D1712151

ENCYCLOPEDIA OF ASSOCIATIONS

REGIONAL, STATE, AND LOCAL ORGANIZATIONS

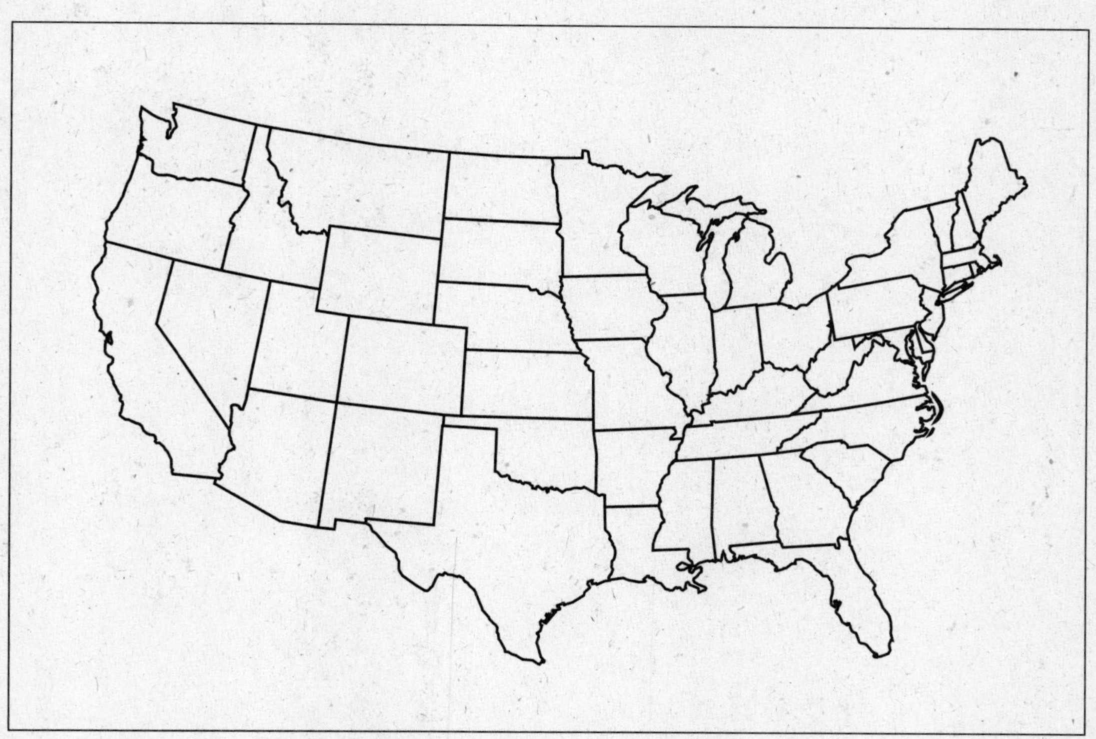

VOLUME I

GREAT LAKES STATES

ISSN 0894-2846

ENCYCLOPEDIA OF ASSOCIATIONS

REGIONAL, STATE, AND LOCAL ORGANIZATIONS

A Guide to Over 100,000 United States Nonprofit Membership Organizations With Regional, State, or Local Scope and Concerned With All Subjects and Areas of Activity

17TH EDITION

VOLUME 1

GREAT LAKES STATES

Includes Illinois, Indiana, Michigan, Minnesota, Ohio, and Wisconsin

THOMSON
GALE

Detroit • New York • San Francisco • New Haven, Conn. • Waterville, Maine • London

Regional, State, and Local Organizations, 17th Edition
Volume 1: Great Lakes States

Product Manager
Jennifer Bernardelli

Project Editor
Verne Thompson

Editorial
Jessica Boguslawski, Bohdan Romaniuk, Amanda D. Sams, Kristy Swartout

Editorial Support Services
Natasha Mikheyeva, Scott Flaugher

Composition and Electronic Prepress
Gary Oudersluys

Manufacturing
Rita Wimberley

For more information, contact
Thomson Gale
27500 Drake Rd.
Farmington Hills, MI 48331-3535
Or you can visit our Internet site at
http://www.gale.com

ISBN-13:	ISBN-10:
978-0-7876-8264-4 (set)	0-7876-8264-0 (set)
978-0-7876-8268-2 (vol. 1)	0-7876-8268-3 (vol. 1)
978-0-7876-8265-1 (vol. 2)	0-7876-8265-9 (vol. 2)
978-0-7876-8266-8 (vol. 3)	0-7876-8266-7 (vol. 3)
978-0-7876-8269-9 (vol. 4)	0-7876-8269-1 (vol. 4)
978-0-7876-8267-5 (vol. 5)	0-7876-8267-5 (vol. 5)

ISSN 0894-2846

Printed in the United States of America
10 9 8 7 6 5 4 3 2 1

Contents

Volume 1: Great Lakes States

Introduction vii
User's Guide ix
Keyword List xiii
Abbreviations xix
Descriptive Listings
1. Illinois 1
2. Indiana 223
3. Michigan 359
4. Minnesota 565
5. Ohio 715
6. Wisconsin 959
Name and Keyword Index 1113

Introduction

For nearly 50 years, the *Encyclopedia of Associations* series has provided detailed and comprehensive information on nonprofit membership organizations. *Regional, State, and Local Organizations (RSL)* covers associations and societies that are organized and function at the regional (both interstate and intrastate), state, county, city, neighborhood, and local levels. Like other volumes in the *Encyclopedia of Associations* series, *RSL* covers:

- Trade and professional associations
- Social welfare and public affairs organizations
- Labor unions
- Fraternal and patriotic organizations
- Religious, sports, and hobby groups
- Many other types of organizations consisting of voluntary members

Describes Over 100,000 Associations

The seventeenth edition of *RSL* covers over 100,000 associations and other nonprofit organizations headquartered in all 50 states, the District of Columbia, and the U.S. territories of Guam, Puerto Rico, and the Virgin Islands. These volumes list contact and descriptive information for local affiliates, chapters, and branches of organizations described in *EA*'s *National Organizations of the U.S.*, as well as independent organizations that function at the regional, state, or local level.

Included are sizable organizations that encompass several states, groups whose membership is limited to residents of a single state, and organizations whose scope is limited to a single city or section of a city. Nonmembership organizations such as resource and referral centers, clearinghouses, information services, projects, and programs are listed if they disseminate information to the public. Some for-profit organizations may be included if their names or activities suggest that they are nonprofit organizations.

Who Uses RSL?

Regional, State, and Local Organizations connects information seekers with highly qualified sources right in their own neighborhoods and states. The associations listed in RSL:

- Provide direct access to information on local subjects and areas of interest in regions throughout the country.
- Offer access to parties responsible for executing plans and programs established by the leadership of national organizations.
- Offer individuals preparing to visit, move to, or conduct business in a specific geographic area a means to easily uncover facts about that area by consulting the appropriate local professional, technical, social, or political organizations.
- Connect members of national associations with local chapters and affiliates.
- Assist individuals seeking local sources of information on subjects of importance or interest.

Published in Five Regional Volumes

The geographic scope of each volume takes into account factors such as shared regional characteristics or interests, and, of course, geography. This allows users to acquire only those volumes that will meet their information needs. Organizations are assigned to a particular volume based on the current location of their headquarters or primary mailing address.

Each of the five regional volumes describes approximately 20,000 groups—numbering over 100,000 total—in the following order:

Volume 1, Great Lakes States: Includes Illinois, Indiana, Michigan, Minnesota, Ohio, and Wisconsin

Volume 2, Northeastern States: Includes Connecticut, Maine, Massachusetts, New Hampshire, New Jersey, New York, Pennsylvania, Rhode Island, and Vermont

Volume 3, Southern and Middle Atlantic States: Includes Alabama, Delaware, District of Columbia, Florida, Georgia, Kentucky, Maryland, Mississippi, North Carolina, Puerto Rico, South Carolina, Tennessee, Virgin Islands, Virginia, and West Virginia

Volume 4, South Central and Great Plains States: Includes Arkansas, Iowa, Kansas, Louisiana, Missouri, Nebraska, North Dakota, Oklahoma, South Dakota, and Texas

Volume 5, Western States: Includes Alaska, Arizona, California, Colorado, Guam, Hawaii, Idaho, Montana, Nevada, New Mexico, Oregon, Utah, Washington, and Wyoming

Content and Arrangement of Entries

Unlike other titles in the *EA* series, each volume of *RSL* is arranged alphabetically by state and city, rather than topically by subject section and keyword. Entries within each state are listed alphabetically by the headquarters' city, and are subclassified alphabetically according to association name. This arrangement facilitates rapid identification of all organizations headquartered within a particular geographic area.

For additional information on the content, format, and arrangement of entries, consult the "User's Guide" on page ix.

Name and Keyword Index

This index lists in alphabetical order the names of all organizations contained in this volume. It also contains references to keywords in organization names, and many subject keywords that have been assigned by the editors. The Keyword List can be found on page xiii.

For complete information on the index, consult the "Name and Keyword Index" section of the "User's Guide" on page xi.

Method of Compilation

Although every attempt is made to achieve accuracy and currency, associations constantly form, disband, and relocate. This is particularly true of regional and local organizations, which tend to be more ephemeral than their larger and better-funded national and international counterparts.

An extensive research effort is conducted to maintain and enrich the *RSL* database: entry information previously listed in *RSL* was sent to the organizations for updating; questionnaires were sent to newly formed or newly identified associations, and efforts were made to contact organizations that did not provide updated information or failed to return questionnaires—these efforts included emailing and faxing organizations, as well as searching organizations' websites; national organizations were contacted for lists of their local affiliates; other databases maintained by Thomson Gale were searched for local organizations; and reliable secondary sources were employed after being checked for accuracy.

Available in Electronic Formats

Licensing. *Regional, State and Local Organizations* is available for licensing. The complete database is provided in a fielded format and is deliverable on such media as disk or CD-ROM. For more information, contact Gale's Business Development Group at 1-800-877-GALE, or visit us on our web site at www.gale.com/bizdev.

Online. The complete *Encyclopedia of Associations (EA)* series (including associations listed in the national and regional, state and local editions) is available online as File 114:Encyclopedia of Associations through The Dialog Corporation's DIALOG service and as File ENASSC through LexisNexis. For more information, contact The Dialog Corporation, 11000 Regency Parkway, Ste. 400, Cary, NC 27511; phone: (919) 462-8600; toll-free: 800-3-DIALOG; or LexisNexis, P.O. Box 933, Dayton, OH 45401-0933; phone (937) 865-6800; toll-free: 800-227-4908.

Associations Unlimited. *Associations Unlimited* is a modular approach to the *Encyclopedia of Associations* database, allowing customers to select the pieces of the series that they want to purchase. The five modules include each of the EA series (national, international, and regional) as well as one module featuring U.S. government data on more than 300,000 nonprofit organizations, and one module providing logos, membership applications, and the entire text of brochures and pamphlets from 3,000 of the most often contacted organizations in the United States. *Associations Unlimited* is available on a subscription basis through InfoTrac, Gale's online information resource that features an easy-to-use end-user interface, powerful search capabilities, and ease of access through the World-Wide Web. For more information, call 800-877-GALE.

The complete *EA* database is also available through InfoTrac as part of *Gale's Ready Reference Shelf.*

Acknowledgments

The editors would like to thank the many individuals who responded to requests for information. Without their cooperation this book would not have been possible.

Comments and Suggestions Welcome

If you have questions, concerns, or comments about the *Encyclopedia of Associations: Regional, State, and Local Organizations (RSL)* or other Gale products, please contact Jennifer Bernardelli, Product Manager. Please write or call:

Encyclopedia of Associations: Regional, State, and Local Organizations
Thomson Gale
27500 Drake Rd.
Farmington Hills, MI 48331-3535
Phone: (248) 699-4253
Toll-free: 800-347-GALE
Fax: (248) 699-8075

Arrangement of Entries

Volumes are arranged geographically by state. Within each state, organizations are arranged alphabetically by the headquarters' city, and subarranged according to association name. The city and state names and entry number from the first entry on each left-hand page and the city name and entry number from the last entry on each right-hand page are listed in the top outer corners of the pages.

Organization name and subject access to entries is provided through the alphabetical Name and Keyword Index. An explanation of this index follows the sample entry.

Sample Entry

The number preceding each portion of the sample entry designates an item of information that is included in an entry when reported by the organization. Each numbered item in the sample entry is explained in the paragraph of the same number following the entry.

■1■ 2243 ■ ■2■ Chicago Society of Earth Sciences ■3■ (CSES)
■4■ 456 Burns Ave.
P.O. Box 2243
Northbrook, IL 60062-2243
■5■ Ph: (312)555-1212
(312)555-1213
■6■ Fax: (312)555-1215
Free: (800)555-1214
■7■ E-mail: jwilson@ses.org
■8■ URL: http://www.cses.org
■9■ Contact: Jason T. Wilson, Pres.

■10■ **Founded:** 1970. ■11■ **Members:** 95. ■12■ **Membership Dues:** individual, $15 (annual) • family, $25 (annual). ■13■ **Staff:** 8. ■14■ **Budget:** $45,000. ■15■ **Local Groups:** 4. ■16■ **Languages:** English, Spanish. ■17■ **Local.** ■18■ Geologists, geological engineers, and geology students. Promotes the study of geology and allied sciences. Conducts seminars on field techniques. Sponsors Chicago Earth Sciences Research Institute. ■19■ **Libraries: Type:** open to the public; lending. **Holdings:** 10,000; books, articles, audio recordings. ■20■ **Awards:** Young Geologist of the Year. **Frequency:** annual. **Type:** scholarship. **Recipient:** Chicago high school student submitting the best geology project proposal. ■21■ **Computer Services:** database • online services. ■22■ **Additional Websites:** http://www.earth.com. ■23■ **Telecommunication Services:** electronic bulletin board • teletype. ■24■ **Divisions:** Research, Program Development. ■25■ **Affiliated With:** American Society of Earth Sciences. ■26■ **Also Known As:** Chicago Earth. ■27■ **Formerly:** (1983) American Society of Earth Sciences, Chicago Chapter. ■28■ **Publications:** *Illinois Geologist*, quarterly. Newsletter. ■29■ **Price:** free to members • *Journal of the CSES*, semi-annual. ■30■ **ISSN:** 1234-5678. ■31■ **Circulation:** 5,000. ■32■ **Advertising:** accepted. ■33■ **Alternate Formats:** online. ■34■ **Also Cited As:** *CSES Review*, Quarterly. ■35■ **Conventions/Meetings:** monthly meeting • annual convention, with speakers (exhibits) - always Chicago, IL. 2004 September 15-17; Avg. Attendance: 300.

Description of Numbered Elements

■1■ **Sequential Entry Number.** The entries in this volume are numbered sequentially, and the entry number (rather than the page number) is used in the indexes to refer to an entry. To facilitate location of the entries in the text, the first entry number on each left-hand page and the last entry number on each right-hand page are provided at the top outer corners of the pages.

■2■ **Organization Name.** The formal name is given; "The" and "Inc." are omitted in most listings, unless they are an integral part of the acronym used by the association.

■3■ **Acronym.** Indicates the short form or abbreviation of the organization's name.

■4■ **Address.** The address is that of the permanent headquarters, or of the executive officer for a group without a permanent office. The headquarters city and state of the first full entry on each left-hand page and the last entry on each right-hand page are provided at the top outer corners of the pages.

■5■ **Telephone Numbers.** These are listed when furnished by the organization.

■6■ **Fax, Telex, Cable, and Toll-Free Numbers.** These are listed when furnished by the organization.

■7■ **E-mail.** This is listed when furnished by the organization.

■8■ **URLs.** The primary web address for the organization, contact person listed, or national affiliate.

■9■ Chief Official and Title. Many organizations employ full-time executives to handle their affairs. If the association does not employ a full-time executive, the name of an elected officer has been provided.

■10■ Founding Date. Indicates the year in which the organization was formed. If the group has changed its name, the founding date is for the earliest name by which it was known. If, however, the group was formed by a merger or supersedes another group, the founding date refers to the year in which this action took place; an attempt is also made to give the founding dates for the predecessor organizations in the body of the description. (See paragraph 27.)

■11■ Number of Members. This figure may represent individuals, firms, institutions, other associations, or a combination of these categories. Since membership constantly fluctuates, the figure should be considered an approximation. If an organization describes itself as nonmembership, a boldfaced notation to that effect appears preceding the descriptive text.

■12■ Membership Dues. Provides the amount, frequency of renewal, and type of membership.

■13■ Staff. Many associations employ a small permanent paid staff. The fact that an organization has no paid staff does not mean it has a limited program. Many groups carry on extensive activities through volunteer workers and committees.

■14■ Budget. This figure represents approximate annual budget for all activities, as reported by the organization, and is rounded off, if necessary, by the editors.

■15■ Regional, State, and Local Groups. Indicates the number of regional, state, and local associations, chapters, clubs, councils, posts, and other subgroups affiliated with the listed association.

■16■ Languages. The official and/or working languages of the organization are listed, if other than English.

■17■ Geographic Scope. The boldface word **Regional** indicates a multistate scope of the organization; **State** indicates a statewide scope; **Local** indicates a local scope.

■18■ Description. Briefly outlines the membership, purpose, and activities of the association. Where no description is given, the title of the group is usually self-explanatory; in some cases, no summary of activities could be obtained.

■19■ Libraries. Provides information for organizations that maintain a library. Includes type of collection, holdings, and a description, if available.

■20■ Awards. If the group offers awards, the names, types, and descriptions are located here.

■21■ Computer Services. Lists computer-based services offered by the organization, including online services and databases, bibliographic or other search services, automated mailing list services, and electronic publishing capabilities.

■22■ Additional Websites. List additional Internet addresses which may be used to access information on or related to the organization. Addresses are organized by type (e.g. FTP, Gopher, Telnet, and World Wide Web.)

■23■ Telecommunication Services. Lists special communications services sponsored by the organization. Services included are additional e-mail addresses, electronic bulletin boards, teleconference capabilities, phone referral systems, teletypes, and TDDs.

■24■ Sections and Divisions. Notes those subgroups, including committees, sections, divisions, councils, departments, etc., that give an indication of the activities of the group, as distinguished from administrative committees such as membership, finance, and convention. This information often supplements the description (paragraph 18) by providing details about the organization's programs and fields of interest.

■25■ Affiliated With. Lists organizations sponsored by or directly related to the listed group. Entries for organizations listed as affiliates are also listed in this or another volume of the Encyclopedia of Associations series.

■26■ Also Known As. If the organization is also known by another name, legally does business under another name, or otherwise operates under a name other than its official title, that name is provided here.

■27■ Supersessions, Mergers, and Changes of Name. If the group superseded another organization or was formed by a merger, the original organization(s) and founding date(s) are listed. Former names and the date of change to a new name are also indicated.

■28■ Publications. The official publication(s)—including magazines, bulletins, journals, proceedings, directories, and similar periodicals—are listed alphabetically, with frequencies. Non-serial publications are also listed, but the listing of such materials is not necessarily complete. If the organization does not issue publications, this is noted at the end of the description. (See paragraph 18.)

■29■ Price. Lists the figure(s) provided by the organization.

■30■ ISSN. The International Standard Serial Number is a unique code for the purpose of identifying specific serial publications. It is listed when provided by the organization; not all publications have been assigned ISSNs.

■31■ Circulation. Provides the figure reported by the organization.

■32■ Advertising. Indicates whether or not the association accepts advertising in its publications.

■33■ Alternate Formats. Notes on-line, CD-ROM, and microform (microfiche and microfilm) availability.

■34■ Also Cited As. Lists any alternate or former names of the publication.

■35■ **Conventions/Meetings.** Gives the frequency, date, location (city and state), and average number of attendees of the association's conventions, meetings, or conferences, if available at the time of publication. If the group does not hold any conventions or meetings, this is stated at the end of the description. (See paragraph 18.)

Name and Keyword Index

A comprehensive alphabetical index to organization names and keywords is provided at the back of this volume. Each organization is listed alphabetically by complete name, by important words contained in the name, and by any added subject keywords, in bold, which may have been assigned by the editors to facilitate subject access. Former and alternate names and the names of important projects and programs are also listed in the same format. All organizations concerned with the same general subjects appear grouped together by those subjects in the index. An alphabetical list of subject keywords follows this User's Guide.

Index references to organizations described in this volume include added geographic information. This information, which consists of the name of the headquarters city and state, appears in brackets following each complete reference to the main association name used for each organization. These geographic scope notations can be used in conjunction with keyword indexing to further refine subject searches. Appended geographic information also distinguishes references to organizations with similar or identical names.

The Name and Keyword index refers the user to an entry number, rather than to the page on which the entry is listed. The number for the first entry on each left-hand page and the last entry on each right-hand page is listed in the top outer corners of the pages. **Index citations marked with a star (★) denote organizations mentioned within the description of another organization's main entry.**

For example, the sample entry appearing near the beginning of this User's Guide would have the following listings in the index:

Amer. Soc. of Earth Sciences, Chicago Chapter **[★2243]**
Chicago Earth **[★2243]**
Chicago Earth Sciences Res. Inst. **[★2243]**
Chicago Soc. of Earth Sciences **[2243]**, Northbrook, IL
Earth; Chicago **[★2243]**
Earth Sciences, Chicago Chapter; Amer. Soc. of **[★2243]**
Earth Sciences; Chicago Soc. of **[2243]**, Northbrook, IL
Earth Sciences Res. Inst.; Chicago **[★2243]**
Geology
Chicago Soc. of Earth Sciences **[2243]**, Northbrook, IL
Res. Inst.; Chicago Earth Sciences **[★2243]**
Sciences; Chicago Chapter; Amer. Soc. of Earth **[★2243]**
Sciences; Chicago Soc. of **[2243]**, Northbrook, IL
Sciences Res. Inst.; Chicago Earth **[★2243]**

Keyword List

A

Academic Freedom
Accountants
Accounting
Accreditation
Acoustics
Actors
Administration
Administrative Services
Admissions
Adoption
Adult Education
Advertising
Aerospace
Aerospace Medicine
AFL-CIO
Africa
African
African-American
Agents
Aging
Agnostic
Agribusiness
Agricultural Development
Agricultural Education
Agricultural Engineering
Agricultural Equipment
Agricultural Science
Agriculture
AIDS
Aikido
Aircraft
Alcohol
Alcohol Abuse
Alcoholic Beverages
Allergy
Alternative Medicine
Alumni
Alzheimer's Disease
Amateur Radio
Ambulatory Care
American Indian
American Legion
American Revolution
Amyotrophic Lateral Sclerosis
Anesthesiology
Animal Breeding
Animal Research
Animal Welfare
Animals
Antiques
Appalachian
Apparel
Apple
Appraisers
Aquaculture
Aquatics
Arbitration and Mediation
Archaeology
Archery
Architecture
Archives
Armed Forces
Army
Art
Art Therapy
Artists
Arts
Arts and Crafts
Arts and Sciences
Asbestos
Asian-American
Associations
Astronomy
Atheist
Athletes
Athletics
Attorneys
Auctions
Authors
Autism
Automobile
Automotive
Automotive Education
Automotive Industries
Automotive Manufacturers
Automotive Services
Aviation
Awards

B

Bakery
Baking
Bands
Banking
Baptist
Baseball
Basketball
Beer
Behavioral Sciences
Bereavement
Bernese Mountain Dog
Beverages
Bible
Bicycle
Bilingualism
Biology
Biotechnology
Bird
Birds of Prey
Birth Defects
Blacksmiths
Blind
Blood
Boating
Bocce
Books
Botany
Bottles
Bowling
Boxing
Breastfeeding
Broadcasters
Broadcasting
Building Industries
Building Trades
Burns
Bus
Business
Business and Commerce
Business Education
Business Products
Business Tourism

C

Camping
Cancer
Canoeing
Capital Punishment
Cardiology
Cartography
Cast Metals
Cat
Catholic
Cattle
Census
Ceramics
Cerebral Palsy
Chambers of Commerce
Cheerleading
Chefs
Chemicals
Chemistry
Chess
Chevrolet
Child Abuse
Child Care
Child Health
Child Welfare
Childhood Education
Children
Chiropractic
Choirs
Christian
Christianity
Church and State
Churches
Circumcision
Citizenship
Civics
Civil Engineering
Civil Law
Civil Rights and Liberties
Civil Service
Civil War
Classical Studies
Climbing
Clinical Studies
Clothing

Clubs
Coaching
Coal
Coast Guard
Coatings
Collectibles
Collectors
Colleges and Universities
Colonial
Commodities
Commodity Exchanges
Communications
Community
Community Action
Community Colleges
Community Development
Community Education
Community Improvement
Community Mental Health
Community Organization
Community Service
Compensation Medicine
Composers
Computer Science
Computer Software
Computer Users
Computers
Concrete
Conflict Resolution
Conservation
Conservationists
Conservative
Constitutional Law
Construction
Consulting
Consumers
Contractors
Cooperative Extension
Cooperatives
Correctional
Cosmetology
Cosmology
Counseling
Country Music
County Government
Court Employees
Crafts
Creation
Credit
Credit Unions
Cricket
Crime
Criminal Justice
Critical Care
Cultural Centers
Cultural Exchange
Cultural Resources
Curling
Curriculum
Cycling

D

Dachshund
Dairies
Dairy Products
Dance
Data Processing
Deaf
Deer
Democratic Party
Dental Hygiene
Dentistry
Design
Developmental Education
Diabetes
Disabilities
Disabled
Disabled Veterans
Disarmament
Discipline
Disease
Distance Running
Diving
Divorce
Doberman Pinscher
Dog
Dog Racing
Dolls
Domestic Violence
Down's Syndrome
Drag Racing
Drug Abuse
Drug Rehabilitation
Drunk Driving
Dry Cleaning
Duck
Dutch
Dyslexia

E

Eagles
Eastern Europe
Ecology
Economic Development
Economics
Ecumenical
Education
Education Youth
Education, Special
Educational Advocacy
Educational Funding
Educational Reform
Educators
Electrical
Electrical Engineering
Electricity
Electronics
Elks
Emergency Aid
Emergency Medicine
Emergency Services
Employee Assistance
  Programs
Employee Benefits
Employee Ownership
Employers
Employment
Energy
Engineering
English
English Toy Spaniel
Entertainers
Entertainment
Entomology
Environment
Environmental Education
Environmental Health
Environmental Law
Environmental Quality
Epilepsy
Ergonomics
Esperanto
Estate Management
Evaluation
Evangelism
Exhibitors
Experiential Education
Exploration
Explosives

F

Fair Agencies
Families
Family Medicine
Family Name Societies
Family Planning
Farm Equipment
Farm Management
Farming
Feed
Feminism
Fencing
Ferret
Fertility
Fertilizer
Film
Film Industry
Finance
Financial Aid
Financial Planning
Finnish
Fire Fighting
Fire Protection
Firearms
Fish
Fishing
Florists
Flowers
Folk
Food
Food and Drugs
Food Service
Football
Foreign Service
Foreign Students
Foreign Trade
Forensic Sciences
Forest Industries
Forest Products
Forestry
Foster Parents
Fraternities and Sororities
Fraternities, Service
Free Enterprise
Freedom
Friends
Fruits and Vegetables
Fuel
Fundraising
Funeral
Future
Futures

G

Gambling
Games
Gardening
Gases
Gastroenterology
Gay/Lesbian
Genealogy
Genetic Disorders
Geography
Geology
German
German Pointer
German Shepherd
Gerontology
Gifted
Gilbert and Sullivan
Girls
Glass
Goats
Golf
Gospel Music
Government
Government Employees
Grain
Graphic Arts
Graphics
Grass
Great Lakes
Greek
Greyhound
Grounds Management
Gymnastics

H

Haiti
Hardware
Head Injury
Health
Health Care
Health Care Products

Health Education
Health Plans
Health Professionals
Health Services
Hearing Impaired
Heart Disease
Heating and Cooling
Helicopter
Hematology
Herbs
Herpetology
Higher Education
Highways
Hiking
Hinduism
Hispanic
Historic Preservation
Historical Societies
History
Hobbies
Hockey
Holistic Medicine
Holocaust
Home
Home Care
Home Economics
Home Repair
Homeless
Honor Societies
Horse Racing
Horseback Riding
Horses
Horseshoes
Horticulture
Hospice
Hospital
Hospitality Industries
Hotel Management
Hound
Housing
Human Engineering
Human Life Issues
Human Relations
Human Resources
Human Rights
Human Services
Humanism
Humanities
Hunger
Hunting
Hunting Dogs
Hypnosis

I

Ichthyology
Immigration
Independent Schools
Industrial Development
Industrial Education
Industrial Engineering
Industrial Equipment
Industrial Security
Industrial Workers
Infants
Infectious Diseases
Information Management
Instructional Media
Insurance
Intercultural Studies
Interior Design
Internal Medicine
International Affairs
International Development
International Law
International Relations
International Standards
International Trade
Inventors
Investigation
Investments
Iranian
Irish
Islamic
Israel
Israeli

J

Japanese
Jaycees
Jazz
Jewelry
Jewish
Journalism
Judiciary
Juvenile

K

Kidney
Kite Flying
Korean War

L

Labor
Labor Management
Labor Studies
Labor Unions
Laboratory
Lacrosse
Lakes
Land Control
Landscaping
Language
Latin
Latin American
Laundry
Laurel and Hardy
Law
Law Enforcement
Leadership
Learning Disabled
Legal
Legal Aid
Legal Services
Lending
Lepidopterology
Leukemia
Libraries
Library Science
Lighting
Lilies
Literacy
Literature
Livestock
Lodgings
Lupus Erythematosus
Lutheran

M

Magic
Maintenance
Maltese
Management
Managers
Manufactured Housing
Manufacturing
Marijuana
Marine
Marine Corps
Marine Industries
Maritime
Marketing
Marriage
Martial Arts
Martinism
Masonry
Masons
Matchcover
Materials
Mathematics
Meat
Mechanics
Media
Medical
Medical Administration
Medical Assistants
Medical Education
Medical Records
Medical Technology
Medicine
Meeting Planners
Men's Rights
Mental Health
Mentally Disabled
Metabolic Disorders
Metal
Metallurgy
Metals
Meteorology
Microscopy
Migrant Workers
Military
Mineralogy
Minerals
Mining
Ministry
Minority Business
Missing-in-Action
Model Trains
Models
Moose
Mortuary Services
Motorcycle
Municipal Government
Museums
Music
Musicians
Mycology

N

Native American
Natural Resources
Natural Sciences
Navy
Nephrology
Networking
Neurological Disorders
Neurology
Neuroscience
Neurosurgery
Newspapers
Nonprofit Organizations
Nonviolence
Norwegian
Nuclear
Nuclear Medicine
Nuclear War and Weapons
Nudism
Numismatic
Nurseries
Nursing
Nursing Homes
Nutrition
Nuts

O

Obesity
Obstetrics and Gynecology
Occupational Medicine
Oceanography
Officers
Opera
Ophthalmology
Opticianry
Optics
Optometry
Orchestras
Organ
Organic Farming
Organization Development
Organizations
Oriental Healing
Orienteering
Ornithology
Orthopedics
Osteopathic Medicine

Osteopathy
Ostomy
Otorhinolaryngology
Outdoor Recreation

P

Packaging
Pain
Paints and Finishes
Paper
Paralegals
Parapsychology
Parasitology
Parents
Parking
Parks and Recreation
Parliaments
Peace
Pediatrics
Performing Arts
Personnel
Pest Control
Petroleum
Pets
Pharmaceuticals
Pharmacy
Phenomena
Philanthropy
Philatelic
Photography
Physical Education
Physical Fitness
Physical Therapy
Physician Assistants
Physicians
Physics
Physiology
Pioneers
Pipes
Placement
Planning
Plumbing
Podiatry
Police
Policy
Polio
Polish
Political Action
Political Parties
Political Prisoners
Politics
Pollution Control
Postal Service
Postal Workers
Poultry
Poverty
Preschool Education
Press
Principals
Prisoners of War
Private Radio
Private Schools
Professionals
Professions
Professors
Property Management
Property Rights
Psychiatry
Psychoanalysis
Psychology
Public Administration
Public Affairs
Public Finance
Public Health
Public Information
Public Policy
Public Relations
Public Service
Public Speaking
Public Welfare
Public Works
Publishing
Puppetry
Purchasing

Q

Quality Assurance
Quality Control

R

Rabbits
Racing
Racquetball
Radio
Radiology
Railroads
Rape
Reading
Real Estate
Recreation
Recreational Vehicles
Recycling
Red Cross
Reform
Refrigeration
Refugees
Regional Government
Rehabilitation
Relief
Religion
Religious Administration
Religious Studies
Religious Understanding
Renaissance
Renting and Leasing
Repair
Reproductive Health
Reproductive Rights
Reptiles
Republican Party
Rescue
Research
Respiratory Diseases
Restaurant
Retail Hardware
Retailing
Retardation, Mental
Retirees
Retirement
Reye's Syndrome
Rheumatic Diseases
Rifles
Right to Life
Robotics
Rodeo
Rowing
Rugby
Runaways
Rural Development
Rural Youth

S

Safety
Safety Education
Sales
Sanitation
Scholarship
Scholarship Alumni
School Boards
School Security
School Services
Schools
Science
Scottish
Scouting
Sculpture
Securities
Security
Seed
Selfhelp
Senility
Service
Service Clubs
Service Sororities
Sexual Abuse
Sheep
Sheepdog
Shelter
Shipping
Shooting
Sickle Cell Anemia
Silent Film
Singles
Skating
Skiing
Slovak
Small Business
Snow Sports
Snowmobiles
Soccer
Social Action
Social Clubs
Social Fraternities
Social Issues
Social Justice
Social Security
Social Service
Social Studies
Social Welfare
Social Work
Social Workers
Socialism
Softball
Soil Conservation
Solar Energy
Space
Special Education
Special Forces
Spectroscopy
Speech
Speech and Hearing
Speleology
Spina Bifida
Spinal Injury
Spiritualist
Sports
Sports Facilities
Sports Officials
Standards
Star Trek
State Government
Statistics
Stone
Stroke
Student Services
Students
Substance Abuse
Sudden Infant Death Syndrome
Suicide
Summer School
Support Groups
Surgery
Surveying
Sweden
Swedish
Swimming
Swine

T

Table Tennis
Tallness
Taxation
Teacher Education
Teachers
Technical Consulting
Technical Education
Technology
Telecommunications
Telephone Service
Temperance
Tennis
Terrorism
Testing
Textiles
Theatre
Theosophical

Therapy
Thoracic Medicine
Tires
Tobacco
Tourism
Track and Field
Trade
Traffic
Trails
Trainers
Translation
Transplantation
Transportation
Trappers
Trapping
Trauma
Travel
Trees
Trees and Shrubs
Trial Advocacy
Triumph
Trucking
Trucks
Turfgrass
Turkish

U

Unemployment
Unions
Urban Affairs
Urology
Utilities

V

Vacuum Technology
Vascular System
Vaulting
Vegetables
Vegetarianism
Vending
Veterans
Veterans of Foreign Wars
Veterinary Medicine
Victims
Vietnam Veterans
Vietnam War
Violence
Visually Impaired
Vocational Education
Volcanology
Volleyball
Voluntarism

W

Walking
Waste
Water
Water Conservation
Water Resources
Weightlifting
Weimaraners
Welding
West Indian
Wetlands
Wholesale
Wholesale Distribution
Wildlife
Wildlife Conservation
Wine
Women
Women's Rights
Women's Studies
Wood
Wood Trades
Woodcarvings
Wool
Workers
World Notables
Wrestling
Writers
Writing

Y

Yoga
Youth

Z

Zoological Gardens
Zoology

Geographic Abbreviations

United States and U.S. Territories

AK	Alaska
AL	Alabama
AR	Arkansas
AZ	Arizona
CA	California
CO	Colorado
CT	Connecticut
DC	District of Columbia
DE	Delaware
FL	Florida
GA	Georgia
GU	Guam
HI	Hawaii
IA	Iowa
ID	Idaho
IL	Illinois
IN	Indiana
KS	Kansas
KY	Kentucky
LA	Louisiana
MA	Massachusetts
MD	Maryland
ME	Maine
MI	Michigan
MN	Minnesota
MO	Missouri
MS	Mississippi
MT	Montana
NC	North Carolina
ND	North Dakota
NE	Nebraska
NH	New Hampshire
NJ	New Jersey
NM	New Mexico
NV	Nevada
NY	New York
OH	Ohio
OK	Oklahoma
OR	Oregon
PA	Pennsylvania
PR	Puerto Rico
RI	Rhode Island
SC	South Carolina
SD	South Dakota
TN	Tennessee
TX	Texas
UT	Utah
VA	Virginia
VI	Virgin Islands
VT	Vermont
WA	Washington
WI	Wisconsin
WV	West Virginia
WY	Wyoming

Table of Abbreviations Used in Addresses and the Index

Acad	Academy
AFB	Air Force Base
Amer	American
APO	Army Post Office
Apt	Apartment
Assn	Association
Ave	Avenue
Bd	Board
Bldg	Building
Blvd	Boulevard
Br	Branch
Bur	Bureau
c/o	Care of
Co	Company
Coll	College
Comm	Committee
Commn	Commission
Conf	Conference
Confed	Confederation
Cong	Congress
Corp	Corporation
Coun	Council
Ct	Court
Dept	Department
Div	Division
Dr	Drive
E	East
Expy	Expressway
Fed	Federation
Fl	Floor
Found	Foundation
FPO	Fleet Post Office
Ft	Fort
Fwy	Freeway
Govt	Government
GPO	General Post Office
Hwy	Highway
Inc	Incorporated
Inst	Institute
Intl	International
Ln	Lane
Ltd	Limited
Mfrs	Manufacturers
Mgt	Management
Mt	Mount
N	North
Natl	National
NE	Northeast
No	Number
NW	Northwest
Pkwy	Parkway
Pl	Place
PO	Post Office
Prof	Professor
Rd	Road
RD	Rural Delivery
RFD	Rural Free Delivery
Rm	Room
RR	Rural Route
Rte	Route
S	South
SE	Southeast
Sect	Section
Soc	Society

Sq	Square
St	Saint, Street
Sta	Station
Ste	Sainte, Suite
Subcomm	Subcommittee
Subcommn	Subcommission
SW	Southwest
Terr	Terrace, Territory
Tpke	Turnpike
T.V.	Television
UN	United Nations
Univ	University
U.S.	United States
U.S.A.	United States of America
W	West

Abingdon

1 ■ Abingdon Chamber of Commerce (AACC)
902 W Jackson St.
Abingdon, IL 61410-1276
Ph: (309)462-3234
E-mail: palmerh1@gallatinriver.net
URL: http://www.abingdon.net
Contact: Hollis Palmer, Treas.
Membership Dues: all, $40 (annual). **Local**. Provides leadership for the community, promotes local resources, enhances local programs, and coordinates development efforts. **Conventions/Meetings:** annual banquet - last Saturday in February • monthly board meeting - every second Thursday. Abingdon, IL.

2 ■ American Legion, Illinois Post 381
c/o Harry E. Wiles
PO Box 53
Abingdon, IL 61410
Ph: (309)465-3623
Fax: (309)663-5783
URL: National Affiliate–www.legion.org
Contact: Harry E. Wiles, Contact
Local. Affiliated With: American Legion.

Addison

3 ■ Addison Chamber of Commerce and Industry (AAIC)
777 Army Trail Rd., Ste.D
Addison, IL 60101
Ph: (630)543-4300
Fax: (630)543-4355
E-mail: addisonchamber@sbcglobal.net
URL: http://www.addisonaic.org
Contact: Bernadette Hanrahan, Exec.Dir.
Founded: 1991. **Members:** 350. **Membership Dues:** Addison business, $185 (annual) • not for profit organization, home based business, $110 (annual) • non-Addison business, $275 (annual). **Budget:** $86,000. **Local**. Promotes the retention and further development of business in Addison, IL, and the representation of businesses to local and national county, state, and national governmental agencies. **Libraries: Type:** reference. **Holdings:** audio recordings, books, video recordings. **Formed by Merger of:** Addison Chamber of Commerce; Addison Industrial Association. **Publications:** *Addison Community Directory*, biennial. Contains member directory. **Price:** free. **Advertising:** accepted • *Shoptalk*, bimonthly. Newsletter. Outlines matters of legislative concern, notices of various business meetings, general information concerning Chamber members. **Advertising:** accepted. **Conventions/Meetings:** annual Five Star Business EXPO - show, combined six area chambers; one day exhibit by business members (exhibits).

4 ■ American Hellenic Educational Progressive Association - DuPage, Chapter 423
c/o Louis Papadakos, Pres.
20 W 444 Lake St.
Addison, IL 60101
Ph: (630)773-2150
Fax: (630)773-2047
E-mail: alpharealty@sbcglobal.net
URL: http://www.ahepafamily.org/d13
Contact: Louis Papadakos, Pres.
Local. Affiliated With: American Hellenic Educational Progressive Association.

5 ■ American Legion, Illinois Post 1969
c/o Dwight D. Eisenhower
PO Box 211
Addison, IL 60101
Ph: (309)663-0361
Fax: (309)663-5783
URL: National Affiliate–www.legion.org
Contact: Dwight D. Eisenhower, Contact
Local. Affiliated With: American Legion.

6 ■ Chicago Association for Healthcare Central Service Professionals
c/o Eloise McCarthy, Treas.
The Suburban Surgery Center of DuPage
1580 W Lake St.
Addison, IL 60101
Ph: (630)694-7519
URL: National Affiliate–www.ashcsp.org
Contact: Eloise McCarthy, Treas.
Local. Promotes healthcare central service, sterile processing and inventory management practices. Provides education, professional and organization development, advocacy and communication to healthcare service professionals. **Affiliated With:** American Society for Healthcare Central Service Professionals.

7 ■ Home Builders Association of Greater Chicago
c/o Peter Schwartz
1841 W Army Trail Rd.
Addison, IL 60101
Ph: (630)627-7575
Fax: (630)627-7580
E-mail: peters@hbagc.com
URL: http://www.hbagc.com
Contact: Peter Schwartz, CEO
Local. Single and multifamily home builders, commercial builders, and others associated with the building industry. **Affiliated With:** National Association of Home Builders.

8 ■ Illinois Computing Educators (ICE)
777 Army Trail Rd.
Addison, IL 60101
Ph: (630)628-1088
Fax: (630)628-5388
URL: http://www.iceberg.org
Contact: Beth Burke, Exec.Dir.
State. Seeks to improve the quality of education through the innovative use of technology. Facilitates the exchange of information and resources between policy makers and professional organizations. Encourages research and evaluation relating to the use of technology in education. **Affiliated With:** International Society for Technology in Education.

9 ■ Kiwanis Club of Addison
PO Box 54
Addison, IL 60101
E-mail: info@addisonkiwanis.org
URL: http://addisonkiwanis.org
Contact: David Williams, Contact
Local.

10 ■ Phi Theta Kappa, Alpha Nu Theta Chapter - DeVry University
c/o Gary Luechtefeld
Dupage Campus
1221 N Swift Rd.
Addison, IL 60101
Ph: (630)953-1300
E-mail: gluechte@dpg.devry.edu
URL: http://www.ptk.org/directories/chapters/IL/2070-1.htm
Contact: Gary Luechtefeld, Advisor
Local.

Albany

11 ■ American Legion, Hanson-Kennedy Post 1079
401 S Church St.
Albany, IL 61230
Ph: (309)663-0361
Fax: (309)663-5783
URL: National Affiliate–www.legion.org
Local. Affiliated With: American Legion.

12 ■ Rock Island Greater Lions Club
1003 S Bluff St.
Albany, IL 61230
Ph: (309)887-5114
URL: http://rockislandgreateril.lionwap.org
Local. Affiliated With: Lions Clubs International.

Albers

13 ■ American Legion, Stukenberg-Eilermann Post 1026
600 N Bertha
Albers, IL 62215
Ph: (618)248-5484
Fax: (309)663-5783
URL: National Affiliate–www.legion.org
Local. Affiliated With: American Legion.

Albion

14 ■ American Legion, Albion-Browns Post 590
239 S 4th St.
Albion, IL 62806
Ph: (618)445-8986
Fax: (309)663-5783
URL: National Affiliate–www.legion.org
Local. Affiliated With: American Legion.

15 ■ Greater Wabash Regional Planning Commission
10 W Main
PO Box 209
Albion, IL 62806
Ph: (618)445-3612
Fax: (618)445-3629
E-mail: gwrpc@midwest.net
Contact: Lisa A. Michels, Exec.Dir.
Founded: 1964. **Members:** 42. **Staff:** 5. **Budget:** $205,256. **Regional Groups:** 5. **State Groups:** 2. **Local Groups:** 5. **Local.** Administers seven county economic development district. **Libraries: Type:** open to the public. **Holdings:** books, periodicals. **Subjects:** planning, economic development. **Publications:** Annual Report. **Conventions/Meetings:** annual meeting; Avg. Attendance: 50.

16 ■ National Active And Retired Federal Employees Association - Little Egypt 1007
RR 1 Box 237
Albion, IL 62806-9778
Ph: (618)445-2887
URL: National Affiliate–www.narfe.org
Contact: Rosie Stennett, Contact
Local. Protects the retirement future of employees through education. Informs members on issues affecting the retirement. **Affiliated With:** National Association of Retired Federal Employees.

Aledo

17 ■ Aledo Area Chamber of Commerce
PO Box 261
Aledo, IL 61231
Ph: (309)582-5373
Fax: (309)582-8822
Contact: Peggy Smith, Sec.
Local.

18 ■ Aledo Main Street
PO Box 209
Aledo, IL 61231
Ph: (309)582-2751
E-mail: aledoms@qconline.com
URL: http://www.aledomainstreet.com
Local.

19 ■ American Legion, Fallerans Post 121
PO Box 121
Aledo, IL 61231
Ph: (309)582-7218
Fax: (309)663-5783
URL: National Affiliate–www.legion.org
Local. Affiliated With: American Legion.

20 ■ Edwards River Earth Science Club
c/o Lyle Kugler, Pres.
612 SE 3rd St.
Aledo, IL 61231
E-mail: l.kugler@mchsi.com
URL: National Affiliate–www.amfed.org
Contact: Kathy Thompson, Sec.
Local. Aims to further the study of Earth Sciences and the practice of lapidary arts and mineralogy. **Affiliated With:** American Federation of Mineralogical Societies.

Alexis

21 ■ American Legion, Illinois Post 189
c/o James Harvey Scott
PO Box 511
Alexis, IL 61412
Ph: (309)663-0361
Fax: (309)663-5783
URL: National Affiliate–www.legion.org
Contact: James Harvey Scott, Contact
Local. Affiliated With: American Legion.

22 ■ Illinois Coaches Association
c/o John K. Elder
PO Box 240
Alexis, IL 61412
Ph: (309)482-5561
Fax: (309)482-5561
E-mail: elder@icacoach.org
URL: http://www.icacoach.org
Contact: John K. Elder, Contact
Founded: 1928. **Members:** 3,000. **Membership Dues:** individual, $20 (annual). **State. Publications:** *Torch*, 3/year. Newsletter.

23 ■ Mercer County Angus Association
c/o Kenneth Shike, Pres.
3096 1st Ave.
Alexis, IL 61412
Ph: (309)482-3438
URL: National Affiliate–www.angus.org
Contact: Kenneth Shike, Pres.
Local. Affiliated With: American Angus Association.

Algonquin

24 ■ Algonquin - Lake in the Hills Chamber of Commerce
106 S Main St.
PO Box 7283
Algonquin, IL 60102
Ph: (847)658-5300
Fax: (847)658-6546
E-mail: info@algonquin-lith-chamber.com
URL: http://www.algonquin-lith-chamber.com
Contact: Sandy Oslance, Exec.Dir.
Membership Dues: primary business, $250-$650 (annual) • municipality, $350 (annual) • school, $275 (annual) • church, religious organization, $175 (annual) • club or non-profit association, $125 (annual) • associate, $150 (annual). **Local.** Aims to bring area businesses and individuals together to improve the business climate and quality of life for all citizen. **Computer Services:** Mailing lists, of members. **Publications:** Newsletter, bimonthly. **Advertising:** accepted.

25 ■ American Legion, Algonquin Post 670
PO Box 121
Algonquin, IL 60102
Ph: (309)663-0361
Fax: (309)663-5783
URL: National Affiliate–www.legion.org
Local. Affiliated With: American Legion.

26 ■ Chlorine Free Products Association
c/o Archie J. Beaton
19 N Main St.
Algonquin, IL 60102
Ph: (847)658-6104
Fax: (847)658-3152
E-mail: info@chlorinefreeproducts.org
URL: http://www.chlorinefreeproducts.org
Regional.

27 ■ Fox River Valley Chapter of Muskies
PO Box 7613
Algonquin, IL 60102
Ph: (847)741-9771
E-mail: joemellott@hotmail.com
URL: http://www.frvmuskie.com
Contact: Rich Gallagher, Pres.
Local.

Alhambra

28 ■ American Legion, Alhambra Post 1147
PO Box 52
Alhambra, IL 62001
Ph: (309)663-0361
Fax: (309)663-5783
URL: National Affiliate–www.legion.org
Local. Affiliated With: American Legion.

Alpha

29 ■ American Legion, Oxford Post 1197
PO Box 414
Alpha, IL 61413
Ph: (309)529-4251
Fax: (309)663-5783
URL: National Affiliate–www.legion.org
Local. Affiliated With: American Legion.

Alsip

30 ■ Alsip Chamber of Commerce and Economic Development
12159 S Pulaski Rd.
Alsip, IL 60803
Ph: (708)597-2668
Fax: (708)597-5962
Free: (800)INA-LSIP
E-mail: info@alsipevents.com
URL: http://www.alsipevents.com
Contact: Mary Schmidt, Exec.Dir.
Members: 300. **Local.**

31 ■ ASIS International, Chicago Chapter
c/o Initial Electronics, Inc.
12838 S Cicero Ave.
Alsip, IL 60803
Ph: (312)627-6689
URL: http://www.asischicago.org
Contact: Jack Plaxe, Chm.
Local. Seeks to increase the effectiveness and productivity of security practices by developing educational programs and materials that address security concerns. **Affiliated With:** ASIS International.

Altamont

32 ■ Altamont Chamber of Commerce
202 N 2nd St.
Altamont, IL 62411
Ph: (618)483-5714
E-mail: chamber@altamontil.net
URL: http://www.altamontil.net
Contact: Butch Roedl, Pres.
Local. Promotes business and community development in Altamont, IL area. **Committees:** Banquet; Economic Development; 5K Run/Walk; Internet Communication; Promote Altamont; Retail; Rodeo; Scholarship.

33 ■ American Legion, Grobengieser-Fischer Post 512
PO Box 64
Altamont, IL 62411
Ph: (618)483-6323
Fax: (309)663-5783
URL: National Affiliate–www.legion.org
Local. Affiliated With: American Legion.

Alton

34 ■ 100 Black Men of Alton
PO Box 321
Alton, IL 62002
Ph: (618)466-3447
Fax: (618)465-9225
URL: National Affiliate–www.100blackmen.org
Local. Affiliated With: 100 Black Men of America.

35 ■ AAA Missouri
217 E Center Dr.
Alton, IL 62002-3964
Ph: (618)462-1091
URL: http://www.aaamissouri.com
Contact: Wanda Bellito, Intravel
State.

36 ■ Alton Market Place Association
100 E Broadway
Alton, IL 62002
Ph: (618)463-1016
Fax: (618)463-1091
E-mail: ampa@altonmarketplace.com
URL: http://www.altonmarketplace.com
Local.

37 ■ Alton Regional Convention and Visitors Bureau
200 Piasa St.
Alton, IL 62002-6271
Ph: (618)465-6676
Fax: (618)465-6151
Free: (800)ALT-ONIL
E-mail: info@visitalton.com
URL: http://www.VisitALton.com
Contact: Mr. Brett Stawar, Pres./CEO
Founded: 1985. **Staff:** 5. **Budget:** $400,000. **Nonmembership. Local.** Serves the three county regions of Northern Madison, Jersey and Calhoun Counties all around Alton. Builds public awareness of the many tourism assets in the area and encourage new tourist to visit the region. **Libraries: Type:** open to the public. **Holdings:** periodicals. **Subjects:** tourism. **Formerly:** (2003) Greater/Alton Twin Rivers Convention and Visitors Bureau. **Publications:** *The Official All Around Alton Visitors Guide*, annual. Magazine. Contains information about Alton. **Price:** free. **Circulation:** 100,000. **Advertising:** accepted.

38 ■ American Hellenic Educational Progressive Association - Alton, Chapter 304
c/o John Siampos, Pres.
234 Alben St.
Alton, IL 62002
Ph: (618)465-8416
URL: http://www.ahepafamily.org/d13
Contact: John Siampos, Pres.
Local. Affiliated With: American Hellenic Educational Progressive Association.

39 ■ American Legion, Allen-Bevnue Post 354
PO Box 8072
Alton, IL 62002
Ph: (309)663-0361
Fax: (309)663-5783
URL: National Affiliate–www.legion.org
Local. Affiliated With: American Legion.

40 ■ American Legion, Alton Post 126
600 George St.
Alton, IL 62002
Ph: (618)462-2644
Fax: (309)663-5783
URL: National Affiliate–www.legion.org
Local. Affiliated With: American Legion.

41 ■ American Red Cross, Southwestern Illinois Chapter
1639 Main St.
Alton, IL 62002
Ph: (618)465-7704
E-mail: sicarc@sbcglobal.net
URL: http://swillinois.redcross.org
Regional.

42 ■ Great Rivers Land Preservation Association
PO Box 821
Alton, IL 62002
Ph: (618)467-2265
Fax: (618)466-6167
E-mail: tcwp@direcway.com
URL: http://www.greatriverslandtrust.com
Contact: Alan Ringhausen, Exec.Dir.
Local.

43 ■ Police and Firemen's Insurance Association - Alton Fire Department
c/o Donald E. Dugan
2318 Birch St.
Alton, IL 62002-4415
Ph: (618)462-6692
URL: National Affiliate–www.pfia.net
Contact: Donald E. Dugan, Contact
Local. Affiliated With: Police and Firemen's Insurance Association.

44 ■ Sierra Club - Illinois Chapter - Piasa Palisades Group
223 Market St.
Alton, IL 62002
Ph: (618)462-6802
Fax: (618)462-0282
E-mail: cfavilla@ezl.com
URL: http://illinois.sierraclub.org/piasapalisades
Contact: Christine Favilla, Contact
State.

Altona

45 ■ American Legion, Ekstedt-Hurr Post 390
1567 Knox Hwy. 4
Altona, IL 61414
Ph: (309)484-2105
Fax: (309)663-5783
URL: National Affiliate–www.legion.org
Local. Affiliated With: American Legion.

46 ■ Galesburg Philatelic Society
c/o Mr. David Nestander
101 S Depot St.
Altona, IL 61414
E-mail: davosales@winco.net
URL: National Affiliate–www.stamps.org
Contact: Mr. David Nestander, Contact
Local. Affiliated With: American Philatelic Society.

Alvin

47 ■ Korean War Veterans Association, Robert Wurtsbaugh Chapter
c/o David Thornsbrough
28869 N 1800 E Rd.
Alvin, IL 61811
Ph: (217)759-7321
E-mail: thorsheep2@aol.com
URL: National Affiliate–www.kwva.org
Contact: David Thornsbrough, Contact
Local. Affiliated With: Korean War Veterans Association.

Amboy

48 ■ Amboy Area Chamber of Commerce
PO Box 163
Amboy, IL 61310
Ph: (815)857-3814 (815)849-5176
Contact: Julie Kessel Jr., Pres.
Local.

49 ■ American Legion, Poths-Lavelle Post 453
224 N Jones St.
Amboy, IL 61310
Ph: (309)663-0361
Fax: (309)663-5783
URL: National Affiliate–www.legion.org
Local. Affiliated With: American Legion.

Andover

50 ■ American Legion, Andover Post 465
5th Elm St.
Andover, IL 61233
Ph: (309)663-0361
Fax: (309)663-5783
URL: National Affiliate–www.legion.org
Local. Affiliated With: American Legion.

Anna

51 ■ American Legion, Illinois Post 344
c/o Townsend F. Dodd
PO Box 24
Anna, IL 62906
Ph: (618)833-6210
Fax: (309)663-5783
URL: National Affiliate–www.legion.org
Contact: Townsend F. Dodd, Contact
Local. Affiliated With: American Legion.

52 ■ Southernmost Illinois Tourism Bureau (SITB)
PO Box 378
Anna, IL 62906
Ph: (618)833-9928
Fax: (618)833-9924
Free: (800)248-4373
E-mail: info@southernmostillinois.com
URL: http://www.southernmostillinois.com
Contact: Carol Hoffman, Sales Mgr.
Local. Seeks to promote the six counties in the southernmost tip of Illinois: Union, Johnson, Pope, Massac, Pulaski, and Alexander.

53 ■ Union County Chamber of Commerce (UCCC)
330 S Main St.
Anna, IL 62906
Ph: (618)833-6311
Fax: (618)833-1903
E-mail: uccc@shawneelink.net
URL: http://www.shawneeheartland.com
Contact: Jeannie Toler, Exec.Dir.
Founded: 1906. **Members:** 126. **Local.** Promotes business and community development in Union County, IL. Sponsors community Christmas decorations and Colorfest. **Formerly:** Anna-Jonesboro Area Chamber of Commerce. **Publications:** *Chamber Notes*, quarterly. Newsletter. Alternate Formats: online. **Conventions/Meetings:** annual meeting.

Annawan

54 ■ American Legion, Mapes-Cathelyn Post 309
PO Box 382
Annawan, IL 61234
Ph: (309)663-0361
Fax: (309)663-5783
URL: National Affiliate–www.legion.org
Local. Affiliated With: American Legion.

Antioch

55 ■ American Legion, Antioch Post 748
PO Box 465
Antioch, IL 60002
Ph: (708)395-9843
Fax: (309)663-5783
URL: National Affiliate–www.legion.org
Local. Affiliated With: American Legion.

56 ■ Antioch Chamber of Commerce and Industry (ACCI)
882 Main St.
Antioch, IL 60002
Ph: (847)395-2233
Fax: (847)395-8954
URL: http://www.antiochchamber.org
Members: 150. **Local.** Promotes business and community development in Antioch, IL. Sponsors art and craft fair, Christmas program, Easter Program, and Taste of Antioch. **Publications:** Newsletter, monthly. **Advertising:** accepted. Alternate Formats: online. **Conventions/Meetings:** semiannual Antioch Arts and Craft Faire - show, features handcrafts (exhibits) - every summer and fall, Antioch, IL • monthly meeting • quarterly Mixer - meeting, with speaker.

57 ■ Antioch Woman's Club
PO Box 282
Antioch, IL 60002
E-mail: golfnutsns@earthlink.net
URL: http://www.antiochwomansclub.org
Contact: Nancy Sorensen, Pres.
Local.

58 ■ Sweet Adelines International, Westosha Lakes Chorus
Antioch VFW Hall
75 North Ave.
Antioch, IL 60002-2491
E-mail: baripol@yahoo.com
URL: http://www.westoshalakes.org
Contact: Polly Merrill, Dir.
Local. Advances the musical art form of barbershop harmony through education and performances. Provides education, training and coaching in the development of women's four-part barbershop harmony. **Affiliated With:** Sweet Adelines International.

Apple River

59 ■ American Legion, Albert-Shelby Post 298
114 W Railroad St.
Apple River, IL 61001
Ph: (815)594-2343
Fax: (309)663-5783
URL: National Affiliate–www.legion.org
Local. **Affiliated With:** American Legion.

Arcola

60 ■ American Legion, Arcola Post 639
c/o C.W. Chancellor
421 N Elm St.
Arcola, IL 61910
Ph: (309)663-0361
Fax: (309)663-5783
URL: National Affiliate–www.legion.org
Contact: C.W. Chancellor, Contact
Local. **Affiliated With:** American Legion.

61 ■ Arcola Chamber of Commerce
PO Box 274
Arcola, IL 61910
Ph: (217)268-4530
Free: (800)336-5456
URL: http://www.arcola-il.org
Contact: Susan Foster, Exec.Dir.
Local. Promotes business and community development in Arcola, IL area.

Arenzville

62 ■ American Legion, Arenzville Post 604
313 W Frederick St.
Arenzville, IL 62611
Ph: (217)997-5958
Fax: (309)663-5783
URL: National Affiliate–www.legion.org
Local. **Affiliated With:** American Legion.

Arlington Heights

63 ■ American Legion, Merle Guild Post 208
121 N Douglas Ave.
Arlington Heights, IL 60006
Ph: (708)398-9713
Fax: (309)663-5783
URL: National Affiliate–www.legion.org
Local. **Affiliated With:** American Legion.

64 ■ American Society of Mechanical Engineers, Chicago Section
c/o A. Thomas Peterson
807 W Catino St.
Arlington Heights, IL 60005-2315
Ph: (708)371-3674
Fax: (708)371-2926
E-mail: petersona3@asme.org
URL: http://sections.asme.org/chicago
Contact: Allan R. Kishpaugh PE, Chm.
Local. Promotes the art, science and practice of Mechanical Engineering and allied arts and sciences. Encourages original research and fosters engineering education. Promotes the technical and societal contribution of engineers. **Affiliated With:** American Society of Mechanical Engineers.

65 ■ Arlington Heights Chamber of Commerce (AHCC)
311 S Arlington Heights Rd., Ste.20
Arlington Heights, IL 60005
Ph: (847)253-1703
Fax: (847)253-9133
E-mail: info@arlingtonhtschamber.com
URL: http://www.arlingtonhtschamber.com
Contact: Jon S. Ridler, Exec.Dir.
Founded: 1946. **Members:** 500. **Membership Dues:** retail/commercial/industrial/professional and service firm, $194-$1,850 (annual) • home-based business, $194 (annual) • financial institution (per million in assets), $30 (annual) • hotel/motel (per room), $1 (annual) • utility, $600 (annual) • hospital/convalescent and nursing home (per bed), $1 (annual) • apartment/condo/retirement community (per unit), $1 (annual) • government/school district, $250 (annual) • religious/charitable organization/associate/civic club/service organization, $165 (annual). **Staff:** 3. **Local**. Promotes business and community development in Arlington Heights, IL. **Committees:** Ambassador; Events and Programs; Finance; Golf Outing and Dinner; Government Affairs; Marketing; Membership. **Councils:** Professional Women's. **Publications:** Directory, periodic • Newsletter, monthly. **Advertising:** accepted. Alternate Formats: online. **Conventions/Meetings:** monthly meeting.

66 ■ Arlington Heights Lions Club
PO Box 513
Arlington Heights, IL 60006-0513
E-mail: helen_anderson@acordia.com
URL: http://www.ahlionsclub.org
Contact: Helen Anderson, Pres.
Local. **Affiliated With:** Lions Clubs International.

67 ■ Chicago-North Romance Writers of America
PO Box 6
Arlington Heights, IL 60006-0006
E-mail: info@chicagonorthrwa.org
URL: http://www.chicagonorthrwa.org
Contact: Simone Elkeles, Pres.
Local. Works to provide networking and support to individuals seriously pursuing a career in romance fiction. Helps writers become published and established in their writing field. **Affiliated With:** Romance Writers of America.

68 ■ Chicago Radiological Society (CRS)
c/o Carl L. Kalbhen, MD, Pres.
Radiology Dept.
Northwest Community Hosp.
800 W Central Rd.
Arlington Heights, IL 60005
Ph: (847)618-5850
Fax: (847)617-5909
E-mail: info@chi-rad-soc.org
URL: http://www.chi-rad-soc.org
Contact: Carl L. Kalbhen MD, Pres.
Local. Promotes the value of radiology, radiation oncology, nuclear medicine, medical physics and other related fields. Seeks to improve the quality of patient care and influence the socio-economics of the practice of radiology. Provides continuing education for radiology and allied health professionals. **Affiliated With:** American College of Radiology.

69 ■ Clinical Laboratory Management Association, Chicago Chapter
c/o Corrine Cagney, Pres.
800 W Central Rd.
Arlington Heights, IL 60005
Ph: (847)618-6890
Fax: (847)618-6889
E-mail: ccagney@nch.org
URL: http://www.cclma.org
Contact: Corrine Cagney, Pres.
Local. Provides clinical laboratory leaders with resources to balance science and technology with the art of management. Promotes efficient, productive, and high quality operations. Enhances the professional, managerial and leadership skills of members. **Affiliated With:** Clinical Laboratory Management Association.

70 ■ Eastland Disaster Historical Society
c/o Ted Wachholz
PO Box 2013
Arlington Heights, IL 60006-2013
Fax: (877)865-6295
Free: (877)865-6295
E-mail: info@eastlanddisaster.org
URL: http://www.eastlanddisaster.org
Local.

71 ■ Illinois Environmental Health Association - North Chapter
33 S Arlington Heights Rd.
Arlington Heights, IL 60005
Ph: (847)202-6612
Fax: (847)359-9040
E-mail: abdullahk@cityrm.org
URL: http://www.ieha.us
Contact: Kerry Abdullah, Dir.
Local. Advances the environmental health and protection profession. Provides educational and training opportunities for members. Works to establish standards of competence and ethics for the profession. **Affiliated With:** National Environmental Health Association.

72 ■ National Audubon Society- Prairie Woods
PO Box 1065
Arlington Heights, IL 60006
Ph: (847)514-4977
E-mail: ezolaezola@hotmail.com
URL: http://www.prairiewoodsaudubon.org/index.html
Contact: Nathan Mitchell, Pres.
Local.

73 ■ National Organization for Women - Northwest Suburban (Chicago)
PO Box 784
Arlington Heights, IL 60006
Ph: (847)604-1913
E-mail: contact@nwsubnow.org
URL: http://www.nwsubnow.org
Local. **Affiliated With:** National Organization for Women.

74 ■ North American Versatile Hunting Dog Association (NAVHDA)
PO Box 520
Arlington Heights, IL 60006
Ph: (847)253-6488
Fax: (847)255-5987
E-mail: navoffice@aol.com
URL: http://navhda.org
Contact: Richard T. St. Amant, Pres.
Members: 40. **Regional**. **Publications:** *Versatile Hunting Dog*, monthly. Magazine. **Price:** included in membership dues. **Circulation:** 40. **Advertising:** accepted.

75 ■ North West Sailing Association (NWSA)
PO Box 921
Arlington Heights, IL 60006
E-mail: membership@nwsail.com
URL: http://www.nwsail.com
Contact: Mike Kenny, Commodore
Local.

76 ■ Prairie Brass Band Association
PO Box 182
Arlington Heights, IL 60006-0182
Ph: (847)523-4467
E-mail: info@prairiebrass.org
URL: http://www.prairiebrass.org
Contact: Clark Niermeyer, Contact
Founded: 1997. **Members:** 35. **Membership Dues:** voluntary, $50 (annual). **Staff:** 1. **Budget:** $20,000. **Local Groups:** 1. **Local**. Part-time brass musicians in the Chicago, IL area interested in playing British brass band music on traditional brass band instruments. Sponsors performances and competitions. **Affiliated With:** North American Brass Band Association. **Publications:** *Prairie Brass Press*, 3/year. Newsletter. Contains news about the band and concert announcements. **Price:** free. **Circulation:** 350. **Advertising:** accepted. Alternate Formats: online; CD-ROM. **Conventions/Meetings:** weekly Rehearsal - meeting.

77 ■ Prairie Woods Audubon Society
c/o Nathan Mitchell, Pres.
PO Box 1065
Arlington Heights, IL 60006
Ph: (847)622-5321
E-mail: ezolaezola@hotmail.com
URL: http://prairiewoodsaudubon.org/
Local. Affiliated With: National Audubon Society.

78 ■ Professional Photographers of America of Northern Illinois (PPANI)
c/o Joseph A. Weber, Exec.Sec.
303 S Donald Ave.
Arlington Heights, IL 60004-6850
Ph: (847)670-9834
Fax: (847)670-9854
E-mail: info@ppani.org
URL: http://www.ppani.org
Contact: Joseph A. Weber, Exec.Sec.
Founded: 1954. **Members:** 350. **Membership Dues:** active voting, $65 (annual) • colleague non-PPA, $65 (annual) • sustaining, $85 (annual). **Local Groups:** 1. **Local**. Professional society of portrait, commercial, industrial, and specialized photographers. Conducts programs; sponsors image competitions. **Libraries: Type:** not open to the public. **Holdings:** video recordings. **Awards:** Print Competition Awards. **Type:** recognition • **Type:** scholarship. **Recipient:** for members. **Affiliated With:** Professional Photographers of America. **Publications:** *Northern Hi-Lites*, monthly. Magazine. Contains technical, business articles and association news. **Price:** $25.00/year. **Advertising:** accepted • Membership Directory, annual. **Price:** included in membership dues. **Conventions/Meetings:** monthly meeting - always second Wednesday; except March, September and December • annual trade show - always in September.

79 ■ Read To Learn
c/o Forest View Ed Center
2121 S Goebbert Rd
Arlington Heights, IL 60005
Ph: (847)718-7724 (847)718-7720
Fax: (847)718-7927
E-mail: esuffrit@d214.org
URL: http://www.readtolearn.org
Contact: Dr. Erica Suffritz PhD, Prog.Coor.
Founded: 1985. **Members:** 800. **Membership Dues:** adult student, $10 (periodic). **Staff:** 5. **Budget:** $70,000. **Languages:** English, Polish, Spanish. **Local**. Volunteer-based adult literacy program. Trained volunteers work one-to-one with adult students to improve reading abilities and basic skills; conversation classes available for advanced non-native English speakers. **Libraries: Type:** reference. **Holdings:** 700. **Subjects:** lifeskills, english vocabulary and comprehension, miscellaneous. **Computer Services:** Information services, literacy teaching. **Affiliated With:** ProLiteracy Worldwide. **Formerly:** (2004) Read To Learn for a Brighter Future. **Publications:** *Tutor Talk*, semiannual. Newsletter. Contains information for volunteer tutors of the association. **Price:** free. **Circulation:** 350.

80 ■ Realtor Association of NorthWest Chicagoland (RANWC)
1114 S Arlington Heights Rd.
Arlington Heights, IL 60004
Ph: (847)506-5002 (847)506-5050
Fax: (847)253-8145
E-mail: info@ranwc.com
URL: http://www.nwar.com
Contact: Peggy Kayser CAE, CEO
Local.

81 ■ Reserve Officers Association - Department of Illinois, O'Hare Chapter 61
c/o Maj. Ronald Landry, Sec.
1014 W Cedar Ln.
Arlington Heights, IL 60005
Ph: (847)398-2613
URL: http://www.ilroa.org
Contact: Col. James Chrysokos, Pres.
Local. Promotes and supports the development and execution of a military policy for the United States. Provides professional development seminars, workshops and programs for its members. **Affiliated With:** Reserve Officers Association of the United States.

82 ■ RSVP of Northern Cook and Northern Dupage Counties
c/o Mary Fitzgibbons, Dir.
2121 S Goebbert Rd.
Arlington Heights, IL 60005-1814
Ph: (847)228-1006
Fax: (847)228-1327
E-mail: rsvp@volunteerinfo.net
URL: http://www.volunteerinfo.net
Contact: Mary Fitzgibbons, Dir.
Local. Affiliated With: Retired and Senior Volunteer Program.

83 ■ Sons of Norway, Skjold Lodge 5-100
c/o Gregg LeDuc, Pres.
PO Box 1364
Arlington Heights, IL 60006-1364
Ph: (847)835-0709
E-mail: postmaster@skjoldlodge.com
URL: http://www.skjoldlodge.com
Contact: Gregg LeDuc, Pres.
Local. Affiliated With: Sons of Norway.

Armington

84 ■ American Legion, Taylor-Eckhardt Post 913
PO Box 49
Armington, IL 61721
Ph: (309)663-0361
Fax: (309)663-5783
URL: National Affiliate–www.legion.org
Local. Affiliated With: American Legion.

Aroma Park

85 ■ American Legion, Aroma Park Post 1019
PO Box 51
Aroma Park, IL 60910
Ph: (309)663-0361
Fax: (309)663-5783
URL: National Affiliate–www.legion.org
Local. Affiliated With: American Legion.

Arrowsmith

86 ■ American Legion, Witt-Webber-Carrell Post 617
13526 N, 3200 E Rd.
Arrowsmith, IL 61722
Ph: (309)727-1120
Fax: (309)663-5783
URL: National Affiliate–www.legion.org
Local. Affiliated With: American Legion.

Arthur

87 ■ American Legion, Arthur Post 479
PO Box 236
Arthur, IL 61911
Ph: (217)543-2017
Fax: (309)663-5783
URL: National Affiliate–www.legion.org
Local. Affiliated With: American Legion.

88 ■ Arthur Association of Commerce
106 E Progress St.
Arthur, IL 61911
Ph: (217)543-2242
Fax: (217)543-2004
Free: (800)722-6474
E-mail: tourismarthur@consolidated.net
URL: http://www.illinoisamishcountry.com
Contact: Jim Jurgens, Pres.
Local. Promotes business and community development in Arthur, IL area. **Additional Websites:** http://www.arthuril.com.

Ashkum

89 ■ American Legion, Peters Post 643
PO Box 87
Ashkum, IL 60911
Ph: (309)663-0361
Fax: (309)663-5783
URL: National Affiliate–www.legion.org
Local. Affiliated With: American Legion.

Ashland

90 ■ American Legion, Illinois Post 498
c/o George H. Pettit
504 W Franklin St., No. 219FR1
Ashland, IL 62612
Ph: (217)476-3997
Fax: (309)663-5783
URL: National Affiliate–www.legion.org
Contact: George H. Pettit, Contact
Local. Affiliated With: American Legion.

Ashley

91 ■ Military Vehicle Collectors of Southern Illinois
c/o John LaBusier, Sr., Pres.
22540 State Rte. 14
Ashley, IL 62808
Ph: (618)493-6115
E-mail: labusier@yahoo.com
URL: National Affiliate–www.mvpa.org
Contact: John LaBusier Sr., Pres.
Local. Affiliated With: Military Vehicle Preservation Association.

Ashton

92 ■ American Legion, Ashton Post 345
704 N First St.
Ashton, IL 61006
Ph: (815)453-2247
Fax: (309)663-5783
URL: National Affiliate–www.legion.org
Local. Affiliated With: American Legion.

93 ■ American Truck Historical Society, Northwest Illinois Chapter
c/o Warren Johnson
7143 E Flagg Rd.
Ashton, IL 61006
Ph: (815)453-2482
URL: National Affiliate–www.aths.org
Contact: Warren Johnson, Contact
Local.

Assumption

94 ■ American Legion, Illinois Post 284
c/o Neil E. Hillabrant
319 W 3rd South St.
Assumption, IL 62510
Ph: (217)226-4220
Fax: (309)663-5783
URL: National Affiliate–www.legion.org
Contact: Neil E. Hillabrant, Contact
Local. Affiliated With: American Legion.

Astoria

95 ■ American Legion, Astoria Post 25
PO Box 297
Astoria, IL 61501
Ph: (309)663-0361
Fax: (309)663-5783
URL: National Affiliate–www.legion.org
Local. Affiliated With: American Legion.

96 ■ Astoria Lions Club
213 S Green St.
Box 525
Astoria, IL 61501
Ph: (309)329-2168
URL: http://frogy40.tripod.com/lions/astorialions.html
Local. Affiliated With: Lions Clubs International.

Athens

97 ■ American Legion, Illinois Post 129
c/o James C. Wade
PO Box 42
Athens, IL 62613
Ph: (309)663-0361
Fax: (309)663-5783
URL: National Affiliate–www.legion.org
Contact: James C. Wade, Contact
Local. Affiliated With: American Legion.

98 ■ Friends of the Athens Municipal Library
PO Box 168
Athens, IL 62613-0168
Ph: (217)636-8047
Fax: (217)636-8763
E-mail: info@athens.lib.il.us
URL: http://www.athens.lib.il.us
Contact: Bev Hoffman, Pres.
Local.

Atkinson

99 ■ American Legion, Charles De Crane Post 724
308 W Henry St., No. 441
Atkinson, IL 61235
Ph: (309)936-7593
Fax: (309)663-5783
URL: National Affiliate–www.legion.org
Local. Affiliated With: American Legion.

Atlanta

100 ■ American Legion, Gresham-Crutchley Post 341
106 6th St.
Atlanta, IL 61723
Ph: (309)663-0361
Fax: (309)663-5783
URL: National Affiliate–www.legion.org
Local. Affiliated With: American Legion.

Atwood

101 ■ American Legion, James Reeder Post 770
PO Box 366
Atwood, IL 61913
Ph: (309)663-0361
Fax: (309)663-5783
URL: National Affiliate–www.legion.org
Local. Affiliated With: American Legion.

Auburn

102 ■ American Legion, Auburn Post 277
412 W Adams St.
Auburn, IL 62615
Ph: (217)438-3433
Fax: (309)663-5783
URL: National Affiliate–www.legion.org
Local. Affiliated With: American Legion.

103 ■ Central Illinois Golf Course Superintendents Association (CIGCSA)
c/o Lisa Mulvey, Exec.Sec.
9 Isabelle Dr.
Auburn, IL 62615
Ph: (217)438-6496
Fax: (217)438-6496
URL: http://www.ci-gcsa.com
Contact: Jeff Boldig, Pres.
Founded: 1954. **Local.** Represents the interests of golf course superintendents. Advances members' profession for career success. Enhances the enjoyment, growth and vitality in the game of golf. Educates members concerning efficient and economical management of golf courses. **Affiliated With:** Golf Course Superintendents Association of America.

104 ■ Illinois Quarter Horse Association, District No. 8
c/o John Boxell, Dir.
16215 Briarwood Trace
Auburn, IL 62615-9534
Ph: (217)438-9145
E-mail: zmbg@richlandranch.com
URL: http://www.ilqha.com
Contact: John Boxell, Dir.
Local. Affiliated With: American Quarter Horse Association.

105 ■ Reserve Officers Association - Department of Illinois, Springfield Chapter 39
c/o LTC Hugh W. Shown, Pres.
120 S 4th St.
Auburn, IL 62615-1452
Ph: (217)438-6579
E-mail: hshown@dickey-john.com
URL: http://www.ilroa.org
Contact: LTC Hugh W. Shown, Pres.
Local. Promotes and supports the development and execution of a military policy for the United States. Provides professional development seminars, workshops and programs for its members. **Affiliated With:** Reserve Officers Association of the United States.

Aurora

106 ■ American Brush Manufacturers Association (ABMA)
c/o David C. Parr, Exec.Dir.
2111 W Plum St., Ste.274
Aurora, IL 60506
Ph: (630)631-5217
Fax: (630)897-9140
E-mail: info@abma.org
URL: http://www.abma.org
Contact: David C. Parr, Exec.Dir.
Local.

107 ■ American Legion, Illinois Post 1105
683 Laurel Dr. F
Aurora, IL 60506
Ph: (708)892-8075
Fax: (309)663-5783
URL: National Affiliate–www.legion.org
Contact: Dorothy V. Gurbal, Financial Officer
Local. Affiliated With: American Legion.

108 ■ American Legion, Roosevelt-Aurora Post 84
PO Box 4784
Aurora, IL 60507
Ph: (309)663-0361
Fax: (309)663-5783
URL: National Affiliate–www.legion.org
Local. Affiliated With: American Legion.

109 ■ American Purchasing Society of Illinois
PO Box 256
Aurora, IL 60506
Ph: (630)859-0250
Fax: (630)859-0270
E-mail: support@american-purchasing.com
URL: http://www.american-purchasing.com
Founded: 1969. **Members:** 4,000. **Membership Dues:** individual, $119 (annual) • company, $235 (annual). **Budget:** $500,000. **State.** Seeks to improve and advance the purchasing profession and certifies qualified professional buyers and purchasing managers. **Affiliated With:** American Purchasing Society. **Publications:** *Benchmarking Report of Purchasing Practices*, annual • *Professional Purchasing*, monthly. Newsletter • *Salary Report of Purchasing Occupations*, annual. **Conventions/Meetings:** periodic seminar.

110 ■ Association for Individual Development of Aurora, IL (AID)
c/o Dave Peterson
309 W New Indian Trail Ct.
Aurora, IL 60506
Ph: (630)966-4000
E-mail: dpeterson@the-association.org
URL: http://www.the-association.org
Local. Telecommunication Services: teletype, (630)884-5063.

111 ■ Aurora Area Convention and Tourism Council (AACVB)
43 W Galena Blvd.
Aurora, IL 60506
Ph: (630)897-5581
Fax: (630)897-5589
Free: (800)477-4369
E-mail: sue@enjoyaurora.com
URL: http://www.enjoyaurora.com
Contact: Sue Vos, Exec.Dir.
Founded: 1987. **Local.**

112 ■ Aurora Community Study Circles
c/o Study Circles
501 Coll. Ave., No. 421-23
Aurora, IL 60505-3561
Ph: (630)898-7515
Fax: (630)898-7525
E-mail: admin@acstudycircles.org
URL: http://auroracommunitystudycircles.org
Contact: Mary Jane Hollis, Exec.Dir.
Founded: 1995. **Staff:** 3. **Budget:** $50,000. **Nonmembership. Local.** Seeks to build a stronger community in Aurora, IL, by expanding the participation of citizens, diverse by race, ethnicity, gender, age, and social economic levels, in dialogue that will foster greater understanding, cooperation, and community participation. Committed to fostering racial justice and working, through positive conflict resolution models, towards solving the local community's social and economic problems. **Publications:** *Study Circle Sun*, quarterly. Newsletter.

113 ■ Aurora Tri-County Association of Realtors
323 W Galena Blvd.
Aurora, IL 60506
Ph: (630)859-1300
Fax: (630)859-1308
E-mail: evpatcar@ameritech.net
URL: National Affiliate–www.realtor.org
Contact: Kristine Hettinger, Exec. Officer
Local. Strives to develop real estate business practices. Advocates the right to own, use and transfer real property. Provides a facility for professional development, research and exchange of information among members and to the general public. **Affiliated With:** National Association of Realtors.

114 ■ Aurora University Biology Club
347 S Gladstone Ave.
Aurora, IL 60506
Ph: (630)892-6431
Fax: (630)844-5535
Free: (800)742-5281
URL: http://www.aurora.edu
Contact: Craig Zimmerman, Prof. of Biology
Local.

115 ■ Chemical Coaters Association International, Northern Illinois
2470 Bradford Dr.
Aurora, IL 60506
Ph: (630)264-7913
Fax: (630)264-7914
E-mail: jsudges@midwestfinishing.com
URL: National Affiliate–www.ccaiweb.com
Contact: John Sudges, Pres.
Local. Provides information and training on surface coating technologies. Raises the standards of finishing operations through educational meetings and seminars, training manuals, certification programs, and outreach programs with colleges and universities. **Affiliated With:** Chemical Coaters Association International.

116 ■ Fox Valley United Way
40 W Downer Pl.
Aurora, IL 60506
Ph: (630)896-4636
Fax: (630)896-4681
E-mail: vstull@ameritech.net
URL: http://www.unitedwayaa.org
Contact: Vicki Stull, Exec.Dir.
Local. Affiliated With: United Way of America.

117 ■ Girl Scouts - Fox Valley Council
200 New Bond St.
Aurora, IL 60506
Ph: (630)897-1565
Fax: (630)466-7018
E-mail: fvgsc@fvgsc.org
URL: http://www.fvgsc.org
Local. Young girls and adult volunteers, corporate, government and individual supporters. Strives to develop potential and leadership skills among its members. Conducts trainings, educational programs and outdoor activities.

118 ■ Greater Aurora Chamber of Commerce (GACC)
43 W Galena Blvd.
Aurora, IL 60506
Ph: (630)897-9214
Fax: (630)897-7002
E-mail: jhenning@aurora-il.org
URL: http://www.aurorachamber.com
Contact: Joseph Henning, Exec.Dir.
Founded: 1920. **Members:** 1,400. **Local**. Promotes business and community development in the Aurora, IL area. **Publications:** Directory, semiannual. Contains information on members businesses. • Newsletter, monthly.

119 ■ Greater Chicago American Orff-Schulwerk Association (GCAOSA)
c/o Janet Tindell
212 Heather Glen Dr.
Aurora, IL 60504
E-mail: jlperneym@aol.com
URL: http://www.gcaosa.org
Contact: Linda Perney, Pres.
Local. Provides a forum for the continued growth and development of Orff Schulwerk. Promotes the value and use of Orff Schulwerk.

120 ■ Illinois Chapter of National Association of Tax Professionals
c/o Barry J. Bellott, Dir.
2600 Beverly Ste.108
Aurora, IL 60504
Ph: (630)236-1750
Fax: (630)236-1664
E-mail: bbellott@sbcglobal.net
URL: National Affiliate–www.natptax.com
Contact: Leonard T. Racine, Pres.
State. Affiliated With: National Association of Tax Professionals.

121 ■ Illinois Science Teachers Association
c/o Raymond Dagenais, Pres.
Illinois Math and Sci. Acad.
1500 W Sullivan Rd.
Aurora, IL 60506-1000
Ph: (630)907-5092
E-mail: rjdag@imsa.edu
URL: http://www.ista-il.org
Contact: Raymond Dagenais, Pres.
State. Promotes excellence and innovation in science teaching and learning for all. Serves as the voice for excellence and innovation in science teaching and learning, curriculum and instruction, and assessment. Promotes interest and support for science education. **Affiliated With:** National Science Teachers Association.

122 ■ Kickers Soccer Club
c/o Mark Pickett, Pres.
2112 W Galena Blvd., Ste.8, PMB 296
Aurora, IL 60506
Ph: (630)375-7459
E-mail: admin@kickerssoccerclub.org
URL: http://kickerssoccerclub.org
Contact: Mark Pickett, Pres.
Members: 200. **Staff:** 1. **Local**. Fields boys' and girls' teams in competitive traveling soccer leagues in Northern Illinois.

123 ■ League of Illinois Bicyclists (LIB)
c/o Ed Barsotti, Exec.Dir.
2550 Cheshire Dr.
Aurora, IL 60504
Ph: (630)978-0583
E-mail: lib@bikelib.org
URL: http://www.bikelib.org
Contact: Ed Barsotti, Exec.Dir.
State. Affiliated With: International Mountain Bicycling Association. **Formerly:** (2000) Folks on Spokes.

124 ■ National Organization of Black Law Enforcement Executives, Northern Illinois Chapter (NOBLE)
c/o Willie Mayes, Sr., Pres.
PO Box 1321
Aurora, IL 60507
E-mail: noble@nic-noble.org
URL: http://www.nic-noble.org
Contact: Willie Mayes Sr., Pres.
Founded: 1999. **Membership Dues:** individual, $25 (annual). **Regional. Affiliated With:** National Organization of Black Law Enforcement Executives.

125 ■ National Technological Honor Society - East Aurora High School - Illinois (EAHS)
500 Tomcat Ln.
Aurora, IL 60505
Ph: (630)299-8000 (630)299-8135
Fax: (630)299-8004
E-mail: mgonzalez@d131.org
Contact: Marin Gonzalez, Contact
Local.

126 ■ National Technological Honor Society - West Aurora High School - Illinois
1201 W New York St.
Aurora, IL 60506
Ph: (630)301-5600
URL: http://www.sd129.org
Contact: LuAnne Kelsey, Contact
Local.

127 ■ PFLAG Aurora/Fox Valley
PO Box 1133
Aurora, IL 60507
Ph: (815)886-6951
E-mail: jvlarson@aol.com
URL: National Affiliate–www.pflag.org
Local. Affiliated With: Parents, Families, and Friends of Lesbians and Gays.

128 ■ Psi Chi, National Honor Society in Psychology - Aurora University
c/o Dept. of Psychology
347 S Gladstone Ave.
Aurora, IL 60506
Ph: (630)844-6531 (630)844-6517
Fax: (630)844-5242
E-mail: jgalezew@aurora.edu
URL: National Affiliate–www.psichi.org
Local. Affiliated With: Psi Chi, National Honor Society in Psychology.

129 ■ Quad County Urban League
808 E Galena, Ste.B
Aurora, IL 60505
Ph: (630)851-2203
E-mail: info@qcul.org
URL: National Affiliate–www.nul.org
Contact: Theodia Gillespie, Pres.
Founded: 1975. **Local**. Multi-racial community-based organization seeking to secure equal opportunities for all disadvantaged persons and minorities. **Publications:** none. **Convention/Meeting:** none. **Affiliated With:** National Urban League.

130 ■ SCORE Fox Valley
1444 N Farnsworth Ave., Rm. 504
Aurora, IL 60505
Ph: (630)692-1162 (630)942-3775
Fax: (630)852-3127
E-mail: mckaydonald@cs.com
URL: http://www.scorefoxvalley.org
Contact: Don McKay, Chm.
Local. Strives for the formation, growth and success of small businesses. Provides professional guidance and information to maximize the success of existing and emerging small businesses. Promotes entrepreneur education in Fox Valley area, Illinois. **Affiliated With:** SCORE.

131 ■ Sons of Norway, Polar Star Lodge 5-472
c/o Donald D. Danielson, Pres.
3130 Cambria Ct.
Aurora, IL 60504-5751
Ph: (630)299-3661
E-mail: ddlcdan@aol.com
URL: National Affiliate–www.sofn.com
Contact: Donald D. Danielson, Pres.
Local. Affiliated With: Sons of Norway.

132 ■ United Association of Journeymen and Apprentices of the Plumbing and Pipe Fitting Industry of the United States and Canada - Local Union 501
1295 Butterfield Rd.
Aurora, IL 60504-8879
Ph: (630)978-4600
Fax: (630)978-4616
E-mail: benefitinfo@nibf501.org
URL: http://www.nibf501.org
Contact: Robert E. Niksa, Admin.Mgr.
Members: 1,942. **Local. Affiliated With:** United Association of Journeymen and Apprentices of the Plumbing, Pipe Fitting, Sprinkler Fitting Industry of the U.S. and Canada.

133 ■ United States Naval Sea Cadet Corps - Aurora Division
411 Bangs St.
Aurora, IL 60505-4821
Ph: (630)898-5297
E-mail: c.o.@auroraseacadets.org
URL: http://www.auroraseacadets.org
Contact: LTJG Jeffrey Dooley, Commanding Officer
Local. Works to instill good citizenship and patriotism in youth. Encourages qualities such as personal neatness, loyalty, obedience, dependability, and responsibility to others. Offers courses in physical fitness and military drill, first aid, water safety, basic seamanship, and naval history and traditions. **Affiliated With:** Naval Sea Cadet Corps.

134 ■ USA Weightlifting - Aurora Weightlifting Club
c/o Thomas A. Kraus
527 California Ave.
Aurora, IL 60506
Ph: (630)897-6738
E-mail: thomas.kraus@sbcglobal.net
URL: National Affiliate–www.usaweightlifting.org
Contact: Thomas A. Kraus, Contact
Local. **Affiliated With:** USA Weightlifting.

135 ■ USA Weightlifting - Fox Valley
c/o Martin Razo
30 S Stolp Ave., Ste.409
Aurora, IL 60506
Ph: (630)721-5116 (630)553-0672
Fax: (630)553-0672
URL: National Affiliate–www.usaweightlifting.org
Contact: Martin Razo, Contact
Local. **Affiliated With:** USA Weightlifting.

Aviston

136 ■ American Legion, Mondt-Lampe Post 1239
PO Box 123
Aviston, IL 62216
Ph: (618)228-7321
Fax: (309)663-5783
URL: National Affiliate–www.legion.org
Local. **Affiliated With:** American Legion.

Baldwin

137 ■ American Legion, Illinois Post 619
c/o Nicholas Laufer
PO Box 2
Baldwin, IL 62217
Ph: (309)663-0361
Fax: (309)663-5783
URL: National Affiliate–www.legion.org
Contact: Nicholas Laufer, Contact
Local. **Affiliated With:** American Legion.

Barrington

138 ■ Adoptive Families Today (AFT)
PO Box 1726
Barrington, IL 60011-1726
Ph: (847)382-0858
Fax: (847)382-0831
E-mail: adopadvo@aol.com
URL: http://www.adoptivefamiliestoday.org
Contact: Kathy Casey, Advisor
Founded: 1988. **Members:** 200. **Membership Dues:** full, $35 (annual) • newsletter only, $25 (annual). **Budget:** $20,000. **Local**. Pre and post adoptive families and adoption professionals. Provides education and support to children. **Awards:** AFT Foster Scholarship. **Frequency:** annual. **Type:** scholarship. **Recipient:** to foster child graduating from high school or getting GED to further their education. **Special Interest Groups:** 5-8; Infant to 4; 9 and older; Parents; Pre-Adoptive; Transracial/Transcultural. **Publications:** *AdoptNews*, monthly. Newsletter. **Price:** $25.00/yr. **Circulation:** 300. Alternate Formats: online. **Conventions/Meetings:** annual Adoption Conference, pre and post adoption and parenting issues (exhibits) - November.

139 ■ American Legion, Barrington Post 158
PO Box 244
Barrington, IL 60011
Ph: (708)428-6363
Fax: (309)663-5783
URL: National Affiliate–www.legion.org
Local. **Affiliated With:** American Legion.

140 ■ American Public Works Association, Chicago Metro Chapter
c/o Rick E. Forner
234 James St., Ste.100
Barrington, IL 60010
Ph: (847)381-1800
Fax: (847)381-1875
URL: http://chicago.apwa.net
Contact: Rick E. Forner, Contact
Local. Promotes professional excellence and public awareness through education, advocacy and the exchange of knowledge. **Affiliated With:** American Public Works Association.

141 ■ Barrington Area Chamber of Commerce (BACC)
325 N Hough St.
Barrington, IL 60010-3026
Ph: (847)381-2525
Fax: (847)381-2540
E-mail: email@barringtonchamber.com
URL: http://www.barringtonchamber.com
Contact: Janet Meyer, Pres.
Members: 725. **Membership Dues:** business, $225-$1,445 (annual) • emeritus, $125 (annual) • not-for-profit, $135 (annual). **Local**. Aims to promote a dynamic business environment for the community. **Divisions:** Business Development; Community Affairs; Legislative Affairs; Membership Development.

142 ■ Barrington Area Character Counts
PO Box 93
Barrington, IL 60011-0093
E-mail: info@charactercountsbarrington.org
URL: http://www.charactercountsbarrington.org
Local.

143 ■ Barrington Area United Way
PO Box 733
Barrington, IL 60011-0733
Ph: (847)382-8778
URL: National Affiliate–national.unitedway.org
Local. **Affiliated With:** United Way of America.

144 ■ Barrington Community Unit School District 220
310 E James St.
Barrington, IL 60010
Ph: (847)381-6300
Fax: (847)381-6337
E-mail: rwhitehouse@cusd220.lake.k12.il.us
URL: http://www.cusd220.lake.k12.il.us
Contact: Deb Etzel, Pres.
Founded: 1972. **Local**. Works to enhance education in District 220 Schools by providing speakers for classes and connecting community members to volunteer opportunities. **Convention/Meeting:** none. **Formerly:** (1998) Volunteer Bureau of Barrington; (2005) School Volunteers of District 220. **Publications:** *FYI*, periodic. Newsletter. Alternate Formats: online.

145 ■ Barrington Swim Club (BSC)
c/o Barrington High School
616 W Main St.
Barrington, IL 60010
Ph: (847)381-1400
Fax: (847)304-3937
E-mail: president@swimbsc.org
URL: http://www.swimbsc.org
Contact: Cyndi Alexander, Pres.
Founded: 1979. **Members:** 250. **Staff:** 8. **Local**. **Awards:** Most Improved Swimmer. **Frequency:** annual. **Type:** recognition • Parents Hall of Fame. **Frequency:** annual. **Type:** recognition. **Boards:** Parent. **Conventions/Meetings:** semiannual competition, tryout - always May and October.

146 ■ Barrington Women's Club
c/o Luisa Bremer
989 Bosworth Fields Rd.
Barrington, IL 60010
Ph: (847)382-1251
Contact: Luisa Bremer, Pres.
Founded: 1914. **Members:** 220. **Membership Dues:** regular, $30 (annual). **Budget:** $5,000. **Local Groups:** 1. **Local**. Conducts fundraising activities to benefit the local community, including annual scholarships and local philanthropic organizations. **Publications:** Newsletter, monthly. **Price:** free for members.

147 ■ Chicago Society for Coatings Technology (CSCT)
c/o Mr. Herb Waltenspiel, Pres.
Neville Chem.
4830 Castaway Ln.
Barrington, IL 60010
Ph: (847)202-9028
Fax: (847)202-9028
E-mail: hwaltenspiel@nevchem.com
URL: http://www.chicagocoatings.org
Contact: Mr. Herb Waltenspiel, Pres.
Local. Represents chemists, chemical engineers, technologists and supervisory production personnel in the decorative and protective coatings industry and allied industries. Works to gather and disseminate practical and technical facts, data and standards fundamental to the manufacturing and use of paints, varnishes, lacquers, related protective coatings and printing inks. **Affiliated With:** Federation of Societies for Coatings Technology.

148 ■ Flat-Coated Retriever Club of Illinois (FCRCI)
27941 W Flynn Creek Dr.
Barrington, IL 60010
E-mail: kistnec@yahoo.com
URL: http://www.fcrci.org
Contact: Cheryl Kistner, Pres.
State. **Affiliated With:** Flat-Coated Retriever Society of America.

149 ■ Institute of Internal Auditors, Chicago Chapter
c/o Kathy Casey
112 Wesley St.
Barrington, IL 60010
Ph: (847)842-1606
Fax: (847)842-1605
E-mail: iiachicago@aol.com
URL: National Affiliate–www.theiia.org
Contact: Kathy Casey, Contact
Membership Dues: regular, $115 (annual) • educator, $65 (annual) • student, retired, $30 (annual) • life, $2,100 • sustainer (government auditors only), $50 (annual) • organization ($65 per staff member over 5; $50 per staff member over 100), $425-$6,600 (annual). **Local**. Serves as an advocate for the internal audit profession. Provides certification, education, research, and technological guidance for the profession. **Committees:** Education; International; Nominating. **Programs:** Certified Internal Auditor. **Affiliated With:** Institute of Internal Auditors. **Publications:** *Chicago Innovator*, monthly. Newsletter. **Price:** included in membership dues. **Advertising:** accepted. Alternate Formats: online • *Internal Auditor*, bimonthly. Magazine. Provides information for professionals who want to keep pace with the diverse, dynamic field of internal auditing. **Price:** included in membership dues. **Advertising:** accepted. Alternate Formats: online.

150 ■ Parents Television Council - Chicago Illinois Chapter
c/o Marti Anderson, Dir.
PO Box 3394
Barrington, IL 60011
Free: (888)241-7201
E-mail: chicagochapter@parentstv.org
URL: National Affiliate–www.parentstv.org
Contact: Marti Anderson, Dir.
Local.

151 ■ Trout Unlimited - Lee Wulff Chapter
25340 W Elm Grove Dr.
Barrington, IL 60010
Contact: Mike McCorcle, Pres.

152 ■ United States Naval Sea Cadet Corps - Manatra Division
Main St.
Barrington, IL 60010
E-mail: co@seacadets911.com
URL: http://dolphin.seacadets.org/US_units/UnitDetails.asp?UnitID=091MAN
Contact: LTJG Jack A. Harrison NSCC, Commanding Officer
Local. Works to instill good citizenship and patriotism in youth. Encourages qualities such as personal neatness, loyalty, obedience, dependability, and responsibility to others. Offers courses in physical fitness and military drill, first aid, water safety, basic seamanship, and naval history and traditions. **Affiliated With:** Naval Sea Cadet Corps.

153 ■ Vintage Chevrolet Club of America, Northern Illinois Region No. 7
c/o Steve Bergin, Dir.
980 Williamsburg Park
Barrington, IL 60010
Ph: (847)356-3684
URL: National Affiliate–www.vcca.org
Contact: Steve Bergin, Dir.
Local. **Affiliated With:** Vintage Chevrolet Club of America.

154 ■ Wagon Wheel Figure Skating Club (WWFSC)
PO Box 173
Barrington, IL 60011-0173
E-mail: skating@nsn.org
URL: http://www.wwfsc.com
Contact: Lanny Nelson, Pres.
Local. Provides programs to encourage participation and achievement in the sport of figure skating on ice. Defines and maintains uniform standards of skating proficiency. Organizes and sponsors competitions and exhibitions for the purpose of stimulating interest in figure skating. **Affiliated With:** United States Figure Skating Association.

Barry

155 ■ American Legion, Barry Post 222
PO Box 154
Barry, IL 62312
Ph: (309)663-0361
Fax: (309)663-5783
URL: National Affiliate–www.legion.org
Local. **Affiliated With:** American Legion.

156 ■ American Truck Historical Society, Mark Twain Chapter
c/o Charles Bruce Kendall
1010 Greene St.
Barry, IL 62312
Ph: (217)335-2417
URL: National Affiliate–www.aths.org
Contact: Charles Bruce Kendall, Contact
Local.

Bartelso

157 ■ American Legion, Hacker-Gebke Post 976
PO Box 181
Bartelso, IL 62218
Ph: (309)663-0361
Fax: (309)663-5783
URL: National Affiliate–www.legion.org
Local. **Affiliated With:** American Legion.

Bartlett

158 ■ American Legion, Bartlett Post 1212
PO Box 8219
Bartlett, IL 60103
Ph: (309)663-0361
Fax: (309)663-5783
URL: National Affiliate–www.legion.org
Local. **Affiliated With:** American Legion.

159 ■ American Legion, Chipilly-131st-Infantry Post 310
c/o James A. Gleason
1055 W Park Pl. Dr.
Bartlett, IL 60103
Ph: (708)837-2319
Fax: (309)663-5783
URL: National Affiliate–www.legion.org
Contact: James A. Gleason, Contact
Local. **Affiliated With:** American Legion.

160 ■ Bartlett Chamber of Commerce
138 S Oak Ave.
Bartlett, IL 60103
Ph: (630)830-0324
Fax: (630)830-9724
E-mail: info@bartlettchamber.com
URL: http://www.bartlettchamber.com
Contact: Diane Hubberts, Exec.Dir.
Founded: 1977. **Members:** 350. **Membership Dues:** business, $135-$275 (annual) • civic organization, $70 (annual). **Staff:** 2. **Local**. Promotes business and community development in Bartlett, IL. **Awards: Frequency:** annual. **Type:** scholarship. **Recipient:** must be associated with a current member. **Publications:** *Bartletter Business and Chamber of Commerce Directory*, annual. Membership Directory. **Circulation:** 14,000. **Advertising:** accepted • *Business Beat*, monthly. Newsletter. **Advertising:** accepted.

161 ■ Bartlett Character Counts
PO Box 8037
Bartlett, IL 60103-8037
E-mail: bartlettcharactercounts@hotmail.com
URL: http://www.bartlettcharactercounts.homestead.com
Local.

162 ■ Bartlett Lions Club
PO Box 8049
Bartlett, IL 60103
Ph: (630)375-7157
E-mail: bartlettlionsclub@yahoo.com
URL: http://www.bartlettlions.org
Local. **Affiliated With:** Lions Clubs International.

163 ■ Izaak Walton League of America, Illinois Division
c/o Joseph F. Hyland
255 E. Cleburne Ave.
Bartlett, IL 60103-5004
Ph: (630)372-6919
E-mail: jhyland19@outdrs.net
URL: National Affiliate–www.iwla.org
Works to educate the public to conserve, maintain, protect, and restore the soil, forest, water, and other natural resources of the U.S; promotes the enjoyment and wholesome utilization of these resources. **Affiliated With:** Izaak Walton League of America.

164 ■ Rogers Park Cricket Club
805 W Appletree Ln.
Bartlett, IL 60103
URL: http://www.usaca.org/Clubs.htm
Contact: Mohtasim Abbasi, Contact
Local.

165 ■ Sons of the Desert, Tree in a Test Tube Society (TITTS)
PO Box 8215
Bartlett, IL 60103-8215
Ph: (630)289-2023
Fax: (630)830-4710
Contact: Mr. Lee J. McBeath, Grand Sheik
Founded: 1978. **Members:** 2. **Local**. Fans of the film comedy team Stan Laurel and Oliver Hardy in suburban Chicago, IL. Seeks to perpetuate the spirit and genius of Laurel and Hardy. Hosts of 10th International Convention: The Laurel and Hardy Cruise. **Libraries: Type:** not open to the public. **Holdings:** 164; audio recordings, books, films, video recordings. **Subjects:** laurel and hardy, comedy, film. **Affiliated With:** American Film Institute; Sons of the Desert. **Publications:** *The Frying Pan*. Newsletter • *The Intra-Tent Journal*, quarterly. **Price:** $18.00/2 years. **Circulation:** 4,000. **Advertising:** accepted. **Conventions/Meetings:** biennial Funfest - convention (exhibits).

166 ■ Sweet Adelines International, Spring Valley Chorus
822 Brookside Dr.
Bartlett, IL 60103
Ph: (224)210-3428
E-mail: info@springvalleychorus.com
URL: http://springvalleychorus.com
Contact: June Berg, Dir.
Local. Advances the musical art form of barbershop harmony through education and performances. Provides education, training and coaching in the development of women's four-part barbershop harmony. **Affiliated With:** Sweet Adelines International.

Bartonville

167 ■ American Legion, Limestone Post 979
4501 Airport Rd.
Bartonville, IL 61607
Ph: (309)697-2423
Fax: (309)663-5783
URL: National Affiliate–www.legion.org
Local. **Affiliated With:** American Legion.

168 ■ Bartonville Lions Club
PO Box 4161
Bartonville, IL 61607
Ph: (309)397-1236
E-mail: vick70@insightbb.com
URL: http://bartonvilleil.lionwap.org
Contact: Greg Mulligan, Pres.
Local. **Affiliated With:** Lions Clubs International.

169 ■ Limestone Area Chamber of Commerce (LACOC)
PO Box 4043
Bartonville, IL 61607
Ph: (309)697-1031
E-mail: email@limestonechamber.com
URL: http://www.limestonechamber.com
Contact: Alan Getz, Pres.
Local. Promotes business and community development in Limestone area.

170 ■ Mohammed Shriners
c/o Richard L. Armstrong
4201 S Indus. Dr.
Bartonville, IL 61607-2844

Ph: (309)633-2808
Fax: (309)633-2820
E-mail: mohammedshrine@sbcglobal.net
URL: http://mohammedshrine.org
Contact: Richard L. Armstrong, Recorder
Local. Affiliated With: Imperial Council of the Ancient Arabic Order of the Nobles of the Mystic Shrine for North America.

Batavia

171 ■ American Cancer Society, Batavia - Fox Valley Regional
143 1st St.
Batavia, IL 60510
Ph: (630)879-9009
Fax: (630)879-9047
Free: (800)942-6985
URL: http://www.cancer.org
Contact: David Riggs, Regional Dir.
Local. Affiliated With: American Cancer Society.

172 ■ American Legion, Batavia Post 504
PO Box 222
Batavia, IL 60510
Ph: (309)663-0361
Fax: (309)663-5783
URL: National Affiliate–www.legion.org
Local. Affiliated With: American Legion.

173 ■ American Society for Quality, Fox Valley Section 1208
c/o Cecilia Clark, Sec.
340 Houston St., Ste.A
Batavia, IL 60510-1960
Ph: (630)845-8473
Fax: (630)208-1881
E-mail: jose.martinez@knowles.com
URL: http://www.asq-foxvalley.org
Contact: Jose Martinez, Chm.
Local. Advances learning, quality improvement and knowledge exchange to improve business results and to create better workplaces and communities worldwide. Provides a forum for information exchange, professional development and continuous learning in the science of quality. **Affiliated With:** American Society for Quality.

174 ■ APICS, The Association for Operations Management - Fox River Chapter No. 207
PO Box 608
Batavia, IL 60510
Ph: (630)406-6278
E-mail: jbarnard18@concast.net
URL: http://www.apics-foxriver.org
Contact: Jeff Barnard CPIM, Publicity Dir./Webmaster
Local. Provides information and services in production and inventory management and related areas to enable members, enterprises and individuals to add value to their business performance. **Affiliated With:** APICS - The Association for Operations Management.

175 ■ Batavia Chamber of Commerce (BCC)
100 N Island Ave.
Batavia, IL 60510-1931
Ph: (630)879-7134
Fax: (630)879-7215
E-mail: chamber@cityofbatavia.net
URL: http://www.bataviachamber.org
Contact: Mr. Roger Breisch, Exec.Dir.
Founded: 1930. **Members:** 260. **Membership Dues:** one-time processing fee (new members), $25 • home based business, $195 (annual) • business, $240-$630 (annual) • premier, $150 (annual) • associate (not involve in a business), $95 (annual) • utility, $445 (annual) • nonprofit civic group, $190 (annual) • government, $325 (annual) • financial institution, $1,000 (annual). **Staff:** 2. **Budget:** $150,000. **Local.** Businesses, organizations, and individuals interested in business and community development in Batavia, IL. Supports community improvement projects. **Affiliated With:** Illinois Association of Chamber of Commerce Executives; Illinois State Chamber of Commerce; U.S. Chamber of Commerce. **Publications:** *Batavia Business*, monthly. Newsletter. Publication of events and topics of interest. **Advertising:** accepted • Directory, annual • Brochures, periodic.

176 ■ Batavia Community Chest/United Way
PO Box 372
Batavia, IL 60510-0372
Ph: (630)406-9219
URL: National Affiliate–national.unitedway.org
Local. Affiliated With: United Way of America.

177 ■ Batavia Mothers Club Foundation (BMCF)
PO Box 91
Batavia, IL 60510
E-mail: bmcinformation@yahoo.com
URL: http://www.bataviamothersclub.org
Local. Formerly: (2005) Batavia Mothers Club.

178 ■ Chicago Area Vascular Association (CAVA)
2324 Crane Ct.
Batavia, IL 60510
Ph: (630)527-7842 (630)406-1952
Fax: (630)527-2840
E-mail: kirkkilker@comcast.net
URL: National Affiliate–www.svunet.org
Contact: Kathryn D. Kilker BS, Contact
Local. Represents vascular technologists and individuals in the field of noninvasive vascular technology. Seeks to establish an information clearinghouse providing reference and assistance in matters relating to noninvasive vascular technology. Facilitates cooperation among noninvasive vascular facilities and other health professions. Provides continuing education for individuals in the field. Represents members on various regulatory issues. **Affiliated With:** Society for Vascular Ultrasound.

179 ■ Chicago Metro Chapter of Association for Healthcare Resource and Materials Management
c/o Rich Burruss, VP
O'Brien Corp.
934 Paramount Pkwy.
Batavia, IL 60510
Ph: (630)879-0010
Fax: (630)879-0303
E-mail: rich@obriencorp.com
URL: National Affiliate–www.ahrmm.org
Contact: Rich Burruss, VP
Local. Represents purchasing agents and materials managers active in the field of purchasing, inventory, distribution and materials management as performed in hospitals, related patient care institutions and government and voluntary health organizations. Provides networking and educational opportunities for members. Develops new business ventures that ensure the financial stability of members. **Affiliated With:** Association for Healthcare Resource and Materials Management.

180 ■ Chicago Space Frontier L5 Society
MS 355, Fermilab Box 500
Batavia, IL 60510
Ph: (630)393-6817
E-mail: higgins@fnal.gov
URL: http://www.astrodigital.org/csfs
Contact: Bill Higgins, Contact
Local. Works for the creation of a spacefaring civilization. Encourages the establishment of self-sustaining human settlements in space. Promotes large-scale industrialization and private enterprise in space.

181 ■ Hoover-Wood Elementary School Parent Teacher Organization
c/o Karen Mulattieri, Principal
1640 Wagner Rd.
Batavia, IL 60510
Ph: (630)879-1636 (630)761-6635
Fax: (630)406-8243
E-mail: karen.mulattieri@bps101.net
URL: http://hws.bps101.net/pto.htm
Contact: Karen Mulattieri, Principal
Local.

182 ■ Illinois Quarter Horse Association, District No. 2
c/o Cheryl LaMaster, Dir.
230 Woodland Hills Rd.
Batavia, IL 60510-9999
Ph: (630)482-9774
E-mail: clamaste@fnal.gov
URL: http://www.ilqha.com
Contact: Cheryl LaMaster, Dir.
Local. Affiliated With: American Quarter Horse Association.

183 ■ Mothers Against Drunk Driving, Kane County
PO Box 36
Batavia, IL 60510
Ph: (630)482-2242
Fax: (630)482-2243
E-mail: maddkanecoil@sbcglobal.net
URL: National Affiliate–www.madd.org
Local. Victims of drunk driving crashes; concerned citizens. Encourages citizen participation in working towards reform of the drunk driving problem and the prevention of underage drinking. Acts as the voice of victims of drunk driving crashes by speaking on their behalf to communities, businesses, and educational groups. **Affiliated With:** Mothers Against Drunk Driving.

184 ■ National Association of Rocketry - Fermilab Association of Rocketry (FAR)
c/o Greg Cisko, Pres.
Fermi Natl. Accelerator Lab
PO Box 500, MS 357
Batavia, IL 60510-0500
Ph: (630)452-3998
E-mail: cisko@fnal.gov
URL: http://www.fnal.gov/orgs/far
Contact: Greg Cisko, Pres.
Local.

185 ■ National Technological Honor Society - Batavia High School - Illinois
1200 W Wilson St.
Batavia, IL 60510
Ph: (630)879-4600
Fax: (630)879-4660
E-mail: webmaster@bps101.net
URL: http://www.bps101.net
Contact: Dough Drexler, Contact
Local.

186 ■ Northwestern Illinois Golf Course Superintendents Association (NWIGCSA)
c/o Daniel Murray, CGCS, Pres.
919 E Fabyan Pkwy.
Batavia, IL 60510
Ph: (630)232-4922
Fax: (630)232-1252
E-mail: mur5213@comcast.net
URL: http://www.nwigcsa.org
Contact: Daniel Murray CGCS, Pres.
Founded: 1963. **Local.** Represents the interests of golf course superintendents. Advances members' profession for career success. Enhances the enjoyment, growth and vitality in the game of golf. Educates members concerning efficient and economical management of golf courses. **Affiliated With:** Golf Course Superintendents Association of America.

Beardstown

187 ■ American Legion, Beardstown Post 605
218 W 3rd St.
Beardstown, IL 62618
Ph: (309)663-0361
Fax: (309)663-5783
URL: National Affiliate–www.legion.org
Local. Affiliated With: American Legion.

188 ■ Beardstown Chamber of Commerce (BCC)
121 S State St.
Beardstown, IL 62618
Ph: (217)323-3271
Fax: (217)323-3271
E-mail: info@beardstownil.org
URL: http://www.beardstownil.org
Members: 94. **Local**. Promotes business and community development in Beardstown, IL.

189 ■ United Way of Greater Beardstown
212-B Washington St.
Beardstown, IL 62618-1149
Ph: (217)323-5660
URL: National Affiliate–national.unitedway.org
Contact: Judith Moore, Exec.Dir.
Founded: 1968. **Budget:** $50,000. **Local. Affiliated With:** United Way of America.

190 ■ Wisconsin-Illinois-Indiana-Michigan State Association of Emblem Club
c/o Elizabeth Gernay, Pres.
5116 US Hwy. 67
Beardstown, IL 62618-8063
E-mail: ronsand@casscomm.com
URL: http://www.emblemclub.com/html/wiim.html
Contact: Elizabeth Gernay, Pres.
Regional. Affiliated With: Supreme Emblem Club of the United States of America.

Beason

191 ■ American Legion, Chestnut-Beason Post 848
2101 1500th St.
Beason, IL 62512
Ph: (217)447-3421
Fax: (309)663-5783
URL: National Affiliate–www.legion.org
Local. Affiliated With: American Legion.

Beaverville

192 ■ American Legion, Beaverville Post 877
PO Box 65
Beaverville, IL 60912
Ph: (815)435-2481
Fax: (309)663-5783
URL: National Affiliate–www.legion.org
Local. Affiliated With: American Legion.

Beckemeyer

193 ■ American Legion, Holthaus-Kampwerth Post 1227
391 Louis
Beckemeyer, IL 62219
Ph: (309)663-0361
Fax: (309)663-5783
URL: National Affiliate–www.legion.org
Local. Affiliated With: American Legion.

Bedford Park

194 ■ Association of Late-Deafened Adults - Chicago
c/o Heidi Adams, Pres.
PO Box 785
Bedford Park, IL 60499
E-mail: adams45@earthlink.net
URL: http://www.deafvision.net/alda-chicago
Contact: Heidi Adams, Pres.
Local. Advocates for the needs of late-deafened people. Provides information, support and social opportunities through self-help groups, meetings and social events. **Affiliated With:** Association of Late-Deafened Adults.

Beecher

195 ■ Beecher Chamber of Commerce
PO Box 292
Beecher, IL 60401
Ph: (708)946-6803
E-mail: bchamber@villageofbeecher.org
URL: http://www.villageofbeecher.org/chamber
Contact: Chuck Hoehn, Pres.
Local. Promotes business and community development in the Beecher, IL area.

Beecher City

196 ■ American Legion, Eva Casstevens Post 535
c/o Don Riley
RR 3, Box 308B
Beecher City, IL 62414
Ph: (618)487-5381
Fax: (309)663-5783
URL: National Affiliate–www.legion.org
Contact: Don Riley, Contact
Local. Affiliated With: American Legion.

Belleville

197 ■ AAA Missouri
2629 N Illinois St.
Belleville, IL 62226
Ph: (618)235-5700
Fax: (618)235-6641
URL: http://www.aaa.com
Contact: Ashley Toennies, Intravel
State.

198 ■ American Legion, Illinois Post 58
c/o George E. Hilgard
PO Box 124
Belleville, IL 62222
Ph: (309)663-0361
Fax: (309)663-5783
URL: National Affiliate–www.legion.org
Contact: George E. Hilgard, Contact
Local. Affiliated With: American Legion.

199 ■ American Legion, Stookey Post 1255
201 Eiler Rd.
Belleville, IL 62223
Ph: (618)538-5445
Fax: (309)663-5783
URL: National Affiliate–www.legion.org
Local. Affiliated With: American Legion.

200 ■ Catholic Alumni Club of Mississippi and Missouri River Valleys
c/o Louis Kappel, Pres.
39 Signal Hill Blvd.
Belleville, IL 62223
Ph: (618)397-2320
URL: http://www.caci.org/cac/mmrv.html
Contact: Louis Kappel, Pres.
Regional. Affiliated With: Catholic Alumni Clubs, International.

201 ■ Epilepsy Foundation of Southwestern Illinois
1931 W Main St.
Belleville, IL 62226-7479
Ph: (618)236-2181
URL: National Affiliate–www.epilepsyfoundation.org
Local. Affiliated With: Epilepsy Foundation.

202 ■ Greater Belleville Chamber of Commerce
216 E A St.
Belleville, IL 62221
Ph: (618)233-2015
Fax: (618)233-2077
E-mail: info@bellevillechamber.org
URL: http://www.bellevillechamber.org
Contact: Garry Reute, Chm.
Local. Works to support and advance business and community interests, as well as the quality of life. **Formerly:** (2002) Belleville Economic Progress.

203 ■ Jewish Federation of Southern Illinois, Southeastern Missouri and Western Kentucky
c/o Steven C. Low, Exec.Dir.
3419 W Main
Belleville, IL 62226
Ph: (618)398-6100
Fax: (618)398-0539
Free: (877)714-6103
URL: http://www.simokyfed.com
Regional.

204 ■ Limelight Players, Not-for-Profit
c/o Jeff Blue, Dir.
PO Box 392
Belleville, IL 62222
Ph: (618)628-9998
E-mail: info@limelightplayers.org
URL: http://www.limelightplayers.org
Contact: Jeff Blue, Dir.
Local.

205 ■ Mackinaw Walkers Volkssport Club
c/o Jim Muma
1706 Pine
Belleville, IL 62226-4256
Ph: (618)234-8706
E-mail: michiganjim@spcglobal.net
URL: National Affiliate–www.ava.org
Contact: Jim Muma, Pres.
Local. Affiliated With: American Volkssport Association.

206 ■ Mathematical Association of America, Illinois Section
c/o Keven Hansen, Dir.
Dept. of Mathematics
Southwestern Illinois Coll.
2500 Carlyle Ave.
Belleville, IL 62221
Ph: (618)235-2700
E-mail: keven.hansen@swic.edu
URL: http://www.maa.org/Illinois
Contact: Keven Hansen, Dir.
State. Promotes the general understanding and appreciation of mathematics. Advances and improves the education in the mathematical sciences at the collegiate level. Provides resources and activities that foster scholarship, professional growth and cooperation among teachers, other professionals and students. **Affiliated With:** Mathematical Association of America.

207 ■ Metro East Coin and Currency Club
c/o Johnny Kicklighter
1121 E Main St.
Belleville, IL 62220
Ph: (618)277-4493
E-mail: kicklighter.johnny@mcleodusa.net
URL: National Affiliate–www.money.org
Contact: Johnny Kicklighter, Sec.
Members: 30. **Membership Dues:** all, $5 (annual). **For-Profit. Local.** Promotes education and collecting of coins and currency. **Affiliated With:** American Numismatic Association. **Formerly:** (2003) St. Clair Numismatic Society.

208 ■ National Sojourners, Charles A. Lindbergh No. 247
557 Pebble Brook Ln.
Belleville, IL 62221-7610
Ph: (618)632-7515
E-mail: ellceekay@juno.com
URL: National Affiliate–www.nationalsojourners.org
Contact: Lester C. King, Contact
Local.

209 ■ Phi Theta Kappa, Theta Epsilon Chapter - Southwestern Illinois College
c/o Helen Clark
2500 Carlyle Rd.
Belleville, IL 62221

Ph: (618)235-2700
E-mail: helen.clark@swic.edu
URL: http://www.ptk.org/directories/chapters/IL/173-1.htm
Contact: Helen Clark, Advisor
Local.

210 ■ St. Clair County Medical Society (SCCMS)
c/o Elaine Hoffmann, Exec.Dir.
6400 W Main St., Ste.3-L
Belleville, IL 62223
Ph: (618)397-5315
E-mail: sccms@peaknet.net
URL: http://www.stclairmed.org
Contact: Elaine Hoffmann, Exec.Dir.
Local. Advances the art and science of medicine. Promotes patient care and the betterment of public health.

211 ■ Southern Illinois District, The Lutheran Church-Missouri Synod
2408 Lebanon Ave.
Belleville, IL 62221-2529
Ph: (618)234-4767
Fax: (618)234-4830
E-mail: sidwebmaster@yahoo.com
URL: http://sid.lcms.org
Contact: Rev. Herbert Mueller Jr., Pres.
Local.

212 ■ Southwestern Illinois RSVP
c/o Penelope Neale, Dir.
201 N Church St.
Belleville, IL 62220-4098
Ph: (618)234-4410
Fax: (618)234-8634
E-mail: penelope.neale@swic.edu
URL: http://www.seniorcorps.gov
Contact: Penelope Neale, Dir.
Local. Affiliated With: Retired and Senior Volunteer Program.

Bellflower

213 ■ American Legion, Grant Post 202
PO Box 63
Bellflower, IL 61724
Ph: (309)722-3305
Fax: (309)663-5783
URL: National Affiliate–www.legion.org
Local. Affiliated With: American Legion.

Bellwood

214 ■ American Legion, Constitution Post 326
4009 Warren Ave.
Bellwood, IL 60104
Ph: (309)663-0361
Fax: (309)663-5783
URL: National Affiliate–www.legion.org
Local. Affiliated With: American Legion.

215 ■ Bellwood Chamber of Commerce and Industry
PO Box 86
Bellwood, IL 60104
Ph: (708)547-5030
Fax: (708)547-5030
E-mail: slthompson73@yahoo.com
URL: http://www.bellwoodchamber.org
Contact: Vera Douglas, Pres.
Local. Promotes business and community development in Bellwood, IL.

216 ■ Chicagoland Sheet Metal Contractors Association (CSMCA)
c/o Tony Adolfs, Exec.Dir.
2703 Van Buren St.
Bellwood, IL 60104-2458
Ph: (708)544-7007
Fax: (708)544-7098
E-mail: info@csmca.org
URL: http://www.csmca.org
Contact: Tony Adolfs, Exec.Dir.
Local. Affiliated With: Sheet Metal and Air Conditioning Contractors' National Association.

217 ■ Plumbing-Heating-Cooling Contractors Association, West Suburban
c/o Mr. James Young, Pres.
4009 Warren Ave.
Bellwood, IL 60104-2066
Ph: (708)544-2070
Fax: (708)544-6806
URL: National Affiliate–www.phccweb.org
Contact: Mr. James Young, Pres.
Local. Represents the plumbing, heating and cooling contractors. Promotes the construction industry. Protects the environment, health, safety and comfort of society. **Affiliated With:** Plumbing-Heating-Cooling Contractors Association.

Belvidere

218 ■ American Legion, Boone Post 77
900 Chrysler Dr.
Belvidere, IL 61008
Ph: (309)663-0361
Fax: (309)663-5783
E-mail: wschup35@insightbb.com
URL: National Affiliate–www.legion.org
Local. Affiliated With: American Legion.

219 ■ Belvidere Area Chamber of Commerce (BACC)
200 S State St.
Belvidere, IL 61008
Ph: (815)544-4357
Fax: (815)547-7654
E-mail: tlassandro@belviderechamber.com
URL: http://www.belviderechamber.com
Contact: Thomas Lassandro, Exec.Dir.
Founded: 1915. **Members:** 320. **Budget:** $100,000. **Local**. Promotes business and community development in the Boone County, IL area. **Convention/Meeting:** none. **Formerly:** (1974) Belvidere +Chamber of Commerce. **Publications:** *Chamber HELP*, annual. Directory • *Chamber News*, monthly. Newsletter. Contains issues affecting the business community.

220 ■ Belvidere Board of Realtors
215 N State St.
Belvidere, IL 61008
Ph: (815)544-2719
Fax: (815)544-2714
E-mail: bbor@insightbb.com
URL: National Affiliate–www.realtor.org
Contact: Kris Schmidt, Exec. Officer
Local. Strives to develop real estate business practices. Advocates the right to own, use and transfer real property. Provides a facility for professional development, research and exchange of information among members and to the general public. **Affiliated With:** National Association of Realtors.

221 ■ Belvidere Lions Club
PO Box 398
Belvidere, IL 61008
Ph: (815)547-8974
E-mail: w.villont@insightbb.com
URL: http://belvidereil.lionwap.org
Contact: William Villont, Sec.
Local. Affiliated With: Lions Clubs International.

222 ■ PFLAG Rock River Valley
136 Garden Dr.
Belvidere, IL 61008
Ph: (815)547-8669
Fax: (815)964-2639
E-mail: gimpyfac@inwave.com
URL: http://www.pflag.org/Illinois.204.0.html
Local. Affiliated With: Parents, Families, and Friends of Lesbians and Gays.

223 ■ United Way of Boone County, Illinois
220 W Locust St.
Belvidere, IL 61008-3621
Ph: (815)544-3144
URL: National Affiliate–national.unitedway.org
Local. Affiliated With: United Way of America.

Bement

224 ■ American Legion, Illinois Post 620
c/o Albert Parker
PO Box 18
Bement, IL 61813
Ph: (217)678-8125
Fax: (309)663-5783
URL: National Affiliate–www.legion.org
Contact: Albert Parker, Contact
Local. Affiliated With: American Legion.

Bensenville

225 ■ Bensenville Chamber of Commerce
PO Box 905
Bensenville, IL 60106-0315
Ph: (630)860-3800
Fax: (630)860-3814
E-mail: info@bensenvillechamber.org
URL: http://www.bensenvillechamber.org
Contact: Rich Johnson, Dir.
Local. Promotes business and community development in Bensenville, IL.

226 ■ Illinois Chapter National Corvette Restorers Society (ILNCRS)
c/o Bill Braun, Chm.
PO Box 7122
Bensenville, IL 60106
Ph: (815)344-8276
E-mail: ilncrs@joltmail.com
URL: http://www.ilncrs.org
Contact: Bill Braun, Chm.
Founded: 1978. **Membership Dues:** individual, $20 (annual). **State. Affiliated With:** National Corvette Restorers Society.

227 ■ Kiwanis Club of Bensenville-Wood Dale
c/o Bill Black
PO Box 524
Bensenville, IL 60106
E-mail: wblack@jrhi7.dupage.k12.il.us
URL: http://users.aol.com/wdsd2/Bensenville/Bensen.htm
Contact: Bill Black, Contact
Local.

228 ■ National Active And Retired Federal Employees Association - Dupage 1771
17 W 343 Hickory
Bensenville, IL 60106
Ph: (630)595-6005
URL: National Affiliate–www.narfe.org
Contact: Elizabeth J. Blaszinski, Contact
Local. Protects the retirement future of employees through education. Informs members on issues affecting the retirement. **Affiliated With:** National Association of Retired Federal Employees.

Benson

229 ■ American Legion, Benson Post 454
PO Box 312
Benson, IL 61516
Ph: (309)394-2273
Fax: (309)663-5783
URL: National Affiliate–www.legion.org
Local. Affiliated With: American Legion.

Benton

230 ■ American Legion, Stanley Mc Collum Post 280
311 S Main St.
Benton, IL 62812
Ph: (618)438-0861
Fax: (309)663-5783
URL: National Affiliate–www.legion.org
Local. Affiliated With: American Legion.

231 ■ Benton Kiwanis Club Foundation
c/o David L. Webster
8976 Carter Ln.
Benton, IL 62812-0000
Local.

232 ■ Benton-West City Area Chamber of Commerce (BACC)
211 N Main St.
PO Box 574
Benton, IL 62812
Ph: (618)438-2121
Fax: (618)438-8011
Free: (866)536-8423
E-mail: chamber@bentonwestcity.com
URL: http://www.bentonwestcity.com
Contact: Gloria Atchison, Exec.Sec.
Founded: 1941. **Members:** 173. **Membership Dues:** individual, $50 (annual) • civic club and organization, $100 (annual) • business and professional, $150 (annual) • industrial and commercial (bronze), $250 (annual) • industrial and commercial (silver), $500 (annual) • industrial and commercial (gold), $1,000 (annual). **Staff:** 1. **Local.** Promotes business and community development in the Benton, IL area. Holds area festival. **Publications:** Newsletter, monthly. **Circulation:** 350. **Advertising:** accepted. **Conventions/Meetings:** monthly board meeting, open to the public - every first Thursday, Benton, IL • monthly executive committee meeting - every first Tuesday • annual Rend Lake Festival and Parade - every spring.

233 ■ Benton-West City Economic Development Corp.
207 N Maple
Benton, IL 62812-1320
Ph: (618)435-8234
Local.

234 ■ Little Egypt Independent Electrical Contractors
c/o David Atchison
114 McFall Ave.
Benton, IL 62812
Ph: (618)439-6006
Fax: (618)439-6022
E-mail: littlegyptiec@onecliq.net
URL: National Affiliate–www.ieci.org
Contact: David Atchison, Contact
Local. Affiliated With: Independent Electrical Contractors.

Berwyn

235 ■ American Legion, Berwyn Post 422
PO Box 62
Berwyn, IL 60402
Ph: (708)788-9422
Fax: (309)663-5783
URL: National Affiliate–www.legion.org
Local. Affiliated With: American Legion.

236 ■ American Legion, Commodore Barry Post 256
6919 W Roosevelt Rd.
Berwyn, IL 60402
Ph: (708)484-9599
Fax: (309)663-5783
URL: National Affiliate–www.legion.org
Local. Affiliated With: American Legion.

237 ■ Berwyn Development Corporation (BCD)
3322 S Oak Park Ave., 2nd Fl.
Berwyn, IL 60402
Ph: (708)788-8100
Fax: (708)788-0966
E-mail: kelly@berwyn.net
URL: http://www.berwyn.net
Contact: Kievan B. Kelly, Exec.Dir.
Founded: 1983. **Members:** 300. **Membership Dues:** individual, nonprofit organization, $100 (annual) • corporate patron, $500-$2,000 (annual) • corporate sponsor, $1,000 (annual) • corporate benefactor, $2,000 (annual) • business (based on number of employees), hospital/utility, financial institution, $100-$350 (annual). **Staff:** 3. **Local.** Promotes business and community development in Berwyn, IL. Conducts charitable activities. **Libraries: Type:** open to the public. **Holdings:** articles, audio recordings, books, periodicals, video recordings. **Subjects:** business development, retention, project funding, and grant sources. **Awards:** Charles E. Piper Award. **Frequency:** annual. **Type:** recognition. **Supersedes:** Berwyn Chamber of Commerce. **Publications:** *Berwyn Business Briefs*, quarterly. Newsletter. **Circulation:** 1,000. **Advertising:** accepted • *Berwyn Community Business Directory*, annual. **Price:** free. **Advertising:** accepted. **Conventions/Meetings:** monthly board meeting - always first Tuesday.

238 ■ International Brotherhood of Teamsters, Chauffeurs, Warehousemen and Helpers of America, AFL-CIO - Local Union 714
6815 W Roosevelt Rd.
Berwyn, IL 60402-1098
Ph: (773)242-3215
Fax: (708)788-4662
URL: http://www.teamsters714.org
Contact: Robert A. Hogan, Sec.-Treas.
Members: 9,200. **Local. Affiliated With:** International Brotherhood of Teamsters.

239 ■ Seguin Retarded Citizens Association
6224 W Ogden Ave.
Berwyn, IL 60402
Ph: (708)788-5777
Fax: (708)788-5784
URL: National Affiliate–www.TheArc.org
Contact: Sheila Ryan-Henry, Exec.Dir.
Local. Parents, professional workers, and others interested in individuals with mental retardation. Works to promote services, research, public understanding, and legislation for people with mental retardation and their families. **Affiliated With:** Arc of the United States.

240 ■ Society of Otorhinolaryngology and Head/Neck Nurses - Chicago Chapter
1421 Wisconsin Ave.
Berwyn, IL 60402
Ph: (708)216-3890
Fax: (708)216-9396
E-mail: bharri2@lumc.edu
URL: National Affiliate–www.sohnnurse.com
Contact: Bethany A. Harris BSN, Contact
Local. Advances the professional growth and development of nurses dedicated to the specialty of Otorhinolaryngology nursing through education and research. Promotes innovations in practice, research and healthcare policy initiatives. **Affiliated With:** Society of Otorhinolaryngology and Head/Neck Nurses.

Bethalto

241 ■ American Legion, Bethalto Post 214
109 S Prairie St.
Bethalto, IL 62010
Ph: (309)663-0361
Fax: (309)663-5783
URL: National Affiliate–www.legion.org
Local. Affiliated With: American Legion.

Bethany

242 ■ American Legion, Bethany Post 507
PO Box 59
Bethany, IL 61914
Ph: (309)663-0361
Fax: (309)663-5783
URL: National Affiliate–www.legion.org
Local. Affiliated With: American Legion.

Big Rock

243 ■ American Legion, Big Rock Post 529
PO Box 43
Big Rock, IL 60511
Ph: (815)286-3856
Fax: (309)663-5783
URL: National Affiliate–www.legion.org
Local. Affiliated With: American Legion.

Biggsville

244 ■ American Legion, Biggsville Memorial Post 1176
206 E Main St.
Biggsville, IL 61418
Ph: (309)663-0361
Fax: (309)663-5783
URL: National Affiliate–www.legion.org
Local. Affiliated With: American Legion.

Blandinsville

245 ■ American Legion, Hicks-Olson Post 424
PO Box 142
Blandinsville, IL 61420
Ph: (309)652-3251
Fax: (309)663-5783
URL: National Affiliate–www.legion.org
Local. Affiliated With: American Legion.

Bloomingdale

246 ■ American Legion, Pat Petrone Post 885
326 Morningside Dr., Unit B
Bloomingdale, IL 60108
Ph: (630)924-0624
Fax: (309)663-5783
URL: National Affiliate–www.legion.org
Local. Affiliated With: American Legion.

247 ■ Bloomingdale Chamber of Commerce
109 W Franklin St.
Bloomingdale, IL 60108
Ph: (630)980-9082
Fax: (630)980-9092
E-mail: bloomcham@sbcglobal.net
URL: http://www.BloomingdaleChamber.com
Contact: Mrs. Richa Wennerholm, Admin.
Founded: 1982. **Members:** 250. **Membership Dues:** business (1-2 employees), $150 (annual) • business (100 or more employees), $500 (annual) • business (3-10 employees), $175 (annual) • business (11-25 employees), $225 (annual) • business (51-99 employees), $300 (annual) • business (26-50 employees), $250 (annual). **Staff:** 2. **Local.** Strives to promote the growth of local business for the benefit of Bloomingdale Chamber of Commerce and the community. **Awards:** Business of the Year. **Frequency:** annual. **Type:** recognition. **Recipient:** to the business/organization that promotes the growth and awareness of the chamber • Business Person of the Year. **Frequency:** annual. **Type:** recognition. **Recipient:** to an individual who has made a significant contribution to the growth of the chamber • Chamber Ambassador. **Frequency:** annual. **Type:** recognition. **Recipient:** to and individual that strive to put the chamber first in their everyday business activities. **Subgroups:**

Bloomingdale ONE Leads Group. **Publications:** *Chamber Outlook*, monthly. Newsletter. **Price:** free to members only. **Circulation:** 400. **Advertising:** accepted.

248 ■ Bloomingdale Character Counts
c/o Barb Weber
201 S Bloomingdale Rd.
Bloomingdale, IL 60108
Ph: (630)671-5613
URL: http://www.geocities.com/character60108
Contact: Barb Weber, Contact
Local.

249 ■ Communication Alliance to Network Thoroughbred Ex-Racehorses (CANTER)
198 Applewood Ln.
Bloomingdale, IL 60108
Ph: (630)341-1582
E-mail: canteril@yahoo.com
URL: http://www.canterusa.org/illinois
Contact: Denise Fillo, Exec.Dir.
Members: 10. **Budget:** $3,000. **Regional Groups:** 7. **Local**. Helps retiring IL racehorses safely transition to non-racing homes.

250 ■ USA Dance - Chicagoland Chapter
c/o D.J. Lawn, Sec./Membership Chair
142 Canterbury Ct.
Bloomingdale, IL 60108
Ph: (630)893-2926
E-mail: chicagochallenge@aol.com
URL: http://usadancechicago.org
Contact: D.J. Lawn, Sec./Membership Chair
Local. Encourages and promotes the physical, mental and social benefits of partner dancing. Organizes and supports programs for the recreational enjoyment of ballroom dancing. Creates opportunities for the general public to participate in ballroom dancing and DanceSport.

Bloomington

251 ■ 100 Black Men of Central Illinois
5 Aster Ct.
Bloomington, IL 61704
E-mail: lee.smith43@gte.net
URL: National Affiliate–www.100blackmen.org
Local. **Affiliated With:** 100 Black Men of America.

252 ■ Alcoholics Anonymous World Services, Bloomington/Normal Intergroup
102 Southeast St., Ste.430
Bloomington, IL 61701
Ph: (309)828-7092
URL: National Affiliate–www.aa.org
Local. Individuals recovering from alcoholism. AA maintains that members can solve their common problem and help others achieve sobriety through a twelve step program that includes sharing their experience, strength, and hope with each other. **Affiliated With:** Alcoholics Anonymous World Services.

253 ■ Alzheimer's Association, Bloomington/Normal Illinois Chapter
2027 S Main St., Ste.3
Bloomington, IL 61704
Ph: (309)827-9508
Fax: (309)827-9520
Free: (800)272-3900
URL: http://www.alzheimers-illinois.org
Founded: 1987. **Local**. Strives to reach out to Alzheimer's victims who have the disease and those who care for them. **Affiliated With:** Alzheimer's Association. **Formerly:** (2005) Alzheimer's Association, East Central Illinois Chapter.

254 ■ American Industrial Hygiene Association - Prairie Local Section
c/o Phillip Miller, Treas.
507 W Seminary
Bloomington, IL 61701
E-mail: phillip_miller@hseworld.com
URL: http://www.aiha.org/LocalSections/html/prairie/index.htm
Contact: Phillip Miller, Treas.
Local. Represents the interests of occupational and environmental health professionals practicing in industry, government, labor and academic institutions and independent organizations. Promotes the certification of industrial hygienists. Administers educational programs for environmental health and safety professionals. **Affiliated With:** American Industrial Hygiene Association.

255 ■ American Industrial Hygiene Association, Prairie Section
c/o Phillip Miller, Treas.
507 W Seminary
Bloomington, IL 61701
E-mail: phillip_miller@hseworld.com
URL: http://www.aiha.org/localsections/html/prairie/index.htm
Contact: Phillip Miller, Treas.
Local. Promotes the study and control of environmental factors affecting the health and well being of workers. Sponsors continuing education courses in industrial hygiene, government affairs, and public relations. Conducts educational and research programs. **Affiliated With:** American Industrial Hygiene Association.

256 ■ American Legion Department Of Illinois
c/o Terry L. Woodburn, Adj.
2720 E Lincoln St.
Bloomington, IL 61704
Ph: (309)663-0361
Fax: (309)663-5783
E-mail: hdqs@illegion.org
URL: http://www.illegion.org
Contact: Terry L. Woodburn, Adj.
Founded: 1919. **Members:** 130,000. **Staff:** 20. **State**. **Affiliated With:** American Legion. **Formerly:** (2055) American Legion Illinois.

257 ■ American Legion, Illinois Headquarters Post 2910
PO Box 2910
Bloomington, IL 61702
Ph: (309)663-0361
Fax: (309)663-5783
URL: National Affiliate–www.legion.org
Local. **Affiliated With:** American Legion.

258 ■ American Legion, Illinois Post 56
c/o Louis E. Davis
PO Box 3263
Bloomington, IL 61704
Ph: (309)663-0361
Fax: (309)663-5783
URL: National Affiliate–www.legion.org
Contact: Louis E. Davis, Contact
Local. **Affiliated With:** American Legion.

259 ■ American Legion, Villa Grove Post 215
2720 E Lincoln St.
Bloomington, IL 61704
Ph: (309)663-0361
Fax: (309)663-5783
URL: National Affiliate–www.legion.org
Local. **Affiliated With:** American Legion.

260 ■ American Rabbit Breeders Association (ARBA)
PO Box 426
Bloomington, IL 61702
Ph: (309)664-7500
Fax: (309)664-0941
E-mail: arbapost@aol.com
URL: National Affiliate–www.arba.net
Contact: Roger Cota, Contact
Founded: 1982. **Members:** 20. **Membership Dues:** $10 (annual). **Local**. Breeders of cavies and rabbits. A local club of members interested in rabbits as pets, for show, and source of Angora wool. **Affiliated With:** American Rabbit Breeders Association. **Formerly:** Mohawk Valley Rabbit and Cavy Breeders Association; (2000) Mohawk Valley Rabbit Breeders Association. **Publications:** *MVRCBA News*, bimonthly. Newsletter. **Price:** free to members. **Circulation:** 1. **Conventions/Meetings:** monthly meeting.

261 ■ American Red Cross, McLean County Chapter, Bloomington
One Westport Ct.
Bloomington, IL 61704
Ph: (309)662-0500
Fax: (309)662-0301
URL: http://www.arcmclean.org
Local.

262 ■ American Wine Society - Bloomington-Normal
c/o C. Frank Shaw III, Co-Chm.
19173 Meander Way
Bloomington, IL 61704-5227
Ph: (309)661-4642
E-mail: cfs-mms@verizon.net
URL: National Affiliate–www.americanwinesociety.org
Contact: C. Frank Shaw III, Co-Chm.
Local. **Affiliated With:** American Wine Society.

263 ■ Association for Computing Machinery, Illinois Wesleyan University (ACM IWU)
c/o Jesse Magenheimer, Chm.
1312 Park St.
Bloomington, IL 61702
Ph: (309)556-3666
Fax: (309)556-3864
E-mail: acm@sun.iwu.edu
URL: http://sun.iwu.edu/~acm/
Contact: Jesse Magenheimer, Chm.
Local. Biological, medical, behavioral, and computer scientists; hospital administrators; programmers and others interested in application of computer methods to biological, behavioral, and medical problems. Stimulates understanding of the use and potential of computers in the Biosciences. **Affiliated With:** Association for Computing Machinery.

264 ■ Association for Women in Science, Heart of Illinois
c/o Zahia Drici, Dr., Pres.
Illinois Wesleyan Univ.
Dept. of Mathematics and Cmpt. Sci.
201 E Beecher St.
Bloomington, IL 61701
Ph: (309)556-3669
E-mail: zdrici@sun.iwu.edu
URL: National Affiliate–www.awis.org
Local. Professional women and students in life, physical, and social sciences and engineering; men are also members. Promotes equal opportunities for women to enter the scientific workforce and to achieve their career goals; provides educational information to women planning careers in science; networks with other women's groups; monitors scientific legislation and the status of women in science. **Affiliated With:** Association for Women in Science.

265 ■ Bloomington Lions Club, IL
PO Box 5045
Bloomington, IL 61702-5045
Ph: (309)452-1800
URL: http://bloomingtonillions.lionwap.org
Local. **Affiliated With:** Lions Clubs International.

266 ■ Bloomington Normal Association of Realtors
902 N Linden St.
Bloomington, IL 61701
Ph: (309)829-3341
Fax: (309)827-3671
E-mail: realtormik@aol.com
URL: National Affiliate–www.realtor.org
Contact: Michael McGaughan, Exec. Officer
Local. Strives to develop real estate business practices. Advocates the right to own, use and transfer real property. Provides a facility for professional development, research and exchange of information among members and to the general public. **Affiliated With:** National Association of Realtors.

267 ■ Bloomington Normal Human Resource Council (BNHRC)
PO Box 1794
Bloomington, IL 61702
E-mail: cshoman@ilstu.edu
URL: http://www.thebabyfold.org/BNHRC/index.htm
Contact: Colette Homan, Pres.
Local. Represents the interests of human resource and industrial relations professionals and executives. Promotes the advancement of human resource management.

268 ■ Building and Construction Trades Department, AFL-CIO - Livingston and Mclean Counties Building and Construction Trades Council
PO Box 1626
Bloomington, IL 61704
Ph: (309)963-3927
Fax: (309)963-3941
E-mail: iptapp@uanet.org
URL: National Affiliate–www.buildingtrades.org
Contact: Rick Terven, Pres.
Members: 25. **Local**. Helps trade unions make job sites safer, deliver apprenticeship and journey-level training, organize new workers, and support legislation that affects working families. **Affiliated With:** Building and Construction Trades Department - AFL-CIO.

269 ■ Central Illinois Association for Computing Machinery Chapter
c/o John Walther, Chair
PO Box 874
Bloomington, IL 61701
Ph: (309)763-3271
Biological, medical, behavioral, and computer scientists; hospital administrators; programmers and others interested in application of computer methods to biological, behavioral, and medical problems. Stimulates understanding of the use and potential of computers in the Biosciences. **Affiliated With:** Association for Computing Machinery.

270 ■ Central Illinois Chapter, American Society for Training and Development (CIC-ASTD)
PO Box 5472
Bloomington, IL 61702
E-mail: bill.d.pence.ara3@statefarm.com
URL: http://www.cic-astd.org
Contact: Bill Pence, Pres.
Local. Promotes workplace learning and the improvement of skills of workplace professionals. Provides resource and professional development to individuals in the field of learning and development. Recognizes and sets standards for learning and performance professionals. **Affiliated With:** American Society for Training and Development.

271 ■ Central Illinois Chapter of the Society of Financial Service Professionals
c/o Laura Zaverdinos, ChFC, Sec.-Treas.
State Farm
Financial Reporting & Anal.
1 State Farm Plz.
Bloomington, IL 61710-0001
Ph: (309)766-6957
E-mail: laura.zaverdinos.hlme@statefarm.com
URL: http://www.sfsp.net/centralillinois
Contact: Laura Zaverdinos ChFC, Sec.-Treas.
Local. Represents the interests of financial advisers. Fosters the development of professional responsibility. Helps clients achieve their personal and business-related financial goals. **Affiliated With:** Society of Financial Service Professionals.

272 ■ Central Illinois Club of Printing House Craftsmen (CICPHC)
c/o Wayne Kreps
810 IAA Dr.
Bloomington, IL 61701
Ph: (309)663-1375
E-mail: wkreps@ilgraphics.com
URL: National Affiliate–www.iaphc.org
Contact: Wayne Kreps, Pres.
Local. Represents individuals employed or interested in any facet of graphic arts. Promotes the printing and graphic arts industry. Works to educate, promote, inform and connect its members and the global graphic community in fostering their growth and success. **Affiliated With:** International Association of Printing House Craftsmen.

273 ■ Central Illinois Jeep Club (CIJC)
PO Box 1932
Bloomington, IL 61702-1932
E-mail: info@cijeep.com
URL: http://www.cijeep.com
Contact: Henry Dawdy, Contact
Local. **Affiliated With:** United Four-Wheel Drive Associations.

274 ■ Central Illinois Paralegal Association (CIPA)
PO Box 1948
Bloomington, IL 61702
E-mail: jackie.mckinnis.sag1@statefarm.com
URL: http://www.ciparalegal.org
Contact: Jackie Mckinnis, Contact
Local. Provides continuing education and professional development programs for paralegal professionals. Works to improve the quality and effectiveness of the delivery of legal services.

275 ■ Central Illinois Planned Giving Council
PO Box 3722
Bloomington, IL 61702-3722
Ph: (217)793-3363
Fax: (309)438-5748
E-mail: larryj@sikich-gardner.com
URL: National Affiliate–www.ncpg.org
Contact: Larry Johnson, Pres.
Local. Development officers, attorneys, CPAs, financial planners and insurance agents. Seeks to promote planned giving and to educate everyone on related methods, techniques and legal issues. Activities include establishing the Leave A Legacy program. **Affiliated With:** National Committee on Planned Giving.

276 ■ Corn Belt Philatelic Society
c/o Janice Jenkins
PO Box 625
Bloomington, IL 61702-0625
Ph: (309)663-2761
E-mail: jackjenk@a5.com
URL: National Affiliate–www.stamps.org
Contact: Janice Jenkins, Contact
Regional. Collectors of stamps and postcards. Hosts two monthly meetings (one for stamps, one for postcards), with programs, auctions, and information for collectors; also hosts a two-day annual show and bourse open to the public, with an awards banquet. **Affiliated With:** American Philatelic Society.

277 ■ Decatur Stamp Club
c/o David Stauffer
14206 Lara Trace
Bloomington, IL 61704
URL: http://www.stamps.org
Contact: Mr. David Stauffer, Contact
Founded: 1854. **Members:** 15. **Local**. Stamp collectors. Seeks to promote the hobby of stamp collecting through education. **Publications:** none. **Affiliated With:** American Philatelic Society. **Conventions/Meetings:** semimonthly meeting - always 1st and 3rd Wednesday.

278 ■ Habitat for Humanity of Mc Lean County Illinois
410 N Prairie St.
Bloomington, IL 61701
Ph: (309)827-3931
Fax: (309)827-5347
E-mail: info@habitatmclean.org
URL: http://www.habitatmclean.org
Contact: Jim Dady, Pres.
Local. **Affiliated With:** Habitat for Humanity International.

279 ■ IAIFA Bloomington
c/o Debra Lynn Wharton, Exec.
PO Box 1691
Bloomington, IL 61702-1691
Ph: (309)821-2150
Fax: (309)820-4345
E-mail: debra.wharton@countryfinancial.com
URL: National Affiliate–naifa.org
Contact: Debra Lynn Wharton, Exec.
Local. Represents the interests of insurance and financial advisors. Advocates for a positive legislative and regulatory environment. Enhances business and professional skills of members. **Affiliated With:** National Association of Insurance and Financial Advisors.

280 ■ Illinois Agricultural Association Foundation
c/o Steve Newman, CAE, Exec.Dir.
1701 N Towanda Ave.
PO Box 2901
Bloomington, IL 61702-2901
Ph: (309)557-2230
Fax: (309)557-2441
E-mail: iaafoundation@ilfb.org
URL: http://www.iaafoundation.org
Contact: Steve Newman CAE, Exec.Dir.
Founded: 1987. **State**.

281 ■ Illinois Association for College Admissions Counseling (IACAC)
PO Box 1666
Bloomington, IL 61702-1666
Ph: (309)662-0176
Fax: (309)662-0176
Free: (800)829-0176
E-mail: iacacgrove@aol.com
URL: http://www.iacac.org
Contact: Sandie Gilbert, Pres.
State. **Affiliated With:** National Association for College Admission Counseling.

282 ■ Illinois Boer Goat Association
c/o Dave Thomas
RR 1, Box 188
Bloomington, IL 61704
E-mail: thomasboers@msn.com
URL: National Affiliate–usbga.org
Contact: Dave Thomas, Contact
State.

283 ■ Illinois Corn Marketing Board (ICMB)
PO Box 487
Bloomington, IL 61702-0487
Ph: (309)827-0912
E-mail: ilcorn@ilcorn.org
URL: http://www.ilcorn.org
Contact: Rodney Weinzierl, Exec.Dir.
Founded: 1982. **State**. Serves the interests of all corn producers in Illinois.

284 ■ Illinois Fertilizer and Chemical Association (IFCA)
c/o Jean Payne, Pres.
PO Box 1326
Bloomington, IL 61702-1326
Ph: (309)827-2774
Fax: (309)827-2779
E-mail: jeanp@ifca.com
URL: http://www.ifca.com
Contact: Robin Schroeder, Chm.
State. **Publications:** *IFCA News*, monthly. Newsletter. **Conventions/Meetings:** annual meeting - always winter.

285 ■ Illinois High School Association (IHSA)
PO Box 2715
Bloomington, IL 61702-2715
Ph: (309)663-6377
Fax: (309)663-7479
E-mail: general@ihsa.org
URL: http://www.ihsa.org
Contact: Jim Woodward, Pres.
State. **Affiliated With:** National Federation of State High School Associations.

286 ■ Illinois Milk Producers' Association (IMPA)
1701 N Towanda Ave.
Bloomington, IL 61701
Ph: (309)557-3703
Fax: (309)557-3729
E-mail: fraley@ilfb.org
URL: http://www.illinoismilk.org
Contact: Doug Scheider, Pres.
Founded: 1933. **State.**

287 ■ Illinois School-Age Child Care Network
c/o Curtis Peace, Coor.
208 W Jefferson, Ste.301
Bloomington, IL 61701
Ph: (309)828-1892
Fax: (309)828-0526
Free: (800)649-1766
E-mail: curtis@ccrrn.com
URL: http://www.ccrrn.com
Contact: Kim Marshall, Asst.Dir.
State. Affiliated With: National AfterSchool Association.

288 ■ Illinois Soybean Association (ISA)
1605 Commerce Pkwy.
Bloomington, IL 61704
Ph: (309)662-3373
Fax: (309)663-6981
E-mail: ilsoy@ilsoy.org
URL: http://www.ilsoy.org
Contact: Lyle Roberts, Exec.Dir.
State. Affiliated With: American Soybean Association.

289 ■ Illinois Specialty Growers Association (ISGA)
1701 N Towanda Ave.
Bloomington, IL 61701
Ph: (309)557-2107
Fax: (309)557-3729
E-mail: handley@ilfb.org
URL: http://www.specialtygrowers.org
Contact: Diane Handley, Admin.Asst.
Founded: 1989. **State.**

290 ■ Illinois State Horticultural Society
c/o Mr. Don H. Naylor, Exec.Sec.
15962 Old Orchard Rd.
Bloomington, IL 61704
Ph: (309)828-8929
E-mail: ilsthortsoc@yahoo.com
URL: http://www.specialtygrowers.org
Contact: Mr. Don H. Naylor, Exec.Sec.
Founded: 1856. **Members:** 87. **Membership Dues:** primary, associate, agri-industry, $70 (annual). **Staff:** 1. **Budget:** $10,000. **State Groups:** 1. **For-Profit. Regional. Libraries: Type:** reference. **Holdings:** 145. **Subjects:** transactions, proceedings. **Awards:** Cider Contest Awards. **Type:** recognition. **Recipient:** selected by committee • Hall of Fame. **Type:** recognition. **Recipient:** selected by committee. **Affiliated With:** Illinois Specialty Growers Association. **Publications:** *Transactions and Proceedings*, annual. Contains organization activities and researches. **Price:** $25.00 domestic; $28.00 international (plus postage). ISSN: 0892-3477.

291 ■ Illinois State Society of Radiologic Technologists (ISSRT)
c/o Linda L. Racki, Exec.Sec.
PO Box 1942
Bloomington, IL 61702-1942
Free: (800)947-7784
E-mail: issrt@msn.com
URL: http://www.issrt.org
Contact: Linda L. Racki, Exec.Sec.
Founded: 1935. **Members:** 1,500. **Membership Dues:** active, associate, $50 (annual) • student, $25 (annual). **Staff:** 2. **Regional Groups:** 16. **State.** Radiologic technologists; students. Provides continuing education; represents members in legislature. Sponsors educational tournament for students. **Libraries: Type:** open to the public. **Subjects:** radiography. **Awards:** Elizabeth Bray Scholarship. **Frequency:** annual. **Type:** scholarship. **Recipient:** for members 60 days prior. **Affiliated With:** American Society of Radiologic Technologists. **Publications:** *The Illini Tech*, bimonthly. Newsletter. **Advertising:** accepted. **Conventions/Meetings:** annual conference (exhibits).

292 ■ International Union, United Automobile, Aerospace and Agricultural Implement Workers of America, AFL-CIO - Local Union 2488
10226 E 1400 N Rd.
Bloomington, IL 61704-5195
Ph: (309)828-2880
Fax: (309)829-2128
E-mail: uaw2488mail@verizon.net
URL: http://www.uaw2488.org
Contact: Ralph Timan, Pres.
Members: 2,773. **Local.** AFL-CIO. **Affiliated With:** International Union, United Automobile, Aerospace and Agricultural Implement Workers of America.

293 ■ John Wesley Powell Audubon Society
c/o Rhea Edge, Pres.
313 N Main St.
Bloomington, IL 61701
Ph: (309)829-2373
URL: National Affiliate–www.audubon.org
Local. Works to conserve and restore natural ecosystems, focusing on birds and other wildlife for the benefit of humanity and the earth's biological diversity. **Affiliated With:** National Audubon Society.

294 ■ Kiwanis Club of Bloomington, Illinois
c/o Andrea Raycraft, Sec.
PO Box 1866
Bloomington, IL 61702-1866
E-mail: andik0728@msn.com
URL: http://www.bloomingtonkiwanis.org
Contact: Katie Klein, Pres.
Local.

295 ■ McLean County Chamber of Commerce (MCC)
210 S East St.
PO Box 1586
Bloomington, IL 61702-1586
Ph: (309)829-6344
Fax: (309)827-3940
E-mail: info@mcleancochamber.org
URL: http://www.mcleancochamber.org
Contact: Michael Malone, Exec.Dir.
Founded: 1900. **Members:** 1,150. **Local.** Represents businesses and individuals investing time and money in a continual community development program. Improves the economic, civic and cultural well-being of McLean County. **Telecommunication Services:** electronic mail, michael@mcleancochamber.org. **Committees:** Ambassadors; Gala; Government Affairs; Marketing; Membership; Stroker Golf Classic; Workforce Development. **Councils:** Agri-Business. **Publications:** *News, Views & Issues*, monthly. Newsletter. Includes a message from the president of the chamber, updates from the MCC women's division, and other chamber membership information. **Circulation:** 35,000. **Advertising:** accepted. Alternate Formats: online. Also Cited As: *NV&I*. **Conventions/Meetings:** monthly Business After Hours - meeting - every third Wednesday • monthly Business Before Hours - meeting - every last Wednesday • annual Stroker Golf Classic - competition.

296 ■ McLean County Historical Society (MCHS)
200 N Main St.
Bloomington, IL 61701
Ph: (309)827-0428
Fax: (309)827-0100
URL: http://www.mchistory.org
Contact: Greg Koos, Exec.Dir.
Founded: 1892. **Members:** 1,400. **Staff:** 7. **Budget:** $525,000. **Local.** Individuals interested in the history of McLean County, IL. Operates McLean County Historical Society Museum and Library. **Libraries: Type:** open to the public. **Holdings:** 8,000; archival material. **Subjects:** local history. **Affiliated With:** American Association of Museums. **Doing business as:** (1999) McLean County Museum of History. **Publications:** *Illustrated History of McLean County* • *Military Buttons of the Land Services, 1787-1902* • *On the Square*, quarterly. Newsletter • *Places of Pride* • Newsletter, quarterly. **Conventions/Meetings:** annual meeting.

297 ■ McLean County Regional Planning Commission (MCRPC)
Govt. Ctr. No. M103
115 E Washington St.
Bloomington, IL 61701
Ph: (309)828-4331
Fax: (309)827-4773
E-mail: paul@mcplan.org
URL: http://www.mcplan.org
Contact: Paul Russell, Exec.Dir.
Local.

298 ■ Mothers Against Drunk Driving, McLean County
PO Box 794
Bloomington, IL 61702-0794
Fax: (309)747-3490
Free: (877)816-6233
E-mail: maddline@maddmclean.org
URL: http://www.maddmclean.org
Local. Victims of drunk driving crashes; concerned citizens. Encourages citizen participation in working towards reform of the drunk driving problem and the prevention of underage drinking. Acts as the voice of victims of drunk driving crashes by speaking on their behalf to communities, businesses, and educational groups. **Affiliated With:** Mothers Against Drunk Driving.

299 ■ National Active And Retired Federal Employees Association Bloomington-Normal 2177
709 E Bissell St.
Bloomington, IL 61701-6801
Ph: (309)828-8284
URL: National Affiliate–www.narfe.org
Contact: Roger E. Atkinson, Contact
Local. Protects the retirement future of employees through education. Informs members on issues affecting the retirement. **Affiliated With:** National Association of Retired Federal Employees.

300 ■ National Association of Home Builders of the U.S., Home Builders Association of Bloomington-Normal
c/o Lisa O'Brien Kohn
Local No. 1411
PO Box 918
Bloomington, IL 61702-0918
Ph: (309)663-6612
Fax: (309)663-6612
E-mail: bnahba@gte.net
URL: National Affiliate–www.nahb.org
Contact: Lisa O'Brien Kohn, Exec. Officer
Local. Single and multifamily home builders, commercial builders, and others associated with the building industry. **Affiliated With:** National Association of Home Builders.

301 ■ National Technological Honor Society - Bloomington Area Vocational Center - Illinois (BAVC)
PO Box 5187
Bloomington, IL 61702-5187
Ph: (309)829-8671
Fax: (309)828-3546
URL: http://www.bloomingtonavc.org
Contact: Dr. Steven Poznic, Dir.
Local.

302 ■ Normal - Young Life
2310 E Oakland Ave., Ste.3, Rm. 102
Bloomington, IL 61701
Ph: (309)661-8885
URL: http://whereis.younglife.org/FriendlyUrlRedirector.aspx?ID=C-849
Local.

303 ■ ParkLands Foundation
PO Box 3132
Bloomington, IL 61702-3132
Ph: (309)527-5636
E-mail: horgan@mcchs.org
URL: http://www.parklands.org
Contact: Mary Horgan, VP
Founded: 1967. **Membership Dues:** student, $10 • regular, $25 • active, $35 • contributing, $50 • sustaining, $100 • supporting, $250 • patron, $500 • life, $1,000. **Local**. Aims to preserve, protect, and ecologically restore historic natural lands in McLean and contiguous counties. These lands are dedicated primarily for preserving the biological diversity of native plants and wildlife, and secondarily for passive public recreation, environmental education and scientific research.

304 ■ People First of Illinois
PO Box 4294
Bloomington, IL 61702-4294
Ph: (309)820-8844
Fax: (309)821-1594
E-mail: ppl1st@peoplefirstofillinois.org
URL: http://www.peoplefirstofillinois.org
State. **Affiliated With:** People First International.

305 ■ PFLAG Bloomington/Normal
PO Box 615
Bloomington, IL 61702
Ph: (309)862-1844
E-mail: jhoward@ilstu.edu
URL: http://www.pflag.org/Illinois.204.0.html
Local. **Affiliated With:** Parents, Families, and Friends of Lesbians and Gays.

306 ■ Plumbing-Heating-Cooling Contractors Association, Bloomington/Normal
c/o Mr. Doug Dodson, Pres.
304 S Mason St.
Bloomington, IL 61701-4956
Ph: (309)828-0459
Fax: (309)829-2162
Free: (800)735-7422
E-mail: mimipbghtg@aol.com
URL: National Affiliate–www.phccweb.org
Contact: Mr. Doug Dodson, Pres.
Local. Represents the plumbing, heating and cooling contractors. Promotes the construction industry. Protects the environment, health, safety and comfort of society. **Affiliated With:** Plumbing-Heating-Cooling Contractors Association.

307 ■ Police and Firemen's Insurance Association - Bloomington Fire and Police Department
c/o Randall T. Wikoff
14554 N 900 E
Bloomington, IL 61704
Ph: (309)936-4463
URL: National Affiliate–www.pfia.net
Contact: Randall T. Wikoff, Contact
Local. **Affiliated With:** Police and Firemen's Insurance Association.

308 ■ Project Management Institute, Central Illinois Chapter (PMI-CIC)
PO Box 1449
Bloomington, IL 61702-1449
Ph: (309)763-3308
E-mail: president@pmi-cic.org
URL: http://www.pmi-cic.org
Contact: Debbie Sheehan, Pres.
Local. Corporations and individuals engaged in the practice of project management; project management students and educators. Seeks to advance the study, teaching, and practice of project management. **Affiliated With:** Project Management Institute.

309 ■ Psi Chi, National Honor Society in Psychology - Illinois Wesleyan University
c/o Dept. of Psychology
PO Box 2900
Bloomington, IL 61702-2900
Ph: (309)556-3940 (309)556-3867
Fax: (309)556-3864
E-mail: jpretz@iwu.edu
URL: National Affiliate–www.psichi.org
Local. **Affiliated With:** Psi Chi, National Honor Society in Psychology.

310 ■ Reserve Officers Association - Department of Illinois, Central Illinois Chapter 33
c/o LTC Terry J. DeHaan, Pres.
19243 Inverness Ct.
Bloomington, IL 61704
Ph: (309)378-5661
E-mail: dehaan68@aol.com
URL: http://www.ilroa.org
Contact: LTC Terry J. DeHaan, Pres.
Local. Promotes and supports the development and execution of a military policy for the United States. Provides professional development seminars, workshops and programs for its members. **Affiliated With:** Reserve Officers Association of the United States.

311 ■ SCORE Central Illinois
402 N Hershey Rd.
Bloomington, IL 61704
Ph: (309)664-0549
Fax: (309)661-1177
URL: http://www.central-illinois-score.org
Contact: John Robinson, Chm.
Local. Provides free consulting services to both start-up and existing small businesses in Central Illinois service area. **Affiliated With:** SCORE.

312 ■ United Way of McLean County
201 E Grove St.
Bloomington, IL 61701
Ph: (309)828-7383
Fax: (309)829-2469
E-mail: unitedwaymc@uwaymc.org
URL: http://www.uwaymc.org
Contact: Greg Cott, Pres.
Local. **Affiliated With:** United Way of America.

313 ■ Young Life McLean County
2310 E Oakland, Ste.3, Rm. 102
Bloomington, IL 61701
Ph: (309)661-8885
URL: http://whereis.younglife.org/FriendlyUrlRedirector.aspx?ID=A-IL36
Local.

Blue Island

314 ■ American Legion, Blue Island Post 50
PO Box 336
Blue Island, IL 60406
Ph: (309)663-0361
Fax: (309)663-5783
URL: National Affiliate–www.legion.org
Local. **Affiliated With:** American Legion.

315 ■ Blue Island Area Chamber of Commerce and Industry
2434 Vermont St.
Blue Island, IL 60406
Ph: (708)388-1000
Fax: (708)388-1062
E-mail: blueislandchamber@sbcglobal.net
URL: http://www.bichamber.org
Contact: Eda Schrimple, Exec.Dir.
Members: 350. **Membership Dues:** individual, not-for-profit, $50 • business, $125-$500. **Local**. Coordinates marketing and networking efforts, as well as acting as a liaison with various municipal bodies. **Publications:** *Chamber Chatter*, quarterly. Newsletter. **Advertising:** accepted. Alternate Formats: online. **Conventions/Meetings:** annual Blue Island Chamber of Commerce Community Expo - meeting, promotes Chamber members and businesses to Blue Island neighbors (exhibits) - every September.

316 ■ Blue Island Citizens For Developmental Disabilities
2155 Broadway
Blue Island, IL 60406
Ph: (708)389-6578
URL: National Affiliate–www.thearc.org
Local. Parents, professional workers, and others interested in individuals with mental retardation. Works to promote services, research, public understanding, and legislation for people with mental retardation and their families. **Affiliated With:** Arc of the United States.

317 ■ Main Street Blue Island
PO Box 476
Blue Island, IL 60406
Ph: (708)388-5735
Fax: (708)388-6532
E-mail: bimain@msn.com
URL: http://www.blueisland.org
Local.

Blue Mound

318 ■ American Legion, Mt. Auburn Post 1057
2592 N 1600 E Rd.
Blue Mound, IL 62513
Ph: (217)676-5621
Fax: (309)663-5783
URL: National Affiliate–www.legion.org
Local. **Affiliated With:** American Legion.

Bluffs

319 ■ American Legion, Illinois Post 441
c/o Charles Wolford
PO Box 14
Bluffs, IL 62621
Ph: (309)663-0361
Fax: (309)663-5783
URL: National Affiliate–www.legion.org
Contact: Charles Wolford, Contact
Local. **Affiliated With:** American Legion.

Bluford

320 ■ American Legion, Bluford Post 1193
15123 N Legion Ln.
Bluford, IL 62814
Ph: (309)663-0361
Fax: (309)663-5783
URL: National Affiliate–www.legion.org
Local. **Affiliated With:** American Legion.

Bolingbrook

321 ■ American Legion, Bolingbrook Post 1288
PO Box 1133
Bolingbrook, IL 60440
Ph: (708)972-9033
Fax: (309)663-5783
URL: National Affiliate–www.legion.org
Local. **Affiliated With:** American Legion.

322 ■ Bolingbrook Area Chamber of Commerce
375 W Briarcliff Rd.
Bolingbrook, IL 60440

Ph: (630)226-8420
Fax: (630)759-9937
E-mail: info@bolingbrookchamber.org
URL: http://www.bolingbrookchamber.org
Contact: Peg Kenyon, Exec.Dir.

Founded: 1978. **Members:** 600. **Membership Dues:** administrative/processing fee (new members), $30 • business, $175-$600 (annual) • developer, $425 (annual) • non-profit/charitable, $100 (annual) • church clergy, $50 (annual) • additional business/store location, $55 (annual). **Staff:** 4. **Local.** Fosters a competitive enterprise system of business and promotes the growth and development of businesses in the community. **Formerly:** (2006) Bolingbrook Chamber of Commerce and Industry. **Publications:** *The Reporter*, monthly. Newsletter. Includes helpful business information, networking tips, recent and upcoming events, recognition of members and a planning calendar. **Advertising:** accepted. Alternate Formats: online. **Conventions/Meetings:** annual Business to Business Showcase - trade show, networking event for businesses that provide products and services to other businesses (exhibits).

Bone Gap

323 ■ American Legion, Bone Gap Post 1041
RR 1
Bone Gap, IL 62815
Ph: (309)663-0361
Fax: (309)663-5783
URL: National Affiliate–www.legion.org
Local. Affiliated With: American Legion.

Bourbonnais

324 ■ American Legion, Illinois Post 1164
c/o Harvey S. Ruel
485 Briarcliff Ln., Apt. 6
Bourbonnais, IL 60914
Ph: (309)663-0361
Fax: (309)663-5783
URL: National Affiliate–www.legion.org
Contact: Harvey S. Ruel, Contact
Local. Affiliated With: American Legion.

325 ■ Antique Automobile Club of America, Illinois Region - Momence Chapter
c/o Shirley Salm, Pres.
1447 Westminster Ln.
Bourbonnais, IL 60914
E-mail: salm1447@comcast.net
URL: http://www.momencecarclub.com
Contact: Shirley Salm, Pres.
Local. Collectors, hobbyists, and others interested in the preservation, maintenance, and restoration of automobiles and in automotive history. **Affiliated With:** Antique Automobile Club of America.

326 ■ Bradley-Bourbonnais Chamber of Commerce (BBCC)
1690 Newtowne Dr.
Bourbonnais, IL 60914
Ph: (815)932-2222
Fax: (815)932-3294
E-mail: bbcc@bbchamber.com
URL: http://bbchamber.com
Contact: Ed Munday, Pres./CEO
Founded: 1989. **Members:** 535. **Staff:** 8. **Local.** Promotes business and community development in Bradley and Bourbonnais, IL. Conducts charitable programs; sponsors Bradley Village Christmas Parade. **Formed by Merger of:** (1989) Bourbannais Chamber of Commerce; (1989) Bradley Association of Commerce and Industry. **Publications:** *Leverage*, monthly. Newsletter. Alternate Formats: online • Membership Directory, annual. **Conventions/Meetings:** annual dinner.

327 ■ Kankakee Area Youth for Christ
70B Ken Hayes Dr.
Bourbonnais, IL 60914
Ph: (815)935-2020
Fax: (815)935-2226
URL: http://www.kayfc.org
Local. Affiliated With: Youth for Christ/U.S.A.

328 ■ Psi Chi, National Honor Society in Psychology - Olivet Nazarene University
c/o Dept. of Psychology
One Univ. Ave.
Bourbonnais, IL 60914-2271
Ph: (815)939-5273
Fax: (815)928-5571
E-mail: igassin@olivet.edu
URL: http://www.psichi.org/chapters/info.asp?chapter_id=928
Contact: Elizabeth Gassin PhD, Advisor
Local.

329 ■ Tri-City REACT
12 St. Michaels Dr.
Bourbonnais, IL 60914
Ph: (815)802-0956
E-mail: tricityreact@aol.com
URL: http://www.reactintl.org/teaminfo/usa_teams/teams-usil.htm
Local. Trained communication experts and professional volunteers. Provides volunteer public service and emergency communications through the use of radios (Citizen Band, General Mobile Radio Service, UHF and HAM). Coordinates with radio industries and government on safety communication matters and supports charitable activities and community organizations.

Bowen

330 ■ American Legion, Bowen Post 1087
PO Box 243
Bowen, IL 62316
Ph: (309)663-0361
Fax: (309)663-5783
URL: National Affiliate–www.legion.org
Local. Affiliated With: American Legion.

Bradford

331 ■ American Legion, Bradford Post 445
RR 2, Box 92
Bradford, IL 61421
Ph: (309)897-8088
Fax: (309)663-5783
URL: National Affiliate–www.legion.org
Local. Affiliated With: American Legion.

Bradley

332 ■ American Hellenic Educational Progressive Association - Kankakee, Chapter 345
c/o Gus A. Costones, Pres.
978 Quail Dr.
Bradley, IL 60915
Ph: (815)932-5194
URL: http://www.ahepafamily.org/d13
Contact: Gus A. Costones, Pres.
Local. Affiliated With: American Hellenic Educational Progressive Association.

333 ■ American Legion, Bradley Post 766
835 W Broadway St.
Bradley, IL 60915
Ph: (815)939-9113
Fax: (309)663-5783
URL: National Affiliate–www.legion.org
Local. Affiliated With: American Legion.

334 ■ Local 60C, Chemical Workers Council of the UFCW
383 South Ctr.
Bradley, IL 60915-2111
Ph: (847)662-6003
URL: National Affiliate–www.ufcw.org
Local. Affiliated With: United Food and Commercial Workers International Union.

Braidwood

335 ■ American Legion, Koca Post 39
248 E Main St.
Braidwood, IL 60408
Ph: (309)663-0361
Fax: (309)663-5783
URL: National Affiliate–www.legion.org
Local. Affiliated With: American Legion.

Breese

336 ■ American Legion, Timmermann-Benhoff Post 252
PO Box 101
Breese, IL 62230
Ph: (618)526-4265
Fax: (309)663-5783
URL: National Affiliate–www.legion.org
Local. Affiliated With: American Legion.

337 ■ Breese Chamber of Commerce
PO Box 132
Breese, IL 62230-0132
Ph: (618)526-7731 (618)526-0280
Contact: Jim Kueper, Pres.
Local.

338 ■ Clinton County Farm Bureau Foundation
c/o Curt Rueter, PR
PO Box 126
1165 N, 4th St.
Breese, IL 62230-0126
Ph: (618)526-4541 (618)526-7235
Fax: (618)526-2156
Contact: Diane Warnecke, Sec.
Local.

Bridgeport

339 ■ American Legion, Bridgeport Post 62
PO Box 273
Bridgeport, IL 62417
Ph: (618)945-4111
Fax: (309)663-5783
URL: National Affiliate–www.legion.org
Local. Affiliated With: American Legion.

Bridgeview

340 ■ Bridgeview Chamber of Commerce
7300 W 87th St.
Bridgeview, IL 60455
Ph: (708)598-1700
Fax: (708)598-1709
E-mail: bvchamber@aol.com
URL: http://www.bridgeviewchamber.com
Contact: Roseann Bautista, Exec.Dir.
Local. Provides information from local, state and federal sources on a variety of issues that may affect the business community. Sponsors community programs such as the Toys for Needy Children Drive at Christmas, scholarships to deserving students, Fire Prevention Poster Contest, and Christmas Tree Lighting Ceremony. **Computer Services:** Information services, membership directory. **Publications:** Newsletter, monthly. Contains information about programs and activities, legislative, business and village information, community news, and member profiles. •

Membership Directory, annual. Contains listing of members both alphabetically and categorically by business service or product.

341 ■ Bridgeview Lions Club
PO Box 1732
Bridgeview, IL 60455
E-mail: dgrogan498@aol.com
URL: http://bridgeviewil.lionwap.org
Local. Affiliated With: Lions Clubs International.

342 ■ National Active And Retired Federal Employees Association - Southwest Chicago Metro 1106
7112 S Oketo Ave.
Bridgeview, IL 60455-1146
Ph: (708)458-4990
URL: National Affiliate–www.narfe.org
Contact: John Altar, Contact
Local. Protects the retirement future of employees through education. Informs members on issues affecting the retirement. **Affiliated With:** National Association of Retired Federal Employees.

Brighton

343 ■ American Legion, Brighton Post 476
PO Box 775
Brighton, IL 62012
Ph: (618)372-3669
Fax: (309)663-5783
URL: National Affiliate–www.legion.org
Local. Affiliated With: American Legion.

344 ■ Brighton BMX
c/o Jacqueline L. Hood
Hwy. 111 Schneider Park
Brighton, IL 62012
Ph: (618)372-7223 (314)799-5878
E-mail: info@brightonbmx.com
URL: http://brightonbmx.com
Contact: Jacqueline L. Hood, Contact
Local.

Brimfield

345 ■ American Legion, Brimfield Post 452
PO Box 573
Brimfield, IL 61517
Ph: (309)446-3020
Fax: (309)663-5783
URL: National Affiliate–www.legion.org
Local. Affiliated With: American Legion.

Brocton

346 ■ American Legion, Illinois Post 977
c/o Robert Willoughby
PO Box 106
Brocton, IL 61917
Ph: (309)663-0361
Fax: (309)663-5783
URL: National Affiliate–www.legion.org
Contact: Robert Willoughby, Contact
Local. Affiliated With: American Legion.

Brookfield

347 ■ American Legion, Illinois Post 190
c/o Edward Feely
PO Box 3
Brookfield, IL 60513
Ph: (309)663-0361
Fax: (309)663-5783
URL: National Affiliate–www.legion.org
Contact: Edward Feely, Contact
Local. Affiliated With: American Legion.

348 ■ Antique Automobile Club of America, Illinois Region
c/o Laura McDonald, Pres.
3633 Vernon Ave.
Brookfield, IL 60513
Ph: (630)852-9893
E-mail: ilregionaaca@aol.com
URL: http://local.aaca.org/illinois
Contact: Laura McDonald, Pres.
Founded: 1946. **Membership Dues:** individual, $23 (annual) • life, $300. **State.** Collectors, hobbyists, and others interested in the preservation, maintenance, and restoration of automobiles and in automotive history. **Affiliated With:** Antique Automobile Club of America.

349 ■ Brookfield Chamber of Commerce
3724 Grand Blvd.
Brookfield, IL 60513
Ph: (708)485-1434
E-mail: matthew.joseph@wamu.net
URL: http://www.brookfieldchamberofcommerce.org
Contact: Mr. Matthew Joseph, Pres.
Founded: 1953. **Members:** 71. **Membership Dues:** business, $115 (annual) • non-profit organization, $65 (annual). **Local. Publications:** Newsletter, monthly. **Price:** free.

350 ■ Brookfield Zoo/Chicago Zoological Society
c/o Keith Winsten
3300 Golf Rd.
Brookfield, IL 60513
Ph: (708)485-0263
Fax: (708)485-3532
Free: (800)201-0784
E-mail: kewinsten@brookfieldzoo.org
URL: http://www.brookfieldzoo.org
Contact: Keith Winsten, Dir. of Comm.
Local.

351 ■ Chicagoland Environmental Network (CEN)
3300 Golf Rd.
Brookfield, IL 60513
Ph: (708)485-0263
E-mail: cen@brookfieldzoo.org
URL: http://www.chicagoenvironment.org
Staff: 1. **Local.** Informs the public about opportunities to get involved in environmental issues in the Greater Chicago metropolitan area. Promotes public participation in environmental activities.

352 ■ Girl Scouts of Whispering Oaks Council
8934 Ogden Ave., 2nd Fl.
Brookfield, IL 60513
Ph: (708)354-4855
Fax: (708)354-5264
E-mail: info@whisperingoaksgs.org
URL: http://www.whisperingoaksgs.org
Local. Young girls and adult volunteers, corporate, government and individual supporters. Strives to develop potential and leadership skills among its members. Conducts trainings, educational programs and outdoor activities.

353 ■ Kiwanis Club of Brookfield, IL
PO Box 225
Brookfield, IL 60513
Ph: (708)485-2847
E-mail: cphall2@aol.com
URL: http://bbrookkiwanis.home.comcast.net
Contact: Swede Klang, Pres.
Local.

354 ■ Salt Creek Watershed Network
c/o Jeff Swano
8738 Washington Ave.
Brookfield, IL 60513-1424
Ph: (708)485-4190
Founded: 1998. **Members:** 350. **Staff:** 2. **Local. Publications:** *Confluence*, quarterly. Newsletter. Contains informational updates and education. **Price:** free. **Advertising:** not accepted.

Brookport

355 ■ American Legion, Lester Reynolds Post 523
PO Box 807
Brookport, IL 62910
Ph: (618)564-3207
Fax: (309)663-5783
URL: National Affiliate–www.legion.org
Local. Affiliated With: American Legion.

Brussels

356 ■ American Legion, Francis Pohlman Post 685
PO Box 65
Brussels, IL 62013
Ph: (309)663-0361
Fax: (309)663-5783
URL: National Affiliate–www.legion.org
Local. Affiliated With: American Legion.

Buckley

357 ■ American Legion, Hickerson Post 432
313 S Walnut
Buckley, IL 60918
Ph: (309)663-0361
Fax: (309)663-5783
URL: National Affiliate–www.legion.org
Local. Affiliated With: American Legion.

Buda

358 ■ American Legion, Illinois Post 261
c/o Frank W. Suggitt
RR 1, Box 41
Buda, IL 61314
Ph: (309)663-0361
Fax: (309)663-5783
URL: National Affiliate–www.legion.org
Contact: Frank W. Suggitt, Contact
Local. Affiliated With: American Legion.

Buffalo Grove

359 ■ American Legion, Board of Education Post 471
820 Weidner Rd., Apt. 407
Buffalo Grove, IL 60089
Ph: (309)663-0361
Fax: (309)663-5783
URL: National Affiliate–www.legion.org
Local. Affiliated With: American Legion.

360 ■ Buffalo Grove Area Chamber of Commerce
50 1/2 Raupp Blvd.
PO Box 7124
Buffalo Grove, IL 60089
Ph: (847)541-7799
Fax: (847)541-7819
E-mail: info@bgacc.org
URL: http://www.bgacc.org
Contact: Lynne Schneider, Exec.Dir.
Founded: 1972. **Members:** 430. **Membership Dues:** business (based on number of employees), $170-$655 (annual) • not-for-profit, school, worship, $115 (annual) • governmental, $170 (annual). **Staff:** 2. **Budget:** $200,000. **Regional Groups:** 1. **State Groups:** 1. **For-Profit. Local.** Promotes business and community development in Buffalo Grove, IL and surrounding communities. **Computer Services:** database • information services • mailing lists. **Committees:** BG Networkers; Buffalo Grove Days; NIBPAC; Restaurants and Retailers. **Councils:** Women in Business. **Formerly:** (1999) Buffalo Grove Chamber of Commerce. **Publications:** *Around Town*, monthly. Newsletter. **Price:** included in membership dues. **Cir-**

culation: 1,200. **Advertising:** accepted. **Conventions/Meetings:** monthly meeting, networking, lunch and program (exhibits) - always 1st Tuesday.

361 ■ Illinois Society of Enrolled Agents - Northwest Chapter
c/o Gregory A. Woitach, Pres.
993 Alden Ln.
Buffalo Grove, IL 60089
Ph: (847)541-4711
Fax: (847)541-4711
E-mail: gawojo@aol.com
Contact: Gregory A. Woitach EA, Pres.
Local. Affiliated With: National Association of Enrolled Agents.

362 ■ International Facility Management Association, Northern Illinois (Suburban Chicago)
c/o Kathy Daloia, Chapter Administrator
PO Box 4893
Buffalo Grove, IL 60089-4893
Ph: (847)821-8243
Fax: (847)821-8248
E-mail: chapteradministrator@ifmani.com
URL: http://www.ifmani.com
Contact: Tom Kapusta AIA, Pres.
Local. Affiliated With: International Facility Management Association.

363 ■ Midwest Stamp Dealers Association (MSDA)
c/o James F. Bardo
PO Box 7437
Buffalo Grove, IL 60089
E-mail: frankb@theramp.net
URL: http://msdastamp.com/
Contact: Mr. James F. Bardo, Contact
Local. Affiliated With: American Philatelic Society.

364 ■ Northwest Suburban Jewish Community Center (NWSJCC)
1250 Radcliffe Rd.
Buffalo Grove, IL 60089
Ph: (847)392-7411
Fax: (847)392-7917
URL: http://www.jccofchicago.org
Contact: Bonnie Greenberg, Exec.Dir.
Founded: 1980. **Members:** 1,000. **Membership Dues:** $185 (annual). **Staff:** 75. **Local.** Provides social, recreational, educational, and cultural activities for Jewish citizens in the Buffalo Grove, IL area. **Publications:** *Newsbreak*, monthly. Newsletter. **Price:** free. **Advertising:** not accepted • Brochure, semiannual. **Price:** free. **Advertising:** not accepted.

Bunker Hill

365 ■ American Legion, Partridge Post 578
319 N Marion
Bunker Hill, IL 62014
Ph: (618)585-4478
Fax: (309)663-5783
URL: National Affiliate–www.legion.org
Local. Affiliated With: American Legion.

366 ■ National Active And Retired Federal Employees Association - Alton 575
419 N East St.
Bunker Hill, IL 62014-1239
Ph: (618)585-4872
URL: National Affiliate–www.narfe.org
Contact: Malvern W. Allen, Contact
Local. Protects the retirement future of employees through education. Informs members on issues affecting the retirement. **Affiliated With:** National Association of Retired Federal Employees.

Burbank

367 ■ American Hellenic Educational Progressive Association - Oaklawn-Englewood, Chapter 323
c/o John Giaouris, Pres.
8030 S McVicker Ave.
Burbank, IL 60459
Ph: (708)599-6880
URL: http://www.ahepafamily.org/d13
Contact: John Giaouris, Pres.
Local. Affiliated With: American Hellenic Educational Progressive Association.

368 ■ Burbank Chamber of Commerce
5501 W 79th St.
Burbank, IL 60459
Ph: (708)425-4668
Fax: (708)424-9492
Contact: Judy M. Balestri, Exec.Sec.
Local.

369 ■ South Side Muskie Hawks (SSMH)
8212 S Mulligan
Burbank, IL 60459
Ph: (708)430-4444
E-mail: fishdaley@aol.com
URL: http://www.muskiesinc.org/chapters/07
Contact: John Martin Daley, Pres.
Local.

Burnside

370 ■ American Legion, Snyder-Turner Post 1163
2064 E C R 2100
Burnside, IL 62330
Ph: (309)663-0361
Fax: (309)663-5783
URL: National Affiliate–www.legion.org
Local. Affiliated With: American Legion.

371 ■ Young Life Tri State
c/o Shawn Whitaker
1875 E County Rd. 2300
Burnside, IL 62330
Ph: (217)755-4204
URL: http://tristate.younglife.org
Contact: Shawn Whitaker, Contact
Local.

Burr Ridge

372 ■ Central Chapter of the Society of Nuclear Medicine (CCSNM)
c/o Bacon-Hedland Mgt.
475 S Frontage Rd., Ste.101
Burr Ridge, IL 60527-6282
Ph: (630)323-7028
Fax: (630)323-6989
E-mail: info@ccsnm.org
URL: http://www.ccsnm.org
Contact: Merle Hedland, Exec.Dir.
Regional. Affiliated With: Society of Nuclear Medicine. **Publications:** *Central Chapter News*, three to four times a year. Newsletter. Alternate Formats: online.

373 ■ Chicago Branch Coast Guard Enlisted Association
215 W 83rd St., Ste.D
Burr Ridge, IL 60527
Ph: (630)986-2151
E-mail: kbrockhouse@msochicago.uscg.mil
URL: http://www.uscgcpoa.org/3-cgea/3-cgea_index.htm
Contact: Kenneth Brockhouse, Pres.
Local. Affiliated With: United States Coast Guard Chief Petty Officers Association.

374 ■ Chicagoland Section of the Mercedes-Benz Club of America
c/o Wendy Brown, Pres.
6750 County Line Ln.
Burr Ridge, IL 60527
Ph: (630)323-4090
E-mail: webmaster@mbclub.com
URL: http://www.mbclub.com/index.htm
Contact: Wendy Brown, Pres.
Local. Affiliated With: Mercedes-Benz Club of America.

375 ■ Illinois Radiological Society (IRS)
c/o Merle Hedland
475 S Frontage Rd., Ste.101
Burr Ridge, IL 60527-6282
Ph: (630)323-5344
Fax: (630)323-6989
E-mail: info@illradsoc.org
URL: http://www.illradsoc.org
Contact: Merle Hedland, Contact
State. Promotes the value of radiology, radiation oncology, nuclear medicine, medical physics and other related fields. Seeks to improve the quality of patient care and influence the socio-economics of the practice of radiology. Provides continuing education for radiology and allied health professionals. **Affiliated With:** American College of Radiology.

376 ■ Murphy Roche Irish Music Club
c/o Michael Chole, Sec. and Regional Delegate
11309 W, 72nd St.
Burr Ridge, IL 60527-4938
Ph: (630)662-8611
Fax: (630)662-8611
E-mail: info@murphyroche.com
URL: http://www.murphyroche.com
Contact: Kell Chole, Contact
Founded: 1997. **Members:** 100. **Membership Dues:** individual, $20 (annual) • family, $40 (annual). **Staff:** 6. **Local.** Works to teach and promote Irish music and culture. **Publications:** *Treoir* (in English and Gaelic), quarterly. Magazine. Features information about traditional Irish music and musicians. **Price:** included in membership dues. **Advertising:** accepted. **Conventions/Meetings:** annual North American Convention of Comheltas Ceoltoiri Eireann; Avg. Attendance: 2000.

377 ■ Professional Convention Management Association, Greater Midwest Chapter
c/o Merle Hedland, Administrator
Bacon-Hedland Mgt., Inc.
476 S Frontage Rd., Ste.101
Burr Ridge, IL 60527
Ph: (630)323-7413
Fax: (630)323-6989
E-mail: gmcpcma@bacon-hedland.com
URL: National Affiliate–www.pcma.org
Regional. Affiliated With: Professional Convention Management Association.

378 ■ Willowbrook - Burr Ridge Chamber of Commerce and Industry
8300 S Madison
Burr Ridge, IL 60527
Ph: (630)654-0909
Fax: (630)654-0922
E-mail: info@wbbrchamber.org
URL: http://www.wbbrchamber.org
Contact: Ron Isdonas, Pres.
Founded: 1985. **Membership Dues:** business (depends upon the number of employees), $175-$290 (annual). **Local.** Provides community leadership, facilitates communication, promotes education, supports local causes and represents the interest and advancement of its members. **Computer Services:** Information services, membership directory. **Committees:** Budget; Business and Industrial Enhancement; Business Expo; By-Laws; Community and Government Relations; Golf Outing; Health and Wellness; Publicity. **Publications:** Newsletter, monthly. **Circulation:** 1,400. **Advertising:** accepted.

Bushnell

379 ■ Bushnell Chamber of Commerce
PO Box 111
Bushnell, IL 61422
Ph: (309)772-2171
Fax: (309)772-3616
E-mail: chamber@bushnellchamber.com
URL: http://www.bushnellchamber.com
Contact: Don Swartzbaugh, Pres.
Local. Works to build a strong economic base through the promotion of local businesses and activities. **Computer Services:** Information services, membership directory. **Conventions/Meetings:** monthly meeting - every 1st Wednesday.

380 ■ Illinois Lamb and Wool Producers
c/o Eugene McGrew, Exec.Sec.
907 Twyman
Bushnell, IL 61422
Ph: (309)772-8064
Fax: (309)772-8064
Contact: Eugene McGrew, Exec.Sec.
State.

Byron

381 ■ American Legion, Illinois Post 209
c/o Philip Cafagna
PO Box 971
Byron, IL 61010
Ph: (815)234-5131
Fax: (309)663-5783
URL: National Affiliate–www.legion.org
Contact: Philip Cafagna, Contact
Local. **Affiliated With:** American Legion.

382 ■ Audubon Council of Illinois
c/o Ed Stirling, Pres.
PO Box 813
Byron, IL 61010-0813
Ph: (815)389-4775
E-mail: stirli@hughestech.net
URL: http://www.audubon.org/chapter/il/il/index.html
Contact: Ed Stirling, Pres.
State.

383 ■ Byron Area Chamber of Commerce
110 N Union
PO Box 405
Byron, IL 61010-0405
Ph: (815)234-5500
Fax: (815)234-7114
E-mail: byronchamber@byronil.net
URL: http://byronchamber.com
Contact: Caryn Huber, Exec.Dir.
Founded: 1958. **Members:** 130. **Membership Dues:** general business/professional (base), $130 • government agency, $200 • church, non-profit club, $115 • individual, $50 • financial (per million asset), $17. **Staff:** 2. **State Groups:** 1. **Local**. Promotes business and community development in Byron, IL. **Libraries: Type:** open to the public. **Awards:** Business of the Year. **Frequency:** annual. **Type:** recognition • Citizen of the Year. **Frequency:** annual. **Type:** recognition. **Publications:** Newsletter, monthly. **Conventions/Meetings:** monthly luncheon - every 1st Tuesday.

384 ■ Byron Lions Club, IL
PO Box 200
Byron, IL 61010
E-mail: president@byronlions.com
URL: http://www.byronlions.com
Local. **Affiliated With:** Lions Clubs International.

Cahokia

385 ■ American Legion, Cahokia Memorial Post 784
16 Delano Dr.
Cahokia, IL 62206
Ph: (618)337-6454
Fax: (309)663-5783
URL: National Affiliate–www.legion.org
Local. **Affiliated With:** American Legion.

386 ■ Cahokia Area Chamber of Commerce
905 Falling Springs Rd.
Cahokia, IL 62206
Ph: (618)332-1900
Fax: (618)332-6690
Contact: Debbie Brockland, Pres.
Local.

387 ■ Local 871C, Chemical Workers Council of the UFCW
1105 Williams St.
Cahokia, IL 62206
Ph: (618)583-1045
E-mail: icwuc871@apci.net
URL: National Affiliate–www.ufcw.org
Local. **Affiliated With:** United Food and Commercial Workers International Union.

388 ■ Madison County Beagle Club
c/o Robert Franey
507 E 5th St.
Cahokia, IL 62206-1712
URL: National Affiliate–clubs.akc.org
Contact: Robert Franey, Contact
Local.

Cairo

389 ■ American Legion, Claude Robinson Post 899
PO Box 25
Cairo, IL 62914
Ph: (618)748-9108
Fax: (309)663-5783
URL: National Affiliate–www.legion.org
Local. **Affiliated With:** American Legion.

390 ■ Cairo Chamber of Commerce (CCC)
220 8th St.
Cairo, IL 62914-2135
Ph: (618)734-2737
E-mail: cairochamber@earthlink.net
Contact: Ms. Mickey Blackburn, Sec.
Founded: 1866. **Members:** 60. **Membership Dues:** business, $100 (annual) • individual, $50 (annual). **Staff:** 1. **State Groups:** 1. **For-Profit**. **Local**. Promotes business and community development in Alexander and Pulaski counties, IL. Sponsors Riverboat Day. **Publications:** none. **Conventions/Meetings:** annual meeting - always March.

Calumet City

391 ■ American Legion, Calumet Memorial Post 330
950 Legion Dr.
Calumet City, IL 60409
Ph: (708)862-8687
Fax: (309)663-5783
URL: National Affiliate–www.legion.org
Local. **Affiliated With:** American Legion.

392 ■ American Legion, Walter Stelmaszek Post 792
312 Warren St.
Calumet City, IL 60409
Ph: (708)730-1883
Fax: (309)663-5783
URL: National Affiliate–www.legion.org
Local. **Affiliated With:** American Legion.

393 ■ Calumet City Chamber of Commerce (CCCC)
1243 Hirsch Ave.
Calumet City, IL 60409
Ph: (708)891-5888
Fax: (708)891-9451
E-mail: ccham2000@aol.com
Contact: Frank Orsini, Pres.
Founded: 1937. **Local**. Promotes business and community development in Calumet City, IL.

394 ■ Izaak Walton League of America, Calumet Region Chapter
c/o Dennis Strych
635 Calhoun
Calumet City, IL 60409
Ph: (708)862-5581
URL: National Affiliate–www.iwla.org
Local. Works to educate the public to conserve, maintain, protect, and restore the soil, forest, water, and other natural resources of the U.S; promotes the enjoyment and wholesome utilization of these resources. **Affiliated With:** Izaak Walton League of America.

Calumet Park

395 ■ American Legion, Calumet Park Post 1156
12633 S Bishop St.
Calumet Park, IL 60827
Ph: (708)385-8446
Fax: (309)663-5783
URL: National Affiliate–www.legion.org
Local. **Affiliated With:** American Legion.

396 ■ National Black United Front, Chicago Chapter
12817 S Ashland Ave.
Calumet Park, IL 60827
Ph: (708)389-9929
Fax: (708)389-9819
E-mail: nbufchi@allways.net
URL: http://www.nbufront.org/html/Chapters/NBUF-Chicago.html
Contact: Conrad Worrill PhD, Chm.
Local. **Affiliated With:** National Black United Front.

Cambridge

397 ■ American Legion, Cambridge Post 417
102 Circle Dr.
Cambridge, IL 61238
Ph: (309)663-0361
Fax: (309)663-5783
URL: National Affiliate–www.legion.org
Local. **Affiliated With:** American Legion.

Camp Point

398 ■ American Legion, Camp Point Post 238
2033 E 2000th St.
Camp Point, IL 62320
Ph: (309)663-0361
Fax: (309)663-5783
URL: National Affiliate–www.legion.org
Local. **Affiliated With:** American Legion.

Campbell Hill

399 ■ American Legion, Campbell Hill Post 1096
PO Box 221
Campbell Hill, IL 62916
Ph: (309)663-0361
Fax: (309)663-5783
URL: National Affiliate–www.legion.org
Local. **Affiliated With:** American Legion.

Canton

400 ■ American Legion, Illinois Post 16
c/o Orlando C. Crowther
550 S 4th St.
Canton, IL 61520

Ph: (309)647-0914
Fax: (309)663-5783
URL: National Affiliate–www.legion.org
Contact: Orlando C. Crowther, Contact
Local. Affiliated With: American Legion.

401 ■ Canton Area Chamber of Commerce (CACC)
45 E Side Sq., Ste.303
Canton, IL 61520
Ph: (309)647-2677
Fax: (309)647-2712
E-mail: cantonareacc@sbcglobal.net
URL: http://www.cantonillinois.org
Contact: Rod Ahitow, Exec.Dir.
Founded: 1925. **Members:** 250. **Membership Dues:** retail/service/manufacturing/professional, $200-$500 (annual) • hospital/nursing home (per bed), $5 (annual) • financial institution, $16 (annual) • utility (major), $500 (annual) • individual (regular), $75 (annual) • individual (retired), $50 (annual) • church/school/nonprofit (based on budget), $75-$200 (annual) • gold level, $350 (annual). **Staff:** 2. **Budget:** $50,000. **Local.** Businesses, organizations, and individuals promoting economic and community development in the Canton, IL area. **Awards:** Business Person of the Year. **Frequency:** annual. **Type:** recognition • Citizen of the Year. **Frequency:** annual. **Type:** recognition • Educator of the Year. **Frequency:** annual. **Type:** recognition. **Affiliated With:** U.S. Chamber of Commerce. **Publications:** *Chamber Courier*, monthly. Newsletter. Contains information on chamber events and member activities. Alternate Formats: online.

402 ■ Christian Camp and Conference Association, Illinois
c/o John Theien, Pres.
Camp Kearney
30000 Mission Camp Rd.
Canton, IL 61520
Ph: (309)389-5375
URL: National Affiliate–www.ccca-us.org
Contact: John Theien, Pres.
State. Affiliated With: Christian Camping International/U.S.A.

403 ■ Elks Lodge
61 W. Elm St.
Canton, IL 61520
Ph: (309)647-0200

404 ■ Illinois School Library Media Association (ISLMA)
c/o Kay Maynard, Exec.Sec.
PO Box 598
Canton, IL 61520
Ph: (309)649-0911
Fax: (309)649-0916
E-mail: islma@islma.org
URL: http://www.islma.org
Contact: Kay Maynard, Exec.Sec.
Founded: 1988. **Members:** 1,100. **Membership Dues:** personal, $50 (annual) • associate or corporate, $75 (annual) • retired, $30 (annual). **Budget:** $175,000. **State.** Elementary and secondary school library media specialists interested in the general improvement and extension of services for children and young people. **Awards:** Abraham Lincoln Illinois High School Book Award. **Frequency:** annual. **Type:** recognition. **Recipient:** designed to encourage high school students to read for personal satisfaction and become familiar with authors of young adult and adult books; to an author selected by young adult readers • ISLMA/Highsmith Award. **Frequency:** annual. **Type:** monetary. **Recipient:** for a school library media center's achievement in planning and implementing an innovative or creative program or service which has a measurable, positive impact on its users • The Monarch Award. **Frequency:** annual. **Type:** recognition. **Recipient:** to an author and/or illustrator of a book voted as their favorite by participating K-3 children in Illinois it is designed to encourage Illinois students to read critically and become familiar with children's books, authors and illustrators • Polestar Award. **Frequency:** annual. **Type:** recognition. **Recipient:** for members of the association who have made outstanding contributions to school library media programs in Illinois. **Affiliated With:** American Association of School Librarians. **Absorbed:** (1988) Illinois Association for Media in Education. **Publications:** *ISLMA News*, bimonthly. Newsletter. **Advertising:** accepted • *Linking for Learning: the Illinois School Library Media Program Guidelines*. **Price:** $18.50 • Membership Directory, annual. **Price:** included in membership dues. **Advertising:** accepted. **Conventions/Meetings:** annual convention, pre-conference presentations, breakout sessions, speakers, exhibits, conference store and meal functions (exhibits) - every fall.

405 ■ Mothers Against Drunk Driving, Fulton County
PO Box 671
Canton, IL 61520
Ph: (309)647-7778
Fax: (309)647-6899
E-mail: ikenmimi@sbcglobal.net
URL: http://www.maddfultonco.org
Local. Victims of drunk driving crashes; concerned citizens. Encourages citizen participation in working towards reform of the drunk driving problem and the prevention of underage drinking. Acts as the voice of victims of drunk driving crashes by speaking on their behalf to communities, businesses, and educational groups. **Affiliated With:** Mothers Against Drunk Driving.

406 ■ Phi Theta Kappa, Nu Delta Chapter - Spoon River College
c/o Diane Taylor
23235 N County 22
Canton, IL 61520
Ph: (309)833-6020
E-mail: dtaylor@spoonrivercollege.edu
URL: http://www.ptk.org/directories/chapters/IL/183-1.htm
Contact: Diane Taylor, Advisor
Local.

407 ■ United Way for Spoon River Country
PO Box 335
Canton, IL 61520-0335
Ph: (309)647-1825
URL: National Affiliate–national.unitedway.org
Local. Affiliated With: United Way of America.

Carbondale

408 ■ AAA Missouri
1260 E Main
Carbondale, IL 62901
Ph: (618)457-8448
Fax: (618)549-8926
Free: (800)554-8820
URL: http://www.aaamissouri.com
State.

409 ■ American Chemical Society, Southern Illinois Section
c/o Dr. Bakul C. Dave, Chm.
Southern Illinois Univ.
1245 Lincoln Dr.
Carbondale, IL 62901-4304
E-mail: dave@chem.siu.edu
URL: National Affiliate–acswebcontent.acs.org
Contact: Dr. Bakul C. Dave, Chm.
Local. Represents the interests of individuals dedicated to the advancement of chemistry in all its branches. Provides opportunities for peer interaction and career development. **Affiliated With:** American Chemical Society.

410 ■ American Institute of Architects Southern Illinois
c/o image Architechs, Inc.
PO Box 850
Carbondale, IL 62901
Ph: (618)457-2128
Fax: (618)549-5725
URL: National Affiliate–www.aia.org
Local. Professional society of architects. Fosters professionalism and accountability among members through continuing education and training; promotes design excellence by influencing change in the industry. **Affiliated With:** American Institute of Architects.

411 ■ American Legion, Illinois Post 514
c/o Donald Forsythe
PO Box 2883
Carbondale, IL 62902
Ph: (618)549-4313
Fax: (309)663-5783
URL: National Affiliate–www.legion.org
Contact: Donald Forsythe, Contact
Local. Affiliated With: American Legion.

412 ■ Association for Computing Machinery, Southern Illinois University Carbondale
1000 Faner Dr.
Carbondale, IL 62901
Ph: (618)453-6039
Fax: (618)453-6044
E-mail: acm@cs.siu.edu
URL: http://www.siu.edu/~acm
Contact: Lucas Utterback, Pres.
Local. Biological, medical, behavioral, and computer scientists; hospital administrators; programmers and others interested in application of computer methods to biological, behavioral, and medical problems. Stimulates understanding of the use and potential of computers in the biosciences. **Affiliated With:** Association for Computing Machinery.

413 ■ Astronomical Association of Southern Illinois
205 S Canterbury Dr.
Carbondale, IL 62901
Ph: (618)529-7713
E-mail: bless@isbe.accessus.net
URL: http://htreece.it.siu.edu/aasi/index.html
Contact: Donald R. Bless, Contact
Local. Promotes the science of astronomy. Works to encourage and coordinate activities of amateur astronomical societies. Fosters observational and computational work and craftsmanship in various fields of astronomy. **Additional Websites:** http://www.astronomy.com/asy/community/groups/group-info.asp?groupid=475. **Affiliated With:** Astronomical League.

414 ■ Big River Appaloosa Horse club
c/o Larry W. Parr
331 Wagon Wheel Rd.
Carbondale, IL 62901
Ph: (618)457-2830
E-mail: parrjean@yahoo.com
URL: National Affiliate–www.appaloosa.com
Contact: Larry W. Parr, Contact
Local. Affiliated With: Appaloosa Horse Club.

415 ■ Carbondale Chamber of Commerce (CCC)
PO Box 877
Carbondale, IL 62903
Ph: (618)549-2146
Fax: (618)529-5063
E-mail: info@carbondalechamber.com
URL: http://www.carbondalechamber.com
Contact: Mary Mechler, Pres.
Founded: 1916. **Members:** 500. **Membership Dues:** general, $180-$1,200 (annual) • financial institution (per million in assets), $31 (annual) • professional (plus $10 for each additional), $180 (annual) • individual/nonprofit/church, $85 (annual). **Local.** Promotes business and community development in the Carbondale, IL area. **Awards:** Athena. **Frequency:** annual. **Type:** recognition. **Recipient:** for individuals who strive toward the highest levels of professional accomplishment • Business Leader of the Year. **Frequency:** annual. **Type:** recognition. **Recipient:** for a member who best exemplifies the

principles of business and community leadership through service to the community, respect for employees, and dedication to customer service • Business of the Year. **Frequency:** annual. **Type:** recognition. **Recipient:** to a business that exemplifies excellence in business growth, innovation in product or service, civic leadership of owners, and employee's impact on community and chamber involvement • Citizen of the Year. **Frequency:** annual. **Type:** recognition. **Recipient:** for a citizen who has made a significant contribution outside of his chosen profession. **Affiliated With:** American Chamber of Commerce Executives; U.S. Chamber of Commerce. **Publications:** *The Communicator*, bimonthly. Newsletter. **Price:** $3.00/year. Alternate Formats: online • *Membership Directory and Buyer's Guide*, annual.

416 ■ Carbondale Convention and Tourism Bureau
1185 E Main St.
Carbondale, IL 62901-3128
Ph: (618)529-4451
Fax: (618)529-5590
Free: (800)526-1500
E-mail: cctb@neondsl.com
URL: http://www.cctb.org
Contact: Debbie Moore, Dir.
Local.

417 ■ Carbondale Main Street
111 S Illinois Ave.
Carbondale, IL 62901
Ph: (618)529-8040
Fax: (618)529-8041
E-mail: info@carbondalemainstreet.com
URL: http://www.carbondalemainstreet.com
Local.

418 ■ Friends of Southern Illinois Regional Social Services (FOS)
604 E Coll.
Carbondale, IL 62901-3309
Ph: (618)457-6703
Fax: (618)457-8377
E-mail: sirss@sirss.org
URL: http://www.sirss.org
Contact: Gordon Plumb, Pres.
Founded: 1960. **Staff:** 140. **Languages:** English, Spanish. **Local. Computer Services:** database, donor database on access. **Telecommunication Services:** TDD, (618)457-7814. **Formerly:** (2004) Jackson Company Health Center. **Publications:** *Collateral*, semiannual. Newsletter. **Price:** free. **Circulation:** 1,500.

419 ■ Jackson-Union County Habitat for Humanity
PO Box 1064
Carbondale, IL 62903-1064
Ph: (618)457-8480
Fax: (618)351-0822
E-mail: lee@brackettinsurancegroup.com
URL: http://www.juchabitat.org
Contact: Lee Brackett, Pres.
Local. Affiliated With: Habitat for Humanity International.

420 ■ Jayco Jafari International Travel Club, Flight 9 Four Rivers Jaycos
c/o Steve Dawson, Pres.
2615 W Kent Dr.
Carbondale, IL 62901
Ph: (618)421-8541
E-mail: dawsonstevejudy@aol.com
URL: http://www.4riversjayco.netfirms.com
Contact: Steve Dawson, Pres.
Regional. Affiliated With: Jayco Travel Club.

421 ■ Military Officers Association of America, Little Egypt Chapter
c/o Lt.Col. Harold Ashby
34 Shawnee Hills Dr.
Carbondale, IL 62902-7239
Ph: (618)457-6874
E-mail: halashby@accessus.net
URL: National Affiliate–www.moaa.org
Contact: Lt.Col. Harold Ashby, Contact
Local. Affiliated With: Military Officers Association of America.

422 ■ Muslim Student Association - Southern Illinois University at Carbondale (MSA-SIU)
c/o Islamic Center of Carbondale
511 S Poplar St.
Carbondale, IL 62901
Ph: (618)457-2770
Fax: (618)549-3868
E-mail: icc511@yahoo.com
URL: http://www.siu.edu/~msa
Local. Muslim students in North America. Seeks to advance the interests of members; works to enable members to practice Islam as a complete way of life. **Affiliated With:** Muslim Students Association of the United States and Canada.

423 ■ National Active And Retired Federal Employees Association - Greater Egypt 1097
2575 W Striegel Rd.
Carbondale, IL 62901-5310
Ph: (618)457-5250
URL: National Affiliate–www.narfe.org
Contact: Edward R. Blair, Contact
Local. Protects the retirement future of employees through education. Informs members on issues affecting the retirement. **Affiliated With:** National Association of Retired Federal Employees.

424 ■ National Association of Insurance and Financial Advisors, Southern Illinois Chapter
c/o John M. Williams, Pres.
PO Box 3932
Carbondale, IL 62902
Ph: (618)993-6100
Fax: (618)998-0586
E-mail: kimblaise@finsvcs.com
URL: National Affiliate–naifa.org
Contact: John M. Williams, Pres.
Local.

425 ■ National Speleological Society, Little Egypt Grotto
c/o Geology Dept.
SIUC Mailcode 4324
Carbondale, IL 62901
Ph: (618)775-6426
E-mail: garyresch@hotmail.com
URL: http://members.ll.net/carbide
Contact: Gary Resch, Pres.
Local. Seeks to study, explore and conserve cave and karst resources. Protects access to caves and promotes responsible caving. Encourages responsible management of caves and their unique environments. **Affiliated With:** National Speleological Society.

426 ■ Parents Television Council - Carbondale, Illinois/Paducah, Kentucky Chapter
c/o Daniele Loyd, Dir.
PO Box 2770
Carbondale, IL 62902-2723
Free: (800)852-9371
E-mail: carbondalepaducahchapter@parentstv.org
URL: National Affiliate–www.parentstv.org
Contact: Daniele Loyd, Dir.
Local.

427 ■ Peace Coalition of Southern Illinois Fellowship of Reconciliation
c/o Margie Parker
1702 Taylor Dr.
Carbondale, IL 62901
Ph: (618)549-7193
E-mail: mparker@srellim.org
URL: http://www.geocities.com/peacecoalitionsouthernillinois
Contact: Margie Parker, Contact
Local. Affiliated With: Fellowship of Reconciliation - USA.

428 ■ PFLAG Carbondale/Southern Illinois
PO Box 2
Carbondale, IL 62903
Ph: (618)977-7953
E-mail: info@pflagcarbondale.org
URL: http://www.pflag.org/Illinois.204.0.html
Local. Affiliated With: Parents, Families, and Friends of Lesbians and Gays.

429 ■ Psi Chi, National Honor Society in Psychology - Southern Illinois University at Carbondale
c/o Dept. of Psychology
1125 Lincoln Dr.
Carbondale, IL 62901-4306
Ph: (618)536-2301 (618)453-3555
Fax: (618)453-3563
E-mail: ugpsych@siu.edu
URL: National Affiliate–www.psichi.org
Local. Affiliated With: Psi Chi, National Honor Society in Psychology.

430 ■ SCORE Southern Illinois
150 E Pleasant Hill Rd.
Carbondale, IL 62901
Ph: (618)453-6654
Fax: (618)453-5040
E-mail: siuscore@siu.edu
URL: http://silscore.org
Local. Provides professional guidance and information to maximize the success of existing and emerging small businesses. Promotes entrepreneur education in Southern Illinois. **Affiliated With:** SCORE.

431 ■ Southern Illinois Chapter for Healthcare Engineering (SICHE)
PO Box 192
Carbondale, IL 62901
Ph: (618)549-0721
Fax: (618)549-4058
E-mail: siche@heartlandit.com
URL: http://www.siche-online.org
Contact: Mike Armstrong, Pres.
Regional. Hospital engineers, facilities managers, directors of buildings and grounds, assistant administrators, directors of maintenance, directors of clinical engineering, design and construction professionals, and safety officers. Works to: promote better patient care by encouraging and assisting members to develop their knowledge and increase their competence in the field of facilities management; cooperate with hospitals and allied associations in matters pertaining to facilities management; bring about closer cooperation among members; provide a medium for interchange of material relative to facilities management. **Affiliated With:** American Society for Healthcare Engineering of the American Hospital Association. **Formerly:** (2005) Southern Illinois Chapter for Hospital Engineering.

432 ■ Southern Illinois Fellowship of Christian Athletes
c/o Roger Lipe, Dir.
828C E Main
Carbondale, IL 62901
Ph: (618)549-2735
E-mail: rlipe@fca.org
URL: http://www.sifca.org
Contact: Roger Lipe, Dir.
Local.

433 ■ Southern Illinois Libertarians (SIL)
c/o John Cogan, Chm.
PO Box 4
Carbondale, IL 62903-0004

Ph: (618)565-1595
E-mail: sil@il.lp.org
URL: http://SIL.LPIllinois.org
Contact: John Cogan, Chm.
Local. Affiliated With: Libertarian National Committee.

434 ■ Southern Illinois Stamp Club
c/o Richard J. Chaklos, APS Representative
Univ. Mall
Carbondale, IL 62901
Ph: (618)985-3041
E-mail: vfelts@siu.edu
URL: http://www.orgsites.com/il/sisc
Contact: Richard J. Chaklos, APS Representative
Founded: 1959. **Members:** 75. **Membership Dues:** individual, $10 (annual). **Local.** Promotes the hobby of philately by serving the needs of the stamp collecting community in Southern Illinois. Sponsors a youth group (Science Center Stampers) and a stamp show (SIRPEX). **Subgroups:** Science Center Stampers (youth). **Affiliated With:** American Philatelic Society. **Publications:** *SISC Newsletter*, semimonthly. Eight-pages newsletter, with color photos. **Price:** $10.00 free to members. **Circulation:** 100.

435 ■ Theta Xi Fraternity, Beta Delta Chapter
c/o Tony Coconate
606 S Univ.
Carbondale, IL 62901
E-mail: me@tonycoconate.com
URL: http://www.siu.edu/~thetaxi
Contact: Tony Coconate, Contact
Local. Affiliated With: Theta Xi.

436 ■ Wildlife Society - Southern Illinois University Student Chapter
c/o Cooperative Wildlife Research Laboratory
Southern Illinois Univ.
251 Life Sci. II
Carbondale, IL 62901-6504
Fax: (618)453-6944
E-mail: siuctws@siu.edu
URL: http://www.siu.edu/~siuctws
Local. Affiliated With: The Wildlife Society.

Carlinville

437 ■ American Legion, Guy Baird Post 554
PO Box 554
Carlinville, IL 62626
Ph: (217)854-7316
Fax: (309)663-5783
URL: National Affiliate–www.legion.org
Local. Affiliated With: American Legion.

438 ■ Carlinville Community Chamber of Commerce (CCCC)
126 E Main St.
Carlinville, IL 62626
Ph: (217)854-2141
Fax: (217)854-8548
E-mail: info@carlinvillechamber.com
URL: http://www.carlinvillechamber.com
Founded: 1953. **Members:** 115. **Local.** Promotes business and community development in Carlinville, IL. **Formerly:** (1995) Carlinville Chamber of Commerce. **Publications:** *Chamber Insider*, monthly. Newsletter. **Price:** free. Alternate Formats: online. **Conventions/Meetings:** annual Christmas Market - festival • annual dinner • annual Super Summer Weekend - meeting - promotional event.

439 ■ Carlinville Lions Club
PO Box 582
Carlinville, IL 62626
Ph: (217)854-2517
URL: http://carlinvilleil.lionwap.org
Local. Affiliated With: Lions Clubs International.

Carlyle

440 ■ American Legion, Ruf-Marcham Post 404
PO Box 44
Carlyle, IL 62231
Ph: (618)594-4042
Fax: (309)663-5783
URL: National Affiliate–www.legion.org
Local. Affiliated With: American Legion.

441 ■ Carlyle Lake Chamber of Commerce
PO Box 246
Carlyle, IL 62231
Ph: (618)594-7666 (618)594-2468
E-mail: resort@onemain.com
URL: http://www.carlyle.il.us
Contact: Mark Sugars, Pres.
Local.

Carmi

442 ■ American Legion, Carmi Post 224
PO Box 302
Carmi, IL 62821
Ph: (309)663-0361
Fax: (309)663-5783
URL: National Affiliate–www.legion.org
Local. Affiliated With: American Legion.

443 ■ Carmi Chamber of Commerce (CCC)
225 E Main St.
Carmi, IL 62821
Ph: (618)382-7606
E-mail: ccc@cityofcarmi.com
URL: http://www.cityofcarmi.com
Contact: Paula Pierson, Exec.Dir.
Founded: 1944. **Members:** 100. **Local.** Aims to sustain and further develop a thriving economy in the area and enhance the community's quality of life. Sponsors several activities including community food basket drives at Thanksgiving and establishes a yearly scholarship. **Awards: Frequency:** annual. **Type:** scholarship. **Recipient:** for a qualified graduating senior from Carmi White County High School.

Carol Stream

444 ■ American Legion, Aaron Post 788
PO Box 2910
Carol Stream, IL 60188
Ph: (708)682-1219
Fax: (309)663-5783
URL: National Affiliate–www.legion.org
Local. Affiliated With: American Legion.

445 ■ Carol Stream Chamber of Commerce
150 S Gary Ave.
Carol Stream, IL 60188-2079
Ph: (630)665-3325
Fax: (630)665-6965
E-mail: info@carolstreamchamber.com
URL: http://www.carolstreamchamber.com
Contact: Ms. Luanne Triolo, Exec.Dir.
Founded: 1992. **Members:** 300. **Membership Dues:** business (1-2 employees), $175 (annual) • business (3-10 employees), $200 (annual) • business (11-24 employees), $250 (annual) • business (25-99 employees), $275 (annual) • business (over 100 employees), $375 (annual) • nonprofit organization, $175 (annual). **Staff:** 2. **For-Profit. Local.** Organization of businesses and professional people. Works to advance the economic well-being of the greater Carol Stream area and its nearby vicinity. Offers a variety of program to keep the members at their competitive best. **Computer Services:** database, of members • mailing lists, of members. **Committees:** Chamber Member Promotion; Community Relations; Community Service Directory; Documents and Procedures; Golf; Holiday Social; Nominations; Programs. **Affiliated With:** Chicagoland Chamber of Commerce; Illinois Association of Chamber of Commerce Executives. **Publications:** *Chamber Connection*, quarterly. Newsletter. Contains news on upcoming events, past events, announcements, new members, and current topics. **Price:** free. **Circulation:** 300. **Advertising:** accepted. Alternate Formats: online. **Conventions/Meetings:** monthly Business After Hours - meeting, with networking - every 3rd Thursday • monthly luncheon, with guest speakers (exhibits) - every 2nd Wednesday.

446 ■ Carol Stream Youth Cheerleading Association (CSYCA)
780 W Army Trail Rd., No. 300
Carol Stream, IL 60188
Ph: (630)830-1639
E-mail: contactus@csyca.com
URL: http://www.csyca.com
Local.

447 ■ Dupage Area AIFA
c/o Francis Michael Nugent, Pres.
350 S Schmale Rd., No. 100
Carol Stream, IL 60188-2789
Ph: (630)268-0030
Fax: (630)268-0329
E-mail: naifadupage@sbcglobal.net
URL: National Affiliate–naifa.org
Contact: Francis Michael Nugent, Pres.
Local. Represents the interests of insurance and financial advisors. Advocates for a positive legislative and regulatory environment. Enhances business and professional skills of members. **Affiliated With:** National Association of Insurance and Financial Advisors.

448 ■ DuPage Libertarians
c/o Crystal Jurczynski, Pres.
PO Box 87465
Carol Stream, IL 60188-7465
Ph: (630)876-1935
E-mail: dpl@dupagelibertarians.org
URL: http://www.dupagelibertarians.org
Contact: Crystal Jurczynski, Pres.
Local. Affiliated With: Libertarian National Committee.

449 ■ Fox Valley German American Team of Educational Sponsors
635 Hiawatha Dr.
Carol Stream, IL 60188
URL: http://www.germanfun.org
Founded: 2001. **Local.**

450 ■ Glenbard North PTSA
c/o Glenbard North High School
990 Kuhn Rd.
Carol Stream, IL 60188
Ph: (630)653-7000
Fax: (630)653-7259
E-mail: depadoo@comcast.net
URL: http://www.glenbardnorthptsa.com
Contact: Maria Depa, Pres.
Local. Parents, teachers, students and others interested in uniting the forces of home, school and community. Promotes the welfare of children and youth.

451 ■ Illinois USA Wrestling
590 Appaloosa Ct.
Carol Stream, IL 60188
Ph: (630)653-6808
URL: http://www.ilusaw.com
Contact: Jim Considine, State Dir.
State. Affiliated With: U.S.A. Wrestling.

452 ■ Sheet Metal Workers' International Association, Local Union 265
205 Alexandra Way
Carol Stream, IL 60188
Ph: (630)668-0110
Fax: (630)668-0932
E-mail: smw265@smw265.org
URL: http://www.smw265.org
Contact: George Slater, Business Mgr./Pres.
Members: 2,521. **Local. Affiliated With:** Sheet Metal Workers' International Association.

Carpentersville

453 ■ Foxview Alliance for Corp. Enhancement
3 Oxford Rd., Apt., 14
Foxview Apartments
Carpentersville, IL 60110-1070
Ph: (847)428-7771
Contact: Sandra Neeley, Mgr.
Local.

454 ■ Independent Order of Odd Fellows, Century Lodge No. 492
50 1/2 E Main St.
Carpentersville, IL 60110
Ph: (847)426-3901
E-mail: joey@direcpc.com
URL: http://www.geocities.com/centurylodge492
Local.

455 ■ National Active And Retired Federal Employees Association - Greater Fox Valley 2181
102 Del Rio Rd.
Carpentersville, IL 60110-1108
Ph: (708)428-0782
URL: National Affiliate–www.narfe.org
Contact: Oscar Eugene Shell, Contact
Local. Protects the retirement future of employees through education. Informs members on issues affecting the retirement. **Affiliated With:** National Association of Retired Federal Employees.

Carrier Mills

456 ■ American Legion, Marion Oshel Post 364
112 Clark St.
Carrier Mills, IL 62917
Ph: (309)663-0361
Fax: (309)663-5783
URL: National Affiliate–www.legion.org
Local. **Affiliated With:** American Legion.

Carrollton

457 ■ American Legion, Carrollton Post 114
9 4th St.
Carrollton, IL 62016
Ph: (217)942-5094
Fax: (309)663-5783
URL: National Affiliate–www.legion.org
Local. **Affiliated With:** American Legion.

458 ■ Carrollton Chamber of Commerce (CCC)
PO Box 69
Carrollton, IL 62016
Ph: (217)942-3187
E-mail: fieldsteve@hotmail.com
Contact: Steve Field, Pres.
Members: 47. **Local**. Businesses interested in promoting business and community development in Carrollton, IL.

Carterville

459 ■ American Brittany Club - Directors Chapter
c/o Mary Jo Trimble, Exec.Sec.
10370 Fleming Rd.
Carterville, IL 62918
Ph: (618)985-2336
Fax: (618)985-5103
E-mail: trimnatchbritts@midamer.net
URL: http://clubs.akc.org/brit
Contact: Mary Jo Trimble, Exec.Sec.
Members: 2,700. **Membership Dues:** $25 (annual). **Staff:** 1. **Local Groups:** 90. **Local**. Purebred Brittany dog owners and breeders. **Awards:** Hall of Fame. **Frequency:** periodic. **Type:** recognition. **Recipient:** for past service. **Affiliated With:** American Brittany Club. **Publications:** *The American Brittany*, monthly. Magazine. **Price:** $25.00/year. **Circulation:** 3,300. **Advertising:** accepted. **Conventions/Meetings:** annual show (exhibits).

460 ■ American Legion, Illinois Post 347
c/o John A. Logan
PO Box 227
Carterville, IL 62918
Ph: (618)985-2541
Fax: (309)663-5783
URL: National Affiliate–www.legion.org
Contact: John A. Logan, Contact
Local. **Affiliated With:** American Legion.

461 ■ Carterville Chamber of Commerce
PO Box 262
Carterville, IL 62918-0262
Ph: (618)985-6942
Fax: (618)985-4205
E-mail: chamber@midamer.net
URL: http://www.cartervillechamber.com
Contact: Tracey Glenn, Exec.Dir.
Membership Dues: business (1-3 employees), $60 (annual) • business (4-9 employees), $85 (annual) • business (10-25 employees), $115 (annual) • business (more than 51 employees), $150 (annual) • associate, $30 (annual). **Staff:** 2. **Local**. Enhances the business and social climate of the Carterville area which helps individual businesses prosper. **Conventions/Meetings:** bimonthly meeting, with an interesting and appropriate speaker or program - every first Wednesday.

462 ■ King City Beagle Club
c/o Bill Halstead
RR1, Box 343Aa
Carterville, IL 62918-9753
URL: National Affiliate–clubs.akc.org
Contact: Bill Halstead, Contact
Local.

463 ■ Phi Theta Kappa, Upsilon Pi Chapter - John A. Logan College
c/o Tom Carroll
700 Logan Coll. Rd.
Carterville, IL 62918
Ph: (618)985-3741
E-mail: tomcarroll@jalc.edu
URL: http://www.ptk.org/directories/chapters/IL/194-1.htm
Contact: Tom Carroll, Advisor
Local.

Carthage

464 ■ American Legion, Illinois Post 74
c/o Phillip Hartzell
1545 Ecr 1800
Carthage, IL 62321
Ph: (309)663-0361
Fax: (309)663-5783
URL: National Affiliate–www.legion.org
Contact: Phillip Hartzell, Contact
Local. **Affiliated With:** American Legion.

465 ■ Carthage Area Chamber of Commerce (CACC)
PO Box 247
Carthage, IL 62321
Ph: (217)357-3024
Fax: (217)357-3024
E-mail: chamber@carthage-il.com
URL: http://www.carthage-il.com
Contact: Cyndi Huffman, Sec.-Treas.
Members: 130. **Membership Dues:** full, $175 (annual) • large nonprofit (with 4 or more paid employees), $175 (annual) • small nonprofit (with 3 or fewer paid employees), $50 (annual) • additional or 2nd business (non-voting), $75 (annual) • individual (non-voting), $50 (annual) • pacesetter high visibility type for major chamber supporter, $500 (annual). **Local**. Promotes business and community development in Hancock County, IL. **Convention/Meeting:** none. **Formerly:** (1999) Carthage Chamber of Commerce. **Publications:** Newsletter, periodic.

466 ■ Hancock County Sheriff Reserve Deputy Corps
98 Buchanan St.
Carthage, IL 62321-1202
Ph: (217)357-2115
Contact: Capt. Steve Shoopman, Contact
Founded: 2000. **Members:** 15. **Local**.

467 ■ West Central Illinois RSVP
c/o Nancy Jameson, Dir.
Carl Sandburg Coll.
604 Wabash Ave.
Carthage, IL 62321-1360
Ph: (217)357-2804
Fax: (217)357-2098
E-mail: rsvp@adams.net
URL: http://www.seniorcorps.gov
Contact: Nancy Jameson, Dir.
Local. **Affiliated With:** Retired and Senior Volunteer Program.

Cary

468 ■ American Legion, Illinois Post 276
c/o Raymond Wascher
208 W Main St.
Cary, IL 60013
Ph: (309)663-0361
Fax: (309)663-5783
URL: National Affiliate–www.legion.org
Contact: Raymond Wascher, Contact
Local. **Affiliated With:** American Legion.

469 ■ American Legion, Illinois Post 768
121 N School St.
Cary, IL 60013
Ph: (708)639-7540
Fax: (309)663-5783
URL: National Affiliate–www.legion.org
Contact: Nick Livas, Contact
Local. **Affiliated With:** American Legion.

470 ■ Cary Basketball Association (CBA)
PO Box 119
Cary, IL 60013
Ph: (847)289-4667
E-mail: info@caryhoops.com
URL: http://www.caryhoops.com
Contact: Jeff Taylor, Pres.
Local.

471 ■ Cary Character Counts
c/o Cary Area Public Library
1606 Three Oaks Rd.
Cary, IL 60013
Ph: (847)639-4210
Fax: (847)639-8890
URL: http://www.cary.lib.il.us/characterabout.htm
Local.

472 ■ Cary/Grove Area Chamber of Commerce (CCC)
27 E Main St.
PO Box 302
Cary, IL 60013
Ph: (847)639-2800
Fax: (847)639-2168
E-mail: info@carygrovechamber.com
URL: http://www.carygrovechamber.com
Contact: Jack Ehlers, Pres.
Founded: 1964. **Members:** 220. **Membership Dues:** sole proprietor, service/non-profit organization, $125 (annual) • business, $160-$325 (annual) • silver, $500 (annual) • gold, $750 (annual) • platinum, $1,000 (annual). **Staff:** 1. **Local**. Promotes business and community development in the Cary, IL area. Holds bimonthly board meeting. Sponsors Home and Business Expo. **Publications:** *Minutes of Board Meeting*, bimonthly • Membership Directory, annual.

473 ■ Counselors of Real Estate, Midwest Chapter
c/o William J. Bornhoff, CRE, Chm.
Strategic Real Estate Solutions
445 High Rd.
Cary, IL 60013
Ph: (847)639-0576
Fax: (847)639-0577
E-mail: bornhoff@comcast.net
URL: National Affiliate–www.cre.org
Contact: William J. Bornhoff CRE, Chm.
Regional. Affiliated With: Counselors of Real Estate.

474 ■ Northwest Human Resources Council
307 Bell Dr.
Cary, IL 60013
Ph: (847)516-1684
E-mail: chapter193@sbcglobal.net
URL: http://www.mynhrc.org
Contact: Chris Stein, Pres.
Local. Represents the interests of human resource and industrial relations professionals and executives. Promotes the advancement of human resource management.

475 ■ Riverbend Benders Snowmobile Club
PO Box 75
Cary, IL 60013-0075
Ph: (847)289-7272
Fax: (815)444-8067
E-mail: jlindberg@ameritech.net
URL: http://www.riverbendbenders.com
Contact: Scott Helmer, Pres.
Founded: 1983. **Members:** 150. **Membership Dues:** individual, $25 (annual) • family, $35 (annual) • associate individual, business, $15 (annual) • associate family, $20 (annual). **Staff:** 1. **Budget:** $5,000. **Regional Groups:** 2. **State Groups:** 1. **Local Groups:** 1. **Local.** Promotes the family sport of snowmobiling, including family snowmobile rides, trips and outings, trail marking, annual kitty cat event, and snowmobile watercross. **Libraries: Type:** open to the public. **Awards:** Chrissy Erickson Award. **Frequency:** annual. **Type:** recognition • George Bates. **Frequency:** annual. **Type:** recognition. **Additional Websites:** http://www.h2ox.com. **Publications:** Newsletter, monthly. **Circulation:** 300. **Conventions/Meetings:** annual convention (exhibits) • semimonthly meeting - always first and third Thursday from September to April.

476 ■ Special Libraries Association, Michigan - Western/Upper Peninsula
c/o Leslie Burke, Pres.-Elect
EBSCO Subscription Services
1140 Silver Lake Rd.
Cary, IL 60013-1129
Fax: (616)361-2080
E-mail: lburke@ebsco.com
URL: http://www.sla.org/chapter/cwmi/index.html
Contact: Leslie Burke, Pres.-Elect
Local. Seeks to advance the leadership role of special librarians. Promotes and strengthens members through learning, advocacy and networking initiatives. **Affiliated With:** Special Libraries Association.

477 ■ Wooden Canoe Heritage Association, Illinois
c/o Doug Phelps, Pres.
408 Crest Dr.
Cary, IL 60013
Ph: (708)639-8712
E-mail: dphelpsemail-wcha1@yahoo.com
URL: National Affiliate–www.wcha.org
Contact: Doug Phelps, Pres.
State. Affiliated With: Wooden Canoe Heritage Association.

Casey

478 ■ American Legion, Victor Hill Post 534
1203 North Dr.
Casey, IL 62420
Ph: (309)663-0361
Fax: (309)663-5783
URL: National Affiliate–www.legion.org
Local. Affiliated With: American Legion.

479 ■ East Central Council of Teachers of Mathematics
506 E Delaware
Casey, IL 62420
Ph: (217)932-0117
E-mail: mareed@rr1.net
URL: http://www.eiu.edu/~ec2tm
Contact: Martha Reed, Contact
Local. Aims to improve the teaching and learning of mathematics. Provides vision, leadership and professional development to support teachers in ensuring mathematics learning of the highest quality for all students. **Affiliated With:** National Council of Teachers of Mathematics.

Caseyville

480 ■ American Legion, East St. Louis Post 53
PO Box 637
Caseyville, IL 62232
Ph: (618)667-9721
Fax: (309)663-5783
URL: National Affiliate–www.legion.org
Local. Affiliated With: American Legion.

481 ■ Caseyville Chamber of Commerce
PO Box 470
Caseyville, IL 62232
Ph: (618)345-2452 (618)345-0660
Fax: (618)345-0188
Contact: Jim Eisele, Pres.
Local.

482 ■ Illinois Thoroughbred Breeders and Owners Foundation (ITBOF)
PO Box 336
Caseyville, IL 62232
Ph: (618)344-3427
Fax: (618)346-1051
E-mail: itboffp@apci.net
URL: http://www.illinoisracingnews.com/itbof.htm
Contact: John Bauman, Pres.
State.

Catlin

483 ■ American Legion, Davis-Busby Post 776
PO Box 583
Catlin, IL 61817
Ph: (309)663-0361
Fax: (309)663-5783
URL: National Affiliate–www.legion.org
Local. Affiliated With: American Legion.

Cedarville

484 ■ American Legion, Cedarville Memorial Post 1224
PO Box 93
Cedarville, IL 61013
Ph: (815)563-4339
Fax: (309)663-5783
URL: National Affiliate–www.legion.org
Local. Affiliated With: American Legion.

Centralia

485 ■ American Association of Physicians of Indian Origin, Downstate Illinois
c/o Narendra Gupta, MD
15 E Calumet St.
Centralia, IL 62801
Ph: (618)532-1155
URL: National Affiliate–www.aapiusa.org
Contact: Narendra Gupta MD, Contact
Local. Represents Indian American physicians. Promotes excellence in patient care, teaching and research. Serves as a forum for scientific, educational and social interaction among members and other medical scientists of Indian heritage. Fosters the availability of medical assistance to indigent people in the United States. **Affiliated With:** American Association of Physicians of Indian Origin.

486 ■ American Legion, Illinois Post 446
c/o George M. Nelms
PO Box 278
Centralia, IL 62801
Ph: (309)663-0361
Fax: (309)663-5783
URL: National Affiliate–www.legion.org
Contact: George M. Nelms, Contact
Local. Affiliated With: American Legion.

487 ■ Greater Centralia Chamber of Commerce
130 S Locust St.
Centralia, IL 62801
Ph: (618)532-6789
Fax: (618)533-7305
Free: (888)533-2600
E-mail: gccoc@centraliail.com
URL: http://www.centraliail.com
Contact: Bob Kelsheimer, Exec.Dir.
Local. Improves the Centralia Area Business Climate by working diligently for positive community planning and change. **Committees:** Ambassadors; Community Image/Charette; Education; Government Action; Special Events; Tourism. **Publications:** *Dateline*. Newsletter. Keeps members informed about current chamber information, meetings, events, activities, business tips, new members and renewing members.

488 ■ Illinois Society of Enrolled Agents - Southern Chapter
c/o Terry Bill, Pres.
501 W Broadway
Centralia, IL 62801
Ph: (618)532-7223
Fax: (618)532-3640
E-mail: billtax@midwest.net
Contact: Terry Bill EA, Pres.
Local. Affiliated With: National Association of Enrolled Agents.

489 ■ National Active And Retired Federal Employees Association - Egyptian Gateway 2190
428 Clarida Dr.
Centralia, IL 62801-6014
Ph: (618)533-1719
URL: National Affiliate–www.narfe.org
Contact: Loren Byrd, Contact
Local. Protects the retirement future of employees through education. Informs members on issues affecting the retirement. **Affiliated With:** National Association of Retired Federal Employees.

490 ■ National Sojourners, Wayne W. Gatewood No. 536
c/o Mr. Herschel O. Thomas
1302 Nelms Ave.
Centralia, IL 62801-4933
Ph: (618)532-3206
E-mail: hotl80@netwitz.net
URL: National Affiliate–www.nationalsojourners.org
Contact: Mr. Herschel O. Thomas, Contact
Local.

491 ■ Phi Theta Kappa, Iota Omicron Chapter - Kaskaskia College
c/o Susie Wurth
27210 Coll. Rd.
Centralia, IL 62801
Ph: (618)545-3385
E-mail: swurth@kaskaskia.edu
URL: http://www.ptk.org/directories/chapters/IL/170-1.htm
Contact: Susie Wurth, Advisor
Local.

Cerro Gordo

492 ■ American Legion, Cerro Gordo Post 117
PO Box 743
Cerro Gordo, IL 61818
Ph: (309)663-0361
Fax: (309)663-5783
URL: National Affiliate–www.legion.org
Local. **Affiliated With:** American Legion.

Chadwick

493 ■ American Legion, Chadwick Post 739
PO Box 1
Chadwick, IL 61014
Ph: (815)684-5461
Fax: (309)663-5783
URL: National Affiliate–www.legion.org
Local. **Affiliated With:** American Legion.

Champaign

494 ■ Alcoholics Anonymous World Services, East Central Illinois Intergroup
PO Box 3293
Champaign, IL 61826
Ph: (217)373-4200
URL: National Affiliate–www.aa.org
Local. Individuals recovering from alcoholism. AA maintains that members can solve their common problem and help others achieve sobriety through a twelve step program that includes sharing their experience, strength, and hope with each other. **Affiliated With:** Alcoholics Anonymous World Services.

495 ■ Alpha Chi Chapter of Sigma Tau Gamma Alumni
47 E Chalmers St.
Champaign, IL 61820-5955
Ph: (217)384-2257
E-mail: alumniax@stg.org
URL: http://www.stg.org
Contact: Chris Grimes, Pres.
Local. **Affiliated With:** Sigma Tau Gamma.

496 ■ American Cancer Society, Champaign - Eastern Regional
2509 S Neil St.
Champaign, IL 61820
Ph: (217)356-9076
Fax: (217)356-7721
URL: National Affiliate–www.cancer.org
Regional. **Affiliated With:** American Cancer Society.

497 ■ American Chemical Society, East Central Illinois Section
c/o Karen Sue Harlin, Sec.
Illinois State Water Survey
2204 Griffith Dr.
Champaign, IL 61820-7463
Ph: (217)244-6413
Fax: (217)333-6540
E-mail: prairiefire7@prairieinet.net
URL: National Affiliate–acswebcontent.acs.org
Contact: Karen Sue Harlin, Sec.
Local. Represents the interests of individuals dedicated to the advancement of chemistry in all its branches. Provides opportunities for peer interaction and career development. **Affiliated With:** American Chemical Society.

498 ■ American Legion, Champaign Post 24
705 Bloomington Rd.
Champaign, IL 61824
Ph: (309)663-0361
Fax: (309)663-5783
URL: National Affiliate–www.legion.org
Local. **Affiliated With:** American Legion.

499 ■ American Legion, Illinois Post 559
c/o William Frank Earnest
704 N Hickory St.
Champaign, IL 61820
Ph: (309)663-0361
Fax: (309)663-5783
E-mail: post559@aol.com
URL: National Affiliate–www.legion.org
Contact: William Frank Earnest, Contact
Local. **Affiliated With:** American Legion.

500 ■ Associated Landscape Contractors of America, Parkland College
c/o Kaizad R. Irani, Faculty Advisor
2400 W Bradley Ave.
Champaign, IL 61821
Ph: (217)351-2406
Fax: (217)373-3896
E-mail: dbergfield@parkland.cc.il.us
URL: National Affiliate–www.alca.org
Contact: Kaizad R. Irani, Faculty Advisor
Local. **Affiliated With:** Professional Landcare Network.

501 ■ Association of Illinois Middle-Level Schools (AIMS)
c/o Deb Schrock, Exec.Dir.
510 Devonshire Dr.
Champaign, IL 61820
Ph: (217)333-7104
Fax: (217)333-2440
E-mail: dlgreen@uiuc.edu
URL: http://www.aims.uiuc.edu
Contact: David Green, Sec.
State.

502 ■ Bricklayers and Allied Craftworkers Local No. 8
2901 Res. Rd.
Champaign, IL 61822
Ph: (217)356-0419
Fax: (217)356-0694
E-mail: info@bac8il.org
URL: http://bac8il.org
Contact: Daniel McCall, Pres.
Founded: 1993. **Members:** 1,489. **Membership Dues:** journeyman (without hourly check-off), $28 (monthly) • journeyman, $23 (monthly) • apprentice, $16 (monthly) • retired, temporary disabled, working outside of the trade, $10 (monthly) • permanently disabled, $5 (monthly). **Staff:** 8. **State**. **Affiliated With:** AFL-CIO. **Formerly:** (2005) Bricklayers AFL-CIO, LU 8. **Conventions/Meetings:** monthly meeting • semiannual meeting - every 1st Saturday of May and November.

503 ■ Central High School PTSA
610 W Univ.
Champaign, IL 61820
Ph: (217)351-3911
E-mail: annc@prairienet.org
URL: http://www.prairienet.org/cpta/CentralHS
Local. Parents, teachers, students, and others interested in uniting the forces of home, school, and community. Promotes the welfare of children and youth.

504 ■ Central Illinois Aerospace (CIA)
5 The Summit
Champaign, IL 61820
Ph: (217)359-8225
E-mail: jsivier@uiuc.edu
URL: http://www.prairienet.org/cia
Contact: Jonathan Sivier, Sec.
Local. People who are interested in building and flying model rockets. **Affiliated With:** National Association of Rocketry.

505 ■ Central Illinois Human Resources Group (CIHRG)
c/o Linda Broerman, Pres.
Advances Filtration Syss., Inc.
3206 Farber Dr.
Champaign, IL 61822
Ph: (217)353-0511
E-mail: lindab@afsifilters.com
URL: http://www.cihrg.org
Contact: Linda Broerman, Pres.
Local. Represents the interests of human resource and industrial relations professionals and executives. Promotes the advancement of human resource management.

506 ■ Champaign Area AIFA
PO Box 1504
Champaign, IL 61824
Ph: (217)359-7100
Fax: (217)239-7100
E-mail: larry.mullins@mchsi.com
URL: National Affiliate–naifa.org
Contact: Carrie J. Cunningham, Pres.
Local. Represents the interests of insurance and financial advisors. Advocates for a positive legislative and regulatory environment. Enhances business and professional skills of members. **Affiliated With:** National Association of Insurance and Financial Advisors.

507 ■ Champaign Area Young Life
313 1/2 Van Doren St.
Champaign, IL 61820
Ph: (217)239-4495
URL: http://IL19.younglife.org
Local.

508 ■ Champaign County Chamber of Commerce
1817 S Neil St., Ste.201
Champaign, IL 61820-7269
Ph: (217)359-1791
Fax: (217)359-1809
E-mail: info@champaigncounty.org
URL: http://www.ccchamber.org
Contact: Laura E. Weis IOM, Exec.Dir.
Members: 1,150. **Staff:** 7. **Budget:** $700,000. **Local**. Works to ensure a healthy economic and socio-economic base to benefit the community. **Awards:** Athena Award. **Frequency:** annual. **Type:** recognition. **Recipient:** for an individual who contributes improvement for others in achieving quality of life in the community • Champaign County Most Valuable Citizen. **Frequency:** annual. **Type:** recognition. **Recipient:** for an individual who shows ongoing commitment to the community and its development that has made a difference • Small Business of the Year. **Frequency:** annual. **Type:** recognition. **Recipient:** for a chamber member who has a solid track record of growth and demonstrated integrity and community involvement • Top Chamber Investors. **Frequency:** annual. **Type:** recognition. **Telecommunication Services:** electronic mail, lauraw@champaigncounty.org. **Committees:** Account Retention; Agribusiness; Chamber Ambassadors; Planning and Infrastructure; Small Business Month; Workforce Development. **Programs:** High Tech Edge Executive Steering; Leadership Institute. **Publications:** *Chamber Connection*, monthly. Newsletter. Contains information on Chamber activities, issues of concern to members, committee reports, special events, and new member updates. **Circulation:** 25,000 • *Images of Champaign County*, annual. Magazine. Features photos and stories that will showcase the people, natural beauty, and progressive business climate of Champaign County. **Circulation:** 15,000. **Advertising:** accepted • Membership Directory, annual. **Advertising:** accepted. **Conventions/Meetings:** monthly Brown Bag - workshop - every 3rd Tuesday • monthly Business After Hours - meeting - every 3rd Thursday.

509 ■ Champaign/Douglas/Piatt RSVP
c/o Vicki Stewart, Dir.
Stevick Senior Ctr.
48 E Main St.
Champaign, IL 61820

Ph: (217)359-6500
Fax: (217)359-6550
E-mail: vsdrsvp@earthlink.net
URL: http://www.seniorcorps.gov/about/programs/rsvp_state.asp?usestateabbr=il&Search4.x=14&Search4.y=5
Contact: Vicki Stewart, Dir.
Local. Affiliated With: Retired and Senior Volunteer Program.

510 ■ Champaign PTA Council
2404 Peppertree Pl.
Champaign, IL 61822
Ph: (217)356-9153
E-mail: nlholm@prairienet.org
URL: http://www.prairienet.org/cpta
Contact: Nancy Holm, Pres.
Local. Parents, teachers, students, and others interested in uniting the forces of home, school, and community. Promotes the welfare of children and youth.

511 ■ Champaign-Urbana Astronomical Society
c/o William Staerkel Planetarium
Parkland Coll.
2400 W Bradley Ave.
Champaign, IL 61821
Ph: (217)351-2567
E-mail: dleake@parkland.edu
URL: http://www.prairienet.org/cuas
Contact: David Leake, Treas.
Local. Created to promote the science of astronomy in an educational as well as recreational climate and to unite those within the community with this common interest.

512 ■ Champaign-Urbana Jewish Federation (CUJF)
c/o Michael Shapiro, Pres.
503 E John St.
Champaign, IL 61820
Ph: (217)367-9872
Fax: (217)344-1540
E-mail: cujf@shalomcu.org
URL: http://www.shalomcu.org
Contact: Lee Melhado, Exec.Dir.
Local. Works to help Jewish people in need. Fosters a vibrant Jewish future, both at home and abroad. Affiliated with the United Jewish Communities.

513 ■ Champaign-Urbana Junior Woman's Club (CUJWC)
PO Box 6526
Champaign, IL 61826-6526
E-mail: info@cujwc.org
URL: http://www.cujwc.org
Local.

514 ■ Champaign-Urbana Stamp Club
c/o Ms. Louise B. Toft
PO Box 11115
Champaign, IL 61826-1115
Ph: (217)265-0314
E-mail: tuchman@uiuc.edu
URL: http://www.prairienet.org/cusc/
Contact: Ms. Louise B. Toft, Contact
Local. Affiliated With: American Philatelic Society.

515 ■ Champaign-Urbana Sweet Adelines
Grace Lutheran Church
313 S Prospect
Champaign, IL 61820
E-mail: info@cusweetadelines.org
URL: http://www.cusweetadelines.org
Contact: Tammy Ziegler, Pres.
Local. Advances the musical art form of barbershop harmony through education and performances. Provides education, training and coaching in the development of women's four-part barbershop harmony. **Affiliated With:** Sweet Adelines International.

516 ■ Champaign WyldLife
PO Box 11313
Champaign, IL 61826-1313
Ph: (217)239-4495
URL: http://ChampaignWyldLife.younglife.org
Local. Represents the interests of individuals committed to impacting kids' lives and preparing them for the future. Helps young people develop their skills, assets and attitudes to reach their full God-given potential. Reaches suburban, urban, multicultural and disabled kids and teenage mothers. **Affiliated With:** Young Life.

517 ■ Champaign Young Life
313 1/2 Van Doren St.
Champaign, IL 61820
Ph: (217)239-4495
URL: http://Champaign.younglife.org
Local.

518 ■ East Central Illinois MOAA
c/o Lt.Col. Charles McGee
3813 Farhills Dr.
Champaign, IL 61822-9304
Ph: (217)352-7390
E-mail: cfmcgee@aol.com
URL: National Affiliate–www.moaa.org
Contact: Lt.Col. Charles McGee, Contact
Local. Affiliated With: Military Officers Association of America.

519 ■ East Central Illinois Youth for Christ
PO Box 1076
Champaign, IL 61824-1076
Ph: (217)356-1176
Fax: (217)356-9749
URL: http://www.yfceci.org
Local. Affiliated With: Youth for Christ/U.S.A.

520 ■ Graduate Employees Organization (GEO)
c/o Mike Stewart
1001 S Wright St.
Champaign, IL 61820
Ph: (217)344-8283
E-mail: geo@shout.net
URL: http://www.shout.net/~geo
Local.

521 ■ Great Lakes Section of the Society for Sedimentary Geology (GLS-SEPM)
c/o C. Pius Weibel, Sec.
Illinois St. Geological Survey
615 E Peabody Dr.
Champaign, IL 61820
Ph: (217)333-5108
Fax: (217)333-2830
E-mail: weibel@isgs.uiuc.edu
URL: http://www.isgs.uiuc.edu/gls-sepm
Contact: C. Pius Weibel, Sec.
Founded: 1971. **Members:** 150. **Membership Dues:** regular, $3 (annual). **Regional**. Represents geologists who work, reside, or have research interests in the Great Lakes area. Aims to promote the science of geology in the Great Lakes area of North America through research in paleontology, sedimentary petrology, sedimentology, and stratigraphy. Exchanges, disseminates and shares experiences/information of mutual interest. **Awards:** Best Paper Student Presentation. **Frequency:** annual. **Type:** monetary. **Recipient:** for best paper by a student on sedimentary geology. **Affiliated With:** Society for Sedimentary Geology. **Publications:** *Fieldtrip Guide*, annual • Newsletters. **Conventions/Meetings:** annual conference - fall.

522 ■ Habitat for Humanity of Champaign County (HFHCC)
111 N Market
Champaign, IL 61820
Ph: (217)355-6460
E-mail: habitat@cuhabitat.org
URL: http://www.cuhabitat.org
Contact: Laura Huth, Exec.Dir.
Local. Affiliated With: Habitat for Humanity International.

523 ■ IEEE Central Illinois Section
Power World Corp.
2001 S First St.
Champaign, IL 61820
Ph: (217)384-6330
E-mail: weber@powerworld.com
URL: http://www.powerworld.com/ieee
Contact: James Weber, Chair
Local. Engineers and scientists in electrical engineering, electronics, and allied fields. Promotes creating, developing, integrating, sharing, and applying knowledge about electro and information technologies and sciences for the benefit of humanity and the profession. Conducts lectures on current engineering and scientific topics.

524 ■ Illinois Association of College Stores (IACS)
Sta. A - Box 2245
Champaign, IL 61825
Ph: (217)586-4414
Fax: (217)586-4414
E-mail: iacs@mchsi.com
URL: http://www.iacs.org
Contact: Lynne Durin, Pres.
State. Promotes the collegiate retailing industry. Enhances the college store industry through service, education and research. Promotes high standards of business practices and ethics within the industry. **Affiliated With:** National Association of College Stores.

525 ■ Illinois Association for Institutional Research (IAIR)
c/o Sharon Kristovich, Membership Chair
Parkland Coll.
2400 W Bradley Ave., Rm. X203
Champaign, IL 61821
E-mail: skristovich@parkland.edu
URL: http://www.pir.ilstu.edu/iair
Contact: Sharon Kristovich, Membership Chair
State. Represents individuals interested in institutional research. Fosters research leading to improved understanding, planning, and operation of institutions of postsecondary education. **Affiliated With:** Association for Institutional Research.

526 ■ Illinois Crop Improvement Association
c/o Dennis R. Thompson, CEO
3105 Res. Rd.
PO Box 9013
Champaign, IL 61826-9013
Ph: (217)359-4053
Fax: (217)359-4075
E-mail: ilcrop@ilcrop.com
URL: http://www.ilcrop.com
Contact: Dennis R. Thompson, CEO
State.

527 ■ Illinois Heritage Association
602-1/2 E Green St.
Champaign, IL 61820
Ph: (217)359-5600
Fax: (877)271-5871
E-mail: plmxiha@prairienet.org
URL: http://illinoisheritage.prairienet.org
Contact: Ms. Patricia L. Miller, Exec.Dir.
Founded: 1981. **Membership Dues:** individual, $30 (annual) • institutional, $35 (annual) • corporate, $75 (annual) • governmental, $100 (annual) • advisory (voting), $100 (annual). **Staff:** 1. **State**. Provides technical assistance to museums, libraries, historical and genealogical societies, preservation associations, and others who work to preserve the cultural heritage of IL. **Libraries: Type:** lending. **Holdings:** 1,000; archival material, audio recordings, books, periodicals, video recordings. **Subjects:** nonprofit administration, collections management, collections care, interpretation, history and historic preservation. **Computer Services:** Information services. **Publications:** Newsletter, bimonthly. Contains four printed news about nonprofit activities. **Price:** $4.00 single copy for nonmembers; included in membership dues. ISSN: 0890-3719. **Circulation:** 500 • Newsletter, monthly. Features online information about current activities of nonprofit organization on national scene.

Price: included in membership dues. Alternate Formats: online.

528 ■ Illinois Quarter Horse Association, District No. 6
c/o Lowell Osterbur, Dir.
2115 CR 1200 E
Champaign, IL 61822-9437
Ph: (217)643-6845
E-mail: obur25@aol.com
URL: http://www.ilqha.com
Contact: Lowell Osterbur, Dir.
Local. Affiliated With: American Quarter Horse Association.

529 ■ Illinois Seed Trade Association
PO Box 9013
Champaign, IL 61826-9013
Ph: (217)359-4053
Fax: (217)359-4075
E-mail: rdenhart_ista@ilcrap.com
Contact: Richard Denhart, Exec.Sec.-Treas.
State.

530 ■ Illinois Volkssport Association
c/o David Bradley
3109 Valerie Dr.
Champaign, IL 61822-1830
Ph: (217)355-6811
E-mail: dybradley@insightbb.com
URL: National Affiliate–www.ava.org
Contact: David Bradley, Contact
State.

531 ■ International Brotherhood of Electrical Workers, AFL-CIO, CFL - Local Union 601
PO Box 3902
Champaign, IL 61826
Ph: (217)352-1741
E-mail: phuls@ibew601.org
URL: http://www.ibew601.org
Contact: Bryan Holderfield, Pres.
Members: 484. **Local.** Works to elevate the moral, intellectual and social conditions of workers. **Affiliated With:** International Brotherhood of Electrical Workers.

532 ■ International Brotherhood of Magicians, Ring 236 - The Magic Wand Ring
c/o Dorothy Schultz
1207 W Univ.
Champaign, IL 61821
Ph: (217)352-7206
E-mail: magiciands@cs.com
URL: http://www.angelfire.com/wizard/cigtg
Contact: Dorothy Schultz, Contact
Founded: 1976. **Members:** 23. **Membership Dues:** individual, $18 (annual). **Local.** Seeks to associate for professional growth, exchange of ideas, and cooperation of individuals sincerely interested in the advancement, promotion, and practice of the art of magic. **Additional Websites:** http://www.magician.org/LocalRings/illinois.htm. **Affiliated With:** International Brotherhood of Magicians. **Publications:** Newsletter, monthly. **Conventions/Meetings:** triennial Central Illinois Magic Get-Together - meeting • monthly meeting - every 4th Thursday at 7 PM.

533 ■ Kenwood Elementary PTA
c/o Kenwood Elementary School
1001 S Stratford
Champaign, IL 61821
Ph: (217)351-3815
E-mail: jgjiufan@aol.com
URL: http://familyeducation.com/IL/KenwoodPTA
Contact: Julie Johnson, Pres.
Local. Parents, teachers, students, and others interested in uniting the forces of home, school, and community. Promotes the welfare of children and youth.

534 ■ Kiwanis Club of Champaign-Urbana
1516 Countryside Pl.
Champaign, IL 61821
E-mail: fbundy@news-gazette.com
URL: http://www.cukiwanis.org
Contact: Floyd Bundy, Pres.
Local.

535 ■ Labor and Employment Relations Association (LERA)
Univ. of Illinois at Urbana-Champaign
121 Labor and Indus. Relations Bldg.
504 E Armory Ave.
Champaign, IL 61820
Ph: (217)333-0072
Fax: (217)265-5130
E-mail: leraoffice@uiuc.edu
URL: http://www.lera.uiuc.edu
Contact: Paula Wells, Exec.Dir.
Founded: 1947. **Members:** 4,000. **Membership Dues:** individual, $85 (annual) • student, $25 (annual) • family (additional member in individual members household), $15 (annual) • emeritus, $50 (annual) • contributing, $175 (annual) • institutional, $110 (annual). **Budget:** $485,000. **Local.** Represents academic, labor, management, and neutral communities committed to the discussion and exchange of ideas between and amongst its broad constituencies through meetings, publications, and its various electronic listservs and website. Encourages research in all aspects of the field of labor, employment, and the workplace. **Publications:** *IRRA Newsletter*, quarterly, March, June, September, and December. Magazine • *IRRA Proceedings of the Annual Meeting*, annual, every September. Book • *IRRA Research Volume*, annual, every October. Book • *Perspectives on Work*, semiannual, every June and December. Magazine. **Conventions/Meetings:** semiannual Executive Board Meeting - January and June • annual meeting, held in conjunction with the Allied Social Science Association annual meeting - first weekend in January • annual National Policy Forum - conference - June.

536 ■ Midwest Region FCA
c/o Stephanie Wetzel, Mgr.
1701 Broadmoor, Ste.210
Champaign, IL 61821
Ph: (217)378-4518
E-mail: ilfca@aol.com
URL: http://www.mwregionfca.org
Contact: Stephanie Wetzel, Mgr.
Regional.

537 ■ National Active And Retired Federal Employees Association - Illini 348
3001 Valley Brook Dr.
Champaign, IL 61822-6113
Ph: (217)359-5974
URL: National Affiliate–www.narfe.org
Contact: Robert P. Bentz, Contact
Local. Protects the retirement future of employees through education. Informs members on issues affecting the retirement. **Affiliated With:** National Association of Retired Federal Employees.

538 ■ National Alliance for the Mentally Ill - Champaign County
PO Box 1514
Champaign, IL 61824
Ph: (217)352-2064
E-mail: namiccprez@sbcglobal.net
URL: http://namichampaign.nami.org
Contact: Fannie Griffin, Pres.
Local. Strives to improve the quality of life of children and adults with severe mental illness through support, education, research and advocacy. **Affiliated With:** National Alliance for the Mentally Ill.

539 ■ National Softball Association - Illinois
c/o Bob Biehl, Dir.
PO Box 3812
Champaign, IL 61826
Ph: (217)356-0244
E-mail: rbiehl@usd116.org
URL: National Affiliate–www.playnsa.com
Contact: Bob Biehl, Dir.
State. Affiliated With: National Softball Association.

540 ■ Nature of Illinois Foundation
701 Devonshire Dr.
Champaign, IL 61820-3321
E-mail: nps@natureillinois.org
URL: http://www.natureillinois.org/
Contact: Nicholas P Schneider, Exec.Dir.
State.

541 ■ North Central Weed Science Society
1508 W Univ. Ave.
Champaign, IL 61821-3133
Ph: (217)352-4212
Fax: (217)352-4241
URL: http://www.ncwss.org
Regional. Affiliated With: Weed Science Society of America.

542 ■ Patton's Woods Nature Preserve Committee
Parkland Coll.
2400 W Bradley Ave.
Champaign, IL 61821
Ph: (217)351-2200
Fax: (217)373-3830
Free: (800)346-8089
URL: http://www.parkland.cc.il.us
Contact: Heidi Leuzler, Contact
Local.

543 ■ Petroleum Technology Transfer Council Midwest Region
c/o David Morse, Dir.
615 E Peabody Dr.
Champaign, IL 61820
Ph: (217)244-9337
Fax: (217)244-2785
E-mail: morse@isgs.uiuc.edu
URL: http://www.isgs.uiuc.edu/pttc/index.html
Contact: David Morse, Dir.
Regional. Assists independent oil company engineers and geologists to learn about new technologies that will improve exploration, drilling and completion, operations and production, reservoir development, and environmental solutions. Provides technical workshops, online data and technical information, case studies, software demos, newsletters, and on-call assistance in providing technical solutions. **Affiliated With:** Petroleum Technology Transfer Council.

544 ■ PFLAG Urbana-Champaign
1916 McDonald Dr.
Champaign, IL 61821
E-mail: cupflag@hotmail.com
URL: http://www.pflag.org/Illinois.204.0.html
Local. Affiliated With: Parents, Families, and Friends of Lesbians and Gays.

545 ■ Phi Theta Kappa, Alpha Psi Eta Chapter - Parkland College
c/o Tom Barnard
2400 W Bradley Ave.
Champaign, IL 61821
Ph: (217)353-2349
E-mail: tbarnard@parkland.edu
URL: http://www.ptk.org/directories/chapters/IL/20580-1.htm
Contact: Tom Barnard, Advisor
Local.

546 ■ Plumbing-Heating-Cooling Contractors Association, East Central Illinois
c/o Henry R. Hart
1513 Grandview Dr.
Champaign, IL 61820-6828

Ph: (217)356-6442
Fax: (217)356-6447
URL: National Affiliate–www.phccweb.org
Contact: Henry R. Hart, Contact
Local. Represents the plumbing, heating and cooling contractors. Promotes the construction industry. Protects the environment, health, safety and comfort of society. **Affiliated With:** Plumbing-Heating-Cooling Contractors Association.

547 ■ Prairie Ensemble
PO Box 295
Champaign, IL 61824-0295
Ph: (217)355-9077
Fax: (217)355-9077
E-mail: contact@prauseensemble.org
URL: http://www.prairieensemble.org
Contact: Kevin Kelly, Music Dir.
Founded: 1996. **Members:** 40. **Membership Dues:** individual, $25 (annual). **Budget:** $61,000. **Local**. Community-professional chamber orchestra bringing high-quality musical entertainment to diverse audiences at minimal cost. Provides four performances throughout the year. **Conventions/Meetings:** monthly board meeting • annual meeting.

548 ■ Prairie Rivers Network
809 S 5th St.
Champaign, IL 61820
Ph: (217)344-2371
Fax: (217)344-2381
E-mail: info@prairierivers.org
URL: http://www.prairierivers.org
Contact: Jean Flemma, Exec.Dir.
Local. Strives to protect the rivers and streams of Illinois and to promote the lasting health and beauty of watershed communities.

549 ■ Primary Purpose Area of Narcotics Anonymous (PPANA)
PO Box 1332
Champaign, IL 61824-1332
Free: (800)539-0475
URL: http://www.ppana.org
Local. **Affiliated With:** Narcotics Anonymous.

550 ■ Psi Chi, National Honor Society in Psychology - University of Illinois at Urbana-Champaign
c/o Dept. of Psychology
10 Psychology Bldg.
603 E Daniel St.
Champaign, IL 61820
Ph: (217)333-0631 (217)333-6478
Fax: (217)244-5876
E-mail: wszalek@s.psych.uiuc.edu
URL: National Affiliate–www.psichi.org
Local. **Affiliated With:** Psi Chi, National Honor Society in Psychology.

551 ■ Puppeteers of America - Central Illinois Puppetry Guild
c/o Ginger Lozar, Pres./Ed.
1708 Salem Rd.
Champaign, IL 61821
Ph: (217)352-1672
E-mail: clozar@aol.com
URL: National Affiliate–www.puppeteers.org
Contact: Ginger Lozar, Pres./Ed.
Local.

552 ■ Ridgewalkers Walking Club
c/o David Bradley
3109 Valerie Dr.
Champaign, IL 61822-1830
Ph: (217)355-6811
Fax: (217)355-9413
E-mail: dybradley@insightbb.com
URL: National Affiliate–www.ava.org
Contact: David Bradley, Contact
Founded: 1989. **Members:** 30. **Membership Dues:** individual, $10 (annual). **Regional Groups:** 1. **State Groups:** 1. **Local**. Chartered member of the American Volkssport Association; affiliate of the Champaign and Urbana Park Districts. **Libraries: Type:** not open to the public. **Holdings:** 30; books. **Subjects:** walking, fitness. **Affiliated With:** American Volkssport Association. **Formerly:** (1995) Rantoul Ridgewalkers. **Publications:** *Ridgewalkers*, monthly. Newsletter. **Circulation:** 30.

553 ■ RSVP Champaign, Douglas, Piatt Counties
c/o Vicki Stewart, Dir.
48 Main
Champaign, IL 61820
Ph: (217)359-6500
Fax: (217)359-6550
E-mail: vsdrsvp@earthlink.net
URL: http://www.seniorcorps.gov/about/programs/rsvp_state.asp?usestateabbr=il&Search4.x=0&Search4.y=0
Contact: Vicki Stewart, Dir.
Local. **Affiliated With:** Retired and Senior Volunteer Program.

554 ■ United Way of Champaign County
404 W Church St.
Champaign, IL 61820
Ph: (217)352-5151
Fax: (217)352-6494
E-mail: tammy@uwayhelps.org
URL: http://www.uwayhelps.org
Contact: Tammy Lemke, Pres./CEO
Local. **Affiliated With:** United Way of America.

555 ■ University of Illinois At Urbana-Champaign Figure Skating Club
406 E Armory Ave.
Champaign, IL 61820
E-mail: magiet@uiuc.edu
URL: National Affiliate–www.usfigureskating.org
Local. Provides programs to encourage participation and achievement in the sport of figure skating on ice. Defines and maintains uniform standards of skating proficiency. Organizes and sponsors competitions and exhibitions for the purpose of stimulating interest in figure skating. **Affiliated With:** United States Figure Skating Association.

556 ■ University of Illinois - Committee on Natural Areas (CNA)
116 Vivarium (MC-444)
606 E Healey St.
Champaign, IL 61820
Ph: (217)333-6458
E-mail: sbuck@uiuc.edu
URL: http://www.uiuc.edu/unit/vcres/cna
Contact: Steve Buck, Research Technologist
Local.

557 ■ Urban League of Champaign County (ULCC)
314 S Neil St.
Champaign, IL 61820
Ph: (217)363-3333
Fax: (217)356-1310
E-mail: lbonnett@urbanleague.net
URL: http://www.urbanleague.net
Contact: Mr. Tracy Parsons, Pres./CEO
Founded: 1961. **Members:** 300. **Membership Dues:** individual and corporate, $25-$10,000 (annual). **Staff:** 50. **Budget:** $4,000,000. **Languages:** English, Spanish. **Local**. Works to enable African Americans secure economic self-reliance, parity, power and civil rights through: Education and Youth Empowerment; Economic Empowerment; Civic Engagement and Leadership Empowerment and Civil Rights and Racial Justice Empowerment. **Awards:** Beautiful People Awards. **Frequency:** annual. **Type:** recognition. **Recipient:** community partners that aid in the urban league mission. **Departments:** Education; Fund Development and Comm.; Housing Programs and Services, Transportation; Workforce Development; Youth Development and Family Support.

558 ■ Urbana Country Dancers (UCD)
5 The Summit
Champaign, IL 61820
Ph: (217)359-8225
E-mail: jsivier@uiuc.edu
URL: http://www.prairienet.org/contra
Contact: Jonathan Sivier, Contact
Local. Represents people interested in traditional American Country music and dance. Holds contra dances twice a month.

Chandlerville

559 ■ American Legion, Chandler Post 694
8 N Main St.
Chandlerville, IL 62627
Ph: (309)663-0361
Fax: (309)663-5783
URL: National Affiliate–www.legion.org
Local. **Affiliated With:** American Legion.

560 ■ Illinois Quarter Horse Association, District No. 7
c/o Lori Jallas, Dir.
23927 Questing Hills Rd.
Chandlerville, IL 62627-9133
Ph: (217)458-2520
E-mail: brianjallas@tworiversfs.com
URL: http://www.ilqha.com
Contact: Lori Jallas, Dir.
Local. **Affiliated With:** American Quarter Horse Association.

Channahon

561 ■ Cat Overpopulation Planned Endeavor (COPE)
PO Box 801
Channahon, IL 60410
Ph: (815)729-4045 (815)725-8777
E-mail: info@copecats.org
URL: http://www.copecats.org
Contact: Joe Bertoglio, Contact
Local.

Chapin

562 ■ American Legion, Chapin Post 878
PO Box 55
Chapin, IL 62628
Ph: (309)663-0361
Fax: (309)663-5783
URL: National Affiliate–www.legion.org
Local. **Affiliated With:** American Legion.

Charleston

563 ■ American Legion, Charleston Memorial Post 1999
2531 Salem Rd.
Charleston, IL 61920
Ph: (309)663-0361
Fax: (309)663-5783
URL: National Affiliate–www.legion.org
Local. **Affiliated With:** American Legion.

564 ■ Central East Alcoholism and Drug Council (CEADC)
635 Div. St.
PO Box 532
Charleston, IL 61920
Ph: (217)348-8108 (217)348-0154
Fax: (217)345-6794
E-mail: ceadbzns@mcleodusa.net
URL: http://www.ceadcouncil.org
Contact: Pamela Irwin PhD, Exec.Dir.
Founded: 1972. **State**. Works for the prevention of alcoholism and substance abuse through programs of public and professional education, community

service, and the promotion of alcohol and substance abuse research. Provides full array of addiction treatment programs including outpatient and residential levels of care. **Programs:** Adult Outpatient; Detoxification; Intensive Outpatient; Men's Residential; Recovery Home for Women with Children; Women's Halfway House; Women's Outpatient; Women's Residential. **Affiliated With:** National Council on Alcoholism and Drug Dependence.

565 ■ Central Illinois Board of Realtors
733 Windsor Rd.
Charleston, IL 61920
Ph: (217)348-7070
Fax: (217)348-8763
E-mail: candy@consolidated.net
URL: http://www.cibor.org
Contact: Candy Vaughan, Association Exec.
Local. Strives to develop real estate business practices. Advocates the right to own, use and transfer real property. Provides a facility for professional development, research and exchange of information among members and to the general public. **Affiliated With:** National Association of Realtors.

566 ■ Charleston Area Chamber of Commerce (CACC)
501 Jackson Ave.
PO Box 77
Charleston, IL 61920-0077
Ph: (217)345-7041 (217)348-0430
Fax: (217)345-7042
E-mail: caccinfo@charlestonchamber.com
URL: http://www.charlestonchamber.com
Contact: Cindy Titus, Exec.Dir.
Founded: 1919. **Membership Dues:** bank/savings & loan (per million in asset with a cap of $1300), $27 (annual) • associate/educator/individual, $86 (annual) • senior/retired person/service organization with no paid staff, $57 (annual) • business (based on number of employees), $185-$865 (annual) • corporate sponsor, $1,300 (annual) • owner/manager, $124 (annual). **Staff:** 3. **Local**. Promotes the economic climate in the greater Charleston, Illinois area. Acts as the marketing/promoting agent for the Charleston area in collaboration with other community organizations. **Computer Services:** Online services, members list. **Publications:** *Chamber Focus*, monthly. Newsletter. Contains information about business issues and Chamber opportunities. **Advertising:** accepted • *Membership Directory & Buyers' Guide*, annual, every January. Serves as an excellent resource for business leads and contacts and a great sales tool. Alternate Formats: online.

567 ■ Coles County Habitat for Humanity
PO Box 945
Charleston, IL 61920
Ph: (217)348-7063
E-mail: cchfh@colescountyhabitat.net
URL: http://www.colescountyhabitat.net
Contact: Sharon Monroe, Pres.
Local. **Affiliated With:** Habitat for Humanity International.

568 ■ Coles County RSVP
c/o Marilyn Strangeman, Dir.
720 6th St.
Charleston, IL 61920-2163
Ph: (217)345-9530
Fax: (217)345-1194
E-mail: ccrsvp@consolidated.net
URL: http://www.seniorcorps.gov/about/programs/rsvp_state.asp?usestateabbr=il&Search4.x=21&Search4.y=4
Contact: Marilyn Strangeman, Dir.
Local. Affiliated With: Retired and Senior Volunteer Program.

569 ■ Eastern Illinois AIFA
c/o Eldon D. Gourley, Pres.
733 Windsor Rd.
Charleston, IL 61920
Ph: (217)345-3832
Fax: (217)756-3210
URL: National Affiliate–naifa.org
Contact: Eldon D. Gourley, Pres.
Local. Represents the interests of insurance and financial advisors. Advocates for a positive legislative and regulatory environment. Enhances business and professional skills of members. **Affiliated With:** National Association of Insurance and Financial Advisors.

570 ■ Psi Chi, National Honor Society in Psychology - Eastern Illinois University
c/o Dept. of Psychology
1151 Physical Scis. Bldg.
600 Lincoln Ave.
Charleston, IL 61920-3099
Ph: (217)581-2127 (217)581-6413
Fax: (217)581-6764
E-mail: glcanivez@eiu.edu
URL: http://www.psichi.org/chapters/info.asp?chapter_id=271
Contact: Gary L. Canivez PhD, Advisor
Local.

571 ■ Reserve Officers Association - Department of Illinois, Eastern Illinois Chapter 12
c/o LTC Murray R. Choate, Pres.
2100 Meadow Lake Dr.
Charleston, IL 61920
Ph: (217)345-4435
URL: http://www.ilroa.org
Contact: LTC Murray R. Choate, Pres.
Local. Promotes and supports the development and execution of a military policy for the United States. Provides professional development seminars, workshops and programs for its members. **Affiliated With:** Reserve Officers Association of the United States.

572 ■ Society of Manufacturing Engineers - Eastern Illinois University S151
c/o Eastern Illinois Univ.
600 Lincoln Ave.
Charleston, IL 61920
Ph: (217)581-7259
Fax: (217)581-6607
E-mail: cfsag@eiu.edu
URL: http://www.eiu.edu/%7Esamgnet/EIU_SME/EIU_SME_Welcome.htm
Contact: Dr. Sam Guccione, Contact
Local. Advances manufacturing knowledge to gain competitive advantage. Improves skills and manufacturing solutions for the growth of economy. Provides resources and opportunities for manufacturing professionals. **Affiliated With:** American Society of Mechanical Engineers Auxiliary.

573 ■ USA Weightlifting - Charleston
c/o Marty Schnorf
PO Box 183
Charleston, IL 61920
Ph: (217)258-6588
E-mail: charlestonweightliftingclub@yahoo.com
URL: National Affiliate–www.usaweightlifting.org
Contact: Marty Schnorf, Contact
Local. Affiliated With: USA Weightlifting.

574 ■ USA Weightlifting - Team Body Club
c/o James DiNaso
618 Jackson Ave.
Charleston, IL 61920
Ph: (217)348-0819
E-mail: bodyclub@worthlink.net
URL: National Affiliate–www.usaweightlifting.org
Contact: James DiNaso, Contact
Local. Affiliated With: USA Weightlifting.

575 ■ Veterans of Foreign Wars
1821 20th St.
Charleston, IL 61920
Ph: (217)345-2707

576 ■ Workforce Opportunities Resource Consortium (WORC)
730 7th St.
Charleston, IL 61920
Ph: (217)348-0151
E-mail: worc@roe11.k12.il.us
URL: http://www.worcetc.com
Contact: Virginia Hayes, Coor.
Founded: 1994. **Members:** 207. **Staff:** 2. **Local**. Works to facilitate and advance the processes whereby all learners will be given opportunities to prepare for successful employment and citizenry. **Awards:** Exemplary Business Education Partnership. **Frequency:** annual. **Type:** recognition. **Conventions/Meetings:** annual MidIllinois Mentoring Conference.

Chatham

577 ■ American Legion, Chatham Post 759
206 W Chestnut
Chatham, IL 62629
Ph: (217)524-1187
Fax: (309)663-5783
URL: National Affiliate–www.legion.org
Local. Affiliated With: American Legion.

578 ■ American Mothers - Illinois Chapter
c/o Paula Staab Polk, Pres.
210 S Main St.
Chatham, IL 62629
E-mail: staabpolk@mwii.net
URL: National Affiliate–www.americanmothers.org
Contact: Paula Staab Polk, Pres.
State. Affiliated With: American Mothers, Inc.

579 ■ Illinois Native Plant Society, Central Chapter
142 Lilac Ln.
Chatham, IL 62629
E-mail: johnlana@netscape.com
URL: http://www.ill-inps.org
Contact: John Benedict, Pres.
Local. Affiliated With: Illinois Native Plant Society.

580 ■ Kiwanis Club of Chatham
c/o Brian R. Davis, Treas.
PO Box 164
Chatham, IL 62629
Ph: (217)241-5771
E-mail: chathamkiwanis@yahoo.com
URL: http://chathamkiwanis.port5.com
Contact: Norm Smith, Pres.
Local.

Chatsworth

581 ■ American Legion, Walter Clemons Post 613
PO Box 186
Chatsworth, IL 60921
Ph: (309)663-0361
Fax: (309)663-5783
URL: National Affiliate–www.legion.org
Local. Affiliated With: American Legion.

582 ■ Illinois State Rifle Association (ISRA)
PO Box 637
Chatsworth, IL 60921
Ph: (815)635-3198
Fax: (815)635-3723
E-mail: president@isra.org
URL: http://www.isra.org
Contact: Richard A. Pearson, Exec.Dir.
Founded: 1903. **State. Affiliated With:** National Rifle Association of America.

Chebanse

583 ■ American Legion, Lauridsen Post 408
PO Box 393
Chebanse, IL 60922
Ph: (309)663-0361
Fax: (309)663-5783
URL: National Affiliate–www.legion.org
Local. Affiliated With: American Legion.

Chenoa

584 ■ American Legion, Illinois Post 234
c/o Ben Roth
215 S Veto St.
Chenoa, IL 61726
Ph: (815)945-3883
Fax: (309)663-5783
URL: National Affiliate–www.legion.org
Contact: Ben Roth, Contact
Local. Affiliated With: American Legion.

Cherry Valley

585 ■ Alpine Kiwanis of Rockford, Illinois
c/o Ron Janecek, Sec.
7588 Wild Oats Trail
Cherry Valley, IL 61016
E-mail: rij46@aol.com
URL: http://www.alpinekiwanis-il.org
Contact: Gary G. Hunt, Pres.
Local.

586 ■ American Youth Soccer Organization, Region 115
PO Box 462
Cherry Valley, IL 61016
Ph: (815)703-7381
Fax: (815)967-0788
E-mail: jflemming_1010@hotmail.com
URL: http://www.rockfordayso.com
Local. Affiliated With: American Youth Soccer Organization.

587 ■ Rockford Area Coin Club (RACC)
c/o Rich Hartzog
PO Box 294
Cherry Valley, IL 61016
Ph: (815)226-0771
E-mail: hartzog@exonumia.com
URL: http://www.exonumia.com/racc.htm
Contact: Rich Hartzog, Contact
Local. Promotes the interests of all collectors of coins, paper money, exonumia, tokens and medals. **Affiliated With:** American Numismatic Association.

Chester

588 ■ American Legion, Alva Courier Post 487
500 Opdyke St.
Chester, IL 62233
Ph: (618)826-3433
Fax: (309)663-5783
URL: National Affiliate–www.legion.org
Local. Affiliated With: American Legion..

589 ■ Chester Chamber of Commerce
PO Box 585
Chester, IL 62233
Ph: (618)826-2721
E-mail: chesterc@egyptian.net
URL: http://www.chesterill.com
Contact: Linda Sympson, Exec.Dir.
Local. Promotes business and community development in Chester, IL.

Chicago

590 ■ 100 Black Men of Chicago
188 W Randolph, Ste.626
Chicago, IL 60601
Ph: (312)461-2673
Fax: (312)765-1750
E-mail: micxmas622@aol.com
URL: http://www.100bmc.org
Local. Affiliated With: 100 Black Men of America.

591 ■ 5600 South Paulina Block Club
c/o Beverly Moores
5611 S. Paulina
Chicago, IL 60636-1221
Ph: (773)737-9644
Local.

592 ■ AARP Illinois
222 N LaSalle St., Ste.710
Chicago, IL 60601
Fax: (312)372-2204
Free: (866)448-3613
E-mail: aarpil@aarp.org
URL: National Affiliate–www.aarp.org
Contact: Evelyn Gooden, Pres.
State. Seeks to improve every aspect of living for older people. Addresses the needs and interests of older people, working or retired. Promotes positive social change and delivers value to members through information, advocacy and service. **Affiliated With:** American Association of Retired Persons.

593 ■ Access Living
614 W Roosevelt Rd.
Chicago, IL 60607
Ph: (312)253-7000
Fax: (312)253-7001
E-mail: generalinfo@accessliving.org
URL: http://www.accessliving.org
Contact: Marca Bristo, Pres./CEO
Founded: 1980. **Membership Dues:** individual, $25 (annual) • sponsor, $50 (annual). **Staff:** 51. **Budget:** $2,900,000. **Languages:** English, Spanish. **For-Profit. Local.** Fosters the dignity, inclusion, and independence of people with disabilities through peer oriented independent living services; public education and awareness; individualized and systematic advocacy; and enforcement of civil rights on behalf of people with disabilities. **Libraries: Type:** open to the public. **Holdings:** artwork, books, periodicals. **Subjects:** disabilities. **Programs:** Nursing Home Transition. **Subgroups:** Civil Rights; Housing; In-home Personal Assistance; Information and Referral; Peer Support; Transportation; Youth and Education. **Affiliated With:** National Council on Independent Living. **Publications:** *The Bullhorn*, 3/year. Newsletter. Contains information about the organizations activities. **Price:** included in membership dues. Alternate Formats: online • *Shunted Aside Hidden And Ignored*. Report. Contains details on Illinois' failure to implement Olmstead. Alternate Formats: online • *Terri Schiavo Brief*. Proceedings. Contains information about the case of Terri Schiavo. Alternate Formats: online • Annual Report. **Price:** free. Alternate Formats: magnetic tape; diskette • Brochures.

594 ■ ACF Windy City Professional Culinarians
c/o Union League Club of Chicago
65 W Jackson Blvd.
Chicago, IL 60604
Ph: (312)435-4822
Fax: (312)435-5962
E-mail: garbimi@ulcc.org
URL: National Affiliate–www.acfchefs.org
Contact: Michael H. Garbin CEC, Pres.
Local. Promotes the culinary profession. Provides on-going educational training and networking for members. Provides opportunities for competition, professional recognition and access to educational forums with other culinarians at local, regional, national and international events. **Affiliated With:** American Culinary Federation.

595 ■ Action for Children
c/o Receptionist
4753 N Broadway, Ste.1200
Chicago, IL 60640
Ph: (773)687-4000
Fax: (773)481-6610
URL: http://www.daycareaction.org
Contact: Maria Whelan, Pres./CEO
Founded: 1970. **State. Formerly:** (2004) Day Care Action Council of Illinois.

596 ■ Actors' Fund of America, Midwestern Region
203 N Wabash, Ste.2104
Chicago, IL 60601
Ph: (312)372-0989
E-mail: dtowne@actorsfund.org
URL: National Affiliate–www.actorsfund.org
Contact: Donald Towne, Contact
Regional. Human service organization of the entertainment industry. **Affiliated With:** Actors' Fund of America.

597 ■ African American Women Evolving (AAWE)
220 S State St., Ste.1330
Chicago, IL 60604-2141
Ph: (312)566-0983
Fax: (312)566-0992
E-mail: askaawe@aaweonline.org
URL: http://www.aaweonline.org
Contact: Ms. Mildred Leggett, Programs Asst.
Founded: 1996. **Members:** 350. **Staff:** 3. **Budget:** $350,000. **Local.**

598 ■ AFSME Council 31
c/o Lorie Scafaro
29 N Wacker Dr., Ste.800
Chicago, IL 60606
Ph: (312)641-6060
Fax: (312)346-1016
E-mail: loreleis@afsmeillinois.org
URL: http://www.afscme31.org
Contact: Lorie Scafaro, Contact
State.

599 ■ AIDS Legal Council of Chicago (ALCC)
c/o Ann Fisher
188 W Randolph St., Ste.2400
Chicago, IL 60601
Ph: (312)427-8990
Fax: (312)427-8419
E-mail: info@aidslegal.com
URL: http://www.aidslegal.com
Contact: Justin Hayford, Case Mgr.
Local. Provides legal services to low-income Chicago-area residents with HIV; promotes legal education and advocacy on HIV-related topics.

600 ■ Albany Park Chamber of Commerce
4745 N Kedzie Ave.
Chicago, IL 60625
Ph: (773)478-0202
Fax: (773)478-0282
E-mail: mmcdaniel@northrivercommission.com
URL: http://www.albanyparkchamber.org
Contact: Melissa McDaniel, Exec.Dir.
Founded: 1976. **Members:** 600. **Local.** Promotes business and community development in the Albany Park area of Chicago, IL. Sponsors promotions. **Convention/Meeting:** none. **Publications:** Newsletter, monthly.

601 ■ Albany Park Neighborhood Council
c/o Kirk Noden
4419 N Kedzie Ave.
Chicago, IL 60625
Ph: (773)583-1387
E-mail: knoden@hotmail.com
URL: National Affiliate–www.npa-us.org
Local. Affiliated With: National People's Action.

602 ■ Alcoholics Anonymous World Services, Chicago Area Service Office
200 N Michigan Ave., Ste.501
Chicago, IL 60601
Ph: (312)346-1475
Fax: (312)346-5477
Free: (800)371-1475
E-mail: caso@chicagoaa.org
URL: http://www.chicagoaa.org
Contact: Bruce Parry, Mgr.
Local. Individuals recovering from alcoholism. AA maintains that members can solve their common problem and help others achieve sobriety through a twelve step program that includes sharing their experience, strength, and hope with each other. **Affiliated With:** Alcoholics Anonymous World Services.

603 ■ Alcoholics Anonymous World Services, Comite De Intergrupos
2814 1/2 W 59th St.
Chicago, IL 60629
Ph: (773)863-0172
URL: National Affiliate–www.aa.org
Local. Individuals recovering from alcoholism. AA maintains that members can solve their common problem and help others achieve sobriety through a twelve step program that includes sharing their experience, strength, and hope with each other. **Affiliated With:** Alcoholics Anonymous World Services.

604 ■ Alliance for the Great Lakes
220 S State St., Ste.1900
Chicago, IL 60604
Ph: (312)939-0838
Fax: (312)939-2708
E-mail: chicago@greatlakes.org
URL: http://www.lakemichigan.org
Contact: Cameron Davis, Exec.Dir.
Founded: 1970. **State**. Works to restore fish and wildlife habitat, conserve land and water and eliminate toxins in the watershed of the largest lake within the United States through education, research, law, science, economics and strategic partnerships. **Formerly:** (2005) Lake Michigan Federation.

605 ■ American Academy of Pediatrics, Illinois Chapter
c/o Scott G. Allen, Exec.Dir.
1358 W Randolph, Ste.2E
Chicago, IL 60607
Ph: (312)733-1026
Fax: (312)733-1791
E-mail: info@illinoisaap.com
URL: http://www.illinoisaap.org
Contact: Scott G. Allen, Exec.Dir.
State. Promotes the right of all children to live happy, safe, and healthy lives, to ensure that children receive quality medical care from pediatricians and to assess and serve the needs of members. Primary activities include advocacy on behalf of children, families, and health professionals in Illinois; the provision of continuing medical education and other resources for child health care providers; and collaboration with other state organizations and agencies on programs and projects that improve the health and well-being of children. **Affiliated With:** American Academy of Pediatrics. **Publications:** *Illinois Pediatrician*, quarterly. Newsletters. **Advertising:** accepted. Alternate Formats: online.

606 ■ American Association of Airport Executives, Illinois
c/o Thomas J. Stastny, AAE
Chicago Midway Airport
5757 S Cicero Ave.
Chicago, IL 60638-3817
Ph: (773)838-0686
Fax: (773)838-0583
E-mail: tstastny@cityofchicago.org
URL: http://www.glcaaae.org
Contact: Thomas J. Stastny AAE, Contact
State. Represents airport management personnel at public airports. Promotes professionalism and financial stability in the administration of airports. Furthers airport safety and operational efficiency. Seeks to develop a systematic exchange of information and experience in the development, maintenance and operation of airports. **Affiliated With:** American Association of Airport Executives.

607 ■ American Association of Critical Care Nurses, Greater Chicago Area Chapter
c/o Sheila Coogan, Pres.
PO Box 301023
Chicago, IL 60630-1023
E-mail: gcac.info@aacn.org
URL: http://www.aacn.org/chapters/gcac.nsf/other/homepage?opendocument
Contact: Sheila Coogan, Pres.
Founded: 1972. **Members:** 50. **Membership Dues:** active, $20 (annual) • active, $35 (biennial). **Local**. Professional critical care nurses. Established to provide continuing education programs for nurses specializing in critical care and to develop standards of nursing care of critically ill patients. **Affiliated With:** American Association of Critical-Care Nurses. **Publications:** *AACN News*, monthly. Newspaper • *The American Journal of Critical Care*, bimonthly. Magazine • *Critical Care Nurse*, bimonthly. Magazine • Newsletter, semiannual. **Conventions/Meetings:** annual Cardiovascular Symposium - January • periodic Educational Program - meeting - from February to June and September through November • periodic workshop.

608 ■ American Association for Laboratory Animal Science - Chicago (CBAALAS)
c/o Maria Lang
1840 W Taylor St.
Chicago, IL 60612
E-mail: cbaalas@yahoo.com
URL: http://www.cbaalas.org
Contact: Maria Lang, Contact
Local. Serves as a clearinghouse for the collection and exchange of information and expertise in the care and use of laboratory animals. Promotes and encourages the highest level of ethics within the profession of laboratory animal science. Provides educational and training programs for members and others who are professionally engaged in the production, care, use and study of laboratory animals. **Affiliated With:** American Association for Laboratory Animal Science.

609 ■ American Association of Legal Nurse Consultants, Greater Chicago Chapter
c/o Pat DiFiglio, RN, Pres.
500 W Superior, No. 705
Chicago, IL 60610
Ph: (847)604-1442 (708)467-1921
E-mail: chicagolnc@hotmail.com
URL: http://www.aalncchicago.org
Contact: Pat DiFiglio RN, Pres.
Founded: 1992. **Membership Dues:** active, associate, $40 (annual) • sustaining, $75 (annual). **Local**. **Libraries: Type:** lending. **Holdings:** audio recordings, books. **Subjects:** anesthesia, accidents, cancer, diagnostic studies, elder care issues, expert witness, forensics, hospital liability, legal nurse consulting practice, life care planning, medication liability and injuries, neurology, nursing negligence, obstetrics, pathology, pediatrics, surgeries. **Affiliated With:** American Association of Legal Nurse Consultants.

610 ■ American Association of Physics Teachers, Chicago Section
c/o Maria K. Udo, Pres.
Loyola Univ. - Chicago, Dept. of Physics
6525 N Sheridan Rd.
Chicago, IL 60626
Ph: (773)508-7723
Fax: (773)508-3534
E-mail: mudo@luc.edu
URL: http://www.aapt-chicago.org
Contact: Maria K. Udo, Pres.
Local. Seeks to enhance the understanding and appreciation of physics through teaching. Aims to improve the pedagogical skills and physics knowledge of teachers at all levels. **Affiliated With:** American Association of Physics Teachers.

611 ■ American Association of Retired Persons, Chicago
223 N La Salle St., Ste.710
Chicago, IL 60601
Fax: (312)372-2204
Free: (866)448-3613
URL: http://www.aarp.org
Contact: Evelyn Gooden, Pres.
Local. Persons 50 years of age or older, working or retired. Seeks to improve every aspect of living for older people. **Affiliated With:** American Association of Retired Persons.

612 ■ American Association of Teachers of Spanish and Portuguese - Chicago Chapter
c/o Mary Ann Hockman, Sec.
4917 N Drake
Chicago, IL 60625
E-mail: mariannehockman@aol.com
URL: http://www.chicagoaatsp.org
Contact: John Finan, Pres.
Local. Promotes the study and teaching of Spanish and Portuguese languages, literatures and cultures at all educational levels. **Affiliated With:** American Association of Teachers of Spanish and Portuguese.

613 ■ American Begonia Society, Greater Chicago Area Chapter
c/o Esther Detliefsen, Representative
3336 N Oak Park Ave.
Chicago, IL 60634
Ph: (773)282-2255
URL: National Affiliate–www.begonias.org
Contact: Esther Detliefsen, Representative
Local. **Affiliated With:** American Begonia Society.

614 ■ American Camping Association - Illinois Section
c/o Gordie Kaplan, Section Exec.
67 E Madison St., Ste.1406
Chicago, IL 60603-3010
Ph: (312)332-0833 (312)332-2497
Fax: (312)332-4011
E-mail: info@acail.org
URL: http://www.acail.org
Contact: Gordie Kaplan, Section Exec.
Members: 250. **State**. Chartered Section of national organization. Accredits youth camps. Provides information to public free of charge to help them find a camp for their child. Professional development for camp leaders. **Affiliated With:** American Camping Association.

615 ■ American Cancer Society Chicago Region
c/o Sherry Howard
225 N Michigan Ave., Ste.1210
Chicago, IL 60601
Ph: (312)372-0471
Fax: (312)372-0910
E-mail: sherry.howard@cancer.org
URL: http://www.cancer.org
Local.

616 ■ American Choral Directors Association - Central Division
c/o Robert Sinclair, Chm.
3140 S Fed. St.
Chicago, IL 60616-3731
Ph: (312)225-6288
E-mail: rsinclair@vandercook.edu
URL: http://www.acdaonline.org/Central
Contact: Gordon Krasupe, Pres.
Membership Dues: associate/active, $75 (annual) • student, $30 (annual) • life, $2,000. **Regional**. Promotes excellence in choral music through performance, composition, publication, research and teaching. Elevates choral music's position in American society. **Subgroups:** Repertoire and Standards. **Affiliated With:** American Choral Directors Association.

617 ■ American Civil Liberties Union of Illinois
c/o Colleen K. Connell, Exec.Dir.
180 N Michigan Ave., Ste.2300
Chicago, IL 60601
Ph: (312)201-9740
Fax: (312)201-9760
E-mail: acluofillinois@aclu-il.org
URL: http://www.aclu-il.org
Contact: Colleen K. Connell, Exec.Dir.
Founded: 1946. **Members:** 22,000. **State.** Protects liberties and freedoms guaranteed by the United States Constitution through litigation, lobbying, and education programs. **Affiliated With:** American Civil Liberties Union. **Publications:** *The Illinois Brief*, quarterly. Newsletter. ISSN: 1044-7725.

618 ■ American Diabetes Association - Northern Illinois (ADA)
c/o Stephanie Cesna, District Mgr.
30 N Michigan, Ste.2015
Chicago, IL 60602
Ph: (312)346-1805
Fax: (312)346-5342
Free: (800)342-2383
URL: http://www.diabetes.org
Contact: Stephanie Cesna, District Mgr.
Local.

619 ■ American Federation of Government Employees, District 7
c/o Dorothy James, Natl.VP
300 S Ashland Ave., Ste.302
Chicago, IL 60607
Ph: (312)421-6245
Fax: (312)421-6283
E-mail: jamesd@afge.org
URL: National Affiliate–www.afge.org
Contact: Dorothy James, Natl.VP
Regional. Affiliated With: American Federation of Government Employees.

620 ■ American Friends Service Committee, Chicago
c/o Michael McConnell, Regional Dir.
637 S Dearborn, Ste.3
Chicago, IL 60605
Ph: (312)427-2533
Fax: (312)427-4171
E-mail: afscchicago@igc.org
URL: http://www.afsc.org/chicago
Contact: Michael McConnell, Regional Dir.
Local. Affiliated With: American Friends Service Committee.

621 ■ American Hellenic Educational Progressive Association - Evanston, Chapter 204
c/o Constantine Kangles, Pres.
6007 N Sheridan Rd.
Chicago, IL 60660
Ph: (773)769-9101
URL: http://www.ahepafamily.org/d13
Contact: Constantine Kangles, Pres.
Local. Affiliated With: American Hellenic Educational Progressive Association.

622 ■ American Hellenic Educational Progressive Association - Milo, Chapter 348
c/o James Mezilson, Pres.
10247 S Oakley Ave.
Chicago, IL 60643
Ph: (773)239-5366
URL: http://www.ahepafamily.org/d13
Contact: James Mezilson, Pres.
Local. Affiliated With: American Hellenic Educational Progressive Association.

623 ■ American Hellenic Educational Progressive Association - Northshore, Chapter 94
c/o George T. Pantazelos, Pres.
233 E Wacker Dr., No. 3413
Chicago, IL 60601
Ph: (312)960-9500
E-mail: premier617@aol.com
URL: http://www.ahepafamily.org/d13
Contact: George T. Pantazelos, Pres.
Local. Affiliated With: American Hellenic Educational Progressive Association.

624 ■ American Hellenic Educational Progressive Association - Northwestern, Chapter 388
c/o James Triantapel, Pres.
3232 N New England Ave.
Chicago, IL 60634
Ph: (773)777-8150
URL: http://www.ahepafamily.org/d13
Contact: James Triantapel, Pres.
Local. Affiliated With: American Hellenic Educational Progressive Association.

625 ■ American Hellenic Educational Progressive Association - Shoreline, Chapter 380
c/o Constantine P. Kiamos, Pres.
7927 W Cortland Pkwy.
Chicago, IL 60607
Ph: (708)452-1957
E-mail: cpkiamos@comcast.net
URL: http://www.ahepafamily.org/d13
Contact: Constantine P. Kiamos, Pres.
Local. Affiliated With: American Hellenic Educational Progressive Association.

626 ■ American Institute of Architects Chicago
222 Merchandise Mart No. 1049
Chicago, IL 60654
Ph: (312)670-7770
Fax: (312)670-2422
E-mail: sinkevitcha@aiachicago.org
URL: National Affiliate–www.aia.org
Local. Professional society of architects. Fosters professionalism and accountability among members through continuing education and training; promotes design excellence by influencing change in the industry. **Affiliated With:** American Institute of Architects.

627 ■ American Legion, Advertising Mens Post 38
PO Box 38
Chicago, IL 60690
Ph: (708)832-4867
Fax: (309)663-5783
URL: National Affiliate–www.legion.org
Local. Affiliated With: American Legion.

628 ■ American Legion, All American Post 1776
5758 N Mulligan Ave.
Chicago, IL 60646
Ph: (312)631-0659
Fax: (309)663-5783
URL: National Affiliate–www.legion.org
Local. Affiliated With: American Legion.

629 ■ American Legion, Archer-Highland Post 698
4871 S Archer Ave.
Chicago, IL 60632
Ph: (312)586-6490
Fax: (309)663-5783
URL: National Affiliate–www.legion.org
Local. Affiliated With: American Legion.

630 ■ American Legion, Board of Trade Post 304
141 W Jackson Blvd., Rm. 1550
Chicago, IL 60604
Ph: (708)398-4863
Fax: (309)663-5783
URL: National Affiliate–www.legion.org
Local. Affiliated With: American Legion.

631 ■ American Legion, Budlong District Post 837
2831 W Lawrence Ave.
Chicago, IL 60625
Ph: (309)663-0361
Fax: (309)663-5783
URL: National Affiliate–www.legion.org
Local. Affiliated With: American Legion.

632 ■ American Legion, C.D. Burton Post 808
5409 S Narragansett Ave.
Chicago, IL 60638
Ph: (309)663-0361
Fax: (309)663-5783
URL: National Affiliate–www.legion.org
Local. Affiliated With: American Legion.

633 ■ American Legion, Central Park Post 1028
4349 S Kedvale Ave.
Chicago, IL 60632
Ph: (708)241-0543
Fax: (309)663-5783
URL: National Affiliate–www.legion.org
Local. Affiliated With: American Legion.

634 ■ American Legion, Chesterfield Post 695
10437 S Ave. F
Chicago, IL 60617
Ph: (309)663-0361
Fax: (309)663-5783
URL: National Affiliate–www.legion.org
Local. Affiliated With: American Legion.

635 ■ American Legion, Chicago Firemen's Post 667
3337 W 109th St.
Chicago, IL 60655
Ph: (312)625-3814
Fax: (309)663-5783
URL: National Affiliate–www.legion.org
Local. Affiliated With: American Legion.

636 ■ American Legion, Chicago Nisei Post 1183
4427 N Clark St.
Chicago, IL 60640
Ph: (312)267-3207
Fax: (309)663-5783
URL: National Affiliate–www.legion.org
Local. Affiliated With: American Legion.

637 ■ American Legion, Chicago Post 170
116 W Kinzie St.
Chicago, IL 60610
Ph: (708)668-1345
Fax: (309)663-5783
URL: National Affiliate–www.legion.org
Local. Affiliated With: American Legion.

638 ■ American Legion, Chinatown Post 1003
267 W Alexander St.
Chicago, IL 60616
Ph: (312)842-0279
Fax: (309)663-5783
URL: National Affiliate–www.legion.org
Local. Affiliated With: American Legion.

639 ■ American Legion, Clearing Post 600
4352 W 63rd St.
Chicago, IL 60629
Ph: (312)767-0230
Fax: (309)663-5783
URL: National Affiliate–www.legion.org
Local. Affiliated With: American Legion.

640 ■ American Legion, Commonwealth Edison Post 118
PO Box 1941
Chicago, IL 60690
Ph: (309)663-0361
Fax: (309)663-5783
URL: National Affiliate–www.legion.org
Local. Affiliated With: American Legion.

641 ■ American Legion, Crispus Attucks Post 1268
3918 W Roosevelt Rd.
Chicago, IL 60624
Ph: (309)663-0361
Fax: (309)663-5783
URL: National Affiliate–www.legion.org
Local. Affiliated With: American Legion.

642 ■ American Legion, Darius-Girenas Post 271
1956 W 35th St.
Chicago, IL 60609
Ph: (309)663-0361
Fax: (309)663-5783
URL: National Affiliate–www.legion.org
Local. Affiliated With: American Legion.

643 ■ American Legion, Dorman-Dunn Post 547
2129 W Cermak Rd.
Chicago, IL 60608
Ph: (312)927-0923
Fax: (309)663-5783
URL: National Affiliate–www.legion.org
Local. Affiliated With: American Legion.

644 ■ American Legion, Draza Mihailovich Post 1946
3737 E 114th St.
Chicago, IL 60617
Ph: (309)663-0361
Fax: (309)663-5783
URL: National Affiliate–www.legion.org
Local. Affiliated With: American Legion.

645 ■ American Legion, Edison Park Post 541
6755 N Northwest Hwy.
Chicago, IL 60631
Ph: (309)663-0361
Fax: (309)663-5783
URL: National Affiliate–www.legion.org
Local. Affiliated With: American Legion.

646 ■ American Legion, Electric Post 769
600 W Washington Blvd.
Chicago, IL 60661
Ph: (309)663-0361
Fax: (309)663-5783
URL: National Affiliate–www.legion.org
Local. Affiliated With: American Legion.

647 ■ American Legion, Enrico Fermi Post 1266
3543 N Pontiac Ave.
Chicago, IL 60634
Ph: (773)625-7284
Fax: (309)663-5783
URL: National Affiliate–www.legion.org
Local. Affiliated With: American Legion.

648 ■ American Legion, Filipino Post 509
3930 N Clark St., Apt. 1630
Chicago, IL 60640
Ph: (309)663-0361
Fax: (309)663-5783
URL: National Affiliate–www.legion.org
Local. Affiliated With: American Legion.

649 ■ American Legion, Franklin D. Roosevelt Post 923
1824 W Cortland St.
Chicago, IL 60622
Ph: (312)278-0093
Fax: (309)663-5783
URL: National Affiliate–www.legion.org
Local. Affiliated With: American Legion.

650 ■ American Legion, Fred Zeplin Post 1005
c/o Matthew J. Kovats
8529 S Keating
Chicago, IL 60652
Ph: (309)663-0361
Fax: (309)663-5783
URL: National Affiliate–www.legion.org
Contact: Matthew J. Kovats, Contact
Local. Affiliated With: American Legion.

651 ■ American Legion, Gage Park Post 959
3208 W Marquette Rd.
Chicago, IL 60632
Ph: (312)436-7945
Fax: (309)663-5783
URL: National Affiliate–www.legion.org
Local. Affiliated With: American Legion.

652 ■ American Legion, Gen. Ike Eisenhower Post 98
3640 W 59th St.
Chicago, IL 60629
Ph: (309)663-0361
Fax: (309)663-5783
URL: National Affiliate–www.legion.org
Local. Affiliated With: American Legion.

653 ■ American Legion, Gladstone Post 777
PO Box 31278
Chicago, IL 60631
Ph: (309)663-0361
Fax: (309)663-5783
URL: National Affiliate–www.legion.org
Local. Affiliated With: American Legion.

654 ■ American Legion, Glendale Post 805
5932 S Sawyer
Chicago, IL 60629
Ph: (312)776-3373
Fax: (309)663-5783
URL: National Affiliate–www.legion.org
Local. Affiliated With: American Legion.

655 ■ American Legion, Hanson Park Post 1177
2258 N Mango Ave.
Chicago, IL 60639
Ph: (309)663-0361
Fax: (309)663-5783
URL: National Affiliate–www.legion.org
Local. Affiliated With: American Legion.

656 ■ American Legion, Harold Washington Post 1987
3840 Gaslight Sq., Apt. 206
Chicago, IL 60649
Ph: (312)436-3552
Fax: (309)663-5783
URL: National Affiliate–www.legion.org
Local. Affiliated With: American Legion.

657 ■ American Legion, Illiana Post 220
10506 S Ewing Ave.
Chicago, IL 60617
Ph: (312)933-9610
Fax: (309)663-5783
URL: National Affiliate–www.legion.org
Local. Affiliated With: American Legion.

658 ■ American Legion, Illinois Dept. of Employment Sec Post 815
33 S State St.
Chicago, IL 60603
Ph: (309)663-0361
Fax: (309)663-5783
URL: National Affiliate–www.legion.org
Local. Affiliated With: American Legion.

659 ■ American Legion, Illinois Post 47
c/o Harold A. Taylor
PO Box 578159
Chicago, IL 60657
Ph: (312)549-8185
Fax: (309)663-5783
URL: National Affiliate–www.legion.org
Contact: Harold A. Taylor, Contact
Local. Affiliated With: American Legion.

660 ■ American Legion, Illinois Post 87
c/o George L. Giles
5745 S State St.
Chicago, IL 60621
Ph: (312)487-5763
Fax: (309)663-5783
URL: National Affiliate–www.legion.org
Contact: George L. Giles, Contact
Local. Affiliated With: American Legion.

661 ■ American Legion, Illinois Post 272
c/o Fred Schweitzer
13304 S Baltimore Ave.
Chicago, IL 60633
Ph: (312)646-3272
Fax: (309)663-5783
URL: National Affiliate–www.legion.org
Contact: Fred Schweitzer, Contact
Local. Affiliated With: American Legion.

662 ■ American Legion, Illinois Post 363
c/o Gen. John Swift
5545 S Meade Ave.
Chicago, IL 60638
Ph: (312)585-6850
Fax: (309)663-5783
URL: National Affiliate–www.legion.org
Contact: Gen. John Swift, Contact
Local. Affiliated With: American Legion.

663 ■ American Legion, Illinois Post 419
c/o James J. Zientek
3647 W 51st St.
Chicago, IL 60632
Ph: (309)663-0361
Fax: (309)663-5783
URL: National Affiliate–www.legion.org
Contact: James J. Zientek, Contact
Local. Affiliated With: American Legion.

664 ■ American Legion, Illinois Post 437
3028 W Birchwood Ave.
Chicago, IL 60645
Ph: (309)663-0361
Fax: (309)663-5783
URL: National Affiliate–www.legion.org
Contact: G. Brown, Contact
Local. Affiliated With: American Legion.

665 ■ American Legion, Illinois Post 716
6940 W Belmont Ave.
Chicago, IL 60634
Ph: (708)453-4472
Fax: (309)663-5783
URL: National Affiliate–www.legion.org
Contact: Gen. George Bell Jr., Contact
Local. Affiliated With: American Legion.

666 ■ American Legion, Illinois Post 746
c/o Stanley F. Sullivan
PO Box 388576
Chicago, IL 60638

Ph: (309)663-0361
Fax: (309)663-5783
URL: National Affiliate–www.legion.org
Contact: Stanley F. Sullivan, Contact
Local. Affiliated With: American Legion.

667 ■ American Legion, Illinois Post 802
c/o Joseph L. Mc Farland
6351 W Peterson Ave.
Chicago, IL 60646
Ph: (309)663-0361
Fax: (309)663-5783
URL: National Affiliate–www.legion.org
Contact: Joseph L. Mc Farland, Contact
Local. Affiliated With: American Legion.

668 ■ American Legion, Illinois Post 806
c/o Billy Caldwell
5116 W Irving Park Rd.
Chicago, IL 60641
Ph: (312)545-2187
Fax: (309)663-5783
URL: National Affiliate–www.legion.org
Contact: Billy Caldwell, Contact
Local. Affiliated With: American Legion.

669 ■ American Legion, Illinois Post 829
c/o Col. John R. Marshall
PO Box 17644
Chicago, IL 60680
Ph: (309)663-0361
Fax: (309)663-5783
URL: National Affiliate–www.legion.org
Contact: Col. John R. Marshall, Contact
Local. Affiliated With: American Legion.

670 ■ American Legion, Illinois Post 915
c/o Dorie Miller
PO Box 20245
Chicago, IL 60620
Ph: (773)667-0210
Fax: (309)663-5783
URL: National Affiliate–www.legion.org
Contact: Dorie Miller, Contact
Local. Affiliated With: American Legion.

671 ■ American Legion, Illinois Post 958
c/o Frank J. Triner
6245 W Cuyler Ave.
Chicago, IL 60634
Ph: (309)663-0361
Fax: (309)663-5783
URL: National Affiliate–www.legion.org
Contact: Frank J. Triner, Contact
Local. Affiliated With: American Legion.

672 ■ American Legion, Illinois Post 984
7132 W Summerdale Ave.
Chicago, IL 60656
Ph: (312)774-7921
Fax: (309)663-5783
URL: National Affiliate–www.legion.org
Contact: Paul Parise, Contact
Local. Affiliated With: American Legion.

673 ■ American Legion, Illinois Post 1017
2658 S Hamlin Ave.
Chicago, IL 60623
Ph: (309)663-0361
Fax: (309)663-5783
URL: National Affiliate–www.legion.org
Contact: Manuel Perez Jr., Contact
Local. Affiliated With: American Legion.

674 ■ American Legion, Illinois Post 1119
c/o Sgt. Roy G. Eriksson
1326 S Ridge
Chicago, IL 60646
Ph: (312)631-0437
Fax: (309)663-5783
URL: National Affiliate–www.legion.org
Contact: Sgt. Roy G. Eriksson, Contact
Local. Affiliated With: American Legion.

675 ■ American Legion, Illinois Post 1990
c/o Col. James M. Cushing
915 W Wilson Ave., Apt. 227
Chicago, IL 60640
Ph: (309)663-0361
Fax: (309)663-5783
URL: National Affiliate–www.legion.org
Contact: Col. James M. Cushing, Contact
Local. Affiliated With: American Legion.

676 ■ American Legion, John Ericsson Post 1042
6400 W Belle Plaine No. 508
Chicago, IL 60634
Ph: (309)663-0361
Fax: (309)663-5783
URL: National Affiliate–www.legion.org
Local. Affiliated With: American Legion.

677 ■ American Legion, Kosciuszko Post 712
c/o Jim Grabowski
5040 W Patterson Ave.
Chicago, IL 60641
Ph: (312)286-9724
Fax: (309)663-5783
URL: National Affiliate–www.legion.org
Contact: Jim Grabowski, Contact
Local. Affiliated With: American Legion.

678 ■ American Legion, Kurdel-Cigoi Post 1110
c/o Anthony J. Letrich
2849 N Springfield Ave.
Chicago, IL 60618
Ph: (312)489-2197
Fax: (309)663-5783
URL: National Affiliate–www.legion.org
Contact: Anthony J. Letrich, Contact
Local. Affiliated With: American Legion.

679 ■ American Legion, La Fayette Post 159
5420 N Ludlam Ave.
Chicago, IL 60647
Ph: (309)663-0361
Fax: (309)663-5783
URL: National Affiliate–www.legion.org
Local. Affiliated With: American Legion.

680 ■ American Legion, Lincoln Square Post 473
4449 N Springfield Ave.
Chicago, IL 60625
Ph: (309)663-0361
Fax: (309)663-5783
URL: National Affiliate–www.legion.org
Local. Affiliated With: American Legion.

681 ■ American Legion, Logan Square Post 405
625 W Madison St., Apt. 513, Tower 4
Chicago, IL 60661
Ph: (309)663-0361
Fax: (309)663-5783
URL: National Affiliate–www.legion.org
Local. Affiliated With: American Legion.

682 ■ American Legion, Lulich-Ogrizovich Post 1001
9845 S Muskegon Ave.
Chicago, IL 60617
Ph: (309)663-0361
Fax: (309)663-5783
URL: National Affiliate–www.legion.org
Local. Affiliated With: American Legion.

683 ■ American Legion, Marine Post 273
3265 W Palmer St.
Chicago, IL 60647
Ph: (708)447-8507
Fax: (309)663-5783
URL: National Affiliate–www.legion.org
Local. Affiliated With: American Legion.

684 ■ American Legion, Marvin Seemann Garfield Ridge Post 1112
5123 S Meade Ave.
Chicago, IL 60638
Ph: (312)735-4780
Fax: (309)663-5783
URL: National Affiliate–www.legion.org
Local. Affiliated With: American Legion.

685 ■ American Legion, Milton Olive Post 1932
5090 W Harrison
Chicago, IL 60644
Ph: (309)663-0361
Fax: (309)663-5783
URL: National Affiliate–www.legion.org
Local. Affiliated With: American Legion.

686 ■ American Legion, Neer-Goudie-Teamsters Post 846
6643 N Northwest Hwy.
Chicago, IL 60631
Ph: (312)733-2724
Fax: (309)663-5783
URL: National Affiliate–www.legion.org
Local. Affiliated With: American Legion.

687 ■ American Legion, North Loop Post 949
c/o Donald J. Gesicki
6233 N Caldwell Ave.
Chicago, IL 60646
Ph: (309)663-0361
Fax: (309)663-5783
URL: National Affiliate–www.legion.org
Contact: Donald J. Gesicki, Contact
Local. Affiliated With: American Legion.

688 ■ American Legion, North Shore Post 21
c/o Commander Joseph Klasen
5653 W Byron St.
Chicago, IL 60634
Ph: (312)685-1498
Fax: (309)663-5783
URL: National Affiliate–www.legion.org
Contact: Commander Joseph Klasen, Contact
Local. Affiliated With: American Legion.

689 ■ American Legion, Norwood Post 740
6027 Northwest Hwy.
Chicago, IL 60631
Ph: (309)663-0361
Fax: (309)663-5783
URL: National Affiliate–www.legion.org
Local. Affiliated With: American Legion.

690 ■ American Legion, O-Donnell-Eddy-Floss Post 714
6136 S Pulaski Rd.
Chicago, IL 60629
Ph: (312)436-4980
Fax: (309)663-5783
URL: National Affiliate–www.legion.org
Local. Affiliated With: American Legion.

691 ■ American Legion, Old Town Chicago Post 184
1448 N Wells St.
Chicago, IL 60610
Ph: (309)663-0361
Fax: (309)663-5783
URL: National Affiliate–www.legion.org
Local. Affiliated With: American Legion.

692 ■ American Legion, Paul Revere Post 623
2509 W Superior St.
Chicago, IL 60612
Ph: (312)278-5067
Fax: (309)663-5783
URL: National Affiliate–www.legion.org
Local. Affiliated With: American Legion.

693 ■ American Legion, Peoples Gas Post 336
130 E Randolph, 19th Fl.
Chicago, IL 60601
Ph: (312)431-4974
Fax: (309)663-5783
URL: National Affiliate–www.legion.org
Local. Affiliated With: American Legion.

694 ■ American Legion, Philippine-American-Veterans Post 1995
1250 W Eddy St., Apt. 3
Chicago, IL 60657
Ph: (309)663-0361
Fax: (309)663-5783
URL: National Affiliate–www.legion.org
Local. Affiliated With: American Legion.

695 ■ American Legion, Pilsen Post 825
PO Box 389141
Chicago, IL 60638
Ph: (309)663-0361
Fax: (309)663-5783
URL: National Affiliate–www.legion.org
Local. Affiliated With: American Legion.

696 ■ American Legion, Portage Park Post 183
4226 N Moody Ave.
Chicago, IL 60634
Ph: (312)663-5510
Fax: (309)663-5783
URL: National Affiliate–www.legion.org
Local. Affiliated With: American Legion.

697 ■ American Legion, Railroad Retirement Board Post 856
844 N Rush St.
Chicago, IL 60611
Ph: (312)751-3396
Fax: (309)663-5783
URL: National Affiliate–www.legion.org
Local. Affiliated With: American Legion.

698 ■ American Legion, Rogers Park Post 108
PO Box 269219
Chicago, IL 60626
Ph: (773)943-9640
Fax: (309)663-5783
URL: National Affiliate–www.legion.org
Local. Affiliated With: American Legion.

699 ■ American Legion, Rome Post 1
c/o Joseph A. Stacy
2509 W Superior St.
Chicago, IL 60612
Ph: (309)663-0361
Fax: (309)663-5783
URL: National Affiliate–www.legion.org
Contact: Joseph A. Stacy, Contact
Local. Affiliated With: American Legion.

700 ■ American Legion, Roy P. Benavidez Memorial Post 226
4514 S Richmond St.
Chicago, IL 60632
Ph: (309)663-0361
Fax: (309)663-5783
URL: National Affiliate–www.legion.org
Local. Affiliated With: American Legion.

701 ■ American Legion, Scudiero Post 1978
c/o F. Orrico, Jr.
1055 S Mayfield Ave.
Chicago, IL 60644
Ph: (309)663-0361
Fax: (309)663-5783
URL: National Affiliate–www.legion.org
Contact: F. Orrico Jr., Contact
Local. Affiliated With: American Legion.

702 ■ American Legion, South Chicago Post 493
11133 S Ave. C
Chicago, IL 60617
Ph: (312)221-9854
Fax: (309)663-5783
URL: National Affiliate–www.legion.org
Local. Affiliated With: American Legion.

703 ■ American Legion, South Deering Post 1238
9721 S Ave. H
Chicago, IL 60617
Ph: (309)663-0361
Fax: (309)663-5783
URL: National Affiliate–www.legion.org
Local. Affiliated With: American Legion.

704 ■ American Legion, South Shore Post 388
13501 Ave. N
Chicago, IL 60633
Ph: (312)646-2665
Fax: (309)663-5783
URL: National Affiliate–www.legion.org
Local. Affiliated With: American Legion.

705 ■ American Legion, Tattler Post 973
4355 N Western Ave.
Chicago, IL 60618
Ph: (312)588-5809
Fax: (309)663-5783
URL: National Affiliate–www.legion.org
Local. Affiliated With: American Legion.

706 ■ American Legion, Theodore Roosevelt Post 627
c/o Carlton M. Mc Carl, Sr.
7555 S Clyde Ave.
Chicago, IL 60649
Ph: (312)955-4349
Fax: (309)663-5783
URL: National Affiliate–www.legion.org
Contact: Carlton M. Mc Carl Sr., Contact
Local. Affiliated With: American Legion.

707 ■ American Legion, Union League Post 758
65 W Jackson Blvd.
Chicago, IL 60604
Ph: (309)663-0361
Fax: (309)663-5783
URL: National Affiliate–www.legion.org
Local. Affiliated With: American Legion.

708 ■ American Legion, Van Buren Post 401
PO Box 5276
Chicago, IL 60680
Ph: (708)257-8689
Fax: (309)663-5783
URL: National Affiliate–www.legion.org
Local. Affiliated With: American Legion.

709 ■ American Legion, Victory Post 7
3504 N Bell Ave.
Chicago, IL 60618
Ph: (309)663-0361
Fax: (309)663-5783
URL: National Affiliate–www.legion.org
Local. Affiliated With: American Legion.

710 ■ American Legion, Wave Post 988
4424 N Sacramento Ave.
Chicago, IL 60625
Ph: (773)539-0949
Fax: (309)663-5783
URL: National Affiliate–www.legion.org
Local. Affiliated With: American Legion.

711 ■ American Legion, Wayne-Wright Post 1052
1258 W Wrightwood Ave.
Chicago, IL 60614
Ph: (312)935-3486
Fax: (309)663-5783
URL: National Affiliate–www.legion.org
Local. Affiliated With: American Legion.

712 ■ American Legion, William Mc Kinley Post 231
1954 W 35th St.
Chicago, IL 60609
Ph: (312)254-4522
Fax: (309)663-5783
URL: National Affiliate–www.legion.org
Local. Affiliated With: American Legion.

713 ■ American Liver Foundation - Illinois Chapter
c/o Volunteer Coor.
180 N Michigan Ave., Ste.1870
Chicago, IL 60601
Ph: (312)377-9030
Fax: (312)377-9035
E-mail: info@illinois-liver.org
URL: http://www.illinois-liver.org
Contact: Ms. Jacqueline A. Dominguez, Exec.Dir.
Founded: 1994. **Membership Dues:** $25 (annual). **State. Libraries: Type:** reference. **Subjects:** liver wellness, diseases, transplantation. **Boards:** Junior. **Committees:** Medical Advisory.

714 ■ American Lung Association of Metropolitan Chicago (ALAMC)
1440 W Washington Blvd.
Chicago, IL 60607
Ph: (312)243-2000
Fax: (312)243-3954
E-mail: jafrick@alamc.org
URL: http://www.lungchicago.org
Contact: Joel Africk, CEO
Local. Aims to prevent lung disease and promote lung health through research, advocacy and education. **Affiliated With:** American Lung Association.

715 ■ American Morgan Horse Association, Region 5
c/o Mark Staehnke, Dir.
1 E Wacker Dr., Ste.2800
Chicago, IL 60607
Ph: (312)832-7253
Fax: (208)275-0434
E-mail: mark@morganhorse.com
URL: National Affiliate–www.morganhorse.com
Contact: Mark Staehnke, Dir.
Regional. Affiliated With: American Morgan Horse Association.

716 ■ American ORT Chicago Chapter
203 N Wabash Ave., Ste.1020
Chicago, IL 60601
Fax: (312)853-3255
Free: (800)364-9678
E-mail: chicago@aort.org
URL: http://www.aort.org
Contact: Roni R. Wallace, Midwest Dir.
Local. Provides technical education and training to over 300,000 people in the U.S. and 60 countries worldwide. Teaches the skills of more than 100 trades and professions. **Affiliated With:** American ORT.

717 ■ American Payroll Association, Chicago Chapter
PO Box 836
Chicago, IL 60690
Ph: (312)474-3221
Fax: (312)474-3032
E-mail: chicago_chapter_apa@hotmail.com
URL: http://www.chicagopayroll.com
Contact: Chris O'Hara CPP, Pres.
Local. Aims to increase the Payroll Professional's skill level through education and mutual support. Represents the Payroll Professional before legislative

bodies. Administers the certified payroll professional program of recognition. Provides public service education on payroll and employment issues. **Affiliated With:** American Payroll Association.

718 ■ American Planning Association Chicago Chapter
122 S Michigan Ave., Ste.1600
Chicago, IL 60603-6107
Ph: (312)431-9100
Fax: (312)431-9985
URL: National Affiliate–www.planning.org
Contact: Myra Stennis, Office Mgr.
Local. Affiliated With: American Planning Association.

719 ■ American Red Cross of Greater Chicago
Rauner Ctr.
2200 W Harrison St.
Chicago, IL 60612
Ph: (312)729-6100
E-mail: chiweb@usa.redcross.org
URL: http://www.chicagoredcross.org
Contact: Francesca M. Maher, CEO
Founded: 1917. **Staff:** 2. **Budget:** $80,000. **State.** Instructors and volunteers who provide health and safety training, disaster relief, and aid to military members and their families. The America Red Cross of Greater Chicago serves the seven county Chicago land area. The McHenry Service Center serves specifically McHenry County for the ARC of Greater Chicago. **Affiliated With:** American Red Cross National Headquarters. **Formerly:** American Red Cross, McHenry County Chapter. **Publications:** Annual Report. Alternate Formats: online • Newsletters. Alternate Formats: online. **Conventions/Meetings:** annual dinner.

720 ■ American Schools Association
c/o Carl M. Dye
PO Box 577820
Chicago, IL 60657-7820
Ph: (773)782-0046
Fax: (773)782-0113
Free: (800)230-2263
E-mail: asaceu@hotmail.com
URL: http://asaceu.com
Founded: 1914. **Regional.**

721 ■ American Society of Business Publication Editors - Chicago Chapter
c/o Ira Pilchen, Treas.
Student Lawyer Amer. Bar Assn.
321 N Clark St.
Chicago, IL 60610
Ph: (312)988-6048
Fax: (312)988-6081
E-mail: pilcheni@staff.abanet.org
URL: National Affiliate–www.asbpe.org
Contact: Tina Grady Barbaccia, Pres.
Local. Promotes the public and professional understanding of business publication. Serves to enhance editorial standards and quality and to raise the level of publication management skills of its members. **Affiliated With:** American Society of Business Publication Editors.

722 ■ American Society of Civil Engineers - Illinois Section
645 N Michigan Ave., Ste.540
Chicago, IL 60611
Ph: (312)649-4600
Fax: (312)649-5840
E-mail: admin@isasce.org
URL: http://www.isasce.org
Contact: Barb Pries, Contact
State. Seeks to advance the profession of engineering to enhance the welfare of humanity. **Affiliated With:** American Society of Civil Engineers.

723 ■ American Society of Directors of Volunteer Service (ASDVS)
c/o Audrey Harris, Exec.Dir.
1 N Franklin, 27th Fl.
Chicago, IL 60606
Ph: (312)422-3939
Fax: (312)422-4579
E-mail: asdvs@aha.org
URL: http://www.asdvs.org
Contact: Audrey Harris, Exec.Dir.
Local.

724 ■ American Society of Interior Designers - Illinois Chapter
1647 Merchandise Mart
Chicago, IL 60654
Ph: (312)467-5080
Fax: (312)467-0888
E-mail: asidil@sbcglobal.net
URL: http://www.asidillinois.com
Contact: Erin Halloran, Administrator
Local. Establishes a common identity for professionals and businesses in the field of interior design. Provides professional education. **Affiliated With:** American Society of Interior Designers.

725 ■ American Society of Media Photographers, Chicago/Midwest
PO Box 804246
Chicago, IL 60680-4104
Ph: (312)733-7798
Fax: (312)733-7109
E-mail: info@chimwasmp.org
URL: http://www.chimwasmp.org
Contact: Yorrick Rydzewski, Pres.
Regional. Affiliated With: American Society of Media Photographers.

726 ■ American Society for Technion-Israel Institute of Technology, West Central Region
111 W Washington, Ste.1220
Chicago, IL 60602
Ph: (312)553-2222
Fax: (312)553-2223
URL: National Affiliate–www.ats.org
Regional. Affiliated With: American Society for Technion-Israel Institute of Technology.

727 ■ American Society for Training and Development, Chicagoland Chapter
5443 N Broadway, Ste.101
Chicago, IL 60640
Ph: (773)561-0907
Fax: (773)561-1343
E-mail: ccastd@aol.com
URL: http://www.ccastd.org
Contact: Micki Lewis, Pres.
Founded: 1947. **Members:** 1,400. **Membership Dues:** individual, corporate, $85 (annual). **Local.** Represents individuals engaged in the training and development of business, industry, education, and government employees. **Affiliated With:** ASTD. **Publications:** *CCASTD Update*, monthly. Newsletter • *Resource Guide*, annual • *Training Today*, bimonthly. Magazine • Membership Directory, annual. **Conventions/Meetings:** monthly board meeting • quarterly Human Resource Development Institute Course - meeting • monthly Programs - meeting • annual University Summit - meeting.

728 ■ American Theatre Organ Society, Chicagoland Chapter
c/o Dennis Scott, Pres.
6448 S Fairfield Ave.
Chicago, IL 60629
Ph: (312)326-5679
E-mail: scotgraph@aol.com
URL: National Affiliate–www.atos.org
Contact: Dennis Scott, Pres.
Local. Aims to restore, preserve and promote the theatre pipe organ and its music. Encourages the youth to learn the instrument. Operates a committee that gathers history and old music from silent film days and information on theatre organists, theaters and organ installations of the silent film era. **Affiliated With:** American Theatre Organ Society.

729 ■ American Women in Radio and Television, Chicago
c/o Lisa Rosengard, Pres.
WCIU-TV
26 N Halstead
Chicago, IL 60661
Ph: (312)705-2668
E-mail: awrtchicago@hotmail.com
URL: http://www.awrtchicago.org
Contact: Lisa Rosengard, Pres.
Local. Affiliated With: American Women in Radio and Television.

730 ■ American Youth Soccer Organization, Region 418
4507 N Ravenswood, Ste.101
Chicago, IL 60640
Ph: (773)929-5425
URL: http://www.ayso418.org
Local. Affiliated With: American Youth Soccer Organization.

731 ■ Amnesty International of the U.S.A., Midwest Regional Office (AIUSAM)
53 W Jackson, Rm. 731
Chicago, IL 60604
Ph: (312)427-2060
Fax: (312)427-2589
Free: (866)A-REGION
E-mail: aiusamw@aiusa.org
URL: http://www.amnesty-usa.org
Contact: Nancy Bothne, Dir.
Founded: 1961. **Members:** 100,000. **Membership Dues:** $25 (annual). **Staff:** 4. **Regional Groups:** 55. **Local Groups:** 70. **Languages:** English, Spanish. **Regional.** Individuals in the midwestern U.S. interested in promoting human rights throughout the world. Participates in letter writing campaigns. **Affiliated With:** Amnesty International of the U.S.A. **Publications:** Newsletter, quarterly. **Price:** free. **Conventions/Meetings:** annual Regional Conference-Midwest - meeting (exhibits).

732 ■ Ancient Coin Club of Chicago
c/o Paul Johnson
PO Box 411933
Chicago, IL 60641
E-mail: gallienus@hotmail.com
URL: http://www.ancient-coin-club-chicago.com
Contact: Paul Johnson, Contact
Local. Affiliated With: American Numismatic Association.

733 ■ Anti-Cruelty Society (ACS)
c/o Darlene Duggan, Volunteer Mgr.
157 W Grand Ave.
Chicago, IL 60610
Ph: (312)644-8338
Fax: (312)644-3878
E-mail: info@anticruelty.org
URL: http://www.anticruelty.org
Contact: Darlene Duggan, Volunteer Mgr.
Founded: 1899. **Local.**

734 ■ Arcade Park Garden Club
c/o Susan James, Pres.
Hotel Florence
11111 S Forrestville Ave.
Chicago, IL 60628
Ph: (773)568-4669
URL: National Affiliate–www.members.aol.com/pullmanil
Contact: Susan James, Pres.
Local.

735 ■ Arthritis Foundation, Greater Chicago Chapter
29 E Madison, Ste.500
Chicago, IL 60602

Ph: (312)372-2080
Fax: (312)372-2081
Free: (800)735-0096
E-mail: info.gc@arthritis.org
URL: http://www.arthritis.org
Contact: Tom Fite, Chapter Pres.

Founded: 1948. **Membership Dues:** individual, $20 (annual). **Staff:** 15. **State Groups:** 2. **Local Groups:** 9. **Regional**. Seeks to: discover the cause and improve the methods for the treatment and prevention of arthritis and other rheumatic diseases; increase the number of scientists investigating rheumatic diseases; provide training in rheumatic diseases for more doctors; extend knowledge of arthritis and other rheumatic diseases to the lay public, emphasizing the socioeconomic as well as medical aspects of these diseases. **Affiliated With:** Arthritis Foundation. **Publications:** *Arthritis Today*, bimonthly. Magazine. **Price:** included in membership dues; $12.95 /year for nonmembers. **Advertising:** accepted. Alternate Formats: online. **Conventions/ Meetings:** annual meeting - early June.

736 ■ Asian American Bar Association of the Greater Chicago Area
PO Box A3782
Chicago, IL 60690
E-mail: aabachicago@yahoo.com
URL: http://www.aabachicago.com
Contact: Maria Kuriakos Ciesil, Pres.

Regional. Represents the interests of Asian Pacific American attorneys and their communities. Promotes justice, equity and opportunity for Asian Pacific Americans. Fosters professional development, legal scholarship, advocacy and community development. **Affiliated With:** National Asian Pacific American Bar Association.

737 ■ Asian American Journalists Association - Chicago Chapter
PO Box 577639
Chicago, IL 60657-9997
E-mail: chiaaja@yahoo.com
URL: http://chapters.aaja.org/Chicago/index.htm
Contact: Lorene Yue, Pres.

Local. Promotes fair and accurate news coverage of Asian American and Pacific Islanders. Encourages Asian American individuals to pursue a career in journalism. Seeks to increase the number of Asian American and Pacific Islander journalists and news managers in the industry. **Affiliated With:** Asian American Journalists Association.

738 ■ Associated Colleges of the Midwest (ACM)
205 W Wacker Dr., Ste.1300
Chicago, IL 60606
Ph: (312)263-5000
Fax: (312)263-5879
E-mail: acm@acm.edu
URL: http://www.acm.edu
Contact: Scott Lewis, Dir. of Publications

Founded: 1958. **Members:** 14. **Staff:** 12. Small, independent, and coeducational liberal arts colleges united to conduct activities that will enrich their programs and increase their operating efficiency. Primary area of cooperation is in off-campus programs that could not profitably be administrated by one college alone. Sponsors extensive activity in professional development for faculty members. Conducts admissions activities, data sharing, and operational research. **Awards:** Nick Adams Short Story Prize. **Frequency:** annual. **Type:** recognition. **Recipient:** for the best story by an ACM college student in good standing. **Publications:** *ACM Notes*, 3/year. Newsletter • *Pre-College Planner*, annual. Booklet. Offers tips for high school students preparing to seek college admission. • Brochures.

739 ■ Association of Black Psychologists, Mid-West Region
c/o Nkechi Townsend, PhD
8515 S Constance
Chicago, IL 60617
Ph: (202)722-0808
Fax: (425)699-6851
E-mail: midwest_rep@abpsi.org
URL: http://hometown.aol.com/nkechit2/myhomepage/profile.html

Regional. **Affiliated With:** Association of Black Psychologists.

740 ■ Association of Community Organizations for Reform Now, Chicago
650 S Clark St., Ste.200
Chicago, IL 60605
Ph: (312)939-7488
Fax: (312)939-6877
E-mail: ilacorn@acorn.org
URL: National Affiliate–www.acorn.org

Local. **Affiliated With:** Association of Community Organizations for Reform Now.

741 ■ Association for Computing Machinery, Chicago Military Academy-Bronzville
c/o Vaughn G. Silverman
3519 S Giles St.
Chicago, IL 60653
Ph: (773)534-9750
Fax: (773)534-9951
E-mail: nswilliam@cps.k12.il.us
URL: National Affiliate–www.acm.org
Contact: Nina William, Librarian

Local. Stimulates understanding of the use and potential of computers in Biosciences. **Affiliated With:** Association for Computing Machinery.

742 ■ Association for Computing Machinery, Columbia College/Chicago
c/o Wade Roberts
600 S Michigan Ave.
Chicago, IL 60605
Ph: (312)344-7750
Fax: (312)344-8084
E-mail: wroberts@colum.edu
Contact: Wate Roberts, Dir.

Local. Biological, medical, behavioral, and computer scientists; hospital administrators; programmers and others interested in application of computer methods to biological, behavioral, and medical problems. Stimulates understanding of the use and potential of computers in the Biosciences. **Affiliated With:** Association for Computing Machinery.

743 ■ Association for Computing Machinery, Illinois Institute of Technology
c/o Steve Beitzel, Chair
10 W 31st St.
Chicago, IL 60616
Ph: (312)567-3075
E-mail: acm@iit.edu
URL: http://www.iit.edu/~acm/

State. **Affiliated With:** Association for Computing Machinery.

744 ■ Association for Computing Machinery, University of Chicago
c/o Ivan Beschastnikh
5801 S Ellis Ave.
Chicago, IL 60637
Ph: (773)702-1234
E-mail: ivan@cs.uchicago.edu
URL: http://www.uchicago.edu
Contact: Ivan Beschastnikh, Contact

Local. Biological, medical, behavioral, and computer scientists; hospital administrators; programmers and others interested in application of computer methods to biological, behavioral, and medical problems. Stimulates understanding of the use and potential of computers in the Biosciences. **Affiliated With:** Association for Computing Machinery.

745 ■ Association for Computing Machinery, University of Illinois/Chicago (ACMUIC)
Rm. 300 CCC (M/C 118), Box 39
750 S Halsted
Chicago, IL 60607
Ph: (312)996-5947
E-mail: acm@acm.cs.uic.edu
URL: http://acm.eecs.uic.edu
Contact: Tom Palarz, Pres.

Founded: 1965. **Membership Dues:** individual, $5 (annual). **Local**. Aims to serve students in learning and research of anything related to computing. Conducts hardware demonstrations, programming contests and engineering week. **Affiliated With:** Association for Computing Machinery.

746 ■ Association of Consultants to Nonprofits (ACN)
c/o Ms. Christine Johnson, Pres.
PO Box 2449
Chicago, IL 60690-2449
Ph: (312)580-1875
E-mail: info@acnconsult.org
URL: http://www.acnconsult.org
Contact: Ms. Christine Johnson, Pres.

Founded: 1989. **Members:** 130. **Membership Dues:** individual consultant, $175 (annual) • consulting firm, $350 (annual). **Budget:** $35,000. **Regional Groups:** 1. **Local**. Develops, strengthens and promotes its members as providers of best practice consulting services to the nonprofit community. **Computer Services:** database, notes on previous professional development seminars, calendar of upcoming events • mailing lists, e-mail to committee chairs and others • online services, access to links and other resources. **Committees:** Board Development; Business Development; Marketing; Newsletter and Program. **Publications:** *Consultants Interactive*, quarterly. Newsletter. Includes notes from professional development seminars, member news, and upcoming events. **Price:** free for members. **Circulation:** 130. Alternate Formats: online • Directory. Alternate Formats: online.

747 ■ Association of Descendents of the Shoah - Illinois
c/o Larry Schwartz and Moshe Hubscher
3034 W Devon, Ste.106
Chicago, IL 60659-1400
Ph: (773)764-6701
E-mail: adsi@hub-data.com
URL: http://chicago2002.Descendants.org
Contact: I. Moshe Hubscher, VP

Founded: 1977. **Members:** 200. **Membership Dues:** regular, $25 (annual) • family, $50 (annual). **Budget:** $10,000. **Regional Groups:** 1. **State Groups:** 1. **Local Groups:** 1. **Languages:** English, Hebrew, Hungarian, Polish, Yiddish. **State**. Sponsors educational, cultural and social events, such as informal discussion groups, panel discussions, lectures, tours and an international conference. **Publications:** *A Brivele*, quarterly. Newsletter. Contains information about the Holocaust and Israel, and related articles, calendar, tidbits. **Price:** $25.00/year to members; $25.00/issue to libraries. **Circulation:** 1,000. **Advertising:** accepted. **Conventions/Meetings:** triennial Living the Legacy - conference, with workshops, panels, lectures, entertainment, history - 2008 June 29-July 1, Chicago, IL - Avg. Attendance: 1200.

748 ■ Association of Energy Engineers, Illinois/Chicago
c/o Michael Peterson, Pres.
DOE, MidWest Regional Off.
1 S Wacker Dr., Ste.2380
Chicago, IL 60606-4614
Ph: (312)886-8577
Fax: (312)886-8561
E-mail: michael.peterson@ee.doe.gov
URL: National Affiliate–www.aeecenter.org
Contact: Michael Peterson, Pres.

Local. **Affiliated With:** Association of Energy Engineers.

749 ■ Association Forum of Chicagoland
c/o Gary LaBranche, CAE, Pres./CEO
20 N Wacker Dr., Ste.3000
Chicago, IL 60606

Ph: (312)236-2288
Fax: (312)236-3771
E-mail: labranche@associationforum.org
URL: http://www.associationforum.org
Contact: Gary LaBranche CAE, Pres./CEO

Founded: 1916. **Members:** 3,000. **Membership Dues:** association CEO, $315 (annual). **Staff:** 16. **Budget:** $3,500,000. **Local**. Chief executive officers and other professionals who manage trade associations, professional societies and other not-for-profit organizations based in the greater Chicago, IL area. Provides essential learning, compelling experiences and powerful resources as it advances the professional practice of association management. Provides educational programs, networking, publications, shared interest groups, governmental relations, professional practice statements, research and online resources. Sponsors "Association Week" annually to celebrate and recognize Chicagoland's association community. **Libraries: Type:** open to the public. **Holdings:** 500; articles, books, clippings, monographs, papers, periodicals. **Subjects:** association and non-profit management. **Awards:** Samuel Shapiro Award for CEO Excellence. **Frequency:** annual. **Type:** recognition. **Recipient:** for distinguished achievement by an association chief executive officer. **Computer Services:** Online services, association job posting service; salary calculator; archived articles and sample documents; podcasts and other resources. **Committees:** Audit; Content; Diversity; Nominating; Professional Practices; Public Policy. **Working Groups:** Annual Meeting; CAE. **Also Known As:** (2005) Association Forum. **Formerly:** (1967) Association Executives Forum of Chicago; (1997) Chicago Society of Association Executives. **Publications:** *Forum*, monthly. Magazine. Features industry related articles and information. ISSN: 1056-0092. **Circulation:** 5,000. **Advertising:** accepted • *This Week - Association Forum*, weekly. Newsletter. **Price:** included in membership dues. **Circulation:** 4,000. **Advertising:** accepted. Alternate Formats: online. Also Cited As: *View Point* • Membership Directory, annual. **Conventions/Meetings:** annual Holiday Showcase - trade show (exhibits).

750 ■ Association of Government Accountants - Chicago Chapter
PO Box 1604
Chicago, IL 60690-1604
Ph: (312)886-4140
E-mail: daniel.eckert@oig.hhs.gov
URL: http://www.agachicago.org
Contact: Dan Eckert, Pres.

Local. Provides quality education, professional development and certification to government accountants. Supports standards and research to advance government accountability. Seeks to encourage the interchange of ideas among financial managers in government service and among government and nongovernmental managers. **Affiliated With:** Association of Government Accountants.

751 ■ Association of Independent Commercial Producers/Midwest
c/o Crossroads Films
10 W Hubbard St.
Chicago, IL 60610
Ph: (312)215-3653
Fax: (312)527-9637
E-mail: midwest@aicp.com
URL: National Affiliate–www.aicp.com
Contact: Mark Egmon, Contact

Regional. **Affiliated With:** Association of Independent Commercial Producers.

752 ■ Association of Professional Researchers for Advancement, Illinois Chapter (APRA-IL)
c/o Kimberly A. Montroy, Pres.
Museum of Sci. and Indus.
57th St., Lake Shore Dr.
Chicago, IL 60637-2093
Ph: (773)947-4167
Fax: (773)684-7141
E-mail: kim.montroy@msichicago.org
URL: http://www.altrue.net/site/apra/
Contact: Kimberly A. Montroy, Pres.

Founded: 1989. **Members:** 90. **Membership Dues:** regular, $30 (annual). **Local**. Seeks to advance the goals of the prospect research profession through professional development, continuing education, information sharing, and advocacy. **Affiliated With:** Association of Professional Researchers for Advancement. **Conventions/Meetings:** annual conference • annual retreat - every November.

753 ■ Association for Professionals in Infection Control and Epidemiology, Chicago
c/o Mary Beth Fry, CIC, Pres.-Elect
Univ. of Illinois Medical Ctr.
820 S Wood St., M/C 770
Chicago, IL 60612
Ph: (312)996-1395
Fax: (312)996-1438
E-mail: info@apicchicago.org
URL: http://www.apicchicago.org
Contact: Mary Beth Fry CIC, Pres.-Elect

Local. Works to influence, support and improve the quality of healthcare through the development of educational programs and standards. Promotes quality research and standardization of practices and procedures. **Affiliated With:** Association for Professionals in Infection Control and Epidemiology.

754 ■ Association for Psychological Type - Chicago
c/o Melody Camp
Melody Camp Gp.
10425 S Hamilton
Chicago, IL 60643
Ph: (773)445-1717
Fax: (773)881-9061
E-mail: melody@melodycamp.com
URL: National Affiliate–www.aptinternational.org
Contact: Melody Camp, Contact

Local. Promotes the practical application and ethical use of psychological type. Provides members with opportunities for continuous learning, sharing experiences and creating understanding and knowledge through research. **Affiliated With:** Association for Psychological Type.

755 ■ ATHENA International
70 E Lake St., Ste.1220
Chicago, IL 60601-5939
Ph: (312)580-0111
Fax: (312)580-0110
Free: (800)548-8247
E-mail: athena@athenainternational.org
URL: http://www.athenainternational.org
Contact: Dorothy Huisman, Exec.Dir.

Founded: 1982. **Local**. **Awards:** ATHENA Award. **Frequency:** annual. **Type:** recognition. **Recipient:** to an individual for outstanding service to their community and for actively assisting women in attainment of their professional goals and leadership skills. **Formerly:** (2005) ATHENA Foundation. **Publications:** *The ATHENAIAN*, 3/year. Newsletters. Provides ATHENA recipients and friends with an overview of current programs and events. **Circulation:** 7,000.

756 ■ Audio Engineering Society, Columbia College Section
c/o Mauricio Ardila
Dept. of Audio Arts & Scis.
33 E Cong. Pkwy., Ste.601K
Chicago, IL 60605
Ph: (312)344-8804
Fax: (312)344-8427
URL: National Affiliate–www.aes.org
Contact: Mauricio Ardila, Contact

Local. Represents the interests of engineers, administrators and technicians for radio, television and motion picture operation. Operates educational and research foundation. **Affiliated With:** Audio Engineering Society.

757 ■ Austin Childcare Providers Network
c/o Ruth Kimble
5831 W Augusta
Chicago, IL 60651-2511
Ph: (773)287-2528
Fax: (773)287-0247
E-mail: quinlan3@prodigy.net
URL: http://www.inkindex.com/members/RUTH%20Kimble/index.asp
Contact: Ruth Kimble, Contact

Local. Provides quality childcare through education and training.

758 ■ Back of the Yards Business Association
c/o Paul J. Lopez, Pres.
1751 W 47th St., 2nd Fl.
Chicago, IL 60609
Ph: (773)247-5100
Fax: (773)254-3525
Contact: Anna Cardoso, Exec.Dir.
Local.

759 ■ BACnet Manufacturers Association
980 N Michigan Ave., Ste.1400
Chicago, IL 60611
Ph: (312)540-1200
Fax: (312)540-9616
E-mail: fc@bacnetassociation.org
URL: http://www.bacnetassociation.org
Contact: Franklin Cooper, Exec.Dir.

Founded: 2000. **Members:** 50. **Membership Dues:** $5,000 (annual). **Staff:** 1. **Budget:** $175,000. **Local**. Works to encourage successful use of the data communications protocol "bacnet" in building automation and control systems, through interoperability testing, educational programs and promotional activities. **Publications:** *Forum*, semiannual. Newsletter. **Conventions/Meetings:** annual conference.

760 ■ Belmont-Central Chamber of Commerce
3250 N Central Ave., 2nd Fl.
Chicago, IL 60634
Ph: (773)202-9923
E-mail: belmontcentralcc@aol.com
URL: http://www.belmontcentral.org
Contact: Larry Lynch, Pres.

Staff: 1. **Local**. Maintains a strong and viable commercial district at Belmont-Central.

761 ■ Best Buddies Illinois
350 N Orleans St., Ste.678
Chicago, IL 60654
Ph: (312)828-9313
Fax: (312)828-9421
E-mail: maryjanemannella@bestbuddies.org
URL: http://bestbuddies.org
Contact: Mary Jane Mannella, State Dir.
State.

762 ■ Bethel New Life
c/o Mildred Wiley
4006 W Lake St.
Chicago, IL 60624
Ph: (773)826-5540
URL: National Affiliate–www.npa-us.org
Local. **Affiliated With:** National People's Action.

763 ■ Better Business Bureau of Chicago and Northern Illinois
330 N Wabash Ave., Ste.2006
Chicago, IL 60611
Ph: (312)832-0500
Fax: (312)832-9985
E-mail: info@chicago.bbb.org
URL: http://www.chicago.bbb.org
Contact: James E. Baumhart, Pres./CEO

Founded: 1926. **Members:** 2,750. **Membership Dues:** consumer, $15 (annual). **Local**. Seeks to promote and foster the highest ethical relationship between businesses and the public through voluntary self-regulation, consumer and business education, and service excellence. Provides information to help consumers and businesses make informed purchasing decisions and avoid costly scams and frauds; settles consumer complaints through arbitration and other means. **Affiliated With:** BBB Wise Giving Alliance. **Publications:** *BBB Alert*, bimonthly. Newsletter • *The Consumer Resource Guide*, semiannual. Newspaper. **Conventions/Meetings:** quarterly board meeting • annual dinner • annual Torch Award for Marketplace Ethics - luncheon.

764 ■ Between Friends
c/o Kathleen Doherty, Exec.Dir.
PO Box 608548
Chicago, IL 60660
Ph: (773)274-5232
Fax: (773)262-2543
Free: (800)603-4357
E-mail: mmowbray@betweenfriendschicago.org
URL: http://www.betweenfriendschicago.org
Contact: Kathleen Doherty, Exec.Dir.
Local. Provides comprehensive domestic violence counseling for women and children, 24-hour crisis line, court advocacy, hospital outreach and education, teen dating violence prevention program, and community prevention/education. **Formerly:** (2006) Friends of Battered Women and Their Children.

765 ■ Bickerdike Redevelopment Corp.
c/o Atanacio Gonzalez, Pres.
2551 W North Ave.
Chicago, IL 60647
Ph: (773)278-5669
Local.

766 ■ Big Brothers Big Sisters of Metropolitan Chicago (BBBSMC)
28 E Jackson Blvd., Ste.1800
Chicago, IL 60604-2215
Ph: (312)427-0637
Fax: (312)427-0760
E-mail: bbbschicag@aol.com
URL: http://www.bbbschgo.org
Contact: Clayton I. Brewer, Interim CEO
Local. Works to provide quality-mentoring relationships between children and qualified adults in Metropolitan Chicago, and promote their development into competent, confident and caring individuals. **Affiliated With:** Big Brothers Big Sisters of America. **Formerly:** (2005) Big Brothers Big Sisters of America of Metropolitan Chicago.

767 ■ Blocks Together
c/o Melissa Spatz, Co-Exec.Dir.
3914 W North Ave.
Chicago, IL 60647
Ph: (773)276-2194
Fax: (773)276-2296
E-mail: btogether@aol.com
URL: http://www.blockstogether.org
Local.

768 ■ Book Worm Angels
c/o Michael P. Ban, Exec.Dir.
3100 N Sheridan Rd., Apt. 4-B
Chicago, IL 60657-4955
Ph: (773)528-4786 (312)259-8087
Fax: (773)477-2207
E-mail: mpban1@ameritech.net
URL: http://www.bookwormangels.org
Contact: Michael P. Ban, Exec.Dir.
Founded: 1999. **Staff:** 6. **Budget:** $50,000. **Nonmembership**. **Local**. Aims to develop regular reading habits among children in schools, with primary focus on schools where 70% or more of students read below grade level. Establishes in-classroom free lending libraries of recreational reading books for children Pre-K through 8th grade. Holds book drives to provide books that are redistributed to qualifying schools. Provides Teacher's Manual with ideas about how to maximize student and parental involvement. Encourages parents/caregivers to read with their children nightly. **Awards:** Angel of the Year. **Frequency:** annual. **Type:** recognition. **Recipient:** to individuals and organizations who have unusually successful results with book drives.

769 ■ Boys and Girls Clubs of Chicago
c/o Andrea Hynes
550 W Van Buren St., Ste.350
Chicago, IL 60607
Ph: (312)235-8000 (312)235-8030
Fax: (312)427-4110
E-mail: ahynes@bgcc.org
URL: http://www.bgcc.org
Local.

770 ■ BPO Elks of the USA
2750 N Lakeview Ave.
Chicago, IL 60614-1889
Ph: (773)755-4700
Fax: (773)755-4790
E-mail: grandlodge@elks.org
URL: http://www.elks.org
Contact: Jack Jensen, Grand Sec.
Founded: 1961. **Members:** 399. **Membership Dues:** $76 (annual). **Local**. Fraternal organization. Conducts community services. **Affiliated With:** Benevolent and Protective Order of Elks. **Formerly:** (2005) Benevolent and Protective Order of Elks Lodge 2243. **Conventions/Meetings:** semimonthly meeting - always second and fourth Tuesdays of the month.

771 ■ Brain Injury Association of Illinois (BIA of IL)
PO Box 64420
Chicago, IL 60664-0420
Ph: (312)726-5699
Fax: (312)630-4011
Free: (800)699-6443
E-mail: info@biail.org
URL: http://www.biail.org
Contact: Philicia L. Deckard, Exec.Dir.
Members: 500. **Membership Dues:** basic, $35 (annual) • professional, $50 (annual) • corporate (includes 2 individual), $200 (annual). **Staff:** 2. **State**. People with brain injuries, family members, friends and professionals. Works to create a better future through brain injury awareness, prevention, education, and advocacy. **Libraries: Type:** open to the public. **Subjects:** brain injury. **Affiliated With:** Brain Injury Association of America. **Publications:** *Ordinary Miracles*, quarterly. Newsletter. **Price:** free to members. **Advertising:** accepted. **Conventions/Meetings:** annual conference (exhibits) - in October.

772 ■ Building and Construction Trades Department AFL-CIO, Chicago and Cook County
c/o Frank O'Lone, Sec.-Treas.
150 N Wacker Dr., Ste.1850
Chicago, IL 60606
Ph: (312)372-2049
Fax: (312)372-7342
E-mail: buildunion@chicagobuildingtrades.org
URL: http://www.buildingtrades.org
Contact: Frank O'Lone, Sec.-Treas.
Members: 62,000. **Local**. **Additional Websites:** http://www.chicagobuildingtrades.org. **Affiliated With:** Building and Construction Trades Department - AFL-CIO.

773 ■ Business Marketing Association, Chicago Chapter
1920 N Clark St., No. 10A
Chicago, IL 60614
Ph: (312)943-8040
Fax: (312)943-6829
E-mail: info@mbachicago.org
URL: http://bmachicago.org
Contact: Paul Lesher, Exec.Dir.
Founded: 1919. **Membership Dues:** individual, $250 (annual) • educator, $210 (annual) • student, $50 (annual) • corporate (per person), $250 (annual). **Local**. Promotes the development of business-to-business marketing and communications professionals through education, training and networking. **Awards:** Proud Award. **Frequency:** annual. **Type:** recognition. **Recipient:** for exceptional and continual service to the organization • Tower Awards. **Frequency:** annual. **Type:** recognition. **Recipient:** for excellence in business to business marketing communications. **Committees:** Auction/Biz Bash; Careerlink; CBC Certification and Training; Educational Programs; Hospitality; Programs; Public Relations; Tower Awards. **Affiliated With:** Business Marketing Association.

774 ■ Cambodian Association of Illinois (CAI)
2831 W Lawrence Ave.
Chicago, IL 60625
Ph: (773)878-7090
Fax: (773)878-5299
E-mail: cai@cambodian-association.org
URL: http://www.cambodian-association.org
Contact: Mr. Kompha Seth, Exec.Dir.
State. Social service organization and United Way member agency. Seeks to help refugees and immigrants from Cambodia who now reside in the state of IL to become self-sufficient, productive participants in U.S. society while preserving and enhancing their cultural heritage and sense of belonging to a community.

775 ■ Camp Fire USA Metropolitan Chicago Council
203 N Wabash Ave., No. 1518
Chicago, IL 60601
Ph: (312)263-6218
Fax: (312)263-6386
E-mail: jean@campfirechicago.org
URL: http://www.campfirechicago.org
Contact: Jean D. Lachowicz, Exec.Dir.
Local. Provides inclusive programs that meet the needs of children, teens and families. **Affiliated With:** Camp Fire USA.

776 ■ Carter Temple Community Development Corp.
c/o Paige McIntosh
7841 S Wabash Ave.
Chicago, IL 60619-2322
Ph: (773)846-2758 (773)874-0175
Fax: (773)874-8620
Local.

777 ■ Chi-Town Squares
5315 N Clark St.
PMB 167
Chicago, IL 60640-2113
E-mail: chi-townsquares@sbcglobal.net
URL: http://www.iagsdc.org/chi-townsquares
Contact: Phil Davis, Pres.
Local. **Affiliated With:** International Association of Gay Square Dance Clubs.

778 ■ Chicago 1st Black Inventors/Entrepreneurs Organization, NFP
10001 S Woodlawn Ave., Ste.1118-F
Chicago, IL 60628
Ph: (773)568-8058
E-mail: cfbieo@yahoo.com
URL: National Affiliate–www.uiausa.org
Contact: Calvin Flowers, Contact
Local. Represents inventors' organizations and providers of services to inventors. Seeks to facilitate the development of innovation conceived by independent inventors. Provides leadership and support services to inventors and inventors' organizations. **Affiliated With:** United Inventors Association of the U.S.A.

779 ■ Chicago Abused Women Coalition (CAWC)
c/o Olga Becker
PO Box 477916
Chicago, IL 60647-7916
Ph: (773)489-9081
Fax: (773)489-6111
E-mail: cawcadmin@mindspring.com
URL: http://www.cawc.org
Contact: Olga Becker, Contact
State. Provides shelter, counseling and support services to abused women and their children.

780 ■ Chicago Accreditation Partnership
c/o Jamilah R. Jordan
228 S Wabash St., Ste.1000
Chicago, IL 60604-2308
Ph: (312)554-1300
Fax: (312)554-1301
E-mail: jjordan@pcca-cap.org
URL: http://www.earlystars.com
Contact: Jamilah R. Jordan, Pres.
Founded: 1995. **Staff:** 11. **Local Groups:** 1. **Languages:** English, Spanish. **Local.**

781 ■ Chicago Ancient Hibernian Order - Division No. 32
PO Box 46276
Chicago, IL 60646
E-mail: kensullivan@aooh.org
URL: http://www.aooh.org
Contact: Ken Sullivan, Pres.
Local. Affiliated With: Ancient Order of Hibernians in America.

782 ■ Chicago/ARC
8 S Michigan Ave., Ste.1700
Chicago, IL 60603
Ph: (312)346-6230
Fax: (312)346-2218
E-mail: relations@chgoarc.org
Contact: Kristine Maclae, Exec.Dir
Local. Parents, professional workers, and others interested in individuals with mental retardation. Works to promote services, research, public understanding, and legislation for people with mental retardation and their families. **Affiliated With:** Arc of the United States.

783 ■ Chicago Area Gay and Lesbian Chamber of Commerce
1210 W Rosedale
Chicago, IL 60660
Ph: (773)303-0167
Fax: (773)303-0168
E-mail: info@glchamber.org
URL: http://www.glchamber.org
Contact: Christee L. Snell, Exec.Dir.
Founded: 1996. **Members:** 600. **Membership Dues:** base, $110 (annual). **Staff:** 2. **Local.** Seeks to help gay, lesbian, bisexual and transgender business community through networking, promotions, marketing and attracting tourism.

784 ■ Chicago Area Health Information Management Association (CAHIMA)
c/o Benjamin Oden, RHIT, Pres.-Elect
Amer. Hosp. Assn.
1 N Franklin St., 29th Fl.
Chicago, IL 60606
Ph: (312)422-3385
E-mail: boden@aha.org
URL: http://www.ilhima.org
Contact: Benjamin Oden RHIT, Pres.-Elect
Local. Represents the interests of individuals dedicated to the effective management of personal health information needed to deliver quality healthcare to the public. Provides career, professional development and practice resources. Sets standards for education and certification. Advocates public policy that advances Health Information Management (HIM) practice. **Affiliated With:** American Health Information Management Association.

785 ■ Chicago Area Translators and Interpreters Association (CHICATA)
c/o John F. Bukacek, Pres.
PO Box 804595
Chicago, IL 60680-4107
Ph: (312)836-0961
E-mail: info@chicata.org
URL: http://www.chicata.org
Contact: John F. Bukacek, Pres.
Local. Affiliated With: American Translators Association.

786 ■ Chicago Association for Computing Machinery Chapter
c/o John Garton, Chm.
PO Box 2381
Chicago, IL 60690
Ph: (773)327-9250
E-mail: jgarton@acm.org
URL: http://www.acm.org/chapters/chicago
Contact: John Garton, Chm.
Membership Dues: $20 (annual). **Local.** Computer professionals and others interested in learning more about the computer field. Objectives are the education of members and the general public on current and emerging topics in the field of computer science. Activities include monthly meetings open to members and the public featuring a social hour and guest speaker on a current topic. **Affiliated With:** Association for Computing Machinery. **Conventions/Meetings:** monthly meeting, with guest speaker and social hour.

787 ■ Chicago Association of Holy Name Societies (CAHNS)
c/o Louis G. Rexing, Pres.
5227 W 63rd Pl.
Chicago, IL 60638-5754
Ph: (773)582-4515 (312)733-1460
E-mail: president@chicagoholyname.org
URL: http://www.chicagoholyname.org
Contact: Louis G. Rexing, Pres.
Founded: 1997. **Members:** 50. **Membership Dues:** parish, $50 (annual). **Budget:** $2,000. **Local.** Catholic organization of men's social clubs. **Awards:** Ed Condon - Man of the Year. **Frequency:** annual. **Type:** recognition. **Publications:** Newsletter, quarterly. **Price:** included in membership dues. **Conventions/Meetings:** annual convention.

788 ■ Chicago Association of Law Libraries (CALL)
PO Box 60690
Chicago, IL 60690
Ph: (312)362-6895
E-mail: mlinnane@condor.depaul.edu
URL: http://www.aallnet.org/chapter/call
Contact: Mary Lu Linnane, VP
Local. Promotes the value of law libraries to the legal and public communities. Aims to advance the profession of law librarianship. Conducts professional development programs for members. **Affiliated With:** American Library Association.

789 ■ Chicago Association of Litigation Support Managers (CALSM)
c/o James B. Salla, VP, Jenner & Block, LLP
One IBM Plz.
Chicago, IL 60611
Ph: (312)558-7909
E-mail: jamessalla@bigfoot.com
URL: http://www.calsm.org
Contact: Barbara Hanahan, Pres.
Local.

790 ■ Chicago Association of Realtors
200 S Michigan Ave., Ste.400
Chicago, IL 60601
Ph: (312)803-4900
Fax: (312)803-4905
E-mail: alex@hsrhomes.com
URL: http://www.chicagorealtor.com
Contact: Alexander R. Chaparro, Pres.
Local. Strives to develop real estate business practices. Advocates the right to own, use and transfer real property. Provides a facility for professional development, research and exchange of information among members and to the general public. **Affiliated With:** National Association of Realtors.

791 ■ Chicago Asthma Consortium (CAC)
4541 N Ravenswood Ave., Ste.303
Chicago, IL 60640
Ph: (773)769-6060
Fax: (773)769-6505
URL: http://www.chicagoasthma.org
Contact: Sandy Cook PhD, Chair
Founded: 1996. **Members:** 300. **Membership Dues:** individual, $35 (annual) • professional, $100 (annual) • organization (with up to 20 employees), $200 (annual) • organization (with more than 20 employees), $300 (annual) • affiliate, sustaining, $500 (annual). **Staff:** 5. **Budget:** $450,000. **Local.** MDs, RNs, RRTs, other health care professionals and institutes, public policy officials, social services, educators, school staff, persons with asthma, caregivers, and interested individuals. Aims to reduce morbidity and mortality due to asthma and improve the quality of life for persons with asthma through education, advocacy, data collection, and analysis. Also looks to improve access to appropriate care, creating new, more appropriate systems of care. **Awards:** Mitch Trubitt Community Asthma Champion Award. **Frequency:** annual. **Type:** grant. **Recipient:** to community resident who has made a difference or improved the situation for persons with asthma in their community. **Committees:** Access to Care; Community; Data; Education; Schools. **Publications:** *Annual Data Workshop Report* • *CAC News*, quarterly • *Educational Pamphlets* (in English, Polish, and Spanish). **Conventions/Meetings:** quarterly meeting, with educational and networking opportunities for persons interested in asthma and related issues - January, April, July, and October.

792 ■ Chicago Astronomical Society (CAS)
PO Box 30287
Chicago, IL 60630-0287
Ph: (773)725-5618
URL: http://www.chicagoastro.org
Contact: Michael F. Barrett, Treas.
Founded: 1862. **Members:** 120. **Membership Dues:** regular, $55 (annual) • student, $47 (annual) • associate, $14 (annual). **Local.** Individuals interested in astronomy. Sponsors charitable and educational activities. Sponsor of "Astrofest", telescope fair attracting over 800 people nationally. **Affiliated With:** Astronomical League. **Absorbed:** (1955) Burnham Astronomical Society. **Publications:** *CAS Observer*, monthly. Newsletter. **Price:** $5.80. **Circulation:** 120. **Advertising:** accepted. **Conventions/Meetings:** annual Astrofest - convention, telescope maker's convention - always September • monthly meeting, two hour meeting usually featuring a speaker - usually the 3rd Friday.

793 ■ Chicago Audubon Society (CAS)
5801-C N Pulaski Rd.
Chicago, IL 60646-6057
Ph: (773)539-6793
Fax: (773)539-6830
E-mail: cas@chicagoaudubon.org
URL: http://www.chicagoaudubon.org
Contact: Joe Lill, Pres.
Founded: 1971. **Local.**

794 ■ Chicago Board Options Exchange (CBOE)
400 S LaSalle
Chicago, IL 60605
Ph: (312)786-5600
Fax: (312)786-7409
Free: (877)THE-CBOE
E-mail: help@cboe.com
URL: http://www.cboe.com
Contact: Ms. Janice Calvin, Contact
Founded: 1973. Individuals, institutions and firms engaged in the buying and selling of various products including stock options, cash-settled index options, options on HOLDRs, options on Exchange Traded Funds and Structured Products. **Publications:** Also publishes rule book (revised as needed), and product brochures.

795 ■ Chicago Board of Trade (CBOT)
141 W Jackson Blvd., Ste.1460
Chicago, IL 60604-2994
Ph: (312)435-3500 (312)435-3590
Fax: (312)341-3392
Free: (800)621-4670
E-mail: lmur10@cbot.com
URL: http://www.cbot.com
Contact: Bernard W. Dan, Pres./CEO
Founded: 1848. **Members:** 3,400. **Staff:** 800. Futures exchange - contracts based on agricultural

products, financial instruments, precious metals, and options on futures. Works for the development and economic justification of existing and new contracts. Sponsors seminars, conferences, and classes for industry and other user or user-oriented groups and the public. Maintains 4000 volume library on futures' trading and economics. Provides market information trading data services. **Departments:** Accounting; Communications; Exchange Floor Service; Human Resources; Information Systems; Investigations and Audits; Market and Product Development; Market Information; Registrar; Telecommunications. **Formerly:** (2004) Board of Trade of the City of Chicago. **Publications:** Catalog • Annual Report, annual • Brochure, semiannual.

796 ■ Chicago Cabaret Professionals (CCP)
c/o Roberta Miles, Treas.
2924 W North Shore Ave.
Chicago, IL 60645-4207
Ph: (312)409-3106
URL: http://www.chicagocabaret.org
Contact: Roberta Miles, Treas.
Local.

797 ■ Chicago Chapter of the American Recorder Society
c/o Esther M. Schechter, Treas.
6747 S Constance Ave.
Chicago, IL 60649
Ph: (773)667-0934
E-mail: alandes@worldnet.att.net
URL: http://www.geocities.com/ars2test
Contact: Esther M. Schechter, Treas.
Local. Promotes the recorder and its music by developing resources and standards to help people of all ages and ability levels to play and study the recorder. Encourages increased career opportunities for professional recorder performers and teachers. **Affiliated With:** American Recorder Society.

798 ■ Chicago Chapter of American Society of Plumbing Engineers
111 W Washington, Ste.2100
Chicago, IL 60602
Ph: (847)328-3555
E-mail: jsm@grummanbutkus.com
URL: http://www.aspe.org/Chicago
Contact: Jason McDonald CPD, Pres.
Local. Represents the interests of individuals dedicated to the advancement of the science of plumbing engineering. Seeks to resolve professional problems in plumbing engineering. Advocates greater cooperation among members and plumbing officials, contractors, laborers and the public. **Affiliated With:** American Society of Plumbing Engineers.

799 ■ Chicago Chapter of the Appraisal Institute (CCAI)
303 E Wacker Dr., Ste.200
Chicago, IL 60601
Ph: (312)616-9400
Fax: (312)616-9404
E-mail: laanderson@ccai.org
URL: http://www.ccai.org
Contact: L.A. Anderson, Exec. Officer
Founded: 1991. **Members:** 1,200. **Membership Dues:** affiliate, $190 (annual) • student affiliate, $50 (annual) • associate (plus applicable chapter dues), $310 (annual). **Local.** Appraises real property, commercial and residential. Offers courses to become a real estate appraiser, as well as continuing education seminars for its members. Seeks to be the global authority providing real estate solutions. **Libraries: Type:** reference. **Subjects:** appraisal. **Computer Services:** Online services, appraisers chat forums. **Telecommunication Services:** electronic mail, melissa@ccai.org. **Committees:** Appraisers Political Action Committee. **Affiliated With:** Appraisal Institute. **Publications:** *Appraisal Institute Directory of Members.* Provides the best source for finding qualified appraisers. **Price:** included in membership dues • *Appraisal Journal.* **Price:** included in membership dues • *MarketSource*, quarterly. Bulletin. Contains real estate market activity. **Price:** included in membership dues.

800 ■ Chicago Chapter Black Nurses Association (09)
PO Box 4612
Chicago, IL 60680-4612
Ph: (773)792-7222
URL: http://www.chicagochapternbna.org
Contact: Marion Summage, VP
Local. Represents registered nurses, licensed practical nurses, licensed vocational nurses, and student nurses. Builds consumer knowledge and understanding of health care issues. Facilitates the professional development and career advancement of nurses in emerging healthcare systems. Promotes economic development of nurses through entrepreneurial and other business initiatives. **Affiliated With:** National Black Nurses Association.

801 ■ Chicago Chapter of the National Association of Black Social Workers
PO Box 208140
Chicago, IL 60620-8140
Local.

802 ■ Chicago Chinatown Chamber of Commerce
c/o Jimmy D. Lee, Exec.Dir.
2169B S China Pl.
Chicago, IL 60616
Ph: (312)326-5320
Fax: (312)326-5668
E-mail: info@chicagochinatown.org
URL: http://www.chicagochinatown.org
Contact: Jimmy D. Lee, Exec.Dir.
Membership Dues: corporate (business with 100 or more employees), $650 (annual) • gold (business with 25-100 employees), $325 (annual) • small business/not for profit organization (business with 24 or less employees), $175 (annual). **Staff:** 5. **State.** Strives to improve and expand business opportunities and to educate others on the history, culture, and customs of the Chinese American community. **Formerly:** (2004) Chinatown Chamber of Commerce. **Publications:** *The Chamber News*, quarterly. Newsletter. **Price:** included in membership dues. **Advertising:** accepted. Alternate Formats: online • Directory, annual. **Price:** included in membership dues.

803 ■ Chicago Coin Club
PO Box 2301
Chicago, IL 60690
E-mail: carlwolfco@msn.com
URL: http://www.chicagocoinclub.org
Contact: Carl F. Wolf, Contact
Local. Affiliated With: American Numismatic Association.

804 ■ Chicago Compensation Association (CCA)
8 S Michigan Ave., No. 1000
Chicago, IL 60603
Ph: (312)541-2667
Fax: (312)580-0165
E-mail: cca@gss.net
URL: http://www.chicagocompensation.org
Contact: Rosa Perez, Dir.
Founded: 1976. **Members:** 350. **Membership Dues:** regular, $80 (annual) • student, $45 (annual). **Local. Affiliated With:** WorldatWork.

805 ■ Chicago Convention and Tourism Bureau
2301 S Lake Shore Dr.
Chicago, IL 60616-1490
Ph: (312)567-8500
Fax: (312)567-8533
URL: http://www.meetinchicago.com
Local.

806 ■ Chicago Democratic Socialists of America (CDSA)
1608 N Milwaukee, Rm. 403
Chicago, IL 60647
Ph: (773)384-0327 (773)384-4291
E-mail: chiildsa@chicagodsa.org
URL: http://www.chicagodsa.org
Contact: Tom Broderick, Co-Chm.
Founded: 1983. **Members:** 500. **Membership Dues:** regular, $45 (annual). **Budget:** $25,000. **Local Groups:** 3. **Local.** Promotes democratic socialism. **Awards:** Debs Thomas Harrington. **Frequency:** annual. **Type:** recognition. **Affiliated With:** Democratic Socialists of America. **Publications:** *New Ground*, bimonthly. Newsletter. **Price:** $10.00. **Circulation:** 1,000. **Advertising:** accepted.

807 ■ Chicago Dental Society (CDS)
401 N Michigan Ave., Ste.300
Chicago, IL 60611
Ph: (312)836-7300
Fax: (312)836-7337
URL: http://www.chicagodentalsociety.org
Contact: Randall B. Grove, Exec.Dir.
Founded: 1864. **Membership Dues:** dental student, $10 (annual) • postgraduate, resident, $35 (annual) • associate (dentists practicing outside Lake, DuPage, or Cook Counties, Illinois), $125 (annual). **Local.** Represents its members; promotes the science and art of dentistry; and aims to improve the dental health of the public.

808 ■ Chicago Elementary Teachers' Mathematics Club
c/o Karen Holly, Representative
3728 W 67th Pl.
Chicago, IL 60629-4132
E-mail: webmaster@ictm.org
URL: National Affiliate–www.nctm.org
Contact: Karen Holly, Representative
Local. Aims to improve the teaching and learning of mathematics. Provides vision, leadership and professional development to support teachers in ensuring mathematics learning of the highest quality for all students. **Affiliated With:** National Council of Teachers of Mathematics.

809 ■ Chicago Federation of Musicians
656 W Randolph St.
Chicago, IL 60661
Ph: (312)782-0063
Fax: (312)782-7880
E-mail: local10-208@afm.org
URL: http://www.livemusicchicago.com
Local. AFL-CIO. Musicians. Seeks to improve the wages and working conditions of professional musicians. **Affiliated With:** American Federation of Musicians of the United States and Canada. **Formerly:** (2005) Chicago Federation of Musicians - Local 10-208, American Federation of Musicians.

810 ■ Chicago Festival Association (CFA)
c/o Philip Purevich, Exec.Dir.
111 N State St., 11th Fl.
Chicago, IL 60602
Ph: (312)781-5681
Fax: (312)781-5407
E-mail: philip.purevich@chicagofestivals.org
URL: http://www.chicagofestivals.org
Local.

811 ■ Chicago Foundation for Women
One E Wacker Dr., Ste.1620
Chicago, IL 60601
Ph: (312)577-2801
Fax: (312)577-2802
E-mail: info@cfw.org
URL: http://www.cfw.org
Contact: Hannah Rosenthal, Exec.Dir.
Local. Aims to expand opportunities and resources, and advocates positive social change for women and girls.

812 ■ Chicago Herpetological Society (CHS)
2430 N Cannon Dr.
Chicago, IL 60614
Ph: (773)281-1800
E-mail: linda_malawy@hotmail.com
URL: http://www.chicagoherp.org
Contact: Linda Malawy, Pres.
Members: 700. **Membership Dues:** individual, $25 • family, $28 • institutional, $38 • sustaining, $50 •

contributing, $100 • corporate, $1,000. **Local.** **Awards:** Herpetological Grants. **Frequency:** annual. **Type:** grant. **Recipient:** for members. **Publications:** *CHS Bulletin*, monthly. Journal. Features original articles, photographs and artworks, columns, books reviews, abstracts of current herpetological activities and classified ads. ISSN: 0009-3564. **Advertising:** accepted. **Conventions/Meetings:** monthly meeting - every last Wednesday.

813 ■ Chicago Jewish Historical Society (CJHS)
618 S Michigan Ave.
Chicago, IL 60605
Ph: (312)663-5634
E-mail: info@chicagojewishhistory.com
URL: http://www.chicagojewishhistory.org
Contact: Walter Roth, Pres.
Founded: 1977. **Local.** **Affiliated With:** American Jewish Historical Society.

814 ■ Chicago Log Cabin Republicans
3712 N Broadway, No. 136
Chicago, IL 60613
Ph: (312)925-3105
E-mail: president@lcrchicago.com
URL: http://www.logcabin.org/lcrchicago
Contact: Erik Linell, Pres.
Local. **Affiliated With:** Log Cabin Republicans.

815 ■ Chicago Map Society (CMS)
c/o Newberry Library
60 W Walton St.
Chicago, IL 60610
Ph: (312)255-3689
E-mail: smithctr@newberry.org
URL: http://www.newberry.org/smith/cms/cms.html
Contact: Jim Ackerman, Contact
Founded: 1976. **Members:** 180. **Membership Dues:** general, $25 (annual) • contributing, $50 (annual) • sustaining, $100 (annual). Teachers, collectors, librarians, dealers, and interested individuals. Supports and encourages the study and preservation of maps and related materials. **Conventions/Meetings:** monthly lecture, includes social gathering.

816 ■ Chicago Medical Society (CMS)
515 N Dearborn St.
Chicago, IL 60610
Ph: (312)670-2550
Fax: (312)670-3646
URL: http://www.cmsdocs.org
Contact: Peter E. Eupierre MD, Pres.
Local.

817 ■ Chicago Memorial Association
PO Box 2923
Chicago, IL 60690
Ph: (773)327-4604
E-mail: chicmem@hotmail.com
URL: http://www.funerals.org/chicago
Contact: Janice Atsaves, Pres.
Local. Promotes a consumer's right to choose a dignified, meaningful, and affordable funeral. Provides educational material to the public and affiliates. Monitors the funeral and cemetery industry for consumers nationwide. Responds to consumer complaints. **Affiliated With:** Funeral Consumers Alliance.

818 ■ Chicago Mercantile Exchange (CME)
20 S Wacker Dr.
Chicago, IL 60606
Ph: (312)930-1000
Fax: (312)648-3625
Free: (800)331-3332
E-mail: info@cme.com
URL: http://www.cme.com
Contact: Craig S. Donohue, CEO
Founded: 1898. **Members:** 2,724. **Staff:** 880. **Budget:** $90,000,000. **Multinational.** Commodity futures exchange for live hogs, feeder cattle, live beef cattle, frozen pork bellies (bacon), lumber, gold, foreign currencies, government securities, bank debt, and equity financial instruments; deals with options on equity futures, interest rates, foreign currencies, and livestock. Maintains speakers' bureau; conducts research programs to help develop new contracts and update existing contracts; compiles statistics. Operates library of 3000 books on various aspects of futures trading. **Committees:** Audit; Compensation; Governance; Market Regulation Oversight; Marketing and Public Relations Advisory. **Divisions:** AG Marketing; Building Operations; Compliance; Financial Instruments Marketing; Government Relations; Legal and Regulatory; Main frame Systems and Programs; Mainframe Software Support; Marketing; Price Quotations; Support Facilities Statistics. **Formerly:** (1919) Chicago Butter and Egg Board. **Publications:** *Bibliography and Information Source Lists*, annual • *Chicago Mercantile Exchange—Annual Report* • *CME Magazine*. Features customer case histories, trend stories, editorials and news briefs. Alternate Formats: online • *Open Outcry*, monthly • *RCR Report*, quarterly • Membership Directory, annual • Newsletter, monthly • Yearbook • Also publishes contract specifications brochures and fundamental factor books. **Conventions/Meetings:** annual meeting - always November.

819 ■ Chicago Metal Finishers Institute (CMFI)
c/o Evelyne A. Hallberg
5048 N Marine Dr.
Chicago, IL 60640
Ph: (773)784-1895
Fax: (773)784-1304
E-mail: cmfi@net0.com
Contact: Evelyne A. Hallberg, Exec.Sec.
Founded: 1935. **Members:** 95. **Staff:** 2. **Budget:** $100,000. **Local.** Promotes the development, efficiency, and general welfare of the metal finishing industry. **Formerly:** (1981) Chicago Electro-Platers Institute. **Publications:** Newsletter, monthly. **Conventions/Meetings:** monthly meeting.

820 ■ Chicago Metropolitan Association for the Education of Young Children
c/o Tom Layman, Exec.Dir.
30 E Adams, Ste.1000
Chicago, IL 60603
Ph: (312)427-5399
Fax: (312)427-5028
E-mail: tlayman@chicagometroaeyc.org
URL: http://www.chicagometroaeyc.org
Contact: Tom Layman, Exec.Dir.
Founded: 1962. **Members:** 2,200. **Membership Dues:** student, $35 (annual) • regular, $70 (annual) • comprehensive, $110 (annual). **Staff:** 8. **Budget:** $1,400,000. **Local Groups:** 2. **Local.** Strives to improve the quality of services to young children and their families through advocacy, public education, and professional development. **Awards:** Service to the Chicago Metro AEYC. **Frequency:** annual. **Type:** recognition • Service to Young Children. **Frequency:** annual. **Type:** recognition. **Computer Services:** Information services, web page on job openings in early childhood education, childcare, and related fields. **Commissions:** Children and Violence; Infant-Toddler; Intergenerational; Kindergarten-Primary; Preschool (3-5); Professional Leadership Development; Public Policy. **Committees:** Program Standing. **Affiliated With:** National Association for the Education of Young Children. **Also Known As:** (2004) Chicago Metro AEYC. **Publications:** *Greatest 500 Books*. Directory. Contains list of books developed as an "Excellence in Teaching" program. Alternate Formats: online. **Conventions/Meetings:** annual conference (exhibits).

821 ■ Chicago Military Academy - Bronzeville Association
3519 S Giles Ave.
Chicago, IL 60653-1105
Ph: (773)534-9750
E-mail: rcgray@cps.k12.il.us
Contact: Mr. Richard Gray, Principal
Local.

822 ■ Chicago National Association of Women Business Owners
330 S Wells St., Ste.1110
Chicago, IL 60606
Ph: (312)322-0990
Fax: (312)461-0238
E-mail: info@nawbochicago.org
URL: http://www.nawbochicago.org
Contact: Kara E.F. Cenar, Pres.
Local. **Affiliated With:** National Association of Women Business Owners.

823 ■ Chicago Police Women's Association
c/o Michele Owens, Pres.
PO Box 7576
Chicago, IL 60680-7576
Ph: (312)458-9683
E-mail: mao390@aol.com
URL: National Affiliate–www.iawp.org
Contact: Michele Owens, Pres.
Local. Seeks to strengthen, unite and raise the profile of women in criminal justice. **Affiliated With:** International Association of Women Police.

824 ■ Chicago Pro Musica NFP
c/o John Bruce Yeh
2045 N Halsted St.
Chicago, IL 60614-4369
Ph: (708)638-6210
Fax: (312)664-6569
E-mail: jyehcondor@aol.com
Founded: 1979. **Local.**

825 ■ Chicago Psychoanalytic Society (CPS)
122 S Michigan Ave.
Chicago, IL 60603
Ph: (312)922-7474
Fax: (312)922-5656
URL: http://www.3b.com/cps/index.htm
Contact: Lucy Wrobel, Administrator
Founded: 1931. **Members:** 225. **Membership Dues:** regular, $400 (annual). **Staff:** 1. **Budget:** $60,000. **Regional.** Professional association of psychoanalysts organized to advance the field of psychoanalysis, maintain professional and ethical standards of its members, and the profession. Promotes professional activities of its members. **Awards:** Chicago Psychoanalytic Society Annual Original Paper Prize. **Frequency:** annual. **Type:** monetary. **Affiliated With:** American Psychoanalytic Association. **Conventions/Meetings:** biennial meeting, scientific - always fourth Tuesday of September, October, January, February, March, May and June.

826 ■ Chicago Radio Controlled Sailing Club No. 181
c/o Mark Watkins
3754 N Lawndale Ave.
Chicago, IL 60618
Ph: (773)583-5810
URL: http://www.chicagorcsailing.org
Contact: Mark Watkins, Contact
Local.

827 ■ Chicago Region PTA
330 N Wabash, Ste.2100
Chicago, IL 60611
Ph: (312)467-0471
Fax: (312)467-0509
E-mail: chicagoregion@ptamail.com
URL: http://myschoolonline.com/Il/ChicagoRegionPTA
Local. Parents, teachers, students, and others interested in uniting the forces of home, school, and community. Promotes the welfare of children and youth.

828 ■ Chicago Roofing Distributors Association
c/o Jim Bone
1950 N Narragansett Ave.
Chicago, IL 60639-3830
Ph: (773)237-9740
Fax: (773)237-9844
E-mail: brsjim@boneroffingsupply.com
Contact: Jim Bone, VP
Local.

829 ■ Chicago SCORES
1847 Pulaski Rd.
Chicago, IL 60623
Ph: (773)522-5500
E-mail: aroberson@americascores.org
URL: http://www.americascores.org
Contact: Artavia Berry-Roberson, Exec.Dir.
Local.

830 ■ Chicago Ski Twisters
PO Box 20414
Chicago, IL 60620
Ph: (773)445-8345
E-mail: rjscott@ix.netcom.com
URL: http://www.nbs.org/clubs/skitwisters
Contact: Raymond Scott, Adj.
Local. **Affiliated With:** National Brotherhood of Skiers.

831 ■ Chicago Sno-Gophers Ski Club
217 E 71st St.
Box No. 95
Chicago, IL 60619
Ph: (312)683-5231 (773)221-5060
E-mail: marlinhowell@yahoo.com
URL: http://www.sno-gophers.org
Contact: Marlin Howell, Pres.
Local. **Affiliated With:** National Brotherhood of Skiers.

832 ■ Chicago Stock Exchange (CHX)
One Financial Pl.
440 S LaSalle St.
Chicago, IL 60605
Ph: (312)663-2222
E-mail: info@chx.com
URL: http://www.chx.com
Contact: David Herron, CEO
Founded: 1882. **Members:** 446. Brokers and dealers in local and national securities. Wholly-owned subsidiaries: Midwest Securities Trust Company; Midwest Clearing Corp; Mortgage Backed Securities Clearing Corp. **Formerly:** (1993) Midwest Stock Exchange. **Publications:** Report, annual. **Conventions/Meetings:** annual meeting - always April, Chicago, IL.

833 ■ Chicago Thoracic Society
c/o Beverlyn Weaver
1440 W Washington Blvd.
Chicago, IL 60607
Ph: (312)243-2000 (708)202-3559
E-mail: bweaver@alamc.org
URL: National Affiliate–www.thoracic.org
Contact: Franco Laghi MD, Pres.
Local. Aims to improve the study and practice of thoracic surgery and related disciplines. Seeks to prevent and fight respiratory diseases through research, education and patient advocacy. **Affiliated With:** American Thoracic Society.

834 ■ Chicago Trendsetters
PO Box 438281
Chicago, IL 60619
E-mail: ntysn@earthlink.net
URL: National Affiliate–www.nbs.org
Contact: Helen Tyson, Pres.
Local. **Affiliated With:** National Brotherhood of Skiers.

835 ■ Chicago Urban League
4510 S Michigan Ave.
Chicago, IL 60653
Ph: (773)285-5800
Fax: (773)285-7772
E-mail: info@cul-chicago.org
URL: http://www.cul-chicago.org
Local.

836 ■ Chicago Women in Business (CWIB)
c/o Sita Sandeep
Univ. of Chicago
Chicago, IL 60615
Ph: (773)742-6020
E-mail: sramasar@gsb.uchicago.edu
URL: http://gsbwww.uchicago.edu/student/cwib/
Local.

837 ■ Chicago Women in Publishing (CWIP)
PO Box 268107
Chicago, IL 60626
Ph: (312)641-6311
Fax: (773)508-5871
E-mail: info@cwip.org
URL: http://www.cwip.org
Contact: Lisa Scacco, Pres.
Founded: 1972. **Local**. Assists members toward their career goals in Chicago's publishing industry.

838 ■ Chicago Women in Trades
c/o Lauren Sugerman, Pres.
1657 W Adams, Ste.401
Chicago, IL 60612
Ph: (312)942-1444
Fax: (312)942-0802
E-mail: cwitinfo@cwit2.org
URL: http://www.chicagowomenintrades.org
Contact: Mrs. Jacquelyn Lyda, Dir. of Finance and Administration
Founded: 1981. **Members:** 500. **Membership Dues:** employed, $30 (annual) • unemployed, $10 (annual). **Staff:** 12. **Budget:** $1,000,000. **Local**. Strives to improve women's economic equity by increasing the number of women working in well-paid, skilled trade jobs traditionally held by men. **Publications:** *Breaking New Ground: Worksite 2000*. Report. **Price:** $10.00 • *Building Equal Opportunity*. Report. **Price:** $10.00 • *Drafting the Blueprint*. Report. **Price:** $10.00 • *Tools for Success*. Manual. **Price:** $10.00 • *Youth Guide, Tradeswomen of Tomorrow*. Report. **Price:** $25.00.

839 ■ Chicago Women in Travel
c/o Sanger Tours, Inc.
332 S. Michigan, Ste.1040
Chicago, IL 60604
Ph: (312)939-3993
Fax: (312)939-3920

840 ■ Chicagoland Bicycle Federation
c/o Dan Korman, Dir. of Membership and Communications
9 W Hubbard St., Ste.402
Chicago, IL 60610-6545
Ph: (312)427-3325
Fax: (312)427-4907
E-mail: cbf@biketraffic.org
URL: http://www.biketraffic.org
Contact: Dan Korman, Dir. of Membership and Communications
Local. Works to improve the bicycling environment and quality of life in the region. Promotes bicycle safety, education and facilities; encourages use of the bicycle as an energy-efficient, economical and non-polluting form of transportation and as a healthful and enjoyable form of recreation.

841 ■ Chicagoland Chamber of Commerce (CCoC)
One IBM Plz.
330 N Wabash, Ste.2800
Chicago, IL 60611-3605
Ph: (312)494-6700
Fax: (312)494-0196
E-mail: staff@chicagolandchamber.org
URL: http://www.chicagolandchamber.org
Contact: Robert Wislow, Pres./CEO
Members: 2,600. **Membership Dues:** business with 1-3 employees, $400 (annual) • business with 4-20 employees, $500 (annual) • business with 21-50 employees, $750 (annual) • business with 51-100 employees, $1,000 (annual). **Local**. Promotes business and community development in Chicago, IL. Conducts drug-free workplace program. **Committees:** Drug-Free Workplace; Education Workforce Quality; Environmental; Government Relations; Political Action; Taxation; Technology Growth; Transportation Infrastructure. **Affiliated With:** National Association of Women Business Owners. **Publications:** *Business Resource Guide and Membership Directory*. Lists of more than 2,600 member companies, civic, professional organizations, and trade associations that are members of the Chamber. **Price:** $50.00 for members; $150.00 for nonmembers • *Relocation Guide for the Chicagoland Area*. Articles. Includes detailed information on each Chicagoland neighborhood and surrounding suburbs, housing, education, recreation, and community resources. **Price:** $25.00 plus 6.05 for 1st class postage • Directory, annual • Newsletter, monthly. Alternate Formats: online • Annual Report, annual. Alternate Formats: online.

842 ■ Chicagoland Rottweiler Club
c/o Bernard Clay
118 S Mayfield Ave.
Chicago, IL 60644-3819
Ph: (773)261-6734
URL: National Affiliate–www.amrottclub.org
Contact: Bernard Clay, Contact
Regional. **Affiliated With:** American Rottweiler Club.

843 ■ Chiesa Nuova (CN)
c/o Fr. Robert M. Hutmacher
230 S Laflin St.
Chicago, IL 60607-5306
Ph: (312)226-0983
Fax: (312)226-0980
E-mail: bobhoot@chiesanuova.org
URL: http://chiesanuova.org
Founded: 1997. **Members:** 6. **Staff:** 30,000. **Local**. Franciscan ministry for the performing arts; hosts artists for recitals, sponsors events elsewhere; performs in Chicago and Italy; offers professional artistic experiences for the less fortunate.

844 ■ Child Welfare League of America, Mid-West Region
c/o Adoption Information Center of Illinois
120 W Madison St., Ste.800
Chicago, IL 60602
Ph: (312)701-0491
Fax: (312)701-0493
E-mail: midwest@cwla.org
URL: National Affiliate–www.cwla.org
Regional. **Affiliated With:** Child Welfare League of America.

845 ■ Children's Place Association
c/o John Connors
3059 W Augusta Blvd.
Chicago, IL 60622
Ph: (773)826-1230
Fax: (773)826-0705
E-mail: info@childrens-place.org
URL: http://childrens-place.org
Contact: Betty Jackson, Chair
Local.

846 ■ Chinese American Service League (CASL)
2141 S Tan Ct.
Chicago, IL 60616
Ph: (312)791-0418
Fax: (312)791-0509
E-mail: adminis@caslservice.org
URL: http://www.caslservice.org
Founded: 1978. **Regional**.

847 ■ Citizen Action/Illinois
c/o Human Resources
28 E Jackson Blvd., Ste.605
Chicago, IL 60604
Ph: (312)427-2114
Fax: (312)427-2307
E-mail: info@citizenaction-il.org
URL: http://www.citizenaction-il.org
State.

848 ■ Citizens for a Better Environment - Illinois
205 W. Monroe, 4th Fl.
Chicago, IL 60606
Ph: (312)346-8870
Fax: (312)346-8871
E-mail: ilcbe@cbemw.org
Contact: Jennifer Li, Contact

849 ■ City Club of Chicago
360 N Michigan Ave., Ste.903
Chicago, IL 60601
Ph: (312)565-6500
Fax: (312)759-8339
E-mail: info@cityclub-chicago.com
URL: http://www.cityclub-chicago.com
Contact: Sarah Badesch, Exec.Dir.
Local.

850 ■ Coalition of African, Asian, European and Latino Immigrants of Illinois (CAAELII)
c/o Dale Asis, Dir
4300 N Hermitage Ave.
Chicago, IL 60613
Ph: (773)248-1019
Fax: (773)248-1179
E-mail: contact@caaelii.org
URL: http://www.caaelii.org
Local.

851 ■ Colored Pencil Society of America, Chicago, Illinois Chapter 103
c/o Tracy Frein
1046 W Byron St., No. 3
Chicago, IL 60613
Ph: (773)327-0795 (312)943-5995
E-mail: chicago-dc103@cpsa.org
URL: National Affiliate–www.cpsa.org
Contact: Tracy Frein, Contact
Local. Promotes colored pencil art as a viable art form. Provides a forum for the education, communication and recognition of colored pencil artists. Conducts exhibitions, workshops and other social activities. **Affiliated With:** Colored Pencil Society of America.

852 ■ Columbia Yacht Club
111 N Lake Shore Dr.
Chicago, IL 60601
Ph: (312)938-3625
Fax: (312)938-3630
E-mail: lynn@colyc.com
URL: http://www.colyc.com
Contact: Lynn Almy, Gen.Mgr.
Local.

853 ■ Commercial Finance Association, Mid-West Chapter
c/o Beverly Gray, Pres.
Bank One
120 S LaSalle St., 8th Fl.
Chicago, IL 60603
Ph: (312)661-6983
Fax: (312)661-5292
E-mail: beverly_gray@bankone.com
URL: National Affiliate–www.cfa.com
Contact: Beverly Gray, Pres.
Local. Affiliated With: Commercial Finance Association.

854 ■ Community Health Charities of Illinois
c/o Gael Mennecke, Pres./CEO
28 E Jackson Blvd., No. 910
Chicago, IL 60604-2211
Ph: (312)939-6275
Fax: (312)939-7590
Free: (800)299-6842
E-mail: info@healthcharitiesillinois.org
URL: http://www.healthcharitiesillinois.org
Contact: Gael Mennecke, Pres./CEO
Founded: 1969. **Members:** 37. **Membership Dues:** nonprofit health agency in IL, $10,000 (annual). **Staff:** 4. **Budget:** $186,000. **State Groups:** 1. **State.** Coordinates fundraising activities and health education programming at public and private work sites. **Affiliated With:** Community Health Charities. **Formerly:** (1999) National Voluntary Health Agencies in Illinois. **Publications:** *Partners in Good Health*, biennial. Newsletter. **Conventions/Meetings:** annual meeting.

855 ■ Community Nutrition Network and Senior Services Association of Cook County (CNNSSA)
208 S LaSalle St., Ste.1900
Chicago, IL 60604-1119
Ph: (312)207-5290
Fax: (312)441-0641
E-mail: pisaacson@mowcookcounty.org
URL: http://www.cnnssacookcounty.org
Contact: Peg Isaacson, Contact
Local. Publications: Annual Report, annual. Alternate Formats: online.

856 ■ Cook County Bar Association (CCBA)
120 W Madison St., Ste.450
Chicago, IL 60602
Ph: (312)630-1157
Fax: (312)630-0983
E-mail: info@cookcountybar.org
URL: http://www.cookcountybar.org
Contact: Bruce Cook, Pres.
Founded: 1914. **Members:** 1,300. **Membership Dues:** 1-3 years, $50 (annual) • 3-5 years, $70 (annual) • 5 years and up, $100 (annual) • student, $10 (annual). **Staff:** 1. **Local.** Attorneys in good standing. Seeks to improve the administration of civil and criminal justice, and the availability of legal services to the public. **Affiliated With:** National Bar Association. **Publications:** Newsletter.

857 ■ CoreNet Global - Chicago Chapter
c/o Peter L. Block
455 N Cityfront Plz. Dr., 28th Fl.
Chicago, IL 60611-5555
Ph: (312)470-1846
Fax: (312)470-3800
E-mail: peter_block@cushwake.com
URL: National Affiliate–www.corenetglobal.org
Contact: Peter L. Block, Pres.
Local. Represents real estate professionals. Encourages professionalism within corporate real estate through education and communication. Protects the interests of corporate realty in dealing with adversaries, public or private. Maintains contact with other real estate organizations. Conducts seminars including concentrated workshops on the corporate real estate field. **Affiliated With:** CoreNet Global.

858 ■ Corporation for National and Community Service - Kansas
c/o John Hosteny
77 W Jackson Blvd., Ste.442, Rm. 457
Chicago, IL 60604-3511
Ph: (312)353-3622
Fax: (312)353-6496
E-mail: il@cns.gov
URL: http://www.nationalservice.gov/about/role_impact/state_profiles_detail.asp?tbl_profiles_state=KS
Contact: John Hosteny, Contact
State.

859 ■ Cosmopolitan Chamber of Commerce (CCC)
560 W Lake St., 5th Fl.
Chicago, IL 60661
Ph: (312)786-0212
Fax: (312)786-9079
E-mail: hildafontaine@cchamber.org
URL: http://www.cchamber.org
Contact: Gloria Bell, Exec.Dir.
Founded: 1933. **Members:** 350. **Staff:** 6. **Local.** Individuals and businesses promoting the growth and development of minority-owned businesses in Chicago, IL. **Convention/Meeting:** none. **Formerly:** (1954) Chicago Negro Chamber of Commerce. **Publications:** *CosmoConnection*, monthly. Newsletter. Alternate Formats: online.

860 ■ Council for Adult and Experiential Learning (CAEL)
c/o Pamela Tate, Pres. and CEO
55 E Monroe St., Ste.1930
Chicago, IL 60603
Ph: (312)499-2600
Fax: (312)499-2601
E-mail: cael@cael.org
URL: http://www.cael.org
Local.

861 ■ Council for Disability Rights
c/o Josephine Holzer
205 W Randolph, Ste.1645
Chicago, IL 60606-1892
Ph: (312)444-9484
Fax: (312)444-1977
E-mail: webmaven@disabilityrights.org
URL: http://www.disabilityrights.org
Contact: Ms. Jo Holzer, Exec.Dir.
Founded: 1980. **Members:** 5,000. **Membership Dues:** individual, $15 (annual) • corporation, $25 (annual). **Staff:** 2. **State.** Strives to advance the rights and responsibilities and enhances the lives of people with disabilities and their families through quality programs. Promotes public policy and legislation, public awareness through education, and provides information and referral services. **Libraries: Type:** not open to the public. **Awards:** Gargoyle Awards. **Frequency:** annual. **Type:** trophy. **Recipient:** advocacy for disability rights. **Publications:** *CDR Reports*, monthly. Newsletter. Features disability advocacy news items/resources. **Circulation:** 5,000. Alternate Formats: online; magnetic tape.

862 ■ Council for Exceptional Children, Illinois
c/o Joan Rog
3856 N Nordica Ave.
Chicago, IL 60634-2378
Ph: (773)534-8230
E-mail: storm2457@worldnet.att.net
URL: http://www.cec.sped.org/ab/federati.html
Contact: Joan Rog, Contact
State.

863 ■ Council For Jewish Elderly (CJE)
3003 W Touhy Ave.
Chicago, IL 60645
Ph: (773)508-1000
Fax: (773)508-1028
E-mail: info@cje.net
URL: http://www.cje.net
Contact: Mark D. Weiner, Pres./CEO
Local. Agency serving elderly people and their families for 30 years.

864 ■ Council of Great Lakes Governors (CGLG)
35 E Wacker Dr., Ste.1850
Chicago, IL 60601
Ph: (312)407-0177
Fax: (312)407-0038
E-mail: dnaftzger@cglg.org
URL: http://www.cglg.org
Contact: David Naftzger, Exec.Dir.
Founded: 1983. **Regional.**

865 ■ Customs Brokers and Foreign Freight Forwarders Association of Chicago (CBFFFAC)
PO Box 66365
Chicago, IL 60666
Ph: (847)759-1600
E-mail: cslaski@cs.com
URL: http://CBFFFAC.org
Contact: Cathy Slaski, Chair
Founded: 1960. **Members:** 175. **Membership Dues:** regular, associate, $195 (annual). **Staff:** 15. **Local.** Treasury-licensed custom house brokers and FMC-licensed independent ocean freight forwarders united to maintain high standards of business practice throughout the industry. **Affiliated With:** National Customs Brokers and Forwarders Association of

America. **Publications:** *CBFFFAC Newsletter*, bimonthly. **Advertising:** accepted.

866 ■ Dearborn Realtist Board (DRB)
8454 S Stony Island Ave.
Chicago, IL 60617
Ph: (773)374-9191
Fax: (773)374-9191
E-mail: info@dearbornreb.com
URL: http://www.dearbornreb.com
Contact: Diane Danzy-Odell, Pres.
Local. Aims to protect the public against unethical, improper, or fraudulent practices connected with the real estate business. **Affiliated With:** National Association of Real Estate Brokers.

867 ■ DePaul University Students In Free Enterprise
Coleman Entrepreneurship Ctr.
1 E Jackson Blvd., Ste.8100
Chicago, IL 60604-2287
Ph: (312)362-8625
Fax: (312)362-8667
E-mail: sife@condor.depaul.edu
URL: http://condor.depaul.edu/~sife
Contact: Ms. Natalia Padalino, Pres.
Local.

868 ■ Depression and Bipolar Support Alliance (DBSA)
730 N Franklin St., Ste.501
Chicago, IL 60610-7225
Fax: (312)642-7243
Free: (800)826-3632
E-mail: questions@dbsalliance.org
URL: http://dbsalliance.org
Contact: Susan Bergeson, VP
Local. Seeks to help people through support and information. Seeks to remove stigma and encourage others to get help. **Affiliated With:** Depression and Bipolar Support Alliance. **Formerly:** (2004) Depressive and Manic-Depressive Association Maine.

869 ■ Design-Build Institute of America - Great Lakes Chapter
c/o Bonnie Henriques, Exec.Dir.
1400 W Devon
Box 368
Chicago, IL 60660
Ph: (773)465-8687
E-mail: bhenriques@rcn.com
URL: National Affiliate–www.dbia.org
Contact: Bonnie Henriques, Exec.Dir.
Regional. Works to advocate and advance single source project delivery within the design and construction community. Promotes the use of innovative design-build teams on non-residential building, civil infrastructure and process industry projects. **Affiliated With:** Design-Build Institute of America.

870 ■ Dignity - Chicago
3023 N Clark St., Ste.237
Chicago, IL 60657-5200
Ph: (312)458-9438
E-mail: dignitychicago@aol.com
URL: http://www.dignitychicago.org
Local.

871 ■ Divine Praise
c/o Sharon Saunders
4128 W Adams St.
Chicago, IL 60624-2701
E-mail: engagements@divinepraise.org
URL: http://www.divinepraise.org
Contact: Sharon Saunders, Contact
Local.

872 ■ Donors Forum of Chicago
208 S LaSalle St., Ste.740
Chicago, IL 60604
Ph: (312)578-0090
Fax: (312)578-0103
E-mail: info@donorsforum.org
URL: http://www.donorsforum.org
Contact: Valerie S. Lies, Pres./CEO
Founded: 1974. **Members:** 1,100. **Budget:** $1,800,000. **Local**. Grantmakers and financial advisors. Promotes effective and responsive philanthropy. Provides resources for grant makers, nonprofit organizations, the media and researchers through education programs, workshops, publications, research projects, a library, and public policy advocacy. **Affiliated With:** National Council of Nonprofit Associations. **Publications:** *Directory of Illinois Foundations*, biennial • *Forum Notes*, monthly. Newsletter • *Giving in Illinois*, biennial. Report • *Members, Associate Members and Forum Partners Directory*, annual. **Conventions/Meetings:** annual luncheon.

873 ■ Dreams for Kids
218 N. Jefferson, Ste.300
Chicago, IL 60622
Ph: (312)669-8859
Fax: (312)669-8856
E-mail: dreams@dreamsforkids.org
URL: http://www.dreamsforkids.org
Contact: Thomas W. Tuohy, Pres.
Founded: 1989. **Membership Dues:** $50 (annual). **Nonmembership**. **For-Profit**. **Regional**. Improving the quality of life of kids with disabilities and those who have suffered hardship.

874 ■ Dress for Success Chicago
7848 S Chappel
Chicago, IL 60649-5005
Ph: (773)753-0942
Fax: (773)753-0947
E-mail: chicago@dressforsuccess.org
URL: National Affiliate–www.dressforsuccess.org
Contact: Shawna Brown, Founder/Exec.Dir.
Local.

875 ■ Duckling Council
c/o John Tucker, Pres.
PO Box 641433
Chicago, IL 60664
Fax: (312)377-3420
Free: (800)591-3466
URL: http://www.duckling.org
Regional.

876 ■ Earth First! Illinois / Last Wizards
3400 W 111th St., No. 154
Chicago, IL 60655
Ph: (708)507-4306
Fax: (708)974-4365
E-mail: info@lastwizards.com
URL: http://www.lastwizards.com
Contact: James John Bell, Organizer
Founded: 1996. **State**. Engages the public on advanced technology issues, like those around biotechnology and the coming "technologic singularity". Explores the connections between environmental defense, ecological philosophy, and scholarly social theory. Organizes around issues of environmental justice, urban sprawl, nuclear waste and indigenous sovereignty. Maintains a code of non-violence. Takes a no-compromise stance in defense of the earth.

877 ■ Earth Share of Illinois
c/o Natalia Petraszczuk, Exec.Dir.
35 E Wacker Dr. Ste.1300
Chicago, IL 60601-2110
Ph: (312)795-3740
Fax: (312)795-3742
E-mail: info@earthshare-illinois.org
URL: http://earthshare-illinois.org
Contact: Natalia Pertaczuk, Exec.Dir.
Local.

878 ■ Earthsave International, Chicago
2417 W Homer St.
Chicago, IL 60647
Ph: (708)531-8910
E-mail: chicago@earthsave.org
URL: http://www.earthsavechicago.com
Contact: Chris Brunn, Chm.
State. **Affiliated With:** EarthSave International.

879 ■ East Side Chamber of Commerce
3658 E 106th St.
Chicago, IL 60617-6611
Ph: (773)721-7948
Fax: (773)721-7446
E-mail: eastsidechamber@aol.com
Contact: Joann Caporale, Exec.Sec.
Members: 174. **Local**. Promotes business and community development on Chicago's east side.

880 ■ Easter Seals Metropolitan Chicago, Illinois
14 E Jackson Blvd., Ste.900
Chicago, IL 60604
Ph: (312)939-5115 (312)408-0268
Fax: (312)939-0283
Free: (866)448-2372
URL: http://chicago.easterseals.com
Contact: F. Timothy Muri, Pres./CEO
Founded: 1969. **Local**. Provides comprehensive services for individuals with disabilities or other special needs and their families to improve quality of life and maximize independence. **Affiliated With:** Easter Seals.

881 ■ Edgebrook Chamber of Commerce
5357 W Devon Ave.
Chicago, IL 60646-4142
Ph: (773)775-0378
Fax: (773)775-0371
Contact: Barbara A. Copeland, Exec.Dir.
Local. Promotes business and community development in the Edgebrook-Sauganash area of Chicago, IL. **Formerly:** (2005) Edgebrook-Sauganash Chamber of Commerce. **Publications:** Newsletter, monthly. **Price:** free to members.

882 ■ Edgewater Community Council (ECC)
6044 N Broadway
Chicago, IL 60660
Ph: (773)334-5609
Fax: (773)334-1871
E-mail: edgecc@core.com
URL: http://www.edgewatercc.org
Local.

883 ■ Electric Service Dealers Association of Illinois
c/o George J. Weiss, Exec.Dir.
4927 W Irving Park Rd.
Chicago, IL 60641
Ph: (773)282-9400
State.

884 ■ Employee Assistance Professionals Association - Northern Illinois Chapter
PO Box 81673
Chicago, IL 60681-0673
Ph: (312)458-9797
Fax: (847)998-6994
E-mail: nieapa@comcast.net
URL: http://www.eapa.info/ChaptBranch/IL01/NorthernIllinois.htm
Contact: William R. Heffernan, Pres.
Regional. **Affiliated With:** Employee Assistance Professionals Association.

885 ■ Epilepsy Foundation of Greater Chicago
17 N State St., Ste.1300
Chicago, IL 60602
Ph: (312)939-8622
Free: (800)273-6027
E-mail: info@epilepsychicago.org
URL: National Affiliate–www.epilepsyfoundation.org
Contact: Paula Fischer, Contact
Local. **Affiliated With:** Epilepsy Foundation.

886 ■ ESOP Association, Illinois
c/o John G. Hommel, Interim Pres.
N Star Trust Co.
500 W Madison, Ste.3630
Chicago, IL 60661

Ph: (312)559-9763
Free: (877)765-3782
E-mail: info@northstartrust.com
URL: http://www.northstartrust.com
Contact: John G. Hommel, Interim Pres.
State. **Affiliated With:** ESOP Association.

887 ■ Esperanto Society of Chicago
828 S Ada St.
Chicago, IL 60607
Ph: (312)271-8673
URL: http://www.esperanto-chicago.org
Contact: Charlie Gunn, Treas.
Membership Dues: youth, limited income, $10 (annual) • individual, $20 (annual) • family, $30 (annual) • sustaining, $40 (annual). **Local**. **Affiliated With:** Esperanto League for North America.

888 ■ Executive Service Corps of Chicago (ESC)
25 E Washington St., Ste.1500
Chicago, IL 60602-1804
Ph: (312)580-1840
Fax: (312)580-0042
E-mail: info@esc-chicago.org
URL: http://www.esc-chicago.org
Founded: 1978. **Local**.

889 ■ Explorers Club - Chicago/Great Lakes Chapter
c/o Cheryl Istvan, Sec.-Treas.
1807 N Fremont St.
Chicago, IL 60614
Ph: (312)640-0741
Fax: (312)640-0731
E-mail: ec.chicago@mac.com
URL: National Affiliate–www.explorers.org
Contact: Mel Surdel, Chm.
Regional. Represents explorers and scientists. Promotes field research and scientific exploration. Encourages public interest in exploration and the sciences. **Affiliated With:** The Explorers Club.

890 ■ Facing History and Ourselves, Chicago
200 E Randolf St., Ste.2100
Chicago, IL 60601
Ph: (312)726-4500
Fax: (312)726-3713
URL: National Affiliate–www.facinghistory.org
Contact: Chuck Meyers, Program Associate
Local. **Affiliated With:** Facing History and Ourselves National Foundation. **Formerly:** (2005) Facing History and Ourselves National Foundation, Chicago.

891 ■ Federation of Women Contractors (FWC)
c/o Beth Doria, Exec.Dir.
5650 S Archer
Chicago, IL 60638
Ph: (312)360-1122
Fax: (312)360-0239
E-mail: fwcchicago@aol.com
URL: http://www.fwcchicago.com
Contact: Beth Doria, Exec.Dir.
Founded: 1986. **Members:** 125. **Staff:** 3. **Local**. Committed to the advancement of entrepreneurial women in the construction industry. **Awards:** Women's Advocate Award. **Frequency:** annual. **Type:** trophy. **Recipient:** for contribution of women business owners in construction industry. **Publications:** Membership Directory, annual. **Circulation:** 2,500. **Conventions/Meetings:** monthly meeting - always third Thursday.

892 ■ Financial Executives International, Chicago Chapter
c/o Ms. Susan Gidley, Administrator
330 S Wells St., Ste.1110
Chicago, IL 60606
Ph: (312)362-9770
Fax: (312)461-0238
E-mail: feichi@aol.com
URL: http://www.fei.org/eWeb/startpage.aspx?site=ch_chi
Contact: Ms. Marie Hollein, Pres.
Founded: 1933. **Members:** 740. **Local**. Promotes personal and professional development of financial executives. Provides peer networking opportunities and advocacy services. **Affiliated With:** Financial Executives International. **Publications:** Membership Directory • Newsletter, monthly. **Conventions/Meetings:** monthly dinner, with guest speaker - every 3rd Thursday of the month; September to March.

893 ■ Financial Managers Society, Chicago Chapter
c/o Larry Davis
Second Fed. Savings
3960 W 26th St.
Chicago, IL 60623
Ph: (773)277-8500
E-mail: ldavis@secondfederal.com
URL: National Affiliate–www.fmsinc.org
Contact: Larry Davis, VP
Local. Provides technical information exchange for financial personnel within financial institutions. **Affiliated With:** Financial Managers Society.

894 ■ Flames Cricket Club
3660 N Lakeshore Dr., No. 4707
Chicago, IL 60613
URL: http://www.usaca.org/Clubs.htm
Contact: Tariq Ahmad, Contact
Local.

895 ■ Foster Grandparent Program of Suburban Cook County
10046 S Western Ave.
Chicago, IL 60643-1943
Ph: (773)429-9381
Fax: (773)429-0200
E-mail: mariont@ucanchicago.org
URL: National Affiliate–www.seniorcorps.org
Contact: Tracee Marion, Dir.
Local. Serves as mentors, tutors and caregivers for at-risk children and youth with special needs. Provides older Americans the opportunity to put their life experiences to work for local communities.

896 ■ Franciscan Outreach Association
c/o Fr. Paul Gallagher, OFM
1645 W LeMoyne St.
Chicago, IL 60622
Ph: (773)278-6724
Fax: (773)278-7120
E-mail: mail@franoutreach.org
URL: http://www.franoutreach.org
Local.

897 ■ Friends of the Farnsworth House
c/o Chris Robling
455 N Cityfront Plz.
Chicago, IL 60611-5503
Ph: (312)343-2026 (708)369-0612
URL: http://www.farnsworthhousefriends.org
Contact: Chris Robling, Contact
Local.

898 ■ Friends of Meigs Field
PO Box 59-7308
Chicago, IL 60659-7308
Ph: (312)458-9250
Fax: (847)966-6168
E-mail: info@friendsofmeigs.org
URL: http://friendsofmeigs.org
Contact: Richard Steinbrecher, Operations Mgr.
Founded: 1995. **Members:** 6,800. **Membership Dues:** basic, $10 (annual) • family, $25 (annual) • cockpit, $50 (annual) • flight leader, $100 (annual) • corporate, $150 (annual) • benefactor, $200 (annual) • patron, $500 (annual) • angel, $1,000 (annual). **Staff:** 2. **Local**. Seeks to educate the public on the value of the last remaining general aviation airport in Chicago, IL. **Publications:** Newsletter, quarterly. **Circulation:** 3,500. **Conventions/Meetings:** annual International Youth Eagle's Day at Meigs - meeting • annual Open House at Meigs Field - meeting, with unusual aircraft and information displays about aviation (exhibits) • monthly Young Eagles Rally - always second Saturday.

899 ■ Friends of the Parks (FOTP)
55 E Washington, Ste.1911
Chicago, IL 60602
Ph: (312)857-2757
Fax: (312)857-0656
E-mail: trantere@fotp.org
URL: http://www.fotp.org
Contact: Erma Tranter, Pres.
Founded: 1975. **Membership Dues:** student/senior, $25-$34 • individual, $35-$49 • family, $50-$100 • patron, $100-$249 • conserver, $250-$499 • benefactor, $500-$999 • Fredrick Law Olmsted Circle, $1,000. **Local**. **Publications:** *The Advocate*, quarterly. Newsletter. **Price:** included in membership dues.

900 ■ Friends of WVON
c/o Melody Spann-Cooper
3350 S Kedzie Ave.
Chicago, IL 60623-5189
Ph: (773)247-6200
Fax: (773)247-5336
E-mail: sharon@wvon.com
URL: http://www.wvon.com
Contact: Sharon McGhee, News Dir.
Local.

901 ■ Garfield Park Conservatory Alliance (GPCA)
300 N Central Park Ave.
Chicago, IL 60624-1996
Ph: (773)638-1766
Fax: (773)638-1777
E-mail: erushing@garfieldpark.org
URL: http://www.garfield-conservatory.org
Contact: Eunita Rushing, Pres.
Founded: 1995. **Members:** 375. **Staff:** 15. **Budget:** $800,000. **Local**. Works in partnership with the Chicago Park District to revitalize the Garfield Park Conservatory through programs in education, community greening, and visitor services.

902 ■ Girl Scouts of Chicago
c/o Gwen Ferguson, Volunteer Services Dir.
222 S Riverside Plz., Ste.2120
Chicago, IL 60606
Ph: (312)416-2500
Fax: (312)416-2932
E-mail: info@girlscouts-chicago.org
URL: http://www.girlscouts-chicago.org
Contact: Gwen Ferguson, Volunteer Services Dir.
Local.

903 ■ Go Veggie!
c/o Kay Stepkin
PO Box 577997
Chicago, IL 60657
Ph: (773)871-7000
Fax: (773)935-3112
E-mail: kstepkin@earthlink.net
URL: http://www.go-veggie.org
Contact: Kay Stepkin, Contact
Local. Seeks to educate individuals to the many benefits of vegetarianism for human health, the environment, and the well being of all life on the planet. Publishes a bimonthly newsletter, brings in speakers, hosts dinners, offers cooking classes and other special events such as the Turkey-free Thanksgiving Dinner.

904 ■ Grand Boulevard Federation
715 E 47th St.
Chicago, IL 60653-4201
Ph: (773)548-8140
Fax: (773)548-6622
Contact: Greg Washington, Pres.
Local.

905 ■ Grassroots Collaborative of Chicago, Illinois
c/o Michael McConnell
59 E. Van Buren, Ste.1400
Chicago, IL 60605
Ph: (312)427-2533
Fax: (312)427-4171
E-mail: mmcconnell-glr@afsc.org

906 ■ Great Lakes Disability and Business Technical Assistance Center
1640 W Roosevelt Rd., Rm. 405
Chicago, IL 60608
Ph: (312)413-1407
Fax: (312)413-1856
Free: (800)949-4232
URL: http://www.adagreatlakes.org
Contact: Robin A. Jones, Dir.
Founded: 1991. **Staff:** 7. **Budget:** $770,000. **Nonmembership**. **Regional**. Provides information, materials, technical assistance and training on the Americans with Disabilities Act of 1990 (ADA) and Accessible Information Technology (IT). **Libraries: Type:** open to the public. **Holdings:** 300. **Subjects:** ADA section 504 of Rehab Act, reasonable accommodation. **Committees:** State Steering Committees. **Also Known As:** Great Lakes ADA Center. **Publications:** *Region V News*, quarterly. Newsletter. **Price:** free. **Circulation:** 12,000. Alternate Formats: magnetic tape; diskette; online.

907 ■ Greater Ashburn Planning Association
c/o Scott Bizewski, Pres.
8136 S Kedzie Ave.
Chicago, IL 60652
Ph: (773)436-2482
Fax: (773)436-9186
E-mail: gapa@bigplanet.com
Local.

908 ■ Greater North Michigan Avenue Association (GNMAA)
625 N Michigan Ave., Ste.401
Chicago, IL 60611
Ph: (312)642-3570
Fax: (312)642-3826
E-mail: gnmaa@gnmaa.com
URL: http://www.themagnificentmile.com
Contact: Mr. John Maxson, Pres./CEO
Founded: 1912. **Members:** 1,000. **Staff:** 9. **Budget:** $1,000,000. **Local.** Works to provide protection and encourage development of commercial and residential property. **Awards:** Beautification Award. **Frequency:** annual. **Type:** recognition. **Additional Websites:** http://www.gnmaa.com. **Publications:** *Greater North*, quarterly. Newsletter. **Price:** free. **Circulation:** 1,200. **Advertising:** accepted. **Conventions/Meetings:** annual meeting - always February • quarterly meeting.

909 ■ Habitat for Humanity - MidWest Region
1920 S Laflin
Chicago, IL 60608
Ph: (312)243-6448
Fax: (312)243-9632
Free: (800)643-7845
URL: National Affiliate–www.habitat.org
Regional.

910 ■ Health and Medicine Policy Research Group (HMPRG)
c/o Margie Schaps, Exec.Dir
29 E Madison St., Ste.602
Chicago, IL 60602-4404
Ph: (312)372-4292
Fax: (312)372-2753
E-mail: info@hmprg.org
URL: http://www.hmprg.org
Local.

911 ■ Heartland Alliance for Human Needs and Human Rights
c/o Sabrina Harkrader
208 S LaSalle St., Ste.1818
Chicago, IL 60604
Ph: (312)660-1500
Fax: (312)660-1510
E-mail: sharkrader@heartlandalliance.org
Contact: Sabrina Harkrader, Contact

912 ■ Hemophilia Foundation of Illinois
332 S Michigan Ave., Ste.1135
Chicago, IL 60604-4305
Ph: (312)427-1495
Fax: (312)427-1602
E-mail: info@hfi-il.org
URL: http://www.hemophiliaillinois.org
Contact: Robert P. Robinson, Exec.Dir.
State. Strives to improve the quality of life for persons affected by inherited bleeding disorders through advocacy, consumer services, education and research. **Affiliated With:** National Hemophilia Foundation.

913 ■ Heritage Community Development Corp.
c/o Dr. Alan V. Ragland
1501 W 95th St.
Chicago, IL 60643-1329
Ph: (773)429-0993
Contact: Dr. Alan Ragland, Pres.
Local.

914 ■ High School Council PTSA
c/o Steve Budde, Corresponding Sec.
3830 N Damen
Chicago, IL 60618-3904
Ph: (773)281-7636
E-mail: super_racenut@juno.com
URL: http://geocities.com/highschoolcouncil/index.htm
Contact: Steve Budde, Corresponding Sec.
Local. Parents, teachers, students, and others interested in uniting the forces of home, school, and community. Promotes the welfare of children and youth.

915 ■ Historic Chicago Bungalow Initiative
1 N LaSalle St., 12th Fl.
Chicago, IL 60602
Ph: (312)642-9900
E-mail: bungalow@chicagobungalow.org
URL: http://www.chicagobungalow.org
Contact: Charles Shanabruch, Exec.Dir.
Founded: 2000. **Members:** 3,100. **Staff:** 2. **Budget:** $400,000. **Local. Awards:** Matching grants. **Type:** grant. **Conventions/Meetings:** annual Historic Chicago Bungalow Expo - meeting, with workshops (exhibits).

916 ■ Horizon Community Services, DBA Center on Halsted
2855 N Lincoln
Chicago, IL 60657-4201
Ph: (773)472-6469
Fax: (773)472-6643
E-mail: mail@centeronhalsted.org
URL: http://www.horizonsonline.org
Contact: Ms. Robbin Burr, Exec.Dir.
Founded: 1973. **Members:** 5,000. **Staff:** 33. **Budget:** $1,750,000. **Local.** Social service agency for lesbians, gays, bisexuals, and transgendered. Focuses on youth programs (14-23), anti-violence project, psychotherapy, education, speaker services, and older adult program (45+). **Additional Websites:** http://www.centeronhalsted.org. **Telecommunication Services:** hotline, state of Illinois HIV/AIDS/STD hotline, (800)243-2437 • hotline, LGBT helpline, (773) 929-4357 • 24-hour hotline, crisis line, (773)871-2273.

917 ■ Horizons for Youth
c/o Audrey George-Griffin
703 W Monroe St.
Chicago, IL 60661
Ph: (312)627-9031
Fax: (312)627-9033
E-mail: georgegriffin@anet.com
URL: http://horizons-for-youth.org
Contact: Audrey George-Griffin, Contact
Local.

918 ■ Hospitality Financial and Technology Professionals - Chicago Chapter
c/o Scott Schippel, CHAE, Pres.
Habitat Co.
555 W Madison St.
Chicago, IL 60661-2514
Ph: (312)902-2427
Fax: (312)902-2070
E-mail: sschippel@habitat.com
URL: http://www.hftpchicago.org
Contact: Scott Schippel CHAE, Pres.
Members: 150. **Local.** Provides opportunities to members through professional and educational development. **Affiliated With:** Hospitality Financial and Technology Professionals. **Conventions/Meetings:** monthly meeting, with guest speaker - every third Tuesday.

919 ■ Hostelling International - American Youth Hostels, Metropolitan Chicago Council
24 E Cong. Pkwy.
Chicago, IL 60605
Ph: (312)360-0300
Fax: (312)360-0313
E-mail: reserve@hichicago.org
URL: http://www.hichicago.org
Contact: Thomas J. Applegate, Exec.Dir.
Founded: 1947. **Members:** 6,000. **Membership Dues:** regular, $25 (annual). **Staff:** 3. **Budget:** $250,000. **Local.** Seeks to help all people, especially the young, gains a greater understanding of the world and its people through hostelling. **Affiliated With:** Hostelling International-American Youth Hostels. **Publications:** *By Ways*, quarterly. Newsletter. **Price:** included in membership dues. **Circulation:** 6,000. **Advertising:** accepted. **Conventions/Meetings:** periodic executive committee meeting.

920 ■ Hull House Association
c/o Maxine Florell
4520 N Beacon St.
Chicago, IL 60640
Ph: (773)561-3500
Fax: (773)561-3507
E-mail: mflorell@hullhouse.org
URL: http://www.hullhouse.org
Local.

921 ■ Hyde Park Chamber of Commerce
5211 S Harper, Ste.D
Chicago, IL 60615
Ph: (773)288-0124
Fax: (773)288-0464
E-mail: hpchamber@juno.com
URL: http://www.hpchamber.com
Contact: Cheryl Heads, Exec.Dir.
Founded: 1939. **Members:** 200. **Local.** Works to represent and assist in promoting local businesses. **Computer Services:** database, membership directory. **Publications:** Newsletter, monthly.

922 ■ Hyde Park Young Life
c/o Aimee Tucker
5421 S Dorchester Ave., Apt. 1
Chicago, IL 60615
Ph: (773)752-2897
URL: http://HydePark.younglife.org
Contact: Aimee Tucker, Contact
Local.

923 ■ Hyderabad Decan Cricket Club
2546 W Devon Ave.
Chicago, IL 60659
URL: http://www.usaca.org/Clubs.htm
Contact: Raees Nizami, Contact
Local.

924 ■ IEEE Chicago Section
Western Soc. of Engineers
28 E Jackson, Ste.1320
Chicago, IL 60604

Ph: (312)253-4333
Free: (800)898-4333
E-mail: aschaefer@owpp.com
URL: http://ewh.ieee.org/r4/chicago
Contact: Angeline Schaefer, Chm.
State. Engineers and scientists in electrical engineering, electronics, and allied fields. Promotes creating, developing, integrating, sharing, and applying knowledge about electro and information technologies and sciences for the benefit of humanity and the profession. Conducts lectures on current engineering and scientific topics.

925 ■ Illinois Arts Alliance (IAA)
200 N Michigan Ave., Ste.404
Chicago, IL 60601
Ph: (312)855-3105
Fax: (312)855-1565
E-mail: info@artsalliance.org
URL: http://www.artsalliance.org
State.

926 ■ Illinois Association of College and Research Libraries (IACRL)
33 W Grand Ave., Ste.301
Chicago, IL 60610-4306
Ph: (312)644-1896
Fax: (312)644-1899
E-mail: ilayes@interaccess.com
URL: http://servercc.oakton.edu/~iacrl
Contact: Barbara Galik, Pres.
State. Enhances the ability of academic library and information professionals to serve the information needs of the higher education community and to improve learning, teaching and research. **Affiliated With:** Association of College and Research Libraries.

927 ■ Illinois Association of Criminal Defense Lawyers
PO Box 2864
Chicago, IL 60690-2864
Ph: (773)643-4225 (312)831-1500
Fax: (312)831-1502
Contact: Nancy E. O'Connor, Exec.Dir.
Founded: 1985. **Members:** 475. **Staff:** 3. **Regional Groups:** 3. **State Groups:** 1. **Local Groups:** 1. **State**. Represents both the public and private sectors of the criminal defense bar; fosters, maintains, educates and encourages the integrity, independence and expertise of lawyers in the field of criminal defense. **Awards: Frequency:** annual. **Type:** recognition. **Affiliated With:** National Association of Criminal Defense Lawyers. **Publications:** *Criminal Defense Quarterly*. Newsletter. Contains topics presented in criminal defense. **Price:** for members only. **Advertising:** accepted. Alternate Formats: online. **Conventions/Meetings:** quarterly seminar • annual seminar, with dinner.

928 ■ Illinois Association of Environmental Professionals (IAEP)
c/o A.J. Pavlick, Pres.
PO Box 81551
Chicago, IL 60681-0551
Ph: (847)934-0370
E-mail: ajpavlick@comcast.net
URL: http://www.iaepnetwork.org
Contact: A.J. Pavlick, Pres.
State.

929 ■ Illinois Association for Infant Mental Health (ILAIMH)
c/o Erikson Institute
420 N Wabash Ave., 6th Fl.
Chicago, IL 60611
Ph: (312)893-7175
E-mail: infant@ilaimh.org
URL: http://ilaimh.org
Contact: Susan Kaplan, Pres.
State. Provides public information on infant mental health. Advocates research on mental disorders that affect infants. Promotes the optimal development of infants and the treatment of mental disorders in the child's early years. **Affiliated With:** World Association for Infant Mental Health.

930 ■ Illinois Association for Mulitcultural Multilingual Education (IAMME)
c/o University of Illinois
Coll. of Educ.
1040 W Harrison
Chicago, IL 60625
Ph: (312)355-4481
Fax: (847)433-1308
E-mail: jane@iamme.org
URL: http://www.iamme.org
Contact: Janes Montes, Pres.
Membership Dues: para-educator, parent, student, retired, $15 (annual) • regular, $30 (annual) • insitution, $50 (annual). **State**. Represents both English language learners and bilingual education professionals. Promotes public understanding and appreciation of the linguistic and cultural needs of language-minority children, youth and adults.

931 ■ Illinois Campaign for Better Health Care
c/o Jim Duffett
1325 S Wabash, Ste.305
Chicago, IL 60605
Ph: (312)913-9449
Fax: (312)913-9559
E-mail: jduffett@cbhconline.org
URL: http://www.cbhconline.org
State. Works to organize individuals and organizations to insure public input in the creation and ongoing oversight of a system that responds to the health care needs of people. Promotes high quality of life, which include community health and wholeness, by understanding the social roots of ill health like poverty, unemployment, poor housing, inadequate education, environment degradation, racism, sexism and homophobia.

932 ■ Illinois Chapter, American Academy of Pediatrics
c/o Jennifer Hurtarte
1358 W. Randolph, Ste.2 E.
Chicago, IL 60607
E-mail: info@illinoisaap.com
URL: http://www.illinoisaap.org
State.

933 ■ Illinois Coalition Against the Death Penalty (ICADP)
c/o Rachael Dietkus
180 N Michigan Ave., Ste.2300
Chicago, IL 60601-7401
Ph: (312)849-2279
Fax: (312)201-9760
E-mail: info@icadp.org
URL: http://www.icadp.org
Contact: Rachael Dietkus, Contact
State.

934 ■ Illinois Coalition for Immigrant and Refugee Rights (ICIRR)
c/o Maricela Garcia
36 S Wabash, Ste.1425
Chicago, IL 60603
Ph: (312)332-7360
Fax: (312)332-7044
E-mail: info@icirr.org
URL: http://www.icirr.org
State.

935 ■ Illinois Council on Developmental Disabilities (ICDD)
100 W Randolph St., Ste.10-600
Chicago, IL 60601
Ph: (312)814-2080
Fax: (312)814-7141
E-mail: vmorris@mail.state.il.us
URL: http://www.state.il.us/agency/icdd
Contact: Vanessa Morris, Admin.Asst.
State. **Affiliated With:** National Association of Councils on Developmental Disabilities. **Formerly:** (2000) Illinois Planning Council on Developmental Disabilities.

936 ■ Illinois Council on Long Term Care
c/o Terrance P. Sullivan, Exec.Dir.
3550 W Peterson, Ste.304
Chicago, IL 60659
Ph: (773)478-6613
Fax: (773)478-0843
E-mail: thisweek@nursinghome.org
URL: http://www.nursinghome.org
State.

937 ■ Illinois Council of Teachers of Mathematics (ICTM)
c/o Ann Hanson, Exec.Dir.
Columbia Coll., Sci./Math Dept.
600 S Michigan Ave.
Chicago, IL 60605-1996
Ph: (312)663-1600
E-mail: robert_urbain@glenbard.org
URL: http://www.ictm.org
Contact: Bob Urbain, Pres.
Founded: 1949. **State**.

938 ■ Illinois CPA Society (ICPAS)
c/o Jane Kelledy, Exec.Asst.
550 W Jackson, Ste.900
Chicago, IL 60661-5716
Ph: (312)993-0407
Fax: (312)993-9954
Free: (800)993-0407
E-mail: illinoiscpasociety@icpas.org
URL: http://www.icpas.org
Contact: Jane Kelledy, Exec.Asst.
State.

939 ■ Illinois Cricket Club
5355 W Newort Ave.
Chicago, IL 60641
URL: http://www.usaca.org/Clubs.htm
Contact: Rup Seenarain, Contact
Local.

940 ■ Illinois Environmental Balancing Bureau
221 N La Salle, Ste.3400
Chicago, IL 60601
Ph: (312)384-1220
Fax: (312)384-1229
E-mail: dbulley@mca.org
URL: National Affiliate–www.nebb.org
Contact: Daniel Bulley, Chapter Coor.
Local. Works to help architects, engineers, building owners, and contractors produce buildings with HVAC systems. Establishes and maintains industry standards, procedures, and specifications for testing, adjusting, and balancing work. **Affiliated With:** National Environmental Balancing Bureau.

941 ■ Illinois Fair Plan Association (IFPA)
PO Box 81469
Chicago, IL 60681-0469
Ph: (312)861-0385
Fax: (312)861-0134
E-mail: info@illinoisfairplan.com
URL: http://www.illinoisfairplan.com
Contact: Douglas A. Jensen, Pres.
State.

942 ■ Illinois Gay Rodeo Association (ILGRA)
PO Box 14878
Chicago, IL 60614
Ph: (312)477-5793
E-mail: ilgra@aol.com
URL: http://www.ilgra.com
Contact: Anthony Adamowski, Trustee
Founded: 1992. **Members:** 100. **Membership Dues:** $40 (annual). **State**. **Publications:** *The Corral*, monthly. Newsletter. **Price:** included in membership dues. **Conventions/Meetings:** Annual Windy City Gay Rodeo - show, charity amateur, IGRA rodeo series (exhibits) • monthly meeting, general membership.

943 ■ Illinois Health Information Management Association (ILHIMA)
233 N Michigan, Ste.2150
Chicago, IL 60601-5519
Ph: (312)233-1521
Fax: (312)233-1522
E-mail: ilhima@ahima.org
URL: http://www.ilhima.org
State. Represents the interests of professionals engaged in health information management. Strives to promote the quality, access and security of health information in all healthcare settings for the benefit of the members, healthcare consumers, providers and other users of clinical data.

944 ■ Illinois Hotel and Lodging Association (IHLA)
27 E Monroe St. Ste.1200
Chicago, IL 60603
Ph: (312)346-3135
Fax: (312)346-6036
Free: (800)603-4624
E-mail: mgordon@illinoishotels.org
URL: http://www.illinoishotels.org
Contact: Mark J. Gordon, Pres./CEO
State. Formerly: (2005) Hotel-Motel Association of Illinois.

945 ■ Illinois Humanities Council (IHC)
c/o Phoebe Stein Davis, Communications Coor.
203 N Wabash Ave., Ste.2020
Chicago, IL 60601-2417
Ph: (312)422-5580
Fax: (312)422-5588
E-mail: ihc@prairie.org
URL: http://www.prairie.org
Founded: 1973. **Members:** 28. **Staff:** 21. **State.** Dedicated to fostering a culture in which the humanities are a vital part of the lives of individuals and communities. **Libraries: Type:** open to the public. **Holdings:** 30; films. **Subjects:** documentaries. **Awards:** Grants Program. **Frequency:** 5/year. **Type:** grant • Studs Terkel Humanities Service Award. **Frequency:** biennial. **Type:** recognition. **Recipient:** for individuals, primarily volunteers, who have championed the humanities in their communities.

946 ■ Illinois Library Association (ILA)
33 W Grand Ave., Ste.301
Chicago, IL 60610-4306
Ph: (312)644-1896
Fax: (312)644-1899
E-mail: ila@ila.org
URL: http://www.ila.org
Contact: Robert P. Doyle, Exec.Dir.
Founded: 1896. **Members:** 3,000. **Membership Dues:** trustee, $75 (annual) • friend, retired, $50 (annual) • student, $35 (annual) • unemployed, $25 (annual) • public library and system (based on population), $55-$7,500 (annual) • higher education (based on total enrollment), $75-$360 (annual) • elementary and secondary school, school district, $90 (annual) • special library, library advocacy, associate, $100 (annual). **Staff:** 3. **Budget:** $900,000. **State.** Provides leadership for the development, promotion, and improvement of library services in Illinois and for the library community, in order to enhance learning and ensure access for all. **Publications:** *Handbook of Organization and Membership Directory*, annual • *ILA Reporter*, bimonthly. Newsletter. Covers legislative topics, current issues, and information on ILA activities. **Price:** $25.00. ISSN: 0018-9979. **Circulation:** 4,000. **Advertising:** accepted. **Conventions/Meetings:** annual conference (exhibits).

947 ■ Illinois Life and Health Insurance Guaranty Association
8420 W Bryn Mawr Ave., Ste.550
Chicago, IL 60631
Ph: (773)714-8052
E-mail: dorth@ilhiga.org
URL: http://www.ilhiga.org
Contact: Daniel A. Orth III, Exec.Dir.
State. Promotes the life and health insurance guaranty industry. Provides coverage for resident policyholders of insurers licensed to do business and in the event of life or health insurer insolvency. **Affiliated With:** National Organization of Life and Health Insurance Guaranty Associations.

948 ■ Illinois Maternal and Child Health Coalition
c/o Laura Leon, Project Dir.
1256 W Chicago Ave.
Chicago, IL 60622
Ph: (312)491-8161
Fax: (312)491-8171
E-mail: ilmaternal@ilmaternal.org
URL: http://www.ilmaternal.org/
State.

949 ■ Illinois Medical Group Management Association (ILMGMA)
20 N Michigan Ave., Ste.700
Chicago, IL 60602
Ph: (312)263-7150
Fax: (312)782-0553
E-mail: jcampbell@midwest-cardiology.com
URL: http://www.ilmgma.com
Contact: Jim Campbell CMPE, Pres.
State. Enhances health care delivery and administration through Group Practice Leadership, Professional Development, Education, Information Exchange, Communication, Advocacy, and Networking Activities. **Affiliated With:** Medical Group Management Association.

950 ■ Illinois Migrant Council (IMC)
c/o Planning Department
28 E Jackson Blvd., No. 1600
Chicago, IL 60604
Ph: (312)663-1522
Fax: (312)663-1994
E-mail: info@illinoismigrant.org
URL: http://www.illinoismigrant.org
Founded: 1966. **State.**

951 ■ Illinois Mortgage Bankers Association (IMBA)
111 W Washington St., Ste.1320
Chicago, IL 60602
Ph: (312)236-6208
Fax: (312)236-7117
E-mail: imba@anet-chi.com
URL: http://www.imba.org
Contact: Barbara Saylor, Pres.
State.

952 ■ Illinois NORML
1573 N Milwaukee Ave.
PMB 446
Chicago, IL 60622-2009
Ph: (773)395-9708
E-mail: info@illinoisnorml.org
URL: http://www.illinoisnorml.org
State. Affiliated With: National Organization for the Reform of Marijuana Laws.

953 ■ Illinois Osteopathic Medical Association (IOMS)
c/o Elizabeth Forkins Harano, Exec.Dir.
142 E Ontario Ave., No. 1023
Chicago, IL 60611-2854
Ph: (312)202-8174
Fax: (312)202-8224
E-mail: ioms@ioms.org
URL: http://www.ioms.org
Contact: Elizabeth Forkins Harano, Exec.Dir.
Local. Affiliated With: American Osteopathic Association.

954 ■ Illinois Parents of Blind Children
c/o Debbie Stein
5817 N Nina Ave.
Chicago, IL 60631
Ph: (773)631-1093
E-mail: dkent5817@worldnet.att.net
URL: National Affiliate–www.nfb.org
Contact: Debbie Stein, Contact
State. Provides information and support to parents of blind children. Develops and expands resources available to parents and their children. Aims to eliminate discrimination and prejudice against the blind. **Affiliated With:** National Organization of Parents of Blind Children.

955 ■ Illinois Peace Action (IPA)
PO Box 2783
Chicago, IL 60690-2783
E-mail: ilpeaceaction@yahoo.com
URL: http://www.webcom.com/ipa
Contact: Jim Senyszyn, Contact
State. Affiliated With: Peace Action.

956 ■ Illinois Podiatric Medical Association (IPMA)
122 S Michigan Ave., Ste.1441
Chicago, IL 60603
Ph: (312)427-5810
Fax: (312)427-5813
E-mail: communications@ipma.net
URL: http://ipma.net
Contact: Mary S. Feeley CAE, Exec.Dir.
Founded: 1917. **Members:** 700. **Membership Dues:** podiatric physician, $725 (annual). **Staff:** 4. **Budget:** $500,000. **Regional Groups:** 3. **State.** Podiatric physicians concerned with the delivery of quality care, access to patients, physician education, public and media education, and legislative activity that protects patients and encourages inclusion of podiatry in health plans. **Affiliated With:** American Podiatric Medical Association. **Publications:** *Memo*, 10/year. Newsletter. Provides legislative updates, insurance advice, and general information. **Price:** included in membership dues. **Circulation:** 700. **Advertising:** accepted. Alternate Formats: online. **Conventions/Meetings:** annual meeting, clinical/scientific sessions and practice management (exhibits).

957 ■ Illinois Pollution Control Board (IPCB)
James R. Thompson Ctr.
100 W Randolph St., Ste.11-500
Chicago, IL 60601
Ph: (312)814-3620 (312)814-3623
Fax: (312)814-3669
E-mail: wiley@ipcb.state.il.us
URL: http://www.ipcb.state.il.us
Contact: Sandra Wiley, Office Mgr.
State.

958 ■ Illinois Primary Health Care Association (IPHCA)
542 S Dearborn St., Ste.900
Chicago, IL 60605-1842
Ph: (312)692-3000
Fax: (312)692-3001
E-mail: info@iphca.org
URL: http://www.iphca.org
Contact: Bruce A. Johnson, Pres./CEO
Founded: 1982. **Members:** 44. **Staff:** 25. **State.**

959 ■ Illinois Psychiatric Society (IPS)
20 N Michigan Ave., Ste.700
Chicago, IL 60602
Ph: (312)263-7391
Fax: (312)782-0553
E-mail: ips@isms.org
URL: http://www.illinoispsychiatricsociety.org
Contact: Joan Anzia MD, Pres.
State.

960 ■ Illinois Psychological Association (IPA)
c/o Terrence J. Koller, PhD, Exec. Officer
203 N Wabash Ave., Ste.1404
Chicago, IL 60601
Ph: (312)372-7610
Fax: (312)372-6787
E-mail: ipaexec@aol.com
URL: http://www.illinoispsychology.org
Contact: Terrence J. Koller PhD, Exec. Officer
State. Affiliated With: American Psychological Association.

961 ■ Illinois Public Interest Research Group (PIRG)
407 S Dearborn, Ste.701
Chicago, IL 60605
Ph: (312)364-0096
Fax: (312)364-0092
E-mail: info@illinoispirg.com
URL: http://www.illinoispirg.org
Contact: Brian Imus, Senior Policy Advocate
State.

962 ■ Illinois Restaurant Association
200 N La Salle St., Ste.880
Chicago, IL 60601
Ph: (312)787-4000
Fax: (312)787-4792
Free: (800)572-1086
E-mail: illinoisrestaurants@illinoisrestaurants.org
URL: http://www.illinoisrestaurants.org
Contact: Colleen McShane, Pres.
State. **Publications:** *Membership News Bulletin*, monthly. **Conventions/Meetings:** annual meeting - always spring.

963 ■ Illinois Retail Merchants Association (IRMA)
19 S LaSalle St., Ste.300
Chicago, IL 60603
Ph: (312)726-4600
Fax: (312)726-9570
E-mail: info@irma.org
URL: http://www.irma.org
Contact: Mr. Dave Vite, Pres./CEO
Founded: 1957. **Membership Dues:** retailer with sales volume of up to $300,000, $75 (annual) • retailer with sales volume of $300,000 to $500,000, $100 (annual) • retailer with sales volume of $500,000 to $1,000,000, $150 (annual). **State**. Helps in representation of the industry and the business community in state government. Provides information on any state law or regulation affecting business operations. Offers group programs in energy purchasing, telecom management, and Bankcard processing. **Committees:** Credit; Loss Prevention; Pharmacy; Tax. **Affiliated With:** Illinois Food Retailers Association; Midwest Hardware Association; National Retail Federation. **Publications:** *Retail Register*, monthly. Newsletter. Covers business and regulatory issues affecting Illinois merchants. **Price:** included in membership dues. Alternate Formats: online • *This Week in Springfield*, weekly, during legislative session. Newsletter. Covers legislative activity in Springfield of direct impact on retail businesses in Illinois. **Price:** included in membership dues. Alternate Formats: online. **Conventions/Meetings:** annual Retail Day - meeting, retailers to meet legislators and voice issues of concern (exhibits) - every April or May • annual Retailer of the Year Award Luncheon, honors excellent Illinois retailer - every September.

964 ■ Illinois Right to Life Committee (IRLC)
65 E Wacker Pl., Ste.800
Chicago, IL 60601-7203
Ph: (312)422-9300
Fax: (312)422-9302
E-mail: illinoisrighttolife@ameritech.net
URL: http://www.illinoisrighttolife.org
Contact: Mr. William Beckman, Exec.Dir.
Founded: 1968. **Members:** 7,000. **Staff:** 3. **State**. Individuals interested in protecting the right to life of human beings, from conception to natural death. Opposes abortion, euthanasia, human cloning, embryonic stem cell research and infanticide. Advertises and seeks to educate through billboards, newspaper and radio ads, and posters on public transportation. Maintains speakers' bureau. **Libraries: Type:** reference. **Holdings:** 300. **Subjects:** abortion, euthanasia, infanticide. **Publications:** *Illinois Right-to-Life News*, quarterly. Newsletter. **Price:** $10.00/year. **Circulation:** 10,000. **Conventions/Meetings:** annual Speakers Workshop, features various speakers.

965 ■ Illinois Society of Enrolled Agents - Tri-Counties Chapter
c/o Fred Toler, EA, Pres.
231 E 79th St.
Chicago, IL 60619
Ph: (773)723-1821
Fax: (773)723-8284
Contact: Fred Toler EA, Pres.
Local. **Affiliated With:** National Association of Enrolled Agents.

966 ■ Illinois Society of Pediatric Dentists (ISPD)
c/o Larry B. Salzmann, DDS, Pres.
801 S Paulina St.
Chicago, IL 60612-7211
Ph: (312)996-7531 (312)996-6414
Fax: (312)996-1981
E-mail: lbs@uic.edu
URL: http://www.ilspd.org
Contact: Larry B. Salzmann DDS, Pres.
State.

967 ■ Illinois Society for the Prevention of Blindness (ISPB)
407 S Dearborn, Ste.1000
Chicago, IL 60605-1117
Ph: (312)922-8710
Fax: (312)922-8713
Free: (800)433-4772
E-mail: ispb@ehil.org
URL: http://www.eyehealthillinois.org
Contact: James A. McKechnie Jr., Exec.Dir.
Founded: 1916. **Staff:** 4. **Budget:** $425,000. **Nonmembership**. **State**. Seeks to further the protection and preservation of sight through educational, informational, eye safety and research programs. **Publications:** *The Visionary*, semiannual. Newsletter. Provides up-to-date information on eye diseases, eye safety and research. **Price:** free • Brochures, periodic.

968 ■ Illinois Speech-Language-Hearing Association (ISHA)
230 E Ohio St., Ste.400
Chicago, IL 60611-3265
Ph: (312)644-0828
Fax: (312)644-8557
E-mail: ishail@bostrom.com
URL: http://www.ishail.org
Contact: Christy Strole, Pres.
Founded: 1960. **Members:** 4,000. **State**.

969 ■ Illinois State Acupuncture Association
c/o Claudette Baker, Pres.
5315 N Clark St., Ste.611
Chicago, IL 60640-2113
Ph: (773)271-4387
Fax: (773)955-9953
E-mail: claudettebaker@sbcglobal.net
URL: http://www.ilaaom.org
Contact: Claudette Baker, Pres.
State. **Affiliated With:** American Association of Oriental Medicine.

970 ■ Illinois State Chamber of Commerce (ISCC)
311 S Wacker Dr., Ste.1500
Chicago, IL 60606-6619
Ph: (312)983-7100
Fax: (312)983-7101
E-mail: info@ilchamber.org
URL: http://www.ilchamber.org
Contact: Douglas L. Whitley, Pres./CEO
Founded: 1919. **Members:** 5,000. **Membership Dues:** sustaining, $365-$2,500 (annual) • local chamber and nonprofit organization, $250-$1,250 (annual). **Staff:** 35. **Budget:** $4,000,000. **State**. Promotes business and community development in Illinois. Seeks to reduce operational costs for employers by providing information on state government regulations through seminars, publications and a member helpline. Lobbies on key business issues; holds legislative briefings. **Councils:** Economic Development; Employment Law; Environment; Government Affairs; Infrastructure; Tax Institute; Transportation Coalition. **Publications:** *ISCC Exec Report*, monthly. Newsletter. Contains issues about human resources, management, business, economy, tax, energy, environment, and chamber news. Alternate Formats: online • *Legislative Directory*, biennial. Includes general assembly, congressional delegation, executive branch, state offices and more. **Price:** $5.00 • *Springfield Scene*, weekly. Newsletter. **Conventions/Meetings:** Annual Legislative Briefing - conference - always January or February • Annual Legislative Conference - always March or April • annual board meeting - always September.

971 ■ Illinois State Fabricare Association (ISFA)
c/o Barbara Boden, Exec.Dir.
307 N Michigan Ave., Ste.800
Chicago, IL 60601
Fax: (312)360-0388
Free: (800)462-4732
E-mail: info@isfa.net
URL: http://www.isfa.net
Contact: Barbara Boden, Exec.Dir.
Founded: 1916. **Members:** 380. **Staff:** 3. **State**. **Publications:** *Press Ahead*, biennial. Newsletter. **Advertising:** accepted. **Conventions/Meetings:** biennial Equipment Trade Show (exhibits) • annual Winter Convention (exhibits).

972 ■ Illinois Tenants Union
c/o Michael Pensack, Exec.Dir.
4616 N Drake
Chicago, IL 60625-5814
Ph: (773)478-1133
E-mail: michael@tenant.org
URL: http://www.tenant.org
State.

973 ■ Imperial Windy City Court of the Prairie State Empire
PO Box 804545
Chicago, IL 60680-4107
Ph: (773)334-3296
E-mail: info@windycityempire.org
URL: http://www.windycityempire.org
Contact: Richard Clough, Dir.
Founded: 2001. **Members:** 42. **Membership Dues:** $20 (annual). **Budget:** $20,000. **Regional Groups:** 4. **State Groups:** 1. **Local Groups:** 1. **Local**. Conducts fundraisers culminating in an annual ball and distribution of money raised to charities. **Awards:** Baron & Baroness. **Frequency:** annual. **Type:** recognition. **Publications:** Newsletter, bimonthly. **Price:** free. **Circulation:** 50. **Conventions/Meetings:** annual Adornment - convention.

974 ■ Independent Schools Association of the Central States (ISACS)
1550 N Dearborn Pkwy.
Chicago, IL 60610
Ph: (312)255-1244
Fax: (312)255-1278
E-mail: jbraman@isacs.org
URL: http://www.isacs.org
Contact: John Braman, Pres.
Founded: 1909. **Members:** 221. **Membership Dues:** corporate sponsor, $500 (annual). **Staff:** 5. Independent schools including, but not limited to, private prep, special education, boarding, religiously affiliated, and day schools. Strives to foster good relations and communication among member schools and between schools and governmental or public education agencies; promotes the interests and positive public image of independent schools; works to ensure that the public interest is being served by member schools; assists member schools in preserving freedoms which enable them to practice their educational philosophies. Maintains and reviews an evaluation/accreditation program (schools are evaluated every seven years). Provides access to other independent school associations and organizations. Monitors relevant federal, state, and regional legislation, regulations, and judicial activity. Maintains speakers' bureau; compiles statistics; sponsors seminars and workshops. **Computer Services:** database. **Telecommunication Services:** phone referral service.

Affiliated With: The College Board; Council for American Private Education; National Association of Independent Schools; North Central Association Commission on Accreditation and School Improvement. **Publications:** *Accreditation Guide*. Features a comprehensive description of ISACS Accreditation Program, 7-year cycle, including a full appendix of forms. **Price:** $18.00 for members; $25.00 for nonmembers. Alternate Formats: online • Membership Directory, annual. Alternate Formats: online. **Conventions/Meetings:** annual Heads Conference - always winter • annual Leaders and Learners - always June • annual Leadership Forum (exhibits) - always November.

975 ■ Industrial Workers of the World - Chicago
PO Box 18387
Chicago, IL 60618
Ph: (815)550-2018
E-mail: chicago@iww.org
URL: National Affiliate–www.iww.org
Local. Affiliated With: Industrial Workers of the World.

976 ■ Inner-City Teaching Corps
c/o Eric B. Johnson, Dir. of Development & Communications
3141 W Jackson Blvd.
Chicago, IL 60612
Ph: (773)265-7240
Fax: (773)265-7259
E-mail: jalexander@ictc-chicago.org
URL: http://www.ictc-chicago.org
Contact: Mr. Jim Alexander, Exec.Dir.
Founded: 1991. **Members:** 42. **Staff:** 11. **Budget:** $1,600,000. **Local.** Strives to transform education in underserved communities. Empowers children in urban schools through innovative people and programs.

977 ■ Institute of Real Estate Management, Region 9
c/o Greg L. Martin, CPM
Draper and Kramer, Inc., AMO
33 W Monroe Ste.1900
Chicago, IL 60603
Ph: (312)795-2242
Fax: (312)795-2742
E-mail: marting@draperandkramer.com
URL: National Affiliate–www.irem.org
Contact: Greg Martin, Contact
Local. Affiliated With: Institute of Real Estate Management.

978 ■ Interfaith Youth Core (IFYC)
c/o Jeff Pinzino
1111 N Wells, Ste.501
Chicago, IL 60610
Ph: (312)573-8825
Fax: (312)573-8850
E-mail: info@ifyc.org
URL: http://www.ifyc.org
Local.

979 ■ International Association of Business Communicators, Chicago Chapter
c/o Tina K. Bowness
4036 N Pioneer Ave.
Chicago, IL 60634
Ph: (773)625-6792
E-mail: t-bowness@alumni.northwestern.edu
URL: National Affiliate–www.iabc.com
Contact: Tina K. Bowness, Pres.
Local. Represents the interests of communication managers, public relations directors, writers, editors and audiovisual specialists. Encourages establishment of college-level programs in organizational communication. Conducts surveys on employee communication effectiveness and media trends. Conducts research in the field of communication. **Affiliated With:** International Association of Business Communicators.

980 ■ International Association of Convention and Visitor Bureau, Charlotte Chicago, Illinois
40 E Chicago Ave.
Chicago, IL 60611-2026
Ph: (312)787-6564
Fax: (312)787-4716
E-mail: norma.taylor@visitcharlotte.org
URL: http://www.visitcharlotte.org
Contact: Norma J. Taylor, Reg.Dir./Sales
State. Affiliated With: International Association of Convention and Visitor Bureaus.

981 ■ International Association of Gay Square Dance Clubs - Chi-Town Squares
PMB 167
5315 N Clark St.
Chicago, IL 60640-2113
E-mail: chi-townsquares@sbcglobal.net
URL: http://www.iagsdc.org/chi-townsquares
Contact: Phil Davis, Pres.
Local. Fosters educational, recreational, and social opportunities within the framework of Modern Western square dancing for the gay and lesbian community. Works to increase the enjoyment of square dancing for everyone. Promotes better understanding between the straight world and the gay and lesbian community. **Affiliated With:** International Association of Gay Square Dance Clubs.

982 ■ International Association of Heat and Frost Insulators and Asbestos Workers, AFL-CIO, CFL - Local Union 17
Hugh Mulligan Center
3850 S Racine Ave.
Chicago, IL 60609
Ph: (773)247-8184
Fax: (773)247-6724
E-mail: local17@email.msn.com
URL: http://www.local17insulators.com
Contact: John Crininon, Contact
Members: 883. **Local. Affiliated With:** International Association of Heat and Frost Insulators and Asbestos Workers.

983 ■ International Association of Physicians in AIDS Care (IAPAC)
33 N LaSalle St., Ste.1700
Chicago, IL 60602-2601
Ph: (312)795-4930
Fax: (312)795-4938
E-mail: iapac@iapac.org
URL: http://www.iapac.org
Regional.

984 ■ International Brotherhood of Electrical Workers, Local 1220
8605 W Bryn Mawr Ave., Ste.309
Chicago, IL 60631
Ph: (773)714-1220
Fax: (773)693-0009
E-mail: info@ibew1220.org
URL: http://www.ibew1220.org
Contact: Madeleine Monaco, Business Mgr./Financial Sec.
Founded: 1939. **Members:** 747. **Regional. Affiliated With:** International Brotherhood of Electrical Workers. **Also Known As:** Radio and Television Broadcast Engineers. **Formerly:** (1998) Electrical Workers IBEW AFL-CIO, LU 1220; (2005) Radio and TV Broadcast Engineers International Brotherhood of Electrical Workers AFL-CIO, LU 1220. **Publications:** *Info Channel*, monthly. Newsletter. **Price:** $10.00.

985 ■ International Brotherhood of Painters and Allied Trades of the United States and Canada AFL-CIO-CFL - District Council 14
1456 W Adams St.
Chicago, IL 60607-2897
Ph: (312)421-0046
Fax: (312)421-7884
E-mail: info@pdc14.com
URL: http://www.pdc14.com
Members: 5,762. **Local.**

986 ■ International Brotherhood of Teamsters, Chauffeurs, Warehousemen and Helpers of America, AFL-CIO - Local Union 710
4217 S Halsted St.
Chicago, IL 60609
Ph: (773)254-3200
URL: http://www.local710.org
Contact: Patrick W. Flynn, Sec.-Treas.
Members: 15,243. **Local. Affiliated With:** International Brotherhood of Teamsters.

987 ■ International Customer Service Association, Chicago
Northwestern Memorial Hosp.
Galter Pavilion 6-101, 251 E Huron
Chicago, IL 60611
Ph: (312)926-0606
E-mail: cwithers@nmh.org
URL: National Affiliate–www.icsa.com
Contact: Cathryn Withers, Contact
Local. Affiliated With: International Customer Service Association.

988 ■ International Dark-Sky - Illinois-Chicago
59 W North Ave.
Chicago, IL 60610
Ph: (312)582-6435
URL: http://www.darksky.org/aboutida/sections
Contact: Dennis Erickson, Contact
Local. Astronomical societies, lighting and engineering groups, professional astronomers. Seeks to inform about the effects of nighttime lighting. Builds awareness about the problems that have effects on astronomy. Presents examples of good lighting design. Conducts speaker's bureau. Documents on good and bad lighting through photos and videos.

989 ■ International Kennel Club of Chicago (IKC)
6222 W North Ave.
Chicago, IL 60639
Ph: (773)237-5100
Fax: (773)237-5126
E-mail: ikcdogshow@ameritech.net
URL: http://www.ikcdogshow.com
Contact: Ms. Dori Auslander, Sec.
Founded: 1938. **Budget:** $500,000. Issues premium lists and catalogs of shows. Manages dog shows and a pet expo held annually for consumers. **Committees:** Agility Liaison; Benching; Building Management; Catalog Advertising; Junior Dog Judging; Media Relations; Obedience and Rally; Show. **Conventions/Meetings:** annual All-Breed Dog Show (exhibits) - always Chicago, IL.

990 ■ International Personnel Management Association, Chicago
c/o Adele De Mooy, Pres.
Metropolitan Water Reclamation District
111 E Erie
Chicago, IL 60611
Ph: (312)751-5174
Fax: (312)751-5171
E-mail: adele.demooy@mwrd.org
URL: National Affiliate–www.ipma-hr.org
Contact: Adele De Mooy, Pres.
Local. Affiliated With: International Public Management Association for Human Resources.

991 ■ International Personnel Management Association, Greater St. Louis, Missouri
c/o Karen Toal, Pres.
Depaul Univ. Public Sers. Graduate Prog.
25 E Jackson - 1250 O'Malley Bldg.
Chicago, IL 60604
Ph: (314)622-3200
Fax: (314)436-7405
E-mail: toalk@stlouiscity.com
URL: National Affiliate–www.ipma-hr.org
Contact: Karen Toal, Pres.
Local. Affiliated With: International Public Management Association for Human Resources.

992 ■ International Thomas Merton Society - Chicago, IL
c/o Michael A. Brennan
4527 N Melvina
Chicago, IL 60630-3013
E-mail: michaelbrennan@ameritech.net
URL: National Affiliate–www.merton.org
Contact: Michael A. Brennan, Contact

Local. Promotes the knowledge of the life and writings of Thomas Merton. Organizes retreats and conferences devoted to Merton and his works. Supports the general writing of general-interest and scholarly books and articles about Merton.

993 ■ International Trade Club of Chicago (ITCC)
PO Box 0638
Chicago, IL 60690-0638
Ph: (312)368-9197
Fax: (312)603-9971
E-mail: membership@itcc.org
URL: http://www.itcc.org
Contact: Sidney Salvadori, Pres.

Founded: 1919. **Members:** 500. **Membership Dues:** individual, $95 (annual) • corporate, $245 (annual) • diplomatic, $85 (annual) • academic/not-for-profit, $75 (annual) • student, $50 (annual). **Staff:** 1. Individuals who are involved in international export and import operations for their firms; representatives of allied service fields. Fosters and seeks to expand international business by removing barriers that may interfere with its development and by providing members with a medium for the discussion of problems and sharing of experience. Promotes a better understanding of U.S. foreign policy and its impact on international business. Conducts trade development and professional training programs, including the monthly ITCC Import Workshop series and the Global Manufacturing Series; conducts seminars on current trade issues, industry sectors, world markets; holds business networking events 4-5 times a year. **Additional Websites:** http://www.itcc-tma.org. **Committees:** Export Expansion; Export Managers Council; Import; International Finance; International Liaison; Publications; Transportation. **Formerly:** (1957) Export Managers Club of Chicago; (1980) International Trade Club of Chicago; (1981) International Business Council; (1987) International Business Council Midamerica. **Publications:** *ITCC Trade News*, annual. Membership Directory. **Price:** $75.00 • *ITCC Trade Report*, monthly. Newsletter. Explores trade issues, spotlighting specific industries, regions, upcoming events and member companies. **Price:** included in membership dues. Alternate Formats: online • Membership Directory. **Price:** $75.00. Alternate Formats: online. **Conventions/Meetings:** annual Chicago World Trade Conference - meeting.

994 ■ International Union of Elevator Constructors, Local 2 - Chicago, Illinois
300 S Ashland Blvd., Ste.308
Chicago, IL 60607
Ph: (312)421-1440
Fax: (312)421-7143
Free: (800)446-IUEC
E-mail: iueclu2@aol.com
URL: http://www.iueclocal2.com
Contact: John Valone, Pres.

Members: 1,645. **Local**. Encourages a higher standard of skill among its members. Cultivates a feeling of friendship among the craft. Obtains and maintains a fair standard of wages and assists members in securing employment. Engages in cultural, civic, legislative, fraternal, educational, charitable, welfare, social and other activities. **Affiliated With:** International Union of Elevator Constructors.

995 ■ International Union of Operating Engineers, Local 143
447 W 31st St.
Chicago, IL 60616
Ph: (312)326-1430 (312)326-0548
Fax: (312)326-6928
E-mail: biacullo@local143.org
URL: http://www.local143.org
Contact: William E. Iacullo, Pres.

Local. AFL-CIO. **Affiliated With:** International Union of Operating Engineers.

996 ■ International Union of Operating Engineers, Local 399
c/o Brian E. Hickey, Pres./Business Mgr.
763 W Jackson Blvd.
Chicago, IL 60661-5411
Ph: (312)372-9870
Fax: (312)372-7055
E-mail: fanning@fan.net
URL: http://www.iuoe399.org
Contact: Brian E. Hickey, Pres./Business Mgr.

Local. Works to bring economic justice to the workplace and to improve the lives of working families. **Affiliated With:** International Union of Operating Engineers.

997 ■ Investment Analysts Society of Chicago (IASC)
307 N Michigan Ave., Ste.800
Chicago, IL 60601
Ph: (312)360-0382
Fax: (312)360-0388
E-mail: info@iaschicago.org
Contact: Barbara Boden, Chief Operating Officer

Local. Security and financial analyst association whose members are practicing investment analysts. Promotes education, uniform performance presentation standards, improved accounting and disclosure of corporate information, and development of improved standards of investment research and portfolio management. **Affiliated With:** CFA Institute.

998 ■ IPMA-HR Chicago Chapter
c/o Adele De Mooy, Pres.
Metropolitan Water Reclamation District
111 E Erie
Chicago, IL 60611
Ph: (312)751-5174
Fax: (312)751-5171
E-mail: adele.demooy@mwrd.org
URL: National Affiliate–www.ipma-hr.org
Contact: Adele De Mooy, Pres.

Local. Seeks to improve human resource practices in government through provision of testing services, advisory service, conferences, professional development programs, research and publications. Sponsors seminars, conferences and workshops on various phases of public personnel administration.

999 ■ IPMA-HR Greater St. Louis, Missouri Chapter
c/o Karen Toal, Pres.
Depaul Univ. Public Sers. Graduate Prog.
25 E Jackson, 1250 O'Malley Bldg.
Chicago, IL 60604
Ph: (314)622-3200
Fax: (314)436-7405
E-mail: toalk@stlouiscity.com
URL: National Affiliate–www.ipma-hr.org
Contact: Karen Toal, Pres.

Local. Seeks to improve human resource practices in government through provision of testing services, advisory service, conferences, professional development programs, research and publications. Sponsors seminars, conferences and workshops on various phases of public personnel administration.

1000 ■ Irish-America Alliance
11134 S Western Ave.
Chicago, IL 60643
Ph: (773)233-5040
Local.

1001 ■ Jackson Park Yacht Club of Chicago (JPYC)
6400 S Promontory Dr.
Chicago, IL 60649
Ph: (773)684-5522
Fax: (773)684-1505
URL: http://www.jacksonparkyachtclub.org
Contact: Stanley L. Hill, Commodore
Local.

1002 ■ Jane Austen Society of North America, Greater Chicago Region (JASNA-GCR)
c/o Jane Davis, Treas.
345 W Fullerton Pkwy., No. 1703
Chicago, IL 60614
Ph: (773)665-1108
E-mail: jasnagcr@sbcglobal.net
URL: http://www.jasnailin.org
Contact: Linda Relias, Outreach Chair

Local. Writers, scholars, educators, and other individuals interested in the life and works of Jane Austen (1775-1817), English novelist. Encourages interest in Austen. **Affiliated With:** Jane Austen Society of North America. **Formerly:** (2006) Jane Austen Society of North America, Illinois / Northern Indiana.

1003 ■ Jefferson Park Chamber of Commerce
4849 N Milwaukee Ave., Ste.305
Chicago, IL 60630-2171
Ph: (773)736-6697
Fax: (773)736-3508
E-mail: carol@jeffersonpark.net
URL: http://www.jeffersonpark.net
Contact: Carol Gawron, Exec.Dir.

Founded: 1934. **Membership Dues:** business, $100-$250 (annual) • nonprofit organization, $100 (annual) • financial institution/major contributor, $250 (annual). **Local**. Helps maintain the viability of the community through promotion and development of business in Jefferson Park. **Publications:** Membership Directory, annual. **Advertising:** accepted. Alternate Formats: online • Newsletter, monthly. Alternate Formats: online. **Conventions/Meetings:** monthly General Business Meetings - every 2nd Tuesday.

1004 ■ Jewish Broadcasting Network Corporation
c/o George D. Hanus
333 W Wacker Dr., Ste.2750
Chicago, IL 60606-1290
Ph: (312)332-4172
Fax: (312)332-2119
E-mail: info@jewishbroadcasting.org
URL: http://www.jewishbroadcasting.org
Contact: Mayrav Newman, Exec.Dir.
Languages: English, Hebrew. **Local**.

1005 ■ Jewish Children's Bureau of Chicago
c/o Yael Reinhold, System of Care Supervisor
216 W Jackson Blvd., Ste.800
Chicago, IL 60606
Ph: (312)444-2090
Fax: (312)855-3754
E-mail: soc@jcbchicago.org
URL: http://www.jcbchicago.org
Local.

1006 ■ Jewish Community Centers Endowment Foundation
c/o David S. Rosen
1 S Franklin St., Ste.2150
Chicago, IL 60606-4609
Ph: (312)357-4700
Fax: (312)855-3283
URL: http://www.gojcc.org
Local.

1007 ■ Jewish Council on Urban Affairs (JCUA)
c/o Molly Bougearel
618 S Michigan Ave., Ste.700
Chicago, IL 60605

Ph: (312)663-0960
Fax: (312)663-5305
E-mail: jcuamail@jcua.org
URL: http://www.jcua.org
Founded: 1964. **Local**.

1008 ■ Jewish United Fund/Jewish Federation of Metropolitan Chicago (JUF/JF)
Ben Gurion Way
1 S Franklin St.
Chicago, IL 60606-4594
Ph: (312)346-6700
URL: http://www.juf.org
Contact: Steven B. Nasatir PhD, Pres.
Founded: 1900. **Members:** 50,000. **Staff:** 150. **Budget:** $85,000,000. **State**. Allocates funds received from the Jewish United Fund, United Way, and other sources to benefit social welfare, health, and education agencies in Chicago, Israel, and in Jewish communities worldwide. **Publications:** *JUF News*, monthly. Newsletter. **Price:** for members. **Circulation:** 50,000. **Advertising:** accepted • Annual Report. **Conventions/Meetings:** annual United Jewish Communities General Assembly (exhibits) - November.

1009 ■ Jobs For Youth/Chicago
50 E Washington St., Fourth Fl.
Chicago, IL 60602-2100
Ph: (312)499-4778
Fax: (312)499-4772
E-mail: info@jfychicago.org
URL: http://www.jfychicago.org
Contact: Robert Barnett, Exec.Dir.
Local.

1010 ■ Junior Achievement of Chicago
c/o Richard W. Ashley, Exec.VP
651 W Washington Blvd., Ste.404
Chicago, IL 60661
Ph: (312)715-1300
Fax: (312)715-0694
URL: http://www.jachicago.org
Contact: W. James Farrell, Chm.
Local. Works to educate and inspire young people to value free enterprise, business and economics to improve the quality of their lives.

1011 ■ Juvenile Diabetes Research Foundation Illinois
500 N Dearborn, Ste.305
Chicago, IL 60610
Ph: (312)670-0313
Fax: (312)670-0250
Free: (800)JDF-CURE
E-mail: afranze@jdrf.org
URL: http://www.jdrfillinois.org
Contact: Amy Franze, Exec.Dir.
Founded: 1974. **Members:** 28,000. **Membership Dues:** regular, $25 (annual). **Staff:** 12. **Budget:** $10,000,000. **Local**. Diabetic children, their families, and others interested in supporting diabetes research. Promotes fundraising activities for diabetes research and supports diabetic children. **Awards:** Man/Woman of the Year. **Frequency:** annual. **Type:** recognition. **Recipient:** for significant contributions to the community/diabetes issues. **Boards:** Medical Advisory. **Committees:** Volunteer. **Affiliated With:** Juvenile Diabetes Research Foundation International. **Formed by Merger of:** Juvenile Diabetes Foundation of Illinois; Juvenile Diabetes Foundation, Chicago Metro Chapter. **Formerly:** (2000) Juvenile Diabetes Foundation of Greater Chicago; (2002) Juvenile Diabetes Research Foundation of Greater Chicago. **Publications:** *JDRF News*, 3/year. Newsletter. **Price:** included in membership dues. **Circulation:** 30,000. Alternate Formats: online • Magazine, quarterly.

1012 ■ Keyhole Players
c/o Matthew David
2003 W Warner, 1st Fl.
Chicago, IL 60618-3029
Ph: (773)525-3683 (773)517-2950
E-mail: keyholeplayers@excite.com
URL: http://www.keyholeplayers.homestead.com/
Contact: Matthew David, Exec.Dir.
Founded: 1999. **Staff:** 4. **Budget:** $11,000. **Local**. Aims to produce plays that explore life by looking "through the keyhole" to obtain an honest perspective on social interaction; seeks to create emotionally and intellectually accessible theater.

1013 ■ Killerspin Multiplex Table Tennis Club
Union Sta. Multiplex
444 W Jackson Blvd.
Chicago, IL 60606
Ph: (312)441-0124
E-mail: rblackwell@killerspin.com
URL: http://www.killerspin.com
Contact: Robert Blackwell Jr., Contact
Local. **Affiliated With:** U.S.A. Table Tennis.

1014 ■ Korean American Merchants Association of Chicago
c/o Seoul Consulting Co.
4404 W Lawrence Ave., Ste.202
Chicago, IL 60630-2513
Ph: (773)685-5551
Local.

1015 ■ Korean War Veterans Association, Greater Chicago Chapter
c/o Niels Larsen
5347 W Waveland Ave.
Chicago, IL 60641-3354
Ph: (773)545-4379
E-mail: niels5347@earthlink.net
URL: National Affiliate–www.kwva.org
Contact: Niels Larsen, Contact
Local. **Affiliated With:** Korean War Veterans Association.

1016 ■ Labor and Employment Relations Association, Chicago
c/o Cathy Kwiatkowski
815 W Van Buren St., No. 214
Chicago, IL 60607
Ph: (312)996-2623
Fax: (312)413-2997
E-mail: cathyk@uic.edu
URL: http://www.lera.uiuc.edu/chapters/Profiles/IL-Chicago.html
Contact: Patricia Simpson, Pres.
Local.

1017 ■ Lake View East Chamber of Commerce (LVECC)
3138 N Broadway
Chicago, IL 60657-5316
Ph: (773)348-8608
Fax: (773)348-7409
E-mail: info@lakevieweast.com
URL: http://www.lakevieweast.com
Contact: Maureen Martino, Exec.Dir.
Membership Dues: business (based on number of employees), $125-$500. **Staff:** 2. **Local**. Promotes business and community development in the Lakeview area of Chicago. **Telecommunication Services:** electronic mail, maureen@lakevieweast.com. **Formerly:** (1999) Lakeview Chamber of Commerce. **Publications:** *Chamber Report*, monthly. Newsletter. Alternate Formats: online • *Lakeview Directory & Neighborhood Guide*, annual • *Official Guide to Lakeview East*, annual. Handbook. Includes membership directory. **Advertising:** accepted.

1018 ■ Lakeview Action Coalition (LAC)
3225 N Sheffield Ave.
Chicago, IL 60657-2210
Ph: (773)549-1947
Fax: (773)549-4639
E-mail: jenrg@lakeviewaction.org
URL: http://www.lakeviewaction.org
Contact: Jennifer Ritter-Gonzalez, Exec.Dir.
Founded: 1993. **Members:** 40. **Local**. Develops leaders through training, action and reflection. **Affiliated With:** National People's Action.

1019 ■ Landmarks Preservation Council of Illinois (LPCI)
53 W Jackson Blvd., Ste.1315
Chicago, IL 60604
Ph: (312)922-1742
Fax: (312)922-8112
E-mail: mail@lpci.org
URL: http://www.landmarks.org
Contact: David Bahlman, Pres.
Founded: 1971. **Local**.

1020 ■ Lane Tech - Young Life
2170 W Warner
Chicago, IL 60618
Ph: (773)327-5262
URL: http://whereis.younglife.org/FriendlyUrlRedirector.aspx?ID=C-826
Local.

1021 ■ LaSalle Street Young Lives - YoungLives
1111 N Wells St., Ste.402
Chicago, IL 60610
Ph: (312)573-8918
URL: http://whereis.younglife.org/FriendlyUrlRedirector.aspx?ID=C-813
Local.

1022 ■ Lawndale Christian Development Corporation
c/o Arthur Turner, Pres.
3843 W Ogden Ave.
Chicago, IL 60623-2451
Ph: (773)762-8889
Fax: (773)762-8893
E-mail: ebrooks@lcdc.net
URL: http://www.lcdc.net
Local.

1023 ■ Lawyers' Committee for Better Housing (LCBH)
c/o Kathleen Clark, J.D., Exec.Dir.
220 S State St., Ste.1700
Chicago, IL 60604
Ph: (312)347-7600
Fax: (312)347-7604
E-mail: lcbhoffice@sbcglobal.net
URL: http://www.lcbh.org
Contact: Kathleen Clark J.D., Exec.Dir.
Local.

1024 ■ League of Women Voters of Chicago
332 S Michigan Ave., Ste.1050
Chicago, IL 60604
Ph: (312)939-5935
E-mail: info@lwvchicago.org
URL: http://www.lwvchicago.org
Local. **Affiliated With:** League of Women Voters of the United States.

1025 ■ League of Women Voters of Cook County (LWVCC)
332 S Michigan, Ste.1050
Chicago, IL 60604
Ph: (312)939-5935
E-mail: info@cookcounty.il.lwvnet.org
URL: http://cookcounty.il.lwvnet.org
Local. **Affiliated With:** League of Women Voters of the United States.

1026 ■ League of Women Voters of Illinois (LWVIL)
332 S Michigan Ave., Ste.1050
Chicago, IL 60604
Ph: (312)939-5935
Fax: (312)939-6887
E-mail: info@lwvil.org
URL: http://www.lwvil.org
Contact: Barbara G. Lippai, Pres.
Founded: 1920. **Members:** 4,500. **Membership Dues:** individual, family, student, $50 (annual). **Staff:** 4. **Local Groups:** 59. **State**. Individuals promoting political responsibility through an informed electorate. Sponsors League of Women Voters of Illinois Education Fund. Encourages the informed and active

participation of citizens in government and works to influence public policy through education and advocacy. Supports no candidates for elected office; acts on issues after study and consensus. **Affiliated With:** League of Women Voters of the United States. **Publications:** *Illinois Voter*, quarterly. Newsletter. **Circulation:** 5,500 • *Legislative Directory*, semiannual • *Making Your Voice Hear: How You Can Influence Government*. Pamphlet • *Running for Office*. Booklet • *Where We Stand: 2001-2003 Program*, semiannual. Booklet. **Conventions/Meetings:** biennial convention - odd-numbered years at the state level; even-numbered years at the national level • annual meeting.

1027 ■ Levy Cares
c/o Lawrence F. Levy
980 N Michigan Ave., Ste.400
Chicago, IL 60611-4518
Ph: (312)664-8200
Fax: (312)280-2739
URL: http://www.levyrestaurant.com
Contact: Natasha Bergeron, Dir.
Local.

1028 ■ Libertarian Party of Chicago (LPC)
PO Box 1746
Chicago, IL 60690-1746
Ph: (312)409-2223
Free: (877)LPC-VOTE
E-mail: chair@lpchicago.org
URL: http://www.lpchicago.org
Local. Affiliated With: Libertarian National Committee.

1029 ■ Licensed Practical Nurses Association of Illinois (LPNAI)
c/o Marie Burris, Pres.
8741 S Greenwood Ave., No. 207
Chicago, IL 60619-7018
Ph: (773)928-8942
E-mail: hojpha@aol.com
URL: National Affiliate–www.nflpn.org
Contact: Marie Burris, Pres.
Founded: 1949. **Members:** 750. **Membership Dues:** student, $17 (annual) • per capita, $80 (annual) • retired, $51 (annual). **Staff:** 1. **State Groups:** 1. **Local Groups:** 25. **State**. Professional organization of licensed practical and vocational nurses. Holds workshops. **Awards:** Educator of the Year. **Frequency:** annual. **Type:** recognition • Student of the Year. **Frequency:** annual. **Type:** recognition. **Affiliated With:** National Federation of Licensed Practical Nurses. **Publications:** *News and Views*, quarterly. Newsletter. **Advertising:** accepted • Yearbook. **Conventions/Meetings:** annual convention, with educational programs.

1030 ■ Lincoln Park Chamber of Commerce
2534 N Lincoln Ave., Ste.301
Chicago, IL 60614-2354
Ph: (773)880-5200
Fax: (773)880-0266
E-mail: info@lincolnparkchamber.com
URL: http://www.lincolnparkchamber.com
Contact: Kim Klausmeier, Pres./CEO
Founded: 1947. **Members:** 550. **Membership Dues:** business (with 1-5 employees), $200 (annual) • business (with 6-25 employees), $250 (annual) • business (with 26-50 employees), $340 (annual) • business (with 51-100 employees), $505 (annual) • business (with 101 or more employees), $670 (annual) • associate, $75 (annual). **Local**. Works to develop and implement membership services and provides essential information. Advocates for the protection and advancement of economic and business development. Promotes the Lincoln Park area and its businesses. Encourages relationships and communication between and among the community and its governmental bodies. **Computer Services:** database, database of available properties • online services, membership listings. **Committees:** Ambassador; Economic and Business Development; Government and Community Affairs; Human Services; Marketing; Membership Outreach. **Task Forces:** Affinity Programs; Service Assessment. **Publications:** *Resident's Guide to Lincoln Park*. Handbook. **Circulation:** 15,000. **Advertising:** accepted • *The Source*, bimonthly. Newsletter. Contains information on business issues and upcoming programs. **Advertising:** accepted. Alternate Formats: online • Membership Directory, annual. Contains listing of members.

1031 ■ Lincoln Park Zoo
2001 N Clark St.
Chicago, IL 60614
Ph: (312)742-2000
E-mail: webmaster@lpzoo.org
URL: http://www.lpzoo.com
Contact: Rebecca Severson, Contact
Founded: 1868. **Local. Formerly:** (2005) Lincoln Park Zoological Society.

1032 ■ Literacy Chicago
17 N State St., Ste.900
Chicago, IL 60602
Ph: (312)870-1100
Fax: (312)870-4488
E-mail: info@literacychicago.org
URL: http://www.literacychicago.org
Contact: Susan D. Kidder M.Ed., Exec.Dir.
Founded: 1992. **Staff:** 13. **Budget:** $750,000. **Local.** Works to improve the literacy skills of Chicago area adults and their families. Conducts programs including Adult Literacy, Adult Basic Education, GED Preparation, Family Literacy, English as a Second Language, Workplace Literacy, Employability Skills Training, Computer Assisted Instruction, EL Civics, and Reach Out and Read. Provides services through credentialed staff and trained volunteer tutors. **Libraries: Type:** reference. **Holdings:** 1,000. **Affiliated With:** Literacy Chicago; ProLiteracy Worldwide. **Formerly:** (1992) Literacy Volunteers of America, Chicago Chapter. **Publications:** *Bookmarks*, quarterly. Newsletter. Alternate Formats: online • *Notes*, monthly. Newsletter. Alternate Formats: online • *Reads*, 3/year. Newsletter. Alternate Formats: online • *Words on Page*, quarterly. Journal. Alternate Formats: online • Annual Report, annual.

1033 ■ Literacy Volunteers of Illinois (LVI)
30 E Adams, Ste.1130
Chicago, IL 60603
Ph: (312)857-1582
Fax: (312)857-1586
E-mail: info@lvillinois.org
URL: http://literacyvolunteersillinois.org
Contact: Dorothy M. Miaso, Exec.Dir.
Founded: 1979. **State**. Develops and supports volunteer literacy programs that help families, adults and out-of-school teens increase their literacy skills. **Affiliated With:** ProLiteracy Worldwide.

1034 ■ Little Village Environmental Justice Organization
c/o John Chavez-Pedersen
2856 S Millard
Chicago, IL 60623-4550
Ph: (773)762-6991
Fax: (773)762-6993
Contact: Kim Wasserman, Coor.
Local.

1035 ■ Loyola Association for Computing Machinery (ACM)
c/o Muhamad Krad, Chm.
6525 N Sheridan Rd. Box No. 5
Assn. for Computing Machinery
Chicago, IL 60626
Ph: (312)915-7979
Fax: (312)508-2123
E-mail: loyola@yahoo.com
Contact: Muhamad Krad, Chm.
Local. Biological, medical, behavioral, and computer scientists; hospital administrators; programmers and others interested in application of computer methods to biological, behavioral, and medical problems. Stimulates understanding of the use and potential of computers in the Biosciences. **Affiliated With:** Association for Computing Machinery.

1036 ■ Lupus Support Group, Logan County
Illinois Chap. of the Lupus Foundation of Am.
20 E Jackson, Ste.1150
Chicago, IL 60604
Ph: (312)542-0002
Fax: (312)542-0003
Free: (800)2LU-PUS2
E-mail: info@lupusil.org
URL: http://www.lupusil.org
Contact: Mrs. Jean Malloy, Interim Exec.Dir.
Founded: 1973. **Members:** 5,000. **Membership Dues:** individual, $35 (annual). **Staff:** 6. **Budget:** $350,000. **State Groups:** 1. **Languages:** English, Spanish. **State**. Assist members and lupus survivors across the state of Illinois. Also sponsors educational meetings, support groups, advocacy efforts, and a toll-free hotline where free information is dispensed along with comforting words of hope.

1037 ■ Make-A-Wish Foundation of Northern Illinois (MAW)
c/o Stephanie Springs, CEO
640 N LaSalle, Ste.280
Chicago, IL 60610
Ph: (312)602-9474
Fax: (312)943-9813
Free: (800)978-9474
E-mail: springs@wishes.org
URL: http://www.wishes.org
Contact: Stephanie Springs, CEO
Founded: 1985. **Staff:** 15. **Budget:** $4,300,000. **Languages:** English, Polish, Spanish. **Local**. Works to fulfill the wishes of children between the ages of 2 1/2 and 18 battling terminal and life-threatening illnesses. **Affiliated With:** Make-A-Wish Foundation of America. **Publications:** *Wishes*, quarterly. Newsletter. Highlights wishes fulfilled and funds raised. **Price:** free. **Circulation:** 35,000. **Conventions/Meetings:** annual National Make-A-Wish Conference - always October.

1038 ■ Math Energy Club of Eastern Illinois University
c/o Mallory Bourke, Representative
10734 S Albany
Chicago, IL 60655
Ph: (708)258-6021
E-mail: bordenk1@aol.com
URL: http://www.eiu.edu/~mathnrgy
Contact: Krissi Borden, Pres.
Local. Aims to improve the teaching and learning of mathematics. Provides vision, leadership and professional development to support teachers in ensuring mathematics learning of the highest quality for all students. **Affiliated With:** National Council of Teachers of Mathematics.

1039 ■ Mathematics Teachers' Association of Chicago and Vicinity
c/o Patrick Fowler, Membership Chm.
9045 S Claremont Ave.
Chicago, IL 60620-6123
E-mail: vande@math.luc.edu
URL: http://www1.math.luc.edu/~mta
Contact: Patrick Fowler, Membership Chm.
Local. Aims to improve the teaching and learning of mathematics. Provides vision, leadership and professional development to support teachers in ensuring mathematics learning of the highest quality for all students. **Affiliated With:** National Council of Teachers of Mathematics.

1040 ■ Maxwell Street Historic Preservation Coalition
c/o Charles K. Cowdery
PMB No. 298, 3712 N Broadway
Chicago, IL 60613-4198
Ph: (773)477-9691
E-mail: cowdery@ix.netcom.com
URL: http://www.maxwellstreet.org
Contact: Charles Cowdery, Pres.
Founded: 1994. **Local**. All volunteer organization that seeks to preserve, study, and celebrate the heritage of the Maxwell Street district in Chicago, IL. Members include those with experience in architec-

ture, restoration, museum exhibits, urban planning, and entrepreneurial economics. Activities include advocacy, collecting documents and artifacts, giving tours, and film-making.

1041 ■ Meals on Wheels of Chicago
111 E Wacker Dr., Ste.2200
Chicago, IL 60601
Ph: (312)673-4411
E-mail: landerson@mealsonwheelschicago.org
URL: http://www.mealsonwheelschicago.org
Contact: Lyle Anderson, Contact
Local. Affiliated With: Meals on Wheels Association of America.

1042 ■ Mechanical Contractors Association Chicago
221 N LaSalle St., Ste.3400
Chicago, IL 60601
Ph: (312)384-1220
Fax: (312)384-1229
E-mail: staff@mca.org
URL: http://www.mca.org
Contact: Stephen L. Lamb, Exec.VP
Founded: 1888. **Members:** 50. **Staff:** 6. **Local.** Piping industry trade association for mechanical contractors. **Affiliated With:** Mechanical Contractors Association of America. **Publications:** *Pipeline*, bimonthly. Newsletter. **Conventions/Meetings:** annual conference.

1043 ■ Media Communications Association International, Chicago
333 N Michigan Ave., No. 932
Chicago, IL 60601
Ph: (630)789-9614
E-mail: cunninghamprod@sbcglobal.net
URL: http://www.mcaichicago.com
Contact: Jim Cunningham, Pres.
Membership Dues: associate, $80 (annual). **Local.** Provides networking and education opportunities to media communications professionals. Facilitates effective communication using new technology and with sound communication principles. **Affiliated With:** Chemical Coaters Association International. **Publications:** *Chicago Chapter News*, monthly. Newsletter. **Circulation:** 400. Alternate Formats: online.

1044 ■ Mediation Council of Illinois
c/o Sharon Walsh
3540 N. Southport, No. 453
Chicago, IL 60657
Ph: (312)641-3000
Fax: (847)462-0385
E-mail: bensharonlucysally@comcast.net
URL: http://MediationCouncilofIllinois.org
Contact: Hon. Benjamin Mackoff, Pres.
State.

1045 ■ Mental Health Association in Illinois (MHAI)
70 E Lake St., Ste.900
Chicago, IL 60601
Ph: (312)368-9070
Fax: (312)368-0283
URL: http://www.mhai.org
Contact: Caryn Curry, Contact
State. Seeks to promote mental health and prevent mental health disorders. Improves mental health of Americans through advocacy, public education, research and service. **Affiliated With:** National Mental Health Association.

1046 ■ Metropolitan Mayors Caucus
c/o David E. Bennett, Exec.Dir.
177 N State St., Ste.500
Chicago, IL 60601
Ph: (312)201-4505
Fax: (312)553-4355
E-mail: dbennett@mayorscaucus.org
URL: http://www.mayorscaucus.org
Contact: David E. Bennett, Exec.Dir.
Local.

1047 ■ Metropolitan Planning Council (MPC)
25 E Washington St., Ste.1600
Chicago, IL 60602
Ph: (312)922-5616
Fax: (312)922-5619
E-mail: info@metroplanning.org
URL: http://www.metroplanning.org
Contact: Ms. MarySue Barrett, Pres.
Founded: 1934. **Members:** 750. **Membership Dues:** individual/corporate, $50 (annual) • senior, student, $30 (annual). **Staff:** 20. **Budget:** $3,109,728. **Languages:** English, Spanish. **Regional. Libraries: Type:** not open to the public. **Holdings:** archival material, articles, books, business records, papers, reports. **Awards:** Burnham Award for Excellence in Planning. **Frequency:** annual. **Type:** monetary. **Recipient:** for innovative and visionary planning efforts in the Chicago metropolitan region. **Committees:** Housing; Regional Development; Transportation; Urban Development. **Conventions/Meetings:** annual luncheon.

1048 ■ Mid-America International Agri-Trade Council (MIATCO)
309 W Washington St., Ste.600
Chicago, IL 60606
Ph: (312)334-9200
Fax: (312)334-9230
E-mail: info@miatco.org
URL: http://www.miatco.org
Contact: Tim Hamilton, Exec.Dir.
Founded: 1969. **Members:** 12. **Staff:** 9. **Regional.** Promotes exports of value added food and agriculture products from Midwestern states. **Publications:** *Global Food Marketer*, bimonthly. Newsletter. Provides export news and information for Midwestern food and agricultural companies. **Price:** free. **Circulation:** 5,000. **Advertising:** accepted.

1049 ■ Mid-South Planning and Development Commission
c/o Mary Steward, Exec.Dir.
4309 S King Dr.
Chicago, IL 60653
Ph: (773)924-1330
Fax: (773)924-3151
E-mail: smidsouth@aol.com
Contact: Mary Steward, Exec.Dir.
Founded: 1993. **Members:** 300. **Membership Dues:** non resident, $25 • resident, $15 (annual). **Staff:** 7. **Local.** Works to improve and enhance the quality of life for residents of the Bronzeville community. **Publications:** *Mid-South Strategic Development Plan*. **Price:** $20.00.

1050 ■ Middle-Atlantic Wholesalers Association
PO Box 3310
Chicago, IL 60654-3310
Ph: (312)464-0314
Fax: (312)464-0091
Free: (800)464-0314
Local.

1051 ■ Midwest Aikido Center (MAC)
4349 N Damen Ave.
Chicago, IL 60618
Ph: (773)477-0123
Fax: (773)477-0449
E-mail: info@midwestaikidocenter.org
URL: http://www.aikidomac.org
Contact: Arthur Wise, Instructor
Local. Affiliated With: United States Aikido Federation.

1052 ■ Midwest Aikido Federation
Midwest Aikido Center
4349 N Damen Ave.
Chicago, IL 60618
Ph: (773)477-0123
URL: http://www.usaikifed.com
Regional. Affiliated With: United States Aikido Federation.

1053 ■ Midwest Antiquarian Booksellers Association (MWABA)
1759 Rosehill Dr.
Chicago, IL 60660
Ph: (773)989-2200
Fax: (773)989-7599
E-mail: info@midwestbookhunters.org
URL: http://www.midwestbookhunters.org
Contact: Joycelyn Merchant, Coor.
Founded: 1971. **Members:** 130. **Membership Dues:** business (with approval from board of directors), $60 (annual). **Regional.** Represents dealers in out-of-print, antiquarian, and rare books who desire to perform their tasks at a professional level. Promotes the love and appreciation of books, maps, prints, and ephemera among the general public. **Formerly:** (2006) Midwest Bookhunters. **Publications:** Newsletter, quarterly. **Conventions/Meetings:** Book Fairs - trade show - 3/year.

1054 ■ Midwest Business Travel Association
PO Box 81238
Chicago, IL 60681-0238
E-mail: grparker@atsohare-midway.com
URL: http://www.midwestbta.org
Contact: Guy Parker CMP, Pres.
Regional. Represents travel managers and providers. Promotes the value of the travel manager in meeting corporate travel needs and financial goals. Cultivates a positive public image of the corporate travel industry. Protects the interests of members and their corporations in legislative and regulatory matters. Promotes safety, security, efficiency and quality travel. Provides a forum for the exchange of information and ideas among members. **Affiliated With:** National Business Travel Association.

1055 ■ Midwest Decoy Collectors Association (MDCA)
6 E Scott St., No. 3
Chicago, IL 60610-2321
Ph: (312)337-7957 (847)842-8847
Fax: (312)337-9679
E-mail: hcdesch@rcn.com
URL: http://www.midwestdecoy.org
Contact: Herb Desch, Pres.
Founded: 1966. **Members:** 1,000. **Membership Dues:** regular, $15 (annual). Decoy collectors. Finds and preserves old decoys; identifies decoy carvers. Provides forum for buying and selling decoys among members. Conducts programs by individual members. **Libraries: Type:** reference; open to the public. **Telecommunication Services:** electronic mail, mdc@midwestdecoy.org. **Publications:** Membership Directory, annual. Lists all members and their collection interests. **Price:** included in membership dues. **Circulation:** 1,000. **Conventions/Meetings:** annual National Antique Decoy and Sporting Collectibles - lecture (exhibits) - always last full weekend in April.

1056 ■ Midwest Energy Efficiency Alliance (MEEA)
c/o Alecia Ward
1 E Erie, Ste.200
Chicago, IL 60611
Ph: (312)587-8390
Fax: (312)587-8391
E-mail: award@mwalliance.org
URL: http://www.mwalliance.org
Contact: Alecia Ward, Exec.Dir.
Founded: 1999. **Members:** 37. **Staff:** 7. **Budget:** $750,000. **Regional.**

1057 ■ Midwest Securities Transfer Association
c/o FirstEnergy Corp.
135 S La Salle St.
La Salle Bank NA
Chicago, IL 60603
Ph: (312)904-2553
Fax: (330)384-3866
E-mail: udoviche@firstenergycorp.com
Contact: Mr. Gregory Malatia, Pres.
Regional.

1058 ■ MIT Enterprise Forum of Chicago
c/o Peter Balbus, Chm.
191 N Wacker Dr., Ste.3700
Chicago, IL 60606
E-mail: info@mitefchicago.org
URL: http://www.mitefchicago.org
Contact: Peter Balbus, Chm.
Local. Promotes the establishment and growth of innovative technology companies through creative programs that educate and entertain entrepreneurs.

1059 ■ Mount Greenwood Chamber of Commerce
3052 W 111th St.
Chicago, IL 60655
Ph: (773)238-6103
Contact: Darlene Larsen, Exec.Dir.
Members: 84. **Local**. Promotes business and community development in the Mt. Greenwood area of Chicago, IL.

1060 ■ Mount Sinai Hospital
c/o Laura Roth
California Ave., 15th St.
Chicago, IL 60608
Ph: (773)542-2000
Fax: (773)257-6289
E-mail: rotl@sinai.org
URL: http://www.sinai.org
Contact: Laura Roth, Contact
Local. **Formerly:** (2005) Mount Sinai Medical Institute Council.

1061 ■ Muslim Students' Association - Loyola University of Chicago
c/o Jawad Pervez, Pres.
Loyola Univ. of Chicago
Dept. of Student Life
6525 N Sheridan Rd.
Chicago, IL 60626
Ph: (773)274-3000
E-mail: jpervez@luc.edu
URL: http://www.luc.edu/orgs/msa
Contact: Jawad Pervez, Pres.
Local. Muslim students in North America. Seeks to advance the interests of members; works to enable members to practice Islam as a complete way of life. **Affiliated With:** Muslim Students Association of the United States and Canada.

1062 ■ Muslim Students' Association - Northeastern Illinois University
c/o Br. Samir Mohammad, Pres.
Student Activities Off.
5500 N St. Louis Ave.
Chicago, IL 60625
Ph: (312)851-4672
Fax: (773)465-MSA5
E-mail: msa-l@neiu.edu
URL: http://www.neiu.edu/~msa/
Contact: Br. Samir Mohammad, Pres.
Regional. Muslim students. Seeks to advance the interests of members; works to enable members to practice Islam as a complete way of life. **Affiliated With:** Muslim Students Association of the United States and Canada.

1063 ■ NACE International, Chicago Section
c/o Sandra Sanchez, Vice Chair
Peoples Energy
1235 Kilbourn
Chicago, IL 60623
Ph: (773)542-7808
E-mail: sa.sanchez@pecorp.com
URL: National Affiliate–www.nace.org
Contact: Sandra Sanchez, Vice Chair
Local. Promotes public safety by advancing the knowledge of corrosion engineering and science. Works to raise awareness of corrosion control and prevention technology among government agencies and legislators, businesses, professional societies and the general public. **Affiliated With:** NACE International: The Corrosion Society.

1064 ■ NALS of Illinois
PO Box 1225
Chicago, IL 60690-1225
E-mail: info@nalsofillinois.org
URL: http://www.nalsofillinois.org
Contact: Alice Rose Stiegler, Pres.
State. Enhances the competencies and contributions of members in the legal services profession. Provides continuing legal education, certifications, information, and training to individuals in the legal services industry. **Affiliated With:** NALS, the Association for Legal Professionals.

1065 ■ NAMES Project Chicago
c/o Center on Halsted
2855 N Lincoln Ave.
Chicago, IL 60657
Ph: (773)472-6469
Fax: (773)472-3945
E-mail: names@centeronhalsted.org
URL: http://www.namesprojectchicago.org
Local. Sponsors Project CANVAS, Youth Council, Saturday Quilting Bees, and Speakers' Bureau. **Affiliated With:** Names Project Foundation - AIDS Memorial Quilt.

1066 ■ National Academy of Television Arts and Sciences, Chicago/Midwest Chapter
c/o Rebekah Cowing, Admin.Dir.
33 E Cong., Ste.505
Chicago, IL 60605
Ph: (312)435-1825
Fax: (312)435-1828
E-mail: infonatas@aol.com
URL: http://www.chicagoemmyonline.org
Contact: Rebekah Cowing, Admin.Dir.
Founded: 1958. **Membership Dues:** regular, $85 (annual) • student, $30 (annual). **Regional**. Promotes excellence in broadcasting. Inspires the next generation of broadcast journalists. Educates television viewers. **Awards:** Emmy Awards. **Frequency:** annual. **Type:** recognition. **Recipient:** for outstanding achievement in broadcasting • Silver Circle Awards Program. **Frequency:** annual. **Type:** recognition. **Recipient:** for significant contributions to Chicago/Midwest broadcasting. **Affiliated With:** National Academy of Television Arts and Sciences. **Publications:** Newsletter.

1067 ■ National Active And Retired Federal Employees Association - Downtown 1878
1122 N Clark St. Apt. 2606
Chicago, IL 60610-7888
Ph: (312)274-0166
URL: National Affiliate–www.narfe.org
Contact: Howard B. Ostmann, Contact
Local. Protects the retirement future of employees through education. Informs members on issues affecting the retirement. **Affiliated With:** National Association of Retired Federal Employees.

1068 ■ National Active And Retired Federal Employees Association - Joseph F.Gore 6
10050 S Carpenter St.
Chicago, IL 60643-2248
Ph: (773)445-5420
URL: National Affiliate–www.narfe.org
Contact: Emma J. Price, Contact
Local. Protects the retirement future of employees through education. Informs members on issues affecting the retirement. **Affiliated With:** National Association of Retired Federal Employees.

1069 ■ National Alliance for the Mentally Ill of Greater Chicago (NAMI-GC)
1536 W Chicago Ave.
Chicago, IL 60622
Ph: (312)563-0445
Fax: (312)563-0467
E-mail: namigc@aol.com
URL: http://www.namigc.org
Contact: Suzanne M. Andriukaitis MA, Exec.Dir.
Local. Strives to improve the quality of life of children and adults with severe mental illness through support, education, research and advocacy. **Affiliated With:** National Alliance for the Mentally Ill.

1070 ■ National Association for the Advancement of Colored People, Chicago Southside Branch
800 E 78th St.
Chicago, IL 60619
Ph: (773)487-9600
Fax: (773)487-9633
URL: http://www.chicagosouthsidenaacp.com
Contact: Phillip O'Bannon, Pres.
Local.

1071 ■ National Association of Artists' Organizations, Midwest
c/o Laura Weathered, Exec.Dir.
Near Northwest Arts Council
Acme Art Works
1741 N Western Ave.
Chicago, IL 60647
Ph: (773)278-7677
Fax: (773)278-8451
E-mail: nnwac@nnwac.org
URL: http://www.nnwac.org
Contact: Laura Weathered, Exec.Dir.
Founded: 1986. **Members:** 200. **Staff:** 2. **Budget:** $140,000. **Local**. Committed to sharing the power of creativity to build community. Provides affordable housing for artists at Acme Artists Community. Manages exhibit, studio and performance space at Acme Art Works, and works with artists of all media and disciplines to create a sustainable environment for creative work. **Affiliated With:** National Association of Artists' Organizations.

1072 ■ National Association of Asian American Professionals, Chicago Chapter
PO Box 81138
Chicago, IL 60681
Ph: (773)918-2454
URL: http://www.naaapchicago.org
Contact: Mitch Schneider, Pres.
Local. Enhances the leadership and professional development of Asian Americans in their careers and in the community. Raises awareness of Asian Americans in corporate America. Seeks to ensure that Asian Americans are included in diversity programs. **Affiliated With:** National Association of Asian American Professionals.

1073 ■ National Association of Black Journalists - Chicago Chapter
PO Box 811132
Chicago, IL 60681
Ph: (773)779-6936
E-mail: nabjchicagochapter1@yahoo.com
URL: National Affiliate–www.nabj.org
Contact: Brenda Butler, Pres.
Local. Advocates the rights of black journalists. Provides informational and training services and professional development to black journalists and to the general public. **Affiliated With:** National Association of Black Journalists.

1074 ■ National Association of Corporate Directors, Chicago Chapter
c/o Michele Hooper, Pres.
875 N Michigan Ave., Ste.2314
Chicago, IL 60610
Ph: (312)335-0871
E-mail: president@chicagonacd.org
URL: http://www.chicagonacd.org
Contact: Michele Hooper, Pres.
Local. **Affiliated With:** National Association of Corporate Directors.

1075 ■ National Association of Industrial and Office Properties, Chicago Chapter
c/o Jack Durburg
CB Richard Ellis, Inc.
311 S Wacker Dr., Ste.400
Chicago, IL 60606

Ph: (312)935-1418
Fax: (312)935-1429
E-mail: jack.durburg@cbre.com
URL: http://www.naiopchicago.org
Contact: Mr. Jack Durburg, Pres.
Members: 300. **Local**. Represents the interests of developers and owners of industrial, office and related commercial estate. Provides communication, networking, business opportunities and a forum to its members. Promotes effective public policy to create, protect and enhance property values. **Awards:** Awards for Excellence. **Frequency:** annual. **Type:** recognition. **Recipient:** for outstanding achievement in industrial and office real estate in the Chicagoland area. **Computer Services:** database, membership directory. **Committees:** Awards for Excellence; Legislative Affairs; Programming; Sponsorship. **Subcommittees:** Nominations. **Affiliated With:** National Association of Industrial and Office Properties. **Conventions/Meetings:** monthly meeting - 4th Thursday of each month.

1076 ■ National Association of Investors Corporation, Greater North Suburban Chapter
PO Box 31943
Chicago, IL 60631
Ph: (847)562-9703
E-mail: dormie@ameritech.net
URL: http://better-investing.org/chapter/gnsuburban
Contact: Dawn Williams, Pres.
Local. Teaches individuals how to become successful strategic long-term investors. Provides highly focused learning resources and investment tools that empower individuals to become better investors. **Affiliated With:** National Association of Investors Corporation.

1077 ■ National Association of Social Workers, Illinois Chapter (NASW-IL)
180 N Michigan Ave., Ste.400
Chicago, IL 60601
Ph: (312)236-8308
Fax: (312)236-8410
Free: (877)9NA-SWIL
E-mail: office@naswil.org
URL: http://www.naswil.org
Contact: Joel L. Rubin, Exec.Dir.
Founded: 1955. **Members:** 8,600. **Membership Dues:** individual, $178 (annual). **Staff:** 7. **Budget:** $675,000. **Local Groups:** 9. **State**. Social workers united to advance the profession of social work. **Awards:** Legislator of the Year. **Frequency:** annual. **Type:** recognition • Lifetime Achievement. **Frequency:** annual. **Type:** recognition • Public Citizen of the Year. **Frequency:** annual. **Type:** recognition • Social Worker of the Year. **Frequency:** annual. **Type:** recognition. **Committees:** Conference; Legislative/Social Policy; Nominations & Leadership Identity; Political Action; Racial and Ethnic Diversity. **Task Forces:** Media; Mental Health. **Affiliated With:** National Association of Social Workers. **Publications:** *Networker*, 10/year. Newsletter. **Price:** $40.00 for nonmembers; included in membership dues. **Advertising:** accepted. **Conventions/Meetings:** Statewide Annual Conference (exhibits).

1078 ■ National Association of Urban Debate Leagues (NAUDL)
c/o Les Lynn, Exec.Dir.
332 S Michigan Ave., Ste.500
Chicago, IL 60604
Ph: (312)427-8101 (312)898-8101
Fax: (312)427-6130
E-mail: leslynn@urbandebate.org
URL: http://www.urbandebate.org
Regional. Exists to improve urban public education by empowering youth to become engaged learners, critical thinkers, and active citizens who are effective advocates for themselves and their communities.

1079 ■ National Council of La Raza-Midwest
c/o Jode Ocampo
203 N Wabash Ave., Ste.918
Chicago, IL 60601
Ph: (312)269-9250
Fax: (312)269-9260
Free: (800)311-NCLR
E-mail: jocampo@nclr.org
URL: http://www.nclr.org
Contact: Jode Ocampo, Office Mgr.
Local.

1080 ■ National Exchange Carrier Association, Midwest
c/o Teri Kessler, Dir.
8755 W Higgins Rd., Ste.1050
Chicago, IL 60631-2702
Ph: (773)693-3210
Fax: (800)323-8402
Free: (800)323-4953
E-mail: tkessle@neca.org
URL: National Affiliate–www.neca.org
Contact: Teri Kessler, Dir.
Regional. **Affiliated With:** National Exchange Carrier Association.

1081 ■ National Forum for Black Public Administrators, Illinois Chapter
c/o Darnetta K. Tyus, Exec.Asst. to Board of Commissioners
626 W Jackson Blvd., No. 700
Chicago, IL 60661
Ph: (312)742-8478
Fax: (312)627-1501
E-mail: dtyus@thecha.org
URL: National Affiliate–www.nfbpa.org
Contact: Darnetta K. Tyus, Exec.Asst.
State. Works to promote, strengthen and expand the role of Blacks in public administration. Seeks to focus the influence of Black administrators toward building and maintaining viable communities. Develops specialized training programs for managers and executives. Works to further communication among Black public, private and academic institutions. Addresses issues that affect the administrative capacity of Black managers. **Affiliated With:** National Forum for Black Public Administrators.

1082 ■ National Hook-up of Black Women, Chicago Chapter
c/o Pamela Howard
11122 S Ashland Ave.
Chicago, IL 60643-3514
Ph: (708)425-1642
E-mail: nhbwdir2@aol.com
URL: http://www.nhbwinc.com/Chicago.htm
Contact: Pamela Howard, Contact
Local. **Affiliated With:** National Hook-Up of Black Women.

1083 ■ National Kidney Foundation of Illinois (NKFI)
215 W Illinois St., Apt. 1C
Chicago, IL 60610
Ph: (312)321-1500
Fax: (312)321-1505
E-mail: kidney@nkfi.org
URL: http://www.nkfi.org
Contact: Kate O'Connor, Assoc.Exec.Dir.
State. Provides educational services and materials for Illinois dialysis patients, transplant recipients and community prevention programs. **Affiliated With:** National Kidney Foundation.

1084 ■ National Multiple Sclerosis Society of Greater Illinois
c/o Pam Swenk, Pres.
910 W Van Buren, 4th Fl.
Chicago, IL 60607
Ph: (312)421-4500
Fax: (312)421-4544
E-mail: cgic@ild.nmss.org
URL: http://www.msillinois.org
Contact: Pam Swenk, Pres.
Founded: 1952. **State**. Stimulates, supports, and coordinates research into the cause, treatment, and cure of multiple sclerosis; provides services for persons with MS and related diseases and their families. **Affiliated With:** National Multiple Sclerosis Society.

1085 ■ National Network of Libraries of Medicine, Greater Midwest Region
Univ. of Illinois at Chicago
Lib. of the Hea. Scis.
1750 W Polk St., MC763
Chicago, IL 60612-4330
Ph: (312)996-2464
Fax: (312)996-2226
Free: (800)338-7657
E-mail: gmr@uic.edu
URL: http://nnlm.gov/gmr
Contact: Susan Jacobson, Dir.
Founded: 1978. **Members:** 800. **Staff:** 7. **State Groups:** 10. **Regional**. Provides all U.S. health professionals with equal access to biomedical information. Seeks to improve the public's access to information to enable them to make informed decisions about their health. Offers interlibrary services and training in PubMed, Docline, and Internet. **Councils:** Regional Advisory. **Publications:** *E Sources*, quarterly. Newsletter.

1086 ■ National Organization of Black Law Enforcement Executives, Chicago Metropolitan Chapter
11223 S Halsten St.
Chicago, IL 60620
Ph: (312)754-2689
Fax: (312)745-3509
E-mail: cmc@noblenational.net
URL: http://www.chicago.noblechapter.org
Contact: Michael Shields, Pres.
Local. **Additional Websites:** http://noblenational.org. **Affiliated With:** National Organization of Black Law Enforcement Executives.

1087 ■ National Organization for Reform of Marijuana Laws, Illinois Chapter
c/o Bryan Brickner
1573 N Milwaukee Ave., PMB No. 446
Chicago, IL 60622-2009
Ph: (773)395-9708
E-mail: info@illinoisnorml.org
URL: http://www.illinoisnorml.org
Contact: Bryan Brickner, Contact
State.

1088 ■ National Organization for Women - Chicago
c/o Jennifer Koehler
200 N Michigan Ave., Ste.602
Chicago, IL 60601
Ph: (312)578-9351
E-mail: jkoehler23@aol.com
URL: http://www.chicagonow.org
Contact: Meghan Streit, Pres.
Local. Furthers the advancement of women and girls in the Chicago area. **Boards:** Educational Fund. **Committees:** Political Action.

1089 ■ National Spa and Pool Institute Midwest Chapter
c/o Angelo Adams, Pres.
Halogen Supply Co.
4653 W Lawrence Ave.
Chicago, IL 60630
Ph: (773)286-6300
Fax: (773)286-1024
E-mail: halogensupply@aol.com
URL: National Affiliate–www.nspi.org
Local. **Affiliated With:** Association of Pool and Spa Professionals.

1090 ■ National Writers Union - Chicago Chapter
PO Box 2537
Chicago, IL 60690-2537
Ph: (773)426-9382
E-mail: info@nwu-chicago.org
URL: National Affiliate–www.nwu.org
Contact: Helena Worthen, Chair
Local. **Affiliated With:** National Writers Union.

1091 ■ NCA of Illinois
c/o Paul Dykstra, Exec.Dir.
401 N Michigan Ave.
Chicago, IL 60611
Ph: (312)245-1555
Fax: (312)245-1080
Free: (800)422-3715
E-mail: membership@isnow.com
URL: http://www.IsNow.com
Contact: Paul Dykstra, Exec.Dir.
State. Formerly: (2004) Illinois Cosmetology Association.

1092 ■ Near North Development Corp.
c/o Elbert Greene, Pres.
1251 N Clybourn Ave.
Chicago, IL 60610
Ph: (312)337-5666
Fax: (312)337-5753
Contact: Rosie Vaughn, Office Mgr.
Local.

1093 ■ Near NorthWest Arts Council (NNWAC)
2418 W Bloomingdale
Chicago, IL 60647
Ph: (773)278-7677
Fax: (773)278-8451
E-mail: nnwac@nnwac.org
URL: http://www.nnwac.org
Contact: Laura Weathered, Exec.Dir.
Founded: 1986. **Membership Dues:** family or individual, $30 (annual) • business, $100 (annual). **Staff:** 3. **Budget:** $100,000. **Nonmembership. Local.** Represents artists in the Chicago, IL area interested in sharing the power of creativity, building community through democratic control, cooperative enterprise, and grassroots investment.

1094 ■ Near Northwest Civic Committee
c/o Anthony Lucafo, Exec.Dir.
1450 W Chicago Ave.
Chicago, IL 60622
Ph: (312)243-2342
Fax: (312)243-8598
E-mail: nearnwciviccommittee@inetmail.att.net
URL: http://chicagoareaproject.org/aff_nrnorthwest.htm
Contact: Anthony Lucafo, Exec.Dir.
Local. Sponsors educational, recreational and other activities, such as in-school tutor/sports programs, after-school tutoring, Scout Troops, Karate classes, Cultural Dance classes, Teen Girl Mentor program, field trips and holiday activities for the youth and community of the near northwest side of Chicago.

1095 ■ Near Northwest Neighborhood Network (NNNN)
2412 W North Ave.
Chicago, IL 60647
Ph: (773)489-0383
Fax: (773)489-6360
E-mail: admin@nnnn.org
URL: http://www.nnnn.org
Contact: Eliud Medina, Exec.Dir.
Founded: 1987. **Members:** 80. **Staff:** 4. **Budget:** $165,000. **Languages:** English, Spanish. **Local.** Works to develop the will and the vision to stabilize and to revitalize the community so that the community provides quality to both family life and work, especially for low to moderate-income families and individuals. **Conventions/Meetings:** biennial Issues Assembly - every third Monday.

1096 ■ Near West Side Community Development Corp. (NWSCDC)
216 S Hoyne Ave.
Chicago, IL 60612
Ph: (312)738-2280
Fax: (312)738-2308
E-mail: msgonzalez616@aol.com
URL: http://www.nearwestsidecdc.org
Contact: LaShunda Gonzalez, Contact
Local. Provides resident support services, loans and grants for home repairs and organizes community members in order to directly involve them in the rebirth of the neighborhood. Builds affordable housing and commercial real estate.

1097 ■ Neighborhood Boys and Girls Club (NBGC)
2501 W Irving Park Rd.
Chicago, IL 60618
Ph: (773)463-4161 (773)463-1848
Fax: (773)463-5392
E-mail: nbgc1931@aol.com
URL: http://www.NBGC.org
Contact: James D. McNulty, Exec.Dir.
Founded: 1931. **Members:** 1,200. **Staff:** 14. **Budget:** $500,000. **Languages:** English, Spanish. **Local.** Boys and girls in the Northcenter/Lakeview/Roscoe Village/Albany Park/Irving Park/Uptown/Logan Square areas of Chicago, IL, ages six through 18. Seeks to create "better men and women" through a program of supervised athletics, social, educational, and inter-generational programs. Sponsors annual Major Family Fest/Carnival and "Leaders of the Future" Scholarship luncheon to raise funds. **Awards:** NBGC Scholarships. **Frequency:** annual. **Type:** scholarship. **Recipient:** for active member with outstanding leadership skills. **Computer Services:** Online services, web site with information and retrieval services. **Working Groups:** Alumni Association; Dads Club; Moms Club. **Affiliated With:** Ravenswood Community Council. **Formerly:** Neighborhood Boys Club. **Publications:** *Alumni Chatter*, quarterly. Newsletter. Contains specific information for the alumni and club activities. **Price:** free. **Circulation:** 2,000. **Advertising:** accepted • *Monkeyshine*, weekly • Directory, annual. **Conventions/Meetings:** quinquennial Anniversary Banquet - assembly, gathering of alumni from the 1930's through the present celebrates the history and accomplishments of the organization • annual meeting - always January.

1098 ■ Net and Paddle Club
Berry Memorial Church
4754 N Leavitt
Chicago, IL 60625
Ph: (773)764-7987
E-mail: paultabten@sbcglobal.net
URL: National Affiliate–www.usatt.org
Contact: Paul Pashuku, Contact
Local. Affiliated With: U.S.A. Table Tennis.

1099 ■ Network of Women Entrepreneurs
330 S Wells St., Ste.1110
Chicago, IL 60606
Ph: (312)461-9492
Fax: (312)461-0238
Contact: Susan Gidley, Admin.Dir.
Local. Educate, facilitate and support women's growth in all aspects of their lives.

1100 ■ News and Letters Committee, Chicago Chapter (NLC-CC)
36 S Wabash, Rm. 1440
Chicago, IL 60603
Ph: (312)236-0799
Fax: (312)236-0725
E-mail: arise@newsandletters.org
URL: http://www.newsandletters.org
Contact: Olga Domanski, Co-Organizer
Founded: 1955. **State.** Marxist-Humanist organization that believes in the abolishment of capitalism and the development of new human relations. Holds weekly educational and editing sessions. **Affiliated With:** News and Letters Committee. **Publications:** *News & Letters*, bimonthly. Newspaper. **Price:** $5.00/year. ISSN: 0028-8969 • *The Power of Negativity: Selected Writings on the Dialectic in Hegel and Marx by Rava Dunayevskaya*. Book. **Price:** $24.95.

1101 ■ Nobel Neighbors
c/o Dean Morris, Exec.Dir.
1345 N Karlov Ave.
Chicago, IL 60651
Ph: (773)252-8524
Fax: (773)252-8548
E-mail: nobelneighbors@aol.com
URL: http://www.neighborhoodlink.com/chicago/nobel
Contact: Dean Morris, Exec.Dir.
Local. Promotes and fosters an environment that allows community residents to solve the problems that affect their lives; through community organizing strategies, educational opportunities, and leadership building. Encourages residents to work towards empowerment. **Affiliated With:** National People's Action.

1102 ■ North River Commission (NRC)
4745 N Kedzie Ave.
Chicago, IL 60625
Ph: (773)478-0202
Fax: (773)478-0282
URL: http://www.northrivercommission.org
Contact: Charles Frederick Daas, Exec.Dir.
Founded: 1962. **Membership Dues:** individual, $50 (annual) • small civic group, block club, $100 (annual) • large civic organization, nonprofit organization, $300 (annual) • small business, $1,000 (annual) • neighborhood institution, $2,500-$5,000 (annual) • bank, $5,000 (annual) • corporation, $10,000 (annual). **Local.**

1103 ■ North Shore Cricket Club
6828 N Clark St.
Chicago, IL 60626
URL: http://www.usaca.org/Clubs.htm
Contact: Shahid Pervaz, Contact
Local.

1104 ■ North Shore Philatelic Society
c/o Mr. Ronald L. Schloss, Sec.-Treas.
PO Box 60223
Chicago, IL 60660-0223
E-mail: 1stsgt33@megsinet.net
URL: National Affiliate–www.stamps.org
Contact: Mr. Ronald L. Schloss, Sec.-Treas.
Founded: 1933. **Members:** 30. **Membership Dues:** $5 (annual). **Local.** Strives to educate stamp collectors and possible collectors on all aspects of stamp collecting. **Affiliated With:** American Philatelic Society. **Publications:** Newsletter, monthly.

1105 ■ Northalsted Area Merchants Association
c/o Gloria J. Shoff, Ex. Dir
3739 N. Halsted St.
Chicago, IL 60613
Ph: (773)883-0500
Contact: Gloria J. Shoff, Exec.Dir.
Founded: 1981. **Members:** 70. **Staff:** 1. **Budget:** $100,000. **Local. Publications:** *Northalsted Street Talk*, quarterly. Newsletter. **Circulation:** 20,000. **Advertising:** accepted.

1106 ■ Northeastern Illinois Planning Commission (NIPC)
Sears Tower, Ste.800
233 S Wacker
Chicago, IL 60606
Ph: (312)454-0400
Fax: (312)454-0411
E-mail: info@nipc.org
URL: http://www.nipc.org
Contact: Ronald L. Thomas, Exec.Dir.
Founded: 1957. **Local.**

1107 ■ Northern Illinois Deaf Golf Association
c/o Bryan Jendra
160 E Illinois St., Ste.600
Chicago, IL 60611-3859
Ph: (312)329-9244
Fax: (312)329-2472
E-mail: nidga2000@yahoo.com
Contact: Kathy Gilbert, Contact
Local. Provides social interaction with deaf and non-deaf people for business and social relations. **Conventions/Meetings:** meeting.

1108 ■ Northside Wyldlife - Wyldlife
2170 W Warner
Chicago, IL 60618
Ph: (773)327-5262
URL: http://sites.younglife.org/_layouts/ylext/default.aspx?ID=C-3407
Local. Represents the interests of individuals committed to impacting kids' lives and preparing them for the future. Helps young people develop their skills, assets and attitudes to reach their full God-given potential. Reaches suburban, urban, multicultural and disabled kids and teenage mothers. **Affiliated With:** Young Life.

1109 ■ Northwest Neighborhood Federation (NNF)
c/o Alex Jimenez, Pres.
3443 N Parkside
Chicago, IL 60634
Ph: (773)545-9300
Fax: (773)545-9966
E-mail: nwnf@nwnf.org
URL: http://www.nwnf.org
Regional.

1110 ■ Norwood Park Chamber of Commerce and Industry
6097 N NW Hwy.
Chicago, IL 60631
Ph: (773)763-3606
Fax: (773)763-3620
E-mail: info@norwoodpark.org
URL: http://www.norwoodpark.org
Contact: Helen I. Brown, Pres.
Local. Works to provide leadership, visions and strategy to the business community. **Publications:** Newsletter, monthly.

1111 ■ O.A. Thorp Scholastic Academy Parent-Teacher Association
6024 W Warwick Ave.
Chicago, IL 60634
Ph: (312)409-4331
E-mail: oathorppta@aol.com
URL: http://myschoolonline.com/site/0,1876,-212037-21-59391,00.html
Contact: Terrie Hayes, Pres.
Local. Parents, teachers, students and others interested in uniting the forces of home, school and community. Promotes the welfare of children and youth.

1112 ■ Obsessive Compulsive Foundation of Metropolitan Chicago
2300 Lincoln Park W
Chicago, IL 60614
Ph: (773)880-1635
Fax: (773)880-1966
E-mail: info@ocfchicago.org
URL: http://www.ocfchicago.org
Contact: Ms. Ellen Sawyer, Exec.Dir.
Founded: 1994. **Membership Dues:** individual, $45 (annual) • professional, $85 (annual) • family, $65 (annual). **Staff:** 1. **Regional**. Provides education, support, and treatment resources for individuals with OCD and their families. **Affiliated With:** Obsessive-Compulsive Foundation. **Also Known As:** (2004) OCF Chicago. **Publications:** *News Update*, semiannual. Newsletter. Timely information about Obsessive Compulsive Disorder. **Price:** free to people on mailing list. Alternate Formats: online.

1113 ■ Oldsmobile Club of America, Illinois Valley Oldsmobile Chapter (IVOC)
c/o Brian M. Lenz, Membership Coor.
PO Box 557903
Chicago, IL 60655
Ph: (708)481-7973 (847)390-8463
E-mail: info@ivoc-olds.com
URL: http://www.ivoc-olds.com
Contact: Richard Barnas, Pres.
Founded: 1980. **Membership Dues:** individual, $18 (annual). **Local. Affiliated With:** Oldsmobile Club of America.

1114 ■ Open Doors Organization (ODO)
c/o Eric Lipp
2551 N Clark St., Ste.301
Chicago, IL 60614
Ph: (773)388-8839
E-mail: info@opendoorsnfp.org
URL: http://opendoorsnfp.org
Founded: 2000. **Local.**

1115 ■ Organization of Chinese Americans - Greater Chicago Chapter
PO Box 365
Chicago, IL 60690-0365
Ph: (202)223-5500
E-mail: ocachicago@yahoo.com
URL: http://www.ocachicago.org
Contact: Michael Chin, Pres.
Local.

1116 ■ Organization Development Network of Chicago
5443 N Broadway, Ste.101
Chicago, IL 60640
Ph: (773)561-4919
Fax: (773)561-1343
E-mail: odnchicago@aol.com
URL: http://www.odnetwork.org/odnc
Contact: Kevin G. Boyer, Administrator
Local. Helps its members develop their effectiveness in improving organizations. Offers opportunities for professional education and development, as well as the active exchange of experience, support and new ideas. **Affiliated With:** Organization Development Network.

1117 ■ Organization of the North East (ONE)
1329 W Wilson Ave.
Chicago, IL 60640
Ph: (773)769-3232
Fax: (773)769-0729
E-mail: sjk@onechicago.org
URL: http://www.onechicago.org
Contact: Sarah Jane Knoy, Exec.Dir.
Founded: 1974. **Local.**

1118 ■ Orthopaedic Technologists Association of Illinois
7241 S Francisco
Chicago, IL 60629
Ph: (773)412-4126 (312)864-5183
URL: National Affiliate–naot.org
Contact: Gerald Cotton OTC, Contact
State. Promotes continued professional education for members and other orthopedic health care providers. Administers certification examinations. Seeks to enhance public understanding of orthopedics. **Affiliated With:** National Association of Orthopaedic Technologists.

1119 ■ Pak Gymkhana
2156 W Devon, Apt. No. 205
Chicago, IL 60659
URL: http://www.usaca.org/Clubs.htm
Contact: Rashid Mohd, Contact
Local.

1120 ■ Pan-African Association
c/o Tiffaney Holcomb
6163 N Broadway
Chicago, IL 60660
Ph: (773)381-9723
Fax: (773)381-9727
E-mail: panafrican@sbcglobal.net
URL: http://www.panafricanassociation.org
Contact: Patrick Agustin, Dir.
Local.

1121 ■ Paramount Tall Club of Chicago
PO Box 661182
Chicago, IL 60666-1182
Ph: (312)853-0183
E-mail: president@tallchicago.org
URL: http://www.tallclubchicago.org
Contact: Laura Cofran, Pres.
Local. Affiliated With: Tall Clubs International.

1122 ■ Parents Anonymous of Chicago, Illinois
217 N Jefferson
Chicago, IL 60661
Ph: (312)669-8200
Fax: (312)669-1512
E-mail: weberc@ucanchicago.org
URL: http://www.uhlich.org
Contact: Courtney Weber, Coor.
Local.

1123 ■ People for the American Way, Illinois
c/o Julie Sweet, Dir.
111 N Wabash Ave., Ste.1403
Chicago, IL 60602
Ph: (312)726-2179
Fax: (312)726-7449
E-mail: pfawch@pfaw.org
URL: National Affiliate–www.pfaw.org
Contact: Julie Sweet, Dir.
State. Affiliated With: People for the American Way.

1124 ■ PFLAG Chicago/Hinsdale/West Suburban
PO Box 11023
Chicago, IL 60611
Ph: (773)472-3079
Fax: (630)415-0622
E-mail: contact@pflagchicago.com
URL: http://www.pflagchicago.com
Local. Affiliated With: Parents, Families, and Friends of Lesbians and Gays.

1125 ■ PFLAG Chicago/Lakeview
PO Box 11023
Chicago, IL 60611
Ph: (773)472-3079
E-mail: pflagchicago@aol.com
URL: http://www.pflagchicago.com
Local. Affiliated With: Parents, Families, and Friends of Lesbians and Gays.

1126 ■ Phi Beta Kappa, University of Illinois (Chicago)
c/o Paul Francuch, Sec.
Off. of Public Affairs
M/C 288
601 S Morgan
1350 Univ. Hall
Chicago, IL 60607
Ph: (312)996-3457
E-mail: francuch@uic.edu
URL: http://www.uic.edu/las/college/info/phibetakappa.shtml
Contact: Paul Francuch, Sec.
Local. Academic honor society for undergraduates in the liberal arts and sciences. Chapter of the Phi Beta Kappa Society. **Affiliated With:** Phi Beta Kappa.

1127 ■ Phi Theta Kappa, Alpha Lambda Iota Chapter - Malcolm X College
c/o David Rice
1900 W Van Buren St.
Chicago, IL 60612
Ph: (312)850-7325
E-mail: drice@ccc.edu
URL: http://www.ptk.org/directories/chapters/IL/216-1.htm
Contact: David Rice, Advisor
Local.

1128 ■ Phi Theta Kappa, Kappa Beta Chapter - Kendall College
c/o Brady Carey
900 N Br. St.
Chicago, IL 60622
Ph: (312)752-2434
E-mail: bcarey@kendall.edu
URL: http://www.ptk.org/directories/chapters/IL/174-1.htm
Contact: Brady Carey, Advisor
Local.

1129 ■ Phi Theta Kappa, Lambda Iota Chapter - Olive-Harvey College
c/o Addie Davis
10001 S Woodlawn Ave.
Chicago, IL 60628
Ph: (773)291-6428
E-mail: addavis@ccc.edu
URL: http://www.ptk.org/directories/chapters/IL/176-1.htm
Contact: Addie Davis, Advisor
Local.

1130 ■ Phi Theta Kappa, Lambda Rho Chapter - Kennedy-King College
c/o Jeanette Williams
6800 S Wentworth Ave.
Chicago, IL 60621
Ph: (773)602-5159
E-mail: jmwilliams@ccc.edu
URL: http://www.ptk.org/directories/chapters/IL/177-1.htm
Contact: Jeanette Williams, Advisor
Local.

1131 ■ Phi Theta Kappa, Mu Pi Chapter - Harold Washington College
c/o Slavinka Spirovska, Advisor
30 E Lake St.
Chicago, IL 60601
Ph: (312)553-5697
E-mail: slavinka.spirovska@ptk.org
URL: http://www.ptk.org/directories/chapters/IL/179-1.htm
Contact: Slavinka Spirovska, Advisor
Local.

1132 ■ Phi Theta Kappa, Nu Lambda Chapter - Harry S. Truman College
c/o Gregory Robinson
1145 W Wilson Ave.
Chicago, IL 60640
Ph: (773)907-4719
E-mail: grobinson@ccc.edu
URL: http://www.ptk.org/directories/chapters/IL/185-1.htm
Contact: Gregory Robinson, Advisor
Local.

1133 ■ Phi Theta Kappa, Pi Rho Chapter - Richard J. Daley College
c/o Gayle Ward
7500 S Pulaski Rd.
Chicago, IL 60652
Ph: (773)838-7582
E-mail: gward@ccc.edu
URL: http://www.ptk.org/directories/chapters/IL/184-1.htm
Contact: Gayle Ward, Advisor
Local.

1134 ■ Phi Theta Kappa, Tau Delta Chapter - MacCormac College
c/o John Tomei
29 E Madison St.
Chicago, IL 60602
Ph: (312)922-1884
E-mail: jtomei@maccormac.edu
URL: http://www.ptk.org/directories/chapters/IL/188-1.htm
Contact: John Tomei, Advisor
Local.

1135 ■ Phi Theta Kappa, Theta Omega Chapter - Wilbur Wright College
c/o Dr. Patricia Williams Lessane, Advisor
4300 N Naragansett Ave.
Chicago, IL 60634
Ph: (773)481-8370
E-mail: plessane@ccc.edu
URL: http://www.ptk.org/directories/chapters/IL/168-1.htm
Contact: Dr. Patricia Williams Lessane, Advisor
Local.

1136 ■ Philalethes Society, Logos Chapter
c/o Richard Lozins
100 E. Huron St., Ste.1604
Chicago, IL 60611
E-mail: iamamason@aol.com
URL: http://members.aol.com/iamamason/logos.html
Founded: 1999. **Local. Affiliated With:** Philalethes Society.

1137 ■ Physicians for Social Responsibility, Chicago
c/o Olga I. Delgado, Exec.Dir.
4750 N Sheridan, No. 439
Chicago, IL 60640
Ph: (773)989-4655
Fax: (773)506-7072
E-mail: info@psrchicago.org
URL: http://www.psrchicago.org
Contact: Olga I. Delgado, Exec.Dir.
Local. Affiliated With: Physicians for Social Responsibility.

1138 ■ Pilsen Neighbors Community Council
c/o Janet Dominguez, FDS Dir.
2026 S Blue Island Ave.
Chicago, IL 60608
Ph: (312)666-2663
Fax: (312)666-4661
E-mail: marty@fiestadelsol.org
URL: http://www.fiestadelsol.org
Contact: Marty Sanchez, Board Pres.
Local.

1139 ■ Planned Parenthood of Chicago Area
18 S Michigan Ave., 6th Fl.
Chicago, IL 60603
Ph: (312)592-6800
URL: National Affiliate–www.plannedparenthood.org
Local. Affiliated With: Planned Parenthood Federation of America.

1140 ■ Police and Firemen's Insurance Association - Chicago Fire Department
c/o John Giordano
2623 W Eastwood Ave.
Chicago, IL 60625
Ph: (773)463-0195
Fax: (773)463-0195
URL: National Affiliate–www.pfia.net
Contact: John Giordano, Contact
Local. Affiliated With: Police and Firemen's Insurance Association.

1141 ■ Polish American Congress, Illinois Division
c/o Mr. Christopher Kurczaba, Pres.
5711 N Milwaukee Ave.
Chicago, IL 60646
Ph: (773)774-0011
Fax: (773)774-0022
E-mail: info@pacil.org
URL: http://www.pacil.org
Contact: Mr. Christopher Kurczaba, Pres.
State. Affiliated With: Polish American Congress.

1142 ■ Portage Park Chamber of Commerce (PPCC)
4849 A Irving Park Rd.
Chicago, IL 60641-2719
Ph: (773)777-2020
Fax: (773)777-0202
Contact: George S. Borovik, Exec.Dir.
Founded: 1937. **Members:** 175. **Local.** Promotes business and community development in the Portage Park area of Chicago, IL. Markets the six corners business district. Sponsors community events and promotional activities. **Publications:** Newsletter, monthly • Newsletter, annual. **Price:** free. **Conventions/Meetings:** monthly meeting.

1143 ■ Prevent Blindness America, Illinois Division
211 W Wacker Dr., Ste.1700
Chicago, IL 60606
Ph: (312)363-6001
Fax: (312)363-6052
E-mail: info@preventblindness.org
URL: http://www.preventblindness.org
State. Affiliated With: Prevent Blindness America.

1144 ■ Prevent Child Abuse America
200 S Michigan Ave., 17th Fl.
Chicago, IL 60604-2404
Ph: (312)663-3520
Fax: (312)939-8962
E-mail: mailbox@preventchildabuse.org
URL: http://www.preventchildabuse.org
Regional.

1145 ■ Printing Industry of Illinois-Indiana Association (PII)
70 E Lake St.
Chicago, IL 60601
Ph: (312)704-5000
Fax: (312)704-5025
E-mail: info@pii.org
URL: http://www.pii.org
Contact: Polly Jensen, Pres./CEO
Founded: 1925. **Members:** 1,000. **Staff:** 25. **Budget:** $2,500,000. **Regional.** Commercial printing firms and allied companies in the graphic arts field. **Affiliated With:** Printing Industries of America. **Publications:** *Galley Proof*, weekly. Newsletter. **Circulation:** 1,700 • *Insights*, bimonthly. Magazine. **Circulation:** 4,000. **Advertising:** accepted. **Conventions/Meetings:** annual meeting.

1146 ■ Project Danztheatre Company
c/o Ellyzabeth Adler Stanke
1028 N. Paulina, Ste.1F
Chicago, IL 60622-3857
Ph: (773)486-8261
URL: http://www.danztheatre.org
Contact: Ellyzabeth Adler, Contact
Founded: 2001. **Staff:** 2. **Budget:** $15,000. **Local.** Organize to provide outreach program,kid project and adult performance group.

1147 ■ Protestants for the Common Good (PCG)
77 W Washington St., Ste.1124
Chicago, IL 60602
Ph: (312)223-9544
Fax: (312)223-9540
E-mail: sharp@thecommongood.org
URL: http://www.thecommongood.org
Contact: Alexander E. Sharp, Exec.Dir.
Founded: 1996. **Members:** 1,000. **Membership Dues:** regular, $35 (annual) • student/senior, $15 (annual). **Staff:** 6. **Budget:** $400,000. **Local.** Brings an informed and strong Protestant voice to public life and offers educational resources and advocacy opportunities to people of faith on matters of public policy. Pursues its educational activities, including the teaching of a Faith and Public Issues discussion series, public events such as forums and town meetings on issues with important moral dimensions, and the dissemination of written materials that prepare the reader to consider the direct moral consequences of public policy. **Publications:** *Common Good*, 8/year. Newsletter. Contains organizational news. **Price:** included in membership dues. **Circulation:** 1,000.

1148 ■ Psi Chi, National Honor Society in Psychology - Adler School of Professional Psychology
65 E Wacker Pl., Ste.2100
Chicago, IL 60601-7203
Ph: (312)201-5900
Fax: (312)201-5917
E-mail: hhm@adler.edu
URL: http://www.psichi.org/chapters/info.asp?chapter_id=758
Contact: Harold H. Mosak PhD, Advisor
Local.

1149 ■ Psi Chi, National Honor Society in Psychology - Chicago State University
c/o Dept. of Psychology
9501 S Dr. Martin L. King Jr. Dr., HWH 328
Chicago, IL 60628-1598
Ph: (773)995-2394 (773)995-2127
Fax: (773)995-3767
E-mail: aw-richardson@csu.edu
URL: http://www.psichi.org/chapters/info.asp?chapter_id=809
Contact: Alesia Williams Richardson PhD, Advisor
Local.

1150 ■ Psi Chi, National Honor Society in Psychology - DePaul University
c/o Dept. of Psychology
420 Byrne Hall
2219 N Kenmore Ave.
Chicago, IL 60614-3298
Ph: (773)325-7887 (773)325-7155
Fax: (773)325-7888
E-mail: jhauskne@depaul.edu
URL: http://www.psichi.org/chapters/info.asp?chapter_id=210
Contact: John Hausknecht PhD, Advisor
Local.

1151 ■ Psi Chi, National Honor Society in Psychology - Illinois Institute of Technology
c/o Inst. of Psychology
3101 S Dearborn St., Ste.252
Chicago, IL 60616
Ph: (312)567-3500 (312)567-3493
Fax: (312)567-3517
E-mail: psychology@iit.edu
URL: http://www.iit.edu/~psichi
Local. Affiliated With: Psi Chi, National Honor Society in Psychology.

1152 ■ Psi Chi, National Honor Society in Psychology - Loyola University Chicago
c/o Dept. of Psychology
6525 N Sheridan Rd.
Chicago, IL 60626
Ph: (773)508-3001
Fax: (773)508-8713
E-mail: rtindal@luc.edu
URL: http://www.luc.edu/psychology/orgs/psichi.shtml
Local. Affiliated With: Psi Chi, National Honor Society in Psychology.

1153 ■ Psi Chi, National Honor Society in Psychology - North Park University
c/o Elizabeth Gray, PhD, Advisor
Box 16
3225 W Foster Ave.
Chicago, IL 60625-4895
Ph: (773)244-5720 (773)244-4844
Fax: (773)244-4952
E-mail: egray@northpark.edu
URL: National Affiliate–www.psichi.org
Contact: Elizabeth Gray PhD, Advisor
Local.

1154 ■ Psi Chi, National Honor Society in Psychology - Northeastern Illinois University
c/o Dept. of Psychology
5500 N St., Louis Ave.
Chicago, IL 60625
Ph: (773)442-5840 (773)442-5842
Fax: (773)442-5850
E-mail: j-parker@neiu.edu
URL: National Affiliate–www.psichi.org
Local. Affiliated With: Psi Chi, National Honor Society in Psychology.

1155 ■ Psi Chi, National Honor Society in Psychology - Roosevelt University
c/o Dept. of Psychology
435 S Michigan Ave.
Chicago, IL 60605-1394
Ph: (312)341-3750 (312)341-6380
Fax: (312)341-6362
E-mail: jchoca@roosevelt.edu
URL: http://www.psichi.org/chapters/info.asp?chapter_id=49
Contact: James P. Choca PhD, Advisor
Local.

1156 ■ Psi Chi, National Honor Society in Psychology - Saint Xavier University
c/o Psychology Dept.
3700 W 103rd St.
Chicago, IL 60655-3105
Ph: (773)298-3471 (773)298-3474
Fax: (773)298-3480
E-mail: deisinger@sxu.edu
URL: National Affiliate–www.psichi.org
Contact: Julie A. Deisinger PhD, Advisor
Local.

1157 ■ Psi Chi, National Honor Society in Psychology - University of Chicago
5848 S Univ. Ave.
Chicago, IL 60637
Ph: (773)834-3072
E-mail: pvisser@uchicago.edu
URL: http://psichi.uchicago.edu
Local. Affiliated With: Psi Chi, National Honor Society in Psychology.

1158 ■ Psi Chi, National Honor Society in Psychology - University of Illinois at Chicago
c/o Dept. of Psychology
1009 Behavioral Sci. Bldg., M/C 285
1007 W Harrison St.
Chicago, IL 60607-7137
Ph: (312)996-3036 (312)355-2501
Fax: (312)413-4122
E-mail: jwiley@uic.edu
URL: National Affiliate–www.psichi.org
Local. Affiliated With: Psi Chi, National Honor Society in Psychology.

1159 ■ Public Health Practitioner Certification Board
c/o Victoria Wiebel
1603 W Taylor St., MC923
Chicago, IL 60612-4336
Ph: (312)996-6531
Fax: (312)996-5768
E-mail: vikki@uic.edu
URL: http://www.phpcb.org
Contact: Victoria Wiebel, Mgr.
Founded: 1998. **Members:** 6. **Staff:** 2. **Local.** Uses competency-based evidence (experiential and/or academic) to approve certification of public health administrators and emergency response coordinators. **Affiliated With:** Illinois Public Health Association. **Formerly:** (2003) Illinois Public Health Administrator Certification Board. **Conventions/Meetings:** quarterly board meeting - January, April, July, October.

1160 ■ Puppeteers of America - Chicagoland Puppetry Guild
c/o Cynthia Von Orthal, Pres.
4316 N Springfield Ave.
Chicago, IL 60618
Ph: (773)463-6373
E-mail: fepmgp@aol.com
URL: http://www.chicagopuppet.org
Contact: Cynthia Von Orthal, Pres.
Local.

1161 ■ Rainbow/PUSH Coalition (RPC)
c/o Denise Dixon, National Field Organizer
930 E 50th St.
Chicago, IL 60615-2702
Ph: (773)373-3366
Fax: (773)373-3571
E-mail: info@rainbowpush.org
URL: http://www.rainbowpush.org
Regional.

1162 ■ Ravenswood Community Council (RCC)
2348 W Irving Park Rd., Ste.106
Chicago, IL 60618
Ph: (773)583-1600
Fax: (773)583-3243
E-mail: ravenswood@core.com
URL: http://www.ravenswoodcommunity.org
Contact: Carolyn M. Bull, Exec.Dir.
Founded: 1958. **Members:** 200. **Membership Dues:** senior, $10 (annual) • community organization/small business/school or church, $30 (annual) • individual, $15 (annual) • family/household, $25 (annual) • large business, $100 (annual). **Staff:** 4. **Budget:** $130,000. **Local.** Promotes interests of the people and community of Ravenswood in areas of housing, street and home security, community improvement and beautification and business development through education, information, volunteer services and other programs. Provides services such as problem building intervention, online apartment searches, court advocacy, CAPS community policing support, emergency-only cell phones, and more. Supports development of affordable housing for seniors and families. **Awards:** Raven Award. **Frequency:** annual. **Type:** trophy. **Recipient:** for outstanding contributor to the Ravenswood community. **Committees:** Housing and Seniors; Membership and Development; Nominating; Planning and Zoning; Public Safety; Youth and Education. **Formerly:** Ravenswood Conservation Commission. **Publications:** Newsletter, bimonthly. Provides information of community interest pertaining to education, housing, and safety and crime topics. **Circulation:** 500. **Advertising:** accepted. **Conventions/Meetings:** annual Community Meeting, membership and open attendance meeting with topic of interest to the community - held 3rd Tuesday of October in Chicago, IL.

1163 ■ Real Presence Association
c/o Richard J. Guzior
7030 W 63rd St.
Chicago, IL 60638-3918
Ph: (773)586-2352
Fax: (773)586-7781
E-mail: trp@svs.com
URL: http://www.therealpresence.org
Local.

1164 ■ Recording for the Blind and Dyslexic Illinois Unit
18 S Michigan Ave., Ste.806
Chicago, IL 60603
Ph: (312)236-8715
E-mail: sfernandez@rfbd.org
URL: National Affiliate–www.rfbd.org
Contact: Sandy Fernandez, Acting Mgr.
State. Serves individuals who cannot effectively read standard print because of visual impairment, dyslexia, or other physical disabilities. Creates educational opportunities for students with print disabilities through educational and outreach services. Provides and promotes the effective use of accessible educational materials. **Affiliated With:** Recording for the Blind and Dyslexic.

1165 ■ Recreation for Individuals Dedicated to the Environment (RIDE)
208 S LaSalle, Ste.1700
Chicago, IL 60604
Ph: (312)853-2820
Free: (800)458-2358
E-mail: rideimba@aol.com
URL: http://www.bike-ride.com
Membership Dues: regular, $38 (annual) • family, $55 (annual) • enthusiast, $100 (annual). **Local.** Aims to preserve and restore the environment. Advocates public access to natural areas for education and recreation, and for spiritual enrichment through contact with nature. **Affiliated With:** International Mountain Bicycling Association.

1166 ■ Rivendell Theatre Ensemble
c/o Ms. Tara Mallen, Artistic Dir.
1711 W Belle Plaine, No. 3B
Chicago, IL 60613-1852

Ph: (773)472-1169
E-mail: info@rivendelltheatre.net
URL: http://www.rivendelltheatre.net
Contact: Ms. Tara Mallen, Artistic Dir.
Founded: 1994. **Members:** 10. **Budget:** $60,000. **Local**. Ensemble of people working in the theatre.

1167 ■ River North Association (RNA)
400 N Wells St., Ste.200
Chicago, IL 60610
Ph: (312)645-1047
Fax: (312)645-1151
E-mail: info@rivernorthassociation.com
URL: http://www.rivernorthassociation.com
Contact: Heather Imhoff, Exec.Dir.
Staff: 2. **Local**. Represents businesses and provides member services to help them succeed. **Publications:** *Destination River North*, annual, September. Article. Contains supplement for Chicago magazine. **Advertising:** accepted • *River North News*, quarterly. Newsletter. **Advertising:** accepted • Membership Directory, annual. Contains a list of members and businesses in River North. **Advertising:** accepted. **Conventions/Meetings:** periodic Business Exchange and Exposition - trade show (exhibits) • periodic Fraud: Preparing for Holiday Business - meeting, offers tips and strategies for consumers and businesses to protect themselves from fraud • annual Holiday Party, with silent auction and entertainment fundraiser - always in December.

1168 ■ Rogers Park Community Action Network
c/o Fran Tobin
1545 W Morse
Chicago, IL 60626
Ph: (773)973-7888
Fax: (773)973-7282
E-mail: fxtobin@earthlink.net
Local.

1169 ■ Rogers Park/West Ridge Historical Society (RP/WR HS)
c/o Mary Jo Doyle, Exec.Dir.
7344 N Western
Chicago, IL 60645-1814
Ph: (773)764-4078 (773)764-2401
Fax: (773)764-2824
E-mail: mjdoyle44@aol.com
URL: http://www.rpwrhs.org
Contact: Mary Jo Doyle, Exec.Dir.
Membership Dues: senior, student, $15 (annual) • individual, $20 (annual) • nonprofit, institutional, $25 (annual) • family, $35 (annual) • sponsor, $50 (annual) • sustaining, business, $100 (annual) • donor, $200 (annual) • business sponsor, $250 (annual) • life, $750. **Local**. Works to gather and preserve the history of Rogers Park and West Ridge, two communities on the Far North Side of Chicago, Illinois. Hosts a holiday party in January, spring event, Founders Day in July, an annual Fall House Tour in September, and various programs during the year. Also publishes two books on the history of the area.

1170 ■ Roseland Business Development Council
11145 S Michigan Ave., 2nd Fl.
Chicago, IL 60628
Ph: (773)995-6200
E-mail: rosebdc1@aol.com
Contact: John Edwards, Pres.
Founded: 1979. **Members:** 29. **Membership Dues:** full, $200 (annual). **Staff:** 2. **Budget:** $30,000. **Local**. **Awards:** CBDG. **Frequency:** annual. **Type:** grant.

1171 ■ RSVP of Hull House Chicago
c/o Jeffrey B. Nelson, Dir.
1712 S Prairie, 4th Fl.
Chicago, IL 60616
Ph: (312)922-2183
Fax: (312)922-2369
E-mail: jnelson@hullhouse.org
URL: http://www.seniorcorps.gov/about/programs/rsvp.asp
Contact: Jeffrey B. Nelson, Dir.
Local. **Affiliated With:** Retired and Senior Volunteer Program.

1172 ■ Salmon Unlimited (SU)
5936 N Manton Ave.
Chicago, IL 60646
Ph: (773)736-5757
Fax: (773)736-8900
E-mail: salmonunlimited@sbcglobal.net
URL: http://www.salmonunlimitedinc.com
Contact: Jean Sliwa, Contact
Local.

1173 ■ Scholarship and Guidance Association (SGA)
11 E Adams St., Ste.1500
Chicago, IL 60603
Ph: (312)663-0305
Fax: (312)663-0644
E-mail: admin@sga-youth.org
URL: http://www.sga-youth.org
Founded: 1911. **Local**.

1174 ■ SCORE Chicago
500 W Madison St., Ste.1250
Chicago, IL 60661-2511
Ph: (312)353-7724
Fax: (312)886-4879
E-mail: scorechi@sbcglobal.net
URL: http://www.chicagoscore.org
Local. Works to strengthen the formation, growth and success of small businesses nationwide. **Affiliated With:** SCORE.

1175 ■ Secular Humanist Society of Chicago
PO Box 7951
Chicago, IL 60680-7951
Ph: (312)226-0420
E-mail: email@chisechum.org
URL: http://www.chisechum.org
Contact: Adam R. Walker, Pres.
Founded: 1999. **Members:** 50. **Staff:** 1. **Local**. An individual and family membership organization for non-religious people. Meets once a month or more for fellowship and to emphasize reason and scientific inquiry, individual freedom and responsibility, and the separation of church and state. A local affiliate of the Council for Secular Humanism. **Conventions/Meetings:** monthly meeting.

1176 ■ SEIU Local 73
1165 N Clark St., Ste.500
Chicago, IL 60610
Ph: (312)787-5868
Fax: (312)337-7768
E-mail: jmisnik@seiu73.org
URL: http://www.seiu73.org
Contact: Joanna Misnik, Communications Dir.
Founded: 1987. **Members:** 967. **Regional**. Represents public service workers in Illinois and Indiana. **Affiliated With:** Service Employees International Union. **Formerly:** (2000) Service Employees AFL-CIO, Indiana/Iowa, D 1199; (2005) District 1199 Indiana/Iowa of Service Employees International Union Local.

1177 ■ SER - Jobs for Progress, Central States
c/o Rachel McDonald, Exec.Dir.
3948 W 26th St., Ste.213
Chicago, IL 60623
Ph: (773)542-9030
Fax: (773)542-9213
E-mail: rmcdonald@centralstatesser.org
URL: National Affiliate–www.ser-national.org
Contact: Rachel McDonald, Exec.Dir.
Regional. **Affiliated With:** SER - Jobs for Progress National.

1178 ■ Service Employees International Union, AFL-CIO, CLC - Illinois Council
111 E Wacker Dr., Ste.2500
Chicago, IL 60601
Ph: (312)233-8879
E-mail: general_email@seiuilcouncil.org
URL: http://www.seiu-illinois.org
Contact: Thomas Balanoff, Pres.
Members: 80,000. **State**. **Affiliated With:** Service Employees International Union.

1179 ■ Service Employees International Union, AFL-CIO, CLC - Local Union 4
7026 W North Ave.
Chicago, IL 60707
Ph: (773)889-7348
Fax: (773)836-9623
E-mail: seiu4@hotmail.com
URL: http://www.seiu4.org
Contact: Ronald Walski, Pres.
Members: 7,978. **Local**. **Affiliated With:** Service Employees International Union.

1180 ■ Service Employees International Union Local 880
c/o Myra Glassman
SEIU Local 880 HQ
650 S Clark St., 2nd Fl.
Chicago, IL 60605
Ph: (312)939-7490
Fax: (312)939-8256
Free: (800)321-7348
E-mail: seiu880ch@acorn.org
URL: http://www.seiulocal880.org
Local.

1181 ■ Shakura Ensemble Ritual Theatre
c/o Blanche Blacke
2936 N. Southpot
Chicago, IL 60657
Ph: (773)743-7372
URL: http://www.shakuraworld.org
Founded: 1999. **Local**. Strives to enhance consciousness and education of intentional theatre productions influenced by the indigenous world cultures. **Formerly:** (2004) Shakura Ensemble.

1182 ■ Sickle Cell Disease Association of Illinois (SCDAI)
200 N Michigan Ave., Ste.605
Chicago, IL 60601-5980
Free: (866)798-1097
E-mail: support@sicklecelldisease-il.org
URL: http://www.sicklecelldisease-il.org
Founded: 1971. **Staff:** 3. **Budget:** $400,000. **Nonmembership**. **State**. Provides information about sickle cell anemia and patient services. Conducts summer camp, gives scholarships to students who have Sickle Cell Disease, emergency patient grants and raises funds for research. Sponsors annual Walk Jog-a Bike-A-Thon. **Awards: Frequency:** periodic. **Type:** scholarship. **Recipient:** for individuals with sickle cell anemia (several each year). **Formerly:** Midwest Assn. for Sickle Cell Anemia. **Publications:** *SCDAI Newsletter*, quarterly.

1183 ■ Sierra Club - Illinois Chapter - Chicago Group
200 N Michigan Ave., Ste.505
Chicago, IL 60601
Ph: (312)251-1680 (773)935-8439
E-mail: birdchris@aol.com
URL: http://illinois.sierraclub.org/Chicago
Contact: Christine Williamson, ExCom Co-Chair
Local.

1184 ■ Silent Film Society of Chicago (SFSC)
c/o Dennis Wolkowicz
The Gateway Theater/Copernicus Ctr.
5216 W Lawrence
Chicago, IL 60631
Ph: (773)250-SFSC
E-mail: pal2775@msn.com
URL: http://www.silentfilmchicago.com
Contact: Dennis Wolkowicz, Contact
Local.

1185 ■ Society of American Military Engineers, Chicago Post (SAME-C)
c/o Mr. Jan S. Plachta, Sec.
U.S. Army Corps of Engineers
111 N Canal St., Ste.600
Chicago, IL 60606-7206

Ph: (312)846-5465
Fax: (312)353-2156
E-mail: jan.s.plachta@lrc02.usace.army.mil
URL: http://posts.same.org/chicago
Contact: Mr. Jan S. Plachta, Sec.
Founded: 1919. **Members:** 400. **Membership Dues:** $49 (annual). **For-Profit**. **State**. Military engineers, engineering firms, and others in allied fields interested in advancing knowledge in the science of military engineering, and increasing the national defense engineering potential of the U.S. **Awards:** Goethals. **Frequency:** annual. **Type:** medal • Gold. **Frequency:** annual. **Type:** medal • Sverdrup. **Frequency:** annual. **Type:** medal • Tudor. **Frequency:** annual. **Type:** medal • Wheeler. **Frequency:** annual. **Type:** medal. **Affiliated With:** Society of American Military Engineers. **Publications:** *Chicago Post Gazette*, periodic. Newsletter. Alternate Formats: online. **Conventions/Meetings:** annual conference - always October • monthly luncheon - always third Wednesday.

1186 ■ Society of Architectural Historians - Chicago Chapter
1365 N Astor St.
Chicago, IL 60610
Ph: (773)368-7137
E-mail: sah_chicago@mac.com
URL: http://www.sah-chicago.org
Contact: Robert Herbst, Pres.
Local. Promotes the preservation of buildings of historical and aesthetic significance. Encourages scholarly research in the field of architectural history. **Affiliated With:** Society of Architectural Historians.

1187 ■ Society of Automotive Engineers - University of Illinois-Chicago
MIE Dept.
842 W Taylor St.
Chicago, IL 60607-7021
E-mail: mghaffar@uic.edu
URL: National Affiliate–www.sae.org
Contact: Mohammad Ghaffarpour, Contact
Local. Advances the engineering mobility systems. Provides technical information and expertise used in designing, building, maintaining and operating self-propelled vehicles, whether land, sea, air or space based. Collects and disseminates information on cars, trucks, aircraft, space vehicles, off-highway vehicles, marine equipment and engine of all types. Fosters information exchange among the worldwide automotive and aerospace communities. **Affiliated With:** SAE International - Society of Automotive Engineers.

1188 ■ Society for College and University Planning, Illinois
c/o Anne Foley, Asst. VP for Institutional Planning and Research
Columbia Coll. Chicago
600 S Michigan
Chicago, IL 60605
Ph: (312)663-1600
Fax: (312)344-8052
E-mail: afoley@popmail.colum.edu
URL: http://www.colum.edu
Contact: Ms. Lorel Vidlund, Regional Program Coor.
State. University and college presidents, vice presidents, directors, deans, and faculty interested in higher education planning; government agencies; corporations; private consultants. **Affiliated With:** Society for College and University Planning.

1189 ■ Society for Healthcare Consumer Advocacy of the American Hospital Association (SHCA AHA)
One N Franklin
Chicago, IL 60606
Ph: (312)422-3851
Fax: (312)422-4575
E-mail: shca@aha.org
URL: http://www.shca-aha.org
Contact: Lindsay Robinson CHE, Exec.Dir.
Founded: 1974. **Members:** 980. **Membership Dues:** student, retired, $125 (annual) • associate, $120 (annual). **Regional**. Provides vital support to professionals joined together to ensure that patients and consumers receive high-quality health care. **Telecommunication Services:** electronic mail, tjohnson@aha.org. **Affiliated With:** Society for Healthcare Consumer Advocacy of the American Hospital Association. **Publications:** *The Patient Advocate*, quarterly. Newsletter. **Conventions/Meetings:** annual conference.

1190 ■ Society of Human Resource Professionals (SHRP)
8 S Michigan Ave., No. 1000
Chicago, IL 60603
Ph: (312)368-0188
Fax: (312)580-0165
E-mail: shrp@gss.net
URL: http://www.shrp.org
Contact: Karen M. Vujtech, Pres.
Local. Represents the interests of human resource and industrial relations professionals and executives. Promotes the advancement of human resource management.

1191 ■ Society for Information Management, Chicago
c/o Cindy Wiertel
401 N. Michigan Ave.
Chicago, IL 60611
Ph: (312)527-6734
Fax: (312)419-8249
E-mail: simchicago@aol.com
URL: http://simnet.org
Contact: Cindy Wiertel, Contact
State. **Affiliated With:** Society for Information Management.

1192 ■ South Chicago Parents And Friends Of Retarded Children
10242 S Commercial Ave.
Chicago, IL 60617
Ph: (773)734-2222
URL: National Affiliate–www.TheArc.org
Contact: Tom Schell, Exec.Dir.
Local. Parents, professional workers, and others interested in individuals with mental retardation. Works to promote services, research, public understanding, and legislation for people with mental retardation and their families. **Affiliated With:** Arc of the United States.

1193 ■ Southeast Chicago Commission (SECC)
1511 E 53rd St.
Chicago, IL 60615
Ph: (773)324-6926
Fax: (773)324-6685
E-mail: secc2@sbcglobal.net
URL: http://www.hydeparksecc.com
Contact: Robert C. Mason, Exec.Dir.
Founded: 1952. **Members:** 75. **Staff:** 4. **Budget:** $498,000. **Local**. Focuses on law enforcement, victim/witness assistance, building code enforcement, zoning code enforcement, business district recruitment and promotion-community maintenance. **Awards:** Special Service Awards. **Frequency:** annual. **Type:** recognition. **Recipient:** to persons in public or private sector for special service to the community. **Publications:** *SECC News*. Newsletter. Alternate Formats: online.

1194 ■ Southern Thoracic Surgical Association (STSA)
633 N St. Clair St., Ste.2320
Chicago, IL 60611-3658
Ph: (312)202-5892
Fax: (312)202-5801
Free: (800)685-7872
E-mail: stsa@stsa.org
URL: http://www.stsa.org
Contact: D. Glenn Pennington, Pres.
Founded: 1954. **Members:** 800. **Membership Dues:** individual, $255 (annual). **Regional**. **Publications:** *The Annals of Thoracic Surgery*, monthly. Journal. **Conventions/Meetings:** quarterly board meeting • annual meeting.

1195 ■ Southwest Guaranteed Home Equity Program
8136 S. Kedzie Ave.
Chicago, IL 60652
Ph: (773)436-9105
Fax: (773)436-4025
E-mail: swguaranteed@earthlink.net
Contact: Charmaine Ramirez, Chairperson
Founded: 1988. **Members:** 700. **Staff:** 1. **Budget:** $42,000. **Local**. Works to further the goal of maintaining and enhancing the value of properties in the Greater Ashburn area. **Publications:** *Guaranteed Source*, quarterly. Newsletter.

1196 ■ Southwest Women Working Together (SWWT)
6845 S Western Ave.
Chicago, IL 60636
Ph: (773)737-2500
Fax: (773)737-1925
E-mail: info@swwt.org
URL: http://swwt.org
Contact: Ms. Doris Jones, Dir. of Marketing & Resource Development
Founded: 1975. **Regional**. Aims to recognize and free the potential of women, children, and their families. Provides tools and resources through direct service and advocacy, to lead empowered, self-sufficient, and violence-free lives. **Additional Websites:** http://thespiritofawoman.com.

1197 ■ Southwestern Surgical Congress
401 N Michigan Ave.
Chicago, IL 60611-4267
Ph: (312)527-6667
Fax: (312)527-6658
E-mail: swsc@sba.com
URL: http://www.swscongress.org
Contact: April Snyder CAE, Exec.Dir.
Regional.

1198 ■ Special Libraries Association, Illinois Chapter
c/o Priscilla Stultz, Pres.-Elect
LexisNexis
70 W Madison St., Ste.2200
Chicago, IL 60602
Ph: (773)755-3814
Fax: (312)984-1600
E-mail: priscilla.stultz@lexisnexis.com
URL: http://www.slaillinois.org
Contact: Priscilla Stultz, Pres.-Elect
State. Seeks to advance the leadership role of special librarians. Promotes and strengthens members through learning, advocacy and networking initiatives. **Affiliated With:** Special Libraries Association.

1199 ■ Special Wish Foundation, Chicago Chapter
PO Box 577248
Chicago, IL 60657
Ph: (773)551-4982
E-mail: info@aswchicago.org
URL: http://www.aswchicago.com
Local. **Affiliated With:** A Special Wish Foundation.

1200 ■ Starlight Children's Foundation Midwest
30 E Adams St., Ste.1020
Chicago, IL 60603
Ph: (312)251-7827
Fax: (312)251-7825
E-mail: starlightmidwest@starlightmidwest.org
URL: http://www.starlightmidwest.org
Contact: Kathleen D. Super, Exec.Dir.
Regional. Works to improve the quality of life for seriously ill children and their families. Provides both hospital-based and out-patient programs that help seriously ill children and their families cope with the stress, isolation, fear and loneliness of hospitalization, and help relieve the daily suffering and coping

challenges associated with serious illness and disability. **Affiliated With:** Starlight Children's Foundation.

1201 ■ Steinmetz HS JROTC Pathfinders
c/o Maj. Roger Seymore
3030 N Mobile Ave.
Chicago, IL 60634
Ph: (773)534-3023
URL: http://www.jrotc-steinmetz.com
Contact: Maj. Roger Seymore, Contact
Local. Affiliated With: United States Orienteering Federation.

1202 ■ Stone Academy PTA
c/o Stone Scholastic Academy
6329 N Leavitt Ave.
Chicago, IL 60659
Ph: (773)534-2045 (773)534-2067
E-mail: p_unger@msn.com
URL: http://www.greenville.k12.sc.us/stone/communit/pta.asp
Contact: Camille Unger, Pres.
Local. Parents, teachers, students, and others interested in uniting the forces of home, school, and community. Promotes the welfare of children and youth.

1203 ■ Streeterville Organization of Active Residents
c/o Carlotta Olson, Asst.Exec.Dir.
215 E Chicago Ave., Ste.212
Chicago, IL 60611
Ph: (312)440-9325
Fax: (312)440-9328
E-mail: soarchicago@aol.com
URL: http://www.soarchicago.org
Contact: Rosalie Harris, Exec.Dir.
Founded: 1975. **Members:** 620. **Membership Dues:** resident, $50 (annual) • condo/co-op/building, $250-$400 (annual) • institution/business/hotel/non-profit, $250 (annual). **Staff:** 1. **Budget:** $60,000. **Local.** Local resident striving to maintain and enhance quality of life in Streetville and to value investments of residents in the community. Activities are quarterly public programs, newsletter and public statements. **Awards:** Beautification Award. **Frequency:** annual. **Type:** recognition. **Recipient:** to the most attractive residence and one to most attractive commercial venue. **Publications:** *SOAR Newsletter & News Briefs*, quarterly. Newsletters. **Price:** free. **Circulation:** 800. Alternate Formats: diskette.

1204 ■ Studebaker Driver's Club, Black Hawk Chapter
c/o Dave Reid, Starliner Ed.
3212 S Lowe Ave.
Chicago, IL 60616-3408
Ph: (312)842-1864
URL: http://www.studebakerclubs.com/blackhawk
Contact: Dave Reid, Starliner Ed.
Local. Works to preserve the Studebaker name and related vehicles produced by the company during its period in the transportation field. Supports the parent Studebaker Drivers Club and provides services to members. **Affiliated With:** Studebaker Driver's Club.

1205 ■ Swedish American Museum Association of Chicago (SAMAC)
5211 N Clark St.
Chicago, IL 60640
Ph: (773)728-8111
Fax: (773)728-8870
E-mail: museum@samac.org
URL: http://www.samac.org
Contact: Kerstin Lane, Exec.Dir.
Founded: 1976. **Members:** 1,600. **Membership Dues:** student/senior, $15 (annual) • senior couple, $25 (annual) • individual, $35 (annual) • spouse/family, $50 (annual) • sustaining/nonprofit organization, $75 (annual) • corporate, $250 (annual) • Sandburg Society, $100-$249 (annual) • Linnaeus Society, $250-$520 (annual) • club, $521-$999 (annual) • 3 Crowns Group members (minimum), $1,000 (annual). **Staff:** 6. **Budget:** $600,000. **Languages:** English, Swedish. Americans of Swedish descent; other interested Swedes. Group is national in scope, but membership is concentrated in the Chicago, IL area. Seeks to preserve the history and culture of Swedish Americans. Maintains speakers' bureau and Swedish Museum and Cultural Center; offers genealogy classes, craft lessons, and language instruction; provides children's services. Sponsors concerts; observes Swedish holidays; holds exhibits. **Awards:** Swedish American Museum Award. **Frequency:** annual. **Type:** recognition. **Publications:** *FLAGGAN*, quarterly. Newsletter. **Price:** included in membership dues. **Circulation:** 1,500. **Advertising:** accepted.

1206 ■ Sweet Adelines International, Edge O' Town Chapter
Irving Park Baptist Church
4401 W Irving Park Rd.
Chicago, IL 60641-2804
Ph: (773)545-1369
E-mail: richard.malczewski@comcast.net
URL: National Affiliate–www.sweetadelineintl.org
Contact: Laura Malczewski, Contact
Local. Advances the musical art form of barbershop harmony through education and performances. Provides education, training and coaching in the development of women's four-part barbershop harmony. **Affiliated With:** Sweet Adelines International.

1207 ■ Theta Xi, Gamma Kappa Chapter — University of Illinois-Chicago
c/o Mike Kelly
UIC Campus Prgs M/118, Rm. 300
750 S Halsted
Chicago, IL 60607
Ph: (312)355-6569
E-mail: mtkelly@neiu.edu
URL: http://www.txgk.com
Local. Affiliated With: Theta Xi.

1208 ■ Tourette Syndrome Camping Organization
c/o Scott B. Loeff
6933 N Kedzie Ave., Ste.816
Chicago, IL 60645-2725
Ph: (773)465-7536
E-mail: scott63@prodigy.net
URL: http://www.tourettecamp.com
Contact: Scott B. Loeff, Contact
Founded: 2002. **Nonmembership. Local.** Runs a summer camp for children with Tourette Syndrome, OCD and ADD/ADHD. Activities include sharing sessions among children with the same disabilities, exchanging coping mechanisms in a fun, safe and positive environment. **Awards:** Camp Scholarships. **Type:** scholarship. **Recipient:** based on need.

1209 ■ Trout Unlimited, Elliott Donnelley
6880 N Wildwood
Chicago, IL 60646
Ph: (773)775-2933
E-mail: jimcoursey@ameritech.net
URL: http://www.edtu.org
Contact: James Coursey, Pres.
Founded: 1960. **Members:** 600. **Local. Affiliated With:** Trout Unlimited.

1210 ■ Turkish American Chamber of Commerce (TACCOMM)
PO Box 06238
Chicago, IL 60606-6238
E-mail: info@turkishchamber.org
URL: http://www.turkishchamber.org
Local.

1211 ■ Turkish American Cultural Alliance of Chicago (TACA)
PO Box 5533
Chicago, IL 60680
Fax: (773)327-3066
E-mail: taca@tacaonline.org
URL: http://www.tacaonline.org
Contact: Mehmet Celebi, Pres.
Founded: 1968. **Membership Dues:** individual, $75 (annual) • family, $150 (annual) • student, $35 (annual). **Local. Affiliated With:** Assembly of Turkish American Associations.

1212 ■ Union Avenue Wyld Life - Wyldlife
4350 S Union Ave.
Chicago, IL 60609
Ph: (773)924-5060
URL: http://sites.younglife.org/_layouts/ylext/default.aspx?ID=C-3402
Local. Represents the interests of individuals committed to impacting kids' lives and preparing them for the future. Helps young people develop their skills, assets and attitudes to reach their full God-given potential. Reaches suburban, urban, multicultural and disabled kids and teenage mothers. **Affiliated With:** Young Life.

1213 ■ United Association of Journeymen and Apprentices of the Plumbing and Pipe Fitting Industry of the United States and Canada - Local Union 597
45 N Ogden Ave.
Chicago, IL 60607
Ph: (312)829-4191
Fax: (312)829-0137
URL: http://www.pf597.org
Contact: Curt L. Cade, Financial Sec.-Treas.
Members: 7,085. **Local. Affiliated With:** United Association of Journeymen and Apprentices of the Plumbing, Pipe Fitting, Sprinkler Fitting Industry of the U.S. and Canada.

1214 ■ United Brotherhood of Carpenters and Joiners of America, Chicago Regional Council of Carpenters
12 E Erie St.
Chicago, IL 60611-2796
Ph: (312)787-3076
Fax: (312)951-1516
URL: http://www.carpentersunion.org
Contact: Martin C. Umlauf, Pres./Exec.Sec.-Treas.
Regional. Affiliated With: United Brotherhood of Carpenters and Joiners of America. **Formerly:** (2005) United Brotherhood of Carpenters and Joiners of America, Milwaukee and Southeast Wisconsin Regional Council 4288.

1215 ■ United Chinese Scholars and Students Association
c/o Jianming Zhang
5455 S Blackstone, No. 1C
Chicago, IL 60615-5437
E-mail: contact@ucssa.org
Contact: Jianming Zhang, Contact
Founded: 2000. **Members:** 7,000. **Membership Dues:** $50 (annual). **Staff:** 12. **Budget:** $5,000. **Regional Groups:** 11. **Languages:** Chinese, English.

1216 ■ United States Naval Sea Cadet Corps - Carl G. Stockholm Battalion
NW Natl. Guard Armory
1551 N Kedzie Ave.
Chicago, IL 60651
E-mail: levvintre@aol.com
URL: http://dolphin.seacadets.org/US_units/UnitDetails.asp?UnitID=091STO
Contact: Lt. Paul E. Levvintre, Commanding Officer
Local. Works to instill good citizenship and patriotism in youth. Encourages qualities such as personal neatness, loyalty, obedience, dependability, and responsibility to others. Offers courses in physical fitness and military drill, first aid, water safety, basic seamanship, and naval history and traditions. **Affiliated With:** Naval Sea Cadet Corps.

1217 ■ United Way of Metropolitan Chicago
560 W Lake
Chicago, IL 60661
Ph: (312)906-2350
Fax: (312)876-0199
E-mail: info@uw-mc.org
URL: http://www.uw-mc.org
Contact: Janet Froetscher, Pres./CEO
Local. Affiliated With: United Way of America.

1218 ■ Upgrade Cycle
1130 W Chicago
Chicago, IL 60622
Ph: (312)226-8650
URL: http://www.upgradecycle.com
Local. Affiliated With: International Mountain Bicycling Association.

1219 ■ Uptown Chamber of Commerce
4753 N Broadway, Ste.822
Chicago, IL 60640
Ph: (773)878-1184
Fax: (773)878-3678
E-mail: info@uptownchamber.com
URL: http://www.uptownchamber.com
Contact: Wally Rozak, Interim Exec.Dir.
Members: 150. **Local.** Promotes business and community development in the uptown area of Chicago, IL. **Awards:** Athena Award. **Frequency:** annual. **Type:** recognition. **Recipient:** to outstanding businesswoman • Stone Award. **Frequency:** annual. **Type:** recognition. **Recipient:** to outstanding businessperson. **Publications:** *Chambergram*, monthly. Newsletter. **Price:** free. **Conventions/Meetings:** bimonthly meeting.

1220 ■ USA Weightlifting - Sayre Park
c/o Charles Nooten
6871 W Belden
Chicago, IL 60707
Ph: (630)587-9363
URL: National Affiliate–www.usaweightlifting.org
Contact: Charles Nooten, Contact
Local. Affiliated With: USA Weightlifting.

1221 ■ Variety of Illinois
One IBM Plz., Ste.2800
Chicago, IL 60611
Ph: (312)822-0660
Fax: (312)822-0661
E-mail: info@varietyclub26.org
URL: http://www.varietyclub26.org
State. Affiliated With: Variety International - The Children's Charity.

1222 ■ Victor C Neumann Association
5548 N Bavenswood
Chicago, IL 60640
Ph: (773)769-4313
Fax: (773)769-1476
URL: National Affiliate–www.TheArc.org
Contact: Eileen Durkin, CEO
Local. Parents, professional workers, and others interested in individuals with mental retardation. Works to promote services, research, public understanding, and legislation for people with mental retardation and their families. **Affiliated With:** Arc of the United States.

1223 ■ Voices for Illinois Children
c/o Julie Parente, Communications Dir.
208 S LaSalle St., Ste.1490
Chicago, IL 60604-1120
Ph: (312)456-0600
Fax: (312)456-0088
E-mail: info@voices4kids.org
URL: http://www.voices4kids.org
Contact: Gaylord Gieseke, VP
State. Affiliated With: Voices for America's Children.

1224 ■ Volunteers of America of Illinois
224 N Des Plaines, Ste.500
Chicago, IL 60661
Ph: (312)707-8707
E-mail: adoran@avoa.org
URL: http://www.voaillinois.com
Contact: Nancy J. Hughes, Pres./CEO
State. Provides local human service programs and opportunities for individual and community involvement. **Affiliated With:** Volunteers of America.

1225 ■ Walk and Roll Chicago - American Cancer Society
225 N Michigan Ave., Ste.1210
Chicago, IL 60601
Ph: (312)372-0471
Fax: (312)372-0910
E-mail: walk.roll@cancer.org
URL: http://www.walkandrollchicago.org
Contact: Tracy May, Senior Income Development Representative
Local. Aims to eliminate cancer as a major health problem through research, education, advocacy and services.

1226 ■ Walkabout Theater Company
c/o Kristan Schmidt, Artistic Dir.
3241 N Ravenswood Ave.
Chicago, IL 60657
Ph: (312)458-0566
URL: http://www.walkabouttheater.org
Contact: Kristan Schmidt, Artistic Dir.
Local.

1227 ■ West Central Association
c/o Michael Ezgur, Pres.
625 W. Madison St., No. 1403
Chicago, IL 60661
Ph: (312)902-4538
Fax: (312)902-4922
E-mail: officewca@aol.com
URL: http://westcentralassociation.com
Contact: Robert Wiggs, Exec.Dir.
Founded: 1929. **Members:** 175. **Membership Dues:** regular level member, $300 (annual) • director level member, $600 (annual) • sustaining level member, $1,200 (annual). **Staff:** 2. **For-Profit. Local.** Works as area chamber of commerce. **Publications:** *Area Service*, annual. Directory. **Price:** no fee. **Circulation:** 5,000 • Newsletter, monthly. **Price:** no fee. **Circulation:** 750.

1228 ■ West Chatham Improvement Association
c/o Jacqueline M. Curry, Pres.
8153 S Harvard Ave.
Chicago, IL 60620-1708
Ph: (773)846-8871
Fax: (773)846-8871
E-mail: jcurry@mbda.gov
Contact: Jacqueline M. Curry, Pres.
Works to promote the civic involvement of the West Chatham community and all those areas which affect the well-being, advancement, improvement and overall stability of the community and all of its residents.

1229 ■ West Lawn Chamber of Commerce
4021 W 63rd St., Unit 2B
Chicago, IL 60629-3711
Ph: (773)735-7690
Fax: (773)284-8110
E-mail: wstlwncc@aol.com
URL: http://www.westlawncc.org
Contact: Mrs. Edie Cavanaugh, Exec.Dir.
Founded: 1972. **Members:** 125. **Membership Dues:** $125 (annual). **Staff:** 1. **Local.** Provides technical assistance to local businesses in the areas of marketing, finance, employment, and public relations. **Publications:** *Members Directory* • Newsletter, monthly • Brochure, periodic. **Conventions/Meetings:** monthly meeting, with guest speakers, workshops - first Tuesday of the month.

1230 ■ West Portage Park Neighborhood Improvement Association
c/o Portage Park Center for the Arts
3914 N Menard Ave.
Chicago, IL 60634-2600
Ph: (773)205-0151
Fax: (773)205-8753
E-mail: jlacivita1@sbcglobal.net
Contact: Jennifer La Civita, Exec.Dir.
Founded: 1999. **Nonmembership. Local.** Seeks to provide and enrich the community with educational programs and neighborhood beautification projects. Highlights all the community has to offer serving as a supportive resource site. Goal is to create a thriving, viable institution that celebrates the arts, promotes aesthetic enlightenment, and appreciation for all things living.

1231 ■ Westridge Chamber of Commerce
2720 W Devon, Ste.B
Chicago, IL 60659
Ph: (773)743-6022
Fax: (773)743-2893
E-mail: westridgechamber@sbcglobal.net
URL: http://westridgechamber.org
Contact: Neal Gallo, Pres.
Founded: 1992. **Members:** 140. **Membership Dues:** $75 (annual). **Staff:** 2. **Local.** Local chamber of commerce. Represents members' interests; holds seminars, workshops, and other promotional activities. **Formerly:** (2005) Devon North Town Business and Professional Association. **Publications:** *International Marketplace Newsletter*. **Price:** free.

1232 ■ Wheelmen, Illinois
PO Box 09075
Chicago, IL 60609-9075
Ph: (773)523-5906
E-mail: wasp3245@aol.com
URL: National Affiliate–www.thewheelmen.org
State.

1233 ■ Windy City Miniature Club
c/o Doris Leftakes
5601 N Menard Ave.
Chicago, IL 60646
Ph: (773)774-7532
URL: http://www.miniatures.org/states/IL.html
Contact: Doris Leftakes, Contact
Local. Affiliated With: National Association of Miniature Enthusiasts.

1234 ■ Windy City Women's Charity Club
c/o Maura McCarthy
2827 N Washtenaw Unit E
Chicago, IL 60618
Ph: (312)474-2033
E-mail: mmccarthy@cwcc.org
URL: http://www.wcwcc.org
Local.

1235 ■ Women in the Director's Chair of Chicago (WIDC)
c/o Lopa Pal
PO Box 11135
Chicago, IL 60611-0135
Ph: (773)235-4301
Fax: (773)235-4302
E-mail: widc@widc.org
URL: http://www.widc.org
Local.

1236 ■ Women Employed
c/o Karen Latimer, Dir. of Finance and Administration
111 N Wabash, Ste.1300
Chicago, IL 60602
Ph: (312)782-3902
Fax: (312)782-5249
E-mail: info@womenemployed.org
URL: http://www.womenemployed.org
Local.

1237 ■ Women In Film Chicago
c/o Jenny Polk
100 W Kinzie, 3rd Fl.
Chicago, IL 60661
Fax: (312)884-0084
E-mail: info@wifchicago.org
URL: http://www.wifchicago.org
Contact: Jenny Polk, Contact
Local. Advances the professional development and achievement of women working in all areas of film, television, video, multimedia and related disciplines. Improves the status of women through education, training, networking and advocacy. **Affiliated With:** Women in Film.

1238 ■ Women's Bar Association of Illinois (WBAI)
321 S Plymouth Ct., Ste.4S
Chicago, IL 60604
Ph: (312)341-8530
Fax: (312)341-8533
E-mail: wbai8530@enteract.com
URL: http://www.wbaillinois.org
Contact: Dawn Gonzalez, Pres.
State.

1239 ■ Wrightwood Community Development Corp.
c/o Stanley Burchette, Pres.
8228 S Kedzie Ave.
Chicago, IL 60652
Ph: (773)476-9880
Fax: (773)476-9887
E-mail: wrightcdc@aol.com
Contact: Anita Norwood, Exec.Dir.
Provides housing information, minor repair program for seniors, technical assistance and after-school program to residents and businesses located in the Southwest area of Chicago.

1240 ■ YMCA Training Alliance
c/o Norma Dreux
YMCA Training Alliance of Chicago
11 E Adams St., Ste.300
Chicago, IL 60603
Ph: (312)913-2150
Fax: (312)913-2157
E-mail: ndreux@ymcachgo.org
URL: http://collaboratory.nunet.net/itrc/ymcata
Contact: Norma Dreux, Contact
Local.

1241 ■ Young Life Chicago Northside
2170 W Warner Ave.
Chicago, IL 60618
Ph: (773)327-5262
URL: http://ChicagoNorthside.younglife.org
Local.

1242 ■ Young Life LaSalle Street
1111 N Wells St., Ste.402
Chicago, IL 60610
Ph: (312)573-8918
Fax: (312)573-8939
URL: http://whereis.younglife.org/FriendlyUrlRedirector.aspx?ID=A-IL20
Local.

1243 ■ Young Life MW Multicultural/Urban
1111 N Wells St., Ste.500
Chicago, IL 60610
Ph: (312)573-8896
Fax: (312)573-8888
URL: http://whereis.younglife.org/FriendlyUrlRedirector.aspx?ID=A-1535
Local.

1244 ■ Young Life Northwest Chicago
Gap Community Ctr.
Chicago, IL 60639
Ph: (773)489-5949
Fax: (773)489-6014
URL: http://whereis.younglife.org/FriendlyUrlRedirector.aspx?ID=A-IL31
Local.

1245 ■ Young Life Union Ave.
4350 S Union Ave.
Chicago, IL 60609
Ph: (773)924-5060
URL: http://sites.younglife.org/_layouts/ylext/default.aspx?ID=C-871
Local. Affiliated With: Young Life.

1246 ■ YWCA of Metropolitan Chicago
360 N Michigan Ave.
Chicago, IL 60601
Ph: (312)372-6600
Fax: (312)372-4673
E-mail: info@ywcachicago.org
URL: http://www.ywcachicago.org
Contact: Martha McGuire, Pres.
Local. Affiliated With: Girls Inc.

Chicago Heights

1247 ■ American Legion, Chicago Heights Post 131
PO Box 54
Chicago Heights, IL 60412
Ph: (709)754-0131
Fax: (309)663-5783
URL: National Affiliate–www.legion.org
Local. Affiliated With: American Legion.

1248 ■ American Legion, Illinois Post 410
c/o Franklin A. Dennison
1523 Halsted
Chicago Heights, IL 60411
Ph: (309)663-0361
Fax: (309)663-5783
URL: National Affiliate–www.legion.org
Contact: Franklin A. Dennison, Contact
Local. Affiliated With: American Legion.

1249 ■ American Legion, Park Forest Post 1198
1631 Western Ave.
Chicago Heights, IL 60411
Ph: (309)663-0361
Fax: (309)663-5783
URL: National Affiliate–www.legion.org
Local. Affiliated With: American Legion.

1250 ■ Habitat for Humanity Chicago South Suburbs
1655 Union Ave.
Chicago Heights, IL 60411
Ph: (708)756-2015
Fax: (708)756-2075
E-mail: dst13@mcihispeed.net
URL: http://www.hfhchgosouth.org
Local. Affiliated With: Habitat for Humanity International.

1251 ■ Phi Theta Kappa, Nu Sigma Chapter - Prairie State College
c/o Velton Lacefield
202 S Halsted Ave.
Chicago Heights, IL 60411
Ph: (708)709-3624
E-mail: vlacefield@prairiestate.edu
URL: http://www.ptk.org/directories/chapters/IL/180-1.htm
Contact: Velton Lacefield, Advisor
Local.

Chicago Ridge

1252 ■ American Legion, Glenn Maker Post 1160
10739 Ridgeland Ave.
Chicago Ridge, IL 60415
Ph: (708)422-5675
Fax: (309)663-5783
URL: National Affiliate–www.legion.org
Local. Affiliated With: American Legion.

1253 ■ American Legion, Triangle Post 933
c/o Emanuel Cosentino
10960 Oxford Ave.
Chicago Ridge, IL 60415
Ph: (309)663-0361
Fax: (309)663-5783
URL: National Affiliate–www.legion.org
Contact: Emanuel Cosentino, Contact
Local. Affiliated With: American Legion.

Chillicothe

1254 ■ American Legion, Chillicothe Post 9
1043 N 2nd St.
Chillicothe, IL 61523
Ph: (309)274-3255
Fax: (309)663-5783
URL: National Affiliate–www.legion.org
Local. Affiliated With: American Legion.

1255 ■ Chillicothe Chamber of Commerce (CCC)
1028 N 2nd St.
Chillicothe, IL 61523
Ph: (309)274-4556
Fax: (309)274-3303
E-mail: info@chillicothechamber.com
URL: http://www.chillicothechamber.com
Contact: Sarah Williamson, Pres.
Local. Promotes business and community development in Chillicothe, IL. **Awards:** Chamber Member of the Year. **Frequency:** annual. **Type:** recognition • Civic Award of the Year. **Frequency:** annual. **Type:** recognition. **Councils:** Chillicothe City. **Conventions/Meetings:** semimonthly Chillicothe City Council - meeting - every second and fourth Monday • monthly General Membership - meeting - always third Wednesday.

1256 ■ Chillicothe Twin City REACT
21729 N Yankee Ln.
Chillicothe, IL 61523
Ph: (309)274-4535
URL: http://www.reactintl.org/teaminfo/usa_teams/teams-usil.htm
Local. Trained communication experts and professional volunteers. Provides volunteer public service and emergency communications through the use of radios (Citizen Band, General Mobile Radio Service, UHF and HAM). Coordinates with radio industries and government on safety communication matters and supports charitable activities and community organizations.

Chrisman

1257 ■ American Legion, Chrisman Post 477
124 N Illinois St.
Chrisman, IL 61924
Ph: (217)269-2421
Fax: (309)663-5783
URL: National Affiliate–www.legion.org
Local. Affiliated With: American Legion.

Christopher

1258 ■ American Legion, Christopher Post 528
217 W Market St.
Christopher, IL 62822
Ph: (618)724-2034
Fax: (309)663-5783
URL: National Affiliate–www.legion.org
Local. Affiliated With: American Legion.

Cicero

1259 ■ American Legion, Cicero Post 96
5820 W 35th St.
Cicero, IL 60804
Ph: (708)652-4341
Fax: (309)663-5783
URL: National Affiliate–www.legion.org
Local. Affiliated With: American Legion.

1260 ■ Cicero Chamber of Commerce and Industry
5801 W Cermak Rd., 2nd Fl.
Cicero, IL 60804
Ph: (708)863-6000
Fax: (708)863-8981
URL: http://www.cicerochamber.org
Contact: Mary Esther Rodriguez, Exec.Dir.
Local. Promotes business and community development in Cicero, IL area.

1261 ■ Phi Theta Kappa, Theta Omicron Chapter - Morton College
c/o Blance Gutierrez
3801 S Central Ave.
Cicero, IL 60804
Ph: (708)656-8000
E-mail: blanca.gutierre@morton.edu
URL: http://www.ptk.org/directories/chapters/IL/175-1.htm
Contact: Blanca Gutierrez, Advisor
Local.

1262 ■ West Towns Board of Realtors
6017 W 26th St.
Cicero, IL 60804-3012
Ph: (708)863-1111
Fax: (708)863-1134
E-mail: wtbr@westtownsboard.com
URL: http://www.westtownsboard.com
Contact: Barbara Novak, Pres.
Local. Strives to develop real estate business practices. Advocates the right to own, use and transfer real property. Provides a facility for professional development, research and exchange of information among members and to the general public. **Affiliated With:** National Association of Realtors.

Cisco

1263 ■ American Legion, Craig-Reed Post 1181
55 Dodge St.
Cisco, IL 61830
Ph: (217)669-2325
Fax: (309)663-5783
URL: National Affiliate–www.legion.org
Local. **Affiliated With:** American Legion.

Cisne

1264 ■ American Legion, Gresham Post 603
PO Box 283
Cisne, IL 62823
Ph: (309)663-0361
Fax: (309)663-5783
URL: National Affiliate–www.legion.org
Local. **Affiliated With:** American Legion.

Cissna Park

1265 ■ American Legion, Cissna Park Post 527
124 S 2nd St.
Cissna Park, IL 60924
Ph: (309)663-0361
Fax: (309)663-5783
URL: National Affiliate–www.legion.org
Local. **Affiliated With:** American Legion.

Clarendon Hills

1266 ■ Clarendon Hills Lions Club
PO Box 62
Clarendon Hills, IL 60514
E-mail: info@chlions.org
URL: http://www.chlions.org
Local. **Affiliated With:** Lions Clubs International.

Clay City

1267 ■ American Legion, Clay City Post 840
RR 1, Box 268
Clay City, IL 62824
Ph: (618)676-1122
Fax: (309)663-5783
URL: National Affiliate–www.legion.org
Local. **Affiliated With:** American Legion.

Clayton

1268 ■ American Legion, Clayton Post 286
PO Box 284
Clayton, IL 62324
Ph: (217)894-7787
Fax: (309)663-5783
URL: National Affiliate–www.legion.org
Local. **Affiliated With:** American Legion.

Clifton

1269 ■ American Legion, Clifton Post 385
PO Box 475
Clifton, IL 60927
Ph: (815)694-2227
Fax: (309)663-5783
URL: National Affiliate–www.legion.org
Local. **Affiliated With:** American Legion.

Clinton

1270 ■ American Legion, Craig-Bennett Post 103
PO Box 23
Clinton, IL 61727
Ph: (217)935-5443
Fax: (309)663-5783
URL: National Affiliate–www.legion.org
Local. **Affiliated With:** American Legion.

1271 ■ American Nuclear Society, Central Illinois Section
c/o Mr. Alan C. Darelius, Chm.
Clinton Power Sta.
RR3 Box 228
Clinton, IL 61727-9351
Ph: (217)937-3162
Fax: (217)935-0761
URL: National Affiliate–www.ans.org
Contact: Mr. Alan C. Darelius, Chm.
Local. Works to advance science and engineering in the nuclear industry. Works with government agencies, educational institutions, and other organizations dealing with nuclear issues. **Affiliated With:** American Nuclear Society.

1272 ■ Central Illinois Health Information Management Association (CIHIMA)
c/o Jeanette Ferguson, RHIA, Treas.
RR 3, Box 207F
Clinton, IL 61727
Ph: (312)233-1520
E-mail: kathy.giannangelo@ahima.org
URL: http://www.ilhima.org
Contact: Kathy Giannangelo RHIA, Pres.-Elect
Local. Represents the interests of individuals dedicated to the effective management of personal health information needed to deliver quality healthcare to the public. Provides career, professional development and practice resources. Sets standards for education and certification. Advocates public policy that advances Health Information Management (HIM) practice. **Affiliated With:** American Health Information Management Association.

1273 ■ Clinton Area Chamber of Commerce (CACC)
100 S Center St., Ste.101
Clinton, IL 61727-1945
Ph: (217)935-3364
Fax: (217)935-0064
Free: (866)4DE-WITT
E-mail: info@clintonilchamber.com
URL: http://www.clintonilchamber.com
Contact: Steve Vandiver, Exec.Dir.
Founded: 1953. **Members:** 200. **Staff:** 3. **Local**. Promotes business and community development in Clinton, IL. Sponsors Clinton May Days Festival and Community Expo. **Telecommunication Services:** electronic mail, clintonillinoischamber@verizon.net. **Affiliated With:** American Chamber of Commerce Executives. **Formerly:** (1999) Clinton +Chamber of Commerce. **Publications:** *Chamber Scoop*. Newsletter. Alternate Formats: online. **Conventions/Meetings:** annual Christmas Candlelight - tour - every Friday in December, De Witt, IL • annual Clinton May Days - festival, with carnival, food and craft vendors, and entertainment - always May, Clinton, IL • annual dinner, with dancing • annual Terror on Washington Street - meeting, Halloween scare event - latter part of October, Clinton, IL.

1274 ■ International Facility Management Association, Central Illinois (Bloomington/Decatur/Champaign)
c/o Ronda E. Piatt, Pres.
Chestnut Hea. Syss.
RR2 Box 243
Clinton, IL 61727
Ph: (309)827-6026
Fax: (309)820-3574
E-mail: rpiatt@chestnut.org
URL: National Affiliate–www.ifma.org
Contact: Ronda E. Piatt, Pres.
Local. **Affiliated With:** International Facility Management Association.

Coal City

1275 ■ American Legion, Coal City Post 796
PO Box 282
Coal City, IL 60416
Ph: (815)634-2787
Fax: (309)663-5783
URL: National Affiliate–www.legion.org
Local. **Affiliated With:** American Legion.

1276 ■ American Rabbit Breeders Association, Illinois Dutch Rabbit Club
c/o Norma Hart
190 N First Ave.
Coal City, IL 60416
E-mail: normahart1@aol.com
URL: http://www.nordickrabbits.com/specialt.htm
Contact: Norma Hart, Contact
Local. **Affiliated With:** American Rabbit Breeders Association.

1277 ■ American Rabbit Breeders Association, Land of Lincoln Satin Rabbit Breeders Association
c/o Jackie Marshall
195 E North St.
Coal City, IL 60416-1056
Ph: (815)634-6627
E-mail: tbmarshall2@aol.com
URL: http://www.nordickrabbits.com/specialt.htm
Contact: Jackie Marshall, Contact
Local. **Affiliated With:** American Rabbit Breeders Association.

Coal Valley

1278 ■ American Legion, Coal Valley Post 1248
108 W 7th St.
Coal Valley, IL 61240

Ph: (309)792-3645
Fax: (309)663-5783
URL: National Affiliate–www.legion.org
Local. Affiliated With: American Legion.

1279 ■ Coal Valley Lions Club
131 W 14 St.
Coal Valley, IL 61240
Ph: (309)799-5675
E-mail: meyer296@mchsi.com
URL: http://coalvalleyil.lionwap.org
Local. Affiliated With: Lions Clubs International.

1280 ■ Quad Cities British Auto Club
c/o Bob Kerr
8323 50th St.
Coal Valley, IL 61240
E-mail: ocikerr@aol.com
URL: http://qcbac.home.mchsi.com
Contact: Bob Kerr, Contact
Local. Affiliated With: Vintage Triumph Register.

Cobden

1281 ■ American Legion, Cobden Post 259
PO Box 466
Cobden, IL 62920
Ph: (309)663-0361
Fax: (309)663-5783
URL: National Affiliate–www.legion.org
Local. Affiliated With: American Legion.

Colchester

1282 ■ Colchester Lions Club
PO Box 333
Colchester, IL 62326
Ph: (309)836-6641
E-mail: elwilhelm04@yahoo.com
URL: http://www.freewebs.com/clions
Local. Affiliated With: Lions Clubs International.

Colfax

1283 ■ American Legion, Davis-Kerber Post 653
PO Box 454
Colfax, IL 61728
Ph: (309)723-5451
Fax: (309)663-5783
URL: National Affiliate–www.legion.org
Local. Affiliated With: American Legion.

1284 ■ American Legion, Erwin Martensen Post 164
36409 E 1800 N Rd.
Colfax, IL 61728
Ph: (309)723-6411
Fax: (309)663-5783
URL: National Affiliate–www.legion.org
Local. Affiliated With: American Legion.

1285 ■ Illinois Angus Association
c/o Chad Hoffman, Pres.
18206 N 3400 E Rd.
Colfax, IL 61728-9567
Ph: (309)723-4006
E-mail: angus21@mindspring.com
URL: National Affiliate–www.angus.org
Contact: Chad Hoffman, Pres.
Local. Affiliated With: American Angus Association.

Collinsville

1286 ■ American Legion, Leighton Evatt Post 365
1022 Vandalia St.
Collinsville, IL 62234
Ph: (618)344-7664
Fax: (309)663-5783
URL: National Affiliate–www.legion.org
Local. Affiliated With: American Legion.

1287 ■ Collinsville Chamber of Commerce
221 W Main St.
Collinsville, IL 62234
Ph: (618)344-2884
Fax: (618)344-7499
E-mail: info@discovercollinsville.com
URL: http://www.discovercollinsville.com
Staff: 2. **Local.** Promotes business and community development in Collinsville, IL.

1288 ■ Collinsville Convention and Visitors Bureau
One Gateway Dr.
Collinsville, IL 62234-6107
Ph: (618)345-4999
Fax: (618)345-9024
Free: (800)289-2388
E-mail: lsmith@discovercollinsville.com
URL: http://www.discovercollinsville.com
Contact: Lisa Smith, Dir. of Tourism
Local. Seeks to promote overnight stays and other tourism-related activities for Collinsville, IL.

1289 ■ Collinsville Memorial Public Library Foundation
c/o William J. Metzger
408 W Main St.
Collinsville, IL 62234-3018
Ph: (618)344-1112
Fax: (618)345-6401
E-mail: barbarrar@lcls.org
URL: http://www.collinsvillelibrary.org
Contact: Barbarra Rhodes, Dir.
Local.

1290 ■ Downtown Collinsville Main Street Program
216 E Main St.
Collinsville, IL 62234
Ph: (618)345-5598
Fax: (618)345-5699
E-mail: info@downtowncollinsville.com
URL: http://www.downtowncollinsville.com
Local.

1291 ■ Midwestern United States Imperial Club (MUSIC)
PO Box 695
Collinsville, IL 62234
Ph: (618)463-2405
E-mail: webmaster@music-il.com
URL: http://www.music-il.com
Contact: Linda McKechan, Pres.
Regional. Promotes and preserves bop, swing, shag and jitterbug dance styles and the heritage of those styles of music that center on the beat and rhythm. Strives to enhance communication and promotional coordination of activities throughout the membership.

1292 ■ Trail of Tears Association - Illinois Chapter
PO Box 631
Collinsville, IL 62234
Ph: (618)993-5114
E-mail: ozkoala@hcis.net
URL: National Affiliate–www.nationaltota.org
Contact: Andrew West, Pres.
State. Supports the creation, development, and interpretation of the Trail of Tears National Historic Trail. Promotes awareness of the Trail of Tear's legacy. Promotes and engages in the protection and preservation of National Historic Trail resources. **Affiliated With:** Trail of Tears Association.

Colona

1293 ■ American Legion, Green-Rock-Colona Post 1233
PO Box 51
Colona, IL 61241
Ph: (309)663-0361
Fax: (309)663-5783
URL: National Affiliate–www.legion.org
Local. Affiliated With: American Legion.

1294 ■ Bi-State Sportsman's Association
PO Box 204
Colona, IL 61241
Ph: (309)792-8455
URL: National Affiliate–www.mynssa.com
Local. Affiliated With: National Skeet Shooting Association.

1295 ■ Colona-Green Rock-Orion United Way
PO Box 398
Colona, IL 61241-0398
Ph: (309)792-3028
URL: National Affiliate–national.unitedway.org
Local. Affiliated With: United Way of America.

1296 ■ National Active And Retired Federal Employees Association - Blackhawk 338
266 Melrose Dr.
Colona, IL 61241-9602
Ph: (309)949-3819
URL: National Affiliate–www.narfe.org
Contact: Linda J. Bass, Contact
Local. Protects the retirement future of employees through education. Informs members on issues affecting the retirement. **Affiliated With:** National Association of Retired Federal Employees.

Columbia

1297 ■ American Legion, Columbia Post 581
375 E Locust St.
Columbia, IL 62236
Ph: (618)281-5556
Fax: (309)663-5783
URL: National Affiliate–www.legion.org
Local. Affiliated With: American Legion.

1298 ■ Kiwanis Club of Columbia, Illinois
c/o Jeff Huch, Membership Chair
2642 Lakeshore Dr.
Columbia, IL 62236
Ph: (618)281-2413
E-mail: jhuch@htc.net
URL: http://www.kiwaniscolumbia.com
Contact: Gary Heath, Pres.
Local.

Compton

1299 ■ American Legion, Brooklyn Post 657
PO Box 28
Compton, IL 61318
Ph: (815)497-2001
Fax: (309)663-5783
URL: National Affiliate–www.legion.org
Local. Affiliated With: American Legion.

Cordova

1300 ■ American Legion, Cordova Post 1033
PO Box 11
Cordova, IL 61242
Ph: (309)663-0361
Fax: (309)663-5783
URL: National Affiliate–www.legion.org
Local. Affiliated With: American Legion.

Cornell

1301 ■ American Legion, Illinois Post 752
c/o Harold N. Shank
PO Box 220
Cornell, IL 61319
Ph: (309)663-0361
Fax: (309)663-5783
URL: National Affiliate–www.legion.org
Contact: Harold N. Shank, Contact
Local. Affiliated With: American Legion.

Cortland

1302 ■ American Trail Horse Association (ATHA)
PO Box 293
Cortland, IL 60112-0293
Fax: (877)266-1678
Free: (877)266-1678
E-mail: atha@trailhorse.com
URL: http://www.trailhorse.com
Founded: 2001. **Members:** 6,500. **Membership Dues:** individual, $25 (annual) • equine registry (life), $35. **Regional Groups:** 9. **State Groups:** 68. **For-Profit**. **Regional**. Dedicated to the registration, identification, certification and acknowledgement of America's Trail Horses, regardless of color, breed, size or bloodiness. **Awards:** Trail Horse of the Year. **Frequency:** annual. **Type:** recognition. **Telecommunication Services:** information service, stolen equine helpline. **Affiliated With:** Illinois Trail Riders; United States Equestrian Federation. **Publications:** *The View from Behind*, monthly. Newsletter. Features ATHA's news and views. **Price:** free to members. **Advertising:** accepted. Alternate Formats: online.

Coulterville

1303 ■ Egyptian Beagle Club
c/o Bob Coil
880 Violet Rd.
Coulterville, IL 62237
URL: National Affiliate–clubs.akc.org
Contact: Bob Coil, Contact
Local.

Countryside

1304 ■ American Legion, Illinois Post 41
720 61st Pl.
Countryside, IL 60525
Ph: (309)663-0361
Fax: (309)663-5783
URL: National Affiliate–www.legion.org
Contact: Rufus La Rue, Contact
Local. **Affiliated With:** American Legion.

1305 ■ Countryside Lions Club
PO Box 395
Countryside, IL 60525
E-mail: rlzavorka@yahoo.com
URL: http://countrysideil.lionwap.org
Local. **Affiliated With:** Lions Clubs International.

1306 ■ International Union of Operating Engineers, Local 150
c/o William E. Dugan, Pres., Business Mgr.
6200 Joliet Rd.
Countryside, IL 60525
Ph: (708)482-8800
URL: http://www.crown.net/~ddurfee/150.html
Contact: William E. Dugan, Pres./Business Mgr.
Local. AFL-CIO. **Affiliated With:** International Union of Operating Engineers.

1307 ■ National Association of Watch and Clock Collectors, Chapter 3
6201 Joliet Rd.
Countryside, IL 60525-3958
Ph: (847)658-1433
E-mail: president@nawcc-chapter3.org
URL: http://www.nawcc-chapter3.org
Contact: Rick Chandler, Pres.
Local.

Cowden

1308 ■ American Legion, Flynn Brown Post 455
PO Box 245
Cowden, IL 62422
Ph: (309)663-0361
Fax: (309)663-5783
URL: National Affiliate–www.legion.org
Local. **Affiliated With:** American Legion.

Crest Hill

1309 ■ ACF Louis Joliet Chapter
c/o Albert Imming
1816 Barthelone Ave.
Crest Hill, IL 60435
Ph: (815)280-2447
Fax: (815)280-2696
E-mail: aimming@jjc.edu
URL: National Affiliate–www.acfchefs.org
Contact: Albert Imming CMPC, Chm. of the Board
Local. Promotes the culinary profession. Provides on-going educational training and networking for members. Provides opportunities for competition, professional recognition and access to educational forums with other culinarians at local, regional, national and international events. **Affiliated With:** American Culinary Federation.

1310 ■ German Shorthaired Pointer Club of Illinois (GSPCI)
1715 Arbor Ln., Apt. 202A
Crest Hill, IL 60435
Ph: (630)420-9015
E-mail: jpcortese@sbcglobal.net
URL: http://www.gspci.org
Contact: Gary Ellinger, Pres.
State.

1311 ■ Will-Grundy Home Builders Association
c/o Debra Perrine
1203 Theodore St., Ste.2 A
Crest Hill, IL 60435-2084
Ph: (815)773-9103
Fax: (815)773-9105
E-mail: wgchba@msn.com
URL: National Affiliate–www.nahb.org
Single and multifamily home builders, commercial builders, and others associated with the building industry. **Affiliated With:** National Association of Home Builders.

Crestwood

1312 ■ National Active And Retired Federal Employees Association - Michael C. Nave 1344
13934 Lavergne Ave. Unit 803
Crestwood, IL 60445-2282
Ph: (708)388-8798
URL: National Affiliate–www.narfe.org
Contact: Norbert F. Lewandowski, Contact
Local. Protects the retirement future of employees through education. Informs members on issues affecting the retirement. **Affiliated With:** National Association of Retired Federal Employees.

Crete

1313 ■ American Legion, South Suburban Post 1291
25346 S Dixie Hwy.
Crete, IL 60417
Ph: (309)663-0361
Fax: (309)663-5783
URL: National Affiliate–www.legion.org
Local. **Affiliated With:** American Legion.

1314 ■ Crete Area Chamber of Commerce
PO Box 263
Crete, IL 60417-0263
Ph: (708)672-9216
Fax: (708)672-7640
E-mail: cretechamber@sbcglobal.net
URL: http://www.cretechamber.com
Contact: Patricia C. Herbert, Exec.Dir.
Founded: 1984. **Members:** 130. **Membership Dues:** general, $75 (annual). **Staff:** 1. **For-Profit**. **Local**. Promotes business and community development in Crete, IL area. Sponsors 2-antique show, Wine Tasting, ribbon cutting, and grants scholarship. **Publications:** *Crete Record*, weekly. Newspaper. **Conventions/Meetings:** monthly meeting - every 2nd Wednesday • monthly meeting - every 4th Thursday.

1315 ■ Crete Lions Club
PO Box 306
Crete, IL 60417
Ph: (708)672-4575
URL: http://creteil.lionwap.org
Local. **Affiliated With:** Lions Clubs International.

1316 ■ First Catholic Slovak Ladies Association - Chicago Junior Branch 174
25726 State Line Rd.
Crete, IL 60417
Ph: (708)672-6275
URL: National Affiliate–www.fcsla.com
Local. **Affiliated With:** First Catholic Slovak Ladies Association.

Crystal Lake

1317 ■ American Legion, William Chandler Peterson Post 171
PO Box 1713
Crystal Lake, IL 60039
Ph: (815)459-0481
Fax: (309)663-5783
URL: National Affiliate–www.legion.org
Local. **Affiliated With:** American Legion.

1318 ■ APICS, The Association for Operations Management - Highlands Chapter 261
PO Box 1168
Crystal Lake, IL 60039-1168
Ph: (815)356-1470
URL: http://www.highlandsapics.com
Contact: Jim DeModica, Pres./VP Education
Local. Provides information and services in production and inventory management and related areas to enable members, enterprises and individuals to add value to their business performance. **Affiliated With:** APICS - The Association for Operations Management.

1319 ■ Bromeliad Society of Greater Chicago (BSGC)
c/o Steve Goode, Sec.
826 Buckingham Ct.
Crystal Lake, IL 60014-7601
Ph: (815)459-1623
E-mail: stevegoodel@ameritech.net
URL: http://www.chicago-bromeliad.org
Contact: Steve Goode, Sec.
Local. **Affiliated With:** Bromeliad Society International.

1320 ■ Crystal Lake Chamber of Commerce
427 Virginia St.
Crystal Lake, IL 60014-5959
Ph: (815)459-1300
Fax: (815)459-0243
E-mail: info@clchamber.com
URL: http://www.clchamber.com
Contact: Bob Blazier, Pres.
Founded: 1940. **Members:** 1,100. **Membership Dues:** business (1-5 employees), $305 (annual) • business (6-15 employees), $320 (annual) • business (16-30 employees), $365 (annual) • business (31-100 employees), $445 (annual) • business (101-200 employees), $590 (annual) • business (201-500 employees), $825 (annual) • business (501-800 employees), $1,165 (annual) • business (801 or more employees), $1,500 (annual) • non-profit, $130 (annual) • associate, $168 (annual). **Staff:** 8. **Local**. Provides businesses, professionals, and community organizations in the area with opportunities to meet, share interests, and develop business relationships. **Libraries: Type:** reference. **Holdings:** audio recordings, books, video recordings. **Awards:** Athena Award. **Frequency:** annual. **Type:** recognition. **Recipient:** to a woman who promotes excellence in leadership and service in business • Business of the Year. **Frequency:** annual. **Type:** recognition. **Recipi-**

ent: for an individual who shows business leadership and honor to the community • Carl Wehde Award. **Frequency:** annual. **Type:** recognition • Eagle Awards. **Frequency:** annual. **Type:** recognition. **Recipient:** for a new member who has shown outstanding leadership and commitment. **Computer Services:** Mailing lists, of members • online services, business directory. **Telecommunication Services:** electronic mail, bblazier@clchamber.com. **Committees:** Committee for Business Support; Sister Cities; Small Office/Home Office Professionals. **Divisions:** Ambassadors; Business Development; Community Services; Finance; Member Benefits. **Publications:** *Community Guide*, annual, in July. Directory. Contains information on the city, education, government, phone numbers, library, post office, park district, restaurants, and churches. • *News & Views*, monthly. Newsletter. Includes chamber information, photos, articles, columns, and calendar of events. **Advertising:** accepted. Alternate Formats: online • *Shopping and Dining Guide*. Brochure. Contains complete restaurant information and map, calendar of events, park information, and Chamber businesses. **Price:** free for members • Membership Directory, annual. Includes Chamber programs, calendar of events, parks and recreation, and business and industry. **Circulation:** 1,100. **Advertising:** accepted. **Conventions/Meetings:** annual Ambassadors Gala Golf Outing - competition, participants enjoy golf, lunch, dinner, and prizes - last Monday in June • annual Awards - dinner, special tributes are presented - usually May • annual Old Fashioned Family - picnic, with food, beverages, games, prizes, entertainment, and fun - every August • annual Staff Appreciation Day - luncheon, opportunity for Chamber members to treat their staff members with prizes and entertainment - during Administrative Professionals Week in April.

1321 ■ Crystal Lake Historical Society
PO Box 1151
Crystal Lake, IL 60039-1151
Ph: (815)455-1151
E-mail: info@cl-hs.org
URL: http://www.cl-hs.org
Contact: Diana L. Kenney, Pres.
Founded: 2000. **Members:** 120. **Local**. Seeks to preserve, present, and promote the history of Crystal Lake, IL.

1322 ■ Crystal Lake Lions Club
PO Box 48
Crystal Lake, IL 60039-0048
Ph: (815)477-0571
E-mail: mcnamarab@fsgrhino.com
URL: http://crystallakeil.lionwap.org
Contact: Brian McNamara, Pres.
Local. Affiliated With: Lions Clubs International.

1323 ■ Faith in Action of McHenry County (FIAMC)
111 S Virginia St.
Crystal Lake, IL 60014
Ph: (815)455-3120
Fax: (815)455-3813
E-mail: staff@fiamchenrycounty.org
URL: http://www.fiamchenrycounty.org
Contact: Rhonda Anderson, Exec.Dir.
Founded: 1998. **Budget:** $22,000. **State Groups:** 32. **Local Groups:** 1. **Does not correspond in English. Local**. Provides volunteer non-medical services to seniors 62 years old and above who live at home, and helps them maintain their independence. **Publications:** *Angel's Wings*, quarterly. Newsletter. Alternate Formats: online. **Conventions/Meetings:** annual National Convention in Washington DC.

1324 ■ Friends of the Fox River (FOFR)
PO Box 1314
Crystal Lake, IL 60039-1314
Ph: (815)356-6605
E-mail: croberts@friendsofthefoxriver.org
URL: http://www.friendsofthefoxriver.org
Contact: Chuck Roberts, Pres.
Founded: 1990. **Members:** 200. **Local**. Works in building a watershed in Fox River Valley. **Subgroups:** Fox River Watershed Monitoring Network. **Publications:** *The Riffle*, quarterly. Newsletter. **Conventions/Meetings:** monthly board meeting • annual meeting.

1325 ■ Illinois Sports Owners Association (ISOA)
c/o Jack Billimack, Dir.
23 Elmhurst Ave.
Crystal Lake, IL 60014
Ph: (815)459-4721
E-mail: jbillimack@isoaaol.com
URL: http://www.snic-braaapp.org
Contact: Jack Billimack, Dir.
Members: 165. **Membership Dues:** all, $25 (annual). **Local**. Persons interested in preserving and enjoying Triumph automobiles. Aims to increase awareness of Triumph automobiles in northern Illinois; train members to make simple repairs; maintain storehouse of special tools required for mechanical repairs. Activities include driving tours, camping, rallies, autocross. Sponsors British car show. **Affiliated With:** Vintage Triumph Register. **Publications:** *Snic Braaapp*, monthly. Newsletter. **Conventions/Meetings:** monthly meeting - 1st Sunday evening.

1326 ■ McHenry County AIFA
c/o Gary R. Bonick, Pres./Exec.
PO Box 103
Crystal Lake, IL 60039-0103
Ph: (815)459-8300
Fax: (815)459-4189
E-mail: a017151@allstate.com
URL: National Affiliate–naifa.org
Contact: Gary R. Bonick, Pres./Exec.
Local. Represents the interests of insurance and financial advisors. Advocates for a positive legislative and regulatory environment. Enhances business and professional skills of members. **Affiliated With:** National Association of Insurance and Financial Advisors.

1327 ■ McHenry County Aikido Club
1401 W Rte. 176
Crystal Lake, IL 60014
Ph: (815)455-5831
E-mail: mushin1@msn.com
URL: http://www.aikidomchenry.org
Local. Affiliated With: United States Aikido Federation.

1328 ■ Mothers Against Drunk Driving, McHenry County
PO Box 1705
Crystal Lake, IL 60039-1705
Ph: (815)334-7775
Fax: (815)356-1715
URL: National Affiliate–www.madd.org
Local. Victims of drunk driving crashes; concerned citizens. Encourages citizen participation in working towards reform of the drunk driving problem and the prevention of underage drinking. Acts as the voice of victims of drunk driving crashes by speaking on their behalf to communities, businesses, and educational groups. **Affiliated With:** Mothers Against Drunk Driving.

1329 ■ National Alliance for the Mentally Ill - McHenry County
PO Box 1391
Crystal Lake, IL 60039-1391
Ph: (815)444-9991
E-mail: namimc@ameritech.net
URL: http://www.namimchenry.com
Contact: Merna Drewno, Contact
Local. Strives to improve the quality of life of children and adults with severe mental illness through support, education, research and advocacy. **Affiliated With:** National Alliance for the Mentally Ill.

1330 ■ Options and Advocacy for McHenry County
365 Millenium Dr., Ste.A
Crystal Lake, IL 60014-3598
Ph: (815)477-4720
Fax: (815)477-4702
URL: National Affiliate–www.TheArc.org
Contact: Janice Prunier-King, Exec.Dir.
Local. Parents, professional workers, and others interested in individuals with mental retardation. Works to promote services, research, public understanding, and legislation for people with mental retardation and their families. **Affiliated With:** Arc of the United States.

1331 ■ Pheasants Forever - Mchenry County Chapter
PO Box 1153
Crystal Lake, IL 60039-1153
Ph: (815)477-4828
E-mail: pheasant@northstarnet.org
URL: http://www.crystallakenet.org/pheasant
Contact: Bob Veugeler Sr., Pres.
Local. Affiliated With: Pheasants Forever.

1332 ■ Phi Theta Kappa, Chi Upsilon Chapter - McHenry County College
c/o David Elder
8900 US Hwy. 14
Crystal Lake, IL 60012
Ph: (815)455-8715
E-mail: delder@mchenry.edu
URL: http://www.ptk.org/directories/chapters/IL/204-1.htm
Contact: David Elder, Advisor
Local.

1333 ■ Stateline Society for Human Resource Management
PO Box 682
Crystal Lake, IL 60039
Ph: (815)344-7117
E-mail: info@statelineshrm.org
URL: http://www.statelineshrm.org
Contact: Carmella Dobler, Pres.
Local. Represents the interests of human resource and industrial relations professionals and executives. Promotes the advancement of human resource management.

1334 ■ Sunburst Corvette Club (SCC)
PO Box 433
Crystal Lake, IL 60039-0433
Ph: (847)658-9532
E-mail: president@sunburstcorvetteclub.com
URL: http://www.sunburstcorvetteclub.com
Contact: Butch Novak, Pres.
Local. Affiliated With: National Council of Corvette Clubs.

Cuba

1335 ■ American Legion, Illinois Post 533
c/o Russell Smith
PO Box 533
Cuba, IL 61427
Ph: (309)785-5456
Fax: (309)663-5783
URL: National Affiliate–www.legion.org
Contact: Russell Smith, Contact
Local. Affiliated With: American Legion.

Cullom

1336 ■ American Legion, Skinner-Trost Post 122
PO Box 122
Cullom, IL 60929
Ph: (815)689-2155
Fax: (309)663-5783
URL: National Affiliate–www.legion.org
Local. Affiliated With: American Legion.

Dakota

1337 ■ Association of Late-Deafened Adults - Freeport
c/o Kathy Schlueter
11038 N Pleasant Hill Rd.
Dakota, IL 61018

Ph: (894)537-8157
E-mail: ksctryln@aol.com
URL: National Affiliate–www.alda.org
Contact: Kathy Schlueter, Contact
Local. Advocates for the needs of late-deafened people. Provides information, support and social opportunities through self-help groups, meetings and social events. **Affiliated With:** Association of Late-Deafened Adults.

Dallas City

1338 ■ American Legion, Gittings-Sandine Post 297
PO Box 342
Dallas City, IL 62330
Ph: (217)852-3844
Fax: (309)663-5783
URL: National Affiliate–www.legion.org
Local. Affiliated With: American Legion.

Dalton City

1339 ■ American Legion, Illinois Post 475
c/o Charles F. Hight
PO Box 367
Dalton City, IL 61925
Ph: (309)663-0361
Fax: (309)663-5783
URL: National Affiliate–www.legion.org
Contact: Charles F. Hight, Contact
Local. Affiliated With: American Legion.

Danforth

1340 ■ American Legion, Danforth Post 367
PO Box 57
Danforth, IL 60930
Ph: (815)269-2593
Fax: (309)663-5783
URL: National Affiliate–www.legion.org
Local. Affiliated With: American Legion.

Danville

1341 ■ American Legion, Bradley-Maberry Post 736
38 N Washington Ave.
Danville, IL 61832
Ph: (217)446-0497
Fax: (309)663-5783
URL: National Affiliate–www.legion.org
Local. Affiliated With: American Legion.

1342 ■ American Legion, Illinois Post 210
c/o Curtis G. Redden
201 Prospect Ave.
Danville, IL 61832
Ph: (217)442-3201
Fax: (309)663-5783
E-mail: legionpost210@hotmail.com
URL: National Affiliate–www.legion.org
Contact: Curtis G. Redden, Contact
Local. Affiliated With: American Legion.

1343 ■ Danville Area Board of Realtors
813 Oak St.
Danville, IL 61832
Ph: (217)443-2170
Fax: (217)443-8237
E-mail: dabr@soltec.net
URL: National Affiliate–www.realtor.org
Contact: Debbie Borgwald, Exec. Officer
Local. Strives to develop real estate business practices. Advocates the right to own, use and transfer real property. Provides a facility for professional development, research and exchange of information among members and to the general public. **Affiliated With:** National Association of Realtors.

1344 ■ Danville Area Convention and Visitors Bureau (DACVB)
100 W Main, No. 146
Danville, IL 61832
Ph: (217)442-2096
Fax: (217)442-2137
Free: (800)383-4386
E-mail: dacvb@cooketech.net
URL: http://www.danvillecvb.com
Contact: Jeanie Cooke, Exec.Dir.
Local.

1345 ■ Danville District Dental Society
1010 N Gilbert St.
Danville, IL 61832-3849
Ph: (217)442-4878
E-mail: kfmuster@sbcglobal.net
URL: http://www.isds.org
Contact: Dr. Karl F. Muster, Pres.
Local. Represents the interests of dentists committed to the public's oral health, ethics, science and professional advancement. Promotes the art and science of dentistry through advocacy, education, research and the development of standards. **Affiliated With:** American Dental Association; Illinois State Dental Society.

1346 ■ Danville Kiwanis' Clubs, Breakfast Club
c/o Lynn Foster, Pres.
1009 Pries
Danville, IL 61832
Ph: (217)442-1861
E-mail: coclerk@soltec.net
URL: http://www.danvillekiwanisclubs.org
Contact: Lynn Foster, Pres.
Local.

1347 ■ Danville Kiwanis' Clubs, Golden K Club
c/o Neicy Hreha, Pres.
2405 N Vermilion
Danville, IL 61832
Ph: (217)443-1644
E-mail: neicymh@aol.com
URL: http://www.danvillekiwanisclubs.org
Contact: Neicy Hreha, Pres.
Local.

1348 ■ Danville Kiwanis' Clubs, Noon Club
c/o Elzer Marx, Pres.
2832 N Vermilion St.
Danville, IL 61832
Ph: (217)442-5527
E-mail: emarx@prof1realty.com
URL: http://www.danvillekiwanisclubs.org
Contact: Elzer Marx, Pres.
Local.

1349 ■ Illinois Audubon Society (IAS)
PO Box 2418
Danville, IL 61834
Ph: (217)446-5085
Fax: (217)446-6375
E-mail: director@pdnt.com
URL: http://www.illinoisaudubon.org
Contact: Marilyn F. Campbell, Exec.Dir.
Founded: 1897. **Members:** 6,000. **Membership Dues:** student, $12 (annual) • family, $30 (annual) • contributing, $50 (annual) • sustaining, $100 (annual) • corporate, $500 (annual) • individual, $25 (annual) • friend, $35 (annual) • supporting, $75 (annual) • Eagle Club, $500 (annual) • Cardinal Club, $1,000 (annual). **Local Groups:** 16. **State**. Individuals interested in conservation. Seeks to educate the public about conservation and preservation of wildlife. Sponsors sanctuary program, acquires land for threatened and endangered species. **Libraries: Type:** not open to the public. **Holdings:** 1,200; books. **Subjects:** natural history. **Awards:** IAS Conservation Award. **Frequency:** annual. **Type:** recognition • IAS Youth Conservation Award. **Frequency:** annual. **Type:** recognition. **Publications:** *Cardinal News*, quarterly. Newsletter • *Illinois Audubon*, quarterly. Magazine. **Conventions/Meetings:** semiannual meet (exhibits).

1350 ■ Phi Theta Kappa, Pi Omega Chapter - Danville Area Community College (PTK)
c/o Lori Garrett, Advisor
2000 E Main St.
Danville, IL 61832
Ph: (217)443-8796
E-mail: scholars@dacc.edu
URL: http://www.dacc.edu/scholars/ptk
Contact: Lori Garrett, Advisor
Membership Dues: student, $65. **Local**. Provides scholarship, leadership, fellowship, and service. Promotes academic excellence and civic engagement. **Telecommunication Services:** electronic bulletin board, open forum for members.

1351 ■ Renaissance Initiative
c/o Thomas M. Goodwin
7 E North St.
Danville, IL 61832-5803
Ph: (217)443-3095
Fax: (217)443-3872
URL: http://www.renaissanceinitiative.org
Contact: Hank Norris, Exec.Dir.
Local.

1352 ■ Sweet Adelines International, Danville Chapter
Harrison Park Club House
W Voorhes St.
Danville, IL 61832
Ph: (217)283-9633
E-mail: ratolch@hoopeston.k12.il.us
URL: National Affiliate–www.sweetadelineintl.org
Contact: Rita Dean, Contact
Local. Advances the musical art form of barbershop harmony through education and performances. Provides education, training and coaching in the development of women's four-part barbershop harmony. **Affiliated With:** Sweet Adelines International.

1353 ■ United Way of the Danville Area
320 N Franklin St.
Danville, IL 61834-0132
Ph: (217)442-3512
Fax: (217)442-2946
E-mail: uwda@insightbb.com
URL: http://www.uwda.org
Contact: Bill Brandenberger, Pres./CPO
Local. Affiliated With: United Way of America.

1354 ■ Vermilion Advantage-Chamber of Commerce Division (VACC)
28 W North St.
Danville, IL 61832-5729
Ph: (217)442-1887
Fax: (217)442-6228
Free: (800)373-6201
E-mail: gkietzmann@vermilionadvantage.com
URL: http://www.vermilionadvantage.com
Contact: Glenda Kietzman, Exec.Dir.
Founded: 1899. **Members:** 500. **Staff:** 4. **State Groups:** 2. **Local**. Promotes business and community development in the Vermilion County, IL area. **Councils:** Agribusiness; Ambassadors; Personnel; Retail Trade; Safety; Technology. **Affiliated With:** U.S. Chamber of Commerce. **Publications:** *Commerce Communicator*, bimonthly. Newsletter • *Danville Is.*, triennial. Book • Membership Directory, annual.

1355 ■ Vermilion AIFA
c/o Gary Carl Erickson, Pres.
PO Box 536
Danville, IL 61834-0536
Ph: (217)443-9137
Fax: (217)443-9623
E-mail: terry@danville.net
URL: National Affiliate–naifa.org
Contact: Gary Carl Erickson, Pres.
Local. Represents the interests of insurance and financial advisors. Advocates for a positive legislative and regulatory environment. Enhances business and

professional skills of members. **Affiliated With:** National Association of Insurance and Financial Advisors.

1356 ■ Vermilion County Museum Society (VCMS)
116 N Gilbert St.
Danville, IL 61832-8506
Ph: (217)442-2922
Fax: (217)442-2001
E-mail: susricht@aol.com
URL: http://www.vermilioncountymuseum.org
Contact: Don Richter, Pres.
Founded: 1964. **Members:** 1,150. **Membership Dues:** individual, $20 (annual) • student, senior, organization, $15 (annual) • life, $250 • family, $25 (annual) • sustaining, $50 (annual) • patron, $75 (annual) • business, $100 (annual). **Staff:** 4. **Budget:** $65,000. **Local.** Individuals interested in preserving the history of Vermilion County, IL. Conducts lectures and guided tours. Operates museum, Lamon House, and Mann's Chapel. **Libraries: Type:** open to the public. **Holdings:** 1,500; books, clippings, periodicals. **Subjects:** local history, Lincoln, Civil War. **Affiliated With:** American Association for State and Local History. **Publications:** *Heritage of Vermilion County*, quarterly. Journal. **Price:** included in membership dues. ISSN: 0018-0718 • Newsletter, bimonthly.

Darien

1357 ■ American Hellenic Educational Progressive Association - West Suburban, Chapter 202
c/o Vasilios Albanos, PDG, Pres.
7129 Beechnut Ln.
Darien, IL 60561
Ph: (630)842-0579
Fax: (630)963-2980
E-mail: psilearning@comcast.net
URL: http://www.ahepafamily.org/d13
Contact: Vasilios Albanos PDG, Pres.
Local. Affiliated With: American Hellenic Educational Progressive Association.

1358 ■ Darien Chamber of Commerce (DCC)
1702 Plainfield Rd.
Darien, IL 60561-5080
Ph: (630)968-0004
Fax: (630)968-2474
E-mail: info@darienchamber.com
URL: http://www.darienchamber.com
Contact: Tom Sailer, Pres.
Founded: 1984. **Members:** 75. **Local.** Promotes business and community development in Darien, IL. Sponsors Easter Gala, tree lighting ceremony, and annual festival. **Formerly:** (1999) Darien Chamber of Commerce and Industry. **Publications:** *Chamber Directory*. **Conventions/Meetings:** semimonthly meeting.

1359 ■ Darien Lions Club, IL
PO Box 2006
Darien, IL 60561
E-mail: info@darienlions.org
URL: http://www.darienlions.org
Local. Affiliated With: Lions Clubs International.

1360 ■ First Catholic Slovak Ladies Association - Berwyn Junior Branch 426
8337 Grandview Ln.
Darien, IL 60561
Ph: (630)910-9250
URL: National Affiliate–www.fcsla.com
Local. Affiliated With: First Catholic Slovak Ladies Association.

1361 ■ First Catholic Slovak Ladies Association - Berwyn Senior Branch 503
8337 Grandview Ln.
Darien, IL 60561
Ph: (630)910-9250
URL: National Affiliate–www.fcsla.com
Local. Affiliated With: First Catholic Slovak Ladies Association.

1362 ■ Kiwanis Club of Darien-Westmont
c/o Ave Obmaces, Pres.
7811 Wakefield Dr.
Darien, IL 60561
Ph: (630)910-1473
E-mail: obmaces630@ameritech.net
URL: http://come.to/kiwanisclub
Contact: Ave Obmaces, Pres.
Local.

1363 ■ Midwest Computer Measurement Group (MCMG)
c/o Donna Folkerts, Chair
IBM Global Services
7510 Farmingdale Dr., No. 309
Darien, IL 60561-4770
Ph: (630)455-0306
E-mail: mcmg@cmg.org
URL: http://regions.cmg.org/regions/mcmg/index.html
Contact: Donna Folkerts, Chair
Regional. Affiliated With: Computer Measurement Group.

1364 ■ National Association of Miniature Enthusiasts - Crazy Eight's
c/o Ruth L. Hacker
705 Maple Ln.
Darien, IL 60561-4070
Ph: (630)968-7891
URL: http://www.miniatures.org/states/IL.html
Contact: Ruth L. Hacker, Contact
Local. Affiliated With: National Association of Miniature Enthusiasts.

1365 ■ Rotary Club of Darien, Illinois
c/o Ron Broida
PO Box 2066
Darien, IL 60561
E-mail: clubservice@darienrotaryclub.org
URL: http://www.darienrotaryclub.org
Contact: Jim Palatine, Pres.
Local.

Davenport

1366 ■ Rock Island County Medical Society
201 W 2nd St.
Davenport, IL 52801
Ph: (563)328-3390
Fax: (563)328-3388
E-mail: qcmso@aol.com
URL: http://www.qcmso.com
Contact: Walter Bradley, Pres.-Elect
Local. Advances the art and science of medicine. Promotes patient care and the betterment of public health.

Davis Junction

1367 ■ Upland Hunt Club and Sporting Clays
14755 Edson Rd.
Davis Junction, IL 61020
Ph: (815)874-7444
Fax: (815)874-8994
E-mail: uplandhuntclub@aol.com
URL: http://www.uplandhuntclub.us
Local. Affiliated With: National Skeet Shooting Association.

Dawson

1368 ■ American Truck Historical Society, Lincoln Trail Chapter
c/o Charles R. Flexter
PO Box 264
Dawson, IL 62520
Ph: (217)364-4162
URL: National Affiliate–www.aths.org
Contact: Charles R. Flexter, Contact
Local. Affiliated With: American Truck Historical Society.

De Land

1369 ■ American Legion, Lincoln Post 102
PO Box 264
De Land, IL 61839
Ph: (217)762-9783
Fax: (309)663-5783
URL: National Affiliate–www.legion.org
Local. Affiliated With: American Legion.

Decatur

1370 ■ Al-Anon Family Group
PO Box 3223
Decatur, IL 62526
Ph: (217)423-8214
E-mail: wso@al-anon.org
URL: http://www.al-anon.org
Regional.

1371 ■ American Chemical Society, Decatur-Springfield Section
c/o Aaron Lee Wilham, Chm.
2200 E Eldorado St.
Decatur, IL 62521-1578
Ph: (217)421-3627
Fax: (309)438-5538
E-mail: alwilham@tlna.com
URL: National Affiliate–acswebcontent.acs.org
Contact: Aaron Lee Wilham, Chm.
Local. Represents the interests of individuals dedicated to the advancement of chemistry in all its branches. Provides opportunities for peer interaction and career development. **Affiliated With:** American Chemical Society.

1372 ■ American Hellenic Educational Progressive Association - Decatur, Chapter 457
c/o Chris Chiligiris, Pres.
121 N Main St.
Decatur, IL 62526
Ph: (217)423-2180
URL: http://www.ahepafamily.org/d13
Contact: Chris Chiligiris, Pres.
Local. Affiliated With: American Hellenic Educational Progressive Association.

1373 ■ American Legion, Castle Williams Post 105
1535 Legion Dr.
Decatur, IL 62521
Ph: (217)423-1411
Fax: (309)663-5783
URL: National Affiliate–www.legion.org
Local. Affiliated With: American Legion.

1374 ■ American Legion, Robinson and Starks Post 1972
1032 W Tuttle St.
Decatur, IL 62522
Ph: (309)663-0361
Fax: (309)663-5783
URL: National Affiliate–www.legion.org
Local. Affiliated With: American Legion.

1375 ■ American Red Cross, Mid-Illinois Chapter
2674 N Main St.
Decatur, IL 62526
Ph: (217)428-7758
Fax: (217)423-8260
URL: http://www.midillinoisredcross.org
Regional.

1376 ■ Arthritis Foundation, Macon County Branch
c/o St. Mary's Hospital
1800 E Lakeshore Dr., Rm. 3025
Decatur, IL 62525

1415 ■ American Legion, Deerfield
849 Waukegan Rd.
Deerfield, IL 60015
Ph: (847)945-9821
URL: National Affiliate–www.legion.org
Local. Affiliated With: American Legion.

1416 ■ American Youth Soccer Organization, Region 1007
PO Box 618
Deerfield, IL 60015
Ph: (847)604-1560
URL: http://www.deerfieldayso.org
Local. Affiliated With: American Youth Soccer Organization.

1417 ■ Apollo VII REACT
215 Mayer Ct.
Deerfield, IL 60015
Ph: (847)236-1955
E-mail: apolloviireact@ameritech.net
URL: http://www.reactintl.org/teaminfo/usa_teams/teams-usil.htm
Local. Trained communication experts and professional volunteers. Provides volunteer public service and emergency communications through the use of radios (Citizen Band, General Mobile Radio Service, UHF and HAM). Coordinates with radio industries and government on safety communication matters and supports charitable activities and community organizations.

1418 ■ Children's Rights Council of Illinois
916 Fountainview Dr.
Deerfield, IL 60015
Ph: (847)207-2791
E-mail: hummelfan7@aol.com
URL: National Affiliate–www.gocrc.com
State. Affiliated With: Children's Rights Council.

1419 ■ Deerfield, Bannockburn, Riverwoods Chamber of Commerce (DBRCC)
601 Deerfield Rd., Ste.200
Deerfield, IL 60015
Ph: (847)945-4660
Fax: (847)940-0381
E-mail: info@dbrchamber.com
URL: http://www.dbrchamber.com
Contact: Victoria Case, Exec.Dir.
Founded: 1925. **Members:** 430. **Staff:** 1. **Local.** Strives to enhance the local business climate and to promote business and community development in the Deerfield, Bannockburn, and Riverwoods, IL areas. **Awards:** College Scholarship. **Frequency:** annual. **Type:** scholarship. **Recipient:** for community service. **Affiliated With:** U.S. Chamber of Commerce. **Formerly:** (1995) Deerfield Chamber of Commerce. **Publications:** *Community Guide and Shopping, Dining, Lodging Guide, and a Street Map*, annual. Directory. **Price:** $5.00/copy. **Conventions/Meetings:** periodic meeting.

1420 ■ Delta Solutions (DSI)
c/o Tommy Davis, Sr.
Four Pkwy. N, Ste.120
Deerfield, IL 60015
Ph: (847)317-9544
URL: http://www.deltasi.com
Local.

1421 ■ Family Firm Institute, Midwest (Chicago) Study Group
c/o David Lansky, PhD
Family Bus. Innovations
102 Wilmot Rd., Ste.140
Deerfield, IL 60015
Ph: (847)444-0705
Fax: (847)444-0706
E-mail: dlansky@familybusinessinnovations.com
URL: http://www.familybusinessinnovations.com
Local. Affiliated With: Family Firm Institute.

1422 ■ Psi Chi, National Honor Society in Psychology - Trinity International University
c/o Dept. of Psychology
2065 Half Day Rd.
Deerfield, IL 60015
Ph: (847)317-7162
E-mail: trobinso@tiu.edu
URL: http://www.tiu.edu/psychology/psichi/psichi.htm
Local. Affiliated With: Psi Chi, National Honor Society in Psychology.

1423 ■ Skokie Valley Skating Club (SVSC)
c/o Denise Jirout, Pres.
504 Sandpiper Ln.
Deerfield, IL 60015
Ph: (847)520-1632 (312)884-0413
E-mail: djirout@jacobsononline.com
URL: http://www.skokievalleyskatingclub.com
Contact: Denise Jirout, Pres.
Local. Provides programs to encourage participation and achievement in the sport of figure skating on ice. Defines and maintains uniform standards of skating proficiency. Organizes and sponsors competitions and exhibitions for the purpose of stimulating interest in figure skating. **Affiliated With:** United States Figure Skating Association.

DeKalb

1424 ■ American Chemical Society, Rock River Section
c/o Dr. Chong Zheng, Chm.
Northern Illinois Univ., Dept. of Chemistry
1425 W Lincoln Hwy.
DeKalb, IL 60115-2828
Ph: (815)753-6871
Fax: (815)753-4802
E-mail: zheng@cz.chem.niu.edu
URL: National Affiliate–acswebcontent.acs.org
Contact: Dr. Chong Zheng, Chm.
Local. Represents the interests of individuals dedicated to the advancement of chemistry in all its branches. Provides opportunities for peer interaction and career development. **Affiliated With:** American Chemical Society.

1425 ■ American Choral Directors Association - Illinois Chapter
c/o Eric Johnson, Pres.
Northern Illinois Univ., School of Music
DeKalb, IL 60115
Ph: (815)753-7984
E-mail: ejohnsn@niu.edu
URL: http://www.il-acda.org
Contact: Eric Johnson, Pres.
Membership Dues: associate/active, $75 (annual) • student, $30 (annual) • life, $2,000. **State.** Promotes excellence in choral music through performance, composition, publication, research and teaching. Elevates choral music's position in American society. **Awards:** Harold Decker Award. **Frequency:** annual. **Type:** recognition. **Computer Services:** Online services, forums. **Subgroups:** Repertoire and Standards. **Affiliated With:** American Choral Directors Association.

1426 ■ American Legion, De Kalb Post 66
1204 S 4th St.
DeKalb, IL 60115
Ph: (309)663-0361
Fax: (309)663-5783
URL: National Affiliate–www.legion.org
Local. Affiliated With: American Legion.

1427 ■ American Meteorological Society, Northern Illinois University (NIU AMS)
c/o Jie Song, Advisor
Dept. of Geography
Davis Hall 118
DeKalb, IL 60115
Ph: (815)753-6837
E-mail: jsong@niu.edu
URL: http://www.ametsoc.org/chapters/noillinois
Contact: Ms. Joi Kwiatkowski, Pres.
Founded: 1971. **Membership Dues:** Northern Illinois student, $15 (annual). **Local.** Faculty and students in the meteorology program at Northern Illinois University. Conducts educational programs. **Affiliated With:** American Meteorological Society. **Conventions/Meetings:** monthly general assembly.

1428 ■ American Red Cross, DeKalb County Chapter
2727 Sycamore Rd., Ste.2A
DeKalb, IL 60115
Ph: (815)756-7339
Fax: (815)756-6627
E-mail: remenk@crossnet.org
URL: http://dekalbillinois.redcross.org
Local.

1429 ■ Chicago Table Tennis Club at Northern Illinois University
Northern Illinois Univ.
1425 W Lincoln Hwy.
DeKalb, IL 60115
Ph: (847)312-0590
E-mail: cttc4u@yahoo.com
URL: http://www.sa.niu.edu/tabletennis
Contact: Engelbert Solis, Contact
Local. Affiliated With: U.S.A. Table Tennis.

1430 ■ Clinton Rosette Middle School PTA (CRMS PTA)
1st St.
DeKalb, IL 60115
E-mail: donpta@djanas1.com
URL: http://dist428.dekalb.k12.il.us/rosette/pta/index.htm
Contact: Misty Haji-Sheikh, Pres.
Local. Parents, teachers, students, and others interested in uniting the forces of home, school, and community. Promotes the welfare of children and youth.

1431 ■ DeKalb Chamber of Commerce
164 E Lincoln Hwy.
DeKalb, IL 60115
Ph: (815)756-6306
Fax: (815)756-5164
E-mail: chamber@dekalb.org
URL: http://www.dekalb.org
Contact: Chuck Siebrasse, Exec.Dir.
Membership Dues: business (1-5 employees), $210 (annual) • business (6-10 employees), $262 (annual) • business (11-15 employees), $315 (annual) • business (16-20 employees), $367 (annual) • business (21-50 employees), $525 (annual) • business (51-100 employees), $682 (annual) • business (101-200 employees), $840 (annual) • business (201-400 employees), $945 (annual) • business (401-1000 employees), $1,260 (annual) • financial institution (per million in local deposit), $12 (annual) • non-profit (with 1-50 employees), $105 (annual) • non-profit (with 51 or more employees), $525 (annual) • individual/service club, $52 (annual). **Local.** Represents retail, commercial, industrial, service, agriculture, education, and not-for-profit business in the greater DeKalb area. **Awards:** ATHENA Awards. **Frequency:** annual. **Type:** recognition. **Telecommunication Services:** electronic mail, manager@dekalb.org. **Committees:** Ambassadors; Athena Awards; Business to Business Expo; Golf Outing; Marketing; Public Policy; Tourism. **Publications:** *Chamber Connection*, quarterly. Newsletter. **Advertising:** accepted. Alternate Formats: online • Membership Directory, annual. **Conventions/Meetings:** annual Business to Business Expo - trade show - usually end of May • annual Golf Outing - competition - always July • monthly luncheon • annual meeting • periodic workshop.

1432 ■ DeKalb County Farmland Foundation (DCFF)
PO Box 375
DeKalb, IL 60115
Ph: (815)756-2580
E-mail: dcff@dcff.org
URL: http://www.dcff.org
Contact: Donna Gorski, Sec.
Local. Citizens dedicated to the preservation of farmland in DeKalb County, IL.

1433 ■ Illinois Association for Educational Communications and Technology (IAECT)
c/oPeter C. West, Dir.
Learning Center
Northern Illinois Univ.
DeKalb, IL 60115-2854
Ph: (815)753-8368
Fax: (815)753-1258
E-mail: pwest@niu.edu
URL: http://www.aect.org
Contact: Peter C. West, Dir.
State. Provides leadership in educational communications and technology by linking professionals holding a common interest in the use of educational technology and its application of the learning process.

1434 ■ Illinois Association of School Business Officials
Northern Illinois Univ., IA-103
108 Caroll Ave.
DeKalb, IL 60115-2829
Ph: (815)753-1276
Fax: (815)753-9367
E-mail: reverett@niu.edu
URL: http://www.iasbo.org
Contact: Ronald E. Everett, Exec.Dir.
Founded: 1952. **Members:** 1,785. **Membership Dues:** active, $190 (annual). **Staff:** 7. **Budget:** $1,000,000. **Regional Groups:** 17. **State**. Seeks advanced school business management. **Awards:** Annual Scholarship Award. **Frequency:** annual. **Type:** monetary. **Recipient:** for a member enrolled in SBM/certification program. **Boards:** IASBO Board of Directors. **Affiliated With:** Association of School Business Officials International. **Publications:** *Journal of School Business Management*, semiannual. **Price:** $4.00/copy. ISSN: 1058-2622. **Circulation:** 2,000. **Advertising:** accepted • *Update*, 10/year. Newsletter. **Conventions/Meetings:** annual conference (exhibits).

1435 ■ Illinois City County Management Association (ILCMA)
Regional Development Inst.
Northern Illinois Univ.
DeKalb, IL 60115
Ph: (815)753-5424
Fax: (815)753-2305
E-mail: dpeters@niu.edu
URL: http://www.ilcma.org
Contact: Jeanette Gray, Program Associate
Founded: 1953. **Members:** 500. **Membership Dues:** manager/administrator, director of councils and regional organizations (with additional 1.75 per $1000 salary), $65 (annual) • cooperating (employee of ICMA recognized local governments and others interested in the field of municipal management), $65 (annual) • consultant (employee of firms working with local government), $325 (annual) • student (individuals studying on a full time basis for a career in public administration), $20 (annual) • retired corporate (former full member now retired), $40 (annual). **Staff:** 2. **Budget:** $160,000. **State**. City and county managers and others who work in management offices of local government organized to support and improve municipal and county management and strengthen local government. **Subgroups:** County Management Association; Illinois Association of County Administrators; Illinois Association of Municipal Management Assistants; Metropolitan Managers Association Downstate City. **Publications:** *City/County Management in Illinois*, 10/year. Newsletter. **Advertising:** accepted • Membership Directory, annual. **Conventions/Meetings:** semiannual conference, presents sessions on the current practices in local government and training sessions to develop managerial skills (exhibits).

1436 ■ Illinois Council on Economic Education (ICEE)
Northern Illinois Univ.
DeKalb, IL 60115-2854
Ph: (815)753-0356
Fax: (815)753-0355
Free: (877)IDO-ECON
E-mail: icee@niu.edu
URL: http://www.econed-il.org
Contact: Joanne R. Dempsey, Pres./Exec.Dir.
State. Strives to prepare all young people to function effectively in the economic system as productive workers, wise consumers, smart savers, and investors and informed voting citizens. Provides workshops and courses for K-12 teachers to help them integrate economics across the curriculum.

1437 ■ Islamic Society - Northern Illinois University (ISNIU)
721 Normal Rd.
DeKalb, IL 60115
Ph: (815)756-9640
Fax: (815)756-1708
E-mail: isniu@iname.com
URL: http://members.tripod.com/~isniu
Contact: Azher Ahmed, Contact
Local. Muslim students in North America. Seeks to advance the interests of members; works to enable members to practice Islam as a complete way of life. **Affiliated With:** Muslim Students Association of the United States and Canada.

1438 ■ Kishwaukee United Way
PO Box 311
DeKalb, IL 60115
Ph: (815)756-7522
Fax: (815)748-5142
E-mail: info@kishwaukeeunitedway.com
URL: http://www.kishwaukeeunitedway.org
Contact: Ms. Dawn Littlefield, Exec.Dir.
Local. **Affiliated With:** United Way of America.

1439 ■ Kishwaukee Valley Habitat for Humanity
2300 Sycamore Rd. No. 44
DeKalb, IL 60115-2067
Ph: (815)758-5055
Fax: (815)758-5525
E-mail: kvhfh@tbc.net
URL: http://www.kishwaukeevalleyhabitat.org
Local. **Affiliated With:** Habitat for Humanity International.

1440 ■ Northern Illinois University Fencing Club
c/o Office of Campus Recreation
Fencing Club
Northern Illinois Univ.
DeKalb, IL 60115
Ph: (815)754-5944
E-mail: niufence@hotmail.com
URL: http://www.sa.niu.edu/fencing/home.htm
Contact: Matt Etherington, Pres.
Regional. Amateur fencers. **Affiliated With:** United States Fencing Association.

1441 ■ Professional Association of Clothiers, Chicago Chapter
c/o Robin Bolton
2120 Monticello Dr.
DeKalb, IL 60115
Ph: (815)716-5450
Fax: (815)357-6393
E-mail: pbolton192@aol.com
Contact: Robin Bolton, Contact
Local. Seeks to meet the needs of custom clothiers; promotes the use of custom clothing to the general public and provides a referral service to potential clients. **Affiliated With:** Professional Association of Custom Clothiers.

1442 ■ Psi Chi, National Honor Society in Psychology - Northern Illinois University
c/o Dept. of Psychology
411 Psychology Bldg.
1425 W Lincoln Hwy.
DeKalb, IL 60115
Ph: (815)753-0372 (815)753-5920
Fax: (815)753-8088
E-mail: horcutt@niu.edu
URL: National Affiliate–www.psichi.org
Local. **Affiliated With:** Psi Chi, National Honor Society in Psychology.

1443 ■ Shawnee Muskie Hunters
PO Box 602
DeKalb, IL 60115
Ph: (815)756-3231
E-mail: crus61@charter.net
URL: National Affiliate–www.muskiesinc.org
Contact: Gary Dew, Pres.
Local.

1444 ■ Society of Manufacturing Engineers - Northern Illinois University S210
103 C Still Hall, Still Gym 204
DeKalb, IL 60115-2854
Ph: (815)753-1754
Fax: (815)753-3702
E-mail: otieno@ceet.niu.edu
URL: National Affiliate–www.sme.org
Contact: Andrew Otieno, Contact
Local. Advances manufacturing knowledge to gain competitive advantage. Improves skills and manufacturing solutions for the growth of economy. Provides resources and opportunities for manufacturing professionals. **Affiliated With:** U.S. National Committee on Theoretical and Applied Mechanics.

1445 ■ Sweet Adelines International, Prairie Echoes Chapter
Hillcrest Covenant Church
1515 N 1st St.
DeKalb, IL 60115-1731
Ph: (815)758-0004
E-mail: lynn78@earthlink.net
URL: National Affiliate–www.sweetadelineintl.org
Contact: Lynn Fillmore, Contact
Local. Advances the musical art form of barbershop harmony through education and performances. Provides education, training and coaching in the development of women's four-part barbershop harmony. **Affiliated With:** Sweet Adelines International.

Delavan

1446 ■ American Legion, Delavan Post 382
118 E 3rd St.
Delavan, IL 61734
Ph: (309)244-7591
Fax: (309)663-5783
URL: National Affiliate–www.legion.org
Local. **Affiliated With:** American Legion.

Depue

1447 ■ American Legion, Illinois Post 327
c/o Lloyd Knowlton
PO Box 332
Depue, IL 61322
Ph: (815)447-2318
Fax: (309)663-5783
URL: National Affiliate–www.legion.org
Contact: Lloyd Knowlton, Contact
Local. **Affiliated With:** American Legion.

Des Plaines

1448 ■ AAA-Chicago Motor Club
1000 E Touhy Ave., No. 125
Des Plaines, IL 60018-2736
Ph: (847)390-9000
Local.

1449 ■ American Institute of Chemical Engineers - Chicago Section
c/o Brian C. Gahan, Chm.
Exploration Production Ctr.
Gas Tech. Inst.
1700 S Mt. Prospect Rd.
Des Plaines, IL 60018
Ph: (847)768-0931
Fax: (847)919-6789
E-mail: brian.gehan@gastechnology.org
URL: http://www.aiche-chicago.org
Contact: Brian C. Gahan, Chm.
Local. Represents the interests of chemical engineering professionals. Aims to contribute to the improvement of chemical engineering curricula offered in universities. Seeks to enhance the lifelong career development and financial security of chemical engineers through products, services, networking and advocacy. **Affiliated With:** American Institute of Chemical Engineers.

1450 ■ American Legion, Cannata-Mcdonough-Curcuru Post 994
1291 Oakwood Ave.
Des Plaines, IL 60016
Ph: (847)824-3236
Fax: (309)663-5783
URL: National Affiliate–www.legion.org
Local. Affiliated With: American Legion.

1451 ■ American Legion, Des Plaines Post 36
1291 Oakwood Ave.
Des Plaines, IL 60016
Ph: (309)663-0361
Fax: (309)663-5783
URL: National Affiliate–www.legion.org
Local. Affiliated With: American Legion.

1452 ■ American Legion, General C. Pulaski Post 86
2083 Fox Ln.
Des Plaines, IL 60018
Ph: (847)827-4155
Fax: (309)663-5783
URL: National Affiliate–www.legion.org
Local. Affiliated With: American Legion.

1453 ■ Cable Television and Communications Association of Illinois
c/o Joan Ellen, Pres.
2400 E Devon, Ste.317
Des Plaines, IL 60018
Ph: (847)297-4520
Fax: (847)297-3865
E-mail: help@ilcampaign.org
State.

1454 ■ Central Educational Network
c/o James Fellows, Pres./CEO
1400 E. Touhy Ave., Ste.260
Des Plaines, IL 60018
Ph: (847)390-8700
Fax: (847)390-9435

1455 ■ Chicago Catalysis Club
c/o J. W. Adriaan Sachtler, Dr., Pres.
25 E Algonquin Rd.
Des Plaines, IL 60017-5016
Ph: (847)391-3177
Fax: (847)391-1274
E-mail: adriaan.sachtler@uop.com
URL: National Affiliate–www.nacatsoc.org
Contact: J. W. Adriaan Sachtler, Dr., Pres.
Local. Affiliated With: North American Catalysis Society.

1456 ■ Crohn's and Colitis Foundation of America, Illinois Carol Fisher Chapter
2250 E Devon Ave., Ste.244
Des Plaines, IL 60018-4509
Ph: (847)827-0404
Fax: (847)827-6563
Free: (800)886-6664
URL: National Affiliate–www.ccfa.org
Contact: Kathleen Durkin, Exec.Dir.
Founded: 1967. **Members:** 1,500. **Membership Dues:** lay, $25 (annual) • physician, $150 (annual). **Staff:** 4. **Budget:** $550,000. **State Groups:** 3. **Local Groups:** 25. **Local**. Support group for persons afflicted with Crohn's and colitis in the midwestern U.S; physicians. Seeks to raise funds for educational and research programs. **Libraries: Type:** open to the public. **Holdings:** articles, books. **Subjects:** health diet, surgery, emotional factors. **Awards: Frequency:** annual. **Type:** grant. **Affiliated With:** Crohn's and Colitis Foundation of America. **Formerly:** Crohn's and Colitis Foundation of America Midwest Region; (1990) National Foundation for Ileitis and Colitis, Midwest Regional. **Publications:** *Foundation Focus*, periodic. Newsletter. **Price:** free with membership • *Inflammatory Bowel Disease*. Journal. **Conventions/Meetings:** annual Lay Education Programs - meeting • annual Professional Education Program - meeting.

1457 ■ Des Plaines Chamber of Commerce and Industry
1401 Oakton St.
Des Plaines, IL 60018
Ph: (847)824-4200
Fax: (847)824-7932
E-mail: info@dpchamber.com
URL: http://www.dpchamber.com
Contact: Barbara Ryan, Exec.Dir.
Membership Dues: business (based on number of employees), $195-$1,725 (annual) • bank/financial institution, $520 (annual) • utility, $335 (annual) • government/education, $310 (annual) • individual (non-business), $180 (annual) • emeritus (retired CEO, Manager, etc.), $128 (annual) • hospital/nursing home (add $1.30/bed), $230 (annual) • hotel/motel (add $1.30/room), $230 (annual) • non-profit/civic/charitable, $210 (annual). **Staff:** 3. **Local**. Promotes, supports, and assists the Des Plaines business community through effective communication and quality service. Improves the quality of life for all citizens of the area. **Divisions:** Education; Industrial; International; Retail; Service. **Publications:** *The Business Advocate*, monthly. Newsletter. Contains chamber news, tips, happenings, advice and other information. **Price:** free for members; $10.00 /year for nonmembers. **Circulation:** 1,000. **Advertising:** accepted. Alternate Formats: online • *Directory and Community Guide*, annual. Brochure.

1458 ■ Des Plaines Historical Society (DPHS)
789 Pearson St.
Des Plaines, IL 60016
Ph: (847)391-5399
Fax: (847)297-4741
E-mail: dphslibrary@juno.com
URL: http://dpkhome.northstarnet.org/DPHS/index.html
Contact: Joy Matthiessen, Dir.
Founded: 1967. **Members:** 450. **Membership Dues:** senior citizen, $9 (annual) • individual, $15 (annual) • family, $20 (annual) • business/organization, $100 (annual) • patron, $50 (annual) • student, $7 (annual) • life, $500. **Staff:** 6. **Budget:** $250,000. **Regional Groups:** 3. **State Groups:** 4. **Local Groups:** 1. **Local**. Individuals and groups interested in the history of the Des Plaines, IL area, including Maine Township in Cook County. Conducts programs, educational tours, and exhibits. Holds annual Ice Cream Social, River Days, Holiday Gala, and other special events. Operates museum and research library. **Libraries: Type:** open to the public. **Holdings:** archival material, business records, maps, photographs. **Subjects:** history of Des Plaines and Maine Township in Cook County, Illinois. **Formerly:** (2004) Des Plaines History Center. **Publications:** *The Cobweb*, bimonthly. Newsletter. Features museum happenings, history articles, and staff articles. **Price:** included in membership dues. **Circulation:** 450. **Conventions/Meetings:** Business & Volunteer Recognition - meeting, with food, awards, silent auction • monthly meeting.

1459 ■ Illinois Chapter of American Medical Billing Association (IL-AMBA)
7500 Elmhurst Rd., No. 593
Des Plaines, IL 60018
Ph: (708)431-0322
Fax: (815)846-0744
E-mail: smhs.brenda@sbcglobal.net
URL: National Affiliate–www.ambanet.net/AMBA.htm
Contact: Brenda Keene, Pres.
State. Promotes the medical billing profession. Assists small and home medical billing professionals. **Affiliated With:** American Medical Billing Association.

1460 ■ Inland Press Association
701 Lee St., Ste.925
Des Plaines, IL 60016
Ph: (847)795-0380
Fax: (847)795-0385
E-mail: inland@inlandpress.org
URL: http://www.inlandpress.org
Contact: Ray Carlsen, Exec.Dir.
Local. Provides training seminars and workshops, confidential business research, publications, conferences, and other services.

1461 ■ International Association of Machinists and Aerospace Workers, AFL-CIO, CLC - Local Lodge 1487
50 W Oakton St.
Des Plaines, IL 60018
Ph: (847)299-8144
E-mail: news1487@yahoo.com
URL: http://www.iamlocal1487.org
Contact: Erik Stenberg, Pres.
Members: 9,394. **Local**. Seeks for the dignity and equality of the workers. Strives to provide contractors with well-trained, productive employees. **Affiliated With:** International Association of Machinists and Aerospace Workers.

1462 ■ Junior Woman's Club of Des Plaines
PO Box 44
Des Plaines, IL 60016
Ph: (847)803-5478
URL: http://dpkhome.northstarnet.org/CO/JrWomen.html
Local.

1463 ■ Kiwanis Club of Des Plaines, Illinois
PO Box 1060
Des Plaines, IL 60017
E-mail: kiwanisd@northstarnet.org
URL: http://dpkhome.northstarnet.org/kiwanisd
Local.

1464 ■ National Association of the Remodeling Industry of Greater Chicagoland
780 Lee St., Ste.108
Des Plaines, IL 60016
Ph: (847)298-6212
Fax: (847)298-2922
E-mail: narichicagoland@aol.com
URL: National Affiliate–www.nari.org
Contact: Matt Hopkins, Pres.
Local. Brings together people who work in the remodeling industry. Provides resources for knowledge and training in the industry. Encourages ethical conduct, 'sound business practices and professionalism. Promotes the remodeling industry's products. **Affiliated With:** National Association of the Remodeling Industry.

1465 ■ Navy League of the United States, Glenview
c/o Barry J. Jacobson
10001 Linda Ln.
Des Plaines, IL 60016-1329

Ph: (847)635-2050
E-mail: bjjacobson60016@aol.com
URL: National Affiliate–www.navyleague.org
Contact: Barry J. Jacobson, Pres.

Local. Civilian organization that supports U.S. capability to keep the sea lanes open through a strong, viable Navy, Marine Corps, Coast Guard, and Merchant Marine. Seeks to awaken interest and cooperation of U.S. citizens in matters serving to aid, improve, and develop the efficiency of U.S. naval and maritime forces and equipment. **Affiliated With:** Navy League of the United States.

1466 ■ Northern Illinois Air Conditioning Contractors of America (NIACCA)
c/o Mimi Makar, Exec.Dir.
780 Lee St., Ste.104A
Des Plaines, IL 60016
Ph: (847)297-7669
Fax: (847)297-7679
E-mail: office@niacca.org
URL: http://www.niacca.org
Contact: Mimi Makar, Exec.Dir.

Regional. **Affiliated With:** Air Conditioning Contractors of America.

1467 ■ Phi Theta Kappa, Alpha Iota Phi Chapter - Oakton Community College
c/o Paul Sanburg
1600 E Golf Rd.
Des Plaines, IL 60016
Ph: (847)635-2649
E-mail: psanburg@oakton.edu
URL: http://www.ptk.org/directories/chapters/IL/211-1.htm
Contact: Paul Sanburg, Advisor

Local.

1468 ■ Scenic Illinois
c/o John Hedrick, Pres./Founder
PO Box 2925
Des Plaines, IL 60017-2925
Ph: (847)767-4018
E-mail: scenicillinois@aol.com
URL: http://www.scenicillinois.org/about.htm
Contact: John Hedrick, Pres./Founder

State. **Affiliated With:** Scenic America.

1469 ■ Transport Workers Union of America, AFL-CIO - Local Union 572
PO Box 1067
Des Plaines, IL 60017-1067
Ph: (773)686-6520
E-mail: twu572@yahoo.com
URL: http://local572.twuatd.org
Contact: Joe Schreiber, Pres.

Members: 197. **Local**. **Affiliated With:** Transport Workers Union of America.

1470 ■ United Food and Commercial Workers, Local 580T, Northcentral Region
2165 Lee St.
Des Plaines, IL 60018
Ph: (847)297-0293
URL: National Affiliate–www.ufcw.org

Local. **Affiliated With:** United Food and Commercial Workers International Union.

1471 ■ U.S.A. Volleyball Great Lakes Region
c/o Lea Wagner
1635 Greenleaf
Des Plaines, IL 60018
Ph: (847)297-3419
Fax: (847)827-2811
E-mail: lwagnerglr@aol.com
URL: http://www.greatlakesvolleyball.org

Local. **Affiliated With:** United States Volleyball Association/United States Volleyball Association.

Dieterich

1472 ■ American Legion, Dieterich Post 628
PO Box 13
Dieterich, IL 62424
Ph: (217)925-5291
Fax: (309)663-5783
URL: National Affiliate–www.legion.org
Local. **Affiliated With:** American Legion.

Dixon

1473 ■ American Counseling Association, Illinois
c/o Richard Longfellow
PO Box 903
Dixon, IL 61021-0903
Fax: (877)284-1521
Free: (877)284-1521
E-mail: dlongfel@essex1.com
URL: National Affiliate–www.counseling.org

State. **Affiliated With:** American Counseling Association.

1474 ■ American Legion, Dixon Post 12
PO Box 401
Dixon, IL 61021
Ph: (815)284-7645
Fax: (309)663-5783
URL: National Affiliate–www.legion.org
Local. **Affiliated With:** American Legion.

1475 ■ American Red Cross, Lee County Chapter
Commerce Towers
215 E First St., Ste.150
Dixon, IL 61021
Ph: (815)284-2829
Fax: (815)284-9260
URL: http://home.grics.net/~redcross
Local.

1476 ■ American Society for Training and Development, Rock Valley Chapter
c/o Christie Mason, Membership Dir./Web Administrator
4083 Timberlane
Dixon, IL 61021
Ph: (815)652-3196
Fax: (815)652-3196
E-mail: cmason@managersforum.com
URL: http://www.managersforum.com/ASTD/index.htm
Contact: Christie Mason, Membership Dir./Web Administrator

Local. Works to enhance personal and professional learning, leadership and performance. **Affiliated With:** ASTD. **Publications:** Newsletter. **Conventions/Meetings:** monthly meeting, with peer interaction and presentations.

1477 ■ Dixon Area Chamber of Commerce and Industry (DACCI)
101 W Second St., Ste.301
Dixon, IL 61021
Ph: (815)284-3361
Fax: (815)284-3675
E-mail: dchamber@essex1.com
URL: http://www.dixonillinoischamber.com
Contact: John R. Thompson, CEO/Pres.

Founded: 1887. **Members:** 380. **Membership Dues:** general business, retail and service (add $3.52/employee above 30), $249-$764 (annual) • manufacturer, general contractor, distributor, publisher (add $3.52/employee over 20), $275 (annual) • professional (add $91.02/principal and $13.99 each professional staff), $275 (annual) • hotel/motel per unit (add $69.99, with restaurant; $140.03, with bar; $217.93, with banquet facility), $3 (annual) • hospital/nursing home per unit (add $91.02/professional directly employed), $3 (annual) • financial institution (base fee up to $5 million in asset), $785 (annual) • retired/clergy and church/individual, educator/civic, official/non-profit, $98 (annual). **Staff:** 3. **Budget:** $100,000. **Local**. Businesspersons, manufacturers, professionals, and non-profit organizations interested in promoting business and community development in the Dixon, IL area. **Telecommunication Services:** electronic mail, info@dixonillinoischamber.com. **Also Known As:** Dixon Chamber of Commerce. **Formerly:** (1915) Citizen's Association. **Publications:** *Dixon Area Business News*, monthly. Newsletter. **Advertising:** accepted. Alternate Formats: online • *Membership and Business Services Directory*, annual. **Conventions/Meetings:** annual meeting.

1478 ■ Gardeners of America/Men's Garden Clubs of America - Dixon Men's Garden Club
c/o Donetta Harnes
201 S Coll. Ave.
Dixon, IL 61021
Ph: (815)284-3646
E-mail: jondon@grics.net
URL: National Affiliate–www.tgoa-mgca.org
Contact: Donetta Harnes, Contact

Local.

1479 ■ Illinois Association of School Nurses (IASN)
c/o Marian Myers, Exec.Sec.
1110 White Rock Dr.
Dixon, IL 61021
Ph: (815)652-5218
Fax: (815)652-6730
E-mail: iasn@grics.net
URL: http://www.iasn.org
Contact: Marian Myers, Exec.Sec.

Founded: 1957. **State**.

1480 ■ Illinois Native Plant Society, Quad City Chapter
3155 52nd Ave.
Dixon, IL 61021
Ph: (563)843-2852
E-mail: bjbryant@netins.net
URL: http://www.ill-inps.org
Contact: Robert Brady, Pres.

Local. **Affiliated With:** Illinois Native Plant Society.

1481 ■ Local 758C, Chemical Workers Council of the UFCW
423 Spruce St.
Dixon, IL 61021
Ph: (815)284-0384
E-mail: abletwo@essex1.com
URL: National Affiliate–www.ufcw.org

Local. **Affiliated With:** United Food and Commercial Workers International Union.

1482 ■ Phi Theta Kappa, Beta Alpha Gamma Chapter - Sauk Valley Community College
c/o Steve Nunez
173 Illinois Rte. 2
Dixon, IL 61021
Ph: (815)288-5511
E-mail: nunezs@svcc.edu
URL: http://www.ptk.org/directories/chapters/IL/20652-1.htm
Contact: Steve Nunez, Advisor

Local.

1483 ■ Rock River Human Resources Professional Association
PO Box 962
Dixon, IL 61021
E-mail: avila@rayovac.com
Contact: Penny Avila, Pres.

Local. Represents the interests of human resource and industrial relations professionals and executives. Promotes the advancement of human resource management.

1484 ■ Society of Physics Students - Sauk Valley College Chapter No. 6390
173 Illinois Rte. 2
Dixon, IL 61021
Ph: (815)288-5511
E-mail: atchlec@svcc.edu
URL: National Affiliate–www.spsnational.org
Local. Offers opportunities for the students to enrich their experiences and skills about physics. Helps students to become professional in the field of physics. **Affiliated With:** Society of Physics Students.

1485 ■ United Way of Lee County, Illinois
PO Box 382
Dixon, IL 61021-0382
Ph: (815)284-3339
URL: National Affiliate–national.unitedway.org
Local. Affiliated With: United Way of America.

1486 ■ Veteran Motor Car Club of America - Reagan Country Classics Chapter
c/o Harold Vail, Pres.
1465 S Coll. Ave.
Dixon, IL 61021
Ph: (815)285-0201
E-mail: hvail@gallatinriver.net
URL: National Affiliate–www.vmcca.org
Contact: Harold Vail, Pres.
Local. Affiliated With: Veteran Motor Car Club of America.

Dolton

1487 ■ 1st Chicago Bottle Club
PO Box 224
Dolton, IL 60419
Ph: (708)841-4068
URL: National Affiliate–www.fohbc.com
Local. Affiliated With: Federation of Historical Bottle Collectors.

1488 ■ Dolton Chamber of Commerce
PO Box 823
Dolton, IL 60419-0823
Ph: (708)841-4810
Fax: (708)841-4833
Contact: Larceeda Jefferson, Admin.Asst.
Founded: 1976. **Members:** 125. **Membership Dues:** $50 (annual). **Staff:** 1. **Budget:** $190,300. **Local.** Promotes business and community development in Dolton, IL. Sponsors 4th of July parade and weekly bingo. **Awards:** Citizen of the Year. **Frequency:** annual. **Type:** recognition. **Publications:** Directory, annual • Newsletter, monthly. **Conventions/Meetings:** monthly dinner - always third Wednesday of the month • annual meeting.

1489 ■ New Hope Association
1625 E 154th St.
Dolton, IL 60419
Ph: (708)841-1071
Fax: (708)841-1053
Contact: Jeff Gajewski, Dir.
Local. Parents, professional workers, and others interested in individuals with mental retardation. Works to promote services, research, public understanding, and legislation for people with mental retardation and their families. **Affiliated With:** Arc of the United States.

Dongola

1490 ■ American Legion, Miller-Manning Post 418
PO Box 143
Dongola, IL 62926
Ph: (618)827-4171
Fax: (309)663-5783
URL: National Affiliate–www.legion.org
Local. Affiliated With: American Legion.

Donovan

1491 ■ American Legion, Donovan Post 633
3084 E 2700 North Rd.
Box 226
Donovan, IL 60931
Ph: (309)663-0361
Fax: (309)663-5783
URL: National Affiliate–www.legion.org
Local. Affiliated With: American Legion.

Dowell

1492 ■ American Legion, Deceased Veterans Post 975
401 Union
Dowell, IL 62927
Ph: (309)663-0361
Fax: (309)663-5783
URL: National Affiliate–www.legion.org
Local. Affiliated With: American Legion.

Downers Grove

1493 ■ American Industrial Hygiene Association - Chicago Local Section
c/o Kevin Aikman, PhD, Treas.
United Analytical Services, Inc.
1515 Centre Cir. Dr.
Downers Grove, IL 60515
Ph: (630)691-8271
E-mail: kaikman@uas1.com
URL: http://www.chicagoaiha.org
Contact: Kevin Aikman PhD, Treas.
Local. Represents the interests of occupational and environmental health professionals practicing in industry, government, labor and academic institutions and independent organizations. Promotes the certification of industrial hygienists. Administers educational programs for environmental health and safety professionals. **Affiliated With:** American Industrial Hygiene Association.

1494 ■ American Legion, Illinois Post 80
c/o Alexander Bradley Burns
4000 Saratoga Ave., No. 9072
Downers Grove, IL 60515
Ph: (630)968-9710
Fax: (309)663-5783
URL: National Affiliate–www.legion.org
Contact: Alexander Bradley Burns, Contact
Local. Affiliated With: American Legion.

1495 ■ American Legion, Illinois Post 957
5513 Washington St.
Downers Grove, IL 60516
Ph: (708)852-4612
Fax: (309)663-5783
URL: National Affiliate–www.legion.org
Contact: Herb Jacobs, Contact
Local. Affiliated With: American Legion.

1496 ■ American Legion, Illinois Post 1974
5120 Belmont Rd., Ste.U
Downers Grove, IL 60515
Ph: (708)776-8776
Fax: (309)663-5783
URL: National Affiliate–www.legion.org
Contact: Frank W. Leahy, Contact
Local. Affiliated With: American Legion.

1497 ■ Brahma Samaj of Greater Chicago (BSGC)
c/o Gaurang Trivedi
1400 Terr. Dr.
Downers Grove, IL 60516
Ph: (630)968-9394 (847)726-1628
E-mail: info@bsgc-il.org
URL: http://www.bsgc-il.org
Contact: Gaurang Trivedi, Contact
Local.

1498 ■ Chicago Local Section of the American Nuclear Society
c/o Jeffrey A. Dunlap
Exelon Nuclear
Nuclear Fuel Mgt.
Fuel Procurement Engineer
1400 Opus Pl., Ste.400
Downers Grove, IL 60515
Ph: (630)663-3061
E-mail: ans_chicago@hotmail.com
URL: http://www.geocities.com/ans_chicago
Contact: Jeffrey A. Dunlap, Contact
Local. Works to advance science and engineering in the nuclear industry. Works with government agencies, educational institutions, and other organizations dealing with nuclear issues. **Affiliated With:** American Nuclear Society.

1499 ■ Chicagoland's Human Resource Association
1400 Opus Pl., Ste.500
Downers Grove, IL 60515
Ph: (630)963-6316
E-mail: info@chicagolandhr.org
URL: http://www.chicagolandhr.org
Contact: Dawn Nijim Hill, Pres.
Local. Represents the interests of human resource and industrial relations professionals and executives. Promotes the advancement of human resource management.

1500 ■ Coin Laundry Association (CLA)
1315 Butterfield Rd., Ste.212
Downers Grove, IL 60515
Ph: (630)963-5547
Fax: (630)963-5864
Free: (877)CLA-IDEA
E-mail: info@coinlaundry.org
URL: http://www.coinlaundry.org
Contact: Brian Wallace, Pres./CEO
Founded: 1965. **Members:** 200. **Membership Dues:** store owner, $175 (annual) • distributor, $499 (annual). **Staff:** 3. **Local.** Owners and operators of coin laundry stores around the nation; equipment distributors and suppliers. Seeks to improve the operation and management of coin operated laundry stores; promotes greater use of coin operated laundry stores. Sponsors educational programs. **Affiliated With:** Coin Laundry Association. **Formerly:** (1983) Midwest Automatic Laundry and Cleaning Council. **Publications:** *The Official Voice of the Coin Laundry Industry*, monthly. Journal. Features the coin laundry and dry cleaning industry. **Price:** free to industry members. **Conventions/Meetings:** bimonthly seminar - except summer; in Chicago, IL.

1501 ■ Downers Grove Area Chamber of Commerce and Industry
1015 Curtiss St.
Downers Grove, IL 60515
Ph: (630)968-4050
Fax: (630)968-8368
E-mail: chamber@downersgrove.org
URL: http://www.downersgrove.org
Contact: Barbara L. Wysocki, Pres./CEO
Members: 700. **Membership Dues:** business, $250-$930 (annual). **Staff:** 4. **Local.** Supports the business community while partnering with the residential, educational and service organizations. Helps to shape the business climate in the Downers Grove area. **Telecommunication Services:** hotline, business referral hotline, (630)968-4051. **Committees:** Ambassadors; Community Awareness; Education; Golf; Health Awareness; Legislative; Membership Services; Programs/Events. **Publications:** *ChamberLine*, monthly. Newsletter. Features upcoming Chamber events, member opportunities, and legislative issues. **Circulation:** 800. **Advertising:** accepted • *Village and Business*, annual. Directory. **Circulation:** 30,000.

1502 ■ Downers Grove South High School Parent Teacher Association
c/o Downers Grove South High School
1436 Norfolk
Downers Grove, IL 60516

Ph: (630)795-8500
E-mail: dcozzo@csd99.org
URL: http://www.csd99.k12.il.us/south/pta
Contact: Dan Cozzo, Asst. Principal
Local. Parents, teachers, students, and others interested in uniting the forces of home, school, and community. Promotes the welfare of children and youth.

1503 ■ IEEE Electromagnetic Compatibility Society, Chicago
c/o Jack Black, Chm.
DLS Electronic Systems
1516 Centre Circle Dr.
Downers Grove, IL 60515
Ph: (847)537-6400
Fax: (847)537-6488
E-mail: jblack@dlsemc.com
URL: http://www.ewh.ieee.org/soc/emcs/chicago
Contact: Jack Black, Chm.
Local. **Affiliated With:** IEEE Electromagnetic Compatibility Society.

1504 ■ Illinois Cochlear Implant Club
c/o Hanna Benioff
6316 Tamiami Dr.
Downers Grove, IL 60516-2108
Ph: (630)964-1229
E-mail: benioff@megsinet.net
URL: http://us.geocities.com/illinoisic
Contact: Hanna Benioff, Pres.
Founded: 1990. **Members:** 60. **Membership Dues:** individual, family, professional, $25 (annual). **State**. **Affiliated With:** Cochlear Implant Association, Inc. **Publications:** *ICIC Newsletter*, quarterly.

1505 ■ Management Association of Illinois (MAI)
c/o Mary Lynn Fayoumi, CAE, Pres./CEO
1400 Opus Pl., Ste.500
Downers Grove, IL 60515
Ph: (630)963-7600
Fax: (630)963-2800
Free: (800)448-4584
E-mail: info@hrsource.org
URL: http://www.hrsource.org
Contact: Mary Lynn Fayoumi CAE, Pres./CEO
Founded: 1898. **Members:** 800. **Staff:** 30. **Budget:** $3,000,000. **State**. Employers. Provides human resource information, training, compensation, consulting, and legal services for employer/employee related concerns. **Libraries: Type:** not open to the public. **Holdings:** articles, books, periodicals. **Subjects:** human resources. **Formed by Merger of:** Associated Employers of Illinois; MIMA, The Management Association. **Publications:** *Policies and Benefits Survey*, biennial • *Resources*, monthly. Newsletter • *Wage, Salary, National Executive Compensation Survey*, annual. Surveys. **Conventions/Meetings:** annual Human Resources Conference - always spring and fall • annual meeting.

1506 ■ National Association of Rocketry - Northern Illinois Rocketry Association (NIRA)
c/o Adam Elliot
4725 Belmont
Downers Grove, IL 60515
Ph: (630)662-1424
E-mail: adamnira@yahoo.com
URL: http://www.nira.chicago.il.us
Contact: Adam Elliot, Contact
Local.

1507 ■ PACT Humane Society
c/o Cherie Travis
PO Box 841
Downers Grove, IL 60515
Ph: (630)375-7017
Fax: (630)497-1672
E-mail: director@pacthumanesociety.org
URL: http://www.pacthumanesociety.org
Founded: 2000. **Languages:** English, German, Spanish. **Local**.

1508 ■ Parents Without Partners, Ogden Trails
PO Box 37
Downers Grove, IL 60515-9998
Ph: (630)932-1615
URL: National Affiliate–www.parentswithoutpartners.org
Local. Custodial and non-custodial parents who are single by reason of widowhood, divorce, separation, or otherwise. Works to alleviate the problems of single parents in relation to the welfare and upbringing of their children and the acceptance into the general social order of single parents and their children. **Affiliated With:** Parents Without Partners.

1509 ■ Perinatal Information Systems User Group (PISUG)
c/o Melissa Dolenga, VP
1202 N 75th St., No. 296
Downers Grove, IL 60517
E-mail: webdiva@pisug.org
URL: http://www.pisug.org/index.html
Contact: Melissa Dolenga, VP
Local.

1510 ■ Ray Graham Association for People with Disabilities
c/o Kristi Athas
2801 Finley Rd.
Downers Grove, IL 60515
Ph: (630)620-2222
Fax: (630)628-2350
E-mail: rgajobs@yahoo.com
URL: http://www.ray-graham.org
Contact: Kristi Athas, Contact
Local.

1511 ■ Realtor Association of West/South Suburban Chicagoland
6655 S Main St.
Downers Grove, IL 60516
Ph: (630)324-8400
Fax: (630)324-8401
E-mail: info@rwssc.com
URL: http://www.rwssc.com
Contact: Pam Krieter, CEO
Local. Strives to develop real estate business practices. Advocates the right to own, use and transfer real property. Provides a facility for professional development, research and exchange of information among members and to the general public. **Affiliated With:** National Association of Realtors.

1512 ■ Sons of Norway, Leif Erikson Lodge 5-97
c/o Joann J. Hansen, Pres.
19 7th St.
Downers Grove, IL 60515-5354
Ph: (630)969-5477
E-mail: joann.hansen@worldnet.att.net
URL: http://www.leiferikson5-097.org
Contact: Joann J. Hansen, Pres.
Local. **Affiliated With:** Sons of Norway.

Downs

1513 ■ American Legion, Lloyd Fleischer Post 1150
215 Seminary St.
Downs, IL 61736
Ph: (309)378-9429
Fax: (309)663-5783
URL: National Affiliate–www.legion.org
Local. **Affiliated With:** American Legion.

1514 ■ Illinois Country Music Association (ICMA)
PO Box 79
Downs, IL 61736-0079
Ph: (309)829-7883
Fax: (309)828-0054
E-mail: icmaillinois@aol.com
URL: http://www.ICMA2002.com
Contact: Ray Prince, Pres.
Founded: 1989. **Members:** 50. **Membership Dues:** general, $12 (annual) • family, $7 (annual) • commercial, $30 (annual). **Staff:** 11. **Budget:** $20,000. **Regional Groups:** 1. **State Groups:** 2. **State**. Promotes country, gospel, bluegrass, and Western music in the state of Illinois. Promotes all forms of country dancing. Sponsors concerts, shows, and other events. Provides information to assist and encourage new and established artists. **Awards:** Fan of the Year. **Frequency:** annual. **Type:** recognition • People's Choice Awards. **Frequency:** annual. **Type:** recognition. **Recipient:** for individuals who have earned the respect of their fellow members in the Illinois country music arena • Pioneer Award. **Frequency:** annual. **Type:** recognition • Richard Brown Memorial Scholarship. **Type:** scholarship. **Recipient:** for students. **Affiliated With:** Country Music Association. **Publications:** Newsletter, bimonthly. **Price:** included in membership dues. **Circulation:** 500. **Advertising:** accepted. **Conventions/Meetings:** monthly State Executive Board Meeting - executive committee meeting - every first Thursday in Mason City, IL.

Du Bois

1515 ■ American Hiking Society - DuBois Center
2651 Quarry Rd.
Du Bois, IL 62831
Ph: (618)787-2202
Fax: (618)787-7701
E-mail: duboiscenter@frontiernet.net
URL: http://www.duboiscenter.org
Contact: Rev. Kerry Bean, Dir.
Local.

Du Quoin

1516 ■ American Legion, Illinois Post 647
c/o Roy Mitchell
900 S Jefferson St.
Du Quoin, IL 62832
Ph: (618)542-2477
Fax: (309)663-5783
URL: National Affiliate–www.legion.org
Contact: Roy Mitchell, Contact
Local. **Affiliated With:** American Legion.

1517 ■ Du Quoin Chamber of Commerce
PO Box 57
Du Quoin, IL 62832-0057
Ph: (618)542-9570
Free: (800)455-9570
E-mail: dqchamber@onecliq.net
URL: http://www.duquoin.org
Contact: Joe Davis, Pres.
Local. Promotes the common interests and community welfare of the residents in Du Quoin, IL. Seeks to enhance the city's image and develop and encourage the various commercial, industrial, professional, financial, and civic interests of the city.

Dundee

1518 ■ American Legion, Dundee-Carpentersville Post 679
PO Box 123
Dundee, IL 60118
Ph: (309)663-0361
Fax: (309)663-5783
URL: National Affiliate–www.legion.org
Local. **Affiliated With:** American Legion.

1519 ■ American Postal Workers Union, AFL-CIO - Crystal Lake Local Union 1879
c/o Michael Daurio, Pres.
10 E Main St., Ste.110
Dundee, IL 60118

Ph: (847)428-3863
Fax: (847)428-4248
E-mail: mickdaurio@neialapwu.org
URL: http://www.neialapwu.org
Contact: Michael Daurio, Pres.

Members: 443. **Local**. AFL-CIO. **Affiliated With:** American Postal Workers Union.

Dunlap

1520 ■ American Legion, Elliott Keller Post 1078
5511 W Legion Hall Rd.
Dunlap, IL 61525
Ph: (309)243-7096
Fax: (309)663-5783
URL: National Affiliate–www.legion.org

Local. Affiliated With: American Legion.

1521 ■ Illinois River Valley Orienteering Club (IRVOC)
c/o Mike Duncan
2201 W Murphy Dr.
Dunlap, IL 61525
Ph: (309)243-9564
E-mail: info@il-orienteering.org
URL: http://www.il-orienteering.org
Contact: Mike Duncan, Contact

Founded: 2000. **Local**.

1522 ■ Peoria Astronomical Society
11307 N Columbine Dr.
Dunlap, IL 61525
E-mail: webmaster@astronomical.org
URL: http://www.astronomical.org
Contact: Scott Swords, Contact

Local. Promotes the science of astronomy. Works to encourage and coordinate activities of amateur astronomical societies. Fosters observational and computational work and craftsmanship in various fields of astronomy. **Affiliated With:** Astronomical League.

Dupo

1523 ■ American Legion, Prairie Du Pont Post 485
200 S 5th St.
Dupo, IL 62239
Ph: (618)286-9585
Fax: (309)663-5783
URL: National Affiliate–www.legion.org

Local. Affiliated With: American Legion.

Durand

1524 ■ American Legion, Gold Star Post 676
211 State St.
Durand, IL 61024
Ph: (309)663-0361
Fax: (309)663-5783
URL: National Affiliate–www.legion.org

Local. Affiliated With: American Legion.

Dwight

1525 ■ American Legion, Dwight Post 486
112 S Franklin St.
Dwight, IL 60420
Ph: (815)584-9860
Fax: (309)663-5783
URL: National Affiliate–www.legion.org

Local. Affiliated With: American Legion.

1526 ■ Dwight Area Chamber of Commerce
119 W Main St.
Dwight, IL 60420
Ph: (815)584-2091
Fax: (815)584-2096
Free: (800)554-6635
E-mail: dwightchamber@fyidwight.net
Contact: Judy Piskule, Admin.

Founded: 1957. **Members:** 98. **Local**. Promotes business and community development and tourism in the Dwight, IL area. Sponsors annual 4th of July fireworks display and annual Dwight Harvest Days Festival. **Publications:** Newsletter, monthly. **Conventions/Meetings:** monthly board meeting - always second Thursday of the month • annual meeting.

Earlville

1527 ■ American Legion, Illinois Post 549
c/o James H. Hamill
PO Box 366
Earlville, IL 60518
Ph: (309)663-0361
Fax: (309)663-5783
URL: National Affiliate–www.legion.org
Contact: James H. Hamill, Contact

Local. Affiliated With: American Legion.

East Alton

1528 ■ American Ex-Prisoners of War, Okaw Chapter
c/o Kenneth V. Bryan
144 Greenview St.
East Alton, IL 62024
Ph: (618)259-4377
URL: National Affiliate–www.axpow.org

Local. Affiliated With: American Ex-Prisoners of War.

1529 ■ American Legion, East Alton Post 794
120 E Alton Ave.
East Alton, IL 62024
Ph: (618)254-7078
Fax: (309)663-5783
URL: National Affiliate–www.legion.org

Local. Affiliated With: American Legion.

1530 ■ International Association of Machinists and Aerospace Workers, Local Lodge 60
161 N Shamrock St.
East Alton, IL 62024
Ph: (618)259-8558
Fax: (618)259-2672
E-mail: ll660@sbcglobal.net
URL: http://www.iamll660.org
Contact: Tim Young, Pres.

Members: 3,307. **Local**. Represents workers. Strives to provide contractors with well-trained and productive employees. **Affiliated With:** International Association of Machinists and Aerospace Workers.

1531 ■ Madison District Dental Society
c/o Dr. Kenneth P. Webb, Exec.Dir.
45 E Haller Dr.
East Alton, IL 62024-1746
Ph: (618)259-6434
E-mail: dental@maconcountyhealth.org
URL: http://www.isds.org
Contact: Dr. Kenneth P. Webb, Exec.Dir.

Local. Represents the interests of dentists committed to the public's oral health, ethics and professional development. Encourages the improvement of the public's oral health and promotes the art and science of dentistry. **Affiliated With:** American Dental Association; Illinois State Dental Society.

East Carondelet

1532 ■ American Legion, Archview Post 1265
PO Box 295
East Carondelet, IL 62240
Ph: (309)663-0361
Fax: (309)663-5783
URL: National Affiliate–www.legion.org

Local. Affiliated With: American Legion.

East Dubuque

1533 ■ American Legion, East Dubuque Post 787
112 Smoke Signal Ln.
East Dubuque, IL 61025
Ph: (815)747-6184
Fax: (309)663-5783
URL: National Affiliate–www.legion.org

Local. Affiliated With: American Legion.

East Dundee

1534 ■ Antique Automobile Club of America, Illinois Region - Fox Valley Chapter
c/o Dan Sobczyk, Pres.
822 Bannock Rd.
East Dundee, IL 60118
Ph: (847)608-2651
E-mail: dansobczyk@netscape.net
URL: http://local.aaca.org/illinois
Contact: Dan Sobczyk, Pres.

Membership Dues: individual, $5 (annual) • life, $300. **Local**. Collectors, hobbyists, and others interested in the preservation, maintenance, and restoration of automobiles and in automotive history. **Affiliated With:** Antique Automobile Club of America.

East Hazel Crest

1535 ■ South Suburban Mayors and Managers Association (SSMMA)
1904 W 174th St.
East Hazel Crest, IL 60429
Ph: (708)206-1155
URL: http://www.ssmma.org
Contact: Karen Hoffschmidt, Deputy Exec.Dir.

Local. Provides information and technical assistance to member towns that work together on issues such as transportation, public safety, legislation, economic development, purchasing, storm water, and housing.

East Moline

1536 ■ American Legion, East Moline Post 227
829 16th Ave.
East Moline, IL 61244
Ph: (309)755-5622
Fax: (309)663-5783
URL: National Affiliate–www.legion.org

Local. Affiliated With: American Legion.

1537 ■ Chemical Coaters Association International, Quad Cities
482 33rd Ave.
East Moline, IL 61244-3170
Ph: (309)755-4179
Fax: (319)263-6587
E-mail: rmascari@aol.com
URL: National Affiliate–www.ccaiweb.com
Contact: Rocci A. Mascari, Contact

Local. Provides information and training on surface coating technologies. Raises the standards of finishing operations through educational meetings and seminars, training manuals, certification programs, and outreach programs with colleges and universities. **Affiliated With:** Chemical Coaters Association International.

1538 ■ Information Systems Audit and Control Association and Foundation, Quad Cities Chapter
c/o Marty Coe
Coe & Associates, LLC
1180 42nd Ave.
East Moline, IL 61244
Fax: (309)792-8390
Free: (800)424-3874
E-mail: mcoe@coeonline.com
URL: National Affiliate–www.isaca.org
Local. Affiliated With: Information Systems Audit and Control Association and Foundation.

East Peoria

1539 ■ American Legion, Creve Coeur Post 1234
216 Marquette St.
East Peoria, IL 61611
Ph: (309)347-1756
Fax: (309)663-5783
URL: National Affiliate–www.legion.org
Local. Affiliated With: American Legion.

1540 ■ American Legion, East Peoria Post 983
PO Box 2116
East Peoria, IL 61611
Ph: (309)694-2435
Fax: (309)663-5783
URL: National Affiliate–www.legion.org
Local. Affiliated With: American Legion.

1541 ■ Association for Accounting Administration, Illinois Chapter
c/o Donna J. Cimino, Pres.
2400 N Main St.
East Peoria, IL 61611
Ph: (309)694-4251
Fax: (309)694-4202
E-mail: dcimino@hbcpas.com
URL: National Affiliate–www.cpaadmin.org
Contact: Donna J. Cimino, Pres.
State. Fosters the professional skills needed as firm administrators. Promotes accounting administration profession. Provides education to enhance the professional and personal competencies of accounting administration. **Affiliated With:** Association for Accounting Administration.

1542 ■ East Peoria Chamber of Commerce and Tourism (EPCCT)
111 W Washington St., Ste.290
East Peoria, IL 61611-2532
Ph: (309)699-6212
Fax: (309)699-6220
E-mail: epcc@epcc.org
URL: http://www.epcc.org
Contact: Charlie Moore, Exec.Dir.
Members: 400. **Local.** Businesses interested in promoting East Peoria, IL. **Awards:** Chamber Distinguished Company of the Year. **Frequency:** annual. **Type:** recognition • East Peoria Distinguished Citizen of the Year. **Frequency:** annual. **Type:** recognition • **Frequency:** annual. **Type:** scholarship. **Recipient:** for an East Peoria Community High School senior who plans to pursue a career in a business related field • Terry Brewer Memorial Scholarship. **Frequency:** annual. **Type:** scholarship. **Recipient:** for an East Peoria High School senior who plans to pursue a course of study in a social work/counseling/community service field at Illinois Central College. **Committees:** Ambassador's Club; Government Affairs; Membership; Networking and Education. **Affiliated With:** U.S. Chamber of Commerce. **Formerly:** (1999) East Peoria +Chamber of Commerce. **Publications:** *East Peoria Business Directory*, periodic • *EP Update*, monthly. Newsletter. Contains valuable information on upcoming events, member news, and legislative issues. **Price:** free for members. **Advertising:** accepted • *The FOLEPI Guide*, annual. Manual. **Circulation:** 40,000. **Advertising:** accepted. **Conventions/Meetings:** monthly Business After Hours - meeting - usually on the third Thursday except December • annual Mayor's Prayer - breakfast, with inspirational speaker and music, hosted by the mayor of East Peoria - usually in May • monthly meeting • annual Mittens for Muffins - breakfast, for members - every December.

1543 ■ Mothers Against Drunk Driving, Heartland Chapter
PO Box 2186
East Peoria, IL 61611
Ph: (309)244-9156
Fax: (309)244-7208
E-mail: madd@flink.com
URL: National Affiliate–www.madd.org/
Contact: Sandra Taylor, Pres.
For-Profit. Local. Victims of drunk driving crashes; concerned citizens. Encourages citizen participation in working towards reform of the drunk driving problem and the prevention of underage drinking. Acts as the voice of victims of drunk driving crashes by speaking on their behalf to communities, businesses, and educational groups. Provides trained victim-advocates to support victims of drunk driving crashes. **Affiliated With:** Mothers Against Drunk Driving.

1544 ■ National Association of Rocketry - Willow Hill Rocketry Group (WHRG)
304 E Far Hills Dr.
East Peoria, IL 61611
Ph: (309)383-2700
E-mail: office@willowhill.org
URL: http://www.willowhill.org
Contact: Greg Blum, Office Mgr.
Local.

1545 ■ Peoria Orchid Society
c/o Barry E. Jones
302 E Eller Dr.
East Peoria, IL 61611
Ph: (309)388-4022
E-mail: orkidj@mtco.com
URL: National Affiliate–www.orchidweb.org
Contact: Barry E. Jones, Contact
Local. Professional growers, botanists, hobbyists, and others interested in extending the knowledge, production, use, and appreciation of orchids. **Affiliated With:** American Orchid Society.

1546 ■ Peoria Skeet and Trap
1470 IL. Rte. 26
East Peoria, IL 61611
Ph: (309)822-8146
URL: http://www.peoriaskeetandtrap.org
Local. Affiliated With: National Skeet Shooting Association.

East St. Louis

1547 ■ Ainad Shriners
c/o Mark Maxwell
609 St. Louis Ave.
East St. Louis, IL 62201-2927
Ph: (618)874-1870
Fax: (618)874-6920
E-mail: admin@ainad.com
URL: http://www.ainad.com
Contact: Mark Maxwell, Administrator
Local. Affiliated With: Imperial Council of the Ancient Arabic Order of the Nobles of the Mystic Shrine for North America.

1548 ■ American Legion, East St. Louis Post 2505
PO Box 623
East St. Louis, IL 62201
Ph: (309)663-0361
Fax: (309)663-5783
URL: National Affiliate–www.legion.org
Local. Affiliated With: American Legion.

1549 ■ American Legion, Willis Hunter Post 378
PO Box 2646
East St. Louis, IL 62202
Ph: (618)271-0080
Fax: (309)663-5783
URL: National Affiliate–www.legion.org
Local. Affiliated With: American Legion.

1550 ■ Greater East St. Louis Chamber of Commerce
327 Missouri Ave., Ste.602
East St. Louis, IL 62201
Ph: (618)271-2855
Fax: (618)271-4622
E-mail: nrosscsac@yahoo.com
Contact: Norman Ross, Exec.Dir.
Founded: 1917. **Members:** 175. **Staff:** 3. **Local.** Promotes business and community development in East St. Louis, IL. Conducts charitable dinner. Sponsors annual golf tournament, Octoberfest, and East St. Louis night at Busch Stadium. Conducts planning and program development/administration in small buiness development, Industrial/manufacturing, industrial/manufacturing and neighborhood. **Affiliated With:** U.S. Chamber of Commerce. **Publications:** *Business Dialogue*, periodic. Newsletter. **Price:** free to members. **Circulation:** 25 • *Chamber Membership Directory*, annual. Magazine • *Industrial Directory*, periodic. **Conventions/Meetings:** quarterly Business After Hours - meeting • Chamber Annual Dinner • periodic conference • periodic workshop.

1551 ■ National Association for the Advancement of Colored People, East St. Louis, Illinois Branch
PO Box 671
East St. Louis, IL 62205-1135
Ph: (618)271-4698
E-mail: eslnaacp@email.com
URL: http://www.eslnaacp.org
Contact: Johnny Scott, Pres.
Local.

1552 ■ RSVP of Saint Clair County
c/o Geretta Bonner, Dir.
1200 N 13th St.
East St. Louis, IL 62205
Ph: (618)874-0777
Fax: (618)874-0511
E-mail: gbonner@peaknet.net
URL: http://www.gbgm-umc.org/lessiebates
Contact: Geretta Bonner, Dir.
Local. Affiliated With: Retired and Senior Volunteer Program.

Edgewood

1553 ■ American Legion, Keeler-Adams Post 1168
810 Rte. 37
Edgewood, IL 62426
Ph: (309)663-0361
Fax: (309)663-5783
URL: National Affiliate–www.legion.org
Local. Affiliated With: American Legion.

Edinburg

1554 ■ American Legion, John Poor Post 717
PO Box 372
Edinburg, IL 62531
Ph: (217)623-5507
Fax: (309)663-5783
URL: National Affiliate–www.legion.org
Local. Affiliated With: American Legion.

Edwards

1555 ■ American Rabbit Breeders Association, Central States Flemish Giant Rabbit Breeders
c/o Myrl Costa
8612 W Schmitt Ln.
Edwards, IL 61528
Ph: (309)692-6589
URL: http://www.nordickrabbits.com/specialt.htm
Contact: Myrl Costa, Contact
Local. Affiliated With: American Rabbit Breeders Association.

Edwardsville

1556 ■ American Legion, Edwardsville Post 199
PO Box 629
Edwardsville, IL 62025
Ph: (309)663-0361
Fax: (309)663-5783
URL: National Affiliate–www.legion.org
Local. Affiliated With: American Legion.

1557 ■ Association for Computing Machinery, Southern Illinois University/Edwardsville
c/o Jerry Weinberg
Dept. of Cmpt. Sci.-CAOS
Box 1656
Edwardsville, IL 62026
Ph: (618)650-2386
Fax: (618)650-2555
E-mail: bwaxman@siue.edu
Contact: Bernard Waxman, Chair
Local. Biological, medical, behavioral, and computer scientists; hospital administrators; programmers and others interested in application of computer methods to biological, behavioral, and medical problems. Stimulates understanding of the use and potential of computers in the Biosciences. **Affiliated With:** Association for Computing Machinery.

1558 ■ Edwardsville - Glen Carbon Chamber of Commerce (EGCCC)
c/o Carol Foreman, Exec.Dir.
200 Univ. Park Dr., Ste.260
Edwardsville, IL 62025
Ph: (618)656-7600
Fax: (618)656-7611
E-mail: cforeman@edglenchamber.com
URL: http://www.edglenchamber.com
Contact: Carol Foreman, Exec.Dir.
Founded: 1924. **Members:** 345. **Membership Dues:** general business, $188-$1,882 (annual) • special investor, $275-$10,000 (annual) • education, $79-$796 (annual) • utility, $1,034 (annual) • city/village, $530 (annual) • organization, service club, church, $106 (annual) • individual, non-business, $72 (annual). **Staff:** 5. **Budget:** $129,000. **Local.** Promotes business and community development in Madison County, IL. Holds monthly Business After Hours party; sponsors annual Halloween Parade, Harvest Hometest and Annual Golf Scramble. Organizes ribbon cutting events for new local businesses. **Awards:** Albert Cassens Community Service Award. **Type:** recognition • Athena Award. **Frequency:** annual. **Type:** recognition. **Committees:** The Alliance; External Affairs; Internal Affairs; Strategic Planning. **Affiliated With:** U.S. Chamber of Commerce. **Formerly:** Edwardsville +Glen Carbon Chamber of Commerce. **Publications:** *Business Directory*. **Advertising:** accepted • *Community Map*, monthly. Newsletter. Includes news about chamber events. **Advertising:** accepted. **Conventions/Meetings:** annual meeting, with auction - last Saturday in January • annual meeting, introduction of new members of the chamber - always spring • annual New Educators Reception - seminar, introduction of new educators to business community - always September.

1559 ■ Friends of the Colonel Benjamin Stephenson House
PO Box 754
Edwardsville, IL 62025
Ph: (618)288-0888
E-mail: stephensonhouse@sbcglobal.net
Contact: Carol K. Wetzel, Pres.
Founded: 2000. **Members:** 100. **Membership Dues:** platinum benefactor, $10,000 • gold benefactor, $5,000 • silver benefactor, $2,500 • bronze benefactor, $1,000 • statesman, $500 • patron, $250 • sponsor, $100 • associate, $50 • friend, $25. **Budget:** $25,000. **Local Groups:** 1. **Local.** Works to restore and furnish the historic Colonel Benjamin Stephenson House, a two-story brick home built in 1820. Seeks to open the house to the public, providing an authentic look at life in the 1820s. Focuses on the restoration of the house and adjoining garden areas; the acquisition of period furnishings; development of educational programs, workshops, and exhibits dealing with the life and times of the 1820s; and providing the general public with guided tours by docents in period dress. **Publications:** *The 1820 Colonel Benjamin Stephenson House Brochure*.

1560 ■ Illinois Innovators and Inventors
PO Box 623
Edwardsville, IL 62025
Ph: (314)892-3478
E-mail: il_inventor@hotmail.com
URL: http://ilinventor.tripod.com
Contact: Joan Brennan, Sec.
State. Represents inventors' organizations and providers of services to inventors. Seeks to facilitate the development of innovation conceived by independent inventors. Provides leadership and support services to inventors and inventors' organizations. **Affiliated With:** United Inventors Association of the U.S.A.

1561 ■ Illinois Trail Riders
c/o Denise Maxwell, Pres.
4873 Indian Hills Dr.
Edwardsville, IL 62025
Ph: (618)656-2591
E-mail: president@illinoistrailriders.com
URL: http://illinoistrailriders.com
Contact: Denise Maxwell, Pres.
Founded: 1994. **Members:** 500. **Membership Dues:** individual, $15 (annual) • family, $20 (annual) • organization, $25 (annual). **Staff:** 10. **State.** Trail advocacy group in the state of IL. Dedicated to acquiring new trails and keeping the trails that are currently in existence. **Publications:** *Illinois Trail Riders Handbook*. Contains information on trails, camps, and services as well as health and safety tips and a few poems and recipes. **Price:** $20.00 plus $3 shipping and handing • Newsletter, quarterly. Contains updates on trail issues, legislation, etc. **Advertising:** accepted. **Conventions/Meetings:** semiannual board meeting • semiannual Illinois Horse Fair - trade show - March in Springfield and August in Belvedere.

1562 ■ Knights of Columbus, Council 1143 - Edwardsville
7132 Marine Rd.
Edwardsville, IL 62025
Ph: (618)656-4985
Fax: (618)656-4985
E-mail: kofc1143@juno.com
URL: http://www.kofc1143.com
Contact: Ryan Grotefendt, Grand Knight
Local. Affiliated With: Knights of Columbus.

1563 ■ Madison County Historical Society Museum and Library
157 N Main St., Ste.109
Edwardsville, IL 62025
Ph: (618)692-6200
Fax: (618)692-8903
URL: http://www.co.madison.il.us
Contact: Suzanne Dietrich, Museum Dir.
Founded: 1920. **Members:** 130. **Membership Dues:** general, $35 (annual) • James Madison's Circle, $100 (annual). **Staff:** 4. **Budget:** $72,000. **State Groups:** 4. **Local Groups:** 1. **Local.** Works to preserve the history of Madison County, IL. **Libraries: Type:** open to the public. **Holdings:** 2,479; articles, books, maps, papers, periodicals, photographs. **Subjects:** local and state history. **Subgroups:** Friends of the Museum. **Also Known As:** Madison County Historical Museum and Library. **Formerly:** Madison County Historical Society and Museum. **Publications:** *Museum News*, 3/year. Newsletter. **Price:** free. **Circulation:** 1,900. **Conventions/Meetings:** monthly meeting, of historical society • meeting, of Friends of the Museum - 3/year • monthly meeting, of Madison County Education Committee.

1564 ■ Metro East Humane Society (MEHS)
c/o Ned Lucco, Exec.Dir.
8495 State Rte. 143
Edwardsville, IL 62025
Ph: (618)656-4405
Fax: (618)659-1613
E-mail: info@mehs.org
URL: http://www.mehs.org
Contact: Ned Lucco, Exec.Dir.
Local. Telecommunication Services: electronic mail, volunteer@mehs.org.

1565 ■ Psi Chi, National Honor Society in Psychology - Southern Illinois University Edwardsville
c/o Dept. of Psychology
Alumni Hall, Rm. 0118
Edwardsville, IL 62026
Ph: (618)650-2202 (618)650-2265
E-mail: cbarnha@siue.edu
URL: http://www.siue.edu/PSYCHOLOGY/psichi
Local. Affiliated With: Psi Chi, National Honor Society in Psychology.

1566 ■ Riverbend Skating Club
2 Sunset Hills Executive Park, No. 4C
Edwardsville, IL 62025
E-mail: debcobb@sbcglobal.net
URL: National Affiliate–www.usfigureskating.org
Local. Provides programs to encourage participation and achievement in the sport of figure skating on ice. Defines and maintains uniform standards of skating proficiency. Organizes and sponsors competitions and exhibitions for the purpose of stimulating interest in figure skating. **Affiliated With:** United States Figure Skating Association.

1567 ■ Society of Manufacturing Engineers - Southern Illinois University Edwardsville S349
Br. Box 1275
Edwardsville, IL 62025-0001
Ph: (618)650-3634
E-mail: khubbar@siue.edu
URL: National Affiliate–www.sme.org
Contact: Dr. Kevin Hubbard, Contact
Local. Advances manufacturing knowledge to gain competitive advantage. Improves skills and manufacturing solutions for the growth of economy. Provides resources and opportunities for manufacturing professionals. **Affiliated With:** American Foundry Society.

1568 ■ Southern Illinois Sheet Metal Contractors Organization
PO Box 310
Edwardsville, IL 62025
Ph: (618)259-3529
Fax: (618)259-3529
E-mail: markknetzer@charter.net
URL: National Affiliate–www.smacna.org
Contact: Debra Hill, Contact
Regional. Affiliated With: Sheet Metal and Air Conditioning Contractors' National Association.

Effingham

1569 ■ American Legion, Effingham Post 120
PO Box 354
Effingham, IL 62401
Ph: (217)342-3655
Fax: (309)663-5783
URL: National Affiliate–www.legion.org
Local. Affiliated With: American Legion.

1570 ■ Greater Effingham Chamber of Commerce and Industry (GECCI)
PO Box 643
Effingham, IL 62401
Ph: (217)342-4147
Fax: (217)342-4228
E-mail: chamber@effinghamchamber.org
URL: http://www.effinghamchamber.org
Contact: Norma Lansing, Pres.
Founded: 1917. **Members:** 380. **Membership Dues:** general retail, wholesale, service business, $200-$1,185 (annual) • church, school, government institution, individual, $200-$500 (annual) • financial institution, motel (plus $15/million in assets), $200 (annual) • professional (base), $225 (annual) • public utility (base), $300 (annual). **Staff:** 3. **Local**. Promotes business and community development in the Effingham, IL area. Sponsors rodeo. **Awards:** Chamber Community Scholarship. **Frequency:** annual. **Type:** scholarship • Member of the Month. **Frequency:** monthly. **Type:** recognition. **Programs:** Gift Certificate; Lead. **Affiliated With:** Illinois Retail Merchants Association; Illinois State Chamber of Commerce; U.S. Chamber of Commerce. **Publications:** *Effingham Business*, quarterly. Report. **Price:** free. **Circulation:** 2,500 • *Take Five*, monthly. Newsletter. **Circulation:** 800. **Conventions/Meetings:** annual banquet - always January • monthly luncheon, with speaker - every 1st Friday.

1571 ■ International Personnel Management Association, Greater Illinois
c/o Rick Goeckner, Pres.
201 E Jefferson
Effingham, IL 62401
Ph: (217)347-7169
Fax: (217)347-2675
E-mail: goeckner@ci.effingham.il.us
URL: National Affiliate–www.ipma-hr.org
Contact: Rick Goeckner, Pres.
Local. Affiliated With: International Public Management Association for Human Resources.

1572 ■ IPMA-HR Greater Illinois Chapter
c/o Rick Goeckner, Pres.
201 E Jefferson
Effingham, IL 62401
Ph: (217)347-7169
Fax: (217)347-2675
E-mail: goeckner@ci.effingham.il.us
URL: National Affiliate–www.ipma-hr.org
Contact: Rick Goeckner, Pres.
Local. Seeks to improve human resource practices in government through provision of testing services, advisory service, conferences, professional development programs, research and publications. Sponsors seminars, conferences and workshops on various phases of public personnel administration.

1573 ■ RSVP Clay/Effingham/Moultrie/Shelby
c/o Rita Schniederjon, Dir.
PO Box 928
Effingham, IL 62401-0928
Ph: (217)342-2193
Fax: (217)342-4701
E-mail: rschniederjon@effingham.net
URL: http://www.seniorcorps.gov/about/programs/rsvp_state.asp?usestateabbr=il&Search4.x=24&Search4.y=2
Contact: Rita Schniederjon, Dir.
Local. Affiliated With: Retired and Senior Volunteer Program.

1574 ■ United Way of Effingham County
PO Box 2
Effingham, IL 62401-0002
Ph: (217)342-3824
Fax: (217)342-6093
E-mail: effunitedway@consolidated.net
URL: http://www.effinghamunitedway.org
Contact: Linda Hemmen, CPO
Founded: 1960. **Members:** 18. **Staff:** 1. **Local**. Businesses and individuals organized to raise funds and aid the underprivileged. **Publications:** Brochure, annual. **Circulation:** 5,000 • Newsletter, quarterly. **Circulation:** 225. **Conventions/Meetings:** monthly board meeting - always 3rd Tuesday.

El Paso

1575 ■ American Legion, El Paso Post 59
PO Box 215
El Paso, IL 61738
Ph: (309)527-6761
Fax: (309)663-5783
URL: National Affiliate–www.legion.org
Local. Affiliated With: American Legion.

1576 ■ El Paso Chamber of Commerce
PO Box 196
El Paso, IL 61738
Ph: (309)527-4005 (309)527-4400
E-mail: adrake@hbtbank.com
URL: http://www.elpasoil.org/chamber/
Contact: Allen Drake, Sec.
Local.

1577 ■ Masonic Lodge
40 W. Main St.
El Paso, IL 61738
Ph: (309)527-2460

Elburn

1578 ■ American Legion, Elburn Post 630
PO Box 774
Elburn, IL 60119
Ph: (309)663-0361
Fax: (309)663-5783
URL: National Affiliate–www.legion.org
Local. Affiliated With: American Legion.

1579 ■ Elburn Lions Club
500 Filmore St.
Elburn, IL 60119
Ph: (630)365-6315
Fax: (630)365-6362
E-mail: info@elburnlions.com
URL: http://www.elburnlions.com
Contact: Louis Gholson, Pres.
Local. Works to improve communities and serves families in need.

1580 ■ Friends of the Town and Country Public Library
c/o Town and Country Public Library
320 N St.
Elburn, IL 60119
Ph: (630)365-2244
URL: http://www.elburnfriends.org
Contact: Joan Hansen, Pres.
Local.

Eldorado

1581 ■ American Legion, Eldorado Post 169
1201 Locust St.
Eldorado, IL 62930
Ph: (618)273-9020
Fax: (309)663-5783
URL: National Affiliate–www.legion.org
Local. Affiliated With: American Legion.

Eldred

1582 ■ American Legion, Eldred Post 1135
PO Box 328
Eldred, IL 62027
Ph: (217)983-2875
Fax: (309)663-5783
URL: National Affiliate–www.legion.org
Local. Affiliated With: American Legion.

Elgin

1583 ■ American Association of Teachers of German - Northern Illinois Chapter
c/o Sabine Woerner, Pres.
Elgin Community Coll.
1700 Spartan Dr.
Elgin, IL 60123
Ph: (847)214-7400
E-mail: woerner@ameritech.net
URL: http://www.northernillinois.aatg.org
Contact: Sabine Woerner, Pres.
Local. Represents teachers of German at all levels of instruction and all those interested in the teaching of German. Advances and improves the teaching of the language, literatures and cultures of the German-speaking countries. Provides members with educational and professional services. **Affiliated With:** American Association of Teachers of German.

1584 ■ American Legion, Elgin Post 57
820 N Liberty St.
Elgin, IL 60120
Ph: (708)741-2358
Fax: (309)663-5783
URL: National Affiliate–www.legion.org
Local. Affiliated With: American Legion.

1585 ■ Congregation Kneseth Israel (CKI)
c/o Perry Pitzele, Pres.
330 Div. St.
Elgin, IL 60120
Ph: (847)741-5656
Fax: (847)741-5679
URL: http://www.ckielgin.org
Contact: Perry Pitzele, Pres.
Local. Formerly: (2005) Elgin Area United Jewish Appeal.

1586 ■ Downtown Neighborhood Association of Elgin
2 Douglas Ave., 1st Fl.
Elgin, IL 60120
Ph: (847)488-1456
Fax: (847)488-1449
E-mail: dna@elginil.org
URL: http://www.elginil.org
Contact: Norma Miess, Exec.Dir.
Local.

1587 ■ Elgin Area Chamber of Commerce (EACC)
31 S Grove Ave.
PO Box 648
Elgin, IL 60120
Ph: (847)741-5660
Fax: (847)741-5677
E-mail: info@elginchamber.com
URL: http://www.elginchamber.com
Contact: Leo Nelson, Pres.
Founded: 1908. **Members:** 700. **Staff:** 8. **Budget:** $452,800. **Local**. Promotes economic and community development in northern Kane County, IL. **Publications:** *Elgin Area Chamber Business Review*, monthly. Newsletter. **Advertising:** accepted. **Conventions/Meetings:** monthly board meeting • periodic meeting • periodic seminar.

1588 ■ Elgin Area Convention and Visitors Bureau
77 Riverside Dr.
Elgin, IL 60120
Ph: (847)695-7540
Fax: (847)695-7668
Free: (800)217-5362
E-mail: elgincvb@northernfoxrivervalley.com
URL: http://www.northernfoxrivervalley.com
Contact: Kimberly Bless, Exec.Dir.
Founded: 1984. **Budget:** $500,000. **Regional**. Promotes Chicagoland's Northern Fox River Valley, including Elgin, IL and 13 surrounding communities as an overnight destination for business and leisure travel. Features superior accommodations and amenities to serve even the most discriminating visitor.

1589 ■ Elgin Children's Chorus
PO Box 725
Elgin, IL 60121-0725
Ph: (847)931-7464
Fax: (847)622-3058
E-mail: akepley@elgin.edu
URL: http://www.elginchch.org
Contact: Ann E. Kepley, Exec.Dir.
Founded: 1986. **Members:** 210. **Membership Dues:** student, $285 (annual). **Staff:** 9. **Budget:** $150,000. **Local**. Strives to teach life through song.

1590 ■ Gardeners of America/Men's Garden Clubs of America - Elgin Gardeners of America
c/o William Ingham
1205 Mohawk Dr.
Elgin, IL 60120
Ph: (847)741-7922
E-mail: billbda@aol.com
URL: National Affiliate–www.tgda-mgca.org
Contact: William Ingham, Contact
Local.

1591 ■ Girl Scouts - Sybaquay Council
12N124 Coombs Rd.
Elgin, IL 60123
Ph: (847)741-5521
Fax: (847)741-5667
E-mail: info@gs-sybaquay.org
URL: http://www.gs-sybaquay.org
Local. Young girls and adult volunteers, corporate, government and individual supporters. Strives to develop potential and leadership skills among its members. Conducts trainings, educational programs and outdoor activities.

1592 ■ Illinois Coalition to End Homelessness
PO Box 1267
Elgin, IL 60121
Ph: (847)742-4227
Fax: (847)742-3260
E-mail: ilhomeless@aol.com
URL: http://illinoiscoalition.org
Contact: Matthew Hanafee, Exec.Dir.
Founded: 1987. **Membership Dues:** individual, $25 (annual) • group, $100 (annual). **State**. A statewide advocacy group whose members are committed to eradicating homelessness. **Publications:** *People Just Like You*. Report. **Price:** $25.00.

1593 ■ Izaak Walton League of America, Elgin Chapter
PO Box 622
Elgin, IL 60121
Ph: (847)741-9393
Fax: (847)741-9480
E-mail: mrdier@wideopenwest.com
URL: http://www.elginikes.org
Contact: Roger Dieringer, State Dir.
Local. Works to educate the public to conserve, maintain, protect, and restore the soil, forest, water, and other natural resources of the U.S; promotes the enjoyment and wholesome utilization of these resources. **Affiliated With:** Izaak Walton League of America.

1594 ■ Joliet Area of Sheet Metal and Air Conditioning Contractors' National Association
1814 Grandstand Pl., Ste.B
Elgin, IL 60123-4981
Ph: (847)741-3788
Fax: (847)741-3791
E-mail: nisca1@sbcglobal.net
URL: National Affiliate–www.smacna.org
Local. Ventilating, air handling, warm air heating, architectural and industrial sheet metal, kitchen equipment, testing and balancing, siding, and decking and specialty fabrication contractors. **Affiliated With:** Sheet Metal and Air Conditioning Contractors' National Association.

1595 ■ League of Women Voters of the Elgin Area
569 Franklin Blvd.
Elgin, IL 60123
Ph: (847)695-7122
E-mail: info@elgin.il.lwvnet.org
URL: http://www.elgin.il.lwvnet.org
Local. **Affiliated With:** League of Women Voters of the United States.

1596 ■ Literacy Connection
270 N Grove Ave.
Elgin, IL 60120
Ph: (847)742-6565
Fax: (847)742-6599
E-mail: info@elginliteracy.org
URL: http://www.elginliteracy.org
Contact: Ms. Karen L. Oswald, Exec.Dir.
Founded: 1983. **Members:** 500. **Staff:** 8. **Budget:** $350,000. **Languages:** English, Spanish. **Local**. Trains and aids individuals to tutor adults in basic reading and conversational English. **Libraries: Type:** not open to the public. **Holdings:** 400; audio recordings, books, periodicals, video recordings. **Subjects:** adult education. **Affiliated With:** ProLiteracy Worldwide. **Formerly:** (2004) Literacy Volunteers of America - Elgin Affiliate. **Publications:** *Connections*, quarterly. Newsletter. **Price:** free.

1597 ■ National Technological Honor Society - Elgin High School - Illinois
1200 Maroon Dr.
Elgin, IL 60120
Ph: (847)888-5100
Fax: (847)888-6997
URL: http://www.u46.k12.il.us
Contact: David Smiley, Contact
Local.

1598 ■ Northeastern Illinois Sheet Metal Contractors Association (NISCA)
1814 Grandstand Pl., Ste.B
Elgin, IL 60123-4981
Ph: (847)741-3788
Fax: (847)741-3791
E-mail: nisca1@sbcglobal.net
URL: National Affiliate–www.smacna.org
Contact: Doug Johnson, Exec.Dir.
Founded: 1983. **Local**. Ventilating, air handling, warm air heating, industrial sheet metal, air conditioning, and specialty fabrication contractors. **Affiliated With:** Sheet Metal and Air Conditioning Contractors' National Association. **Publications:** Newsletter, monthly.

1599 ■ Phi Theta Kappa, Rho Kappa Chapter - Elgin Community College
c/o Amybeth Maurer
1700 Spartan Dr.
Elgin, IL 60123
Ph: (847)214-7423
E-mail: amaurer@elgin.edu
URL: http://www.ptk.org/directories/chapters/IL/189-1.htm
Contact: Amybeth Maurer, Advisor
Local.

1600 ■ Psi Chi, National Honor Society in Psychology - Judson College
c/o Dept. of Psychology
1151 N State St.
Elgin, IL 60123-1498
Ph: (847)628-1141 (847)628-1120
Fax: (847)628-1134
E-mail: mvaughn@judsoncollege.edu
URL: http://www.psichi.org/chapters/info.asp?chapter_id=1036
Local.

1601 ■ SBC Pioneers Illinois Chapter
c/o John Artinghelli, Pres.
790 N Waverly Dr.
Elgin, IL 60120
Ph: (847)888-3551
Fax: (847)622-9196
E-mail: johnarti@wideopenwest.com
URL: http://sbcpioneers.org/chapters/illinois/illinois.html
Contact: Fonda Bradford, Sec.
State. **Affiliated With:** TelecomPioneers.

1602 ■ United Way of Elgin
2022 Larkin Ave.
Elgin, IL 60123
Ph: (847)741-2259
Fax: (847)741-2270
E-mail: info@uwelgin.org
URL: http://www.uwelgin.org
Contact: Lynne Bosley, Pres.
Local. **Affiliated With:** United Way of America.

Elizabeth

1603 ■ Elizabeth Chamber of Commerce
PO Box 371
Elizabeth, IL 61028
Ph: (815)858-2221
Fax: (815)858-3881
E-mail: info@elizabeth-il.com
URL: http://www.elizabeth-il.com
Contact: Lyndsay Plath, Pres.
Founded: 1986. **Members:** 80. **Membership Dues:** general, $60 (annual). **Local**. Promotes business and community development in Elizabeth, IL area. **Conventions/Meetings:** monthly meeting - every 1st Thursday.

1604 ■ Safe Haven Humane Society for Jo Daviess County
PO Box 305
Elizabeth, IL 61028-0305
Ph: (815)858-2265
E-mail: petifon@safehavenforpets.org
URL: http://www.safehavenforpets.org
Membership Dues: senior, student, $10 (annual) • individual, $15 (annual) • family, $25 (annual) • patron, $100 (annual) • life, $1,000. **Local**.

Elk Grove Village

1605 ■ American Legion, Elk Grove Village Memorial Post 216
1001 Wellington Ave.
Elk Grove Village, IL 60007
Ph: (309)663-0361
Fax: (309)663-5783
URL: National Affiliate–www.legion.org
Local. **Affiliated With:** American Legion.

1606 ■ Associated Builders and Contractors Illinois Chapter (ABCIL)
1691 Elmhurst Rd.
Elk Grove Village, IL 60007
Ph: (847)709-2960
Fax: (847)709-2970
E-mail: info@abcil.org
URL: http://www.abcni.org
Contact: Kevin B. Kelly, Pres.
Founded: 1975. **State**. **Affiliated With:** Associated Builders and Contractors.

1607 ■ Chicago Figure Skating Club
1232 Berkenshire Ln.
Elk Grove Village, IL 60007
E-mail: gordondevlyn@aol.com
URL: http://www.chicagofsc.org
Contact: Dolores Devlyn, Contact
Local. Provides programs to encourage participation and achievement in the sport of figure skating on ice. Defines and maintains uniform standards of skating proficiency. Organizes and sponsors competitions and exhibitions for the purpose of stimulating interest in figure skating. **Affiliated With:** United States Figure Skating Association.

1608 ■ IAMAW Air Transport District Lodge 141
1771 Commerce Dr., Ste.103
Elk Grove Village, IL 60007
Ph: (847)640-2222
Fax: (847)640-2277
URL: http://www.iam141.org
Contact: Jerry Moore, District Organizer
Local.

1609 ■ Illinois Coin Laundry Association (ILCLA)
c/o Wally Makowsky
2700 United Ln.
Elk Grove Village, IL 60007-6823
Ph: (847)766-3322
URL: National Affiliate–www.coinlaundry.org
Contact: Wally Makowsky, Contact
State. **Affiliated With:** Coin Laundry Association.

1610 ■ Illinois Quarter Horse Association (ILQHA)
2513 E Higgins Rd.
Elk Grove Village, IL 60007
Ph: (847)437-7896
E-mail: kbingham@ilqha.com
URL: http://www.ilqha.com
Contact: Lea Ann Koch-Bingham, Pres.
State. **Affiliated With:** American Quarter Horse Association.

1611 ■ International Association of Machinists and Aerospace Workers, AFL-CIO, CLC - District Lodge 141
1771 Commerce Dr., Ste.103
Elk Grove Village, IL 60007
Ph: (847)640-2222
Fax: (847)640-2277
E-mail: dl141desplaines@aol.com
URL: http://www.iam141.org
Contact: S.R. Canale, Pres./Gen. Chair
Members: 31,300. **Regional**. Represents workers. Strives to provide contractors with well-trained and productive employees. **Affiliated With:** International Association of Machinists and Aerospace Workers.

1612 ■ National Ornamental and Miscellaneous Metals Association Upper Midwest Chapter
c/o Lynn Parquette
655 Lively Blvd.
Elk Grove Village, IL 60007-2015
Ph: (847)758-9941
Fax: (847)758-9941
E-mail: mueller@ornamental.net
URL: National Affiliate–www.nomma.org
Contact: Lynn Parquette, Pres.
Local. Promotes greater recognition, use, and sales of ornamental and miscellaneous metal fabricators; educates craftsmen, designers, and managers through support of and participation in educational and training programs; encourages quality production by suggesting voluntary guidelines for fabrication to meet building codes and other regulations; fosters friendly relations among members of the industry and works to keep them informed. Conducts seminars. Sponsors insurance programs; organizes competitions. **Affiliated With:** National Ornamental and Miscellaneous Metals Association.

1613 ■ Reel Hang Glider Pilots Association
502 Shadywood
Elk Grove Village, IL 60007
Ph: (847)640-0171
E-mail: peterb@ameritech.net
URL: National Affiliate–www.ushga.org
Local. **Affiliated With:** U.S. Hang Gliding Association.

1614 ■ Society for Marketing Professional Services, Chicago Chapter
c/o Tracy Mathieu, Pres.
25 NW Point Blvd., Ste.100
Elk Grove Village, IL 60007
Ph: (847)981-8600
Fax: (847)981-8667
E-mail: tracy.mathieu@mortenson.com
URL: http://www.smps-chi.org
Contact: Tracy Mathieu, Pres.
Local. Offers educational programs, professional development seminars and network opportunities to marketing professionals from architectural, engineering, planning, interior design, construction and consulting firms serving the Chicago region. **Affiliated With:** Society for Marketing Professional Services.

1615 ■ Village Cycle Sport MTB Club (VCSMTB)
c/o Village CycleSport
45 Arlington Heights Rd.
Elk Grove Village, IL 60007
E-mail: vcsmtb@yahoo.com
URL: http://vcsmtb.tripod.com
Local. **Affiliated With:** International Mountain Bicycling Association.

Elkhart

1616 ■ American Legion, Elkhart Post 616
301 Kennedy Rd.
Elkhart, IL 62634
Ph: (217)947-2790
Fax: (309)663-5783
URL: National Affiliate–www.legion.org
Local. **Affiliated With:** American Legion.

Ellsworth

1617 ■ American Legion, Ellsworth Post 1244
PO Box 12
Ellsworth, IL 61737
Ph: (309)724-8208
Fax: (309)663-5783
URL: National Affiliate–www.legion.org
Local. **Affiliated With:** American Legion.

Elmhurst

1618 ■ American Legion, T.H.B. Post 187
310 W Butterfield Rd.
Elmhurst, IL 60126
Ph: (630)833-7800
Fax: (309)663-5783
URL: National Affiliate–www.legion.org
Local. **Affiliated With:** American Legion.

1619 ■ Elmhurst Chamber of Commerce and Industry
113 Adell Pl.
PO Box 752
Elmhurst, IL 60126-0752
Ph: (630)834-6060
Fax: (630)834-6002
E-mail: info@elmhurstchamber.org
URL: http://www.elmhurstchamber.org
Contact: John R. Quigley, Pres.
Founded: 1918. **Members:** 600. **Membership Dues:** profit business (based on number of employees), $205-$1,000 (annual) • non-profit business (based on number of employees), $110-$550 (annual) • charitable organization, $100 (annual) • bank, savings & loan, financial institution within Elmhurst (based on million dollar deposits), $250-$5,000 (annual) • bank, savings & loan, financial institution outside Elmhurst (based on million dollar deposits), $250-$5,000 (annual). **Staff:** 5. **Budget:** $250,000. **For-Profit**. **Local**. Business and professional men and women. Sponsors annual Elmfest. Offers services, programs and events that provide opportunities for networking and referral, business education, development and promotion, governmental representation and community involvement. **Committees:** Governmental Affairs; Marketing; Ways and Means. **Affiliated With:** U.S. Chamber of Commerce. **Publications:** *Elmhurst Community*, annual. Directory. **Circulation:** 20,000 • *Focus*, monthly. Newsletter.

1620 ■ Elmhurst Choral Union (ECU)
PO Box 1493
Elmhurst, IL 60126
Ph: (630)758-1100
E-mail: sings2@sbcglobal.net
URL: http://www.elmhurst.edu/mus/ensembles/choralunion
Contact: James MacDonald, Dir.
Local.

1621 ■ Great Lakes Sport Fishing Council (GLSFC)
c/o Dan Thomas
PO Box 297
Elmhurst, IL 60126
Ph: (630)941-1351
Fax: (630)941-1196
E-mail: staff@great-lakes.org
URL: http://www.great-lakes.org
Contact: Dan Thomas, Pres.
Founded: 1973. **Members:** 325,000. **Membership Dues:** individual, in U.S., $15 (annual) • individual, charter captain in Canada, small business in U.S., $25 (annual) • charter captain, small business in Canada, $35 (annual) • associate, club, $75 (annual) • corporate, $100 (annual). Great Lakes regional sport fishermen and their families. Disseminates information and provides educational programs on conservation and sport fishing in the Great Lakes. Represents the interests of members before regional and federal agencies. Award winning web site with over 400 pages offers weekly news and is open to the public. **Committees:** Finance; Legal; Legislative; Membership; Safety; Steelhead. **Publications:** *Great Lakes Basin Report*, monthly. Newsletter. **Price:** $15.00/year; $25.00 in Canada. **Advertising:** accepted. Alternate Formats: online. **Conventions/Meetings:** periodic meeting (exhibits).

1622 ■ Illinois Orchid Society (IOS)
c/o Anne Kotowski, Membership Dir.
430 Addison
Elmhurst, IL 60126-2310
Ph: (630)833-8042
E-mail: wswesley1@aol.com
URL: http://www.iosoc.com
Contact: Wendy Wesley, Pres.
Founded: 1952. **Members:** 360. **Membership Dues:** household, $25 (annual). **Local**. Professional growers, botanists, hobbyists, and others interested in extending the knowledge, production, conservation, and appreciation of orchids. **Affiliated With:** American Orchid Society.

1623 ■ Illinois Professional Firefighters Association (IPFA)
c/o Timothy S. Clemens, Exec.Dir.
188 Indus. Dr., Ste.18-A
Elmhurst, IL 60126-1609
Ph: (630)833-2405
Fax: (630)833-2412
E-mail: ipfa@aol.com
URL: http://www.ipfaonline.org
Contact: Timothy S. Clemens, Exec.Dir.
Founded: 1959. **Members:** 2,600. **Membership Dues:** individual, $50 (annual). **Staff:** 4. **Budget:** $125,000. **State**. Professional firefighters in Illinois. Seeks to improve firefighting techniques. Introduces and supports legislation designed to aid firefighters and citizens. **Awards:** J. Eugene Baker Honorary Scholarship. **Frequency:** annual. **Type:** scholarship. **Publications:** *The Size Up*, quarterly. Newsletter. **Circulation:** 3,200. **Advertising:** accepted • *Wage Survey*, annual. **Conventions/Meetings:** annual Pension Seminar (exhibits) - always 1st Friday of November.

1624 ■ International Association of Torch Clubs, Region 6
248 Arlington Ave.
Elmhurst, IL 60126

Ph: (630)832-8217
Fax: (612)831-3999
E-mail: jcjsr@aol.com
URL: National Affiliate–www.torch.org
Contact: Jack C. Jones, Dir.

Regional. Represents the interests of men and women of diverse professions. Fosters high standards of professional ethics and civic well-being. **Affiliated With:** International Association of Torch Clubs.

1625 ■ International Union of Police Associations, AFL-CIO - Illinois Council of Police and Sherif Local Union 7
227 W Spangler Ave.
Elmhurst, IL 60126-1523
Ph: (630)832-6772
Free: (800)832-7501
E-mail: icops7@aol.com
URL: http://www.icops.org
Contact: Norm Frese, Pres.

Members: 300. **State**. **Affiliated With:** International Union of Police Associations.

1626 ■ Prairie Club
c/o Jacquie Dziak
110 E Schiller, Ste.302
Elmhurst, IL 60126
Ph: (630)516-1277
Fax: (630)516-1278
E-mail: info@prairieclub.org
URL: http://www.prairieclub.org
Contact: Jacquie Dziak, Contact

Local. Seeks to promote outdoor recreation such as walks, outings, camping, and canoeing; to establish and maintain permanent and temporary camps; to encourage love of nature; to disseminate knowledge of the environment; to preserve outdoor recreational areas; and to conserve the land, water, air, and wildlife.

1627 ■ Psi Chi, National Honor Society in Psychology - Elmhurst College
c/o Dept. of Psychology
190 Prospect Ave.
Elmhurst, IL 60126-3296
Ph: (630)617-3587
Fax: (630)617-3735
E-mail: packles@elmhurst.edu
URL: http://www.psichi.org/chapters/info.asp?chapter_id=209
Contact: Patrick Ackles PhD, Advisor

Local.

1628 ■ Society of Tribologists and Lubrication Engineers - Chicago Section
c/o Jack McKenna, Chm.
364 Sherman Ave.
Elmhurst, IL 60126
Ph: (630)279-4265
Fax: (630)279-7704
E-mail: jack.mckenna@sbcglobal.net
URL: National Affiliate–www.stle.org
Contact: Jack McKenna, Chm.

Local. Promotes the advancement of tribology and the practice of lubrication engineering. Stimulates the study and development of lubrication tribology techniques. Promotes higher standards in the field. **Affiliated With:** Society of Tribologists and Lubrication Engineers.

Elmwood

1629 ■ American Legion, Elmwood Post 638
PO Box 574
Elmwood, IL 61529
Ph: (309)742-8094
Fax: (309)663-5783
URL: National Affiliate–www.legion.org

Local. **Affiliated With:** American Legion.

1630 ■ Korean War Veterans Association, Peoria Chapter
c/o W. Gene Wilson
8220 N McClellan Rd.
Elmwood, IL 61529
Ph: (309)742-8151
E-mail: swilson@elmnet.net
URL: National Affiliate–www.kwva.org
Contact: W. Gene Wilson, Contact

Local. **Affiliated With:** Korean War Veterans Association.

Elmwood Park

1631 ■ American Legion, Illinois Post 495
c/o Raymond J. Hagamann
2931 76th Ct.
Elmwood Park, IL 60707
Ph: (312)585-5223
Fax: (309)663-5783
URL: National Affiliate–www.legion.org
Contact: Raymond J. Hagamann, Contact

Local. **Affiliated With:** American Legion.

1632 ■ Illinois Police Association (IPA)
7508 North Ave.
Elmwood Park, IL 60707
Ph: (708)452-8332
Fax: (708)452-1618
URL: http://www.ipacops.org
Contact: Edward W. Hoes, Exec.Dir.

State.

1633 ■ Mont Clare - Elmwood Park Chamber of Commerce
c/o Barbara Melnyk, Exec.Dir.
11 Conti Pkwy.
Elmwood Park, IL 60707
Ph: (708)456-8000
Fax: (708)456-8680
E-mail: info@mcepchamber.org
URL: http://www.mcepchamber.org
Contact: Walter Saranecki Jr., Pres.

Membership Dues: non-profit/school/individual, $25 (annual) • silver (under 25 employees), $100 (annual) • gold (25-50 employees), $200 (annual) • platinum (over 50 employees), $300 (annual). **Local**. Works on bridging the gap between the business community, political community, community organizations, and the area residents. **Publications:** *The Chamber Chatter*, bimonthly. Newsletter. Contains information on what's happening in the community, upcoming events, tips from other members and much more. **Advertising:** accepted • *Mont Clare/Elmwood Park Chamber of Commerce Community Guide*. Book. Contains information on the community and local businesses.

1634 ■ Women in Direct Marketing International, Chicago Chapter
PO Box 350068
Elmwood Park, IL 60707
Ph: (847)952-6319
E-mail: wdmichic@aol.com
URL: http://www.wdmi.org/chicago
Contact: Marge Lipuma-Helms, Pres.

Local. Seeks to: advance the interests and influence of women in the direct response industry; provide for communication and career education; assist in advancement of personal career objectives; serve as professional network to develop business contacts and foster mutual goals. Maintains career talent bank. **Affiliated With:** Women in Direct Marketing International.

Elsah

1635 ■ Community Cultivators
c/o Blair Campbell
12865 Joywood Dr.
Elsah, IL 62028-3011
Ph: (618)462-6802
Contact: Christine Faulla, Pres.

Founded: 2002. **Staff:** 1. **Local**. Volunteer group that teaches organic gardening methods to children and adults. **Conventions/Meetings:** monthly Garden Work Day - workshop - every first Saturday of the month.

Emden

1636 ■ American Legion, Emden Post 506
PO Box 111
Emden, IL 62635
Ph: (217)376-3494
Fax: (309)663-5783
URL: National Affiliate–www.legion.org

Local. **Affiliated With:** American Legion.

Emington

1637 ■ American Legion, Flynn-Eick Post 451
26521 E 2200 N Rd.
Emington, IL 60934
Ph: (309)663-0361
Fax: (309)663-5783
URL: National Affiliate–www.legion.org

Local. **Affiliated With:** American Legion.

Energy

1638 ■ Illinois Broadcasters' Association (IBA)
300 N Pershing Ave., Ste.B
Energy, IL 62933
Ph: (618)942-2139 (217)793-2636
Fax: (618)988-9056
E-mail: iba@ilba.org
URL: http://www.ilba.org
Contact: Dennis Lyle, Pres./CEO

Founded: 1948. **Members:** 245. **Membership Dues:** statewide radio (based on number of stations and population), $100-$1,050 (annual) • Chicago radio (based on gross revenue), $500-$1,500 (annual) • Chicago television (based on gross revenue), $1,500-$6,200 (annual) • medium market television, $1,100 (annual) • small market television, $600 (annual) • other television, $225-$1,050 (annual) • associate, $100-$325 (annual). **Staff:** 2. **State**. Television and radio stations, telecommunications companies, ad agencies, and colleges. Provides training seminars and workshops. **Awards:** Silver Dome Awards. **Frequency:** annual. **Type:** recognition. **Recipient:** for accomplished work that aired in the previous year • Vincent T. Wasilewski Award. **Frequency:** annual. **Type:** recognition. **Recipient:** to an Illinois broadcaster who has achieved a lifetime of excellence in broadcasting. **Publications:** *Transmitter*, monthly. Newsletter. **Advertising:** accepted • Membership Directory, biennial. **Price:** $25.00. **Advertising:** accepted. **Conventions/Meetings:** annual Silver Dome Awards - convention (exhibits) - always fall.

Equality

1639 ■ American Legion, Mc-Lain-Glover Post 595
RR 1, Box 19
Equality, IL 62934
Ph: (618)276-4311
Fax: (309)663-5783
URL: National Affiliate–www.legion.org

Local. **Affiliated With:** American Legion.

1640 ■ Back Country Horsemen of Illinois
3250 High Knob Rd.
Equality, IL 62934
Ph: (618)275-4412
URL: National Affiliate–www.backcountryhorse.com

State. **Affiliated With:** Back Country Horsemen of America.

Erie

1641 ■ American Legion, Denton-Schreiner Post 582
PO Box 273
Erie, IL 61250
Ph: (309)659-2926
Fax: (309)663-5783
URL: National Affiliate–www.legion.org
Local. Affiliated With: American Legion.

Eureka

1642 ■ American Legion, Eureka Post 466
2000 S Main St.
Eureka, IL 61530
Ph: (309)467-2783
Fax: (309)663-5783
URL: National Affiliate–www.legion.org
Local. Affiliated With: American Legion.

1643 ■ Association for the Developmentally Disabled in Woodford County
200 Moody St.
Eureka, IL 61530
Ph: (309)467-3015
Fax: (309)467-5206
E-mail: addwc@mtco.com
URL: National Affiliate–www.TheArc.org
Contact: Mr. Keith McArdle, Pres./CEO
Local. Parents, professional workers, and others interested in individuals with mental retardation. Works to promote services, research, public understanding, and legislation for people with mental retardation and their families. **Affiliated With:** Arc of the United States.

1644 ■ International Dark-Sky - Illinois-Central
1247 County Rd., 1300 N
Eureka, IL 61530
URL: http://www.darksky.org/aboutida/sections
Contact: Mr. Richard Tennis, Contact
State. Astronomical societies, lighting and engineering groups, professional astronomers. Seeks to inform about the effects of nighttime lighting. Builds awareness about the problems that have effects on astronomy. Presents examples of good lighting design. Conducts speaker's bureau. Documents on good and bad lighting through photos and videos.

1645 ■ RSVP of Woodford, Marshall, and Livingston Counties
c/o Marian Egli, Dir.
700 N Main St.
Eureka, IL 61530-1066
Ph: (309)467-9059
Fax: (309)467-9097
E-mail: marian@maple-lawn.com
URL: http://www.seniorcorps.gov
Contact: Marian Egli, Dir.
Local. Affiliated With: Retired and Senior Volunteer Program.

Evanston

1646 ■ American Cancer Society, Evanston - North Shore Regional
820 Davis St., Ste.340
Evanston, IL 60201
Ph: (847)328-5147
Fax: (847)570-6043
Free: (800)ACS-2345
URL: National Affiliate–www.cancer.org
Contact: Lea Morgan, Regional Dir.
Local. Affiliated With: American Cancer Society.

1647 ■ American Legion, Evanston Post 42
PO Box 42
Evanston, IL 60204
Ph: (708)475-9076
Fax: (309)663-5783
URL: National Affiliate–www.legion.org
Local. Affiliated With: American Legion.

1648 ■ American Legion, Illinois Post 236
PO Box 6084
Evanston, IL 60204
Ph: (309)663-0361
Fax: (309)663-5783
URL: National Affiliate–www.legion.org
Contact: Gen. Benjamin O. Davis Sr., Contact
Local. Affiliated With: American Legion.

1649 ■ Association for Computing Machinery, Northern Chicago Student Chapter
c/o Kenneth Forbus, Sponsor
Northwestern Univ.
Dept. of Cmpt. Sci.
2145 Sheridan
Evanston, IL 60201
Ph: (847)491-7379
Fax: (847)491-5341
E-mail: acm@nwu.edu
Contact: Vlada Breiburg, Pres.
Founded: 1996. **Members:** 100. **Membership Dues:** individual, $5 (annual). **Local.** Everyone interested in computing and information technologies. United to share experience, knowledge and ideas about computing and information technologies. **Affiliated With:** Association for Computing Machinery.

1650 ■ Association of Engineering Geologists - North Central Section
c/o Mark T. White, Chm.
3034 Isabella St.
Evanston, IL 60201
Ph: (847)869-7624
Fax: (847)346-4781
E-mail: whitemt@bv.com
URL: National Affiliate–www.aegweb.org
Contact: Mark T. White, Chm.
Regional. Promotes professional success by providing leadership, advocacy, and applied research in environmental and engineering geology. Fosters public understanding of the engineering geology profession. **Affiliated With:** Association of Environmental and Engineering Geologists.

1651 ■ Ayla's Originals International Bead Bazaar
1511 Sherman Ave.
Evanston, IL 60201
Ph: (847)328-4040
Fax: (847)733-0086
Free: (877)328-2952
URL: http://www.aylasoriginals.com
Contact: Ayla Phillips, Exec. Officer
Membership Dues: $18 (annual). **Local.** Gathers and disseminates information pertaining to the bead business. **Awards:** Beck Scholarship Fund. **Frequency:** periodic. **Type:** scholarship. **Recipient:** for bead research. **Affiliated With:** Bead Society of Los Angeles. **Publications:** Newsletter, quarterly. **Conventions/Meetings:** semiannual Spring and Holiday Bead Bazaar - trade show, with 50-60 bead and jewelry vendors (exhibits) - always March and November • periodic workshop.

1652 ■ Chicago Barn Dance Company
c/o Paul Watkins
PMB 195, 2859 Central St.
Evanston, IL 60201
Ph: (847)329-9173
E-mail: info@chicagobarndance.com
URL: http://www.chicagobarndance.com
Contact: Paul Watkins, Contact
Local. Affiliated With: Country Dance and Song Society.

1653 ■ Chicago Table Tennis Club at Evanston
Evanston 1255 Hartrey Ave.
Evanston, IL 60202
Ph: (847)312-0590
E-mail: cttc4u@yahoo.com
URL: http://www.usatt.org/clubs
Contact: Engelbert Solis, Contact
Local. Affiliated With: U.S.A. Table Tennis.

1654 ■ Children's Home and Aid Society of Illinois - Metropolitan Region
c/o Les Inch, PhD
Rice Child & Family Center
1101 Washington
Evanston, IL 60202
Ph: (847)424-5170 (847)866-3800
Fax: (847)866-8581
E-mail: linch@rcc.chasi.org
URL: http://www.chasi.org
Local.

1655 ■ Evanston Chamber of Commerce (ECC)
1 Rotary Ctr.
1560 Sherman Ave., Ste.860
Evanston, IL 60201
Ph: (847)328-1500
Fax: (847)328-1510
E-mail: info@evchamber.com
URL: http://www.evchamber.com
Contact: Jonathan D. Perman, Exec.Dir.
Founded: 1921. **Members:** 725. **Staff:** 5. **Budget:** $500,000. **Local.** Promotes business and community development in Evanston, IL. Sponsors Fountain Square Arts Festival and The World's Largest Garage Sale. **Awards:** Business Person of the Year. **Frequency:** annual. **Type:** recognition • Community Leadership Award. **Frequency:** annual. **Type:** recognition. **Committees:** Ambassador; City/Chamber; Community Issues; Fountain Square Arts Festival; Golf Outing; Home Based Business Network; Small Business; Transportation/Parking. **Publications:** *Destination Evanston*, annual. Brochures • *Evanston Community Guide*, annual. Directory • *Evanston Marketplace*, bimonthly. Magazine • Brochures, periodic. **Conventions/Meetings:** annual meeting.

1656 ■ Evanston Historical Society (EHS)
225 Greenwood
Evanston, IL 60201
Ph: (847)475-3410
Fax: (847)475-3599
E-mail: evanstonhs@northwestern.edu
URL: http://www.evanstonhistorical.org
Contact: Eden Juron Pearlman, Curator of Collections
Founded: 1898. **Members:** 1,000. **Membership Dues:** individual, $30 (annual) • family/dual, $45 (annual) • sustainer, $100 (annual) • patron, $250 (annual) • Curey Club Conservator, $500 (annual) • Curey Club Circle, $1,000 (annual). **Staff:** 4. **Budget:** $250,000. **Local.** Aims to preserve and share the history of Evanston and vicinity. Maintains a research library and the restored, furnished National Historic Landmark Charles Dawes House. Organizes historical exhibits mounted on site and at other locations. **Libraries: Type:** reference. **Holdings:** archival material, books, periodicals, photographs. **Subjects:** local history, genealogy, architecture, blueprints. **Publications:** *TimeLines*, quarterly. Newsletter. Features events, announcements and historical articles. **Price:** free for members and museum visitors. **Circulation:** 1,200. Alternate Formats: online.

1657 ■ Evanston-Skokie District 65 Education Foundation
1500 Mcdaniel Ave.
Evanston, IL 60201
Ph: (847)859-8000
Fax: (847)859-8707
URL: http://www.district65.net
Contact: Ms. Jan Fisher, Coor.
Local.

1658 ■ Evanston United Way/Community Service
1811 Benson Ave.
Evanston, IL 60201
Ph: (847)475-2400
Fax: (847)475-2469
E-mail: afitzpatrick@uw-mc.org
URL: http://www.evanstonuw.org
Contact: Anne Fitzpatrick, CPO
Local. Affiliated With: United Way of America.

1659 ■ Illinois African Violet Society
c/o Anna Jean Landgren
20 Calvin Cir.
Evanston, IL 60201
Ph: (847)492-2879
E-mail: geoajl@aol.com
URL: National Affiliate–www.avsa.org
Contact: Anna Jean Landgren, Contact
State. Affiliated With: African Violet Society of America.

1660 ■ Illinois Athletic Trainers' Association (IATA)
c/o Tory Lindley, Pres.-Elect
Northwestern Univ.
1501 Central St.
Evanston, IL 60208
Ph: (847)491-8867
Fax: (847)491-8865
E-mail: tory@northwestern.edu
URL: http://www.illinoisathletictrainers.org
Contact: Tory Lindley, Pres.-Elect
State. Affiliated With: National Athletic Trainers' Association.

1661 ■ Illinois Chapter of the National Association of Telecommunications Officers and Advisors (ILNATOA)
c/o Max Rubin, Treas.
2100 Ridge Ave.
Evanston, IL 60201
Ph: (847)781-2607
Fax: (847)882-2621
E-mail: admin@ilnatoa.org
URL: http://www.ilnatoa.org
Contact: Gary White, Pres.
Founded: 1986. **Members:** 70. **Membership Dues:** full, $60 (annual). **State.** Represents municipal telecommunications officers, advisors and related consultants and industry members. Seeks to assist members in the development, regulation and administration of cable television and other telecommunications systems through education, training and the sharing of information. **Affiliated With:** National Association of Telecommunications Officers and Advisors.

1662 ■ Illinois Jaguar Club (IJC)
c/o Allan Price, Pres.
704 Main St., 2nd Fl.
Evanston, IL 60202
Ph: (847)492-3460
E-mail: pricemktg@aol.com
URL: http://www.illinoisjaguarclub.com
Contact: Allan Price, Pres.
Members: 175. **State.** Individuals in the state of IL interested in the care, maintenance, and history of Jaguar automobiles. Conducts social meetings, driving and concours events. **Affiliated With:** Jaguar Clubs of North America.

1663 ■ Juvenile Justice Initiative (JJI)
c/o Paula Goedert
PO Box 1833
Evanston, IL 60204-1833
Ph: (847)864-1567
E-mail: info@jjustice.org
URL: http://www.jjustice.org
Contact: Frank Kopecky, Chair
Local.

1664 ■ Kidney Cancer Association (KCA)
1234 Sherman Ave.
Evanston, IL 60202
Ph: (847)332-1051
Fax: (847)332-2978
Free: (800)850-9132
E-mail: office@curekidneycancer.org
URL: http://www.curekidneycancer.org
Contact: William P. Bro, CEO
Local. Funds kidney cancer research and helps kidney cancer patients through patient meetings, information, and advocacy.

1665 ■ Kingsley PTA
c/o Kingley Elementary School
2300 Green Bay Rd.
Evanston, IL 60201
E-mail: s3jones@home.com
URL: http://familyeducation.com/IL/KingsleyPTA
Contact: Patty Sprague, Pres.
Local. Parents, teachers, students, and others interested in uniting the forces of home, school, and community. Promotes the welfare of children and youth.

1666 ■ Lake Shore African Violet Society
c/o Morgan Simmons
2210 Hartzell St.
Evanston, IL 60201
Ph: (847)869-1697
E-mail: msimmevan@aol.com
URL: National Affiliate–www.avsa.org
Contact: Morgan Simmons, Contact
Local. Affiliated With: African Violet Society of America.

1667 ■ League of Women Voters of Evanston
2100 Ridge Ave.
Evanston, IL 60201
Ph: (847)869-7844
E-mail: lwvevanston@att.net
URL: http://www.lwve.org
Local. Affiliated With: League of Women Voters of the United States.

1668 ■ Masonic Lodge
1453 Maple Ave.
Evanston, IL 60201
Ph: (847)475-9420

1669 ■ Midwest Cricket Conference
PO Box 251
Evanston, IL 60202
URL: http://www.midwestcricket.org
Contact: Tariq Ahmad, Pres.
Regional.

1670 ■ Muslim-cultural Students Association - Northwestern University (McSA)
Multicultural Ctr.
1936 Sheridan Rd.
Evanston, IL 60208
Ph: (847)467-2348
E-mail: a-siddiqui-1@northwestern.edu
URL: http://groups.northwestern.edu/mcsa
Contact: Amir Bari Siddiqui, Pres.
Regional. Muslim students in North America. Seeks to advance the interests of members; works to enable members to practice Islam as a complete way of life. **Affiliated With:** Muslim Students Association of the United States and Canada.

1671 ■ National Active And Retired Federal Employees Association - North West Chicago Area 852
2022 Lake St.
Evanston, IL 60201-3926
Ph: (847)864-3626
URL: National Affiliate–www.narfe.org
Contact: Charlie P. Booker, Contact
Local. Protects the retirement future of employees through education. Informs members on issues affecting the retirement. **Affiliated With:** National Association of Retired Federal Employees.

1672 ■ Palliative CareCenter and Hospice of the North Shore (PCCHNS)
c/o Sharon Madderom, Exec.Dir.
2821 Central St.
Evanston, IL 60201
Ph: (847)467-7423
Fax: (847)866-6023
Free: (800)331-5484
E-mail: careinfo@carecenter.org
URL: http://www.carecenter.org
Contact: Sharon Madderom, Exec.Dir.
Regional. Provides individuals and families with support to cope with illness, disability and death.

1673 ■ Rotary International (RI)
One Rotary Ctr.
1560 Sherman Ave.
Evanston, IL 60201
Ph: (847)866-3000
Fax: (847)328-8554
E-mail: councilservices@rotaryintl.org
URL: http://www.rotary.org
Regional.

1674 ■ Sheridan Chamber Players
c/o Dileep Gangolli, Artistic Director
1570 Ashland Ave.
Evanston, IL 60201-4070
Ph: (847)902-0733
E-mail: k622@yahoo.com
URL: http://www.sheridanchamberplayers.org
Contact: Dileep Gangolli, Artistic Dir.
Founded: 2001. **Members:** 1. **Staff:** 1. **Budget:** $10,000. **Regional Groups:** 1. **Local.** Presents classical chamber music concerts.

1675 ■ Sigma Alpha Epsilon
1856 Sheridan Rd.
Evanston, IL 60201-3837
Ph: (847)475-1856
Fax: (847)475-2250
E-mail: info@sae.net
URL: http://www.sae.net
Contact: Dan Brunnert, Dir. of Educ. Programs
Local.

1676 ■ Society for the Advancement of Material and Process Engineering, Chicago Chapter
c/o Barbara J. Mueller, Dir.
Northwestern Univ.
2145 Sheridan Rd., Rm. L370
Evanston, IL 60208
Ph: (847)476-6392
Fax: (847)467-3033
E-mail: bjmueller@northwestern.edu
URL: National Affiliate–www.sampe.org
Contact: Barbara J. Mueller, Dir.
Local. Represents individuals engaged in the development of advanced materials and processing technology in airframe, missile, aerospace, propulsion, electronics, life sciences, management, and related industries. Provides scholarships for science students seeking financial assistance. Provides placement services for members. **Affiliated With:** Society for the Advancement of Material and Process Engineering.

Evansville

1677 ■ American Legion, Evansville Post 1172
1001 Booster St.
Evansville, IL 62242
Ph: (618)853-7347
Fax: (309)663-5783
URL: National Affiliate–www.legion.org
Local. Affiliated With: American Legion.

Evergreen Park

1678 ■ American Legion, Evergreen Park Post 854
9701 S Kedzie Ave.
Evergreen Park, IL 60805
Ph: (312)239-0604
Fax: (309)663-5783
URL: National Affiliate–www.legion.org
Local. Affiliated With: American Legion.

1679 ■ American Society of Heating, Refrigerating and Air-Conditioning Engineers - Illinois Chapter
PO Box 42-8020
Evergreen Park, IL 60805-8020
Ph: (708)636-5819
Fax: (708)636-5847
E-mail: dkdoherty@chicagosite.org
URL: http://www.illinoisashrae.org
Contact: Tony Ranallo, Pres.
State. Advances the arts and sciences of heating, ventilation, air-conditioning and refrigeration. Provides a source of technical and educational information, standards and guidelines. Conducts seminars for professional growth. **Affiliated With:** American Society of Heating, Refrigerating and Air-Conditioning Engineers.

1680 ■ Austin Philatelic Club
c/o Mr. James L. Kobelt
9347 S Avers
Evergreen Park, IL 60805-1856
E-mail: wsgm71a@hotmail.com
URL: National Affiliate–www.stamps.org
Contact: Mr. James L. Kobelt, Contact
Local. Affiliated With: American Philatelic Society.

1681 ■ Chicago Beverly Ridge Lions Club
9116 S Albany
Evergreen Park, IL 60805
Ph: (708)636-1286
URL: http://dennismaloney.lionwap.org
Local. Affiliated With: Lions Clubs International.

1682 ■ Evergreen Park Chamber of Commerce
3960 W 95th St., 3rd Fl.
Evergreen Park, IL 60805-1905
Ph: (708)423-1118
Fax: (708)423-1859
E-mail: epchamber@sbcglobal.net
URL: http://www.evergreenparkchamber.com
Contact: Timothy J. Clark, Pres.
Members: 170. **Membership Dues:** residential/service organization/home-based business, $85 (annual) • business, $105-$335 (annual) • taxing body, $125 (annual). **Local**. Serves the business community by creating a positive business environment. Promotes commerce by developing and providing information and advocacy in a responsive and ethical manner. **Publications:** Membership Directory, annual. Contains list of all of members with their business name, address, phone, fax, e-mail and hours of operation. **Conventions/Meetings:** annual Harvest Ball - meeting - late autumn • annual Installation Dinner Dance - every January • monthly meeting - every first Tuesday.

1683 ■ Evergreen Park Lions Club
10141 S Homan
Evergreen Park, IL 60805
Ph: (708)425-8172
URL: http://lionsclubofevergreenparkil.lionwap.org
Local. Affiliated With: Lions Clubs International.

Fairbury

1684 ■ American Legion, Illinois Post 54
c/o John Joda
PO Box 84
Fairbury, IL 61739
Ph: (309)663-0361
Fax: (309)663-5783
URL: National Affiliate–www.legion.org
Contact: John Joda, Contact
Local. Affiliated With: American Legion.

1685 ■ Fairbury Chamber of Commerce
101 E Locust
PO Box 86
Fairbury, IL 61739
Ph: (815)692-3899
Fax: (815)692-4273
E-mail: fac@fairburyil.org
URL: http://www.fairburyil.org
Contact: Cathi Coppinger, Exec.Sec.
Founded: 1951. **Members:** 135. **Membership Dues:** by business type, $88 (annual). **Staff:** 1. **Local**. Advances the commercial, industrial, civic and professional interest of the City of Fairbury by supporting the growth of existing industries and assisting those firms or individuals seeking to locate in the area. **Formerly:** (2005) Fairbury Association of Commerce. **Publications:** *Member Directory & Community Guide*. **Circulation:** 525 • Newsletter, quarterly. **Conventions/Meetings:** monthly board meeting - every second Monday.

Fairfield

1686 ■ American Legion, Illinois Post 176
c/o Anthony Wayne
PO Box 14
Fairfield, IL 62837
Ph: (309)663-0361
Fax: (309)663-5783
URL: National Affiliate–www.legion.org
Contact: Anthony Wayne, Contact
Local. Affiliated With: American Legion.

1687 ■ Frontier Community College Students In Free Enterprise
Frontier Community Coll.
2 Frontier Dr.
Fairfield, IL 62837-2601
E-mail: fccsife@hotmail.com
URL: http://www.iecconline.net/sife
Local.

1688 ■ Greater Fairfield Area Chamber of Commerce (GFACC)
121 E Main St.
Fairfield, IL 62837
Ph: (618)842-6116
E-mail: chamber@wabash.net
URL: http://www.fairfieldillinoischamber.com
Contact: Patsy J. Cooper, Exec.Sec.
Members: 160. **Membership Dues:** individual, $50 (annual) • retail, service, small business, lodging, $115-$300 (annual) • civic, fraternal organization, professional, government, education, nonprofit, $115 (annual) • media, $150 (annual) • financial institution, $350-$550 (annual) • industrial/manufacturing, $300-$600 (annual). **Staff:** 1. **Local**. Business, professionals, and interested others. Promotes agricultural, business, community, and industrial development in the Fairfield, IL area. **Telecommunication Services:** electronic mail, chamber@fairfieldwireless.net. **Formerly:** (1973) Fairfield Chamber of Commerce. **Publications:** *Greater Fairfield Area Chamber of Commerce News*, quarterly. Newsletter. **Conventions/Meetings:** monthly meeting - always third Tuesday.

1689 ■ Phi Theta Kappa, Beta Alpha Lambda Chapter - Frontier Community College
c/o Jan Wiles
2 Frontier Dr.
Fairfield, IL 62837
Ph: (618)842-3711
E-mail: wilesj@iecc.edu
URL: http://www.ptk.org/directories/chapters/IL/20640-1.htm
Contact: Jan Wiles, Advisor
Local.

Fairmont City

1690 ■ American Legion, Fairmont City Post 961
2870 N 44th St.
Fairmont City, IL 62201
Ph: (618)874-5900
Fax: (309)663-5783
URL: National Affiliate–www.legion.org
Local. Affiliated With: American Legion.

Fairmount

1691 ■ Illinois Native Plant Society, Forest Glen Chapter
8310 E 1425 N Rd.
Fairmount, IL 61841
Ph: (217)733-2660
E-mail: carrollc@inhs.uiuc.edu
URL: http://www.ill-inps.org
Contact: Connie Carroll, Pres.
Local. Affiliated With: Illinois Native Plant Society.

Fairview

1692 ■ American Legion, Roy Miller Post 644
PO Box 47
Fairview, IL 61432
Ph: (309)778-2235
Fax: (309)663-5783
URL: National Affiliate–www.legion.org
Local. Affiliated With: American Legion.

Fairview Heights

1693 ■ American Legion, Fairview Heights Post 978
PO Box 3098
Fairview Heights, IL 62208
Ph: (618)397-5179
Fax: (309)663-5783
URL: National Affiliate–www.legion.org
Local. Affiliated With: American Legion.

1694 ■ American Public Works Association, Illinois Chapter
c/o Mr. Robert D. Hotz, PE, Pres.
10025 Bunkum Rd.
Fairview Heights, IL 62208-1703
Ph: (618)489-2020
Fax: (618)489-2029
E-mail: hotzrd@ci.fairview-heights.il.us
URL: http://illinois.apwa.net
Contact: Mr. Robert D. Hotz PE, Pres.
State. Promotes professional excellence and public awareness through education, advocacy and the exchange of knowledge. **Affiliated With:** American Public Works Association.

1695 ■ Dupo Coin Club
c/o Harry Niccum
1017 Harris Dr.
Fairview Heights, IL 62208
Ph: (618)632-3331
E-mail: kawon@htc.net
URL: National Affiliate–www.money.org
Contact: Harry Niccum, Contact
Local. Affiliated With: American Numismatic Association.

1696 ■ Fairview Heights Chamber of Commerce (FHCOC)
10003 Bunkum Rd.
Fairview Heights, IL 62208-1703
Ph: (618)397-3127
Fax: (618)397-5563
E-mail: office@fairviewheightschamber.org
URL: http://www.fairviewheightschamber.org
Contact: Ms. Terri Isenhart, Exec.Dir.
Membership Dues: individual, $75 (annual) • non-profit, $150 (annual) • business (based on number of

employees), $150-$425 (annual). **Local**. Brings together the private sector, non-profit entities, educational institutions and government in Fairview Heights. Integrates the agendas of many organizations working toward similar economic, educational, and quality of life goals. **Publications:** *Chamber Communicator*, monthly. Newsletter. Contains information about business events in the community. **Advertising:** accepted.

1697 ■ Gateway Riders BMW Club No. 22
c/o Jay Green, Membership Dir.
95 Peachtree Ln.
Fairview Heights, IL 62208
E-mail: jay.green@dcma.mil
URL: http://www.gatewayriders.com
Contact: Marilyn Roberts, Pres.
Local. Represents BMW motorcycle owners organized for pleasure, recreation, safety, and dissemination of information concerning BMW motorcycles. **Affiliated With:** BMW Motorcycle Owners of America.

1698 ■ Plumbing-Heating-Cooling Contractors Association, Greater SW Illinois
c/o Ronald W. Wilson, CAE, Exec.Mgr.
10314 Lincoln Trail, Ste.106
Fairview Heights, IL 62208-1801
Ph: (618)397-7422
Fax: (618)397-5822
E-mail: thegreatsouthwest@yahoo.com
URL: National Affiliate–www.phccweb.org
Contact: Ronald W. Wilson CAE, Exec.Mgr.
Local. Represents the plumbing, heating and cooling contractors. Promotes the construction industry. Protects the environment, health, safety and comfort of society. **Affiliated With:** Plumbing-Heating-Cooling Contractors Association.

Farina

1699 ■ American Legion, Farina Post 411
PO Box 268
Farina, IL 62838
Ph: (618)349-6247
Fax: (309)663-5783
URL: National Affiliate–www.legion.org
Local. **Affiliated With:** American Legion.

Farmer City

1700 ■ American Legion, Illinois Post 55
c/o Joe Williams
PO Box 133
Farmer City, IL 61842
Ph: (309)928-3055
Fax: (309)663-5783
URL: National Affiliate–www.legion.org
Contact: Joe Williams, Contact
Local. **Affiliated With:** American Legion.

Farmington

1701 ■ American Legion, Farmington Post 140
PO Box 49
Farmington, IL 61531
Ph: (309)245-4140
Fax: (309)663-5783
URL: National Affiliate–www.legion.org
Local. **Affiliated With:** American Legion.

Fisher

1702 ■ AMVETS, Fisher Post 52
PO Box 52
Fisher, IL 61843
Ph: (217)897-6265
URL: http://amvetspost52.home.mchsi.com
Local. **Affiliated With:** AMVETS - American Veterans.

Flanagan

1703 ■ American Legion, Flanagan Post 456
PO Box 10
Flanagan, IL 61740
Ph: (309)663-0361
Fax: (309)663-5783
URL: National Affiliate–www.legion.org
Local. **Affiliated With:** American Legion.

Flat Rock

1704 ■ American Legion, Illinois Post 132
301 S Main St.
Flat Rock, IL 62427
Ph: (309)663-0361
Fax: (309)663-5783
URL: National Affiliate–www.legion.org
Contact: David B. Reavill, Contact
Local. **Affiliated With:** American Legion.

Flora

1705 ■ American Legion, Clay County Post 14
PO Box 214
Flora, IL 62839
Ph: (618)662-8626
Fax: (309)663-5783
URL: National Affiliate–www.legion.org
Local. **Affiliated With:** American Legion.

1706 ■ Flora Chamber of Commerce (FCC)
122 N Main St.
Flora, IL 62839
Ph: (618)662-5646
Fax: (618)662-5646
E-mail: fchamber@bspeedy.com
URL: http://www.florachamber.com
Contact: Belinda Davis, Pres.
Founded: 1940. **Members:** 130. **Local**. Promotes business and community development in Flora, IL. Sponsors annual fall festival and Halloween parade. Conducts charitable activities, including a D.A.R.E. program with a country singer from Nashville. **Publications:** *Chamber Connection*, quarterly. Newsletter • Directory, annual. **Conventions/Meetings:** monthly meeting.

Flossmoor

1707 ■ Glenwood Figure Skating Club (GFSC)
3134 Monterey Dr.
Flossmoor, IL 60422
E-mail: mayfsc@aol.com
URL: http://www.gfsc.org
Local. Provides programs to encourage participation and achievement in the sport of figure skating on ice. Defines and maintains uniform standards of skating proficiency. Organizes and sponsors competitions and exhibitions for the purpose of stimulating interest in figure skating. **Affiliated With:** United States Figure Skating Association.

1708 ■ Illiana Jewish Genealogical Society (IJGS)
PO Box 384
Flossmoor, IL 60422-0384
E-mail: ijgs@comcast.net
Founded: 1984. **Members:** 40. **Membership Dues:** individual/family, $20 (annual). **Local**. Promotes general and Jewish genealogy in southern Chicago suburbs and northwestern Indiana. Holds annual summer indoor picnics. **Libraries: Type:** not open to the public. **Affiliated With:** International Association of Jewish Genealogical Societies. **Publications:** Newsletter, quarterly. **Advertising:** accepted. **Conventions/Meetings:** monthly meeting - third Sunday.

Forest Park

1709 ■ American Legion, Forest Park Post 414
500 Circle Ave.
Forest Park, IL 60130
Ph: (708)366-4732
Fax: (309)663-5783
URL: National Affiliate–www.legion.org
Local. **Affiliated With:** American Legion.

1710 ■ Concerned Black Men of Cook County Chicago
PO Box 462
Forest Park, IL 60130
Free: (888)395-7816
E-mail: cbmchicago@verizon.net
URL: National Affiliate–www.cbmnational.org
Local.

1711 ■ Forest Park Chamber of Commerce
7344 W Madison St.
PO Box 617
Forest Park, IL 60130
Ph: (708)366-2543
Fax: (708)366-3373
E-mail: more@forestparkchamber.org
URL: http://www.forestparkchamber.org
Contact: Laurie Kokenes, Exec.Dir.
Founded: 1912. **Members:** 200. **Membership Dues:** bank/financial institution, $200-$250 (annual) • non-profit/church, $30 (annual) • retired, $15 (annual) • small business (less than 10 employees), $75 (annual) • large business (10 or more employees), $125 (annual) • supporting, $500 (annual) • contributing, $1,000 (annual) • sustaining, $2,000 (annual). **Local**. Local businesses, organizations and community-minded individuals working together to promote business and a sense of community. Provides a climate where business can grow by strengthening, supporting, and promoting the economic viability, social needs and community cohesion of the Village of Forest Park. **Telecommunication Services:** electronic mail, info@forestparkchamber.org. **Publications:** *Forest Park Community Guide*, annual. Directory. Distributed to new, prospective and existing businesses and residents. **Advertising:** accepted. **Conventions/Meetings:** monthly Networking - luncheon, members make new business contacts with other chamber members - every second Tuesday.

1712 ■ Forest Park Main Street
7344 W Madison St.
Forest Park, IL 60130-1575
Ph: (708)771-4777
Fax: (708)771-8131
E-mail: info@forestparkmainstreet.org
URL: http://www.forestparkmainstreet.org
Local.

1713 ■ Greater Chicagoland Futurists (GCF)
c/o Robert Jene, Pres.
Land/Scape
850 Des Plaines Ave., No. 201
Forest Park, IL 60130-2051
Ph: (708)771-8641
E-mail: gcfinquiry@chicagofuturists.org
URL: http://www.chicagofuturists.org
Contact: Robert Jene, Pres.
Membership Dues: individual, $25 (annual). **Local**. Promotes foresight for tomorrow through conferences, meetings and newsletters. **Affiliated With:** World Future Society.

1714 ■ Partners in Play
7209 W Roosevelt Rd.
Forest Park, IL 60130
Ph: (708)366-2888
E-mail: webmaster@partners-in-play.org
URL: http://www.partners-in-play.org
Contact: Penny Murad, Dir.
Local.

1715 ■ West Suburban Bar Association (WSBA)
320 Circle Ave.
Forest Park, IL 60130
Ph: (708)366-1122
Fax: (708)366-1159
E-mail: wsbalaw@aol.com
Contact: Lois L. Bugajsky, Exec.Dir.
Founded: 1943. **Members:** 350. **Membership Dues:** general, $85 (annual). **Staff:** 2. **Budget:** $90,000. **Local.** Attorneys in good standing. Seeks to improve the administration of civil and criminal justice, and the availability of legal services to the public. **Publications:** Directory, biennial • Newsletter, monthly. **Conventions/Meetings:** monthly board meeting, with dinner and a featured speaker - always 3rd Thursday of the month, LaGrange Park, IL.

Forreston

1716 ■ American Legion, Forreston Post 308
PO Box 314
Forreston, IL 61030
Ph: (815)233-5750
Fax: (309)663-5783
URL: National Affiliate–www.legion.org
Local. Affiliated With: American Legion.

1717 ■ Illinois Haflinger Association (IHA)
c/o Karen Weegens, Sec.
4422 N Union Rd.
Forreston, IL 61030
Ph: (815)938-3642
E-mail: kaweegens@aeroinc.net
URL: http://www.illinoishaflinger.org
Contact: Karen Weegens, Sec.
Founded: 1990. **Members:** 63. **Membership Dues:** family, $25 (annual). **For-Profit. State.** Promotes the Haflinger with sales, shows, and a yearly raffle of a yearling filly. **Computer Services:** Online services, email information on horses. **Affiliated With:** American Haflinger Registry. **Publications:** *The Illinois Haflinger Post*, quarterly. Newsletter. Features updates on the association. **Price:** included in membership dues; $12.50 /year for nonmembers. **Circulation:** 63. **Advertising:** accepted. **Conventions/Meetings:** semiannual meeting, includes board meeting - January and July.

Fox Lake

1718 ■ American Legion, Lake Region Post 703
703 N Rte. 12
Fox Lake, IL 60020
Ph: (708)587-2323
Fax: (309)663-5783
URL: National Affiliate–www.legion.org
Local. Affiliated With: American Legion.

1719 ■ Fox Lake Area Chamber of Commerce and Industry (FLACCI)
PO Box 203
Fox Lake, IL 60020
Ph: (847)587-7474
Fax: (847)587-1725
E-mail: discoverfoxlake@yahoo.com
URL: http://www.discoverfoxlake.com
Contact: Mary Randall, Exec.Sec.
Members: 159. **Membership Dues:** business (based on number of employees), $150-$250 (annual) • utility, $300 (annual) • school, local government agency, $85 (annual) • second business, $75 (annual) • nonprofit, retired senior, $60 (annual). **Local.** Promotes business and community development in the Fox Lake, IL area. Sponsors area festival, Miss Fox Lake competition, and trade fair; conducts fundraising activities. **Publications:** Newsletter, monthly. **Conventions/Meetings:** monthly meeting.

Fox River Grove

1720 ■ American Legion, Bank of America Post 383
514 Skyline Dr.
Fox River Grove, IL 60021
Ph: (309)663-0361
Fax: (309)663-5783
URL: National Affiliate–www.legion.org
Local. Affiliated With: American Legion.

1721 ■ American Legion, Illinois Post 119
228 Foxmoor Rd.
Fox River Grove, IL 60021
Ph: (309)663-0361
Fax: (309)663-5783
URL: National Affiliate–www.legion.org
Contact: Frank H. Nagel Jr., Contact
Local. Affiliated With: American Legion.

Frankfort

1722 ■ Chicago/Midwest Chapter of the Turnaround Management Association
PO Box 33
Frankfort, IL 60423
Ph: (815)469-2935
Fax: (815)469-1901
E-mail: cglatz@managementservices.org
URL: http://www.chicago.turnaround.org
Contact: Ms. Christine Glatz, Administrator
Founded: 1988. **Members:** 900. **Membership Dues:** regular, $275 (annual) • academic, $150 (annual) • student, $85 (annual). **Staff:** 1. **Budget:** $600,000. **Regional.** Practitioners, bankers, attorneys, accountants, appraisers, and liquidators. Involved in helping financially distressed businesses. **Awards:** Transaction of the Year. **Frequency:** annual. **Type:** recognition • Turnaround of the Year. **Frequency:** annual. **Type:** recognition. **Recipient:** for financial success. **Affiliated With:** Turnaround Management Association. **Formerly:** (1998) Chicago - Midwest Chapter of the Turnaround Management Association. **Publications:** *Newsletter of Corporate Renewal*, bimonthly. **Price:** included in membership dues. **Circulation:** 1,000. **Advertising:** accepted. Alternate Formats: online. **Conventions/Meetings:** monthly meeting, business and educational topics - 2-3 times.

1723 ■ Chicago (SPIE/OSC) Optical Group
c/o Imaging Technology Consultants
PO Box 725
Frankfort, IL 60423-0725
Ph: (815)469-7104
Fax: (815)469-7105
E-mail: admin@chicago-optgrp.org
URL: http://www.chicago-optgrp.org
Contact: Dr. Lahsen Assoufid, Pres.
Founded: 1996. **Members:** 300. **Membership Dues:** individual (not a national member of SPIE/OSA), $15 (annual) • corporate, $100 (annual) • individual (national member of SPIE/OSA), $10 (annual). **For-Profit. Local.** Provides educational programs for members and the public in all fields related to the science and technology of light and applications. **Libraries: Type:** reference. **Subjects:** educational materials for teachers. **Awards:** Student Science Fair Awards. **Frequency:** annual. **Type:** monetary. **Recipient:** for outstanding projects related to light, electro-optics/optical engineering. **Committees:** Education. **Affiliated With:** Optical Society of America.

1724 ■ Frankfort Chamber of Commerce
123 Kansas St.
Frankfort, IL 60423
Ph: (815)469-3356
Fax: (815)469-4352
Free: (877)469-3356
E-mail: info@frankfortchamber.com
URL: http://www.frankfortchamber.com
Contact: Lynne Doogan, Exec.Dir.
Founded: 1967. **Members:** 600. **Membership Dues:** general, $125-$350 (annual) • utility, $350 (annual) • individual/political organization/taxing body, $150 (annual) • civic organization, $100 (annual). **Local.** Promotes the commercial, industrial, and civic welfare of the Frankfort area. Provides many civic and business development programs. Sponsors fund-raising events like Labor Day Weekend Festival and Frankfort Fall Festival. **Computer Services:** Mailing lists, of members. **Telecommunication Services:** electronic mail, lynne@frankfortchamber.com. **Affiliated With:** Chicago Southland Convention and Visitors Bureau; Illinois Association of Chamber of Commerce Executives; Illinois State Chamber of Commerce. **Publications:** *Frankfort Business*, monthly. Newsletter. **Price:** free for members; $15.00 each, for nonmembers. **Circulation:** 550. **Advertising:** accepted. **Conventions/Meetings:** annual Business Expo - meeting, networking event with product presentations (exhibits) - every spring • annual Frankfort Fall - festival, with crafters from over thirty-six states and Canada - on Labor Day Weekend • annual Golf Outing - competition, starts with a full breakfast buffet, shot gun scramble and ends with a short program and picnic dinner - always July.

1725 ■ International Facility Management Association, Chicago
PO Box 83
Frankfort, IL 60423
Ph: (312)236-0900
Fax: (815)469-1901
E-mail: admin@ifma-chicago.org
URL: http://www.ifma-chicago.org
Contact: Christine Glatz, Mgr.
Membership Dues: individual, $275 (annual). **Local.** Provides ongoing education and networking opportunities for professionals who work in the facilities management industry and/or support the industry by providing a product or service. **Affiliated With:** International Facility Management Association. **Publications:** *FM Broadcast*, bimonthly. Newsletter. **Conventions/Meetings:** monthly meeting, board and educational.

1726 ■ International Interior Design Association, Illinois Chapter
c/o Christine M. Glatz
IIDA Illinois Chap.
20400 Green Meadow Ln.
Frankfort, IL 60423
Ph: (815)464-0785
Fax: (815)469-1901
E-mail: cglatz@managementservices.org
URL: http://www.iida.org
Contact: Christine Glatz, Exec.Admin.
State. Offers educational programs and networking opportunities throughout the year to further promote the professional growth of the interior design community. **Affiliated With:** International Interior Design Association.

1727 ■ LW Central - Young Life
8122 W Sauk Trl
Frankfort, IL 60423
Ph: (815)464-5152
URL: http://whereis.younglife.org/FriendlyUrlRedirector.aspx?ID=C-803
Local.

1728 ■ LW East - Young Life
8122 W Sauk Trl
Frankfort, IL 60423
Ph: (815)464-5152
URL: http://whereis.younglife.org/FriendlyUrlRedirector.aspx?ID=C-804
Local.

1729 ■ National School Public Relations Association, Illinois
c/o Christine Glatz, Mgr.
PO Box 47
Frankfort, IL 60423

Ph: (815)464-3275
Fax: (815)469-1901
E-mail: vstewart@elmhurst.k12.il.us
URL: http://www.inspra.org
Contact: Christine Glatz, Mgr.
State. Promotes professional development of school public relations professionals through monthly educational programs and special events. **Affiliated With:** National School Public Relations Association.

1730 ■ Palos Sportsman's Club
24038 S Harlem
Frankfort, IL 60423
Ph: (815)469-4446
URL: National Affiliate–www.mynssa.com
Local. **Affiliated With:** National Skeet Shooting Association.

1731 ■ Young Life Lincoln-Way
8122 W Sauk Trl
Frankfort, IL 60423
Ph: (815)464-5152
Fax: (815)469-8459
URL: http://whereis.younglife.org/FriendlyUrlRedirector.aspx?ID=A-IL102
Local.

Franklin

1732 ■ American Legion, Franklin Post 1089
308 Wyatt Ave.
Franklin, IL 62638
Ph: (217)675-2094
Fax: (309)663-5783
URL: National Affiliate–www.legion.org
Local. **Affiliated With:** American Legion.

Franklin Grove

1733 ■ American Legion, Altenberg Post 497
139 N Elm St.
Franklin Grove, IL 61031
Ph: (815)456-2319
Fax: (309)663-5783
URL: National Affiliate–www.legion.org
Local. **Affiliated With:** American Legion.

1734 ■ Dixon Coin Club
c/o James LaBonte
PO Box 218
Franklin Grove, IL 61031
E-mail: jlabonte@essex1.com
URL: National Affiliate–www.money.org
Contact: James LaBonte, Contact
Local. **Affiliated With:** American Numismatic Association.

Franklin Park

1735 ■ American Legion, Franklin Park Post 974
9757 Pacific Ave.
Franklin Park, IL 60131
Ph: (309)663-0361
Fax: (309)663-5783
URL: National Affiliate–www.legion.org
Local. **Affiliated With:** American Legion.

1736 ■ Chicago Table Tennis Club at Franklin Park 9560 Franklin Ave.
Franklin Park, IL 60131
Ph: (847)312-0590
E-mail: cttc4u@yahoo.com
URL: http://www.geocities.com/fpttc4u
Contact: Engelbert Solis, Contact
Local. **Affiliated With:** U.S.A. Table Tennis.

1737 ■ Chicago Windy City Jitterbug Club (CWCJC)
PO Box 713
Franklin Park, IL 60131
Ph: (630)616-2100
E-mail: cwcjc@jitterbugchicago.com
URL: http://www.jitterbugchicago.com
Contact: Sue Duzenski Mlynski, Pres.
Local. Promotes and preserves bop, swing, shag and jitterbug dance styles and the heritage of those styles of music that center on the beat and rhythm. Strives to enhance communication and promotional coordination of activities throughout the membership.

1738 ■ Franklin Park Manila Lions Club
2549 Scott St.
Franklin Park, IL 60131
Ph: (847)288-1921
URL: http://franklinparkil.lionwap.org
Local. **Affiliated With:** Lions Clubs International.

1739 ■ Franklin Park/Schiller Park Chamber of Commerce
PO Box 186
Franklin Park, IL 60131
Ph: (708)865-9510
Fax: (708)865-9520
E-mail: info@chamberbyohare.org
URL: http://www.chamberbyohare.org
Contact: Patricia Letarte, Pres.
Membership Dues: business (1-5 employees), $75 (annual) • business (6 or more employees), $150 (annual) • individual/non-profit, $75 (annual). **Local**. Creates a strong association between two villages that have a similar industrial and residential community base. Works toward the integration of resources and a strong presence through community event participation, consistent programs for business leaders, educational opportunities and networking for continued business interaction. **Affiliated With:** Illinois State Chamber of Commerce. **Formerly:** (2002) Franklin Park Chamber of Commerce and Industry. **Publications:** Newsletter, quarterly. Alternate Formats: online. **Conventions/Meetings:** annual Superior Golf Outing - competition - every third Tuesday in June.

Freeburg

1740 ■ American Legion, Locklar-Smith Post 550
203 S Richland St.
Freeburg, IL 62243
Ph: (618)234-9515
Fax: (309)663-5783
URL: National Affiliate–www.legion.org
Local. **Affiliated With:** American Legion.

1741 ■ Freeburg Area Community Development Association
14 Southgate Ct.
Freeburg, IL 62243-1541
Ph: (618)539-5545 (618)539-5705
Fax: (618)539-5590
URL: http://www.freeburg.com
Contact: Billie Louthan, Admin.Asst.
Founded: 1836. **Members:** 4. **Staff:** 35. **Budget:** $5,000,000. **Local**.

1742 ■ Freeburg Chamber of Commerce
PO Box 179
Freeburg, IL 62243
Ph: (618)539-6075
Contact: Mr. Gregory Nold, Pres.
Local.

Freeman Spur

1743 ■ American Legion, Freeman Spur Post 1273
PO Box 126
Freeman Spur, IL 62841
Ph: (309)663-0361
Fax: (309)663-5783
URL: National Affiliate–www.legion.org
Local. **Affiliated With:** American Legion.

Freeport

1744 ■ American Legion, Freeport Post 139
PO Box 26
Freeport, IL 61032
Ph: (309)663-0361
Fax: (309)663-5783
URL: National Affiliate–www.legion.org
Local. **Affiliated With:** American Legion.

1745 ■ American Red Cross, Northwest Illinois Chapter
27 W Main St.
Freeport, IL 61032
Ph: (815)233-0011
Fax: (815)233-0019
URL: http://northwestillinois.redcross.org
Regional.

1746 ■ Blackhawk Orchid Society
c/o Brian Lang
3509 S Baileyvile Rd.
Freeport, IL 61032
Ph: (815)233-0757
E-mail: langfam@aeroinc.net
URL: National Affiliate–www.orchidweb.org
Contact: Brian Lang, Contact
Local. Professional growers, botanists, hobbyists, and others interested in extending the knowledge, production, use, and appreciation of orchids. **Affiliated With:** American Orchid Society.

1747 ■ Freeport Area Chamber of Commerce (FACC)
27 W Stephenson St.
Freeport, IL 61032
Ph: (815)233-1350
Fax: (815)233-3226
E-mail: kim.grimes@aeroinc.net
URL: http://www.freeportilchamber.com
Contact: Mr. Kim Grimes, Exec.Dir.
Founded: 1947. **Members:** 400. **Local**. Promotes business and community development in the Freeport, IL area. Conducts annual Tutty Baker Days festival. **Publications:** *Communicator*, monthly. Newsletter. Alternate Formats: online • Membership Directory, periodic.

1748 ■ Freeport Galena Area Association of Realtors
24 W Stephenson St.
Freeport, IL 61032
Ph: (815)235-3068
Fax: (815)235-3060
E-mail: fgaar@cjrinc.com
URL: National Affiliate–www.realtor.org
Contact: Roger L. Kerr, Exec. Officer
Local. Strives to develop real estate business practices. Advocates the right to own, use and transfer real property. Provides a facility for professional development, research and exchange of information among members and to the general public. **Affiliated With:** National Association of Realtors.

1749 ■ Illinois Association of Meat Processors (IAMP)
c/o Jeri Nieman
1177 S Springfield Rd.
Freeport, IL 61032
Ph: (815)232-1006
Fax: (815)233-6299
E-mail: iamp@mwci.net
URL: National Affiliate–www.aamp.com
Contact: Jeri Nieman, Exec.Sec.
Founded: 1970. **Members:** 250. **Membership Dues:** owner, operator, supplier, $100 (annual). **Staff:** 2. **Budget:** $10,000. **State**. Independent meat processors. Seeks to provide a better consumer

product. Provides technical and service support. **Awards:** Cured Meat Awards. **Frequency:** annual. **Type:** recognition. **Recipient:** based upon judging at product competition. **Affiliated With:** American Association of Meat Processors. **Publications:** *IAMP Update*, quarterly. Newsletter. **Price:** free to members. **Circulation:** 400. **Advertising:** accepted. **Conventions/Meetings:** annual convention, with booths displaying meat processing equipment and supplies (exhibits).

1750 ■ Korean War Veterans Association, Northwest Illinois Chapter
c/o Clyde G. Fruth
3060 W Prairie Rd.
Freeport, IL 61032
Ph: (815)233-0242
E-mail: farklr@insightbb.com
URL: National Affiliate–www.kwva.org
Contact: Clyde G. Fruth, Contact
Local. Affiliated With: Korean War Veterans Association.

1751 ■ Northern Illinois Dairy Goat Association
c/o Beverly Mueller
4410 Hillcrest Rd.
Freeport, IL 61032
Ph: (815)449-2500
URL: National Affiliate–adga.org
Contact: Beverly Mueller, Contact
Local. Affiliated With: American Dairy Goat Association.

1752 ■ Phi Theta Kappa, Nu Mu Chapter - Highland Community College
c/o Victoria Jensen
2998 W Pearl City Rd.
Freeport, IL 61032
Ph: (815)599-3531
E-mail: vicki.jensen@highland.edu
URL: http://www.ptk.org/directories/chapters/IL/178-1.htm
Contact: Victoria Jensen, Advisor
Local.

1753 ■ RSVP Northwest Illinois
c/o Mike Shore, Dir.
Highland Community Coll. Bldg. R
2998 W Pearl City Rd.
Freeport, IL 61032-6130
Ph: (815)599-3491
Fax: (815)233-9277
E-mail: mike.shore@highland.edu
URL: http://www.seniorcorps.gov/about/programs/rsvp_state.asp?usestateabbr=il&Search4.x=0&Search4.y=0
Contact: Mike Shore, Dir.
Local. Affiliated With: Retired and Senior Volunteer Program.

1754 ■ Stephenson County Historical Society (SCHS)
1440 S Carroll Ave.
Freeport, IL 61032
Ph: (815)232-8419
Fax: (815)297-0313
E-mail: director@stephcohs.org
URL: http://www.stephcohs.org
Founded: 1944. **Members:** 300. **Membership Dues:** student, $10 (annual) • individual, $20 (annual) • family, $30 (annual) • Addams, $100 (annual) • Lincoln, $250 (annual) • Taylor, $500 (annual) • Tutty, $50 (annual). **Staff:** 1. **Budget:** $40,000. **Local.** Individuals interested in preserving the history of the area. Disseminates historical information about Stephenson County, IL. Operates Historical Museum in former Oscar Taylor home, on the national register of historic places. **Affiliated With:** Illinois State Historical Society. **Publications:** Newsletter, periodic. Lists of upcoming events and volunteering opportunities, also tidbits of local history. **Price:** included in membership dues. **Circulation:** 300. **Conventions/Meetings:** annual meeting.

1755 ■ U.S. Grant Dental Society
c/o Dr. Dale A. Johnson, Pres.
1717 W Church St.
Freeport, IL 61032-4695
Ph: (815)233-9777
E-mail: johnsdc4@aol.com
URL: http://www.isds.org
Contact: Dr. Dale A. Johnson, Pres.
Local. Represents the interests of dentists committed to the public's oral health, ethics and professional development. Encourages the improvement of the public's oral health and promotes the art and science of dentistry. **Affiliated With:** American Dental Association; Illinois State Dental Society.

1756 ■ United Way of Northwest Illinois
524 W Stephenson St., Ste.101
Freeport, IL 61032
Ph: (815)232-5184
Fax: (815)232-5185
E-mail: smills@aeroinc.net
URL: http://www.uwni.org
Contact: Steven W. Mills, Exec.Dir.
Local. Affiliated With: United Way of America.

Fulton

1757 ■ American Legion, Fulton Post 402
PO Box 93
Fulton, IL 61252
Ph: (815)589-2114
Fax: (309)663-5783
URL: National Affiliate–www.legion.org
Local. Affiliated With: American Legion.

1758 ■ Fulton Chamber of Commerce
PO Box 253
Fulton, IL 61252-0253
Ph: (815)589-4545
E-mail: chamber@cityoffulton.us
URL: http://www.cityoffulton.us/chamber.php
Contact: Heather Bennett, Exec.Dir.
Membership Dues: business (1-10 employees), $125 (annual) • business (11-50 employees), $150 (annual) • business (51 or more employees), $250 (annual) • individual/retired/non-profit, $100 (annual). **Local.** Small business owners, individuals and large corporations. Enhances the economic climate and promotes the business community for the benefit of the greater Fulton area. **Publications:** Newsletter, quarterly, every October, February, May, and August. **Conventions/Meetings:** monthly meeting - every 2nd Tuesday.

Fults

1759 ■ Okaw Valley Beagle Club
c/o Herschel Riddle, Jr.
3444 Sutterville Rd.
Fults, IL 62244-1418
URL: National Affiliate–clubs.akc.org
Contact: Herschel Riddle Jr., Contact
Local.

Galena

1760 ■ American Legion, Fickbohm-Hissem Post 193
100 S Main St.
Galena, IL 61036
Ph: (309)663-0361
Fax: (309)663-5783
URL: National Affiliate–www.legion.org
Local. Affiliated With: American Legion.

1761 ■ Galena Area Chamber of Commerce
101 Bouthillier St.
Galena, IL 61036
Ph: (815)777-9050
Fax: (815)777-8465
E-mail: office@galenachamber.com
URL: http://www.galenachamber.com
Contact: Nancy Lewis, Exec.Dir.
Founded: 1838. **Members:** 530. **Membership Dues:** base (business, industry, professional, lodging), $210 • utility, $310 • nonprofit organization, $75 • associate, $50 • second business, $110. **Staff:** 10. **Budget:** $300,000. **Local.** Organized on behalf of its members to promote the economic welfare of the business community and contribute to the quality of life in the Galena area. Events sponsored include a business and trade showcase, 2 golf outings, Festival of Quilts, Ladies Getaway, Business After Hours, Business A.M., Halloween Parade, Night of the Luminaria, and various community education meetings. **Committees:** Ambassadors; Fundraising; Marketing. **Publications:** *Community Development Guide and Membership Directory*, annual • *Galenian*, semiannual. Journal • *Nexus*, monthly. Newsletter. Alternate Formats: online • Brochures, periodic. **Conventions/Meetings:** annual meeting - always November.

1762 ■ Galena and Jo Daviess County Convention and Visitors Bureau
101 Bouthillier St.
Galena, IL 61036
Ph: (815)777-3557
Fax: (815)777-3566
Free: (877)464-2536
E-mail: info@galena.org
URL: http://www.galena.org
Contact: Betsy Eaton, Interim Exec.Dir./Services Mgr.
Founded: 1983. **Local.** Works to develop year-round sustainable tourism for Jo Daviess County, Illinois, in a manner which will favorably impact the resident's quality of life and economic well-being.

1763 ■ Galena/Jo Daviess County Historical Society (G/JOCHS)
211 S Bench St.
Galena, IL 61036
Ph: (815)777-9129
Fax: (815)777-9131
E-mail: ghmuseum@galenalink.net
URL: http://www.galenahistorymuseum.org
Contact: Daryl Watson, Dir.
Founded: 1938. **Members:** 560. **Membership Dues:** guardian, $1,000 (annual) • benefactor, $500 (annual) • patron, $250 (annual) • business/sustaining, $100 (annual) • single, $20 (annual) • family, $30 (annual) • single (senior), $15 (annual). **Staff:** 4. **Local.** Collects, preserves and interprets the history of Galena and Jo Daviess County, Illinois. Operates the Galena History Museum. **Publications:** *Miner's Journal*, quarterly. **Price:** included in membership dues. **Circulation:** 560. **Advertising:** accepted.

1764 ■ Habitat for Humanity of Jo Daviess County
309 Hill St.
Galena, IL 61036-1803
Ph: (815)777-2594
Fax: (815)777-3384
E-mail: habjdc@hotmail.com
URL: National Affiliate–www.habitat.org
Local. Provides housing projects for citizens of Jo Daviess County. **Affiliated With:** Habitat for Humanity International.

1765 ■ International Dark-Sky - Illinois-Northwest
16 Hawthorne Ln.
Galena, IL 61036
Ph: (815)777-1264
E-mail: jgarrity@galenalink.com
URL: http://www.darksky.org/aboutida/sections
Contact: Bonnie Garrity, Contact
Local. Astronomical societies, lighting and engineering groups, professional astronomers. Seeks to inform about the effects of nighttime lighting. Builds awareness about the problems that have effects on astronomy. Presents examples of good lighting

design. Conducts speaker's bureau. Documents on good and bad lighting through photos and videos.

Galesburg

1766 ■ Alcoholics Anonymous World Services, District 91 Central Office
PO Box 1058
Galesburg, IL 61402-1058
Ph: (309)343-1530
URL: National Affiliate–www.aa.org
Local. Individuals recovering from alcoholism. AA maintains that members can solve their common problem and help others achieve sobriety through a twelve step program that includes sharing their experience, strength, and hope with each other. **Affiliated With:** Alcoholics Anonymous World Services.

1767 ■ American Legion, Illinois Post 285
c/o Ralph M. Noble
PO Box 285
Galesburg, IL 61402
Ph: (309)663-0361
Fax: (309)663-5783
URL: National Affiliate–www.legion.org
Contact: Ralph M. Noble, Contact
Local. Affiliated With: American Legion.

1768 ■ Becca's Karing Individuals for Disabilities (bKids)
PO Box 1126
Galesburg, IL 61401
Ph: (309)341-2394
Fax: (309)341-2394
E-mail: knaack@galesburg.net
URL: National Affiliate–www.ndss.org
Contact: Becca Knaack, Pres.
Founded: 1999. **Local**. Raises funds, awareness and acceptance for children with Down's Syndrome and other developmental disabilities. **Affiliated With:** National Down Syndrome Society. **Conventions/ Meetings:** annual bKids Buddy Walk - meeting, fundraiser.

1769 ■ Carl Sanburg College Literacy Coalition
c/o Gwen Kohler
Carl Sandburg Coll.
2400 Tom L. Wilson Blvd.
Galesburg, IL 61401
Ph: (309)341-5330 (309)341-5469
Fax: (309)344-1951
E-mail: kavalos@sandburg.edu
URL: http://www.sandburg.edu
Contact: Karen Avalos, Contact
Local. Trains and places volunteer tutors to work with adults who have inadequate literacy skills. **Affiliated With:** ProLiteracy Worldwide.

1770 ■ Celtic Cross Pipes and Drums
c/o Karen Engstrom, Band Mgr.
1468 Clark St.
Galesburg, IL 61401
Ph: (309)342-1150
E-mail: engstrom@grics.net
URL: http://celticcrossillinois.com
Founded: 1965. **Members:** 47. **Local**. Highland bagpipe band.

1771 ■ Galesburg Area Chamber of Commerce
471 E Main St.
PO Box 749
Galesburg, IL 61402-0749
Ph: (309)343-1194
Fax: (309)343-1195
E-mail: chamber@galesburg.org
URL: http://www.galesburg.org
Contact: Robert C. Maus, CEO/Pres.
Local.

1772 ■ Galesburg Area Convention and Visitors Bureau (GACVB)
2163 E Main St.
Galesburg, IL 61401
Ph: (309)343-2485
Fax: (309)343-2521
Free: (800)916-3330
E-mail: visitors@visitgalesburg.com
URL: http://www.visitgalesburg.com
Contact: Diane Bruening, Dir.
Founded: 1984. **Staff:** 3. **Budget:** $204,000. **Nonmembership**. **Local**. Promotes tourism in the Galesburg/Knox County, IL area. **Affiliated With:** American Bus Association; International Association of Convention and Visitor Bureaus; National Tour Association; Society of Government Meeting Professionals. **Publications:** *Getaway to Galesburg*. Directory. **Price:** free. **Conventions/Meetings:** monthly Stories Alive - meeting, story telling and other related activities for kids and adult companions.

1773 ■ Galesburg Downtown Council
471 E Main St.
Galesburg, IL 61401
Ph: (309)343-1194
Fax: (309)343-1195
E-mail: chamber@galesburg.org
URL: http://www.galesburg.org
Local.

1774 ■ Illinois Environmental Health Association - Central Chapter
c/o Knox County Health Dept.
1361 W Fremont St.
Galesburg, IL 61401
Ph: (309)344-2224
Fax: (309)344-5049
E-mail: whayes@knoxcountyhealth.org
URL: http://www.ieha.us
Contact: Wil Hayes, Dir.
Local. Advances the environmental health and protection profession. Provides educational and training opportunities for members. Works to establish standards of competence and ethics for the profession. **Affiliated With:** National Environmental Health Association.

1775 ■ Independent Accountants Association of Illinois (IAAI)
PO Box 1506
Galesburg, IL 61402-1506
Ph: (309)342-5400
Fax: (309)342-2557
Free: (800)222-2270
E-mail: iaai@grics.net
URL: http://www.illinoisaccountants.com
Contact: Cathy Olson, Admin.Asst.
Founded: 1949. **Members:** 1,000. **Membership Dues:** regular, active, $175 (annual) • associate, $140 (annual) • employee, $75 (annual) • student, $20 (annual) • affiliated state, $85 (annual) • prairie state, $25 (annual). **Staff:** 2. **Budget:** $250,000. **State Groups:** 16. **State**. Professional society of accountants. **Awards:** Independent Accountants Scholarship Award. **Frequency:** annual. **Type:** scholarship. **Recipient:** for college students pursuing a career in accounting and maintaining a B average. **Affiliated With:** National Society of Accountants. **Publications:** *Debits and Credits*, 8/year. Newsletter. **Price:** included in membership dues. **Circulation:** 1,200. **Advertising:** accepted. Alternate Formats: diskette. **Conventions/Meetings:** annual Accounting - seminar, 2-day seminar on accounting related topics, 12 cpe credits (exhibits) • annual meeting (exhibits) • annual Tax Seminar (exhibits).

1776 ■ Knox County Genealogical Society (KCGS)
PO Box 13
Galesburg, IL 61402-0013
E-mail: ptthomas@hbci.com
URL: http://www.rootsweb.com/~ilknox/home/kcgs.htm
Contact: Pat Thomas, Contact
Founded: 1971. **Members:** 220. **Membership Dues:** ordinary, $14 (annual) • contributing, $10 (annual) • life, $150. **Budget:** $7,000. **Local**. Researching family history. **Libraries: Type:** open to the public. **Subjects:** genealogy. **Publications:** *Knox County Genealogical*, quarterly. Newsletter. **Price:** included in membership dues. **Circulation:** 225. **Conventions/ Meetings:** annual workshop (exhibits).

1777 ■ Mid Illinois Retriever Club
c/o Brenda Carver, Corresponding Sec.
988 N Farnham St.
Galesburg, IL 61401-3159
Ph: (217)774-5677
E-mail: tbrach@midirc.com
URL: http://www.midirc.com
Contact: Matt Carver, Pres.
Local.

1778 ■ National Association of Home Builders, Western Illinois Building Authority
c/o Joann Johnson
PO Box 565
Galesburg, IL 61402-0565
Ph: (309)343-2116
Fax: (309)343-2116
E-mail: wiba@gries.net
URL: National Affiliate–www.nahb.org
Local. Single and multifamily home builders, commercial builders, and others associated with the building industry. **Affiliated With:** National Association of Home Builders.

1779 ■ Phi Theta Kappa, Chi Kappa Chapter - Carl Sandburg College
c/o Diane Kroll
2232 S Lake Storey Rd.
Galesburg, IL 61401
Ph: (309)341-5332
E-mail: dkroll@sandburg.edu
URL: http://www.ptk.org/directories/chapters/IL/203-1.htm
Contact: Diane Kroll, Advisor
Local.

1780 ■ Prairie Valley District Dental Society
c/o Dr. Charles A. Fifield, Exec.Dir./Sec.-Treas.
70 Circle Dr.
Galesburg, IL 61401-1827
Ph: (309)344-2889
URL: http://www.isds.org
Contact: Dr. Charles A. Fifield, Exec.Dir./Sec.-Treas.
Local. Represents the interests of dentists committed to the public's oral health, ethics and professional development. Encourages the improvement of the public's oral health and promotes the art and science of dentistry. **Affiliated With:** American Dental Association; Illinois State Dental Society.

1781 ■ Psi Chi, National Honor Society in Psychology - Knox College
c/o Dept. of Psychology
2 E South St.
Galesburg, IL 61401-4999
Ph: (309)341-1905 (309)341-7334
Fax: (309)341-7718
URL: National Affiliate–www.psichi.org
Local. Affiliated With: Psi Chi, National Honor Society in Psychology.

1782 ■ United Way of Knox County, Illinois
PO Box 807
Galesburg, IL 61402-0807
Ph: (309)343-4434
URL: National Affiliate–national.unitedway.org
Local. Affiliated With: United Way of America.

1783 ■ West Central Illinois Association of Realtors
2101 Windish Dr., Ste.103
Galesburg, IL 61401
Ph: (309)342-6225
Fax: (309)342-8075
E-mail: dlhallstrom@grics.net
URL: National Affiliate–www.realtor.org
Contact: Diana L. Hallstrom, Exec. Officer
Local. Strives to develop real estate business practices. Advocates the right to own, use and

transfer real property. Provides a facility for professional development, research and exchange of information among members and to the general public. **Affiliated With:** National Association of Realtors.

Galva

1784 ■ American Legion, Hagberg-Hamlin Post 45
PO Box 64
Galva, IL 61434
Ph: (309)663-0361
Fax: (309)663-5783
URL: National Affiliate–www.legion.org
Local. Affiliated With: American Legion.

Gardner

1785 ■ American Legion, Danner-Madsen Post 663
426 Indus. Ave.
Gardner, IL 60424
Ph: (309)663-0361
Fax: (309)663-5783
URL: National Affiliate–www.legion.org
Local. Affiliated With: American Legion.

1786 ■ Chicago Beagle Club
c/o Joanne McMillan
6755 S Filman Rd.
Gardner, IL 60424-6030
URL: National Affiliate–clubs.akc.org
Contact: Joanne McMillan, Contact
Local.

Geneseo

1787 ■ American Legion, Shearer Post 350
PO Box 155
Geneseo, IL 61254
Ph: (309)663-0361
Fax: (309)663-5783
URL: National Affiliate–www.legion.org
Local. Affiliated With: American Legion.

1788 ■ Geneseo Chamber of Commerce (GCC)
100 W Main
Geneseo, IL 61254-1518
Ph: (309)944-2686
Fax: (309)944-2647
E-mail: geneseo@geneseo.net
Contact: Dawn Tubbs, Exec.Dir.
Local. Promotes business and community development in Geneseo, IL. Sponsors festival. **Formerly:** Geneseo Development Group. **Publications:** Newsletter, monthly.

1789 ■ Izaak Walton League of America - Blackhawk Chapter
c/o Cherie Larimer
919 S Spring St.
Geneseo, IL 61254-1831
Ph: (309)944-4126
URL: http://www.iwla.org
Contact: Cherie Larimer, Contact
Local. Educates the public to conserve, maintain, protect, and restore the soil, forest, water, and other natural resources of the U.S. Promotes the utilization of these resources. Sponsors environmental programs.

1790 ■ Quad Cities African Violet Society
c/o John Jugenheimer
14 Hickory Hills
Geneseo, IL 61254
Ph: (309)441-6849
E-mail: qcavs@yahoo.com
URL: http://www.carrollsweb.com/xenson
Contact: John Jugenheimer, Contact
Regional. Affiliated With: African Violet Society of America.

Geneva

1791 ■ American Legion, Fox-River-Geneva Post 75
22 S 2nd St.
Geneva, IL 60134
Ph: (309)663-0361
Fax: (309)663-5783
URL: National Affiliate–www.legion.org
Local. Affiliated With: American Legion.

1792 ■ Fox River Valley Dental Society
718 McKinley Ave.
Geneva, IL 60134
Ph: (630)232-4229
E-mail: frvds@aol.com
URL: http://www.isds.org
Contact: Maureen Emma, Exec.Dir.
Local. Represents the interests of dentists committed to the public's oral health, ethics, science and professional advancement. Promotes the art and science of dentistry through advocacy, education, research and the development of standards. **Affiliated With:** American Dental Association; Illinois State Dental Society.

1793 ■ Geneva Chamber of Commerce (GCC)
8 S 3rd St.
PO Box 481
Geneva, IL 60134-0481
Ph: (630)232-6060
Fax: (630)232-6083
Free: (866)4-GENEVA
E-mail: chamberinfo@genevachamber.com
URL: http://www.genevachamber.com
Contact: Jean Gaines, Pres.
Founded: 1950. **Members:** 536. **Staff:** 8. **Local.** Promotes business and community development in Geneva, IL. Sponsors local festivals. **Publications:** *Soundings*, monthly. Newsletter. Alternate Formats: online • Directory, periodic.

1794 ■ Geneva Lions Club
c/o Martha Talley, Pres.
PO Box 382
Geneva, IL 60134
Ph: (630)208-7611
URL: http://www.genevalionsclub.org
Contact: Martha Talley, Pres.
Local. Affiliated With: Lions Clubs International.

1795 ■ Geneva - Young Life
PO Box 545
Geneva, IL 60134
Ph: (630)262-3939
URL: http://whereis.younglife.org/FriendlyUrlRedirector.aspx?ID=C-857
Local.

1796 ■ Kane County Bar Association (KCBA)
c/o Jan Wade, Exec.Dir.
PO Box 571
Geneva, IL 60134
Ph: (630)762-1900
Fax: (630)762-9395
E-mail: director@kanecountybar.org
URL: http://www.kanecountybar.org
Contact: Jan Wade, Exec.Dir.
Founded: 1858. **Members:** 853. **Membership Dues:** voting, $105 (biennial). **Staff:** 3. **Budget:** $200,000. **State Groups:** 1. **Local.** Attorneys in good standing. Seeks to improve the administration of civil and criminal justice, and the availability of legal services to the public. **Publications:** *Bar Briefs*, monthly. Magazine. Features substantive legal articles, continuing legal education seminars, social events, etc. **Circulation:** 900. **Advertising:** accepted. **Conventions/Meetings:** monthly board meeting - 3rd Thursday • monthly Continuing Legal Education Seminar, with different topic each month; free to members - from September through June.

1797 ■ National Alliance for the Mentally Ill - Kane County South
PO Box 541
Geneva, IL 60134
Ph: (630)896-6264
E-mail: info@namidkk.org
URL: http://www.namidkk.org
Contact: Lynda Rivers, Exec.Dir.
Local. Strives to improve the quality of life of children and adults with severe mental illness through support, education, research and advocacy. **Affiliated With:** National Alliance for the Mentally Ill.

1798 ■ National Speakers Association/Illinois Chapter (NSA-IL)
c/o Sue Black, Exec.Dir.
2306 Brookway
Geneva, IL 60134
Ph: (630)208-0776
Fax: (630)208-4935
E-mail: sueblack@nsa-il.org
URL: http://www.nsa-il.org
Contact: Sue Black, Exec.Dir.
Local. Affiliated With: National Speakers Association.

1799 ■ National Technological Honor Society - Geneva Community High School Illinois
416 McKinley Ave.
Geneva, IL 60134
Ph: (630)463-3800
Fax: (630)463-3809
E-mail: gfantozzi@geneva304.org
URL: http://www.geneva.k12.il.us
Contact: Greg Fantozzi, Contact
Local.

1800 ■ St. Charles - Young Life
PO Box 545
Geneva, IL 60134
Ph: (630)262-3939
URL: http://whereis.younglife.org/FriendlyUrlRedirector.aspx?ID=C-2867
Local.

1801 ■ Young Life Kane County
PO Box 545
Geneva, IL 60134
Ph: (630)262-3939
Fax: (630)262-3939
URL: http://whereis.younglife.org/FriendlyUrlRedirector.aspx?ID=A-IL41
Local.

1802 ■ Young Life Youth Center St. Charles - Department of Corrections
321 Hamilton St., Ste.B
Geneva, IL 60134
Ph: (630)262-3939
URL: http://sites.younglife.org/_layouts/ylext/default.aspx?ID=C-858
Local. Affiliated With: Young Life.

Genoa

1803 ■ American Legion, Bayard Brown Post 337
311 S Washington St.
Genoa, IL 60135
Ph: (815)784-5967
Fax: (309)663-5783
URL: National Affiliate–www.legion.org
Local. Affiliated With: American Legion.

1804 ■ Genoa Chamber of Commerce (GCC)
327 W Main St., Upper Level
Genoa, IL 60135
Ph: (815)784-2212
Fax: (815)784-2212
E-mail: genoachamb@tbcnet.com
Contact: Susan J. Drendel, Exec.Dir.
Founded: 1956. **Members:** 85. **Staff:** 1. **Local**. Businesses, associations, and individuals interested in advancing the commercial, civic, industrial, and agricultural interests of Genoa, IL. Sponsors Genoa Days Queen Contest. **Publications:** *Chamber News*, monthly. Newsletter.

1805 ■ Genoa-Kingston United Way
PO Box 5
Genoa, IL 60135-0005
Ph: (414)263-8100
E-mail: paul.weil@unitedway.org
URL: National Affiliate–national.unitedway.org
Contact: Paul Weil, Dir.
Local. Affiliated With: United Way of America.

Georgetown

1806 ■ American Legion, Dornblaser Post 203
106 E West St.
Georgetown, IL 61846
Ph: (217)662-8211
Fax: (309)663-5783
URL: National Affiliate–www.legion.org
Local. Affiliated With: American Legion.

Germantown

1807 ■ American Legion, Diesen-Winkler Post 325
1105 Sycamore St.
Germantown, IL 62245
Ph: (618)523-4504
Fax: (309)663-5783
URL: National Affiliate–www.legion.org
Local. Affiliated With: American Legion.

Gibson City

1808 ■ American Legion, Lee Lowery Post 568
203 N Sangamon Ave.
Gibson City, IL 60936
Ph: (217)784-8517
Fax: (309)663-5783
URL: National Affiliate–www.legion.org
Local. Affiliated With: American Legion.

1809 ■ Gibson Area Chamber of Commerce (GACC)
126 N Sangamon Ave.
Gibson City, IL 60936
Ph: (217)784-5217
Fax: (217)784-4119
E-mail: chamber@gibsoncityillinois.com
URL: http://gibsoncityillinois.com/default.asp
Contact: Pam Bradbury, Sec.-Treas.
Members: 138. **Local**. Promotes business and community development in the Gibson, IL area. **Formerly:** (1999) Gibson Chamber of Commerce. **Publications:** Newsletter. Alternate Formats: online.

Gillespie

1810 ■ Cahokia Beagle Club
c/o Freida M. Price
RR 2, Box 55
Gillespie, IL 62033-9615
URL: National Affiliate–www.akc.org
Contact: Freida M. Price, Contact
Local.

Gilman

1811 ■ American Legion, Speicher Post 499
125 N Central St.
Gilman, IL 60938
Ph: (815)265-7245
Fax: (309)663-5783
URL: National Affiliate–www.legion.org
Local. Affiliated With: American Legion.

1812 ■ Gilman Chamber of Commerce
PO Box 13
Gilman, IL 60938
Ph: (815)265-4818
Contact: Jeff McMillan, Pres.
Local.

Girard

1813 ■ American Legion, Illinois Post 115
c/o David Hart
608 W Mill St.
Girard, IL 62640
Ph: (217)627-2539
Fax: (309)663-5783
URL: National Affiliate–www.legion.org
Contact: David Hart, Contact
Local. Affiliated With: American Legion.

1814 ■ Girard Chamber of Commerce
PO Box 92
Girard, IL 62640
Ph: (217)627-3441 (217)627-2045
Fax: (217)627-3528
E-mail: girardchamber@girardilusa.com
URL: http://www.girardilusa.com
Contact: Debra Burnett, Sec.
Local. Promotes business and community development in the Girard, IL area.

Glasford

1815 ■ American Legion, Illinois Post 35
c/o Charles D. Looger
PO Box 346
Glasford, IL 61533
Ph: (309)389-4101
Fax: (309)663-5783
URL: National Affiliate–www.legion.org
Contact: Charles D. Looger, Contact
Local. Affiliated With: American Legion.

1816 ■ American Rabbit Breeders Association, Illinois Standard Chinchilla RC
c/o Walter Grebner
15902 W Riekena Rd.
Glasford, IL 61533
Ph: (309)565-7188
E-mail: waltjg30@wmconnect.com
URL: http://www.nordickrabbits.com/specialt.htm
Contact: Walter Grebner, Contact
Local. Affiliated With: American Rabbit Breeders Association.

1817 ■ American Truck Historical Society, Central Illinois Chapter
c/o Ken Nolte
14205 W Canton Glasford Rd.
Glasford, IL 61533
Ph: (309)389-2257
URL: National Affiliate–www.aths.org
Contact: Ken Nolte, Contact
Local.

Glen Carbon

1818 ■ American Legion, Illinois Post 435
c/o Harry G. Seaton
PO Box 265
Glen Carbon, IL 62034
Ph: (309)663-0361
Fax: (309)663-5783
URL: National Affiliate–www.legion.org
Contact: Harry G. Seaton, Contact
Local. Affiliated With: American Legion.

1819 ■ East Side AIFA
c/o Michael A. Babcock, Pres.
11 Glen Ed Professional Park
Glen Carbon, IL 62034
Ph: (618)659-8744
E-mail: eastsideaifa@yahoo.com
URL: http://www.naifanet.com/eastside
Contact: Michael A. Babcock, Pres.
Local. Represents the interests of insurance and financial advisors. Advocates for a positive legislative and regulatory environment. Enhances business and professional skills of members. **Affiliated With:** National Association of Insurance and Financial Advisors.

1820 ■ Girl Scouts of River Bluff's Council
4 Ginger Creek Pkwy.
Glen Carbon, IL 62034
Ph: (618)692-0692
Fax: (618)692-0685
Free: (800)345-6858
E-mail: gsrbc@riverbluffs.org
URL: http://www.riverbluffs.org
Contact: Mary Griggs, CEO
Founded: 1912. **Members:** 2,800. **Budget:** $28,000. **Local**. Informal educational organization for girls ages 5-17 that inspires girls to the highest ideals of character, conduct, patriotism and service; serving over 9000 girls in a five county area in southwest Illinois.

1821 ■ Greater Gateway Association of Realtors
10 Ginger Creek Pkwy.
Glen Carbon, IL 62034
Ph: (618)692-8300
Fax: (618)692-8307
E-mail: general@gatewayrealtors.com
URL: http://www.gatewayrealtors.com
Contact: Al Suguitan, Pres.
Local. Strives to develop real estate business practices. Advocates the right to own, use and transfer real property. Provides a facility for professional development, research and exchange of information among members and to the general public. **Affiliated With:** National Association of Realtors.

1822 ■ Ties, Needles, and Threads Guild
c/o Wendy Gergen
PO Box 85
Glen Carbon, IL 62034-0085
Local.

1823 ■ United States Army Warrant Officers Association, St. Louis Gateway Chapter 0312/3312
c/o Walter B. Harris , CW3, Pres.
213 Star Ln.
Glen Carbon, IL 62034-1152
Ph: (618)288-0928
E-mail: walter.harris@us.army.mil
URL: http://www.geocities.com/stlouis_metro_warrants
Contact: Walter B. Harris, Pres.
Founded: 1982. **Members:** 35. **Membership Dues:** regular, $45 (annual) • retired, $30 (annual). **Regional**. Active duty, National Guard, Reserve, and retired U.S. Army warrant officers. Works to promote the technical and social welfare of warrant officers. **Affiliated With:** United States Army Warrant Officers Association.

Glen Ellyn

1824 ■ American Association for Women in Community Colleges, College of DuPage
Coll. of DuPage
425 Fawell Blvd.
Glen Ellyn, IL 60137-6599

Ph: (630)942-2380 (630)942-2689
E-mail: masters@cdnet.cod.edu
URL: http://www.cod.edu/dept/aawcc
Contact: Stacey Masters-Rolle, Pres.

Local. Fosters the development of comprehensive educational, career and life opportunities for all persons. Encourages and supports professional development and advancement of all women in community, junior and technical colleges. **Affiliated With:** American Association for Women in Community Colleges.

1825 ■ American Legion, Glen Ellyn Post 3
PO Box 122
Glen Ellyn, IL 60138
Ph: (708)469-5060
Fax: (309)663-5783
URL: National Affiliate–www.legion.org

Local. Affiliated With: American Legion.

1826 ■ Ben Franklin Parent Teacher Association
c/o Ben Franklin School
350 Bryant Ave.
Glen Ellyn, IL 60137
E-mail: ptaboard@benfranklinpta.org
URL: http://myschoolonline.com/IL/benfranklinpta

Local. Parents, teachers, students, and others interested in uniting the forces of home, school, and community. Promotes the welfare of children and youth. **Additional Websites:** http://www.benfranklinpta.org.

1827 ■ Chicago Society of Clinical Hypnosis
257 Chesterfield Ave.
Glen Ellyn, IL 60137-4921
Ph: (630)249-1983
E-mail: drlow@pobox.com
URL: National Affiliate–www.asch.net
Contact: Carol B. Low PsyD, Contact

Local. Represents health and mental health care professionals using clinical hypnosis. Provides and encourages education programs to further the knowledge, understanding and application of hypnosis in health care. Works for the recognition and acceptance of hypnosis as an important tool in clinical health care. **Affiliated With:** American Society of Clinical Hypnosis.

1828 ■ Glen Crest Wyld Life - Wyldlife
PO Box 67
Glen Ellyn, IL 60138
Ph: (630)469-5060
URL: http://glencrest.younglife.org

Local. Represents the interests of individuals committed to impacting kids' lives and preparing them for the future. Helps young people develop their skills, assets and attitudes to reach their full God-given potential. Reaches suburban, urban, multicultural and disabled kids and teenage mothers. **Affiliated With:** Young Life.

1829 ■ Glen Ellyn Chamber of Commerce (GECOC)
490 Pennsylvania Ave.
Glen Ellyn, IL 60137
Ph: (630)469-0907
Fax: (630)469-0426
E-mail: kay@glenellynchamber.com
URL: http://www.glenellynchamber.com
Contact: Kay C. Kendall, Exec.Dir.

Founded: 1949. **Members:** 290. **Membership Dues:** business (based on number of employees), $235-$550 (annual) • citizen, $75 (annual) • gold sponsor, $5,000 (annual). **Staff:** 1. **Budget:** $52,000. **Local**. Promotes business and community development in the Glen Ellyn, IL area. **Publications:** *Chamber Goods and Services Guide*, annual. Directory • *Navigator*, monthly. Newsletter. **Advertising:** accepted. Alternate Formats: online. **Conventions/Meetings:** semiannual seminar.

1830 ■ Glen Ellyn Lions Club
PO Box 278
Glen Ellyn, IL 60138-0278
Fax: (630)790-0647
URL: http://www.glen-ellyn.com/lions

Local. Affiliated With: Lions Clubs International.

1831 ■ Glen Ellyn Lions Foundation
c/o Ray Campbell
PO Box 278
Glen Ellyn, IL 60138-0278
Ph: (630)462-1188
E-mail: lions@glen-ellyn.net
URL: http://www.glen-ellyn.com/lions/
Contact: R.C. Newsome, Treas.

Founded: 2000. **Members:** 35. **Local**.

1832 ■ Glen Ellyn Philatelic Club
c/o Bob Arundale, III
PO Box 217
Glen Ellyn, IL 60138
E-mail: robertkarundaleiii@avenew.com
URL: http://www.glenellynstampclub.org/
Contact: Al Dlhy, Pres.

Local. Affiliated With: American Philatelic Society.

1833 ■ Hadley Wyld Life
PO Box 67
Glen Ellyn, IL 60138
Ph: (630)469-5060
E-mail: dan@ylchicago.com
URL: http://hadley.younglife.org
Contact: Dan Nicholas, Staff Intern

Local. Represents the interests of individuals committed to impacting kids' lives and preparing them for the future. Helps young people develop their skills, assets and attitudes to reach their full God-given potential. Reaches suburban, urban, multicultural and disabled kids and teenage mothers. **Affiliated With:** Young Life.

1834 ■ Hill BMX Elgin Association
c/o Mark Knasko
Elgin Community Coll.
Rte. 20 McLean Blvd., Spartan Dr.
Glen Ellyn, IL 60137-3562
Ph: (630)469-5290
E-mail: thehillbmx@aol.com
URL: http://www.ababmx.com
Contact: Mark Knasko, Dir.

Founded: 1990. **Members:** 300. **Membership Dues:** $45 (annual). **Staff:** 35. **Local Groups:** 1. **Local**. Provides organized bicycle racing and gives national prominence to the sport of BMX. **Additional Websites:** http://www.thehillbmx.com. **Publications:** *ABA BMXer*, monthly. Magazine. **Advertising:** accepted.

1835 ■ Illinois Association for Marriage and Family Therapy (IAMFT)
c/o E. Maurlea Babb, EdD, Exec.Dir.
PO Box 665
Glen Ellyn, IL 60138
Ph: (630)260-9010
Fax: (630)260-9072
E-mail: iamft@aol.com
URL: http://www.IAMFT.org
Contact: E. Maurlea Babb EdD, Exec.Dir.

State. Professional association.

1836 ■ Kiwanis Club of Glen Ellyn
PO Box 440
Glen Ellyn, IL 60138-0440
Ph: (630)790-1545
E-mail: kiwanis@glen-ellyn.com
URL: http://www.glen-ellyn.com/kiwanis
Contact: Glen Scott, Contact

Local.

1837 ■ League of Women Voters of Glen Ellyn
PO Box 2391
Glen Ellyn, IL 60138-2391
Ph: (630)881-1490
URL: http://www.glen-ellyn.com/lwv

Local. Affiliated With: League of Women Voters of the United States.

1838 ■ Penn State Alumni Association, Greater Chicago Chapter
PO Box 2176
Glen Ellyn, IL 60138
E-mail: president@psuchicago.com
URL: http://www.psuchicago.com
Contact: Sally Anderson, Pres.

Local.

1839 ■ Phi Theta Kappa, Phi Beta Chapter - College of DuPage
c/o Shannon Hernandez
425 Fawell St.
Glen Ellyn, IL 60137
Ph: (630)942-3054
E-mail: shannon.hernandez@ptk.org
URL: http://www.ptk.org/directories/chapters/IL/196-1.htm
Contact: Shannon Hernandez, Advisor

Local.

1840 ■ Prairie State Bonsai Society
PO Box 2634
Glen Ellyn, IL 60138-2634
E-mail: president@prairiestatebonsai.com
URL: http://www.prairiestatebonsai.com
Contact: Dahn Lindstrom, Pres.

Founded: 1975. **Members:** 100. **Membership Dues:** individual, $30 (annual) • family, $35 (annual). **Staff:** 5. **Local**. Promotes interest in and knowledge of bonsai, an art that is part horticulture, part pruning, shaping, and container-growing to produce dwarfed, three-dimensional forms suggesting natural trees or landscapes. **Libraries: Type:** open to the public. **Holdings:** 75; books, periodicals. **Subjects:** bonsai, flowers, shrubs, trees. **Affiliated With:** American Bonsai Society. **Publications:** *Bulletin*, monthly. Newsletter. Contains information, vendor ads, and schedule of events. **Price:** included in membership dues. **Circulation:** 100.

1841 ■ Solid Waste Association of North America, Illinois Land of Lincoln Chapter
PO Box 2037
Glen Ellyn, IL 60138
Ph: (312)251-8705 (708)952-1895
Fax: (312)346-5228
E-mail: martelcm@cdm.com
URL: http://www.swanaillinois.org
Contact: Mr. Christopher Martel PE, Pres.

Local. Works to advance the practice of environmentally and economically sound management of municipal solid waste. Provides private and public representation, including waste haulers, MRF operators, municipal coordinators, consultants and state officials. **Affiliated With:** Solid Waste Association of North America. **Conventions/Meetings:** monthly dinner • symposium.

1842 ■ Tourette Syndrome Association of Illinois (TSA)
800 Roosevelt Rd.
Bldg. A, Ste.10
Glen Ellyn, IL 60137
Ph: (630)790-8083
Fax: (630)790-8084
Free: (877)TSA-IL55
E-mail: tsail2001@sbcglobal.net
URL: http://www.tsa-illinois.org/default.asp?TOCID=2083225691
Contact: Norma Okada, Chair

Founded: 1976. **Members:** 900. **Membership Dues:** individual, $45 (annual) • family/allied professional, $60 (annual) • physician, $100 (annual). **Staff:** 1. **State**. Health care and educational professionals, individuals, and families in Illinois intimately involved with Tourette Syndrome. Seeks to increase awareness and disseminate information about TS and to assist health care professionals and individuals and families dealing with the disease. Sponsors speaker's bureau and workshops. Provides physician referrals. **Affiliated With:** Tourette Syndrome Association. **Publications:** *Physician's Referral List*, periodic. Directory • *Tourette Syndrome: A Young Man's Poetic Journey Through Childhood*. Booklet • *TSA-IL News-Briefs*, quarterly. Newsletter. **Conventions/Meetings:** monthly board meeting • annual Children's Summer Camp - meeting • periodic conference • quarterly General Membership Meeting.

1843 ■ Willowbrook Wildlife Foundation (WWF)
525 S Park Blvd.
Glen Ellyn, IL 60137-6932
Ph: (630)942-6200
E-mail: willowbrook@dupageforest.com
URL: http://willowbrookwildlife.org
Contact: Celeste Mancini, Pres.
Local.

1844 ■ Young Life Glenbard South
PO Box 67
Glen Ellyn, IL 60138
Ph: (630)469-5060
URL: http://gs.younglife.org
Local.

1845 ■ Young Life Glenbard West
PO Box 67
Glen Ellyn, IL 60138
Ph: (630)469-5060 (630)730-5451
E-mail: dan@ylchicago.com
URL: http://gw.younglife.org
Contact: Dan Nicholas, GW Staff Intern
Local.

1846 ■ Young Life Northwest DuPage
PO Box 67
Glen Ellyn, IL 60138
Ph: (630)469-5060
Fax: (630)604-5658
URL: http://nwdupage.younglife.org
Local.

1847 ■ Young Life Wheaton North
PO Box 67
Glen Ellyn, IL 60138
Ph: (630)469-5060
URL: http://wn.younglife.org
Local.

1848 ■ Young Life Wheaton Warrenville South
PO Box 67
Glen Ellyn, IL 60138
Ph: (630)469-5060
URL: http://wws.younglife.org
Local.

Glencoe

1849 ■ Glencoe Chamber of Commerce
PO Box 575
Glencoe, IL 60022
Ph: (847)835-3333
Fax: (847)835-9823
E-mail: info@glencoechamber.org
URL: http://www.glencoechamber.org
Contact: Lenna Scott, Exec.Dir.
Founded: 1965. **Members:** 100. **Membership Dues:** business (based on number of employees), $150-$500 (annual) • home business, $50 (annual) • nonprofit, $150 (annual) • governmental organization, $250 (annual). **Staff:** 1. **Local**. Promotes business and community development in Glencoe, IL area. **Committees:** Farmer's Market; Marketing; Sidewalk Sale; Web Site. **Publications:** Newsletter, monthly.

1850 ■ Glencoe PTO
PO Box 243
Glencoe, IL 60022
Fax: (847)835-1064
E-mail: info@glencoepto.org
URL: http://familyeducation.com/IL/Glencoe_PTA
Contact: Wendy Serrino, Pres.
Local. Parents, teachers, students, and others interested in uniting the forces of home, school, and community. Promotes the welfare of children and youth. **Additional Websites:** http://www.glencoepto.org.

Glendale Heights

1851 ■ Glendale Heights Barangay Lions Club
PO Box 5510
Glendale Heights, IL 60139
E-mail: barangay44@hotmail.com
URL: http://www.glendaleheightsbarangay.lionwap.org
Local. **Affiliated With:** Lions Clubs International.

1852 ■ Glendale Heights Junior Woman's Club
PO Box 5584
Glendale Heights, IL 60139
Ph: (630)464-0209
E-mail: joyce@svs.com
URL: http://ghjwc.org
Contact: Joyce Hundhausen, Pres.
Local.

1853 ■ Polo Cricket Club
717 Nolan Ave.
Glendale Heights, IL 60139
URL: http://www.usaca.org/Clubs.htm
Contact: Yasoob Ahmed, Contact
Local.

Glenview

1854 ■ American Hellenic Educational Progressive Association - Chicago/Logan, Chapter 260
c/o Elias Matsakis, Pres.
3601 Ari Ln.
Glenview, IL 60025
Ph: (312)715-5731
URL: http://www.ahepafamily.org/d13
Contact: Elias Matsakis, Pres.
Local. **Affiliated With:** American Hellenic Educational Progressive Association.

1855 ■ American Legion, Illinois Post 166
c/o Joseph M. Sesterhenn
PO Box 104
Glenview, IL 60025
Ph: (708)913-8621
Fax: (309)663-5783
URL: National Affiliate–www.legion.org
Contact: Joseph M. Sesterhenn, Contact
Local. **Affiliated With:** American Legion.

1856 ■ American Legion, Illinois Post 1009
c/o Carl Lindberry
1427 Brandon Rd.
Glenview, IL 60025
Ph: (708)724-7970
Fax: (309)663-5783
URL: National Affiliate–www.legion.org
Contact: Carl Lindberry, Contact
Local. **Affiliated With:** American Legion.

1857 ■ American Parkinson Disease Association, Midwest Chapter
c/o Mary Anne Ostrenga, Pres.
2050 Pfingsten Rd., Ste.127
Glenview, IL 60025
Ph: (847)724-7087
E-mail: mao961@aol.com
URL: National Affiliate–www.apdaparkinson.org
Contact: Mary Anne Ostrenga, Pres.
Local. **Affiliated With:** American Parkinson Disease Association.

1858 ■ American Youth Soccer Organization, Region 362
PO Box 772
Glenview, IL 60025-0772
Ph: (847)729-2976
URL: http://www.glenviewayso.org
Local. **Affiliated With:** American Youth Soccer Organization.

1859 ■ APICS, The Association for Operations Management - Chicago Chapter
PO Box 2007
Glenview, IL 60025-6007
Ph: (847)604-3161
Fax: (773)442-0416
Free: (800)982-7427
E-mail: info@apics-chicago.org
URL: http://www.apics-chicago.org
Contact: Timothy R. Wilson CPIM, Pres.
Local. Provides information and services in production and inventory management and related areas to enable members, enterprises and individuals to add value to their business performance. **Affiliated With:** APICS - The Association for Operations Management.

1860 ■ Association of Insurance Compliance Professionals, Great Lakes Chapter
c/o Michael J. Hollar, Treas.
Combined Insurance Co. of Am.
1000 N Milwaukee Ave., 5th Fl.
Glenview, IL 60025-2423
Ph: (847)953-1531
Fax: (847)953-1557
URL: National Affiliate–www.aicp.net
Contact: Michael J. Hollar, Treas.
Regional. Promotes regulatory competence and awareness for the improvement of regulatory compliance within the insurance industry. Serves the insurance compliance community by promoting relationships, exchanging information, and providing learning opportunities within a regulatory environment.

1861 ■ BMW Car Club of America, Windy City Chapter
PO Box 133
Glenview, IL 60025
Ph: (847)729-5268
E-mail: adams2002@aol.com
URL: http://windycitybmw.com
Contact: Barbara Adams, Newsletter Ed.
Founded: 1971. **Members:** 2,050. **Membership Dues:** general, $35 (annual). **Local**. Owners of BMW (Bavarian Motor Works) automobiles and other interested persons. Promotes interest in BMW automobiles through technical, social, and driving events; encourages the exchange of information among members. **Affiliated With:** BMW Car Club of America. **Publications:** *Breeze*, monthly. Newsletter. **Price:** available to members only. **Circulation:** 2,200. **Advertising:** accepted. **Conventions/Meetings:** annual Oktoberfest - festival.

1862 ■ Chicago Table Tennis Club at Glenview
Glenview Park District
2400 Chestnut Ave.
Glenview, IL 60025
Ph: (847)312-0590
E-mail: cttc4u@yahoo.com
URL: http://www.geocities.com/cttc4u
Contact: Engelbert Solis, Contact
Local. **Affiliated With:** U.S.A. Table Tennis.

1863 ■ Executive Women International, Chicago Chapter
c/o Terry Muglia
Illinois Tool Works Inc.
3600 W Lake Ave.
Glenview, IL 60026-1215
Ph: (847)657-4036
Fax: (847)402-1904
E-mail: info@ewichicago.org
URL: http://www.ewichicago.org
Contact: Peggy Quade, Pres.
Founded: 1952. **Members:** 32. **Local**. Works to promote member firms and improve their communities. Provides opportunities for business and personal growth. **Committees:** By-Laws; External Affairs; Nominating; Program; Publications; Ways & Means. **Subgroups:** Hospitality; Strategic Planning. **Affiliated With:** Executive Women International. **Publications:** *Pulse*, monthly. Newsletter. Alternate Formats: online.

1864 ■ Glenview Area Historical Society (GAHS)
1121 Waukegan Rd.
Glenview, IL 60025
Ph: (847)724-2235
E-mail: berdaw@juno.com
URL: http://gvkhome.northstarnet.org/gvhist
Contact: Beverly Dawson, Pres.
Founded: 1966. **Members:** 250. **Membership Dues:** family, $20 (annual) • life, $400 • contributor, $35 (annual) • business (1-49 employees), $25 (annual) • patron/business (50 or more employees), $50 (annual). **Local**. Preserves the cultural heritage and Glenview and its people. Identifies and preserves all aspects of the area history and perpetuates a protected environment for perishable documents and records. Develops educational programs to enhance Glenview cultural heritage. Maintains museum and library. **Libraries: Type:** reference. **Holdings:** papers, photographs. **Subjects:** Glenview history. **Affiliated With:** Glenview Chamber of Commerce; Illinois State Historical Society. **Publications:** Newsletter, quarterly. **Price:** included in membership dues.

1865 ■ Glenview Chamber of Commerce
2320 Glenview Rd.
Glenview, IL 60025-2711
Ph: (847)724-0900
Fax: (847)724-0202
E-mail: gcstaff@glenviewchamber.com
URL: http://glenviewchamber.com
Contact: Kathleen Miles, Pres.
Founded: 1923. **Members:** 425. **Membership Dues:** one-time application (new members), $25 • business within Glenview (based on number of employees), $174-$753 (annual) • non-Glenview business (based on number of employees), $201-$828 (annual). **Staff:** 2. **Local**. Works for the advancement of commercial, industrial, professional and civic interests of Glenview. Provides programs that increase visibility, customers and education. **Awards:** Business Person of the Year. **Frequency:** annual. **Type:** recognition. **Recipient:** to a member for outstanding contributions to the community. **Computer Services:** database, list of all members. **Committees:** Ambassadors; Golf Outing; Holiday in the Park & Parade; Local Government Affairs; Silent Auction; Summer Festival; Technology Council. **Publications:** *Community Resource Directory*, biennial. Membership Directory. Contains valuable community information and recognizes members whose committed to a better community. **Price:** $10.00 each. **Conventions/Meetings:** monthly Business After Hours - meeting, networking event for chamber members - every 2nd Wednesday • annual Business Person of the Year - luncheon, awarding of the chamber's highest recognition • annual Glenview Art Fair - meeting, with works in painting, sculpture, ceramics, photography, jewelry and mixed media, face-painting for kids, food and entertainment (exhibits) • annual Golf Classic - competition - every summer • annual Holiday in the Park & Parade - festival, includes a visit with Santa, hayrides, and munch on cookies, hot apple cider, hot chocolate and popcorn.

1866 ■ Glenview/North Shore African Violet Society
c/o Barbara Goodsell
429 Cherry Ln.
Glenview, IL 60025
Ph: (847)729-1690
E-mail: r.goodsell@eradoetsch.com
URL: National Affiliate–www.avsa.org
Contact: Barbara Goodsell, Contact
Local. **Affiliated With:** African Violet Society of America.

1867 ■ Illinois American Saddlebred Horse Association
c/o Cindie Kozeluh
1444 Magnolia St.
Glenview, IL 60025
Ph: (847)699-5961
E-mail: iaspha@comcast.net
URL: http://www.iaspha.com
Contact: Cindie Kozeluh, Contact
State. **Affiliated With:** American Saddlebred Horse Association.

1868 ■ Illinois Chapter of the American College of Cardiology
4242 Commercial Way
Glenview, IL 60025
Ph: (847)391-9777
Fax: (847)391-9711
E-mail: ilacc@ilacc.org
URL: http://www.ilacc.org
Contact: David J. Hale MD, Pres.
State. **Affiliated With:** American College of Cardiology.

1869 ■ Illinois Curling Association - North Shore Curling Club
1340 Glenview Rd.
Glenview, IL 60025
Ph: (847)724-9762
E-mail: curldeb@sbcglobal.net
URL: http://www.northshorecurling.org
Contact: Deb Murray, Contact
Local. **Affiliated With:** United States Curling Association.

1870 ■ Illinois Home Care Council (IHCC)
1926 Waukegan Rd., Ste.1
Glenview, IL 60025
Ph: (847)657-6960
Fax: (847)657-6963
E-mail: ihcc-hq@tcaq.com
URL: http://www.ilhomecare.org
Contact: Debbie T. Witt, Governmental Relations Mgr.
Founded: 1960. **Members:** 350. **Membership Dues:** provider, $5,000 (annual) • allied, associate, $500. **Staff:** 7. **Budget:** $800,000. **State**. Home health care providers and suppliers united for mutual education and legislative action. Holds educational conferences and workshops. **Awards:** Helen Heyrman Award. **Frequency:** annual. **Type:** recognition. **Recipient:** to individual who has made a significant contribution towards the advancement of the Illinois home care industry through outstanding leadership. **Committees:** Awards; Bylaws/Policy; Home Infusion; Leadership Development; Legislative Affairs; Regulatory / Reimbursement; Strategic Planning. **Working Groups:** Private Duty. **Affiliated With:** Illinois Hospital Association; National Association for Home Care and Hospice. **Publications:** *Best of Q & A: A Guide to Regulatory Resources* • *Council Communicator*, bimonthly. Newsletter. **Circulation:** 650. **Advertising:** accepted • Directory, annual. **Advertising:** accepted. **Conventions/Meetings:** annual conference (exhibits).

1871 ■ Midwest Pain Society (MPS)
c/o Amy Sherwood, Administrator
4700 W Lake Ave.
Glenview, IL 60025
Ph: (847)375-4855
E-mail: asherwood@connect2amc.com
URL: National Affiliate–www.ampainsoc.org
Contact: Amy Sherwood, Administrator
Regional. Advances pain-related research, education, treatment and professional practice. Promotes control, management and understanding of pain. Develops standards for training and ethical management of pain patients. **Affiliated With:** American Pain Society.

1872 ■ PFLAG Glenview/North Suburban Chicago
901 Milwaukee Ave.
Glenview, IL 60025
Ph: (773)477-3079
E-mail: contact@pflagchicago.com
URL: http://www.pflagchicago.com
Local. **Affiliated With:** Parents, Families, and Friends of Lesbians and Gays.

Godfrey

1873 ■ American Legion, Godfrey Post 2506
PO Box 661
Godfrey, IL 62035
Ph: (309)663-0361
Fax: (309)663-5783
URL: National Affiliate–www.legion.org
Local. **Affiliated With:** American Legion.

1874 ■ Growth Association of Southwestern Illinois
c/o Monica J. Bristow, Pres.
5800 Godfrey Rd.
Alden Hall, LCCC
Godfrey, IL 62035
Ph: (618)467-2280
Fax: (618)466-8289
E-mail: info@growthassociation.com
URL: http://www.growthassociation.com
Contact: Monica J. Bristow, Pres.
Founded: 1878. **Members:** 700. **Staff:** 5. **Budget:** $400,000. **Regional**. Members include those in education, unions, businesses, and government. **Awards:** Ambassador of the Month Award. **Frequency:** monthly. **Type:** recognition • Captains of the River Bend, Chairman's Award. **Frequency:** annual. **Type:** recognition. **Recipient:** to members with most contributions to regions. **Also Known As:** Chamber of Commerce; Economic Development Organization. **Formerly:** (2004) River Bend Growth Association. **Publications:** *Business Edge*, monthly. Newsletter. **Advertising:** accepted.

1875 ■ Phi Theta Kappa, Eta Psi Chapter - Lewis and Clark Community College
c/o Dennis Delfert, PhD
5800 Godfrey Rd.
Godfrey, IL 62035
Ph: (618)468-4833
E-mail: ddelfert@lc.edu
URL: http://www.ptk.org/directories/chapters/IL/171-1.htm
Contact: Dennis Delfert PhD, Advisor
Local.

1876 ■ SCORE SW Illinois
c/o Ned Wuellner, Chm.
5800 Godfrey Rd.
Alden Hall
Godfrey, IL 62035-2466
Ph: (618)467-2280
Fax: (618)466-8289
E-mail: score@lc.edu
Contact: Mr. Ned H. Wuellner, Chapter Chm.
Members: 50. **Budget:** $3,000. **For-Profit**. **Local**. **Computer Services:** Information services, advice in setting up. **Committees:** Banking Rel.; Legislative; Marketing; Recruiting; Technology; Training. **Affiliated With:** SCORE. **Publications:** *Illinois Gazette*, monthly. Newsletter. **Price:** free.

Golconda

1877 ■ American Legion, Pope County Post 719
c/o Carol W. Gibbs
RR 2, Box 126
Golconda, IL 62938
Ph: (618)949-3734
Fax: (309)663-5783
URL: National Affiliate–www.legion.org
Contact: Carol W. Gibbs, Contact
Local. Affiliated With: American Legion.

Golf

1878 ■ Western Golf Association (WGA)
1 Briar Rd.
Golf, IL 60029
Ph: (847)724-4600
Fax: (847)724-7133
E-mail: evansscholars@wgaesf.com
URL: http://www.westerngolfassociation.com
Contact: Donald D. Johnson, Exec.Dir.
Founded: 1899. **Members:** 500. **Budget:** $5,000,000. More than 500 golf and country clubs. Conducts three national golf championships: the Western Open, Western Amateur, and Western Junior. Supports and administers the Evans Scholars Foundation, which awards four-year college scholarships to caddies on a competitive basis. **Awards:** Evans. **Frequency:** annual. **Type:** scholarship. **Recipient:** for high school students. **Publications:** Annual Report • Brochure, annual. **Conventions/Meetings:** annual meeting - always May, Golf, IL.

Goreville

1879 ■ Thimble Collectors International, ILMO Thimblers
c/o Peggy Carroll
2369 Goreville Rd.
Goreville, IL 62939
Ph: (618)995-9013
E-mail: carroll@midamer.net
URL: National Affiliate–www.thimblecollectors.com
Contact: Peggy Carroll, Contact
Local. Affiliated With: Thimble Collectors International.

Grafton

1880 ■ American Legion, Whalen-Hill Post 648
PO Box 143
Grafton, IL 62037
Ph: (309)663-0361
Fax: (309)663-5783
URL: National Affiliate–www.legion.org
Local. Affiliated With: American Legion.

Granite City

1881 ■ American Legion, Tri-City Post 113
1825 State St.
Granite City, IL 62040
Ph: (618)876-2902
Fax: (309)663-5783
URL: National Affiliate–www.legion.org
Local. Affiliated With: American Legion.

1882 ■ International Union, United Automobile, Aerospace and Agricultural Implement Workers of America, AFL-CIO - Local Union 3206
2014A State St., Rm. 306
Granite City, IL 62040
Ph: (618)452-2620
Fax: (618)452-2624
URL: http://www.local3206.com
Contact: Anthony H. Collins, Financial Sec.
Members: 431. **Local.** AFL-CIO. **Affiliated With:** International Union, United Automobile, Aerospace and Agricultural Implement Workers of America.

1883 ■ National Alliance for the Mentally Ill - Madison County
Gateway Regional Medical Ctr., 4th Fl.
2100 Madison Ave.
Granite City, IL 62040
Ph: (618)656-6781
E-mail: pattyr6@charter.net
URL: http://madisoncty.nami.org
Contact: Pat Rudloff, Pres.
Local. Strives to improve the quality of life of children and adults with severe mental illness through support, education, research and advocacy. **Affiliated With:** National Alliance for the Mentally Ill.

1884 ■ Phi Theta Kappa, Alpha Kappa Rho Chapter - Southwestern Illinois College
c/o Lynne Cross
4950 Maryville Rd.
Granite City, IL 62040
Ph: (618)931-0600
E-mail: lynne.cross@swic.edu
URL: http://www.ptk.org/directories/chapters/IL/215-1.htm
Contact: Lynne Cross, Advisor
Local.

1885 ■ Southwestern Madison County Chamber of Commerce
PO Box 370
Granite City, IL 62040-0370
Ph: (618)876-6400
Fax: (618)876-6448
E-mail: chamber@chamberswmadisoncounty.com
URL: http://www.chamberswmadisoncounty.com
Contact: Rosemarie Brown, Exec.Dir.
Local. Formerly: (2002) Tri-Cities Area Chamber of Commerce.

1886 ■ United Transportation Union, AFL-CIO - Local Union 469
c/o Dave
1400 20th St.
Granite City, IL 62040
Ph: (618)452-0775
Fax: (618)452-0778
E-mail: utulocal469@aol.com
URL: http://www.angelfire.com/il3/utulocal469/index.html
Contact: Tom Kennedy, Pres.
Members: 135. **Local. Affiliated With:** United Transportation Union.

Grant Park

1887 ■ American Legion, Grant Park Star Post 295
PO Box 402
Grant Park, IL 60940
Ph: (815)465-6171
Fax: (309)663-5783
URL: National Affiliate–www.legion.org
Local. Affiliated With: American Legion.

Granville

1888 ■ American Legion, Granville Post 180
PO Box 180
Granville, IL 61326
Ph: (309)663-0361
Fax: (309)663-5783
URL: National Affiliate–www.legion.org
Local. Affiliated With: American Legion.

Grayslake

1889 ■ American Legion, Garnett-Foch Post 684
126 Gulfstream Ct.
Grayslake, IL 60030
Ph: (312)271-0960
Fax: (309)663-5783
URL: National Affiliate–www.legion.org
Local. Affiliated With: American Legion.

1890 ■ American Legion, Grayslake Post 659
PO Box 247
Grayslake, IL 60030
Ph: (708)223-4303
Fax: (309)663-5783
URL: National Affiliate–www.legion.org
Local. Affiliated With: American Legion.

1891 ■ Chain-O-Lakes Sail and Power Squadron
c/o Ron Herbig, Exec. Officer
244 Carters Grove Ct.
Grayslake, IL 60030-1196
E-mail: rorqual@sbcglobal.net
URL: http://www.uspsd20.org/spage/chain_o_lakes.html
Contact: Ron Herbig, Exec. Officer
Local. Affiliated With: United States Power Squadrons.

1892 ■ Exchange Club of Grayslake
PO Box 113
Grayslake, IL 60030
E-mail: info@exchangeofgrayslake.com
URL: http://www.exchangeofgrayslake.com
Contact: Bob Wegge, Pres.
Local.

1893 ■ Grayslake Area Chamber of Commerce
10 S Seymour Ave.
PO Box 167
Grayslake, IL 60030
Ph: (847)223-6888
Fax: (847)223-6895
E-mail: business@grayslakechamber.com
URL: http://www.grayslakechamber.com
Contact: Shirley A. Christian, Exec.Dir.
Founded: 1950. **Members:** 240. **Membership Dues:** business (3 or less employees), $205 (annual) • business (4 or more employees), $260 (annual) • business (10 or more employees), $300 (annual). **Local.** Commercial, industrial, professional service and retail businesses. Acts as a liaison between the Village of Grayslake, the Township, Lake County, the State and local citizens on matters concerning the well-being of the Grayslake business community. Plans, organizes and funds community events that are designed to promote the Village and the businesses in it. **Awards:** Joanne W. Lawrence Scholarship. **Frequency:** annual. **Type:** scholarship. **Recipient:** to two graduating seniors from Grayslake Community High School. **Computer Services:** Mailing lists, of members. **Commissions:** Economic Development. **Publications:** *Community Resource Guide*. Directory. Contains list of Chamber businesses alphabetically and categorically. **Circulation:** 13,000. **Advertising:** accepted • Newsletter, monthly. Highlights new members, lists latest Chamber events and provides up-to-date business news. **Advertising:** accepted. **Conventions/Meetings:** annual Arts - festival, a celebration of fine arts and music - every June • annual Golf Outing - competition - usually the first Wednesday in June • annual Grayslake Summer Days - festival, includes parade, games, and a wide variety of food, business and craft booths and activities for the entire family - third weekend in August • annual Tree Lighting Ceremony - meeting, featuring carriage rides, visits with Santa, caroling and refreshments - every November.

1894 ■ Handshake Beagle Club
c/o Oscar Calanca
18753 W Casey Rd.
Grayslake, IL 60030-9554
URL: National Affiliate–clubs.akc.org
Contact: Oscar Calanca, Contact
Local.

1895 ■ Illinois Quarter Horse Association, District No. 3
c/o Brad Kearns, Dir.
PO Box 7076A
Grayslake, IL 60030
Ph: (847)223-9440
E-mail: bradkearns@aol.com
URL: http://www.ilqha.com
Contact: Brad Kearns, Dir.
Local. Affiliated With: American Quarter Horse Association.

1896 ■ Northbrook Sports Club
PO Box 766
Grayslake, IL 60030
Ph: (847)223-5700
Fax: (847)223-3443
URL: http://www.northbrooksportsclub.org
Local. Affiliated With: National Skeet Shooting Association.

1897 ■ Phi Theta Kappa, Alpha Alpha Pi Chapter - College of Lake County
c/o Felicia Ganther
19351 W Washington St.
Grayslake, IL 60030
Ph: (847)543-2288
E-mail: fganther@clcillinois.edu
URL: http://www.ptk.org/directories/chapters/IL/202-2.htm
Contact: Felicia Ganther, Advisor
Local.

Grayville

1898 ■ American Legion, Illinois Post 696
c/o James M. Helm
PO Box 215
Grayville, IL 62844
Ph: (309)663-0361
Fax: (309)663-5783
URL: National Affiliate–www.legion.org
Contact: James M. Helm, Contact
Local. Affiliated With: American Legion.

1899 ■ Grayville Chamber of Commerce (GCC)
PO Box 117
Grayville, IL 62844
Ph: (618)375-7518
Contact: Steve Hartsock, Pres.
Members: 60. **Local**. Promotes business and community development in Grayville, IL. Sponsors annual Grayville Days. **Awards:** Business of Year. **Frequency:** annual. **Type:** recognition • Citizen of the Year. **Frequency:** annual. **Type:** recognition. **Conventions/Meetings:** annual meeting.

Great Lakes

1900 ■ Lake County Gem and Mineral Society
c/o Olen Hartman, Pres.
2620 A Pennsylvania Ave.
Great Lakes, IL 60088
E-mail: mbeverly45@aol.com
URL: National Affiliate–www.amfed.org
Contact: Eleanor Pocius, Sec.
Local. Aims to further the study of Earth Sciences and the practice of lapidary arts and mineralogy. **Affiliated With:** American Federation of Mineralogical Societies.

Green Oaks

1901 ■ Compassionate Friends - Northern Lake County Illinois Chapter
c/o Vicki Szech
31023 Prairie Ridge Rd.
Green Oaks, IL 60048
E-mail: rottiecd@aol.com
URL: http://www.itcf.org
Contact: Marilyn Grace, Chapter Leader
Local.

Greenfield

1902 ■ American Legion, Fitzsimmons Post 225
202 Pine St.
Greenfield, IL 62044
Ph: (217)368-2252
Fax: (309)663-5783
URL: National Affiliate–www.legion.org
Local. Affiliated With: American Legion.

Greenup

1903 ■ American Legion, Nichols-Goleman-Boggs Post 566
PO Box 696
Greenup, IL 62428
Ph: (309)663-0361
Fax: (309)663-5783
URL: National Affiliate–www.legion.org
Local. Affiliated With: American Legion.

Greenview

1904 ■ American Legion, Lawrence Rayburn Post 116
RR 1, Box 115
Greenview, IL 62642
Ph: (217)968-5400
Fax: (309)663-5783
URL: National Affiliate–www.legion.org
Local. Affiliated With: American Legion.

Greenville

1905 ■ American Legion, Greenville Post 282
PO Box 101
Greenville, IL 62246
Ph: (618)664-0286
Fax: (309)663-5783
URL: National Affiliate–www.legion.org
Local. Affiliated With: American Legion.

1906 ■ Beta Beta Beta, Gamma Gamma Chapter
c/o Dr. Eugene Dunkley
Greenville Coll.
Dept. of Biology
Greenville, IL 62246
Ph: (618)664-1840 (618)664-2800
Fax: (618)664-9880
Free: (800)345-4440
E-mail: edunkley@greenville.edu
URL: National Affiliate–tri-beta.org
Contact: Dr. Eugene Dunkley, Contact
Founded: 1957. **Members:** 20. **Budget:** $100. **Local**. Honorary society for biology majors at Greenville College. Promotes interest and research in biological sciences; sponsors educational and social events. **Affiliated With:** Beta Beta Beta. **Conventions/Meetings:** annual District Conference.

1907 ■ Greenville Chamber of Commerce
PO Box 283
Greenville, IL 62246
Ph: (618)664-9272
Free: (888)862-8201
E-mail: greenville@gcctv.com
URL: http://greenvilleusa.org
Contact: Ms. Julia Jenner, Exec.Dir.
Membership Dues: basic business with 1 - 4 people, $60 (annual). **Local**.

1908 ■ Libertarian Party of Illinois (LPI)
c/o Jan Stover, Exec.Dir.
515 W Main
Greenville, IL 62246-1616
Fax: (217)531-8854
Free: (800)735-1776
E-mail: director@lpillinois.org
URL: http://www.il.lp.org
Contact: Jan Stover, Exec.Dir.
State. Affiliated With: Libertarian National Committee.

1909 ■ Psi Chi, National Honor Society in Psychology - Greenville College
c/o Dept. of Psychology
PO Box 159
Greenville, IL 62246-0159
Ph: (618)664-6825
Fax: (618)664-6841
E-mail: jim.zahniser@greenville.edu
URL: http://www.psichi.org/chapters/info.asp?chapter_id=1025
Contact: James H. Zahniser PhD, Advisor
Local.

Gridley

1910 ■ American Legion, Gridley Post 218
212 W 2nd St.
Gridley, IL 61744
Ph: (309)663-0361
Fax: (309)663-5783
URL: National Affiliate–www.legion.org
Local. Affiliated With: American Legion.

1911 ■ McLean County Dental Society
c/o Dr. Timothy D. Supan, Pres.
PO Box 197
Gridley, IL 61744
Ph: (309)747-2213
E-mail: gridleydental@gridcom.net
URL: http://www.isds.org
Contact: Dr. Timothy D. Supan, Pres.
Local. Represents the interests of dentists committed to the public's oral health, ethics and professional development. Encourages the improvement of the public's oral health and promotes the art and science of dentistry. **Affiliated With:** American Dental Association; Illinois State Dental Society.

Griggsville

1912 ■ American Legion, Griggsville Post 213
PO Box 261
Griggsville, IL 62340
Ph: (217)833-9909
Fax: (309)663-5783
URL: National Affiliate–www.legion.org
Local. Affiliated With: American Legion.

Gurnee

1913 ■ American Legion, Gurnee Post 771
PO Box 71
Gurnee, IL 60031
Ph: (309)663-0361
Fax: (309)663-5783
URL: National Affiliate–www.legion.org
Local. Affiliated With: American Legion.

1914 ■ American Sewing Guild, Chicago Chapter
c/o Chris Abrams
7622 Mendocino Dr.
Gurnee, IL 60031
Ph: (847)548-8223
E-mail: u_sew_grl@yahoo.com
URL: http://www.asgchicago.org
Contact: Chris Abrams, Contact
Local. Affiliated With: American Sewing Guild.

1915 ■ Big Brothers Big Sisters of Lake County
c/o Jim Kales, CEO
3701-G Grand Ave.
Gurnee, IL 60031
Ph: (847)360-0770
Fax: (847)360-0784
E-mail: mentor@bbbslc.org
URL: http://www.bbbslc.org
Contact: Jim Kales, CEO
Local. Offers one to one youth mentoring.

1916 ■ Blue Devil Swim Club (BDSC)
34203 N Horseshoe Ln.
Gurnee, IL 60031-4200
Ph: (847)722-8841
E-mail: joryblauer@bluedevilswimclub.org
URL: http://www.bluedevilswimclub.org
Contact: Barb Conway, Pres.
Local.

1917 ■ Chicago Coach Federation (CCF)
c/o Sandy Mitsch
531 Old Walnut Cir.
Gurnee, IL 60031-5332
Ph: (847)223-7668
E-mail: s.mitsch@rthcoaching.com
URL: http://www.chicagocoaches.com
Contact: Cindy Nappi, Co-Pres.
Local. Formerly: (2005) International Coach Federation, Chicago Chapter.

1918 ■ Firewalker Four Wheel Drive Club
242 Pilgrims Path
Gurnee, IL 60031
Ph: (847)249-5091
E-mail: information@firewalker4x4.org
URL: http://www.firewalker4x4.org
Contact: Scott DePauw, Pres.
Local. Affiliated With: United Four-Wheel Drive Associations.

1919 ■ Healthy Communities Healthy Youth (HCHY)
c/o Sue Simpson, Treas.
17801 W Washington St.
Gurnee, IL 60031-5311
E-mail: ssimpson@warrentownship.net
URL: http://www.building4success.org
Contact: Sue Simpson, Treas.
Local.

1920 ■ Humanists of North Eastern Illinois (HNEI)
745 Cohasset Ct.
Gurnee, IL 60031-5809
Ph: (847)625-0745
E-mail: hnei@comcast.net
URL: http://hnei.home.comcast.net
Contact: Ted Sanders, Contact
Local.

1921 ■ Lake County Chamber of Commerce (LCCC)
5221 W Grand Ave.
Gurnee, IL 60031-1818
Ph: (847)249-3800
Fax: (847)249-3892
E-mail: info@lakecountychamber.com
URL: http://www.lakecounty-il.org
Contact: Mr. Steve Robinson, Pres.
Founded: 1915. **Members:** 785. **Staff:** 3. **Budget:** $165,000. **Local.** Businesses and individuals in Lake County, IL. Promotes: tourism; trade between local and foreign businesses; community and county development; friendly relations between local industry and business leaders. **Libraries: Type:** reference. **Holdings:** books, periodicals. **Subjects:** business, community development. **Computer Services:** Information services, member search. **Additional Websites:** http://www.lakecountychamber.com. **Formerly:** (1946) Waukegan Chamber of Commerce; (1974) Waukegan-North Chicago Chamber of Commerce; (1975) Waukegan-North Chicago Area Chamber of Commerce; (1993) Waukegan/Lake County. **Publications:** *E-Newsletter*, monthly • *Future Forum*, quarterly. Newsletter. **Advertising:** accepted. Alternate Formats: online.

1922 ■ Lake County Illinois Convention and Visitors Bureau
5455 W Grand Ave., Ste.302
Gurnee, IL 60031-5906
Ph: (847)662-2700
Fax: (847)662-2702
Free: (800)LAK-ENOW
E-mail: tourism@lakecounty.org
URL: http://www.lakecounty.org
Contact: Maureen Riedy, Pres.
Local. Publications: *Spaces*, annual. Magazine. Contains visitor planning guide. **Circulation:** 250,000. **Advertising:** accepted.

1923 ■ Lake County Philatelic Society
c/o Howard Shaughnessy, Sec.
6834 W Monticello Ct.
Gurnee, IL 60031
E-mail: clprr@aol.com
URL: http://lacopex.netfirms.com/
Contact: Fred Schaefer, Pres.
Local. Affiliated With: American Philatelic Society.

1924 ■ Plumbing-Heating-Cooling Contractors Association, Lake and McHenry Counties
c/o Mr. Tom Swartz, Pres.
4997 Carriage Dr.
Gurnee, IL 60031
Ph: (847)360-8906
Fax: (847)360-8905
E-mail: swartzplumbing@comcast.net
URL: National Affiliate–www.phccweb.org
Contact: Mr. Tom Swartz, Pres.
Local. Represents the plumbing, heating and cooling contractors. Promotes the construction industry. Protects the environment, health, safety and comfort of society. **Affiliated With:** Plumbing-Heating-Cooling Contractors Association.

1925 ■ Southport Skating Club
PO Box 8792
Gurnee, IL 60031
Ph: (847)336-1176
URL: http://www.southportskatingclub.org
Contact: Sarah Mahan, Membership Chair
Local. Provides programs to encourage participation and achievement in the sport of figure skating on ice. Defines and maintains uniform standards of skating proficiency. Organizes and sponsors competitions and exhibitions for the purpose of stimulating interest in figure skating. **Affiliated With:** United States Figure Skating Association.

1926 ■ United Way of Lake County, Illinois
330 S Greenleaf St.
Gurnee, IL 60031-3389
Ph: (847)775-1000
Fax: (847)775-1001
E-mail: uwlc@uwlakeco.org
URL: http://www.uwlakeco.org
Contact: Kristi Long, Pres./CEO
Local. Affiliated With: United Way of America.

Hamilton

1927 ■ American Legion, Hamilton Post 629
1258 N Hwy. 96
Hamilton, IL 62341
Ph: (309)663-0361
Fax: (309)663-5783
URL: National Affiliate–www.legion.org
Local. Affiliated With: American Legion.

1928 ■ Hamilton Community Development Coalition
c/o Brandy Garrett
1010 Broadway St.
Hamilton, IL 62341
Ph: (217)847-2906
Fax: (217)847-2936
URL: http://www.hamiltonillinois.org/cdc.htm
Contact: Brandy Garrett, Contact
Local.

Hampshire

1929 ■ American Legion, Haderer-Eineke Post 680
PO Box 801
Hampshire, IL 60140
Ph: (309)663-0361
Fax: (309)663-5783
URL: National Affiliate–www.legion.org
Local. Affiliated With: American Legion.

1930 ■ Hampshire Area Chamber of Commerce (HACC)
PO Box 157
Hampshire, IL 60140
Ph: (847)683-1122
Fax: (847)683-1146
URL: http://www.hampshireillinois.com
Contact: Jeanmarie Sullivan, Pres.
Members: 25. **Local.** Promotes business and community development in Hampshire, IL. Organizes annual Coon Creek Day. **Formerly:** (1999) Hampshire Chamber of Commerce. **Conventions/Meetings:** monthly meeting, networking opportunities - 2nd wednesday of each month.

Hampton

1931 ■ Muskies Mississippi Valley Chapter
93 Kennelworth Cir.
Hampton, IL 61256
Ph: (309)797-1803
E-mail: qcca@aol.com
URL: National Affiliate–www.muskiesinc.org
Contact: Sonny Stephens, Pres.
Local.

Hanna City

1932 ■ American Legion, Thrush-Parry Post 212
PO Box 156
Hanna City, IL 61536
Ph: (309)565-4464
Fax: (309)663-5783
URL: National Affiliate–www.legion.org
Local. Affiliated With: American Legion.

Hanover

1933 ■ American Legion, S.C.S. Post 707
PO Box 63
Hanover, IL 61041
Ph: (309)663-0361
Fax: (309)663-5783
URL: National Affiliate–www.legion.org
Local. Affiliated With: American Legion.

Hanover Park

1934 ■ German Shepherd Dog Training Club of Chicago (GSDTC)
4925 County Farm Rd.
Hanover Park, IL 60133
Ph: (630)830-6226
E-mail: bchilders@speakeasy.net
URL: http://www.gsdtcchgo.com
Contact: Bill Childers, Pres.
Local.

Hardin

1935 ■ American Legion, Calhoun Post 636
PO Box 91
Hardin, IL 62047
Ph: (217)983-2876
Fax: (309)663-5783
URL: National Affiliate–www.legion.org
Local. Affiliated With: American Legion.

Harrisburg

1936 ■ American Hiking Society - River to River Trail Society
1142 Winkleman Rd.
Harrisburg, IL 62946
Ph: (618)252-6789
Fax: (618)438-2915
E-mail: trails444@hotmail.com
URL: http://www.americanhiking.org
Local.

1937 ■ American Legion, Carrier Mills Post 1140
US RR 45, 2nd St.
Harrisburg, IL 62946
Ph: (309)663-0361
Fax: (309)663-5783
URL: National Affiliate–www.legion.org
Local. Affiliated With: American Legion.

1938 ■ American Legion, Illinois Post 167
c/o George Hart
600 E Logan
Harrisburg, IL 62946
Ph: (618)252-6444
Fax: (309)663-5783
URL: National Affiliate–www.legion.org
Contact: George Hart, Contact
Local. Affiliated With: American Legion.

1939 ■ Phi Theta Kappa, Mu Psi Chapter - Southeastern Illinois College
c/o Kellye Whitler
3575 Coll. Rd.
Harrisburg, IL 62946
Ph: (618)252-5400
E-mail: kellye.whitler@sic.edu
URL: http://www.ptk.org/directories/chapters/IL/181-1.htm
Contact: Kellye Whitler, Advisor
Local.

1940 ■ Saline County Chamber of Commerce
303 S Commercial St.
Harrisburg, IL 62946
Ph: (618)252-4192
Fax: (618)252-0210
E-mail: chamber@salinecountychamber.org
URL: http://www.salinecountychamber.org
Contact: Katrinka Stevers, Dir.
Membership Dues: individual, $50 (annual) • non-profit organization, $75 (annual) • senior citizen, $25 (annual) • business (based on number of employees), $100-$200 (annual). **Local.** Promotes business and community development in Harrisburg, IL. **Publications:** Newsletter, quarterly.

1941 ■ Society of American Foresters, Illinois Chapter
c/o J. Daniel Price, Chair
3575 Coll. Rd.
Harrisburg, IL 62946-4925
Ph: (618)252-5400
Fax: (618)252-2941
E-mail: wildland@winco.net
URL: http://www.siu.edu/~ilsaf
Contact: J. Daniel Price, Chair
State. Affiliated With: Society of American Foresters.

1942 ■ Society of American Foresters, Southeast Illinois Student Chapter
c/o Reid Alan Bitner, Chair
4449 Muddy Rd., Apt. 2D
Harrisburg, IL 62946
Ph: (217)482-3653
E-mail: pheasant16@yahoo.com
URL: http://www.siu.edu/~ilsaf
Contact: Reid Alan Bitner, Chair
Local. Affiliated With: Society of American Foresters.

1943 ■ Southeastern Illinois Regional Planning and Development Commission (SIRP&DC)
PO Box 606
Harrisburg, IL 62946
Ph: (618)252-7463
Fax: (618)252-7464
E-mail: sirpdc@midamer.net
URL: http://www.sirpdc.org
Contact: Julie Patera, Exec.Dir.
Founded: 1968. **Members:** 25. **Staff:** 5. **State Groups:** 1. **Local.** Works to serve the people, businesses, communities and local government units within the Illinois counties of Gallatin, Hamilton, Hardin, Pope and Saline as liaison with the State and Federal agencies concerned with comprehensive planning and development of the District. **Awards:** Harrisburg Chamber of Commerce 1997 Community Service Award. **Frequency:** annual. **Type:** recognition • NADO Innovation Award. **Frequency:** annual. **Type:** recognition. **Publications:** *Southeastern Messenger*, quarterly. Newsletter. Alternate Formats: online. **Conventions/Meetings:** annual Economic Development Administration - conference • annual NADO - conference.

Hartsburg

1944 ■ American Legion, Hartsburg Post 1146
PO Box 17
Hartsburg, IL 62643
Ph: (309)663-0361
Fax: (309)663-5783
URL: National Affiliate–www.legion.org
Local. Affiliated With: American Legion.

1945 ■ American Rabbit Breeders Association, Californian Rabbit Specialty Club of Illinois
c/o Wayne Coffey
313 W Front St.
Hartsburg, IL 62643
Ph: (217)642-5350
E-mail: tcoffey2@mchsi.com
URL: http://www.nordickrabbits.com/specialt.htm
Contact: Wayne Coffey, Contact
Local. Affiliated With: American Rabbit Breeders Association.

1946 ■ American Rabbit Breeders Association, Illinois Netherland Dwarf Specialty Club
c/o Twila Coffey
313 W Front St.
Hartsburg, IL 62643
Ph: (217)642-5350
E-mail: tcoffey2@mchsi.com
URL: http://www.nordickrabbits.com/specialt.htm
Contact: Twila Coffey, Contact
Local. Affiliated With: American Rabbit Breeders Association.

Harvard

1947 ■ Aikido of Harvard
39 N Ayer
Harvard, IL 60033
Ph: (815)943-8141
E-mail: tleonard@aikidoharvard.org
URL: http://www.aikidoharvard.org
Local. Affiliated With: United States Aikido Federation.

1948 ■ American Legion, Illinois Post 265
c/o William J. Metzen
PO Box 36
Harvard, IL 60033
Ph: (815)943-5041
Fax: (309)663-5783
URL: National Affiliate–www.legion.org
Contact: William J. Metzen, Contact
Local. Affiliated With: American Legion.

1949 ■ Free Spirit Siberian Rescue
PO Box 626
Harvard, IL 60033
Ph: (815)245-2972
Fax: (815)943-5738
E-mail: info@huskyrescue.org
URL: http://www.huskyrescue.org
Local.

1950 ■ Greater Harvard Area Chamber of Commerce (GHACC)
62 N Ayer St., Ste.B
Harvard, IL 60033
Ph: (815)943-4404
Fax: (815)943-4410
E-mail: info@harvcc.net
URL: http://www.harvcc.net
Contact: Pamela Hayes, Exec.Dir.
Members: 165. **Local.** Promotes business and community development in the Harvard, IL area. **Committees:** Ambassadors; Budget; Building and Maintenance; Golf Outing; Greeter Service; Industrial; Recognition; Website.

1951 ■ Northern Illinois Saint Bernard Club
9504 Mansion Heights Dr.
Harvard, IL 60033
Ph: (815)648-4549
Fax: (815)648-2135
E-mail: vanrijn@worldnet.att.net
URL: National Affiliate–www.saintbernardclub.org
Contact: Sara Sykora, Sec.
Local. Affiliated With: Saint Bernard Club of America.

1952 ■ Ruffed Grouse Society, T. Stanton Armour Chapter
c/o John A. Clemetsen
19317 Stateline Rd.
Harvard, IL 60033
Ph: (815)943-7790
E-mail: printim@aol.com
URL: National Affiliate–www.ruffedgrousesociety.org
Contact: John A. Clemetsen, Contact
Local. Affiliated With: Ruffed Grouse Society.

Harvey

1953 ■ American Legion, Phoenix Post 1254
PO Box 2910
Harvey, IL 60426
Ph: (309)663-0361
Fax: (309)663-5783
URL: National Affiliate–www.legion.org
Local. Affiliated With: American Legion.

1954 ■ Healthcare Financial Management Association, First Illinois Chapter
c/o Vincent E. Pryor, CPA, Pres.
Ingalls Hea. Sys.
1 Ingalls Dr.
Harvey, IL 60426
Ph: (708)915-6110
Fax: (708)915-2099
E-mail: firstillinois@firstillinoishfma.org
URL: http://www.firstillinoishfma.org
Contact: Vincent E. Pryor CPA, Pres.
Local. Provides education, analysis and guidance to healthcare finance professionals. Helps members and other individuals in advancing the financial management of health care and in improving the business performance of organizations serving the healthcare field. **Affiliated With:** Healthcare Financial Management Association.

1955 ■ Ingalls Stroke Club
Ingalls Memorial Hosp.
One Ingalls Dr.
Harvey, IL 60426
Ph: (708)333-2300
E-mail: contact@ingalls.org
URL: http://www.ingalls.org
Contact: Sheila Bender, Coor.
Founded: 1985. **Members:** 55. **Staff:** 1. **Local Groups:** 1. **Local**. Stroke survivors and families. Helps members retain confidence, increase self-esteem, and share ideas on ways to cope with individual problems. **Conventions/Meetings:** monthly meeting, with presentations - always 1st Monday of every month, March through Nov. Harvey, IL - Avg. Attendance: 25.

1956 ■ National Association of Investors Corporation, Chicago South Chapter
PO Box 1875
Harvey, IL 60426
E-mail: robmoe_2000@yahoo.com
URL: http://better-investing.org/chapter/south-chicago
Contact: Robert Moore, Pres.
Local. Teaches individuals how to become successful strategic long-term investors. Provides highly focused learning resources and investment tools that empower individuals to become better investors. **Affiliated With:** National Association of Investors Corporation.

Harwood Heights

1957 ■ Muslim Student Association - University of Illinois - Chicago
4412 N. Oak Park Ave.
Harwood Heights, IL 60656
Ph: (708)867-7131
Fax: (708)867-7131
URL: http://www2.uic.edu/stud_orgs/religion/msa
Muslim students in North America. Seeks to advance the interests of members; works to enable members to practice Islam as a complete way of life. **Affiliated With:** Muslim Students Association of the United States and Canada.

Havana

1958 ■ American Legion, Havana Post 138
215 E Dearborn St.
Havana, IL 62644
Ph: (309)663-0361
Fax: (309)663-5783
URL: National Affiliate–www.legion.org
Local. Affiliated With: American Legion.

1959 ■ Havana Area Chamber of Commerce
PO Box 116
Havana, IL 62644
Ph: (309)543-7385
Free: (888)236-8406
E-mail: mcdemo@havanaprint.com
URL: http://www.havanail.net
Contact: Mary Layton, Pres.
Local. Works with other community resources to promote local tourism, create jobs, and recruit new businesses in Havana, IL. Sponsors community events.

1960 ■ Mason County Farm Bureau Foundation
c/o Tim Urish
PO Box 318
127 S High St.
Havana, IL 62644-0318
Ph: (309)543-4451 (309)543-4452
Fax: (309)543-2486
E-mail: masonfb@casscomm.com
Contact: Deedee Gellerman, Mgr.
Local.

1961 ■ Wildlife Society - Illinois Chapter
c/o Aaron Yetter, Pres.
PO Box 590
Havana, IL 62644
Ph: (309)543-3950
E-mail: mgeorgi@mail.inhs.uiuc.edu
URL: http://home.grics.net/forbes/ICTWS
Contact: Aaron Yetter, Pres.
State. Affiliated With: The Wildlife Society.

Hazel Crest

1962 ■ American Legion, Hazel Crest Post 398
17034 Page Ave.
Hazel Crest, IL 60429
Ph: (309)663-0361
Fax: (309)663-5783
URL: National Affiliate–www.legion.org
Local. Affiliated With: American Legion.

1963 ■ Nation Council for GeoCosmic Research, Southwest Suburban Chicago Chapter
16963 Page Ave.
Hazel Crest, IL 60429
Ph: (708)335-2277
E-mail: patriciahanus@aol.com
URL: National Affiliate–www.geocosmic.org
Contact: Pat Hanus-Dussman, Pres.
Local. Raises the standards of astrological education and research. Works to foster and publish research of a geocosmic nature and to pursue educational programs in various interdisciplinary fields related to geocosmic studies. **Affiliated With:** National Council for GeoCosmic Research.

Hazel Dell

1964 ■ American Legion, Glidewell-Yelton Post 1230
128 N Pine St.
Hazel Dell, IL 62428
Ph: (309)663-0361
Fax: (309)663-5783
URL: National Affiliate–www.legion.org
Local. Affiliated With: American Legion.

Hebron

1965 ■ American Legion, Eugene Drill Post 606
PO Box 36
Hebron, IL 60034
Ph: (309)663-0361
Fax: (309)663-5783
URL: National Affiliate–www.legion.org
Local. Affiliated With: American Legion.

Hennepin

1966 ■ American Legion, Putnam County Seat Post 1044
421 E Court
Hennepin, IL 61327
Ph: (309)663-0361
Fax: (309)663-5783
URL: National Affiliate–www.legion.org
Local. Affiliated With: American Legion.

1967 ■ Putnam County Historical Society
327 Old Hwy. 26
PO Box 74
Hennepin, IL 61327-0074
Ph: (815)925-7560
E-mail: pchs61327@yahoo.com
Contact: Mrs. Karen Bailey, Pres.
Founded: 1963. **Members:** 600. **Membership Dues:** individual, $10 (annual) • husband and wife, $15 (annual) • student, $8 (annual) • contributing, $25 (annual) • family, $40 (annual) • business, $50 (annual) • life, $100 • gold, $500 • platinum, $1,000. **Staff:** 21. **Budget:** $27,000. **Regional Groups:** 1. **Local**. Assists genealogy research and those seeking local history. Collects, preserves, and disseminates local history through the restoration and preservation of the Edward Pulsifer House in Hennepin and the establishment of Agricultural Museum. Hosts quarterly and annual programs to educate and entertain the public in the history and culture of county, area and State. **Libraries: Type:** reference; open to the public. **Holdings:** 400; biographical archives, books, business records, papers, periodicals, photographs. **Subjects:** Illinois. **Awards:** Whitaker Key History Award. **Frequency:** annual. **Type:** recognition. **Recipient:** for outstanding history student in District 535. **Computer Services:** database, early Putnam County marriages, newspaper indexes, scrapbook indexes and genealogy research information. **Publications:** *Putnam Past Times*, semiannual. Newsletter. Contains news and history of society. **Price:** included in membership dues. **Circulation:** 1,000. **Conventions/Meetings:** quarterly meeting, for public and membership.

Henry

1968 ■ American Legion, Henry Post 323
PO Box 195
Henry, IL 61537
Ph: (309)663-0361
Fax: (309)663-5783
URL: National Affiliate–www.legion.org
Local. Affiliated With: American Legion.

1969 ■ Henry Area Chamber of Commerce
514 Front St.
River Park Ctr.
Henry, IL 61537-0211
Ph: (309)364-3261 (309)364-2384
Fax: (309)364-3261
E-mail: s1939@ocslink.com
URL: http://www.cc.henry.il.us
Contact: Jerry Read, Pres.
Local. Promotes business and community development in Henry, IL area.

1970 ■ Illinois Dietetic Association (IDA)
PO Box 26
Henry, IL 61537
Ph: (309)364-2919
Fax: (309)364-2954
E-mail: headquarters@eatrightillinois.org
URL: http://www.eatrightillinois.org
Contact: Terry McBride, Contact
State. Dietetic professionals, registered dietitians and dietetic technicians serving the public through promotion of optimal nutrition, health and well being. Seeks to shape the food choices and impact the nutritional status of the public in hospitals, colleges, universi-

ties, schools, day care centers, research, business and industry. **Affiliated With:** American Dietetic Association.

Herrick

1971 ■ American Legion, Sarver-Guthrie Post 839
PO Box 13
Herrick, IL 62431
Ph: (618)428-5748
Fax: (309)663-5783
URL: National Affiliate–www.legion.org
Local. Affiliated With: American Legion.

Herrin

1972 ■ American Legion, Herrin Prairie Post 645
213 E Madison St.
Herrin, IL 62948
Ph: (618)942-3313
Fax: (309)663-5783
URL: National Affiliate–www.legion.org
Local. Affiliated With: American Legion.

1973 ■ Girl Scouts of Shagbark Council
c/o Lana Bardo, Asst.Exec.Dir.
304 N 14th St.
Herrin, IL 62948
Ph: (618)942-3164
E-mail: girlscouts@shagbark.org
URL: http://www.shagbark.org
Contact: Lana Bardo, Asst.Exec.Dir.
Local. Seeks to inspire girls, aged 5 to 17, with the highest ideals of character, conduct, patriotism, and service so that they may become happy and resourceful citizens. Covers 24 counties in southern IL and Knox County, IN. Focuses on leadership development and real life skills.

1974 ■ Herrin Chamber of Commerce
3 S Park Ave.
Herrin, IL 62948
Ph: (618)942-5163
E-mail: herrincc@herrinillinois.com
URL: http://www.herrinillinois.com
Contact: Sue Douglas, Exec.Dir.
Membership Dues: business (first member), $160 (annual) • business (for each additional member), $130 (annual) • individual (not associated with a business), $105 (annual). **Local.** Serves and supports the economic good of the greater Herrin area with priority given to economic development and the assistance necessary to acquire and retain business and industry in Herrin and the surrounding region. **Publications:** *Chamber Chat*, monthly. Newsletter. **Advertising:** accepted. **Conventions/Meetings:** annual dinner, distinguished citizens and businesses are recognized - every January • annual Herrinfesta Italiana - festival, includes a showcase of entertainment, authentic Italian food, an art gallery, a carnival, Pasta Eating contests and others - always on Memorial Day weekend • annual Herrin's Homecoming Celebration - meeting, includes a parade, golf tournament, football game, queen's court and class reunions - every October.

Herscher

1975 ■ American Legion, Herscher Post 795
102 N Oak St.
Herscher, IL 60941
Ph: (815)426-2264
Fax: (309)663-5783
URL: National Affiliate–www.legion.org
Local. Affiliated With: American Legion.

1976 ■ Herscher Chamber of Commerce
PO Box 437
Herscher, IL 60941
Ph: (815)426-2685 (815)426-6542
Contact: Dawn Deany, Member
Local.

Heyworth

1977 ■ American Legion, Illinois Post 624
PO Box 295
Heyworth, IL 61745
Ph: (309)663-0361
Fax: (309)663-5783
URL: National Affiliate–www.legion.org
Contact: Carl E. Miller, Contact
Local. Affiliated With: American Legion.

1978 ■ American Rabbit Breeders Association, Illinois Checkered Giant Rabbit Club
c/o Jean Martin
RR 2 Box 59
Heyworth, IL 61745
Ph: (309)473-3869
URL: http://www.nordickrabbits.com/specialt.htm
Contact: Jean Martin, Contact
Local. Affiliated With: American Rabbit Breeders Association.

1979 ■ Central Illinois Chapter of American Society of Plumbing Engineers
15040 E 425N Rd.
Heyworth, IL 61745
Ph: (309)473-2984
E-mail: pres@centralillinoisaspe.org
URL: http://www.centralillinoisaspe.org
Contact: Scott Leopold CPD, Pres.
Local. Represents the interests of individuals dedicated to the advancement of the science of plumbing engineering. Seeks to resolve professional problems in plumbing engineering. Advocates greater cooperation among members and plumbing officials, contractors, laborers and the public. **Affiliated With:** American Society of Plumbing Engineers.

Hickory Hills

1980 ■ American Legion, Ours For Victory Post 971
8751 Hillside Dr.
Hickory Hills, IL 60457
Ph: (309)663-0361
Fax: (309)663-5783
URL: National Affiliate–www.legion.org
Local. Affiliated With: American Legion.

1981 ■ First Catholic Slovak Ladies Association - Chicago Junior Branch 370
8801 Willow Rd.
Hickory Hills, IL 60457
Ph: (708)430-5023
URL: National Affiliate–www.fcsla.com
Local. Affiliated With: First Catholic Slovak Ladies Association.

1982 ■ First Catholic Slovak Ladies Association - Chicago Senior Branch 225
8801 Willow Rd.
Hickory Hills, IL 60457
Ph: (708)430-5023
URL: National Affiliate–www.fcsla.com
Local. Affiliated With: First Catholic Slovak Ladies Association.

1983 ■ Hickory Hills Chamber of Commerce
8652 W 95th St.
Hickory Hills, IL 60457
Ph: (708)598-4800
Fax: (708)430-6245
Contact: Arlene Kasper, Pres.
Local.

Highland

1984 ■ American Legion, Lee Iten Post 439
1130 New Trenton Rd.
Highland, IL 62249
Ph: (618)654-3450
Fax: (309)663-5783
URL: National Affiliate–www.legion.org
Local. Affiliated With: American Legion.

1985 ■ Highland Chamber of Commerce (HCC)
907 Main St.
Highland, IL 62249
Ph: (618)654-3721
Fax: (618)654-8966
E-mail: jami@highlandillinois.com
URL: http://www.highlandillinois.com
Contact: Jami Jansen, Exec.Dir.
Founded: 1924. **Members:** 125. **Staff:** 1. **Budget:** $35,000. **Local.** Promotes business, tourism, and community development in Highland, IL. **Committees:** Building Maintenance; Business Education; Industrial Affairs; Signage. **Publications:** *Available Site Location Guide*, annual. Directory • *Chamber News*, monthly. Newsletter. Alternate Formats: online • Brochures, monthly. **Conventions/Meetings:** monthly board meeting • quarterly general assembly.

Highland Park

1986 ■ American Legion, Highland Park Post 145
PO Box 145
Highland Park, IL 60035
Ph: (309)663-0361
Fax: (309)663-5783
URL: National Affiliate–www.legion.org
Local. Affiliated With: American Legion.

1987 ■ Antique Automobile Club of America, Illinois Region - North Shore Chapter
c/o Robert Grutza, Pres.
2880 Idlewood Ln.
Highland Park, IL 60035
Ph: (847)432-0698
E-mail: jrubensteinalert@aol.com
URL: http://clubs.hemmings.com/frameset.cfm?club=illinoisnorthshoreaaca
Contact: Robert Grutza, Pres.
Membership Dues: individual, $5 (annual). **Local.** Collectors, hobbyists, and others interested in the preservation, maintenance, and restoration of automobiles and in automotive history. **Affiliated With:** Antique Automobile Club of America.

1988 ■ Chicago Action for Jews in the Former Soviet Union
555 Vine St., Ste.111
Highland Park, IL 60035
Ph: (847)433-0144
Fax: (847)433-5530
E-mail: officecasj@ameritech.net
URL: http://www.chicagoaction.org
Contact: Marillyn Tallman, Chair
Founded: 1972. **Staff:** 10. **Languages:** English, Russian. **Multinational.** Seeks to give humanitarian aid to Jews in the former Soviet Union; funds soup kitchens, meals on wheels, medicine, visiting nurses, meals for school children, heating for homes and schools, and security systems for synagogues. Communicates daily with Jewish communities in towns and villages in the former Soviet Union for information, and also informs members in the U.S. of anti-Semitic incidents there; created and supervised a program, Yad L'Yad (Hand to Hand), which pairs synagogues in the Chicago area and the Midwest with Jewish communities in the former Soviet Union. **Telecommunication Services:** electronic mail, chicagoaction@ameritech.net. **Formerly:** (1998) International Physicians Commission. **Publications:** *Lifeline*, periodic. Newsletter. Alternate Formats: online.

1989 ■ Highland Park Chamber of Commerce (HPCC)
508 Central Ave., Ste.206
Highland Park, IL 60035
Ph: (847)432-0284
Fax: (847)432-2802
E-mail: chamber@ehighlandpark.com
URL: http://www.ehighlandpark.com/default2.asp
Contact: Ginny Anzelmo Glasner, Exec.Dir.
Founded: 1910. **Members:** 350. **Membership Dues:** restaurant, retail, service (based on number of employees), $225-$675 (annual) • auto sale, hotel, media, utility, $475 (annual) • commercial and residential estate, $375 (annual) • hospital, clinic, $775 (annual) • financial institution (based on total assets), $375-$925 (annual) • nonprofit, $150 (annual). **Local**. Promotes business and community development in Highland Park, IL. Conducts charitable activities. Sponsors festival. **Committees:** Government Affairs; Retail; Special Events/Fundraising. **Publications:** Directory, annual • Newsletter, monthly. **Advertising:** accepted.

1990 ■ Highland Park Historical Society (HPHS)
326 Central Ave.
PO Box 56
Highland Park, IL 60035
Ph: (847)432-7090
E-mail: hphistorical@sbcglobal.net
URL: http://www.highlandpark.org/historic
Contact: Ellsworth Mills II, Managing Dir.
Founded: 1966. **Members:** 1,500. **Membership Dues:** family, $30 (annual) • supporting, $50 (annual) • sustaining, $100 (annual) • benefactor, $250 (annual) • patron, $500 (annual). **Staff:** 4. **Budget:** $40,000. **Local**. Residents of Highland Park, IL. Seeks to preserve local history and artifacts. Maintains Francis Stupey Log Cabin, Jean Butz James Museum, Walt Durbahn Tool Museum, and Bob Robinson Bandstand. Sponsors open houses, housewalk and meetings. **Libraries: Type:** reference. **Holdings:** 250; archival material. **Subjects:** local history. **Affiliated With:** Illinois State Historical Society. **Publications:** *The Lamplighter*, quarterly. Brochures. Contains news of the Society. **Circulation:** 800. **Conventions/Meetings:** periodic meeting.

1991 ■ Highland Park Public Library
494 Laurel Ave.
Highland Park, IL 60035
Ph: (847)432-0216
E-mail: hpplweb@nslsilus.org
URL: http://www.hppl.lib.il.us
Contact: Donna Fletcher, Pres.
Founded: 1947. **Members:** 30. **Local**. Strives to enhance the services of the Highland Park Public Library. Makes equipment and other contributions; sponsors lecture series. **Libraries: Type:** open to the public. **Holdings:** 200,000. **Subjects:** broad cultural nature, business, arts, etc. **Additional Websites:** http://www.highlandpark.org. **Publications:** *The Laurels*, semiannual. Newsletter. Contains library news and program schedules. **Price:** free. **Circulation:** 30,575. **Conventions/Meetings:** quarterly meeting • quarterly meeting - March, June, September, and December.

1992 ■ Illinois Curling Association - Exmoor Curling Club
700 Vine St.
Highland Park, IL 60035
Ph: (847)432-9520
Fax: (847)432-3661
E-mail: tolucabird@attbi.com
URL: http://www.goodcurling.net/basics/U.S.%20clubs/illinois.html
Contact: John Beckwith, Pres.
Local. Affiliated With: United States Curling Association.

1993 ■ League of Women Voters of Highland Park
PO Box 396
Highland Park, IL 60035
Ph: (847)433-8855
URL: http://www.highlandpark.org/lwvhp
Local. Affiliated With: League of Women Voters of the United States.

Highwood

1994 ■ American Legion, Highwood Post 501
PO Box 91
Highwood, IL 60040
Ph: (309)663-0361
Fax: (309)663-5783
URL: National Affiliate–www.legion.org
Local. Affiliated With: American Legion.

1995 ■ Chicago Vegetarian Society
c/o Sonya M Kugler, Pres.
PO Box 223
Highwood, IL 60040
Ph: (312)420-8344
E-mail: edkugler@millardgroup.com
URL: http://www.vegetarianusa.com/city/Chicago.html
Contact: Sonia M Kugler, Pres.
State.

Hillsboro

1996 ■ American Legion, Mc-Lain-Chandler Post 153
805 Montgomery Ave.
Hillsboro, IL 62049
Ph: (309)663-0361
Fax: (309)663-5783
URL: National Affiliate–www.legion.org
Local. Affiliated With: American Legion.

1997 ■ American Legion, Moncravie Post 425
10120 Coffeen Rd.
Hillsboro, IL 62049
Ph: (217)533-4380
Fax: (309)663-5783
URL: National Affiliate–www.legion.org
Local. Affiliated With: American Legion.

1998 ■ Hillsboro Area Chamber of Commerce
PO Box 6
Hillsboro, IL 62049-0006
Ph: (217)532-3711
Fax: (217)532-5567
E-mail: hillsborochamber@consolidated.net
Contact: Yvonne Purcell, Exec.Sec.
Local.

Hillsdale

1999 ■ American Legion, Hillsdale Post 1144
PO Box 111
Hillsdale, IL 61257
Ph: (309)663-0361
Fax: (309)663-5783
URL: National Affiliate–www.legion.org
Local. Affiliated With: American Legion.

Hillside

2000 ■ American Legion, Berkeley Post 1016
PO Box 714
Hillside, IL 60162
Ph: (708)544-3773
Fax: (309)663-5783
URL: National Affiliate–www.legion.org
Local. Affiliated With: American Legion.

2001 ■ American Legion, Broadview-Hillside Post 626
4941 Butterfield Rd.
Hillside, IL 60162
Ph: (708)449-2923
Fax: (309)663-5783
URL: National Affiliate–www.legion.org
Local. Affiliated With: American Legion.

2002 ■ American Legion, Evzones Post 1039
4400 Frontage Rd.
Hillside, IL 60162
Ph: (309)663-0361
Fax: (309)663-5783
URL: National Affiliate–www.legion.org
Local. Affiliated With: American Legion.

2003 ■ American Legion, Hillside Post 863
5156 Madison St.
Hillside, IL 60162
Ph: (309)663-0361
Fax: (309)663-5783
URL: National Affiliate–www.legion.org
Local. Affiliated With: American Legion.

2004 ■ American Legion, Illinois Post 500
4722 Butterfield Rd.
Hillside, IL 60162
Ph: (309)663-0361
Fax: (309)663-5783
URL: National Affiliate–www.legion.org
Contact: John W. Sullivan, Contact
Local. Affiliated With: American Legion.

2005 ■ Construction Safety Council (CSC)
4100 Madison St.
Hillside, IL 60162
Ph: (708)544-2082
Fax: (708)544-2371
Free: (800)552-7744
E-mail: csc@buildsafe.org
URL: http://buildsafe.org
Contact: Thomas A. Broderick, Exec.Dir.
Founded: 1989. **Members:** 800. **Membership Dues:** individual, $150 (annual). **Staff:** 10. **Regional**. Promotes safe working conditions in the construction workplace. Conducts education and training programs. **Libraries: Type:** open to the public. **Holdings:** articles, books, periodicals, video recordings. **Subjects:** safety, health. **Formerly:** CSCI. **Publications:** *Construction Safety News*, quarterly. Newsletter. **Price:** $50.00/year. **Circulation:** 10,000 • *Executive Update*, monthly. Newsletter. **Conventions/Meetings:** annual Construction Safety Conference (exhibits) • periodic Construction Safety Related Courses and Seminars.

2006 ■ Hillside Coin Club (HCC)
PO Box 750
Hillside, IL 60162-0750
E-mail: hcccoin@aol.com
URL: http://www.worksandwords.com/hcc
Contact: Merrill Drake, Pres.
Local. Affiliated With: American Numismatic Association.

2007 ■ Sheet Metal Workers' Union Local 73, AFL-CIO
c/o Stanley F. Karczynski, Pres./Business Mgr.
4550 W Roosevelt Rd.
Hillside, IL 60162
Ph: (708)449-0073
Fax: (708)449-7337
E-mail: unionoffice@smw73.org
URL: http://www.smw73.org
Contact: Stanley F. Karczynski, Pres./Business Mgr.
Members: 6,135. **Local. Affiliated With:** Sheet Metal Workers' International Association.

Hinckley

2008 ■ American Legion, Wade Post 598
PO Box 230
Hinckley, IL 60520
Ph: (309)663-0361
Fax: (309)663-5783
URL: National Affiliate–www.legion.org
Local. Affiliated With: American Legion.

2009 ■ Chicago Regional Search and Rescue
c/o Brian Kilpatrick, Pres.
15607 Phillips Rd.
Hinckley, IL 60520
Ph: (847)799-1010
E-mail: ardaillinois@comcast.net
URL: http://www.crsardogs.com
Contact: Brian Kilpatrick, Pres.
Local. Affiliated With: American Rescue Dog Association.

2010 ■ Windy City Soaring Association
12637 US Rte. 30 W
Hinckley, IL 60520
Ph: (815)286-7200
E-mail: makerley@mindspring.com
Contact: Mark Akerley, Pres.
Local. Affiliated With: Soaring Society of America.

Hindsboro

2011 ■ American Legion, Illinois Post 194
c/o Ray Freeman
1777 E, RR 133
Hindsboro, IL 61930
Ph: (309)663-0361
Fax: (309)663-5783
URL: National Affiliate–www.legion.org
Contact: Ray Freeman, Contact
Local. Affiliated With: American Legion.

Hinsdale

2012 ■ American Legion, Hinsdale Post 250
PO Box 92
Hinsdale, IL 60522
Ph: (708)654-4979
Fax: (309)663-5783
URL: National Affiliate–www.legion.org
Local. Affiliated With: American Legion.

2013 ■ American Wine Society - Suburban Cook County
c/o Theodore J. Schulze, Chm.
919 S Quincy
Hinsdale, IL 60521
Ph: (630)323-4301
URL: National Affiliate–www.americanwinesociety.org
Contact: Theodore J. Schulze, Chm.
Local. Affiliated With: American Wine Society.

2014 ■ Assistance League of Chicagoland West
930 York Rd., Ste.12
Hinsdale, IL 60521
Ph: (630)321-2529
E-mail: alcw60@northstarnet.org
URL: http://www.assistance-league.org
Local. Affiliated With: Assistance League.

2015 ■ Christians Golfers' Association - Hinsdale
c/o Ed Vesely, Pres.
930 N York Rd., Ste.220
Hinsdale, IL 60521
Ph: (630)325-6477
URL: National Affiliate–www.christiangolfer.org
Contact: Ed Vesely, Pres.
Local.

2016 ■ Hinsdale Central - Young Life
18 E 4th St.
Hinsdale, IL 60521
Ph: (630)325-5212
URL: http://hinsdalecentral.younglife.org
Local.

2017 ■ Hinsdale Chamber of Commerce (HCC)
22 E 1st St.
Hinsdale, IL 60521
Ph: (630)323-3952
Fax: (630)323-3953
E-mail: hinsdalechamber@earthlink.net
URL: http://www.hinsdalechamber.com
Contact: Jim Slonoff, Pres.
Founded: 1925. **Members:** 260. **Staff:** 1. **Budget:** $100,000. **State Groups:** 2. **Local.** Promotes business and community development in Hinsdale, IL. Holds annual Fine Arts Fair, Farmers' Market, and other social events. Sponsors Christmas walk, annual garage, Halloween Parade, sidewalk sales. Operates welcome service. **Publications:** *Guide Book*, annual • *Hinsdale Community Directory*, annual • Newsletter, monthly. **Conventions/Meetings:** monthly luncheon.

2018 ■ Hinsdale South - Young Life
18 E 4th St.
Hinsdale, IL 60521
Ph: (630)325-5212
URL: http://hinsdalesouth.younglife.org
Local.

2019 ■ Hinsdale WyldLife
18 E 4th St.
Hinsdale, IL 60521
Ph: (630)325-5212
E-mail: jrooney@ylchicago.com
URL: http://wl.younglife.org
Contact: Justin Rooney, Contact
Local. Represents the interests of individuals committed to impacting kids' lives and preparing them for the future. Helps young people develop their skills, assets and attitudes to reach their full God-given potential. Reaches suburban, urban, multicultural and disabled kids and teenage mothers. **Affiliated With:** Young Life.

2020 ■ Illinois State Racquetball Association
464 Old Surrey
Hinsdale, IL 60521
Ph: (630)954-3135 (630)325-6410
E-mail: auntlollyd@aol.com
URL: http://www.illinoisracquetball.com
Contact: Laurel Davis, Contact
State. Affiliated With: United States Racquetball Association.

2021 ■ Life Services Network of Illinois (LSN)
c/o Mr. Dennis R. Bozzi, Pres.
911 N Elm St., Ste.228
Hinsdale, IL 60521-3634
Ph: (630)325-6170
Fax: (630)325-0749
E-mail: info@lsni.org
URL: http://www.lsni.org
Contact: Mr. Dennis R. Bozzi, Pres.
State. State affiliate of the American Association of Homes and Services for the Aging (AAHSA) and the Assisted Living Federation of America (ALFA). **Affiliated With:** Assisted Living Federation of America. **Publications:** Newsletter, weekly. **Conventions/Meetings:** annual conference.

2022 ■ Navy League of the United States, Chicago
c/o Camilla B. Ross
5502 S Madison St., No. 3
Hinsdale, IL 60521-5149
Ph: (630)325-1852
E-mail: camillab@juno.com
URL: National Affiliate–www.navyleague.org
Contact: Camilla B. Ross, Pres.
Local. Civilian organization that supports U.S. capability to keep the sea lanes open through a strong, viable Navy, Marine Corps, Coast Guard, and Merchant Marine. Seeks to awaken interest and cooperation of U.S. citizens in matters serving to aid, improve, and develop the efficiency of U.S. naval and maritime forces and equipment. **Affiliated With:** Navy League of the United States.

2023 ■ Resolve of Illinois Chapter
PO Box 56
Hinsdale, IL 60521
Ph: (773)743-1623
Free: (800)395-5522
E-mail: info@resolveofillinois.org
URL: http://www.resolveofillinois.org
Contact: Kari Skloot, Exec.Dir.
Founded: 1979. **Membership Dues:** consumer, $55 (annual) • professional, $150 (annual). **State. Affiliated With:** Resolve, The National Infertility Association. **Formerly:** (2005) Resolve of Illinois.

2024 ■ Timothy Christian - Young Life
18 E 4th St.
Hinsdale, IL 60521
Ph: (630)325-5212
URL: http://timothy.younglife.org
Local.

2025 ■ United Brotherhood of Carpenters and Joiners of America, Chicago Local Union No. 1185
930 N York Rd., Ste.202
Hinsdale, IL 60521
Ph: (630)325-4132
Fax: (630)325-8062
E-mail: unionfloor@aol.com
URL: http://www.chicagofloorcovering.com
Local. Affiliated With: United Brotherhood of Carpenters and Joiners of America.

2026 ■ United Brotherhood of Carpenters and Joiners of America, Chicago Local Union No. 9074
930 N York Rd., Ste.202
Hinsdale, IL 60521
Ph: (630)325-1584
Fax: (630)325-6052
E-mail: lathers74l@ubchinsdale.com
URL: National Affiliate–www.carpenters.org/home.html
Local. Affiliated With: United Brotherhood of Carpenters and Joiners of America.

2027 ■ Western Lights Chorus of Sweet Adelines International
Seventh Day Adventist Church Hall
201 N Oak St.
Hinsdale, IL 60521-3830
Ph: (630)553-1736
E-mail: westernlightschorus@hotmail.com
URL: http://www.westernlightschorus.com
Contact: Vernell Wyeth, Contact
Local. Advances the musical art form of barbershop harmony through education and performances. Provides education, training and coaching in the development of women's four-part barbershop harmony. **Affiliated With:** Sweet Adelines International.

2028 ■ York and Willowbrook - Young Life
18 E 4th St.
Hinsdale, IL 60521
Ph: (630)325-5212 (847)691-9740
E-mail: lgorter@ylchicago.com
URL: http://york.younglife.org
Contact: Lucretia Gorter, Contact
Local. Represents the interests of individuals committed to impacting kids' lives and preparing them for the future. Helps young people develop their skills, assets and attitudes to reach their full God-given

potential. Reaches suburban, urban, multicultural and disabled kids and teenage mothers. **Affiliated With:** Young Life.

2029 ■ York - Young Life
18 E 4th St.
Hinsdale, IL 60521
Ph: (630)325-5212
URL: http://york.younglife.org
Local.

2030 ■ Young Life Eastern DuPage
18 E 4th St.
Hinsdale, IL 60521
Ph: (630)325-5212
Fax: (630)325-5282
URL: http://easterndupage.younglife.org
Local.

Hodgkins

2031 ■ American Legion, Electro-Motive-Diesel Post 992
c/o Ollen Patrick
6801 S Lagrange Rd., Unit E20
Hodgkins, IL 60525
Ph: (312)586-4408
Fax: (309)663-5783
URL: National Affiliate–www.legion.org
Contact: Ollen Patrick, Contact
Local. Affiliated With: American Legion.

Hoffman Estates

2032 ■ Bereaved Parents of the USA, Woodfield Chapter
c/o Jan Kendra
1225 W Dovington Dr.
Hoffman Estates, IL 60194
Ph: (847)882-4727
E-mail: bereavedparents@surfersnet.com
URL: National Affiliate–www.bereavedparentsusa.org
Contact: Jan Kendra, Contact
Local.

2033 ■ Coalition on Abortion/Breast Cancer
c/o Karen Malec
PO Box 957133
Hoffman Estates, IL 60195
Ph: (847)421-4000
Free: (877)803-0102
E-mail: response@abortionbreastcancer.com
URL: http://abortionbreastcancer.com
Contact: Karen Malec, Pres.
Local. Seeks to protect the health and save the lives of women by educating and providing information on abortion as a risk factor for breast cancer. Distributes brochures; provides speakers; issues press releases; circulates an internet newsletter; and acts as a clearinghouse by maintaining a website exploring the research, women's legal rights and public policy. Maintains an extensive library consisting of epidemiological, biological and experimental research.

2034 ■ Far Northwest Suburban United Way
2200 W Higgins, Ste.135
Hoffman Estates, IL 60195
Ph: (847)884-8186
E-mail: farnorthwest@uw-mc.org
URL: http://www.farnwuw.org
Contact: Jennifer Orban, CPO
Local. Affiliated With: United Way of America.

2035 ■ Hoffman Estates Chamber of Commerce
2200 W Higgins Rd., Ste.201
Hoffman Estates, IL 60195-2400
Ph: (847)781-9100
Fax: (847)781-9172
E-mail: info@hechamber.com
URL: http://www.hechamber.com
Contact: Ms. Jill Blodgett, Exec.Dir.
Founded: 1990. **Members:** 350. **Membership Dues:** business (based on number of employees), $210-$605 (annual). **Staff:** 3. **Local.** Promotes business and community development in Hoffman Estates, IL area. **Awards: Frequency:** annual. **Type:** scholarship. **Recipient:** for academic performance and community service. **Publications:** *Community Guide*, annual. Directory. Features lists of business and highlights of the Hoffman Estates community. **Circulation:** 16,000 • Newsletter, monthly.

2036 ■ Institute of Internal Auditors, Northwest Metro Chicago Chapter
c/o Michael T. Ryan
Career Educ. Corp.
2895 Greenspoint Pkwy., Ste.600
Hoffman Estates, IL 60195
Ph: (847)585-3803
E-mail: cec404mtr@yahoo.com
URL: National Affiliate–www.theiia.org
Contact: Michael T. Ryan, Pres.
Membership Dues: regular, $115 (annual) • educator, $65 (annual) • student, retired, $30 (annual) • life, $2,100 • sustainer (government auditors only), $50 (annual) • organization ($65 per staff member over 5; $50 per staff member over 100), $425-$6,600 (annual). **Local.** Serves as an advocate for the internal audit profession. Provides certification, education, research, and technological guidance for the profession. **Affiliated With:** Institute of Internal Auditors.

2037 ■ John Muir PTA
c/o John Muir School
1973 Kensington Ln.
Hoffman Estates, IL 60195
Ph: (847)885-6778
E-mail: john.muir.pta@ptamail.com
URL: http://familyeducation.com/IL/JohnMuirPTA
Contact: Sheryl Walter, Pres.
Local. Parents, teachers, students, and others interested in uniting the forces of home, school, and community. Promotes the welfare of children and youth.

2038 ■ Lincoln Prairie PTSA
c/o Lincoln Prairie School
500 W Hillcrest Blvd.
Hoffman Estates, IL 60195
Ph: (847)885-6766 (847)882-7429
E-mail: vdbleek5@comcast.net
URL: http://web54.sd54.k12.il.us/schools/Lincoln/ptsa
Contact: Lisa Van Der Bleek, Pres.
Local. Parents, teachers, students, and others interested in uniting the forces of home, school, and community. Promotes the welfare of children and youth.

2039 ■ National Recreation and Park Association - Central Region
c/o Walter C. Johnson, CAE, Regional Dir.
650 W. Higgins Rd.
Hoffman Estates, IL 60195-3402
Ph: (847)843-7529
Fax: (847)843-3058
E-mail: aqnrpa@aol.com
URL: National Affiliate–www.nrpa.org
Affiliated With: National Recreation and Park Association.

Homer

2040 ■ American Legion, Homer Post 290
PO Box 134
Homer, IL 61849
Ph: (309)663-0361
Fax: (309)663-5783
URL: National Affiliate–www.legion.org
Local. Affiliated With: American Legion.

2041 ■ Southeastern Illinois Beagle Club
c/o Wm. R. Edwards
202 N Waverly St.
Homer, IL 61849-1033
URL: National Affiliate–www.akc.org
Contact: Wm. R. Edwards, Contact
Local. Affiliated With: American Kennel Club.

Homer Glen

2042 ■ Club Corvo
14107 W Dublin Dr.
Homer Glen, IL 60441
Ph: (630)257-2954
E-mail: dp6001@earthlink.net
URL: National Affiliate–www.bocce.com
Local. Affiliated With: United States Bocce Federation.

Homewood

2043 ■ American Legion, East Hazel Crest Post 1139
PO Box 1256
Homewood, IL 60430
Ph: (309)663-0361
Fax: (309)663-5783
URL: National Affiliate–www.legion.org
Local. Affiliated With: American Legion.

2044 ■ American Legion, Homewood Post 483
PO Box 1571
Homewood, IL 60430
Ph: (708)799-7755
Fax: (309)663-5783
URL: National Affiliate–www.legion.org
Local. Affiliated With: American Legion.

2045 ■ ARC of Illinois
18207-A-Dixie Hwy.
Homewood, IL 60430-1739
Ph: (708)206-1930
Fax: (708)206-1171
Free: (800)588-7002
E-mail: tony@thearcofil.org
URL: http://www.thearcofil.org
Contact: Mr. Anthony Paulauski, Exec.Dir.
Founded: 1949. **Members:** 3,000. **Membership Dues:** $25 (annual). **Budget:** $100,000. **Local Groups:** 75. **Languages:** English, Spanish. **State.** Parents, professionals, and other interested individuals. Promotes services, research, public understanding, and legislation for persons with developmental disabilities and their families. **Formerly:** Association for Retarded Citizens of Illinois. **Publications:** *The ARC of Illinois Today*, semimonthly. Newsletter. **Price:** included in membership dues via e-mail. **Circulation:** 2,000. **Advertising:** accepted. Alternate Formats: online. **Conventions/Meetings:** annual convention (exhibits).

2046 ■ Citywide Drag Racing Association
c/o Troy Donahue
PO Box 2493
Homewood, IL 60430-7493
URL: http://www.cdracing.org
Local.

2047 ■ Girl Scouts of South Cook County (SCCGS)
1005 W 175th St.
Homewood, IL 60430-4603
Ph: (708)957-8100
Fax: (708)957-8506
E-mail: gsinfo@girlscouts-scc.org
URL: http://www.girlscouts-scc.org
Contact: Carol Kocan, Communication Dir.
Founded: 1948. **Members:** 12,000. **Membership Dues:** regular, $7 (annual). **Staff:** 27. **Budget:** $1,400,000. **Local Groups:** 750. **Local.** Girls ages 5 to 17 and adult volunteers. Provides an informal, educational program for girls in the south suburbs of Chicago. Sponsors training workshops for leaders. **Affiliated With:** Girl Scouts of the U.S.A. **Publications:** *Signpost*, 4-5/year. **Conventions/Meetings:** annual meeting - always 3rd Thursday of May.

2048 ■ Homewood Area Chamber of Commerce (HACC)
18300 Dixie Hwy.
Charter One Bank Bldg.
Homewood, IL 60430
Ph: (708)206-3384
Fax: (708)206-3605
E-mail: kyle@homewoodareachamber.com
URL: http://www.homewoodareachamber.com
Contact: Mr. Kyle Storjohann IOM, Administrator
Founded: 1962. **Members:** 190. **Staff:** 1. **Local.** Promotes business and community development in the area. Sponsors Fine Art Fair; conducts charitable activities. **Publications:** Newsletter, monthly.

Hoopeston

2049 ■ American Legion, Ira Owen Kreager Post 384
PO Box 423
Hoopeston, IL 60942
Ph: (217)283-6312
Fax: (309)663-5783
URL: National Affiliate–www.legion.org
Local. Affiliated With: American Legion.

2050 ■ Women Making a Difference
c/o Kathy Noland
728 S. Market St.
Hoopeston, IL 60942-1848
Ph: (217)283-9730 (217)283-6429
Fax: (217)283-9730
E-mail: kathyn7@copper.net
Contact: Kathy Noland, VP
Founded: 2001. **Members:** 49. **Membership Dues:** female, $25 (annual). **Local Groups:** 1. **Local. Awards:** WMD. **Type:** scholarship. **Recipient:** financial need 75%;grades 25%.

Hopedale

2051 ■ American Legion, Hopedale Post 1157
PO Box 173
Hopedale, IL 61747
Ph: (309)449-3247
Fax: (309)663-5783
URL: National Affiliate–www.legion.org
Local. Affiliated With: American Legion.

Hoyleton

2052 ■ American Legion, Claude Earl Post 887
PO Box 55
Hoyleton, IL 62803
Ph: (309)663-0361
Fax: (309)663-5783
URL: National Affiliate–www.legion.org
Local. Affiliated With: American Legion.

Huntley

2053 ■ American Legion, Huntley Post 673
11712 Coral St.
Huntley, IL 60142
Ph: (309)663-0361
Fax: (309)663-5783
URL: National Affiliate–www.legion.org
Local. Affiliated With: American Legion.

2054 ■ Huntley Area Chamber of Commerce and Industry
PO Box 157
Huntley, IL 60142
Ph: (847)669-0166
Fax: (847)669-0170
E-mail: info@huntleychamber.org
URL: http://www.huntleychamber.org
Contact: Rita Slawek, Exec.Dir.
Founded: 1992. **Members:** 295. **Membership Dues:** regular, $250 (annual) • executive club, $775 (annual) • not-for-profit, $150 (annual). **Staff:** 2. **Local.** Promotes business and community development in Huntley, IL area. **Computer Services:** Mailing lists, of members. **Telecommunication Services:** electronic mail, rita@huntleychamber.org. **Committees:** Community Guide; Home & Business Expo; Miss Huntley. **Publications:** *The Chamber Review*, monthly. Newsletter. **Price:** included in membership dues. **Circulation:** 295. **Advertising:** accepted • *Community Guide*, annual. Directory. **Advertising:** accepted.

2055 ■ McHenry County Dental Society
c/o Dr. Kevin M. Anderson, Pres.
PO Box 156
Huntley, IL 60142-0156
Ph: (847)669-5421
E-mail: hda@mc.net
URL: http://www.isds.org
Contact: Dr. Kevin M. Anderson, Pres.
Local. Represents the interests of dentists committed to the public's oral health, ethics and professional development. Encourages the improvement of the public's oral health and promotes the art and science of dentistry. **Affiliated With:** American Dental Association; Illinois State Dental Society.

2056 ■ United States Power Squadrons - District 20
c/o William Myers, Commander
11903 Ludbury Ridge
Huntley, IL 60142
Ph: (847)961-6888
E-mail: myerswilliamm@sbcglobal.net
URL: http://www.uspsd20.org
Contact: William Myers, Commander
Regional. Affiliated With: United States Power Squadrons.

Hurst

2057 ■ American Legion, Noel Robison Post 664
PO Box 515
Hurst, IL 62949
Ph: (618)987-2684
Fax: (309)663-5783
URL: National Affiliate–www.legion.org
Local. Affiliated With: American Legion.

Illiopolis

2058 ■ American Legion, Illiopolis Post 508
402 5th St.
Illiopolis, IL 62539
Ph: (309)663-0361
Fax: (309)663-5783
URL: National Affiliate–www.legion.org
Local. Affiliated With: American Legion.

Ina

2059 ■ Great Rivers Athletic Conference
468 N Ken Gray Pkwy.
Rend Lake Coll.
Ina, IL 62846
Ph: (618)437-5321
E-mail: kelley@rlc.cc.il.us
URL: http://www.rlc.cc.il.us
Contact: Mr. Neil Fiala, Pres.
Founded: 1982. **Members:** 8. **Regional.** Community college athletic programs in southern Illinois competing in 5 sports. **Affiliated With:** National Junior College Athletic Association. **Formerly:** Southern Illinois College Conference. **Conventions/Meetings:** quarterly meeting.

2060 ■ Phi Theta Kappa, Rho Xi Chapter - Rend Lake College
c/o Cheri Rushing
468 N Ken Gray Pkwy.
Ina, IL 62846
Ph: (618)437-5321
E-mail: rushing@rlc.cc.il.us
URL: http://www.ptk.org/directories/chapters/IL/191-1.htm
Contact: Cheri Rushing, Advisor
Local.

Indian Head Park

2061 ■ Northern Illinois Chapter of the Military Vehicle Association
c/o John Ayers, Pres.
6218 S Wolf Rd.
Indian Head Park, IL 60525-3746
Ph: (708)246-3497
E-mail: jayres@afmetals.com
URL: http://www.nicmvpa.com
Contact: John Ayers, Pres.
Local. Affiliated With: Military Vehicle Preservation Association.

Ingleside

2062 ■ Friends of Volo Bog
28478 W Brandenburg Rd.
Ingleside, IL 60041
Ph: (815)344-1294
Contact: Daniel Haller, Chm.
Local.

2063 ■ Great Pyrenees Rescue of Greater Chicago
24320 Blackcherry Ln.
Ingleside, IL 60041-9553
Ph: (847)668-7297
E-mail: whitegentlegiants@yahoo.com
URL: http://www.gpcgc.org/rescue.htm
Founded: 1999. **Members:** 100. **Local Groups:** 1. **Local.** Volunteers placing orphaned or displaced Great Pyrenees in responsible loving homes, and educating the public about the Great Pyrenees breed. **Affiliated With:** Great Pyrenees Club of America.

2064 ■ NAIFA-Chicago Region
c/o Kris Nobilio, Exec.
35478 Sheridan Dr.
Ingleside, IL 60041
Ph: (847)587-0282
Fax: (847)587-2248
E-mail: naifachicago@comcast.net
URL: National Affiliate–naifa.org
Contact: Kris Nobilio, Exec.
Local. Represents the interests of insurance and financial advisors. Advocates for a positive legislative and regulatory environment. Enhances business and professional skills of members. **Affiliated With:** National Association of Insurance and Financial Advisors.

Ipava

2065 ■ American Legion, Illinois Post 17
c/o Harold C. Hoopes
PO Box 110
Ipava, IL 61441
Ph: (309)753-8666
Fax: (309)663-5783
URL: National Affiliate–www.legion.org
Contact: Harold C. Hoopes, Contact
Local. Affiliated With: American Legion.

Irving

2066 ■ National Christmas Tree Association, Mid America
c/o Hazel Redman
15073 Seven Sisters Ave.
Irving, IL 62051
Ph: (217)533-4382
E-mail: bangus@ccipost.net
URL: National Affiliate–www.realchristmastrees.org
Contact: Hazel Redman, Contact
Local. Affiliated With: National Christmas Tree Association.

Itasca

2067 ■ Illinois Road and Transportation Builders Association
500 Park Blvd., Ste.1250
Itasca, IL 60143
Ph: (630)773-1220
Fax: (630)773-1231
E-mail: irtba@irtba.org
URL: http://www.irtba.org
Contact: William G. Grams, Exec.Dir.
Founded: 1938. **Members:** 300. **Staff:** 4. **Budget:** $250,000. **State.** Highway construction contractors and suppliers of goods and services. **Affiliated With:** American Road and Transportation Builders Association. **Publications:** *Contractor's Directory*, biennial. **Price:** $35.00 /year for nonmembers. **Circulation:** 600. **Advertising:** accepted • *Road Builder Magazine*, 3/year. **Circulation:** 750. **Advertising:** accepted. **Conventions/Meetings:** annual convention - always February or March.

2068 ■ National Safety Council, Chicago Chapter
1121 Spring Lake Dr., Ste.100
Itasca, IL 60143-3201
Ph: (630)775-2213
Fax: (630)775-2136
Free: (800)621-2855
E-mail: chicago@nsc.org
URL: National Affiliate–www.nsc.org
Local. Affiliated With: National Safety Council.

2069 ■ Society for Mitral Valve Prolapse Syndrome
c/o Jim Durante
PO Box 431
Itasca, IL 60143-0431
Ph: (630)250-9327
Fax: (630)773-0478
E-mail: bonnie0107@aol.com
URL: http://www.mitralvalveprolapse.com
Contact: Bonnie Durante, VP
Founded: 1991. **Members:** 500. **Staff:** 3. **Local. Publications:** *And the Beat Goes On*, bimonthly. Newsletter. **Price:** $14.00/year. **Conventions/Meetings:** annual seminar (exhibits) - September • monthly support group meeting.

2070 ■ Underground Contractors Association (UCA)
500 Park Blvd., Ste.154C
Itasca, IL 60143
Ph: (630)467-1919
Fax: (630)773-4873
E-mail: dbenjamin@uca.org
URL: http://www.uca.org
Contact: David J. Benjamin, Exec.Dir.
Founded: 1956. **State.** Association of self-employed contractors.

2071 ■ Village of Itasca Chamber of Commerce
550 W Irving Park Rd.
Itasca, IL 60143
Ph: (630)773-0835
Fax: (630)773-2505
URL: http://www.itasca.com
Contact: Claudia Gruber, Contact
Local.

Jacksonville

2072 ■ ACF Central Illinois Culinary Arts Association
c/o Charles Rivers, Pres.
1006 E Independence
Jacksonville, IL 62650
Ph: (217)245-2134
E-mail: cechef@csj.net
URL: National Affiliate–www.acfchefs.org
Contact: Charles Rivers CEC, Pres.
Local. Promotes the culinary profession. Provides on-going educational training and networking for members. Provides opportunities for competition, professional recognition and access to educational forums with other culinarians at local, regional, national and international events. **Affiliated With:** American Culinary Federation.

2073 ■ American Legion, Illinois Post 279
c/o Edward F. Brennan
903 W Superior Ave.
Jacksonville, IL 62650
Ph: (217)245-1827
Fax: (309)663-5783
URL: National Affiliate–www.legion.org
Contact: Edward F. Brennan, Contact
Local. Affiliated With: American Legion.

2074 ■ American Legion, Moss-Walton Post 953
432 S West St.
Jacksonville, IL 62650
Ph: (217)243-8500
Fax: (309)663-5783
URL: National Affiliate–www.legion.org
Local. Affiliated With: American Legion.

2075 ■ American Rabbit Breeders Association, Illinois New Zealand Rabbit Breeders Specialty Club
c/o Roger Walker
1960 Arcadia Rd.
Jacksonville, IL 62650
Ph: (217)245-7851
URL: http://www.nordickrabbits.com/specialt.htm
Contact: Roger Walker, Contact
Local. Affiliated With: American Rabbit Breeders Association.

2076 ■ Bereaved Parents of the USA, Jacksonville Chapter
c/o Betty M. Still
1337 S East St.
Jacksonville, IL 62650
Ph: (217)243-6947
URL: National Affiliate–www.bereavedparentsusa.org
Contact: Betty M. Still, Contact
Local.

2077 ■ Big Brothers Big Sisters of West Central Illinois
220 E Morgan
Jacksonville, IL 62650
Ph: (217)243-3821
Fax: (217)245-6499
E-mail: bganz@bbbsmorgan.org
URL: http://www.bbbsmorgan.org
Contact: Brian J. Ganz, Exec.Dir.
Regional. Matches community volunteers to serve as positive role models and mentors in one-to-one relationships with youth providing guidance, professional supervision and support to parents, volunteers and youth. **Affiliated With:** Big Brothers Big Sisters of America.

2078 ■ Illinois Association for Health, Physical Education, Recreation, and Dance (IAHPERD)
1713 SW St.
Jacksonville, IL 62650
Ph: (217)245-6413
Fax: (217)245-5261
E-mail: iahperd@iahperd.org
URL: http://iahperd.org
Contact: Beth Verner, Pres.
Founded: 1931. **Members:** 3,500. **Staff:** 1. **State.** Physical education teachers, health educators, and individuals involved in recreation and dance. Promotes, supports, and encourages personal development through programs in health, physical education, and recreation. Holds board meetings. **Affiliated With:** American Alliance for Health, Physical Education, Recreation and Dance. **Publications:** *Governmental Action News*, quarterly. Newsletter • *Illinois Journal for Health, Physical Education, Recreation, and Dance*, semiannual • *On the Move*, 3/year. Newsletter. **Conventions/Meetings:** annual conference (exhibits) - always November.

2079 ■ Jacksonville Area Association of Realtors
PO Box 969
Jacksonville, IL 62651
Ph: (217)243-2611
Fax: (217)243-2611
E-mail: jaar1935@netzero.com
URL: National Affiliate–www.realtor.org
Contact: Amy Little, Exec. Officer
Local. Strives to develop real estate business practices. Advocates the right to own, use and transfer real property. Provides a facility for professional development, research and exchange of information among members and to the general public. **Affiliated With:** National Association of Realtors.

2080 ■ Jacksonville Area Chamber of Commerce
c/o Ginny Fanning, Pres.
155 W Morton
Jacksonville, IL 62650
Ph: (217)245-2174
Fax: (217)245-0661
E-mail: chamber@jacksonvilleareachamber.org
URL: http://www.jacksonvilleareachamber.org
Contact: Ginny Fanning, Pres.
Founded: 1888. **Members:** 584. **Membership Dues:** regular, professional and business, $190 (annual) • civic and retiree, $95 (annual). **Staff:** 3. **Budget:** $212,000. **Local.** Promotes business and community development in the Jacksonville, IL area. **Awards:** Business of the Year 25 or More Employees. **Frequency:** annual. **Type:** trophy • Business of the Year Under 25 Employees. **Frequency:** annual. **Type:** trophy • Not-For-Profit Organization of the Year. **Frequency:** annual. **Type:** trophy. **Computer Services:** database • mailing lists. **Divisions:** Agri-Industry; Business; Education; Government; Health and Community Services; Internal Affairs; Membership Services; Quality of Life. **Publications:** *Chamber Review*, monthly. Newsletter. Contains information on current chamber issues and activities. **Price:** included in membership dues. **Circulation:** 850. **Advertising:** accepted. **Conventions/Meetings:** annual conference.

2081 ■ Jacksonville Main Street
PO Box 152
Jacksonville, IL 62651-0152
Ph: (217)245-6884
Fax: (217)479-4002
E-mail: info@jacksonvillemainstreet.com
URL: http://www.jacksonvillemainstreet.com
Contact: Judy Tighe, Program Manager
Local.

2082 ■ Kiwanis Club of Jacksonville, Illinois
c/o Roger Deem, Pres.
134 Prospect
Jacksonville, IL 62650
Ph: (217)245-9188
E-mail: admiraldeem@mchsi.com
URL: http://www.jaxkiwanis.com
Contact: Roger Deem, Pres.
Local.

2083 ■ Land of Lincoln Thunderbirds
1020 W Walnut St.
Jacksonville, IL 62650
Ph: (217)245-5468
URL: National Affiliate–www.vintagethunderbirdclub.org
Local. Affiliated With: Vintage Thunderbird Club International.

2084 ■ National Federation of the Blind of Illinois
c/o Catherine Lois Montgomery, Pres.
3527-12th Ave.
Jacksonville, IL 62650-2266
Ph: (309)762-6324
E-mail: lmm3527@aol.com
URL: http://www.nfbofillinois.org
Contact: Catherine Lois Montgomery, Pres.
State. Works to help blind persons achieve self-confidence and self-respect. Acts as a vehicle for collective self-expression by the blind. Provides education, information and referral services, scholarships, literature, and publications about blindness.

2085 ■ Prairieland United Way
PO Box 244
Jacksonville, IL 62651-0244
Ph: (217)245-4557
URL: National Affiliate–national.unitedway.org
Local. **Affiliated With:** United Way of America.

2086 ■ Psi Chi, National Honor Society in Psychology - Illinois College
c/o Dept. of Psychology
18 C Baxter Hall
1101 W Coll. Ave.
Jacksonville, IL 62650-2299
Ph: (217)245-3408
Fax: (217)245-3034
E-mail: relling@hilltop.ic.edu
URL: http://www.psichi.org/chapters/info.asp?chapter_id=910
Contact: Elizabeth Rellinger PhD, Advisor
Local.

2087 ■ Psi Chi, National Honor Society in Psychology - MacMurray College
c/o Dept. of Psychology
447 E Coll. Ave.
Jacksonville, IL 62650-2590
Ph: (217)479-7106
Fax: (217)479-7097
E-mail: chris.schmidt@mac.edu
URL: http://www.psichi.org/chapters/info.asp?chapter_id=149
Contact: Chris Schmidt PhD, Advisor
Local.

Jerseyville

2088 ■ American Legion, Worthey Post 492
Rte. 4, Box 338
Jerseyville, IL 62052
Ph: (618)498-5757
Fax: (309)663-5783
URL: National Affiliate–www.legion.org
Local. **Affiliated With:** American Legion.

2089 ■ Healthcare Financial Management Association, Southern Illinois Chapter
c/o Timothy A. Bartels, Pres.-Elect
Jersey Community Hosp.
400 Maple Summit Rd.
Jerseyville, IL 62052
Ph: (618)498-8320
Fax: (618)498-8492
URL: http://www.sihfma.org
Contact: Timothy A. Bartels, Pres.-Elect
Local. Provides education, analysis and guidance to healthcare finance professionals. Helps members and other individuals in advancing the financial management of health care and in improving the business performance of organizations serving the healthcare field. **Affiliated With:** Healthcare Financial Management Association.

2090 ■ Jersey County Business Association
209 N State St.
Jerseyville, IL 62052-1755
Ph: (618)639-5222
E-mail: ann@jcba-il.us
URL: http://www.jerseycounty.org
Contact: Ann Rice, Admin.Asst.
Founded: 1955. **Membership Dues:** $175 (annual). **Local**. Promotes business and community development in Jersey County, IL. Sponsors golf day, car show, and craft shows. **Formerly:** (2005) Jersey County Chamber of Commerce. **Publications:** *The Business News*, monthly. Newsletter.

2091 ■ Post Oak Flats Resource Conservation and Development Council
RR1, Box 10
Jerseyville, IL 62052
Ph: (618)548-3654
Fax: (618)548-2341
URL: National Affiliate–www.rcdnet.org
Contact: John Schuler, Coor.
Local. **Affiliated With:** National Association of Resource Conservation and Development Councils.

2092 ■ Southern Illinois Healthcare Materials Management Association
c/o Sandy Long, Materials Mgr.
Jersey Community Hosp.
400 Maple Summit Rd.
Jerseyville, IL 62052
Ph: (618)498-8334
Fax: (618)498-8334
E-mail: slong@jch.org
URL: National Affiliate–www.ahrmm.org
Contact: Sandy Long, Materials Mgr.
Local. Represents purchasing agents and materials managers active in the field of purchasing, inventory, distribution and materials management as performed in hospitals, related patient care institutions and government and voluntary health organizations. Provides networking and educational opportunities for members. Develops new business ventures that ensure the financial stability of members. **Affiliated With:** Association for Healthcare Resource and Materials Management.

Johnsonville

2093 ■ Bereaved Parents of the USA, Wayne County Illinois
c/o Hollie Kelly, Chapter Leader
RR1 Box 23 A
Johnsonville, IL 62850
E-mail: holliernfnp1@hotmail.com
URL: National Affiliate–www.bereavedparentsusa.org
Contact: Hollie Kelly, Chapter Leader
Local.

Johnston City

2094 ■ American Legion, Illinois Post 563
c/o Arlie B. Lawrence
1709 Follis Ave.
Johnston City, IL 62951
Ph: (309)663-0361
Fax: (309)663-5783
URL: National Affiliate–www.legion.org
Contact: Arlie B. Lawrence, Contact
Local. **Affiliated With:** American Legion.

Joliet

2095 ■ American Association for Women in Community Colleges, Region V
c/o Dr. Terry Irby, Dir.
Joliet Junior Coll.
Adult Educ. and Family Services
214 N Ottawa St.
Joliet, IL 60436
Ph: (815)280-1317
E-mail: tirby@jjc.edu
URL: National Affiliate–www.aims.edu/aawcc
Contact: Dr. Terry Irby, Dir.
Regional. Fosters the development of comprehensive educational, career and life opportunities for all persons. Encourages and supports professional development and advancement of all women in community, junior and technical colleges. **Affiliated With:** American Association for Women in Community Colleges.

2096 ■ American Legion, Buffalo Soldier Memorial Post 241
15 S Raynor Ave.
Joliet, IL 60436
Ph: (309)663-0361
Fax: (309)663-5783
URL: National Affiliate–www.legion.org
Local. **Affiliated With:** American Legion.

2097 ■ American Legion, Harwood Post 5
705 S Larkin Ave.
Joliet, IL 60436
Ph: (815)725-4333
Fax: (309)663-5783
URL: National Affiliate–www.legion.org
Local. **Affiliated With:** American Legion.

2098 ■ American Legion, Joliet Post 1284
5 NW Circle Dr.
Joliet, IL 60433
Ph: (815)723-7513
Fax: (309)663-5783
URL: National Affiliate–www.legion.org
Local. **Affiliated With:** American Legion.

2099 ■ American Legion, St. Josephs Park Post 1080
2625 Ingalls Ave.
Joliet, IL 60435
Ph: (309)663-0361
Fax: (309)663-5783
URL: National Affiliate–www.legion.org
Local. **Affiliated With:** American Legion.

2100 ■ Associated Landscape Contractors of America, Joliet Junior College
c/o Lisa Perkins, Faculty Advisor
Ag Hort Dept.
1215 Houbolt Rd.
Joliet, IL 60431
Ph: (815)729-9020
Fax: (815)280-6650
URL: National Affiliate–www.alca.org
Contact: Lisa Perkins, Faculty Advisor
Local. **Affiliated With:** Professional Landcare Network.

2101 ■ Big Brothers Big Sisters of Will and Grundy Counties
2322 Plainfield Rd.
Joliet, IL 60435
Ph: (815)725-4324
Fax: (815)725-4489
E-mail: llas@bbbswillgrundy.org
URL: http://www.bbbswillgrundy.org
Contact: Ms. Lisa Morel Las, CEO
Founded: 1973. **Staff:** 8. **Nonmembership**. **Local**. Matches volunteers with children who would benefit from extra guidance, friendship, and role modeling. **Affiliated With:** Big Brothers Big Sisters of America.

2102 ■ Dress for Success Joliet
214 N Ottawa St.
Joliet, IL 60432
Ph: (815)280-1317
E-mail: joliet@dressforsuccess.org
URL: National Affiliate–www.dressforsuccess.org
Local.

2103 ■ Easter Seals-Joliet
212 Barney Dr.
Joliet, IL 60435-2830
Ph: (815)725-2194
Fax: (815)725-5150
URL: http://www.il-wg.easter-seals.org
Contact: Mary Beth Clausen, Chair
Local. Works to help individuals with disabilities and special needs, and their families. Conducts programs to assist people of all ages with disabilities. Provides outpatient medical rehabilitation services. Advocates for the passage of legislation to help people with dis-

abilities achieve independence, including the Americans with Disabilities Act (ADA). **Affiliated With:** Easter Seals.

2104 ■ Eastern Illinois Chapter National Electrical Contractors Association
1050 Essington Rd., No. B
Joliet, IL 60435-2841
Ph: (815)729-2288
Fax: (815)729-2280
E-mail: tconner@necaeil.com
URL: http://www.necaeil.com
Contact: Thomas L. Conner, Exec.VP
Founded: 1972. **Members:** 35. **Budget:** $400,000. **Local.** Represents contractors erecting, installing, repairing, servicing, and maintaining electric wiring, equipment, and appliances. **Affiliated With:** National Electrical Contractors Association. **Publications:** *NECA Chapter Report and Newsletter*, monthly. **Conventions/Meetings:** monthly board meeting • annual meeting • annual Summer Outing - meeting.

2105 ■ First Catholic Slovak Ladies Association - Joliet Senior Branch 053
2617 Crescenzo Rd.
Joliet, IL 60436-1052
Ph: (815)741-4996
URL: National Affiliate–www.fcsla.com
Local. Affiliated With: First Catholic Slovak Ladies Association.

2106 ■ Illinois Native Plant Society, Northeast Chapter
321 Marigold Pl.
Joliet, IL 60433
Ph: (815)724-1267
E-mail: fcatchpole@fpdwc.org
URL: http://www.ill-inps.org
Contact: Floyd Catchpole, Co-Pres.
Local. Affiliated With: Illinois Native Plant Society.

2107 ■ Illinois Polygraph Society
515 Woodruff Rd.
Joliet, IL 60432
Ph: (815)740-5361
E-mail: reedhar@isp.state.il.us
URL: National Affiliate–www.polygraph.org
Contact: Harry C. Reed, Contact
State. Represents individuals dedicated to providing a valid and reliable means to verify the truth and establish the highest standards of moral, ethical, and professional conduct in the polygraph field. Establishes standards of ethical practices, techniques, instrumentation, research, advanced training and continuing educational programs. Provides a forum for the presentation and exchange of information derived from such research, training and education. **Affiliated With:** American Polygraph Association.

2108 ■ Industrial Workers of the World - Joliet
PO Box 3658
Joliet, IL 60434
Ph: (815)483-8299
E-mail: joliet@iww.org
URL: National Affiliate–www.iww.org
Local. Affiliated With: Industrial Workers of the World.

2109 ■ International Association of Machinists and Aerospace Workers, District Lodge 55
113 Republic Ave.
Joliet, IL 60435-3279
Ph: (815)846-6458
Fax: (815)846-6459
Free: (800)273-5563
E-mail: dodonnelliam55@aol.com
Contact: Dan O'Donnell, Contact
Members: 8,000. **Local Groups:** 19. **Local. Affiliated With:** International Association of Machinists and Aerospace Workers.

2110 ■ Izaak Walton League of America, Walter Sherry Memorial Chapter
409 Oakview Ave.
Joliet, IL 60433-2027
Ph: (815)723-5065
URL: National Affiliate–www.iwla.org
Contact: Cindy Campbell, Pres.
Local. Works to educate the public to conserve, maintain, protect, and restore the soil, forest, water, and other natural resources of the U.S; promotes the enjoyment and wholesome utilization of these resources. **Affiliated With:** Izaak Walton League of America.

2111 ■ Joliet ALU
PO Box 2426
Joliet, IL 60434
Ph: (815)254-7900
Fax: (815)254-7339
URL: National Affiliate–www.naifa.org
Local. Represents the interest of insurance and financial advisors. Advocates for a positive legislative and regulatory environment. Enhances business and professional skills of members. **Affiliated With:** National Association of Insurance and Financial Advisors.

2112 ■ Joliet Area Theatre Organ Enthusiasts (JATOE)
PO Box 212
Joliet, IL 60434
Ph: (708)562-8538
E-mail: jpatak@comcast.net
URL: http://www.organman.com/jatoe
Contact: Jim Patak, Pres.
Local. Aims to restore, preserve and promote the theatre pipe organ and its music. Encourages the youth to learn the instrument. Operates a committee that gathers history and old music from silent film days and information on theatre organists, theaters and organ installations of the silent film era. **Affiliated With:** American Theatre Organ Society.

2113 ■ Joliet Region Chamber of Commerce and Industry
63 N Chicago St.
PO Box 752
Joliet, IL 60434-0752
Ph: (815)727-5371
Fax: (815)727-5374
E-mail: info@jolietchamber.com
URL: http://www.jolietchamber.com
Contact: Russ Slinkard, Pres./CEO
Founded: 1914. **Membership Dues:** business (based on number of employees), $225-$3,000 (annual) • government body (serving less than 50000 people), $350 (annual) • government body (serving more than 50000 people), $500 (annual) • grade school/high school, $350 (annual) • college/university, $500 (annual) • charitable/non-profit, $225 (annual). **Local.** Promotes business environment to enhance the quality of life in Joliet Region, IL. Serves as the voice in governmental and social affairs in the community. **Computer Services:** Information services, membership directory. **Telecommunication Services:** electronic mail, rslinkard@jolietchamber.com • electronic mail, mpaone@jolietchamber.com. **Councils:** Council for Working Women. **Programs:** Greeter. **Affiliated With:** U.S. Chamber of Commerce. **Publications:** *Vision*, monthly. Newsletter. **Circulation:** 2,000. **Advertising:** accepted.

2114 ■ Knights of Columbus, Council 4400
1813 E Cass St.
Joliet, IL 60432
Ph: (815)723-3827
E-mail: kc4400@yahoo.com
URL: http://www.kofc4400.com
Contact: Rev. John T. McGeean, Chaplain
Local. Affiliated With: Knights of Columbus. **Also Known As:** (2005) Knights of Columbus, Joliet.

2115 ■ National Hook-up of Black Women, Joliet Chapter
c/o Bettye Gavin, Pres.
PO Box 1084
Joliet, IL 60434
Ph: (815)724-0547
E-mail: bg7349@sbcglobal.net
URL: http://www.nhbwjoliet.com
Contact: Bettye Gavin, Pres.
Local. Affiliated With: National Hook-Up of Black Women.

2116 ■ National Technological Honor Society - Joliet Junior College - Illinois
1215 Houbolt Rd.
Joliet, IL 60431-8938
Ph: (815)729-9020
E-mail: president@jjc.edu
URL: http://www.jjc.edu
Contact: J. Ross, Pres.
Local.

2117 ■ Phi Theta Kappa, Alpha Lambda Phi Chapter - Joliet Junior College
c/o Patricia Shue, Advisor
1215 Houbolt Ave.
Joliet, IL 60431
Ph: (815)280-2519
E-mail: pshue@jjc.edu
URL: http://www.ptk.org/directories/chapters/IL/218-1.htm
Contact: Patricia Shue, Advisor
Local.

2118 ■ Psi Chi, National Honor Society in Psychology - University of St. Francis
c/o Dept. of Psychology
500 Wilcox St.
Joliet, IL 60435
Ph: (815)740-3594
Fax: (815)740-4285
E-mail: lzhou@stfrancis.edu
URL: National Affiliate–www.psichi.org
Local. Affiliated With: Psi Chi, National Honor Society in Psychology.

2119 ■ RSVP of Joliet Area
c/o Ellen Thomas, Dir.
203 N Ottawa St.
Joliet, IL 60432-4350
Ph: (815)723-3405
Fax: (815)723-3452
E-mail: srethomas@cc-doj.org
URL: http://www.seniorcorps.gov/about/programs/rsvp.asp
Contact: Ellen Thomas, Dir.
Local. Affiliated With: Retired and Senior Volunteer Program.

2120 ■ Three Rivers Association of Realtors
303 Springfield Ave.
Joliet, IL 60435
Ph: (815)744-4520
Fax: (815)744-7677
E-mail: realtorkeith5491@comcast.net
URL: http://www.trarealtors.net
Contact: Keith M. Alberico, Pres.
Local. Strives to develop real estate business practices. Advocates the right to own, use and transfer real property. Provides a facility for professional development, research and exchange of information among members and to the general public. **Affiliated With:** National Association of Realtors.

2121 ■ United Cerebral Palsy of Will County
311 S Reed St.
Joliet, IL 60436
Ph: (815)744-3500
Fax: (815)744-3504
E-mail: ucpwill@ucpwill.org
URL: http://www.ucpwill.org
Contact: Samuel Mancuso, Exec.Dir.
Local. Works to improve the quality of life of people with developmental disabilities. Provides support and

direct services to individuals and their families impacted by the challenges of developmental disabilities. **Affiliated With:** United Cerebral Palsy Associations. **Publications:** *Connections*. Newsletter. Contains information on the association and its members. Alternate Formats: online.

2122 ■ United Way of Will County
54 N Ottawa St., Ste.300
Joliet, IL 60432-4394
Ph: (815)723-2500
Fax: (815)723-2814
Free: (800)526-0844
E-mail: unitedwaywillcounty@yahoo.com
URL: http://www.unitedwaywillcounty.org
Contact: Michael D. Hennessy, Pres./CEO
Founded: 1935. **Local**. Supports human care agencies and their operations. Conducts fundraising activities. Volunteer Referral Program. **Affiliated With:** United Way of America.

2123 ■ Will County Center for Economic Development (CED)
116 N Chicago St., Ste.101
Joliet, IL 60432-4204
Ph: (815)774-6060
Fax: (815)723-6972
E-mail: john.greuling@willcountyced.com
URL: http://www.willcountyced.com
Contact: Mr. John E. Greuling, Pres./CEO
Founded: 1981. **Members:** 300. **Staff:** 15. **Budget:** $1,400,000. **State**. Provides information and assistance in locating or expanding a business in Will County. Offers services such as county development data, business incentive programs and government relations. **Divisions:** Will County Chamber of Commerce. **Formerly:** (2005) Will County Chamber of Commerce.

2124 ■ Will County Dental Society
c/o Sue Ciarlette, Exec.Sec.
3033 W Jefferson St., Ste.220
Joliet, IL 60435
Ph: (815)744-5676
E-mail: sciarlette@aol.com
URL: http://www.isds.org
Contact: Sue Ciarlette, Exec.Sec.
Local. Represents the interests of dentists committed to the public's oral health, ethics and professional development. Encourages the improvement of the public's oral health and promotes the art and science of dentistry. **Affiliated With:** American Dental Association; Illinois State Dental Society.

Jonesboro

2125 ■ Illinois Native Plant Society, Southern Chapter
521 N Main St.
Jonesboro, IL 62952
Ph: (618)833-8576
E-mail: scalloway@fs.fed.us
URL: http://www.ill-inps.org
Contact: Sarah Calloway, Pres.
Local. Affiliated With: Illinois Native Plant Society.

Kampsville

2126 ■ American Legion, Kampsville Post 1083
PO Box 134-185
Kampsville, IL 62053
Ph: (309)663-0361
Fax: (309)663-5783
URL: National Affiliate–www.legion.org
Local. Affiliated With: American Legion.

Kane

2127 ■ American Legion, Crawford Post 1038
PO Box 69
Kane, IL 62054
Ph: (309)663-0361
Fax: (309)663-5783
URL: National Affiliate–www.legion.org
Local. Affiliated With: American Legion.

Kankakee

2128 ■ American Legion, Kankakee Post 85
855 N Kennedy Dr.
Kankakee, IL 60901
Ph: (815)932-4413
Fax: (309)663-5783
URL: National Affiliate–www.legion.org
Local. Affiliated With: American Legion.

2129 ■ American Red Cross, Kankakee County Chapter
1432 S 4th Ave.
Kankakee, IL 60901
Ph: (815)933-2286
Fax: (815)933-2677
URL: http://www.kankakeeredcross.org
Local.

2130 ■ American Welding Society, J.A.K. Section
c/o John Willard, Chm.
Ironworkers Local No. 465
220 W Ct. St.
Kankakee, IL 60901
Ph: (815)954-4838
Fax: (815)939-3821
E-mail: kustom_bilt@msn.com
URL: National Affiliate–www.aws.org
Contact: John Willard, Chm.
Local. Professional engineering society in the field of welding. **Affiliated With:** American Welding Society.

2131 ■ Arthritis Foundation, Kankakee County Branch
c/o Provena East Side Medical Center
1777 E Court St.
Kankakee, IL 60901
Ph: (815)937-2461
Fax: (815)928-6098
E-mail: tcardosi@arthritis.org
URL: http://www.arthritis.org
Contact: Therese Cardosi, Dir.
Local. Seeks to: discover the cause and improve the methods for the treatment and prevention of arthritis and other rheumatic diseases; increase the number of scientists investigating rheumatic diseases; provide training in rheumatic diseases for more doctors; extend knowledge of arthritis and other rheumatic diseases to the lay public, emphasizing the socioeconomic as well as medical aspects of these diseases. **Affiliated With:** Arthritis Foundation.

2132 ■ Home Builders Association of Kankakee
c/o Sally Schmidt
PO Box 801
Kankakee, IL 60901-0801
Ph: (815)482-4131
Fax: (815)937-0555
URL: National Affiliate–www.nahb.org
Contact: Sally Schmidt, CEO
Local. Single and multifamily home builders, commercial builders, and others associated with the building industry. **Affiliated With:** National Association of Home Builders.

2133 ■ Illinois Learning Specialists and Developmental Educators (ILSADE)
c/o Bruce Myers, Pres.
PO Box 888
Kankakee, IL 60901-0888
Ph: (815)802-8454
E-mail: bmyers@kcc.edu
URL: http://www.ilsade.org
Contact: Bruce Myers, Pres.
State. Exists to promote the improvement of learning assistance and developmental education for adult learners at various levels of ability and in a variety of educational institutions throughout IL. **Affiliated With:** National Association for Developmental Education. **Formerly:** (2001) Illinois Association of Learning Assistance Professionals.

2134 ■ Kankakee County Association of Realtors
256 S Washington Ave.
Kankakee, IL 60901
Ph: (815)937-5551
Fax: (815)937-0882
E-mail: kristietubbs@speckmanrealty.com
URL: http://www.kcarweb.com
Contact: Rhonda Tatom, Pres.
Local. Strives to develop real estate business practices. Advocates the right to own, use and transfer real property. Provides a facility for professional development, research and exchange of information among members and to the general public. **Affiliated With:** National Association of Realtors.

2135 ■ Kankakee County Regional Planning Commission
190 E Court St.
Kankakee, IL 60901
Ph: (815)937-2940
Fax: (815)937-2974
URL: http://www.k3county.net
Contact: Michael J. Van Mill, Exec.Dir.
Staff: 15. **Budget:** $250,000. **Local**.

2136 ■ Kankakee District Dental Society
c/o Dr. Raffi K. Leblebijian, Pres.
401 N Wall St., Ste.203
Kankakee, IL 60901-2949
Ph: (815)933-4121
URL: http://www.isds.org
Contact: Dr. Raffi K. Leblebijian, Pres.
Local. Represents the interests of dentists committed to the public's oral health, ethics and professional development. Encourages the improvement of the public's oral health and promotes the art and science of dentistry. **Affiliated With:** American Dental Association; Illinois State Dental Society.

2137 ■ Kankakee River Valley Chamber of Commerce (KRVCC)
PO Box 905
Kankakee, IL 60901
Ph: (815)933-7721
Fax: (815)933-7675
E-mail: sara.segur@krvcc.org
URL: http://www.kankakee.org
Contact: Sara Segur Barzantny, Contact
Founded: 1904. **Members:** 500. **Local**. Promotes business and community development in the Kankakee County, IL area. **Awards:** Athena Award. **Frequency:** annual. **Type:** recognition. **Recipient:** for an outstanding business woman • Citizen of the Year. **Frequency:** annual. **Type:** recognition. **Recipient:** for outstanding service to the community. **Committees:** Accreditation; Health and Safety; Legislative Affairs; Nominations; Public Relations; Transportation Issues. **Councils:** Business/Education. **Programs:** Retention. **Affiliated With:** U.S. Chamber of Commerce. **Formerly:** (1999) Kankakee Area +Chamber of Commerce. **Publications:** *News and Views*, monthly. Newsletter. Includes chamber activities and programs. **Price:** $10.00/year. Alternate Formats: online.

2138 ■ Kankakee Valley AIFA
c/o Eugene E. Boelte, Pres.
PO Box 761
Kankakee, IL 60901
Ph: (815)469-5266
Fax: (815)469-5871
E-mail: lchilders@ggmic.com
URL: National Affiliate–naifa.org
Contact: Eugene E. Boelte, Pres.
Local. Represents the interests of insurance and financial advisors. Advocates for a positive legislative and regulatory environment. Enhances business and

professional skills of members. **Affiliated With:** National Association of Insurance and Financial Advisors.

2139 ■ Kankakee Valley REACT
465 S Nelson Ave.
Kankakee, IL 60901
Ph: (815)933-5697
URL: http://www.reactintl.org/teaminfo/usa_teams/teams-usil.htm
Local. Trained communication experts and professional volunteers. Provides volunteer public service and emergency communications through the use of radios (Citizen Band, General Mobile Radio Service, UHF and HAM). Coordinates with radio industries and government on safety communication matters and supports charitable activities and community organizations.

2140 ■ Local 872C, Chemical Workers Council of the UFCW
1795 S Schuyler Ave., Apt. A
Kankakee, IL 60901
Ph: (815)936-1848
URL: National Affiliate–www.ufcw.org
Local. Affiliated With: United Food and Commercial Workers International Union.

2141 ■ National Active And Retired Federal Employees Association - Kankakee 1109
1544 S 7th Ave.
Kankakee, IL 60901-4716
Ph: (815)933-7530
URL: National Affiliate–www.narfe.org
Contact: Eugene Wood, Contact
Local. Protects the retirement future of employees through education. Informs members on issues affecting the retirement. **Affiliated With:** National Association of Retired Federal Employees.

2142 ■ Phi Theta Kappa, Alpha Delta Eta Chapter - Kankakee Community College
c/o Susan LaMore
PO Box 888
Kankakee, IL 60901
Ph: (815)802-8208
E-mail: slamore@kcc.edu
URL: http://www.ptk.org/directories/chapters/IL/206-1.htm
Contact: Susan LaMore, Advisor
Local.

2143 ■ United Food and Commercial Workers, Local 1281P, Northcentral Region
PO Box 2291
Kankakee, IL 60901
Ph: (815)939-3631
URL: National Affiliate–www.ufcw.org
Local. Affiliated With: United Food and Commercial Workers International Union.

2144 ■ United Way of Kankakee County
PO Box 1286
Kankakee, IL 60901
Ph: (815)932-7476
Fax: (815)932-7506
E-mail: info@myunitedway.org
URL: http://www.myunitedway.org
Contact: Matt McBurnie, Exec.Dir.
Local. Affiliated With: United Way of America.

Kansas

2145 ■ American Legion, Coral Hall Post 539
PO Box 342
Kansas, IL 61933
Ph: (217)948-5361
Fax: (309)663-5783
URL: National Affiliate–www.legion.org
Local. Affiliated With: American Legion.

Karnak

2146 ■ RSVP of the Pennisula
c/o Georgia Smith, Dir.
PO Box 298
Karnak, IL 62956-0298
Ph: (618)634-2201
Fax: (618)634-9551
E-mail: sdcrsvp@starband.net
URL: http://www.joinseniorservice.org
Contact: Georgia Smith, Dir.
Local. Affiliated With: Retired and Senior Volunteer Program.

Kempton

2147 ■ American Legion, Olson-Bute-Malone Post 737
212 S First St.
Kempton, IL 60946
Ph: (815)253-6495
Fax: (309)663-5783
URL: National Affiliate–www.legion.org
Local. Affiliated With: American Legion.

Kenilworth

2148 ■ Chicago Council on Planned Giving
PO Box 350
Kenilworth, IL 60043-0350
Ph: (847)251-1400
Fax: (847)256-5601
E-mail: chicagocpg@aol.com
URL: http://www.chicagocpg.org
Contact: Walter L. Keats, Administrator
Local. Affiliated With: National Committee on Planned Giving.

2149 ■ Chicago Health Executives Forum
PO Box 350
Kenilworth, IL 60043-0350
Ph: (847)256-9454 (312)525-8153
Fax: (847)256-5601
E-mail: info@chefchicago.org
URL: http://www.chefchicago.org
Contact: Ogan Gurel MD, Pres.
Local. Works to improve the health status of society by advancing healthcare leadership and management excellence. Conducts research, career development and public policy programs. **Affiliated With:** American College of Healthcare Executives.

2150 ■ Illinois Association for Healthcare Quality (IAHQ)
PO Box 350
Kenilworth, IL 60043-0350
Ph: (217)223-8400
Fax: (217)228-3097
E-mail: jspeckhart@blessinghospital.com
Founded: 1975. **Members:** 301. **Membership Dues:** individual, $40 (annual). **State.** Strives to promote quality health care through education and professional collaboration. **Affiliated With:** National Association for Healthcare Quality. **Publications:** *IAHQ.net*, quarterly. Newsletter. Alternate Formats: online. **Conventions/Meetings:** annual conference • annual convention.

2151 ■ Suburban Chicago Planned Giving Council
c/o David S. Terrill, CFRE, Dir. of Gift Planning
PO Box 350
Kenilworth, IL 60043-0350
Ph: (847)251-1400
Fax: (847)256-5601
E-mail: associationsvcs@aol.com
URL: National Affiliate–www.ncpg.org
Local. Development officers with non-profit organizations and allied professionals who assist their donors and clients with charitable estate planning. Sponsors breakfast meetings and one all-day seminar per year. **Affiliated With:** National Committee on Planned Giving.

2152 ■ Women Health Executives Network (WHEN)
c/o Laurie Gibbons, Pres.
PO Box 350
Kenilworth, IL 60043
Ph: (847)251-1400 (847)292-6716
Fax: (847)256-5601
E-mail: lgibbons@phcs.com
URL: http://www.whenchicago.org
Contact: Nancy A. Peterman, Pres.
Founded: 1981. **Members:** 210. **Membership Dues:** senior, $100 (annual) • regular, $70 (annual) • student, $50 (annual). **Budget:** $20,000. **Local Groups:** 1. **Local.** Offers networking opportunities and educational programs for leaders in women's healthcare in the Chicago, Illinois area. **Awards:** Achievement in Health Care Management. **Frequency:** annual. **Type:** recognition. **Recipient:** for contribution to health care management and promotion of women executives. **Publications:** *WHEN Executive Notes*, quarterly. Newsletter. **Circulation:** 300. **Conventions/Meetings:** monthly board meeting - Chicago, IL • annual meeting - Chicago, IL • Program/Networking - meeting - 10/year. Chicago, IL.

Kenney

2153 ■ American Legion, Kenney-Hallsville Post 1133
110 S Johnston
Kenney, IL 61749
Ph: (309)663-0361
Fax: (309)663-5783
URL: National Affiliate–www.legion.org
Local. Affiliated With: American Legion.

Kewanee

2154 ■ American Legion, Kewanee Post 31
PO Box 252
Kewanee, IL 61443
Ph: (309)853-5508
Fax: (309)663-5783
URL: National Affiliate–www.legion.org
Local. Affiliated With: American Legion.

2155 ■ Independent Construction Equipment Builders Union (ICEBU)
PO Box 834
Kewanee, IL 61443-1714
Ph: (309)853-5051
E-mail: icebu@inw.net
Contact: Bob Curry, Contact
Members: 150. **Local.**

2156 ■ Kewanee Area United Way
315 W 1st St.
Kewanee, IL 61443-2103
Ph: (309)853-5158
URL: National Affiliate–national.unitedway.org
Local. Affiliated With: United Way of America.

2157 ■ Kewanee Chamber of Commerce (KCC)
113 E 2nd St.
Kewanee, IL 61443
Ph: (309)852-2175
Fax: (309)852-2176
E-mail: chamber@kewanee-il.com
URL: http://www.kewanee-il.com
Contact: Mark Mikenas, Exec.VP
Members: 175. **Staff:** 2. **Budget:** $75,000. **Local.** Promotes business and community development in Kewanee, IL. **Publications:** Newsletter, quarterly.

2158 ■ Mid Valley Association of Realtors
305 N Main St.
Kewanee, IL 61443
Ph: (309)852-5002
Fax: (309)853-4132
E-mail: info@midvalleymls.com
URL: National Affiliate–www.realtor.org
Contact: Carol Wager, Exec. Officer
Local. Strives to develop real estate business practices. Advocates the right to own, use and transfer real property. Provides a facility for professional development, research and exchange of information among members and to the general public. **Affiliated With:** National Association of Realtors.

2159 ■ Phi Theta Kappa, Alpha Phi Beta Chapter - Black Hawk College
c/o Carla Hillman
1501 State Hwy. 78
Kewanee, IL 61443
Ph: (309)852-5671
E-mail: hillmanc@bhc.edu
URL: http://www.ptk.org/directories/chapters/IL/20510-1.htm
Contact: Carla Hillman, Advisor
Local.

2160 ■ Red Witch R/C Yacht Club No. 152
c/o Ken Wegener
716 Henry St.
Kewanee, IL 61443
Ph: (309)853-9953
URL: National Affiliate–www.amya.org
Contact: Ken Wegener, Contact
Local.

Keyesport

2161 ■ American Legion, Jay H. Findley Memorial Post 1994
PO Box 36
Keyesport, IL 62253
Ph: (309)663-0361
Fax: (309)663-5783
URL: National Affiliate–www.legion.org
Local. Affiliated With: American Legion.

Kincaid

2162 ■ American Legion, Edwin Corpin Post 905
800 Railroad Ave.
Kincaid, IL 62540
Ph: (309)663-0361
Fax: (309)663-5783
URL: National Affiliate–www.legion.org
Local. Affiliated With: American Legion.

Kingston

2163 ■ American Legion, Illinois Post 1010
c/o Willard Aves
PO Box 38
Kingston, IL 60145
Ph: (815)784-5208
Fax: (309)663-5783
URL: National Affiliate–www.legion.org
Contact: Willard Aves, Contact
Local. Affiliated With: American Legion.

Kinmundy

2164 ■ American Legion, Kinmundy Post 519
PO Box 52
Kinmundy, IL 62854
Ph: (309)663-0361
Fax: (309)663-5783
URL: National Affiliate–www.legion.org
Local. Affiliated With: American Legion.

Knoxville

2165 ■ American Legion, Illinois Post 749
c/o Harry W. Philblad
PO Box 173
Knoxville, IL 61448
Ph: (309)289-2653
Fax: (309)663-5783
URL: National Affiliate–www.legion.org
Contact: Harry W. Philblad, Contact
Local. Affiliated With: American Legion.

2166 ■ AMVETS, Knoxville Post 8
111 N Market St.
Knoxville, IL 61448
Ph: (309)289-4524
E-mail: 6shelties@insightbb.com
URL: http://amvetspost8.homestead.com
Contact: Don Dredge, Sr. Vice Commander
Local. Affiliated With: AMVETS - American Veterans.

La Fayette

2167 ■ American Legion, Illinois Post 948
RR 1
La Fayette, IL 61449
Ph: (309)663-0361
Fax: (309)663-5783
URL: National Affiliate–www.legion.org
Contact: Fred J. Wilkins, Contact
Local. Affiliated With: American Legion.

La Grange

2168 ■ American Legion, Illinois Post 1941
900 S La Grange Rd.
La Grange, IL 60525
Ph: (708)352-1814
Fax: (309)663-5783
URL: National Affiliate–www.legion.org
Contact: Robert E. Coulter Jr., Contact
Local. Affiliated With: American Legion.

2169 ■ Chicago Table Tennis Club at La Grange
Richport YMCA
31 E Ogden
La Grange, IL 60525
Ph: (847)312-0590
E-mail: cttc4u@yahoo.com
URL: http://www.usatt.org/clubs
Contact: Engelbert Solis, Contact
Local. Affiliated With: U.S.A. Table Tennis.

2170 ■ Kiwanis Club of La Grange, Illinois
PO Box 97
La Grange, IL 60525
URL: http://www.kiwanis-lagrange-ill.org
Contact: Joe Dudley, Pres.
Local.

2171 ■ Religious Coalition for Reproductive Choice - Illinois Chapter
PO Box 2198
La Grange, IL 60525
E-mail: rcrc_il@hotmail.com
URL: National Affiliate–www.rcrc.org
State. Affiliated With: Religious Coalition for Reproductive Choice.

2172 ■ Spinal Cord Injury Association of Illinois
c/o Mercedes Rauen, Exec.Dir.
1032 S LaGrange Rd.
La Grange, IL 60525
Ph: (708)352-6223
Fax: (708)352-9065
E-mail: sciinjury@aol.com
URL: http://www.SCI-Illinois.org
Contact: Mercedes Rauen, Exec.Dir.
Membership Dues: individual or family, $15-$20 (annual) • professional, $25-$50 (annual) • business or corporate, $50-$100 (annual). **State**. Works as a comprehensive resource center for individuals with spinal cord injury, family members and professionals working in related fields. **Affiliated With:** National Spinal Cord Injury Association. **Publications:** *SCI Life*, quarterly. Magazine. Contains articles of interest to members and other disability community. **Price:** included in membership dues • Newsletters, quarterly. **Price:** included in membership dues.

2173 ■ West Suburban Chamber of Commerce and Industry (WSCCI)
47 S 6th Ave.
La Grange, IL 60525
Ph: (708)352-0494
Fax: (708)352-0620
E-mail: info@westsuburbanchamber.org
URL: http://www.westsuburbanchamber.org
Contact: Lisa Zeigler, Exec.Dir.
Founded: 1901. **Members:** 400. **Membership Dues:** business (1-250 employees), $195-$630 • individual, $130 • nonprofit, $130-$500 • financial institution (base rate), $225. **Local**. Advocates for business by striving to enhance and promote the stability and well-being of the community. Sponsors job fair, golf outing, awards gala, and New Teachers' Welcome Breakfast. **Awards:** Business of the Year. **Frequency:** annual. **Type:** recognition • Man of the Year. **Frequency:** annual. **Type:** recognition • Public Servant of the Year. **Frequency:** annual. **Type:** recognition • Woman of the Year. **Frequency:** annual. **Type:** recognition • Youth of the Year. **Frequency:** annual. **Type:** recognition. **Computer Services:** Information services, membership directory • mailing lists, of members. **Committees:** Annual Awards Gala; Golf Outing; Holiday Luncheon. **Councils:** Ambassadors/Membership Development; Legislative Affairs; Tourism. **Subgroups:** Business-Education Partnership. **Formerly:** (2006) West Suburban Chamber of Commerce. **Publications:** *Community Resource Guide*. Book. **Advertising:** accepted • *Outlook*. Newsletter • *Regional Map*, biennial. Book. **Advertising:** accepted • Membership Directory, annual. **Advertising:** accepted. **Conventions/Meetings:** monthly meeting.

2174 ■ West Suburban Chicago Chapter, MOAA
c/o CW3 Donald Sender
219 Wildflower Ln.
La Grange, IL 60525-5295
Ph: (630)668-1897
E-mail: donsender1@msn.com
URL: National Affiliate–www.moaa.org
Contact: CW3 Donald Sender, Contact
Local. Affiliated With: Military Officers Association of America.

La Grange Park

2175 ■ CATNAP from the Heart
c/o Roberta Meyer
1101 Beach Ave.
La Grange Park, IL 60526-1677
Ph: (708)352-3914
Fax: (708)352-3941
URL: http://www.catnapfromtheheart.org
Contact: Bobbi Meyer, Pres.
Founded: 1997. **Local. Formerly:** (2004) From The Heart.

2176 ■ Project Management Institute, Chicagoland Chapter
c/o Mr. Jeffrey D. Stewart, PMP, Pres.
PO Box 1183
La Grange Park, IL 60526-9283

Ph: (708)387-1201
E-mail: president@pmi-chicagoland.org
URL: National Affiliate–www.pmi.org
Contact: Mr. Jeffrey D. Stewart PMP, Pres.
Local. Corporations and individuals engaged in the practice of project management; project management students and educators. Seeks to advance the study, teaching, and practice of project management. **Affiliated With:** Project Management Institute. **Formerly:** PMI Midwest Chapter.

2177 ■ West Suburban United Way
555 N Kensington
La Grange Park, IL 60526
Ph: (708)352-7614
Fax: (708)352-7896
E-mail: westuw@uw-mc.org
URL: http://www.westuw.org
Contact: Sharon Alberts, CPO
Local. Affiliated With: United Way of America.

La Harpe

2178 ■ American Legion, La Harpe Post 301
PO Box 35
La Harpe, IL 61450
Ph: (217)659-3660
Fax: (309)663-5783
URL: National Affiliate–www.legion.org
Local. Affiliated With: American Legion.

La Moille

2179 ■ American Legion, La Moille Post 1043
PO Box 437
La Moille, IL 61330
Ph: (309)663-0361
Fax: (309)663-5783
URL: National Affiliate–www.legion.org
Local. Affiliated With: American Legion.

La Salle

2180 ■ American Legion, Romulus Meehan Post 426
PO Box 196
La Salle, IL 61301
Ph: (309)663-0361
Fax: (309)663-5783
URL: National Affiliate–www.legion.org
Local. Affiliated With: American Legion.

2181 ■ Habitat for Humanity of La Salle, Bureau, and Putnam Counties
PO Box 235
La Salle, IL 61301
Ph: (815)434-2041
Fax: (815)434-2064
E-mail: habitat@udnet.net
URL: http://www.habitat.org/local/affiliate_detail.asp?affiliate=2392-8109
Contact: CiCi Fisher Chalus, Exec.Dir.
Local. Affiliated With: Habitat for Humanity International.

2182 ■ Illinois Valley Area Chamber of Commerce and Economic Development (IVAC)
300 Bucklin
PO Box 446
La Salle, IL 61301-0446
Ph: (815)223-0227
Fax: (815)223-4827
E-mail: ivaced@ivaced.org
URL: http://www.ivaced.org
Contact: Ms. Barb Koch, Exec.Dir./CEO
Founded: 1911. **Members:** 425. **Staff:** 3. **Budget:** $315,000. **For-Profit. Local.** Promotes business and community development in portions of Bureau, LaSalle, Marshall, and Putnam counties, IL. **Affiliated With:** American Chamber of Commerce Executives; International Economic Development Council; U.S. Chamber of Commerce. **Publications:** *Agri-Business Brochure* • *Airport Brochure* • *The Illinois Valley* (in Chinese, English, German, and Japanese). Video • *Industrial Guide*, annual. Directory. **Price:** $5.00 • *Major Annual Events*, annual • *Membership Memo*, monthly. Brochure • *Transportation Brochure*. **Conventions/Meetings:** annual dinner • monthly Small Business Seminar.

2183 ■ United Way of Illinois Valley
c/o Dixie M. Reed, Exec.Dir.
1157 First St.
La Salle, IL 61301-3285
Ph: (815)223-8339
Fax: (815)224-4956
E-mail: uwiv.whatmatters@sbcglobal.net
URL: National Affiliate–national.unitedway.org
Contact: Dixie M. Reed, Exec.Dir.
Founded: 1966. **Members:** 27. **Staff:** 3. **Budget:** $400,000. **Regional Groups:** 1. **State Groups:** 1. **Local Groups:** 1. **Languages:** English, Spanish. **Local. Awards:** Venture Grants. **Frequency:** annual. **Type:** monetary. **Recipient:** for new initiatives and not for profit organizations in La Salle, Buriace, and Putnam Counties. **Publications:** *Information and Referral Guide of Human Services* (in English and Spanish), annual. Book. Lists human service providers in Bureace, La Salle, and Putnam Counties. **Price:** free. **Circulation:** 2,000. **Advertising:** accepted.

Lacon

2184 ■ American Legion, Walter Guede Post 593
110 4th St.
Lacon, IL 61540
Ph: (309)246-3077
Fax: (309)663-5783
URL: National Affiliate–www.legion.org
Local. Affiliated With: American Legion.

Ladd

2185 ■ American Legion, Illinois Post 938
c/o Harold E. Russell
121 S Main St.
Ladd, IL 61329
Ph: (815)894-2551
Fax: (309)663-5783
URL: National Affiliate–www.legion.org
Contact: Harold E. Russell, Contact
Local. Affiliated With: American Legion.

2186 ■ American Legion, Illinois Post 1056
PO Box 50
Ladd, IL 61329
Ph: (312)463-8577
Fax: (309)663-5783
URL: National Affiliate–www.legion.org
Contact: Dominick P. Nuccio Jr., Contact
Local. Affiliated With: American Legion.

Lake Bluff

2187 ■ American Legion, Lake Bluff Post 510
PO Box 142
Lake Bluff, IL 60044
Ph: (708)295-8468
Fax: (309)663-5783
URL: National Affiliate–www.legion.org
Local. Affiliated With: American Legion.

2188 ■ Child Care Coalition of Lake County (CCCLC)
c/o Barbara Haley
655 Rockland Rd.
Lake Bluff, IL 60044
Ph: (847)735-9945
Fax: (847)735-9645
E-mail: info@childcarecoalition.org
URL: http://www.childcarecoalition.org
Local.

2189 ■ Illinois High School and College Driver Education Association (IHSCDEA)
c/o Raymond Kracik, Exec.Sec.
104 Kohl Dr.
Lake Bluff, IL 60044
Ph: (847)234-4085
E-mail: raykracikvet60@comcast.net
URL: http://www.ihscdea.org
Founded: 1952. **State.**

2190 ■ National Sojourners, Lake Michigan No. 289
c/o Mr. B. Ralph Edwards
1130 Foster Ave.
Lake Bluff, IL 60044-1406
Ph: (847)234-6894
E-mail: sredwgen@sbcglobal.net
URL: National Affiliate–www.nationalsojourners.org
Contact: Mr. B. Ralph Edwards, Contact
Local.

2191 ■ Young Life Lake County
803 Jenkisson
Lake Bluff, IL 60044
Ph: (847)561-8232
Fax: (847)615-2755
URL: http://whereis.younglife.org/FriendlyUrlRedirector.aspx?ID=A-IL30
Local.

Lake Forest

2192 ■ American Chesapeake Club, Illinois
c/o Carol Andersen
373 Stafford Ct.
Lake Forest, IL 60045
Ph: (847)234-8655
E-mail: caroway@aol.com
URL: National Affiliate–www.amchessieclub.org
Contact: Carol Andersen, Contact
State. Affiliated With: American Chesapeake Club.

2193 ■ American Legion, Mc Kinlock Post 264
801 N Mckinley Rd.
Lake Forest, IL 60045
Ph: (708)295-6523
Fax: (309)663-5783
E-mail: post264600@sbcglobal.net
URL: National Affiliate–www.legion.org
Local. Affiliated With: American Legion.

2194 ■ American Society of Sanitary Engineering, Illinois Chapter
c/o Albert Gehrke, Pres.
1735 Wimbledon Ct.
Lake Forest, IL 60045
E-mail: pipedds@aol.com
URL: National Affiliate–www.asse-plumbing.org
Contact: Albert Gehrke, Pres.
State. Represents plumbing officials, sanitary engineers, plumbers, plumbing contractors, building officials, architects, engineers, designing engineers, physicians, and others interested in health. Conducts research on plumbing and sanitation and develops performance standards for components of the plumbing system. Sponsors disease research programs and other studies of water-borne epidemics. **Affiliated With:** American Society of Sanitary Engineering.

2195 ■ American Youth Soccer Organization, Region 163
PO Box 693
Lake Forest, IL 60045
Ph: (847)557-2976
E-mail: ayso163@aol.com
URL: http://www.ayso163.org
Local. Affiliated With: American Youth Soccer Organization.

2196 ■ DuPage Figure Skating Club
730 S Ridge Rd.
Lake Forest, IL 60045
E-mail: dupagefsc@hotmail.com
URL: http://www.dupagefsc.org
Contact: Joseph Serafine, Contact
Local. Provides programs to encourage participation and achievement in the sport of figure skating on ice. Defines and maintains uniform standards of skating proficiency. Organizes and sponsors competitions and exhibitions for the purpose of stimulating interest in figure skating. **Affiliated With:** United States Figure Skating Association.

2197 ■ Great Lakes Adaptive Sports Association (GLASA)
c/o Cindy Hounser
400 E Illinois Rd.
Lake Forest, IL 60045
Ph: (847)283-0908
Fax: (847)283-0973
E-mail: info@glasa.org
URL: http://home.wi.rr.com/glasa/
Regional. **Affiliated With:** Wheelchair Sports, USA.

2198 ■ Illinois Curling Association (ICA)
c/o Scott Rahn, Pres.
466 Circle Ln.
Lake Forest, IL 60045
Ph: (847)735-1541
Fax: (847)735-1371
E-mail: gail.spreen@wilmettecurling.org
URL: http://www.curlillinois.org
Contact: Scott Rahn, Pres.
State. **Affiliated With:** United States Curling Association.

2199 ■ Lake County Medical Society - Illinois (LCMS)
222 E Wisconsin Ave., Ste.214
Lake Forest, IL 60045
Ph: (847)482-0222
Fax: (847)574-0445
E-mail: lakedocs@aol.com
URL: http://www.lakecountymedicalsociety.com
Contact: Erik Nelson MD, Pres.
Local. Advances the art and science of medicine. Promotes patient care and the betterment of public health.

2200 ■ Lake Forest - Lake Bluff Chamber of Commerce
695 N Western Ave.
Lake Forest, IL 60045
Ph: (847)234-4282
E-mail: info@lflbchamber.com
URL: http://www.lakeforestonline.com
Contact: Joanna Rolek, Exec.Dir.
Membership Dues: base, $220 (annual). **Local**. Promotes the economic and civic interest of the community. **Computer Services:** Information services, business directory. **Additional Websites:** http://www.lflbchamber.com. **Publications:** *Community Guide*, annual. Handbook • *Shopping and Dining Guide*, annual. Handbook • Newsletter, monthly.

2201 ■ Midwest Daffodil Society
c/o Al Champ, Treas.
1546 Willow
Lake Forest, IL 60045
Ph: (847)438-5309
E-mail: george@dorners.net
URL: http://www.lzarea.org/daffodil
Contact: Al Champ, Treas.
Local. **Affiliated With:** American Daffodil Society.

2202 ■ National Active And Retired Federal Employees Association - Marion Payne 1309
21 E Linden Ave.
Lake Forest, IL 60045-2932
Ph: (847)295-0805
URL: National Affiliate–www.narfe.org
Contact: Allen F. Goldberg, Contact
Local. Protects the retirement future of employees through education. Informs members on issues affecting the retirement. **Affiliated With:** National Association of Retired Federal Employees.

2203 ■ Psi Chi, National Honor Society in Psychology - Lake Forest College
c/o Dept. of Psychology
555 N Sheridan Rd.
Lake Forest, IL 60045
Ph: (847)735-5040 (847)735-5262
Fax: (847)735-6190
E-mail: kelley@lfc.edu
URL: National Affiliate–www.psichi.org
Local. **Affiliated With:** Psi Chi, National Honor Society in Psychology.

2204 ■ Risk and Insurance Management Society, Chicago Chapter
c/o Ron Cooley
100 Grainger Pkwy.
Lake Forest, IL 60045
Ph: (847)535-4614
Fax: (847)535-9231
E-mail: cooley.r@grainger.com
URL: http://chicago.rims.org
Contact: Ron Cooley, Contact
Local. Seeks to promote the discipline of risk management and enhance the image of professional risk managers. Fosters the educational and professional development of risk managers and others involved in the risk management and insurance industry. **Affiliated With:** Risk and Insurance Management Society.

2205 ■ United Way of the North Shore
400 E Illinois Rd.
Lake Forest, IL 60045
Ph: (847)234-5843
E-mail: uwnorthshore@uw-mc.org
URL: http://www.uwnorthshore.org
Contact: Jean Gibbons, CPO
Local. **Affiliated With:** United Way of America.

Lake in the Hills

2206 ■ American Legion, Lake in the Hills Post 1231
1101 W Algonquin Rd.
Lake in the Hills, IL 60156
Ph: (708)658-2010
Fax: (309)663-5783
E-mail: adjutant@post1231.org
URL: National Affiliate–www.legion.org
Local. **Affiliated With:** American Legion.

2207 ■ American Wine Society - Cork Club Chicago
c/o Danica Fuller Katelan, Co-Chair
5010 Princeton Ln.
Lake in the Hills, IL 60156
E-mail: danikat@comcast.net
URL: National Affiliate–www.americanwinesociety.org
Contact: Danica Fuller Katelan, Co-Chair
Local. **Affiliated With:** American Wine Society.

Lake Zurich

2208 ■ American Legion, Lake Zurich Post 964
PO Box 331
Lake Zurich, IL 60047
Ph: (708)438-9477
Fax: (309)663-5783
URL: National Affiliate–www.legion.org
Local. **Affiliated With:** American Legion.

2209 ■ Lake Zurich Area Chamber of Commerce (LZACC)
1st Bank Plz., Ste.304
Lake Zurich, IL 60047
Ph: (847)438-5572
Fax: (847)438-5574
E-mail: info@lzacc.com
URL: http://www.lzacc.com
Contact: Dale Perrin, Exec.Dir.
Founded: 1915. **Members:** 400. **Membership Dues:** business (depends on the number of employees), $195-$500 (annual) • government, hospital, $275 (annual) • utility, $385 (annual) • non-profit, $125 (annual). **Staff:** 2. **Budget:** $110,000. **Local**. Retailers, industrial concerns, professionals, and service organizations that promote business and industry in Lake Zurich, IL. Sponsors Business After Hours seminars, retail promotions, and community recognition and beautification programs. Offers group insurance plans; conducts social activities. Donates to youth services and library. Sponsors Community Recognition Program and a trade fair. **Awards: Type:** scholarship. **Computer Services:** database, list of members • information services, facts about the local communities. **Committees:** Continuing Education Programs; Governmental Relations/Economic Development; Lake Zurich Invitational Networking; Retail; Scholarship; School Mentoring. **Subcommittees:** Lake Zurich Area Networking. **Affiliated With:** American Chamber of Commerce Executives. **Formerly:** (1924) Lake Zurich Commercial Club. **Publications:** *Chatter*, monthly. Newsletter. **Circulation:** 500. **Advertising:** accepted. Alternate Formats: online • *Guide to Lake Zurich*, annual. Directory. **Conventions/Meetings:** annual banquet • periodic luncheon • periodic meeting • periodic seminar.

2210 ■ Libertarian Party of Lake County (LPLC)
c/o Eric Dubiel, Chm.
PO Box 703
Lake Zurich, IL 60047
Ph: (847)438-7776
E-mail: chair@lake.il.lp.org
URL: http://lake.il.lp.org
Contact: Eric Dubiel, Chm.
Local. **Affiliated With:** Libertarian National Committee.

2211 ■ Mid-States Morgan Horse Club
c/o Sheryl L. Hurley, Sec.
25880 N Anna Ct.
Lake Zurich, IL 60047-8414
Ph: (847)526-1777
E-mail: sherhurley@juno.com
URL: http://www.midstatesmorgan.org
Contact: Sheryl L. Hurley, Sec.
Local. **Affiliated With:** American Morgan Horse Association.

2212 ■ Reserve Officers Association - Department of Illinois, Cook County Chapter 6
c/o CW4 Richard E. Johnson, Pres.
23231 Hillcrest Dr.
Lake Zurich, IL 60047-9058
Ph: (847)438-1920
URL: http://www.ilroa.org
Contact: CW4 Richard E. Johnson, Pres.
Local. Promotes and supports the development and execution of a military policy for the United States. Provides professional development seminars, workshops and programs for its members. **Affiliated With:** Reserve Officers Association of the United States.

Lanark

2213 ■ American Legion, Crouse-Engles Post 357
527 Hanabarger
Lanark, IL 61046
Ph: (309)663-0361
Fax: (309)663-5783
URL: National Affiliate–www.legion.org
Local. **Affiliated With:** American Legion.

Lansing

2214 ■ American Legion, Edward Schultz Post 697
PO Box 709
Lansing, IL 60438
Ph: (708)474-5906
Fax: (309)663-5783
URL: National Affiliate–www.legion.org
Local. **Affiliated With:** American Legion.

2215 ■ American Legion, Russell Square Post 1006
c/o John A. Ziolkowski
3680 186th St., No. 302
Lansing, IL 60438
Ph: (708)849-1914
Fax: (309)663-5783
URL: National Affiliate–www.legion.org
Contact: John A. Ziolkowski, Contact
Local. Affiliated With: American Legion.

2216 ■ Chicago Southland Convention and Visitors Bureau (CSCVB)
2304 173rd St.
Lansing, IL 60438-6006
Ph: (708)895-8200
Fax: (708)895-8288
Free: (888)895-8233
E-mail: info@visitchicagosouthland.com
URL: http://www.visitchicagosouthland.com
Local. Assists meeting planners with site selection, bids/proposals, transportation coordination, registration, and more.

2217 ■ Connecting Business Men to Christ - Chicagoland
18228 Torrence Ave.
Lansing, IL 60438
Ph: (708)474-4744
Fax: (708)474-4745
E-mail: chicagoland@cbmc.com
URL: http://www.cbmcchicago.com/
Local.

2218 ■ Greater Midwest Rotorcraft - Popular Rotocraft Association Chapter 18
3441 Washington
Lansing, IL 60438
Ph: (708)895-0398
E-mail: gyroplanes@aol.com
URL: http://www.gyroclub.com
Local. Affiliated With: Popular Rotorcraft Association.

2219 ■ Izaak Walton League of America - Chicago Chapter No. 1
3651 Monroe St.
Lansing, IL 60438-2416
Ph: (708)895-0850
E-mail: tpreid@mindspring.com
URL: National Affiliate–www.iwla.org
Contact: Wendy A. Reid, Contact
Local. Educates the public to conserve, maintain, protect and restore the soil, forest, water and other natural resources of the United States.

2220 ■ Lansing Chamber of Commerce
3404 Lake St.
Lansing, IL 60438
Ph: (708)474-4170
Contact: Joyce Tiltges, Exec.Dir.
Local.

2221 ■ Lansing Junior Woman's Club
PO Box 564
Lansing, IL 60438-0564
E-mail: president@lansingjrs.com
URL: http://www.lansingjrs.com
Local.

Latham

2222 ■ American Association of Teachers of German - Southern Illinois Chapter
c/o Joe Scanavino, Pres.
PO Box 88
Latham, IL 62543
Ph: (217)668-2392
E-mail: jscanavino@yahoo.com
URL: http://southernillinois.aatg.org
Contact: Joe Scanavino, Pres.
Local. Represents teachers of German at all levels of instruction and all those interested in the teaching of German. Advances and improves the teaching of the language, literatures and cultures of the German-speaking countries. Provides members with educational and professional services. **Affiliated With:** American Association of Teachers of German.

Lawrenceville

2223 ■ American Legion, Lawrence Post 28
PO Box 87
Lawrenceville, IL 62439
Ph: (618)943-4414
Fax: (309)663-5783
URL: National Affiliate–www.legion.org
Local. Affiliated With: American Legion.

2224 ■ Illinois Environmental Health Association - South Chapter
c/o Lawrence County Health Dept.
RR No. 3, Box 414
Lawrenceville, IL 62439
Ph: (618)943-3302
Fax: (618)943-3657
E-mail: egpaulin@shawneelink.net
URL: http://www.ieha.us
Contact: Eric Paulen, Dir.
Local. Advances the environmental health and protection profession. Provides educational and training opportunities for members. Works to establish standards of competence and ethics for the profession. **Affiliated With:** National Environmental Health Association.

2225 ■ Lawrence County Chamber of Commerce (LCCC)
619 12th St.
Lawrenceville, IL 62439
Ph: (618)943-3516
Fax: (618)943-4748
E-mail: lccc@midwest.net
URL: http://www.lawrencecountyillinois.com/chamber.html
Contact: Delilah Gray, Exec.Dir.
Members: 175. **Local.** Promotes business and community development in Lawrence County, IL. festivities; conducts annual Basketball Capital Classic. Sponsors the Lawrenceville Fall Festival. **Affiliated With:** Illinois State Chamber of Commerce. **Publications:** *Let Us Point You in the Right Direction*, annual. Directory. **Price:** free.

2226 ■ National Active And Retired Federal Employees Association Lawrenceville 1041
PO Box 624
Lawrenceville, IL 62439-0624
Ph: (618)943-4133
URL: National Affiliate–www.narfe.org
Contact: John T. Howard, Contact
Local. Protects the retirement future of employees through education. Informs members on issues affecting the retirement. **Affiliated With:** National Association of Retired Federal Employees.

2227 ■ Wabash Valley Resource Conservation and Development Council
2808A W Haven R
Lawrenceville, IL 62439
Ph: (618)943-2621
Fax: (618)943-2969
E-mail: betty.joubert@il.usda.gov
URL: National Affiliate–www.rcdnet.org
Contact: Betty Joubert, Coor.
Local. Affiliated With: National Association of Resource Conservation and Development Councils.

Le Roy

2228 ■ American Legion, Ruel Neal Post 79
100 N Main St.
Le Roy, IL 61752
Ph: (309)962-3341
Fax: (309)663-5783
URL: National Affiliate–www.legion.org
Local. Affiliated With: American Legion.

Leaf River

2229 ■ American Legion, Jerry Wickham Post 1148
PO Box 371
Leaf River, IL 61047
Ph: (309)663-0361
Fax: (309)663-5783
URL: National Affiliate–www.legion.org
Local. Affiliated With: American Legion.

Lebanon

2230 ■ American Legion, Schuetz-Hermann Post 283
c/o Lloyd A. Vrell, Adj.
111 E Wesley St.
Lebanon, IL 62254
Ph: (309)663-0361
Fax: (309)663-5783
URL: National Affiliate–www.legion.org
Contact: Lloyd A. Vrell, Adj.
Local. Affiliated With: American Legion.

2231 ■ Lebanon Chamber of Commerce
23 W St. Louis St.
Lebanon, IL 62254
Ph: (618)537-8420
Contact: Carrie Christ, Pres.
Local.

Lee

2232 ■ American Legion, Lee Post 1253
PO Box 95
Lee, IL 60530
Ph: (815)824-2070
Fax: (309)663-5783
URL: National Affiliate–www.legion.org
Local. Affiliated With: American Legion.

Leland

2233 ■ American Legion, Leland Post 570
168 N Main St.
Leland, IL 60531
Ph: (815)495-2281
Fax: (309)663-5783
URL: National Affiliate–www.legion.org
Local. Affiliated With: American Legion.

Lemont

2234 ■ American Hellenic Educational Progressive Association - South Chicago, Chapter 351
c/o Thomas Cosmos, Pres.
1397 St. Vincents Dr.
Lemont, IL 60439
Ph: (312)738-1552
URL: http://www.ahepafamily.org/d13
Contact: Thomas Cosmos, Pres.
Local. Affiliated With: American Hellenic Educational Progressive Association.

2235 ■ American Legion, Cornell Post 928
432 Ashbury Ct.
Lemont, IL 60439
Ph: (309)663-0361
Fax: (309)663-5783
URL: National Affiliate–www.legion.org
Local. Affiliated With: American Legion.

2236 ■ American Legion, Lemont Post 243
PO Box 151
Lemont, IL 60439
Ph: (708)458-7097
Fax: (309)663-5783
URL: National Affiliate–www.legion.org
Local. Affiliated With: American Legion.

2237 ■ American Vacuum Society, Prairie Chapter
c/o Richard Rosenberg
Argonne Natl. Lab.
9700 S Cass Ave., Bldg. 401
Lemont, IL 60439
Ph: (630)252-6112
Fax: (630)252-8742
E-mail: lhanley@uic.edu
URL: National Affiliate–www.avs.org
Contact: Luke Hanley, Chm.
Local. Affiliated With: AVS Science and Technology Society. **Conventions/Meetings:** semiannual meeting.

2238 ■ American Youth Soccer Organization, Region 458
PO Box 148
Lemont, IL 60439-0148
Ph: (630)621-8405
E-mail: commissioner@lemontayso.com
URL: http://www.lemontayso.org
Local. Affiliated With: American Youth Soccer Organization.

2239 ■ Chicago District Golf Association (CDGA)
11855 Archer Ave.
Lemont, IL 60439
Ph: (630)257-2005
Fax: (630)257-2088
E-mail: rmarkionni@cdga.org
URL: http://www.cdga.org
Contact: Robert Markionni, Exec.Dir.
Regional. Affiliated With: International Association of Golf Administrators.

2240 ■ Global Grid Forum (GGF)
c/o Charlie Catlett
9700 S Cass Ave., Bldg. 221/A142
Lemont, IL 60439
Ph: (630)252-4300
Fax: (630)252-4466
E-mail: office@ggf.org
URL: http://www.gridforum.org
Contact: Charlie Catlett, Pres.
Local.

2241 ■ Illinois Junior Golf Association (IJGA)
c/o Dan McGuire, Exec.Dir.
Midwest Golf House Complex
11855 Archer Ave., Ste.200
Lemont, IL 60439
Ph: (630)257-9806
Fax: (630)257-9830
E-mail: info@ijga.org
URL: http://www.ijga.org
Contact: Ms. Elaine Pope, Governing Board Pres.
Founded: 1967. **Members:** 2,300. **Membership Dues:** junior golfer (ages 7-18), $55 (annual). **Staff:** 15. **Budget:** $800,000. **State. Affiliated With:** International Association of Golf Administrators.

2242 ■ Illinois Mycological Association (IMA)
c/o Jim Lamb, Treas.
20W 075 98th
Lemont, IL 60439-9661
E-mail: lshernof@uchicago.edu
URL: http://www.ilmyco.gen.chicago.il.us
Contact: Leon Shernoff, Contact
State. Amateur and professional mycologists, mycophagists, devotees of mushroom lore, students, and botanists. Promotes amateur mycology (the study of fungi, such as mushrooms, puffballs, molds, rusts, and smuts). **Affiliated With:** North American Mycological Association.

2243 ■ Illinois Turfgrass Foundation (ITF)
The Midwest Golf House Complex
11855 Archer Ave.
Lemont, IL 60439
Ph: (630)243-9483
Fax: (630)257-0362
E-mail: info@illinoisturfgrassfoundation.org
URL: http://www.turf.uiuc.edu
Contact: Luke Cella, Exec.Dir.
State.

2244 ■ International Association of Machinists and Aerospace Workers, Local Lodge 2458
PO Box 291
Lemont, IL 60439
URL: http://www.iamawll2458.org
Contact: Richard Prien, Pres.
Members: 237. **Local. Affiliated With:** International Association of Machinists and Aerospace Workers.

2245 ■ Lemont Area Chamber of Commerce
101 Main St.
Lemont, IL 60439-3675
Ph: (630)257-5997
Fax: (630)257-3238
E-mail: lacc@core.com
URL: http://www.lemontchamber.com
Contact: Mr. Pat O'Brien, Pres.
Founded: 1948. **Members:** 257. **Membership Dues:** business (depends upon the number of employees), $130-$500 (annual) • church, $100 (annual). **Staff:** 1. **Local.** Aims to promote the community and make it a better place to live, work, and conduct business. **Awards:** Citizen of the Year. **Frequency:** annual. **Type:** recognition. **Recipient:** for a person's contribution to a community's interest. **Computer Services:** Information services, membership directory. **Publications:** *Chamber Chords*, monthly. Newsletter. Includes upcoming events. **Price:** free for members. **Circulation:** 325. **Advertising:** accepted.

2246 ■ Lemont Junior Woman's Club (LJWC)
PO Box 563
Lemont, IL 60439
E-mail: ljwc2000@excite.com
URL: http://www.lemontjuniorwomansclub.org
Local.

2247 ■ Midwest Association Golf Course Superintendents
11855 Archer Ave.
Lemont, IL 60439
Ph: (847)622-4823
E-mail: zeinert5@tbcnet.com
URL: http://www.magcs.org
Contact: Phil Zeinert, Pres.
Membership Dues: class A, $160 • class B, $160 • class C, $110. **Local.** Represents the interests of golf course superintendents. Advances members' profession for career success. Enhances the enjoyment, growth and vitality in the game of golf. Educates members concerning efficient and economical management of golf courses. **Affiliated With:** Golf Course Superintendents Association of America. **Publications:** *On Course*, monthly. Newsletter.

Lena

2248 ■ American Legion, Sprague-Inman Post 577
PO Box 500
Lena, IL 61048
Ph: (309)663-0361
Fax: (309)663-5783
URL: National Affiliate–www.legion.org
Local. Affiliated With: American Legion.

Lewistown

2249 ■ American Legion, Bishop Post 1
260 W Lincoln Ave.
Lewistown, IL 61542
Ph: (309)547-7209
Fax: (309)663-5783
URL: National Affiliate–www.legion.org
Local. Affiliated With: American Legion.

2250 ■ Lewistown Chamber of Commerce
119 S Adams
Lewistown, IL 61542
Ph: (309)547-4300
Contact: Anna Raines, Pres.
Local.

Lexington

2251 ■ American Legion, Illinois Post 291
c/o Elmo F. Hill
PO Box 171
Lexington, IL 61753
Ph: (309)663-0361
Fax: (309)663-5783
URL: National Affiliate–www.legion.org
Contact: Elmo F. Hill, Contact
Local. Affiliated With: American Legion.

2252 ■ Central Illinois Angus Association
c/o Gary Dameron, Pres.
R.R. 2, Box 74
Lexington, IL 61753
Ph: (309)365-8288
URL: National Affiliate–www.angus.org
Contact: Gary Dameron, Pres.
Local. Affiliated With: American Angus Association.

2253 ■ Farrier Industry Association No. 37
c/o Steve Hoselton, Pres.
Anvil Brand Shoe Co.
PO Box 198
Lexington, IL 61753
Ph: (309)365-8207
Fax: (309)365-3341
E-mail: steve@anvilbrand.com
URL: National Affiliate–www.americanfarriers.org
Contact: Steve Hoselton, Pres.
Local. Affiliated With: American Farrier's Association.

Liberty

2254 ■ American Legion, Blentlinger-Tournear Post 640
RR 1
Liberty, IL 62347
Ph: (217)645-3365
Fax: (309)663-5783
URL: National Affiliate–www.legion.org
Local. Affiliated With: American Legion.

Libertyville

2255 ■ American Hellenic Educational Progressive Association - Waukegan, Chapter 218
c/o Stavros Frangos, Pres.
511 Juniper Pkwy.
Libertyville, IL 60048
Ph: (847)362-9494
E-mail: sfrangos@yahoo.com
URL: http://www.ahepafamily.org/d13
Contact: Stavros Frangos, Pres.
Local. Affiliated With: American Hellenic Educational Progressive Association.

2256 ■ American Legion, Libertyville Post 329
715 N Milwaukee Ave.
Libertyville, IL 60048
Ph: (309)663-0361
Fax: (309)663-5783
URL: National Affiliate–www.legion.org
Local. Affiliated With: American Legion.

2257 ■ American Society for Quality, Northeastern Illinois Section 1212
c/o Thomas Hannan, Chm.
PO Box 93
Libertyville, IL 60048
Ph: (630)776-6366
E-mail: thomas.hannan@precisetech.com
URL: http://www.asq1212.org
Contact: Thomas Hannan, Chm.
Local. Advances learning, quality improvement and knowledge exchange to improve business results and to create better workplaces and communities worldwide. Provides a forum for information exchange, professional development and continuous learning in the science of quality. **Affiliated With:** American Society for Quality.

2258 ■ Gardeners of America/Men's Garden Clubs of America - Gardeners of Central Lake County
c/o Tony Kirch, Pres.
30908 N Pinehurst Ct.
Libertyville, IL 60048
Ph: (847)816-7602
E-mail: tkirch30@aol.com
URL: National Affiliate–www.tgoa-mgca.org
Contact: Tony Kirch, Pres.
Local.

2259 ■ GLMV Area Chamber of Commerce
1123 S Milwaukee Ave.
Libertyville, IL 60048
Ph: (847)680-0750
Fax: (847)680-0760
E-mail: info@glmvchamber.org
URL: http://glmvchamber.org
Contact: B. Dwight Houchins, Pres.
Membership Dues: all (base rate), $240 (annual). **Local. Computer Services:** Information services, membership directory. **Formerly:** (2005) Green Oaks - Libertyville - Mundelein - Vernon Hills Area Chamber of Commerce and Liberty. **Publications:** *Action News*, monthly. Newsletter. **Advertising:** accepted. Alternate Formats: online • *Images*. Magazine. Contains full colored pages with photos and stories about GLMV area. **Advertising:** accepted. Alternate Formats: online • Membership Directory. Provides alphabetical and categorical listings of member businesses. **Advertising:** accepted.

2260 ■ Illinois Emergency Services Management Association (IESMA)
c/o Louise Bryner, Exec.Sec.
1303 N Milwaukee Ave.
Libertyville, IL 60048
Ph: (847)984-5230
Fax: (847)367-4907
E-mail: iesma@aol.com
URL: http://www.iesma.org
State.

2261 ■ Lake County Audubon Society
PO Box 332
Libertyville, IL 60048
Ph: (847)362-0472
E-mail: underbrink.f@district128.org
URL: http://www.audubon.org/chapter/il/index.html
Contact: Frank K. Underbrink, Contact
Local. **Formerly:** (2005) National Audubon Society - Lake County.

2262 ■ Libertyville Junior Woman's Club (LJWC)
PO Box 893
Libertyville, IL 60048
E-mail: libertyvillejuniors@yahoo.com
URL: http://www.libertyvillejuniors.org
Local.

2263 ■ Libertyville-Mundelein Historical Society (LMHS)
c/o Cook Memorial Public Library District
413 N Milwaukee Ave.
Libertyville, IL 60048
Ph: (847)362-2330
Fax: (847)362-0006
E-mail: likref@cooklib.org
URL: http://www.cooklib.org
Contact: Jerrold L. Schulkin, Pres.
Founded: 1955. **Members:** 174. **Local**. Individuals interested in the history of Libertyville and Mundelein, Lake County, IL. Maintains Ansel B. Cook Home, Victorian museum, and archives. Sponsors Victorian Christmas, Summer Open House, and tours. Provides tours of homes listed on the national register of historic places. **Affiliated With:** Illinois State Historical Society. **Publications:** Newsletter, monthly. **Conventions/Meetings:** periodic meeting • monthly symposium - always third Monday; except June, July, August, and December.

2264 ■ Main Street Libertyville
133 E Cook Ave.
Libertyville, IL 60048
Ph: (847)680-0336
Fax: (847)680-0370
URL: http://www.mainstreetlibertyville.org
Local.

2265 ■ NAIFA-Lake County
PO Box 683
Libertyville, IL 60048
Ph: (847)356-8900
Fax: (847)356-6065
URL: National Affiliate–www.naifa.org
Local. Represents the interest of insurance and financial advisors. Advocates for a positive legislative and regulatory environment. Enhances business and professional skills of members. **Affiliated With:** National Association of Insurance and Financial Advisors.

2266 ■ National Alliance for the Mentally Ill - Lake County
PO Box 6356
Libertyville, IL 60048
Ph: (847)249-1515
E-mail: namisupport@hotmail.com
URL: http://www.namilake-il.org
Contact: Lori Lewis, Co-Pres.
Local. Strives to improve the quality of life of children and adults with severe mental illness through support, education, research and advocacy. **Affiliated With:** National Alliance for the Mentally Ill.

2267 ■ North Shore and Chicago Chapter of the MOAA
406 Juniper Pkwy.
Libertyville, IL 60048-3529
Ph: (847)831-5614
E-mail: duane_ute@earthlink.net
URL: National Affiliate–www.moaa.org
Contact: LTC Duane Golvach, Contact
Local. Affiliated With: Military Officers Association of America.

2268 ■ Society for Applied Spectroscopy, Chicago
c/o Michael F. Jankowski, Chair
USG Corp.
700 N Hwy. 45
Libertyville, IL 60048
Ph: (847)970-5061
E-mail: mjankowski@usg.com
URL: http://www.sas-chicago.org
Contact: Michael F. Jankowski, Chair
Local. Affiliated With: Society for Applied Spectroscopy.

2269 ■ USA Weightlifting - Windy City
c/o Mike Gattone
332 Kenloch Ave.
Libertyville, IL 60048
Ph: (847)309-4809
Fax: (847)458-2073
E-mail: mgatone@aol.com
URL: National Affiliate–www.usaweightlifting.org
Contact: Mike Gattone, Contact
Local. Affiliated With: USA Weightlifting.

Lincoln

2270 ■ Abraham Lincoln Tourism Bureau of Logan County
303 S Kickapoo St.
Lincoln, IL 62656
Ph: (217)732-8687
Fax: (217)732-6293
E-mail: tourlogancounty@ccaonline.com
URL: http://www.logancountytourism.org/
Contact: Thressia Usherwood, Exec.Dir.
Founded: 1987. **Staff:** 1. **Budget:** $80,000. **Local**. Promotes increased economic development through tourism. **Awards:** Awards from Illinois Gov. Conference. **Frequency:** annual. **Type:** recognition. **Recipient:** advertising.

2271 ■ American Legion, Logan Post 263
PO Box 425
Lincoln, IL 62656
Ph: (217)732-3743
Fax: (309)663-5783
URL: National Affiliate–www.legion.org
Local. Affiliated With: American Legion.

2272 ■ American Meteorological Society, Central Illinois
c/o Christopher J. Miller, Pres.
Natl. Weather Ser.
1362 State Rte. 10
Lincoln, IL 62656
Ph: (217)333-0850
E-mail: chris.miller@noaa.org
URL: http://www.c-il-ams.org/
Contact: Christopher J. Miller, Pres.
Regional. Professional meteorologists, oceanographers, and hydrologists; interested students and nonprofessionals. **Affiliated With:** American Meteorological Society.

2273 ■ American Welding Society, Sangamon Valley Section 070
c/o Brian Huff, Chm.
Midwest Tech. Inst.
PO Box 506
Lincoln, IL 62656
Ph: (217)735-3105
Free: (800)804-8882
URL: National Affiliate–www.aws.org
Contact: Mike Casper, VP
Local. Professional engineering society in the field of welding. **Affiliated With:** American Welding Society.

2274 ■ BMW Car Club of America, Illini Chapter
c/o Denny M. Smith
PO Box 253
Lincoln, IL 62656-0253
Ph: (309)828-1492
E-mail: barhop12@yahoo.com
URL: http://www.illinibmw.com/
Contact: Denny M. Smith, Contact
Local. Affiliated With: BMW Car Club of America.

2275 ■ Lincoln Junior Woman's Club
PO Box 152
Lincoln, IL 62656
Ph: (217)376-3222
E-mail: nwesten1@abelink.com
URL: http://userweb.abelink.com/tbarcalo/LJWCindex.htm
Contact: Ms. Nina Westen, Pres.
Local.

2276 ■ Lincoln - Logan County Chamber of Commerce
1555 Fifth St.
Lincoln, IL 62656
Ph: (217)735-2385
Fax: (217)735-9205
E-mail: chamber@lincolnillinois.com
URL: http://www.lincolnillinois.com
Contact: Bobbi Abbott, Exec.Dir.
Founded: 1903. **Members:** 250. **Membership Dues:** private business or organization (base), $350 (an-

nual) • associate (retired), $75 (annual) • financial firm (base), $250 (annual). **Staff:** 3. **Local**. Strives to enhance the general welfare and prosperity of the Lincoln and Logan County area. **Committees:** Agriculture; Ambassadors; Community Awards; Government/Education; Marketing; Technology. **Affiliated With:** U.S. Chamber of Commerce. **Publications:** *Update*, monthly. Newsletter.

2277 ■ Lincoln and Logan County Development Partnership
c/o Mark L. Smith, Exec. Officer
1555 5th St.
Lincoln, IL 62656
Ph: (217)735-2385 (217)732-8739
Fax: (217)735-9205
URL: http://www.lincolnlogan.com
Contact: Rob Orr, Exec.Dir.
Local.

2278 ■ Lincoln-Railsplitter REACT
911 Pekin St.
Lincoln, IL 62656
Ph: (217)732-9488
URL: http://www.reactintl.org/teaminfo/usa_teams/teams-usil.htm
Local. Trained communication experts and professional volunteers. Provides volunteer public service and emergency communications through the use of radios (Citizen Band, General Mobile Radio Service, UHF and HAM). Coordinates with radio industries and government on safety communication matters and supports charitable activities and community organizations.

2279 ■ Main Street Lincoln
229 S Kickapoo
Lincoln, IL 62656
Ph: (217)732-2929
E-mail: manager@mainstreetlincoln.com
URL: http://www.mainstreetlincoln.com
Local.

2280 ■ Phi Theta Kappa, Iota Chi Chapter - Lincoln College
c/o June Burke
300 Keokuk St.
Lincoln, IL 62656
Ph: (217)732-3155
E-mail: jburke@lincolncollege.edu
URL: http://www.ptk.org/directories/chapters/IL/172-1.htm
Contact: June Burke, Advisor
Local.

2281 ■ United Way of Logan County
PO Box 684
Lincoln, IL 62656-0684
Ph: (217)735-4499 (405)236-8441
Fax: (217)735-1599
E-mail: jliles@unitedwayokc.org
URL: http://www.unitedwayokc.org/partnerships_uwlc.htm
Contact: Jim Liles, Dir. of Resource Development Operations
Founded: 1961. **Staff:** 1. **Budget:** $100,000. **Nonmembership**. **Local**. Conducts fundraising to support non-profit groups meeting specific criteria. **Affiliated With:** United Way of America. **Conventions/Meetings:** annual meeting - January.

Lincolnshire

2282 ■ American Cancer Society, Highland Park - Lake County Regional
100 Tristate Intl., Ste.125
Lincolnshire, IL 60069
Ph: (847)317-0025
Fax: (847)317-0366
URL: http://www.cancer.org
Contact: Catherine Sawyer, Regional VP
Local. **Affiliated With:** American Cancer Society.

2283 ■ American Statistical Association, Northeastern Illinois Chapter
c/o Melvin Munsaka, Pres.
Takeda Pharmacological North Amer., Inc.
475 Half Day Rd.
Lincolnshire, IL 60069
Ph: (847)383-7390
E-mail: mmunsaka@tpna.com
URL: National Affiliate–www.amstat.org
Contact: Melvin Munsaka, Pres.
Local. Promotes statistical practice, applications and research. Works for the improvement of statistical education at all levels. Seeks opportunities to advance the statistics profession. **Affiliated With:** American Statistical Association.

2284 ■ Greater Lincolnshire Chamber of Commerce (GLCC)
175 Olde Half Day Rd., Ste.125
Lincolnshire, IL 60069-3061
Ph: (847)793-2409
Fax: (847)793-2405
E-mail: tglcc@aol.com
URL: http://www.lincolnshirechamber.org
Contact: Jane Meloy, Exec.Dir.
Founded: 1973. **Membership Dues:** business, $205-$1,890 (annual) • hospital, hotel and motel (per room), $2 (annual) • financial institution, $525 (annual) • nonprofit, $200 (annual). **Local**. Works to serve the needs of businesses in the Greater Lincolnshire area. Provides a community and business guide for all area residents and businesses. **Computer Services:** Online services, member listings. **Affiliated With:** Better Business Bureau; Chicagoland Chamber of Commerce. **Publications:** Newsletter. **Conventions/Meetings:** monthly luncheon, with speakers - every 2nd Tuesday • bimonthly meeting - every 3rd Wednesday.

2285 ■ Illinois Association of Occupational Health Nurses (IAOHN)
c/o Patricia Hovany, Ed.
8 Yorkshire Dr.
Lincolnshire, IL 60069
Ph: (773)975-8773
E-mail: phovany@hotmail.com
URL: http://www.iaohn.org
Contact: Ellen Pyrek, Pres.
State. Advances the profession of occupational and environmental health nursing. Promotes public awareness of occupational health nursing. **Affiliated With:** American Association of Occupational Health Nurses.

2286 ■ International Graphic Arts Education Association - Region 1, North Central
c/o Thomas Loch, VP
Stevenson HS District 125
One Stevenson Dr.
Lincolnshire, IL 60069
Ph: (847)634-4000
Fax: (847)634-0983
E-mail: aloch@district125.k12.il.us
URL: National Affiliate–www.igaea.org
Contact: Thomas Loch, VP
Regional. Provides leadership for professional growth and development in graphic communications education and related subjects. Fosters scholarship, research and information sharing through partnership with educational and industrial associations, companies and individuals. Promotes the graphic communications industry and its career opportunities. **Affiliated With:** International Graphic Arts Education Association.

Lincolnwood

2287 ■ American Legion, Lincolnwood Post 1226
4170 W Morse Ave.
Lincolnwood, IL 60712
Ph: (708)674-4157
Fax: (309)663-5783
URL: National Affiliate–www.legion.org
Local. **Affiliated With:** American Legion.

2288 ■ Illinois State Bowling Proprietors Association (ISBPA)
7356 N Cicero Ave.
Lincolnwood, IL 60712
Ph: (847)982-1305
Fax: (847)982-9048
E-mail: bill@bowlillinois.com
URL: http://www.bowlillinois.com
Contact: R. William Duff Jr., Exec.Dir.
Members: 200. **State**.

2289 ■ Lincolnwood Chamber of Commerce and Industry
7001 N Lawndale Ave.
Lincolnwood, IL 60712
Ph: (847)679-5760
Fax: (847)679-5790
E-mail: dlass@lincolnwoodchamber.org
URL: http://www.lincolnwoodchamber.org
Contact: Diana Lass, Exec.Dir.
Founded: 1978. **Members:** 255. **Membership Dues:** business (based on number of employees), $160-$900 (annual). **Local**. Promotes business and community development in Lincolnwood, IL. **Awards:** Madeleine Grant Memorial College Scholarship. **Frequency:** annual. **Type:** scholarship. **Recipient:** for high school seniors. **Computer Services:** database, list of members • information services, profile of the local community. **Telecommunication Services:** electronic mail, lwdcci@aol.com. **Affiliated With:** U.S. Chamber of Commerce. **Formerly:** (2005) Lincolnwood Chamber of Commerce. **Publications:** Directory, annual • Newsletter, quarterly. **Circulation:** 700. **Advertising:** accepted.

Lindenhurst

2290 ■ American Legion, Lake Villa Township Post 1219
1901 Hazelwood Dr.
Lindenhurst, IL 60046
Ph: (708)356-6635
Fax: (309)663-5783
URL: National Affiliate–www.legion.org
Local. **Affiliated With:** American Legion.

2291 ■ Chicago Model Yacht Club No. 7
c/o Tom Lenhart
925 Sumac Ct.
Lindenhurst, IL 60046
Ph: (847)265-5586
URL: http://www.chicago-rc-model-yacht-club.org
Contact: Tom Lenhart, Contact
Local.

2292 ■ Lindenhurst - Lake Villa Chamber of Commerce
500 Grand Ave.
PO Box 6075
Lindenhurst, IL 60046-6075
Ph: (847)356-8446
Fax: (847)356-8561
E-mail: llvchamber@llvchamber.com
URL: http://www.llvchamber.com
Contact: Connie Meadie, Exec.Dir.
Members: 260. **Membership Dues:** sustaining, $200 (annual) • gold, $500 (annual) • corporate, $1,000 (annual). **Local**. Helps to promote a sound economic climate in Northeastern Illinois. **Computer Services:** Information services, member listing. **Telecommunication Services:** electronic mail, llvcoc@mc.net. **Publications:** *On the Move*, monthly. Newsletter. **Advertising:** accepted. Alternate Formats: online.

Lisle

2293 ■ American Legion, First National Post 985
824 Maple Ave.
Lisle, IL 60532
Ph: (312)732-2167
Fax: (309)663-5783
URL: National Affiliate–www.legion.org
Local. **Affiliated With:** American Legion.

2294 ■ Chicago Chapter of the International Society for Performance Improvement (CISPI)
6382 Hastings Ln.
Lisle, IL 60532
Ph: (630)585-3681
Fax: (630)524-9033
E-mail: info@cispi.com
URL: http://www.cispi.com
Contact: Gretchen Hartke, Pres.
Local. Performance technologists, training directors, human resource managers, instructional designers, human factors practitioners, and organizational development consultants who work in a variety of industries such as automotive, communications and telecommunications, computer, financial services, government agencies, health services, manufacturing, the military, travel/hospitality, and education. Dedicated to improving productivity and performance in the workplace through the application of performance and instructional technologies.

2295 ■ Girl Scouts of DuPage County Council
c/o Melody Thompson
2400 Ogden Ave., Ste.400
Lisle, IL 60532-3933
Ph: (630)544-5900
Fax: (630)544-5999
E-mail: info@girlscoutsofdupage.org
URL: http://www.girlscoutsofdupage.org
Local.

2296 ■ Illinois Academy of Family Physicians (IAFP)
c/o Vincent D. Keenan, CAE, Exec.VP
4756 Main St.
Lisle, IL 60532-1724
Ph: (630)435-0257
Fax: (630)435-0433
Free: (800)826-7944
E-mail: vkeenan@iafp.com
URL: http://www.aafp.org/cgi-bin/chapterlookup.pl?chapter=il
Contact: Vincent D. Keenan CAE, Exec.VP
Founded: 1948. **Members:** 4,000. **Membership Dues:** active, $350 (annual). **Staff:** 10. **Budget:** $3,900,000. **Local Groups:** 28. **State**. Promotes excellence in the health and well-being of the people of Illinois through support and education of family physicians, and the families and communities they serve. **Awards:** Distinguished Service Award. **Frequency:** annual. **Type:** recognition • Family Physician of the Year. **Frequency:** annual. **Type:** recognition. **Recipient:** for IAFP member in active practice • Family Practice Teacher of the Year. **Frequency:** annual. **Type:** recognition • Media Award. **Frequency:** annual. **Type:** recognition. **Affiliated With:** American Academy of Family Physicians. **Publications:** *Family Physician*, bimonthly. Newsletter. **Price:** $35.00/year. **Circulation:** 4,000. **Advertising:** accepted • Membership Directory, annual. **Price:** free for members; $150.00 for nonmembers. **Advertising:** accepted. **Conventions/Meetings:** annual Family Practice Weekend - meeting, includes continuing medical education programs, committee and board meetings, and family fun activities (exhibits).

2297 ■ Illinois Spina Bifida Association
3080 Ogden Ave., Ste.103
Lisle, IL 60532
Ph: (630)637-1050 (773)581-2426
Fax: (630)637-1066
Free: (800)969-ISBA
E-mail: ilsba1@aol.com
URL: http://illinoisspinabifidaassociation.com
Contact: Mr. Adam Rappaport MS, Exec.Dir.
Founded: 1969. **Members:** 900. **Membership Dues:** $35 (annual). **Staff:** 2. **Budget:** $400,000. **Languages:** English, Spanish. **State**. Members are comprised of families with Spina Bifida, professionals, and interested individuals. Activities offered include a summer residential camp, family outreach program, newsletter, family picnic, holiday party, information and referral. The mission of the ISBA is to improve the quality of life of people with Spina Bifida through direct services, information and referral and public awareness. **Libraries:** **Type:** open to the public. **Holdings:** 150. **Subjects:** spina bifida - development. **Awards:** **Frequency:** annual. **Type:** scholarship. **Recipient:** for post secondary education, must have spina bifida, be a member and resident of Illinois. **Publications:** *Crossroads*, quarterly. Newsletter. **Price:** free. **Circulation:** 1,100. **Advertising:** accepted. **Conventions/Meetings:** seminar - 3/year.

2298 ■ Institute of Real Estate Management - Chicago Chapter No. 23
c/o TTC Realty Group
801 Warrenville Rd., Ste.222
Lisle, IL 60532
Ph: (630)353-0700
Fax: (630)353-0600
E-mail: admin@iremchicago.org
URL: http://www.iremchicago.org
Contact: Louis G. Lutz Jr., Pres.
Local. Represents real property and asset management professionals. Works to promote professional ethics and standards in the field of property management. Strives to keep its members informed on the latest legislative activities and current industry trends. Provides classroom training, continuing education seminars, job referral service and candidate assistance services to enhance the effectiveness and professionalism of its members. **Affiliated With:** Institute of Real Estate Management.

2299 ■ Lisle Chamber of Commerce (LCC)
4733 Main St.
Lisle, IL 60532
Ph: (630)964-0052
Fax: (630)964-2726
E-mail: info@lislechamber.com
URL: http://www.lislechamber.com
Contact: Tom Althoff, Pres./CEO
Founded: 1983. **Members:** 400. **Staff:** 5. **Budget:** $125,000. **Local**. Promotes business and community development in the Lisle, IL area. **Affiliated With:** U.S. Chamber of Commerce. **Publications:** *Community Profile on Village of Lisle*, biennial. Directory • *Membership Directory and Product/Services Guide*, annual. Newsletter • Newsletter, bimonthly. **Conventions/Meetings:** monthly meeting.

2300 ■ Lucent Humanist League
Lucent Technologies
Greg Spahn NWN 7B-214
2701 Lucent Ln.
Lisle, IL 60532
Ph: (630)224-7479
E-mail: gspahn@lucent.com
URL: National Affiliate–www.americanhumanist.org
Local.

2301 ■ Mothers Against Drunk Driving, Dupage County
2900 Ogden Ave.
Lisle, IL 60532-1676
Ph: (630)369-6233
Fax: (630)369-8033
E-mail: madd_dupage@juno.com
Contact: Mary Gall, Chapter Admin.
Founded: 1987. **Members:** 300. **Membership Dues:** individual, $20 (annual) • family, $40 (annual). **Local**. Victims of drunk driving crashes; concerned citizens. Encourages citizen participation in working towards reform of the drunk driving problem and the prevention of underage drinking. Acts as the voice of victims of drunk driving crashes by speaking on their behalf to communities, businesses, and educational groups. **Affiliated With:** Mothers Against Drunk Driving.

2302 ■ Psi Chi, National Honor Society in Psychology - Benedectine University
c/o Dept. of Psychology
5700 Coll. Rd.
Lisle, IL 60532-0900
Ph: (630)829-6230 (630)829-6485
Fax: (630)829-6231
E-mail: jiaccino@ben.edu
URL: http://www.psichi.org/chapters/info.asp?chapter_id=467
Contact: James F. Iaccino PhD, Advisor
Local.

2303 ■ Romance Writers of America, Windy City Chapter
c/o Laura Renken, Pres.
PO Box 3523
Lisle, IL 60532
E-mail: melody@melodythomas.com
URL: http://www.windycityrwa.com
Contact: Laura Renken, Pres.
Founded: 1992. **Members:** 75. **Membership Dues:** individual, $20 (annual). **Local**. Strives to promote excellence in romantic fiction, to help writers become published and to establish careers in their writing field, while maintaining a safe, supportive environment. **Affiliated With:** Romance Writers of America. **Conventions/Meetings:** semimonthly workshop, with guest speaker - every 2nd and 4th Wednesday of the month.

2304 ■ U.S.A. Track and Field, Illinois
1213 Maple Ave., Fl. 2, Unit E
Lisle, IL 60532
Ph: (630)512-0727
Fax: (630)512-0728
E-mail: usatfil@sbcglobal.net
URL: http://www.usatfillinois.org
Contact: Eldon Bastian, Office Mgr.
State. **Affiliated With:** U.S.A. Track and Field.

Litchfield

2305 ■ American Legion, Kniery-Knagg Post 436
PO Box 1
Litchfield, IL 62056
Ph: (217)324-6213
Fax: (309)663-5783
URL: National Affiliate–www.legion.org
Local. **Affiliated With:** American Legion.

2306 ■ Hearts United Association
c/o Vicki G. Shaffer
107 W Ryder St.
Litchfield, IL 62056-0000
Ph: (217)324-2876
Fax: (217)324-2937
E-mail: hearts@consolidated.net
Contact: Vicki Shaffer, Admin.
Founded: 1999. **Staff:** 1. **Budget:** $70,000. **Local Groups:** 1. **Local**. Serves 15 local churches; operates as a charitable clearinghouse to mobilize Christians to care for others. Runs a thrift store; limited funds are available for basic requirement assistance, such as food, clothing or housing; development of a transitional housing program projected to start January 2004.

2307 ■ Litchfield Chamber of Commerce
311 N Madison
PO Box 334
Litchfield, IL 62056
Ph: (217)324-2533
Fax: (217)324-3559
E-mail: chamber@litchfieldil.com
URL: http://www.litchfieldil.com/chamber
Contact: Charlene Pigg, Exec.VP
Founded: 1936. **Members:** 160. **Budget:** $35,000. **Local**. Assumes a leadership role to promote and stimulate the economic growth within the greater Litchfield area by mobilizing the talents and energies of the chamber's members. **Computer Services:** Information services, membership directory. **Publications:** *Chamber World*, monthly. Newsletter. **Conventions/Meetings:** monthly board meeting • periodic meeting.

Livingston

2308 ■ American Legion, Illinois Post 1984
c/o John J. Slifka
PO Box 314
Livingston, IL 62058
Ph: (618)637-2527
Fax: (309)663-5783
URL: National Affiliate–www.legion.org
Contact: John J. Slifka, Contact
Local. Affiliated With: American Legion.

Lockport

2309 ■ American Legion, Illinois Post 18
c/o John Olson
15052 Archer Ave.
Lockport, IL 60441
Ph: (815)838-2559
Fax: (309)663-5783
URL: National Affiliate–www.legion.org
Contact: John Olson, Contact
Local. Affiliated With: American Legion.

2310 ■ American Legion, Illinois Post 123
c/o Leroy A. Mc Cullough
13020 Woodland Dr.
Lockport, IL 60441
Ph: (309)663-0361
Fax: (309)663-5783
URL: National Affiliate–www.legion.org
Contact: Leroy A. Mc Cullough, Contact
Local. Affiliated With: American Legion.

2311 ■ American Welding Society, Chicago Section 002
c/o Bob Zimny, Chm.
Welders Unlimited
16146 W Blackhawk Dr.
Lockport, IL 60441
Ph: (773)802-2572
E-mail: bzimny@yahoo.com
URL: National Affiliate–www.aws.org
Local. Professional engineering society in the field of welding. **Affiliated With:** American Welding Society.

2312 ■ Antique Automobile Club of America, Illinois Region - Des Plaines Valley Chapter
c/o Lee E. Nelson, Pres.
522 S Washington St.
Lockport, IL 60441
Ph: (815)729-0366
E-mail: l-n522@juno.com
URL: http://local.aaca.org/illinois
Contact: Lee E. Nelson, Pres.
Founded: 1959. **Local.** Collectors, hobbyists, and others interested in the preservation, maintenance, and restoration of automobiles and in automotive history. **Affiliated With:** Antique Automobile Club of America.

2313 ■ Christians Golfers' Association - Lockport
c/o Beth Ragona, Pres.
16833 Deer Path Dr.
Lockport, IL 60491-6904
Ph: (815)485-5569
URL: National Affiliate–www.christiangolfer.org
Contact: Beth Ragona, Pres.
Local.

2314 ■ Joliet Archery Club
c/o Carrie Hooper, Membership Chm.
15027 Arboretum Dr.
Lockport, IL 60441-7101
Ph: (708)301-5321
E-mail: jacmembership@hotmail.com
URL: http://www.jolietarcheryclub.org
Contact: Carrie Hooper, Membership Chm.
Local.

2315 ■ Lockport Area Exchange Club
PO Box 94
Lockport, IL 60441
Ph: (815)838-0790
E-mail: frankaexch@aol.com
URL: http://hometown.aol.com/frankaexch/Overview.html
Local.

2316 ■ Lockport Chamber of Commerce (LCC)
921 S State St.
Lockport, IL 60441-3435
Ph: (815)838-3357
Fax: (815)838-2653
E-mail: office@lockportchamber.com
URL: http://www.lockportchamber.com
Contact: Ms. Sharon Hannah, Exec.Dir.
Founded: 1974. **Members:** 240. **Staff:** 2. **Local.** Promotes business and community development in Lockport, IL. Sponsors parades as well as a variety of social and promotional activities. **Awards:** Dollars for Scholars. **Frequency:** annual. **Type:** scholarship. **Recipient:** for college-bound Lockport students. **Telecommunication Services:** information service, pertinent business information to members. **Affiliated With:** Illinois Retail Merchants Association; Illinois State Chamber of Commerce. **Publications:** *Lockport*, biennial. Directory. Contains listing of member businesses as well as local information; distributed to new residents and businesses. **Circulation:** 1,500. **Advertising:** accepted • *Lockport Connections*, monthly. Newsletter. **Price:** free for members. **Circulation:** 300 • *Lockport Map*, biennial. Brochure. **Conventions/Meetings:** annual Business After Hours - meeting • annual Business Expo - trade show • annual Golf Outing - competition • monthly meeting, monthly updates from local government officials and informational programming - always 2nd Monday.

2317 ■ Midwest Crossroad Chorus of Sweet Adelines International
St. Dennis Church
1214 S Hamilton St.
Lockport, IL 60441
Free: (866)LUV-SING
E-mail: chorus@midwestcrossroad.com
URL: http://www.midwestcrossroad.com
Contact: Tori Hicks, Dir.
Regional. Advances the musical art form of barbershop harmony through education and performances. Provides education, training and coaching in the development of women's four-part barbershop harmony. **Affiliated With:** Sweet Adelines International.

2318 ■ Pontiac-Oakland Club International, Illinois Chapter
c/o Carla Knotek, Membership Admin./Ed.
15456 Scott Ct.
Lockport, IL 60441
E-mail: info@il-chapter-poci.org
URL: http://www.il-chapter-poci.org
Contact: Ken Bauco, Pres.
Membership Dues: individual, $20 (annual). **State. Affiliated With:** Pontiac-Oakland Club International.

2319 ■ Williana Clumber Spaniel Club
c/o Judy Sutfin, Dir.
12549 Hadley Rd.
Lockport, IL 60441
Ph: (815)485-8160
E-mail: sumerstraw@aol.com
URL: http://www.williana.org
Contact: Sharon Holland, Pres.
Local.

Loda

2320 ■ American Legion, Iroquois Post 503
107 E Adams St.
Loda, IL 60948
Ph: (309)663-0361
Fax: (309)663-5783
URL: National Affiliate–www.legion.org
Local. Affiliated With: American Legion.

2321 ■ Loda Lions Club
PO Box 188
Loda, IL 60948
Ph: (217)386-2748
URL: http://www.angelfire.com/il2/lodalionsclub
Local. Affiliated With: Lions Clubs International.

Lomax

2322 ■ American Legion, Henderson County Post 765
RR 1, Box 131
Lomax, IL 61454
Ph: (309)924-1766
Fax: (309)663-5783
URL: National Affiliate–www.legion.org
Local. Affiliated With: American Legion.

Lombard

2323 ■ American Legion, Illinois Post 135
c/o Hiram J. Slifer
700 S Fairfield Ave.
Lombard, IL 60148
Ph: (309)663-0361
Fax: (309)663-5783
URL: National Affiliate–www.legion.org
Contact: Hiram J. Slifer, Contact
Local. Affiliated With: American Legion.

2324 ■ American Legion, Lombard Post 391
218 E St. Charles Rd.
Lombard, IL 60148
Ph: (708)279-4723
Fax: (309)663-5783
URL: National Affiliate–www.legion.org
Local. Affiliated With: American Legion.

2325 ■ American Legion, Riverside Post 488
2600 S Finley Rd., Apt. 3509
Lombard, IL 60148
Ph: (309)663-0361
Fax: (309)663-5783
URL: National Affiliate–www.legion.org
Local. Affiliated With: American Legion.

2326 ■ Camp Fire USA Illinois Prairie Council
270 N Eisenhower Ln., No. 3A
Lombard, IL 60148
Ph: (630)629-5160
Fax: (630)629-6324
E-mail: info@campfireusa-illinois.org
URL: http://www.campfireusa-illinois.org
Contact: Joseph P. Haines, Exec.Dir.
Founded: 1993. **Members:** 200. **Membership Dues:** individual, $15 (annual) • family, $30 (annual). **Budget:** $250,000. **State.** Builds caring, confident youth and future leaders through a variety of programs including clubs, camping, in-school programs, after-school programs, and community empowerment programs. **Affiliated With:** Camp Fire USA. **Formerly:** (2001) Illinois Prairie Council of Camp Fire. **Publications:** *The Prairie Post*, quarterly. Newsletter. **Conventions/Meetings:** monthly board meeting • annual meeting.

2327 ■ Chicago Whitewater Association (CWA)
c/o Frank Jakubowski
473 N La Londe Ave.
Lombard, IL 60148-1837
Ph: (847)328-0145
Fax: (847)328-0359
E-mail: cwa@chicagowhitewater.org
URL: http://www.chicagowhitewater.org
Contact: Steve Paolini, Pres.
Founded: 1970. **Members:** 300. **Membership Dues:** individual to join CWA, $20 (annual) • individual to join both CWA and ACA, $35 (annual) • family to join both CWA and ACA, $40 (annual). **Local.** Works to promote fun, safety, and awareness on the river. Members include individuals interested in kayaking

and canoeing. **Affiliated With:** American Canoe Association; American Whitewater. **Publications:** *The Gradient*, 10/year. Newsletter. Includes trip reports, event schedules. **Conventions/Meetings:** monthly meeting - first Wednesday.

2328 ■ Chicagoland Evaluation Association (CEA)
c/o Matthew Hanson
1064 Kufrin Way
Lombard, IL 60148
Ph: (630)253-4465
E-mail: mrhanson@uiuc.edu
URL: National Affiliate–www.eval.org
Contact: Matthew Hanson, Contact
Regional. Seeks to improve evaluation practices and methods. Provides a forum for professional development, networking and exchange of practical, methodological and theoretical knowledge in the field of evaluation. Promotes evaluation as a profession. **Affiliated With:** American Evaluation Association.

2329 ■ Chicagoland Thunderbirds
PO Box 565
Lombard, IL 60148
Ph: (630)865-3461
E-mail: president@thunderbirds.org
URL: http://www.thunderbirds.org
Local. **Affiliated With:** Vintage Thunderbird Club International.

2330 ■ Council of State Governments Midwestern Office (CSG)
701 E 22nd St., Ste.110
Lombard, IL 60148
Ph: (630)925-1922
Fax: (630)925-1930
E-mail: csgm@csg.org
URL: http://www.csgmidwest.org
Contact: Michael H. McCabe, Dir.
Founded: 1933. **Regional**. **Affiliated With:** Council of State Governments. **Formerly:** (2005) Midwestern Legislative Conference of the Council of State Governments.

2331 ■ DuPage Senior Citizens Council (DSCC)
1919 S Highland Ave., Bldg. A, Ste.210
Lombard, IL 60148
Ph: (630)620-0804
Fax: (630)620-1158
E-mail: info@dupageseniorcouncil.org
URL: http://www.dupageseniorcouncil.org
Contact: Greg Weider, Exec.Dir.
Local.

2332 ■ Illinois Association of Mortgage Brokers (IAMB)
c/o Marve Stockert, Exec.Dir.
350 W 22nd St.
Lombard, IL 60148
Ph: (630)916-7720
Fax: (630)396-3501
E-mail: mstocker@iamb.org
URL: http://www.iamb.org
Contact: Marve Stockert, Exec.Dir.
State.

2333 ■ Illinois Food Retailers Association
c/o Brian R. Jordan, CAE, Pres. & C.E.O.
1919 S Highland Ave.
Lombard, IL 60148-0000
Ph: (630)627-8100
Fax: (630)627-8106
E-mail: ilfood@ilfood.org
State.

2334 ■ Illinois Neurofibromatosis
PO Box 1923
Lombard, IL 60148
Ph: (630)932-8111
Fax: (630)932-8119
Free: (800)322-6363
E-mail: ilnfinc@sbcglobal.net
URL: http://www.nfinc.org
Contact: Kim Bischoff, Exec.Dir.
Founded: 1982. **Members:** 3,000. **Membership Dues:** individual, $25 (annual). **Staff:** 1. **Budget:** $100,000. **Local Groups:** 1. **State**. Persons with neurofibromatosis, their relatives, and medical professionals. Seeks to promote public awareness of the disease. Provides support for patients and their families. Promotes and funds research on the causes, treatments, and eventual cure for neurofibromatosis. **Affiliated With:** Neurofibromatosis. **Publications:** *Understanding Neurofibromatosis*, periodic. Booklet • Newsletter, quarterly. **Conventions/Meetings:** quarterly meeting • annual symposium - always fall.

2335 ■ International Association of Ministers Wives and Ministers Widows, Illinois
10 17 Beverly Ct.
Lombard, IL 60148
Ph: (630)932-3211
URL: National Affiliate–www.iamwmw.org
Contact: Mrs. Gladys Piper, Pres.
State. **Affiliated With:** International Association of Ministers Wives and Ministers Widows.

2336 ■ Kiwanis Club of Lombard
c/o Jay Wojcik
PO Box 321
Lombard, IL 60148
Ph: (630)827-4426
E-mail: j.wojcik@sbcglobal.net
URL: http://myschoolonline.com/site/0,1876,16836-145896-21-24828,00.html
Contact: Susan Friend, Pres.
Local.

2337 ■ Lombard Area Chamber of Commerce and Industry
225 W St. Charles Rd.
Lombard, IL 60148
Ph: (630)627-5040
Fax: (630)627-5519
E-mail: info@lombardchamber.com
URL: http://www.lombardchamber.com
Contact: Tom Ploke, Pres.
Members: 180. **Membership Dues:** business - standard (depends on the number of employees), $150-$900 (annual) • business - silver (depends on the number of employees), $225-$1,200 (annual) • business - gold (depends on the number of employees), $300-$1,500 (annual) • not for profit, $150 (annual). **Staff:** 2. **Budget:** $52,000. **Regional Groups:** 1. **State Groups:** 1. **Local Groups:** 1. **Local**. Promotes business and community development in the Lombard, IL area. Sponsors Lilac Festival and Lilac Ball. Sponsors golf outing. **Awards:** Business Pride Award. **Frequency:** annual. **Type:** recognition. **Recipient:** for successful and responsible companies • Jim Bell Distinguished Developer Award. **Frequency:** annual. **Type:** recognition. **Recipient:** for the construction of high quality projects • Major Milestone Award. **Frequency:** annual. **Type:** recognition. **Recipient:** for significant contribution to business and community • Property Improvement Award. **Frequency:** annual. **Type:** recognition. **Recipient:** for improvement in properties • Property Stewardship Award. **Frequency:** annual. **Type:** recognition. **Recipient:** for excellent maintenance of properties. **Computer Services:** database, list of members • information services, facts about the local community. **Telecommunication Services:** electronic mail, lacci@lombardchamber.com. **Formerly:** (1999) Lombard Area Chamber of Commerce and Industry. **Publications:** *Lombard Community Directory*, annual • *The Sourcebook: Directory of Goods and Services* • *Village*. Directory • Newsletter, monthly. **Price:** free. **Circulation:** 180. **Advertising:** accepted. **Conventions/Meetings:** periodic conference.

2338 ■ Lombard Junior Woman's Club
c/o Cheryl Schroeder, Pres.
PO Box 512
Lombard, IL 60148
Ph: (630)495-3121
E-mail: ndkohl@msn.com
Contact: Nancy Kohl, Pres.

2339 ■ Medinah Shriners
c/o John Martin
78 Eisenhower Ln. N
Lombard, IL 60148
Ph: (630)705-9901
Fax: (630)705-9907
E-mail: info@medinah.org
URL: http://medinah.org
Contact: John Martin, Potentate
Local. **Affiliated With:** Imperial Council of the Ancient Arabic Order of the Nobles of the Mystic Shrine for North America.

2340 ■ Midwestern Governors Association (MGA)
c/o Ilene K. Grossman, Asst.Dir.
701 E 22nd St., Ste.110
Lombard, IL 60148-5095
Ph: (630)925-1922
Fax: (630)925-1930
E-mail: igrossman@csg.org
URL: http://www.midwestgovernors.org
Contact: Ilene K. Grossman, Asst.Dir.
Regional. **Affiliated With:** Council of State Governments. **Formerly:** (2005) Midwestern Governors' Conference of the Council of State Governments.

2341 ■ Wilmington Illinois Beagle Club
c/o Thomas A. Samas
342 Garfield Terr.
Lombard, IL 60148-2716
URL: National Affiliate–www.akc.org
Contact: Thomas A. Samas, Contact
Local. **Affiliated With:** American Kennel Club.

London Mills

2342 ■ American Legion, London Mills Post 470
RR 1
London Mills, IL 61544
Ph: (309)663-0361
Fax: (309)663-5783
URL: National Affiliate–www.legion.org
Local. **Affiliated With:** American Legion.

2343 ■ Illinois Quarter Horse Association, District No. 4
c/o Valerie Watson, Dir.
12860 E Lyons Rd.
London Mills, IL 61544
Ph: (309)778-2436
E-mail: dvwqhp@winco.net
URL: http://www.ilqha.com
Contact: Valerie Watson, Dir.
Local. **Affiliated With:** American Quarter Horse Association.

2344 ■ Spoon River Valley Pheasants Forever
8766 E Young Rd.
London Mills, IL 61544
Ph: (309)647-0348
Contact: Mike Dorethy, Pres.
Local. **Affiliated With:** Pheasants Forever.

Long Point

2345 ■ American Legion, Long Point Post 1217
4th St.
Long Point, IL 61333
Ph: (815)854-2662
Fax: (309)663-5783
URL: National Affiliate–www.legion.org
Local. **Affiliated With:** American Legion.

Lostant

2346 ■ American Legion, Lostant Post 173
216 S Main St.
Lostant, IL 61334
Ph: (309)663-0361
Fax: (309)663-5783
URL: National Affiliate–www.legion.org
Local. Affiliated With: American Legion.

Louisville

2347 ■ American Legion, Louisville Post 914
590 S Main St.
Louisville, IL 62858
Ph: (618)665-4555
Fax: (309)663-5783
URL: National Affiliate–www.legion.org
Local. Affiliated With: American Legion.

Loves Park

2348 ■ Access Services of Northern Illinois
7399 Forest Hills Rd.
Loves Park, IL 61111-3974
Ph: (815)282-8824
Fax: (815)282-8835
E-mail: info@accessni.com
URL: http://www.accessni.com
Contact: Matthew Toohey, Exec.Dir.
State. Works to empower and assist individuals with developmental disabilities to participate as full citizens in their community by coordination and advocating for community services and supports of their choice. **Affiliated With:** United Cerebral Palsy Associations.

2349 ■ Illinois Council of Health System Pharmacists (ICHP)
4055 N Perryville Rd.
Loves Park, IL 61111
Ph: (815)227-9292
Fax: (815)227-9294
E-mail: scottm@ichpnet.org
URL: http://www.ichpnet.org
Contact: Scott Meyers, Exec.VP
State.

2350 ■ Loves Park Lions Club
100 Heart Blvd.
Loves Park, IL 61111
Ph: (815)987-3557
URL: http://lovesparkil.lionwap.org
Contact: Gary Binicewicz, Pres.
Local. Affiliated With: Lions Clubs International.

2351 ■ Loves Park - Machesney Park Chamber of Commerce
100 Heart Blvd.
Loves Park, IL 61111
Ph: (815)633-3999
Fax: (815)633-4057
URL: http://www.parkschamber.com
Contact: Kurt Cottier, Pres.
Members: 282. **Local.** Works to build a healthy economy and improve the quality of life in the community. **Committees:** Ambassadors; Community Projects; Fundraising; Legislative; Membership Services; Nominating; Young at Heart Festival. **Also Known As:** (2005) Parks Chamber of Commerce. **Publications:** *Chamber Chatter*, monthly. Newsletter. Alternate Formats: online.

2352 ■ Missouri Society of Health-System Pharmacists (MSHP)
4055 N Perryville Rd.
Loves Park, IL 61111
Ph: (815)227-9292
Fax: (815)227-9294
E-mail: amy.sipe@med.va.gov
URL: http://www.moshp.com/index.asp
Contact: Amy Sipe, Pres.
State. Advances and supports the professional practice of pharmacists in hospitals and health systems. Serves as the collective voice on issues related to medication use and public health. **Affiliated With:** American Society of Health System Pharmacists.

2353 ■ Rockford Area Habitat for Humanity (RAHFH)
c/o Ed McCaskey, Pres.
5183 Harlem Rd.
Loves Park, IL 61111
Ph: (815)636-4573
Fax: (815)636-4574
E-mail: homes@rockfordhabitat.org
URL: http://www.rockfordhabitat.org
Contact: Ed McCaskey, Pres.
Local. Works in partnership with people in need to build decent, affordable housing. Volunteers provide most of the labor, and individual and corporate donors provide money and materials to build Habitat houses.

2354 ■ Rockford Area Society for Human Resource Management
PO Box 2453
Loves Park, IL 61132-0453
E-mail: rockfordshrm@rockfordshrm.org
URL: http://www.rockfordshrm.org
Contact: Jim Schmitt, Pres.
Local. Represents the interests of human resource and industrial relations professionals and executives. Promotes the advancement of human resource management.

2355 ■ Rockford "Noon" Lions Club
6227 Parkridge Rd.
Loves Park, IL 61111
Ph: (815)633-7546
URL: http://rockfordilnoon.lionwap.org
Local. Affiliated With: Lions Clubs International.

Lovington

2356 ■ American Legion, Community Post 429
RR 1, Box 111
Lovington, IL 61937
Ph: (309)663-0361
Fax: (309)663-5783
URL: National Affiliate–www.legion.org
Local. Affiliated With: American Legion.

Ludlow

2357 ■ American Legion, Ludlow Post 518
PO Box 176
Ludlow, IL 60949
Ph: (309)663-0361
Fax: (309)663-5783
URL: National Affiliate–www.legion.org
Local. Affiliated With: American Legion.

2358 ■ Loda Sportsmen's Club
PO Box 211
Ludlow, IL 60949
Ph: (217)396-5621
Fax: (217)379-9064
URL: National Affiliate–www.mynssa.com
Local. Affiliated With: National Skeet Shooting Association.

Lynn Center

2359 ■ American Legion, Ophiem Post 1077
PO Box 28
Lynn Center, IL 61262
Ph: (309)663-0361
Fax: (309)663-5783
URL: National Affiliate–www.legion.org
Local. Affiliated With: American Legion.

Lyons

2360 ■ American Legion, Illinois Post 699
c/o Emil Scheive
PO Box 186
Lyons, IL 60534
Ph: (309)663-0361
Fax: (309)663-5783
URL: National Affiliate–www.legion.org
Contact: Emil Scheive, Contact
Local. Affiliated With: American Legion.

2361 ■ Lyons Lions Club, IL
PO Box 144
Lyons, IL 60534
E-mail: ljmfish@chilitech.com
URL: http://lyonsil.lionwap.org
Contact: Edward J. Chodl, Pres.
Local. Affiliated With: Lions Clubs International.

Machesney Park

2362 ■ American Legion, Illinois Post 60
c/o Walter R. Craig
325 Sycamore Ln.
Machesney Park, IL 61115
Ph: (815)654-1333
Fax: (309)663-5783
URL: National Affiliate–www.legion.org
Contact: Walter R. Craig, Contact
Local. Affiliated With: American Legion.

Mackinaw

2363 ■ American Legion, Emery Whisler Post 607
511 E Fast St.
Mackinaw, IL 61755
Ph: (309)663-0361
Fax: (309)663-5783
URL: National Affiliate–www.legion.org
Local. Affiliated With: American Legion.

2364 ■ Society of Tribologists and Lubrication Engineers - Central Illinois Section
c/o Larry Wegman, Chm.
30456 Grandview Terr.
Mackinaw, IL 61755
Ph: (309)359-8697
Fax: (309)353-1288
E-mail: melagrensis@hotmail.com
URL: National Affiliate–www.stle.org
Contact: Larry Wegman, Chm.
Local. Promotes the advancement of tribology and the practice of lubrication engineering. Stimulates the study and development of lubrication tribology techniques. Promotes higher standards in the field. **Affiliated With:** Society of Tribologists and Lubrication Engineers.

Macomb

2365 ■ American Chemical Society, Mark Twain Section
c/o Mark William Moore, Chm.
110 N Yorktown Rd.
Macomb, IL 61455-9398
Ph: (217)224-6900
Fax: (217)224-4208
E-mail: moore@jwcc.edu
URL: National Affiliate–acswebcontent.acs.org
Contact: Mark William Moore, Chm.
Local. Represents the interests of individuals dedicated to the advancement of chemistry in all its branches. Provides opportunities for peer interaction and career development. **Affiliated With:** American Chemical Society.

2366 ■ American Legion, Mc Donough County Post 6
221 E Washington St.
Macomb, IL 61455
Ph: (309)833-2951
Fax: (309)663-5783
URL: National Affiliate–www.legion.org
Local. Affiliated With: American Legion.

2367 ■ Association for Computing Machinery, Western Illinois University (WIU ACM)
c/o Zach Malmgren, Chm.
447 Stipes Hall
1 University Cir.
Macomb, IL 61455
Ph: (309)298-7437
E-mail: micsa@wiu.edu
URL: http://www.wiu.edu/users/micsa
Contact: Zach Malmgren, Chm.
Regional. Biological, medical, behavioral, and computer scientists; hospital administrators; programmers and others interested in application of computer methods to biological, behavioral, and medical problems. Stimulates understanding of the use and potential of computers in the Biosciences. **Affiliated With:** Association for Computing Machinery.

2368 ■ Centrill West LUA
c/o Bryce Dexter
131 S Randolph
Macomb, IL 61455
Ph: (309)836-5675
Fax: (309)836-5696
URL: National Affiliate–www.naifa.org
Local. Represents the interest of insurance and financial advisors. Advocates for a positive legislative and regulatory environment. Enhances business and professional skills of members. **Affiliated With:** National Association of Insurance and Financial Advisors.

2369 ■ Illinois Groundwater Association (IGA)
c/o Steve Bennett, Treas.
Western Illinois Univ.
Dept. of Geology
1 Univ. Cir.
Macomb, IL 61455
Ph: (309)298-1256
Fax: (309)298-3399
E-mail: sw-bennett1@wiu.edu
URL: http://www.iga.uiuc.edu
Contact: Steve Bennett, Treas.
Founded: 1984. **Membership Dues:** regular, $15 (annual) • student, $5 (annual). **Local**. Representatives of federal, state, county and municipal organizations, consulting engineers, water well contractors, industries concerned with groundwater resources and anyone interested in the groundwater resources of Illinois. Seeks to advance the knowledge of groundwater resources in Illinois and functions exclusively for charitable and educational purposes. Sponsors student grants each year for students attending an Illinois college and performing groundwater research. **Affiliated With:** National Ground Water Association. **Publications:** Newsletter, semiannual. **Conventions/Meetings:** semiannual meeting, with speakers and discussions of current groundwater issues and research - spring and fall.

2370 ■ Lamoine Valley Association of Realtors
1336 E Pierce
Macomb, IL 61455
Ph: (309)837-2546
Fax: (309)837-4632
E-mail: wollbrin@macomb.com
URL: National Affiliate–www.realtor.org
Contact: Nan Wollbrink, Exec. Officer
Local. Strives to develop real estate business practices. Advocates the right to own, use and transfer real property. Provides a facility for professional development, research and exchange of information among members and to the general public. **Affiliated With:** National Association of Realtors.

2371 ■ Macomb Area Chamber of Commerce & Downtown Development Corporation
214 N. Lafayette St.
PO Box 274
Macomb, IL 61455-0274
Ph: (309)837-4855
Fax: (309)837-4857
E-mail: chamber@macomb.com
Contact: Becky Paulsen, Pres.
Founded: 1933. **Members:** 300. **Staff:** 4. **Budget:** $79,000. **State Groups:** 1. **For-Profit. Local**. Promotes the development and growth of Macomb, IL. Strives to serve as catalyst for the business, professional and educational community's collective efforts to enhance the economic climate and quality of life. **Libraries: Type:** lending. **Holdings:** 75; books, video recordings. **Subjects:** economic development, small businesses. **Boards:** Government Relations; Transportation. **Committees:** Ambassadors; Community Promotions; Retail. **Formerly:** (2004) Macomb Area Chamber of Commerce. **Publications:** *The Macomb Advantage*, monthly. Newsletter. **Price:** free. **Circulation:** 600. **Advertising:** accepted. **Conventions/Meetings:** annual dinner - always January.

2372 ■ Masonic Lodge
133 S. Randolph St.
Macomb, IL 61455
Ph: (309)837-1276

2373 ■ McDonough County United Way
119 N Randolph St., Ste.A
Macomb, IL 61455
Ph: (309)837-9180
URL: http://www.macomb.com/unitedway
Contact: Melanie Falk, Pres.
Founded: 1946. **Staff:** 2. **Budget:** $188,000. **Local Groups:** 16. **Local. Awards: Frequency:** annual. **Type:** monetary. **Affiliated With:** United Way of America. **Publications:** Brochure, annual. Contains an overview of agencies funded and process used. **Circulation:** 3,700.

2374 ■ Mosaic
221 N LaFayette
Macomb, IL 61455
Ph: (309)837-5506
URL: National Affiliate–www.TheArc.org
Contact: Rodessa Heaton, Exec.Dir.
Local. Parents, professional workers, and others interested in individuals with mental retardation. Works to promote services, research, public understanding, and legislation for people with mental retardation and their families. **Affiliated With:** Arc of the United States. **Formerly:** (2005) Bethphage.

2375 ■ Prairie Hills Resource Conservation and Development Council
321 W Univ. Dr.
Macomb, IL 61455
Ph: (309)833-4747
Fax: (309)833-4019
E-mail: david.king@il.usda.gov
URL: http://www.prairiehillsrcd.org
Contact: David King, Coor.
Local. Affiliated With: National Association of Resource Conservation and Development Councils.

2376 ■ Psi Chi, National Honor Society in Psychology - Western Illinois University
c/o Dept. of Psychology
162 Waggoner Hall
Macomb, IL 61455
Ph: (309)298-2672
Fax: (309)298-2179
E-mail: psichi@wiu.edu
URL: http://www.wiu.edu/users/psichi
Local. Affiliated With: Psi Chi, National Honor Society in Psychology.

2377 ■ Western Illinois Youth for Christ
PO Box 126
Macomb, IL 61455
Ph: (309)833-3026
Fax: (309)833-3022
URL: National Affiliate–www.yfc.net
Local. Affiliated With: Youth for Christ/U.S.A.

Magnolia

2378 ■ American Legion, Illini Post 254
123 N Chicago St.
Magnolia, IL 61336
Ph: (815)869-7295
Fax: (309)663-5783
URL: National Affiliate–www.legion.org
Local. Affiliated With: American Legion.

Mahomet

2379 ■ American Legion, Mahomet Post 1015
412 E Main St.
Mahomet, IL 61853
Ph: (309)663-0361
Fax: (309)663-5783
URL: National Affiliate–www.legion.org
Local. Affiliated With: American Legion.

2380 ■ Mahomet Chamber of Commerce
PO Box 1031
Mahomet, IL 61853-1031
Ph: (217)586-3165
E-mail: mahchbrcomm@netscape.net
URL: http://www.mahometchamberofcommerce.com
Contact: Jim Fialkowski, Pres.
Founded: 1985. **Members:** 90. **Membership Dues:** business, $125 (annual). **Staff:** 1. **Local**. Works to advance the general welfare and prosperity of the Mahomet area. **Awards:** Mahomet Chamber of Commerce Scholarship. **Frequency:** annual. **Type:** scholarship. **Recipient:** for a graduate of Mahomet/Seymour high school. **Publications:** *Mahomet Connection*, monthly. Newsletter. Contains current and upcoming events and other items of the chamber. • Brochure. **Conventions/Meetings:** annual banquet - January • monthly meeting - every 3rd Thursday.

Malta

2381 ■ Phi Theta Kappa, Alpha Rho Eta Chapter - Kishwaukee College
c/o Beth Parks
21193 Malta Rd.
Malta, IL 60150
Ph: (815)825-2086
E-mail: bethpark@ns1.kishwaukeecollege.edu
URL: http://www.ptk.org/directories/chapters/IL/190-2.htm
Contact: Beth Parks, Advisor
Local.

Manchester

2382 ■ American Legion, South Scott County Post 751
PO Box 148
Manchester, IL 62663
Ph: (217)587-2916
Fax: (309)663-5783
URL: National Affiliate–www.legion.org
Local. Affiliated With: American Legion.

Manhattan

2383 ■ American Legion, Manhattan Post 935
PO Box 171
Manhattan, IL 60442
Ph: (815)725-2318
Fax: (309)663-5783
URL: National Affiliate–www.legion.org
Local. Affiliated With: American Legion.

2384 ■ Manhattan Chamber of Commerce
PO Box 357
Manhattan, IL 60442-0357
Ph: (815)478-3811
Fax: (815)478-7761
E-mail: chamber@manhattan-il.com
URL: http://www.manhattan-il.com
Contact: Jeane Wade, Pres.
Local. Promotes business and community development in Manhattan, IL.

Manito

2385 ■ American Legion, Hill-Palmer Post 561
402 S Washington St.
Manito, IL 61546
Ph: (309)663-0361
Fax: (309)663-5783
URL: National Affiliate–www.legion.org
Local. Affiliated With: American Legion.

2386 ■ Compassionate Friends - Pekin Area Chapter
c/o Nina Schacherbauer
13529 Cedar St.
Manito, IL 61546
E-mail: tcfpekin@dpc.net
URL: http://www.homestead.com/TCFPekin/TCF_Home.html
Contact: Janet Knight, Chapter Leader
Local.

2387 ■ Manito Area Chamber of Commerce
PO Box 143
Manito, IL 61546
Ph: (309)968-7200
Contact: Rayeann Meeker, Board Member
Local.

Mansfield

2388 ■ American Legion, Illinois Post 650
c/o Kelso M. Garver
PO Box 585
Mansfield, IL 61854
Ph: (309)663-0361
Fax: (309)663-5783
URL: National Affiliate–www.legion.org
Contact: Kelso M. Garver, Contact
Local. Affiliated With: American Legion.

2389 ■ Land of Lincoln Horseshoer's Association No. 30
c/o Andy Jansen
416 E Newton
Mansfield, IL 61854
Ph: (217)871-0779
E-mail: jansen@ilshoer.com
URL: http://www.ilshoer.com/
Contact: Andy Jansen, Pres.
Local. Affiliated With: American Farrier's Association.

Manteno

2390 ■ American Legion, Manteno Post 755
PO Box 641
Manteno, IL 60950
Ph: (815)468-6397
Fax: (309)663-5783
URL: National Affiliate–www.legion.org
Local. Affiliated With: American Legion.

Maple Park

2391 ■ American Legion, Maple Park Post 312
PO Box 97
Maple Park, IL 60151
Ph: (309)663-0361
Fax: (309)663-5783
URL: National Affiliate–www.legion.org
Local. Affiliated With: American Legion.

2392 ■ Jayco Jafari International Travel Club, Flight 32 Holi-Jays
c/o Dan Cain, Pres.
PO Box 155
Maple Park, IL 60151
E-mail: dgrecain@aol.com
URL: National Affiliate–www.jaycorvclub.com
Contact: Dan Cain, Pres.
Local. Affiliated With: Jayco Travel Club.

2393 ■ National Technological Honor Society - Fox Valley Career Center Illinois
47W326 Keslinger Rd.
Maple Park, IL 60151
Ph: (630)365-5113
Fax: (630)365-9088
E-mail: limel@kaneland.org
URL: http://www.kaneland.org
Contact: Larry Imel, Dir.
Local.

2394 ■ National Technological Honor Society - Kaneland High School - Illinois
47W326 Keslinger Rd.
Maple Park, IL 60151
Ph: (630)365-5100
Fax: (630)365-8421
E-mail: dbertrand@kaneland.org
URL: http://www.kaneland.org
Contact: Dan Bertrand, Contact
Local.

Maquon

2395 ■ American Legion, Maquon Post 1099
c/o James Cecil
PO Box 205
Maquon, IL 61458
Ph: (309)663-0361
Fax: (309)663-5783
URL: National Affiliate–www.legion.org
Contact: James Cecil, Contact
Local. Affiliated With: American Legion.

Marengo

2396 ■ American Legion, Kishwaukee Post 192
315 Park Dr.
Marengo, IL 60152
Ph: (815)568-6937
Fax: (309)663-5783
URL: National Affiliate–www.legion.org
Local. Affiliated With: American Legion.

2397 ■ Marengo-Union Chamber of Commerce
116 S State St.
Marengo, IL 60152
Ph: (815)568-6680
Fax: (815)568-6879
E-mail: info@marengo-union.com
URL: http://www.marengo-union.com
Contact: Candice W. Delger, Exec.Dir.
Founded: 1970. **Members:** 220. **Membership Dues:** business (based on number of employees), $200-$710 (annual) • service organization, district, $100 (annual). **Local.** Promotes business and community development in McHenry County, IL. Sponsors annual Settlers Day. **Computer Services:** database, list of members • information services, facts about Marengo, IL. **Telecommunication Services:** electronic mail, webcommittee@marengo-union.com. **Committees:** Annual Dinner; Budget; Clean Sweep; Community Guide; Economic Development; Executive; Personnel; Santa Visits; Settler's Day Parade; Strategic Planning; Website. **Divisions:** Retail. **Publications:** *Chamber Talk*, monthly. Newsletter. **Advertising:** accepted. Alternate Formats: online.

Marine

2398 ■ American Legion, Becker-Reding Post 702
PO Box 431
Marine, IL 62061
Ph: (309)663-0361
Fax: (309)663-5783
URL: National Affiliate–www.legion.org
Local. Affiliated With: American Legion.

Marion

2399 ■ American Cancer Society, Marion - Southern Regional
805 W DeYoung St., Ste.B
Marion, IL 62959
Ph: (618)998-9898
Fax: (618)997-8456
Free: (800)642-7792
URL: http://www.cancer.org
Contact: Carolyn Grear, Regional VP
Local. Affiliated With: American Cancer Society.

2400 ■ American Legion, Williamson Post 147
11720 Longstreet Rd.
Marion, IL 62959
Ph: (618)997-6168
Fax: (309)663-5783
URL: National Affiliate–www.legion.org
Local. Affiliated With: American Legion.

2401 ■ American Lung Association of Illinois, Southern Illinois Region
1616 W Main St., Ste.506
Marion, IL 62959
Ph: (618)997-8160
Free: (800)LUNG-USA
E-mail: info@lungil.org
URL: National Affiliate–www.lungusa.org
Contact: Betty Needling, Dir.
Local. Voluntary organization concerned with the control of lung disease. **Affiliated With:** American Lung Association.

2402 ■ Arthritis Foundation, Southern Illinois Branch
4501 W DeYoung, Ste.B104
Marion, IL 62959
Ph: (618)993-1777
Fax: (618)993-1779
E-mail: greaterillinois@arthritis.org
URL: National Affiliate–www.arthritis.org
Local. Seeks to: discover the cause and improve the methods for the treatment and prevention of arthritis and other rheumatic diseases; increase the number of scientists investigating rheumatic diseases; provide training in rheumatic diseases for more doctors; extend knowledge of arthritis and other rheumatic diseases to the lay public, emphasizing the socioeconomic as well as medical aspects of these diseases. **Affiliated With:** Arthritis Foundation.

2403 ■ Greater Marion Area United Way
PO Box 1901
Marion, IL 62959-8101
Ph: (618)997-7744
URL: National Affiliate–national.unitedway.org
Local. Affiliated With: United Way of America.

2404 ■ Habitat for Humanity of the Greater Marion Area
PO Box 754
Marion, IL 62959-0754
Ph: (618)997-3134
E-mail: marionhabitat@hotmail.com
URL: National Affiliate–www.habitat.org
Local. Affiliated With: Habitat for Humanity International.

2405 ■ Marion Chamber of Commerce
PO Box 307
Marion, IL 62959
Ph: (618)997-6311
Fax: (618)997-4665
Free: (800)699-1760
E-mail: marionchamber@marionillinois.com
URL: http://www.marionillinois.com
Contact: Rose Mary Crear, Exec.Sec.
Members: 650. **Staff:** 2. **Local.** Promotes business and community development in the Marion, IL area. **Committees:** Ambassador; Business/Education; Information Technology; Marketing; Retention; Special Events. **Publications:** Newsletter.

2406 ■ Marion Main Street
PO Box 535
Marion, IL 62959
Ph: (618)993-5299
E-mail: marionmainst@midamer.net
URL: http://www.marionmainstreet.org
Local.

2407 ■ Plumbing-Heating-Cooling Contractors Association, Egyptian
c/o Mr. Bill Atkisson, Pres.
PO Box 576
Marion, IL 62959-0576
Ph: (618)997-5355
Fax: (618)997-5426
E-mail: aaplbg@hotmail.com
URL: National Affiliate–www.phccweb.org
Contact: Mr. Bill Atkisson, Pres.
Local. Represents the plumbing, heating and cooling contractors. Promotes the construction industry. Protects the environment, health, safety and comfort of society. **Affiliated With:** Plumbing-Heating-Cooling Contractors Association.

2408 ■ Quail Unlimited, Shawnee Chapter
22258 Buffalo Lick Rd.
Marion, IL 62959
Ph: (618)982-2749
E-mail: ronaldsims11@hotmail.com
URL: National Affiliate–www.qu.org
Local. Affiliated With: Quail Unlimited.

2409 ■ Regional Economic Development Corp. (REDCO)
2305 W Main St.
Marion, IL 62959
Ph: (618)998-8252
Fax: (618)997-4665
E-mail: redco@redco.org
URL: http://www.redco.org
Founded: 1999. **Members:** 36. **Staff:** 1. **Budget:** $300,000. **Local.** Regional economic development corporation consisting of the municipalities of Williamson County, IL, and Chambers of Commerce of Marion, Herrin and Carterville, IL.

2410 ■ Shawnee Resource Conservation and Development Council
502 Comfort Dr.
Marion, IL 62959
Ph: (618)993-5396
Fax: (618)993-2924
E-mail: roscoe.allen@il.usda.gov
URL: National Affiliate–www.rcdnet.org
Contact: Roscoe Allen, Coor.
Local. Affiliated With: National Association of Resource Conservation and Development Councils.

2411 ■ United Way of Southern Illinois
PO Box 1901
Marion, IL 62959-8101
Ph: (618)997-7744
Fax: (618)993-0141
Free: (866)894-3577
URL: National Affiliate–national.unitedway.org
Local.

2412 ■ Williamson County Events Commission Corp.
c/o Robert Toupal
PO Box 1088
8588 Rte. 148 S
Marion, IL 62959-7588
Ph: (618)993-2637
Local.

2413 ■ Williamson County Tourism Bureau
PO Box 1088
8588 Rte. 148 S.
Marion, IL 62959-7588
Ph: (618)997-3690
Fax: (618)997-1874
Free: (800)433-7399
E-mail: wctb@midamer.net
Founded: 1986. **Staff:** 3. **Local.**

Marissa

2414 ■ American Legion, Illinois Post 172
c/o Robert F. Arnold
PO Box 172
Marissa, IL 62257
Ph: (618)295-2231
Fax: (309)663-5783
URL: National Affiliate–www.legion.org
Contact: Robert F. Arnold, Contact
Local. Affiliated With: American Legion.

2415 ■ Belclair Beagle Club
c/o Henry Phillips
444 State Rte. 13
Marissa, IL 62257-1416
URL: National Affiliate–clubs.akc.org
Contact: Henry Phillips, Contact
Local.

Markham

2416 ■ American Legion, Markham Manor Post 828
16258 Lathrop Ave.
Markham, IL 60426
Ph: (309)663-0361
Fax: (309)663-5783
URL: National Affiliate–www.legion.org
Local. Affiliated With: American Legion.

Maroa

2417 ■ American Legion, Weilepp-Cramer Post 660
PO Box 72
Maroa, IL 61756
Ph: (217)794-5547
Fax: (309)663-5783
URL: National Affiliate–www.legion.org
Local. Affiliated With: American Legion.

Marseilles

2418 ■ American Legion, Bushnell-Prairie-City Post 2004
2898 E 24th Rd.
Marseilles, IL 61341
Ph: (309)663-0361
Fax: (309)663-5783
URL: National Affiliate–www.legion.org
Local. Affiliated With: American Legion.

2419 ■ American Legion, Marseilles Post 235
571 Rutland St.
Marseilles, IL 61341
Ph: (309)663-0361
Fax: (309)663-5783
URL: National Affiliate–www.legion.org
Local. Affiliated With: American Legion.

2420 ■ Illinois River Area Chamber of Commerce (IRACC)
135 Washington St.
Marseilles, IL 61341-0326
Ph: (815)795-2323 (815)357-1080
Fax: (815)795-4546
E-mail: iracc@mtco.com
Contact: John F. Henning, Exec.Dir.
Founded: 1968. **Members:** 160. **Membership Dues:** church, clergy, $15 (annual) • large area bank, $1,000 (annual). **Staff:** 2. **Budget:** $60,000. **For-Profit. Local.** Promotes business and community development in Marseilles and Seneca, IL. Conducts community social and promotional activities. **Libraries: Type:** reference. **Holdings:** books, periodicals. **Subjects:** economic development. **Awards:** Citizen of the Year. **Frequency:** annual. **Type:** recognition. **Publications:** *Business & Organizational Directory for Seneca & Marseilles*, periodic. **Price:** free. **Advertising:** accepted • *Caboose News*, monthly. Newsletter. **Conventions/Meetings:** annual Auction - meeting • annual meeting • annual Pig Roast - banquet.

2421 ■ Illinois Suffolk Sheep Association
c/o Cheryl Roelfsema, Sec.-Treas.
3129 E 27th Rd.
Marseilles, IL 61341
Ph: (815)795-5030
URL: National Affiliate–www.u-s-s-a.org
Contact: Cheryl Roelfsema, Sec.-Treas.
State. Affiliated With: United Suffolk Sheep Association.

2422 ■ Marseilles Volunteer Firefighters Association
PO Box 4
205 Lincoln St.
Marseilles, IL 61341-0004
Local.

Marshall

2423 ■ American Legion, Clark County Post 90
PO Box 147
Marshall, IL 62441
Ph: (217)826-2713
Fax: (309)663-5783
URL: National Affiliate–www.legion.org
Local. Affiliated With: American Legion.

2424 ■ Marshall Area Chamber of Commerce (MACC)
708 Archer Ave.
Marshall, IL 62441
Ph: (217)826-2034
Fax: (217)826-2034
E-mail: marshall.chamber@abcs.com
URL: http://www.marshall-il.com
Contact: George Dallmier, Pres.
Founded: 1940. **Members:** 86. **Staff:** 1. **Local.** Industries and businesses organized to promote agricultural, business, community, and tourism development in the Marshall, IL area. **Committees:** Education; Events. **Publications:** *Chamber Chatter*, monthly. Newsletter. Alternate Formats: online. **Conventions/Meetings:** annual dinner.

Martinsville

2425 ■ American Legion, Martinsville Post 515
PO Box 273
Martinsville, IL 62442

Ph: (217)382-5240
Fax: (309)663-5783
URL: National Affiliate–www.legion.org
Local. **Affiliated With:** American Legion.

2426 ■ Martinsville Chamber of Commerce
PO Box 429
Martinsville, IL 62442-0429
Ph: (217)382-4323
Fax: (217)382-4726
Contact: Sheila Higginbothom, Pres.
Local.

Maryville

2427 ■ American Legion, Illinois Post 917
c/o Julius Zupan
122 S Donk Ave.
Maryville, IL 62062
Ph: (309)663-0361
Fax: (309)663-5783
URL: National Affiliate–www.legion.org
Contact: Julius Zupan, Contact
Local. **Affiliated With:** American Legion.

2428 ■ Home Builders Association of Greater Southwest Illinois
c/o Jerry Rombach
6100 W Main St.
Maryville, IL 62062-6688
Ph: (618)343-6331
Fax: (618)343-6335
E-mail: jrombach@hbaswil.org
URL: National Affiliate–www.nahb.org
Local. Single and multifamily home builders, commercial builders, and others associated with the building industry. **Affiliated With:** National Association of Home Builders. **Formerly:** (2004) Home Builders Association of Southwest Illinois.

2429 ■ International Union of Operating Engineers, Local 148
148 Wilma
Maryville, IL 62062
Ph: (618)271-1807
Fax: (618)345-0035
E-mail: dgiljum@oe148.org
URL: http://www.oe148.org
Contact: Don Giljum, Business Mgr.
Local. Works to bring economic justice to the workplace and to improve the lives of working families. **Affiliated With:** International Union of Operating Engineers.

Mascoutah

2430 ■ American Legion, Illinois Post 292
c/o Clarence V. Scheel
1414 W Main St.
Mascoutah, IL 62258
Ph: (618)566-9470
Fax: (309)663-5783
URL: National Affiliate–www.legion.org
Contact: Clarence V. Scheel, Contact
Local. **Affiliated With:** American Legion.

2431 ■ St. Clair District Dental Society
c/o Dr. Randy A. Parmlee, Pres.
PO Box 142
Mascoutah, IL 62258-2135
Ph: (618)566-7384
URL: http://www.isds.org
Contact: Dr. Randy A. Parmlee, Pres.
Local. Represents the interests of dentists committed to the public's oral health, ethics and professional development. Encourages the improvement of the public's oral health and promotes the art and science of dentistry. **Affiliated With:** American Dental Association; Illinois State Dental Society.

2432 ■ Southwestern Illinois Resource Conservation and Development Council
406 Main St.
Mascoutah, IL 62258
Ph: (618)566-4451
Fax: (618)566-4452
E-mail: ed.weilbacher@swircd.org
URL: http://www.swircd.org
Contact: Ed Weilbacher, Coor.
Local. **Affiliated With:** National Association of Resource Conservation and Development Councils.

Mason City

2433 ■ American Legion, Jackson-Keen Post 496
PO Box 126
Mason City, IL 62664
Ph: (309)663-0361
Fax: (309)663-5783
URL: National Affiliate–www.legion.org
Local. **Affiliated With:** American Legion.

Matherville

2434 ■ Mothers Against Drunk Driving, Mercer County
PO Box 635
Matherville, IL 61263
Ph: (309)754-8845
Fax: (309)754-8748
E-mail: marlam@winco.net
Local. Victims of drunk driving crashes; concerned citizens. Encourages citizen participation in working towards reform of the drunk driving problem and the prevention of underage drinking. Acts as the voice of victims of drunk driving crashes by speaking on their behalf to communities, businesses, and educational groups. **Affiliated With:** Mothers Against Drunk Driving.

Matteson

2435 ■ American Legion, Rehfeldt-Meyer Post 474
3539 214th St.
Matteson, IL 60443
Ph: (309)663-0361
Fax: (309)663-5783
URL: National Affiliate–www.legion.org
Local. **Affiliated With:** American Legion.

2436 ■ Folks on Spokes Bicycle Club
c/o Barbara Sturges, VP
PO Box 763
Matteson, IL 60443
Ph: (708)585-7672 (708)481-3429
E-mail: president@folksonspokes.com
URL: http://www.folksonspokes.com
Contact: Salie Vloedman, Pres.
Founded: 1976. **Members:** 230. **Membership Dues:** individual, $15 (annual) • family, $20 (annual). **Local**. Strives to organize and promote recreational interest in bicycling for members of the corporation and the public. Encourages and facilitates touring, bicycle outings, and other recreational bicycling. Educates individuals and groups about the maintenance and care of their bicycles, bicycle safety and courtesy. Works to promote, defend, and protect the rights of bicyclists. Encourages and secures the provisions of safe and desirable facilities for bicycling. Promotes intergovernmental cooperation in the development and implementation of an area-wide bicycle plan. **Affiliated With:** Chicagoland Bicycle Federation; Indiana Bicycle Coalition; International Mountain Bicycling Association; League of American Bicyclists; League of Illinois Bicyclists. **Formerly:** (2004) Folks on Spokes. **Publications:** *Spokin' Word*, monthly, January to November. Newsletter.

2437 ■ Illinois School Transportation Association (ISTA)
c/o Linda Long, Exec.Dir
PO Box 195
Matteson, IL 60443
Ph: (708)720-9863
Fax: (708)720-2163
URL: National Affiliate–www.schooltrans.com
Founded: 1950. **Members:** 155. **Membership Dues:** associate, $100 (annual). **Budget:** $55,000. **State Groups:** 1. **State**. Companies dedicated to improving the transportation industry for school children. **Libraries: Type:** reference. **Holdings:** video recordings. **Subjects:** safety, training. **Awards:** Pownall Award. **Frequency:** annual. **Type:** recognition. **Affiliated With:** National School Transportation Association. **Formerly:** National School Transportation Association, Illinois Chapter. **Publications:** Newsletter, quarterly. **Conventions/Meetings:** annual board meeting (exhibits) - 3rd week of June • annual convention (exhibits).

2438 ■ Matteson Area Chamber of Commerce (MACC)
600 Holiday Plaza Dr., Ste.110
PO Box 106
Matteson, IL 60443
Ph: (708)747-6000
Fax: (708)747-6054
URL: http://www.macclink.com
Contact: Georgia C. O'Neill, Pres./CEO
Membership Dues: business (based on number of employees), $150-$450 (annual) • school district, $320 (annual) • bank, $475 (annual) • hospital, $475 (annual) • municipality, $475 (annual) • utility, $475 (annual). **Local**. Promotes business and community development in University Park, IL. **Computer Services:** Information services, business directory • mailing lists, of members. **Committees:** Expo; Fundraising; Golf Outing; Legislative/Economic Development; Links Club; Programs; Public Relations. **Affiliated With:** Chicago Southland Convention and Visitors Bureau; Illinois State Chamber of Commerce; U.S. Chamber of Commerce. **Formerly:** (1999) University Park Business League Chamber of Commerce. **Publications:** *MaccLink*, bimonthly. Newsletter. **Advertising:** accepted.

2439 ■ Rich Rattlers Wrestling Club
c/o David Argue
5326 Drake Ln.
Matteson, IL 60443
Ph: (708)720-0768
E-mail: bludoc@aol.com
URL: http://www.eteamz.com/richrattlers
Founded: 1970. **Local**.

Mattoon

2440 ■ American Legion, Lawrence Riddle Post 88
PO Box 693
Mattoon, IL 61938
Ph: (217)234-7155
Fax: (309)663-5783
URL: National Affiliate–www.legion.org
Local. **Affiliated With:** American Legion.

2441 ■ Illinois Agricultural Aviation Association (IAAA)
c/o Scott Schurtz, Exec.Dir.
490 Airport Rd.
Mattoon, IL 61938
Ph: (217)234-9439
Fax: (217)234-2700
E-mail: youakido@agaviation.com
URL: http://www.agaviation.com/
Founded: 1966. **Members:** 40. **Membership Dues:** $100 (annual). **State**.

2442 ■ Masonic Lodge
116 N. 1st St.
Mattoon, IL 61938
Ph: (217)234-6933

2443 ■ Mattoon Chamber of Commerce
500 Broadway Ave.
Mattoon, IL 61938-3911
Ph: (217)235-5661
Fax: (217)234-6544
E-mail: matchamber@consolidated.net
URL: http://www.mattoonchamber.com
Contact: Mary Wetzel, Exec.Dir.
Founded: 1905. **Members:** 450. **Membership Dues:** professional (plus $68/associate), $180 (annual) • financial institution (plus $25/million in deposits), $100 (annual) • continuing retired, $54 (annual) • business (depends upon the number of employees), $193-$1,280 (annual). **Staff:** 3. **Budget:** $90,000. **Local.** Business and professional firms. Seeks to support community and economic development in Coles County, IL. Sponsors Bagelfest. **Awards:** Citizen of the Year. **Frequency:** annual. **Type:** recognition • Education Award. **Frequency:** annual. **Type:** recognition. **Recipient:** for a teacher or educational support person. **Computer Services:** Information services, membership directory • mailing lists, of members. **Publications:** *Briefings*, monthly. Newsletter. **Advertising:** accepted • *Business Directory and Buyer's Guide*, annual. **Advertising:** accepted • *Mattoon Image Book* • Book, annual.

2444 ■ Mattoon Public Action to Deliver Shelter
c/o Bob Beall, Pres.
2017 Broadway Ave.
Mattoon, IL 61938-3809
Ph: (217)234-7237
URL: http://www.mattoonchamber.com
Contact: Ms. Amy Clarida, Exec.Dir.
Local. Also Known As: (2005) Mattoon Area PADs Community Organization.

2445 ■ Phi Theta Kappa, Alpha Theta Psi Chapter - Lake Land College
c/o Gregory Capitosti
5001 Lakeland Blvd.
Mattoon, IL 61938
Ph: (217)234-5320
E-mail: gcapitos@lakeland.cc.il.us
URL: http://www.ptk.org/directories/chapters/IL/214-1.htm
Contact: Gregory Capitosti, Advisor
Local.

2446 ■ Planned Giving Information Consortium of East Central Illinois
c/o Vallery E. Mullens, Dir.
PO Box 372
Mattoon, IL 61938
Ph: (217)258-4177 (217)348-4177
E-mail: vmullens@sblhs.org
URL: http://pgic.org
Founded: 1999. **Members:** 69. **Membership Dues:** individual, $125 (annual). **Local Groups:** 1. **Local.** Strives to provide education on planned giving. Hosts quarterly membership luncheons and public seminars and a quarterly newsletter. **Publications:** Brochure • Newsletter.

2447 ■ United Way of Coles County
PO Box 868
Mattoon, IL 61938-0868
Ph: (217)234-8022
URL: National Affiliate–national.unitedway.org
Local. Affiliated With: United Way of America.

Maywood

2448 ■ American Legion, Illinois Post 838
c/o John H. Shelton
1219 Madison St.
Maywood, IL 60153
Ph: (309)663-0361
Fax: (309)663-5783
URL: National Affiliate–www.legion.org
Contact: John H. Shelton, Contact
Local. Affiliated With: American Legion.

2449 ■ Maywood Chamber of Commerce (MCC)
PO Box 172
Maywood, IL 60153
Ph: (708)345-7077
Fax: (708)345-9455
Contact: Edwin H. Walker IV, Pres.
Founded: 1935. **Members:** 200. **Membership Dues:** business, $50 (annual) • individual, $25 (annual). **Staff:** 1. **Local.** Businesses, churches, organizations, government agencies, and individuals interested in promoting business and community development in Maywood, IL. Conducts charitable activities. **Publications:** *Business Guide*, biennial • *Community Guide*, annual. Directory • Newsletter, monthly • Newsletter, annual. **Conventions/Meetings:** monthly luncheon - usually 3rd Monday of the month.

Mazon

2450 ■ American Legion, Mazon Post 352
PO Box 96
Mazon, IL 60444
Ph: (815)448-2550
Fax: (309)663-5783
URL: National Affiliate–www.legion.org
Local. Affiliated With: American Legion.

Mc Clure

2451 ■ American Legion, Mc Clure Post 900
PO Box 103
Mc Clure, IL 62957
Ph: (309)663-0361
Fax: (309)663-5783
URL: National Affiliate–www.legion.org
Local. Affiliated With: American Legion.

Mc Connell

2452 ■ American Legion, Mc Connell Post 1225
PO Box 12
Mc Connell, IL 61050
Ph: (815)868-2354
Fax: (309)663-5783
URL: National Affiliate–www.legion.org
Local. Affiliated With: American Legion.

Mc Lean

2453 ■ American Legion, Burger-Benedict Post 573
213 E Spencer
Mc Lean, IL 61754
Ph: (309)663-0361
Fax: (309)663-5783
URL: National Affiliate–www.legion.org
Local. Affiliated With: American Legion.

Mc Nabb

2454 ■ American Legion, Mc Nabb Post 1242
Sr 89 S
Mc Nabb, IL 61335
Ph: (309)663-0361
Fax: (309)663-5783
URL: National Affiliate–www.legion.org
Local. Affiliated With: American Legion.

McHenry

2455 ■ American Legion, Mc Henry Post 491
PO Box 447
McHenry, IL 60050
Ph: (815)334-4036
Fax: (309)663-5783
URL: National Affiliate–www.legion.org
Local. Affiliated With: American Legion.

2456 ■ Big Brothers Big Sisters of McHenry County
1600 N Indus. Dr.
McHenry, IL 60050
Ph: (815)385-3855
Fax: (815)385-3852
E-mail: info@bbbsmchenry.org
URL: http://www.bbbsmchenry.org
Local. Affiliated With: Big Brothers Big Sisters of America. **Formerly:** (2005) Big Brothers Big Sisters of America of McHenry County.

2457 ■ Country Quilters Society of McHenry
PO Box 114
McHenry, IL 60051-0114
Founded: 2002. **Members:** 75. **Local.**

2458 ■ Illinois Society of Enrolled Agents
1415 Matanuska Trail
McHenry, IL 60050
Ph: (815)385-6889 (630)759-5070
Fax: (815)363-1623
E-mail: ilsea1@msn.com
URL: http://www.naea.org/MemberPortal/StateAffiliates/Listing
Contact: Karen Miller EA, Contact
State. Affiliated With: National Association of Enrolled Agents.

2459 ■ Kane/McHenry Counties RSVP
c/o Deborah Danitz, Dir.
McHenry Township Cntr.
3519 N Richmond Rd.
McHenry, IL 60050-1447
Ph: (815)344-3555
Fax: (815)344-3593
E-mail: ddanitz@seniorservicesassoc.org
URL: http://www.seniorcorps.gov/about/programs/rsvp_state.asp?usestateabbr=il&Search4.x=0&Search4.y=0
Contact: Deborah Danitz, Dir.
Local. Affiliated With: Retired and Senior Volunteer Program.

2460 ■ McHenry Area Chamber of Commerce (MACC)
1257 N Green St.
McHenry, IL 60050
Ph: (815)385-4300
Fax: (815)385-9142
E-mail: info@mchenrychamber.com
URL: http://www.mchenrychamber.com
Contact: Kay Rial Bates, Membership Dir.
Founded: 1952. **Membership Dues:** business (based on number of employees), $215-$1,300 (annual) • home based business, $115 (annual) • not-for-profit, $95 (annual). **Local.** Business and professional men and women working together to provide support to the growth and development of the business community and continually improve the quality of life for those who work and live in McHenry. **Awards:** FELA - Frank E. Low Award. **Type:** recognition. **Committees:** Downtown Revitalization; Fiesta Days; Golf Outing; Seminar; Special Events. **Councils:** Business; Retail/Merchants. **Affiliated With:** Community Leadership Association; U.S. Chamber of Commerce. **Publications:** *Community Guide*, annual. Includes organization lists, calendar of events, and editorials. • *Up Front*, monthly. Newsletter. **Circulation:** 900. **Advertising:** accepted. **Conventions/Meetings:** monthly Business Council - meeting • Country Meadows Craft Show (exhibits) • annual Dinner Dance, gives recognition to long-time chamber members - always 3rd Saturday in January • annual Home and Recreation Show/Trade Fair - trade show (exhibits).

2461 ■ McHenry County Table Tennis Club
McHenry Township Recreation Center
3703 N Richmond Rd.
McHenry, IL 60050

Ph: (815)653-9015
Fax: (815)653-7455
E-mail: mcttclub@nsn.org
URL: http://www.crystallakenet.org/mcttclub
Contact: Dennis Palys, Contact
Founded: 1990. **Local. Affiliated With:** U.S.A. Table Tennis.

2462 ■ Sons of Norway, Fjordland Lodge 5-606
c/o Ervin T. Staveteig, Pres.
1414 W Lincoln Rd.
McHenry, IL 60050-7813
Ph: (815)385-6255
E-mail: erv1@mindspring.com
URL: http://user.mc.net/~norbie/son
Contact: Ervin T. Staveteig, Pres.
Local. Affiliated With: Sons of Norway.

2463 ■ South of the Border Chapter of Muskies
c/o Len Szule
28926 W Big Hollow Rd.
McHenry, IL 60050
Ph: (815)385-9026
Fax: (847)392-9779
E-mail: wefishn@aol.com
URL: http://www.muskiesinc.org
Contact: Len Szule, Pres.
Local.

2464 ■ United Way of McHenry County
4508 Prime Pkwy.
McHenry, IL 60050
Ph: (815)363-1377
Fax: (815)363-1878
E-mail: info@uwmchenry.org
URL: http://www.uwmchenry.org
Contact: Carlos Acosta, Contact
Local. Affiliated With: United Way of America.

McLeansboro

2465 ■ American Legion, Illinois Post 106
c/o John H. Stelle
409 W Market St.
McLeansboro, IL 62859
Ph: (618)643-9004
Fax: (309)663-5783
URL: National Affiliate–www.legion.org
Contact: John H. Stelle, Contact
Local. Affiliated With: American Legion.

2466 ■ Hamilton County Chamber of Commerce and Economic Development Commission
PO Box 456
McLeansboro, IL 62859
Ph: (618)643-3971
URL: http://www.mcleansboro.com
Contact: Chris Howten, Pres.
Local.

McNabb

2467 ■ McNabb Magnolia Junior Woman's Club
PO Box 224
McNabb, IL 61335
URL: http://mmjrs.tripod.com
Local.

Medora

2468 ■ American Legion, Medora Post 399
129 S Jefferson St.
Medora, IL 62063
Ph: (309)663-0361
Fax: (309)663-5783
URL: National Affiliate–www.legion.org
Local. Affiliated With: American Legion.

Melrose Park

2469 ■ American Legion, Iwaszuk-Cetwinski Post 943
5000 N Cumberland Ave.
Melrose Park, IL 60164
Ph: (309)663-0361
Fax: (309)663-5783
URL: National Affiliate–www.legion.org
Local. Affiliated With: American Legion.

2470 ■ American Legion, Maywood Post 133
1704 N 17th Ave.
Melrose Park, IL 60160
Ph: (309)663-0361
Fax: (309)663-5783
URL: National Affiliate–www.legion.org
Local. Affiliated With: American Legion.

2471 ■ American Legion, Sarlo-Sharp Post 368
200 Concord Dr.
Melrose Park, IL 60160
Ph: (708)941-3294
Fax: (309)663-5783
URL: National Affiliate–www.legion.org
Local. Affiliated With: American Legion.

2472 ■ Melrose Park Chamber of Commerce
1718 W Lake St.
Melrose Park, IL 60160-3819
Ph: (708)338-1007
Fax: (708)338-9924
E-mail: info@melroseparkchamber.org
URL: http://www.melroseparkchamber.org
Contact: Mrs. Cathy K. Stenberg, Exec.Dir.
Founded: 1925. **Members:** 269. **Membership Dues:** individual, church, $75 (annual) • business (depends upon the number of employees), $75-$425 (annual) • school, government, $125 (annual) • utility, $225 (annual). **Staff:** 1. **Local**. Helps different companies to recognize their business. **Libraries: Type:** by appointment only. **Computer Services:** Information services, business directory • mailing lists, of members. **Publications:** *Chamber Business and Community Guide*, annual. Directory • *Chamber Chit-Chat*, quarterly. Newsletter. **Advertising:** accepted.

Melvin

2473 ■ American Legion, Melvin Post 642
PO Box 45
Melvin, IL 60952
Ph: (217)388-2373
Fax: (309)663-5783
URL: National Affiliate–www.legion.org
Local. Affiliated With: American Legion.

Mendon

2474 ■ American Legion, Bear Creek Post 823
RR 2, Box 75
Mendon, IL 62351
Ph: (309)663-0361
Fax: (309)663-5783
URL: National Affiliate–www.legion.org
Local. Affiliated With: American Legion.

Mendota

2475 ■ American Legion, Mendota Post 540
PO Box 182
Mendota, IL 61342
Ph: (815)539-9757
Fax: (309)663-5783
URL: National Affiliate–www.legion.org
Local. Affiliated With: American Legion.

2476 ■ Mendota Area Chamber of Commerce
800 Washington St.
PO Box 620
Mendota, IL 61342-0620
Ph: (815)539-6507
Fax: (815)539-6025
E-mail: mendotachamber@yahoo.com
URL: http://mendotachamber.com
Contact: Valerie Corrigan, Exec.Dir.
Local. Promotes business and community development in Mendota, IL.

Meredosia

2477 ■ American Legion, Meredosia Post 516
PO Box 31
Meredosia, IL 62665
Ph: (309)663-0361
Fax: (309)663-5783
URL: National Affiliate–www.legion.org
Local. Affiliated With: American Legion.

Metamora

2478 ■ American Legion, Illinois Post 89
c/o Fred Herring
205 E Partridge St.
Metamora, IL 61548
Ph: (309)367-2237
Fax: (309)663-5783
URL: National Affiliate–www.legion.org
Contact: Fred Herring, Contact
Local. Affiliated With: American Legion.

2479 ■ Crusaders for Kids
c/o Robert D. Hirsch
303 Hickory Point Rd.
Metamora, IL 61548-8735
Ph: (309)688-5318
Fax: (309)688-5369
URL: http://www.crusaders4kids.com
Contact: Mike Loveless, Dir.
Founded: 1999. **Staff:** 7. **Budget:** $100,000. **State Groups:** 1. **Local Groups:** 1. **Nonmembership. Local. Conventions/Meetings:** monthly general assembly - 3rd Sunday; Avg. Attendance: 40.

2480 ■ Izaak Walton League of America, Peoria Chapter
1677 State Rte. 26
Metamora, IL 61548-9576
Ph: (309)822-8207
URL: National Affiliate–www.iwla.org
Contact: Dwaine Sharp, Pres.
Local. Works to educate the public to conserve, maintain, protect, and restore the soil, forest, water, and other natural resources of the U.S; promotes the enjoyment and wholesome utilization of these resources. **Affiliated With:** Izaak Walton League of America.

Metropolis

2481 ■ American Legion, Illinois Post 306
c/o Overton P. Morris
321 Market St.
Metropolis, IL 62960
Ph: (618)524-2043
Fax: (309)663-5783
URL: National Affiliate–www.legion.org
Contact: Overton P. Morris, Contact
Local. Affiliated With: American Legion.

2482 ■ Antique Automobile Club of America, Southern Illinois Region - Ohio Valley Chapter
c/o Michael Hausman
1001 Metropolis St.
Metropolis, IL 62960
E-mail: mmhaus@hcis.net
URL: http://www.aaca.org/southernillinois/
Contact: Michael Hausman, Pres.
Local. Collectors, hobbyists, and others interested in the preservation, maintenance, and restoration of

automobiles and in automotive history. **Affiliated With:** Antique Automobile Club of America.

2483 ■ Massac County United Way
PO Box 735
Metropolis, IL 62960-0735
Ph: (618)524-8185
URL: National Affiliate–national.unitedway.org
Local. Affiliated With: United Way of America.

2484 ■ Metropolis Area Chamber of Commerce
607 Market St.
PO Box 188
Metropolis, IL 62960-0188
Ph: (618)524-2714
Fax: (618)524-4780
Free: (800)949-5740
E-mail: metrochamber@hcis.net
URL: http://www.metropolischamber.com
Contact: Lindsay Pankey, Sec.
Membership Dues: business, $100-$300 • associate, $35. **Local.** Promotes business and community development in Metropolis, IL area. **Computer Services:** Information services, membership directory • mailing lists, of members. **Committees:** Ambassadors; Annual Banquet; ASA-Archery Tournament; Business Expo; Golf Outing; Parades and Events; Publication and Tourism; Superman Celebration. **Formerly:** (2006) Metropolis Area Chamber of Commerce, Tourism and Economic Development. **Publications:** *Chamberlink*, monthly. Newsletter. **Advertising:** accepted. **Conventions/Meetings:** monthly luncheon - every 2nd Wednesday in Metropolis, IL.

Middletown

2485 ■ American Legion, Six Gold Star Post 672
PO Box 138
Middletown, IL 62666
Ph: (309)663-0361
Fax: (309)663-5783
URL: National Affiliate–www.legion.org
Local. Affiliated With: American Legion.

Midlothian

2486 ■ American Legion, Milton W. Mager Memorial Post 691
14817 Pulaski Rd.
Midlothian, IL 60445
Ph: (309)663-0361
Fax: (309)663-5783
URL: National Affiliate–www.legion.org
Local. Affiliated With: American Legion.

2487 ■ Illinois Four Wheel Drive Association (ILFWDA)
PO Box 923
Midlothian, IL 60445
Ph: (630)220-9820
E-mail: president@ilfwda.org
URL: http://www.ilfwda.org
Contact: Phil Dawkins, Pres.
Founded: 1998. **Members:** 1,800. **Membership Dues:** club, $25-$100 (annual) • individual, $20 (annual) • business, $40-$150 (annual). **State Groups:** 18. **For-Profit. State. Affiliated With:** United Four-Wheel Drive Associations.

Milan

2488 ■ American Legion, Milan Post 569
515 1st Ave. W
Milan, IL 61264
Ph: (309)787-4149
Fax: (309)663-5783
URL: National Affiliate–www.legion.org
Local. Affiliated With: American Legion.

2489 ■ Humane Society of Rock Island County
724 W 2nd Ave.
Milan, IL 61264
Ph: (309)787-6830
Fax: (309)787-0685
E-mail: hsric@netexpress.net
URL: http://www.qcawc.org
Contact: Patti Lahn, Exec.Dir.
Founded: 1977. **Members:** 1,000. **Membership Dues:** general, $25 (annual). **Staff:** 15. **Budget:** $325,000. **Regional.** Humane organization representing agencies and individuals seeking to prevent cruelty to animals.

2490 ■ Interstate Resource Conservation and Development Council
3020 E First Ave.
Milan, IL 61264
Ph: (309)764-1486
Fax: (309)764-1830
E-mail: mark.jackson@il.usda.gov
URL: http://www.interstatercd.org
Contact: Mark Jackson, Coor.
Regional. Affiliated With: National Association of Resource Conservation and Development Councils.

2491 ■ Midwest Corvette Club (MWCC)
PO Box 111
Milan, IL 61264-0111
Ph: (309)593-2587
E-mail: rjc820@frontiernet.net
URL: http://www.midwest-corvette-club.net
Contact: Ron Johnson, Pres.
Local. Affiliated With: National Council of Corvette Clubs.

Milford

2492 ■ American Legion, Forrest Ballard Post 723
2081 E 920 N Rd.
Milford, IL 60953
Ph: (309)663-0361
Fax: (309)663-5783
URL: National Affiliate–www.legion.org
Local. Affiliated With: American Legion.

2493 ■ Jayco Jafari International Travel Club, Flight 5 Heart of Illinois Jaytrackers
c/o Debbie Beer, Pres.
120 S Woodworth Rd.
Milford, IL 60953
E-mail: beer@colint.com
URL: National Affiliate–www.jaycorvclub.com
Contact: Debbie Beer, Pres.
State. Affiliated With: Jayco Travel Club.

Milledgeville

2494 ■ American Legion, Duggar Post 553
PO Box 724
Milledgeville, IL 61051
Ph: (815)225-7764
Fax: (309)663-5783
URL: National Affiliate–www.legion.org
Local. Affiliated With: American Legion.

2495 ■ Northern Illinois Angus Association
c/o Darrel DeGraff, Pres.
4708 Hitt Rd.
Milledgeville, IL 61051
Ph: (815)225-5090
URL: National Affiliate–www.angus.org
Contact: Darrel DeGraff, Pres.
Local. Affiliated With: American Angus Association.

Millstadt

2496 ■ American Legion, Millstadt Post 502
PO Box 25
Millstadt, IL 62260
Ph: (618)476-1460
Fax: (309)663-5783
URL: National Affiliate–www.legion.org
Local. Affiliated With: American Legion.

Mineral

2497 ■ American Legion, Clark-Carrington Post 1031
PO Box 216
Mineral, IL 61344
Ph: (309)663-0361
Fax: (309)663-5783
URL: National Affiliate–www.legion.org
Local. Affiliated With: American Legion.

Minier

2498 ■ American Legion, Harry Riddle Post 448
33498 Legion Rd.
Minier, IL 61759
Ph: (309)663-0361
Fax: (309)663-5783
URL: National Affiliate–www.legion.org
Local. Affiliated With: American Legion.

Minonk

2499 ■ American Legion, Minonk Post 142
PO Box 152
Minonk, IL 61760
Ph: (309)663-0361
Fax: (309)663-5783
URL: National Affiliate–www.legion.org
Local. Affiliated With: American Legion.

Minooka

2500 ■ American Legion, Minooka Post 1188
PO Box 278
Minooka, IL 60447
Ph: (309)663-0361
Fax: (309)663-5783
URL: National Affiliate–www.legion.org
Local. Affiliated With: American Legion.

2501 ■ Chicago Glider Club
26045 W Airport Rd.
Minooka, IL 60447
Ph: (815)467-9861
URL: http://aerotow.evl.uic.edu/cgc
Local. Affiliated With: Soaring Society of America.

2502 ■ Greater Channahon-Minooka Area Chamber of Commerce
c/o Linda Fritz
408 Mondamin
PO Box 444
Minooka, IL 60447
Ph: (815)521-9999
Free: (877)878-1314
E-mail: fritz.s@worldnet.att.net
URL: http://chamber.minooka.com
Contact: Linda Fritz, Contact
Local.

Mode

2503 ■ Twin Oak Sporting Clays
RR 1, Box 239
Mode, IL 62444
Ph: (217)774-4196
URL: National Affiliate–www.mynssa.com
Local. Affiliated With: National Skeet Shooting Association.

Mokena

2504 ■ American Industrial Hygiene Association, Chicago Section
c/o Eugene A. Satrun, CIH, Pres.
Exxon Mobil Corp.
18825 Marjorie Pkwy.
Mokena, IL 60448
Ph: (815)521-7739
E-mail: eugene.a.satrun@exxonmobil.com
URL: http://www.chicagoaiha.org
Contact: Eugene A. Satrun CIH, Pres.
Local. Promotes the study and control of environmental factors affecting the health and well being of workers. Sponsors continuing education courses in industrial hygiene, government affairs, and public relations. Conducts educational and research programs. **Affiliated With:** American Industrial Hygiene Association.

2505 ■ American Legion, Frankfort-Mokena Post 2000
PO Box 115
Mokena, IL 60448
Ph: (309)663-0361
Fax: (309)663-5783
URL: National Affiliate–www.legion.org
Local. Affiliated With: American Legion.

2506 ■ Association of Certified Fraud Examiners - Greater Chicago Chapter
c/o Management Services
19102 Blackhawk Pkwy., Unit 25
Mokena, IL 60448
Ph: (815)663-7283
Fax: (815)469-1901
E-mail: cglatz@managementservices.org
URL: http://www.acfechicago.org
Contact: Christine Glatz, Admin.
Local. Works to promote improved fraud detection and deterrence through the expansion of knowledge and the interaction of its members and represent the highest standards and traditions to the Association of Certified Fraud Examiners. **Affiliated With:** Association of Certified Fraud Examiners.

2507 ■ DKY Developers Association
c/o Dorothy Appiah
19912 Everett Ln.
Mokena, IL 60448-7762
Fax: (708)479-3279
E-mail: dkydevelopers60448@msn.com
Local.

2508 ■ Frankfort Sportsman Club
PO Box 7
Mokena, IL 60448
Ph: (815)469-9887
E-mail: mrussell@frankfortsportsmanclub.com
URL: http://www.frankfortsportsmanclub.com
Contact: Mike Russell, Contact
Local.

2509 ■ Illinois Music Educators Association
c/o Randolph F. Kummer, Exec.Dir.
19747 Wolf Rd., Ste.201
Mokena, IL 60448-1362
Ph: (708)479-4000
Fax: (708)479-5638
E-mail: stateoffice@ilmea.org
URL: http://www.ilmea.org
Contact: Randolph F. Kummer, Exec.Dir.
State. Supports and advances a comprehensive and sequential program of music education. **Publications:** *Illinois Music Educator Journal*, 3/year. Contains materials and information of interest and concern to the Illinois music education community. **Price:** $14.00 for nonmembers. **Circulation:** 3,000. **Advertising:** accepted.

2510 ■ Mokena Chamber of Commerce
B 19820 Wolf Rd.
PO Box 67
Mokena, IL 60448-9998
Ph: (708)479-2468
Fax: (708)479-7144
E-mail: joann@mokena.com
URL: http://www.mokena.com
Contact: Jo Ann McGowan, Exec.Dir.
Membership Dues: platinum, $1,200 (annual) • gold, $1,000 (annual) • silver, $800 (annual) • 2003 renewal, $135 (annual) • 2004 new, $140 (annual) • home based, $50 (annual). **Local. Computer Services:** Mailing lists, listing of membership. **Publications:** *Chambergram*, quarterly.

2511 ■ SkillsUSA Illinois
PO Box 15
Mokena, IL 60448
Ph: (708)479-8422
Fax: (708)479-8444
E-mail: ilskillsusa@aol.com
URL: http://www.illinoisskillsusa.org
Contact: Donald Bauc, Dir.
State. Represents high school and college students enrolled in training programs in technical, skilled, service and health occupations. Teaches the importance of developing leadership skills, positive attitudes and pride in workmanship. Promotes understanding of the free enterprise system and involvement in community service activities. **Affiliated With:** Skills USA - VICA.

Moline

2512 ■ 100 Black Men of the Quad Cities, Davenport
2601 15th St.
Moline, IL 61265
Ph: (309)764-7694
E-mail: revgrimes1@aol.com
URL: National Affiliate–www.100blackmen.org
Local. Affiliated With: 100 Black Men of America.

2513 ■ Alcoholics Anonymous World Services, Illowa Intergroup
1702 15th St. Pl.
Moline, IL 61265
Ph: (309)764-1016
URL: http://www.aaquadcities.com
Local. Individuals recovering from alcoholism. AA maintains that members can solve their common problem and help others achieve sobriety through a twelve step program that includes sharing their experience, strength, and hope with each other. **Affiliated With:** Alcoholics Anonymous World Services.

2514 ■ American Ex-Prisoners of War, Western Illinois Chapter
c/o Martin Parisot
3555 8th St.
Moline, IL 61265-7157
Ph: (309)764-5060
URL: National Affiliate–www.axpow.org
Local. Affiliated With: American Ex-Prisoners of War.

2515 ■ American Legion, Moline
1623 15th St.
Moline, IL 61265
Ph: (309)762-1126
URL: National Affiliate–www.legion.org
Local. Affiliated With: American Legion.

2516 ■ American Red Cross of the Quad Cities Area
PO Box 888
Moline, IL 61266-0888
Ph: (309)743-2166
URL: http://www.qcredcross.org
Local.

2517 ■ American Theatre Organ Society, Quad Cities Chapter
c/o Barbara Christiansen, Sec.
2815 53rd St.
Moline, IL 61265
Ph: (309)797-3255
URL: National Affiliate–www.atos.org
Contact: Barbara Christiansen, Sec.
Regional. Aims to restore, preserve and promote the theatre pipe organ and its music. Encourages the youth to learn the instrument. Operates a committee that gathers history and old music from silent film days and information on theatre organists, theaters and organ installations of the silent film era. **Affiliated With:** American Theatre Organ Society.

2518 ■ Child Abuse Council (CAC)
c/o Sue Swisher, Exec.Dir.
525 16th St.
Moline, IL 61265
Ph: (309)764-7017
Fax: (309)757-8554
E-mail: info@childabuseqc.org
URL: http://www.childabuseqc.org
Contact: Sue Swisher, Exec.Dir.
Local.

2519 ■ Credit Professionals International, West Central Illinois
c/o Linda Bridgeford, Pres.
Moline Dispatch Publishing Co.
1720 5th Ave.
Moline, IL 61265
Ph: (309)757-4906
E-mail: racerat@qconline.com
URL: http://www.creditprofessionals.org/5/WCentral.html
Contact: Linda Bridgeford, Pres.
Local. Supports members through networking, career development and community involvement. Promotes and contributes to the innovation of the credit industry. Provides education in the practice and procedure of credit. **Affiliated With:** Credit Professionals International. **Conventions/Meetings:** monthly meeting - every 3rd Tuesday.

2520 ■ Illinois Numismatic Association
c/o Donald Keopple, II, Pres.
3319 23rd Ave.
Moline, IL 61265-4304
Ph: (309)797-5066
E-mail: acecoins3319@aol.com
URL: http://www.ilnaclub.org
Contact: Donald Keopple II, Pres.
State. Affiliated With: American Numismatic Association.

2521 ■ Illinois Quad City Chamber of Commerce
622 19th St.
Moline, IL 61265-2142
Ph: (309)757-5416
Fax: (309)757-5435
E-mail: rbaker@quadcitychamber.com
URL: http://www.quadcitychamber.com
Contact: Rick L. Baker, Pres./CEO
Membership Dues: business (up to 200 employees), $235-$821 (annual) • realtor (up to 200 agents/associates), $235-$1,200 (annual) • professional office (1-50 professionals), $235-$1,110 (annual) • lodging

(base rate), $235 (annual) • financial institution (base rate), $390 (annual) • utility (base rate), $235 (annual) • retiree, $78 (annual) • student, $78 (annual). **Local**. Promotes business and community development in Illinois Quad City, IL. **Computer Services:** Information services, business directory. **Publications:** *Business Directory and Partners Resource Guide*, annual, in March. **Advertising:** accepted • *Business News Monthly*, 8/year. Newsletter • *Business News Quarterly*. Magazine • *QC Direct Quality of Life Guide*, annual. Handbook. Profiles the communities and direct newcomers to Chamber partners. **Price:** free.

2522 ■ Junior Achievement, Quad-Cities Area
c/o Christy Kunz, Pres.
800 12th Ave.
Moline, IL 61265
Ph: (309)736-1630
Fax: (309)736-1762
E-mail: ckunz@jaqca.org
URL: http://www.jaqca.org
Contact: Natasha Sottos, Marketing Mgr.
Local. Educates and inspires young people to value free enterprise, business, and economics. Programs include JA Exchange City, and JA Job Shadow Day. **Affiliated With:** Junior Achievement.

2523 ■ Military Officers Association of America, Quad Cities Chapter
950 46th St. Dr.
Moline, IL 61265-2649
Ph: (309)736-3131
E-mail: jnorton785@sbcglobal.net
URL: National Affiliate–www.moaa.org
Contact: Col. John Norton, Contact
Local. **Affiliated With:** Military Officers Association of America.

2524 ■ Moline - Young Life
PO Box 1487
Moline, IL 61266
Ph: (309)757-7123
URL: http://whereis.younglife.org/FriendlyUrlRedirector.aspx?ID=C-847
Local.

2525 ■ National Association of Miniature Enthusiasts - Metro Mini Makers
c/o Karen Cockerill
1030 42nd St.
Moline, IL 61265
Ph: (309)797-6489
URL: http://www.miniatures.org/states/IL.html
Contact: Karen Cockerill, Contact
Local. **Affiliated With:** National Association of Miniature Enthusiasts.

2526 ■ PFLAG Moline
3732 40th St. Ct.
Moline, IL 61265
Ph: (309)797-7986
Fax: (309)797-5669
E-mail: joycewiley@mchsi.com
URL: http://www.pflag.org/Illinois.204.0.html
Local. **Affiliated With:** Parents, Families, and Friends of Lesbians and Gays.

2527 ■ Phi Theta Kappa, Eta Kappa Chapter - Black Hawk College
c/o Holly Smith
6600 34th Ave.
Moline, IL 61265
Ph: (309)796-5051
E-mail: smithh@bhc.edu
URL: http://www.ptk.org/directories/chapters/IL/169-1.htm
Contact: Holly Smith, Advisor
Local.

2528 ■ Public Relations Society of America, Quad Cities
c/o Wendy Davies-Popelka, Pres.
PO Box 553
Moline, IL 61266
Ph: (563)355-4310
Fax: (563)355-3308
E-mail: prsaqc@yahoo.com
URL: National Affiliate–www.prsa.org
Contact: Jennifer Nolin, Pres.
Provides professional development and networking opportunities to public relations professionals in the Quad City (IA/IL) area. **Affiliated With:** Public Relations Society of America.

2529 ■ Quad Cities Convention and Visitors Bureau, Illinois-Iowa
2021 River Dr.
Moline, IL 61265-1472
Ph: (309)788-7800
Free: (800)747-7800
E-mail: cvb@quadcities.com
Contact: Joe Taylor, Pres./CEO
Founded: 1990. **Members:** 400. **Budget:** $1,300,000. **Regional**. **Publications:** *Destination Quad Cities*, annual.

2530 ■ Quad City Area Youth for Christ
2420 41 St.
Moline, IL 61265
Ph: (309)764-1405
Fax: (309)764-1472
URL: http://www.qcayfc.com
Local. **Affiliated With:** Youth for Christ/U.S.A.

2531 ■ Quad City Stamp Club
c/o Mr. Milton J. Schober
PO Box 1301
Moline, IL 61266-1301
E-mail: pmats5@aol.com
URL: http://members.aol.com/pmats5/qcsc.html
Contact: Mr. Milton J. Schober, Contact
Local. **Affiliated With:** American Philatelic Society.

2532 ■ Rock Island District Dental Society
c/o Dr. Bryan C. Blew, Sec.
604 35th Ave.
Moline, IL 61265-6174
Ph: (309)797-4336
E-mail: bblew2@yahoo.com
URL: http://www.isds.org
Contact: Dr. Bryan C. Blew, Sec.
Local. Represents the interests of dentists committed to the public's oral health, ethics and professional development. Encourages the improvement of the public's oral health and promotes the art and science of dentistry. **Affiliated With:** American Dental Association; Illinois State Dental Society.

2533 ■ SCORE Quad Cities
622 19th St.
Moline, IL 61265
Ph: (309)797-0082
Fax: (309)757-5435
E-mail: info@quadcitiesscore.org
URL: http://www.qconline.com/business/score
Contact: Richard Weeks, Chm.
Founded: 1978. **Local**. Provides professional guidance and information to maximize the success of existing and emerging small businesses. Develops business plans and evaluate financial projections. Promotes entrepreneur education in Moline, IL. **Affiliated With:** SCORE. **Publications:** Newsletter, bimonthly. **Conventions/Meetings:** monthly seminar - every 2nd Saturday.

2534 ■ Society for Technical Communication, Quad Cities Chapter
c/o Kathy Black, Pres.
KONE, Inc.
1 Montgomery Ct.
Moline, IL 61265
Ph: (309)764-6771
E-mail: katherine.black@kone.com
URL: http://www.stc-qc.org
Contact: Kathy Black, Pres.
Regional. Seeks to advance the theory and practice of technical communication in all media. Enhances the professionalism of the members and the status of the profession. Promotes the education of members and supports research activities in the field. **Affiliated With:** Society for Technical Communication.

2535 ■ Studebakers Driver's Club, Big Six River Bend Chapter
c/o David Kahn, Pres.
2948 11th Ave. B
Moline, IL 61265
Ph: (309)764-6100
E-mail: avantir4@msn.com
URL: National Affiliate–www.studebakerdriversclub.com
Contact: David Kahn, Pres.
Local. Owners of Studebaker automobiles and trucks. Attempts to aid in the restoration of, procure parts for, and reproduce old instruction manuals of the Studebaker car. **Affiliated With:** Studebaker Driver's Club.

2536 ■ Young Life Rock Island County
PO Box 1487
Moline, IL 61266
Ph: (309)757-7123
URL: http://whereis.younglife.org/FriendlyUrlRedirector.aspx?ID=A-IL35
Local.

Momence

2537 ■ American Legion, Momence-Ganeer Post 40
PO Box 363
Momence, IL 60954
Ph: (309)663-0361
Fax: (309)663-5783
URL: National Affiliate–www.legion.org
Local. **Affiliated With:** American Legion.

2538 ■ Momence Chamber of Commerce
203 E River
Momence, IL 60954
Ph: (815)472-4620
Fax: (815)472-6453
E-mail: membership@momence.net
URL: http://www.momence.net
Contact: Patrick Dryer, Pres.
Local. Provides its members with the opportunity to network and make business contacts. **Computer Services:** Information services, membership directory. **Publications:** Newsletter, quarterly.

Monee

2539 ■ American Legion, Doss-Malone Post 1200
PO Box 521
Monee, IL 60449
Ph: (708)534-8172
Fax: (309)663-5783
URL: National Affiliate–www.legion.org
Local. **Affiliated With:** American Legion.

Monmouth

2540 ■ American Legion, Illinois Post 136
c/o Marion B. Fletcher
PO Box 136
Monmouth, IL 61462
Ph: (309)734-2976
Fax: (309)663-5783
URL: National Affiliate–www.legion.org
Contact: Marion B. Fletcher, Contact
Local. **Affiliated With:** American Legion.

2541 ■ Monmouth Area Chamber of Commerce (MACC)
90 Public Sq.
PO Box 857
Monmouth, IL 61462-0857

Ph: (309)734-3181
E-mail: macc@maplecity.com
URL: http://www.ci.monmouth.il.us/coc
Contact: Angie McElwee, Exec.Dir.
Founded: 1912. **Members:** 225. **Staff:** 2. **Budget:** $52,000. **Local**. Business and professional persons interested in promoting business and community development in the Monmouth, IL area. Sponsors prime beef festival. **Computer Services:** database, list of members. **Committees:** Ambassadors; Community Affairs; Education; Executive; Legislation; Tourism; Transportation. **Councils:** Downtown Business. **Programs:** Business Assistance. **Affiliated With:** U.S. Chamber of Commerce. **Formerly:** (1950) Monmouth Commercial Club. **Publications:** *Chamber Chatter*, monthly. Directory • *Chamber Communicator*, monthly. Newsletter. **Advertising:** accepted • Membership Directory, annual. **Conventions/Meetings:** annual dinner - always April • monthly Good Morning Monmouth - breakfast, with speaker - every 1st Wednesday.

2542 ■ Psi Chi, National Honor Society in Psychology - Monmouth College
c/o Dept. of Psychology
700 E Broadway Ave.
Monmouth, IL 61462
Ph: (309)457-2385 (309)457-2164
Fax: (309)457-7500
E-mail: klarson@monm.edu
URL: National Affiliate–www.psichi.org
Local. Affiliated With: Psi Chi, National Honor Society in Psychology.

2543 ■ Warren County United Way, Illinois
PO Box 85
Monmouth, IL 61462-0085
Ph: (309)734-6364
URL: National Affiliate–national.unitedway.org
Local. Affiliated With: United Way of America.

Montgomery

2544 ■ Illinois Young Democrats
c/o Martin Flowers, Pres.
68 Red Fox Run
Montgomery, IL 60538-2911
Ph: (630)897-1627
E-mail: mflowers1993@aol.com
URL: http://www.yda.org/CMS/State/17
State.

2545 ■ Thimblefools of Northern Illinois
c/o Brooks Popowitch
112 Circle Dr. W
Montgomery, IL 60538
Ph: (630)859-2584
E-mail: thimcoll@aol.com
URL: National Affiliate–www.thimblecollectors.com
Contact: Brooks Popowitch, Contact
Local. Affiliated With: Thimble Collectors International.

Monticello

2546 ■ American Legion, Roy-Hamm-Robert-Burke Post 101
PO Box 551
Monticello, IL 61856
Ph: (217)762-5011
Fax: (309)663-5783
URL: National Affiliate–www.legion.org
Local. Affiliated With: American Legion.

2547 ■ Central Illinois Muskie Hunters
c/o Lorin Nevling
1191 Sandra Ln.
Monticello, IL 61856
Ph: (217)762-8070
E-mail: lnevling@monticello.net
Contact: Lorin Nevling, Pres.
Local.

2548 ■ Monticello Chamber of Commerce
PO Box 313
Monticello, IL 61856-0313
Ph: (217)762-7921
Fax: (217)762-2711
Free: (800)952-3396
E-mail: info@monticellochamber.org
URL: http://www.monticellochamber.org
Contact: Sue Gortner, Exec.Dir.
Members: 170. **Local**. Works to create an environment where businesses can succeed. **Computer Services:** Information services, member listing. **Additional Websites:** http://www.monticelloillinois.net. **Committees:** Christmas Parade; Expo; Lunch with Santa; Marketing; Program, Annual Banquet, Lunch, After-Hours; Special Events; Tourism; Web. **Publications:** *Business*, annual. Directory. **Conventions/Meetings:** annual Lunch with Santa on the Train - luncheon, with treats - 2006 Dec. 2-3, Monticello, IL.

2549 ■ Monticello Lions Club, IL
PO Box 85
Monticello, IL 61856
Ph: (217)762-7921
Fax: (217)762-7259
Free: (800)952-3396
E-mail: gnix@pdnt.com
URL: http://www.monticellolions.org
Local. Affiliated With: Lions Clubs International.

2550 ■ Monticello Main Street
PO Box 392
Monticello, IL 61856
Ph: (217)762-9318
Fax: (217)762-9713
E-mail: info@monticellomainstreet.org
URL: http://www.monticellomainstreet.org
Contact: Linda Miller, Program Dir.
Local.

Morris

2551 ■ American Legion, Morris Post 294
212 W Washington St.
Morris, IL 60450
Ph: (815)942-0183
Fax: (309)663-5783
URL: National Affiliate–www.legion.org
Local. Affiliated With: American Legion.

2552 ■ American Red Cross, Grundy County Chapter
117 W Washington St.
Morris, IL 60450
Ph: (815)942-1046
Fax: (815)942-1243
E-mail: amercross@sbcglobal.net
URL: http://grundycounty.redcross.org
Local.

2553 ■ Bernese Mountain Dog Club of Northeastern Illinois (BMDCNI)
c/o Elaine Squires, Pres.
1995 W Southmor Rd.
Morris, IL 60450-8247
Ph: (815)941-2492
E-mail: info@bmdcni.org
URL: http://www.bmdcni.org
Regional.

2554 ■ Fox Valley Payroll Association
c/o Sandee Vicena, CPP, HR/Payroll Administrator
Aux Sable Liquid Prdts.
6155 E US Rte. 6
Morris, IL 60450
Ph: (630)719-7292
Fax: (630)719-2076
E-mail: pschwichtenberg@gknna.com
URL: http://www.foxvalleypayroll.org
Contact: Pat Schwichtenberg CPP, Pres.
Local. Aims to increase the Payroll Professional's skill level through education and mutual support. Represents the Payroll Professional before legislative bodies. Administers the certified payroll professional program of recognition. Provides public service education on payroll and employment issues. **Affiliated With:** American Payroll Association.

2555 ■ United Way of Grundy County, Illinois
105 E Main St., Ste.204
Morris, IL 60450-2138
Ph: (815)942-4430
URL: National Affiliate–national.unitedway.org
Local. Affiliated With: United Way of America.

Morrison

2556 ■ American Legion, Morrison Post 328
PO Box 322
Morrison, IL 61270
Ph: (309)663-0361
Fax: (309)663-5783
URL: National Affiliate–www.legion.org
Local. Affiliated With: American Legion.

2557 ■ American Rabbit Breeders Association, Illinois Florida White Specialty Club
c/o Don Dudley
18112 Folkers Rd.
Morrison, IL 61270
Ph: (815)336-2126
URL: http://www.nordickrabbits.com/specialt.htm
Contact: Don Dudley, Contact
Local. Affiliated With: American Rabbit Breeders Association.

2558 ■ Barbershop Harmony Society - Illinois District
c/o William Thorndike, Pres.
405 W Wall St.
Morrison, IL 61270-2137
Ph: (815)772-7936
E-mail: watjn@mchsi.com
URL: http://www.harmonize.ws/ILL
Contact: William Thorndike, Pres.
State. Encourages and preserves barbershop harmony through the support of vocal music education. Serves members by sharing fellowship, performance skills and leadership development. **Affiliated With:** Society for the Preservation and Encouragement of Barber Shop Quartet Singing in America.

2559 ■ Morrison Chamber of Commerce
202 E Lincoln Way
Morrison, IL 61270
Ph: (815)772-3757
Fax: (815)772-3757
E-mail: morrcham@essex1.com
URL: http://www.thecity1.com/biz/morrisoncc/index.php
Contact: Roann Porter, Administrator
Local. Aims to promote Morrison and support its members through structure and events that unite the community. **Computer Services:** Information services, membership directory. **Committees:** Christmas Walk; Discount Card; Dollars for Scholars; Downtown Development; Food Vendor Booth at Paint the Town; Glow Ball Golf; Halloween Parade; Morrison Fest.

2560 ■ Society of Manufacturing Engineers - Morrison Institute of Technology S321
701 Postland Ave.
Morrison, IL 61270
Ph: (815)772-7218
Fax: (815)772-7584
E-mail: sbahulekar@morrison.tec.il.us
URL: National Affiliate–www.sme.org
Contact: Sumukh Bahulekar, Contact
Local. Advances manufacturing knowledge to gain competitive advantage. Improves skills and manufacturing solutions for the growth of economy. Provides resources and opportunities for manufacturing professionals. **Affiliated With:** International Society for the Interaction of Mechanics and Mathematics.

Morrisonville

2561 ■ American Legion, Leslie-Reddick Post 721
PO Box 634
Morrisonville, IL 62546
Ph: (217)526-3611
Fax: (309)663-5783
URL: National Affiliate–www.legion.org
Local. Affiliated With: American Legion.

Morton

2562 ■ American Legion, Morton Post 318
PO Box 220
Morton, IL 61550
Ph: (309)266-6778
Fax: (309)663-5783
URL: National Affiliate–www.legion.org
Local. Affiliated With: American Legion.

2563 ■ Illinois Valley BMW MOA No. 70
c/o Paul Boyd
54 Hyde Park Dr.
Morton, IL 61550
Ph: (309)266-6603
E-mail: k12rs@mtco.com
URL: National Affiliate–www.bmwmoa.org
Contact: Paul Boyd, Contact
Local. BMW motorcycle owners organized for pleasure, recreation, safety, and dissemination of information concerning BMW motorcycles. **Affiliated With:** BMW Motorcycle Owners of America. **Formerly:** (2005) Illinois Valley BMW No. 70.

2564 ■ Morton Chamber of Commerce (MCC)
415 W Jefferson
Morton, IL 61550-1817
Ph: (309)263-2491
Fax: (309)263-2401
Free: (888)765-6588
E-mail: pumpkin@mtco.com
URL: http://mortonchamber.org
Contact: Mike Badgerow, Exec.Dir.
Founded: 1955. **Members:** 260. **Staff:** 3. **Budget:** $95,000. **Local.** Businesses. Promotes business and community development in Morton, IL. Sponsors retail promotions and annual Pumpkin Festival. **Publications:** *Morton Matters*, monthly. Newsletter.

Morton Grove

2565 ■ American Legion, Morton Grove Post 134
6140 Dempster St.
Morton Grove, IL 60053
Ph: (708)965-9503
Fax: (309)663-5783
URL: National Affiliate–www.legion.org
Local. Affiliated With: American Legion.

2566 ■ American Legion, Niles-Northtown Post 29
9354 Octavia Ave.
Morton Grove, IL 60053
Ph: (708)724-2028
Fax: (309)663-5783
URL: National Affiliate–www.legion.org
Local. Affiliated With: American Legion.

2567 ■ Citizens for Legal Responsibility (CLR)
c/o Dave Roberts
PO Box 232
Morton Grove, IL 60053-0232
Ph: (847)429-0311
Fax: (847)429-0311
E-mail: clr@clr.org
URL: http://www.clr.org
Contact: Dave Roberts, Contact
Local. Works to inform members of legal, civil and Constitutional Rights. Promotes ethical standards of conduct for individuals practicing in the commercial business of law; exposes misconduct of attorneys and judges.

2568 ■ Golf School District 67 PTA
c/o Golf School District 67
9401 Waukegan Rd.
Morton Grove, IL 60053
Ph: (847)966-8200
Fax: (847)966-8290
E-mail: smeyer@abanet.org
URL: http://www.golf67.net
Contact: Susan Meyer, Pres.
Local. Parents, teachers, students and others interested in uniting the forces of home, school and community. Promotes the welfare of children and youth.

2569 ■ Morton Grove Chamber of Commerce and Industry (MGCCI)
6101 Capulina Ave., Lower Level
Morton Grove, IL 60053
Ph: (847)965-0330
Fax: (847)965-0349
E-mail: info@mgcci.org
URL: http://www.mgcci.org
Contact: Suzanne Archer, Acting Exec.Dir.
Founded: 1920. **Members:** 220. **Membership Dues:** business (based on number of employees), $180-$995 (annual). **Staff:** 1. **Budget:** $50,000. **Local.** Promotes business and community development in Morton Grove, IL. **Computer Services:** database, listing of members. **Publications:** *MGCCI It's Your Business*, monthly. Newsletter. **Advertising:** accepted. Alternate Formats: online • *Morton Grove Community Guide*, biennial. Directory. **Price:** $3.00. **Advertising:** accepted. **Conventions/Meetings:** monthly Business After Hours - meet • annual Golf Outing - meet • annual Installation of Officers/Directors - meeting • quarterly luncheon • annual VIP Business Person of the Year Reception - meeting.

2570 ■ Muslim Gymkhana
727 Golf Rd.
Morton Grove, IL 60053
URL: http://www.usaca.org/Clubs.htm
Contact: Azhar Iqbal, Contact
Local.

Mounds

2571 ■ American Legion, Illinois Post 1960
c/o Joe Neill
789 Bucher Rd.
Mounds, IL 62964
Ph: (309)663-0361
Fax: (309)663-5783
URL: National Affiliate–www.legion.org
Contact: Joe Neill, Contact
Local. Affiliated With: American Legion.

Mount Carmel

2572 ■ American Legion, Wabash Post 423
PO Box 536
Mount Carmel, IL 62863
Ph: (309)663-0361
Fax: (309)663-5783
URL: National Affiliate–www.legion.org
Local. Affiliated With: American Legion.

2573 ■ Mount Carmel Public Library Foundation
727 Mulberry St.
Mount Carmel, IL 62863-2047
Ph: (618)263-3531
Fax: (618)263-4542
Contact: Louise Taylor, Library Dir.
Local.

2574 ■ Phi Theta Kappa, Rho Psi Chapter - Wabash Valley College
c/o Brenda Phegley
2200 Coll. Dr.
Mount Carmel, IL 62863
Ph: (618)262-8641
E-mail: phegleyb@iecc.edu
URL: http://www.ptk.org/directories/chapters/IL/193-1.htm
Contact: Brenda Phegley, Advisor
Local.

2575 ■ Wabash County Chamber of Commerce
219 Market St., Ste.1A
Mount Carmel, IL 62863-1698
Ph: (618)262-5116
Fax: (618)262-2424
E-mail: mtcarmelchamber@mt-carmel.net
Contact: Tanja Bingham, Exec.Dir.
Founded: 1947. **Members:** 322. **Staff:** 2. **Budget:** $48,000. **Local.** Promotes business, tourism and community development in Mt. Carmel and Wabash County, IL. **Awards:** Business of the Year. **Frequency:** annual. **Type:** recognition. **Affiliated With:** Community Development Society.

Mount Carroll

2576 ■ American Legion, Mt. Carroll Post 67
PO Box 54
Mount Carroll, IL 61053
Ph: (815)244-6352
Fax: (309)663-5783
URL: National Affiliate–www.legion.org
Local. Affiliated With: American Legion.

2577 ■ Mount Carroll Chamber of Commerce
PO Box 94
Mount Carroll, IL 61053
Ph: (815)244-2255 (815)244-4424
URL: http://www.mount-carroll.il.us
Contact: Kathy Cyr, Pres.
Local. Promotes business and community development in Mt. Carroll, IL.

Mount Morris

2578 ■ American Legion, Mount Morris Post 143
PO Box 12
Mount Morris, IL 61054
Ph: (815)734-4641
Fax: (309)663-5783
URL: National Affiliate–www.legion.org
Local. Affiliated With: American Legion.

Mount Olive

2579 ■ American Legion, Yurkovich-Beck Post 594
21294 RR 138
Mount Olive, IL 62069
Ph: (219)999-6271
Fax: (309)663-5783
URL: National Affiliate–www.legion.org
Local. Affiliated With: American Legion.

2580 ■ First Catholic Slovak Ladies Association - Mount Olive Junior Branch 140
309 E Putnam St.
Mount Olive, IL 62069
Ph: (217)999-7455
URL: National Affiliate–www.fcsla.com
Local. Affiliated With: First Catholic Slovak Ladies Association.

2581 ■ First Catholic Slovak Ladies Association - Mount Olive Senior Branch 049
309 E Putnam St.
Mount Olive, IL 62069
Ph: (217)999-7455
URL: National Affiliate–www.fcsla.com
Local. Affiliated With: First Catholic Slovak Ladies Association.

Mount Prospect

2582 ■ American Hellenic Educational Progressive Association - Chicago, Chapter 46
c/o Peter Poulopoulos, Pres.
1110 Greenwood Dr.
Mount Prospect, IL 60056
Ph: (773)743-2100
Fax: (773)743-6551
E-mail: peterjp@realpoul.com
URL: http://www.ahepafamily.org/d13
Contact: Peter Poulopoulos, Pres.
Local. Affiliated With: American Hellenic Educational Progressive Association.

2583 ■ American Legion, Mount Prospect Post 525
PO Box 173
Mount Prospect, IL 60056
Ph: (708)255-3220
Fax: (309)663-5783
URL: National Affiliate–www.legion.org
Local. Affiliated With: American Legion.

2584 ■ American Legion, Robert Woodburn Post 1037
1326 N Peartree Ln.
Mount Prospect, IL 60056
Ph: (312)792-2726
Fax: (309)663-5783
URL: National Affiliate–www.legion.org
Local. Affiliated With: American Legion.

2585 ■ Friends of the Mount Prospect Public Library
c/o Marilyn Genther, Exec.Dir.
Mt. Prospect Public Lib.
10 S Emerson St.
Mount Prospect, IL 60056
Ph: (847)253-5675
Fax: (847)253-0642
E-mail: mgenther@mppl.org
URL: http://www.mtprospect.org/friends
Contact: Marilyn Genther, Exec.Dir.
Founded: 1983. **Members:** 350. **Membership Dues:** individual, $5 (annual) • family, $10 (annual) • good friend, $25 (annual) • life, $100. **Local.** Supports and promotes the public library of Mt. Prospect, IL. Conducts used book sales. **Libraries: Type:** open to the public. **Holdings:** 370,000. **Affiliated With:** Friends of Libraries U.S.A. **Publications:** *The Friends*, quarterly. Newsletter. **Price:** included in membership dues. **Conventions/Meetings:** monthly board meeting - always second Monday.

2586 ■ Greater Wheeling Area Youth Outreach
c/o Philip Berman
550 Bus. Ctr. Dr.
Mount Prospect, IL 60056
Ph: (847)759-0679
Fax: (847)759-0687
URL: http://www.gwayo.org
Contact: Philip Herman, Dir.
Local.

2587 ■ Illinois Fencers Club (IFC)
c/o Diane Baia, Adult and Teen Program Coor.
411 S Maple St.
Mount Prospect, IL 60056
Ph: (847)356-5395
E-mail: davesaint@comcast.net
URL: http://www.totheescrime.org/ifc
Contact: David St. George, Pres.
State. Amateur fencers. **Affiliated With:** United States Fencing Association.

2588 ■ International Dark-Sky - Illinois At-Large Section
409 S HiLusi Ave.
Mount Prospect, IL 60056
Ph: (847)255-2255
URL: http://www.darksky.org/aboutida/sections
Contact: Dave Toeppen, Contact
State. Astronomical societies, lighting and engineering groups, professional astronomers. Seeks to inform about the effects of nighttime lighting. Builds awareness about the problems that have effects on astronomy. Presents examples of good lighting design. Conducts speaker's bureau. Documents on good and bad lighting through photos and videos.

2589 ■ Mount Prospect Chamber of Commerce
107 S Main St.
Mount Prospect, IL 60056
Ph: (847)398-6616
Fax: (847)398-6780
E-mail: jim@mountprospect.com
URL: http://www.mountprospectchamber.org
Contact: James Uszler, Exec.Dir.
Founded: 1926. **Members:** 397. **Local.** Promotes business and community development in Mt. Prospect, IL. **Publications:** *Communique*, monthly. Newsletter • *Community Guide and Business Listing*, annual. Directory. **Conventions/Meetings:** monthly board meeting.

2590 ■ Northwest Suburban United Way
PO Box 294
Mount Prospect, IL 60056
Ph: (847)768-1074
E-mail: uwnorthwest@uw-mc.org
URL: http://www.uwnorthwest.org
Contact: Mike Thompson, Pres.
Local. Affiliated With: United Way of America.

Mount Sterling

2591 ■ American Legion, Mt. Sterling Post 374
PO Box 94
Mount Sterling, IL 62353
Ph: (309)663-0361
Fax: (309)663-5783
URL: National Affiliate–www.legion.org
Local. Affiliated With: American Legion.

2592 ■ United Way of Brown County, Illinois
PO Box 132
Mount Sterling, IL 62353-0132
Ph: (217)773-3327
URL: National Affiliate–national.unitedway.org
Local. Affiliated With: United Way of America.

Mount Vernon

2593 ■ American Legion, Jefferson Post 141
816 Main St.
Mount Vernon, IL 62864
Ph: (618)242-4561
Fax: (309)663-5783
URL: National Affiliate–www.legion.org
Local. Affiliated With: American Legion.

2594 ■ AMVETS, Mount Vernon Post 4
1207 Main St.
Mount Vernon, IL 62864
Ph: (618)244-1375
E-mail: lghoffman@charter.net
URL: http://geocities.com/ilamvetspost4
Contact: Clay McDaniel, Commander
Local. Affiliated With: AMVETS - American Veterans.

2595 ■ Bereaved Parents of the USA, Southern Illinois
c/o Martha Honn
1407 N Shadow Lake Ln.
Mount Vernon, IL 62864
Ph: (618)244-1203
URL: National Affiliate–www.bereavedparentsusa.org
Contact: Martha Honn, Contact
Local.

2596 ■ Egyptian Board of Realtors
123 S 10th St., Ste.315
Mount Vernon, IL 62864
Ph: (618)244-3301
Fax: (618)244-4261
E-mail: hills@midamer.net
URL: http://mvn.net/ebrinc/index.htm
Contact: Paula Hill, Pres.
Local. Strives to develop real estate business practices. Advocates the right to own, use and transfer real property. Provides a facility for professional development, research and exchange of information among members and to the general public. **Affiliated With:** National Association of Realtors.

2597 ■ Illinois Court Reporters Association (ILCRA)
c/o Nancy C. Davis, CPE, Exec.Dir.
41 SW Crescent Dr.
Mount Vernon, IL 62864
Ph: (618)242-2142
Fax: (618)242-2143
Free: (800)656-2467
E-mail: ilcraoffice@aol.com
URL: http://www.ilcra.org
Contact: Nancy C. Davis CPE, Exec.Dir.
State. Assumes responsibility for leadership and enlightenment of the users of verbatim shorthand reporting of proceedings and of the public regarding the special competency, importance and value of the shorthand reporting system. **Affiliated With:** National Court Reporters Association.

2598 ■ Illinois Elks Association
c/o Marvin G. Leathers, Sec.
PO Box 984
Mount Vernon, IL 62864
E-mail: marvin.leathers@illinois-elks.org
URL: http://www.illinois-elks.org
Contact: Paul Ronzani, Pres.
State. Promotes the principles of charity, justice, brotherhood and loyalty among members. Fosters the spirit of American Patriotism. Seeks to stimulate pride and respect toward patriotism. **Affiliated With:** Benevolent and Protective Order of Elks.

2599 ■ Jefferson County Chamber of Commerce (JCCC)
200 Potomac Blvd.
Mount Vernon, IL 62864
Ph: (618)242-5725
Fax: (618)242-5130
E-mail: chamber@mvn.net
URL: http://www.southernillinois.com
Contact: Floyd Brookman, Exec.Dir.
Founded: 1921. **Members:** 500. **Staff:** 2. **Budget:** $70,000. **For-Profit. Local.** Promotes business and community development in Jefferson County, IL. Holds Business After Hours parties and board meetings. **Councils:** Ambassadors; Educational Clearing House; Small Business; Special Events. **Affiliated With:** U.S. Chamber of Commerce. **Publications:** *Business News*, monthly. Newsletter. **Advertising:** accepted. **Conventions/Meetings:** annual dinner.

2600 ■ Kiwanis Club of Mt. Vernon
PO Box 1601
Mount Vernon, IL 62864
E-mail: danwevers@mvn.net
URL: http://kiwanis.mvn.net
Contact: Steve Swofford, Pres.
Local.

2601 ■ National Active And Retired Federal Employees Association - Jefferson 688
8555 E Bakerville Rd.
Mount Vernon, IL 62864-7309
Ph: (618)244-0048
URL: National Affiliate–www.narfe.org
Contact: Virgil L. Ford, Contact
Local. Protects the retirement future of employees through education. Informs members on issues affecting the retirement. **Affiliated With:** National Association of Retired Federal Employees.

2602 ■ National Association of Home Builders of the U.S., South Central Home Builders Association
c/o Doris Troutt
Local No. 1441
PO Box 216
11636 E Goshen Meadows Rd.
Mount Vernon, IL 62864-0005
Ph: (618)266-7230
Fax: (618)266-7848
E-mail: troutt@mvn.net
URL: National Affiliate–www.nahb.org
Contact: Doris Troutt, Contact
Local. Single and multifamily home builders, commercial builders, and others associated with the building industry. **Affiliated With:** National Association of Home Builders.

2603 ■ United Cerebral Palsy of Southern Illinois
9 Cusumano Professional Plaza
Mount Vernon, IL 62864
Ph: (618)244-2505
Fax: (618)244-3568
Free: (800)332-9745
E-mail: ucpsi@onemain.com
Contact: Sharon Hale, Exec.Dir.
Founded: 1957. **Staff:** 4. **Budget:** $190,000. **Local**. Aids persons with cerebral palsy and other disabilities, and their families. Goals are to prevent cerebral palsy, minimize its effects, and improve the quality of life for persons with cerebral palsy and other disabilities, and their families. **Affiliated With:** United Cerebral Palsy Associations.

2604 ■ United Way of Jefferson County, Illinois
PO Box 2506
Mount Vernon, IL 62864
Ph: (618)242-8000
Fax: (618)242-8048
E-mail: uwjc@mvn.net
URL: http://unitedway.mvn.net
Contact: Cindy B. Vincent, Exec.Dir.
Local. Affiliated With: United Way of America.

Mount Zion

2605 ■ Decatur AMBUCS
c/o Phillip R. Sturgeon, Pres.
6417 Derby Dr.
Mount Zion, IL 62549
Ph: (217)475-4576 (217)864-9256
E-mail: psturgeon@insightbb.com
URL: National Affiliate–www.ambucs.org
Contact: Phillip R. Sturgeon, Pres.
Founded: 1946. **Members:** 50. **Membership Dues:** individual, $60 (bimonthly). **Budget:** $10,000. **Local**. Creates opportunities for independence for individuals with disabilities by providing community service, AmTrykes for children with disabilities, and scholarships for therapists. **Affiliated With:** AMBUCS. **Publications:** *Decatur Noon AMBUC Newsletter*, monthly. **Conventions/Meetings:** annual convention.

2606 ■ Mount Zion Chamber of Commerce (ZCC)
PO Box 84
Mount Zion, IL 62549
Ph: (217)864-2526
Fax: (217)864-6115
E-mail: contact@mtzionchamberofcommerce.com
Contact: Judy Kaiser, Admin.
Founded: 1987. **Members:** 160. **Local**. Promotes business and community development in the Mt. Zion, IL area. Participates in Pony Express Days; sponsors Small Business Expo. **Formerly:** (1999) Village of Mt. Zion Chamber of Commerce. **Publications:** *Directory of Members*, annual. **Conventions/Meetings:** monthly meeting.

Moweaqua

2607 ■ American Legion, Illinois Post 370
c/o Remann H. Harlan
101 N Main St.
Moweaqua, IL 62550
Ph: (309)663-0361
Fax: (309)663-5783
URL: National Affiliate–www.legion.org
Contact: Remann H. Harlan, Contact
Local. Affiliated With: American Legion.

Mulberry Grove

2608 ■ American Legion, Mulberry Grove Post 1180
20290 Mt. Moriah Ave.
Mulberry Grove, IL 62262
Ph: (217)534-2307
Fax: (309)663-5783
URL: National Affiliate–www.legion.org
Local. Affiliated With: American Legion.

2609 ■ Technology Student Association, Illinois
c/o Mr. Thomas Dooly, Exec.Dir.
Mulberry Grove High School
801 W Wall St.
Mulberry Grove, IL 62262
Ph: (618)326-8222
Fax: (618)326-7504
E-mail: tdooly@swetland.net
URL: http://www.iltsa.org
Contact: Mr. Thomas Dooly, Exec.Dir.
State. Affiliated With: Technology Student Association.

Mundelein

2610 ■ American Legion, Mundelein Post 867
145 N Seymour Ave.
Mundelein, IL 60060
Ph: (708)566-0552
Fax: (309)663-5783
URL: National Affiliate–www.legion.org
Local. Affiliated With: American Legion.

2611 ■ American Youth Soccer Organization, Region 372
PO Box 783
Mundelein, IL 60060
Ph: (847)949-6320
URL: http://www.ayso372.org
Local. Affiliated With: American Youth Soccer Organization.

2612 ■ Catholics United for the Faith - Blessed John XXIII Chapter
c/o James and Colleen Sheehan
PO Box 421
Mundelein, IL 60060
Ph: (847)838-0344
E-mail: blessedjohn23@juno.com
URL: National Affiliate–www.cuf.org
Contact: Colleen Sheehan, Contact
Local.

2613 ■ Fil-Am Association of Mundelein, Illinois
c/o Yolanda G. Rodrigo
308 W. Orchard
Mundelein, IL 60060-2777
Local.

2614 ■ Lake County Illinois Genealogical Society (LCIGS)
1170 N Midlothian Rd.
Mundelein, IL 60060
Ph: (847)918-3208
E-mail: lcigs@yahoo.com
Contact: Jim Swab, Pres.
Founded: 1978. **Members:** 215. **Membership Dues:** regular, $20 (annual) • family, $22 (annual). **Staff:** 8. **Local Groups:** 1. **State**. Individuals interested in the research and preservation of the genealogy of Lake County, IL. Offers research trips and programs; provides for indexing and printing of various records. **Libraries: Type:** reference. **Holdings:** 3,000. **Publications:** *Quarterly*. Magazine. Update of society events, history of Lake County, IL. **Price:** free to members. **Advertising:** accepted. **Conventions/Meetings:** annual workshop (exhibits).

2615 ■ Mundelein MainStreet
16 E Park St.
Mundelein, IL 60060
Ph: (847)970-9235
Fax: (847)970-9282
E-mail: mundeleinmainstreet@tds.net
URL: http://www.mundeleinmainstreet.org
Contact: Ms. Marian O. Rodriguez, Exec.Dir.
Founded: 1993. **Members:** 100. **Staff:** 1. **Budget:** $70,000. **Local**.

2616 ■ National Alliance of Methadone Advocates of Chicago
205 N Seymour Ave.
Mundelein, IL 60060
Ph: (847)949-4682
E-mail: andyr02311@aol.com
URL: National Affiliate–www.methadone.org
Contact: Andrew Richardson CMA, Contact
Local. Promotes quality methadone maintenance treatment as the most effective modality for the treatment of opiate addiction. Eliminates discrimination toward methadone patients. **Affiliated With:** National Alliance of Methadone Advocates.

Murphysboro

2617 ■ American Legion, Paul Stout Post 127
1700 Gartside St.
Murphysboro, IL 62966
Ph: (618)684-3561
Fax: (309)663-5783
URL: National Affiliate–www.legion.org
Local. Affiliated With: American Legion.

2618 ■ Jackson County Historical Society
1616 Edith St.
Murphysboro, IL 62966
Ph: (618)684-6989
E-mail: jchs@globaleyes.net
URL: http://mysite.verizon.net/jchs
Contact: Kenneth Cochran, Pres.
Founded: 1969. **Members:** 320. **Membership Dues:** $16 (annual). **Local**. Supports preservation of local history. **Libraries: Type:** open to the public. **Holdings:** 5,000. **Subjects:** history, genealogy. **Publications:** *The Ventilator*, quarterly. Newsletter.

2619 ■ Murphysboro Chamber of Commerce
PO Box 606
Murphysboro, IL 62966
Ph: (618)684-6421
Fax: (618)684-2010
E-mail: executive@globaleyes.net
URL: http://www.murphysboro.com/chamber/index.html
Contact: Robert Wurster MS Ed., Exec.Dir.
Founded: 1923. **Membership Dues:** business (based on number of employees), $150-$275 (an-

nual) • associate (individual, nonprofit organization), $30 (annual) • individual/self-employed, $100 (annual) • gold key, $400 (annual) • multiple business (additional), $75 (annual). **Staff:** 2. **Local**. Promotes business and community development in Murphysboro, IL. **Computer Services:** database, list of members. **Publications:** *Chamber Directory*, periodic • *City Directory*, periodic • Newsletter, periodic. **Advertising:** accepted. **Conventions/Meetings:** annual meeting.

2620 ■ National Association of Housing and Redevopment Officials, Illinois Association
c/o Tyler Young, Jr., PHM, Exec.Dir.
PO Box 1209
Murphysboro, IL 62966-1209
Ph: (618)684-3185
Fax: (618)684-3222
E-mail: tyjr@midwest.net
URL: National Affiliate–www.nahro.org
Contact: Tyler Young, Exec.Dir.
State. **Affiliated With:** National Association of Housing and Redevelopment Officials.

2621 ■ Society of American Foresters, Southern Illinois University Student Chapter
c/o Charles Michael Ruffner, Faculty Representative
321 N 14th St.
Murphysboro, IL 62966-2011
Ph: (618)453-7469
Fax: (618)453-7475
E-mail: ruffner@siu.edu
URL: http://www.siu.edu/~ilsaf
Contact: Charles Michael Ruffner, Faculty Representative
Local. **Affiliated With:** Society of American Foresters.

Murrayville

2622 ■ American Legion, Murrayville Post 311
PO Box 136
Murrayville, IL 62668
Ph: (217)882-4151
Fax: (309)663-5783
URL: National Affiliate–www.legion.org
Local. **Affiliated With:** American Legion.

Naperville

2623 ■ American Associates of Blacks in Energy, Chicago
c/o Janet Jones, Pres.
State Govt. Relations NICOR
1844 Ferry Rd.
Naperville, IL 60563
Ph: (630)388-3747
Fax: (630)548-3574
E-mail: jjones1@nicor.com
URL: National Affiliate–www.aabe.org
Contact: Janet Jones, Pres.
Local. **Affiliated With:** American Association of Blacks in Energy.

2624 ■ American Institute of Architects Northeast Illinois
c/o Corda Murphy, Exec.Dir.
412 Green Valley Dr.
Naperville, IL 60540
Ph: (630)527-8550
Fax: (630)357-4818
E-mail: exec@aianei.org
URL: http://www.aianei.com
Contact: Corda Murphy, Exec.Dir.
Founded: 1978. **Members:** 480. **Local**. Works to celebrate and promote the profession of architecture and provide opportunities for professional growth. **Awards:** Honor Awards. **Frequency:** biennial. **Type:** recognition. **Recipient:** for submittal • Service Awards. **Frequency:** biennial. **Type:** recognition. **Recipient:** for submittal • Student Scholarship. **Frequency:** annual. **Type:** monetary. **Recipient:** for application. **Committees:** Design/Build; Golf Outing; Long Range Planning; Small Practice Management; Young Architects. **Affiliated With:** American Institute of Architects. **Publications:** *Architalk*, monthly. Newsletter. **Advertising:** accepted. Alternate Formats: online. **Conventions/Meetings:** monthly meeting, dinner meeting with featured topic (exhibits).

2625 ■ American Legion, Naperville Post 43
PO Box 4
Naperville, IL 60566
Ph: (708)420-9744
Fax: (309)663-5783
URL: National Affiliate–www.legion.org
Local. **Affiliated With:** American Legion.

2626 ■ Associated Illinois Milk, Food and Environmental Sanitarians (AIMFES)
1733 Park St., Ste.220
Naperville, IL 60563
Ph: (217)785-2439
Free: (800)222-6455
URL: http://www.aimfes.org
Contact: Jayne Nosari, Pres.
State. Provides food safety professionals with a forum to exchange information on protecting the food supply. Promotes sanitary methods and procedures for the development, production, processing, distribution, preparation and serving of food. **Affiliated With:** International Association for Food Protection.

2627 ■ Bikeline of Naperville
1277 S Naper Blvd.
Naperville, IL 60540
E-mail: bikeline1277@aol.com
URL: http://napervillebikeline.com
Local. **Affiliated With:** International Mountain Bicycling Association.

2628 ■ Chicago Area Association for Computing Machinery SIGCHI
c/o Kay Burnett, Chair
622 S Main St.
Naperville, IL 60540
Ph: (630)588-0442
E-mail: kburnett@acm.org
URL: http://www.acm.org/chapters/chi-sqrd
Contact: Kay Burnett, Chair
Local. Biological, medical, behavioral, and computer scientists; hospital administrators; programmers and others interested in application of computer methods to biological, behavioral, and medical problems. Stimulates understanding of the use and potential of computers in the Biosciences. **Affiliated With:** Association for Computing Machinery.

2629 ■ Chicago Terminal Chapter, Pennsylvania Railroad Technical and Historical Society
c/o Marvin Cadwell, Pres.
28 W 046 Country View Dr.
Naperville, IL 60564-9643
E-mail: ld_mlc43@comcast.net
URL: National Affiliate–www.prrths.com
Contact: Marvin Cadwell, Pres.
Local. Brings together people who are interested in the history of the Pennsylvania Railroad. Promotes the preservation and recording of all information regarding the organization, operation, facilities and equipment of the Pennsylvania Railroad. **Affiliated With:** Pennsylvania Railroad Technical and Historical Society.

2630 ■ Chicagoland Sky Liners
1532 77th St.
Naperville, IL 60565
Ph: (630)369-6834
E-mail: herbs@interaccess.com
URL: http://thebigkiteguy.com/skyliners/index.html
Local. **Affiliated With:** American Kitefliers Association.

2631 ■ DuPage Society for Human Resource Management
PO Box 4134
Naperville, IL 60567
E-mail: drust@drbusinessconsultant.com
URL: http://www.dshrm.org
Contact: Roger Hart, Pres.
Local. Represents the interests of human resource and industrial relations professionals and executives. Promotes the advancement of human resource management.

2632 ■ DuPage Unitarian Universalist Church
4 S 535 Old Naperville Rd.
Naperville, IL 60563
Ph: (630)505-9408
E-mail: office@duuc.org
URL: http://www.duuc.org
Contact: Neil Lichtman, Pres.
Local. Persons who are devoted to humanism as a way of life. Humanism presupposes humanity's sole dependence on natural and social resources and acknowledges no supernatural power. Humanists believe that morality is based on the knowledge that humans are interdependent and, therefore, responsible to one another. **Affiliated With:** American Humanist Association.

2633 ■ East Aurora Young Life
711 Oswego Rd.
Naperville, IL 60540
Ph: (630)428-3023
URL: http://eastaurora.younglife.org
Local.

2634 ■ East West Corporate Corridor Association (EWCCA)
c/o Shaye Mandle
1120 E Diehl Rd., Ste.140
Naperville, IL 60563
Ph: (630)505-7730
Fax: (630)505-7732
E-mail: smandle@ewcca.org
Contact: Shaye Mandle, Exec.Dir.
Founded: 1983. **Members:** 170. **Membership Dues:** institutional and corporate, $900 (annual). **Staff:** 5. **Budget:** $200,000. **For-Profit**. **State**. Businesses. Provides a unified voice for members' concerns in matters of transportation, government relations, human resources, education, and economic development. **Awards:** Illinois Legislator of the Year. **Frequency:** annual. **Type:** recognition. **Programs:** Public Safety Coalition. **Publications:** *Economic Forecast Survey of Members*, biennial • *EWCCA Newsletter*, quarterly. **Price:** included in membership dues. **Conventions/Meetings:** bimonthly board meeting • annual Economic Forecasting - breakfast - December • monthly meeting (exhibits) • bimonthly meeting, on topics current to the business community.

2635 ■ Fox Valley African Violet Society
c/o Dixie Williams, Membership Chm.
3211 White Eagle Dr.
Naperville, IL 60564
Ph: (630)904-1698
E-mail: dixw@aol.com
URL: http://www.foxvalleyavsociety.org
Contact: Dixie Williams, Membership Chm.
Regional. **Affiliated With:** African Violet Society of America.

2636 ■ Fox Valley Aikikai
12 S 076 Robert Dr.
Naperville, IL 60563
Ph: (630)778-6600
E-mail: danzanryu@aol.com
URL: http://www.martialartstraining.com
Local. **Affiliated With:** United States Aikido Federation.

2637 ■ Humane Society of the United States, Central State Regional Office (CSRO)
800 W 5th Ave., Ste.110
Naperville, IL 60563
Ph: (630)357-7015
Fax: (630)357-5725
URL: National Affiliate–www.hsus.org

Membership Dues: individual, $25 (annual) • family, $35 (annual) • supporting, $50 (annual) • sustaining, $100 (annual) • sponsor, $500 (annual) • patron, $1,000 (annual). **Regional**. **Affiliated With:** Humane Society of the United States. **Formerly:** (2005) Humane Society of the United States, Great Lakes Regional Office 2.

2638 ■ IEEE Communications Society, Chicago Chapter
c/o Dr. Yigang Cai, Chm.
1919 Nutmeg Cir.
Naperville, IL 60565-6809
Ph: (630)979-3303
Fax: (630)224-1415
E-mail: ycai@lucent.com
URL: National Affiliate–www.comsoc.org
Contact: Dr. Yigang Cai, Chm.

Members: 900. **Membership Dues:** regular/student, $120 (annual). **Local**. Industry professionals with a common interest in advancing all communications technologies. Seeks to foster original work in all aspects of communications science, engineering, and technology and encourages the development of applications that use signals to transfer voice, data, image, and/or video information between locations. Promotes the theory and use of systems involving all types of terminals, computers, and information processors; all pertinent systems and operations that facilitate transfer; all transmission media; switched and unswitched networks; and network layout, protocols, architectures, and implementations. **Affiliated With:** IEEE Communications Society.

2639 ■ Illinois Association for Medical Equipment Services (IAMES)
c/o Tom Renk, Exec.Dir.
1801 N Mill St., Ste.R
Naperville, IL 60563
Ph: (630)369-7782
Fax: (630)369-3773
E-mail: admin@iames.org
URL: http://www.iames.org
Contact: Tom Renk, Exec.Dir.

State. **Telecommunication Services:** electronic mail, tom@aeinc.org.

2640 ■ Illinois Credit Union League (ICUL)
c/o Dan Plauda, Pres./CEO
PO Box 3107
Naperville, IL 60566-7107
Ph: (630)983-3400
Fax: (630)983-4284
Free: (800)942-7124
E-mail: dan.plauda@ilcusys.org
URL: http://www.iculeague.org
Contact: Ms. Vicki Ponzo, Senior VP, Member Services

Founded: 1930. **Members:** 480. **Staff:** 22. **Budget:** $500,000,000. **State**. Provides education, information and legislation to assist Illinois credit unions to thrive and prosper. **Affiliated With:** Illinois Credit Union League. **Publications:** *E-News Direct, Weekly Governmental News*, periodic. Newsletters. **Circulation:** 500. Alternate Formats: online • *In Depth*, quarterly. Newsletter. **Price:** included in membership dues. **Circulation:** 2,000. **Conventions/Meetings:** annual convention (exhibits).

2641 ■ Illinois Dental Laboratory Association (IDLA)
c/o Karen Sharpe, Exec.Dir.
443 Newport Dr.
Naperville, IL 60565
Ph: (630)355-7912
Free: (800)942-4352
E-mail: idla@wideopenwest.com
URL: http://www.idla.com
Contact: Karen Sharpe, Exec.Dir.
Founded: 1946. **State**.

2642 ■ Illinois Division of the International Association for Identification
3108 S Rte. 59, Ste.No. 124
Naperville, IL 60564
E-mail: debmcgarry@comcast.net
URL: http://www.feinc.net/idiai.htm
Contact: Deborah McGarry, Sec.-Treas.
State. Organizes people in the profession of forensic identification, investigation and scientific examination of physical evidence, through education, training and research. Advances the scientific techniques of forensic identification and crime detection.

2643 ■ Illinois Hospital Association (IHA)
c/o Kenneth C. Robbins, Pres.
PO Box 3015
Naperville, IL 60566
Ph: (630)505-7777
Fax: (630)505-9457
E-mail: falbrecht@ihastaff.org
URL: http://www.ihatoday.org
Contact: Flora Albrecht, Contact
Founded: 1923. **State**.

2644 ■ Illinois State Society of American Medical Technologists (ILSSAMT)
c/o Susan Brooks, MT, Pres.
1367 Auburn Ave.
Naperville, IL 60565
Ph: (630)595-3888 (630)527-1948
E-mail: suebrook@wideopenwest.com
URL: http://www.il-amt.org
Contact: Susan Brooks MT, Pres.
State. Works to manage, promote and improve certification programs for allied health professionals who work in a variety of disciplines and settings. Administers certification examinations in accordance with the highest standards of accreditation. Provides continuing education, information and advocacy services to members. **Affiliated With:** American Medical Technologists.

2645 ■ Literacy Volunteers of DuPage
24W500 Maple Ave., Ste.217
Naperville, IL 60540-6057
Ph: (630)416-6699
Fax: (630)416-9465
E-mail: lvadupage@aol.com
URL: http://www.literacyvolunteersdupage.org
Contact: Ms. Lisa Thackeray, Program Mgr.
Founded: 1972. **Members:** 400. **Membership Dues:** adult student, $25. **Staff:** 7. **Local**. Trains and supports volunteers to tutor adult learner in English literacy skills. **Subgroups:** Advisory. **Affiliated With:** ProLiteracy Worldwide. **Formerly:** Literacy Volunteers of America - Central Du Page, Affiliate; (2004) LVA Dupage. **Publications:** *Literacy Volunteers of DuPage News*, quarterly. Newsletter. Provides news for members and supporters. **Circulation:** 100. **Advertising:** accepted. Alternate Formats: online. **Conventions/Meetings:** monthly board meeting - 2nd Monday evening.

2646 ■ Midwest Healthcare Marketing Association (MHMA)
1755 Park St., Ste.260
Naperville, IL 60563
Ph: (630)416-1166
Fax: (630)416-9798
E-mail: mscott@wmrhq.com
URL: http://www.mhma.com
Contact: Damon Schultz, Pres.
Regional. Exists to enhance the professional value of healthcare marketers and to increase their opportunities for success within the healthcare industry. Provides education programs, personal and professional networking opportunities, client relationship-building forums, dialogue and/or debate on current trends and issues, industry news, social events and new friendships.

2647 ■ Naperville Area Chamber of Commerce
55 S Main St., Ste.351
Naperville, IL 60540
Ph: (630)355-4141
Fax: (630)355-8335
E-mail: chamber@naperville.net
URL: http://www.naperville.net
Contact: Mike Skarr, Pres./CEO
Founded: 1913. **Membership Dues:** basic plan, $450 (annual) • classic plan, $750 (annual) • premier plan, $1,250 (annual) • executive premier plan, $3,000 (annual). **Local**. Promotes business and community development in Naperville, IL area. **Awards:** Anniversary Recognition. **Type:** recognition. **Recipient:** for members of 5 years • Small Business of the Year. **Frequency:** annual. **Type:** recognition. **Recipient:** for companies that set the standards of excellence among small businesses in the community. **Computer Services:** database, downtown shopping directory • information services, business directory. **Committees:** Focus: Women in Business. **Councils:** International Business; Small Office/Home Office; South Business Relations. **Subgroups:** Business Introduction Alliance; Power Partners. **Task Forces:** Expos. **Affiliated With:** U.S. Chamber of Commerce. **Publications:** *Commerce*, monthly. Newsletter. Contains articles and information about members and events. **Advertising:** accepted. Alternate Formats: online • *Community Resource Guide and Relocation Handbook*. Provides directory of area businesses, community information, service organizations and demographics. • *Membership Directory and Buyer's Guide*, annual. Contains member listing alphabetically and by category. **Advertising:** accepted • *Shopping and Dining Guide*. Handbook. Provides lists of restaurants and shopping centers and map.

2648 ■ Naperville Area Humane Society (NAHS)
1620 W Diehl Rd.
Naperville, IL 60563
Ph: (630)420-8989
Fax: (630)420-9380
E-mail: info@napervillehumanesociety.org
URL: http://www.napervillehumanesociety.org
Contact: Linda Linford, Exec.Dir.
Founded: 1979. **Local**. Develops and implements animal welfare programs and services in Naperville and surrounding communities.

2649 ■ Naperville Astronomical Association
c/o Drew Carhart
29W304 103rd St.
Naperville, IL 60564-5719
Ph: (630)922-1651
E-mail: info@naperastro.org
URL: http://www.naperastro.org
Contact: Mitchell Gerdisch, Pub.Rel.Off.
Founded: 1973. **Local**. Amateur astronomy society of the Chicago, Illinois area. Sponsors two monthly public programs, open public evenings at Glen D. Riley Observatory, plus activities and services for members.

2650 ■ Naperville Central Young Life
711 Oswego Rd.
Naperville, IL 60540
Ph: (630)428-3023
URL: http://napervillecentral.younglife.org
Local.

2651 ■ Naperville Junior Woman's Club
PMB 329, 1807 S Washington St., Ste.110
Naperville, IL 60565-2050
E-mail: info@napervillejuniors.org
URL: http://www.napervillejuniors.org
Contact: Denise Petty, Pres.
Local.

2652 ■ Naperville Noon Lions Club
PO Box 282
Naperville, IL 60566-0282
Ph: (630)375-7809
E-mail: info@napervillenoonlions.org
URL: http://napervillenoonlions.org
Local. Affiliated With: Lions Clubs International.

2653 ■ Naperville North Young Life
711 Oswego Rd.
Naperville, IL 60540
Ph: (630)428-3023
URL: http://napervillenorth.younglife.org
Local.

2654 ■ Naperville United Way
29 S Webster Ave., Ste.106B
Naperville, IL 60540
Ph: (630)369-2508
Fax: (630)369-5492
E-mail: napervilleunitedway@uw-mc.org
URL: http://www.napervilleunitedway.org
Contact: Susan Fritz, Exec.Dir.
Local. Affiliated With: United Way of America.

2655 ■ National Association of Church Business Administration, Chicago Chapter
c/o Lauralyn J. Theodore, Pres.
Community United Methodist Church
20 N Center St.
Naperville, IL 60540-4611
Ph: (630)355-1483
Fax: (630)778-2011
E-mail: ltheodore@communityunitedmethodist.org
URL: National Affiliate–www.nacba.net
Contact: Lauralyn J. Theodore, Pres.
Local. Affiliated With: National Association of Church Business Administration.

2656 ■ National Sojourners, Chicago
c/o Maj. Mark W. Johnson
457 Valley Dr., No. 302
Naperville, IL 60563
Ph: (630)627-3221
E-mail: major8411@msn.com
URL: National Affiliate–www.nationalsojourners.org
Contact: Maj. Mark W. Johnson, Contact
Local.

2657 ■ Neuqua Valley Young Life
711 Oswego Rd.
Naperville, IL 60540
Ph: (630)428-3023
URL: http://neuqua.younglife.org
Local.

2658 ■ Northern Illinois Chapter Association of Rehabilitation Nurses (NIARN)
c/o Donna Vittorio, Pres.
24466 Blvd. De John
Naperville, IL 60564
Ph: (630)904-0510
E-mail: boardmember@niarn.org
URL: http://www.niarn.org
Contact: Donna Vittorio, Pres.
Local. Works to advance the quality of rehabilitation nursing practice. Provides educational opportunities and facilitates the exchange of ideas among members. **Affiliated With:** Association of Rehabilitation Nurses.

2659 ■ Northern Illinois Fiero Enthusiasts
c/o Jim Hallman
2039 Yellow Daisy Ct.
Naperville, IL 60563
Ph: (630)305-9806
E-mail: jjh93@juno.com
URL: http://www.fierofocus.com
Contact: Mr. Jim Hallman, Pres./Founder
Founded: 1991. **Members:** 350. **Membership Dues:** $25 (annual). **Regional.** Individuals in the Chicago and metropolitan area dedicated to preserving the excitement of the Pontiac Fiero that was manufactured from 1984 through 1988. Attends area car-related events. **Publications:** *Fiero Focus*, bimonthly. Newsletter. **Circulation:** 350. **Advertising:** accepted. **Conventions/Meetings:** annual Fierorama - show, car show that focuses on members vehicles.

2660 ■ Organization of Islamic Speakers, Midwest (OISM)
c/o Seema A. Imam
608 S Washington St., Ste.302
Naperville, IL 60540
Ph: (630)848-1475
Fax: (630)848-1495
E-mail: admin@oismidwest.org
URL: http://www.oismidwest.org
Contact: Seema A. Imam, Contact
Regional.

2661 ■ Psi Chi, National Honor Society in Psychology - North Central College
c/o Dept. of Psychology
30 N Brainard St.
Naperville, IL 60540
Ph: (630)637-5100
E-mail: smdavis@noctrl.edu
URL: http://www.noctrl.edu/x7926.xml
Local. Affiliated With: Psi Chi, National Honor Society in Psychology.

2662 ■ Vintage Chevrolet Club of America, Great Lakes Region No. 7
c/o William Anderson, Dir.
28 W 103 Lakeview Dr.
Naperville, IL 60564
Ph: (815)498-1146 (630)420-2127
URL: National Affiliate–www.vcca.org
Contact: William Anderson, Dir.
Regional. Affiliated With: Vintage Chevrolet Club of America.

2663 ■ Waubonsie Valley Young Life
711 Oswego Rd.
Naperville, IL 60540
Ph: (630)428-3023
URL: http://waubonsie.younglife.org
Local.

2664 ■ Wheel Fast Racing
2308 Flambeau Dr.
Naperville, IL 60564
Ph: (630)728-5277
E-mail: wheelfast@megsinet.net
URL: http://members.core.com/~wheelfast
Contact: Scott Thielsen, Pres.
Local. Affiliated With: International Mountain Bicycling Association.

2665 ■ Windy City Z Club
3812 Mallard Ln.
Naperville, IL 60565
E-mail: rosecran@anet.com
URL: National Affiliate–www.zcca.org
Contact: Ty Ozgen, Pres.
Local. Affiliated With: Z Car Club Association.

2666 ■ WyldLife Naperville and Aurora
711 Oswego Rd.
Naperville, IL 60540
Ph: (630)428-3023
URL: http://napervillewyldlife.younglife.org
Local. Represents the interests of individuals committed to impacting kids' lives and preparing them for the future. Helps young people develop their skills, assets and attitudes to reach their full God-given potential. Reaches suburban, urban, multicultural and disabled kids and teenage mothers. **Affiliated With:** Young Life.

2667 ■ Xilin Table Tennis Club
Xilin Asian Community Ctr.
1163 E Ogden Ave., Ste.300
Naperville, IL 60563
Ph: (630)773-8887
E-mail: phil@big-ball.com
URL: http://www.catta.org
Contact: Phil Moy, Contact
Local. Affiliated With: U.S.A. Table Tennis.

2668 ■ Young Life Chicagoland Region
711 Oswego Rd.
Naperville, IL 60540
Ph: (630)428-4230
Fax: (630)428-4255
URL: http://chicago.younglife.org
Local.

2669 ■ Young Life Naperville and Aurora
711 Oswego Rd.
Naperville, IL 60540
Ph: (630)428-3023
Fax: (630)428-3024
URL: http://naperville.younglife.org
Local.

Nashville

2670 ■ American Legion, Illinois Post 110
c/o John C. Atchison
PO Box 26
Nashville, IL 62263
Ph: (618)327-3063
Fax: (309)663-5783
URL: National Affiliate–www.legion.org
Contact: John C. Atchison, Contact
Local. Affiliated With: American Legion.

Nauvoo

2671 ■ American Legion, Nauvoo Post 711
PO Box 87
Nauvoo, IL 62354
Ph: (309)663-0361
Fax: (309)663-5783
URL: National Affiliate–www.legion.org
Local. Affiliated With: American Legion.

2672 ■ Nauvoo Chamber of Commerce
PO Box 41
1295 Mulholland St.
Nauvoo, IL 62354
Ph: (217)453-6648
Fax: (217)453-2032
Free: (877)NAUVOO-1
E-mail: chamber@nauvoo.net
URL: http://www.nauvoochamber.org
Contact: David C. Miller, Pres.
Local. Works to advance the general welfare and prosperity of Nauvoo. Promotes the economic, civic, commercial, cultural, industrial, and education interest of the area. **Computer Services:** Information services, community information. **Publications:** Membership Directory. **Conventions/Meetings:** monthly meeting - every 2nd Monday • annual meeting - every 2nd Monday of September.

Neoga

2673 ■ American Legion, Votaw-Swank Post 458
PO Box 636
Neoga, IL 62447
Ph: (309)663-0361
Fax: (309)663-5783
URL: National Affiliate–www.legion.org
Local. Affiliated With: American Legion.

2674 ■ American Society of Dowsers, Central Illiana Dowsers
c/o Doris McKay
88CR 1400N
Neoga, IL 62447
Ph: (217)895-3488
URL: National Affiliate–dowsers.new-hampshire.net
Local. Amateur and professional dowsers and others interested in locating water, oil, mineral deposits, and various objects and information with or without the use of forked sticks, pendulums, and rods. Promotes fellowship and the teaching of dowsing skills. Informs

the public on the significance and uses of dowsing. **Affiliated With:** American Society of Dowsers.

Neponset

2675 ■ American Legion, Neponset Post 875
PO Box 229
Neponset, IL 61345
Ph: (309)663-0361
Fax: (309)663-5783
URL: National Affiliate–www.legion.org
Local. Affiliated With: American Legion.

New Athens

2676 ■ American Legion, Illinois Post 565
c/o Albert Krupp
406 Chester
New Athens, IL 62264
Ph: (309)663-0361
Fax: (309)663-5783
URL: National Affiliate–www.legion.org
Contact: Albert Krupp, Contact
Local. Affiliated With: American Legion.

New Baden

2677 ■ American Legion, Poelker Post 321
105 E Illinois St.
New Baden, IL 62265
Ph: (309)663-0361
Fax: (309)663-5783
URL: National Affiliate–www.legion.org
Local. Affiliated With: American Legion.

2678 ■ Lebanon Cedar Cruisers
c/o William Malina
5 Joan Dr.
New Baden, IL 62265-0000
Ph: (618)588-4097
E-mail: pmalina@ezeeweb.com
URL: National Affiliate–www.ava.org
Contact: William Malina, Pres.
Local. Affiliated With: American Volkssport Association.

New Berlin

2679 ■ American Legion, West Sangamon Post 743
PO Box 377
New Berlin, IL 62670
Ph: (309)663-0361
Fax: (309)663-5783
URL: National Affiliate–www.legion.org
Local. Affiliated With: American Legion.

2680 ■ American Rabbit Breeders Association, Illinois Mini Rex Rabbit Club
c/o Jerry Hicks
10698 Prairie Creek Rd.
New Berlin, IL 62670
Ph: (217)626-1811
E-mail: jerry@agrivestlnc.com
URL: http://www.nordickrabbits.com/specialt.htm
Contact: Jerry Hicks, Contact
Local. Affiliated With: American Rabbit Breeders Association.

New Boston

2681 ■ American Legion, Eliza Post 1971
1512 65th St.
New Boston, IL 61272
Ph: (309)537-3327
Fax: (309)663-5783
URL: National Affiliate–www.legion.org
Local. Affiliated With: American Legion.

2682 ■ American Legion, New Boston Post 48
PO Box 475
New Boston, IL 61272
Ph: (309)663-0361
Fax: (309)663-5783
URL: National Affiliate–www.legion.org
Local. Affiliated With: American Legion.

New Douglas

2683 ■ Silvercreek Glider Club (SGC)
c/o Jim Pitcher
7410 Rockwell Rd.
New Douglas, IL 62074
Ph: (636)346-4657
Fax: (815)425-2121
E-mail: infosgc@yahoo.com
URL: http://www.silvercreekgliderclub.com
Contact: Jim Pitcher, Contact
Languages: English, French, Spanish. **Local. Affiliated With:** Soaring Society of America.

New Haven

2684 ■ American Legion, New Haven Post 1141
PO Box 206
New Haven, IL 62867
Ph: (309)663-0361
Fax: (309)663-5783
URL: National Affiliate–www.legion.org
Local. Affiliated With: American Legion.

New Holland

2685 ■ American Legion, Porter Bell Post 715
PO Box 234
New Holland, IL 62671
Ph: (217)732-2254
Fax: (309)663-5783
URL: National Affiliate–www.legion.org
Local. Affiliated With: American Legion.

2686 ■ Logan County Angus Association
c/o Lynn Miller, Pres.
1848 400th Ave.
New Holland, IL 62671
Ph: (217)445-2442
URL: National Affiliate–www.angus.org
Contact: Lynn Miller, Pres.
Local. Affiliated With: American Angus Association.

New Lenox

2687 ■ American Legion, Illinois Post 1977
c/o Tom E. Hartung
14414 Ford Dr.
New Lenox, IL 60451
Ph: (309)663-0361
Fax: (309)663-5783
URL: National Affiliate–www.legion.org
Contact: Tom E. Hartung, Contact
Local. Affiliated With: American Legion.

2688 ■ American Shetland Sheepdog Association Sheltie Rescue Network
c/o Dorothy K. Christiansen
PO Box 819
New Lenox, IL 60451
Ph: (815)485-3726
E-mail: dchristiansen@tco.com
URL: http://www.assa.org
Contact: Dorothy Christiansen, Coor.
Local. Acts as coordinating body for the Sheltie rescue groups throughout the country; provides financial assistance to rescue groups needing help; assists possible adopters in locating a rescue near them; helps owners surrendering a sheltie to find a contact to help.

2689 ■ Greater Chicagoland Basenji Club
c/o Arnieta Kurtz
1402 Cherrywood Ln.
New Lenox, IL 60451
E-mail: sjoyner@ameritech.net
URL: http://www.basenji.org/chicagoland/
Contact: Sue Joyner, Show Sec.
Founded: 1964. **Members:** 23. **Membership Dues:** $10 (annual). **Local.** Owners of basenji dogs; interested individuals. Encourages and promotes the basenji breed. **Affiliated With:** American Kennel Club; Basenji Club of America. **Publications:** *The Basenji*, monthly. Magazine. Contains club column. • *What is the Basenji*, monthly. **Conventions/Meetings:** monthly meeting - always 3rd Friday of the month • annual specialty show - always June.

2690 ■ Illinois Paralegal Association (IPA)
PO Box 452
New Lenox, IL 60451-0452
Ph: (815)462-4620
Fax: (815)462-4696
E-mail: ipa@ipaonline.org
URL: http://www.ipaonline.org
Contact: Yvonne L. Olsson, Exec.Dir.
Founded: 1972. **Members:** 1,500. **Membership Dues:** regular, $65 (annual) • associate, $55 (annual) • student, $40 (annual) • sustaining, $95 (annual). **Staff:** 1. **State.** Promotes the paralegal profession. Provides continuing education opportunities for paralegals. **Publications:** *Outlook*, quarterly. Magazine. Contains substantive information for paralegals. **Circulation:** 1,600. **Advertising:** accepted. **Conventions/Meetings:** annual Education Seminar, two day continuing education seminar - every fall.

2691 ■ Illinois Sporting Clay Association (ISCA)
c/o Ron Delimata
353 W Francis Rd.
New Lenox, IL 60451
E-mail: rondelimata@il-sportingclays.com
URL: http://www.il-sportingclays.com
Contact: Ron Delimata, Pres.
State.

2692 ■ Interlocking Shetland Sheepdog Club of Monee (ISSCM)
c/o Dorothy Christiansen
PO Box 819
New Lenox, IL 60451
Ph: (815)485-3726
E-mail: dchristiansen@tco.com
URL: http://www.geocities.com/interlockingssc
Contact: Rebecca Sallay, Corresponding Sec.
Founded: 1971. **Members:** 25. **Membership Dues:** full, $25 (annual). **Local.** Promotes the Shetland sheepdog via shows, rescue, educational and social activities. **Libraries: Type:** not open to the public. **Holdings:** photographs. **Subjects:** dog show catalogs. **Awards:** Merit Award. **Frequency:** annual. **Type:** recognition. **Recipient:** to individuals with any AKC recognized title. **Affiliated With:** American Kennel Club; American Shetland Sheepdog Association. **Publications:** *Packaged Goodies*, monthly. Newsletter. Contains news and articles pertinent to shelties. **Price:** $7.00/year. **Circulation:** 40. **Advertising:** accepted. **Conventions/Meetings:** annual Dog Shows - every 1st Friday and Saturday of April in New Lenox, IL • monthly meeting - every 1st Wednesday, except July and August.

2693 ■ New Lenox Chamber of Commerce
PO Box 42
New Lenox, IL 60451-0042
Ph: (815)485-4241
Fax: (815)485-5001
E-mail: bev@newlenoxchamber.com
URL: http://www.newlenoxchamber.com
Contact: Beverly J. Ferris, Exec.Dir.
Founded: 1960. **Members:** 240. **Membership Dues:** business (based on number of employees), $140-

$350 (annual) • school, government, $200 (annual) • nonprofit, $100 (annual) • retiree, $75 (annual). **Local**. Promotes business and community development in New Lenox Township, IL. Sponsors area festival; conducts community awards, scholarships and partnership with schools. **Awards:** Business of the Year. **Frequency:** annual. **Type:** recognition • Citizen of the Year. **Frequency:** annual. **Type:** recognition. **Computer Services:** database, list of members. **Telecommunication Services:** electronic mail, doris@newlenoxchamber.com. **Committees:** Advisory. **Publications:** *Business Bulletin*. Newsletter. **Advertising:** accepted. Alternate Formats: online • *New Lenox, IL: The Community With the Ability to Grow*. Newsletter • *Welcome to New Lenox* • Newsletter, monthly • Directory, periodic. **Conventions/Meetings:** monthly meeting.

2694 ■ Will County Coin Club
c/o Mark Wieclaw
175 W Wood St.
New Lenox, IL 60451
Ph: (815)485-4137
E-mail: ramrodivs@hotmail.com
URL: National Affiliate–www.money.org
Contact: Mark Wieclaw, Contact
Local. Affiliated With: American Numismatic Association.

Newark

2695 ■ American Legion, Irwin Knudson Post 459
PO Box 555
Newark, IL 60541
Ph: (815)695-5750
Fax: (309)663-5783
URL: National Affiliate–www.legion.org
Local. Affiliated With: American Legion.

Newman

2696 ■ American Legion, Stanton Burgett Post 201
PO Box 186
Newman, IL 61942
Ph: (309)663-0361
Fax: (309)663-5783
URL: National Affiliate–www.legion.org
Local. Affiliated With: American Legion.

Newton

2697 ■ American Ex-Prisoners of War, Kickapoo Chapter
c/o Merl Vanderhoof
507 W End Ave.
Newton, IL 62448
Ph: (618)783-2793
URL: National Affiliate–www.axpow.org
Contact: Merl Vanderhoof, Commander
Local. Affiliated With: American Ex-Prisoners of War.

2698 ■ American Legion, Jasper Post 20
108 E Jourdan St.
Newton, IL 62448
Ph: (618)783-2622
Fax: (309)663-5783
URL: National Affiliate–www.legion.org
Local. Affiliated With: American Legion.

2699 ■ Jasper County Chamber of Commerce (JCCC)
c/o Beverly Worthey, Exec.Dir.
207 1/2 Jourdan St.
Newton, IL 62448
Ph: (618)783-3399
Fax: (618)783-4556
E-mail: jasperchamber@psbnewton.com
URL: http://www.newtonillinois.com
Contact: Beverly Worthey, Exec.Dir.
Founded: 1986. **Members:** 60. **Membership Dues:** retail, wholesale, service, education, health care (1-500 employees), $100-$700 • bank (per million in assets), $30 • agricultural producer, $100 • manufacturer, $100-$700 • professional, real estate, insurance, $100 • governmental organization, $75 • nonprofit, $50 • sole proprietor (based on number of employees), $50-$400. **Staff:** 2. **Local**. Promotes business and community development in Jasper County, IL. **Computer Services:** Information services, member listing. **Committees:** Community Relations; Industrial; Public Relations; Retail/Services. **Formerly:** (1996) Jasper County Improvement Association.

Niles

2700 ■ American Chemical Society, Chicago Section
7173 N Austin Ave.
Niles, IL 60714-4617
Ph: (847)647-4805
Fax: (847)647-8364
E-mail: chicagoacs@ameritech.net
URL: National Affiliate–acswebcontent.acs.org
Contact: Barbara Elizabeth Moriarty, Chair/Councilor
Local. Represents the interests of individuals dedicated to the advancement of chemistry in all its branches. Provides opportunities for peer interaction and career development. **Affiliated With:** American Chemical Society.

2701 ■ American Legion, Palmer Post 65
8603 Oriole
Niles, IL 60714
Ph: (309)663-0361
Fax: (309)663-5783
URL: National Affiliate–www.legion.org
Local. Affiliated With: American Legion.

2702 ■ Niles Chamber of Chamber of Commerce and Industry (NCCI)
8060 Oakton St.
Niles, IL 60714
Ph: (847)268-8180
Fax: (847)268-8186
E-mail: info@nileschamber.org
URL: http://www.nileschamber.org
Contact: Katie DiMaria, Exec.Dir.
Founded: 1967. **Members:** 475. **Staff:** 3. **Budget:** $100,000. **Local**. Promotes business and community development in Niles, IL. **Libraries: Type:** reference. **Subjects:** audio, written. **Awards:** Business of the Year. **Frequency:** annual. **Type:** recognition • Citizen of the Year. **Frequency:** annual. **Type:** recognition • Employee of the Year. **Frequency:** annual. **Type:** recognition • Ken Scheel Award. **Type:** recognition. **Committees:** Ambassadors; Golf Outing; Recognition Dinner/Dance; Technology. **Publications:** *Chamber Scene*, quarterly. Newsletter • *NCCI Community Guide*, annual. Directory. **Conventions/Meetings:** quarterly seminar.

2703 ■ Prader-Willi Syndrome Association Illinois
c/o Jeffrey S. Fender, Pres.
PO Box 48-0472
Niles, IL 60714-0472
Ph: (630)508-7355
E-mail: pwsillinois@sbcglobal.net
URL: http://www.pwsausa.org/IL
Contact: Jeffrey S. Fender, Pres.
State. Affiliated With: Prader-Willi Syndrome Association (U.S.A.).

Noble

2704 ■ American Legion, Illinois Post 572
PO Box 39
Noble, IL 62868
Ph: (309)663-0361
Fax: (309)663-5783
URL: National Affiliate–www.legion.org
Contact: Clifford M. Sanderson, Contact
Local. Affiliated With: American Legion.

2705 ■ Richland County Illinois Beagle Club
c/o Ted Rule
1638 N Freedom Rd.
Noble, IL 62868-2703
URL: National Affiliate–www.akc.org
Contact: Ted Rule, Contact
Local. Affiliated With: American Kennel Club.

Nokomis

2706 ■ American Legion, Waples-Bauer Post 94
215 S Spruce St.
Nokomis, IL 62075
Ph: (309)663-0361
Fax: (309)663-5783
URL: National Affiliate–www.legion.org
Local. Affiliated With: American Legion.

Normal

2707 ■ American Dairy Science Association - Illinois State University Dairy Club
c/o Dr. Aaron S. Moore
Illinois State Univ.
Dept. of Agriculture
Campus Box 5020
Normal, IL 61790-5020
E-mail: amoore@ilstu.edu
URL: National Affiliate–www.adsa.org
Contact: Dr. Aaron S. Moore, Contact
Local. Affiliated With: American Dairy Science Association.

2708 ■ American Legion, Illinois Post 635
c/o Carl S. Martin
PO Box 402
Normal, IL 61761
Ph: (309)452-1671
Fax: (309)663-5783
URL: National Affiliate–www.legion.org
Contact: Carl S. Martin, Contact
Local. Affiliated With: American Legion.

2709 ■ Arthritis Foundation, McLean County Branch
108 Boeyekens Pl., Ste.115
Normal, IL 61761
Ph: (309)451-0785
Fax: (309)454-5769
E-mail: greaterillinois@arthritis.org
URL: http://www.arthritis.org
Contact: Jennifer Kamps, Dir.
Local. Seeks to: discover the cause and improve the methods for the treatment and prevention of arthritis and other rheumatic diseases; increase the number of scientists investigating rheumatic diseases; provide training in rheumatic diseases for more doctors; extend knowledge of arthritis and other rheumatic diseases to the lay public, emphasizing the socioeconomic as well as medical aspects of these diseases. **Affiliated With:** Arthritis Foundation.

2710 ■ Association for Computing Machinery, Illinois State University
c/o Brandon Windham, Chm.
Campus Box 5150
School of Info. Tech.
Normal, IL 61790-5150

Ph: (309)438-8147
E-mail: tdennis@ilstu.edu
URL: http://www.acs.ilstu.edu/studentclub
State. Biological, medical, behavioral, and computer scientists; hospital administrators; programmers and others interested in application of computer methods to biological, behavioral, and medical problems. Stimulates understanding of the use and potential of computers in the Biosciences. **Awards:** ITSA CC Award. **Frequency:** semiannual. **Type:** recognition. **Recipient:** to the winner of a computer competition • ITSA Teacher of the year award. **Frequency:** annual. **Type:** recognition. **Recipient:** to the best teacher of the year, selected by IT student. **Committees:** ITSA Public Services. **Subgroups:** NET. **Affiliated With:** Association for Computing Machinery. **Absorbed:** (2003) Information Technology Student Association. **Also Known As:** (2003) ITSA. **Formerly:** (1999) ACS club.

2711 ■ Bloomington Wyldlife - Wyldlife
304 Jersey Ave.
Normal, IL 61761
Ph: (309)661-8885
URL: http://sites.younglife.org/_layouts/ylext/default.aspx?ID=C-4305
Local. Represents the interests of individuals committed to impacting kids' lives and preparing them for the future. Helps young people develop their skills, assets and attitudes to reach their full God-given potential. Reaches suburban, urban, multicultural and disabled kids and teenage mothers. **Affiliated With:** Young Life.

2712 ■ Bloomington - Young Life
304 Jersey Ave.
Normal, IL 61761
Ph: (309)661-8885
URL: http://sites.younglife.org/_layouts/ylext/default.aspx?ID=C-4307
Local. Represents the interests of individuals committed to impacting kids' lives and preparing them for the future. Helps young people develop their skills, assets and attitudes to reach their full God-given potential. Reaches suburban, urban, multicultural and disabled kids and teenage mothers. **Affiliated With:** Young Life.

2713 ■ Heart and Scroll Romance Writers of America
1617 Barton Dr.
Normal, IL 61761
E-mail: info@heartandscroll.com
URL: http://www.heartandscroll.com
Contact: Ms. Laurie Larsen, Treas.
Membership Dues: $12 (annual). **Local**. Works to provide networking and support to individuals seriously pursuing a career in romance fiction. Helps writers become published and established in their writing field. **Libraries: Type:** lending; not open to the public. **Holdings:** 500; audio recordings, books. **Subjects:** craft of writing, career information, research, publishing, writer's life. **Awards:** Madcap Award for Excellence in Romantic Comedy. **Frequency:** annual. **Type:** trophy. **Recipient:** published authors of romantic comedy • Magic Moments Award. **Frequency:** annual. **Type:** monetary. **Recipient:** best 10-page manuscript of a romance novel. **Affiliated With:** Romance Writers of America.

2714 ■ Hearts At Home
900 W Coll. Ave.
Normal, IL 61761
Ph: (309)888-MOMS
Fax: (309)888-4525
E-mail: hearts@hearts-at-home.org
URL: http://www.hearts-at-home.org
Contact: Jill Savage, Dir.
Founded: 1994. **Regional**.

2715 ■ Illinois Association for Supervision and Curriculum Development
c/o Donald Kachur, Exec.Dir.
Campus Box 8650
Normal, IL 61790-8650
Ph: (309)438-5479
Fax: (309)438-5358
E-mail: dskachu@ilstu.edu
URL: http://www.illinoisascd.org
Contact: Donald Kachur, Exec.Dir.
State. Advocates policies and practices that positively influence learning, teaching and leadership in education. Provides programs, services and professional development for effective teaching and learning. **Affiliated With:** Association for Supervision and Curriculum Development.

2716 ■ Illinois Association of Teachers of English (IATE)
4240-English
Illinois State Univ.
Normal, IL 61790-4240
Ph: (309)438-7858 (309)452-6844
E-mail: jneuleib@ilstu.edu
URL: http://www.wiu.edu/users/mfwc/wiu/iatehome.html
Contact: Janice Neuleib, Exec.Sec.
Founded: 1907. **Members:** 900. **Membership Dues:** general, $20 (annual). **Staff:** 2. **State**. English and Communication teachers. Seeks to further English education. Sponsors Illinois Poetry and Prose Contest. **Libraries: Type:** not open to the public. **Affiliated With:** National Council of Teachers of English. **Publications:** *IATE Newsletter*, semiannual • *Illinois English Bulletin*, bimonthly, except June-September. **Conventions/Meetings:** annual conference (exhibits) - always October.

2717 ■ Illinois Geographical Society
c/o Illinois State University
Campus Box 4400
Normal, IL 61790-4400
Ph: (309)438-7649 (309)438-5808
Fax: (309)438-5310
E-mail: mdsuble@ilstu.edu
URL: http://lilt.ilstu.edu/igs
Contact: Dr. Michael D. Sublett, Central Office Dir.
Founded: 1939. **Members:** 250. **Membership Dues:** regular, $25 (annual). **Budget:** $5,000. **State**. Promotes geography teaching and research. **Awards:** Community College. **Frequency:** annual. **Type:** monetary. **Recipient:** to outstanding students of geography attending two-year/community colleges in Illinois • Distinguished Geographer. **Frequency:** annual. **Type:** recognition. **Recipient:** for long and loyal service to the organization and to the discipline of geography • Senior College. **Frequency:** annual. **Type:** monetary. **Recipient:** to each of the outstanding geography majors at four-year colleges in Illinois. **Publications:** *Bulletin of the Illinois Geographical Society*, semiannual. Journal. **Price:** included in membership dues. **Circulation:** 250. **Advertising:** accepted. **Conventions/Meetings:** annual conference.

2718 ■ Illinois Reading Council
1210 Ft. Jesse Rd., Ste.B2
Normal, IL 61761-1836
Ph: (309)454-1341
Fax: (309)454-3512
Free: (888)454-1341
E-mail: ircread@dave-world.net
URL: http://www.illinoisreadingcouncil.org
Contact: Ms. Arlene Pennie, Exec.Dir.
Founded: 1968. **Members:** 6,000. **Membership Dues:** all, $35 (annual) • full-time student, $25 (annual). **Staff:** 3. **State Groups:** 5. **Local Groups:** 27. **State**. **Affiliated With:** International Reading Association. **Publications:** *Illinois Reading Council Journal*, quarterly. **Price:** $35.00 for nonmembers; included with membership dues. **Advertising:** accepted.

2719 ■ Illinois Ready Mixed Concrete Association (IRMCA)
303 Landmark Dr., Ste.1A
Normal, IL 61761
Ph: (309)862-2144
Fax: (309)862-3404
Free: (800)235-4055
E-mail: irmca@irmca.org
URL: http://www.irmca.org
Contact: Bruce Grohne, Exec.Dir.
State.

2720 ■ Illinois School Health Association
Dept. of Hea. Sciences
5220 Illinois State Univ.
Normal, IL 61790-5220
Ph: (309)438-8285
E-mail: mmicke@ilstu.edu
URL: National Affiliate–www.ashaweb.org
Contact: Marion M. Micke PhD, Contact
State. Protects and promotes the health of children and youth by supporting coordinated school health programs as a foundation for school success. **Affiliated With:** American School Health Association.

2721 ■ Illinois State University FarmHouse Fraternity
805 S Franklin
Normal, IL 61761
Ph: (309)452-3306
E-mail: isufarmhouse@hotmail.com
URL: http://www.studentclubs.ilstu.edu/farmhouse
Contact: Kyle Deutsche, Pres.
Local. Promotes good fellowship and studiousness. Encourages members to seek the best in their chosen lines of study as well as in life. Works for the intellectual, spiritual, social, moral and physical development of members. **Affiliated With:** Farmhouse.

2722 ■ Institute of Management Accountants, Illinois State University Chapter
c/o Harlan Fuller, Advisor
Illinois State Univ.
Campus Box 5520
Normal, IL 61790-5520
Ph: (309)438-5192
E-mail: hjfulle@ilstu.edu
URL: http://www.acc.ilstu.edu/ima/centill.htm
Contact: Harlan Fuller, Advisor
Local. Promotes professional and ethical standards. Equips members and students with knowledge and training required for the accounting profession. **Affiliated With:** Institute of Management Accountants. **Publications:** *Footnotes*. Newsletter. Alternate Formats: online.

2723 ■ McLean County RSVP
c/o Tarry Plattner, Dir.
RSVP-YWCA Senior Sers.
905 N Main St.
Normal, IL 61761-1599
Ph: (309)454-1451
Fax: (309)454-1454
E-mail: ywcaseniors@ywcamclean.org
URL: http://www.seniorcorps.gov/about/programs/rsvp_state.asp?usestateabbr=il&Search4.x=0&Search4.y=0
Contact: Tarry Plattner, Dir.
Local. **Affiliated With:** Retired and Senior Volunteer Program.

2724 ■ National Association of College Auxiliary Services, Central
c/o Jim Carlson, Pres.
Illinois State Univ.
2640 Illinois State Ctr.
Normal, IL 61790-2640
Ph: (309)438-2008
Fax: (309)438-5167
E-mail: jhcarlso@ilstu.edu
URL: http://www.nacas.org/Content/NavigationMenu/Regions/Central_Region.htm
Contact: Jim Carlson, Pres.
Regional. Enhances the profession of auxiliary and campus support services. Provides revenue and learning support to higher education institutions. Offers education, information and networking opportuni-

ties to members. **Affiliated With:** National Association of College Auxiliary Services.

2725 ■ National Association of Miniature Enthusiasts - Midstate Minimakers of Illinois
c/o Sara C. Paterson
1300 Schroeder Dr.
Normal, IL 61761
Ph: (309)452-1292
E-mail: repat1@insightbb.com
URL: http://www.miniatures.org/states/IL.html
Contact: Sara C. Paterson, Contact
Local. Affiliated With: National Association of Miniature Enthusiasts.

2726 ■ National Speleological Society, Near Normal Grotto
c/o Troy J. Simpson
PO Box 813
Normal, IL 61761
Ph: (815)432-3814
E-mail: tsimpson@mailcity.com
URL: National Affiliate–www.caves.org
Contact: Troy J. Simpson, Contact
Local. Seeks to study, explore and conserve cave and karst resources. Protects access to caves and promotes responsible caving. Encourages responsible management of caves and their unique environments. **Affiliated With:** National Speleological Society.

2727 ■ Normal Wyldlife - Wyldlife
304 Jersey Ave.
Normal, IL 61761
Ph: (309)661-8885
URL: http://sites.younglife.org/_layouts/ylext/default.aspx?ID=C-850
Local. Represents the interests of individuals committed to impacting kids' lives and preparing them for the future. Helps young people develop their skills, assets and attitudes to reach their full God-given potential. Reaches suburban, urban, multicultural and disabled kids and teenage mothers. **Affiliated With:** Young Life.

2728 ■ North Central Illinois FCA
c/o Joyce Gibs, Admin.Asst.
705 E Lincoln, Ste.102
Normal, IL 61761
Ph: (309)454-6920
E-mail: tgaumer@fca.org
URL: http://www.ncilfca.org
Contact: Joyce Gibs, Admin.Asst.
Local.

2729 ■ Penn State Alumni Association, Central Illinois
1600 Surrey St.
Normal, IL 61761
Ph: (309)862-2472
E-mail: dqthoma@ilstu.edu
Contact: Dave Thomas, Pres.

2730 ■ Phi Theta Kappa, Alpha Omega Xi Chapter - Heartland Community College
c/o Rachel Hills
1500 W Raab Rd.
Normal, IL 61761
Ph: (309)268-8415
E-mail: rachel@heartland.edu
URL: http://www.ptk.org/directories/chapters/IL/20603-1.htm
Contact: Rachel Hills, Advisor
Local.

2731 ■ Psi Chi, National Honor Society in Psychology - Illinois State University
c/o Dept. of Psychology
Illinois State Univ.
435 DeGarmo Hall
Campus Box 4620
Normal, IL 61790
Ph: (309)438-7439 (309)438-7278
Fax: (309)438-5789
E-mail: kspfost@ilstu.edu
URL: National Affiliate–www.psichi.org
Local. Affiliated With: Psi Chi, National Honor Society in Psychology.

2732 ■ Society of Manufacturing Engineers - Illinois State University S203
Illinois State Univ., Indus. Tech. Dept.
210 Turner Hall
Normal, IL 61790-5100
Ph: (309)438-2384
Fax: (309)438-8626
E-mail: stier@ilstu.edu
URL: National Affiliate–www.sme.org
Contact: Kenneth Stier, Contact
Local. Advances manufacturing knowledge to gain competitive advantage. Improves skills and manufacturing solutions for the growth of economy. Provides resources and opportunities for manufacturing professionals. **Affiliated With:** International Council for Pressure Vessel Technology.

2733 ■ Special Olympics Illinois
605 E Willow St.
Normal, IL 61761-2682
Ph: (309)888-2551
Fax: (309)888-2570
Free: (800)394-0562
E-mail: soill@soill.org
URL: http://www.soill.org
Contact: Doug Snyder, Pres./CEO
Founded: 1968. **Members:** 19,000. **Staff:** 55. **State**. Provides year-round sports training and competition in a variety of Olympic-type sports for children (ages 8 years and older) and adults with mental retardation or closely related developmental disabilities, giving them continuing opportunities to develop physical fitness, demonstrate courage, experience joy and participate in a sharing of gifts, skills and friendship with their families, other athletes, and the community. **Awards: Frequency:** annual. **Type:** recognition. **Recipient:** for outstanding athlete, coach, family, volunteer, media, organization, and facility. **Formerly:** (1999) Illinois Special Olympics. **Publications:** *Special Olympics Illinois Connection*, quarterly. Newsletter. Publication for the friends, families, and athletes of Illinois Special Olympics. **Price:** free. **Circulation:** 22,000. **Conventions/Meetings:** State Sports Competitions - 9/year.

2734 ■ Twin City Amateur Astronomers
508 Normal Ave.
Normal, IL 61761
Ph: (309)452-3936
E-mail: mprogers@mail.millikin.edu
URL: http://www.twincityamateurastronomers.org
Contact: L. Duane Yockey, Contact
Local. Promotes the science of astronomy. Works to encourage and coordinate activities of amateur astronomical societies. Fosters observational and computational work and craftsmanship in various fields of astronomy. **Affiliated With:** Astronomical League.

2735 ■ Voice of the Retarded, Illinois
113 Marie Way
Normal, IL 61761
Ph: (309)664-1175
E-mail: enewmi@ilstu.edu
URL: National Affiliate–www.vor.net
Contact: Eleanor Newmister, Dir.
State. Affiliated With: Voice of the Retarded.

Norridge

2736 ■ African Violet Society of Northern Illinois
c/o Edward Johnson
4901 N Azanam Ave.
Norridge, IL 60634
Ph: (708)457-0661
URL: National Affiliate–www.avsa.org
Contact: Edward Johnson, Contact
Local. Affiliated With: African Violet Society of America.

2737 ■ American Legion, Cameron-Butler Post 130
c/o William F. Brinlee, Sr.
4844 N Ozanam Ave.
Norridge, IL 60706
Ph: (309)663-0361
Fax: (309)663-5783
URL: National Affiliate–www.legion.org
Contact: William F. Brinlee Sr., Contact
Local. Affiliated With: American Legion.

2738 ■ American Legion, Hellenic Post 343
c/o George Bakis
4105 N Osceola Ave.
Norridge, IL 60634
Ph: (708)562-2747
Fax: (309)663-5783
URL: National Affiliate–www.legion.org
Contact: George Bakis, Contact
Local. Affiliated With: American Legion.

2739 ■ American Legion, Norridge Post 1263
4009 N Ozark Ave.
Norridge, IL 60706
Ph: (309)663-0361
Fax: (309)663-5783
URL: National Affiliate–www.legion.org
Local. Affiliated With: American Legion.

2740 ■ Anjuman Cricket Club
8242 W Lawrence Ave.
Norridge, IL 60656
URL: http://www.usaca.org/Clubs.htm
Contact: Khalid Dadabhai, Contact
Local.

Norris City

2741 ■ American Legion, Indian Creek Post 109
PO Box 286
Norris City, IL 62869
Ph: (618)378-9953
Fax: (309)663-5783
URL: National Affiliate–www.legion.org
Local. Affiliated With: American Legion.

North Aurora

2742 ■ Midwestern Gilbert and Sullivan Society (MGS)
c/o Sarah Cole
613 W State St.
North Aurora, IL 60542-1538
Ph: (630)896-8860
Fax: (630)896-4422
E-mail: midwestgs@yahoo.com
Contact: Sarah Cole, Sec.
Founded: 1984. **Members:** 150. Individuals interested in the works of Sir William Schwenck Gilbert (1836-1911) and Sir Arthur Seymour Sullivan (1842-1900), whose collaborative compositions include comic operas such as H.M.S. Pinafore, The Pirates of Penzance, and The Mikado. Promotes knowledge of Gilbert and Sullivan and encourages production of their works. Keeps members abreast of current productions and news relating to Gilbert and Sullivan. Conducts charitable activities; donates materials related to Gilbert and Sullivan to libraries. **Publications:** *Precious Nonsense*, quarterly. Newsletter. Contains new findings related to Gilbert and Sullivan and announcements of productions of their works. **Circulation:** 200. **Advertising:** not accepted. **Conventions/Meetings:** annual meeting.

2743 ■ North Aurora Lions Club
PO Box 35
North Aurora, IL 60542
E-mail: northauroralions@yahoo.com
URL: http://www.geocities.com/northauroralions
Local. Affiliated With: Lions Clubs International.

North Barrington

2744 ■ Biltmore Country Club Scholarship Foundation
c/o Biltmore Country Club
160 Biltmore Dr.
North Barrington, IL 60010-2002
Ph: (847)381-1960
Fax: (847)381-5295
URL: http://www.biltmore-cc.com
Contact: Chuck Goss, Controller
Local.

North Chicago

2745 ■ American Legion, Sharvin Post 397
717 17th St.
North Chicago, IL 60064
Ph: (708)336-4767
Fax: (309)663-5783
URL: National Affiliate–www.legion.org
Local. Affiliated With: American Legion.

2746 ■ Society for Neuroscience, Chicago Chapter
c/o Daniel A. Peterson, PhD, Pres.
Rosalind Franklin University
The Chicago Medical School
Dept. of Neuroscience
3333 Green Bay Rd.
North Chicago, IL 60064
Ph: (847)578-3411
Fax: (847)578-8545
E-mail: daniel.peterson@rosalindfranklin.edu
URL: http://www.chicagosfn.org
Contact: Daniel A. Peterson PhD, Pres.
Local. Provides a forum for the exchange of ideas and information between Chicago-area neuroscientists and offers an educational resource for teachers, students and the public at large. **Affiliated With:** Society for Neuroscience.

North Riverside

2747 ■ American Legion, Illinois Post 1109
c/o Ervin A. Borlick
7856 W 26th St.
North Riverside, IL 60546
Ph: (309)663-0361
Fax: (309)663-5783
URL: National Affiliate–www.legion.org
Contact: Ervin A. Borlick, Contact
Local. Affiliated With: American Legion.

2748 ■ Chicago Society for Space Studies
PO Box 1454
North Riverside, IL 60546
Ph: (708)788-1336
E-mail: larryberwy@aol.com
URL: http://www.chicagospace.org
Contact: Larry Boyle, Contact
Local. Works for the creation of a spacefaring civilization. Encourages the establishment of self-sustaining human settlements in space. Promotes large-scale industrialization and private enterprise in space.

Northbrook

2749 ■ American Legion, George William Benjamin Post 791
1435 Pfingsten Rd.
Northbrook, IL 60062
Ph: (309)663-0361
Fax: (309)663-5783
URL: National Affiliate–www.legion.org
Local. Affiliated With: American Legion.

2750 ■ American Society for Quality, Chicago Section 1201
c/o Ron Tozydlo, Sec.
PO Box 2008
Northbrook, IL 60065-2008
Ph: (847)957-2879
URL: http://www.asqchicago.org
Contact: Ron Tozydlo, Sec.
Local. Advances learning, quality improvement and knowledge exchange to improve business results and to create better workplaces and communities worldwide. Provides a forum for information exchange, professional development and continuous learning in the science of quality. **Affiliated With:** American Society for Quality.

2751 ■ Chicago Curling Club (CCC)
555 Dundee Rd.
Northbrook, IL 60062
Ph: (847)564-9877
E-mail: chicagocurling@hotmail.com
URL: http://www.curlingchicago.org
Contact: Bob Sorensen, Pres.
Local. Affiliated With: United States Curling Association.

2752 ■ Chicago Woodturners
c/o Paul Shotola, Pres.
1865 Western Ave.
Northbrook, IL 60062
Ph: (847)412-9781
E-mail: p.shotola@comcast.net
URL: http://www.chicagowoodturners.com
Contact: Paul Shotola, Pres.
Local. Represents amateur and professional woodturners, gallery owners, wood and equipment suppliers, and collectors. **Affiliated With:** American Association of Woodturners.

2753 ■ Chusy Region United Synagogue Youth
601 Skokie Blvd., Ste.402
Northbrook, IL 60062
Ph: (847)714-9130
Fax: (847)714-9133
E-mail: chusy@uscj.org
URL: http://www.chusy.org
Contact: Lisa Alter Krule, Dir.
Regional. Gives Jewish teens a chance to learn and grow as a Jew and most of all to have fun with other Jews. **Affiliated With:** United Synagogue Youth. **Formerly:** (2005) United Synagogue Youth.

2754 ■ Illinois Quarter Horse Association, District No. 12
c/o Francine Barnes, Dir.
1945 Phillips Ave.
Northbrook, IL 60062-5121
Ph: (847)498-6529
E-mail: lopeem1952@aol.com
URL: http://www.ilqha.com
Contact: Francine Barnes, Dir.
Local. Affiliated With: American Quarter Horse Association.

2755 ■ Jewish Genealogical Society of Illinois (JGSI)
PO Box 515
Northbrook, IL 60065-0515
Ph: (312)666-0100 (847)679-1995
Fax: (847)679-3268
E-mail: hrudnit@yahoo.com
URL: http://www.jewishgen.org/JGSI
Contact: Harriet Rudnit, Pres.
Founded: 1981. **Members:** 200. **Membership Dues:** general, $25 (annual). **Local.** Provides forum to share experiences and research methods and learn new techniques and sources in tracing Jewish ancestry. **Libraries: Type:** open to the public. **Holdings:** 400; books. **Affiliated With:** International Association of Jewish Genealogical Societies. **Publications:** *Morasha Heritage*, quarterly. Newsletter. Provides information about Jewish genealogy. **Price:** included in membership dues. **Circulation:** 300. **Advertising:** accepted • *Translation Guide to 19th Century Polish Language Civil-Registration Documents*. **Price:** $25. 00. **Conventions/Meetings:** semiannual Beginners Workshop - always June and January • lecture - 10/ year.

2756 ■ Mid-America Speed Skating - The Long Track Club of USA
1850 Oakwood
Northbrook, IL 60062
Ph: (847)498-0820
E-mail: sam@speedskate.org
URL: http://www.speedskate.org
Contact: Sam Poulos, Pres.
Founded: 1987. **Local.** Ice speedskating enthusiasts. **Affiliated With:** Amateur SpeedSkating Union of the United States. **Formerly:** (1998) Amateur +Skating Union - Mid-America Club.

2757 ■ Model A Restorers Club, Illinois Region
c/o Mort Drexler, Dir.
4116 Bristol Ct.
Northbrook, IL 60062
Ph: (847)564-5668
E-mail: contact@illinoisregionmarc.com
URL: http://www.illinoisregionmarc.com
Contact: Mort Drexler, Dir.
State. Affiliated With: Model "A" Restorers Club.

2758 ■ National Association of Miniature Enthusiasts - A1 Minis R Us
c/o Dee Dee Whipple
945 Huckleberry Ln.
Northbrook, IL 60062-3420
Ph: (847)564-0738
E-mail: whip10@aol.com
URL: http://www.miniatures.org/states/IL.html
Contact: Dee Dee Whipple, Contact
Local. Affiliated With: National Association of Miniature Enthusiasts.

2759 ■ North Shore-Barrington Association of Realtors
450 Skokie Blvd., Bldg. 1200
Northbrook, IL 60062
Ph: (847)480-7177
Fax: (847)480-7362
E-mail: dawn.mcananey@bairdwarner.com
URL: http://www.nsbar.org
Contact: Dawn McAnaney, Chair
Local. Strives to develop real estate business practices. Advocates the right to own, use and transfer real property. Provides a facility for professional development, research and exchange of information among members and to the general public. **Affiliated With:** National Association of Realtors.

2760 ■ North Suburban United Way
3330 Dundee Rd., Ste.N6
Northbrook, IL 60062-2328
Ph: (847)509-8743
URL: National Affiliate–national.unitedway.org
Local. Affiliated With: United Way of America.

2761 ■ Northbrook Chamber of Commerce and Industry (NCCI)
2002 Walters Ave.
Northbrook, IL 60062
Ph: (847)498-5555
Fax: (847)498-5510
E-mail: info@northbrookchamber.com
URL: http://www.northbrookchamber.org
Contact: Tensley Garris, Pres.
Members: 675. **Staff:** 4. **Local.** Promotes business and economic development in Northbrook, IL. **Computer Services:** Information services, business directory. **Telecommunication Services:** electronic mail, tensley@northbrookchamber.org. **Formerly:** (1999) Northbrook Chamber of Commerce. **Publica-**

tions: *Membership Directory and Buyer's Guide.* Provides description and contact information for member businesses. **Advertising:** accepted • Newsletter, monthly. Highlights new members, posts the latest chamber events and business news. • Articles. Alternate Formats: online.

2762 ■ Sweet Adelines International, Melodeers Chorus
St. Peter Community Church
2700 Willow Rd.
Northbrook, IL 60062
Free: (800)ACA-PLLA
E-mail: pmcole18@aol.com
URL: http://www.melodeers.com
Contact: Lisa Cole, Membership Coor.
Local. Advances the musical art form of barbershop harmony through education and performances. Provides education, training and coaching in the development of women's four-part barbershop harmony. **Affiliated With:** Sweet Adelines International.

Northfield

2763 ■ Chicagoland Military Vehicle Club
PO Box 8024
Northfield, IL 60093
Ph: (847)446-3390
E-mail: m151man@sbcglobal.net
URL: National Affiliate–www.mvpa.org
Regional. Affiliated With: Military Vehicle Preservation Association.

Northlake

2764 ■ American Legion, Illinois Post 888
c/o Howard H. Rohde
241 E North Ave.
Northlake, IL 60164
Ph: (309)663-0361
Fax: (309)663-5783
URL: National Affiliate–www.legion.org
Contact: Howard H. Rohde, Contact
Local. Affiliated With: American Legion.

2765 ■ National Technological Honor Society - West Leyden High School - Illinois
1000 Wolf Rd.
Northlake, IL 60164
Ph: (847)451-3000
Contact: Wil Wagner, Contact
Local.

2766 ■ Northlake Chamber of Commerce
PO Box 2067
Northlake, IL 60164
Ph: (708)562-3110
Contact: Natalie Bradford, Pres.
Local.

O Fallon

2767 ■ American Legion, Fischer-Sollis Post 137
109 N Penn St.
O Fallon, IL 62269
Ph: (309)663-0361
Fax: (309)663-5783
URL: National Affiliate–www.legion.org
Local. Affiliated With: American Legion.

2768 ■ Association of Women's Health, Obstetric and Neonatal Nurses, Southern Illinois Chapter
c/o Brelinda Kern, RN, Coor.
744 Carol Ann Dr.
O Fallon, IL 62269
E-mail: bre_kern@yahoo.com
URL: National Affiliate–www.awhonn.org
Contact: Brelinda Kern RN, Coor.
Local. Represents registered nurses and other health care providers who specialize in obstetric, women's health, and neonatal nursing. Advances the nursing profession by providing nurses with information and support to help them deliver quality care for women and newborns. **Affiliated With:** Association of Women's Health, Obstetric and Neonatal Nurses.

Oak Brook

2769 ■ Chicago Philatelic Society
c/o Reuben A. Ramkissoon, Dr.
3011 White Oak Ln.
Oak Brook, IL 60523-2513
Ph: (630)963-1439
Fax: (630)963-1439
E-mail: rramkissoon@juno.com
URL: http://www.chicagopex.com
Contact: Dr. Reuben A. Ramkissoon MD, Pres.
Founded: 1886. **Members:** 125. **Membership Dues:** $10 (annual). **Regional.** Works to promote the pursuit of philately through education. Holds annual exhibition. **Awards:** Aubrey Berman Award. **Frequency:** periodic. **Type:** recognition. **Recipient:** for outstanding service to the society and its annual exhibition CHICAGOPEX • Sail Newbury. **Frequency:** annual. **Type:** medal. **Recipient:** with outstanding contribution for philately. **Committees:** Berman Award Committee; CHICAGOPEX Organizing Committee; Committees for Russo Award; Newbury Award Committee; Nominating Committee. **Affiliated With:** American Philatelic Society. **Publications:** *Chicago Philatelic Society Bulletin*, monthly. Newsletter. Contains timely philatelic articles. **Price:** included in annual dues payment. **Circulation:** 125. **Conventions/Meetings:** monthly general assembly, featured programs; business (exhibits); Avg. Attendance: 20.

2770 ■ The Compassionate Friends U.S.A. National Organization (TCF)
c/o Mr. Wayne Loder
PO Box 3696
Oak Brook, IL 60522
Ph: (630)990-0010
Fax: (630)990-0246
Free: (877)969-0010
E-mail: public_awareness_coordinator@compassionatefriends.org
URL: http://www.compassionatefriends.org
Contact: Mr. Wayne Loder, Public Awareness Coor.
Founded: 1978. **Staff:** 6. **Budget:** $674,450. **Local Groups:** 600. **Languages:** English, Spanish. **Regional.** Assists families toward the positive resolution of grief following the death of a child of any age, provides information to help others be supportive. National organization sponsors The Worldwide Candle Lighting second Sunday in December at 7p.m. worldwide and the Walk to Remember final morning of the annual TCF National Conference. Most chapters have monthly meetings as well as local activities. **Libraries: Type:** reference. **Subjects:** grief and death of a child, sibling, or grandchild. **Awards:** Compassionate Employer Recognition. **Frequency:** annual. **Type:** recognition. **Recipient:** employer who has bestowed an exemplary level of compassion and support to employee who experienced death of a child, grandchild, or sibling • Compassionate Friends Appreciation Award. **Frequency:** annual. **Type:** recognition. **Recipient:** for significant contribution on promoting TCF goals • Compassionate Friends Chapter Leadership Award. **Frequency:** annual. **Type:** recognition. **Recipient:** chapter leader or member who made outstanding contributions to furthering TCF mission • Compassionate Friends Professional Service Award. **Frequency:** annual. **Type:** recognition. **Recipient:** professional psychologist, counselor, or other practicing professional who has contributed in supporting, assisting or educating others • Compassionate Friends Recognition Award. **Frequency:** annual. **Type:** recognition. **Recipient:** bereaved parent, grandparent or sibling who has contributed outstanding service to TCF at a national level over a period of years. **Publications:** *We Need Not Walk Alone*, quarterly. Magazine. Contains bereavement support for families. **Price:** $20.00. **Circulation:** 7,500. **Conventions/Meetings:** annual Compassionate Friends National Conference, with workshops, speakers, sharing sessions, pre-conference Professionals Day.

2771 ■ DuPage Convention and Visitors Bureau
915 Harger Rd., Ste.240
Oak Brook, IL 60523-1476
Ph: (630)575-8070
Fax: (630)575-8078
Free: (800)232-0502
E-mail: visitor@magmileswest.com
URL: http://www.dupagecvb.com
Contact: Ms. Jo Ellen Strittmatter, Exec.Dir.
Local.

2772 ■ Eastern Neuroradiological Society (ENRS)
c/o Ken Cammarata, Business Mgr.
2210 Midwest Rd., Ste.207
Oak Brook, IL 60523-8205
Ph: (630)574-0220
Fax: (630)574-0661
E-mail: kcammarata@asnr.org
URL: http://www.enrs.org
Contact: Ken Cammarata, Business Mgr.
Founded: 1991. **Members:** 184. **Membership Dues:** individual, $125 (annual). **Regional.** Strives to develop and support standards for the training and practice of neuroradiology and head and neck radiology. Conducts annual meeting for the reading and discussion of papers and the dissemination of knowledge in neuroradiology and head and neck radiology. **Awards:** Norman E. Leeds Award. **Frequency:** annual. **Type:** recognition. **Recipient:** for the best scientific paper presented by a resident at the annual meeting • Stephen A. Kieffer Award. **Frequency:** annual. **Type:** recognition. **Recipient:** for the best scientific paper presented by a trainee at the annual meeting. **Conventions/Meetings:** annual meeting, for physicians with interest and/or background in diagnostic imaging of the spine, brain, head and neck, and peripheral nervous system in children and adults as well as interventional neuroradiology (exhibits) - 2007 Apr. 23-25, Stowe, VT • annual Scientific Meeting.

2773 ■ Elgin AIFA
c/o Timothy W. Stellick, Pres.
616 Enterprise No. 110
Oak Brook, IL 60523
Ph: (847)888-8858
Fax: (847)888-9185
E-mail: walter.sundberg@countryfinancial.com
Contact: Timothy W. Stellick, Pres.
Local. Represents the interests of insurance and financial advisors. Advocates for a positive legislative and regulatory environment. Enhances business and professional skills of members. **Affiliated With:** National Association of Insurance and Financial Advisors.

2774 ■ Greater Chicago Chapter of the Society of Financial Service Professionals
c/o M. Linda Failing, Exec.Dir.
616 Enterprise Dr., No. 110
Oak Brook, IL 60523
Ph: (630)571-8030
Fax: (630)571-0253
E-mail: chicagosfsp@sfsp.net
URL: http://www.sfsp.net/chicago
Contact: M. Linda Failing, Exec.Dir.
Local. Represents the interests of financial advisers. Fosters the development of professional responsibility. Helps clients achieve their personal and business-related financial goals. **Affiliated With:** Society of Financial Service Professionals.

2775 ■ Human Resource Association of Greater Oak Brook
PO Box 4793
Oak Brook, IL 60522
E-mail: hraob@aol.com
URL: http://hraoakbrook.org
Contact: KC Lewis, Pres.
Local. Represents the interests of human resource and industrial relations professionals and executives.

Promotes the advancement of human resource management.

2776 ■ Illinois Chapter of the American Society of Landscape Architects (ILASLA)
PO Box 4566
Oak Brook, IL 60522
Ph: (630)833-4516
E-mail: info@il-asla.org
URL: http://www.il-asla.org
Contact: Brian Hopkins, Pres.
State. Promotes the growth of the landscape architecture profession. Fosters high standards of quality in design, planning, development, and conservation in the field. Promotes the exchange of technical information and supports scientific research in all aspects of landscape architecture. **Telecommunication Services:** electronic mail, brian@landworkslimited.com. **Affiliated With:** American Society of Landscape Architects.

2777 ■ Illinois Landscape Contractors Association (ILCA)
c/o Patricia Cassady, Exec.Dir.
2625 Butterfield Rd., Ste.204 W
Oak Brook, IL 60523
Ph: (630)472-2851
Fax: (630)472-3150
E-mail: pcassady@ilca.net
URL: http://www.ilca.net
Contact: Patricia Cassady, Exec.Dir.
Founded: 1959. **Members:** 873. **Staff:** 4. **State**. Promotes to foster a greater degree of public appreciation for the landscaping profession. Serves as a forum for exchange of information; seeks to educate members and the public regarding landscape contracting. **Affiliated With:** Professional Landcare Network. **Publications:** *The Landscape Contractor*, monthly. Magazine. **Price:** $65.00/year. **Advertising:** accepted • Membership Directory, annual. **Price:** free for members. **Conventions/Meetings:** annual Mid-America Horticultural Trade Show - always January. 2007 Jan. 17-19, Chicago, IL • annual Summer Field Day - meeting - August.

2778 ■ Illinois Landscape Contractors Educational and Charitable Organization (ILCA)
2625 Butterfield Rd., Ste.204W
Oak Brook, IL 60523-1234
Ph: (630)472-2851
Fax: (630)472-3150
E-mail: pcassady@ilca.net
URL: http://www.ilca.net
Contact: Patricia Cassady, Exec.Dir.
Founded: 1959. **Membership Dues:** class A, D and G (for-profit/out-of-state for-profit firms engaged in installing or maintaining plant materials), $355 • class B (firms engaged in providing materials, equipment or consultation needed by the industry), $455 • class C and E (employees of member firms, educators, researchers and retired members), $95 • class F (full-time/part-time students), $35. **Staff:** 4. **State**. **Awards:** Excellence in Landscape. **Frequency:** annual. **Type:** recognition. **Recipient:** for member landscape professionals who exhibit skills and expertise in landscaping. **Publications:** *The Landscape Contractor*, monthly. Magazine. Provides news and developments of the association with emphasis on regional concerns. **Price:** $65.00 /year for individuals in U.S.; $150.00 /year for individuals outside U.S. **Advertising:** accepted • Membership Directory. Contains information on landscape contractor, member types, products and services.

2779 ■ Illinois Manufacturers Association (IMA)
1211 W 22nd St., Ste.620
Oak Brook, IL 60523
Ph: (630)368-5300
Fax: (630)218-7467
Free: (800)482-0462
E-mail: ima@ima-net.org
URL: http://ima-net.org
Contact: Stan Zielinski, Exec.Dir.
State. Seeks to strengthen the economic, social, environmental, and governmental conditions for manufacturing and allied enterprises in the state of IL, resulting in an enlarged business base and increased employment.

2780 ■ Illinois Physical Therapy Association (IPTA)
1010 Jorie Blvd., Ste.134
Oak Brook, IL 60523
Ph: (630)571-1400
Fax: (630)571-1406
Free: (800)552-4782
E-mail: ipta@ipta.org
URL: http://www.ipta.org
Contact: Celeste Kirschner, Exec.Dir.
Founded: 1948. **State**. Aims to empower its members as publicly recognized providers of quality physical therapy and to advance the ethical and professional practice of physical therapy through advocacy and education. **Formerly:** (1998) American Physical Therapy Association, Illinois. **Publications:** *PT Priority*, bimonthly. Newsletter. **Advertising:** accepted.

2781 ■ National Fraternal Congress of America (NFCA)
c/o Anthony Snyder
1315 W 22nd St., Ste.400
Oak Brook, IL 60523
Ph: (630)522-6322
Fax: (630)522-6326
E-mail: nfca@nfcanet.org
URL: http://www.nfcanet.org
Contact: Anthony Snyder, Dir., Fraternal & Commun.
State. Works to unite 76 not-for-profit fraternal benefit societies who provide their members with leadership, social, educational, spiritual, scholarship, financial and volunteer service opportunities.

2782 ■ Sweet Adelines International, Choral-Aires Chorus
Christ Church of Oak Brook
31st St.
Oak Brook, IL 60523
Ph: (630)964-0792
E-mail: barbehst@hotmail.com
URL: http://www.choral-aires.org
Contact: Barb Ehst, Pres.
Local. Advances the musical art form of barbershop harmony through education and performances. Provides education, training and coaching in the development of women's four-part barbershop harmony. **Affiliated With:** Sweet Adelines International.

2783 ■ Trout Unlimited - Illinois Council
c/o Edward Michael
PO Box 5046
Oak Brook, IL 60522-5046
Ph: (847)831-4159
Fax: (847)831-1035
E-mail: e1Michael@cs.com
URL: http://www.tu.org
Contact: Joseph D Hammon, Chm.
Local.

2784 ■ Trout Unlimited - Oak Brook Chapter
c/o Doug Greenwood
PO Box 5046
Oak Brook, IL 60522-5046
Ph: (630)852-9621
E-mail: greenwooddg@hotmail.com
URL: http://www.tu.org
Contact: Walter J Bock, Pres.
Local.

2785 ■ United Way of the DuPage Area
PO Box 5317
Oak Brook, IL 60522
Ph: (630)645-6339
Fax: (630)729-3157
E-mail: uwdupage@uw-mc.org
URL: http://www.uwdupage.org
Contact: Tana Tatnall, CPO
Local. **Affiliated With:** United Way of America.

2786 ■ United Way of Illinois
900 Jorie Blvd., Ste.260
Oak Brook, IL 60523
Ph: (630)645-6300
E-mail: ronmelka@uw-mc.org
URL: http://www.unitedwayillinois.org
Contact: Ron Melka, Pres.
State. **Affiliated With:** United Way of America.

Oak Forest

2787 ■ American Legion, Illinois Post 1976
14904 S Cicero Ave., Apt. 416
Oak Forest, IL 60452
Ph: (309)663-0361
Fax: (309)663-5783
URL: National Affiliate–www.legion.org
Contact: Richard J. Daley, Contact
Local. **Affiliated With:** American Legion.

2788 ■ American Society for Microbiology - Illinois Branch
c/o John S. Hunter, Pres.
15542 Lockwood Ave.
Oak Forest, IL 60452
Ph: (708)687-8269
Fax: (847)349-7191
E-mail: john.hunter@advocatehealth.com
URL: National Affiliate–www.asm.org
Contact: John S. Hunter, Pres.
State. Advances the knowledge in the field of microbiology. Improves educational programs and encourages fundamental and applied research in microbiological sciences. Supports training and public information. **Affiliated With:** American Society for Microbiology.

2789 ■ Bears Cricket Club
5830 Peggy Ln., No. 3
Oak Forest, IL 60452
URL: http://www.usaca.org/Clubs.htm
Contact: Humayun Mirza, Contact
Local.

2790 ■ Oak Forest Chamber of Commerce
15440 S Central Ave.
Oak Forest, IL 60452
Ph: (708)687-4600
Fax: (708)687-7878
E-mail: ofchamber@oakforest.org
URL: http://www.oakforest.org
Contact: Mr. Terence Quinn, Interim Exec.Dir.
Founded: 1964. **Members:** 200. **Membership Dues:** all, $175 (annual). **Staff:** 1. **Budget:** $44,000. **For-Profit**. **Local**. Aims to protect and enhance the investments of the Oak Forest businesses. **Libraries: Type:** reference. **Holdings:** 50; articles, books, periodicals. **Subjects:** business, taxes, local area, history. **Awards:** Scholarship for Oak Forest High School Business Students. **Frequency:** annual. **Type:** monetary. **Recipient:** for students who are pursuing a business degree and/or are attending a business school. **Computer Services:** Mailing lists, of members. **Telecommunication Services:** information service, monthly newsfax sent with info for new members, upcoming events, and community news. **Affiliated With:** Chicagoland Chamber of Commerce; Illinois State Chamber of Commerce. **Publications:** *FYI*. Newspaper. Informs members and businesses about the organization and its upcoming events. Alternate Formats: online • *Oak Leaf*, monthly. Newsletter. Informs members and businesses about the organization and its upcoming events. Alternate Formats: online.

2791 ■ Oak Forest Numismatic Society
c/o Howard Ribbentrop
14849 Park Ave.
Oak Forest, IL 60452-0287

Ph: (708)687-2919
E-mail: dianhow@aol.com
URL: National Affiliate–www.money.org
Contact: Howard Ribbentrop, Contact
Local. Affiliated With: American Numismatic Association.

Oak Lawn

2792 ■ American Legion, Don Varnas Post 986
9619 Kedvale Ave.
Oak Lawn, IL 60453
Ph: (309)663-0361
Fax: (309)663-5783
URL: National Affiliate–www.legion.org
Local. Affiliated With: American Legion.

2793 ■ American Legion, Green Oak Post 757
9514 S 52nd Ave.
Oak Lawn, IL 60453
Ph: (309)663-0361
Fax: (309)663-5783
URL: National Affiliate–www.legion.org
Local. Affiliated With: American Legion.

2794 ■ American Legion, Jackson Park Post 555
PO Box 853
Oak Lawn, IL 60454
Ph: (708)868-2942
Fax: (309)663-5783
URL: National Affiliate–www.legion.org
Local. Affiliated With: American Legion.

2795 ■ American Legion, Naval Post 372
PO Box 746
Oak Lawn, IL 60454
Ph: (309)663-0361
Fax: (309)663-5783
URL: National Affiliate–www.legion.org
Local. Affiliated With: American Legion.

2796 ■ American Legion, Women Veterans Post 919
213 N Preston Ave.
Oak Lawn, IL 60453
Ph: (708)839-5521
Fax: (309)663-5783
URL: National Affiliate–www.legion.org
Local. Affiliated With: American Legion.

2797 ■ Bike Psychos Cycling Club
PO Box 652
Oak Lawn, IL 60454
Ph: (708)802-1804 (708)974-9132
E-mail: admin@bikepsychos.org
URL: http://www.bikepsychos.org
Contact: Russell Apitz, Contact
Local. Affiliated With: International Mountain Bicycling Association.

2798 ■ National Alliance for the Mentally Ill - Southwest
PO Box 23
Oak Lawn, IL 60454-0023
Ph: (708)425-0925
Fax: (708)598-5077
E-mail: celticadventure@ireland.com
URL: http://namisw.nami.org
Contact: Michael Guilfoyle, Contact
Membership Dues: consumer, $1 (annual) • individual, $35 (annual) • family, $40 (annual) • agency, $45 (annual). **Local**. Aims to improve the lives of persons with severe mental illness and their families. **Publications:** *NAMI Southwest*, bimonthly. Newsletter. **Price:** included in membership dues. **Conventions/Meetings:** monthly Sunshine Club - meet, with meals and social activities - every 3rd Friday at Oakview Center in Oak Lawn, IL.

2799 ■ Oak Lawn Chamber of Commerce
5314 W 95th St.
Oak Lawn, IL 60453
Ph: (708)424-8300
Fax: (708)229-2236
E-mail: oaklawnchamber@sbcglobal.net
URL: http://www.oaklawnchamber.com
Contact: Jennifer Busk, Exec.Dir.
Membership Dues: business, $120-$365 (annual). **Local**. Works to represent and advance the Oak Lawn business community; strives with constant integrity, fairness and cooperation to promote and to improve the economic atmosphere, business climate and image of Oak Lawn. **Publications:** *The Networker*. Newsletter. Alternate Formats: online.

2800 ■ Park Lawn Arc
10833 S Laporte Ave.
Oak Lawn, IL 60453
Ph: (708)425-3344
URL: National Affiliate–www.thearc.org
Local. Parents, professional workers, and others interested in individuals with mental retardation. Works to promote services, research, public understanding, and legislation for people with mental retardation and their families. **Affiliated With:** Arc of the United States.

2801 ■ West Highland White Terrier Club of Northern Illinois (WHWTCNI)
c/o Susan Chapman, Ed.
9548 S Brandt Ave.
Oak Lawn, IL 60453-3023
E-mail: westieinfo@westieclub.org
URL: http://www.westieclub.org
Contact: Penny Dubernat, Sec.
Regional. Affiliated With: American Kennel Club.

2802 ■ Windy City Walkers
c/o Therese Glatzhofer
9725 S Karlov Ave., No. 610
Oak Lawn, IL 60453-3341
Ph: (708)425-0211
E-mail: tglatzhofer@fryelouis.com
URL: National Affiliate–www.ava.org
Contact: Therese Glatzhofer, Contact
Local. Affiliated With: American Volkssport Association.

Oak Park

2803 ■ American Historical Society of Germans from Russia, Northern Illinois Chapter
c/o Jerry Amen, Pres.
847 S Home Ave.
Oak Park, IL 60304
Ph: (708)386-2238
E-mail: stametzil@yahoo.com
URL: http://www.ahsgr.org/northern_illinois_chapter.htm
Contact: Jerry Amen, Pres.
Founded: 1978. **Members:** 108. **Membership Dues:** individual, $7 (annual) • family/couple, $14 (annual). **Local**. Individuals who are generally of Russian German ancestry who share an interest in their cultural and historic heritage by keeping the floodways and folklore alive for future generations. Works to collect the history and genealogy of Germans from Russia and share this information with others. **Libraries: Type:** open to the public; lending. **Holdings:** 100; audio recordings, books, video recordings. **Subjects:** history, reference, fiction, music. **Affiliated With:** American Historical Society of Germans From Russia. **Publications:** *Germans from Russia Death Extractions Years 1914-1999*. From the John V. May Funeral Home in Chicago, IL. • *NIC AHSGR 2001*, quarterly. Newsletter • *Unser Leute: Settlers in Northern Illinois*. Contains church records from selected churches in the Chicago area where Germans from Russia either chartered or attended. **Conventions/Meetings:** annual convention.

2804 ■ American Legion, Illinois Post 692
c/o Charles Roth
PO Box 3096
Oak Park, IL 60303
Ph: (708)383-4142
Fax: (309)663-5783
URL: National Affiliate–www.legion.org
Contact: Charles Roth, Contact
Local. Affiliated With: American Legion.

2805 ■ Call to Action Chicagoland
c/o Margaret Field
PO Box 770
Oak Park, IL 60304-2222
Ph: (312)409-7425
E-mail: ctachgo@geocities.com
URL: http://www.geocities.com/Athens/Parthenon/9753
Contact: Margaret Field, Pres.
Founded: 1995. **Members:** 200. **Membership Dues:** regular, $20 (annual). **Budget:** $10,000. **Regional Groups:** 1. **Regional**. Liberal Roman Catholics working for social justice, church reform, and personal spiritual development. **Publications:** *CTA Chicagoland News*, quarterly. Newsletter. **Circulation:** 400. **Conventions/Meetings:** annual CTA Chicagoland Conference (exhibits) - April; Avg. Attendance: 250.

2806 ■ Catholic Physicians' Guild of Chicago
PO Box 214
Oak Park, IL 60303
Ph: (312)948-2506
E-mail: chicago@illinoiscma.org
URL: http://www.illinoiscma.org/Chicago.html
Contact: Patrick Guinan MD, Pres.
Local. Seeks to uphold the principles of the Catholic faith in the science and practice of medicine. **Affiliated With:** Catholic Medical Association.

2807 ■ Chicago Highlanders Pipe Band (CHPB)
c/o Art Skwerski, Band Mgr.
810 N Euclid Ave.
Oak Park, IL 60302
Ph: (708)383-2994
E-mail: bandmanager@chicagohighlanders.org
URL: http://www.chicagohighlanders.org
Contact: Art Skwerski, Band Mgr.
Founded: 1921. **Members:** 30. **State**. Available for community, civic and corporate functions.

2808 ■ Chicagoland Region of Narcotics Anonymous
c/o Public Information
212 S Marion, Ste.27
Oak Park, IL 60302
Ph: (708)848-2211
Fax: (708)848-2263
E-mail: info@chicagona.org
URL: http://www.chicagona.org
Local. Affiliated With: Narcotics Anonymous.

2809 ■ Friends of the Oak Park Conservatory
615 Garfield St.
Oak Park, IL 60304
Ph: (708)386-4700
Contact: John Seaton, Supervisor of Conservatory Operations
Local.

2810 ■ Germany Philatelic Society, Chapter 5 (GPS-CC)
PO Box 980
Oak Park, IL 60303-0980
Ph: (773)685-9700
Fax: (773)685-4590
E-mail: bobglass@aol.com
URL: National Affiliate–www.gps.nu
Contact: Bernard A. Hennig, Sec.
Local. Philatelists interested in collecting and studying German postal issues and postal history. **Libraries: Type:** reference. **Affiliated With:** Germany Philatelic Society. **Publications:** *German Postal Specialist*, monthly. Magazine. **Price:** $18.00 for

nonmembers. **Advertising:** accepted. **Conventions/Meetings:** annual symposium (exhibits).

2811 ■ Harrison Street Cooperative of Performing and Fine Arts
c/o Stefanie Graves
208 Harrison
Oak Park, IL 60304-1534
Ph: (708)386-7019
URL: http://www.harrisonart.com
Contact: Stefanie Graves, Admin.
Founded: 2000. **Members:** 25. **Budget:** $30,000. **Local**. Promotes artists.

2812 ■ Historical Society of Oak Park and River Forest (HSOPRF)
PO Box 771
Oak Park, IL 60303-0771
Ph: (708)848-6755
Fax: (708)848-0246
E-mail: oprfhistorymatters@sbcglobal.net
URL: http://www.oprf.com/oprfhist
Contact: Frank Lipo, Exec.Dir.
Founded: 1969. **Members:** 800. **Membership Dues:** individual, $35 (annual) • patron, $100 (annual) • life, $1,000 • family, $45 (annual) • benefactor, $250 (annual) • senior/student, $20 (annual) • business, $75 (annual). **Staff:** 1. **Local**. Individuals interested in preserving the history of Oak Park and River Forest, IL. Maintains a museum and research center in Pleasant Home. **Libraries: Type:** open to the public. **Publications:** *Nature's Choicest Spot: A Guide to Foreset Home and German Waldheim Cemeteries*. Book. **Price:** $8.00 each • *Village Yesteryears*, bimonthly. Newsletter. Alternate Formats: online • *The Woman Who Never Fails: Grace Wilbur Trout and Suffrage* • Membership Directory, periodic. **Advertising:** accepted. **Conventions/Meetings:** bimonthly meeting, with lecture and slide presentation.

2813 ■ Illinois Association for Family Child Care (IAFCC)
c/o Constance Johnson
PO Box 344
Oak Park, IL 60303
Ph: (773)237-7377
E-mail: iafcc@aol.com
URL: http://www.Illinoisafcc.org
Contact: Ida Butler, Pres.
Membership Dues: principal, $35 (annual). **State**. Advocates for excellence in family child care. Promotes optimal child development through support of the family and surrounding community through consultation, education, resource sharing, and leadership development; provides support to family child care professionals, establishes links with local associations and raises community awareness of the importance of excellence in child care.

2814 ■ Illinois Occupational Therapy Association (ILOTA)
715 Lake St., Ste.710
Oak Park, IL 60301
Ph: (708)386-9393
Fax: (708)386-9820
E-mail: office@ilota.org
URL: http://www.ilota.org
Contact: Patrick Bloom, Pres.
State. Advances the quality, availability, use and support of occupational therapy through standard-setting, advocacy, education and research. **Affiliated With:** American Occupational Therapy Association.

2815 ■ Illinois Recycling Association (IRA)
c/o Mike Mitchell, Exec.Dir.
PO Box 3717
Oak Park, IL 60303-3717
Ph: (708)358-0050
Fax: (708)358-0051
E-mail: executivedirector@illinoisrecycles.org
URL: http://www.illinoisrecycles.org/index.html
Contact: Mike Mitchell, Exec.Dir.
Founded: 1980. **Membership Dues:** business, $200 • educational, $125 • government, $175 • nonprofit, $100 • individual, $75. **State**. Encourages the responsible make use of waste materials. Promotes waste reduction, re-use and recycling through community education. **Conventions/Meetings:** annual conference and trade show.

2816 ■ Illinois Vaccine Awareness Coalition (IVAC)
PO Box 946
Oak Park, IL 60303
Ph: (847)836-0488
E-mail: info@vaccineawareness.org
URL: http://www.vaccineawareness.org
State.

2817 ■ Jaguars Cricket Club
454 N Austin Blvd., No. 1S
Oak Park, IL 60302
URL: http://www.usaca.org/Clubs.htm
Contact: Praveen Maramreddy, Contact
Local.

2818 ■ Literacy Volunteers of Western Cook County
125 N Marion St., Ste.203
Oak Park, IL 60301-1067
Ph: (708)848-8499
Fax: (708)848-9564
E-mail: info@lvwcc.org
URL: http://www.lvwcc.org
Contact: Ms. Angela West Blank, Exec.Dir.
Founded: 1986. **Staff:** 3. **Nonmembership**. **Local**. Dedicated to increasing the literacy levels of adults in the community through a network of trained volunteer tutors. **Libraries: Type:** open to the public; by appointment only. **Holdings:** 1,200; articles, books, periodicals, video recordings. **Subjects:** literacy, ESL, GED preparation. **Committees:** Program Services Committee. **Affiliated With:** ProLiteracy Worldwide. **Publications:** *Literacy Lines*, quarterly. Newsletter. Contains news about the organization and updates on literacy. **Price:** free. **Circulation:** 600.

2819 ■ Metropolitan Mathematics Club of Chicago
c/o Mary Wiltjer, Membership Chair
415 S Ridgeland Ave., No. 2
Oak Park, IL 60302-4009
E-mail: mwiltjer@oprfhs.org
URL: http://www.MMCChicago.org
Contact: Mary Wiltjer, Membership Chair
Local. Aims to improve the teaching and learning of mathematics. Provides vision, leadership and professional development to support teachers in ensuring mathematics learning of the highest quality for all students. **Affiliated With:** National Council of Teachers of Mathematics.

2820 ■ National Association of Professional Mortgage Women - Chicagoland
c/o Terri Konajeski
6821 W North Ave.
Oak Park, IL 60302
Ph: (708)386-7900
Fax: (708)386-1152
E-mail: tkonajeski@prairietitle.com
URL: National Affiliate–www.napmw.org
Contact: Terri Konajeski, Contact
Local. Encourages women to pursue careers in mortgage banking. Aims to maintain high standards of professional conduct. Works for equal recognition and professional opportunities for women. **Affiliated With:** National Association of Professional Mortgage Women.

2821 ■ Oak Park Area Convention and Visitors Bureau
c/o Rich Carollo, Pres./CEO
1118 Westgate
Oak Park, IL 60301
Ph: (708)524-7800
Fax: (708)524-7473
Free: (888)OAK-PARK
E-mail: info@visitoakpark.com
URL: http://www.visitoakpark.com
Contact: Rich Carollo, Pres./CEO
State. Promotes Oak Park area, IL as a tourist destination. **Formerly:** (2005) Oak Park Visitors Bureau.

2822 ■ Oak Park Board of Realtors
212 S Marion St.
Oak Park, IL 60302
Ph: (708)386-0150
Fax: (708)386-0187
E-mail: info@oakparkrealtors.org
URL: http://www.oakparkrealtors.org
Contact: Steven Nasralla, Pres.
Local. Strives to develop real estate business practices. Advocates the right to own, use and transfer real property. Provides a facility for professional development, research and exchange of information among members and to the general public. **Affiliated With:** National Association of Realtors.

2823 ■ Oak Park-River Forest Chamber of Commerce (OPRFCC)
1110 N Blvd.
Oak Park, IL 60301
Ph: (708)848-8151
Fax: (708)848-8182
E-mail: oprf@oprfchamber.org
URL: http://www.oprfchamber.org
Contact: Jim Doss, Exec.Dir.
Founded: 1895. **Members:** 500. **Membership Dues:** business (based on number of employees), $190-$1,500 • branch office, $50 • financial institution (base), $800 • Oak Park-River Forest based financial institution (base dues), $600 • Oak Park-River Forest based college and university, public utility, $600. **Staff:** 3. **Local**. Promotes economic and community development in Oak Park and River Forest, IL. **Awards:** Athena Award. **Type:** recognition • Blue Chip Business of the year. **Frequency:** annual. **Type:** recognition. **Telecommunication Services:** electronic mail, jdoss@oprdchamber.org. **Committees:** Business Advocacy; Events and Activities; Marketing Communications. **Publications:** *Business Connection*, bimonthly. Newsletter • *Community Guide*, annual. Directory • *Portrait*, biennial. Magazine • *Restaurant Guide*, annual. Newsletter. **Conventions/Meetings:** annual Consumer Expo - trade show.

2824 ■ Oak Park-River Forest Community Foundation
1049 Lake St., Ste.No. 204
Oak Park, IL 60301
Ph: (708)848-1560
Fax: (708)848-1531
E-mail: advisors@oprfcommfd.org
URL: http://www.oprfcommfd.org
Contact: David Weindling, Dir. of Donor Services
Founded: 1958. **Members:** 34. **Staff:** 4. **Budget:** $225,000. **Local Groups:** 1. **Local**. Aims to strengthen the community through philanthropy. Stimulates and facilitates individual philanthropy. Provides resources to address community priorities and interests. **Awards: Frequency:** annual. **Type:** grant. **Recipient:** for Oak Park and River Forest projects • **Frequency:** annual. **Type:** grant • **Frequency:** annual. **Type:** scholarship. **Recipient:** for Oak Park and River Forest graduating seniors • **Frequency:** annual. **Type:** scholarship. **Telecommunication Services:** electronic mail, csaxton@oprfcommfd.org. **Affiliated With:** Council on Foundations. **Publications:** *Annual Report to the Community*, annual. **Circulation:** 10,000 • *Building the Community Trust*. Newsletter. **Circulation:** 10,000.

2825 ■ Oak Park/River Forest - Young Life
544 S Harvey
Oak Park, IL 60304

Ph: (708)386-7501
URL: http://sites.younglife.org/_layouts/ylext/default.aspx?ID=C-825
Local. Represents the interests of individuals committed to impacting kids' lives and preparing them for the future. Helps young people develop their skills, assets and attitudes to reach their full God-given potential. Reaches suburban, urban, multicultural and disabled kids and teenage mothers. **Affiliated With:** Young Life.

2826 ■ PFLAG Oak Park Area
306 Wesley Ave.
Oak Park, IL 60302
Ph: (708)386-3016
E-mail: oakpark.pflag@gmail.com
URL: http://www.oakpark-pflag.blogspot.com
Local. **Affiliated With:** Parents, Families, and Friends of Lesbians and Gays.

2827 ■ United Way of Oak Park, River Forest and Forest Park
1042 Pleasant St.
Oak Park, IL 60302
Ph: (708)386-4885
Fax: (708)386-4918
URL: http://www.unitedwayoprffp.org
Contact: Kate Wenzel, CPO
Founded: 1935. **Local**. **Affiliated With:** United Way of America. **Publications:** Annual Report. Alternate Formats: online.

2828 ■ West Suburban Access News Association (WSANA)
c/o Joel Sheffel
PO Box 3221
Oak Park, IL 60302-3221
Ph: (708)383-6258
Fax: (708)383-6291
E-mail: info@wsana.org
URL: http://www.wsana.org
Contact: Mr. Tim Mantz, Pres.
Founded: 2000. **Membership Dues:** individual (fixed income, social security, public aid), $6 (annual) • regular, $12 (annual) • organizational, $25 (annual) • organizational (with free ad each month in newsletter), $40 (annual). **Local**. Provides information on topics of interest to persons with disability. **Publications:** *WSANA*, monthly. Newsletter. **Price:** included in membership dues. **Advertising:** accepted. Alternate Formats: online.

2829 ■ West Suburbs REACT
129 S Lombard Ave.
Oak Park, IL 60302
Ph: (708)848-6152
E-mail: react@westsuburbsreact.com
URL: http://www.reactintl.org/teaminfo/usa_teams/teams-usil.htm
Local. Trained communication experts and professional volunteers. Provides volunteer public service and emergency communications through the use of radios (Citizen Band, General Mobile Radio Service, UHF and HAM). Coordinates with radio industries and government on safety communication matters and supports charitable activities and community organizations.

2830 ■ Young Life Oak Park and River Forest
544 S Harvey
Oak Park, IL 60304
Ph: (708)386-7501
URL: http://oprfyl.younglife.org
Local.

Oakbrook Terrace

2831 ■ American Association of Candy Technologists - Chicago Section
c/o Katie Mulcrone, Sec.
Dawson Sales Co.
One Tower Ln., Ste.330
Oakbrook Terrace, IL 60181
Ph: (630)574-8100
E-mail: katiemulcrone@dawsonsales.com
URL: National Affiliate–www.aactcandy.org
Contact: Katie Mulcrone, Sec.
Local. Seeks to further the education of the technical community of the confectionery industry. Promotes the application of science and engineering to the manufacturing, handling and distribution of confectionery products. **Affiliated With:** American Association of Candy Technologists.

2832 ■ American Cancer Society, Glen Ellyn - Du Page County Regional
1801 S Myers Rd., Ste.100
Oakbrook Terrace, IL 60181
Ph: (630)932-1141
Fax: (630)932-1171
URL: http://www.cancer.org
Contact: Karen Woronicz, Regional Dir.
Local. **Affiliated With:** American Cancer Society.

2833 ■ Chicago Automobile Trade Association
c/o Jerry H. Cizek, III, Pres.
18W200 Butterfield Rd.
Oakbrook Terrace, IL 60181
Ph: (630)495-2282
Fax: (630)495-2260
E-mail: jcizek3rd@drivechicago.com
URL: http://chicagoautoshow.com
Contact: Jerry H. Cizek III, Pres.
Local. **Affiliated With:** National Automobile Dealers Association.

2834 ■ Illinois College of Emergency Physicians (ICEP)
1 S 280 Summit Ave., Ct. B-2
Oakbrook Terrace, IL 60181
Ph: (630)495-6400
Fax: (630)495-6404
Free: (888)495-ICEP
E-mail: info@icep.org
URL: http://www.icep.org
Contact: Virginia Kennedy Palys JD, Exec.Dir.
Membership Dues: active, $765 (annual). **State**. **Affiliated With:** American College of Emergency Physicians.

2835 ■ Illinois Park and Recreation Association (IPRA)
c/o Bill Wald, CEO
1815 S Meyers Rd., Ste.400
Oakbrook Terrace, IL 60181
Ph: (630)376-1911
E-mail: bill@ilipra.org
URL: http://www.il-ipra.org
Contact: Bill Wald, CEO
State. Professional association of park and recreation employees.

2836 ■ National Association of Fleet Administrators, Central Region
c/o Ms. Ruth Alfson
Exelon Corp.
3 Lincoln Ctr., 4th Fl.
Oakbrook Terrace, IL 60181-4204
Ph: (630)576-6327
Fax: (630)576-6324
E-mail: ruth.alfson@exeloncorp.com
URL: National Affiliate–www.nafa.org
Contact: Ms. Ruth Alfson, Contact
Regional. Promotes the professional management of vehicles through education, government and industry relations and services to members. **Affiliated With:** National Association of Fleet Administrators.

2837 ■ Oak Brook Area Association of Commerce and Industry (OBAACI)
c/o Lauri Teschner Adams, Pres./CEO
One Lincoln Ctr., 10th Fl., Ste.1000
18 W 140 Butterfield Rd.
Oakbrook Terrace, IL 60181
Ph: (630)705-9991
Fax: (630)705-9992
E-mail: ltadams@oakbrookbiz.com
Contact: Laurie Teschner Adams, Pres. & CEO
Membership Dues: one time processing fee for new members, $25 • non-profit company (under 25 employees), $185 (annual) • home-based independent contractor, $240 (annual) • with 1-5 employees, $250 (annual) • with 6-10 employees, $325 (annual) • with 11-20 employees, $385 (annual) • with 21-50 employees, $475 (annual) • with 51-100 employees, $565 (annual) • with 101-150 employees, $670 (annual) • with over 150 employees, $885 (annual). **Local**. Offers countless opportunities to network, showcase services, and further professional development. Provides significant ways to become more rooted in the exceptional local business community. **Telecommunication Services:** electronic mail, info@oakbrookbiz.com. **Subgroups:** Businesswomen's Network; OBAACI Leads Group.

2838 ■ Planned Parenthood Federation of America
1 Oakbrook Terr. No. 808
Oakbrook Terrace, IL 60181-4476
Ph: (630)627-9270
Fax: (630)627-9549
E-mail: communications@ppfa.org
URL: http://www.plannedparenthood.org
Regional.

Oakwood

2839 ■ American Legion, Vincent Hays Post 610
PO Box 603
Oakwood, IL 61858
Ph: (309)663-0361
Fax: (309)663-5783
URL: National Affiliate–www.legion.org
Local. **Affiliated With:** American Legion.

2840 ■ Kickapoo Mountain Bike Club (KMBC)
c/o Andy Warren, Pres.
PO Box 475
Oakwood, IL 61858
Ph: (217)678-3624
E-mail: awarren@mchsi.com
URL: http://www.kickapoombc.org
Contact: Andy Warren, Pres.
Membership Dues: individual, $10 (annual) • family, $15 (annual) • junior, $5 (annual). **Local**. **Affiliated With:** International Mountain Bicycling Association.

Oblong

2841 ■ American Legion, Oblong Post 219
PO Box 231
Oblong, IL 62449
Ph: (309)663-0361
Fax: (309)663-5783
URL: National Affiliate–www.legion.org
Local. **Affiliated With:** American Legion.

Oconee

2842 ■ American Legion, Roy Ireland Post 317
PO Box 145
Oconee, IL 62553
Ph: (309)663-0361
Fax: (309)663-5783
URL: National Affiliate–www.legion.org
Local. **Affiliated With:** American Legion.

Odell

2843 ■ American Legion, Odell Post 666
PO Box 101
Odell, IL 60460

Ph: (309)663-0361
Fax: (309)663-5783
URL: National Affiliate–www.legion.org
Local. Affiliated With: American Legion.

2844 ■ American Rabbit Breeders Association, Illinois Mini Lop Club
c/o Bonnie Bolen
19155 E 2500 N Rd.
Odell, IL 60460
Ph: (815)998-2168
E-mail: bbolen@bwsys.net
URL: http://www.nordickrabbits.com/specialt.htm
Contact: Bonnie Bolen, Contact
Local. Affiliated With: American Rabbit Breeders Association.

O'Fallon

2845 ■ East Side Association of Insurance and Financial Advisors
c/o Ray Farmer Jr., Association Exec.
PO Box 1601
O'Fallon, IL 62269-8601
Ph: (618)624-4355
Fax: (618)624-4355
E-mail: eastsideaifa@yahoo.com
URL: http://www.naifanet.com/eastside
Contact: Michael A. Babcock, Pres.
Founded: 1940. **Members:** 125. **Staff:** 1. **Local. Formerly:** (2004) East Side Life Underwriters Association.

2846 ■ Illinois State Grange
955 Keller Ln.
O'Fallon, IL 62269-4218
Ph: (618)632-4322
E-mail: nkelfar@aol.com
URL: http://www.ilgrange.org
Contact: Henrietta Keller, Master
Founded: 1872. **Members:** 2,300. **State Groups:** 1. **Local Groups:** 50. **State.** Centers on farm, family, community service, legislation and fraternity. **Publications:** *Illinois Granger*, monthly. **Conventions/Meetings:** annual Illinois State Grange Conversion - convention, youth, agriculture, and women's activities - always Sept; Avg. Attendance: 200.

2847 ■ Korean War Veterans Association, Imjin Chapter
c/o Coy Baker
PO Box 211
O'Fallon, IL 62269-0211
Ph: (618)877-0893
E-mail: rklein27@peaknet.net
URL: National Affiliate–www.kwva.org
Contact: Coy Baker, Contact
Local. Affiliated With: Korean War Veterans Association.

2848 ■ Main Street O'Fallon
101 W State St.
O'Fallon, IL 62269
Ph: (618)624-4503
URL: http://www.mainstreetofallon.org
Local.

2849 ■ National Active And Retired Federal Employees Association - Alvin G Bohley 1019
108 Red Pine
O'Fallon, IL 62269-2506
Ph: (618)624-8007
URL: National Affiliate–www.narfe.org
Contact: Benjamin S. Brown, Contact
Local. Protects the retirement future of employees through education. Informs members on issues affecting the retirement. **Affiliated With:** National Association of Retired Federal Employees.

2850 ■ O'Fallon Chamber of Commerce (OCC)
PO Box 371
O'Fallon, IL 62269
Ph: (618)632-3377
Fax: (618)632-8162
E-mail: chamber@ofallonchamber.com
URL: http://www.ofallonchamber.com
Contact: Kathy Federico, Pres.
Founded: 1946. **Members:** 300. **Membership Dues:** individual, non-business, $85 (annual) • church, school, club, organization, home business, $100 (annual) • business (based on the number of employees), $140-$275 (annual) • financial institution, major employer, $385 (annual). **Staff:** 2. **Local.** Promotes business and community development in O'Fallon, IL. Sponsors annual Christmas Walk festival. **Committees:** Economic Development; Military Affairs; Nominating Awards. **Publications:** Newsletter, monthly. Alternate Formats: online • Directory, periodic. **Conventions/Meetings:** monthly Business Luncheon - always second Tuesday.

Ogden

2851 ■ American Legion, Ogden Post 998
c/o Louie Karlau
PO Box 302
Ogden, IL 61859
Ph: (309)663-0361
Fax: (309)663-5783
URL: National Affiliate–www.legion.org
Contact: Louie Karlau, Contact
Local. Affiliated With: American Legion.

Oglesby

2852 ■ American Legion, Illinois Post 237
c/o Thomas Larkin
410 Clark St.
Oglesby, IL 61348
Ph: (815)883-8380
Fax: (309)663-5783
URL: National Affiliate–www.legion.org
Contact: Thomas Larkin, Contact
Local. Affiliated With: American Legion.

2853 ■ Illinois Valley Community College Students In Free Enterprise
815 N Orlando Smith Ave.
Oglesby, IL 61348
Ph: (815)224-2720
Fax: (815)224-3033
E-mail: sankovic@ivcc.edu
URL: http://www.ivcc.edu/steljes/SIFE/sife_list.htm
Contact: Mike Sankovich, SIFE Advisor
Local.

2854 ■ Phi Theta Kappa, Rho Omega Chapter - Illinois Valley Community College
c/o Tara Coburn
815 N Orlando Smith Ave.
Oglesby, IL 61348
Ph: (815)224-0335
E-mail: tara_coburn@ivcc.edu
URL: http://www.ptk.org/directories/chapters/IL/195-1.htm
Contact: Tara Coburn, Advisor
Local.

Okawville

2855 ■ American Legion, Illinois Post 233
c/o Ralph G. Mc Ilwain
PO Box 278
Okawville, IL 62271
Ph: (309)663-0361
Fax: (309)663-5783
URL: National Affiliate–www.legion.org
Contact: Ralph G. Mc Ilwain, Contact
Local. Affiliated With: American Legion.

2856 ■ Okawville Chamber of Commerce
PO Box 142
Okawville, IL 62271
Ph: (618)243-5694
Contact: Jeff Rabenort, Pres.
Local.

Olmsted

2857 ■ American Legion, Illinois Post 178
c/o Louis Phares
685 2nd St.
Olmsted, IL 62970
Ph: (618)742-6492
Fax: (309)663-5783
URL: National Affiliate–www.legion.org
Contact: Louis Phares, Contact
Local. Affiliated With: American Legion.

Olney

2858 ■ American Legion, Richland Post 30
303 S Fair
Olney, IL 62450
Ph: (618)392-3121
Fax: (309)663-5783
URL: National Affiliate–www.legion.org
Local. Affiliated With: American Legion.

2859 ■ Olney and the Greater Richland County Chamber of Commerce (OCC)
201 E Chestnut
Olney, IL 62450
Ph: (618)392-2241
Fax: (618)392-4179
E-mail: olneychamber@otbnet.com
URL: http://www.olneychamber.com
Contact: Gwen Gassmann, Exec.Dir.
Founded: 1946. **Members:** 140. **Staff:** 2. **Budget:** $60,000. **Local.** Promotes business and community development in Olney, IL. Sponsors festival. **Affiliated With:** U.S. Chamber of Commerce. **Publications:** Newsletter, monthly. **Circulation:** 245. **Advertising:** accepted. Also Cited As: *Olney Chamber Report*. **Conventions/Meetings:** annual banquet.

2860 ■ Phi Theta Kappa, Alpha Theta Eta Chapter - Olney Central College
c/o Carmen Allen
305 N West St.
Olney, IL 62450
Ph: (618)395-7777
E-mail: allenc@iecc.edu
URL: http://www.ptk.org/directories/chapters/IL/212-1.htm
Contact: Carmen Allen, Advisor
Local.

2861 ■ Southeastern Illinois AIFA
c/o Frank S. Ladner, Pres.
PO Box 367
Olney, IL 62450
Ph: (618)395-8484
Fax: (217)342-2757
URL: National Affiliate–naifa.org
Contact: Frank S. Ladner, Pres.
Local. Represents the interests of insurance and financial advisors. Advocates for a positive legislative and regulatory environment. Enhances business and professional skills of members. **Affiliated With:** National Association of Insurance and Financial Advisors.

2862 ■ Stopping Woman Abuse Now (SWAN)
PO Box 176
Olney, IL 62450
Ph: (618)392-3556
Fax: (618)392-5514
Free: (888)715-6260
E-mail: four@wworld.com
Contact: Linda Bookwalter, Exec.Dir.
Founded: 1981. **Staff:** 20. **Budget:** $454,000. **State Groups:** 1. **Local.** Victim advocates, social service

workers, and interested individuals in southeastern Illinois. Provides services to victims of domestic violence. Promotes public education on domestic violence. Sponsors shelter service for the homeless and elder abuse program. Abuser intervention program and medical advocacy program. Transitional housing for victims of domestic violence and homeless. **Publications:** Newsletter, periodic. **Conventions/Meetings:** monthly Board Meeting • annual meeting.

Onarga

2863 ■ American Legion, Onarga Post 551
PO Box 108
Onarga, IL 60955
Ph: (815)268-7642
Fax: (309)663-5783
URL: National Affiliate–www.legion.org
Local. Affiliated With: American Legion.

Oneida

2864 ■ American Legion, Rylander-Milroy Post 727
131 W Pine St.
Oneida, IL 61467
Ph: (309)483-6445
Fax: (309)663-5783
URL: National Affiliate–www.legion.org
Local. Affiliated With: American Legion.

Orangeville

2865 ■ American Legion, Ewert-Kline Post 720
10501 N Henderson Rd.
Orangeville, IL 61060
Ph: (309)663-0361
Fax: (309)663-5783
URL: National Affiliate–www.legion.org
Local. Affiliated With: American Legion.

Oregon

2866 ■ American Legion, Oregon Post 97
1310 W Washington
Oregon, IL 61061
Ph: (309)663-0361
Fax: (309)663-5783
URL: National Affiliate–www.legion.org
Local. Affiliated With: American Legion.

2867 ■ Illinois Renewable Energy Association
c/o Sonia Vogl
1230 E. Honey Creek Rd.
Oregon, IL 61061-9709
Ph: (815)732-7332
E-mail: sonia@csscx1.com
URL: http://www.illinoisrenew.org
Founded: 1999. **Members:** 100. **State. Conventions/Meetings:** annual Illinois Renewable Energy Fair - show - 2nd weekend in August.

2868 ■ Northwest Illinois Rock Club
c/o Gary Christensen, Pres.
3325 E Rte. 64
Oregon, IL 61061
E-mail: sherry.maves@highland.edu
URL: National Affiliate–www.amfed.org
Contact: Sherry Maves, Sec.
Local. Aims to further the study of Earth Sciences and the practice of lapidary arts and mineralogy. **Affiliated With:** American Federation of Mineralogical Societies.

2869 ■ Oregon Chamber of Commerce (OCC)
124 1/2 N 4th St.
Oregon, IL 61061
Ph: (815)732-2100
Fax: (815)732-2177
E-mail: ococ@oglecom.com
URL: http://www.oregonil.com
Contact: Dr. Michael Nelson, Contact
Members: 200. **Membership Dues:** professional, $110-$135 • financial institution, $110-$125 • business, manufacturing, industry, $110-$550. **Local.** Promotes business and community development in Oregon, IL. Sponsors Autumn on Parade Festival. **Publications:** *The Chamber Update*, monthly. Newsletter. **Circulation:** 300.

2870 ■ Oregon Lions Club
c/o Jerry Hinrichs
501 S 5th St.
Oregon, IL 61061
Ph: (815)732-2958
E-mail: jhinrich@essex1.com
URL: http://home.insightbb.com/~jerryhinrichs
Contact: Jerry Hinrichs, Contact
Local. Affiliated With: Lions Clubs International.

Orient

2871 ■ American Legion, Philip Whiteside Post 1961
PO Box 196
Orient, IL 62874
Ph: (309)663-0361
Fax: (309)663-5783
URL: National Affiliate–www.legion.org
Local. Affiliated With: American Legion.

Orion

2872 ■ American Legion, Orion Post 255
409 11th Ave.
Orion, IL 61273
Ph: (309)799-5640
Fax: (309)663-5783
URL: National Affiliate–www.legion.org
Local. Affiliated With: American Legion.

2873 ■ Main Street Orion
PO Box 693
Orion, IL 61273
Ph: (309)526-3331
Fax: (309)526-3137
E-mail: kcobra@qconline.com
URL: http://www.mainstreetorion.org
Local.

Orland Park

2874 ■ American Hellenic Educational Progressive Association - Beverly Hills, Chapter 350
c/o Peter Gianakas, Pres.
10 Rugles Ct.
Orland Park, IL 60462
Ph: (773)737-3203
URL: http://www.ahepafamily.org/d13
Contact: Peter Gianakas, Pres.
Local. Affiliated With: American Hellenic Educational Progressive Association.

2875 ■ American Legion, Aviation Post 651
17920 Settlers Pond Way No. 2a
Orland Park, IL 60467
Ph: (312)326-2757
Fax: (309)663-5783
URL: National Affiliate–www.legion.org
Local. Affiliated With: American Legion.

2876 ■ American Legion, Beverly Hills Post 407
PO Box 825
Orland Park, IL 60462
Ph: (708)429-5441
Fax: (309)663-5783
URL: National Affiliate–www.legion.org
Local. Affiliated With: American Legion.

2877 ■ American Legion, Orland Memorial Post 111
PO Box 413
Orland Park, IL 60462
Ph: (708)429-0365
Fax: (309)663-5783
URL: National Affiliate–www.legion.org
Local. Affiliated With: American Legion.

2878 ■ Association of Women's Health, Obstetric and Neonatal Nurses, Illinois Section
11911 Windemere Ct., No. 201
Orland Park, IL 60467
Ph: (312)567-2472
E-mail: pacreehan@aol.com
URL: National Affiliate–www.awhonn.org
Contact: Patricia Creehan, Chair
State. Represents registered nurses and other health care providers who specialize in obstetric, women's health, and neonatal nursing. Advances the nursing profession by providing nurses with information and support to help them deliver quality care for women and newborns. **Affiliated With:** Association of Women's Health, Obstetric and Neonatal Nurses. **Publications:** Newsletter.

2879 ■ Azalea Society of America, Lake Michigan Chapter
c/o Tadeusz Dauksza
11726 Springbrook Ct.
Orland Park, IL 60467
Ph: (708)479-8130
E-mail: iltkyao@yahoo.com
URL: http://www.azaleas-lake-michigan.org
Contact: Tadeusz Dauksza, Contact
Local. Affiliated With: Azalea Society of America.

2880 ■ Korean War Veterans Association, South Suburban Chapter
c/o Arnold Feinberg
6914 W Leslie Dr.
Orland Park, IL 60467
Ph: (708)460-6914
URL: National Affiliate–www.kwva.org
Contact: Arnold Feinberg, Contact
Local. Affiliated With: Korean War Veterans Association.

2881 ■ Medallion Rottweiler Club
c/o Cindy Childers, Corresponding Sec.
8424 Thorngate Ct.
Orland Park, IL 60462-5928
Ph: (708)873-9877
E-mail: cindyfive0@aol.com
URL: http://www.mrcrottweiler.com/navbar.htm
Contact: Cindy Childers, Corresponding Sec.
Local.

2882 ■ Northern Ice Skating Club (NISC)
11729 Kristoffer Ct.
Orland Park, IL 60467-6863
Ph: (708)528-1134
E-mail: lynn@northernice.org
URL: http://www.northernice.org
Contact: Lyn Balaskas, Pres.
Local. Provides programs to encourage participation and achievement in the sport of figure skating on ice. Defines and maintains uniform standards of skating proficiency. Organizes and sponsors competitions and exhibitions for the purpose of stimulating interest in figure skating. **Affiliated With:** United States Figure Skating Association.

2883 ■ Orland Park Area Chamber of Commerce
8799 W 151st St.
Orland Park, IL 60462
Ph: (708)349-2972
Fax: (708)349-7454
E-mail: info@orlandparkchamber.org
URL: http://www.orlandparkchamber.org
Contact: Keloryn Putnam, Exec.Dir.
Founded: 1958. **Members:** 550. **Membership Dues:** business (based on number of employees), $165-$395 (annual) • charitable not-for-profit, $115 (annual). **Local.** Serves as the primary resource in helping businesses and the community grow and prosper. **Computer Services:** Information services, directory of members. **Publications:** *Chambergram*, monthly. Newsletter. **Advertising:** accepted. Alternate Formats: online.

2884 ■ Orland Park Open Lands Corp.
14700 S Ravinia Ave.
Orland Park, IL 60462-3134
Ph: (708)403-6115
Fax: (708)403-6124
Contact: Lou Mule, Pres.
Founded: 1996. **Members:** 8. **Budget:** $800,000. **Local.** Orland Park residents with interests or expertise in areas related to land preservation. Raises funds for acquisition of open space and seeks out properties to acquire and preserve. **Conventions/Meetings:** monthly meeting - 2nd Tuesday of each month. Orland Park, IL.

2885 ■ Southwest Suburban United Way
PO Box 31
Orland Park, IL 60462
Ph: (708)371-1328
E-mail: uwsouthwest@uw-mc.org
URL: http://www.telecompioneers.org
Contact: Terry Flynn, CPO
Local. Affiliated With: United Way of America.

2886 ■ Special Forces Association Chapter XXXVII
c/o Ed Lacey, Pres
13600 Kristoffer Ln.
Orland Park, IL 60467-6870
Ph: (630)736-0388
E-mail: edlaceyjr@myexcel.com
URL: http://www.geocities.com/sfaxxxvii
Contact: Ed Lacey, Pres.
Local. Perpetuates the Special Forces traditions and honors Special Forces troop members who have died. Active and retired military men who are now, or who have been, assigned or attached to any U.S. Army Special Forces unit or units. **Affiliated With:** Special Forces Association.

2887 ■ Windy City Corvettes
PO Box 353
Orland Park, IL 60462-0353
E-mail: shadowlp@comcast.net
URL: http://windycitycorvettes.com
Contact: Larry Pagliaro, Pres.
Local. Affiliated With: National Council of Corvette Clubs.

Oswego

2888 ■ American Legion, Oswego Post 675
19 W Washington St.
Oswego, IL 60543
Ph: (708)554-8751
Fax: (309)663-5783
URL: National Affiliate–www.legion.org
Local. Affiliated With: American Legion.

2889 ■ Habitat for Humanity of Illinois
323 Grape Vine Trail
Oswego, IL 60543
Ph: (630)551-0160
Fax: (630)551-4040
E-mail: hfhillinois@aol.com
URL: http://www.habitatillinois.org
Contact: Bobbi Burgstone, Exec.Dir.
State. Affiliated With: Habitat for Humanity International.

2890 ■ Humanists of West Suburban Chicagoland
c/o Jack Sechrest
452 Burr Oak Dr.
Oswego, IL 60543-7504
Ph: (630)554-8058
E-mail: jack@skognet.com
URL: http://www.humanistswestofchicago.org
Contact: Jack Sechrest, Contact
Local. Persons who are devoted to humanism as a way of life. Humanism presupposes humanity's sole dependence on natural and social resources and acknowledges no supernatural power. Humanists believe that morality is based on the knowledge that humans are interdependent and, therefore, responsible to one another. **Affiliated With:** American Humanist Association.

2891 ■ Knollwood Gun Club
PO Box 711
Oswego, IL 60543
Ph: (630)553-7585
URL: National Affiliate–www.mynssa.com
Local. Affiliated With: National Skeet Shooting Association.

2892 ■ National Technological Honor Society - Oswego High School - Illinois
4250 Rt. 71
Oswego, IL 60543
Ph: (630)636-2000
Fax: (630)554-7160
E-mail: tcolvin@oswego308.org
URL: http://www.oswego308.org
Contact: Todd Colvin, Contact
Local.

2893 ■ Oswego Chamber of Commerce
22 W VanBuren
Oswego, IL 60543-0863
Ph: (630)554-3505
Fax: (630)554-0050
E-mail: info@oswegochamber.org
URL: http://www.oswegochamber.org
Contact: Kim Rosebraugh, Exec.Dir.
Members: 300. **Membership Dues:** general business, $150-$750 (annual) • associate, church, social service organization, $75 (annual) • government, utility, education, $250 (annual) • club, association, retired citizen, $50 (annual) • elite (depends upon the category), $1,000-$2,500 (annual). **Local.** Aims to make business in Oswego grow and succeed. **Computer Services:** Information services, business directory. **Committees:** Ambassadors; Business and Job Fair; Christmas Walk; Education; Golf Outing; Government Affairs; Nominating; Programs. **Publications:** *Chamber News*, monthly. Newsletter. **Advertising:** accepted. Alternate Formats: online.

Ottawa

2894 ■ American Institute of Architects Eastern Illinois
c/o James J. Prybys
620 W Lafayette St.
Ottawa, IL 61350
Ph: (815)434-0108
Fax: (815)434-1603
E-mail: gcary@bca-architects.com
URL: http://www.aiaeic.org
Contact: George Cary, Pres.
Local. Provides exposure to superior design through advocacy, information and advancement. **Additional Websites:** http://www.aia.org. **Affiliated With:** American Institute of Architects.

2895 ■ American Legion, Ottawa Post 33
901 La Salle St.
Ottawa, IL 61350
Ph: (815)433-1191
Fax: (309)663-5783
URL: National Affiliate–www.legion.org
Local. Affiliated With: American Legion.

2896 ■ AMVETS, Ottawa Post 30
Amer. Legion Post 33
901 Lasalle St.
Ottawa, IL 61350
Ph: (815)434-7756
URL: http://www.amvets.org/HTML/for_our_members/illinois.htm
Local. Affiliated With: AMVETS - American Veterans.

2897 ■ Easter Seals of LaSalle and Bureau Counties, Illinois
1013 Adams St.
Ottawa, IL 61350-4399
Ph: (815)434-0857
URL: National Affiliate–www.easter-seals.org
State. Affiliated With: Easter Seals.

2898 ■ Illinois Valley Dental Society
c/o Dr. Mitchell B. Myers, Pres.
1300 Starfire Dr.
Ottawa, IL 61350-1624
Ph: (815)433-3413
E-mail: drmyers@starfiredental.com
URL: http://www.isds.org
Contact: Dr. Mitchell B. Myers, Pres.
Local. Represents the interests of dentists committed to the public's oral health, ethics and professional development. Encourages the improvement of the public's oral health and promotes the art and science of dentistry. **Affiliated With:** American Dental Association; Illinois State Dental Society.

2899 ■ Ottawa Area Chamber of Commerce and Industry
100 W Lafayette St.
Ottawa, IL 61350
Ph: (815)433-0084
Fax: (815)433-2405
E-mail: info@ottawachamberillinois.com
URL: http://www.ottawachamberillinois.com
Contact: Boyd Palmer, Exec.Dir.
Founded: 1916. **Members:** 350. **Membership Dues:** retired, clergy, $52 (annual) • individual, $103 (annual) • not for profit, $155 (annual) • home-based business, $195 (annual) • general business, manufacturing, $222-$836 (annual) • insurance, investment, real state, professional, $279-$529 (annual). **Staff:** 3. **Budget:** $140,000. **Local.** Retailers, professionals, corporations, and individuals united to promote tourism, generate new business, aid downtown merchants, and improve the quality of life in the Ottawa, IL area. Sponsors Welcomburger festival, Farmers Market, Legislative and State of the City Luncheons, Small Business Seminars and IVLead Leadership Series. **Libraries: Type:** reference. **Holdings:** books. **Subgroups:** Communications; Downtown Events and Promotions; Public Policy. **Task Forces:** Economic Development. **Publications:** *Manufacturer's Guide*, periodic. Directory • Newsletter, bimonthly. **Conventions/Meetings:** monthly board meeting • annual meeting - always April.

2900 ■ Sons of Norway, Cleng Peerson Lodge 5-525
c/o Orion L. Carlson, Pres.
818 King Arthur Ln.
Ottawa, IL 61350-4222
Ph: (815)434-7235
E-mail: ocarlson@aol.com
URL: National Affiliate–www.sofn.com
Contact: Orion L. Carlson, Pres.
Local. Affiliated With: Sons of Norway.

2901 ■ United Way of Eastern La Salle County
1400 La Salle St.
Ottawa, IL 61350-1910
Ph: (815)434-4003
URL: National Affiliate–national.unitedway.org
Local. Affiliated With: United Way of America.

Ozark

2902 ■ American Legion, K.M.B.B. Post 400
200 Thunderhawk Rd.
Ozark, IL 62972
Ph: (618)994-2367
Fax: (309)663-5783
URL: National Affiliate–www.legion.org
Local. Affiliated With: American Legion.

Palatine

2903 ■ American Cancer Society, Palatine - Northwest Suburban Regional
100 W Palatine Rd., Ste.150
Palatine, IL 60067
Ph: (847)358-3965
Fax: (847)358-9218
URL: http://www.cancer.org
Contact: Catherine Sawyer, Regional VP
Local. Affiliated With: American Cancer Society.

2904 ■ American Legion, Palatine Post 690
122 W Palatine Rd.
Palatine, IL 60067
Ph: (309)663-0361
Fax: (309)663-5783
URL: National Affiliate–www.legion.org
Local. Affiliated With: American Legion.

2905 ■ American Society for Healthcare Food Service Administrators, Chicago Midwest Chapter
c/o Nina Dubman, RD, Pres.
Apostolic Christian Rest Haven
1258 Conway Bay
Palatine, IL 60074
Ph: (847)741-4543
Fax: (847)741-4562
E-mail: ndubman@sbcglobal.net
URL: National Affiliate–www.ashfsa.org
Contact: Nina Dubman RD, Pres.
Local. Advances healthcare foodservice leadership through education, networking and advocacy. **Affiliated With:** American Society for Healthcare Food Service Administrators.

2906 ■ American Statistical Association, Chicago Chapter
c/o Kathleen Morrissey, Pres.
PO Box 2419
Palatine, IL 60078
Ph: (847)927-5307
E-mail: kmorrissey@strategy2market.com
URL: National Affiliate–www.amstat.org
Contact: Kathleen Morrissey, Pres.
Local. Promotes statistical practice, applications and research. Works for the improvement of statistical education at all levels. Seeks opportunities to advance the statistics profession. **Affiliated With:** American Statistical Association.

2907 ■ ASIS International, Illinois North Shore Chapter
c/o Rich Keyworth, CFPO, Vice Chm.
Sears & Anderson
245 Eric Dr.
Palatine, IL 60067
Ph: (847)341-6051
E-mail: keysafcon@aol.com
URL: http://www.northshoreasis.com
Contact: Rich Keyworth CFPO, Vice Chm.
Local. Seeks to increase the effectiveness and productivity of security practices by developing educational programs and materials that address security concerns. **Affiliated With:** ASIS International.

2908 ■ Chicago Playing Card Collectors (CPCC)
1319 E Sanborn
Palatine, IL 60067
Ph: (770)992-7478
Fax: (847)966-1044
E-mail: altxcc@aol.com
URL: http://www.cpccinc.org
Contact: Betsy Behrendt, Contact
Founded: 1951. **Members:** 600. **Membership Dues:** individual, $20 (annual). Persons interested in the collecting and study of playing cards. Members participate in card trading, discussions, exhibits, films, and other activities covering the history, lore, manufacture, and use of playing cards. Conducts lectures, exhibits, and question-and-answer sessions for libraries, schools, television and radio, and other educational organizations. **Libraries: Type:** reference. **Holdings:** 4. **Subjects:** history of playing cards. **Publications:** *Playing Card Mail Auctions*, quarterly • *Reference Guides and Classification Listings*, semiannual • Bulletin, quarterly. **Price:** included in membership dues • Membership Directory, annual • Prepares monthly article on playing cards for *Hobbies Magazine* and has published a 500-year history of playing cards. **Conventions/Meetings:** annual meeting (exhibits).

2909 ■ Fremd - Young Life
PO Box 712
Palatine, IL 60078
Ph: (847)670-1855
URL: http://Fremd.younglife.org
Local.

2910 ■ Gray M. Sanborn PTA
c/o Gray M. Sanborn Elementary School
101 Oak St.
Palatine, IL 60067
Ph: (847)359-8789
URL: http://myschoolonline.com/il/sanbornpta
Contact: Lisa VorBroker, Pres.
Local. Parents, teachers, students, and others interested in uniting the forces of home, school, and community. Promotes the welfare of children and youth.

2911 ■ Illinois Association for Gifted Children (IAGC)
800 E, NW Hwy., Ste.610
Palatine, IL 60074
Ph: (847)963-1892
Fax: (847)963-1893
URL: http://www.iagcgifted.org
Contact: Sally Walker, Exec.Dir.
Founded: 1989. **Membership Dues:** individual, $50 (annual) • affiliate, $120 (annual). **State.** Advances interest in programs for the gifted. Seeks to further education of the gifted and enhances their potential creativity. Unites to address the unique needs of children and youth with demonstrated gifts and talents as well as those children who may be able to develop their talent potentials with appropriate educational experiences. Encourages and responds to the diverse expressions of gifts and talents in children and youth from all cultures, racial and ethnic backgrounds, and socioeconomic groups. **Affiliated With:** National Association for Gifted Children.

2912 ■ Illinois Mathematics Association of Community Colleges
Harper Coll.
1200 W Algonquin Rd.
Palatine, IL 60067
Ph: (847)925-6728
URL: http://www.imacc.org
Contact: Dave Clydesdale, Contact
State. Aims to improve the teaching and learning of mathematics. Provides vision, leadership and professional development to support teachers in ensuring mathematics learning of the highest quality for all students. **Affiliated With:** National Council of Teachers of Mathematics.

2913 ■ Independent Computer Consultants Association, Chicago
PO Box 2121
Palatine, IL 60078-2121
Ph: (847)920-9066
Free: (877)804-4222
E-mail: info@icca-chicago.org
URL: http://www.icca-chicago.org
Contact: Jeffrey Ring, Pres.
Local. Affiliated With: Independent Computer Consultants Association.

2914 ■ International Association of Convention and Visitor Bureaus, Kansas City - Palatine, Illinois
c/o Mary Lou Newbold, Midwest Regional Sales Mgr.
853 N Quentin Rd., PMB No. 347
Palatine, IL 60067
Ph: (847)202-4331
Fax: (847)202-4349
E-mail: mnewbold@visitkc.com
URL: http://www.visitkc.com
Contact: Mary Lou Newbold, Midwest Reg. Sales Mgr.
Affiliated With: International Association of Convention and Visitor Bureaus.

2915 ■ International Brotherhood of Trail Workers
155 N NW, Hwy.
Palatine, IL 60067
Ph: (847)358-0948
E-mail: wmikesbikes@aol.com
URL: http://groups.yahoo.com/group/imbc/
Local. Affiliated With: International Mountain Bicycling Association. **Formerly:** (2005) Illinois Mountain Bike Association.

2916 ■ Izaak Walton League of America - Des Plaines Chapter (IWLA)
721 N Glenn Dr.
Palatine, IL 60074-7193
Ph: (847)358-9023
E-mail: robie721@sbcglobal.net
URL: National Affiliate–www.iwla.org
Contact: Donald K. Johanson, Contact
Local. Educates the public to conserve, maintain, protect and restore the soil, forest, water and other natural resources of the United States.

2917 ■ Jayco Jafari International Travel Club, Flight 13 Ja Triskaidekka
c/o John Blyth, Pres.
223 N Greenwood Ave.
Palatine, IL 60067
E-mail: j-d-blyth@earthlink.net
URL: National Affiliate–www.jaycorvclub.com
Contact: John Blyth, Pres.
Local. Affiliated With: Jayco Travel Club.

2918 ■ Lake Michigan Air and Waste Management Association
11 Pleasant Hill Blvd.
Palatine, IL 60067
Ph: (847)202-0418
Fax: (847)202-0427
E-mail: lm_awma@ameritech.net
URL: http://www.lmawma.org
Local. Affiliated With: Air and Waste Management Association.

2919 ■ National Speleological Society, Windy City Grotto
c/o Fred Schumann, Chm.
2252 A. Baldwin Way
Palatine, IL 60074
Ph: (847)963-0823
E-mail: ericcoy@aol.com
URL: http://www.windycitygrotto.org
Contact: Fred Schumann, Chm.
Local. Seeks to study, explore and conserve cave and karst resources. Protects access to caves and promotes responsible caving. Encourages respon-

sible management of caves and their unique environments. **Affiliated With:** National Speleological Society.

2920 ■ North Shore Musicians Club
c/o Roy Houck
950 E. Wilmette Ave., Ste.416
Palatine, IL 60067-6479
Local.

2921 ■ Palatine Area Chamber of Commerce (PACC)
625 North Ct., Ste.320
Palatine, IL 60067
Ph: (847)359-7200
Fax: (847)359-7246
E-mail: info@palatinechamber.com
URL: http://www.palatinechamber.com
Contact: Mindy Phillips, Dir.
Founded: 1950. **Members:** 500. **Membership Dues:** business (based on number of employees), $270-$600 (annual) • utility company, $460 (annual) • financial institution/bank, $760 (annual) • hospital, government, $380 (annual) • non-profit organization, $140 (annual). **Staff:** 5. **Local.** Promotes business and community development in Palatine, IL. **Awards:** Ehlenfeldt Memorial Scholarship. **Frequency:** annual. **Type:** scholarship. **Recipient:** for community participation and school involvement. **Formerly:** (2003) Greater Palatine Chamber of Commerce and Industry. **Publications:** *The Chamber Guide*, annual. Magazine • *Community Guide*, monthly. Newsletter. Contains profile of Palatine. **Price:** $3.00. Alternate Formats: online • *The Key*, bimonthly. Newsletter. **Advertising:** accepted • Membership Directory, annual. **Circulation:** 32,000. Alternate Formats: online.

2922 ■ Palatine/Fremd - Young Life
PO Box 712
Palatine, IL 60078
Ph: (847)670-1855
URL: http://Palatine.younglife.org
Contact: Chris Fanning, Contact
Local.

2923 ■ Palatine Historical Society (PHS)
224 E Palatine Rd.
PO Box 134
Palatine, IL 60078-0134
Ph: (847)991-6460
Fax: (847)963-0605
E-mail: claysonmus@aol.com
URL: http://www.palatineparkdistrict.com/clayson.html
Contact: Marilyn Pedersen, Dir.
Founded: 1955. **Members:** 350. **Membership Dues:** $15 (annual). **Staff:** 1. **Local.** Residents and local businesses and organizations. Seeks to preserve local history; disseminates information. Operates Clayson House Library and Museum, a restored 1873 Victorian House and furnishings of that period, and local history library. **Libraries: Type:** reference. **Subjects:** genealogy. **Awards:** National Register of Historic Places. **Type:** recognition. **Publications:** *Census of Palatine Township, 1900, 10, 20* • *Hillside Cemetery* • *Palatine 125 Yrs., History Book* • *Palatine 1929 - Biography of Residents Living in Palatine in 1929* • *Palaver*, quarterly. Newsletter. **Price:** free for members • *Slice of Life, NW Newspapers of 1901.*

2924 ■ Palatine Lions Club
c/o Paul Pioch
PO Box 441
Palatine, IL 60078
Ph: (847)609-5805
E-mail: ppioch@comcast.net
URL: http://www.palatinelions.org
Contact: Paul Pioch, Contact
Local. Affiliated With: Lions Clubs International.

2925 ■ PFLAG Palatine
248 N Ashland Ave.
Palatine, IL 60074
Ph: (847)358-3994
E-mail: dixiel622@hotmail.com
URL: http://www.pflag-palatine.org
Contact: Dixie LoCicero, Pres.
Local. Affiliated With: Parents, Families, and Friends of Lesbians and Gays.

2926 ■ Phi Theta Kappa, Phi Phi Chapter - William Rainey Harper College
c/o Jennifer Puente
1200 Algonquin Rd.
Palatine, IL 60067
Ph: (847)925-6344
E-mail: jpuente@harpercollege.edu
URL: http://www.ptk.org/directories/chapters/IL/199-1.htm
Contact: Jennifer Puente, Advisor
Local.

2927 ■ Reserve Officers Association - Department of Illinois
c/o Col. Michael P. Peck, Sec./Webmaster
55 S Greeley St., Apt. 109
Palatine, IL 60067
Ph: (847)991-4700
Fax: (847)991-5742
E-mail: colpeck@yahoo.com
URL: http://www.ilroa.org
Contact: Capt. Barbara Brake, Pres.
State. Promotes and supports the development and execution of a military policy for the United States. Provides professional development seminars, workshops and programs for its members. **Affiliated With:** Reserve Officers Association of the United States.

2928 ■ Society for Technical Communication, Chicago Chapter
PO Box 1745
Palatine, IL 60078-1745
Ph: (312)630-0110
Fax: (815)425-3838
E-mail: info@stc-chicago.org
URL: http://www.stc-chicago.org
Contact: Judy Rosenberg, Pres.
Local. Seeks to advance the theory and practice of technical communication in all media. Enhances the professionalism of the members and the status of the profession. Promotes the education of members and supports research activities in the field. **Affiliated With:** Society for Technical Communication.

2929 ■ Virginia Lake PTA (VLPTA)
c/o Virginia Lake School
925 N Glenn Dr.
Palatine, IL 60074
Ph: (847)202-8712
URL: http://www.virginialakepta.org
Contact: Lizzie Falkenberg, Pres.
Local. Parents, teachers, students, and others interested in uniting the forces of home, school, and community. Promotes the welfare of children and youth.

2930 ■ Young Life NW Suburban Chicago
PO Box 712
Palatine, IL 60078
Ph: (847)670-1855
URL: http://211214.younglife.org
Local.

Palestine

2931 ■ Palestine Chamber of Commerce (PCC)
PO Box 155
Palestine, IL 62451
Ph: (618)586-2222
Fax: (618)586-9477
E-mail: plstnecc@shawneelink.net
URL: http://www.pioneercity.com/chamberofcommerce
Contact: Brad Surrells, Pres.
Founded: 1950. **Members:** 80. **Membership Dues:** business, $25 (annual) • organization, $20 (annual) • individual, $15 (annual). **Local.** Promotes business and community development in Crawford County, IL. Sponsors annual professional rodeo and Labor Day Weekend Festival. **Publications:** Newsletter, monthly. **Conventions/Meetings:** monthly meeting.

2932 ■ Palestine Development Association (PDA)
c/o James Ellis
PO Box 101
Palestine, IL 62451
E-mail: pda@pioneercity.com
URL: http://pioneercity.com/pda
Founded: 1998. **Local.**

Palmyra

2933 ■ American Legion, Palmyra Post 1034
PO Box 202
Palmyra, IL 62674
Ph: (309)663-0361
Fax: (309)663-5783
URL: National Affiliate–www.legion.org
Local. Affiliated With: American Legion.

Palos Heights

2934 ■ American Hellenic Educational Progressive Association - Woodlawn, Chapter 93
c/o Richard Yukich, Sec.
6420 W 126th Pl.
Palos Heights, IL 60463
Ph: (708)957-3333
E-mail: yukich@msn.com
URL: http://www.ahepafamily.org/d13
Contact: Richard Yukich, Sec.
Local. Affiliated With: American Hellenic Educational Progressive Association.

2935 ■ American Legion, Chicago Police Post 207
1520 N Monticello Ave.
Palos Heights, IL 60463
Ph: (708)448-2963
Fax: (309)663-5783
URL: National Affiliate–www.legion.org
Local. Affiliated With: American Legion.

2936 ■ American Legion, Square Post 232
6860 W Highland Dr.
Palos Heights, IL 60463
Ph: (708)422-3718
Fax: (309)663-5783
URL: National Affiliate–www.legion.org
Local. Affiliated With: American Legion.

2937 ■ Concerned Women for America - Illinois
c/o Kathy Valente, Dir.
PO Box 188
Palos Heights, IL 60463
Ph: (708)371-7810
Fax: (708)371-7896
E-mail: director@illinois.cwfa.org
URL: National Affiliate–www.cwfa.org
Contact: Kathy Valente, Dir.
State. Affiliated With: Concerned Women for America.

Palos Hills

2938 ■ First Catholic Slovak Ladies Association - Chicago Junior Branch 308
9024 Del Prado Dr., No.1-S
Palos Hills, IL 60465
Ph: (708)598-1468
URL: National Affiliate–www.fcsla.com
Local. Affiliated With: First Catholic Slovak Ladies Association.

2939 ■ First Catholic Slovak Ladies Association - Chicago Senior Branch 352
9024 Del Prado Dr., No.1-S
Palos Hills, IL 60465
Ph: (708)598-1468
URL: National Affiliate–www.fcsla.com
Local. Affiliated With: First Catholic Slovak Ladies Association.

2940 ■ Learning Disabilities Association of Illinois
c/o Sharon Schussler
10101 S Roberts Rd., Ste.205
Palos Hills, IL 60465-1556
Ph: (708)430-7532
Fax: (708)430-7592
E-mail: ldaofil@ameritech.net
URL: http://www.ldail.org
Contact: Sharon Schussler, Admin.Asst.
State. Dedicated to the advancement of the education and general welfare of children and youth of normal or potentially normal intelligence who have learning disabilities of a perceptual, conceptual or coordinative nature or related problems. Present an annual fall conference. Members receive 4 newsletters a year from state LDA and 6 newsletters a year of national LDA. **Affiliated With:** Learning Disabilities Association of America.

2941 ■ Palos Hills Chamber of Commerce
PO Box 110
Palos Hills, IL 60465
Ph: (708)598-3400
Contact: Phyllis Majka, Pres.
Local.

2942 ■ Phi Theta Kappa, Alpha Iota Lambda Chapter - Moraine Valley Community College
c/o Jennifer Langland
10900 S 88th Ave.
Palos Hills, IL 60465
Ph: (708)974-5353
URL: http://www.ptk.org/directories/chapters/IL/209-1.htm
Contact: Jennifer Langland, Advisor
Local.

Palos Park

2943 ■ American Legion, Palos Memorial Post 1993
PO Box 538
Palos Park, IL 60464
Ph: (309)663-0361
Fax: (309)663-5783
URL: National Affiliate–www.legion.org
Local. Affiliated With: American Legion.

Pana

2944 ■ American Legion, Kerr-Mize Post 168
6 S State St.
Pana, IL 62557
Ph: (217)567-3614
Fax: (309)663-5783
URL: National Affiliate–www.legion.org
Local. Affiliated With: American Legion.

2945 ■ Pana Chamber of Commerce
City Hall
120 E 3rd St.
Pana, IL 62557-1646
Ph: (217)562-4240
Fax: (217)562-3823
E-mail: panail@consolidated.net
URL: http://www.panaillinois.com
Contact: Jim Deere, Sec.-Treas.
Founded: 1943. **Members:** 120. **Membership Dues:** business, professional, associate, $110 (annual). **Staff:** 1. **Budget:** $20,787. **For-Profit. Local**. Promotes business and community development in Pana, IL. Sponsors annual Pana Heritage Days, Chamber Week, Downtown Block Party, Car Show, Illinois State Championship Antique Bicycle Show, Blacksmith Hammer in & Antique Tractor Show and Christmas Week. **Libraries: Type:** open to the public. **Additional Websites:** http://www.panaindustrial.com. **Committees:** Retail Promotions. **Publications:** *Business and Professional Memo*, quarterly. Newsletter. **Price:** included in membership dues. **Circulation:** 250. **Advertising:** accepted. **Conventions/Meetings:** monthly board meeting - every third Tuesday.

Paris

2946 ■ East Central Illinois Bluebird Society
c/o Loren Hughes
1234 Tucker Beach Rd.
Paris, IL 61944
Ph: (217)463-7175
E-mail: suziq@comwares.net
URL: National Affiliate–www.nabluebirdsociety.org
Contact: Loren Hughes, Contact
Local. Affiliated With: North American Bluebird Society.

2947 ■ Edgar County Genealogical Society (ECGS)
PO Box 304
Paris, IL 61944-0304
Ph: (217)463-4209
E-mail: ecgl@tigerpaw.com
URL: http://www.comwares.net/ecgl/
Contact: A. Joyce Brown, Past Pres.
Founded: 1984. **Members:** 200. **Membership Dues:** individual, $12 (annual) • life, $150. **Local**. Preservation of local archives, dissemination of genealogical and historical information, education of interested persons (including children and adults) acquisition of pertinent materials for Edgar County Genealogy Library and staffing of same. **Libraries: Type:** open to the public; by appointment only. **Holdings:** 2,770; audio recordings, books, business records, periodicals, video recordings. **Subjects:** Edgar and adjoining counties. **Awards:** Edythe Stevens Family History Award. **Frequency:** annual. **Type:** recognition. **Recipient:** for service to the genealogical community. **Publications:** *Edgar Co. Genealogical Society Quarterly*. Newsletter. Contains queries, bible records, family charts, newspaper excerpts on marriages, deaths and births. **Price:** included in membership dues. ISSN: 361 R27. **Circulation:** 200. **Advertising:** not accepted. **Conventions/Meetings:** bimonthly general assembly, brief business, then informational and educational program (exhibits) - always August, October, December, February, April, June; usually at 7 PM, 2nd Tuesday of month. Paris, IL - Avg. Attendance: 20.

2948 ■ Edgar County Sportsman's Club
420 Prairie St.
Paris, IL 61944
Ph: (217)465-5044
E-mail: hoashooter@yahoo.com
URL: National Affiliate–www.mynssa.com
Local. Affiliated With: National Skeet Shooting Association.

2949 ■ Main Street Paris
222 N Main St.
Paris, IL 61944
Ph: (217)463-2611
E-mail: mainstparis@joink.com
URL: http://www.mainstreetparis.com
Local.

2950 ■ Paris Area Chamber of Commerce and Tourism (PACCT)
c/o Brenda Buckley, Exec.Dir.
105 N Central Ave.
Paris, IL 61944
Ph: (217)465-4179
URL: http://www.parisilchamber.com
Contact: Brenda Buckley, Exec.Dir.
Founded: 1903. **Members:** 275. **Membership Dues:** government, associate, $70 (annual) • financial institution (plus $10/million in assets), $130 (annual) • insurance, realtor (base), $135 (annual) • hotel, motel, nursing home, professional, $160 (annual) • utility company, $815 (annual) • industrial, $160-$790 (annual) • service, retail, wholesale, $145-$525 (annual). **Staff:** 2. **Budget:** $80,000. **Local**. Promotes business and community development in Paris, IL. Sponsors Honey Bee Festival. **Awards:** Parisian. **Frequency:** annual. **Type:** recognition • SBA. **Frequency:** annual. **Type:** recognition. **Formerly:** (1999) Paris Area +Chamber of Commerce. **Publications:** Newsletter, monthly. **Circulation:** 275. **Advertising:** accepted.

2951 ■ United Way of Edgar County
PO Box 400
Paris, IL 61944-0400
Ph: (217)465-4154
URL: National Affiliate–national.unitedway.org
Local. Affiliated With: United Way of America.

Park Forest

2952 ■ Illinois Association for Floodplain and Stormwater Management (IAFSM)
153 Nanti St.
Park Forest, IL 60466
Ph: (708)747-5273
Fax: (708)747-5279
E-mail: iafsm@aol.com
URL: http://www.illinoisfloods.org
Contact: Mary Lu Wetmore, Exec.Sec.
Founded: 1986. **Members:** 300. **Membership Dues:** student, $25 (annual) • individual, $90 (annual) • agency, $250 (annual). **State**. Promotes the common interest in floodplain and stormwater management; enhances cooperation among various local, state, and federal agencies; encourages effective and innovative approaches to manage the state's floodplain and stormwater management systems. **Affiliated With:** Association of State Floodplain Managers. **Publications:** Newsletter. **Conventions/Meetings:** bimonthly board meeting • annual dinner.

2953 ■ NAIFA-South Cook Region
c/o Sylvia Lindecker, Sec.
353 Oswego St.
Park Forest, IL 60466
Ph: (708)747-9796
Fax: (708)748-9756
E-mail: slindecker@aol.com
URL: National Affiliate–naifa.org
Contact: Sylvia Lindecker, Sec.
Local. Represents the interests of insurance and financial advisors. Advocates for a positive legislative and regulatory environment. Enhances business and professional skills of members. **Affiliated With:** National Association of Insurance and Financial Advisors.

2954 ■ Park Forest Historical Society (PFHS)
400 Lakewood Blvd.
Park Forest, IL 60466
Ph: (708)748-3731
Fax: (708)748-8829
E-mail: jnicoll@sslic.net
URL: http://www.lincolnnet.net/users/lrpfhs
Contact: Jane Nicoll, Archivist
Founded: 1985. **Members:** 224. **Membership Dues:** $10 (annual) • $25 (annual). **Local**. Promotes public awareness of the history of Park Forest, IL and the preservation of local historical materials. Presents panel discussions, videotapes, and television programming. **Libraries: Type:** open to the public. **Awards:** Park Forest Hall of Fame. **Frequency:** annual. **Type:** recognition. **Publications:** *Prologue*, periodic. Newsletter.

2955 ■ Park Forest Table Tennis Club
Faith United Protestant Church
10 Hemlock
Park Forest, IL 60466

Ph: (708)748-8476
URL: National Affiliate–www.usatt.org
Contact: Dewey Helmick, Contact
Local. Affiliated With: U.S.A. Table Tennis.

2956 ■ Thorn Creek Audubon Society
PO Box 895
Park Forest, IL 60466
E-mail: rrinersprint5@earthlink.net
URL: http://www.thorncreekaudubon.org
Contact: Dick Riner, Pres.
Local. Formerly: (2005) National Audubon Society - Thorn Creek.

Park Ridge

2957 ■ American Legion, General-Schwengel-Seagram Post 807
c/o Patrick H. Kewin
1580 Habberton
Park Ridge, IL 60068
Ph: (309)663-0361
Fax: (309)663-5783
URL: National Affiliate–www.legion.org
Contact: Patrick H. Kewin, Contact
Local. Affiliated With: American Legion.

2958 ■ American Legion, Illinois Post 247
c/o Mel Tierney
2017 Glenview Ave.
Park Ridge, IL 60068
Ph: (309)663-0361
Fax: (309)663-5783
URL: National Affiliate–www.legion.org
Contact: Mel Tierney, Contact
Local. Affiliated With: American Legion.

2959 ■ American Society of Appraisers, Chicago Chapter
c/o Michael R. Crismyre, Pres.
907 N Knight Ave.
Park Ridge, IL 60068-2519
Ph: (847)823-2810
Fax: (312)298-7664
E-mail: chicago@apo.com
URL: http://www.appraisers.org/chicago
Contact: Michael R. Crismyre, Pres.
Local. Serves as a professional appraisal educator, testing and accrediting society. Sponsors mandatory recertification program for all members. Offers consumer information service to the public. **Affiliated With:** American Society of Appraisers.

2960 ■ American Society of Women Accountants, Chicago Chapter No. 002
c/o Dawn Schoene, CGFM, Pres.
US Dept. of Labor
209 Stanley Ave.
Park Ridge, IL 60068
Ph: (312)353-8367 (847)823-5943
Fax: (312)353-2328
E-mail: dhschoene@msn.com
URL: National Affiliate–www.aswa.org
Contact: Dawn Schoene CGFM, Pres.
Local. Affiliated With: American Society of Women Accountants.

2961 ■ Avenues to Independence
515 Busse Hwy.
Park Ridge, IL 60068
Ph: (847)292-0870
Fax: (847)292-0873
E-mail: avenues@avenuesonline.org
URL: http://www.avenuestoindependence.org
Local.

2962 ■ Counselors of Real Estate, Chesapeake Chapter
c/o Michael S. MaRous, CRE, Chm.
300 S Northwest Hwy., Ste.204
Park Ridge, IL 60068-4257
Ph: (847)384-2030
Fax: (847)692-5498
E-mail: mmarous@marous.com
URL: National Affiliate–www.cre.org
Contact: Michael S. MaRous CRE, Chm.
Local. Affiliated With: Counselors of Real Estate.

2963 ■ Kiwanis Club of Park Ridge - Noon
PO Box 249
Park Ridge, IL 60068
E-mail: jvandcar@prpl.org
URL: http://www.park-ridge.il.us/prkiwanis
Contact: Janet Van De Carr, Pres.
Local.

2964 ■ Park Ridge Chamber of Commerce (PRCC)
140 Euclid
Park Ridge, IL 60068
Ph: (847)825-3121
Fax: (847)825-3122
E-mail: email@parkridgeilchamber.com
URL: http://www.parkridgeilchamber.com
Contact: Richard E. Brayer, Exec.Dir.
Membership Dues: base (hotel, motel), $240 • base (physician, dentist, attorney), $195 • public body (schools, parks, municipal), $550 • financial institution (base), $615 • civic (base), $100. **Local.** Promotes business and community development in Park Ridge, IL. **Committees:** Budget; Business Exposition; Communications; Program; Retail; Service Business; Uptown Development; Women in Business. **Publications:** *Community Guide*, annual. Directory. **Circulation:** 14,000 • Newsletter, bimonthly.

2965 ■ Tooling and Manufacturing Association (TMA)
c/o Bruce Braker, Pres.
1177 S Dee Rd.
Park Ridge, IL 60068
Ph: (847)825-1120
Fax: (847)825-0041
E-mail: bbraker@tmanet.com
URL: http://www.tmanet.com
Founded: 1925. **Local.**

Patoka

2966 ■ American Legion, Illinois Post 543
c/o Edgar R. Rogier
405 N Washington St.
Patoka, IL 62875
Ph: (309)663-0361
Fax: (309)663-5783
URL: National Affiliate–www.legion.org
Contact: Edgar R. Rogier, Contact
Local. Affiliated With: American Legion.

2967 ■ Illinois Quarter Horse Association, District No. 9
c/o Trent Adams, Dir.
260 Wisher Rd.
Patoka, IL 62875-9999
Ph: (618)432-5609
E-mail: trentadamspatoka@yahoo.com
URL: http://www.ilqha.com
Contact: Trent Adams, Dir.
Local. Affiliated With: American Quarter Horse Association.

Paw Paw

2968 ■ American Legion, Smith-Reynolds Post 511
PO Box 93
Paw Paw, IL 61353
Ph: (309)663-0361
Fax: (309)663-5783
URL: National Affiliate–www.legion.org
Local. Affiliated With: American Legion.

2969 ■ National Technological Honor Society - Paw Paw High School - Illinois
511 N Chapman St.
Paw Paw, IL 61353
Ph: (815)627-2841
Fax: (815)627-2971
URL: http://www.2paws.net
Local.

Pawnee

2970 ■ American Legion, Pawnee Post 586
PO Box 1144
Pawnee, IL 62558
Ph: (217)625-7923
Fax: (309)663-5783
URL: National Affiliate–www.legion.org
Local. Affiliated With: American Legion.

2971 ■ Chinese Shar-Pei Club of America (CSPCA)
c/o Karen Kleinhans, Pres.
7803 N Pawnee Rd.
Pawnee, IL 62558-4628
Ph: (217)498-6850
E-mail: cspcapres@aol.com
URL: http://www.cspca.com
Contact: Karen Kleinhans, Pres.
State. Affiliated With: American Kennel Club.

Paxton

2972 ■ American Legion, Prairie Post 150
763 E Pells St.
Paxton, IL 60957
Ph: (309)663-0361
Fax: (309)663-5783
URL: National Affiliate–www.legion.org
Local. Affiliated With: American Legion.

2973 ■ Illinois Central Railroad Historical Society (ICHS)
PO Box 288
Paxton, IL 60957
E-mail: membership@icrrhistorical.org
URL: http://icrrhistorical.org
Contact: Don Horn, Pres.
Founded: 1979. **Members:** 1,034. **Membership Dues:** regular, $25 (annual) • sustaining, $35 (annual). **Regional Groups:** 1. Individuals interested in the history of the Illinois Central Railroad. Dedicated to the preservation of historical and educational information about the Illinois Central Railroad and its predecessor lines. Strives to preserve the memories of the people who worked for the railroad, the places it went, and the affect it had on the communities through which it passed. Purchased the former Lake Erie & Western Railway freighthouse to house the group's headquarters and archives. Conducts educational programs. **Libraries: Type:** reference. **Holdings:** archival material, audio recordings, business records, video recordings. **Subjects:** Illinois Central Railroad history. **Departments:** Company Store; Depot at Paxton; Internet Operations; Publications. **Publications:** *Green Diamond*, quarterly. Magazine. Contains articles and stories about the railroad. **Price:** $6.50/issue for nonmembers; included in membership dues. **Circulation:** 2,000 • Newsletter, quarterly. Includes information on upcoming society events. **Price:** included in membership dues. **Conventions/Meetings:** annual meeting and show.

2974 ■ National Active And Retired Federal Employees Association - East Central 854
2 Meridian Terr.
Paxton, IL 60957-1850
Ph: (217)379-4935
URL: National Affiliate–www.narfe.org
Contact: Gwen E. Ennen, Contact
Local. Protects the retirement future of employees through education. Informs members on issues af-

fecting the retirement. **Affiliated With:** National Association of Retired Federal Employees.

2975 ■ Paxton Area Chamber of Commerce
PO Box 75
148 N Market
Paxton, IL 60957
Ph: (217)379-4655
Contact: Madge Mullinax, Exec.Sec.
Local.

2976 ■ Paxton Lions Club
787 E Summer St.
Paxton, IL 60957
Ph: (217)379-2262
URL: http://paxtonil.lionwap.org
Local. Affiliated With: Lions Clubs International.

2977 ■ Pheasants Forever Illinois Pioneer Chapter
PO Box 70
Paxton, IL 60957
Ph: (217)388-2442
URL: http://pheasantsforever-ill-pioneer-69.com
Contact: Dennis Lee, Chm.
Local. Affiliated With: Pheasants Forever.

Payson

2978 ■ Illinois National Barrel Horse Association
205 E 1300th St.
Payson, IL 62360
Ph: (618)723-3081
E-mail: lpatrick@socket.net
URL: National Affiliate–www.nbha.com
Contact: Lisa Patrick, Dir.
State. Promotes the sport of barrel horse racing. Conducts barrel racing competitions. Establishes standard rules for the sport. **Affiliated With:** National Barrel Horse Association.

Pearl City

2979 ■ American Legion, Pearl City Post 1014
PO Box 124
Pearl City, IL 61062
Ph: (309)663-0361
Fax: (309)663-5783
URL: National Affiliate–www.legion.org
Local. Affiliated With: American Legion.

2980 ■ Northwest Illinois Audubon Society
13476 W Loran Rd.
Pearl City, IL 61062-9204
Ph: (815)443-9102
E-mail: sjsimpson@msn.com
URL: http://www.audubon.org/chapter/il/index.html
Contact: Steve Simpson, Pres.
Local. Formerly: (2005) National Audubon Society - Northwest Illinois.

Pecatonica

2981 ■ American Legion, Illinois Post 197
c/o Eugene J. Barloga
PO Box 338
Pecatonica, IL 61063
Ph: (309)663-0361
Fax: (309)663-5783
URL: National Affiliate–www.legion.org
Contact: Eugene J. Barloga, Contact
Local. Affiliated With: American Legion.

Pekin

2982 ■ AMBUCS, Pekin Club
c/o Jim Deverman, Pres.
531 Ct. St.
Pekin, IL 61554
Ph: (309)346-1194
Fax: (309)346-0511
E-mail: jim@deverman.com
URL: National Affiliate–www.ambucs.org
Contact: Jim Deverman, Pres.
Local. Affiliated With: AMBUCS.

2983 ■ American Legion, William Schaefer Post 44
718 Court St.
Pekin, IL 61554
Ph: (309)346-6483
Fax: (309)663-5783
URL: National Affiliate–www.legion.org
Local. Affiliated With: American Legion.

2984 ■ American Rabbit Breeders Association, Midwest Champagn D'Argent Rabbit Club
c/o Wayne Cleer
1704 Heisel Ave.
Pekin, IL 61554
Ph: (309)347-1347
E-mail: cleerchamp@grics.net
URL: http://www.nordickrabbits.com/specialt.htm
Contact: Wayne Cleer, Contact
Local. Affiliated With: American Rabbit Breeders Association.

2985 ■ Central Illinois Mountain Bicycling Association
1502 S 6th St.
Pekin, IL 61554
E-mail: mtnjak@hotmail.com
URL: National Affiliate–www.imba.com
State. Affiliated With: International Mountain Bicycling Association.

2986 ■ Dream Factory of Central Illinois
c/o Victoria Buckley, Area Coor.
PO Box 1431
Pekin, IL 61554
Ph: (309)353-7326
Fax: (309)246-2011
E-mail: centralillinois@dreamfactoryinc.com
URL: http://www.dreamfactoryci.com
Contact: Victoria Buckley, Area Coor.
Local. Affiliated With: Dream Factory.

2987 ■ National Association of Investors Corporation, Heart of Illinois Chapter
c/o Bobbie Kincaid, Pres.
2220 Mayflower Dr.
Pekin, IL 61554
Ph: (309)925-3075
E-mail: bkincaid@insightbb.com
URL: http://better-investing.org/chapter/heart
Contact: Bobbie Kincaid, Pres.
Local. Teaches individuals how to become successful strategic long-term investors. Provides highly focused learning resources and investment tools that empower individuals to become better investors. **Affiliated With:** National Association of Investors Corporation.

2988 ■ Pekin Area Board of Realtors
511 Elizabeth St.
Pekin, IL 61554-4215
Ph: (309)346-4020
Fax: (309)346-5260
E-mail: paar@pekinrealtors.net
URL: National Affiliate–www.realtor.org
Contact: Gina McKinley, Exec. Officer
Local. Strives to develop real estate business practices. Advocates the right to own, use and transfer real property. Provides a facility for professional development, research and exchange of information among members and to the general public. **Affiliated With:** National Association of Realtors.

2989 ■ Pekin Area Chamber of Commerce
402 Court St.
PO Box 636
Pekin, IL 61555-0636
Ph: (309)346-2106
Fax: (309)346-2104
E-mail: chamber@pekin.net
URL: http://www.pekin.net
Contact: Bill Fleming, Exec.Dir.
Founded: 1893. **Membership Dues:** business (1-500 employees), $185-$1,255 (annual) • governmental agency (based on number of employees), $265-$525 (annual) • non-profit, $55 (annual) • non-business individual, $50 (annual) • retired businessperson, $35 (annual). **Local.** Promotes the growth of the Pekin area through collective efforts. **Computer Services:** Information services, membership directory. **Committees:** Leadership Academy; Marigold Festival; Marigold Golf; Pekin 1st. **Divisions:** Business Environment; Marketing; Member Promotion; Quality of Life. **Publications:** *Focus*, monthly. Newsletter. **Advertising:** accepted. Alternate Formats: online. **Conventions/Meetings:** monthly Business After Hours - meeting - every 1st Thursday in Pekin, IL • monthly luncheon - every 3rd Wednesday in Pekin, IL.

2990 ■ Pekin Lions Club
PO Box 751
Pekin, IL 61555-0751
E-mail: dvronna@insightbb.com
URL: http://www.pekinlionsclub.org
Local. Affiliated With: Lions Clubs International.

2991 ■ Pekin Main Street
PO Box 371
Pekin, IL 61555-0371
Ph: (309)353-3100
Fax: (309)353-3101
E-mail: mainstreet@grics.net
URL: http://www.pekinmainstreet.com
Local.

2992 ■ Professional Towing and Recovery Operators of Illinois (PTROI)
851 Brenkman Dr.
Pekin, IL 61554
Ph: (309)347-2375
Fax: (309)347-2375
Free: (800)286-0519
E-mail: ptroi@ntslink.net
URL: http://towingillinois.com
Contact: Melanie Matthews, Admin.
Founded: 1979. **Members:** 200. **Membership Dues:** regular (based on number of trucks), $150-$300 (annual) • associate, $250 (annual) • affiliate, $100 (annual) • employee, $35 (annual). **Staff:** 1. **Budget:** $110,000. **State Groups:** 1. **State.** Tow truck owners and operators organized to upgrade and promote the industry. **Awards:** High Standards Award. **Frequency:** annual. **Type:** recognition • Longevity Award. **Frequency:** annual. **Type:** recognition • Safety Award. **Frequency:** annual. **Type:** recognition. **Committees:** Convention. **Affiliated With:** Professional Towing and Recovery Operators of Illinois; Towing and Recovery Association of America. **Publications:** *Beacon*, 10/year. Newsletter. Contains up-to-date information and ideas. **Price:** included in membership dues. **Circulation:** 250. **Advertising:** accepted. Alternate Formats: diskette • Directory, semiannual. **Conventions/Meetings:** annual convention, trade show (exhibits).

2993 ■ Tazewell County Genealogical and Historical Society (TCGHS)
PO Box 312
Pekin, IL 61555-0312
Ph: (309)477-3044
E-mail: tcghs@tcghs.org
URL: http://www.tcghs.org
Contact: David Perkins, Pres.
Members: 450. **Membership Dues:** regular, charter family, $15 (annual) • regular, family in Canada, $18

(annual) • life, individual, $175 • life, family, $250 • student, $13 (annual). **Local**. Seeks to preserve Tazewell County local history. **Libraries: Type:** open to the public. **Holdings:** 4,200; articles, books, periodicals. **Subjects:** genealogy, history. **Publications:** *Tazewell Genealogical & Historical Monthly*. Newsletter. **Conventions/Meetings:** monthly meeting (exhibits) - every 2nd Tuesday in Pekin, IL.

2994 ■ Tazewell County S.T.A.R. (Student-Tutor-Adult Reading)
c/o YWCA
315 Buena Vista Ave.
Pekin, IL 61554-4227
Ph: (309)347-2104
Fax: (309)347-7457
E-mail: jgronewoldywca@grics.net
URL: National Affiliate–www.proliteracy.org
Contact: Ms. Jean G. Gronewold, Program Dir. Adult Literacy
Founded: 1985. **Members:** 50. **Staff:** 2. **Budget:** $35,000. **Local**. Strives to teach adults in basic reading and math skills and non-English-speaking adults in English language skills. **Libraries: Type:** not open to the public. **Holdings:** books. **Subjects:** adult learners ABE/ESL. **Boards:** Advisory; YWCA. **Affiliated With:** ProLiteracy Worldwide; United Way. **Formerly:** (2004) YWCA Student Tutor Adult Reading.

2995 ■ United Way of Pekin
PO Box 324
Pekin, IL 61555-0324
Ph: (309)346-2433
URL: National Affiliate–national.unitedway.org
Local. Affiliated With: United Way of America.

2996 ■ World Future Society, Pekin
c/o Charles Patrick Galvin
1607 Sommerset St.
Pekin, IL 61554
Ph: (309)346-8758
URL: National Affiliate–www.wfs.org
Contact: Charles Patrick Galvin, Contact
Local. Affiliated With: World Future Society.

Penfield

2997 ■ American Legion, Penfield-Gifford-Memorial Post 1153
PO Box 124
Penfield, IL 61862
Ph: (309)663-0361
Fax: (309)663-5783
URL: National Affiliate–www.legion.org
Local. Affiliated With: American Legion.

Peoria

2998 ■ ACF Heart of Illinois Professional Chefs Association
PO Box 688
Peoria, IL 61615
Ph: (309)266-3627
E-mail: jbonnette@sommerproducts.com
URL: National Affiliate–www.acfchefs.org
Contact: James M. Petruska, Pres.
Local. Promotes the culinary profession. Provides on-going educational training and networking for members. Provides opportunities for competition, professional recognition and access to educational forums with other culinarians at local, regional, national and international events. **Affiliated With:** American Culinary Federation.

2999 ■ Alcoholics Anonymous World Services, Peoria Area Intergroup Association
610 W Main St.
Peoria, IL 61606
Ph: (309)673-1456
E-mail: information@aapeoria.org
URL: http://www.aapeoria.com
Local. Individuals recovering from alcoholism. AA maintains that members can solve their common problem and help others achieve sobriety through a twelve step program that includes sharing their experience, strength, and hope with each other. **Affiliated With:** Alcoholics Anonymous World Services.

3000 ■ Alzheimer's Association, Central Illinois Chapter
606 W Glen Ave.
Peoria, IL 61614
Ph: (309)681-1100
Fax: (309)681-1101
Free: (800)272-3900
E-mail: jackie.bowers@alz.org
URL: http://www.alz.org
Contact: Jackie Bowers, Program Dir.
Local. Family members of sufferers of Alzheimer's disease. Combats Alzheimer's disease and related disorders. (Alzheimer's disease is a progressive, degenerative brain disease in which changes occur in the central nervous system and outer region of the brain causing memory loss and other changes in thought, personality, and behavior.) Promotes research to find the cause, treatment, and cure for the disease. **Affiliated With:** Alzheimer's Association.

3001 ■ American Cancer Society, Peoria - West Central Regional
4234 N Knoxville, Ste.B
Peoria, IL 61614
Ph: (309)688-3488
Fax: (309)688-9493
Free: (800)322-4577
URL: http://www.cancer.org
Contact: Ms. Tonda Thompson, Regional VP
Local. Affiliated With: American Cancer Society.

3002 ■ American Legion, Peoria Post 2
PO Box 298
Peoria, IL 61650
Ph: (309)676-2691
Fax: (309)663-5783
URL: National Affiliate–www.legion.org
Local. Affiliated With: American Legion.

3003 ■ American Legion, Peoria Post 1151
1520 W Garden St.
Peoria, IL 61605
Ph: (309)663-0361
Fax: (309)663-5783
URL: National Affiliate–www.legion.org
Local. Affiliated With: American Legion.

3004 ■ American Red Cross, Central Illinois Chapter
311 W John Gwynn Ave.
Peoria, IL 61605
Ph: (309)677-7272
Fax: (309)677-7283
URL: http://www.redcrossillinois.org
Regional.

3005 ■ Arthritis Foundation, Greater Illinois Chapter
2621 N Knoxville Ave.
Peoria, IL 61604
Ph: (309)682-6600
Fax: (309)682-6732
Free: (800)795-9115
E-mail: greaterillinois@arthritis.org
URL: http://arthritis.org
Contact: Gary Dutro, Chapter Pres.
Staff: 12. **Local Groups:** 13. **Local**. Seeks to: discover the cause and improve the methods for the treatment and prevention of arthritis and other rheumatic diseases; increase the number of scientists investigating rheumatic diseases; provide training in rheumatic diseases for more doctors; extend knowledge of arthritis and other rheumatic diseases to the lay public, emphasizing the socioeconomic as well as medical aspects of these diseases. **Affiliated With:** Arthritis Foundation.

3006 ■ Arthritis Foundation, Tri-County Branch
2622 N Knoxville Ave.
Peoria, IL 61604
Ph: (309)682-6600
Fax: (309)682-6732
Free: (800)795-9115
E-mail: greaterillinois@arthritis.org
URL: National Affiliate–www.arthritis.org
Local. Seeks to: discover the cause and improve the methods for the treatment and prevention of arthritis and other rheumatic diseases; increase the number of scientists investigating rheumatic diseases; provide training in rheumatic diseases for more doctors; extend knowledge of arthritis and other rheumatic diseases to the lay public, emphasizing the socioeconomic as well as medical aspects of these diseases. **Affiliated With:** Arthritis Foundation.

3007 ■ Associated Landscape Contractors of America, Illinois Central College
c/o Randey Wall, Faculty Advisor
Horticultural Prog.
One Coll. Dr. TK 5
Peoria, IL 61635
Ph: (309)694-5414
Fax: (309)694-5799
E-mail: rwall@icc.cc.il.us
URL: National Affiliate–www.alca.org
Contact: Randey Wall, Faculty Advisor
Local. Affiliated With: Professional Landcare Network.

3008 ■ Association of Legal Administrators, Cyber Chapter
c/o Paul J. Sullivan, Pres.
Quinn Johnston Henderson & Pretorius
227 NE Jefferson St.
Peoria, IL 61602
Ph: (309)636-7252
Fax: (309)674-6503
E-mail: president@cyberala.org
URL: http://www.cyberala.org
Contact: Paul J. Sullivan, Pres.
Local. Affiliated With: Association of Legal Administrators.

3009 ■ Better Business Bureau of Central Illinois
112 Harrison
Peoria, IL 61602
Ph: (309)688-3741
Fax: (309)681-7290
E-mail: bbb@heart.net
URL: http://www.peoria.bbb.org
Contact: Bonnie Bakin, CEO
Local. Seeks to promote and foster the highest ethical relationship between businesses and the public through voluntary self-regulation, consumer and business education, and service excellence. Provides information to help consumers and businesses make informed purchasing decisions and avoid costly scams and frauds; settles consumer complaints through arbitration and other means. **Affiliated With:** BBB Wise Giving Alliance.

3010 ■ Bradley University Students In Free Enterprise
Bradley Univ.
1501 W Bradley Ave.
Peoria, IL 61625
E-mail: sife@hotmail.com
URL: http://www.bradley.edu/campusorg/sife
Contact: Rahul Jain, Pres.
Local.

3011 ■ Central Illinois Chapter National Electrical Contractors Association
c/o James E. Gardner, Governor
707 NE Jefferson
Peoria, IL 61603-3843

Ph: (309)673-6900
Fax: (309)673-6322
E-mail: ceilneca@sbcglobal.net
URL: National Affiliate–www.necanet.org
Contact: Mr. Alan Koener, Pres
Regional. Contractors erecting, installing, repairing, servicing, and maintaining electric wiring, equipment, and appliances. **Affiliated With:** National Electrical Contractors Association.

3012 ■ Central Illinois Chapter of Sheet Metal and Air Conditioning Contractors' National Association
c/o Vicki Bahr
5200 N Knoxville Ave., 303N
Peoria, IL 61614-5057
Ph: (309)692-2997
Fax: (309)692-2947
E-mail: cilsmacna@sbcglobal.net
URL: National Affiliate–www.smacna.org
Contact: Vicki Bahr, Contact
Founded: 1918. **Local**. Represents sheet metal contracters in ten counties of central Illinois. **Awards:** Multi-Service Chapter Designation. **Frequency:** triennial. **Type:** recognition. **Affiliated With:** Sheet Metal and Air Conditioning Contractors' National Association. **Formerly:** Peoria Sheet Metal, Air Conditioning and Roofing Contractors Association.

3013 ■ Charitable Classics
c/o Joseph D. O'Brien, Jr.
411 N Hamilton Blvd., Ste.2002
Peoria, IL 61602
Ph: (309)637-1222
Fax: (309)674-1222
URL: http://www.charitableclassics.org
Contact: John Elias, Sec.
Founded: 1997. **Local**.

3014 ■ Citizens for Animal Rights
PO Box 5131
Peoria, IL 61601
Ph: (309)446-9772
E-mail: cfar_il@yahoo.com
Contact: Raymond Curry, Pres.
Founded: 1980. **Members:** 10. **Local**. Seeks to inform the public about animal issues. **Publications:** Newsletter, quarterly. **Conventions/Meetings:** monthly meeting - every last Tuesday in Peoria, IL.

3015 ■ Dress for Success Peoria
Peoria Friendship House
800 NE Madison
Peoria, IL 61603-3999
Ph: (309)671-5200
Fax: (309)671-5206
E-mail: peoria@dressforsuccess.org
URL: National Affiliate–www.dressforsuccess.org
Contact: Laura Clark, Program Dir.
Local.

3016 ■ Employers Association (EA)
401 NE Jefferson Ave.
Peoria, IL 61603-3725
Ph: (309)637-3333
Fax: (309)637-3300
Free: (800)948-5700
E-mail: staff@eaconnect.com
URL: http://www.eaconnect.com
Contact: Cindy Hamilton, Dir. of Operations
Founded: 1917. **Regional**. **Affiliated With:** Employers Association. **Formerly:** (1999) Employers Association, Peoria.

3017 ■ Fellowship of Freethinkers, Bradley University
c/o Paul Turack, Founder
912 N Elmwood Ave.
Heitz Hall, Rm. 112
Peoria, IL 61606
Ph: (309)677-1421
E-mail: aspphilosopher@hotmail.com
URL: National Affiliate–www.atheists.org
Contact: Paul Turack, Founder
Local. **Affiliated With:** American Atheists.

3018 ■ Financial Planning Association of Illinois
416 Main St.
Peoria, IL 61602
Ph: (309)999-3334
E-mail: mumchi@ameritech.net
URL: http://www.fpaillinois.org
Contact: Kathleen L. Leson CFP, Pres.
State. Supports the financial planning process in order to help people achieve their goals and dreams. Promotes the legislative, regulatory and professional interests of the financial service industry. Fosters the value of financial planning and advances the financial planning profession. **Affiliated With:** Financial Planning Association.

3019 ■ Forest Park Foundation
5823 N Forest Park Dr.
Peoria, IL 61614
Ph: (309)688-6631 (309)676-8910
Contact: William L Rutherford, Contact
Local.

3020 ■ Foster Grandparent Program of Peoria/Tazewell Counties
2219 S Idaho St.
Peoria, IL 61605-3023
Ph: (309)671-3950
Fax: (309)673-0052
E-mail: fgp@pcceo.org
URL: http://www.pcceo.org
Contact: Malinda K. Duncan, Dir.
Local. Serves as mentors, tutors and caregivers for at-risk children and youth with special needs. Provides older Americans the opportunity to put their life experiences to work for local communities. **Councils:** Foster Grandparent Program Advisory. **Also Known As:** (2005) Peoria Citizens Committee for Economic Opportunity.

3021 ■ Girl Scouts-Kickapoo Council
1103 W Lake Ave.
Peoria, IL 61614
Ph: (309)688-8671
E-mail: girlscouts@girlscouts-kickapoocouncil.org
URL: http://www.girlscouts-kickapoocouncil.org
Contact: Molly T. Fuller, CEO
Local. Young girls and adult volunteers, corporate, government and individual supporters. Strives to develop potential and leadership skills among its members. Conducts trainings, educational programs and outdoor activities.

3022 ■ Greater Peoria Contractors and Suppliers Association (GPCSA)
PO Box 3416
Peoria, IL 61612-3416
Ph: (309)692-5710
Fax: (309)692-5790
E-mail: info@gpcsa.org
URL: http://www.gpcsa.org
Contact: Bernie Koch, Pres.
Local. Represents general contractors, subcontractors, suppliers, manufacturers' representatives and individual firms related to the construction industry. Provides information on construction and building procedures. **Affiliated With:** International Builders Exchange Executives. **Publications:** Newsletter.

3023 ■ Habitat for Humanity of the Greater Peoria Area
931 N Douglas
Peoria, IL 61606
Ph: (309)676-6729
Fax: (309)676-6409
E-mail: hfhfred@sbcglobal.net
URL: http://www.habitatpeoria.org
Contact: Fred Kowalske, Exec.Dir.
Local. **Affiliated With:** Habitat for Humanity International.

3024 ■ Hamilton Park Neighborhood Association
c/o Melvina Haynes, Pres.
2619 N Mission
Peoria, IL 61604-2305
Ph: (309)685-7007
Founded: 1997. **Members:** 650. **Local**.

3025 ■ Heart of Illinois Chapter - MOAA
PO Box 10762
Peoria, IL 61612-0762
E-mail: pilot61571@yahoo.com
URL: http://heartofillinoismoaa.org
Contact: Tom Zentz, Pres.
Founded: 2003. **Local**. **Affiliated With:** Military Officers Association of America.

3026 ■ Heart of Illinois United Way
509 W High St.
Peoria, IL 61606
Ph: (309)674-5181
Fax: (309)674-1056
E-mail: michael.stephan@unitedway.org
URL: http://www.hoiunitedway.org
Contact: Michael Stephan, Pres.
Local. **Affiliated With:** United Way of America.

3027 ■ Heartland Water Resources Council
Commerce Bldg.
416 Main St., No. 828
Peoria, IL 61602
Ph: (309)637-5253
Fax: (309)637-5254
Contact: Tom Tincher, Exec.Dir.
Local.

3028 ■ Illinois Valley Figure Skating Club (IVFSC)
PO Box 10631
Peoria, IL 61612-0631
E-mail: benann@gries.net
URL: http://www.ivfsc.org
Contact: Ann Rahn, Sec.
Local. Provides programs to encourage participation and achievement in the sport of figure skating on ice. Defines and maintains uniform standards of skating proficiency. Organizes and sponsors competitions and exhibitions for the purpose of stimulating interest in figure skating. **Affiliated With:** United States Figure Skating Association.

3029 ■ Institute of Real Estate Management - Central Illinois Chapter No. 78
c/o Dave Paskert
Chase Property Mgt., Inc.
219 Fulton St.
Peoria, IL 61602
Ph: (309)999-5501
E-mail: dpaskert@chasepm.com
URL: National Affiliate–www.irem.org
Contact: Dave Paskert CPM, Treas.
Local. Represents real property and asset management professionals. Works to promote professional ethics and standards in the field of property management. Strives to keep its members informed on the latest legislative activities and current industry trends. Provides classroom training, continuing education seminars, job referral service and candidate assistance services to enhance the effectiveness and professionalism of its members. **Affiliated With:** Institute of Real Estate Management.

3030 ■ International Edsel Club, Illinois Chapter
6617 W Jones Rd.
Peoria, IL 61604-4327
E-mail: ntryon@adams.net
URL: National Affiliate–www.internationaledsel.com
State. **Affiliated With:** International Edsel Club.

3031 ■ International Union of Operating Engineers, Local 649
6408 W Plank Rd.
Peoria, IL 61604
Ph: (309)697-0070
Fax: (309)697-0025
URL: http://www.iuoe649.org
Contact: James Schultheis, Pres.
Local. AFL-CIO. **Affiliated With:** International Union of Operating Engineers.

3032 ■ InterVarsity Christian Fellowship in Downstate Illinois
c/o John Egleston, Communications and Systems Specialist
923 N Western Ave.
Peoria, IL 61604
Ph: (309)673-8500
Fax: (309)673-8505
E-mail: ivcfdill@insightbb.com
URL: http://www.ivcfdill.org
Contact: John Egleston, Communications and Systems Specialist
State. Acts as a resource for the Downstate staff and campus chapters of IVCF-USA.

3033 ■ Korean War Veterans Association, Department of Illinois
c/o Paul W. Sutphin
5307 S Mid Ct.
Peoria, IL 61607-9537
Ph: (309)697-0659
URL: National Affiliate–www.kwva.org
Contact: Paul W. Sutphin, Contact
State. **Affiliated With:** Korean War Veterans Association.

3034 ■ Mental Health Association of Illinois Valley
5407 N Univ. St.
Peoria, IL 61614
Ph: (309)692-1766
Fax: (309)692-2966
E-mail: mhaiv@mhaiv.org
URL: http://www.mhaiv.org
Contact: Katie Jones MSW, Exec.Dir.
Local. Seeks to promote mental health and prevent mental health disorders. Improves mental health of Americans through advocacy, public education, research and service. **Affiliated With:** National Mental Health Association.

3035 ■ Muscular Dystrophy Association Support Groups
2424 W Nebraska
Peoria, IL 61604
Ph: (309)693-8653
Fax: (309)693-8657
Contact: Lisa Holloway, District Dir.
Local.

3036 ■ National Active And Retired Federal Employees Association - Greater Peoria 268
1108 W Macqueen Ave.
Peoria, IL 61604-3310
Ph: (309)688-4657
URL: National Affiliate–www.narfe.org
Contact: Raymond L. Cunningham, Contact
Local. Protects the retirement future of employees through education. Informs members on issues affecting the retirement. **Affiliated With:** National Association of Retired Federal Employees.

3037 ■ National Alliance for the Mentally Ill - Tri-County
5407 N Univ. St.
Peoria, IL 61614
Ph: (309)693-0541
URL: http://www.nami.org/sites/namitri-county
Contact: Keith Stone, Pres.
Local. Strives to improve the quality of life of children and adults with severe mental illness through support, education, research and advocacy. **Affiliated With:** National Alliance for the Mentally Ill.

3038 ■ National Association of Student Personnel Administrators, Illinois
c/o Alan Galsky, Coor.
Bradley Univ.
1501 W Bradley Ave.
Sisson Hall 100
Peoria, IL 61625
Ph: (309)677-3140
Fax: (309)677-3789
E-mail: apsa@bradley.edu
URL: National Affiliate–www.naspa.org
Contact: Alan Galsky, Coor.
State. Provides professional development and advocacy for student affairs educators and administrators. Seeks to promote, assess and support student learning through leadership. **Affiliated With:** National Association of Student Personnel Administrators.

3039 ■ National Technological Honor Society - Illinois Central College Illinois (ICC)
1 Coll. Dr.
Peoria, IL 61635-0001
Ph: (309)694-5422
E-mail: jerwin@icc.edu
URL: http://www.icc.edu
Contact: Dr. John Erwin, Pres.
Local.

3040 ■ Pathfinders Ski Club
1113 W Groveland Ave.
Peoria, IL 61604
E-mail: wam4208@aol.com
URL: National Affiliate–www.nbs.org
Contact: Winston A. Mitchell, Pres.
Local. **Affiliated With:** National Brotherhood of Skiers.

3041 ■ Peoria Academy Of Science - Geology Section
PO Box 10294
Peoria, IL 61612-0294
Ph: (309)745-5429
E-mail: lilbrownbat13@yahoo.com
URL: http://www.pasgeology.com
Contact: Kathy Travis, Sec.
Local. Aims to further the study of Earth Sciences and the practice of lapidary arts and mineralogy. **Affiliated With:** American Federation of Mineralogical Societies.

3042 ■ Peoria AIFA
c/o Jerry D. Jackson, Pres.
2214 N Univ., No. 140
Peoria, IL 61604-3168
Ph: (309)685-2470
Fax: (309)682-8840
E-mail: paifa1@sbcglobal.net
URL: http://www.naifanet.com/peoria
Contact: Jerry D. Jackson, Pres.
Local. Represents the interests of insurance and financial advisors. Advocates for a positive legislative and regulatory environment. Enhances business and professional skills of members. **Affiliated With:** National Association of Insurance and Financial Advisors.

3043 ■ Peoria Area Association of Realtors (PAAR)
7307 Willowlake Ct.
Peoria, IL 61614
Ph: (309)688-8591
Fax: (309)688-3120
E-mail: paar@paarealtors.com
URL: http://www.paarealtors.com
Contact: Shara Manning, Pres.
Local. Strives to develop real estate business practices. Advocates the right to own, use and transfer real property. Provides a facility for professional development, research and exchange of information among members and to the general public. **Affiliated With:** National Association of Realtors.

3044 ■ Peoria Area Chamber of Commerce (PACC)
124 SW Adams St., Ste.300
Peoria, IL 61602-1388
Ph: (309)676-0755
Fax: (309)676-7534
E-mail: chamber@chamber.h-p.org
URL: http://www.peoriachamber.org
Contact: Roberta M. Parks, Senior VP/COO
Founded: 1911. **Members:** 1,200. **Local**. Promotes business and community development in the Peoria, IL area. **Telecommunication Services:** electronic mail, dgraves@chamber.h-p.org. **Committees:** Business Advocacy; Education; Marketing; Transportation. **Publications:** *Chamber Communicator*, weekly. Newsletter. Alternate Formats: online. **Conventions/Meetings:** monthly Business After Hours - meeting, with networking opportunities - every 2nd Thursday.

3045 ■ Peoria Area Convention and Visitors Bureau (PACVB)
456 Fulton St., Ste.300
Peoria, IL 61602
Ph: (309)676-0303
Fax: (309)676-6916
Free: (800)747-0302
E-mail: spowell@peoria.org
URL: http://www.peoria.org
Contact: Steve Powell, Exec.Dir.
Local.

3046 ■ Peoria Area Miniature Society (PAMS)
c/o Sandy Staker
7417 N Knoxville Ave.
Peoria, IL 61614
Ph: (309)689-1943
E-mail: sandyslace@juno.com
URL: http://www.miniatures.org/states/IL.html
Contact: Sandy Staker, Contact
Local. **Affiliated With:** National Association of Miniature Enthusiasts.

3047 ■ Peoria Area Mountain Bike Association (PAMBA)
c/o Terry Carter
4506 N Nelson Dr.
Peoria, IL 61614
Ph: (309)689-6224
E-mail: terry@pambamtb.org
URL: http://www.pambamtb.org
Contact: Terry Carter, Contact
Local. Aims to promote off-road bicycling through education, trail creation, trail maintenance, and social events. **Affiliated With:** International Mountain Bicycling Association.

3048 ■ Peoria Area Youth for Christ
4100 N Brandywine Dr.
Peoria, IL 61614
Ph: (309)688-6685
Fax: (309)688-6686
URL: http://www.yfcpeoria.org
Local. **Affiliated With:** Youth for Christ/U.S.A.

3049 ■ Peoria Association For Retarded Citizens
PO Box 3418
Peoria, IL 61612
Ph: (309)691-3800
URL: National Affiliate–www.TheArc.org
Contact: Roy Rickitts, CEO
Local. Parents, professional workers, and others interested in individuals with mental retardation. Works to promote services, research, public understanding, and legislation for people with mental retardation and their families. **Affiliated With:** Arc of the United States.

3050 ■ Peoria County Bar Association (PCBA)
411 Hamilton Blvd., Ste.1618
Peoria, IL 61602

Ph: (309)674-6049
Fax: (309)674-4047
E-mail: pcba@mtco.com
URL: http://www.abanet.org
Contact: Linda Raineri, Exec.Sec.

Founded: 1879. **Members:** 564. **Membership Dues:** $140 (annual). **Staff:** 1. **Budget:** $70,000. **Local**. Attorneys in good standing. Seeks to improve the administration of civil and criminal justice, and the availability of legal services to the public. **Convention/Meeting:** none. **Publications:** *Legal Ease*, monthly. Newsletter. **Circulation:** 564.

3051 ■ Peoria District Dental Society (PDDS)
809 E Nebraska Ave.
Peoria, IL 61603-2621
Ph: (309)685-5339
Fax: (309)685-5591
E-mail: info@pdds.org
URL: http://www.pdds.org
Contact: Mrs. Georgana Donnelly, Exec.Sec.

Local. Represents the interests of dentists committed to the public's oral health, ethics and professional development. Encourages the improvement of the public's oral health and promotes the art and science of dentistry. **Affiliated With:** American Dental Association; Illinois State Dental Society.

3052 ■ Peoria Girls Sports League (PGSL)
c/o Jerry Robertson
PO Box 120091
Peoria, IL 61614-0900
Ph: (309)693-9473 (309)624-5152
Fax: (309)693-9479
E-mail: pgsl@insightbb.com
Contact: Mr. Jerry Robertson, Pres.

Founded: 1982. **Members:** 890. **Membership Dues:** individual, $50 (annual). **Budget:** $25,000. **Local**. Girls sports league for ages 7 through 17 designed to build skill level in basketball, softball and volleyball. Emphasis is placed on the social and sportsmanship aspects of each sport. **Conventions/Meetings:** annual board meeting.

3053 ■ Peoria Heights Chamber of Commerce
1203 E Kingman
Peoria, IL 61616
Ph: (309)685-4812
E-mail: phcc@bwsys.net
Contact: Susan Watters, Sec.

Local.

3054 ■ Peoria Lions Club
PO Box 1492
Peoria, IL 61655
Ph: (309)692-3946
URL: http://peoriail.lionwap.org

Local. Affiliated With: Lions Clubs International.

3055 ■ Peoria Medical Society
7700 N Harker Dr., Ste.D
Peoria, IL 61615
Ph: (309)692-1192
Fax: (309)692-2502
E-mail: megw@peomedsoc.org
URL: http://www.isms.org
Contact: Meg Williams, Exec.Dir.

Local. Advances the art and science of medicine. Promotes patient care and the betterment of public health.

3056 ■ Peoria Obedience Training Club (POTC)
PO Box 183
Peoria, IL 61650
Ph: (309)676-9472
URL: http://www.potcdogs.com
Contact: Jean Auer, Pres.

Local. Affiliated With: American Kennel Club.

3057 ■ Peoria Youth Hockey Association (PYHA)
PO Box 3692
Peoria, IL 61612-3692
Ph: (309)673-8328
E-mail: pyha@pyha.org
URL: http://www.pyha.org
Contact: Randall M. Jacobs, Pres.

Members: 500. **Local**. Youth hockey association. Promotes the growth of ice hockey in the Peoria, IL area by encouraging, developing, and administering the sport. Endeavors to develop and prepare players and coaches to achieve optimum performance at all levels, providing essential information, quality instruction, and a positive experience through participation in the programs.

3058 ■ Phi Theta Kappa, Upsilon Mu Chapter - Illinois Central College
c/o Jen Richrath, Advisor
English Dept.
1 Coll. Dr.
Peoria, IL 61635
Ph: (309)694-5101
E-mail: jrichrath@icc.edu
URL: http://www.ptk.org/directories/chapters/IL/192-1.htm
Contact: Jen Richrath, Advisor

Local.

3059 ■ Police and Firemen's Insurance Association - Peoria Fire Department
c/o Tom C. Jackson
3726 W Eagle Point Dr.
Peoria, IL 61615
Ph: (309)691-6075
URL: National Affiliate–www.pfia.net
Contact: Tom C. Jackson, Contact

Local. **Affiliated With:** Police and Firemen's Insurance Association.

3060 ■ Psi Chi, National Honor Society in Psychology - Bradley University
c/o Dept. of Psychology
Comstock Hall
1501 W Bradley Ave.
Peoria, IL 61625-0001
Ph: (309)677-2580
Fax: (309)677-3763
E-mail: ffiles@bradley.edu
URL: http://www.psichi.org/chapters/info.asp?chapter_id=249
Contact: Forrest J. Files PhD, Advisor

Local.

3061 ■ Public Relations Society of America, Central Illinois
c/o Karen Korsgard, Account Exec.
Hult Fritz Matuszak Integrated Communs.
401 SW Water St., Ste.601
Peoria, IL 61603
Ph: (309)673-8191
Fax: (309)674-5530
E-mail: kkorsgard@hfma.com
URL: http://www.geocities.com/prsa_ci
Contact: Ms. Karen Korsgard APR, Pres.

Founded: 1979. **Members:** 50. **Membership Dues:** full membership, $290 (annual) • full membership - local, $35 (annual). **State**. Strives to promote ethics and professionalism in the field of public relations. **Affiliated With:** Public Relations Society of America.

3062 ■ Retired and Senior Volunteer Program of Peoria and Tazewell Counties
3100 N Knoxville Ave., Ste.15
Peoria, IL 61603-1038
Ph: (309)682-8521
Fax: (309)682-8524
E-mail: rsvp@rsvpvolunteers.org
URL: http://www.rsvpvolunteers.org
Contact: Jan Sweikert, Dir.

Local. Affiliated With: Retired and Senior Volunteer Program.

3063 ■ Saint Bernard Club of Greater St. Louis
925 Oakview
Peoria, IL 61615
Ph: (309)692-4673
URL: National Affiliate–www.saintbernardclub.org
Contact: Cathy Hewitt, Sec.

Local. **Affiliated With:** Saint Bernard Club of America.

3064 ■ SCORE Peoria
c/o Peoria Chamber of Commerce
124 SW Adams, Ste.300
Peoria, IL 61602
Ph: (309)676-0755
Fax: (309)676-7534
E-mail: score@score.h-p.org

Local. Strives for the formation, growth and success of small businesses. Provides professional guidance and information to maximize the success of existing and emerging small businesses. Promotes entrepreneur education in Peoria area, Illinois. **Affiliated With:** SCORE.

3065 ■ Tazewell Numismatic Society
c/o Gerry Gerber
6013 N Heather Oak Dr.
Peoria, IL 61615
Ph: (309)691-5692
URL: National Affiliate–www.money.org
Contact: Gerry Gerber, Contact

Local. **Affiliated With:** American Numismatic Association.

3066 ■ Theta Xi, Alpha Sigma Chapter — Bradley University
c/o Terry Nighswanger, Advisor
1317 W Fredonia
Peoria, IL 61606
Ph: (309)694-2831
URL: http://www.thetaxionline.com
Contact: Terry Nighswanger, Advisor

Membership Dues: associate, $275 (annual) • active (living out of house), $550 • active (living in house), $2,000. **Local. Affiliated With:** Theta Xi.

3067 ■ Tri-County Regional Planning Commission (TCRPC)
411 Hamilton Rd., Ste.2001
Peoria, IL 61602
Ph: (309)673-9330
Fax: (309)673-9802
E-mail: info@tricountyrpc.org
URL: http://www.tricountyrpc.org
Contact: Terry D. Kohlbuss, Exec.Dir.

Founded: 1958. **Members:** 22. **Staff:** 11. **Budget:** $968,475. **Local**. Serves the residents of the Tri-County Region through the creation of a forum for leaders of local government to develop a vision for the future and to implement plans. **Libraries: Type:** open to the public. **Holdings:** 200. **Subjects:** transportation planning, water resources.

3068 ■ United Food and Commercial Workers, Local 536, Northcentral Region
2200 E War Memorial Dr.
Peoria, IL 61614
Ph: (309)686-0304
URL: National Affiliate–www.ufcw.org

Local. Affiliated With: United Food and Commercial Workers International Union.

3069 ■ Women for Humanity
c/o Razia Hameed Ahmed
2015 W Cimarron Dr.
Peoria, IL 61614
E-mail: info@womenforhumanity.org
URL: http://womenforhumanity.org

Local.

Peoria Heights

3070 ■ Junior Achievement of Central Illinois
c/o Larry Timm, Pres.
4450 N Propsect Rd., Ste.C4
Peoria Heights, IL 61616
Ph: (309)682-1800
Fax: (309)673-0115
E-mail: ltimm@juniorachievement.biz
URL: http://www.juniorachievement.biz
Contact: Larry Timm, Pres.
Local.

Peotone

3071 ■ American Legion, Peotone Post 392
109 E North St.
Peotone, IL 60468
Ph: (708)258-6952
Fax: (309)663-5783
URL: National Affiliate–www.legion.org
Local. Affiliated With: American Legion.

3072 ■ Peotone Woman's Club
PO Box 1083
Peotone, IL 60468
E-mail: terrycare@aol.com
URL: http://careconnections.kwiatkowski.com/club
Contact: Terry Kwiatkowski, Contact
Local.

Percy

3073 ■ American Legion, Percy Post 1145
1064 E Broadway
Percy, IL 62272
Ph: (309)663-0361
Fax: (309)663-5783
URL: National Affiliate–www.legion.org
Local. Affiliated With: American Legion.

Perry

3074 ■ American Legion, Perry Post 1040
Box 188
Perry, IL 62362
Ph: (309)663-0361
Fax: (309)663-5783
URL: National Affiliate–www.legion.org
Local. Affiliated With: American Legion.

Peru

3075 ■ American Legion, Peru Post 375
1018 Henry St.
Peru, IL 61354
Ph: (309)663-0361
Fax: (309)663-5783
URL: National Affiliate–www.legion.org
Local. Affiliated With: American Legion.

3076 ■ American Postal Workers Union, AFL-CIO - Local Union 1701
c/o Janice Studer
1500 4th St.
Peru, IL 61354
Ph: (815)223-0320
Free: (800)275-8777
URL: http://www.usps.com
Contact: Janet Wamhoff, Postmaster
Members: 6. **Local**. AFL-CIO. **Affiliated With:** American Postal Workers Union.

3077 ■ Arthritis Foundation, Illinois Valley Branch
1301 Peoria St.
Peru, IL 61354
Ph: (815)224-2799
Fax: (815)224-2710
E-mail: greaterillinois@arthritis.org
URL: National Affiliate–www.arthritis.org
Local. Seeks to: discover the cause and improve the methods for the treatment and prevention of arthritis and other rheumatic diseases; increase the number of scientists investigating rheumatic diseases; provide training in rheumatic diseases for more doctors; extend knowledge of arthritis and other rheumatic diseases to the lay public, emphasizing the socioeconomic as well as medical aspects of these diseases. **Affiliated With:** Arthritis Foundation.

3078 ■ Hospital Engineers Society of Northern Illinois (HESNI)
c/o Jeffrey Arthurs, CHFM, Pres.
Illinois Valley Community Hosp.
925 West St.
Peru, IL 61354-2757
Ph: (815)780-3281
Fax: (815)780-3107
E-mail: jeff.arthurs@ivch.org
URL: http://www.hesni.org
Contact: Jeffrey Arthurs CHFM, Pres.
Local. Promotes better patient care by encouraging members to develop their knowledge and increase their competence in the field of facilities management. Cooperates with hospitals and allied associations in matters pertaining to facilities management. **Affiliated With:** American Society for Healthcare Engineering of the American Hospital Association.

3079 ■ Illini Valley Association of Realtors
1125 Peoria St.
Peru, IL 61354
Ph: (815)224-1868
E-mail: mellis@illinivalleyrealtors.org
URL: http://www.illinivalleyrealtors.org
Contact: Marcia Ellis, Exec.VP
Local. Strives to develop real estate business practices. Advocates the right to own, use and transfer real property. Provides a facility for professional development, research and exchange of information among members and to the general public. **Affiliated With:** National Association of Realtors.

3080 ■ Illinois Valley AIFA
c/o Diane Noder, Sec.
809 21st St.
Peru, IL 61354
Ph: (815)224-4170
Fax: (815)224-4117
E-mail: diane.noder@countryfinancial.com
URL: National Affiliate–naifa.org
Contact: Diane Noder, Sec.
Local. Represents the interests of insurance and financial advisors. Advocates for a positive legislative and regulatory environment. Enhances business and professional skills of members. **Affiliated With:** National Association of Insurance and Financial Advisors.

3081 ■ Mothers from Hell 2
PO Box 62
Peru, IL 61354
Ph: (815)224-4568
E-mail: kim@mothersfromhell2.org
URL: http://www.mothersfromhell2.org
Founded: 1999. **Members:** 400. **Membership Dues:** general, $10 (annual). **Staff:** 4. **Budget:** $3,000. **Regional**. Fights for the appropriate education, community acceptance, desperately needed services, rights of, and entitlements for individuals with disabilities. Offers support and empowerment for families of individuals with special needs. **Publications:** *The Brimstone Bulletin*, quarterly. Newsletter. Contains support and other information related to group's mission. **Price:** included in membership dues. **Circulation:** 400.

3082 ■ Retail, Wholesale and Department Store Union District Council, UFCW, AFL-CIO, CLC Local Union 17
2111 Plum St.
Peru, IL 61354
Ph: (815)223-4835
URL: http://www.rwdsu-cs.org/Local17.html
Contact: Dan Witalka, Pres.
Members: 123. **Local. Affiliated With:** Retail, Wholesale and Department Store Union.

Pesotum

3083 ■ American Legion, Pesotum Post 580
PO Box 166
Pesotum, IL 61863
Ph: (309)663-0361
Fax: (309)663-5783
URL: National Affiliate–www.legion.org
Local. Affiliated With: American Legion.

Petersburg

3084 ■ American Legion, Kirby-Watkins Post 198
111 N 7th St.
Petersburg, IL 62675
Ph: (309)663-0361
Fax: (309)663-5783
URL: National Affiliate–www.legion.org
Local. Affiliated With: American Legion.

3085 ■ Illinois B.A.S.S. Federation (IBF)
c/o Stan Leach
183 Cedar Ln.
Petersburg, IL 62675
Ph: (217)632-3110
E-mail: president@ilbassfed.com
URL: http://www.ilbassfed.com
Contact: Sue Bixler, Sec.
State.

3086 ■ Petersburg Chamber of Commerce (PCC)
PO Box 452
Petersburg, IL 62675
Ph: (217)632-7363
Fax: (217)632-7363
E-mail: dsk@petersburgil.com
URL: http://www.petersburgil.com/pcoc
Contact: Betty Winchester, Pres.
Members: 80. **Membership Dues:** individual, $50 (annual) • business, $125 (annual). **Local.** Promotes business and community development in Menard County, IL. Sponsors Petersburg Harvest Fest and Christmas in Petersburg.

Philo

3087 ■ American Legion, Philo Post 1171
1085 Harrison
Philo, IL 61864
Ph: (309)663-0361
Fax: (309)663-5783
URL: National Affiliate–www.legion.org
Local. Affiliated With: American Legion.

3088 ■ Police and Firemen's Insurance Association - Urbana Fire Department
Box 180
Philo, IL 61864
Ph: (217)684-2753
URL: National Affiliate–www.pfia.net
Contact: James G. Kingston, Contact
Local. Affiliated With: Police and Firemen's Insurance Association.

Pinckneyville

3089 ■ American Legion, Daffron-Presswood Post 2504
PO Box 207
Pinckneyville, IL 62274
Ph: (309)663-0361
Fax: (309)663-5783
URL: National Affiliate–www.legion.org
Local. Affiliated With: American Legion.

3090 ■ Perry County Historical Society
108 W Jackson St.
Pinckneyville, IL 62274
Ph: (618)357-2225
URL: http://www.fnbpville.com/perrycounty.html
Contact: William E. Timpner, Contact
Members: 130. **Membership Dues:** $10 (annual). **Local.** Individuals interested in preserving the history of Perry County, IL. Operates the Perry County Old Jail Museum and Perry County genealogy research. **Committees:** Genealogy Branch; Perry County Museum. **Publications:** *Journal of the Perry County Historical Society*, monthly. Newsletter. **Price:** included in membership dues, free sample upon request. **Conventions/Meetings:** monthly meeting - second Tuesday, public invited.

3091 ■ Pinckneyville Chamber of Commerce
4 S Walnut St.
Pinckneyville, IL 62274-0183
Ph: (618)357-3243
E-mail: pvllecoc@midwest.net
URL: http://chamber.pinckneyville.com
Contact: Joan Smith, Exec.Coor.
Membership Dues: business, $90 • associate, $25 • individual, $35. **Local.** Provides a venue in which people can take effective action for the progress of the community. Organizes convention, sales meetings and other gatherings. **Awards:** Business of the Year. **Frequency:** annual. **Type:** recognition • Person of the Year. **Frequency:** annual. **Type:** recognition • **Frequency:** annual. **Type:** scholarship. **Recipient:** for graduating seniors at PCHS. **Computer Services:** Information services, membership directory. **Committees:** Beautification; Golf Scramble; Mardi Gras Festival; Pinckeyville Online. **Conventions/Meetings:** monthly board meeting - every 4th Wednesday in Pinckeyville, IL.

Piper City

3092 ■ American Legion, Gibb Post 588
43 W Main St.
Piper City, IL 60959
Ph: (309)663-0361
Fax: (309)663-5783
URL: National Affiliate–www.legion.org
Local. Affiliated With: American Legion.

Pittsfield

3093 ■ American Legion, Pittsfield Post 152
1302 W Washington St.
Pittsfield, IL 62363
Ph: (217)285-2819
Fax: (309)663-5783
URL: National Affiliate–www.legion.org
Local. Affiliated With: American Legion.

3094 ■ Lamoine Valley Angus Association
c/o Andy Musgrave, Pres.
R.R. 3, Box 3218
Pittsfield, IL 62363
Ph: (217)833-3985
URL: National Affiliate–www.angus.org
Contact: Andy Musgrave, Pres.
Local. Affiliated With: American Angus Association.

3095 ■ Pike County Chamber of Commerce
224 W Washington
PO Box 283
Pittsfield, IL 62363
Ph: (217)285-2971
Fax: (217)285-5251
E-mail: info@pikeil.org
URL: http://www.pikeil.org
Contact: Ms. Alicia Smith, Exec.Dir.
Founded: 1955. **Members:** 200. **Staff:** 1. **Local.** Promotes business and community development in Pike County, IL.

3096 ■ Pittsfield Lions Club
PO Box 255
Pittsfield, IL 62363
E-mail: wrightplace@adams.net
URL: http://pittsfieldlionsclubil.lionwap.org
Contact: Peter Wright, Pres.
Local. Affiliated With: Lions Clubs International.

Plainfield

3097 ■ American Chemical Society, Joliet Section
c/o William John Peacy, Chm.
4302 Thornwood Ln.
Plainfield, IL 60586-5021
Ph: (630)942-2014
E-mail: peacyw@cdnet.cod.edu
URL: National Affiliate–acswebcontent.acs.org
Contact: William John Peacy, Chm.
Local. Represents the interests of individuals dedicated to the advancement of chemistry in all its branches. Provides opportunities for peer interaction and career development. **Affiliated With:** American Chemical Society.

3098 ■ American Hellenic Educational Progressive Association - Joliet, Chapter 131
c/o Elefterios Saravinos, Pres.
15317 Dan Patch Dr.
Plainfield, IL 60544
Ph: (815)436-3055
URL: http://www.ahepafamily.org/d13
Contact: Elefterios Saravinos, Pres.
Local. Affiliated With: American Hellenic Educational Progressive Association.

3099 ■ American Legion, Marne Post 13
24741 Renwick Rd.
Plainfield, IL 60544
Ph: (309)663-0361
Fax: (309)663-5783
URL: National Affiliate–www.legion.org
Local. Affiliated With: American Legion.

3100 ■ Kiwanis Club of Plainfield
c/o Jim Lindamood, Pres.
PO Box 642
Plainfield, IL 60544
E-mail: president@plainfieldkiwanis.org
URL: http://www.plainfieldkiwanis.org
Contact: Jim Lindamood, Pres.
Local.

3101 ■ Main Street Plainfield
506 W Lockport St.
Plainfield, IL 60544
Ph: (815)436-5510
E-mail: msplainfield@sbcglobal.net
URL: http://www.mainstreetplainfield.org
Local.

3102 ■ MOAA Illinois Council of Chapters
21740 W Empress Ln.
Plainfield, IL 60544-6322
Ph: (815)407-1404
E-mail: ajwolff34@aol.com
URL: National Affiliate–www.moaa.org
Contact: Col. Aaron Wolff, Contact
State. Affiliated With: Military Officers Association of America.

3103 ■ National Active And Retired Federal Employees Association - Louis Joliet 655
13800 S Mandarin Ct.
Plainfield, IL 60544-9337
Ph: (815)372-7229
URL: National Affiliate–www.narfe.org
Contact: Norman L. Sherpan, Contact
Local. Protects the retirement future of employees through education. Informs members on issues affecting the retirement. **Affiliated With:** National Association of Retired Federal Employees.

3104 ■ National Association of Miniature Enthusiasts - Town Hall Minis
c/o Darlene Wilkinson
13738 S Ironwood Dr.
Plainfield, IL 60544
Ph: (815)372-1020
E-mail: billndar@core.com
URL: http://www.miniatures.org/states/IL.html
Contact: Darlene Wilkinson, Contact
Local. Affiliated With: National Association of Miniature Enthusiasts.

3105 ■ Plainfield Area Chamber of Commerce
530 W Lockport St., No. 108
Plainfield, IL 60544-1583
Ph: (815)436-4431
Fax: (815)436-0520
E-mail: etcollins@plainfieldchamber.com
URL: http://www.plainfieldchamber.com
Contact: Liz Collins, Pres./CEO
Local.

3106 ■ Plainfield South High School Parent Teacher Student Organization
c/o Paulette Aldis
7800 W Caton Farm Rd.
Plainfield, IL 60544-0000
Ph: (815)436-3200 (815)439-5555
URL: http://www.learningcommunity202.org
Contact: Cathy Noa, Pres.
Local.

3107 ■ Society of Antique Modelers - Illinois 117
23546 Fern St.
Plainfield, IL 60544-2324
Ph: (815)842-6703
E-mail: mgmrcfly@davesworld.net
URL: National Affiliate–www.antiquemodeler.org
Local. Affiliated With: Society of Antique Modelers.

Plano

3108 ■ American Legion, Leon Burson Post 395
510 E Dearborn St.
Plano, IL 60545
Ph: (708)552-8313
Fax: (309)663-5783
URL: National Affiliate–www.legion.org
Local. Affiliated With: American Legion.

3109 ■ American Rottweiler Club (ARC)
c/o Pam Grant, Pres.
43 Huntsman Dr.
Plano, IL 60545
Ph: (630)552-8740
E-mail: quailrdg@comcast.net
URL: http://www.amrottclub.org
Contact: Pam Grant, Pres.
Regional.

3110 ■ Plano Commerce Association
101 W Main St.
PO Box 81
Plano, IL 60545-0081

Ph: (630)552-7272
Fax: (630)552-0165
E-mail: pedco@indianvalley.com
URL: http://planocommerce.org
Contact: William Negley, Exec.Dir.
Local. Strives to promote and perpetuate the business, civic, and agricultural interests of the Plano area. **Awards: Frequency:** annual. **Type:** recognition. **Recipient:** for physical building enhancements and contributions to the community.

3111 ■ Quad County Hawg Hunters
PO Box 185
Plano, IL 60545
Ph: (815)695-1494
E-mail: danaws@msn.com
URL: http://www.muskiesinc.org/chapters/17
Contact: Dana Smith, Contact
Local.

Pleasant Hill

3112 ■ American Legion, Pleasant Hill Post 1048
104 W Clay St.
Pleasant Hill, IL 62366
Ph: (309)663-0361
Fax: (309)663-5783
URL: National Affiliate–www.legion.org
Local. Affiliated With: American Legion.

Pleasant Plains

3113 ■ American Legion, Pleasant Plains Post 599
5716 Altmans Rd.
Pleasant Plains, IL 62677
Ph: (217)626-1003
Fax: (309)663-5783
URL: National Affiliate–www.legion.org
Local. Affiliated With: American Legion.

Plymouth

3114 ■ American Legion, Plymouth Post 912
West Side Sq.
Plymouth, IL 62367
Ph: (309)458-6505
Fax: (309)663-5783
URL: National Affiliate–www.legion.org
Local. Affiliated With: American Legion.

Pocahontas

3115 ■ American Legion, Pocahontas Memorial Post 1104
379 Illinois RR 143
Pocahontas, IL 62275
Ph: (309)663-0361
Fax: (309)663-5783
URL: National Affiliate–www.legion.org
Local. Affiliated With: American Legion.

Polo

3116 ■ American Legion, Illinois Post 83
c/o Patrick Fegan
610 S Div. St.
Polo, IL 61064
Ph: (815)946-2814
Fax: (309)663-5783
URL: National Affiliate–www.legion.org
Contact: Patrick Fegan, Contact
Local. Affiliated With: American Legion.

3117 ■ Polo Chamber of Commerce
115 S Franklin Ave.
Polo, IL 61064
Ph: (815)946-3131
Fax: (815)946-2004
E-mail: webmaster@poloil.net
URL: http://www.poloil.net
Contact: Susie Corbitt, Sec.
Members: 130. **Local Groups:** 1. **Local**. Promotes business and community development in Polo, IL. Sponsors festivals. **Publications:** none. **Conventions/Meetings:** annual meeting, for membership.

Pontiac

3118 ■ American Legion, Aarvig-Campbell Post 78
17602 Billet Rd.
Pontiac, IL 61764
Ph: (309)663-0361
Fax: (309)663-5783
URL: National Affiliate–www.legion.org
Local. Affiliated With: American Legion.

3119 ■ Arthritis Foundation, Livingston County Branch
c/o Saint James Hospital/Resource Center
2501 W Reynolds St.
Pontiac, IL 61764
Ph: (815)842-2828
E-mail: greaterillinois@arthritis.org
URL: National Affiliate–www.arthritis.org
Local. Seeks to: discover the cause and improve the methods for the treatment and prevention of arthritis and other rheumatic diseases; increase the number of scientists investigating rheumatic diseases; provide training in rheumatic diseases for more doctors; extend knowledge of arthritis and other rheumatic diseases to the lay public, emphasizing the socioeconomic as well as medical aspects of these diseases. **Affiliated With:** Arthritis Foundation.

3120 ■ Pontiac Area Chamber of Commerce (PACC)
PO Box 534
Pontiac, IL 61764
Ph: (815)844-5131
Fax: (815)844-2600
E-mail: clambert@pontiacchamber.org
URL: http://www.pontiacchamber.org/
Contact: Cheri Lambert, Pres. & CEO
Founded: 1917. **Members:** 219. **Local**. Promotes business and community development in the Pontiac, IL area. Jointly sponsors annual Bluegrass Festival. **Affiliated With:** U.S. Chamber of Commerce. **Publications:** *Chamber Plus*, quarterly. Newsletter.

3121 ■ Sweet Adelines International, Vermillion Valley Show Chapter
Futures Unlimited
210 E Torrance
Pontiac, IL 61764
Ph: (815)796-3288
E-mail: ruth_311@hotmail.com
URL: National Affiliate–www.sweetadelineintl.org
Contact: Ruth Finney, Contact
Local. Advances the musical art form of barbershop harmony through education and performances. Provides education, training and coaching in the development of women's four-part barbershop harmony. **Affiliated With:** Sweet Adelines International.

3122 ■ United Way of Pontiac
PO Box 534
Pontiac, IL 61764-0534
Ph: (815)844-5131
URL: National Affiliate–national.unitedway.org
Local. Affiliated With: United Way of America.

Pontoon Beach

3123 ■ American Legion, Venice-Madison Post 307
3801 Pontoon Rd.
Pontoon Beach, IL 62040
Ph: (618)876-0121
Fax: (309)663-5783
URL: National Affiliate–www.legion.org
Local. Affiliated With: American Legion.

Poplar Grove

3124 ■ American Legion, North Boone Post 205
PO Box 326
Poplar Grove, IL 61065
Ph: (309)663-0361
Fax: (309)663-5783
URL: National Affiliate–www.legion.org
Local. Affiliated With: American Legion.

3125 ■ North Boone High School Chess Club (NBHSCC)
c/o Tom Seeger
17641 Poplar Grove Rd.
Poplar Grove, IL 61065
Ph: (815)765-3311
Fax: (815)765-3316
Contact: Glen Gratz, Chess Adviser
Founded: 1965. **Members:** 25. **Membership Dues:** single, $2 (annual). **Local**. Chess players enrolled at North Boone High School. Promotes the game of chess; holds matches and tournaments. **Awards:** Lehers. **Frequency:** annual. **Type:** recognition. **Affiliated With:** United States Chess Federation. **Conventions/Meetings:** weekly meeting.

Port Byron

3126 ■ American Legion, Coe-Lamb Post 421
PO Box 421
Port Byron, IL 61275
Ph: (309)663-0361
Fax: (309)663-5783
URL: National Affiliate–www.legion.org
Local. Affiliated With: American Legion.

Posen

3127 ■ American Legion, Posen Post 990
PO Box 64
Posen, IL 60469
Ph: (309)663-0361
Fax: (309)663-5783
URL: National Affiliate–www.legion.org
Local. Affiliated With: American Legion.

Potomac

3128 ■ American Legion, Harry Carpenter Post 428
PO Box 245
Potomac, IL 61865
Ph: (217)442-9018
Fax: (309)663-5783
URL: National Affiliate–www.legion.org
Local. Affiliated With: American Legion.

Prairie City

3129 ■ Illinois Draft Horse and Mule Breeders Association
23595 E 1800 St.
Prairie City, IL 61470
Ph: (309)772-3436
E-mail: belgians@arends-sons.com
URL: National Affiliate–www.nasdha.net/RegionalAssoc.htm
Contact: Bill McGrew, Contact
State.

Prairie Du Rocher

3130 ■ American Legion, Illinois Post 622
c/o Joseph Park
PO Box 322
Prairie Du Rocher, IL 62277
Ph: (309)663-0361
Fax: (309)663-5783
URL: National Affiliate–www.legion.org
Contact: Joseph Park, Contact
Local. Affiliated With: American Legion.

Prairie Grove

3131 ■ Wee 'c' Mini Club
c/o Cathy Kalte, Show Chair
4508 Barreville Rd.
Prairie Grove, IL 60012
Ph: (815)477-4241
E-mail: info@weecminiclub.com
URL: http://www.weecminiclub.com
Contact: Cathy Kalte, Show Chair
Local. Affiliated With: National Association of Miniature Enthusiasts.

Prairie du Rocher

3132 ■ Southwestern Illinois Angus Breeders Association
c/o Stephen Gonzalez, Pres.
6784 Bluff Rd.
Prairie du Rocher, IL 62277
Ph: (618)284-7702
URL: National Affiliate–www.angus.org
Contact: Stephen Gonzalez, Pres.
Local. Affiliated With: American Angus Association.

Princeton

3133 ■ American Legion, Princeton Post 125
1549 W Peru St.
Princeton, IL 61356
Ph: (815)875-2794
Fax: (309)663-5783
URL: National Affiliate–www.legion.org
Local. Affiliated With: American Legion.

3134 ■ Bureau County Historical Society (BCHS)
109 Park Ave. W
Princeton, IL 61356
Ph: (815)875-2184
Contact: Mrs. Pam Lange, Dir.
Founded: 1911. **Members:** 500. **Staff:** 6. **Local.** Individuals interested in local history organized to collect and maintain historical artifacts. Operates museum and genealogical library. Conducts genealogical research. Holds two annual open houses; participates in Homestead Festival. **Awards:** Maude C. Trimble History Award. **Frequency:** annual. **Type:** monetary. **Recipient:** for 8th grader with best essay on some aspect of county history. **Absorbed:** (1920) Early Settlers Association. **Conventions/Meetings:** annual dinner.

3135 ■ Bureau County United Way
PO Box 308
Princeton, IL 61356-0308
Ph: (815)872-0821
URL: National Affiliate–national.unitedway.org
Local. Affiliated With: United Way of America.

3136 ■ National Association for Home Care and Hospice, Region V
c/o Gail F. Greene
In-Home Care VNA
33 W Crown St.
Princeton, IL 61356
Ph: (815)875-4114
Fax: (815)875-4112
E-mail: gailgreene@inhomecarevna.com
URL: National Affiliate–www.nahc.org
Contact: Gail F. Greene, Contact
Regional. Develops and promotes high standards of patient care in home care services. Gathers and disseminates home care industry data. Develops public relations strategies. Works to increase the political visibility of home care services. Interprets home care services to governmental and private sector bodies affecting the delivery and financing of such services. **Affiliated With:** National Association for Home Care and Hospice.

3137 ■ Princeton Area Chamber of Commerce and Main Street (PACCMS)
435 S Main St.
Princeton, IL 61356
Ph: (815)875-2616
Fax: (815)875-1156
Free: (877)730-4306
E-mail: ptoncham@theramp.net
URL: http://www.princeton-il.com
Contact: Woody Wendt, Exec.Dir.
Local. Serves as a clearinghouse of business and community information, to legislative issues and reliable business referrals. **Computer Services:** Information services, membership directory. **Formerly:** (2005) Princeton Chamber of Commerce. **Publications:** Newsletter, monthly. **Advertising:** accepted.

Princeville

3138 ■ American Legion, Princeville Post 248
PO Box 136
Princeville, IL 61559
Ph: (309)385-2162
Fax: (309)663-5783
URL: National Affiliate–www.legion.org
Local. Affiliated With: American Legion.

Prophetstown

3139 ■ American Legion, Eshelman-Talley-Doye Post 1191
PO Box 124
Prophetstown, IL 61277
Ph: (309)663-0361
Fax: (309)663-5783
URL: National Affiliate–www.legion.org
Local. Affiliated With: American Legion.

3140 ■ American Legion, Prophetstown Post 522
PO Box 34
Prophetstown, IL 61277
Ph: (815)537-2818
Fax: (309)663-5783
URL: National Affiliate–www.legion.org
Local. Affiliated With: American Legion.

3141 ■ Prophetstown-Lyndon Area Chamber of Commerce
5 Victoria Dr.
Prophetstown, IL 61277-1401
Ph: (815)499-0201
E-mail: ptownms@frontiernet.net
URL: http://www.prophetstownil.com/organizations.html
Contact: Sena Warkins, Contact
Local. Promotes business and community development in the Prophetstown, IL area.

3142 ■ Prophetstown's Main Street Program
306 Washington St.
Prophetstown, IL 61277
Ph: (815)537-5139
Fax: (815)537-5139
E-mail: bbmainstreet@frontiernet.net
URL: http://www.prophetstown.net
Local.

Prospect Heights

3143 ■ Chicago's North Suburbs, Prospect Heights CVB
8 N Elmhurst Rd., Ste.100
Prospect Heights, IL 60070-1567
Ph: (847)577-3666
Fax: (847)590-8490
Free: (800)955-7259
E-mail: info@chicagonorthsuburbs.com
URL: http://www.chicagonorthsuburbs.com
Contact: Ms. Patricia Wharton, Exec.Dir.
Founded: 1986. **Members:** 35. **Membership Dues:** recreation/sports facility, transportation, attraction, banquet facility, entertainment venue, restaurant, shopping, hotel, $100-$500 (annual). **Staff:** 4. **Budget:** $643,651. **For-Profit. Regional.** Mission is to market Chicago's North Suburbs as a meeting and leisure destination; solicit convention and group business; engage in visitor promotions that generate overnight stays in the hotels, retail, food and beverage sales, expenditures at attractions, festivals, events and other visitor related businesses; thereby enhancing the economic stability of the area. **Computer Services:** Information services. **Committees:** Marketing Committee. **Affiliated With:** Hospitality Sales and Marketing Association International; International Association of Convention and Visitor Bureaus; National Tour Association; Ohio Travel Association. **Formerly:** (2004) Prospect Heights Convention and Visitors Bureau. **Publications:** *Chicago's North Suburbs Getaway Guide*, annual. Brochure. Serves as an area visitor's guide. **Price:** free. Alternate Formats: online.

Quincy

3144 ■ Adams County Pork Producers
c/o Robert Gray
639 York St.
Quincy, IL 62301
Ph: (217)228-0557
Fax: (217)592-3602
E-mail: sdarnell@wciagingnetwork.org
Contact: Shay Darnell, Dir.
Local.

3145 ■ Adams County RSVP
c/o Carla Gosney, Dir.
1301 S 48th St.
Quincy, IL 62305
Ph: (217)641-4961
Fax: (217)641-4900
E-mail: gosney@jwcc.edu
URL: http://www.quincynet.com/analists/npmessag/n5395.htm
Contact: Carla Gosney, Dir.
Local. Affiliated With: Retired and Senior Volunteer Program.

3146 ■ American Legion, Quincy Post 37
116 N 8th St.
Quincy, IL 62301
Ph: (217)222-8210
Fax: (309)663-5783
URL: National Affiliate–www.legion.org
Local. Affiliated With: American Legion.

3147 ■ American Postal Workers Union, AFL-CIO - Quincy Area Local Union 77
PO Box 3034
Quincy, IL 62305-3034
Ph: (217)224-8228 (217)224-9227
Fax: (217)224-8228
E-mail: apwuqcy@adams.net
URL: http://users.adams.net/~apwuqcy/
Contact: Don Brown, Pres.
Members: 108. **Local.** AFL-CIO. **Affiliated With:** American Postal Workers Union.

3148 ■ American Welding Society, Mississippi Valley Section 194
c/o Dave Essig, Chm.
Ill-Mo Welding Prdts.
400 Gardner Expy.
Quincy, IL 62301
Ph: (217)222-0603
Fax: (217)222-1312
URL: National Affiliate–www.aws.org
Contact: Jason Carver, Store Mgr.
Local. Professional engineering society in the field of welding. **Affiliated With:** American Welding Society.

3149 ■ Arthritis Foundation, Adams County Branch
c/o Blessing Hospital
Blessing at 14th
Quincy, IL 62301
Ph: (217)228-3208
Fax: (217)228-3213
E-mail: arthritis@adams.net
URL: National Affiliate–www.arthritis.org
Contact: Mary Alice Bybee, Dir.
Local. Seeks to: discover the cause and improve the methods for the treatment and prevention of arthritis and other rheumatic diseases; increase the number of scientists investigating rheumatic diseases; provide training in rheumatic diseases for more doctors; extend knowledge of arthritis and other rheumatic diseases to the lay public, emphasizing the socioeconomic as well as medical aspects of these diseases. **Affiliated With:** Arthritis Foundation.

3150 ■ Girl Scouts of Two Rivers Council
PO Box 809
Quincy, IL 62306-0809
Ph: (217)222-1030
Fax: (217)222-8433
E-mail: girlscouts@gstworivers.org
URL: http://www.gstworivers.org
Contact: Victoria Huntley, Pres.
Local. Young girls and adult volunteers, corporate, government and individual supporters. Strives to develop potential and leadership skills among its members. Conducts trainings, educational programs and outdoor activities.

3151 ■ Historic Quincy Business District
510 Maine St., Ste.300
Quincy, IL 62301
Ph: (217)228-8696
Fax: (217)228-8698
E-mail: quincy@ksni.net
URL: http://www.downtownquincy.com
Local.

3152 ■ Historical Society of Quincy and Adams County (HSQAC)
425 S 12th
Quincy, IL 62301
Ph: (217)222-1835
Contact: Philip Germann, Exec.Dir.
Founded: 1896. **Members:** 500. **Local.** Individuals interested in the history of Adams County, IL. Operates Governor John Wood Mansion Museum. **Libraries: Type:** reference. **Holdings:** 1,150. **Subjects:** Illinois history. **Affiliated With:** Illinois State Historical Society. **Publications:** Newsletter, periodic. **Conventions/Meetings:** annual meeting - always June.

3153 ■ Korean War Veterans Association, Lester Hammond Chapter
c/o Donald W. Goerlich
2929 S 48th St.
Quincy, IL 62305
Ph: (217)224-4251
E-mail: kb9zfknorb@msn.com
URL: National Affiliate–www.kwva.org
Contact: Donald W. Goerlich, Contact
Local. **Affiliated With:** Korean War Veterans Association.

3154 ■ Mothers Against Drunk Driving, Quinsippi Chapter
2901 Broadway No. 135
Quincy, IL 62301
Ph: (217)641-6233
Fax: (217)221-0968
E-mail: ssweetbratdebi@aol.com
URL: National Affiliate–www.madd.org
Contact: Doris Mitchelle, Contact
Local. Victims of drunk driving crashes; concerned citizens. Encourages citizen participation in working towards reform of the drunk driving problem and the prevention of underage drinking. Acts as the voice of victims of drunk driving crashes by speaking on their behalf to communities, businesses, and educational groups. **Affiliated With:** Mothers Against Drunk Driving.

3155 ■ National Active And Retired Federal Employees Association - West Central Ill. 361
2130 Harrison Cot 21A
Quincy, IL 62301
Ph: (217)222-2557
URL: National Affiliate–www.narfe.org
Contact: Charlotte F. Berman, Contact
Local. Protects the retirement future of employees through education. Informs members on issues affecting the retirement. **Affiliated With:** National Association of Retired Federal Employees.

3156 ■ National Technological Honor Society - Vatterrott College - Quincy Illinois
501 N 3rd St.
Quincy, IL 62301
Ph: (217)224-0600
Fax: (217)223-6771
Free: (800)438-5621
E-mail: quincy@vatterott-college.edu
URL: http://www.vatterott-college.edu
Local.

3157 ■ PFLAG Quincy
333 N 6th St.
Quincy, IL 62301
Ph: (217)222-8440
Fax: (217)233-2030
E-mail: kspring@co.adams.il.us
URL: http://www.pflag.org/Illinois.204.0.html
Local. **Affiliated With:** Parents, Families, and Friends of Lesbians and Gays.

3158 ■ Phi Theta Kappa, Alpha Tau Gamma Chapter - John Wood Community College
c/o Sandi Jett, Advisor
1301 S 48th St.
Quincy, IL 62305
Ph: (217)641-4530
E-mail: sjett@jwcc.edu
URL: http://www.ptk.org/directories/chapters/IL/12613-1.htm
Contact: Sandi Jett, Advisor
Local.

3159 ■ Psi Chi, National Honor Society in Psychology - Quincy University
c/o Dept. of Psychology
1800 Coll. Ave.
Quincy, IL 62301
Ph: (217)222-8020
E-mail: bellewe@quincy.edu
URL: National Affiliate–www.psichi.org
Local. **Affiliated With:** Psi Chi, National Honor Society in Psychology.

3160 ■ Quincy Area Chamber of Commerce (QACC)
300 Civic Center Plz., Ste.245
Quincy, IL 62301
Ph: (217)222-7980
Fax: (217)222-3033
E-mail: amyl@adams.net
URL: http://www.quincychamber.org
Contact: Amy Looten, Exec.Dir.
Founded: 1887. **Members:** 500. **Staff:** 4. **Local.** Promotes issues and activities for members who enhance the economic well being and quality of life in the Quincy area. **Committees:** Agri-Business; Ambassador; Leadership; Legislative; Marketing; Technology. **Formerly:** (1897) Young Men's Business Association. **Publications:** *Update*, weekly. Newsletter. Alternate Formats: online.

3161 ■ Quincy Area Chapter of the Society for Human Resource Management
PO Box 715
Quincy, IL 62301
URL: http://www.riverbnd.com/org/shrm
Contact: Darla Rischar, Pres.
Local. Represents the interests of human resource and industrial relations professionals and executives. Promotes the advancement of human resource management.

3162 ■ Quincy Area Convention and Visitors Bureau
300 Civic Ctr. Plz., Ste.237
Quincy, IL 62301
Ph: (217)223-1000
Free: (800)978-4748
E-mail: hcain@quincy-cvb.org
URL: http://www.quincy-cvb.org
Contact: Holly Cain, Dir. of Tourism
Local. **Formerly:** (2005) Quincy Convention and Visitors Bureau.

3163 ■ Quincy Association of Realtors (QAR)
1535 Broadway
Quincy, IL 62301
Ph: (217)228-0652
Fax: (217)228-0670
E-mail: qar@adams.net
URL: http://www.quincyrealtors.com
Contact: Steve Flesner, Pres.
Local. Strives to develop real estate business practices. Advocates the right to own, use and transfer real property. Provides a facility for professional development, research and exchange of information among members and to the general public. **Affiliated With:** National Association of Realtors.

3164 ■ Quincy Citizens Police Academy Alumni Association (QCPAAA)
c/o Quincy Police Dept.
110 S 8th St.
Quincy, IL 62301-4002
Ph: (217)222-9360 (217)228-4470
URL: http://www.ci.quincy.il.us/PublicSafety/police/programs/citizenpolice.htm
Local.

3165 ■ Quincy Exchange Club
PO Box 1163
Quincy, IL 62306
E-mail: niemann7@aol.com
URL: http://www.quincyexchangeclub.org
Contact: Rich Zeidler, Pres.
Local.

3166 ■ Quincy Gun Club
930 Maine St.
Quincy, IL 62301
Fax: (217)222-0759
URL: National Affiliate–www.mynssa.com
Local. **Affiliated With:** National Skeet Shooting Association.

3167 ■ Quincy Noon Kiwanis
PO Box 57
Quincy, IL 62306
E-mail: quincynoonkiwanis@yahoo.com
URL: http://www.kiwanisofquincy.org
Local.

3168 ■ Quincy University Students In Free Enterprise
Quincy Univ.
1800 Coll. Ave.
Quincy, IL 62301
E-mail: blueth@quincy.edu
URL: http://websites.quincy.edu/orgs/sife
Contact: Dr. Tom Blue, SIFE Advisor
Local.

3169 ■ Quincy Wyldlife - Wyldlife
436 S 6th St., Ste.202
Quincy, IL 62301
Ph: (217)223-5470
URL: http://sites.younglife.org/_layouts/ylext/default.aspx?ID=C-4045
Local. Represents the interests of individuals committed to impacting kids' lives and preparing them for the future. Helps young people develop their skills, assets and attitudes to reach their full God-given potential. Reaches suburban, urban, multicultural and disabled kids and teenage mothers. **Affiliated With:** Young Life.

3170 ■ Quincy Young Lives - YoungLives
436 S 6th St., Ste.202
Quincy, IL 62301
Ph: (217)223-5470
URL: http://whereis.younglife.org/FriendlyUrlRedirector.aspx?ID=C-805
Local.

3171 ■ Reserve Officers Association - Department of Illinois, Quincy Chapter 35
c/o CW4 Richard E. Veihl, Pres.
1 Deveron Cir.
Quincy, IL 62301
Ph: (217)228-8566
URL: http://www.ilroa.org
Contact: CW4 Richard E. Veihl, Pres.
Local. Promotes and supports the development and execution of a military policy for the United States. Provides professional development seminars, workshops and programs for its members. **Affiliated With:** Reserve Officers Association of the United States.

3172 ■ SCORE Quincy Tri-State
c/o Quincy Area Chamber of Commerce
300 Civic Center Plz., Ste.245
Quincy, IL 62301
Ph: (217)222-8093
Fax: (217)222-3033
E-mail: score@adams.net
URL: http://www.score-tristate.org
Contact: Ralph Mortimore, Chm.
Founded: 1980. **Regional**. Provides counseling to persons wanting to go into business as well as those already in the business. Sponsors seminars and workshops. **Affiliated With:** SCORE.

3173 ■ United Way of Adams County
300 Civic Ctr. Plz., Ste.260
Quincy, IL 62301
Ph: (217)222-5020
Fax: (217)222-0911
E-mail: info@unitedwayadamsco.org
URL: http://www.unitedwayadamsco.org
Contact: Cheryl Waterman, Exec.Dir.
Founded: 1937. **Local**. **Affiliated With:** United Way of America.

3174 ■ West Central Illinois AIFA
731 Washington St.
Quincy, IL 62301
Ph: (217)224-9533
Fax: (217)224-9536
URL: National Affiliate–www.naifa.org
Local. Represents the interest of insurance and financial advisors. Advocates for a positive legislative and regulatory environment. Enhances business and professional skills of members. **Affiliated With:** National Association of Insurance and Financial Advisors.

3175 ■ Young Life Quincy
436 S 6th St., Ste.202
Quincy, IL 62301
Ph: (217)223-5470
URL: http://whereis.younglife.org/FriendlyUrlRedirector.aspx?ID=A-IL117
Local.

Ramsey

3176 ■ American Legion, Anderson-scroggins Post 460
120 E 5th St.
Ramsey, IL 62080
Ph: (309)663-0361
Fax: (309)663-5783
URL: National Affiliate–www.legion.org
Local. **Affiliated With:** American Legion.

3177 ■ National Active And Retired Federal Employees Association - Effingham 849
PO Box 173
Ramsey, IL 62080-0173
Ph: (618)423-2509
URL: National Affiliate–www.narfe.org
Contact: David W. Hinton, Contact
Local. Protects the retirement future of employees through education. Informs members on issues affecting the retirement. **Affiliated With:** National Association of Retired Federal Employees.

Rankin

3178 ■ American Legion, Lost Five Post 444
113 S Main St.
Rankin, IL 60960
Ph: (309)663-0361
Fax: (309)663-5783
URL: National Affiliate–www.legion.org
Local. **Affiliated With:** American Legion.

Ransom

3179 ■ American Legion, Oscar-Lee-Thomas-Moran Post 674
105 N Lincoln St.
Ransom, IL 60470
Ph: (309)663-0361
Fax: (309)663-5783
URL: National Affiliate–www.legion.org
Local. **Affiliated With:** American Legion.

Rantoul

3180 ■ American Legion, Rantoul Post 287
1132 N Century Blvd.
Rantoul, IL 61866
Ph: (217)893-3401
Fax: (309)663-5783
URL: National Affiliate–www.legion.org
Local. **Affiliated With:** American Legion.

3181 ■ Home School Children's Club
c/o Elizabeth Cothen
Rantoul Public Lib.
106 W Flessner
Rantoul, IL 61866
Ph: (217)893-3955
Fax: (217)893-3961
E-mail: ecothe@ltnet.ltls.org
URL: http://www.rantoul.lib.il.us
Contact: Elizabeth Cothen, Chdns.Libn.
Local. Informal meeting gives homeschooling families an opportunity to interact and teaches children information literacy skills.

3182 ■ Rantoul Area Chamber of Commerce (RACC)
100 W Sangamon Ave., Ste.101
Rantoul, IL 61866
Ph: (217)893-3323
E-mail: dir@pdnt.com
URL: http://www.rantoulchamber.com/RACC
Contact: Joe Bolser, Exec.Dir.
Members: 260. **Staff:** 2. **Local**. Promotes business and community development in Rantoul, IL. Sponsors Fourth of July celebration. **Committees:** Business After Hours; Education; Golf Outing; Governmental Affairs; Leadership Rantoul; Rantoul Revitalization. **Councils:** Industrial. **Programs:** Welcome Ambassador. **Affiliated With:** U.S. Chamber of Commerce. **Publications:** Directory, annual • Newsletter, monthly.

Raymond

3183 ■ American Legion, Triple Star Post 299
PO Box 281
Raymond, IL 62560
Ph: (309)663-0361
Fax: (309)663-5783
URL: National Affiliate–www.legion.org
Local. **Affiliated With:** American Legion.

Red Bud

3184 ■ American Legion, Illinois Post 524
c/o George A. Siegfried
116 E South 1st St.
Red Bud, IL 62278
Ph: (618)282-2251
Fax: (309)663-5783
URL: National Affiliate–www.legion.org
Contact: George A. Siegfried, Contact
Local. **Affiliated With:** American Legion.

3185 ■ Lower Kaskaskia Stakeholders, Inc. (LKSI)
c/o Kaskaskia Regional Port Dist.
154 S. Main St.
Red Bud, IL 62278-1103
Ph: (618)282-3807
Founded: 1999. **Members:** 150. **Membership Dues:** $20 (annual). **Local**.

3186 ■ Phi Theta Kappa, Beta Iota Iota Chapter - Southwestern Illinois College
c/o Judith Quimby
Red Bud Campus
500 W South 4th St.
Red Bud, IL 62278
Ph: (618)282-6682
E-mail: judi.white-quimby@swic.edu
URL: http://www.ptk.org/directories/chapters/IL/21637-1.htm
Contact: Judith Quimby, Advisor
Local.

Renault

3187 ■ American Legion, Renault Post 1215
PO Box 34
Renault, IL 62279
Ph: (309)663-0361
Fax: (309)663-5783
URL: National Affiliate–www.legion.org
Local. **Affiliated With:** American Legion.

Reynolds

3188 ■ American Legion, Community Post 1166
PO Box 376
Reynolds, IL 61279
Ph: (309)372-8990
Fax: (309)663-5783
URL: National Affiliate–www.legion.org
Local. **Affiliated With:** American Legion.

3189 ■ Police and Firemen's Insurance Association - Rock Island Fire Department
c/o Patrick Behr
15019 70th St. W
Reynolds, IL 61279
Ph: (309)372-8273
URL: National Affiliate–www.pfia.net
Contact: Patrick Behr, Contact
Local. Affiliated With: Police and Firemen's Insurance Association.

Richmond

3190 ■ American Legion, Illinois Post 253
c/o Paul C. Hoffman
PO Box 14
Richmond, IL 60071
Ph: (309)663-0361
Fax: (309)663-5783
URL: National Affiliate–www.legion.org
Contact: Paul C. Hoffman, Contact
Local. Affiliated With: American Legion.

3191 ■ Chicagoland Chapter of Avanti Owners Association International
c/o Jerry Thielen, Pres.
9622 Hideaway Ln.
Richmond, IL 60071
Ph: (815)382-7266
E-mail: mandskolish@yahoo.com
URL: National Affiliate–www.aoai.org
Contact: Jerry Thielen, Pres.
Local. Affiliated With: Avanti Owners Association International.

3192 ■ Richmond/Spring Grove Area Chamber of Commerce
10906 Main St.
PO Box 475
Richmond, IL 60071
Ph: (815)678-7742
Fax: (815)678-2070
E-mail: chamber@rsg.org
URL: http://www.rsgchamber.com
Contact: Loretta Podeszwa, Exec.Dir.
Local.

Richton Park

3193 ■ Police and Firemen's Insurance Association - Chicago Southern Suburbs
c/o Jeffery A. Duhoski
5104 Imperial Dr.
Richton Park, IL 60471
Ph: (708)748-0960
URL: National Affiliate–www.pfia.net
Contact: Jeffery A. Duhoski, Contact
Local. Affiliated With: Police and Firemen's Insurance Association.

Ridge Farm

3194 ■ Vintage Chevrolet Club of America, Central Illinois Region No. 7
c/o Wallace Deck, Dir.
PO Box 380
Ridge Farm, IL 61870
Ph: (217)247-2162
URL: National Affiliate–www.vcca.org
Contact: Wallace Deck, Dir.
Local. Affiliated With: Vintage Chevrolet Club of America.

Ridgway

3195 ■ American Legion, Ridgway Post 596
PO Box 267
Ridgway, IL 62979
Ph: (618)272-8561
Fax: (309)663-5783
URL: National Affiliate–www.legion.org
Local. Affiliated With: American Legion.

Ringwood

3196 ■ Upper Midwest Horseshoer's Association No. 21
c/o James H. Woods, Pres.
5312 N Ridgeway Rd.
Ringwood, IL 60072-9608
Ph: (815)728-1960
Fax: (815)653-9496
E-mail: farrier@equus.com
URL: National Affiliate–www.americanfarriers.org
Contact: James H. Woods, Pres.
Local. Affiliated With: American Farrier's Association.

Rio

3197 ■ Classical Association of Illinois
3376 30th Ave.
Rio, IL 61472
Ph: (309)734-2166
E-mail: winev@bhc.edu
URL: http://www.camws.org
Contact: Vicki A. Wine, VP
State. Represents university, college, secondary and elementary teachers of Latin, Greek and all other studies which focus on the world of classical antiquity. Supports and promotes the study of classical languages.

River Forest

3198 ■ American Hellenic Educational Progressive Association - Garfield, Chapter 203
c/o James Tsiolis, Pres.
7918 W Oak Ave.
River Forest, IL 60305
Ph: (708)366-4321
URL: http://www.ahepafamily.org/d13
Contact: James Tsiolis, Pres.
Local. Affiliated With: American Hellenic Educational Progressive Association.

3199 ■ American Library Association, Dominican University
c/o Bethany Bottoms, Pres.
Graduate School of Lib. and Info. Sci.
Dominican Univ.
7900 W Div. St.
River Forest, IL 60305
Ph: (708)524-6541
Fax: (708)366-5360
E-mail: lissa@dom.edu
URL: National Affiliate–www.ala.org
Contact: Bethany Bottoms, Pres.
Founded: 1989. **Local. Affiliated With:** American Library Association.

3200 ■ Chicagoland Gerontological Advanced Practice Nurses
c/o Anna Treinkman, Pres.
744 Keystone Ave.
River Forest, IL 60305-1602
E-mail: anna_d_treinkman@rush.edu
URL: http://www.ncgnp.org
Contact: Anna Treinkman, Pres.
Founded: 1997. **Members:** 60. **Membership Dues:** $20 (annual). **Regional Groups:** 1. **Local.**

3201 ■ Illinois Association of Community Care Program Homecare Providers (IACCPHP)
PO Box 5378
River Forest, IL 60305
Ph: (708)488-8995 (708)218-3110
Fax: (708)488-8922
E-mail: iaccphp@yahoo.com
URL: http://www.idoahomecare.org
Contact: Sue Bohenstengel, Exec.Dir.
Founded: 1988. **Members:** 60. **State.**

3202 ■ Illinois Association of Groundwater Professionals (IAGP)
c/o Sue Bohenstengel, Exec.Dir.
PO Box 5378
River Forest, IL 60305
Ph: (708)488-8993
Fax: (708)488-8922
Free: (800)990-2209
E-mail: iagp2002@yahoo.com
URL: http://www.iagp.org
Contact: Sue Bohenstengel, Exec.Dir.
Membership Dues: contractor, $180 (annual) • firm/corporation, $150 (annual) • individual, $45 (annual). **State. Affiliated With:** National Ground Water Association.

3203 ■ Illinois Curling Association - Oak Park Curling Club
c/o Tom Michael, Pres.
1227 Ashland Ave.
River Forest, IL 60305
Ph: (708)366-8228
E-mail: bigguylor@comcast.net
URL: http://www.goodcurling.net/basics/U.S.%20clubs/illinois.html
Contact: Tom Michael, Pres.
Local. Affiliated With: United States Curling Association.

3204 ■ Psi Chi, National Honor Society in Psychology - Concordia University
c/o Dept. of Psychology
7400 Augusta St.
River Forest, IL 60305-1499
Ph: (708)771-8300 (708)209-3481
Fax: (708)209-3176
E-mail: crfvenzkeb@curf.edu
URL: http://www.psichi.org/chapters/info.asp?chapter_id=889
Contact: Beth Venzke PhD, Advisor
Local.

3205 ■ Psi Chi, National Honor Society in Psychology - Dominican University
c/o Dept. of Psychology
7900 W Div. St.
River Forest, IL 60305-1099
Ph: (708)524-6915 (708)524-6909
Fax: (708)524-5990
E-mail: tschultz@dom.edu
URL: http://www.psichi.org/chapters/info.asp?chapter_id=495
Contact: Theresa M. Schultz PhD, Advisor
Local.

River Grove

3206 ■ American Legion, River Grove Post 335
8664 W Grand Ave.
River Grove, IL 60171
Ph: (708)453-0075
Fax: (309)663-5783
URL: National Affiliate–www.legion.org
Local. Affiliated With: American Legion.

3207 ■ Phi Theta Kappa, Chi Zeta Chapter - Triton College
c/o Charles Fuller
2000 5th Ave.
River Grove, IL 60171
Ph: (708)456-0300
E-mail: cfuller3@triton.edu
URL: http://www.ptk.org/directories/chapters/IL/201-1.htm
Contact: Charles Fuller, Advisor
Local.

3208 ■ West Suburban Cook and Southern Du Page County RSVP
c/o Katherine Deresinski, Dir.
2000 5th Ave.
River Grove, IL 60171

Ph: (708)456-0300
Fax: (708)583-3778
E-mail: kderesin@triton.cc.il.us
URL: http://www.seniorcorps.gov
Contact: Katherine Deresinski, Dir.
Local. **Affiliated With:** Retired and Senior Volunteer Program.

Riverdale

3209 ■ American Legion, Illinois Post 303
c/o Paul Gall
PO Box 278248
Riverdale, IL 60827
Ph: (309)663-0361
Fax: (309)663-5783
URL: National Affiliate–www.legion.org
Contact: Paul Gall, Contact
Local. **Affiliated With:** American Legion.

3210 ■ Illinois Society for Respiratory Care
c/o Douglas McQueary
13932 Michigan Ave.
Riverdale, IL 60827
Ph: (217)522-5558
Fax: (217)522-5557
Free: (800)698-6248
E-mail: phatcher@kishhospital.org
URL: http://www.isrc.org
Contact: Pam Hatcher, Pres.
State. Fosters the improvement of educational programs in respiratory care. Advocates research in the field of respiratory care. **Affiliated With:** American Association for Respiratory Care.

3211 ■ Riverdale Chamber of Commerce (RCC)
208 W 144th St.
Riverdale, IL 60827
Ph: (708)841-3311
Fax: (708)841-1805
E-mail: rdpl2@earthlink.net
URL: http://www.district148.net/rcoc
Contact: Adelle Swanson, Sec.
Founded: 1958. **Members:** 85. **Local**. Promotes business and community development in Riverdale, IL. **Publications:** none.

3212 ■ United States Naval Sea Cadet Corps - Gen. Colin L. Powell Division
PO Box 277847
Riverdale, IL 60827-5713
Ph: (708)275-9194
E-mail: ltjgwls@aol.com
Contact: LTJG Abe Wilson, Contact
Local. Works to instill good citizenship and patriotism in youth. Encourages qualities such as personal neatness, loyalty, obedience, dependability, and responsibility to others. Offers courses in physical fitness and military drill, first aid, water safety, basic seamanship, and naval history and traditions. **Affiliated With:** Naval Sea Cadet Corps.

Riverside

3213 ■ American Cancer Society, Riverside Regional Office
7234 W Ogden Ave., Ste.3 S
Riverside, IL 60546
Ph: (708)484-8541
Fax: (708)484-3179
URL: http://www.cancer.org
Contact: Lea Morgan, Regional VP
Local. **Affiliated With:** American Cancer Society.

3214 ■ Riverside Chamber of Commerce
PO Box 7
Riverside, IL 60546
Ph: (708)802-1631 (708)447-2261
E-mail: business@riversidechamberofcommerce.com
URL: http://www.riversidechamberofcommerce.com
Contact: David Moravecek, Pres.
Membership Dues: active (with active business), $100 (annual) • associate (without an active business), $60 (annual). **Local**. Promotes business and community development in Riverside, IL area. **Computer Services:** Information services, membership directory. **Formerly:** (2005) Riverside Township Chamber of Commerce.

Riverwoods

3215 ■ Reserve Officers Association - Department of Illinois, Fort Sheridan Chapter 48
c/o Col. Marshall J. Goby, Pres.
592 Eagle Ct.
Riverwoods, IL 60015-3866
Ph: (847)940-0353
URL: http://www.ilroa.org
Contact: Col. Marshall J. Goby, Pres.
Local. Promotes and supports the development and execution of a military policy for the United States. Provides professional development seminars, workshops and programs for its members. **Affiliated With:** Reserve Officers Association of the United States.

Roanoke

3216 ■ American Legion, Roanoke Post 463
PO Box 377
Roanoke, IL 61561
Ph: (309)923-7092
Fax: (309)663-5783
URL: National Affiliate–www.legion.org
Local. **Affiliated With:** American Legion.

3217 ■ Central Illinois Woodturners (CIW)
c/o Terry Quiram, Pres.
301 East Ct.
Roanoke, IL 61561
Ph: (309)923-7500
E-mail: walnut1950@yahoo.com
URL: http://www.centralillinoiswoodturners.com
Contact: Terry Quiram, Pres.
Local. Represents amateur and professional woodturners, gallery owners, wood and equipment suppliers, and collectors. **Affiliated With:** American Association of Woodturners.

Robinson

3218 ■ American Legion, Illinois Post 69
c/o Ernest M. Coulter
308 E Main St.
Robinson, IL 62454
Ph: (618)546-1418
Fax: (309)663-5783
URL: National Affiliate–www.legion.org
Contact: Ernest M. Coulter, Contact
Local. **Affiliated With:** American Legion.

3219 ■ Crawford County Genealogical Society
PO Box 120
Robinson, IL 62454
URL: http://www.rootsweb.com/~ilcrawfo
Contact: Sue Jones, Pres.
Founded: 1976. **Members:** 175. **Membership Dues:** $10 (annual). **Local**. Individuals interested in the family history of Crawford County in IL. Does such things as update research materials and repair tombstones. **Libraries:** **Type:** reference. **Holdings:** 3,000; audiovisuals. **Subjects:** aspects of general research and genealogy. **Publications:** *Genealogy Newsletter*, 3/year. Full of Crawford Co. records. **Price:** included with membership. **Circulation:** 200. **Advertising:** accepted. **Conventions/Meetings:** quarterly workshop - February, May, August, November.

3220 ■ Crawford County Habitat for Humanity
PO Box 957
Robinson, IL 62454
Ph: (618)546-0171
E-mail: prairie1@shawneelink.net
URL: http://www.geocities.com/cchfh
Local. **Affiliated With:** Habitat for Humanity International.

3221 ■ Phi Theta Kappa, Alpha Iota Epsilon Chapter - Lincoln Trail College
c/o Ms. Susan Polgar, Advisor
11220 State Hwy. 1
Robinson, IL 62454
Ph: (618)544-8657
E-mail: polgars@iecc.edu
URL: http://www.ptk.org/directories/chapters/IL/207-1.htm
Contact: Ms. Susan Polgar, Advisor
Membership Dues: life (student), $58. **Staff:** 2. **Regional Groups:** 1. **State Groups:** 1. **Local Groups:** 1. **Local**.

Rochelle

3222 ■ American Legion, Rochelle Post 403
900 Carrie Ave., Apt. 9
Rochelle, IL 61068
Ph: (815)562-6117
Fax: (309)663-5783
URL: National Affiliate–www.legion.org
Local. **Affiliated With:** American Legion.

3223 ■ American Rabbit Breeders Association, Midwest Holland Lop Club
c/o Bob Bemis
111 E Orchard Hills Dr.
Rochelle, IL 61068
Ph: (815)562-1729
E-mail: coyotesprings@attbi.com
URL: http://www.nordickrabbits.com/specialt.htm
Contact: Bob Bemis, Contact
Local. **Affiliated With:** American Rabbit Breeders Association.

3224 ■ Gardeners of America/Men's Garden Clubs of America - Rochelle Gardeners of America
c/o Robert Jacobs, Pres.
1105 N Main St.
Rochelle, IL 61068
Ph: (815)562-6365
URL: National Affiliate–www.tgoa-mgca.org
Contact: Robert Jacobs, Pres.
Local.

3225 ■ Illinois Environmental Health Association (IEHA)
PO Box 609
Rochelle, IL 61068
Ph: (815)562-1040
Fax: (815)562-6448
E-mail: ieha2001@aol.com
URL: http://www.ieha.us
Contact: Diana Rawlings, Pres.
State. Advances the environmental health and protection profession. Provides educational and training opportunities for members. Works to establish standards of competence and ethics for the profession. **Affiliated With:** National Environmental Health Association.

3226 ■ Retail, Wholesale and Department Store Union District Council, UFCW, AFL-CIO, CLC Local Union 578
106 Winward Ln.
Rochelle, IL 61068
Ph: (815)562-5808
URL: http://www.rwdsu-cs.org/local578.html
Contact: Michael Williams, Sec.-Treas.
Members: 117. **Local**. **Affiliated With:** Retail, Wholesale and Department Store Union.

3227 ■ Rochelle Area Chamber of Commerce
350 May Mart Dr.
Rochelle, IL 61068-0220
Ph: (815)562-4189
Fax: (815)562-4180
E-mail: chamber@rochelle.net
URL: http://www.rochellechamber.org
Contact: Jeana Abbott, Exec.Dir.
Membership Dues: retail (based on number of employees), $210-$1,050 (annual) • financial institution (per million in deposits), $12 (annual) • association, $105 (annual) • nonprofit, $105 (annual) • individual, $105 (annual). **Local**. Represents, educates and supports member businesses, promoting economic vitality and enhancing the quality of life. **Computer Services:** Information services, member listing. **Publications:** *Community Guide*, annual. Membership Directory • Newsletter, monthly. Alternate Formats: online.

Rochester

3228 ■ American Legion, Harry Fogle Post 274
PO Box 485
Rochester, IL 62563
Ph: (309)663-0361
Fax: (309)663-5783
URL: National Affiliate–www.legion.org
Local. **Affiliated With:** American Legion.

3229 ■ Illinois Mountain Bicyclists Coalition
517 Burberry Ln.
Rochester, IL 62563
Ph: (217)899-5125
E-mail: slmrides@yahoo.com
URL: http://sports.groups.yahoo.com/group/imbc
State. **Affiliated With:** International Mountain Bicycling Association.

3230 ■ Illinois Professional Land Surveyors Association (IPLSA)
c/o Robert E. Church, Exec.Dir.
PO Box 588
Rochester, IL 62563
Ph: (217)498-8102
Fax: (217)498-8489
E-mail: mchurch245@aol.com
URL: http://www.iplsa.org
Contact: Robert E. Church, Exec.Dir.
Founded: 1928. **Members:** 1,050. **Staff:** 2. **State**. Represents individuals and firms engaged in land surveying. Establishes and maintains survey standards; acts as the single reference source for survey information unique to Illinois. **Affiliated With:** American Congress on Surveying and Mapping. **Publications:** *Illinois Surveyor*, quarterly. Newsletter. **Circulation:** 1,200. **Advertising:** accepted • Directory, annual. **Conventions/Meetings:** annual conference.

3231 ■ Illinois Stewardship Alliance (ISA)
PO Box 648
Rochester, IL 62563
Ph: (217)498-9707
Fax: (217)498-9235
E-mail: isa@illinoisstewardshipalliance.org
URL: http://www.illinoisstewardshipalliance.org
Contact: Gayle Keiser, Exec.Dir.
State. Promotes a safe and nutritious food system.

3232 ■ Lincoln Orbit Earth Science Society
c/o Judith Washburn, Pres.
107 Deer Creek Rd.
Rochester, IL 62563
E-mail: jrwashburn2@msn.com
URL: National Affiliate–www.amfed.org
Contact: Janice Bryant, Sec.
Local. Aims to further the study of Earth Sciences and the practice of lapidary arts and mineralogy. **Affiliated With:** American Federation of Mineralogical Societies.

Rock Falls

3233 ■ American Legion, Rock Falls Post 902
PO Box 303
Rock Falls, IL 61071
Ph: (309)663-0361
Fax: (309)663-5783
URL: National Affiliate–www.legion.org
Local. **Affiliated With:** American Legion.

3234 ■ Blackhawk Hills Resource Conservation and Development Council
102 E Rte. 30
Canal Plz., Ste.2
Rock Falls, IL 61071
Ph: (815)625-3854
Fax: (815)625-4072
E-mail: dave.dornbusch@il.usda.gov
URL: http://www.blackhawkhills.com/rcd.shtml
Contact: Dave Dornbusch, Coor.
Local. **Affiliated With:** National Association of Resource Conservation and Development Councils.

3235 ■ Brotherhood of Maintenance of Way Employees, AFL-CIO, CLC - Chicago and Northwestern System Federation
c/o K. L. Bushman, Gen.Chm.
28151 Buena Vista Dr.
Rock Falls, IL 61071
Ph: (815)626-6636
E-mail: kbushman@insightbb.com
URL: National Affiliate–www.bmwe.org
Contact: K. L. Bushman, Gen.Chm.
Members: 23. **Regional**. **Affiliated With:** Brotherhood of Maintenance of Way Employees.

3236 ■ Rock Falls Chamber of Commerce (RFCC)
601 W 10th St.
Rock Falls, IL 61071-1576
Ph: (815)625-4500
Fax: (815)625-4558
E-mail: rockfallschamber@essex1.com
URL: http://www.rockfallschamber.com/index.html
Contact: Doug Wiersema, Pres./CEO
Founded: 1956. **Members:** 360. **Membership Dues:** family, $75 (annual) • individual, $50 (annual). **Staff:** 3. **Local**. Promotes business and community development in Whiteside County, IL. **Awards:** Shoulder to the Wheel. **Frequency:** annual. **Type:** recognition. **Recipient:** work for better places in which to live. **Publications:** *Chamber News Highlights*, monthly. Newsletter. **Advertising:** accepted. **Conventions/Meetings:** annual dinner • quarterly luncheon • meeting - 3/year.

Rock Island

3237 ■ AGC of The Quad Cities
520 24th St.
Rock Island, IL 61201
Ph: (309)788-7406
Fax: (309)794-0568
E-mail: tondi@agcqc.org
URL: http://agcqc.org
Contact: Mr. Steven P. Tondi, Pres./CEO
Founded: 1935. **Members:** 12. **Staff:** 2. **Budget:** $175,000. **Local**. Construction General contractors in southeastern Iowa and northeastern Illinois. **Formerly:** Quad City Builders Association. **Publications:** *Bulletins*, periodic.

3238 ■ American Cancer Society, Rock Island - Northwest Regional
3727 Blackhawk Rd.
Rock Island, IL 61201
Ph: (309)794-0601
Fax: (309)793-3251
Free: (800)322-4337
URL: http://www.cancer.org
Contact: Tonda Thompson, Regional VP
Local. **Affiliated With:** American Cancer Society.

3239 ■ American Legion, Illinois Post 591
1326 4th Ave.
Rock Island, IL 61201
Ph: (309)663-0361
Fax: (309)663-5783
URL: National Affiliate–www.legion.org
Contact: Charles A. Young, Contact
Local. **Affiliated With:** American Legion.

3240 ■ American Legion, Rock Island Post 200
PO Box 6621
Rock Island, IL 61201
Ph: (309)788-4009
Fax: (309)663-5783
URL: National Affiliate–www.legion.org
Local. **Affiliated With:** American Legion.

3241 ■ Bi-State Regional Commission
1504 Third Ave.
Rock Island, IL 61204
Ph: (309)793-6300 (309)793-6302
Fax: (309)793-6305
E-mail: dbulat@bistateonline.org
URL: http://www.bistateonline.org
Contact: Denise Bulat, Exec.Dir.
Regional.

3242 ■ Central Illinois TAM Users Group
c/o Cleaveland Insurance Group
1617 2nd Ave., No. 200
Rock Island, IL 61201
Ph: (309)794-9700
Fax: (309)786-9603
E-mail: taylor@cleavelandinsurance.com
URL: National Affiliate–www.ascnet.org
Contact: Deborah Taylor, Pres.
Local. Represents insurance agents and brokers using the Agency Manager software. Promotes successful automation and business practices through communication, education, and advocacy. **Affiliated With:** Applied Systems Client Network.

3243 ■ Friends of Off-Road Cycling (FORC)
1255 37th St.
Rock Island, IL 61201
E-mail: centuryelectric@mchsi.com
URL: http://www.qcforc.org
Contact: Rick Wren, Coor.
Local. **Affiliated With:** International Mountain Bicycling Association.

3244 ■ Girl Scouts of The Mississippi Valley
2011 Second Ave.
Rock Island, IL 61201
Ph: (309)788-0833
Fax: (309)788-0836
Free: (800)798-0833
E-mail: info@girlscouts-mvc.org
URL: http://www.girlscouts-mvc.org
Contact: Diane Koster, Contact
Local. Young girls and adult volunteers, corporate, government and individual supporters. Strives to develop potential and leadership skills among its members. Conducts trainings, educational programs and outdoor activities.

3245 ■ Illinois Prairie State Chiropractic Association (IPSCA)
PO Box 4147
Rock Island, IL 61204-4174
Ph: (309)732-3233
Fax: (309)732-3227
E-mail: jreyes@illinoischiropractors.org
URL: http://www.illinoischiropractors.org
Contact: Eric Anderson DC, Pres.
Founded: 1950. **State**.

3246 ■ Jewish Federation of the Quad Cities
c/o Allan Ross, Exec. Dir.
1705 2nd Ave., Ste.405
Rock Island, IL 61201
Ph: (309)793-1300
Fax: (309)793-1345
Contact: Allan Ross, Exec.Dir.

3247 ■ Korean War Veterans Association, Quad Cities Chapter
c/o Ronald Sears
1301 2nd Ave., No. 3W Apt. 1
Rock Island, IL 61201
Ph: (309)786-5391
E-mail: f131sgt@mchsi.com
URL: National Affiliate–www.kwva.org
Contact: Ronald Sears, Contact
Local. Affiliated With: Korean War Veterans Association.

3248 ■ Phi Theta Kappa, Beta Zeta Beta Chapter - Trinity College of Nursing
c/o Cathy Konrad
2122 25th Ave.
Rock Island, IL 61201
Ph: (309)779-7724
E-mail: konradc@trinityqc.com
URL: http://www.ptk.org/directories/chapters/IL/20764-1.htm
Contact: Cathy Konrad, Advisor
Local.

3249 ■ Popular Astronomy Club
2232-24th St.
Rock Island, IL 61201
Ph: (309)786-6844
E-mail: prc29@aol.com
URL: http://pacastronomy.50megs.com
Contact: Lee Farrar, Contact
Local. Promotes the science of astronomy. Works to encourage and coordinate activities of amateur astronomical societies. Fosters observational and computational work and craftsmanship in various fields of astronomy. **Affiliated With:** Astronomical League.

3250 ■ Psi Chi, National Honor Society in Psychology - Augustana College
c/o Dept. of Psychology
639 38th St.
Rock Island, IL 61201-2296
Ph: (309)794-7300 (309)794-7355
Fax: (309)794-7431
E-mail: psfenwick@augustana.edu
URL: National Affiliate–www.psichi.org
Local. Affiliated With: Psi Chi, National Honor Society in Psychology.

3251 ■ Quad City Chapter of the Society of Financial Service Professionals
c/o Willard Gombert, CLU, Pres.
Financial Architects Inc.
1800 3rd Ave., Ste.515
Rock Island, IL 61201-1201
Ph: (309)788-1970
Fax: (309)788-1958
E-mail: bill@tfausa.com
URL: http://www.sfsp.net/quadcity
Contact: Willard Gombert CLU, Pres.
Regional. Represents the interests of financial advisers. Fosters the development of professional responsibility. Helps clients achieve their personal and business-related financial goals. **Affiliated With:** Society of Financial Service Professionals.

3252 ■ Quad City Conservation Alliance (QCCA)
c/o Richard Miller, Pres.
2621 4th Ave.
Rock Island, IL 61201
Ph: (309)788-5912
Fax: (309)788-9619
Free: (877)734-1565
E-mail: qcca@qconline.com
URL: http://www.qccaexpocenter.com
Contact: Craig Elvert, Facility Mgr.
Local. Presents shows to support conservation projects within a 75 mile radius of the Quad Cities. Provides facility that can be rented for shows and expositions.

3253 ■ Quad City Development Group (QCDG)
c/o Thomas W. Hart, Pres.
1830 2nd Ave., Ste.200
Rock Island, IL 61201
Ph: (309)788-7436 (563)326-1005
Fax: (309)788-4964
E-mail: thart@quadcities.org
URL: http://www.quadcities.org
Contact: Thomas W. Hart, Pres.
Founded: 1962. **Members:** 135. **Staff:** 9. **Regional Groups:** 1. **State Groups:** 3. **Languages:** English, German. **Regional.** Retains local companies and helps them grow. Markets the Quad Cities to targeted companies across the nation and throughout the world to attract jobs and investment. **Publications:** *Update*, monthly. Newsletter. Features the activities of Development Group. **Price:** free. **Circulation:** 635.

3254 ■ Quad City Estate Planning Council (QCEPC)
c/o Lori Duffy
7907 7th St. W
Rock Island, IL 61201
Ph: (309)732-5042
Fax: (309)794-6488
E-mail: lduffy@ambankqc.com
URL: http://councils.naepc.org
Contact: Mr. Roger Schemmel, Pres.
Founded: 1962. **Members:** 130. **Membership Dues:** professional, $150 (annual). **Regional.** Advances the goal of estate planning in Scott, Clinton, Jackson and Muscatine counties in Iowa and Rock Island, Henry, Knox, Mercer and Whiteside counties in Illinois. Provides educational opportunities to members comprised of attorneys, CPAs, chartered life underwriters, trust officers and others who are actively practicing estate planning. Strives to keep the members abreast of changes in the estate planning arena. **Affiliated With:** National Association of Estate Planners and Councils.

3255 ■ Quad City Illinois and Iowa Federation of Labor (QCIIFL)
311 1/2 21st. St.
Rock Island, IL 61201
Ph: (309)788-1303
Contact: Jerry Messer, Pres.
Regional. Labor unions. Represents the interests of labor; lobbies for favorable legislation. **Affiliated With:** AFL-CIO.

3256 ■ Rock Island County Arc
4016 Ninth St.
Rock Island, IL 61201
Ph: (309)786-6474
Fax: (309)786-9861
E-mail: arcricil@arcric.org
URL: http://www.arcric.org
Contact: Art McElhaney, Exec.Dir.
Local. Parents, professional workers, and others interested in individuals with mental retardation. Works to promote services, research, public understanding, and legislation for people with mental retardation and their families. **Affiliated With:** Arc of the United States.

3257 ■ Rock Island County Chapter of Pheasants Forever
c/o Denny Hild
2221-39th St.
Rock Island, IL 61201
Ph: (309)786-2191
E-mail: pf4ever98@qconline.com
Contact: Chuck Wahlberg, Sec.
Local. Affiliated With: Pheasants Forever.

3258 ■ RSVP of Scott IA and Rock Island IL
c/o Suzy Hartung, Dir.
729-34th Ave.
Rock Island, IL 61201-5950
Ph: (309)793-6800
Fax: (309)793-6807
E-mail: shartung@wiaaa.org
URL: http://www.wiaaa.org/rsvp_home.htm
Contact: Suzy Hartung, Dir.
Local. Affiliated With: Retired and Senior Volunteer Program.

3259 ■ Society of American Military Engineers, Rock Island Post
Clock Tower Bldg.
Rock Island, IL 61204-2004
Ph: (309)794-5790
E-mail: duane.p.gapinski.col@usace.army.mil
URL: http://posts.same.org/rockisland
Contact: Col. Duane Gapinski, Pres.
Local. Works to advance the science of military engineering. Promotes and facilitates engineering support for national security. Develops and enhances relationships and competencies among uniformed services, public and private sector engineers and related professionals.

3260 ■ Upper Mississippi River Conservation Committee (UMRCC)
4469 48th Avenue Ct.
Rock Island, IL 61201
Ph: (309)793-5800
Fax: (309)793-5804
E-mail: umrcc@mississippi-river.com
URL: http://www.mississippi-river.com/umrcc
Contact: Martin Konrad, Chm.
Founded: 1943. **Members:** 200. **Staff:** 1. **Budget:** $10,000. **Regional Groups:** 1. Natural resources managers and biologists. Objectives are: to promote the preservation and wise use of the natural and recreational resources of the upper Mississippi River; to formulate policies, plans, and programs for conducting cooperative studies. Creates cooperative projects that include creel census, commercial fishing statistics, waterfowl and wildlife censuses, hunter surveys, fish tagging, and collection of boating and other recreational use data. Helps to define land management for public properties such as public hunting grounds, wildlife refuges, flood plain reserves, and recreational lands. Works as an advisory body on all technical aspects of fish, wildlife, and recreation. Makes recommendations on conservation laws, programs, and legislation to state and federal governments. Maintains a continuing evaluation of the effects of water control regulation and recreational resources. Sponsors research programs. **Libraries: Type:** reference. **Holdings:** 5,000. **Subjects:** Mississippi River resources management. **Awards:** UMRCC Conservation Award. **Frequency:** annual. **Type:** recognition. **Computer Services:** database, Upper Mississippi River issues • online services. **Working Groups:** Fisheries; Law Enforcement; Recreation; Water Quality; Wildlife. **Publications:** *UMRCC Annual Proceedings*, annual. **Price:** $15.00 • Newsletter, bimonthly. **Price:** free. **Circulation:** 700. Alternate Formats: online • Reports. Alternate Formats: online. **Conventions/Meetings:** annual meeting and conference (exhibits) - always March.

Rockford

3261 ■ Alcoholics Anonymous World Services, Rockford Area Intergroup
229 N Church St.
Rockford, IL 61101
Ph: (815)968-0333
Fax: (815)968-6733
URL: National Affiliate–www.aa.org
Contact: John Dunn, Contact
Local. Individuals recovering from alcoholism. AA maintains that members can solve their common problem and help others achieve sobriety through a twelve step program that includes sharing their experience, strength, and hope with each other. **Affiliated With:** Alcoholics Anonymous World Services.

3262 ■ Alzheimer's Association - Greater Illinois Chapter, Rockford Regional Program Center
4777 E State St.
Rockford, IL 61108
Ph: (815)484-1300
Fax: (815)484-9286
Free: (800)272-3900
E-mail: erna.colborn@alz.org
URL: http://www.alzheimers-illinois.org
Contact: Erna Colborn, Senior VP
Founded: 1980. **Staff:** 41. **Regional Groups:** 6. **State Groups:** 1. **Languages:** English, Polish, Spanish. **Nonmembership**. **State**. Serves Winnebago, Boone, DeKalb, Ogle, Stephenson and McHenry counties in Illinois. **Libraries: Type:** open to the public; lending; reference. **Holdings:** 150; articles, books, periodicals, video recordings. **Subjects:** dementia, grief, caregiving, Alzheimer's disease.

3263 ■ American Cancer Society, Rockford - Northern Regional
4312 E State St.
Rockford, IL 61108
Ph: (815)229-1287
Fax: (815)229-1363
Free: (800)892-9296
URL: http://www.cancer.org
Contact: David Riggs, Regional VP
Local. Affiliated With: American Cancer Society.

3264 ■ American Hiking Society - Atwood Outdoor Education Center - Rockford Park District
2685 New Milford School Rd.
Rockford, IL 61109
Ph: (815)874-7576
Fax: (815)874-2467
E-mail: katietownsend@rockfordparkdistrict.org
URL: http://www.rockfordparkdistrict.org
Contact: Harris Agnew, Contact
Local.

3265 ■ American Legion, Daniel Post 864
5419 Garden Plain Ave.
Rockford, IL 61125
Ph: (309)663-0361
Fax: (309)663-5783
URL: National Affiliate–www.legion.org
Local. Affiliated With: American Legion.

3266 ■ American Legion, Illinois Post 904
c/o William R. Marks
3715 Tennessee Dr.
Rockford, IL 61108
Ph: (309)663-0361
Fax: (309)663-5783
URL: National Affiliate–www.legion.org
Contact: William R. Marks, Contact
Local. Affiliated With: American Legion.

3267 ■ American Legion, Illinois Post 1207
c/o Lt. Robert C.A. Carlson
3835 Broadway
Rockford, IL 61108
Ph: (815)397-6672
Fax: (309)663-5783
URL: National Affiliate–www.legion.org
Contact: Lt. Robert C.A. Carlson, Contact
Local. Affiliated With: American Legion.

3268 ■ American Legion, Jefferson-Horton Post 340
1010 S Main St.
Rockford, IL 61101
Ph: (309)663-0361
Fax: (309)663-5783
URL: National Affiliate–www.legion.org
Local. Affiliated With: American Legion.

3269 ■ American Red Cross, Rock River Chapter
727 N Church St.
Rockford, IL 61103
Ph: (815)963-8471
Fax: (815)963-0407
URL: http://chapters.redcross.org/il/rockriver
Local.

3270 ■ American Welding Society, Blackhawk Section 113
c/o Victor Hunter
Carpenters L.U. 792
213 S First St.
Rockford, IL 61104
Ph: (815)963-8675
URL: National Affiliate–www.aws.org
Local. Professional engineering society in the field of welding. **Affiliated With:** American Welding Society.

3271 ■ APICS, The Association for Operations Management - Rock Valley Chapter
PO Box 6021
Rockford, IL 61125
Ph: (815)226-2869
E-mail: president@apics-rockvalley.org
URL: http://www.apics-rockvalley.org
Contact: Shannon Euclide, Pres.
Local. Provides information and services in production and inventory management and related areas to enable members, enterprises and individuals to add value to their business performance. **Affiliated With:** APICS - The Association for Operations Management.

3272 ■ Arc of Winnebago, Boone and Ogle
401 N First St.
Rockford, IL 61107-3978
Ph: (815)965-3455
Fax: (815)965-3678
URL: http://www.arcwbo.org
Contact: Jackie Neil Boss, Exec.Dir.
Local. Parents, professional workers, and others interested in individuals with mental retardation. Works to promote services, research, public understanding, and legislation for people with mental retardation and their families. **Affiliated With:** Arc of the United States.

3273 ■ Arthritis Foundation, Winnebago County Branch
c/o Rockford Health System
2400 Rockton Ave., Ste.207
Rockford, IL 61103
Ph: (815)971-6380
Fax: (815)971-6455
E-mail: greaterillinois@arthritis.org
URL: National Affiliate–www.arthritis.org
Contact: Zickie Fogel, Dir.
Local. Seeks to: discover the cause and improve the methods for the treatment and prevention of arthritis and other rheumatic diseases; increase the number of scientists investigating rheumatic diseases; provide training in rheumatic diseases for more doctors; extend knowledge of arthritis and other rheumatic diseases to the lay public, emphasizing the socioeconomic as well as medical aspects of these diseases. **Affiliated With:** Arthritis Foundation.

3274 ■ Blackhawk Bicycle and Ski Club
c/o Bill Tucker, Pres.
PO Box 6443
Rockford, IL 61125-1443
Ph: (815)874-9862
E-mail: wepedl1@msn.com
URL: http://www.aeroinc.net/users/bbsc
Contact: Bill Tucker, Pres.
Local. Affiliated With: International Mountain Bicycling Association.

3275 ■ Catholic League for Religious and Civil Rights, Rockford, IL Chapter
c/o John Boreen, Dir. of Communications
322 W State St., Ste.1100
Rockford, IL 61101
Ph: (815)962-6088
Fax: (815)962-0034
URL: National Affiliate–www.catholicleague.org
Contact: John Boreen, Contact
Local. Affiliated With: Catholic League for Religious and Civil Rights.

3276 ■ Epilepsy Foundation of North/Central Illinois
321 W State St., Ste.208
Rockford, IL 61101-1119
Ph: (815)964-2689
Fax: (815)964-2731
Free: (800)221-2689
E-mail: efncil@efncil.org
URL: http://www.efncil.org
Contact: Vic Verni, Exec.Dir.
State. Strives to prevent and control epilepsy and improve the lives of those who have it. **Boards:** Advisory. **Affiliated With:** Epilepsy Foundation. **Publications:** *Wavelength*, quarterly. Newsletter. Contains national news, epilepsy education and news on county service area. **Price:** free.

3277 ■ Figure Skating Club of Rockford
2591 Hickory Ave.
Rockford, IL 61114
E-mail: csio@membersalliance.org
URL: National Affiliate–www.usfigureskating.org
Contact: Cheryl Sio, Contact
Local. Provides programs to encourage participation and achievement in the sport of figure skating on ice. Defines and maintains uniform standards of skating proficiency. Organizes and sponsors competitions and exhibitions for the purpose of stimulating interest in figure skating. **Affiliated With:** United States Figure Skating Association.

3278 ■ Gardeners of America/Men's Garden Clubs of America - Boone County Gardeners of America
c/o Bruce Campbell, Pres.
9524 Roanoak Dr.
Rockford, IL 61107
Ph: (815)332-4089
URL: National Affiliate–www.tgoa-mgca.org
Contact: Bruce Campbell, Pres.
Local.

3279 ■ Gardeners of America/Men's Garden Clubs of America - Rockford Area Gardeners of America
c/o James Campobello, Pres.
2086 Azure Ct.
Rockford, IL 61108
Ph: (815)398-1916
URL: National Affiliate–www.tgoa-mgca.org
Contact: James Campobello, Pres.
Local.

3280 ■ Girl Scouts - Rock River Valley
2101 Auburn St.
Rockford, IL 61103
Ph: (815)962-5591
Fax: (815)962-5658
Free: (800)242-5591
E-mail: ahamaker@girlscoutsrrv.org
URL: http://www.girlscoutsrrv.org
Contact: Amanda Hamaker, Dir. of Community Support
Local.

3281 ■ IEEE Computer Society, Rock River Valley Chapter (RRVS CS/CSS)
c/o Robert Parro
5922 Thatcher Dr.
Rockford, IL 61114-5568
Ph: (815)877-6670
E-mail: b.parro@ieee.org
URL: http://ieee.flask.com/rrvs/css.htm
Contact: Robert Parro, Contact
Local. Affiliated With: IEEE Computer Society.

3282 ■ International Association of Machinists and Aerospace Workers, LL-1553
1553 9th St. S
Rockford, IL 61104
Ph: (815)965-6701
E-mail: webmaster_1@charter.net
URL: http://www.iam1553.org
Contact: Lloyd Jefferson, Pres.
Members: 448. **Local**. **Affiliated With:** International Association of Machinists and Aerospace Workers.

3283 ■ International Union of Bricklayers and Allied Craftworkers, AFL-CIO-CLC Local Union 6
661 Southrock Dr.
Rockford, IL 61102
Ph: (815)963-5311
E-mail: local6@rockriver.net
URL: http://www.bac6il.org
Contact: Ed Tegland, Pres.
Members: 1,450. **Local**. **Affiliated With:** International Union of Bricklayers and Allied Craftworkers.

3284 ■ Junior Achievement, Rock River Valley
c/o Kathy Siedenburg, Pres.
1040 N 2nd St.
Rockford, IL 61107
Ph: (815)963-8413
Fax: (815)966-2034
E-mail: ksiedenburgja@choiceonemail.com
URL: http://rockford.ja.org
Local. **Affiliated With:** Junior Achievement.

3285 ■ Kiwanis Club of Rockford
c/o Robert J. McLaughlin, Sec.
PO Box 1573
Rockford, IL 61110
Ph: (815)229-5864
E-mail: contact@rockfordkiwanisclub.org
URL: http://www.rockfordkiwanisclub.org
Contact: John Crandall, Pres.
Local.

3286 ■ Korean War Veterans Association, Greater Rockford Chapter
c/o Jack F. Philbrick
1601 Scottswood Rd.
Rockford, IL 61107-2069
Ph: (815)226-1601
E-mail: felbrigge@insightbb.com
URL: National Affiliate–www.kwva.org
Contact: Jack F. Philbrick, Contact
Local. **Affiliated With:** Korean War Veterans Association.

3287 ■ Literacy Council
982 N Main St.
Rockford, IL 61103-7061
Ph: (815)963-7323
Fax: (815)963-7347
E-mail: read@theliteracycouncil.org
URL: http://www.theliteracycouncil.org
Contact: Karen Scheffels, Exec.Dir.
Local. Works to strengthen communities by providing literacy instruction to individuals and families. **Affiliated With:** ProLiteracy Worldwide.

3288 ■ Military Officers Association of America, Northern Illinois Chapter
c/o Cdr. Donald Campbell
1543 Rural St.
Rockford, IL 61107-3165
Ph: (815)877-7905
URL: National Affiliate–www.moaa.org
Contact: Cdr. Donald Campbell, Contact
Local. **Affiliated With:** Military Officers Association of America.

3289 ■ National Active And Retired Federal Employees Association - Rockford 415
1463 Woodcreek Bend
Rockford, IL 61108-1521
Ph: (815)226-1610
URL: National Affiliate–www.narfe.org
Contact: Raymond R. Moser, Contact
Local. Protects the retirement future of employees through education. Informs members on issues affecting the retirement. **Affiliated With:** National Association of Retired Federal Employees.

3290 ■ National Association of Catholic Family Life Ministers, Region No. 7
c/o Lorrie Gramer, Region Representative
Off. of Family Life
7708 E McGregor Rd.
Rockford, IL 61102-9655
Ph: (815)965-5011
Fax: (815)965-5811
E-mail: lorriegramer@aol.com
URL: National Affiliate–www.nacflm.org
Contact: Lorrie Gramer, Representative
State. Catholic Family Life Ministers who work to assist families in Church and society and who also provide mutual support and professional development for those who minister with families. **Affiliated With:** National Association of Catholic Family Life Ministers.

3291 ■ Navy Club of Rockford - Ship No. 1
5840 Garrett Ln., No. 4
Rockford, IL 61107
Ph: (815)484-9282
URL: National Affiliate–www.navyclubusa.org
Contact: John Bichl, Commander
Local. Represents individuals who are, or have been, in the active service of the U.S. Navy, Naval Reserve, Marine Corps, Marine Corps Reserve, and Coast Guard. Promotes and encourages further public interest in the U.S. Navy and its history. Upholds the spirit and ideals of the U.S. Navy. Acts as a public forum for members' views on national defense. Assists the Navy Recruiting Command whenever and wherever possible. Conducts charitable activities. **Affiliated With:** Navy Club of the United States of America.

3292 ■ Northern Illinois Association of Teachers of Mathematics
c/o Gerry Davies, Representative
4000 St. Francis Dr.
Rockford, IL 61103-1661
E-mail: webmaster@ictm.org
URL: National Affiliate–www.nctm.org
Contact: Gerry Davies, Representative
Local. Aims to improve the teaching and learning of mathematics. Provides vision, leadership and professional development to support teachers in ensuring mathematics learning of the highest quality for all students. **Affiliated With:** National Council of Teachers of Mathematics.

3293 ■ Northern Illinois Building Contractors Association (NIBCA)
1111 S Alpine Rd., Ste.No. 202
Rockford, IL 61108
Ph: (815)229-5636
Fax: (815)226-4856
E-mail: glen@nibca.net
URL: http://www.nibca.net
Contact: Glen Turpoff, Exec.Dir.
Local. Works to improve businesses of members through political actions and programs.

3294 ■ Northern Illinois Chapter National Electrical Contractors Association
4864 Colt Rd.
Rockford, IL 61109
Ph: (815)874-8400
Fax: (815)874-7701
E-mail: info@nilneca.org
URL: http://www.nilneca.org
Contact: Carl Ballard, Pres.
Founded: 1964. **Local**. Electrical and technical contractors erecting, installing, repairing, servicing, and maintains electrical and systems wiring, appliances, and devices. **Affiliated With:** National Electrical Contractors Association. **Publications:** Newsletter, periodic.

3295 ■ Northern Illinois Corvette Club (NICC)
PO Box 573
Rockford, IL 61105
E-mail: niccmail@nicccorvette.com
URL: http://nicccorvette.com
Contact: Ted Amlong, Pres.
Local. **Affiliated With:** National Council of Corvette Clubs.

3296 ■ Northern Illinois Estate Planning Council
c/o Tracy Beard, CFP, Pres.
190 Buckley Dr.
Rockford, IL 61107
Ph: (815)227-0300
Fax: (815)226-2195
E-mail: tbeard@savantcapital.com
URL: National Affiliate–councils.naepc.org
Contact: Tracy Beard CFP, Pres.
Local. Fosters understanding of the proper relationship between the functions of professionals in the estate planning field. Provides forum for estate planning professionals in Northern Illinois. Encourages cooperation among members. **Affiliated With:** National Association of Estate Planners and Councils.

3297 ■ Northern Illinois Woodturners
c/o Bruce Dearborn
5995 Spring Creek Rd., No. 201
Rockford, IL 61114
Free: (800)333-2300
E-mail: bdearborn@rwbaird.com
URL: National Affiliate–woodturner.org
Contact: Bruce Dearborn, Contact
Local. Amateur and professional woodturners, gallery owners, wood and equipment suppliers, and collectors. **Affiliated With:** American Association of Woodturners.

3298 ■ Phi Theta Kappa, Omicron Eta Chapter - Rock Valley College
c/o Tim Spielman
3301 N Mulford Rd.
Rockford, IL 61114
Ph: (815)921-3501
E-mail: tspielman@ednet.rvc.cc.il.us
URL: http://www.ptk.org/directories/chapters/IL/182-1.htm
Contact: Tim Spielman, Advisor
Local.

3299 ■ Polish Falcons of America, Nest 507
126 15th Ave.
Rockford, IL 61104
Ph: (815)962-6511
URL: http://www.polishfalcons.org/nest/507/index.html
Contact: Toni L. Cooper, Pres.
Local. **Affiliated With:** Polish Falcons of America.

3300 ■ Psi Chi, National Honor Society in Psychology - Rockford College
c/o Dept. of Psychology
5050 E State St.
Rockford, IL 61108-2393
Ph: (815)226-4172
Fax: (815)226-4119
E-mail: stousman@aol.com
URL: http://www.psichi.org/chapters/info.asp?chapter_id=903
Contact: Stuart Tousman PhD, Advisor
Local.

3301 ■ Rock Cut Trail Crew (RCTC)
c/o Andy Garrison, Pres.
PO Box 5271
Rockford, IL 61125
E-mail: rctrailcrew@sbcglobal.net
URL: http://www.rctrailcrew.org
Contact: Andy Garrison, Pres.
Local. **Affiliated With:** International Mountain Bicycling Association.

3302 ■ Rock Valley College Students In Free Enterprise
Rock Valley Coll.
3301 N Mulford Rd.
CL II Rm. 139
Rockford, IL 61114
E-mail: krkilgore@ednet.rvc.cc.il.us
URL: http://rvcsife.org
Contact: Kevin Kilgore, Exec.Dir.
Local.

3303 ■ Rockford AIFA
c/o Ned M. Burns, VP
PO Box 6544
Rockford, IL 61125
Ph: (815)332-6700
Fax: (815)332-6701
E-mail: holly@massinofinancial.com
URL: http://www.raifa.org
Contact: Ned M. Burns, VP
Local. Represents the interests of insurance and financial advisors. Advocates for a positive legislative and regulatory environment. Enhances business and professional skills of members. **Affiliated With:** National Association of Insurance and Financial Advisors.

3304 ■ Rockford Aikikai
Gymnastic Acad. of Rockford
6630 Springbrook Rd.
Rockford, IL 61114
Ph: (815)654-3867
URL: http://gbit.com/ra
Contact: William VonGlockner, Instructor
Local. **Affiliated With:** United States Aikido Federation.

3305 ■ Rockford Area Association of Realtors (RAAR)
6776 E State St.
Rockford, IL 61108
Ph: (815)395-6776
Fax: (815)395-6770
E-mail: terrieceo@aol.com
URL: http://www.raarnet.com
Contact: Ginger Sreenan, Pres.
Local. Strives to develop real estate business practices. Advocates the right to own, use and transfer real property. Provides a facility for professional development, research and exchange of information among members and to the general public. **Affiliated With:** National Association of Realtors.

3306 ■ Rockford Area Chapter of the American Payroll Association
c/o Stephanie Holm, Membership Coor.
Janet Wattles Ctr.
526 W State St.
Rockford, IL 61101
Ph: (815)720-4919
E-mail: sholm@janetwattles.org
URL: http://www.rockfordpayroll.org
Contact: Stephanie Holm, Membership Coor.
Local. Aims to increase the Payroll Professional's skill level through education and mutual support. Represents the Payroll Professional before legislative bodies. Administers the certified payroll professional program of recognition. Provides public service education on payroll and employment issues. **Affiliated With:** American Payroll Association.

3307 ■ Rockford Area Convention and Visitors Bureau (RACVB)
102 N Main St.
Rockford, IL 61101-1102
Ph: (815)963-8111
Fax: (815)963-4298
Free: (800)521-0849
E-mail: info@gorockford.com
URL: http://www.gorockford.com
Contact: Wendy Perks Fisher, Pres./CEO
Founded: 1984. **Local**. Official tourism promotion agency for Rockford, Illinois and Winnebago County. **Publications:** *Go To Rockford News*, quarterly. Newsletter. **Price:** free. Alternate Formats: online • *GoRockford.Report*, quarterly. Newsletter. **Price:** free. Alternate Formats: online.

3308 ■ Rockford Area Libertarians
c/o Kathy Kelley, Chair
PO Box 4775
Rockford, IL 61110
Ph: (815)874-6345
E-mail: liberty@lprockford.8m.com
URL: http://lprockford.8m.com
Contact: Kathy Kelley, Chair
Local. **Affiliated With:** Libertarian National Committee.

3309 ■ Rockford Regional Chamber of Commerce
515 N Court St.
Rockford, IL 61103
Ph: (815)987-8100
Fax: (815)987-8122
E-mail: cservice@rockfordchamber.com
URL: http://www.rockfordchamber.com
Contact: Verla Sterett, Customer Service
Founded: 1910. **Members:** 1,850. **Membership Dues:** $250 (annual). **Staff:** 15. **Local**. Members help other members increase sales, control costs, network effectively, advocate improvements in the business climate. **Libraries: Type:** reference. **Holdings:** 4. **Subjects:** yearbook, membership directory, manufacturing directory, map. **Telecommunication Services:** phone referral service, 815963-8123 • phone referral service, 815963-8123. **Committees:** Ambassador. **Councils:** Business Women; Communications; International Business; Manufacturing; Minority Business; Nonprofit; Professional Sales. **Formerly:** (2005) Rockford Area Chamber of Commerce. **Publications:** *Manufacturers Directory*, annual • *Membership and Business Directory*, annual • *Rockford Area Map*, annual • *The Voice*, monthly. Newspaper. **Circulation:** 200. **Advertising:** accepted. Alternate Formats: online. **Conventions/Meetings:** annual meeting.

3310 ■ Rockford Regional Chamber of Commerce Business Women's Council
PO Box 1747
Rockford, IL 61110-0247
Ph: (815)987-8100
Fax: (815)987-8122
E-mail: teriwatts@rockfordchamber.com
URL: http://www.rockfordchamber.com
Contact: Teri Watts, Contact
Members: 200. **For-Profit**. **Regional**. **Formerly:** (2004) Rockford Area Chamber of Commerce Business Women's Council. **Conventions/Meetings:** annual luncheon, networking, lunch and program.

3311 ■ Rockford Sail and Power Squadron
c/o Judi Gerstein, Ed.
3220 Gunflint Trail
Rockford, IL 61109
E-mail: judik1@aol.com
URL: http://www.usps.org/localusps/rockford
Contact: Judi Gerstein, Ed.
Local. **Affiliated With:** United States Power Squadrons.

3312 ■ Rockford Skeet Club
7801 Wagon Wheel Ln.
Rockford, IL 61109
Ph: (815)873-8773
URL: National Affiliate–www.mynssa.com
Local. **Affiliated With:** National Skeet Shooting Association.

3313 ■ Rockford Table Tennis Club
Flodin Boys and Girls Club
1000 Mill Rd.
Rockford, IL 61108
Ph: (815)965-8505
E-mail: ldk-bsi@worldnet.att.net
URL: National Affiliate–www.usatt.org
Contact: Ed Hogshead, Contact
Local. **Affiliated With:** U.S.A. Table Tennis.

3314 ■ Rockford - Wyldlife
5450 Wansford Way Ste.241
Rockford, IL 61109
Ph: (815)226-8131
URL: http://sites.younglife.org/_layouts/ylext/default.aspx?ID=C-856
Local. Represents the interests of individuals committed to impacting kids' lives and preparing them for the future. Helps young people develop their skills, assets and attitudes to reach their full God-given potential. Reaches suburban, urban, multicultural and disabled kids and teenage mothers. **Affiliated With:** Young Life.

3315 ■ Rockfordland Youth for Christ
316 Wood Rd.
Rockford, IL 61107
Ph: (815)399-7203
Fax: (815)399-7204
URL: National Affiliate–www.yfc.net
Local. **Affiliated With:** Youth for Christ/U.S.A.

3316 ■ RSVP of Winnebago/Boone Counties
c/o Diana Burke, Dir.
705 Kilburn Ave.
Rockford, IL 61101
Ph: (815)490-1112
Fax: (815)962-6009
E-mail: rsvp@lifescapeservices.com
URL: http://www.joinseniorservice.org
Contact: Diana Burke, Dir.
Local. **Affiliated With:** Retired and Senior Volunteer Program.

3317 ■ SCORE Northern Illinois
c/o Marion Wilke, Chm.
515 N Court St.
Rockford, IL 61103-6807
Ph: (815)962-0122
Fax: (815)962-0806
E-mail: marwid@juno.com
URL: http://www.northernillinoisscore.org
Contact: Ms. Marion Wilke, Chm.
Members: 40. **Budget:** $3,500. **State Groups:** 14. **Local Groups:** 1. **Regional**. Counsels small businesses on start-up, writing a business plan, addressing problems with cash flow, inventory control, and other business-related issues. **Affiliated With:** SCORE. **Publications:** *Scoreboard*, monthly. Newsletter. Contains news about the local organization and its members. **Circulation:** 40. Alternate Formats: online. **Conventions/Meetings:** monthly Starting a Small Business/Writing a Business Plan - workshop, presents materials of interest to potential or actual small businesses.

3318 ■ Sheet Metal and Air Conditioning Contractors' National Association of Northern Illinois
c/o Deb Sullivan
4010 E State St., Ste.204
Rockford, IL 61108-2044
Ph: (815)226-1764
Fax: (815)226-1775
E-mail: nilsmacna@msn.com
URL: National Affiliate–www.smacna.org
Contact: Debra Sullivan, Contact
Founded: 1958. **Members:** 26. **Staff:** 1. **Local**. Ventilating, air handling, warm air heating, industrial sheet metal, and specialty fabrication contractors. **Affiliated With:** Sheet Metal and Air Conditioning Contractors' National Association.

3319 ■ Sierra Club - Illinois Chapter - Blackhawk Group
PO Box 8976
Rockford, IL 61126-8976
Ph: (815)964-7111
E-mail: peaceman50@aol.com
URL: http://illinois.sierraclub.org/Blackhawk
Contact: Stanley Campbell, Conservation Chm.
Local.

3320 ■ Sinnissippi Audubon Society
c/o Jack Armstrong, Pres.
PO Box 7544
Rockford, IL 61126
Ph: (815)398-2974
URL: National Affiliate–www.audubon.org
Local. Works to conserve and restore natural ecosystems, focusing on birds and other wildlife for the benefit of humanity and the earth's biological diversity. **Affiliated With:** National Audubon Society.

3321 ■ Society of Manufacturing Engineers - Rock Valley College S269
3301 N Mulford Rd.
Rockford, IL 61114
Ph: (815)921-3055
Fax: (815)654-4459
E-mail: r.avery@ednet.ruc.cc.il.us
URL: National Affiliate–www.sme.org
Contact: Raymon Avery, Contact
Local. Advances manufacturing knowledge to gain competitive advantage. Improves skills and manufacturing solutions for the growth of economy. Provides resources and opportunities for manufacturing professionals. **Affiliated With:** Vibration Institute.

3322 ■ Sons of the American Revolution, Illinois Society
c/o Dr. Ken Griswold, State Pres.
3901 Spring Creek Rd.
Rockford, IL 61107
Ph: (815)398-8955
E-mail: robngrs@aol.com
URL: http://www.sar.org/ilssar
Contact: Ken Griswold Dr., State Pres.
State. **Affiliated With:** National Society, Sons of the American Revolution.

3323 ■ STARFLEET: USS Black Hawk
c/o Jeffery Higdon
2803 Ridgeway Ave.
Rockford, IL 61101
E-mail: blackhawk@rockriver.net
URL: http://www.region12.org
Contact: Jeffery Higdon, Pres.
Local. **Affiliated With:** STARFLEET.

3324 ■ Sweet Adelines International, River City Sound Chapter
2927 Hanford Dr.
Rockford, IL 61114
Ph: (815)874-2916
URL: http://www.rivercitysound.org
Contact: Maureen Brzinski, Dir.
Local. Advances the musical art form of barbershop harmony through education and performances. Provides education, training and coaching in the development of women's four-part barbershop harmony. **Affiliated With:** Sweet Adelines International.

3325 ■ Tebala Shriners
c/o Thomas L. Runge
7910 Newburg Rd.
Rockford, IL 61108
Ph: (815)332-2010
Fax: (815)332-5923
E-mail: shriners@tebala.com
URL: http://mastermason.com/Tebala
Contact: Thomas L. Runge, Potentate
Local. **Affiliated With:** Imperial Council of the Ancient Arabic Order of the Nobles of the Mystic Shrine for North America.

3326 ■ United States Naval Sea Cadet Corps - Maj. Gen. John L. Borling Division
Rockford East High School
2929 Charles St.
Rockford, IL 61108
E-mail: morrow85@tds.net
URL: http://dolphin.seacadets.org/US_units/UnitDetails.asp?UnitID=091JLB
Contact: LTJG Steven D. Morrow NSCC, Commanding Officer
Local. Works to instill good citizenship and patriotism in youth. Encourages qualities such as personal neatness, loyalty, obedience, dependability, and responsibility to others. Offers courses in physical fitness and military drill, first aid, water safety, basic seamanship, and naval history and traditions. **Affiliated With:** Naval Sea Cadet Corps.

3327 ■ United Way of Rock River Valley
612 N Main St., Ste.300
Rockford, IL 61103
Ph: (815)968-5400
Fax: (815)968-5878
E-mail: michael@unitedwayrrv.org
URL: http://www.unitedwayrrv.org
Contact: Michael Call, Pres./CEO
Local. **Affiliated With:** United Way of America.

3328 ■ Visiting Nurses Association (VNA)
4223 E State St.
Rockford, IL 61108
Ph: (815)971-3550
E-mail: vnaweb@rhsnet.org
URL: http://www.rhsnet.org
Regional. Nursing professionals specializing in Older Adult Care, Case Management, Elder Abuse, Circuit Breaker, Money Management, Caregiver Services, and Health Promotion.

3329 ■ Winnebago County Dental Society - Illinois
c/o Vanie Hildreth-Hatch, Exec.Dir.
4312 E State St.
Rockford, IL 61108
Ph: (815)399-1797
URL: http://www.isds.org
Contact: Vanie Hildreth-Hatch, Exec.Dir.
Local. Represents the interests of dentists committed to the public's oral health, ethics and professional development. Encourages the improvement of the public's oral health and promotes the art and science of dentistry. **Affiliated With:** American Dental Association; Illinois State Dental Society.

3330 ■ Winnebago County Medical Society
6991 Redansa Dr.
Rockford, IL 61107
Ph: (815)395-9267
Fax: (815)484-4109
E-mail: wcms1@aol.com
URL: http://www.wcmsonline.com
Contact: John P. Holden MD, Pres.
Local. Advances the art and science of medicine. Promotes patient care and the betterment of public health.

3331 ■ Wood Truss Council of America - Illinois (WTCA-IL)
c/o Mike Karceski, Pres.
PO Box 6536
Rockford, IL 61125
Ph: (815)332-4904
Fax: (815)332-5311
E-mail: mkarceski@atlasci.com
URL: National Affiliate–www.sbcindustry.com
Contact: Mike Karceski, Pres.
State. Represents manufacturers and suppliers of structural wood components. Protects and advances the interests of members, manufacturers and suppliers of related products. Encourages the use of structural wood components. Supports research, development and testing of wood trusses. **Affiliated With:** Wood Truss Council of America.

3332 ■ Young Life Rockford
5450 Wansford Way, Ste.241
Rockford, IL 61109
Ph: (815)226-8131
Fax: (815)226-8135
URL: http://Rockford.younglife.org
Local.

3333 ■ YWCA of Rockford
4990 E State St.
Rockford, IL 61108
Ph: (815)968-9681
Fax: (815)968-9858
E-mail: theresa@ywca-rockford.org
URL: http://www.ywca-rockford.org
Contact: Theresa Merriman, CEO
Local. Promotes the self-sufficiency of women and girls through job readiness, self-esteem, confidence, math and science, life skills, career exploration programs, and advocacy and leadership development. Assists in finding and paying for child care, recruits and trains childcare providers. **Affiliated With:** Girls Inc.

Rockton

3334 ■ American Legion, Walter Graham Post 332
219 W Main St.
Rockton, IL 61072
Ph: (815)624-7350
Fax: (309)663-5783
URL: National Affiliate–www.legion.org
Local. **Affiliated With:** American Legion.

3335 ■ Hononegah High School Key Club (HHS)
307 Salem St.
Rockton, IL 61072
E-mail: gooseyluci43@hotmail.com
URL: http://www.keyclub.org/club/hhs
Contact: Amanda Volz, Pres.
Local.

3336 ■ Rockton Chamber of Commerce
119 Blackhawk Blvd.
PO Box 237
Rockton, IL 61072
Ph: (815)624-7625 (815)624-8535
Fax: (815)624-7385
E-mail: info@rocktonchamber.com
URL: http://www.rocktonchamber.com
Contact: Ms. Carol Lamb, Exec.Dir.
Founded: 1951. **Members:** 160. **Membership Dues:** 1 to 5 employees, $75 (annual) • 6 to 10 employees, $100 (annual) • 11 to 20 employees, $150 (annual) • over 20 employees, $300 (annual). **Staff:** 1. **For-Profit**. **Regional**. **Awards:** **Frequency:** annual. **Type:** scholarship. **Recipient:** for Hononegah High School graduate. **Conventions/Meetings:** monthly meeting, general membership (exhibits) - every 1st Wednesday.

Rolling Meadows

3337 ■ American Legion, Rolling Meadows Post 1251
3001 Dove St.
Rolling Meadows, IL 60008
Ph: (309)663-0361
Fax: (309)663-5783
URL: National Affiliate–www.legion.org
Local. **Affiliated With:** American Legion.

3338 ■ Association of Old Crows, Windy City Chapter
c/o Mr. Joe Duthie, Pres.
Northrop Grumman
600 Hicks Rd., M/S L3200
Rolling Meadows, IL 60008
Ph: (847)259-9600
E-mail: joseph.duthie@ngc.com
URL: National Affiliate–www.myaoc.org
Contact: Mr. Joe Duthie, Pres.
Local. Works for the advancement of electronic warfare and information superiority. Provides a means for communicating and disseminating new developments in electronic warfare technology, training, operations, and doctrines. **Affiliated With:** Association of Old Crows.

3339 ■ Huntington's Disease Society of America, Illinois Chapter
c/o Barry Kahn, Pres.
PO Box 8383
Rolling Meadows, IL 60008
Ph: (630)443-9876
E-mail: barrykahn1@comcast.net
URL: http://www.lib.uchicago.edu/~rd13/hd/illinois.html
Contact: Barry Kahn, Pres.

Membership Dues: individual, $15 (annual) • benefactor, $25 (annual) • angel, $50 (annual) • century club, $100 (annual) • patron, $250 (annual). **State**. Individuals and groups of volunteers concerned with Huntington's disease, an inherited and terminal neurological condition causing progressive brain and nerve deterioration. Goals are to: identifies HD families; educates the public and professionals, with emphasis on increasing consumer awareness of HD; promotes and supports basic and clinical research into the causes and cure of HD; assists families in meeting the social, economic, and emotional problems resulting from HD. Works to change the attitude of the working community toward the HD patient, enhance the HD patient's lifestyle, and promote better health care and treatment, both in the community and in facilities. **Affiliated With:** Huntington's Disease Society of America. **Publications:** *Hopes and Dreams*. Newsletter. Contains items of interest relating to individuals with HD, their families, health care professionals and supporters.

3340 ■ National Association of Credit Management - Chicago/Midwest (NACM)
3005 Tollview Dr.
Rolling Meadows, IL 60008
Ph: (847)483-6400
Fax: (847)253-6685
E-mail: info@nacmchicago.org
URL: http://www.nacmchicago.org
Contact: Larry Grogan CCE, Chm.

Local. Works to educate its members in credit, collections and related matters while working toward the continuing professionalization of the credit management field. **Affiliated With:** National Association of Credit Management.

3341 ■ Northwest Cultural Council (NWCC)
5999 New Wilke Rd., Ste.308
Rolling Meadows, IL 60008
Ph: (847)956-7966
E-mail: nwcc@northwestculturalcouncil.org
URL: http://northwestculturalcouncil.org
Contact: Kathy Umlauf, Exec.Dir.

Founded: 1989. **Staff:** 2. **Regional**. Promotes public awareness and appreciation of the arts in the area from O'Hare International Airport through Elgin, IL. **Publications:** *Spotlights*, quarterly. Newsletter. Includes event calendar. **Circulation:** 7,000. **Advertising:** accepted. **Conventions/Meetings:** periodic Arts Walk - meeting • annual Literary and Artists' Workshop • monthly Poetry Workshop - 2nd Saturday.

3342 ■ Northwest Suburban Alliance for Commerce and Industry (NSACI)
2220 Hicks Rd., Ste.201
Rolling Meadows, IL 60008
Ph: (847)259-8774
Fax: (847)259-8775
E-mail: thomas.menzel@nsaci.org
URL: http://www.nsaci.org
Contact: Thomas Menzel, Pres.

Membership Dues: general company/professional firm (plus $5 per additional full-time employee), $330 (annual) • government, $350 (annual) • utility, $750 (annual) • shopping center (plus $15 per store), $330 (annual) • retail store not at a mall/stand alone, restaurant, $400 (annual) • hotel, minimum (plus $4.50 per room), $300 (annual) • legislator, $225 (annual) • independent contractor, $330 (annual) • nonprofit organization (based on per million budget), $195-$310 (annual). **State**. **Publications:** *Networker*, bimonthly. Newsletter.

3343 ■ Rainbows, Illinois State Chapter
c/o Suzy Y. Marta
2100 Golf Rd., No. 370
Rolling Meadows, IL 60008
Ph: (847)952-1770
Fax: (847)952-1774
E-mail: suzy@rainbows.org
URL: National Affiliate–www.rainbows.org
Contact: Suzy Y. Marta, Contact
State. **Affiliated With:** RAINBOWS.

3344 ■ Rolling Meadows Chamber of Commerce (RMCC)
2775 Algonquin Rd., Ste.310
Rolling Meadows, IL 60008
Ph: (847)398-3730
Fax: (847)398-3745
E-mail: office@rmchamber.org
URL: http://www.rmchamber.org
Contact: Linda Liles Ballantine, Exec.Dir.

Founded: 1961. **Members:** 275. **Staff:** 2. **Local**. Promotes business, industrial, professional, cultural, and civic development in the Rolling Meadows, IL area. Monitors legislation; partners with city to oversee economic development. **Awards:** Business Beautification. **Frequency:** annual. **Type:** recognition • Business Leader of the Year. **Frequency:** annual. **Type:** recognition • Community Leader of the Year. **Frequency:** annual. **Type:** recognition • Small Business of the Year. **Frequency:** annual. **Type:** recognition. **Affiliated With:** U.S. Chamber of Commerce. **Publications:** *The Connector*, bimonthly. Newsletter • *Dining Guide*, semiannual. Journal • *Legislative Guide to Elected & Appointed Officials*, annual • Membership Directory, annual • Journal, annual. **Conventions/Meetings:** annual Golf Outing - meeting • periodic Networking/Social Function - meeting • annual Recognition Dinner.

3345 ■ United Cricket Club
2800 S Hampton Dr., No. 203
Rolling Meadows, IL 60008
URL: http://www.usaca.org/Clubs.htm
Contact: Adnan Baig, Contact
Local.

Romeoville

3346 ■ Psi Chi, National Honor Society in Psychology - Lewis University
c/o Dept. of Psychology
1 Univ. Pkwy. 1056
Romeoville, IL 60446-2200
Ph: (815)836-5594 (815)836-5364
Fax: (815)836-5032
E-mail: jihch@lewisu.edu
URL: http://www.psichi.org/chapters/info.asp?chapter_id=512
Contact: Chwan-Shyang Jih PhD, Advisor
Local.

3347 ■ Romeoville Chamber of Commerce
27 Montrose Dr.
Romeoville, IL 60446-1329
Ph: (815)886-2076
Fax: (815)886-2096
E-mail: info@romeovillechamber.org
URL: http://www.romeovillechamber.org
Contact: Tony Marquez, Pres.

Founded: 1975. **Membership Dues:** business (based on number of employees), $150-$650 • nonprofit, $100. **Local**. Serves as communication vehicle of business, professional and service organization in governmental and social affairs in Romeoville. **Computer Services:** Information services, business classified ads • information services, membership directory. **Programs:** Greeter. **Publications:** Newsletter, bimonthly. Contains new business highlights, legislative update and chamber activities. **Advertising:** accepted. Alternate Formats: online. **Conventions/Meetings:** monthly luncheon - every 2nd Tuesday in Lockport, IL.

3348 ■ Society of Consumer Affairs Professionals in Business, Chicago Chapter
c/o Dorothy Nicholson
Sharp Electronics Corp.
1300 Naperville Dr.
Romeoville, IL 60446
Ph: (630)378-3377
E-mail: chicago@socap.org
URL: National Affiliate–www.socap.org
Affiliated With: Society of Consumer Affairs Professionals in Business.

Roodhouse

3349 ■ American Legion, Roodhouse Post 373
321 E Rowe St.
Roodhouse, IL 62082
Ph: (309)663-0361
Fax: (309)663-5783
URL: National Affiliate–www.legion.org
Local. **Affiliated With:** American Legion.

Roscoe

3350 ■ National Active and Retired Federal Employees Association - Janesville 44
12355 Love Rd.
Roscoe, IL 61073-7309
Ph: (815)389-4666
URL: National Affiliate–www.narfe.org
Contact: Donald W. Owens, Contact

Local. Protects the retirement future of employees through education. Informs members on issues affecting the retirement. **Affiliated With:** National Association of Retired Federal Employees.

3351 ■ National Alliance for the Mentally Ill - Rock County
c/o Larry Bergen, Pres.
6747 Lynnhurst Ln.
Roscoe, IL 61073
Ph: (815)389-7902
URL: http://www.namiwisconsin.org/library/directory
Contact: Larry Bergen, Pres.

Local. Strives to improve the quality of life of children and adults with severe mental illness through support, education, research and advocacy. **Affiliated With:** National Alliance for the Mentally Ill.

Roselle

3352 ■ American Legion, Northwest Du Page Post 1084
334 E Maple Ave.
Roselle, IL 60172
Ph: (309)663-0361
Fax: (309)663-5783
URL: National Affiliate–www.legion.org
Local. **Affiliated With:** American Legion.

3353 ■ American Society of Safety Engineers, Northeastern Illinois Chapter (ASSE NEIL)
PO Box 72698
Roselle, IL 60172-0698
Ph: (847)925-6923
E-mail: sgibson@harpercollege.edu
URL: http://neil.asse.org
Contact: Sara Gibson, Pres.

Local. Enhances the advancement of the safety profession and the safety professional. Promotes the technical, societal and economic well-being of safety practitioners. **Affiliated With:** American Society of Safety Engineers.

3354 ■ Community Associations Institute - Illinois Chapter (CAI)
480 W Lake St., Ste.1B
Roselle, IL 60172
Ph: (630)307-0659
Fax: (630)307-3641
E-mail: info@cai-illinois.org
URL: http://www.cai-illinois.org
Contact: Jessica Fortich, Interim Exec.Dir.
State. Affiliated With: Community Associations Institute.

3355 ■ Roselle Chamber of Commerce and Industry
81 E Devon Ave.
Roselle, IL 60172
Ph: (630)894-3010
Fax: (630)894-3042
E-mail: execdir@rosellechamber.com
URL: http://www.rosellechamber.com
Contact: Gail Croson, Exec.Dir.
Founded: 1949. **Members:** 215. **Membership Dues:** regular, $160. **Local.** Promotes business and community development in Roselle, IL. Conducts networking, social activities and business seminars; sponsors community parade, entertainment tents at annual festival and business expo; participates in or contributes to other business and community projects and events. **Awards:** Brian K. Healy Service Award. **Type:** recognition • Business Person of the Year Award. **Frequency:** annual. **Type:** recognition. **Publications:** *Roselle Chamber Business News*, monthly. Newsletter. **Advertising:** accepted. **Conventions/ Meetings:** monthly board meeting • monthly Business After Hours - meeting • annual meeting, with officer installation • monthly meeting - every 3rd Tuesday.

3356 ■ Roselle Historical Foundation
102 S Prospect
Roselle, IL 60172-2026
Ph: (630)351-5300
URL: http://www.roselle.il.us/community/historicaloverview.html
Contact: Kay Cahill, Pres.
Founded: 1987. **Members:** 250. **Membership Dues:** regular, $20 (annual). **Staff:** 1. **Budget:** $25,000. **Regional Groups:** 2. **State Groups:** 2. **Local Groups:** 1. **Local.** Represents individuals interested in the history of Roselle, IL. Operates museum. **Libraries: Type:** reference. **Subjects:** local genealogy-limited. **Affiliated With:** Illinois State Historical Society. **Supersedes:** Roselle Historical Society. **Publications:** *Etched in Time*, quinquennial. Journal. Highlights the history of Roselle. **Price:** $20.00 • Newsletter, bimonthly. **Conventions/Meetings:** monthly meeting - always 2nd Sunday in Roselle, IL.

3357 ■ Roselle Lions Club
PO Box 72092
Roselle, IL 60172
E-mail: kathie.fitzpatrick@rosellelionsclub.org
URL: http://www.rosellelionsclub.org
Contact: Kathie Fitzpatrick, Pres.
Local. Affiliated With: Lions Clubs International.

3358 ■ Skokie Valley Kennel Club
c/o Corinne Kehoe, Treas.
160 N Garden Ave.
Roselle, IL 60172-1764
Ph: (630)893-5796
Fax: (630)893-6438
E-mail: cjk@skokievalleykc.org
URL: http://www.skokievalleykc.org
Contact: Corinne Kehoe, Treas.
Local. Affiliated With: American Kennel Club.

Rosemont

3359 ■ Associated Roofing Contractors of Maryland (ARCOM)
c/o NRCA
10255 W Higgins Rd., Ste.600
Rosemont, IL 60018
Ph: (847)493-7582
Fax: (847)299-1183
E-mail: jgolike@nrca.net
URL: http://www.arcom.org
Contact: Dave Taylor, Pres.
Founded: 1948. **Members:** 95. **Membership Dues:** roofing contractor, manufacturer, distributor, $350 (annual). **Staff:** 1. **State Groups:** 1. **State. Libraries: Type:** not open to the public. **Holdings:** 50. **Subjects:** roofing, application, management. **Awards: Frequency:** annual. **Type:** scholarship. **Publications:** *Roof Topics*, quarterly. Newsletter. **Price:** free. **Advertising:** accepted. **Conventions/ Meetings:** annual convention (exhibits).

3360 ■ United Food and Commercial Workers International Union, AFL-CIO, CLC -Local Union 881, Northcentral Region
10400 W Higgins Rd., Ste.500
Rosemont, IL 60018-3705
Ph: (847)294-5064
URL: http://www.local881ufcw.org
Contact: Ronald E. Powell, Pres./VP
Members: 37,891. **Local. Affiliated With:** United Food and Commercial Workers International Union.

Roseville

3361 ■ American Legion, Lawson Babbitt Post 614
175 W Penn
Roseville, IL 61473
Ph: (309)663-0361
Fax: (309)663-5783
URL: National Affiliate–www.legion.org
Local. Affiliated With: American Legion.

Rosiclare

3362 ■ American Legion, Illinois Post 571
c/o Paul C. Rowan
PO Box 163
Rosiclare, IL 62982
Ph: (618)287-3278
Fax: (309)663-5783
URL: National Affiliate–www.legion.org
Contact: Paul C. Rowan, Contact
Local. Affiliated With: American Legion.

3363 ■ Goshen Trail Beagle Club
c/o Carl Buchanan
PO Box 548
Rosiclare, IL 62982-0548
URL: National Affiliate–www.akc.org
Contact: Carl Buchanan, Contact
Local.

Rossville

3364 ■ American Legion, Spears-Dukes Post 733
PO Box 194
Rossville, IL 60963
Ph: (309)663-0361
Fax: (309)663-5783
URL: National Affiliate–www.legion.org
Local. Affiliated With: American Legion.

Round Lake Beach

3365 ■ Round Lake Area Chamber of Commerce and Industry
1777 N Cedar Lake Rd.
Round Lake Beach, IL 60073
Ph: (847)546-2002
E-mail: rlchamber@sbcglobal.net
URL: http://www.rlchamber.org
Contact: Monica Marr, Exec.Dir.
Founded: 1947. **Members:** 174. **Membership Dues:** full, $175 (annual). **Local.** Promotes business and community development in the Round Lake, IL area. Conducts annual Home and Trade Fair. **Awards: Type:** scholarship. **Recipient:** to Round Lake High School seniors. **Affiliated With:** Illinois State Chamber of Commerce. **Publications:** *Chamber News*, monthly. Newsletter. **Conventions/Meetings:** monthly meeting - always third Thursday.

Round Lake Park

3366 ■ American Legion, Round Lake Post 1170
111 E Main St.
Round Lake Park, IL 60073
Ph: (309)663-0361
Fax: (309)663-5783
URL: National Affiliate–www.legion.org
Local. Affiliated With: American Legion.

Royal

3367 ■ American Legion, Royal Post 996
PO Box 121
Royal, IL 61871
Ph: (309)663-0361
Fax: (309)663-5783
URL: National Affiliate–www.legion.org
Local. Affiliated With: American Legion.

Royalton

3368 ■ American Legion, Illinois Post 963
c/o Edward Teffertiller
PO Box 251
Royalton, IL 62983
Ph: (309)663-0361
Fax: (309)663-5783
URL: National Affiliate–www.legion.org
Contact: Edward Teffertiller, Contact
Local. Affiliated With: American Legion.

Rushville

3369 ■ American Legion, Schuyler Post 4
PO Box 473
Rushville, IL 62681
Ph: (217)322-9000
Fax: (309)663-5783
URL: National Affiliate–www.legion.org
Local. Affiliated With: American Legion.

3370 ■ Illinois Meat Goat Producers
RR 2, Box 220B
Rushville, IL 62681
E-mail: cjmagmills@yahoo.com
URL: National Affiliate–www.abga.org
Contact: Clause J. Miller, Contact
State.

3371 ■ Rushville Area Chamber of Commerce and Main Street (RACC & MST)
PO Box 171
117 S Cong. St.
Rushville, IL 62681
Ph: (217)322-3689
Fax: (217)322-3689
E-mail: racc_mst@frontiernet.net
URL: http://www.rushville.org
Contact: Ms. Kathy Love, Chamber Office Mgr./Exec. Dir.
Members: 109. **Staff:** 1. **Local.** Businesses, manufacturers, and interested individuals. Promotes business and community development in the Rushville, IL area. **Convention/Meeting:** none. **Libraries: Type:** reference; by appointment only. **Holdings:** articles, books, clippings, papers, photographs, reports. **Boards:** Chamber; Main Street. **Formed by Merger of:** Rushville Chamber of Commerce. **Publications:** Membership Directory, quarterly.

3372 ■ Rushville Area C.O.C. and Main Street
PO Box 171
Rushville, IL 62681
Ph: (217)322-3689
URL: http://www.rushville.org
Local.

3373 ■ T.L. Gilmer Dental Society
c/o Dr. David A. Naff, Jr., Pres.
PO Box 288
Rushville, IL 62681-1436
Ph: (217)322-3928
E-mail: naff@casscomm.com
URL: http://www.isds.org
Contact: Dr. David A. Naff Jr., Pres.
Local. Represents the interests of dentists committed to the public's oral health, ethics and professional development. Encourages the improvement of the public's oral health and promotes the art and science of dentistry. **Affiliated With:** American Dental Association; Illinois State Dental Society.

Rutland

3374 ■ American Legion, Rutland Memorial Post 1121
PO Box 33
Rutland, IL 61358
Ph: (815)863-5156
Fax: (309)663-5783
URL: National Affiliate–www.legion.org
Local. Affiliated With: American Legion.

Sailor Springs

3375 ■ American Legion, Sailor Springs Post 230
PO Box 24
Sailor Springs, IL 62879
Ph: (618)689-9951
Fax: (309)663-5783
URL: National Affiliate–www.legion.org
Local. Affiliated With: American Legion.

St. Anne

3376 ■ American Legion, St. Anne Post 842
PO Box 302
St. Anne, IL 60964
Ph: (309)663-0361
Fax: (309)663-5783
URL: National Affiliate–www.legion.org
Local. Affiliated With: American Legion.

St. Charles

3377 ■ American Board of Trial Advocates - Illinois
7 S Second Ave.
St. Charles, IL 60174
Ph: (630)584-7666
Fax: (630)584-1649
E-mail: wclancy@clancylaw.com
Contact: Wendell W. Clancy, Pres.
State. Improves the ethical and technical standards of practice in the field of advocacy. Elevates the standards of integrity, honor and courtesy in the legal profession. Promotes the efficient administration of justice and improvement of the law. **Affiliated With:** American Board of Trial Advocates.

3378 ■ American Legion, St. Charles Post 342
PO Box 245
St. Charles, IL 60174
Ph: (309)663-0361
Fax: (309)663-5783
URL: National Affiliate–www.legion.org
Local. Affiliated With: American Legion.

3379 ■ American Red Cross, Fox River Chapter
121 N Second St., Ste.G
St. Charles, IL 60174
Ph: (630)443-8844
Fax: (630)443-8875
E-mail: stuph@foxriver.org
URL: http://foxriver.redcross.org
Local.

3380 ■ Downtown St. Charles Partnership
213 Walnut St.
St. Charles, IL 60174
Ph: (630)513-5386
E-mail: info@dtown.org
URL: http://www.dtown.org
Local.

3381 ■ Fox Valley Dog Training Club (FVDTC)
PO Box 992
St. Charles, IL 60174
Ph: (630)575-WOOF
URL: http://www.fvdtc.org
Contact: Carolyn Pearson, Sec.
Founded: 1948. **Members:** 170. **Membership Dues:** basic, $90 (annual). **Local Groups:** 1. **Local.** Individuals who love dogs. Trains owners to train their dogs to develop their intelligence as well as their physical ability. **Libraries: Type:** not open to the public. **Holdings:** 35; books, video recordings. **Subjects:** dogs. **Affiliated With:** American Kennel Club. **Publications:** *Waggin' Tales*, monthly. Newsletter. Alternate Formats: online.

3382 ■ Fox Valley General Contractors Association
PO Box 478
St. Charles, IL 60174
Ph: (630)443-0055
Fax: (630)443-0057
E-mail: barbh@fvgca.org
Contact: Barbara Hayboer, Office Mgr.
Local. Works to improve businesses of members through political actions and programs.

3383 ■ Home Builders Association of Greater Fox Valley
555 S Randall Rd., Ste.201
St. Charles, IL 60174
Ph: (630)587-1700
Fax: (630)587-1800
E-mail: hba@inil.com
URL: http://www.buildfoxvalley.com
Contact: Ray Budde, CEO
Local. Single and multifamily home builders, commercial builders, and others associated with the building industry. **Affiliated With:** National Association of Home Builders.

3384 ■ Illinois Art Education Association (IAEA)
c/o Becky Blane
PO Box 825
St. Charles, IL 60174
Ph: (630)377-4852
Fax: (630)513-5751
E-mail: bblaine@d303.org
URL: http://www.ilaea.org
Contact: Heather Shore, Sec.
State. Promotes art education through professional development, service, advancement of knowledge, and leadership.

3385 ■ Illinois National Emergency Number Association (INENA)
c/o David Tuttle, ENP, Pres.
PO Box 911
St. Charles, IL 60174-0911
Ph: (309)494-8035
Fax: (309)494-8034
E-mail: dtuttle@ci.peoria.il.us
URL: http://www.illinoisnena.org
Contact: David Tuttle ENP, Pres.
State. Promotes the technical advancement, availability, and implementation of a universal emergency telephone number system. **Affiliated With:** National Emergency Number Association.

3386 ■ International Brotherhood of Painters and Allied Trades of the United States and Canada AFL-CIO-CFL - District Council 30
3813 Illinois Ave., Ste.101
St. Charles, IL 60174
Ph: (630)377-2120
Fax: (630)377-2384
E-mail: cealma@ix.netcom.com
URL: http://www.paintersdc30.com
Contact: Charles E. Anderson, Sec.-Treas.
Members: 3,366. **Local.**

3387 ■ Kane County Medical Society (KCMS)
2320 Dean St., Ste.106
St. Charles, IL 60175
Ph: (630)584-6129
Fax: (630)584-6703
E-mail: info@kcmsdocs.org
URL: http://www.kcmsdocs.org
Contact: D. Andrew McNamara MD, Pres.
Local. Advances the art and science of medicine. Promotes patient care and the betterment of public health.

3388 ■ McHenry County Medical Society
2320 Dean St., Ste.106
St. Charles, IL 60175
Ph: (630)584-7173
Fax: (630)584-7179
E-mail: info@mchenrymed.com
URL: http://www.mchenrymed.org
Contact: Paul DeHaan MD, Pres.
Local. Advances the art and science of medicine. Promotes patient care and the betterment of public health.

3389 ■ Midwest Environmental Enforcement Association
c/o James Triner, Exec.Dir.
525 S Tyler Rd., Unit N-1B
St. Charles, IL 60174
Ph: (630)762-8610
Fax: (630)762-8615
Regional.

3390 ■ National Organization for Women - Fox Valley
c/o Teri Waters
PO Box 3505
St. Charles, IL 60174
E-mail: foxvalleynow@hotmail.com
URL: http://www.foxvalleynow.org
Contact: Teri Waters, Contact
Local. Affiliated With: National Organization for Women.

3391 ■ Public Relations Society of America, Suburban Chicagoland Chapter
PO Box 3023
St. Charles, IL 60174-3023
Ph: (630)992-0081
Fax: (630)922-0085
E-mail: prsasuburbanchicagoland@hotmail.com
URL: http://www.prsasuburbanchicagoland.org
Contact: Cynthia Lamb APR, Pres.
Local. Affiliated With: Public Relations Society of America.

3392 ■ St. Charles Area Chamber of Commerce
10 State Ave.
St. Charles, IL 60174
Ph: (630)584-8384
Fax: (630)584-6065
E-mail: info@stcharleschamber.com
URL: http://www.stcharleschamber.com
Contact: Lori G. Hewitt, Exec.Dir.
Founded: 1922. **Members:** 525. **Local.** Promotes business and community development in St. Charles, IL area. **Awards:** Charlemagne Award. **Frequency:** annual. **Type:** recognition. **Recipient:** for continuous voluntary service to the community. **Divisions:** Am-

bassador Club; Community; Industrial; Leads & Leads $ II; Professional; Small Business; Women's Business Council. **Affiliated With:** U.S. Chamber of Commerce. **Formerly:** St. Charles Chamber of Commerce. **Publications:** *Fox Fax*, monthly. Newsletter.

3393 ■ St. Charles Illinois Convention and Visitors Bureau
311 N 2nd St., Ste.100
St. Charles, IL 60174
Ph: (630)377-6161
Fax: (630)513-0566
Free: (800)777-4373
E-mail: info@visitstcharles.com
URL: http://www.visitstcharles.com
Contact: Kathy Loubsky, Exec.Dir.
Founded: 1983. **Local.** Promotes tourism and overnight visitors to the city of St. Charles, IL. **Publications:** *St. Charles Visitors Magazine*, annual.

3394 ■ St. Charles Sportsmen Club
PO Box 534
St. Charles, IL 60174
Ph: (630)365-9881 (630)375-7184
URL: http://www.saintcharles-sc.org
Contact: Robert Scherf, Pres.
Local.

3395 ■ United Way of St. Charles and Elburn
475 Dunham Rd., Ste.1C
PO Box 473
St. Charles, IL 60174-0473
Ph: (630)377-1930
Fax: (630)377-1950
E-mail: stcuw@aol.com
URL: http://www.unitedwayofstcharles.org
Contact: Mary Ann Subleski, Exec.Dir.
Staff: 1. **Local.** Members include every citizen in the St. Charles community. Provides funding to member agencies that serve the health and human care needs of St. Charles area residents. Participates in the United Way Drive. **Awards:** Agency Allocations. **Frequency:** quarterly. **Type:** monetary. **Recipient:** must be an approved 501 (c) (3) member agency. **Affiliated With:** United Way of America. **Formerly:** Community Chest/United Way of St. Charles. **Conventions/Meetings:** quarterly board meeting.

St. Elmo

3396 ■ American Legion, Weakly-Rowland Post 420
PO Box 132
St. Elmo, IL 62458
Ph: (309)663-0361
Fax: (309)663-5783
URL: National Affiliate–www.legion.org
Local. Affiliated With: American Legion.

St. Francisville

3397 ■ American Legion, St. Francisville Post 947
PO Box 325
St. Francisville, IL 62460
Ph: (309)663-0361
Fax: (309)663-5783
URL: National Affiliate–www.legion.org
Local. Affiliated With: American Legion.

St. Jacob

3398 ■ American Legion, Bussong-Mersinger Post 665
PO Box 214
St. Jacob, IL 62281
Ph: (309)663-0361
Fax: (309)663-5783
URL: National Affiliate–www.legion.org
Local. Affiliated With: American Legion.

3399 ■ River Bend Astronomy Club
132 Jessica Dr.
St. Jacob, IL 62281
E-mail: riverbendastro@att.net
URL: http://www.riverbendastro.org
Contact: Gary Kronk, Contact
Local. Promotes the science of astronomy. Works to encourage and coordinate activities of amateur astronomical societies. Fosters observational and computational work and craftsmanship in various fields of astronomy. **Affiliated With:** Astronomical League.

St. Joseph

3400 ■ American Legion, St. Joseph Post 634
PO Box 466
St. Joseph, IL 61873
Ph: (309)663-0361
Fax: (309)663-5783
URL: National Affiliate–www.legion.org
Local. Affiliated With: American Legion.

3401 ■ Prairie Hearts Romance Writers of America Chapter 43
c/o Nancy Finney, Pres.
PO Box 106
St. Joseph, IL 61873
E-mail: prairiehearts@yahoo.com
URL: http://www.geocities.com/prairiehearts
Contact: Nancy Finney, Pres.
Local. Works to provide networking and support to individuals seriously pursuing a career in romance fiction. Helps writers become published and established in their writing field. **Affiliated With:** Romance Writers of America.

St. Libory

3402 ■ American Legion, Illinois Post 683
c/o Henry Schmitz
PO Box 211
St. Libory, IL 62282
Ph: (309)663-0361
Fax: (309)663-5783
URL: National Affiliate–www.legion.org
Contact: Henry Schmitz, Contact
Local. Affiliated With: American Legion.

3403 ■ Illinois Christmas Tree Association (ICTA)
7223 State Rte. 15
St. Libory, IL 62282
Ph: (618)768-4221
E-mail: info@ilchristmastrees.com
URL: http://www.ilchristmastrees.com
State. Affiliated With: National Christmas Tree Association. **Formerly:** (2005) National Christmas Tree Association, Illinois.

Ste. Marie

3404 ■ American Legion, Sainte Marie Post 932
PO Box 66
Ste. Marie, IL 62459
Ph: (309)663-0361
Fax: (309)663-5783
URL: National Affiliate–www.legion.org
Local. Affiliated With: American Legion.

St. Peter

3405 ■ American Legion, Wodtka-Rothe-Reiss Post 380
PO Box 9
St. Peter, IL 62880
Ph: (309)663-0361
Fax: (309)663-5783
URL: National Affiliate–www.legion.org
Local. Affiliated With: American Legion.

3406 ■ Southern Illinois Health Information Management Association (SILHIMA)
c/o Evelyn Hencke, RHIT, Pres.
PO Box 13
St. Peter, IL 62880
E-mail: evelyn_hencke@yahoo.com
URL: http://www.ilhima.org
Contact: Evelyn Hencke RHIT, Pres.
Local. Represents the interests of individuals dedicated to the effective management of personal health information needed to deliver quality healthcare to the public. Provides career, professional development and practice resources. Sets standards for education and certification. Advocates public policy that advances Health Information Management (HIM) practice. **Affiliated With:** American Health Information Management Association.

Salem

3407 ■ American Legion, Illinois Post 128
c/o Luther B. Easley
212 E Main St.
Salem, IL 62881
Ph: (309)663-0361
Fax: (309)663-5783
URL: National Affiliate–www.legion.org
Contact: Luther B. Easley, Contact
Local. Affiliated With: American Legion.

3408 ■ Brotherhood of Locomotive Engineers and Trainmen, AFL-CIO - Division 724 (BLET)
4712 C J Heck Rd.
Salem, IL 62881
Ph: (618)548-4410
E-mail: edmike@blet724.org
URL: National Affiliate–www.ble.org
Contact: D.E. Michael, Pres.
Members: 88. **Local. Affiliated With:** Brotherhood of Locomotive Engineers and Trainmen, A Division of the Rail Conference of the International Brotherhood of Teamsters. **Formerly:** (2005) International Brotherhood of Locomotive Engineers, AFL-CIO - Division 724.

3409 ■ Greater Salem Chamber of Commerce
615 W Main St.
Salem, IL 62881
Ph: (618)548-3010
Fax: (618)548-3014
E-mail: visitus@salemilchamber.com
URL: http://www.salemilchamber.com
Contact: Jon Ashby, Pres.
Members: 300. **Local.** Promotes business and community development in Salem, IL. **Telecommunication Services:** phone referral service, (618)548-5565. **Affiliated With:** U.S. Chamber of Commerce. **Formerly:** (1999) Salem +Chamber of Commerce. **Publications:** Newsletter, monthly. Contains listings of current events. **Price:** free for members.

3410 ■ Quail Unlimited, Skillet Fork Chapter
616 Lovell
Salem, IL 62881
Ph: (618)548-3363
E-mail: skilletforkqu602@hotmail.com
URL: National Affiliate–www.qu.org
Local. Affiliated With: Quail Unlimited.

3411 ■ Shawnee Hills Appaloosa Horse Club
c/o Sheron Lemmons
2414 Paul Rd.
Salem, IL 62881
E-mail: roadapples@mvn.net
URL: National Affiliate–www.appaloosa.com
Works to promote and preserve the Appaloosa breed. **Affiliated With:** Appaloosa Horse Club.

3412 ■ South Central Illinois Regional Planning and Development Commission (SCIRP&DC)
c/o Dana Hosick - Economic Development Planner
120 Delmar Ave., Ste.A
Salem, IL 62881-2006
Ph: (618)548-4234 (618)548-4235
Fax: (618)548-4236
E-mail: scirpdc@accessus.net
URL: http://www.scirpdc.com
Contact: Fred W. Walker, Exec.Dir.

Founded: 1972. **Members:** 31. **Staff:** 5. **Budget:** $836,500. **Regional Groups:** 2. **State Groups:** 1. **Local**. Provides planning and technical assistance. Offers grant writing/management services; business development financing services. **Libraries: Type:** reference. **Holdings:** 50. **Subjects:** planning related documents. **Committees:** Area Wide Loan Review; CEO's Advisory.

3413 ■ Wabash River Dental Society
c/o Dr. Steven B. Light, Pres.
500 N Broadway
Salem, IL 62881-1516
Ph: (618)548-0774
E-mail: dlhanks@ussonet.net
URL: http://www.isds.org
Contact: Dr. Steven B. Light, Pres.

Local. Represents the interests of dentists committed to the public's oral health, ethics and professional development. Encourages the improvement of the public's oral health and promotes the art and science of dentistry. **Affiliated With:** American Dental Association; Illinois State Dental Society.

San Jose

3414 ■ American Legion, San Jose Memorial Post 1269
301 S 2nd St.
San Jose, IL 62682
Ph: (309)247-3309
Fax: (309)663-5783
URL: National Affiliate–www.legion.org

Local. Affiliated With: American Legion.

Sandwich

3415 ■ American Legion, Brown-Miller Post 181
PO Box 21
Sandwich, IL 60548
Ph: (815)786-2437
Fax: (309)663-5783
URL: National Affiliate–www.legion.org

Local. Affiliated With: American Legion.

3416 ■ Sandwich Chamber of Commerce
PO Box 214
128 E Railroad St.
Sandwich, IL 60548
Ph: (815)786-9075
Fax: (815)786-2505
E-mail: info@sandwich-il.org
URL: http://www.sandwich-il.org
Contact: Pat Voga, Admin.

Membership Dues: business, $110-$550 (annual) • government/education/utility, $220 (annual) • nonprofit/retired, $55 (annual) • financial institution, $165-$550 (annual). **Local**. Works to provide a favorable business climate by acting as a vehicle to help promote the area's economic progress. Supports the development of the business community and to improve the quality of life for those that live and work in the area. **Committees:** Dinner Dance; Trade Fair. **Publications:** *Business Connection*, monthly. Newsletter.

Sauk Village

3417 ■ American Legion, Sauk Village Post 1259
21542 Cynthia Ave.
Sauk Village, IL 60411
Ph: (708)758-4648
Fax: (309)663-5783
URL: National Affiliate–www.legion.org

Local. Affiliated With: American Legion.

Saunemin

3418 ■ American Legion, Saunemin Verdun Post 531
PO Box 202
Saunemin, IL 61769
Ph: (309)663-0361
Fax: (309)663-5783
URL: National Affiliate–www.legion.org

Local. Affiliated With: American Legion.

Savanna

3419 ■ American Legion, Van-Bibber-Hansen Post 148
313 1/2 Main St.
Savanna, IL 61074
Ph: (309)663-0361
Fax: (309)663-5783
URL: National Affiliate–www.legion.org

Local. Affiliated With: American Legion.

3420 ■ National Active And Retired Federal Employees Association - Palisades 604
11573 Oakton Rd.
Savanna, IL 61074-8621
Ph: (815)273-7513
URL: National Affiliate–www.narfe.org
Contact: Thomas J. Michels, Contact

Local. Protects the retirement future of employees through education. Informs members on issues affecting the retirement. **Affiliated With:** National Association of Retired Federal Employees.

3421 ■ Savanna Chamber of Commerce (SCC)
PO Box 315
Savanna, IL 61074
Ph: (815)273-2722
Fax: (815)273-2754
E-mail: savchamber@grics.net
URL: http://www.savanna-il.com
Contact: Karen Wallace, Exec.Dir.

Founded: 1949. **Members:** 100. **Staff:** 1. **Local**. Promotes business and community development in Savanna, IL. Sponsors annual trade shows and seminars, annual Car Cruise and Beach Party, annual Gingerbread Christmas and Cookie Walk, and other social and promotional activities. **Publications:** *Outlook*, monthly. Newsletter. **Conventions/Meetings:** monthly board meeting.

Savoy

3422 ■ Champaign County Association of Realtors
305 Burwash
Savoy, IL 61874
Ph: (217)356-1389
Fax: (217)356-3684
E-mail: lindag01@aol.com
URL: National Affiliate–www.realtor.org
Contact: Linda J. Green, Exec. Officer

Local. Strives to develop real estate business practices. Advocates the right to own, use and transfer real property. Provides a facility for professional development, research and exchange of information among members and to the general public. **Affiliated With:** National Association of Realtors.

3423 ■ Illinois Pilots Association (IPA)
PO Box 481
Savoy, IL 61874
E-mail: webmaster@illinoispilots.com
URL: http://www.illinoispilots.com
Contact: Ruth Frantz, Contact

State. Promotes aviation safety and pilot education. Improves and strengthens the aviation industry. Facilitates communication among members. **Affiliated With:** United States Pilots Association.

3424 ■ Mid-State Sheet Metal and Air Conditioning Contractors Association
c/o Ralph E. Patzke
100 Parkview Ln., Apt. 127
Savoy, IL 61874-8107
Ph: (217)356-0841
Fax: (217)356-0142
E-mail: rpatzke@insightbb.com
URL: National Affiliate–www.smacna.org
Contact: Ralph E. Patzke, Contact

Local. Affiliated With: Sheet Metal and Air Conditioning Contractors' National Association.

3425 ■ National Association of Rocketry - Central Illinois Aerospace (CIA)
c/o Robert Brunner
507 Buttercup Dr.
Savoy, IL 61874
Ph: (217)344-5723
E-mail: rbrunner@uiuc.edu
URL: http://www.prairienet.org/cia
Contact: Robert Brunner, Contact

Local.

3426 ■ Navy League of the United States, Champaign
c/o Michael D. Barker
705 W Church St.
Savoy, IL 61874-9702
Ph: (217)398-4889
E-mail: mdbarker42@aol.com
URL: National Affiliate–www.navyleague.org
Contact: Michael D. Barker, Pres.

Local. Civilian organization that supports U.S. capability to keep the sea lanes open through a strong, viable Navy, Marine Corps, Coast Guard, and Merchant Marine. Seeks to awaken interest and cooperation of U.S. citizens in matters serving to aid, improve, and develop the efficiency of U.S. naval and maritime forces and equipment. **Affiliated With:** Navy League of the United States.

Saybrook

3427 ■ American Legion, David Humphrey Daniel Post 427
PO Box 11
Saybrook, IL 61770
Ph: (309)475-6231
Fax: (309)663-5783
URL: National Affiliate–www.legion.org

Local. Affiliated With: American Legion.

3428 ■ Illinois Dairy Goat Association
c/o Richard Hudson
Rte. 1, Box 88
Saybrook, IL 61770
Ph: (309)475-2921
URL: National Affiliate–adga.org
Contact: Richard Hudson, Contact

State. Affiliated With: American Dairy Goat Association.

Schaumburg

3429 ■ American Legion, Ellsworth Meinke Post 1983
PO Box 68213
Schaumburg, IL 60194
Ph: (309)663-0361
Fax: (309)663-5783
URL: National Affiliate–www.legion.org
Local. Affiliated With: American Legion.

3430 ■ ASTD, South Central Wisconsin Chapter
c/o Kimberly LaBounty
1901 N Roselle Rd., Ste.800
Schaumburg, IL 60195
Ph: (847)592-7080
Fax: (630)563-9181
Free: (866)717-7292
E-mail: astdscwc@astdscwc.org
URL: http://www.astdscwc.org
Local. Works to provide learning and networking opportunities for professionals dedicated to improving individual and organizational performance. **Affiliated With:** ASTD.

3431 ■ Autism Society of America, Northwest Suburban Chapter
300 Fleming Ln.
Schaumburg, IL 60193
Ph: (847)885-8006
E-mail: autismillinois@aol.com
URL: http://www.Autismillinois.com
Local. Works to improve the quality of life of all individuals with autism and their families through education, research and advocacy. Promotes public awareness and understanding of the symptoms and problems of individuals with autism.

3432 ■ Chicago Divorce Association
1450 E Amer. Ln.
Zurich Towers, Ste.1400
Schaumburg, IL 60173
Ph: (630)860-2100
E-mail: info@chicagodivorce.com
Contact: Dr. Richard A. Delorto, Exec.Dir.
Founded: 1986. **Members:** 5,000. **Membership Dues:** life, $125. **Staff:** 7. **For-Profit. Regional.** Provides services and information to people before, during and after divorce, including 24-hour educational counseling, legal information, private investigators, meditation, certified child custody evaluations, and attorney referrals. **Publications:** *Child Custody Evaluations and Procedures*. **Price:** $29.95. **Conventions/Meetings:** periodic support group meeting.

3433 ■ Chicago Rocks and Minerals Society
c/o Craig Heinze, Pres.
1131 Hampton Harbor
Schaumburg, IL 60193-4219
E-mail: fgutkowski@chicagorocks.org
URL: http://www.chicagorocks.org
Contact: Ron Gutkowski, Sec.
Local. Aims to further the study of Earth Sciences and the practice of lapidary arts and mineralogy. **Affiliated With:** American Federation of Mineralogical Societies.

3434 ■ Eagles Cricket Club
1120 E Algonquin Rd., No. 30
Schaumburg, IL 60173
URL: http://www.usaca.org/Clubs.htm
Contact: Chandra Warrier, Contact
Local.

3435 ■ Florida Urological Society (FUS)
c/o Wendy J. Weiser, Exec.Dir.
1111 N Plaza Dr., Ste.550
Schaumburg, IL 60173
Ph: (847)571-7249
Fax: (847)517-7229
E-mail: info@flaurological.org
URL: http://www.flaurological.org
Contact: Wendy J. Weiser, Exec.Dir.
State.

3436 ■ Greater Woodfield Convention and Visitors Bureau (GWCVB)
1430 N Meacham Rd., Ste.1400
Schaumburg, IL 60173
Ph: (847)490-1010
Free: (800)VIS-ITGW
E-mail: info@chicagonorthwest.com
URL: http://www.chicagonorthwest.com
Contact: Tom Dahlquist, Dir. of Sales
Local. Represents the hotels and attractions in the northwest suburbs of Chicago.

3437 ■ Illinois Association of Collegiate Registrars and Admissions Officers
c/o Gwen E. Kanelos, Asst.VP for Enrollment/ Student Services
Roosevelt Univ.
1400 N Roosevelt Blvd.
MS SCH110-A
Schaumburg, IL 60173
Ph: (847)619-7300 (847)619-8620
Fax: (847)619-8636
Free: (877)APP-LYRU
E-mail: gkanelos@roosevelt.edu
URL: http://www.roosevelt.edu
Contact: Gwen E. Kanelos, Asst.VP for Enrollment/ Student Services
Founded: 1922. **Membership Dues:** institutional, $110 (annual) • individual, $10 (annual). **State. Affiliated With:** American Association of Collegiate Registrars and Admissions Officers. **Publications:** *The Chronicle*, quarterly. Newsletter. **Conventions/Meetings:** annual meeting.

3438 ■ Illinois Regional Insulation Contractors Association (IRIC)
1515 E Woodfield Rd., No. 118
Schaumburg, IL 60173
Ph: (847)619-9528
Fax: (847)619-9556
E-mail: info@iricinsulation.org
URL: http://www.iricinsulation.org
Contact: Steve Wanaski Jr., Pres.
State. Affiliated With: National Insulation Association.

3439 ■ Midwest Business Brokers and Intermediaries (MBBI)
869 E Schaumburg Rd., No. 365
Schaumburg, IL 60194
Ph: (847)882-8230
Fax: (847)882-0362
E-mail: twhipple@falconmanda.com
URL: http://www.mbbi.org
Contact: Tom Whipple, Pres.
Regional. Disseminates industry information; encourages growth of sales; assists in new industry developments. Represents members in legislative matters and lobbies for recognition of the industry. Coordinates activity among business brokerages and cooperates with other types of brokerages. Conducts educational and promotional programs for members. **Affiliated With:** International Business Brokers Association.

3440 ■ North Central Section of the American Urological Association
1111 N Plaza Dr., Ste.550
Schaumburg, IL 60173-4950
Ph: (847)517-1544
Fax: (847)517-7229
E-mail: info@ncsaua.org
URL: http://www.ncsaua.org
Contact: Ms. Wendy Weiser, Exec.Dir.
Regional. Represents the interests of physicians specializing in urology. Formulates healthcare policies for urologists. **Affiliated With:** American Urological Association.

3441 ■ Northwest Suburban Astronomers
PO Box 68265
Schaumburg, IL 60168
Ph: (815)759-3812
E-mail: jskuban@comcast.net
URL: http://www.nsaclub.org
Contact: Jay Skuban, Contact
Local. Promotes the science of astronomy. Works to encourage and coordinate activities of amateur astronomical societies. Fosters observational and computational work and craftsmanship in various fields of astronomy. **Affiliated With:** Astronomical League.

3442 ■ Ohio Urological Society (OUS)
1111 N Plaza Dr., Ste.550
Schaumburg, IL 60173
Ph: (847)517-2801
Fax: (847)517-7229
E-mail: contactus@ousweb.org
URL: http://www.ousweb.org
Contact: Mark Daniel Stovsky MD, Pres.
State. Stimulates interest in the science and practice of urology. Promotes understanding of socioeconomic and political affairs affecting medical practice. Formulates healthcare policies for urologists.

3443 ■ Psi Chi, National Honor Society in Psychology - Illinois School of Professional Psychology at Argosy University-Schaumburg (ISPP)
1000 N Plaza Dr., Ste.100
Schaumburg, IL 60173-4990
Ph: (847)290-7400 (847)598-6180
Fax: (847)598-6158
E-mail: pdodzik@argosyu.edu
URL: http://auschaumburg.net
Contact: Dr. Peter Dodzik, Advisor
Local.

3444 ■ Psi Chi, National Honor Society in Psychology - Roosevelt University Albert A. Robin Campus
c/o Dept. of Psychology
1400 N Roosevelt Blvd.
Schaumburg, IL 60173-4348
Ph: (847)619-8542 (847)619-8543
Fax: (847)619-8555
E-mail: mhelford@aol.com
URL: http://www.psichi.org/chapters/info.asp?chapter_id=993
Contact: Mike Helford PhD, Advisor
Local.

3445 ■ Schaumburg Business Association (SBA)
c/o Laurie Stone, Pres.
28 W Schaumburg Rd.
Schaumburg, IL 60194
Ph: (847)885-8800
Fax: (847)885-9099
E-mail: info@schaumburgbusiness.com
URL: http://www.schaumburgbusiness.com
Contact: Laurie Stone, Pres.
Local.

3446 ■ Schaumburg Table Tennis Club
Community Rec. Center
505 N Springinsguth Rd.
Schaumburg, IL 60194
Ph: (847)343-1616
E-mail: hackie_honda@yahoo.com
URL: http://www.sttc.net
Contact: Spenser Lam, Contact
Local. Affiliated With: U.S.A. Table Tennis.

3447 ■ Singles Pleasing the Lord
c/o Debra Powell
PO Box 59131
Schaumburg, IL 60159
Ph: (847)640-1878
URL: http://www.singlespleasingthelord.com
Contact: Debra Powell, Pres.
Local.

3448 ■ Society of Incentive and Travel Executives, Chicago Chapter
c/o Summit Event Management, Inc.
636 Remington Rd., Ste.A
Schaumburg, IL 60173

Ph: (847)908-0183
Fax: (847)908-0184
E-mail: jfeldman@itcheque.com
URL: http://sitechicago.org
Contact: James Feldman CITE, Co-Pres.
Local. Increases the level of professionalism of the incentive industry. Serves members and other incentive industry professionals by providing educational programs, information services and networking opportunities. **Affiliated With:** Society of Incentive and Travel Executives.

3449 ■ South Central Section of the American Urological Association
1111 N Plaza Dr., Ste.550
Schaumburg, IL 60173-4950
Ph: (847)605-0850
Fax: (847)517-7229
E-mail: info@scsauanet.org
URL: http://www.scsauanet.org
Contact: Ms. Wendy Weiser, Exec.Dir.
Regional. Represents the interests of physicians specializing in urology. Formulates healthcare policies for urologists. **Affiliated With:** American Urological Association.

3450 ■ Southeastern Section of the American Urological Association
1111 N Plaza Dr., Ste.550
Schaumburg, IL 60173-4950
Ph: (847)969-0248
Fax: (847)517-7229
E-mail: ses@wjweiser.com
URL: http://www.sesaua.org
Contact: Ms. Wendy Weiser, Exec.Sec.
Regional. Represents the interests of physicians specializing in urology. Formulates healthcare policies for urologists. **Affiliated With:** American Urological Association.

3451 ■ Tiger Cricket Club
1110 E Algonquin Rd., No. 2R
Schaumburg, IL 60173
URL: http://www.usaca.org/Clubs.htm
Contact: Praveen Tammana, Contact
Local.

3452 ■ United Transportation Union, AFL-CIO - Local Union 1258
326 Br.wood Ct.
Schaumburg, IL 60193
E-mail: utu1258@aol.com
URL: http://hometown.aol.com/utu1258/UTUMain.htm
Contact: L.E. Vicars, Contact
Members: 56. **Local. Affiliated With:** United Transportation Union.

3453 ■ Wildcats Cricket Club
1251 Olde Farm Rd., No. 205
Schaumburg, IL 60173
URL: http://www.usaca.org/Clubs.htm
Contact: Sanjay Barretto, Contact
Local.

Schiller Park

3454 ■ ACF Chicago Chefs of Cuisine
c/o Joe Aiello
4318 River Rd.
Schiller Park, IL 60176
Ph: (847)671-6095
Fax: (847)671-6128
E-mail: apropo_chef@juno.com
URL: National Affiliate–www.acfchefs.org
Contact: Joe Aiello, Office Dir.
Local. Promotes the culinary profession. Provides on-going educational training and networking for members. Provides opportunities for competition, professional recognition and access to educational forums with other culinarians at local, regional, national and international events. **Affiliated With:** American Culinary Federation.

3455 ■ American Legion, Schiller Park Post 104
PO Box 2031
Schiller Park, IL 60176
Ph: (708)678-5197
Fax: (309)663-5783
URL: National Affiliate–www.legion.org
Local. Affiliated With: American Legion.

Scott AFB

3456 ■ American Meteorological Society, Greater St. Louis
c/o James E. Rogers Jr., VP
4609B Patrick Henry Cir.
Scott AFB, IL 62225
Ph: (618)628-1719
E-mail: theriaux@charter.net
URL: National Affiliate–www.ametsoc.org/AMS
Contact: James E. Rogers Jr., VP
Local. Affiliated With: American Meteorological Society.

3457 ■ Illinois Trekkers Volkssport Club
c/o Charles Botula
PO Box 25063
Scott AFB, IL 62225-0063
Ph: (618)236-9521
E-mail: packysuba@juno.com
URL: http://www.illinois-trekkers.org
Contact: Charles Botula, Pres.
Founded: 1980. **Members:** 200. **Membership Dues:** family, $10 (annual) • single, $6 (annual). **State**. Persons in southwestern Illinois interested in the sport of walking. Promotes individual physical fitness through education. Hosts trekking events. **Affiliated With:** American Volkssport Association. **Publications:** *Footnotes*, quarterly. Newsletter. **Conventions/Meetings:** biennial meeting (exhibits).

3458 ■ Military Officers Association of America, Southwest Illinois Chapter
c/o Col. Richard Smith
PO Box 25122
Scott AFB, IL 62225-0122
Ph: (618)624-6113
E-mail: richardsmith26@charter.net
URL: National Affiliate–www.moaa.org
Contact: Col. Richard Smith, Contact
Local. Affiliated With: Military Officers Association of America.

Seneca

3459 ■ American Legion, Kasal Post 457
PO Box 354
Seneca, IL 61360
Ph: (309)663-0361
Fax: (309)663-5783
URL: National Affiliate–www.legion.org
Local. Affiliated With: American Legion.

Sesser

3460 ■ American Legion, Bates Post 560
302 W Coal St.
Sesser, IL 62884
Ph: (309)663-0361
Fax: (309)663-5783
URL: National Affiliate–www.legion.org
Local. Affiliated With: American Legion.

Seymour

3461 ■ American Legion, Seymour Post 1256
PO Box 158
Seymour, IL 61875
Ph: (217)687-4690
Fax: (309)663-5783
URL: National Affiliate–www.legion.org
Local. Affiliated With: American Legion.

Shannon

3462 ■ American Legion, Boyle-Hoy Post 379
22 E Market St.
Shannon, IL 61078
Ph: (309)663-0361
Fax: (309)663-5783
URL: National Affiliate–www.legion.org
Local. Affiliated With: American Legion.

Shawneetown

3463 ■ American Legion, St. Mihiel Post 585
PO Box 407
Shawneetown, IL 62984
Ph: (309)663-0361
Fax: (309)663-5783
URL: National Affiliate–www.legion.org
Local. Affiliated With: American Legion.

Sheffield

3464 ■ American Legion, H.F. Hortz Post 415
c/o Sheffield Fire Hall
PO Box 696
Sheffield, IL 61361
Ph: (815)454-2731
Fax: (309)663-5783
URL: National Affiliate–www.legion.org
Local. Affiliated With: American Legion.

Shelbyville

3465 ■ American Legion, Roy Vanderpool Post 81
121 2nd St.
Shelbyville, IL 62565
Ph: (217)774-4329
Fax: (309)663-5783
URL: National Affiliate–www.legion.org
Local. Affiliated With: American Legion.

3466 ■ Mothers Against Drunk Driving, Shelby County
PO Box 14
Shelbyville, IL 62565
Ph: (217)774-2030
Fax: (217)774-2040
URL: National Affiliate–www.madd.org
Local. Victims of drunk driving crashes; concerned citizens. Encourages citizen participation in working towards reform of the drunk driving problem and the prevention of underage drinking. Acts as the voice of victims of drunk driving crashes by speaking on their behalf to communities, businesses, and educational groups. **Affiliated With:** Mothers Against Drunk Driving.

3467 ■ Shelbyville Area Chamber of Commerce (SCC)
124 N Morgan St.
Shelbyville, IL 62565
Ph: (217)774-2221
Fax: (217)774-2221
E-mail: chamber01@consolidated.net
URL: http://www.shelbyvillechamberofcommerce.com
Contact: Joe Hampton, Contact
Founded: 1930. **Members:** 350. **Budget:** $18,000. **Local**. Promotes business and community development in Shelbyville, IL. **Libraries: Type:** open to the public. **Publications:** *Chamber Chatter*, bimonthly. Newsletter. **Price:** free. **Circulation:** 15 • *Chamber of Commerce*. Brochure. **Conventions/Meetings:** monthly board meeting.

Sheldon

3468 ■ American Legion, Sheldon Post 393
159 S 4th St.
Sheldon, IL 60966
Ph: (309)663-0361
Fax: (309)663-5783
URL: National Affiliate–www.legion.org
Local. Affiliated With: American Legion.

Sheridan

3469 ■ American Legion, Illinois Post 729
c/o La Verne W. Anderson
PO Box 206
Sheridan, IL 60551
Ph: (815)496-2210
Fax: (309)663-5783
URL: National Affiliate–www.legion.org
Contact: La Verne W. Anderson, Contact
Local. Affiliated With: American Legion.

Sherman

3470 ■ Illinois Sheriffs Association
c/o Greg Sullivan, Exec.Dir.
PO Box 263
2626 E. Andrew Rd.
Sherman, IL 62684-0263
Ph: (217)496-2371
Fax: (217)496-2373
E-mail: greg@ilsheriff.org
URL: http://www.ilsheriff.org
Contact: Mr. Greg S. Sullivan, Exec.Dir.
Founded: 1928. **Members:** 33,000. **Staff:** 6. **Budget:** $1,200,000. **Regional Groups:** 3. **State Groups:** 1. **State.**

3471 ■ Sons of Norway, Lincolnland Lodge 5-598
c/o Cora Elizabeth Muench, Pres.
6257 Sherman Rd.
Sherman, IL 62684-8133
Ph: (217)566-3440
E-mail: eemuench@earth.link.net
URL: National Affiliate–www.sofn.com
Contact: Cora Elizabeth Muench, Pres.
Local. Affiliated With: Sons of Norway.

Shipman

3472 ■ Illinois Valley Angus Breeders Association
c/o Jeff Bagley, Pres.
PO Box 235
Shipman, IL 62685-0235
Ph: (618)836-7770
URL: National Affiliate–www.angus.org
Contact: Jeff Bagley, Pres.
Local. Affiliated With: American Angus Association.

3473 ■ Quail Unlimited, Quad County Chapter
PO Box 140
Shipman, IL 62685
Ph: (618)836-5439
URL: National Affiliate–www.qu.org
Local. Affiliated With: Quail Unlimited.

Sibley

3474 ■ American Legion, Illinois Post 244
c/o Martin H. Suntken
235 N Franklin St.
Sibley, IL 61773
Ph: (309)663-0361
Fax: (309)663-5783
URL: National Affiliate–www.legion.org
Contact: Martin H. Suntken, Contact
Local. Affiliated With: American Legion.

Sidell

3475 ■ American Legion, Harvey Stunkard Post 530
PO Box 381
Sidell, IL 61876
Ph: (217)288-9076
Fax: (309)663-5783
URL: National Affiliate–www.legion.org
Local. Affiliated With: American Legion.

Sidney

3476 ■ American Legion, Sidney Post 433
212 S David
Sidney, IL 61877
Ph: (309)663-0361
Fax: (309)663-5783
URL: National Affiliate–www.legion.org
Local. Affiliated With: American Legion.

3477 ■ Illinois Mathematics Teacher Educators
PO Box 266
Sidney, IL 61877-0266
Ph: (217)688-2728
URL: National Affiliate–www.nctm.org
Contact: Carol Castellon, Contact
State. Aims to improve the teaching and learning of mathematics. Provides vision, leadership and professional development to support teachers in ensuring mathematics learning of the highest quality for all students. **Affiliated With:** National Council of Teachers of Mathematics.

Sigel

3478 ■ American Legion, Sigel Post 1134
503 S Church St.
Sigel, IL 62462
Ph: (217)844-3690
Fax: (309)663-5783
URL: National Affiliate–www.legion.org
Local. Affiliated With: American Legion.

Silvis

3479 ■ Midwest Central Service Association
c/o Nancy Hunt, Pres.
Illini Hosp.
704 Fourth Ave.
Silvis, IL 61282
Ph: (309)792-4293
Fax: (309)792-4338
E-mail: huntn@genesishealth.com
URL: National Affiliate–www.ashcsp.org
Contact: Nancy Hunt, Pres.
Regional. Promotes healthcare central service, sterile processing and inventory management practices. Provides education, professional and organization development, advocacy and communication to healthcare service professionals. **Affiliated With:** American Society for Healthcare Central Service Professionals.

Skokie

3480 ■ American Hellenic Educational Progressive Association - Lincolnwood, Chapter 396
c/o George Houmpavlis, Pres.
6845 N Lavergne St.
Skokie, IL 60076
Ph: (847)674-2135
E-mail: baba727@aol.com
URL: http://www.ahepafamily.org/d13
Contact: George Houmpavlis, Pres.
Local. Affiliated With: American Hellenic Educational Progressive Association.

3481 ■ American Legion, Skokie Post 320
PO Box 292
Skokie, IL 60077
Ph: (708)674-0320
Fax: (309)663-5783
URL: National Affiliate–www.legion.org
Local. Affiliated With: American Legion.

3482 ■ American Society of Dowsers, Northern Illinois Chapter
8129 Kilpatrick
Skokie, IL 60076
Ph: (847)674-3490
E-mail: gemschneider@earthlink.net
URL: National Affiliate–dowsers.new-hampshire.net
Contact: Arettha Schneider, Sec.
Local. Affiliated With: American Society of Dowsers.

3483 ■ Chicagoland Muskie Hunters
7600 Kilbourn Ave.
Skokie, IL 60076
Ph: (847)677-0017
E-mail: dondublin@hotmail.com
URL: http://www.chicagolandmuskiehunters.org
Contact: Don Dublin, Pres.
Local.

3484 ■ East Prairie School Educational Foundation
c/o Marlene S. Kamm
3907 W Dobson St.
Skokie, IL 60076-3718
Ph: (847)673-1141
URL: http://www.eps.n-cook.k12.il.us
Contact: Marlene S. Kamm, Contact
Founded: 1998. **Members:** 14. **Local.**

3485 ■ Estate Planning Council of Lake County
c/o Richard Rosenbaum, CPA, Pres.
5014 Greenwood
Skokie, IL 60077
Ph: (847)673-4010
Fax: (847)673-4012
E-mail: richard.rosenbaum@gsbpop.uchicago.edu
URL: http://councils.naepc.org
Contact: Richard Rosenbaum CPA, Pres.
Members: 60. **Local.** Fosters understanding of the proper relationship between the functions of professionals in the estate planning field. Provides forum for estate planning professionals in Lake County, IL. Encourages cooperation among members. **Affiliated With:** National Association of Estate Planners and Councils.

3486 ■ Ethical Humanist Society of Greater Chicago
7574 N Lincoln Ave.
Skokie, IL 60077-3334
Ph: (847)677-3334
E-mail: admin@ethicalhuman.org
URL: http://www.ethicalhuman.org
Local.

3487 ■ Evanston Community Tennis Association (ECTA)
c/o Mr. Alan Soell, Pres.
8228 Ridgeway Ave.
Skokie, IL 60076
Ph: (847)982-1414
E-mail: alansoell@comcast.net
URL: http://www.evanstontennis.org
Contact: Mr Alan Soell, Pres.
Founded: 2001. **Members:** 200. **Membership Dues:** adult, $15 (annual) • child, $5 (annual). **Budget:** $8,000. **Local Groups:** 1. **Local.** Aims to sustain, develop, and promote tennis for all ages in the community by providing and coordinating league, tourna-

ment and other recreational tennis opportunities to and for its membership.

3488 ■ Mail Systems Management Association, Chicago Chapter
c/o Drop Ship Express
9434 Latrobe Ave.
Skokie, IL 60077-1112
Ph: (847)967-8925
Fax: (847)967-8935
URL: National Affiliate–www.msmanational.org
Contact: Barbara Creinin, Pres.
Local. Provide a forum for people involved in the management, supervision and support of mail systems in business, industry, government and institutions. Raises the level of management prestige and esteem for managers employed in mail management.

3489 ■ North Shore Dog Training Club (NSDTC)
c/o Hope Saidel
4923 Oakton St.
Skokie, IL 60077
Ph: (847)677-0680
E-mail: trainer@nsdtc.com
URL: http://www.nsdtc.com
Contact: Colleen Tsuji, Corresponding Sec.
Local. Affiliated With: American Kennel Club.

3490 ■ Skokie Chamber of Commerce (SCC)
5002-5006 Oakton St.
Skokie, IL 60077
Ph: (847)673-0240
Fax: (847)673-0249
E-mail: chamber@skokiechamber.org
URL: http://www.skokiechamber.org
Contact: Sandi Stamp, Sec.
Founded: 1925. **Members:** 550. **Membership Dues:** business (based on number of employees), $185-$900 • school district, $200 • financial institution (base), $500 • retailer, $275 • hotel/nursing home (per bed), $3. **Staff:** 2. **Budget:** $140,000. **Local**. Promotes business and community development in the Skokie, IL area. **Convention/Meeting:** none. **Committees:** Ambassadors; Golf; Marketing; Program/Education. **Roundtables:** Industry. **Publications:** *Business and Professional Directory*, annual • *Chamber Connection*, monthly. Newsletter • *Industrial Directory*, annual.

Smithton

3491 ■ American Legion, Gem Post 937
102 N Main St., No. 266
Smithton, IL 62285
Ph: (618)235-2303
Fax: (309)663-5783
URL: National Affiliate–www.legion.org
Local. Affiliated With: American Legion.

Somonauk

3492 ■ American Legion, M.R.L. Post 772
345 S Cherry St.
Somonauk, IL 60552
Ph: (309)663-0361
Fax: (309)663-5783
URL: National Affiliate–www.legion.org
Local. Affiliated With: American Legion.

3493 ■ Antique Automobile Club of America, Illinois Region - Silver Springs Chapter
c/o Rick Shaw, Pres.
320 N Sycamore St.
PO Box 713
Somonauk, IL 60552
E-mail: ricks@indianvalley.com
URL: http://www.aaca.org/illinois/
Contact: Rick Shaw, Pres.
Local. Collectors, hobbyists, and others interested in the preservation, maintenance, and restoration of automobiles and in automotive history. **Affiliated With:** Antique Automobile Club of America.

Sorento

3494 ■ American Legion, Kessinger Post 713
PO Box 286
Sorento, IL 62086
Ph: (309)663-0361
Fax: (309)663-5783
URL: National Affiliate–www.legion.org
Local. Affiliated With: American Legion.

South Beloit

3495 ■ American Legion, Holtz-Hirst Post 288
PO Box 97
South Beloit, IL 61080
Ph: (608)365-2764
Fax: (309)663-5783
URL: National Affiliate–www.legion.org
Local. Affiliated With: American Legion.

3496 ■ Muskies Flatlanders Chapter
5776 Vesper Dr.
South Beloit, IL 61080
Ph: (815)389-4622
E-mail: muskejunke@aol.com
URL: National Affiliate–www.muskiesinc.org
Contact: Steve Ruhmann, Pres.
Local.

South Elgin

3497 ■ Elgin Coin Club (ECC)
PO Box 561
South Elgin, IL 60177
E-mail: ecc1@worksandwords.com
URL: http://www.prairienet.com/coins/ecc
Contact: Doug Nelson, Pres.
Membership Dues: full, $10 (annual) • junior, $5 (annual) • family, $15 (annual). **Local**. Collectors in the Elgin, Illinois area who get together on the first Wednesday of the month to celebrate collecting coins and paper money. **Affiliated With:** American Numismatic Association.

3498 ■ Refrigeration Service Engineers Society, Fox Valley Chapter
c/o Rich Hoke, CMS
21 Laurel Ct.
South Elgin, IL 60177
Ph: (847)742-4377
URL: National Affiliate–www.rses.org
Contact: Rich Hoke CMS, Pres.
Local. Represents individuals engaged in refrigeration, air-conditioning and heating installation, service, sales and maintenance. Conducts training courses and certification testing. **Affiliated With:** Refrigeration Service Engineers Society.

3499 ■ South Elgin Lions Club
PO Box 221
South Elgin, IL 60177
Ph: (847)888-9575
URL: http://www.southelginlions.com
Local. Affiliated With: Lions Clubs International.

3500 ■ Trips for Kids-Fox Valley
587 Arlington Ln.
South Elgin, IL 60177
Ph: (847)927-0759
E-mail: tfkoxvalley@sbcglobal.net
URL: http://www.bicyclesetc-il.com/tfkfoxvalley
Contact: Laura Andersen, Dir.
Local. Affiliated With: International Mountain Bicycling Association.

South Holland

3501 ■ American Legion, South Holland Post 883
PO Box 251
South Holland, IL 60473
Ph: (708)333-6601
Fax: (309)663-5783
URL: National Affiliate–www.legion.org
Local. Affiliated With: American Legion.

3502 ■ American Society for Quality, Illiana Section 1213
c/o Mike Boothe
17035 Westview Ave.
South Holland, IL 60473
Ph: (708)596-5800
E-mail: quality@callabco.com
URL: http://www.asq-illiana.org
Contact: Mike Boothe, Contact
Local. Advances learning, quality improvement and knowledge exchange to improve business results and to create better workplaces and communities worldwide. Provides a forum for information exchange, professional development and continuous learning in the science of quality. **Affiliated With:** American Society for Quality.

3503 ■ Association for Iron and Steel Technology Midwest Chapter
c/o Thomas H. Cipich, Sec.
823 E 168th St.
South Holland, IL 60473
Ph: (708)596-8361
Fax: (708)596-1421
E-mail: ositom84@aol.com
URL: http://www.aistech.org/chapters/mc_midwest.htm
Contact: Thomas H. Cipich, Sec.
Regional. Seeks to provide a medium of communication and cooperation among those interested in any phase of ferrous metallurgy and materials science and technology. Encourages interest in and the advancement of education in metallurgical and materials science and engineering related to the iron and steel industry. Conducts short continuing education courses. **Affiliated With:** Association for Iron and Steel Technology.

3504 ■ Homewood-Flossmoor - Young Life
PO Box 1125
South Holland, IL 60473
Ph: (708)331-7922
URL: http://whereis.younglife.org/FriendlyUrlRedirector.aspx?ID=C-3061
Local.

3505 ■ McKinley Jr. High - Wyldlife
PO Box 1125
South Holland, IL 60473
Ph: (708)331-7922
URL: http://sites.younglife.org/_layouts/ylext/default.aspx?ID=C-824
Local. Represents the interests of individuals committed to impacting kids' lives and preparing them for the future. Helps young people develop their skills, assets and attitudes to reach their full God-given potential. Reaches suburban, urban, multicultural and disabled kids and teenage mothers. **Affiliated With:** Young Life.

3506 ■ Phi Theta Kappa, Psi Pi Chapter - South Suburban College of Cook County
c/o Herman Stark
15800 S State St.
South Holland, IL 60473
Ph: (708)596-2000
E-mail: hstark@southsuburbancollege.edu
URL: http://www.ptk.org/directories/chapters/IL/198-1.htm
Contact: Herman Stark, Advisor
Local.

3507 ■ South Holland Business Association (SHBA)
PO Box 334
South Holland, IL 60473
Ph: (708)596-0065
Fax: (708)596-6696
E-mail: info@shba.org
URL: http://www.shba.org
Contact: Patricia A. Bohacik, Exec.Dir.
Founded: 1979. **Members:** 300. **Regional**. Promotes business and community development. **Awards:** Beautification Awards. **Frequency:** annual. **Type:** recognition. **Publications:** *Intercom*, monthly. Newsletter. **Circulation:** 400. **Advertising:** accepted • Directory, annual. **Conventions/Meetings:** monthly meeting - always fourth Thursday.

3508 ■ South Holland Historical Society (SHHS)
PO Box 48
South Holland, IL 60473
Ph: (708)596-2722
URL: National Affiliate–www.nationaltrust.org
Contact: Pauline Schaap, Pres.
Founded: 1969. **Members:** 115. **Membership Dues:** individual, $5 (annual). **Staff:** 1. **Local**. Individuals and organizations interested in the history of South Holland, IL. Disseminates historical information; conducts social programs. Maintains museum, Paarlberg Farm Homestead, and Van Oosterbrugge Centennial Home. Sponsors Labor Day festival and barn sale. **Affiliated With:** National Trust for Historic Preservation. **Publications:** *Onion Skin*, quarterly. Newsletter. **Conventions/Meetings:** monthly meeting - always 3rd Tuesday of the month.

3509 ■ South Holland Professional Firefighters Association
c/o Peter L. Renz
PO Box 304
South Holland, IL 60473
Ph: (708)331-3123
E-mail: sstegenga@iaff4109.org
URL: http://www.iaff4109.org
Contact: Scott Stegenga, Pres.
Local.

3510 ■ Thornwood High School - Young Life
PO Box 1125
South Holland, IL 60473
Ph: (708)331-7922
URL: http://thornwood.younglife.org
Local.

3511 ■ Young Life Chicago South
PO Box 1125
South Holland, IL 60473
Ph: (708)331-7922
Fax: (708)331-7922
URL: http://chicagosouth.younglife.org
Local.

South Roxana

3512 ■ American Legion, South Roxana Post 1167
PO Box 358
South Roxana, IL 62087
Ph: (618)254-2408
Fax: (309)663-5783
URL: National Affiliate–www.legion.org
Local. **Affiliated With:** American Legion.

Sparta

3513 ■ American Legion, Illinois Post 396
c/o Edwin Alexander
112 Fox Run No. 432
Sparta, IL 62286
Ph: (618)443-5022
Fax: (309)663-5783
URL: National Affiliate–www.legion.org
Contact: Edwin Alexander, Contact
Local. **Affiliated With:** American Legion.

3514 ■ Sparta Area Chamber of Commerce (SCC)
PO Box 93
Sparta, IL 62286-0093
Ph: (618)443-2151
Contact: Nathan Lee, Pres.
Founded: 1940. **Members:** 105. **Membership Dues:** business/service, $30 (annual) • individual, $15 (annual) • institution, $100 (annual). **Staff:** 1. **State Groups:** 1. **Local**. Individuals united to advance the industrial, business, social, and civic life of Sparta, IL and the surrounding area. Aids and encourages the establishment of new business in the area. **Awards:** Outstanding Citizens Award. **Frequency:** annual. **Type:** recognition. **Formerly:** (1980) Sparta Chamber of Commerce. **Publications:** Report, annual. **Conventions/Meetings:** monthly board meeting - always first Wednesday of the month • annual dinner - always April.

Spring Bay

3515 ■ American Legion, Spring Bay Post 1115
500 Legion Ln.
Spring Bay, IL 61611
Ph: (309)663-0361
Fax: (309)663-5783
URL: National Affiliate–www.legion.org
Local. **Affiliated With:** American Legion.

Spring Grove

3516 ■ Mathematics Department Heads of Western Chicago Suburbs
c/o Sharon Mallo, Representative
10814 Red Hawk Ln.
Spring Grove, IL 60081-9278
E-mail: webmaster@ictm.org
URL: National Affiliate–www.nctm.org
Contact: Sharon Mallo, Representative
Local. Aims to improve the teaching and learning of mathematics. Provides vision, leadership and professional development to support teachers in ensuring mathematics learning of the highest quality for all students. **Affiliated With:** National Council of Teachers of Mathematics.

Spring Valley

3517 ■ American Legion, Illinois Post 182
c/o Dominic Oberto
131 W Iowa St.
Spring Valley, IL 61362
Ph: (815)664-4982
Fax: (309)663-5783
URL: National Affiliate–www.legion.org
Contact: Dominic Oberto, Contact
Local. **Affiliated With:** American Legion.

3518 ■ Spring Valley Mine and Historical Society
c/o Millie Mautino
529 W. St. Paul St.
Spring Valley, IL 61362-1755
Local.

Springerton

3519 ■ American Legion, Springerton Post 1126
314 N Main St.
Springerton, IL 62887
Ph: (618)963-9005
Fax: (309)663-5783
URL: National Affiliate–www.legion.org
Local. **Affiliated With:** American Legion.

Springfield

3520 ■ Alcoholics Anonymous World Services, Springfield Intergroup
PO Box 1744
Springfield, IL 62705
Ph: (217)525-5795
Free: (866)525-5795
E-mail: soberone@aaspringfield.org
URL: http://www.aaspringfield.org
Local. Individuals recovering from alcoholism. AA maintains that members can solve their common problem and help others achieve sobriety through a twelve step program that includes sharing their experience, strength, and hope with each other. **Affiliated With:** Alcoholics Anonymous World Services.

3521 ■ Alliance of Automotive Service Providers, Illinois
c/o Mike Lane
225 E Cook St.
Springfield, IL 62704
Ph: (217)528-5230
Fax: (217)241-4683
E-mail: m.lane@aaspi.org
URL: National Affiliate–www.autoserviceproviders.com
Contact: Mike Lane, Contact
State. Advances professionalism and excellence in the automotive repair industry through education and member services. **Affiliated With:** Alliance of Automotive Service Providers of Minnesota.

3522 ■ Alzheimer's Association, Greater Illinois Chapter
6 Drawbridge, Ste.4
Springfield, IL 62704
Ph: (217)726-5184
Fax: (217)726-5185
Free: (800)272-3900
E-mail: brian.schwarberg@alz.org
URL: http://www.alzheimers-illinois.org
Contact: Brian Schwarberg, Regional Dir.
Local. Works to research for the prevention, cure, and treatment of Alzheimer's disease and related disorders. Provides support and assistance to patients, their families, and caregivers. **Affiliated With:** Alzheimer's Association.

3523 ■ American Cancer Society, Springfield - Western Regional
1305 Wabash
Springfield, IL 62704
Ph: (217)546-7586
Fax: (217)546-7631
Free: (800)252-5302
URL: http://www.cancer.org
Local. **Affiliated With:** American Cancer Society.

3524 ■ American Institute of Architects - Illinois
c/o Michael Waldinger, Exec.VP
1 Old State Capital Plz. N, Ste.300
Springfield, IL 62701-1323
Ph: (217)522-2309
Fax: (217)522-5370
E-mail: aiaillinois@ameritech.net
URL: http://www.aiail.org
Contact: Michael Waldinger, Exec.VP
Members: 3,300. **State**. Strives to advocate a livable built environment by advancing the profession of architecture in Illinois. **Affiliated With:** American Institute of Architects.

3525 ■ American Legion, Illinois Post 809
c/o Col. Otis B. Duncan
PO Box 5867
Springfield, IL 62705
Ph: (309)663-0361
Fax: (309)663-5783
URL: National Affiliate–www.legion.org
Contact: Col. Otis B. Duncan, Contact
Local. **Affiliated With:** American Legion.

3526 ■ American Legion, Springfield Post 32
505 Amer. Legion Ave.
Springfield, IL 62701
Ph: (309)663-0361
Fax: (309)663-5783
URL: National Affiliate–www.legion.org
Local. Affiliated With: American Legion.

3527 ■ American Lung Association of Illinois (ALA-NCI)
3000 Kelly Ln.
Springfield, IL 62711
Fax: (217)787-5916
Free: (800)LUNG-USA
E-mail: info@lungil.org
URL: http://www.lungil.org
Contact: Harold Wimmer, CEO
State. Voluntary health organization concerned with controlling, preventing, and curing lung disease through research, education, and advocacy. **Affiliated With:** American Lung Association. **Publications:** *Breathing Matters*. Newsletter. Alternate Formats: online • Annual Report, annual. Alternate Formats: online.

3528 ■ American Red Cross, Illinois Capital Area Chapter
PO Box 1058
Springfield, IL 62705
Ph: (217)522-3357
Free: (888)343-5766
URL: http://www.il-redcross.org
Local.

3529 ■ American Red Cross, Sangamon Valley Chapter
PO Box 1058
Springfield, IL 62705
Ph: (217)522-3357
Fax: (217)522-9842
Free: (888)343-5766
E-mail: oglem@il-redcross.org
URL: http://www.il-redcross.org
Contact: Mary Ogle, Exec.Dir.
Founded: 1917. **Members:** 2,500. **Staff:** 10. **Budget:** $650,000. **Local.** Provides relief to victims of disaster and helps people prevent, prepare for, and respond to emergencies. Offers training in first aid and CPR; and supports other community services. **Formed by Merger of:** American Red Cross, Sangamon County Chapter; American Red Cross, Menard County Chapter.

3530 ■ American Society for Public Administration, Central Illinois Chapter (ASPA)
c/o Gregory Michaud
Johnson, Depp, and Quisenberry
6417 Cherylwood Dr.
Springfield, IL 62704
Ph: (217)529-4534
Fax: (217)529-8278
E-mail: grmichaud@jdq-engineers.com
URL: National Affiliate–www.aspanet.org
Contact: Gregory Michaud, Pres.
Local. Affiliated With: American Society for Public Administration. **Conventions/Meetings:** monthly luncheon - always last Monday • monthly meeting - always first Monday.

3531 ■ Ansar Shriners
c/o Richard H. Chesnut
PO Box 5090
Springfield, IL 62705
Ph: (217)525-1771
Fax: (217)525-1745
E-mail: ansar@motion.net
URL: http://www.webruler.com/shriners/ansar.htm
Contact: Richard H. Chesnut, Contact
Local. Affiliated With: Imperial Council of the Ancient Arabic Order of the Nobles of the Mystic Shrine for North America.

3532 ■ Arthritis Foundation, Sangamon County Branch
802 E Carpenter
Springfield, IL 62702
Ph: (217)523-2200
Fax: (217)757-6455
E-mail: greaterillinois@arthritis.org
URL: National Affiliate–www.arthritis.org
Local. Seeks to: discover the cause and improve the methods for the treatment and prevention of arthritis and other rheumatic diseases; increase the number of scientists investigating rheumatic diseases; provide training in rheumatic diseases for more doctors; extend knowledge of arthritis and other rheumatic diseases to the lay public, emphasizing the socioeconomic as well as medical aspects of these diseases. **Affiliated With:** Arthritis Foundation.

3533 ■ Associated Beer Distributors of Illinois (ABDI)
c/o William D. Olson, Exec.VP
PO Box 396
Springfield, IL 62705-0396
Ph: (217)528-4371
Fax: (217)528-4376
E-mail: abdi@abdi.org
URL: http://www.abdi.org
Contact: William D. Olson, Exec.VP
State.

3534 ■ Associated Firefighters of Illinois (AFFI)
132 W Allen
Springfield, IL 62704
Ph: (217)522-8180
Fax: (217)522-8244
URL: http://www.affi-iaff.org
Contact: Rick Merrill, Pres.
State.

3535 ■ Associated General Contractors - Central Illinois Chapter
PO Box 2266
Springfield, IL 62705
Ph: (217)744-2100
Fax: (217)744-2104
E-mail: info@cibagc.org
URL: http://www.cibagc.org
Contact: Carolyn Brown, Office Mgr.
Local. Works to improve businesses of members through political actions and programs.

3536 ■ Associated General Contractors of Illinois (AGCI)
3219 Executive Park Dr.
Springfield, IL 62703
Ph: (217)789-2650
Fax: (217)789-1048
E-mail: sdokey@agcil.org
URL: http://www.agcil.org
Contact: Eric D. Fields, Exec.Dir.
Founded: 1907. **Members:** 295. **Membership Dues:** associate, $875 (annual) • active (District 1, home chapter), $1,600 (annual) • active (District 1, non-home chapter), $1,250 (annual) • active (Downstate, home chapter), $1,200 (annual) • active (Downstate, non-home chapter), $850 (annual). **Staff:** 8. **Budget:** $1,060,500. **State.** Represents contractors, subcontractors, and associates. Serves its members by promoting the interests of the heavy-highway industry in Illinois. **Affiliated With:** Associated General Contractors of America. **Formerly:** (1920) Association of Municipal Contractors. **Publications:** *Builder Magazine*, quarterly. **Advertising:** accepted • *Illinois Construction Directory & Buyer's Guide*, weekly. Bulletin • Directory, annual. **Conventions/Meetings:** annual convention • annual Mid-Winter Seminar.

3537 ■ Association of Community Organizations for Reform Now, Springfield, Illinois
2445 S Fifth St., No. 101
Springfield, IL 62703
Ph: (217)744-7352
Fax: (217)744-7353
E-mail: ilacornspr@acorn.org
URL: National Affiliate–www.acorn.org
Local. Affiliated With: Association of Community Organizations for Reform Now.

3538 ■ Association of Illinois Soil and Water Conservation Districts (AISWCD)
2520 Main St.
Springfield, IL 62702
Ph: (217)744-3414
Fax: (217)744-3420
E-mail: tdavis@winco.net
URL: http://www.aiswcd.org
Contact: Mr. Terry Davis, Pres.
Founded: 1948. **State.**

3539 ■ Automotive Wholesalers of Illinois (AWOI)
6450 S 6th St. Rd.
Springfield, IL 62712
Ph: (217)786-2850
Fax: (217)529-3705
Free: (800)369-2964
E-mail: membership@awoi.com
URL: http://www.awoi.com
Contact: Jan Firth, Exec.VP
Founded: 1958. **State.** Person, firm or corporation whose principal business is the wholesaling, and/or retailing, manufacture and sales, or servicing of motor vehicle parts, accessories and equipment. **Also Known As:** (2005) Automotive Parts and Service Association of Illinois.

3540 ■ Bereaved Parents of the USA, Springfield Chapter
c/o Jim Dixon
PO Box 914
Springfield, IL 62705
Ph: (217)691-4906
E-mail: bpspringfield@famvid.com
URL: National Affiliate–www.bereavedparentsusa.org
Contact: Jim Dixon, Contact
Local.

3541 ■ Capital Area Association of Realtors
3149 Robbins Rd.
Springfield, IL 62704
Ph: (217)698-7000
E-mail: info@caaronline.com
URL: http://www.seehouses.com
Contact: Cheryl L. Dambacher, Pres.
Local. Strives to develop real estate business practices. Advocates the right to own, use and transfer real property. Provides a facility for professional development, research and exchange of information among members and to the general public. **Affiliated With:** National Association of Realtors.

3542 ■ Centerline Dressage
c/o Paula Thoroman, Pres.
1500 W Edwards
Springfield, IL 62704
Ph: (217)793-1590
E-mail: thoroman@fgi.net
URL: http://www.irtc.net/~gnbecker
Contact: Paula Thoroman, Pres.
Local. Affiliated With: United States Dressage Federation.

3543 ■ Central Illinois Corvette Club
PO Box 9445
Springfield, IL 62791-9445
E-mail: randrew525@aol.com
URL: http://www.centralillinoiscorvettes.com
Contact: Shari Andrew, Pres.
Local. Affiliated With: National Council of Corvette Clubs.

3544 ■ Chemical Industry Council of Illinois (CICI)
400 W Monroe, Ste.205
Springfield, IL 62704
Ph: (217)522-5805
Fax: (217)522-5815
URL: http://www.cicil.net
Founded: 1951. **Members:** 201. **State**.

3545 ■ Community Bankers Association of Illinois (CBAI)
c/o Mr. Robert J. Wingert, Pres.
901 Community Dr.
Springfield, IL 62703-5184
Ph: (217)529-2265
Fax: (217)529-9484
Free: (800)736-2224
E-mail: bobw@cbai.com
URL: http://www.cbai.com
Contact: Mr. Robert J. Wingert, Pres.
Founded: 1974. **Members:** 506. **Membership Dues:** corporate (based on total assets), $330-$7,500 (semiannual). **Staff:** 29. **Budget:** $5,000,000. **State Groups:** 11. **State**. Provide services to keep community banks competitive and profitable so that their respective communities will continue to receive dedicated financial services. **Libraries: Type:** not open to the public. **Holdings:** 300; archival material, articles, books, periodicals, reports, software. **Subjects:** bank regulatory (Federal Reserve, FDIC, Federal Home Loan Bank, Comptroller of the Currency, State Commissioner); banking law; financial; economics. **Awards:** BKD Award. **Frequency:** annual. **Type:** recognition. **Recipient:** to financial institution for innovative community service program offered during the year • Outstanding Member. **Frequency:** annual. **Type:** recognition • Patron of Community Banking. **Frequency:** annual. **Type:** recognition • Service of the Year. **Frequency:** annual. **Type:** recognition. **Recipient:** to a marketing partner of the association for outstanding service/ performance during the year. **Computer Services:** Online services, hosting service for member banks • record retrieval services, access to the Illinois secretary of state database for records searches. **Boards:** CBAI Services Marketing Group; Community BancInsurance Services; Community BancService Corporation. **Committees:** Agriculture; Communications; Education; Legislation and Regulation; Special Events. **Publications:** *Associate Member Directory*, semiannual. Lists all associate member firms with descriptions and contact information. **Circulation:** 800 • *CBAI Annual Report*, annual. Contains complete review of association's performance for the year ending 6/30 (by corporation and department). **Circulation:** 3,500 • *CBAI Banknotes*, bimonthly. Magazine. Emphasizes on banking articles, member news, and association events. **Price:** $35.00 for members and their directors. **Circulation:** 3,500. **Advertising:** accepted • *CBAI Education Catalog*, annual. Contains complete listing of all educational seminars, schools, and teleweb workshops. • *Illinois Financial Institutions Directory & Fact Book*, annual. Contains complete detailed listing of all financial institutions in Illinois; detailed information on CBAI. **Price:** $49.00. **Circulation:** 800. **Advertising:** accepted • *Legislative Ledger*, periodic. Bulletin. Contains brief update on state legislative/regulatory issues. **Circulation:** 700. **Conventions/Meetings:** annual convention (exhibits) - 2007 Sept. 27-29, Memphis, TN - Avg. Attendance: 800.

3546 ■ Community Behavioral Healthcare Association of Illinois (CBHA)
3085 Stevenson Dr., Ste.308
Springfield, IL 62703
Ph: (217)585-1600
Fax: (217)585-1601
E-mail: info@cbha.net
URL: http://www.cbha.net
Contact: Frank Anselmo MPA, CEO
State.

3547 ■ Consulting Engineers Council of Illinois
5221 S 6th St. Rd., Ste.120
Springfield, IL 62703
Ph: (217)529-7430
Fax: (217)529-2742
E-mail: acec-il@acec-il.org
URL: http://www.cec-il.org
Contact: David E. Kennedy, Exec.Dir.
Founded: 1921. **Members:** 225. **Membership Dues:** business, $193 (annual). **Staff:** 3. **Budget:** $400,000. **State**. Private practice consulting engineering firms. **Awards:** Engineering Excellence Award. **Frequency:** annual. **Type:** recognition. **Affiliated With:** American Council of Engineering Companies. **Publications:** *CE Reporter*, quarterly. Newsletter.

3548 ■ Democratic Party of Illinois
PO Box 518
Springfield, IL 62705
Ph: (217)546-7404
Fax: (217)546-8847
E-mail: jgyure@ildems.com
URL: http://www.ildems.com
Contact: Michael J. Madigan, Chm.
State. **Affiliated With:** Democratic National Committee.

3549 ■ Enos Park Neighborhood Improvement Association
c/o Marilyn Piland
1007 N 7th St.
Springfield, IL 62702
Ph: (217)522-9381
Fax: (217)522-3060
E-mail: mpiland@juno.com
URL: http://www.springfieldpartners.com
Contact: Marilyn R. Piland, Exec.Dir.
Founded: 1989. **Members:** 102. **Membership Dues:** $20 (annual). **Staff:** 1. **Budget:** $15,000. **Local**. Residents working to restore historic area to its former grandeur. Publishes newsletter.

3550 ■ Family, Career and Community Leaders of America, Illinois
100 N First St. N-242
Springfield, IL 62777-0000
Ph: (217)782-2827 (217)782-2826
Fax: (217)785-9210
E-mail: sburg@isbe.net
URL: National Affiliate–www.fcclainc.org
Contact: Martha Rockwood, Exec.Dir.
State. Young men and women studying family and consumer sciences and related occupational courses in public and private schools through grade 12. Youth assume social roles in areas of personal growth, family life, vocational preparation, and community involvement. **Affiliated With:** Family, Career and Community Leaders of America.

3551 ■ Federation of Independent Illinois Colleges and Universities
c/o David W. Tretter, Pres.
1123 S 2nd St.
Springfield, IL 62704
Ph: (217)789-1400
Fax: (217)789-6259
E-mail: info@federationedu.org
URL: http://www.federationedu.org
Contact: David W. Tretter, Pres.
State. **Affiliated With:** National Association of Independent Colleges and Universities.

3552 ■ Fraternal Order of Police, Illinois State Lodge (ILFOP)
4341 Acer Grove, Ste.B
Springfield, IL 62711
Ph: (217)726-8880
Fax: (217)726-8881
Free: (800)522-2677
E-mail: statelodge@ilfop.org
URL: http://www.ilfop.org
Contact: Fred Scholl, State Sec.
Founded: 1963. **Members:** 35,000. **Local Groups:** 240. **State**. Promotes and fosters the enforcement of law and order. Improves the individual and collective proficiency of its members in the performance of their duties. Encourages fraternal, educational, charitable and social activities among law enforcement officers. **Affiliated With:** Fraternal Order of Police, Grand Lodge.

3553 ■ Girl Scouts, Land of Lincoln Council
3020 Baker Dr.
Springfield, IL 62703-5918
Ph: (217)523-8159
Fax: (217)523-8321
Free: (877)231-1446
E-mail: webmaster@girlscoutsllc.org
URL: http://www.girlscoutsllc.org
Contact: Sue Clark, CEO
Local. Young girls and adult volunteers, corporate, government and individual supporters. Strives to develop potential and leadership skills among its members. Conducts trainings, educational programs and outdoor activities.

3554 ■ Grain and Feed Association of Illinois (GFAI)
c/o Mr. Jeff Adkission, CAE, Exec.VP/Treas.
3521 Hollis Dr.
Springfield, IL 62711-9440
Ph: (217)787-2417
Fax: (217)787-8671
E-mail: info@gfai.org
URL: http://www.gfai.org
Contact: Mr. Jeffrey Adkisson CAE, Exec.VP/Treas.
Staff: 4. **State**. Represents, promotes and advances the common interests of a viable grain and feed industry through an involved and informed membership. **Awards: Frequency:** annual. **Type:** scholarship. **Recipient:** junior college and university students are screened on their academic ability, financial need and a career goal in the area of the agri-business side of the grain and feed industry. **Affiliated With:** National Grain and Feed Association.

3555 ■ Grand Lodge Ancient Free and Accepted Masons Illinois
2866 Via Verde St.
Springfield, IL 62703
Ph: (217)529-8900

3556 ■ Greater Springfield Chamber of Commerce
3 S Old State Capitol Plaza
Springfield, IL 62701-1593
Ph: (217)525-1173
Fax: (217)525-8768
E-mail: gplummer@gscc.org
URL: http://www.gscc.org
Contact: Gary Plummer, CEO/Pres.
Membership Dues: individual, $140 (annual) • professional (per firm and only 1 professional), $240 (annual) • real estate (per firm and only 1 contractor), $240 (annual) • nonprofit, $240 (annual) • bank (per million of local assets), $34 (annual) • retail (1-20 employees), $240-$490 (annual). **Local**. **Awards:** Small Business Person of the Year. **Frequency:** annual. **Type:** recognition. **Computer Services:** database, member search. **Committees:** Infrastructure; Leadership Springfield. **Publications:** *Membership Directory and Buyer's Guide*, annual, distributed every summer. **Price:** $35.00 for nonmembers; $25.00 for members. **Advertising:** accepted • *Update*, monthly. Newsletter. **Price:** for members. **Advertising:** accepted. Alternate Formats: online.

3557 ■ G.V. Black District Dental Society
c/o Dr. Myron M. Sternstein, Pres.-Elect
997 Clock Tower Dr.
Springfield, IL 62704-1301
Ph: (217)546-9600
E-mail: tuthmvr@tuthmvr.com
URL: http://www.isds.org
Contact: Dr. Myron M. Sternstein, Pres.-Elect
Local. Represents the interests of dentists committed to the public's oral health, ethics, science and professional advancement. Promotes the art and science of dentistry through advocacy, education, research and the development of standards. **Affiliated With:** American Dental Association; Illinois State Dental Society.

3558 ■ Habitat for Humanity Sangamon County
918 E Enos Ave.
Springfield, IL 62702
Ph: (217)523-2710
E-mail: habitat@cityscape.net
URL: http://www.habitatsangamon.com
Contact: Dan Frachey, Resource Dir.
Local. **Affiliated With:** Habitat for Humanity International.

3559 ■ Home Builders Association of Illinois (HBAI)
c/o J. Mark Harrison, Exec.VP
112 W Edwards St.
Springfield, IL 62704-1902
Ph: (217)753-3963
Fax: (217)753-3811
Free: (800)255-6047
E-mail: markharrison@hbai.org
URL: http://www.hbai.org
Contact: J. Mark Harrison, Exec.VP
Founded: 1956. **Members:** 211,000. **Staff:** 5. **State Groups:** 1. **Local Groups:** 23. **State**. Home building companies. Supports the industry; seeks to portray favorable image of the industry to the public and the legislature. Conducts educational programs. **Publications:** *Illinois Builder Journal*, bimonthly. Newspaper. **Circulation:** 4,000. **Advertising:** accepted. **Conventions/Meetings:** annual meeting.

3560 ■ Illinois Academy of Physician Assistants (IAPA)
c/o Kari Anderson, Exec.Dir.
225 E Cook St.
Springfield, IL 62704-2509
Ph: (217)241-0232
Fax: (217)789-4664
Free: (800)975-9344
E-mail: kari@ampka.com
URL: http://www.illinoispa.org
Contact: Ann Browning PA-C, Pres.
State. Physician assistants who have graduated from an accredited program and/or are certified by the National Commission on Certification of Physician Assistants; individuals who are enrolled in an accredited PA educational program. Purposes are to: enhance public access to quality, cost-effective health care, educate the public about the physician assistant profession; represent physician assistants' interests before Congress, government agencies, and health-related organizations; assure the competence of physician assistants through development of educational curricula and accreditation programs; provide services for members. **Affiliated With:** American Academy of Physician Assistants.

3561 ■ Illinois AIFA
c/o Lawrence E. Mullins, Pres.
60 Adloff Ln.
Springfield, IL 62703
Ph: (217)529-0126
Fax: (217)529-0977
E-mail: sara@iaifa.com
URL: http://www.iaifa.com
Contact: Lawrence E. Mullins, Pres.
State. Represents the interests of insurance and financial advisors. Advocates for a positive legislative and regulatory environment. Enhances business and professional skills of members. **Affiliated With:** National Association of Insurance and Financial Advisors.

3562 ■ Illinois Alcoholism and Drug Dependence Association (IADDA)
c/o Angela M. Bowman, CEO
937 S 2nd St.
Springfield, IL 62704-2701
Ph: (217)528-7335
Fax: (217)528-7340
Free: (800)252-6301
E-mail: iadda@iadda.org
URL: http://www.iadda.org
Contact: Angela M. Bowman, CEO
State.

3563 ■ Illinois Asphalt Pavement Association (IAPA)
c/o William F. Cellini, Exec.VP
241 N Fifth St.
Springfield, IL 62701
Ph: (217)523-2208 (217)523-2241
Fax: (217)544-0086
E-mail: info@il-asphalt.org
URL: http://www.il-asphalt.org
Contact: William F. Cellini, Exec.VP
State.

3564 ■ Illinois Association of Aggregate Producers (IAAP)
1115 S 2nd St.
Springfield, IL 62704
Ph: (217)241-1639
Fax: (217)241-1641
E-mail: iaap@hansoninfosys.com
URL: http://www.iaap-aggregates.org
Contact: John Henriksen, Exec.Dir.
State.

3565 ■ Illinois Association for Career and Technical Education (IACTE)
c/o Jim Stubblefield, Pres.
2450 Found. Dr., Ste.500
Springfield, IL 62703
Ph: (217)585-9430
Fax: (217)585-9435
E-mail: info@iacte.org
URL: http://www.iacte.org
Contact: Jim Stubblefield, Pres.
Staff: 1. **State**. Strives to provide unified, visionary leadership to advance and promote learning in career and technical education. **Affiliated With:** Association for Career and Technical Education.

3566 ■ Illinois Association of Chamber of Commerce Executives (IACCE)
215 E Adams St.
Springfield, IL 62701
Ph: (217)522-5512
Fax: (217)522-5518
E-mail: info@iacce.org
URL: http://www.iacce.org
Contact: Elizabeth D. Fiala, Pres.
Founded: 1915. **Membership Dues:** chamber (depends upon the number of members), $100-$350. **State**. Serves as an access and valued resource for the professional development of Chamber of Commerce executives and staff in Illinois. **Awards:** Distinguished Chamber of the Year. **Frequency:** annual. **Type:** recognition. **Recipient:** for those who distinguish themselves through their management of the chamber. **Computer Services:** Information services, membership directory. **Committees:** Communications; Membership Development; Professional Development. **Publications:** *IACCE News*, monthly. Newsletter. Contains current articles on important issues, new member services, and other chamber programs. • *Resource Guide*, annual. Membership Directory. Includes list of all chamber executives' members as well as the associate staff members together with the by-laws and board of directors.

3567 ■ Illinois Association of Chiefs of Police
c/o Giacomo A. Pecoraro, Exec.Dir.
426 S 5th St., No. 200
Springfield, IL 62701-1824
Ph: (217)523-3765
Fax: (217)523-8352
E-mail: gapecoraro@ilchiefs.org
URL: http://www.ilchiefs.org
State.

3568 ■ Illinois Association of County Engineers (IACE)
c/o Molly Rockford, Exec.Dir.
712 S Second St.
Springfield, IL 62704
Ph: (217)523-1146
E-mail: mrockford@illinoisstrategies.com
URL: http://www.iaceng.org
Contact: Molly Rockford, Exec.Dir.
Founded: 1914. **Members:** 102. **Membership Dues:** associate, $250 (annual) • regular, assessment based on MFT received, $240. **Budget:** $100,000. **State**. County superintendents working to promote the need for better roads in Illinois. **Awards: Type:** scholarship. **Affiliated With:** National Association of County Engineers. **Publications:** *Committee Report*, annual. Newsletter • *Legislative Report*, periodic. Newsletter • *Minutes*, periodic. **Conventions/Meetings:** semiannual conference (exhibits) - always spring and fall.

3569 ■ Illinois Association of Defense Trial Counsel (IDC)
c/o Shirley A. Stevens, Exec.Dir.
PO Box 7288
Springfield, IL 62791
Ph: (217)636-7960 (217)636-7814
Fax: (217)636-8812
Free: (800)232-0169
E-mail: idcoffice@gcctv.com
URL: http://www.iadtc.org
Contact: Shirley A. Stevens, Exec.Dir.
Founded: 1964. **Members:** 1,100. **Membership Dues:** individual (based on number of years in practice), $90-$195 (annual). **Budget:** $300,000. **State**. Promotes improvements in the administration of justice and enhances the service of the legal profession to the public. Supports and works for the improvement of the adversary system of jurisprudence in the operation of the courts. Encourages the prompt, fair, and just disposition of tort litigation. Enhances the knowledge and improvement of the skills of defense lawyers. Advances the equitable and expeditious handling of disputes arising under all forms of insurance and surety contracts. Works for the elimination of court congestion and delays in civil litigations. Carries on other relation and similar activities in the public interest. **Publications:** *IDC Quarterly*. Magazine. **Conventions/Meetings:** annual seminar - spring • annual seminar - fall • annual seminar, for rookies • annual Trial Academy - meeting.

3570 ■ Illinois Association for the Education of Young Children
c/o Donetta Braner, Office Mgr.
3180 Adloff Ln., Ste.302
Springfield, IL 62703
Ph: (217)529-7732
Fax: (217)529-7738
E-mail: donetta836@illinoisaeyc.org
URL: http://www.illinoisaeyc.org
Contact: Donetta Braner, Off.Mgr.
State. Advocates for the best childcare and education for all children in the state of Illinois. **Affiliated With:** National Association for the Education of Young Children.

3571 ■ Illinois Association of Fire Protection Districts (IAFPD)
901 S Second St., Ste.201
Springfield, IL 62704
Ph: (217)525-6620
Fax: (217)525-6627
Free: (800)524-6620
E-mail: info@iafpd.org
URL: http://www.iafpd.org
Contact: Cheri Breneman, Administrator
Founded: 1943. **State**.

3572 ■ Illinois Association of Museums (IAM)
1 Old State Capitol Plz.
Springfield, IL 62701
Ph: (217)524-7080 (217)524-6977
Fax: (217)558-1512
E-mail: mary.turner@illinois.gov
URL: http://www.illinoismuseums.org
Contact: David Oberg, Pres.
State. Promotes professional standards and development within the museum community. Promotes understanding of the state history, culture and natural history through public education.

3573 ■ Illinois Association of Mutual Insurance Companies (IAMIC)
PO Box 7083
Springfield, IL 62791-7083
Ph: (217)787-8383
Fax: (217)787-8389
E-mail: leadership@iamic.org
URL: http://www.iamic.org
Contact: Sandra J. Wulf CAE, Pres.
Founded: 1881. **Members:** 115. **Staff:** 2. **Budget:** $300,000. **State**. Promotes leadership; committed to the growth and development of the mutual insurance industry. **Publications:** *Lautum News*, quarterly. Newsletter. **Price:** $5.00. **Circulation:** 1,000. **Advertising:** accepted. **Conventions/Meetings:** annual convention (exhibits).

3574 ■ Illinois Association for Parents of Children with Visual Impairments (IPVI)
PO Box 7477
Springfield, IL 62791-7477
Free: (877)411-IPVI
E-mail: ipvi@ipvi.org
URL: http://www.ipvi.org
Contact: Rich Zabelski, Pres.
State. Represents individuals committed to providing support to the parents of children who have visual impairments. Promotes public understanding of the needs and rights of children who are visually impaired. **Affiliated With:** National Association for Parents of Children With Visual Impairments.

3575 ■ Illinois Association of Park Districts (IAPD)
c/o Ted Flickinger, PhD, Pres./CEO
211 E Monroe St.
Springfield, IL 62701
Ph: (217)523-4554
Fax: (217)523-4273
E-mail: iapd@ilparks.org
URL: http://www.ilparks.org
Contact: Ted Flickinger PhD, Pres./CEO
Founded: 1928. **Members:** 2,500. **Staff:** 9. **Budget:** $1,500,000. **State**. Strives to promulgate, foster, promote and carry into effect a continuing civic and educational program for the improvement and extension of park, recreation and conservation facilities and programs and the efficient administration thereof. Membership is by agency, but includes elected board members, board secretary and attorney and director. **Publications:** *Illinois Parks & Recreation*, bimonthly. Magazine. **Price:** $25.00. ISSN: 0019-2155. **Circulation:** 5,500. **Advertising:** accepted. **Conventions/Meetings:** annual conference (exhibits).

3576 ■ Illinois Association of Plumbing-Heating-Cooling Contractors
c/o Beverly A. Potts, Exec.Dir.
821 S Grand Ave., W
Springfield, IL 62704
Ph: (217)522-7219
Fax: (217)522-4315
Free: (800)795-7422
E-mail: bev@ilphcc.com
URL: http://www.ilphcc.com
Contact: Beverly A. Potts, Exec.Dir.
State.

3577 ■ Illinois Association of Realtors (IAR)
c/o Gary L. Clayton, CAE, CEO
PO Box 19451
Springfield, IL 62794-9451
Ph: (217)529-2600
Fax: (217)529-3904
E-mail: iaraccess@iar.org
URL: http://www.illinoisrealtor.org
Contact: Gary L. Clayton CAE, CEO
Founded: 1916. **Members:** 55,000. **State**.

3578 ■ Illinois Association of Rehabilitation Facilities (IARF)
206 S Sixth St.
Springfield, IL 62701
Ph: (217)753-1190
Fax: (217)525-1271
E-mail: jstover@hso.net
URL: http://www.iarf.org
Contact: Janet S. Stover, Exec.Dir.
State.

3579 ■ Illinois Association of School Administrators (IASA)
c/o Dr. Walter H. Warfield, PhD, Exec.Dir.
2020 Timberbrook Dr.
Springfield, IL 62702-4627
Ph: (217)787-9306
Fax: (217)787-9362
E-mail: warfield@iasaedu.org
URL: http://www.iasaedu.org
Contact: Dr. Walter H. Warfield PhD, Exec.Dir.
State.

3580 ■ Illinois Association of School Boards (IASB)
2921 Baker Dr.
Springfield, IL 62703-5429
Ph: (217)528-9688
Fax: (217)528-2831
E-mail: mjohnson@iasb.com
URL: http://www.iasb.com
Contact: Dr. Michael D. Johnson, Exec.Dir.
Founded: 1913. **Members:** 860. **Staff:** 48. **Budget:** $5,500,000. **Regional Groups:** 21. **State**. Voluntary association of local school boards. Provides workshops, publications, and direct consulting. **Libraries: Type:** not open to the public. **Holdings:** 2,000; articles, audiovisuals, books, periodicals. **Subjects:** education issues, public school governance. **Publications:** *IASB School Board News Bulletin*, monthly • *Illinois School Board Journal*, bimonthly • *Legislative Bulletin* • *School PR Service*, quarterly. **Conventions/Meetings:** annual conference (exhibits) - always the weekend before Thanksgiving.

3581 ■ Illinois Association of Tobacco and Candy Distributors
217 E Monroe St., Ste.102
Springfield, IL 62707
Ph: (217)535-2282
Fax: (217)544-0874
Contact: Eric Irvin, Pres.
State.

3582 ■ Illinois Association of Vocational Agriculture Teachers
3221 Northfield Dr.
Springfield, IL 62702
Ph: (217)753-6628 (217)784-5525
Fax: (217)753-3359
E-mail: larrl@gcms.k12.il.us
URL: http://www.iavat.org
Contact: Larry Littlefield, Pres.
State. Seeks to advance agricultural education and promotes the professional interests and growth of agriculture teachers. Provides agricultural education through visionary leadership, advocacy and service. **Affiliated With:** National Association of Agricultural Educators.

3583 ■ Illinois Association of Wastewater Agencies (IAWA)
c/o William F. Cellini, Exec.Dir.
241 N 5th St.
Springfield, IL 62701
Ph: (217)523-1814
Fax: (217)544-0086
E-mail: info@ilwastewater.org
URL: http://www.ilwastewater.org
Contact: William F. Cellini, Exec.Dir.
State.

3584 ■ Illinois Automobile Dealers Association (IADA)
300 W Edwards St.
PO Box 3045
Springfield, IL 62708
Ph: (217)753-0220
Fax: (217)753-3424
Free: (800)252-8944
E-mail: info@illinoisdealers.com
URL: http://www.illinoisdealers.com
Contact: Mr. Peter J. Sander, Pres.
State.

3585 ■ Illinois Bankers Association (IBA)
133 S 4th St., Ste.300
Springfield, IL 62701
Ph: (217)789-9340
Fax: (217)789-5410
E-mail: djemison@ilbanker.com
URL: http://www.ilbanker.com
Contact: Deborah Jemison, VP of Communications/ Marketing
State.

3586 ■ Illinois Beef Association (IBA)
2060 W Iles Ave., Ste.B
Springfield, IL 62704-4191
Ph: (217)787-4280
Fax: (217)793-3605
E-mail: maraleemj@aol.com
URL: http://www.illinoisbeef.com
Contact: Maralee Johnson, Exec.VP
Local. Promotes and markets Illinois beefs. Delivers detailed analysis and presentation on beef industry by giving up-to-date news, important issues and other beef-related information that are essential for beef producers and consumers in the region. **Affiliated With:** Cattlemen's Beef Promotion and Research Board.

3587 ■ Illinois Cast Metals Association (ICMA)
220 E Adams St.
Springfield, IL 62705
Ph: (217)528-8238
Fax: (217)523-0309
Free: (800)875-4462
E-mail: stanz@ilcastmetals.org
URL: http://www.ilcastmetals.org
Contact: Stan Zielinski, Exec.Dir.
State.

3588 ■ Illinois Chapter National Electrical Contractors Association
3701 S 6th St.
Springfield, IL 62703
Ph: (217)585-9500
Fax: (217)585-9600
Free: (800)252-8922
E-mail: info@ilneca.org
URL: http://www.ilneca.org
Contact: William C. Belforte, Exec.VP
State. Contractors erecting, installing, repairing, servicing, and maintaining electric wiring, equipment, and appliances. **Affiliated With:** National Electrical Contractors Association.

3589 ■ Illinois Chiropractic Society
1143 S Spring St.
Springfield, IL 62704
Ph: (217)525-1200
Fax: (217)525-1205
Free: (800)424-0121
E-mail: ics@ilchiro.org
URL: http://www.ilchiro.org
Contact: Roger J. Mills, Exec.Dir.
Founded: 1926. **Members:** 950. **State**. Unites to advance the chiropractic profession. **Publications:** *ICS News*, bimonthly. Newsletter • *Members Only*, bimonthly. Newsletter. **Conventions/Meetings:** semiannual meeting - spring and fall.

3590 ■ Illinois Coal Association (ICA)
212 S 2nd St.
Springfield, IL 62701
Ph: (217)528-2092
Fax: (217)523-5191
E-mail: philgonet@springnet1.com
URL: http://www.ilcoalassn.com
Contact: Phillip M. Gonet, Pres.
State.

3591 ■ Illinois Coalition Against Domestic Violence
801 S 11th St.
Springfield, IL 62703
Ph: (217)789-2830
Fax: (217)789-1939
E-mail: ilcadv@ilcadv.org
URL: http://www.ilcadv.org
State. Affiliated With: National Coalition Against Domestic Violence.

3592 ■ Illinois Coalition Against Sexual Assault (ICASA)
100 N 16th St.
Springfield, IL 62703
Ph: (217)753-4117
Fax: (217)753-8229
E-mail: sblack@icasa.org
URL: http://www.icasa.org
Contact: Polly Poskin, Exec.Dir.
Founded: 1979. **Members:** 29. **Budget:** $14,000,000. **State**. Coalition of community-based sexual assault crisis centers. Provides counseling and advocacy for victims of sexual assault and conducts educational programs in IL communities. Contracts with the IL Department of Human Services and the IL Criminal Justice Information Authority to allocate state and federal funds to the sexual assault crisis centers and to monitor those services for programmatic and fiscal compliance. Supports survivors of sexual assault, child sexual abuse, acquaintance rape, and sexual harassment through counseling and advocacy services as well as friends and family members of victims. Provides educational and training programs for students, teachers, social service workers, criminal justice and medical personnel, and other audiences. **Formerly:** (2001) Illinois CASA. **Publications:** *A Guide to Advocacy Services* (in English and Spanish) • *A Guide to Civil Lawsuits* • *Acquaintance Rape* (in English and Spanish) • *After Sexual Assault* (in English, Korean, Polish, and Spanish) • *Coalition Community*, quarterly. Newsletter • *How Can I Help?* (in English, Korean, Polish, and Spanish) • *Illinois Criminal Sexual Assault Act* • *Male Survivors* • *Men Responding to Sexual Violence* (in English and Spanish) • *Parent Pamphlet* (in English and Spanish) • *What Do I Need to Know?*.

3593 ■ Illinois Coin Machine Operators Association (ICMOA)
600 S 2nd, Ste.403
Springfield, IL 62704
Ph: (630)369-3772
Fax: (630)369-3773
E-mail: director@icmoa.org
URL: http://www.icmoa.org
Contact: Adonna Jerman, Exec.Dir.
State. Provides a forum for the exchange of ideas, opportunities, and education in the coin-operated industry. **Conventions/Meetings:** Annual Illinois State Pool, Dart, and Electronic Golf Tournament - conference, for members • annual meeting, offers seminars and equipment display.

3594 ■ Illinois Community Action Association (ICAA)
c/o Dalitso Sulamoyo, Pres./CEO
3435 Liberty Dr.
Springfield, IL 62704
Ph: (217)789-0125
Fax: (217)789-0139
URL: http://www.icaanet.org
Contact: Dalitso Sulamoyo, Pres./CEO
State.

3595 ■ Illinois Community College Trustees Association (ICCTA)
401 E Capitol Ave., Ste.200
Springfield, IL 62701-1711
Ph: (217)528-2858
Fax: (217)528-8662
E-mail: iccta@communitycolleges.org
URL: http://www.communitycolleges.org
Contact: Michael S. Monaghan, Exec.Dir.
Founded: 1970. **Members:** 300. **Staff:** 5. **Budget:** $500,000. **State**. Community college trustees. Lobbies; conducts trustee educational seminars; disseminates information. **Libraries: Type:** not open to the public. **Holdings:** 1,000; articles, books, periodicals, reports. **Subjects:** education, government. **Awards:** Alumnus Award. **Frequency:** annual. **Type:** recognition • Outstanding Legislator. **Frequency:** annual. **Type:** recognition • Student Essay Contest. **Frequency:** annual. **Type:** recognition • Trustee Achievement Award. **Frequency:** annual. **Type:** recognition. **Publications:** *Illinois Trustee*, quarterly. Newsletter • Directory, periodic. **Price:** $10.00. **Circulation:** 600. **Conventions/Meetings:** annual convention (exhibits) - always June • meeting - 7/year.

3596 ■ Illinois Concrete Pipe Association
c/o William F. Cellini, Exec.Dir.
241 N 5th St.
Springfield, IL 62701
Ph: (217)523-7473
Fax: (217)544-0086
E-mail: info@il-concretepipe.org
State.

3597 ■ Illinois Conference of Churches (ICC)
c/o Rev. David A. Anderson, Exec.Dir.
522 E Monroe, Ste.208
Springfield, IL 62701
Ph: (217)522-7099
Fax: (217)529-7105
E-mail: davidanderson@ilconfchurches.org
URL: http://www.ilconfchurches.org
Contact: Rev. David A. Anderson, Exec.Dir.
Founded: 1930. **Members:** 31. **Staff:** 3. **Budget:** $224,000. **State**. Brings together religious leaders, judicatory staff, clergy, and lay representatives from the member churches to foster Christian unity. Represents the Protestant, Anglican, Catholic, and Orthodox traditions of the Christian faith. **Awards:** Local Ecumenical Award for Christian Unity and Mission. **Frequency:** triennial. **Type:** recognition. **Recipient:** for initiatives that nurture growing relationships among Christian churches and/or generate ecumenical witness and mission. **Councils:** Judicatory Executives. **Publications:** *Ecumenical Courier*, periodic. Newsletter. Contains reports. **Advertising:** accepted • *Public Policy Alert*, periodic. Paper • *Public Policy Profile*, bimonthly. Paper. Alternate Formats: online. **Conventions/Meetings:** triennial Ecumenical Assembly, related to the work of the ICC statewide (exhibits).

3598 ■ Illinois Conservation Foundation (ICF)
1 Natural Resources Way
Springfield, IL 62702-1270
Ph: (217)785-2003
Fax: (217)785-9236
E-mail: jhansen@dnrmail.state.il.us
URL: http://www.ilcf.org
Contact: Jess Hansen, Exec.Dir.
State. Works to preserve and enhance natural resources by supporting ecological, educational and recreational programs.

3599 ■ Illinois Council of the Blind (ICB)
c/o Dick Bledsoe, Pres.
PO Box 1336
Springfield, IL 62705-1336
Ph: (217)523-4967
Fax: (217)523-4302
Free: (888)698-1862
E-mail: icb@icbonline.org
URL: http://www.icbonline.org
Contact: Dick Bledsoe, Pres.
State. Strives to improve the well being of all blind and visually impaired people. Aims to elevate the social, economic and cultural levels of blind people. Cooperates with the public and private institutions and organizations concerned with blind services. Conducts a public education program to promote greater understanding of blindness and the capabilities of blind people. **Affiliated With:** American Council of the Blind.

3600 ■ Illinois Dental Hygienists' Association (IDHA)
4 Lawrence Sq.
Springfield, IL 62704
Free: (800)550-4342
E-mail: info@idha.net
URL: http://www.idha.net
Contact: Gina M. Strelecki RDH, Pres.
State.

3601 ■ Illinois Education Association (IEA)
100 E Edwards St.
Springfield, IL 62704-1999
Ph: (217)544-0706 (217)544-3081
Fax: (217)544-7383
Free: (800)252-8076
URL: http://www.ieanea.org
Contact: Clayton K. Marquardt, Exec.Dir.
Founded: 1853. **Members:** 102,000. **Membership Dues:** full or part-time educational employee, $314 (annual). **Staff:** 200. **Budget:** $28,300,000. **Regional Groups:** 22. **State Groups:** 1,100. **State**. Aims to improve the quality of public education in Illinois and protect the rights of educational employees. **Awards:** IEA Scholarships. **Frequency:** annual. **Type:** scholarship. **Recipient:** dependents of members only. **Publications:** *The Advocate*, 8/year. **Conventions/Meetings:** annual meeting - always March.

3602 ■ Illinois Environmental Council (IEC)
107 W Cook St., Ste.E
Springfield, IL 62704-2527
Ph: (217)544-5954
Fax: (217)544-5958
E-mail: iec@ilenviro.org
URL: http://www.ilenviro.org
Contact: Jonathan Goldman, Exec.Dir.
Founded: 1975. **Members:** 200. **Membership Dues:** individual, $30 (annual) • organization, $300 (annual). **Staff:** 4. **State Groups:** 50. **Local Groups:** 100. **State**. Seeks to advocate sound environmental policies and facilitate a statewide network. Works with its educational fund to provide information on environmental issues. Promotes environmental quality and protecting air, land, water and wildlife in the state of Illinois. **Awards:** Environmental Leadership Award. **Frequency:** annual. **Type:** recognition. **Recipient:** for environmental leaders in Illinois • Michael J. Scully Lifetime Achievement Award. **Frequency:** periodic. **Type:** recognition • 100% Environmental Voting Record. **Frequency:** annual. **Type:** recognition. **Recipient:** for state legislators who have earned a 100% on IECs environmental voting scorecard. **Programs:** Mercury Free Illinois; Partners for Parks and Wildlife. **Publications:** *Environmental Voting Scorecard*, annual. Report • *Illinois EnviroNews*, quarterly. Newsletter. **Price:** included in membership dues • *2005-2006 Environmental Issues Briefing Book*, biennial.

3603 ■ Illinois Farmers Union
40 Adloff Ln., Ste.1
Springfield, IL 62703
Ph: (217)786-4220
Fax: (217)585-1486
E-mail: gordy@ilfu.net
URL: http://www.ilfu.org
Contact: Gordy Stine, Pres.
Founded: 1954. **Members:** 2,000. **Membership Dues:** farmer, $50 (annual). **Staff:** 4. **State**. Gives support for area farmers. Provides effective grassroots leadership to build a sustainable economic system in which family farms and rural communities thrive and prosper. **Publications:** *Illinois Union Farmer*, quarterly. Newsletter. **Circulation:** 2,500. **Advertising:** accepted. **Conventions/Meetings:** annual meeting - always winter.

3604 ■ Illinois Federation of Business and Professional Women Clubs (IFBPW)
c/o Mary Ann Gould, Pres.
2743 S Veterans Pkwy.
Springfield, IL 62704

Ph: (217)557-0885
Fax: (212)293-1100
E-mail: bpwil@bpw-il.org
URL: http://bpw-il.org
Contact: Mary Ann Gould, Pres.
Founded: 1921. **Members:** 3,000. **Membership Dues:** regular, $100 (annual) • national level (for individual from local level), $50 (annual) • national level (for student from local level), $15 (annual). **Staff:** 1. **Local Groups:** 95. **State**. Working women. Promotes women's advancement in the workplace. Lobbies and disseminates information; conducts training seminars. **Awards:** Celia M. Howard Fellowship. **Frequency:** annual. **Type:** grant. **Recipient:** for a deserving Illinois woman's study in the field of diplomacy. **Publications:** *Illinois Bulletin*, quarterly. **Price:** included in membership dues • Directory, annual • Newsletter, quarterly. **Conventions/Meetings:** annual convention (exhibits) - always mid-April.

3605 ■ Illinois Funeral Directors Association
215 S Grand Ave. W
Springfield, IL 62704
Ph: (217)525-2000
Fax: (217)525-8342
Free: (800)240-4332
E-mail: info@ifda.org
URL: http://www.ifda.org
Contact: Mr. Paul G. Dixon, Exec.Dir.
Founded: 1881. **Members:** 1,100. **Staff:** 13. **State**. Seeks to provide the public and the profession continuous education and improved understanding of funeral service, its values and community contributions made by funeral directors and services to the living while properly caring for the dead. **Publications:** *Connections*, monthly. Newsletter • *I.D.*, quarterly. Magazine. Informs and entertains regarding the funeral profession in Illinois. **Circulation:** 2,000. **Advertising:** accepted • *IFDA Yearbook*, annual. **Circulation:** 1,300. **Advertising:** accepted. **Conventions/Meetings:** annual conference (exhibits) - always June.

3606 ■ Illinois Health Care Association (IHCA)
c/o William L. Kempiners
1029 S 4th St.
Springfield, IL 62703-2224
Ph: (217)528-6455
Fax: (217)528-0452
Free: (800)252-8988
E-mail: info@ihca.com
URL: http://www.ihca.com
Contact: William L. Kempiners, Exec.Dir.
Founded: 1950. **Members:** 495. **Membership Dues:** associate, $895 (annual). **Staff:** 19. **Budget:** $2,000,000. **State**. **Publications:** *Info Park*, monthly • *Members Only*, weekly. Newsletter. **Price:** included in membership dues. **Circulation:** 925. **Advertising:** accepted • *Quest Journal*, quarterly. Magazine. **Conventions/Meetings:** annual Charting Our Course: Tools for Navigating the Future - convention, vendors who service long term care industry (exhibits).

3607 ■ Illinois Jewelers Association (IJA)
225 E Cook St.
Springfield, IL 62704
Ph: (217)241-0232
Fax: (217)789-4664
Free: (800)975-9344
E-mail: info@illinoisjewelers.org
URL: http://www.illinoisjewelers.org
Contact: Kari Anderson, Exec.Dir.
Members: 272. **Membership Dues:** regular jewelry store, $125-$225 (annual) • associate, $200 (annual) • student, retired jeweler, $25 (annual). **Staff:** 1. **Budget:** $48,000. **State**.

3608 ■ Illinois Lake Management Association (ILMA)
c/o Richard Hilton, Administration Asst.
PO Box 20655
Springfield, IL 62708
Fax: (815)653-5097
Free: (800)338-6976
E-mail: ilma@ilma-lakes.org
URL: http://www.ilma-lakes.org
Contact: Joe Marencik, Pres.
State. **Affiliated With:** North American Lake Management Society.

3609 ■ Illinois Land Title Association (ILTA)
c/o Michael R. Lane, Exec.Dir.
225 E Cook St.
Springfield, IL 62704
Ph: (217)528-5230
Fax: (217)241-4683
E-mail: m.lane@illinoislandtitle.org
URL: http://www.illinoislandtitle.org
Contact: Michael R. Lane, Exec.Dir.
Founded: 1908. **Members:** 147. **Staff:** 3. **Budget:** $200,000. **State**. **Publications:** *Title Record*, quarterly. Newsletter. **Conventions/Meetings:** annual convention - July • Title School - seminar.

3610 ■ Illinois League of Financial Institutions (ILFI)
133 S 4th St., Ste.206
Springfield, IL 62701
Ph: (217)522-5575
Fax: (217)789-9115
E-mail: info@ilfi.org
URL: http://ilfi.org
Contact: Mr. Jay R. Stevenson, Pres.
Founded: 1880. **Members:** 160. **Membership Dues:** affiliate, $1,750 (annual). **Staff:** 8. **Budget:** $1,500,000. **State**. Represents the thrift and community banking institutions. Serves the Illinois financial institutions and the public by fostering thrift and homeownership and by sustaining and promoting the legislative, regulatory and business interests of its members. **Libraries:** **Type:** not open to the public. **Holdings:** articles, books, periodicals. **Subjects:** lending, depository accounts, accounting, financial institution operations. **Awards:** Arnold J. Rauen Award. **Frequency:** annual. **Type:** recognition. **Recipient:** for legislative activities • Commendation of Service. **Frequency:** annual. **Type:** recognition. **Recipient:** for years of service and regulatory. **Affiliated With:** America's Community Bankers. **Publications:** *Illinois Reporter*, bimonthly. Magazine. Contains articles impacting financial institutions. **Price:** included in membership dues. **Circulation:** 500. **Advertising:** accepted. Alternate Formats: CD-ROM; online. **Conventions/Meetings:** annual convention, for CEOs, senior staff members, and directors of Illinois financial institutions (exhibits).

3611 ■ Illinois Licensed Beverage Association (ILBA)
c/o Steve Riedl, Exec.Dir.
1127 S Second St.
Springfield, IL 62704
Ph: (217)523-3232
Fax: (217)523-3242
Free: (800)336-4752
E-mail: ilba@springnet1.com
URL: http://www.ilba.net
Contact: Steve Riedl, Exec.Dir.
Founded: 1880. **Members:** 2,500. **Membership Dues:** retail and individual, $150 (annual) • platinum affiliate company, $5,000 (annual) • gold affiliate company, $3,000 (annual). **Staff:** 2. **Budget:** $450,000. **Regional Groups:** 30. **State Groups:** 1. **Local Groups:** 30. **State**. Retail business trade association for all Illinois businesses that serve or sell beverage alcohol at retail level. **Awards:** Life Member. **Frequency:** annual. **Type:** recognition. **Recipient:** as selected by peers • Lifetime Achievement. **Frequency:** annual. **Type:** recognition. **Recipient:** as selected by peers • Outstanding Board Member. **Frequency:** annual. **Type:** recognition. **Recipient:** as selected by peers • Outstanding Secretary. **Frequency:** annual. **Type:** recognition. **Recipient:** as selected by peers. **Computer Services:** Online services, training. **Affiliated With:** American Beverage Licensees. **Publications:** *Respect Magazine*, quarterly. **Price:** free. **Circulation:** 22,000. **Advertising:** accepted. Alternate Formats: online. **Conventions/Meetings:** annual convention, with speakers (exhibits) - from 2nd Monday to 2nd Wednesday of September • annual trade show, with speakers (exhibits) - from 2nd Monday to 2nd Wednesday of September.

3612 ■ Illinois Life Insurance Council
c/o Larry Barry, Pres.
600 S Second St., Ste.401
Springfield, IL 62704-2542
Ph: (217)544-1637
Fax: (217)544-6604
State.

3613 ■ Illinois Lumber and Materials Dealers Association
c/o J. Barry Johnson, Exec.Dir.
932 S Spring St.
Springfield, IL 62704
Ph: (217)544-5405
Fax: (217)544-4206
E-mail: ilmda@ilmda.com
URL: http://www.ilmda.com
Contact: J. Barry Johnson, Exec.Dir.
State. **Publications:** *Advantage*, monthly • *Directory and Buyers Guide*, biennial.

3614 ■ Illinois Manufactured Housing Association (IMHA)
3888 Peoria Rd.
Springfield, IL 62702
Ph: (217)528-3423
Fax: (217)528-4642
E-mail: info@imha.org
URL: http://www.imha.org
Contact: Mr. Robert W. Thieman Jr., Exec.Dir.
Founded: 1949. **Members:** 450. **Staff:** 3. **Budget:** $150,000. **Regional Groups:** 16. **State Groups:** 4. **State**. Represents manufacturers, retailers, suppliers, and owners of manufactured housing communities. Promotes professionalism and positive business climate in the manufactured housing industry. **Publications:** *FOCUS*, monthly. Newsletter • Membership Directory, annual. **Conventions/Meetings:** annual meeting.

3615 ■ Illinois Mini Storage Association
225 E Cook St.
Springfield, IL 62704
Ph: (217)528-5230
Fax: (217)241-4683
E-mail: member@p-a-m-s.com
URL: http://www.ilministorage.org
Contact: Michael Lane, Exec.Dir.
State. Represents owners and operators of self storage facilities. Works to improve the quality of management, customer service and facilities. Promotes public awareness of the self storage industry. Conducts educational meetings on management, marketing, security, and related topics. Lobbies for state legislation protecting and recognizing self storage owners and operators. **Affiliated With:** Self Storage Association.

3616 ■ Illinois Motorcycle Dealers Association (IMDA)
2000 E Cornell Ave.
Springfield, IL 62703
Ph: (217)753-8866
Fax: (217)753-8897
E-mail: info@illinoismda.com
URL: http://www.illinoismda.com
Contact: Karl Kegel, Pres.
Founded: 1971. **Members:** 75. **Membership Dues:** business, $360 (annual). **Staff:** 2. **State**. Motorcycle dealers; associate members are companies within the motorcycle industry. Seeks to promote the sport of on- and off-road cycling. **Awards:** Illinois M/C (Racer) Rider of the Year. **Frequency:** annual. **Type:** monetary. **Publications:** *Cycle Digest*, monthly. Newsletter. **Price:** free for members. **Circulation:** 200. **Advertising:** accepted. **Conventions/Meetings:** annual meeting (exhibits) - always January.

3617 ■ Illinois Movers' and Warehousemen's Association (IMAWA)
c/o Patricia McLaughlin, Exec.Dir.
40 Adloff Ln., Ste.2
Springfield, IL 62703-4441

Ph: (217)585-2470
Fax: (217)585-2472
Free: (888)791-2516
E-mail: imawa@imawa.com
URL: http://www.imawa.com
Contact: Patricia McLaughlin, Exec.Dir.
Founded: 1953. **State**.

3618 ■ Illinois Municipal League
c/o Kenneth A. Alderson, Exec.Dir.
500 E Capitol Ave.
PO Box 5180
Springfield, IL 62705-5180
Ph: (217)525-1220
Fax: (217)525-7438
E-mail: kalderson@iml.org
URL: http://www.iml.org
Contact: Kenneth A. Alderson, Exec.Dir.
Founded: 1914. **Members:** 1,092. **Budget:** $2,500,000. **State**. United for education, assistance and representation for municipalities in Illinois. Serves as a common meeting ground for all municipalities and municipal officials of the state. Provides a formal voice for IL municipalities in matters involving common interests, particularly legislative issues. Promotes competence and integrity in the administration of municipal government. Seeks a just balance between federal, state, and municipal government. Offers services and programs that provide municipal officials the knowledge, experience, and assistance necessary to best administer their duties. **Publications:** *Illinois Municipal Review*, monthly. Magazine. **Conventions/Meetings:** annual conference.

3619 ■ Illinois Municipal Utilities Association (IMUA)
919 S Spring St.
Springfield, IL 62704
Ph: (217)241-3027
Fax: (217)241-3037
E-mail: imua@imea.org
URL: http://www.ilmua.org
Contact: Ronald D. Earl, Gen.Mgr./CEO
Founded: 1948. **State**.

3620 ■ Illinois National Congress of Parents and Teachers
901 S Spring St.
Springfield, IL 62704-2790
Ph: (217)528-9617
Fax: (217)528-9490
E-mail: il_office@pta.org
URL: National Affiliate–www.pta.org
State. **Affiliated With:** National PTA - National Congress of Parents and Teachers.

3621 ■ Illinois Nurserymen's Association (INA)
1717 S 5th St.
Springfield, IL 62703
Ph: (217)525-6222
Fax: (217)525-6257
Free: (888)525-3900
E-mail: info@ina-online.org
URL: http://www.ina-online.org
Contact: Dave Bender, Exec.Dir.
Founded: 1925. **State**.

3622 ■ Illinois Optometric Association (IOA)
c/o Michael G. Horstman, Exec.Dir.
304 W Washington St.
Springfield, IL 62701
Ph: (217)525-8012
Fax: (217)525-8018
Free: (800)933-7289
E-mail: ioa@ioaweb.org
URL: http://www.ioaweb.org
Contact: Michael G. Horstman, Exec.Dir.
Staff: 5. **State**. Makes optometry as stronger profession in Illinois. Ensures a voice in legislation that affect the profession and ability of Optometrist to care for patients to the fullest extent of their training and licensure. **Affiliated With:** American Optometric Association. **Conventions/Meetings:** annual convention.

3623 ■ Illinois Optometric Licensing and Disciplinary Board
c/o Sheila Powers, Liaison for the Illinois Optometric Board
320 W Washington, 3rd Fl.
Springfield, IL 62786
Ph: (217)785-0800
Fax: (217)782-7645
URL: http://www.idfpr.com
Contact: Gary W. Lasken OD, Chair
State. **Affiliated With:** Association of Regulatory Boards of Optometry.

3624 ■ Illinois Petroleum Council
c/o David Sykuta, Dir.
400 W Monroe
Springfield, IL 62704
Ph: (217)544-7404
Fax: (217)523-5131
E-mail: illinois@api.org
State.

3625 ■ Illinois Petroleum Marketers Association (IPMA)
PO Box 12020
112 W Cook St.
Springfield, IL 62791
Ph: (217)544-4609
Fax: (217)789-0222
E-mail: judi@ipma-iacs.org
URL: http://www.ipma-iacs.org
Contact: Judi Kren, Exec.Asst.
Founded: 1921. **Members:** 500. **Staff:** 9. **Budget:** $750,000. **Regional Groups:** 5. **State**. Represents the interests of convenience stores, equipment companies, oil companies, petroleum jobbers, and truck stops. Works to ensure a favorable competitive climate in petroleum distribution and to encourage an adequate supply of petroleum products in order to best serve the customer. **Affiliated With:** Petroleum Marketers Association of America. **Publications:** *Gallonage Book*, annual • *Information Bulletin*, weekly • *Legislative Bulletin* • *Oil Can Magazine*, bimonthly • Membership Directory, annual. **Conventions/Meetings:** annual conference (exhibits).

3626 ■ Illinois Pharmacists Association (IPhA)
204 W Cook St.
Springfield, IL 62704
Ph: (217)522-7300
Fax: (217)522-7349
E-mail: ipha@ipha.org
URL: http://www.ipha.org
Contact: J. Michael Patton, Exec.Dir.
Founded: 1880. **Members:** 2,200. **Membership Dues:** regular, $200 (annual) • recent graduate/out-of-state/retired/joint, $100 (annual) • student, $15 (annual) • technician, $35 (annual) • corporate, $650 (annual) • associate, $200 (annual). **Staff:** 4. **Budget:** $750,000. **State**. Strives to enhance the professional competency of registered pharmacists. Provides legislative and regulatory advocacy. Offers continuing education programs. Creates and provides programs to educate and inform the public. **Libraries: Type:** reference; by appointment only. **Holdings:** 1,000; archival material, books, periodicals, video recordings. **Subjects:** pharmacy, legislation. **Awards:** Allan Granat Memorial Scholarship. **Frequency:** annual. **Type:** monetary. **Recipient:** for interest in writing on professional issues • Leadership Award. **Frequency:** annual. **Type:** monetary. **Recipient:** for leadership based on GPA and involvement in profession. **Computer Services:** Bibliographic search • database • electronic publishing • information services • mailing lists • online services • record retrieval services. **Committees:** Standing. **Formerly:** (1979) Illinois Pharmaceutical Association. **Publications:** *Illinois Pharmacist*, bimonthly. Journal. Provides pharmacy legislation information, updates, and continuing education. **Price:** $36.00 /year for nonmembers; free for members. **Circulation:** 2,200. **Advertising:** accepted. Alternate Formats: CD-ROM • *Information Exchange*, biweekly. Newsletter. Alternate Formats: online. **Conventions/Meetings:** annual conference (exhibits) - always spring.

3627 ■ Illinois Pork Producers Association (IPPA)
6411 S 6th St. Rd.
Springfield, IL 62712-6817
Ph: (217)529-3100
Fax: (217)529-1771
E-mail: info@ilpork.com
URL: http://www.ilpork.com
Contact: Jim Kaitschuk, Exec.Dir.
State. **Publications:** *Hot Sheet*, monthly • *Pork Press*, quarterly. Magazine. **Conventions/Meetings:** annual meeting - always February.

3628 ■ Illinois Press Association (IPA)
900 Community Dr.
Springfield, IL 62703
Ph: (217)241-1300
Fax: (217)241-1301
E-mail: dporter@il-press.com
URL: http://www.il-press.com
Contact: David Porter, Communications and Marketing Dir.
Members: 600. **State**.

3629 ■ Illinois Principals Association (IPA)
2940 Baker Dr.
Springfield, IL 62703
Ph: (217)525-1383
Fax: (217)525-7264
E-mail: brian@ilprincipals.org
URL: http://www.ilprincipals.org
Contact: Brian Schwartz, Acting Exec.Dir./Gen. Counsel
State. Dedicated to improvement of elementary and secondary education.

3630 ■ Illinois Propane Gas Association (IPGA)
c/o Rhonda Turner, Exec.Dir.
5240 S 6th St. Rd.
Springfield, IL 62703
Ph: (217)525-8000
Fax: (217)529-8482
Free: (800)727-6207
E-mail: alawson@ilpga.org
URL: http://www.ilpga.org
Contact: Rhonda Turner, Exec.Dir.
Founded: 1959. **Members:** 355. **Membership Dues:** associate, $300 (annual) • cylinder, $370 (annual) • individual, $150 (annual) • retail marketer (minimum; depending on previous year's gallonage), $820 (annual). **Staff:** 2. **State**. Liquid propane gas retailers, marketers, producers; shipping and transport companies; distributors and manufacturers of equipment used in the LP gas industry. Promotes the safe use of LP gas. **Publications:** *Illinois Bobtail*, bimonthly. Magazine • *Illinois Propane Marketers*, annual. Directory. **Conventions/Meetings:** annual meeting - always July in St. Louis, MO • monthly meeting, with educational presentation.

3631 ■ Illinois Public Airports Association
c/o Vince Waters, Pres.
600 S Second St., Ste.400
Springfield, IL 62704
Ph: (217)523-4200
Fax: (217)523-4215
State.

3632 ■ Illinois Public Health Association (IPHA)
c/o James R. Nelson, Exec.Dir.
223 S Third St.
Springfield, IL 62701
Ph: (217)522-5687
Fax: (217)522-5689
E-mail: ipha@ipha.com
URL: http://www.ipha.com
Contact: James R. Nelson, Exec.Dir.
Founded: 1940. **Members:** 6,000. **Membership Dues:** retired, student, sustaining individual, $20 (annual) • individual, $50 (annual) • regular affiliate, $250 (annual) • sustaining affiliate (1-25 employees), $500 (annual) • sustaining affiliate (26-50 employees), $1,000 (annual) • sustaining affiliate (51 or more

employees), $2,000-$4,000 (annual). **Staff:** 16. **State.** Strives to enhance the health of Illinois residents through leadership and improvement of the practice of public health. **Libraries: Type:** reference. **Holdings:** audio recordings, books, periodicals, video recordings. **Subjects:** health, educational and developmental concerns of infancy and early childhood. **Committees:** Annual Meeting/Conference; Continuing Education; Marketing and Communications; Nominating; Policy and Legislative; Strategic Planning Implementation. **Sections:** Academia; Environmental Health. **Affiliated With:** American Public Health Association. **Publications:** *Viewpoint.* Magazines. Contains information about the current and upcoming events of the association and contributed articles of the members. Alternate Formats: online. **Conventions/Meetings:** annual NACCHO-ASTHO - meeting.

3633 ■ Illinois Rural Health Association (IRHA)
PO Box 7387
Springfield, IL 62791-7387
Fax: (217)793-0041
Free: (800)500-1560
E-mail: info@ilruralhealth.org
URL: http://www.ilruralhealth.org
Contact: Pat Bickoff, Pres.

Founded: 1989. **Membership Dues:** individual, $50 (annual) • student, $15 (annual) • organization, $200 (annual). **State.** Improves access to quality health care for residents of rural Illinois. Advocates for health interests of rural residents in public and private policy issues. Enhances the public awareness on rural health issues. **Awards:** IRHA Presidential Award. **Frequency:** annual. **Type:** recognition. **Recipient:** for outstanding contributions to the association • Rural Health Practitioner of the Year. **Frequency:** annual. **Type:** recognition. **Recipient:** for special contribution to rural health • Rural Health Worker of the Year. **Frequency:** annual. **Type:** recognition. **Recipient:** for serving the interests of rural healthcare communities • Special Project Award. **Frequency:** annual. **Type:** recognition. **Recipient:** for exemplary performance in establishing project for rural health. **Committees:** Annual Conference; Awards; Education and Research; Public Policy/Legislative; Public Relations; Strategic Planning. **Subgroups:** Professional Medical Liability; Rural Medical Emergency. **Affiliated With:** National Rural Health Association. **Publications:** *Highlights*, monthly. Newsletter. Alternate Formats: online.

3634 ■ Illinois Small Business Development Center
c/o Mark Petrilli, State Dir.
620 E Adams St., 4th Fl.
Springfield, IL 62701
Ph: (217)524-5856
Fax: (217)524-0171
Free: (800)252-2923
E-mail: mpetrill@illinoisbiz.biz
URL: http://www.ilsbdc.biz
Contact: Mark Petrilli, State Dir.

Founded: 1984. **State.** Statewide network of centers providing information, counseling, and training to existing small business and pre-venture entrepreneurs. **Affiliated With:** Association of Small Business Development Centers.

3635 ■ Illinois Society of Association Executives (ISAE)
c/o Pamela J. Tolson, CAE, Exec.Dir.
PO Box 7513
Springfield, IL 62791
Ph: (217)793-5420
Fax: (217)793-0041
E-mail: pam@isae.com
URL: http://www.isae.com
Contact: Ms. Pamela Tolson CAE, Exec.Dir.

State. Publications: *Inside ISAE*, monthly • Newsletter, 9/year. **Conventions/Meetings:** annual meeting - always July.

3636 ■ Illinois Society of Professional Engineers (ISPE)
c/o Kim Robinson, Exec.Dir.
600 S Second St., Ste.403
Springfield, IL 62704-2504
Ph: (217)544-7424
Fax: (217)528-6545
E-mail: kimrobinson@illinoisengineer.com
URL: http://www.eosinc.com/ispe
Contact: Kim Robinson, Exec.Dir.

Founded: 1886. **Members:** 3,000. **Staff:** 4. **Local Groups:** 21. **State.** Licensed professional and structural engineers, engineer interns, and graduate students. Seeks to advance the professional, social, and economic interests of members and the engineering profession. **Publications:** *Illinois Engineer*, bimonthly. Journal • Directory, annual, August • Newsletter, periodic. **Conventions/Meetings:** annual conference.

3637 ■ Illinois Standardbred Owners and Breeders Association
c/o John Cisna, Exec.Dir.
Illinois Fairgrounds, Box 576
Springfield, IL 62705
Ph: (217)522-8781
Fax: (217)522-4201
Contact: John Cisna, Contact
State.

3638 ■ Illinois State Bar Association (ISBA)
c/o Robert E. Craghead, Exec.Dir.
Illinois Bar Ctr.
424 S 2nd St.
Springfield, IL 62701
Ph: (217)525-1760
Fax: (217)525-0712
Free: (800)252-8908
E-mail: rcraghead@isba.org
URL: http://www.isba.org
Contact: Robert E. Craghead, Exec.Dir.
State.

3639 ■ Illinois State Data Center Cooperative (ISDCC)
Illinois Dept. of Commerce and Community Affairs
620 E Adams St.
Springfield, IL 62701
Ph: (217)782-7500
Fax: (217)524-3701
E-mail: sebetsch@commerce.state.il.us
URL: http://www.commerce.state.il.us
Contact: Suzanne Ebetsch, Coor.

Founded: 1979. **Staff:** 2. **Local Groups:** 35. **State.** Local affiliates include regional and local planning commissions, libraries, universities, and health research groups. **Libraries: Type:** reference. **Holdings:** 1,000; books. **Subjects:** federal statistics including data from census bureau, bureau of economic analysis and bureau of labor statistics. **Publications:** *Illinois Population Trends, 1990 to 2020*, biennial. Population projections for state of Illinois and counties by age and gender.

3640 ■ Illinois State Dental Society (ISDS)
1010 S 2nd St.
PO Box 376
Springfield, IL 62704
Ph: (217)525-1406
Free: (800)475-4737
E-mail: info@isds.org
URL: http://www.isds.org
Contact: Robert A. Rechner, Exec.Dir.

Founded: 1865. **Members:** 6,300. **Membership Dues:** individual, $220 (annual). **Staff:** 14. **Budget:** $2,000,000. **State.** Dentists working to further the profession and the oral health of the public. **Awards:** Distinguished Member Award. **Frequency:** annual. **Type:** recognition. **Recipient:** for achievements in civic, cultural, religious, humanitarian, academic and/or professional areas • Paul Clopper Memorial. **Frequency:** annual. **Type:** scholarship • William J. Greek Memorial Leadership Award. **Frequency:** annual. **Type:** recognition. **Recipient:** to a member who has been out of dental school for less than 10 years and demonstrates leadership qualities while promoting the profession. **Publications:** *Illinois Dental News*, monthly. Newsletter. **Price:** $25.00 for members; $45.00 for nonmembers; $75.00 outside U.S.; $5.00 single issue. ISSN: 1084-8282. **Circulation:** 7,000. **Advertising:** accepted. **Conventions/Meetings:** annual convention.

3641 ■ Illinois State Historical Society (ISHS)
210 1/2 S Sixth St.
Springfield, IL 62701-1503
Ph: (217)525-2781
Fax: (217)525-2783
E-mail: ishs@eosinc.com
URL: http://www.historyillinois.org
Contact: William Furry, Exec.Dir.

Founded: 1899. **Members:** 2,300. **Membership Dues:** student, $30 (annual) • general, $50 (annual) • family, $60 (annual) • sustaining, $75 (annual) • donor, $250-$499 (annual) • patron, $500 (annual) • Lincoln Silver, $1,000 (annual). **Staff:** 5. **Budget:** $300,000. **State.** History professors and teachers, historical agencies, libraries, and businesses. Promotes the study of Illinois history and the collection and preservation of historical artifacts and landmarks. Encourages research. Sponsors centennial business recognition and historic site markers. **Awards:** Centennial Award. **Frequency:** annual. **Type:** recognition. **Recipient:** for 100 years of operation in Illinois • Hostick Award. **Frequency:** annual. **Type:** scholarship. **Recipient:** for PhD in history or library science • ISHS Award Program. **Frequency:** annual. **Type:** recognition. **Recipient:** for outstanding work or publication project • Olive S. Foster Award. **Frequency:** annual. **Type:** monetary. **Recipient:** for outstanding educator in grades 6 to 12 • Pratt Award. **Frequency:** annual. **Type:** monetary. **Recipient:** for best article in Journal of the Illinois State Historical Society. **Formerly:** (1984) Congress of Illinois Historical Societies and Museums. **Publications:** *Dispatch/News*, quarterly. Newsletter. Includes news, activities, calendar, and features. **Price:** included in membership dues. ISSN: 1069-451X. **Circulation:** 2,700 • *Illinois Heritage*, bimonthly. Magazine. **Price:** included in membership dues • *Journal of the Illinois State Historical Society*, quarterly. **Conventions/Meetings:** annual Illinois History Symposium - convention, with speakers and banquet (exhibits) - always weekend closest to December 2 • annual meeting, with business meeting, speakers, tours (exhibits) - always spring.

3642 ■ Illinois State Museum Society
Spring and Edwards St.
Springfield, IL 62706
Ph: (217)782-7386
Fax: (217)782-1254
E-mail: director@museum.state.il.us
URL: http://www.museum.state.il.us
Contact: Bonnie W. Styles, Museum Dir.

State. Represents the interests of museums and galleries serving the people of Illinois.

3643 ■ Illinois Telecommunications Association (ITA)
300 E Monroe St., Rm. 306
Springfield, IL 62701
Ph: (217)525-1044
Fax: (217)525-1103
E-mail: illtelecom@ameritech.net
URL: http://www.il-ita.com
Contact: Douglas A. Dougherty, Pres./Sec.
Founded: 1905. **State.**

3644 ■ Illinois Thoracic Society
c/o Lori Younker, Administrator
3000 Kelly Ln.
Springfield, IL 62707
Free: (800)586-4872
E-mail: lyounker@lungil.org
URL: National Affiliate–www.thoracic.org
Contact: Lori Younker, Administrator

State. Aims to improve the study and practice of thoracic surgery and related disciplines. Seeks to prevent and fight respiratory diseases through research, education and patient advocacy. **Affiliated With:** American Thoracic Society.

3645 ■ Illinois Trial Lawyers Association
c/o James M. Collins, Exec.Dir.
PO Box 5000
401 W Edwards St.
Springfield, IL 62705
Ph: (217)789-0755
Fax: (217)789-0810
Free: (800)252-8501
E-mail: iltla@aol.com
URL: http://www.iltla.com
Contact: James M. Collins, Exec.Dir.
State. Commits to the utilization of the experience and knowledge of the members to the furtherance of the public interest. Encourages the continuing professional education of the lawyer practicing in the field of personal injury law, worker's compensation, civil litigation and general torts.

3646 ■ Institute of Internal Auditors, Springfield Chapter
c/o Stephen D. Kirk, Pres.
PO Box 205
Springfield, IL 62705-0205
Ph: (217)782-4843
E-mail: stephen_kirk@ioia.state.il.us
URL: National Affiliate–www.theiia.org
Contact: Stephen D. Kirk, Pres.
Founded: 1978. **Membership Dues:** regular, $115 (annual) • educator, $65 (annual) • student, retired, $30 (annual) • life, $2,100 • sustainer (government auditors only), $50 (annual) • organization ($65 per staff member over 5; $50 per staff member over 100), $425-$6,600 (annual). **Local**. Serves as an advocate for the internal audit profession. Provides certification, education, research, and technological guidance for the profession. **Committees:** Nominating. **Programs:** Certified Internal Auditor. **Subgroups:** Academic Relations; Audit; Awards; Distribution/Public Relations; Newsletter; Programs, Seminars, and Continuing Education. **Affiliated With:** Institute of Internal Auditors. **Publications:** *Springfield Audit Trails*, monthly. Newsletter. **Advertising:** accepted. Alternate Formats: online.

3647 ■ Life Services Network of Illinois - Springfield
2 Lawrence Sq.
Springfield, IL 62704
Ph: (217)789-1677
Fax: (217)789-1778
E-mail: dbildilli@lsni.org
URL: http://www.lsni.org
Contact: Donna L. Bildilli, Sec.
Local. Provides information, education and innovative services for older adults. **Affiliated With:** American Association of Homes and Services for the Aging.

3648 ■ Mid-West Truckers Association (MTA)
2727 N Dirksen Pkwy.
Springfield, IL 62702
Ph: (217)525-0310
Fax: (217)525-0342
E-mail: info@mid-westtruckers.com
URL: http://www.mid-westtruckers.com
Contact: Donald Schaefer, Exec.VP
Founded: 1961. **Members:** 2,616. **Membership Dues:** $230 (annual). **Staff:** 10. **Budget:** $12,000,000. **Regional Groups:** 3. **State Groups:** 3. **For-Profit**. Owners and operators of trucking companies. Serves as a unified voice for truckers nationwide; conducts lobbying. Sponsors services to members including: mass purchasing program, whereby members may purchase parts at wholesale rates; drug and alcohol testing program; assistance with international registration; license plate procurement; group insurance programs self-funded worker's Compensation Program. Conducts seminars and educational programs; maintains speakers' bureau. **Libraries: Type:** reference. **Holdings:** 102; video recordings. **Subjects:** safety, drugs, alcohol, truck and trailer maintenance. **Awards:** Safe and Courteous Driver Award. **Frequency:** annual. **Type:** recognition. **Recipient:** for most miles driven without accidents or violations • Truck of the Year Award. **Frequency:** annual. **Type:** recognition. **Computer Services:** database, internal • mailing lists, for associate business members. **Telecommunication Services:** electronic mail, truckers@iname.com. **Committees:** Political Action (TRK-PAC). **Publications:** *Cost Summary Booklet*. Contains cost summaries. • *Keep on Truckin' News*, monthly. Magazine. Includes legislative developments, safety issues, and equipment news. Contains semiannual associate business member listing. **Price:** $5.00/year, for members only. **Circulation:** 4,000. **Advertising:** accepted • Also publishes rate tariffs, designated highway map, safety programs, videos, books and pamphlets. **Conventions/Meetings:** annual Mid-West Truck Show, trucking industry services and supplies (exhibits).

3649 ■ Military Officers Association of America, Lincolnland Chapter
c/o Col. John Raschke
PO Box 9174
Springfield, IL 62791-9174
Ph: (217)793-8346
E-mail: foxwilson1@aol.com
Contact: Col. John Raschke, Contact
Local. **Affiliated With:** Military Officers Association of America.

3650 ■ Mississippi Valley Morgan Horse Club (MVMHC)
c/o Kathy Firch, Sec.
6009 Old Salem Rd.
Springfield, IL 62707
Ph: (217)793-0723
E-mail: rockinghorsemorgans@springnet1.com
URL: http://www.geocities.com/mvmhc
Contact: Kathy Firch, Sec.
State. **Affiliated With:** American Morgan Horse Association.

3651 ■ Mothers Against Drunk Driving, Illinois State
2070 W Monroe
Springfield, IL 62704
Ph: (217)523-6233
Fax: (217)523-7079
E-mail: maddilsm@motion.net
URL: http://www.maddillinois.org
Contact: Susan McKinney, Exec.Dir.
State. Victims of drunk driving crashes; concerned citizens. Encourages citizen participation in working towards reform of the drunk driving problem and the prevention of underage drinking. Acts as the voice of victims of drunk driving crashes by speaking on their behalf to communities, businesses, and educational groups. **Affiliated With:** Mothers Against Drunk Driving.

3652 ■ National Active And Retired Federal Employees Association - Lincoln Home 402
2701 Bennington Dr.
Springfield, IL 62704-4224
Ph: (217)546-7567
URL: National Affiliate–www.narfe.org
Contact: Barbara Howard, Contact
Local. Protects the retirement future of employees through education. Informs members on issues affecting the retirement. **Affiliated With:** National Association of Retired Federal Employees.

3653 ■ National Association of State Foresters, Illinois
c/o Mike Mason
1 Natural Resources Way
Springfield, IL 62702-1271
Ph: (217)785-8774
E-mail: michael.r.mason@illinois.gov
URL: National Affiliate–www.stateforesters.org
Contact: Mike Mason, Contact
State. **Affiliated With:** National Association of State Foresters.

3654 ■ National Federation of Independent Business - Illinois (NFIB)
c/o Kim Clark Maisch, State Dir.
600 S Second St., Ste.101
Springfield, IL 62704
Ph: (217)523-5471
Fax: (217)523-3850
E-mail: kim.maisch@nfib.org
Contact: Kim Clark Maisch, State Dir.
State. **Affiliated With:** National Federation of Independent Business.

3655 ■ National Organization for Women - Illinois
PO Box 474
Springfield, IL 62705
E-mail: illinoisnow@juno.com
URL: http://www.illinoisnow.org
State. **Affiliated With:** National Organization for Women.

3656 ■ National Technological Honor Society - Capital Area Career Center Illinois
2201 Toronto Rd.
Springfield, IL 62707-8645
Ph: (217)529-5431
Fax: (217)529-7861
E-mail: jbailey@caccschool.org
URL: http://www.capital.tec.il.us
Contact: John Bailey, Dir.
Local.

3657 ■ Navy Club of Sangamon - Ship No. 32
2426 Tamaroa Trail
Springfield, IL 62702
Ph: (217)528-6906
URL: National Affiliate–www.navyclubusa.org
Contact: Robert E. Wiltshire, Commander
Local. Represents individuals who are, or have been, in the active service of the U.S. Navy, Naval Reserve, Marine Corps, Marine Corps Reserve, and Coast Guard. Promotes and encourages further public interest in the U.S. Navy and its history. Upholds the spirit and ideals of the U.S. Navy. Acts as a public forum for members' views on national defense. Assists the Navy Recruiting Command whenever and wherever possible. Conducts charitable activities. **Affiliated With:** Navy Club of the United States of America.

3658 ■ Owen Marsh Elementary School Parent Teacher Organization
1100 Avon Dr.
Springfield, IL 62704-2133
Ph: (217)525-3242
Local.

3659 ■ Parents Television Council - Central Illinois Chapter
c/o Dayton A. Loyd, Dir.
PO Box 2553
Springfield, IL 62708-2553
Free: (800)852-9321
E-mail: centralillinoischapter@parentstv.org
URL: National Affiliate–www.parentstv.org
Contact: Dayton A. Loyd, Dir.
Local.

3660 ■ Phi Theta Kappa, Alpha Epsilon Kappa Chapter - Alpha Epsilon Kappa Chapter
c/o Sherry Montgomery
PO Box 19256
Springfield, IL 62794
Ph: (217)786-4502
E-mail: sherry.montgomery@llcc.edu
URL: http://www.ptk.org/directories/chapters/IL/210-1.htm
Contact: Sherry Montgomery, Advisor
Local.

3661 ■ Phi Theta Kappa, Delta Theta Chapter - Springfield College
c/o Beata Knoedler
1500 N 5th St.
Springfield, IL 62702

Ph: (217)525-1420
E-mail: knoedler@sci.edu
URL: http://www.ptk.org/directories/chapters/IL/167-1.htm
Contact: Beata Knoedler, Advisor
Local.

3662 ■ Planned Parenthood of Springfield Area
1000 E Washington St.
Springfield, IL 62703-1048
Ph: (217)544-2744
URL: http://www.planparent.org
Local. **Affiliated With:** Planned Parenthood Federation of America.

3663 ■ Prairie Art Alliance
420 S 6th St.
Springfield, IL 62701
Ph: (217)544-2787
Fax: (217)544-4035
E-mail: pshavloske@prairieart.org
URL: http://www.prairieart.org
Contact: Patrick Shavloske, Exec.Dir.
Founded: 1979. **Members:** 200. **Membership Dues:** full, $150 (annual) • associate, $35 (annual) • sponsor, $50-$1,000 (annual). **Staff:** 4. **Budget:** $139,000. **Local**. Strives to serve the public through exhibits, classes and community outreach programs. Encourages the development of member artists. **Formerly:** (1995) Women's Art Alliance.

3664 ■ Prairie Capital Corvair Association (PCCA)
PO Box 954
Springfield, IL 62705
E-mail: prairiecapital@corvair.org
URL: http://www.corvair.org/chapters/chapter627
Contact: Sue Biggs, Pres.
Founded: 1977. **Members:** 50. **Membership Dues:** regular, $18 (annual). **Local**. Enthusiasts of Corvair automobiles. **Affiliated With:** Corvair Society of America. **Publications:** *Flat Six*, monthly. Newsletter. **Advertising:** accepted. Alternate Formats: online. **Conventions/Meetings:** annual convention (exhibits) • monthly meeting - every 1st Tuesday.

3665 ■ Prairie State Orchid Society
c/o Tom Gephart
17 Shetland Dr.
Springfield, IL 62702
E-mail: tomgephart@hotmail.com
URL: National Affiliate–www.orchidweb.org
Local. Professional growers, botanists, hobbyists, and others interested in extending the knowledge, production, use, and appreciation of orchids. **Affiliated With:** American Orchid Society.

3666 ■ Prevent Child Abuse Illinois
528 S 5th St., Ste.211
Springfield, IL 62701
Ph: (217)522-1129
Fax: (217)522-0655
E-mail: rharley@preventchildabuseillinois.org
URL: http://www.preventchildabuseillinois.org
Contact: Roy Harley, Exec.Dir.
Founded: 1990. **Budget:** $1,000,000. **State**. Works to prevent all forms of child abuse and neglect throughout the state, accomplishing this through public awareness campaigns, parent education and support programs, training and technical assistance and community prevention services. Campaigns include Shaken Baby Syndrome prevention, Who's Caring for your Kids?, Make It Stop and Teaming Up to Keep Kids.Safe at Home. **Affiliated With:** Prevent Child Abuse. **Publications:** Report, annual • Brochures. **Conventions/Meetings:** quarterly board meeting • annual Child Abuse Conference • annual Child Death Review Team - symposium.

3667 ■ Professional Independent Insurance Agents of Illinois (PIIAI)
c/o Michael Tate, CAE
4360 Wabash Ave.
Springfield, IL 62711
Ph: (217)793-6660 (630)655-9112
Fax: (217)793-6744
Free: (800)628-6436
E-mail: info@piiai.org
URL: http://www.piiai.org
Contact: James W. Ander, Chm.
Founded: 1993. **Members:** 1,500. **Membership Dues:** property and casualty agency, $500-$2,300 (annual) • associate (individual company), $750 (annual) • associate (based on level), $3,500-$20,000 (annual). **State**. Strives to provide the educational, political, and business needs of the members by recommending and promoting legislation. **Programs:** New Producer Development; PIIAI Bond; Small Risk Workers Comp. **Sections:** Education; Government Affairs. **Affiliated With:** National Association of Professional Insurance Agents. **Formerly:** (2004) Professional Insurance Agents of Illinois. **Publications:** *Association Brief*, weekly. Newsletter. Discusses about the industry and association information. Alternate Formats: online • *Insurance Insight*, monthly. Magazine. Features articles about the organization that includes industry news, markets and coverages, financial planning and agency management. **Advertising:** accepted • *The Young Agents Advocate*, monthly. Newsletter. Contains marketing tips and articles of interest to young agents. Alternate Formats: online. **Conventions/Meetings:** trade show, networking opportunities (exhibits).

3668 ■ Psi Chi, National Honor Society in Psychology - University of Illinois at Springfield
c/o Dept. of Psychology
1 Univ. Plz.
Springfield, IL 62703-5404
Ph: (217)206-6696 (217)206-8226
Fax: (217)206-6217
E-mail: jbark4@uis.edu
URL: National Affiliate–www.psichi.org
Local. **Affiliated With:** Psi Chi, National Honor Society in Psychology.

3669 ■ Route 66 Association of Illinois
c/o John Miller, Pres.
2743 Veterans Pkwy., Rm. 166
Springfield, IL 62704
Ph: (708)528-7866 (708)479-9317
E-mail: kixonrte66@hotmail.com
URL: http://www.il66assoc.org
Contact: John Miller, Pres.
Founded: 1989. **Members:** 1,100. **Membership Dues:** individual, $15 (annual) • business, $30 (annual) • family, $25 (annual) • life, $200 • foreign, $35 (annual). **State Groups:** 1. **State**. Works to educate, preserve, and promote Route 66 in Illinois. Holds Annual Motor Tour in June and preservation projects. **Publications:** *The 66 News*, quarterly. Newsletter. **Conventions/Meetings:** quarterly meeting (exhibits) - January, April, July and October.

3670 ■ RSVP of Sangamon, Menard and Logan Counties
c/o Judy Donath, Dir.
701 W Mason St.
Springfield, IL 62702-2499
Ph: (217)528-4035
Fax: (217)528-1759
E-mail: jdonath@ssoci.org
URL: http://www.ssoci.org/page3.html
Contact: Judy Donath, Dir.
Local. **Affiliated With:** Retired and Senior Volunteer Program.

3671 ■ Sangamon Astronomical Society
3904 Rocky Falls Rd.
Springfield, IL 62707
E-mail: sas_sky@hotmail.com
URL: http://www.sas-sky.org
Contact: Larry Hardy, Contact
Local. Promotes the science of astronomy. Works to encourage and coordinate activities of amateur astronomical societies. Fosters observational and computational work and craftsmanship in various fields of astronomy. **Affiliated With:** Astronomical League.

3672 ■ Sangamon County Medical Society (SCMS)
230 W Carpenter St.
Springfield, IL 62702-4940
Ph: (217)525-0765
Fax: (217)525-0334
E-mail: exec@cillnet.com
URL: http://www.scmsdocs.org
Contact: Sumanta M. Mitra MD, Pres.-Elect
Local. Advances the art and science of medicine. Promotes patient care and the betterment of public health.

3673 ■ Sangamon - Menard County Agricultural Education Partnership
2449 N. Dirksen Pkwy.
Springfield, IL 62702-1443
Ph: (217)753-4611
Local.

3674 ■ SCORE Springfield
3330 Ginger Creek Dr., Ste.B, S
Springfield, IL 62711
Ph: (217)793-5020
Fax: (217)793-5027
E-mail: score571@aol.com
URL: http://www.scorespi.org
Local. **Affiliated With:** SCORE.

3675 ■ Springfield Area Mountain Bike Association (SAMBA)
400 Old Tippecanoe Dr.
Springfield, IL 62711
Ph: (217)899-5125
Fax: (708)570-6797
E-mail: slmrides@yahoo.com
URL: http://www.sambariders.org
Contact: Shawn McKinney, Pres.
Founded: 1989. **Members:** 100. **Local**. **Affiliated With:** International Mountain Bicycling Association.

3676 ■ Springfield Association for Retarded Citizens (SPARC)
One SPARCenter Plz.
232 Bruns Ln.
Springfield, IL 62702
Ph: (217)793-2100
E-mail: devtrn@spfldsparc.org
URL: http://www.springfieldsparc.org
Contact: Carlissa Puckett, Sec.
Founded: 1951. **Members:** 70. **Membership Dues:** $25 (annual). **Staff:** 215. **Budget:** $8,300,000. **For-Profit**. **Local**. Helps individuals with developmental disabilities improve the quality of their lives. **Awards:** Adele Karlson Lifetime Achievement Award. **Frequency:** annual. **Type:** recognition. **Recipient:** for lifelong support of and/or advocacy for individuals with developmental disabilities. **Publications:** *Change Matters*, quarterly. Newsletter. **Circulation:** 5,000. **Conventions/Meetings:** annual meeting - usually October in Springfield, IL.

3677 ■ Springfield Figure Skating Club (SFSC)
868 S Park
Springfield, IL 62704
E-mail: lluster@cdb.state.il.us
URL: http://www.sfsc4u.com
Contact: Lynn Luster, Contact
Local. Provides programs to encourage participation and achievement in the sport of figure skating on ice. Defines and maintains uniform standards of skating proficiency. Organizes and sponsors competitions and exhibitions for the purpose of stimulating interest in figure skating. **Affiliated With:** United States Figure Skating Association.

3678 ■ Springfield Home Builders Association
c/o Sue Scaife
112 W Edwards St.
Springfield, IL 62704-1902
Ph: (217)698-4941
Fax: (217)698-4942
URL: National Affiliate–www.nahb.org
Local. Single and multifamily home builders, commercial builders, and others associated with the building industry. **Affiliated With:** National Association of Home Builders.

3679 ■ Springfield Illinois Convention and Visitors Bureau (SCVB)
109 N 7th St.
Springfield, IL 62701
Ph: (217)789-2360
Fax: (217)544-8711
Free: (800)545-7300
E-mail: mailbox@springfield.il.us
URL: http://www.springfield.il.us
Local.

3680 ■ Springfield Jaycees
PO Box 662
Springfield, IL 62707
Ph: (217)528-8669
E-mail: spfldjcs@family-net.net
URL: http://www.springfieldjaycees.org
Contact: Donna Baker, Pres.
Local.

3681 ■ Springfield Jewish Federation (SJF)
c/o Gloria Schwartz, Exec.Dir.
2815 Old Jacksonville Rd., Ste.103A
Springfield, IL 62704
Ph: (217)787-7223
Fax: (217)787-7470
E-mail: gschwartz@shalomspringfield.org
URL: http://www.shalomspringfield.org
Contact: Gloria Schwartz, Exec.Dir.
Founded: 1941. **Local**.

3682 ■ Springfield Milers BMW Motorcycle Club No. 121
c/o James S. Oliver, Sec.
2336 Cherry Hills Dr. B5
Springfield, IL 62704
Ph: (217)546-5282 (217)625-7346
E-mail: milers@geocities.com
URL: http://www.geocities.com/MotorCity/Speedway/6077/
Contact: James S. Oliver, Sec.
Local. BMW motorcycle owners organized for pleasure, recreation, safety, and dissemination of information concerning BMW motorcycles. **Affiliated With:** BMW Motorcycle Owners of America.

3683 ■ Springfield Parents for Public Schools
PO Box 7452
Springfield, IL 62791
Ph: (217)787-2596
E-mail: contactus@springfieldpps.org
URL: http://www.springfieldpps.org
Contact: Linda Tarr, Contact
Local.

3684 ■ Springfield and Vicinity Sheet Metal Contractors' Association (SVSMCA)
c/o Deborah Garber
917 Click Tower Dr., Ste.100
Springfield, IL 62704-6041
Ph: (217)698-1384
Fax: (217)698-1385
E-mail: deb987a@yahoo.com
URL: National Affiliate–www.smacna.org
Contact: Deborah Smith, Contact
Founded: 1962. **Members:** 9. **Membership Dues:** contractor, $100 (annual). **Staff:** 1. **Budget:** $54,000. **State Groups:** 2. **Local**. Sheet metal and air conditioning contractors in central Illinois. Engages in labor relations activities; acts as an information resource; sponsors seminar and other educational activities. **Libraries: Type:** reference. **Holdings:** 50. **Subjects:** industry topics. **Affiliated With:** Sheet Metal and Air Conditioning Contractors' National Association.

3685 ■ Sweet Adelines International, Sound Celebration Chorus
Center for the Arts
420 S 6th St., 3rd Fl.
Springfield, IL 62701-1808
Ph: (217)529-6839
URL: http://www.soundcelebrationchorus.org
Contact: Linda Russell, Pres.
Local. Advances the musical art form of barbershop harmony through education and performances. Provides education, training and coaching in the development of women's four-part barbershop harmony. **Affiliated With:** Sweet Adelines International.

3686 ■ Taxpayers' Federation of Illinois (TFI)
300 W Edwards St., Ste.201
Springfield, IL 62704
Ph: (217)522-6818
E-mail: tfi@hansoninfosys.com
URL: http://www.taxpayfedil.org
Contact: Timothy S. Bramlet, Pres.
Founded: 1940. **Members:** 400. **Staff:** 5. **Budget:** $500,000. **State**. Individual taxpayers, small businesses, and large corporations. Monitors Illinois government financial activities. Conducts lobbying efforts and research. **Publications:** *Illinois Tax Facts*, monthly. Newsletter. Contains research and analyses on areas of taxation, with special emphasis on how changes might affect the average taxpayer. • *Legislative Manual and Fiscal Facts*, biennial. Booklet. **Price:** free. **Conventions/Meetings:** annual board meeting - always March • periodic Tax Advisory Meeting • annual Tax Conference - always September.

3687 ■ Teamsters Local 916
2701 N Dirksen Pkwy.
Springfield, IL 62703
Ph: (217)522-7932
Fax: (217)522-9492
Free: (877)349-4916
E-mail: mail@teamsters916.org
URL: http://www.teamsters916.org
Contact: Tony Barr, Pres.
Members: 2,900. **Staff:** 7. **Local**. Works to improve the economy of the community by safeguarding the livelihood of its members. Protects each member's right to fair wages, good working conditions, and dignity and respect in the workplace. **Affiliated With:** International Brotherhood of Teamsters. **Formerly:** (2005) Teamsters AFL-CIO, LU 916. **Publications:** *The Hall Report*. Newsletter. Alternate Formats: online.

3688 ■ Toby Tire Safety and Illinois Not-for-Profit Organization
118 W Edwards St., Ste.103
Springfield, IL 62704
Ph: (217)753-8629
E-mail: safety@tobytire.org
URL: http://www.tobytire.org
State.

3689 ■ Township Officials of Illinois (TOI)
408 S 5th St.
Springfield, IL 62701
Ph: (217)744-2212
Fax: (217)744-7419
Free: (866)897-4688
E-mail: questions@toi.org
URL: http://www.toi.org
Contact: Bryan E. Smith, Exec.Dir.
Founded: 1907. **Members:** 11,000. **Staff:** 4. **State**. Elected local government officials, representing 1397 governments, organized to strengthen local government. Provides assistance for the indigent, assessment of property for local taxation and maintenance of roads and bridges. **Awards: Frequency:** annual. **Type:** scholarship. **Recipient:** average or above, graduating senior from Illinois High School. **Publications:** *Township Perspective*, 11/year. Magazine • Journal, periodic • Directory, periodic. **Advertising:** accepted. **Conventions/Meetings:** annual conference (exhibits) - always November.

3690 ■ Troopers Lodge 41
2651 S 5th St.
Springfield, IL 62703
Ph: (217)522-4238
Fax: (217)522-1107
Free: (800)252-5634
E-mail: rmullen@iltroopers41.org
URL: http://www.iltroopers41.org
Contact: Rita Mullen, Office Mgr.
State. Acts as the voice for people who dedicate their lives to protecting and serving the citizens of Illinois. Improves the working conditions of the Illinois State Police through legislation and employee representation.

3691 ■ United Brotherhood of Carpenters and Joiners of America, Mid-Central Illinois Regional Council of Carpenters
No. 1 Kalmia Way
Springfield, IL 62702
Ph: (217)744-1831
Fax: (217)744-1849
E-mail: jdalluge@cityscape.net
URL: National Affiliate–www.carpenters.org
Contact: Dan Smallwood, Pres.
Regional. **Affiliated With:** United Brotherhood of Carpenters and Joiners of America. **Formerly:** (2005) United Brotherhood of Carpenters and Joiners of America, Mid-Central Illinois District Council 4281.

3692 ■ United Cerebral Palsy of Illinois (UCPI)
310 E. Adams
Springfield, IL 62701
Ph: (217)528-9681
Fax: (217)528-9739
Free: (877)550-8274
E-mail: ucpil@aol.com
URL: http://www.ucpillinois.com
Contact: Susan Jennings, Conf.Coor.
State. Aids persons with cerebral palsy and other disabilities, and their families. Goals are to prevent cerebral palsy, minimize its effects, and improve the quality of life for persons with cerebral palsy and other disabilities, and their families. **Affiliated With:** United Cerebral Palsy Associations.

3693 ■ United Counties Council of Illinois
c/o W. Michael McCreery, Exec.Dir.
217 E Monroe, Ste.101
Springfield, IL 62701-1743
Ph: (217)544-5585
Fax: (217)544-5571
E-mail: wmmccreery@hotmail.com
URL: National Affiliate–www.naco.org
Contact: W. Michael McCreery, Exec.Dir.
State. **Affiliated With:** National Association of Counties. **Formerly:** (2005) Urban Counties Council of Illinois.

3694 ■ United Way of Central Illinois
730 E Vine St., Ste.114
Springfield, IL 62703
Ph: (217)789-7000
Fax: (217)789-7120
E-mail: unitedway@uwcil.org
URL: http://www.uwcil.org
Contact: John Kelker, Pres./CPO
Local. **Affiliated With:** United Way of America.

Staunton

3695 ■ American Legion, Illinois Post 362
PO Box 118
Staunton, IL 62088
Ph: (618)635-2470
Fax: (309)663-5783
URL: National Affiliate–www.legion.org
Contact: George Oehler Jr., Contact
Local. **Affiliated With:** American Legion.

3696 ■ Macoupin County Genealogical Society (MCGS)
PO Box 95
Staunton, IL 62088
Ph: (618)635-3852
E-mail: woof8609@sbcglobal.net
URL: http://www.rootsweb.com/~ilmacoup/mcgs
Contact: Mary McKenzie, Coor.
Founded: 1980. **Members:** 250. **Membership Dues:** family, individual, $15 (annual) • charter, $14 (annual) • student, $10 (annual) • life, $150. **Local.** Collects and shares genealogy and history of Macoupin County, IL. **Libraries: Type:** open to the public. **Holdings:** 1,000. **Subjects:** genealogy. **Publications:** *Macoupin County Searcher*, quarterly. Newsletter. Provides information pertaining to the history and genealogy of Macoupin County. **Price:** included in membership dues. **Circulation:** 250.

3697 ■ Staunton Chamber of Commerce
229 W Main St.
Staunton, IL 62088
Ph: (618)635-8356
URL: http://www.stauntonil.com
Contact: Ray Duda, Pres.
Local. Promotes business and community development in Staunton, IL area. **Computer Services:** Information services, business directory.

3698 ■ Staunton Main Street USA
106 N Wood St.
Staunton, IL 62088
Ph: (618)635-2418
E-mail: mainstr@madisontelco.com
URL: http://www.stauntonil.com
Contact: Melanie Sherer, Program Mgr.
Local.

Steeleville

3699 ■ American Legion, Beisner-Brueggemann-Knop Post 480
303 S Sparta St.
Steeleville, IL 62288
Ph: (618)965-3362
Fax: (309)663-5783
URL: National Affiliate–www.legion.org
Local. Affiliated With: American Legion.

3700 ■ RSVP Western Egyptian EOC
c/o Donna Wolters, Dir.
PO Box 7
Steeleville, IL 62288-0007
Ph: (618)965-9523
Fax: (618)965-9421
E-mail: rsvp@egyptian.net
URL: http://www.weeoc.org/Volunteer/rsvp.htm
Contact: Donna Wolters, Dir.
Local. Affiliated With: Retired and Senior Volunteer Program.

Steger

3701 ■ American Legion, Steger Post 521
PO Box 223
Steger, IL 60475
Ph: (708)754-9056
Fax: (309)663-5783
URL: National Affiliate–www.legion.org
Local. Affiliated With: American Legion.

Sterling

3702 ■ American Legion, Sterling Post 296
601 1st Ave.
Sterling, IL 61081
Ph: (815)625-1212
Fax: (309)663-5783
URL: National Affiliate–www.legion.org
Local. Affiliated With: American Legion.

3703 ■ Sauk Valley Area Chamber of Commerce
211 Locust St.
Sterling, IL 61081-3536
Ph: (815)625-2400
Fax: (815)625-9361
E-mail: chamber@essex1.com
URL: http://www.saukvalleyareachamber.com
Contact: Heather Sotelo, Exec.Dir.
Founded: 1912. **Members:** 450. **Staff:** 3. **Local.** Promotes business and community development in the Sauk Valley Area. Conducts Business Expo, Seasonal Sights and Sounds, and Community Carnival. **Formerly:** (2003) Sterling Area Chamber of Commerce. **Publications:** *Action Report*, periodic. Newsletter • *Membership List*, periodic. Membership Directory • *Sterling/Rock Falls Restaurant and Lodging Guide*, periodic. Brochure • *What the Chamber does for You*, periodic.

3704 ■ Sauk Valley Association of Realtors
2605 Woodlawn Rd., Ste.4
Sterling, IL 61081
Ph: (815)626-8148
Fax: (815)626-4026
E-mail: wcar@essex1.com
URL: http://www.nirealtor.com
Contact: Darlene Dodd, Pres.
Local. Strives to develop real estate business practices. Advocates the right to own, use and transfer real property. Provides a facility for professional development, research and exchange of information among members and to the general public. **Affiliated With:** National Association of Realtors.

3705 ■ United Brotherhood of Carpenters and Joiners of America, Heartland Regional Council of Carpenters 4274
218 First Ave.
Sterling, IL 61081-3933
Ph: (815)626-2177
Fax: (815)626-2190
E-mail: ottawa@essex1.com
URL: http://www.heartlandcouncil.org
Contact: Gary Grabowski, Pres.
Local. Affiliated With: United Brotherhood of Carpenters and Joiners of America.

3706 ■ United Way of Whiteside County
PO Box 806
Sterling, IL 61081-0806
Ph: (815)625-7973
URL: National Affiliate–national.unitedway.org
Local. Affiliated With: United Way of America.

3707 ■ Whiteside Co. Emergency REACT
PO Box 857
Sterling, IL 61081
Ph: (815)336-2230
E-mail: blcox@frontiernet.net
URL: http://www.reactintl.org/teaminfo/usa_teams/teams-usil.htm
Local. Trained communication experts and professional volunteers. Provides volunteer public service and emergency communications through the use of radios (Citizen Band, General Mobile Radio Service, UHF and HAM). Coordinates with radio industries and government on safety communication matters and supports charitable activities and community organizations.

3708 ■ Whiteside-Lee County Dental Society
c/o Dr. John T. Readel, Sec.-Treas.
1006 Gregdon Shores Dr.
Sterling, IL 61081-9657
Ph: (815)626-5718
URL: http://www.isds.org
Contact: Dr. John T. Readel, Sec.-Treas.
Local. Represents the interests of dentists committed to the public's oral health, ethics and professional development. Encourages the improvement of the public's oral health and promotes the art and science of dentistry. **Affiliated With:** American Dental Association; Illinois State Dental Society.

Stewardson

3709 ■ American Legion, Wilbur Braughton Post 611
RR 1, Box 1
Stewardson, IL 62463
Ph: (309)663-0361
Fax: (309)663-5783
URL: National Affiliate–www.legion.org
Local. Affiliated With: American Legion.

Stickney

3710 ■ American Legion, Stickney Post 687
6431 W Pershing Rd.
Stickney, IL 60402
Ph: (708)788-8203
Fax: (309)663-5783
URL: National Affiliate–www.legion.org
Local. Affiliated With: American Legion.

3711 ■ Chicago Area Mountain Bikers (CAMBR)
6618 W 41st St.
Stickney, IL 60402
Ph: (708)749-8488
E-mail: edbartunek@msn.com
URL: http://www.cambr.org
State. Affiliated With: International Mountain Bicycling Association. **Formerly:** (2000) Trail Users Rights Foundation.

Stillman Valley

3712 ■ American Legion, Illinois Post 1072
c/o Paul Johnson
PO Box 401
Stillman Valley, IL 61084
Ph: (309)663-0361
Fax: (309)663-5783
URL: National Affiliate–www.legion.org
Contact: Paul Johnson, Contact
Local. Affiliated With: American Legion.

Stockton

3713 ■ American Legion, Stockton Post 449
322 N Main St.
Stockton, IL 61085
Ph: (815)947-2553
Fax: (309)663-5783
URL: National Affiliate–www.legion.org
Local. Affiliated With: American Legion.

3714 ■ Northern Illinois Orienteering Club (NIOC)
c/o Nancy Breed
11512 Rte. 20 E
Stockton, IL 61085
Ph: (815)947-3771
E-mail: breed@jisp.net
URL: http://www.o-galena.org
Contact: Nancy Breed, Contact
Local. Affiliated With: United States Orienteering Federation.

Stonington

3715 ■ American Legion, Zue-Vandeveer Post 257
PO Box 274
Stonington, IL 62567
Ph: (309)663-0361
Fax: (309)663-5783
URL: National Affiliate–www.legion.org
Local. Affiliated With: American Legion.

Strasburg

3716 ■ American Legion, Liberty Post 289
RR 1, Box 20
Strasburg, IL 62465
Ph: (309)663-0361
Fax: (309)663-5783
URL: National Affiliate–www.legion.org
Local. Affiliated With: American Legion.

Streamwood

3717 ■ American Meteorological Society, Chicago
c/o William J. Johnson Sr.
820 E Streamwood Blvd.
Streamwood, IL 60107-1735
Ph: (630)603-1440 (630)293-6800
E-mail: stwclimate@home.com
URL: National Affiliate–www.ametsoc.org/AMS
Contact: William J. Johnson Sr., Sec.
Local. Professional meteorologists, oceanographers, and hydrologists; interested students and nonprofessionals. **Affiliated With:** American Meteorological Society.

3718 ■ Awana Clubs International
One E Bode Rd.
Streamwood, IL 60107
Ph: (630)213-2000
URL: http://www.awana.org
Contact: Deby Ammons, Exec.Sec.
State.

3719 ■ Illinois Dressage and Combined Training Association (IDCTA)
c/o Gail Gardner
124 Locksley Dr.
Streamwood, IL 60107
Ph: (630)830-0790
E-mail: idcta@idcta.org
URL: http://www.idcta.org
Contact: Amy Grahn, Pres.
State. Affiliated With: United States Dressage Federation.

3720 ■ Kiwanis Club of Streamwood
PO Box 1011
Streamwood, IL 60107
Ph: (630)213-3660
E-mail: contact@streamwoodkiwanis.com
URL: http://www.streamwoodkiwanis.org
Contact: John Tampir, Pres.
Local.

3721 ■ Streamwood Chamber of Commerce (SCC)
22 W Streamwood Blvd.
Streamwood, IL 60107
Ph: (630)837-5200
Fax: (630)837-5251
E-mail: staff@streamwoodchamber.com
URL: http://www.streamwoodchamber.com
Contact: Ann Townsend, Exec.Sec.
Founded: 1981. **Members:** 170. **Membership Dues:** retail, commercial, industrial, professional, service firm (base on number of employees), $175-$225 (annual) • nonprofit organization, individual, $50 (annual) • government body/school, $330 (annual) • corporate, $400 (annual). **Staff:** 1. **Local.** Promotes business and community development in Streamwood, IL. Sponsors Summer Celebration, community festivals, and other community events. **Awards:** Business of the Year. **Frequency:** annual. **Type:** recognition • Business Person of the Year. **Frequency:** annual. **Type:** recognition • **Type:** scholarship. **Boards:** Ambassador; Golf; Legislative; Program; Summer Celebration. **Committees:** By-Laws; Fund Raising; Membership; Scholarship. **Publications:** *Chamber News*, bimonthly. Newsletter. **Advertising:** accepted • *Community Guide*, annual. Directory. **Circulation:** 17,000. **Advertising:** accepted. **Conventions/Meetings:** monthly Business After Hours - meeting • quarterly seminar.

3722 ■ Streamwood Guns 'n Hoses Association
c/o Gary Jacobs
PO Box 381
Streamwood, IL 60107-0381
Ph: (630)213-6300
E-mail: mnabor@streamwood.org
Contact: Michelle Nabor, Admin.Exec.
Founded: 1999. **Members:** 25. **Local.** Off-duty police and firefighters dedicated to giving back to the community they serve; provides donations to needy families during holidays and throughout the year. Sponsors annual charity basketball game, police versus fire department.

3723 ■ United Food and Commercial Workers, Local 200T, Northcentral Region
606 Hayward Ave.
Streamwood, IL 60107
Ph: (630)543-4952
URL: National Affiliate–www.ufcw.org
Local. Affiliated With: United Food and Commercial Workers International Union.

Streator

3724 ■ American Legion, Illinois Post 217
c/o Leslie G. Woods
218 W Main St.
Streator, IL 61364
Ph: (815)672-6701
Fax: (309)663-5783
URL: National Affiliate–www.legion.org
Contact: Leslie G. Woods, Contact
Local. Affiliated With: American Legion.

3725 ■ American Red Cross, Streator Chapter
204 S Bloomington
Streator, IL 61364
Ph: (815)672-2682
Fax: (815)673-2331
E-mail: redcross@crtelco.com
URL: http://streator.redcross.org
Local.

3726 ■ First Catholic Slovak Ladies Association - Streator Junior Branch 077
209 W Stanton St.
Streator, IL 61364
Ph: (815)672-7920
URL: National Affiliate–www.fcsla.com
Local. Affiliated With: First Catholic Slovak Ladies Association.

3727 ■ First Catholic Slovak Ladies Association - Streator Senior Branch 007
1104 N Otter Creek St.
Streator, IL 61364
Ph: (815)672-8325
URL: National Affiliate–www.fcsla.com
Local. Affiliated With: First Catholic Slovak Ladies Association.

3728 ■ First Catholic Slovak Ladies Association - Streator Senior Branch 066
3 Liz Mar Pl.
Streator, IL 61364
Ph: (815)673-1700
URL: National Affiliate–www.fcsla.com
Local. Affiliated With: First Catholic Slovak Ladies Association.

3729 ■ National Active And Retired Federal Employees Association - Hardscrabble 2202
1004 Elliott St.
Streator, IL 61364-2410
Ph: (815)672-7308
URL: National Affiliate–www.narfe.org
Contact: Irene M. Berg, Contact
Local. Protects the retirement future of employees through education. Informs members on issues affecting the retirement. **Affiliated With:** National Association of Retired Federal Employees.

3730 ■ Streator Area Chamber of Commerce (SACC)
PO Box 360
Streator, IL 61364
Ph: (815)672-2921
Fax: (815)672-1768
E-mail: streator@streatoril.com
URL: http://www.streatoril.com
Contact: Stephen A. Jonland, Exec.Dir.
Founded: 1915. **Members:** 240. **Membership Dues:** $250 (annual). **Staff:** 2. **Budget:** $154,000. **Local.** Businesses organized to promote economic and community development in Streator, IL. **Formerly:** (1999) Streator Area +Chamber of Commerce and +Industry. **Publications:** Newsletter, monthly.

3731 ■ Streator Area United Way
122 N Bloomington St.
Streator, IL 61364-2208
Ph: (815)672-6721
URL: National Affiliate–national.unitedway.org
Local. Affiliated With: United Way of America.

3732 ■ Streator Lions Club
PO Box 243
Streator, IL 61364
Ph: (815)672-6795
URL: http://streatoril.lionwap.org
Contact: Pam Podkanowicz, Pres.
Local. Affiliated With: Lions Clubs International.

Sublette

3733 ■ Bureau County Angus Association
c/o Steve Florschuetz, Pres.
2212 Maytown Rd.
Sublette, IL 61367
Ph: (815)849-5587
URL: National Affiliate–www.angus.org
Contact: Steve Florschuetz, Pres.
Local. Affiliated With: American Angus Association.

3734 ■ Gardeners of America/Men's Garden Clubs of America - Gardeners Club of Mendota
c/o Tom Palmer
PO Box 101
Sublette, IL 61367
Ph: (815)849-5149
URL: National Affiliate–www.tgoa-mgca.org
Contact: Tom Palmer, Contact
Local.

Sugar Grove

3735 ■ American Legion, Sugar Grove Post 1271
PO Box 68
Sugar Grove, IL 60554
Ph: (708)466-9700
Fax: (309)663-5783
URL: National Affiliate–www.legion.org
Local. Affiliated With: American Legion.

3736 ■ Depression and Bipolar Support Alliance Fox Valley
c/o Judith Kramer
PO Box 158
Sugar Grove, IL 60554
Ph: (630)466-4851
E-mail: judykramer@mchsi.com
URL: National Affiliate–www.dbsalliance.org
Contact: Judith Kramer, Pres.
Founded: 1991. **Members:** 300. **Membership Dues:** patient with mood disorders, $1. **Local.** Seeks to educate patients, families, professionals, and the public concerning the nature of depressive and manic-depressive illnesses as treatable medical diseases; to foster self-help for patients and families;

to eliminate discrimination and stigma; to improve access to care; and to advocate for research toward the elimination of these illnesses and improve the lives of people living with Mood Disorders. **Affiliated With:** Depression and Bipolar Support Alliance. **Publications:** *Depressive Bipolar Support Alliance-Fox Valley Newsletter*, quarterly. Contains information about mood disorders. **Price:** free after joining. **Circulation:** 250. **Conventions/Meetings:** semimonthly lecture, mental health professionals discuss mood disorders - every 2nd and 4th Tuesday except December, Winfield, IL.

3737 ■ Phi Theta Kappa, Phi Omicron Chapter - Waubonsee Community College
c/o Cherie Westfall
4S783 State Rte. 47
Sugar Grove, IL 60554
Ph: (630)466-7900
E-mail: cwestfall@waubonsee.edu
URL: http://www.ptk.org/directories/chapters/IL/197-1.htm
Contact: Cherie Westfall, Advisor
Local.

Sullivan

3738 ■ American Legion, Sullivan Post 68
PO Box 526
Sullivan, IL 61951
Ph: (217)728-4612
Fax: (309)663-5783
URL: National Affiliate–www.legion.org
Local. Affiliated With: American Legion.

3739 ■ Blackhawk Appaloosa Horse Club
c/o Rachel L. Marx
RR1 Box 265d
Sullivan, IL 61951
Ph: (217)728-7244
E-mail: rmarx@effinghamequity.com
URL: National Affiliate–www.appaloosa.com
Contact: Rachel L. Marx, Contact
Local. Affiliated With: Appaloosa Horse Club.

3740 ■ Moultrie County United Way
PO Box 224
Sullivan, IL 61951-0224
Ph: (217)728-2522
URL: National Affiliate–national.unitedway.org
Local. Affiliated With: United Way of America.

3741 ■ Sullivan Chamber and Economic Development (SCED)
112 W Harrison St.
Sullivan, IL 61951
Ph: (217)728-4223
Fax: (217)728-4064
E-mail: info@sullivanchamber.com
URL: http://www.sullivanchamber.com
Contact: Kathy Woodworth, Administrator
Founded: 1957. **Members:** 112. **Staff:** 1. **Local.** Promotes business and community development in Moultrie County, IL. Promotes tourism. Sponsors annual Christmas parade, Christmas lighting contest, Safe Trick or Treat, and Festival of Stars in May. **Formerly:** (2006) Sullivan Area Chamber of Commerce. **Publications:** *News-Notes*, monthly. Newsletter. **Conventions/Meetings:** monthly board meeting - every 3rd Wednesday • annual dinner.

Summit

3742 ■ American Legion, Argo-Summit Post 735
PO Box 235
Summit, IL 60501
Ph: (708)458-0735
Fax: (309)663-5783
URL: National Affiliate–www.legion.org
Local. Affiliated With: American Legion.

Sumner

3743 ■ Wabash Valley Angus Association
c/o Reid Thacker, Pres.
R.R. 2, Box 136
Sumner, IL 62466
Ph: (618)947-2415
URL: National Affiliate–www.angus.org
Contact: Reid Thacker, Pres.
Local. Affiliated With: American Angus Association.

Swansea

3744 ■ Swansea Chamber of Commerce
1501 Caseyville Ave.
Swansea, IL 62226
Ph: (618)233-3938
Fax: (618)233-3936
E-mail: swansea@swanseachamber.org
URL: http://www.swanseachamber.org
Contact: Amy Melinder, Exec.Dir.
Founded: 1969. **Members:** 150. **Staff:** 1. **Local.** Aims to bring businesses together for the purpose of developing and promoting balanced economic growth and business opportunities that in harmony with the objectives of the entire community. Welcomes all businesses, organizations, and individuals regardless of race, religion, color, or national origin who demonstrate an interest in maintaining and promoting a healthy economic climate in the Village of Swansea, Illinois. **Awards:** Swansea Chamber of Commerce Scholarship Award. **Frequency:** annual. **Type:** scholarship. **Recipient:** to high school seniors/recent high school graduates who are Swansea residents. **Committees:** Ambassadors Club; Economic Development. **Affiliated With:** Illinois Association of Chamber of Commerce Executives; Illinois State Chamber of Commerce. **Publications:** *E-Chamber Update*, weekly. Newsletter. **Price:** e-mail update for members only. Alternate Formats: online • Newsletters, monthly. **Price:** available for members only. **Advertising:** accepted. Alternate Formats: online.

Sycamore

3745 ■ American Legion, Sycamore Post 99
3640 W 59th St.
Sycamore, IL 60178
Ph: (815)895-2931
Fax: (309)663-5783
URL: National Affiliate–www.legion.org
Local. Affiliated With: American Legion.

3746 ■ Association for Conflict Resolution, Chicago Area Chapter
PO Box 461
Sycamore, IL 60178-0461
Ph: (847)639-9622
E-mail: acr_chicagoarea@yahoo.com
URL: http://www.acrchicago.org
Contact: Danielle Loevy, Pres.
Membership Dues: individual, $50 (annual). **Local.** Mediators, arbitrators, advocates, consultants and academics interested in employment/labor, family, civil, consumer issues and all areas of practice. Works to bring together the local dispute resolution community. **Committees:** Administrative; Diversity and Equity; Legislative; Professional Development; Program; Public Awareness. **Affiliated With:** Association for Conflict Resolution. **Publications:** *Practitioner*. Directory. Contains information about the chapter members.

3747 ■ DeKalb Area Association of Realtors, Illinois
1430 DeKalb Ave.
Sycamore, IL 60178
Ph: (815)899-3301
Fax: (815)899-3309
E-mail: heather@nirealtor.com
URL: http://www.nirealtor.com
Contact: Sue Elsner, Pres.
Local. Strives to develop real estate business practices. Advocates the right to own, use and transfer real property. Provides a facility for professional development, research and exchange of information among members and to the general public. **Affiliated With:** National Association of Realtors.

3748 ■ Sycamore Chamber of Commerce
407 W State St., Ste.10
Sycamore, IL 60178
Ph: (815)895-3456
Fax: (815)895-0125
E-mail: info@sycamorechamber.com
URL: http://www.sycamorechamber.com
Contact: Rose Treml, Exec.Dir.
Founded: 1915. **Membership Dues:** retail (based on number of employees), $185-$900 • financial institution (per million in deposits), $12 • associate, $100 • non-profit, civic club, $100 • patron, $55 • school, government body, park, $100. **Local.** Promotes economic and social development in Sycamore, IL. **Computer Services:** Information services, business directory. **Formerly:** (2005) Greater Sycamore Chamber of Commerce. **Publications:** *Chamber Focus*. Newsletter. **Advertising:** accepted. Alternate Formats: online.

Table Grove

3749 ■ American Legion, Table Grove Post 413
PO Box 218
Table Grove, IL 61482
Ph: (309)758-5250
Fax: (309)663-5783
URL: National Affiliate–www.legion.org
Local. Affiliated With: American Legion.

Tallula

3750 ■ Illinois Appaloosa Association
c/o Frances Lange
RR 1 Box 92
Tallula, IL 62688
Ph: (217)632-3398
URL: National Affiliate–www.appaloosa.com
Contact: Frances Lange, Contact
Local. Affiliated With: Appaloosa Horse Club.

Tamaroa

3751 ■ American Legion, Tamaroa Memorial Post 1277
PO Box 115
Tamaroa, IL 62888
Ph: (618)496-5412
Fax: (309)663-5783
URL: National Affiliate–www.legion.org
Local. Affiliated With: American Legion.

Tamms

3752 ■ American Legion, Winifred Fairfax Warder Post 406
34th & Sycamore Sts.
Tamms, IL 62988
Ph: (618)734-1286
Fax: (309)663-5783
URL: National Affiliate–www.legion.org
Local. Affiliated With: American Legion.

Tampico

3753 ■ American Legion, Tampico Post 574
c/o John Taets
PO Box 11
Tampico, IL 61283

Ph: (309)663-0361
Fax: (309)663-5783
URL: National Affiliate–www.legion.org
Contact: John Taets, Contact
Local. Affiliated With: American Legion.

Taylorville

3754 ■ American Legion, J. Ivan Dappert Post 73
110 W Franklin St.
Taylorville, IL 62568
Ph: (217)287-1212
Fax: (309)663-5783
URL: National Affiliate–www.legion.org
Local. Affiliated With: American Legion.

3755 ■ Korean War Veterans Association, Sangamon County Chapter
c/o Bernard Scott
3712 E Lakeshore Dr.
Taylorville, IL 62568
Ph: (217)824-6847
URL: National Affiliate–www.kwva.org
Contact: Bernard Scott, Contact
Local. Affiliated With: Korean War Veterans Association.

3756 ■ Taylorville Main Street
PO Box 526
Taylorville, IL 62568-9105
Ph: (217)824-3555
E-mail: tvillemainst@consolidated.net
URL: http://www.downtowntaylorville.com
Contact: Michelle Merker, Prog.Dir.
Founded: 2002. **Members:** 100. **Staff:** 1. **Budget:** $68,000. **State Groups:** 55. **Local Groups:** 1. **Local.** Dedicated to promoting downtown enterprise and building a vital future by strengthening the bonds of community and preserving the past. **Publications:** *Downtown Matters*, bimonthly. Newsletter. Alternate Formats: online.

3757 ■ United Way of Christian County
PO Box 372
Taylorville, IL 62568-0372
Ph: (217)824-8404
URL: National Affiliate–national.unitedway.org
Local. Affiliated With: United Way of America.

Teutopolis

3758 ■ American Legion, Teutopolis Post 924
106 N Plum St.
Teutopolis, IL 62467
Ph: (217)857-3095
Fax: (309)663-5783
URL: National Affiliate–www.legion.org
Local. Affiliated With: American Legion.

Thawville

3759 ■ American Legion, Illinois Post 700
c/o Tracy Smith
106 W Main St.
Thawville, IL 60968
Ph: (309)663-0361
Fax: (309)663-5783
URL: National Affiliate–www.legion.org
Contact: Tracy Smith, Contact
Local. Affiliated With: American Legion.

Thomson

3760 ■ American Legion, Illinois Post 1025
c/o Donald J. Ashpole
PO Box 404
Thomson, IL 61285
Ph: (309)663-0361
Fax: (309)663-5783
URL: National Affiliate–www.legion.org
Contact: Donald J. Ashpole, Contact
Local. Affiliated With: American Legion.

3761 ■ National Active And Retired Federal Employees Association - Prairie 2332
4955 Whispering Pines Cir.
Thomson, IL 61285-7614
Ph: (815)259-2910
URL: National Affiliate–www.narfe.org
Contact: Barbara J. Overton, Contact
Local. Protects the retirement future of employees through education. Informs members on issues affecting the retirement. **Affiliated With:** National Association of Retired Federal Employees.

Thornton

3762 ■ American Legion, Roseland Post 49
PO Box 103
Thornton, IL 60476
Ph: (309)663-0361
Fax: (309)663-5783
URL: National Affiliate–www.legion.org
Local. Affiliated With: American Legion.

3763 ■ American Legion, Thornton Post 1070
109 N Williams St.
Thornton, IL 60476
Ph: (309)663-0361
Fax: (309)663-5783
URL: National Affiliate–www.legion.org
Local. Affiliated With: American Legion.

Timewell

3764 ■ American Legion, Timewell Post 1059
PO Box 8
Timewell, IL 62375
Ph: (309)663-0361
Fax: (309)663-5783
URL: National Affiliate–www.legion.org
Local. Affiliated With: American Legion.

Tinley Park

3765 ■ American Cancer Society, Tinley Park - Prairie Land Regional
17060 Oak Park Ave.
Tinley Park, IL 60477
Ph: (708)633-7770
Fax: (708)633-7773
Free: (800)920-1441
URL: http://www.cancer.org
Contact: Chris Hensley, Regional VP
Local. Affiliated With: American Cancer Society.

3766 ■ American Legion, Gold Star Post 1102
c/o John Riffice
117 Iliad Dr.
Tinley Park, IL 60477
Ph: (708)923-0342
Fax: (309)663-5783
URL: National Affiliate–www.legion.org
Contact: John Riffice, Contact
Local. Affiliated With: American Legion.

3767 ■ American Legion, Illinois Post 1531
c/o Gen. Lewis Chesty Puller
8158 W 169th St.
Tinley Park, IL 60477
Ph: (708)448-2627
Fax: (309)663-5783
URL: National Affiliate–www.legion.org
Contact: Gen. Lewis Chesty Puller, Contact
Local. Affiliated With: American Legion.

3768 ■ American Legion, Tinley Park Post 615
17423 67th Ct.
Tinley Park, IL 60477
Ph: (309)663-0361
Fax: (309)663-5783
URL: National Affiliate–www.legion.org
Local. Affiliated With: American Legion.

3769 ■ Diabetes Educators of Chicago Area American Association of Diabetes Educators (DECAADE)
c/o Sue Bettenhausen, Membership Chair
17619 Dover Ct.
Tinley Park, IL 60477
E-mail: suebettenhausen@comcast.net
URL: http://www.decaade.org
Contact: Sue Bettenhausen, Membership Chair
Local. Promotes the development of quality diabetes education for the diabetic consumer. Fosters communication and cooperation among individuals and organizations involved in diabetes patient education. Provides educational opportunities for the professional growth and development of members. **Affiliated With:** American Association of Diabetes Educators.

3770 ■ Kiwanis Club of Tinley Park
PO Box 153
Tinley Park, IL 60477
E-mail: tpkiwains@hotmail.com
URL: http://www.angelfire.com/il3/tpkiwanis
Contact: Celeste Hayward, Pres.
Local.

3771 ■ Model A Restorers Club, Calumet Region
c/o Charles Vetteri
18444 Lakeview Cir. W
Tinley Park, IL 60477
Ph: (708)532-4946
E-mail: calumetregion@aol.com
URL: http://www.thechatteronline.com
Contact: Charles Vetteri, Contact
Local. Affiliated With: Model "A" Restorers Club.

3772 ■ National Association to Advance Fat Acceptance, Chicago Chapter
PO Box 595
Tinley Park, IL 60477
Ph: (708)802-0860
E-mail: chicagonaafa@aol.com
URL: http://geocities.com/bbw_carolyn
Contact: Lisa Breisch, Pres.
Founded: 1975. **Local. Affiliated With:** National Association to Advance Fat Acceptance.

3773 ■ Skokie Valley Kennel Club
7401 173rd St.
Tinley Park, IL 60477-3250
Fax: (630)893-6438
E-mail: cjk@skokievalleykc.org
URL: http://www.skokievalleykc.org
Contact: Marleene Hovanes, Corresponding Sec.
Local.

3774 ■ Tinley Park Chamber of Commerce (TPCC)
17316 S Oak Park Ave.
Tinley Park, IL 60477
Ph: (708)532-5700
Fax: (708)532-1475
E-mail: info@tinleychamber.org
URL: http://www.tinleychamber.org
Contact: Ms. Bernadette Shanahan-Haas, Exec.Dir.
Founded: 1962. **Members:** 500. **Membership Dues:** platinum, $3,500 (annual) • gold, $2,000 (annual) • silver, $800 (annual) • charitable nonprofit, $50 (annual) • shared account, $30 (annual). **Local.** Promotes business and community development in Tinley Park, IL. **Awards:** Youth in Business Award. **Frequency:** periodic. **Type:** scholarship. **Publications:** *Chamber News and Views*, monthly. Newsletter. **Advertising:** accepted. Alternate Formats: online • Directory, annual. **Conventions/Meet-**

ings: monthly board meeting - every last Thursday • annual Community Awards Dinner.

Tiskilwa

3775 ■ American Legion, Tiskilwa Post 346
635 W Brewster St.
Tiskilwa, IL 61368
Ph: (815)646-4778
Fax: (309)663-5783
URL: National Affiliate–www.legion.org
Local. Affiliated With: American Legion.

Toledo

3776 ■ American Legion, Wiley-Mumford Post 764
PO Box 309
Toledo, IL 62468
Ph: (309)663-0361
Fax: (309)663-5783
URL: National Affiliate–www.legion.org
Local. Affiliated With: American Legion.

Toluca

3777 ■ American Legion, Illinois Post 440
c/o John Rolinski
PO Box 463
Toluca, IL 61369
Ph: (309)663-0361
Fax: (309)663-5783
URL: National Affiliate–www.legion.org
Contact: John Rolinski, Contact
Local. Affiliated With: American Legion.

Tonica

3778 ■ American Legion, Russell-Zenor Post 260
PO Box 62
Tonica, IL 61370
Ph: (309)663-0361
Fax: (309)663-5783
URL: National Affiliate–www.legion.org
Local. Affiliated With: American Legion.

Toulon

3779 ■ American Legion, Toulon Post 416
PO Box 351
Toulon, IL 61483
Ph: (309)995-3529
Fax: (309)663-5783
URL: National Affiliate–www.legion.org
Local. Affiliated With: American Legion.

3780 ■ Heartland Dairy Goat Club
c/o Donna Onley
RR 2, Box 89
Toulon, IL 61483
Ph: (309)852-0485
URL: National Affiliate–adga.org
Contact: Donna Onley, Contact
Regional. Affiliated With: American Dairy Goat Association.

3781 ■ Izaak Walton League of America, Kewanee Chapter
c/o John D. Turnbull
Rte. 2, Box 60
Toulon, IL 61483-9523
Ph: (309)896-3506
URL: National Affiliate–www.iwla.org
Local. Works to educate the public to conserve, maintain, protect, and restore the soil, forest, water, and other natural resources of the U.S; promotes the enjoyment and wholesome utilization of these resources. **Affiliated With:** Izaak Walton League of America.

Towanda

3782 ■ American Legion, Marion Lee Miller Post 931
207 W Hely St.
Towanda, IL 61776
Ph: (309)728-2384
Fax: (309)663-5783
URL: National Affiliate–www.legion.org
Local. Affiliated With: American Legion.

Tremont

3783 ■ American Legion, Tremont Post 1236
24584 E Lake Windermere Rd.
Tremont, IL 61568
Ph: (309)925-5495
Fax: (309)663-5783
URL: National Affiliate–www.legion.org
Local. Affiliated With: American Legion.

Trenton

3784 ■ American Legion, Stahl Post 778
108 S Oak St.
Trenton, IL 62293
Ph: (618)224-9814
Fax: (309)663-5783
URL: National Affiliate–www.legion.org
Local. Affiliated With: American Legion.

Triumph

3785 ■ Illinois Curling Association - Waltham Curling Club
PO Box 11
Triumph, IL 61371-0011
E-mail: info@walthamcurling.org
URL: http://www.walthamcurling.org
Contact: Lance Yednock, Pres.
Local. Affiliated With: United States Curling Association.

Troy

3786 ■ American Legion, Troy Post 708
PO Box 91
Troy, IL 62294
Ph: (618)667-9650
Fax: (309)663-5783
URL: National Affiliate–www.legion.org
Local. Affiliated With: American Legion.

3787 ■ Friends of the Park
c/o Laura Wise
PO Box 433
Troy, IL 62294-0433
Local.

3788 ■ Jordan Hall Research Associates
c/o Robert W. Ridlon, Jr.
8037 Roberts Ln.
Troy, IL 62294-2825
Ph: (618)667-9956
E-mail: jhra@mindspring.com
Contact: Robert W. Ridlon Jr., VP
Founded: 1997. **Staff:** 4. Promotes scientific education and research guided by Biblical models. **Publications:** *Creation or Evolution: Does It Matter?*. Book. **Price:** $15.00.

3789 ■ Scott AFB Rod and Gun Club
944 Ivy Ct.
Troy, IL 62294
Ph: (618)256-2052
E-mail: umpmarr@aol.com
URL: National Affiliate–www.mynssa.com
Local. Affiliated With: National Skeet Shooting Association.

3790 ■ Troy Area Chamber of Commerce
647 E US Hwy. 40
Troy, IL 62294
Ph: (618)667-8769
Fax: (618)667-8759
Free: (888)667-8769
E-mail: info@troycoc.com
URL: http://www.troycoc.com
Contact: Dawn Mushill, Exec.Dir.
Founded: 1984. **Members:** 300. **Membership Dues:** civic organization, $75 • friend of the chamber, $75 • government, school, city, township, library, park, $110 • individual, $140 • business (plus $2/employee over 76), $140-$385 • hotel, $195 • financial institution, $450 • utility, $450. **Staff:** 2. **Local.** Promotes business development and networking in order to enhance the growth and self sufficiency within the community and surrounding areas. **Computer Services:** Information services, business directory. **Telecommunication Services:** electronic mail, dawn@troycoc.com. **Formerly:** (2005) Troy Chamber of Commerce. **Publications:** Newsletter, monthly. **Circulation:** 350. Alternate Formats: online.

Tuscola

3791 ■ American Legion, Douglas County Post 27
PO Box 452
Tuscola, IL 61953
Ph: (309)663-0361
Fax: (309)663-5783
URL: National Affiliate–www.legion.org
Local. Affiliated With: American Legion.

3792 ■ American Rabbit Breeders Association, District 5
c/o Butch Hall, Dir.
571E CR 1250N
Tuscola, IL 61953
Ph: (217)253-2966
E-mail: butch.hall@netcare-il.com
URL: http://www.geocities.com/arbadistrict5
Contact: Butch Hall, Dir.
Regional. Affiliated With: American Rabbit Breeders Association.

3793 ■ Eastern Illinois Dental Society
703 N Niles Ave.
Tuscola, IL 61953-1059
Ph: (217)253-5216
E-mail: richard.davidson@netcare-il.com
URL: http://www.isds.org
Contact: Dr. Richard D. Davidson, Pres.
Local. Represents the interests of dentists committed to the public's oral health, ethics, science and professional advancement. Promotes the art and science of dentistry through advocacy, education, research and the development of standards. **Affiliated With:** American Dental Association; Illinois State Dental Society.

3794 ■ Main Street Tuscola
PO Box 145
Tuscola, IL 61953
Ph: (217)253-2552
E-mail: tedi@tuscola.org
URL: http://www.tuscola.org
Local.

3795 ■ Reserve Officers Association - Department of Illinois, Champaign Chapter 4
c/o BG William R. Smith, Pres.
RR No. 1, Box 172
Tuscola, IL 61953-9725

Ph: (217)253-3626 (217)253-3468
URL: http://www.ilroa.org
Contact: BG William R. Smith, Pres.
Local. Promotes and supports the development and execution of a military policy for the United States. Provides professional development seminars, workshops and programs for its members. **Affiliated With:** Reserve Officers Association of the United States.

3796 ■ Tuscola Chamber of Commerce
PO Box 434
Tuscola, IL 61953
Ph: (217)253-5013
E-mail: tourism@tuscola.org
URL: http://www.tuscola.org
Contact: Dedee Hoel, Pres.
Local. Promotes business and community development in Tuscola, IL area.

Ullin

3797 ■ Phi Theta Kappa, Alpha Lambda Epsilon Chapter - Shawnee Community College
c/o Craig Bradley
8364 Shawnee Coll. Rd.
Ullin, IL 62992
Ph: (618)634-3345
E-mail: craigb@shawneecc.edu
URL: http://www.ptk.org/directories/chapters/IL/217-1.htm
Contact: Craig Bradley, Advisor
Local.

Union

3798 ■ American Legion, Illinois Post 482
c/o Henry F. Miller
PO Box 65
Union, IL 60180
Ph: (309)663-0361
Fax: (309)663-5783
URL: National Affiliate–www.legion.org
Contact: Henry F. Miller, Contact
Local. Affiliated With: American Legion.

3799 ■ McHenry County Historical Society (MCHS)
PO Box 434
Union, IL 60180
Ph: (815)923-2267
Fax: (815)923-2271
E-mail: info@mchsonline.org
URL: http://www.mchsonline.org
Contact: John Hammer, Pres.
Founded: 1963. **Members:** 800. **Membership Dues:** senior, $10 (annual) • individual, $20 (annual) • couple, $30 (annual) • organization, $25 (annual) • business, $100 (annual) • life, $500. **Staff:** 3. **Budget:** $168,000. **Regional Groups:** 3. **State Groups:** 3. **Local Groups:** 1. **Local.** Individuals, families, organizations, and businesses wishing to preserve and promote an interest in the history of McHenry County, IL. Maintains museum, log cabin, town-hall, one-room schoolhouse, and library. Sponsors school and adult education programs; erects historical plaques. **Libraries: Type:** open to the public. **Holdings:** 3,000; books, maps, photographs. **Subjects:** local history, genealogy. **Awards:** Leta Clark Elementary Teacher Scholarship. **Frequency:** annual. **Type:** monetary. **Recipient:** to McHenry County High School senior planning to become elementary teacher. **Roundtables:** McHenry County Antique Farm Equipment Assoc.; McHenry County Civil War. **Working Groups:** McHenry County Historic Barn Preservation Association. **Affiliated With:** American Association of Museums; American Association for State and Local History; Illinois State Historical Society. **Publications:** *Society's Page*, 8/year. Newsletter. Details the society's business. • *Tracer*, quarterly. Newsletter. **Advertising:** accepted. **Conventions/Meetings:** annual meeting - always 4th Monday in June.

University Park

3800 ■ Psi Chi, National Honor Society in Psychology - Governors State University
c/o Dept. of Psychology
Off. of Student Life
B Bldg. Second Fl.
1 Univ. Pkwy.
University Park, IL 60466
Ph: (708)534-4840 (708)534-8951
Fax: (708)534-8451
E-mail: d-wright@govst.edu
URL: National Affiliate–www.psichi.org
Local. Affiliated With: Psi Chi, National Honor Society in Psychology.

Urbana

3801 ■ Alzheimer's Family Support Group
c/o Cindy Cunningham
Champaign County Nursing Home/Adult Day Ctr.
1702 E Main St.
Urbana, IL 61802
Ph: (217)384-3784
Fax: (217)337-0120
E-mail: ljkoty@aol.com
Contact: Linda Kotynek RN, Contact
Members: 30. **Staff:** 1. **Local. Libraries: Type:** not open to the public. **Holdings:** 150; articles, books, periodicals, video recordings. **Subjects:** Alzheimer's disease.

3802 ■ American Institute of Aeronautics and Astronautics, Illinois
c/o Harry Hilton
Univ. of Illinois at Urbana-Champaign
Aerospace Engg. and NCSA
104 S Wright St.
Urbana, IL 61801-2935
E-mail: h-hilton@uiuc.edu
URL: National Affiliate–www.aiaa.org/
Contact: Harry Hilton, Contact
State. Affiliated With: American Institute of Aeronautics and Astronautics.

3803 ■ American Legion, Urbana Post 71
107 N Broadway Ave.
Urbana, IL 61801
Ph: (217)367-3121
Fax: (309)663-5783
URL: National Affiliate–www.legion.org
Local. Affiliated With: American Legion.

3804 ■ American Red Cross, Illini Prairie Chapter
507 W Springfield
Urbana, IL 61801
Ph: (217)344-2800
E-mail: redcross@soltec.net
URL: http://illiniprairie.redcross.org
Local.

3805 ■ American Society of Agricultural and Biological Engineers, District 3 - Central Illinois
c/o Prasanta Kalita, Chair
Univ. of Illinois
Dept. of Agricultural Engg.
1304 W Pennsylvania Ave.
Urbana, IL 61801
Ph: (217)333-0945
E-mail: pkalita@age.uiuc.edu
URL: http://www.asabe.org/membership/sections/ci/index.html
Contact: Prasanta Kalita, Chair
Local. Promotes the science and art of engineering in agricultural, food and biological systems. Encourages the professional improvement of members. Fosters education and develops engineering standards used in agriculture, food and biological systems. **Affiliated With:** American Society of Agricultural and Biological Engineers.

3806 ■ Arthritis Foundation, Champaign County Branch
200 Lincoln Sq.
Urbana, IL 61801
Ph: (217)398-7815
Fax: (217)398-7815
E-mail: greaterillinois@arthritis.org
URL: National Affiliate–www.arthritis.org
Local. Seeks to: discover the cause and improve the methods for the treatment and prevention of arthritis and other rheumatic diseases; increase the number of scientists investigating rheumatic diseases; provide training in rheumatic diseases for more doctors; extend knowledge of arthritis and other rheumatic diseases to the lay public, emphasizing the socioeconomic as well as medical aspects of these diseases. **Affiliated With:** Arthritis Foundation.

3807 ■ Association for Computing Machinery, University of ILL/Urbana-Champaign (ACM/UIUC)
1104 Siebel Center for Cmpt. Sci.
201 N Goodwin Ave.
Urbana, IL 61801
Ph: (217)333-5828
E-mail: acm@uiuc.edu
URL: http://www.acm.uiuc.edu
Contact: Anthony Philipp, Chm.
Founded: 1965. **Local.** Represents dedicated individuals interested in exploring the possibilities of computers and learning more about how to use and develop them; made up of several interactive components: special interest groups, core meetings, general meetings, and social activities; activities are open to the entire University community, regardless of computer experience and background. **Affiliated With:** Association for Computing Machinery.

3808 ■ Central Illinois Aikikai
2112 S Vine St.
Urbana, IL 61801
Ph: (217)384-6370
Fax: (217)344-1071
URL: http://www.aikidocia.org
Contact: Knut Bauer, Instructor
Local.

3809 ■ Central Illinois Association of Diabetes Educators (CIDE)
c/o Cathy Faulstich, BSN, Pres.
Carle Clinic Endocrinology
602 W Univ. Ave.
Urbana, IL 61801
Ph: (217)383-5918
Fax: (217)383-3439
E-mail: cathy.faulstich@carle.com
URL: http://www.cidenet.org
Contact: Cathy Faulstich BSN, Pres.
Local. Promotes the development of quality diabetes education for the diabetic consumer. Fosters communication and cooperation among individuals and organizations involved in diabetes patient education. Provides educational opportunities for the professional growth and development of members. **Affiliated With:** American Association of Diabetes Educators.

3810 ■ Central Illinois English Country Dancers (CIECD)
505 W Stoughton
Urbana, IL 61801
Ph: (217)359-8225
E-mail: jsivier@uiuc.edu
URL: http://www.prairienet.org/ciecd
Contact: Jonathan Sivier, Contact
Local. People interested in English Country music and dance. Holds monthly dances and a ball twice a year.

3811 ■ Champaign County Audubon Society
c/o Beth Chato, Pres.
PO Box 882
Urbana, IL 61803

Ph: (217)367-6766
URL: National Affiliate–www.audubon.org
Local. Works to conserve and restore natural ecosystems, focusing on birds and other wildlife for the benefit of humanity and the earth's biological diversity. **Affiliated With:** National Audubon Society.

3812 ■ Champaign County Humane Society
c/o Katie Widlacki
1911 E Main St.
Urbana, IL 61802
Ph: (217)344-7297
Fax: (217)344-7299
E-mail: volunteer@cuhumane.org
URL: http://www.cuhumane.org
Founded: 1951. **Local.**

3813 ■ Employee Assistance Professionals Association - Central Illinois Chapter
c/o Terrance Jobin, Pres.
1011 W Univ. Ave.
Urbana, IL 61801
Ph: (217)244-5312
E-mail: jobin@uiuc.edu
URL: http://www.eapa.info/ChaptBranch/IL03/CentralIllinois.htm
Contact: Terrance Jobin, Pres.
Local. Affiliated With: Employee Assistance Professionals Association.

3814 ■ FarmHouse Fraternity - Illinois FarmHouse
809 W Pennsylvania
Urbana, IL 61801
Ph: (217)344-4069
URL: National Affiliate–www.farmhouse.org
State. Promotes good fellowship and studiousness. Encourages members to seek the best in their chosen lines of study as well as in life. Works for the intellectual, spiritual, social, moral and physical development of members. **Affiliated With:** Farmhouse.

3815 ■ Flossie Wiley Elementary School PTA
c/o Flossie Wiley Elementary
1602 S Anderson
Urbana, IL 61801
Ph: (217)384-3670
URL: http://familyeducation.com/IL/WileyPTA
Local. Parents, teachers, students, and others interested in uniting the forces of home, school, and community. Promotes the welfare of children and youth.

3816 ■ Funeral Consumers Alliance of Champaign County (FCA-CC)
309 W Green St.
Urbana, IL 61801
E-mail: g.schoedel@insightbb.com
URL: National Affiliate–www.funerals.org
Local. Works to protect consumers right to choose a meaningful dignified funeral. Provides information on low cost cremations and funerals. **Affiliated With:** Funeral Consumers Alliance.

3817 ■ Girl Scouts - Green Meadows Council
1405 N Lincoln Ave.
Urbana, IL 61801
Ph: (217)328-5112
Fax: (217)328-1548
E-mail: gmstaff@pdnt.com
URL: http://www.gsgmc.org
Contact: Traci Nally, Pres.
Local. Young girls and adult volunteers, corporate, government and individual supporters. Strives to develop potential and leadership skills among its members. Conducts trainings, educational programs and outdoor activities.

3818 ■ Grand Prairie Friends of Illinois (GPF)
PO Box 36
Urbana, IL 61803-0036
Ph: (217)265-0831
E-mail: gpf@prairienet.org
URL: http://www.prairienet.org/gpf
Contact: Jamie Ellis, Pres.
Membership Dues: student/low income, $15 • individual, $20 (annual) • family, $25 (annual) • sustaining, $35 (annual) • patron, $50 (annual) • benefactor, $100 (annual) • life, $500. **Local.** Preserves and restores native tallgrass prairie habitat in central Illinois. Acquires and manages prairie remnants, conducts prescribed burns, propagates and plants prairie plants in reconstructions, and generates interest in prairies through a variety of educational programs. **Publications:** *A Prairie Rendezvous*, quarterly. Newsletter.

3819 ■ Griefshare
c/o Chris Thais
Vineyard Christian Fellowship
1500 N Lincoln Ave.
Urbana, IL 61801-1550
Ph: (217)384-3070 (217)687-2824
E-mail: cthais7@hotmail.com
URL: http://www.griefshare.org
Contact: Chris Thais, Contact
Local.

3820 ■ Illini Space Development Society
314 Talbot Lab.
104 S Wright St.
Urbana, IL 61801
Ph: (214)244-4263
E-mail: isds@hotmail.com
Contact: Joannah Metz, Contact
Local. Works for the creation of a spacefaring civilization. Encourages the establishment of self-sustaining human settlements in space. Promotes large-scale industrialization and private enterprise in space.

3821 ■ Illinois Association of Collegiate Registrars and Admissions Officers (IACRAO)
c/o Peter Hood, Archivist
1303 E McHenry St.
Urbana, IL 61801
Ph: (217)367-5616
Fax: (217)244-3173
E-mail: phood@uiuc.edu
URL: http://www.iacrao.org
State.

3822 ■ Illinois Council on Food and Agricultural Research (C-FAR)
1101 W Peabody
Urbana, IL 61801
Ph: (217)244-4232
Fax: (217)244-8594
Free: (800)232-7991
E-mail: cfar@aces.uiuc.edu
URL: http://www.ilcfar.org
Contact: Kraig A. Wagenecht, Exec. Administrator
Founded: 1993. **Members:** 218. **Membership Dues:** organizational, $250 (annual) • affiliate, $100 (annual) • individual, $50 (annual). **Staff:** 5. **State.** Works to secure additional resources to adequately fund relevant and high-quality research and related outreach programs that lead to profitable, consumer-sensitive, and environmentally sound food and agricultural systems in Illinois and the nation. Fosters public confidence in food and agricultural research through public participation in planning and evaluating the process and impact of research activities. **Publications:** *C-FAR Annual Report*, annual • *C-FAR Connection*, semiannual. Newsletter. **Conventions/Meetings:** board meeting • annual meeting • semiannual meeting.

3823 ■ Illinois Poultry Industry Council
c/o Dave Thompson, Pres.
282 ASL
1207 W Gregory Dr.
Urbana, IL 61801
Ph: (217)244-0195
Fax: (217)333-7861
State.

3824 ■ Illinois Society for Histotechnologists (ISH)
c/o Jane Chladny
Univ. of Illinois
Coll. of Veterinary Medicine
2001 S Lincoln, 1609 VMBSB
Urbana, IL 61802
Ph: (217)333-8708
E-mail: mchladny@uiuc.edu
URL: http://www.ilhisto.org
Contact: Jane Chladny, Pres.
State. Histology laboratory technicians, pathologists, laboratory equipment manufacturers' representatives, and interested individuals. Dedicated to the advancement of histotechnology and related sciences such as immunohistochemistry and molecular biology. Works to strengthen personal growth, leadership, education, and quality service to the medical community. Investigates health hazards in the laboratory and ensures the safety of the laboratory.

3825 ■ Illinois Student Environment Network (ISEN)
110 S. Race, Ste.202
Urbana, IL 61801-3297
Ph: (217)384-0830
E-mail: isen@isenonline.org
URL: http://isenonline.org
Contact: Barbara Sego, Exec.Dir.
Founded: 1994. **Members:** 3,500. **Staff:** 3. **State.**

3826 ■ Izaak Walton League of America, Champaign County Chapter
c/o James G. Sternburg
107 E Florida Ave.
Urbana, IL 61801
Ph: (217)367-9857
URL: National Affiliate–www.iwla.org
Contact: James G. Sternburg, Contact
Local. Works to educate the public to conserve, maintain, protect, and restore the soil, forest, water, and other natural resources of the U.S; promotes the enjoyment and wholesome utilization of these resources. **Affiliated With:** Izaak Walton League of America.

3827 ■ League of Women Voters of Champaign County (LWVCC)
PO Box 201
Urbana, IL 61803-0201
Ph: (217)384-4478
Fax: (312)939-6887
E-mail: lwv@prairienet.org
URL: http://www.prairienet.org/lwv
Local. Affiliated With: League of Women Voters of the United States.

3828 ■ Muslim Students Association - University of Illinois at Urbana-Champaign (MSA-UIUC)
280 Illini Union
Urbana, IL 61801
Ph: (217)344-0022
E-mail: msa@uiuc.edu
URL: http://www.msauiuc.org
Contact: Shaz Kaiseruddin, Pres.
Local. Muslim students in North America. Seeks to advance the interests of members; works to enable members to practice Islam as a complete way of life. **Affiliated With:** Muslim Students Association of the United States and Canada.

3829 ■ National Audubon Society - Champaign County
c/o Jeff Courson, Pres.
PO Box 882
Urbana, IL 61803
Ph: (217)581-5110
E-mail: h-parker@uiuc.edu
Contact: Helen Parker, Conservation Chair
Local.

3830 ■ National Organization of Black Law Enforcement Executives, Central Illinois Land of Lincoln Chapter
c/o Eddie Adair, Chief of Police
Urbana Police Dept.
400 Vine St.
Urbana, IL 61801
Ph: (217)384-2321
Fax: (217)384-2372
E-mail: adaireb@city.urbana.il.us
Contact: Eddie Adair, Chief of Police
Local. Affiliated With: National Organization of Black Law Enforcement Executives.

3831 ■ National Society of Black Engineers - University of Illinois, Urbana-Champaign
103A Engg. Hall
1308 W Green St.
Urbana, IL 61801
Ph: (217)333-3558
E-mail: uiucpres@netscape.net
URL: http://nsbe.ec.uiuc.edu
Contact: Brandon Middleton, Pres.
Local. Strives to increase the number of culturally responsible Black engineers who excel academically, succeed professionally and positively impact the community. **Affiliated With:** National Society of Black Engineers.

3832 ■ New Mexico Council of Teachers of English (NMCTE)
1111 W Kenyon Rd.
Urbana, IL 61801-1096
Ph: (217)328-3870
Fax: (217)328-9645
Free: (877)369-6283
URL: National Affiliate–www.ncte.org
Contact: Kyoko Sato, Pres.
Founded: 1963. **Members:** 60,000. **Membership Dues:** individual, $40 (annual) • student/emeritus, $20 (annual). **State.** Teachers of English language arts. Promotes the teaching of English language arts; stimulates professional development; provides a forum for the exchange of ideas among members. Conducts workshops; sponsors student contests. **Awards:** Excellence in English Education. **Frequency:** annual. **Type:** recognition. **Affiliated With:** National Council of Teachers of English. **Publications:** *Forum*, quarterly. Newsletter. **Circulation:** 300 • *New Mexico English Journal*, semiannual. **Conventions/Meetings:** annual conference (exhibits) - always September or October in Albuquerque, NM.

3833 ■ Society of American Foresters, University of Illinois Student Chapter
c/o Jeffrey O. Dawson, Faculty Representative
Univ. of Illinois
1102 S Goodwin W 503 Turner Hall
Urbana, IL 61801
Ph: (217)333-9281
Fax: (217)244-3219
E-mail: jdawson2@uiuc.edu
URL: http://www.siu.edu/~ilsaf
Contact: Jeffrey O. Dawson, Faculty Representative
Local. Affiliated With: Society of American Foresters.

3834 ■ Society for Healthcare Consumer Advocacy, Illinois
c/o Marilyn Kennedy, Pres.
Carle Found. Hosp.
611 W. Park St.
Urbana, IL 61801-2595
Ph: (217)383-3406
Fax: (217)326-1605
E-mail: marilyn.kennedy@carle.com
URL: National Affiliate–www.shca-aha.org
Contact: Marilyn Kennedy, Pres.
Affiliated With: Society for Healthcare Consumer Advocacy of the American Hospital Association.

3835 ■ Society of Manufacturing Engineers - University of Illinois S219
Univ. of Illinois, Mech. and Indus. Engg.
1206 W Green St.
Urbana, IL 61801
Ph: (217)244-7762
E-mail: jastori@uiuc.edu
URL: National Affiliate–www.sme.org
Contact: James Stori, Contact
Local. Advances manufacturing knowledge to gain competitive advantage. Improves skills and manufacturing solutions for the growth of economy. Provides resources and opportunities for manufacturing professionals. **Affiliated With:** ASM International.

3836 ■ Society for Technical Communication, Central Illinois Chapter
PO Box 993
Urbana, IL 61803-0993
E-mail: cil_stc@prairienet.org
URL: http://www.prairienet.org/cil_stc
Contact: Nancee Moster, Pres.
Local. Seeks to advance the theory and practice of technical communication in all media. Enhances the professionalism of the members and the status of the profession. Promotes the education of members and supports research activities in the field. **Affiliated With:** Society for Technical Communication.

3837 ■ STARFLEET: USS Bortas
c/o Capt. Allen Glenn
PO Box 2
Urbana, IL 61803
E-mail: bortasco@ussbortas.net
URL: http://www.region12.org
Contact: Capt. Allen Glenn, Contact
Local. Affiliated With: STARFLEET.

3838 ■ Students for Individual Liberty - University of Illinois, Urbana/Champaign
c/o Justin Doran, Pres.
1401 W Green St.
Rm. 280, Mailbox No. 70
Urbana, IL 61801
E-mail: liberty@uiuc.edu
URL: http://www.lpillinois.org/LPIinfo/local_affiliates.php
Contact: Justin Doran, Pres.
Local. Affiliated With: Libertarian National Committee.

3839 ■ University of Illinois Urbana Champaign National Organization for the Reform of Marijuana Laws (UIUCNORML)
c/o Matthew King
305 N Lincoln Ave., No. 120
Urbana, IL 61801
Ph: (309)303-6497
E-mail: mdking@uiuc.edu
URL: http://www.uiucnorml.org
Local. Affiliated With: National Organization for the Reform of Marijuana Laws.

3840 ■ Urbana Free Library Foundation
201 S Race St.
Urbana, IL 61801-3283
Ph: (217)367-4057
URL: http://urbanafreelibrary.org/uflfound.htm
Contact: Dr. Frederick A. Schlipf, Dir.
Founded: 1995. **Staff:** 1. **Local.** Works to raise funds and accepts charitable gifts in support of the facilities, programs, and collections of the Urbana Free Library in Urbana, IL.

Utica

3841 ■ American Legion, Pierce-Davis Post 731
764 N 3450 Rd.
Utica, IL 61373
Ph: (309)663-0361
Fax: (309)663-5783
URL: National Affiliate–www.legion.org
Local. Affiliated With: American Legion.

3842 ■ Illinois Alpaca Owners and Breeders Association (IAOBA)
c/o Karen Rogers, Sec.
3037 E 11th Rd.
Utica, IL 61373
E-mail: info@iaoba.com
URL: http://www.iaoba.com
Contact: Karen Rogers, Sec.
State. Affiliated With: Alpaca Owners and Breeders Association.

Valier

3843 ■ American Legion, Valier Post 82
400 Main St.
Valier, IL 62891
Ph: (618)724-7012
Fax: (309)663-5783
URL: National Affiliate–www.legion.org
Local. Affiliated With: American Legion.

3844 ■ Franklin County Beagle Club
c/o Rob Vercellino
PO Box G
Valier, IL 62891-0381
URL: National Affiliate–clubs.akc.org
Contact: Rob Vercellino, Contact
Local.

Valmeyer

3845 ■ American Legion, Valmeyer Post 901
618 S Meyer Ave.
Valmeyer, IL 62295
Ph: (309)663-0361
Fax: (309)663-5783
URL: National Affiliate–www.legion.org
Local. Affiliated With: American Legion.

Vandalia

3846 ■ American Legion, Crawford-Hale Post 95
PO Box 66
Vandalia, IL 62471
Ph: (618)283-0832
Fax: (309)663-5783
URL: National Affiliate–www.legion.org
Local. Affiliated With: American Legion.

3847 ■ Mothers Against Drunk Driving, Fayette County
1303 N Seventh
Vandalia, IL 62471
Ph: (618)283-9077
Fax: (618)283-9077
E-mail: maddfayette@earthlink.net
URL: National Affiliate–www.madd.org
Local. Victims of drunk driving crashes; concerned citizens. Encourages citizen participation in working towards reform of the drunk driving problem and the prevention of underage drinking. Acts as the voice of victims of drunk driving crashes by speaking on their behalf to communities, businesses, and educational groups. **Affiliated With:** Mothers Against Drunk Driving.

3848 ■ Okaw Valley Libertarians (OVL)
c/o Jeff Jones, Chm.
420 W Gallatin St.
Vandalia, IL 62471
Ph: (618)283-0888
E-mail: sunman23@fgi.net
URL: http://www.okawvalleylibertarians.com
Contact: Jeff Jones, Chm.
Local. Affiliated With: Libertarian National Committee.

3849 ■ Vandalia Chamber of Commerce
1408 N 5th St.
PO Box 238
Vandalia, IL 62471
Ph: (618)283-2728
Fax: (618)283-4439
URL: http://www.vandaliaillinois.com
Contact: Julie Francis, Dir.
Founded: 1914. **Members:** 200. **Membership Dues:** business, $125 • individual, non-profit organization, $50. **Local.** Aims to advance the interest of business, professional, and service organizations in the Vandalia area through acting as their voice in governmental and social affairs, communicating their needs and enhancing the quality of life. **Committees:** Banquet; Building Grounds; Bylaws and Nominating; Community Improvement; Job Shadowing; Program; Tourism; Ways and Means.

3850 ■ Vandalia Main Street Program
219 S Fifth St., 2nd Fl.
Vandalia, IL 62471
Ph: (618)283-8751
Fax: (618)283-3642
E-mail: kim@vandaliamainstreet.com
URL: http://www.vandaliamainstreet.com
Local.

Vermont

3851 ■ American Legion, Illinois Post 26
c/o Carroll Rankin
PO Box 154
Vermont, IL 61484
Ph: (309)784-4791
Fax: (309)663-5783
URL: National Affiliate–www.legion.org
Contact: Carroll Rankin, Contact
Local. Affiliated With: American Legion.

Vernon Hills

3852 ■ American Legion, Vernon Post 1247
PO Box 5971
Vernon Hills, IL 60061
Ph: (847)367-4153
Fax: (309)663-5783
URL: National Affiliate–www.legion.org
Local. Affiliated With: American Legion.

3853 ■ Girl Scouts - Illinois Crossroads Council
PO Box 8116
Vernon Hills, IL 60061-8116
Ph: (847)573-0500
Fax: (847)573-0500
E-mail: webmaster@ilcrossroads.org
URL: http://www.girlscouts-kickapoocouncil.org
Contact: Stephanie Springs, Chm.
Local. Young girls and adult volunteers, corporate, government and individual supporters. Strives to develop potential and leadership skills among its members. Conducts trainings, educational programs and outdoor activities.

3854 ■ Midwest Association for Employment in Education
c/o Dr. Youssef Yomtoob, Superintendent
Hawthorn School District No. 73
201 Hawthorn Pkwy.
Vernon Hills, IL 60061-1497
Ph: (847)990-4200
Fax: (847)367-6290
E-mail: yomtooby@hawthorn73.org
URL: National Affiliate–www.aaee.org
Contact: Dr. Youssef Yomtoob, Superintendent
Regional. Serves the staffing needs of education professionals at colleges, universities and school districts whose members are school personnel/HR administrators and college and university career center administrators. Promotes ethical standards and practices in the employment processes. **Affiliated With:** American Association for Employment in Education.

3855 ■ Special Needs Network
c/o Mary Ann Ehlert, Pres.
50 Lakeview Pkwy., Ste.102
Vernon Hills, IL 60061
Ph: (847)522-7546
Free: (800)344-7725
E-mail: info@tsnn.org
URL: http://www.tsnn.org
Contact: Mary Anne Ehlert, Pres.
Local.

Versailles

3856 ■ Versailles Area Genealogical and Historical Society (VAGHS)
PO Box 92
Versailles, IL 62378-0092
Ph: (217)225-3401
E-mail: vaghs83@yahoo.com
URL: http://vaghs.tripod.com
Contact: Mark Oldham, Pres.
Founded: 1983. **Members:** 200. **Membership Dues:** $12 (annual). **Staff:** 6. **Local. Libraries: Type:** open to the public. **Holdings:** 100; books, films, periodicals, reports. **Subjects:** history, genealogy. **Publications:** Newsletter, quarterly. Contains local historical and genealogical articles, etc. **Price:** $3.00 for nonmembers; included in membership dues. **Circulation:** 200. **Conventions/Meetings:** bimonthly meeting, museum of historical area items, clothing, business items, farm machinery, antique fire engine, kitchen display, school items, etc (exhibits) - every 3rd Thursday of April, June, August, October, and December at 7:30 P.M. in Versailles, IL.

Victoria

3857 ■ American Legion, Illinois Post 726
c/o Charles A. Warrensford
1675 Knox Hwy. 7
Victoria, IL 61485
Ph: (309)663-0361
Fax: (309)663-5783
URL: National Affiliate–www.legion.org
Contact: Charles A. Warrensford, Contact
Local. Affiliated With: American Legion.

Vienna

3858 ■ American Legion, Illinois Post 536
c/o Harry Sullins
PO Box 733
Vienna, IL 62995
Ph: (618)658-9381
Fax: (309)663-5783
URL: National Affiliate–www.legion.org
Contact: Harry Sullins, Contact
Local. Affiliated With: American Legion.

3859 ■ Illinois Federation of Families
104 E Main St.
Vienna, IL 62995
Ph: (847)336-0115
Fax: (847)336-2557
E-mail: iffcmh@msn.com
URL: http://www.iffcmh.net
Contact: Patti Leppala-Bardell, Contact
State. Affiliated With: Federation of Families for Children's Mental Health.

3860 ■ Illinois Quarter Horse Association, District No. 11
c/o Cherylann Easley, Dir.
230 Concord Church Ln.
Vienna, IL 62995
Ph: (618)658-2051
E-mail: ctd@shawneelink.net
URL: http://www.ilqha.com
Contact: Cherylann Easley, Dir.
Local. Affiliated With: American Quarter Horse Association.

3861 ■ Southern Illinois Dental Society
c/o Dr. Robin A. Wetherell, Sec.-Treas.
PO Box 397
Vienna, IL 62995-0397
Ph: (618)658-8361
E-mail: drwetherell@hotmail.com
URL: http://www.isds.org
Contact: Dr. Robin A. Wetherell, Sec.-Treas.
Local. Represents the interests of dentists committed to the public's oral health, ethics and professional development. Encourages the improvement of the public's oral health and promotes the art and science of dentistry. **Affiliated With:** American Dental Association; Illinois State Dental Society.

Villa Park

3862 ■ American Legion, Villa Park Post 652
39 E St. Charles Rd.
Villa Park, IL 60181
Ph: (309)663-0361
Fax: (309)663-5783
URL: National Affiliate–www.legion.org
Local. Affiliated With: American Legion.

3863 ■ American Society of Professional Estimators, Chicago Chapter
PO Box 6811
Villa Park, IL 60181
E-mail: info@aspenational.org
URL: http://www.aspechicago.org
Contact: Bill Carey, Pres.
Local. Serves construction estimators through education, fellowship and opportunity for professional development.

3864 ■ Bereaved Parents of the USA, Hinsdale Chapter
c/o Donna Corrigan
561 N Yale, No. 1
Villa Park, IL 60181
Ph: (630)279-6148
E-mail: silks6@aol.com
URL: National Affiliate–www.bereavedparentsusa.org
Contact: Donna Corrigan, Contact
Local.

3865 ■ Buick Club of America - Chicagoland Chapter
PO Box 6660
Villa Park, IL 60181-6660
Ph: (847)566-7456
E-mail: scott@earlmich.com
URL: http://www.buickclub.org/chicagoland
Contact: Scott Mich, Dir.
Regional. Represents individuals who are interested in Buick automobiles. Promotes the development, publication and interchange of technical, historical, and other information among members. Encourages the maintenance, restoration, and preservation of Buick automobiles. **Affiliated With:** Buick Club of America.

3866 ■ Villa Park Chamber of Commerce
10 W Park Blvd.
Villa Park, IL 60181
Ph: (630)941-9133
Fax: (630)941-9134
E-mail: vpchamber@sbcglobal.net
URL: http://www.villaparkchamber.org
Contact: Rhonda M. Hartman, Exec.Dir.
Founded: 1948. **Membership Dues:** non-profit, $100 (annual) • business, $150-$300 (annual). **Local.** Promotes business and community development in Villa Park, IL area. **Publications:** *Chamber Connections*, monthly. Newsletter. **Advertising:** accepted • Directory, annual. **Circulation:** 7,000.

3867 ■ Willowbrook Key Club
1250 S Ardmore Ave.
Villa Park, IL 60181
Ph: (630)530-3400
Fax: (630)530-3401
URL: http://www.keyclub.org/club/willowbrook
Local.

Viola

3868 ■ American Legion, Irvin Lee Terrey Post 229
1703 14th Ave.
Viola, IL 61486
Ph: (309)596-2709
Fax: (309)663-5783
URL: National Affiliate–www.legion.org
Local. Affiliated With: American Legion.

Virden

3869 ■ Air Conditioning Contractors of America, Southern Illinois Chapter
c/o Glen Gobel
PO Box 147
Virden, IL 62690
Ph: (217)965-1409
Fax: (217)965-1409
E-mail: acca-si@royell.org
URL: National Affiliate–www.acca.org
Contact: Glen Gobel, Contact
Local. Works to represent contractors involved in installation and service of heating, air conditioning, and refrigeration systems. **Affiliated With:** Air Conditioning Contractors of America.

3870 ■ American Legion, Illinois Post 386
c/o Elmer E. Vance
118 S Dye St.
Virden, IL 62690
Ph: (217)965-4114
Fax: (309)663-5783
URL: National Affiliate–www.legion.org
Contact: Elmer E. Vance, Contact
Local. Affiliated With: American Legion.

3871 ■ Jacksonville Area AIFA
c/o David O'Dell, Sec.
145 W Jackson
Virden, IL 62690
Ph: (217)965-5888
Fax: (217)965-3353
E-mail: david.odell@countryfinancial.com
URL: National Affiliate–naifa.org
Contact: David O'Dell, Sec.
Local. Represents the interests of insurance and financial advisors. Advocates for a positive legislative and regulatory environment. Enhances business and professional skills of members. **Affiliated With:** National Association of Insurance and Financial Advisors.

Virginia

3872 ■ American Legion, Charles Walter Reid Post 258
262 S Cass St.
Virginia, IL 62691
Ph: (309)663-0361
Fax: (309)663-5783
URL: National Affiliate–www.legion.org
Local. Affiliated With: American Legion.

Waggoner

3873 ■ American Legion, Illinois Post 701
c/o Everett C. Burton
PO Box 137
Waggoner, IL 62572
Ph: (309)663-0361
Fax: (309)663-5783
URL: National Affiliate–www.legion.org
Contact: Everett C. Burton, Contact
Local. Affiliated With: American Legion.

Walnut

3874 ■ American Legion, Walnut Post 179
North St.
Walnut, IL 61376
Ph: (309)663-0361
Fax: (309)663-5783
URL: National Affiliate–www.legion.org
Local. Affiliated With: American Legion.

3875 ■ Walnut Chamber of Commerce (WCC)
PO Box 56
Walnut, IL 61376-0056
Ph: (815)379-2141
Fax: (815)379-9375
Contact: Ms. Donna L. Manak, Exec.Dir.
Founded: 1972. **Members:** 100. **Membership Dues:** single member, $25 (annual) • couple membership, $40 (annual) • business, $100 (annual). **Staff:** 1. **Local.** Promotes business and community development in the Walnut, IL area. **Awards:** Hall of Fame. **Frequency:** annual. **Type:** recognition. **Recipient:** interest in and support of community. **Publications:** *Chamber Corner*, WEE. Article. **Advertising:** accepted. Alternate Formats: CD-ROM. Also Cited As: *Walnut Leader*.

Warren

3876 ■ American Legion, Wickler-Copeland Post 464
PO Box 411
Warren, IL 61087
Ph: (309)663-0361
Fax: (309)663-5783
URL: National Affiliate–www.legion.org
Local. Affiliated With: American Legion.

Warrenville

3877 ■ National Association of Home Builders of the U.S., Northern Illinois Home Builders Association
c/o Paulette Buczko
Local No. 1434
29 W 140 Butterfield Rd., Ste.101
Warrenville, IL 60555-2812
Ph: (630)393-4490
Fax: (630)393-4090
E-mail: pbuczko@nihba.com
URL: http://NIHBA.com
Contact: Paulette Buczko, Contact
Founded: 1956. **Members:** 350. **Local.** Single and multifamily home builders, commercial builders, and others associated with the building industry. **Affiliated With:** National Association of Home Builders.

3878 ■ National Speleological Society, Sub-Urban Chicago Grotto
c/o Gary Gibula
3S511 4th St.
Warrenville, IL 60555-3313
Ph: (630)393-6746
E-mail: ggibula@aol.com
URL: http://members.aol.com/GGibula/SUCG.html
Contact: Gary Gibula, Contact
Local. Seeks to study, explore and conserve cave and karst resources. Protects access to caves and promotes responsible caving. Encourages responsible management of caves and their unique environments. **Affiliated With:** National Speleological Society.

3879 ■ Skokie Valley Astronomers
c/o Mrs. Gretchen L.T. Patti
1 S 751 Avon Dr.
Warrenville, IL 60555
Ph: (630)393-7929
E-mail: gpatti@tezzaron.com
URL: http://ourworld.compuserve.com/homepages/E_Neuzil
Contact: Mrs. Gretchen L.T. Patti, Contact
Founded: 1980. **Members:** 45. **Membership Dues:** all, $20 (annual). **Local.** Exists to share enjoyment of astronomy, the sky, and all things space-related. **Publications:** *Star Gazette*, monthly. Newsletter. Contains 2 or 3 pages announcements, schedule, ephemeris and 1 or 2 brief articles. **Conventions/Meetings:** monthly meeting, one hour presentation followed by observation - every 2nd Friday.

3880 ■ Warrenville Firemen
c/o Dennis L. Rogers
PO Box 90
Warrenville, IL 60555-0090
Ph: (630)393-1381
Fax: (630)393-4608
URL: http://www.warrenvillefire.com
Contact: Jerry Kleinwachater, Chief
Founded: 1936. **Local.**

Wasco

3881 ■ American Legion, Wesley Johnson Memorial Post 1195
PO Box 12
Wasco, IL 60183
Ph: (708)584-3010
Fax: (309)663-5783
URL: National Affiliate–www.legion.org
Local. Affiliated With: American Legion.

3882 ■ Chicago Sun Club (CSC)
PO Box 133
Wasco, IL 60183
Ph: (630)377-3719
Fax: (630)377-9914
E-mail: morrison@inil.com
URL: http://www.midwestsun.com/csc
Contact: Mr. George E. Morrison III, Owner
Founded: 1983. **Members:** 150. **Membership Dues:** individual, family, $50 (annual). **Local.** Clothes-optional recreation organization. **Affiliated With:** American Association for Nude Recreation; The Naturist Society. **Formerly:** (2004) North American Naturists. **Publications:** *Bare Facts*, monthly. Newsletter. **Circulation:** 150. **Conventions/Meetings:** semimonthly meeting.

3883 ■ Fox Valley Astronomical Society (FVAS)
PO Box 38
Wasco, IL 60183
Ph: (630)881-0172
Fax: (630)810-7868
E-mail: information@fvastro.org
URL: http://www.fvastro.org
Contact: Herman Zwirn, Pres.
Local. Promotes the science of astronomy. Works to encourage and coordinate activities of amateur astronomical societies. Fosters observational and computational work and craftsmanship in various fields of astronomy. **Affiliated With:** Astronomical League.

Washburn

3884 ■ American Legion, Washburn Post 661
PO Box 325
Washburn, IL 61570
Ph: (309)248-7497
Fax: (309)663-5783
URL: National Affiliate–www.legion.org
Local. Affiliated With: American Legion.

Washington

3885 ■ American Legion, Washington Post 100
211 Legion Rd.
Washington, IL 61571
Ph: (309)444-9859
Fax: (309)663-5783
URL: National Affiliate–www.legion.org
Local. Affiliated With: American Legion.

3886 ■ Dunlap - Central Illinois - Young Life
23 Valley Forge Plz.
Washington, IL 61571
Ph: (309)886-2400
URL: http://dunlap.younglife.org
Local.

3887 ■ Dunlap Wyldlife - Wyldlife
23 Valley Forge Plz.
Washington, IL 61571
Ph: (309)886-2400
URL: http://DunlapWyldlife.younglife.org
Local. Represents the interests of individuals committed to impacting kids' lives and preparing them for the future. Helps young people develop their skills, assets and attitudes to reach their full God-given potential. Reaches suburban, urban, multicultural and disabled kids and teenage mothers. **Affiliated With:** Young Life.

3888 ■ East Peoria - Young Life
23 Valley Forge Plz.
Washington, IL 61571
Ph: (309)886-2400
URL: http://EastPeoria.younglife.org
Local. Represents the interests of individuals committed to impacting kids' lives and preparing them for the future. Helps young people develop their skills, assets and attitudes to reach their full God-given potential. Reaches suburban, urban, multicultural and disabled kids and teenage mothers. **Affiliated With:** Young Life.

3889 ■ Morton - Central Illinois - Young Life
23 Valley Forge Plz.
Washington, IL 61571
Ph: (309)886-2400
URL: http://morton.younglife.org
Local.

3890 ■ Richwoods - Central Illinois - Young Life
23 Valley Forge Plz.
Washington, IL 61571
Ph: (309)886-2400
E-mail: ksletten@insightbb.com
URL: http://richwoods.younglife.org
Contact: Kevin Sletten, Contact
Local.

3891 ■ Sweet Adelines International, Heart of Illinois Chorus
PO Box 103
Washington, IL 61571
Ph: (309)689-3538
E-mail: hoiheartschorus@yahoo.com
URL: http://www.hoichorus.org
Contact: Rhonda Flottmann, Contact
Local. Advances the musical art form of barbershop harmony through education and performances. Provides education, training and coaching in the development of women's four-part barbershop harmony. **Affiliated With:** Sweet Adelines International.

3892 ■ Washington - Central Illinois - Young Life
23 Valley Forge Plz.
Washington, IL 61571
Ph: (309)886-2400
URL: http://washington.younglife.org
Local.

3893 ■ Washington Chamber of Commerce
112 Washington Sq.
Washington, IL 61571-2657
Ph: (309)444-9921
E-mail: wcoc@mtco.com
Contact: Denise Magnuson, Dir.
Founded: 1959. **Members:** 240. **Staff:** 3. **For-Profit. Local.** Promotes business and community development in Washington, IL. **Publications:** *Window on Washington*, monthly. Newsletter. **Advertising:** accepted. **Conventions/Meetings:** annual Washington Day Banquet - always in February.

3894 ■ WyldLife - Morton, Illinois
23 Valley Forge Plz.
Washington, IL 61571
Ph: (309)886-2400
URL: http://mortonwyldlife.younglife.org
Local. Represents the interests of individuals committed to impacting kids' lives and preparing them for the future. Helps young people develop their skills, assets and attitudes to reach their full God-given potential. Reaches suburban, urban, multicultural and disabled kids and teenage mothers. **Affiliated With:** Young Life.

3895 ■ WyldLife - Washington, Illinois
23 Valley Forge Plz.
Washington, IL 61571
Ph: (309)886-2400
URL: http://washingtonwyldlife.younglife.org
Local. Represents the interests of individuals committed to impacting kids' lives and preparing them for the future. Helps young people develop their skills, assets and attitudes to reach their full God-given potential. Reaches suburban, urban, multicultural and disabled kids and teenage mothers. **Affiliated With:** Young Life.

3896 ■ Young Life Central Illinois
23 Valley Forge Plz.
Washington, IL 61571
Ph: (309)886-2400
Fax: (309)886-2142
URL: http://centralillinois.younglife.org
Local.

3897 ■ Young Life - Youth Farm
23 Valley Forge Plz.
Washington, IL 61571
Ph: (309)886-2400
URL: http://sites.younglife.org/sites/youthfarm/default.aspx
Local. Affiliated With: Young Life.

Waterloo

3898 ■ American Legion, Waterloo Post 747
PO Box 82
Waterloo, IL 62298
Ph: (618)939-9990
Fax: (309)663-5783
URL: National Affiliate–www.legion.org
Local. Affiliated With: American Legion.

3899 ■ Great River REACT
314 E 4th St.
Waterloo, IL 62298
Ph: (618)939-6531
URL: http://www.reactintl.org/teaminfo/usa_teams/teams-usil.htm
Local. Trained communication experts and professional volunteers. Provides volunteer public service and emergency communications through the use of radios (Citizen Band, General Mobile Radio Service, UHF and HAM). Coordinates with radio industries and government on safety communication matters and supports charitable activities and community organizations.

3900 ■ Monroe Actors Stage Company (MASC)
c/o Michael D. Hemmer, Pres.
PO Box 89
202 S Main St.
Waterloo, IL 62298
Ph: (618)939-7469
E-mail: mike.hemmer@masctheatre.org
URL: http://www.masctheatre.org
Contact: Michael D. Hemmer, Pres.
Local.

3901 ■ National Active And Retired Federal Employees Association - Granite 1067
711 Willow Ln.
Waterloo, IL 62298-1811
Ph: (618)939-6390
URL: National Affiliate–www.narfe.org
Contact: Margaret A. Tempel, Contact
Local. Protects the retirement future of employees through education. Informs members on issues affecting the retirement. **Affiliated With:** National Association of Retired Federal Employees.

3902 ■ Southern Illinois Haflinger Association
c/o Roger Marcum, Pres.
6521 Old Orchard Ln.
Waterloo, IL 62298
Ph: (618)242-3630
URL: National Affiliate–www.haflingerhorse.com
Contact: Roger Marcum, Pres.
Local. Affiliated With: American Haflinger Registry.

3903 ■ Waterloo Chamber of Commerce
PO Box 1
Waterloo, IL 62298
Ph: (618)939-5300
Fax: (618)939-1805
E-mail: chamber@enjoywaterloo.com
URL: http://www.enjoywaterloo.com
Contact: Debbie Ruggeri, Exec.Dir.
Membership Dues: business, $150-$480 • financial institution (plus $14.50 per $1 million deposit base), $250 • utility, city of waterloo (per employee), $12 • friend of the chamber, $50. **Local.** Helps promote a prosperous business climate and quality of life for the businesses and people of Waterloo. **Publications:** Newsletter, monthly.

3904 ■ Waterloo Lions Club
404 Hillcrest Dr.
Waterloo, IL 62298
Ph: (618)939-3214
URL: http://waterlooil.lionwap.org
Local. Affiliated With: Lions Clubs International.

Waterman

3905 ■ American Legion, Waterman Post 654
PO Box 122
Waterman, IL 60556
Ph: (815)264-3366
Fax: (309)663-5783
URL: National Affiliate–www.legion.org
Local. Affiliated With: American Legion.

3906 ■ Waterman Lions Club
10211 Lee Rd.
Waterman, IL 60556
Ph: (815)264-3215
URL: http://watermanil.lionwap.org
Local. Affiliated With: Lions Clubs International.

Watseka

3907 ■ American Legion, Watseka Post 23
PO Box 98
Watseka, IL 60970
Ph: (309)663-0361
Fax: (309)663-5783
URL: National Affiliate–www.legion.org
Local. Affiliated With: American Legion.

3908 ■ Iroquois County Genealogical Society
103 W Cherry St.
Watseka, IL 60970
Ph: (815)432-3730
Fax: (815)432-2215
E-mail: iroqgene@techinter.com
URL: http://www.rootsweb.com/~ilicgs/index.htm
Contact: Carol Rench, Librarian
Founded: 1972. **Members:** 500. **Membership Dues:** individual, $18 (annual). **Staff:** 2. **Languages:** English, Flemish, French. **Regional.** Provides resource materials for persons with ancestry in Iroquois County, Illinois. **Libraries: Type:** open to the public; reference. **Holdings:** 800; archival material, biographical archives, books, business records, clippings, periodicals. **Subjects:** family genealogies, state histories, county histories, cemetery records, marriage records, death records, immigrant indexes, church records. **Awards:** Certificate of Merit. **Frequency:** annual. **Type:** recognition. **Recipient:** to members who have donated their time and effort towards a library project in the past year. **Computer Services:** database, various databases relating to the county • online services, publication subscriptions and memberships information. **Publications:** *The Stalker*, quarterly.

3909 ■ Iroquois Valley Youth for Christ
PO Box 127
Watseka, IL 60970
Ph: (815)432-4932
Fax: (815)432-4986
URL: http://www.ivyfc.org
Local. Affiliated With: Youth for Christ/U.S.A.

3910 ■ Lucky Hearts Support Group
c/o Marsha Hubert
Iroquois Memorial Hosp.
200 E Fairman
Watseka, IL 60970
Ph: (815)432-5841
Free: (800)242-2731
E-mail: icu@iroquoismemorial.com
URL: http://www.iroquoismemorial.com
Contact: Marsha Hubert, Contact
Local.

3911 ■ Watseka Area Chamber of Commerce (WACC)
206 E Walnut St.
Watseka, IL 60970
Ph: (815)432-2416
Fax: (815)432-2762
E-mail: office@watsekachamber.org
URL: http://www.watsekachamber.org
Contact: Darcey Smith, Exec.Dir.
Founded: 1945. **Members:** 220. **Membership Dues:** business, $160 (annual). **Local Groups:** 3. **Local.** Promotes business and community development in the Watseka, IL area. **Publications:** *WACC Report*, monthly. Newsletter. **Conventions/Meetings:** semiannual Business Showcase - meeting (exhibits).

Wauconda

3912 ■ American Legion, Wauconda Post 911
PO Box 146
Wauconda, IL 60084
Ph: (708)526-9718
Fax: (309)663-5783
URL: National Affiliate–www.legion.org
Local. Affiliated With: American Legion.

3913 ■ Barrington Bloomers African Violet Society
c/o Nikki Collard
27457 N Forest Garden Rd.
Wauconda, IL 60084
Ph: (847)526-6055
URL: National Affiliate–www.avsa.org
Contact: Nikki Collard, Contact
Local. Affiliated With: African Violet Society of America.

3914 ■ Behavior Analysis Society of Illinois (BASIL)
c/o ABA Chicago
361 Oakwood Rd.
Wauconda, IL 60084-2811
Ph: (847)997-7157
E-mail: basil@abachicago.com
URL: http://abachicago.com/abachicago/basil2006.htm
Contact: Selma Martinez, Pres.
State. Affiliated With: Association for Behavior Analysis.

3915 ■ Public Relations Society of America, Chicago Chapter
1000 N Rand Rd., Ste.214
Wauconda, IL 60084
Ph: (847)526-2010
Fax: (847)526-3993
E-mail: mail@prsachicago.com
URL: http://www.prsachicago.com
Contact: William H. Parke, Pres.
Local. Affiliated With: Public Relations Society of America.

3916 ■ Wauconda Chamber of Commerce (WCC)
100 Main St.
Wauconda, IL 60084
Ph: (847)526-5580
Fax: (847)526-3059
E-mail: info@waucondachamber.org
URL: http://www.waucondachamber.org
Contact: Debra Ogorzaly, Exec.Dir.
Founded: 1948. **Members:** 200. **Membership Dues:** business (based on number of employees), $129-$499 (annual) • salesperson, realtor, utility, $149 (annual) • residential/commercial developer, $349 (annual) • taxing body, $299 (annual) • base (hotel, motel, apartment, condo, healthcare, nursing home, hospital), $150 (annual) • nonprofit, $99 (annual) • emeritus, social, $79 (annual). **Staff:** 1. **Local.** Businesses and industries united to promote and foster the commercial, industrial, professional, civic, and general interests of Wauconda Township, IL. Provides information to the public and business community about the area. Sponsors Miss Wauconda Pageant and the Wauconda Rodeo; holds dinner meetings; conducts Thanksgiving and Christmas community activities. Awards scholarships to local students. **Publications:** *Wauconda Community Guide*, annual. Magazine. Contains annual publication of community information, contact numbers and Chamber member directory. **Circulation:** 5,000. **Advertising:** accepted • *Wauconda Wave*, bimonthly. Newsletter. Contains 12 page newsletter of Chamber activities, new member listings and upcoming events. **Circulation:** 350. **Advertising:** accepted.

Waukegan

3917 ■ Alexian Brothers The Harbor
c/o Wendy Massie Ulmer
826 N Ave.
Waukegan, IL 60085
Ph: (847)782-8015
Fax: (847)782-0822
E-mail: information@theharborwaukegan.org
URL: http://www.TheHarborWaukegan.org
Local.

3918 ■ American Hiking Society - Youth Conservation Corps (YCC)
1020 Glen Rock Ave., Ste.No. 32
Waukegan, IL 60085
Ph: (847)623-0900
Fax: (847)623-0909
E-mail: yccbob@aol.com
URL: http://www.youthconservation.org
Contact: Bob McCammon, Exec.Dir.
Local.

3919 ■ American Legion, Homer Dahringer Post 281
PO Box 740
Waukegan, IL 60085
Ph: (847)662-9589
Fax: (309)663-5783
URL: National Affiliate–www.legion.org
Local. Affiliated With: American Legion.

3920 ■ American Legion, Lake County Post 1122
317 Cory Ave.
Waukegan, IL 60085
Ph: (708)662-0976
Fax: (309)663-5783
URL: National Affiliate–www.legion.org
Local. Affiliated With: American Legion.

3921 ■ American Legion, Winnetka Post 10
128 Washington No. 5
Waukegan, IL 60085
Ph: (309)663-0361
Fax: (309)663-5783
URL: National Affiliate–www.legion.org
Local. Affiliated With: American Legion.

3922 ■ Antique Bottle Club of Northern Illinois
c/o Dan Puzzo, Pres.
270 Stanley Ave.
Waukegan, IL 60085
Ph: (815)338-2567
URL: National Affiliate–www.fohbc.com
Contact: Dan Puzzo, Pres.
Local. Affiliated With: Federation of Historical Bottle Collectors.

3923 ■ Habitat for Humanity Lake County, Illinois
315 N Martin Luther King Jr. Ave.
Waukegan, IL 60085
Ph: (847)623-1020
Fax: (847)623-1038
E-mail: info@habitatlc.org
URL: http://www.habitatlc.org
Contact: Julie Donovan, Exec.Dir.
Local. Telecommunication Services: electronic mail, jdonovan@habitatlc.org. **Affiliated With:** Habitat for Humanity International.

3924 ■ Industrial Workers of the World - Waukegan
PO Box 507
Waukegan, IL 60079
E-mail: waukeganiww@iww.org
URL: National Affiliate–www.iww.org
Local. Affiliated With: Industrial Workers of the World.

3925 ■ International Union of Bricklayers and Allied Craftworkers, AFL-CIO-CLC Local Union 20
2751 Washington St.
Waukegan, IL 60085
Ph: (847)336-8130 (847)244-3685
Fax: (847)244-0556
URL: http://www.bacillinoisdistrictcouncil.org/20_il.htm
Contact: Joe Gagliardo, Business Mgr.
Members: 458. **Local. Affiliated With:** International Union of Bricklayers and Allied Craftworkers.

3926 ■ Lake County Coin Club
c/o Leslie A. Hannula
2210 Crescent Pl.
Waukegan, IL 60085
E-mail: gkefsen@juno.com
URL: National Affiliate–www.money.org
Contact: Leslie A. Hannula, Contact
Local. Affiliated With: American Numismatic Association.

3927 ■ Lake County Contractors Association
1312 Washington St.
Waukegan, IL 60085
Ph: (847)623-2345
Fax: (847)623-2349
E-mail: gdowty@lcca-il.org
URL: http://www.lcca-il.org
Contact: Gary Dowty, Exec.VP

Local. Represents general contractors, subcontractors, suppliers, manufacturers' representatives and individual firms related to the construction industry. Provides information on construction and building procedures. **Affiliated With:** International Builders Exchange Executives.

3928 ■ Lake County RSVP
c/o Jan Beck, Dir.
Lake County Cap
106 S Sheridan Rd.
Waukegan, IL 60085-5682
Ph: (847)249-4330
Fax: (847)249-4393
E-mail: janbec@prodigy.net
URL: http://www.seniorcorps.gov/about/programs/rsvp_state.asp?usestateabbr=il&Search4.x=31&Search4.y=9
Contact: Jan Beck, Dir.

Local. **Affiliated With:** Retired and Senior Volunteer Program.

3929 ■ National Active And Retired Federal Employees Association - Lake County 441
2605 W Grove Ave.
Waukegan, IL 60085-1420
Ph: (847)244-5983
URL: National Affiliate–www.narfe.org
Contact: Bernard F. Zastrow, Contact

Local. Protects the retirement future of employees through education. Informs members on issues affecting the retirement. **Affiliated With:** National Association of Retired Federal Employees.

3930 ■ Retired Enlisted Association, 90
c/o Al Ballok
PO Box 8311
Waukegan, IL 60079
Ph: (847)662-2840
Fax: (847)662-2353
E-mail: skcaeb@comcast.net
URL: http://www.agelesswarriors.org
Contact: Al Ballok, Pres.

Local. Works to enhance the quality of life of uniformed service enlisted personnel, families, and survivors; to stop the erosion of earned benefits through legislative efforts; to maintain esprit de corps, dedication, patriotism, and allegiance to country. **Affiliated With:** The Retired Enlisted Association.

3931 ■ SER - Jobs for Progress, Lake County
c/o Katherine Harris, Exec.Dir.
117 N Genesee St.
Waukegan, IL 60085
Ph: (847)336-1004
Fax: (847)336-1050
E-mail: kharris@serlake.org
URL: National Affiliate–www.ser-national.org
Contact: Katherine Harris, Exec.Dir.

Local. **Affiliated With:** SER - Jobs for Progress National.

3932 ■ Waukegan Main Street
221 N Genesee St.
Waukegan, IL 60085
Ph: (847)623-6650
Fax: (847)623-6620
URL: http://www.waukegandowntown.org

Local.

Waverly

3933 ■ American Legion, Waverly Post 262
136 E State St.
Waverly, IL 62692
Ph: (309)663-0361
Fax: (309)663-5783
URL: National Affiliate–www.legion.org

Local. **Affiliated With:** American Legion.

Wayne City

3934 ■ American Legion, Wayne City Post 1132
PO Box 25
Wayne City, IL 62895
Ph: (618)895-2127
Fax: (309)663-5783
URL: National Affiliate–www.legion.org

Local. **Affiliated With:** American Legion.

Waynesville

3935 ■ American Legion, Waynesville Post 1189
PO Box 38
Waynesville, IL 61778
Ph: (217)949-3301
Fax: (309)663-5783
URL: National Affiliate–www.legion.org

Local. **Affiliated With:** American Legion.

Weldon

3936 ■ American Legion, Hiter-Wene Post 1049
PO Box 284
Weldon, IL 61882
Ph: (309)663-0361
Fax: (309)663-5783
URL: National Affiliate–www.legion.org

Local. **Affiliated With:** American Legion.

Wenona

3937 ■ American Legion, Wenona Post 8
PO Box 40
Wenona, IL 61377
Ph: (309)663-0361
Fax: (309)663-5783
URL: National Affiliate–www.legion.org

Local. **Affiliated With:** American Legion.

West Chicago

3938 ■ American Legion, West Chicago Post 300
PO Box 28
West Chicago, IL 60186
Ph: (708)231-9853
Fax: (309)663-5783
URL: National Affiliate–www.legion.org

Local. **Affiliated With:** American Legion.

3939 ■ DuKane A.B.A.T.E.
PO Box 188
West Chicago, IL 60186-0188
Ph: (630)688-8428
E-mail: dukaneabate@core.com
URL: http://www.abate-il.org/Dukane
Contact: Mark Garrison, Pres.

Local. Works as a politically active group aimed toward the rights of motorcyclists in the state of Illinois. Promotes safety and awareness through drivers' education classes.

3940 ■ Greater Chicago Insulator Club
c/o Mr. Robert Stahr, Pres.
515 Carriage Dr., Unit 2D
West Chicago, IL 60185
Ph: (630)231-4171
E-mail: gcic@clubs.insulators.com
URL: http://www.insulators.com/clubs/gcic.htm
Contact: Mr. Robert Stahr, Pres.

Founded: 1992. **Members:** 60. **Membership Dues:** regular adult, $10 (annual) • junior (under 16 years of age), $5 (annual). **Budget:** $1,000. **Local**. **Libraries: Type:** not open to the public. **Holdings:** 420; books, periodicals. **Subjects:** antique telegraph, telephone, power insulators and collecting. **Awards: Frequency:** annual. **Type:** trophy. **Recipient:** for best use of power insulators display at the NIA National Show. **Affiliated With:** National Insulator Association. **Publications:** Newsletter, bimonthly. **Price:** free for members.

3941 ■ Northeastern Illinois Chapter, National Electrical Contractors Association
31W007 N Ave., Ste.100
West Chicago, IL 60185
Ph: (630)876-5360
Fax: (630)876-5364
E-mail: bcreen@neca-web.org
URL: http://neca-web.org
Contact: Bruce Creen, Exec.Dir.

Local. Aims to promote and advance the interests of the electrical contracting industry. **Affiliated With:** National Electrical Contractors Association.

3942 ■ Northern Illinois BMW Riders No. 271
c/o Gerhard Pilz, Pres.
29W473 Lee Rd.
West Chicago, IL 60185
Ph: (630)231-4673
E-mail: gpilz@jglinc.com
URL: http://members.aol.com/nibmwriders/index.html
Contact: Gerhard Pilz, Pres.

Founded: 1997. **Regional**. BMW motorcycle owners organized for pleasure, recreation, safety, and dissemination of information concerning BMW motorcycles. **Affiliated With:** BMW Motorcycle Owners of America.

3943 ■ West Chicago Chamber of Commerce and Industry
306 Main St.
West Chicago, IL 60185-2839
Ph: (630)231-3003
Fax: (630)231-3009
E-mail: wchicagochamber@cs.com
Contact: Joe Castelluccio, Pres.

Founded: 1952. **Members:** 240. **Membership Dues:** $60-$4,950 (annual). **Staff:** 2. **Local**. Works to provide training, networking, community visibility, and government policy engagement. **Telecommunication Services:** electronic mail, director@wegochamber.org • electronic mail, secretary@wegochamber.org. **Committees:** Governmental Affairs; Marketing; Member Benefits; Ways and Means. **Subgroups:** Special Events. **Formerly:** (1999) West Chicago Chamber of Commerce.

3944 ■ Wycliffe Bible Translators, North Central
100 Wycliffe Dr.
West Chicago, IL 60185-4002
Ph: (630)876-0876
Fax: (630)876-0882
Free: (877)876-4876
E-mail: wnc@wycliffe.org
URL: National Affiliate–www.wycliffe.org

Regional. Works as partners in Bible translation. **Affiliated With:** Wycliffe Bible Translators.

West Dundee

3945 ■ Habitat for Humanity of Northern Fox Valley
c/o Barbara Beckman
411 W Main St.
West Dundee, IL 60118

Ph: (847)836-1432
Fax: (847)836-1495
E-mail: barb.beckman@hfhnfv.org
URL: http://local.habitat.org/northernfoxvalley
Founded: 1990. **Local.**

3946 ■ Mchenry Wyldlife
516 Washington
West Dundee, IL 60118
Ph: (847)844-1662
URL: http://mchenrywildlife.younglife.org
Local. Represents the interests of individuals committed to impacting kids' lives and preparing them for the future. Helps young people develop their skills, assets and attitudes to reach their full God-given potential. Reaches suburban, urban, multicultural and disabled kids and teenage mothers. **Affiliated With:** Young Life.

3947 ■ Partners in Charity (PIC)
c/o Charles Konkus
613 W Main St.
West Dundee, IL 60118
Ph: (630)953-7112
Fax: (800)514-9848
Free: (800)705-8350
E-mail: info@partnersincharity.org
URL: http://partnersincharity.org
Contact: Charles Korkus, Dir.
Founded: 2000. **Staff:** 16. **Local.** Provides down payment grants for residential buyers with no restrictions. **Awards:** Down Payment Assistance. **Type:** grant.

3948 ■ Riverside Chorus of Sweet Adelines International
Bethlehem Lutheran Church
401 W Main St.
West Dundee, IL 60118-2022
Ph: (630)377-2477
E-mail: sunnyporter@hotmail.com
URL: http://www.riversidechorus.com
Contact: Sunny Porter, Team Leader
Local. Advances the musical art form of barbershop harmony through education and performances. Provides education, training and coaching in the development of women's four-part barbershop harmony. **Affiliated With:** Sweet Adelines International.

3949 ■ Young Life McHenry
516 Washington
West Dundee, IL 60118
Ph: (847)844-1662
Fax: (847)844-1662
URL: http://YoungLifeMcHenry.younglife.org
Local.

West Frankfort

3950 ■ Chicago Social Security Management Association (CSSMA)
c/o Hugh Stempfley, Pres.
1005 Factory Outlet Dr.
West Frankfort, IL 62896
Ph: (618)937-2435
Fax: (618)932-2448
E-mail: hugh.stempfley@ssa.gov
URL: http://www.ncssma.org/cssma
Contact: Hugh Stempfley, Pres.
Founded: 1971. **Members:** 520. **Membership Dues:** associate, $78 (annual). **Budget:** $50,000. **Regional.** Supervisors and managers working at the Social Security Administration. Seeks to create dialogue with agency executives to further the mission of the agency. **Libraries: Type:** not open to the public. **Awards:** All 1 Agency Award. **Frequency:** annual. **Type:** recognition. **Recipient:** staff employee who provides outstanding service to front line employees • Public Service Award. **Frequency:** annual. **Type:** recognition. **Recipient:** for promoting the stature of social security management through public service • Robert Fleminger Award. **Frequency:** annual. **Type:** recognition. **Recipient:** for making advancements in the goals of the association. **Publications:** *New Forum*, quarterly. Newsletter. Details association activities. **Price:** included in membership dues. **Circulation:** 600. **Conventions/Meetings:** annual meeting - September.

West Salem

3951 ■ American Legion, Mc Cormack Post 658
113 W North St.
West Salem, IL 62476
Ph: (309)663-0361
Fax: (309)663-5783
URL: National Affiliate–www.legion.org
Local. Affiliated With: American Legion.

West Union

3952 ■ American Legion, Illinois Post 1130
18903 E 350th Rd.
West Union, IL 62477
Ph: (309)663-0361
Fax: (309)663-5783
URL: National Affiliate–www.legion.org
Contact: Dale Poorman, Contact
Local. Affiliated With: American Legion.

Westchester

3953 ■ American Legion, Col. A.L. Brodie Post 1437
15324 Treetop Dr.
Westchester, IL 60154
Ph: (708)343-2499
Fax: (309)663-5783
URL: National Affiliate–www.legion.org
Local. Affiliated With: American Legion.

3954 ■ American Theater Organ Society, Joliet
c/o Jim Patak, Pres.
1406 Mandel Ave.
Westchester, IL 60154-3435
Ph: (708)562-8538
E-mail: jpatak@comcast.net
URL: http://www.organman.com/jatoe
Contact: Jim Patak, Pres.
Local. Affiliated With: American Theatre Organ Society.

3955 ■ Cook County Chamber of Commerce
One Westbrook Corporate Center, Ste.300
Westchester, IL 60154-5701
Ph: (708)531-1117
Fax: (630)968-9038
E-mail: gmurph@xnet.com
Contact: Gerald L. Murphy, Pres.
Founded: 1993. **Members:** 25. **Regional Groups:** 5. **Local Groups:** 134. **Regional.** Business owners, managers and organization leaders. Strives to improve the business climate through property tax reform,economic development initiatives, retention and expansion of existing businesses.Disseminates information to business executives and to the public, facilitates networking among business executives and testifies before local, regional and state governments on matters that affect the Cook County business community. local, regional and state governments on matters that affect the Cook County business community. **Libraries: Type:** not open to the public. **Holdings:** 1; books. **Subjects:** businesses, economic data. **Publications:** Bulletin, bimonthly.

3956 ■ Electrical Contractors' Association of City of Chicago
Five Westbrook Corporate Ctr., Ste.940
Westchester, IL 60154
Ph: (708)531-0022
Fax: (708)531-0071
E-mail: chineca@ecachicago.com
URL: http://www.ecachicago.com
Contact: Mark A. Nemshick, Exec.VP/CEO
Local. Serves as trade association representing electrical contractors in the Chicago Metropolitan Area, Cook County, Illinois. **Affiliated With:** National Electrical Contractors Association.

3957 ■ Paralyzed Veterans of America, Vaughan Chapter
2235 Enterprise Dr., Ste.3501
Westchester, IL 60154
Ph: (708)947-9790
Fax: (708)947-9755
Free: (800)727-2234
E-mail: pvachvaug@mindspring.com
URL: http://www.vaughanpva.org
Contact: Gary E. McDermott, Pres.
Founded: 1947. **Members:** 773. **Membership Dues:** associate, $20 (annual) • life (associate), $100. **Staff:** 2. **Budget:** $821,720. **State Groups:** 1. **Local.** Veterans from Illinois, northwestern Indiana, eastern Iowa, southwest Michigan, northern Missouri, and southwest Wisconsin with spinal cord injury or disease. Advocates for rights of veterans, their families, and other disabled individuals. **Libraries: Type:** open to the public. **Subjects:** barrier-free design, veterans benefits, legislation. **Awards:** Certificate of Appreciation. **Frequency:** annual. **Type:** recognition. **Computer Services:** Online services, web pages that pertain exclusively to spinal cord injury, spinal cord injury resources, and spinal cord injury rehabilitation facilities. **Committees:** Chapter Representative to Hines VA Sports. **Subgroups:** Advocacy/Legislative; Corn Beef & Cabbage Dinner; Hospital Liaison; Newsletter; Sports; Team Sports. **Affiliated With:** Access Living; National Spinal Cord Injury Association; Paralyzed Veterans of America. **Publications:** *Getting It Done, A Future Together* (in English and Spanish). Brochures. **Advertising:** accepted • *PN/Paraplegia News*, monthly. Magazine. Covers PVA news and all aspects of life related to spinal cord injury or disease. **Price:** free for members; $23.00 /year for nonmembers; $39.00 for 24 issues; $32.00/year, non USA. **Advertising:** accepted • *Sports 'N Spokes*, bimonthly. Magazine. Contains information about wheelchair sports and recreational activities. **Price:** $21.00/year, in U.S.; $38.00 for 12 issues, in U.S.; $27.00/year, non USA; $50.00 for 12 issues, non USA. **Advertising:** accepted • Newsletter, monthly. Contains information and reports of the organization. **Advertising:** accepted. **Conventions/Meetings:** monthly board meeting - 1st Tuesday in Hines, IL.

3958 ■ Westchester Chamber of Commerce
PO Box 7309
Westchester, IL 60154
Ph: (708)562-7747
Fax: (708)223-8475
E-mail: brat6169@aol.com
URL: http://www.westchesterchamber.org
Contact: Ms. Kathy Sheldon, Pres.
Founded: 1954. **Membership Dues:** financial institution, professional, retailer, restaurant, manufacturer, $140 (annual) • individual, nonprofit organization, $115 (annual). **Local.** Promotes growth and health of businesses in the community of Westchester. **Telecommunication Services:** electronic mail, pastorjoemills@email.com.

Western Springs

3959 ■ American Truck Historical Society, Windy City Chapter
c/o Bill Schutt
4106 Gilbert Ave.
Western Springs, IL 60558
Ph: (708)246-2406
URL: National Affiliate–www.aths.org
Contact: Bill Schutt, Contact
Local.

3960 ■ American Youth Soccer Organization, Region 300
PO Box 74
Western Springs, IL 60558
Ph: (708)930-3034
E-mail: hotline@ayso300.org
URL: http://www.ayso300.org
Local. Affiliated With: American Youth Soccer Organization.

3961 ■ LaGrange - Wyldlife
812 Hillgrove Ave.
Western Springs, IL 60558-1767
Ph: (708)784-9595
URL: http://sites.younglife.org/_layouts/ylext/default.aspx?ID=C-818
Local. Represents the interests of individuals committed to impacting kids' lives and preparing them for the future. Helps young people develop their skills, assets and attitudes to reach their full God-given potential. Reaches suburban, urban, multicultural and disabled kids and teenage mothers. **Affiliated With:** Young Life.

3962 ■ Lyons Township Young Life
812 Hillgrove Ave.
Western Springs, IL 60558
Ph: (708)784-9595
URL: http://LT.younglife.org
Contact: Seth Holzwarth, Contact
Local.

3963 ■ Sons of Norway, Elvesund Lodge 5-593
c/o John D. Myhre, Pres.
1341 Ogden Ave.
Western Springs, IL 60558-1060
Ph: (708)246-5991
E-mail: john.myhre@bigfoot.com
URL: National Affiliate–www.sofn.com
Contact: John D. Myhre, Pres.
Local. Affiliated With: Sons of Norway.

3964 ■ Young Life Metro SW
812 Hillgrove Ave.
Western Springs, IL 60558
Ph: (708)784-9595
Fax: (708)784-9599
URL: http://MetroSW.younglife.org
Local.

Westfield

3965 ■ American Legion, Weeden-Zeller Post 609
PO Box 186
Westfield, IL 62474
Ph: (309)663-0361
Fax: (309)663-5783
URL: National Affiliate–www.legion.org
Local. Affiliated With: American Legion.

Westmont

3966 ■ Aga Khan Gymkhana Cricket Club
52 W 60th St., No. 110
Westmont, IL 60559
URL: http://www.usaca.org/Clubs.htm
Contact: Naeem Bhaidani, Contact
Local.

3967 ■ American Legion, Westmont Post 338
55 E Richmond St.
Westmont, IL 60559
Ph: (309)663-0361
Fax: (309)663-5783
URL: National Affiliate–www.legion.org
Local. Affiliated With: American Legion.

3968 ■ Association for Corporate Growth, Chicago Chapter
c/o Terry D. Cobb, Administrator
PO Box 220
Westmont, IL 60559
Ph: (630)455-1740
Fax: (630)455-1741
E-mail: chicagoacg@acg.org
URL: http://www.acg.org/chicago
Contact: Terry D. Cobb, Administrator
Local. Affiliated With: Association for Corporate Growth. **Publications:** Newsletter, quarterly. Alternate Formats: online.

3969 ■ DuPage Power Squadron
c/o Joyce I. Bousquet, Exec. Officer
307 E Des Moines St.
Westmont, IL 60559
Ph: (630)963-4832
E-mail: jyc985@cs.com
URL: http://www.uspsdupage.org
Contact: Joyce I. Bousquet, Exec. Officer
Local. Affiliated With: United States Power Squadrons.

3970 ■ Illinois Federation of Teachers (IFT)
PO Box 390
Westmont, IL 60559
Ph: (630)571-0100
Fax: (630)571-1204
Free: (800)942-9242
E-mail: info@ift-aft.org
URL: http://www.ift-aft.org
Contact: James F. Dougherty, Pres.
Members: 90,000. **State.**

3971 ■ Illinois Government Finance Officers Association (IGFOA)
Westmont Ctre.
1 S Cass Ave., Ste.202
Westmont, IL 60559
Ph: (630)663-0019
Fax: (630)663-0162
E-mail: info@igfoa.org
URL: http://www.igfoa.org
Contact: Marianne C. Shank, Exec.Dir.
State. Promotes improved methods of governmental finance in the State of Illinois; advances the use of common terminology, classification and principles in governmental finance; encourage the use of independent periodic audits; analyzes and resolves financial problems arising under the Illinois Statutes; and develops closer understanding and cooperation among those concerned with public finance in Illinois.

3972 ■ Mudslingers 4x4 Club
c/o Brian Frank
234 S Adams St.
Westmont, IL 60559
Ph: (630)968-7751
Fax: (630)968-9671
E-mail: bkconst@comcast.net
URL: http://www.mudslingers.org
Contact: Brian Frank, Pres.
Local. Affiliated With: United Four-Wheel Drive Associations.

3973 ■ West Suburban ALANO Club
PO Box 618
Westmont, IL 60559-0618
Ph: (630)968-4694
URL: National Affiliate–www.aa.org
Contact: William R. Punzio, Exec. Officer
Founded: 1951. **Members:** 165. **Membership Dues:** private, $50 (annual). **Staff:** 12. **Budget:** $42,000. **Local Groups:** 1. **Local.** Members of Alcoholics Anonymous. **Affiliated With:** Alcoholics Anonymous World Services.

3974 ■ Westmont Chamber of Commerce and Tourism Bureau
1 S Cass Ave.
Westmont, IL 60559
Ph: (630)960-5553
Fax: (630)960-5554
E-mail: information@westmontchamber.com
URL: http://www.westmontchamber.com
Contact: Janelle Fallan, Exec.Dir.
Membership Dues: business (depends upon the number of employees), $140-$550 (annual). **Local.** Works to improve the economic environment of Westmont by fostering the development of business growth and prosperity of the entire community. **Awards:** Business of the Month. **Frequency:** monthly. **Type:** recognition. **Computer Services:** Information services, membership directory. **Committees:** Business Development and Growth; Education Awards; Tourism and Events. **Publications:** Newsletter, bimonthly. Contains industry tips and local business news and updates. **Advertising:** accepted. Alternate Formats: online.

Westville

3975 ■ American Legion, Illinois Post 51
c/o Martin F. Vutrick
115 S State St.
Westville, IL 61883
Ph: (217)267-2342
Fax: (309)663-5783
URL: National Affiliate–www.legion.org
Contact: Martin F. Vutrick, Contact
Local. Affiliated With: American Legion.

3976 ■ Illinois Native Plant Society (INPS)
20301 E 900 North Rd.
Westville, IL 61883
Ph: (217)662-2142 (217)442-1691
Fax: (217)662-2146
E-mail: ilnps@aol.com
URL: http://www.ill-inps.org
Contact: Ken Konsis, Ed.
Founded: 1981. **Members:** 450. **Membership Dues:** regular, institutional, $15 (annual) • patron, $50 (annual) • life, $200. **Budget:** $7,000. **Local Groups:** 5. **State.** Works to protect native flora and its habitats. Offers educational programs and field trips. **Libraries: Type:** open to the public. **Holdings:** 100; books, periodicals. **Subjects:** botany. **Awards: Frequency:** annual. **Type:** scholarship. **Publications:** *Erigenia*, annual. Journal. Contains information on local native flora, habitats, endangered species, exotics, and taxonomic lists. **Price:** $5.00 plus shipping and handling. ISSN: 1094-9607. **Circulation:** 500 • *The Harbinger*, quarterly. Newsletter. **Price:** included in membership dues. **Conventions/Meetings:** annual meeting - May or June.

3977 ■ Illinois Walnut Council
Forest Glen Preserve
20301 E. 900 N. Rd.
Westville, IL 61883
Ph: (217)662-2142
E-mail: kenkonsis@aol.com
URL: http://www.vccd.org
Contact: Bob Trimble, Pres.
State.

Wheaton

3978 ■ American Legion, First Division Cantigny Post 556
1st 151 Winfield Rd.
Wheaton, IL 60187
Ph: (708)260-8184
Fax: (309)663-5783
URL: National Affiliate–www.legion.org
Local. Affiliated With: American Legion.

3979 ■ American Legion, Perrottet-Nickerson Post 76
PO Box 463
Wheaton, IL 60189
Ph: (708)682-0076
Fax: (309)663-5783
URL: National Affiliate–www.legion.org
Local. Affiliated With: American Legion.

3980 ■ Association of Pool and Spa Professionals (APSP)
214 N Hale St.
Wheaton, IL 60187
Ph: (630)510-4572
Fax: (630)510-4501
E-mail: llenard@association-mgmt.com
URL: http://www.spa-pool.org
Contact: Liz Lenard, Admin.Dir.
Local. Works to advance the business, images and welfare of members. Strives to increase the number of pool and spa buyers. **Affiliated With:** Association of Pool and Spa Professionals. **Formerly:** (2005) National Spa and Pool Institute - Region V.

3981 ■ Chicago Area Orienteering Club (CAOC)
PO Box 4591
Wheaton, IL 60189
Ph: (847)604-4419
E-mail: secretary@chicago-orienteering.org
URL: http://www.chicago-orienteering.org
Local. Affiliated With: United States Orienteering Federation.

3982 ■ Chicago Area Theatre Organ Enthusiasts (CATOE)
c/o Paul Van Der Molen, Membership Dir.
468 Willow Rd.
Wheaton, IL 60187-2934
E-mail: info@catoe.org
URL: http://www.catoe.org
Contact: John Peters, Pres.
Founded: 1962. **Membership Dues:** regular, $25 (annual) • supporting, $75 (annual) • sponsoring, $175 (annual) • sustaining, $300 (annual) • life, $1,000. **Local. Affiliated With:** American Theatre Organ Society.

3983 ■ Du Page County Historical Society (DCHS)
PO Box 1460
Wheaton, IL 60189
Ph: (630)682-7343
E-mail: bookedit1@yahoo.com
URL: http://www.dupagehistory.org
Contact: Catherine Bruck, Pres.
Founded: 1929. **Members:** 300. **Membership Dues:** basic individual, $15 (annual). **Budget:** $10,000. **Local.** Represents individuals interested in the history of Du Page County, IL. Provides support group for the Du Page County Historical Museum which is operated by the County of Du Page. **Publications:** *DuPage History*, annual. Magazine • *Now and Then*, quarterly. Newsletter. **Conventions/Meetings:** bimonthly meeting - always 3rd Monday.

3984 ■ Du Page County (IL) Genealogical Society (DCGS)
PO Box 3
Wheaton, IL 60189-0003
E-mail: membersdcgs@aol.com
URL: http://www.dcgs.org
Contact: Judy Gaddess, Pres.
Founded: 1974. **Members:** 300. **Membership Dues:** individual, $18 (annual) • family, $27 (annual) • youth, $9 (annual). **Local.** Individuals interested in the study of family history and genealogy and the preservation of Du Page County, IL records. Offers genealogy classes to encourage the study of family history and genealogy. **Affiliated With:** Federation of Genealogical Societies. **Formerly:** (1980) Lombard Suburban Genealogical Society; (1987) Du Page Genealogical Society. **Publications:** *Review of the Du Page County Illinois Genealogical Society*, 8/year. Newsletter. **Circulation:** 360 • Journal, quarterly. **Conventions/Meetings:** annual conference • bimonthly meeting.

3985 ■ DuPage Habitat for Humanity
213 S Wheaton Ave.
Wheaton, IL 60187
Ph: (630)510-3737
Fax: (630)682-4881
E-mail: dhfh@dupagehabitat.org
URL: http://www.dupagehabitat.org
Local. Affiliated With: Habitat for Humanity International.

3986 ■ Fox Valley Electric Auto Association (FVEAA)
c/o Ted Lowe, Pres.
PO Box 214
Wheaton, IL 60189-0214
Ph: (630)260-0424
E-mail: contact@fveaa.org
URL: http://www.fveaa.org
Contact: Ted Lowe, Pres.
Local. Affiliated With: Electric Auto Association.

3987 ■ Greater Chicago Chapter of the Association of Legal Administrators
c/o Diane M. Brummel
Norton Mancini Weiler & DeAno
109 N Hale St.
Wheaton, IL 60187
Ph: (630)668-9440
Fax: (630)668-9489
E-mail: dbrummel@nortonmancini.com
URL: http://www.alachicago.org
Contact: Diane M. Brummel, Contact
Local. Affiliated With: Association of Legal Administrators.

3988 ■ Illinois School Psychologists Association (ISPA)
PO Box 664
Wheaton, IL 60189-0664
Ph: (630)871-0670
Fax: (630)524-9030
E-mail: ilispa@sbcglobal.net
URL: http://www.ilispa.org
Contact: Christy Budt, Pres.
State. Represents and supports school psychology through leadership. Enhances the mental health and educational competence of children. Informs the public on the services and practice of school psychology. **Affiliated With:** National Association of School Psychologists.

3989 ■ Illinois Solar Energy Association (ISEA)
c/o Mark Burger, Pres.
PO Box 634
Wheaton, IL 60189-0634
Ph: (630)260-0424
E-mail: info@illinoissolar.org
URL: http://www.iseanetwork.org
Contact: Mark Burger, Pres.
Founded: 1975. **Membership Dues:** student and senior, $20 (annual) • individual, $25 (annual) • family, $30 (annual) • business, $100-$500 (annual). **State.** Works to educate the public and promote the appropriate use of solar energy and other renewable energy sources. **Affiliated With:** American Solar Energy Society. **Publications:** *ISEA's Heliograph*, quarterly. Newsletter. **Price:** included in membership dues. Alternate Formats: online. **Conventions/Meetings:** annual Illinois Renewable Energy Fair - trade show.

3990 ■ Infusion Nurses Society, Illinois
717 Pershing Ave.
Wheaton, IL 60187
Ph: (630)668-9294
E-mail: patricia_beck@cdh.org
URL: National Affiliate–www.ins1.org
Contact: Patricia Beck, Pres.
State. Represents the interests of healthcare professionals who are involved with the practice of infusion therapy. Seeks to advance the delivery of quality therapy to patients. Promotes research and education in the practice of infusion nursing. **Affiliated With:** Infusion Nurses Society.

3991 ■ Metro Chicago Youth for Christ
324 E Roosevelt Rd.
Wheaton, IL 60187
Ph: (630)588-0700
Fax: (630)871-0978
URL: http://www.mcyfc.org
Local. Affiliated With: Youth for Christ/U.S.A.

3992 ■ National Alliance for the Mentally Ill of DuPage County
1403 N Main St., Ste.301
Wheaton, IL 60187
Ph: (630)752-0066
Fax: (630)752-1064
E-mail: il@namidupage.org
URL: http://www.namidupage.org
Contact: Mary Lou Lowry, Exec.Dir.
Local. Strives to improve the quality of life of children and adults with severe mental illness through support, education, research and advocacy. **Affiliated With:** National Alliance for the Mentally Ill.

3993 ■ National Association for the Advancement of Colored People, Du Page County Branch
PO Box 475
Wheaton, IL 60189-0475
Ph: (630)585-4633
Free: (800)439-4394
URL: http://www.dupagenaacp.org
Contact: Theresa Dear, Pres.
Local.

3994 ■ Northern Illinois Commercial Association of Realtors
214 N Hale St.
Wheaton, IL 60187
Ph: (630)510-4566
Fax: (630)510-4501
E-mail: tstevenson@association-mgmt.com
URL: http://www.nicar.com
Contact: Terry Stevenson, Contact
Local. Strives to develop real estate business practices. Advocates the right to own, use and transfer real property. Provides a facility for professional development, research and exchange of information among members and to the general public. **Affiliated With:** National Association of Realtors.

3995 ■ Nuzzled Network
PO Box 5352
Wheaton, IL 60189
E-mail: info@nuzzled.net
URL: http://nuzzled.net
Local.

3996 ■ PFLAG DuPage
PO Box 1333
Wheaton, IL 60189
Ph: (630)375-7756
E-mail: sknox1974@aol.com
URL: http://www.pflagdupage.org
Local. Affiliated With: Parents, Families, and Friends of Lesbians and Gays.

3997 ■ Reserve Officers Association - Department of Illinois, DuPage County Chapter 11
c/o Lt.Col. Jamet M. Kamer, Pres.
2236 Blacksmith Dr.
Wheaton, IL 60187-8974
Ph: (630)510-0064
URL: http://www.ilroa.org
Contact: Lt.Col. Jamet M. Kamer, Pres.
Local. Promotes and supports the development and execution of a military policy for the United States. Provides professional development seminars, workshops and programs for its members. **Affiliated With:** Reserve Officers Association of the United States.

3998 ■ Sotos Syndrome Support Association (SSSA)
PO Box 4626
Wheaton, IL 60189
Free: (888)246-7772
E-mail: sssa@well.com
URL: http://www.well.com/user/sssa
Contact: Mrs. Joanne Weick, Pres.

Founded: 1985. **Members:** 300. **Membership Dues:** family, $25 (annual). **Regional**. Seeks to provide a social support environment for professionals and families of individuals with a range of diagnoses from Sotos Syndrome to Sotos-like and including other overgrowth syndromes; provide understanding of the condition through education; and give opportunity for professionals working with individuals affected by Sotos Syndrome. **Affiliated With:** Sotos Syndrome Support Association. **Publications:** *SSSA Notes*, quarterly. Newsletter. **Conventions/Meetings:** annual conference, with experts in genetics, neurology, psychology and education • annual meeting.

3999 ■ Theosophical Society in America
c/o Jeff Gresko
1926 N Main St.
PO Box 270
Wheaton, IL 60189
Ph: (630)668-1571
Fax: (630)668-4976
E-mail: olcott@theosmail.net
URL: http://www.theosophical.org

Regional.

4000 ■ Wheaton Chamber of Commerce (WCC)
108 E Wesley St.
Wheaton, IL 60187
Ph: (630)668-6464
Fax: (630)668-2744
E-mail: wccinfo@ewheaton.com
URL: http://www.ewheaton.com
Contact: Glenn Keller, Chm.

Membership Dues: business (based on number of employees), $295-$795 (annual) • nonprofit (charitable), $145 (annual) • nonprofit (non-charitable; plus $1/employee over 5), $295 (annual) • realtor, $155 (annual) • citizen, $85 (annual). **Local**. Fosters meaningful business relationships, advocates on issues impacting the local economy, and develops business education and marketing opportunities. **Computer Services:** Information services, business directory. **Committees:** Autumn Fest; Chamber Connection; Chamber Leads; Education; Golf Outing; Government Affairs; TIF Advocacy; Women in Business. **Publications:** *Advantage*, monthly. Newsletter. **Circulation:** 800. **Advertising:** accepted. Alternate Formats: online • *Business and Community Directory*, annual. Membership Directory. **Circulation:** 18,000 • *Wheaton Map*, annual. Brochure. Includes information on Wheaton, area attractions, shopping opportunities and list of area golf courses. **Circulation:** 2,000. **Advertising:** accepted.

4001 ■ Wheaton Junior Woman's Club
PO Box 460
Wheaton, IL 60189-0460
Ph: (630)367-0783
E-mail: info@wheatonjrs.com
URL: http://www.wheatonjrs.com
Contact: Lisa Bock, Pres.

Local.

4002 ■ Wheaton Lions Club
c/o Joel Riley, Pres.
PO Box 296
Wheaton, IL 60189
E-mail: jriley@trustcoil.com
URL: http://www.wheatonlions.org
Contact: Joel Riley, Pres.

Local. **Affiliated With:** Lions Clubs International.

4003 ■ Windy City Matchcover Club
c/o Annie Johnson
1307 Coll. Ave., No. 12
Wheaton, IL 60187
E-mail: ltlb1t@aol.com
URL: National Affiliate–www.matchcover.org
Contact: Annie Johnson, Contact

Local. **Affiliated With:** Rathkamp Matchcover Society.

Wheeling

4004 ■ American Legion, Wheeling Memorial Post 221
100 Capri Terr., No. 15
Wheeling, IL 60090
Ph: (309)663-0361
Fax: (309)663-5783
URL: National Affiliate–www.legion.org

Local. **Affiliated With:** American Legion.

4005 ■ Chicago Metro REACT
1047 Kingsport Dr.
Wheeling, IL 60090
Ph: (847)595-1920
E-mail: ulmspec@aol.com
URL: http://www.reactintl.org/teaminfo/usa_teams/teams-usil.htm

Local. Trained communication experts and professional volunteers. Provides volunteer public service and emergency communications through the use of radios (Citizen Band, General Mobile Radio Service, UHF and HAM). Coordinates with radio industries and government on safety communication matters and supports charitable activities and community organizations.

4006 ■ Wheeling - Prospect Heights Area Chamber of Commerce and Industry (WPHACCI)
395 E Dundee Rd., Ste.300
Wheeling, IL 60090
Ph: (847)541-0170
Fax: (847)541-0296
E-mail: info@wphchamber.com
URL: http://www.wphchamber.com
Contact: Catherine Powers, Exec.Dir.

Founded: 1927. **Members:** 380. **Membership Dues:** business (regular), $185-$1,040 (annual) • business (plus members), $275-$1,560 (annual) • utility, $550 (annual) • civic/educational/nonprofit group/religious (regular), $170 (annual) • civic/educational/nonprofit group/religious (plus members), $255 (annual). **Local**. Promotes business and community development in the Wheeling and Prospect Heights, IL area. **Affiliated With:** U.S. Chamber of Commerce. **Publications:** *Buying Guide*, annual. Directory. **Advertising:** accepted • *Chamber Connections*, bimonthly. Newsletter. **Advertising:** accepted. **Conventions/Meetings:** annual Business EXPO - trade show • annual meeting (exhibits).

White Hall

4007 ■ American Legion, White Hall Post 70
130 N Main
White Hall, IL 62092
Ph: (309)663-0361
Fax: (309)663-5783
URL: National Affiliate–www.legion.org

Local. **Affiliated With:** American Legion.

Wildwood

4008 ■ Rand Park Dog Training Club
c/o Lois Breslow
18017 Winnebago Dr.
Wildwood, IL 60030-0000
Ph: (847)966-7908
E-mail: l.breslow@gte.net
URL: http://www.randparkdtc.org
Contact: Marion Meseth, Chm.

Local.

Williamsfield

4009 ■ American Legion, Williamsfield Post 371
PO Box 182
Williamsfield, IL 61489
Ph: (309)663-0361
Fax: (309)663-5783
URL: National Affiliate–www.legion.org

Local. **Affiliated With:** American Legion.

Willow Springs

4010 ■ American Legion, Illinois Post 832
c/o William R. Edmondson
PO Box 23
Willow Springs, IL 60480
Ph: (309)663-0361
Fax: (309)663-5783
URL: National Affiliate–www.legion.org
Contact: William R. Edmondson, Contact

Local. **Affiliated With:** American Legion.

4011 ■ Technical Association of the Pulp and Paper Industry - Chicago Section
c/o Ernie Moon, Chm.
8526 Bucki Ln.
Willow Springs, IL 60480
Ph: (708)738-2933
Fax: (708)839-6927
E-mail: info@chicagotappi.com
URL: http://www.chicagotappi.com
Contact: Ernie Moon, Chm.

Local. Furthers the application of science, engineering and technology in paper and other related industries. Serves as a forum for the collection, dissemination and interchange of technical concepts and information about the pulp and paper industry. Provides education, training and professional growth opportunities to members. **Affiliated With:** TAPPI - Technical Association of the Pulp and Paper Industry.

Willowbrook

4012 ■ First Catholic Slovak Ladies Association - Chicago Senior Branch 421
7525 Sheridan Dr., Apt. 2-E
Willowbrook, IL 60527-2673
Ph: (630)325-8963
URL: National Affiliate–www.fcsla.com

Local. **Affiliated With:** First Catholic Slovak Ladies Association.

4013 ■ LHV Model Yacht Club No. 168
c/o James R. Reid
17 Lakeshore Dr.
Willowbrook, IL 60527
Ph: (708)729-0204
URL: National Affiliate–www.amya.org
Contact: James R. Reid, Contact

Local.

4014 ■ USA Weightlifting - Team Velocity Willowbrook
c/o Mary Dempsey
7051 S Adams St.
Willowbrook, IL 60527
Ph: (630)301-1466
E-mail: mdempsey@velocitysp.com
URL: National Affiliate–www.usaweightlifting.org
Contact: Mary Dempsey, Contact

Local. **Affiliated With:** USA Weightlifting.

4015 ■ Visiting Nurses Association First
6855 Kingery Hwy.
Willowbrook, IL 60527
Ph: (630)455-2130
Fax: (630)455-4537
Free: (800)678-7875
E-mail: vnaf@vnaf.org
URL: http://www.vnaf.org
State. Provides home health services for all ages. **Affiliated With:** National Association for Home Care and Hospice.

Wilmette

4016 ■ American Legion, Huerter-Wilmette Post 46
1925 Wilmette Ave.
Wilmette, IL 60091
Ph: (309)663-0361
Fax: (309)663-5783
URL: National Affiliate–www.legion.org
Local. Affiliated With: American Legion.

4017 ■ Bead Society of Greater Chicago
PO Box 8103
Wilmette, IL 60091-8103
Ph: (312)458-0519 (847)699-7959
E-mail: info@bsgc.org
URL: http://bsgc.org
Contact: Judith Schwab, Pres.
Founded: 1989. **Members:** 370. **Membership Dues:** individual, $35 (annual) • business, $45 (annual). **Local Groups:** 1. **Local**. Sponsors lectures and workshops on subjects relating to artistic and historic importance of beads and beadwork. **Libraries: Type:** not open to the public. **Holdings:** 200; books, periodicals, video recordings. **Subjects:** beads and beadwork. **Awards:** Bead Society of Greater Chicago Grant. **Frequency:** periodic. **Type:** monetary. **Recipient:** determined on individual basis by committee. **Affiliated With:** Bead Society of Los Angeles. **Publications:** *Bead Words*, quarterly. Newsletter. Chicago area and national news events. **Price:** included in membership dues. **Advertising:** accepted. **Conventions/Meetings:** monthly lecture, lecture or a discussion and a slide show - usually second Thursday of the month • monthly meeting - always second Thursday of the month.

4018 ■ Boys Hope Girls Hope of Chicago (BHGH)
c/o Erin Lockley, Business Mgr.
1100 N Laramie Ave.
Wilmette, IL 60091-1021
Ph: (847)920-2783 (847)920-2786
Fax: (847)256-8213
E-mail: chicago@bhgh.org
URL: http://www.Chicagobhgh.org
Contact: Erin Lockley, Business Mgr.
Founded: 1979. **Local**.

4019 ■ Mystery Writers of America, Midwest Chapter
c/o David J. Walker
1009 Oakwood Ave.
Wilmette, IL 60091
E-mail: dvdjwlkr@aol.com
URL: http://www.mysterywriters.org
Contact: David J. Walker, Contact
Regional. Affiliated With: Mystery Writers of America.

4020 ■ North Suburban Gays (NSG)
PO Box 465
Wilmette, IL 60091
Ph: (847)251-8853
E-mail: info@northsuburbangays.org
URL: http://www.northsuburbangays.org
Contact: Albert D., Pres.
Founded: 1981. **Members:** 90. **Membership Dues:** single, $28 (annual) • couple, $45 (annual). **Local**. Gay men and lesbians from the northern suburbs of Chicago, IL. Serves as a social and educational forum. **Publications:** *Northern Lites*, monthly. Newsletter. **Price:** included in membership dues; $18.00 /year for nonmembers.

4021 ■ Northwest Passage Outing Club
1130 Greenleaf Ave.
Wilmette, IL 60091
Ph: (847)256-4409
Fax: (847)256-4476
Free: (800)732-7328
E-mail: info@nwpassage.com
URL: http://www.nwpassage.com
Contact: Rick Sweitzer, Exec.Dir.
Founded: 1984. **Members:** 228. **Membership Dues:** regular, $35 (annual) • renewal, $25 (annual) • family, $75 (annual). **Staff:** 13. **Local Groups:** 1. **For-Profit. Regional**. Works to enhance personal development, promote self-confidence and teach skills through adventure challenge while providing a safe and exciting environment for every participant. **Affiliated With:** American Canoe Association; Professional Paddlesports Association. **Publications:** *The Northwest NEWS*, bimonthly. Newsletter. **Price:** $5.00/year. **Circulation:** 350. **Conventions/Meetings:** Kayak Symposiums - seasonal • Leadership Workshops - seasonal.

4022 ■ Olinga Productions Association
c/o Joyce Owen Olinga
PO Box 8121
Wilmette, IL 60091
Ph: (847)804-6690
E-mail: olingaproduction@aol.com
Contact: Ms. Joyce Olinga, Pres. and Video Producer
Members: 5. **Regional**. Focuses on documentaries, capturing workshops, and special events. **Libraries: Type:** open to the public; by appointment only. **Holdings:** books, video recordings. **Subjects:** interviews, nature and cities; documentary on African Bahai, Enoch Olinga, Hand of the Cause of God.

4023 ■ Wilmette Chamber of Commerce (WCC)
1150 Wilmette Ave., Ste.A
Wilmette, IL 60091
Ph: (847)251-3800
Fax: (847)251-6321
E-mail: info@wilmettechamber.org
URL: http://www.wilmettechamber.org
Contact: Julie Yusim, Exec.Dir.
Founded: 1957. **Members:** 370. **Local**. Promotes business and community development in the Wilmette, IL area. Sponsors sidewalk sale. **Awards:** Business of the Year Awards. **Frequency:** annual. **Type:** recognition • Citizens of th'e Year Awards (Youth, Adult, Senior). **Frequency:** annual. **Type:** recognition. **Publications:** *WCC Community Guide*, annual. Directory. **Price:** free • *Wilmette Chamber Headline News*. Newsletter. Alternate Formats: online • Newsletter, monthly.

4024 ■ Wilmette Golf Club
3900 Fairway Dr.
Wilmette, IL 60091-1043
Ph: (847)256-9777
Fax: (847)251-5627
E-mail: jaime@golfwilmette.com
URL: http://www.golfwilmette.com
Contact: Jaime Locke, Contact
Local.

Wilmington

4025 ■ American Legion, Illinois Post 191
c/o Lester Smith
PO Box 577
Wilmington, IL 60481
Ph: (309)663-0361
Fax: (309)663-5783
URL: National Affiliate–www.legion.org
Contact: Lester Smith, Contact
Local. Affiliated With: American Legion.

4026 ■ Wilmington Chamber of Commerce
PO Box 724
Wilmington, IL 60481
Ph: (815)476-5991
Fax: (815)476-7002
E-mail: fpnads@cbcast.com
URL: http://www.wilmingtonchamberofcommerce.org
Contact: Eric Fisher, Pres.
Membership Dues: base, $100 (annual). **Local**. Promotes business and community development in Wilmington, IL area. **Awards:** Business Person of the Year. **Frequency:** annual. **Type:** recognition • Employee of the Month. **Frequency:** monthly. **Type:** recognition • **Frequency:** annual. **Type:** scholarship. **Recipient:** for a graduating senior of Wilmington High School. **Computer Services:** Information services, member listing. **Publications:** *Newsbriefs*, monthly. Newsletter. Alternate Formats: online. **Conventions/Meetings:** annual Chamber Christmas Party - every 1st Monday of December • monthly meeting - every 2nd Thursday in Wilmington, IL.

Winchester

4027 ■ American Legion, Illinois Post 442
c/o Julian Wells
24 S Hill St.
Winchester, IL 62694
Ph: (309)663-0361
Fax: (309)663-5783
URL: National Affiliate–www.legion.org
Contact: Julian Wells, Contact
Local. Affiliated With: American Legion.

4028 ■ Two Rivers Jeep Club (TRJC)
870 State Rte. 106
Winchester, IL 62694-8160
Ph: (630)717-5337
Free: (866)483-3982
E-mail: trjc1@trjc.com
URL: http://www.trjc.com
Contact: Lee Altor, Pres.
Local. Affiliated With: United Four-Wheel Drive Associations.

Windsor

4029 ■ American Legion, Garrett-Baldridge Post 725
RR 1, Box 125
Windsor, IL 61957
Ph: (309)663-0361
Fax: (309)663-5783
URL: National Affiliate–www.legion.org
Local. Affiliated With: American Legion.

Winfield

4030 ■ Society for Healthcare Consumer Advocacy of the American Hospital Association
c/o Kate Clarke, Pres.
Central DuPage Hospital
25 N. Winfield Rd.
Winfield, IL 60190
Ph: (630)933-6328
Fax: (630)933-2700
E-mail: kate_clarke@cdh.org
URL: National Affiliate–www.shca-aha.org
Members: 36. **State Groups:** 1. **State**. Provides an organized structure that advances and develops healthcare consumer advocacy services in health organizations and agencies by providing members with education, information, and networking opportunities, to enhance personal growth and professional skills; conducting educational programs and activities to strengthen and develop healthcare consumer advocacy programs; disseminating information pertinent to healthcare consumer advocacy. **Affiliated With:** Society for Healthcare Consumer Advocacy of the American Hospital Association.

4031 ■ Winfield Chamber of Commerce (WCC)
OS 125 Church St.
PO Box 209
Winfield, IL 60190
Ph: (630)682-3712
Fax: (630)682-3726
E-mail: winfieldchamber@sbcglobal.net
URL: http://www.winfield-chamber.com
Contact: Rich Bysina, Exec.Dir.
Founded: 1975. **Members:** 142. **Staff:** 1. **Local.** Retail businesses, banks, professional service organizations, and individuals. Promotes business and community development in the Winfield, IL area. Sponsors festival. **Publications:** Newsletter, bimonthly. **Conventions/Meetings:** monthly board meeting - always second Tuesday of the month • monthly meeting, for membership - always third Tuesday of the month.

Winnebago

4032 ■ Winnebago County Pheasants Forever
PO Box 322
Winnebago, IL 61088-0322
Ph: (815)399-4610
E-mail: edruef@inwave1.com
URL: http://www.pfwcil.org
Contact: Ed Ruef, Pres.
Local. Affiliated With: Pheasants Forever.

Winnetka

4033 ■ American Youth Soccer Organization, Region 425
PO Box 575
Winnetka, IL 60093
Free: (877)297-6425
URL: http://www.playsoccer.org
Local. Affiliated With: American Youth Soccer Organization.

4034 ■ Association of the United States Army, Fort Sheridan - Chicago
c/o Bill Powell
693 Walden Rd.
Winnetka, IL 60093-2034
Ph: (847)446-7977
E-mail: wlpowell@enteract.com
URL: National Affiliate–www.ausa.org
Local. Represents the interests and concerns of American Soldiers. Fosters public support of the Army's role in national security. Provides professional education and information programs.

4035 ■ Catholic League for Religious and Civil Rights, Chicago Chapter
c/o Patrick Cremin
PO Box 729
Winnetka, IL 60093
Ph: (312)464-6144
Fax: (312)371-3394
E-mail: cl@catholicleague.org
Local. Affiliated With: Catholic League for Religious and Civil Rights.

4036 ■ E Angel Community
c/o Roger Winship
560 Green Bay Rd., Ste.408
Winnetka, IL 60093-2243
Ph: (312)636-4114
E-mail: eangelcommunity@yahoo.com
URL: http://www.eangel.org
Contact: Roger Winship, Pres.
Local.

4037 ■ Illinois Curling Association - Indian Hill Curling Club
c/o Jim Smith, Pres.
550 Ridge Rd.
Winnetka, IL 60093
Ph: (847)256-2436
URL: http://www.goodcurling.net/basics/U.S.%20clubs/illinois.html
Contact: Jim Smith, Pres.
Local. Affiliated With: United States Curling Association.

4038 ■ Illinois North Shore North Shore Society
1364 Edgewood Ln.
Winnetka, IL 60093
Ph: (847)446-8343
E-mail: jgljgl@aol.com
URL: National Affiliate–www.nss.org
Contact: Jeffrey Liss, Contact
Local. Works for the creation of a spacefaring civilization. Encourages the establishment of self-sustaining human settlements in space. Promotes large-scale industrialization and private enterprise in space.

4039 ■ National Alliance on Mental Illness - Cook County North Suburban (NAMI CCNS)
PO Box 612
Winnetka, IL 60093
Ph: (847)724-1460
E-mail: namiccns@earthlink.net
URL: http://www.namiccns.org
Contact: Candice Hughes, Co-Pres.
Local. Strives to improve the quality of life of children and adults with severe mental illness through support, education, research and advocacy. **Affiliated With:** National Alliance for the Mentally Ill.

4040 ■ Winnetka Chamber of Commerce (WCC)
841 Spruce St., Ste.204
Winnetka, IL 60093
Ph: (847)446-4451
Fax: (847)446-4452
E-mail: wcc@winnetkachamber.com
URL: http://www.winnetkachamber.com
Contact: Cicely Clarke Michalak, Exec.Dir.
Founded: 1923. **Members:** 265. **Staff:** 2. **Local.** Seeks to serve as the principal representative of area businesses; to ensure a favorable business climate; and to promote economic development. Sponsors Winnetka Days, a recognition luncheon and holiday lighting program. **Awards:** Crystal Plate Award. **Type:** recognition. **Subgroups:** By-laws; Development; Promotion. **Publications:** *Shoppe Talk*, biennial. Newsletter. **Advertising:** accepted • *Win-net-work*, biennial. Newsletter. **Advertising:** accepted • Directory, annual. **Conventions/Meetings:** monthly Recognition Lunches - board meeting.

Winslow

4041 ■ American Legion, Stewart-Schneider Post 592
9204 Babler Rd.
Winslow, IL 61089
Ph: (815)367-4701
Fax: (309)663-5783
URL: National Affiliate–www.legion.org
Local. Affiliated With: American Legion.

Winthrop Harbor

4042 ■ North Point Charter Boat Association
PO Box 164
Winthrop Harbor, IL 60096
Free: (800)247-6727
E-mail: npcba@sbcglobal.net
URL: http://www.salmonoid.com/npcba/index.html
Local.

Wood Dale

4043 ■ American Legion, Illinois Post 1205
c/o Robert D. Clark
203 N Edgewood Ave.
Wood Dale, IL 60191
Ph: (708)595-1606
Fax: (309)663-5783
URL: National Affiliate–www.legion.org
Contact: Robert D. Clark, Contact
Local. Affiliated With: American Legion.

4044 ■ Wood Dale Chamber of Commerce
PO Box 353
Wood Dale, IL 60191-0353
Ph: (630)595-0505
Fax: (630)595-0677
E-mail: info@wooddalechamber.com
URL: http://www.wooddalechamber.com
Contact: Lorrie Heggaton, Pres.
Local. Works for the advancement of the economic, industrial, professional, cultural and civic welfare of businesses while giving all proper assistance to any new firms or individuals seeking to locate in Wood Dale. Supports beneficial activity for the community. **Awards:** Business Person of the Year. **Frequency:** annual. **Type:** recognition. **Computer Services:** Information services, membership directory • mailing lists, of members. **Affiliated With:** U.S. Chamber of Commerce. **Publications:** *Chamber Update*. Newsletter • Directory, annual.

Wood River

4045 ■ American Legion, Wood River Post 204
PO Box 505
Wood River, IL 62095
Ph: (309)663-0361
Fax: (309)663-5783
URL: National Affiliate–www.legion.org
Local. Affiliated With: American Legion.

Woodhull

4046 ■ American Legion, Illinois Post 546
c/o Miles S. Sturgeon
PO Box 242
Woodhull, IL 61490
Ph: (309)663-0361
Fax: (309)663-5783
URL: National Affiliate–www.legion.org
Contact: Miles S. Sturgeon, Contact
Local. Affiliated With: American Legion.

Woodridge

4047 ■ American Legion, Burlington Route Post 387
6312 Maxwell Dr.
Woodridge, IL 60517
Ph: (309)663-0361
Fax: (309)663-5783
URL: National Affiliate–www.legion.org
Local. Affiliated With: American Legion.

4048 ■ American Society of Agricultural and Biological Engineers, District 3 - Chicago
c/o David Bartimus, Chm.
2715 Davey Rd.
Woodridge, IL 60517
Ph: (630)972-9300
Fax: (630)972-9392
E-mail: david_bartimus@yahoo.com
URL: National Affiliate–www.asabe.org
Contact: David Bartimus, Chm.
Local. Promotes the science and art of engineering in agricultural, food and biological systems. Encourages the professional improvement of members. Fosters education and develops engineering standards used in agriculture, food and biological systems. **Affiliated With:** American Society of Agricultural and Biological Engineers.

4049 ■ Chicago Lakeside Lawn Bowling Club
c/o Cal Wright, Sec.
6906 Prarieview
Woodridge, IL 60517
Ph: (630)969-0890
URL: http://hometown.aol.com/lawnbowling/welcome1a.htm
Contact: Cal Wright, Sec.
Local. Affiliated With: United States Lawn Bowls Association.

4050 ■ Woodridge Area Chamber of Commerce (WACC)
5 Plaza Dr., Ste.212
Woodridge, IL 60517-5014
Ph: (630)960-7080
Fax: (630)852-2316
E-mail: chamber@woodridgechamber.org
URL: http://www.woodridgechamber.org
Contact: Shawnna Donovan, Pres./CEO
Founded: 1978. **Members:** 270. **Membership Dues:** nonprofit (standard), $100 (annual) • business (standard), $150-$550 (annual) • business (emerald), $195-$715 (annual) • business (diamond), $260-$950 (annual). **Staff:** 2. **Local.** Promotes business and community development in the Woodridge, IL area. Sponsors annual Jubilee Festival. **Publications:** *Chamber Connections*, monthly. Newsletter. Alternate Formats: online • *Chamber Directory*, annual. **Conventions/Meetings:** monthly meeting.

4051 ■ Woodridge Junior Woman's Club (WJWC)
PO Box 5221
Woodridge, IL 60517
E-mail: woodridgejuniors@hotmail.com
URL: http://www.woodridgejuniors.com
Contact: Kathy Erpenbach, Pres.
Local.

Woodson

4052 ■ American Legion, Illinois Post 249
c/o Raymond Baxter
301 E Main St.
Woodson, IL 62695
Ph: (309)663-0361
Fax: (309)663-5783
URL: National Affiliate–www.legion.org
Contact: Raymond Baxter, Contact
Local. Affiliated With: American Legion.

Woodstock

4053 ■ American Legion, Peter Umathum Post 412
240 N Throop St.
Woodstock, IL 60098
Ph: (815)338-5624
Fax: (309)663-5783
URL: National Affiliate–www.legion.org
Local. Affiliated With: American Legion.

4054 ■ American Youth Soccer Organization, Region 726
PO Box 854
Woodstock, IL 60098
Ph: (815)334-7007
URL: http://www.wayso.net
Local. Affiliated With: American Youth Soccer Organization.

4055 ■ Family Health Partnership Clinic (FHPC)
c/o Suzanne Hoban, Health Center Dir.
13707 W Jackson
Woodstock, IL 60098
Ph: (815)334-8987
Fax: (815)334-9013
E-mail: hpclinic@mc.net
URL: http://www.hpclinic.org
Contact: Suzanne Hoban, Health Center Dir.
Local. Individuals and organizations concerned with parenting, child development, and family issues. Works to provide primary health care to the uninsured and underinsured residents of McHenry County, Illinois. **Formerly:** (2005) Family Health Partnership.

4056 ■ Hooved Animal Humane Society (HAHS)
10804 McConnell Rd.
Woodstock, IL 60098
Ph: (815)337-5563
Fax: (815)337-5569
E-mail: info@hahs.org
URL: http://www.hahs.org
Founded: 1971. **Local.**

4057 ■ Illinois Association of Conservation Districts
9313 Bull Valley Rd.
Woodstock, IL 60098
Ph: (815)338-7664
Fax: (815)338-2773
Contact: Kathy Merner, Pres.
State.

4058 ■ Jayco Jafari International Travel Club, Flight 101 Jayco Big Birds
c/o Donna Jensen, Pres.
1204 Wheeler St.
Woodstock, IL 60098
E-mail: we_love_camping@sbcglobal.net
URL: National Affiliate–www.jaycorvclub.com
Contact: Donna Jensen, Pres.
Local. Affiliated With: Jayco Travel Club.

4059 ■ McHenry County Association of Realtors
666 W Jackson St.
Woodstock, IL 60098
Ph: (815)338-3660
Fax: (815)338-4122
E-mail: info@mchcar.com
URL: http://www.mchcar.com
Contact: Nancy Sobol, Pres.
Local. Strives to develop real estate business practices. Advocates the right to own, use and transfer real property. Provides a facility for professional development, research and exchange of information among members and to the general public. **Affiliated With:** National Association of Realtors.

4060 ■ McHenry County Audubon Society (MCAS)
PO Box 67
Woodstock, IL 60098
Ph: (815)356-1710
E-mail: audubon@nsn.org
URL: http://www.crystallakenet.org/audubon
Contact: Randy Schietzelt, Pres.
Members: 200. **Membership Dues:** general, $6 (annual). **Local.** Individuals in the McHenry County, IL area interested in the preservation and conservation of wildlife in the area. Promotes the appreciation of birds and other wildlife. Increases the knowledge of the environment and of the wildlife it supports. Seeks to preserve wildlife and its habitat. Supports conservation actions at the local, state, and national levels. **Also Known As:** (2006) Audubon Society, Illinois - McHenry County. **Publications:** Newsletter, monthly. **Price:** included in membership dues. **Circulation:** 200. **Conventions/Meetings:** monthly meeting.

4061 ■ McHenry County Defenders
124 Cass St., Ste.3
Woodstock, IL 60098
Ph: (815)338-0393
Fax: (815)338-0394
E-mail: mcdef@owc.net
URL: http://www.mcdef.org
Contact: Christopher T. Paluch, Exec.Dir.
Founded: 1970. **Local.** Helps in the preservation and improvement of the environment.

4062 ■ McHenry County Regional Planning Commission
2200 N Seminary Ave.
Woodstock, IL 60098
Ph: (815)334-4560 (815)334-4000
Fax: (815)337-3720
E-mail: plandev@co.mchenry.il.us
URL: http://www.co.mchenry.il.us
Contact: Sue Ehardt, Dir.
Founded: 1963. **Members:** 11. **Staff:** 3. **Local.** Works to enhance the quality of life in McHenry County by promoting a balance between the preservation of existing resources and the orderly development of the region through sound comprehensive planning practices and intergovernmental cooperation.

4063 ■ PFLAG Woodstock/McHenry County
Congregational Unitarian Church
221 Dean St.
Woodstock, IL 60098
Ph: (815)385-9068
E-mail: pflagwoodstock@earthlink.net
URL: http://www.pflag.org/Illinois.204.0.html
Local. Affiliated With: Parents, Families, and Friends of Lesbians and Gays.

4064 ■ USA Dance - Greater Fox Valley of Illinois Chapter No. 2042
c/o Walt Fink, Newsletter Ed.
8804 Bull Run Trail
Woodstock, IL 60098-7784
Ph: (815)337-6860
Fax: (815)337-7759
E-mail: info@dancefoxvalley.org
URL: http://dancefoxvalley.org
Contact: Walt Fink, Newsletter Ed.
Local. Encourages and promotes the physical, mental and social benefits of partner dancing. Organizes and supports programs for the recreational enjoyment of ballroom dancing. Creates opportunities for the general public to participate in ballroom dancing and DanceSport.

4065 ■ Woodstock Chamber of Commerce and Industry (WCCI)
136 Cass St.
Woodstock, IL 60098
Ph: (815)338-2436
Fax: (815)338-2927
E-mail: chamber@woodstockilchamber.com
URL: http://www.woodstockilchamber.com
Contact: Quinn Keefe, Exec.Dir.
Local. Promotes business and community development in Woodstock, IL. Sponsors festivals; hosts art fairs, craft fairs, and business exposition. Conducts charitable activities. **Committees:** Education/Leadership; Programming; Retail; Service/Industry. **Publications:** *Connection*, monthly. Newsletter. Alternate Formats: online • Directory, annual.

Worden

4066 ■ American Legion, Worden Post 564
PO Box 107
Worden, IL 62097
Ph: (618)459-3222
Fax: (309)663-5783
URL: National Affiliate–www.legion.org
Local. Affiliated With: American Legion.

Worth

4067 ■ American Ex-Prisoners of War, Greater Chicago Chapter
c/o Robert Hubley
11225 S Natoma Ave.
Worth, IL 60482
Ph: (708)448-1657
URL: National Affiliate–www.axpow.org
Local. Affiliated With: American Ex-Prisoners of War.

4068 ■ American Legion, Marrs-Meyer Post 991
11001 S Depot St.
Worth, IL 60482
Ph: (708)448-7006
Fax: (309)663-5783
URL: National Affiliate–www.legion.org
Local. Affiliated With: American Legion.

4069 ■ American Legion, Mt. Greenwood Post 844
PO Box 403
Worth, IL 60482
Ph: (309)663-0361
Fax: (309)663-5783
URL: National Affiliate–www.legion.org
Local. Affiliated With: American Legion.

4070 ■ Chicago Ridge - Worth Business Association
PO Box 356
Worth, IL 60482
Ph: (708)923-2050
Contact: Jack Murray, Pres.
Local.

Wyanet

4071 ■ Wyanet Chamber of Commerce
PO Box 125
Wyanet, IL 61379
Ph: (815)699-2631
Fax: (815)699-2631
Contact: John Gordon, Contact
Local.

Wyoming

4072 ■ American Legion, Wyoming Post 91
PO Box 17
Wyoming, IL 61491
Ph: (309)695-9994
Fax: (309)663-5783
URL: National Affiliate–www.legion.org
Local. Affiliated With: American Legion.

Yorkville

4073 ■ American Legion, Yorkville Post 489
PO Box 79
Yorkville, IL 60560
Ph: (309)663-0361
Fax: (309)663-5783
URL: National Affiliate–www.legion.org
Local. Affiliated With: American Legion.

4074 ■ Howell Shooting Club
10712 Church Rd.
Yorkville, IL 60560
E-mail: info@howellshooting.com
URL: http://www.howellshootingclub.com
Contact: David Lombardo, Pres.
Local.

4075 ■ Illinois Federation of Republican Women
7437 Rte. 71
Yorkville, IL 60560
Ph: (630)553-1599 (630)217-7437
Fax: (630)217-7437
E-mail: gophatcher@ameritech.net
Contact: Ms. Kay Hatcher, Pres.
Founded: 1939. **State.**

4076 ■ Navy League of the United States, Aurora
c/o Kenneth D. Williams, II
525 W Barberry Cir.
Yorkville, IL 60560
Ph: (630)553-5314
Fax: (630)553-5316
E-mail: kenneth.williams@kroeschellinc.com
URL: National Affiliate–www.navyleague.org
Contact: Kenneth D. Williams II, Pres.
Local. Civilian organization that supports U.S. capability to keep the sea lanes open through a strong, viable Navy, Marine Corps, Coast Guard, and Merchant Marine. Seeks to awaken interest and cooperation of U.S. citizens in matters serving to aid, improve, and develop the efficiency of U.S. naval and maritime forces and equipment. **Affiliated With:** Navy League of the United States.

4077 ■ Yorkville Area Chamber of Commerce
26 W Countryside Pkwy., Ste.101
Yorkville, IL 60560
Ph: (630)553-6853
Fax: (630)553-0702
E-mail: yorkvillechamber@sbcglobal.net
URL: http://www.yorkvillechamber.org
Local. Promotes the business and community development in Yorkville, IL.

Zeigler

4078 ■ American Legion, Illinois Post 177
c/o Patrick Mc Clellen, Adj.
104 S Main St.
Zeigler, IL 62999
Ph: (618)596-6011
Fax: (309)663-5783
URL: National Affiliate–www.legion.org
Contact: Patrick Mc Clellen, Adj.
Local. Affiliated With: American Legion.

Zion

4079 ■ American Guild of Organists, Moody Bible Institute (595)
c/o Prof. Elizabeth M. Naegele, D.Mus.
2516 Edina Blvd.
Zion, IL 60099-2702
Ph: (312)329-4089 (847)746-6547
Fax: (847)662-0801
E-mail: socratesnaegele@att.net
URL: National Affiliate–www.agohq.org
Contact: Prof. Elizabeth M. Naegele D.Mus., Dean
Members: 5. **Membership Dues:** student, $20 (annual). **Local. Telecommunication Services:** electronic mail, elizabeth.naegele@moody.edu. **Affiliated With:** American Guild of Organists. **Publications:** *The American Organist*, monthly. Magazine. Contains information on organ scholarship and performance, and reports of activities in the AGO. **Price:** included in membership dues.

4080 ■ American Legion, Zion-Benton Post 865
PO Box 114
Zion, IL 60099
Ph: (708)872-4638
Fax: (309)663-5783
URL: National Affiliate–www.legion.org
Local. Affiliated With: American Legion.

4081 ■ Zion Chamber of Commerce
2671 Sheridan Rd.
Zion, IL 60099
Ph: (847)872-5405
Fax: (847)872-9309
E-mail: info@zionchamber.com
URL: http://www.zionchamber.com
Contact: Diana Gornik, Exec.Dir.
Membership Dues: general, $110-$660 • financial institution, bank, $330 • construction company, $275 • educational institution, $198 • hotel, motel, apartment, $192 • municipality, $220 • utility, $550 • not for profit, $55 • real estate, insurance, land development, $110. **Local.** Enhances the economic environment of its local business community. **Computer Services:** Information services, membership directory. **Publications:** *News and Views*, quarterly. Newsletter. **Price:** included in membership dues.

Advance

4082 ■ American Legion, Nicely-Brindle Post 201
PO Box 21
Advance, IN 46102
Fax: (317)237-9891
URL: National Affiliate–www.legion.org
Local. Affiliated With: American Legion.

Albany

4083 ■ American Legion, Albany Post 167
128 W State St.
Albany, IN 47320
Ph: (317)630-1300
Fax: (317)237-9891
URL: National Affiliate–www.legion.org
Local. Affiliated With: American Legion.

Albion

4084 ■ American Legion, Albion Post 246
410 E Park Dr.
Albion, IN 46701
Ph: (219)636-2226
Fax: (317)237-9891
URL: National Affiliate–www.legion.org
Local. Affiliated With: American Legion.

4085 ■ National Association of Miniature Enthusiasts - Now and Again Club
c/o Jan Redfield
312 S Hickory St.
Albion, IN 46701-1266
Ph: (260)636-6234
E-mail: gramajan@ligtel.com
URL: http://www.miniatures.org/states/IN.html
Contact: Jan Redfield, Contact
Local. Affiliated With: National Association of Miniature Enthusiasts.

4086 ■ Noble County Genealogical Society (NCGS)
c/o Linda J. Shultz, Pres.
PO Box 162
Albion, IN 46701
E-mail: rmbdlb@aol.com
URL: http://www.nobgensoc.org
Contact: Linda J. Shultz, Pres.
Founded: 1980. **Members:** 75. **Membership Dues:** student, $1 (annual) • individual, $10 (annual) • family, $15 (annual) • sustaining/non-profit, $20 (annual) • business, $25 (annual) • life (single), $50 • life (couple), $75. **Local.** Amateur and professional genealogists and libraries interested in the genealogy of Northeastern Indiana. Provides assistance to individuals researching their own genealogy. **Libraries: Type:** open to the public. **Holdings:** 500. **Subjects:** Noble County history. **Publications:** *Noble News*, quarterly. Newsletter. **Price:** included in membership dues. **Circulation:** 125. **Conventions/Meetings:** annual Beginners Night - meeting - usually March or April in Albion, IN • annual dinner, with speaker - usually September • meeting - 11/year; usually 3rd Monday, except December.

4087 ■ United Way of Noble County
2094 N State Rd. 9
Albion, IN 46701
Ph: (260)636-8929
Fax: (260)636-2624
E-mail: info@uwnoble.org
URL: http://www.uwnoble.org
Contact: Nona Leatherman, Exec.Dir.
Local. Affiliated With: United Way of America.

Alexandria

4088 ■ Achieva Resources First Steps - Madison County
407 Park Ave., Ste.A
Alexandria, IN 46001
Ph: (765)724-9602
Fax: (765)724-9603
URL: http://www.achievaresources.org
Contact: Dan Stewart, Pres./CEO
Membership Dues: single, $20 • family, $30 • consumer, $2. **Local.**

4089 ■ Alexandria - Monroe Chamber of Commerce (ACC)
c/o Kimberly Kirtley, Dir./Pres.
119 N Harrison St.
Alexandria, IN 46001-2017
Ph: (765)724-3144
Fax: (765)724-3144
E-mail: kimberly.chamber@sbcglobal.net
URL: http://alexandriachamber.com
Contact: Kimberly Kirtley, Dir./Pres.
Founded: 1960. **Members:** 85. **Membership Dues:** business, $100 (annual) • organization, $50 (annual) • civic, $30 (annual). **Staff:** 1. **Local.** Promotes business and community development in Alexandria, IN. Conducts business development and management training courses. **Libraries: Type:** open to the public. **Publications:** Newsletter, monthly. **Conventions/Meetings:** annual banquet • monthly luncheon.

4090 ■ American Legion, Alexander Bright Post 87
215 E Water St.
Alexandria, IN 46001
Ph: (317)724-3558
Fax: (317)237-9891
URL: National Affiliate–www.legion.org
Local. Affiliated With: American Legion.

4091 ■ Indiana Amateur Softball Association, Region 6
c/o Leon Zachary, VP
226 E Benton St.
Alexandria, IN 46001
Ph: (765)643-2279
URL: http://www.indiana-asa.org
Contact: Leon Zachary, VP
Local. Affiliated With: Amateur Softball Association of America.

4092 ■ Izaak Walton League of America, Alexandria Chapter
c/o Julie A. Etchison
407 Walnut St.
Alexandria, IN 46001-1614
Ph: (765)724-3353
URL: National Affiliate–www.iwla.org
Local. Works to educate the public to conserve, maintain, protect, and restore the soil, forest, water, and other natural resources of the U.S; promotes the enjoyment and wholesome utilization of these resources. **Affiliated With:** Izaak Walton League of America.

Amboy

4093 ■ American Legion, Amboy Post 429
PO Box 213
Amboy, IN 46911
Ph: (317)630-1300
Fax: (317)237-9891
URL: National Affiliate–www.legion.org
Local. Affiliated With: American Legion.

Anderson

4094 ■ Alcoholics Anonymous World Services, Madison County Intergroup
PO Box 326
Anderson, IN 46015
Ph: (765)644-3212
URL: National Affiliate–www.aa.org
Local. Individuals recovering from alcoholism. AA maintains that members can solve their common problem and help others achieve sobriety through a twelve step program that includes sharing their experience, strength, and hope with each other. **Affiliated With:** Alcoholics Anonymous World Services.

4095 ■ American Cancer Society, Mid-Indiana Area Service Center
1220 Meridian St.
Anderson, IN 46016
Ph: (765)642-6603
Fax: (765)642-6711
URL: National Affiliate–www.cancer.org
Local. Affiliated With: American Cancer Society.

4096 ■ American Legion, Indiana Post 127
c/o George H. Hockett
4118 Columbus Ave.
Anderson, IN 46013
Ph: (317)644-9895
Fax: (317)237-9891
URL: National Affiliate–www.legion.org
Contact: George H. Hockett, Contact
Local. Affiliated With: American Legion.

4097 ■ American Legion, William Hall Post 282
2237 Arrow Ave.
Anderson, IN 46016
Ph: (317)630-1300
Fax: (317)237-9891
URL: National Affiliate–www.legion.org
Local. Affiliated With: American Legion.

4098 ■ American Red Cross, Madison County Chapter
914 Chase St.
Anderson, IN 46016
Ph: (765)643-6621
E-mail: madcoredcross@insightbb.com
URL: http://www.madisoncounty-redcross.org
Contact: Sheryl Delaplane, Exec.Dir.
Founded: 1917. **Staff:** 2. **Local**. Aims to improve the quality of human life. Helps people avoid, prepare for, and cope with emergencies. Performs services that are governed and directed by volunteers and are consistent with congressional charter and the principles of the International Red Cross. Serves members of the armed forces, veterans, and their families. Assists disaster victims, collects and distributes blood, and supports other community services. Trains community members in CPR, first aid, and swimming. **Telecommunication Services:** electronic mail, madisona@ecicnet.org. **Affiliated With:** American Red Cross National Headquarters. **Formerly:** (1991) American Red Cross, Norfolk Chapter.

4099 ■ Anderson/Madison County Association of Realtors (AMCAR)
205 W 11th St.
Anderson, IN 46016
Ph: (765)649-8106
Fax: (765)642-0266
E-mail: pkuhn@andersonarearealtors.com
URL: http://www.andersonarearealtors.com
Contact: Patty Kuhn, Exec. Officer
Local. Strives to develop real estate business practices. Advocates the right to own, use and transfer real property. Provides a facility for professional development, research and exchange of information among members and to the general public. **Affiliated With:** National Association of Realtors.

4100 ■ Anderson/Madison County Visitors and Convention Bureau
6335 S Scatterfield Rd.
Anderson, IN 46013
Ph: (765)643-5633
Fax: (765)643-9083
Free: (800)533-6569
E-mail: info@heartlandspirit.com
URL: http://www.heartlandspirit.com
Contact: Ralph L. Day, Exec.Dir.
Founded: 1982. **Members:** 85. **Membership Dues:** individual, $10 (annual) • business/civic, $25 (annual) • president, $100 (annual). **Staff:** 6. **Local**. Promotes conventions and tourism in Madison County, Indiana. **Publications:** Newsletter, quarterly.

4101 ■ Anderson University Students In Free Enterprise
Hardacre Hall Rm. 226
Anderson, IN 46012
Ph: (765)641-3823
E-mail: sife@andeson.edu
URL: http://sife.anderson.edu
Contact: John VanDrunen, Pres.
Local.

4102 ■ Association for Computing Machinery, Anderson University
c/o Kevin Joiner, Sponsor
1100 E 5th St.
Cmpt. Sci. Dept.
Anderson, IN 46012-3462
Ph: (765)649-9071
Fax: (765)641-3851
E-mail: joiner@anderson.edu
URL: National Affiliate–www.acm.org
Contact: Kevin Joiner, Contact
Local. Biological, medical, behavioral, and computer scientists; hospital administrators; programmers and others interested in application of computer methods to biological, behavioral, and medical problems. Stimulates understanding of the use and potential of computers in the Biosciences. **Affiliated With:** Association for Computing Machinery.

4103 ■ Central Indiana Rotorwing Club
614 W Vineyard St.
Anderson, IN 46011-3420
URL: http://torchs.org/clubs/clubs.htm
Contact: John C. Zankl, Contact
Local.

4104 ■ Chamber of Commerce for Anderson and Madison County
PO Box 469
205 W 11th St.
Anderson, IN 46015-0469
Ph: (765)642-0264
Fax: (765)642-0266
E-mail: andersonchamber@ameritech.net
URL: http://www.andersoninchamber.com
Contact: Keith J. Pitcher, Pres./CEO
Founded: 1914. **Members:** 505. **Membership Dues:** business, $250 (annual). **Staff:** 5. **Budget:** $206,321. **Local**. Represents retail, commercial, manufacturing, and professional firms promoting community and economic development in the Anderson, IN area. **Telecommunication Services:** electronic mail, info@andersoninchamber.com. **Publications:** *The Business Edge*, monthly. Newsletter.

4105 ■ East Central Indiana Youth for Christ
PO Box 123
Anderson, IN 46015
Ph: (765)608-3058
Fax: (765)608-3056
URL: National Affiliate–www.yfc.net
Local. Affiliated With: Youth for Christ/U.S.A.

4106 ■ Indiana Federation of Families for Children's Mental Health
2205 Costello Dr.
Anderson, IN 46011
Ph: (765)643-4357
E-mail: indianafedfam@insightbb.com
URL: National Affiliate–www.ffcmh.org
Contact: Brenda Hamilton, Contact
State. Affiliated With: Federation of Families for Children's Mental Health.

4107 ■ Indiana State Numismatic Association (ISNA)
c/o Joyce Fischer, Corresponding Sec.
1123 Historic W 8th St.
Anderson, IN 46016-2616
E-mail: kycolonels@insightbb.com
URL: http://www.theisna.org
Contact: Joyce Fischer, Corresponding Sec.
State. Affiliated With: American Numismatic Association.

4108 ■ International Union of Bricklayers and Allied Craftworkers, AFL-CIO-CLC Indiana and Kentucky Local Union 4
2041 Broadway
Anderson, IN 46012
Fax: (765)683-9225
Free: (800)322-2830
E-mail: tedchamp@baclocal4.org
URL: http://www.baclocal4.org
Contact: Ted Champ, Pres.
Members: 4,373. **Local. Affiliated With:** International Union of Bricklayers and Allied Craftworkers.

4109 ■ International Union, United Automobile, Aerospace and Agricultural Implement Workers of America, AFL-CIO - Local Union 663
2840 Madison Ave.
Anderson, IN 46016
Ph: (765)643-6921
Fax: (765)644-6697
E-mail: dave@uawlocal663.com
URL: http://www.uawlocal663.com
Contact: Kelly Gaskill, Financial Sec.
Members: 1,637. **Local**. AFL-CIO. **Affiliated With:** International Union, United Automobile, Aerospace and Agricultural Implement Workers of America.

4110 ■ Madison County Council of Governments (MCCOG)
16 E 9th St., Rm. 100
Anderson, IN 46016
Ph: (765)641-9482
Fax: (765)641-9486
E-mail: mccog@aol.com
Contact: Jerrold Bridges, Exec.Dir.
Founded: 1969. **Staff:** 8. **Budget:** $700,000. **State Groups:** 1. **Local**. Local government units. Promotes city development in Madison County, IN. Metropolitan Planning Organization (MPO). **Libraries: Type:** not open to the public. **Holdings:** 2,000; articles, books, periodicals. **Subjects:** transportation, housing, land use, landscape design, economic development, finance, environment. **Committees:** Citizen; Policy; Technical. **Publications:** *OWP*, *TIP*, *Corridor Studies*, *Park Plans*, *Comprehensive Plans*, semiannual. Newsletter • *Special Studies*, monthly. **Conventions/Meetings:** annual workshop (exhibits); Avg. Attendance: 37.

4111 ■ Madison County REACT
818 Eastgate Dr.
Anderson, IN 46012
Ph: (765)649-2569
E-mail: jrparker@iquest.net
URL: http://www.reactintl.org/teaminfo/usa_teams/teams-usin.htm
Local. Trained communication experts and professional volunteers. Provides volunteer public service and emergency communications through the use of radios (Citizen Band, General Mobile Radio Service, UHF and HAM). Coordinates with radio industries and government on safety communication matters and supports charitable activities and community organizations.

4112 ■ Mothers Against Drunk Driving, East Central Indiana
PO Box 1054
Anderson, IN 46015-1054
Ph: (765)649-2958
Fax: (765)649-2958
E-mail: eastcentralindiana@sbcglobal.net
URL: http://www.madd.org/in/eastcentral
Contact: Stephanie Stevens, Pres.
Local. Victims of drunk driving crashes; concerned citizens. Encourages citizen participation in working towards reform of the drunk driving problem and the prevention of underage drinking. Acts as the voice of victims of drunk driving crashes by speaking on their behalf to communities, businesses, and educational groups. **Affiliated With:** Mothers Against Drunk Driving.

4113 ■ National Active and Retired Federal Employees Association - Madison County 36
4326 Rutgers Dr.
Anderson, IN 46013-4439
Ph: (765)643-8843
URL: National Affiliate–www.narfe.org
Contact: Haskell Counts, Contact
Local. Protects the retirement future of employees through education. Informs members on issues affecting the retirement. **Affiliated With:** National Association of Retired Federal Employees.

4114 ■ National Association of Home Builders of the U.S., Madison County Home Builders Association
c/o Jim Stuart
Local No. 1504
1905 Woodview Ln.
Anderson, IN 46011-1054
Ph: (765)521-7509
Fax: (765)521-7516
E-mail: jim.stuart@ameriana.com
URL: National Affiliate–www.nahb.org
Contact: Jim Stuart, Contact
Local. Single and multifamily home builders, commercial builders, and others associated with the building industry. **Affiliated With:** National Association of Home Builders. **Formerly:** (2005) National Association of Home Builders of the U.S., Anderson Home Builders Association.

4115 ■ Phi Theta Kappa, Alpha Omega Delta Chapter - Ivy Tech State College
c/o Obrin Griffin
Anderson Campus
104 W 53rd St.
Anderson, IN 46013
Ph: (765)643-7133
E-mail: ogriffin@ivytech.edu
URL: http://www.ptk.org/directories/chapters/IN/20601-1.htm
Contact: Obrin Griffin, Advisor
Local.

4116 ■ Police and Firemen's Insurance Association - Anderson Fire Department
c/o Dennis A. Jones
823 W 1st St.
Anderson, IN 46016
Ph: (765)649-6720
URL: National Affiliate–www.pfia.net
Contact: Dennis A. Jones, Contact
Local. Affiliated With: Police and Firemen's Insurance Association.

4117 ■ Psi Chi, National Honor Society in Psychology - Anderson University
c/o Dept. of Psychology
1100 E 5th St.
Anderson, IN 46012-3495
Ph: (765)641-4470 (765)641-4471
Fax: (765)641-3851
E-mail: iks@anderson.edu
URL: http://www.psichi.org/chapters/info.asp?chapter_id=942
Contact: Linda K. Swindell PhD, Advisor
Local.

4118 ■ Queens of the Court
c/o Louis Lacy
1711 Silver St.
Anderson, IN 46012
Ph: (765)644-6315
E-mail: loulacy@lquest.net
URL: http://eteamz.com/queens_of_the_court/
Contact: Lou Lacey, Pres.
Founded: 1999. **Members:** 75. **Staff:** 10. **Local**. Promotes girl's basketball.

4119 ■ RSVP Volunteer Resources of Madison County
c/o Judith Kratzner
125 E 13th St.
Anderson, IN 46016-0000
Ph: (765)641-2470 (765)641-2193
Fax: (765)641-2194
E-mail: rsvp@and.lib.in.us
URL: http://www.and.lib.in.us
Contact: Judith Kratzner, Dir.
Founded: 1989. **Members:** 400. **Staff:** 2. **Budget:** $70,000. **State Groups:** 24. **Local**. Provides listings of volunteer opportunities and contacts for persons of all ages, assists with volunteer selection, registration and volunteer recognition.

4120 ■ SCORE Anderson
c/o Anderson Chamber of Commerce
PO Box 469
Anderson, IN 46015
Ph: (765)642-0264
E-mail: postmaster@scoreanderson.org
URL: http://www.scoreanderson.org
Contact: Jim Alexander, Contact
Local. Provides counseling to persons wanting to go into business as well as those already in the business. Sponsors seminars and workshops. **Affiliated With:** SCORE.

4121 ■ United Way of Madison County
PO Box 1200
Anderson, IN 46015-1200
Ph: (765)643-7493
Fax: (765)608-3065
E-mail: office@unitedwaymadisonco.org
URL: http://www.unitedwaymadisonco.org
Contact: Bill Pitts, Pres.
Local. Affiliated With: United Way of America.

4122 ■ Urban League of Madison County
c/o William Raymore, Pres.
1210 W 10th St.
Anderson, IN 46015
Ph: (765)649-7126
E-mail: wraymore@aol.com
URL: National Affiliate–www.nul.org
Contact: William Raymore, Pres.
Local. Affiliated With: National Urban League.

Angola

4123 ■ American Legion, Angola Post 31
PO Box 331
Angola, IN 46703
Ph: (317)630-1300
Fax: (317)237-9891
URL: National Affiliate–www.legion.org
Local. Affiliated With: American Legion.

4124 ■ Angola Area Chamber of Commerce (AACC)
211 E Maumee St., Ste.B
Angola, IN 46703
Ph: (260)665-3512
Fax: (260)665-7418
E-mail: info@angolachamber.org
URL: http://www.angolachamber.org
Contact: Jill Boggs, Exec.Dir.
Members: 310. **Membership Dues:** business (based on the number of employees), $152-$495 (annual) • church, non-profit, elected official, $70 (annual) • individual (retired), $25 (annual) • motel, hospital, nursing home (based on the number of beds), $152-$271 (annual). **Local**. Promotes business and community development in Angola, IN. Maintains industrial committee. **Computer Services:** Online services, membership directory. **Committees:** Issues Management; Planning; Public Relations; Specific Event. **Affiliated With:** U.S. Chamber of Commerce. **Publications:** *Business to Business*, monthly. Newsletter. **Price:** free • *Industrial Directory*, periodic. **Price:** $10.00 • Membership Directory, annual. **Price:** $10.00. **Conventions/Meetings:** monthly meeting.

4125 ■ Indiana Lake Management Society (ILMS)
207 S Wayne, Ste.B
Angola, IN 46703
E-mail: president@indianalakes.org
URL: http://www.indianalakes.org
Contact: Mark Mongin, Pres.
State. Affiliated With: North American Lake Management Society.

4126 ■ Indiana Marine Trade Association
c/o John McLaughlin
2860 W. Orland Rd.
Angola, IN 46703-9042
Ph: (260)833-2114
Fax: (260)833-4950
E-mail: nautalease@locl.net
Contact: John McLaughlin, Contact
Founded: 2000. **Members:** 37. **Membership Dues:** $250 (annual). **Staff:** 3. **State. Publications:** Newsletter, semiannual. **Price:** free.

4127 ■ Maumee Valley St. Bernard Club
c/o Janice Green, Sec.
3785 W Orland Rd.
Angola, IN 46703
Ph: (260)833-2947
E-mail: jkgjlg@msn.com
URL: National Affiliate–www.saintbernardclub.org
Contact: Janice Green, Sec.
Local. Affiliated With: Saint Bernard Club of America.

4128 ■ Mental Health Association in Steuben County
c/o Ms. Betty Bemesderfer, Exec.Dir.
PO Box 372
Angola, IN 46703-0372
Ph: (260)665-5981
URL: http://www.mentalhealthassociation.com
Contact: Ms. Betty Bemesderfer, Exec.Dir.
Local. Seeks to promote mental health and prevent mental health disorders. Improves mental health of Americans through advocacy, public education, research and service. **Affiliated With:** Mental Health Association in Indiana; National Mental Health Association.

4129 ■ Society of Manufacturing Engineers - Tri-State University U173
Allen School of Engg. and Tech., Engg. Tech. Dept.
1 Univ. Ave.
Angola, IN 46703
Ph: (260)665-4264
Fax: (260)665-4188
E-mail: ertekiny@tristate.edu
URL: National Affiliate–www.sme.org
Contact: Dr. Yalcin Ertekin, Contact
Local. Advances manufacturing knowledge to gain competitive advantage. Improves skills and manufacturing solutions for the growth of economy. Provides resources and opportunities for manufacturing professionals. **Affiliated With:** American Meteorological Society.

4130 ■ Steuben County United Way
c/o Karma Austin, Exec.Dir.
317 S Wayne St., Ste.3D
Angola, IN 46703
Ph: (260)665-6196
Fax: (260)665-6196
E-mail: scuw@locl.net
URL: http://www.unitedwaysteuben.org
Contact: Karma Austin, Exec.Dir.
Founded: 1957. **Staff:** 2. **Local**. Strives to unite the community through visionary leadership, assessment of needs, and the mobilization and dispersion of resources to positively impact the quality of life for the citizens of Steuben County. **Awards: Type:** grant. **Recipient:** for Steuben County residents. **Affiliated With:** Angola Area Chamber of Commerce; United Way of America. **Conventions/Meetings:** monthly board meeting, discusses policy, governance and community needs assessment discussions - every Wednesday at 7:00 AM.

4131 ■ Sweet Adelines International, Little River Chapter
Angola Middle School
E Maumee St.
Angola, IN 46703
Ph: (260)833-4350
E-mail: rjwells11550@wmconnect.com
URL: National Affiliate–www.sweetadelineintl.org
Contact: Rita Wells, Contact
Local. Advances the musical art form of barbershop harmony through education and performances. Provides education, training and coaching in the

development of women's four-part barbershop harmony. **Affiliated With:** Sweet Adelines International.

4132 ■ Wood-Land-Lakes Resource Conservation and Development Council
1220 N 200 W, Ste.J
Peachtree Plz.
Angola, IN 46703
Ph: (260)665-3211
Fax: (260)668-8887
E-mail: kathleen.latz@in.rcdnet.org
URL: http://www.wood-land-lakes.org/council.htm
Contact: Kathleen Latz, Coor.
Local. Affiliated With: National Association of Resource Conservation and Development Councils.

Arcadia

4133 ■ American Legion, Indiana Post 344
c/o Harry C. Leeman
PO Box 174
Arcadia, IN 46030
Ph: (317)630-1300
Fax: (317)237-9891
URL: National Affiliate–www.legion.org
Contact: Harry C. Leeman, Contact
Local. Affiliated With: American Legion.

Argos

4134 ■ American Legion, James Lowell Corey Post 68
120 N 1st St.
Argos, IN 46501
Ph: (317)630-1300
Fax: (317)237-9891
URL: National Affiliate–www.legion.org
Local. Affiliated With: American Legion.

Attica

4135 ■ American Legion, Attica Post 52
122 W Mill St.
Attica, IN 47918
Ph: (317)764-4713
Fax: (317)237-9891
URL: National Affiliate–www.legion.org
Local. Affiliated With: American Legion.

Auburn

4136 ■ American Legion, De Kalb Post 97
1729 Sprott
Auburn, IN 46706
Ph: (317)630-1300
Fax: (317)237-9891
URL: National Affiliate–www.legion.org
Local. Affiliated With: American Legion.

4137 ■ American Truck Historical Society, Auburn Heritage Truck Chapter
c/o John Martin Smith
PO Box 686
Auburn, IN 46706
Ph: (260)925-5714
E-mail: inmemories@mchsi.com
URL: National Affiliate–www.aths.org
Contact: John Martin Smith, Contact
Local.

4138 ■ Auburn Chamber of Commerce (ACC)
PO Box 168
208 S Jackson St.
Auburn, IN 46706-0168
Ph: (260)925-2100
Fax: (260)925-2199
E-mail: chamber@locl.net
URL: http://www.chamberinauburn.com
Contact: Kelly Knox, Exec.Dir.
Founded: 1903. **Members:** 300. **Membership Dues:** non-profit (less than 10 employees), $125 (annual) • non-profit (over 10 employees), associate (no site or employees in DeKalb County), $199 (annual) • full, $35 (annual) • second business, $80 (annual) • full, associate (based on number of employees), $199-$945 (annual). **Staff:** 2. **Budget:** $125,000. **Regional Groups:** 2. **State Groups:** 1. **Local Groups:** 5. **Local.** Promotes business and community development in Auburn, IN. Supports art competitions and annual Auburn-Cord-Duesenberg Festival. Sponsors Auburn Sidewalk Sale Days and Dekalb Free Fall Fair. **Libraries: Type:** not open to the public. **Holdings:** 25; articles, books, periodicals, video recordings. **Subjects:** business, law, training. **Awards:** Business of the Year. **Frequency:** annual. **Type:** recognition • Citizen of the Year. **Frequency:** annual. **Type:** recognition • College Scholarships. **Type:** scholarship • Member of the Month. **Frequency:** monthly. **Type:** recognition • Member of the Year. **Frequency:** annual. **Type:** recognition. **Publications:** Directory, annual • Newsletter, quarterly. Alternate Formats: online. **Conventions/Meetings:** annual Fox-Tail Drive - meeting - always Memorial Day Weekend.

4139 ■ Izaak Walton League of America, DeKalb County Chapter
1957 County Rd. 68
Auburn, IN 46706-9521
Ph: (260)925-4637
E-mail: mary-anna.feitler@ge.com
URL: National Affiliate–www.iwla.org
Contact: Ms. Mary Anna Feitler, Pres.
Founded: 1972. **Members:** 9. **Local.** Works to educate the public to conserve, maintain, protect, and restore the soil, forest, water, and other natural resources of the U.S; promotes the enjoyment and wholesome utilization of these resources. **Affiliated With:** Izaak Walton League of America.

4140 ■ Mental Health Association in Dekalb County
c/o Ms. Cheryl Taylor, Exec.Dir.
902 Deer Ridge Crossing
Auburn, IN 46706-1494
Ph: (260)925-8309
Fax: (260)925-1733
URL: http://www.mentalhealthassociation.com
Contact: Ms. Cheryl Taylor, Exec.Dir.
Local. Seeks to promote mental health and prevent mental health disorders. Improves mental health of Americans through advocacy, public education, research and service. **Affiliated With:** Mental Health Association in Indiana; National Mental Health Association.

4141 ■ Northeast Indiana Youth for Christ
PO Box 424
Auburn, IN 46706
Ph: (260)925-1058
Fax: (260)925-1101
URL: http://www.yfcweb.com
Local. Affiliated With: Youth for Christ/U.S.A.

4142 ■ Pheasants Forever Northeast Indiana Chapter 182
4615 CR 19
Auburn, IN 46706
E-mail: ronaldlong@comcast.net
URL: http://www.pheasantsforever182.com
Contact: Ron Long, Pres.
Local. Affiliated With: Pheasants Forever.

4143 ■ RSVP of Dekalb/Noble/Steuben Counties
c/o Patti Sheppard, Dir.
107 W 5th St.
Auburn, IN 46706
Ph: (260)925-0917
Fax: (260)925-1732
E-mail: rsvp@locl.net
URL: http://www.seniorcorps.gov/about/programs/rsvp.asp
Contact: Patti Sheppard, Dir.
Local. Affiliated With: Retired and Senior Volunteer Program.

4144 ■ United Way of DeKalb County
c/o Amy Truesdell, Exec.Dir.
PO Box 307
Auburn, IN 46706
Ph: (260)927-0995
Fax: (260)927-0996
E-mail: caring@unitedwaydekalb.org
URL: http://www.unitedwaydekalb.org
Contact: Amy Truesdell, Exec.Dir.
Local.

Aurora

4145 ■ American Legion, Indiana Post 231
c/o Keith Ross
119 Bridgeway St.
Aurora, IN 47001
Ph: (317)630-1300
Fax: (317)237-9891
URL: National Affiliate–www.legion.org
Contact: Keith Ross, Contact
Local. Affiliated With: American Legion.

4146 ■ Hillforest Historical Foundation (HHF)
PO Box 127
Aurora, IN 47001
Ph: (812)926-0087
Fax: (812)926-1075
E-mail: hillforest@seidata.com
URL: http://hillforest.org
Contact: Linda Early, Curator
Founded: 1956. **Members:** 500. **Membership Dues:** individual, $25 (annual). **Staff:** 1. **Budget:** $100,000. **Local.** Individuals interested in the preservation and interpretation of the Hillforest Mansion. Conducts educational programs, fundraisers, and tours. Sponsors Victorian Christmas festival. **Publications:** *Calendar of Events*, annual • *Hillforest Happenings*, quarterly. Newsletter • Brochures.

4147 ■ Korean War Veterans Association, Southeastern Indiana No. 4 Chapter
c/o Luther E. Rice
414 Water St.
Aurora, IN 47001-1242
Ph: (812)926-2790
E-mail: lerice@one.net
URL: National Affiliate–www.kwva.org
Contact: Luther E. Rice, Contact
Local. Affiliated With: Korean War Veterans Association.

4148 ■ Southeastern Indiana Board of Realtors
218 Fourth St.
Aurora, IN 47001
Ph: (812)926-4644
E-mail: info@seibr.com
URL: http://www.seibr.com
Contact: Sue Page, Exec. Officer
Local. Strives to develop real estate business practices. Advocates the right to own, use and transfer real property. Provides a facility for professional development, research and exchange of information among members and to the general public. **Affiliated With:** National Association of Realtors.

Austin

4149 ■ Silver Creek Beagle Club
c/o Gerald D. Hickman
1421 W Booe Rd.
Austin, IN 47102-1067
URL: National Affiliate–www.akc.org
Contact: Gerald D. Hickman, Contact
Local.

Avilla

4150 ■ American Legion, Avilla Post 240
PO Box 434
Avilla, IN 46710
Ph: (219)897-2225
Fax: (317)237-9891
URL: National Affiliate–www.legion.org
Local. Affiliated With: American Legion.

4151 ■ Indiana Appaloosa Association
c/o Margaret Keim, Pres.
9038 E 200 S
Avilla, IN 46710
Ph: (260)897-2033
URL: http://www.indaphc.com
Contact: Margaret Keim, Pres.
Local. Affiliated With: Appaloosa Horse Club.

Avon

4152 ■ Greater Avon Chamber of Commerce (ACOC)
8244 E Hwy. 36, Ste.140
Avon, IN 46123
Ph: (317)272-4333
Fax: (317)272-7217
E-mail: info@avonchamber.org
URL: http://www.avonchamber.org
Contact: Tom Downard, Exec.Dir.
Members: 190. **Membership Dues:** business (based on number of employees), $275-$450 (annual) • financial institution, $350 (annual) • nonprofit, $200 (annual) • individual, $150 (annual). **Local.** Promotes the continuous improvement of the quality of life in the Avon community through the pursuit of new business, cultural, social and economic education of the citizen by providing accurate and timely assistance to the business community. **Computer Services:** Information services, business directory.

4153 ■ Indiana Amateur Softball Association, Region 8
c/o Steve Boone, VP
8103 E US Hwy., 36 Rm. 222
Avon, IN 46123
Ph: (317)902-8243
E-mail: booney@avonsoftballpark.com
URL: http://www.indiana-asa.org
Contact: Steve Boone, VP
Local. Affiliated With: Amateur Softball Association of America.

4154 ■ National Corvette Restorers Society, Indiana Chapter
c/o Ron Stoner
6534 Lake Forest Dr.
Avon, IN 46123
Ph: (317)839-7127
E-mail: rwstoner@iquest.net
URL: http://www.ncrs.org/in
Contact: Ron Stoner, Contact
Membership Dues: family, $20 (annual). **Local.** Dedicated to the same principles as the national society which is the restoration, preservation, history, and enjoyment of Corvettes made from the model years 1953 through 1982. **Affiliated With:** National Corvette Restorers Society. **Publications:** *Points and Plugs*, quarterly. Newsletter. **Conventions/Meetings:** periodic meeting, judging meet, seminars, road tour, and business meeting - 5/year.

4155 ■ Public Relations Society of America, Hoosier (PRSA)
c/o Deanna Lepsky, APR, Pres.
779 Weeping Way Ln.
Avon, IN 46123
Ph: (317)265-4887
E-mail: deannalepsky@hotmail.com
URL: http://www.hoosierprsa.org
Local. Affiliated With: Public Relations Society of America.

Batesville

4156 ■ American Legion, Prell Bland Post 271
PO Box 74
Batesville, IN 47006
Ph: (812)934-2228
Fax: (317)237-9891
URL: National Affiliate–www.legion.org
Local. Affiliated With: American Legion.

4157 ■ Batesville Area Chamber of Commerce
132 S Main St.
Batesville, IN 47006
Ph: (812)934-3101
Fax: (812)932-0202
E-mail: chamberexec@batesvillein.com
URL: http://www.batesvillein.com
Contact: Lydia S. Woodward, Exec.Dir.
Local. Provides its members with networking, marketing and advertising opportunities, and business counseling and referral services. **Publications:** *Chamber Chatter*, monthly. Newsletter. Contains information about business issues, legislative updates, local events, chamber member news, and chamber events.

4158 ■ Batesville - Wyld Life
PO Box 224
Batesville, IN 47006
Ph: (812)934-4254
URL: http://sites.younglife.org/sites/Batesvillewyldlife/default.aspx
Local. Affiliated With: Young Life.

4159 ■ Batesville - Young Life
PO Box 224
Batesville, IN 47006
Ph: (812)934-4254
URL: http://Batesville.younglife.org
Local.

4160 ■ Institute of Internal Auditors, Indianapolis Chapter
c/o Jeffrey T. Kendall
Hillenbrand Indus.
700 State Rte. 46 E
Mailcode Y27
Batesville, IN 47006
Ph: (812)934-1066
Fax: (812)934-7657
E-mail: jeff.kendall@hillenbrand.com
URL: http://indianapolis.vchapters.org
Contact: Jeffrey T. Kendall, Pres.
Local. Serves as an advocate for the internal audit profession. Provides certification, education, research, and technological guidance for the profession. **Affiliated With:** Institute of Internal Auditors. **Publications:** Newsletter, periodic. Alternate Formats: online.

4161 ■ Southeast Indiana Young Life
PO Box 224
Batesville, IN 47006
Ph: (812)934-4254 (812)569-7185
URL: http://southeastindiana.younglife.org
Contact: Ozzie Smith, Area Dir.
Local.

4162 ■ Tri-County Coonhunters Conservation Club
PO Box 81
Batesville, IN 47006
E-mail: mkick@nalu.net
URL: National Affiliate–www.mynssa.com
Local. Affiliated With: National Skeet Shooting Association.

Battle Ground

4163 ■ PFLAG Lafayette/Tippecanoe County
PO Box 59
Battle Ground, IN 47920
Ph: (765)567-2478
Fax: (765)491-6357
E-mail: randm@insightbb.com
URL: http://www.pflag.org/Indiana.205.0.html
Local. Affiliated With: Parents, Families, and Friends of Lesbians and Gays.

Bedford

4164 ■ American Legion, Gillen Post 33
515 X St.
Bedford, IN 47421
Ph: (812)275-4273
Fax: (317)237-9891
URL: National Affiliate–www.legion.org
Local. Affiliated With: American Legion.

4165 ■ American Red Cross Hoosier Hills Chapter
2119 29th St.
Bedford, IN 47421
Ph: (812)275-5162
Fax: (812)275-5120
E-mail: chapter@hhredcross.org
URL: http://www.hhredcross.org
Contact: Don Waterman, Chm.
Founded: 1917. **Staff:** 2. **Local.** Works to help people prevent, prepare for, and respond to emergencies through disaster services and health and safety education. Provides an emergency communication link between members of the armed forces and their families, and frequently holds blood drives to help secure the area's blood supply. **Affiliated With:** American Red Cross National Headquarters. **Formerly:** (1998) American Red Cross, Lawrence County Chapter; (2001) American Red Cross of Lawrence and Orange Counties; (2005) American Red Cross of Lawrence County, Hoosier Hills Chapter. **Publications:** Newsletter, annual.

4166 ■ Association for Accounting Administration, Indiana Chapter
c/o Treva Olson, Pres.
1725 M St.
Bedford, IN 47421
Ph: (812)275-4858
Fax: (812)275-4871
E-mail: tolson@olsoncpafirm.com
URL: National Affiliate–www.cpaadmin.org
Contact: Treva Olson, Pres.
State. Fosters the professional skills needed as firm administrators. Promotes accounting administration profession. Provides education to enhance the professional and personal competencies of accounting administration. **Affiliated With:** Association for Accounting Administration.

4167 ■ Bedford Area Chamber of Commerce
1116 16th St.
Bedford, IN 47421
Ph: (812)275-4493
Fax: (812)279-5998
E-mail: bedford@bedfordchamber.com
URL: http://www.bedfordchamber.com
Contact: Adele Bowden-Purlee, Pres.
Founded: 1916. **Members:** 430. **Membership Dues:** regular, $175 (annual). **Staff:** 3. **Budget:** $75,000. **State Groups:** 1. **Local.** Promotes business and community development in the Bedford, IN area. **Publications:** *Chamber Advantage*, monthly. Newsletter. **Advertising:** accepted.

4168 ■ Bedford Board of Realtors
PO Box 9
Bedford, IN 47421

Ph: (812)277-1861
Fax: (812)277-1575
E-mail: bbr@quik.com
URL: National Affiliate–www.realtor.org
Contact: Greg Taylor, Exec. Officer
Local. Strives to develop real estate business practices. Advocates the right to own, use and transfer real property. Provides a facility for professional development, research and exchange of information among members and to the general public. **Affiliated With:** National Association of Realtors.

4169 ■ Bedford Hiking Club
c/o Linda Gates
PO Box 1555
Bedford, IN 47421-0000
Ph: (812)279-3397
E-mail: hikerusa@insightbb.com
URL: http://www.kiva.net/~jeskewic/hike.html
Contact: Linda Gates, Contact
Local. Affiliated With: American Volkssport Association.

4170 ■ Fraternal Order of Eagles, Bedford No. 654
1312 'J' St.
Bedford, IN 47421
Ph: (812)275-3773
Fax: (812)275-3930
E-mail: eagles_654@sbcglobal.net
URL: National Affiliate–www.foe.org
Founded: 1948. **Members:** 700. **Membership Dues:** $10 (annual). **State Groups:** 93. **Local Groups:** 1. **Local**. Fraternal society. **Affiliated With:** Grand Aerie, Fraternal Order of Eagles. **Conventions/Meetings:** annual meeting - 2nd week of June, Indianapolis, IN • bimonthly Regular Aerie Meeting, regular membership - every 2nd and 4th Tuesday.

4171 ■ Indiana Dietary Managers Association
c/o Mary Staggs, CDM, Pres.
2118 Old Farm Rd.
Bedford, IN 47421
Ph: (812)279-4437
URL: http://www.dmaonline.org/IN
Contact: Mary Staggs CDM, Pres.
State. Represents dietary managers. Maintains a high level of competency and quality in dietary departments through continuing education. Provides optimum nutritional care through foodservice management. **Affiliated With:** Dietary Managers Association.

4172 ■ Indiana Limestone Institute of America (ILI)
Stone City Bank Bldg., Ste.400
1502 I St.
Bedford, IN 47421
Ph: (812)275-4426
Fax: (812)279-8682
E-mail: jim@iliai.com
URL: http://www.iliai.com
Contact: James P. Owens, Exec.Dir.
Founded: 1928. **Members:** 70. **Staff:** 3. Conducts promotional and technical services for the Indiana limestone industry; sponsors research; establishes standards; offers technical service in product use to architects, builders, and owners. Maintains speakers' bureau; conducts specialized education. **Absorbed:** National Association for Indiana Limestone. **Publications:** *Indiana Limestone Handbook*, biennial • Pamphlets. **Conventions/Meetings:** semiannual meeting.

4173 ■ Lawrence County Homebuilders Association
PO Box 292
Bedford, IN 47421
Ph: (812)275-7718
Fax: (812)275-7718
E-mail: hoosdoor@kiva.net
Contact: Laquita Jennings, Contact
Founded: 1970. **Members:** 76. **Membership Dues:** $310 (annual). **For-Profit. Local.** Contributes to local organizations within the community. **Publications:** *Builders' Connection*, monthly. Newsletter. **Price:** for members. **Advertising:** accepted. **Conventions/Meetings:** monthly meeting - always second Monday of each month. Bedford, IN - Avg. Attendance: 60.

4174 ■ National Active and Retired Federal Employees Association - Bedford 578
2408 Windwood Dr.
Bedford, IN 47421-3956
Ph: (812)275-3738
URL: National Affiliate–www.narfe.org
Contact: John G. Martis, Contact
Local. Protects the retirement future of employees through education. Informs members on issues affecting the retirement. **Affiliated With:** National Association of Retired Federal Employees.

4175 ■ Society of Antique Modelers - Indiana 112, Hoosier Bombers
1194 Art Gallery Rd.
Bedford, IN 47421
Ph: (812)277-0695
E-mail: richardmonie@yahoo.com
URL: National Affiliate–www.antiquemodeler.org
Local. Affiliated With: Society of Antique Modelers.

4176 ■ Society of Antique Modelers - Variety Group
2556 Old St., Rd. 37 N
Bedford, IN 47421
Ph: (812)275-8678
E-mail: dale_hannum@yahoo.com
URL: National Affiliate–www.antiquemodeler.org
Local. Affiliated With: Society of Antique Modelers.

4177 ■ Stonebelt Stargazers
PO Box 1112
Bedford, IN 47421
Ph: (812)279-5012
E-mail: klein62@tima.com
URL: http://mainbyte.com/stargazers/index.html
Contact: Mike Pritchett, Contact
Local. Promotes the science of astronomy. Works to encourage and coordinate activities of amateur astronomical societies. Fosters observational and computational work and craftsmanship in various fields of astronomy. **Affiliated With:** Astronomical League.

4178 ■ United Way of Lawrence County, Indiana
PO Box 671
Bedford, IN 47421-0671
Ph: (812)277-0493
URL: National Affiliate–national.unitedway.org
Local. Affiliated With: United Way of America.

4179 ■ White River Humane Society (WRHS)
PO Box 792
Bedford, IN 47421
Ph: (812)279-2457
E-mail: thewrhs@yahoo.com
URL: http://www.whiteriverhumanesociety.com
Contact: Don Harrison, Pres.
Founded: 1975. **Members:** 275. **Membership Dues:** junior, $2 (annual) • individual, $10 (annual) • family, $25 (annual) • business, club, $50 (annual) • supporting, $50 (annual) • benefactor, $100 (annual) • life, $400. **Staff:** 3. **Budget:** $120,000. **Local**. Works for animal rights. Fosters a humane ethic and philosophy through educational, legislative, investigative, and legal activities. Makes presentations to community service groups and schools. Sponsors fundraisers. Operates shelter. **Libraries: Type:** open to the public. **Awards:** Coleman Award. **Type:** recognition • Humanitarian Award. **Frequency:** annual. **Type:** recognition. **Formerly:** (1990) Lawrence County Humane Society. **Publications:** *Purrs & Paws*, semiannual. Newsletter. **Circulation:** 5,000. **Advertising:** accepted. **Conventions/Meetings:** annual meeting - January.

4180 ■ White River Resource Conservation and Development Council
1919 Steven Ave.
Bedford, IN 47421
Ph: (812)279-8117
Fax: (812)279-1394
E-mail: catrina.perkinson@in.usda.gov
URL: National Affiliate–www.rcdnet.org
Contact: Catrina Perkinson, Coor.
Local. Affiliated With: National Association of Resource Conservation and Development Councils.

Beech Grove

4181 ■ American Legion, Beech Grove Post 276
327 Main St.
Beech Grove, IN 46107
Ph: (317)787-5547
Fax: (317)237-9891
URL: National Affiliate–www.legion.org
Local. Affiliated With: American Legion.

4182 ■ Indiana State Wrestling Association (ISWA)
PO Box 157
Beech Grove, IN 46107
Ph: (317)780-1885
E-mail: iswa@sbcglobal.net
URL: http://www.iswa.com
Contact: Mike Dowden, State Dir.
State. Affiliated With: U.S.A. Wrestling.

4183 ■ Mothers Against Drunk Driving, Central Indiana
707 Main St.
Beech Grove, IN 46107
Ph: (317)783-4199
Fax: (317)783-4941
E-mail: maddmom@sbcglobal.net
URL: National Affiliate–www.madd.org/
Local. Victims of drunk driving crashes; concerned citizens. Encourages citizen participation in working towards reform of the drunk driving problem and the prevention of underage drinking. Acts as the voice of victims of drunk driving crashes by speaking on their behalf to communities, businesses, and educational groups. **Affiliated With:** Mothers Against Drunk Driving.

4184 ■ Mothers Against Drunk Driving, Indiana State
711 Main
Beech Grove, IN 46107
Ph: (317)781-6233
Fax: (317)781-6236
Free: (800)247-6233
E-mail: maddin@prodigy.net
URL: National Affiliate–www.madd.org
Contact: Melody Stevens, Exec.Dir.
State. Victims of drunk driving crashes; concerned citizens. Encourages citizen participation in working towards reform of the drunk driving problem and the prevention of underage drinking. Acts as the voice of victims of drunk driving crashes by speaking on their behalf to communities, businesses, and educational groups. **Affiliated With:** Mothers Against Drunk Driving.

4185 ■ National Active and Retired Federal Employees Association - Eastside 2197
322 N 15th Ave.
Beech Grove, IN 46107-1122
Ph: (317)787-8484
URL: National Affiliate–www.narfe.org
Contact: Sherman N. Mcclellan, Contact
Local. Protects the retirement future of employees through education. Informs members on issues affecting the retirement. **Affiliated With:** National Association of Retired Federal Employees.

Berne

4186 ■ American Legion, Berne Post 468
PO Box 312
Berne, IN 46711
Ph: (219)589-2798
Fax: (317)237-9891
URL: National Affiliate–www.legion.org
Local. Affiliated With: American Legion.

4187 ■ Berne Chamber of Commerce (BCC)
PO Box 85
175 W Main St.
Berne, IN 46711-0085
Ph: (260)589-8080
Fax: (260)589-8384
E-mail: tourism@bernein.com
URL: http://www.bernein.com
Contact: Connie Potter, Exec.Dir.
Founded: 1914. **Members:** 175. **Staff:** 3. **Budget:** $61,000. **Local.** Represents industries, professional service firms, and retailers interested in promoting business and community development in Berne, IN. Sponsors Swiss Day Festival. Conducts tours and provides tourist information for sites throughout the U.S. and Switzerland. **Awards: Type:** recognition. **Recipient:** to businesses who have remodeled their buildings to have a Swiss look. **Publications:** *Briefs*, monthly. Newsletter. **Price:** free for members • *Swiss Days*. Brochure • Membership Directory, annual. **Conventions/Meetings:** monthly board meeting - always second Thursday • monthly meeting • annual meeting.

Beverly Shores

4188 ■ American Welding Society, Chicago Section
c/o Paul Burys, Chm.
PO Box 182
Beverly Shores, IN 46301
Ph: (312)296-9553
E-mail: pab.stv@juno.com
URL: National Affiliate–www.aws.org
Contact: Paul Burys, Chm.
Local. Exists to support education, certification, and publishing of welding related documents and specifications. **Affiliated With:** American Welding Society.

Bicknell

4189 ■ American Legion, Indiana Post 32
c/o John T. Miller
118 Washington St.
Bicknell, IN 47512
Ph: (812)735-3388
Fax: (317)237-9891
URL: National Affiliate–www.legion.org
Contact: John T. Miller, Contact
Local. Affiliated With: American Legion.

Bloomfield

4190 ■ American Legion, Memorial Post 196
125 S Washington St.
Bloomfield, IN 47424
Ph: (812)854-1569
Fax: (317)237-9891
URL: National Affiliate–www.legion.org
Local. Affiliated With: American Legion.

4191 ■ Bloomfield Chamber of Commerce
PO Box 144
Bloomfield, IN 47424
Ph: (812)384-9286 (812)659-3778
Fax: (812)384-8936
Contact: Terri Coker, Pres.
Local.

4192 ■ Greene County Coin Club
c/o Donald Nelson
278 W Davis St.
Bloomfield, IN 47424
Ph: (812)384-3916
E-mail: littlek14@hotmail.com
URL: National Affiliate–www.money.org
Contact: Donald Nelson, Contact
Local. Affiliated With: American Numismatic Association.

4193 ■ National Active and Retired Federal Employees Association - Bloomfield 847
RR 7, Box 1554
Bloomfield, IN 47424-8010
Ph: (812)384-4748
URL: National Affiliate–www.narfe.org
Contact: Phyllis J. Parkes, Contact
Local. Protects the retirement future of employees through education. Informs members on issues affecting the retirement. **Affiliated With:** National Association of Retired Federal Employees.

Bloomington

4194 ■ Acacia, Indiana Chapter
702 E Third St.
Bloomington, IN 47406
Ph: (812)331-4100
URL: http://www.indianaacacia.org
State. Affiliated With: Acacia.

4195 ■ American Board of Trial Advocates - Indiana
123 S Coll. Ave.
Bloomington, IN 47404
Ph: (812)332-9451
Fax: (812)331-5321
E-mail: bkgreene@kiva.net
Contact: Betsy K. Greene, Pres.
State. Improves the ethical and technical standards of practice in the field of advocacy. Elevates the standards of integrity, honor and courtesy in the legal profession. Promotes the efficient administration of justice and improvement of the law. **Affiliated With:** American Board of Trial Advocates.

4196 ■ American Chemical Society, Southern Indiana Section
c/o Dr. Cathrine E. Reck, Chair
Indiana Univ., Dept. of Chemistry
800 E Kirkwood Ave.
Bloomington, IN 47405-7102
Ph: (812)855-3972
E-mail: creck@indiana.edu
URL: National Affiliate–acswebcontent.acs.org
Contact: Dr. Cathrine E. Reck, Chair
Local. Represents the interests of individuals dedicated to the advancement of chemistry in all its branches. Provides opportunities for peer interaction and career development. **Affiliated With:** American Chemical Society.

4197 ■ American Legion, Burton Woolery Post 18
1800 W 3rd St.
Bloomington, IN 47404
Ph: (812)334-0500
Fax: (317)237-9891
URL: National Affiliate–www.legion.org
Local. Affiliated With: American Legion.

4198 ■ American Library Association Student Chapter, Indiana University (ALA-SC)
c/o Arianne Hartsell, Pres.
School of Lib. and Info. Sci.
Indiana Univ.
1320 E 10th St.
Bloomington, IN 47405-3907
Ph: (812)855-2018
Fax: (812)855-6166
E-mail: ahartsel@indiana.edu
URL: http://ella.slis.indiana.edu/g/alasc
Contact: Arianne Hartsell, Pres.
Local. Strives to provide the students in the School of Library and Information Science (SLIS) at Indiana University with a variety of beneficial activities. Promotes a sense of community in the organization and within SLIS itself. Supports the professional goals of members. **Telecommunication Services:** electronic bulletin board. **Affiliated With:** American Library Association.

4199 ■ AMVETS, Bloomington Post 2000
5227 W Airport Rd.
Bloomington, IN 47403
Ph: (812)825-2200
URL: http://amvetspost2000.com
Contact: Les Compton, Contact
Local. Affiliated With: AMVETS - American Veterans.

4200 ■ Association for Computing Machinery, Indiana University (ACM)
c/o Bryan Reinicke, Chm.
School of Lib. & Info. Sci.
Maim Lib. 011
Bloomington, IN 47405-1801
Ph: (812)855-1490
Fax: (812)855-6166
E-mail: iubacm@indiana.edu
URL: http://www.acm.indiana.edu
Contact: Bryan Reinicke, Chm.
State. Biological, medical, behavioral, and computer scientists; hospital administrators; programmers and others interested in application of computer methods to biological, behavioral, and medical problems. Stimulates understanding of the use and potential of computers in the Biosciences. **Affiliated With:** Association for Computing Machinery.

4201 ■ Association for Women in Science, Bloomington
c/o Rosemary Hart, Treas.
1422 Elliston Dr.
Bloomington, IN 47401
Fax: (812)335-0365
E-mail: rhart@indiana.edu
URL: http://php.indiana.edu/~awis/awis
Contact: Rosemary Hart, Treas.
Local. Represents professional women and students in life, physical, and social sciences and engineering. Promotes equal opportunities for women to enter the scientific workforce and to achieve their career goals; provides educational information to women planning careers in science; networks with other women's groups; monitors scientific legislation and the status of women in science. **Affiliated With:** Association for Women in Science.

4202 ■ Association of Women's Health, Obstetric and Neonatal Nurses - Bloomington Chapter
c/o Cathy Greene
310 Sewell Rd.
Bloomington, IN 47408
E-mail: cathygreene2@aol.com
URL: National Affiliate–www.awhonn.org
Contact: Andrea Headdy, Coor.
Local. Represents registered nurses and other health care providers who specialize in obstetric, women's health, and neonatal nursing. Advances the nursing profession by providing nurses with information and support to help them deliver quality care for women and newborns. **Affiliated With:** Association of Women's Health, Obstetric and Neonatal Nurses.

4203 ■ Bloomington Bicycle Club (BBC)
PO Box 463
Bloomington, IN 47402
E-mail: edmonds@indiana.edu
URL: http://www.bloomington.in.us/~bbc
Contact: Allan Edmonds, Pres.
Founded: 1976. **Members:** 120. **Membership Dues:** single, $15 (annual). **Local.** Promotes bicycling in

Monroe County, IN. **Additional Websites:** http://bloomingtonbicycleclub.org. **Affiliated With:** International Mountain Bicycling Association. **Publications:** *Bloomington Bicycle Club Map Packet*. Directory. Contains 20 maps of 27 routes that originate in Bloomington, IN.

4204 ■ Bloomington Board of Realtors
PO Box 1478
Bloomington, IN 47402
Ph: (812)339-1301
Fax: (812)333-7497
E-mail: sgraham@homefinder.org
URL: National Affiliate–www.realtor.org
Contact: Susie Graham, Exec. Officer
Local. Strives to develop real estate business practices. Advocates the right to own, use and transfer real property. Provides a facility for professional development, research and exchange of information among members and to the general public. **Affiliated With:** National Association of Realtors.

4205 ■ Bloomington Community Park and Recreation Foundation
PO Box 848
Bloomington, IN 47402
Ph: (812)349-3700
Fax: (812)349-3705
Contact: Theodore R. Deppe, Pres.
Founded: 1967. **Members:** 20. **Budget:** $89,954. **Local.** Supports parks and recreation programs and activities. **Conventions/Meetings:** annual meeting, for Total Foundation Board - always December. Bloomington, IN - Avg. Attendance: 30.

4206 ■ Bloomington Convention and Visitors Bureau
2855 N Walnut St.
Bloomington, IN 47404
Ph: (812)334-8900
Fax: (812)334-2344
Free: (866)333-0088
E-mail: cvb@visitbloomington.com
URL: http://www.visitbloomington.com
Contact: Valerie Pena, Exec.Dir.
Founded: 1976. **Nonmembership. Local.** Promotes convention business and tourism in Monroe County, IN. **Additional Websites:** http://www.visitgaybloomington.com. **Publications:** *Visitor's Guides*, periodic.

4207 ■ Bloomington FlyingFish Walking Club
c/o Margaret Dalle-Ave
3114 N Ramble Rd. W
Bloomington, IN 47408-1079
Ph: (812)339-7549
E-mail: dalleave@sbcglobal.net
URL: http://www.bloomington.in.us/~flyinfsh/index.html
Contact: Margaret Dalle-Ave, Contact
Local. Affiliated With: American Volkssport Association. **Formerly:** (2005) Bloomington Flying Fish Volkssports.

4208 ■ Bloomington Meals on Wheels
714 S Rogers St.
Bloomington, IN 47403
Ph: (812)323-4982
URL: http://www.bloomington.in.us/~meals
Local. Affiliated With: Meals on Wheels Association of America.

4209 ■ Bloomington Old Time Music and Dance Group (BOTMDG)
PO Box 3238
Bloomington, IN 47402
E-mail: botmdg@bloomington.in.us
URL: http://www.bloomington.in.us/~botmdg
Contact: David Ernst, Board Coor.
Membership Dues: regular, $12 (annual) • senior, student, $1 (annual). **Local.** Dedicated to the preservation of the Contra dance tradition. **Affiliated With:** Country Dance and Song Society.

4210 ■ Bloomington Volunteer Network
c/o Ms. Bet Savich, Dir.
401 N Morton St., Ste.260
PO Box 100
Bloomington, IN 47402
Ph: (812)349-3472
Fax: (812)349-3483
E-mail: volunteer@bloomington.in.gov
URL: http://www.bloomington.in.gov/volunteer
Contact: Ms. Bet Savich, Dir.
Founded: 1980. **Staff:** 3. **Local.** Volunteer center for Bloomington and Monroe County, IN. Promotes and facilitates volunteer activities throughout the community. Functions as an umbrella agency, cooperating with other agencies, non-profits corporations, businesses, and Indiana University to mobilize the effective use of volunteers in resolving community problems. Supports, guides, and assists agencies in recruiting, utilizing, and managing volunteers.

4211 ■ Bloomington - Wyldlife
4111 W Broadway Ave.
Bloomington, IN 47404
Ph: (812)345-3352
URL: http://sites.younglife.org/_layouts/ylext/default.aspx?ID=C-911
Local. Affiliated With: Young Life.

4212 ■ Children's Organ Transplant Association
2501 Cota Dr.
Bloomington, IN 47403
Ph: (812)336-8872
Free: (800)366-2682
URL: http://www.cota.org
Local.

4213 ■ Downtown Bloomington Commission
302 S Coll. Ave.
Bloomington, IN 47403
Ph: (812)336-3681
E-mail: downtown@downtownbloomington.com
URL: http://www.downtownbloomington.com
Local.

4214 ■ Downtown Kiwanis Club of Bloomington
PO Box 2121
Bloomington, IN 47402
Ph: (765)342-2915
URL: http://www.monroe.lib.in.us/databases/cominfo/B10004816.html
Contact: Bob Nelson, Treas.
Local.

4215 ■ EarthSave, Bloomington
PO Box 1764
Bloomington, IN 47402-1764
Ph: (812)33-EARTH
Fax: (801)457-8687
E-mail: earthsave@yahoo.com
Contact: Scot Curry, Chm.
Founded: 1997. **Members:** 12. **Membership Dues:** individual, $35 (annual) • family, $50 (annual) • student, senior, $20 (annual). **Affiliated With:** EarthSave International.

4216 ■ Eastern (Greene) - Young Life
4111 W Broadway Ave.
Bloomington, IN 47404
Ph: (812)345-3352
URL: http://sites.younglife.org/_layouts/ylext/default.aspx?ID=C-2999
Local. Affiliated With: Young Life.

4217 ■ Eastern - Young Life
4111 W Broadway Ave.
Bloomington, IN 47404
Ph: (812)336-9091
URL: http://whereis.younglife.org/FriendlyUrlRedirector.aspx?ID=C-2999
Local.

4218 ■ Edgewood - Young Life
4111 W Broadway Ave.
Bloomington, IN 47404
Ph: (812)336-9091
URL: http://whereis.younglife.org/FriendlyUrlRedirector.aspx?ID=C-4208
Local.

4219 ■ Funeral Consumers Alliance of Bloomington, Indiana
PO Box 7232
Bloomington, IN 47407-7232
Ph: (812)335-6633
E-mail: fcab@atsbloomington.in.us
URL: http://www.bloomington.in.us/~fcab
Nonmembership. Local. Group of individuals engaged in the funeral business who dedicate themselves to informing the public about state regulations and local options concerning burials, alternative funeral services options and promoting the dignity of funeral rites and memorial services.

4220 ■ Girl Scouts of Tulip Trace Council
PO Box 5485
Bloomington, IN 47407-5485
Ph: (812)336-6804
Fax: (812)333-1606
Free: (800)467-6804
E-mail: gscouts@tuliptrace.org
URL: http://www.tuliptrace.org
Local. Young girls and adult volunteers, corporate, government and individual supporters. Strives to develop potential and leadership skills among its members. Conducts trainings, educational programs and outdoor activities.

4221 ■ Girls Incorporated of Monroe County
1108 W 8th St.
Bloomington, IN 47404
Ph: (812)336-7313
Fax: (812)336-7317
E-mail: info@girlsinc-monroe.org
URL: http://www.bloomington.in.us/~girlsinc
Contact: Dorothy Granger, Exec.Dir.
Local. Conducts daily programs in careers and life planning, health and sexuality, leadership and communication, sports and adventure, and life skills and self-reliance. Works to create an environment in which girls can learn and grow to their fullest potential. **Affiliated With:** Girls Inc.

4222 ■ Graduate Program in Neural Science, Indiana University, Bloomington Chapter
Prog. in Neural Sci.
Indiana Univ.
Psychology Bldg., Rm. 343
1101 E 10th St.
Bloomington, IN 47405-7007
Ph: (812)855-7756
Fax: (812)855-4520
E-mail: iuneuron@indiana.edu
URL: http://www.indiana.edu/~neurosci
Contact: J. Michael Walker, Dir.
Local. Affiliated With: Society for Neuroscience. **Formerly:** (2005) Society for Neuroscience, Indiana University, Bloomington Chapter.

4223 ■ Greater Bloomington Chamber of Commerce (GBCC)
400 W 7th St., Ste.102
PO Box 1302
Bloomington, IN 47402-1302
Ph: (812)336-6381
Fax: (812)336-0651
E-mail: showard@chamber.bloomington.in.us
URL: http://www.chamber.bloomington.in.us
Contact: Steve Howard, Pres.
Founded: 1915. **Members:** 1,050. **Staff:** 7. **Budget:** $800,000. **Local.** Promotes business and community development in the Bloomington, IN area. **Affiliated With:** U.S. Chamber of Commerce. **Publications:** *Business Network*, monthly. Newspaper • Directory, annual. Contains a business network and a listing of all chamber members. **Price:** included in membership dues; $10.00 for nonmembers. **Conventions/**

Meetings: annual meeting • periodic Tech Exposition • annual trade show.

4224 ■ Habitat for Humanity of Monroe County, Indiana
1119 N Lindbergh Dr.
Bloomington, IN 47404
Ph: (812)331-4069
E-mail: habitat@bloomington.in.us
URL: http://www.bloomington.in.us/~habitat
Contact: Doug Booher, Pres.
Local. Affiliated With: Habitat for Humanity International.

4225 ■ Hoosier Hills Estate Planning Council (HHEPC)
c/o Eric Slotegraaf, Pres.
400 W 7th St., Ste.104
Bloomington, IN 47404
Ph: (812)339-8537 (812)332-4200
Fax: (812)331-4511
E-mail: kmcconahay@yahoo.com
URL: National Affiliate–councils.naepc.org
Contact: Eric Slotegraaf, Pres.
Local. Fosters understanding of the relationship between the functions of professionals in the estate planning field. Engages in study, discussions, meetings and additional activities which will continuously improve the services the members deliver to clients. Encourages cooperation among members. Advances public knowledge of the concept of estate planning in Bloomington area, IN. **Affiliated With:** National Association of Estate Planners and Councils.

4226 ■ Indiana Association on Higher Education and Disability
c/o Margaret Londergan, Pres.-Elect/VP
Indiana Univ.
2711 E 10th St.
Bloomington, IN 47401
E-mail: londerga@indiana.edu
URL: http://www.ahead.org/about/regional_affiliates/indiana1.htm
Contact: Margaret Londergan, Pres.-Elect/VP
State. Represents individuals interested in promoting the equal rights and opportunities of disabled post-secondary students, staff, faculty and graduates. Provides educational and professional development opportunities for persons with disabilities in postsecondary education. Encourages and supports legislation for the benefit of disabled students. **Affiliated With:** Association on Higher Education and Disability.

4227 ■ Indiana Association of Scholars (IAS)
c/o Robert H. Heidt, Pres.
Indiana Univ.
School of Law, Rm. 266
211 S Indiana Ave.
Bloomington, IN 47405-7001
Ph: (812)855-7272
Fax: (812)855-0555
E-mail: heidt@indiana.edu
URL: http://rasmusen.org/ias
Contact: Robert H. Heidt, Pres.
State. Works to enrich the substance and to strengthen the integrity of scholarship and teaching. Provides a forum for the discussion of curricular issues and trends in higher education.

4228 ■ Indiana Mortgage Bankers Association, South Central Chapter
The Peoples State Bank
200 E Kirkwood Ave.
Bloomington, IN 47408
Ph: (812)323-3221
Fax: (812)323-3219
E-mail: jjohnson@peoples-bank.com
URL: http://www.indianamba.org/Chapters/South_Central.htm
Contact: Janet Johnson, Pres.
Local. Promotes fair and ethical lending practices and fosters professional excellence among real estate finance employees. Seeks to create an environment that enables members to invest in communities and achieve their business objectives. **Affiliated With:** Mortgage Bankers Association.

4229 ■ Indiana Recycling Coalition (IRC)
PO Box 7108
Bloomington, IN 47407-7108
Free: (877)283-9550
E-mail: info@indianarecycling.org
URL: http://www.indianarecycling.org
Contact: Michelle Cohen, Exec.Dir.
Founded: 1989. **Members:** 150. **Staff:** 1. **Budget:** $90,000. **Regional Groups:** 2. **State Groups:** 1. **State.** Concerned citizens, state and local government officials, business, industry, and environmental groups. Promotes increased use of reusable, recyclable, and recycled materials. Serves as an information clearinghouse and networking service. **Publications:** Newsletter, quarterly • Manuals, periodic. **Conventions/Meetings:** annual conference (exhibits) - always spring.

4230 ■ Indiana Student Public Interest Research Group (INPIRG)
IMU 470A
Indiana Univ.
Bloomington, IN 47405
Ph: (812)856-4128
Fax: (812)856-4128
E-mail: info@inpirg.org
URL: http://www.inpirg.org
Founded: 1996. **Members:** 3,500. **Membership Dues:** regular, $10 (annual). **Staff:** 1. **Budget:** $36,000. **State.**

4231 ■ Indiana Transportation Association
c/o Kent McDaniel, Exec.Dir.
826 E 8th St.
Bloomington, IN 47408-3891
Ph: (812)855-8143
State.

4232 ■ Indiana University College Democrats
c/o Jared Fallick, Pres.
107 S Indiana Ave.
Bloomington, IN 47405-7000
Ph: (812)855-4848
E-mail: iudems@indiana.edu
URL: http://www.indiana.edu/~iudems
Local.

4233 ■ Indiana University - Environmental Law Society
Indiana Univ. School of Law
211 S Indiana Ave., Rm. 003
Bloomington, IN 47405
Ph: (812)856-5277
E-mail: els@indiana.edu
URL: http://www.law.indiana.edu/students/groups/els/index.shtml
Contact: Matthew Melick, Pres.
Local. Seeks to improve the educational experience of all Indiana University law students interested in environmental law.

4234 ■ Indiana University Figure Skating Club
IUFSC - Student Activities Off.
IMU Rm. 371
Bloomington, IN 47405
E-mail: iufigureskating@yahoo.com
URL: National Affiliate–www.usfigureskating.org
Local. Provides programs to encourage participation and achievement in the sport of figure skating on ice. Defines and maintains uniform standards of skating proficiency. Organizes and sponsors competitions and exhibitions for the purpose of stimulating interest in figure skating. **Affiliated With:** United States Figure Skating Association.

4235 ■ Indiana University Student Association (IUSA)
107 S Indiana Ave. Memorial Union, Rm. No. 387
Bloomington, IN 47405
Ph: (812)855-4872
Fax: (812)855-2846
E-mail: iusa@indiana.edu
URL: http://www.indiana.edu/~iusa/
Contact: Casey B. Cox, Student Body Pres.
Local. Student government of Indiana University. Serves as the voice of students to the administration and provides resources and services to students.

4236 ■ Indiana Young Democrats
c/o John Zody, Pres.
807 W 6th St., No. 1
Bloomington, IN 47404-3633
Ph: (812)330-6037
E-mail: johnczody@aol.com
URL: http://www.yda.org/CMS/State/18
State.

4237 ■ International Alliance of Theatrical Stage Employees, Moving Picture Technicians, Artists, M 618
1600 N Willis Dr., No. 192
Bloomington, IN 47404
Ph: (812)331-7472
Fax: (812)331-8949
E-mail: ba618@iatse618.com
URL: http://www.iatse618.com
Contact: Mark Serris, Sec.
Founded: 1920. **Members:** 50. **Local. Affiliated With:** International Alliance of Theatrical Stage Employees, Moving Picture Technicians, Artists and Allied Crafts of the United States, Its Territories and Canada.

4238 ■ IUB Latino Faculty and Staff Council
c/o Belinda De La Rosa, PhD, Chair Latino Faculty
1800 10th St.
Bloomington, IN 47406-7511
Ph: (812)856-0347
Fax: (812)856-5152
E-mail: lfasc@indiana.edu
URL: http://www.iub.edu/~lfasc
Contact: Belinda De La Rosa PhD, Chair Latino Faculty
Founded: 2002. **Members:** 135. **Membership Dues:** faculty, $15 (annual) • staff, $10 (annual). **Staff:** 4. **Languages:** English, Portuguese, Spanish. **Local.** Individuals interested in promoting a forum for understanding the issues concerning the Latino academic community; builds fellowship and strengthens communication through collaboration with the university administration, faculty, students and staff to address and improve the issues regarding recruitment, retention and promotion of members. **Computer Services:** database, maintains current directory of Latino faculty and professional staff • mailing lists.

4239 ■ Mental Health Alliance of Monroe County
120 W 7th St., Ste.21
Bloomington, IN 47404
Ph: (812)339-1551
Fax: (812)339-3025
E-mail: mha@bloomington.in.us
URL: http://www.mentalhealthassociation.com
Contact: Ms. Donna Graves, Exec.Dir.
Local. Seeks to promote mental health and prevent mental health disorders. Improves mental health of Americans through advocacy, public education, research and service. **Affiliated With:** Mental Health Association in Indiana; National Mental Health Association.

4240 ■ Military Officers Association of America, Bloomington Area Chapter
711 Whitehorn Pl.
Bloomington, IN 47403
Ph: (812)824-2818
E-mail: dickworsena@yahoo.com
URL: National Affiliate–www.moaa.org
Contact: CDR Richard Worsena, Contact
Local. Affiliated With: Military Officers Association of America.

4241 ■ Monroe County Apartment Association (MCAA)
PO Box 202
Bloomington, IN 47402
Ph: (812)331-7368
E-mail: director@mcaaonline.org
URL: http://www.mcaaonline.org
Contact: Linda Brown, Pres.
Local. Affiliated With: National Apartment Association.

4242 ■ Mother Hubbard's Cupboard (MHC)
1010 S Walnut, Ste.G
Bloomington, IN 47401
Ph: (812)355-6843
E-mail: mhc@bloomington.in.us
URL: http://www.bloomington.in.us/~mhc
Contact: Libby Yarnelle, Dir.
Founded: 1998. **Local.** Works as a volunteer-run food pantry that aims to provide healthful, wholesome foods to people in need. Coordinates area community garden projects.

4243 ■ Muslim Student Union - Indiana University, Bloomington
Indiana Memorial Union No. 476
Bloomington, IN 47405
E-mail: msuweb@indiana.edu
URL: National Affiliate–www.msa-natl.org
Local. Muslim students in North America. Seeks to advance the interests of members; works to enable members to practice Islam as a complete way of life. **Affiliated With:** Muslim Students Association of the United States and Canada. **Formerly:** (2005) Muslim Students' Association - Indiana University, Bloomington.

4244 ■ NAIFA-Bloomington
c/o Ryan A. Pitner, Pres.
PO Box 123
Bloomington, IN 47402-0123
Ph: (812)332-1000
Fax: (812)332-1033
E-mail: lydiabr1@sbcglobal.net
URL: National Affiliate–naifa.org
Contact: Ryan A. Pitner, Pres.
Local. Represents the interests of insurance and financial advisors. Advocates for a positive legislative and regulatory environment. Enhances business and professional skills of members. **Affiliated With:** National Association of Insurance and Financial Advisors.

4245 ■ National Active and Retired Federal Employees Association - Bloomington 580
604 W Guy Ave.
Bloomington, IN 47403-2919
Ph: (812)332-4023
URL: National Affiliate–www.narfe.org
Contact: Dorothy M. Riensch, Contact
Local. Protects the retirement future of employees through education. Informs members on issues affecting the retirement. **Affiliated With:** National Association of Retired Federal Employees.

4246 ■ National Association for the Advancement of Colored People, Monroe County Branch
PO Box 243
Bloomington, IN 47402-0243
Ph: (812)332-1513
E-mail: wavdlv@sbcglobal.net
URL: http://www.bloomington.in.us/~mcbnaacp
Contact: Clarence W. Gilliam, Pres.
Local.

4247 ■ National Association of Home Builders of the U.S., Monroe County Builders Association
c/o Nancy Baldwin
Local No. 1508
409 S Walnut St., Ste.C
Bloomington, IN 47401-4613
Ph: (812)332-7480
Fax: (812)332-7482
E-mail: mcba@bluemarble.net
URL: National Affiliate–www.nahb.org
Contact: Nancy Baldwin, Contact
Local. Single and multifamily home builders, commercial builders, and others associated with the building industry. **Affiliated With:** National Association of Home Builders.

4248 ■ National Speleological Society, Bloomington, Indiana Grotto
c/o Sam Frushour, Treas.
513 W Dixie St.
Bloomington, IN 47403-4707
Ph: (812)339-2130
E-mail: frushour@indiana.edu
URL: http://www.caves.org/grotto/big/big.html
Contact: Sam Frushour, Treas.
Local. Seeks to study, explore and conserve cave and karst resources. Protects access to caves and promotes responsible caving. Encourages responsible management of caves and their unique environments. **Affiliated With:** National Speleological Society.

4249 ■ North - Young Life
4111 W Broadway Ave.
Bloomington, IN 47404
Ph: (812)336-9091
URL: http://whereis.younglife.org/FriendlyUrlRedirector.aspx?ID=C-909
Local.

4250 ■ PFLAG Bloomington
PO Box 8152
Bloomington, IN 47407
Ph: (812)332-5057
E-mail: pflag@indiana.edu
URL: http://www.geocities.com/pflagbloomington
Contact: Judy Schroeder, Co-Chair
Local. Affiliated With: Parents, Families, and Friends of Lesbians and Gays.

4251 ■ Phi Theta Kappa, Alpha Rho Sigma Chapter - Ivy Tech State College
c/o Jennie Vaughan
200 Daniels Way
Bloomington, IN 47404
Ph: (812)332-1559
E-mail: jvaughan@ivytech.edu
URL: http://www.ptk.org/directories/chapters/IN/9739-1.htm
Contact: Jennie Vaughan, Advisor
Local.

4252 ■ Psi Chi, National Honor Society in Psychology - Indiana University Bloomington
c/o Dept. of Psychology
1101 E 10th St.
Bloomington, IN 47405-7007
Ph: (812)855-2012 (812)856-5551
Fax: (812)855-4691
E-mail: scthomps@indiana.edu
URL: National Affiliate–www.psichi.org
Local. Affiliated With: Psi Chi, National Honor Society in Psychology.

4253 ■ Rental Purchase Dealers Association (RPDA)
c/o Christy Kuntz
5109 N Hwy. 37
Bloomington, IN 47404
Ph: (812)333-7496
Fax: (812)331-5527
E-mail: ckwingnut@aol.com
URL: http://www.rpda.org
State.

4254 ■ RSVP of Monroe and Owen Counties
7500 W Reeves Rd.
Bloomington, IN 47404
Ph: (812)876-3383
Fax: (812)876-9922
Free: (800)844-1010
E-mail: ssarin-rsvp@area10.bloomington.in.us
URL: http://www.bloomington.in.us/~rsvp
Members: 450. **Staff:** 4. **Local. Awards:** Presidential Volunteer Service Award. **Frequency:** annual. **Type:** recognition. **Recipient:** to volunteers who serve a particular number of hours qualify to receive a volunteer service award from the president of the united states. **Affiliated With:** Retired and Senior Volunteer Program. **Publications:** *RSVP Newsletter*, bimonthly. Newsletters. Newsletter designed for people 55 and over. **Circulation:** 600.

4255 ■ Sassafras Audubon Society (SAS)
PO Box 85
Bloomington, IN 47402-0085
E-mail: contactsas@yahoo.com
URL: http://www.bloomington.in.us/~audubon
Local. Works to conserve and restore natural ecosystems, focusing on birds and other wildlife for the benefit of humanity and the earth's biological diversity. **Affiliated With:** National Audubon Society.

4256 ■ SCORE Bloomington
c/o James Rusie, Chm.
216 W Allen St., Ste.133
Bloomington, IN 47403
Ph: (812)335-7344
E-mail: score527@sbcglobal.net
URL: http://www.bloomingtonscore.org
Local. Affiliated With: SCORE.

4257 ■ Society for Applied Spectroscopy, Indiana (ISSAS)
Indiana Univ.
Dept. of Chemistry
Bloomington, IN 47405
Ph: (812)855-7905
E-mail: issas@indiana.edu
URL: http://www.indiana.edu/~issas
Contact: Gerardo Gamez, Chm.
Local. Affiliated With: Society for Applied Spectroscopy.

4258 ■ South - Young Life
4111 W Broadway Ave.
Bloomington, IN 47404
Ph: (812)336-9091
URL: http://whereis.younglife.org/FriendlyUrlRedirector.aspx?ID=C-910
Local.

4259 ■ Southern Hills Youth for Christ
PO Box 1854
Bloomington, IN 47402
Ph: (812)331-2366
Fax: (812)331-2358
URL: National Affiliate–www.yfc.net
Local. Affiliated With: Youth for Christ/U.S.A.

4260 ■ Southern Indiana Daylily, Hosta, Daffodil, and Iris Society
5289 S Harrell Rd.
Bloomington, IN 47401
Ph: (812)824-9216
E-mail: mecline@insightbb.com
URL: National Affiliate–www.daylilies.org
Contact: Marilla Schowmeyer, Past Pres.
Membership Dues: individual, $10 (annual) • family, $15 (annual). **Local.**

4261 ■ Stone Belt Arc - Monroe County
2815 E Tenth St.
Bloomington, IN 47408
Ph: (812)332-2168
URL: National Affiliate–www.thearc.org
Local. Parents, professional workers, and others interested in individuals with mental retardation. Works to promote services, research, public understanding, and legislation for people with mental

retardation and their families. **Affiliated With:** Arc of the United States.

4262 ■ United Way Community Service of Monroe County
441 S Coll. Ave.
Bloomington, IN 47403
Ph: (812)334-8370
Fax: (812)334-8387
E-mail: uw@monroeunitedway.org
URL: http://www.monroeunitedway.org
Contact: Barry Lessow, Exec.Dir.
Local. Affiliated With: United Way of America.

4263 ■ USA Dance - Heartland Chapter
c/o Larry Gogel
PO Box 2085
Bloomington, IN 47402-2085
Ph: (812)272-6102
E-mail: heartlandreg@hotmail.com
URL: http://indyusabda.org
Contact: Larry Gogel, Contact
Local. Encourages and promotes the physical, mental and social benefits of partner dancing. Organizes and supports programs for the recreational enjoyment of ballroom dancing. Creates opportunities for the general public to participate in ballroom dancing and DanceSport.

4264 ■ USA Diving - Indiana Diving
1601 Law Ln.
Bloomington, IN 47405-2111
Ph: (812)855-5710
E-mail: jhuber@indiana.edu
URL: National Affiliate–www.usdiving.org
Contact: Jeff Huber, Contact
State. Affiliated With: USA Diving.

4265 ■ Wildlife Society - Indiana Chapter
c/o Zack Walker
Div. of Fish and Wildlife
553 E Miller Rd.
Bloomington, IN 47401
Ph: (317)232-4098
E-mail: wfaatz@dnr.in.gov
URL: http://www.agriculture.purdue.edu/fnr/itws/index.htm
Contact: Wayne Faatz, Pres.
State. Affiliated With: The Wildlife Society.

4266 ■ Young Life Southern Hills
4111 W Broadway Ave.
Bloomington, IN 47404
Ph: (812)336-9091
URL: http://whereis.younglife.org/FriendlyUrlRedirector.aspx?ID=A-IN35
Local.

Bluffton

4267 ■ Adams, Jay and Wells County Youth for Christ
PO Box 431
Bluffton, IN 46714
Ph: (260)824-1330
Fax: (260)824-1374
URL: National Affiliate–www.yfc.net
Local. Affiliated With: Youth for Christ/U.S.A.

4268 ■ American Legion, Grover Sheets Post 111
111 W Washington St.
Bluffton, IN 46714
Ph: (219)824-3815
Fax: (317)237-9891
URL: National Affiliate–www.legion.org
Local. Affiliated With: American Legion.

4269 ■ Mental Health Association in Wells County
c/o B.J. Gray
223 W Washington St.
Bluffton, IN 46714-1996
Ph: (219)824-1514
URL: http://www.mentalhealthassociation.com
Contact: B.J. Gray, Contact
Local. Seeks to promote mental health and prevent mental health disorders. Improves mental health of Americans through advocacy, public education, research and service. **Affiliated With:** Mental Health Association in Indiana; National Mental Health Association.

4270 ■ United Way of Wells County
112 S Main St.
Bluffton, IN 46714
Ph: (260)824-5589
Fax: (260)824-2217
E-mail: mail@unitedwaywells.org
URL: http://www.unitedwaywells.org
Contact: Pamela Beckford, Exec.Dir.
Local. Affiliated With: United Way of America.

4271 ■ Wells County Chamber of Commerce
211 W Water St.
Bluffton, IN 46714
Ph: (260)824-0510
Fax: (260)824-5871
E-mail: coc@blufftonwellschamber.com
URL: http://www.blufftonwellschamber.com
Contact: Suzanne Huffman, Dir.
Local. Promotes the civic and economic development in Wells County. **Computer Services:** Information services, membership directory. **Formerly:** (1999) Bluffton Chamber of Commerce. **Publications:** Newsletter, monthly. Contains updates in the community and in the chamber. **Advertising:** accepted.

Boonville

4272 ■ American Ex-Prisoners of War, Southern Indiana Chapter
c/o Guy M. Stephens
5477 Yankeetown Rd.
Boonville, IN 47601
Ph: (812)853-8223
URL: National Affiliate–www.axpow.org
Local. Affiliated With: American Ex-Prisoners of War.

4273 ■ American Legion, Warrick Post 200
PO Box 524
Boonville, IN 47601
Ph: (812)893-2200
Fax: (317)237-9891
URL: National Affiliate–www.legion.org
Local. Affiliated With: American Legion.

4274 ■ Antique Automobile Club of America, Lower Ohio Valley Evansville Region (AACA LOVER)
c/o Jerry D. Smith, Pres.
855 Mt. Gilead Rd.
Boonville, IN 47601
Ph: (812)897-3995
E-mail: jwolf@vinu.edu
URL: http://beaver.vinu.edu/lover.htm
Contact: Jerry D. Smith, Pres.
Local. Collectors, hobbyists, and others interested in the preservation, maintenance, and restoration of automobiles and in automotive history. **Affiliated With:** Antique Automobile Club of America.

4275 ■ Navy Club of Warrick County - Ship No. 237
445 State Rd. 261
Boonville, IN 47601
Ph: (812)897-5464
URL: National Affiliate–www.navyclubusa.org
Contact: Jack Forester, Commander
Local. Represents individuals who are, or have been, in the active service of the U.S. Navy, Naval Reserve, Marine Corps, Marine Corps Reserve, and Coast Guard. Promotes and encourages further public interest in the U.S. Navy and its history. Upholds the spirit and ideals of the U.S. Navy. Acts as a public forum for members' views on national defense. Assists the Navy Recruiting Command whenever and wherever possible. Conducts charitable activities. **Affiliated With:** Navy Club of the United States of America.

4276 ■ Warrick County Chamber of Commerce
224 W Main St.
PO Box 377
Boonville, IN 47601-0377
Ph: (812)897-2340
Fax: (812)897-2360
E-mail: warco@sigecom.net
URL: http://www.warrickcounty.com
Contact: Tracy Holder, Exec.Dir.
Local. Promotes business and community development in Warrick County, IL.

4277 ■ Young Life Boonville
PO Box 436
Boonville, IN 47601
Ph: (812)853-9052
Fax: (812)853-9690
URL: http://whereis.younglife.org/FriendlyUrlRedirector.aspx?ID=A-IN40
Local.

Borden

4278 ■ Indiana Optometric Association, Southeastern District
c/o Polly E. Hendricks, OD, Trustee
207 Money Hollow Rd.
Borden, IN 47106
Ph: (812)288-8566
Fax: (812)284-2326
E-mail: phendricksod@insightbb.com
URL: http://www.ioa.org
Contact: Polly E. Hendricks OD, Trustee
Local. Aims to improve the quality, availability and accessibility of eye and vision care. Promotes high standards of patient care. Monitors and promotes legislation concerning the scope of optometric practice and other issues relevant to eye/vision care. **Affiliated With:** American Optometric Association; Indiana Optometric Association.

Boswell

4279 ■ American Legion, Boswell Post 476
PO Box 476
Boswell, IN 47921
Ph: (317)869-5018
Fax: (317)237-9891
URL: National Affiliate–www.legion.org
Local. Affiliated With: American Legion.

Bourbon

4280 ■ American Legion, Bourbon Post 424
202 S Main St.
Bourbon, IN 46504
Ph: (219)342-9125
Fax: (317)237-9891
URL: National Affiliate–www.legion.org
Local. Affiliated With: American Legion.

4281 ■ Bourbon Lions Club
510 Maplewood Dr.
Bourbon, IN 46504
Ph: (574)858-2245
E-mail: bourbonlions@yahoo.com
URL: http://bourbonlionsin.lionwap.org
Local. Affiliated With: Lions Clubs International.

Brazil

4282 ■ American Legion, Clay County Post 2
1013 S Forest Ave.
Brazil, IN 47834
Ph: (812)443-8611
Fax: (317)237-9891
URL: National Affiliate–www.legion.org
Local. **Affiliated With:** American Legion.

4283 ■ Clay County Chamber of Commerce
PO Box 23
Brazil, IN 47834-0023
Ph: (812)448-8457
Fax: (812)448-9957
E-mail: claycoc@claynet.com
Contact: Cheryl Myers, Sec.
Local.

4284 ■ Mental Health Association in Clay County
c/o Pat Heffner
1211 E Natl. Ave.
Brazil, IN 47834
Ph: (812)448-8801
URL: http://www.mentalhealthassociation.com
Contact: Pat Heffner, Contact
Local. Seeks to promote mental health and prevent mental health disorders. Improves mental health of Americans through advocacy, public education, research and service. **Affiliated With:** Mental Health Association in Indiana; National Mental Health Association.

4285 ■ Terre Haute Kennel Club
8141 S Fallen Rock Rd.
Brazil, IN 47834-9528
URL: http://home.earthlink.net/~superdoo71/thkc
Contact: Judy Proctor, Corresponding Sec.
Local.

Bremen

4286 ■ American Legion, Indiana Post 191
c/o Otho B. Place
PO Box 351
Bremen, IN 46506
Ph: (219)546-4959
Fax: (317)237-9891
URL: National Affiliate–www.legion.org
Contact: Otho B. Place, Contact
Local. **Affiliated With:** American Legion.

4287 ■ Bremen Chamber of Commerce (BCC)
PO Box 125
Bremen, IN 46506
Ph: (574)546-2044
Fax: (574)546-5487
E-mail: townbremenin@skyenet.net
Contact: D. Elliott, Operations Dir.
Members: 100. **Local**. Promotes business and community development in Bremen, IN. Conducts charitable programs. **Publications:** Directory, annual • Newsletter, bimonthly. **Conventions/Meetings:** annual meeting - always fall.

4288 ■ Michiana Miniature Guild
c/o Carol Hudson
3782 W Shores Dr.
Bremen, IN 46506
Ph: (574)546-2046
E-mail: jpcdhudson@myvine.com
URL: http://www.miniatures.org/states/IN.html
Contact: Carol Hudson, Contact
Regional. **Affiliated With:** National Association of Miniature Enthusiasts.

4289 ■ Pheasants Forever Central Indiana, Marshall County
339 Hope Blvd.
Bremen, IN 46506
Ph: (219)546-5470
URL: http://pfcic.org
Contact: Dennis Enbrecht, Pres.
Local. **Affiliated With:** Pheasants Forever.

Bristol

4290 ■ ADEC Resources for Independence
PO Box 398
Bristol, IN 46507
Ph: (574)848-7451
Fax: (574)848-5917
Free: (877)342-8954
URL: http://www.adecinc.com
Contact: Dennis Blyly, Chairperson
Founded: 1952. **Local**.

4291 ■ American Legion, Charles Harker Post 143
905 Maple St.
Bristol, IN 46507
Ph: (317)630-1300
Fax: (317)237-9891
URL: National Affiliate–www.legion.org
Local. **Affiliated With:** American Legion.

4292 ■ Pheasants Forever Central Indiana, Elkhart County
19911 Willowbend Blvd.
Bristol, IN 46507
URL: http://pfcic.org
Contact: Derrick Hendricks, Pres.
Local. **Affiliated With:** Pheasants Forever.

Brook

4293 ■ American Legion, Brook Post 364
PO Box 68
Brook, IN 47922
Ph: (219)275-7252
Fax: (317)237-9891
URL: National Affiliate–www.legion.org
Local. **Affiliated With:** American Legion.

Brookston

4294 ■ American Legion, Indiana Post 251
c/o James R. Currie
304 N Indiana 43
Brookston, IN 47923
Ph: (317)563-3776
Fax: (317)237-9891
URL: National Affiliate–www.legion.org
Contact: James R. Currie, Contact
Local. **Affiliated With:** American Legion.

Brookville

4295 ■ Achieva Resources Center Plant 3 - Franklin County
437 Mill St.
Brookville, IN 47012
Ph: (765)647-6055
Fax: (765)647-4044
URL: http://www.achievaresources.org
Contact: Dan Stewart, Pres./CEO
Membership Dues: single, $20 • family, $30 • consumer, $2. **Local**.

4296 ■ American Legion, Indiana Post 77
c/o Bernard Hurst
1290 Fairfield Ave.
Brookville, IN 47012
Ph: (317)647-4613
Fax: (317)237-9891
URL: National Affiliate–www.legion.org
Contact: Bernard Hurst, Contact
Local. **Affiliated With:** American Legion.

4297 ■ American Legion, St. Joseph Post 464
28866 Post 464 Rd.
Brookville, IN 47012
Ph: (812)537-2900
Fax: (317)237-9891
URL: National Affiliate–www.legion.org
Local. **Affiliated With:** American Legion.

4298 ■ Brookville-Franklin County Chamber of Commerce
c/o Lois E. Clark
PO Box 211
Brookville, IN 47012-0211
Ph: (765)647-3177 (765)647-4150
E-mail: fcedc@cnz.com
Contact: Lois E. Clark, Exec.Dir.
Founded: 1889. **Members:** 250. **Staff:** 1. **Local**.

4299 ■ Mental Health Association in Franklin County, Indiana
PO Box 94
Brookville, IN 47012-0094
Ph: (765)647-2737
URL: http://www.mentalhealthassociation.com
Contact: Ms. Paula Holloway, Exec.Dir.
Local. Seeks to promote mental health and prevent mental health disorders. Improves mental health of Americans through advocacy, public education, research and service. **Affiliated With:** Mental Health Association in Indiana; National Mental Health Association.

4300 ■ United Way of Franklin County, Indiana
PO Box 105
Brookville, IN 47012-0105
Ph: (765)647-2789
URL: National Affiliate–national.unitedway.org
Local. **Affiliated With:** United Way of America.

4301 ■ Youth for Christ of Southeast Indiana
PO Box 159
Brookville, IN 47012
Ph: (765)647-3074
Fax: (765)647-3074
URL: National Affiliate–www.yfc.net
Local. **Affiliated With:** Youth for Christ/U.S.A.

Brownsburg

4302 ■ American Legion, Brownsburg Lincoln Post 331
636 E Main St.
Brownsburg, IN 46112
Ph: (317)852-3200
Fax: (317)237-9891
URL: National Affiliate–www.legion.org
Local. **Affiliated With:** American Legion.

4303 ■ Brownsburg Chamber of Commerce (BCoC)
104 E Main St.
PO Box 82
Brownsburg, IN 46112-0082
Ph: (317)852-7885
Fax: (317)852-8688
E-mail: chamber@brownsburg.com
URL: http://www.brownsburg.com
Contact: Walter Duncan, Exec.Dir.
Founded: 1983. **Members:** 314. **Membership Dues:** business (based on the number of employee), $250-$500 (annual) • non-profit, $135 (annual) • associate, $65 (annual). **Staff:** 1. **Budget:** $65,000. **Local**. Promotes business and community development in the Brownsburg, IN area. Sponsors annual Olde

Fashioned Fall Festival and annual golf tournament. **Publications:** Directory, semiannual • Newsletter, monthly.

4304 ■ Vintage Thunderbird Club of Indiana
8575 N CR 650 E
Brownsburg, IN 46112
Ph: (317)852-7669
E-mail: serc1mp@iquest.net
URL: National Affiliate–www.vintagethunderbirdclub.org
State. Affiliated With: Vintage Thunderbird Club International.

Brownstown

4305 ■ American Legion, Camp Jackson Post 112
PO Box 221
Brownstown, IN 47220
Ph: (317)630-1300
Fax: (317)237-9891
URL: National Affiliate–www.legion.org
Local. Affiliated With: American Legion.

Bunker Hill

4306 ■ National Hot Rod Association, Division 3
c/o Jay Hullinger, Dir.
5 W State, Rd. 218
Bunker Hill, IN 46914
Ph: (765)689-8727
Fax: (765)689-7956
E-mail: jhullinger@nhra.com
URL: http://www.nhradiv3.com
Contact: Jay Hullinger, Dir.
Membership Dues: individual (first-class mail), $185 (annual) • individual (periodical postage), $59 (annual). **Regional. Affiliated With:** National Hot Rod Association.

Burlington

4307 ■ American Legion, Burlington Post 414
PO Box 291
Burlington, IN 46915
Ph: (317)630-1300
Fax: (317)237-9891
URL: National Affiliate–www.legion.org
Local. Affiliated With: American Legion.

Burns Harbor

4308 ■ Rescue A Shar-Pei (RASP)
c/o Deborah Cooper, Chair
2912 State
Burns Harbor, IN 46304
Ph: (219)395-9019
E-mail: dcooper@frontenac.com
URL: http://www.rescueasharpei.com
Contact: Deborah Cooper, Chair
Founded: 1992. **Regional.** Works to rescue abandoned and abused Shar-Pei in Illinois, Indiana, Wisconsin and surrounding areas. **Affiliated With:** Chinese Shar-Pei Club of America. **Formerly:** (2004) Rasp, Chinese Shar-Pei Rescue Group.

Butler

4309 ■ American Legion, Charles Foster Blaker Post 202
PO Box 61
Butler, IN 46721
Ph: (219)868-2260
Fax: (317)237-9891
URL: National Affiliate–www.legion.org
Local. Affiliated With: American Legion.

Cambridge City

4310 ■ American Legion, Indiana Post 169
c/o Lawrence H. Bertsch
25 W Church St.
Cambridge City, IN 47327
Ph: (317)478-3877
Fax: (317)237-9891
URL: National Affiliate–www.legion.org
Contact: Lawrence H. Bertsch, Contact
Local. Affiliated With: American Legion.

Camden

4311 ■ American Legion, Camden Post 413
PO Box 121
Camden, IN 46917
Ph: (219)686-2551
Fax: (317)237-9891
URL: National Affiliate–www.legion.org
Local. Affiliated With: American Legion.

Campbellsburg

4312 ■ American Legion, Patton-Chastain Post 195
PO Box 176
Campbellsburg, IN 47108
Ph: (317)630-1300
Fax: (317)237-9891
URL: National Affiliate–www.legion.org
Local. Affiliated With: American Legion.

Cannelton

4313 ■ American Legion, Indiana Post 142
c/o Harry G. Myers
516 Knight St.
Cannelton, IN 47520
Ph: (317)630-1300
Fax: (317)237-9891
URL: National Affiliate–www.legion.org
Contact: Harry G. Myers, Contact
Local. Affiliated With: American Legion.

4314 ■ Lincoln Hills Resource Conservation and Development Council
125 S 8th St.
Cannelton, IN 47520
Ph: (812)547-7028
Fax: (812)547-6775
E-mail: karen.dearlove@in.usda.gov
URL: National Affiliate–www.rcdnet.org
Contact: Karen Dearlove, Coor.
Local. Affiliated With: National Association of Resource Conservation and Development Councils.

Carmel

4315 ■ American Legion, Carmel Post 155
852 W Main St.
Carmel, IN 46032
Ph: (317)846-0001
Fax: (317)237-9891
URL: National Affiliate–www.legion.org
Local. Affiliated With: American Legion.

4316 ■ American Society of Heating, Refrigerating and Air-Conditioning Engineers Region 5
c/o James K. Willson, Dir.
Honeywell Intl.
129 Maple Crest Dr.
Carmel, IN 46033-1938
Ph: (317)582-0549 (317)506-1156
Fax: (317)582-0549
E-mail: jimwill@indy.net
URL: http://region5.ashraeregions.org
Contact: James K. Willson, Pres.
Regional. Advances the arts and sciences of heating, ventilation, air-conditioning and refrigeration. Provides a source of technical and educational information, standards and guidelines. Conducts seminars for professional growth. **Affiliated With:** American Society of Heating, Refrigerating and Air-Conditioning Engineers.

4317 ■ Carmel Clay Chamber of Commerce (CCCC)
41 E Main St.
PO Box 1
Carmel, IN 46032
Ph: (317)846-1049
Fax: (317)844-6843
E-mail: chamberinfo@carmelchamber.com
URL: http://www.carmelchamber.com
Contact: Mo Merhoff, Pres.
Founded: 1970. **Members:** 525. **Membership Dues:** bronze, $500 (annual) • silver, $1,000 (annual) • gold, $2,500 (annual). **Staff:** 3. **Budget:** $150,000. **Local.** Businesses and individuals interested in community and economic development in Clay Township, IN. Purpose is to inform members and residents about legislative issues and community activities. Acts as information center for businesses and residents. Sponsors Carmel Business Fair and Chamber Golf Classic. **Committees:** Business After Hours and Big Business After Hours; Business Issues; Business Over Bagels and Networking Breakfast; Civic Pride; Education; Golf; Luncheon. **Affiliated With:** U.S. Chamber of Commerce. **Publications:** *Business Bulletin*, monthly • *Community Directory*, biennial • *Map of Carmel-Clay*, biennial. **Conventions/Meetings:** monthly luncheon (exhibits) - usually first Wednesday • periodic seminar • periodic workshop.

4318 ■ Carmel Clay Veterans Memorial Corporation (CCVMC)
c/o Willis A. Ensign
PO Box 1224
Carmel, IN 46082
URL: http://www.ccvmc.org
Contact: W.A. Ensign, Pres.
Founded: 2002. **Budget:** $600,000. **Local.** Aims to develop a memorial in the City of Carmel to honor all veterans who have served American freedom in peace or war.

4319 ■ Compensation and Benefits Professionals of Indiana (CBPI)
c/o Dan Diebolt
14213 Joshua Dr.
Carmel, IN 46033
Ph: (317)467-1564
E-mail: generalinfo@cbpi.org
URL: http://www.cbpi.org
Contact: Mary Kay Conley, Pres.
State. Affiliated With: WorldatWork.

4320 ■ Hoosier Sail and Power Squadron
c/o George D. Herrington, Commander
143 Chadwick Ct.
Carmel, IN 46033
Ph: (317)843-1084
E-mail: george@handy.pair.com
URL: http://www.usps.org/localusps/hoosier
Contact: George D. Herrington, Commander
Local. Affiliated With: United States Power Squadrons.

4321 ■ Ice Skating Club of Indianapolis
Carmel Ice Skadium
1040 3rd Ave. SW
Carmel, IN 46032
E-mail: isciemail@aol.com
URL: National Affiliate–www.usfigureskating.org
Local. Provides programs to encourage participation and achievement in the sport of figure skating on ice. Defines and maintains uniform standards of skating

proficiency. Organizes and sponsors competitions and exhibitions for the purpose of stimulating interest in figure skating. **Affiliated With:** United States Figure Skating Association.

4322 ■ Indiana American Saddlebred Horse Association (IASHA)
c/o Mrs. Linda Beltz, Pres.
1510 Prestwick Cir.
Carmel, IN 46032
E-mail: nierliho@aol.com
URL: http://www.indianasaddlebred.com
Contact: Mrs. Linda Beltz, Pres.

State. Affiliated With: American Saddlebred Horse Association.

4323 ■ Indiana Association for the Gifted (IAG)
PO Box 641
Carmel, IN 46082
Ph: (317)818-0073
URL: http://www.iag-online.org
Contact: Virginia Burney, Legislative Project Chair

Membership Dues: individual, $25 (annual) • individual, $45 (biennial) • institutional (5 members), $100 (annual). **State**. Advances interest in programs for the gifted. Seeks to further education of the gifted and enhances their potential creativity. Unites to address the unique needs of children and youth with demonstrated gifts and talents as well as those children who may be able to develop their talent potentials with appropriate educational experiences. Encourages and responds to the diverse expressions of gifts and talents in children and youth from all cultures, racial and ethnic backgrounds, and socioeconomic groups. **Affiliated With:** National Association for Gifted Children.

4324 ■ Indiana Crossroads Orienteering (ICO)
c/o Linda Jones, Membership Dir.
211 Concord Ln.
Carmel, IN 46032
E-mail: ljones@indyo.org
URL: http://www.indyo.org
Contact: Linda Jones, Membership Dir.

Local. Affiliated With: United States Orienteering Federation.

4325 ■ Indiana Federation of Ambulatory Surgical Centers (IFASC)
PO Box 3183
Carmel, IN 46082-3183
Ph: (317)848-5255
E-mail: mkoeh40303@aol.com
URL: http://www.ifasc.com
Contact: Mary Anne Koehler, Admin.Asst.

State. Assists physicians, corporations, healthcare administrators to provide excellence in ambulatory care; provides information to build free-standing surgery center by addressing legal, accreditation and leadership issues.

4326 ■ Indiana Mineral Aggregates Association (IMMA)
11711 N Coll. Ave., Ste.180
Carmel, IN 46032-5601
Ph: (317)580-9100
Fax: (317)580-9183
E-mail: staff@indmaa.org
URL: http://www.indmaa.org
Contact: Robert G. Jones, Exec.Dir.

State. Represents crushed stone, sand and gravel, and slag companies in Indiana. **Additional Websites:** http://www.aglime.org.

4327 ■ Indiana Society of Public Accountants
c/o James E. Tilford, Exec.VP
PO Box 3035
Carmel, IN 46082
Ph: (317)581-1143
Fax: (317)581-1173
Free: (800)854-1040
E-mail: jtilford@stoughtongroup.com
Contact: Jim Tilford, VP

Founded: 1946. **Members:** 375. **Staff:** 3. **State**. **Publications:** *Indiana Public Accountant*, monthly. Newsletter. **Conventions/Meetings:** annual Tax and Management Seminar (exhibits) - June and November; Avg. Attendance: 100.

4328 ■ Indiana Wildlife Federation
950 N Rangeline Rd., Ste.A
Carmel, IN 46032
Ph: (317)571-1220
Fax: (317)571-1223
E-mail: info@indianawildlife.org
URL: http://www.indianawildlife.org
Contact: John R. Goss, Exec.Dir.

Founded: 1949. **Membership Dues:** individual, family, $25 (annual) • business sponsor, $500 (annual) • sponsor, $100 (annual) • sustaining, $50 (annual). **Staff:** 2. **Budget:** $116,000. **State**. Individuals and corporations with an interest in environmental protection and wildlife conservation. Promotes wise management of natural resources. **Affiliated With:** National Wildlife Federation. **Publications:** *Hoosier Conservation*, quarterly. Magazine. **Price:** included in membership dues. **Advertising:** accepted. **Conventions/Meetings:** annual meeting (exhibits) - 2nd week of June.

4329 ■ National Association of Miniature Enthusiasts (NAME)
PO Box 69
Carmel, IN 46082-0069
Ph: (317)571-8094
Fax: (317)571-8105
Free: (800)571-6263
E-mail: name@miniatures.org
URL: http://www.miniatures.org
Contact: John Purcell, Exec.VP/COO

Founded: 1972. **Membership Dues:** family, $30 (annual) • youth, $15 (annual). **Local**. Represents collectors and crafters of scale miniatures promoting the craft of miniature making.

4330 ■ Navy Club of USS Indianapolis - Ship No. 35
13630 Eglin Dr.
Carmel, IN 46032
Ph: (317)574-0498
URL: http://www.ship35ncusa.org
Contact: Bruce E. Backofen, Commander

Local. Represents individuals who are, or have been, in the active service of the U.S. Navy, Naval Reserve, Marine Corps, Marine Corps Reserve, and Coast Guard. Promotes and encourages further public interest in the U.S. Navy and its history. Upholds the spirit and ideals of the U.S. Navy. Acts as a public forum for members' views on national defense. Assists the Navy Recruiting Command whenever and wherever possible. Conducts charitable activities. **Affiliated With:** Navy Club of the United States of America.

4331 ■ Pheasants Forever Central Indiana Chapter
c/o Jim Horton, Pres.
1240 Clay Springs Dr.
Carmel, IN 46032
Ph: (317)571-9698
URL: http://pfcic.org
Contact: Jim Horton, Pres.

Local. Affiliated With: Pheasants Forever.

4332 ■ Printing Industry of Illinois/Indiana Association
c/o Cathy Mendonca, Dir. of Operations
PO Box 3443
Carmel, IN 46082
Ph: (317)733-8512
Fax: (317)733-8594
E-mail: cmendonca@pii.org
URL: http://www.pii.org

For-Profit. Regional. Commercial printing firms (lithography, letterpress, gravure, platemakers, typographic houses); allied firms in the graphic arts. **Affiliated With:** Printing Industries of America.

4333 ■ White River Chapter MOAA
c/o Lt.Col. Paul May
PO Box 404
Carmel, IN 46082-0404
Ph: (317)842-4994
E-mail: r1l1habn@aol.com
URL: National Affiliate–www.moaa.org
Contact: Lt.Col. Paul May, Contact

Local. Affiliated With: Military Officers Association of America.

Cayuga

4334 ■ American Legion, Rainbow Post 263
922 W Ferry St.
Cayuga, IN 47928
Ph: (317)492-3971
Fax: (317)237-9891
URL: National Affiliate–www.legion.org

Local. Affiliated With: American Legion.

Cedar Lake

4335 ■ American Legion, Cedar Lake Post 261
13050 Washington St.
Cedar Lake, IN 46303
Ph: (219)374-9815
Fax: (317)237-9891
URL: National Affiliate–www.legion.org

Local. Affiliated With: American Legion.

4336 ■ Cedar Lake Chamber of Commerce
PO Box 101
Cedar Lake, IN 46303-0101
Ph: (219)374-6157
Fax: (219)374-6157
E-mail: clchamber@eternalisp.com
Contact: Diane Jostes, Exec.Dir.

Local.

Centerpoint

4337 ■ Little Creek Special Equestrians
c/o Penny Akers
Centerpoint Stables
1799 N Sonnefield Rd.
Centerpoint, IN 47840
Ph: (812)986-3097
URL: http://www.littlecreekinc.org
Contact: Penny Akers, Contact

Local.

4338 ■ Southwestern Indiana Angus Association
c/o Mike Kittle, Pres.
1622 S SR 59
Centerpoint, IN 47840
Ph: (812)835-3610
URL: National Affiliate–www.angus.org
Contact: Mike Kittle, Pres.

Local. Affiliated With: American Angus Association.

Centerville

4339 ■ American Legion, Hunt-Trouse Post 287
106 N Morton Ave.
Centerville, IN 47330
Ph: (317)630-1300
Fax: (317)237-9891
URL: National Affiliate–www.legion.org

Local. Affiliated With: American Legion.

4340 ■ Centerville Lions Club, IN
401 N 1st St.
Centerville, IN 47330
E-mail: centervillelionsclub@yahoo.com
URL: http://centervillelionsclub.tripod.com
Local. Affiliated With: Lions Clubs International.

4341 ■ Easter Seals Wayne and Union Counties
5632 U.S. Hwy. 40 E
Centerville, IN 47330-0086
Ph: (765)855-2482
E-mail: easterseals@juno.com
URL: http://www.easterseaIscrossroads.org
Local. Affiliated With: Easter Seals.

4342 ■ Eastern Indiana Beagle Club
c/o Susie Geiling
1065 Kellam Rd.
Centerville, IN 47330-9756
URL: National Affiliate–www.akc.org
Contact: Susie Geiling, Contact
Founded: 1942. **Members:** 39. **Membership Dues:** $20 (annual). **Local. Affiliated With:** American Kennel Club.

Chalmers

4343 ■ American Legion, Chalmers Post 268
1st and Main Sts.
Chalmers, IN 47929
Ph: (317)630-1300
Fax: (317)237-9891
URL: National Affiliate–www.legion.org
Local. Affiliated With: American Legion.

Chandler

4344 ■ International Brotherhood of Magicians, Ring 56
c/o Bruce Mabis
10655 Heim Rd.
Chandler, IN 47610
Ph: (812)925-7258
E-mail: magicbyfranklin@hotmail.com
URL: http://welcome.to/ring56
Contact: Bruce Mabis, Contact
Local. Professional and semiprofessional magicians; suppliers, assistants, agents, and others interested in magic. Seeks to advance the art of magic in the field of amusement, entertainment, and culture. Promotes proper means of discouraging false or misleading advertising of effects, tricks, literature, merchandise, or actions appertaining to the magical arts; opposes exposures of principles of the art of magic, except in books on magic and magazines devoted to such art for the exclusive use of magicians and devotees of the art; encourages humane treatment and care of live animals whenever employed in magical performances. **Affiliated With:** International Brotherhood of Magicians.

4345 ■ Kiwanis Club of Chandler
PO Box 151
Chandler, IN 47610
E-mail: chandlerkiwanis@yahoo.com
Contact: Bill Carroll, Pres.
Membership Dues: $85 (annual). **Local.** Members come from the Chandler community. Focuses on needs of children, scholarships, and support of the local community. Participates with the state organization in its support of Riley Hospital, and the international organization in IDD and other worldwide projects. Fundraisers include pancake breakfasts, car shows, citrus sales, rummage sales and similar functions. **Awards:** Memorial Scholarships. **Frequency:** annual. **Type:** scholarship. **Recipient:** to two graduating seniors from the Chandler School District each year • Mental Attitude Awards. **Frequency:** 3/year. **Type:** recognition. **Recipient:** to Castle high school student-athletes for mental attitude in fall, winter and spring sports. **Affiliated With:** Kiwanis International. **Also Known As:** (2005) Chandler Kiwanis.

Charlestown

4346 ■ American Legion, Red Greissel Post 335
PO Box 156
Charlestown, IN 47111
Ph: (317)630-1300
Fax: (317)237-9891
URL: National Affiliate–www.legion.org
Local. Affiliated With: American Legion.

4347 ■ Indiana Boer Goat Association
c/o Pam Obertate
3410 Bottorff Rd.
Charlestown, IN 47111
E-mail: wobertate@msn.com
URL: National Affiliate–usbga.org
Contact: Pam Obertate, Contact
State.

Chesterfield

4348 ■ American Legion, Indiana Post 408
c/o John T. Clendenen
5100 Mounds Rd.
Chesterfield, IN 46017
Ph: (317)378-0333
Fax: (317)237-9891
URL: National Affiliate–www.legion.org
Contact: John T. Clendenen, Contact
Local. Affiliated With: American Legion.

Chesterton

4349 ■ American Legion, Chesterton Post 170
798 Wabash Ave.
Chesterton, IN 46304
Ph: (219)926-4577
Fax: (317)237-9891
URL: National Affiliate–www.legion.org
Local. Affiliated With: American Legion.

4350 ■ American Legion, William C. Lee Memorial Post 503
320 Lincoln St.
Chesterton, IN 46304
Ph: (219)926-2680
Fax: (317)237-9891
URL: National Affiliate–www.legion.org
Local. Affiliated With: American Legion.

4351 ■ Association of Artists and Craftsmen of Porter County (AACPC)
c/o Judy Gregurich, Exec.Dir.
115 S 4th St.
Chesterton, IN 46304
Ph: (219)926-4711
E-mail: gallery@chestertonart.com
URL: http://www.chestertonart.com
Contact: Judy Gregurich, Exec.Dir.
Founded: 1955. **Members:** 600. **Membership Dues:** family, $25 (annual) • patron, $50 (annual) • benefactor, $100 (annual) • sponsor, $1,000 (annual). **Staff:** 2. **Budget:** $150,000. **Local.** Promotes public awareness and appreciation of the arts in northern Indiana. Operates Chesterton Art Gallery. Sponsors biennial ART COMP art competition, annual Chesterton Arts and Crafts Fair, and 14 annual exhibitions. **Libraries: Type:** lending; reference. **Holdings:** books. **Subjects:** art. **Publications:** Newsletter, monthly. **Circulation:** 750. **Conventions/Meetings:** monthly meeting, regional and national artists.

4352 ■ Chesterton and Duneland Chamber of Commerce (DCC)
220 Broadway
Chesterton, IN 46304
Ph: (219)926-5513
Fax: (219)926-7593
E-mail: info@chestertonchamber.org
URL: http://www.chestertonchamber.org
Contact: Ms. Bonnie Trout, Exec.Dir.
Founded: 1955. **Members:** 500. **Membership Dues:** business (based on number of employees), $172-$1,362 (annual) • home based business, $172 (annual) • bank/financial institution (plus $50 for every million dollars deposit), $172 (annual) • charitable and service organization, $172 (annual) • single, $73 (annual) • couple, $103 (annual). **Staff:** 3. **Budget:** $200,000. **Local.** Businesses and firms organized to promote tourism and industry in northwestern Indiana. Sponsors Festival of the Dunes and Wizard of Oz Festival; conducts Community Cleanup and Planting Days. **Awards:** Athena Award. **Frequency:** annual. **Type:** recognition • Community and Service Leadership. **Frequency:** annual. **Type:** recognition. **Computer Services:** Mailing lists, members name & addresses to other members for invitation purposes. **Affiliated With:** U.S. Chamber of Commerce. **Publications:** *Duneland Digest*, monthly. Newsletter. **Price:** included in membership dues • Bulletin, monthly • Directory, annual. **Conventions/Meetings:** monthly meeting.

4353 ■ Izaak Walton League of America, Porter County Chapter
1429 N Tremont Rd.
Chesterton, IN 46304-1135
Ph: (219)926-1323
URL: National Affiliate–www.iwla.org
Local. Works to educate the public to conserve, maintain, protect, and restore the soil, forest, water, and other natural resources of the U.S; promotes the enjoyment and wholesome utilization of these resources. **Affiliated With:** Izaak Walton League of America.

4354 ■ Porter County Convention Bureau (PCCRVC)
1120 S Calumet Rd., Ste.1
Chesterton, IN 46304
Ph: (219)926-2255
Fax: (219)929-5395
Free: (800)283-8687
E-mail: info@indianadunes.com
URL: http://www.indianadunes.com
Contact: Lorelei Weimer, Exec.Dir.
Local. Encourages economic growth by promoting Porter County as a destination for leisure and business travelers.

Chrisney

4355 ■ Spencer County REACT
PO Box 83
Chrisney, IN 47611-0083
Ph: (812)362-7561
URL: http://www.reactintl.org/teaminfo/usa_teams/teams-usin.htm
Local. Trained communication experts and professional volunteers. Provides volunteer public service and emergency communications through the use of radios (Citizen Band, General Mobile Radio Service, UHF and HAM). Coordinates with radio industries and government on safety communication matters and supports charitable activities and community organizations.

Churubusco

4356 ■ American Legion, Gilbert Davis Post 157
115 S Main St.
Churubusco, IN 46723
Ph: (317)630-1300
Fax: (317)237-9891
URL: National Affiliate–www.legion.org
Local. Affiliated With: American Legion.

4357 ■ National Speleological Society, Northern Indiana Grotto
c/o Karen Tadsen, Chair/Ed.
8518 State Rd. 205
Churubusco, IN 46723
Ph: (260)249-0924
E-mail: bentbat@hotmail.com
URL: http://www.caves.org/grotto/nig
Contact: Karen Tadsen, Chair/Ed.
Local. Seeks to study, explore and conserve cave and karst resources. Protects access to caves and promotes responsible caving. Encourages responsible management of caves and their unique environments. **Affiliated With:** National Speleological Society.

Cicero

4358 ■ American Legion, James Evans Post 341
PO Box 256
Cicero, IN 46034
Ph: (317)984-4441
Fax: (317)237-9891
URL: National Affiliate–www.legion.org
Local. Affiliated With: American Legion.

4359 ■ Cicero Area Chamber of Commerce
70 N Byron St.
PO Box 466
Cicero, IN 46034
Ph: (317)984-4079
Fax: (317)984-4079
E-mail: jane@hamiltonnorthchamber.com
URL: http://www.belong2it.com/cicerochamber
Contact: Jane Hunter, Exec.Dir.
Founded: 1981. **Local**. Promotes business and community development in Hamilton County.

4360 ■ Indiana Draft Horse Breeders
23210 Anthony Rd.
Cicero, IN 46034
Ph: (317)758-6328
URL: National Affiliate–www.nasdha.net/RegionalAssoc.htm
Contact: Bob Whisman, Sec.-Treas.
State.

4361 ■ Indiana Dressage Society
c/o Paula Bruveris
2830 Stringtown Pike
Cicero, IN 46034
Ph: (317)984-9289
E-mail: bonna@volte.org
URL: http://www.indianadressage.org
Contact: Bonna McCuiston, Pres.
State. Affiliated With: United States Dressage Federation.

4362 ■ Indiana Glass Association (IGA)
c/o Peggy Georgi, Exec.Dir.
PO Box 27
Cicero, IN 46034-0027
Fax: (317)984-2167
Free: (888)442-4420
State. Affiliated With: National Glass Association.

Clarksville

4363 ■ American Association of Neuroscience Nurses, Kentuckiana Chapter
1038 Centralia Ct.
Clarksville, IN 47129
E-mail: leahphillipsblack@alumni.indiana.edu
URL: http://www.geocities.com/ldpb/NeuroNurse.html
Contact: Leah Phillips Black, Contact
Founded: 1999. **Local**. Provides a means of communication between neuroscience nurses. Serves as an educational resource in neuroscience nursing. **Affiliated With:** American Association of Neuroscience Nurses.

4364 ■ American Cancer Society, Southeast Indiana Area Service Center
230 E Montgomery Ave., Ste.105
Clarksville, IN 47129
Ph: (812)282-4266
Fax: (812)282-5334
Free: (888)635-9254
URL: National Affiliate–www.cancer.org
Local. Affiliated With: American Cancer Society.

4365 ■ Home Builders Association of Southern Indiana
c/o Donna Gibson
1601 Greentree Ct.
Clarksville, IN 47129
Ph: (812)280-1600
Fax: (812)280-1700
E-mail: donna@hbasi.com
URL: National Affiliate–www.nahb.org
Local. Single and multifamily home builders, commercial builders, and others associated with the building industry. **Affiliated With:** National Association of Home Builders.

4366 ■ Local 15C, Chemical Workers Council of the UFCW
1201 Woerner Ave.
Clarksville, IN 47129
Ph: (812)283-7284
E-mail: local15c@aol.com
URL: National Affiliate–www.ufcw.org
Local. Affiliated With: United Food and Commercial Workers International Union.

4367 ■ National Active and Retired Federal Employees Association Jeffersonville 381
1889 Gutford Ct.
Clarksville, IN 47129-9064
Ph: (812)944-4327
URL: National Affiliate–www.narfe.org
Contact: Patricia A. Cress, Contact
Local. Protects the retirement future of employees through education. Informs members on issues affecting the retirement. **Affiliated With:** National Association of Retired Federal Employees.

4368 ■ Southern Indiana Realtors Association
Hwy. 131, Lincoln Dr.
Clarksville, IN 47129
Ph: (812)941-7472
Fax: (812)941-7272
E-mail: sslayton@sira.org
URL: http://www.sira.org
Contact: Suzanne Slayton, Pres.
Local. Strives to develop real estate business practices. Advocates the right to own, use and transfer real property. Provides a facility for professional development, research and exchange of information among members and to the general public. **Affiliated With:** National Association of Realtors.

4369 ■ STARFLEET: USS Indiana
c/o Capt. Jeff Davis
PO Box 2292
Clarksville, IN 47129-2292
E-mail: capt_ncc_79158@insightbb.com
URL: http://www.regionone.net
Contact: Capt. Jeff Davis, Contact
State. Affiliated With: STARFLEET.

Clay City

4370 ■ American Legion, Clay City Post 225
706 White St.
Clay City, IN 47841
Ph: (317)630-1300
Fax: (317)237-9891
URL: National Affiliate–www.legion.org
Local. Affiliated With: American Legion.

Clinton

4371 ■ American Legion, Clinton Post 140
248 S Main St.
Clinton, IN 47842
Ph: (317)832-5183
Fax: (317)237-9891
URL: National Affiliate–www.legion.org
Local. Affiliated With: American Legion.

4372 ■ Vermillion County Chamber of Commerce (CCC)
PO Box 7
Clinton, IN 47842-0007
Ph: (765)832-3844
Fax: (765)828-1619
Contact: Chadwanna Jukes, Exec.Asst.
Members: 92. **Local**. Businesspersons promoting community and economic development in Clinton, IN. **Convention/Meeting:** none. **Publications:** none. **Formerly:** (2003) Clinton Chamber of Commerce.

Cloverdale

4373 ■ American Legion, Hurst-Collins Post 281
501 S Main St.
Cloverdale, IN 46120
Ph: (317)795-3472
Fax: (317)237-9891
URL: National Affiliate–www.legion.org
Local. Affiliated With: American Legion.

4374 ■ Cloverdale Area Chamber of Commerce (CACC)
PO Box 83
Cloverdale, IN 46120
Ph: (765)795-3993
E-mail: chamber@ccrtc.com
URL: http://www.cloverdale.in.us/chamber/index.htm
Contact: Steve Walters, Contact
Founded: 1985. **Membership Dues:** individual, non-profit organization, $20 (annual) • business (depends upon the number of employees), $60-$200 (annual). **Local**. Promotes business and community development in Cloverdale, IN area. **Computer Services:** Information services, membership list.

4375 ■ Indiana Orchid Society
c/o Dick Wells
1151 E County Rd. 800 S
Cloverdale, IN 46120
Ph: (765)795-6016
E-mail: rwells@ccrtc.com
URL: National Affiliate–www.orchidweb.org
Contact: Dick Wells, Contact
Local. Professional growers, botanists, hobbyists, and others interested in extending the knowledge, production, use, and appreciation of orchids. **Affiliated With:** American Orchid Society.

Coatesville

4376 ■ Hoosier Appaloosas
c/o Faith Heiss
8869 E 100 N
Coatesville, IN 46121
Ph: (765)386-7259
Fax: (765)386-8059
E-mail: heiss@ccrtc.com
URL: National Affiliate–www.appaloosa.com
Contact: Faith Heiss, Sec.
Local. Promotes the Appaloosa horse; conducts horse shows and activities to promote the Appaloosa breed. **Affiliated With:** Appaloosa Horse Club.

Colfax

4377 ■ American Legion, Colfax Post 439
PO Box 234
Colfax, IN 46035
Ph: (317)324-2636
Fax: (317)237-9891
URL: National Affiliate–www.legion.org
Local. Affiliated With: American Legion.

Columbia City

4378 ■ American Legion, Columbia City Post 98
430 W Bus. 30
Columbia City, IN 46725
Ph: (317)630-1300
Fax: (317)237-9891
URL: National Affiliate–www.legion.org
Local. Affiliated With: American Legion.

4379 ■ Columbia City Area Chamber of Commerce (CCACC)
201 N Line St.
PO Box 166
Columbia City, IN 46725-0166
Ph: (260)248-8131
Fax: (260)248-8162
E-mail: chamber@columbiacity.org
URL: http://www.columbiacity.org
Contact: Patricia Hatcher, Exec.Dir.
Founded: 1952. **Members:** 281. **Membership Dues:** basic membership for small businesses or out of county businesses, $155 (annual) • individuals, retirees, $75. **Staff:** 2. **Budget:** $165,000. **Local.** Promotes business and community development in the Columbia City, IN area. **Formerly:** (1958) Columbia City Commercial Club. **Publications:** *The Chamber Impact*, monthly. Newsletter. Stories about members and chamber activities.

4380 ■ Goshen Old-Time Dancing
c/o Barry Dupen
3286 N 50 W
Columbia City, IN 46725
Ph: (574)552-1037
E-mail: olinzuercher@comcast.net
URL: http://www.godancing.org
Contact: Barry Dupen, Contact
Local. Affiliated With: Country Dance and Song Society.

4381 ■ Habitat for Humanity of Whitley County
PO Box 803
Columbia City, IN 46725-0803
Ph: (260)244-4479
Fax: (603)909-7689
E-mail: csiler@whitleynet.org
Founded: 1994. **Staff:** 1. **Budget:** $200,000. **Local.** Builds simple, decent, affordable houses in partnership with those who lack decent shelter. **Affiliated With:** Habitat for Humanity International.

4382 ■ Indiana Council of Teachers of English (ICTE)
c/o Laurel Steill
516 E Jefferson St.
Columbia City, IN 46725
E-mail: ejevans@isuqw.indstate.edu
URL: http://web.indstate.edu/english/icte/index.html
Contact: Laurel Steill, Contact
Founded: 1911. **Membership Dues:** student, $3 (annual) • new, $15 (annual) • life, $100. **State.** Works to promote literacy in schools, homes, and public life. **Affiliated With:** National Council of Teachers of English.

4383 ■ Jayco Jafari International Travel Club, Flight 3 Tri-State Jaybirds
c/o Thomas Smith, Pres.
1890 W SR 205
Columbia City, IN 46725
E-mail: pwjohnson@hoosierlink.com
URL: National Affiliate–www.jaycorvclub.com
Contact: Thomas Smith, Pres.
Regional. Affiliated With: Jayco Travel Club.

4384 ■ Pheasants Forever Central Indiana, Eel River
2842 S 150 E
Columbia City, IN 46725
Ph: (219)248-8368
URL: http://pfcic.org
Contact: Darren Simmons, Pres.
Local. Affiliated With: Pheasants Forever.

4385 ■ United Way of Whitley County
333 N Oak St., Ste.K
PO Box 464
Columbia City, IN 46725
Ph: (260)244-6454
Fax: (260)244-5377
E-mail: unitedway@whitleynet.org
URL: http://www.unitedwaywhitley.org
Local.

4386 ■ Whitley County Literacy Council
c/o Lisa Harris, Coor.
PO Box 922
Columbia City, IN 46725-0922
Ph: (260)244-5772
E-mail: wcliteracy@yahoo.com
URL: http://www.wcliteracy.org
Contact: Tracey Peterson, Dir.
Local. Affiliated With: ProLiteracy Worldwide.

Columbus

4387 ■ Air Force Association, Columbus-Bakalar Chapter No. 288
c/o Atterbury-Bakalar Air Museum
4742 Ray Boll Blvd.
Columbus, IN 47203
E-mail: afachapter288@indy.rr.com
URL: http://www.atterburybakalarairmuseum.org/afa.htm
Contact: Robert J. Goedl, Pres.
Local. Promotes public understanding of aerospace power and the role it plays in the security of the nation. Sponsors symposia and disseminates information through outreach programs. **Affiliated With:** Air Force Association.

4388 ■ American Legion, Columbus Post 24
2515 25th St.
Columbus, IN 47202
Ph: (812)372-6559
Fax: (317)237-9891
URL: National Affiliate–www.legion.org
Local. Affiliated With: American Legion.

4389 ■ American Society for Quality, South Central Indiana Section 0920
PO Box 1244
Columbus, IN 47202-1244
Ph: (812)375-4619 (812)377-2567
E-mail: info@asq0920.org
URL: http://www.asq0920.org
Contact: Glenn Gee, Sec.
Local. Advances learning, quality improvement and knowledge exchange to improve business results and to create better workplaces and communities worldwide. Provides a forum for information exchange, professional development and continuous learning in the science of quality. **Affiliated With:** American Society for Quality.

4390 ■ Columbus Area AIFA
c/o Albert C. Furlani, Exec.
1720 Central Ave.
Columbus, IN 47201
Ph: (812)372-8459
Fax: (812)372-8546
E-mail: al@alfurlani.com
URL: National Affiliate–naifa.org
Contact: Albert Furlani, Exec.
Local. Represents the interests of insurance and financial advisors. Advocates for a positive legislative and regulatory environment. Enhances business and professional skills of members. **Affiliated With:** National Association of Insurance and Financial Advisors.

4391 ■ Columbus Area Arts Council (CAAC)
302 Washington St.
Columbus, IN 47201
Ph: (812)376-2539
Fax: (812)376-2589
E-mail: caac@artsincolumbus.org
URL: http://www.artsincolumbus.org
Contact: Mr. Warren Baumgart Jr., Exec.Dir.
Founded: 1972. **Members:** 45. **Staff:** 9. **Budget:** $500,000. **Regional.** Provides visionary leadership in the arts. Works to foster, support and promote growth in arts that educate and enrich the cultural environment of Bartholomew County and Region Nine. Provides a variety of quality arts and entertainment events, exhibits, and programs in the Columbus area. **Computer Services:** Electronic publishing, monthly electronic newsletter that contains news of upcoming community events (subscription available from web site). **Publications:** *E-Newsletter*, monthly. Contains news of upcoming community events. **Price:** free. Alternate Formats: online.

4392 ■ Columbus Area Chamber of Commerce (CACC)
500 Franklin St.
Columbus, IN 47201-6214
Ph: (812)379-4457
Fax: (812)378-7308
E-mail: info@columbusareachamber.com
URL: http://www.columbusareachamber.com
Contact: Richard A. Stenner, Pres.
Local. Promotes business and community development in the Columbus, IN area. **Awards:** Achievement of Excellence Award. **Frequency:** annual. **Type:** recognition • Athena Award. **Frequency:** annual. **Type:** recognition • Community Service Award. **Frequency:** annual. **Type:** recognition • Edna V. Folger Outstanding Teacher Award. **Frequency:** annual. **Type:** recognition • Growth and Expansion Award. **Frequency:** annual. **Type:** recognition. **Publications:** *Chamber Connection*, monthly. Newsletter.

4393 ■ Columbus Area Miniature Enthusiasts
c/o Lee Humphries
2050 Kingdom Dr.
Columbus, IN 47201
Ph: (812)372-7426
E-mail: l34eeh@tls.net
URL: http://www.miniatures.org/states/IN.html
Contact: Lee Humphries, Contact
Local. Affiliated With: National Association of Miniature Enthusiasts.

4394 ■ Columbus Area Table Tennis Association
Donner Center
22nd and Sycamore Sts.
Columbus, IN 47202
Ph: (812)342-0783
E-mail: btbrewer@sbcglobal.net
URL: http://www.usatt.org/clubs
Contact: Brad Tempest, Pres.
Local. Affiliated With: U.S.A. Table Tennis.

4395 ■ Columbus Board of Realtors, Indiana
430 5th St.
Columbus, IN 47201
Ph: (812)378-2626
Fax: (812)378-5720
E-mail: colbor@iquest.net
URL: http://www.columbusinhomes.com
Contact: Janet Brinkman, Pres.
Local. Strives to develop real estate business practices. Advocates the right to own, use and

transfer real property. Provides a facility for professional development, research and exchange of information among members and to the general public. **Affiliated With:** National Association of Realtors.

4396 ■ Columbus Evening Kiwanis Club
c/o Golden Corral
1250 N Natl. Rd.
Columbus, IN 47201
E-mail: columbuseveningkiwanis.org@domainsbyproxy.com
URL: http://www.columbuseveningkiwanis.org
Contact: Deryl Denney, Pres.
Local.

4397 ■ Columbus Lions Club, IN
PO Box 1052
Columbus, IN 47202-1052
Ph: (812)314-0806
E-mail: shanept@yahoo.com
URL: http://columbuslion25f.lionwap.org
Local. Affiliated With: Lions Clubs International.

4398 ■ Columbus Wellness Walkers
c/o Carol Bussell
2400 E 17th St.
Columbus, IN 47201-0000
Ph: (812)372-9352
E-mail: cbussell@crh.org
URL: National Affiliate–www.ava.org
Contact: Carol Bussell, Contact
Local. Non-competitive sports enthusiasts. **Affiliated With:** American Volkssport Association.

4399 ■ First Call for Help
1531 13th St.
Columbus, IN 47201
Ph: (812)376-3001 (812)376-6666
Fax: (812)376-0019
URL: National Affiliate–www.airs.org
Contact: Anne Tolan, Administrator
Founded: 1968. **Staff:** 3. **Budget:** $92,000. **Nonmembership. Local.** Links people in need to community resources. **Affiliated With:** Alliance of Information and Referral Systems; Points of Light Foundation. **Formerly:** (1984) Volunteer Services of Bartholomew County; (1987) Volunteer Services/Information and Referral. **Publications:** *Resource Guide*, annual. Contains community resource information. **Price:** $12.00/year.

4400 ■ Indiana Volkssport Association
c/o Carol Bussell
CRH Wellness Prog.
2400 E 17th St.
Columbus, IN 47201
Ph: (812)372-9352
E-mail: cbussell@crh.org
URL: National Affiliate–www.ava.org
Contact: Carol Bussell, Contact
Founded: 1985. **Members:** 750. **Staff:** 5. **Budget:** $2,000. **Regional Groups:** 5. **State Groups:** 1. **State.** Non-competitive sports enthusiasts. **Affiliated With:** American Volkssport Association. **Publications:** *Calendar of Events and Club Listing*, annual. Brochure. Lists all clubs and sanctioned events in Indiana. **Price:** free, send self addressed envelope. **Conventions/Meetings:** quarterly State Meeting.

4401 ■ International Brotherhood of Magicians, Ring 336 (IBM 336)
c/o Lee Tieche, Pres.
4362 River Rd.
Columbus, IN 47203
Ph: (812)378-6227
E-mail: leetieche@hotmail.com
URL: http://www.ibmring336.bravehost.com/index.htm
Contact: Lee Tieche, Pres.
Local. Professional and semi-professional magicians; suppliers, assistants, agents, and others interested in magic. Seeks to advance the art of magic in the field of amusement, entertainment, and culture. Promotes proper means of discouraging false or misleading advertising of effects, tricks, literature, merchandise, or actions appertaining to the magical arts; opposes exposures of principles of the art of magic, except in books on magic and magazines devoted to such art for the exclusive use of magicians and devotees of the art; encourages humane treatment and care of live animals whenever employed in magical performances. **Affiliated With:** International Brotherhood of Magicians.

4402 ■ Lincoln Center Figure Skating Club
2009 Iroquois Trail
Columbus, IN 47203
Ph: (812)379-4613
E-mail: mackey1@kiva.net
URL: National Affiliate–www.usfigureskating.org
Contact: Paula Jean Mackey, Contact
Local. Provides programs to encourage participation and achievement in the sport of figure skating on ice. Defines and maintains uniform standards of skating proficiency. Organizes and sponsors competitions and exhibitions for the purpose of stimulating interest in figure skating. **Affiliated With:** United States Figure Skating Association.

4403 ■ National Active and Retired Federal Employees Association - Columbus 1052
1811 Dawnshire Dr.
Columbus, IN 47203-4032
Ph: (812)379-4640
URL: National Affiliate–www.narfe.org
Contact: Danny W. Jarrard, Contact
Local. Protects the retirement future of employees through education. Informs members on issues affecting the retirement. **Affiliated With:** National Association of Retired Federal Employees.

4404 ■ Phi Theta Kappa, Alpha Rho Tau Chapter - Ivy Tech State College
c/o Rebecca Allen, Advisor
4475 Central Ave.
Columbus, IN 47203
Ph: (812)372-9925
E-mail: rallen@ivytech.edu
URL: http://www.ptk.org/directories/chapters/IN/9738-1.htm
Contact: Rebecca Allen, Advisor
Local.

4405 ■ Police and Firemen's Insurance Association - Columbus Fire Department
c/o L. David Allmon
3946 E Norris Ln.
Columbus, IN 47203
Ph: (812)379-2624
E-mail: allmon679@comcast.net
URL: National Affiliate–www.pfia.net
Contact: L. David Allmon, Contact
Local. Affiliated With: Police and Firemen's Insurance Association.

4406 ■ SCORE South East Indiana
500 Franklin St.
Columbus, IN 47201
Ph: (812)379-4457
E-mail: score419@tls.net
URL: http://www.score.org
Local. Affiliated With: SCORE.

4407 ■ United Way of Bartholomew County
1531 13th St., Ste.1100
Columbus, IN 47201
Ph: (812)376-3001
Fax: (812)376-0019
E-mail: info@uwbarthco.org
URL: http://www.uwbarthco.org
Contact: Doug Otto, Pres.
Local. Affiliated With: United Way of America.

4408 ■ Young Life South Central Indiana
3304 Grove Pkwy.
Columbus, IN 47203
Ph: (812)372-7976
URL: http://whereis.younglife.org/FriendlyUrlRedirector.aspx?ID=A-IN19
Local.

Connersville

4409 ■ Achieva Resources - Healthy Families and Employment Services - Fayette County
1455 E 5th St.
Connersville, IN 47331
Ph: (765)827-4402
Fax: (765)827-6330
URL: http://www.achievaresources.org
Contact: Dan Stewart, Pres./CEO
Membership Dues: single, $20 • family, $30 • consumer, $2. **Local.**

4410 ■ American Legion, Reginald Fisher Post 1
PO Box 447
Connersville, IN 47331
Ph: (317)825-3781
Fax: (317)237-9891
URL: National Affiliate–www.legion.org
Local. Affiliated With: American Legion.

4411 ■ Community Education Coalition (CEC)
PO Box 225
Connersville, IN 47331
Ph: (765)825-7633
Fax: (765)825-1693
E-mail: info@comedcoalition.org
URL: http://www.comedcoalition.org
Contact: Cindy Bernzott, Exec.Dir.
Staff: 11. **Local. Publications:** *CEC News and Notes*, monthly. Newsletter. Alternate Formats: online.

4412 ■ Connersville - Fayette County Chamber of Commerce
115 E 6th St.
Connersville, IN 47331-2046
Ph: (765)825-2561
Fax: (765)825-4613
E-mail: chamber@ydial.com
Contact: Katrina Griffin, Exec.Dir.
Local.

4413 ■ Connersville Lions Club
PO Box 581
Connersville, IN 47331
Ph: (765)827-5409
E-mail: connersvillelionsclub@yahoo.com
URL: http://connersvillein.lionwap.org
Contact: Craig Brown, Pres.
Local. Affiliated With: Lions Clubs International.

4414 ■ East Central Indiana Board of Realtors
PO Box 263
Connersville, IN 47331
Ph: (765)825-0094
Fax: (765)825-0094
E-mail: ecibor@si-net.com
URL: National Affiliate–www.realtor.org
Contact: Lawrence J. Rosenberger, Exec. Officer
Local. Strives to develop real estate business practices. Advocates the right to own, use and transfer real property. Provides a facility for professional development, research and exchange of information among members and to the general public. **Affiliated With:** National Association of Realtors.

4415 ■ Korean War Veterans Association, Gene A. Sturgeon Memorial Chapter
c/o Loren E. Sturgeon
827 Earl Dr.
Connersville, IN 47331-1728

Ph: (765)825-5427
E-mail: amvetjohn@amvets.us
URL: National Affiliate–www.kwva.org
Contact: Loren E. Sturgeon, Contact
Local. Affiliated With: Korean War Veterans Association.

4416 ■ United Way of Fayette County, Indiana
428 Water St.
Connersville, IN 47331
Ph: (765)825-8667
URL: National Affiliate–national.unitedway.org
Local. Affiliated With: United Way of America.

Corydon

4417 ■ American Legion, Harrison Post 123
PO Box 372
Corydon, IN 47112
Ph: (812)949-9853
Fax: (317)237-9891
URL: National Affiliate–www.legion.org
Local. Affiliated With: American Legion.

4418 ■ Chamber of Commerce of Harrison County (CCHC)
310 N Elm St.
Corydon, IN 47112
Ph: (812)738-2137
Fax: (812)738-6438
Free: (888)738-2137
E-mail: dvoelker@harrisonchamber.org
URL: http://www.harrisonchamber.org
Contact: Darrell R. Voelker, Exec.Dir.
Founded: 1933. **Members:** 380. **Staff:** 8. **Budget:** $150,000. **Local.** Promotes business and community development in Harrison County, IN. **Awards:** Chamber of Commerce Scholarship Award. **Frequency:** annual. **Type:** scholarship. **Recipient:** for graduating senior in Harrison County • President's Award. **Frequency:** annual. **Type:** recognition. **Recipient:** for outstanding community service. **Affiliated With:** U.S. Chamber of Commerce. **Publications:** *Directory/Business Profile Booklet*, annual. **Price:** free • Newsletter, quarterly. **Conventions/Meetings:** monthly meeting.

4419 ■ Corydon Noon Lions Club
840 Forest Glen Rd.
Corydon, IN 47112
Ph: (812)941-6348 (812)923-1989
E-mail: roger.ellis@wslife.com
URL: http://corydonin.lionwap.org
Contact: Roger L. Ellis, Membership Chm.
Local. Affiliated With: Lions Clubs International.

Covington

4420 ■ American Legion, Fulton-Banta Post 291
PO Box 286
Covington, IN 47932
Ph: (317)630-1300
Fax: (317)237-9891
URL: National Affiliate–www.legion.org
Local. Affiliated With: American Legion.

4421 ■ ASIS International, Central Illinois Chapter 158
11778 S 600 W
Covington, IN 47932
Ph: (217)255-5010
E-mail: asis158@security-zone.com
URL: http://www.security-zone.com/asis158/index.htm
Contact: Christopher Evangelisti, Chm.
Local. Seeks to increase the effectiveness and productivity of security practices by developing educational programs and materials that address security concerns. **Affiliated With:** ASIS International.

4422 ■ National Active And Retired Federal Employees Association - Danville 332
916 6th St.
Covington, IN 47932-1036
Ph: (765)793-2342
URL: National Affiliate–www.narfe.org
Contact: John R. Bodine, Contact
Local. Protects the retirement future of employees through education. Informs members on issues affecting the retirement. **Affiliated With:** National Association of Retired Federal Employees.

Crane

4423 ■ Association of Old Crows, Crane Roost
c/o Mr. Robert L. Walker, Pres.
Code 80EW, NSWC Crane
300 Hwy. 361
Crane, IN 47522
Ph: (812)854-3921
E-mail: walker_rob@crane.navy.mil
URL: National Affiliate–www.myaoc.org
Contact: Mr. Robert L. Walker, Pres.
Local. Works for the advancement of electronic warfare and information superiority. Provides a means for communicating and disseminating new developments in electronic warfare technology, training, operations, and doctrines. **Affiliated With:** Association of Old Crows.

Crawfordsville

4424 ■ American Legion, Byron Cox Post 72
101 Walter Remley Dr.
Crawfordsville, IN 47933
Ph: (317)362-9921
Fax: (317)237-9891
URL: National Affiliate–www.legion.org
Local. Affiliated With: American Legion.

4425 ■ Crawfordsville - Montgomery County Chamber of Commerce (CMCCC)
309 N Green St.
Crawfordsville, IN 47933
Ph: (765)362-6800
Fax: (765)362-6900
E-mail: info@crawfordsvillechamber.com
URL: http://www.crawfordsvillechamber.com
Contact: Dave Long, Exec.VP
Founded: 1918. **Members:** 385. **Staff:** 3. **Budget:** $111,000. **Local.** Businesses promoting economic development, tourism, and community and political involvement in Montgomery County, IN. **Committees:** Ambassador; Education; Legislative. **Affiliated With:** U.S. Chamber of Commerce. **Formerly:** (1985) Montgomery County +Chamber of Commerce. **Publications:** *Chamber Newsletter*, monthly • *Community Information Directory*, biennial. **Conventions/Meetings:** annual dinner.

4426 ■ Indiana Amateur Softball Association, Region 4
c/o Larry Utz, VP
1824 A Elmore St.
Crawfordsville, IN 47933
Ph: (765)362-8939
URL: http://www.indiana-asa.org
Contact: Larry Utz, VP
Local. Affiliated With: Amateur Softball Association of America.

4427 ■ Pheasants Forever Central Indiana, Coal Greek
Rte. 6, Box 86
Crawfordsville, IN 47933
Ph: (765)794-4352
URL: http://pfcic.org
Contact: Brian Holt, Pres.
Local. Affiliated With: Pheasants Forever.

4428 ■ Psi Chi, National Honor Society in Psychology - Wabash College
c/o Dept. of Psychology
PO Box 352
Crawfordsville, IN 47933-0352
Ph: (765)361-6324 (765)361-6248
Fax: (765)361-6277
E-mail: bostp@wabash.edu
URL: National Affiliate–www.psichi.org
Local. Affiliated With: Psi Chi, National Honor Society in Psychology.

Crown Point

4429 ■ American Legion, Indiana Post 20
c/o Fred Schmidt
PO Box 119
Crown Point, IN 46308
Ph: (219)663-6235
Fax: (317)237-9891
URL: National Affiliate–www.legion.org
Contact: Fred Schmidt, Contact
Local. Affiliated With: American Legion.

4430 ■ GFWC Indiana
1168 N Main St.
Crown Point, IN 46307
Ph: (219)661-4840
E-mail: gfwclord@yahoo.com
URL: http://www.gfwcindiana.org
State.

4431 ■ Indiana Amateur Softball Association, Region 1
c/o Dick Zurbriggen, VP
925 S Indiana St.
Crown Point, IN 46307
Ph: (219)663-3408
URL: http://www.indiana-asa.org
Contact: Dick Zurbriggen, VP
Local. Affiliated With: Amateur Softball Association of America.

4432 ■ Lake County Bar Association
2293 N Main
Crown Point, IN 46307
Ph: (219)738-1905
Contact: Vernita Cole, Exec.Dir.
Local.

4433 ■ Lake County Historical Society
Courthouse Sq., Ste.202
Crown Point, IN 46307
Ph: (219)794-1259 (219)942-4641
E-mail: bwoods_mhs@yahoo.com
URL: http://www.cpcourthouse.com
Contact: Bruce L. Woods, Pres.
Founded: 1875. **Members:** 50. **Membership Dues:** $5 (annual). **Staff:** 5. **Local.** Preserves the history Lake County. Operates Lake County Historical museum. **Libraries: Type:** open to the public. **Holdings:** 100. **Subjects:** history of Lake county. **Publications:** *Reports & Papers - Lake County Historical Society*. Book. **Price:** $4.00. **Conventions/Meetings:** bimonthly meeting - always second Saturday in December.

4434 ■ Meals On Wheels of Northwest Indiana
211 S East St.
Crown Point, IN 46307
Ph: (219)663-6078
Fax: (219)662-9206
E-mail: info@mealsonwheelsnwindiana.org
URL: http://www.mealsonwheelsnwindiana.org
Local. Affiliated With: Meals on Wheels Association of America.

4435 ■ Midwest Weightlifting
c/o Frank Eksten
399 Ellendale Pkwy.
Crown Point, IN 46307

Ph: (219)865-6969
E-mail: eksten_f@yahoo.com
URL: http://www.midwestweightlifting.com
Contact: Frank Eksten, Contact
Local.

4436 ■ National Association of Home Builders of the U.S., Building Industries Association of Northwest Indiana
1103 Broadway, Ste.C
Crown Point, IN 46307
Ph: (219)663-4475
Fax: (219)663-4482
E-mail: bia@bianwi.org
URL: http://www.bianwi.org
Contact: Sharon Carlotta, Exec. Officer
Local. Single and multifamily home builders, commercial builders, and others associated with the building industry. **Affiliated With:** National Association of Home Builders.

4437 ■ Southlake Young Men's Christian Association
1450 S Court St.
Crown Point, IN 46307
Ph: (219)663-5810
E-mail: info@slymca.com
URL: http://www.slymca.com
Contact: Phillip Mallers, Exec.Dir.
Founded: 1975. **Members:** 5,000. **Staff:** 65. **Budget:** $750,000. **Local**. Seeks to develop and improve the spiritual, social, mental, and physical life of youth and adults in Southern Lake County, IN. **Publications:** *Program Brochure*, 3/year.

Culver

4438 ■ Culver Chamber of Commerce
PO Box 129
Culver, IN 46511-0129
Ph: (574)842-5253
Fax: (574)842-5253
Free: (888)252-5253
E-mail: djdodge@culcom.net
URL: http://www.culverchamber.com
Contact: Judi Dodge, Pres.
Founded: 1925. **Members:** 126. **Local**. Promotes business and community development in the Culver, IN area.

Dale

4439 ■ American Legion, Abe Lincoln Post 444
309 E Medcalf St.
Dale, IN 47523
Ph: (317)630-1300
Fax: (317)237-9891
URL: National Affiliate–www.legion.org
Local. **Affiliated With:** American Legion.

Daleville

4440 ■ American Legion, Indiana Post 446
c/o John F. Hurley
14708 W 6th St.
Daleville, IN 47334
Ph: (317)378-0320
Fax: (317)237-9891
URL: National Affiliate–www.legion.org
Contact: John F. Hurley, Contact
Local. **Affiliated With:** American Legion.

4441 ■ Girl Scouts of Wapehani Council (GSWC)
PO Box 587
Daleville, IN 47334
Ph: (765)378-3373
Free: (800)686-6465
E-mail: girlscouts@gswc.ws
URL: http://www.gswc.ws
Contact: Deborah Beckman, CEO
Founded: 1956. **Local**. Strives to develop potential and leadership skills among its members. Conducts trainings, educational programs and outdoor activities.

4442 ■ Madison County AIFA
c/o Clyde J. House, Pres.
PO Box 551
Daleville, IN 47334
Ph: (765)378-6100
Fax: (765)378-6875
E-mail: toniawainscott@yahoo.com
URL: National Affiliate–naifa.org
Contact: Clyde J. House, Pres.
Local. Represents the interests of insurance and financial advisors. Advocates for a positive legislative and regulatory environment. Enhances business and professional skills of members. **Affiliated With:** National Association of Insurance and Financial Advisors.

Danville

4443 ■ American Legion, Avon Post 145
377 S State Rd. 267
Danville, IN 46122
Ph: (317)630-1300
Fax: (317)237-9891
URL: National Affiliate–www.legion.org
Local. **Affiliated With:** American Legion.

4444 ■ American Legion, Hendricks County Post 118
846 S State Rd. 39
Danville, IN 46122
Ph: (317)745-4736
Fax: (317)237-9891
URL: National Affiliate–www.legion.org
Local. **Affiliated With:** American Legion.

4445 ■ Greater Danville Chamber of Commerce (DCC)
56 W Main St.
PO Box 273
Danville, IN 46122
Ph: (317)745-0670
Fax: (317)745-0682
E-mail: chamber@danville.org
URL: http://www.danville.org
Contact: Sandy Teer, Exec.Dir.
Members: 120. **Membership Dues:** business (based on the number of employee), $150-$350 (annual) • civic/service/social/fraternal organization, $75 (annual) • private investor/non-commercial/retired, $50 (annual). **Local**. Promotes business and community development in Danville, IN. Holds monthly board meeting. **Publications:** Newsletter. Contains membership information. **Conventions/Meetings:** monthly board meeting.

4446 ■ Indiana Society of Enrolled Agents (ISEA)
c/o Helen (Casey) Juza
202 E Main St.
Danville, IN 46122
Ph: (317)745-6051
Fax: (317)745-1735
E-mail: execserv@aol.com
URL: http://www.naea.org/MemberPortal/StateAffiliates/Listing
Contact: Helen Juza EA, Contact
State. **Additional Websites:** http://www.indianaenrolledagents.com. **Affiliated With:** National Association of Enrolled Agents.

4447 ■ Meals on Wheels of Hendricks County
c/o Sandy Pickett, Dir.
PO Box 409
Danville, IN 46122
Ph: (317)745-3469
Fax: (317)718-4060
Contact: Sandy Pickett, Contact
Delivers meals to home-bound senior citizens. All volunteer drivers deliver hot meals Monday through Friday to those who have difficulty preparing meals themselves.

Darlington

4448 ■ American Legion, Darlington Post 302
PO Box 43
Darlington, IN 47940
Ph: (317)794-9482
Fax: (317)237-9891
URL: National Affiliate–www.legion.org
Local. **Affiliated With:** American Legion.

4449 ■ Friends of Sugar Creek
PO Box 171
Darlington, IN 47940
Ph: (765)362-5351
E-mail: dford@tds.net
Contact: R. Dean Ford, Pres.
Dedicated to the restoration and preservation of the Sugar Creek watershed in West Central Indiana.

Decatur

4450 ■ American Legion, Adams Post 43
101 Madison St.
Decatur, IN 46733
Ph: (219)724-3705
Fax: (317)237-9891
URL: National Affiliate–www.legion.org
Local. **Affiliated With:** American Legion.

4451 ■ Decatur Chamber of Commerce (DCC)
125 E Monroe St.
Decatur, IN 46733-1732
Ph: (260)724-2604
Fax: (260)724-3104
E-mail: lmacklin@decaturchamber.org
URL: http://www.decaturchamber.org
Contact: Larry D. Macklin, Exec.Dir.
Founded: 1903. **Local**. Promotes business, economic, workforce development, and community in Decatur, IN. Sponsors Callithumpian parade, community smorgasbord, Riverside Festival, city-wide sidewalk sale, golf outing, and Holiday Open House. **Affiliated With:** U.S. Chamber of Commerce. **Publications:** *Chamber Charger*, monthly. Newsletter • *Community Service Directory*, periodic • *Industrial Directory*, periodic • Brochure, periodic. **Conventions/Meetings:** annual dinner - always March • annual Industrial Appreciation Dinner - always October.

4452 ■ United Way of Adams County, Indiana
115 N 3rd St.
Decatur, IN 46733
Ph: (260)728-2056
Fax: (260)728-4601
E-mail: unitedway@decaturdirectory.com
URL: http://www.unitedwayofadamscounty.com
Contact: Janet Macklin, Exec.Dir.
Founded: 1991. **Staff:** 2. **Budget:** $237,180. **Local**. Improves health, human, and social conditions in Adams County by: promoting organizational cooperation, stimulating volunteer participation, mobilizing and deploying community resources, and seeking solutions to urgent community problems. **Affiliated With:** United Way of America.

Delphi

4453 ■ American Legion, Indiana Post 75
c/o Harry Bohannon
111 S Washington St.
Delphi, IN 46923
Ph: (317)564-3575
Fax: (317)237-9891
URL: National Affiliate–www.legion.org
Contact: Harry Bohannon, Contact
Local. Affiliated With: American Legion.

4454 ■ Carroll County Historical Society Museum
c/o Mrs. Don R. Moore, Museum Curator
PO Box 277
Delphi, IN 46923-0277
Ph: (765)564-3152
Fax: (765)564-6161
E-mail: phyllismoore@ffni.com
URL: http://www.carrollcountymuseum.org
Contact: Mrs. Don R. Moore, Museum Curator
Founded: 1921. **Membership Dues:** junior (under 18), $1 (annual) • active, $10 (annual) • patron, $25 (annual) • life, $100. **Staff:** 3. **Local.** Individuals and others interested in the historic preservation and genealogy of Carroll County. **Libraries: Type:** open to the public. **Subjects:** genealogy material. **Conventions/Meetings:** annual board meeting • monthly meeting - always first Monday.

4455 ■ Kiwanis Club Delphi Chapter
c/o Stone House Restaurant
1433 S Washington St.
Delphi, IN 46923
URL: http://www.geocities.com/kiwanisdelphi/Kiwanisdelphi.html
Contact: Jean Logan, Pres.
Local.

4456 ■ Wabash Valley Gem and Mineral Society
c/o Nancy Mattox, Pres.
423 Front St.
Delphi, IN 46923
E-mail: wilson@purdue.edu
URL: National Affiliate–www.amfed.org
Contact: Anna Wilson, Sec.
Local. Aims to further the study of Earth Sciences and the practice of lapidary arts and mineralogy. **Affiliated With:** American Federation of Mineralogical Societies.

Demotte

4457 ■ American Legion, Demotte Post 440
1011 15th St. SE
Demotte, IN 46310
Ph: (219)987-2961
Fax: (317)237-9891
URL: National Affiliate–www.legion.org
Local. Affiliated With: American Legion.

4458 ■ Demotte Chamber of Commerce (DCC)
PO Box 721
Demotte, IN 46310
Ph: (219)987-5800
Contact: Pat Kopanda, Outreach Dir.
Founded: 1981. **Local.** Promotes business and community development in DeMotte, IN.

4459 ■ Pheasants Forever Central Indiana, Iroquois River
6250 W 1000 N
Demotte, IN 46310
Ph: (219)987-3256
URL: http://pfcic.org
Contact: Clem Grover, Pres.
Local. Affiliated With: Pheasants Forever.

Dillsboro

4460 ■ American Legion, Northcutt-Laaker Post 292
PO Box 292
Dillsboro, IN 47018
Ph: (812)432-9200
Fax: (317)237-9891
URL: National Affiliate–www.legion.org
Local. Affiliated With: American Legion.

4461 ■ Vending Machine Servicemen's Union
c/o Darren Thayer
8834 Davies Rd.
Dillsboro, IN 47018-9034
Local.

Donaldson

4462 ■ Phi Theta Kappa, Beta Beta Beta Chapter - Ancilla College
c/o Sara Grubbs
PO Box 1
Donaldson, IN 46513
Ph: (574)936-8898
E-mail: sgrubbs@ancilla.edu
URL: http://www.ptk.org/directories/chapters/IN/20661-1.htm
Contact: Sara Grubbs, Advisor
Local.

Dublin

4463 ■ American Legion, Leroy Tout Post 338
214 Harrison St.
Dublin, IN 47335
Ph: (317)630-1300
Fax: (317)237-9891
URL: National Affiliate–www.legion.org
Local. Affiliated With: American Legion.

Dugger

4464 ■ American Legion, Rexford Ballard Post 224
815 E Main St.
Dugger, IN 47848
Ph: (812)648-2666
Fax: (317)237-9891
URL: National Affiliate–www.legion.org
Local. Affiliated With: American Legion.

Dunkirk

4465 ■ American Legion, Indiana Post 227
c/o Ralph Burgess
118 W Commerce St.
Dunkirk, IN 47336
Ph: (317)768-6281
Fax: (317)237-9891
URL: National Affiliate–www.legion.org
Contact: Ralph Burgess, Contact
Local. Affiliated With: American Legion.

4466 ■ Dunkirk Area Chamber of Commerce (DACC)
Box 291
Dunkirk, IN 47336
Ph: (765)768-6225
E-mail: samjhub@aol.com
Contact: Sam J. Hubbard, Exec.Dir
Local. Promotes business and community development in Dunkirk, IN. Conducts charitable activities; sponsors festivals. **Formerly:** (1999) Dunkirk Chamber of Commerce.

Dyer

4467 ■ Dyer Chamber of Commerce
PO Box 84
Dyer, IN 46311
Ph: (219)865-1045
E-mail: chamber@townofdyer.com
Contact: Ms. Tammy Hedrick, Contact
Members: 100. **Membership Dues:** business, $125 (annual). **Staff:** 1. **Local.** Promotes business and community development in Dyer, IN. **Awards:** Business Person of the Year. **Frequency:** annual. **Type:** recognition. **Committees:** Super. **Publications:** Newsletter, monthly. **Price:** free. **Circulation:** 100. **Conventions/Meetings:** monthly luncheon - always first Thursday of the month.

4468 ■ Plumbing-Heating-Cooling Contractors Association, Northwest
c/o Mr. Pete Bultema, Pres.
PO Box 488
Dyer, IN 46311-0488
Ph: (219)365-1811
Fax: (219)365-1813
URL: National Affiliate–www.phccweb.org
Contact: Mr. Pete Bultema, Pres.
Local. Represents the plumbing, heating and cooling contractors. Promotes the construction industry. Protects the environment, health, safety and comfort of society. **Affiliated With:** Plumbing-Heating-Cooling Contractors Association.

4469 ■ Veterans of Foreign Wars/Auxiliary Unit 6448
PO Box 272
Dyer, IN 46311
Ph: (219)865-9730
Contact: Fred Tobias, Commander
Local.

Earl Park

4470 ■ American Legion, Earl Park Post 455
PO Box 85
Earl Park, IN 47942
Ph: (219)474-5090
Fax: (317)237-9891
URL: National Affiliate–www.legion.org
Local. Affiliated With: American Legion.

East Chicago

4471 ■ American Legion, Casimer Pulaski Post 78
4003 Alder St.
East Chicago, IN 46312
Ph: (219)398-9678
Fax: (317)237-9891
URL: National Affiliate–www.legion.org
Local. Affiliated With: American Legion.

4472 ■ American Legion, East Chicago Allied Post 369
1401 W Chicago Ave.
East Chicago, IN 46312
Ph: (219)398-1802
Fax: (317)237-9891
URL: National Affiliate–www.legion.org
Local. Affiliated With: American Legion.

4473 ■ American Legion, Indiana Post 508
c/o Emilio Albert De La Garza, Jr.
610 W Chicago Ave.
East Chicago, IN 46312
Ph: (317)630-1300
Fax: (317)237-9891
URL: National Affiliate–www.legion.org
Contact: Emilio Albert De La Garza Jr., Contact
Local. Affiliated With: American Legion.

4474 ■ American Legion, Twin City Post 266
513 W Chicago Ave.
East Chicago, IN 46312
Ph: (317)630-1300
Fax: (317)237-9891
URL: National Affiliate–www.legion.org
Local. Affiliated With: American Legion.

4475 ■ Korean War Veterans Association, Sgt. William E. Windrich No. 3 Chapter
c/o Eliseo Castaneda
1314 E Columbus Dr.
East Chicago, IN 46312
Ph: (219)398-2083
URL: National Affiliate–www.kwva.org
Contact: Eliseo Castaneda, Contact
Local. Affiliated With: Korean War Veterans Association.

Eaton

4476 ■ American Legion, O Leara Quirk Post 90
PO Box 482
Eaton, IN 47338
Ph: (317)396-3552
Fax: (317)237-9891
URL: National Affiliate–www.legion.org
Local. Affiliated With: American Legion.

Economy

4477 ■ Compassionate Friends - East Central Indiana Chapter
c/o Jackie Wesley
13515 US 35
Economy, IN 47339
Ph: (765)886-5643
E-mail: tcfjackie@hotmail.com
URL: http://www.ecitcf.com
Contact: Jackie Wesley, Chapter Leader
Local.

4478 ■ Compassionate Friends - Miami-WhiteWater Chapter
13515 US 35
Economy, IN 47339
Ph: (765)886-5643 (765)966-6253
E-mail: jackiewesley@peoplepc.com
URL: http://www.miamiwhitewater.org
Contact: Jackie Wesley, Chapter Leader
Local.

Edinburgh

4479 ■ American Legion, Edinburg Post 233
500 Memorial Dr.
Edinburgh, IN 46124
Ph: (812)526-9001
Fax: (317)237-9891
URL: National Affiliate–www.legion.org
Local. Affiliated With: American Legion.

4480 ■ Edinburgh Lions Club
112 S Walnut St.
Edinburgh, IN 46124
Ph: (812)526-8622
URL: http://edinburghlionind.lionwap.org
Local. Affiliated With: Lions Clubs International.

4481 ■ Greater Edinburgh Community Chamber of Commerce (GECCC)
PO Box 128
Edinburgh, IN 46124
Ph: (812)373-4016
URL: http://www.edinburgh-in.com
Contact: Kathy Richmond, Pres.
Founded: 1983. **Members:** 55. **Local.** Promotes business and community development in the Edinburgh, IN area. **Publications:** *Chamber News*, monthly. Newsletter. **Conventions/Meetings:** monthly board meeting - always second Monday of the month • monthly meeting - always second Thursday of the month.

4482 ■ Indiana American Eskimo Dog Club
c/o Joseph Allen
8767 S Edinburg Rd.
Edinburgh, IN 46124
Ph: (812)526-6682
URL: National Affiliate–www.eskie.com/naeda
Contact: Joseph Allen, Contact
State.

Edwardsport

4483 ■ American Legion, Chauncey-Barr-Rex-Boyer Post 192
PO Box 172
Edwardsport, IN 47528
Ph: (812)847-4997
Fax: (317)237-9891
URL: National Affiliate–www.legion.org
Local. Affiliated With: American Legion.

Elberfeld

4484 ■ American Legion, Elberfeld Post 351
350 N 4th St.
Elberfeld, IN 47613
Ph: (317)630-1300
Fax: (317)237-9891
URL: National Affiliate–www.legion.org
Local. Affiliated With: American Legion.

4485 ■ Indiana Dietetic Association (IDA)
c/o Debbie Denton, Office Mgr.
150 N Illinois St.
Elberfeld, IN 47613
Ph: (812)983-9911
Fax: (812)983-9911
E-mail: dsdenton90@aol.com
URL: http://www.dietetics.com/ida
Contact: Debbie Denton, Office Mgr.
State. Dietetic professionals, registered dietitians and dietetic technicians serving the public through promotion of optimal nutrition, health and well being. Seeks to shape the food choices and impact the nutritional status of the public in hospitals, colleges, universities, schools, day care centers, research, business and industry. **Affiliated With:** American Dietetic Association.

Elizabeth

4486 ■ American Legion, Hornickel Post 379
5365 Amer. Legion Ln. SE
Elizabeth, IN 47117
Ph: (812)969-2751
Fax: (317)237-9891
URL: National Affiliate–www.legion.org
Local. Affiliated With: American Legion.

Elizabethtown

4487 ■ American Legion, Kent Voyls Post 322
6800 S, 750 E
Elizabethtown, IN 47232
Ph: (812)579-6944
Fax: (317)237-9891
URL: National Affiliate–www.legion.org
Local. Affiliated With: American Legion.

Elkhart

4488 ■ American Legion, Indiana Post 74
c/o Thomas Mc Coy
PO Box 4822
Elkhart, IN 46514
Ph: (317)630-1300
Fax: (317)237-9891
URL: National Affiliate–www.legion.org
Contact: Thomas Mc Coy, Contact
Local. Affiliated With: American Legion.

4489 ■ American Legion, Indiana Post 93
c/o Edward E. Mabie
PO Box 2653
Elkhart, IN 46515
Ph: (317)630-1300
Fax: (317)237-9891
URL: National Affiliate–www.legion.org
Contact: Edward E. Mabie, Contact
Local. Affiliated With: American Legion.

4490 ■ Better Business Bureau of Elkhart County
722 W Bristol St.
Elkhart, IN 46514
Ph: (219)262-8996
Fax: (219)266-2026
Free: (800)552-4631
E-mail: info@neindianabbb.org
URL: http://www.elkhart.bbb.org
Contact: Dreama Jensen, Contact
Local. Seeks to promote and foster the highest ethical relationship between businesses and the public through voluntary self-regulation, consumer and business education, and service excellence. Provides information to help consumers and businesses make informed purchasing decisions and avoid costly scams and frauds; settles consumer complaints through arbitration and other means. **Affiliated With:** BBB Wise Giving Alliance.

4491 ■ Connecting Business Men to Christ - Elkhart
PO Box 4654
Elkhart, IN 46514-0654
URL: http://www.cbmcelkhart.com
Local.

4492 ■ Elkhart County Board of Realtors
3801 S Main
Elkhart, IN 46517-3510
Ph: (574)875-3283
Fax: (574)875-7174
E-mail: info@ecbor.com
URL: http://www.ecbor.com
Contact: Tona Ambrosen, Pres.
Local. Strives to develop real estate business practices. Advocates the right to own, use and transfer real property. Provides a facility for professional development, research and exchange of information among members and to the general public. **Affiliated With:** National Association of Realtors.

4493 ■ Elkhart County Chess Club (ECCC)
c/o Thomas R. Smith
Unitarian Universalist Church
1732 Garden St.
Elkhart, IN 46514
Ph: (574)262-4023 (574)257-9033
E-mail: r.blaine@mppl.lib.in.us
URL: National Affiliate–www.uschess.org
Contact: Thomas R. Smith, Pres.
Founded: 1980. **Members:** 40. **Membership Dues:** adult, $10 (annual) • junior, $8 (annual). **Budget:** $500. **Local.** Individuals interested in the game of chess. Promotes chess play; conducts tournaments; participates in chess events at shopping malls. **Awards:** Club Champion. **Frequency:** annual. **Type:** recognition. **Affiliated With:** United States Chess Federation. **Publications:** *Elkhart County Chess Club Newsletter*, bimonthly. **Circulation:** 50. **Advertising:** accepted. **Conventions/Meetings:** weekly meeting - always Tuesdays. Elkhart, IN - Avg. Attendance: 15.

4494 ■ Elkhart County RSVP
c/o Barbara Miller, Dir.
200 E Jackson Blvd.
Elkhart, IN 46516

Ph: (574)389-3399
Fax: (574)293-6359
E-mail: rsvp@ywcaelkhartcounty.org
URL: http://www.seniorcorps.gov/about/programs/rsvp_state.asp?usestateabbr=in&Search4.x=28&Search4.y=4
Contact: Barbara Miller, Dir.
Local. Affiliated With: Retired and Senior Volunteer Program.

4495 ■ Elkhart County Youth for Christ
PO Box 73
Elkhart, IN 46515
Ph: (574)294-7407
Fax: (574)294-6926
URL: National Affiliate–www.yfc.net
Local. Affiliated With: Youth for Christ/U.S.A.

4496 ■ Elkhart Lions Club
PO Box 81
Elkhart, IN 46515
E-mail: mmow@elkhart.k12.in.us
URL: http://www.elkhartlions.org
Contact: Mark Mow, Pres.
Local. Affiliated With: Lions Clubs International.

4497 ■ Greater Elkhart County Chamber of Commerce
418 S Main St.
Elkhart, IN 46515-0428
Ph: (574)293-1531
Fax: (574)294-1859
E-mail: info@elkhart.org
URL: http://www.elkhart.org
Contact: Philip Penn, Pres./CEO
Founded: 1926. **Members:** 1,100. **Local.** Represents the business community in problem solving, promoting economic development, transportation issues, and downtown development. **Awards:** Eartha Award. **Type:** recognition. **Recipient:** for companies who go above and beyond the call of duty environmentally • Fairbanks Award. **Type:** recognition • Outstanding Not for Profit Businesses. **Type:** recognition • Small Business of the Month. **Frequency:** annual. **Type:** recognition • Small Business of the Year. **Frequency:** annual. **Type:** recognition. **Computer Services:** Information services, business directory. **Councils:** Annual Outing; Business Recognition; Economic Development; Education; Minority Business Development; OSHA; Technology; Transportation. **Publications:** *Business Resource Guide*. Membership Directory. Contains list of chamber members alphabetically, by category and by representative/s of each organization. **Price:** free for members (first copy); $25.00 for members; $50.00 for nonmembers • *Elkhart Area Recreational Vehicle Directory*. Provides an up to date listing of RV manufacturers, dealers, park models and more. **Price:** $20.00 for members; $40.00 for nonmembers • *Elkhart County Manufacturers Directory*. Contains list of all manufacturers in Elkhart County alphabetically, by category and by SIC codes. **Price:** $30.00 for members; $60.00 for nonmembers • *Elkhart County Wage and Benefit Report*. Summarizes the wage and salary practices of Elkhart County employers. **Price:** $75.00 for members; $150.00 for nonmembers • Newsletter, monthly. **Advertising:** accepted. Alternate Formats: online.

4498 ■ Indiana Division - IAAP
Metalworking Machinery Syss., Inc.
PO Box 1421
Elkhart, IN 46515-1421
Ph: (574)522-3800
E-mail: sales@metalworking-machinery.com
URL: http://www.indiana-iaap.org
Contact: Sally Biller, Pres.
State. Professionals, corporations, academic institutions and students. Develops research and educational projects for administrative professionals. Provides training, seminars, conferences and educational programs.

4499 ■ Junior Achievement of Elkhart County
c/o Ms. Karen A. Shackle, Pres.
530 E Lexington Ave.
Elkhart, IN 46516
Ph: (574)293-4554
Fax: (574)294-2450
E-mail: toot@npcc.net
URL: http://www.ja.org/nested/elkhart
Contact: Ms. Karen Shackle, Pres.
Local. Strives to ensure that every child in America will gain a fundamental understanding of the free enterprise system. Educates and inspires young people in grades K-12 to value free enterprise, business and economics to improve quality of life. **Affiliated With:** Junior Achievement.

4500 ■ Mental Health Association in Elkhart County
401 S 2nd St.
Elkhart, IN 46516
Ph: (574)295-8935
Fax: (574)295-1460
E-mail: execdirector@mhaec.org
URL: http://www.mhaec.org
Contact: Lori L. Harrington MSW, Exec.Dir.
Local. Seeks to promote mental health and prevent mental health disorders. Improves mental health of Americans through advocacy, public education, research and service. **Affiliated With:** Mental Health Association in Indiana; National Mental Health Association.

4501 ■ Michiana Emmaus Community (MEC)
c/o Deb Blacklaw, Treas.
PO Box 1026
Elkhart, IN 46515-1026
Ph: (574)264-0100
E-mail: mecboard@michianaemmauscommunity.org
URL: http://www.michianaemmauscommunity.org
Contact: Deb Blacklaw, Treas.
Local.

4502 ■ Michiana R/C Choppers (MRCC)
54768 Bradley
Elkhart, IN 46514
Ph: (574)264-6756
E-mail: miked@mrcc.info
URL: http://www.mrcc.info
Contact: Mike DeMetz, Contact
Founded: 1987. **Membership Dues:** general, $30 (annual). **Regional. Affiliated With:** Academy of Model Aeronautics. **Publications:** *The Sideframes*, monthly. Newsletters. Contains minutes of last meeting and upcoming events.

4503 ■ National Association of Insurance and Financial Advisors, Elkhart County Chapter
c/o Jackie R. Clindaniel, Pres.
PO Box 1911
Elkhart, IN 46515
Ph: (574)206-8844
Fax: (574)206-8866
E-mail: cfarmer@hri-dho.com
URL: http://www.naifaelkhart.com
Contact: Jackie R. Clindaniel, Pres.
Local.

4504 ■ Phi Theta Kappa, Beta Beta Alpha Chapter - Ivy Tech State College
c/o Liana Legus
Elkhart Campus
2521 Indus. Pkwy.
Elkhart, IN 46516
Ph: (574)389-7732
E-mail: llegus@ivytech.edu
URL: http://www.ptk.org/directories/chapters/IN/20662-1.htm
Contact: Liana Legus, Advisor
Local.

4505 ■ Quail Unlimited, Northern Indiana Chapter
3530 Oak Ridge Dr.
Elkhart, IN 46517
Ph: (574)294-3844
E-mail: sheley@hi-techhousing.com
URL: National Affiliate–www.qu.org
Local. Affiliated With: Quail Unlimited.

4506 ■ SCORE Elkhart
c/o Greater Elkhart Chamber of Commerce
418 S Main St.
Elkhart, IN 46515
Ph: (574)293-1531
Fax: (219)294-1859
E-mail: score@elkhart.org
URL: National Affiliate–www.score.org
Local. Provides professional guidance and information to America's small businesses. **Affiliated With:** SCORE.

4507 ■ Trillium Land Conservancy
1717 E Lusher Ave.
Elkhart, IN 46516-4967
Ph: (574)293-5070
Fax: (574)970-0593
E-mail: eecmail@coelkhartindiana.org
URL: National Affiliate–www.lta.org
Local.

4508 ■ United Way of Elkhart County
222 Middlebury St.
Elkhart, IN 46516
Ph: (574)295-1650
E-mail: quatmanj@unitedwayec.org
URL: http://www.unitedwayec.org
Contact: Jerome M. Quatman, Pres.
Local. Affiliated With: United Way of America.

4509 ■ U.S.A. Volleyball Hoosier Region
c/o Charles Stemm, Commissioner/Pres./Treas.
52428 Winding Waters Ln.
Elkhart, IN 46514-5725
Ph: (574)262-9211
Fax: (574)266-1892
E-mail: hoosiervba@comcast.net
URL: http://www.indianavolleyball.org
Contact: Charles Stemm, Commissioner/Pres./Treas.
Regional. Affiliated With: United States Volleyball Association/United States Volleyball Association. **Formerly:** (2005) U.S.A. Volleyball Michiana Region.

Ellettsville

4510 ■ Ellettsville Main Street
c/o Jeana Kapczynski
PO Box 143
Ellettsville, IN 47429-0143
Founded: 1999. **Local.**

Elnora

4511 ■ American Legion, Indiana Post 245
c/o Clarence R. White
PO Box 276
Elnora, IN 47529
Ph: (812)692-5533
Fax: (317)237-9891
URL: National Affiliate–www.legion.org
Contact: Clarence R. White, Contact
Local. Affiliated With: American Legion.

Elwood

4512 ■ American Legion, Louis Monroe Post 53
114 S Anderson St.
Elwood, IN 46036
Ph: (317)630-1300
Fax: (317)237-9891
URL: National Affiliate–www.legion.org
Local. Affiliated With: American Legion.

4513 ■ Elwood Chamber of Commerce (ECC)
108 S Anderson St.
Elwood, IN 46036
Ph: (765)552-0180
Fax: (765)552-1277
E-mail: elwoodchamber@yahoo.com
URL: National Affiliate–www.uschamber.com
Contact: Jerry Mendenhall, Exec.Dir.
Founded: 1938. **Local**. Promotes business and community development in Elwood, IN. Sponsors Home Show, Sparkle N' Shine town clean-up, Chili Cook-Off-Breakfast with Santa, Elwood Glass Festival and annual Dinner. Sponsors quarterly networking meetings. **Affiliated With:** U.S. Chamber of Commerce. **Publications:** *Chamber Minute*, monthly. Newsletter.

4514 ■ National Technical Honor Society - John H. Hinds Career Center - Indiana
1105 N 19th St.
Elwood, IN 46036
E-mail: jpearson@hindscc.k12.in.us
URL: http://www.elwood.k12.in.us
Contact: Ms. Tami Davis, Instructor
Local.

Evansville

4515 ■ ACF Tri-State Chefs and Cooks Chapter
c/o Edwards Ellis III
8410 Kneer Rd.
Evansville, IN 47720
Ph: (812)963-3259
E-mail: chefed@insightbb.com
URL: National Affiliate–www.acfchefs.org
Contact: Edward W. Ellis III, Chm. of the Board
Regional. Promotes the culinary profession. Provides on-going educational training and networking for members. Provides opportunities for competition, professional recognition and access to educational forums with other culinarians at local, regional, national and international events. **Affiliated With:** American Culinary Federation.

4516 ■ Alcoholics Anonymous, Southwestern Indiana Central Office
PO Box 132
Evansville, IN 47701
Ph: (812)464-2219
Fax: (812)464-3161
Free: (800)266-5584
E-mail: southwesternindiana@southwesternindianaaa.com
URL: http://www.southwesternindianaaa.com
Regional. Individuals recovering from alcoholism. Maintains that members can solve their common problem and help others achieve sobriety through a twelve step program that includes sharing their experience, strength, and hope with each other. **Affiliated With:** Alcoholics Anonymous World Services.

4517 ■ American Association of Airport Executives, Indiana
c/o Robert H. Working, AAE
Evansville Regional Airport
7801 Bussing Dr.
Evansville, IN 47725-6728
Ph: (812)421-4401
Fax: (812)421-4412
E-mail: ruworking@aol.com
URL: http://www.glcaaae.org
Contact: Robert H. Working AAE, Contact
State. Represents airport management personnel at public airports. Promotes professionalism and financial stability in the administration of airports. Furthers airport safety and operational efficiency. Seeks to develop a systematic exchange of information and experience in the development, maintenance and operation of airports. **Affiliated With:** American Association of Airport Executives.

4518 ■ American Cancer Society, Vanderburgh County Unit
1510 W Franklin St.
Evansville, IN 47710
Ph: (812)424-8281 (812)424-8282
Fax: (812)424-1059
Free: (800)543-5245
URL: http://www.cancer.org/docroot/COM/COM_0.asp
Contact: Rhoda Martin, Regional Exec.Dir.
Founded: 1945. **Staff:** 9. **Local**. Seeks to eliminate cancer. Conducts research, educational, service, and advocacy programs. **Affiliated With:** American Cancer Society. **Publications:** *Cancer Facts and Figures*, periodic • Annual Report, annual.

4519 ■ American Chemical Society, Indiana-Kentucky Border Section
c/o Dr. Ihab N. Odeh, Chm.
636 Silver Lake
Evansville, IN 47712-3140
Ph: (812)421-0036
E-mail: ihabnizar@aol.com
URL: National Affiliate–acswebcontent.acs.org
Contact: Dr. Ihab N. Odeh, Chm.
Regional. Represents the interests of individuals dedicated to the advancement of chemistry in all its branches. Provides opportunities for peer interaction and career development. **Affiliated With:** American Chemical Society.

4520 ■ American Legion, Eugene Pate Post 265
1301 N Fares Ave.
Evansville, IN 47711
Ph: (812)423-6470
Fax: (317)237-9891
URL: National Affiliate–www.legion.org
Local. Affiliated With: American Legion.

4521 ■ American Legion, Everette Burdette Post 187
300 Court St.
Evansville, IN 47736
Ph: (317)630-1300
Fax: (317)237-9891
URL: National Affiliate–www.legion.org
Local. Affiliated With: American Legion.

4522 ■ American Legion, Funkhouser Post 8
6001 New Harmony Rd.
Evansville, IN 47720
Ph: (812)963-5391
Fax: (317)237-9891
URL: National Affiliate–www.legion.org
Local. Affiliated With: American Legion.

4523 ■ American Legion, Otis Stone Post 354
1127 Chestnut St.
Evansville, IN 47713
Ph: (317)630-1300
Fax: (317)237-9891
URL: National Affiliate–www.legion.org
Local. Affiliated With: American Legion.

4524 ■ American Sewing Guild, Evansville Chapter (ASG)
c/o Patti Dee Wazny
2630 Anthony Dr.
Evansville, IN 47711-6703
Ph: (812)477-2517
E-mail: pattidee100@aol.com
Contact: Patti Dee Wazny, Contact
Founded: 1995. **Members:** 74. **Membership Dues:** individual, $35 (annual). **Regional Groups:** 21. **State Groups:** 7. **Local Groups:** 1. **Local**. Works to increase members' knowledge about skills in sewing. Sponsors annual style show, community projects, charity sewing activities, and fabric shopping bus tours. **Libraries: Type:** lending; not open to the public. **Holdings:** 100; books, video recordings. **Subjects:** clothing, fitting, home decorating, sergers, heirloom sewing, quilting, purses, accessories, gifts, fabric bowls and boxes, machine embroidery, numerous video tapes on all aspects of sewing and fitting, children's clothing, sashiko, machine beading. **Boards:** Chapter Advisory. **Committees:** Special Events. **Programs:** Annual Style Show. **Projects:** Community Service. **Subgroups:** Sew-N-Sews Neighborhood. **Affiliated With:** American Sewing Guild.

4525 ■ American Society of Heating, Refrigerating and Air-Conditioning Engineers Evansville
c/o Tom Slaats, Pres.
5401 US Hwy. 41 N
Evansville, IN 47711
Ph: (812)426-4685
Fax: (812)426-4106
E-mail: thomas_m_slaats@email.whirlpool.com
URL: http://www.evansvilleashrae.org
Contact: Tom Slaats, Pres.
Local. Advances the arts and sciences of heating, ventilation, air-conditioning and refrigeration. Provides a source of technical and educational information, standards and guidelines. Conducts seminars for professional growth. **Affiliated With:** American Society of Heating, Refrigerating and Air-Conditioning Engineers.

4526 ■ American Society for Quality, Evansville-Owensboro Section 0915
c/o Rita Wade, Sec.
2425 US Hwy. 41 N, Ste.402
Evansville, IN 47711
Ph: (812)482-1041
E-mail: rwade@jasperengines.com
URL: http://www.psci.net/asq915
Contact: Rita Wade, Sec.
Local. Advances learning, quality improvement and knowledge exchange to improve business results and to create better workplaces and communities worldwide. Provides a forum for information exchange, professional development and continuous learning in the science of quality. **Affiliated With:** American Society for Quality.

4527 ■ American Society for Training and Development, River Cities Chapter
c/o Kevin H. Kennedy, Pres.
501 John St., Ste.5
Evansville, IN 47713
Ph: (812)423-4914
Fax: (812)423-5269
E-mail: khkennedy@sigecom.net
URL: http://www.astd-evv.org
Contact: Kevin H. Kennedy, Pres.
Local. Represents individuals engaged in the training and development of business, industry, education, and government employees. **Affiliated With:** ASTD.

4528 ■ American Welding Society, Tri-River Section 107
c/o Earl Young, Chm.
PO Box 208
Evansville, IN 47702
Ph: (812)464-7239
E-mail: eyoung@industrialcontractors.com
URL: National Affiliate–www.aws.org
Contact: Earl Young, Chm.
Local. Advances the science, technology and application of welding and related joining disciplines. **Affiliated With:** American Welding Society.

4529 ■ Apartment Association of Southern Indiana
c/o Kara Hohne, Association Exec.
PO Box 5526
Evansville, IN 47716-5526
Ph: (812)473-0917
Fax: (812)473-6401
E-mail: info@aaosi.com
URL: National Affiliate–www.naahq.org
Contact: Kara Hohne, Association Exec.
Regional. **Affiliated With:** National Apartment Association.

4530 ■ Arthritis Foundation, Southern Indiana Branch
700 N Weinbach, Ste.102
Evansville, IN 47711
Ph: (812)474-1381
Fax: (812)474-1390
E-mail: info.in@arthritis.org
URL: National Affiliate–www.arthritis.org
Local. Seeks to: discover the cause and improve the methods for the treatment and prevention of arthritis and other rheumatic diseases; increase the number of scientists investigating rheumatic diseases; provide training in rheumatic diseases for more doctors; extend knowledge of arthritis and other rheumatic diseases to the lay public, emphasizing the socioeconomic as well as medical aspects of these diseases. **Affiliated With:** Arthritis Foundation.

4531 ■ Association for Computing Machinery, University of Evansville
c/o Deborah Hwang, Dr., Faculty Advisor
Cmpt. Sci. Dept.
1800 Lincoln Ave.
Evansville, IN 47714
Ph: (812)479-2193
Fax: (812)479-2780
E-mail: acm@csserver.evansville.edu
URL: http://csserver.evansville.edu/~acm
Local. Affiliated With: Association for Computing Machinery.

4532 ■ Association for Retarded Citizens - Vanderburgh County
PO Box 4089
Evansville, IN 47724-0089
Ph: (812)428-4500
URL: National Affiliate–www.thearc.org
Local. Parents, professional workers, and others interested in individuals with mental retardation. Works to promote services, research, public understanding, and legislation for people with mental retardation and their families. **Affiliated With:** Arc of the United States.

4533 ■ Azalea Society of America, Tri-State Chapter
c/o Larry Miller
10 Chandler Ave.
Evansville, IN 47713
Ph: (812)422-2864
E-mail: elar1946@sbcglobal.net
URL: National Affiliate–www.azaleas.org
Contact: Larry Miller, Contact
Regional. Affiliated With: Azalea Society of America.

4534 ■ Big Brothers Big Sisters of the Ohio Valley
PO Box 3071
713 N Second Ave.
Evansville, IN 47730-3071
Ph: (812)425-6076
Fax: (812)425-2522
E-mail: bbbs@sigecom.net
URL: http://www.bbbsevansville.org
Contact: Frank Howard, Exec.Dir.
Local. Provides adult mentors to children in both site based programs, such as schools and Boys and Girls Clubs, and in the general community. **Affiliated With:** Big Brothers Big Sisters of America.

4535 ■ Carver of Evansville Community Development Corp.
c/o David Wagner
400 SE 8th St.
Evansville, IN 47713-1819
Ph: (812)423-2612
Local.

4536 ■ Community Marriage Builders (CMB)
1229 Bellemeade Ave.
Evansville, IN 47714
Ph: (812)477-2260
Fax: (812)473-2912
Free: (800)443-8594
E-mail: office@marryright.org
URL: http://www.marryright.org
Contact: Rev. Carl J. Mann Jr., Pres.
Local.

4537 ■ Community Worship Arts
c/o James Peterson
4016 Oxmoor Rd.
Evansville, IN 47715-1310
Ph: (812)437-5811 (812)453-0631
E-mail: jcworshiparts@worldnet.att.net
Contact: James Peterson, Contact
Founded: 2000. **Members:** 63. **Staff:** 2. **Budget:** $24,000. **Regional Groups:** 1. **State Groups:** 2. **Local Groups:** 1. **Local.**

4538 ■ Compassionate Friends - Southern Indiana Chapter
PO Box 2336
Evansville, IN 47728-2336
Ph: (812)477-3085
E-mail: bfliesarefree@hotmail.com
URL: http://members.evansville.net/ktsembrd/index.html
Local.

4539 ■ Downtown Evansville
209 Main St.
Evansville, IN 47708
Ph: (812)424-2986
Fax: (812)424-4772
E-mail: tiffany@downtownevansville.org
URL: http://www.downtownevansville.org
Local.

4540 ■ Evansville Area 4C
5115 Oak Grove Rd., Ste.A
Evansville, IN 47715
Ph: (812)423-4008
Fax: (812)423-3399
Free: (866)200-5909
E-mail: 4c@child-care.org
URL: http://www.child-care.org
Contact: Erin Ramsey, Exec.Dir.
Local.

4541 ■ Evansville Area Association of Realtors
2225 N Cullen Ave.
Evansville, IN 47715
Ph: (812)473-3333
Fax: (812)475-6789
E-mail: eaar@evansvillerealtors.com
URL: National Affiliate–www.realtor.org
Contact: Sherry Tilley, Exec. Officer
Local. Strives to develop real estate business practices. Advocates the right to own, use and transfer real property. Provides a facility for professional development, research and exchange of information among members and to the general public. **Affiliated With:** National Association of Realtors.

4542 ■ Evansville Area Council of Parent Teacher Associations
One SE Ninth St.
Evansville, IN 47708
Ph: (812)435-8453
E-mail: colleen.317@insightbb.com
URL: http://www.evsc.k12.in.us/evscinfo/pta/ptahome.htm
Contact: Jeff Devine, Pres.
Local. Parents, teachers, students, and others interested in uniting the forces of home, school, and community. Promotes the welfare of children and youth.

4543 ■ Evansville Area Human Resource Association (EHRA)
PO Box 6491
Evansville, IN 47719
E-mail: ehra@ehranet.org
URL: http://www.ehranet.org
Contact: Angie J. Brawdy, Pres.
Local. Represents the interests of human resource and industrial relations professionals and executives. Promotes the advancement of human resource management.

4544 ■ Evansville Audubon Society
c/o Wesselman Woods
Nature Preserve
551 N Boeke Rd.
Evansville, IN 47711
E-mail: pcbennett1@mindspring.com
URL: http://www.evvaudubon.org
Contact: Ted Hitch, Pres.
Local. Works to conserve and restore natural ecosystems, focusing on birds and other wildlife for the benefit of humanity and the earth's biological diversity. **Affiliated With:** National Audubon Society.

4545 ■ Evansville Coin Club
c/o Dan Bevers
1313 Stinson Ave.
Evansville, IN 47712
Ph: (812)524-8433
E-mail: danms65@yahoo.com
URL: National Affiliate–www.money.org
Contact: Dan Bevers, Contact
Local. Affiliated With: American Numismatic Association.

4546 ■ Evansville Convention and Visitors Bureau
401 SE Riverside Dr.
Evansville, IN 47713
Ph: (812)421-2200
Fax: (812)421-2207
Free: (800)433-3025
E-mail: info@evansvillecvb.org
URL: http://www.evansvillecvb.org
Contact: Marilee Fowler, Exec.Dir.
Staff: 5. **Budget:** $750,000. **Nonmembership. Local.** Promotes business and tourism in the Evansville, IN area.

4547 ■ Evansville Lapidary Society
1304 N Willow Rd.
Evansville, IN 47711
E-mail: gemlady2000@hotmail.com
URL: National Affiliate–www.amfed.org
Contact: Don Lambert, Sec.
Local. Aims to further the study of Earth Sciences and the practice of lapidary arts and mineralogy. **Affiliated With:** American Federation of Mineralogical Societies.

4548 ■ First District Dental Society
PO Box 2226
Evansville, IN 47728-0226
Ph: (812)454-4732
Fax: (270)826-6919
E-mail: firstdistrictdental@hotmail.com
URL: National Affiliate–www.ada.org
Contact: Ms. Shelly Schmelzer, Exec.Dir.
Local. Represents the interests of dentists committed to the public's oral health, ethics and professional development. Encourages the improvement of the public's oral health and promotes the art and science of dentistry. **Affiliated With:** American Dental Association; Indiana Dental Association.

4549 ■ Greater Evansville Figure Skating Club
PO Box 2506
Evansville, IN 47728-0506
E-mail: vbobsmom@aol.com
URL: National Affiliate–www.usfigureskating.org
Local. Provides programs to encourage participation and achievement in the sport of figure skating on ice. Defines and maintains uniform standards of skating

proficiency. Organizes and sponsors competitions and exhibitions for the purpose of stimulating interest in figure skating. **Affiliated With:** United States Figure Skating Association.

4550 ■ Hadi Shriners
c/o Gary Hudson
6 Walnut St.
Evansville, IN 47708
Ph: (812)423-4285
Fax: (812)421-4477
E-mail: recorder@hadishrine.org
URL: http://www.hadishrine.org
Contact: Gary Hudson, Recorder
Local. Affiliated With: Imperial Council of the Ancient Arabic Order of the Nobles of the Mystic Shrine for North America.

4551 ■ Independent Electrical Contractors, Southern Indiana/Evansville Chapter
c/o Dottie Happe
PO Box 4104
Evansville, IN 47724
Ph: (812)963-8261
Fax: (812)963-8261
E-mail: iecsie@juno.com
URL: National Affiliate–www.ieci.org
Contact: Dottie Happe, Contact
Regional. Affiliated With: Independent Electrical Contractors.

4552 ■ Indiana Amateur Softball Association, Region 12
c/o Stacy Kueber, VP
7020 Arla Jane Dr.
Evansville, IN 47710
Ph: (812)204-0561
E-mail: iasajo@aol.com
URL: http://www.indiana-asa.org
Contact: Stacy Kueber, VP
Local. Affiliated With: Amateur Softball Association of America.

4553 ■ Indiana Mortgage Bankers Association, Southwest Chapter
Wells Fargo Home Mortgage
4400 Washington Ave.
Evansville, IN 47714
Ph: (812)228-3751
Fax: (812)475-8879
E-mail: lafe.a.ransom@wellsfargo.com
URL: http://www.indianamba.org/Chapters/Southwest.htm
Contact: Lafe Ransom, Pres.
Local. Promotes fair and ethical lending practices and fosters professional excellence among real estate finance employees. Seeks to create an environment that enables members to invest in communities and achieve their business objectives. **Affiliated With:** Mortgage Bankers Association.

4554 ■ Indiana Sporting Clays Association (ISCA)
PO Box 3437
Evansville, IN 47733-3437
E-mail: jdbagger@aol.com
URL: http://www.indianasportingclays.org
Contact: JD Mendenhall, Pres.
State.

4555 ■ Institute of Internal Auditors, Tri-State Chapter
c/o Shawn Otto
Harding, Shymanski & Co.
21 SE 3rd St., Ste.500
PO Box 3677
Evansville, IN 47735-3677
Ph: (812)491-1393
E-mail: sotto@hsccpa.com
URL: National Affiliate–www.theiia.org
Contact: Sherry Hancock, Sec.
Membership Dues: regular, $115 (annual) • educator, $65 (annual) • student, retired, $30 (annual) • life, $2,100 • sustainer (government auditors only), $50 (annual) • organization ($65 per staff member over 5; $50 per staff member over 100), $425-$6,600 (annual). **Local.** Promotes the internal auditing profession. Offers affordable continuing professional education. Provides local professional development opportunities. **Telecommunication Services:** electronic mail, sherry_hancock@oldnational.com. **Affiliated With:** Institute of Internal Auditors. **Publications:** Newsletter, bimonthly. **Price:** included in membership dues.

4556 ■ Institute of Management Accountants, Evansville Chapter
c/o Melanie Hinton, Newsletter Dir.
Gaither Rutherford and Co., LLP
PO Box 8408
Evansville, IN 47716-8408
E-mail: evillewebmaster@theima.org
URL: http://www.evansville.imanet.org
Contact: Gary Skie, Pres.
Members: 300. **Local.** Promotes professional and ethical standards. Equips members and students with knowledge and training required for the accounting profession. **Affiliated With:** Institute of Management Accountants. **Publications:** *Spotlight*, monthly. Newsletter. Alternate Formats: online.

4557 ■ International Union of Painters and Allied Trades AFL-CIO, Local 156
409 Millner Indus. Dr.
Evansville, IN 47710
Ph: (812)425-4414 (812)425-4415
Fax: (812)425-4890
Free: (877)325-4414
E-mail: srs@dc91.org
URL: http://www.dc91.org
Contact: Donald Vincent, Business Rep.
Founded: 1890. **Members:** 395. **Membership Dues:** $18 (monthly). **Regional. Affiliated With:** AFL-CIO; International Union of Painters and Allied Trades/ Joint Apprenticeship and Training Fund. **Formerly:** (2005) Painters AFL-CIO, LU 156. **Conventions/ Meetings:** monthly General Membership Meeting - every 3rd Monday in Evansville, IN.

4558 ■ La Leche League Northside of Evansville
750 N Park Dr.
Evansville, IN 47711
Ph: (812)402-0192
E-mail: heilman@sigecom.net
Contact: Bonnie Heilman, Ldr.
Founded: 1970. **Members:** 50. **Membership Dues:** individual, $30 (annual) • family, $40 (annual). **Staff:** 3. **Regional Groups:** 3. **State Groups:** 25. **Local Groups:** 3. **Local.** Dedicated to providing education, information, support, and encouragement to women who want to breastfeed. **Libraries: Type:** reference. **Holdings:** 35; books. **Subjects:** breast-feeding, childbirth, pregnancy, nutrition, fitness, child rearing, child care. **Affiliated With:** La Leche League International. **Formerly:** (2002) La Leche League of Warrick County. **Publications:** *Leaven Breastfeeding Abstracts*, quarterly. Newsletter. Reviews articles of medical interest. • *New Beginnings*, bimonthly. Magazine. Contains articles by mothers about breast feeding, experiences, and regular features. **Price:** included in membership dues. **Advertising:** accepted. **Conventions/Meetings:** annual conference, with numerous panels on breastfeeding and childrearing topics (exhibits) - always November or October.

4559 ■ Mental Health Association in Vanderburgh County
713 N 2nd Ave., Box 5
Evansville, IN 47710
Ph: (812)426-2640
Fax: (812)422-3995
E-mail: mentalhealth@sigecom.net
URL: http://www.mhavanderburgh.org
Contact: Ms. Donna Carr, Exec.Dir.
Local. Seeks to promote mental health and prevent mental health disorders. Improves mental health of Americans through advocacy, public education, research and service. **Affiliated With:** Mental Health Association in Indiana; National Mental Health Association.

4560 ■ Metropolitan Evansville Chamber of Commerce (MECC)
100 NW 2nd St., Ste.100
Evansville, IN 47706-2101
Ph: (812)425-8147
Fax: (812)421-5883
E-mail: info@evansvillechamber.com
URL: http://www.evansvillechamber.com
Contact: Matt Meadors, Pres./CEO
Founded: 1915. **Members:** 900. **Membership Dues:** company (with 5 employees or less), $380 (annual). **Staff:** 13. **Budget:** $1,000,000. **Local.** Promotes business and community development in the Evansville, IN area. **Awards:** Equal TQ Annual Award. **Frequency:** annual. **Type:** recognition. **Committees:** Ambassadors; Environmental; Governmental Affairs; Marketing; Retention; Small Business Development Center Advisory Board; Transportation. **Councils:** Small Business. **Publications:** *Impact*, monthly. Newsletter. **Circulation:** 1,500. **Advertising:** accepted • *Manufacturing and Mining Directory (1993-1994)* • Membership Directory. **Conventions/Meetings:** annual Business Outlook Luncheon - always in November • annual E=Qual Total Quality Conference - always March.

4561 ■ National Active and Retired Federal Employees Association - Evansville 326
1400 Tupman Rd.
Evansville, IN 47720-3331
Ph: (812)425-4452
URL: National Affiliate–www.narfe.org
Contact: Kathleen D. Clancy, Contact
Local. Protects the retirement future of employees through education. Informs members on issues affecting the retirement. **Affiliated With:** National Association of Retired Federal Employees.

4562 ■ National Association of Investors Corporation, Evansville Tri-State Chapter
c/o Rita Eades
3469 Manhattan Blvd.
Evansville, IN 47711-7909
Ph: (812)475-9249
E-mail: rae3469@insightbb.com
URL: http://better-investing.org/chapter/evtri
Contact: Rita Eades, Treas.
Regional. Teaches individuals how to become successful strategic long-term investors. Provides highly focused learning resources and investment tools that empower individuals to become better investors. **Affiliated With:** National Association of Investors Corporation.

4563 ■ National Press Photographers Association, Region 4
c/o Denny Simmons, Dir.
Evansville Courier & Press
300 E Walnut
Evansville, IN 47713
Ph: (812)490-0186
Free: (800)288-3200
E-mail: den4life@yahoo.com
URL: National Affiliate–www.nppa.org
Contact: Denny Simmons, Dir.
Local. Promotes the advancement of photojournalism, creation, editing and distribution in all news media. Encourages photojournalists to reflect high standards of quality of performance and personal code of ethics. Provides continuing educational programs and fraternalism.

4564 ■ Ohio Valley Central Service Professionals
c/o Cheryl Ellerbrook, Pres.
St. Mary's Medical Ctr.
3700 Washington Ave.
Evansville, IN 47750

Ph: (812)485-4886
E-mail: cherbear1@sigecom.net
URL: National Affiliate–www.ashcsp.org
Contact: Cheryl Ellerbrook, Pres.
Local. Promotes healthcare central service, sterile processing and inventory management practices. Provides education, professional and organization development, advocacy and communication to healthcare service professionals. **Affiliated With:** American Society for Healthcare Central Service Professionals.

4565 ■ Phi Theta Kappa, Alpha Phi Theta Chapter - Ivy Tech State College
c/o Susan Jindrich
3501 1st Ave.
Evansville, IN 47710
Ph: (812)429-1421
E-mail: sjindric@ivytech.edu
URL: http://www.ptk.org/directories/chapters/IN/20524-1.htm
Contact: Susan Jindrich, Advisor
Local.

4566 ■ Police and Firemen's Insurance Association - Evansville Fire Department
c/o Joseph R. Greenwell
5024 Stratford Rd.
Evansville, IN 47710
Ph: (812)425-2521
URL: National Affiliate–www.pfia.net
Contact: Joseph R. Greenwell, Contact
Local. Affiliated With: Police and Firemen's Insurance Association.

4567 ■ Psi Chi, National Honor Society in Psychology - University of Evansville
c/o Dept. of Psychology
1800 Lincoln Ave.
Evansville, IN 47722-0001
Ph: (812)479-2520 (812)479-2698
Fax: (812)474-4054
E-mail: bw6@evansville.edu
URL: http://www.psichi.org/chapters/info.asp?chapter_id=186
Contact: William U. Weiss PhD, Advisor
Local.

4568 ■ Psi Chi, National Honor Society in Psychology - University of Southern Indiana
c/o Dept. of Psychology
8600 Univ. Blvd.
Evansville, IN 47712
Ph: (812)464-1855
Fax: (812)465-7152
E-mail: jjpallad@usi.edu
URL: http://www.usi.edu/libarts/psychology/index.htm
Local. Affiliated With: Psi Chi, National Honor Society in Psychology.

4569 ■ River City Ramblers
c/o Linda Neu
2003 N Heidelbach Ave.
Evansville, IN 47711
Ph: (812)425-3886
E-mail: stan-linda.n@juno.com
URL: http://home.insightbb.com/~jgvf65/rivercityramblers.htm
Contact: Linda Neu, Contact
Local. Affiliated With: American Volkssport Association.

4570 ■ Rivercity High Society
PO Box 2671
Evansville, IN 47728-0671
Ph: (812)476-5788 (812)424-4563
E-mail: rivercity@tall.org
URL: http://www.tall.org/clubs/in/evansville
Local. Affiliated With: Tall Clubs International.

4571 ■ SCORE Evansville
c/o Tom Koetting, Chm.
1100 W Lloyd Expy., Ste.314
Evansville, IN 47708-1146
Ph: (812)426-6144
Fax: (812)426-6144
E-mail: scoreevv@aol.com
URL: http://www.scoreevansville.com
Local. Affiliated With: SCORE.

4572 ■ Sheet Metal Contractors Association of Evansville
2556 Waterbridge Way
Evansville, IN 47710-3200
Ph: (812)423-2926
Fax: (812)423-4884
E-mail: evsmca@sbcglobal.net
URL: National Affiliate–www.smacna.org
Contact: Denise Hull, Exec.Dir.
Local. Represents contractors specializing in: ventilating, air handling, warm air heating, architectural and industrial sheet metal, kitchen equipment, testing and balancing, siding, and decking and specialty fabrication contractors. **Affiliated With:** Sheet Metal and Air Conditioning Contractors' National Association.

4573 ■ Society for Information Management, Evansville Area
c/o Vic Baillargeon
110 Walnut St.
Evansville, IN 47708
Ph: (812)425-4880
E-mail: vpbaillargeon@rscquality.com
URL: National Affiliate–www.simnet.org
Affiliated With: Society for Information Management.

4574 ■ Southern Indiana Beagle Club
c/o Tom Nalin
4116 Keenland Blvd.
Evansville, IN 47715-1952
URL: National Affiliate–clubs.akc.org
Contact: Tom Nalin, Contact
Regional.

4575 ■ Southern Indiana Chapter National Electrical Contractors Association
c/o Tom Millay, Exec.Mgr.
PO Box 3075
Evansville, IN 47730-3075
Ph: (812)422-3259
Fax: (812)423-3425
Free: (866)202-2448
E-mail: tommillay@sicneca.com
URL: http://www.sicneca.com
Contact: Tom Millay, Exec.Mgr.
Local. Affiliated With: National Electrical Contractors Association.

4576 ■ Southwest Indiana Council of Teachers of Mathematics
c/o Deborah Hartz, Representative
Evansville-Vanderburgh School Corp.
1 SE 9th St.
Evansville, IN 47708
Ph: (812)435-8427
E-mail: debor1300@aol.com
URL: National Affiliate–www.nctm.org
Contact: Deborah Hartz, Representative
Local. Aims to improve the teaching and learning of mathematics. Provides vision, leadership and professional development to support teachers in ensuring mathematics learning of the highest quality for all students. **Affiliated With:** National Council of Teachers of Mathematics.

4577 ■ Southwestern Indiana AIFA
c/o Dorothy McIntosh, Sec./Treas.
4900 Shamrock Dr., Ste.200A
Evansville, IN 47715
Ph: (812)476-2856
Fax: (812)476-2823
E-mail: dorothymcintosh@sigecom.net
URL: National Affiliate–naifa.org
Contact: Dorothy McIntosh, Sec./Treas.
Local. Represents the interests of insurance and financial advisors. Advocates for a positive legislative and regulatory environment. Enhances business and professional skills of members. **Affiliated With:** National Association of Insurance and Financial Advisors.

4578 ■ Southwestern Indiana Daylily Society (SWIDS)
c/o Peg Michas, Pres.
PO Box 3254
Evansville, IN 47731-3254
Ph: (812)385-5326
E-mail: nickm@gibsoncounty.net
URL: http://www.swids.org
Contact: Peg Michas, Pres.
Local.

4579 ■ Southwestern Indiana Master Gardener Association (SWIMGA)
c/o Purdue Extension Service-Vanderburgh County
13301 Darmstadt Rd., Ste.A
Evansville, IN 47725-9593
Ph: (812)435-5287
Fax: (812)867-4944
URL: http://www.ces.purdue.edu/vanderburgh/mastergardener/
Founded: 1999. **Members:** 250. **Membership Dues:** single, master gardener status, $20 (annual) • couple, master gardener status, $35 (annual). **Budget:** $13,000. **Local.** Seeks to train and educate the community in horticultural activities.

4580 ■ Southwestern Indiana Regional Council on Aging (SWIRCA)
c/o Steve Patrow, Exec.Dir.
PO Box 3938
Evansville, IN 47737-3938
Ph: (812)464-7800
Free: (800)253-2188
E-mail: swirca@swirca.org
URL: http://www.swirca.org
Contact: Steve Patrow, Exec.Dir.
Regional. In-home services for the elderly and disabled. **Affiliated With:** National Senior Games Association.

4581 ■ Sweet Adelines International, Spirit of Evansville Chapter
Good Samaritan Home
601 Boeke Rd.
Evansville, IN 47711
Ph: (812)479-5445
E-mail: hsheets@workable.com
URL: National Affiliate–www.sweetadelineintl.org
Contact: Harriet Sheets, Contact
Local. Advances the musical art form of barbershop harmony through education and performances. Provides education, training and coaching in the development of women's four-part barbershop harmony. **Affiliated With:** Sweet Adelines International.

4582 ■ Tri State Beagle Club
c/o Brenda Hulsey
900 N Red Bank Rd.
Evansville, IN 47712-3743
Ph: (812)768-6900
URL: National Affiliate–www.akc.org
Contact: Brenda Hulsey, Contact
Local. Affiliated With: American Kennel Club.

4583 ■ Tri-State Better Business Bureau
1139 Washington Sq.
Evansville, IN 47715
Ph: (812)473-0202
Fax: (812)473-3080
E-mail: info@evansville.bbb.org
URL: http://www.evansville.bbb.org
Contact: Cathy Eichele, Pres.
Regional. Seeks to promote and foster the highest ethical relationship between businesses and the public through voluntary self-regulation, consumer and business education, and service excellence. Provides information to help consumers and businesses make informed purchasing decisions and avoid costly scams and frauds; settles consumer

complaints through arbitration and other means. **Affiliated With:** BBB Wise Giving Alliance.

4584 ■ United Association of Journeymen and Apprentices of the Plumbing and Pipe Fitting Industry of the United States and Canada - Local Union 136
2300 St. Joe Indus. Park Dr.
Evansville, IN 47720
Ph: (812)423-8043
Fax: (812)423-5517
URL: http://www.ualocal136.org
Contact: Kenny Kurzendoerfer, Pres.
Members: 1,261. **Local. Affiliated With:** United Association of Journeymen and Apprentices of the Plumbing, Pipe Fitting, Sprinkler Fitting Industry of the U.S. and Canada.

4585 ■ United Way of Southwestern Indiana
PO Box 18
Evansville, IN 47701-0018
Ph: (812)422-4100
Fax: (812)421-7474
E-mail: unitedway@unitedwayswi.org
URL: http://www.unitedwayswi.org
Contact: Carol Braden Clarke, Exec.Dir.
Local. Affiliated With: United Way of America.

4586 ■ Vanderburgh County 4-H Council
13301 Darmstadt Rd.
Evansville, IN 47725-9593
Ph: (812)435-5287 (812)867-4935
Fax: (812)867-4944
URL: http://www.ces.purdue.edu/vanderburgh
Contact: Randy Brown, Extension Educator
Local.

4587 ■ Vanderburgh County Medical Society (VCMS)
3116 E Morgan Ave., Ste.F
Evansville, IN 47711
Ph: (812)475-9001
Fax: (812)475-9129
E-mail: cwhitehouse@vcmsdocs.org
URL: http://www.vcmsdocs.org
Contact: Monty Lackey MD, Pres.-Elect
Local. Advances the art and science of medicine. Promotes patient care and the betterment of public health. **Affiliated With:** Indiana State Medical Association.

4588 ■ Vanderburgh County REACT
PO Box 3226
Evansville, IN 47731
Ph: (812)424-8566
E-mail: vandcoreact@aol.com
URL: http://www.reactintl.org/teaminfo/usa_teams/teams-usin.htm
Local. Trained communication experts and professional volunteers. Provides volunteer public service and emergency communications through the use of radios (Citizen Band, General Mobile Radio Service, UHF and HAM). Coordinates with radio industries and government on safety communication matters and supports charitable activities and community organizations.

4589 ■ Vanderburgh County RSVP
c/o Bob Regel, Dir.
PO Box 3938
Evansville, IN 47737-3938
Ph: (812)464-7787
E-mail: vccarsvp@sigecom.net
URL: http://www.seniorcorps.gov
Contact: Bob Regel, Dir.
Local. Affiliated With: Retired and Senior Volunteer Program.

Fairland

4590 ■ Indiana U.S.A. Track and Field (IN USATF)
c/o Cheryl Sunman, Pres.
7060 N Woodnotes
Fairland, IN 46126
Ph: (317)276-9137
Fax: (812)855-5977
E-mail: ianms@iquest.net
URL: http://www.inusatf.org
Contact: Cheryl Sunman, Pres.
State. Affiliated With: U.S.A. Track and Field.

4591 ■ USA Track and Field, Indiana
c/o Cheryl Sunman, Pres.
7060 N Woodnotes
Fairland, IN 46126
Ph: (317)276-9137 (317)835-0161
Fax: (260)347-9484
E-mail: ianms@iquest.net
URL: http://www.inusatf.org
Contact: Cheryl Sunman, Pres.
State. Affiliated With: U.S.A. Track and Field.

Fairmount

4592 ■ American Legion, Fairmount Post 313
522 E 8th St., No. 164
Fairmount, IN 46928
Ph: (317)948-4431
Fax: (317)237-9891
URL: National Affiliate–www.legion.org
Local. Affiliated With: American Legion.

Farmersburg

4593 ■ Wabash Valley Antique Glass and Pottery Club
c/o Ron Glasscock, Pres.
PO Box 690
Farmersburg, IN 47850
E-mail: ronsan@ccrtc.com
URL: National Affiliate–www.fohbc.com
Contact: Ron Glasscock, Pres.
Local. Affiliated With: Federation of Historical Bottle Collectors.

Farmland

4594 ■ American Legion, West Randolph Post 353
PO Box 321
Farmland, IN 47340
Ph: (317)630-1300
Fax: (317)237-9891
URL: National Affiliate–www.legion.org
Local. Affiliated With: American Legion.

Ferdinand

4595 ■ American Legion, Ferdinand Post 124
425 Main St.
Ferdinand, IN 47532
Ph: (317)630-1300
Fax: (317)237-9891
URL: National Affiliate–www.legion.org
Local. Affiliated With: American Legion.

4596 ■ Ferdinand Chamber of Commerce
PO Box 101
Ferdinand, IN 47532-0101
Ph: (812)367-0550
Fax: (812)367-1303
E-mail: btretter@psci.net
URL: http://www.ferdinandinchamber.org
Contact: Brian Tretter, Exec.Dir.
Local. Promotes business and community development in the Ferdinand, IN area.

Fishers

4597 ■ Admirals No. 144
c/o Peter Pippen
7129 Koldyke Dr.
Fishers, IN 46038
Ph: (317)845-5520
E-mail: simba2@iquest.net
URL: National Affiliate–www.amya.org
Contact: Peter Pippen, Contact
Local.

4598 ■ Alliance for Responsible Pet Ownership (ARPO)
PO Box 6385
Fishers, IN 46038
Ph: (317)774-8292
E-mail: info@adoptarpo.org
URL: http://www.adoptarpo.org
Contact: Kelley Hinkle, Pres.
Founded: 1998. **Members:** 50. **Membership Dues:** individual, $35 (annual). **Regional Groups:** 1. **Local Groups:** 1. **Regional.** Promotes the adoption and placement of stray and surrendered companion animals.

4599 ■ American Legion, Indiana Post 510
c/o Frank E. Mc Kinney, Sr.
12004 Corbin Dr.
Fishers, IN 46038
Ph: (317)630-1300
Fax: (317)237-9891
URL: National Affiliate–www.legion.org
Contact: Frank E. Mc Kinney Sr., Contact
Local. Affiliated With: American Legion.

4600 ■ American Legion, Lowell Beaver Post 470
9091 E 126th St.
Fishers, IN 46038
Ph: (317)842-5944
Fax: (317)237-9891
URL: National Affiliate–www.legion.org
Local. Affiliated With: American Legion.

4601 ■ Art Libraries Society of North America - Midstates Chapter
c/o Shelley Quattrocchi, Sec.-Treas.
11809 Ledgerock Ct.
Fishers, IN 46037
Ph: (317)920-2647
E-mail: squattrocchi@ima-art.org
URL: http://www.indiana.edu/~arlismid/index.html
Contact: Shelley Quattrocchi, Sec.-Treas.
Regional. Aims to address the needs of art libraries and other professionals. Serves as a means of communication between art librarians and other notable groups and individuals in the industry. Strives to assist in the publishing of articles on art. Advocates art appreciation. **Affiliated With:** Art Libraries Society/North America.

4602 ■ Autism Advocates of Indiana (AAI)
c/o Colleen Krauss, Board of Dir.
10223 Caliburn Ct.
Fishers, IN 46038
Ph: (317)596-0098 (317)482-0032
E-mail: dkrauss1@prodigy.net
URL: http://www.aaiwalk.org
Contact: Colleen Krauss, Board of Dir.
State.

4603 ■ Creating Hope
c/o Jeanette G. Shamblen
10955 Windermere Blvd.
Fishers, IN 46038-8987
Ph: (317)842-2946
Fax: (317)842-3541
E-mail: jeanette@creating-hope.org
URL: http://www.creating-hope.org
Contact: Jeanette Shamblen, Pres.
Founded: 2000. **Nonmembership. Local.** Committed to helping people cope with cancer through self-expression and creativity and inspiring them to find their way through each day toward survival. Activities

include providing watercolor kits, demonstrations and seminars free of charge to cancer patients and survivors.

4604 ■ Fishers Chamber of Commerce (FCC)
11601 Municipal Dr.
PO Box 353
Fishers, IN 46038-0353
Ph: (317)578-0700
Fax: (317)578-1097
E-mail: info@fisherschamber.com
URL: http://www.fisherschamber.com
Contact: Christi J. Wolf, Pres.
Members: 700. **Membership Dues:** business (based on number of employees), $175-$1,200 (annual) • financial institution (plus $125/additional branch), $450 (annual) • apartment complex (plus $.25/unit), $150 (annual) • land developer, $500 (annual) • utility, $500 (annual) • school corporation, $300 (annual) • church, civic, retiree, $75 (annual). **Staff:** 6. **Local.** Promotes business and community development in Fishers, IN. **Awards:** Business of the Year. **Frequency:** annual. **Type:** recognition. **Recipient:** for a business that employs over 25 employees • Curb Appeal Award. **Frequency:** annual. **Type:** recognition. **Recipient:** for a business that contributed to the beautification of Fishers • Emerging Growth. **Frequency:** annual. **Type:** recognition. **Recipient:** for a business that has an annual 15% gross sales increase • Small Business of the Year. **Frequency:** annual. **Type:** recognition. **Recipient:** for a business that employs less than 25 employees and provides positive economic impact. **Telecommunication Services:** electronic mail, cwolf@fisherschamber.com. **Councils:** Community; Economic Development; Education; Marketing; Public Policy. **Publications:** *FishersChamber.Com*, monthly. Newsletter. **Price:** included in membership dues. **Advertising:** accepted. Alternate Formats: online. **Conventions/Meetings:** monthly meeting - every last Wednesday • monthly meeting - every 4th Thursday.

4605 ■ Indiana Academy of Ophthalmology (IAO)
c/o Kimberly Williams, MBA, Exec.Dir.
9959 Allisonville Rd.
Fishers, IN 46038
Ph: (317)577-3062
Fax: (317)578-7718
E-mail: iao@indianaeyemds.com
URL: http://www.indianaeyemds.com
Contact: Kimberly Williams MBA, Exec.Dir.
Members: 236. **Membership Dues:** ordinary fellow, advocate fellow, $795 (annual) • junior/senior fellow, $250 (annual) • resident-in-training, fellow-in-training, $100 (annual) • out-of-state, $150 (annual). **State.** Strives to promote the highest quality, comprehensive vision, medical and surgical eye care.

4606 ■ Indiana Chapter American Concrete Institute
c/o Thomas J. Grisinger, Sec.-Treas.
Lehigh Portland Cement Co.
7905 S Dawson Dr.
Fishers, IN 46038
Ph: (317)469-4660
Fax: (317)469-4901
E-mail: tgrisinger@lehighcement.com
URL: National Affiliate–www.aci-int.org
Contact: Virgil Mabrey, Pres.
State. Affiliated With: American Concrete Institute.

4607 ■ Indiana Healthcare Executives Network
PO Box 670
Fishers, IN 46038-0670
Ph: (317)442-9966
E-mail: barbarabroadbridge@hotmail.com
URL: http://ihen.ache.org
Contact: Barbara T. Broadbridge, Exec.Dir./Pres.
State. Works to improve the health status of society by advancing healthcare leadership and management excellence. Conducts research, career development and public policy programs. **Affiliated With:** American College of Healthcare Executives.

4608 ■ Indiana Township Association (ITA)
PO Box 611
Fishers, IN 46038
Ph: (317)813-3240
Fax: (317)813-3187
E-mail: itaindy@yahoo.com
URL: http://www.indianatownshipassoc.org
Contact: Deborah R. Driskell, Pres.
State.

4609 ■ Kiwanis Club of Fishers Station
PO Box 152
Fishers, IN 46038-0152
Ph: (317)847-0061
E-mail: gashley@clarian.org
URL: http://home.insightbb.com/~fisherskiwanis/index.html
Contact: Graham Ashley, Pres.
Local.

4610 ■ National Association of Miniature Enthusiasts - Miniature Dream Builders
c/o Roberta Waugh
542 Conner Creek Dr.
Fishers, IN 46038
Ph: (317)845-5902
E-mail: rwaugh2845@aol.com
URL: http://www.miniatures.org/states/IN.html
Contact: Roberta Waugh, Contact
Local. Affiliated With: National Association of Miniature Enthusiasts.

4611 ■ Southeastern Swim Club (SSC)
PO Box 327
Fishers, IN 46038
Ph: (317)579-0164
Fax: (317)579-9809
E-mail: joinssc@southeasternswim.org
URL: http://southeasternswim.org
Contact: Andy Pederson, Head Coach
Founded: 1989. **Members:** 225. **Staff:** 6. **Local.** Assists swimmers in finding competitive opportunities. **Publications:** Newsletter, monthly. **Price:** free. **Circulation:** 230.

Flat Rock

4612 ■ Midwest Antique Fruit Jar and Bottle Club
c/o Norm Barnett, Pres.
PO Box 38
Flat Rock, IN 47234
Ph: (812)587-5560
URL: http://www.fruitjar.org
Contact: Norm Barnett, Pres.
Local. Affiliated With: Federation of Historical Bottle Collectors.

Flora

4613 ■ American Legion, Clarence Wiles Post 222
911 S Div. St.
Flora, IN 46929
Ph: (219)967-4661
Fax: (317)237-9891
URL: National Affiliate–www.legion.org
Local. Affiliated With: American Legion.

4614 ■ Arc of Carroll County
216 W Clem St.
Flora, IN 46929
Ph: (574)967-4252
E-mail: kinzer@tds.net
URL: National Affiliate–www.TheArc.org
Local. Parents, professional workers, and others interested in individuals with mental retardation. Works to promote services, research, public understanding, and legislation for people with mental retardation and their families. **Affiliated With:** Arc of the United States.

Floyds Knobs

4615 ■ American Legion, William Zeb Longest Post 42
4530 Paoli Pike
Floyds Knobs, IN 47119
Ph: (812)923-9842
Fax: (317)237-9891
URL: National Affiliate–www.legion.org
Local. Affiliated With: American Legion.

Forest

4616 ■ Pheasants Forever Central Indiana, Clinton County
3936 N 1000 E
Forest, IN 46039
Ph: (765)249-2621
URL: http://pfcic.org
Contact: Charles Davis, Pres.
Local. Affiliated With: Pheasants Forever.

Fort Wayne

4617 ■ 3 Rivers Velo Sport
PO Box 11391
Fort Wayne, IN 46857-1391
Ph: (260)410-7847
E-mail: president@3rvs.com
URL: http://www.3rvs.com
Local. Affiliated With: International Mountain Bicycling Association. **Formerly:** (2005) Three Rivers Velo Sport.

4618 ■ ACF Fort Wayne Professional Chefs Association
c/o George Eyler, Pres.
Ivy Tech State Coll.
3800 N Anthony Blvd.
Fort Wayne, IN 46805
Ph: (260)480-4240
Fax: (260)480-2051
E-mail: aeyler@ivytech.edu
URL: National Affiliate–www.acfchefs.org
Contact: George A. Eyler, Pres.
Local. Promotes the culinary profession. Provides on-going educational training and networking for members. Provides opportunities for competition, professional recognition and access to educational forums with other culinarians at local, regional, national and international events. **Affiliated With:** American Culinary Federation.

4619 ■ Acres Land Trust
2000 N Wells St.
Fort Wayne, IN 46808-2474
Ph: (260)422-1004
Fax: (260)422-1004
E-mail: acres@acreslandtrust.org
URL: http://www.acres-land-trust.org
Contact: Carolyn McNagny, Exec.Dir.
Founded: 1960. **Members:** 1,100. **Membership Dues:** individual, $20 (annual) • family, $30 (annual) • senior citizen, student, $15 (annual) • life, $1,500 • share-the-expense, club/organization, $50 (annual) • patron, $100 (annual). **Staff:** 4. **Budget:** $100,000. Promotes the preservation and acquisition of natural areas in northeastern Indiana. Seeks to acquire and administer natural areas as living museums for educational and scientific purposes and for public enjoyment. Maintains 53 nature preserves in 13 counties in Northeast Indiana. Works to protect other natural areas. Conducts guided field trips, concerts, canoe trips and special events. **Libraries: Type:** reference. **Formerly:** ACRES, Inc. **Publications:** *ACRES Quarterly*. Newsletter. **Price:** included in membership dues. **Circulation:** 2,500.

4620 ■ Alcoholics Anonymous World Services, Fort Wayne Area Intergroup
2118 Inwood Dr., Ste.112
Fort Wayne, IN 46815
Ph: (260)471-6262
URL: National Affiliate–www.aa.org
Local. Individuals recovering from alcoholism. AA maintains that members can solve their common problem and help others achieve sobriety through a twelve step program that includes sharing their experience, strength, and hope with each other. **Affiliated With:** Alcoholics Anonymous World Services.

4621 ■ Allen County Genealogical Society of Indiana (ACGSI)
PO Box 12003
Fort Wayne, IN 46862
Ph: (260)421-1245
E-mail: kathrynabloom@verizon.net
URL: http://www.ipfw.edu/ipfwhist/historgs/acgsi.htm
Contact: Kathryn Bloom, Pres.
Founded: 1976. **Members:** 350. **Membership Dues:** single, $15 (annual) • family, $18 (annual). **Local**. Collects and preserves genealogical information about Allen County, IN families. Encourages genealogical research. **Publications:** *Allen County Lines*, quarterly. Newsletter. **Price:** included in membership dues; $3.00/issue for nonmembers. **Conventions/Meetings:** monthly meeting - always 2nd Wednesday; except July and August.

4622 ■ Alpha Parent Support Group
c/o Marta Meade Desimone
4824 Homestead Rd.
Fort Wayne, IN 46804

4623 ■ American Association of Blacks in Energy, Indiana
c/o Lafayette Jordan, Pres./Operations Mgr.
PO Box 12041
Fort Wayne, IN 46862-2041
Ph: (219)439-1237 (260)439-1237
Fax: (219)439-1230
E-mail: ljordan@nisource.com
URL: http://aabe.org
Contact: Lafayette Jordan, Pres./Operations Mgr.
Local. **Affiliated With:** American Association of Blacks in Energy.

4624 ■ American Association of Critical Care Nurses, Northeast Indiana Chapter (AACCN)
c/o Cheryl Rockwell, Pres.
PO Box 11048
Fort Wayne, IN 46855
Ph: (260)460-4747
E-mail: neic.info@aacn.org
URL: http://www.aacn.org/chapters/nic.nsf/other/homepage?opendocument
Contact: Cheryl Rockwell, Pres.
State. Professional critical care nurses. Established to provide continuing education programs for nurses specializing in critical care and to develop standards of nursing care of critically ill patients. **Affiliated With:** American Association of Critical-Care Nurses.

4625 ■ American Cancer Society, Northeast Indiana Area Service Center
2420 N Coliseum Blvd., Ste.200
Fort Wayne, IN 46805
Ph: (260)471-3911
Fax: (260)483-5344
URL: National Affiliate–www.cancer.org
Local. **Affiliated With:** American Cancer Society.

4626 ■ American Chemical Society, Northeastern Indiana Section
c/o Pamela Lord, Chair
Univ. of St. Francis
2701 Spring St.
Fort Wayne, IN 46808-3939
Ph: (260)434-7565
E-mail: plord@sf.edu
URL: National Affiliate–acswebcontent.acs.org
Contact: Pamela Lord, Chair
Local. Represents the interests of individuals dedicated to the advancement of chemistry in all its branches. Provides opportunities for peer interaction and career development. **Affiliated With:** American Chemical Society.

4627 ■ American Legion, Allen County Post 499
4830 Hillegas Rd.
Fort Wayne, IN 46818
Ph: (219)483-1368
Fax: (317)237-9891
URL: National Affiliate–www.legion.org
Local. **Affiliated With:** American Legion.

4628 ■ American Legion, David Parrish Post 296
130 W Tillman Rd.
Fort Wayne, IN 46807
Ph: (219)456-2988
Fax: (317)237-9891
URL: National Affiliate–www.legion.org
Local. **Affiliated With:** American Legion.

4629 ■ American Legion, Fort Wayne Post 47
6424 St. Joe Rd.
Fort Wayne, IN 46835
Ph: (219)485-0993
Fax: (317)237-9891
URL: National Affiliate–www.legion.org
Local. **Affiliated With:** American Legion.

4630 ■ American Legion, Indiana Post 148
c/o Charles C. Anderson
705 E Lewis St.
Fort Wayne, IN 46802
Ph: (317)630-1300
Fax: (317)237-9891
URL: National Affiliate–www.legion.org
Contact: Charles C. Anderson, Contact
Local. **Affiliated With:** American Legion.

4631 ■ American Legion, Lincoln Post 82
3501 Harris Rd.
Fort Wayne, IN 46808
Ph: (219)484-8276
Fax: (317)237-9891
URL: National Affiliate–www.legion.org
Local. **Affiliated With:** American Legion.

4632 ■ American Legion, Waynedale Post 241
7605 Bluffton Rd.
Fort Wayne, IN 46809
Ph: (219)747-7851
Fax: (317)237-9891
URL: National Affiliate–www.legion.org
Local. **Affiliated With:** American Legion.

4633 ■ American Lung Association of Indiana, Northern
c/o Brett Aschliman, Mgr. of Youth Development
802 W Wayne St.
Fort Wayne, IN 46802
Ph: (260)426-1170
Fax: (260)422-4924
E-mail: baschliman@lungin.org
URL: http://www.lungin.org
Contact: Brett Aschliman, Mgr. of Youth Development
Local. Physicians, nurses, and laymen interested in the prevention and control of lung disease. Conducts patient education, advocacy, and research; major areas of focus are asthma, tobacco control and environmental health. **Programs:** Better Breathers Club; Camp Superkids; Freedom From Smoking. **Affiliated With:** American Lung Association.

4634 ■ American Red Cross Blood Services Indiana-Ohio Region
1212 E California Rd.
Fort Wayne, IN 46825
Ph: (260)480-8145
URL: http://chapters.redcross.org/br/indianaoh
Regional.

4635 ■ American Society for Quality, Northeastern Indiana Section 0905
c/o John Chalmers, Sec.
PO Box 11887
Fort Wayne, IN 46861-1887
Ph: (260)587-9155
E-mail: jchalmers@ashinmold.com
URL: http://www.asq0905.org
Contact: John Chalmers, Sec.
Local. Advances learning, quality improvement and knowledge exchange to improve business results and to create better workplaces and communities worldwide. Provides a forum for information exchange, professional development and continuous learning in the science of quality. **Affiliated With:** American Society for Quality.

4636 ■ American Society of Women Accountants, Fort Wayne Chapter No. 046
c/o Brigitte Godwin, CPA, Pres.
Indiana State Bd. of Accounts
7031 Hawksnest Trail
Fort Wayne, IN 46835
Ph: (317)232-2507 (260)486-8929
E-mail: bgodwin@sboafe.in.gov
URL: National Affiliate–www.aswa.org
Contact: Brigitte Godwin CPA, Pres.
Local. **Affiliated With:** American Society of Women Accountants.

4637 ■ Anthony Wayne Stamp Society
c/o Mr. James A. Mowrer
1301 E State Blvd.
Fort Wayne, IN 46805-4421
E-mail: stamp@gte.net
URL: National Affiliate–www.stamps.org
Contact: Mr. James A. Mowrer, Contact
Local. **Affiliated With:** American Philatelic Society.

4638 ■ Apartment Association of Fort Wayne-Northeast Indiana (AAFW-NEI)
3106 Lake Ave.
Fort Wayne, IN 46805
Ph: (260)482-2916
Fax: (260)482-5187
URL: http://www.apartmentsfortwayne.com
Contact: Jay Scott, Exec.Dir.
Founded: 1978. **Members:** 22,000. **Membership Dues:** associates, $300 (annual). **Staff:** 3. **Budget:** $380,000. **State Groups:** 1. **Local**. Represents owners, managers, maintenance technicians and those who supply goods and services to the home rental industry. **Awards:** Summit Award. **Frequency:** annual. **Type:** recognition. **Committees:** Associate Activities and Events; Education; Fundraising; Legislative; Membership; Standing. **Councils:** Independent Owners. **Affiliated With:** National Apartment Association. **Publications:** *Annual Membership Directory/Buyer's Guide*, annual • *Apartment Guide*, quarterly. Features apartment homes promoted, advertised. **Price:** free. **Circulation:** 18,000. **Advertising:** accepted • *On Site*, monthly. Magazine. **Price:** included in membership dues. **Circulation:** 500. **Advertising:** accepted. Alternate Formats: CD-ROM; magnetic tape. **Conventions/Meetings:** monthly meeting, with industry topics, education addressed - always second Tuesday • annual trade show, with full day of recognition education and product displays (exhibits).

4639 ■ APICS, The Association for Operations Management - Fort Wayne Chapter 139
PO Box 11768
Fort Wayne, IN 46860

Ph: (260)496-1073
E-mail: jnoblitt@digimarc.com
URL: http://www.apics-fortwayne.org
Contact: James Noblitt, Pres.
Local. Provides information and services in production and inventory management and related areas to enable members, enterprises and individuals to add value to their business performance. **Affiliated With:** APICS - The Association for Operations Management.

4640 ■ Arthritis Foundation, Northeast Indiana Branch
11119 Parkview Plz. Dr., Ste.103
Fort Wayne, IN 46845
Ph: (260)672-6570
Fax: (260)672-6571
E-mail: gdodd@arthritis.org
URL: National Affiliate–www.arthritis.org
Contact: Mrs. Ginger Dodd, Exec.Dir.
Founded: 1998. **Staff:** 1. **State Groups:** 4. **Languages:** English, Spanish. **Local**. Aims to improve lives through leadership in the prevention, control and cure of arthritis and related diseases. Raises funds for research, patient, service and education. Conducts presentations where information regarding the disease is discussed and disseminated by physicians and other medical personnel. Makes available exercise classes, self help groups and support groups to aid those suffering from the disease. **Libraries: Type:** open to the public. **Holdings:** articles, books, periodicals, video recordings. **Subjects:** arthritis and related diseases. **Awards: Type:** recognition. **Recipient:** for service to the branch. **Committees:** Forum; JBR; Walk; Wine/Auction. **Affiliated With:** Arthritis Foundation; Arthritis Foundation, Indiana Chapter. **Publications:** *Arthritis Today*, monthly. Magazine. Contains information for those interested in or suffering from the effects of arthritis and related diseases. **Price:** $3.99 for nonmembers; included in membership dues. **Advertising:** accepted • *Arthritis Update*, quarterly. Newsletters. Gives information about the 3 branches and the chapter office regarding events, new research information, etc. **Price:** free. **Conventions/Meetings:** monthly meeting, board of directors meeting.

4641 ■ Assistance League of Fort Wayne
PO Box 40071
Fort Wayne, IN 46804
Ph: (260)749-9551
E-mail: mfsomerville@earthlink.net
URL: http://fortwayne.assistanceleague.org
Local. Affiliated With: Assistance League.

4642 ■ Association for Computing Machinery, Indiana Institute of Technology
c/o Thomas E. Brownridge, Faculty Adv.
1600 E Washington Blvd.
Fort Wayne, IN 46803
Ph: (260)422-5561
Fax: (260)422-7696
E-mail: mfmansfield@indianatech.edu
URL: National Affiliate–www.acm.org
Contact: Martin F. Mansfield, Sponsor
Local. Works to promote an increased knowledge of science, design, development construction, language, and application of modern computing machinery; promotes a greater interest in computing machinery and its applications; and provides a means of communication between persons having interest in computing machinery. Common activities include preparing for and attending programming contests, and attending conferences in neighboring states and universities. **Affiliated With:** Association for Computing Machinery.

4643 ■ Bach Collegium- Fort Wayne
c/o Dr. Daniel G. Reuning, Artistic Dir.
202 W Rudisill Blvd.
Fort Wayne, IN 46807
Ph: (260)744-2585
Fax: (260)744-2585
URL: http://www.bachcollegium.org
Contact: Dr. Daniel G. Reuning, Artistic Dir.
Local.

4644 ■ Better Business Bureau of Northeastern Indiana
4011 Parnell Ave.
Fort Wayne, IN 46805
Ph: (260)423-4433
Fax: (260)423-3301
Free: (800)552-4631
E-mail: info@neindianabbb.org
URL: http://www.neindiana.bbb.org
Contact: Mike Coil, Pres.
Local. Strives to establish a relationship between businesses and the public through self-regulation, service, and consumer and business education. **Councils:** Council of Better Business Bureaus. **Affiliated With:** BBB Wise Giving Alliance. **Publications:** Directory, annual. **Circulation:** 65,000.

4645 ■ Big Brothers Big Sisters of America of Northeast Indiana
2439 Fairfield Ave.
Fort Wayne, IN 46807
Ph: (219)456-1600
Fax: (219)456-2009
Free: (888)456-1600
URL: http://www.bbbsnei.org
Contact: Josette Rider, Exec.Dir.
Local. Affiliated With: Big Brothers Big Sisters of America.

4646 ■ Canal Society of Indiana (CSI)
PO Box 40087
Fort Wayne, IN 46804
E-mail: indcanal@aol.com
URL: http://www.indcanal.org
Contact: Robert F. Schmidt, Pres.
Founded: 1982. **Members:** 550. **Membership Dues:** individual and/or family, $22 (annual) • institution/non-profit, $15 (annual) • contributor, $30 (annual) • patron, $50 (annual). **State**. Persons interested in historic and operating canals. Encourages the preservation, restoration, and use of navigation canals. **Publications:** *Canal Society of Indiana Newsletter*, periodic • *Indiana Canals*, quarterly. Journal. **Conventions/Meetings:** semiannual conference, meeting plus bus tour of canal sites (exhibits) - always spring and fall.

4647 ■ Canterbury - Wyldlife
701 W Rudisill Ave.
Fort Wayne, IN 46807
Ph: (260)745-3492
URL: http://sites.younglife.org/_layouts/ylext/default.aspx?ID=C-913
Local. Affiliated With: Young Life.

4648 ■ Council for Exceptional Children, Indiana
c/o June Robinson
2015 Lawndale Dr.
Fort Wayne, IN 46805
Ph: (260)467-1110
E-mail: junesped@msn.com
URL: http://www.cec.sped.org/ab/federati.html
Contact: June Robinson, Contact
State.

4649 ■ Easter Seals ARC of Northeast Indiana
c/o Chris Ford
4919 Coldwater Rd.
Fort Wayne, IN 46825
Ph: (260)456-4534
Fax: (260)745-5200
Free: (800)234-7811
E-mail: cford@esarc.org
URL: http://www.eastersealsarcnein.org
Contact: Chris Ford, Contact
Founded: 1954. **Local**. **Committees:** Annual Giving; Assistive Technology; Grants; Planned Giving; Product Sales; Special Events. **Affiliated With:** Easter Seals.

4650 ■ Fort Wayne AIFA
c/o George Danusis, Pres.
10319 Dawson's Creek Blvd., Ste.A
Fort Wayne, IN 46825-1911
Ph: (260)489-9884
Fax: (260)482-7687
E-mail: stanley.koehl@nmfn.com
URL: National Affiliate–naifa.org
Contact: George Danusis, Pres.
Local. Represents the interests of insurance and financial advisors. Advocates for a positive legislative and regulatory environment. Enhances business and professional skills of members. **Affiliated With:** National Association of Insurance and Financial Advisors.

4651 ■ Fort Wayne/Allen County Convention and Visitors Bureau
1021 S Calhoun St.
Fort Wayne, IN 46802
Ph: (260)424-3700
Fax: (260)424-3914
Free: (800)767-7752
E-mail: visitorinfo@visitfortwayne.com
URL: http://www.visitfortwayne.com
Contact: Dan O'Connell CAE, Pres.
Founded: 1990. **Members:** 330. **Local**. Seeks to promote Fort Wayne as a destination for conventions, tournaments, and leisure travel.

4652 ■ Fort Wayne Area Association of Realtors
3403 E Dupont Rd.
Fort Wayne, IN 46825
Ph: (260)426-4700
Fax: (260)422-9966
E-mail: karan@fwaar.com
URL: http://www.fwaar.com
Contact: Karan Ford, CEO
Local. Strives to develop real estate business practices. Advocates the right to own, use and transfer real property. Provides a facility for professional development, research and exchange of information among members and to the general public. **Affiliated With:** National Association of Realtors.

4653 ■ Fort Wayne Area Youth for Christ
PO Box 8068
Fort Wayne, IN 46898
Ph: (260)484-4551
Fax: (260)484-4374
URL: http://www.fwayfc.org
Local. Affiliated With: Youth for Christ/U.S.A.

4654 ■ Fort Wayne Astronomical Society
c/o Larry Clifford
PO Box 11093
Fort Wayne, IN 46855
Ph: (260)824-2655
E-mail: clifford@adamswells.com
URL: http://www.members.aol.com/theFWAS/index.html
Local.

4655 ■ Fort Wayne Beagle Club
c/o Stormy A. Weldon
3012 S Clinton St.
Fort Wayne, IN 46806-1064
URL: National Affiliate–clubs.akc.org
Contact: Stormy A. Weldon, Contact
Local.

4656 ■ Fort Wayne Corvette Club
PO Box 10902
Fort Wayne, IN 46854-0902
E-mail: robertthomas.bbk@earthlink.net
URL: http://www.fwcc-in.org
Contact: Robert Thomas, Pres.
Local. Affiliated With: National Council of Corvette Clubs.

4657 ■ Fort Wayne Habitat for Humanity
c/o Chris Knight, Admin.Mgr.
629 E Washington Blvd.
Fort Wayne, IN 46802
Ph: (260)420-9919 (260)422-4828
Fax: (260)424-9272
E-mail: cknight@fortwaynehabitat.org
URL: http://www.fortwaynehabitat.org
Local.

4658 ■ Fort Wayne Hi-Lites
c/o Tom Cashman
15808 Canyon Glen Pkwy.
Fort Wayne, IN 46845-9730
Ph: (219)637-0000
E-mail: ftwayne@tall.org
URL: National Affiliate–www.tall.org
Contact: Tom Cashman, Contact
Local. Affiliated With: Tall Clubs International.

4659 ■ Fort Wayne Medical Society
709 Clay St., Ste.300
Fort Wayne, IN 46802
Ph: (260)420-1011
URL: http://www.fwms.org
Contact: Tom Gutwein MD, Pres.
Local. Advances the art and science of medicine. Promotes patient care and the betterment of public health. **Affiliated With:** Indiana State Medical Association.

4660 ■ Fort Wayne Table Tennis Club
1724 Getz Rd.
Fort Wayne, IN 46804
Ph: (260)432-2294
URL: http://www.usatt.org/clubs
Contact: Max Salisbury, Contact
Local. Affiliated With: U.S.A. Table Tennis.

4661 ■ Fort Wayne Urban League
2135 S Hanna St.
Fort Wayne, IN 46803
Ph: (260)745-3100
Fax: (260)745-0405
E-mail: ftwuleague@aol.com
URL: http://www.fwurbanleague.org
Contact: Jonathan C. Ray, Pres./CEO
Local. Affiliated With: National Urban League.

4662 ■ Ft. Wayne Young Life Club
701 W Rudisill Ave.
Fort Wayne, IN 46807
Ph: (260)745-3492
URL: http://sites.younglife.org/sites/fortwayneyl/default.aspx
Local. Affiliated With: Young Life.

4663 ■ Friends of the Parks of Allen County, Indiana
c/o Julie Donnell
PO Box 9303
Fort Wayne, IN 46899
Founded: 2000. **Members:** 60. **Local. Publications:** *A Walk in the Park*, quarterly. Newsletter.

4664 ■ Friends of the Third World (FOTW)
c/o Mr. Jim Goetsch
611 W Wayne St.
Fort Wayne, IN 46802-2167
Ph: (260)422-6821
Fax: (260)422-1650
E-mail: fotw@igc.org
URL: http://www.friendsofthethirdworld.org
Contact: Mr. Jim Goetsch, Contact
Founded: 1972. **Members:** 400. **Membership Dues:** general, $5 (annual). **Staff:** 4. **Budget:** $400,000. **Local Groups:** 6. **Languages:** English, French, Spanish. **Regional.** Voluntary action against poverty, marketing of handicrafts, public education about the root causes of poverty, both international and domestic. **Libraries: Type:** by appointment only. **Subjects:** poverty and related issues. **Publications:** *Friends in Action*. Newsletter. **Price:** included in membership dues.

4665 ■ Gardeners of America/Men's Garden Clubs of America - Gardeners of America Fort Wayne
c/o Robert Novak, Pres.
1913 Falcon Hill Pl.
Fort Wayne, IN 46825
Ph: (260)497-0461
E-mail: thebobnovak@aol.com
URL: National Affiliate–www.tgoa-mgca.org
Contact: Robert Novak, Pres.
Local.

4666 ■ Girl Scouts of Limberlost Council
2135 Spy Run Ave.
Fort Wayne, IN 46805
Ph: (219)422-3417
Fax: (260)422-0084
Free: (800)283-4812
URL: http://www.gslimberlost.org
Contact: Laura Bush, Pres.
Local. Young girls and adult volunteers, corporate, government and individual supporters. Strives to develop potential and leadership skills among its members. Conducts trainings, educational programs and outdoor activities.

4667 ■ Greater Fort Wayne Chamber of Commerce (GFWCC)
826 Ewing St.
Fort Wayne, IN 46802
Ph: (260)424-1435
Fax: (260)426-7232
E-mail: ppl@fwchamber.org
URL: http://www.fwchamber.org
Contact: Philip P. Laux, Pres. & CEO
Membership Dues: general business firm (plus $5 per full-time employee), $315 (annual) • professional firm (plus $5 per full-time employee/plus $20 for each professional), $315 (annual) • branch/additional location (plus $5 per full-time employee), $215 (annual) • affiliate (plus $5 per full-time employee), $215 (annual) • non-profit (based on the number of employee), $315-$995 (annual). **Local.** Promotes business and community development in the Ft. Wayne, IN area. **Divisions:** Communication; Economic Development; Government; Small Business; Workforce Development. **Publications:** *Emphasis*, periodic. Magazine • *Update*, biweekly. Newsletter • Membership Directory, periodic.

4668 ■ Home Builders Association of Fort Wayne (HBAFW)
305 W Main St.
Fort Wayne, IN 46802
Ph: (260)420-2020
Fax: (260)426-0640
E-mail: homeb@fortwayne.infi.net
URL: http://www.hbafortwayne.com
Contact: Bob Buescher, Pres.
Founded: 1944. **Members:** 530. **Membership Dues:** builder, $450 (annual) • associate, $400 (annual). **Staff:** 3. **Budget:** $450,000. **Local.** Home builders, land developers, and building suppliers united for mutual cooperation and information sharing; sponsors building shows and events. **Libraries: Type:** not open to the public. **Holdings:** 100; books, periodicals. **Subjects:** construction, development. **Computer Services:** database, member directory. **Committees:** Codes; Developers; Education; Legislative; Marketing; Parade of Homes; Policies and Procedures. **Councils:** Remodelors' Council of Fort Wayne. **Affiliated With:** Indiana Builders Association; National Association of Home Builders. **Publications:** *Impact*, monthly. Newsletter • *New Homes, Developments, and Remodeling Magazine* • Directory, annual. **Advertising:** accepted. **Conventions/Meetings:** monthly Code Seminar, for members; held at Allen County Building Department • annual Parade of Homes - festival.

4669 ■ Hoosier Bird Buddies
c/o Deb Nay
1020 Westerly Rd.
Fort Wayne, IN 46845-9333
Ph: (219)637-3490
E-mail: birdnut@gateway.net
URL: http://home.mchsi.com/~tmaldrich/
Contact: Tom Aldrich, Pres.
Local.

4670 ■ Hoosier Vintage Thunderbird Club
303 E Sherwood Terr.
Fort Wayne, IN 46806-2260
Ph: (260)456-3623
E-mail: funbyrd62@aol.com
URL: http://hoosierthunderbird.com
Local. Affiliated With: Vintage Thunderbird Club International.

4671 ■ Indiana Amateur Softball Association, Region 3
c/o Jim Markland, VP
3908 South Dr.
Fort Wayne, IN 46815
Ph: (260)486-7187
E-mail: jim@pyromation.com
URL: http://www.indiana-asa.org
Contact: Jim Markland, VP
Local. Affiliated With: Amateur Softball Association of America.

4672 ■ Indiana Applied Users Group
c/o SourceOne Group
6628 Constitution Dr.
Fort Wayne, IN 46804-1575
Ph: (260)436-3544
Fax: (260)432-8086
E-mail: deb.amstutz@sourceoneinsurance.com
URL: National Affiliate–www.ascnet.org
Contact: Deborah Amstutz, Pres.
State. Represents insurance agents and brokers using the Agency Manager software. Promotes successful automation and business practices through communication, education, and advocacy. **Affiliated With:** Applied Systems Client Network.

4673 ■ Indiana Association of School Nurses (IASN)
7014 Windshire Dr.
Fort Wayne, IN 46814
Ph: (260)672-9280
E-mail: csnyder@tctc.com
URL: http://www.inasn.org
Contact: Carolyn Snyder, Exec.Dir.
State. Advances the delivery of professional school health services. Increases the awareness of students on the necessity of health and learning. Improves the health of children by developing school nursing practices. **Affiliated With:** National Association of School Nurses.

4674 ■ Indiana Chapter of the Association of Air Medical Services (INAAMS)
c/o Rex Alexander, Pres.
7950 W Jefferson Blvd.
Fort Wayne, IN 46804
Ph: (260)435-6651
E-mail: president@inaams.com
URL: http://www.inaams.com
Contact: Rex Alexander, Pres.
State. Represents the interests of manufacturers and distributors of air medical transport equipment and supplies. Provides quality medical care during rapid air transport. Seeks to develop standards for aircraft configuration, minimum professional and educational requirements for personnel on board, medical and communications equipment, and operations. **Affiliated With:** Association of Air Medical Services.

4675 ■ Indiana District, The Lutheran Church-Missouri Synod
1145 S Barr St.
Fort Wayne, IN 46802-3180
Fax: (260)423-1514
Free: (800)837-1145
E-mail: jan.koenig@in.lcms.org
URL: http://www.in.lcms.org
Contact: Rev. Daniel May, Pres.
Regional.

4676 ■ Indiana Division of the International Association for Identification
9908 Shadow Lake Ln.
Fort Wayne, IN 46835
E-mail: ericb277@comcast.net
URL: http://www.iniai.org
Contact: Eric Black, Sec.-Treas.
State. Organizes people in the profession of forensic identification, investigation and scientific examination of physical evidence, through education, training and research. Advances the scientific techniques of forensic identification and crime detection.

4677 ■ Indiana Genealogical Society (IGS)
PO Box 10507
Fort Wayne, IN 46852-0507
Ph: (317)862-2426
E-mail: blwarren49@aol.com
URL: http://www.indgensoc.org
Contact: Betty L. Warren, Pres.
Founded: 1988. **Members:** 900. **Membership Dues:** individual, organization, $30 (annual) • joint, $35 (annual) • life - individual or organization, $1,000 • life - joint, $1,050. **State**. Promotes genealogical and historical research and education; preserves and safeguard manuscripts, books, cemeteries, and memorabilia relating to Indiana and its people; and assists in the publication of materials about the people, place, institutions, and organizations of Indiana. **Awards:** The Elaine Spires Smith Family History Writing Award. **Frequency:** annual. **Type:** recognition. **Recipient:** to honor the memory of Elaine Spires Smith • The IGS Honors & Awards. **Frequency:** annual. **Type:** recognition. **Recipient:** to deserving individuals for their contributions and service • Librarian's Scholarship. **Frequency:** annual. **Type:** scholarship. **Recipient:** to any librarian serving genealogical patrons in a library in the state of Indiana. **Affiliated With:** Federation of Genealogical Societies. **Publications:** *Indiana Genealogical Society Newsletter*, bimonthly. Contains list of news of interest to genealogists in Indiana as well as queries. **Price:** included in membership dues • *Indiana Genealogist*, quarterly. Journal. Contains primary source documents transcribed dealing with Indiana and research methodology. **Price:** included in membership dues. **Conventions/Meetings:** annual conference (exhibits) - always spring • periodic workshop.

4678 ■ Indiana Mortgage Bankers Association, Northeast Chapter
Grabill Bank
5525 Oak Valley Pl.
Fort Wayne, IN 46845
Ph: (260)496-8801
Fax: (260)496-8331
E-mail: douglasf@grabillbank.com
URL: http://www.indianamba.org/Chapters/Northeast.htm
Contact: Doug Fyock, Pres.
Local. Promotes fair and ethical lending practices and fosters professional excellence among real estate finance employees. Seeks to create an environment that enables members to invest in communities and achieve their business objectives. **Affiliated With:** Mortgage Bankers Association.

4679 ■ Indiana Northeast Development
PO Box 11099
Fort Wayne, IN 46855-1099
Ph: (260)426-7649
Fax: (260)426-7232
E-mail: lschrock@innedev.org
URL: http://www.innedev.org
Contact: Lincoln S. Schrock, Dir.
Founded: 1982. **Members:** 20. **Membership Dues:** appointed, $5,000 (annual). **Staff:** 2. **Budget:** $170,000. **Regional Groups:** 9. **Local**. Serves as the economic development agency for a 9-county region and promotes industrial growth in Northeast Indiana. **Conventions/Meetings:** annual Pokagon Industrial - conference, provides information for industrialists considering new or expanded operations in Northeast Indiana (exhibits).

4680 ■ Institute of Internal Auditors, Fort Wayne Chapter
c/o Jerry Danielson
Lincoln Financial Gp.
Mailstop 5H14
1300 S Clinton St.
Fort Wayne, IN 46802
Ph: (260)455-3984
E-mail: jdanielson@lnc.com
URL: National Affiliate–www.theiia.org
Contact: Jerry Danielson, Pres.
Founded: 1965. **Membership Dues:** regular, $115 (annual) • educator, $65 (annual) • student, retired, $30 (annual) • life, $2,100 • sustainer (government auditors only), $50 (annual) • organization ($65 per staff member over 5; $50 per staff member over 100), $425-$6,600 (annual). **Local**. Serves as an advocate for the internal audit profession. Provides certification, education, research, and technological guidance for the profession. **Awards: Frequency:** annual. **Type:** scholarship. **Recipient:** for student. **Committees:** Academic Relations; Certification; Web Site. **Affiliated With:** Institute of Internal Auditors. **Publications:** *Inside IIA*, periodic. Newsletter. Alternate Formats: online • Membership Directory. Alternate Formats: online.

4681 ■ International Alliance of Theatrical Stage Employees, Moving Picture Technicians, Artists, S 146
c/o James Seely
PO Box 13354
Fort Wayne, IN 46868
Ph: (260)484-3288 (260)403-1033
E-mail: jhinen49@verizon.net
URL: National Affiliate–www.iatse.lm.com
Contact: John Hinen, Business Agent
Local. **Affiliated With:** International Alliance of Theatrical Stage Employees, Moving Picture Technicians, Artists and Allied Crafts of the United States, Its Territories and Canada.

4682 ■ International Brotherhood of Electrical Workers, AFL-CIO, CFL - Local Union 723
5401 Keystone Dr.
Fort Wayne, IN 46825
Ph: (260)484-0373
Fax: (260)484-0609
E-mail: ibew723@ibew723.org
URL: National Affiliate–www.ibew.org
Contact: Ted J. Rolf, Pres.
Members: 1,868. **Local**. AFL-CIO. **Affiliated With:** International Brotherhood of Electrical Workers.

4683 ■ International Facility Management Association, North Indiana
c/o Stephen G. Goodman, Pres. and Account Exec.
Irmscher Inc.
1030 Osage St.
Fort Wayne, IN 46808
Ph: (260)422-5572
Fax: (260)424-1487
URL: National Affiliate–www.ifma.org
Contact: Stephen G. Goodman, Pres. and Account Exec.
Regional. Facility managers representing all types of organizations including banks, insurance companies, hospitals, colleges and universities, utility companies, electronic equipment manufacturers, petroleum companies, museums, auditoriums, and federal, state, provincial, and local governments. Works to enhance the professional goals of persons involved or interested in the field of facility management (the planning, designing, and managing of workplaces). **Affiliated With:** International Facility Management Association.

4684 ■ Isaac Knapp District Dental Society
6415 Constitution Dr.
Fort Wayne, IN 46804-1549
Ph: (260)459-9441
Fax: (260)459-9442
E-mail: ikdds@fwi.com
URL: National Affiliate–www.ada.org
Contact: Mr. John Trautman, Exec.Dir.
Local. Represents the interests of dentists committed to the public's oral health, ethics and professional development. Encourages the improvement of the public's oral health and promotes the art and science of dentistry. **Affiliated With:** American Dental Association; Indiana Dental Association.

4685 ■ Korean War Veterans Association, Indiana No. 1 Chapter
6612 Goodrich Dr.
Fort Wayne, IN 46804-2020
Ph: (260)432-1106
E-mail: mrenbarger@renbarger.com
URL: National Affiliate–www.kwva.org
Contact: Ms. Marilyn (Rinn) Krueger Renbarger, Admin. Aide to Pres.
Local. **Affiliated With:** Korean War Veterans Association.

4686 ■ Korean War Veterans Association, Quiet Warrior Chapter
1730 Kinsmoor Ave.
Fort Wayne, IN 46809
Ph: (260)747-0601
E-mail: alohamarcosjoan@juno.com
URL: National Affiliate–www.kwva.org
Contact: Marcos Botas, Contact
Local. **Affiliated With:** Korean War Veterans Association.

4687 ■ Lane Middle School - Wyldlife
701 W Rudisill Ave.
Fort Wayne, IN 46807
Ph: (260)745-3492
URL: http://sites.younglife.org/_layouts/ylext/default.aspx?ID=C-3309
Local. **Affiliated With:** Young Life.

4688 ■ Leadership Fort Wayne (LFW)
2101 E Coliseum Blvd.
Fort Wayne, IN 46805-1499
Ph: (260)481-6119
Fax: (260)481-4116
E-mail: wilks@leadershipfortwayne.org
URL: http://www.leadershipfortwayne.org
Contact: Jane Wilks, Exec.Dir.
Founded: 1983. **Members:** 700. **Membership Dues:** program graduate, $30 (annual). **Staff:** 3. **Budget:** $200,000. **For-Profit**. **Local**. Provides programs to develop leadership skills and community trusteeship in adults and youth. **Awards:** Youth as Resources. **Frequency:** semiannual. **Type:** grant. **Recipient:** for community service projects by youth. **Affiliated With:** Community Leadership Association. **Publications:** *Leader Links*, quarterly. Newsletter • Directory, annual. **Conventions/Meetings:** monthly Program Sessions - workshop - always September through May.

4689 ■ League for the Blind and Disabled
c/o Mr. David Nelson, CRC, Pres./CEO
5821 S Anthony Blvd.
Fort Wayne, IN 46816
Ph: (260)441-0551
Fax: (260)441-7760
Free: (800)889-3443
E-mail: the.league@verizon.net
URL: http://www.the-league.org
Contact: Mr. David Nelson CRC, Pres./CEO
Founded: 1950. **Members:** 400. **Staff:** 16. **Budget:** $1,000,000. **Languages:** English, Spanish. **Regional**. Promotes full inclusion of people with disabilities in every aspect of community life. **Telecommunication Services:** teletext, text telephone or relay capable. **Publications:** *Independence Online*, bimonthly. Newsletter. Contains information of interest to all people about disability issues. **Price:** free. **Circulation:** 31,500. Alternate Formats: diskette; online • *The Voice of Opportunity*, semiannual. Newsletter. Contains information of interest to all people about disability issues. **Price:** free. **Circulation:** 31,500.

4690 ■ Lindley Elementary PTA
2201 Ardmore Ave.
Fort Wayne, IN 46802
Ph: (260)425-7404
URL: http://familyeducation.com/IN/Lindley
Local. Parents, teachers, students, and others interested in uniting the forces of home, school, and community. Promotes the welfare of children and youth.

4691 ■ Mad Anthony Corvair Club
5401 Lower Huntington Rd.
Fort Wayne, IN 46809
Ph: (260)478-3574
E-mail: kcmill@netzero.net
URL: http://clubs.hemmings.com/madanthony
Contact: Keith A. Miller, Contact
Members: 25. **Membership Dues:** family, $15 (annual). **Regional Groups:** 4. **State Groups:** 3. **Local Groups:** 1. **Local.** Enthusiasts of the Corvair automobile united for technical assistance and parts availability. **Libraries: Type:** reference. **Holdings:** books. **Subjects:** mechanics, restoration, hot rodding. **Affiliated With:** Corvair Society of America. **Publications:** *Oversteer*, monthly. Newsletter. **Price:** included in membership dues. **Circulation:** 30. **Advertising:** accepted. **Conventions/Meetings:** annual convention • periodic Regional Meet.

4692 ■ Mental Health Association in Allen County
c/o Ms. Ruth Anne Sprunger, Exec.Dir.
227 E Washington Blvd., Ste.100
Fort Wayne, IN 46802-3137
Ph: (260)422-6441
Fax: (219)423-3400
E-mail: sscheer@mhaac.com
URL: http://www.mentalhealthassociation.com
Contact: Ms. Ruth Anne Sprunger, Exec.Dir.
Local. Seeks to promote mental health and prevent mental health disorders. Improves mental health of Americans through advocacy, public education, research and service. **Affiliated With:** Mental Health Association in Indiana; National Mental Health Association.

4693 ■ Midwest Waterways Flat-coated Retriever Club (MWFCRC)
c/o Kate Barton, Membership Sec.
5325 Ann Hackley Dr.
Fort Wayne, IN 46835-1413
E-mail: ezawodny@buckeye-express.com
URL: http://www.mwfcrc.org
Contact: Ed Zawodny, Pres.
Regional. Affiliated With: Flat-Coated Retriever Society of America.

4694 ■ Midwestern Psychological Association (MPA)
c/o Elaine Blakemore, Sec.-Treas.
Dept. of Psychology
Indiana Univ. Purdue Univ.
Fort Wayne, IN 46805
Ph: (260)481-6400
Fax: (260)481-6972
E-mail: mpa@ipfw.edu
URL: http://www.midwesternpsych.org
Contact: Dr. Elaine Blakemore PhD, Sec.-Treas.
Founded: 1927. **Members:** 2,000. **Membership Dues:** full, $30 (annual) • graduate student, $15 (annual). **Budget:** $70,000. **Regional.** Scientific and professional society of psychologists. Works to advance psychology as a science, a profession, and as a means of promoting human welfare. **Affiliated With:** American Psychological Association. **Publications:** *Program Book*, annual. **Conventions/Meetings:** annual meeting, scientific meeting where research is presented and addresses given (exhibits).

4695 ■ Mizpah Shriners
c/o Ronald J. Harruff, P.P.
407 W Berry St.
Fort Wayne, IN 46802
Ph: (260)426-4543
Fax: (260)426-4544
E-mail: recorder@mizpahshriners.org
URL: http://www.mizpahshriners.com
Contact: Ronald J. Harruff P.P., Contact
Local. Affiliated With: Imperial Council of the Ancient Arabic Order of the Nobles of the Mystic Shrine for North America.

4696 ■ National Active and Retired Federal Employees Association - Fort Wayne 223
2125 Meridian St.
Fort Wayne, IN 46808-2413
Ph: (260)422-7925
URL: National Affiliate–www.narfe.org
Contact: Allen R. Lauer, Contact
Local. Protects the retirement future of employees through education. Informs members on issues affecting the retirement. **Affiliated With:** National Association of Retired Federal Employees.

4697 ■ National Association of Investors Corporation, Northeast Hoosier Chapter
PO Box 11672
Fort Wayne, IN 46859-1672
Ph: (260)497-0572
E-mail: martinkoko@comcast.net
URL: National Affiliate–www.betterinvesting.org
Contact: Joe Kokosa, Associate Dir.
Founded: 1998. **Members:** 700. **Local Groups:** 90. **Local.** Members of investment clubs or individual members of NAIC. **Affiliated With:** National Association of Investors Corporation. **Conventions/Meetings:** workshop - 8-9/year.

4698 ■ National Association of Miniature Enthusiasts - Metro Minis
c/o Andrea Tichenor
11020 Summer Chase Rd.
Fort Wayne, IN 46818
Ph: (219)489-1772
URL: http://www.miniatures.org/states/IN.html
Contact: Andrea Tichenor, Contact
Local. Affiliated With: National Association of Miniature Enthusiasts.

4699 ■ National Association of Rocketry - Summit City Aerospace Modelers (SCAM)
c/o Joseph J. Isca
14022 Linday Ct.
Fort Wayne, IN 46814
Ph: (260)625-3306
E-mail: joseph8255@aol.com
URL: http://www.mixi.net/~bobhart
Contact: Joseph J. Isca, Contact
Local.

4700 ■ Navy Club of Fort Wayne - Ship No. 48
3222 Cedar Run
Fort Wayne, IN 46818
Ph: (260)480-4849
URL: National Affiliate–www.navyclubusa.org
Contact: Tom R. Ralston, Commander
Local. Represents individuals who are, or have been, in the active service of the U.S. Navy, Naval Reserve, Marine Corps, Marine Corps Reserve, and Coast Guard. Promotes and encourages further public interest in the U.S. Navy and its history. Upholds the spirit and ideals of the U.S. Navy. Acts as a public forum for members' views on national defense. Assists the Navy Recruiting Command whenever and wherever possible. Conducts charitable activities. **Affiliated With:** Navy Club of the United States of America.

4701 ■ Northcrest Elementary School PTA
5301 Archwood Ln.
Fort Wayne, IN 46825
Ph: (260)225-7421 (260)482-6275
E-mail: t-hartman@worldnet.att.net
URL: http://familyeducation.com/IN/NorthcrestPTA
Contact: Tina Hartman, Pres.
Local. Parents, teachers, students, and others interested in uniting the forces of home, school, and community. Promotes the welfare of children and youth.

4702 ■ Northeast Indiana Construction Alliance
2930 W Ludwig Rd.
Fort Wayne, IN 46818
Ph: (260)490-5688
E-mail: info@neica.org
URL: http://neica.org
Contact: John E. Hampton, Pres.
Founded: 1977. **Members:** 1,900. **Staff:** 4. **Local.** Helps different companies and residents of Northeast Indiana achieve standard of living. **Affiliated With:** AFL-CIO. **Formerly:** (2005) Building and Construction Trades Department AFL-CIO, Northeastern Indiana, BCTC.

4703 ■ Northeast Indiana Human Resource Association (NIHRA)
PO Box 13142
Fort Wayne, IN 46867
E-mail: reuben.mendez@nihra.com
URL: http://www.nihra.com
Contact: Reuben Mendez, Pres.
Local. Represents the interests of human resource and industrial relations professionals and executives. Promotes the advancement of human resource management.

4704 ■ Northeastern Indiana Kennel Club
c/o Mary Osbun
1315 Westerly Rd.
Fort Wayne, IN 46845-9755
E-mail: info@neikc.org
URL: http://www.neikc.org/
Contact: Deborah Ward, Corresponding Sec.
State. Affiliated With: American Kennel Club.

4705 ■ Northern Indiana Chapter of Associated Locksmiths of America
c/o Jeremy B. Rodocker, CPL, CPS, Chm.
Rodocker's Architectural Security Co.
807 Timberlake Trail
Fort Wayne, IN 46804-5933
Ph: (260)459-1500
E-mail: wendybeau@aol.com
URL: National Affiliate–www.aloa.org
Local. Affiliated With: Associated Locksmiths of America.

4706 ■ Northwood Middle School PTSA
1201 E Washington Ctr. Rd.
Fort Wayne, IN 46825
Ph: (260)425-7424
URL: http://familyeducation.com/IN/Northwood_Middle_School
Contact: Lisa Parker, Pres.
Local. Parents, teachers, students, and others interested in uniting the forces of home, school, and community. Promotes the welfare of children and youth.

4707 ■ Old Fort Coin Club
c/o William L. Hines
PO Box 11051
Fort Wayne, IN 46855
E-mail: fairfieldcoins@aol.com
URL: National Affiliate–www.money.org
Contact: William L. Hines, Contact
Local. Affiliated With: American Numismatic Association.

4708 ■ PFLAG Fort Wayne
PO Box 5086
Fort Wayne, IN 46805
Ph: (260)497-8528
E-mail: pflagftwayne@aol.com
URL: http://members.aol.com/pflagfw
Local. Affiliated With: Parents, Families, and Friends of Lesbians and Gays.

4709 ■ Phi Theta Kappa, Alpha Kappa Nu Chapter - Indiana University - Purdue University Fort Wayne
c/o Sarah Beckman
2101 Coliseum Blvd. E
Fort Wayne, IN 46805

Ph: (260)481-6274
E-mail: beckmans@ipfw.edu
URL: http://www.ptk.org/directories/chapters/IN/219-1.htm
Contact: Sarah Beckman, Advisor
Local.

4710 ■ Phi Theta Kappa ,Alpha Tau Xi Chapter - Ivy Tech State College
c/o John Lynch
3800 N Anthony Blvd.
Fort Wayne, IN 46805
Ph: (219)480-4257
URL: http://www.ptk.org/directories/chapters/IN/16134-1.htm
Contact: John Lynch, Advisor
Local.

4711 ■ Plumbing-Heating-Cooling Contractors Association, Fort Wayne
c/o Tammy Koontz, Exec.Mgr.
919 Charlotte Ave.
Fort Wayne, IN 46805-2512
Ph: (260)484-3890
Fax: (260)484-7511
E-mail: tamarafwaphcc@msn.com
URL: National Affiliate–www.phccweb.org
Contact: Tammy Koontz, Exec.Mgr.
Local. Represents the plumbing, heating and cooling contractors. Promotes the construction industry. Protects the environment, health, safety and comfort of society. **Affiliated With:** Plumbing-Heating-Cooling Contractors Association.

4712 ■ Project Management Institute, Northeast Indiana Chapter
PO Box 11293
Fort Wayne, IN 46857-1293
E-mail: president@pmi-neic.org
URL: http://www.pmi-neic.org
Contact: Paula Felver PMP, Pres.
Local. Corporations and individuals engaged in the practice of project management; project management students and educators. Seeks to advance the study, teaching, and practice of project management. **Affiliated With:** Project Management Institute.

4713 ■ Psi Chi, National Honor Society in Psychology - Indiana University-Purdue University Fort Wayne
c/o Dept. of Psychology
Neff Hall, Rm. 388
2101 Coliseum Blvd. E
Fort Wayne, IN 46805-1499
Ph: (260)481-6403
Fax: (260)481-6972
E-mail: psichi@holmes.ipfw.edu
URL: http://www.ipfw.edu/psyc
Local. **Affiliated With:** Psi Chi, National Honor Society in Psychology.

4714 ■ SCORE Chapter 50
0130 Fed. Bldg.
1300 S Harrison St.
Fort Wayne, IN 46802
Ph: (260)422-2601
Fax: (260)422-2601
E-mail: score@fwi.com
URL: http://www.score-fortwayne.org
Contact: Al Kruetzman, Chm.
Founded: 1976. **Members:** 60. **Staff:** 1. **Local**. Volunteer businessmen and women. Provides free small business management assistance to individuals in Northeast Indiana. **Conventions/Meetings:** monthly meeting - every 3rd Tuesday in Ft. Wayne, IN.

4715 ■ Society of Antique Modelers - Old Fort Flyers
11206 Trentman Rd.
Fort Wayne, IN 46816
Ph: (219)639-6510
E-mail: bjhart@infionline.net
URL: National Affiliate–www.antiquemodeler.org
Local. **Affiliated With:** Society of Antique Modelers.

4716 ■ Society of Manufacturing Engineers - Indiana Institute of Technology S345
1600 E Washington Blvd.
Fort Wayne, IN 46803
Ph: (260)422-5561
Fax: (260)422-7696
E-mail: pcanales@indtech.edu
URL: National Affiliate–www.sme.org
Contact: Peggy Canales, Contact
Local. Advances manufacturing knowledge to gain competitive advantage. Improves skills and manufacturing solutions for the growth of economy. Provides resources and opportunities for manufacturing professionals. **Affiliated With:** Foundry Educational Foundation.

4717 ■ Society of Manufacturing Engineers - Indiana Purdue University-Ft. Wayne S292
Indiana Purdue Univ., IPFW-SME Student Chap.
2101 E Coliseum Blvd.
Fort Wayne, IN 46805-1499
Ph: (260)481-6384
E-mail: narang@ipfw.edu
URL: National Affiliate–www.sme.org
Contact: Remesh Narang, Contact
Local. Advances manufacturing knowledge to gain competitive advantage. Improves skills and manufacturing solutions for the growth of economy. Provides resources and opportunities for manufacturing professionals. **Affiliated With:** International Metallographic Society.

4718 ■ Society of Manufacturing Engineers - ITT - Ft. Wayne S214
ITT - Ft. Wayne, Automated Mfg. Tech.
4919 Coldwater Rd.
Fort Wayne, IN 46825-5532
Ph: (219)484-4107
E-mail: jretnier@yahoo.com
URL: National Affiliate–www.sme.org
Contact: Jerry Etnier, Contact
Local. Advances manufacturing knowledge to gain competitive advantage. Improves skills and manufacturing solutions for the growth of economy. Provides resources and opportunities for manufacturing professionals. **Affiliated With:** International Precious Metals Institute.

4719 ■ Society of Manufacturing Engineers - Ivy Tech State College S265
3800 N Anthony Blvd.
Fort Wayne, IN 46805
Ph: (219)480-4278
Fax: (219)480-2052
E-mail: rmartin@ivytech.edu
URL: National Affiliate–www.sme.org
Contact: Richard S. Martin, Contact
Local. Advances manufacturing knowledge to gain competitive advantage. Improves skills and manufacturing solutions for the growth of economy. Provides resources and opportunities for manufacturing professionals. **Affiliated With:** Minerals, Metals, and Materials Society.

4720 ■ Sons of Norway, Tre Elver Lodge 5-628
c/o Louise A. Larsen, Sec.
10024 Hibiscus Dr.
Fort Wayne, IN 46804-4005
Ph: (260)432-7314
E-mail: john.larsen@juno.com
URL: National Affiliate–www.sofn.com
Contact: Louise A. Larsen, Sec.
Local. **Affiliated With:** Sons of Norway.

4721 ■ Sweet Adelines International, Towns of Harmony Chapter
Harmony Hall
5120 Speedway Dr.
Fort Wayne, IN 46825-5247
Ph: (260)422-9782
E-mail: jwftw2@msn.com
URL: National Affiliate–www.sweetadelineintl.org
Contact: Jane Ward, Contact
Local. Advances the musical art form of barbershop harmony through education and performances. Provides education, training and coaching in the development of women's four-part barbershop harmony. **Affiliated With:** Sweet Adelines International.

4722 ■ Three Rivers Fly Fishers (TRFF)
PO Box 8548
Fort Wayne, IN 46898-8548
E-mail: blowden@3rff.org
URL: http://www.3rff.org
Contact: Bob Lowden, Pres.
Local. **Affiliated With:** Federation of Fly Fishers.

4723 ■ Three Rivers Gem and Mineral Society
c/o Byron Thomas, Pres.
8105 Lakeside Ct. No. 1B
Fort Wayne, IN 46816
Ph: (260)580-2541
E-mail: lancelotblue1@msn.com
URL: http://3riversgem_mineral.tripod.com
Contact: Byron Thomas, Pres.
Local. Aims to further the study of Earth Sciences and the practice of lapidary arts and mineralogy. **Affiliated With:** American Federation of Mineralogical Societies.

4724 ■ Three Rivers Orchid Society, Fort Wayne
c/o Sue Holm, Sec.
4634 Doenges Dr.
Fort Wayne, IN 46815
Ph: (260)485-0164
E-mail: bgholmmg@earthlink.net
URL: National Affiliate–www.orchidweb.org
Contact: Ms. Rose Poehler, Pres.
Founded: 1967. **Members:** 70. **Membership Dues:** individual, $15 (annual) • family, $20 (annual) • student, $7 (annual). **Local**. Strives to promote the culture and interest in the preservation of orchid species and hybrids by educating, teaching, and learning. **Affiliated With:** American Orchid Society. **Publications:** *Three Rivers Orchid Society Newsletter*, monthly. Informs members of upcoming events; provides minutes of the last meeting, treasurer's report, committee reports and other pertinent information. **Price:** included in membership fee. **Circulation:** 60. Alternate Formats: online. **Conventions/Meetings:** monthly general assembly, discusses program on some aspect of orchid growing and/or cultivation, talks about business (exhibits) - every second Sunday of the month except June, July, August and December. Fort Wayne, IN - Avg. Attendance: 40.

4725 ■ Three Rivers Strollers
c/o Edward S. Masloob
4710 Aboite Lake Dr.
Fort Wayne, IN 46804-0000
Ph: (260)432-9370
E-mail: emasloob@aol.com
URL: http://www.3riversstrollers.150m.com
Contact: Edward S. Masloob, Pres.
Founded: 1981. **Members:** 40. **Membership Dues:** individual, $5 (annual) • family, $5 (annual). **Regional Groups:** 1. **State Groups:** 1. **Local Groups:** 1. **Regional**. Promotes the sport of walking in the Ft. Wayne, IN area. Holds Volkmarches and outings. Participates in Three Rivers Festival. **Libraries: Type:** open to the public. **Holdings:** 1; books. **Subjects:** Volksmarches. **Computer Services:** Online services. **Affiliated With:** American Volkssport Association. **Publications:** *Walk and Talk*, quarterly. Newsletter. Contains club information. **Price:** included in membership dues. **Advertising:** accepted. **Conventions/Meetings:** biennial National - convention (exhibits).

4726 ■ Three Rivers Table Tennis Club
Messiah Lutheran Church
7211 Stellhorn Rd.
Fort Wayne, IN 46835
Ph: (260)485-7039
E-mail: td100951@aol.com
URL: http://www.trttc.org
Contact: Tom Dannenfelser, Contact
Local. Affiliated With: U.S.A. Table Tennis.

4727 ■ Tri-County REACT
742 N Coliseum, Apt. 89
Fort Wayne, IN 46805
Ph: (260)420-8664
E-mail: react6026@yahoo.com
URL: http://www.reactintl.org/teaminfo/usa_teams/teams-usin.htm
Local. Trained communication experts and professional volunteers. Provides volunteer public service and emergency communications through the use of radios (Citizen Band, General Mobile Radio Service, UHF and HAM). Coordinates with radio industries and government on safety communication matters and supports charitable activities and community organizations.

4728 ■ United Hispanic-Americans
1210 Broadway
Fort Wayne, IN 46802
Ph: (219)422-2651
Fax: (219)420-2272
E-mail: rosa.gerra@verizon.net
Contact: Rosa A. Gerra, Exec.Dir.
Founded: 1970. **Staff:** 11. **Languages:** English, Spanish. **For-Profit. Regional.** Promotes professional and social advancement of Hispanic-Americans. Provides educational programs, job placement program, youth social development, referrals, translations, outreach activities, and mental health programs. **Awards:** College Scholarships. **Frequency:** annual. **Type:** scholarship. **Recipient:** to Latino students. **Publications:** *La Voy Newsletter*. **Price:** free. **Circulation:** 2,500. **Conventions/Meetings:** annual meeting - in May.

4729 ■ United Way of Allen County
227 E Washington Blvd.
Fort Wayne, IN 46802
Ph: (260)422-4776
Fax: (260)422-4782
E-mail: jerryp@uwacin.org
URL: http://www.unitedwayallencounty.org
Contact: Stephanie Kaskel McCormick, Pres./CEO
Local. Affiliated With: United Way of America.

4730 ■ Young Life Fort Wayne
701 W Rudisill Ave.
Fort Wayne, IN 46807
Ph: (260)745-3492
URL: http://fortwayne.younglife.org
Local.

Fortville

4731 ■ American Legion, Fortville Post 391
PO Box 206
Fortville, IN 46040
Ph: (317)485-4992
Fax: (317)237-9891
URL: National Affiliate–www.legion.org
Local. Affiliated With: American Legion.

4732 ■ National Association of Rocketry - A Method of Reaching Extreme Altitudes (AMOREA)
c/o Carlton Simmons
PO Box 395
Fortville, IN 46040
E-mail: simmonscarl@hotmail.com
URL: http://www.indyrockets.org/amorea.html
Contact: Carlton Simmons, Contact
Local.

4733 ■ National Technical Honor Society - Mt. Vernon High School - Indiana
8112 N 200 W
Fortville, IN 46040
Ph: (317)485-3131
Fax: (317)485-3154
Free: (800)418-6423
E-mail: joe.loomis@mvcsc.k12.in.us
Contact: Joe Loomis, Contact
Local.

Fowler

4734 ■ American Legion, Fowler Post 57
PO Box 147
Fowler, IN 47944
Ph: (317)884-9961
Fax: (317)237-9891
URL: National Affiliate–www.legion.org
Local. Affiliated With: American Legion.

4735 ■ Benton County Association for Retarded Citizens
PO Box 12
Fowler, IN 47944
Ph: (765)884-0092
URL: National Affiliate–www.TheArc.org
Local. Parents, professional workers, and others interested in individuals with mental retardation. Works to promote services, research, public understanding, and legislation for people with mental retardation and their families. **Affiliated With:** Arc of the United States.

4736 ■ Fowler Chamber of Commerce
PO Box 293
Fowler, IN 47944-0293
Ph: (765)884-1780 (765)884-0232
Contact: Mike Brewer, Pres.
Local.

Francesville

4737 ■ American Legion, Indiana Post 228
c/o Jesse Engle
10296 W 350 S
Francesville, IN 47946
Ph: (317)630-1300
Fax: (317)237-9891
URL: National Affiliate–www.legion.org
Contact: Jesse Engle, Contact
Local. Affiliated With: American Legion.

Frankfort

4738 ■ American Legion, Indiana Post 12
c/o Walter T. Cohee
451 W Clinton St.
Frankfort, IN 46041
Ph: (317)654-7144
Fax: (317)237-9891
URL: National Affiliate–www.legion.org
Contact: Walter T. Cohee, Contact
Local. Affiliated With: American Legion.

4739 ■ Clinton County Chamber of Commerce (CCCC)
259 E Walnut St.
Frankfort, IN 46041
Ph: (765)654-5507
Fax: (765)654-9592
E-mail: chamber@ccinchamber.org
URL: http://ccinchamber.org
Contact: Gina L. Sheets, CEO
Founded: 1913. **Local.** Promotes business and community development in Clinton County, IN. **Affiliated With:** U.S. Chamber of Commerce. **Publications:** Newsletter, periodic • Directory, annual. Contains list of members of organization. **Price:** $25.00/year.

4740 ■ Clinton County Historical Society and Historical Museum
301 E Clinton St.
Frankfort, IN 46041
Ph: (765)659-2030 (765)659-4079
Fax: (765)654-7773
E-mail: cchsm@geetel.net
URL: http://www.cchsm.org
Contact: Nancy J. Hart, Curator/Exec.Dir.
Founded: 1921. **Members:** 200. **Membership Dues:** individual, $25 (annual) • senior, $20 (annual) • student, $5 (annual). **Budget:** $25,000. **Languages:** English, Spanish. **Local.** Individuals interested in the history of Clinton County, IN. Operates Clinton County Museum. **Libraries: Type:** open to the public. **Holdings:** 1,500. **Computer Services:** Information services • online services • record retrieval services. **Publications:** *Historical Notes*, 10/year. Newsletter. Contains family histories, photographs, new donations, volunteers and experiences, new members, and letters from visiting students. **Price:** included in membership dues. **Circulation:** 400. **Conventions/Meetings:** monthly meeting (exhibits) - always first Tuesday.

4741 ■ Frankfort Board of Realtors, Indiana
PO Box 518
Frankfort, IN 46041
Ph: (765)654-4456
Fax: (765)654-4457
E-mail: goar@netusa1.net
URL: National Affiliate–www.realtor.org
Contact: C. Steven Frey, Exec. Officer
Local. Strives to develop real estate business practices. Advocates the right to own, use and transfer real property. Provides a facility for professional development, research and exchange of information among members and to the general public. **Affiliated With:** National Association of Realtors.

4742 ■ Frankfort Main Street
301 E Clinton St.
Frankfort, IN 46041
Ph: (765)654-4081
Fax: (765)654-7773
URL: http://www.accs.net/mainstreet
Local.

4743 ■ Mental Health Association in Clinton County
c/o Ms. Cathy Wills, Exec.Dir.
51 W Clinton St., Ste.101
Frankfort, IN 46041-1931
Ph: (765)659-3825
URL: http://www.mentalhealthassociation.com
Contact: Ms. Cathy Wills, Exec.Dir.
Local. Seeks to promote mental health and prevent mental health disorders. Improves mental health of Americans through advocacy, public education, research and service. **Affiliated With:** Mental Health Association in Indiana; National Mental Health Association.

4744 ■ National Active and Retired Federal Employees Association - Frankfort 1989
758 Catterlin St.
Frankfort, IN 46041-1462
Ph: (317)659-2092
URL: National Affiliate–www.narfe.org
Contact: Donald L. Dorsey, Contact
Local. Protects the retirement future of employees through education. Informs members on issues affecting the retirement. **Affiliated With:** National Association of Retired Federal Employees.

4745 ■ United Way for Clinton County
51 W Clinton St., Ste.102
Frankfort, IN 46041
Ph: (765)654-5573
Fax: (765)654-6970
URL: http://www.ftimes.com/unitedway
Contact: Gena Arehart, Exec.Dir.
Local. Affiliated With: United Way of America.

Franklin

4746 ■ American Legion, Franklin Post 205
1200 Park Ave.
Franklin, IN 46131
Ph: (317)738-9934
Fax: (317)237-9891
URL: National Affiliate–www.legion.org
Local. Affiliated With: American Legion.

4747 ■ Franklin Chamber of Commerce (FCC)
370 E Jefferson St.
Franklin, IN 46131
Ph: (317)736-6334
Fax: (317)736-9553
URL: http://www.franklincoc.org
Contact: Tricia E. Bechman, Exec.Dir.
Local. Promotes business and community development in the Franklin, IN area. Sponsors Heritage Festival. **Convention/Meeting:** none. **Publications:** *Depot Signal*, monthly. Newsletter • *Franklin Chamber of Commerce Directory*, annual.

4748 ■ Hoosier Back Country Horsemen, Indiana
851 W 300 S
Franklin, IN 46131
Ph: (317)439-3835
E-mail: hoosierhorsemen@yahoo.com
URL: National Affiliate–www.backcountryhorse.com
Local. Affiliated With: Back Country Horsemen of America.

4749 ■ Indiana Golf Association (IGA)
c/o Mike David, Exec.Dir.
PO Box 516
Franklin, IN 46131
Ph: (317)738-9696
Fax: (317)738-9436
Free: (800)779-7271
E-mail: mdavid@indianagolf.org
URL: http://www.indianagolf.org
Contact: Mike David, Exec.Dir.
Founded: 1972. **State. Affiliated With:** International Association of Golf Administrators.

4750 ■ Johnson County Association for Retarded Citizens
PO Box 216
Franklin, IN 46131
Ph: (317)738-5500
Fax: (317)738-5522
Free: (888)494-8069
URL: National Affiliate–www.TheArc.org
Contact: Karen Luehanan, Exec.Dir.
Local. Affiliated With: Arc of the United States.

4751 ■ Johnson County Historical Museum and Society (JCHMS)
136 N Main
Franklin, IN 46131
Ph: (317)736-4655
Fax: (317)736-5451
E-mail: jcmuseum@netdirect.net
URL: National Affiliate–www.aaslh.org
Contact: Mary Plummer, Exec. Officer
Founded: 1931. **Members:** 430. **Staff:** 5. **Budget:** $111,000. **Local.** Individuals interested in preserving the history of Johnson County, IN. Operates Johnson County Historical Museum. **Libraries: Type:** open to the public. **Holdings:** articles, books, periodicals. **Subjects:** genealogy and history of Johnson County. **Affiliated With:** American Association for State and Local History. **Publications:** *Nostalgia News*, quarterly. Newsletter. Features articles of Johnson County, the people and history of Johnson County. **Price:** included with membership. **Circulation:** 500. **Conventions/Meetings:** semiannual dinner - always spring and fall; Avg. Attendance: 125.

4752 ■ Johnson County REACT
1620 Graham Rd.
Franklin, IN 46131
Ph: (317)738-0268
E-mail: meecewl@walmart.com
URL: http://www.reactintl.org/teaminfo/usa_teams/teams-usin.htm
Local. Trained communication experts and professional volunteers. Provides volunteer public service and emergency communications through the use of radios (Citizen Band, General Mobile Radio Service, UHF and HAM). Coordinates with radio industries and government on safety communication matters and supports charitable activities and community organizations.

4753 ■ National Active and Retired Federal Employees Association - Johnson County 1612
400 Reagan Cir.
Franklin, IN 46131-7291
Ph: (317)736-5498
URL: National Affiliate–www.narfe.org
Contact: Charlotte M. Michelfelder, Contact
Local. Protects the retirement future of employees through education. Informs members on issues affecting the retirement. **Affiliated With:** National Association of Retired Federal Employees.

4754 ■ National Farmers Union, Indiana
c/o Larry Coomer, Pres.
5417 E 300 N
Franklin, IN 46131
Ph: (317)736-6960
Fax: (317)834-9976
E-mail: infarmu@in-motion.net
URL: National Affiliate–www.nfu.org
Contact: Larry Coomer, Pres.
State. Affiliated With: National Farmers Union.

4755 ■ National Sojourners, Indiana Masonic Home No. 541
c/o CPO Douglas C. Fraker
PO Box 307
Franklin, IN 46131-0307
Ph: (317)738-0791
E-mail: douglascfraker@prodigy.net
URL: National Affiliate–www.nationalsojourners.org
Contact: CPO Douglas C. Fraker, Contact
Local.

4756 ■ National Speleological Society, Eastern Indiana Grotto (EIG)
c/o Mark Webb, Chm.
350 W King St.
Franklin, IN 46131
Ph: (317)738-9646
E-mail: mtwebb96@hotmail.com
URL: http://www.caves.org/grotto/eig
Contact: Mark Webb, Chm.
Local. Seeks to study, explore and conserve cave and karst resources. Protects access to caves and promotes responsible caving. Encourages responsible management of caves and their unique environments. **Affiliated With:** National Speleological Society.

4757 ■ United Way of Johnson County, Indiana
PO Box 153
Franklin, IN 46131-0153
Ph: (317)736-7840
URL: National Affiliate–national.unitedway.org
Local. Affiliated With: United Way of America.

Frankton

4758 ■ American Legion, May Berry Post 469
116 Washington St.
Frankton, IN 46044
Ph: (317)754-7384
Fax: (317)237-9891
URL: National Affiliate–www.legion.org
Local. Affiliated With: American Legion.

Freedom

4759 ■ American Legion, Putoff-Lautenschlager Post 141
2268 Steubenville Rd.
Freedom, IN 47431
Ph: (812)859-4311
Fax: (317)237-9891
URL: National Affiliate–www.legion.org
Local. Affiliated With: American Legion.

Fremont

4760 ■ American Legion, Cassel Post 257
PO Box 610
Fremont, IN 46737
Ph: (219)495-9329
Fax: (317)237-9891
URL: National Affiliate–www.legion.org
Local. Affiliated With: American Legion.

4761 ■ Fremont Area Chamber of Commerce
PO Box 462
Fremont, IN 46737
Ph: (260)495-9010
Fax: (260)495-2070
E-mail: fremontc@locl.net
URL: http://www.fremontchamber.org
Contact: Darci Gaff, Exec.Dir.
Members: 60. **Local.** Promotes business and economic development in Fremont Area, IN. **Telecommunication Services:** electronic mail, darci@fremontchamber.org.

French Lick

4762 ■ American Legion, Indiana Post 76
c/o Walter W. Benson
8595 W Main St.
French Lick, IN 47432
Ph: (317)630-1300
Fax: (317)237-9891
URL: National Affiliate–www.legion.org
Contact: Walter W. Benson, Contact
Local. Affiliated With: American Legion.

4763 ■ French Lick - West Baden Chamber of Commerce (FLWBCC)
PO Box 347
French Lick, IN 47432
Ph: (812)936-2405
E-mail: trichardson@flwbcc.com
URL: http://www.frenchlick-westbadencc.org
Contact: Teresa Richardson, Contact
Members: 50. **Local.** Promotes business and community development in French Lick, IN. **Publications:** Newsletter, monthly • Brochure. **Conventions/Meetings:** monthly meeting.

4764 ■ Orange County Convention and Visitor's Bureau
c/o Robert Denbo, Exec.Dir.
PO Box 71
French Lick, IN 47432
Ph: (812)936-3418
Fax: (812)936-7112
Free: (877)422-9925
E-mail: info@orangecountyin.com
URL: http://www.historicsouthernindiana.com
Contact: Robert Denbo, Exec.Dir.
Founded: 2000. **Staff:** 1. **Budget:** $140,000. **Regional Groups:** 2. **State Groups:** 2. **Local.** Promotes tourism. **Awards:** Advertising Grants. **Frequency:** annual. **Type:** grant. **Committees:** Marketing.

Friendship

4765 ■ American Legion, Brown Township Post 247
PO Box 95
Friendship, IN 47021

Ph: (317)630-1300
Fax: (317)237-9891
URL: National Affiliate–www.legion.org
Local. Affiliated With: American Legion.

Galveston

4766 ■ American Legion, Scott-Lambert Post 415
c/o Scott Lambert
PO Box 145
Galveston, IN 46932
Ph: (219)699-6133
Fax: (317)237-9891
URL: National Affiliate–www.legion.org
Contact: Scott Lambert, Contact
Local. Affiliated With: American Legion.

Garrett

4767 ■ American Legion, Aaron Scisinger Post 178
515 W 5th Ave.
Garrett, IN 46738
Ph: (219)357-5133
Fax: (317)237-9891
URL: National Affiliate–www.legion.org
Local. Affiliated With: American Legion.

4768 ■ Garrett Chamber of Commerce (GCC)
111 W Keyser St.
Garrett, IN 46738-1462
Ph: (260)357-4600
Fax: (260)357-5634
Contact: Sandra Arvin, Exec.Dir.
Founded: 1927. **Local.** Promotes business and community development in Garrett, IN. Sponsors social and promotional events. **Awards:** Business of the Year. **Frequency:** biennial. **Type:** recognition • Citizen of the Year. **Frequency:** biennial. **Type:** recognition. **Publications:** *Tracks*, quarterly. Newsletter. **Price:** free. **Conventions/Meetings:** quarterly Industrial Forum Luncheon - meeting.

Gary

4769 ■ 100 Black Men of Gary
650 S Lake St.
Gary, IN 46403
Ph: (219)977-0225
Fax: (219)938-0230
E-mail: kchap54491@aol.com
URL: National Affiliate–www.100blackmen.org
Local. Affiliated With: 100 Black Men of America.

4770 ■ American Legion, American Slovak Post 367
3926 Wright Cir.
Gary, IN 46408
Ph: (219)980-9413
Fax: (317)237-9891
URL: National Affiliate–www.legion.org
Local. Affiliated With: American Legion.

4771 ■ American Legion, Black Oak Post 393
2467 Wheeler St.
Gary, IN 46406
Fax: (317)237-9891
URL: National Affiliate–www.legion.org
Local. Affiliated With: American Legion.

4772 ■ American Legion, Calumet Post 99
2312 Adams St.
Gary, IN 46407
Ph: (317)630-1300
Fax: (317)237-9891
URL: National Affiliate–www.legion.org
Local. Affiliated With: American Legion.

4773 ■ American Legion, Indiana Post 279
c/o Miller Dunes
6601 Hobart Rd.
Gary, IN 46403
Ph: (219)938-9856
Fax: (317)237-9891
URL: National Affiliate–www.legion.org
Contact: Miller Dunes, Contact
Local. Affiliated With: American Legion.

4774 ■ American Legion, Indiana Post 498
c/o Edward M. Page
2270 Broadway
Gary, IN 46407
Ph: (317)630-1300
Fax: (317)237-9891
URL: National Affiliate–www.legion.org
Contact: Edward M. Page, Contact
Local. Affiliated With: American Legion.

4775 ■ American Legion, Tolleston Post 270
5117 Broadway
Gary, IN 46409
Ph: (219)980-9710
Fax: (317)237-9891
URL: National Affiliate–www.legion.org
Local. Affiliated With: American Legion.

4776 ■ Boys and Girls Clubs of Northwest Indiana
839 Broadway, 3rd Fl.
Gary, IN 46402
Ph: (219)881-1060
Fax: (219)881-7850
E-mail: ahensell@bgcnwi.org
URL: http://www.nwipositiveplace.org
Contact: Lincoln D. Ellis, Exec.Dir.
Local.

4777 ■ Credit Professionals International, Illiana
c/o Freya Churchwell, PCE, Pres.
3637 Grant St.
Gary, IN 46408
Ph: (219)980-4800
E-mail: f.churhwell@comcast.net
URL: http://www.creditprofessionals.org/5/illiana.html
Contact: Freya Churchwell PCE, Pres.
Local. Supports members through networking, career development and community involvement. Promotes and contributes to the innovation of the credit industry. Provides education in the practice and procedure of credit. **Affiliated With:** Credit Professionals International.

4778 ■ Gary Chamber of Commerce (GCC)
504 Broadway, No. 328
Gary, IN 46402
Ph: (219)885-7407
Fax: (219)885-7408
E-mail: info@garychamber.com
URL: http://www.garychamber.com
Contact: Jeffrey Q. Williams, Exec.Dir.
Founded: 1907. **Local.** Promotes business and community development in the Gary, IN area. **Affiliated With:** U.S. Chamber of Commerce. **Formerly:** (1999) Greater Gary Chamber of Commerce.

4779 ■ Gary-East Chicago-Hammond Empowerment Zone
c/o Venus Cobb
840 Broadway, 1st Fl.
Gary, IN 46402-2412
Ph: (219)886-9047 (219)886-4997
Fax: (219)886-9051
E-mail: venus@gechezone.com
URL: http://www.gechezone.com
Local. Committees: Northwest Indiana Minority Business Opportunity. **Publications:** *The Power Zone Report*, quarterly. Contains local newsletter of empowernment zone activities. **Conventions/Meetings:** annual Minority Enterprise Development Week - conference (exhibits).

4780 ■ Indiana Optometric Association, Northwestern District
c/o Sheila K. Bogart, OD, Trustee
701 W 5th Ave.
Gary, IN 46402
Ph: (219)881-0655
Fax: (219)881-1104
E-mail: sbogart9@comcast.net
URL: http://www.ioa.org
Contact: Sheila K. Bogart OD, Trustee
Local. Aims to improve the quality, availability and accessibility of eye and vision care. Promotes high standards of patient care. Monitors and promotes legislation concerning the scope of optometric practice and other issues relevant to eye/vision care. **Affiliated With:** American Optometric Association; Indiana Optometric Association.

4781 ■ Indiana University Northwest Student Nurses' Association (IUNSNA)
c/o Indiana University Northwest
3400 Broadway
Gary, IN 46408-1197
Ph: (219)980-6500
Free: (888)968-7486
E-mail: gfrog12@aol.com
URL: http://www.iun.edu/~sna
Contact: Gina Connolly, Pres.
Local. Promotes the nursing profession. Encourages programs and learning opportunities connected with nursing and health. Advocates the participation of nursing students in developing health care methods offered to the public. **Affiliated With:** National Student Nurses' Association.

4782 ■ James Kimbrough Law Association
c/o Jerry Jarrett, Pres.
2148 W 11th Ave.
Gary, IN 46404
Ph: (219)944-2755
Fax: (219)944-2764
E-mail: jjarr5747@aol.com
URL: National Affiliate–www.nationalbar.org
Contact: Jerry Jarrett, Pres.
Local. Affiliated With: National Bar Association.

4783 ■ National Organization of Black Law Enforcement Executives, Northern Indiana Chapter
c/o Richard Ligon
US Postal Inspection Ser.
PO Box 64006
Gary, IN 46401-0006
Ph: (219)886-8239 (219)944-8727
Fax: (219)886-8230
E-mail: richarddligon@aol.com
URL: National Affiliate–www.noblenational.org
Contact: Richard Ligon, Postal Insperctor/Team Leader
Founded: 1998. **Members:** 40. **Membership Dues:** regular, $50 (annual). **Local. Awards:** Scholarship. **Frequency:** annual. **Type:** monetary. **Affiliated With:** National Organization of Black Law Enforcement Executives.

4784 ■ National Spinal Cord Injury Association - Calumet Region Chapter
2109 Cleveland St.
Gary, IN 46404
Ph: (219)944-8037
E-mail: rjackson@ci.gary.in.us
URL: National Affiliate–www.spinalcord.org
Contact: Rita Renae Jackson, Contact
Local. Empowers individuals who are suffering from spinal cord injury. Provides information on the causes and prevention of spinal cord injuries. **Affiliated With:** National Spinal Cord Injury Association.

4785 ■ Phi Theta Kappa ,Alpha Phi Omega Chapter - Ivy Tech State College
c/o Lisa Feuerbach
1440 E 35th Ave.
Gary, IN 46409

Ph: (219)392-3600
URL: http://www.ptk.org/directories/chapters/IN/20530-1.htm
Contact: Lisa Feuerbach, Advisor
Local.

4786 ■ Psi Chi, National Honor Society in Psychology - Indiana University Northwest
c/o Dept. of Psychology
141 Raintree
3400 Broadway
Gary, IN 46408-1101
Ph: (219)980-6680 (219)980-6684
Fax: (219)980-6756
E-mail: mfischer@iun.edu
URL: http://www.psichi.org/chapters/info.asp?chapter_id=436
Contact: Mary Ann Fischer PhD, Advisor
Local.

4787 ■ Urban League of NW Indiana
c/o Eloise Gentry, Pres.
3101 Broadway
Gary, IN 46408
Ph: (219)887-9621
E-mail: jigibonitaj@aol.com
URL: National Affiliate–www.nul.org
Contact: Eloise Gentry, Pres.
Local. Affiliated With: National Urban League.

Gas City

4788 ■ National Active and Retired Federal Employees Association - Marion 503
314 E South B St.
Gas City, IN 46933-1814
Ph: (317)674-5325
URL: National Affiliate–www.narfe.org
Contact: Harold W. Mccollum, Contact
Local. Protects the retirement future of employees through education. Informs members on issues affecting the retirement. **Affiliated With:** National Association of Retired Federal Employees.

Gaston

4789 ■ American Legion, Gaston Post 387
101 N Sycamore St.
Gaston, IN 47342
Ph: (765)358-8346
Fax: (317)237-9891
URL: National Affiliate–www.legion.org
Local. Affiliated With: American Legion.

Georgetown

4790 ■ National Speleological Society, Harrison-Crawford Grotto (HCG)
c/o David L. Black, Treas.
PO Box 147
Georgetown, IN 47122-0147
Ph: (812)951-3886
E-mail: dblack@venus.net
URL: http://www.caves.org/grotto/hcg
Contact: David L. Black, Treas.
Local. Seeks to study, explore and conserve cave and karst resources. Protects access to caves and promotes responsible caving. Encourages responsible management of caves and their unique environments. **Affiliated With:** National Speleological Society.

4791 ■ Quail Unlimited, Southern Indiana Chapter
8005 Dale Ct.
Georgetown, IN 47122
Ph: (812)951-3699
URL: National Affiliate–www.qu.org
Local. Affiliated With: Quail Unlimited.

Goshen

4792 ■ American Legion, Goshen Post 30
123 S 5th St.
Goshen, IN 46528
Ph: (219)533-3600
Fax: (317)237-9891
URL: National Affiliate–www.legion.org
Local. Affiliated With: American Legion.

4793 ■ Credit Professionals International, Goshen
c/o Darla Kauffman, Pres.
First State Bank
PO Box 804
Goshen, IN 46527
Ph: (574)533-8277 (574)825-4041
Fax: (574)533-8640
E-mail: dkkauffman@fsbmiddlebury.com
URL: http://www.creditprofessionals.org/5/goshen.html
Contact: Darla Kauffman, Pres.
Local. Supports members through networking, career development and community involvement. Promotes and contributes to the innovation of the credit industry. Provides education in the practice and procedure of credit. **Affiliated With:** Credit Professionals International.

4794 ■ Environmental Education Association of Indiana (EEAI)
c/o Krista Daniels, VP
218 Queen St.
Goshen, IN 46528
Ph: (574)875-7422
E-mail: krista@elkhartcountyparks.org
URL: http://www.goshen.edu/eeai
Contact: Krista Daniels, VP
Membership Dues: life, $200 • institution, $50 (annual) • family, $30 (annual) • individual, $25 (annual) • student, $10 (annual). **State**. Provides curriculum resources for environmental education development.

4795 ■ Goshen Chamber of Commerce (GCC)
232 S Main St.
Goshen, IN 46526-3723
Ph: (574)533-2102
Fax: (574)533-2103
Free: (800)307-4204
E-mail: info@goshen.org
URL: http://www.goshen.org
Contact: Brent Randall, Membership Services Dir.
Local. Promotes business and community development in Goshen, IN. **Committees:** Economic Development; Public Policy; Quality of Life. **Publications:** *Image*. Magazine • Newsletter, monthly.

4796 ■ Goshen Historical Society/Museum (GHS)
Box 701
Goshen, IN 46526
Ph: (219)533-1053
E-mail: rnofziger@aol.com
Contact: Earlene Nofziger, Pres.
Founded: 1981. **Members:** 140. **Membership Dues:** individual, $10 (annual) • senior/student, $8 (annual) • life, $250. **Local**. Individuals interested in preserving the history and artifacts of Goshen, IN. **Libraries: Type:** not open to the public. **Awards:** Historian of the Year. **Frequency:** annual. **Type:** trophy. **Recipient:** for contribution to the community throughout history. **Committees:** FACE of the City; Historic Landmarks Foundation of Indiana. **Publications:** Newsletter, bimonthly. **Price:** free. **Circulation:** 225. **Conventions/Meetings:** annual Historian of the Year - Elections - dinner - held in May.

4797 ■ Goshen Noon Kiwanis Club
PO Box 287
Goshen, IN 46527-0287
E-mail: brandall@goshen.org
URL: http://www.goshennoonkiwanis.org/index.html
Contact: Brent Randall, Pres.
Local.

4798 ■ Indiana Haflinger Horse Association (IHHA)
60770 County Rd. 35
Goshen, IN 46528
Ph: (574)646-3225
E-mail: secretary@indianahaflingers.com
URL: http://www.indianahaflingers.com
Contact: Glenn Yoder, Pres.
State. Affiliated With: American Haflinger Registry.

4799 ■ Indiana Lakeland Girl Scout Council
2400 Elkhart Rd.
Goshen, IN 46526
Ph: (219)533-8881
Fax: (574)534-7371
Free: (866)223-7740
E-mail: lakegs@verizon.net
URL: http://www.indianalakeland.org
Contact: Suzanne Abel, Pres.
Local. Young girls and adult volunteers, corporate, government and individual supporters. Strives to develop potential and leadership skills among its members. Conducts trainings, educational programs and outdoor activities.

4800 ■ Indiana State Grange
16105 CR 22
Goshen, IN 46528
Ph: (574)533-7638
Fax: (574)533-7638
URL: National Affiliate–www.nationalgrange.org
Contact: Gordon Groves, Master
State. Rural family service organization with a special interest in agriculture. Promotes mission and goals through legislative, social, educational, community service, youth, and member services programs. **Affiliated With:** National Grange.

4801 ■ Mennonite Nurses Association
c/o Merlin Becker-Hoover, Treas.
406 Alana Dr.
Goshen, IN 46526
Ph: (574)534-6225
E-mail: becker-hoover@juno.com
URL: http://mna.mennonite.net
Contact: Phyllis Miller RN, Pres.
Founded: 1942. **Members:** 340. **Membership Dues:** regular, $60 (annual) • retired nurse, $40 (annual). **Budget:** $12,410. **Regional**. Promotes nursing and provides support to Christian nurses within the Anabaptist tradition. **Affiliated With:** Mennonite Medical Association. **Publications:** *Mennonite Health Journal*, quarterly. Exists to feature healthcare workers, discuss biomedical ethics, facilitate relationships, and report on events. **Price:** $15.00. ISSN: 1525-6766.

4802 ■ Michiana Master Gardeners Association
c/o Faye E. Lutz
Purdue Extension Elkhart County
17746-E C R 34
Goshen, IN 46528
E-mail: mmga@michianamastergardeners.com
URL: http://www.michianamastergardeners.com
Local.

4803 ■ National Active and Retired Federal Employees Association - Elkhart 539
59867 County Rd. 117
Goshen, IN 46528-9085
Ph: (574)875-6055
URL: National Affiliate–www.narfe.org
Contact: Richard Wayne Cassel, Contact
Local. Protects the retirement future of employees through education. Informs members on issues affecting the retirement. **Affiliated With:** National Association of Retired Federal Employees.

4804 ■ Old Town Neighborhood Association
c/o Margaret Payne
204 S 6th St.
Goshen, IN 46526

Ph: (574)534-9099
URL: http://eyedart.com/otna
Contact: Phyllis Stutzman, Co-Chm.
Founded: 2000. **Members:** 250. **Budget:** $5,000. **Local Groups:** 1. **Local**. Promotes sound transportation decisions in local community. **Awards:** Neighborhood Preservation. **Frequency:** annual. **Type:** recognition.

4805 ■ Views on Learning/The Learning Society
c/o Joseph A. Rueff
2008 Wakefield Cir.
Goshen, IN 46528
Ph: (574)226-1011
E-mail: jrueff@viewsonlearning.org
URL: http://www.viewsonlearning.org
Contact: Joseph A. Rueff, Exec.Dir.
Founded: 1991. **Members:** 100. **Membership Dues:** individual, $25 (annual) • business, $50 (annual). **Staff:** 2. **Budget:** $160,000. **Local Groups:** 1. **Local**. Secures licenses from the Federal Communications Commission to offer telecommunications services to schools in the U.S. Operates in partnership with commercial telecommunications companies that provide the infrastructure for transmission of television and/or broadband services to interested schools. **Formerly:** (1998) Learning Society of Elkhart; (2001) Learning Society of Elkhart/Views on Learning. **Publications:** *Footprints in Cyberspace*. Newsletter. Alternate Formats: online • *Multicultural Resources Directory for Elkhart County*, biennial. **Price:** free to schools, churches, and service clubs. Alternate Formats: online • *Tabloid*, annual. Article. Found in the Elkhart TRUTH. **Conventions/Meetings:** annual meeting.

Gosport

4806 ■ Central Indiana Beagle Club
c/o Floyd A. Burns
RR, Box 486
Gosport, IN 47433-8135
URL: National Affiliate–clubs.akc.org
Contact: Floyd A. Burns, Contact
Local.

Granger

4807 ■ American Legion, Granger Post 151
c/o Bill Fries, Adj.
51039 Placid Pointe
Granger, IN 46530
Ph: (219)272-1314
Fax: (317)237-9891
URL: National Affiliate–www.legion.org
Contact: Bill Fries, Adj.
Local. **Affiliated With:** American Legion.

4808 ■ Association of Women's Health, Obstetric and Neonatal Nurses - Michiana Chapter
c/o Mary Lou Farr
52142 Mallard Point Dr.
Granger, IN 46530
E-mail: jfarr@cbd.net
URL: National Affiliate–www.awhonn.org
Contact: Lori Bauer, Coor.
Local. Represents registered nurses and other health care providers who specialize in obstetric, women's health, and neonatal nursing. Advances the nursing profession by providing nurses with information and support to help them deliver quality care for women and newborns. **Affiliated With:** Association of Women's Health, Obstetric and Neonatal Nurses.

4809 ■ CISG Chapter of Northern Indiana and Southwestern Michigan
c/o Fred Kantner
50630 Tecumseh Dr.
Granger, IN 46530
Ph: (574)277-4632
Fax: (574)277-4624
E-mail: fredk@mymailstation.com
URL: National Affiliate–www.cici.org
Contact: Fred Kantner, Contact
Regional. Educates and supports cochlear implant recipients and their families. Works to secure the rights of people with hearing loss. Aims to improve public and private financial support for individuals receiving cochlear implants. **Affiliated With:** Cochlear Implant Association, Inc.

4810 ■ Indiana Amateur Softball Association, Region 2
c/o John R. Byers, VP
52233 Tammy Ln.
Granger, IN 46530
Fax: (574)282-1446
URL: http://www.indiana-asa.org
Contact: John R. Byers, VP
Local. **Affiliated With:** Amateur Softball Association of America.

4811 ■ National Association of the Remodeling Industry of Michiana Chapter
12412 Campfire Dr.
Granger, IN 46530
Ph: (574)271-9156
E-mail: rholson49@cs.com
URL: National Affiliate–www.nari.org
Contact: Robert H. Olson, Pres.
Local. Brings together people who work in the remodeling industry. Provides resources for knowledge and training in the industry. Encourages ethical conduct, sound business practices and professionalism. Promotes the remodeling industry's products. **Affiliated With:** National Association of the Remodeling Industry.

4812 ■ National Speleological Society, St. Joseph Valley Grotto (SJVG)
c/o Tony Cunningham, Sec.
PO Box 617
Granger, IN 46530
Ph: (574)293-7492
E-mail: tony@weedpatrol.com
URL: http://www.caves.org/grotto/sjvg
Contact: Tony Cunningham, Sec.
Local. Seeks to study, explore and conserve cave and karst resources. Protects access to caves and promotes responsible caving. Encourages responsible management of caves and their unique environments. **Affiliated With:** National Speleological Society.

4813 ■ Police and Firemen's Insurance Association - South Bend Fire and Police Department
c/o Richard Switalski
51777 Purdue Ct.
Granger, IN 46530
Ph: (574)272-4768
URL: National Affiliate–www.pfia.net
Contact: Richard Switalski, Contact
Local. **Affiliated With:** Police and Firemen's Insurance Association.

Greencastle

4814 ■ American Legion, Indiana Post 58
c/o Cassell C. Tucker
1401 E Indianapolis Rd.
Greencastle, IN 46135
Ph: (317)653-8939
Fax: (317)237-9891
URL: National Affiliate–www.legion.org
Contact: Cassell C. Tucker, Contact
Local. **Affiliated With:** American Legion.

4815 ■ Association for Computing Machinery, Central Indiana Association for Computing Machinery-W Student Chapter
c/o Gloria Childress Townsend
620 S Coll. Ave.
Greencastle, IN 46135
Ph: (765)658-4726
Fax: (765)658-4732
E-mail: gct@depauw.edu
URL: http://www.acm.org
Contact: Gloria Townsend, Sponsor
Founded: 2000. **Members:** 50. **Regional Groups:** 4. **Regional**. Biological, medical, behavioral, and computer scientists; hospital administrators; programmers and others interested in application of computer methods to biological, behavioral, and medical problems. Stimulates understanding of the use and potential of computers in the Biosciences. **Affiliated With:** Association for Computing Machinery.

4816 ■ Association for Computing Machinery, Depauw University
c/o Dr. Carl P. Singer
Julian Sci. Ctr. and Mathematics Ctr.
602 S Coll. Ave.
Greencastle, IN 46135-0037
Ph: (765)658-4294
E-mail: helpdesk@depauw.edu
URL: National Affiliate–www.acm.org
Contact: Dr. Carl P. Singer, Contact
Local. Biological, medical, behavioral, and computer scientists; hospital administrators; programmers and others interested in application of computer methods to biological, behavioral, and medical problems. Stimulates understanding of the use and potential of computers in the Biosciences. **Affiliated With:** Association for Computing Machinery.

4817 ■ Greater Greencastle Chamber of Commerce (GGCC)
2 S Jackson St.
PO Box 389
Greencastle, IN 46135
Ph: (765)653-4517
E-mail: gchamber@ccrtc.com
URL: http://www.gogreencastle.com
Contact: Tammy Amor, Exec.Dir.
Founded: 1908. **Members:** 250. **Staff:** 1. **Budget:** $47,122. **Local**. Promotes and stimulates business, increasing the value of chamber membership to create more opportunities through economic growth and the improved quality of life in the Greencastle, IN area. **Affiliated With:** U.S. Chamber of Commerce. **Formerly:** (1999) Greencastle Chamber of Commerce. **Publications:** *Chamber Chimes*, monthly. Newsletter. **Conventions/Meetings:** monthly Business After Hours - meeting • quarterly luncheon • semiannual seminar.

4818 ■ Indiana Electronic Service Association (IESA)
5 Depot St.
Greencastle, IN 46135-1035
Ph: (765)653-4301 (765)653-5592
Fax: (765)653-4287
Free: (800)288-3824
E-mail: eta@eta-i.org
URL: http://www.eta-sda.com
Contact: Dick Glass, Exec.Dir.
Founded: 1958. **Members:** 120. **Membership Dues:** individual and business, $25 (annual). **Staff:** 7. **Budget:** $10,000. **State Groups:** 1. **State**. Electronic service companies. Provides technical and business management training and industry news and employment assistance. **Libraries: Type:** not open to the public. **Holdings:** 400; books. **Subjects:** radio, television, FCC license, engineering. **Awards:** Outstanding Service. **Frequency:** annual. **Type:** recognition. **Publications:** *High Tech News*, monthly. Journal. **Price:** $12.00. ISSN: 1092-9592. **Advertising:** accepted. **Conventions/Meetings:** annual convention.

4819 ■ Indiana Optometric Association, Western District
c/o Daryl W. Hodges, OD, Trustee
814 E Washington St.
Greencastle, IN 46135
Ph: (765)653-5896
Fax: (765)653-4554
E-mail: dhodges1@airhop.com
URL: http://www.ioa.org
Contact: Daryl W. Hodges OD, Trustee
Local. Aims to improve the quality, availability and accessibility of eye and vision care. Promotes high standards of patient care. Monitors and promotes legislation concerning the scope of optometric practice and other issues relevant to eye/vision care. **Affiliated With:** American Optometric Association; Indiana Optometric Association.

4820 ■ Indiana Society, Sons of the American Revolution, William Knight Chapter
c/o Donald B. Brattain, Pres.
94 Pin Oak Rd.
Greencastle, IN 46135
Ph: (765)653-6834
URL: http://www.geocities.com/inssar-south/willknig.html
Contact: Donald B. Brattain, Pres.
Local. Affiliated With: National Society, Sons of the American Revolution.

4821 ■ Mental Health Association in Putnam County, Indiana
c/o Ms. Eileen Johnson, Exec.Dir.
10 1/2 N Jackson St.
Greencastle, IN 46135-1585
Ph: (765)653-3310
Fax: (765)653-0048
E-mail: mhapc2@ccrtc.com
URL: http://www.mentalhealthassociation.com
Contact: Ms. Eileen Johnson, Exec.Dir.
Local. Seeks to promote mental health and prevent mental health disorders. Improves mental health of Americans through advocacy, public education, research and service. **Affiliated With:** Mental Health Association in Indiana; National Mental Health Association.

4822 ■ National Active and Retired Federal Employees Association - Greencastle 1024
917 Evensview Dr.
Greencastle, IN 46135-1105
Ph: (765)653-6670
URL: National Affiliate–www.narfe.org
Contact: Darrel Thomas, Contact
Local. Protects the retirement future of employees through education. Informs members on issues affecting the retirement. **Affiliated With:** National Association of Retired Federal Employees.

4823 ■ National Association of Student Personnel Administrators, Indiana
c/o James Lincoln, Coor.
DePauw Univ.
313 S Locust St.
Greencastle, IN 46135
Ph: (765)658-4199
Fax: (765)658-4207
E-mail: jlincoln@depauw.edu
URL: National Affiliate–www.naspa.org
Contact: James Lincoln, Coor.
State. Provides professional development and advocacy for student affairs educators and administrators. Seeks to promote, assess and support student learning through leadership. **Affiliated With:** National Association of Student Personnel Administrators.

4824 ■ Psi Chi, National Honor Society in Psychology - DePauw University
c/o Dept. of Psychology
7 E Larabee St.
Greencastle, IN 46135-1625
Ph: (765)658-4566 (765)658-4609
Fax: (765)658-4572
E-mail: mhertenstein@depauw.edu
URL: National Affiliate–www.psichi.org
Local. Affiliated With: Psi Chi, National Honor Society in Psychology.

4825 ■ Putnam County Board of Realtors
PO Box 746
Greencastle, IN 46135
Ph: (765)653-6998
Fax: (765)653-6998
E-mail: pcbr-eo@direcway.com
URL: National Affiliate–www.realtor.org
Contact: Diane Ummel, Exec. Officer
Local. Strives to develop real estate business practices. Advocates the right to own, use and transfer real property. Provides a facility for professional development, research and exchange of information among members and to the general public. **Affiliated With:** National Association of Realtors.

4826 ■ Sycamore Trails Resource Conservation and Development Council
1007 Mill Pond Ln.
Greencastle, IN 46135
Ph: (765)653-5716
Fax: (765)653-9455
E-mail: william.beard@in.usda.gov
URL: http://www.sycamoretrails.org
Contact: William Beard, Coor.
Local. Affiliated With: National Association of Resource Conservation and Development Councils.

4827 ■ United Way of Putnam County, Indiana
PO Box 365
Greencastle, IN 46135-0365
Ph: (765)653-5638
URL: National Affiliate–national.unitedway.org
Local. Affiliated With: United Way of America.

Greenfield

4828 ■ American Dairy Science Association - Midwest Branch
c/o Dr. Deana L. Hancock, Pres.
2001 W Main St.
Greenfield, IN 46140
Ph: (317)277-8638
Fax: (317)277-4288
E-mail: hancock_deana_l@lilly.com
URL: National Affiliate–www.adsa.org
Contact: Dr. Deana L. Hancock, Pres.
Regional. Affiliated With: American Dairy Science Association.

4829 ■ American Legion, Hancock Post 119
119 Amer. Legion Pl.
Greenfield, IN 46140
Ph: (317)462-5352
Fax: (317)237-9891
URL: National Affiliate–www.legion.org
Local. Affiliated With: American Legion.

4830 ■ American Red Cross, Hancock County
715 E Lincoln St.
Greenfield, IN 46140-2169
Ph: (317)462-4343
E-mail: archanco@redcross-indy.org
URL: http://www.redcross-indy.org
Contact: Terri Held, Sec.
Local. Provides communication and counseling services and emergency food, clothing and shelter to victims of natural and manmade disasters, members of the military service(s) and their families. Provides a full range of education programs including disaster prevention and mitigation, first aid, CPR, water safety and lifeguarding and HIV/AIDS education. Programs for youth include babysitting and lifeguarding. Provides transportation for referred clients with special emphasis on those with medical needs.

4831 ■ Avanti Owners Association International, Indiana Chapter
c/o Mike Baker, Pres.
1468 Pippen Dr.
Greenfield, IN 46140-8562
Ph: (317)467-4260
E-mail: mikebaker@aoai.org
URL: National Affiliate–www.aoai.org
Contact: Mike Baker, Pres.
State. Affiliated With: Avanti Owners Association International.

4832 ■ Boys and Girls Club of Hancock County
PO Box 115
715 E Lincoln St.
Greenfield, IN 46140
Ph: (317)462-3704
Fax: (317)462-0664
E-mail: adminoffice@bgchc.com
URL: http://www.bgchc.com
Contact: Darren Turner, Exec.Dir.
Founded: 1938. **Members:** 1,201. **Membership Dues:** individual, $35 (annual). **Staff:** 16. **Budget:** $428,000. **Local.** Provides a positive environment which seeks to inspire and enable all young people to realize their full potential as productive, responsible, and caring citizens. Arranges program areas like character development and leadership development; education and career development; health and life skills; sports, fitness and recreation; the arts. **Libraries: Type:** lending. **Holdings:** 50; books.

4833 ■ Greater Greenfield Chamber of Commerce (GGCC)
1 Courthouse Plz.
Greenfield, IN 46140-2300
Ph: (317)477-4188
Fax: (317)477-4189
E-mail: gfdchamb@greenfieldcc.org
URL: http://www.greenfieldcc.org
Contact: Linda Imel, Pres.
Founded: 1957. **Members:** 350. **Membership Dues:** business (based on the number of employee), $165-$2,200 • non-profit organization & retired citizen (one-half of the base rate), $82 • subcontractor, $55. **Local.** Promotes business and community development in the Greenfield, IN area. **Awards:** Community Service Award. **Frequency:** annual. **Type:** recognition. **Publications:** *Connection*, monthly. Newsletter • *Greater Greenfield Chamber of Commerce*, annual. Membership Directory. **Price:** $10.00. **Conventions/Meetings:** annual Awards Dinner - always April • monthly board meeting - always first Tuesday of each month.

4834 ■ Indiana Angus Association (IAA)
c/o Julia Wickard, Pres.
8267 E 300 N
Greenfield, IN 46140
Ph: (765)785-6297
E-mail: preid@purdue.edu
URL: http://www.indianaangus.com
Contact: Julia Wickard, Pres.
Membership Dues: auxiliary - life, $20 • auxiliary, $5 (annual) • junior, $10 (annual) • Indiana Angus breeder, $30 (annual). **State. Affiliated With:** American Angus Association.

4835 ■ Mental Health Association in Hancock County (MHAHC)
98 E North St.
Greenfield, IN 46140-2198
Ph: (317)462-2877
Fax: (317)462-2877
E-mail: help@mhahc.org
URL: http://www.mhahc.org
Contact: Ms. Ann Osborne, Exec.Dir.
Local. Seeks to promote mental health and prevent mental health disorders. Improves mental health of Americans through advocacy, public education, research and service. **Affiliated With:** Mental Health Association in Indiana; National Mental Health Association.

4836 ■ Police and Firemen's Insurance Association - Marion County Fire Department
c/o Steven M. Kemp
1318 N Westminster Ct.
Greenfield, IN 46140
Ph: (317)250-9933
E-mail: k3706@indygov.org
URL: National Affiliate–www.pfia.net
Contact: Steven M. Kemp, Contact
Local. Affiliated With: Police and Firemen's Insurance Association.

4837 ■ Southeastern Indiana Angus Association
c/o Chris Wickard, Pres.
8267 E 300 N
Greenfield, IN 46140
Ph: (765)785-6297
E-mail: cowsrus@hrtc.net
URL: National Affiliate–www.angus.org
Contact: Chris Wickard, Pres.
Local. Affiliated With: American Angus Association.

Greens Fork

4838 ■ Indiana Holstein Association
c/o Myron Moyer
11594 Ted Davis Rd.
Greens Fork, IN 47345
Ph: (765)478-4509
Fax: (765)478-5294
E-mail: sjmoyer@infocom.com
Contact: Myron Moyer, Exec. Officer
Founded: 1900. **Members:** 425. **Membership Dues:** basic, $34 (annual). **Staff:** 1. **Budget:** $40,000. **State Groups:** 1. Breeders and owners of Holstein cattle. **Awards:** Scholarship Award. **Frequency:** annual. **Type:** scholarship. **Recipient:** for college applicant. **Committees:** Homemakers Association; Junior Association. **Publications:** *Michigan-Indiana Holstein News*, monthly. Magazine. Contains information on Holstein breeders. **Price:** $10.00. **Circulation:** 4,900. **Advertising:** accepted. **Conventions/Meetings:** annual State Convention, dairy industry related (exhibits) - always February; Avg. Attendance: 150.

Greensburg

4839 ■ American Legion, Welsh-Crawley-Kramer Post 129
326 E Main St.
Greensburg, IN 47240
Ph: (812)663-2199
Fax: (317)237-9891
URL: National Affiliate–www.legion.org
Local. Affiliated With: American Legion.

4840 ■ City of Greensburg Public Safety Facilities Building Corporation
c/o Greensburg Clerk, Treas.
314 N Michigan
Greensburg, IN 47240-1433
Ph: (812)663-8582
Fax: (812)663-6314
E-mail: greensburgmayor@insightbb.com
Contact: Frank Manus, Mayor
Local.

4841 ■ Decatur County Board of Realtors, Indiana
PO Box 103
Greensburg, IN 47240
Ph: (812)663-2114
Fax: (812)663-8072
E-mail: dshginc@aol.com
URL: National Affiliate–www.realtor.org
Contact: Helen R. Gardner, Exec. Officer
Local. Strives to develop real estate business practices. Advocates the right to own, use and transfer real property. Provides a facility for professional development, research and exchange of information among members and to the general public. **Affiliated With:** National Association of Realtors.

4842 ■ Decatur County Historical Society (DCHS)
PO Box 163
Greensburg, IN 47240
Ph: (812)663-2764
E-mail: dgreiwe@ffsg.net
URL: http://www.greensburgchamber.com/historical.html
Contact: Deborah Greiwe, Contact
Founded: 1959. **Members:** 371. **Membership Dues:** individual, $10 (annual) • family, $15 (annual) • contributor, $30 (annual). **Local.** Individuals interested in the history of Decatur County, IN. Operates Decatur County Historical Society Museum. **Publications:** Bulletin, quarterly. Contains local history, museum news and society announcements. **Price:** included in membership dues. **Conventions/Meetings:** quarterly meeting.

4843 ■ Greensburg Decatur County Chamber of Commerce (GACC)
115 E North St.
Greensburg, IN 47240
Ph: (812)663-2832
Fax: (812)663-4275
E-mail: info@greensburgchamber.com
URL: http://www.greensburgchamber.com
Contact: Jennifer Sturges, Exec.Dir.
Founded: 1906. **Members:** 277. **Membership Dues:** individual, public official, non-profit, school, church, $88 (annual) • industrial (based on the number of employees), $145-$275 (annual) • apartment (depends on the number of units), $250-$560 (annual) • retiree, $43 (annual). **Staff:** 2. **Budget:** $70,000. **Local.** Local businesses and individuals united to promote economic and community development in the Greensburg, IN area. **Publications:** *Annual Business Directory*, annual • Newsletter, monthly.

Greentown

4844 ■ American Legion, Indiana Post 317
c/o Lowell E. Symons
PO Box 317
Greentown, IN 46936
Ph: (317)628-3943
Fax: (317)237-9891
URL: National Affiliate–www.legion.org
Contact: Lowell E. Symons, Contact
Local. Affiliated With: American Legion.

4845 ■ Eastern Howard Performing Arts Society (EHPAS)
c/o Kelli Austin, Exec.Dir.
120 S Green St.
Greentown, IN 46936-1118
Ph: (765)628-4025 (765)628-4026
Fax: (765)628-5017
Free: (888)649-ARTS
E-mail: questions@ehpas.com
URL: http://www.ehpas.com
Contact: Kelli Austin, Exec.Dir.
Founded: 2000. **Members:** 26. **Staff:** 3. **Local.** Works to foster interest and development of the arts in the local school systems. Presents performing arts program for the cultural enrichment of the community.

Greenwood

4846 ■ American Culinary Federation - Greater Indianapolis Chapter
c/o Carl L. Huckaby II, Pres.
1259 Easton Point Dr.
Greenwood, IN 46142
Ph: (317)882-7998
Fax: (317)878-4394
E-mail: acf.indianapolis@ameritech.net
URL: National Affiliate–www.acfchefs.org
Contact: Carl L. Huckaby II, Pres.
Local. Promotes the culinary profession. Provides on-going educational training and networking for members. Provides opportunities for competition, professional recognition and access to educational forums with other culinarians at local, regional, national and international events. **Affiliated With:** American Culinary Federation.

4847 ■ American Hiking Society - Indianapolis Hiking Club
3871 W Fairview Rd.
Greenwood, IN 46142
Ph: (317)881-8416
E-mail: malayman@earthlink.net
URL: http://www.indyhike.org
Contact: Anna Buckholtz, Pres.
Local.

4848 ■ American Legion, Greenwood Post 252
334 US Hwy. 31 S
Greenwood, IN 46142
Ph: (317)881-1752
Fax: (317)237-9891
URL: National Affiliate–www.legion.org
Local. Affiliated With: American Legion.

4849 ■ Greater Greenwood Chamber of Commerce (GGCC)
550 U.S. Hwy. 31 S
Greenwood, IN 46142-3063
Ph: (317)888-4856
Fax: (317)865-2609
E-mail: info@greenwoodchamber.us
URL: http://www.greenwood-chamber.com
Contact: Gail W. Richards, Exec.Dir.
Membership Dues: social organization, $175 • motel/hotel/apartment (plus $1 per room), $230 • real estate agency and insurance agency (plus $15 per agent), $230 • real estate developer, $230 • financial institution, $50 • shopping center and mall, $230 • licensed professional, $230 • utility (per meter/hookup), $0 • civic, $90. **Local.** Promotes business and community development in the Greenwood, IN area. **Awards:** Ernest Mishler Community Service Award. **Frequency:** annual. **Type:** recognition. **Recipient:** for outstanding community service • Pride & Progress Award. **Frequency:** annual. **Type:** recognition. **Recipient:** for deserving business. **Publications:** *Direction*, monthly. Newsletter. **Price:** members free. **Conventions/Meetings:** monthly workshop.

4850 ■ Humanist Friendship Group of Central Indiana
c/o Reba Boyd Wooden
113 Severn Dr.
Greenwood, IN 46142
Ph: (317)885-1612
E-mail: hfgci@webtv.net
URL: http://community.webtv.net/hfgci/HUMANISTFRIENDSHIP
Contact: Reba Boyd Wooden, Coor.
Local. Provides group support, discussions and social activities for freethinkers of all ages. **Affiliated With:** American Humanist Association.

4851 ■ National Technical Honor Society - Central Nine Career Center - Indiana
1999 US 31 S
Greenwood, IN 46143
Ph: (317)888-4401
E-mail: cfrey@central9.k12.in.us
URL: http://www.central9.k12.in.us
Contact: Cindy Frey, Dir.
Local.

4852 ■ Penn State Alumni Association, Central Indiana Chapter
c/o Phyllis Meek
508 Gatewood Dr.
Greenwood, IN 46143
Ph: (317)889-3559
E-mail: pnmeek@psualum.com
URL: http://www.psualum.com/chapter/cindiana
Contact: Phyllis Meek, Pres.
Local.

Griffith

4853 ■ American Legion Post 66
c/o Bill Snyder
PO Box 136
Griffith, IN 46319
Ph: (219)924-1415
URL: National Affiliate–www.legion.org
Local. Affiliated With: American Legion.

4854 ■ Calumet Astronomical Society (CAS)
PO Box 851
Griffith, IN 46319-0851
E-mail: info@casonline.org
URL: http://www.casonline.org
Contact: Chris Brownewell, Pres.
Local.

4855 ■ Calumet Stamp Club
PO Box 83
Griffith, IN 46319
Ph: (219)924-4836 (708)333-7947
E-mail: z28468@aol.com
URL: http://www.virtualstampclub.com/apscalumet.html
Membership Dues: $5 (annual). **Local. Affiliated With:** American Philatelic Society.

4856 ■ Dunes Calumet Audubon Society
529 S Broad St.
Griffith, IN 46319
E-mail: bergamot@datamine.net
URL: http://www.dunes-calumetaudubon.org
Contact: Donna Gonzalez, Pres.
Local. Works to conserve and restore natural ecosystems, focusing on birds and other wildlife for the benefit of humanity and the earth's biological diversity. **Affiliated With:** National Audubon Society.

4857 ■ Griffith Chamber of Commerce (GCC)
PO Box 204
Griffith, IN 46319-0204
Ph: (219)924-2155
Fax: (219)838-2661
E-mail: griffithchamber@dopplerexpress.net
Contact: Michael Longmiller, Pres.
Members: 120. **Membership Dues:** full, $100 (annual) • associate, $50 (annual). **Staff:** 1. **Local.** Promotes business and community development in Griffith, IN. Conducts annual sidewalk sale; sponsors annual golf outing; sponsors school Santa Poster Contest. Also a Family Steak Fry. **Publications:** *Business Directory and Guide to Buying*, periodic • *Griffith Chamber of Commerce Newsletter*, monthly. **Conventions/Meetings:** monthly luncheon, with speaker - always third Tuesday of the month.

4858 ■ Lake Area United Way, Indiana
221 W Ridge Rd.
Griffith, IN 46319
Ph: (219)923-2302 (219)923-0050
Fax: (219)923-8601
E-mail: info@lauw.net
URL: http://www.lauw.org
Contact: Louis Martinez, Pres.
Local. Affiliated With: United Way of America.

4859 ■ Road Runners Club of America - Calumet Region Striders (CRS)
PO Box 225
Griffith, IN 46319
Ph: (219)712-1715
Fax: (219)762-7535
E-mail: striders@verizon.net
URL: http://www.calstrider.org
Contact: Ms. Cassandra Rozycki, Pres.
Founded: 1978. **Members:** 500. **Membership Dues:** household (plus $7.50 additional family member with same address), $15 (annual). **Local.** Promotes the sport of road racing. Sponsors races, banquets, parties and fun runs. **Awards:** Jim Cox Scholarship. **Frequency:** annual. **Type:** scholarship. **Recipient:** graduating high school member attending a university, college, or trade school based on participation, volunteer efforts, membership status, and application essay. **Affiliated With:** Road Runners Club of America. **Also Known As:** (2005) Striders. **Publications:** *Instep*, monthly. Newsletter. **Conventions/Meetings:** monthly board meeting - every second Thursday at 7:00 pm.

4860 ■ Veterans of Foreign Wars/Griffith Memorial Auxiliary Unit 9982
302 E Main St.
Griffith, IN 46319
Ph: (219)924-6102
Contact: Marlin Crame, Commander
Local.

4861 ■ Wadsworth School PTA
601 N Jay St.
Griffith, IN 46319
Ph: (219)923-4488
Fax: (219)838-6770
URL: http://www.griffith.k12.in.us
Contact: Therese Schoon, Principal
Local.

Hagerstown

4862 ■ American Legion, Indiana Post 333
c/o William O. Frazier
615 W Main St.
Hagerstown, IN 47346
Ph: (317)489-5414
Fax: (317)237-9891
URL: National Affiliate–www.legion.org
Contact: William O. Frazier, Contact
Local. Affiliated With: American Legion.

4863 ■ Hagerstown Lions Club
PO Box 172
Hagerstown, IN 47346
Ph: (765)489-4344 (765)489-5443
URL: http://hagerstownin.lionwap.org
Contact: Jana Murray, Pres.
Local. Affiliated With: Lions Clubs International.

Hamilton

4864 ■ Hamilton Area Chamber of Commerce (HACC)
PO Box 66
Hamilton, IN 46742
Ph: (205)921-7786
Fax: (205)921-2220
E-mail: chamber@hamiltonchamber.com
URL: http://www.hamiltonchamber.com
Contact: Holly Law, Pres.
Founded: 1987. **Members:** 74. **Membership Dues:** business (over 10 employees), $100 • business (under 10 employees), $75 • individual, nonprofit, $50. **Local.** Promotes business and community development in the Hamilton, AL area. **Publications:** Newsletter. **Price:** free. **Conventions/Meetings:** monthly board meeting.

4865 ■ Hamilton Chamber of Commerce
PO Box 66
Hamilton, IN 46742
Ph: (260)488-3607
E-mail: chamber@hamiltonchamber.com
URL: http://www.hamiltonchamber.com
Contact: Tracy Thornbrugh, Pres.
Members: 105. **Membership Dues:** business (10 or more employees), $100 (annual) • business (less than 10 employees), $75 (annual) • patron and other non-profit organization, $50 (annual). **Budget:** $22,000. **For-Profit. Local.** Promotes business and community growth and development in Hamilton Area. **Awards:** Carl Akers Jr. Outstanding Achievement Award. **Frequency:** annual. **Type:** recognition • Hamilton Area Chamber of Commerce Business of the Year. **Frequency:** annual. **Type:** recognition • President's Appreciation Award. **Frequency:** annual. **Type:** recognition. **Conventions/Meetings:** monthly board meeting - every 3rd Tuesday.

Hamlet

4866 ■ American Legion, Clifford Garbison Post 356
PO Box 260
Hamlet, IN 46532
Ph: (812)867-8831
Fax: (317)237-9891
URL: National Affiliate–www.legion.org
Local. Affiliated With: American Legion.

Hammond

4867 ■ American Ex-Prisoners of War, Northern Indiana Chapter
c/o Glenda Mounts
7019 Arkansas Ave.
Hammond, IN 46323
Ph: (219)844-3170
URL: National Affiliate–www.axpow.org
Local. Affiliated With: American Ex-Prisoners of War.

4868 ■ American Legion, Hammond Post 16
6634 Calumet Ave.
Hammond, IN 46324
Ph: (219)933-9363
Fax: (317)237-9891
URL: National Affiliate–www.legion.org
Local. Affiliated With: American Legion.

4869 ■ American Legion Hammond Victory Post 168
c/o Terry Peirson
721 State St.
Hammond, IN 46320
Ph: (219)937-4262
URL: National Affiliate–www.legion.org
Local. Affiliated With: American Legion.

4870 ■ American Legion, Indiana Post 428
c/o Gen. John J. Pershing
617 Gostlin St.
Hammond, IN 46327
Ph: (317)630-1300
Fax: (317)237-9891
URL: National Affiliate–www.legion.org
Contact: Gen. John J. Pershing, Contact
Local. Affiliated With: American Legion.

4871 ■ American Legion, Maywood Post 126
6744 Columbia Ave.
Hammond, IN 46324
Ph: (219)937-9307
Fax: (317)237-9891
URL: National Affiliate–www.legion.org
Local. Affiliated With: American Legion.

4872 ■ American Legion Post 232
c/o Ken Maxie
6523 Kennedy Ave.
Hammond, IN 46323
Ph: (219)844-0230
E-mail: alpost232@peoplepc.com
URL: National Affiliate–www.legion.org
Contact: Ed Batsle, Contact
Local. Affiliated With: American Legion.

4873 ■ American Legion, Riders Memorial Post 17
4840 S Oak Ave.
Hammond, IN 46327
Ph: (219)885-9445
Fax: (317)237-9891
URL: National Affiliate–www.legion.org
Local. Affiliated With: American Legion.

4874 ■ Books, Brushes, and Bands for Education, LLC
c/o Michelle A. Golden
11 Warren St.
Hammond, IN 46320-2340
Ph: (219)937-3737
Fax: (219)937-3789
Contact: Michelle Golden, Pres.
Founded: 2000. **Staff:** 1. **Budget:** $70,000. **Nonmembership. Local.** Provides custom literary, visual and music arts education directly into school and pre-school sites. All projects provide community-wide culminating activity open to the public. Conducts fundraising activities. **Conventions/Meetings:** monthly board meeting.

4875 ■ Caldwell Elementary School PTA
3105 173rd St.
Hammond, IN 46323-2302
Ph: (219)845-7013 (219)845-5279
URL: http://familyeducation.com/IN/Caldwell_Elementary_PTA
Contact: Jennifer Medwetz, Pres.
Local. Parents, teachers, students, and others interested in uniting the forces of home, school, and community. Promotes the welfare of children and youth.

4876 ■ Calumet Area Literacy Council (CALC)
c/o Joanne Broderick
564 State St.
Hammond, IN 46320
Ph: (219)852-2226
Fax: (219)931-3474
Contact: Joanne Broderick, Exec.Dir.
Founded: 1968. **Members:** 100. **Membership Dues:** $5 (annual). **Staff:** 4. **Budget:** $12,675. **Local.** Trained tutors and other interested individuals working to reduce illiteracy and publicize the problem of illiteracy. Trains individuals in the Laubach method of literacy tutoring. **Affiliated With:** Laubach Literacy International. **Publications:** Newsletter, bimonthly.

4877 ■ Calumet Corner Chorus of Sweet Adelines International
Christian Fellowship Church
605 165th St.
Hammond, IN 46324-1310
Ph: (219)365-0160
E-mail: singers@calumetcornerchorus.org
URL: http://www.calumetcornerchorus.org
Contact: Sharon Hovezak, Contact
Local. Advances the musical art form of barbershop harmony through education and performances. Provides education, training and coaching in the development of women's four-part barbershop harmony. **Affiliated With:** Sweet Adelines International.

4878 ■ Eggers Middle School PTSA
5825 Blaine Ave.
Hammond, IN 46320
Ph: (219)931-7448 (219)933-2449
E-mail: phillipsy2k@msn.com
URL: http://familyeducation.com/IN/Eggers_Middle_PTSA
Contact: Barb Phillips, Pres.
Local. Parents, teachers, students, and others interested in uniting the forces of home, school, and community. Promotes the welfare of children and youth.

4879 ■ Family Action Network of Lake County
5720 Sohl Ave., Rm. 113
Hammond, IN 46320
Ph: (219)933-1700
Fax: (219)933-1453
E-mail: familyactionnetwork@msn.com
URL: National Affiliate–www.ffcmh.org
Contact: Nancy Cloonan, Contact
Local. Affiliated With: Federation of Families for Children's Mental Health.

4880 ■ Gavit PTSA
1670 175th St.
Hammond, IN 46324
Ph: (219)989-7325
E-mail: gavitvp1@hotmail.com
URL: http://familyeducation.com/IN/Gavit_PTSA
Contact: Karen Holland, Pres.
Local. Parents, teachers, students and others interested in uniting the forces of home, school and community. Promotes the welfare of children and youth.

4881 ■ Hammond Urban Enterprise Association (HUEA)
649 Conkey St.
Hammond, IN 46324
Ph: (219)853-6512
Fax: (219)853-6515
E-mail: info@helpinghammond.com
URL: http://www.helpinghammond.com
Contact: Patrick J. Reardon, Exec.Dir.
Local.

4882 ■ IEEE Computer Society, Calumet
c/o Nasser Houshangi
Dept. of Engg.
Purdue Univ. Calumet
2200 169th St.
Hammond, IN 46323
Ph: (219)989-2461
Fax: (219)989-2898
E-mail: hnasser@calumet.purdue.edu
URL: http://www.ewh.ieee.org/r4/calumet/
Local. Affiliated With: IEEE Computer Society.

4883 ■ International Association of Women Police, Region 6
c/o Donna C. Wright, Coor.
Purdue Univ. Calumet Police Dept.
2200 169th St.
Hammond, IN 46323-2094
E-mail: wright@calumet.purdue.edu
URL: http://www.iawp.org/region6.htm
Contact: Donna C. Wright, Coor.
Founded: 1915. **Regional.** Composed of women and men in all areas and ranks of the criminal justice field. Strives to increase professionalism in police work, furthers the utilization of women in the field, and provides a forum for sharing developments. Holds annual training conferences. **Affiliated With:** International Association of Women Police.

4884 ■ Izaak Walton League of America - Griffith
6735 Nebraska Ave.
Hammond, IN 46323-1945
Ph: (219)845-8595
E-mail: ruston3@aol.com
URL: National Affiliate–www.iwla.org
Contact: Kimberly Russell, Contact
Local. Educates the public to conserve, maintain, protect and restore the soil, forest, water and other natural resources of the U.S. and other lands.

4885 ■ Lake County Convention and Visitors Bureau (LCCVB)
7770 Corinne Dr., Ste 425
Hammond, IN 46323
Ph: (219)989-7770
Free: (800)ALL-LAKE
E-mail: lccvb@allake.org
URL: http://www.alllake.org
Contact: Speros A. Batistatos CDME, Pres./CEO
Founded: 1983. **Members:** 13. **Staff:** 35. **Budget:** $2,500,000. **State Groups:** 1. **Local Groups:** 1. **Local.** Promotes business and tourism in Lake County, IN. **Publications:** *Lake County Visitors Guide*, annual. Magazine. Lists attractions, restaurants, lodging, outdoor recreation and festivals and events. **Price:** free. **Circulation:** 300,000. **Advertising:** accepted.

4886 ■ Lake County REACT Team
7409 Harrison Ave.
Hammond, IN 46324
Ph: (219)931-0238
E-mail: margaretgetts@yahoo.com
URL: http://www.reactintl.org/teaminfo/usa_teams/teams-usin.htm
Local. Trained communication experts and professional volunteers. Provides volunteer public service and emergency communications through the use of radios (Citizen Band, General Mobile Radio Service, UHF and HAM). Coordinates with radio industries and government on safety communication matters and supports charitable activities and community organizations.

4887 ■ Lakeshore Chamber of Commerce (HCC)
5246 Hohman Ave. Ste.100
Hammond, IN 46320
Ph: (219)931-1000
Fax: (219)937-8778
E-mail: info@lakeshorechamber.com
URL: http://www.lakeshorechamber.com
Contact: Joseph A. Kosina, Pres.
Founded: 1912. **Members:** 436. **Staff:** 3. **Local.** Promotes business and community development in Hammond, IN. **Committees:** Ambassador; Manufacturer; Referral; Special Events. **Formerly:** (2001) Hammon Chamber of Commerce. **Publications:** *Community Directory and Buyers Guide*, biennial • *Greater Hammond Community Map* • *Greater Hammond Transit Map*. Newsletter • *Progress*, monthly • *Summer Events Tabloid*, annual. **Conventions/Meetings:** monthly meeting.

4888 ■ Northwest Indiana Habitat for Humanity
6219 Calumet Ave.
Hammond, IN 46324
Ph: (219)937-2292
Fax: (219)937-2317
E-mail: habitat@nwihabitat.com
URL: http://habitatnwi.bizland.com
Contact: Mike Schrage, Pres.
Local. Affiliated With: Habitat for Humanity International.

4889 ■ Orchard Drive PTA
3640 Orchard Dr.
Hammond, IN 46323
Ph: (219)989-0104 (219)989-7355
E-mail: wkmonthego@comcast.net
URL: http://familyeducation.com/IN/Orchard_Drive_PTA
Contact: Jennifer Sandoval, Pres.
Local. Parents, teachers, students, and others interested in uniting the forces of home, school, and community. Promotes the welfare of children and youth.

4890 ■ Parents As Teachers of Hammond Lake County
2450 169th St.
Hammond, IN 46323

Ph: (219)554-1710
Fax: (219)554-1720
E-mail: pathammond@surfnetinc.com
URL: http://www.lakenetnwi.net/org/pat
Contact: Kimberly Smith, Program Dir.

Founded: 2000. **Members:** 12. **Staff:** 7. **Budget:** $155,000. **Local**. Early childhood parent education; supports program for Hammond families who are expecting or have a child ages newborn-3 years old.

4891 ■ PFLAG Hammond
7143 Olcott Ave.
Hammond, IN 46323
Ph: (219)845-2195
E-mail: hammondpflag@aol.com
URL: http://members.aol.com/DrKcrusher/pflag.htm

Local. **Affiliated With:** Parents, Families, and Friends of Lesbians and Gays.

4892 ■ Police and Firemen's Insurance Association - Hammond Fire Department
c/o Wayne Hargrove
22 Coolidge St.
Hammond, IN 46324
Ph: (219)937-1781
URL: National Affiliate–www.pfia.net
Contact: Wayne Hargrove, Contact

Local. **Affiliated With:** Police and Firemen's Insurance Association.

4893 ■ Psi Chi, National Honor Society in Psychology - Purdue University Calumet
c/o Dept. of Psychology
2200 169th St.
Hammond, IN 46323-2094
Ph: (219)989-2384 (219)989-2712
Fax: (219)989-2008
E-mail: dnalbone@calumet.purdue.edu
URL: http://www.psichi.org/chapters/info.asp?chapter_id=805
Contact: David P. Nalbone PhD, Advisor

Local.

4894 ■ Purdue University Calumet Student Association for Computing Machinery SIGGRAPH
c/o Jana Whittington, Sponsor
2200 169th St.
Hammond, IN 46323
Ph: (219)989-2354
Fax: (219)989-2062
E-mail: whitting@calumet.purdue.edu
URL: http://life.calumet.purdue.edu/siggraph/index.htm
Contact: Brandi Collier, Chair

Local. Biological, medical, behavioral, and computer scientists; hospital administrators; programmers and others interested in application of computer methods to biological, behavioral, and medical problems. Stimulates understanding of the use and potential of computers in the Biosciences. **Affiliated With:** Association for Computing Machinery.

4895 ■ Society of Manufacturing Engineers - Purdue University - Calumet S161
Purdue Univ. - Calumet, Dept. of Mfg. Engg. and Tech.
2200 169th St.
Hammond, IN 46323
Ph: (219)989-2465
Fax: (219)989-2062
E-mail: gneff@purdue.edu
URL: National Affiliate–www.sme.org
Contact: Gregory Neff, Contact

Local. Advances manufacturing knowledge to gain competitive advantage. Improves skills and manufacturing solutions for the growth of economy. Provides resources and opportunities for manufacturing professionals.

4896 ■ Veterans of Foreign Wars/Memorial Post 7881
6831 Kennedy Ave.
Hammond, IN 46323
Ph: (219)844-9616
Contact: Mark Rincon, Commander

Local.

Hanover

4897 ■ Psi Chi, National Honor Society in Psychology - Hanover College
c/o Dept. of Psychology
PO Box 890
Hanover, IN 47243-0890
Ph: (812)866-7307 (812)866-7316
Fax: (812)866-2164
E-mail: krantzj@hanover.edu
URL: National Affiliate–www.psichi.org

Local. **Affiliated With:** Psi Chi, National Honor Society in Psychology.

Harlan

4898 ■ Greater Harlan Business Association
c/o Rick Hullinger
PO Box 201
Harlan, IN 46743-0201
Ph: (260)657-5877
Contact: Rick Hullinger, Sec.

Membership Dues: $50 (annual). **Local**.

Hartford City

4899 ■ American Legion, Moyer-Pooler Post 159
PO Box 462
Hartford City, IN 47348
Ph: (317)348-2900
Fax: (317)237-9891
URL: National Affiliate–www.legion.org

Local. **Affiliated With:** American Legion.

4900 ■ Blackford County Civil War Re-enactment Club (BCCWRCI)
c/o Orville Uggen, Jr., Pres.
3219 S State Rd. 3
Hartford City, IN 47348-9777
Ph: (765)348-4319 (765)348-1981
E-mail: 34ind@insightbb.com
URL: http://www.hartfordcitycwdays.com
Contact: Orville Uggen Jr., Pres.

Founded: 1990. **Members:** 20. **Membership Dues:** individual, $1 (annual). **Staff:** 5. **Budget:** $10,000. **Local**. Updates the records of all Civil War soldiers who were residents of Blackford County, enlisted in Blackford County, or moved to Blackford County after the War. Sells red clay bricks and rose mountain granite blocks around the Civil War Monument. **Conventions/Meetings:** monthly meeting.

4901 ■ Blackford County Historical Society (BCHS)
PO Box 264
Hartford City, IN 47348
Ph: (765)348-1130
E-mail: at@bchs-in.org
URL: http://www.bchs-in.org
Contact: Sinuard Castelo, Pres.

Founded: 1954. **Members:** 50. **Membership Dues:** individual, $10 (annual). **Local**. Individuals interested in the history of Blackford County, IN. Maintains Blackford Historical Museum. **Libraries: Type:** reference. **Holdings:** 300; books, periodicals. **Subjects:** local history. **Publications:** *Gas Belt Review*. Book. **Price:** $7.00/copy • *Marriage Books* • *WW II, Blackford County Remembers*. **Price:** $20.00. **Conventions/Meetings:** monthly meeting - always fourth Tuesday in Hartford City, IN.

4902 ■ Blackford United Way
PO Box 286
Hartford City, IN 47348-0286
Ph: (765)348-1118
URL: National Affiliate–national.unitedway.org

Local. **Affiliated With:** United Way of America.

4903 ■ Hartford City Chamber of Commerce (HCCC)
PO Box 286
Hartford City, IN 47348
Ph: (765)348-1905
Fax: (765)348-4945
E-mail: cbrown@blackfordcounty.com
URL: National Affiliate–www.uschamber.com
Contact: Chris Brown, Sec.Mgr.

Local. Promotes business and community development in Hartford City, IN. **Affiliated With:** U.S. Chamber of Commerce.

4904 ■ Mental Health Association in Blackford County
c/o Ms. Diana Mitchell, Exec.Dir.
814 N Richmond St.
Hartford City, IN 47348-1541
Ph: (765)348-7040
Fax: (765)348-7046
E-mail: dmitchell@towfin.com
URL: http://www.mentalhealthassociation.com
Contact: Ms. Diana Mitchell, Exec.Dir.

Local. Seeks to promote mental health and prevent mental health disorders. Improves mental health of Americans through advocacy, public education, research and service. **Affiliated With:** Mental Health Association in Indiana; National Mental Health Association.

Haubstadt

4905 ■ American Legion, Haubstadt Post 194
200 S Race St.
Haubstadt, IN 47639
Ph: (812)768-6809
Fax: (317)237-9891
URL: National Affiliate–www.legion.org

Local. **Affiliated With:** American Legion.

4906 ■ Evansville Gun Club
RR 2, Box 89-H
Haubstadt, IN 47639
Ph: (812)768-6370
Fax: (812)768-5100
URL: National Affiliate–www.mynssa.com

Local. **Affiliated With:** National Skeet Shooting Association.

Hazleton

4907 ■ American Legion, White River Post 114
PO Box 155
Hazleton, IN 47640
Ph: (317)630-1300
Fax: (317)237-9891
URL: National Affiliate–www.legion.org

Local. **Affiliated With:** American Legion.

Henryville

4908 ■ American Legion, Henryville Post 105
305 N Ferguson St.
Henryville, IN 47126
Ph: (812)294-1338
Fax: (317)237-9891
URL: National Affiliate–www.legion.org

Local. **Affiliated With:** American Legion.

4909 ■ Project Management Institute, Kentuckiana Chapter
c/o Mr. Charles L. Johnson, MPM, PMP, Pres.
5405 Henryville-otisco Rd.
Henryville, IN 47126
Ph: (502)580-1741
Fax: (502)508-1741
E-mail: charlesj@digicove.com
URL: http://www.pmi-kentuckianachapter.org
Contact: Mr. Charles L. Johnson MPM, Pres.
Local. Corporations and individuals engaged in the practice of project management; project management students and educators. Seeks to advance the study, teaching, and practice of project management. **Affiliated With:** Project Management Institute.

Highland

4910 ■ American Legion, Highland Memorial Post 180
PO Box 1682
Highland, IN 46322
Ph: (219)972-3948
Fax: (317)237-9891
URL: National Affiliate–www.legion.org
Local. Affiliated With: American Legion.

4911 ■ Girl Scouts of The Calumet Council
2906 Hwy. Ave.
Highland, IN 46322-1631
Ph: (219)838-3171
Fax: (219)923-6832
E-mail: onmyhonor@gscalumet.org
URL: http://www.gscalumet.org
Local. Young girls and adult volunteers, corporate, government and individual supporters. Strives to develop potential and leadership skills among its members. Conducts trainings, educational programs and outdoor activities.

4912 ■ Highland Chamber of Commerce (HCC)
8536 Kennedy Ave.
Highland, IN 46322
Ph: (219)923-3666
E-mail: mary@highlandchamber.com
URL: http://www.highlandchamber.com
Contact: Mary Luptak, Exec.Dir.
Membership Dues: business (based on the number of employee), $189-$641. **Local**. Promotes business and community development in Highland, IN. **Committees:** Breakfast with the Easter Bunny; Chamber Building; Christmas Treat Bags/Santa Lunch; Fall Festival; Golf Outing; Midwest Zest Festival; Spring Diaper Seminar.

4913 ■ Highland Soccer Club
PO Box 1864
Highland, IN 46322
Ph: (219)922-2656
E-mail: members@highlandsoccer.org
URL: http://www.highlandsoccer.org
Contact: Paul Kyriakides, Pres.
Local.

4914 ■ Highland Table Tennis Club
2450 Lincoln St.
Highland, IN 46322
Ph: (219)838-0114
URL: http://www.highlandparks.org/Brochure/HTTC/httc.htm
Contact: Keith Jones, Contact
Local. Affiliated With: U.S.A. Table Tennis.

4915 ■ Indiana Society, Sons of the American Revolution, William Van Gordon Chapter
c/o Timothy J. Wolf, Pres.
3047 Lake Side Dr.
Highland, IN 46322
Ph: (219)924-0416
URL: http://www.geocities.com/inssar-south/willgord.html
Contact: Timothy J. Wolf, Pres.
Local. Affiliated With: National Society, Sons of the American Revolution.

4916 ■ Lake County Right to Life
PO Box 9103
Highland, IN 46322
Ph: (219)756-4219
E-mail: lakertl@rocketmail.com
URL: http://www.icongrp.com/~rtl
Contact: John Ronald Manfred, Contact
Local.

4917 ■ Mental Health Association in Lake County
9722 Parkway Dr.
Highland, IN 46322-2779
Ph: (219)922-3822
Fax: (219)922-3825
E-mail: info@mhalakecounty.org
URL: http://www.mhalakecounty.org
Contact: William R. Sellers MS, Exec.Dir.
Local. Seeks to promote mental health and prevent mental health disorders. Improves mental health of Americans through advocacy, public education, research and service. **Affiliated With:** Mental Health Association in Indiana; National Mental Health Association.

4918 ■ Northern Indiana TAM Users Group
c/o Regnier Insurance Services
PO Box 9039
Highland, IN 46322
Ph: (219)972-1330
Fax: (219)972-7574
E-mail: jan@ris-ins.com
URL: National Affiliate–www.ascnet.org
Contact: Jan Regnier, Pres.
Local. Represents insurance agents and brokers using the Agency Manager software. Promotes successful automation and business practices through communication, education, and advocacy. **Affiliated With:** Applied Systems Client Network.

4919 ■ Our Lady of Grace School Home and School Association
c/o Margie Dian
3025 Hwy. Ave.
Highland, IN 46322
Ph: (219)838-2901
URL: http://www.olgraceschool.org
Contact: Debbie Lund, Sec.
Local.

Hillsboro

4920 ■ American Legion, Memorial Post 188
PO Box 405
Hillsboro, IN 47949
Ph: (317)798-4190
Fax: (317)237-9891
URL: National Affiliate–www.legion.org
Local. Affiliated With: American Legion.

Hillsdale

4921 ■ Clay County Beagle Club
c/o David Short
9716 S Co. Rd., 275 E
Hillsdale, IN 47854
URL: National Affiliate–clubs.akc.org
Contact: David Short, Contact
Local.

Hobart

4922 ■ American Legion, Paul Leon Wolek Memorial Post 454
3139 Michigan St.
Hobart, IN 46342
Ph: (219)962-1583
Fax: (317)237-9891
URL: National Affiliate–www.legion.org
Local. Affiliated With: American Legion.

4923 ■ Fellowship of Orthodox Christians United in Service Focus (FOCUS)
c/o FOCUS Inc.
4526 16th St.
Hobart, IN 46342-5706
Local.

4924 ■ Hobart Chamber of Commerce
1001 Lillian St.
Hobart, IN 46342
Ph: (219)942-5774
Fax: (219)942-4928
E-mail: info@hobartchamber.com
URL: http://www.hobartchamber.com
Contact: Brenda Clemmons, Exec.Dir.
Membership Dues: business (1-100 employees), $110-$495 (annual) • non-profit, $55 (annual) • associate, $55 (annual). **Local**. Strives to support and advance the best interests, commercial and industrial, of the members of this organization; to promote trade; to further industrial, professional and other worthy activities; and to serve constructively for the public welfare of the city, county, state and nation; and for these purposes to cooperate with other agencies and organizations. **Computer Services:** Information services, membership listing. **Publications:** *Business Directory*. Provides composite listing key elements pertaining to Hobart. • *Hobart Horizons*, monthly. Newsletter. Contains business and community news briefs. Alternate Formats: online. **Conventions/Meetings:** monthly General Membership Meeting, with speaker - every 3rd Thursday in Hobart, IN.

4925 ■ Hobart Historical Society (HHS)
706 E. 4th St.
PO Box 24
Hobart, IN 46342
Ph: (219)942-0970
Contact: Dorothy Ballantyne, Museum Dir.
Founded: 1965. **Members:** 400. **Local**. Individuals interested in preserving the history of Hobart, IN. Operates museum. **Libraries: Type:** reference. **Publications:** *Hobart History News*, periodic. **Conventions/Meetings:** annual meeting - always November.

4926 ■ Indiana First Judicial District Pro Bono Committee
c/o Judith H. Stanton, Plan Admin.
PO Box 427
651 E 3rd St.
Hobart, IN 46342-0427
Ph: (219)945-1799
Fax: (219)945-0995
Free: (866)945-1799
E-mail: probono@hobartlaw.net
Contact: Judith H. Stanton, Plan Administrator
Founded: 2001. **Staff:** 1. **Nonmembership**. **For-Profit**. **Local**. Provides pro bono legal representation by volunteer attorneys to eligible clients; recruiting volunteers; provides technical support; outreach to clients and relevant agencies and organizations. **Awards:** Richard P. Komyatte Excellence in Pro Bono Award. **Frequency:** annual. **Type:** recognition.

4927 ■ Northern Indiana Sheet Metal Contractors Association
c/o Maynard A. Krueger, Exec.VP
111 W. 10th St., Ste.98
Hobart, IN 46342-5990

Ph: (219)947-7447
Fax: (219)947-4115
Free: (888)999-9633
E-mail: nismca@aol.com
URL: National Affiliate–www.smacna.org
Contact: Maynard A. Krueger, Exec.VP
Founded: 1946. **Members:** 23. **Membership Dues:** $300 (annual). **Staff:** 2. **Budget:** $175,000. **Local.** Local chapter of the Sheet Metal and Air Conditioning Contractors' National Association. Represents employers who hire members of the SMWIA (Sheet Metal Workers International Association). Cover the seven northwest counties of the State of Indiana, and bargain on behalf of our member employers with the Union for the pay rates and benefit packages. Also provides educational training to members on many business, safety, and trade practice subjects. Promotes the public merits of using properly trained Union Sheet Metal Workers for construction and service project needs. **Affiliated With:** Sheet Metal and Air Conditioning Contractors' National Association. **Conventions/Meetings:** monthly board meeting • quarterly General Membership Meeting.

4928 ■ Northwestern Indiana Nurserymen's Association
PO Box 277
Hobart, IN 46342-0277
Ph: (219)942-3917
Fax: (219)942-3917
Contact: Jerry Zelenka, Exec.Sec.
Founded: 1960. **Members:** 80. **Membership Dues:** active, $40 (annual) • associate, $40 (annual). **Staff:** 1. **Regional.** Local organization of horticultural professions. Strives to professionally practice and promote horticulture while strongly upholding the ethics and practices of the industry. **Conventions/Meetings:** annual Appreciation Night - dinner, with entertainment - always November • annual Summer Field Day Trip - tour - always summer • annual Winter Educational Seminar - always winter.

4929 ■ Outback Trail Commission
PO Box 431
Hobart, IN 46342
E-mail: inquiries@outbacktrail.org
URL: http://www.outbacktrail.org
Local. Affiliated With: International Mountain Bicycling Association.

4930 ■ Sierra Club - Hoosier Chapter - Dunelands Group
5500 S Liverpool Rd.
Hobart, IN 46342
Ph: (219)942-2956
E-mail: ecorealm@msn.com
URL: http://www.hoosier.sierraclub.org
Contact: Sandy O'Brien, Co-Chm., Conservation
Members: 800. **Membership Dues:** introductory, $25 (annual) • regular, $39 (annual). **Budget:** $1,000. **Local.** Activities include hiking, canoeing, service, picnic outings, solid conservation work. **Conventions/Meetings:** monthly General Membership with Program - meeting - 3rd or 4th Thursday of the month. Hobart, IN.

4931 ■ United Brotherhood of Carpenters and Joiners of America, Hobart Local Union No. 1005
780 Union St.
Hobart, IN 46342-2536
Ph: (219)942-8896
Fax: (219)942-1325
E-mail: phf714@aol.com
URL: National Affiliate–www.carpenters.org
Contact: Paul Hernandez, Pres.
Local. Affiliated With: United Brotherhood of Carpenters and Joiners of America.

4932 ■ Veterans of Foreign Wars/Hobart Post 5365
540 S Indiana St.
Hobart, IN 46342
Ph: (219)942-6474
E-mail: terriluedtke@msn.com
URL: http://www.vfw5365.com
Contact: Joe Barry, Commander
Local. Provides assistance to veterans and their families. Promotes fraternalism and patriotism.

Holland

4933 ■ American Legion, Harmeyer Post 343
PO Box 73
Holland, IN 47541
Ph: (812)536-3096
Fax: (317)237-9891
URL: National Affiliate–www.legion.org
Local. Affiliated With: American Legion.

4934 ■ National Association of Rocketry - Launch Crue
8991 W 900 S
Holland, IN 47541
Ph: (812)683-3288
E-mail: rdwoebke@hotmail.com
URL: http://www.geocities.com/launchcrue
Contact: Ryan Woebkenberg, Pres.
Local.

Hope

4935 ■ American Legion, Hope Post 229
PO Box 203
Hope, IN 47246
Ph: (812)372-3424
Fax: (317)237-9891
URL: National Affiliate–www.legion.org
Local. Affiliated With: American Legion.

Howe

4936 ■ ARC Opportunities - Lagrance County
0235 W 300 N
Howe, IN 46746
Ph: (260)463-2653
Fax: (260)463-2046
E-mail: info@arcopportunities.org
URL: http://www.arcopportunities.org
Contact: Debra Seman, CEO
Founded: 1966. **Staff:** 40. **Nonmembership. Local.** Parents, professional workers, and others interested in individuals with mental retardation. Works to promote services, research, public understanding, and legislation for people with mental retardation and their families. **Affiliated With:** Arc of the United States.

Huntertown

4937 ■ Auburn Duesey Walkers
c/o Kathy Thompson
15216 Hedgebrook Dr.
Huntertown, IN 46748-9328
Ph: (260)710-7294
E-mail: wwguru_@excite.com
URL: National Affiliate–www.ava.org
Contact: Kathy Thompson, Contact
Members: 25. **Membership Dues:** $5 (annual). **Local. Affiliated With:** American Volkssport Association.

4938 ■ Fort Wayne Bonsai Club
c/o Mrs. Darlene Kittle, Pres./Newsletter Ed.
17725 Lima Rd.
Huntertown, IN 46748
Ph: (260)637-5104
Fax: (260)335-1235
E-mail: plantlady6@aol.com
Contact: Mrs. Darlene Kittle, Pres./Newsletter Ed.
Founded: 1980. **Members:** 30. **Membership Dues:** adult, $25 (annual) • family, $30 (annual). **Local Groups:** 1. **Local.** Promotes interest in and knowledge of bonsai, an art which is part horticulture, part art-pruning, shaping, and container-growing to produce dwarfed, three-dimensional forms suggesting natural trees or landscapes. **Libraries: Type:** not open to the public; by appointment only; lending. **Holdings:** 25; articles, books, video recordings. **Subjects:** bonsai. **Computer Services:** Electronic publishing, newsletter • mailing lists, of members. **Affiliated With:** American Bonsai Society. **Publications:** *Fort Wayne Bonsai Club Newsletter*, monthly. Contains notices of meetings, review of previous meetings and educational information about the art of bonsai. **Price:** $6.00 /year for members. **Circulation:** 30. **Advertising:** accepted. Alternate Formats: CD-ROM; online.

4939 ■ Izaak Walton League of America, Fort Wayne Chapter
17100 Griffin Rd.
Huntertown, IN 46748
Ph: (260)637-6735
URL: National Affiliate–www.iwla.org
Local. Works to educate the public to conserve, maintain, protect, and restore the soil, forest, water, and other natural resources of the U.S; promotes the enjoyment and wholesome utilization of these resources. **Affiliated With:** Izaak Walton League of America.

Huntingburg

4940 ■ Huntingburg Chamber of Commerce
309 N Geiger St.
Huntingburg, IN 47542
Ph: (812)683-5699
Fax: (812)683-3524
E-mail: info@huntingburgchamber.org
URL: http://www.huntingburgchamber.org
Contact: Christine Prior, Exec.Dir.
Local. Promotes economic and social development in Huntingburg, IN.

4941 ■ Mental Health Association in Dubois County
809 Hickory Dr.
Huntingburg, IN 47542-9675
Ph: (812)482-9010
URL: http://www.mentalhealthassociation.com
Contact: Ms. Leah Hayworth, Exec.Dir.
Local. Seeks to promote mental health and prevent mental health disorders. Improves mental health of Americans through advocacy, public education, research and service. **Affiliated With:** Mental Health Association in Indiana; National Mental Health Association.

4942 ■ Quail Unlimited, Patoka Hills
2674 W 750 S
Huntingburg, IN 47542
Ph: (812)683-4477
URL: National Affiliate–www.qu.org
Local. Affiliated With: Quail Unlimited.

Huntington

4943 ■ American Legion, Indiana Post 85
c/o Donald E. Converse
1410 S Jefferson St.
Huntington, IN 46750
Ph: (219)358-1206
Fax: (317)237-9891
URL: National Affiliate–www.legion.org
Contact: Donald E. Converse, Contact
Local. Affiliated With: American Legion.

4944 ■ American Legion, Mike and George Bustos Post 7
1330 Etna Ave.
Huntington, IN 46750
Ph: (219)356-9985
Fax: (317)237-9891
URL: National Affiliate–www.legion.org
Local. Affiliated With: American Legion.

4945 ■ American Mothers - Indiana Chapter
c/o Martha Barker, Pres.
980 Ray St.
Huntington, IN 46750
Ph: (260)355-0229
E-mail: mbvioln@sbcglobal.net
URL: National Affiliate–www.americanmothers.org
Contact: Martha Barker, Pres.
State. Affiliated With: American Mothers, Inc.

4946 ■ Association for Professionals in Infection Control and Epidemiology, Indiana Chapter
c/o Ann Carmien
Huntington Memorial Hosp.
2001 Sluts Rd.
Huntington, IN 46750
Ph: (317)962-2639
E-mail: theim@psci.net
URL: http://www.apicin.com
Contact: Laurie Fish, Pres.-Elect
State. Works to influence, support and improve the quality of healthcare through the development of educational programs and standards. Promotes quality research and standardization of practices and procedures. **Affiliated With:** Association for Professionals in Infection Control and Epidemiology.

4947 ■ Huntington Area Association of Realtors
PO Box 226
Huntington, IN 46750
Ph: (260)358-1200
Fax: (260)358-1577
E-mail: jlandrum-haar@sbcglobal.net
URL: National Affiliate–www.realtor.org
Contact: Jill Landrum, Exec. Officer
Local. Strives to develop real estate business practices. Advocates the right to own, use and transfer real property. Provides a facility for professional development, research and exchange of information among members and to the general public. **Affiliated With:** National Association of Realtors.

4948 ■ Huntington Chapter of the American Red Cross
354 N Jefferson St., Ste.203
Huntington, IN 46750
Ph: (260)356-2910
Fax: (260)356-2111
E-mail: red.cross@huntington.in.us
URL: http://chapters.redcross.org/in/huntington
Contact: Karen Bennett, Exec.Dir.
Local.

4949 ■ Huntington County Chamber of Commerce (HCCC)
305 Warren St.
Huntington, IN 46750
Ph: (260)356-5300
Fax: (260)356-5434
E-mail: manager@huntington-chamber.com
URL: http://www.huntington-chamber.com
Contact: Robert C. Brown Jr., Pres.
Founded: 1924. **Members:** 380. **Staff:** 3. **Budget:** $214,000. **Local**. Promotes economic and industrial development in Huntington, IN. Works to retain and improve present business and industry. Recruits industry through Lime City Development Corp. (LCDC). Sponsors golf tournament, annual Heritage Days, and Expo. **Affiliated With:** U.S. Chamber of Commerce. **Publications:** *Chamber Spirit*, monthly. Newsletter • *Civic and Organization Guide*. Directory • *Huntington City and County Map*, triennial. Directory • *Huntington County Retail-Service Guide*, annual • *Industrial Guide* • *Personnel Management Association: Wage and Benefit Study*, annual.

4950 ■ Huntington County Habitat for Humanity
1454 Etna Ave.
Huntington, IN 46750
Ph: (260)356-7425
Fax: (260)356-7102
E-mail: hchabitat@onlyinternet.net
URL: http://habitat.huntingtoncounty.org
Contact: Norris Friesen, Pres.
Local. Affiliated With: Habitat for Humanity International.

4951 ■ Huntington County Visitor and Convention Bureau
407 N Jefferson St.
Huntington, IN 46750
Ph: (260)359-8687
Free: (800)848-4282
E-mail: info@visithuntington.org
URL: http://www.visithuntington.org
Contact: Rose Meldrum, Exec.Dir.
Local. Promotes tourism in Huntington County area. **Awards:** Tourism Promotion Grant. **Frequency:** semiannual. **Type:** grant. **Recipient:** for increased promotions and attractions that draw visitors from outside the county.

4952 ■ International Brotherhood of Electrical Workers AFL-CIO, LU 983
PO Box 5141
Huntington, IN 46750
Ph: (260)358-3473
Fax: (260)358-3207
E-mail: pres983ibew@say.union-yes.cc
URL: http://ibew983online.org
Contact: Tyler Brown, Pres./Business Mgr.
Founded: 1991. **Members:** 550. **Staff:** 23. **Local**. Seeks to: promote reasonable methods of work; cultivate feelings of friendship among different industries; settle all disputes between employers and employees; secure employment; reduce the hours of daily labor; secure adequate pay among workers; promote higher standard of living; and elevate the moral, intellectual and social conditions of everyone. **Affiliated With:** International Brotherhood of Electrical Workers.

4953 ■ Masonic Cemetery Association
c/o George C. Allen
5625 S 100 E.
Huntington, IN 46750-9221
Ph: (260)375-3704
Contact: Jerry Piqune, Sexton/Treas.
Local.

4954 ■ PFLAG Huntington
306 E Washington St.
Huntington, IN 46750
Ph: (260)356-7983
Fax: (260)982-9977
E-mail: kenrieman@hoosierlink.net
URL: http://www.pflag.org/Indiana.205.0.html
Local. Affiliated With: Parents, Families, and Friends of Lesbians and Gays.

4955 ■ United Way of Huntington County
PO Box 347
Huntington, IN 46750-0347
Ph: (219)356-6160
Fax: (260)356-6164
E-mail: unitedway@onlyinternet.net
URL: http://www.unitedwayhuntingtoncounty.org
Contact: Patricia Horoho, Exec.Dir.
Local. Affiliated With: United Way of America.

4956 ■ Youth Service Bureau of Huntington County
c/o Jan Williams, Dir.
1344 Maple Dr.
Huntington, IN 46750
Ph: (260)356-9681
Fax: (260)356-9683
E-mail: ysbadm@choiceonemail.com
URL: http://www.indysb.org
Contact: Jan Williams, Dir.
Local. Offers services to enhance and empower youth and their families.

Hymera

4957 ■ American Legion, Shepherd-Russell Post 298
PO Box 324
Hymera, IN 47855
Ph: (317)630-1300
Fax: (317)237-9891
URL: National Affiliate–www.legion.org
Local. Affiliated With: American Legion.

Idaville

4958 ■ Helping Hands Dairy Goat Club
c/o Lena Sue Schroeder
12562 N 600 W
Idaville, IN 47950
Ph: (219)943-3358
URL: National Affiliate–adga.org
Contact: Lena Sue Schroeder, Contact
Local. Affiliated With: American Dairy Goat Association.

4959 ■ Indiana Dairy Goat Association
c/o Lena Sue Schroeder
12562 N 600 W
Idaville, IN 47950
Ph: (219)943-3358
URL: National Affiliate–adga.org
Contact: Lena Sue Schroeder, Contact
State. Affiliated With: American Dairy Goat Association.

Indianapolis

4960 ■ 100 Black Men of Indianapolis
3901 N Meridian St.
Indianapolis, IN 46208
Ph: (317)921-1276
Fax: (317)921-1355
E-mail: blkmenipls@aol.com
URL: National Affiliate–www.100blackmen.org
Local. Affiliated With: 100 Black Men of America.

4961 ■ AAA Hoosier Motor Club
3750 Guion Rd.
Indianapolis, IN 46222
Ph: (317)923-1500
Fax: (317)924-4669
Free: (800)874-7317
E-mail: tfarias@aaahoosier.com
URL: http://www.aaa.com
Contact: Julie Bigham, Exec.Asst.
Local.

4962 ■ Adoption Support of Indianapolis
c/o Julie Craft
6331 N. Carrollton Ave.
Indianapolis, IN 46220-1754
Ph: (317)255-5916 (317)253-8335
Fax: (317)235-8838
Free: (800)274-1084
E-mail: info@adoptionsupportcenter.com
URL: http://adoptionsupportcenter.com
Contact: Julie Craft, Founder/Pres.
Founded: 1986. **Staff:** 10. **Budget:** $900,000. **Languages:** English, Spanish. **For-Profit. Local. Telecommunication Services:** electronic mail, jcraft77@msn.com. **Subgroups:** Indiana Adoption Support United.

4963 ■ African University Foundation (AUF)
3737 N Meridian St., Ste.204
Indianapolis, IN 46208
Ph: (317)926-2175
Fax: (317)926-2176
E-mail: auf@aufoundation.org
URL: http://www.aufoundation.org
Contact: Baiyee-Mbi Agbor-Baiyee PhD, Pres./CEO
Founded: 1994. **Local. Conventions/Meetings:** annual board meeting.

4964 ■ Aikido of Indianapolis
Eastgate Consumer Mall - Entrance D
7150 E Washington St.
Indianapolis, IN 46219
URL: http://www.indy-aikido.com
Local.

4965 ■ Air Conditioning Contractors of America, Indiana Chapter
c/o Linda C. Compton, Exec.Dir.
3003 E 98th St., Ste.161
Indianapolis, IN 46280
Ph: (317)573-0277
Fax: (317)573-0895
E-mail: accaindiana@aol.com
URL: National Affiliate–www.acca.org
Contact: Linda C. Compton, Exec.Dir.
State. Works to represent contractors involved in installation and service of heating, air conditioning, and refrigeration systems. **Affiliated With:** Air Conditioning Contractors of America.

4966 ■ Air and Waste Management Association, Indiana Chapter
c/o Wade Kohlmann, Treas.
2020 N Meridian St.
Indianapolis, IN 46202-1306
Ph: (317)927-4541
E-mail: admrwk@cgcu.com
URL: http://www.inawma.org
Contact: Wade Kohlmann, Treas.
State.

4967 ■ Alcoholics Anonymous, Indianapolis Intergroup
136 E Market St., Ste.1030
Indianapolis, IN 46204
Ph: (317)632-7864
Fax: (317)632-2155
E-mail: intergroupmail@indyaa.org
URL: http://indyaa.com
Contact: Mr. James A. Bredle, Office Mgr.
Founded: 1935. **Local Groups:** 410. **Nonmembership. Local.** Works to promote fellowship of men and women, who share their experience, strength, and hope with each other that they may solve their common problem and help others recover from alcoholism.

4968 ■ Alpha Kappa Alpha, Alpha Mu Omega
PO Box 88097
Indianapolis, IN 46208
E-mail: president@akaamo.org
URL: http://www.akaamo.org
Contact: Victoria Clark, Pres.
Local. Affiliated With: Alpha Kappa Alpha.

4969 ■ ALS Association of Indiana
PO Box 50129
Indianapolis, IN 46250
Ph: (317)915-9888
Fax: (317)915-9889
Free: (888)508-3232
E-mail: info@alsaindiana.org
URL: http://www.alsaindiana.org
Contact: Ana Stark, Exec.Dir.
Founded: 1997. **Local.** Aims to find cure for, and improve living with, Amyotrophic Lateral Sclerosis (ALS). **Affiliated With:** Amyotrophic Lateral Sclerosis Association.

4970 ■ Alzheimer's Association, Central Indiana Chapter
9135 N Meridian St., Ste.B-4
Indianapolis, IN 46260
Ph: (317)575-9620
Fax: (317)582-0669
Free: (888)575-9624
E-mail: heather.hershberger@alz.org
URL: http://www.standbyyou.org
Contact: Heather Allen Hershberger, Exec.Dir.
Local. Assists people with Alzheimer's disease and related dementia. **Affiliated With:** Alzheimer's Association.

4971 ■ American Academy of Pediatrics, Indiana Chapter
c/o Carolyn Downing, Exec.Dir.
322 Canal Walk
Indianapolis, IN 46202-3268
Ph: (317)261-2060
Fax: (317)261-2076
Free: (800)257-4762
E-mail: cdowning@ismanet.org
URL: http://www.indiana.edu/~iaap
Contact: Carolyn Downing, Exec.Dir.
State. Affiliated With: American Academy of Pediatrics.

4972 ■ American Association for Laboratory Animal Science - Indiana
c/o Cheryl Kantmann-Higgins
1121 W Michigan St., Rm. S507
Indianapolis, IN 46202
Ph: (317)274-5415
E-mail: ckantman@iupui.edu
URL: http://in.d5aalas.org
Contact: Cheryl Kantmann-Higgins, Contact
State. Serves as a clearinghouse for the collection and exchange of information and expertise in the care and use of laboratory animals. Promotes and encourages the highest level of ethics within the profession of laboratory animal science. Provides educational and training programs for members and others who are professionally engaged in the production, care, use and study of laboratory animals. **Affiliated With:** American Association for Laboratory Animal Science.

4973 ■ American Association of Legal Nurse Consultants, Greater Indianapolis Chapter
c/o Cathy Waldron, Pres.
PO Box 1702
Indianapolis, IN 46206-1702
Ph: (317)846-8999
E-mail: cathy@3333law.com
URL: http://www.greaterindyaalnc.org
Contact: Cathy Waldron, Pres.
Founded: 1991. **Membership Dues:** $35 (annual). **Local.** Promotes the professional development of registered nurses practicing in a consulting capacity in the legal field. Consists of nurses and paralegals who practice in the field of medical-legal concerns. **Libraries: Type:** lending. **Holdings:** books, papers, video recordings, audio recordings. **Subjects:** legal nursing issues, medical issues. **Affiliated With:** American Association of Legal Nurse Consultants.

4974 ■ American Association of Physics Teachers, Indiana Section
c/o Timothy A. Duman, Treas.
Univ. of Indianapolis, Dept. of Physics
1400 E Hanna Ave.
Indianapolis, IN 46227-3697
Ph: (317)209-9658
Fax: (317)788-3569
E-mail: tduman@uindy.edu
URL: National Affiliate–www.aapt.org
Contact: Timothy A. Duman, Treas.
State. Seeks to enhance the understanding and appreciation of physics through teaching. Aims to improve the pedagogical skills and physics knowledge of teachers at all levels. **Affiliated With:** American Association of Physics Teachers.

4975 ■ American Association of Retired Persons, Indiana (AARP)
One N. Capitol Ave., Ste.1275
Indianapolis, IN 46204
Fax: (317)423-2211
Free: (866)448-3618
E-mail: inaarp@aarp.org
URL: http://www.aarp.org/in
Members: 800,000. **Membership Dues:** anyone age 50 or older, $12 (annual). **State.** Persons 50 years of age or older, working or retired. Seeks to improve every aspect of living for older people. **Awards:** Andrus Award. **Frequency:** annual. **Type:** recognition. **Affiliated With:** American Association of Retired Persons. **Publications:** *AARP Bulletin*, monthly. **Price:** free • *The Magazine*, bimonthly. **Price:** free.

4976 ■ American Cancer Society - Central Indiana Area Service Center
c/o Kelly Graham
6030 W 62nd St.
Indianapolis, IN 46278
Ph: (317)347-6670
Fax: (317)347-6679
Free: (800)ACS-2345
URL: http://www.cancer.org
Contact: Kelly Graham, Contact
Local. Community-based voluntary health organization dedicated to eliminating cancer as a major health problem by preventing cancer, saving lives and diminishing suffering from cancer, through research, education, advocacy and service.

4977 ■ American Chemical Society, Indiana Section
c/o Mr. Brian M. Mathes, Chm.
7840 Fawnwood Dr.
Indianapolis, IN 46278-9595
Ph: (317)277-7720
E-mail: mathes@lilly.com
URL: National Affiliate–acswebcontent.acs.org
Contact: Mr. Brian M. Mathes, Chm.
State. Represents the interests of individuals dedicated to the advancement of chemistry in all its branches. Provides opportunities for peer interaction and career development. **Affiliated With:** American Chemical Society.

4978 ■ American Council of the Blind of Indiana (ACBI)
c/o Gerry Koors, Pres.
5885 Central Ave.
Indianapolis, IN 46220
Ph: (317)251-2562
E-mail: gerrykoors@aol.com
URL: http://indianaacb.tripod.com
Contact: Gerry Koors, Pres.
State. Strives to improve the well being of all blind and visually impaired people. Aims to elevate the social, economic and cultural levels of blind people. Cooperates with the public and private institutions and organizations concerned with blind services. Conducts a public education program to promote greater understanding of blindness and the capabilities of blind people. **Affiliated With:** American Council of the Blind.

4979 ■ American Council of Engineering Companies of Indiana
55 Monument Cir., Ste.819
Indianapolis, IN 46204
Ph: (317)637-3563
Fax: (317)637-9968
E-mail: staff@acecindiana.org
URL: http://www.acecindiana.org
Contact: Stephanie Morse, Exec.Dir.
State. Advances the profession of consulting engineers in private practice. **Awards:** Engineering Excellence. **Frequency:** annual. **Type:** recognition • **Frequency:** annual. **Type:** scholarship. **Affiliated With:** American Council of Engineering Companies. **Publications:** *The Consultant*, bimonthly. Newsletter. **Price:** free. **Conventions/Meetings:** annual convention - always June • monthly meeting.

4980 ■ American Council on Gift Annuities
233 McCrea St., Ste.400
Indianapolis, IN 46225
Ph: (317)269-6271
Fax: (317)269-6276
E-mail: acga@acga-web.org
URL: http://www.acga-web.org
Contact: Gloria Kermeen, Administrator
Founded: 1927. **Members:** 1,200. **Membership Dues:** organizational sponsorship, $100 (annual). **Staff:** 1. **Local.** Provides educational and other services to charities regarding gift annuities and other forms of planned gifts. Publishes suggested charitable gift annuity rates. **Formerly:** (2000) Committee on

Gift Annuities. **Conventions/Meetings:** biennial conference (exhibits).

4981 ■ American Counseling Association, Indiana
PO Box 40065
Indianapolis, IN 46240-0065
Ph: (317)846-0499
E-mail: icaindiana@aol.com
URL: http://www.indianacounseling.org
Founded: 1962. **Members:** 950. **Staff:** 3. **Budget:** $150,000. **Regional Groups:** 14. **State**. Promotes the profession of counseling by providing opportunities for personal growth and professional development. **Affiliated With:** American Counseling Association. **Publications:** *Hoosier Counselor*, quarterly. Newsletter. **Price:** included in membership dues. **Circulation:** 950. **Conventions/Meetings:** annual conference (exhibits) - 2007 Feb., Indianapolis, IN - Avg. Attendance: 450.

4982 ■ American Dairy Association of Indiana
c/o Sue Branes, Gen.Mgr.
9360 Castlegate Dr.
Indianapolis, IN 46256
Ph: (317)842-7955
Fax: (317)842-3065
Free: (800)225-6455
E-mail: hardin@mpsiinc.com
URL: http://www.indianadairycouncil.org
State.

4983 ■ American Diabetes Association, Central Indiana Area
6415 Castleway W Dr.
Indianapolis, IN 46250
Ph: (317)352-9226
Fax: (317)594-0748
Free: (888)DIABETES
E-mail: askada@diabetes.org
URL: National Affiliate–www.diabetes.org
Contact: Renea Marsh, Contact
Local. Comprises of physicians, laypersons, and health professionals interested in diabetes mellitus. Promotes research, information and advocacy to find a prevention and cure for diabetes and to improve the lives of all people with diabetes. Promotes public awareness of diabetes as a serious disease. Conducts educational programs and provides information to people with diabetes and the health professionals who care for them. **Affiliated With:** American Diabetes Association.

4984 ■ American Family Association of Indiana
c/o Micah Clark
PO Box 26208
Indianapolis, IN 46226
Ph: (317)541-9287
Fax: (317)541-9707
E-mail: micah@afain.net
URL: http://www.afain.net
State.

4985 ■ American Federation of Government Employees, District 6
c/o Arnold R. Scott, Natl.VP
5664 Caito Dr., Ste.100
Indianapolis, IN 46226
Ph: (317)542-0428
Fax: (317)542-0519
E-mail: cinnamonh@sbcglobal.net
URL: http://www.afgedistrict6.org
Contact: Arnold R. Scott, Natl.VP
Regional. **Affiliated With:** American Federation of Government Employees.

4986 ■ American Institute of Aeronautics and Astronautics, Indiana
c/o Kurt Weber
Rolls-Royce Corp.
M/S T14A
PO Box 420
Indianapolis, IN 46206-0420
Ph: (317)230-4591
Fax: (317)230-3691
E-mail: kurt.f.weber@rolls-royce.com
URL: National Affiliate–www.aiaa.org/
Contact: Robert A. Delaney, Contact
Affiliated With: American Institute of Aeronautics and Astronautics.

4987 ■ American Institute of Architects Indiana
47 S Pennsylvania St., Ste.201
Indianapolis, IN 46204-3731
Ph: (317)634-6993
Fax: (317)266-0515
E-mail: aiaindiana@ameritech.net
URL: http://www.aiaindiana.org
Contact: Ken Englund, Exec.Dir.
Founded: 1892. **State**. Strives to promote the aesthetic, scientific, and practical efficiency of the profession of architecture. Works to improve the science and art of planning and building by advancing the standards of architectural education, training, and practice. **Awards:** Citation Awards. **Type:** recognition • Merit Awards. **Type:** recognition • Outstanding Indiana Architecture Award. **Type:** recognition. **Committees:** Agriculture and Small Business; Appointments and Claims; Commerce and Consumer Affairs; Criminal, Civic and Public Policy; Economic Development and Technology; Education and Career Development; Elections and Civic Affairs; Environmental Affairs. **Affiliated With:** American Institute of Architects.

4988 ■ American Legion, Acton-Bunker-Hill Post 220
5440 Senour Rd.
Indianapolis, IN 46239
Ph: (317)862-6995
Fax: (317)237-9891
URL: National Affiliate–www.legion.org
Local. **Affiliated With:** American Legion.

4989 ■ American Legion, Atkins Saw Post 355
7610 S Meridian St.
Indianapolis, IN 46217
Ph: (317)784-0841
Fax: (317)237-9891
URL: National Affiliate–www.legion.org
Local. **Affiliated With:** American Legion.

4990 ■ American Legion, Baltimore Ohio Post 466
217 N Traub Ave.
Indianapolis, IN 46222
Ph: (317)635-2189
Fax: (317)237-9891
URL: National Affiliate–www.legion.org
Local. **Affiliated With:** American Legion.

4991 ■ American Legion, Big Four Railway Post 116
2241 W 79th St.
Indianapolis, IN 46260
Ph: (317)630-1300
Fax: (317)237-9891
URL: National Affiliate–www.legion.org
Local. **Affiliated With:** American Legion.

4992 ■ American Legion, Broad Ripple Post 3
6379 N Coll. Ave.
Indianapolis, IN 46220
Ph: (317)255-0574
Fax: (317)237-9891
URL: National Affiliate–www.legion.org
Local. **Affiliated With:** American Legion.

4993 ■ American Legion, Celtic Post 372
4107 E Washington
Indianapolis, IN 46201
Ph: (317)375-1436
Fax: (317)237-9891
URL: National Affiliate–www.legion.org
Local. **Affiliated With:** American Legion.

4994 ■ American Legion, Central Post 132
802 Weghorst St.
Indianapolis, IN 46204
Ph: (317)630-1300
Fax: (317)237-9891
URL: National Affiliate–www.legion.org
Local. **Affiliated With:** American Legion.

4995 ■ American Legion, Eli Lilly Post 374
4939 E 72nd St.
Indianapolis, IN 46250
Ph: (317)630-1300
Fax: (317)237-9891
URL: National Affiliate–www.legion.org
Local. **Affiliated With:** American Legion.

4996 ■ American Legion, Garfield Park Post 88
1446 S Olive St.
Indianapolis, IN 46203
Ph: (317)632-0417
Fax: (317)237-9891
URL: National Affiliate–www.legion.org
Local. **Affiliated With:** American Legion.

4997 ■ American Legion of Indiana
c/o Ron Martin, Commander
777 N Meridian St.
Indianapolis, IN 46204
Ph: (317)630-1200
Fax: (317)237-9891
E-mail: members@indlegion.org
URL: http://www.indlegion.org
Founded: 1919. **Members:** 135,000. **Staff:** 18. **State Groups:** 1. **State**. Honorably discharged wartime veterans, both male and female, of World Wars I and II, the Korean and Vietnam Wars, and the Grenada, Panama, Lebanon, Bosnia, and Desert Storm conflicts. **Affiliated With:** American Legion. **Publications:** *Hoosier Legionaire*, quarterly. Newsletter. **Conventions/Meetings:** quarterly conference.

4998 ■ American Legion, Indiana Post 26
c/o Paul Coble
5311 N Pennsylvania St.
Indianapolis, IN 46220
Ph: (317)630-1300
Fax: (317)237-9891
URL: National Affiliate–www.legion.org
Contact: Paul Coble, Contact
Local. **Affiliated With:** American Legion.

4999 ■ American Legion, Indiana Post 34
c/o Robert E. Kennington
6440 E Westfield Blvd.
Indianapolis, IN 46220
Ph: (317)259-8311
Fax: (317)237-9891
URL: National Affiliate–www.legion.org
Contact: Robert E. Kennington, Contact
Local. **Affiliated With:** American Legion.

5000 ■ American Legion, Indiana Post 186
c/o John H. Holliday, Jr.
6049 Harlescott Rd.
Indianapolis, IN 46220
Ph: (317)251-7513
Fax: (317)237-9891
URL: National Affiliate–www.legion.org
Contact: John H. Holliday, Contact
Local. **Affiliated With:** American Legion.

5001 ■ American Legion, Indiana Post 249
c/o Tillman H. Harpole
2523 Dr. Martin Luther King St.
Indianapolis, IN 46208
Ph: (317)923-0874
Fax: (317)237-9891
URL: National Affiliate–www.legion.org
Contact: Tillman H. Harpole, Contact
Local. **Affiliated With:** American Legion.

5002 ■ American Legion, Indiana Post 438
c/o Indianapolis Womens Inc.
PO Box 51632
Indianapolis, IN 46251
Ph: (317)881-5990
Fax: (317)237-9891
URL: National Affiliate–www.legion.org
Local. Affiliated With: American Legion.

5003 ■ American Legion, Indiana Post 495
c/o Leo F. Welch, Jr.
8725 E 38th St.
Indianapolis, IN 46226
Ph: (317)898-0652
Fax: (317)237-9891
URL: National Affiliate–www.legion.org
Contact: Leo F. Welch Jr., Contact
Local. Affiliated With: American Legion.

5004 ■ American Legion, Indiana Post 911
c/o Oliver H. Perry
6530 Yellowstone Pkwy.
Indianapolis, IN 46217
Ph: (317)630-1300
Fax: (317)237-9891
URL: National Affiliate–www.legion.org
Contact: Oliver H. Perry, Contact
Local. Affiliated With: American Legion.

5005 ■ American Legion, Indianapolis Power Light Post 300
3605 Parrish Ct.
Indianapolis, IN 46227
Ph: (317)784-8211
Fax: (317)237-9891
URL: National Affiliate–www.legion.org
Local. Affiliated With: American Legion.

5006 ■ American Legion, Madden-Nottingham Post 348
108 E St. Clair St.
Indianapolis, IN 46204
Ph: (317)630-1300
Fax: (317)237-9891
URL: National Affiliate–www.legion.org
Local. Affiliated With: American Legion.

5007 ■ American Legion, Mc-Ilvaine-Kothe Post 153
4102 Central Ave.
Indianapolis, IN 46205
Ph: (317)283-2708
Fax: (317)237-9891
URL: National Affiliate–www.legion.org
Local. Affiliated With: American Legion.

5008 ■ American Legion, New Directions Post 511
2401 E 25th St.
Indianapolis, IN 46218
Ph: (317)630-1300
Fax: (317)237-9891
URL: National Affiliate–www.legion.org
Local. Affiliated With: American Legion.

5009 ■ American Legion, New Indianapolis Post 4
5924b E 10th St.
Indianapolis, IN 46219
Ph: (317)359-0235
Fax: (317)237-9891
URL: National Affiliate–www.legion.org
Local. Affiliated With: American Legion.

5010 ■ American Legion, Northwest Post 497
3011 Guion Rd.
Indianapolis, IN 46222
Ph: (317)925-8503
Fax: (317)237-9891
URL: National Affiliate–www.legion.org
Local. Affiliated With: American Legion.

5011 ■ American Legion, Police Post 56
1431 E Washington St.
Indianapolis, IN 46253
Ph: (317)293-5251
Fax: (317)237-9891
URL: National Affiliate–www.legion.org
Local. Affiliated With: American Legion.

5012 ■ American Legion, Sahara Grotto Post 264
3918 Ivory Way
Indianapolis, IN 46237
Ph: (317)896-2042
Fax: (317)237-9891
URL: National Affiliate–www.legion.org
Local. Affiliated With: American Legion.

5013 ■ American Legion, Service Post 128
PO Box 128
Indianapolis, IN 46236
Ph: (317)630-1300
Fax: (317)237-9891
URL: National Affiliate–www.legion.org
Local. Affiliated With: American Legion.

5014 ■ American Legion, Wayne Post 64
601 S Holt Rd.
Indianapolis, IN 46241
Ph: (317)244-8007
Fax: (317)237-9891
URL: National Affiliate–www.legion.org
Local. Affiliated With: American Legion.

5015 ■ American Lung Association of Indiana
9445 Delegates Row
Indianapolis, IN 46240
Ph: (317)573-3900
Fax: (317)573-3909
Free: (800)LUNG-USA
E-mail: info@lungin.org
URL: http://www.lungin.org
Contact: Nancy Turner, Pres./CEO
State. Physicians, nurses, and laymen interested in the prevention and control of lung disease. Conducts patient education, advocacy, and research; major areas of focus are asthma, tobacco control and environmental health. **Affiliated With:** American Lung Association.

5016 ■ American Physical Therapy Association, Indiana Chapter
PO Box 26692
Indianapolis, IN 46226-0692
Ph: (317)823-3681
Fax: (317)823-3681
E-mail: schroeder@inapta.org
Contact: Teresa Schroeder, Contact
Founded: 1940. **Members:** 1,600. **State Groups:** 5. **Local.** Licensed physical therapists and certified physical therapist assistants. Promotes physical therapy services; offers professional education and information. **Affiliated With:** American Physical Therapy Association. **Publications:** *Issues in Indiana*, bimonthly. Newsletter. **Price:** included in membership dues. **Circulation:** 1,600. **Advertising:** accepted. **Conventions/Meetings:** annual State Conference (exhibits) - spring. Indianapolis, IN.

5017 ■ American Postal Workers Union, AFL-CIO - Indianapolis Local Union 130 (APWU)
1509 E Prospect St.
Indianapolis, IN 46203
Ph: (317)634-1783
Fax: (371)634-1871
URL: http://www.indyapwu.org
Contact: James Guynn, Gen.Pres.
Members: 1,720. **Local.** AFL-CIO. **Affiliated With:** American Postal Workers Union.

5018 ■ American Public Works Association, Indiana Chapter
c/o Mr. Charles B. Bardonner, PE, Pres.
5111 Marble Ct.
Indianapolis, IN 46237-3023
Ph: (317)639-7178
Fax: (317)639-7600
E-mail: charles.bardonner@unitedwater.com
URL: http://indiana.apwa.net
Contact: Mr. Charles B. Bardonner PE, Pres.
State. Promotes professional excellence and public awareness through education, advocacy and the exchange of knowledge. **Affiliated With:** American Public Works Association.

5019 ■ American Red Cross Amateur Radio Club
442 E 10th St.
Indianapolis, IN 46202
Ph: (317)247-1464
E-mail: n9ekm@yahoo.com
URL: http://www.redcross-indy.org/join/radio.asp
Contact: Jerome Harrington, Dir.
Local. Works to provide emergency communication in the event of a major disaster in the Indianapolis area or upon request of the American Red Cross.

5020 ■ American Red Cross of Greater Indianapolis
c/o John B. Lyter, CEO
441 E Tenth St.
Indianapolis, IN 46202-3388
Ph: (317)684-1441
E-mail: arc@redcross-indy.org
URL: http://www.redcross-indy.org
Contact: John B. Lyter, CEO
Local. Provides communication and counseling services and emergency food, clothing and shelter to victims of natural and manmade disasters, members of the military service(s) and their families. Provides a full range of education programs including disaster prevention and mitigation, first aid, CPR, water safety and lifeguarding and HIV/AIDS education. Programs for youth include babysitting and lifeguarding. Provides transportation for referred clients with special emphasis on those with medical needs. **Telecommunication Services:** TDD, (317)684-4359. **Publications:** *Indy Insights*, quarterly. Newsletter.

5021 ■ American Society of Heating, Refrigerating and Air-Conditioning Engineers Central Indiana Chapter
c/o Kevin Token, Pres.
Odle McGuire & Shook Corp.
5875 Castle Creek Pkwy., Ste.440
Indianapolis, IN 46250
Fax: (317)722-0930
E-mail: ktoken@omscorp.net
URL: http://www.indyashrae.org
Contact: Kevin Token, Pres.
Local. Advances the arts and sciences of heating, ventilation, air-conditioning and refrigeration. Provides a source of technical and educational information, standards and guidelines. Conducts seminars for professional growth. **Affiliated With:** American Society of Heating, Refrigerating and Air-Conditioning Engineers.

5022 ■ American Society of Interior Designers, Indiana
1908 E 64th St., South Dr.
Indianapolis, IN 46220-2186
Ph: (317)257-2351
Fax: (317)259-4191
E-mail: chapadmin@asidindiana.org
URL: http://www.members.tripod.com/inasid
Contact: Karen Y. Pfeiffer, Pres.
State. Affiliated With: American Society of Interior Designers.

5023 ■ American Society for Quality, Indianapolis Section 0903
PO Box 441709
Indianapolis, IN 46244-1709
Free: (877)300-8364
E-mail: asqcincinnati@onebox.com
URL: http://www.indyasq.org
Contact: Louis Ripberger, Sec.
Local. Advances learning, quality improvement and knowledge exchange to improve business results and to create better workplaces and communities worldwide. Provides a forum for information exchange, professional development and continuous learning in the science of quality. **Affiliated With:** American Society for Quality.

5024 ■ American Society for Training and Development, Central Indiana Chapter
9840 Westpoint Dr., Ste.200
Indianapolis, IN 46256
Ph: (317)841-1395
Fax: (317)841-8206
E-mail: ciastd@mprecords.com
URL: http://www.ciastd.org
Contact: Mark W. Records CAE, Exec.Dir./Mgr./Administrator
Members: 380. **Membership Dues:** regular, $65 (annual). **Staff:** 3. **Budget:** $65,000. **Local**. Represents individuals engaged in the training and development of business, industry, education, and government employees. **Affiliated With:** ASTD.

5025 ■ American Society of Women Accountants, Indianapolis Chapter No. 001
c/o Jeanne Brady, CPA, Pres.
Vanguard Sers. Inc.
9100 Keystone Crossing, No. 600
Indianapolis, IN 46240-2161
Ph: (317)571-4177 (317)773-8729
Fax: (317)571-4170
E-mail: jbrady@vanguardservices.net
URL: http://www.aswa.org
Contact: Jeanne Brady CPA, Pres.
Founded: 1938. **Members:** 80. **Membership Dues:** regular and affiliate, $113 (annual) • associate, $44 (annual) • retired, $32 (annual). **Local**. Professional society of women accountants, educators, and others in the field of accounting dedicated to the achievement of personal, professional, and economic potential. Assists women accountants in their careers and promotes development in the profession. **Affiliated With:** American Society of Women Accountants. **Publications:** *Footnotes*, monthly. Newsletter. **Conventions/Meetings:** annual conference • monthly meeting, local chapter.

5026 ■ American Statistical Association, Central Indiana Chapter
c/o Lang Li, PhD
1050 Wishard Blvd., RG4101
Div. of Biostatistics
Indianapolis, IN 46202-2872
Ph: (317)274-2661
Fax: (317)274-2678
E-mail: ochain@lilly.com
URL: http://www.math.iupui.edu/~indyasa
Contact: Susan Perkins, Contact
Membership Dues: $5 (annual). **Local**. Promotes statistical studies. **Affiliated With:** American Statistical Association. **Conventions/Meetings:** monthly luncheon - always September through May.

5027 ■ American Theatre Organ Society, Central Indiana Chapter
5440 N Meridian St.
Indianapolis, IN 46206
E-mail: jyoung1208@insightbb.com
URL: http://www.theatreorgans.com/cicatos
Contact: Tim Needler, Business Agent
Local. Works for the preservation and enhancement of theatre organ in Central Indiana. Promotes public appreciation of the theatre pipe organ and music through educational programs and concerts. Strives to encourage talented musicians to preserve the art of theatre organ playing. **Affiliated With:** American Theatre Organ Society.

5028 ■ American Women in Radio and Television, Indiana
c/o Sue Trotman, Pres. WISH-TV
1950 N Meridian St.
Indianapolis, IN 46202
Ph: (317)956-8506
Fax: (317)926-1144
E-mail: strotman@wishtv.com
URL: National Affiliate–www.awrt.org
Contact: Sue Trotman, Pres.
State. **Affiliated With:** American Women in Radio and Television.

5029 ■ Americans United for Separation of Church and State, Greater Indianapolis Chapter (AUINDY)
PO Box 1792
Indianapolis, IN 46206-1792
E-mail: auindy@aol.com
URL: http://www.auindy.org
Local. **Affiliated With:** Americans United for Separation of Church and State.

5030 ■ Amos W. Butler Audubon Society
c/o Ray Shortridge, Pres.
PO Box 80024
Indianapolis, IN 46280
Ph: (317)767-4690
URL: National Affiliate–www.audubon.org
Local. Works to conserve and restore natural ecosystems, focusing on birds and other wildlife for the benefit of humanity and the earth's biological diversity. **Affiliated With:** National Audubon Society.

5031 ■ Ancient Order of Hibernians - Kevin Barry, Division No. 3
c/o Robert Boyle
421 Daffon Dr.
Indianapolis, IN 46227
Ph: (317)882-1700
E-mail: kevinbarryindy@yahoo.com
URL: http://www.aohindy.org
Contact: Robert Boyle, Contact
Local. **Affiliated With:** Ancient Order of Hibernians in America.

5032 ■ APICS, The Association for Operations Management - Central Indiana Chapter
8470 Allison Pointe Blvd., Ste.100
Indianapolis, IN 46250
Ph: (317)713-2964
E-mail: apics-cind@apics-cind.org
URL: http://www.apics-cind.org
Contact: Susan Gentry CPIM, Pres.
Local. Provides information and services in production and inventory management and related areas to enable members, enterprises and individuals to add value to their business performance. **Affiliated With:** APICS - The Association for Operations Management.

5033 ■ APMI Dayton
c/o Dave Lilly
6107 Churchman Rd. Bypass
Indianapolis, IN 46203
Ph: (317)788-4114
Fax: (317)788-0220
E-mail: dlilly@elmco-press.com
URL: National Affiliate–www.mpif.org
Contact: Dave Lilly, Chm.
Local. Maintains speakers' bureau and placement service. Serves the technical and informational needs of individuals interested or involved in the science and art of powder metallurgy. Provides the best source of information about the most up-to-date developments and advances in this dynamic, expanding technology through its publications, conferences and local section activities. **Affiliated With:** APMI International.

5034 ■ Arc of Indiana
108 N Pennsylvania St., Ste.300
Indianapolis, IN 46204
Ph: (317)977-2375
Fax: (317)977-2385
Free: (800)382-9100
E-mail: thearc@arcind.org
URL: http://www.arcind.org
Contact: John Dickerson, Exec.Dir.
State. Works to promote services, research, public understanding, and legislation for people with mental retardation and their families. **Affiliated With:** Arc of the United States.

5035 ■ Art Education Association of Indiana (AEAI)
c/o Despi Ray
Indiana State Museum
650 W Washington St.
Indianapolis, IN 46204-2725
Ph: (317)234-1804
E-mail: homested@dmrtc.net
URL: http://www.aeai.org
Contact: Leah Morgan, Pres.
State. Promotes art education through professional development, service, advancement of knowledge, and leadership.

5036 ■ Arthritis Foundation, Indiana Chapter
8660 Guion Rd.
Indianapolis, IN 46268
Ph: (317)879-0321
Fax: (317)876-5608
Free: (800)783-2342
E-mail: info.in@arthritis.org
URL: http://www.arthritis.org
Contact: Edward Wills Jr., Pres./CEO
Founded: 1948. **Members:** 9,000. **Membership Dues:** $20 (annual). **Staff:** 15. **State**. Serves as information resource site for people with arthritis. Provides an exercise and disease management program. Also offers scholarships. Public health Programs/Speakers Bureau available. **Affiliated With:** Arthritis Foundation. **Publications:** *Arthritis Action*, quarterly. Newsletter. Covers all the local news for the state of Indiana. Alternate Formats: online • *Arthritis Today*, annual. Magazine. **Price:** free. **Circulation:** 10,000. **Advertising:** accepted. **Conventions/Meetings:** annual board meeting.

5037 ■ Arts Council of Indianapolis
20 N Meridian St., Ste.500
Indianapolis, IN 46204
Ph: (317)631-3301
Fax: (317)624-2559
E-mail: gregc@indyarts.org
URL: http://www.indyarts.org
Contact: Greg Charleston, Pres./CEO
Founded: 1987. **Staff:** 15. **Local**. Promotes public awareness and appreciation of the arts in Indianapolis, IN. **Awards:** ARTI Business and Arts Awards. **Frequency:** annual. **Type:** recognition. **Recipient:** to outstanding business and arts partnership • **Type:** grant. **Publications:** *Artists Directory*, annual. Contains listing of individual artists in Indianapolis. **Price:** free • *Arts Education Resource Guide*, annual. Directory. Contains listings of arts organizations that offer educational programming. **Price:** free • *Arts Organizations Directory*, annual. Contains listing of all arts organizations in Indianapolis; other arts information. **Price:** free • *Economic Impact of the Arts*. **Conventions/Meetings:** annual Start with Art Luncheon, with awards presentation - always early September.

5038 ■ Asphalt Pavement Association of Indiana
c/o Lloyd Bandy, Exec.Dir.
107 S Pennsylvania St., Ste.401
Indianapolis, IN 46204
Ph: (317)632-2441
Fax: (317)269-8204
E-mail: lbandyapai@aol.com
URL: http://www.ind-asphalt.com
Contact: Lloyd Bandy, Exec.Dir.
State.

5039 ■ Assistance League of Indianapolis
1475 W 86th St., Ste.E
Indianapolis, IN 46260
Ph: (317)872-1010
Fax: (317)872-1452
URL: http://www.alindy.org
Local. Affiliated With: Assistance League.

5040 ■ Associated Builders and Contractors of Indiana (ABC)
6825 Hillsdale Ct.
Indianapolis, IN 46250
Ph: (317)596-4950
Fax: (317)596-4957
Free: (800)333-9844
E-mail: jr@abc-indy.org
URL: http://www.abc-indy.org
Contact: J.R. Gaylor, Pres./CEO
State. Affiliated With: Associated Builders and Contractors.

5041 ■ Associated General Contractors of Indiana
10 W Market St., Ste.1050
Indianapolis, IN 46204
Ph: (317)656-8899
Fax: (317)656-8889
Free: (800)899-8823
E-mail: jyaist@agcin.org
URL: http://www.agcin.org
Contact: Joyce Yaist, Office Mgr.
Members: 385. **Membership Dues:** regular (based on annual volume), $2,500-$10,000 (annual) • associate, $900 (annual) • affiliate, $625 (annual). **Staff:** 9. **Budget:** $1,000,000. **State**. General construction contractors, subcontractors, industry suppliers, and service firms. **Awards:** Amerisure Safety Awards. **Frequency:** annual. **Type:** recognition. **Recipient:** for regular and associate members who have excelled in safety performance • BKD Build Indiana Awards. **Frequency:** annual. **Type:** recognition. **Recipient:** for contractors whose construction projects demonstrate quality, innovation and excellence in project management and teamwork. **Affiliated With:** Associated General Contractors of America. **Publications:** *AGC of Indiana e-Newsletter*, weekly. Alternate Formats: online • *Indiana Constructor*, bimonthly. Magazine.

5042 ■ Association of Certified Fraud Examiners, Central Indiana Chapter No. 52
PO Box 44182
Indianapolis, IN 46244-0182
Ph: (317)269-6697
Fax: (317)635-6127
E-mail: bbuetow@crowechizek.com
URL: National Affiliate–www.acfe.com
Contact: Brenda Buetow CFE, Pres.
Local. Works to reduce the incidence of fraud and white-collar crime and to assist the members in its detection and deterrence. Sponsors training seminars on fraud and loss prevention. Administers credentialing programs for Certified Fraud Examiners. **Affiliated With:** Association of Certified Fraud Examiners.

5043 ■ Association of Clinical Research Professionals - Circle City
22 E 46th St.
Indianapolis, IN 46205
Ph: (317)521-7126
E-mail: liz.pertile@roche.com
URL: http://www.acrpnet.org/chapters/circ/index.html
Contact: Elizabeth Pertile, Pres.
Local. Promotes professional growth in the field of clinical research. Provides networking opportunities for members. Advocates for the enhancement of education and knowledge in the field of clinical research. **Affiliated With:** Association of Clinical Research Professionals.

5044 ■ Association of Community Organizations for Reform Now, Indianapolis
520 E 12th St.
Indianapolis, IN 46202
Ph: (317)635-6277
Fax: (317)635-9419
E-mail: inacorn@acorn.org
URL: National Affiliate–www.acorn.org
Local. Affiliated With: Association of Community Organizations for Reform Now.

5045 ■ Association for Computing Machinery, Butler University
c/o Jonathan Sorenson, Dr.
Dept. of Cmpt. Sci.
4600 Sunset Ave.
Indianapolis, IN 46208
Ph: (317)940-9269
Fax: (317)940-9363
E-mail: phenders@butler.edu
URL: http://campus.acm.org
Contact: Zhi-hong Chen, Faculty Adviser
Local. Affiliated With: Association for Computing Machinery.

5046 ■ Association of Government Accountants - Indianapolis Chapter
PO Box 269528
Indianapolis, IN 46226-9528
Ph: (317)510-7410
E-mail: donna.cox@dfas.mil
URL: http://www.againdy.org
Contact: Ms. Donna Cox, Pres.
Local. Provides quality education, professional development and certification to government accountants. Supports standards and research to advance government accountability. Seeks to encourage the interchange of ideas among financial managers in government service and among government and nongovernmental managers. **Affiliated With:** Association of Government Accountants.

5047 ■ Association of Indiana Counties (AIC)
c/o David Bottorff, Exec.Dir.
10 W Market St., Ste.1060
Indianapolis, IN 46204-2986
Ph: (317)684-3710
Fax: (317)684-3713
E-mail: aic@indianacounties.org
URL: http://www.indianacounties.org
Contact: David Bottorff, Exec.Dir.
Founded: 1957. **Members:** 1,600. **Staff:** 7. **Budget:** $700,000. **Regional Groups:** 1. **State Groups:** 9. **State**. Promotes the welfare of the 92 counties in Indiana. Provides legislative advocacy, training, and technical assistance for county elected officials. **Awards:** County Achievement Award. **Frequency:** annual. **Type:** recognition. **Publications:** *County Factbook, News 92*, 6/yr. Newsletter • *Directory of County Officials*, biennial • *Legislative Bulletin*, periodic • *News 92*, bimonthly. Newsletter. **Conventions/Meetings:** annual conference (exhibits) - always fall • annual Legislative Conference - always winter.

5048 ■ Association of Indiana Museums (AIM)
PO Box 1883
Indianapolis, IN 46206
Ph: (317)685-0288
Fax: (317)685-0386
E-mail: coordinator@indianamuseums.org
URL: http://www.indianamuseums.org
Contact: Corrie E. Cook, Coor.
State. Promotes professional standards and development within the museum community. Promotes understanding of the state history, culture and natural history through public education.

5049 ■ Association for Psychological Type - Indiana
c/o Henry Merrill
Indiana Univ.
620 Union Dr., Rm. 129-D
Indianapolis, IN 46202
Ph: (317)278-0546
Fax: (317)278-2280
E-mail: hmerrill@iupui.edu
URL: National Affiliate–www.aptinternational.org
Contact: Henry Merrill, Contact
State. Promotes the practical application and ethical use of psychological type. Provides members with opportunities for continuous learning, sharing experiences and creating understanding and knowledge through research. **Affiliated With:** Association for Psychological Type.

5050 ■ Association of the United States Army, Indiana
c/o Doug Gibbens
6237 Winford Dr.
Indianapolis, IN 46236
Ph: (317)891-0100
E-mail: dgibbens@tuckermortgage.com
URL: National Affiliate–www.ausa.org
State. Represents the interests and concerns of American Soldiers. Fosters public support of the Army's role in national security. Provides professional education and information programs.

5051 ■ Association for Women in Science, Indianapolis
c/o Joan Esterline Lafuze, Dr., Pres.
Ped. Hem/Onc Riley Hospital for Children
702 Barnhill Dr.
Indianapolis, IN 46202
Ph: (317)274-2276
E-mail: jlafuze@indiana.edu
URL: National Affiliate–www.awis.org
Professional women and students in life, physical, and social sciences and engineering; men are also members. Promotes equal opportunities for women to enter the scientific workforce and to achieve their career goals; provides educational information to women planning careers in science; networks with other women's groups; monitors scientific legislation and the status of women in science. **Affiliated With:** Association for Women in Science.

5052 ■ Association of Women's Health, Obstetric and Neonatal Nurses, Indiana Section
c/o Kitty Herndon, Chair
7804 S Oak Dr.
Indianapolis, IN 46227
E-mail: herndons76@hotmail.com
URL: National Affiliate–www.awhonn.org
Contact: Kitty Herndon, Chair
State. Represents registered nurses and other health care providers who specialize in obstetric, women's health, and neonatal nursing. Advances the nursing profession by providing nurses with information and support to help them deliver quality care for women and newborns. **Affiliated With:** Association of Women's Health, Obstetric and Neonatal Nurses.

5053 ■ Association of Women's Health, Obstetric and Neonatal Nurses - Indianapolis Chapter
c/o Renee Oswalt
8864 Rahke Rd.
Indianapolis, IN 46217
E-mail: renee.oswalt@comcast.net
URL: National Affiliate–www.awhonn.org
Contact: Cher Boys-Fore, Coor.
Local. Represents registered nurses and other health care providers who specialize in obstetric, women's health, and neonatal nursing. Advances the nursing profession by providing nurses with information and support to help them deliver quality care for women and newborns. **Affiliated With:** Association of Women's Health, Obstetric and Neonatal Nurses.

5054 ■ Autism Society of Indiana (ASI)
107 N Pennsylvania St., No. 300
Indianapolis, IN 46204
Ph: (317)685-9730
E-mail: lizff@inautismcoalition.org
URL: http://www.autismindiana.org
State. Works to improve the quality of life of all individuals with autism and their families through

education, research and advocacy. Promotes public awareness and understanding of the symptoms and problems of individuals with autism.

5055 ■ Automobile Dealer's Association of Indiana (ADAI)
c/o Mr. Timothy J. Dowling, Exec.VP
150 W Market St., Ste.812
Indianapolis, IN 46204
Ph: (317)635-1441
Fax: (317)685-1028
Free: (800)872-0363
E-mail: dkb-adai@indy.rr.com
URL: http://www.adai-inc.org
Contact: Mr. Timothy J. Dowling, Exec.VP
State.

5056 ■ Ben Davis High School Key Club
1200 N Girls School Rd.
Indianapolis, IN 46214
Ph: (317)244-7691
Fax: (317)243-5506
E-mail: class.webdesign@wayne.k12.in.us
URL: http://www.wayne.k12.in.us/bdkeyc/index2.htm
Contact: Anthony Lahr, Pres.
Local.

5057 ■ Better Business Bureau of Central Indiana
c/o Linda R. Carmody, Pres./CEO
22 E Washington St., Ste.200
Indianapolis, IN 46204
Ph: (317)488-2222
Fax: (317)488-2224
Free: (866)INDYBBB
E-mail: info@central-in.bbb.org
URL: http://www.indybbb.org
Contact: Linda R. Carmody, Pres./CEO
Founded: 1916. **Local**. Seeks to promote and foster the highest ethical relationship between businesses and the public through voluntary self-regulation, consumer and business education, and service excellence. Provides information to help consumers and businesses make informed purchasing decisions and avoid costly scams and frauds; settles consumer complaints through arbitration and other means. **Also Known As:** (2004) Better Business Bureau.

5058 ■ Big Brothers Big Sisters of Central Indiana (BBBSCI)
2960 N Meridian, Ste.150
Indianapolis, IN 46208-4715
Ph: (317)921-2201
Fax: (317)921-2202
Free: (877)921-2201
E-mail: mentoringismagic@bbbsci.org
URL: http://www.bbbsci.org
Contact: Charlie Brown, Pres.
Local. Works to provide quality-mentoring relationships between children and qualified adults in Central Indiana, and promote their development into competent, confident and caring individuals. **Affiliated With:** Big Brothers Big Sisters of America.

5059 ■ BMW Car Club of America, Hoosier Chapter
c/o Tami Reamer
PO Box 20775
Indianapolis, IN 46220-0775
Ph: (317)738-2658
E-mail: president@hoosierbmw.com
URL: http://www.hoosierbmw.com
Contact: Richard Johnson, Pres.
Local. **Affiliated With:** BMW Car Club of America.

5060 ■ Boys and Girls Club of Indianapolis
c/o Mark Branch, Exec.Dir.
300 E Fall Creek Pkwy. North Dr., No. 400
Indianapolis, IN 46205
Ph: (317)920-4700
Fax: (317)920-4701
E-mail: bgcinfo@bgcindy.org
URL: http://www.bgcindy.org
Contact: Mark Branch, Exec.Dir.
Local.

5061 ■ Brain Injury Association of Indiana (BIAI)
c/o Lindsay A. Meyer, Exec.Dir.
9531 Valparaiso Ct., Ste.A
Indianapolis, IN 46268
Ph: (317)356-7722
Fax: (317)808-7770
Free: (866)854-4246
E-mail: info@biai.org
URL: http://www.biausa.org/Indiana
Contact: Lindsay A. Meyer, Exec.Dir.
Founded: 1981. **Members:** 400. **Membership Dues:** individual (consumer), $20 (annual) • family (consumer), $45 (annual) • individual (professional), $75 (annual) • business/corporate, $200 (annual) • sustaining, $500 (annual). **Staff:** 5. **Budget:** $100,000. **Local Groups:** 15. **State**. Dedicated to serving individuals living with brain injury and their families and caretakers by providing information, resources, and advocacy. **Libraries: Type:** open to the public. **Holdings:** 500; articles, books, periodicals, video recordings. **Subjects:** brain injury, rehabilitation, trends, research, recovery. **Awards:** Founders Award. **Frequency:** annual. **Type:** recognition • Jackson Leadership Award. **Frequency:** annual. **Type:** recognition. **Committees:** Education; Fund Development; Publication. **Affiliated With:** Brain Injury Association of America. **Also Known As:** (2000) Head Injury Foundation - Indiana. **Publications:** *Corporate & Professional Network Directory*, quarterly. Features list of companies working in brain injury by location, services provided. • *Perseverance, Living Life with Brain Injury*, quarterly. Newsletter. Educational newsletter. **Conventions/Meetings:** monthly board meeting - every 3rd Tuesday in Indianapolis, IN • annual conference (exhibits) - always fall.

5062 ■ Brebeuf - Young Life
418 E 34th St.
Indianapolis, IN 46205
Ph: (317)923-1319
URL: http://whereis.younglife.org/FriendlyUrlRedirector.aspx?ID=C-888
Local.

5063 ■ Brickyard Boogie Dancers (BBD)
Robert L. Sterrett Ctr.
5700 N Post Rd.
Indianapolis, IN 46216-2006
Ph: (317)881-3750 (317)443-4462
E-mail: ischaeffer@made2manage.com
URL: http://www.brickyardboogiedancers.org
Contact: Ron Fentz, Pres.
Local. Promotes and preserves bop, swing, shag and jitterbug dance styles and the heritage of those styles of music that center on the beat and rhythm. Strives to enhance communication and promotional coordination of activities throughout the membership.

5064 ■ Burn Survivors Support Group
c/o Kellee Blanchard, MSW, LSW
Wishard Memorial Hosp.
1001 W. 10th St.
Indianapolis, IN 46202-2859
Ph: (317)630-8632 (317)630-6471
Fax: (317)630-6851
Contact: Kellee Blanchard MSW, LSW
Forum for burn survivors to discuss current issues and concerns facing them. Meets once a month on the first Saturday of every month.

5065 ■ Business Marketing Association, Indianapolis Chapter
c/o Nila Nealy, Pres.
8650 Commerce Park Pl., Ste.D
Indianapolis, IN 46268
Ph: (317)767-9080
E-mail: info@bmaindy.org
URL: http://www.bmaindy.org
Contact: Nila Nealy, Pres.
Membership Dues: individual, $225 (annual) • educator, $150 (annual) • corporate (per person; 3-4 members), $175 (annual) • corporate (per person; 5-9 members), $160 (annual) • corporate (per person; 10 or more members), $150 (annual). **Local**. Promotes the development of business-to-business marketing and communications professionals through education, training and networking. **Affiliated With:** Business Marketing Association. **Publications:** Newsletter. Alternate Formats: online.

5066 ■ Camp Fire USA Indiana Heartland Council
1410 S Post Rd.
Indianapolis, IN 46239
Ph: (317)898-6831
Fax: (317)898-2917
E-mail: info@campfireusaihc.org
URL: http://www.campfireusaihc.org
Contact: Amanda Green, Program Coor.
Local. Builds caring, confident youth and future leaders. **Affiliated With:** Camp Fire USA.

5067 ■ Carmel High School - Young Life
418 E 34th St.
Indianapolis, IN 46205
Ph: (317)923-1319
URL: http://whereis.younglife.org/FriendlyUrlRedirector.aspx?ID=C-3268
Local.

5068 ■ Carmel - Wyldlife
418 E 34th St.
Indianapolis, IN 46205
Ph: (317)923-1319
URL: http://sites.younglife.org/_layouts/ylext/default.aspx?ID=C-4076
Local. **Affiliated With:** Young Life.

5069 ■ Catholics United for the Faith - Abba, Father Chapter
c/o Holy Rosary Catholic Church
520 Stevens St.
Indianapolis, IN 46203
Ph: (812)342-9550
E-mail: cuf-abba@comcast.com
URL: http://cuf-abba.home.comcast.net
Contact: Eric Slaughter, Chm.
Local.

5070 ■ CBMC Indiana (CBMC)
PO Box 68208
Indianapolis, IN 46268-0208
Ph: (317)871-4098
Fax: (317)871-4094
E-mail: ekibbey@cbmc.com
URL: http://www.cbmcindiana.com
Contact: Eldon Kibbey, State Dir.
State. Focuses on bringing business and professional men into an abiding relationship with God through Jesus Christ. **Affiliated With:** Christian Business Men's Committee. **Conventions/Meetings:** Fort Wayne Business Prayer Breakfast, with speaker.

5071 ■ Central Indiana Better Business Bureau
22 E Washington St., Ste.200
Indianapolis, IN 46204
Ph: (317)488-2222
Fax: (317)488-2224
E-mail: info@central-in.bbb.org
URL: http://www.indybbb.org
Contact: Linda Carmody, Pres./CEO
Founded: 1916. **Local**. Seeks to promote and foster the highest ethical relationship between businesses and the public through voluntary self-regulation, consumer and business education, and service excellence. Provides information to help consumers and businesses make informed purchasing decisions and avoid costly scams and frauds; settles consumer complaints through arbitration and other means. **Affiliated With:** BBB Wise Giving Alliance.

5072 ■ Central Indiana Bicycling Association (CIBA)
PO Box 55405
Indianapolis, IN 46205-0405
Ph: (317)767-7765
E-mail: marcfreeman1@yahoo.com
URL: http://www.cibaride.org
Contact: Marc Freeman, Pres.
Founded: 1971. **Members:** 2,300. **Membership Dues:** individual (first year), $20 • individual (after

first year), $15 (annual) • family (first year), $25 • family (after first year), $20 (annual). **Budget:** $400,000. **Local**. Encourages the use of the bicycle as a means for touring, exercising, and commuting. Sponsors daily rides between March and November and rides every month of the year. Conducts activities such as NITE ride (Indiana's only nighttime ride) and the Hilly Hundred (one of the premier weekend tours in the country). Gives emphasis on safety and the proper use of the bicycle. Supports educational events and developmental activities for younger riders and is active in pursuing adoption of bicycle-related legislation within the local community. **Affiliated With:** International Mountain Bicycling Association. **Publications:** *CIBA News*, 11/year. Newsletter. **Conventions/Meetings:** monthly board meeting • annual meeting, membership.

5073 ■ Central Indiana Cage Bird Club
c/o Terri Wheeler, Pres.
PO Box 24159
Indianapolis, IN 46224
Ph: (317)892-4158
E-mail: president@cicbc.info
URL: http://www.cicbc.info
Local.

5074 ■ Central Indiana Chapter of the Association for Computing Machinery (ACM)
PO Box 2661
Indianapolis, IN 46206-2661
Ph: (317)767-4600
E-mail: central_indiana_chapter@acm.org
URL: http://www.acm.org/chapters/indy
Contact: Jeff Smucker, Chm.
Local. Represents biological, medical, behavioral, and computer scientists; hospital administrators; programmers and others interested in application of computer methods to biological, behavioral, and medical problems. Stimulates understanding of the use and potential of computers in biosciences. **Affiliated With:** Association for Computing Machinery.

5075 ■ Central Indiana Chapter National Electrical Contractors Association
c/o Governor M. Thomas Cummins
8900 Keystone Crossing, Ste.1000
Indianapolis, IN 46240
Ph: (317)846-5680
Fax: (317)574-6865
URL: http://www.necanet.org
Contact: Larry E. VanTries, Contact
Local. Contractors erecting, installing, repairing, servicing, and maintaining electric wiring, equipment, and appliances. **Affiliated With:** National Electrical Contractors Association.

5076 ■ Central Indiana Chapter of the Society of Financial Service Professionals
3009 E 96th St.
Indianapolis, IN 46240
Ph: (317)844-6268
E-mail: indysfsp@yahoo.com
URL: http://www.sfsp.net/Indianapolis
Contact: Kim B. Stoneking CAE, Exec.Dir.
Local. Represents the interests of financial advisers. Fosters the development of professional responsibility. Helps clients achieve their personal and business-related financial goals. **Affiliated With:** Society of Financial Service Professionals.

5077 ■ Central Indiana Fellowship of Christian Athletes
7168 Zionsville Rd.
Indianapolis, IN 46268
Ph: (317)347-1280
Fax: (317)347-1068
E-mail: clong@fca.org
URL: http://www.centralinfca.org/AboutFCA.lsp
Contact: Carol Long, Dir.
Local.

5078 ■ Central Indiana National Space Society
7354 Oakland Hills Ct.
Indianapolis, IN 46236
Ph: (317)823-4805
E-mail: clarkspace@aol.com
URL: National Affiliate–www.nss.org
Contact: Debbie Clark, Contact
Local. Works for the creation of a spacefaring civilization. Encourages the establishment of self-sustaining human settlements in space. Promotes large-scale industrialization and private enterprise in space.

5079 ■ Central Indiana Pug Club
151 E Pleasant Run Pkwy.
Indianapolis, IN 46225
E-mail: centrali@centralindpugclub.org
URL: http://www.centralindpugclub.org
Contact: Carla Ryan, Corresponding Sec.
Local.

5080 ■ Central Indiana Saint Bernard Club
6322 S Sherman Dr.
Indianapolis, IN 46227
Ph: (317)787-4334
E-mail: cleentooth@aol.com
URL: National Affiliate–www.saintbernardclub.org
Contact: Kay Wessar, Chm.
Local. **Affiliated With:** Saint Bernard Club of America.

5081 ■ Central Indiana Soaring Society
2043 Mystic Bay Ct.
Indianapolis, IN 46240
E-mail: darren_bedwel@iquest.net
URL: http://www.centralindianasoaringsociety.org
Contact: Darren Bedwell, Pres.
Local. **Affiliated With:** Soaring Society of America.

5082 ■ Central Indiana Youth for Christ
PO Box 68695
Indianapolis, IN 46268-0695
Ph: (317)925-2828
Fax: (317)472-1128
URL: http://www.ciyfc.org
Local. **Affiliated With:** Youth for Christ/U.S.A.

5083 ■ Character Council of Indiana (CCI)
9951 Crosspoint Blvd., Ste.300
Indianapolis, IN 46256
Ph: (317)770-9051
Fax: (317)770-9052
Free: (877)543-4870
E-mail: jfrisby@charactercouncil.org
URL: http://www.charactercouncil.org
Contact: Jack Frisby, Pres.
Founded: 2000. **Staff:** 2. **State**. **Conventions/Meetings:** periodic Character First Leadership Training - meeting • monthly Leadership Breakfast - 3rd Tuesday in Indianapolis, IN.

5084 ■ Children's Bureau of Indianapolis
c/o Ron Duke Carpenter, Pres./CEO
615 N Alabama St., Rm. 426
Indianapolis, IN 46204
Ph: (317)264-2700
Fax: (317)264-2714
E-mail: info@childrensbureau.org
URL: http://www.childrensbureau.org
Contact: Ron Duke Carpenter, Pres./CEO
Local. Works to serve high-risk children and their families. Makes available services to all children and families.

5085 ■ Christian Leaders for Africa (CLA)
c/o Paul Heidebrecht, Dr., Exec.Dir.
PO Box 1642
Indianapolis, IN 46206
E-mail: info@clafrica.com
URL: http://www.clafrica.com
Contact: Rev. Dick Robinson, Chm.
Local.

5086 ■ Church Federation of Greater Indianapolis
c/o Rev.Dr. Angelique Walker-Smith, Exec.Dir.
1100 W 42nd St., Ste.345
Indianapolis, IN 46208
Ph: (317)926-5371
Fax: (317)926-5373
E-mail: churches@churchfederationindy.org
URL: http://www.churchfederationindy.org
Contact: Rev.Dr. Angelique Walker-Smith, Exec.Dir.
Founded: 1912. **Members:** 200. **Local**. Serves the Greater Indianapolis area through ministries, programs, and resources. **Publications:** *Federation Forecast*, quarterly.

5087 ■ Church World Service/CROP, Indiana-Kentucky
1100 W 42nd St.
Indianapolis, IN 46208
Ph: (317)923-2938
Fax: (317)923-2956
Free: (888)297-2767
E-mail: jdunson@churchworldservice.org
URL: http://www.churchworldservice.org
Contact: Rev. Judy Dunson, Dir.
Founded: 1948. **Staff:** 2. **Budget:** $1,400,000. **Nonmembership**. **Regional**. Volunteers working to increase global awareness about hunger/poverty issues, and raise funds for programs of self-help, refugee resettlement, and disaster relief primarily in developing countries. Assembles self-help kits for distribution worldwide. **Libraries: Type:** reference; lending. **Holdings:** audiovisuals, films, video recordings. **Subjects:** hunger, poverty. **Affiliated With:** National Council of Churches of Christ in the U.S.A. **Publications:** *CROPWALKER*, semiannual. Newsletter. **Price:** free • *Service Illustrated*, semiannual. Newsletter. **Conventions/Meetings:** annual Meeting Hunger, Hands on - workshop.

5088 ■ Circle City Corvairs
PO Box 17325
Indianapolis, IN 46217-0325
E-mail: valveclatter@aol.com
URL: http://circlecitycorvairs.tripod.com
Contact: Pam Ray, Pres.
Local. Enthusiasts of the Corvair automobile united for technical assistance and parts availability. **Affiliated With:** Corvair Society of America.

5089 ■ Circle City Corvette Club
PO Box 68444
Indianapolis, IN 46268
E-mail: 65vette@insightbb.com
URL: http://members.aol.com/cgait60698/index.html
Contact: Frank Sheasley, Pres.
Local. **Affiliated With:** National Council of Corvette Clubs.

5090 ■ Circle City REACT
PO Box 39303
Indianapolis, IN 46239
Ph: (317)359-7000
E-mail: react@indy.rr.com
URL: http://www.reactintl.org/teaminfo/usa_teams/teams-usin.htm
Local. Trained communication experts and professional volunteers. Provides volunteer public service and emergency communications through the use of radios (Citizen Band, General Mobile Radio Service, UHF and HAM). Coordinates with radio industries and government on safety communication matters and supports charitable activities and community organizations.

5091 ■ Citizens Action Coalition of Indiana (CAC)
5420 N Colorado Ave., Ste.100
Indianapolis, IN 46220
Ph: (317)205-3535
Fax: (317)205-3599
E-mail: gsmith@citact.org
URL: http://www.citact.org
Contact: Grant Smith, Exec.Dir.
State.

5092 ■ Columbia Club
121 Monument Cir.
Indianapolis, IN 46204
Ph: (317)767-1361
Fax: (317)638-3137
Free: (800)635-1361
E-mail: eda@columbia-club.org
URL: http://www.columbia-club.org
Contact: Edward M. Albany CCM, Gen.Mgr.
Founded: 1889. **Local.**

5093 ■ Community Associations Institute, Central Indiana Chapter (CAI)
10 W Market St., Ste.1720
Indianapolis, IN 46204
Ph: (317)464-5359
Fax: (317)464-5146
E-mail: matt@cai-indiana.org
URL: http://www.cai-indiana.org
Contact: Matt Englert, Pres.
Staff: 2. **Local. Affiliated With:** Community Associations Institute.

5094 ■ Community Bankers Association of Indiana (CBAI)
c/o S. Joe DeHaven, Pres./CEO
6666 E 75th St., Ste.250
Indianapolis, IN 46250
Ph: (317)595-6810
Fax: (317)595-6820
E-mail: dehaven@cbai.org
URL: http://www.cbai.org
Contact: S. Joe DeHaven, Pres./CEO
State.

5095 ■ Community Choice Federal Credit Union, Indianapolis, Indiana
c/o Cheryl Moss, Ameri/Corp Vista Volunteer
2811 E 10th St., Ste.A
Indianapolis, IN 46201
Ph: (317)633-3100
Fax: (317)264-1845
Contact: Barbara Black, Dir.
Local.

5096 ■ Connecting Business Men to Christ - Indiana
PO Box 68208
Indianapolis, IN 46268-0208
Ph: (317)871-4098
Fax: (317)871-4094
URL: http://www.cbmcindiana.com
State.

5097 ■ Council of Volunteers and Organizations for Hoosiers with Disabilities
c/o Cris Fulford, State Chair
445 N Pennsylvania, Ste.521
Indianapolis, IN 46204
Ph: (317)262-8632
Fax: (317)262-0685
Free: (800)262-8630
E-mail: cfulford@covoh.org
Contact: Cris Fulford, Exec.Dir.

5098 ■ Crohn's and Colitis Foundation of America, Indiana Chapter
8555 Cedar Place Dr., Ste.112
Indianapolis, IN 46240
Ph: (317)259-8071
Fax: (317)259-8091
Free: (800)332-6029
E-mail: indiana@ccfa.org
URL: National Affiliate–www.ccfa.org
Contact: Pat Dudley, Office Mgr.
Local. Provides professional education and fundraising to fuel research for an eventual cure for IBD. **Affiliated With:** Crohn's and Colitis Foundation of America.

5099 ■ Dairy and Nutrition Council, Inc. (DNCI)
9360 Castlegate Dr.
Indianapolis, IN 46256
Ph: (317)842-3060
Fax: (317)842-3065
Free: (800)225-6455
E-mail: olson@mpsiinc.com
URL: http://www.indianadairycouncil.org
Contact: Sue Brames, Gen.Mgr.
Local.

5100 ■ Defense Trial Counsel of Indiana (DTCI)
c/o Lisa Mortier, Exec.Dir.
9505 Copley Dr.
Indianapolis, IN 46260
Ph: (317)580-1233
Fax: (317)580-1235
E-mail: lmortier@dtci.org
URL: http://www.dtci.org
Contact: Lisa Mortier, Exec.Dir.
State.

5101 ■ Delta Sigma Phi Fraternity, SDSU
c/o Justin Spees, Pres.
1331 N Delaware St.
Indianapolis, IN 46202-4439
Ph: (317)634-1899
Fax: (317)634-1410
E-mail: justinspees@yahoo.com
URL: http://www.deltasig.org
Contact: Justin Spees, Pres.
Local.

5102 ■ Dignity - Indianapolis
PO Box 431
Indianapolis, IN 46206
Ph: (317)767-4273
E-mail: dignityindy@rocketmail.com
URL: http://www.gayindy.org/dignity
Local.

5103 ■ Dress for Success Indianapolis
850 N Meridian St.
Indianapolis, IN 46204
Ph: (317)940-3737
Fax: (317)940-3641
E-mail: indianapolis@dressforsuccess.org
URL: National Affiliate–www.dressforsuccess.org
Contact: Dana Harrison, Exec.Dir.
Local.

5104 ■ Drug-Free Marion County
c/o Randy Miller, Exec.Dir.
2506 Willowbrook Pkwy., Ste.100
Indianapolis, IN 46205
Ph: (317)254-2815
Fax: (317)254-2800
E-mail: rmiller@drugfreemc.org
URL: http://www.drugfreemarioncounty.org
Contact: Randy Miller, Exec.Dir.
Founded: 1998. **Members:** 25. **Staff:** 2. **Budget:** $190,000. **Local.** Promotes, implements and coordinates community efforts to prevent and reduce the abuse of alcohol, tobacco and other drugs among youth and adults. **Committees:** Criminal Justice; Finance/Development; Prevention/Education; Public Awareness; Treatment.

5105 ■ Eastwood - Wyldlife
418 E 34th St.
Indianapolis, IN 46205
Ph: (317)923-1319
URL: http://sites.younglife.org/_layouts/ylext/default.aspx?ID=C-893
Local. Affiliated With: Young Life.

5106 ■ Electric League of Indiana (ELI)
c/o Susan Crow Jones, Exec.Dir.
9801 Fall Creek Rd., No. 416
Indianapolis, IN 46256
Ph: (317)823-5628
Fax: (317)823-9545
URL: http://www.elinews.org
Contact: Susan Crow Jones, Exec.Dir.
State.

5107 ■ Electronics Representatives Association - Indiana/Kentucky Chapter (ERA)
c/o James D. Montoya, CAE, Exec.Dir.
7150 Winton Dr., No. 300
Indianapolis, IN 46268
Ph: (317)328-4421
Fax: (317)280-8527
E-mail: jmontoya@raybourn.com
URL: National Affiliate–www.era.org
Contact: James D. Montoya CAE, Exec.Dir.
Members: 54. **Staff:** 5. **Regional.** Provides programs of timely interest plus an ideal environment for profitable interest with customers, principals and peers. **Affiliated With:** Electronics Representatives Association. **Publications:** *The Communicator*, quarterly. Newsletter. **Advertising:** accepted. Alternate Formats: diskette.

5108 ■ Emerald Valley Rottweiler Club of Greater Cleveland, Ohio
c/o Gwen Chaney
5014 Granger Ct.
Indianapolis, IN 46268-5633
Ph: (317)280-1235
E-mail: ejchaneyjr@aol.com
URL: National Affiliate–www.akc.org
Contact: Gwen Chaney, Contact
Local.

5109 ■ Englewood Community Development Corp. (ECDC)
57 N Rural St.
Indianapolis, IN 46201
Ph: (317)639-1541
E-mail: englewood@indy.rr.com
URL: http://www.englewoodcc.com
Local.

5110 ■ ESOP Association, Indiana
c/o Mr. Andrew J. Manchir, Pres.
Goelzer Investment Banking
111 Monument Cir., Ste.500
Indianapolis, IN 46204-5171
Ph: (317)264-2609
Fax: (317)264-2601
E-mail: amanchir@goelzerinc.com
URL: National Affiliate–www.esopassociation.org
Contact: Mr. Andrew J. Manchir, Pres.
Local. Affiliated With: ESOP Association.

5111 ■ Exchange Club of Speedway
PO Box 24745
Indianapolis, IN 46224
Ph: (317)727-2040
URL: http://www.speedwayexchange.com
Contact: Matthew Simpson, Pres.
Local.

5112 ■ Executive Women in HealthCare (EWHC)
c/o Susan Darwent, Exec.Dir.
PO Box 68829
Indianapolis, IN 46268-0829
Ph: (317)733-2380
Fax: (317)733-2385
E-mail: info@ewhc.org
URL: http://www.ewhc.org
Contact: Susan Darwent, Exec.Dir.
Local.

5113 ■ Executive Women International, Indianapolis Chapter
c/o Kimberly Stakelbeck, Pres.
Thermal Air Systems, Inc.
7301 E 90th St., Ste.112
Indianapolis, IN 46256

Ph: (317)598-9900
Fax: (317)598-9909
E-mail: kimberlys@thermalairsystems.net
URL: http://www.indyewi.org
Contact: Kimberly Stakelbeck, Pres.

Founded: 1965. **Local**. Works to promote member firms and improve their communities. Provides opportunities for business and personal growth. **Awards: Frequency:** annual. **Type:** scholarship. **Recipient:** for secondary school junior enrolled in a public, private or parochial school • **Frequency:** annual. **Type:** scholarship. **Recipient:** to adult students at transition points in their lives. **Committees:** Advisory; Budget; Bylaws; Civic Development/ Philanthropy; Courtesy; Nominating; Publications; Sergeant-at-Arms/Hospitality. **Affiliated With:** Executive Women International. **Publications:** *Pulse*, monthly. Newsletter. **Advertising:** accepted. Alternate Formats: online. **Conventions/Meetings:** monthly meeting - every 2nd Monday.

5114 ■ Families Reaching for Rainbows Federation of Families for Children's Mental Health
4701 N Keystone Ave., Ste.150, Rm. 423
Indianapolis, IN 46205
Ph: (317)205-8281
Fax: (317)205-8343
Free: (888)543-9727
E-mail: kwilliams@choicesteam.org
URL: http://www.kidwrap.org
Contact: Kimberly Williams, Contact

Local. Affiliated With: Federation of Families for Children's Mental Health.

5115 ■ Family Service Association of Central Indiana
615 N Alabama St., Ste.320
Indianapolis, IN 46204
Ph: (317)634-6341
Fax: (317)464-9575
E-mail: edieo@family-service-inc.org
URL: http://www.family-service-inc.org
Contact: Edie Olson, Pres.

Local.

5116 ■ Federalist Society for Law and Public Policy Studies - Indianapolis Chapter
c/o Mr. Mark I. Shublak
One Amer. Sq.
Box 82001
Indianapolis, IN 46282-0200
Ph: (317)236-5981
Fax: (317)592-4889
E-mail: mark.shublak@icemiller.com
URL: National Affiliate–www.fed-soc.org
Contact: Mr. Mark I. Shublak, Contact

Local. Seeks to bring about a reordering of priorities within the U.S. legal system that will emphasize individual liberty, traditional values, and the rule of law. **Affiliated With:** Federalist Society for Law and Public Policy Studies.

5117 ■ Financial Planning Association of Greater Indiana
c/o Liz Hoover
Pyramid 1, Third Fl.
3500 DePauw Blvd., Ste.1031
Indianapolis, IN 46268
Ph: (317)871-8578
E-mail: lh@hooverfinancialadvisors.com
URL: http://www.fpagrindiana.org
Contact: Liz Hoover, Pres.

Local. Promotes the legislative, regulatory and professional interests of the financial service industry. Fosters the value of financial planning and advances the financial planning profession. Seeks to foster the financial planning process, with high ethical standards, continuing education, and community awareness. **Affiliated With:** Financial Planning Association.

5118 ■ Franklin Township Education Foundation
c/o Tracey Willard Myers, Exec.Dir.
6141 S Franklin Rd.
Indianapolis, IN 46259-1320
Ph: (317)862-2411 (317)803-5037
Fax: (317)862-7238
E-mail: tracey.myers@ftcsc.k12.in.us
URL: http://www.ftcsc.k12.in.us
Contact: Tracey Willard Myers, Exec.Dir.

Founded: 1997. **Members:** 13. **Staff:** 1. **Local**. Grants award education to teachers to enhance education in the community. **Awards:** Annual Grant Awards. **Frequency:** annual. **Type:** grant. **Boards:** 13 Members of a Volunteer Board of Directors. **Affiliated With:** Indiana Association of Public Education Foundations.

5119 ■ Fraternal Order of Police Lodge 86
1427 E Washington St.
Indianapolis, IN 46201
Ph: (317)637-1195 (317)636-1285
Fax: (317)267-0114
E-mail: lodge@fop86.org
URL: http://fop86.org
Contact: Vince Huber, Pres.

Founded: 1938. **Members:** 3,000. **Membership Dues:** individual, $35 (annual). **Staff:** 6. **Budget:** $500,000. **State Groups:** 1. **Local**. Seeks to benefit law enforcement. **Awards:** FOP86 Scholarship Fund. **Frequency:** annual. **Type:** scholarship. **Recipient:** for children and grandchildren of active, retired, or deceased members of Lodge No. 86. **Publications:** *Siren*, bimonthly. Newsletter. **Price:** included in membership dues. **Circulation:** 3,000. **Conventions/ Meetings:** annual conference (exhibits) - every June.

5120 ■ Friends of the White River
PO Box 90171
Indianapolis, IN 46290
Ph: (317)767-4140
E-mail: fowr@crittur.com
URL: http://www.fowr.org
Contact: Kevin Hardie, Exec.Dir.

Local.

5121 ■ Girl Scouts of Hoosier Capital Council
c/o Mrs. Deborah A. Hearn Smith, CEO
1800 N Meridian St.
Indianapolis, IN 46202
Ph: (317)924-3450
Fax: (317)924-2976
E-mail: dsmith@gshcc.org
URL: http://www.gshcc.org
Contact: Mrs. Deborah A. Hearn Smith, CEO

Founded: 1987. **Members:** 26,000. **Membership Dues:** all, $10 (annual). **Staff:** 54. **Languages:** English, Spanish. **Local**. Dedicated to inspire girls with the highest ideals of character, conduct, patriotism, and service so that they may become happy and resourceful citizens. **Libraries: Type:** reference. **Holdings:** books, video recordings. **Subjects:** girl scouts and badges they can earn. **Awards:** Marie A. Pickens Scholarship. **Frequency:** annual. **Type:** scholarship. **Recipient:** for a graduating senior whose criteria matches the scholarship. **Affiliated With:** Girl Scouts of the U.S.A. **Publications:** *Happenings*, 5/year. Newsletter. Features council and community programs.

5122 ■ Girls Incorporated of Indianapolis
3959 N Central Ave.
Indianapolis, IN 46205
Ph: (317)283-0086
Fax: (317)283-0301
E-mail: info.indy@girls-inc.org
URL: http://www.girlsincindy.org
Contact: Tonja Eagan, Pres./CEO

Founded: 1969. **Local**. Works to create an environment in which girls can learn and grow to their fullest potential. **Affiliated With:** Girls Inc.

5123 ■ Glass Menagerie Corvette Club
c/o Steve Blackwell
2457 N Sharon Ave.
Indianapolis, IN 46222-2360
Ph: (317)926-7496
E-mail: bud@comteck.com
URL: http://www.indianaregion.com
Contact: Steve Blackwell, Contact

Local. Affiliated With: National Council of Corvette Clubs.

5124 ■ Gold Wing Touring Association (GWTA)
PO Box 42403
Indianapolis, IN 46242-0403
Ph: (317)243-6822
Fax: (317)243-6833
Free: (800)960-4982
E-mail: gwtaoffice@gwta.org
URL: http://www.gwta.org
Contact: Bruce Keenon, Exec.Dir.

Membership Dues: individual, $35 (annual) • family, $45 (annual) • life (individual), $600 • life (family), $750. **Local**. Seeks to provide the environment and organizational structure around which its members may enjoy well-coordinated social gatherings and events without political endorsements or religious affiliations. Creates a positive image of tour motorcycling to the public; encourages good riding habits; and involved in civic and charitable affairs.

5125 ■ Goodtime Trailblazers
c/o Tom Martin
5958 Cross Creek Blvd.
Indianapolis, IN 46217-3700
Ph: (317)787-9776
E-mail: fritzmartin@mw.net
URL: National Affiliate–www.ava.org
Contact: Tom Martin, Pres.

Local. Affiliated With: American Volkssport Association.

5126 ■ Governor's Planning Council for People with Disabilities, Indiana
c/o Brenda Wade
150 W Market St., Ste.628
Indianapolis, IN 46204
Ph: (317)232-7770
Fax: (317)233-3712
E-mail: gpcpd@gpcpd.org
URL: http://www.gpcpd.org
Contact: Suellen Jackson-Boner, Exec.Dir.

State. Federally funded council whose members are appointed by the governor to promote public policy which leads to the independence, productivity and inclusion of citizens with disabilities in all aspects of society. **Affiliated With:** National Association of Councils on Developmental Disabilities.

5127 ■ Great Lakes Region Youth for Christ
5160 E 65th St.
Indianapolis, IN 46220
Ph: (317)585-0717
Fax: (317)585-0485
URL: http://www.yfcglr.org

Regional. Affiliated With: Youth for Christ/U.S.A.

5128 ■ Greater Indianapolis Chamber of Commerce
Chase Tower
111 Monument Cir., Ste.1950
Indianapolis, IN 46204
Ph: (317)464-2200
Fax: (317)464-2217
E-mail: rdorson@indylink.com
URL: http://www.indychamber.com
Contact: Roland M. Dorson, Pres.

Founded: 1890. **Members:** 3,800. **Staff:** 33. **Budget:** $3,900,000. **Local**. Promotes business and community development in Indianapolis, IN. **Libraries: Type:** not open to the public. **Holdings:** articles, books, periodicals. **Subjects:** demographics. **Also Known As:** (2005) Indianapolis Chamber of Commerce. **Publications:** *Catalyst*, quarterly. Newsletter. **Circulation:** 5,000. **Advertising:** accepted • *Indianapolis Monthly City Guide*, annual. Magazine • *Manufacturers Directory CD*. Contains information on manufacturers in the nine counties of Indianapolis. **Price:** $260.00 for members; $360.00 for nonmembers. Alternate Formats: CD-ROM • *Monday Morning Memo*, weekly. Articles. **Advertising:** accepted. Alternate Formats: online • *Newcomer Booklet*. **Price:** free (first copy); $1.00 for nonmembers.

5129 ■ Greater Indianapolis Council on Alcoholism and Drug Dependence
2511 E. 46th St., Ste.A-1
Indianapolis, IN 46205
Ph: (317)542-7128
E-mail: indianapolis.in@ncadd.org
URL: National Affiliate–www.ncadd.org
Local. Affiliated With: National Council on Alcoholism and Drug Dependence.

5130 ■ Greater Indianapolis Literacy League - Indy Reads
c/o Linda Gabrielson
Indianapolis-Marion County Public Lib.
PO Box 211
Indianapolis, IN 46206
Ph: (317)274-4040
Fax: (317)269-5220
E-mail: lgabrielson@imcpl.org
URL: http://www.indyreads.org
Contact: Linda Gabrielson, Contact
Founded: 1984. **Staff:** 5. **Local**. Works for providing Adult Basic Literacy and tutoring of English as a second language in Marion County.

5131 ■ Habitat for Humanity of Greater Indianapolis
PO Box 1252
Indianapolis, IN 46206-1252
Ph: (317)921-2121
Fax: (317)921-2126
E-mail: info@indyhabitat.org
URL: http://www.indyhabitat.org
Contact: Frank Hartman, Exec.Dir.
Founded: 1987. **Staff:** 14. **Local**. Provides home ownership opportunities and builds communities of hope as an expression of God's love.

5132 ■ Hamilton County Alliance
10333 N Meridian St., Ste.110
Indianapolis, IN 46290
Ph: (317)573-4950
Fax: (317)573-4959
Free: (800)790-6610
E-mail: aeverson@hcalliance.com
URL: http://www.hcalliance.com
Contact: Amy Everson, Admin.Mgr.
Local. Assists expansion projects of businesses in Hamilton County. Provides assistance with skill enhancement training funds.

5133 ■ Hemophilia of Indiana
c/o Michelle Rice, Exec.Dir.
4905 E 56th St.
Indianapolis, IN 46220
Ph: (317)396-0065
Fax: (317)396-0318
Free; (800)241-2873
E-mail: mrice@hemophiliaofindia.org
URL: http://www.hemophiliaofindiana.org
Contact: Michelle Rice, Exec.Dir.
State. Aims to reduce the stresses and restrictions that are imposed upon individuals and families with hemophilia and von Willibrand Disease. **Affiliated With:** National Hemophilia Foundation.

5134 ■ Hindu Temple of Central Indiana
3350 German Church Rd.
Indianapolis, IN 46236
Ph: (317)875-8905
URL: http://www.htci.org
Contact: Dr. Girdhar Lal Ahuja, Contact
Founded: 1999. **Local**. Works to build a temple with the broad-based needs of the community. Provides religious services and creates a focus for spiritual enrichment. Promotes educational and cultural opportunities for children.

5135 ■ Historic Irvington Community Council
PO Box 19721
Indianapolis, IN 46219
E-mail: president@irvingtoncouncil.com
URL: http://www.irvingtoncouncil.com
Local.

5136 ■ Historic Landmarks Foundation of Indiana
340 W Michigan St.
Indianapolis, IN 46202
Ph: (317)639-4534
Fax: (317)639-6734
Free: (800)450-4534
E-mail: info@historiclandmarks.org
URL: http://www.historiclandmarks.org
Contact: John T. Watson, Chm.
Founded: 1960. **Members:** 10,500. **Membership Dues:** senior/student, $15 (annual) • active, $20 (annual) • non-profit, $25 (annual) • contributor, $30 (annual) • sponsor, $50 (annual) • sustaining/corporate, $100 (annual) • Founder's Club, $250 (annual). **Staff:** 45. **State**. Saves and protects buildings and places of architectural and historical significance; leads and assists individuals, organizations and communities in preserving, adapting and revitalizing Indiana's endangered landmarks; educates the public, restores buildings, advocates preservation, and provides financial support for preservation efforts to enrich contemporary life and leave a legacy of landmarks. **Libraries: Type:** open to the public. **Holdings:** 1,500; artwork, books, clippings, periodicals, video recordings. **Subjects:** historic preservation, architecture, planning. **Awards:** Servaas Award. **Frequency:** annual. **Type:** monetary. **Recipient:** for outstanding contributions to historic preservation in Indiana. **Publications:** *The Indiana Preservationist*, bimonthly. Magazine. **Price:** included in membership dues. **Advertising:** accepted. **Conventions/Meetings:** annual regional meeting • annual Statewide Membership Meeting.

5137 ■ Hoosier Association of Science Teachers
c/o Edward Frazier, Exec.Dir.
5007 W 14th St.
Indianapolis, IN 46224
Ph: (317)243-0107
E-mail: elfrazier@comcast.net
URL: http://www.hasti.org
Contact: Edward Frazier, Exec.Dir.
Local. Promotes excellence and innovation in science teaching and learning for all. Serves as the voice for excellence and innovation in science teaching and learning, curriculum and instruction, and assessment. Promotes interest and support for science education. **Affiliated With:** National Science Teachers Association.

5138 ■ Hoosier Corvette Club
8424 US 31 S
Indianapolis, IN 46227
E-mail: hoosiercorvetteclub@yahoo.com
URL: http://hoosiercorvetteclub.zoomshare.com
Contact: Ed Rudisell, Pres.
Local. Affiliated With: National Council of Corvette Clubs.

5139 ■ Hoosier Environmental Council (HEC)
1915 W 18th St., Ste.A
Indianapolis, IN 46202
Ph: (317)685-8800
E-mail: hec@hecweb.org
URL: http://www.hecweb.org
Contact: Tim Maloney, Exec.Dir.
Local. Advocates for the environment on key issues before the Indiana legislature and regulatory boards.

5140 ■ Hoosier Heartland Resource Conservation and Development Council
5995 Lakeside Blvd., Ste.B
Indianapolis, IN 46278-1996
Ph: (317)290-3250
Fax: (317)290-3150
E-mail: rebecca.fletcher@in.usda.gov
URL: http://www.hhrcd.org
Contact: Rebecca Fletcher, Coor.
Local. Affiliated With: National Association of Resource Conservation and Development Councils.

5141 ■ Hoosier Kitefliers Society (HKS)
c/o Danna Korak, Membership Dir.
8113 Talliho Dr.
Indianapolis, IN 46256
Ph: (317)849-5986
E-mail: dmkorak@comcast.net
URL: http://www.hoosierkite.org
Contact: Danna Korak, Membership Dir.
Local. Affiliated With: American Kitefliers Association.

5142 ■ Hoosier Mountain Bike Association (HMBA)
PMB No. 194
1508 E 86th St.
Indianapolis, IN 46240
E-mail: info@hmba.org
URL: http://www.hmba.org
Contact: Mike Hufhand, Pres.
Local. Affiliated With: International Mountain Bicycling Association.

5143 ■ Hoosier Mountain Bike Club Association
8150 Crook Dr. N
Indianapolis, IN 46256
Ph: (317)590-7511
E-mail: mhufhand@aol.com
URL: http://www.hmba.org
Local. Affiliated With: International Mountain Bicycling Association.

5144 ■ Hoosier Muskie Hunters
PO Box 501371
Indianapolis, IN 46250
Ph: (765)278-2567
E-mail: vancebell@hotmail.com
URL: http://www.hoosiermuskiehunters.com
Contact: Vance Bell, Pres.
Local.

5145 ■ Hoosier Orchid Society
8440 W 82nd St.
Indianapolis, IN 46278
Ph: (317)291-6269
Fax: (317)291-8949
Free: (888)291-6569
E-mail: orchids@hoosierorchid.com
URL: http://www.hoosierorchid.com
Contact: Patty Enders, Office Mgr.
Founded: 1989. **Local**. Professional growers, botanists, hobbyists, and others interested in extending the knowledge, production, use, and appreciation of orchids. **Affiliated With:** American Orchid Society.

5146 ■ Hoosier Salon Patrons Association and Galleries
c/o Karen Seltzer, Asst.Dir.
714 E 65th St.
Indianapolis, IN 46220
Ph: (317)253-5340
Fax: (317)253-5468
E-mail: hoosiersalon@iquest.net
URL: http://www.hoosiersalon.org
Local. Supports Hoosier artists and their art.

5147 ■ Hoosier State Press Association (HSPA)
c/o David M. Stamps, Exec.Dir.
1 Virginia Ave., Ste.701
Indianapolis, IN 46204

Ph: (317)803-4772
Fax: (317)624-4428
E-mail: dstamps@hspa.com
URL: http://www.hspa.com
Founded: 1933. **State.**

5148 ■ Hoosiers Concerned about Gun Violence (HCGV)
2511 E, 46th St., Ste.A-6
Indianapolis, IN 46205
Ph: (317)377-0700
E-mail: hcagv@sbcglobal.net
URL: http://www.HCGV.org
Contact: Kathy George, Pres.
State. Promotes gun violence prevention and education.

5149 ■ House Rabbit Society, Indiana Chapter
c/o Dawn E. Sailer
PO Box 533243
Indianapolis, IN 46253
Ph: (317)767-7636
E-mail: info@indianahrs.org
URL: http://www.indianahrs.org
State.

5150 ■ Human Resource Association of Central Indiana (HRACI)
9840 Westpoint Dr., Ste.200
Indianapolis, IN 46256
Ph: (317)841-3236
Fax: (317)841-8206
E-mail: cmp@hraci.org
URL: http://www.hraci.org
Contact: Cherilyn Stephens, Pres.
Local. Represents the interests of human resource and industrial relations professionals and executives. Promotes the advancement of human resource management.

5151 ■ Human Resource Professional Development Association (HRPDA)
PO Box 441173
Indianapolis, IN 46244
E-mail: kathym@crystal-flash.com
URL: http://www.hrpda.com
Contact: Kathy Marra Wert, Pres.
Local. Represents the interests of human resource and industrial relations professionals and executives. Promotes the advancement of human resource management.

5152 ■ Huntington's Disease Society of America, Indiana Chapter
c/o Michael Lewis, Pres.
PO Box 2101
Indianapolis, IN 46206
Ph: (317)271-0624
Fax: (317)722-7614
E-mail: info@hdsaindiana.org
URL: http://www.hdsaindiana.org
Contact: Michael Lewis, Pres.
Founded: 1969. **State.** Individuals and groups of volunteers concerned with Huntington's disease, an inherited and terminal neurological condition causing progressive brain and nerve deterioration. Goals are to: identifies HD families; educates the public and professionals, with emphasis on increasing consumer awareness of HD; promotes and supports basic and clinical research into the causes and cure of HD; assists families in meeting the social, economic, and emotional problems resulting from HD. Works to change the attitude of the working community toward the HD patient, enhance the HD patient's lifestyle, and promote better health care and treatment, both in the community and in facilities. **Affiliated With:** Huntington's Disease Society of America. **Publications:** *Hoosier Highlights*. Newsletter. **Conventions/Meetings:** annual conference.

5153 ■ I-69 Mid-Continent Highway Coalition
10401 N Meridian St., Ste.300
Indianapolis, IN 46290
Ph: (317)581-6320
Fax: (317)581-6110
E-mail: jimnewland@hotmail.com
Contact: James G. Newland, Exec.Dir.
Regional.

5154 ■ IABC/Indianapolis
PO Box 44108
Indianapolis, IN 46244
Ph: (317)767-4446
E-mail: tsiefert@salliemae.com
URL: http://www.indyiabc.com
Contact: Tina Siefert, Pres.
Local. Public relations and communication professionals. Committed to improve the effectiveness of organizations through strategic, interactive and integrated business communication management. Provides products, services, and networking activities to help people and organizations excel in public relations, employee communication, marketing communication, public affairs and other forms of communication.

5155 ■ IEEE Central Indiana Section
799 W Michigan St.
Indianapolis, IN 46202
Ph: (317)274-0044
URL: http://www.cis-ieee.org
Contact: Jose Ramos, Chair
Local. Engineers and scientists in electrical engineering, electronics, and allied fields. Promotes creating, developing, integrating, sharing, and applying knowledge about electro and information technologies and sciences for the benefit of humanity and the profession. Conducts lectures on current engineering and scientific topics.

5156 ■ Independent Colleges of Indiana (ICI)
101 W Ohio St., Ste.440
Indianapolis, IN 46204-1970
Ph: (317)236-6090
Fax: (317)236-6086
E-mail: info@icindiana.org
URL: http://www.icindiana.org
Contact: Hans Giesecke PhD, Pres.
State. Affiliated With: National Association of Independent Colleges and Universities.

5157 ■ Independent Insurance Agents of Indiana
c/o Roger Ronk, Exec.VP
3435 W 96th St.
Indianapolis, IN 46268
Ph: (317)824-3780
Fax: (317)824-3786
Free: (800)438-4424
E-mail: bigiinfo@bigi.org
URL: National Affiliate–www.iii.org
Contact: Jane A. Perry, Mgt.Serv. Analyst
Membership Dues: agency, $385 (annual) • associate, $500 (annual). **State.** Offers continuing education, a lobbyist to help lobby for insurance laws, and a financing department for members, conference center and banquet space available to members and the public. **Awards:** Agency of the Year. **Frequency:** annual. **Type:** recognition • Agent of the Year. **Frequency:** annual. **Type:** recognition • Company of the Year. **Frequency:** annual. **Type:** recognition • Company Professional of the Year. **Frequency:** annual. **Type:** recognition • Director of the Year. **Frequency:** annual. **Type:** recognition • Distinguished Customer Service of the Year. **Frequency;** annual. **Type:** recognition • H.P. Cooper, Jr.-Industry/Public. **Frequency:** annual. **Type:** recognition • Young Agent of the Year. **Frequency:** annual. **Type:** recognition. **Affiliated With:** Insurance Information Institute. **Publications:** *Focus*, monthly. Magazine. **Advertising:** accepted.

5158 ■ Indiana 4-H Foundation
225 SE St., Ste.760
Indianapolis, IN 46202
Ph: (317)692-7044
Fax: (317)692-7042
E-mail: info@4h.org
URL: http://www.4h.org
Contact: Steve Ingram CAE, Exec.VP
Founded: 1961. **Members:** 2,500. **Staff:** 4. **Budget:** $640,000. **State.** Seeks to create and enhance growth and recognition opportunities for 4-H'ers and their leaders so that they may develop the hallmarks of successful citizens with responsibility, leadership, and integrity. **Awards: Type:** grant • **Type:** scholarship. **Conventions/Meetings:** quarterly board meeting • annual meeting.

5159 ■ Indiana Academy of Family Physicians (IAFP)
c/o Kevin P. Speer, JD, Exec.VP
55 Monument Cir., Ste.400
Indianapolis, IN 46204
Ph: (317)237-4237
Fax: (317)237-4006
Free: (888)422-4237
E-mail: iafp@in-afp.org
URL: http://www.in-afp.org
Contact: Kevin P. Speer JD, Exec.VP
State. Affiliated With: American Academy of Family Physicians.

5160 ■ Indiana Academy of Osteopathy
c/o Michael H. Claphan, Exec.Dir.
3521 Guion Rd., Ste.202
Indianapolis, IN 46222-1672
Ph: (317)926-3009
URL: National Affiliate–www.academyofosteopathy.org
Founded: 1982. **Members:** 50. **Membership Dues:** $50 (annual). **State.** Osteopathic physicians. Promotes improved professional practice. Sponsors continuing medical educational programs. **Publications:** none. **Affiliated With:** American Academy of Osteopathy. **Conventions/Meetings:** annual symposium - always August.

5161 ■ Indiana Amusement and Music Operators Association (IAMOA)
5613 W 74th St.
Indianapolis, IN 46278-1753
Fax: (317)387-0999
Free: (877)463-2662
E-mail: info@iamoa.org
URL: http://www.iamoa.org
Contact: Leslie Murphy, Exec.Dir.
State. Aims to further the interests of those engaged in the sales, marketing, distribution and manufacturing of coin operated equipment. Fosters and promotes goodwill, mutual respect and fair dealing among those engaged in the business of coin-operated amusement devices. **Affiliated With:** Amusement and Music Operators Association.

5162 ■ Indiana Apartment Association (IAA)
9202 N Meridian St., Ste.250
Indianapolis, IN 46260
Ph: (317)816-8900
Fax: (317)816-8911
E-mail: iaa@iaaonline.net
URL: http://www.aaionline.net
Contact: Lynne Sullivan CAE, Exec.Dir.
State.

5163 ■ Indiana Arts Commission
150 W Market St., Ste.618
Indianapolis, IN 46204
Ph: (317)232-1268
Fax: (317)232-5595
E-mail: indianaartscommission@iac.in.gov
URL: http://www.in.gov/arts
Contact: Dorothy L. Ilgen, Exec.Dir.
Founded: 1969. **Staff:** 12. **Budget:** $3,600,000. **Regional Groups:** 12. **State Groups:** 15. **State.** State government agency funded by the Indiana General Assembly and the National Endowment for the Arts.

Helps in funding, encouraging, promoting, and expanding the arts in Indiana. **Awards:** Indiana Governor's Arts Awards. **Frequency:** biennial. **Type:** recognition. **Recipient:** to individuals, groups, businesses, and communities for their contributions to furthering public awareness of the arts. **Publications:** *Arts INform*, quarterly. Newsletter. **Price:** free.

5164 ■ Indiana Assisted Living Federation of America (IALFA)
5120 Aspen Talon Ct.
Indianapolis, IN 46254
Ph: (317)388-8725
Fax: (317)388-8726
E-mail: exdir@ialfa.org
URL: http://www.ialfa.org
Contact: Ms. Susan L. Albers MSM, Exec.Dir.

Founded: 1999. **Members:** 105. **Staff:** 1. **Budget:** $120,000. **Regional Groups:** 5. **State Groups:** 1. **State**. Serves the assisted living industry by promoting quality services and a healthy business client for providers, suppliers, and related service partners. **Affiliated With:** Assisted Living Federation of America. **Publications:** *IALFA Advisory*, quarterly. Newsletter. **Conventions/Meetings:** annual conference • quarterly District Meeting.

5165 ■ Indiana Association of Beverage Retailers
200 S Meridian St., Ste.350
Indianapolis, IN 46225
Ph: (317)684-7580
Fax: (317)673-4210
Free: (888)838-4227
E-mail: jlivengood@livengood-associates.com
Contact: John Livengood, Pres./CEO

State.

5166 ■ Indiana Association of Chiefs of Police (IACP)
c/o Michael F. Ward, Exec.Dir.
10293 N Meridian St., Ste.175
Indianapolis, IN 46290
Ph: (317)816-1619
Fax: (317)816-1633
E-mail: info@iacop.org
URL: http://www.iacop.org
Contact: Michael F. Ward, Exec.Dir.

State.

5167 ■ Indiana Association of Cities and Towns (IACT)
c/o Matthew C. Greller, Exec.Dir.
200 S Meridian St., Ste.340
Indianapolis, IN 46225
Ph: (317)237-6200
Fax: (317)237-6206
E-mail: mgreller@citiesandtowns.org
URL: http://www.citiesandtowns.org
Contact: Matthew C. Greller, Exec.Dir.

Founded: 1899. **Members:** 476. **Staff:** 12. **State**. Cities, towns, companies, and organizations. Acts as a lobbyist before the Indiana Legislature. Conducts training seminars. Sponsors exhibitor programs. **Affiliated With:** National League of Cities. **Formerly:** Indiana Municipal League. **Publications:** *Actionlines*, monthly. Magazine. **Price:** $30.00/year. ISSN: 1092-6259. **Circulation:** 3,800. **Advertising:** accepted. Alternate Formats: online • *Budget Bulletin*, annual • *Final Statehouse Report*, annual. Bulletin • *Indiana Elected Municipal Officials' Handbook*, quadrennial • *Roster of Indiana City and Town Officials*, quadrennial • *Statehouse Report*, biweekly. **Conventions/Meetings:** annual conference (exhibits).

5168 ■ Indiana Association for Community Economic Development (IACED)
c/o Christie L. Gillespie, Exec.Dir.
324 W Morris St., Ste.104
Indianapolis, IN 46225
Ph: (317)423-1070
Fax: (317)423-1075
E-mail: iaced@iaced.org
URL: http://www.iaced.org
Contact: Christie L. Gillespie, Exec.Dir.

Founded: 1986. **Members:** 150. **Membership Dues:** voting, $250 (annual) • associate, $500 (annual). **Budget:** $1,000,000. **State**. Represents community development organizations and affiliates. **Affiliated With:** National Congress for Community Economic Development. **Conventions/Meetings:** annual conference.

5169 ■ Indiana Association of Credit Management (IACM)
415 S Shortridge Rd.
Indianapolis, IN 46219
Fax: (317)636-5720
Free: (800)888-4359
E-mail: iacm@iacm.ws
URL: http://www.iacm.org
Contact: Onda Williams, Contact

State.

5170 ■ Indiana Association for the Education of Young Children
4755 Kingsway Dr., Ste.107
Indianapolis, IN 46205
Ph: (317)356-6884
Fax: (317)259-9489
Free: (800)657-7577
URL: http://www.asyc.org

State. **Affiliated With:** National Association for the Education of Young Children.

5171 ■ Indiana Association for Employment in Education
c/o Joseph O. Erne, Dir.
Metropolitan S.D. of Washington Twp.
8550 Woodfield Crossing Blvd.
Indianapolis, IN 46240-2478
Ph: (317)845-9400
Fax: (317)205-3385
E-mail: jerne@msdwt.k12.in.us
URL: National Affiliate–www.aaee.org
Contact: Joseph O. Erne, Dir.

State. Serves the staffing needs of education professionals at colleges, universities and school districts whose members are school personnel/HR administrators and college and university career center administrators. Promotes ethical standards and practices in the employment processes. **Affiliated With:** American Association for Employment in Education.

5172 ■ Indiana Association for Floodplain and Stormwater Management (INAFSM)
115 W Washington St., Ste.1368 S
Indianapolis, IN 46204
Ph: (317)796-2359
Fax: (317)632-3306
E-mail: info@inafsm.net
URL: http://www.inafsm.net
Contact: Maria Cisco, Exec.Sec.

Founded: 1996. **Members:** 300. **State**. Promotes awareness of proper floodplain and stormwater management; augments the professional status of floodplain and stormwater management and secure all benefits resulting there from; and informs individual concerned through educational and professional seminars. **Affiliated With:** Association of State Floodplain Managers.

5173 ■ Indiana Association for Home and Hospice Care (IAHHC)
c/o Todd Stallings, Exec.Dir.
8604 Allisonville Rd., Ste.260
Indianapolis, IN 46250
Ph: (317)844-6630
Fax: (317)575-8751
E-mail: todd@iahhc.org
URL: http://www.ind-homecare.org
Contact: Todd Stallings, Exec.Dir.

Founded: 1978. **Members:** 150. **Staff:** 3. **Budget:** $600,000. **State**. Providers of home health care, hospice, and homemaker-home health aide services; interested individuals and organizations. Develops and promotes high standards of patient care in home care services. **Affiliated With:** National Association for Home Care and Hospice.

5174 ■ Indiana Association of Homes and Services for the Aging (IAHSA)
c/o Mr. James M. Leich, Pres.
PO Box 68829
Indianapolis, IN 46268-0829
Ph: (317)733-2380
Fax: (317)733-2385
E-mail: jimleich@iahsa.com
URL: http://www.iahsa.com
Contact: Mr. James M. Leich, Pres.

State.

5175 ■ Indiana Association for Infant and Toddler Mental Health (IAITMH)
55 Monument Cir., Ste.455
Indianapolis, IN 46204
Ph: (317)638-3501
Fax: (317)638-3540
Free: (800)555-6424
E-mail: sschwegman@mentalhealthassociation.com
URL: http://www.mentalhealthassociation.com
Contact: Shawna Schwegman, Contact

State. Provides public information on infant mental health. Advocates research on mental disorders that affect infants. Promotes the optimal development of infants and the treatment of mental disorders in the child's early years. **Affiliated With:** World Association for Infant Mental Health.

5176 ■ Indiana Association of Insurance and Financial Advisors (IAIFA)
3009 E 96th St.
Indianapolis, IN 46240
Ph: (317)844-6268
Fax: (317)844-7659
E-mail: stonekingk@sbcglobal.net
URL: National Affiliate–www.naifa.org
Contact: Mr. Kim B. Stoneking, Exec.Dir.

Founded: 1887. **Members:** 3,500. **Staff:** 3. **Budget:** $300,000. **Local Groups:** 27. **State**. Life and health insurance agents. Provides education and legislative advocacy. **Awards:** Hoosier Life Underwriter Award. **Frequency:** annual. **Type:** recognition. **Affiliated With:** National Association of Insurance and Financial Advisors. **Formerly:** (2001) Indiana State Association of Life Underwriters. **Publications:** *ISALU Directory*, annual • *ISALU Review*, quarterly. Newsletter. **Conventions/Meetings:** annual meeting (exhibits).

5177 ■ Indiana Association of Mortgage Brokers (INAMB)
c/o Kelly Miller, Exec.Dir.
5980 W 71st St., Ste.200
Indianapolis, IN 46278
Ph: (317)964-1225
Fax: (317)964-1224
E-mail: kelly@inamb.com
URL: http://www.inamb.com
Contact: Kelly Miller, Exec.Dir.

Founded: 1991. **State**.

5178 ■ Indiana Association of Nonprofit Organizations
c/o Harriet O'Connor, Pres.
10 W Market St., Site 1720
Indianapolis, IN 46204
Ph: (317)464-5324
Fax: (317)464-5146
E-mail: hoconnor@npteam.org
URL: National Affiliate–www.ncna.org
Contact: Harriet O'Connor, Pres.

State. **Affiliated With:** National Council of Nonprofit Associations.

5179 ■ Indiana Association of Plumbing, Heating, Cooling Contractors
c/o Brenda A. Dant, CAE
9595 Whitley Dr., Ste.208
Indianapolis, IN 46240

Ph: (317)575-9292
Fax: (317)575-9378
Free: (888)717-4835
E-mail: bradisley@isleyplumbing.com
URL: http://www.iaphcc.com
Contact: Brenda A. Dant CAE, Contact
State.

5180 ■ Indiana Association of Private Career Schools
c/o Richard H. Weiss, Pres.
7302 Woodland Dr.
Indianapolis, IN 46278-1736
Ph: (317)299-6001
Fax: (317)298-6342
URL: http://www.pcicareers.com
State.

5181 ■ Indiana Association of Public School Superintendents (IAPSS)
c/o Dr. John G. Ellis, Exec.Dir.
One N Capitol, Ste.1215
Indianapolis, IN 46204
Ph: (317)639-0336
Fax: (317)639-3591
E-mail: jellis@iapss-in.org
URL: http://www.iapss-in.org
Contact: Dr. John G. Ellis, Exec.Dir.
State.

5182 ■ Indiana Association of Realtors (IAR)
7301 N Shadeland Ave.
Indianapolis, IN 46250
Ph: (317)842-0890
Fax: (317)842-1076
Free: (800)284-0084
E-mail: rcnye@indianarealtors.com
URL: http://www.indianarealtors.com
Contact: Richard C. Nye CAE, Exec.VP
Founded: 1913. **Members:** 16,000. **Membership Dues:** realtor, $84 (annual). **Staff:** 13. **Budget:** $1,700,000. **Local Groups:** 46. **State.** Real state professionals dedicated to the protection and preservation of the free enterprise system and the right of the individual to own real property. Seeks to sustain a healthy real state market in Indiana. **Affiliated With:** National Association of Realtors. **Publications:** *Indiana Realtor*, monthly. Magazine. **Conventions/Meetings:** annual meeting (exhibits) - always September.

5183 ■ Indiana Association of Rehabilitation Facilities (INARF)
615 N Alabama St., Ste.410
Indianapolis, IN 46204
Ph: (317)634-4957
Fax: (317)634-3221
E-mail: inarf@inarf.org
URL: http://www.inarf.org
Contact: James M. Hammond III, Pres./CEO
State.

5184 ■ Indiana Association of Residential Child Care Agencies (IARCCA)
5519 E 82nd St., Ste.A
Indianapolis, IN 46250-0000
Ph: (317)849-8497
Fax: (317)576-5498
E-mail: iarcca@aol.com
Contact: K. Graham, Exec.Dir.
State. Provides services to children and families, including long-term residential care, foster care, transitional living, home-based services, crisis stabilization, shelter care, and other comprehensive services to improve the quality of life for children and families. Provides individual and group therapy, behavior modification programs and services that promote self-sufficiency. Seeks to encourage family preservation and/or permanency options for children and families.

5185 ■ Indiana Association of School Principals (IASP)
11025 E 25th St.
Indianapolis, IN 46229-1523
Ph: (317)891-9900
Fax: (317)894-9807
Free: (800)285-2188
E-mail: sheck@iasp.org
URL: http://www.iasp.org
Contact: Sharon Pitts, Pres.
Membership Dues: individual, $250 (annual) • associate, retired, aspiring administrator, $50 (annual) • new administrator, $125 (annual). **State.** Supports the commitment of all school principals.

5186 ■ Indiana Association of School Psychologists (IASP)
135 N Pennsylvania St., No. 2350
Indianapolis, IN 46204
Ph: (317)684-5411
Fax: (317)223-0438
Free: (866)518-4472
E-mail: jmelnyk@bosetreacy.com
URL: http://www.iaspweb.org
Contact: Greg Eaken, Pres.
State. Represents and supports school psychology through leadership. Enhances the mental health and educational competence of children. Informs the public on the services and practice of school psychology. **Affiliated With:** National Association of School Psychologists.

5187 ■ Indiana Association of Soil and Water Conservation Districts (IASWCD)
225 SE St., Ste.740
Indianapolis, IN 46202
Ph: (317)692-7325
Fax: (317)423-0756
E-mail: iaswcd@iaswcd.org
URL: http://iaswcd.org
Contact: Gene Weaver, Pres.
State. Represents the interests of Soil and Water Conservation Districts in Indiana.

5188 ■ Indiana Association for Supervision and Curriculum Development
c/o Kay Kelly, EdD
4600 Sunset Ave.
Indianapolis, IN 46208
Ph: (317)940-9824
Fax: (317)872-7808
E-mail: indianaascd@comcast.net
URL: http://indiana.ascd.org
Contact: Kay Kelly EdD, Contact
State. Advocates policies and practices that positively influence learning, teaching and leadership in education. Provides programs, services and professional development for effective teaching and learning. **Affiliated With:** Association for Supervision and Curriculum Development.

5189 ■ Indiana Association of United Way
3901 N Meridian St., Ste.306
Indianapolis, IN 46208-4026
Ph: (317)923-2377
Fax: (317)921-1397
E-mail: roger.frick@iauw.org
URL: http://www.iauw.org
Contact: Roger Frick, Contact
State. Affiliated With: United Way of America.

5190 ■ Indiana Athletic Trainers' Association (IATA)
PO Box 24167
Indianapolis, IN 46224
Ph: (317)231-2825
Fax: (317)481-1825
E-mail: ann@centraloffice1.com
URL: http://www.iata-usa.org
Contact: Joanne Klossner, Sec.
State. Affiliated With: National Athletic Trainers' Association.

5191 ■ Indiana Auto Body Association
c/o Tony Passwater
PO Box 532364
Indianapolis, IN 46253
Ph: (317)290-0611
URL: http://www.scrs.com/affiliateassociations.htm
Contact: Tony Passwater, Contact
State. Seeks to promote the auto body industry and improve the standards of automotive repair services. **Affiliated With:** Society of Collision Repair Specialists.

5192 ■ Indiana Bankers Association (IBA)
3135 N Meridian St.
Indianapolis, IN 46208
Ph: (317)921-3135
Fax: (317)921-3131
E-mail: jcousins@indianabankers.org
URL: http://www.indianabankers.org
Contact: James H. Cousins, Pres.
State. Publications: *Hoosier Banker*, monthly • *IBA General*, biweekly. Bulletin. **Conventions/Meetings:** annual meeting - always June.

5193 ■ Indiana Beef Cattle Association (IBCA)
8770 Guion Rd., Ste.A
Indianapolis, IN 46268
Ph: (317)872-2333
Fax: (317)872-2364
E-mail: sbradway@indianabeef.org
URL: http://www.indianabeef.org
Contact: Julia Wickard, Exec.VP
State.

5194 ■ Indiana Beef Council
c/o Phil Anderson, Exec.VP
8770 Guion Rd., Ste.A
Indianapolis, IN 46268-3017
Ph: (317)872-2333
Fax: (317)872-2364
E-mail: sbradway@indianabeef.org
URL: http://www.indianabeef.org
Contact: Shelley Bradway, Information Support Coor.
Founded: 1965. **Members:** 1,300. **State.** Beef producers. Works to increase profit opportunities and build stronger rural communities. **Affiliated With:** Cattlemen's Beef Promotion and Research Board. **Publications:** *Indiana Beef*, bimonthly. Magazine. **Advertising:** accepted. **Conventions/Meetings:** annual convention - always February • annual Hoosier Beef Congress, with expo (exhibits) - December.

5195 ■ Indiana Beverage Alliance
c/o Marc Carmichael, Pres.
150 W Market St., Ste.812
Indianapolis, IN 46204
Ph: (317)687-9615
Fax: (317)685-1028
URL: National Affiliate–www.nbwa.org
Contact: Marc Carmichael, Pres.
Local. Represents the interests of Independent wholesalers of malt beverages. **Affiliated With:** National Beer Wholesalers Association.

5196 ■ Indiana Bicycle Coalition
c/o Ms. Connie Szabo Schmucker, Exec.Dir.
PO Box 20243
Indianapolis, IN 46220
Ph: (317)466-9701
Fax: (317)466-9701
Free: (800)BIKE110
E-mail: info@bicycleindiana.org
URL: http://www.bicycleindiana.org
Contact: Ms. Connie Szabo Schmucker, Exec.Dir.
Founded: 1993. **Members:** 750. **Membership Dues:** member, $25 (annual) • advocate, $100 (annual) • patron, $250 (annual). **Staff:** 2. **Budget:** $100,000. **State Groups:** 1. **State.** Bicyclists, bicycle clubs, businesses, communities and organizations. Works to promote bicycling and advocacy for cyclists in Indiana. **Libraries: Type:** reference. **Holdings:** 100; articles, books, video recordings. **Subjects:** bicycle safety, transportation planning. **Awards:** Visionary Partner Award. **Frequency:** annual. **Type:** recognition. **Recipient:** for individuals or organiza-

tions that benefit and improve bicycling in Indiana. **Affiliated With:** International Mountain Bicycling Association. **Publications:** *Bicycle Event Calendar*, annual. Magazine. Contains listing of all Indiana bicycle events, organizations and resources. **Price:** free. **Circulation:** 50,000. **Advertising:** accepted. Alternate Formats: online • Newsletter, quarterly. **Conventions/Meetings:** annual Indiana BikeFest - festival, with bicycle rides, ice cream social, tours of unique sites, bicycle movies (exhibits).

5197 ■ Indiana Black Expo (IBE)
3145 N Meridian St.
Indianapolis, IN 46208
Ph: (317)925-2702
Fax: (317)925-6624
Free: (800)897-2702
E-mail: jrogers@ibeonline.com
URL: http://www.indianablackexpo.com
Contact: Alpha Garrett, Dir. of Communication
Founded: 1970. **State**. Serves as a channel for communication and a catalyst for greater harmony within communities throughout the nation and Indiana. Hosts the African-American cultural event, Summer Celebration and an African-American sporting event, Circle City Classic.

5198 ■ Indiana Bowling Centers Association (IBCA)
5455 W 86th St., Ste.100
Indianapolis, IN 46268
Ph: (317)874-2695
Fax: (317)874-2698
Free: (800)424-8962
E-mail: info@indianagobowl.com
URL: http://www.indianagobowl.com
Contact: Sarah Brown, Exec.Dir.
State. Formerly: (2000) Indiana Bowling Proprietors' Association.

5199 ■ Indiana Broadcasters Association (IBA)
3003 E 98th St., Ste.161
Indianapolis, IN 46280
Ph: (317)573-0119
Fax: (317)573-0895
Free: (800)342-6276
E-mail: indba@aol.com
URL: http://www.indianabroadcasters.org
Contact: Linda C. Compton, Pres./CEO
State.

5200 ■ Indiana Builders Association
c/o A. William Carson
Local No. 1500
PO Box 44670
Indianapolis, IN 46244-0670
Ph: (317)236-6334
Fax: (317)236-6342
Free: (800)377-6334
E-mail: inbuild@aol.com
URL: http://www.buildindiana.org
State. Single and multifamily home builders, commercial builders, and others associated with the building industry. **Affiliated With:** National Association of Home Builders.

5201 ■ Indiana Building and Construction Trades Council
1701 W 18th St.
Indianapolis, IN 46202
Ph: (317)636-0806
Fax: (317)638-1217
Contact: Patti Miller, Asst.Dir.
State.

5202 ■ Indiana Cable Telecommunications Association (ICTA)
201 N Illinois St., Ste.1560
Indianapolis, IN 46204
Ph: (317)237-2288
Fax: (317)237-2290
E-mail: toaoks@incable.org
URL: http://www.incable.org
Contact: Tim Oakes, Exec.Dir./Gen. Counsel
State.

5203 ■ Indiana Canine Assistant and Adolescent Network (ICAAN)
c/o Sally J. Irvin, PhD, Exec.Dir.
PO Box 53174A
Indianapolis, IN 46253-0174
Ph: (317)250-6450 (317)299-7678
E-mail: contact@icaan.net
URL: http://icaan.net
Contact: Sally J. Irvin PhD, Exec.Dir.
Founded: 2001. **Staff:** 3. **Budget:** $84,000. **Nonmembership**. **State**. Provides dog training as assistance dogs for people with physical disabilities while helping at-risk youth learn many valuable life skills. **Affiliated With:** Assistance Dogs of America. **Publications:** Report, annual. Alternate Formats: online.

5204 ■ Indiana Cast Metals Association (INCMA)
c/o Blake R. Jeffery, CAE, Exec.Dir.
PO Box 441743
Indianapolis, IN 46244
Ph: (317)974-1830
Fax: (317)974-1832
E-mail: incmaoffice@ameritech.net
URL: http://www.incma.org
Contact: Blake R. Jeffery CAE, Exec.Dir.
Founded: 1990. **State**. Educates and protects Indian foundries and foundry-related businesses.

5205 ■ Indiana Central Association of Diabetes Educators (ICADE)
1427 W 86th St., Ste.No. 126
Indianapolis, IN 46260
Ph: (317)398-5328
Fax: (317)472-0107
E-mail: dmiller@majorhospital.com
URL: http://www.icadegroup.org
Contact: Christy Parkin RN, Pres.
Local. Promotes the development of quality diabetes education for the diabetic consumer. Fosters communication and cooperation among individuals and organizations involved in diabetes patient education. Provides educational opportunities for the professional growth and development of members. **Affiliated With:** American Association of Diabetes Educators.

5206 ■ Indiana Chamber of Commerce (ICC)
115 W Washington St., Ste.850 S
Indianapolis, IN 46204-3420
Ph: (317)264-3110
Fax: (317)264-6855
E-mail: inchamber@indianachamber.com
URL: http://www.indianachamber.com
Contact: Kevin Brinegar, Pres.
Founded: 1922. **Members:** 5,500. **Staff:** 49. **State**. Businesses and other organizations. Promotes free enterprise, and the preservation and advancement of the business climate. Monitors legislative activity. Holds seminars and workshops. **Libraries: Type:** not open to the public. **Holdings:** 500. **Subjects:** business, economics. **Telecommunication Services:** electronic mail, kbrinegar@indianachamber.com. **Publications:** *ADA Guide*. Book. Guide for employers about their rights and responsibilities under the Americans With Disabilities Act. **Price:** $51.75 for members; $69.00 for nonmembers • *BizVoice*, bimonthly. Magazine. Features the Indiana business environment. **Advertising:** accepted. Alternate Formats: online • *Executive Quickline*, monthly. Newsletter • *Legislative Report*, weekly, during Indiana General Assembly. Newsletter • *Model Employee Policies for Indiana Employers*. Book. **Price:** $66.75 for members; $89.00 for nonmembers. Alternate Formats: CD-ROM • *Outlook*, bimonthly. Magazine • Annual Report, annual. **Conventions/Meetings:** semiannual board meeting • periodic conference.

5207 ■ Indiana Chapter of the American Society of Landscape Architects (INASLA)
PO Box 441777
Indianapolis, IN 46244
Ph: (317)767-9375
E-mail: emailinfo@inasla.org
URL: http://www.inasla.org
Contact: Scott Siefker, Pres.
State. Promotes the growth of the landscape architecture profession. Fosters high standards of quality in design, planning, development, and conservation in the field. Promotes the exchange of technical information and supports scientific research in all aspects of landscape architecture. **Telecommunication Services:** electronic mail, ssiefker@hntb.com. **Affiliated With:** American Society of Landscape Architects.

5208 ■ Indiana Chapter, Association of Legal Administrators
c/o Roz Hazzard, Pres.
Bingham McHale, LLP
2700 Market Tower
10 W Market St.
Indianapolis, IN 46204-2982
Ph: (317)968-5353
Fax: (317)236-9007
E-mail: rhazzard@binghammchale.com
URL: http://www.alaindiana.org
Contact: Roz Hazzard, Pres.
Local. **Affiliated With:** Association of Legal Administrators.

5209 ■ Indiana Chapter of the Names Project Foundation
The Damien Ctr.
1350 N Pennsylvania St.
Indianapolis, IN 46202
Ph: (317)632-0123
Fax: (317)632-4362
Free: (800)213-1163
E-mail: info@damien.org
URL: http://www.damien.org
Contact: Steve Thornton, Pres.
State. **Affiliated With:** Names Project Foundation - AIDS Memorial Quilt.

5210 ■ Indiana Chapter of the National Association of Drug Diversion Investigators
c/o Robert Bloss, Pres.
Indiana State Bd. of Pharmacy
402 W Washington St., Rm. W006
Indianapolis, IN 46204
Ph: (317)753-4025
E-mail: bobkoth@aol.com
URL: National Affiliate–www.naddi.org
Contact: Robert Bloss, Pres.
State. Represents the interests of individuals who are responsible for investigating and prosecuting pharmaceutical drug diversion. Seeks to improve the members' ability to investigate and prosecute pharmaceutical drug diversion. **Affiliated With:** National Association of Drug Diversion Investigators.

5211 ■ Indiana Civil Liberties Union (ICLU)
1032 E Washington St.
Indianapolis, IN 46202
Ph: (317)635-4059
Fax: (317)635-4105
E-mail: info@iclu.org
URL: http://www.iclu.org
Contact: Fran Quigley, Exec.Dir.
State. Champions the rights set forth in the Bill of Rights of the U.S. Constitution: freedom of speech, press, assembly, and religion; due process of law and fair trial; equality before the law regardless of race, color, sexual orientation, national origin, political opinion, or religious belief. Activities include litigation, advocacy, and public education. **Affiliated With:** American Civil Liberties Union.

5212 ■ Indiana Coal Council
c/o J. Nathan Noland, Pres.
144 W Market St., Ste.310
Indianapolis, IN 46204
Ph: (317)638-6997
Fax: (317)638-7031
E-mail: incoalco@in.net
State.

5213 ■ Indiana Coalition Against Domestic Violence (ICADV)
1915 W 18th St.
Indianapolis, IN 46202
Ph: (317)917-3685
Fax: (317)917-3695
Free: (800)332-7385
E-mail: icadv@violenceresource.org
URL: http://www.violenceresource.org
Contact: Jeffrey J. Gulley, Pres.
Founded: 1980. **Members:** 150. **Membership Dues:** organization, $100 (annual) • individual, $50 (annual). **Staff:** 7. **Budget:** $450,000. **State**. Unites to eradicate family violence through education and public awareness. Provides technical assistance, information, and referrals. **Libraries: Type:** open to the public. **Subjects:** all violence against women. **Awards:** Outstanding Service Awards. **Frequency:** annual. **Type:** recognition. **Telecommunication Services:** electronic mail, legalta@violenceresource.org. **Publications:** *Coalition Connection*, quarterly. Newsletter. **Advertising:** accepted. **Conventions/Meetings:** annual conference (exhibits) - always October in Indianapolis, IN.

5214 ■ Indiana Collie Club
c/o Patty Fox
9060 Nautical Watch Dr.
Indianapolis, IN 46236
URL: http://www.indianacollieclub.com/index.htm
Contact: Carter Corbrey, Corresponding Sec.
State. **Affiliated With:** American Kennel Club.

5215 ■ Indiana Commercial Board of Realtors
7150 Winton Dr., Ste.300
Indianapolis, IN 46268
Ph: (317)328-5259
Fax: (317)328-4629
E-mail: jwilliams@icbor.com
URL: http://www.icbor.com
Contact: Jackie Williams, Exec. Officer
State. Strives to develop real estate business practices. Advocates the right to own, use and transfer real property. Provides a facility for professional development, research and exchange of information among members and to the general public. **Affiliated With:** National Association of Realtors.

5216 ■ Indiana Constructors
c/o Charles V. Kahl, Exec.Dir.
One N Capitol Ave., Ste.300
Indianapolis, IN 46204-2026
Ph: (317)634-7547
Fax: (317)637-8791
E-mail: ici@indianaconstructors.org
State. **Affiliated With:** American Road and Transportation Builders Association.

5217 ■ Indiana Consumer Finance Association
c/o Louis Mahern, Exec.Dir.
One N Capitol, Ste.545
Indianapolis, IN 46204
Ph: (317)634-0374
Fax: (317)267-9694
Contact: Louis Mahern, Exec.Dir.
State.

5218 ■ Indiana Council of Community Mental Health Centers (ICCMHC)
c/o James F. Jones, Exec.Dir.
101 W Ohio St., Ste.610
Indianapolis, IN 46204
Ph: (317)684-3684
Fax: (317)684-3686
E-mail: iccmhc@iccmhc.org
URL: http://www.iccmhc.org
Contact: James F. Jones, Exec.Dir.
State.

5219 ■ Indiana Council on Outdoor Lightning Education (ICOLE)
PO Box 17351
Indianapolis, IN 46217
Ph: (812)988-0820
URL: http://icole.home.att.net/contact.html
Contact: Kevin Fleming, Contact
State. Astronomical societies, lighting and engineering groups, professional astronomers. Seeks to inform about the effects of nighttime lighting. Builds awareness about the problems that have effects on astronomy. Presents examples of good lighting design. Conducts speaker's bureau. Documents on good and bad lighting through photos and videos.

5220 ■ Indiana Counselors Association on Alcohol and Drug Abuse (ICAADA)
c/o Lynne Calaway, Office Mgr.
1800 N Meridian St., Ste.507
Indianapolis, IN 46202
Ph: (317)923-8800
Fax: (317)923-8860
E-mail: info@icaada.org
URL: http://www.icaada.org
Contact: Lynne Calaway, Office Mgr.
State. **Affiliated With:** NAADAC The Association for Addiction Professionals.

5221 ■ Indiana CPA Society (INCPAS)
8250 Woodfield Crossing Blvd., No. 100
Indianapolis, IN 46240-4348
Ph: (317)726-5000
Fax: (317)726-5005
E-mail: info@incpas.org
URL: http://www.incpas.org
Contact: Gary Bolinger CAE, Pres./CEO
State.

5222 ■ Indiana Credit Union League (ICUL)
c/o John McKenzie, Pres.
PO Box 50425
Indianapolis, IN 46250
Ph: (317)594-5300
Fax: (317)594-5301
Free: (800)285-5300
E-mail: email@icul.org
URL: http://www.icul.org
Contact: John McKenzie, Pres.
State.

5223 ■ Indiana Crime Prevention Coalition
c/o Scott Minier, Exec.Dir.
1229 N Delaware St.
Indianapolis, IN 46202
Ph: (317)464-1200
Fax: (317)464-1211
Free: (800)241-BITE
E-mail: info@indianamcgruff.com
Contact: Chari Burke, Contact
State.

5224 ■ Indiana Democratic Party
1 N Capitol Ave., Ste.200
Indianapolis, IN 46204
Ph: (317)231-7100
Free: (800)223-3387
E-mail: dparker@indems.org
URL: http://www.indems.org
Contact: Dan Parker, Chm.
State. **Affiliated With:** Democratic National Committee.

5225 ■ Indiana Dental Association (IDA)
401 W Michigan St., Ste.1000
PO Box 2467
Indianapolis, IN 46206-2467
Ph: (317)634-2610
Fax: (317)634-2612
E-mail: doug@indental.org
URL: http://www.indental.org
Contact: Douglas M. Bush, Exec.Dir.
Founded: 1858. **Members:** 2,600. **Staff:** 9. **State**. Dentists and dental students working to further the profession. **Publications:** *Indiana Dentist*, quarterly. Newsletter. **Price:** $10.00/year • Journal, quarterly. **Price:** $25.00 in U.S.; $40.00 outside U.S. **Conventions/Meetings:** annual convention (exhibits).

5226 ■ Indiana Dental Hygienists' Association (IDHA)
PO Box 24167
Indianapolis, IN 46224-0167
Ph: (317)634-2610
Fax: (317)634-2612
E-mail: doug@indental.org
URL: http://www.indental.org
Contact: Douglas M. Bush, Exec.Dir.
State.

5227 ■ Indiana District Amateur Athletic Union
c/o Emily Taylor
1420 Sadlier Cir., East Dr.
Indianapolis, IN 46239
Ph: (317)357-8790
Fax: (317)357-8791
URL: National Affiliate–aausports.org
Contact: Emily Taylor, Contact
State. **Affiliated With:** Amateur Athletic Union.

5228 ■ Indiana District of Precision Metalforming Association
c/o Dietra Rosenkoetter, Administrator
Mfg. Extension Partnership Center
6640 Intech Blvd., INTECH 10, Ste.120
Indianapolis, IN 46278-2012
Ph: (317)275-6812
Fax: (317)275-2375
E-mail: dietra@purdue.edu
URL: http://indiana.pma.org
Contact: Dietra Rosenkoetter, Administrator
State. Promotes and safeguards the interests of the metalforming industry. Conducts technical and educational programs. Provides legislative and regulatory assistance to members. **Affiliated With:** Precision Metalforming Association.

5229 ■ Indiana Energy Association
c/o Edwin J. Simcox, Pres.
1375 One Amer. Sq., Box 82065
Indianapolis, IN 46282
Ph: (317)632-4406
Fax: (317)262-4940
Contact: Ed Simcox, Pres.
State. **Formerly:** (2005) Indiana Electric Association.

5230 ■ Indiana Environmental Balancing Bureau
c/o SMACNA of Indiana
1 N Pennsylvania St., Ste.600
Indianapolis, IN 46204
Ph: (317)686-1180
Fax: (317)686-1890
E-mail: smcjo@aol.com
URL: National Affiliate–www.nebb.org
Contact: Phillip Gillespie, Chapter Coor.
State. Works to help architects, engineers, building owners, and contractors produce buildings with HVAC systems. Establishes and maintains industry standards, procedures, and specifications for testing, adjusting, and balancing work. **Affiliated With:** National Environmental Balancing Bureau.

5231 ■ Indiana Environmental Health Association (IEHA)
PO Box 457
Indianapolis, IN 46206-0457
Ph: (317)233-7168 (812)597-4778
Fax: (317)233-7387
E-mail: info@iehaind.org
URL: http://www.iehaind.org
Contact: Margaret Voyles, Sec.
Founded: 1951. **Members:** 430. **Membership Dues:** student, $5 (annual) • general, active, $25 (annual) • sustaining, $100 (annual). **Staff:** 1. **Regional Groups:** 8. **State**. Environmental health specialists and others involved in environmental health. **Awards: Frequency:** annual. **Type:** recognition. **Affiliated With:** International Association for Food Protection; National Environmental Health Association. **For-**

merly: (1986) Indiana Association of Sanitarians. **Publications:** *Indiana Journal of Environmental Health*, quarterly. **Price:** included in membership dues. **Circulation:** 430. **Advertising:** accepted. **Conventions/Meetings:** semiannual conference, educational (exhibits) - spring, fall.

5232 ■ Indiana Equipment Distributors
c/o Dave Ball, Pres.
PO Box 68555
Indianapolis, IN 46268-0555
Ph: (317)872-8410
URL: National Affiliate–www.aednet.org
Contact: Dave Ball, Pres.

State. Represents the interests of companies that sell, rent and service equipment used in construction, mining, forestry, power generation and industrial applications. Helps members enhance their success through networking, industry knowledge and education. **Affiliated With:** Associated Equipment Distributors.

5233 ■ Indiana Evaluation Association (IEA)
c/o Deborah Bonnet
D. Bonnet Associates
5325 Olympia Dr.
Indianapolis, IN 46228
Ph: (317)259-0071
E-mail: dbonnet@aol.com
URL: National Affiliate–www.eval.org
Contact: Deborah Bonnet, Contact

State. Seeks to improve evaluation practices and methods. Provides a forum for professional development, networking and exchange of practical, methodological and theoretical knowledge in the field of evaluation. Promotes evaluation as a profession. **Affiliated With:** American Evaluation Association.

5234 ■ Indiana Family, Career and Community Leaders of America (FCCLA)
c/o Ms. Jen Staley, State Adviser
Indiana Dept. of Educ.
State House, Rm. 229
Indianapolis, IN 46204
Ph: (317)232-9174
Fax: (317)232-9121
E-mail: jstaley@doe.state.in.us
URL: http://indianafccla.org
Contact: Ms. Jen Staley, State Adviser

Founded: 1946. **Members:** 4,900. **Membership Dues:** $700 (annual). **Local Groups:** 150. **State**. Boys and girls, grades 6-12, enrolled in family and consumer science classes. Prepares young people for balancing work and family in adult life and focuses on families, careers, and communities. Promotes leadership development. Conducts competitions. **Awards:** Hurst Scholarship. **Frequency:** annual. **Type:** monetary. **Recipient:** to a senior Indiana FCCLA member who will be entering college and planning to major in Family and Consumer Sciences related field of study • Jeremy K. Jackson Memorial Scholarship. **Frequency:** annual. **Type:** monetary. **Recipient:** to FCCLA member. **Formerly:** (1999) Future Homemakers of America, Indiana Association. **Publications:** *The Exchange*, semiannual. Newsletter. Includes chapter happenings. **Price:** free • Directory, annual. **Conventions/Meetings:** annual conference (exhibits) - always in Indianapolis, IN • State Leadership Conference (exhibits).

5235 ■ Indiana Farm Bureau
c/o Donald B. Villwock
PO Box 1290
Indianapolis, IN 46206
Ph: (317)692-7851
Fax: (317)692-7854
Free: (800)327-6287
E-mail: askus@infarmbureau.org
URL: http://www.infarmbureau.org
Contact: Donald B. Villwock, Pres.
State.

5236 ■ Indiana Federation of Republican Women
47 S Meridian St., Ste.200
Indianapolis, IN 46204
Ph: (317)635-7561
Fax: (317)632-8510
Free: (800)466-1087
E-mail: jsmith@indgop.org
URL: http://www.ifrw.net
Contact: Joyce Smith, Pres.
State.

5237 ■ Indiana Funeral Directors Association (IFDA)
c/o Curtis Rostad, Exec.Dir.
1305 W 96th St., Ste.A
Indianapolis, IN 46260-1193
Ph: (317)846-2448
Fax: (317)846-6534
Free: (800)458-0746
E-mail: info@indiana-fda.org
URL: http://www.indiana-fda.org
Contact: Curtis Rostad, Exec.Dir.

Founded: 1880. **Members:** 480. **State**. **Publications:** *Confidential Newsletter*, periodic • *IN-FU-DI-AS*, bimonthly. **Conventions/Meetings:** annual meeting - always May.

5238 ■ Indiana Gas Association
54 Monument Cir., Ste.500
Indianapolis, IN 46204
Ph: (317)639-5418
Fax: (317)639-6509
URL: http://www.indgasassoc.org
State.

5239 ■ Indiana German Heritage Society
401 E Michigan St.
Indianapolis, IN 46204
Ph: (317)464-9004
Fax: (317)630-0035
E-mail: mcgac@iupui.edu
URL: http://www-lib.iupui.edu/kade/
Contact: Dr. Giles Hoyt, Pres.

Founded: 1984. **Members:** 300. **Membership Dues:** individual, $20 (annual). **Regional Groups:** 2. **Languages:** English, German. **State**. Individuals interested in preserving the history of the German heritage in Indiana. Conducts research in conjunction with Max Kade German-American Center, Indianapolis. **Awards:** IGHS Scholarship. **Frequency:** annual. **Type:** scholarship. **Recipient:** for successful application and essay. **Committees:** Preservation. **Affiliated With:** Society for German-American Studies. **Publications:** *SIGA*, periodic. Monographs • Newsletter, quarterly. **Advertising:** not accepted. **Conventions/Meetings:** monthly assembly - always second Wednesday • annual symposium - always March.

5240 ■ Indiana Grant Makers Alliance
c/o Carol Simonetti, Pres./CEO
32 E Washington St., Ste.1100
Indianapolis, IN 46204-3583
Ph: (317)630-5200
Fax: (317)630-5210
E-mail: info@indianagrantmakers.org
URL: http://www.indianagrantmakers.org
Contact: Carol Simonetti, Pres./CEO

State. **Formerly:** (2005) Indiana Donors Alliance.

5241 ■ Indiana Grocery and Convenience Store Association (IGCSA)
PO Box 2186
Indianapolis, IN 46206-2186
Ph: (317)878-4231
Fax: (317)878-4251
Free: (800)222-4742
E-mail: igcsa@ix.netcom.com
URL: http://www.igcsa.net
State.

5242 ■ Indiana Ground Water Association
c/o Patty Conrad
7829 Prairie View Dr.
Indianapolis, IN 46256
E-mail: ingroundwater@msn.com
URL: National Affiliate–www.ngwa.org
Contact: Patty Conrad, Contact

State. Ground water drilling contractors; manufacturers and suppliers of drilling equipment; ground water scientists such as geologists, engineers, public health officials, and others interested in the problems of locating, developing, preserving, and using ground water supplies. **Affiliated With:** National Ground Water Association.

5243 ■ Indiana Hardwood Lumbermen's Association (IHLA)
c/o Ray Moistner, Exec.Dir.
3600 Woodview Trace, Ste.101
Indianapolis, IN 46268
Ph: (317)875-3660
Fax: (317)875-3661
Free: (800)640-4452
E-mail: info@ihla.org
URL: http://www.ihla.org
Contact: Ray Moistner, Exec.Dir.
State.

5244 ■ Indiana Health Care Association
c/o Arthur Logsdon
One N Capitol, Ste.1116
Indianapolis, IN 46204
Ph: (317)636-6406
Fax: (317)638-3749
E-mail: info@ihca.org
URL: http://www.ihca.org

State. **Affiliated With:** American Health Care Association.

5245 ■ Indiana High School Athletic Association (IHSAA)
c/o Blake Ress, Commissioner
PO Box 40650
Indianapolis, IN 46260
Ph: (317)846-6601
Fax: (317)575-4244
E-mail: brees@ihsaa.org
URL: http://www.ihsaa.org
Contact: Blake Ress, Commissioner

State. **Affiliated With:** National Federation of State High School Associations.

5246 ■ Indiana Horse Council (IHC)
225 S East St., Ste.738
Indianapolis, IN 46202
Ph: (317)692-7115 (317)692-7141
Fax: (317)692-7153
E-mail: inhorsecouncil@aol.com
URL: http://www.indianahorsecouncil.org
Contact: Mindi Vaughn, Development Dir.

Membership Dues: individual without insurance, $25 (annual) • family without insurance, $35 (annual) • youth, $15 (annual) • business, $100 (annual) • association, $75 (annual) • life, $200 • individual with insurance, $45 (annual) • family with insurance, $75 (annual). **State**. Promotes the interests of the horse industry in Indiana and aims to unite the said industry. **Publications:** *Take the Lead*, quarterly. Newsletter. **Price:** included in membership dues.

5247 ■ Indiana Hospital and Health Association (IHHA)
PO Box 82063
Indianapolis, IN 46282
Ph: (317)633-4870
Fax: (317)633-4875
E-mail: carmold@inhha.org
URL: http://www.inhha.org
Contact: Cathleen A. Arnold, Dir. of Member Services
State.

5248 ■ Indiana Hospital Purchasing and Materials Management Association
c/o Larry Gossman, Dir. of Supply Chain Management
Wishard Hea. Services
1001 W 10th St.
Indianapolis, IN 46202
Ph: (317)630-6217
Fax: (317)630-6187
E-mail: lawrence.gossman@wishard.edu
URL: National Affiliate–www.ahrmm.org
Contact: Larry Gossman, Dir. of Supply Chain Management
State. Represents purchasing agents and materials managers active in the field of purchasing, inventory, distribution and materials management as performed in hospitals, related patient care institutions and government and voluntary health organizations. Provides networking and educational opportunities for members. Develops new business ventures that ensure the financial stability of members. **Affiliated With:** Association for Healthcare Resource and Materials Management.

5249 ■ Indiana Hotel and Lodging Association (IHLA)
200 S Meridian St., Ste.350
Indianapolis, IN 46225
Ph: (317)673-4207
Fax: (317)673-4210
Free: (800)455-4468
E-mail: info@indianahotels.org
URL: http://www.indianahotels.org
Contact: Mr. John Livengood, Pres./CEO
Members: 200. **Membership Dues:** state and national association (35 or fewer rooms, with on-premise food service), $255 (annual) • state and national association (35 or fewer rooms without on-premise food service), $250 (annual) • per room, for state and national association (36-75 rooms with on-premise food service), $7 • per room, for state and national association (36-75 rooms without on-premise food service), $7 • per room, for state and national association (75 or more rooms with on-premise food service), $8 • per room, for state and national association (75 or more rooms without on-premise food service), $7 • per room, chapter add, $2 • regular/state membership only (for hotels with less than 35 rooms), $140 (annual) • allied (for state), $300 (annual) • allied (Indianapolis chapter), $100 (annual) • convention and visitors bureau (for state), $200 (annual) • convention and visitors bureau (Indianapolis chapter), $100 (annual). **Staff:** 10. **State**. Serves, promotes and represents the industry in the state by providing governmental affair services, training, and information to its members. Encourages professionalism and high ethical behavior. **Libraries: Type:** reference; open to the public; lending. **Holdings:** articles, books, periodicals, video recordings. **Subjects:** hotel and lodging industry, economics, training, education. **Awards:** Allied Member of the Year. **Frequency:** annual. **Type:** recognition. **Recipient:** nominated by peers for exemplary service and commitment to Indiana's hotel and lodging industry and/or the association • General Manager of the Year. **Frequency:** annual. **Type:** recognition. **Recipient:** nominated by peers for exemplary service and commitment to Indiana's hotel and lodging industry and/or the association • Legislator of the Year. **Frequency:** annual. **Type:** recognition. **Recipient:** nominated by peers for exemplary service and commitment to Indiana's hotel & lodging industry and/or the association • Star of the Industry. **Frequency:** annual. **Type:** recognition. **Recipient:** nominated by peers for exemplary service and commitment to Indiana's hotel and lodging industry and/or the association. **Computer Services:** database • electronic publishing • information services • mailing lists • online services. **Committees:** Executive; Governmental Affairs; Membership; Nominating. **Publications:** *InnSite Online*, monthly. Newsletter. Contains news about the association, members, industry issues, etc. **Price:** free. **Advertising:** accepted. Alternate Formats: online. **Conventions/Meetings:** annual Hoosier Hospitality - conference, educational and networking conference for all Indiana hospitality professionals (exhibits) - typically every March.

5250 ■ Indiana Humanities Council (IHC)
1500 N Delaware St.
Indianapolis, IN 46202-2419
Ph: (317)638-1500
Fax: (317)634-9503
Free: (800)675-8897
E-mail: ihc@iupui.edu
URL: http://www.ihc4u.org
Contact: Scott T. Massey, Pres./CEO
State. Encourages public understanding and utilization of the humanities. Promotes the application of the humanities in American life. **Affiliated With:** Federation of State Humanities Councils.

5251 ■ Indiana Industrial Energy Consumers (INDIEC)
c/o Jack Wickes, Exec.Dir./Counsel
1 Amer. Sq., Ste.2500
Indianapolis, IN 46282
Ph: (317)639-1210
Fax: (317)639-4882
E-mail: jwickes@lewis-kappes.com
URL: http://www.indiec.com
Contact: Jack Wickes, Exec.Dir./Counsel
State.

5252 ■ Indiana Karst Conservancy (IKC)
PO Box 2401
Indianapolis, IN 46206-2401
URL: http://www.caves.org/conservancy/ikc
Contact: Kriste Lindberg, Pres.
State.

5253 ■ Indiana Land Title Association (ILTA)
PO Box 20896
Indianapolis, IN 46220
Ph: (317)257-0360
Fax: (317)257-0362
Free: (800)929-4582
E-mail: inlta@aol.com
URL: http://www.indianalandtitle.org
Contact: Diana S. Nichols, Exec.Dir.
State. Represents the interests of abstracters, title insurance companies and attorneys specializing in real property law. Improves the skills and knowledge of providers in real property transactions.

5254 ■ Indiana Library Federation (ILF)
941 E 86th St., Ste.260
Indianapolis, IN 46240
Ph: (317)257-2040
Fax: (317)257-1389
E-mail: lkolb@ilfonline.org
URL: http://www.ilfonline.org
Contact: Linda D. Kolb, Exec.Dir.
Founded: 1891. **Members:** 3,000. **Membership Dues:** personal, active (based on annual income), $30-$75 (annual) • institutional (based on operating budget), $25-$150 (annual) • public library trustee, $25 (annual). **Staff:** 3. **Budget:** $400,000. **State**. Represents library and media center professionals and supporters. Fosters the professional growth of its members and the promotion of all libraries in Indiana. Works to create a strong sense of unity within the library community. **Awards:** Citizen's Award. **Frequency:** annual. **Type:** recognition. **Recipient:** for individual, corporate entity or group who has rendered outstanding services to Indiana libraries or media centers in the local community • Collaboration Award. **Frequency:** annual. **Type:** recognition. **Recipient:** for a corporation, organization, individual library or group of libraries that made significant contributions in promoting library services in the community, region, or at the statewide level • Outstanding Librarian Award. **Frequency:** annual. **Type:** recognition. **Recipient:** for excellence and innovative leadership in the development of library service • Outstanding Library Award. **Frequency:** annual. **Type:** recognition. **Recipient:** for outstanding library service that consistently exceeds the expectations of the users and serves as an exemplary model for other libraries. **Affiliated With:** American Library Association. **Formerly:** Indiana Library Trustee Association. **Publications:** *Focus on Indiana Libraries*, monthly. Newspaper. Features articles written by members and leaders. **Price:** $15.00. **Circulation:** 3,000. **Advertising:** accepted • *Indiana Libraries*, biennial. Journal. **Price:** $10.00. **Advertising:** accepted. **Conventions/Meetings:** annual conference.

5255 ■ Indiana Licensed Beverage Association (ILBA)
c/o Ronna Chappell, Exec.Dir.
48 S Pennsylvania, Ste.702
Indianapolis, IN 46204
Ph: (317)634-4384
Fax: (317)686-9812
Free: (800)843-5288
E-mail: ilba@aol.com
URL: National Affiliate–www.nlba.org
Founded: 1938. **Membership Dues:** $150 (annual). **Staff:** 2. **State Groups:** 1. **Local Groups:** 20. **State**. Bars, taverns, restaurants, cocktail lounges, and hotels selling alcoholic beverages for on-premises consumption. **Awards:** Legislators of the Year. **Frequency:** annual. **Type:** recognition • Tavern Owner of the Year. **Frequency:** annual. **Type:** recognition. **Affiliated With:** National Licensed Beverage Association. **Publications:** *ILBA News*, bimonthly. Newsletter. **Price:** included in membership dues. **Circulation:** 1,200. **Advertising:** accepted. **Conventions/Meetings:** annual meeting (exhibits).

5256 ■ Indiana Life and Health Insurance Guaranty Association
251 E Ohio St., Ste.1070
Indianapolis, IN 46204-2143
Ph: (317)692-0574
E-mail: jfunk@quadassoc.org
URL: http://www.inlifega.org
Contact: Jan Funk, Exec.Dir.
State. Promotes the life and health insurance guaranty industry. Provides coverage for resident policyholders of insurers licensed to do business and in the event of life or health insurer insolvency. **Affiliated With:** National Organization of Life and Health Insurance Guaranty Associations.

5257 ■ Indiana Lumber and Builders' Supply Association (ILBSA)
c/o Timothy J. Murphy, Exec.Dir.
3600 Woodview Trace, Ste.305
Indianapolis, IN 46268
Ph: (317)875-3737
Fax: (317)875-3717
Free: (877)465-8627
E-mail: info@ilbsa.org
URL: http://www.ilbsa.org
Contact: Timothy J. Murphy, Exec.Dir.
State.

5258 ■ Indiana Manufacturers Association (IMA)
1 Amer. Sq., Ste.2400
Box 82012
Indianapolis, IN 46282
Ph: (317)632-2474
Fax: (317)231-2320
Free: (800)462-7762
E-mail: ima@imaweb.com
URL: http://www.imaweb.com
Contact: Patrick J. Kiely, Pres.
State.

5259 ■ Indiana Medical Device Manufacturers Council (IMDMC)
Administrative Off.
PO Box 441385
Indianapolis, IN 46244
Ph: (317)951-1388
Fax: (317)974-1832
E-mail: imdmcoffice@ameritech.net
URL: http://www.imdmc.org
Contact: Blake Jeffery Sr., Exec.Dir.
Founded: 1991. **Members:** 60. **Membership Dues:** full (based on annual sales revenue), $700-$1,200 (annual) • associate, $475 (annual) • start up company, government employee, $300 (annual). **State**.

Companies and individuals involved in the manufacture of medical equipment. Serves as a spokesperson before legislatures and regulatory agencies. Provides training and information to the industry. Work to foster economic growth to benefit member companies and Indiana. **Committees:** Advocacy; Business Development; Education; Membership. **Publications:** *IMDMC News Update*, quarterly. Newsletter. Contains council and industry information. **Price:** included in membership dues. **Circulation:** 400. Alternate Formats: online. **Conventions/Meetings:** meeting - as scheduled • quarterly Regulatory Roundtable - meeting • periodic seminar.

5260 ■ Indiana Medical Group Management Association
9041 Colgate St.
Indianapolis, IN 46268-1210
Ph: (317)872-6156
Fax: (317)872-0795
E-mail: info@imgma.net
URL: http://www.imgma.net
Contact: Sarah Killion, Admin.Asst.
State. Promotes professional growth and development and visibility of the medical group managers. Provides variety of targeted educational opportunities to members of the organization. Provides opportunities for members to share and disseminate information of mutual interest. Maintains an active liaison with other key public and private organizations that affect the management, funding, and delivery of quality health care services. **Affiliated With:** Medical Group Management Association.

5261 ■ Indiana Mortgage Bankers Association (IMBA)
c/o Karen G. Burch, Exec.Dir.
1908 E 64th St., South Dr.
Indianapolis, IN 46220-2186
Ph: (317)251-0682
Fax: (317)259-4191
E-mail: imba@sbcglobal.net
URL: http://www.indianamba.org
Contact: Ms. Karen G. Burch, Exec.Dir.
Founded: 1958. **Members:** 155. **Membership Dues:** lender, $675 (annual) • vendor, $475 (annual) • not-for-profit, $250 (annual). **Staff:** 1. **Budget:** $200,000. **State Groups:** 1. **Local Groups:** 7. **State**. Provides services, support, and information to its members and promotes sound and ethical business practices consistent with industry standards. **Awards:** Distinguished Service Award. **Frequency:** annual. **Type:** recognition. **Recipient:** for an individual who has rendered years of consistent and exceptional service to the association. **Subgroups:** Duneland Chapter; Greater Indianapolis Chapter; North Central Chapter; Northeast Chapter; South Central Chapter; Southwest Chapter; Wabash Valley Chapter. **Affiliated With:** Mortgage Bankers Association. **Formerly:** (2004) Indiana Mortgage Bankers. **Conventions/Meetings:** annual convention, sponsors may display tables.

5262 ■ Indiana Mortgage Bankers Association, Greater Indianapolis Chapter (GIMBA)
Colonial Natl. Mortgage
9880 Westpoint Dr., Ste.500
Indianapolis, IN 46256
Ph: (317)842-9422
Fax: (317)570-5927
E-mail: darlis@colonialsavings.com
URL: http://www.indianamba.org/Chapters/GIMBA.htm
Contact: Darli Stoughton, Pres.
Local. Promotes fair and ethical lending practices and fosters professional excellence among real estate finance employees. Seeks to create an environment that enables members to invest in communities and achieve their business objectives. **Affiliated With:** Mortgage Bankers Association.

5263 ■ Indiana Motorcycle Dealers Association
c/o Timothy J. Dowling, Exec.VP
150 W Market St., Ste.812
Indianapolis, IN 46204
Ph: (317)635-1441
State.

5264 ■ Indiana National Congress of Parents and Teachers
2525 N Shadeland Ave., D-4
Indianapolis, IN 46219-1770
Ph: (317)357-5881
Fax: (317)357-3751
E-mail: pta@spitfire.net
URL: National Affiliate–www.pta.org
State. **Affiliated With:** National PTA - National Congress of Parents and Teachers.

5265 ■ Indiana Native Plant and Wildflower Society (INPAWS)
PO Box 30317
Indianapolis, IN 46230-0317
Ph: (317)263-9655
E-mail: kbhartlep@interdesign.com
URL: http://www.inpaws.org
Contact: Karen Hartlep, Pres.
State.

5266 ■ Indiana Non-Public Education Association (INPEA)
c/o Derek Redelman, Exec.Dir.
1400 N Meridian St.
Indianapolis, IN 46202-2367
Ph: (317)236-7329
Fax: (317)236-7328
E-mail: inpea@archindy.org
URL: http://www.inpea.org
Contact: Derek Redelman, Exec.Dir.
State. Provides representation to the Indiana State Department of Education, the Indiana General Assembly and other state, federal and private agencies that affect non-public education. Facilitates communications between non-public schools and government agencies, community leaders and private organizations. Affords opportunities for professional growth through educational conferences. Serves as an initiator and a clearinghouse for data and research. Advocates the right of parents to choose the appropriate formal education for their children.

5267 ■ Indiana Nonprofit Resource Network
c/o Indiana Association of United Ways
3901 N Meridian St., Ste.306
Indianapolis, IN 46208-4026
Fax: (317)921-1397
Free: (800)457-1450
E-mail: statewide@inrn.org
URL: http://www.INRN.org
Contact: Lisa Hanger, Contact
Founded: 1994. **Staff:** 8. **Budget:** $292,000. **Regional Groups:** 5. **Nonmembership**. **Local**. **Libraries: Type:** open to the public; lending. **Holdings:** 500; articles, books, video recordings. **Subjects:** governance, fund raising, personnel, volunteer management, community development. **Affiliated With:** United Way of America.

5268 ■ Indiana Norml
c/o Stephen W. Dillon
3601 N Pennsylvania St.
Indianapolis, IN 46205-3435
Ph: (317)923-9391
Fax: (317)924-2920
E-mail: inorml@inorml.org
URL: http://www.inorml.org
State. **Affiliated With:** National Organization for the Reform of Marijuana Laws.

5269 ■ Indiana Nursery and Landscape Association (INLA)
c/o Donna Sheets, CMP
6533 Margaret Ct.
Indianapolis, IN 46237
Ph: (317)889-2382
Fax: (317)889-3935
Free: (800)443-7336
E-mail: info@inla1.org
URL: http://www.inla1.org/
Founded: 1938. **Members:** 400. **Budget:** $250,000. **State**. **Formerly:** (1998) Indiana Association of Nurserymen.

5270 ■ Indiana Optometric Association (IOA)
c/o Todd J. Fettig, Pres.
201 N Illinois St., Ste.1920
Indianapolis, IN 46204
Ph: (317)237-3560
Fax: (317)237-3564
E-mail: todd@eyeassociates.com
URL: http://www.ioa.org
Contact: Todd J. Fettig, Pres.
Founded: 1897. **State**. Works to fulfill the vision and eye care needs of the public through clinical care, research, and education. **Affiliated With:** American Optometric Association.

5271 ■ Indiana Optometry Board
c/o Cindy Vaught, Board Dir.
Professional Licensing Agency
402 W Washington St., Rm. W072
Indianapolis, IN 46204
Ph: (317)234-2054
Fax: (317)233-4236
Free: (888)333-7515
E-mail: pla8@pla.in.gov
URL: http://www.in.gov/pla/bandc/iob
Contact: Cindy Vaught, Board Dir.
State. **Affiliated With:** Association of Regulatory Boards of Optometry.

5272 ■ Indiana Organization of Nurse Executives (IONE)
PO Box 82063
Indianapolis, IN 46282
Ph: (317)633-4870
E-mail: mrs@mail2maria.com
URL: http://www.indianaone.org
Contact: Marijane Smallwood, Pres.
State. Represents nurse leaders who improve healthcare. Provides leadership, professional development, advocacy and research. Advances the nursing administration practice and patient care. **Affiliated With:** American Organization of Nurse Executives.

5273 ■ Indiana Osteopathic Association
c/o Michael H. Claphan, CAE, Exec.Dir.
3520 Guion Rd., Ste.202
Indianapolis, IN 46222-1672
Ph: (317)926-3009
Fax: (317)926-3984
E-mail: info@inosteo.org
URL: http://www.inosteo.org
Contact: Michael H. Claphan CAE, Exec.Dir.
Founded: 1897. **Members:** 400. **Membership Dues:** active, $400 (annual) • associate, $50 (annual). **Staff:** 2. **Budget:** $300,000. **Regional Groups:** 6. **State**. Works to serve the Osteopathic Physicians of Indiana by providing quality continuing medical education and by working with the AOA to create a positive public and legislative awareness of osteopathic medicine. Provides a forum for practicing D.O.'s to initiate and implement changes that improve quality of care to the people of Indiana. **Awards:** Kinsinger Plaque. **Frequency:** annual. **Type:** recognition. **Recipient:** for outstanding contributions to the profession in Indiana. **Publications:** *Hoosier DO*, quarterly. Magazine. **Price:** included in membership dues. **Circulation:** 1,100. **Advertising:** accepted. **Conventions/Meetings:** annual meeting, educational program (exhibits).

5274 ■ Indiana Parents of Blind Children
c/o Tammy Hollingsworth
101 N Delbrick Ln.
Indianapolis, IN 46229
Ph: (317)899-1580
E-mail: parentime@comcast.net
URL: National Affiliate–www.nfb.org
Contact: Tammy Hollingsworth, Contact
State. Provides information and support to parents of blind children. Develops and expands resources available to parents and their children. Aims to eliminate discrimination and prejudice against the blind. **Affiliated With:** National Organization of Parents of Blind Children.

5275 ■ Indiana Perinatal Network (IPN)
2835 N Illinois St.
Indianapolis, IN 46208
Ph: (317)924-0825
Fax: (317)924-0831
E-mail: ipn@indianaperinatal.org
URL: http://www.indianaperinatal.org
Contact: Julia Brillhart RN, Exec.Dir.
State. Improves the health and safety of mothers, babies and families through education and collaborative partnerships of public and private organizations. **Affiliated With:** National Healthy Mothers, Healthy Babies Coalition.

5276 ■ Indiana Petroleum Marketers and Convenience Store Association
101 W Washington St., Ste.805E
Indianapolis, IN 46204-3413
Ph: (317)633-4662
Fax: (317)630-1827
E-mail: kbaber@ipca.org
URL: http://www.ipca.org
Contact: Scot Imus, Exec.Dir.
State.

5277 ■ Indiana Pharmacists Alliance (IPA)
729 N Pennsylvania St.
Indianapolis, IN 46204-1128
Ph: (317)634-4968
Fax: (317)632-1219
E-mail: ipalary@indianapharmacists.org
URL: http://www.indianapharmacists.org
Contact: Lawrence J. Sage, Exec.VP
Founded: 1998. **Members:** 1,700. **Membership Dues:** new active, new graduate, $135 (annual) • associate, $215 (annual) • technician, $35 (annual). **Staff:** 3. **State**. Promotes the interests of pharmacists and pharmacy technicians in Indiana. **Publications:** *ImPAct News*, monthly. Newsletter • *Indiana Pharmacist*, quarterly. Magazine. **Conventions/Meetings:** semiannual convention (exhibits).

5278 ■ Indiana Plant Food and Agricultural Chemicals Association (IPFACA)
c/o Cresswell Hizer, Pres.
2350 First Indiana Plz.
135 N Pennsylvania St.
Indianapolis, IN 46204
Ph: (317)632-4028
Fax: (317)687-9650
Free: (866)222-6943
E-mail: chizer@inagribiz.org
URL: http://www.inagribiz.org
State.

5279 ■ Indiana Podiatric Medical Association (IPMA)
201 N. Illinois St., No. 1910
Indianapolis, IN 46204
Ph: (317)237-3569
Fax: (317)237-3567
E-mail: inpma@tcon.net
URL: National Affiliate–www.apma.org
Contact: Virginia Jewell, Exec.Dir.
Founded: 1920. **Members:** 195. **Staff:** 3. **Regional Groups:** 2. Professional society of podiatrists. **Affiliated With:** American Podiatric Medical Association. **Formerly:** (1985) Indiana State Podiatry Association. **Publications:** *IPMA Newsletter*, monthly. **Conventions/Meetings:** annual meeting - always October, Indianapolis, IN.

5280 ■ Indiana Polygraph Association
8500 E 21st St.
Indianapolis, IN 46219
Ph: (317)899-8241
E-mail: mjames@isp.state.in.us
URL: http://www.indianapolygraphassociation.com
Contact: Mark James, Contact
State. Represents individuals dedicated to providing a valid and reliable means to verify the truth and establish the highest standards of moral, ethical, and professional conduct in the polygraph field. Establishes standards of ethical practices, techniques, instrumentation, research, advanced training and continuing educational programs. Provides a forum for the presentation and exchange of information derived from such research, training and education. **Affiliated With:** American Polygraph Association.

5281 ■ Indiana Primary Health Care Association (IPHCA)
1006 E Washington St., Ste.200
Indianapolis, IN 46202
Ph: (317)630-0845
Fax: (317)630-0849
E-mail: ddobbs@indianapca.org
URL: http://www.indianapca.org
Contact: Lisa Winternheimer, Exec.Dir.
Founded: 1982. **Membership Dues:** affiliate, $500 (annual). **State**. Advocates for quality health care for all those residing in Indiana. Supports the development of community oriented primary care initiatives that are affordable, available, accessible, appropriate and acceptable.

5282 ■ Indiana Professional Educators (IPE)
6919 E 10th St., Ste.E-3
Indianapolis, IN 46219
Ph: (317)356-2878
Fax: (317)356-2883
Free: (800)673-4734
E-mail: ipe@indy.net
URL: http://www.ipeteachers.org
Contact: H. Jane Ping, Pres.
State.

5283 ■ Indiana Psychiatric Society (IPS)
631 E New York St.
Indianapolis, IN 46202
Ph: (317)639-3406
Fax: (317)262-5609
E-mail: ims@imsonline.org
URL: http://www.indianapsych.org
Contact: Frederick Rauscher MD, Pres.
Local. **Affiliated With:** American Psychiatric Association.

5284 ■ Indiana Psychological Association
c/o Carol A. Caldwell, Exec.Dir.
1431 N Delaware St.
Indianapolis, IN 46202
Ph: (317)686-5348
Fax: (317)638-3540
E-mail: ipa@indy.net
URL: http://www.indianapsychologist.org
Contact: Carol A. Caldwell, Exec.Dir.
State. **Affiliated With:** American Psychological Association. **Publications:** *Indiana Psychologist*, quarterly. Newsletter • Membership Directory, annual. **Conventions/Meetings:** semiannual meeting - always spring and fall.

5285 ■ Indiana PTA
2525 N Shadeland Ave. D4
Indianapolis, IN 46219-1787
Ph: (317)357-5881
Fax: (317)357-3751
E-mail: pta@indianapta.org
URL: http://www.indianapta.org
Contact: Marilyn Jones, Pres.
State. Parents, teachers, students, and others interested in uniting the forces of home, school, and community. Promotes the welfare of children and youth.

5286 ■ Indiana Public Health Association
c/o Mary Beth Riner, DNS, Pres.
3838 N Rural St., Rm. No. 214
Indianapolis, IN 46205
Ph: (317)221-2392
Fax: (317)221-3006
E-mail: ipha@indy.net
URL: http://www.InPHA.org
Contact: Jerry King, Exec.Dir.
Practitioners and advocates for public health in Indiana, focusing on workforce development, improvements to the public health infrastructure and community awareness of public health policy priorities. **Affiliated With:** American Public Health Association.

5287 ■ Indiana Radiological Society
c/o Dotty Martens
322 Canal Walk
Indianapolis, IN 46202
Ph: (317)261-2060
Fax: (317)261-2076
E-mail: dmartens@ismanet.org
URL: http://www.inrad.org
Contact: Dotty Martens, Contact
State. Promotes the value of radiology, radiation oncology, nuclear medicine, medical physics and other related fields. Seeks to improve the quality of patient care and influence the socio-economics of the practice of radiology. Provides continuing education for radiology and allied health professionals. **Affiliated With:** American College of Radiology.

5288 ■ Indiana Ready-Mixed Concrete Association (IRMCA)
3500 DePauw Blvd., Ste.1081
Indianapolis, IN 46268-1136
Ph: (317)872-6302
Fax: (317)872-6313
E-mail: irmca@irmca.com
URL: http://www.irmca.com
Contact: Patrick Kiel, Exec.Dir.
Founded: 1943. **Members:** 74. **Budget:** $500,000. **Regional Groups:** 7. **Local**. Ready-mixed concrete producers and cement manufacturers. Seeks to extend the use of concrete by developing marketing aids and promotional materials. Conducts educational programs promoting the technology and economy of concrete construction. **Formerly:** (2005) Indiana Concrete Council. **Publications:** *Concrete Mixer*, periodic. Newsletter • *Directory of Organization and Membership*, annual • *Marketing Letter*, monthly. **Conventions/Meetings:** annual Concrete Workshop and Expo, multi-tube educational workshop - foam concrete contractor, specifying agency and engineer - always in February • annual meeting - in February and March.

5289 ■ Indiana Retail Council
c/o Grant Monahan, Pres.
One N Capitol, Ste.430
Indianapolis, IN 46204
Ph: (317)632-7391
Fax: (317)632-7399
E-mail: inretail@indy.net
URL: http://www.indianaretailers.com
Contact: Grant M. Monahan, Pres.
State. **Affiliated With:** National Retail Federation.

5290 ■ Indiana Retired Teachers Association
c/o Stephen C. Moberly, Exec.Dir.
150 W Market St., Ste.610
Indianapolis, IN 46204-2812
Ph: (317)637-7481
Fax: (317)637-9671
Free: (888)454-9333
E-mail: irta@iquest.net
URL: http://www.retiredteachers.org
Contact: Stephen C. Moberly, Exec.Dir.
Founded: 1950. **Members:** 23,192. **Membership Dues:** individual, $25 (annual). **State**. Promotes the welfare of Indiana's retired educators and encourages and perpetuates education within the state. Provides community leadership, service, and guidance. **Publications:** *The Bulletin Board*, quarterly. Newsletter. **Conventions/Meetings:** annual meeting, business meeting with representatives - always May.

5291 ■ Indiana Right to Life
55 Monument Cir., Ste.325
Indianapolis, IN 46204
Ph: (812)474-3195
Fax: (866)241-4681
E-mail: irtl@lovethemboth.com
URL: http://www.indianalife.org
Contact: Mike Fichter, Exec.Dir.
State. **Affiliated With:** National Right to Life Committee.

5292 ■ Indiana Romance Writers of America (IRWA)
PO Box 269038
Indianapolis, IN 46226
E-mail: absolute@indianarwa.com
URL: http://www.indianarwa.com
Contact: Rebecca Reagan, Pres.
State. Works to provide networking and support to individuals seriously pursuing a career in romance fiction. Helps writers become published and established in their writing field. **Affiliated With:** Romance Writers of America.

5293 ■ Indiana School-Age Consortium (ISAC)
c/o Roger Bower, Pres.
4755 Kingsway Dr., Ste.101
Indianapolis, IN 46205
Ph: (317)259-9491
Free: (888)704-8536
E-mail: rbower@ayskids.org
URL: http://www.indianasac.org
Contact: Roger Bower, Pres.
Founded: 1987. **State**.

5294 ■ Indiana School Boards Association (ISBA)
c/o Dr. Frank A. Bush, Exec.Dir.
1 N Capitol Ave., Ste.1215
Indianapolis, IN 46204-2026
Ph: (317)639-0330
Fax: (317)639-3591
E-mail: fbush@isba-ind.org
URL: http://www.isba-ind.org
Contact: Dr. Frank A. Bush, Exec.Dir.
State. Provides instruction to individual public school board members for the purpose of developing their ability to serve in that capacity.

5295 ■ Indiana Seed Trade Association
PO Box 441710
Indianapolis, IN 46244
Ph: (317)423-0307
Fax: (317)253-1668
Free: (888)572-2900
E-mail: sam@indianaseed.com
URL: http://www.indianaseed.com
Contact: Sam Turpin, Exec.Dir.
Local.

5296 ■ Indiana Self Storage Association
c/o Mike Lane
8605 Allisonville Rd., No. 208
Indianapolis, IN 46250
Fax: (217)241-4683
Free: (866)528-5230
E-mail: mike@p-a-m-s.com
URL: National Affiliate–www.selfstorage.org
Contact: Michael Lane, Contact
State. Represents owners and operators of self storage facilities. Works to improve the quality of management, customer service and facilities. Promotes public awareness of the self storage industry. Conducts educational meetings on management, marketing, security, and related topics. Lobbies for state legislation protecting and recognizing self storage owners and operators. **Affiliated With:** Self Storage Association.

5297 ■ Indiana Sheriffs' Association (ISA)
c/o D. Michael Eslinger, Exec.Dir.
PO Box 19127
Indianapolis, IN 46219
Ph: (317)356-3633
Fax: (317)356-3996
Free: (800)622-4779
E-mail: mike_eslinger@hotmail.com
URL: http://www.indianasheriffs.org
Contact: D. Michael Eslinger, Exec.Dir.
Founded: 1930. **Membership Dues:** associate, $24 (annual). **Staff:** 5. **State**. Educational and service organization comprised of the 92 county sheriffs, their deputies and other law-abiding citizens throughout the state. Formed to provide assistance to sheriffs of Indiana, their deputies and other department personnel, thereby enabling them to improve the delivery of law enforcement services to the citizens of the state.

5298 ■ Indiana SkillsUSA
c/o David Lechleitner, Dir.
State House, Rm. 229
Indianapolis, IN 46204
Ph: (317)232-9167 (260)639-6881
Fax: (317)232-9121
E-mail: dlech@doe.state.in.us
URL: http://www.indianaskillsusa.org
Contact: David Lechleitner, Dir.
State. Affiliated With: Skills USA - VICA. **Formerly:** (2006) Skills USA-VICA, Indiana.

5299 ■ Indiana Small Business Council
Indiana Chamber of Commerce
115 W Washington St., Ste.850 S
Indianapolis, IN 46244-0926
Ph: (317)264-3110
Fax: (317)264-6855
E-mail: jelkin@indianachamber.com
URL: http://www.indianachamber.com
Contact: Kevin Brinegar, Pres.
Local. Works to proactively and favorably impact the Indiana small business environment. **Affiliated With:** National Small Business Association.

5300 ■ Indiana Small Business Development Center
c/o Debbie Bishop Trocha, Exec.Dir.
One N Capitol, Ste.900
Indianapolis, IN 46204
Ph: (317)234-2082
Fax: (317)232-8872
E-mail: dtrocha@isbdc.org
URL: http://www.isbdc.org
Founded: 1985. **State**. **Affiliated With:** Association of Small Business Development Centers.

5301 ■ Indiana Society of Association Executives (ISAE)
c/o Sharon R. Gorup, CAE, Exec.Dir.
7150 Winton Dr., Ste.300
Indianapolis, IN 46268
Ph: (317)328-4569
Fax: (317)280-8527
E-mail: info@isae.org
URL: http://www.isae.org
Contact: Sharon R. Gorup CAE, Exec.Dir.
Founded: 1960. **Members:** 450. **Membership Dues:** master, $205 (annual) • secondary, $145 (annual) • associate, $245 (annual) • student, retired, $25 (annual). **Staff:** 2. **Budget:** $180,000. **State**. Professional trade association serving professionals within and affiliated to the association management industry in Indiana. **Awards:** ISAE Awards of Excellence. **Frequency:** annual. **Type:** recognition. **Recipient:** for members who are displaying excellence in association management. **Publications:** *Synergy*, quarterly. Newsletter. **Price:** included in membership dues. **Advertising:** accepted. Alternate Formats: online. **Conventions/Meetings:** annual convention (exhibits).

5302 ■ Indiana Society of Health-System Pharmacists (ISHP)
c/o Indiana Pharmacists Alliance
729 N Pennsylvania St.
Indianapolis, IN 46204-1128
Ph: (317)634-4968
Fax: (317)632-1219
E-mail: kbarker@theduponthospital.com
URL: http://www.indianapharmacists.org/ishp.html
Contact: Ken Barker, Pres.
State. Advances and supports the professional practice of pharmacists in hospitals and health systems. Serves as the collective voice on issues related to medication use and public health. **Affiliated With:** American Society of Health System Pharmacists.

5303 ■ Indiana Society for Healthcare Engineering (ISHE)
c/o William Matthews, Pres.
PO Box 40727
Indianapolis, IN 46240-0727
Ph: (219)738-5583
Fax: (219)738-5625
E-mail: wmatthews@methodisthospitals.org
URL: http://www.isheweb.org
Contact: William Matthews, Pres.
State. Hospital engineers, facilities managers, directors of buildings and grounds, assistant administrators, directors of maintenance, directors of clinical engineering, design and construction professionals, and safety officers. Works to: promote better patient care by encouraging and assisting members to develop their knowledge and increase their competence in the field of facilities management; cooperate with hospitals and allied associations in matters pertaining to facilities management; bring about closer cooperation among members; provide a medium for interchange of material relative to facilities management. **Affiliated With:** American Society for Healthcare Engineering of the American Hospital Association.

5304 ■ Indiana Society for Histotechnology (ISH)
c/o Cecelia Dodson
3510 Lesley Ave.
Indianapolis, IN 46218
Ph: (317)274-3438
E-mail: cdodson@clarian.org
URL: http://www.ish.iupui.edu
Contact: Cecelia Dodson, Pres.
State. Histology laboratory technicians, pathologists, laboratory equipment manufacturers' representatives, and interested individuals. Dedicated to the advancement of histotechnology and related sciences such as immunohistochemistry and molecular biology. Works to strengthen personal growth, leadership, education, and quality service to the medical community. Investigates health hazards in the laboratory and ensures the safety of the laboratory.

5305 ■ Indiana Society of Internal Medicine (ISIM)
c/o Richard R. King, Exec.Dir.
322 Canal Walk
Indianapolis, IN 46202-3252
Ph: (317)261-2060
Fax: (317)261-2076
Free: (800)257-4762
E-mail: rking@ismanet.org
URL: http://www.ismanet.org
State.

5306 ■ Indiana Society of Professional Engineers (ISPE)
c/o Lauraine M. Howe, Admin.Dir.
PO Box 20806
Indianapolis, IN 46220
Ph: (317)255-2267
Fax: (317)255-2530
E-mail: ispe@sbcglobal.net
URL: http://www.indspe.org
Contact: Lauraine M. Howe, Admin.Dir.
State.

5307 ■ Indiana Society of Professional Land Surveyors
c/o Dianne S. Bennett, Exec.Dir.
55 Monument Cir., Ste.1222
Indianapolis, IN 46204
Ph: (317)687-8859
Fax: (317)687-5053
E-mail: ispls@aol.com
URL: http://www.ispls.org
Contact: Dianne S. Bennett, Exec.Dir.
State. Works to provide the membership a professional identity, professional guidelines and direction, educational services and to promote the interests of the profession.

5308 ■ Indiana Society of Radiologic Technologists (ISORT)
c/o Karen M. Katz, Pres.
8330 Briarhill Way
Indianapolis, IN 46236-8181
Ph: (317)823-8440 (317)355-5488
Fax: (317)351-5487
E-mail: isort@comcast.net
URL: National Affiliate–www.asrt.org
State. Represents the interests of professionals working in the field of radiologic technology. Advances the science of radiologic technology through education, research and advocacy. Strengthens professional standards.

5309 ■ Indiana Soybean Growers Association (ISGA)
c/o Chris Novak, Exec.Dir.
5757 W 74th St.
Indianapolis, IN 46278-1755
Ph: (317)347-3620
Fax: (317)347-3626
E-mail: info@indianasoybeans.com
URL: http://www.indianasoybeans.com
Contact: Chris Novak, Exec.Dir.
State. Develops and implements policies to increase the profitability of its members and the entire soybean industry. **Affiliated With:** American Soybean Association.

5310 ■ Indiana Speech-Language-Hearing Association (ISHA)
c/o Ann Ninness, Exec.Dir.
PO Box 24167
Indianapolis, IN 46224-0167
Ph: (317)916-4146
Fax: (317)481-1825
E-mail: ann@centraloffice1.com
URL: http://www.islha.org
Contact: Kay Olges, Pres.
State.

5311 ■ Indiana Stamp Club (ISC)
PO Box 20005
Indianapolis, IN 46220-0005
E-mail: info@indianastampclub.org
URL: http://indianastampclub.org
Contact: Randy Marcy, VP
Members: 130. **Membership Dues:** individual, $15 (annual). **State**. Sponsors INDYPEX and Spring Stamp Fair. **Affiliated With:** American Philatelic Society. **Publications:** *Kicking Mule*, monthly. Newsletter. **Price:** included in membership dues. **Advertising:** accepted. **Conventions/Meetings:** monthly meeting - every 1st Monday.

5312 ■ Indiana State Assembly of the Association of Surgical Technologists
PO Box 421673
Indianapolis, IN 46242-1673
E-mail: weitlander@insightbb.com
URL: http://www.astindiana.com
Contact: Stephanie Ashley CST, Pres.
State. Represents surgical technologists. Aims to study, discuss, and exchange knowledge, experience, and ideas in the field of surgical technology. Promotes a high standard of surgical technology performance in the community for quality patient care. **Affiliated With:** Association of Surgical Technologists.

5313 ■ Indiana State Bar Association (ISBA)
c/o Thomas A. Pyrz, Exec.Dir.
1 Indiana Sq., Ste.530
Indianapolis, IN 46204
Ph: (317)639-5465
Fax: (317)266-2588
Free: (800)266-2581
E-mail: isbaadmin@inbar.org
URL: http://www.inbar.org
Contact: Thomas A. Pyrz, Exec.Dir.
State.

5314 ■ Indiana State Chiropractic Association (ISCA)
135 N Pennsylvania St., Ste.1600
Indianapolis, IN 46204
Ph: (317)684-5410
Fax: (317)684-5432
E-mail: jlhall@bosetreacy.com
URL: http://www.indianastatechiros.org
Contact: Joy Melnyk, Administrator
Founded: 1959. **Members:** 514. **Staff:** 4. **State**. Legislative advocacy organization for chiropractors. Conducts seminars. **Publications:** *ISCA Report*, bimonthly. Newsletter. **Advertising:** accepted. **Conventions/Meetings:** semiannual conference (exhibits) - always spring and fall, Indianapolis, IN.

5315 ■ Indiana State Employees Association (ISEA)
c/o David R. Larson, Exec.Dir.
1430 Sadlier Cir., Dr. E
Indianapolis, IN 46239-1054
Ph: (317)353-8675
Fax: (317)353-8679
E-mail: aesipleh@aol.com
URL: http://members.tripod.com/s4000employees
Contact: David R. Larson, Exec.Dir.
Founded: 1953. **Members:** 1,500. **Membership Dues:** life, $10,000. **Staff:** 3. **Budget:** $150,000. **Local Groups:** 63. **For-Profit**. **State**. Active retired local and state government employees. Seeks to improve career benefits, retirement benefits, and working conditions of state employees. **Publications:** *ISEA Legislative Newsbrief*, biweekly. Newsletter. **Advertising:** accepted • *ISEA MEMBERandum*, bimonthly • *ISEA Voice*, bimonthly. Newsletter. **Conventions/Meetings:** annual assembly - always September or October.

5316 ■ Indiana State Hispanic Chamber of Commerce (ISHCC)
c/o Manuel T. Gonzalez, Pres./CEO
2511 E 46th St.
Corporate Sq., S-U3
Indianapolis, IN 46205
Ph: (317)547-0200
Fax: (317)547-0210
E-mail: mgon@ishcc.com
URL: http://www.ishcc.com
Contact: Manuel T. Gonzalez, Pres./CEO
State.

5317 ■ Indiana State Library and Historical Bureau Foundation
c/o Pamela J. Bennett, Dir.
140 N Senate Ave.
Indianapolis, IN 46204
Ph: (317)232-2535
Fax: (317)232-3728
E-mail: pbennett@statelib.lib.in.us
URL: http://www.statelib.lib.in.us/www/ihb/giving
Contact: Pamela J. Bennett, Dir.
Founded: 2000. **Budget:** $50,000. **State**. Supports the purposes of the Indiana State Library and the Indiana Historical Bureau.

5318 ■ Indiana State Medical Association (ISMA)
c/o Richard R. King, II, Exec.Dir.
322 Canal Walk
Indianapolis, IN 46202-3268
Ph: (317)261-2060
Fax: (317)261-2076
Free: (800)257-4762
E-mail: rking@ismanet.org
URL: http://www.ismanet.org
Contact: Richard R. King II, Exec.Dir.
Founded: 1849. **State**.

5319 ■ Indiana State Museum Foundation
c/o J. Ronald Newlin, Exec.Dir.
650 W Washington St.
Indianapolis, IN 46204
Ph: (317)232-1637
Fax: (317)685-8320
URL: http://www.indianamuseum.org
State. Works to support the activities of the Indiana State Museum, a publicly-funded museum of natural and cultural history.

5320 ■ Indiana State Museum Volunteers
c/o Debbie Specht, Dir. of Volunteer Services
650 W Washington St.
Indianapolis, IN 46204-2725
Ph: (317)232-8351 (317)232-1637
Fax: (317)232-7090
E-mail: dspecht@dnr.state.in.us
URL: http://www.in.gov/ism
Contact: Debbie Specht, Dir. of Volunteer Services
Local. Works to further the mission and policies of the Department of Natural Resources and the Division of Indiana State Museum and Historic Sites, offering skills and services to all phases of the museum's functions.

5321 ■ Indiana State Nurses Association (ISNA)
2915 N High School Rd.
Indianapolis, IN 46224-2969
Ph: (317)299-4575
Fax: (317)297-3525
E-mail: info@indiananurses.org
URL: http://www.indiananurses.org
Contact: Ernest C. Klein Jr., Exec.Dir.
Founded: 1903. **Members:** 2,000. **Membership Dues:** employed, $261 (annual) • not employed, $130 (annual) • full-time student, individual (62 years or older and not earning more than the Social Security allows), $130 (annual) • individual (62 years or older and not employed or disabled), $65 (annual). **Staff:** 3. **Local Groups:** 20. **State**. Professional organization for registered nurses. **Awards:** Ethel Mae Payne Scholar Loan Program. **Frequency:** annual. **Type:** scholarship. **Recipient:** for a registered nurse member of ISNA. **Telecommunication Services:** electronic mail, klein@indiananurses.org. **Affiliated With:** American Nurses Association. **Publications:** *ISNA Bulletin*, quarterly. Newsletter • Survey. Alternate Formats: online. **Conventions/Meetings:** biennial convention (exhibits) - always fall.

5322 ■ Indiana State Racquetball Association
9507 Maple Way
Indianapolis, IN 46268
Ph: (317)847-6563
E-mail: ryan@insra.org
URL: http://www.insra.org
Contact: Ryan Griffin, Contact
State. **Affiliated With:** United States Racquetball Association.

5323 ■ Indiana State Rifle and Pistol Association (ISRPA)
c/o Jerry Wehner, Pres.
PO Box 24299
Indianapolis, IN 46224-0299
Ph: (219)462-0138
E-mail: membership@isrpa.org
URL: http://www.isrpa.org
Contact: Jerry Wehner, Pres.
Founded: 1966. **Local Groups:** 25. **State**. Promotes shooting sports activities in the state of Indiana. **Affiliated With:** National Rifle Association of America.

5324 ■ Indiana State Teachers Association (ISTA)
150 W Market St., Ste.900
Indianapolis, IN 46204
Ph: (317)263-3400
Free: (800)382-4037
E-mail: wwiliams@ista-in.org
URL: http://www.ista-in.org
Contact: Warren L. Williams, Exec.Dir.
State.

5325 ■ Indiana Statewide Association of Rural Electric Cooperatives
c/o Elmer Stocker, CEO, Exec.Dir.
PO Box 24517
Indianapolis, IN 46224
Ph: (317)487-2230
Fax: (317)247-5220
Free: (800)340-7362
E-mail: estocker@indremcs.org
URL: http://www.indremcs.org
Founded: 1935. **Members:** 37. **Budget:** $4,000,000. **State**. Service organization for rural electric cooperatives. **Publications:** *Electric Consumer*, periodic. **Conventions/Meetings:** bimonthly board meeting • periodic meeting • periodic workshop.

5326 ■ Indiana Subcontractors Association (ISA)
c/o Gary A. Price, Exec.Dir.
1209 Polk St.
Indianapolis, IN 46202
Ph: (317)685-0002
Fax: (317)684-9457
E-mail: gprice@mattisoncorp.com
URL: http://www.indianasubcontractors.org
Contact: Gary A. Price, Exec.Dir.
State.

5327 ■ Indiana Supreme Court Historical Society
c/o John R. Schaibley, III, Chm.
300 N Meridian St., Ste.2700
Indianapolis, IN 46204
Ph: (317)237-1283
Fax: (317)237-1000
E-mail: jrschaib@bakerd.com
URL: National Affiliate–www.supremecourthistory.org
Contact: John R. Schaibley III, Chm.
State. Collects and preserves the history of the Supreme Court of the United States. Conducts educational programs and supports historical research. Collects antiques and artifacts related to the Court's history. Increases public awareness of the Court's contributions to the nation's constitutional heritage. **Affiliated With:** Supreme Court Historical Society.

5328 ■ Indiana Telecommunications Association (ITA)
c/o John E. Koppin, CAE, Pres.
54 Monument Cir., Ste.200
Indianapolis, IN 46204
Ph: (317)635-1272
Fax: (317)635-0285
E-mail: john@itainfo.org
URL: http://www.itainfo.org
Contact: John E. Koppin CAE, Pres.
State.

5329 ■ Indiana Thoracic Society
c/o Sally Shewmaker, Administrator
9445 Delegates Row
Indianapolis, IN 46240
Ph: (317)573-3900
E-mail: sshewmaker@lungin.org
URL: National Affiliate–www.thoracic.org
Contact: Sally Shewmaker, Administrator
State. Aims to improve the study and practice of thoracic surgery and related disciplines. Seeks to prevent and fight respiratory diseases through research, education and patient advocacy. **Affiliated With:** American Thoracic Society.

5330 ■ Indiana Trial Lawyers Association (ITLA)
150 W Market St., Ste.210
Indianapolis, IN 46204
Ph: (317)634-8841
Fax: (317)634-4898
Free: (800)395-4852
E-mail: office@i-t-l-a.org
URL: http://www.i-t-l-a.org
Contact: Michealle B. Wilson, Exec.Dir.
State.

5331 ■ Indiana Triumph Cars (ITC)
7510 Allison Rd.
Indianapolis, IN 46250
Ph: (317)841-7677
Fax: (317)849-2001
E-mail: trrestore@aol.com
URL: http://www.geocities.com/motorcity/5270
Contact: Dan Miller, Pres.
State. **Affiliated With:** Vintage Triumph Register.

5332 ■ Indiana University Purdue University Association for Computing Machinery Student Siggraph
c/o Ed Sullivan
Dept. of Mechanical Engg. Tech.
723 W. Michigan St.
Indianapolis, IN 46202
Ph: (317)278-3814
Fax: (317)274-9702
E-mail: tldowell@uiupui.edu
URL: http://campus.acm.org
Affiliated With: Association for Computing Machinery.

5333 ■ Indiana Veterinary Medical Association (IVMA)
201 S Capitol Ave., Ste.405
Indianapolis, IN 46225
Ph: (317)974-0888
Fax: (317)974-0985
Free: (800)270-0747
E-mail: info@invma.org
URL: http://www.invma.org
Contact: Lisa A. Perius, Exec.Dir.
State. Represents state's veterinarian. Seeks to advance organized veterinary medicine in Indiana. **Affiliated With:** American Veterinary Medical Association.

5334 ■ Indiana Water Resources Association (IWRA)
8204 Claridge Rd.
Indianapolis, IN 46260-4914
Ph: (765)494-1194
E-mail: frankenb@purdue.edu
URL: http://www.valpo.edu/organization/xiwra
Contact: Jane Frankenberger, Pres.
State. Seeks to advance water resources research, planning, development, and management. Collects, organizes and disseminates ideas and information in the field of water resources science and technology. **Affiliated With:** American Water Resources Association.

5335 ■ Indiana Wholesale Distributors
c/o Paul A. Scali
603 E Washington St.
Indianapolis, IN 46204
Ph: (317)423-7087
Fax: (317)921-0740
E-mail: iwdainc@hotmail.com
Contact: Paul Scali, Exec.Dir.
State.

5336 ■ Indiana Youth Group (IYG)
PO Box 20716
Indianapolis, IN 46220-0716
Ph: (317)541-8726
Fax: (317)545-8594
E-mail: info@indianayouthgroup.org
URL: http://www.indianayouthgroup.org
Contact: Ms. Jill Thomas, Program Coor.
Founded: 1987. **Members:** 250. **Staff:** 6. **Budget:** $200,639. **Regional Groups:** 3. **State**. Supports and educates self-identified gay, lesbian and bisexual young people aged 12-20. **Formerly:** (1998) Indianapolis Youth Group. **Publications:** *Reachout*, quarterly. Newsletter. **Circulation:** 2,000. **Advertising:** accepted. **Conventions/Meetings:** annual seminar, leadership training - September.

5337 ■ Indiana Youth Institute (IYI)
603 E Washington St., Ste.800
Indianapolis, IN 46204-2647
Ph: (317)396-2700
Fax: (317)396-2701
Free: (800)343-7060
E-mail: iyi@iyi.org
URL: http://www.iyi.org
Contact: Bill Stanczykiewicz, Pres./CEO
Founded: 1988. **Staff:** 15. **State**. Promotes the healthy development of children and youth by serving the institutions and people of Indiana who work on their behalf. **Libraries: Type:** open to the public. **Holdings:** 17,000. **Subjects:** social science, youth, community development. **Awards:** Youth Investment Award. **Frequency:** annual. **Type:** scholarship. **Publications:** *Blueprint*, quarterly. Newsletter. ISSN: 1085-0562. **Circulation:** 5,000 • *Building Relationships with Parents and Families in School-Age Programs*. Manual. **Price:** $17.50/copy • *Kids Count in Indiana*, annual. Journal • *Youth Worker Booklet* • Annual Report. **Conventions/Meetings:** annual workshop (exhibits).

5338 ■ Indianapolis Ambassadors
c/o Angela Shores, Pres.
PO Box 502067
Indianapolis, IN 46250-7067
Ph: (317)767-5990
E-mail: info@indyambassadors.org
URL: http://www.indyambassadors.org
Contact: Angela Shores, Pres.
Local. Coordinates volunteer efforts throughout central Indianapolis. Provides volunteer opportunities including: Pacers, Fever and Firebird games, Indiana Repertory Theater events, tutoring, Goodwill, Julian Center, and Children's Museum.

5339 ■ Indianapolis Association of Black Journalists
PO Box 441795
Indianapolis, IN 46244
Ph: (317)444-2814
E-mail: mbdabney@yahoo.com
URL: National Affiliate–www.nabj.org
Contact: Michael Dabney, Pres.
Local. Advocates the rights of black journalists. Provides informational and training services and professional development to black journalists and to the general public. **Affiliated With:** National Association of Black Journalists.

5340 ■ Indianapolis BMW Club No. 17
c/o Dom LoDuca, Treas.
417 Buckingham Dr.
Indianapolis, IN 46208
Ph: (317)283-4010
E-mail: dloduca@indy.rr.com
URL: http://www.geocities.com/motorcity/garage/8514/
Contact: Lew Mumford, Pres.
Local. BMW motorcycle owners organized for pleasure, recreation, safety, and dissemination of information concerning BMW motorcycles. **Affiliated With:** BMW Motorcycle Owners of America.

5341 ■ Indianapolis Chapel Hill Lions Club
8206 Rockville Rd., No. 215
Indianapolis, IN 46214
Ph: (317)246-7306 (317)290-9343
E-mail: rsnyder@thesnydergroup.com
URL: http://indianapolischapelhill.lionwap.org
Contact: Bob Snyder, Pres.
Local. **Affiliated With:** Lions Clubs International.

5342 ■ Indianapolis Children's Choir (ICC)
4600 Sunset Ave.
Indianapolis, IN 46208
Ph: (317)940-9640
Fax: (317)940-6129
E-mail: info@icchoir.org
URL: http://www.icchoir.org
Contact: Steven Stolen, Exec.Dir.
Local. Promotes artistic excellence especially in choral performance.

5343 ■ Indianapolis Coin Club
c/o Gail Phillips
PO Box 2897
Indianapolis, IN 46206
E-mail: indianapoliscoinclub@yahoo.com
URL: National Affiliate–www.money.org
Contact: Gail Phillips, Contact

Local. Affiliated With: American Numismatic Association.

5344 ■ Indianapolis Convention and Visitors Association (ICVA)
One RCA Dome, Ste.100
Indianapolis, IN 46225
Ph: (317)639-4282
Fax: (317)639-5273
Free: (800)958-INDY
E-mail: icva@indianapolis.org
URL: http://www.indy.org
Contact: Robert F. Bedell, Pres./CEO

Founded: 1923. **Members:** 835. **Staff:** 45. **Budget:** $9,100,000. **Local.** Serves directly or indirectly visitors' or delegates' needs with a positive impact on the guests' experience. Promotes business and tourism in the Indianapolis, IN area. **Publications:** *Inside Indy*, quarterly. Newsletter. Contains sales and group tour information. • *Member Update*, quarterly. Newsletter • *This is Indianapolis Visitors Guide*, semiannual. Magazine. Contains listing of attractions, maps, stories, and calendar of events. **Price:** free. **Circulation:** 300,000. **Advertising:** accepted.

5345 ■ Indianapolis Corvette Club
c/o Alan Smith
9647 E 96th St.
Indianapolis, IN 46256-9323
Ph: (317)841-9877
URL: http://www.indianaregion.com
Contact: Alan Smith, Contact

Local. Affiliated With: National Council of Corvette Clubs.

5346 ■ Indianapolis District Dental Society (IDDS)
8780 Purdue Rd., Ste.8
Indianapolis, IN 46268-1173
Ph: (317)471-8131
Fax: (317)471-8147
E-mail: sperry@indydentalsociety.org
URL: http://www.indydentalsociety.org
Contact: Ms. Carolyn Hansen, Exec.Dir.

Local. Represents the interests of dentists committed to the public's oral health, ethics and professional development. Encourages the improvement of the public's oral health and promotes the art and science of dentistry. **Affiliated With:** American Dental Association; Indiana Dental Association.

5347 ■ Indianapolis Fencing Club (IFC)
c/o Tim Mills, Sec.
9455 Intl. Ln.
Indianapolis, IN 46268
E-mail: tim@indyfencing.com
URL: http://www.indyfencing.com
Contact: Tim Mills, Sec.

State. Amateur fencers. **Affiliated With:** United States Fencing Association.

5348 ■ Indianapolis Foundation
c/o Brian Payne, Pres.
615 N Alabama St., Ste.119
Indianapolis, IN 46204
Ph: (317)634-2423
Fax: (317)684-0943
E-mail: info@cicf.org
URL: http://www.cicf.org
Contact: Brian Payne, Pres.

Founded: 1916. **Local.**

5349 ■ Indianapolis Franklin Township Lions Club
PO Box 39223
Indianapolis, IN 46239
Ph: (317)861-0755
E-mail: indyftlions@mac.com
URL: http://homepage.mac.com/franklintwpchamber/indyftlions.htm

Local. Affiliated With: Lions Clubs International.

5350 ■ Indianapolis Historic Preservation Commission (IHPC)
City-County Bldg.
200 E Washington St., Ste.1801
Indianapolis, IN 46204
Ph: (317)327-4406
Fax: (317)327-4407
E-mail: dbaker@indygov.org
URL: http://www.indygov.org/eGov/City/DMD/IHPC/home.htm
Contact: David L. Baker, Administrator

Local. Provides approval, design and zoning review for historically designated local districts.

5351 ■ Indianapolis Medical Society (IMS)
631 E New York St.
Indianapolis, IN 46202
Ph: (317)639-3406
Fax: (317)262-5609
E-mail: ims@imsonline.org
URL: http://www.imsonline.org
Contact: Beverly Hurt, Exec.VP

Founded: 1848. **Local.**

5352 ■ Indianapolis Memorial Society
5806 E 56th St.
Indianapolis, IN 46226
Ph: (317)844-1371 (317)545-6005
URL: National Affiliate–www.funerals.org
Contact: Mary Hirsch, Pres.

Local. Affiliated With: Funeral Consumers Alliance.

5353 ■ Indianapolis Musicians - Local 3, American Federation of Musicians
325 N Delaware St.
Indianapolis, IN 46204
Ph: (317)636-3595
Fax: (317)636-3596
E-mail: indymusicians@sbcglobal.net
URL: http://www.indymusicians.com
Contact: J. Michael Lucas, Pres.

Local. AFL-CIO. Musicians. Seeks to improve the wages and working conditions of professional musicians. **Affiliated With:** American Federation of Musicians of the United States and Canada. **Formerly:** (2005) Indianapolis Musicians' Association - Local 3, American Federation of Musicians.

5354 ■ Indianapolis Organization Development Network
c/o Kim Chesky
8622 Sargent Creek Ln.
Indianapolis, IN 46256
Ph: (317)979-0777
Fax: (317)570-0435
E-mail: kimchesky@netscape.net
URL: National Affiliate–www.odnetwork.org
Contact: Kim Chesky, Contact

Local. Affiliated With: Organization Development Network.

5355 ■ Indianapolis RSVP
c/o Kyle Ciresi, Dir.
901 S Shelby St., Rm. 324
Indianapolis, IN 46203
Ph: (317)791-5941
Fax: (317)791-5945
E-mail: cac-rsvp@uindy.edu
URL: http://www.seniorcorps.gov/about/programs/rsvp_state.asp?usestateabbr=in&Search4.x=12&Search4.y=4
Contact: Kyle Ciresi, Dir.

Local. Affiliated With: Retired and Senior Volunteer Program.

5356 ■ Indianapolis Traditional Music and Dance Group (ITMDG)
c/o Fiona Solkowski, Pres.
PO Box 44284
Indianapolis, IN 46244
Ph: (317)373-3631
E-mail: fsolkowski@tnc.org
URL: http://www.indycontra.org
Contact: Fiona Solkowski, Pres.

Founded: 1970. **Members:** 60. **Membership Dues:** individual, $12 (annual). **Local.** Supports and promotes the history, artistry and enjoyment of American traditional folk dance and music, provides demonstration and teaches dances for festivals, events, and schools. **Publications:** Newsletter, quarterly. Contains a schedule of bands and callers. **Conventions/Meetings:** bimonthly board meeting • annual Gypsy Moon Ball - meeting, weekend costume contra dance - last weekend in October.

5357 ■ Indianapolis Urban League
777 Indiana Ave.
Indianapolis, IN 46202
Ph: (317)693-7603
Fax: (317)693-7613
E-mail: gneal@indplsul.org
URL: http://www.indplsul.org
Contact: Mr. Joseph A. Slash, Pres./CEO

Founded: 1965. **Members:** 450. **Membership Dues:** student, $5 (annual) • organization, $30-$500 (annual) • corporation, $1,000 (annual). **Staff:** 25. **Budget:** $18,000,000. **State Groups:** 5. **Local Groups:** 1. **Local.** Assists African-Americans, other minorities and the disadvantaged to achieve social and economic equality. **Libraries: Type:** open to the public. **Holdings:** 50; articles, books, video recordings. **Subjects:** economics, youth, education, health, public policy, civil rights, politics, housing. **Awards: Frequency:** annual. **Type:** recognition. **Recipient:** for supporting the IUL's advocacy and programs • **Frequency:** annual. **Type:** scholarship. **Recipient:** scholastic achievement. **Affiliated With:** National Urban League. **Publications:** *Equality*, semiannual. Newsletter. Covers programs and services. **Circulation:** 1,500. **Conventions/Meetings:** annual meeting, yearly report to membership and election of board members.

5358 ■ Indianapolis Zoo
c/o Michael I. Crowther, Pres./CEO
1200 W Washington St.
Indianapolis, IN 46222
Ph: (317)630-2001
Fax: (317)630-5153
E-mail: info@indyzoo.com
URL: http://www.indianapoliszoo.com
Contact: Michael I. Crowther, Pres./CEO

Local. Additional Websites: http://www.whiterivergardens.com.

5359 ■ Indy African Violet Club
c/o Laurie Mitchell
8430 Christiana Ln.
Indianapolis, IN 46201
Ph: (317)570-9643
E-mail: turtles2@att.net
URL: National Affiliate–www.avsa.org
Contact: Laurie Mitchell, Contact

Local. Affiliated With: African Violet Society of America.

5360 ■ Indy 'G' Walkers
c/o Clarence Wright
PO Box 269001
Indianapolis, IN 46226-9001
Ph: (317)357-8464
E-mail: cgt152@aol.com
URL: National Affiliate–www.ava.org
Contact: Clarence Wright, Contact

Founded: 1981. **Membership Dues:** single, $5 (annual) • family, $8 (annual). **State Groups:** 1. **Regional.** Non-competitive sports enthusiasts. **Affiliated With:** American Volkssport Association. **Publications:** Brochure. Contains information on walking events. **Conventions/Meetings:** monthly general assembly (exhibits) - always third Monday.

5361 ■ Indy South Association of Insurance and Financial Advisors
c/o Barbara Anne Williams, Pres.
PO Box 17486
Indianapolis, IN 46227
Ph: (317)889-3333
Fax: (317)883-4834
E-mail: gtaphorn@famersagent.com
URL: National Affiliate–naifa.org
Contact: Barbara Anne Williams, Pres.
Local.

5362 ■ Indy Swing Dance Club
PO Box 68361
Indianapolis, IN 46268
Ph: (317)691-1239
E-mail: isdc@indyswing.org
URL: http://www.indyswing.org
Contact: Cary Petite, Pres.
Local. Promotes Swing Dancing to the general public as a form of recreation and rehabilitation. Seeks to further communication, profile informational services and keep records for the Swing Dance community.

5363 ■ Indy West Daybreakers Kiwanis Club
55 N Mission Dr.
Indianapolis, IN 46214
URL: http://www.indy-kiwanis.com/index.html
Contact: Dan Gammon, Pres.
Local.

5364 ■ Indy Z Car Club
c/o Jeff Caldwell, Pres./Ed.
1447 S Beulah Ave.
Indianapolis, IN 46241-3903
Ph: (317)240-1071
E-mail: izccinfo@indyzcar.com
URL: http://members.aol.com/KarlWS/IndyZCar.html
Contact: Jeff Caldwell, Pres./Ed.
Local. Affiliated With: Z Car Club Association.

5365 ■ Information and Referral Network (IRN)
PO Box 30530
Indianapolis, IN 46230
Ph: (317)920-4850 (317)926-4357
Fax: (317)920-4885
E-mail: irnadmin@irni.org
URL: http://www.irni.org
Contact: Scott Burns, Chm.
Local. Facilitates connections between people who need human service and those who provide them.

5366 ■ Information Systems Audit and Control Association, Central Indiana Chapter
PO Box 441257
Indianapolis, IN 46244-1257
Ph: (317)715-7352
E-mail: president@indyisaca.org
URL: http://www.indyisaca.org
Contact: Dennis Hattabaugh CISA, Pres.
Local. Affiliated With: Information Systems Audit and Control Association and Foundation.

5367 ■ Information Systems Security Association, Central Indiana Chapter
1427 W 86th St., Box 168
Indianapolis, IN 46260
E-mail: general.kearney@va.gov
URL: http://www.ci-issa.org
Contact: General Kearney, Pres.
Local. Represents information security professionals and practitioners. Enhances the knowledge, skill and professional growth of members. Provides educational forums and peer interaction opportunities. **Affiliated With:** Information Systems Security Association.

5368 ■ Inroads, Indiana
c/o Randall E. Flagg, Managing Dir.
9465 Counselor's Row
Indianapolis, IN 46204
Ph: (317)634-0111 (317)805-4747
Fax: (317)632-2170
E-mail: rflagg@inroads.org
URL: http://www.inroads.org
Contact: Randall E. Flagg, Managing Dir.
Founded: 1987. **Local.** Prepares black, Hispanic, and Native American high school and college students for leadership positions within major American business corporations and in their own communities. **Affiliated With:** INROADS.

5369 ■ Institute of Packaging Professionals, Central Indiana Chapter
c/o Caesar E. Watkins
6823 Eagles Ct.
Indianapolis, IN 46214
Ph: (317)299-6636
Fax: (317)297-1279
E-mail: ioppcentralindiana@sbcglobal.net
URL: National Affiliate–www.iopp.org
Contact: Greg Etzler, Pres.
Local. Affiliated With: Institute of Packaging Professionals.

5370 ■ Institute of Real Estate Management - Indianapolis Chapter No. 24
c/o Julie Dowrey
PO Box 90403
Indianapolis, IN 46290-0403
Ph: (317)815-0163
Fax: (317)706-0281
E-mail: iremoffice@aol.com
URL: National Affiliate–www.irem.org
Contact: Michael E. Gorman CPM, Pres.
Local. Represents real property and asset management professionals. Works to promote professional ethics and standards in the field of property management. Strives to keep its members informed on the latest legislative activities and current industry trends. Provides classroom training, continuing education seminars, job referral service and candidate assistance services to enhance the effectiveness and professionalism of its members. **Affiliated With:** Institute of Real Estate Management.

5371 ■ Insurance Institute of Indiana
c/o Stephen A. Williams, Pres.
201 N Illinois St., Ste.1410
Indianapolis, IN 46204
Ph: (317)464-2450
Fax: (317)464-2460
E-mail: saw@insuranceinstitute.org
URL: http://www.insuranceinstitute.org
Contact: Stephen A. Williams, Pres.
State.

5372 ■ International Association of Business Communicators, Indianapolis Chapter
PO Box 44108
Indianapolis, IN 46244
Ph: (317)767-4446
E-mail: tsiefert@salliemae.com
Contact: Tina Siefert, Pres.
Local. Represents the interests of communication managers, public relations directors, writers, editors and audiovisual specialists. Encourages establishment of college-level programs in organizational communication. Conducts surveys on employee communication effectiveness and media trends. Conducts research in the field of communication. **Affiliated With:** International Association of Business Communicators.

5373 ■ International Association of Heat and Frost Insulators and Asbestos Workers, Local 18
3302 S East St.
Indianapolis, IN 46227
Ph: (317)786-3216
E-mail: local18@sbcglobal.net
URL: http://www.insulators18.org
Local.

5374 ■ International Association of Machinists and Aerospace Workers, AFL-CIO, CLC - District Lodge 90
5638 Professional Cir., Ste.201
Indianapolis, IN 46241-5022
Ph: (317)247-8488
E-mail: sillime@insightbb.com
URL: http://home.comcast.net/~iamawd90
Contact: Ron Butler, Pres.
Members: 8,158. **Regional. Affiliated With:** International Association of Machinists and Aerospace Workers.

5375 ■ International Coach Federation, Greater Indianapolis Chapter
c/o Jim Patton, Treas.
7945 Midlothian Way
Indianapolis, IN 46214
Ph: (317)319-3523
E-mail: treasurer@icfindy.com
URL: http://www.icfindy.com
Contact: Jim Patton, Treas.
Local.

5376 ■ International Facility Management Association, Indianapolis (IFMA)
c/o Norman E. Smiley, CFM, Bldg.Mgr., VP
PO Box 40303
Indianapolis, IN 46240
Ph: (317)514-8114
Fax: (317)581-1594
E-mail: indyifma@aol.com
Contact: Norman E. Smiley, CFM, Bldg.Mgr., VP
State. Facility managers representing all types of organizations including banks, insurance companies, hospitals, colleges and universities, utility companies, electronic equipment manufacturers, petroleum companies, museums, auditoriums, and federal, state, provincial, and local governments. Works to enhance the professional goals of persons involved or interested in the field of facility management (the planning, designing, and managing of workplaces). **Affiliated With:** International Facility Management Association.

5377 ■ International Interior Design Association, Indiana Chapter
c/o Melissa E. Rogers, Exec.Dir.
IIDA Off.
PO Box 20726
Indianapolis, IN 46220
Ph: (317)255-4980
Fax: (317)259-4810
E-mail: iidaoffice@aol.com
URL: National Affiliate–www.iida.org
Contact: Melissa E. Rogers, Exec.Dir.
Committed to enhancing the quality of life through excellence in interior design and advancing interior design through knowledge. **Affiliated With:** International Interior Design Association.

5378 ■ International Union of Elevator Constructors, Local 34 - Indianapolis, Indiana
2206 E Werges Ave.
Indianapolis, IN 46237-1025
Ph: (317)536-8173
E-mail: joea@iuec34.org
URL: http://www.iuec34.org
Contact: Joe Albertson, Business Agent
Members: 156. **Local. Affiliated With:** International Union of Elevator Constructors.

5379 ■ International Union, United Automobile, Aerospace and Agricultural Implement Workers of America, AFL-CIO - Local Union 1111
431 S Shortridge Rd.
Indianapolis, IN 46219
Ph: (317)359-9585
E-mail: jlewis56@visteon.com
URL: http://www.uaw1111.org
Contact: Jim Lewis, Pres.
Members: 2,230. **Local.** Seeks for the dignity and equality of the workers. Strives to provide contractors with well-trained, productive employees. **Affiliated**

With: International Union, United Automobile, Aerospace and Agricultural Implement Workers of America.

5380 ■ IUPUI Association for Computing Machinery Student SIGGRAPH
c/o Douglas C. Acheson
723 W Michigan St.
Indianapolis, IN 46202-5160
Ph: (317)274-4186
Fax: (317)278-3669
E-mail: bdean@indy.rr.com
URL: http://cpt.engr.iupui.edu/acmweb
Contact: Douglas C. Acheson, Contact
Local. Biological, medical, behavioral, and computer scientists; hospital administrators; programmers and others interested in application of computer methods to biological, behavioral, and medical problems. Stimulates understanding of the use and potential of computers in the Biosciences. **Affiliated With:** Association for Computing Machinery.

5381 ■ Jewish Federation of Greater Indianapolis (JFGI)
6705 Hoover Rd.
Indianapolis, IN 46260
Ph: (317)726-5450
Fax: (317)205-0307
E-mail: info@jfgi.org
URL: http://www.jfgi.org
Contact: Dick Leventhal, Pres.
Local.

5382 ■ Jobs Partnership of Greater Indianapolis
c/o Rev. Frank Alexander, Chm.
3549 Blvd. Pl.
Indianapolis, IN 46208
Ph: (317)925-1003
Fax: (317)925-1033
URL: http://www.jpindy.org
Contact: Rev. Frank Alexander, Chm.
Local.

5383 ■ Junior Achievement of Central Indiana
7435 N Keystone Ave.
Indianapolis, IN 46240
Ph: (317)252-5900
Fax: (317)252-5700
Free: (877)252-5224
E-mail: jeff@jaindy.org
URL: http://www.jaindy.org
Contact: Jeff Miller, Pres./CEO
Local. K-12 education organization teaching business understanding and financial literacy. **Affiliated With:** Junior Achievement.

5384 ■ Junior League of Indianapolis
3050 N Meridian St.
Indianapolis, IN 46208
Ph: (317)925-4600
Fax: (317)926-7658
E-mail: jlioffice@sbcglobal.net
Founded: 1922. **Members:** 1,200. **Membership Dues:** active, $120 (annual) • provisional, $170 (annual) • sustaining, $80 (annual). **Staff:** 7. **Local**. Committed to promoting voluntarism, developing the potential of women, and improving the community through the effective action and leadership of trained volunteers. **Awards:** Community Assistance Grant. **Frequency:** annual. **Type:** grant.

5385 ■ Juvenile Diabetes Research Foundation, Indiana State Chapter
8465 Keystone Crossing, Ste.235
Indianapolis, IN 46240
Ph: (317)202-0352
Fax: (317)202-0357
E-mail: indianastate@jdrf.org
URL: National Affiliate–www.jdrf.org
Contact: Linda Gann, Exec.Dir.
Founded: 1983. **Members:** 300. **Budget:** $400,000. **State**. Sponsors fundraising events for diabetes research. **Affiliated With:** Juvenile Diabetes Research Foundation International. **Formerly:** (1998) Juvenile Diabetes Foundation, Indiana State Chapter. **Publications:** *Discoveries*, quarterly. Newsletter. Features the latest information on diabetes research and upcoming chapter events. **Price:** free. **Advertising:** accepted. **Conventions/Meetings:** annual conference.

5386 ■ Keep Indianapolis Beautiful (KIB)
445 N Pennsylvania St., Ste.910
Indianapolis, IN 46204
Ph: (317)264-7555
Fax: (317)264-7565
E-mail: info@kibi.org
URL: http://www.kibi.org
Contact: David Forsell, Pres.
Founded: 1976. **Local**. Strives to have a viable, sustainable impact on lives of residents in the Indianapolis area and the neighborhoods in which they live. Engages citizens in beautifying the city, improving the quality of the environment and fostering pride in the community.

5387 ■ Kiwanis Club of Indianapolis
c/o Nancy Hershman, Office Admin.
320 N Meridian St., Ste.1020
Indianapolis, IN 46204
Ph: (317)636-9700
Fax: (317)636-9709
E-mail: office@indykiwanis.org
URL: http://www.indykiwanis.org
Contact: Nancy Hershman, Office Admin.
Founded: 1916. **Members:** 350. **Local**. Provides service with an emphasis on serving the needs of children.

5388 ■ Korean War Veterans Association, Central Indiana Chapter
c/o Tine P. Martin, Sr.
9137 Timpani Way
Indianapolis, IN 46231
Ph: (317)243-0927
E-mail: tmartinsr@earthlink.net
URL: National Affiliate–www.kwva.org
Contact: Tine P. Martin Sr., Contact
Local. **Affiliated With:** Korean War Veterans Association.

5389 ■ Lacrosse Club of Pike Township
c/o Summex Corp.
6201 Corporate Dr.
Indianapolis, IN 46278
Ph: (317)713-3901
Fax: (317)713-3950
E-mail: robplank@pikelacrosse.org
URL: http://www.pikelacrosse.org
Contact: J. Robert Plankenhorn, Pres.
Local.

5390 ■ League of Professionally Managed Theaters
c/o Robert B. Zehr
749 N Park Ave.
Indianapolis, IN 46202-3432
Ph: (317)923-4597
Contact: Bob Sorbera, Pres.
Local.

5391 ■ Legal Secretaries of Indiana
6699 E 11th St.
Indianapolis, IN 46219
E-mail: joyce.eden@comcast.net
URL: National Affiliate–www.legalsecretaries.org
Contact: Joyce C. Eden PLS, Interim Pres.
State. Works to respond to the educational and networking needs of legal secretaries. **Affiliated With:** Legal Secretaries International.

5392 ■ Leukemia and Lymphoma Society, Indiana Chapter
941 E 86th St., Ste.100
Indianapolis, IN 46240
Ph: (317)726-2270
Fax: (317)726-2280
Free: (800)846-7764
E-mail: spahrp@in-ftw.leukemia-lymphoma.org
URL: National Affiliate–www.leukemia-lymphoma.org
Contact: Pat Spahr, Dir.
Founded: 1945. **Staff:** 10. **Local**. **Affiliated With:** Leukemia and Lymphoma Society. **Formerly:** (2000) Leukemia Society of America, Indiana.

5393 ■ Libertarian Party of Indiana (LPIN)
c/o Brad Klopfenstein, Exec.Dir.
156 E Market St., Ste.405
Indianapolis, IN 46204
Ph: (317)920-1994
Fax: (317)924-2920
Free: (800)814-1776
E-mail: lpinhq@lpin.org
URL: http://www.lpin.org/
Contact: Brad Klopfenstein, Exec.Dir.
Founded: 1972. **Members:** 700. **Membership Dues:** individual, $25 (annual). **Budget:** $50,000. **State**. Dedicated to electing candidates who believe in reducing the size of government. **Affiliated With:** Libertarian National Committee. **Publications:** *Liberty Beacon*, quarterly. Newsletter. **Conventions/Meetings:** annual convention.

5394 ■ Little Red Door Cancer Agency
1801 N Meridian St.
Indianapolis, IN 46202-1411
Ph: (317)925-5595
Fax: (317)925-5597
E-mail: mail@littlereddoor.org
URL: http://www.littlereddoor.org
Contact: David Warshauer, Pres.
Founded: 1945. **Local**. Works to reduce the physical, emotional and financial burdens of cancer by providing free-of-charge patient services, cancer screenings and education.

5395 ■ Make-A-Wish Foundation of Indiana
6325 Digital Way, Ste.150
Indianapolis, IN 46278-1697
Ph: (317)636-6060
Fax: (317)636-2445
Free: (877)872-2756
URL: http://www.makeawishohio.org
Contact: Rhett Cecil, Exec.Dir.
State. Grants wishes of children with life-threatening medical conditions to enrich the human experience with hope, strength and joy. **Affiliated With:** Make-A-Wish Foundation of America.

5396 ■ Mapleton-Fall Creek Neighborhood Association/mid North Weed and Seed
c/o Al Polin, Coor.
401 E. 34th St.
Indianapolis, IN 46205
Ph: (317)926-5740
Fax: (317)926-0887
Contact: Al Polin, Contact

5397 ■ March of Dimes Birth Defects Foundation, Indiana Chapter
c/o Janet Estes, State Dir.
136 E Market St., Ste.500
Indianapolis, IN 46204
Ph: (317)262-4668
Fax: (317)262-4669
Free: (800)844-9255
E-mail: in354@marchofdimes.com
URL: http://www.marchofdimes.com/indiana
Contact: Janet Estes, State Dir.
State. Works to improve the health of babies by preventing birth defects and infant mortality. **Affiliated With:** March of Dimes Birth Defects Foundation.

5398 ■ Marion County Master Gardener Association
c/o Purdue Extension-Marion County
6640 Intech Blvd., Ste.120
Indianapolis, IN 46278-2012

Ph: (317)275-9305
URL: http://www.ces.purdue.edu/CES/Marion/HortConMG07.htm
Local.

5399 ■ Meals on Wheels of Marion County
1099 N Meridian St., Ste.650
Indianapolis, IN 46204-1041
Ph: (317)633-6325
Fax: (317)633-6320
E-mail: mowfood@aol.com
URL: http://www.mealsonwheelsindy.org
Contact: Kim Arvidson, Client Coor.
Local. Delivers two physician prescribed meals each weekday in the greater Indianapolis area.

5400 ■ Mechanical Contractors Association of Central Indiana
c/o John Rayburn
PO Box 20425
Indianapolis, IN 46220-0425
Ph: (317)255-4126
Local.

5401 ■ Mechanical Contractors Association of Indiana (MCAI)
c/o John Rayburn, Exec.VP
PO Box 20425
Indianapolis, IN 46220
Ph: (317)255-4126
Fax: (317)251-9883
E-mail: mcaiinfo@mcai.com
URL: http://www.mcai.com
Local. **Affiliated With:** Mechanical Contractors Association of America. **Formerly:** (2005) Mechanical Contractors Association of America - Indiana Chapter.

5402 ■ Mental Health Association in Indiana (MHAI)
1431 N Delaware St.
Indianapolis, IN 46202
Ph: (317)638-3501
Fax: (317)638-3540
Free: (800)555-MHAI
E-mail: mha@mentalhealthassociation.com
URL: National Affiliate–www.nmha.org
Contact: Stephen C. McCaffrey JD, Pres./CEO
Membership Dues: individual, $25 (annual) • corporate, $100-$1,000 (annual). **Local Groups:** 60. **State**. Works to widen public understanding of mental illness. Advocates for society's acceptance of people with mental problems. Promotes mental health of Indiana citizens.

5403 ■ Mental Health Association in Marion County (MHAMC)
2506 Willowbrook Pkwy., Ste.100
Indianapolis, IN 46205
Ph: (317)251-0005
Fax: (317)254-2800
E-mail: mcmha@mcmha.org
URL: http://www.mcmha.org
Contact: Carson A. Soule, Exec.Dir.
Local.

5404 ■ Mercedes Benz Club of America - 500 Section
c/o Steven Rae, Pres.
7202 Tappan Dr.
Indianapolis, IN 46268
Ph: (317)328-8451
E-mail: smrae2@comcast.net
URL: http://www.mbca500section.org
Contact: Steven Rae, Pres.
Local. **Affiliated With:** Mercedes-Benz Club of America.

5405 ■ Metropolitan Indianapolis Board of Realtors (MIBOR)
c/o Stephen J. Sullivan, CEO
1912 N Meridian St.
Indianapolis, IN 46202
Ph: (317)956-1912 (317)956-5000
Fax: (317)956-5050
E-mail: clairebelby@mibor.com
URL: http://www.mibor.com
Contact: Claire Belby, Communications Dir.
Local.

5406 ■ Mid-America Equipment Retailers Association (MAERA)
9302 N Meridian St., Ste.100
Indianapolis, IN 46260
Ph: (317)844-5259
Fax: (317)843-1964
E-mail: info@maera.org
URL: http://www.maera.org
Contact: Kim Rominger, Exec.VP
Founded: 1916. **Members:** 300. **Membership Dues:** regular, $300 (annual) • associate individual, $95 (annual) • corporate associate, $450 (annual). **Staff:** 4. **Budget:** $800,000. **Regional**. Represents farm, industrial, construction, outdoor power, and agribusiness products and services retailers in Kentucky and Indiana area. Provides insurance programs, wage and salary information, cost of doing business information, trade-in guides, management seminars, wholesale and retail finance programs, credit card processing services, and lobbying and legislative services to members. **Publications:** *The Pinion*, bimonthly. Magazine. **Circulation:** 600. **Advertising:** accepted.

5407 ■ Military Officers' Association of America, Indianapolis Chapter
c/o Lt.Col. Gerald Ell
PO Box 55974
Indianapolis, IN 46205-0974
Ph: (317)787-4157
E-mail: gell@iquest.net
URL: National Affiliate–www.moaa.org
Contact: Lt.Col. Gerald Ell, Contact
Founded: 1958. **Members:** 410. **Membership Dues:** $20 (annual). **Budget:** $5,000. **State Groups:** 1. **Local**. **Awards:** TRVA College Scholarships. **Frequency:** annual. **Type:** scholarship. **Publications:** Newsletter, monthly. **Circulation:** 600. **Conventions/Meetings:** monthly luncheon - always third Thursday, Indianapolis, IN.

5408 ■ Milk Promotion Services of Indiana
c/o Sue Brames, Gen.Mgr.
9360 Castlegate Dr.
Indianapolis, IN 46256
Ph: (317)842-7133
Fax: (317)842-3065
Free: (800)225-6455
E-mail: hardin@mpsiinc.com
URL: http://www.indianadairycouncil.org
Contact: Sue Brames, Gen.Mgr.
State. Promotes the sale and consumption of dairy foods. Carries out studies and research. **Affiliated With:** Dairy Management, Inc.

5409 ■ Murat Shriners
c/o Gordon J. Husk
510 N New Jersey St.
Indianapolis, IN 46204
Ph: (317)635-2433
Fax: (317)686-4199
E-mail: info@muratshrine.org
URL: http://www.muratshrine.org
Contact: Gordon J. Husk, Recorder
Local. **Affiliated With:** Imperial Council of the Ancient Arabic Order of the Nobles of the Mystic Shrine for North America.

5410 ■ NAIFA-Indianapolis
c/o Byron E. Foley, Pres.
3009 E 96th
Indianapolis, IN 46240
Ph: (317)844-6268
Fax: (317)844-7659
E-mail: stonekingk@sbcglobal.net
URL: National Affiliate–naifa.org
Contact: Byron E. Foley, Pres.
Local. Represents the interests of insurance and financial advisors. Advocates for a positive legislative and regulatory environment. Enhances business and professional skills of members. **Affiliated With:** National Association of Insurance and Financial Advisors.

5411 ■ National Active and Retired Federal Employees Association - Indianapolis 151
5350 N Pennsylvania St.
Indianapolis, IN 46220-3059
Ph: (317)255-4928
URL: National Affiliate–www.narfe.org
Contact: Leo J. Hahn, Contact
Local. Protects the retirement future of employees through education. Informs members on issues affecting the retirement. **Affiliated With:** National Association of Retired Federal Employees.

5412 ■ National Alliance for the Mentally Ill Indiana
PO Box 22697
Indianapolis, IN 46222-0697
Ph: (317)925-9399
Fax: (317)925-9398
Free: (800)677-6442
E-mail: lgay@nami.org
URL: http://www.namiindiana.org
Contact: Leslie Gay, Coor.
State. Provides support groups and education programs for people with mental illness and their families and education for the general public. **Affiliated With:** National Alliance for the Mentally Ill.

5413 ■ National Association for the Advancement of Colored People, Indianapolis Branch
PO Box 88676
Indianapolis, IN 46208
Ph: (317)925-5127
URL: http://www.indynaacp.org
Contact: Daryl Mickens, Pres.
Local.

5414 ■ National Association of Air Medical Communication Specialists, Region 5
c/o Kathy Ward
PO Box 1367
Indianapolis, IN 46206
Ph: (317)962-8350
Fax: (317)962-8017
E-mail: kward6112@cs.com
URL: National Affiliate–www.naacs.org
Contact: Kathy Ward, Contact
Regional. Enhances the professionalism of the Air Medical Communications Specialists through education, recognition, and standardization. **Affiliated With:** National Association of Air Medical Communication Specialists.

5415 ■ National Association of Black Accountants, Indianapolis Chapter
c/o Ms. Williamson
PO Box 2631
Indianapolis, IN 46206
Ph: (317)575-7844
E-mail: indynaba@hotmail.com
URL: National Affiliate–www.nabainc.org
Local. **Affiliated With:** National Association of Black Accountants.

5416 ■ National Association of Home Builders, Building Authority of Greater Indianapolis
c/o Steven Lains
PO Box 44670
Indianapolis, IN 46244-0670
Ph: (317)236-6330
Fax: (317)236-6340
E-mail: stevel@bagi.com
URL: http://www.bagi.com
Local. Single and multifamily home builders, commercial builders, and others associated with the building industry. **Affiliated With:** National Association of Home Builders.

5417 ■ National Association for Interpretation - Region 4
c/o Ginger Murphy, Dir.
402 W Washington, Rm. W298
Indianapolis, IN 46204
Ph: (317)232-4143
E-mail: gmurphy@dnr.in.gov
URL: http://www.nairegions.org/4
Contact: Ginger Murphy, Dir.

Regional. Advances the profession of interpretation through on site informal education programs at parks, zoos, nature centers, historic sites, museums and aquaria. **Affiliated With:** National Association for Interpretation.

5418 ■ National Association of Investors Corporation, Central Indiana Chapter
PO Box 19779
Indianapolis, IN 46219
Ph: (317)535-7244
E-mail: rbrouse2@hotmail.com
URL: http://better-investing.org/chapter/indiana
Contact: Roger Brouse, Pres.

Local. Teaches individuals how to become successful strategic long-term investors. Provides highly focused learning resources and investment tools that empower individuals to become better investors. **Affiliated With:** National Association of Investors Corporation.

5419 ■ National Association of Miniature Enthusiasts - Hoosier Mini-Mizers
c/o Susan Durfee
5627 Indianola Ave.
Indianapolis, IN 46220
Ph: (317)253-5494
URL: http://www.miniatures.org/states/IN.html
Contact: Susan Durfee, Contact

Local. **Affiliated With:** National Association of Miniature Enthusiasts.

5420 ■ National Association for Multicultural Education, Indiana Chapter
c/o Patricia Payne, Pres.
Indianapolis Public Schools
1140 Dr. Martin Luther King Jr. St.
Indianapolis, IN 46202
Ph: (317)226-2431
Fax: (317)226-4611
E-mail: paynep@mail.ips.k12.in.us
URL: http://www.nameorg.org/Chapters/Indiana/Indiana.htm
Contact: Patricia Payne, Pres.

State. Represents individuals and groups with an interest in multicultural education from all levels of education, different academic disciplines and from diverse educational institutions and occupations. Provides leadership in national and state dialogues on equity, diversity and multicultural education. Works to fight injustices in schools and in communities. Seeks to ensure that all students receive an equitable education. **Affiliated With:** National Association for Multicultural Education.

5421 ■ National Association of the Remodeling Industry of Central Indiana
827 N Capitol Ave.
Indianapolis, IN 46204
Ph: (317)638-3717
Fax: (317)634-6057
E-mail: dorfmandesigns@sbcglobal.net
URL: National Affiliate–www.nari.org
Contact: Sandi Perlman, Pres.

Local. Brings together people who work in the remodeling industry. Provides resources for knowledge and training in the industry. Encourages ethical conduct, sound business practices and professionalism. Promotes the remodeling industry's products. **Affiliated With:** National Association of the Remodeling Industry.

5422 ■ National Association of Rocketry - Rocketeers of Central Indiana (ROCI)
c/o Bill Scott
6336 E 82nd St.
Indianapolis, IN 46250
Ph: (317)845-4106
E-mail: wmscott@htindy.com
URL: http://www.indyrockets.org/roci.html
Contact: Bill Scott, Contact
Local.

5423 ■ National Association of State Foresters, Indiana
c/o Jack Seifert
Div. of Forestry, Dept. of Natural Resources
402 W Washington St., Rm. W296
Indianapolis, IN 46204
Ph: (317)232-4116
E-mail: jseifert@dnr.in.gov
URL: National Affiliate–www.stateforesters.org
Contact: Jack Seifert, Contact
State. **Affiliated With:** National Association of State Foresters.

5424 ■ National Association of Watch and Clock Collectors, Chapter 18
5301 N Franklin Rd.
Indianapolis, IN 46226-2084
E-mail: johncote@indianachapter18.org
URL: http://www.nawcc.org
Contact: John Cote, Contact
Local.

5425 ■ National Association of Women Business Owners, Indianapolis (NAWBO-Indy)
PO Box 20120
Indianapolis, IN 46220
Ph: (317)466-2768
Fax: (317)578-2876
E-mail: info@nawboindy.org
URL: http://nawboindy.org
Contact: Billie Dragoo, Pres.
Local. Represents the interests of all women business owner. **Affiliated With:** National Association of Women Business Owners.

5426 ■ National Federation of Independent Business - Indiana (NFIB)
c/o Jason Shelley, State Dir.
101 W Ohio St., Ste.470
Indianapolis, IN 46204
Ph: (317)638-4447
Fax: (317)638-4450
E-mail: jason.shelley@nfib.org
Contact: Jason Shelley, State Dir.
State. **Affiliated With:** National Federation of Independent Business.

5427 ■ National Kidney Foundation of Indiana (NKFI)
911 E 86th St., Ste.100
Indianapolis, IN 46240
Ph: (317)722-5640
Fax: (317)722-5650
Free: (800)382-9971
E-mail: nkfi@myvine.com
URL: http://www.kidneyindiana.org
Contact: Heather Gallagher, Communications Dir.
State. Supports research, patient services, professional and public education, organ and tissue donor program, and community service. **Affiliated With:** National Kidney Foundation.

5428 ■ National Multiple Sclerosis Society, Indiana State Chapter
7301 Georgetown Rd., Ste.112
Indianapolis, IN 46268
Ph: (317)870-2500
Fax: (317)870-2520
Free: (800)344-4867
E-mail: astevenson@msindiana.org
URL: http://www.msindiana.org
Contact: Connie Molland, Pres.
Founded: 1954. **Membership Dues:** minimum, $25 (annual). **Staff:** 12. **State**. Stimulates, supports, and coordinates research into the cause, treatment, and cure of multiple sclerosis; provides services and aid for persons with MS and related diseases and their families. **Libraries: Type:** open to the public; lending. **Holdings:** audio recordings, books, video recordings. **Subjects:** multiple sclerosis, related issues. **Affiliated With:** National Multiple Sclerosis Society. **Publications:** *MS Connection*, quarterly. Newsletter. **Price:** free to members. Alternate Formats: online.

5429 ■ National Organization of Black Law Enforcement Executives, Southern Indiana Chapter
c/o Frank Anderson, Sheriff
PO Box 441784
Indianapolis, IN 46244-1784
Ph: (317)231-8200
Fax: (317)231-8596
E-mail: sh20728@indygov.org
URL: National Affiliate–www.noblenational.org
Contact: Frank Anderson, Sheriff
Local. **Affiliated With:** National Organization of Black Law Enforcement Executives.

5430 ■ National Organization for Women - Indiana
PO Box 2264
Indianapolis, IN 46206
E-mail: indiananow@comcast.net
URL: http://indiananow.home.comcast.net
State. **Affiliated With:** National Organization for Women.

5431 ■ National Society of Black Engineers - Indianapolis Alumni Extension (NSBE-IAE)
c/o Ladonia Striver, Vice Chair
PO Box 364
Indianapolis, IN 46206-0364
E-mail: vchair@nsbe-iae.org
URL: http://www.nsbe-iae.org
Contact: Ladonia Striver, Vice Chair
Local. Strives to increase the number of culturally responsible Black engineers who excel academically, succeed professionally and positively impact the community. **Affiliated With:** National Society of Black Engineers.

5432 ■ National Softball Association - Southern Indiana
c/o Richard Foltz, Dir.
3466 N Raceway Rd.
Indianapolis, IN 46234
Ph: (317)293-1776
E-mail: rbfoltz1@cs.com
URL: http://www.indianansa.com
Contact: Richard Foltz, Dir.
Local. **Affiliated With:** National Softball Association.

5433 ■ National Sojourners, Indiana - Fort Harrison No. 66
c/o Lt.Col. Stephen M. Proctor, Jr.
11102 Bayridge Cir. W
Indianapolis, IN 46236-8750
Ph: (317)823-0444
E-mail: sml2o364@aol.com
URL: National Affiliate–www.nationalsojourners.org
Contact: Lt.Col. Stephen M. Proctor Jr., Contact
Local.

5434 ■ National Speleological Society, Central Indiana Grotto (CIG)
PO Box 153
Indianapolis, IN 46206-0153
Ph: (317)844-2415
E-mail: cig@exploringearth.com
URL: http://www.caves.org/grotto/cig
Contact: Ron Adams, Vice Chm.
Local. Seeks to study, explore and conserve cave and karst resources. Protects access to caves and promotes responsible caving. Encourages responsible management of caves and their unique environments. **Affiliated With:** National Speleological Society.

5435 ■ National Technical Honor Society - ITT Technical Institute - Indiana
9511 Angola Ct.
Indianapolis, IN 46268-1119
Ph: (317)875-8640
Free: (800)937-4488
URL: http://www.itt-tech.edu
Local.

5436 ■ National Utility Contractors Association of Indiana
3840 Prospect St.
Indianapolis, IN 46203
Ph: (765)429-4800
Fax: (317)357-6822
E-mail: jasonw@nucaofindiana.com
URL: http://www.nucaofindiana.com
Contact: Elizabeth Goldin, Contact
State. Represents contractors, suppliers, and manufacturers involved in water, sewer, gas, electric, telecommunications, site work, and other segments of the industry across the US. Provides safety training and education for all underground utility construction professionals. Unites and strengthens construction markets. Improves the business environment for the utility construction community through dedicated involvement in legislative action, networking and communication. **Affiliated With:** National Utility Contractors Association. **Publications:** Newsletter, monthly.

5437 ■ Nature Conservancy, Indiana Field Office
1505 N. Delaware St., Ste.200
Indianapolis, IN 46202
Ph: (317)951-8818
Fax: (317)917-2478
Free: (800)YES-LAND
E-mail: csutton@tnc.org
URL: http://www.nature.org/indiana
Contact: Mr. Chip Sutton, Dir. of Communications
Founded: 1959. **Members:** 14,000. **Membership Dues:** subscriber, $25 (annual). **Staff:** 48. **Regional Groups:** 7. **Regional.** Dedicated to the preservation of ecological diversity through the protection of natural areas. **Affiliated With:** Nature Conservancy. **Publications:** *Guide to Indiana Preserves*, biennial. Booklet. **Price:** $20.00. **Advertising:** not accepted • *Indiana Chapter Newsletter*, semiannual. **Conventions/Meetings:** annual meeting - June; Avg. Attendance: 150.

5438 ■ Newborns In Need Indianapolis Chapter
c/o Jo St. John
8247 Braeburn N Dr.
Indianapolis, IN 46219
Ph: (317)362-8028
E-mail: indianapolis@newbornsinneed.org
URL: http://www.newbornsinneed.org/indianapolis
Local.

5439 ■ Noble Arc of Central Indiana - Hamilton, Howard, Marion, Shelby and Tipton Counties
7702 E 21st St.
Indianapolis, IN 46219
Ph: (317)375-2700
URL: National Affiliate–www.TheArc.org
Contact: Monica Barnett, Contact
Local. Parents, professional workers, and others interested in individuals with mental retardation. Works to promote services, research, public understanding, and legislation for people with mental retardation and their families. **Affiliated With:** Arc of the United States.

5440 ■ Noble ARC of Greater Indianapolis
7701 E 21th St.
Indianapolis, IN 46219
Ph: (317)375-2700
URL: http://www.nobleofindiana.org
Contact: Michael Howland, Pres.
Local.

5441 ■ North Central - Young Life
418 E 34th St.
Indianapolis, IN 46205
Ph: (317)923-1319
URL: http://whereis.younglife.org/FriendlyUrlRedirector.aspx?ID=C-889
Local.

5442 ■ Northview - Wyldlife
418 E 34th St.
Indianapolis, IN 46205
Ph: (317)923-1319
URL: http://sites.younglife.org/_layouts/ylext/default.aspx?ID=C-894
Local. Affiliated With: Young Life.

5443 ■ Operation Lifesaver, Indiana
c/o Tom Kinser
31 E Georgia St.
Indianapolis, IN 46204
Ph: (317)267-4357
E-mail: kinserinol@prodigy.net
URL: National Affiliate–www.oli.org
State. Affiliated With: Operation Lifesaver.

5444 ■ Organization for a New Eastside
c/o Ken Moran
PO Box 11454
Indianapolis, IN 46201
Ph: (317)917-8922
URL: National Affiliate–www.npa-us.org
Local. Affiliated With: National People's Action.

5445 ■ Original Circle City Corvette Club
9320 E Prospect St.
Indianapolis, IN 46239-9335
Ph: (317)898-2222
Fax: (317)898-3883
E-mail: president@circlecitycorvetteclub.com
URL: http://www.circlecitycorvetteclub.com
Contact: Phil Harris, Pres.
Local. Affiliated With: National Council of Corvette Clubs.

5446 ■ Overseas Council International (OCI)
PO Box 17368
Indianapolis, IN 46217-0368
Ph: (317)788-7250
Fax: (317)788-7257
Free: (877)788-7250
E-mail: info@overseas.org
URL: http://www.overseas.org
Contact: Ken Jones, VP
Founded: 1974. **Regional. Also Known As:** (1999) Overseas Council.

5447 ■ Parkinson's Awareness Association of Central Indiana (PAACI)
4755 Kingsway Dr., Ste.333
Indianapolis, IN 46205-1560
Ph: (317)255-1993
Fax: (317)254-3670
E-mail: support@paaci.org
URL: http://www.paaci.org
Contact: Edwin Schulz, Founder
Founded: 1981. **Members:** 2,159. **Membership Dues:** regular, $25 (annual). **Budget:** $47,400. **Local.** Provides support and education to those afflicted with Parkinson's disease, their families and friends. Seeks to improve treatments and find a cure for the disease. **Publications:** Newsletter, quarterly. **Price:** included in membership dues. Alternate Formats: online. **Conventions/Meetings:** monthly Administrative Board - board meeting • monthly Educational Meeting • quarterly Executive Board - board meeting • Free Speech and Physical Therapy - meeting - 4/week • annual symposium.

5448 ■ PFLAG Indianapolis
PO Box 441633
Indianapolis, IN 46244
Ph: (317)545-7034
E-mail: info@indypflag.org
URL: http://www.indypflag.org
Local. Affiliated With: Parents, Families, and Friends of Lesbians and Gays.

5449 ■ Phi Theta Kappa, Alpha Upsilon Tau Chapter - Ivy Tech State College
c/o Sharon Dunn
Indianapolis Campus
1 W 26th St.
Indianapolis, IN 46208
Ph: (317)921-4908
URL: http://www.ptk.org/directories/chapters/IN/20506-1.htm
Contact: Sharon Dunn, Advisor
Local.

5450 ■ Phi Theta Kappa, Beta Alpha Omega Chapter - University of Indianapolis
c/o Lisa Berger
1400 E Hanna Ave.
Indianapolis, IN 46227
Ph: (317)788-3200
URL: http://www.ptk.org/directories/chapters/IN/20665-1.htm
Contact: Lisa Berger, Advisor
Local.

5451 ■ Pike - Young Life
418 E 34th St.
Indianapolis, IN 46205
Ph: (317)923-1319
URL: http://whereis.younglife.org/FriendlyUrlRedirector.aspx?ID=C-891
Local.

5452 ■ Planned Giving Group of Indiana
PO Box 2232
Indianapolis, IN 46206
Ph: (317)767-9893
E-mail: pggi@prairieinet.net
URL: http://www.plannedgivingindiana.org
Contact: Cheryl Cooper, Pres.
State. Increases the quality and quantity of charitable planned gifts. Serves as the voice and professional resource for the gift planning community.

5453 ■ Planned Parenthood of Indiana
PO Box 397
Indianapolis, IN 46206
Ph: (317)637-4343
Fax: (317)637-4344
Free: (800)230-PLAN
E-mail: askme@ppin.org
URL: http://ppin.org
Contact: Theresa Browning, Contact
State. Provides reproductive health services to women and men in counties through more than 38 health centers. Offers educational services to bring accurate information to men and women. **Formerly:** (2001) Planned Parenthood of Central and Southern Indiana.

5454 ■ Plumbing-Heating-Cooling Contractors Association, Greater Indianapolis
c/o Ann Booth, Exec.Mgr.
PO Box 68375
Indianapolis, IN 46268-0375
Ph: (317)297-2106
Fax: (317)328-0359
Free: (888)518-4729
URL: National Affiliate–www.phccweb.org
Contact: Ann Booth, Exec.Mgr.
Local. Represents the plumbing, heating and cooling contractors. Promotes the construction industry. Protects the environment, health, safety and comfort of society. **Affiliated With:** Plumbing-Heating-Cooling Contractors Association.

5455 ■ Police and Firemen's Insurance Association - Indianapolis Police Department
c/o Steve D. Murphy
5262 S McFarland Rd.
Indianapolis, IN 46227
Ph: (317)786-8198 (317)368-6939
E-mail: pfiasmurphy@famvid.com
URL: National Affiliate–www.pfia.net
Contact: Steve D. Murphy, Contact
Local. Affiliated With: Police and Firemen's Insurance Association.

5456 ■ Police and Firemen's Insurance Association - Marion County Sheriff
c/o Richard A. Edgemon
5504 Straw Hat Dr.
Indianapolis, IN 46237
Ph: (317)783-4760 (317)761-7469
URL: National Affiliate–www.pfia.net
Contact: Richard A. Edgemon, Contact
Local. Affiliated With: Police and Firemen's Insurance Association.

5457 ■ Prevent Blindness Indiana
c/o John Wagner, Pres./CEO
603 E Washington St., Ste.502
Indianapolis, IN 46204-2620
Ph: (317)955-9580
Fax: (317)955-9583
Free: (800)232-2551
E-mail: jwagner@pbeye.org
URL: http://www.pbeye.org
Contact: John Wagner, Pres./CEO
Founded: 1950. **Staff:** 6. **Budget:** $500,000. **Nonmembership. For-Profit. State.** Provides vision screening. Conducts safety education, vision screening training and services.

5458 ■ Prevent Child Abuse Indiana
9130 E Otis Ave.
Indianapolis, IN 46216
Ph: (317)542-7002
Fax: (317)542-7003
E-mail: generalinfo@pcain.org
URL: http://www.pcain.org
Contact: Ms. Andrea L. Marshall, Exec.Dir.
Founded: 1977. **Members:** 3,076. **Membership Dues:** regular, $35 (annual). **Budget:** $850,000. **Regional Groups:** 40. **State.** Seeks to make it unacceptable for any child to be abused or neglected in Indiana. Sponsors and presents a variety of educational forums, workshops and conferences to better educate all who have contact or responsibility for children. Focuses on prevention of any form of child abuse and neglect. **Affiliated With:** Prevent Child Abuse. **Publications:** *Council Courier*, 3/year. Newsletter • *What's News*, quarterly. Newsletter. **Conventions/Meetings:** annual Breaking the Cycle - conference - mid-April.

5459 ■ Professional Geologists of Indiana
c/o Don Neely, Pres.
PO Box 30165
Indianapolis, IN 46230
E-mail: dneeley@aeeindy.com
URL: http://www.geology.iupui.edu/Outreach/pgi/index.htm
Contact: Don Neely, Pres.
State. Fosters scientific research and advances the science of geology. Promotes technology and inspires high professional conduct. **Affiliated With:** American Association of Petroleum Geologists.

5460 ■ Project Management Institute, Central Indiana
c/o Mr. David C. Daily, PMP President
12119 Emerald Bluff
Indianapolis, IN 46236
Ph: (317)823-7132
E-mail: daily_david@lilly.com
Local. Corporations and individuals engaged in the practice of project management; project management students and educators. Seeks to advance the study, teaching, and practice of project management. **Affiliated With:** Project Management Institute.

5461 ■ Psi Chi, National Honor Society in Psychology - Butler University
c/o Dept. of Psychology
4600 Sunset Ave.
Indianapolis, IN 46208-3485
Ph: (317)940-9266 (317)940-8707
Fax: (317)940-8044
E-mail: kmorris@butler.edu
URL: http://www.psichi.org/chapters/info.asp?chapter_id=905
Contact: Kathryn A. Morris PhD, Advisor
Local.

5462 ■ Psi Chi, National Honor Society in Psychology - Indiana University-Purdue University Indianapolis
c/o Dept. of Psychology
402 N Blackford St.
Indianapolis, IN 46202
Ph: (317)274-6943 (317)278-2237
Fax: (317)274-6756
E-mail: cyclark@iupui.edu
URL: National Affiliate–www.psichi.org
Local. Affiliated With: Psi Chi, National Honor Society in Psychology.

5463 ■ Psi Chi, National Honor Society in Psychology - Marian College
c/o Dept. of Psychology
3200 Cold Spring Rd.
Indianapolis, IN 46222-1997
Ph: (317)955-6075
Fax: (317)955-6448
E-mail: icamp@marian.edu
URL: http://www.psichi.org/chapters/info.asp?chapter_id=574
Contact: Laurel Camp PhD, Advisor
Local.

5464 ■ Psi Chi, National Honor Society in Psychology - University of Indianapolis
c/o School of Psych Sciences
1400 E Hanna Ave.
Indianapolis, IN 46227-3697
Ph: (317)788-3353 (317)788-6142
Fax: (317)788-2120
E-mail: jwall@uindy.edu
URL: http://www.psichi.org/chapters/info.asp?chapter_id=886
Contact: Jacqueline Wall PhD, Advisor
Local.

5465 ■ Quality for Indiana Taxpayers (QFIT)
c/o Jerry Musich, PhD, Exec.Dir.
1040 E 86th St., Ste.46-J
Indianapolis, IN 46240
E-mail: qfit429@aol.com
Contact: Jerry Musich PhD, Exec.Dir.
State. Partnership of the IRS and State of Indiana government entities, corporations, and professional associations operating to serve nonprofits, start-up small businesses, and the tax community. Offers workshops throughout Indiana on the steps in forming a nonprofit and on nonprofit effectiveness, operates a resource center, and hosts meetings for tax professionals. Also works to educate staff members and trustees of nonprofits about best practices and about compliance issues.

5466 ■ Rebuilding The Wall (RTW)
c/o Chris Provence, Exec.Dir.
2401 N Guilford Ave.
Indianapolis, IN 46205
Ph: (317)250-7090
URL: http://www.rebuildingthewall.org
Contact: Chris Provence, Exec.Dir.
Local.

5467 ■ Right to Life of Indianapolis
1060 E 86th St., Ste.61B
Indianapolis, IN 46240
Ph: (317)582-1526
Fax: (317)582-5045
E-mail: life@rtlindy.org
URL: http://www.rtlindy.org
Local.

5468 ■ Rotary Club of Indianapolis
Historic Athenaeum Found. Bldg.
401 E Michigan St., Ste.A
Indianapolis, IN 46204
Ph: (317)631-3733
Fax: (317)631-4530
E-mail: indyrotary@sbcglobal.net
URL: http://www.indyrotary.org
Contact: Susan S. Harmless, Exec.Dir.
Local.

5469 ■ Rural Rental Housing Association of Indiana (RRHAI)
9202 N Meridian St., Ste.250
Indianapolis, IN 46260
Fax: (888)471-8475
Free: (866)546-7742
E-mail: info@rrhain.org
URL: http://www.rrhain.org
Contact: Mark Valenti, Pres.
Founded: 1983. **State.**

5470 ■ Service Corps of Retired Executives-Chapter 6 (SCORE)
8500 Keystone Crossing, Ste.401
Indianapolis, IN 46240
Ph: (317)226-7264
Fax: (317)226-7259
E-mail: score@indyscore.org
URL: http://www.score-indianapolis.org
Members: 35. **Local.** Consults those who want to start a new business or grow an existing business. **Affiliated With:** Indiana Small Business Development Center; National Score Foundation. **Conventions/Meetings:** monthly seminar - every 3rd Thursday.

5471 ■ Service Station Dealers Association of Indiana
6801 Lake Plaza Dr.
Indianapolis, IN 46220
Ph: (317)849-4099
Fax: (317)849-4491
Contact: Roy Schwettman, Exec.Dir.
Membership Dues: $99 (annual). **State.**

5472 ■ Sheet Metal Contractors Association of Central Indiana (SMACNA)
One N Pennsylvania St., Ste.600
Indianapolis, IN 46204
Ph: (317)686-1180
Fax: (317)686-1890
E-mail: smacnaindy@msn.com
URL: http://www.smacnaindiana.com
Local. Affiliated With: Sheet Metal and Air Conditioning Contractors' National Association.

5473 ■ Sigma Theta Tau International Honor Society of Nursing
550 W North St.
Indianapolis, IN 46202
Ph: (317)634-8171
Free: (888)634-7575
URL: http://www.nursingsociety.org
Contact: Nancy Dickenson Hazard, CEO
Local.

5474 ■ Society of Bioprocessing Professionals (SBP)
c/o Roger V. Brunkow
1020 W. 72nd St.
Indianapolis, IN 46260-4037
Ph: (317)257-0845
Fax: (317)257-8986
E-mail: rbrunkow@bioprocessingprofessionals.org
URL: http://www.bioprocessingprofessionals.org
Contact: Roger Brunkow, Pres.
Founded: 2002. **Members:** 165. **Membership Dues:** $90 (annual). **Staff:** 1. Provides educational networking opportunities for Bioprocessing Professionals from all relevant disciplines to share and advance bioprocessing technology through the application of science, engineering, quality principles, and experience in manufacturing. **Conventions/Meetings:** annual Bioprocessing Institute - workshop, with 10

parallel training sessions related to bioprocessing/biomanufacturing (exhibits).

5475 ■ Society of Broadcast Engineers, Chapter 25, Indianapolis
9247 N Meridian St., Ste.305
Indianapolis, IN 46260
Ph: (317)846-9000
Fax: (317)846-9120
URL: http://www.broadcast.net/~sbe25
Contact: Phil Alexander, Chm.

Local. Serves the interests of broadcast engineers. Promotes the profession and related fields for both theoretical and practical applications. Advocates for technical advancement of the industry. **Computer Services:** Mailing lists, of members. **Affiliated With:** Society of Broadcast Engineers.

5476 ■ Society of Consumer Affairs Professionals in Business, Indiana Chapter
c/o Roger Reeves, CRM Consultant
Cross Telecom
12032 Kingfisher Ct.
Indianapolis, IN 46236
Ph: (317)823-0895
Fax: (317)823-0969
E-mail: indiana@socap.org
URL: National Affiliate–www.socap.org

State. Affiliated With: Society of Consumer Affairs Professionals in Business.

5477 ■ Society of Indiana Pioneers (SIP)
140 N Senate Ave.
Indianapolis, IN 46204-2207
Ph: (317)233-6588
E-mail: jreveritt@aol.com
URL: http://www.indianapioneers.com
Contact: Ms. Jamia Jacobsen, Pres.

Founded: 1916. **Members:** 950. **Membership Dues:** regular, associate, $20 (annual) • junior (17 years or younger), $10 (annual) • life, $500. **Staff:** 1. Individuals having at least one ancestor who was a resident of Indiana during the pioneer period, lasting from 1825-1850. Seeks to honor the memory of Indiana pioneers and their work, which opened Indiana to settlement. Works with other historical agencies to disseminate information on the history of Indiana, its leaders, and its residents. Sponsors trips for members within Indiana or to adjoining states. **Awards: Frequency:** annual. **Type:** recognition. **Recipient:** for an outstanding member of the Indiana Junior Historical Society. **Publications:** *Yearbook of the Society of Indiana Pioneers*, annual. **Price:** $5.00 • Book. **Conventions/Meetings:** annual meeting and dinner - always November, in Indianapolis, IN.

5478 ■ Society of Manufacturing Engineers - ITT - Indianapolis S178
ITT - Indianapolis, Automated Mfg. Tech.
6744 Caribou Cir.
Indianapolis, IN 46278
Ph: (317)875-8640
Fax: (317)875-8641
E-mail: mboudaia@itt-tech.edu
URL: National Affiliate–www.sme.org
Contact: Mohammed Boudaia, Contact

Local. Advances manufacturing knowledge to gain competitive advantage. Improves skills and manufacturing solutions for the growth of economy. Provides resources and opportunities for manufacturing professionals. **Affiliated With:** Materials Properties Council.

5479 ■ Society of Manufacturing Engineers - Purdue University - Indianapolis S098
799 W Michigan St.
Indianapolis, IN 46202
Ph: (317)274-0829
Fax: (317)278-3669
E-mail: rennels@engr.iupui.edu
URL: National Affiliate–www.sme.org
Contact: Kenneth Rennels, Contact

Local. Advances manufacturing knowledge to gain competitive advantage. Improves skills and manufacturing solutions for the growth of economy. Provides resources and opportunities for manufacturing professionals.

5480 ■ Society of Professional Journalists (SPJ)
c/o Patty Mengers (VOL)
3909 N Meridian St.
Indianapolis, IN 46208
Ph: (317)927-8000
Fax: (317)920-4789
URL: http://www.spj.org

Regional. **Formerly:** (2005) Society of Professional Journalists, Greater Philadelphia Chapter.

5481 ■ Southern Indiana, National Association of Women Business Owners
PO Box 20120
Indianapolis, IN 46220
Ph: (317)466-2768
Fax: (317)578-2876
E-mail: info@nawboindy.org
URL: http://www.nawboindy.org
Contact: Billie Dragoo, Pres..

Regional. **Affiliated With:** National Association of Women Business Owners.

5482 ■ Special Libraries Association, Indiana Chapter
c/o Christina Bennett-McNew, Pres.-Elect
Lib. Services Infotrieve Inc.
355 E Merrill Bldg. 58/3
Indianapolis, IN 46225
Ph: (317)276-9278
E-mail: cbennett_librarian@yahoo.com
URL: http://www.in-sla.org
Contact: Christina Bennett-McNew, Pres.-Elect

State. Seeks to advance the leadership role of special librarians. Promotes and strengthens members through learning, advocacy and networking initiatives. **Affiliated With:** Special Libraries Association.

5483 ■ Special Olympics Indiana
6100 W 96th St., Ste.270
Indianapolis, IN 46278
Ph: (317)328-2000
Fax: (317)328-2018
Free: (800)742-0612
E-mail: information@soindiana.org
URL: http://www.specialolympicsindiana.org
Contact: Deborah J. Hesse, Pres./CEO

Founded: 1968. **Staff:** 13. **Budget:** $1,625,019. **State Groups:** 1. **Local Groups:** 225. **State**. Provides year-round sports training and competition opportunities for children and adults with mental retardation. **Publications:** *In Reach*, quarterly. Newsletters • *Sports Page*, annual. Newsletter. **Circulation:** 7,500 • *Sports Report*, quarterly. Newsletter. **Conventions/Meetings:** annual conference.

5484 ■ State Guard Association of the United States, Indiana
c/o Scott R. Collins, LTC
Indiana Guard Reserve
2002 S Holt Rd.
Indianapolis, IN 46241-4839
Ph: (317)786-2327 (317)244-7173
URL: National Affiliate–www.sgaus.org
Contact: Scott R. Collins LTC, Contact

State. **Affiliated With:** State Guard Association of the United States.

5485 ■ Sweet Adelines International, Capital City Chorus
All Soul's Unitarian Church
5805 E 56th St.
Indianapolis, IN 46226-1526
Ph: (317)241-7664
E-mail: general@capitalcitychorus.net
URL: http://www.capitalcitychorus.net
Contact: Bev Miller, Dir.

Local. Advances the musical art form of barbershop harmony through education and performances. Provides education, training and coaching in the development of women's four-part barbershop harmony. **Affiliated With:** Sweet Adelines International.

5486 ■ Sycamore Ice Skating Club (SISC)
Perry Park Ice Rink
451 E Stop, 11 Rd.
Indianapolis, IN 46217-4424
E-mail: sycamoreisc@yahoo.com
URL: http://www.geocities.comsiscfigure8index.htm
Contact: Barbara Rector, Contact

Local. Provides programs to encourage participation and achievement in the sport of figure skating on ice. Defines and maintains uniform standards of skating proficiency. Organizes and sponsors competitions and exhibitions for the purpose of stimulating interest in figure skating. **Affiliated With:** United States Figure Skating Association.

5487 ■ Table Tennis Club of Indianapolis
8009-B E Washington St.
Indianapolis, IN 46219
Ph: (317)895-8394
E-mail: craig.teegarden@indytabletennis.com
URL: http://www.indytabletennis.com
Contact: Craig Teegarden, Contact

Local. **Affiliated With:** U.S.A. Table Tennis.

5488 ■ United Cerebral Palsy Association of Greater Indiana
1915 W 18th St., Ste.C
Indianapolis, IN 46202-1016
Ph: (317)632-3561
Fax: (317)632-3338
Free: (800)723-7620
E-mail: donnar@ucpaindy.org
URL: National Affiliate–www.ucp.org
Contact: Donna Roberts, Exec.Dir.

Founded: 1953. **Members:** 15. **Membership Dues:** board, $40 (annual). **Staff:** 2. **Budget:** $324,000. **Regional Groups:** 1. **State**. Aids persons with cerebral palsy, and their families. Goals are to prevent cerebral palsy, minimizes its effects, and improves the quality of life for persons with cerebral palsy, and their families. **Libraries: Type:** reference. **Subjects:** cerebral palsy, treatment, general disability issues. **Awards:** Book-Coleman Scholarship. **Frequency:** annual. **Type:** scholarship. **Recipient:** to an Indiana high school senior. **Committees:** Finance; Fund Development; Program. **Affiliated With:** United Cerebral Palsy Associations. **Publications:** Newsletter. **Conventions/Meetings:** annual luncheon.

5489 ■ United Federation of Doll Clubs - Region 12
10195 E 86th St.
Indianapolis, IN 46256
E-mail: lindacdolls@yahoo.com
URL: http://www.ufdc.org/ufdcregion12.htm
Contact: Linda Cantwell, Dir.

Regional. **Affiliated With:** United Federation of Doll Clubs.

5490 ■ United States Naval Sea Cadet Corps - Cruiser Indianapolis (CA 35) Division
NMCRC Indianapolis
3010 N White River Pkwy., East Dr.
Indianapolis, IN 46208-4983
E-mail: ca35dewitt@aol.com
URL: http://dolphin.seacadets.org/US_units/UnitDetails.asp?UnitID=091IND
Contact: LTJG Eddie L. Dewitt NSCC, Commanding Officer

Local. Works to instill good citizenship and patriotism in youth. Encourages qualities such as personal neatness, loyalty, obedience, dependability, and responsibility to others. Offers courses in physical fitness and military drill, first aid, water safety, basic seamanship, and naval history and traditions. **Affiliated With:** Naval Sea Cadet Corps.

5491 ■ United Way of Central Indiana
PO Box 88409
Indianapolis, IN 46208-0409
Ph: (317)923-1466
Fax: (317)921-1355
E-mail: community@uwci.org
URL: http://www.uwci.org
Contact: Ellen K. Annala, Pres./CEO
Founded: 1918. **Staff:** 85. **Local**. Seeks to mobilize people in the community to care for one another. **Councils:** Community Service. **Affiliated With:** United Way of America. **Publications:** Annual Report, annual. Contains a review of the year's accomplishments and a financial statement. **Circulation:** 2,000.

5492 ■ Variety of Indiana
6919 E 10th St., Ste.B5
Indianapolis, IN 46219-4811
Ph: (317)357-3660
Fax: (317)357-3379
E-mail: varietyindiana@usvariety.org
URL: National Affiliate–www.usvariety.org
State. **Affiliated With:** Variety International - The Children's Charity.

5493 ■ Veterans of Foreign Wars, Indiana Department
c/o David Havely, Adj./Quartermaster
PO Box 361370
Indianapolis, IN 46236
Ph: (317)377-1795
Fax: (317)377-1797
E-mail: have313@aol.com
URL: http://hometown.aol.com/vfwin/index.html
Contact: David Havely, Adj./Quartermaster
State. Provides assistance to veterans and their families. Promotes fraternalism and patriotism.

5494 ■ Vietnam Veterans of America, Chapter 295
PO Box 269279
Indianapolis, IN 46226-9279
Ph: (317)547-4748
E-mail: info@vva295.org
URL: http://www.vva295.org
Local. **Affiliated With:** Vietnam Veterans of America.

5495 ■ Village of Turner Trace
c/o Darrell Brosius, Developer
PO Box 53232
Indianapolis, IN 46253
Ph: (317)341-0364
E-mail: darrell@turnertrace.com
URL: http://www.turnertrace.com
Contact: Darrell Brosius, Developer
Local. **Formerly:** (2005) Village of Turner Trace Property Owners Association.

5496 ■ Volunteers of America of Indiana
927 N Pennsylvania St.
Indianapolis, IN 46204
Ph: (317)686-5800
E-mail: information@voain.org
URL: http://www.voain.org
Contact: Timothy R. Campbell, Pres./CEO
State. Provides local human service programs and opportunities for individual and community involvement. **Affiliated With:** Volunteers of America.

5497 ■ VSA arts of Indiana (VSAI)
c/o Gayle Holtman, Dir. of Districts and Residencies
Harrison Center for the Arts
1505 N Delaware St., Ste.100
Indianapolis, IN 46202
Ph: (317)974-4123
Fax: (317)974-4117
Free: (800)484-8055
E-mail: gholtman@vsai.org
URL: http://www.vsai.org
Contact: Jim Nulty, Pres./CEO
Founded: 1974. **State**. Works to educate through quality arts experiences, advocates for children with disabilities, and provides access to the arts to all individuals. **Affiliated With:** VSA arts.

5498 ■ Warren Arts and Education Foundation (WAEF)
c/o Kevin Weinman, Pres.
975 N Post Rd.
Indianapolis, IN 46219
Ph: (317)869-4383
Fax: (317)869-4385
E-mail: mmckinle@warren.k12.in.us
URL: http://www.warrenfoundation.org
Contact: Mary McKinley, Exec.Dir.
Local. Provides opportunities and recognition for students and staff in education and the arts.

5499 ■ White River Sound Chorus of Sweet Adelines International
Hope Community Church
7440 Hague Rd.
Indianapolis, IN 46256-1930
Ph: (317)408-1139
E-mail: director@whiteriversoundchorus.org
URL: http://www.whiteriversoundchorus.org
Contact: Debbie Thistle, Dir.
Local. Advances the musical art form of barbershop harmony through education and performances. Provides education, training and coaching in the development of women's four-part barbershop harmony. **Affiliated With:** Sweet Adelines International.

5500 ■ Wine and Spirits Wholesalers of Indiana (WSWI)
c/o James A. Purucker, Exec.Dir.
1 Indiana Sq., Ste.150
Indianapolis, IN 46204-2004
Ph: (317)656-8600
Fax: (317)656-8610
URL: http://www.wswi.com
State.

5501 ■ Winter Club of Indianapolis
Indiana State Fairgrounds
Pepsi Coliseum
1202 E 38th
Indianapolis, IN 46224
E-mail: kdp9@yahoo.com
URL: http://www.winterclubindy.com
Contact: Katie Patterson, Pres.
Local. Provides programs to encourage participation and achievement in the sport of figure skating on ice. Defines and maintains uniform standards of skating proficiency. Organizes and sponsors competitions and exhibitions for the purpose of stimulating interest in figure skating. **Affiliated With:** United States Figure Skating Association.

5502 ■ Wooden Canoe Heritage Association, Indiana
c/o Scott Verbarg, Pres.
5216 Limestone Ct.
Indianapolis, IN 46237
E-mail: ssverbarg@yahoo.com
URL: National Affiliate–www.wcha.org
Contact: Scott Verbarg, Pres.
State. **Affiliated With:** Wooden Canoe Heritage Association.

5503 ■ YMCA - Arthur Jordan
c/o Christopher Butler, Exec.Dir.
8400 Westfield Blvd.
Indianapolis, IN 46240
Ph: (317)253-3206
Fax: (317)259-5652
URL: http://www.indymca.org
Contact: Christopher Butler, Exec.Dir.
Local.

5504 ■ YMCA - Benjamin Harrison Branch
c/o Tim McCoy, Exec.Dir.
5736 Lee Rd.
Indianapolis, IN 46216
Ph: (317)547-9622
Fax: (317)547-9640
URL: http://www.indymca.org
Contact: Tim McCoy, Exec.Dir.
Local. Strives to put Christian principles into practice through programs that enhance personal growth and improve health of spirit, mind, and body for all.

5505 ■ Young Audiences of Indiana
3921 N Meridian St., Ste.46208
Indianapolis, IN 46208
Ph: (317)925-4043
Fax: (317)925-0654
E-mail: office@yaindy.org
URL: http://www.yaindy.org
Contact: M. Travis Dinicola, Dir. of PR & Technology
Founded: 1961. **Local**. Seeks to have professional ensembles present live educational programs in music, dance, and theatre to children (grades K-12) during school hours. Works to increase the creative and imaginative capacities of children through listening and participating in live performing arts experiences; to help build future audiences for the performing arts; to develop the performing arts resources of communities by training ensembles in educational techniques. Trains musicians, dancers, and actors to present performances, demonstrations, workshops, and residencies in each of the art forms. **Affiliated With:** Young Audiences.

5506 ■ Young Life Carmel
418 E 34th St.
Indianapolis, IN 46205
Ph: (317)923-1319
Fax: (317)941-5045
URL: http://whereis.younglife.org/FriendlyUrlRedirector.aspx?ID=A-IN84
Local.

5507 ■ Young Life Greater Muncie
1010 N Capitol Ave., Ste.A100
Indianapolis, IN 46204
Ph: (317)684-7005
Fax: (317)684-7007
URL: http://sites.younglife.org/_layouts/ylext/default.aspx?ID=A-IN94
Local. **Affiliated With:** Young Life.

5508 ■ Young Life Greencastle
1010 N Capitol Ave., Ste.A100
Indianapolis, IN 46204
Ph: (317)684-7005
Fax: (317)684-7007
URL: http://Greencastle.younglife.org
Local.

5509 ■ Young Life Hamilton-Southeastern
418 E 34th St.
Indianapolis, IN 46205
Ph: (317)923-1319
Fax: (317)941-5045
URL: http://whereis.younglife.org/FriendlyUrlRedirector.aspx?ID=A-IN85
Local.

5510 ■ Young Life Indiana Region
1010 N Capitol Ave., Ste.A100
Indianapolis, IN 46204
Ph: (317)684-7005
Fax: (317)684-7007
URL: http://indiana.younglife.org
Regional.

5511 ■ Young Life Indianapolis Urban Initiative
418 E 34th St.
Indianapolis, IN 46205
Ph: (317)923-1319
Fax: (317)941-5045
URL: http://sites.younglife.org/_layouts/ylext/default.aspx?ID=A-IN89
Local. **Affiliated With:** Young Life.

5512 ■ Young Life Lawrence
418 E 34th St.
Indianapolis, IN 46205
Ph: (317)923-1319
Fax: (317)941-5045
URL: http://whereis.younglife.org/FriendlyUrlRedirector.aspx?ID=A-IN87
Local.

5513 ■ Young Life Northwest Indianapolis
418 E 34th
Indianapolis, IN 46205
Ph: (317)923-1319
Fax: (317)941-5045
URL: http://whereis.younglife.org/FriendlyUrlRedirector.aspx?ID=A-IN83
Local.

5514 ■ Young Life Washington Township
418 E 34th St.
Indianapolis, IN 46205
Ph: (317)923-1319
Fax: (317)941-5045
URL: http://whereis.younglife.org/FriendlyUrlRedirector.aspx?ID=A-IN24
Local.

5515 ■ Young Life Zionsville
418 E 34th St.
Indianapolis, IN 46205
Ph: (317)923-1319
Fax: (317)941-5045
URL: http://whereis.younglife.org/FriendlyUrlRedirector.aspx?ID=A-IN86
Local.

5516 ■ Young Women's Christian Association of Indianapolis
c/o Grace Ketchum, Exec.Dir.
4460 Guion Rd.
Indianapolis, IN 46254
Ph: (317)299-2750
Fax: (317)298-0641
E-mail: gketchum@ywca-indy.org

5517 ■ Zeta Beta Tau Fraternity
3905 Vincennes Rd., Ste.300
Indianapolis, IN 46268
Ph: (317)334-1898
Fax: (317)334-1899
E-mail: zbt@zbtnational.org
URL: http://www.zetabetatau.org
Contact: Jonathan I. Yulish, Exec.Dir.
Local.

Ireland

5518 ■ Indiana Health Information Management Association (IHIMA)
c/o IHIMA Central Office Coor.
PO Box 96
Ireland, IN 47545-0096
Ph: (812)630-3598
Fax: (812)634-2430
E-mail: centraloffice@ihima.org
URL: http://www.ihima.org
Contact: Cheryl Barbee RHIA, Pres.
Founded: 1948. **Members:** 900. **Membership Dues:** non-AHIMA members, $50 (annual) • corporate, $175 (annual). **State**. Committed to quality of health information for the benefit of patients, providers and other users of health care information. Seeks to advance health information technologies and professional standards; advocate patient privacy rights and confidentiality of health information; influence public and private policies and educate the public regarding health; provide leadership in education and professional development. **Affiliated With:** American Health Information Management Association. **Conventions/Meetings:** annual meeting.

Jamestown

5519 ■ American Legion, Jamestown Post 395
PO Box 310
Jamestown, IN 46147
Ph: (317)676-5937
Fax: (317)237-9891
URL: National Affiliate–www.legion.org
Local. Affiliated With: American Legion.

5520 ■ Jackson Township Historical Society
c/o Marilyn S. Kernodle
PO Box 297
41 W Main St.
Jamestown, IN 46147-0297
Ph: (765)676-5114
E-mail: jths@countyhistory.com
URL: http://www.countyhistory.com/jths.html
Contact: Marilyn Kernodle, Pres.
Founded: 2001. **Members:** 87. **Membership Dues:** single or family, $10 (annual). **Staff:** 4. **Local.** Purchased building housing local newspaper operation which includes presses, linotype machines, etc. Plans to open as a printing museum and depository for artifacts from local area.

Jasonville

5521 ■ American Legion, Jasonville Post 172
231 W Main St.
Jasonville, IN 47438
Ph: (812)665-9002
Fax: (317)237-9891
URL: National Affiliate–www.legion.org
Local. Affiliated With: American Legion.

5522 ■ Shakamak Chamber of Commerce
PO Box 101
Jasonville, IN 47438
Ph: (812)665-3622
Contact: Diane Ellis, Pres.
Local.

Jasper

5523 ■ American Cancer Society, Mid-Southwestern Area Service Center
1500 Meridian Rd.
Jasper, IN 47546
Ph: (812)482-7545
Fax: (812)482-6962
URL: National Affiliate–www.cancer.org
Regional. Affiliated With: American Cancer Society.

5524 ■ American Guild of Organists, University of Evansville C592
c/o Timothy Weisman, Chapter Dean
4544 Baden Strasse
Jasper, IN 47546-9176
Ph: (812)488-3485
E-mail: tw49@evansville.edu
URL: http://www.evansvilleago.org
Contact: Timothy Weisman, Chapter Dean
Local. Affiliated With: American Guild of Organists.

5525 ■ American Legion, Dubois County Post 147
1220 Newton St.
Jasper, IN 47546
Ph: (812)482-3454
Fax: (317)237-9891
URL: National Affiliate–www.legion.org
Local. Affiliated With: American Legion.

5526 ■ Daguerre Club of Indiana
c/o Robert McCarty
PO Box 1050
Jasper, IN 47546
Ph: (812)482-5542
E-mail: rpmcarty@fullnet.com
URL: National Affiliate–ppa.com
Contact: Robert McCarty, Contact
Local. Affiliated With: Professional Photographers of America.

5527 ■ Dubois/Pike and Warrick County RSVP
c/o Mary E. Beckman, Dir.
PO Box 729
Jasper, IN 47547-0729
Ph: (812)482-2233
Fax: (812)482-1071
E-mail: rsvptricap@psci.net
URL: http://www.seniorcorps.gov/about/programs/rsvp_state.asp?usestateabbr=in&Search4.x=29&Search4.y=10
Contact: Mary E. Beckman, Dir.
Local. Affiliated With: Retired and Senior Volunteer Program.

5528 ■ Jasper Chamber of Commerce (JCC)
302 W 6th St.
PO Box 307
Jasper, IN 47547-0307
Ph: (812)482-6866
Fax: (812)482-1883
E-mail: chamber@jasperin.org
URL: http://www.jasperin.org
Founded: 1954. **Membership Dues:** business (based on the number of employees), $165-$315 (annual) • church, club, organization, $100 (annual) • retiree, $35 (annual). **Local.** Promotes business and community development in Jasper, IN. Sponsors annual Strassenfest. **Affiliated With:** U.S. Chamber of Commerce. **Publications:** *Jasper Fact Book/Membership Directory*, periodic • *Manufacturing and Business Directory*, periodic.

5529 ■ Jasper - Wyldlife
1180 Wernsing Rd.
Jasper, IN 47546
Ph: (812)482-2000
URL: http://sites.younglife.org/sites/jasperwyldlife/default.aspx
Local. Affiliated With: Young Life.

5530 ■ Kids of the Kingdom
c/o Whitney Ruff
13 Rolling Ridge Ct.
Jasper, IN 47546-9098
E-mail: kidsofthekingdom@neo.rr.com
URL: http://kidsofthekingdom.tripod.com
Contact: Whitney Ruff, Contact
Local.

5531 ■ National Association of Home Builders of the U.S., Dubois County Builders Association
c/o Judy Mehringer
Local No. 1511
2246 W. Skyview Dr.
Jasper, IN 47546-8216
Ph: (812)482-1184
Fax: (812)634-6793
E-mail: rlmsales@psci.net
URL: National Affiliate–www.nahb.org
Contact: Ms. Judy A. Mehringer, Exec. Officer
Founded: 1987. **Members:** 164. **Membership Dues:** all, $320 (annual). **Staff:** 1. **Local.** Single and multifamily home builders, commercial builders, and others associated with the building industry. **Awards: Frequency:** annual. **Type:** scholarship. **Affiliated With:** National Association of Home Builders.

5532 ■ National Speleological Society, Evansville Metropolitan Grotto
c/o Bob Sergesketter
1090 Hopf Ave.
Jasper, IN 47546-3822

Ph: (812)482-5517
E-mail: emg@caves.org
URL: http://www.caves.org/grotto/emg
Contact: Bob Sergesketter, Contact
Local. Seeks to study, explore and conserve cave and karst resources. Protects access to caves and promotes responsible caving. Encourages responsible management of caves and their unique environments. **Affiliated With:** National Speleological Society.

5533 ■ Navy Club of Dubois County - Ship No. 90
1810 W 5th Ave.
Jasper, IN 47546
Ph: (812)482-3512
URL: National Affiliate–www.navyclubusa.org
Contact: Kenneth Schuetter, Commander
Local. Represents individuals who are, or have been, in the active service of the U.S. Navy, Naval Reserve, Marine Corps, Marine Corps Reserve, and Coast Guard. Promotes and encourages further public interest in the U.S. Navy and its history. Upholds the spirit and ideals of the U.S. Navy. Acts as a public forum for members' views on national defense. Assists the Navy Recruiting Command whenever and wherever possible. Conducts charitable activities. **Affiliated With:** Navy Club of the United States of America.

5534 ■ Phi Theta Kappa, Beta Zeta Rho Chapter - Vincennes University-Jasper
c/o Debbie Kowalchuk
850 Coll. Ave.
Jasper, IN 47546
Ph: (812)481-5910
URL: http://www.ptk.org/directories/chapters/IN/20953-1.htm
Contact: Debbie Kowalchuk, Advisor
Local.

5535 ■ Plumbing-Heating-Cooling Contractors Association, South Central Indiana
c/o Kevin Gudorf, Pres.
1280 3rd Ave.
Jasper, IN 47546-3706
Ph: (812)634-5101
Fax: (812)634-5104
URL: National Affiliate–www.phccweb.org
Contact: Kevin Gudorf, Pres.
Local. Represents the plumbing, heating and cooling contractors. Promotes the construction industry. Protects the environment, health, safety and comfort of society. **Affiliated With:** Plumbing-Heating-Cooling Contractors Association.

5536 ■ YL of Dubois Co - Young Life
1180 Wernsing Rd.
Jasper, IN 47546
Ph: (812)482-2000
URL: http://sites.younglife.org/_layouts/ylext/default.aspx?ID=C-914
Local. **Affiliated With:** Young Life.

5537 ■ Young Life Jasper
1180 Wernsing Rd.
Jasper, IN 47546
Ph: (812)482-2000
Fax: (812)482-9784
URL: http://whereis.younglife.org/FriendlyUrlRedirector.aspx?ID=A-IN57
Local.

Jeffersonville

5538 ■ American Legion, Lawrence Capehart Post 35
217 W Court Ave.
Jeffersonville, IN 47130
Ph: (812)283-8020
Fax: (317)237-9891
URL: National Affiliate–www.legion.org
Local. **Affiliated With:** American Legion.

5539 ■ American Society for Quality, Louisville Section 0912
c/o Kelly Roggenkamp
PO Box 1144
Jeffersonville, IN 47131-1144
Ph: (812)923-1787
E-mail: kelrog@att.net
URL: http://www.asqlouisville.org
Contact: Kelly Roggenkamp, Contact
Local. Advances learning, quality improvement and knowledge exchange to improve business results and to create better workplaces and communities worldwide. Provides a forum for information exchange, professional development and continuous learning in the science of quality. **Affiliated With:** American Society for Quality.

5540 ■ Clark County Historical Society/Howard Steamboat Museum
c/o Yvonne Knight, Administrator
PO Box 606
Jeffersonville, IN 47131-0606
Ph: (812)283-3728
Fax: (812)283-6049
Free: (888)472-0606
E-mail: hsmsteam@aol.com
URL: http://www.steamboatmuseum.org
Contact: Yvonne Knight, Administrator
Founded: 1958. **Members:** 460. **Membership Dues:** senior citizen (65 and older), student, $10 (annual) • adult, $15 (annual) • family, $25 (annual) • contributor, $26-$99 (annual) • friend, $100-$199 (annual) • benefactor, $200-$499 (annual) • James E. and Loretta Howard Society, $500 (annual). **Staff:** 6. **Budget:** $50,000. **Local**. Individuals interested in the history of Clark County, IN, and steamboat and river history. Conducts tours. Sponsors festival. Operates Howard Steamboat Museum. **Libraries: Type:** open to the public. **Holdings:** 2,000. **Subjects:** steamboat history, river history, general interest. **Publications:** *Bitts and Pieces*, semiannual. Newsletter. **Conventions/Meetings:** annual meeting - always last Saturday in September.

5541 ■ Clark - Floyd Counties Convention and Tourism Bureau
315 Southern Indiana Ave.
Jeffersonville, IN 47130
Ph: (812)282-6654
Fax: (812)282-1904
Free: (800)552-3842
E-mail: tourism@sunnysideoflouisville.org
URL: http://www.sunnysideoflouisville.org
Contact: James P. Keith CAE, Exec.Dir.
Staff: 7. **Local**. Promotes business and tourism in Clark and Floyd counties, IN. **Formerly:** (2005) Southern Indiana, Clark-Floyd Counties Convention and Tourism Bureau.

5542 ■ Jeffersonville Main Street
PO Box 1474
Jeffersonville, IN 47131-1474
Ph: (812)283-0301
Fax: (812)283-5892
E-mail: info@jeffmainstreet.org
URL: http://www.jeffmainstreet.org
Contact: Jay Coursey Ellis, Exec.Dir.
Local.

5543 ■ Kentuckiana Golf Course Superintendents Association (KGCSA)
3310 E Hwy. 62, Ste.4
PMB 107
Jeffersonville, IN 47130
Ph: (812)282-3305
E-mail: max_golf@msn.com
URL: http://www.kigcsa.org
Contact: Max Mercer, Pres.
Founded: 1948. **Local**. Represents the interests of golf course superintendents. Advances members' profession for career success. Enhances the enjoyment, growth and vitality in the game of golf. Educates members concerning efficient and economical management of golf courses. **Affiliated With:** Golf Course Superintendents Association of America.

5544 ■ South Central Indiana AIFA
2004 Charlestown-New Albany PK
Jeffersonville, IN 47130
Ph: (813)283-7975
Fax: (812)284-7295
URL: National Affiliate–www.naifa.org
Local. Represents the interest of insurance and financial advisors. Advocates for a positive legislative and regulatory environment. Enhances business and professional skills of members. **Affiliated With:** National Association of Insurance and Financial Advisors.

Jonesboro

5545 ■ American Legion, Mississinewa Post 95
PO Box 95
Jonesboro, IN 46938
Ph: (317)674-8623
Fax: (317)237-9891
URL: National Affiliate–www.legion.org
Local. **Affiliated With:** American Legion.

5546 ■ Christmas City REACT
604 S Corder St.
Jonesboro, IN 46938
Ph: (765)674-2992
URL: http://www.reactintl.org/teaminfo/usa_teams/teams-usin.htm
Local. Trained communication experts and professional volunteers. Provides volunteer public service and emergency communications through the use of radios (Citizen Band, General Mobile Radio Service, UHF and HAM). Coordinates with radio industries and government on safety communication matters and supports charitable activities and community organizations.

Kempton

5547 ■ Indiana State Trappers Association (ISTA)
c/o Tom Morelock, Pres.
PO Box 234
Kempton, IN 46049
Ph: (765)947-5425
E-mail: longspring@aol.com
URL: http://www.indianatrappers.org
Contact: Tom Morelock, Pres.
State. **Affiliated With:** National Trappers Association.

5548 ■ National Active and Retired Federal Employees Association - Kokomo 562
2589 S 1050 W
Kempton, IN 46049-9378
Ph: (765)947-5272
URL: National Affiliate–www.narfe.org
Contact: Louis R. Tragesser, Contact
Local. Protects the retirement future of employees through education. Informs members on issues affecting the retirement. **Affiliated With:** National Association of Retired Federal Employees.

Kendallville

5549 ■ American Legion, Kendallville Post 86
322 S Main St.
Kendallville, IN 46755
Ph: (219)347-9978
Fax: (317)237-9891
URL: National Affiliate–www.legion.org
Local. **Affiliated With:** American Legion.

5550 ■ Kendallville Area Chamber of Commerce
122 S Main St.
Kendallville, IN 46755-1716

Ph: (260)347-1554
Fax: (260)347-1575
Free: (877)347-1554
E-mail: kchamber@locl.net
URL: http://www.kendallvillechamber.com
Contact: Kimm Hunt, Exec.Dir.
Founded: 1925. **Local**. Promotes business and community development in Kendallville, IN. **Publications:** *Chamber Connection*, bimonthly. Newsletter. **Advertising:** accepted.

5551 ■ Northeastern Indiana Association of Realtors
521 Professional Way
Kendallville, IN 46755
Ph: (260)347-1593
Fax: (260)347-1081
Free: (800)373-8119
E-mail: niaor1@mchsi.com
URL: http://www.neiaor.org
Contact: Saundra Bultemeier, Exec.VP
Local. Strives to develop real estate business practices. Advocates the right to own, use and transfer real property. Provides a facility for professional development, research and exchange of information among members and to the general public. **Affiliated With:** National Association of Realtors.

Kentland

5552 ■ American Legion, Hedrick-Brandt Post 23
PO Box 66
Kentland, IN 47951
Ph: (219)474-6113
Fax: (317)237-9891
URL: National Affiliate–www.legion.org
Local. **Affiliated With:** American Legion.

5553 ■ Kentland Area Chamber of Commerce
PO Box 273
Kentland, IN 47951-0273
Ph: (219)474-6665
Fax: (219)474-5071
E-mail: knochel@kentlandbank.com
URL: http://www.kentlandindiana.org/Business/kaindex.html
Contact: Sue Knochel, Membership/Welcoming Committee
Local. Promotes business and community development in Kentland, IN.

5554 ■ Newton County Historical Society
c/o Yvonne Kay
PO Box 303
Kentland, IN 47951
Ph: (219)474-6944
E-mail: newtonhs@ffni.com
URL: http://www.rootsweb.com/~innewton
Contact: Yvonne Kay, Pres.
Founded: 1991. **Members:** 148. **Membership Dues:** family, $10 (annual) • individual, $6 (annual). **Budget:** $10,000. **Local**. Seeks to record and preserve local history and family history as it relates to the larger context of Indiana history. Fosters research and preserves artifacts relating to the area. **Libraries: Type:** reference. **Holdings:** 150; articles, books, periodicals. **Subjects:** Indiana and local history, family history. **Divisions:** Family History. **Publications:** *Morocco Sesquicentennial Historical Collection & Newcomer*. Newsletter. Features local history. **Price:** included in membership dues; $3.00/issue. **Circulation:** 200. Alternate Formats: online. **Conventions/Meetings:** monthly meeting - 4th Monday of month; Avg. Attendance: 60.

Kingman

5555 ■ American Legion, Kingman Post 384
PO Box 443
Kingman, IN 47952
Ph: (317)397-8122
Fax: (317)237-9891
URL: National Affiliate–www.legion.org
Local. **Affiliated With:** American Legion.

Kingsford Heights

5556 ■ American Legion, Zook-Farrington Post 434
500 Grayton Rd.
Kingsford Heights, IN 46346
Ph: (219)393-9288
Fax: (317)237-9891
URL: National Affiliate–www.legion.org
Local. **Affiliated With:** American Legion.

Kirklin

5557 ■ American Legion, Indiana Post 310
c/o Clifton E. Peterson
PO Box 217
Kirklin, IN 46050
Ph: (317)630-1300
Fax: (317)237-9891
URL: National Affiliate–www.legion.org
Contact: Clifton E. Peterson, Contact
Local. **Affiliated With:** American Legion.

Knightstown

5558 ■ American Legion, Knightstown Post 152
22 S Franklin St.
Knightstown, IN 46148
Ph: (317)345-5227
Fax: (317)237-9891
URL: National Affiliate–www.legion.org
Local. **Affiliated With:** American Legion.

5559 ■ Knightstown Indiana Chamber of Commerce
PO Box 44
Knightstown, IN 46148-0044
Ph: (765)345-5290
Free: (800)668-1895
E-mail: info@knightstownchamber.com
URL: http://www.knightstownchamber.com
Contact: Rex Pasco, Pres.
Founded: 1950. **Members:** 75. **Membership Dues:** business, $50 (annual). **Local**. Promotes business and community development in Knightstown, IN area. **Computer Services:** Information services, member listing. **Formerly:** (2005) Knightstown Area Chamber of Commerce.

Knox

5560 ■ American Legion, Albert Williams Post 131
707 S Heaton St.
Knox, IN 46534
Ph: (219)772-4393
Fax: (317)237-9891
URL: National Affiliate–www.legion.org
Local. **Affiliated With:** American Legion.

5561 ■ Starke County Chamber of Commerce
PO Box 5
Knox, IN 46534
Ph: (574)772-5548
Fax; (574)772-0867
E-mail: info@explorestarkecounty.com
URL: http://www.explorestarkecounty.com
Contact: Theda Salmon, Exec.Sec.
Founded: 1984. **Members:** 125. **Local**. Promotes business and community development in the Knox, IN area. Sponsors annual Business fair. Maintains Starke County Fine Arts Commission. Conducts Harvest Days Festival and Harvest Day Parade. **Awards:** Henry F. Schricker. **Type:** scholarship. **Formerly:** (2000) Greater Knox Area Chamber of Commerce. **Publications:** Newsletter, quarterly • Membership Directory, annual. **Conventions/Meetings:** annual dinner - April.

5562 ■ Starke/Pulaski Board of Realtors
0035 E 250 N
Knox, IN 46534
Ph: (574)772-5300
Fax: (574)772-4968
E-mail: beckypulver@nitline.net
URL: National Affiliate–www.realtor.org
Contact: Becky L. Pulver, Exec. Officer
Local. Strives to develop real estate business practices. Advocates the right to own, use and transfer real property. Provides a facility for professional development, research and exchange of information among members and to the general public. **Affiliated With:** National Association of Realtors.

Kokomo

5563 ■ American Legion, Indiana Post 177
c/o Worley David Gaskin
800 N Purdum St.
Kokomo, IN 46901
Ph: (317)459-0363
Fax: (317)237-9891
URL: National Affiliate–www.legion.org
Contact: Worley David Gaskin, Contact
Local. **Affiliated With:** American Legion.

5564 ■ American Legion, James De Armond Golliday Post 6
2604 S Lafountain St.
Kokomo, IN 46902
Ph: (317)453-2501
Fax: (317)237-9891
URL: National Affiliate–www.legion.org
Local. **Affiliated With:** American Legion.

5565 ■ American Society for Microbiology - Indiana Branch
c/o Christian Chauret, Sec.-Treas.
Biology Dept.
Indiana Univ. - Kokomo
2300 S Washington St.
Kokomo, IN 46904
Ph: (765)455-9290
E-mail: cchauret@iuk.edu
URL: http://users.ipfw.edu/merkel/IndianaASM.html
Contact: Jeanne K. Barnett, Pres.
State. Advances the knowledge in the field of microbiology. Improves educational programs and encourages fundamental and applied research in microbiological sciences. Supports training and public information. **Affiliated With:** American Society for Microbiology.

5566 ■ Big Brothers Big Sisters of America of North Central Indiana
207 N Buckeye St.
Kokomo, IN 46902
Ph: (765)452-9638
Fax: (765)454-5577
E-mail: bbbsnciar@sbcglobal.net
URL: http://www.bbbsnci.org
Contact: Ron Powell, Exec.Dir.
Founded: 1977. **Members:** 500. **Staff:** 11. **Budget:** $279,478. **Local**. Consists of adult volunteers who meet regularly with children aged 5 to 15 at time of intake to engage in a variety of activities aimed at broadening their horizons. Emphasizes on the use of positive friendship to help build strengths in young people in order to grow into caring, competent, and confident adults. **Affiliated With:** Big Brothers Big Sisters of America. **Formerly:** Big Brother/Big Sisters of Miami/Fulton Counties. **Publications:** Newsletter, quarterly. **Conventions/Meetings:** bimonthly board meeting.

5567 ■ Howard County Breastfeeding Coalition
c/o Cynthia L Myers
4769 S. 200 E.
Kokomo, IN 46902-9785
Ph: (765)453-0989
Contact: Cynthia L. Myers, Contact
Founded: 2001. **Members:** 15. **Local**. Strives to promote breastfeeding in the home and in public and to educate professionals and the community about the value of human milk and the importance of the breastfeeding relationship.

5568 ■ Howard County Convention and Visitors Commission
1504 N. Reed Rd.
Kokomo, IN 46901
Ph: (765)457-6802
Fax: (765)457-1572
Free: (800)837-0971
E-mail: kokomoin@iquest.net
URL: http://www.kokomo-in.org
Contact: Peggy Ragland Hobson, Exec.Dir.
Founded: 1982. **Staff:** 4. **Budget:** $220,000. **Local**. Promotes tourism in Howard County, IN. **Doing business as:** Kokomo Visitors Bureau; Kokomo Indiana Visitors Bureau. **Publications:** *Dining Guide*, periodic. Brochure • *Meeting Planners Guide*, periodic. Brochure • *Visitor's Guide*, periodic. Brochure. **Price:** free.

5569 ■ Indiana Society of Radiologic Technologists, District 4
c/o Heidi Thomason, BSRT, Pres.
PO Box 9003
Kokomo, IN 46904-9003
Ph: (765)455-9565
E-mail: hthomaso@iuk.edu
URL: http://www.isort.org
Contact: Heidi Thomason BSRT, Pres.
Local. Represents the professional society of radiologic technologists. Advances education and research in the radiologic sciences. Evaluates quality patient care. Improves the welfare and socioeconomics of radiologic technologists. **Affiliated With:** American Society of Radiologic Technologists.

5570 ■ International Union, United Automobile, Aerospace and Agricultural Implement Workers of America, AFL-CIO - Local Union 685
929 E Hoffer St.
Kokomo, IN 46902
Ph: (765)459-3133
Fax: (765)454-5464
E-mail: doc47@insightbb.com
URL: http://www.uawlocal685.org
Contact: Matt Amsbury, Financial Sec.
Members: 6,285. **Local**. AFL-CIO. **Affiliated With:** International Union, United Automobile, Aerospace and Agricultural Implement Workers of America.

5571 ■ Izaak Walton League of America, Howard County Chapter
2629 S County Rd. 200 E
Kokomo, IN 46902
Ph: (765)453-2800
URL: National Affiliate–www.iwla.org
Contact: Mr. Patrick Graham, Membership Dir.
Local. Works to educate the public to conserve, maintain, protect, and restore the soil, forest, water, and other natural resources of the U.S; promotes the enjoyment and wholesome utilization of these resources. **Affiliated With:** Izaak Walton League of America.

5572 ■ Kokomo AIFA
c/o Larry J. Lamp, Sec.
150 E Alto Rd.
Kokomo, IN 46902
Ph: (765)453-0067
Fax: (765)453-1579
E-mail: lamplar@msn.com
Contact: Larry J. Lamp, Sec.
Local. Represents the interests of insurance and financial advisors. Advocates for a positive legislative and regulatory environment. Enhances business and professional skills of members. **Affiliated With:** National Association of Insurance and Financial Advisors.

5573 ■ Kokomo Area Chapter of the United Ostomy Association (KACUOA)
PO Box 2272
Kokomo, IN 46904
Ph: (765)459-5805 (765)452-7113
E-mail: dgdell@netusa1.net
URL: National Affiliate–www.uoa.org
Contact: Dianna Dell, Sec.
Founded: 1975. **Members:** 60. **Membership Dues:** local, $10 (annual) • national, $25 (annual). **Regional Groups:** 1. **Local Groups:** 1. **Local**. Paramedical service organization for ostomates and others interested in ostomy rehabilitation. Offers aid and support to ostomates. Conducts rehabilitation programs. Provides home and hospital visitation services. **Libraries: Type:** open to the public. **Holdings:** 20. **Subjects:** surgery, recovery, anatomy. **Affiliated With:** United Ostomy Association. **Publications:** *Rosebud Gazette*, bimonthly. Newsletter. **Price:** included in membership dues. **Circulation:** 250. **Advertising:** accepted. **Conventions/Meetings:** annual Christmas Party - convention, regional and national, visitor training, health fair (exhibits) • bimonthly meeting, appliances, surgical procedures (exhibits) - first Tuesday of February, April, June, August, October, and December. Kokomo, IN.

5574 ■ Kokomo - Howard County Chamber of Commerce (KHCCC)
325 N Main St.
Kokomo, IN 46901-4621
Ph: (765)457-5301
E-mail: info@kokomochamber.com
URL: http://www.kokomochamber.com
Contact: Rick Hamilton, Pres.
Founded: 1914. **Members:** 650. **Local**. Promotes business and community development in Howard County, IN. **Committees:** Ambassadors; Community Beautification Team; Community Promotional Campaign; Existing Business Assistance; Leadership Kokomo Steering; Legislative Affairs. **Councils:** Small Business. **Task Forces:** Community Guide.

5575 ■ Kokomo Howard County Development Corporation (KHDC)
700 E Firmin, Ste.200
Kokomo, IN 46902
Ph: (765)457-2000
E-mail: info@khdc.org
URL: http://khdc.org
Contact: Greg Aaron, Pres.
Founded: 1980. **Local**. Promotes community and economic development.

5576 ■ Kokomo Main Street Association
325 N Main St.
Kokomo, IN 46901
Ph: (765)454-7926
Fax: (765)452-4564
URL: http://www.kokomomainstreet.org
Contact: Kim Moyers, Exec.Dir.
Local.

5577 ■ Kokomo Shrine Club
PO Box 474
Kokomo, IN 46901
Ph: (765)452-5506 (765)437-1675
Fax: (765)628-0118
Contact: Joseph A. Buckley, Pres.
Founded: 1948. **Members:** 400. **Membership Dues:** $20 (annual). **Staff:** 15. **Budget:** $1,200,000. **Local**. Supports Shriners Hospitals where disabled and burned children are treated for free. **Committees:** Clown Unit; Hillbilly Unit; Mini-T Unit. **Publications:** *Kokomo Shrine Club News*, monthly. Newsletter. **Price:** $15.00/year. **Circulation:** 1,400. **Advertising:** accepted. **Conventions/Meetings:** monthly meeting (exhibits) - always 1st Monday of the month; Avg. Attendance: 100.

5578 ■ Kokomo Table Tennis Club
Johanning Civic Center
1500 N Reed Rd., (U.S. 31 N)
Kokomo, IN 46901
Ph: (765)628-3544 (765)451-1813
E-mail: don.r.mccreary@delphi.com
URL: http://www.usatt.org/clubs
Contact: Don McCreary, Contact
Local. Affiliated With: U.S.A. Table Tennis.

5579 ■ Mental Health Association in Howard County
c/o Ms. Jennifer Mason, Exec.Dir.
PO Box 2221
Kokomo, IN 46904-2221
Ph: (765)459-0309
Fax: (765)459-0300
E-mail: mhahowardco@sbcglobal.net
URL: http://www.mentalhealthassociation.com
Contact: Ms. Jennifer Mason, Exec.Dir.
Local. Seeks to promote mental health and prevent mental health disorders. Improves mental health of Americans through advocacy, public education, research and service. **Affiliated With:** Mental Health Association in Indiana; National Mental Health Association.

5580 ■ Pheasants Forever Central Indiana, Wildcat Creek
3460 Ginger Ct.
Kokomo, IN 46901
Ph: (765)457-9558
URL: http://pfcic.org
Contact: Chris Baer, Pres.
Local. Affiliated With: Pheasants Forever.

5581 ■ Phi Theta Kappa, Alpha Phi Pi Chapter - Ivy Tech State College
c/o Alayne Cook
Kokomo Campus
1815 E Morgan St.
Kokomo, IN 46901
Ph: (765)459-0561
URL: http://www.ptk.org/directories/chapters/IN/20522-1.htm
Contact: Alayne Cook, Advisor
Local.

5582 ■ Police and Firemen's Insurance Association - Kokomo Fire Department
c/o Randel G. Abney
621 Somerset Dr.
Kokomo, IN 46902-3334
Ph: (765)271-1880
URL: National Affiliate–www.pfia.net
Contact: Randel G. Abney, Contact
Local. Affiliated With: Police and Firemen's Insurance Association.

5583 ■ Psi Chi, National Honor Society in Psychology - Indiana University Kokomo
c/o Dept. of Psychology
PO Box 9003
Kokomo, IN 46904-9003
Ph: (765)455-9447
Fax: (765)455-0846
E-mail: abecker@iuk.edu
URL: http://www.psichi.org/chapters/info.asp?chapter_id=857
Contact: Angela H. Becker PhD, Advisor
Local.

5584 ■ Realtors Association of Central Indiana (RACI)
1620 E Hoffer St.
Kokomo, IN 46902
Ph: (765)457-0089
Fax: (765)457-0096
E-mail: kathy@raci.org
URL: http://www.raci.org
Contact: Kathy P. Harbaugh, Association Exec.
Local. Strives to develop real estate business practices. Advocates the right to own, use and

transfer real property. Provides a facility for professional development, research and exchange of information among members and to the general public. **Affiliated With:** National Association of Realtors.

5585 ■ Ruffed Grouse Society, Indiana Chapter
c/o Michael Shipley
3009 Zartman Rd.
Kokomo, IN 46902
Ph: (219)872-8556
URL: National Affiliate–www.ruffedgrousesociety.org
Contact: Michael Shipley, Contact
State. Affiliated With: Ruffed Grouse Society.

5586 ■ SCORE Kokomo/Howard Counties
325 N Main St.
Kokomo, IN 46901
Ph: (765)457-5301
Fax: (765)452-4564
E-mail: chair543@kokomoscore.org
URL: National Affiliate–www.score.org
Contact: Mr. Bob Straub, Chm.
Founded: 1984. **Members:** 17. **State Groups:** 18. **Local Groups:** 1. **Local**. Represents Business professionals and Counselors. Seeks to provide assistant and counsel to existing and newly opened small businesses. **Computer Services:** Online services, web links assistance in starting a business and assisting small business. **Affiliated With:** SCORE. **Publications:** *Score eNews*, monthly. Newsletter. Offers latest trends and resources to help small business succeed. **Price:** free. Alternate Formats: online • *SCORE Expert Answers*, monthly. Newsletter. Brings marketplace trends and advice from small business experts and industry leaders. **Price:** free. Alternate Formats: online.

5587 ■ SMA Support
c/o Laura Stants
PO Box 6301
Kokomo, IN 46904-6301
Ph: (317)536-6063
Fax: (801)460-2813
E-mail: laura@smasupport.com
URL: http://www.smasupport.com
Contact: Laura Stants, Contact
Founded: 2002. **State Groups:** 2. **Languages:** English, Spanish. **Nonmembership. Regional**. Provides information and support to any and all families affected by the disease Spinal Muscular Atrophy. Gives support consists of medical equipment, funeral expenses, medical supplies, flight costs to required appointments, educational funding, equipment to maintain quality of life, live and internet supports, and other forms of information as well as support not covered by insurance that such families may need. Aims to improve both the quality and quantity of life for those children afflicted with Spinal Muscular Atrophy. **Libraries: Type:** reference. **Computer Services:** Information services • mailing lists, for grief, palliative care families and general SMA population • online services, website for families dealing with SMA and message board for family support. **Telecommunication Services:** electronic bulletin board, message board.

5588 ■ United Way of Howard County
210 W Walnut St.
Kokomo, IN 46901
Ph: (765)457-6691
E-mail: swidland@unitedwayhoco.org
URL: http://www.unitedwayhoco.org
Contact: Sonie Widland, Exec.Sec.
Local. Affiliated With: United Way of America.

5589 ■ Western Beagle Club
c/o Mark Hornstein
1221 Belvedere Dr.
Kokomo, IN 46902-5602
URL: National Affiliate–clubs.akc.org
Contact: Mark Hornstein, Contact
Local.

Kouts

5590 ■ American Legion, Indiana Post 301
c/o William Redilyack
PO Box 307
Kouts, IN 46347
Ph: (317)630-1300
Fax: (317)237-9891
URL: National Affiliate–www.legion.org
Contact: William Redilyack, Contact
Local. Affiliated With: American Legion.

5591 ■ Kankakee Valley Historical Society (KVHS)
c/o John P. Hodson
22 W 1050 S
Kouts, IN 46347
Ph: (219)766-2302
E-mail: president@kankakeevallyhistoricalsociety.org
URL: http://www.kankakeevalleyhistoricalsociety.org
Contact: John P. Hodson, Contact
Local.

5592 ■ Kouts Chamber of Commerce (KCC)
PO Box 330
Kouts, IN 46347
Ph: (219)766-2867
Fax: (219)766-3152
E-mail: koutschamber@verizon.net
URL: http://www.kouts.org
Contact: Julie Jones, Exec.Dir.
Founded: 1921. **Membership Dues:** general, $75 (annual). **Local**. Promotes business and community development in Kouts, IN area.

La Crosse

5593 ■ National Alliance of Methadone Advocates of Indiana
PO Box 65
La Crosse, IN 46348
Ph: (219)896-2402
E-mail: carmpear@csinet.net
URL: National Affiliate–www.methadone.org
Contact: Carmen Pearman CMA, Contact
State. Promotes quality methadone maintenance treatment as the most effective modality for the treatment of opiate addiction. Eliminates discrimination toward methadone patients. **Affiliated With:** National Alliance of Methadone Advocates.

La Porte

5594 ■ American Legion, Hamon Gray Post 83
228 E Lincolnway
La Porte, IN 46350
Ph: (317)630-1300
Fax: (317)237-9891
URL: National Affiliate–www.legion.org
Local. Affiliated With: American Legion.

5595 ■ City of La Porte Urban Enterprise Zone
801 Michigan Ave.
La Porte, IN 46350-3568
Ph: (219)326-1976
URL: National Affiliate–www.ci.la-porte.in.us
Contact: Ron Gigliotti, Pres.
Local.

5596 ■ Greater La Porte Chamber of Commerce (GLCC)
414 Lincolnway
PO Box 486
La Porte, IN 46352-0486
Ph: (219)362-3178
Fax: (219)324-7349
E-mail: info@lpchamber.com
URL: http://www.lpchamber.com
Contact: Michael B. Seitz, Pres.
Founded: 1913. **Members:** 350. **Membership Dues:** commercial (plus $7.50 per employee), $235 (annual) • financial institution (plus $35 per 1 million in assets), $235 (annual) • home-based, $175 (annual) • manufacturing (plus $5 per employee), $235 (annual) • non-profit ($1.50 per employee), $235 (annual) • professional (plus $35 per professional staff/partner), $235 (annual) • real estate (plus $7.50 per agent), $235 (annual). **Staff:** 5. **Budget:** $450,000. **Local**. Businesses, professional firms, and individuals who promote business and economic development in La Porte, IN. Seeks to retain and expand business and industry in the area. **Divisions:** Government & Community Development; Retention & Expansion. **Affiliated With:** U.S. Chamber of Commerce. **Publications:** *Business Today*, quarterly. Newsletter • *LaPorte Business Resource Guide*, annual. Directory. Includes members listings. **Conventions/Meetings:** annual meeting - always spring, La Porte, IN.

5597 ■ La Porte County 4-H Council
c/o Purdue Cooperative Extension
La Porte County Off.
2358 N US Hwy. 35
La Porte, IN 46350
Ph: (219)324-9407
Fax: (219)326-7362
Free: (888)EXT-INFO
E-mail: laporteces@purdue.edu
URL: http://www.ces.purdue.edu/laporte
Contact: Hugh Tonagel, Contact
State. Works as a policy and decision making organization for the LaPorte County 4-H program.

5598 ■ LaPorte County Association of Realtors
PO Box 248
La Porte, IN 46352
Ph: (219)324-8120
Fax: (219)324-9323
Free: (888)343-0478
E-mail: info@lpcar.org
URL: http://www.lpcar.org
Contact: Joy W. Pawlak, Pres.
Local. Strives to develop real estate business practices. Advocates the right to own, use and transfer real property. Provides a facility for professional development, research and exchange of information among members and to the general public. **Affiliated With:** National Association of Realtors.

5599 ■ National Softball Association - Northern Indiana
c/o Jim Kemmel, Dir.
1015 S Westwood Dr.
La Porte, IN 46350
Ph: (219)362-4525
Fax: (219)362-6150
E-mail: jameskimmel@comcast.net
URL: http://www.nsaindiananorth.com
Contact: Jim Kemmel, Dir.
Local. Affiliated With: National Softball Association.

5600 ■ Northwestern Indiana Beagle Club
c/o Shirley Perz
3607 W 400 N St.
La Porte, IN 46350
URL: National Affiliate–clubs.akc.org
Contact: Shirley Perz, Contact
Regional.

5601 ■ Pheasants Forever Central Indiana, Door Prairie
1322 S 300 E
La Porte, IN 46350
Ph: (219)362-2921
URL: http://pfcic.org
Contact: Jack Arnett, Pres.
Local. Affiliated With: Pheasants Forever.

5602 ■ Potawatomi Audubon Society
c/o Mary Jo Pflum, Pres.
PO Box 1632
La Porte, IN 46352
Ph: (219)324-0649 (219)872-0052
E-mail: mjpflum@csinet.net
URL: http://www.alco.org/audubon
Contact: Mary Jo Pflum, Pres.
Local. Works to conserve and restore natural ecosystems, focusing on birds and other wildlife for the benefit of humanity and the earth's biological diversity. **Affiliated With:** National Audubon Society.

5603 ■ United Way of Greater La Porte County
800 Lincolnway, Ste.306
La Porte, IN 46350
Ph: (219)362-6256
Fax: (219)362-9405
Free: (800)399-7222
E-mail: unitedway@unitedwaylpc.org
URL: http://www.unitedwaylpc.org
Contact: Thomas A. Clark, Exec.Dir.
Local. Affiliated With: United Way of America.

Ladoga

5604 ■ American Sewing Guild, Indianapolis Chapter
c/o Patricia Cline
10643 S 875 E
Ladoga, IN 47954-7269
Ph: (765)942-2072
E-mail: pacline@tds.net
URL: http://www.indyasg.com
Contact: Patricia Cline, Contact
Local. Affiliated With: American Sewing Guild.

Lafayette

5605 ■ American Institute of Architects Central/Southern Indiana
c/o Wahl Architecture, PC
1815 Underwood St.
Lafayette, IN 47904-1129
Ph: (765)429-5880
Fax: (765)429-6668
E-mail: wahlarch@gte.net
URL: National Affiliate–www.aia.org
Local. Professional society of architects. Fosters professionalism and accountability among members through continuing education and training; promotes design excellence by influencing change in the industry. **Affiliated With:** American Institute of Architects.

5606 ■ American Legion, Lafayette Post 11
1801 S 9th St.
Lafayette, IN 47905
Ph: (317)474-5851
Fax: (317)237-9891
URL: National Affiliate–www.legion.org
Local. Affiliated With: American Legion.

5607 ■ American Rabbit Breeders Association, Indiana
c/o Max Harrison Jr., Pres.
2323 Poland Hill Dr.
Lafayette, IN 47905
Ph: (765)471-8140
E-mail: amysrabbitranch@wideopenwest.com
URL: http://www.arba.net/district/8/indiana.htm
Contact: Max Harrison Jr., Pres.
State. Affiliated With: American Rabbit Breeders Association.

5608 ■ American Society for Quality, Lafayette Section 0917
c/o Sara Samudio, Sec.
PO Box 5261
Lafayette, IN 47903-5261
Ph: (765)494-1549
E-mail: ssamudio@asq0917.org
URL: http://www.asq0917.org
Contact: Sara Samudio, Sec.
Local. Advances learning, quality improvement and knowledge exchange to improve business results and to create better workplaces and communities worldwide. Provides a forum for information exchange, professional development and continuous learning in the science of quality. **Affiliated With:** American Society for Quality.

5609 ■ Big Brothers Big Sisters of Wabash Valley
1118 State St.
Lafayette, IN 47905
Ph: (765)742-8045
Fax: (765)429-5921
E-mail: info@bbbslaf.com
URL: http://www.bbbslaf.com
Contact: Ronda McKinnis, Exec.Dir.
Local. Works to provide quality-mentoring relationships between children and qualified adults and promote their development into competent, confident and caring individuals. **Affiliated With:** Big Brothers Big Sisters of America. **Formerly:** (2005) Big Brothers Big Sisters of America of Wabash Valley.

5610 ■ Compassionate Friends - Lafayette, Indiana Chapter
PO Box 4781
Lafayette, IN 47903
E-mail: chaptermail@tcflafayette.org
URL: http://www.tcflafayette.org
Contact: Rick Munn, Chapter Leader
Local.

5611 ■ Girl Scouts of Sycamore Council
PO Box 6568
Lafayette, IN 47903-6568
Ph: (765)449-4009
Free: (800)875-0059
E-mail: girlscouts@sycamorecouncil.org
URL: http://www.sycamorecouncil.org
Contact: Mary L. Reece, Chm.
Local. Young girls and adult volunteers, corporate, government and individual supporters. Strives to develop potential and leadership skills among its members. Conducts trainings, educational programs and outdoor activities.

5612 ■ Greater Lafayette Community Development Corporation (GLCDC)
c/o Sanders W. Howse, Jr., Pres.
PO Box 227
337 Columbia St.
Lafayette, IN 47902-0227
Ph: (765)742-1984
Fax: (765)742-6276
E-mail: showse@glcdc.org
URL: http://glcdc.org
Contact: Sanders W. Howse Jr., Pres.
Founded: 2001. **Members:** 25. **Staff:** 3. **Local**. Offers programs to stimulate business and real estate projects that advance community and economic development objectives in Tippecanoe County. Programs include finance and development resources and assistance with environmental property assessments.

5613 ■ Habitat for Humanity of Lafayette
420 S 1st St.
Lafayette, IN 47905
Ph: (765)423-4590
Fax: (765)742-5870
E-mail: habitat@dcwi.com
URL: http://www.dcwi.com/~habitat
Contact: Doug Taylor, Exec.Dir.
Local. Affiliated With: Habitat for Humanity International.

5614 ■ Indiana Council of Teachers of Mathematics
c/o Donna Osborn, Pres.
Lafayette Jefferson High School
1801 S 18th St.
Lafayette, IN 47905
Ph: (765)772-4700
E-mail: dmo@bilbo.bio.purdue.edu
URL: http://indianamath.org
Contact: Donna Osborn, Pres.
State. Aims to improve the teaching and learning of mathematics. Provides vision, leadership and professional development to support teachers in ensuring mathematics learning of the highest quality for all students. **Affiliated With:** National Council of Teachers of Mathematics.

5615 ■ Indiana Crop Improvement Association (ICIA)
c/o Larry Svajgr, Exec.Dir.
7700 Stockwell Rd.
Lafayette, IN 47909-9336
Ph: (765)523-2535
Fax: (765)523-2536
Free: (866)899-2518
E-mail: svajgr@indianacrop.org
URL: http://www.indianacrop.org
Contact: Larry Svajgr, Exec.Dir.
State.

5616 ■ Indiana Junior Golf Association
PO Box 4454
Lafayette, IN 47903
Ph: (765)447-1992
Fax: (765)447-1992
URL: National Affiliate–www.iaga.org
State. Affiliated With: International Association of Golf Administrators.

5617 ■ Indiana Mathematical Association of Two-Year Colleges (IRMC)
c/o Diann Robinson
PO Box 6299
Lafayette, IN 47903
Ph: (765)269-5174
E-mail: drobinso@ivytech.edu
URL: http://www.math.iupui.edu/irmc
Contact: Diann Robinson, Contact
State. Promotes and increases awareness of the role of two-year colleges in mathematics education. Provides a forum for the improvement of mathematics instruction in the first two years of college. Provides professional development opportunities for educators interested in the first two years of collegiate mathematics instruction. **Affiliated With:** American Mathematical Association of Two-Year Colleges.

5618 ■ Indiana Optometric Association, West Central District
c/o Steven C. Mather, OD, Trustee
1401 Union St.
Lafayette, IN 47904
Ph: (765)742-1955
Fax: (765)742-2020
E-mail: steve@aeyecare.net
URL: http://www.ioa.org
Contact: Steven C. Mather OD, Trustee
Local. Aims to improve the quality, availability and accessibility of eye and vision care. Promotes high standards of patient care. Monitors and promotes legislation concerning the scope of optometric practice and other issues relevant to eye/vision care. **Affiliated With:** American Optometric Association; Indiana Optometric Association.

5619 ■ Korean War Veterans Association, Indiana No. 2 Chapter
c/o John M. Rutledge
208 Eastland Dr.
Lafayette, IN 47905

Ph: (765)447-5296
E-mail: robert.schoonover@verizon.net
URL: National Affiliate–www.kwva.org
Contact: John M. Rutledge, Contact
Local. **Affiliated With:** Korean War Veterans Association.

5620 ■ Lafayette Lions Club, IN
PO Box 613
Lafayette, IN 47902
E-mail: clubinformation@lafayettelions.org
URL: http://www.lafayettelionsclub.org
Local. **Affiliated With:** Lions Clubs International.

5621 ■ Lafayette Regional Association of Realtors
1415 Union St.
Lafayette, IN 47904
Ph: (765)429-5411
Fax: (765)429-5637
URL: http://www.lbor.net
Contact: Cheryl Butcher, Pres.
Local. Strives to develop real estate business practices. Advocates the right to own, use and transfer real property. Provides a facility for professional development, research and exchange of information among members and to the general public. **Affiliated With:** National Association of Realtors.

5622 ■ Lafayette - West Lafayette Chamber of Commerce
337 Columbia St.
PO Box 348
Lafayette, IN 47902-0348
Ph: (765)742-4041
Fax: (765)742-6276
E-mail: dana@lafayettechamber.com
URL: http://www.lafayettechamber.com
Contact: Mr. David Williams, Chm.
Founded: 1927. **Members:** 1,000. **Membership Dues:** business (based on number of employees), $235-$1,650 (annual) • student, retired, $90 (annual) • civic/non-profit, $150 (annual) • individual (with no business affiliation), $115 (annual) • professional, $235 (annual). **Local**. Promotes business and community development in the Lafayette, IN area. **Formerly:** (2004) Greater Lafayette Chamber of Commerce. **Publications:** Directory, annual. **Price:** $20.00 • Newsletter, monthly.

5623 ■ Lafayette - West Lafayette Convention and Visitors Bureau
301 Frontage Rd.
Lafayette, IN 47905
Ph: (765)447-9999
Free: (800)872-6648
E-mail: info@homeofpurdue.com
URL: http://www.lafayette-in.com
Contact: Joann L. Wade, Pres.
Founded: 1978. **Staff:** 10. **Budget:** $740,000. **Local**. Promotes tourism and meeting business in the Lafayette, IN area. **Formerly:** (2005) Greater Lafayette Convention and Visitors Bureau. **Publications:** *Greater Lafayette Visitor Magazine*, annual. **Price:** free.

5624 ■ Lafayette - West Lafayette Economic Development Corporation
337 Columbia St.
PO Box 311
Lafayette, IN 47902-0311
Ph: (765)742-0095
Fax: (765)742-6276
E-mail: info@lwledc.org
URL: http://glpi.org
Contact: Gary Henriott, Chm.
Founded: 1984. **Members:** 100. **Staff:** 5. **Budget:** $390,000. **Local**. Works to retain and expand existing business and industry, to capitalize on technology innovations and initiatives from Purdue University, and to promote entrepreneurship. **Formerly:** (2005) Greater Lafayette Progress.

5625 ■ NAIFA-Lafayette Indiana
c/o Cecilia Pierson, Exec.
14 N Second St., Ste.200B
Lafayette, IN 47901
Ph: (765)742-2707
Fax: (765)429-5780
E-mail: mrscp@msn.com
URL: National Affiliate–naifa.org
Contact: Cecilia Pierson, Exec.
Local. Represents the interests of insurance and financial advisors. Advocates for a positive legislative and regulatory environment. Enhances business and professional skills of members. **Affiliated With:** National Association of Insurance and Financial Advisors.

5626 ■ National Active and Retired Federal Employees Association - Lafayette 330
4415 Sugar Maple Dr.
Lafayette, IN 47905-4615
Ph: (765)448-4776
URL: National Affiliate–www.narfe.org
Contact: William K. Kerr, Contact
Local. Protects the retirement future of employees through education. Informs members on issues affecting the retirement. **Affiliated With:** National Association of Retired Federal Employees.

5627 ■ National Association of the Remodeling Industry of Wabash Valley
PO Box 5627
Lafayette, IN 47903
Ph: (317)536-2712
Fax: (317)536-2714
E-mail: tdschrock@tds.net
URL: National Affiliate–www.nari.org
Contact: Tony Batta, Pres.
Local. Brings together people who work in the remodeling industry. Provides resources for knowledge and training in the industry. Encourages ethical conduct, sound business practices and professionalism. Promotes the remodeling industry's products. **Affiliated With:** National Association of the Remodeling Industry.

5628 ■ Navy Club of Lafayette - Ship No. 12
1905 Elmwood Ave.
Lafayette, IN 47904
Ph: (765)538-2509 (765)447-0500
E-mail: ship12co@verizon.net
URL: http://www.ship12.com
Contact: Eric Newman, Commander
Local. Represents individuals who are, or have been, in the active service of the U.S. Navy, Naval Reserve, Marine Corps, Marine Corps Reserve, and Coast Guard. Promotes and encourages further public interest in the U.S. Navy and its history. Upholds the spirit and ideals of the U.S. Navy. Acts as a public forum for members' views on national defense. Assists the Navy Recruiting Command whenever and wherever possible. Conducts charitable activities. **Affiliated With:** Navy Club of the United States of America.

5629 ■ Navy Club of Tippecanoe County - Ship No. 11
3623 Winter St.
Lafayette, IN 47909
Ph: (765)564-6147
URL: National Affiliate–www.navyclubusa.org
Contact: Tom Welcher, Commander
Local. Represents individuals who are, or have been, in the active service of the U.S. Navy, Naval Reserve, Marine Corps, Marine Corps Reserve, and Coast Guard. Promotes and encourages further public interest in the U.S. Navy and its history. Upholds the spirit and ideals of the U.S. Navy. Acts as a public forum for members' views on national defense. Assists the Navy Recruiting Command whenever and wherever possible. Conducts charitable activities. **Affiliated With:** Navy Club of the United States of America.

5630 ■ Phi Theta Kappa, Alpha Sigma Kappa Chapter - Ivy Tech State College
c/o John Laws
3101 S Creasy Ln.
Lafayette, IN 47903
Ph: (765)772-9117
URL: http://www.ptk.org/directories/chapters/IN/11165-1.htm
Contact: John Laws, Advisor
Local.

5631 ■ Plumbing-Heating-Cooling Contractors Association, West Central Indiana
c/o Dave Mecklenburg, Pres.
PO Box 4982
Lafayette, IN 47904-3032
Ph: (765)447-7555
E-mail: dmecko@verizonmail.com
URL: National Affiliate–www.phccweb.org
Contact: Dave Mecklenburg, Pres.
Local. Represents the plumbing, heating and cooling contractors. Promotes the construction industry. Protects the environment, health, safety and comfort of society. **Affiliated With:** Plumbing-Heating-Cooling Contractors Association.

5632 ■ Religious Coalition for Reproductive Choice - Indiana Chapter
PO Box 723
Lafayette, IN 47902-0723
Free: (877)441-5797
E-mail: info@ircrc.org
URL: http://www.ircrc.org
State. **Affiliated With:** Religious Coalition for Reproductive Choice.

5633 ■ STARFLEET: Shuttle Armageddon
c/o Teresa Remaly
324 N 24th St.
Lafayette, IN 47904
E-mail: tdremaly@yahoo.com
URL: http://www.sfi.org/shoc/shuttles/r1.htm
Contact: Teresa Remaly, Contact
Local. **Affiliated With:** STARFLEET.

5634 ■ Sycamore Audubon Society
PO Box 2716
Lafayette, IN 47996
E-mail: info@sycamoreaudubon.org
URL: National Affiliate–www.audubon.org
Local. **Affiliated With:** National Audubon Society.

5635 ■ Tippecanoe County Historical Association - Alameda McCollough Library (TCHA)
1001 S St.
Lafayette, IN 47901
Ph: (765)476-8407 (765)476-8411
Fax: (765)476-8414
E-mail: library@tcha.mus.in.us
URL: http://www.tcha.mus.in.us
Contact: Kevin O'Brien, Exec.Dir.
Founded: 1970. **Members:** 150. **Membership Dues:** individual, $12 (annual) • family, $15 (annual). **Local**. Assists persons searching for ancestors in Tippecanoe County. Provides local history services and a fee-based research service. **Libraries: Type:** open to the public. **Holdings:** 7,000; archival material, books. **Subjects:** Tippecanoe County history, public records, family histories. **Also Known As:** TIPCOA. **Publications:** *TIPCOA Newsletter*, quarterly. **Price:** included in membership dues. **Circulation:** 200. **Conventions/Meetings:** monthly meeting.

5636 ■ United Way of Greater Lafayette
PO Box 677
Lafayette, IN 47902-0677
Ph: (765)742-9077
Fax: (765)742-9079
E-mail: unitedway@uw.lafayette.in.us
URL: http://www.uw.lafayette.in.us
Contact: Jim Smyth, Exec.Dir.
Local. **Affiliated With:** United Way of America.

5637 ■ Wabash Wanderers
c/o Susan Tapia
3331 Crosspoint Ct. S
Lafayette, IN 47909
Ph: (765)474-0881
E-mail: susan_tapia@msn.com
URL: National Affiliate–www.ava.org
Contact: Susan Tapia, Contact
Local. Affiliated With: American Volkssport Association.

Lagrange

5638 ■ American Legion, La Grange Post 215
100 Indus. Pkwy.
Lagrange, IN 46761
Ph: (219)463-4172
Fax: (317)237-9891
URL: National Affiliate–www.legion.org
Local. Affiliated With: American Legion.

5639 ■ Friends of Lagrange County Library
203 W Spring St.
Lagrange, IN 46761-1845
Ph: (260)463-2841
E-mail: info@lagrange.lib.in.us
URL: http://www.lagrange.lib.in.us
Founded: 2000. **Local.**

5640 ■ Lagrange County Cancer Society
c/o Lois Miller
300 S. Detriot St.
Lagrange, IN 46761-1833
Ph: (260)463-3126
Local.

5641 ■ Lagrange County Chamber of Commerce
901 S Detroit St., Ste.A
Lagrange, IN 46761
Ph: (260)463-2443
Fax: (260)463-2683
Free: (877)735-0340
E-mail: info@lagrangechamber.org
URL: http://www.lagrangechamber.org
Contact: Jack Dold, Exec.Dir.
Staff: 2. **Local.** Provides leadership for the promotion and advancement of economic vitality and quality of life in LaGrange County. **Computer Services:** Mailing lists, of members. **Publications:** *Chamber News*, monthly. Newsletter. **Advertising:** accepted. Alternate Formats: online.

5642 ■ Pheasants Forever Central Indiana, Lagrange County
2580 E 250 N
Lagrange, IN 46761
Ph: (219)463-4299
URL: http://pfcic.org
Contact: Dennis Demara, Pres.
Local. Affiliated With: Pheasants Forever.

Lagro

5643 ■ American Legion, Hansel Roberts Post 248
PO Box 66
Lagro, IN 46941
Ph: (219)782-2344
Fax: (317)237-9891
URL: National Affiliate–www.legion.org
Local. Affiliated With: American Legion.

Lake Station

5644 ■ Lake Station Chamber of Commerce
PO Box 5191
Lake Station, IN 46405
Ph: (219)962-4878 (219)962-5779
Contact: Jim Bradford, Sec.
Local.

5645 ■ Veterans of Foreign Wars/Post 9323
2750 Central Ave.
Lake Station, IN 46405
Ph: (219)962-3522
Contact: Norm Fontiane, Commander
Local.

Lake Village

5646 ■ American Legion, Lake Village Post 375
9455 N 300 W
Lake Village, IN 46349
Ph: (317)630-1300
Fax: (317)237-9891
URL: National Affiliate–www.legion.org
Local. Affiliated With: American Legion.

Laketon

5647 ■ American Legion, Sunset Post 402
132 Main St.
Laketon, IN 46943
Ph: (219)982-2896
Fax: (317)237-9891
URL: National Affiliate–www.legion.org
Local. Affiliated With: American Legion.

Lakeville

5648 ■ American Legion, Lakeville Community Post 363
PO Box 93
Lakeville, IN 46536
Ph: (219)784-8012
Fax: (317)237-9891
URL: National Affiliate–www.legion.org
Local. Affiliated With: American Legion.

Laotto

5649 ■ Pheasants Forever Central Indiana, Northeast Indiana
0305 County Rd. 60
Laotto, IN 46763
Ph: (219)357-4918
URL: http://pfcic.org
Contact: Jack V. Ruger, Pres.
Local. Affiliated With: Pheasants Forever.

Lapaz

5650 ■ American Legion, Lapaz Post 385
100 W Randolph St.
Lapaz, IN 46537
Ph: (219)784-9938
Fax: (317)237-9891
URL: National Affiliate–www.legion.org
Local. Affiliated With: American Legion.

Lapel

5651 ■ American Legion, Bartholomew-Whetsel Post 212
PO Box 789
Lapel, IN 46051
Ph: (317)534-4801
Fax: (317)237-9891
URL: National Affiliate–www.legion.org
Local. Affiliated With: American Legion.

Lawrenceburg

5652 ■ American Legion, Indiana Post 239
c/o David Mc Allister
201 2nd St.
Lawrenceburg, IN 47025
Ph: (812)537-0349
Fax: (317)237-9891
URL: National Affiliate–www.legion.org
Contact: David Mc Allister, Contact
Local. Affiliated With: American Legion.

5653 ■ Arc of Dearborn County
947 Primrose Dr.
Lawrenceburg, IN 47025
URL: National Affiliate–www.TheArc.org
Local. Parents, professional workers, and others interested in individuals with mental retardation. Works to promote services, research, public understanding, and legislation for people with mental retardation and their families. **Affiliated With:** Arc of the United States.

5654 ■ Dearborn Community Foundation (DCF)
204 Short St.
Lawrenceburg, IN 47025
Ph: (812)539-4115
Fax: (812)539-4119
E-mail: info@dearborncf.org
URL: http://www.dearborncounty.org/dccf
Contact: Fred McCarter, Exec.Dir.
Founded: 1997. **Members:** 16. **Staff:** 3. **Local.** Aims to advance social, educational and cultural opportunities while preserving the community's heritage. **Awards: Frequency:** periodic. **Type:** grant. **Recipient:** for nonprofit organizations serving the residents in Dearborn County. **Publications:** Annual Report, annual.

5655 ■ Dearborn County Chamber of Commerce (DCC)
320 Walnut St.
Lawrenceburg, IN 47025
Ph: (812)537-0814
Fax: (812)537-0845
Free: (800)322-8198
E-mail: maryc@seidata.com
URL: http://www.dearborncountychamber.org
Contact: Debbie Smith, Dir.
Founded: 1987. **Members:** 400. **Membership Dues:** individual, $95 • business (based on number of employees), $175-$2,160. **Staff:** 4. **Local.** Promotes business and community development in Dearborn County, IN. Holds monthly board meeting. **Committees:** Economic Growth; Events Advisory; Governmental Affairs; Networking Team; Workforce Development. **Publications:** *Chamber Express*, monthly. Newsletter. Alternate Formats: online. **Conventions/Meetings:** bimonthly meeting.

5656 ■ Dearborn County Home Builders Association
303 Walnut St.
Lawrenceburg, IN 47025
Ph: (812)926-3375
Fax: (812)926-3375
E-mail: dchba@suscom.net
URL: National Affiliate–www.nahb.org
Contact: Melanie Smith, Exec. Officer
Local. Single and multifamily home builders, commercial builders, and others associated with the building industry. **Affiliated With:** National Association of Home Builders.

5657 ■ Dearborn County RSVP
c/o Mary Lewis, Dir.
PO Box 4194
Lawrenceburg, IN 47025-0201

Ph: (812)539-4005
Fax: (812)539-2362
E-mail: rsvp@seidata.com
URL: http://www.dearborncounty.org/rsvp.html
Contact: Mary Lewis, Dir.
Local. **Affiliated With:** Retired and Senior Volunteer Program.

5658 ■ Dearborn and Ohio County Prevent Child Abuse Council
230 Mary Ave., Ste.150
Lawrenceburg, IN 47025-2106
Ph: (812)537-5131
Fax: (812)537-8890
URL: http://www.pcain.org
Contact: Randy Hildebrand, Contact
Founded: 1996. **Members:** 10. **Membership Dues:** individual, $30 (annual) • corporation, $50 (annual). **Budget:** $2,000. **State Groups:** 1. **Local Groups:** 1. **For-Profit**. **Local**. Individuals and others interested in the prevention of child abuse. Seeks to inform, educate, and advocate to stop all forms of child abuse. Activities include local fairs, workshops, and seminars. **Affiliated With:** Prevent Child Abuse Indiana. **Formerly:** (2001) Dearborn and Ohio County Child Abuse Prevention Council. **Conventions/Meetings:** monthly board meeting - 1st Wednesday of the month.

5659 ■ Lawrenceburg Lions Club
365 Beckett Landing
Lawrenceburg, IN 47025
Ph: (812)537-2048 (812)926-6298
E-mail: andreamarine@yahoo.com
URL: http://lawrenceburgin.lionwap.org
Contact: Andrea Marine, Pres.
Local. **Affiliated With:** Lions Clubs International.

5660 ■ LHS Key Club
100 Tiger Blvd.
Lawrenceburg, IN 47025
Ph: (812)537-7219
Fax: (812)537-7221
E-mail: president@lhskeyclub.org
URL: http://www.lhskeyclub.org
Contact: Michael Brauer, Pres.
Local.

5661 ■ Phi Theta Kappa, Beta Gamma Tau Chapter - Ivy Tech State College
c/o Beth Goodwin
Lawrenceburg Campus
500 Indus. Dr.
Lawrenceburg, IN 47025
Ph: (812)537-4010
URL: http://www.ptk.org/directories/chapters/IN/20704-1.htm
Contact: Beth Goodwin, Advisor
Local.

5662 ■ Southeast Indiana Healthy Mothers, Healthy Babies Coalition
PO Box 3537
Lawrenceburg, IN 47025
Ph: (812)432-3318
E-mail: jasciarobinson@hotmail.com
URL: National Affiliate–www.hmhb.org
Contact: Jascia Robinson, Contact
Local. Improves the health and safety of mothers, babies and families through education and collaborative partnerships of public and private organizations. **Affiliated With:** National Healthy Mothers, Healthy Babies Coalition.

Leavenworth

5663 ■ American Legion, Indiana Post 133
c/o Ralph E. Parr
407 S Frog St.
Leavenworth, IN 47137
Ph: (317)630-1300
Fax: (317)237-9891
URL: National Affiliate–www.legion.org
Contact: Ralph E. Parr, Contact
Local. **Affiliated With:** American Legion.

5664 ■ Crawford County Chamber of Commerce (CCCC)
6225 E Indus. Ln., Ste.C
Leavenworth, IN 47137
Ph: (812)365-2443
Fax: (812)739-4180
Free: (888)739-7911
E-mail: stroud1942@aol.com
URL: http://www.cccn.net
Contact: Patricia A. Stroud, Pres.
Founded: 1981. **Local**.

Lebanon

5665 ■ American Legion, Brown-Dolson Post 113
1020 Hendricks Dr.
Lebanon, IN 46052
Ph: (317)482-4986
Fax: (317)237-9891
URL: National Affiliate–www.legion.org
Local. **Affiliated With:** American Legion.

5666 ■ ARC Rehab Services
900 W Main St.
Lebanon, IN 46052
Ph: (765)482-6815
Fax: (765)482-6964
URL: http://www.arcrehab.org
Contact: Paul Bowman, Pres.
Founded: 1970. **Local**.

5667 ■ Boone County Cancer Society
c/o Jayn Allen, Dir.
210 E. Main St., No. 100
Lebanon, IN 46052
Ph: (765)482-2043
Fax: (765)482-2043

5668 ■ Boone County Chamber of Commerce (BCCC)
221 N Lebanon St.
Lebanon, IN 46052
Ph: (765)482-1320
Fax: (765)482-3114
E-mail: info@boonechamber.org
URL: http://www.boonechamber.org
Contact: Christa Childers, Exec.VP
Founded: 1919. **Local**. Promotes business and community development in Boone County, IN. **Affiliated With:** U.S. Chamber of Commerce. **Publications:** *C of C News*, bimonthly. Newsletter. **Conventions/Meetings:** annual meeting.

5669 ■ Habitat for Humanity of Boone County
111 W North St.
Lebanon, IN 46052
Ph: (765)483-5134
URL: http://www.bccn.boone.in.us/habitat
Founded: 1984. **Local**. **Affiliated With:** Habitat for Humanity International.

5670 ■ Lebanon Kiwanis
PO Box 1
Lebanon, IN 46052
E-mail: dave8602@netzero.com
URL: http://bccn.boone.in.us/lk/index.htm
Contact: Dave Rose, Pres.
Local.

5671 ■ Mental Health Association in Boone County
c/o Ms. Jane Taylor, Exec.Dir.
1122 N Lebanon St., Ste.A
Lebanon, IN 46052-1759
Ph: (765)482-1599
Fax: (765)482-9001
E-mail: mhabc@in-motion.net
URL: http://www.mentalhealthassociation.com
Contact: Ms. Jane Taylor, Exec.Dir.
Local. Seeks to promote mental health and prevent mental health disorders. Improves mental health of Americans through advocacy, public education, research and service. **Affiliated With:** Mental Health Association in Indiana; National Mental Health Association.

5672 ■ National Active and Retired Federal Employees Association - Plainfield 2141
212 Tahoe Dr.
Lebanon, IN 46052-3140
Ph: (765)483-0326
URL: National Affiliate–www.narfe.org
Contact: Thomasita R. Russell, Contact
Local. Protects the retirement future of employees through education. Informs members on issues affecting the retirement. **Affiliated With:** National Association of Retired Federal Employees.

5673 ■ National Speakers Association, Indiana
c/o Margie Thomas
4080 E 750 N
Lebanon, IN 46052
Ph: (765)325-2482
Fax: (530)453-2990
E-mail: margie@matconsulting.com
URL: http://www.nsa-indiana.com
Contact: Mr. David Lewis, Pres.
Founded: 1974. **State Groups:** 38. **For-Profit**. **State**. **Affiliated With:** National Speakers Association.

Leo

5674 ■ American Legion, Jack Brinker Post 409
14133 State Rd. 1
Leo, IN 46765
Ph: (219)627-2628
Fax: (317)237-9891
URL: National Affiliate–www.legion.org
Local. **Affiliated With:** American Legion.

5675 ■ Association of Women's Health, Obstetric and Neonatal Nurses - Northeast Chapter
c/o Amy Knepp, Coor.
15231 Rolling Oaks Pl.
Leo, IN 46765
E-mail: lknepp@gte.net
URL: National Affiliate–www.awhonn.org
Contact: Amy Knepp, Coor.
Local. Represents registered nurses and other health care providers who specialize in obstetric, women's health, and neonatal nursing. Advances the nursing profession by providing nurses with information and support to help them deliver quality care for women and newborns. **Affiliated With:** Association of Women's Health, Obstetric and Neonatal Nurses.

Lexington

5676 ■ National Active and Retired Federal Employees Association - Jefferson County 1677
8298 West St., Rd. 356
Lexington, IN 47138-7612
Ph: (812)866-2650
URL: National Affiliate–www.narfe.org
Contact: Norman Arbuckle, Contact
Local. Protects the retirement future of employees through education. Informs members on issues affecting the retirement. **Affiliated With:** National Association of Retired Federal Employees.

Liberty

5677 ■ Achieva Resources Healthy Families - Union County
14 Market St.
Liberty, IN 47353
Ph: (765)458-9151
URL: http://www.achievaresources.org
Contact: Dan Stewart, Pres./CEO
Membership Dues: single, $20 • family, $30 • consumer, $2. **Local**.

5678 ■ American Legion, Simon Ethelbert Snyder Post 122
4 W High St.
Liberty, IN 47353
Ph: (317)458-5545
Fax: (317)237-9891
URL: National Affiliate–www.legion.org
Local. **Affiliated With:** American Legion.

5679 ■ Liberty - Union County Chamber of Commerce
5 W High St.
Liberty, IN 47353-1121
Ph: (765)458-5976
Fax: (765)458-5976
E-mail: ucdc@dslmyway.com
URL: http://www.ucdc.us
Contact: Blanche G. Stelle, Exec.Dir.
Local.

Ligonier

5680 ■ American Legion, West Noble Post 243
100 S Main St.
Ligonier, IN 46767
Ph: (219)894-3430
Fax: (317)237-9891
URL: National Affiliate–www.legion.org
Local. **Affiliated With:** American Legion.

5681 ■ Ligonier Chamber of Commerce (LCC)
PO Box 121
Ligonier, IN 46767-0121
Ph: (260)894-3619
URL: http://www.ligonierindianachamber.org
Contact: Jolene Durham, Pres.
Founded: 1935. **Members:** 64. **Local**. Promotes business and community development in Ligonier, IN. Helps sponsor Legionier festival. **Awards:** New Business Plaque. **Type:** recognition. **Publications:** Newsletter, periodic. **Conventions/Meetings:** annual banquet • monthly meeting.

Linton

5682 ■ American Legion, Frank Courtney Post 22
139 S Main St.
Linton, IN 47441
Ph: (812)847-2906
Fax: (317)237-9891
URL: National Affiliate–www.legion.org
Local. **Affiliated With:** American Legion.

5683 ■ Greene County Board of Realtors
PO Box 511
Linton, IN 47441-0511
Ph: (812)847-3300
Fax: (812)847-1900
E-mail: rrandallbaker@insightbb.com
URL: National Affiliate–www.realtor.org
Contact: R. Randall Baker, Exec. Officer
Local. Strives to develop real estate business practices. Advocates the right to own, use and transfer real property. Provides a facility for professional development, research and exchange of information among members and to the general public. **Affiliated With:** National Association of Realtors.

5684 ■ Linton-Stockton Chamber of Commerce (LSCC)
159 1st St. NW
PO Box 208
Linton, IN 47441
Ph: (812)847-4846
Fax: (812)847-0246
E-mail: chamber@joink.com
URL: http://www.lintonchamber.org
Contact: Tammy Martin, Exec.Dir.
Founded: 1929. **Members:** 140. **Membership Dues:** business (based on the number of employee), $100-$375 (annual) • service organization, $50 (annual) • church, $50 (annual) • individual, $25 (annual) • family, $35 (annual). **Staff:** 1. **Local**. Businesses, civic clubs, fraternal organizations, and interested individuals. Promotes business and community development in Stockton Township, IN. Sponsors Linton Freedom Festival. **Committees:** Ambassadors; Program; Technology; Tourism. **Task Forces:** Economic Development; Nominating; Outreach; Publicity. **Formerly:** (1982) Linton Chamber of Commerce. **Publications:** *Chamber of Commerce Newsletter*, monthly. **Conventions/Meetings:** annual meeting • monthly meeting.

5685 ■ National Active and Retired Federal Employees Association - Linton 1688
RR1, Box 508
Linton, IN 47441-9586
Ph: (812)847-4668
URL: National Affiliate–www.narfe.org
Contact: Jimmy Anderson, Contact
Local. Protects the retirement future of employees through education. Informs members on issues affecting the retirement. **Affiliated With:** National Association of Retired Federal Employees.

5686 ■ Quail Unlimited, Sullivan County Chapter
RR 2, Box 832
Linton, IN 47441
Ph: (812)847-8535
E-mail: mstacy@osmre.com
URL: National Affiliate–www.qu.org
Local. **Affiliated With:** Quail Unlimited.

Logansport

5687 ■ American Legion, Cass County Post 60
PO Box 737
Logansport, IN 46947
Ph: (219)753-6916
Fax: (317)237-9891
URL: National Affiliate–www.legion.org
Local. **Affiliated With:** American Legion.

5688 ■ Association of the United States Army, South Bend
c/o Kelly Rosenberger
1232 Tower Dr.
Logansport, IN 46947
Ph: (219)753-0518
E-mail: cptr2293in@msn.com
URL: National Affiliate–www.ausa.org
Local. Represents the interests and concerns of American Soldiers. Fosters public support of the Army's role in national security. Provides professional education and information programs.

5689 ■ Cass County Board of Realtors
601 North St.
Logansport, IN 46947
Ph: (574)722-3648
Fax: (574)725-3198
E-mail: cassboardofrealtors@hotmail.com
URL: National Affiliate–www.realtor.org
Contact: Debra A. Drinkwine, Pres.
Local. Strives to develop real estate business practices. Advocates the right to own, use and transfer real property. Provides a facility for professional development, research and exchange of information among members and to the general public. **Affiliated With:** National Association of Realtors.

5690 ■ Cass County REACT Team
719 Plum St.
Logansport, IN 46947
Ph: (574)753-4213
E-mail: s.forker@verizon.net
URL: http://www.reactintl.org/teaminfo/usa_teams/teams-usin.htm
Local. Trained communication experts and professional volunteers. Provides volunteer public service and emergency communications through the use of radios (Citizen Band, General Mobile Radio Service, UHF and HAM). Coordinates with radio industries and government on safety communication matters and supports charitable activities and community organizations.

5691 ■ Indiana Amateur Softball Association, Region 5
c/o Don Lombardi, VP
1911 E Broadway
Logansport, IN 46947
Ph: (574)753-8392
E-mail: drjlom@netzero.com
URL: http://www.indiana-asa.org
Contact: Don Lombardi, VP
Local. **Affiliated With:** Amateur Softball Association of America.

5692 ■ Logan's Landing
PO Box 473
Logansport, IN 46947
Ph: (574)722-9345
E-mail: pwihebrink@logansianding.com
URL: http://www.logansianding.com
Local.

5693 ■ Logansport - Cass County Chamber of Commerce
300 E Broadway, Ste.103
Logansport, IN 46947-3185
Ph: (574)753-6388
E-mail: info@logan-casschamber.com
URL: http://www.logan-casschamber.com
Contact: Brain Shafer, Pres.
Founded: 1938. **Local**. Promotes business and community development in Cass County, IN. **Committees:** Ambassadors; Business Advocacy; Business/Education; Business Solutions Group; Community Marketing; Events; Hospitality. **Programs:** Leadership. **Affiliated With:** U.S. Chamber of Commerce. **Publications:** *On Target*, monthly. Newsletter. **Conventions/Meetings:** annual general assembly.

5694 ■ Mental Health Association in Cass County
c/o Ms. Karen Waldron, Exec.Dir.
421 12th St.
Logansport, IN 46947-3539
Ph: (574)722-3984
E-mail: karenwaldronmha@yahoo.com
URL: http://www.mentalhealthassociation.com
Contact: Ms. Karen Waldron, Exec.Dir.
Local. Seeks to promote mental health and prevent mental health disorders. Improves mental health of Americans through advocacy, public education, research and service. **Affiliated With:** Mental Health Association in Indiana; National Mental Health Association.

5695 ■ National Active and Retired Federal Employees Association - Logansport 1046
4823 E Div. Rd.
Logansport, IN 46947-7962
Ph: (574)753-6799
URL: National Affiliate–www.narfe.org
Contact: Daniel J. Guckien, Contact
Local. Protects the retirement future of employees through education. Informs members on issues af-

fecting the retirement. **Affiliated With:** National Association of Retired Federal Employees.

5696 ■ Phi Theta Kappa, Beta Gamma Zeta Chapter - Ivy Tech State College
c/o Sheila Wiggins
Logansport Campus
2815 E Market St.
Logansport, IN 46947
Ph: (574)753-5101
URL: http://www.ptk.org/directories/chapters/IN/20696-1.htm
Contact: Sheila Wiggins, Advisor
Local.

5697 ■ Police and Firemen's Insurance Association - Logansport Fire and Police Department
c/o Arthur L. Hess
225 N Cicott St.
Logansport, IN 46947
Ph: (219)732-1665
URL: National Affiliate–www.pfia.net
Contact: Arthur L. Hess, Contact
Local. Affiliated With: Police and Firemen's Insurance Association.

5698 ■ SCORE Logansport
2815 E Market St., Rm. 112
Logansport, IN 46947
Ph: (574)753-5101
Fax: (574)735-5103
Free: (866)753-5102
E-mail: score@clss.net
URL: http://www.score615logansport.org
Contact: Mrs. Chris Coon, Chair
Founded: 1986. **Members:** 17. **Local. Affiliated With:** SCORE.

5699 ■ United Way of Cass County (UWCC)
c/o Joyce Gebhardt, Exec.Dir.
401 E Broadway
Logansport, IN 46947
Ph: (574)753-3533
Fax: (574)737-7803
E-mail: unitedway@cqc.com
URL: http://www.unitedway.cqc.com
Contact: Joyce Gebhardt, Exec.Dir.
Staff: 2. **Budget:** $80,000. **Local.** Works to assist in fundraising by conducting company-wide employee campaigns and by encouraging corporate contributions. **Publications:** none. **Affiliated With:** United Way of America.

Long Beach

5700 ■ PFLAG Michigan City/Indiana Dunes
1602 Hidden Hills Trail
Long Beach, IN 46360
Ph: (219)873-4961
E-mail: bdefuniak@aol.com
URL: http://www.pflag.org/Indiana.205.0.html
Local. Affiliated With: Parents, Families, and Friends of Lesbians and Gays.

Loogootee

5701 ■ Alfordsville-Reeve Township Schools Organization
c/o L. Oenone Bradley
RR 1
Box 91
Loogootee, IN 47553-9627
Ph: (812)644-7199 (812)644-7617
E-mail: alfordsvilleindreevestownshipschools@communities.msn.com
Contact: Larry A. Ray, Pres.
Founded: 2001. **Members:** 380. **Staff:** 7. **Budget:** $3,000. **Local Groups:** 1. **Local.** Provides a base of history for the Alfordsville-Reeve Township schools; promotes understanding of the history of education for the area. **Publications:** *Remembering Our Past.* Magazine. Contains pictures and historical items about the school. **Advertising:** not accepted. **Conventions/Meetings:** biennial Alfordsville-Reeve Township Schools Homecoming • annual meeting.

5702 ■ American Legion, Loogootee Post 120
112 Church St.
Loogootee, IN 47553
Ph: (812)295-2085
Fax: (317)237-9891
URL: National Affiliate–www.legion.org
Local. Affiliated With: American Legion.

5703 ■ Martin County Chamber of Commerce
PO Box 447
Loogootee, IN 47553
Ph: (812)295-4142
Fax: (812)295-5425
Contact: Laura Albertson, Pres.
Local.

Lowell

5704 ■ American Legion, Lowell Post 101
108 E Commercial Ave.
Lowell, IN 46356
Ph: (219)696-9120
Fax: (317)237-9891
URL: National Affiliate–www.legion.org
Local. Affiliated With: American Legion.

5705 ■ Lowell Chamber of Commerce (LCC)
428 E Commercial Ave.
Lowell, IN 46356
Ph: (219)696-0231
Fax: (219)696-0383
E-mail: lowellchamber@xvi.net
URL: http://Lowell.net
Contact: Ruth Dunn, Office Mgr.
Founded: 1952. **Members:** 111. **Local.** Promotes business and community development in the Lowell, IN area. Sponsors festival. Operates Visitors Center. **Publications:** Newsletter, monthly. **Conventions/Meetings:** semiannual meeting • quarterly meeting.

5706 ■ Veterans of Foreign Wars/Post 6841
c/o Dave Zander, Commander
PO Box 4
Lowell, IN 46356
Ph: (219)696-8121
E-mail: vfw-6841@webtv.net
URL: http://community-2.webtv.net/VFW-6841/webpage
Contact: Dave Zander, Commander
Local. Provides assistance to veterans and their families. Promotes fraternalism and patriotism.

Lynn

5707 ■ American Legion, Indiana Post 274
c/o Harry Howell
PO Box 498
Lynn, IN 47355
Ph: (317)630-1300
Fax: (317)237-9891
URL: National Affiliate–www.legion.org
Contact: Harry Howell, Contact
Local. Affiliated With: American Legion.

Lynnville

5708 ■ Greater Evansville Bonsai Society
c/o David Bogan
101 Terry Ln.
Lynnville, IN 47619
E-mail: dbogan@scvl.com
URL: National Affiliate–www.bonsai-bci.com
Contact: David Bogan, Contact
Local. Affiliated With: Bonsai Clubs International.

Lyons

5709 ■ American Legion, James Gastineau Post 479
PO Box 178
Lyons, IN 47443
Ph: (317)630-1300
Fax: (317)237-9891
URL: National Affiliate–www.legion.org
Local. Affiliated With: American Legion.

Madison

5710 ■ American Legion, Jefferson Post 9
707 Jefferson St.
Madison, IN 47250
Ph: (812)265-4417
Fax: (317)237-9891
URL: National Affiliate–www.legion.org
Local. Affiliated With: American Legion.

5711 ■ Big Ring Adventure Team
PO Box 622
Madison, IN 47250
Fax: (812)265-4203
E-mail: info@bigringadventure.com
URL: http://www.bigringadventure.com
Local. Affiliated With: International Mountain Bicycling Association.

5712 ■ Clinical Laboratory Management Association, Greater Indiana Chapter (GICLMA)
c/o Angela Lauster
King's Daughters' Hosp. and Hea. Services
1 King's Daughters' Hosp.
Madison, IN 47250
Ph: (812)265-5099
Fax: (812)265-0573
E-mail: adlauster@yahoo.com
URL: http://www.giclma.org
Contact: Angela Lauster, Contact
Local. Provides clinical laboratory leaders with resources to balance science and technology with the art of management. Promotes efficient, productive, and high quality operations. Enhances the professional, managerial and leadership skills of members. **Affiliated With:** Clinical Laboratory Management Association.

5713 ■ Indiana Chapter of National Emergency Number Association
c/o Harold Williams, Pres.
1223 Wells Dr.
Madison, IN 47250
Ph: (219)866-4991
E-mail: cptwms@hotmail.com
URL: http://www.innena.org
Contact: Harold Williams, Pres.
State. Promotes the technical advancement, availability, and implementation of a universal emergency telephone number system. **Affiliated With:** National Emergency Number Association.

5714 ■ Jefferson County Board of Realtors, Indiana
975 Indus. Dr., Ste.7
Madison, IN 47250
Ph: (812)574-1101
Fax: (812)574-1102
E-mail: eojcbor@seidata.com
URL: National Affiliate–www.realtor.org
Contact: Vivian L. Shatley, Exec. Officer
Local. Strives to develop real estate business practices. Advocates the right to own, use and transfer real property. Provides a facility for professional development, research and exchange of information among members and to the general public. **Affiliated With:** National Association of Realtors.

5715 ■ Jefferson County United Way, Indiana
PO Box 193
Madison, IN 47250-0193
Ph: (812)265-2036
URL: National Affiliate–national.unitedway.org
Local. Affiliated With: United Way of America.

5716 ■ Jefferson Switzerland Association for Retarded Citizens
3355 N SR 7
Madison, IN 47250
Ph: (812)273-6872
URL: National Affiliate–www.TheArc.org
Local. Parents, professional workers, and others interested in individuals with mental retardation. Works to promote services, research, public understanding, and legislation for people with mental retardation and their families. **Affiliated With:** Arc of the United States.

5717 ■ Madison Area Chamber of Commerce (MACC)
975 Indus. Dr., Ste.1
Madison, IN 47250
Ph: (812)265-3135
Fax: (812)265-5544
E-mail: info@madisonchamber.org
URL: http://www.madisonchamber.org
Contact: Mr. Galen L. Bremmer, Exec.VP
Founded: 1924. **Members:** 390. **Local.** Retail businesses, educational and professional organizations, and clubs. Promotes business and community development in the Jefferson County, IN area. Sponsors Annual Job Fair, Chamber Annual Golf Outing, Soup, Stew, Chili & Brew Festival, Business Expo. **Publications:** *Chamber Insight*, monthly. Newsletters. **Circulation:** 650. **Advertising:** accepted. Alternate Formats: online • *Community Information Directory*, annual. **Conventions/Meetings:** annual dinner.

5718 ■ Madison Main Street Program
301 E Main St.
Madison, IN 47250
Ph: (812)265-3270
URL: http://www.madisonindiana.org/mainstreet
Local.

5719 ■ Phi Theta Kappa, Alpha Psi Lambda Chapter - Ivy Tech State College
c/o Barbara Sigmon
Southeast Campus
590 IVY Tech Dr.
Madison, IN 47250
Ph: (812)265-2580
URL: http://www.ptk.org/directories/chapters/IN/20586-1.htm
Contact: Barbara Sigmon, Advisor
Local.

5720 ■ RSVP of Jefferson County
c/o Vickie Copeland, Dir.
512 W Main St.
Madison, IN 47250-3718
Ph: (812)265-3950
Fax: (812)273-6676
E-mail: vcopelan@tls.net
URL: http://www.seniorcorps.gov/about/programs/rsvp.asp
Contact: Vickie Copeland, Dir.
Local. Affiliated With: Retired and Senior Volunteer Program.

5721 ■ Save the Valley
PO Box 813
Madison, IN 47250
Ph: (812)265-4577
E-mail: richardhill@savethevalley.org
URL: http://www.savethevalley.org
Contact: Richard Hill, Pres.
Founded: 1974. **Members:** 60. **Membership Dues:** regular, $15 (annual) • senior, student, $5 (annual) • life, $200. **Budget:** $50,000. **For-Profit. Regional.** Works to prevent further pollution of air, water, and land in the Valley of the Ohio River between Lawrenceburg, Indiana and Louisville, Kentucky. Represents environmental and public interest before regulatory agencies.

Marengo

5722 ■ American Legion, Crawford County Post 84
PO Box 155
Marengo, IN 47140
Ph: (317)630-1300
Fax: (317)237-9891
URL: National Affiliate–www.legion.org
Local. Affiliated With: American Legion.

Marion

5723 ■ American Cancer Society, Mid-Indiana Area Service Center
1315 Gillespie
Marion, IN 46952
Ph: (765)668-7188
URL: National Affiliate–www.cancer.org
Contact: Kaye Bochert, Contact
Local. Affiliated With: American Cancer Society.

5724 ■ American Legion, Indiana Post 10
c/o Byron W. Thornburg
1700 S Pennsylvania St.
Marion, IN 46953
Ph: (317)662-1008
Fax: (317)237-9891
URL: National Affiliate–www.legion.org
Contact: Byron W. Thornburg, Contact
Local. Affiliated With: American Legion.

5725 ■ American Legion, Russell Weaver Post 166
3709 S Alabama Ave.
Marion, IN 46953
Ph: (317)630-1300
Fax: (317)237-9891
URL: National Affiliate–www.legion.org
Local. Affiliated With: American Legion.

5726 ■ American Society of Women Accountants, Marion Chapter No. 108
c/o Bobbi Hendey, Pres.
Ewer and Moritz, PC
PO Box 1029
Marion, IN 46952
Ph: (765)664-6201 (765)384-5118
Fax: (765)664-8329
E-mail: bobbi@hendeyfamily.com
URL: National Affiliate–www.aswa.org
Contact: Bobbi Hendey, Pres.
Local. Affiliated With: American Society of Women Accountants.

5727 ■ AMVETS, Marion Post 5
841 E 38th St.
Marion, IN 46953
Ph: (765)674-2400
E-mail: rbpiper@prodigy.net
URL: http://geocities.com/amvetspost5
Contact: Ronald Piper, Commander
Local. Affiliated With: AMVETS - American Veterans.

5728 ■ Association for Indiana Media Educators (AIME)
c/o Rick Jones, Pres.
560 S 900 E
Marion, IN 46953-9629
Ph: (765)664-1214
Fax: (765)664-1216
E-mail: rajones@eastbrook.k12.in.us
URL: http://www.ilfonline.org/AIME
Contact: Rick Jones, Pres.
State. Works to encourage the professional growth of its members and to undertake, sponsor, and promote programs for the improvement of education in Indiana through the effective and efficient use of educational media. Sponsors programs like Media Fair, Young Hoosier Book Award, Eliot Rosewater High School Book Award, and the Read-Aloud Books Too Good to Miss. **Publications:** *Focus on Indiana Libraries*, monthly. Newsletter • *Indiana Libraries*, semiannual. Journal. **Conventions/Meetings:** annual conference.

5729 ■ Court Appointed Special Advocates of Grant County (CASA)
c/o Roland L. Auble
110 W. 4th St.
Marion, IN 46952-4018.
Local.

5730 ■ Garden Club of Marion
c/o Judy Fornshell, Pres.
706 Macalan Dr.
Marion, IN 46952-2043
Ph: (765)664-4720
E-mail: judy@gardenclubmarionindiana.org
URL: http://www.gardenclubmarionindiana.org
Contact: Judy Fornshell, Pres.
Local.

5731 ■ Grant County Literacy Council
c/o Co-Presidents
112 E 35th St.
Marion, IN 46953-4343
Ph: (765)674-9250
E-mail: ddhartma@netscape.net
URL: National Affiliate–www.proliteracy.org
Contact: Mr. David D. Hartman, Co-Pres.
Founded: 1987. **Members:** 91. **Membership Dues:** all, $5 (annual). **Budget:** $12,000. **Local Groups:** 1. **Local.** Provides one-on-one tutoring at no charge for functionally illiterate adults. **Libraries: Type:** not open to the public. **Holdings:** books. **Subjects:** learning to read. **Affiliated With:** ProLiteracy Worldwide. **Formerly:** Grant County Literacy.

5732 ■ Indiana Inventors Association
c/o Robert Humbert
5514 S Adams
Marion, IN 46953
Ph: (765)674-2845
Fax: (765)733-0579
E-mail: arhumbert@bpsinet.com
URL: National Affiliate–www.uiausa.org
Contact: Robert Humbert, Contact
Local. Affiliated With: United Inventors Association of the U.S.A.

5733 ■ Indiana Society for Healthcare Consumer Advocacy (ISHCA)
c/o Randy Deffenbaugh, Pres.
Marion Gen. Hosp.
441 N Wabash Ave.
Marion, IN 46952
Ph: (765)662-4113
Fax: (765)662-4717
E-mail: rdeffenb@mgh.net
URL: National Affiliate–www.shca-aha.org
Contact: Randy Deffenbaugh, Pres.
State. Healthcare professionals. Represents and advocates for healthcare consumers in Indiana. **Affiliated With:** Society for Healthcare Consumer Advocacy of the American Hospital Association.

5734 ■ Indiana Wesleyan University Association for Computing Machinery Student Chapter
c/o Dr. Connie D. Lightfoot
4201 S Washington St.
Marion, IN 46953
Ph: (765)677-2554
Fax: (765)677-2455
E-mail: connie.lightfoot@indwes.edu
URL: http://cas.indwes.edu/Natural_Sciences_Mathematics/CIS.htm
Contact: Ms. Sara Turskey, Pres.
Local. Biological, medical, behavioral, and computer scientists; hospital administrators; programmers and others interested in application of computer methods

to biological, behavioral, and medical problems. Stimulates understanding of the use and potential of computers in the Biosciences. **Affiliated With:** Association for Computing Machinery.

5735 ■ Izaak Walton League of America, Grant County Chapter
4030 N Wilshire Dr.
Marion, IN 46952-8610
Ph: (765)664-0790
URL: National Affiliate–www.iwla.org
Local. Works to educate the public to conserve, maintain, protect, and restore the soil, forest, water, and other natural resources of the U.S; promotes the enjoyment and wholesome utilization of these resources. **Affiliated With:** Izaak Walton League of America.

5736 ■ Marion Area Board of Realtors
1330 W 1st St.
Marion, IN 46952
Ph: (765)664-3232
Fax: (765)662-3903
E-mail: exec@marionrealtors.com
URL: http://www.marionrealtors.com
Contact: Karen Wood, Pres.
Local. Strives to develop real estate business practices. Advocates the right to own, use and transfer real property. Provides a facility for professional development, research and exchange of information among members and to the general public. **Affiliated With:** National Association of Realtors.

5737 ■ Marion Coin Club
c/o Ray Lockwood
2075 E Bocock Rd.
Marion, IN 46952
Ph: (765)664-6520
E-mail: sunrayofmarion@aol.com
URL: http://www.members.tripod.com/marioncoinclub
Contact: Ray Lockwood, Contact
Local. **Affiliated With:** American Numismatic Association.

5738 ■ Marion-Grant County Chamber of Commerce
215 S Adams St.
Marion, IN 46952-3895
Ph: (765)664-5107
Fax: (765)668-5443
E-mail: info@marionchamber.org
URL: http://www.marionchamber.org
Contact: Aaron DeWeese, Pres.
Founded: 1935. **Members:** 500. **Local**. Promotes business and community development in Grant County, IN. **Awards:** Athena Award. **Frequency:** annual. **Type:** recognition • Chairman's Award. **Frequency:** annual. **Type:** recognition • Special Recognition Awards. **Frequency:** annual. **Type:** recognition. **Divisions:** Education; Governmental Affairs; Member Services. **Affiliated With:** U.S. Chamber of Commerce. **Publications:** *Momentum*, monthly. Newsletter. **Price:** free for members • Membership Directory, semiannual. **Conventions/Meetings:** annual Business Trade Fair - trade show - always first Wednesday in May • periodic meeting • monthly meeting - always second Tuesday • annual meeting - always August • annual meeting - always October • monthly seminar.

5739 ■ Marion-Grant County Convention and Visitors Bureau
217 S Adams St.
Marion, IN 46952
Ph: (765)668-5435
Fax: (765)668-5424
Free: (800)662-9474
E-mail: geninfo@jamesdeancountry.com
URL: http://www.jamesdeancountry.com
Contact: Karen Lentz, Exec.Dir.
Local. Promotes business and tourism in Grant County, IN. **Formerly:** (2005) Grant County Convention and Visitors Bureau. **Publications:** *Cool Times*, periodic. Newsletter. Provides hospitality news and information on local events. **Circulation:** 3,500.

5740 ■ North Central Indiana Youth for Christ
PO Box 1184
Marion, IN 46952
Ph: (765)674-7735
Fax: (765)674-7736
URL: http://www.youthforchrist.tv
Local. **Affiliated With:** Youth for Christ/U.S.A.

5741 ■ Psi Chi, National Honor Society in Psychology - Indiana Wesleyan University
c/o Dept. of Psychology
4201 S Washington St.
Marion, IN 46953-4999
Ph: (765)677-2231 (765)677-2993
Fax: (765)677-2487
E-mail: kpuffer@indwes.edu
URL: http://www.psichi.org/chapters/info.asp?chapter_id=977
Contact: Keith A. Puffer PhD, Advisor
Local.

5742 ■ Salamonie AIFA
c/o David L. Mann, Pres.
1317 W 5th St.
Marion, IN 46953
Ph: (260)563-6381
Fax: (765)664-7539
E-mail: dave.mann@nmfn.com
URL: National Affiliate–naifa.org
Contact: David L. Mann, Pres.
Local. Represents the interests of insurance and financial advisors. Advocates for a positive legislative and regulatory environment. Enhances business and professional skills of members. **Affiliated With:** National Association of Insurance and Financial Advisors.

5743 ■ SCORE Marion/Grant Co
215 S Adams St.
Marion, IN 46952
Ph: (765)664-5107
E-mail: score550@nxco.com
URL: http://www.bloomington.in.us/~mscore
Local. Provides free business counseling and management training programs for small business owners/managers, and for those who plan to start a new business. **Affiliated With:** SCORE.

5744 ■ Society for Healthcare Consumer Advocacy, Indiana
c/o Randy Deffenbaugh, Pres.
Marion Gen. Hospital
441 N. Wabash Ave.
Marion, IN 46952
Ph: (765)662-4113
Fax: (765)662-4717
E-mail: rdeffenb@mgh.net
URL: National Affiliate–www.shca-aha.org
Affiliated With: Society for Healthcare Consumer Advocacy of the American Hospital Association.

5745 ■ United Way of Grant County, Indiana
PO Box 61
Marion, IN 46952-0061
Ph: (765)662-9811
URL: National Affiliate–national.unitedway.org
Local. **Affiliated With:** United Way of America.

Markle

5746 ■ American Rabbit Breeders Association, District 8
c/o Bruce Ormsby, Dir.
PO Box 283
Markle, IN 46770-0283
Ph: (260)758-9255
E-mail: rabbitjudge@excite.com
URL: http://www.arba.net/district/8
Contact: Bruce Ormsby, Dir.
Regional. **Affiliated With:** American Rabbit Breeders Association.

Marshall

5747 ■ Young Life Indiana Camp
4215 E Landry Ln.
Marshall, IN 47859
Ph: (765)597-2272
URL: http://sites.younglife.org/_layouts/ylext/default.aspx?ID=A-5280
State. **Affiliated With:** Young Life.

Martinsville

5748 ■ American Chesapeake Club, Indiana
c/o Channa Beth Butcher
2000 Pumpkinvine Hill
Martinsville, IN 46151
Ph: (765)342-7327
E-mail: cbbut@reliable-net.net
URL: National Affiliate–www.amchessieclub.org
Contact: Channa Beth Butcher, Contact
State. **Affiliated With:** American Chesapeake Club.

5749 ■ American Hiking Society - Hoosiers Hikers Council (HHC)
PO Box 1327
Martinsville, IN 46151
Ph: (765)349-0204
E-mail: hikers@scican.net
URL: http://www.HoosierHikersCouncil.org
Contact: Suzanne Mittenthal, Exec.Dir.
Local.

5750 ■ American Legion, Martinsville Post 230
701 E Morgan St.
Martinsville, IN 46151
Ph: (317)342-2799
Fax: (317)237-9891
URL: National Affiliate–www.legion.org
Local. **Affiliated With:** American Legion.

5751 ■ American Society for Healthcare Food Service Administrators, Hoosier Chapter
c/o Becky Amt, RHSO, Pres.
Morgan Hosp. & Medical Ctr.
2209 John R. Wooden Dr.
Martinsville, IN 46151
Ph: (765)349-6500
Fax: (765)349-6446
E-mail: bamt@mcmh.net
URL: National Affiliate–www.ashfsa.org
Contact: Becky Amt RHSO, Pres.
Local. Advances healthcare foodservice leadership through education, networking and advocacy. **Affiliated With:** American Society for Healthcare Food Service Administrators.

5752 ■ Greater Martinsville Chamber of Commerce (MCC)
20 W. Washington St.
PO Box 1378
Martinsville, IN 46151
Ph: (765)342-8110
Fax: (765)342-5713
E-mail: gmcofc@reliable-net.net
URL: http://www.scican.net/~chamber/
Contact: Bill Cunningham, Pres.
Members: 200. **Membership Dues:** large manufacturing, bank, utility, hospital, $500 (annual) • retail, restaurant, lodging, entertainment, $200 (annual) • small business, contractor, professional, non-profit, $125 (annual) • associate, church, community service club, $50 (annual). **Budget:** $40,000. **Local**. Promotes business and community development in Martinsville, IN.

5753 ■ Habitat for Humanity of Morgan County, Indiana
PO Box 1929
Martinsville, IN 46151
Ph: (765)349-9003
E-mail: habitatoffice@morgancountyhabitat.org
URL: http://www.morgancountyhabitat.org
Contact: Joe Skvarenina, Exec.Dir.
Local. **Affiliated With:** Habitat for Humanity International.

5754 ■ Hoosier Hikers Council (HHC)
c/o Suzanne Mittenthal, Exec.Dir.
PO Box 1327
Martinsville, IN 46151
Ph: (765)349-0204
E-mail: hikers@scican.net
URL: http://www.hoosierhikerscouncil.org
Contact: Suzanne Mittenthal, Exec.Dir.
Founded: 1994. **Local**. Statewide hikers, runners, and backpackers promoting, protecting, and building hiking trails and natural resources that support them.

5755 ■ Independent Funeral Directors of Indiana
c/o Mack Porter
PO Box 1494
Martinsville, IN 46151-0494
Ph: (765)349-6285
Fax: (765)349-2355
Free: (800)880-9861
E-mail: admin@ifdofi.org
Contact: Mr. Mack Porter, Exec.Dir.
Founded: 1999. **Members:** 136. **Membership Dues:** regular, $300 (annual). **Staff:** 2. **State Groups:** 1. **For-Profit. State**. Family, independently owned funeral homes located in the State of Indiana and the suppliers of goods and services to these funeral homes. **Computer Services:** database. **Publications:** *Independent Informer*, quarterly. Newsletter. **Price:** included in membership dues. **Circulation:** 150. **Advertising:** accepted. Alternate Formats: CD-ROM; diskette. **Conventions/Meetings:** annual convention - always fall.

5756 ■ International Edsel Club, Indiana Chapter
4280 Abner Ln.
Martinsville, IN 46151-6878
E-mail: nanapap@rnetinc.net
URL: National Affiliate–www.internationaledsel.com
State. Affiliated With: International Edsel Club.

5757 ■ Vintage Chevrolet Club of America, Indiana Region No. 7
c/o Don Guthrie, Dir.
9340 Old State Rd., 37 N
Martinsville, IN 46151-7661
E-mail: jburnes@vintagechevrolet.org
URL: http://www.vintagechevrolet.org/indiana
Contact: Don Guthrie, Dir.
State. Affiliated With: Vintage Chevrolet Club of America.

Medaryville

5758 ■ American Legion, Harold Kripisch Post 96
PO Box 353
Medaryville, IN 47957
Ph: (219)843-6696
Fax: (317)237-9891
URL: National Affiliate–www.legion.org
Local. Affiliated With: American Legion.

Medora

5759 ■ American Legion, Medora Post 453
PO Box 477
Medora, IN 47260
Ph: (317)630-1300
Fax: (317)237-9891
URL: National Affiliate–www.legion.org
Local. Affiliated With: American Legion.

Memphis

5760 ■ American Legion, Lexington Post 352
208 Appletree Ln.
Memphis, IN 47143
Ph: (317)630-1300
Fax: (317)237-9891
URL: National Affiliate–www.legion.org
Local. Affiliated With: American Legion.

Mentone

5761 ■ Mentone Chamber of Commerce
PO Box 366
Mentone, IN 46539
Ph: (574)353-7417
Contact: Rita Simpson, Pres.
Local.

Merrillville

5762 ■ American Cancer Society, Northwest Indiana Area Service Center
1551 E 85th Ave.
Merrillville, IN 46410
Ph: (219)793-1030
Fax: (219)793-1033
Free: (888)635-9255
URL: http://www.cancer.org
Contact: Jim Puente, Exec.Dir.
Local. Works to support education and research in cancer prevention, diagnosis, detection, and treatment. **Affiliated With:** American Cancer Society.

5763 ■ American Legion, Glen Park Post 214
PO Box 11151
Merrillville, IN 46411
Ph: (317)630-1300
Fax: (317)237-9891
URL: National Affiliate–www.legion.org
Local. Affiliated With: American Legion.

5764 ■ American Legion, Merrillville Post 430
7430 Broadway
Merrillville, IN 46410
Ph: (219)769-3071
Fax: (317)237-9891
URL: National Affiliate–www.legion.org
Local. Affiliated With: American Legion.

5765 ■ American Legion, Tadeusz Kosciuszko Post 207
6920 Broadway
Merrillville, IN 46411
Ph: (219)924-8456
Fax: (317)237-9891
URL: National Affiliate–www.legion.org
Local. Affiliated With: American Legion.

5766 ■ American Legion, Vytautas Post 289
1804 E 73rd Ave.
Merrillville, IN 46410
Ph: (219)942-8998
Fax: (317)237-9891
URL: National Affiliate–www.legion.org
Local. Affiliated With: American Legion.

5767 ■ American Red Cross of Northwest Indiana
791 E 83rd Ave.
Merrillville, IN 46410-6204
Ph: (219)756-5360
Fax: (219)756-5371
Free: (800)589-8502
E-mail: zone2@nwindiana-redcross.org
URL: http://www.nwindiana-redcross.org
Contact: Gordon Johnson, Exec.Dir.
Local. Works to provide relief to victims of disasters and helps people prevent, prepare for, and respond to emergencies. **Publications:** Annual Report, annual. Alternate Formats: online.

5768 ■ Better Business Bureau of Northwest Indiana
6111 Harrison St., Ste.101
Merrillville, IN 46410
Ph: (219)980-1511
Fax: (219)884-2123
E-mail: info@nwin.bbb.org
URL: http://www.nwin.bbb.org
Contact: Morris W. Cochran, Pres./CEO
Local. Seeks to promote and foster the highest ethical relationship between businesses and the public through voluntary self-regulation, consumer and business education, and service excellence. Provides information to help consumers and businesses make informed purchasing decisions and avoid costly scams and frauds; settles consumer complaints through arbitration and other means. **Affiliated With:** BBB Wise Giving Alliance.

5769 ■ Drifting Dunes Girl Scout Council
899 Broadway
Merrillville, IN 46410
Ph: (219)795-9640
Free: (800)654-4711
E-mail: msmith@ddgsc.com
URL: http://www.ddgsc.com
Contact: Melissa Thompson, Dir. of Communications and Development
Local. Helps girls build character and skills for success in the real world.

5770 ■ Greater Northwest Indiana Association of Realtors
8672 Broadway
Merrillville, IN 46410
Ph: (219)795-3600
Fax: (219)795-3611
E-mail: smith@gniar.com
URL: National Affiliate–www.realtor.org
Contact: Nancy Smith, Exec. Officer
Local. Strives to develop real estate business practices. Advocates the right to own, use and transfer real property. Provides a facility for professional development, research and exchange of information among members and to the general public. **Affiliated With:** National Association of Realtors.

5771 ■ Indiana Structural Engineers Association (ISEA)
c/o James M. Kirk, PE, Pres.
Enspect, Inc.
8896 Louisiana St.
Merrillville, IN 46410
Ph: (219)736-6002
E-mail: enspectinc@cs.com
URL: http://www.indianasea.org
Contact: James M. Kirk PE, Pres.
Founded: 2002. **Members:** 50. **Membership Dues:** professional engineer, $100 (annual). **State**. Registered professional engineers, specifically students, practicing and studying structural engineering. Promotes, monitors, and research for the enhancement of the practice of structural engineering. **Committees:** Codes; Education; Government Relations; Professional Practices. **Affiliated With:** National Council of Structural Engineers Associations. **Conventions/Meetings:** monthly meeting - every first Tuesday.

5772 ■ Lake County Medical Society - Indiana
8006 Tyler St.
Merrillville, IN 46410
Ph: (219)769-3551
Fax: (219)769-3564
E-mail: kathylcms@sbcglobal.net
URL: http://www.lcmedsoc.org
Contact: Heratch Doumanian MD, Pres.
Local. Advances the art and science of medicine. Promotes patient care and the betterment of public health. **Affiliated With:** Indiana State Medical Association.

5773 ■ Lake County Public Library Staff Association
1919 W. 81st Ave.
Merrillville, IN 46410
Ph: (219)769-3541
Fax: (219)769-0690
URL: http://www.lakeco.lib.in.us
Members: 237. **Membership Dues:** full-time, $5 (annual) • part-time, $2 (annual). **Local Groups:** 1. **Local. Libraries: Type:** not open to the public. **Holdings:** 1,175,131; audio recordings, books, periodicals, software, video recordings.

5774 ■ Merrillville Chamber of Commerce
255 W 80th Pl.
Merrillville, IN 46410
Ph: (219)769-8180
Fax: (219)736-6223
E-mail: geninq@merrillvillecoc.org
URL: http://www.merrillvillecoc.org
Contact: John J. Janik, Pres./CEO
Founded: 1954. **Staff:** 5. **Local.** Promotes business and economic development in Merrillville, IN. **Computer Services:** Mailing lists, of members. **Publications:** Newsletter, monthly.

5775 ■ Michiana Professional Photographers (MPP)
c/o John Bir, Pres.
John Giolas Photo., Inc.
7994 Broadway
Merrillville, IN 46410-5540
Ph: (219)769-7934 (219)769-7935
E-mail: jbir@giolas.com
URL: http://www.mppofi.org
Contact: John Bir, Pres.
Local. Affiliated With: Professional Photographers of America.

5776 ■ National Active and Retired Federal Employees Association - Hammond 546
89 E 70th Ave.
Merrillville, IN 46410-3611
Ph: (219)738-2438
URL: National Affiliate–www.narfe.org
Contact: Edward F. Spanier, Contact
Local. Protects the retirement future of employees through education. Informs members on issues affecting the retirement. **Affiliated With:** National Association of Retired Federal Employees.

5777 ■ Northwest Indiana AIFA
c/o George G. Ross, Pres.
PO Box 10207
Merrillville, IN 46411
Ph: (219)764-9728
Fax: (219)764-7039
E-mail: heftyinsurances@comcast.net
URL: National Affiliate–naifa.org
Contact: George G. Ross, Pres.
Local. Represents the interests of insurance and financial advisors. Advocates for a positive legislative and regulatory environment. Enhances business and professional skills of members. **Affiliated With:** National Association of Insurance and Financial Advisors.

5778 ■ Northwest Indiana Dental Society
8006 Tyler St.
Merrillville, IN 46410
Ph: (219)769-3504
Fax: (219)769-3564
E-mail: knelson@netnitco.net
URL: National Affiliate–www.ada.org
Contact: Ms. Kathy Nelson, Exec.Dir.
Local. Represents the interests of dentists committed to the public's oral health, ethics and professional development. Encourages the improvement of the public's oral health and promotes the art and science of dentistry. **Affiliated With:** American Dental Association; Indiana Dental Association.

5779 ■ Wellness Council of Indiana
PO Box 1405
Merrillville, IN 46411
Ph: (219)962-6613
URL: http://www.wellnessin.org
Contact: Phil Huffine, Exec.Dir.
State. Formerly: (2005) Wellness Council of Northwest Indiana.

Michigan City

5780 ■ ACF Chefs of Northwest Indiana
PO Box 9140
Michigan City, IN 46360
Ph: (708)485-2383
E-mail: chefpeteccc@sbcglobal.net
URL: National Affiliate–www.acfchefs.org
Contact: Peter E. Jeschke CCC, Pres.
Local. Promotes the culinary profession. Provides on-going educational training and networking for members. Provides opportunities for competition, professional recognition and access to educational forums with other culinarians at local, regional, national and international events. **Affiliated With:** American Culinary Federation.

5781 ■ Acme Lodge 83 Free and Accepted Masons
c/o Larry Harris
105 Ruby Ct.
Michigan City, IN 46360
E-mail: lapat697@ameritech.net

5782 ■ American Legion, Indiana Post 37
c/o John Franklin Miller
756 E US Hwy. 20
Michigan City, IN 46360
Ph: (219)879-9801
Fax: (317)237-9891
URL: National Affiliate–www.legion.org
Contact: John Franklin Miller, Contact
Local. Affiliated With: American Legion.

5783 ■ American Legion, Indiana Post 451
c/o Frank Edward Skwiat
PO Box 451
Michigan City, IN 46361
Ph: (219)874-8563
Fax: (317)237-9891
URL: National Affiliate–www.legion.org
Contact: Frank Edward Skwiat, Contact
Local. Affiliated With: American Legion.

5784 ■ American Legion, La Porte, County Post 130
PO Box 41
Michigan City, IN 46361
Ph: (317)630-1300
Fax: (317)237-9891
URL: National Affiliate–www.legion.org
Local. Affiliated With: American Legion.

5785 ■ LaPorte County Convention and Visitors Bureau (LPCCVB)
1503 S Meer Rd.
Michigan City, IN 46360
Ph: (219)872-5055
Fax: (219)872-3660
Free: (800)634-2650
E-mail: lpccvb@netnitco.net
Contact: Dionne Wisniewski, Exec.Dir.
Founded: 1979. **Local.** Promotes travel and tourism and promotion to Northern Indiana Harbor Country. Assists in planning of meetings, conventions, family reunions, group trips and special events in the county. **Publications:** *Dune-Line*, quarterly. Newsletter.

5786 ■ Michigan City Area Chamber of Commerce
200 E Michigan Blvd.
Michigan City, IN 46360-3270
Ph: (219)874-6221
Fax: (219)873-1204
E-mail: info@mcachamber.com
URL: http://www.michigancitychamber.com
Contact: Tim Bietry, Pres.
Founded: 1918. **Members:** 451. **Staff:** 5. **Local.** Promotes business and community development in the Michigan City, IN area. **Divisions:** Community Improvement; Economic Development; Government/Legislative. **Affiliated With:** U.S. Chamber of Commerce. **Publications:** *The Beacon*, weekly. Newsletter. Contains information, hot topics, current projects and deadlines. • *Lakeview*, bimonthly. Newsletter. **Price:** free. **Circulation:** 14,000. **Advertising:** accepted.

5787 ■ Michigan City Exchange Club
Elks Lodge 432
416 E US Hwy. 20
Michigan City, IN 46360
Ph: (219)874-1158
Fax: (219)874-2121
E-mail: leweber@home.com
URL: http://www.promonational.com/mcexchange
Contact: Lou Weber, Treas.
Local.

5788 ■ Michigan City Historical Society (MCHS)
PO Box 512
Michigan City, IN 46361
Ph: (219)872-6133
URL: http://www.michigancity.com/MCHistorical/
Contact: June M. Jaques, Dir.
Founded: 1927. **Members:** 284. **Membership Dues:** individual, $8 (annual) • family, $10 (annual) • patron, $25 (annual) • sponsor, $50 (annual) • life, $150. **For-Profit. Local.** Individuals interested in preserving the history of Michigan City, IN. Maintains Old Lighthouse Museum, maritime exhibits on Lake Michigan, and special exhibits. **Publications:** *Old Lighthouse Museum News*, quarterly. Newsletter. **Circulation:** 284. **Conventions/Meetings:** quarterly meeting.

5789 ■ Michigan Indiana Thimble Society
c/o Mary Jo Stoll
316 Derby St.
Michigan City, IN 46360
Ph: (219)879-8134
E-mail: mjstoll8@yahoo.com
URL: National Affiliate–www.thimblecollectors.com
Contact: Mary Jo Stoll, Contact
Regional. Affiliated With: Thimble Collectors International.

5790 ■ Northern Indiana Chapter, National Electrical Contractors Association
PO Box 2006
Michigan City, IN 46361-8006
Ph: (219)872-3151
Fax: (219)872-3916
Free: (800)642-9334
E-mail: info@necani.org
URL: http://www.necani.org
Contact: Mr. Edward J. Shikany, Pres.
Founded: 1944. **Local.** Aims to promote and advance the interests of the electrical contracting industry. **Affiliated With:** National Electrical Contractors Association.

5791 ■ Orak Shriners
c/o Thomas J. Rutkowski
3848 N Frontage Rd.
Michigan City, IN 46360-9264
Ph: (219)872-0485
Fax: (219)872-0490
Free: (800)276-6725
E-mail: orakshrn@csinet.net
URL: http://www.orakshrine.org
Contact: Thomas J. Rutkowski, Recorder
Local. Affiliated With: Imperial Council of the Ancient Arabic Order of the Nobles of the Mystic Shrine for North America.

5792 ■ RSVP of Laporte/Starke Counties
c/o Thomas J. Szawara, Dir.
321 W 11th st.
Michigan City, IN 46360-3709
Ph: (219)874-8195
Fax: (219)879-9073
E-mail: mcrsvp@catholic-charities.org
URL: http://www.volunteersolutions.org/uwpc/org/6249582.html
Contact: Thomas J. Szawara, Dir.
Local. Additional Websites: http://www.seniorcorps.gov/about/programs/rsvp.asp. **Affiliated With:** Retired and Senior Volunteer Program.

5793 ■ Ruffed Grouse Society, Hoosier Chapter
c/o Tony Hofstetter
H & D Tree Ser.
2500 Shorewood Dr.
Michigan City, IN 46360
Ph: (219)872-8556
URL: National Affiliate–www.ruffedgrousesociety.org
Contact: Tony Hofstetter, Contact
Local. Affiliated With: Ruffed Grouse Society.

5794 ■ Save the Dunes Council
c/o Thomas R. Anderson, Exec.Dir.
444 Barker Rd.
Michigan City, IN 46360
Ph: (219)879-3937
Local.

Middlebury

5795 ■ American Legion, Indiana Post 210
c/o Mark L. Wilt
103 York Dr.
Middlebury, IN 46540
Ph: (219)825-5121
Fax: (317)237-9891
URL: National Affiliate–www.legion.org
Contact: Mark L. Wilt, Contact
Local. Affiliated With: American Legion.

Middletown

5796 ■ American Legion, Charles Mundell Post 216
450 N 10th St.
Middletown, IN 47356
Ph: (317)354-4892
Fax: (317)237-9891
URL: National Affiliate–www.legion.org
Local. Affiliated With: American Legion.

Milan

5797 ■ American Legion, Smith-Ashcraft-Kissell Post 235
318 E Indian Trail
Milan, IN 47031
Ph: (812)654-9233
Fax: (317)237-9891
URL: National Affiliate–www.legion.org
Local. Affiliated With: American Legion.

5798 ■ Ghetto Grouse Gun Club
PO Box 728
Milan, IN 47031
Ph: (812)654-3322
URL: National Affiliate–www.mynssa.com
Local. Affiliated With: National Skeet Shooting Association.

Milford

5799 ■ American Legion, Ancil Geiger Post 226
PO Box 121
Milford, IN 46542
Ph: (317)630-1300
Fax: (317)237-9891
URL: National Affiliate–www.legion.org
Local. Affiliated With: American Legion.

5800 ■ Northeast Indiana Angus Association
c/o Jim Amsden, Pres.
PO Box 574
Milford, IN 46542
Ph: (574)658-4474
URL: National Affiliate–www.angus.org
Contact: Jim Amsden, Pres.
Local. Affiliated With: American Angus Association.

5801 ■ Tippecanoe Audubon Society
c/o Paul Steffan, Pres.
PO Box 488
Milford, IN 46542-0488
Ph: (574)658-4504
E-mail: ecoexpo@earthlink.net
URL: National Affiliate–www.audubon.org
Contact: Paul Steffen, Contact
Local. Works to conserve and restore natural ecosystems, focusing on birds and other wildlife for the benefit of humanity and the earth's biological diversity. **Affiliated With:** National Audubon Society.

Millersburg

5802 ■ American Legion, Richard Hoffman Post 484
111 E Washington St.
Millersburg, IN 46543
Ph: (219)642-3511
Fax: (317)237-9891
URL: National Affiliate–www.legion.org
Local. Affiliated With: American Legion.

5803 ■ Northern Indiana Draft Horse Breeders
11513 County Rd. 42
Millersburg, IN 46543
Ph: (574)642-1300
URL: National Affiliate–www.nasdha.net/RegionalAssoc.htm
Contact: Marion L. Bontrager, Contact
State.

Milltown

5804 ■ American Legion, Milltown Post 332
PO Box 265
Milltown, IN 47145
Ph: (812)739-2359
Fax: (317)237-9891
URL: National Affiliate–www.legion.org
Local. Affiliated With: American Legion.

5805 ■ Comfort House
c/o R.A.P.E. Treatment Center
PO Box 125
Milltown, IN 47145
Ph: (812)633-2500
Fax: (812)633-2500
E-mail: contact@comfort-house.org
URL: http://www.comfort-house.org
Contact: Lola Ratterman, Exec.Dir.
Founded: 2001. **Staff:** 1. **Local.** Provides education and treatment to minimize harm from sexual exploitation. **Formerly:** (2005) Southern Indiana Regional Alliance to Prevent Exploitation.

Mishawaka

5806 ■ American Legion, Mishawaka Post 161
133 E Mishawaka Ave.
Mishawaka, IN 46545
Ph: (219)255-8319
Fax: (317)237-9891
URL: National Affiliate–www.legion.org
Local. Affiliated With: American Legion.

5807 ■ Chapter 81 - Mentone Aero Club
c/o Bernard Ernst, Sec.
60350 Cedar Rd.
Mishawaka, IN 46544
Ph: (574)633-4675 (574)268-9974
E-mail: mikeernst@datacruz.com
URL: http://www.geocities.com/mentoneaeroclub
Contact: Tim Blackwell, Pres.
Local. Affiliated With: Popular Rotorcraft Association.

5808 ■ Home Builders Association of St. Joseph Valley
c/o Dianna DeWitt
105 E Grove St.
Mishawaka, IN 46545-6647
Ph: (574)258-0411
Fax: (574)255-6705
E-mail: hbaofstjoevalley@aol.com
URL: http://www.hbaofstjoevalley.com
Local. Single and multifamily home builders, commercial builders, and others associated with the building industry. **Affiliated With:** National Association of Home Builders.

5809 ■ Michigan Health Information Management Association, Michiana
c/o Darlene Lindsey, Pres.
114 E 9th St.
Mishawaka, IN 46544
Ph: (574)237-7435 (574)256-1153
E-mail: lindseyd@sjrmc.com
URL: http://www.mhima.org
Contact: Darlene Lindsey, Pres.
Regional. Represents the interests of individuals dedicated to the effective management of personal health information needed to deliver quality healthcare to the public. Provides career, professional development and practice resources. Sets standards for education and certification. Advocates public policy that advances Health Information Management (HIM) practice. **Affiliated With:** American Health Information Management Association; Michigan Health Information Management Association.

5810 ■ National Association of Investors Corporation, Northwest Indiana Chapter
c/o Pat Benford, Treas.
144 W Marion St.
Mishawaka, IN 46545
E-mail: benfordpat@sbcglobal.net
URL: http://better-investing.org/chapter/nw-indiana
Contact: Pat Benford, Treas.
Local. Teaches individuals how to become successful strategic long-term investors. Provides highly focused learning resources and investment tools that empower individuals to become better investors. **Affiliated With:** National Association of Investors Corporation.

5811 ■ North Central Indiana AIFA
c/o Rex A. Sallak, Pres.
3900 Edison Lakes Pkwy., Ste.120
Mishawaka, IN 46545
Ph: (574)273-5665
Fax: (574)273-5680
E-mail: rsallak@jhnetwork.com
URL: http://www.nciaifa.com
Contact: Rex A. Sallak, Pres.
Local. Represents the interests of insurance and financial advisors. Advocates for a positive legislative and regulatory environment. Enhances business and professional skills of members. **Affiliated With:** National Association of Insurance and Financial Advisors.

5812 ■ Plumbing-Heating-Cooling Contractors Association, St. Joseph Valley
c/o Kathy Jonas, Exec.Mgr.
4609 Grape Rd.
Mishawaka, IN 46545-2649
Ph: (574)243-0400
Fax: (574)243-8220
E-mail: stjoevalleyphcc@ameritech.net
URL: National Affiliate–www.phccweb.org
Contact: Kathy Jonas, Exec.Mgr.
Local. Represents the plumbing, heating and cooling contractors. Promotes the construction industry. Protects the environment, health, safety and comfort of society. **Affiliated With:** Plumbing-Heating-Cooling Contractors Association.

5813 ■ South Bend-Elkhart Audubon Society (SBEAS)
PO Box 581
Mishawaka, IN 46546
Ph: (574)243-8739
E-mail: southbendaudubon@aol.com
URL: http://www.sbeaudubon.org
Contact: John Bentley, Recording Sec.
Founded: 1944. **Members:** 800. **Membership Dues:** combined/local, $20. **Local.** Works to promote habitat conservation and environmental education in St. Joseph and Elkhart Counties. **Formerly:** (2004) National Audubon Society - South Bend. **Publications:** *Audubon Leaves*, 8/year. Newsletter. **Price:** included in membership dues. **Circulation:** 750.

Mitchell

5814 ■ American Legion, Indiana Post 250
c/o Cecil C. Martin
PO Box 154
Mitchell, IN 47446
Ph: (812)849-3872
Fax: (317)237-9891
URL: National Affiliate–www.legion.org
Contact: Cecil C. Martin, Contact
Local. Affiliated With: American Legion.

5815 ■ Greater Mitchell Chamber of Commerce (GMCC)
PO Box 216
Mitchell, IN 47446
Ph: (812)849-4441
Fax: (812)849-4619
Free: (800)580-1985
E-mail: mitchell@kiva.net
Contact: Debra Webster, Exec.Dir.
Members: 100. **Staff:** 1. **Local.** Promotes business and community development in Mitchell, IN. **Affiliated With:** U.S. Chamber of Commerce. **Formerly:** (1999) Mitchell Chamber of Commerce. **Publications:** *Chamber Report*, monthly. Newsletter. **Conventions/Meetings:** annual meeting - always January.

5816 ■ Indiana Amateur Softball Association, Region 10
c/o Dave Nolan, VP
PO Box 223
Mitchell, IN 47446
Ph: (812)849-4442
E-mail: dave@cpainbluejeans.com
URL: http://www.indiana-asa.org
Contact: Dave Nolan, VP
Local. Affiliated With: Amateur Softball Association of America.

Monon

5817 ■ American Legion, Eugene Hughes Post 319
478 W 900 N
Monon, IN 47959
Ph: (219)253-8266
Fax: (317)237-9891
URL: National Affiliate–www.legion.org
Local. Affiliated With: American Legion.

5818 ■ Monon Chamber of Commerce (MCC)
PO Box 777
Monon, IN 47959
Ph: (219)253-6441
Contact: Troy Geisler, Pres.
Members: 40. **Local.** Promotes business and community development in Monon, IN.

Monroeville

5819 ■ American Legion, Keith Brown Post 420
112 W South St.
Monroeville, IN 46773
Ph: (219)623-6679
Fax: (317)237-9891
URL: National Affiliate–www.legion.org
Local. Affiliated With: American Legion.

Monrovia

5820 ■ State Florist Association of Indiana
c/o Carole Snyder, Exec.Dir.
PO Box 133
Monrovia, IN 46157
Ph: (317)996-2241
Fax: (317)996-8090
URL: http://www.sfainow.com
State.

Monterey

5821 ■ American Legion, Collins-Tasch Post 399
PO Box 133
Monterey, IN 46960
Ph: (219)842-2541
Fax: (317)237-9891
URL: National Affiliate–www.legion.org
Local. Affiliated With: American Legion.

Monticello

5822 ■ American Legion, Indiana Post 81
c/o Thornton Williams
405 E Washington St.
Monticello, IN 47960
Ph: (317)630-1300
Fax: (317)237-9891
URL: National Affiliate–www.legion.org
Contact: Thornton Williams, Contact
Local. Affiliated With: American Legion.

5823 ■ Greater Monticello Chamber of Commerce and Visitors Bureau
116 N Main St.
Monticello, IN 47960
Ph: (574)583-7220
E-mail: janet.dold@monticelloin.com
URL: http://www.monticelloin.com
Contact: Janet Dold, Exec.Dir.
Local. Strives to build a favorable business government and community environment to enhance the quality of life in Greater Monticello, IN.

5824 ■ Hoosier Praire ARC
5053 Norway Rd.
Monticello, IN 47960
Ph: (574)583-8227
Fax: (574)583-6454
URL: http://www.cdcresources.org
Contact: Michael Cruz, Exec.Dir.
Local.

5825 ■ Meadowlawn Parent Teacher Organization
c/o Daryl R. Smith
715 W. Ohio St.
Monticello, IN 47960-2264
Local.

5826 ■ Mental Health Association in White County
c/o Ms. Pam Ashton, Exec.Dir.
1120 N Main St.
Monticello, IN 47960-1500
Ph: (219)583-7073
URL: http://www.mentalhealthassociation.com
Contact: Ms. Pam Ashton, Exec.Dir.
Local. Seeks to promote mental health and prevent mental health disorders. Improves mental health of Americans through advocacy, public education, research and service. **Affiliated With:** Mental Health Association in Indiana; National Mental Health Association.

5827 ■ Pheasants Forever Central Indiana, Twin Lakes
226 N Illinois St.
Monticello, IN 47960
Ph: (219)583-9116
URL: http://pfcic.org
Contact: Joe Maudlin, Pres.
Local. Affiliated With: Pheasants Forever.

5828 ■ White County Association of Realtors
PO Box 59
Monticello, IN 47960
Ph: (574)583-4507
Fax: (574)583-0178
E-mail: wcar@pwrtc.com
URL: National Affiliate–www.realtor.org
Contact: Carol A. Hendress, Exec. Officer
Local. Strives to develop real estate business practices. Advocates the right to own, use and transfer real property. Provides a facility for professional development, research and exchange of information among members and to the general public. **Affiliated With:** National Association of Realtors.

5829 ■ White County United Way
PO Box 580
Monticello, IN 47960-0580
Ph: (574)583-6544
URL: National Affiliate–national.unitedway.org
Local. Affiliated With: United Way of America.

Montmorenci

5830 ■ American Legion, Wallace Sniffin Post 506
PO Box 53
Montmorenci, IN 47962
Ph: (317)583-2043
Fax: (317)237-9891
URL: National Affiliate–www.legion.org
Local. Affiliated With: American Legion.

Montpelier

5831 ■ American Legion, Millard-Brown Post 156
PO Box 44
Montpelier, IN 47359
Ph: (317)630-1300
Fax: (317)237-9891
URL: National Affiliate–www.legion.org
Local. Affiliated With: American Legion.

Moores Hill

5832 ■ American Legion, Floyd Becker Post 209
14656 Wood St.
Moores Hill, IN 47032
Ph: (812)744-3403
Fax: (317)237-9891
URL: National Affiliate–www.legion.org
Local. Affiliated With: American Legion.

5833 ■ Greater Cincinnati Health Information Management Association (GCHIMA)
c/o Carrie Newport, Sec.
11631 Long Br. Rd.
Moores Hill, IN 47032-9683
Ph: (513)948-5960
E-mail: pamela.greenstone@cchmc.org
URL: http://www.ohima.org/reg.associations/regassocgchima.html
Contact: Pam Greenstone, Pres.
Local. Represents the interests of individuals dedicated to the effective management of personal health information needed to deliver quality healthcare to the public. Provides career, professional development and practice resources. Sets standards for education and certification. Advocates public policy

that advances Health Information Management (HIM) practice. **Affiliated With:** American Health Information Management Association; Ohio Health Information Management Association.

Mooresville

5834 ■ American Legion, Mooresville Post 103
350 E Main St.
Mooresville, IN 46158
Ph: (317)630-1300
Fax: (317)237-9891
URL: National Affiliate–www.legion.org
Local. Affiliated With: American Legion.

5835 ■ American Legion, Zook-Scott Post 325
PO Box 144
Mooresville, IN 46158
Ph: (317)630-1300
Fax: (317)237-9891
URL: National Affiliate–www.legion.org
Local. Affiliated With: American Legion.

5836 ■ Healthcare Financial Management Association, Indiana Pressler Memorial Chapter
c/o D. Keith Jewell, CPA, Pres.-Elect
St. Francis Hosp. and Hea. Ctr.
1201 Hadley Rd.
Mooresville, IN 46158-1737
Ph: (317)834-5835 (317)834-9612
E-mail: keith.jewell@ssfhs.org
URL: http://www.hfma-indiana.org
Contact: D. Keith Jewell CPA, Pres.-Elect
State. Provides education, analysis and guidance to healthcare finance professionals. Helps members and other individuals in advancing the financial management of health care and in improving the business performance of organizations serving the healthcare field. **Affiliated With:** Healthcare Financial Management Association.

5837 ■ Mooresville Chamber of Commerce (MCC)
26 S Indiana St.
PO Box 62
Mooresville, IN 46158
Ph: (317)831-6509
Fax: (317)831-9548
E-mail: mrsvlcoc@mooresvillechamber.org
Contact: Julie Kyle-Lee, Ofc.Admin.
Local. Promotes business and community development in Mooresville, IN. **Formerly:** (1999) Mooresville Chamber of Commerce and Economic Development Commission.

5838 ■ Studebakers Driver's Club, Indy Chapter
c/o David Neitzel, Treas.
5543 Neitzel Rd.
Mooresville, IN 46158
Ph: (317)831-0825
E-mail: jhwilli@nlci.com
URL: National Affiliate–www.studebakerdriversclub.com
Contact: Harold Williams, Pres.
Local. Works to preserve the vehicles produced by the Studebaker Corp. during its period in the transportation field. Provides services to members. **Affiliated With:** Studebaker Driver's Club.

Morgantown

5839 ■ Christian Camp and Conference Association, Indiana
c/o Scott Smith, Pres.
Walnut Hills Retreat
4500 Bear Creek Church Rd.
Morgantown, IN 46160
Ph: (812)597-4455
URL: National Affiliate–www.ccca-us.org
Contact: Scott Smith, Pres.
State. Affiliated With: Christian Camping International/U.S.A.

5840 ■ Indiana B.A.S.S. Federation (IBF)
c/o Dan Pardue
7244 N Homestead Rd.
Morgantown, IN 46160
Ph: (812)988-8763 (574)457-5328
E-mail: xreebockx@aol.com
URL: http://www.indianabass.com
Contact: Doug Bradley, Pres.
State.

5841 ■ Spiritual Fellowship
c/o Nancy Long
9554 Lick Creek Rd.
Morgantown, IN 46160-9436
E-mail: nlong@thespiritualfellowship.org
URL: http://www.thespiritualfellowship.org
Contact: Nancy Long, Contact
Local.

Morocco

5842 ■ American Legion, William Chizum Post 146
402 N Waker St.
Morocco, IN 47963
Ph: (219)285-6286
Fax: (317)237-9891
URL: National Affiliate–www.legion.org
Local. Affiliated With: American Legion.

Morristown

5843 ■ American Legion, Indiana Post 102
c/o Willard E. Hensley
PO Box 102
Morristown, IN 46161
Ph: (317)763-7175
Fax: (317)237-9891
URL: National Affiliate–www.legion.org
Contact: Willard E. Hensley, Contact
Local. Affiliated With: American Legion.

Mount Vernon

5844 ■ 21st Century Leadership, Posey County
c/o Nancy L. Burns
PO Box 633915
E Fourth St.
Mount Vernon, IN 47620-0633
Ph: (812)838-3639
Fax: (812)838-6358
E-mail: chamber@poseynet.com
URL: National Affiliate–www.mtvernonposeycochamber.com
Contact: Nancy L. Burns, Contact
Local.

5845 ■ American Legion, Owen Dunn Post 5
203 Walnut St.
Mount Vernon, IN 47620
Ph: (812)838-5122
Fax: (317)237-9891
URL: National Affiliate–www.legion.org
Local. Affiliated With: American Legion.

5846 ■ American Red Cross, Posey County Chapter (ARCPCC)
c/o Connie K. Gibbs, Exec.Dir.
402 Mill St.
Mount Vernon, IN 47620
Ph: (812)838-3671
Fax: (812)838-3903
E-mail: arcposeyin@insightbb.com
URL: http://www.poseycounty.redcross.org
Contact: Connie K. Gibbs, Exec.Dir.
Founded: 1917. **Members:** 228. **Membership Dues:** donation, $1 (annual). **Staff:** 2. **Budget:** $101,254. **Regional Groups:** 1. **State Groups:** 1. **Local Groups:** 1. **For-Profit. Local.** Seeks to serve members of the armed forces, veterans, and their families; to assist disaster victims; to support other community services. Offers training in areas including lifeguarding, CPR, First Aid, disaster preparedness, disaster response, and basic water safety. Sponsors infant and baby car safety program, classes in babysitting, Preventing Disease Transmission, HIV/AIDS Prevention Facts, Disaster Preparedness, and Disaster Response. **Libraries: Type:** open to the public. **Subjects:** child safety, HIV/AIDS, health, disaster education, biomedical issues, water safety. **Awards:** Volunteer of the Year Award (Anton F. Boehm Award). **Frequency:** annual. **Type:** recognition. **Recipient:** Red Cross service to the needy. **Affiliated With:** American Red Cross National Headquarters. **Publications:** *Safe Kids and You*, quarterly. Newsletter. Contains safety and injury prevention information. Also information on Red Cross Services. **Circulation:** 3,750. **Advertising:** accepted. **Conventions/Meetings:** monthly board meeting - always 2nd Tuesday of the month • annual meeting (exhibits) - August.

5847 ■ Big River Bend Appaloosa Horse Club
c/o Beverly J. Utley
4225 Copperline Rd.
Mount Vernon, IN 47620
Ph: (812)783-2201
URL: National Affiliate–www.appaloosa.com
Contact: Beverly J. Utley, Contact
Local. Affiliated With: Appaloosa Horse Club.

5848 ■ Classical Association of Indiana
Mt. Vernon High School
700 Harriet St.
Mount Vernon, IN 47620
Ph: (812)838-4356
E-mail: grebejm@msdmv.k12.in.us
URL: http://www.camws.org
Contact: Judy M. Grebe, VP
State. Represents university, college, secondary and elementary teachers of Latin, Greek and all other studies which focus on the world of classical antiquity. Supports and promotes the study of classical languages.

5849 ■ Indiana Association of Agricultural Educators
c/o David Reese, Pres.
10421 S Eastgate Dr.
Mount Vernon, IN 47620
Ph: (812)833-5927
Fax: (812)985-9512
E-mail: reesede@msdmv.k12.in.us
URL: http://www.indianaaged.org/iaae.html
Contact: David Reese, Pres.
State. Seeks to advance agricultural education and promotes the professional interests and growth of agriculture teachers. Provides agricultural education through visionary leadership, advocacy and service. **Affiliated With:** National Association of Agricultural Educators.

5850 ■ Indiana Society of Radiologic Technologists, District 8
4221 Joyce Ln.
Mount Vernon, IN 47620
Ph: (812)461-5212 (812)985-5296
Fax: (812)465-7092
E-mail: alwilson2@usi.edu
URL: http://www.isort.org
Contact: Amy Wilson RT, Pres.-Elect
Local. Represents the professional society of radiologic technologists. Advances education and research in the radiologic sciences. Evaluates quality patient care. Improves the welfare and socioeconomics of

radiologic technologists. **Affiliated With:** American Society of Radiologic Technologists.

5851 ■ Indiana Society, Sons of the American Revolution, General Thomas Posey Chapter
c/o Albert Gibbs, Pres.
624 W 6th St.
Mount Vernon, IN 47620
E-mail: wmagibbs@peoplepc.com
URL: http://www.geocities.com/inssar-south/thospose.htm
Contact: Albert Gibbs, Pres.
Local. Affiliated With: National Society, Sons of the American Revolution.

5852 ■ Mt. Vernon - Young Life
PO Box 951
Mount Vernon, IN 47620-0951
Ph: (812)454-4786
URL: http://whereis.younglife.org/FriendlyUrlRedirector.aspx?ID=C-3534
Local.

5853 ■ Plumbing-Heating-Cooling Contractors Association, Southwestern
c/o Mr. Robert McBride, Pres.
324 W Lincoln Ave.
Mount Vernon, IN 47620-1252
Ph: (812)643-0076
Fax: (812)643-0076
URL: National Affiliate–www.phccweb.org
Contact: Mr. Robert McBride, Pres.
Local. Represents the plumbing, heating and cooling contractors. Promotes the construction industry. Protects the environment, health, safety and comfort of society. **Affiliated With:** Plumbing-Heating-Cooling Contractors Association.

5854 ■ Posey County Association for Retarded Citizens
7285 Sauerkraut Ln. N
Mount Vernon, IN 47620
Ph: (812)838-2550
URL: National Affiliate–www.TheArc.org
Local. Parents, professional workers, and others interested in individuals with mental retardation. Works to promote services, research, public understanding, and legislation for people with mental retardation and their families. **Affiliated With:** Arc of the United States.

5855 ■ Posey County Chamber of Commerce
915 E 4th St.
PO Box 633
Mount Vernon, IN 47620-0633
Ph: (812)838-3639
Fax: (812)838-6358
E-mail: poseychamber@sbcglobal.net
URL: http://www.mtvernonposeycochamber.com
Contact: Sally A. Dennning, Admin.Dir.
Founded: 1921. **Members:** 225. **Budget:** $89,000. **Local.** Seeks to maintain the economic stability of Posey County to help bring about selective growth and development; and to improve Posey County's product through careful analysis and concerted action to remove any obstacle which might make the area less attractive than competitive areas. **Computer Services:** database, membership. **Telecommunication Services:** electronic mail, chamber@poseynet.com. **Formerly:** (1999) Mt. Vernon Chamber of Commerce. **Publications:** *Chamber News*, monthly. Newsletter. **Conventions/Meetings:** monthly board meeting • quarterly seminar.

5856 ■ Posey County Young Life
PO Box 951
Mount Vernon, IN 47620-0951
Ph: (812)454-4786
Fax: (812)838-9456
URL: http://PoseyCounty.younglife.org
Local.

5857 ■ Project Management Institute, Southwest Indiana Chapter
1511 Main St.
Mount Vernon, IN 47620
Ph: (812)833-2274
Fax: (812)838-6000
E-mail: jadamait@qualex.com
URL: http://chapter.pmi.org/swindiana
Contact: Mr. John J. Adamaitis, Pres.
Local. Corporations and individuals engaged in the practice of project management; project management students and educators. Seeks to advance the study, teaching, and practice of project management. **Affiliated With:** Project Management Institute.

5858 ■ United Way of Posey County
PO Box 562
Mount Vernon, IN 47620-0562
Ph: (812)838-3637
URL: National Affiliate–national.unitedway.org
Local. Affiliated With: United Way of America.

Muncie

5859 ■ AAA Hoosier Motor Club
4351 W Clara Ln.
Muncie, IN 47304
Ph: (765)289-7161
Free: (800)822-2490
E-mail: dtirey@aaahoosier.com
Contact: Jill Watson, Office Mgr.
Local.

5860 ■ American Hiking Society - Delaware Greenways
700 E Wysor St.
Muncie, IN 47305
Ph: (765)287-0399
Fax: (765)287-0396
E-mail: info@delgreenways.org
URL: http://www.delgreenways.org
Contact: Lenette Freeman, Exec.Dir.
Local.

5861 ■ American Legion, Buss Waters Post 299
3520 S Meeker Ave.
Muncie, IN 47302
Ph: (765)286-8947
Fax: (317)237-9891
URL: National Affiliate–www.legion.org
Local. Affiliated With: American Legion.

5862 ■ American Legion, Cammack Post 327
9113 W Jackson St.
Muncie, IN 47304
Ph: (317)630-1300
Fax: (317)237-9891
URL: National Affiliate–www.legion.org
Local. Affiliated With: American Legion.

5863 ■ American Legion, Delaware Post 19
418 N Walnut St.
Muncie, IN 47305
Ph: (317)282-8371
Fax: (317)237-9891
URL: National Affiliate–www.legion.org
Local. Affiliated With: American Legion.

5864 ■ American Legion, John B. Lotz Memorial Post 91
PO Box 555
Muncie, IN 47308
Ph: (317)288-3049
Fax: (317)237-9891
URL: National Affiliate–www.legion.org
Local. Affiliated With: American Legion.

5865 ■ American Legion, Lester Newton Hensley Post 55
3210 S Madison St.
Muncie, IN 47302
Ph: (317)630-1300
Fax: (317)237-9891
URL: National Affiliate–www.legion.org
Local. Affiliated With: American Legion.

5866 ■ American Society for Quality, East Central Indiana Section 0904
c/o Henry Peresie, Sec.
PO Box 3147
Muncie, IN 47307-1147
Ph: (765)432-5138
E-mail: peresieh@comcast.net
URL: http://www.ASQ904.org
Contact: Henry Peresie, Sec.
Local. Advances learning, quality improvement and knowledge exchange to improve business results and to create better workplaces and communities worldwide. Provides a forum for information exchange, professional development and continuous learning in the science of quality. **Affiliated With:** American Society for Quality.

5867 ■ AMVETS, Muncie Post 12
7621 N State Rd. 3
Muncie, IN 47303
Ph: (765)287-9054
URL: http://amvetspost12.homestead.com
Contact: Gene Farmer, Commander
Local. Affiliated With: AMVETS - American Veterans.

5868 ■ Association for Computing Machinery, Ball State University Chapter (ACM)
c/o Alex B Chalmers, Chm.
Dept. of Cmpt. Sci.
2000 W Univ. Ave.
Muncie, IN 47306
Ph: (765)285-8643
Fax: (765)285-2614
E-mail: acm@cs.bsu.edu
URL: http://www.cs.bsu.edu/~acm
Contact: Alex B Chalmers, Chm.
Local. Biological, medical, behavioral, and computer scientists; hospital administrators; programmers and others interested in application of computer methods to biological, behavioral, and medical problems. Stimulates understanding of the use and potential of computers in the Biosciences. **Affiliated With:** Association for Computing Machinery.

5869 ■ Association of Women's Health, Obstetric and Neonatal Nurses - Marian/Anderson/Muncie Chapter
c/o Margie Pyron, Coor.
2713 W Ashbrook Ln.
Muncie, IN 47304
E-mail: mpyron@chs.cami3.com
URL: National Affiliate–www.awhonn.org
Contact: Margie Pyron, Coor.
Local. Represents registered nurses and other health care providers who specialize in obstetric, women's health, and neonatal nursing. Advances the nursing profession by providing nurses with information and support to help them deliver quality care for women and newborns. **Affiliated With:** Association of Women's Health, Obstetric and Neonatal Nurses.

5870 ■ Audio Engineering Society, Ball State University Section
c/o Michael Pounds
Ball State Univ., MET Studios
2520 W Bethel Ave.
Muncie, IN 47306
Ph: (765)285-5537
Fax: (765)285-8768
URL: National Affiliate–www.aes.org
Contact: Michael Pounds, Contact
Local. Represents the interests of engineers, administrators and technicians for radio, television and mo-

tion picture operation. Operates educational and research foundation. **Affiliated With:** Audio Engineering Society.

5871 ■ Community Alliance to Promote Education (CAPE)
c/o Pat Shoemaker, Exec.Asst.
201 E Jackson St., 200A
Muncie, IN 47305
Ph: (765)741-1020
Fax: (765)741-1030
E-mail: pshoemaker@prodigy.net
URL: http://www.capedelco.org
Contact: Pat Shoemaker, Exec.Asst.
Local.

5872 ■ Delaware County Historical Society
120 E Washington St.
Muncie, IN 47305-1734
Ph: (765)282-1550
E-mail: dchs@tmcsmail.com
URL: http://www.dchsmuncein.org/index.htm
Contact: Robin Odle, Exec.Dir.
Founded: 1987. **Members:** 420. **Membership Dues:** individual, $20 (annual) • family, $30 (annual) • student, $5 (annual) • corporate, $50 (annual). **Staff:** 3. **Budget:** $35,000. **Local**. Seeks to enrich the lives of the people of Delaware County through the preservation and interpretation of its heritage and to enhance the general public's knowledge, understanding and appreciation of the history of Delaware County. Provides research and queries regarding Delaware County and its history. **Libraries: Type:** open to the public. **Holdings:** 2,500; books, periodicals. **Subjects:** Delaware, some counties and states. **Committees:** Journal; Library, Moore-Youse Collection; Moore-Youse Collection; Old Barn Publication. **Publications:** *Delaware County Genealogist and Historian*, quarterly. Journal. Contains informative articles, query section, and surname section. **Price:** $13.00/year. **Circulation:** 175 • *Delaware County Newsletter*, bimonthly. Contains information on events and general home news. **Price:** $20. 00/year. **Conventions/Meetings:** annual Business Meeting and Dinner.

5873 ■ East Central Indiana AIFA
c/o Andrea C. Guerrero, Admin.Asst.
PO Box 753
Muncie, IN 47308
Ph: (765)287-8310
Fax: (765)287-8518
E-mail: naifaeci@comcast.net
URL: National Affiliate–naifa.org
Contact: Andrea C. Guerrero, Admin.Asst.
Local. Represents the interests of insurance and financial advisors. Advocates for a positive legislative and regulatory environment. Enhances business and professional skills of members. **Affiliated With:** National Association of Insurance and Financial Advisors.

5874 ■ East Central Indiana Human Resources Association (ECIHRA)
PO Box 1915
Muncie, IN 47308
E-mail: ddouglass@mfsbank.com
URL: http://www.ecihra.com
Contact: Dorothy Douglass, Pres.
Local. Represents the interests of human resource and industrial relations professionals and executives. Promotes the advancement of human resource management.

5875 ■ East Central Indiana Payroll Association
2903 W Jackson St.
Muncie, IN 47304
Ph: (765)747-9500
Fax: (765)741-1424
E-mail: snicholas@pdpcorp.com
URL: http://www.apaecipa.org
Contact: Shirley Nicholas, Pres.
Local. Aims to increase the Payroll Professional's skill level through education and mutual support. Represents the Payroll Professional before legislative bodies. Administers the certified payroll professional program of recognition. Provides public service education on payroll and employment issues. **Affiliated With:** American Payroll Association.

5876 ■ Greater Muncie Indiana Habitat for Humanity
PO Box 1119
Muncie, IN 47308
Ph: (765)286-5739
E-mail: bhubbard@munciehabitat.org
URL: http://www.munciehabitat.org
Contact: Barbara Hubbard, Exec.Dir.
Local. **Affiliated With:** Habitat for Humanity International.

5877 ■ Home Builders Association of Muncie
1711 W Royale Dr.
Muncie, IN 47304-2241
Ph: (765)282-9617
Fax: (765)282-1592
E-mail: munciehomebuilders@comcast.net
URL: National Affiliate–www.nahb.org
Contact: Dave Donahune, Exec. Officer
Local. Single and multifamily home builders, commercial builders, and others associated with the building industry. **Affiliated With:** National Association of Home Builders.

5878 ■ Indiana Fireworks Distributors Association
c/o Richard B. Shields, Pres.
PO Box 2623
Muncie, IN 47307-0623
Ph: (765)284-7122
Fax: (765)284-5788
Free: (800)800-2264
Contact: Richard B. Shields, Pres.
State. Involved in regulatory issues pertaining to fireworks and fireworks legislation. Special emphasis on public education and safety issues.

5879 ■ Indiana Fireworks Users Association
PO Box 746
Muncie, IN 47305
Ph: (765)287-1869
Fax: (765)287-1850
Free: (800)535-7477
Contact: Carol Phillips, Mgr.
State.

5880 ■ Indiana Music Educators Association (IMEA)
c/o JoDee Marshall, Exec.Mgr.
School of Music
Ball State Univ.
Muncie, IN 47306
Ph: (765)285-5496
Fax: (765)285-1139
E-mail: manager@imeamusic.org
URL: http://www.imeamusic.org
Contact: JoDee Marshall, Exec.Mgr.
Founded: 1946. **Members:** 1,100. **Membership Dues:** individual, $88 (annual) • corporate, $150 (annual) • collegiate music education major, $20 (annual). **Staff:** 15. **Budget:** $400,000. **For-Profit**. **State**. Professional membership association for music educators K-collegiate. Supports and advances music education in Indiana by representing the united interests of music educators and students and by providing professional leadership and service in music education to enhance the arts in schools. Functions as the federated state unit of the Music Education National Conference. **Awards:** Hoosier Musician. **Frequency:** annual. **Type:** recognition. **Recipient:** teacher and administrator recommendation; accomplishments in the music education field • Outstanding Administrator. **Frequency:** annual. **Type:** recognition. **Recipient:** teacher and administrator recommendation; accomplishments in the music education field • Outstanding Music Educators of Elementary, Middle School, High School and University Levels. **Frequency:** annual. **Type:** recognition. **Recipient:** teacher and administrator recommendation; accomplishments in the music education field. **Committees:** IMEA Executive. **Affiliated With:** MENC: The National Association for Music Education. **Publications:** *Indiana Musicator*, quarterly, September, November, March, May. Journal. Features information for music educators who are members of the association. **Price:** $20.00. ISSN: 0273-9933. **Circulation:** 1,500. **Advertising:** accepted. Alternate Formats: online; CD-ROM • Brochures. **Conventions/Meetings:** annual conference, professional development for Indiana music teachers and students (exhibits).

5881 ■ Indiana Society, Sons of the American Revolution, Continental Chapter
c/o Mark R. Kreps
1611 N Tillotson Ave.
Muncie, IN 47304-2500
E-mail: mjkreps@gmail.com
URL: http://www.geocities.com/inssar-south/cont.html
Contact: Mark R. Kreps, Contact
Local. Affiliated With: National Society, Sons of the American Revolution.

5882 ■ Jay County Beagle Club
c/o Derrick Clark
8013 E Devonshire Rd.
Muncie, IN 47302-9047
URL: National Affiliate–www.akc.org
Contact: Derrick Clark, Contact
Local. Affiliated With: American Kennel Club.

5883 ■ Media Communications Association International, Ball State University (BSU/MCA-I)
2000 W Univ. Ave.
Muncie, IN 47306
Ph: (765)285-1485
Fax: (765)285-9278
E-mail: arichard@bsu.edu
URL: National Affiliate–www.mca-i.org
Contact: John Dailey, Contact
Local. Provides networking and education opportunities to media communications professionals. Facilitates effective communication using new technology and with sound communication principles. **Affiliated With:** Chemical Coaters Association International.

5884 ■ Mental Health Association in Delaware County
413 S Liberty St.
Muncie, IN 47305-2341
Ph: (765)288-1924
Fax: (765)288-1956
E-mail: delcomha@aol.com
URL: http://www.mentalhealthassociation.com
Contact: Ms. Kay Walker, Exec.Dir.
Local. Seeks to promote mental health and prevent mental health disorders. Improves mental health of Americans through advocacy, public education, research and service. **Affiliated With:** Mental Health Association in Indiana; National Mental Health Association.

5885 ■ Mid-Eastern Indiana Association of Realtors
3908 N Rosewood Ave.
Muncie, IN 47304
Ph: (765)747-7197
Fax: (765)741-2707
E-mail: nancy.meiar@comcast.net
URL: National Affiliate–www.realtor.org
Contact: Nancy Hartley, Exec. Officer
Local. Strives to develop real estate business practices. Advocates the right to own, use and transfer real property. Provides a facility for professional development, research and exchange of information among members and to the general public. **Affiliated With:** National Association of Realtors.

5886 ■ Muncie Area Youth for Christ
PO Box 99
Muncie, IN 47308
Ph: (765)287-9518
Fax: (765)287-9520
URL: National Affiliate–www.yfc.net
Local. Affiliated With: Youth for Christ/U.S.A.

5887 ■ Muncie-Delaware County Chamber of Commerce (MDCCC)
401 S High St.
PO Box 842
Muncie, IN 47308-0842
Ph: (765)288-6681
Fax: (765)751-9151
Free: (800)336-1373
E-mail: chamber@muncie.com
URL: http://www.muncie.com
Contact: Dan Allen, Pres.
Founded: 1937. **Members:** 850. **Membership Dues:** individual with no business affiliation, $220 (annual) • non-profit, home-based business, $157 (annual) • retiree, $135 (annual) • business (based on number of employees), $220-$822 (annual) • church (based on average attendance), $55-$135 (annual) • associate, $105 (annual). **Staff:** 25. **Local.** Promotes business and community development in Delaware County, IN. **Affiliated With:** U.S. Chamber of Commerce. **Formerly:** Muncie Chamber of Commerce. **Publications:** *Community Profile*, biennial. Newsletter • *Horizons*, monthly. Directory. Tabloid. • *Manufacturer Directory for Muncie-Delaware County*, annual • *Membership Directory/Buyer's Guide*, annual. Brochure • *Newcomer's Guide for Muncie-Delaware County Indiana*, biennial. Video • *Quality of Life*, triennial. **Conventions/Meetings:** annual meeting.

5888 ■ Muncie Obedience Training Club (MOTC)
2200 E Memorial Dr. 12th St., Ste.B
Muncie, IN 47302
Ph: (765)282-5959
E-mail: info@munciedogtraining.com
URL: http://groups.msn.com/MuncieObedienceTrainingClub
Contact: Susan Armstrong, Sec.
Founded: 1946. **Members:** 50. **Membership Dues:** individual, $40 (annual) • family, $50 (annual). **Local.** Promotes the training of all breeds of dogs. Seeks to protect and advance the interests of all breeds of dogs; to sponsor and conduct classes for the training of dogs; and to conduct performance competitions under the rules of the AKC. **Awards:** May McCommon Memorial Trophy. **Frequency:** annual, **Type:** trophy. **Recipient:** for top score at obedience trial. **Additional Websites:** http://www.munciedogtraining.com. **Affiliated With:** American Kennel Club. **Publications:** *Newsletter of the Muncie Obedience Training Club*, bimonthly. **Circulation:** 200. **Conventions/Meetings:** bimonthly meeting - every 1st Wednesday of even-numbered months in Muncie, IN • annual Obedience Trial - specialty show - every 1st weekend of April in Yorktown, IN.

5889 ■ Muncie Sailing Club
PO Box 390
Muncie, IN 47308
E-mail: sail@munciesailingclub.org
URL: http://www.munciesailingclub.org
Local.

5890 ■ Muncie - Young Life
1201 N Wheeling Ave., Ste.2
Muncie, IN 47303
Ph: (765)289-6695
URL: http://whereis.younglife.org/FriendlyUrlRedirector.aspx?ID=C-887
Local.

5891 ■ National Active and Retired Federal Employees Association - Muncie 125
1002 E 22nd St.
Muncie, IN 47302-5319
Ph: (765)282-2405
URL: National Affiliate–www.narfe.org
Contact: Geneva G. Greenlee, Contact
Local. Protects the retirement future of employees through education. Informs members on issues affecting the retirement. **Affiliated With:** National Association of Retired Federal Employees.

5892 ■ National Association of Miniature Enthusiasts - Mini Construction Company
c/o Linda Farris
4908 N Holborn Dr.
Muncie, IN 47304
Ph: (765)284-5313
E-mail: lindajfarris@comcast.net
URL: http://www.miniatures.org/states/IN.html
Contact: Linda Farris, Contact
Local. Affiliated With: National Association of Miniature Enthusiasts.

5893 ■ PFLAG Muncie
PO Box 566
Muncie, IN 47308
Ph: (765)683-2145
E-mail: munciepflag@yahoo.com
URL: http://www.pflag.org/Indiana.205.0.html
Local. Affiliated With: Parents, Families, and Friends of Lesbians and Gays.

5894 ■ Phi Theta Kappa, Alpha Upsilon Lambda Chapter - Ivy Tech State College
c/o Michael Eppards
4301 S Cowan Rd.
Muncie, IN 47302
Ph: (765)289-2291
URL: http://www.ptk.org/directories/chapters/IN/20497-1.htm
Contact: Michael Eppards, Advisor
Local.

5895 ■ Police and Firemen's Insurance Association - Muncie Fire Department
c/o James Osborne
1314 N Alden Rd.
Muncie, IN 47304
Ph: (765)282-1465
URL: National Affiliate–www.pfia.net
Contact: James Osborne, Contact
Local. Affiliated With: Police and Firemen's Insurance Association.

5896 ■ Psi Chi, National Honor Society in Psychology - Ball State University
c/o Dept. of Psychological Science
2000 W Univ. Ave.
Muncie, IN 47306
Ph: (765)285-1690
Fax: (765)285-8980
E-mail: bwhitley@bsu.edu
URL: http://www.bsu.edu/psysc/psichi
Local. Affiliated With: Psi Chi, National Honor Society in Psychology.

5897 ■ RSVP of Delaware County
c/o Susie Cooper, Dir.
310 E Charles St.
Muncie, IN 47305-2415
Ph: (765)288-5876
Fax: (765)289-0416
E-mail: rsvpmuncie@voyager.net
URL: http://www.seniorcorps.gov/about/programs/rsvp.asp
Contact: Susie Cooper, Dir.
Local. Affiliated With: Retired and Senior Volunteer Program.

5898 ■ Theta Xi, Kappa Kappa Chapter — Ball State University
c/o Michael Catlin
904 Riverside Ave.
Muncie, IN 47303
Ph: (765)282-8412
E-mail: mcatlin@midwestiso.org
URL: http://www.thetaxifraternity.com
Contact: Michael Catlin, Advisor
Local. Affiliated With: Theta Xi.

5899 ■ United Way of Delaware County, Indiana
PO Box 968
Muncie, IN 47305
Ph: (765)288-5586
Fax: (765)288-5588
E-mail: unitedway@uwctl.org
URL: http://www.uwctl.org
Contact: Sam Abram, Chair
Local. Affiliated With: United Way of America.

5900 ■ White River Ramblers
c/o LaVerna Balser
5609 Pineridge Rd.
Muncie, IN 47304
Ph: (765)284-0259
E-mail: jehendee42@msn.com
URL: National Affiliate–www.ava.org
Contact: LaVerna Balser, Treas.
Local. Affiliated With: American Volkssport Association.

Munster

5901 ■ American Society for Quality, Northwest Indiana Section 1011
c/o Scott Markovich, Sec.
PO Box 3255
Munster, IN 46321
E-mail: marko41159@yahoo.com
URL: http://www.asq-nwi.org
Contact: Scott Markovich, Sec.
Local. Advances learning, quality improvement and knowledge exchange to improve business results and to create better workplaces and communities worldwide. Provides a forum for information exchange, professional development and continuous learning in the science of quality. **Affiliated With:** American Society for Quality.

5902 ■ Jewish Federation Northwest Indiana
585 Progress Ave.
Munster, IN 46321
Ph: (219)922-4024
Fax: (219)972-4779
E-mail: defwej@airbaud.net
Contact: Michael Steinberg, Exec.Dir.
Local.

5903 ■ Munster Chamber of Commerce
1040 Ridge Rd.
Munster, IN 46321
Ph: (219)836-5549
Fax: (219)836-5551
E-mail: info@munsterchamber.com
URL: http://www.munsterchamber.com
Contact: Rhonda Damjanovich, Pres.
Founded: 1955. **Members:** 273. **Membership Dues:** business (based on the number of employees), $200-$775 (annual) • associate, $75 (annual) • spirit, $50 (annual). **Staff:** 2. **Budget:** $50,000. **Local.** Business, industry, and professional individuals interested in promoting business and community development in Munster, IN. Sponsors annual Breakfast with Santa, Blues, Jazz and Arts on the Ridge Festival. **Awards:** Beautification and Appearance. **Frequency:** annual. **Type:** recognition • Citizen of the Year. **Frequency:** annual. **Type:** recognition. **Computer Services:** database, list of members. **Committees:** Annual Banquet; Breakfast with Santa; Business After Hours; Golf Outing; Legislative; Winetasting Dinners. **Publications:** *Chamber Newsletter*, monthly • *Munster Business Handbook*, annual. **Conventions/Meetings:** annual meeting.

5904 ■ Munster High School PTO
8808 Columbia Ave.
Munster, IN 46321
Ph: (219)836-3200
URL: http://www.munster.k12.in.us
Contact: Kathy Howard, Pres.
Local.

5905 ■ Northern Indiana Arts Association (NIAA)
1040 Ridge Rd.
Munster, IN 46321
Ph: (219)836-1839
Fax: (219)836-1863
E-mail: johnc@niaaonline.org
URL: http://niaaonline.org
Contact: John M. Cain, Exec.Dir.
Local.

Nabb

5906 ■ Henryville Beagle Club
c/o Kevin A. Cole
PO Box 35
Nabb, IN 47147-0035
URL: National Affiliate–clubs.akc.org
Contact: Kevin A. Cole, Contact
Local.

Nappanee

5907 ■ American Legion, Nappanee Post 154
201 W Lincoln St.
Nappanee, IN 46550
Ph: (219)773-7686
Fax: (317)237-9891
URL: National Affiliate–www.legion.org
Local. Affiliated With: American Legion.

5908 ■ Nappanee Area Chamber of Commerce
451 N Main St.
Nappanee, IN 46550
Ph: (574)773-7812
Fax: (574)773-4961
E-mail: info@nappaneechamber.com
URL: http://www.nappaneechamber.com
Contact: Larry Andrews, Exec.Dir.
Members: 150. **Membership Dues:** business (1-50 employees), $155-$465 (annual) • business (51-250 employees), $566-$775 (annual) • business (251-1000 employees), $1,025-$1,545 (annual) • business (1001-2000 employees), $2,060 (annual) • business (more than 2000 employees), $2,575 (annual) • individual, service club, non-profit, church, $80 (annual). **Local.** Promotes business, community, and industrial development in the Nappanee, IN area. Sponsors Apple Festival. **Telecommunication Services:** electronic mail, nappaneecofc@kconline.com • electronic mail, landrews@nappaneechamber.com. **Committees:** Education and Workforce Development; Infrastructure Environment, Transportation; Local County and State Government; Quality of Life and Human Services; Resource Development and Community Marketing. **Publications:** *Embrace the Pace*, bimonthly. Newsletter. Alternate Formats: online.

Nashville

5909 ■ American Legion, Indiana Post 13
PO Box 1335
Nashville, IN 47448
Ph: (317)630-1300
Fax: (317)237-9891
URL: National Affiliate–www.legion.org
Local. Affiliated With: American Legion.

5910 ■ Brown County Bluebird Society
c/o Dan Sparks
PO Box 660
Nashville, IN 47448
Ph: (812)988-1876
Fax: (360)361-3704
E-mail: b4bluebirds@yahoo.com
URL: National Affiliate–www.nabluebirdsociety.org
Contact: Dan Sparks, Contact
Local. Affiliated With: North American Bluebird Society.

5911 ■ Brown County Chamber of Commerce
37 W Main St.
PO Box 164
Nashville, IN 47448-0164
Ph: (812)988-6647
Fax: (812)988-1547
E-mail: commerce@browncounty.org
URL: http://www.browncounty.org
Local. Promotes business and community development in Brown County, IL. **Computer Services:** Information services, membership directory.

5912 ■ Brown County Convention and Visitors Bureau
PO Box 840
Nashville, IN 47448
Ph: (812)988-7303
Fax: (812)988-1070
Free: (800)753-3255
E-mail: info@browncounty.com
URL: http://www.browncounty.com
Contact: Teresa Anderson, Pres./CEO
Local.

5913 ■ Brown County Lions Club
PO Box 716
Nashville, IN 47448
E-mail: rnixonlionsclub@aol.com
URL: http://www.browncountylions.org
Local. Affiliated With: Lions Clubs International.

5914 ■ Central Illinois District Amateur Athletic Union
4080 Freeman Ridge Ln.
Nashville, IN 47448
Ph: (847)293-5504 (812)988-2375
E-mail: info@centralillinoisaau.org
URL: http://centralillinoisaau.org
Local. Affiliated With: Amateur Athletic Union.

New Albany

5915 ■ American Legion, Indiana Post 28
c/o Bonnie Sloan
1930 Mcdonald Ln.
New Albany, IN 47151
Ph: (812)945-1944
Fax: (317)237-9891
URL: National Affiliate–www.legion.org
Contact: Bonnie Sloan, Contact
Local. Affiliated With: American Legion.

5916 ■ American Society of Women Accountants, Louisville Chapter No. 018
c/o Carol Flynn, CPA, Pres.
3025 Shady Brook Ln.
New Albany, IN 47150
Ph: (502)417-4761 (812)948-1826
Fax: (812)948-9798
E-mail: ccfcpa@insightbb.com
URL: National Affiliate–www.aswa.org
Contact: Carol Flynn CPA, Pres.
Local. Strives to enable women and men in all accounting and related fields to achieve their full personal, professional, and economic potential and to contribute to the future development of their profession. **Affiliated With:** American Society of Women Accountants.

5917 ■ Knob and Valley Audubon Society (KAVAS)
PO Box 556
New Albany, IN 47150
E-mail: dcoyte@juno.com
URL: http://www.kavaudubon.org
Contact: David Coyte, Pres.
Local. Formerly: (2005) National Audubon Society - Knob and Valley.

5918 ■ Mental Health Association in Floyd County
c/o Mr. David Mullineaux, Exec.Dir.
PO Box 63
New Albany, IN 47151-0063
Ph: (812)941-0308
URL: http://www.mentalhealthassociation.com
Contact: Mr. David Mullineaux, Exec.Dir.
Local. Seeks to promote mental health and prevent mental health disorders. Improves mental health of Americans through advocacy, public education, research and service. **Affiliated With:** Mental Health Association in Indiana; National Mental Health Association.

5919 ■ National Active and Retired Federal Employees Association - New Albany 1777
2619 W Robin Rd.
New Albany, IN 47150-3783
Ph: (812)945-6872
URL: National Affiliate–www.narfe.org
Contact: Dorothy D. Weber, Contact
Local. Protects the retirement future of employees through education. Informs members on issues affecting the retirement. **Affiliated With:** National Association of Retired Federal Employees.

5920 ■ New Albany/Floyd County Habitat for Humanity
PO Box 1814
New Albany, IN 47150
Ph: (812)948-1235
Fax: (812)948-1235
E-mail: info@newalbanyhfh.org
URL: http://www.newalbanyhfh.org
Local. Affiliated With: Habitat for Humanity International.

5921 ■ Professional Photographers of Greater Louisville
c/o Karen Carmickle
PO Box 85
New Albany, IN 47151
Ph: (812)944-3779
E-mail: karenphoto@aol.com
URL: National Affiliate–ppa.com
Contact: Karen Carmickle, Contact
Local. Affiliated With: Professional Photographers of America.

5922 ■ Psi Chi, National Honor Society in Psychology - Indiana University Southeast
c/o Dept. of Psychology
140 Crestview Hall/Soc. Scs. Div.
4201 Grant Line Rd.
New Albany, IN 47150-6405
Ph: (812)941-2391 (812)941-2300
Fax: (812)941-2591
E-mail: dwille@ius.edu
URL: http://www.psichi.org/chapters/info.asp?chapter_id=686
Contact: Diane Wille PhD, Advisor
Local.

5923 ■ SCORE South Central Indiana
702 E Market St.
New Albany, IN 47150
Ph: (812)944-9178
E-mail: 522score@netpointe.com
URL: National Affiliate–www.score.org
Local. Provides counseling to persons wanting to go into business as well as those already in the business. Sponsors seminars and workshops. **Affiliated With:** SCORE.

5924 ■ Society of Broadcast Engineers, Chapter 35 - Kentucky
410 Mt. Tabor Rd.
New Albany, IN 47150
E-mail: info@sbe35.org
URL: http://www.sbe35.org
Contact: Jerry May, Chm.
State. Serves the interests of broadcast engineers. Promotes the profession and related fields for both theoretical and practical applications. Advocates for technical advancement of the industry. **Affiliated With:** Society of Broadcast Engineers.

5925 ■ Society of Manufacturing Engineers - Purdue University - New Albany S351
4201 Grant Line Rd.
New Albany, IN 47150
Ph: (812)941-2399
Fax: (812)941-2629
E-mail: trcooley@purdue.edu
URL: National Affiliate–www.sme.org
Contact: Tim Cooley, Contact
Local. Advances manufacturing knowledge to gain competitive advantage. Improves skills and manufacturing solutions for the growth of economy. Provides resources and opportunities for manufacturing professionals. **Affiliated With:** American Association of State Climatologists.

5926 ■ South Central Indiana RSVP
c/o Ceil Sperzel, Dir.
702 E Market St.
New Albany, IN 47150-2916
Ph: (812)948-1815
Fax: (812)948-9249
E-mail: rsvp1815@aol.com
URL: http://www.seniorcorps.gov
Contact: Ceil Sperzel, Dir.
Local. Affiliated With: Retired and Senior Volunteer Program.

5927 ■ Southern Indiana Chamber of Commerce (SICC)
c/o Greg Fitzloff, Pres.
4100 Charlestown Rd.
New Albany, IN 47150-9538
Ph: (812)945-0266
Fax: (812)948-4664
E-mail: greg@sicc.org
URL: http://www.sicc.org
Contact: Greg Fitzloff, Pres.
Founded: 1985. **Members:** 1,000. **Staff:** 9. **Budget:** $200,000. **Local**. Promotes economic and community development in Clark and Floyd counties, IN. **Affiliated With:** U.S. Chamber of Commerce. **Formed by Merger of:** CLark County Chamber of Commerce; Floyd County Chamber of Commerce. **Publications:** *Report from the Chamber*, monthly. **Conventions/Meetings:** annual meeting.

5928 ■ Southern Indiana Table Tennis Association
c/o New Albany-Floyd Co.
Dept. of Parks and Rec.
1721 Ekin Ave.
New Albany, IN 47150
Ph: (812)952-3800 (812)952-3826
URL: http://www.sitta.org
Contact: John Riley, Contact
Local. Affiliated With: U.S.A. Table Tennis.

5929 ■ Southern Seven Workforce Investment Board
c/o James W. Bye
PO Box 6712
New Albany, IN 47150-2155
Ph: (812)944-7793
Contact: Ron McKulick, Dir.
Local.

New Carlisle

5930 ■ American Legion, New Carlisle Post 297
PO Box 181
New Carlisle, IN 46552
Ph: (219)654-7438
Fax: (317)237-9891
URL: National Affiliate–www.legion.org
Local. Affiliated With: American Legion.

New Castle

5931 ■ American Association for Medical Transcription, 500 Central Indiana Chapter
c/o Amanda K. Clark, CMT, Pres.
1702 Irvin St.
New Castle, IN 47362-2354
E-mail: amandamt@sbcglobal.net
URL: http://www.aamt.org/ca/centralindy
Contact: Amanda K. Clark CMT, Pres.
Local. Works to represent and advance the profession of medical transcription and its practitioners. **Affiliated With:** American Association for Medical Transcription.

5932 ■ American Legion, Indiana Post 137
c/o Howard R. Smith
419 New York Ave.
New Castle, IN 47362
Ph: (317)529-3259
Fax: (317)237-9891
URL: National Affiliate–www.legion.org
Contact: Howard R. Smith, Contact
Local. Affiliated With: American Legion.

5933 ■ American Society of Women Accountants, Anderson/Muncie Chapter No. 077
c/o Shirley New, Pres.
Harper Hotels Inc.
7178 W State Rd. 38
New Castle, IN 47362
Ph: (765)288-8422 (765)533-6452
Fax: (765)288-8424
E-mail: harperhinc@sbcglobal.net
URL: http://www.aswa.org
Contact: Shirley New EA, Pres.
Local. Strives to enable women in all fields of accounting to achieve their personal, professional and economic potential, and to contribute to the future development of the profession. Encourages and assists qualified women entering the accounting profession. Informs the public and the profession of the abilities and achievements of women in accounting. Urges members to continue their education. Assists women accountants returning to the labor market. Encourages members to develop leadership skills and participate actively in other professional organizations. Cooperates with the American Women's Society of Certified Public Accountants in the common objectives of the two societies. **Affiliated With:** American Society of Women Accountants.

5934 ■ Daughters of the American Revolution, Sarah Winston Henry Chapter
204 S 11th St.
New Castle, IN 47362
Ph: (765)529-3586
Fax: (765)529-3586
E-mail: melbaj@usa.com
Contact: Melba McLane McKnight, Regent
Founded: 1927. **Members:** 63. **Membership Dues:** $35 (annual). **State Groups:** 1. **Local**. Women in Henry County, IN whose ancestors fought in the American Revolutionary War. Helps foster patriotism. Sponsors patriotic, historical, and educational contests for school children and American History Month. **Libraries: Type:** open to the public. **Subjects:** genealogy. **Awards:** Good Citizens Award. **Frequency:** annual. **Type:** recognition • History Awards. **Frequency:** annual. **Type:** recognition. **Recipient:** for American history students. **Affiliated With:** National Society, Daughters of the American Revolution. **Publications:** *Daughters of the American Revolution Magazine*, monthly. **Price:** $13.00/y. **Conventions/Meetings:** annual Continental Congress, promoting sales within the group (exhibits) - always April.

5935 ■ Henry County Historical Society (HCHS)
c/o Marianne Hughes, Curator
606 S 14th St.
New Castle, IN 47362
Ph: (765)529-4028
E-mail: hchisoc@kiva.net
URL: http://www.kiva.net/~hchisoc/museum.htm
Contact: Marianne Hughes, Curator
Founded: 1887. **Members:** 640. **Membership Dues:** single/family/non-profit group, $20 (annual) • business patron, $50 (annual) • life, $500. **Staff:** 4. **Regional**. Individuals interested in the history and genealogy of Henry County, Indiana. **Libraries: Type:** open to the public. **Publications:** *Henry County Historicalog*, semiannual. Catalog. **Price:** included in membership dues. **Conventions/Meetings:** semiannual general assembly - usually third Thursday of April and October, in New Castle, IN • annual Summer Lawn Social - festival • annual Victorian Christmas Tea - festival - always second Sunday in December.

5936 ■ Indiana Optometric Association, Central District
c/o Jennifer R. Bailey, OD, Trustee
PO Box 645
New Castle, IN 47362
Ph: (765)529-9364
Fax: (765)529-2030
E-mail: drjbailey@sbcglobal.net
URL: http://www.ioa.org
Contact: Jennifer R. Bailey OD, Trustee
Local. Aims to improve the quality, availability and accessibility of eye and vision care. Promotes high standards of patient care. Monitors and promotes legislation concerning the scope of optometric practice and other issues relevant to eye/vision care. **Affiliated With:** American Optometric Association; Indiana Optometric Association.

5937 ■ Mental Health Association in Henry County
PO Box 449
New Castle, IN 47362-0449
Ph: (765)529-4403
Fax: (765)593-2510
E-mail: mhahcin@yahoo.com
URL: http://www.mentalhealthassociation.com
Contact: Mr. O. Kenneth Pew Jr., Exec.Dir.
Local. Seeks to promote mental health and prevent mental health disorders. Improves mental health of Americans through advocacy, public education, research and service. **Affiliated With:** Mental Health Association in Indiana; National Mental Health Association.

5938 ■ New Castle Area - Young Life
PO Box 397
New Castle, IN 47362
Ph: (765)593-2653
URL: http://whereis.younglife.org/FriendlyUrlRedirector.aspx?ID=C-884
Local.

5939 ■ New Castle-Henry County Chamber of Commerce (NCACC)
100 S Main St., Ste.108
New Castle, IN 47362
Ph: (765)529-5210
Fax: (765)521-7404
E-mail: info@nchcchamber.com
URL: http://www.nchcchamber.com
Contact: Betty Lou Heintz, Exec.Dir.
Founded: 1889. **Local**. Promotes business and community development in the New Castle and Henry County, IN area. **Awards:** Business of the Year. **Frequency:** annual. **Type:** recognition • Citizen of the

Year. **Frequency:** annual. **Type:** recognition. **Computer Services:** Mailing lists, of members. **Formerly:** (1995) New Castle Area Chamber of Commerce. **Publications:** *Chamber Commentary*, monthly. Newsletter. Contains Chamber functions, local business happenings, and timely business information. **Price:** free for members. **Conventions/Meetings:** monthly board meeting - every 3rd Thursday • monthly meeting, chamber ambassadors - every 2nd Tuesday.

5940 ■ RSVP of Hancock, Henry, and Rush
c/o Susan McAmis, Dir.
PO Box 449
New Castle, IN 47362-0449
Ph: (765)521-7414
Fax: (765)521-7415
E-mail: smcamis@icapcaa.org
URL: http://www.seniorcorps.gov/about/programs/rsvp.asp
Contact: Susan McAmis, Dir.
Local. Affiliated With: Retired and Senior Volunteer Program.

5941 ■ Young Life Henry County
PO Box 397
New Castle, IN 47362
Ph: (765)593-2653
Fax: (765)529-0078
URL: http://henrycounty.younglife.org
Local.

New Goshen

5942 ■ New Goshen-West Vigo Lions Club
PO Box 69
New Goshen, IN 47863
E-mail: jflow123@aol.com
URL: http://newgoshenwestvigoin.lionwap.org
Local. Affiliated With: Lions Clubs International.

New Harmony

5943 ■ American Legion, New Harmony Post 370
PO Box 293
New Harmony, IN 47631
Ph: (317)630-1300
Fax: (317)237-9891
URL: National Affiliate–www.legion.org
Local. Affiliated With: American Legion.

5944 ■ American Truck Historical Society, Wabash Valley Chapter
c/o Brian Blaylock
3060 Hidbrader Rd.
New Harmony, IN 47631
Ph: (812)682-5103
URL: National Affiliate–www.aths.org
Contact: Brian Blaylock, Contact
Local.

New Haven

5945 ■ American Legion, New Haven Post 330
330 Entrance Way
New Haven, IN 46774
Ph: (219)749-0313
Fax: (317)237-9891
URL: National Affiliate–www.legion.org
Local. Affiliated With: American Legion.

5946 ■ International Brotherhood of Magicians, Ring 221 - A.H. Stoner Ring
c/o Jim Reams
1421 Dundee Dr.
New Haven, IN 46774
Ph: (260)484-2757
E-mail: magicmolar@aol.com
URL: http://ibmring221.welcome.to
Contact: Jim Reams, Contact
Local. Professional and semiprofessional magicians; suppliers, assistants, agents, and others interested in magic. Seeks to advance the art of magic in the field of amusement, entertainment, and culture. Promotes proper means of discouraging false or misleading advertising of effects, tricks, literature, merchandise, or actions appertaining to the magical arts; opposes exposures of principles of the art of magic, except in books on magic and magazines devoted to such art for the exclusive use of magicians and devotees of the art; encourages humane treatment and care of live animals whenever employed in magical performances. **Affiliated With:** International Brotherhood of Magicians.

5947 ■ Navy Club of New Haven - Ship No. 245
1705 Woodmere
New Haven, IN 46774
Ph: (260)493-4030
URL: National Affiliate–www.navyclubusa.org
Contact: Scott Strong, Commander
Local. Represents individuals who are, or have been, in the active service of the U.S. Navy, Naval Reserve, Marine Corps, Marine Corps Reserve, and Coast Guard. Promotes and encourages further public interest in the U.S. Navy and its history. Upholds the spirit and ideals of the U.S. Navy. Acts as a public forum for members' views on national defense. Assists the Navy Recruiting Command whenever and wherever possible. Conducts charitable activities. **Affiliated With:** Navy Club of the United States of America.

5948 ■ New Haven Chamber of Commerce
428 Broadway
PO Box 66
New Haven, IN 46774-0066
Ph: (260)749-4484
Fax: (260)749-4484
E-mail: nhchamber@aol.com
Contact: Ron Oetting, Pres.
Founded: 1945. **Members:** 192. **Staff:** 1. **Budget:** $60,000. **Local.** Promotes business and community development in eastern Allen County, IN. Holds annual banquet, sponsors special events and promotions, conducts business referrals and provides new resident packets to individuals and corporations. **Publications:** *Business Update*, quarterly. Newsletter • Directory, annual. **Conventions/Meetings:** annual banquet • monthly meeting.

New Palestine

5949 ■ American Legion, New Palestine Post 182
4611 S 700 W
New Palestine, IN 46163
Ph: (317)861-4730
Fax: (317)237-9891
URL: National Affiliate–www.legion.org
Local. Affiliated With: American Legion.

5950 ■ Indianapolis Professional Photographers Guild
c/o Norman Dingle
7239 W Timer Dr.
New Palestine, IN 46163
Ph: (317)861-9047
E-mail: ndingle@treasuredmemoriesphoto.com
URL: National Affiliate–ppa.com
Contact: Norman Dingle, Contact
Local. Affiliated With: Professional Photographers of America.

5951 ■ New Palestine Area Chamber of Commerce (NPACC)
PO Box 541
New Palestine, IN 46163
Ph: (317)861-2345
Fax: (317)861-4201
E-mail: info@newpalchamber.com
URL: http://www.newpalchamber.com
Contact: Rebecca Gaines, Sec.
Local. Promotes business and community development in the New Palestine, IN area.

5952 ■ Police and Firemen's Insurance Association - Indianapolis Fire Department
c/o Bradd T. Roembke
6215 Caribou Cir.
New Palestine, IN 46163
Ph: (317)861-8614
URL: National Affiliate–www.pfia.net
Contact: Bradd T. Roembke, Contact
Local. Affiliated With: Police and Firemen's Insurance Association.

New Paris

5953 ■ Alcoholics Anonymous World Services, Original Recipe Intergroup
PO Box 72
New Paris, IN 46553-0072
URL: National Affiliate–www.aa.org
Local. Individuals recovering from alcoholism. AA maintains that members can solve their common problem and help others achieve sobriety through a twelve step program that includes sharing their experience, strength, and hope with each other. **Affiliated With:** Alcoholics Anonymous World Services.

5954 ■ New Paris Lions Club
PO Box 138
New Paris, IN 46553
E-mail: dave@mapletronics.com
URL: http://www.newparislionsclub.org
Local. Affiliated With: Lions Clubs International.

5955 ■ Society for Technical Communication, St. Joseph Valley Chapter
c/o Mark Stucky, Pres.
KMC Controls
19476 Indus. Dr.
New Paris, IN 46553
Ph: (574)831-8111
E-mail: cyberspirit99@hotmail.com
URL: http://www.stc-sjvc.org
Contact: Mark Stucky, Pres.
Local. Seeks to advance the theory and practice of technical communication in all media. Enhances the professionalism of the members and the status of the profession. Promotes the education of members and supports research activities in the field. **Affiliated With:** Society for Technical Communication.

New Richmond

5956 ■ Indiana Land Improvement Contractors Association (INLICA)
c/o Kathy Peevler, Exec.Dir.
PO Box 120
New Richmond, IN 47967
Ph: (765)339-7343
Fax: (765)366-2912
E-mail: kpeevler@inlica.org
URL: http://www.inlica.org
Contact: Kathy Peevler, Exec.Dir.
Founded: 1954. **Members:** 150. **Membership Dues:** active contractor, $230 (annual) • associate (vendor), $145 (annual) • affiliate (friend of LICA), retired contractor, $45 (annual). **Staff:** 1. **State.** Represents land improvement contractors. Seeks to encourage development of high standards for quality work in land and water conservation contracting. Encourages members to help "sell" land improvement to all and to cooperate with industry and with local, state and federal agencies in education and service. **Awards:** $1000 Scholarship. **Frequency:** annual. **Type:** monetary. **Recipient:** to a member, spouse, son, daughter, or grandchild of a contractor member. **Pub-**

lications: Newsletter, 8-9 times per year. **Price:** included in membership dues. **Advertising:** accepted.

New Ross

5957 ■ American Legion, Robert Turner Post 427
PO Box 39
New Ross, IN 47968
Ph: (317)630-1300
Fax: (317)237-9891
URL: National Affiliate–www.legion.org
Local. Affiliated With: American Legion.

New Whiteland

5958 ■ National Association of Miniature Enthusiasts - Madison Avenue Miniaturists
c/o Christine Benham
631 Princeton Dr.
New Whiteland, IN 46184
Ph: (317)535-8076
E-mail: benham2@aol.com
URL: http://www.miniatures.org/states/IN.html
Contact: Christine Benham, Contact
Local. Affiliated With: National Association of Miniature Enthusiasts.

Newburgh

5959 ■ American Legion, Kapperman Post 44
711 State St.
Newburgh, IN 47629
Ph: (812)858-1020
Fax: (317)237-9891
URL: National Affiliate–www.legion.org
Local. Affiliated With: American Legion.

5960 ■ Historic Newburgh (HNI)
PO Box 543
Newburgh, IN 47629-0543
Ph: (812)853-2815
E-mail: director@historicnewburgh.org
URL: http://www.historicnewburgh.org
Contact: Ms. Nancy Lybarger, Exec.Dir.
Founded: 1980. **Local.** Represents members who are dedicated to the preservation, improving quality of life and revitalization of the downtown historic district. Continues to hold special events, such as the July 4th Fireworks, Ghost Walks and regular walking tours of the historic district, to inform and interest the public in the pursuit of the mission. **Awards:** Preservation Award. **Frequency:** annual. **Type:** recognition. **Recipient:** to a home owner, a business and an HNI member, for their efforts in preservation and revitalization in the downtown area.

5961 ■ Izaak Walton League of America - Evansville
8466 Kingston Dr.
Newburgh, IN 47630
Ph: (812)853-2025
E-mail: chihawks01@sbcglobal.net
URL: National Affiliate–www.iwla.org
Contact: Bill Reinert, Contact
Local. Educates the public to conserve, maintain, protect and restore the soil, forest, water and other natural resources of the United States.

5962 ■ Newburgh - Wyldlife
4333 State Rd. 261
Newburgh, IN 47630
Ph: (812)853-9906
URL: http://sites.younglife.org/_layouts/ylext/default.aspx?ID=C-883
Local. Affiliated With: Young Life.

5963 ■ PFLAG Evansville/Tri-State
7444 Capri Ct.
Newburgh, IN 47630
Ph: (812)490-2454
URL: http://www.pflag.org/Indiana.205.0.html
Regional. Affiliated With: Parents, Families, and Friends of Lesbians and Gays.

5964 ■ Tri-State Corvette Club
PO Box 771
Newburgh, IN 47629
E-mail: info@tristatecorvetteclub.com
URL: http://www.tristatecorvetteclub.com
Regional. Affiliated With: National Council of Corvette Clubs.

5965 ■ Young Life Indiana-Kentucky Region
PO Box 335
Newburgh, IN 47629
Ph: (812)853-9052
Fax: (812)853-9690
URL: http://whereis.younglife.org/FriendlyUrlRedirector.aspx?ID=A-AG76
Regional.

5966 ■ Young Life Newburgh
4333 State Rd. 261
Newburgh, IN 47630
Ph: (812)853-9906
Fax: (812)853-9907
URL: http://Newburgh.younglife.org
Local.

Newport

5967 ■ American Legion, Reveille Post 184
PO Box 11
Newport, IN 47966
Ph: (317)630-1300
Fax: (317)237-9891
URL: National Affiliate–www.legion.org
Local. Affiliated With: American Legion.

Noblesville

5968 ■ American Legion, Indiana Post 45
c/o Frank E. Huntzinger
1094 Conner St.
Noblesville, IN 46060
Ph: (317)773-9985
Fax: (317)237-9891
URL: National Affiliate–www.legion.org
Contact: Frank E. Huntzinger, Contact
Local. Affiliated With: American Legion.

5969 ■ American Red Cross, Hamilton County Service Center
15325 Herriman Blvd.
Noblesville, IN 46060-4214
Ph: (317)773-0380
E-mail: archc@redcross-indy.org
URL: http://www.redcross-indy.org
Contact: Angela Holliday, Contact
Local. Works to provide relief to victims of disasters and help people prevent, prepare for, and respond to emergencies.

5970 ■ Crooked Creek Conservation and Gun Club
13203 E 246th St.
Noblesville, IN 46060
Ph: (765)552-8925 (765)552-6210
E-mail: datrice@insightbb.com
URL: http://crookedcreekgunclub.org
Contact: Dennis A. Trice, Pres.
Local. Affiliated With: National Skeet Shooting Association.

5971 ■ Hamilton County First Steps Council
c/o Lisa Kopka
942 N 10th St.
Noblesville, IN 46060
Ph: (317)776-1313
Fax: (317)776-2090
E-mail: steps29@ori.net
URL: http://www.hamiltoncountyfirststeps.com
Contact: Lisa Kopka, Coor.
Founded: 1991. **Members:** 36. **Staff:** 1. **Budget:** $35,760. **Local.**

5972 ■ Hamilton County Sertoma Club
PO Box 501
Noblesville, IN 46061
URL: http://www.ori.net/eclipse/serthome.htm
Contact: Paul von Wiegant, Pres.
Local.

5973 ■ Hamilton County Sheriffs Department Chaplaincy
18100 Cumberland Rd.
Noblesville, IN 46060-1624
Ph: (317)773-1872
Fax: (317)776-9835
URL: http://www.indianasheriffs.org
Contact: Mr. Doug Carter, Sheriff
Local.

5974 ■ Humane Society for Hamilton County (HSHC)
18102 Cumberland Rd.
Noblesville, IN 46060
Ph: (317)773-4974
Fax: (317)773-2131
E-mail: hshc@hamiltonhumane.com
URL: http://hamiltonhumane.com
Contact: Rebecca Stevens, Exec.Dir.
Local.

5975 ■ Institute of Management Accountants, Indianapolis Chapter
c/o Rebecca L. Dixon, Pres.
18530 Windstone Cir.
Noblesville, IN 46062
Ph: (317)275-4850
E-mail: bdixon@imcpl.org
URL: http://www.indyima.org
Contact: Rebecca L. Dixon, Pres.
Founded: 1927. **Local.** Promotes professional and ethical standards. Equips members and students with knowledge and training required for the accounting profession. **Affiliated With:** Institute of Management Accountants. **Publications:** *The Spreadsheet*, monthly. Newsletter. Alternate Formats: online.

5976 ■ Meals on Wheels of Hamilton County
c/o Margaret Lukes, Dir.
395 Westfield Rd.
Noblesville, IN 46060
Ph: (317)776-7159
Fax: (317)770-2971
E-mail: mlukes@riverview.org
Contact: Margaret Lukes, Dir.
Founded: 1975. **Membership Dues:** individual - basic, $25 (annual) • individual - gold, family - basic, $50 (annual) • family - gold, $100 (annual) • corporate - basic, $200 (annual) • corporate - gold, $500 (annual). **Staff:** 1. **Budget:** $100,000. **Local.** Delivers nutritional meals to residents who are unable to provide such for themselves because of physical or other disabilities without regard to race, age, color, religion, sex, disability, national origin or ancestry. **Committees:** Community Affairs; Internal Affairs; Volunteer. **Publications:** *The Meal Wheeler*, annual. Newsletter. Contains information about special events. **Price:** free. **Advertising:** accepted. Alternate Formats: online.

5977 ■ MOAA Indiana Council of Chapters
c/o Col. Joseph Ryan
124 Pine Tree Ln.
Noblesville, IN 46060-2401
Ph: (317)773-2275
E-mail: noblesvillej@msn.com
URL: National Affiliate–www.moaa.org
Contact: Col. Joseph Ryan, Contact
State. Affiliated With: Military Officers Association of America.

5978 ■ Noblesville Chamber of Commerce (NCC)
54 N 9th St., Ste.100
Noblesville, IN 46060
Ph: (317)773-0086
Fax: (317)773-1966
E-mail: info@noblesvillechamber.com
URL: http://www.noblesvillechamber.com
Contact: Sharon McMahon, Pres.
Founded: 1935. **Members:** 300. **Membership Dues:** business (based on number of full-time employees), $175-$1,000 (annual) • financial institution, $500 (annual) • utility, $800 (annual) • education/government, $300 (annual) • hospital, $400 (annual) • individual, church, civic, service club, $80 (annual). **Staff:** 2. **Budget:** $70,000. **Local**. Businesses, organizations, industries, and individuals promoting business and community development in the Noblesville, IN area. **Computer Services:** database, list of members and local institutions. **Affiliated With:** U.S. Chamber of Commerce. **Publications:** *The Chamber Enterprise*, monthly. Newsletter • *Community Information Directory*, biennial • *Monthly Memo*. **Conventions/Meetings:** monthly luncheon • annual meeting.

5979 ■ Noblesville Main Street
876 1/2 Logan St.
Noblesville, IN 46060
Ph: (317)776-0205
Fax: (317)776-2688
E-mail: mainstrt@sbcglobal.net
URL: http://www.noblesvillemainstreet.org
Local.

5980 ■ Remember the Children
c/o Andy Baker
17039 Mercantile Blvd., PMB 301
Noblesville, IN 46060
Ph: (317)774-3222
Fax: (317)774-3293
E-mail: info@remember-the-children.org
URL: http://www.remember-the-children.org
Contact: Andrew A. Baker, Dir.
Founded: 2001. **Staff:** 3. **Budget:** $200,000. **Nonmembership**. **Local**. Strives to provide humanitarian aid. **Publications:** Newsletter, 3/year. **Price:** free. **Circulation:** 3,600. Alternate Formats: online.

5981 ■ Wayne-Fall Lions Club
11940 E 191st St.
Noblesville, IN 46060
E-mail: waynefallin@lionwap.org
URL: http://waynefallin.lionwap.org
Local. **Affiliated With:** Lions Clubs International.

North Judson

5982 ■ American Legion, Indiana Post 92
c/o Harry L. Keller
208 Collins St.
North Judson, IN 46366
Ph: (219)896-2011
Fax: (317)237-9891
URL: National Affiliate–www.legion.org
Contact: Harry L. Keller, Contact
Local. **Affiliated With:** American Legion.

5983 ■ Kankakee Valley Astronomical Society
408 Luken St.
North Judson, IN 46366
Ph: (574)896-3300
E-mail: upham@nitline.net
URL: http://www.heartlandsystemsoftware.com/kvas
Contact: Thomas Upham, Contact
Local. Promotes the science of astronomy. Works to encourage and coordinate activities of amateur astronomical societies. Fosters observational and computational work and craftsmanship in various fields of astronomy. **Affiliated With:** Astronomical League.

North Liberty

5984 ■ American Legion, Indiana Post 365
c/o Edward Sousley
PO Box 705
North Liberty, IN 46554
Ph: (219)656-8012
Fax: (317)237-9891
URL: National Affiliate–www.legion.org
Contact: Edward Sousley, Contact
Local. **Affiliated With:** American Legion.

5985 ■ St. Joseph Valley Beagle Club
c/o James H. Davis
68341 Sr 23 SW
North Liberty, IN 46554
URL: National Affiliate–clubs.akc.org
Contact: James H. Davis, Contact
Local.

North Manchester

5986 ■ American Legion, Eel River Post 286
215 E Main St.
North Manchester, IN 46962
Ph: (219)982-8114
Fax: (317)237-9891
URL: National Affiliate–www.legion.org
Local. **Affiliated With:** American Legion.

5987 ■ Mental Health Association in Wabash County
c/o Ms. Mary Ann Mast, Exec.Dir.
PO Box 310
North Manchester, IN 46962-0310
Ph: (260)982-7766
Fax: (260)982-6868
E-mail: mamast@kconline.com
URL: http://www.mentalhealthassociation.com
Contact: Ms. Mary Ann Mast, Exec.Dir.
Local. Seeks to promote mental health and prevent mental health disorders. Improves mental health of Americans through advocacy, public education, research and service. **Affiliated With:** Mental Health Association in Indiana; National Mental Health Association.

5988 ■ North Manchester Chamber of Commerce
109 N Market St.
North Manchester, IN 46962-1518
Ph: (260)982-7644
Fax: (260)982-8718
E-mail: nmcc@kconline.com
URL: http://www.northmanchesterchamber.com
Contact: Kathy Roberts, Exec.Dir.
Founded: 1944. **Staff:** 2. **Local**. Serves as a community leader fostering projects and programs that will promote the economic health, welfare and development of business in North Manchester area. **Awards:** Business of the Year. **Frequency:** annual. **Type:** recognition • Citizen of the Year. **Frequency:** annual. **Type:** recognition • Industry of the Year. **Frequency:** annual. **Type:** recognition. **Computer Services:** Information services, membership listing. **Telecommunication Services:** electronic mail, nmcc@northmanchesterchamber.com • electronic mail, ksroberts@kconline.com. **Publications:** *Chamber Notes*, monthly. Newsletter. Alternate Formats: online.

5989 ■ North Manchester Fellowship of Reconciliation
PO Box 25
North Manchester, IN 46962
E-mail: nmfor@nmfor.org
URL: http://www.nmfor.org
Contact: Heidi Gross, Contact
Local. **Affiliated With:** Fellowship of Reconciliation - USA. **Publications:** *Climate Changer*, quarterly. Newsletter. Alternate Formats: online.

5990 ■ Psi Chi, National Honor Society in Psychology - Manchester College
c/o Dept. of Psychology
Box 121
604 E Coll. Ave.
North Manchester, IN 46962
Ph: (260)982-5944
Fax: (260)982-5043
E-mail: mlcoulter-kern@manchester.edu
URL: National Affiliate–www.psichi.org
Local. **Affiliated With:** Psi Chi, National Honor Society in Psychology.

5991 ■ Tippecanoe Audubon Society
c/o Wilson B. Lutz, Membership Chm.
806 E Second St.
North Manchester, IN 46962
Ph: (260)982-2471 (574)658-4504
E-mail: mwlutz@kconline.com
URL: http://www.tippeaudubon.org
Contact: Wilson Lutz, Membership Chm.
Local. **Formerly:** (2005) National Audubon Society - Tippecanoe. **Publications:** *Tippe Topics*, monthly. Newsletter. Alternate Formats: online.

North Salem

5992 ■ American Legion, Kurtz-Booker Post 217
PO Box 206
North Salem, IN 46165
Ph: (317)630-1300
Fax: (317)237-9891
URL: National Affiliate–www.legion.org
Local. **Affiliated With:** American Legion.

North Vernon

5993 ■ American Legion, Indiana Post 199
3614 Townsend St.
North Vernon, IN 47265
Ph: (317)630-1300
Fax: (317)237-9891
URL: National Affiliate–www.legion.org
Local. **Affiliated With:** American Legion.

5994 ■ Heartland Peruvian Horse Club
c/o Bob Taylor
155 E County Rd. 175 N
North Vernon, IN 47265-8336
E-mail: rapsley@seidata.com
URL: National Affiliate–www.aaobpph.org
Contact: Bob Taylor, Contact
Local. **Affiliated With:** American Association of Owners and Breeders of Peruvian Paso Horses.

5995 ■ Jennings County Chamber of Commerce
PO Box 340
North Vernon, IN 47265
Ph: (812)346-2339
Fax: (812)346-2065
E-mail: jheath@jenningscountychamber.org
URL: http://www.jenningscountychamber.org
Contact: Judy Heath, Admin.Asst.
Founded: 1955. **Members:** 270. **Membership Dues:** business, $150 (annual) • associate, $62 (annual) • out of county business, $250 (annual). **Local**. Promotes business and community development in Jennings County, IN. **Computer Services:** database, list of members • information services, facts about Jennings County. **Committees:** Ambassadors; Education/Government; Programs. **Affiliated With:** U.S. Chamber of Commerce. **Formerly:** (1999) Jennings County Chamber of Commerce/Economic Development. **Publications:** *Chamber News*, monthly. Newsletter. Provides current issues and chamber news. **Price:** free for members. **Advertising:** accepted. **Conventions/Meetings:** monthly Business After Hours - meeting, networking - every 3rd Thursday.

5996 ■ Jennings County United Way
PO Box 446
North Vernon, IN 47265
Ph: (812)346-5257
Fax: (812)352-9578
E-mail: cheri@jcunitedway.com
URL: http://www.jcunitedway.com
Local. Affiliated With: United Way of America.

5997 ■ Muscatatuck Board of Realtors
PO Box 559
North Vernon, IN 47265
Ph: (812)346-4982
Fax: (812)346-3745
E-mail: tlawson@seidata.com
URL: National Affiliate–www.realtor.org
Contact: Susan M. Page, Exec. Officer
Local. Strives to develop real estate business practices. Advocates the right to own, use and transfer real property. Provides a facility for professional development, research and exchange of information among members and to the general public. **Affiliated With:** National Association of Realtors.

North Webster

5998 ■ American Camp Association Indiana
PO Box 260
North Webster, IN 46555
Ph: (574)457-4379
Fax: (574)834-2183
Free: (888)620-2267
E-mail: info@acaindiana.org
URL: http://www.acacamps.org/in
Contact: Brigitta Adkins, Exec.Dir.
State. Camp and youth professionals dedicated to enriching the lives of children and adults through the camp experience. Activities include: public policy, public education, knowledge center, conferences, professional development, vendors and supplies, library, bookstore, bi-monthly publication, risk management, newsletters, and local support. **Affiliated With:** American Camping Association.

5999 ■ American Legion, Indiana Post 253
c/o Herbert Kuhn
756 S St., Rd. 13
North Webster, IN 46555
Ph: (219)834-4297
Fax: (317)237-9891
URL: National Affiliate–www.legion.org
Contact: Herbert Kuhn, Contact
Local. Affiliated With: American Legion.

6000 ■ North Webster - Tippecanoe Township Chamber of Commerce
PO Box 95
North Webster, IN 46555
Ph: (574)834-7076
Contact: Chris Bruno, Pres.
Local.

6001 ■ Webster Musky Club
PO Box 670
North Webster, IN 46555
Ph: (260)385-0623
E-mail: chae@maplenet.net
URL: http://www.websterlakemuskyclub.org
Contact: Chae Dolsen, Pres.
Local.

Notre Dame

6002 ■ American Association of Teachers of German - Indiana Chapter
Univ. of Notre Dame
320 Decio Hall
Notre Dame, IN 46556
Ph: (219)631-7751
Fax: (574)272-9248
E-mail: weber.15@nd.edu
URL: http://www.bsu.edu/xtranet/IFLTA/german
Contact: Hannelore Weber, Pres.
State. Represents teachers of German at all levels of instruction and all those interested in the teaching of German. Advances and improves the teaching of the language, literatures and cultures of the German-speaking countries. Provides members with educational and professional services. **Affiliated With:** American Association of Teachers of German.

6003 ■ Association for Computing Machinery, University of Notre Dame
c/o Jef Fox, Chm.
Dept. of Cmpt. Sci. and Engg.
384 Fitzpatrick Hall
Notre Dame, IN 46556
Ph: (574)631-8320
Fax: (574)631-9260
E-mail: cse@cse.nd.edu
URL: http://www.cse.nd.edu
Contact: Jef Fox, Chm.
Local. Biological, medical, behavioral, and computer scientists; hospital administrators; programmers and others interested in application of computer methods to biological, behavioral, and medical problems. Stimulates understanding of the use and potential of computers in the biosciences. **Affiliated With:** Association for Computing Machinery.

6004 ■ Institute of Internal Auditors, Michiana Chapter
c/o Matt Riem
Univ. of Notre Dame
Audit and Advisory Sers.
402 Grace Hall
Notre Dame, IN 46556
Ph: (574)631-3686
E-mail: matthew.s.riem.1@nd.edu
URL: National Affiliate–www.theiia.org
Contact: Matt Riem, Pres.
Membership Dues: regular, $115 (annual) • educator, $65 (annual) • student, retired, $30 (annual) • life, $2,100 • sustainer (government auditors only), $50 (annual) • organization ($65 per staff member over 5; $50 per staff member over 100), $425-$6,600 (annual). **Local**. Serves as an advocate for the internal audit profession. Provides certification, education, research, and technological guidance for the profession. **Affiliated With:** Institute of Internal Auditors. **Publications:** *Eyes and Ears*, monthly. Newsletter. Alternate Formats: online.

6005 ■ Phi Theta Kappa, Beta Epsilon Rho Chapter - Holy Cross College
c/o Sandra Ohlund
54515 State Rd. 933 N
Notre Dame, IN 46556
Ph: (574)239-8400
E-mail: sohlund@csinet.net
URL: http://www.ptk.org/directories/chapters/IN/20758-1.htm
Contact: Sandra Ohlund, Advisor
Local.

6006 ■ Psi Chi, National Honor Society in Psychology - Saint Mary's College
c/o Dept. of Psychology
PO Box 84
Notre Dame, IN 46556-5001
Ph: (574)284-4534 (574)284-4530
Fax: (574)284-4716
E-mail: stoddart@saintmarys.edu
URL: http://www.psichi.org/chapters/info.asp?chapter_id=417
Contact: Rebecca Stoddart PhD, Advisor
Local.

6007 ■ Psi Chi, National Honor Society in Psychology - University of Notre Dame
c/o Dept. of Psychology
118 Haggar Hall
Notre Dame, IN 46556
Ph: (574)631-7675 (574)631-6619
Fax: (574)631-8883
E-mail: aventer@nd.edu
URL: National Affiliate–www.psichi.org
Local. Affiliated With: Psi Chi, National Honor Society in Psychology.

Oakford

6008 ■ Howard County Genealogical Society
PO Box 2
Oakford, IN 46965-0002
URL: http://www.rootsweb.com/~inhoward/hcgs/index.html
Contact: Margaret Cardwell, Pres.
Founded: 1972. **Members:** 150. **Membership Dues:** single, family, $15 (annual). **Local**. Individuals interested in genealogy. Gathers and disseminates information. **Awards: Frequency:** annual. **Type:** recognition. **Recipient:** for outstanding 4 H genealogical exhibit. **Publications:** *Family History Book*. **Price:** $57.75/copy, plus $5 for mailing • *Howard County Genealogical Newsletter*, quarterly. **Price:** included in membership dues. **Conventions/Meetings:** monthly meeting - always first Monday.

Oakland City

6009 ■ American Legion, Johnson Curd Post 256
211 E Washington St.
Oakland City, IN 47660
Ph: (812)749-7844
Fax: (317)237-9891
URL: National Affiliate–www.legion.org
Local. Affiliated With: American Legion.

Odon

6010 ■ American Legion, Odon Post 293
504 N Spring St.
Odon, IN 47562
Ph: (317)630-1300
Fax: (317)237-9891
URL: National Affiliate–www.legion.org
Local. Affiliated With: American Legion.

Oolitic

6011 ■ National Association of Home Builders of the U.S., Home Builders Association of Lawrence County
c/o LaQuita Jennings, Sec.
Local No. 1535
201 Main St.
Hoosier Door
Oolitic, IN 47451
Ph: (812)275-7718
Fax: (812)275-7718
E-mail: hoosdoor@kiva.net
URL: National Affiliate–www.nahb.org
Contact: LaQuita Jennings, Sec.
Local. Single and multifamily home builders, commercial builders, and others associated with the building industry. **Affiliated With:** National Association of Home Builders.

Orland

6012 ■ American Legion, Orland Post 423
PO Box 448
Orland, IN 46776
Ph: (219)829-6544
Fax: (317)237-9891
URL: National Affiliate–www.legion.org
Local. Affiliated With: American Legion.

Orleans

6013 ■ American Legion, Warren Brock Post 69
116 N Washington St.
Orleans, IN 47452
Ph: (812)865-2916
Fax: (317)237-9891
URL: National Affiliate–www.legion.org
Local. Affiliated With: American Legion.

6014 ■ Orleans Chamber of Commerce
PO Box 9
Orleans, IN 47452-0009
Ph: (812)865-9930 (812)865-3190
URL: http://www.town.orleans.in.us
Contact: Robert F. Henderson, Pres./CEO
Local. Promotes business and community development in Orleans, IN area.

Osceola

6015 ■ American Legion, Osceola Post 308
PO Box 36
Osceola, IN 46561
Ph: (317)630-1300
Fax: (317)237-9891
URL: National Affiliate–www.legion.org
Local. Affiliated With: American Legion.

Osgood

6016 ■ American Legion, Indiana Post 267
c/o William A. Gilland
120 S Elm St.
Osgood, IN 47037
Ph: (317)630-1300
Fax: (317)237-9891
URL: National Affiliate–www.legion.org
Contact: William A. Gilland, Contact
Local. Affiliated With: American Legion.

Otterbein

6017 ■ American Legion, Indiana Post 125
c/o Martin Kennedy
PO Box 82
Otterbein, IN 47970
Ph: (317)583-4852
Fax: (317)237-9891
URL: National Affiliate–www.legion.org
Contact: Martin Kennedy, Contact
Local. Affiliated With: American Legion.

Owensville

6018 ■ American Legion, Owensville Post 51
RR 1, Box 310h
Owensville, IN 47665
Ph: (317)630-1300
Fax: (317)237-9891
URL: National Affiliate–www.legion.org
Local. Affiliated With: American Legion.

Paoli

6019 ■ American Legion, Indiana Post 63
c/o Clarence A. Keith
PO Box No. 7
Paoli, IN 47454
Ph: (812)723-3260
Fax: (317)237-9891
URL: National Affiliate–www.legion.org
Contact: Clarence A. Keith, Contact
Local. Affiliated With: American Legion.

6020 ■ Paoli Chamber of Commerce
210 SW Court St.
Paoli, IN 47454
Ph: (812)723-4769
E-mail: paolichamber@verizon.net
URL: http://www.paolichamber.com
Contact: Beverly Dillard, Pres.
Founded: 1984. **Membership Dues:** business, $50-$300 (annual) • personal, $20 (annual). **Staff:** 1. **Budget:** $55,000. **State Groups:** 1. **Local.** Promotes business and industry in and around Paoli, IN.

Pekin

6021 ■ American Legion, Pekin Post 203
578 W Main St.
Pekin, IN 47165
Ph: (812)967-2154
Fax: (317)237-9891
URL: National Affiliate–www.legion.org
Local. Affiliated With: American Legion.

6022 ■ Newborn Lifeline Network
c/o Kathryn Satow
PO Box 220
Pekin, IN 47165-0220
Ph: (812)967-1234
URL: http://www.newbornlifeline.org
Contact: Cathy Satow, Contact
Local.

Pendleton

6023 ■ American Legion, Pendleton Post 117
PO Box 179
Pendleton, IN 46064
Ph: (317)778-7661
Fax: (317)237-9891
URL: National Affiliate–www.legion.org
Local. Affiliated With: American Legion.

6024 ■ Chamber of Commerce in Pendleton
PO Box 542
Pendleton, IN 46064-0542
Ph: (765)778-1741
Fax: (765)778-1741
Contact: Suzanne Hagan, Mgr.
Local.

6025 ■ Korean War Veterans Association, Department of Indiana
c/o George A. Ellwood
8770 Carriage Ln.
Pendleton, IN 46064
Ph: (765)778-8735
E-mail: dandc2k@webtv.net
URL: National Affiliate–www.kwva.org
Contact: George A. Ellwood, Contact
State. Affiliated With: Korean War Veterans Association.

6026 ■ Moms Club of Pendleton, IN
PO Box 2
Pendleton, IN 46064-8528
URL: National Affiliate–www.momsclub.org
Founded: 1999. **Members:** 35. **Membership Dues:** stay-at-home mom, $20 (annual). **Local. Affiliated With:** International MOMS Club.

6027 ■ Prairie Creek Beagle Club
c/o Robert Harvey
7882 S 650 W
Pendleton, IN 46064-9762
URL: National Affiliate–clubs.akc.org
Contact: Robert Harvey, Contact
Local.

Pennville

6028 ■ American Legion, Pennville Post 482
PO Box 212
Pennville, IN 47369
Ph: (317)630-1300
Fax: (317)237-9891
URL: National Affiliate–www.legion.org
Local. Affiliated With: American Legion.

Perrysville

6029 ■ American Legion, Walter Hoyt Post 350
PO Box 245
Perrysville, IN 47974
Ph: (317)793-2653
Fax: (317)237-9891
URL: National Affiliate–www.legion.org
Local. Affiliated With: American Legion.

Peru

6030 ■ American Legion, Glen Owens Post 14
PO Box 1164
Peru, IN 46970
Ph: (317)472-3857
Fax: (317)237-9891
URL: National Affiliate–www.legion.org
Local. Affiliated With: American Legion.

6031 ■ Daleville Skeet and Trap Club
6146 E 100 S
Peru, IN 46970
Ph: (765)378-5122
E-mail: g.gardineer@att.net
URL: National Affiliate–www.mynssa.com
Local. Affiliated With: National Skeet Shooting Association.

6032 ■ Izaak Walton League of America, Miami Chapter
700 W. 10th St.
Peru, IN 46970
Ph: (765)473-4073
E-mail: ikemiami@aol.com
URL: National Affiliate–www.iwla.org
Contact: Mr. Daniel Wilson, Pres.
Founded: 1946. **Members:** 130. **Membership Dues:** $70. **Budget:** $2,000. **State Groups:** 24. **Local.** Works to educate the public to conserve, maintain, protect, and restore the soil, forest, water, and other natural resources of the U.S; promotes the enjoyment and wholesome utilization of these resources. **Affiliated With:** Izaak Walton League of America; Izaak Walton League of America, Indiana Division.

6033 ■ Peru - Miami County Chamber of Commerce
13 E Main St.
Peru, IN 46970
Ph: (765)472-1923
Fax: (765)472-7099
E-mail: info@miamicochamber.com
URL: http://www.miamicochamber.com
Contact: Denise Day, Exec.Dir.
Founded: 1916. **Members:** 220. **Staff:** 2. **Budget:** $88,575. **Local.** Promotes business, community development, and tourism in the Miami County, IN area. **Publications:** *Chamber Newsletter*, quarterly • *Directory of Clubs and Organizations*. **Price:** $5.00 • *Industrial Directory*. **Price:** $15.00 • Membership Directory. **Price:** $15.00. **Conventions/Meetings:** annual Board Retreat - always third Thursday of October • annual meeting - always third Thursday in January.

6034 ■ United Way of Miami County
13 E Main St.
Peru, IN 46970-2210
Ph: (765)473-4240
URL: National Affiliate–national.unitedway.org
Local. Affiliated With: United Way of America.

Petersburg

6035 ■ American Legion, Conrad Post 179
PO Box 433
Petersburg, IN 47567
Ph: (317)630-1300
Fax: (317)237-9891
URL: National Affiliate–www.legion.org
Local. Affiliated With: American Legion.

6036 ■ Four Rivers Resource Conservation and Development Council
112 S Lakeview Dr.
Petersburg, IN 47567-9040
Ph: (812)345-6808
Fax: (812)345-2785
E-mail: dave.elgin@in.usda.gov
URL: National Affiliate–www.rcdnet.org
Contact: Dave Elgin, Coor.
Local. Affiliated With: National Association of Resource Conservation and Development Councils.

6037 ■ Pike County Chamber of Commerce
714 E Main St.
PO Box 291
Petersburg, IN 47567-0291
Ph: (812)354-8155
Fax: (812)354-2335
E-mail: chamber@verizon.net
URL: http://pikecountyin.org
Contact: Alycia Church, Exec.Dir.
Local. Promotes business and community development in Pike County, IN.

6038 ■ Professional Photographers of Indiana
c/o Jeff Harting, Pres.
Harting Studio
575 River Rd.
Petersburg, IN 47567
Ph: (812)354-8037
E-mail: hartingstudio@email.com
URL: http://www.ppofi.org
Contact: Jeff Harting, Pres.
State. Dedicated to promoting the highest level of professionalism and ethical practices within the photographic industry; seeks to advance recognition of the field of photography as an art form, science, recorder of history as a profession; provides educational forums, publications, fellowship and general public awareness to enhance the role of the professional photographer. **Affiliated With:** Professional Photographers of America.

6039 ■ United Way of Pike County, Indiana
PO Box 321
Petersburg, IN 47567
Ph: (812)789-2557
URL: National Affiliate–national.unitedway.org
Local. Affiliated With: United Way of America.

Pierceton

6040 ■ American Legion, Menzie-Reece Post 258
PO Box 535
Pierceton, IN 46562
Ph: (317)630-1300
Fax: (317)237-9891
URL: National Affiliate–www.legion.org
Local. Affiliated With: American Legion.

Pittsboro

6041 ■ American Legion, Pittsboro Post 426
52b E Main St.
Pittsboro, IN 46167
Ph: (317)630-1300
Fax: (317)237-9891
URL: National Affiliate–www.legion.org
Local. Affiliated With: American Legion.

Plainfield

6042 ■ American Legion, Nysewander-Bayliff Post 329
PO Box 131
Plainfield, IN 46168
Ph: (317)839-4284
Fax: (317)237-9891
URL: National Affiliate–www.legion.org
Local. Affiliated With: American Legion.

6043 ■ Plainfield Chamber of Commerce
210 W Main St.
PO Box 14
Plainfield, IN 46168-0014
Ph: (317)839-3800
Fax: (317)839-9670
E-mail: plainfieldchamber@ameritech.net
URL: http://www.plainfield-in.com
Contact: Jeff Banning, Pres.
Founded: 1967. **Membership Dues:** nonprofit, $50 (annual) • commercial developer, $500 (annual) • apartment, $300 (annual) • financial institution (per million in local assets), $20 (annual) • hotel (plus $2/unit), $225 (annual) • business (based on number of employees), $175-$1,500 (annual). **Local.** Promotes continuous improvement of commerce in Plainfield by taking leadership in community development through actively supporting and promoting social, economic, cultural, and educational activities. **Awards:** Member Service Award. **Frequency:** annual. **Type:** recognition • **Type:** scholarship. **Recipient:** for high school seniors. **Computer Services:** Information services, member listing. **Publications:** Newsletter, monthly. Alternate Formats: online. **Conventions/Meetings:** monthly General Membership Meeting, with guest speaker - every 3rd Thursday.

6044 ■ Wheelmen, Indiana
559 Gibbs St.
Plainfield, IN 46168-1309
Ph: (317)839-1621
E-mail: carolynremax1@aol.com
URL: National Affiliate–www.thewheelmen.org
State.

Plymouth

6045 ■ American Legion, Indiana Post 27
c/o Charles B. Reeve
PO Box 279
Plymouth, IN 46563
Ph: (219)936-8827
Fax: (317)237-9891
URL: National Affiliate–www.legion.org
Contact: Charles B. Reeve, Contact
Local. Affiliated With: American Legion.

6046 ■ Indiana Morgan Horse Club
c/o Danielle Kiefer, Sec.-Treas.
16779 Lincoln Hwy.
Plymouth, IN 46563
Ph: (574)941-2035
E-mail: daniellekiefer@skyenet.net
Contact: Danielle Kiefer, Sec.-Treas.
State. Affiliated With: American Morgan Horse Association.

6047 ■ Indiana Quarter Horse Association (IQHA)
c/o Lorna Shively, Sec.
17677 W Lincoln Hwy.
Plymouth, IN 46563
Ph: (574)936-9975
Fax: (574)936-9976
E-mail: shivelyiqha@earthlink.net
URL: http://www.iqha.com
Contact: Lorna Shively, Sec.
State. Affiliated With: American Quarter Horse Association.

6048 ■ Marshall County Convention and Visitors Bureau
PO Box 669
220 N Center
Plymouth, IN 46563-0669
Ph: (574)936-1882
Fax: (574)936-9845
Free: (800)626-5353
E-mail: mccvb@blueberrycountry.org
URL: http://www.blueberrycountry.org
Contact: Mike Woolfington, Exec.Dir.
Founded: 1991. **Members:** 7. **Staff:** 2. **Budget:** $140,000. **Regional Groups:** 1. **State Groups:** 3. **Local Groups:** 3. **Local.** Promotes Marshall County, IN as a tourist destination. Members are county appointed. **Libraries: Type:** not open to the public. **Holdings:** 10. **Awards: Frequency:** semiannual. **Type:** grant. **Publications:** *Visitors Guide*, annual.

6049 ■ Marshall County Historical Society (MCHS)
123 N Michigan St.
Plymouth, IN 46563
Ph: (574)936-2306
Fax: (574)936-9306
E-mail: mchistory@mchistoricalsociety.org
URL: http://www.mchistoricalsociety.org
Contact: Linda Rippy, Exec.Dir.
Founded: 1957. **Members:** 536. **Membership Dues:** regular, $10 (annual) • life, $100. **Staff:** 3. **Local.** Individuals interested in preserving the history of Marshall County, IN. Maintains museum. **Libraries: Type:** reference. **Subjects:** history of Marshall County. **Publications:** Journal, quarterly. Contains articles on Marshall County History. **Price:** included in membership dues. **Circulation:** 550. **Conventions/Meetings:** annual general assembly.

6050 ■ North Central Indiana Association of Realtors
409 N Michigan St.
Plymouth, IN 46563
Ph: (574)935-3940
Fax: (574)935-3960
E-mail: nciar@earthlink.net
URL: National Affiliate–www.realtor.org
Contact: Mary J. Yates, Exec. Officer
Local. Strives to develop real estate business practices. Advocates the right to own, use and transfer real property. Provides a facility for professional development, research and exchange of information among members and to the general public. **Affiliated With:** National Association of Realtors.

6051 ■ Plumbing-Heating-Cooling Contractors Association, North Central Indiana
c/o Betty Leverett, Exec.Mgr.
PO Box 474
Plymouth, IN 46563-0474
Fax: (574)935-4478
Free: (866)577-7422
E-mail: phccncia@earthlink.net
URL: National Affiliate–www.phccweb.org
Contact: Betty Leverett, Exec.Mgr.
Local. Represents the plumbing, heating and cooling contractors. Promotes the construction industry. Protects the environment, health, safety and comfort of society. **Affiliated With:** Plumbing-Heating-Cooling Contractors Association.

6052 ■ Plymouth Area Chamber of Commerce (PACC)
120 N Michigan St.
Plymouth, IN 46563
Ph: (574)936-2323
Fax: (574)936-6584
E-mail: plychamber@plychamber.org
URL: http://www.plychamber.org
Contact: Doug Anspach, Exec.Dir.
Founded: 1924. **Members:** 400. **Local**. Promotes business and community development in the Plymouth, IN area. **Awards:** Distinguished Citizen. **Frequency:** annual. **Type:** recognition. **Recipient:** for positive contributions to quality of life in Plymouth area • Public Servant. **Frequency:** annual. **Type:** recognition. **Recipient:** for outstanding leadership in the public sector • Volunteer. **Frequency:** annual. **Type:** recognition. **Recipient:** for volunteering to worthwhile organizations • Youth Service. **Frequency:** annual. **Type:** recognition. **Recipient:** for exemplary service to the youth. **Computer Services:** database, list of members • information services, facts about Plymouth, IN. **Affiliated With:** U.S. Chamber of Commerce. **Publications:** *Industrial Directory*, annual. **Price:** $25.00/year • *NewsMonth*, monthly. Newsletter. Alternate Formats: online • Membership Directory, annual. **Price:** $25.00/year. **Conventions/ Meetings:** annual dinner.

6053 ■ United Way of Marshall County, Indiana
PO Box 392
Plymouth, IN 46563
Ph: (574)936-3366
Fax: (574)936-8040
E-mail: uwinfo@marshallcountyuw.org
URL: http://www.marshallcountyuw.org
Local. Affiliated With: United Way of America.

Poneto

6054 ■ Fort Wayne Area Sheet Metal Contractors Association
c/o Debra Smith
PO Box 127
Poneto, IN 46781-0127
Ph: (260)694-6518
Fax: (260)694-6556
E-mail: fwasmca@citznet.com
URL: National Affiliate–www.smacna.org
Contact: Debra Smith, Contact
Members: 6. **Staff:** 1. **Local**. Promotes the sheet metal industry. **Affiliated With:** Sheet Metal and Air Conditioning Contractors' National Association.

Portage

6055 ■ American Legion, Port City Post 260
5675 Mulberry Ave.
Portage, IN 46368
Ph: (219)762-3541
Fax: (317)237-9891
URL: National Affiliate–www.legion.org
Local. Affiliated With: American Legion.

6056 ■ Greater Portage Chamber of Commerce
2642 Eleanor St.
PO Box 1098
Portage, IN 46368-3634
Ph: (219)762-3300
Fax: (219)763-2450
E-mail: gpcoc@netnitco.net
Contact: Terry A. Hufford, Exec.Dir.
Local.

6057 ■ Hoosier African Violet Society
c/o Gary Mikita
2842 Brown St.
Portage, IN 46368
Ph: (219)763-4861
E-mail: garymikita@cs.com
URL: http://www.hoosieravs.com
Contact: Gary Mikita, Contact
Local. Affiliated With: African Violet Society of America.

6058 ■ Izaak Walton League of America, Indiana Division
c/o Charles Siar
2173 Pennsylvania St.
Portage, IN 46368-2448
Ph: (219)762-4876
E-mail: res08mep@verizon.net
URL: http://www.in-iwla.org/
Affiliated With: Izaak Walton League of America.

6059 ■ Nativity Home and School Association
c/o John Kobitz
2949 Willowcreek Rd.
Portage, IN 46368-3519
Contact: Joann Abbott, Prin.
Local. Provides support to Nativity of Our Savior Catholic School.

6060 ■ Portage Exchange Club
PO Box 255
Portage, IN 46368
E-mail: baclapp1@comcast.net
URL: http://www.portage-exchange.com
Contact: Mr. Brad Clapp, Past District Pres.
Founded: 1970. **Members:** 70. **Membership Dues:** active, $10 (monthly). **Budget:** $23,000. **Regional Groups:** 12. **State Groups:** 37. **Local**. Provides local community service programs including Service to Seniors, Youth, Americanism and National Program of Service The Prevention of Child Abuse.

Porter

6061 ■ Association of Women's Health, Obstetric and Neonatal Nurses - Northwest Chapter
c/o Aleda Waggoner, Coor.
551 N River Road Dr.
Porter, IN 46304
E-mail: aleda@bluedotweb.com
URL: National Affiliate–www.awhonn.org
Contact: Aleda Waggoner, Coor.
Local. Represents registered nurses and other health care providers who specialize in obstetric, women's health, and neonatal nursing. Advances the nursing profession by providing nurses with information and support to help them deliver quality care for women and newborns. **Affiliated With:** Association of Women's Health, Obstetric and Neonatal Nurses.

Portland

6062 ■ American Legion, Indiana Post 211
c/o Robert Guy Ayers
211 W Walnut St.
Portland, IN 47371
Ph: (219)726-4449
Fax: (317)237-9891
URL: National Affiliate–www.legion.org
Contact: Robert Guy Ayers, Contact
Local. Affiliated With: American Legion.

6063 ■ Mental Health Association in Jay County
c/o Sheron McClung
964 S Meridian St.
Portland, IN 47371-2846
Ph: (219)726-8614
URL: http://www.mentalhealthassociation.com
Contact: Sheron McClung, Contact
Local. Seeks to promote mental health and prevent mental health disorders. Improves mental health of Americans through advocacy, public education, research and service. **Affiliated With:** Mental Health Association in Indiana; National Mental Health Association.

6064 ■ Portland Area Chamber of Commerce (PACC)
118 S Meridian St., Ste.A
Portland, IN 47371
Ph: (260)726-4481
Fax: (260)726-3372
E-mail: chamber@jayco.net
URL: http://portlandchamber.jayco.net
Contact: Vicki L. Tague, Exec.Dir.
Members: 275. **Membership Dues:** regular based on number of full time employees beginning at $150, $150 (annual). **Local**. Promotes business and community development in the Portland, IN area. **Libraries: Type:** not open to the public. **Holdings:** video recordings. **Subjects:** safety training. **Awards:** Business of the Year. **Frequency:** annual. **Type:** trophy. **Recipient:** for outstanding achievement in the award area • Citizen of the Year. **Frequency:** annual. **Type:** trophy. **Recipient:** for outstanding achievement in the award area • Industry of the Year. **Frequency:** annual. **Type:** recognition. **Recipient:** for outstanding achievement in the award area • Lifetime Achievement. **Frequency:** annual. **Type:** recognition. **Recipient:** for outstanding achievement in the award area. **Computer Services:** Mailing lists, of members. **Telecommunication Services:** information service, community information. **Publications:** *Chamber Update*, monthly. Newsletter.

6065 ■ Portland Economic Development Corporation
c/o William W. Hinkle
118 S Meridian St., Ste.B
Portland, IN 47371-1905
Ph: (260)726-9395 (260)726-9311
Contact: Bob Quadrozi, Contact
Local.

6066 ■ United Way of Jay County
PO Box 204
Portland, IN 47371-0204
Ph: (260)726-7010
Fax: (260)726-4434
E-mail: uwjay@jayco.net
URL: National Affiliate–national.unitedway.org
Contact: Susan D. Reichard, Exec.Dir.
Founded: 1958. **Members:** 23. **Staff:** 2. **Local**. Promotes fundraising in the local communities; funds health, human and social service needs in the communities they represent. **Awards:** Lee G. Hall Memorial Award. **Frequency:** annual. **Type:** trophy. **Recipient:** leadership contributing. **Affiliated With:** United Way of America.

Poseyville

6067 ■ American Legion, Indiana Post 278
c/o Oliver Marquis
PO Box 344
Poseyville, IN 47633
Ph: (812)874-2420
Fax: (317)237-9891
URL: National Affiliate–www.legion.org
Contact: Oliver Marquis, Contact
Local. Affiliated With: American Legion.

Princeton

6068 ■ American Legion, Princeton Post 25
501 W Broadway St.
Princeton, IN 47670
Ph: (812)385-5247
Fax: (317)237-9891
URL: National Affiliate–www.legion.org
Local. Affiliated With: American Legion.

6069 ■ Domestic Violence Task Force of Gibson County
c/o Darcy C. Norton
225 N. Hart St., Ste.2
Princeton, IN 47670-1558
Local.

6070 ■ Indiana Suffolk Sheep Association
c/o Rachel Thompson, Sec.-Treas.
107 S Spring St.
Princeton, IN 47670
Ph: (812)385-2929
URL: National Affiliate–www.u-s-s-a.org
Contact: Rachel Thompson, Sec.-Treas.
State. **Affiliated With:** United Suffolk Sheep Association.

6071 ■ Princeton Area Chamber of Commerce (PACC)
202 E Broadway
Princeton, IN 47670
Ph: (812)385-2134
Fax: (812)385-2401
E-mail: paccoffice@insightbb.com
URL: http://www.princetonin.org
Contact: B. Todd Mosby, Exec.Dir.
Members: 180. **Local**. Promotes business and community development in the Princeton, IN area. **Computer Services:** database, of members • information services, facts about Princeton area. **Affiliated With:** U.S. Chamber of Commerce. **Publications:** Newsletter, monthly. Alternate Formats: online.

6072 ■ South Gibson Wrestling Club
c/o Kevin Trible
PO Box 1300
Princeton, IN 47670
Ph: (812)386-1223
Fax: (812)385-0525
E-mail: sunins@gibsoncounty.net
URL: http://www.southgibsonwrestlingclub.50megs.com
Contact: Kevin Trible, Pres.
Founded: 1982. **Members:** 100. **Membership Dues:** $20 (annual). **Staff:** 10. **Local**. Teaches wrestling skills to children in order to wrestle with other clubs. **Awards:** Lloyd Wallace Memorial. **Frequency:** annual. **Type:** recognition. **Recipient:** to someone promoting wrestling and volunteers time to club. **Formerly:** (2005) South Gibson Wrestling Boosters Club.

6073 ■ United Way of Gibson County
PO Box 235
Princeton, IN 47670-0235
Ph: (812)386-6120
URL: National Affiliate–national.unitedway.org
Local. **Affiliated With:** United Way of America.

Redkey

6074 ■ American Legion, Williamson-Smiley Post 401
PO Box 657
Redkey, IN 47373
Ph: (317)369-2177
Fax: (317)237-9891
URL: National Affiliate–www.legion.org
Local. **Affiliated With:** American Legion.

Remington

6075 ■ American Legion, Dewey Mc Glynn Post 280
PO Box 348
Remington, IN 47977
Ph: (219)297-3101
Fax: (317)237-9891
URL: National Affiliate–www.legion.org
Local. **Affiliated With:** American Legion.

Rensselaer

6076 ■ American Legion, Indiana Post 29
c/o Dewey Biggs
1565 N Mckinley
Rensselaer, IN 47978
Ph: (219)866-9934
Fax: (317)237-9891
URL: National Affiliate–www.legion.org
Contact: Dewey Biggs, Contact
Local. **Affiliated With:** American Legion.

6077 ■ Birthright of Rensselaer
216 W Washington, Ste.A
Rensselaer, IN 47978-2822
Ph: (219)866-4555
Free: (800)550-4900
URL: http://www.birthright.org
Contact: Germaine Schenk, Dir.
Founded: 1988. **Nonmembership**. **Local**. Seeks to help pregnant women find alternatives to abortion. Offers free pregnancy tests and maternity and baby clothing. **Publications:** Newsletter, quarterly. **Price:** free. **Circulation:** 750.

6078 ■ Indiana Bluebird Society (IBS)
PO Box 134
Rensselaer, IN 47978-0134
Ph: (219)866-3081
E-mail: ibs@indianabluebirdsociety.org
URL: http://indianabluebirdsociety.org
Contact: Ted Vesa, Pres.
State. **Affiliated With:** North American Bluebird Society.

6079 ■ Indiana Society, Sons of the American Revolution, Simon Kenton Chapter
c/o W. Craig Jackson, Pres.
470 E Amsler Rd.
Rensselaer, IN 47978
Ph: (219)886-5200
E-mail: craigj@netnitco.net
URL: http://www.geocities.com/inssar-south/simokent.html
Contact: W. Craig Jackson, Pres.
Local. **Affiliated With:** National Society, Sons of the American Revolution.

6080 ■ Psi Chi, National Honor Society in Psychology - Saint Joseph's College
c/o Dept. of Psychology
PO Box 905
Rensselaer, IN 47978-0905
Ph: (219)866-6000
E-mail: chauw@saintjoe.edu
URL: http://www.psichi.org/chapters/info.asp?chapter_id=461
Contact: Chau Wong PhD, Advisor
Local.

6081 ■ Rensselaer - Remington Chamber of Commerce (RRACC)
PO Box 194
Rensselaer, IN 47978
Ph: (219)866-8223
Fax: (219)866-8593
E-mail: chamber@nwiis.com
Contact: Renee Bruscemi, Dir.
Founded: 1967. **Local**. Promotes business and community development in Rensselaer, IN. Sponsors annual Duck Float, as well as July 4th Fireworks Festival. **Awards: Type:** scholarship. **Recipient:** for local High School students matriculating to St. Joseph College. **Formerly:** (2005) Rensselaer - Remington Area Chamber of Commerce. **Publications:** *In Focus*, monthly. Newsletter • *Jasper County Business Directory*, quadrennial. **Conventions/Meetings:** monthly Board Meeting - always second Wednesday of the month • biennial Home and Garden Show.

Richland

6082 ■ Time Out 4 Youth
c/o Sandra R. Helms
PO Box 87
Richland, IN 47634-9543
Ph: (812)359-4341 (812)449-2142
E-mail: admin@timeout4youth.org
URL: http://www.TimeOut4Youth.org
Contact: Sandra R. Helms, Pres.
Founded: 2001. **Members:** 5. **Budget:** $7,000. **Local**. Works to pass down knowledge of God's Word to the next generation. Conducts weekly community service projects, annual cookouts for Christian Talent and Karaoke. **Formerly:** (2005) T and O Outreach. **Publications:** Brochure.

Richmond

6083 ■ Achieva Resources Corporation - Wayne County
PO Box 1252
Richmond, IN 47375
Ph: (765)966-0502
Fax: (765)962-3179
URL: http://www.achievaresources.org
Contact: Dan Stewart, Pres./CEO
Membership Dues: single, $20 • family, $30 • consumer, $2. **Local**.

6084 ■ American Association of Collegiate Registrars and Admissions Officers, Indiana (IACRAO)
c/o Dennis Hicks
Indiana Univ. East
2325 Chester Blvd., WZ 116
Richmond, IN 47374
Ph: (765)973-8270
Fax: (765)973-8288
E-mail: dehicks@indiana.edu
URL: http://www.iupui.edu/~iacrao
Contact: Dennis Hicks, Contact
State. **Affiliated With:** American Association of Collegiate Registrars and Admissions Officers.

6085 ■ American Legion, Harry Ray Post 65
109 N 6th St.
Richmond, IN 47374
Ph: (317)966-1280
Fax: (317)237-9891
URL: National Affiliate–www.legion.org
Local. **Affiliated With:** American Legion.

6086 ■ American Legion, Indiana Post 315
c/o Howard Thomas
1214 S 8th St.
Richmond, IN 47374
Ph: (317)630-1300
Fax: (317)237-9891
URL: National Affiliate–www.legion.org
Contact: Howard Thomas, Contact
Local. **Affiliated With:** American Legion.

6087 ■ American Legion, Moore-Irvin Post 359
400 N 8th St.
Richmond, IN 47374
Ph: (317)630-1300
Fax: (317)237-9891
URL: National Affiliate–www.legion.org
Local. **Affiliated With:** American Legion.

6088 ■ Association of Indiana College Stores
Indiana Univ. E
2325 Chester Blvd.
Richmond, IN 47374
Ph: (765)973-8273
E-mail: mparrish@indiana.edu
URL: http://www.iubookstore.com/outerweb/aics.asp
Contact: Barbara Biddle, Pres.
State. Promotes the collegiate retailing industry. Enhances the college store industry through service, education and research. Promotes high standards of

business practices and ethics within the industry. **Affiliated With:** National Association of College Stores.

6089 ■ Centerville High School - Young Life
4444 Natl. Rd. E
Richmond, IN 47374
Ph: (765)973-9191
URL: http://whereis.younglife.org/FriendlyUrlRedirector.aspx?ID=C-917
Local.

6090 ■ Eastern Indiana Human Resource Association (EIHRA)
PO Box 2184
Richmond, IN 47375
E-mail: kimberly.parker@belden.com
URL: http://www.eihra.com
Contact: Kim Parker, Membership Dir.
Local. Represents the interests of human resource and industrial relations professionals and executives. Promotes the advancement of human resource management.

6091 ■ Girl Scouts of Treaty Line Council (TLCGS)
4245 S A St.
Richmond, IN 47374
Ph: (765)962-0225
Fax: (765)966-8870
Free: (800)595-4353
E-mail: sharlene@gstlc.org
URL: http://www.gstlc.org
Contact: Sharlene George, Exec.Dir.
Founded: 1960. **Members:** 2,000. **Membership Dues:** individual, $7 (annual). **Staff:** 7. **Budget:** $414,860. **Regional.** Girls 5 to 17 years old and adult leaders in east central Indiana and west central Ohio organized for educational programs and activities. **Affiliated With:** Girl Scouts of the U.S.A. **Formed by Merger of:** Wayne County Girl Scouts; Fayette County Girl Scouts. **Publications:** *Communique*, semiannual • *Treaty Liner*, quarterly. **Conventions/Meetings:** semiannual meeting - always 1st Thursday in May and November.

6092 ■ Indiana Four Wheel Drive Association (IFWDA)
c/o Scott Sperling, Pres.
2500 Wernle Rd.
Richmond, IN 47374
Ph: (765)966-7887
E-mail: president@ifwda.org
URL: http://www.ifwda.org
Contact: Jayson Soliday, Sec.
State. Affiliated With: United Four-Wheel Drive Associations.

6093 ■ Indiana Hospital Purchasing and Material Management Association
1401 Chester Blvd.
Richmond, IN 47374
Ph: (765)983-3074
Fax: (765)983-3176
Contact: William Stitt, Dir.
State.

6094 ■ International Brotherhood of Magicians, Ring 310 - Muncie Mystifiers (IBM RING 310)
c/o Richard Anderson, Pres.
3325 NW C St.
Richmond, IN 47374
Ph: (765)962-2076
Fax: (765)939-2183
E-mail: dick.anderson@insightbb.com
URL: http://woodencigars.com/muncie/muncie.html
Contact: Richard Anderson, Pres.
Members: 40. **Membership Dues:** full time, $20 (annual). **State.** Professional and semi-professional magicians; suppliers, assistants, agents, and others interested in magic. Seeks to advance the art of magic in the field of amusement, entertainment, and culture. Promotes proper means of discouraging false or misleading advertising of effects, tricks, literature, merchandise, or actions appertaining to the magical arts; opposes exposures of principles of the art of magic, except in books on magic and magazines devoted to such art for the exclusive use of magicians and devotees of the art; encourages humane treatment and care of live animals whenever employed in magical performances. **Affiliated With:** International Brotherhood of Magicians.

6095 ■ Junior Achievement of Eastern Indiana
c/o Christina J. Hilkert, Pres.
300 Hub Etchinson Pkwy.
Richmond, IN 47374
Ph: (765)962-0503
Fax: (765)973-3718
E-mail: jaei@globalsite.net
URL: http://easternindiana.ja.org
Local. Affiliated With: Junior Achievement.

6096 ■ Main Street Richmond-Wayne County
814 E Main St.
Richmond, IN 47374
Ph: (765)962-8151
Fax: (765)935-6197
E-mail: uptown@uptownrichmond.com
URL: http://www.uptownrichmond.com
Contact: Renee Oldham, Exec.Dir.
Local.

6097 ■ Mental Health Association in Wayne County, Indiana
c/o Ms. Kristy McKee, Mgr.
750 NW 13th St.
Richmond, IN 47374-2882
Ph: (765)966-0221
Fax: (765)966-5915
URL: http://www.mentalhealthassociation.com
Contact: Ms. Kristy McKee, Mgr.
Local. Seeks to promote mental health and prevent mental health disorders. Improves mental health of Americans through advocacy, public education, research and service. **Affiliated With:** Mental Health Association in Indiana; National Mental Health Association.

6098 ■ National Active and Retired Federal Employees Association - Richmond 536
57 Mid Dr.
Richmond, IN 47374-2033
Ph: (765)939-3421
URL: National Affiliate–www.narfe.org
Contact: Joseph R. Mcgill, Contact
Local. Protects the retirement future of employees through education. Informs members on issues affecting the retirement. **Affiliated With:** National Association of Retired Federal Employees.

6099 ■ PFLAG Richmond/Whitewater Valley
24 S 21st St.
Richmond, IN 47374
Ph: (765)935-5762
Fax: (765)966-4458
E-mail: barryc44@go.com
URL: http://www.pflag.org/Indiana.205.0.html
Local. Affiliated With: Parents, Families, and Friends of Lesbians and Gays.

6100 ■ Phi Theta Kappa, Alpha Upsilon Omega Chapter - Ivy Tech State College
c/o Leanna Angi-White
Whitewater Region
2325 Chester Blvd.
Richmond, IN 47374
Ph: (765)966-2656
URL: http://www.ptk.org/directories/chapters/IN/20513-1.htm
Contact: Leanna Angi-White, Advisor
Local.

6101 ■ Police and Firemen's Insurance Association - Richmond Fire Department
c/o James A. Sticco
87 Edwards Pl.
Richmond, IN 47374
Ph: (765)962-6637
E-mail: mijoccits61@insight.bb.com
URL: National Affiliate–www.pfia.net
Contact: James A. Sticco, Contact
Local. Affiliated With: Police and Firemen's Insurance Association.

6102 ■ Psi Chi, National Honor Society in Psychology - Earlham College
c/o Dept. of Psychology
801 Natl. Rd. W
Richmond, IN 47374-4095
Ph: (765)983-1227 (765)983-1558
Fax: (765)983-1897
E-mail: punzodi@earlham.edu
URL: http://www.psichi.org/chapters/info.asp?chapter_id=960
Contact: Diana Punzo PhD, Advisor
Local.

6103 ■ Psi Chi, National Honor Society in Psychology - Indiana University East
c/o Dept. of Psychology
Middle Fork Hall
2325 Chester Blvd.
Richmond, IN 47374-1289
Ph: (765)973-8222 (765)973-8344
Fax: (765)973-8504
E-mail: wwagor@indiana.edu
URL: http://www.psichi.org/chapters/info.asp?chapter_id=856
Contact: Walter F. Wagor PhD, Advisor
Local.

6104 ■ Richmond Area AIFA
c/o James A. Haskins, Pres.
1119 NW 5th St.
Richmond, IN 47374
Ph: (765)962-1431
Fax: (765)966-9312
E-mail: jim.haskins.byz6@statefarm.com
URL: National Affiliate–naifa.org
Contact: James A. Haskins, Pres.
Local. Represents the interests of insurance and financial advisors. Advocates for a positive legislative and regulatory environment. Enhances business and professional skills of members. **Affiliated With:** National Association of Insurance and Financial Advisors.

6105 ■ Richmond Association of Realtors, Indiana (RAR)
3108 Backmeyer Rd.
Richmond, IN 47374
E-mail: info@richmondassnofrealtors.com
URL: http://www.richmondassnofrealtors.com
Contact: Mary Grimes, Pres.
Local. Strives to develop real estate business practices. Advocates the right to own, use and transfer real property. Provides a facility for professional development, research and exchange of information among members and to the general public. **Affiliated With:** National Association of Realtors.

6106 ■ Richmond-Wayne County Chamber of Commerce (RWCCC)
33 S 7th St., Ste.2
Richmond, IN 47374
Ph: (765)962-1511
Fax: (765)966-0882
E-mail: info@rwchamber.org
URL: http://www.rwchamber.org
Contact: Frank Mazzei, CEO & Pres.
Founded: 1955. **Members:** 755. **Staff:** 10. **Budget:** $357,000. **Local.** Promotes business, industrial, civic, and community development in the Richmond-Wayne County IN area. Maintains small business development, regional manufacturing extension, and export assistance centers; sponsors professional women's network. **Libraries: Type:** reference. **Holdings:** periodicals. **Subjects:** business. **Committees:** Agribusiness; Community Development; Education; Learning Corporation; Legislative Affairs; Local Government. **Task Forces:** Business Medical Educa-

tion Linkages; Buy Local. **Affiliated With:** U.S. Chamber of Commerce. **Publications:** *Chamber NewsLink*, monthly. Newsletter • *Industrial and Wholesale Directory*, annual • *Membership Directory and Buyers Guide*, annual. **Price:** $25.00 for non-members; free to members. **Conventions/Meetings:** monthly board meeting - every 3rd Monday of the month • bimonthly Chamber Network Night - meeting - 2nd Thursday of every other month • annual Midwestern Professional Women's Conference - Richmond, IN.

6107 ■ Richmond - Young Life
4444 Natl. Rd. E
Richmond, IN 47374
Ph: (765)973-9191
URL: http://whereis.younglife.org/FriendlyUrlRedirector.aspx?ID=C-916
Local.

6108 ■ Small Business Development Center Network
c/o Cliff Fry, Regional Dir.
33 S 7th St., No. 3
Richmond, IN 47374-5462
Ph: (765)962-2887
Fax: (765)966-0882
E-mail: jkraft@isbdc.org
URL: http://www.isbdc.org
Contact: Jim Kraft, Reg.Dir.
Staff: 5. **Nonmembership**. **State**. Strives to enhace the success rate of new business formation and contribute to the growth and prosperity of existing businesses in Wayne, Union, Franklin, Fayette, and Rush counties. **Libraries: Type:** open to the public. **Holdings:** artwork, books, periodicals, video recordings. **Subjects:** all business. **Conventions/Meetings:** meeting (exhibits).

6109 ■ United Way of Whitewater Valley
33 S 7th St., Ste.5
Richmond, IN 47374
Ph: (765)962-2700
Fax: (765)966-6272
E-mail: contactus@givetheunitedway.com
URL: http://www.givetheunitedway.com
Contact: Tom Bivens, Exec.Dir.
Staff: 5. **Local**. **Affiliated With:** United Way of America.

6110 ■ Wandering Wheels Volkssports Club
c/o Thelma Goris
705 SW 18th St.
Richmond, IN 47374
Ph: (765)966-0391
E-mail: thelmajg@infocom.com
URL: National Affiliate–www.ava.org
Contact: Thelma Goris, Contact
Local. Non-competitive sports enthusiasts. **Affiliated With:** American Volkssport Association.

6111 ■ Wayne County RSVP
c/o Martha Young, Dir.
1600 S 2nd St.
Richmond, IN 47374
Ph: (765)983-7309
Fax: (765)983-7386
E-mail: myoung@ci.richmond.in.us
URL: http://www.seniorcorps.gov
Contact: Martha Young, Dir.
Local. Affiliated With: Retired and Senior Volunteer Program.

6112 ■ Wayne County Veterans Memorial Committee
PO Box 2401
Richmond, IN 47375
Local.

6113 ■ Whitewater Valley Wanderers
c/o Mary Parker
1030 S 23rd, Apt. 156
Richmond, IN 47374-0000
Ph: (765)962-0444
URL: National Affiliate–www.ava.org
Contact: Mary Parker, Contact
Membership Dues: first year, $10 (annual) • family, $5 (annual). **Local**. Non-competitive sports enthusiasts. **Affiliated With:** American Volkssport Association.

6114 ■ Young Life Greater Richmond
4444 Natl. Rd. E
Richmond, IN 47374
Ph: (765)973-9191
Fax: (765)973-9191
URL: http://whereis.younglife.org/FriendlyUrlRedirector.aspx?ID=A-IN63
Local.

Ridgeville

6115 ■ American Legion, Indiana Post 507
c/o Abe Miller
4th & Camden Sts.
Ridgeville, IN 47380
Ph: (317)857-2515
Fax: (317)237-9891
URL: National Affiliate–www.legion.org
Contact: Abe Miller, Contact
Local. Affiliated With: American Legion.

Riley

6116 ■ American Legion, Indiana Post 328
c/o Charles Raymond Fagg
PO Box 31
Riley, IN 47871
Ph: (317)630-1300
Fax: (317)237-9891
URL: National Affiliate–www.legion.org
Contact: Charles Raymond Fagg, Contact
Local. Affiliated With: American Legion.

6117 ■ Riley Township Lions Club
PO Box 109
Riley, IN 47871
Ph: (812)894-3530
URL: http://rileylions.org
Local. Affiliated With: Lions Clubs International.

Rising Sun

6118 ■ American Legion, Noah O'bannion Post 59
110 Main St.
Rising Sun, IN 47040
Ph: (317)630-1300
Fax: (317)237-9891
URL: National Affiliate–www.legion.org
Local. Affiliated With: American Legion.

Roann

6119 ■ American Legion, Indiana Post 419
c/o Robert H. Bowman
7365 W State Rd. 16
Roann, IN 46974
Ph: (317)630-1300
Fax: (317)237-9891
URL: National Affiliate–www.legion.org
Contact: Robert H. Bowman, Contact
Local. Affiliated With: American Legion.

Roanoke

6120 ■ American Legion, Indiana Post 160
c/o Robert M. Mayne
1122 N Main St.
Roanoke, IN 46783
Ph: (317)630-1300
Fax: (317)237-9891
URL: National Affiliate–www.legion.org
Contact: Robert M. Mayne, Contact
Local. Affiliated With: American Legion.

Rochester

6121 ■ American Legion, Indiana Post 36
c/o Leroy C. Shelton
PO Box 703
Rochester, IN 46975
Ph: (317)630-1300
Fax: (317)237-9891
URL: National Affiliate–www.legion.org
Contact: Leroy C. Shelton, Contact
Local. Affiliated With: American Legion.

6122 ■ Fulton County United Way
PO Box 583
Rochester, IN 46975-0583
Ph: (574)223-8929
URL: National Affiliate–national.unitedway.org
Local. Affiliated With: United Way of America.

6123 ■ Mental Health Association in Fulton County
c/o Ms. Carol Joy Holloway, Exec.Dir.
401 E 8th St., Ste.C
Rochester, IN 46975
Ph: (574)223-6870
Fax: (574)224-6870
E-mail: mhafc@rtcol.com
URL: http://www.mentalhealthassociation.com
Contact: Ms. Carol Joy Holloway, Exec.Dir.
Local. Seeks to promote mental health and prevent mental health disorders. Improves mental health of Americans through advocacy, public education, research and service. **Affiliated With:** Mental Health Association in Indiana; National Mental Health Association.

6124 ■ Pheasants Forever Central Indiana, Fulton County
725 S 650 W
Rochester, IN 46975
Ph: (219)223-6161
URL: http://pfcic.org
Contact: Troy Cowles, Pres.
Local. Affiliated With: Pheasants Forever.

6125 ■ Rochester and Lake Manitou Chamber of Commerce
822 Main St.
Rochester, IN 46975
Ph: (574)224-2666
Fax: (574)224-2329
E-mail: chamber@rtcol.com
Contact: Alison Heyde, Exec.Dir.
Members: 204. **Local**. Promotes business and community development in the Rochester, IN area. **Awards:** Community Service Award. **Frequency:** annual. **Type:** recognition • New Business Award. **Frequency:** annual. **Type:** recognition. **Formerly:** (1988) Rochester +Chamber of Commerce. **Publications:** *Rochester and Lake Manitou Chamber of Commerce Newsletter*, monthly. **Conventions/Meetings:** monthly Educational Lunches - board meeting.

6126 ■ RSVP of Fulton County
c/o Phyllis Triplett, Dir.
625 Pontiac St.
Rochester, IN 46975-1340
Ph: (574)223-3716
Fax: (574)223-4962
E-mail: phyllisrsvp@yahoo.com
URL: http://www.seniorcorps.gov/about/programs/rsvp.asp
Contact: Phyllis Triplett, Dir.
Local. Affiliated With: Retired and Senior Volunteer Program.

Rockport

6127 ■ American Legion, Jenkins Post 254
1804 S State Rd. 45
Rockport, IN 47635
Ph: (317)630-1300
Fax: (317)237-9891
URL: National Affiliate–www.legion.org
Local. Affiliated With: American Legion.

6128 ■ Spencer County ARC
PO Box 197
Rockport, IN 47635
Ph: (812)649-9538
E-mail: scarc@psci.net
URL: http://www.spencercountyarc.org
Contact: Jim Howard, Pres.
Local. Provides leadership and resources for mentally handicapped individuals of Spencer County. Reduces the incidence and limiting the consequence of mental retardation through education, research, advocacy and the support of families, friends and community. Strives to provide leadership in the field of mental retardation and physical disabilities to develop necessary human and financial resources to attain its goals. **Affiliated With:** Arc of the United States. **Conventions/Meetings:** monthly meeting - every second Tuesday.

6129 ■ Spencer County Regional Chamber of Commerce
2792 N U.S. Hwy. 231, Ste.100
Rockport, IN 47635
Ph: (812)649-2186
Fax: (812)649-2246
E-mail: scrcc@psci.net
URL: http://www.spencercoin.org
Contact: Barbie Brown, Exec.Dir.
Membership Dues: business (1-10 employees), $150 (annual) • business (11-49 employees), $250 (annual) • business (50 or more employees), $500 (annual) • individual/non-profit organization, $75 (annual). **Local.** Regional businesses in Spencer County, IN dedicated to the progress and growth of the area. **Formerly:** (1999) Rockport Chamber of Commerce.

Rockville

6130 ■ American Legion, Fellenzer Post 48
115 E Ohio St.
Rockville, IN 47872
Ph: (317)630-1300
Fax: (317)237-9891
URL: National Affiliate–www.legion.org
Local. Affiliated With: American Legion.

6131 ■ American Wine Society - Wabash Valley Chapter (AWS)
100 W. York St.
Rockville, IN 47872
Ph: (765)569-5099
Fax: (765)569-5199
Free: (888)965-WINE
URL: http://www.ticz.com/~terrevin/aws.html
Founded: 1995. **Local.** Consumer organization. Seeks to educate people on all aspects of wine. Activities include tastings, dinners, lectures, picnics, winery tours, amateur wine judging events and other wine-related social events. **Affiliated With:** American Wine Society.

6132 ■ AMVETS, Rockville Post 61
PO Box 305
Rockville, IN 47872
Ph: (765)569-3312
URL: http://webspawner.com/users/USVets
Contact: John Garland, Commander
Local. Affiliated With: AMVETS - American Veterans.

6133 ■ Mental Health Association in Parke County
c/o Ms. Nancy Swain, Exec.Dir.
3851 S 200 W
Rockville, IN 47872-7334
Ph: (765)245-2719
URL: http://www.mentalhealthassociation.com
Contact: Ms. Nancy Swain, Exec.Dir.
Local. Seeks to promote mental health and prevent mental health disorders. Improves mental health of Americans through advocacy, public education, research and service. **Affiliated With:** Mental Health Association in Indiana; National Mental Health Association.

6134 ■ National Active and Retired Federal Employees Association - Rockville 1660
229 S Hillcrest
Rockville, IN 47872-7401
Ph: (765)569-2311
URL: National Affiliate–www.narfe.org
Contact: Alan R. Ader, Contact
Local. Protects the retirement future of employees through education. Informs members on issues affecting the retirement. **Affiliated With:** National Association of Retired Federal Employees.

6135 ■ Parke County Chamber of Commerce
105 N Market St., Ste.A
Rockville, IN 47872
Ph: (765)569-5565
E-mail: info@parkecountychamber.com
URL: http://www.parkecountychamber.com
Contact: Chris Leach, Exec.Dir.
Founded: 1966. **Local.** Promotes business and community development in the Parke County, IN area. **Publications:** *Chamber Check*, bimonthly. Newsletter.

Rolling Prairie

6136 ■ Share Foundation with the Handicapped
PO Box 400
Rolling Prairie, IN 46371
Ph: (219)778-2585
Fax: (219)778-2582
E-mail: share@sharefoundation.org
URL: http://www.sharefoundation.org
Contact: Kathleen Kelly, Exec.Dir.
Founded: 1982. **Staff:** 8. **Budget:** $600,000. **Local.** Provides housing, recreation, socialization, personal growth opportunities, advocacy, and referral services to adults who are developmentally disabled. **Publications:** *The Good News*, monthly. Newsletter. **Circulation:** 11,000. Alternate Formats: online. **Conventions/Meetings:** annual meeting.

Rome City

6137 ■ American Legion, Indiana Post 381
c/o Robert W. Schermerhorn
611 Kelly St. Extension
Rome City, IN 46784
Ph: (219)854-2477
Fax: (317)237-9891
URL: National Affiliate–www.legion.org
Contact: Robert W. Schermerhorn, Contact
Local. Affiliated With: American Legion.

Rosedale

6138 ■ American Legion, Tony Kashon Post 290
10522 S Coxville Rd.
Rosedale, IN 47874
Ph: (312)548-2660
Fax: (317)237-9891
URL: National Affiliate–www.legion.org
Local. Affiliated With: American Legion.

Roselawn

6139 ■ American Legion, Roselawn Post 238
PO Box 135
Roselawn, IN 46372
Ph: (219)345-3857
Fax: (317)237-9891
URL: National Affiliate–www.legion.org
Local. Affiliated With: American Legion.

6140 ■ North Newton Area Chamber of Commerce
PO Box 268
Roselawn, IN 46372
Ph: (219)345-2525
Fax: (219)345-2121
Contact: John Morgin, Pres.
Local.

Rossville

6141 ■ American Legion, Homer Cameron Post 342
PO Box 106
Rossville, IN 46065
Ph: (317)589-8341
Fax: (317)237-9891
URL: National Affiliate–www.legion.org
Local. Affiliated With: American Legion.

Rushville

6142 ■ American Legion, Indiana Post 150
c/o Robert L. Jenkins
113 S Morgan St.
Rushville, IN 46173
Ph: (317)932-3415
Fax: (317)237-9891
URL: National Affiliate–www.legion.org
Contact: Robert L. Jenkins, Contact
Local. Affiliated With: American Legion.

6143 ■ Mental Health Association in Rush County
Rush County Courthouse, 3rd Fl.
Rushville, IN 46173
Ph: (765)932-2004
URL: http://www.mentalhealthassociation.com
Contact: Ms. Pat Springman, Exec.Dir.
Local. Seeks to promote mental health and prevent mental health disorders. Improves mental health of Americans through advocacy, public education, research and service. **Affiliated With:** Mental Health Association in Indiana; National Mental Health Association.

6144 ■ National Active and Retired Federal Employees Association - Shelbyville 813
1454 E Dover Dr.
Rushville, IN 46173
Ph: (765)932-3734
URL: National Affiliate–www.narfe.org
Contact: Sue A. Huber, Contact
Local. Protects the retirement future of employees through education. Informs members on issues affecting the retirement. **Affiliated With:** National Association of Retired Federal Employees.

6145 ■ Rush County Chamber of Commerce
315 N Main St.
Rushville, IN 46173-1635
Ph: (765)932-2880
E-mail: rccc@lightbound.com
URL: http://www.rushcounty.com/chamber
Contact: Pamela C. Leisure, Exec.Dir.
Membership Dues: apartment (plus $2/unit), $155 • automotive, agriculture, construction, manufacturing (plus $5/employee), $155 • insurance, restaurant, retail, service, wholesaler (plus $5/employee), $155 • education, $155 • finance (plus $15/million in deposit), $155 • hospital, nursing home (plus $2.50/bed), $155 • residential care (plus $2/bed), $155 • motel, hotel

(plus $4/room), $155 • real estate (plus $15/broker & $5/employee), $155. **Local**. Promotes business and community development in Rush County, IN. **Publications:** *Chamber Made*, quarterly. Newsletter.

Russellville

6146 ■ American Legion, Indiana Post 255
c/o C.W. Scribner
8433 W St., Rd. 236
Russellville, IN 46175
Ph: (317)435-2535
Fax: (317)237-9891
URL: National Affiliate–www.legion.org
Contact: C.W. Scribner, Contact
Local. Affiliated With: American Legion.

Russiaville

6147 ■ American Legion, Floyd Marshall Post 412
PO Box 22
Russiaville, IN 46979
Ph: (317)883-7354
Fax: (317)237-9891
URL: National Affiliate–www.legion.org
Local. Affiliated With: American Legion.

6148 ■ Indiana Skeet Shooting Association
PO Box 37
Russiaville, IN 46979
Ph: (765)883-5039
E-mail: wainscottw@aol.com
URL: National Affiliate–www.mynssa.com
State. Affiliated With: National Skeet Shooting Association.

St. Anthony

6149 ■ American Legion, St. Anthony Post 493
4545 S Cross
St. Anthony, IN 47575
Ph: (317)630-1300
Fax: (317)237-9891
URL: National Affiliate–www.legion.org
Local. Affiliated With: American Legion.

St. Bernice

6150 ■ American Legion, Osborn Post 108
PO Box 63
St. Bernice, IN 47875
Ph: (317)832-7333
Fax: (317)237-9891
URL: National Affiliate–www.legion.org
Local. Affiliated With: American Legion.

6151 ■ Izaak Walton League of America, Clinton Chapter
PO Box 258
St. Bernice, IN 47875-0258
E-mail: clarawalters@worldnet.att.net
URL: National Affiliate–www.iwla.org
Contact: Clara R. Walters, Contact
Local. Works to educate the public to conserve, maintain, protect, and restore the soil, forest, water, and other natural resources of the U.S; promotes the enjoyment and wholesome utilization of these resources. **Affiliated With:** Izaak Walton League of America.

St. Joe

6152 ■ Saint Joe Valley Conservation
5871 CR 60
St. Joe, IN 46785
Ph: (260)337-1011
Fax: (260)837-8101
URL: National Affiliate–www.mynssa.com
Local. Affiliated With: National Skeet Shooting Association.

St. John

6153 ■ St. John Chamber of Commerce
PO Box 592
St. John, IN 46373
Ph: (219)365-4686
Fax: (219)365-4602
E-mail: boricrs@jorsm.com
URL: http://www.stjohnchamber.com
Contact: Jim Betowski, Pres.
Membership Dues: $100 (annual). **Local**. Promotes business and community development in the St. John, IN area.

St. Meinrad

6154 ■ American Legion, St. Meinrad Post 366
PO Box 104
St. Meinrad, IN 47577
Ph: (812)357-5583
Fax: (317)237-9891
URL: National Affiliate–www.legion.org
Local. Affiliated With: American Legion.

6155 ■ Mental Health Association in Spencer County
c/o Ms. Sharon Schaefer, Exec.Dir.
1416 St. Meinrad Rd.
St. Meinrad, IN 47577-9746
E-mail: sschaefer@psci.net
URL: http://www.mentalhealthassociation.com
Contact: Ms. Sharon Schaefer, Exec.Dir.
Local. Seeks to promote mental health and prevent mental health disorders. Improves mental health of Americans through advocacy, public education, research and service. **Affiliated With:** Mental Health Association in Indiana; National Mental Health Association.

St. Paul

6156 ■ Indiana Amateur Softball Association, Region 9
c/o Don Kanouse, VP
PO Box 237
St. Paul, IN 47272
Ph: (765)525-9792
URL: http://www.indiana-asa.org
Contact: Don Kanouse, VP
Local. Affiliated With: Amateur Softball Association of America.

Salem

6157 ■ American Legion, Indiana Post 41
c/o Cecil Grimes
209 S Main St.
Salem, IN 47167
Ph: (317)630-1300
Fax: (317)237-9891
URL: National Affiliate–www.legion.org
Contact: Cecil Grimes, Contact
Local. Affiliated With: American Legion.

6158 ■ Indiana County Assessors Association
Washington County Ct. House, Ste.105
Salem, IN 47167
Ph: (812)883-4000
URL: http://www.icul.org
Contact: Eugene Trueblood, Treas.
Local.

Santa Claus

6159 ■ American Legion, Santa Claus Post 242
41 N Holiday Blvd.
Santa Claus, IN 47579
Ph: (812)937-2611
Fax: (317)237-9891
URL: National Affiliate–www.legion.org
Local. Affiliated With: American Legion.

6160 ■ National Active and Retired Federal Employees Association - Patoka Valley 1847
PO Box 491
Santa Claus, IN 47579-0491
Ph: (812)544-3320
URL: National Affiliate–www.narfe.org
Contact: Gerald Cunningham, Contact
Local. Protects the retirement future of employees through education. Informs members on issues affecting the retirement. **Affiliated With:** National Association of Retired Federal Employees.

6161 ■ Spencer County Tourism Commission
c/o Spencer Co.Visitors Bureau
PO Box 202
Santa Claus, IN 47579-0202
Ph: (812)937-4199
Fax: (812)937-4199
Free: (888)444-9252
E-mail: tourinfo@psct.net
URL: http://www.legendaryplaces.org
Founded: 1994. **Local.**

Schererville

6162 ■ American Legion, Brunswick Post 485
7485 Burr St.
Schererville, IN 46375
Ph: (219)322-5485
Fax: (317)237-9891
URL: National Affiliate–www.legion.org
Local. Affiliated With: American Legion.

6163 ■ Indiana Chapter of American Medical Billing Association
228 W Lincoln Hwy., No. 169
Schererville, IN 46375
Ph: (219)769-7785
E-mail: indianaamba@yahoo.com
URL: National Affiliate–www.ambanet.net/AMBA.htm
Contact: Patricia J. Lecyk CMRS, Pres.
State. Promotes the medical billing profession. Assists small and home medical billing professionals. **Affiliated With:** American Medical Billing Association.

6164 ■ Indiana Mortgage Bankers Association, Duneland Chapter
Countrywide Home Loans
1525 US Rte. 41, Ste.C-26
Schererville, IN 46375
Ph: (219)322-2802
Fax: (219)322-5538
E-mail: pamela_hiller@countrywide.com
URL: http://www.indianamba.org/Chapters/Duneland.htm
Contact: Pamela Hiller, Pres.
Local. Promotes fair and ethical lending practices and fosters professional excellence among real estate finance employees. Seeks to create an environment that enables members to invest in communities and achieve their business objectives. **Affiliated With:** Mortgage Bankers Association.

6165 ■ Midwest Crossroads Emmaus Community
c/o Roseanne Piercy, Registrar
2135 Robin Hood Blvd.
Schererville, IN 46375

Ph: (219)322-8038
E-mail: rrpiercy@mail.icongrp.com
URL: http://www.members.tripod.com/mwcemmaus
Contact: Roseanne Piercy, Registrar
Local.

6166 ■ Midwest Independent Electrical Contractors
c/o John Evorik, Apprenticeship Chm.
PO Box 921
Schererville, IN 46375
Ph: (219)226-0954
Fax: (219)226-0954
E-mail: gdykstra@dgelectric.com
URL: National Affiliate–www.ieci.org
Contact: Mr. Harry Stariha, Pres.
Founded: 1998. **Members:** 21. **Membership Dues:** regular/associate (based on number of employees), $790 (annual). **Staff:** 4. **Regional Groups:** 1. **State Groups:** 3. **Regional. Affiliated With:** Alaska Independent Electrical Contractors Association; Independent Electrical Contractors; Independent Electrical Contractors Association of Arizona; Independent Electrical Contractors Association, Ashland and Tri-State Area Chapter; Independent Electrical Contractors Association, Kentucky and Southern Indiana Chapter; Independent Electrical Contractors Association Redwood Empire Chapter; Independent Electrical Contractors of the Builders Association of Northwest Pennsylvania; Independent Electrical Contractors Dallas; Independent Electrical Contractors, Nashville; Independent Electrical Contractors San Antonio Chapter; Northwest Washington Chapter Independent Electrical Contractors. **Formerly:** (2005) Northwest Indiana Independent Electrical Contractors. **Publications:** Newsletter. **Advertising:** accepted.

6167 ■ Project Management Institute, Calumet Chapter
PO Box 357
Schererville, IN 46375
Ph: (708)387-1201
E-mail: admin@pmi-camulet.org
URL: http://chapter.pmi.org/calumet
Contact: John Hudson, Pres.
Local. Affiliated With: Project Management Institute. **Formerly:** (2005) Project Management Institute, Calumet.

6168 ■ Schererville Chamber of Commerce (SCC)
13 W Joliet St.
Schererville, IN 46375
Ph: (219)322-5412
Fax: (219)322-0598
E-mail: info@scherervillechamber.com
URL: http://www.scherervillechamber.com
Contact: Mary Watson, Pres.
Membership Dues: business (based on number of employees), $165-$420 (annual). **Local.** Promotes business and economic development in Schererville, IN. **Telecommunication Services:** electronic mail, mmpmary@comcast.net. **Committees:** Ambassadors; Business After Hours; Golf Outing; Government Affairs; Legislative Issues; Nominations; Ribbon Cutting Ceremonies; Spotlight Speakers. **Conventions/Meetings:** monthly luncheon - every 3rd Wednesday.

6169 ■ Society for Human Resource Management - Northwest Indiana Chapter
PO Box 662
Schererville, IN 46375
E-mail: shrmnwi@shrmnwi.org
URL: http://www.shrmnwi.org
Contact: Ms. Chrisanne Christ, Pres.
Local. Represents the interests of human resource and industrial relations professionals and executives. Promotes the advancement of human resource management.

Scipio

6170 ■ Indiana Amateur Softball Association, Region 11
c/o LeAnne Eberts, VP
4835 W 600 N
Scipio, IN 47273
Ph: (812)392-2226
E-mail: leanneeberts@yahoo.com
URL: http://www.indiana-asa.org
Contact: LeAnne Eberts, VP
Local. Affiliated With: Amateur Softball Association of America.

Scottsburg

6171 ■ American Legion, Mount-Wilson Post 473
10514 E Old State Rd. 56
Scottsburg, IN 47170
Ph: (317)630-1300
Fax: (317)237-9891
URL: National Affiliate–www.legion.org
Local. Affiliated With: American Legion.

6172 ■ American Legion, Scott Post 234
PO Box 151
Scottsburg, IN 47170
Ph: (317)630-1300
Fax: (317)237-9891
URL: National Affiliate–www.legion.org
Local. Affiliated With: American Legion.

6173 ■ Greater Scott County Chamber of Commerce
PO Box 404
Scottsburg, IN 47170
Ph: (812)752-4080
Fax: (812)752-4307
E-mail: scottcom@c3bb.com
URL: http://www.greatscottindiana.org/Scott_County/chamber/chamber.htm
Contact: Keith Colbert, Exec.Dir.
Membership Dues: gold sponsor, $500 • silver sponsor, $325 • bronze sponsor, $200. **Local.** Promotes business, industry, and agriculture through the advancement of education, quality of life, environmental awareness, and tourism in Scott County, IN. **Awards: Frequency:** annual. **Type:** scholarship. **Recipient:** for students who are chamber members or children of chamber members. **Additional Websites:** http://scottchamber.org. **Telecommunication Services:** electronic mail, info@scottchamber.org. **Programs:** Character Counts!; Scott County Leadership Academy. **Publications:** *Chamber Exchange*, monthly. Newsletter. **Advertising:** accepted.

6174 ■ United Way of Scott County
PO Box 227
Scottsburg, IN 47170
Ph: (812)752-2586
URL: National Affiliate–national.unitedway.org
Local. Affiliated With: United Way of America.

Sellersburg

6175 ■ American Legion, Indiana Post 204
c/o Wilbur M. Ruby
412 N New Albany Ave.
Sellersburg, IN 47172
Ph: (812)246-4064
Fax: (317)237-9891
URL: National Affiliate–www.legion.org
Contact: Wilbur M. Ruby, Contact
Local. Affiliated With: American Legion.

6176 ■ Kilroy Military Vehicle Preservation Association
c/o Charles Ridenour, Pres.
832 Beechwood Dr.
Sellersburg, IN 47172
Ph: (812)246-9144
URL: National Affiliate–www.mvpa.org
Contact: Charles Ridenour, Pres.
Local. Affiliated With: Military Vehicle Preservation Association.

6177 ■ Mental Health Association in Clark County
6815 Hwy. 311
Sellersburg, IN 47172-1801
Ph: (812)246-9860
Fax: (812)284-9811
URL: http://www.mentalhealthassociation.com
Contact: Ms. Mary Grimes, Exec.Dir.
Local. Seeks to promote mental health and prevent mental health disorders. Improves mental health of Americans through advocacy, public education, research and service. **Affiliated With:** Mental Health Association in Indiana; National Mental Health Association.

6178 ■ Phi Theta Kappa, Alpha Tau Sigma Chapter - Ivy Tech State College
c/o Twila Yaste
8204 Hwy. 311
Sellersburg, IN 47172
Ph: (812)246-3301
URL: http://www.ptk.org/directories/chapters/IN/16074-1.htm
Contact: Twila Yaste, Advisor
Local.

Selma

6179 ■ American Legion, Selma Post 437
PO Box 547
Selma, IN 47383
Ph: (317)282-7020
Fax: (317)237-9891
URL: National Affiliate–www.legion.org
Local. Affiliated With: American Legion.

Seymour

6180 ■ American Legion, Seymour Post 89
PO Box 907
Seymour, IN 47274
Ph: (812)522-1883
Fax: (317)237-9891
URL: National Affiliate–www.legion.org
Local. Affiliated With: American Legion.

6181 ■ Greater Seymour Chamber of Commerce (GSCC)
105 S Chestnut St.
Seymour, IN 47274
Ph: (812)522-3681
Fax: (812)524-1800
E-mail: seycoc@comcast.net
URL: http://www.seymourchamber.org
Contact: Bill Bailey, Pres.
Founded: 1944. **Members:** 460. **Staff:** 3. **Budget:** $185,000. **Local.** Promotes business and community development in the Seymour, IN area. Sponsors art show. **Publications:** Membership Directory, periodic. **Price:** free for members; $10.00 for nonmembers.

6182 ■ Jackson County Mental Health Association
PO Box 51
Seymour, IN 47274-0051
Ph: (812)522-3480
URL: http://www.mentalhealthassociation.com
Contact: Ms. Shanell Clayton, Exec.Dir.
Local. Seeks to promote mental health and prevent mental health disorders. Improves mental health of Americans through advocacy, public education, research and service. **Affiliated With:** Mental Health Association in Indiana; National Mental Health Association.

6183 ■ Jackson County United Way, Indiana
PO Box 94
Seymour, IN 47274-0094
Ph: (816)522-5450
URL: National Affiliate–national.unitedway.org
Local. Affiliated With: United Way of America.

6184 ■ National Active and Retired Federal Employees Association - Jackson County 944
3579 N 975 E
Seymour, IN 47274-9265
Ph: (812)522-5369
URL: National Affiliate–www.narfe.org
Contact: Lois M. Scheffe, Contact
Local. Protects the retirement future of employees through education. Informs members on issues affecting the retirement. **Affiliated With:** National Association of Retired Federal Employees.

6185 ■ PFLAG Seymour
PO Box 997
Seymour, IN 47274
Ph: (812)522-9515
E-mail: rmurray@hsonline.net
URL: http://www.seymour.org/community/pflag
Local. Affiliated With: Parents, Families, and Friends of Lesbians and Gays.

6186 ■ Seymour Main Street
PO Box 92
Seymour, IN 47274-2105
Ph: (812)522-2897
Contact: Nick Greemann, Chairman
Founded: 2001. **Members:** 50. **Budget:** $15,000. **Local.** Promotes the downtown area of Seymour.

Sharpsville

6187 ■ American Legion, Sharpsville Post 443
PO Box 108
Sharpsville, IN 46068
Ph: (317)630-1300
Fax: (317)237-9891
URL: National Affiliate–www.legion.org
Local. Affiliated With: American Legion.

Shelburn

6188 ■ American Legion, Stewart-Norris Post 197
824 N Washington St.
Shelburn, IN 47879
Ph: (812)397-5110
Fax: (317)237-9891
URL: National Affiliate–www.legion.org
Local. Affiliated With: American Legion.

Shelbyville

6189 ■ 4 Wheels to Freedom 4WD Club
PO Box 342
Shelbyville, IN 46176
Ph: (317)729-5752
Fax: (317)729-5930
E-mail: nascar3297@aol.com
URL: http://www.4wtf.org
Contact: Steve Tam, Pres.
Local. Affiliated With: United Four-Wheel Drive Associations.

6190 ■ American Legion, Victory Post 70
PO Box 113
Shelbyville, IN 46176
Ph: (317)392-3158
Fax: (317)237-9891
URL: National Affiliate–www.legion.org
Local. Affiliated With: American Legion.

6191 ■ Association of the United States Army, 19th Star Chapter
c/o Bernard Kruse
3556 N Michigan Rd.
Shelbyville, IN 46176-9414
Ph: (317)392-8270
E-mail: bernard.kruse@in.ngb.army.mil
URL: National Affiliate–www.ausa.org
Local. Represents the interests and concerns of American Soldiers. Fosters public support of the Army's role in national security. Provides professional education and information programs.

6192 ■ Girls Incorporated of Shelbyville and Shelby County
904 S Miller St.
Shelbyville, IN 46176
Ph: (317)392-1190
E-mail: girlsinc@girlsincshelbycounty.org
URL: http://www.girlsincshelbycounty.org
Contact: Barbara Anderson, Pres./CEO
Local. Affiliated With: Girls Inc.

6193 ■ Indiana Elks Association
c/o Harry E. Smith, Pres.
Shelbyville Lodge No. 457
321 N Knightstown Rd.
Shelbyville, IN 46176-9574
Ph: (317)392-3271
E-mail: hsmith@lightbound.com
URL: http://www.indianaelks.org
Contact: Harry E. Smith, Pres.
State. Promotes the principles of charity, justice, brotherhood and loyalty among members. Fosters the spirit of American Patriotism. Seeks to stimulate pride and respect toward patriotism. **Affiliated With:** Benevolent and Protective Order of Elks.

6194 ■ Kiwanis Club of Shelbyville
PO Box 1081
Shelbyville, IN 46176
E-mail: president@kiwanisofshelbyville.org
URL: http://www.kiwanisofshelbyville.org
Contact: Tom Reuter, Pres.
Local.

6195 ■ Shelby County Chamber of Commerce (SCCC)
501 N Harrison St.
Shelbyville, IN 46176
Ph: (317)398-6647
Fax: (317)392-3901
Free: (800)318-4083
E-mail: chamberinfo@shelbychamber.net
URL: http://www.shelbychamber.net
Contact: Tim Barrick, Pres.
Founded: 1948. **Members:** 310. **Staff:** 3. **Local.** Promotes business and community development in Shelby County, IN. **Committees:** Ambassadors; Beautification; Public Relations. **Affiliated With:** U.S. Chamber of Commerce. **Publications:** *Industrial Directory*, periodic • Newsletter, monthly. Alternate Formats: online. **Conventions/Meetings:** annual dinner - every last Tuesday of February • monthly luncheon - every 2nd Wednesday • annual Trade Fair - trade show - last Saturday of April.

6196 ■ South Central Indiana Corvette Club
824 S 500 W
Shelbyville, IN 46176-9035
E-mail: gr8vett@insightbb.com
URL: http://clubs.hemmings.com/clubsites/scicc
Contact: Dick Duvall, Pres.
Local. Affiliated With: National Council of Corvette Clubs.

6197 ■ Tri-County AIFA
c/o Owen R. Menchhofer, Pres.
406 S Harrison St.
Shelbyville, IN 46176
Ph: (812)934-4593
Fax: (317)835-7062
E-mail: insuranceguy@lightbound.com
URL: National Affiliate–naifa.org
Contact: Owen R. Menchhofer, Pres.
Local. Represents the interests of insurance and financial advisors. Advocates for a positive legislative and regulatory environment. Enhances business and professional skills of members. **Affiliated With:** National Association of Insurance and Financial Advisors.

Sheridan

6198 ■ American Legion, Indiana Post 67
c/o Kenneth V. Elliott
406 E 10th St.
Sheridan, IN 46069
Ph: (317)630-1300
Fax: (317)237-9891
URL: National Affiliate–www.legion.org
Contact: Kenneth V. Elliott, Contact
Local. Affiliated With: American Legion.

6199 ■ American Morgan Horse Association, Region 3
c/o Sharon A. Cole, Dir.
501 W 261st St.
Sheridan, IN 46069
Ph: (317)758-6245
Fax: (317)758-0075
E-mail: sherry@morganhorse.com
URL: National Affiliate–www.morganhorse.com
Contact: Fred Braden, Exec.Dir.
Regional. Affiliated With: American Morgan Horse Association.

Shoals

6200 ■ American Legion, Hanson Mc Fee Post 61
206 S High St.
Shoals, IN 47581
Ph: (812)247-2821
Fax: (317)237-9891
URL: National Affiliate–www.legion.org
Local. Affiliated With: American Legion.

6201 ■ National Sojourners, Southern Indiana No. 328
c/o SGM. Paul E. Shaw
PO Box 381
Shoals, IN 47581-0381
Ph: (812)247-2838
URL: National Affiliate–www.nationalsojourners.org
Contact: SGM. Paul E. Shaw, Contact
Local.

Silver Lake

6202 ■ American Legion, Silver Lake Post 431
PO Box 235
Silver Lake, IN 46982
Ph: (317)630-1300
Fax: (317)237-9891
URL: National Affiliate–www.legion.org
Local. Affiliated With: American Legion.

Solsberry

6203 ■ American Legion, Solsberry Post 450
RR 2, Box 279
Solsberry, IN 47459
Ph: (317)630-1300
Fax: (317)237-9891
URL: National Affiliate–www.legion.org
Local. Affiliated With: American Legion.

6204 ■ Mental Health Association in Greene County
c/o Mr. Norman Sullivan, Exec.Dir.
RR 2, Box 132
Solsberry, IN 47459-9420
Ph: (812)825-7108
URL: http://www.mentalhealthassociation.com
Contact: Mr. Norman Sullivan, Exec.Dir.
Local. Seeks to promote mental health and prevent mental health disorders. Improves mental health of Americans through advocacy, public education, research and service. **Affiliated With:** Mental Health Association in Indiana; National Mental Health Association.

Somerville

6205 ■ American Legion, Wilson-Oliver-Riley Post 462
PO Box 325
Somerville, IN 47683
Ph: (317)630-1300
Fax: (317)237-9891
URL: National Affiliate–www.legion.org
Local. Affiliated With: American Legion.

South Bend

6206 ■ ACF South Bend Chefs and Cooks Association
PO Box 1431
South Bend, IN 46624
Ph: (574)277-8636
Fax: (574)243-1207
E-mail: chefk@sbcglobal.net
URL: National Affiliate–www.acfchefs.org
Contact: Kathy M. Haney, Sec.
Local. Promotes the culinary profession. Provides on-going educational training and networking for members. Provides opportunities for competition, professional recognition and access to educational forums with other culinarians at local, regional, national and international events. **Affiliated With:** American Culinary Federation.

6207 ■ Adams - Young Life
PO Box 563
South Bend, IN 46624
Ph: (574)287-3596
URL: http://whereis.younglife.org/FriendlyUrlRedirector.aspx?ID=C-905
Local.

6208 ■ Alcohol and Addictions Resource Center
818 Jefferson Blvd.
South Bend, IN 46617
Ph: (574)234-6024
E-mail: southbend.in@ncadd.org
URL: National Affiliate–www.ncadd.org
Local. Works for the prevention and treatment of alcoholism and other drug dependence through programs of public education, information, and public policy advocacy. **Affiliated With:** National Council on Alcoholism and Drug Dependence.

6209 ■ Alcoholics Anonymous, Michiana Central Service Office
814 E Jefferson Blvd.
South Bend, IN 46617
Ph: (574)234-7007
Fax: (574)234-7043
E-mail: info@michianasober.org
URL: http://www.michianasober.org
Contact: Mable Vanett, Office Mgr.
Local. Represents individuals recovering from alcoholism. AA maintains that members can solve their common problem and help others achieve sobriety through a twelve step program that includes sharing their experience, strength, and hope with each other. **Affiliated With:** Alcoholics Anonymous World Services.

6210 ■ Alzheimer's Services of Northern Indiana
922 E Colfax Ave.
South Bend, IN 46617
Ph: (574)232-4121
Fax: (574)232-4235
Free: (888)303-0180
E-mail: alzservicesni@sbcglobal.net
URL: http://www.alz-nic.org
Local. Family members of sufferers of Alzheimer's disease. Combats Alzheimer's disease and related disorders. (Alzheimer's disease is a progressive, degenerative brain disease in which changes occur in the central nervous system and outer region of the brain causing memory loss and other changes in thought, personality, and behavior.) Promotes research to find the cause, treatment, and cure for the disease. **Affiliated With:** Alzheimer's Association.

6211 ■ American Legion, Bendix Aviation Post 284
23571 Grant Rd.
South Bend, IN 46619
Ph: (219)289-4459
Fax: (317)237-9891
URL: National Affiliate–www.legion.org
Local. Affiliated With: American Legion.

6212 ■ American Legion, Indiana Post 309
c/o Robert Johnson
726 Johnson St.
South Bend, IN 46628
Ph: (219)234-1396
Fax: (317)237-9891
URL: National Affiliate–www.legion.org
Contact: Robert Johnson, Contact
Local. Affiliated With: American Legion.

6213 ■ American Legion, Pulaski Post 357
5414 W Sample St.
South Bend, IN 46619
Ph: (219)234-5073
Fax: (317)237-9891
URL: National Affiliate–www.legion.org
Local. Affiliated With: American Legion.

6214 ■ American Legion, River Park Post 303
2503 Mishawaka Ave.
South Bend, IN 46615
Ph: (219)237-9055
Fax: (317)237-9891
URL: National Affiliate–www.legion.org
Local. Affiliated With: American Legion.

6215 ■ American Legion, South Bend Post 50
1633 N Bendix Dr.
South Bend, IN 46628
Ph: (219)287-2696
Fax: (317)237-9891
URL: National Affiliate–www.legion.org
Local. Affiliated With: American Legion.

6216 ■ American Society of Heating, Refrigerating and Air-Conditioning Engineers Northern Indiana Chapter
c/o Bob Gehrlich, Pres.
Havel Bros.
3210 Sugar Maple Ct.
South Bend, IN 46628
Ph: (574)232-6908
Fax: (574)232-3560
E-mail: bgehrlich@shambaugh.com
URL: http://home.aol.com/noindashrae/index.htm
Contact: Bob Gehrlich, Pres.
Local. Advances the arts and sciences of heating, ventilation, air-conditioning and refrigeration. Provides a source of technical and educational information, standards and guidelines. Conducts seminars for professional growth. **Affiliated With:** American Society of Heating, Refrigerating and Air-Conditioning Engineers.

6217 ■ American Society for Training and Development - Michiana Chapter
c/o Melinda Clark, Treas.
PO Box 1743
South Bend, IN 46634
E-mail: treasurer@michiana-astd.org
URL: http://www.michiana-astd.org
Contact: Lisa Malkewicz, Pres.
Regional. Promotes workplace learning and the improvement of skills of workplace professionals. Provides resource and professional development to individuals in the field of learning and development. Recognizes and sets standards for learning and performance professionals. **Affiliated With:** American Society for Training and Development.

6218 ■ American Truck Historical Society, Northwest Indiana Chapter
c/o Bryan Webster
24621 W Roosevelt Rd.
South Bend, IN 46614
Ph: (574)287-8702
URL: National Affiliate–www.aths.org
Contact: Bryan Webster, Contact
Local.

6219 ■ APICS, The Association for Operations Management - Michiana Chapter No. 57
PO Box 673
South Bend, IN 46624
Ph: (574)239-2444
Fax: (219)273-2230
E-mail: president@apics-michiana.org
URL: http://www.apics-michiana.org
Contact: Alan Chell CPIM, Pres.
Regional. Provides information and services in production and inventory management and related areas to enable members, enterprises and individuals to add value to their business performance. **Affiliated With:** APICS - The Association for Operations Management.

6220 ■ Arthritis Foundation, Northern Indiana Branch
300 N Michigan St., Ste.412
South Bend, IN 46601
Ph: (574)251-1424
Fax: (574)251-1425
E-mail: mbryan@arthritis.org
URL: National Affiliate–www.arthritis.org
Local. Seeks to: discover the cause and improve the methods for the treatment and prevention of arthritis and other rheumatic diseases; increase the number of scientists investigating rheumatic diseases; provide training in rheumatic diseases for more doctors; extend knowledge of arthritis and other rheumatic diseases to the lay public, emphasizing the socioeconomic as well as medical aspects of these diseases. **Affiliated With:** Arthritis Foundation.

6221 ■ Association for Computing Machinery, Indiana University South Bend
c/o Michael R. Scheessele
PO Box 7111
South Bend, IN 46634
Ph: (574)520-4872
E-mail: acm@iusb.edu
URL: http://www.iusb.edu/~sbacm
Contact: Michael R. Scheessele, Contact
Local. Biological, medical, behavioral, and computer scientists; hospital administrators; programmers and others interested in application of computer methods to biological, behavioral, and medical problems. Stimulates understanding of the use and potential of computers in the Biosciences. **Affiliated With:** Association for Computing Machinery.

6222 ■ Camp Fire USA River Bend Council
2828 E Jefferson Blvd.
South Bend, IN 46615
Ph: (574)234-4145
E-mail: info@campfireusarbc.org
URL: http://www.tannadoonah.org
Contact: Elaine Veevaete, Exec.Dir.
Local. Provides programs that include mentoring opportunities, environmental education, camping, and

direct child care services. **Additional Websites:** http://www.campfireusarbc.org. **Affiliated With:** Camp Fire USA.

6223 ■ Chamber of Commerce of St. Joseph County
c/o The Commerce Center
401 E Colfax Ave., Ste.310
PO Box 1677
South Bend, IN 46634-1677
Ph: (574)234-0051
Fax: (574)289-0358
E-mail: info@sjchamber.org
URL: http://www.sjchamber.org
Contact: Mark N. Eagan CCE, Pres./CEO
Founded: 1909. **Members:** 1,300. **Membership Dues:** business, $295 (annual). **Staff:** 8. **Local**. Seeks to serve the interests of member businesses through progressive leadership, advocacy and services. **Computer Services:** Online services, business directory. **Committees:** Education; Legislative Affairs. **Task Forces:** Environmental; Human Resources and Health; Taxation and Public Finance; Transportation. **Affiliated With:** South Bend/Mishawaka Convention and Visitors Bureau. **Publications:** *Book for Business*, annual. Membership Directory • *Chamber@Work*, monthly. Newsletter. **Conventions/Meetings:** bimonthly board meeting.

6224 ■ Children Need the Lord (CNL)
4600 S Michigan St.
South Bend, IN 46614-2556
Ph: (219)291-7086
Fax: (219)291-7086
URL: http://www.cnlbookstore.com
Contact: Phillip Layman, Chm.
Founded: 1944. **Staff:** 3. **Budget:** $60,000. **Nonmembership**. **Local**. Seeks to evangelize children; trains children's workers; operates bookstore. **Libraries: Type:** open to the public. **Holdings:** 200; video recordings. **Subjects:** children's stories. **Formerly:** Child Evangelism of St. Joseph County; (1998) Child Evangelism Ministries of St. Joseph County. **Publications:** Newsletter, 5/year • Newsletter, bimonthly. **Conventions/Meetings:** monthly workshop, teacher training workshop - always third Tuesday.

6225 ■ Christ Child Society of South Bend, Indiana
PO Box 1286
South Bend, IN 46624
Ph: (219)288-6028
E-mail: officer@christchildsb.org
URL: http://christchildsb.org
Contact: Teddi Murray, Pres.
Local. **Affiliated With:** National Christ Child Society.

6226 ■ Citizens Action Coalition of Indiana - North Office (CAC)
2015 W Western Ave., No. 101
South Bend, IN 46629
Ph: (574)232-7905
Fax: (574)232-7945
E-mail: cac.sbend@prodigy.net
URL: http://www.citact.org
Contact: Grant Smith, Exec.Dir.
Founded: 1974. **Members:** 300,000. **Membership Dues:** individual/organizational, $15 (annual). **Staff:** 75. **Budget:** $2,500,000. **State**. Consumer, environmental, and labor organizations; interested individuals. Represents residents of Indiana in utility, home care, farm, environmental, and other issues. Conducts research and lobbying activities. Holds Lobby Day and meetings between citizens and lawmakers. **Formerly:** (2005) Citizens Action Coalition. **Publications:** *Citizen Power*, quarterly. Newsletter. **Circulation:** 175,000. **Conventions/Meetings:** bimonthly board meeting • annual Consumer Rights Banquet • annual convention.

6227 ■ Clay - Young Life
PO Box 563
South Bend, IN 46624
Ph: (574)287-3596
URL: http://whereis.younglife.org/FriendlyUrlRedirector.aspx?ID=C-904
Local.

6228 ■ Girl Scouts of Singing Sands Council
3620 Deahl Ct.
South Bend, IN 46628
Ph: (574)273-3021
Fax: (574)273-4944
Free: (800)272-7755
E-mail: heather@gsssc.org
URL: http://www.gsssc.org
Contact: Ms. Lesa Garrison, Exec.Sec.
Local. Strives to develop potential and leadership skills among its members. Conducts trainings, educational programs and outdoor activities.

6229 ■ Greater South Bend-Mishawaka Association of Realtors
1357 Northside Blvd.
South Bend, IN 46615
Ph: (574)289-6378
E-mail: chuck@sbmaor.com
URL: http://www.sbmaor.com
Contact: Chuck Stultz, Exec. Officer
Local. Strives to develop real estate business practices. Advocates the right to own, use and transfer real property. Provides a facility for professional development, research and exchange of information among members and to the general public. **Affiliated With:** National Association of Realtors.

6230 ■ Habitat for Humanity of St. Joseph County, IN
c/o David Hatch, Exec.Dir.
402 E South St.
South Bend, IN 46601
Ph: (574)288-6967
Fax: (574)289-1954
E-mail: habitat@habitat-for-humanity.org
URL: http://www.habitat-for-humanity.org
Contact: David Hatch, Exec.Dir.
Local.

6231 ■ Indiana Association of College and Research Libraries
c/o Scott Opasik, Chm.
PO Box 7111
South Bend, IN 46634-7111
Ph: (574)520-4446
E-mail: sopasik@iusb.edu
URL: http://www.ilfonline.org/Units/Associations/IALA/index.html
Contact: Scott Opasik, Chm.
State. Enhances the ability of academic library and information professionals to serve the information needs of the higher education community and to improve learning, teaching and research. **Affiliated With:** Association of College and Research Libraries.

6232 ■ Information Systems Audit and Control Association and Foundation, Michiana Chapter
c/o Craig D. Sullivan, CISA, CPA
Crowe, Chizek and Co.
330 E Jefferson Blvd.
PO Box 7
South Bend, IN 46624
Ph: (574)232-3992
Fax: (219)236-8692
URL: National Affiliate–www.isaca.org
Contact: Mr. Craig D. Sullivan, Contact
Local. **Affiliated With:** Information Systems Audit and Control Association and Foundation.

6233 ■ Institute of Real Estate Management - Northern Indiana Chapter No. 100
c/o Sharon Piechorowski
Holladay Properties
227 S Main St., Ste.210
South Bend, IN 46601
Ph: (574)234-2860
Fax: (574)284-3799
E-mail: speach@holladayproperties.com
URL: National Affiliate–www.irem.org
Contact: Sharon Piechorowski, Contact
Local. Represents real property and asset management professionals. Works to promote professional ethics and standards in the field of property management. Strives to keep its members informed on the latest legislative activities and current industry trends. Provides classroom training, continuing education seminars, job referral service and candidate assistance services to enhance the effectiveness and professionalism of its members. **Affiliated With:** Institute of Real Estate Management.

6234 ■ Jewish Federation of St. Joseph Valley
c/o Debra Barton Grant, Exec.VP
3202 Shalom Way
South Bend, IN 46615-2955
Ph: (574)233-1164
Fax: (574)288-4103
E-mail: dbartongrant@thejewishfed.org
URL: http://www.jfedsjv.org
Contact: Debra Barton Grant, Exec.VP
Local. Serves the Jewish people-locally, in Israel, and throughout the world-through coordinated fund raising, community-wide programming, social services, and educational activities. **Additional Websites:** http://www.thejewishfed.org.

6235 ■ John Young - Wyldlife
PO Box 563
South Bend, IN 46624
Ph: (574)287-3596
URL: http://sites.younglife.org/sites/jywyldlife/default.aspx
Local. **Affiliated With:** Young Life.

6236 ■ Kiwanis Club of Potowatomi-South Bend
PO Box 4171
South Bend, IN 46634-0171
E-mail: rbernardc@aol.com
URL: http://users.michiana.org/pkiwanis/hometmpl.htm
Contact: Jerry Oberly, Pres.
Local.

6237 ■ Mental Health Association in St. Joseph County
c/o Ms. Ann Thomas, Exec.Dir.
711 E Colfax Ave.
South Bend, IN 46601-2801
Ph: (574)234-1049
Fax: (574)234-8177
E-mail: athomas@uhs-in.org
URL: http://www.mentalhealthassociation.com
Contact: Ms. Ann Thomas, Exec.Dir.
Local. Seeks to promote mental health and prevent mental health disorders. Improves mental health of Americans through advocacy, public education, research and service. **Affiliated With:** Mental Health Association in Indiana; National Mental Health Association.

6238 ■ Michiana Astronomical Society
PO Box 262
South Bend, IN 46624-0262
Ph: (574)546-3889
E-mail: ripariansmith@skyenet.net
URL: http://home.comcast.net/~michiana_astro
Contact: Dan Smith, Contact
Regional. Promotes the science of astronomy. Works to encourage and coordinate activities of amateur astronomical societies. Fosters observational and computational work and craftsmanship in various fields of astronomy. **Affiliated With:** Astronomical League.

6239 ■ Michiana Chapter of Society for Human Resource Management
c/o Terry Bush
PO Box 1921
South Bend, IN 46634
E-mail: tbush@klcpas.com
URL: http://www.michianashrm.com
Contact: Terry Bush, Contact
Local. Represents the interests of human resource and industrial relations professionals and executives.

Promotes the advancement of human resource management.

6240 ■ Michiana Corvette Club (MCC)
PO Box 4056
South Bend, IN 46634-4056
E-mail: mccsec@hotmail.com
URL: http://clubs.hemmings.com/frameset.cfm?club=mcc
Contact: Connie Fowler, Sec.
Local. Affiliated With: National Council of Corvette Clubs.

6241 ■ Michiana Free-Net Society
c/o Steve Ross, Exec.Dir.
PO Box 1054
South Bend, IN 46624
Ph: (574)280-4850
Fax: (574)282-4651
E-mail: director@michiana.org
URL: http://michiana.org
Local.

6242 ■ Michiana Gem and Mineral Society
c/o Diane Gram, Pres.
3921 Eastmont
South Bend, IN 46628
E-mail: gram@3rd.edu
URL: National Affiliate–www.amfed.org
Contact: Jeanne Finske, Sec.
Local. Aims to further the study of Earth Sciences and the practice of lapidary arts and mineralogy. **Affiliated With:** American Federation of Mineralogical Societies.

6243 ■ Michiana Peace and Justice Coalition (MPJC)
702 E South St.
South Bend, IN 46601
Ph: (574)289-2126
E-mail: michpeacejust@yahoo.com
URL: http://community.michiana.org/justice
Contact: Glenda Rae Hernandez, Contact
Founded: 1991. **Members:** 2. **Local.** Helps organize vigils, rallies, and marches against war and military spending. **Affiliated With:** War Resisters League. **Formerly:** Michiana War Resistors League.

6244 ■ Military Officers Association of America, Michiana Chapter
c/o Maj. John Romano
PO Box 6454
South Bend, IN 46660-6454
Ph: (574)272-6534
E-mail: john.romano@amgeneral.com
URL: http://www.moaa.org/Chapters/customchapter.asp?chaptcode=IN0
Contact: Maj. John Romano, Contact
Local. Affiliated With: Military Officers Association of America.

6245 ■ Mishawaka - Young Life
PO Box 563
South Bend, IN 46624
Ph: (574)287-3596
URL: http://whereis.younglife.org/FriendlyUrlRedirector.aspx?ID=C-907
Local.

6246 ■ National Active and Retired Federal Employees Association - South Bend-Mishawaka 145
18261 Farm Ln.
South Bend, IN 46637-4379
Ph: (574)273-1125
URL: National Affiliate–www.narfe.org
Contact: Eldon G. Kronewitter, Contact
Local. Protects the retirement future of employees through education. Informs members on issues affecting the retirement. **Affiliated With:** National Association of Retired Federal Employees.

6247 ■ National Association of Miniature Enthusiasts - My Favorite Things
c/o Marcia Suvelza
1891 Riverside Dr.
South Bend, IN 46616
Ph: (574)289-4274
E-mail: mmsuvelza@aol.com
URL: http://www.miniatures.org/states/MI.html
Contact: Marcia Suvelza, Contact
Local. Affiliated With: National Association of Miniature Enthusiasts.

6248 ■ North Central Dental Society
919 E Jefferson Blvd., Ste.105
South Bend, IN 46617
Ph: (574)288-4401
Fax: (574)288-4402
E-mail: sjcmedsoc@aol.com
URL: National Affiliate–www.ada.org
Contact: Ms. Kathy Karczewski, Exec.Dir.
Local. Represents the interests of dentists committed to the public's oral health, ethics and professional development. Encourages the improvement of the public's oral health and promotes the art and science of dentistry. **Affiliated With:** American Dental Association; Indiana Dental Association.

6249 ■ Northern Indiana Mountain Bicycling Association
PO Box 6383
South Bend, IN 46660
Ph: (574)257-7947
E-mail: kerian@earthlink.net
URL: http://www.nimbabike.org
Local. Affiliated With: International Mountain Bicycling Association.

6250 ■ Parents Television Council - South Bend, Indiana Chapter
c/o Mike Conway, Dir.
PO Box 1274
South Bend, IN 46624
Free: (800)848-0314
E-mail: southbendchapter@parentstv.org
URL: National Affiliate–www.parentstv.org
Contact: Mike Conway, Dir.
Local.

6251 ■ Penn - Young Life
PO Box 563
South Bend, IN 46624
Ph: (574)287-3596
URL: http://whereis.younglife.org/FriendlyUrlRedirector.aspx?ID=C-2992
Local.

6252 ■ PFLAG South Bend/Michiana
PO Box 4195
South Bend, IN 46634
Ph: (574)277-2684
E-mail: pflag@gaymichiana.org
URL: http://www.gaymichiana.org/pflag.html
Regional. Affiliated With: Parents, Families, and Friends of Lesbians and Gays.

6253 ■ Phi Theta Kappa, Alpha Tau Omicron Chapter - Ivy Tech State College
c/o Barb Schwartz
220 Dean Johnson Blvd.
South Bend, IN 46601
Ph: (574)289-7001
URL: http://www.ptk.org/directories/chapters/IN/16142-1.htm
Contact: Barb Schwartz, Advisor
Local.

6254 ■ Polish Falcons of America, Nest 4
3212 Keller St.
South Bend, IN 46628
Ph: (219)288-1090
URL: http://www.polishfalcons.org/nest/4/index.html
Contact: Paul E. Pluta, Pres.
Local. Affiliated With: Polish Falcons of America.

6255 ■ Polish Falcons of America, Nest 80
325 S Sheriden St.
South Bend, IN 46619
Ph: (219)288-3335
URL: http://www.polishfalcons.org/nest/80/index.html
Contact: Kenneth E. Staszewski, Pres.
Local. Affiliated With: Polish Falcons of America.

6256 ■ Psi Chi, National Honor Society in Psychology - Indiana University South Bend
c/o Dept. of Psychology
1700 Mishawaka Ave., DW 2134
South Bend, IN 46615-1400
Ph: (574)237-4393 (574)237-4889
Fax: (574)237-4538
E-mail: kritchie@iusb.edu
URL: http://www.psichi.org/chapters/info.asp?chapter_id=387
Contact: Kathy L. Ritchie PhD, Advisor
Local.

6257 ■ Riley - Young Life
PO Box 563
South Bend, IN 46624
Ph: (574)287-3596
URL: http://whereis.younglife.org/FriendlyUrlRedirector.aspx?ID=C-4203
Local.

6258 ■ RSVP of Saint Joseph County
c/o Pam Claeys, Dir.
1817 Miami St.
South Bend, IN 46613
Ph: (574)234-3111
Fax: (574)289-1034
E-mail: pclaeys@ccfwsb.org
URL: http://www.joinseniorservice.org
Contact: Pam Claeys, Dir.
Local. Affiliated With: Retired and Senior Volunteer Program.

6259 ■ St. Joseph County Medical Society
919 E Jefferson Blvd., Ste.105
South Bend, IN 46617
Ph: (574)288-4401
Fax: (574)288-4402
E-mail: sjcmedsoc@aol.com
URL: http://www.sjcmedsoc.org
Contact: Kathy Karczewski, Exec.Dir.
Local. Advances the art and science of medicine. Promotes patient care and the betterment of public health. **Affiliated With:** Indiana State Medical Association.

6260 ■ St. Joseph River Basin Commission
227 W Jefferson Blvd.
County-City Bldg., No. 1120
South Bend, IN 46601-1802
Ph: (574)287-1829
Fax: (574)287-1840
E-mail: sjrbcdir@macog.com
URL: http://www.sjrbc.com
Contact: Karen Mackowiak, Water Quality Mgr.
Local. Seeks to conserve, enhance and promote the natural resources and benefits of the St. Joseph River Basin watershed for present and future generations by providing vision, leadership and means.

6261 ■ St. Joseph River Valley Fly Fishers (SJRVFF)
PO Box 933
South Bend, IN 46624
Ph: (574)522-0735
E-mail: m3plus2@hotmail.com
URL: http://www.sjrvff.com
Contact: Todd Ezzell, Pres.
Local. Affiliated With: Federation of Fly Fishers.

6262 ■ St. Joseph Valley REACT
PO Box 389
South Bend, IN 46624-0389
Ph: (269)684-4609
E-mail: ajp11123@aol.com
URL: http://www.reactintl.org/teaminfo/usa_teams/teams-usin.htm
Local. Trained communication experts and professional volunteers. Provides volunteer public service and emergency communications through the use of radios (Citizen Band, General Mobile Radio Service, UHF and HAM). Coordinates with radio industries and government on safety communication matters and supports charitable activities and community organizations.

6263 ■ SCORE South Bend
401 E Colfax Ave., Ste.120
South Bend, IN 46601
Ph: (574)282-4350
Fax: (574)236-1056
E-mail: chair@southbend-score.org
URL: http://www.southbend-score.org
Contact: George Stump, Chm.
Local. Provides counseling to persons wanting to go into business as well as those already in the business. Sponsors seminars and workshops. **Affiliated With:** SCORE.

6264 ■ Sheet Metal and Air Conditioning Contractors' National Association of Michiana
3215-A Sugar Maple Ct.
South Bend, IN 46628
Ph: (574)289-7785
Fax: (574)289-7786
E-mail: smacna@constructionsite.org
URL: http://www.constructionsite.org
Contact: Kevin Smith, Pres.
Local. Affiliated With: Sheet Metal and Air Conditioning Contractors' National Association.

6265 ■ Sons of Norway, Knute Rockne Lodge 5-634
c/o Ellsworth B. Frankson, Pres.
1388 Berkshire Dr.
South Bend, IN 46614-6050
Ph: (574)291-2498
E-mail: ellsfran@aol.com
URL: National Affiliate–www.sofn.com
Contact: Ellsworth B. Frankson, Pres.
Local. Affiliated With: Sons of Norway.

6266 ■ South Bend Federation of Musicians - Local 278, American Federation of Musicians
c/o William T. Engeman, Pres.
120 W LaSalle Ave., Ste.305
South Bend, IN 46601
Ph: (574)233-8111
Fax: (574)233-9797
E-mail: sbmusic@michiana.org
URL: http://community.michiana.org/sbmusic
Contact: William T. Engeman, Pres.
Founded: 1903. **Local**. Represents musicians. Seeks to improve the wages and working conditions of professional musicians. **Affiliated With:** American Federation of Musicians of the United States and Canada.

6267 ■ South Bend Lions Club
c/o Robert A. Kord, Pres.
PO Box 867
South Bend, IN 46624-0867
Ph: (574)235-2252
E-mail: kord@1stsource.com
URL: http://www.southbendlionsclub.org
Contact: Robert A. Kord, Pres.
Local. Affiliated With: Lions Clubs International.

6268 ■ South Bend/Mishawaka Convention and Visitors Bureau
401 E Colfax Ave., Ste.310
South Bend, IN 46617
Fax: (574)289-0358
Free: (800)519-0577
E-mail: info@exploresouthbend.org
URL: http://www.livethelegends.org
Contact: Greg Ayers, Exec.Dir.
Local. Promotes tourism in the South Bend, Mishawaka, and Notre Dame, IN area. **Publications:** Newsletter. Alternate Formats: online.

6269 ■ South Bend SCORE
401 E Colfax Ave., Ste.120
South Bend, IN 46601
Ph: (574)282-4350
Fax: (574)236-1056
E-mail: chair@southbend-score.org
URL: http://www.southbendbcg.com
Contact: George Stump, Chm.
Local. Provides professional guidance, mentoring services and financial assistance to maximize the success of existing and merging small businesses. **Libraries: Type:** reference; by appointment only. **Holdings:** books, video recordings. **Additional Websites:** http://www.southbend-score.org.

6270 ■ South Bend Table Tennis Club
Brown Intermediate School
737 W Beale St.
South Bend, IN 46616
Ph: (574)261-4545 (574)233-3830
E-mail: philipms@aol.com
URL: http://www.sbttc.org
Contact: Philip Schmucker, Contact
Local. Affiliated With: U.S.A. Table Tennis.

6271 ■ Sweet Adelines International, River Bend Chorus
River Park United Methodist Church
920 S 23rd St.
South Bend, IN 46615-1702
Ph: (574)293-7460
E-mail: information@riverbendchorus.org
URL: http://www.riverbendchorus.org
Contact: Sherry Berkley, Dir.
Local. Advances the musical art form of barbershop harmony through education and performances. Provides education, training and coaching in the development of women's four-part barbershop harmony. **Affiliated With:** Sweet Adelines International.

6272 ■ United Way of St. Joseph County
PO Box 6396
South Bend, IN 46660-6396
Ph: (574)232-8201
URL: http://www.uwsjc.com
Contact: Hollis E. Hughes, Pres./CEO
Local. Affiliated With: United Way of America.

6273 ■ Urban League of South Bend and St. Joseph County
c/o Michael Patton, Interim Pres.
1555 W Western Ave.
South Bend, IN 46619
Ph: (574)287-2800
E-mail: sburbanleague@aol.com
URL: National Affiliate–www.nul.org
Contact: Michael Patton, Interim Pres.
Local. Affiliated With: National Urban League.

6274 ■ USA Weightlifting - Lynch's Gym
c/o Tom Lentych
745 S Walnut
South Bend, IN 46619
Ph: (219)289-3071
URL: National Affiliate–www.usaweightlifting.org
Contact: Tom Lentych, Contact
Local. Affiliated With: USA Weightlifting.

6275 ■ Young Life Michiana
PO Box 563
South Bend, IN 46624
Ph: (574)287-3596
Fax: (574)287-2005
URL: http://whereis.younglife.org/FriendlyUrlRedirector.aspx?ID=A-IN31
Local.

South Milford

6276 ■ Indiana Chapter of National Association of Tax Professionals
c/o Peggy Willits, EA, Pres.
Willits Tax Ser.
PO Box 8
South Milford, IN 46786-0008
Ph: (260)351-2051
Fax: (260)351-4202
E-mail: pwillits@kuntrynet.com
URL: National Affiliate–www.natptax.com
Contact: Peggy Willits EA, Pres.
State. Affiliated With: National Association of Tax Professionals.

Speedway

6277 ■ American Legion, Speedway Post 500
1926 Georgetown Rd.
Speedway, IN 46224
Ph: (317)244-9625
Fax: (317)237-9891
URL: National Affiliate–www.legion.org
Local. Affiliated With: American Legion.

6278 ■ Speedway Kiwanis Club
PO Box 24678
Speedway, IN 46224
E-mail: lpurichia@gscocpa.com
URL: http://speedwaykiwanis.org
Contact: Lisa Purichia, Pres.
Local.

6279 ■ Speedway Lions Club
c/o Jerry Ridge, Pres.
PO Box 24205
Speedway, IN 46224
E-mail: president@speedwaylions.org
URL: http://speedwaylions.tripod.com
Contact: Jerry Ridge, Pres.
Local. Affiliated With: Lions Clubs International.

Spencer

6280 ■ American Legion, Call-Payton Post 285
154 S Main St.
Spencer, IN 47460
Ph: (812)829-9088
Fax: (317)237-9891
URL: National Affiliate–www.legion.org
Local. Affiliated With: American Legion.

6281 ■ Arc of Owen County
36 Concord Rd.
Spencer, IN 47460
Ph: (812)829-3978
URL: National Affiliate–www.TheArc.org
Local. Parents, professional workers, and others interested in individuals with mental retardation. Works to promote services, research, public understanding, and legislation for people with mental retardation and their families. **Affiliated With:** Arc of the United States.

6282 ■ Owen County Chamber of Commerce and Economic Development Corporation
205 E Morgan St., Ste.D
PO Box 87
Spencer, IN 47460
Ph: (812)829-3245
Fax: (812)829-0936
E-mail: oced@ccrtc.com
URL: http://www.owencountyindiana.org
Contact: Denise Shaw, Exec.Dir.
Members: 125. **Membership Dues:** civic group and individual, $35 (annual) • employer with less than 10 employees, $120 (annual) • employer with more than 10 employees, $150 (annual). **Staff:** 1. **Budget:** $30,000. **Local**. Promotes existing businesses, community & economic development and tourism in

Owen County, Indiana. **Libraries: Type:** open to the public. **Awards: Type:** scholarship. **Formerly:** (1991) Spencer Chamber of Commerce; (1999) Spencer-Owen Chamber of Commerce. **Publications:** *News Letter*. Brochures • *Owen County Business Directory*. **Conventions/Meetings:** annual meeting - always November, Spencer, IN.

Spiceland

6283 ■ American Legion, Ralph Test Post 269
PO Box 297
Spiceland, IN 47385
Ph: (317)987-7259
Fax: (317)237-9891
URL: National Affiliate–www.legion.org
Local. Affiliated With: American Legion.

Springport

6284 ■ Indiana Christmas Tree Growers Association
c/o Gail Ratliff
8650 N 100 E
Springport, IN 47386
Ph: (765)755-3345
Fax: (765)755-3637
URL: http://www.indianachristmastree.com
Contact: Gail Ratliff, Contact
State. Affiliated With: National Christmas Tree Association. **Formerly:** (2005) National Christmas Tree Association, Indiana.

Stanford

6285 ■ Citizens for Appropriate Rural Roads (CARR)
PO Box 54
Stanford, IN 47463
Ph: (812)825-9555
Free: (800)515-6936
E-mail: carr@bloomington.in.us
URL: http://www.carri69.org
State. Works to promote fiscally conservative and environmentally sound transportation policy.

Sullivan

6286 ■ American Legion, Sullivan Post 139
PO Box 183
Sullivan, IN 47882
Ph: (812)268-5937
Fax: (317)237-9891
URL: National Affiliate–www.legion.org
Local. Affiliated With: American Legion.

6287 ■ Sullivan County Chamber of Commerce (SCCC)
4 N. Court St.
PO Box 325
Sullivan, IN 47882
Ph: (812)268-4836
Fax: (812)268-4836
E-mail: bunny@abcs.com
Contact: Joan Smith, Coor.
Founded: 1962. **Members:** 125. **Staff:** 1. **Local**. Promotes business and community development in Sullivan County, IN. **Publications:** none. **Conventions/Meetings:** monthly meeting.

Sunman

6288 ■ American Legion, Indiana Post 337
c/o Kenneth L. Diver
PO Box 184
Sunman, IN 47041
Ph: (317)630-1300
Fax: (317)237-9891
URL: National Affiliate–www.legion.org
Contact: Kenneth L. Diver, Contact
Local. Affiliated With: American Legion.

6289 ■ American Legion, North Dearborn Post 452
PO Box 30
Sunman, IN 47041
Ph: (812)623-2727
Fax: (317)237-9891
URL: National Affiliate–www.legion.org
Local. Affiliated With: American Legion.

Syracuse

6290 ■ American Legion, Wawasee Post 223
1806 S Huntington
Syracuse, IN 46567
Ph: (219)457-3261
Fax: (317)237-9891
URL: National Affiliate–www.legion.org
Local. Affiliated With: American Legion.

6291 ■ Dollhouse and Miniature Society of Elkhart
c/o Marcia B. Hicks
10011 N Wild Cherry Ln.
Syracuse, IN 46567
Ph: (260)856-2821
E-mail: chicks@ligtel.com
URL: http://www.miniatures.org/states/IN.html
Contact: Marcia B. Hicks, Contact
Local. Affiliated With: National Association of Miniature Enthusiasts.

6292 ■ Syracuse Municipal Building Corporation
311 N Huntington St.
Syracuse, IN 46567-1309
Ph: (574)457-3229
Fax: (574)457-8485
Contact: Client Houseworth, Dir.
Local.

6293 ■ Syracuse-Wawasee Chamber of Commerce (SWCC)
PO Box 398
Syracuse, IN 46567-0398
Ph: (574)457-5637
Fax: (574)528-6040
E-mail: info@swchamber.com
URL: http://www.swchamber.com
Contact: Kristi E. Plikerd, Exec.Dir.
Founded: 1972. **Members:** 135. **Membership Dues:** business ($1.50 for each employee over 50), $135-$450 (annual) • nonprofit/individual, $100 (annual). **Staff:** 1. **Local**. Promotes business and community development in Syracuse, IN. Sponsors annual Syracuse Days and Holiday Magic. **Publications:** Newsletter. Alternate Formats: online. **Conventions/Meetings:** semiannual meeting.

6294 ■ Wawasee Area Conservancy Foundation (WACF)
PO Box 548
Syracuse, IN 46567
Ph: (574)457-4549
Fax: (574)457-4432
URL: http://wacf.com
Contact: David Brandes, Chm.
Founded: 1992. **Local**. Promotes the protection of water quality in the Wawasee Watershed for today and future generations.

Tell City

6295 ■ American Legion, Perry County Post 213
Hwy. 66 W
Tell City, IN 47586
Ph: (812)547-8201
Fax: (317)237-9891
URL: National Affiliate–www.legion.org
Local. Affiliated With: American Legion.

6296 ■ Crawford/Perry/Spencer RSVP
c/o Sharon Jean Schulte, Dir.
PO Box 336
Tell City, IN 47586-0336
Ph: (812)547-3435
Fax: (812)547-3466
E-mail: rsvp@lhdc.dubois.net
URL: http://www.seniorcorps.gov/about/programs/rsvp_state.asp?usestateabbr=in&Search4.x=34&Search4.y=15
Contact: Sharon Jean Schulte, Dir.
Local. Affiliated With: Retired and Senior Volunteer Program.

6297 ■ Perry County Chamber of Commerce
645 Main St., Ste.200
PO Box 82
Tell City, IN 47586-0082
Ph: (812)547-2385
Fax: (812)547-8378
E-mail: info@perrycountychamber.com
URL: http://www.perrycountychamber.com
Contact: Cheri Cronin, Admin.Asst.
Founded: 1903. **Members:** 340. **Staff:** 1. **Budget:** $120,000. **Local**. Promotes local business and community development in Perry County, IN. **Computer Services:** Information services, business directory. **Telecommunication Services:** electronic mail, perrychamber@psci.net. **Publications:** *Chamber Business*, monthly. Newsletter. Contains articles pertinent to business growth and synopsis of chamber events for the month. **Advertising:** accepted • *Perry County Community Profile Magazine*, triennial. **Advertising:** accepted. **Conventions/Meetings:** monthly board meeting - every 1st Thursday.

6298 ■ Perry County Convention and Visitor's Bureau
c/o Jeremy W. Yackle
PO Box 721
645 Main St.
Tell City, IN 47586-0721
Ph: (812)547-7933
Fax: (812)547-8378
Free: (888)343-6262
E-mail: perrycountycvb@psci.net
URL: http://www.perrycountyindiana.org
Contact: Jeremy W. Yackle, Exec.Dir.
Founded: 1995. **Members:** 11. **Staff:** 2. **Budget:** $100,000. **Regional Groups:** 1. **State Groups:** 1. **Local Groups:** 1. **Local**. Promotes Perry County, Indiana for tourism. **Publications:** *Ohio River Highlands*. Brochure. Visitor guide.

6299 ■ Perry County Development Corporation (PCDC)
645 Main, Ste.200
PO Box 731
Tell City, IN 47586-0731
Ph: (812)547-8377
Fax: (812)547-8378
E-mail: pcdcgw@psci.net
URL: http://www.pcdcorp.com
Contact: J. Gregory Wathen, Exec.Dir.
Founded: 1990. **Members:** 15. **Staff:** 4. **Regional Groups:** 1. **Local**. Promotes business and community development in Perry County, IN.

6300 ■ United Way of Perry County
PO Box 73
Tell City, IN 47586-0073
Ph: (812)547-2577
URL: National Affiliate–national.unitedway.org
Local. Affiliated With: United Way of America.

Tennyson

6301 ■ American Legion, Tennyson Post 463
PO Box 134
Tennyson, IN 47637
Ph: (317)630-1300
Fax: (317)237-9891
URL: National Affiliate–www.legion.org
Local. Affiliated With: American Legion.

Terre Haute

6302 ■ AAA Hoosier Motor Club
1400 S Third St.
Terre Haute, IN 47802-1092
Ph: (812)232-2338
Local.

6303 ■ Air Conditioning Contractors of America, Wabash Valley Chapter
c/o Jeff Paitson, Chapter Exec.
741 S Dobbs Glenn Ct.
Terre Haute, IN 47803
Ph: (812)232-2347
Fax: (812)232-3933
E-mail: pb.heat@gte.net
URL: National Affiliate–www.acca.org
Contact: Jeff Paitson, Chapter Exec.
Local. Works to represent contractors involved in installation and service of heating, air conditioning, and refrigeration systems. **Affiliated With:** Air Conditioning Contractors of America.

6304 ■ Alcoholics Anonymous, Wabash Valley Intergroup
PO Box 8102
Terre Haute, IN 47808
Ph: (812)234-0827 (812)460-4311
E-mail: penniwel@feverdream.com
URL: http://www.feverdream.com/aa.htm
Local. Individuals recovering from alcoholism. Strives to maintain that members can solve their common problem and help others achieve sobriety through a twelve step program that includes sharing their experience, strength, and hope with each other. **Affiliated With:** Alcoholics Anonymous World Services.

6305 ■ American Cancer Society, Wabash Valley Indiana Area Service Center
705 Putnam St.
Terre Haute, IN 47802
Ph: (812)232-2679
Fax: (812)232-2741
URL: National Affiliate–www.cancer.org
Local. Affiliated With: American Cancer Society.

6306 ■ American Chemical Society, Wabash Valley Section
c/o Jonathan Oswald Brooks, Chm.
909 Barton Ave.
Terre Haute, IN 47803-2749
Ph: (812)238-9828
E-mail: j.o.brooks@att.net
URL: National Affiliate–acswebcontent.acs.org
Contact: Jonathan Oswald Brooks, Chm.
Local. Represents the interests of individuals dedicated to the advancement of chemistry in all its branches. Provides opportunities for peer interaction and career development. **Affiliated With:** American Chemical Society.

6307 ■ American Guild of Organists, Wabash Valley (527)
c/o Gary L. Jenkins
382 Francis Ave. Ct.
Terre Haute, IN 47804-1080
Ph: (812)466-1584
E-mail: garyjenkins@juno.com
URL: http://www.wabashvalleyago.org
Contact: Gary L. Jenkins, Dean
Local. Affiliated With: American Guild of Organists.

6308 ■ American Legion, Carl Mount Post 104
2690 Ft. Harrison Rd.
Terre Haute, IN 47805
Ph: (812)232-6506
Fax: (317)237-9891
URL: National Affiliate–www.legion.org
Local. Affiliated With: American Legion.

6309 ■ American Legion, Fort Harrison Post 40
2150 N 3rd St.
Terre Haute, IN 47807
Ph: (317)630-1300
Fax: (317)237-9891
URL: National Affiliate–www.legion.org
Local. Affiliated With: American Legion.

6310 ■ American Legion, Pioneer Post 340
2149 Tippecanoe St.
Terre Haute, IN 47807
Ph: (812)232-3581
Fax: (317)237-9891
URL: National Affiliate–www.legion.org
Local. Affiliated With: American Legion.

6311 ■ American Legion, Prairie Creek Post 404
14766 S State Rd. 63
Terre Haute, IN 47802
Ph: (812)898-2255
Fax: (317)237-9891
URL: National Affiliate–www.legion.org
Local. Affiliated With: American Legion.

6312 ■ American Legion, Wayne Newton Post 346
1346 Wabash Ave.
Terre Haute, IN 47807
Ph: (317)630-1300
Fax: (317)237-9891
URL: National Affiliate–www.legion.org
Local. Affiliated With: American Legion.

6313 ■ American Society of Women Accountants, Terre Haute Chapter No. 008
c/o Judy Roby, EA, Pres.
Roby Tax Ser.
817 S Prospect St.
Terre Haute, IN 47802
Ph: (812)234-4619
Fax: (812)234-4619
E-mail: robypauljudy@aol.com
URL: National Affiliate–www.aswa.org
Contact: Judy Roby EA, Pres.
Local. Affiliated With: American Society of Women Accountants.

6314 ■ Arc of Vigo County
89 Cherry St.
Terre Haute, IN 47807
Ph: (812)232-4112
URL: National Affiliate–www.TheArc.org
Contact: Pam Hunter, Contact
Local. Parents, professional workers, and others interested in individuals with mental retardation. Works to promote services, research, public understanding, and legislation for people with mental retardation and their families. **Affiliated With:** Arc of the United States.

6315 ■ Association for Computing Machinery, Rose-Hulman Institute of Technology
c/o Andy Kinley, Sponsor
Campus Mail No. 102
5500 Wabash Ave.
Terre Haute, IN 47803-3999
Ph: (812)877-8974
Fax: (812)872-6060
E-mail: acm@cs.rose-hulman.edu
URL: National Affiliate–www.acm.org
Contact: Sarah White, Chair
Local. Biological, medical, behavioral, and computer scientists; hospital administrators; programmers and others interested in application of computer methods to biological, behavioral, and medical problems. Stimulates understanding of the use and potential of computers in the Biosciences. **Affiliated With:** Association for Computing Machinery.

6316 ■ Association of Women's Health, Obstetric and Neonatal Nurses - Evansville Chapter
c/o Kim Butcher, Coor.
302 Welworth Ave.
Terre Haute, IN 47804
E-mail: dcochran@uhhg.org
URL: National Affiliate–www.awhonn.org
Contact: Kim Butcher, Coor.
Local. Represents registered nurses and other health care providers who specialize in obstetric, women's health, and neonatal nursing. Advances the nursing profession by providing nurses with information and support to help them deliver quality care for women and newborns. **Affiliated With:** Association of Women's Health, Obstetric and Neonatal Nurses.

6317 ■ Association of Women's Health, Obstetric and Neonatal Nurses - West Central Illiana Chapter
c/o Dena Cochran, Coor.
1606 N 7th St.
Terre Haute, IN 47804
E-mail: dcochran@uhhg.org
URL: National Affiliate–www.awhonn.org
Contact: Dena Cochran, Coor.
Local. Represents registered nurses and other health care providers who specialize in obstetric, women's health, and neonatal nursing. Advances the nursing profession by providing nurses with information and support to help them deliver quality care for women and newborns. **Affiliated With:** Association of Women's Health, Obstetric and Neonatal Nurses.

6318 ■ Covered Bridge Girl Scout Council
1100 Girl Scout Ln.
Terre Haute, IN 47807
Ph: (812)232-0104
Fax: (812)232-8738
Free: (800)232-0104
E-mail: info@girlscoutlane.org
URL: http://www.coveredbridgegirlscouts.org
Local. Young girls and adult volunteers, corporate, government and individual supporters. Strives to develop potential and leadership skills among its members. Conducts trainings, educational programs and outdoor activities.

6319 ■ Exchange Club of Terre Haute
PO Box 10296
Terre Haute, IN 47801
Ph: (812)235-1518
Fax: (812)234-2330
E-mail: linda@exchangeclubofterrehaute.com
URL: http://www.exchangeclubofterrehaute.com
Contact: Lynn May, Pres.
Local.

6320 ■ Flat-Coated Retriever Society of America (FCRSA)
c/o Nancy Schenck, Pres.
3652 N Country Rd.
Terre Haute, IN 47805
Ph: (812)877-0425
E-mail: desteny@abcs.com
URL: http://www.fcrsainc.org
Contact: Nancy Schenck, Pres.
State. Affiliated With: American Kennel Club.

6321 ■ Greater Terre Haute Chamber of Commerce
643 Wabash Ave.
PO Box 689
Terre Haute, IN 47808-0689
Ph: (812)232-2391
Fax: (812)232-2905
E-mail: kcraig@terrehautechamber.com
URL: http://www.terrahaute.com/chamber
Contact: G. Roderick Henry, Pres./CEO
Founded: 1906. **Members:** 800. **Budget:** $380,000. **Local.** Businesses, individuals, and professionals. Promotes business and community development in Wabash Valley, including west central Indiana and east central Illinois. **Publications:** *Valley Business Review*, monthly. Newsletter. **Price:** free.

6322 ■ Greater Wabash Valley SCORE
c/o David Mirchell, Chm.
CINERY Ser. Bldg.
301 Home Ave.
Terre Haute, IN 47803
Ph: (812)231-6763
Fax: (812)231-6777
E-mail: scorechapter661@aol.com
URL: http://www.scorechapter661.org/index.htm

Local. Promotes business and community development in the Terre Haute, IN area. Conducts business education seminars and workshops to those wanting to start a business.

6323 ■ Home Builders Association of Greater Terre Haute
c/o Executive Officer
2747 Sidenbender Rd
Terre Haute, IN 47802
Ph: (812)234-5736
Fax: (812)234-3066
E-mail: hba@thnet.com
URL: National Affiliate–www.nahb.org

Members: 250. **Membership Dues:** all, $320 (annual). **Staff:** 1. **Budget:** $150,000. **Local**. Single and multifamily home builders, commercial builders, and others associated with the building industry. **Awards: Frequency:** annual. **Type:** scholarship. **Recipient:** student in construction. **Affiliated With:** National Association of Home Builders. **Publications:** *Under Construction*, monthly. Newsletter. **Advertising:** accepted.

6324 ■ Indiana Amateur Softball Association
c/o Wayne Myers, Commissioner
3300 S 5th St.
Terre Haute, IN 47802
Ph: (812)234-0339
Fax: (812)234-6369
E-mail: inasacomm@aol.com
URL: http://www.indiana-asa.org
Contact: Wayne Myers, Commissioner

State. **Affiliated With:** Amateur Softball Association of America.

6325 ■ Indiana Amateur Softball Association, Region 7
c/o John Benton, VP
8033 E Acorn St.
Terre Haute, IN 47803
Ph: (812)877-2566
URL: http://www.indiana-asa.org
Contact: John Benton, VP

Local. **Affiliated With:** Amateur Softball Association of America.

6326 ■ Indiana Fox Trotter Association
c/o Charla McCullough
7382 E Devonald Ave.
Terre Haute, IN 47805
E-mail: cmdomino2000@aol.com
URL: http://www.indianafoxtrotter.com

State. **Affiliated With:** Missouri Fox Trotting Horse Breed Association.

6327 ■ Indiana Mortgage Bankers Association, Wabash Valley Chapter
Wells Fargo Home Mortgage
403 Wabash Ave.
Terre Haute, IN 47807
Ph: (812)478-6224
Fax: (812)234-6331
E-mail: janice.l.robinson@wellsfargo.com
URL: http://www.indianamba.org/Chapters/Wabash_Valley.htm
Contact: Jan Robinson CRMP, Pres.

Local. Promotes fair and ethical lending practices and fosters professional excellence among real estate finance employees. Seeks to create an environment that enables members to invest in communities and achieve their business objectives. **Affiliated With:** Mortgage Bankers Association.

6328 ■ Indiana Rural Health Association (IRHA)
PO Box 10366
Terre Haute, IN 47801
Ph: (812)478-3919
Fax: (812)232-8602
E-mail: mcrhscs@uhhg.org
URL: http://www.indianaruralhealth.org
Contact: Sarah Snider MBA, Pres.

Founded: 1997. **Membership Dues:** individual, $25 (annual) • student/community, $10 (annual) • organization, $200 (annual). **Staff:** 5. **State**. Provides leadership for the improvement of rural health. Sets a forum for assessing health care system and leadership resources. Identifies the needs and problems of rural health communities in Indiana. **Awards:** Outstanding Educator Award. **Frequency:** annual. **Type:** recognition. **Recipient:** for outstanding contributions to the body of knowledge of rural health. **Projects:** Bioterrorism; Rural Health Outreach. **Affiliated With:** National Rural Health Association. **Publications:** *IRHA News*, quarterly. Newsletter. Alternate Formats: online. **Conventions/Meetings:** annual conference, with speakers - always June.

6329 ■ Indiana Society, Sons of the American Revolution, John Martin Chapter
c/o Gene Printz, Pres.
7707 Sycamore Knolls St.
Terre Haute, IN 47802
Ph: (812)299-2577
E-mail: printz@gte.net
URL: http://www.geocities.com/inssar-south/johnmart.html
Contact: Gene Printz, Pres.

Local. **Affiliated With:** National Society, Sons of the American Revolution.

6330 ■ Indiana Student Financial Aid Association (ISFAA)
c/o Melinda Middleton, Pres.
Rose-Hulman Inst. of Tech.
5500 Wabash Ave.
Terre Haute, IN 47803
Ph: (812)877-8259
Fax: (812)877-8746
E-mail: melinda.middleton@rose-hulman.edu
URL: http://www.isfaa.org
Contact: Melinda Middleton, Pres.

State. Represents the interests and needs of students, faculties and other persons involved in student financial aid. Promotes student aid legislation, regulatory analysis and professional development of financial aid legislators. Seeks to improve activities relating to the quality and improvement of student financial assistance in Higher Education institutions. **Affiliated With:** National Association of Student Financial Aid Administrators.

6331 ■ Institute of Management Accountants, Wabash Valley Chapter
2306 N 7th St.
Terre Haute, IN 47804
Ph: (812)231-7108
Fax: (812)231-7294
E-mail: tsullivan@tri-industries.com
URL: http://www.imawabashvalley.imanet.org
Contact: Tim Sullivan, Sec.

Founded: 1944. **Members:** 58. **Local**. Promotes professional and ethical standards. Equips members and students with knowledge and training required for the accounting profession. **Affiliated With:** Institute of Management Accountants. **Publications:** *The Analyst*. Newsletter. Alternate Formats: online.

6332 ■ Junior Achievement of the Wabash Valley
c/o Veronica L. Dougherty, Pres.
35 Southland Shopping Ctr.
Terre Haute, IN 47802
Ph: (812)232-6230
Fax: (812)234-9044
E-mail: jaterreh@gte.net
URL: http://jawv.ja.org
Contact: Veronica L. Dougherty, Pres.

Founded: 1965. **Regional**. Provides economic and free enterprise education for students in grades K-12 as they prepare for futures in the U.S. economy. **Affiliated With:** Junior Achievement. **Also Known As:** (2005) JA of the Wabash Valley.

6333 ■ Mental Health Association in Vigo County
c/o Ms. Myra Wilkey, Exec.Dir.
620 8th Ave.
Terre Haute, IN 47804-2744
Ph: (812)232-5681
Fax: (812)232-9467
URL: http://www.mentalhealthassociation.com
Contact: Ms. Myra Wilkey, Exec.Dir.

Local. Seeks to promote mental health and prevent mental health disorders. Improves mental health of Americans through advocacy, public education, research and service. **Affiliated With:** Mental Health Association in Indiana; National Mental Health Association.

6334 ■ Military Officers Association of America, Ernie Pyle Chapter
c/o Lt.Col. Harry James
3637 Emarquette Ave.
Terre Haute, IN 47805-1049
Ph: (812)299-4601
URL: National Affiliate–www.moaa.org
Contact: Lt.Col. Harry James, Contact

Local. **Affiliated With:** Military Officers Association of America.

6335 ■ Mothers Against Drunk Driving, Wabash Valley Chapter (MADD)
PO Box 3265
Terre Haute, IN 47803
Ph: (812)238-2280
Free: (877)478-0125
E-mail: maddwabv@gte.net
URL: National Affiliate–www.madd.org
Contact: Marcia Stevens, Pres.

Founded: 1983. **Members:** 100. **Membership Dues:** individual, $20 (annual) • family, $40 (annual). **State Groups:** 1. **Local Groups:** 1. **Local**. Victims of drunk driving and other concerned citizens in Clay, Parke, Putnam, Sullivan, Vermillion, and Vigo counties, IN. Mobilizes victims and their allies to establish that impaired driving is unacceptable and a criminal offense. Works to increase public awareness of the problem and to educate the public about the drinking and driving problem. Seeks to improve the laws and the judicial system and promote corresponding policies, programs, and personal accountability. Works with first time offenders. **Affiliated With:** Mothers Against Drunk Driving. **Publications:** Newsletter, quarterly. Contains information and meeting notices. **Price:** free. **Circulation:** 450. **Conventions/Meetings:** monthly meeting - every 3rd Saturday.

6336 ■ NAIFA-Terre Haute
c/o Dewayne Hauck, Sec.
3000 Poplar
Terre Haute, IN 47803
Ph: (812)478-9748
Fax: (812)232-7573
E-mail: seburr912@aol.com
URL: National Affiliate–naifa.org
Contact: Dewayne Hauck, Sec.

Local. Represents the interests of insurance and financial advisors. Advocates for a positive legislative and regulatory environment. Enhances business and professional skills of members. **Affiliated With:** National Association of Insurance and Financial Advisors.

6337 ■ National Active and Retired Federal Employees Association - Terre Haute 327
1910 S 19 St.
Terre Haute, IN 47802-2532
Ph: (812)235-3571
URL: National Affiliate–www.narfe.org
Contact: Burt Mains, Contact
Local. Protects the retirement future of employees through education. Informs members on issues affecting the retirement. **Affiliated With:** National Association of Retired Federal Employees.

6338 ■ Pheasants Forever Central Indiana, Wabash Valley
4600 Lafayette Ave. N
Terre Haute, IN 47805
Ph: (812)466-6719
URL: http://pfcic.org
Contact: Kevin Smith, Pres.
Local. **Affiliated With:** Pheasants Forever.

6339 ■ Phi Theta Kappa, Alpha Phi Eta Chapter - Ivy Tech State College
c/o Leslie Stultz
Terre Haute Campus
7999 US Hwy. 41 S
Terre Haute, IN 47802
Ph: (812)299-2227
URL: http://www.ptk.org/directories/chapters/IN/20518-1.htm
Contact: Leslie Stultz, Advisor
Local.

6340 ■ Police and Firemen's Insurance Association - Terre Haute Fire Department
c/o Robert L. Kiefner
2304 N 11th St.
Terre Haute, IN 47804
Ph: (812)460-1279
URL: National Affiliate–www.pfia.net
Contact: Robert L. Kiefner, Contact
Local. **Affiliated With:** Police and Firemen's Insurance Association.

6341 ■ Psi Chi, National Honor Society in Psychology - Indiana State University
c/o Dept. of Psychology
Root Hall
Indiana State Univ.
200 N Seventh St.
Terre Haute, IN 47809
Ph: (812)237-2445 (812)237-2455
Fax: (812)237-4378
E-mail: lizo@indstate.edu
URL: National Affiliate–www.psichi.org
Local. **Affiliated With:** Psi Chi, National Honor Society in Psychology.

6342 ■ Risk and Insurance Management Society, Indiana Chapter
c/o William Chattin
403 Jones
Terre Haute, IN 47809
Ph: (812)230-2893
E-mail: isstu1@isugw.indstate.edu
URL: http://indiana.rims.org
Contact: David Lacey, Pres.
State. Seeks to promote the discipline of risk management and enhance the image of professional risk managers. Fosters the educational and professional development of risk managers and others involved in the risk management and insurance industry. **Affiliated With:** Risk and Insurance Management Society.

6343 ■ Society of Automotive Engineers - Indiana State University-Terre Haute
N 6th St.
Terre Haute, IN 47809-0001
Ph: (812)237-3353
E-mail: wncastner@msn.com
URL: National Affiliate–www.sae.org
Contact: N. Wayne Castner, Contact
Local. Advances the engineering mobility systems. Provides technical information and expertise used in designing, building, maintaining and operating self-propelled vehicles, whether land, sea, air or space based. Collects and disseminates information on cars, trucks, aircraft, space vehicles, off-highway vehicles, marine equipment and engine of all types. Fosters information exchange among the worldwide automotive and aerospace communities. **Affiliated With:** SAE International - Society of Automotive Engineers.

6344 ■ Terre Haute Area Association of Realtors, Indiana
1616 S 13th St.
Terre Haute, IN 47802
Ph: (812)234-8732
Fax: (812)238-2213
E-mail: thaar@thaar.com
URL: http://www.thaar.com
Contact: Mary Strickland, Exec. Officer
Local. Strives to develop real estate business practices. Advocates the right to own, use and transfer real property. Provides a facility for professional development, research and exchange of information among members and to the general public. **Affiliated With:** National Association of Realtors.

6345 ■ Terre Haute Convention and Visitors Bureau
643 Wabash Ave.
Terre Haute, IN 47807
Ph: (812)234-5555
Fax: (812)234-6750
Free: (800)366-3043
E-mail: info@terrehaute.com
URL: http://www.terrehaute.com
Contact: David A. Patterson, Exec.Dir.
Founded: 1980. **Staff:** 5. **Budget:** $593,000. **Nonmembership**. **Local**. Promotes the development and growth of the Convention & Visitors industry in Vigo County. Serves as a catalyst to stimulate new interest and awareness of Terre Haute and Vigo County as a visitor destination, providing services to major group markets such as conventions, meetings, sporting events, motorcoaches and other special events. Provides information about local lodging facilities, restaurants, attractions, events to all visitors.

6346 ■ Theta Xi, Kappa Chapter — Rose-Hulman Institute of Technology
902 S 6th St.
Terre Haute, IN 47807
Ph: (812)235-3262
E-mail: officers@thetaxi.rose-hulman.edu
URL: http://thetaxi.rose-hulman.edu
Founded: 1907. **Local**. **Affiliated With:** Theta Xi.

6347 ■ United Way of the Wabash Valley
PO Box 3094
Terre Haute, IN 47803-0094
Ph: (812)235-6287
Fax: (812)235-3901
Free: (800)823-9301
E-mail: joan.kutlu@unitedway.org
URL: http://www.uwwv.org
Contact: Joan Kutlu, Office Mgr.
Local. **Affiliated With:** United Way of America.

6348 ■ Vigo Parke Vermillion Medical Society (VPVMS)
PO Box 986
Terre Haute, IN 47808
E-mail: vpvmed@vpvmed.org
URL: http://www.vpvmed.org
Contact: Durga Guha MD, Pres.-Elect
Local. Advances the art and science of medicine. Promotes patient care and the betterment of public health. **Affiliated With:** Indiana State Medical Association.

6349 ■ Wabash Valley Audubon Society
PO Box 2338
Terre Haute, IN 47802-2338
URL: National Affiliate–www.audubon.org
Local. Works to conserve and restore natural ecosystems, focusing on birds and other wildlife for the benefit of humanity and the earth's biological diversity. **Affiliated With:** National Audubon Society.

6350 ■ Wabash Valley Coin Club (WVCC)
PO Box 3
Terre Haute, IN 47808-0003
Ph: (812)235-0884
E-mail: wvcoinclub@aol.com
URL: http://wvccol.tripod.com
Contact: Robert Randolph, Pres.
Regional. **Affiliated With:** American Numismatic Association.

6351 ■ Wabash Valley REACT
1447 S 19th St.
Terre Haute, IN 47803
Ph: (812)238-0063
E-mail: joyjuli8@juno.com
URL: http://www.reactintl.org/teaminfo/usa_teams/teams-usin.htm
Local. Trained communication experts and professional volunteers. Provides volunteer public service and emergency communications through the use of radios (Citizen Band, General Mobile Radio Service, UHF and HAM). Coordinates with radio industries and government on safety communication matters and supports charitable activities and community organizations.

6352 ■ Wabash Valley Youth for Christ
PO Box 3052
Terre Haute, IN 47803
Ph: (812)232-3781
Fax: (812)232-2009
URL: National Affiliate–www.yfc.net
Local. **Affiliated With:** Youth for Christ/U.S.A.

6353 ■ WICAA RSVP in Clay/Putnam and Vigo Counties
c/o Jeraldine H. Sowards, Dir.
PO Box 1018
Terre Haute, IN 47808
Ph: (812)232-1264
Fax: (812)232-9634
E-mail: jsowards@wicaa.org
URL: http://www.seniorcorps.gov
Contact: Jeraldine H. Sowards, Dir.
Local. **Affiliated With:** Retired and Senior Volunteer Program.

6354 ■ Zorah Shriners
c/o William E. Knauer
420 N 7th St.
Terre Haute, IN 47807
Ph: (812)232-8232
Fax: (812)232-8233
URL: http://zorahtemple.org
Contact: William E. Knauer, Potentate
Local. **Affiliated With:** Imperial Council of the Ancient Arabic Order of the Nobles of the Mystic Shrine for North America.

Thorntown

6355 ■ American Legion, Thorntown Post 218
PO Box 44
Thorntown, IN 46071
Ph: (317)630-1300
Fax: (317)237-9891
URL: National Affiliate–www.legion.org
Local. **Affiliated With:** American Legion.

Tipton

6356 ■ American Legion, Charles Sturdevant Post 46
129 N Independence St.
Tipton, IN 46072
Ph: (317)675-4180
Fax: (317)237-9891
URL: National Affiliate–www.legion.org
Local. **Affiliated With:** American Legion.

6357 ■ Puppeteers of America - Indiana Puppetry Guild
c/o Dan Cox, Pres./Ed.
446 N Main St.
Tipton, IN 46072
Ph: (765)675-6233
E-mail: dcox@nupoint.net
URL: National Affiliate–www.puppeteers.org
Contact: Dan Cox, Pres./Ed.
State.

6358 ■ Tipton County Chamber of Commerce (TCCC)
136 E Jefferson St.
Tipton, IN 46072
Ph: (765)675-7533
Fax: (765)675-8917
E-mail: ditimm@tds.net
URL: http://www.tiptonchamber.com
Contact: Diane R. Timm, Exec.Dir.
Founded: 1889. **Members:** 150. **Membership Dues:** business (plus $5 per employee), $100 (annual) • financial service/professional/public utility, $100 (annual) • church/library/school/club and organization/nonprofit, $100 (annual) • individual, $50 (annual) • retiree, $25 (annual) • associate, $250 (annual). **Staff:** 1. **Budget:** $25,000. **Local.** Businesses and individuals organized to promote economic and community development in Tipton County, IN. Sponsors community activities. **Convention/Meeting:** none. **Publications:** *Tipton County News and Views*, quarterly. Newsletter. Contains news from the Tipton County Chamber of Commerce and Tipton County Economic Development Corporation. Alternate Formats: online.

Trafalgar

6359 ■ American Legion, Trafalgar Post 416
4632 Cardinal Point
Trafalgar, IN 46181
Ph: (317)630-1300
Fax: (317)237-9891
URL: National Affiliate–www.legion.org
Local. Affiliated With: American Legion.

Union City

6360 ■ American Legion, Indiana Post 158
c/o Orville N. Stover
PO Box 148
Union City, IN 47390
Ph: (317)964-4455
Fax: (317)237-9891
URL: National Affiliate–www.legion.org
Contact: Orville N. Stover, Contact
Local. Affiliated With: American Legion.

6361 ■ Art Association of Randolph County (AARC)
115 N Howard St.
Union City, IN 47390
Ph: (765)964-7227
Fax: (765)964-4569
E-mail: jan@artsdepot.org
URL: http://artsdepot.org
Contact: Teri Boxell, Exec.Dir.
Founded: 1954. **Members:** 250. **Membership Dues:** individual, $15 (annual) • family, $25 (annual) • business, $50 (annual). **Staff:** 1. **Budget:** $45,000. **Local.** Individuals working to promote visual and performing arts in the community. Teaches art appreciation in schools through hands-on projects; promotes local artists through individual art shows and workshops. Holds 18-24 events per year. **Publications:** *Artracks*, monthly. Newsletter. **Price:** free. **Conventions/Meetings:** monthly meeting - always second Thursday in Union City, IN.

6362 ■ Indiana SADD
401 N Plum St.
Union City, IN 47390
Ph: (765)964-4683
Fax: (765)964-7233
E-mail: jnoffsinger1@woh.rr.com
URL: http://www.homestead.com/indianasadd
Contact: Jim Noffsinger, Coor.
State. Affiliated With: Students Against Destructive Decisions, Students Against Drunk Driving.

6363 ■ Mental Health Association in Randolph County, Indiana
c/o Mr. Jim Noffsinger, Exec.Dir.
524 Park Ave.
Union City, IN 47390-1021
Ph: (765)964-4683
URL: http://www.mentalhealthassociation.com
Contact: Mr. Jim Noffsinger, Exec.Dir.
Local. Seeks to promote mental health and prevent mental health disorders. Improves mental health of Americans through advocacy, public education, research and service. **Affiliated With:** Mental Health Association in Indiana; National Mental Health Association.

6364 ■ Union City Chamber of Commerce
PO Box 424
Union City, IN 47390
Ph: (765)964-5409
Fax: (765)964-5409
E-mail: ucchamber@jayco.net
Contact: Darlene Wymer, Exec.Dir.
Local.

Union Mills

6365 ■ American Legion, Hanna Post 472
8907 S 600 W
Union Mills, IN 46382
Ph: (317)630-1300
Fax: (317)237-9891
URL: National Affiliate–www.legion.org
Local. Affiliated With: American Legion.

6366 ■ American Legion, Union Mills Post 295
710 Water St.
Union Mills, IN 46382
Ph: (317)630-1300
Fax: (317)237-9891
URL: National Affiliate–www.legion.org
Local. Affiliated With: American Legion.

Unionville

6367 ■ Benton Township of Monroe County Volunteer Fire Department
c/o Don Glass
7606 E State Rd. 45
Unionville, IN 47468-9701
Ph: (812)332-2637
Fax: (812)332-2637
Founded: 1979. **Members:** 13. **Local.**

6368 ■ Bloomington Bonsai Club
c/o Dolores Freiburger
7636 Hilltop Dr.
Unionville, IN 47468
Ph: (812)331-2611
E-mail: doloresrfr@aol.com
URL: National Affiliate–www.bonsai-bci.com
Contact: Dolores Freiburger, Contact
Local. Affiliated With: Bonsai Clubs International.

Upland

6369 ■ American Legion, Orville Bidwell Post 138
164 W Railroad
Upland, IN 46989
Ph: (317)630-1300
Fax: (317)237-9891
URL: National Affiliate–www.legion.org
Local. Affiliated With: American Legion.

6370 ■ Mathematical Association of America, Indiana Section
c/o Jeremy Case, Vice Chm.
Mathematics Dept., Taylor Univ.
236 W Reade Ave.
Upland, IN 46989-1002
Ph: (765)998-4845
E-mail: jrcase@tayloru.edu
URL: http://www.maa.org/Indiana
Contact: Jeremy Case, Vice Chm.
State. Promotes the general understanding and appreciation of mathematics. Advances and improves the education in the mathematical sciences at the collegiate level. Provides resources and activities that foster scholarship, professional growth and cooperation among teachers, other professionals and students. **Affiliated With:** Mathematical Association of America.

6371 ■ Upland Chamber of Commerce
PO Box 157
Upland, IN 46989
Ph: (765)998-2579 (765)998-7439
Contact: Kevin Crawford, Pres.
Local.

Urbana

6372 ■ American Legion, Indiana Post 175
c/o Claude Wilcox
310 E Mill St.
Urbana, IN 46990
Ph: (219)774-3410
Fax: (317)237-9891
URL: National Affiliate–www.legion.org
Contact: Claude Wilcox, Contact
Local. Affiliated With: American Legion.

Vallonia

6373 ■ American Fisheries Society, Indiana Chapter President
c/o Jim Luttrell, Pres.
Driftwood State Fish Hatchery
Div. of Fish and Wildlife
5013 S CR 250 W
Vallonia, IN 47281
Ph: (812)358-4110
E-mail: jluttrell@dnr.state.in.us
URL: http://www.bsu.edu/csh/bio/inafs
Contact: Jim Luttrell, Pres.
State. Affiliated With: American Fisheries Society.

6374 ■ Southern Indiana Angus Association
c/o Troy Thompson, Pres.
2493 W Co. Rd. 275 S
Vallonia, IN 47281
Ph: (812)358-9072
E-mail: troyth@voyager.net
URL: National Affiliate–www.angus.org
Contact: Troy Thompson, Pres.
Local. Affiliated With: American Angus Association.

Valparaiso

6375 ■ American Cancer Society, Porter County Unit
410 E Lincolnway
Valparaiso, IN 46383
Ph: (219)464-2895
Fax: (219)465-1044
Free: (800)227-2345
E-mail: judithrooney-davis@cancer.org
URL: http://www.cancer.org
Contact: Judy Rooney-Davis, Exec.Dir.
Founded: 1913. **Members:** 37. **Staff:** 1. **Local Groups:** 1. **Local.** Volunteers supporting education

and research in cancer prevention, diagnosis, detection, and treatment. **Libraries: Type:** open to the public. **Subjects:** cancer detection, treatment, support. **Awards:** Great Lakes Division Foundation. **Frequency:** annual. **Type:** scholarship. **Recipient:** survivor of cancer under 18. **Committees:** Detection and Treatment; GASO and Comprehensive School Health Education; Porter County Breast Cancer Control Team; Porter County Tobacco Control Team. **Affiliated With:** American Cancer Society. **Publications:** *Voices*, quarterly. Newsletter. Updates to the public on ongoing in IN and MI. **Price:** free. **Advertising:** accepted. **Conventions/Meetings:** annual workshop, volunteers and staff together in planning - always fall in Indiana.

6376 ■ American Legion, Indiana Post 94
c/o Charles Pratt
PO Box 268
Valparaiso, IN 46384
Ph: (219)462-4452
Fax: (317)237-9891
URL: National Affiliate–www.legion.org
Contact: Charles Pratt, Contact
Local. Affiliated With: American Legion.

6377 ■ American Legion, Paul Robert Strange Post 502
429 W 750 N
Valparaiso, IN 46385
Ph: (219)759-4327
Fax: (317)237-9891
URL: National Affiliate–www.legion.org
Local. Affiliated With: American Legion.

6378 ■ American Red Cross, Porter County Chapter (ARCPC)
755 W Lincolnway
Valparaiso, IN 46384
Ph: (219)462-8543
Fax: (219)464-8189
E-mail: pcarc@netnitco.net
URL: http://portercountyredcross.org
Contact: Deb Williams, Exec.Dir.
Founded: 1917. **Members:** 150. **Staff:** 2. **Local.** Works to serve members of the armed forces, veterans, and their families; to assist disaster victims; and to support other community services. **Affiliated With:** American Red Cross National Headquarters. **Publications:** *Care Line*, quarterly. Newsletter. **Price:** free. **Circulation:** 3,000. **Conventions/Meetings:** monthly board meeting - second Tuesday.

6379 ■ Association of Certified Fraud Examiners, Northern Indiana Chapter No. 79
497 Wexford Rd.
Valparaiso, IN 46385
Ph: (219)464-9938
E-mail: topollgh@aol.com
URL: National Affiliate–www.acfe.com
Contact: George H. Topoll CFE, Pres.
Local. Works to reduce the incidence of fraud and white-collar crime and to assist the members in its detection and deterrence. Sponsors training seminars on fraud and loss prevention. Administers credentialing programs for Certified Fraud Examiners. **Affiliated With:** Association of Certified Fraud Examiners.

6380 ■ Boys and Girls Clubs of Porter County
PO Box 254
Valparaiso, IN 46384-0254
Ph: (219)464-7282
Fax: (219)462-1081
E-mail: mjones@bgcpoco.org
URL: http://www.bgcpoco.org
Contact: Chuck Leer, Pres.
Local.

6381 ■ Epsilon Sigma Phi, Alpha Lambda
c/o Emily Remster
368 E 400 St.
Valparaiso, IN 46383
Ph: (219)462-0352
Fax: (219)477-6499
E-mail: emilyremster@aol.com
URL: National Affiliate–espnational.org
Local. Affiliated With: Epsilon Sigma Phi.

6382 ■ Great Lake Sound Chorus of Sweet Adelines International
First Presbyterian Church
3401 N Valparaiso St.
Valparaiso, IN 46383
Ph: (219)464-9627
E-mail: janbooboo@comcast.net
URL: http://www.geocities.com/greatlakesound
Contact: Debbie Kardos, Contact
Regional. Advances the musical art form of barbershop harmony through education and performances. Provides education, training and coaching in the development of women's four-part barbershop harmony. **Affiliated With:** Sweet Adelines International.

6383 ■ Greater Valparaiso Chamber of Commerce (GVCC)
PO Box 330
Valparaiso, IN 46384-0330
Ph: (219)462-1105
Fax: (219)462-5710
E-mail: info@valparaisochamber.org
URL: http://www.valparaisochamber.org
Contact: Rex G. Richards, Pres.
Members: 600. **Membership Dues:** business (based on the number of employees), $291-$2,820 (annual) • non-profit, $156 (annual) • subsidiary, $73 (annual) • associate, civic, $117 (annual). **Staff:** 5. **Local.** Promotes business and community development in the Valparaiso, IN area. **Publications:** *Valparaiso Magazine*, quarterly. Features community highlights, people, community event calendar and chamber information. **Circulation:** 16,500.

6384 ■ Indiana Association for Institutional Research (INAIR)
c/o Ann Trost, Treas.
Valparaiso Univ.
1700 Chapel Dr.
Kretzmann Hall
Valparaiso, IN 46383
E-mail: wtobin@depauw.edu
URL: http://www.bsu.eduwebinairdefault.htm
Contact: Bill Tobin, Pres.
State. Represents individuals interested in institutional research. Fosters research leading to improved understanding, planning, and operation of institutions of postsecondary education. **Affiliated With:** Association for Institutional Research.

6385 ■ Mental Health Association in Porter County
c/o Ms. Mary Hodson, Exec.Dir.
402 Indiana Ave.
Valparaiso, IN 46383-5716
Ph: (219)462-6267
Fax: (219)464-7483
E-mail: mha@netnitco.net
URL: http://www.mentalhealthassociation.com
Contact: Ms. Mary Hodson, Exec.Dir.
Local. Seeks to promote mental health and prevent mental health disorders. Improves mental health of Americans through advocacy, public education, research and service. **Affiliated With:** Mental Health Association in Indiana; National Mental Health Association.

6386 ■ Northwest Indiana Youth for Christ
PO Box 1064
Valparaiso, IN 46384
Ph: (219)462-3000
Fax: (219)477-5646
URL: National Affiliate–www.yfc.net
Local. Affiliated With: Youth for Christ/U.S.A.

6387 ■ One by One Civic Club
PO Box 2102
Valparaiso, IN 46384-2102
Local.

6388 ■ Porter County Home Builders Association
552 Vale Park Rd., Ste.B
Valparaiso, IN 46385-2547
Ph: (219)464-2944
Fax: (219)465-7220
E-mail: buildpcba@aol.com
URL: National Affiliate–www.nahb.org
Contact: Avilyn White, Contact
Local. Single and multifamily home builders, commercial builders, and others associated with the building industry. **Affiliated With:** National Association of Home Builders.

6389 ■ Psi Chi, National Honor Society in Psychology - Valparaiso University
c/o Dept. of Psychology
Dickmeyer Hall
Union St.
Valparaiso, IN 46383-6493
Ph: (219)464-5440 (219)464-5497
Fax: (219)464-6878
E-mail: stanley.hughes@valpo.edu
URL: http://www.psichi.org/chapters/info.asp?chapter_id=711
Contact: Stanley L. Hughes PhD, Advisor
Local.

6390 ■ Sons of Norway, Scandiana Lodge 5-600
c/o Jerry E. Moe, Pres.
3501 Coventry Cir.
Valparaiso, IN 46383-2005
Ph: (219)465-4176
E-mail: jerrymoe@netnitco.net
URL: National Affiliate–www.sofn.com
Contact: Jerry E. Moe, Pres.
Local. Affiliated With: Sons of Norway.

6391 ■ Sons of Norway, Trollhaugen Lodge 5-417
c/o Shirley Gronlund, Pres.
69 Deer Meadow Trail
Valparaiso, IN 46385-8948
Ph: (219)464-7551
E-mail: fli-by@msn.com
URL: National Affiliate–www.sofn.com
Contact: Shirley Gronlund, Pres.
Local. Affiliated With: Sons of Norway.

6392 ■ United Way of Porter County Indiana
c/o Sharon Kish, Pres.
PO Box 2028
Valparaiso, IN 46384-2028
Ph: (219)464-3583
Fax: (219)477-5845
Free: (877)464-3583
E-mail: info@unitedwaypc.org
URL: http://www.unitedwaypc.org
Contact: Sharon Kish, Pres.
Founded: 1957. **Members:** 30. **Staff:** 6. **Budget:** $2,000,000. **Local.** Seeks to improve lives and mobilizes the 'caring power' of the Porter County community.

6393 ■ Valparaiso Community Festivals and Events
PO Box 189
Valparaiso, IN 46384-0189
Ph: (219)464-8332
Fax: (219)464-2343
E-mail: popcorn@netnitco.net
URL: http://www.popcornfest.org
Local.

6394 ■ Valparaiso High School Key Club
2727 N Campbell
Valparaiso, IN 46385
Ph: (219)537-3070
URL: http://www.keyclub.org/club/valparaiso
Contact: Jill M., Pres.
Local.

6395 ■ Valparaiso RSVP
c/o Joyce Bolin, Dir.
1005 Campbell
Valparaiso, IN 46385
Ph: (219)464-1028
Fax: (219)464-0012
E-mail: jbolin@niia.net
URL: http://www.seniorcorps.gov
Contact: Joyce Bolin, Dir.
Local. Affiliated With: Retired and Senior Volunteer Program.

Van Buren

6396 ■ American Legion, Brown-Doyle Post 368
759 E 450 N
Van Buren, IN 46991
Ph: (765)934-2700
Fax: (317)237-9891
URL: National Affiliate–www.legion.org
Local. Affiliated With: American Legion.

6397 ■ Van Buren Chamber of Commerce
PO Box 484
Van Buren, IN 46991
Ph: (765)934-4646
Contact: Dean Baker, Pres.
Local.

Veedersburg

6398 ■ American Legion, Charles Forrest Post 288
301 N Newlin St.
Veedersburg, IN 47987
Ph: (317)630-1300
Fax: (317)237-9891
URL: National Affiliate–www.legion.org
Local. Affiliated With: American Legion.

6399 ■ American Legion, Quigle-Palin Post 394
2718 E 400 N
Veedersburg, IN 47987
Ph: (317)630-1300
Fax: (317)237-9891
URL: National Affiliate–www.legion.org
Local. Affiliated With: American Legion.

6400 ■ Fountain County Association for Retarded Citizens
1500 E State, Rd. 32
Veedersburg, IN 47987
Ph: (765)798-2743
URL: National Affiliate–www.TheArc.org
Local. Parents, professional workers, and others interested in individuals with mental retardation. Works to promote services, research, public understanding, and legislation for people with mental retardation and their families. **Affiliated With:** Arc of the United States.

Versailles

6401 ■ American Legion, Leora Weare Post 173
PO Box 173
Versailles, IN 47042
Ph: (812)689-5202
Fax: (317)237-9891
URL: National Affiliate–www.legion.org
Local. Affiliated With: American Legion.

6402 ■ Historic Hoosier Hills Resource Conservation and Development Council
PO Box 407
Versailles, IN 47042-0407
Ph: (812)689-6410
Fax: (812)689-3141
E-mail: terry.stephenson@in.usda.gov
URL: http://www.hhhills.org
Contact: Terry Stephenson, Coor.
Local. Affiliated With: National Association of Resource Conservation and Development Councils.

6403 ■ Ripley County Chamber of Commerce
c/o Jean Nichols, Admin.Asst.
102 N Main St.
PO Box 576
Versailles, IN 47042
Ph: (812)689-6654
Fax: (812)689-3934
E-mail: ripleycc@ripleycountychamber.org
URL: http://ripleycountychamber.org
Contact: Darla Westerfield, Pres.
Local. Promotes business and community development in Ripley County Versailles, IN area. **Publications:** *Chamber Page in the Versailles Republican*, quarterly, every 1st Thursday of the new quarter. Newspaper • Newsletter, quarterly. Highlights current business issues, legislative updates, local events, new Chamber members, and events. **Conventions/Meetings:** monthly board meeting - every 2nd Thursday.

6404 ■ Ripley County, Indiana Historical Society (RCIHS)
PO Box 525
Versailles, IN 47042
Ph: (812)689-3031
E-mail: rchslib@seidata.com
URL: http://seidata.com/~rchslib
Contact: Betty Reopke, Pres.
Founded: 1924. **Members:** 200. **Membership Dues:** renewal, $5 (annual) • life, $100 • new, $10 (annual). **Regional.** Individuals interested in the history and genealogy of Ripley County, IN. Maintains the archives building, the museum and the log cabin. **Libraries: Type:** reference; open to the public. **Holdings:** archival material, books, maps, papers, photographs, software. **Subjects:** genealogy, history. **Publications:** *Quarterly Bulletin of the Ripley County Indiana Historical Society*. **Price:** included in membership dues. **Circulation:** 200 • *Ripley County History Book, 1989 Vol I & Vol II* • Newsletter, quarterly. **Price:** $5.00. **Conventions/Meetings:** quarterly meeting - always January, April, July, and October.

Vevay

6405 ■ American Legion, Indiana Post 185
c/o Edwin C. Danner
213 Ferry St.
Vevay, IN 47043
Ph: (812)427-9144
Fax: (317)237-9891
URL: National Affiliate–www.legion.org
Contact: Edwin C. Danner, Contact
Local. Affiliated With: American Legion.

6406 ■ United Fund of Switzerland County
PO Box 221
Vevay, IN 47043
Ph: (812)594-2182
E-mail: gce@direcway.com
URL: National Affiliate–www.iauw.org
Contact: Mr. Fred R Stave, Pres.
Founded: 2000. **Members:** 500. **Budget:** $100,000. **Local.** Collects resources using United Way principles, concepts and practices and disperse those resources to qualified charitable organizations in Switzerland County such that quality of life will be enhanced for all people in Switzerland County.

Vincennes

6407 ■ American Cancer Society, MidSouthwestern Area Service Center
318 Main St.
Vincennes, IN 47591
Ph: (812)886-9007
Fax: (812)886-9008
URL: National Affiliate–www.cancer.org
Regional. Affiliated With: American Cancer Society.

6408 ■ American Legion, Vincennes Post 73
PO Box 823
Vincennes, IN 47591
Ph: (812)882-5608
Fax: (317)237-9891
URL: National Affiliate–www.legion.org
Local. Affiliated With: American Legion.

6409 ■ Illiana Watermelon Association
2924 E Nowaski Rd.
Vincennes, IN 47591
Ph: (812)886-1051
Fax: (812)886-1814
E-mail: sjn@illianawatermelon.org
URL: http://www.illianawatermelon.org
Contact: John Nowaskie, Pres.
Local.

6410 ■ Indiana Society, Sons of the American Revolution, George Rogers Clark Chapter
c/o Marshall E. Miller, Sec.-Treas.
1314 Weed Ln.
Vincennes, IN 47591-5051
Ph: (812)882-9646
E-mail: memiller2@charter.net
URL: http://www.geocities.com/inssar-south/georclar.html
Contact: Marshall E. Miller, Sec.-Treas.
Local. Affiliated With: National Society, Sons of the American Revolution.

6411 ■ Knox County Association for Retarded Citizens
2830 E Arc Ave.
Vincennes, IN 47591
Ph: (812)886-4312
URL: National Affiliate–www.thearc.org
Local. Parents, professional workers, and others interested in individuals with mental retardation. Works to promote services, research, public understanding, and legislation for people with mental retardation and their families. **Affiliated With:** Arc of the United States.

6412 ■ Knox County Board of Realtors
PO Box 221
Vincennes, IN 47591
Ph: (812)895-5669
Fax: (812)882-2248
E-mail: rtpoole@wvc.net
URL: National Affiliate–www.realtor.org
Contact: Richard Poole, Exec. Officer
Local. Strives to develop real estate business practices. Advocates the right to own, use and transfer real property. Provides a facility for professional development, research and exchange of information among members and to the general public. **Affiliated With:** National Association of Realtors.

6413 ■ Knox County Chamber of Commerce
102 N 3rd St.
PO Box 553
Vincennes, IN 47591-0553
Ph: (812)882-6440
Fax: (812)882-6441
Free: (888)895-6622
E-mail: chamber@knoxchamber.com
URL: http://www.accessknoxcounty.com
Contact: Mark A. McNeece, Pres./CEO
Local. Promotes business and community development in Knox County, IN. **Formerly:** (1999) Vincennes Area Chamber of Commerce.

6414 ■ Knox County RSVP
c/o Patty Dreiman, Dir.
PO Box 314
Vincennes, IN 47591
Ph: (812)888-5879
Fax: (812)888-4566
E-mail: pdreiman@vinu.edu
URL: http://www.seniorcorps.gov/about/programs/rsvp_state.asp?usestateabbr=in&Search4.x=12&Search4.y=7
Contact: Patty Dreiman, Dir.
Local. Affiliated With: Retired and Senior Volunteer Program.

6415 ■ Masonic Lodge
501 Broadway St.
Vincennes, IN 47591
Ph: (812)882-5973
Founded: 1809. **Local.**

6416 ■ Mental Health Association in Knox County
PO Box 859
Vincennes, IN 47591-0859
Ph: (812)895-1007
Fax: (812)885-2723
E-mail: kevans@wvc.net
URL: http://www.mentalhealthassociation.com
Contact: Ms. Kathy Evans, Exec.Dir.
Local. Seeks to promote mental health and prevent mental health disorders. Improves mental health of Americans through advocacy, public education, research and service. **Affiliated With:** Mental Health Association in Indiana; National Mental Health Association.

6417 ■ Mutual UFO Network, Indiana
c/o Jerry L. Sievers, State Dir.
1395 E Ramsey Rd.
Vincennes, IN 47591
Ph: (812)882-1862
E-mail: mufon_in@hotmail.com
URL: http://indianamufon.homestead.com/
Contact: Jerry L. Sievers, State Dir.
Founded: 1970. **Members:** 40. **Membership Dues:** $30 (annual). **Staff:** 1. **State Groups:** 1. **State.** Systematically collects and analyzes UFO data, with ultimate goal of learning the origin and nature of the UFO phenomena. **Libraries: Type:** not open to the public. **Subjects:** UFO and related phenomena. **Affiliated With:** Mutual UFO Network. **Conventions/Meetings:** semiannual meeting - always spring and fall.

6418 ■ National Active and Retired Federal Employees Association Washington/Vincennes 527
2115 Montclair Ave.
Vincennes, IN 47591-5972
Ph: (812)895-1524
URL: National Affiliate–www.narfe.org
Contact: Roy A. Bear, Contact
Local. Protects the retirement future of employees through education. Informs members on issues affecting the retirement. **Affiliated With:** National Association of Retired Federal Employees.

6419 ■ Paper, Allied-Industrial, Chemical and Energy Workers International Union, AFL-CIO, CLC - Local Union 555
PO Box 95
Vincennes, IN 47591-0095
E-mail: pacelocal4555@cox-internet.com
URL: http://www.geocities.com/pace4555
Contact: Mike Ayer, Contact
Members: 73. **Local. Affiliated With:** Pace International Union.

6420 ■ Phi Theta Kappa, Zeta Psi Chapter - Vincennes University
c/o Donna Clinkenbeard
Career Center
1002 N 1st St.
Vincennes, IN 47591
Ph: (812)888-4354
URL: http://www.ptk.org/directories/chapters/IN/5486-1.htm
Contact: Donna Clinkenbeard, Advisor
Local.

6421 ■ Police and Firemen's Insurance Association - Vincennes Fire Department
PO Box 1445
Vincennes, IN 47591
Ph: (812)895-0382
URL: National Affiliate–www.pfia.net
Contact: Robert A. Jarrell, Contact
Local. Affiliated With: Police and Firemen's Insurance Association.

6422 ■ United Way of Knox County, Indiana
PO Box 198
Vincennes, IN 47591-0198
Ph: (812)882-3624
URL: National Affiliate–national.unitedway.org
Local. Affiliated With: United Way of America.

Wabash

6423 ■ American Legion, Indiana Post 15
c/o Thomas Stineman
188 W Market St.
Wabash, IN 46992
Ph: (219)563-3932
Fax: (317)237-9891
URL: National Affiliate–www.legion.org
Contact: Thomas Stineman, Contact
Local. Affiliated With: American Legion.

6424 ■ Halderman Real Estate Services - Halderman Farm Management
PO Box 297
Wabash, IN 46992
Ph: (260)563-8888
Free: (800)424-2324
E-mail: info@halderman.com
URL: http://www.halderman.com
Contact: Howard Halderman, Pres.
Founded: 1930. **Local. Affiliated With:** American Society of Farm Managers and Rural Appraisers. **Formerly:** (2005) American Society of Farm Managers and Rural Appraisers Indiana Chapter.

6425 ■ Izaak Walton League of America, Wabash Chapter
c/o Ned Vandegrift, Membership Sec.
10439 Old State Rd.
Wabash, IN 46992-3711
Ph: (260)563-6069
E-mail: nvande@hotmail.com
URL: http://www.iwla.org
Contact: Ned Vandegrift, Membership Sec.
Membership Dues: individual, $36 (annual) • family, $54 (annual). **Local.** Promotes environmental resources conservation. **Affiliated With:** Izaak Walton League of America.

6426 ■ Wabash Area Chamber of Commerce (WACC)
111 S Wabash St.
PO Box 371
Wabash, IN 46992-0371
Ph: (260)563-1168
Fax: (260)563-6920
E-mail: wacc@wabashchamber.org
URL: http://www.wabashchamber.org
Contact: Ms. Kimberly A. Pinkerton, Pres.
Founded: 1942. **Members:** 265. **Staff:** 3. **Budget:** $130,000. **Local.** Promotes business and community development in the Wabash, IN area. Sponsors festival; conducts annual Wabash Showcase - A Business Expo. **Awards:** Business of the Year. **Frequency:** annual. **Type:** recognition • Distinguished Citizen. **Frequency:** annual. **Type:** recognition • Small Business of the Year. **Frequency:** annual. **Type:** recognition. **Publications:** *Buyers Guide*, annual. Directory • *Industrial and Business Directory*, periodic • Newsletter, monthly. **Conventions/Meetings:** periodic meeting.

6427 ■ Wabash County Board of Realtors
PO Box 641
Wabash, IN 46992
Ph: (260)563-8009
Fax: (260)563-8009
E-mail: wabcaor@verizion.net
URL: National Affiliate–www.realtor.org
Contact: Vita E. Miller, Exec. Officer
Local. Strives to develop real estate business practices. Advocates the right to own, use and transfer real property. Provides a facility for professional development, research and exchange of information among members and to the general public. **Affiliated With:** National Association of Realtors.

6428 ■ Wabash Marketplace
PO Box 420
Wabash, IN 46992
Ph: (260)563-0975
Fax: (260)563-7957
E-mail: info@wabashmarketplace.org
URL: http://www.wabashmarketplace.org
Contact: Ms. Holly Kendall, Exec.Dir.
Local. Fosters historic preservation and encourage community cooperation to ensure the future of active and vital downtown of Wabash, Indiana. **Committees:** Design; Economic Restructuring; Organization; Promotion. **Affiliated With:** Historic Landmarks Foundation of Indiana; National Trust Main Street Center.

Wakarusa

6429 ■ American Legion, Indiana Post 307
c/o William A. Reed
PO Box 177
Wakarusa, IN 46573
Ph: (219)862-2655
Fax: (317)237-9891
URL: National Affiliate–www.legion.org
Contact: William A. Reed, Contact
Local. Affiliated With: American Legion.

6430 ■ Holiday Rambler Recreational Vehicle Club (HRRVC)
PO Box 587
Wakarusa, IN 46573
Ph: (574)862-7330
Fax: (574)862-7390
Free: (877)702-5415
E-mail: hrclub@monacohr.com
URL: http://www.hrrvc.org
Contact: Ardith Christensen, Sec.
Local. Formerly: (2005) Holiday Rambler Recreational.

6431 ■ Wakarusa Chamber of Commerce
c/o Doris Biller, Exec.Sec.
100 W Waterford St.
PO Box 291
Wakarusa, IN 46573
Ph: (574)862-4344
Fax: (574)862-2245
E-mail: chamber@wakarusachamber.com
URL: http://www.wakarusachamber.com
Contact: Doris Biller, Exec.Sec.
Membership Dues: individual/association, $25 (annual) • employer with 1-50 employees, $50 (annual) • employer with 51-100 employees, $100 (annual) • employer with 101-200 employees, $200 (annual) • employer with 201-300 employees, $300 (annual) • employer with over 300 employees, $500 (annual). **Local.** Strives to render constructive services for the promotion of the welfare of the community and citizens of Wakarusa, Indiana. **Publications:** *Chamber News*, monthly. Newsletter. Alternate Formats: online.

Walkerton

6432 ■ American Legion, Orville Easterday Post 189
407 Indiana St.
Walkerton, IN 46574
Ph: (219)586-2001
Fax: (317)237-9891
URL: National Affiliate–www.legion.org
Local. Affiliated With: American Legion.

6433 ■ American Legion, Wilbur Bud Crane Post 400
302 Lakeside Dr.
Walkerton, IN 46574
Ph: (219)369-1242
Fax: (317)237-9891
URL: National Affiliate–www.legion.org
Local. Affiliated With: American Legion.

6434 ■ Mental Health Association in Marshall County
c/o Ms. Dee Martin, Exec.Dir.
2112 W County Line Rd.
Walkerton, IN 46574-8695
Ph: (574)935-5314
E-mail: mhamc@kconline.com
URL: http://www.mentalhealthassociation.com
Contact: Ms. Dee Martin, Exec.Dir.
Local. Seeks to promote mental health and prevent mental health disorders. Improves mental health of Americans through advocacy, public education, research and service. **Affiliated With:** Mental Health Association in Indiana; National Mental Health Association.

6435 ■ National Active and Retired Federal Employees Association - Herbert L. Gabel 565
69497 State Rd. 23
Walkerton, IN 46574-9709
Ph: (574)586-3377
URL: National Affiliate–www.narfe.org
Contact: Thomas W. Osowski, Contact
Local. Protects the retirement future of employees through education. Informs members on issues affecting the retirement. **Affiliated With:** National Association of Retired Federal Employees.

6436 ■ Northwest Indiana Angus Breeders Association
c/o Ted Stull, Pres.
4005 Tamarack Rd.
Walkerton, IN 46574
Ph: (574)586-3281
E-mail: ted.stull@hydro.com
URL: National Affiliate–www.angus.org
Contact: Ted Stull, Pres.
Local. Affiliated With: American Angus Association.

6437 ■ Walkerton Area Chamber of Commerce (WACC)
612 Roosevelt Rd.
Walkerton, IN 46574-1218
Ph: (574)586-3100
Fax: (574)586-3469
E-mail: louzons@1stsource.com
URL: http://www.walkerton.org
Contact: Phil Buckmaster, Pres.
Membership Dues: individual, $35 (annual) • school, $270 (annual) • utility/financial, $315 (annual) • self-employed/non profit, $50 (annual) • business (based on number of employees), $110-$260 (annual). **Local.** Promotes business and community development in Walkerton, IN. **Formerly:** (1999) Walkerton Chamber of Commerce. **Publications:** Membership Directory, annual.

Walton

6438 ■ American Legion, Walton Post 418
PO Box 424
Walton, IN 46994
Ph: (219)626-2625
Fax: (317)237-9891
URL: National Affiliate–www.legion.org
Local. Affiliated With: American Legion.

Wanatah

6439 ■ American Legion, Koselke Mayfield Post 403
PO Box 5
Wanatah, IN 46390
Ph: (219)733-2349
Fax: (317)237-9891
URL: National Affiliate–www.legion.org
Local. Affiliated With: American Legion.

Warsaw

6440 ■ American Legion, Indiana Post 49
c/o John C. Peterson
301 N Buffalo St.
Warsaw, IN 46580
Ph: (219)267-5549
Fax: (317)237-9891
URL: National Affiliate–www.legion.org
Contact: John C. Peterson, Contact
Local. Affiliated With: American Legion.

6441 ■ American Payroll Association, Northeast Indiana Chapter
c/o Ms. Cindy Shelton, Pres.
Dalton Corp.
PO Box 230
Warsaw, IN 46580-0230
Ph: (574)371-5257
Fax: (574)371-5258
E-mail: cshelton@daltonfoundries.com
URL: http://www.fwapa.org
Contact: Ms. Cindy Shelton, Pres.
Members: 35. **Membership Dues:** $25 (annual). **State Groups:** 4. **Local Groups:** 1. **Local.** Aims to increase the Payroll Professional's skill level through education and mutual support. Represents the Payroll Professional before legislative bodies. Administers the certified payroll professional program of recognition. Provides public service education on payroll and employment issues. **Affiliated With:** American Payroll Association.

6442 ■ Indiana Farrier's Association No. 15
c/o Matthew G. Gillis, Pres.
1317 E 300 N
Warsaw, IN 46582
Ph: (574)269-7733
Fax: (574)269-7733
E-mail: lcf@kconline.com
URL: National Affiliate–www.americanfarriers.org
Contact: Matthew G. Gillis, Pres.
State. Affiliated With: American Farrier's Association.

6443 ■ Indiana Lakes Area Youth for Christ
PO Box 1221
Warsaw, IN 46581
Ph: (574)936-2325
Fax: (574)936-2304
URL: http://www.yfcinlakes.org
Local. Affiliated With: Youth for Christ/U.S.A.

6444 ■ Kosciusko AIFA
c/o Brad K. Skiles, Pres.
PO Box 1988
Warsaw, IN 46581
Ph: (574)267-6252
Fax: (574)269-6220
E-mail: pjenkins@kconline.com
URL: National Affiliate–naifa.org
Contact: Brad K. Skiles, Pres.
Local. Represents the interests of insurance and financial advisors. Advocates for a positive legislative and regulatory environment. Enhances business and professional skills of members. **Affiliated With:** National Association of Insurance and Financial Advisors.

6445 ■ Kosciusko Board of Realtors
120 S Lake St., Ste.220
Warsaw, IN 46580
Ph: (574)269-6706
Fax: (574)268-1763
E-mail: kbor@kbor.com
URL: http://www.kbor.com
Contact: Bev Ganshorn, Pres.
Local. Strives to develop real estate business practices. Advocates the right to own, use and transfer real property. Provides a facility for professional development, research and exchange of information among members and to the general public. **Affiliated With:** National Association of Realtors.

6446 ■ Kosciusko County Convention and Visitors Bureau
111 Capital Dr.
Warsaw, IN 46582
Ph: (574)269-6090
Free: (800)800-6090
E-mail: info@koscvb.org
URL: http://www.koscvb.org
Contact: Linda L. Arnold, Contact
Founded: 1986. **Members:** 17. **Staff:** 2. **Budget:** $325,000. **Regional Groups:** 1. **State Groups:** 1. **Local.** Promotes business and tourism in Kosciusko County, IN. **Publications:** *Visitors Guide*, annual. Magazine. **Price:** free.

6447 ■ Kosciusko County Historical Society (KCHS)
PO Box 1071
Warsaw, IN 46581-1071
Ph: (574)269-1078
E-mail: sue.zellers@kconline.com
URL: http://culture.kconline.com/kchs
Founded: 1966. **Members:** 480. **Membership Dues:** individual, $15 (annual) • family, $25 (annual) • student, $8 (annual) • contributing, $30 (annual) • sustaining, corporate, $150 (annual). **Staff:** 3. **Budget:** $60,000. **Local.** Individuals interested in the genealogy and history of Kosciusko County, IN. Operates Kosciusko County Jail Museum and Pound Museum, and Chinworth Tippecanoe Bridge. Sponsors Genealogy Section, Junior Historical Society. Collects, preserves and exhibits materials of history, especially those for Kosciusko County. Initiates and encourages historical research and to participate in the cultural life of the community. **Libraries: Type:** open to the public. **Holdings:** 6,000; articles, books. **Subjects:** area history, genealogy. **Affiliated With:** American Association for State and Local History. **Publications:** *Kosciusko County Historical Society Newsletter*, quarterly. **Price:** included in membership dues. **Circulation:** 40 • *Our Missing Links*, quarterly. **Price:** $10.00 /year for members. **Conventions/Meetings:** periodic Genealogy Section Meeting • periodic Reenactment - meeting • periodic workshop.

6448 ■ Kosko Conservation
PO Box 801
Warsaw, IN 46580
Ph: (574)267-7599
E-mail: gasser@kconline.com
URL: National Affiliate–www.mynssa.com
Local. Affiliated With: National Skeet Shooting Association.

6449 ■ Mental Health Association in Kosciusko County
920 Fisher Ave.
Warsaw, IN 46580-4700
Ph: (574)269-2102
Fax: (574)269-3554
URL: http://www.mentalhealthassociation.com
Contact: Ms. Sandra Frush, Exec.Dir.
Local. Seeks to promote mental health and prevent mental health disorders. Improves mental health of Americans through advocacy, public education, research and service. **Affiliated With:** Mental Health Association in Indiana; National Mental Health Association.

6450 ■ National Association of Home Builders, Building Authority of Kosciusko-Fulton County
c/o Carol Huffer
PO Box 1600
Warsaw, IN 46581-1600
Ph: (574)267-6125
Fax: (574)267-3836
E-mail: bakfc@kconline.com
URL: National Affiliate–www.nahb.org
Local. Single and multifamily home builders, commercial builders, and others associated with the building industry. **Affiliated With:** National Association of Home Builders.

6451 ■ National Sojourners, Northern Indiana No. 544
c/o GMCS Albert H. McClelland
350 S Eastridge North Dr.
Warsaw, IN 46582
Ph: (574)267-7485
Fax: (574)268-2831
E-mail: ahmcclelland@hotmail.com
URL: National Affiliate–www.nationalsojourners.org
Contact: GMCS Albert H. McClelland, Contact
Local.

6452 ■ Pheasants Forever Central Indiana, Tippe River Basin
5559 W Wallace Rd.
Warsaw, IN 46580
Ph: (219)858-9456
URL: http://pfcic.org
Contact: Emerson Poort, Pres.
Local. **Affiliated With:** Pheasants Forever.

6453 ■ Phi Theta Kappa, Beta Zeta Kappa Chapter - Ivy Tech State College
c/o Dennis Kambs
Warsaw Campus
3755 Lake City Hwy.
Warsaw, IN 46580
Ph: (574)267-5428
URL: http://www.ptk.org/directories/chapters/IN/20775-1.htm
Contact: Dennis Kambs, Advisor
Local.

6454 ■ United Way of Kosciusko County
PO Box 923
Warsaw, IN 46581-0923
Ph: (574)269-2592
Fax: (574)269-3713
E-mail: unitedway@kconline.com
URL: http://unitedway.kconline.com
Contact: Patricia Coy, Exec.Dir.
Founded: 1958. **Members:** 27. **Staff:** 2. **Local**. **Affiliated With:** United Way of America.

6455 ■ Warsaw - Kosciusko County Chamber of Commerce
313 S Buffalo St.
Warsaw, IN 46580-4304
Ph: (574)267-6311
Fax: (574)267-7762
Free: (800)776-6311
E-mail: jmccarthy-sessing@wkchamber.com
URL: http://www.wkchamber.com
Contact: Joy McCarthy-Sessing, Pres.
Founded: 1911. **Members:** 500. **Membership Dues:** business (1-5 employees), $235 (annual) • business (6-15 employees), $320 (annual) • business (16-30 employees), $440 (annual) • business (31-60 employees), $640 (annual) • business (61-90 employees), $880 (annual) • business (91-150 employees), $1,120 (annual) • business (151-250 employees), $1,680 (annual) • business (251-500 employees), $2,230 (annual) • business (more than 501 employees), $2,710 (annual) • family business, $125 (annual) • seasonal business, $105 (annual) • non-profit classification I (small nonprofit organization), $125 (annual). **Staff:** 4. **Local**. Promotes business and community development in Warsaw, IN area. **Committees:** Ambassadors; Education Steering; Golf Outings; Health Care; Workforce Development. **Councils:** Education; Small Business. **Task Forces:** Internal Operations. **Publications:** *The Kosciusko Business Insights*, monthly. Newsletter. Alternate Formats: online • Membership Directory, annual. Contains members' business information and community activities.

Washington

6456 ■ American Legion, Burch-Wood Post 121
501 E Main St.
Washington, IN 47501
Ph: (812)254-9859
Fax: (317)237-9891
URL: National Affiliate–www.legion.org
Local. **Affiliated With:** American Legion.

6457 ■ Daviess County Chamber of Commerce (DCCC)
1 Train Depot St.
PO Box 430
Washington, IN 47501-0430
Ph: (812)254-5262
Fax: (812)254-4003
Free: (800)449-5262
E-mail: chamber@dmrtc.net
Contact: Elke Guratzsch, Exec.Asst.
Founded: 1961. **Membership Dues:** business (based on number of employees), $175-$450 • church, non-profit, $150 • individual, $100. **Local**. Professional, service, agricultural, industrial and retail related. Strives to make Daviess County a better place in which to live and visit. **Affiliated With:** U.S. Chamber of Commerce. **Publications:** Newsletter, periodic. **Conventions/Meetings:** monthly board meeting • annual meeting.

6458 ■ Daviess County Growth Council
PO Box 191
Washington, IN 47501
Ph: (812)254-1500
Fax: (812)254-2550
Free: (800)449-5262
E-mail: rarnold@dcedc.net
URL: http://www.dcgc.org
Contact: Ron Arnold, Exec.Dir.
Local.

6459 ■ Mental Health Association in Daviess County
c/o Ms. Beth Nord-Kirsch, Exec.Dir.
PO Box 183
Washington, IN 47501-0183
Ph: (812)254-8366
URL: http://www.mentalhealthassociation.com
Contact: Ms. Beth Nord-Kirsch, Exec.Dir.
Local. Seeks to promote mental health and prevent mental health disorders. Improves mental health of Americans through advocacy, public education, research and service. **Affiliated With:** Mental Health Association in Indiana; National Mental Health Association.

6460 ■ RSVP of Daviess County Indiana
c/o Susan Ballengee, Dir.
PO Box 648
Washington, IN 47501-0648
Ph: (812)254-1996
Fax: (812)254-1996
E-mail: rsvp1@rtccom.net
URL: http://www.seniorcorps.gov/about/programs/rsvp.asp
Contact: Susan Ballengee, Dir.
Local. **Affiliated With:** Retired and Senior Volunteer Program.

6461 ■ United Way of Daviess County
PO Box 224
Washington, IN 47501-0224
Ph: (812)254-1038
URL: National Affiliate–national.unitedway.org
Local. **Affiliated With:** United Way of America.

Waveland

6462 ■ American Legion, Raymond Todd Post 323
PO Box 176
Waveland, IN 47989
Ph: (317)435-2296
Fax: (317)237-9891
URL: National Affiliate–www.legion.org
Local. **Affiliated With:** American Legion.

Waynetown

6463 ■ American Legion, Waynetown Post 445
PO Box 83
Waynetown, IN 47990
Ph: (317)234-2724
Fax: (317)237-9891
URL: National Affiliate–www.legion.org
Local. **Affiliated With:** American Legion.

6464 ■ Indiana National Barrel Horse Association
1769 N 875 W
Waynetown, IN 47990
Ph: (765)234-0602
URL: National Affiliate–www.nbha.com
Contact: Cindy Harlan, Dir.
State. Promotes the sport of barrel horse racing. Conducts barrel racing competitions. Establishes standard rules for the sport. **Affiliated With:** National Barrel Horse Association.

West Baden Springs

6465 ■ American Legion, Phillips-Grigsby Post 149
PO Box 115
West Baden Springs, IN 47469
Ph: (317)630-1300
Fax: (317)237-9891
URL: National Affiliate–www.legion.org
Local. **Affiliated With:** American Legion.

West Harrison

6466 ■ AMVETS, West Harrison Post 13
515 S State St.
West Harrison, IN 47060
Ph: (812)637-2024
E-mail: amvets13@amvets13.org
URL: http://www.amvets13.org
Contact: Allan Wileman, Commander
Local. **Affiliated With:** AMVETS - American Veterans.

6467 ■ Dearborn County Beagle Club
c/o Larry Roberts
26552 Wiedeman Rd., No. Harrison
West Harrison, IN 47060-8818
URL: National Affiliate–www.akc.org
Contact: Larry Roberts, Contact
Local.

West Lafayette

6468 ■ ACM Siggraph Purdue University Chapter (ACM)
c/o Brian Dalcorobbo, Chm.
Dept. of Cmpt. Graphics Tech.
1419 Knoy Hall, Rm. 363
West Lafayette, IN 47906

Ph: (765)463-3690
Fax: (765)494-9267
E-mail: siggraph@tech.purdue.edu
URL: http://www.purdue.edu/siggraph
Contact: Brian Dalcorobbo, Chm.
Founded: 1998. **Members:** 56. **Membership Dues:** individual, $10 (annual) • individual, per semester, $6. **Local**. Biological, medical, behavioral, and computer scientists; hospital administrators; programmers and others interested in application of computer methods to biological, behavioral, and medical problems. Stimulates understanding of the use and potential of computers in the Biosciences. **Affiliated With:** Association for Computing Machinery. **Publications:** *Announcement Listserv*, weekly. Newsletter. **Conventions/Meetings:** biweekly meeting.

6469 ■ American Chemical Society, Purdue Section
c/o Beatriz Cisneros, Chair
3227 Jasper St.
West Lafayette, IN 47906-1238
Ph: (765)494-5310
E-mail: cisneros@purdue.edu
URL: National Affiliate–acswebcontent.acs.org
Contact: Beatriz Cisneros, Chair
Local. Represents the interests of individuals dedicated to the advancement of chemistry in all its branches. Provides opportunities for peer interaction and career development. **Affiliated With:** American Chemical Society.

6470 ■ American Legion, First United Methodist Church Post 38
1700 W State St.
West Lafayette, IN 47906
Ph: (317)743-1339
Fax: (317)237-9891
URL: National Affiliate–www.legion.org
Local. **Affiliated With:** American Legion.

6471 ■ American Legion, West Lafayette Post 492
PO Box 2015
West Lafayette, IN 47996
Ph: (317)630-1300
Fax: (317)237-9891
URL: National Affiliate–www.legion.org
Local. **Affiliated With:** American Legion.

6472 ■ American Payroll Association, Greater Lafayette Chapter
PO Box 2775
West Lafayette, IN 47996
Ph: (765)463-4300
Fax: (765)463-0588
E-mail: brian@automatedpayroll.net
URL: http://www.apalafayette.org
Contact: Brian Barrett CPP, Pres. Elect
Local. Aims to increase the Payroll Professional's skill level through education and mutual support. Represents the Payroll Professional before legislative bodies. Administers the certified payroll professional program of recognition. Provides public service education on payroll and employment issues. **Affiliated With:** American Payroll Association.

6473 ■ American Society of Appraisers, Indiana Chapter
c/o Sharon A. Smith-Theobald, Pres.
Appraisal Associates Intl.
2167 Tecumseh Park Ln.
West Lafayette, IN 47906-2118
Ph: (765)463-1270
Fax: (765)463-1270
E-mail: aaiappraisals@insightbb.com
URL: http://www.appraisers.org/indiana
Contact: Sharon A. Smith-Theobald, Pres.
State. Serves as a professional appraisal educator, testing and accrediting society. Sponsors mandatory recertification program for all members. Offers consumer information service to the public. **Affiliated With:** American Society of Appraisers.

6474 ■ American Society for Enology and Viticulture - Eastern Section (ASEV-ES)
c/o Ellen Harkness, Treas.
Purdue Univ.
745 Agriculture Mall Dr.
West Lafayette, IN 47907-2009
Ph: (765)494-6704
Fax: (765)494-7953
E-mail: harkness@purdue.edu
URL: http://www.nysaes.cornell.edu/fst/asev
Contact: Ellen Harkness, Treas.
Founded: 1974. **Members:** 255. **Membership Dues:** regular, $15 (annual). **Regional**. Winemakers, grape growers, extension specialists, and university faculty and staff. Encourages, stimulates, and supports research and education in enology, viticulture, and other directly related sciences. **Awards: Frequency:** annual. **Type:** scholarship. **Recipient:** for university students in wine related programs. **Affiliated With:** American Society for Enology and Viticulture. **Conventions/Meetings:** annual conference, with symposium (exhibits).

6475 ■ American Wine Society - Tippie Tasters
c/o Brenton W. Russell, Co-Chm.
2018 Wind Flower Pl.
West Lafayette, IN 47906
Ph: (765)463-3620
E-mail: brent.russell@insightbb.com
URL: National Affiliate–www.americanwinesociety.org
Contact: Brenton W. Russell, Co-Chm.
Local. **Affiliated With:** American Wine Society.

6476 ■ Associated Landscape Contractors of America, Purdue University
c/o Paul Siciliano, Faculty Advisor
Dept. of Horticulture & Landscape Arch.
1165 Horticulture Bldg.
West Lafayette, IN 47907-1165
Ph: (765)494-1300
Fax: (765)494-0391
E-mail: siciliano@hort.purdue.edu
URL: National Affiliate–www.alca.org
Contact: Paul Siciliano, Faculty Advisor
Local. **Affiliated With:** Professional Landcare Network.

6477 ■ Association for Computing Machinery, Purdue University Chapter (ACM)
c/o Christian Mattix, Chm.
CompSci. Dept. Rm. 319, Knoy Hall
401 N. Grant St.
West Lafayette, IN 47906
Ph: (765)494-7818
Fax: (765)494-0739
E-mail: acm@cs.purdue.edu
URL: http://www.cs.purdue.edu/acm
Contact: Christian Mattix, Chm.
Local. Biological, medical, behavioral, and computer scientists; hospital administrators; programmers and others interested in application of computer methods to biological, behavioral, and medical problems. Stimulates understanding of the use and potential of computers in the Biosciences. **Affiliated With:** Association for Computing Machinery.

6478 ■ Association of Women's Health, Obstetric and Neonatal Nurses - Lafayette/Sagamore Chapter
c/o Joyce Medorna, Coor.
3049 Greenbrier Ave.
West Lafayette, IN 47906
E-mail: jners@msn.com
URL: National Affiliate–www.awhonn.org
Contact: Joyce Medorna, Coor.
Local. Represents registered nurses and other health care providers who specialize in obstetric, women's health, and neonatal nursing. Advances the nursing profession by providing nurses with information and support to help them deliver quality care for women and newborns. **Affiliated With:** Association of Women's Health, Obstetric and Neonatal Nurses.

6479 ■ Catalina 22 Fleet 158, Lafayette, Indiana
c/o Lewie J. Wallace
1701 Woodland Ave.
West Lafayette, IN 47906
Ph: (765)463-6069
E-mail: ljwallace@purdue.edu
URL: http://www.kv.k12.in.us/LSC/nc22.htm
Contact: Lewie J. Wallace, Fleet Capt.
Local. Organized to coordinate Catalina 22 one-design class racing, interfleet and interclub cruising activities, and to serve as a central media for distribution of information and publicity pertinent to Catalina 22 yachts. Members are comprised of Catalina 22 owners in the central Indiana area. Currently, members sail primarily with Eagle Creek Sailing Club in Indianapolis and Lafayette Sailing Club in Lafayette. **Affiliated With:** Catalina 22 National Sailing Association.

6480 ■ Club Managers Association of America - Purdue University
c/o Renee Ebert, Pres.
700 W State St.
West Lafayette, IN 47907
E-mail: ebertr@purdue.edu
URL: http://web.ics.purdue.edu/~cmaa
Contact: Renee Ebert, Pres.
Local. Promotes and advances friendly relations between and among persons connected with the management of clubs. Encourages the education and advancement of members in the field of club management. **Affiliated With:** Club Managers Association of America.

6481 ■ FarmHouse - Purdue University Chapter
1028 State St.
West Lafayette, IN 47906
Ph: (765)743-4681
URL: http://web.ics.purdue.edu/~fhouse
Contact: Jaret Wicker, Pres.
Local. Promotes good fellowship and studiousness. Encourages members to seek the best in their chosen lines of study as well as in life. Works for the intellectual, spiritual, social, moral and physical development of members. **Affiliated With:** Farmhouse.

6482 ■ Greater Lafayette Young Life
PO Box 2630
West Lafayette, IN 47996
Ph: (765)429-8988
URL: http://GreaterLafayette.younglife.org
Local.

6483 ■ Harrison High School - Young Life
PO Box 2630
West Lafayette, IN 47996
Ph: (765)429-8988
URL: http://whereis.younglife.org/FriendlyUrlRedirector.aspx?ID=C-901
Local.

6484 ■ Indiana Auctioneers Association (IAA)
PO Box 2881
West Lafayette, IN 47996
Ph: (765)463-4188
Fax: (765)497-1399
E-mail: info@indianaauctioneers.com
URL: http://indianaauctioneers.org
Contact: Georgia Jones, Exec.Dir.
State.

6485 ■ Indiana Occupational Therapy Association (IOTA)
PO Box 2702
West Lafayette, IN 47996-2702
Ph: (765)471-7604
Fax: (765)474-4324
Free: (800)688-4682
E-mail: inota@inota.com
URL: http://www.inota.com
Contact: Kathleen Foley, Pres.
State.

6486 ■ Indiana State Dairy Association (ISDA)
c/o Bob Albrecht, Exec.Sec.
Poultry Bldg., Rm. 120
125 S Russell St.
West Lafayette, IN 47907-2042
Ph: (765)494-8025
Fax: (765)494-9347
Free: (800)973-5753
E-mail: albrecht@purdue.edu
URL: http://www.ansc.purdue.edu/dairy/isda
Contact: Bob Albrecht, Exec.Sec.
State. Provides dairy management record services.

6487 ■ Indiana State Poultry Association (ISPA)
c/o Paul Wm. Brennan, Exec.VP
Purdue Univ., Animal Sciences
915 W State St.
West Lafayette, IN 47907-2054
Ph: (765)494-8517
Fax: (765)496-1600
URL: http://ag.ansc.purdue.edu/ispa
State. **Publications:** *Wings, Webs, and Wattles*, periodic. Newsletter. **Conventions/Meetings:** quarterly board meeting.

6488 ■ Jefferson High School - Young Life
PO Box 2630
West Lafayette, IN 47996
Ph: (765)429-8988
URL: http://whereis.younglife.org/FriendlyUrlRedirector.aspx?ID=C-3890
Local.

6489 ■ McCutcheon High School - Young Life
PO Box 2630
West Lafayette, IN 47996
Ph: (765)429-8988
URL: http://whereis.younglife.org/FriendlyUrlRedirector.aspx?ID=C-899
Local.

6490 ■ Michiana Orchid Society
c/o Rick Hendrickson
3605 U.S.Hwy. 52 W.
West Lafayette, IN 47906-8863
Ph: (765)463-3500
E-mail: hendr@ecn.purdue.edu
URL: National Affiliate–www.orchidweb.org
Professional growers, botanists, hobbyists, and others interested in extending the knowledge, production, use, and appreciation of orchids. **Affiliated With:** American Orchid Society.

6491 ■ Military Officers Association of America, Lafayette Chapter
c/o Maj. Jerry Brown
2413 Trace 24
West Lafayette, IN 47906-1887
Ph: (765)743-3816
E-mail: ccbrown@gte.net
URL: National Affiliate–www.moaa.org
Contact: Maj. Jerry Brown, Contact
Local. **Affiliated With:** Military Officers Association of America.

6492 ■ Muslim Student Association - Purdue University
c/o Islamic Society of Greater Lafayette
1022 First St.
West Lafayette, IN 47906
Ph: (765)743-8650
URL: http://expert.ics.purdue.edu/~msa
Contact: Hany Gabal, Pres.
Local. Muslim students in North America. Seeks to advance the interests of members; works to enable members to practice Islam as a complete way of life. **Affiliated With:** Muslim Students Association of the United States and Canada.

6493 ■ National Association for Multicultural Education, Region 5
c/o Pamala V. Morris, Dir.
Purdue Univ.
615 W State St.
West Lafayette, IN 47907-2053
Ph: (765)494-8293
Fax: (765)496-1152
E-mail: pmorris@purdue.edu
URL: National Affiliate–www.nameorg.org
Contact: Pamala V. Morris, Dir.
Regional. Represents individuals and groups with an interest in multicultural education from all levels of education, different academic disciplines and from diverse educational institutions and occupations. Provides leadership in national and state dialogues on equity, diversity and multicultural education. Works to fight injustices in schools and in communities. Seeks to ensure that all students receive an equitable education. **Affiliated With:** National Association for Multicultural Education.

6494 ■ National Society of Black Engineers - Purdue University Chapter
550 Stadium Mall Dr., Civil Engg. Bldg. 1246
West Lafayette, IN 47907
Ph: (765)494-7047
E-mail: nsbe@ecn.purdue.edu
URL: http://www.ecn.purdue.edu/NSBE
Contact: John Wright, Pres.
Local. Strives to increase the number of culturally responsible Black engineers who excel academically, succeed professionally and positively impact the community. **Affiliated With:** National Society of Black Engineers.

6495 ■ Pheasants Forever Central Indiana, Sagamore
3461 Woodmar Ct.
West Lafayette, IN 47906
Ph: (765)463-6932
URL: http://pfcic.org
Contact: Darren Unland, Pres.
Local. **Affiliated With:** Pheasants Forever.

6496 ■ Psi Chi, National Honor Society in Psychology - Purdue University
c/o Dept. of Psychological Sciences
703 Third St.
West Lafayette, IN 47907
E-mail: agroth@purdue.edu
URL: http://web.ics.purdue.edu/~amtaylor/psichi/psichimainpage.html
Local. **Affiliated With:** Psi Chi, National Honor Society in Psychology.

6497 ■ Purdue NORML
c/o Conrad Golbov, Pres.
108 S River Rd., No. 307
West Lafayette, IN 47906-3712
Ph: (775)813-7408
E-mail: cgolbov@purdue.edu
URL: http://expert.ics.purdue.edu/~norml
Contact: Conrad Golbov, Pres.
Local. Practices campus activism for the repeal and reform of harmful marijuana laws. **Affiliated With:** National Organization for the Reform of Marijuana Laws.

6498 ■ Purdue University Meteorological Association (PUMA)
Dept. of Earth/Atmospheric Sci.
550 Stadium Mall Dr.
West Lafayette, IN 47907
E-mail: kklockow@purdue.edu
Contact: Kim Klockow, Pres.
Local. Professional meteorologists, oceanographers, and hydrologists; interested students and nonprofessionals. **Affiliated With:** American Meteorological Society. **Formerly:** (2001) American Meteorological Society, Purdue University.

6499 ■ Society of Manufacturing Engineers - Purdue University - Lafayette S006
1417 Knoy Hall - Rm. 131
West Lafayette, IN 47907
Ph: (765)494-7515
Fax: (765)494-6219
E-mail: bcharriger@tech.purdue.edu
URL: National Affiliate–www.sme.org
Contact: Bradley C. Harriger, Contact
Local. Advances manufacturing knowledge to gain competitive advantage. Improves skills and manufacturing solutions for the growth of economy. Provides resources and opportunities for manufacturing professionals.

6500 ■ Sycamore Audubon Society
PO Box 2716
West Lafayette, IN 47996-2716
Ph: (765)583-2275
E-mail: sas@sycamoreaudubon.org
URL: http://www.audubon.org/chapter/in/sycamore/
Local. **Formerly:** (2005) National Audubon Society - Sycamore.

6501 ■ Theta Xi Fraternity, Theta Chapter
c/o John Nofli, Sr., Alumni Advisor
1051 David Ross Rd.
West Lafayette, IN 47906
Ph: (765)532-3036 (765)474-0078
Free: (888)722-2148
E-mail: nolfijg@ecn.purdue.edu
URL: http://www.thetaxipurdue.org
Contact: Nik Rooney, Pres.
Local. **Affiliated With:** Theta Xi.

6502 ■ Turkey Market Development Council
c/o Indiana State Poultry Association
Purdue University, Animal Sciences
915 W State St.
West Lafayette, IN 47907-2054
Ph: (765)494-8517
Fax: (765)496-1600
E-mail: pbrennan@purdue.edu
Contact: Paul Brennan, Exec.Dir.
Founded: 1976. **State**. Promotes turkey products, market development, research, and education. **Publications:** *Wings Webs Wattles*, quarterly. **Advertising:** accepted. **Conventions/Meetings:** quarterly board meeting • periodic workshop.

6503 ■ Wabash Valley Astronomical Society (WVAS)
PO Box 2020
West Lafayette, IN 47996-2020
E-mail: wyncott@verizon.net
URL: http://www.stargazing.net/wvas
Contact: George Wyncott, Treas.
Founded: 1972. **Members:** 40. **Membership Dues:** regular, $25 (annual). **Budget:** $1,000. **Local**. Individuals in Tippecanoe County, IN interested in astronomy. Seeks to further the knowledge of astronomy and promote interest in the science. Sponsors open houses and star parties. **Affiliated With:** Astronomical League. **Publications:** *The Nebula*, monthly. Newsletter • Directory, quarterly.

6504 ■ Walnut Council
c/o Nancy F. Gunning
Walnut Coun. Intl. Off.
Wright Forestry Ctr.
1011 N 725 W
West Lafayette, IN 47906-9431
Ph: (765)583-3501
Fax: (765)583-3512
E-mail: walnutcouncil@walnutcouncil.org
URL: http://www.walnutcouncil.org
Contact: Nancy F. Gunning, Contact
Founded: 1970. **Members:** 900. **Membership Dues:** $25 (annual). **Staff:** 1. **State Groups:** 12. **Local**. **Awards:** Black Walnut Achievement Award. **Frequency:** annual. **Type:** monetary. **Publications:** *Walnut Council Bulletin*, quarterly. Newsletter. **Price:** included in membership dues. **Advertising:** accepted. **Conventions/Meetings:** annual meeting, with workshops (exhibits).

6505 ■ West Lafayette High School Alumni Association
c/o Ronald P. Moore
PO Box 2186
West Lafayette, IN 47996-2186
E-mail: cbs@insightbb.com
URL: http://www.wlhsalumni.org
Founded: 2000. **Members:** 400. **Budget:** $10,000. **Local Groups:** 1. **Local. Publications:** *WL Alumni News*, 3/year. Newsletter. **Price:** free. **Circulation:** 2,800. **Conventions/Meetings:** annual reunion.

6506 ■ West Lafayette High School - Young Life
PO Box 2630
West Lafayette, IN 47996
Ph: (765)429-8988
URL: http://whereis.younglife.org/FriendlyUrlRedirector.aspx?ID=C-900
Local.

West Terre Haute

6507 ■ American Legion, Indiana Post 501
c/o John E. Heyen
1001 W US 40
West Terre Haute, IN 47885
Ph: (812)533-0025
Fax: (317)237-9891
URL: National Affiliate–www.legion.org
Contact: John E. Heyen, Contact
Local. Affiliated With: American Legion.

6508 ■ American Society for Quality, Wabash Valley Section 0919
c/o Wil Decker, Vice Chm.
PO Box 360
West Terre Haute, IN 47885
Ph: (317)230-5906
E-mail: wabashadmin@asqwabashvalley.org
URL: http://www.asqwabashvalley.org
Contact: Wil Decker, Vice Chm.
Local. Advances learning, quality improvement and knowledge exchange to improve business results and to create better workplaces and communities worldwide. Provides a forum for information exchange, professional development and continuous learning in the science of quality. **Affiliated With:** American Society for Quality.

Westfield

6509 ■ American Legion, Hochstedler Post 318
420 N Union St.
Westfield, IN 46074
Ph: (317)896-2453
Fax: (317)237-9891
URL: National Affiliate–www.legion.org
Local. Affiliated With: American Legion.

6510 ■ Habitat for Humanity Hamilton County
PO Box 247
Westfield, IN 46074-0247
Ph: (317)896-9423
URL: http://www.hfhhc.org
Local. Affiliated With: Habitat for Humanity International.

6511 ■ Indiana Military Vehicle Preservation Association
c/o Ted Ponius, Pres./Newsletter Ed.
13141 West Rd.
Westfield, IN 46074-9593
Ph: (317)873-2994
URL: National Affiliate–www.mvpa.org
Contact: Ted Ponius, Pres./Newsletter Ed.
State. Affiliated With: Military Vehicle Preservation Association.

6512 ■ Mutual Insurance Companies Association of Indiana
c/o Susan M. Andrews, Exec.VP/Gen. Mgr.
PO Box 787
Westfield, IN 46074-0787
Ph: (317)848-5067
Fax: (317)571-1089
Contact: Susan M. Andrews, Exec.VP/Gen.Mgr.
Founded: 1897. **Members:** 47. **Staff:** 2. **State. Awards:** Sherlock Award. **Frequency:** annual. **Type:** monetary. **Recipient:** for most outstanding action fighting insurance fraud or arson. **Computer Services:** database. **Publications:** *MICAI Monitor*, quarterly. Newsletter. **Price:** free. **Conventions/Meetings:** Annual State Convention, small trade show (exhibits) - every December.

6513 ■ Westfield Washington Chamber of Commerce (WWCC)
322 W Main St.
PO Box 534
Westfield, IN 46074
Ph: (317)896-2378 (317)867-8066
Fax: (317)867-2523
E-mail: info@westfield-chamber.org
URL: http://www.westfield-chamber.org
Contact: Julieann Sole, Exec.Dir.
Founded: 1981. **Members:** 350. **Staff:** 2. **For-Profit. Local.** Promotes business and community development in the Westfield-Washington Township, IN area. **Affiliated With:** U.S. Chamber of Commerce. **Publications:** *Directory of Community*, biennial • Newsletter, monthly. **Conventions/Meetings:** annual Community Night - meeting - always September • monthly Membership Meeting - workshop - always third Thursday.

Westport

6514 ■ American Legion, Meredith Low Post 134
PO Box 711
Westport, IN 47283
Ph: (317)630-1300
Fax: (317)237-9891
URL: National Affiliate–www.legion.org
Local. Affiliated With: American Legion.

Westville

6515 ■ American Legion, Rhen Hilkert Post 21
PO Box 24
Westville, IN 46391
Ph: (219)785-2923
Fax: (317)237-9891
URL: National Affiliate–www.legion.org
Local. Affiliated With: American Legion.

6516 ■ Indiana Association for Developmental Education (INADE)
c/o Dr. Linda Duttlinger, Pres.
1401 S US 421
Westville, IN 46391
Ph: (219)785-5217
E-mail: lduttlinger@pnc.edu
URL: http://faculty.ivytech.edu/~rmetzger/inade
Contact: Dr. Linda Duttlinger, Pres.
State. Seeks to improve the theory and practice of developmental education. Enhances the professional capabilities of development educators. Supports student learning and provides public leadership. **Affiliated With:** National Association for Developmental Education.

6517 ■ International Association of Machinists and Aerospace Workers, LL-2903
PO Box 180
Westville, IN 46391
Ph: (219)785-4097
Fax: (219)785-1528
E-mail: smiller168@cpmail.ivytech.edu
URL: http://www.locallodge2903.com
Contact: Tim Ward, Pres.
Members: 260. **Local.** Seeks for the dignity and equality of the workers. Strives to provide contractors with well-trained, productive employees. **Affiliated With:** International Association of Machinists and Aerospace Workers.

6518 ■ Westville Area Chamber of Commerce (WACC)
PO Box 215
Westville, IN 46391-0215
Ph: (219)785-2824
URL: National Affiliate–www.uschamber.com
Contact: Yvonne Lundwall, Pres.
Founded: 1982. **Members:** 74. **Membership Dues:** open, $50. **Staff:** 1. **Budget:** $15,000. **Local.** Promotes business and community development in LaPorte County, IN. Sponsors fall pumpkin festival. **Affiliated With:** U.S. Chamber of Commerce.

Wheatfield

6519 ■ American Legion, Wheatfield Post 406
17658 N 80 W
Wheatfield, IN 46392
Ph: (219)956-3365
Fax: (317)237-9891
URL: National Affiliate–www.legion.org
Local. Affiliated With: American Legion.

Whiteland

6520 ■ American Red Cross, Johnson County Office
41 N U.S. 31
Whiteland, IN 46184
Ph: (317)535-5959
Local.

Whitestown

6521 ■ American Legion, Indiana Post 410
c/o Donald E. Pipes
PO Box 163
Whitestown, IN 46075
Ph: (317)769-3232
Fax: (317)237-9891
URL: National Affiliate–www.legion.org
Contact: Donald E. Pipes, Contact
Local. Affiliated With: American Legion.

6522 ■ Tails a' Waggin' Rescue
c/o Jane A. Heine
PO Box 37
Whitestown, IN 46075
Ph: (317)769-2543
Fax: (317)769-4007
E-mail: jane@tailsawaggin.org
URL: http://www.tailsawaggin.org
Local.

6523 ■ West Central Indiana Angus Association
c/o Mark Smith, Pres.
2463 N 675 E
Whitestown, IN 46075
Ph: (317)769-6789
E-mail: mnm87smith@aol.com
URL: National Affiliate–www.angus.org
Contact: Mark Smith, Pres.
Local. Affiliated With: American Angus Association.

Whiting

6524 ■ American Legion Post 80
c/o John J. Beno
2003 Indianapolis Blvd.
Whiting, IN 46394
Ph: (219)659-0215
URL: National Affiliate–www.legion.org
Contact: Jack Banko, Contact
Local. Affiliated With: American Legion.

6525 ■ Compassionate Friends - Lake Porter County Chapter
c/o Patti Ward
1737 Lincoln Ave.
Whiting, IN 46394
Ph: (219)464-1516
E-mail: lake_portertcf@yahoo.com
URL: http://www.geocities.com/lake_portertcf
Contact: Chris McDonald, Contact
Local.

6526 ■ Whiting - Robertsdale Chamber of Commerce
1442 119th St.
Whiting, IN 46394
Ph: (219)659-0292
Fax: (219)659-5851
E-mail: puccini99@aol.com
URL: http://www.whitingindiana.com
Contact: Gayle Faulkner-Kosalko, Exec.Dir.
Founded: 1923. **Membership Dues:** resident/non-profit, $36 (annual) • business (based on number of employees), $144-$4,320 (annual). **Local.** Promotes business and community development in Whiting-Robertsdale, IN area. **Additional Websites:** http://www.pierogifest.net/info.html. **Publications:** *Write Stuff*, monthly. Magazine. **Circulation:** 13,000. **Advertising:** accepted.

Williamsburg

6527 ■ American Legion, Williamsburg Post 442
7213 Morgan Creek Rd.
Williamsburg, IN 47393
Ph: (317)874-1419
Fax: (317)237-9891
URL: National Affiliate–www.legion.org
Local. Affiliated With: American Legion.

Williamsport

6528 ■ American Legion, Warren Post 259
408 State Rd. 28 E
Williamsport, IN 47993
Ph: (317)630-1300
Fax: (317)237-9891
URL: National Affiliate–www.legion.org
Local. Affiliated With: American Legion.

6529 ■ Warren County Community Foundation (WCCF)
31 N Monroe St.
Williamsport, IN 47993-1117
Ph: (765)764-1501
E-mail: wccf@warrenco.net
URL: http://wccf.warrenco.net
Contact: Susan Stratman, Exec.Dir.
Local.

6530 ■ Warren County Local Economic Development Organization
c/o Carol C. Clark, Dir.
31 N Monroe St.
Williamsport, IN 47993-1117
Ph: (765)762-6055
Fax: (765)764-1501
E-mail: ledo@warrenadvantage.com
URL: http://www.warrenadvantage.com
Contact: Carol C. Clark, Dir.
Local.

Winamac

6531 ■ American Legion, Pulaski County Post 71
110 N Franklin St.
Winamac, IN 46996
Ph: (219)946-4443
Fax: (317)237-9891
URL: National Affiliate–www.legion.org
Local. Affiliated With: American Legion.

6532 ■ Arrowhead Country Resource Conservation and Development Council
311 Northwest St.
Winamac, IN 46996
Ph: (574)946-3022
Fax: (574)946-7391
E-mail: randy.moore@in.usda.gov
URL: National Affiliate–www.rcdnet.org
Contact: Randy Moore, Coor.
Local. Affiliated With: National Association of Resource Conservation and Development Councils.

6533 ■ International Chiropractors Association of Indiana (ICAI)
c/o Bruce Hermann, Treas.
439 E Old State Rd. 14
Winamac, IN 46996
Ph: (574)946-6111
Free: (800)662-4224
E-mail: hrmchiro@pwrtc.com
URL: http://www.icai.net
Contact: James Thwaits, Pres.
Membership Dues: full, $175 (annual) • 2nd year in practice, $100 (annual) • 2nd year in practice (former student member), $50 (annual) • 1st year in practice, $50 (annual) • 1st year in practice (former student member), $25 (annual) • retired, $50 (annual) • out of state, $30 (annual). **State.** Promotes the science, philosophy and art of the chiropractic profession by advocating the highest standard of ethics in practice; by working united in the advancement of the profession; by developing close cooperation among the doctors with the Association for the welfare of all doctors of chiropractic and the public they serve; and by promoting desirable relationships with other entities for the benefit of the chiropractic profession. **Affiliated With:** International Chiropractors Association.

6534 ■ Pulaski County REACT
PO Box 293
Winamac, IN 46996
Ph: (219)946-3857
URL: http://www.reactintl.org/teaminfo/usa_teams/teams-usin.htm
Local. Trained communication experts and professional volunteers. Provides volunteer public service and emergency communications through the use of radios (Citizen Band, General Mobile Radio Service, UHF and HAM). Coordinates with radio industries and government on safety communication matters and supports charitable activities and community organizations.

Winchester

6535 ■ American Legion, Randolph Post 39
304 S East St.
Winchester, IN 47394
Ph: (317)584-2941
Fax: (317)237-9891
URL: National Affiliate–www.legion.org
Local. Affiliated With: American Legion.

6536 ■ Randolph County Board of Realtors
400 W Franklin St.
Winchester, IN 47394
Ph: (765)584-1011
Fax: (765)584-3819
E-mail: nanceandsandifar@aol.com
URL: National Affiliate–www.realtor.org
Contact: James R. Nance, Exec. Officer
Local. Strives to develop real estate business practices. Advocates the right to own, use and transfer real property. Provides a facility for professional development, research and exchange of information among members and to the general public. **Affiliated With:** National Association of Realtors.

6537 ■ United Way of Randolph County
109 W Franklin St.
Winchester, IN 47394-1821
Ph: (765)584-4483
E-mail: rcuway@jayco.net
URL: National Affiliate–national.unitedway.org
Founded: 1998. **Staff:** 1. **Local.** Provides funding programs to benefit residents of Randolph County. **Affiliated With:** United Way of America. **Formerly:** (2004) United Way of the Greater Union City Area.

6538 ■ Winchester Area Chamber of Commerce
112 W Washington St.
Winchester, IN 47394
Ph: (765)584-3731
Fax: (765)584-5544
E-mail: chamber@globalsite.net
URL: http://www.winchesterchamber.org
Contact: Vicki Phenis, Exec.Dir.
Membership Dues: retail, wholesale, service, agriculture (based on number of employees), $100-$600 (annual) • finance (based on million net assets), $330-$770 (annual) • industry (based on number of employees), $165-$880 (annual) • professional, $100 (annual) • non-profit club or organization, $50 (annual) • civic, $20-$30 (annual). **Local.** Promotes business and community development in Winchester, IN area. **Committees:** Annual Banquet; Business Development; Education; Government Relations; Home & Garden Show; Membership Development; Public Relations & Marketing; Randolph County Tourism. **Publications:** Newsletter, quarterly.

Windfall

6539 ■ American Legion, Jesse Rogers Post 483
213 N Windfall
Windfall, IN 46076
Ph: (317)630-1300
Fax: (317)237-9891
URL: National Affiliate–www.legion.org
Local. Affiliated With: American Legion.

Wingate

6540 ■ American Legion, Wingate Post 174
PO Box 21
Wingate, IN 47994
Ph: (317)275-2477
Fax: (317)237-9891
URL: National Affiliate–www.legion.org
Local. Affiliated With: American Legion.

Winona Lake

6541 ■ Warsaw Astronomical Society
c/o James D. Tague, Treas.
1308 Sunset Dr.
Winona Lake, IN 46590
Ph: (574)269-1856
E-mail: jtague@kconline.com
URL: http://clubs.kconline.com/was/
Local.

Winslow

6542 ■ American Legion, Winslow Post 115
PO Box 361
Winslow, IN 47598
Ph: (812)789-5228
Fax: (317)237-9891
URL: National Affiliate–www.legion.org
Local. Affiliated With: American Legion.

Wolcott

6543 ■ American Legion, Wolcott Post 294
PO Box 128
Wolcott, IN 47995
Ph: (219)984-5579
Fax: (317)237-9891
URL: National Affiliate–www.legion.org
Local. Affiliated With: American Legion.

Wolcottville

6544 ■ American Legion, Verner Hanes Post 110
601 W County Line Rd.
Wolcottville, IN 46795
Ph: (317)630-1300
Fax: (317)237-9891
URL: National Affiliate–www.legion.org
Local. Affiliated With: American Legion.

Woodburn

6545 ■ American Legion, Woodburn Post 377
22115 Woodburn Dr.
Woodburn, IN 46797
Ph: (219)632-4711
Fax: (317)237-9891
URL: National Affiliate–www.legion.org
Local. Affiliated With: American Legion.

Worthington

6546 ■ American Legion, Bashaw-Roth Post 106
109 S Commercial St.
Worthington, IN 47471
Ph: (812)875-2271
Fax: (317)237-9891
URL: National Affiliate–www.legion.org
Local. Affiliated With: American Legion.

Yorktown

6547 ■ American Legion, Yorktown Post 321
2110 S Broadway
Yorktown, IN 47396
Ph: (317)759-7916
Fax: (317)237-9891
URL: National Affiliate–www.legion.org
Local. Affiliated With: American Legion.

Zionsville

6548 ■ American Legion, Indiana Post 79
c/o Francis Neidlinger
9950 E 600 S
Zionsville, IN 46077
Ph: (317)873-3105
Fax: (317)237-9891
URL: National Affiliate–www.legion.org
Contact: Francis Neidlinger, Contact
Local. Affiliated With: American Legion.

6549 ■ Boys and Girls Club of Zionsville
1575 Mulberry St.
Zionsville, IN 46077-1146
Ph: (317)873-6670
Fax: (317)873-9176
E-mail: info@bagcoz.org
URL: http://bagcoz.org
Contact: Chuck Smitha, Exec.Dir.
Founded: 1990. **Members:** 1,250. **Membership Dues:** individual, $45 (annual). **Staff:** 10. **Budget:** $320,000. **Local.** Provides social development, recreational, and educational programs to youth ages 5 to 18. **Publications:** *Z-Club Newsletter*, quarterly. **Price:** free. **Advertising:** accepted. **Conventions/ Meetings:** monthly board meeting - always fourth Wednesday except July.

6550 ■ Greater Zionsville Chamber of Commerce (GZCC)
135 S Elm St.
PO Box 148
Zionsville, IN 46077
Ph: (317)873-3836
Fax: (317)873-3836
E-mail: info@zionsvillechamber.org
URL: http://www.zionsvillechamber.org
Contact: Debbie Cranfill, Exec.Dir.
Founded: 1961. **Members:** 270. **Local.** Promotes business and community development in the Zionsville, IN area. Sponsors annual country market, street dance, and village tour of homes. **Publications:** *Greater Zionsville Chamber of Commerce Newsletter*, quarterly. **Price:** free for members • *Membership Directory and Research Guide*, annual. **Conventions/Meetings:** monthly board meeting.

6551 ■ Indiana Choral Directors Association (ICDA)
c/o Marie Palmer, Pres.
Zionsville Middle School
900 N Ford Rd.
Zionsville, IN 46077
Ph: (317)873-2426
E-mail: mpalmer@zcs.k12.in.us
URL: http://www.in-acda.org
Contact: Marie Palmer, Pres.
Membership Dues: associate/active, $75 (annual) • student, $30 (annual) • life, $2,000. **State.** Promotes excellence in choral music through performance, composition, publication, research and teaching. Elevates choral music's position in American society. **Subgroups:** Repertoire and Standards. **Affiliated With:** American Choral Directors Association. **Publications:** *ICDA Notations*, quarterly. Newsletter. **Advertising:** accepted. Alternate Formats: online.

6552 ■ Indiana Pork Producers Association (IPPA)
4649 Northwestern Dr.
Zionsville, IN 46077-9248
Ph: (317)872-7500
Fax: (317)872-6675
Free: (800)535-2405
E-mail: info@inpork.org
URL: http://www.inpork.org
Contact: Rick Wagner, Office Administrator
Founded: 1963. **Members:** 6,300. **Staff:** 5. **State.** Represents the interests of Indiana pork producers. **Publications:** *Check Off*, biennial. Newsletter. **Conventions/Meetings:** annual conference - always January in Indianapolis, IN.

6553 ■ Sons of Norway, Circle City Lodge 5-614
c/o Alma T. Lathrop, Sec.
1250 S 950 E
Zionsville, IN 46077-9543
Ph: (317)769-4647
E-mail: mom@lathrop.com
URL: National Affiliate–www.sofn.com
Contact: Alma T. Lathrop, Sec.
Local. Affiliated With: Sons of Norway.

6554 ■ Zionsville Kiwanis Club
c/o John Wallace
675 S Ford Rd.
Zionsville, IN 46077
Ph: (765)482-2390
URL: http://www.bccn.boone.in.us/zk
Contact: John Wallace, Contact
Local.

6555 ■ Zionsville Lions Club
PO Box 252
Zionsville, IN 46077
Ph: (317)873-5540
URL: http://www.zionsvillelions.com
Local. Affiliated With: Lions Clubs International.

Ada

6556 ■ Air and Waste Management Association - West Michigan Chapter
PO Box 465
Ada, MI 49301
Fax: (616)261-2740
URL: http://www.wmawma.org
Local. Affiliated With: Air and Waste Management Association.

6557 ■ Cannonsburg Challenged Ski Association (CCSA)
c/o Craig Wallace
PO Box 352
Ada, MI 49301
Ph: (616)335-9869 (616)874-3060
Fax: (616)874-8581
E-mail: ski_ccsa@hotmail.com
URL: http://www.skiccsa.org
Contact: Mr. Craig Wallace, Pres.
Founded: 1980. **Local. Affiliated With:** Disabled Sports USA.

6558 ■ Kent County Conservation League
PO Box 397
Ada, MI 49301
Ph: (616)676-1056
Fax: (616)676-9884
E-mail: info@kccl.org
URL: http://www.kccl.org
Local. Affiliated With: National Skeet Shooting Association.

Addison

6559 ■ American Legion, Chauncey Curtis Smith Post 118
17335 Manitou Beach Rd.
Addison, MI 49220
Ph: (517)371-4720
Fax: (517)371-2401
URL: National Affiliate–www.legion.org
Local. Affiliated With: American Legion.

Adrian

6560 ■ Adrian Breakfast Lions Club
c/o Terry Hicks, Pres.
152 E Siena Heights Dr.
Adrian, MI 49221
Ph: (517)263-7173
URL: http://www.lionsdistrict11b1.org/lc_adrian_breakfast.htm
Contact: Terry Hicks, Pres.
Local. Affiliated With: Lions Clubs International.

6561 ■ Adrian Evening Lions Club
c/o Lawrence Richardson, Sec.
3030 Marvin Dr.
Adrian, MI 49221
Ph: (517)265-8010 (517)265-2963
E-mail: larryrichardson@lenawee.mi.us
URL: http://www.lionsdistrict11b1.org/lc_adrian_evening.htm
Contact: Lawrence Richardson, Sec.
Local. Affiliated With: Lions Clubs International.

6562 ■ Adrian - Young Life
PO Box 904
Adrian, MI 49221
Ph: (517)264-5437
URL: http://sites.younglife.org/_layouts/ylext/default.aspx?ID=C-1135
Local. Affiliated With: Young Life.

6563 ■ American Legion, G. Chandler Bond Post 275
543 W Maple Ave.
Adrian, MI 49221
Ph: (517)371-4720
Fax: (517)371-2401
URL: National Affiliate–www.legion.org
Local. Affiliated With: American Legion.

6564 ■ American Legion, Michigan Post 97
c/o William C. Stark
904 N Main St.
Adrian, MI 49221
Ph: (517)371-4720
Fax: (517)371-2401
URL: National Affiliate–www.legion.org
Contact: William C. Stark, Contact
Local. Affiliated With: American Legion.

6565 ■ American Red Cross, Lenawee County Chapter
204 N Broad
Adrian, MI 49221
Ph: (517)263-1904
URL: http://www.lenaweecounty.redcross.org
Local.

6566 ■ Ancient Order of Hibernians of Lenawee County - St. Patrick, Division No. 1
c/o George Brown, Pres.
1072 Orchard Ct.
Adrian, MI 49221
Ph: (517)263-8372 (517)266-1063
URL: http://www.geocities.com/lenaweeaoh
Contact: George Brown, Pres.
Local. Affiliated With: Ancient Order of Hibernians in America.

6567 ■ Ancient Order of Hibernians - Michigan State Board
c/o Patrick E. Maguire, Pres.
574 Hawthorne Dr.
Adrian, MI 49221
Ph: (517)263-5556
E-mail: pmam@tc3net.com
URL: http://www.michiganaoh.com
Contact: Patrick E. Maguire, Pres.
State. Affiliated With: Ancient Order of Hibernians in America.

6568 ■ Gardeners of America/Men's Garden Clubs of America - Maple City Men's Garden Club
c/o Marlin Caris, Pres.
2558 Airport Hwy.
Adrian, MI 49221-3606
Ph: (517)263-6137
URL: National Affiliate–www.tgoa-mgca.org
Contact: Marlin Caris, Pres.
Local.

6569 ■ Habitat for Humanity of Lenawee County (HFHLC)
1205 E Beecher St.
Adrian, MI 49221
Ph: (517)265-6157
Fax: (517)265-3827
E-mail: hfhlc@tc3net.com
URL: http://www.habitat-lenawee.org
Contact: Dick Drabek, Exec.Dir.
Founded: 1989. **Members:** 25. **Staff:** 3. **Local.** Ecumenical Christian organization devoted to making available decent, affordable housing to be purchased by low income families that are in need. **Affiliated With:** Habitat for Humanity International. **Publications:** *Partners*, quarterly. Newsletter. Contains current activities of the local affiliate. **Price:** free. **Circulation:** 1,000. **Conventions/Meetings:** monthly Working Meeting - board meeting - always third Monday.

6570 ■ Home Builders Association of Lenawee County
c/o Tommie Sprague
PO Box 119
Adrian, MI 49221-0119
Ph: (517)264-2545
Fax: (517)436-6485
URL: National Affiliate–www.nahb.org
Local. Single and multifamily home builders, commercial builders, and others associated with the building industry. **Affiliated With:** National Association of Home Builders.

6571 ■ Kiwanis Club of Adrian
PO Box 179
Adrian, MI 49221
E-mail: info@adriankiwanis.org
URL: http://www.adriankiwanis.org
Contact: Mark Gasche, Pres.
Local.

6572 ■ Lenawee Community REACT
1510 Village Green Ln.
Adrian, MI 49221
Ph: (517)260-3303
URL: http://www.reactintl.org/teaminfo/usa_teams/teams-usmi.htm
Local. Trained communication experts and professional volunteers. Provides volunteer public service and emergency communications through the use of radios (Citizen Band, General Mobile Radio Service, UHF and HAM). Coordinates with radio industries and government on safety communication matters and supports charitable activities and community organizations.

6573 ■ Lenawee County Association of Realtors
PO Box 425
Adrian, MI 49221
Ph: (517)263-0325
Fax: (517)263-0821
E-mail: info@lenaweerealtors.com
URL: http://www.lenaweecountyrealtors.com
Contact: Jim Palmer, Pres.
Local. Strives to develop real estate business practices. Advocates the right to own, use and transfer real property. Provides a facility for professional development, research and exchange of information among members. **Affiliated With:** National Association of Realtors.

6574 ■ Lenawee County Chamber of Commerce
5282 W US Hwy. 223, Ste.A
Adrian, MI 49221
Ph: (517)265-5141
Fax: (517)263-6065
E-mail: cphipp@lenaweechamber.com
URL: http://www.lenaweechamber.com
Contact: David B. Munson CEE, Pres./CEO
Founded: 1916. **Membership Dues:** non-profit, $240 • small business partnership, $365. **Local**. Partnership of 800 businesses, organizations and individuals. Strives to strengthen the regional economy and improve Lenawee County as a place to live, work and raise a family. **Awards:** Maple Leaf Award. **Type:** recognition. **Recipient:** for outstanding community service, leadership and citizenship. **Councils:** Area Business Connection; Corporate CEO.

6575 ■ Lenawee County Chamber of Foundation
5285 W US Hwy. 223, Ste.A
Adrian, MI 49221
Ph: (517)265-5141
Fax: (517)263-6065
E-mail: dmunson@lenaweechamber.com
URL: http://www.lenaweechamber.com
Contact: Margaret Noe, Chair
Founded: 1990. **Budget:** $250,000. **Nonmembership**. **Local**. Conducts fundraising activities to support leadership-training programs for volunteers serving nonprofit community service organizations in Lenawee County. Supports local economic development programs.

6576 ■ Lenawee County Chapter of National Alliance for the Mentally Ill
PO Box 3113
Adrian, MI 49221
Ph; (517)547-4825
E-mail: kiknbkk@aol.com
URL: http://mi.nami.org/lcc.html
Contact: James Nicholson, Pres.
Local. Strives to improve the quality of life of children and adults with severe mental illness through support, education, research and advocacy. **Affiliated With:** National Alliance for the Mentally Ill.

6577 ■ Lenawee County Conference and Visitors Bureau (LCCVB)
209 N Main St.
Adrian, MI 49221
Ph: (517)263-7747
Fax: (517)265-2242
Free: (800)536-2933
E-mail: lccvb@tc3net.com
URL: http://www.visitlenawee.com
Contact: Marilyn Schebil, Exec.Dir.
Founded: 1991. **Staff:** 1. **Budget:** $75,000. **Nonmembership**. **Local**. Promotes conference, travel and tourism business for the Lenawee County area. **Committees:** LCCUB Advisory. **Publications:** *Lenawee County CVB Visitor Guide*, annual. Brochure. Contains visitor information and descriptions of tourism-related businesses and events in Lenawee County. **Advertising:** accepted.

6578 ■ Lenawee Noon Lions Club
c/o Christine Wheaton, Pres.
9875 Stoddard Rd.
Adrian, MI 49221
Ph: (517)264-5300 (517)467-7650
E-mail: chritine.wheaton@lenawee.mi.us
URL: http://www.lionsdistrict11b1.org/lc_lenawee_noon.htm
Contact: Christine Wheaton, Pres.
Local. **Affiliated With:** Lions Clubs International.

6579 ■ Lenawee United Way and Volunteer Center
1354 N Main St.
Adrian, MI 49221
Ph: (517)263-4696
Fax: (517)265-3039
E-mail: uway@tc3net.com
URL: http://www.lenaweeunitedway.org
Contact: Kathleen Schanz, Exec.Dir.
Founded: 1942. **Local**. **Affiliated With:** United Way of America. **Formerly:** United Way of the Lenawee Area.

6580 ■ National Active and Retired Federal Employees Association - Lenawee 1953
2763 Drexel Blvd.
Adrian, MI 49221-3520
Ph: (517)265-6512
URL: National Affiliate–www.narfe.org
Contact: Sharon A. Williams, Contact
Local. Protects the retirement future of employees through education. Informs members on issues affecting the retirement. **Affiliated With:** National Association of Retired Federal Employees.

6581 ■ North Central LUGAS
c/o Kapnick & Co. Inc.
PO Box 1801
Adrian, MI 49221
Ph: (517)263-4600
Fax: (517)263-6658
E-mail: kevincrow@kapnick.com
URL: National Affiliate–www.ascnet.org
Contact: Kevin Crow, Pres.
Regional. Represents insurance agents and brokers using the Agency Manager software. Promotes successful automation and business practices through communication, education, and advocacy. **Affiliated With:** Applied Systems Client Network.

6582 ■ Psi Chi, National Honor Society in Psychology - Adrian College
c/o Dept. of Psychology
302B N Hall
110 S Madison St.
Adrian, MI 49221-2575
Ph: (517)264-3191 (517)264-3955
Fax: (517)264-3827
E-mail: ghammerle@adrian.edu
URL: http://www.psichi.org/chapters/info.asp?chapter_id=341
Contact: Gordon C. Hammerle PhD, Advisor
Local.

6583 ■ Psi Chi, National Honor Society in Psychology - Siena Heights University
c/o Dept. of Social and Behavioral Sciences
1247 E Siena Heights Dr.
Adrian, MI 49221
Ph: (517)264-7850 (517)264-7856
Fax: (517)264-7731
E-mail: pmotsch@sienahts.edu
URL: National Affiliate–www.psichi.org
Local. **Affiliated With:** Psi Chi, National Honor Society in Psychology.

6584 ■ Sweet Adelines International, Irish Hills Chapter
Joe Ann Steele Bldg.
130 N Main St.
Adrian, MI 49221-2745
Ph: (419)822-4292
E-mail: csgi@bright.net
URL: National Affiliate–www.sweetadelineintl.org
Contact: Irene Shelt, Contact
Local. Advances the musical art form of barbershop harmony through education and performances. Provides education, training and coaching in the development of women's four-part barbershop harmony. **Affiliated With:** Sweet Adelines International.

6585 ■ Tecumseh - Young Life
PO Box 904
Adrian, MI 49221
Ph: (517)264-5437
URL: http://sites.younglife.org/_layouts/ylext/default.aspx?ID=C-2811
Local. **Affiliated With:** Young Life.

6586 ■ Young Life Lenawee County
PO Box 904
Adrian, MI 49221
Ph: (517)264-5437
URL: http://sites.younglife.org/sites/lenawee/default.aspx
Local. **Affiliated With:** Young Life.

Albion

6587 ■ Albion-Homer United Way
203 S Superior St.
Albion, MI 49224-1774
Ph: (601)545-7141
URL: National Affiliate–national.unitedway.org
Local. **Affiliated With:** United Way of America.

6588 ■ Albion Volunteer Service Organization
203 S Superior St.
Albion, MI 49224
Ph: (517)629-5574
E-mail: avso@forks.org
URL: http://www.avso.forks.org
Contact: Alfredia Dysart-Drake, Contact
Local.

6589 ■ American Legion, Michigan Post 55
c/o Patrick Leo Hanlon
1230 Edwards St.
Albion, MI 49224
Ph: (517)371-4720
Fax: (517)371-2401
URL: National Affiliate–www.legion.org
Contact: Patrick Leo Hanlon, Contact
Local. **Affiliated With:** American Legion.

6590 ■ Greater Albion Chamber of Commerce (GACC)
416 S Superior St.
PO Box 238
Albion, MI 49224
Ph: (517)629-5533
Fax: (517)629-4284
E-mail: gacoc@forks.org
URL: http://www.greateralbionchamber.org
Contact: Sue Marcos, Pres.
Founded: 1923. **Members:** 190. **Membership Dues:** base, $175 (annual). **Staff:** 2. **Budget:** $90,000. **Local**. Promotes business and community development in the Albion, MI area. **Awards:** Small Business of the Year. **Frequency:** annual. **Type:** recognition. **Publications:** *Greater Albion Business News*, monthly. Newsletter. **Conventions/Meetings:** annual

Cardboard Classic Sled Race - competition - every 3rd Sunday of January • annual Festival of the Forks - every 3rd weekend of September.

6591 ■ Michigan Safety Conference (MSC)
c/o Sandra Irion, Exec.Dir.
3511 Country Club Way
Albion, MI 49224
Ph: (517)630-8340
Fax: (517)630-8341
E-mail: sandy@michsafetyconference.org
URL: http://www.michsafetyconference.org
Contact: Sandra Irion, Exec.Dir.
State. Provides safety, health, and environmental education to the citizens of Michigan. Puts on an annual safety conference in Lansing each year with 130 seminars on all types of safety and includes over 200 exhibitors.

6592 ■ Psi Chi, National Honor Society in Psychology - Albion College
c/o Dept. of Psychology
Olin Hall
203 S Huron St.
Albion, MI 49224-1880
Ph: (517)629-0279 (517)629-0395
Fax: (517)629-0407
E-mail: aotto@albion.edu
URL: http://www.psichi.org/chapters/info.asp?chapter_id=181
Contact: Amy L. Otto PhD, Advisor
Local.

6593 ■ Veteran Motor Car Club of America - Jackson Cascades Chapter
c/o Richard Porter, Pres.
28650 H Dr. N
Albion, MI 49224
Ph: (517)629-2774
URL: National Affiliate–www.vmcca.org
Contact: Richard Porter, Pres.
Local. Affiliated With: Veteran Motor Car Club of America.

6594 ■ Woodlands Library Cooperative
415 S Superior, Ste.A
Albion, MI 49224-2174
Ph: (517)629-9469
Fax: (517)629-3812
E-mail: jseidl@monroe.lib.mi.us
URL: http://woodlands.lib.mi.us
Contact: James C. Seidl, Dir.
Founded: 1978. **Members:** 36. **Membership Dues:** associate (schools, academic, special libraries), $150 (annual). **Staff:** 2. **Budget:** $451,292. **Regional**. Public libraries (36) and school, academic, and special libraries (40) in southern Michigan. Coordinates resource sharing programs, continuing education, group discounts, and information dissemination. **Publications:** *News Notes*, 5/year. Newsletter.

Alger

6595 ■ Collie Club of America, Michigan
c/o Shirley A. Schaffer, District Dir.
5735 S M-76
Alger, MI 48610
Ph: (989)942-6265
E-mail: heatherhill@m33access.com
URL: National Affiliate–www.collieclubofamerica.org
Contact: Shirley A. Schaffer, District Dir.
State. "Encourages the breeding of true type collies, both rough and smooth"; works to promote these two varieties of collies; and disseminates information to members on owning, raising and caring for collies. **Affiliated With:** Collie Club of America.

Algonac

6596 ■ ACF Chefs 200 Club Detroit Michigan
c/o Jeffrey Heinzman, Pres.
2225 Pointe Tremble
Algonac, MI 48001
Ph: (810)394-2331
Fax: (586)791-0823
E-mail: jeffheinzman@comcast.net
URL: National Affiliate–www.acfchefs.org
Contact: Jeffrey Heinzman CEC, Pres.
Local. Promotes the culinary profession. Provides on-going educational training and networking for members. Provides opportunities for competition, professional recognition and access to educational forums with other culinarians at local, regional, national and international events. **Affiliated With:** American Culinary Federation.

6597 ■ Algonac Firefighters Association
c/o Charles Johnson
805 St. Clair Dr.
Algonac, MI 48001-0000
Ph: (810)794-3431
E-mail: afd@i-if.com
Contact: Charles Johnson, Chief
Local.

6598 ■ American Legion, Algonac Post 278
734 Pleasant St.
Algonac, MI 48001
Ph: (517)371-4720
Fax: (517)371-2401
URL: National Affiliate–www.legion.org
Local. Affiliated With: American Legion.

6599 ■ Greater Algonac Chamber of Commerce
1396 St. Clair River Dr.
PO Box 375
Algonac, MI 48001
Ph: (810)794-5511
Fax: (810)794-5511
E-mail: execdirector@algonacchamber.com
URL: http://www.algonacchamber.com
Contact: Lisa M. Edwards, Exec.Dir.
Members: 50. **Membership Dues:** business, $150 (annual) • nonprofit organization, $100 (annual) • friend, $50 (annual). **Local**. Promotes business and community development in the Algonac, MI area. **Publications:** *The Chamber Connection*, bimonthly. Newsletter. Alternate Formats: online. **Conventions/Meetings:** monthly board meeting - starts at 9 AM, Algonac, MI.

Allegan

6600 ■ Allegan Area Chamber of Commerce (AACC)
882 Marshall St., Ste.B
Allegan, MI 49010
Ph: (269)673-2479
Fax: (269)673-7190
E-mail: chamber@allegan.net
URL: http://www.chamber.allegan.net
Contact: Lynda Ferris, Dir.
Members: 210. **Staff:** 3. **Budget:** $95,000. **Local**. Promotes business and community development in the Allegan, MI area. **Affiliated With:** U.S. Chamber of Commerce. **Publications:** Directory, annual. **Price:** free • Newsletter, monthly. **Conventions/Meetings:** monthly general assembly.

6601 ■ Allegan County United Way
650 Grand St.
Allegan, MI 49010
Ph: (269)673-6545
Fax: (269)686-5912
E-mail: acuw@chartermi.net
URL: http://www.acuw.org
Contact: Bob Ells, Exec.Dir.
Local. Affiliated With: United Way of America.

6602 ■ Allegan Resource Center
219 Hubbard St.
Allegan, MI 49010
Ph: (269)673-8841
Fax: (269)673-1669
E-mail: arcallegan@datawise.net
URL: National Affiliate–www.TheArc.org
Contact: Pamela Wenzer Wisner, Exec.Dir.
Founded: 1956. **Membership Dues:** $20 (annual) • $50 (annual) • $100 (annual). **Staff:** 2. **Nonmembership**. **Local**. Advocates for people with developmental disabilities so they may live, learn, work, and play with respect, dignity, and meaningful involvement in their communities. Helps parents, professional workers, and others interested in individuals with mental retardation. Works to promote services, research, public understanding, and legislation for people with mental retardation and their families. **Affiliated With:** Arc of the United States. **Formerly:** (2004) Arc Allegan.

6603 ■ American Legion, Michigan Post 89
c/o Oscar Briggs
632 Eastern Ave.
Allegan, MI 49010
Ph: (517)371-4720
Fax: (517)371-2401
URL: National Affiliate–www.legion.org
Contact: Oscar Briggs, Contact
Local. Affiliated With: American Legion.

6604 ■ Arc/Allegan County
219 Hubbard St.
Allegan, MI 49010-1320
Ph: (269)673-8841
Fax: (269)673-1669
E-mail: arcallegan@datawise.net
URL: National Affiliate–www.thearc.org
Contact: Pamela Wisner, Exec.Dir.
Founded: 1956. **Members:** 100. **Membership Dues:** support, $20 (annual). **Staff:** 2. **Budget:** $80,000. **State Groups:** 1. **State**. Advocates for the rights of adults and children who are developmentally disabled and their families. Makes available educational and community advocacy services. **Also Known As:** Association for Retarded Citizens/Allegan County. **Publications:** *The Advocate*, semiannual. Newsletter. **Price:** free for members. **Circulation:** 300. **Conventions/Meetings:** annual meeting - May.

6605 ■ Ruffed Grouse Society, Southwestern Michigan Chapter
c/o Mark Janke
2676 111th Ave.
Allegan, MI 49010
Ph: (269)692-6867
E-mail: 48forest@menasha.com
URL: National Affiliate–www.ruffedgrousesociety.org
Contact: Mark Janke, Contact
Local. Affiliated With: Ruffed Grouse Society.

Allen

6606 ■ American Legion, Allen Post 538
PO Box 112
Allen, MI 49227
Ph: (517)371-4720
Fax: (517)371-2401
URL: National Affiliate–www.legion.org
Local. Affiliated With: American Legion.

Allen Park

6607 ■ AAA Michigan, Allen Park Office
15220 Southfield Rd.
Allen Park, MI 48101
Ph: (313)386-7000
Contact: Robert Williams, Gen.Mgr.
State. Formerly: (2005) AAA Michigan.

6608 ■ American Legion, Allen Park Post 409
6737 Allen Rd.
Allen Park, MI 48101
Ph: (517)371-4720
Fax: (517)371-2401
URL: National Affiliate–www.legion.org
Local. Affiliated With: American Legion.

6609 ■ Bennie PTA
17401 Champaign
Allen Park, MI 48101
Ph: (313)383-7512
URL: http://familyeducation.com/MI/Bennie_PTA
Contact: Linda Fitzgerald, Pres.
Local. Parents, teachers, students, and others interested in uniting the forces of home, school, and community. Promotes the welfare of children and youth.

6610 ■ First Catholic Slovak Ladies Association - Detroit Junior Branch 232
16959 Cambridge
Allen Park, MI 48101
Ph: (313)278-8816
URL: National Affiliate–www.fcsla.com
Local. **Affiliated With:** First Catholic Slovak Ladies Association.

6611 ■ First Catholic Slovak Ladies Association - Detroit Senior Branch 334
16959 Cambridge
Allen Park, MI 48101
Ph: (313)278-8816
URL: National Affiliate–www.fcsla.com
Local. **Affiliated With:** First Catholic Slovak Ladies Association.

6612 ■ Institute of Management Accountants, Detroit Metro Chapter
9920 Niver
Allen Park, MI 48101
Ph: (313)262-2223
Fax: (313)262-2239
E-mail: gkapanowski@williams-int.com
URL: http://www.imamichigan.org/detroit
Contact: Gary Kapanowski, Pres.
Membership Dues: regular, $175 (annual) • academic, $88 (annual) • student, $35 (annual). **Local**. Promotes professional and ethical standards. Equips members and students with knowledge and training required for the accounting profession. **Councils:** Michigan IMA. **Affiliated With:** Institute of Management Accountants. **Publications:** *The Monthly Metro*. Newsletter. Alternate Formats: online.

6613 ■ International Association for the Retractable Awning Industry, Michigan Chapter
9705 Sterling
Allen Park, MI 48101
E-mail: wagco1@yahoo.com
Founded: 1996. **Members:** 150. **Membership Dues:** individual, $35 (annual). **Staff:** 5. **Local**. **Libraries: Type:** reference. **Publications:** Handbooks. **Conventions/Meetings:** biennial conference.

6614 ■ Metro Detroit Chapter of Falcon Club of America
14909 Cleophus Ave.
Allen Park, MI 48101
Ph: (313)382-2993
E-mail: gogofalcon@wowway.com
URL: http://www.geocities.com/detroitfca
Contact: Gordon Leslie, Pres.
Local.

6615 ■ Rainbows, Michigan Chapter
c/o Connie Gladhill
18803 Grey
Allen Park, MI 48101
Ph: (313)383-2353
E-mail: conniegmk@surfmk.com
URL: National Affiliate–www.rainbows.org
Contact: Connie Gladhill; Contact
State. **Affiliated With:** RAINBOWS.

6616 ■ Water Wonderland Thunderbirds
15207 Philomene Blvd.
Allen Park, MI 48101
Ph: (313)928-7692
E-mail: nrzuch@hotmail.com
URL: National Affiliate–www.vintagethunderbirdclub.org
Local. **Affiliated With:** Vintage Thunderbird Club International.

Allendale

6617 ■ Allendale Chamber of Commerce
PO Box 539
Allendale, MI 49401
Ph: (616)895-6295
Fax: (616)895-6670
E-mail: aacc@allendalechamber.org
URL: http://www.allendalechamber.org
Contact: Julie Van Dyke, Exec.Dir.
Founded: 1978. **Members:** 150. **Membership Dues:** $125 (annual). **Staff:** 1. **Local**. Provides networking for area businesses. Sponsors monthly events.

6618 ■ Allendale Middle School - Wyldlife
PO Box 511
Allendale, MI 49401-0511
Ph: (616)895-7994
URL: http://sites.younglife.org/sites/ams/default.aspx
Local. **Affiliated With:** Young Life.

6619 ■ Baldwin St. MS - Wyldlife
PO Box 511
Allendale, MI 49401-0511
Ph: (616)895-7994
URL: http://sites.younglife.org/sites/bsms/default.aspx
Local. **Affiliated With:** Young Life.

6620 ■ Classical Association of Michigan
Grand Valley State Univ.
Dept. of Classics
263 Lake Huron Hall
Allendale, MI 49401
Ph: (616)331-3611
E-mail: anderspe@gvsu.edu
URL: http://www.camws.org
Contact: Peter J. Anderson, VP
State. Represents university, college, secondary and elementary teachers of Latin, Greek and all other studies which focus on the world of classical antiquity. Supports and promotes the study of classical languages.

6621 ■ Eastern Ottawa Young Life
PO Box 511
Allendale, MI 49401-0511
Ph: (616)895-7994
URL: http://sites.younglife.org/sites/EasternOttawa/default.aspx
Contact: Chris Theule-VanDam, Contact
Local. **Affiliated With:** Young Life.

6622 ■ Freethought Association of West Michigan
c/o Jeff Seaver, Chm.
PO Box 101
Allendale, MI 49401
Ph: (616)892-9300
E-mail: info@freethoughtassociation.org
URL: http://www.freethoughtassociation.com
Contact: Jeff Seaver, Chm.
Founded: 1997. **Members:** 250. **Budget:** $5,000. **Regional Groups:** 1. **State**. Provides a community for free thinkers to explore ideas from a rational, critical and non-theistic perspective. **Awards:** Freethinker of the Year. **Frequency:** annual. **Type:** recognition. **Affiliated With:** American Humanist Association.

6623 ■ Hudsonville High - Young Life
PO Box 511
Allendale, MI 49401-0511
Ph: (616)895-7994
E-mail: warnesn@hotmail.com
URL: http://sites.younglife.org/sites/hhs/default.aspx
Contact: Nick Warnes, Contact
Local. **Affiliated With:** Young Life.

6624 ■ Jenison High - Young Life
PO Box 511
Allendale, MI 49401-0511
Ph: (616)895-7994
URL: http://sites.younglife.org/sites/Jhs/default.aspx
Local. **Affiliated With:** Young Life.

6625 ■ Jenison Junior High - Wyldlife
PO Box 511
Allendale, MI 49401-0511
Ph: (616)895-7994
URL: http://sites.younglife.org/sites/jjh/default.aspx
Local. **Affiliated With:** Young Life.

6626 ■ Ottawa County Economic Development Office (OCEDO)
c/o Kenneth J. Rizzio, Exec.Dir.
PO Box 539
6676 Lake Michigan Dr.
Allendale, MI 49401
Ph: (616)892-4120
Fax: (616)895-6670
E-mail: info@ocedo.com
URL: http://www.ocedo.org
Contact: Kenneth J. Rizzio, Exec.Dir.
Founded: 1991. **Members:** 12. **Staff:** 1. **Budget:** $100,000. **Local**. Promotes business and industrial development in Ottawa County, MI. **Libraries: Type:** open to the public. **Holdings:** 100. **Subjects:** small business development. **Publications:** *County Profile*, triennial • *Manufacturers' Directory*, annual. **Price:** $15.00 • *Prospectus*, triennial.

6627 ■ Psi Chi, National Honor Society in Psychology - Grand Valley State University
c/o Dept. of Psychology
1 Campus Dr.
2106 Ausable Hall
Allendale, MI 49401
Ph: (616)331-2195 (616)331-3798
Fax: (616)331-2480
E-mail: burnsl@gvsu.edu
URL: National Affiliate–www.psichi.org
Local. **Affiliated With:** Psi Chi, National Honor Society in Psychology.

6628 ■ Riley St. MS - Wyldlife
PO Box 511
Allendale, MI 49401-0511
Ph: (616)895-7994
URL: http://sites.younglife.org/sites/rsms/default.aspx
Contact: Scott Nielsen, Contact
Local. **Affiliated With:** Young Life.

6629 ■ Unity Christian High - Young Life
PO Box 511
Allendale, MI 49401-0511
Ph: (616)895-7994
E-mail: becker11_1999@yahoo.com
URL: http://sites.younglife.org/sites/uchs/default.aspx
Contact: Justin Beck, Contact
Local. **Affiliated With:** Young Life.

Alma

6630 ■ American Musicological Society - Midwest Chapter
c/o Scott Messing, Pres.
Alma Coll.
535 Wright Ave., No. 23
Alma, MI 48801
Ph: (989)463-7215
Fax: (989)463-7979
E-mail: messing@alma.edu
URL: http://www-personal.umich.edu/~claguem/amsmidwest
Contact: Scott Messing PhD, Pres.
Regional. Aims to advance research in the field of music as a branch of learning and scholarship. **Affiliated With:** American Musicological Society.

6631 ■ Central Michigan Youth for Christ
PO Box 757
Alma, MI 48801
Ph: (989)463-4274
Fax: (989)463-4471
URL: National Affiliate–www.yfc.net
Local. **Affiliated With:** Youth for Christ/U.S.A.

6632 ■ Gratiot Area Chamber of Commerce (GACC)
110 W Superior St.
PO Box 516
Alma, MI 48801
Ph: (989)463-5525
Fax: (989)463-6588
E-mail: chamber@gratiot.org
URL: http://www.gratiot.org/chamber/chamber.html
Contact: Patricia F. Nelson, Exec.Dir.

Founded: 1994. **Members:** 450. **Membership Dues:** business (based on number of employees), $160-$1,280 (annual) • business with no employee, $110 (annual) • associate (non-business), $45 (annual). **Staff:** 2. **Budget:** $140,000. **Local.** Businesses in Gratiot County, Michigan united to promote the economic growth of the area. Also home of the Alma Highland Festival and Games. **Committees:** Ambassadors; Business School Alliance; Education; Hospitality Tent; Legislative; Marketing; Showcase; Web Site. **Affiliated With:** U.S. Chamber of Commerce. **Formerly:** Alma Area Chamber of Commerce; Ithaca Chamber; St. Louis Chamber. **Publications:** *Chamber Connections*, monthly. Newsletter. Features news, new member articles, and calendar of events. • *Gratiot Area Community Guide*, annual. Directory • Membership Directory, monthly. **Conventions/Meetings:** annual dinner.

6633 ■ Michigan Academy of Science, Arts, and Letters
Alma Coll.
Centennial House
614 W Superior St.
Alma, MI 48801-1504
Ph: (989)463-7969
Fax: (989)463-7970
E-mail: michiganacademy@alma.edu
URL: http://www.umich.edu/~michacad
Contact: Edward Hansen, Pres.

Founded: 1894. **Members:** 450. **Membership Dues:** affiliated with a member organization (regular), $65 (annual) • affiliated with a member organization (retired), $45 (annual) • not affiliated (regular), $80 (annual) • not affiliated (retired), $55 (annual). **Staff:** 3. **Budget:** $105,000. **State.** Individuals in education, government, and business promoting research. **Awards:** Cohn Prize in Law and Public Policy. **Frequency:** annual. **Type:** scholarship. **Recipient:** for outstanding paper that best contributes to the existing scholarly literature on the topic of law or public policy • Ronald O. Kapp Undergraduate Award. **Frequency:** annual. **Type:** monetary. **Recipient:** for most outstanding paper presented by an undergraduate student. **Committees:** Executive. **Affiliated With:** American Association for the Advancement of Science; National Association of Academies of Science. **Publications:** *Academy Letter*, 3/year. Newsletter. **Price:** included in membership dues. **Circulation:** 800. **Advertising:** accepted • *Michigan Academician*, quarterly. Journal. Contains peer-reviewed articles authored by members as well as reports on research projects in various Michigan college and universities. **Conventions/Meetings:** annual meeting, book exhibits especially welcome (exhibits) - usually March.

6634 ■ National Technical Honor Society - Alma High School - Michigan (AHS)
1500 N Pine Ave.
Alma, MI 48801
Ph: (989)463-3111
URL: http://www.almaschools.net
Contact: Donald Everhart, Contact
Local.

6635 ■ Psi Chi, National Honor Society in Psychology - Alma College
c/o Dept. of Psychology
Swanson Academic Ctr. B-28
614 W Superior St.
Alma, MI 48801
Ph: (989)463-7308 (989)463-7386
Fax: (989)463-7277
E-mail: setter@alma.edu
URL: National Affiliate–www.psichi.org
Local. Affiliated With: Psi Chi, National Honor Society in Psychology.

6636 ■ United Way of Gratiot County
110 W Superior St.
Alma, MI 48801
Ph: (989)463-6245
Fax: (989)463-6588
E-mail: unitedway@gratiot.com
URL: http://www.gratiotunitedway.com
Contact: Sharon Fenton, Exec.Dir.
Local. Affiliated With: United Way of America.

Almont

6637 ■ American Legion, Almont Post 479
PO Box 567
Almont, MI 48003
Ph: (517)371-4720
Fax: (517)371-2401
URL: National Affiliate–www.legion.org
Local. Affiliated With: American Legion.

Alpena

6638 ■ Alpena Alcona Presque Isle Board of Realtors
212 River St.
Alpena, MI 49707
Ph: (989)356-3772
Fax: (989)356-5128
E-mail: aapiboard@yahoo.com
URL: National Affiliate–www.realtor.org
Contact: Patricia J. Denial, Exec. Officer
Local. Strives to develop real estate business practices. Advocates the right to own, use and transfer real property. Provides a facility for professional development, research and exchange of information among members. **Affiliated With:** National Association of Realtors.

6639 ■ Alpena Area Convention and Visitors Bureau (AACVB)
235 W Chisholm St.
Alpena, MI 49707
Ph: (989)354-4181
Free: (800)4AL-PENA
E-mail: info@alpenacvb.com
URL: http://www.alpenacvb.com
Contact: Deborah Pardike, Dir.

Founded: 1984. **Members:** 70. **Staff:** 1. **Budget:** $105,000. **Local.** Owners of motels and tourism businesses. Promotes tourism and conventions in the Alpena, MI area. **Formerly:** (1997) Convention and Visitors Bureau of the Thunder Bay Region. **Supersedes:** Alpena Tourist Association. **Publications:** Brochures, periodic.

6640 ■ Alpena Youth Sailing Club
c/o Peter B. Wilson
102 S 3rd
Alpena, MI 49707-2502
Ph: (989)354-2175
Fax: (989)354-8974
E-mail: pwilson@alpenaagency.com
Contact: Pete Wilson, Pres.

Founded: 2001. **Members:** 50. **Membership Dues:** donation, $25 (annual). **Budget:** $20,000. **Local Groups:** 1. **Local.** Sailing school for children ages 9-16.

6641 ■ American Legion, Michigan Post 65
c/o William F. Weine
4162 Long Rapids Rd.
Alpena, MI 49707
Ph: (517)371-4720
Fax: (517)371-2401
URL: National Affiliate–www.legion.org
Contact: William F. Weine, Contact
Local. Affiliated With: American Legion.

6642 ■ Habitat for Humanity Alpena Area (HFHAAI)
1600 W Chisholm St.
Alpena, MI 49707-1298
Ph: (989)356-3509
Fax: (989)356-9643
E-mail: hfhaai@freeway.net
Contact: Karen Thompson, Exec.Dir.

Founded: 1990. **Members:** 17. **Staff:** 6. **Budget:** $305,000. **Local.** Builds and renovates simple, decent houses in partnership with people in need. **Libraries: Type:** not open to the public. **Holdings:** 20; books, business records, clippings, photographs, reports, video recordings. **Subjects:** business operations, resource development, family nurturing and support, family selection, church relations, construction, site selection, volunteer recruitment/coordination/training, construction safety, public relations, Habitat for Humanity history and development, non-profit operations and development, board development, bylaws, business and payroll records. **Awards:** Outstanding Volunteer or Donor. **Frequency:** periodic. **Type:** recognition. **Recipient:** for outstanding contribution of time and talent or funds towards the purpose and work of the organization. **Committees:** Church Relations; Construction; Executive; Family Selection; Family Support; Finance; Personnel; PR; Resource; Site; Volunteer Development. **Affiliated With:** Habitat for Humanity International.

6643 ■ Michigan National Wild Turkey Federation, Alpena Longbeards
14046 Parnell Ave.
Alpena, MI 49707
E-mail: tuckerj@voyager.net
URL: http://www.mi-nwtf.org/AlpenaLongbeards.htm
Contact: Jack Tucker, Contact
Local.

6644 ■ Michigan Society for Histotechnologists (MSH)
c/o Beth Cox
144 Colorado
Alpena, MI 49707
Ph: (989)356-7594
Fax: (989)356-7756
E-mail: wedgett@yahoo.com
URL: http://www.mshonline.org
Contact: Wendi Edgett, Pres.
State. Histology laboratory technicians, pathologists, laboratory equipment manufacturers' representatives, and interested individuals. Dedicated to the advancement of histotechnology and related sciences such as immunohistochemistry and molecular biology. Works to strengthen personal growth, leadership, education, and quality service to the medical community. Investigates health hazards in the laboratory and ensures the safety of the laboratory.

6645 ■ National Active and Retired Federal Employees Association - Thunder Bay 1487
2032 N Bagley Apt. 8
Alpena, MI 49707
Ph: (989)358-1533
URL: National Affiliate–www.narfe.org
Contact: Neil T. Campau, Contact
Local. Protects the retirement future of employees through education. Informs members on issues affecting the retirement. **Affiliated With:** National Association of Retired Federal Employees.

6646 ■ Northeast Michigan Community Partnership (NEMCPI)
2284 Diamond Point Rd.
Alpena, MI 49707
Ph: (517)356-2880
Fax: (517)354-6939
E-mail: nemcpi@deepnet.com
URL: http://nemcpi.deepnet.com
Contact: Carlene Przykucki, Exec.Dir.

Founded: 1996. **Members:** 30. **Staff:** 2. **Budget:** $51,162. **Regional Groups:** 1. **State Groups:** 1. Local Groups: 1. **Regional**. Promotes substance abuse prevention through promotion of community health, coalition building and collaboration. **Libraries: Type:** open to the public. **Holdings:** 1,000. **Awards: Type:** recognition. **Recipient:** for collaborative prevention efforts. **Formerly:** (1966) Community Partnership for Prevention. **Publications:** *Community Partnership Issues*, quarterly. Newsletter. Contains updates about the organization. **Circulation:** 600. **Conventions/ Meetings:** annual conference (exhibits).

6647 ■ Northeastern District Dental Society, Michigan
176 N Ripley Blvd.
Alpena, MI 49707
Ph: (989)356-3655
Fax: (989)356-2204
URL: National Affiliate–www.ada.org
Contact: Dr. James Vedder, Pres.
Local. Represents the interests of dentists committed to the public's oral health, ethics and professional development. Encourages the improvement of the public's oral health and promotes the art and science of dentistry. **Affiliated With:** American Dental Association; Michigan Dental Association.

6648 ■ Phi Theta Kappa, Nu Omicron Chapter - Alpena Community College
c/o Tom Ray
666 Johnson St.
Alpena, MI 49707
Ph: (989)358-7250
URL: http://www.ptk.org/directories/chapters/MI/253-1.htm
Contact: Tom Ray, Advisor
Local.

6649 ■ Plumbing-Heating-Cooling Contractors Association, North Central
c/o Walter Weinkauf, Sr., Pres.
1411 M 32
Alpena, MI 49707-8194
Ph: (989)354-5427
Fax: (989)356-3483
URL: National Affiliate–www.phccweb.org
Contact: Walter Weinkauf Sr., Pres.
Local. Represents the plumbing, heating and cooling contractors. Promotes the construction industry. Protects the environment, health, safety and comfort of society. **Affiliated With:** Plumbing-Heating-Cooling Contractors Association.

6650 ■ RSVP of Crawford and Roscommon Counties
c/o Barbara E. Dault, Dir.
2375 Gordon Rd.
Alpena, MI 49707-4627
Ph: (989)356-3474
Fax: (989)354-7693
E-mail: daultb@nemcsa.org
URL: http://www.seniorcorps.gov/about/programs/rsvp.asp
Contact: Barbara E. Dault, Dir.
Local. Affiliated With: Retired and Senior Volunteer Program.

6651 ■ United Way of Northeast Michigan
3022 US 23 S, Ste.A
Alpena, MI 49707-4824
Ph: (989)354-2221
Fax: (989)356-5782
E-mail: gpstoppa@alpena.cc.mi.us
URL: National Affiliate–national.unitedway.org
Contact: Germaine P. Stoppa, Exec.Dir.
Founded: 1955. **Staff:** 2. **Budget:** $77,490. **Local**. Assists in fundraising by conducting company-wide employee campaigns and encouraging corporate contributions. Conducts annual fall fund drive. **Affiliated With:** United Way of America. **Publications:** *Local City Directory*, annual. **Conventions/Meetings:** monthly board meeting - always 2nd Tuesday.

Alto

6652 ■ American Legion, Alto Post 528
PO Box 131
Alto, MI 49302
Ph: (517)371-4720
Fax: (517)371-2401
URL: National Affiliate–www.legion.org
Local. Affiliated With: American Legion.

Ann Arbor

6653 ■ Alzheimer's Association, Michigan Great Lakes Chapter
107 Aprill Dr., Ste.1
Ann Arbor, MI 48103-1903
Ph: (734)677-3081
Fax: (734)677-3091
Free: (800)272-3900
E-mail: patricia.bridgham@alz.org
URL: http://www.alzmigreatlakes.org
Contact: Mary Frenza, Pres./CEO
Founded: 1981. **Staff:** 21. **Budget:** $1,300,000. **Nonmembership. Local**. Provides high quality education, training and support services in 21 Michigan counties to those with Alzheimer's disease and related dementias, their families and care partners. Offers education programs and support groups. Maintains speakers' bureau. Supports research efforts. **Libraries: Type:** open to the public; lending. **Holdings:** 250; books, video recordings. **Subjects:** Alzheimer's disease, related dementias, caregiving. **Affiliated With:** Alzheimer's Association. **Also Known As:** Alzheimer's Disease and Related Disorders Association. **Formerly:** (2004) Alzheimer's Association, South Central Michigan Chapter. **Publications:** Newsletter, quarterly. Offers practical, up-to-date information and the latest research news for caregivers. **Circulation:** 2,100. **Conventions/Meetings:** quarterly workshop.

6654 ■ Amazon Africa Aid Organization (3AO)
c/o Dan Weiss, Exec.Dir.
PO Box 7776
Ann Arbor, MI 48107
Ph: (734)769-5778
Fax: (734)769-5779
E-mail: info@amazonafrica.org
URL: http://www.amazonafrica.org
Contact: Daniel A. Weiss, Exec.Dir.
Local.

6655 ■ American Association of Pharmaceutical Scientists, University of Michigan Student Chapter
c/o Sachin Mittal, Chm.
Coll. of Pharmacy
428 Church St., Rm. 2063
Ann Arbor, MI 48109
Ph: (734)763-6319
Fax: (734)615-6162
URL: http://www.umich.edu/~pharmsci/index.htm
Contact: Sachin Mittal, Chm.
Local. Provides a forum for the exchange of knowledge among scientists to enhance their contributions to public health. Offers scientific programs, on-going education, opportunities for networking and professional development. **Affiliated With:** American Association of Pharmaceutical Scientists.

6656 ■ American Cancer Society
2010 Hogback Rd., Ste.6
Ann Arbor, MI 48105
Ph: (734)971-4300
Fax: (734)971-2818
Free: (800)ACS-2345
URL: http://www.cancer.org
Contact: Tamara Rummel, Dir.
Local. Strives to eliminate cancer as a major health problem by preventing cancer, saving lives and diminishing suffering from cancer. Conducts research, education, advocacy and service.

6657 ■ American Chemical Society, Huron Valley Section
c/o Bruce Paul De Maine, Chm.
789 N Dixboro Rd.
Ann Arbor, MI 48105-9723
Ph: (313)769-0109
URL: National Affiliate–acswebcontent.acs.org
Contact: Bruce Paul De Maine, Chm.
Local. Represents the interests of individuals dedicated to the advancement of chemistry in all its branches. Provides opportunities for peer interaction and career development. **Affiliated With:** American Chemical Society.

6658 ■ American Friends Service Committee, Ann Arbor
c/o Susan Hansen , Admin. Associate
1414 Hill St.
Ann Arbor, MI 48104
Ph: (734)761-8283
Fax: (734)761-6022
E-mail: shansen@afsc.org
URL: http://www.afsc.org/greatlakes/ANNARBOR.HTM
Contact: Susan Hansen, Admin. Associate
Local. Affiliated With: American Friends Service Committee.

6659 ■ American Friends Service Committee, Michigan Area Office (AFSC)
c/o Susan Hansen, Admin. Associate
1414 Hill St.
Ann Arbor, MI 48104
Ph: (734)761-8283
Fax: (734)761-6022
E-mail: shansen@afsc.org
URL: National Affiliate–www.afsc.org
Contact: Susan Hansen, Admin. Associate
Staff: 4. **Nonmembership. For-Profit. Local**. Addresses prisoner rights issues; provides education and training in nonviolently addressing lesbian, gay, and bisexual rights issues. **Affiliated With:** American Friends Service Committee.

6660 ■ American Institute of Architects, Huron Valley Chapter
c/o Dan Mooney, Pres.
255 E Liberty, Ste.277
Ann Arbor, MI 48104
Ph: (734)997-9444
Fax: (734)997-7004
E-mail: dmooney@lzarch.com
URL: http://www.aiami.com/chapter_huron_valley_home.htm
Contact: Dan Mooney, Pres.
Members: 169. **Membership Dues:** local, $75 (annual). **Local**. Works to advance the profession of architecture and support membership. **Affiliated With:** American Institute of Architects. **Publications:** *Architrane*, bimonthly. Newsletter. Contains items of interest to architects in Ann Arbor, MI area. **Advertising:** accepted. Alternate Formats: online.

6661 ■ American Legion, Erwin Prieskorn Post 46
PO Box 2192
Ann Arbor, MI 48106
Ph: (517)371-4720
Fax: (517)371-2401
URL: National Affiliate–www.legion.org
Local. Affiliated With: American Legion.

6662 ■ American Library Association, Student Chapter, University of Michigan School of Information
c/o Karen Markey, Group Faculty Advisor
304 W Hall
550 E Univ. Ave.
Ann Arbor, MI 48109-1092

Ph: (734)763-3851
Fax: (734)764-2475
E-mail: alaofficers@umich.edu
URL: http://www.si.umich.edu/ala
Contact: Karen Markey, Group Faculty Advisor
Local. Affiliated With: American Library Association. **Formerly:** (2005) American Library Association, Student Chapter, University of Michigan at Ann Arbor.

6663 ■ American Red Cross, Washtenaw County Chapter
4624 Packard Rd.
Ann Arbor, MI 48108
Ph: (734)971-5300
Fax: (734)971-5303
URL: http://www.wc-redcross.org
Local.

6664 ■ American Society of Business Publication Editors - Michigan Chapter
c/o Judi Lintott, Pres.
Michigan Municipal Rev.
1675 Green Rd.
Ann Arbor, MI 48105
Ph: (734)669-6325
Fax: (734)663-4496
E-mail: jlintott@mml.org
URL: National Affiliate–www.asbpe.org
Contact: Judi Lintott, Pres.
State. Promotes the public and professional understanding of business publication. Serves to enhance editorial standards and quality and to raise the level of publication management skills of its members. **Affiliated With:** American Society of Business Publication Editors.

6665 ■ American Society for Training and Development - Ann Arbor, Michigan Chapter
PO Box 8203
Ann Arbor, MI 48107
E-mail: dwong@emich.edu
URL: http://www.astdannarbor.org
Contact: Diana J. Wong, Pres.
Local. Promotes workplace learning and the improvement of skills of workplace professionals. Provides resource and professional development to individuals in the field of learning and development. Recognizes and sets standards for learning and performance professionals. **Affiliated With:** American Society for Training and Development.

6666 ■ American Statistical Association, Ann Arbor Chapter
c/o Kevin K. Chartier, Sec.-Treas.
Pfizer
2399 Marquis Ct.
Ann Arbor, MI 48103-8935
Ph: (734)622-1260
E-mail: kchartier@aol.com
URL: National Affiliate–www.amstat.org
Contact: Kevin K. Chartier, Sec.-Treas.
Local. Promotes statistical practice, applications and research. Works for the improvement of statistical education at all levels. Seeks opportunities to advance the statistics profession. **Affiliated With:** American Statistical Association.

6667 ■ American Truck Historical Society, Southeast Michigan Chapter
c/o Bob Ludwig
2737 Aspen Rd.
Ann Arbor, MI 48108
Ph: (734)302-3335
URL: National Affiliate–www.aths.org
Contact: Bob Ludwig, Contact
Local.

6668 ■ Ann Arbor Area Chamber of Commerce (AAACC)
425 S Main St., Ste.103
Ann Arbor, MI 48104-2303
Ph: (734)665-4433
Fax: (734)665-4191
E-mail: info@annarborchamber.org
Contact: Ms. Sabrina Keeley, Pres.
Founded: 1919. **Members:** 1,400. **Local.** Promotes business and community development in the Ann Arbor, MI area. **Publications:** *Ann Arbor Business-to-Business*, periodic. Newsletter • *Directory of Firms, Products, and Services*, periodic.

6669 ■ Ann Arbor Area Convention and Visitors Bureau (AAACVB)
120 W Huron St.
Ann Arbor, MI 48104-1318
Ph: (734)995-7281
Fax: (734)995-7283
Free: (800)888-9487
E-mail: info@annarbor.org
URL: http://www.annarbor.org
Contact: Mary A. Kerr, Pres.
Membership Dues: individual, $75 (annual) • business/organization, $100 (annual) • hotel, $125 (annual). **Staff:** 8. **Local.** Promotes Ann Arbor, MI as a tourist destination. **Awards:** Ambassador Award. **Frequency:** annual. **Type:** recognition. **Publications:** *Ann Arbor/Ypsilanti/Washtenaw County Visitors Guide*, annual. Brochure. **Advertising:** accepted.

6670 ■ Ann Arbor Chapter of Optical Society of America
c/o Prof. Almantas Galvanauskas
2646 Traver
Ann Arbor, MI 48105
Ph: (734)615-7166
Fax: (734)647-2718
E-mail: almantas@umich.edu
URL: http://www.osa.org/localsections/aaosa/aaosaindex.htm
Contact: Almantas Galvanauskas, Contact
Local. Affiliated With: Optical Society of America.

6671 ■ Ann Arbor Council for Traditional Music and Dance (AACTMAD)
c/o Joan Hellmann
208 Murray Ave.
Ann Arbor, MI 48103-4359
Ph: (734)769-1052
E-mail: info@aactmad.org
URL: http://www.aactmad.org
Local. Sponsors contra and English country dances, occasional folk music concerts, informal singing group, southeast Michigan Dance Calendar, dance phone hotline and Dancing in the Streets on Labor Day weekend. Strives to foster traditional music and dance in the Ann Arbor area. **Affiliated With:** Country Song and Dance Society; North American Folk Music and Folk Dance Alliance.

6672 ■ Ann Arbor Evening Lions Club
c/o Ruby Fritis, Pres.
3043 Williamsburg Rd.
Ann Arbor, MI 48108
Ph: (734)973-8392
URL: http://www.lionsdistrict11b1.org/lc_ann_arbor_evening.htm
Contact: Ruby Fritis, Pres.
Local. Affiliated With: Lions Clubs International.

6673 ■ Ann Arbor Federation of Musicians - Local 625, American Federation of Musicians (AAFM)
c/o Barbara M. Zmich, Sec.-Treas.
1327 Jones Dr., Ste.102B
Ann Arbor, MI 48105
Ph: (734)668-8041
Fax: (734)668-9625
E-mail: local625@afm.org
URL: http://www.annarbormusicians.org
Contact: Barbara M. Zmich, Sec.-Treas.
Founded: 1912. **Members:** 286. **Membership Dues:** regular, $145 (annual). **Local.** Represents musicians. Seeks to improve the wages and working conditions of professional musicians. **Affiliated With:** American Federation of Musicians of the United States and Canada. **Publications:** *The Score*, quarterly. Newsletter. **Price:** included in membership dues.

6674 ■ Ann Arbor Figure Skating Club (AAFSC)
2121 Oak Valley
Ann Arbor, MI 48103
E-mail: aaskating@yahoo.com
URL: http://www.annarborfsc.com
Contact: Bud Collins, Pres.
Local. Provides programs to encourage participation and achievement in the sport of figure skating on ice. Defines and maintains uniform standards of skating proficiency. Organizes and sponsors competitions and exhibitions for the purpose of stimulating interest in figure skating. **Affiliated With:** United States Figure Skating Association.

6675 ■ Ann Arbor Garden Club
c/o Kathleen M. Fojtik
2271 Placid Way
Ann Arbor, MI 48105-1205
Ph: (734)995-2532
E-mail: cookie4860@aol.com
Contact: Kathy Fojtik, Pres.
Local.

6676 ■ Ann Arbor Huron Highschool Skating Club
3005 Exmoor Rd.
Ann Arbor, MI 48104
Ph: (734)973-8642
E-mail: paul_b748@yahoo.com
URL: National Affiliate–www.usfigureskating.org
Contact: Jeanne Berkowitz, Contact
Local. Provides programs to encourage participation and achievement in the sport of figure skating on ice. Defines and maintains uniform standards of skating proficiency. Organizes and sponsors competitions and exhibitions for the purpose of stimulating interest in figure skating. **Affiliated With:** United States Figure Skating Association.

6677 ■ Ann Arbor Orchid Society
c/o Neal R. Foster, PhD
2115 Georgetown Blvd.
Ann Arbor, MI 48105-1534
Ph: (734)663-0756
E-mail: nealfrost@umich.edu
Contact: Nail Foster, Founder
Local. Professional growers, botanists, hobbyists, and others interested in extending the knowledge, production, use, and appreciation of orchids. **Affiliated With:** American Orchid Society.

6678 ■ Ann Arbor Space Society
1531 Jones Dr.
Ann Arbor, MI 48105-1871
Ph: (734)665-1263
E-mail: johnswolter@wolterworks.com
URL: National Affiliate–www.nss.org
Contact: John S. Wolter, Contact
Local. Works for the creation of a spacefaring civilization. Encourages the establishment of self-sustaining human settlements in space. Promotes large-scale industrialization and private enterprise in space.

6679 ■ Ann Arbor Tenants Union
c/o Melissa Danforth
Trotter House Room, No. 220
1443 Washtenaw Ave.
Ann Arbor, MI 48104-2473
Ph: (734)998-7550
URL: http://www.umich.edu/~aatu/

6680 ■ Association for Community Advocacy
1100 N Main St., No. 205
Ann Arbor, MI 48104
Ph: (734)662-1256
URL: National Affiliate–www.thearc.org
Local. Parents, professional workers, and others interested in individuals with mental retardation. Works to promote services, research, public understanding, and legislation for people with mental retardation and their families. **Affiliated With:** Arc of the United States.

6681 ■ Association for Computing Machinery, University of Michigan
c/o Joey Dravec, Chm.
1301 Beal Ave.
Ann Arbor, MI 48109-2122
Ph: (734)764-2017
Fax: (734)763-6725
E-mail: acmo@engin.umich.edu
Biological, medical, behavioral, and computer scientists; hospital administrators; programmers and others interested in application of computer methods to biological, behavioral, and medical problems. Stimulates understanding of the use and potential of computers in the Biosciences. **Affiliated With:** Association for Computing Machinery.

6682 ■ Association for Corporate Growth, Southeast Michigan Chapter
c/o Sharon M. Kimble
115 E Ann St.
Ann Arbor, MI 48104
Fax: (734)662-9936
Free: (877)894-2754
E-mail: acgsemichigan@acg.org
Contact: Ms. Sharon M. Kimble, Administrator
Founded: 1984. **Members:** 200. **Membership Dues:** $285 (annual). **Staff:** 2. **Local**. Promotes business growth and provides business opportunities in southeast Michigan. **Affiliated With:** Association for Corporate Growth. **Formerly:** (2005) Association for Corporate Growth, Detroit Chapter.

6683 ■ Association for Women in Science, Detroit
c/o Noemi Mirkin
Biophysics Res. Div.
Univ. of Michigan
930 N Univ.
Ann Arbor, MI 48109-1055
Ph: (734)647-1834
E-mail: nmirkin@umich.edu
URL: National Affiliate–www.awis.org
Contact: Dr. Noemi Mirkin, Pres.
Founded: 1975. **Regional Groups:** 1. **State Groups:** 3. **Local**. Professional women and students in life, physical, and social sciences and engineering; men are also members. Promotes equal opportunities for women to enter the scientific workforce and to achieve their career goals; provides educational information to women planning careers in science; networks with other women's groups; monitors scientific legislation and the status of women in science. **Affiliated With:** Association for Women in Science.

6684 ■ Association for Women in Science, University of Michigan-Ann Arbor
Univ. of Michigan
Dept. of Chemistry
930 N Univ. Ave.
Ann Arbor, MI 48109
Ph: (734)763-4923
E-mail: nmelcer@umich.edu
URL: National Affiliate–www.awis.org
Contact: Natalia Melcer, Pres.
Local. Promotes equal opportunities for women to enter the scientific workforce and to achieve their career goals. Provides educational information to women planning careers in science. **Affiliated With:** Association for Women in Science.

6685 ■ Association for Women in Science, Washtenaw Community College
c/o Kathleen Strnad
Div. of Mathematics, Natl. Sci., and Behavioral Sci.
Wastenaw Community Coll.
Ann Arbor, MI 48106
Ph: (734)677-5067
E-mail: kstrnad@wccnet.org
URL: National Affiliate–www.awis.org
Contact: Kathleen Strnad, Contact
Local. Professional women and students in life, physical, and social sciences and engineering; men are also members. Promotes equal opportunities for women to enter the scientific workforce and to achieve their career goals; provides educational information to women planning careers in science; networks with other women's groups; monitors scientific legislation and the status of women in science. **Affiliated With:** Association for Women in Science.

6686 ■ Bereaved Parents of the USA, Southeastern (Ann Arbor) Michigan
c/o Monica Martin
2535 Russell St.
Ann Arbor, MI 48103
Ph: (734)929-9521
E-mail: johnie192004@yahoo.com
URL: National Affiliate–www.bereavedparentsusa.org
Contact: Monica Martin, Contact
Local.

6687 ■ BKS Iyengar Yoga Association of the Midwest Bioregions (IYAMW)
PO Box 8051
Ann Arbor, MI 48107
Ph: (734)662-5026
E-mail: bksiyamw@aol.com
URL: http://hometown.aol.com/bksiyamw
Contact: Donna Pointer, Pres.
Regional. **Affiliated With:** B.K.S. Iyengar Yoga National Association of the U.S.

6688 ■ Boy Scouts of America-Great Sauk Trail Council
c/o Robert F. Poole, Jr., Scout Exec.
1979 Huron Pkwy.
Ann Arbor, MI 48104-4199
Ph: (734)971-7100
URL: http://www.gstcbsa.org/
Contact: Robert F. Poole Jr., Scout Exec.
Local. **Affiliated With:** Boy Scouts of America.

6689 ■ Catholic Alumni Club of Detroit
1077 Joyce Ln.
Ann Arbor, MI 48103
E-mail: cacdetroit@yahoo.com
URL: http://cacd.hypermart.net
Contact: Teresa Walczyk, Pres.
Local. **Affiliated With:** Catholic Alumni Clubs, International.

6690 ■ Catholic League for Religious and Civil Rights, Ann Arbor Chapter
c/o Al Kresta
PO Box 374
Ann Arbor, MI 48106
Ph: (313)930-5210
Fax: (313)930-3179
E-mail: cl@catholicleague.org
URL: National Affiliate–www.catholicleague.org
Local. **Affiliated With:** Catholic League for Religious and Civil Rights.

6691 ■ Clague Middle School Parent-Teachers-Students Organization
c/o Arnold Geldermans
2616 Nixon Rd.
Ann Arbor, MI 48105-1420
Ph: (734)994-1976
Fax: (734)994-1645
E-mail: 2xmichelle@sbcglobal.net
URL: http://clague.aaps.k12.mi.us
Contact: Michelle Machiele, Pres.
Local.

6692 ■ Credit Professionals International of Ann Arbor
c/o Kathryn Greiner, Pres.
First of Washtenaw
305 E Eisenhower Pkwy., Ste.200
Ann Arbor, MI 48108
Ph: (734)663-7900 (734)994-4572
Fax: (734)929-6564
E-mail: donna.daugherty@53.com
URL: http://www.creditprofessionals.org/5/ann_arbor.html
Contact: Kathryn Greiner, Pres.
Local. Supports members through networking, career development and community involvement. Promotes and contributes to the innovation of the credit industry. Provides education in the practice and procedure of credit. **Affiliated With:** Credit Professionals International. **Conventions/Meetings:** monthly breakfast - every 2nd Tuesday.

6693 ■ Dexter HS - Young Life
230 Collingwood, Ste.160A
Ann Arbor, MI 48103
Ph: (734)665-2378
URL: http://sites.younglife.org/sites/dexterhs/default.aspx
Local. **Affiliated With:** Young Life.

6694 ■ Dexter - Wyldlife
230 Collingwood, Ste.160A
Ann Arbor, MI 48103
Ph: (734)665-2378
URL: http://sites.younglife.org/sites/dexterwyldlife/default.aspx
Local. **Affiliated With:** Young Life.

6695 ■ Forsythe - Wyldlife
230 Collingwood, Ste.160A
Ann Arbor, MI 48103
Ph: (734)665-2378
URL: http://sites.younglife.org/_layouts/ylext/default.aspx?ID=C-4462
Local. **Affiliated With:** Young Life.

6696 ■ Gay, Lesbian and Straight Education Network, Ann Arbor-Ypsilanti Area
1893 Chicory Ridge Rd.
Ann Arbor, MI 48103-9238
Ph: (734)930-0357
E-mail: smaksman_sverige@hotmail.com
URL: National Affiliate–www.glsen.org
Local. Creates an environment at school in which every member of the school community is valued and respected, regardless of sexual orientation. Addresses homophobia and heterosexism in schools. **Affiliated With:** Gay, Lesbian, and Straight Education Network.

6697 ■ Genealogical Society of Washtenaw County
PO Box 7155
Ann Arbor, MI 48107-7155
Ph: (734)944-4789
URL: http://www.hvcn.org/info/gswc
Contact: Marcia McCrary, Pres.
Founded: 1974. **Members:** 350. **Membership Dues:** individual, $14 (annual) • family, $15 (annual) • sustaining, $25 (annual). **Local**. Individuals interested in Washtenaw County, MI interested in local history and genealogy. Promotes study of history and genealogy. Assists genealogical research efforts. **Libraries: Type:** reference. **Holdings:** biographical archives. **Publications:** *Family History Capers*, quarterly. Journal • Membership Directory, annual • Newsletter, monthly. **Conventions/Meetings:** monthly meeting - always fourth Sunday.

6698 ■ Gray Panthers of Huron Valley
c/o June Rusten
1733 Dunmore
Ann Arbor, MI 48103
Ph: (734)996-2596
E-mail: junealice@earthlink.net
URL: National Affiliate–www.graypanthers.org
Contact: June Rusten, Contact
Local. Grassroots activists dedicated to advancing social and economic justice. **Affiliated With:** Gray Panthers.

6699 ■ Great Lakes Aikikai
2030 Commerce Dr.
Ann Arbor, MI 48103
Ph: (734)761-6012
Fax: (734)741-9177
E-mail: rpark@mail.cfigroup.com
URL: http://gla-aikido.com
Local. **Affiliated With:** United States Aikido Federation.

6700 ■ Great Lakes Colleges Association (GLCA)
535 W William, Ste.301
Ann Arbor, MI 48103
Ph: (734)761-4833
Fax: (734)761-3939
E-mail: detweiler@glca.org
URL: http://www.glca.org
Contact: Richard Detweiler, Pres.
Founded: 1962. **Members:** 12. **Staff:** 8. **Budget:** $700,000. Independent, liberal arts and sciences colleges in Indiana, Michigan, and Ohio. Seeks to enable members to collaborate on activities that are more effectively done as a group, including off-campus study programs for students, professional development programs for faculty and administrators, sharing management data, and instructional technology. Sponsors women's studies and black studies conferences. **Awards:** New Writers Award. **Frequency:** annual. **Type:** recognition. **Recipient:** for the best fiction and poetry by a first-published author. **Committees:** Institutional Commitment to Educational Equity; International and Off-Campus Education; Technology Advisory Group; Women's Studies. **Councils:** Academic; Deans'. **Affiliated With:** Associated Colleges of the Midwest. **Publications:** *The Bulletin*, monthly. Newsletter • *Great Lakes Colleges Association—Faculty Newsletter*, 4/year. Includes calendar of events. **Price:** included in membership dues. ISSN: 0738-3622.

6701 ■ Great Lakes Commission (GLC)
2805 S Indus. Hwy., Ste.100
Ann Arbor, MI 48104-6791
Ph: (734)971-9135
Fax: (734)971-9150
E-mail: glc@glc.org
URL: http://www.glc.org
Contact: Dr. Michael J. Donahue PhD, Pres./CEO
Founded: 1955. **Members:** 26. **Membership Dues:** Great Lake State, $60,000 (annual). **Staff:** 32. **Budget:** $6,000,000. Interstate Compact Commission. Designated or appointed officials (according to state statutes) in 8 states party to the Great Lakes Basin Compact. Serves as a research, coordinating, advisory, and advocacy agency on the development, use, and protection of the water and related land resources of the Great Lakes Basin. Compiles statistics and information on state, federal, and regional programs and projects. **Awards:** Carol A. Ratza Memorial Scholarship. **Frequency:** annual. **Type:** scholarship. **Recipient:** for outstanding achievement and vision in electronic communications technology • Outstanding Service. **Frequency:** annual. **Type:** recognition. **Recipient:** for organizational leadership. **Computer Services:** database, Great Lakes Regional Water Use and Repository. **Programs:** Administration; Communications and Internet Technology; Data and Information Management; Environmental Quality; Regional Coordination; Resource Management; Transportation and Sustainable Development. **Task Forces:** Air Toxics; Aquatic Nuisance Species; Coast Guard Funding; Ecosystem Charter; Emergency Preparedness; Great Lakes Circle Tour; Great Lakes Information; Network Advisory Board; Soil Erosion and Sedimentation; Soo Locks Funding; Tourism and Outdoor Recreation; Water Resources Management. **Publications:** *Advisor*, bimonthly. Newsletter. **Price:** free. **Circulation:** 3,500. Alternate Formats: online • *Great Lakes Research Checklist*, periodic • *Membership List*, periodic. Membership Directory • *Minutes of Regular Meeting*, semiannual • *Special Publications*, periodic • Annual Report, annual. **Price:** free. Alternate Formats: online. **Conventions/Meetings:** semiannual meeting • annual meeting • periodic meeting, for task forces • seminar.

6702 ■ Great Lakes Fishery Commission (GLFC)
2100 Commonwealth Blvd., Ste.100
Ann Arbor, MI 48105
Ph: (734)662-3209
Fax: (734)741-2010
E-mail: info@glfc.org
URL: http://www.glfc.org
Contact: Chris Goddard, Exec.Sec.
Founded: 1956. **Members:** 12. **Staff:** 9. **Budget:** $12,100,000. **Regional**. Representatives of the governments of Canada and the United States develops coordinated research programs in the Great Lakes and recommends measures permitting the maximum sustained productivity of the lakes. Runs a sea lamprey control program and facilities implementation of the joint strategic plan for management of Great Lakes Fisheries. **Boards:** Habitat Advisory; Technical Experts. **Committees:** Council of Lake; Sea Lamprey Integration. **Publications:** *Forum*, periodic. Newsletter. **Price:** free. Alternate Formats: online • *Technical Report Series*, periodic. **Price:** free. **Conventions/Meetings:** annual meeting (exhibits) - June.

6703 ■ GriefNet
c/o Cendra Lynn, PhD
PO Box 3272
Ann Arbor, MI 48106
Ph: (734)761-1960
E-mail: cendra@griefnet.org
URL: http://griefnet.org
Contact: Cendra Lynn PhD, Dir.
Local.

6704 ■ Habitat for Humanity of Huron Valley (HHHV)
715 Ellsworth Rd., Ste.B
Ann Arbor, MI 48108
Ph: (734)677-1558
Fax: (734)677-1572
E-mail: huronvalley@h4h.org
URL: http://www.h4h.org
Contact: Sarah Stanton, Exec.Dir.
Founded: 1989. **Staff:** 2. **Budget:** $500,000. **Nonmembership**. **Local**. Works as an ecumenical Christian organization devoted to providing low-cost, non-profit housing to low-income people and families.

6705 ■ Home Builders Association of Washtenaw County
c/o Maureen Sloan
179 Little Lake Dr.
Ann Arbor, MI 48103-6200
Ph: (734)996-0100
Fax: (734)996-1008
E-mail: hba@glis.net
URL: http://www.hbawc.com
Local. Single and multifamily home builders, commercial builders, and others associated with the building industry. **Affiliated With:** National Association of Home Builders.

6706 ■ Huron High - Young Life
230 Collingwood, Ste.160A
Ann Arbor, MI 48103
Ph: (734)665-2378
URL: http://sites.younglife.org/_layouts/ylext/default.aspx?ID=C-1079
Local. **Affiliated With:** Young Life.

6707 ■ Huron River Watershed Council (HRWC)
c/o Ms. Laura Rubin, Exec.Dir.
1100 N Main St., Ste.210
Ann Arbor, MI 48104
Ph: (734)769-5123
E-mail: lrubin@hrwc.org
URL: http://www.hrwc.org
Contact: Ms. Laura Rubin, Exec.Dir.
Founded: 1965. **Members:** 650. **Staff:** 10. **Budget:** $750,000. **Regional**. **Libraries:** **Type:** open to the public. **Holdings:** 2,000; articles, books, periodicals, video recordings.

6708 ■ Institute of Management Accountants, Ann Arbor Chapter
c/o Bill Ebright, Pres.
Production Services Mgt.
Ann Arbor Commerce Park
1777 Highland Dr., No. E
Ann Arbor, MI 48108
Ph: (734)677-0454
E-mail: bebright@comcast.net
URL: http://www.imamichigan.org/annarbor
Contact: Bill Ebright, Pres.
Local. Promotes professional and ethical standards. Equips members and students with knowledge and training required for the accounting profession. **Councils:** Michigan. **Affiliated With:** Institute of Management Accountants. **Publications:** *Qualified Opinion*, monthly. Newsletter. **Advertising:** accepted. Alternate Formats: online. **Conventions/Meetings:** monthly meeting - every third Thursday.

6709 ■ Interfaith Council for Peace and Justice (ICPJ)
c/o Chuck Warpehoski, Dir.
730 Tappan
Ann Arbor, MI 48104
Ph: (734)663-1870
Fax: (734)663-9458
E-mail: info@icpj.net
URL: http://www.icpj.net
Contact: Chuck Warpehoski, Dir.
Local.

6710 ■ International Association for Great Lakes Research (IAGLR)
2205 Commonwealth Blvd.
Ann Arbor, MI 48105
Ph: (734)665-5303
Fax: (734)741-2055
E-mail: office@iaglr.org
URL: http://www.iaglr.org
Contact: Wendy L. Foster, Business Mgr.
Membership Dues: individual print subscription, $70 (quarterly) • library print subscription, $250 (quarterly). **Regional**. Research objectives include the promotion of all aspects of Great Lakes research and dissemination of research through publications, meetings, awards, and scholarships. **Publications:** Journal, quarterly. **Price:** included in membership dues. ISSN: 0380-1330. **Circulation:** 1,000. Alternate Formats: online.

6711 ■ Jewish Federation of Washtenaw County
2939 Birch Hollow Dr.
Ann Arbor, MI 48108
Ph: (734)677-0100
Fax: (734)677-0109
E-mail: ellisha@jewishnnarbor.org
URL: http://www.jewishannarbor.org
Contact: Jeffrey Y. Levin, Exec.Dir.
Local. Fosters Jewish life by initiating, coordinating and preserving activities that strengthen Jewish communal life locally, in Israel and throughout the world. **Affiliated With:** United Jewish Communities.

6712 ■ John Allen Parent Council
2560 Towner Blvd.
Ann Arbor, MI 48104-5035
Ph: (734)971-5901
URL: http://www.aaps.k12.mi.us
Contact: Denise Murphy, Pres.
Local.

6713 ■ Kiwanis Club of Ann Arbor
c/o Bob Carr
542 Heritage Dr.
Ann Arbor, MI 48105

Ph: (734)665-8287
Fax: (734)665-1737
E-mail: ricarr@ricarr.com
URL: http://www.aakiwanis.org
Contact: George J. Gilligan, Pres.
Local.

6714 ■ Lutherans Concerned/Great Lakes
c/o Lord of Light Lutheran Church
801 S Forest Ave.
Ann Arbor, MI 48104
Ph: (734)996-2439
E-mail: lcgreatlakes@lcna.org
URL: http://www.lcna.org
Founded: 1971. **Members:** 30. **Membership Dues:** individual, $40 (annual). **Local Groups:** 1. **Local.** Serves the Southeast Michigan and Northwest Ohio. **Awards:** Angel Award. **Frequency:** biennial. **Type:** recognition. **Recipient:** for efforts on behalf of lesbian and gay Lutherans. **Affiliated With:** Lutherans Concerned/North America. **Publications:** *Outer Court*, monthly. Newsletters. **Price:** $15.00. **Advertising:** accepted. **Conventions/Meetings:** biennial assembly, joint assembly of gay Lutherans.

6715 ■ Make-A-Wish Foundation of Michigan
230 Huron View Blvd.
Ann Arbor, MI 48103-2948
Ph: (734)994-8620
Fax: (734)994-8025
Free: (888)857-9474
E-mail: wish@wishmich.org
URL: http://wishmich.org
Contact: Susan Lerch, Pres./CEO
Founded: 1984. **Budget:** $3,800,000. **State.** Grants wishes of children with life-threatening conditions to enrich the human experience with hope, strength and joy. **Affiliated With:** Make-A-Wish Foundation of America. **Publications:** *With Our Best Wishes*, quarterly. Newsletter.

6716 ■ Mathematical Association of America, Michigan Section
c/o Norman Richert, Ed.
PO Box 8604
Ann Arbor, MI 48107-8604
E-mail: nrichert@ams.org
URL: http://www.maa.org/michigan
Contact: Norman Richert, Ed.
State. Promotes the general understanding and appreciation of mathematics. Advances and improves the education in the mathematical sciences at the collegiate level. Provides resources and activities that foster scholarship, professional growth and cooperation among teachers, other professionals and students. **Affiliated With:** Mathematical Association of America.

6717 ■ Memorial Advisory and Planning Society (MAPS)
2030 Chaucer Dr.
Ann Arbor, MI 48103-6106
Ph: (734)665-9516
URL: http://www.aamaps.org
Founded: 1965. **Members:** 700. **Membership Dues:** life, individual, $25 • life, family, $35. **Budget:** $2,000. **Local.** Promotes dignified funeral and/or memorial services. Makes available information and counseling to the bereaved. **Libraries:** **Type:** not open to the public. **Holdings:** 20; books, periodicals. **Subjects:** death, dying, memorials. **Affiliated With:** Funeral Consumers Alliance. **Publications:** *Helping You Plan for Tomorrow Today*, upon request. Brochure. **Price:** free • Newsletter, semiannual. 4-6 pages newsletter. **Price:** free to members. **Conventions/Meetings:** annual meeting - always November in Ann Arbor, MI.

6718 ■ MichBio
PO Box 7944
Ann Arbor, MI 48107
Ph: (734)615-9670
Fax: (734)623-8289
E-mail: info@michbio.org
URL: http://www.michbio.org
Contact: Stephen Rapundalo, Exec.Dir.
State. Supports growth of the biosciences industry in Michigan. Provides services to Michigan's bioscience companies, universities, research institutes and affiliates that serve the bioscience community. **Formerly:** (2003) Michigan Biosciences Industry Association. **Conventions/Meetings:** monthly meeting.

6719 ■ Michigan Association of Municipal Attorneys (MAMA)
c/o Michigan Municipal League
1675 Green Rd.
Box 1487
Ann Arbor, MI 48105
Ph: (734)662-3246
Fax: (734)662-8083
Free: (800)653-2483
E-mail: wcm@mml.org
URL: http://www.mml.org
Contact: William C. Mathewson, Sec.-Treas.
Founded: 1935. **Members:** 549. **Staff:** 2. **State.** City and village attorneys. **Libraries:** **Type:** not open to the public. **Holdings:** 2,000. **Subjects:** state, government. **Awards:** Distinguished Municipal Attorney. **Frequency:** annual. **Type:** recognition. **Publications:** *Municipal Legal Briefs*, bimonthly. Newsletter. **Price:** $60.00 for nonmembers; $25.00 for members. ISSN: 0076-8014. **Circulation:** 850. Alternate Formats: online. **Conventions/Meetings:** annual meeting, program and business meeting.

6720 ■ Michigan Association of Nurse Anesthetists (MANA)
3300 Washtenaw Ave., Ste.220
Ann Arbor, MI 48104-4200
Ph: (734)477-0328
Fax: (734)677-2407
E-mail: miana@miana.org
URL: http://www.miana.org
Contact: Kenneth Kawa CRNA, Pres.-Elect
State. Advances the art and science of anesthesiology. Promotes research in anesthesia. Develops educational standards and techniques for the administration of anesthesia. **Affiliated With:** American Association of Nurse Anesthetists.

6721 ■ Michigan Association of Planning (MAP)
219 S Main St., Ste.300
Ann Arbor, MI 48104
Ph: (734)913-2000
Fax: (734)913-2061
E-mail: info@planningmi.org
URL: http://www.planningmi.org
Contact: Andrea L. Brown, Exec.Dir.
State. Formerly: (2005) Michigan Society of Planning Officials.

6722 ■ Michigan Athletic Trainers' Society (MATS)
c/o Mark Stoessner, VP
Univ. of Michigan
1000 S State St.
Ann Arbor, MI 48109
Ph: (734)763-6890
Fax: (517)432-2137
E-mail: vice-president@matsonline.org
URL: http://www.matsonline.org
Contact: Jeff Monroe, Pres.-Elect
State. Affiliated With: National Athletic Trainers' Association.

6723 ■ Michigan Council of Teachers of Mathematics (MCTM)
3300 Washtenaw Ave., Ste.220
Ann Arbor, MI 48104-4200
Ph: (734)477-0421
Fax: (734)677-2407
E-mail: alecia@ucia2.com
URL: http://www.mictm.org
Contact: Judy Wheeler, Pres.
Founded: 1949. **Members:** 2,500. **Membership Dues:** regular, $35 (annual) • undergraduate student, retired, $17 (annual) • institutional, $30 (annual). **Budget:** $175,000. **State. Publications:** *Mathematics in Michigan*, quarterly • Newsletter, semiannual.

6724 ■ Michigan District, The Lutheran Church-Missouri Synod
3773 Geddes Rd.
Ann Arbor, MI 48105-3098
Ph: (734)665-3791
Fax: (734)665-0255
E-mail: info@michigandistrict.org
URL: http://www.michigandistrict.org
Contact: Rev. C. William Hoesman, Pres.
State.

6725 ■ Michigan Forest Association (MFA)
c/o McClain B. Smith, Jr., Exec.Dir.
1558 Barrington
Ann Arbor, MI 48103
Ph: (734)665-8279
Fax: (734)913-9167
E-mail: info@michiganforests.com
URL: http://www.michiganforests.com
Contact: McClain B. Smith Jr., Exec.Dir.
Founded: 1972. **Members:** 700. **Membership Dues:** individual (participating), $35 (annual) • individual (contributing), $45 (annual) • associate, $85 (annual). **Budget:** $30,000. **Local Groups:** 13. **State.** Private woodland owners, professional foresters, and members of related industries. Seeks to educate members and the general public on good forest practices and wise usage of resources. **Telecommunication Services:** electronic mail, mfa@i-star.com. **Publications:** *Green Gold: Michigan Forest History*. **Price:** $2.00 • *Leaves*, monthly. Newsletter. **Price:** included in membership dues • *Michigan Famous and Historic Trees* • *Michigan Forests*, quarterly. Magazine. **Price:** included in membership dues. ISSN: 1088-7814. **Advertising:** accepted • *Oil and Gas Leasing and Your Land*. **Conventions/Meetings:** annual convention - usually August.

6726 ■ Michigan Foundation for Exceptional Children
c/o Janis Gaubatz, VP
2725 Bd.walk
Ann Arbor, MI 48104
Ph: (734)994-2318 (734)213-2063
Fax: (734)994-1826
E-mail: gaubatz@aaps.k12.mi.us
URL: http://www.michigancec.org
Contact: Janis Gaubatz, VP
State.

6727 ■ Michigan Guild of Artists and Artisans
119 N Fourth Ave.
Ann Arbor, MI 48104-1402
Ph: (734)662-3382
URL: http://www.michiganguild.org
Contact: Debora Clayton, Exec.Dir.
State.

6728 ■ Michigan Interscholastic Forensic Association (MIFA)
2011 S State St., Ste.A
Ann Arbor, MI 48104
Ph: (734)764-1131
Fax: (734)998-6779
E-mail: jonfitz@themifa.org
URL: http://www.themifa.org
Contact: Jon Fitzgerald, Exec.Dir.
Founded: 1917. **Members:** 400. **Membership Dues:** middle school, $165 (annual) • high school, $300 (annual). **Staff:** 2. **Budget:** $200,000. **State.** Secondary schools in the state of MI that promotes interscholastic speech activities, including debate, individual events, legislative simulations, and theatre, through diverse tournaments and workshops. **Councils:** Forensic. **Publications:** *Forensic News*, periodic. Newsletter. **Price:** free • *Speech Activities*. Book.

6729 ■ Michigan Mortgage Brokers Association (MMBA)
3300 Washtenaw Ave., Ste.220
Ann Arbor, MI 48104
Ph: (734)975-4426
Fax: (734)677-2407
E-mail: mmba@mmbaonline.com
URL: http://www.mmbaonline.com
Contact: David Porter, Pres.
State. Promotes the mortgage broker industry through education, programs, professional certifica-

tion and government affairs representation. Seeks to increase professionalism and to foster business relationships among members. **Affiliated With:** National Association of Mortgage Brokers.

6730 ■ Michigan Municipal League (MML)
PO Box 1487
1675 Green Rd.
Ann Arbor, MI 48105
Ph: (734)662-3246
Fax: (734)662-8083
Free: (800)653-2483
E-mail: info@mml.org
URL: http://www.mml.org
Contact: Mr. Daniel Gilmartin, Exec.Dir.
Founded: 1899. **Staff:** 47. **Local**. State association for cities and villages. Advocates on behalf of the member communities in Lansing, Washington and the Courts. Provides different and unique forums and formats to educate local elected and appointed officials; assists local government leaders in administering services through League conceived programs and products. **Libraries: Type:** not open to the public. **Holdings:** 1,000; articles, books, clippings, papers, periodicals, reports. **Subjects:** state, local government. **Awards:** Achievement Awards. **Frequency:** annual. **Type:** recognition. **Recipient:** for innovative program in member communities. **Publications:** *Michigan Municipal Review*, 10/year. Magazine. **Price:** $24.00/year. **Circulation:** 10,300. **Advertising:** accepted. **Conventions/Meetings:** annual meeting (exhibits) - September or October.

6731 ■ Michigan Mushroom Hunters Club (MMHC)
c/o Kenneth W. Cochran
3556 Oakwood
Ann Arbor, MI 48104-5213
Ph: (734)971-2552
E-mail: kwcee@umich.edu
URL: http://www.sph.umich.edu/~kwcee/mmhc
Contact: Mr. Mickey Kulha, Pres.
State. Affiliated With: North American Mycological Association.

6732 ■ Michigan Natural Areas Council (MNAC)
c/o Matthaei Botanical Gardens
1800 N Dixboro
Ann Arbor, MI 48109-9741
Ph: (313)461-9390
E-mail: mnac@cyberspace.org
URL: http://www.cyberspace.org/~mnac
Contact: Phyllis Higman, Chm.
Founded: 1947. **Members:** 100. **Membership Dues:** individual, $25 (annual). **Budget:** $2,000. **Local**. Professional biologists and interested individuals who seek to preserve natural and scenic areas. Sponsors periodic field trips. **Publications:** *Michigan Natural Areas Views and News*, quarterly. Newsletter. **Price:** free. **Circulation:** 150. Alternate Formats: online • *Studies and Papers*, periodic. **Conventions/Meetings:** periodic conference • biennial meeting - April and November • periodic symposium.

6733 ■ Michigan Physical Therapy Association (MPTA)
3300 Washtenaw Ave., Ste.220
Ann Arbor, MI 48104-4200
Ph: (734)929-6075
Fax: (734)677-2407
Free: (800)242-8131
E-mail: mpta@mpta.com
URL: http://www.mpta.com
Contact: Marcy Dwyer CMP, Exec.Dir.
State. Physical therapists united to foster the development and improvement of physical therapy, services, education, and research. **Affiliated With:** American Physical Therapy Association.

6734 ■ Michigan Science Teachers Association (MSTA)
3300 Washtenaw Ave., Ste.220
Ann Arbor, MI 48104
Ph: (734)973-0433
E-mail: paul_drummond@msta-mich.org
URL: http://www.msta-mich.org
Contact: Paul Drummond, Co-Assistant Conference Chm.
State.

6735 ■ Michigan Section of the American Nuclear Society (MI-ANS)
c/o Advent Engineering Services
PO Box 555
Ann Arbor, MI 48106-0555
Ph: (734)930-7500
Fax: (734)327-7501
E-mail: mi-ans@adventengineering.com
URL: http://local.ans.org/mi
Contact: Peter Smith, Chm.
State. Works to advance science and engineering in the nuclear industry. Works with government agencies, educational institutions, and other organizations dealing with nuclear issues. **Affiliated With:** American Nuclear Society.

6736 ■ Michigan Society for Medical Research (MISMR)
PO Box 3237
Ann Arbor, MI 48106-3237
Ph: (734)763-8029
Fax: (734)930-1568
E-mail: mismr@umich.edu
URL: http://www.mismr.org
Contact: Rebecca Ellish-Stengle MPH, Exec.Dir.
Founded: 1981. **Members:** 324. **Staff:** 1. **Budget:** $60,000. **State**. Educational organization of research universities, hospitals, voluntary health organizations, corporations, and interested individuals. Seeks to support biomedical research and inform the public of its everyday applications. Supports humane use of animals in research. Sponsors essay contests. **Publications:** *Animals in Resource: A Resource Guide*. **Price:** $50.00. **Conventions/Meetings:** annual Educational Symposium - conference (exhibits) - always spring.

6737 ■ Michigan Society for Respiratory Care (MSRC)
3300 Washenaw Ave., Ste.220
Ann Arbor, MI 48104
Ph: (734)677-6772
Fax: (734)677-2407
E-mail: info@michiganrc.org
URL: http://www.michiganrc.org
Contact: Carl Haas, Pres.
State. Fosters the improvement of educational programs in respiratory care. Advocates research in the field of respiratory care. **Affiliated With:** American Association for Respiratory Care.

6738 ■ MIT Enterprise Forum of the Great Lakes (MITEFGL)
c/o Grace Lee, Treas.
2929 Plymouth Rd., Ste.207
Ann Arbor, MI 48105
E-mail: grace@logiclink.com
URL: http://www.mitgreatlakes.org
Contact: Grace Lee, Treas.
Regional. Promotes the establishment and growth of innovative technology companies through creative programs that educate and entertain entrepreneurs.

6739 ■ Mothers Against Drunk Driving, Washtenaw County
2409 Haisley
Ann Arbor, MI 48103
Ph: (734)665-5638
URL: National Affiliate–www.madd.org
Contact: Robin Black, Volunteer
Local. Victims of drunk driving crashes; concerned citizens. Encourages citizen participation in working towards reform of the drunk driving problem and the prevention of underage drinking. Acts as the voice of victims of drunk driving crashes by speaking on their behalf to communities, businesses, and educational groups. **Affiliated With:** Mothers Against Drunk Driving.

6740 ■ Muslim Students' Association - University of Michigan - Ann Arbor
530 S State St.
Ann Arbor, MI 48104
Ph: (313)665-5424
Fax: (313)669-6416
E-mail: msa-eboard@umich.edu
URL: http://www.umich.edu/~muslims
Contact: Abdur-Rahman Blauvelt, Pres.
Local. Muslim students in North America. Seeks to advance the interests of members; works to enable members to practice Islam as a complete way of life. **Affiliated With:** Muslim Students Association of the United States and Canada.

6741 ■ NASCO Member Forums (NASCO)
PO Box 7715
Ann Arbor, MI 48107
Ph: (734)663-0889
Fax: (734)663-5072
E-mail: info@nasco.coop
URL: http://www.umich.edu/~nasco
Local.

6742 ■ National Association for Multicultural Education, Michigan Chapter
c/o Thomas Hoetger, Pres.
1760 David Ct.
Ann Arbor, MI 48105
Ph: (734)663-3911
E-mail: tomhoetger@yahoo.com
URL: National Affiliate–www.nameorg.org
Contact: Thomas Hoetger, Pres.
State. Represents individuals and groups with an interest in multicultural education from all levels of education, different academic disciplines and from diverse educational institutions and occupations. Provides leadership in national and state dialogues on equity, diversity and multicultural education. Works to fight injustices in schools and in communities. Seeks to ensure that all students receive an equitable education. **Affiliated With:** National Association for Multicultural Education.

6743 ■ National Association of Pastoral Musicians, Lansing
c/o Dr. Robert Wolf, DMA
2226 Vinewood Blvd.
Ann Arbor, MI 48104-2764
Ph: (734)662-1509
E-mail: musicdir@stpatchurch.org
URL: National Affiliate–www.npm.org
Local. Affiliated With: National Association of Pastoral Musicians.

6744 ■ National Association of the Remodeling Industry of Southeast Michigan
122 W Huron
Ann Arbor, MI 48104-1318
Ph: (734)622-9999
Fax: (734)769-2007
E-mail: jan@jjadvpub.com
URL: http://www.narisemich.org
Contact: Paul LaRoe, Pres.
Local. Brings together people who work in the remodeling industry. Provides resources for knowledge and training in the industry. Encourages ethical conduct, sound business practices and professionalism. Promotes the remodeling industry's products. **Affiliated With:** National Association of the Remodeling Industry. **Publications:** Newsletter.

6745 ■ National Audubon Society - Washtenaw
PO Box 130923
Ann Arbor, MI 48113-0923
Ph: (734)572-0333
E-mail: mabryant@umich.edu
URL: http://www.washtenawaudubon.org
Contact: Mary Ann Bryant, Pres.
Founded: 1950. **Members:** 150. **Membership Dues:** individual/household, $20 (annual) • student/senior, $10 (annual) • individual life/couple life, $200-$250. **Local**. Works to promote the conservation of wildlife and the natural beauty. Cooperates with other

organizations whose aims correspond to those of Washtenaw Audubon Society. Holds monthly meetings that are open to the public, with speakers who present wide variety of birds, wildlife and natural history topics. Conducts natural history field trip. Sponsors bird count and migration count. Works with local school group for volunteer educational programs.

6746 ■ National Kidney Foundation of Michigan
1169 Oak Valley Dr.
Ann Arbor, MI 48108
Ph: (734)222-9800
Fax: (734)222-9801
Free: (800)482-1455
E-mail: mgerlach@nkfm.org
URL: http://www.nkfm.org
State. Affiliated With: National Kidney Foundation.

6747 ■ National Society of Black Engineers - University of Michigan
1232 EECS
1301 Beal Ave.
Ann Arbor, MI 48109
E-mail: nsbe.president@umich.edu
URL: http://www.umich.edu/~nsbe
Contact: Maurice Telesford, Pres.
Local. Strives to increase the number of culturally responsible Black engineers who excel academically, succeed professionally and positively impact the community. **Affiliated With:** National Society of Black Engineers.

6748 ■ National Wildlife Federation - Great Lakes Natural Resource Center
213 W Liberty St., Ste.200
Ann Arbor, MI 48104-1398
Ph: (734)769-3351
Fax: (734)769-1449
E-mail: greatlakes@nwf.org
URL: http://www.nwf.org/greatlakes
Founded: 1982. **Staff:** 26. **Regional.** Strives to educate, inspire and assist individuals and organizations of diverse cultures to conserve wildlife and other natural resources. Works to protect the Earth's environment in order to achieve a peaceful, equitable, and sustainable future.

6749 ■ Optical Society of America, Ann Arbor (AAOSA)
c/o Glen Bolling, Sec.
Kaiser Optical Systems
371 Parkland Plz.
Ann Arbor, MI 48106
E-mail: bolling@kosi.com
URL: http://www.osa.org/localsections/aaosa/aaosaindex.htm
Contact: Prof. Stephen Rand, Contact
Members: 108. **Membership Dues:** regular, $8 (annual) • corporate sponsor, $75 (annual). **Languages:** English, French. **Local.** Works to promote improved understanding of fundamental aspects and applications of optical science, not only among governmental, industrial and university researchers, but also among students of all ages, primarily in southeast Michigan. Organizes a regular monthly seminar, an annual tour of local industry and an industrial snapshot night for networking, and overview presentations by local companies. **Affiliated With:** Optical Society of America.

6750 ■ Parents Television Council - Southeast Michigan Chapter
c/o Rich Coleman, Dir.
PO Box 13052
Ann Arbor, MI 48113
Free: (800)849-5631
E-mail: southeastmichiganchapter@parentstv.org
URL: National Affiliate–www.parentstv.org
Contact: Rich Coleman, Dir.
Local.

6751 ■ Parents Without Partners, Ann Arbor Chapter 38
PO Box 2115
Ann Arbor, MI 48106
Ph: (734)973-1933
E-mail: ltfarah@cs.com
URL: http://www.aapwp.org
Contact: Lou Farah, Pres.
Membership Dues: single parent, $30 (annual). **Local.** Custodial and noncustodial parents who are single by reason of widowhood, divorce, separation, or otherwise. Works to alleviate the problems of single parents in relation to the welfare and upbringing of their children and the acceptance into the general social order of single parents and their children. **Affiliated With:** Parents Without Partners. **Publications:** *The Tree*, monthly. Newsletter. Contains information of interests to single parents. Includes news on upcoming events of the organization. **Price:** included in membership dues.

6752 ■ Performance Network Theatre
c/o David Wolber, Exec.Dir.
120 E Huron St.
Ann Arbor, MI 48104-1437
Ph: (734)663-0696
Fax: (734)663-7367
E-mail: david@performancenetwork.org
URL: http://www.performancenetwork.org
Contact: David Wolber, Exec.Dir.
Founded: 1981. **Members:** 500. **Staff:** 11. **Budget:** $750,000. **Regional Groups:** 1. **Regional.**

6753 ■ PFLAG Ann Arbor
PO Box 7471
Ann Arbor, MI 48107
Ph: (734)741-0659
E-mail: president@pflagaa.org
URL: http://www.pflagaa.org
Local. Affiliated With: Parents, Families, and Friends of Lesbians and Gays.

6754 ■ Phi Theta Kappa, Beta Gamma Alpha Chapter - Washtenaw Community College
c/o Heather Byrne
4800 E Huron River Dr.
Ann Arbor, MI 48106
Ph: (734)973-3729
E-mail: hbyrne@wccnet.org
URL: http://www.ptk.org/directories/chapters/MI/20688-1.htm
Contact: Heather Byrne, Advisor
Local.

6755 ■ Pioneer High - Young Life
230 Collingwood, Ste.160A
Ann Arbor, MI 48103
Ph: (734)665-2378
URL: http://sites.younglife.org/sites/pioneerhs/default.aspx
Local. Affiliated With: Young Life.

6756 ■ Pittsfield Township Historical Society
c/o Betty L. Leclair, Pres.
PO Box 6013
Ann Arbor, MI 48106
Ph: (734)971-2384
E-mail: donbet@comcast.net
URL: http://www.pittsfieldhistory.org
Contact: Betty L. Leclair, Pres.
Founded: 1998. **Members:** 56. **Membership Dues:** individual, $12 (annual) • family, $18 (annual). **Local.**

6757 ■ Plumbing-Heating-Cooling Contractors Association, Flint
c/o Sandra Miller, Exec.Mgr.
58 Parkland Plz., Ste.600
Ann Arbor, MI 48103-6209
Ph: (734)665-4681
Fax: (734)665-5051
URL: National Affiliate–www.phccweb.org
Contact: Sandra Miller, Exec.Mgr.
Local. Represents the plumbing, heating and cooling contractors. Promotes the construction industry. Protects the environment, health, safety and comfort of society. **Affiliated With:** Plumbing-Heating-Cooling Contractors Association.

6758 ■ Police and Firemen's Insurance Association - Ann Arbor Fire and Police Department
c/o John M. Schnur
520 N Wagner Rd.
Ann Arbor, MI 48103
Ph: (734)665-2652
URL: National Affiliate–www.pfia.net
Contact: John M. Schnur, Contact
Local. Affiliated With: Police and Firemen's Insurance Association.

6759 ■ Potawatomi MMBA (MMBA)
1606 Pontiac Trail
Ann Arbor, MI 48105
E-mail: poto@mmba.org
URL: http://www.mmba.org
Founded: 1987. **Members:** 500. **Local. Affiliated With:** International Mountain Bicycling Association.

6760 ■ Psi Chi, National Honor Society in Psychology - University of Michigan
c/o Dept. of Psychology
Undergrad Psychology Off.
525 E Univ. Ave.
Ann Arbor, MI 48109-1109
Ph: (734)764-2580
Fax: (734)764-3520
E-mail: psichi2005_exec@umich.edu
URL: National Affiliate–www.psichi.org
Local. Affiliated With: Psi Chi, National Honor Society in Psychology.

6761 ■ RSVP of Washtenaw County
c/o Jill Kind, Dir.
PO Box 995
Ann Arbor, MI 48106
Ph: (734)712-3625
Fax: (734)712-7765
E-mail: bchaudhry@csswashtenaw.org
URL: http://www.csswashtenaw.org
Contact: Jill Kind, Dir.
Local. Affiliated With: Retired and Senior Volunteer Program.

6762 ■ Saline High - Young Life
230 Collingwood, Ste.160A
Ann Arbor, MI 48103
Ph: (734)665-2378
URL: http://sites.younglife.org/sites/salinehs/default.aspx
Local. Affiliated With: Young Life.

6763 ■ Sandhill Soaring Club
PO Box 2021
Ann Arbor, MI 48106
E-mail: orrinbeckham@hotmail.com
URL: http://www.sandhillsoaring.org
Contact: Orrin Beckham, Contact
Local. Affiliated With: Soaring Society of America.

6764 ■ SCORE Ann Arbor Area Chapter
c/o Karl Hauser, Chm.
425 S Main St., Ste.103
Ann Arbor, MI 48104
Ph: (734)665-4434
Fax: (734)665-4191
URL: http://www.score.org
Contact: Karl Hauser, Chm.
Founded: 2000. **Members:** 24. **Local.** Provides free experienced counseling for small business by volunteers. **Affiliated With:** SCORE. **Formerly:** (2005) SCORE Ann Arbor Area.

6765 ■ Sierra Club - Mackinac Chapter - Huron Valley Group
1117 Brooks St.
Ann Arbor, MI 48103
E-mail: dcow2@yahoo.com
URL: http://www.michigan.sierraclub.org/huron
Contact: Doug Cowherd, Co-Chm.
Local. Works to explore, enjoy, and protect nature in the Michigan counties of Washtenaw, Lenawee, and Monroe.

6766 ■ Society of Antique Modelers - Michigan 40
319 Lexington Dr.
Ann Arbor, MI 48105
Ph: (734)761-9304
E-mail: chutton@mediaone.net
URL: National Affiliate–www.antiquemodeler.org
Local. Affiliated With: Society of Antique Modelers.

6767 ■ Society of Manufacturing Engineers - University of Michigan S001
Dept. of Mech. Engg., 2250 G.G. Brown Lab
2350 Hayward Ave.
Ann Arbor, MI 48109-2125
URL: National Affiliate–www.sme.org
Local. Advances manufacturing knowledge to gain competitive advantage. Improves skills and manufacturing solutions for the growth of economy. Provides resources and opportunities for manufacturing professionals. **Affiliated With:** Linnaean Society of New York.

6768 ■ Society for Technical Communication, Southeastern Michigan Chapter
PO Box 1289
Ann Arbor, MI 48106
Ph: (419)531-1270
E-mail: president@stc-sm.org
URL: http://www.stc-sm.org
Contact: Lanette Cornwell, Pres.
Local. Seeks to advance the theory and practice of technical communication in all media. Enhances the professionalism of the members and the status of the profession. Promotes the education of members and supports research activities in the field. **Affiliated With:** Society for Technical Communication.

6769 ■ Sons of Norway, Nordkap Lodge 5-378
c/o Stephen L. Landes, Pres.
1260 Barrister Dr.
Ann Arbor, MI 48105-2820
Ph: (734)604-8146
E-mail: chieftobac@yahoo.com
URL: National Affiliate–www.sofn.com
Contact: Stephen L. Landes, Pres.
Local. Affiliated With: Sons of Norway.

6770 ■ Southern Michigan Northern Ohio Association for Computing Machinery SIGCHI
c/o Jack Zaientz, Chm.
315 W Huron, No. 140
Ann Arbor, MI 48103
Ph: (734)647-6437
Fax: (734)765-9353
E-mail: jzaientz@soartech.com
Regional. Affiliated With: Association for Computing Machinery.

6771 ■ Southern Michigan Orienteering Club (SMOC)
c/o Bill Luitje
2677 Wayside Dr.
Ann Arbor, MI 48103
Ph: (734)769-7820
E-mail: gsarnecki@online.emich.edu
URL: http://www.michigano.org
Contact: Bill Luitje, Contact
Local. Affiliated With: United States Orienteering Federation.

6772 ■ Special Libraries Association, Michigan Chapter
c/o Charlene Stachnik, Pres.
Museums Lib., Univ. of Michigan
2500 Museums Bldg.
Ann Arbor, MI 48109
Ph: (734)764-0467
Fax: (734)763-9813
E-mail: sta@umich.edu
URL: http://www.sla.org/chapter/cmi/index.html
Contact: Charlene Stachnik, Pres.
Regional. Seeks to advance the leadership role of special librarians. Promotes and strengthens members through learning, advocacy and networking initiatives. **Affiliated With:** Special Libraries Association.

6773 ■ Tasters Guild International - Ann Arbor, Chapter No. 037
601 S Forest
Ann Arbor, MI 48104
Ph: (734)995-1818
E-mail: winerat@villagecorner.com
URL: http://www.villagecorner.com
Contact: Richard Scheer, Contact
Local. Aims to educate consumers and spread the word of responsible wine and food consumption. Provides opportunity to encounter the best in wine and culinary delights. **Affiliated With:** Tasters Guild International.

6774 ■ Theta Xi Fraternity, Sigma Chapter
1345 Washtenaw Ave.
Ann Arbor, MI 48104-2587
Ph: (248)722-1671
E-mail: akulpa@engin.umich.edu
URL: http://www.umich.edu/~thetaxi
Contact: David Mayseless, Pres.
Local. Affiliated With: Theta Xi.

6775 ■ Thimble Collectors International, Great Lakes
c/o Ruth Primas
1743 Broadview Ln., No. 507
Ann Arbor, MI 48105
Ph: (734)665-6774
E-mail: ruthp@umich.edu
URL: National Affiliate–www.thimblecollectors.com
Contact: Ruth Primas, Contact
Regional. Affiliated With: Thimble Collectors International.

6776 ■ Trout Unlimited - Ann Arbor Chapter 127
c/o Leo Landis, Pres.
527 S Seventh St.
Ann Arbor, MI 48103
Ph: (734)663-4957
E-mail: landis@tir.com
URL: http://www.aaatu.org/
Contact: Leo Landis, Pres.
Local.

6777 ■ University of Michigan ACM SIGGRAPH Student Chapter
c/o Jon Harris
2101 Boinsteel Blvd.
Ann Arbor, MI 48109-2090
E-mail: siggraph.info@umich.edu
URL: http://campus.acm.org
Contact: Jon Harris, Contact
Local. Promotes computer graphics, including visual effects, modeling, animation, computer games, virtual reality, and more. Holds workshops to teach techniques for creating computer graphics, particularly graphics programming libraries and use of industry-standard modeling and animation software. Brings in professionals to speak on various topics in the field, serves as a communication hub for all things on the U-M campus related to graphics, and provides support and outlets for students' projects and ideas. **Affiliated With:** Association for Computing Machinery.

6778 ■ University of Michigan Skating Club
1000 S State St.
Ann Arbor, MI 48109
Ph: (734)904-4344
E-mail: skateblue@umich.edu
URL: http://www.umich.edu/~umsst
Local. Provides programs to encourage participation and achievement in the sport of figure skating on ice. Defines and maintains uniform standards of skating proficiency. Organizes and sponsors competitions and exhibitions for the purpose of stimulating interest in figure skating. **Affiliated With:** United States Figure Skating Association.

6779 ■ University Musical Society (UMS)
Burton Memorial Tower
881 N Univ. Ave.
Ann Arbor, MI 48109-1011
Ph: (734)764-2538
Fax: (734)647-1171
Free: (800)221-1229
E-mail: umstix@umich.edu
URL: http://www.ums.org
Contact: Kenneth C. Fischer, Pres.
Founded: 1879. **Members:** 3,000. **Staff:** 24. **Budget:** $8,000,000. **Regional.** Music, dance, and theatre enthusiasts. Sponsors concerts, educational events, and social events. **Convention/Meeting:** none. **Awards:** UMS Distinguished Artist Award. **Frequency:** annual. **Type:** recognition. **Recipient:** for internationally recognized performer. **Affiliated With:** Association of Performing Arts Presenters; Chamber Music America; International Society for the Performing Arts. **Publications:** *Bravo! A Cookbook Celebration: 120 years of the University Musical Society.* Books. Contains recipes, legends, and love. • *Notes*, semiannual. Newsletter. Contains anecdotes about performances, performers, UMS donors and special events. **Price:** free for members • Booklets.

6780 ■ Vanezetti Hamilton Bar Association
c/o Francois Nabwangu, Pres.
McCoy & Associates
2381 E Stadium Blvd.
Ann Arbor, MI 48104
Ph: (734)665-8496
Fax: (734)769-0056
URL: National Affiliate–www.nationalbar.org
Contact: Francois Nabwangu, Pres.
Local. Affiliated With: National Bar Association.

6781 ■ Vietnam Veterans of America, Washtenaw County - Chapter 310
c/o John Kinzinger
PO Box 3221
Ann Arbor, MI 48106-3221
Ph: (734)222-4743
E-mail: president@vva310.org
URL: http://www.vva310.org
Contact: John Kinzinger, Contact
Local. Affiliated With: Vietnam Veterans of America.

6782 ■ Washtenaw Bicycling and Walking Coalition (WBWC)
c/o The Ecology Center
117 N Div. St.
Ann Arbor, MI 48104
Ph: (734)913-8604 (734)487-9058
E-mail: info@wbwc.org
URL: http://www.wbwc.org
Contact: Kris Talley, Chair
Local.

6783 ■ Washtenaw Contractors Association (WCA)
3135 S State St., Ste.210
Ann Arbor, MI 48108
Ph: (734)662-2570
Fax: (734)662-1695
E-mail: info@wcaonline.org
URL: http://www.wcaonline.org
Contact: Gretchen A. Waters, Exec.Dir.
Founded: 1949. **Members:** 120. **Membership Dues:** corporate/associate, $575 (annual). **Staff:** 2. **Local.** Supports and promotes the professional interests of member contractors. **Awards:** Nelson VanderHyden Award. **Frequency:** annual. **Type:** recognition. **Recipient:** for a contractor exemplifying high standards of professionalism and community involvement • Pyramid Awards. **Frequency:** annual. **Type:** recognition. **Recipient:** for outstanding project teams; for safety; for innovation; for outstanding subcontractors. **Publications:** *Contractor Connection*, bimonthly. Newsletter. Provides Washtenaw construction related news. **Price:** included in membership dues. **Circulation:** 600. **Advertising:** accepted. **Conventions/Meetings:** bimonthly meeting, membership.

6784 ■ Washtenaw County Bar Association (WCBA)
c/o Judith Van Amburg, Exec.Dir.
PO Box 8645
110 N Fourth Ave.
Ann Arbor, MI 48107
Ph: (734)994-4912
Fax: (734)663-2430
E-mail: vanamburgj@ewashtenaw.org
URL: http://www.washbar.org
Contact: Judith Van Amburg, Exec.Dir.
Founded: 1894. **Members:** 725. **Budget:** $160,000. **Local. Publications:** *Res Ipsa Loquitur*, monthly. Newsletter. **Conventions/Meetings:** monthly board meeting • monthly meeting.

6785 ■ Washtenaw County Coalition on Gender Violence and Safety
c/o Domestic Violence Project Inc./SAFEHouse
PO Box 7052
Ann Arbor, MI 48107-7052
Ph: (734)973-0242
Fax: (734)973-7817
E-mail: barbaran@dvpsh.org
URL: http://www.ci.ann-arbor.mi.us/police/index.html
Contact: Ms. Barbara Niess, Chairwoman
Founded: 1985. **Members:** 26. **Local.** Coalition of twenty-eight member organizations in Washtenaw County and includes local agencies serving survivors and local agency serving perpetrators, two major health systems, law enforcement and criminal justice system agencies, local government, religious organizations and businesses. Collaborative county-wide effort to address and prevent sexual assault, dating and domestic violence, and stalking. **Formerly:** (2001) Ann Arbor Mayor's Task Force.

6786 ■ Washtenaw County Historical Society
PO Box 3336
Ann Arbor, MI 48106-3336
Ph: (734)662-9092
E-mail: wchs-500@ameritech.net
URL: http://www.hvcn.org/info/gswc/society/socwashtenaw.htm
Contact: Pauline V. Walters, Pres.
Founded: 1857. **Members:** 400. **Membership Dues:** individual, $15 (annual) • couple, family, $25 (annual) • patron, business patron, $100 (annual) • student, senior, $10 (annual) • senior couple, $19 (annual) • business, $50 (annual). **Budget:** $8,000. **Local.** Collects, displays, and interprets the history of Washtenaw County. **Additional Websites:** http://www.washtenawhistory.org. **Formerly:** Washtenaw Historical Society. **Publications:** *Washtenaw Impressions*, 7/year. Newsletter. **Price:** included in membership dues. **Conventions/Meetings:** monthly board meeting • Public Program - meeting - 8/year.

6787 ■ Washtenaw County Medical Society
123 N Ashley, No. 121
Ann Arbor, MI 48104
Ph: (734)668-6241
Fax: (734)668-8928
E-mail: wcms@msms.org
URL: http://www.msms.org
Contact: Sallie Schiel, Exec.Dir.
Local. Advances the art and science of medicine. Promotes patient care and the betterment of public health. **Affiliated With:** Michigan State Medical Society.

6788 ■ Washtenaw County Pheasants Forever
PO Box 3478
Ann Arbor, MI 48106
Free: (800)298-9987
E-mail: info@washtenawpf.com
URL: http://www.washtenawpf.org
Contact: Steve Schneider, Pres.
Local. Affiliated With: Pheasants Forever.

6789 ■ Washtenaw District Dental Society
169 Barton Dr.
Ann Arbor, MI 48105
Ph: (734)761-2445
Fax: (734)668-2089
E-mail: nini2go@sbcglobal.net
URL: National Affiliate–www.ada.org
Contact: Ms. Amalia Gobetti, Exec.Dir.
Local. Represents the interests of dentists committed to the public's oral health, ethics and professional development. Encourages the improvement of the public's oral health and promotes the art and science of dentistry. **Affiliated With:** American Dental Association; Michigan Dental Association.

6790 ■ Washtenaw Sierra Club Inner City Outings
c/o Susan Hollar
1109 Pomona
Ann Arbor, MI 48103
E-mail: washtenawico@yahoo.com
URL: http://michigan.sierraclub.org/ico/washtenaw/ico.html
Local.

6791 ■ Washtenaw United Way
2305 Platt Rd.
Ann Arbor, MI 48104
Ph: (734)971-8200
Fax: (734)971-6230
E-mail: dbratkovich@wuway.org
URL: http://www.wuway.org
Contact: Deb Bratkovich, Contact
Local. Affiliated With: United Way of America.

6792 ■ WAUG
14 Payeur Rd.
Ann Arbor, MI 48108
Ph: (313)971-8576
E-mail: harvey@ic.net
URL: http://ic.net/~harvey/waug.htm
Contact: Craig Harvey, Exec. Officer
Founded: 1985. **Members:** 20. **Membership Dues:** regular, $15 (annual). **Local.** Promotes the use and understanding of computers. **Libraries: Type:** reference. **Subjects:** programs for Atari, IBM and other computers. **Formerly:** Wastenaws Atari Users Group. **Publications:** *WAUG Newsletter*, monthly. **Price:** included in membership dues. **Conventions/Meetings:** monthly meeting - every 2nd Tuesday.

6793 ■ Women's International League for Peace and Freedom - Ann Arbor/Ypsilanti (WILPF)
c/o Odile Hugonot-Haber, Chm.
531 Third St.
Ann Arbor, MI 48103-4956
Ph: (734)761-7967
Fax: (734)769-2971
E-mail: od4life@aol.com
URL: http://www.wilpf.org
Contact: Odile Hugonot-Haber, Co-Coor.
Local. Works to build bridges for racial justice and advocates disarmament. Organizes educational programs on national or international issues. Advocates redirecting defense spending towards human needs.

6794 ■ Young Life Washtenaw County
230 Collingwood, Ste.160A
Ann Arbor, MI 48103
Ph: (734)665-2378
Fax: (734)665-9447
URL: http://sites.younglife.org/sites/washtenawcounty/default.aspx
Local. Affiliated With: Young Life.

L'Anse

6795 ■ Baraga County Tourist and Recreation Association (BCTRA)
755 E Broad St.
L'Anse, MI 49946-1311
Ph: (906)524-7444
Fax: (906)524-7454
Free: (800)743-4908
E-mail: bctra@up.net
URL: http://www.baragacountytourism.com
Contact: Tracey E. Barrett, Exec.Dir.
Founded: 1985. **Members:** 100. **Membership Dues:** business, $125 (annual). **Staff:** 1. **Budget:** $46,000. **Local.** Promotes convention business and tourism in the area. **Publications:** Newsletter, bimonthly. **Price:** free. **Conventions/Meetings:** annual meeting - always October.

Arcadia

6796 ■ Arcadia Lions Club
c/o Tom McChaner, Pres.
PO Box 258
Arcadia, MI 49613
Ph: (231)889-4416
E-mail: wesbetty@yahoo.com
URL: http://lions.silverthorn.biz/11-e1
Contact: Tom McChaner, Pres.
Local. Affiliated With: Lions Clubs International.

Armada

6797 ■ ACF Blue Water Chefs Association
c/o Francine Salvatore, Pres.
15309 34 Mile Rd.
Armada, MI 48005
Ph: (586)752-7782
E-mail: pamelascatering@hotmail.com
URL: National Affiliate–www.acfchefs.org
Contact: Francine Salvatore CC, Pres.
Local. Promotes the culinary profession. Provides on-going educational training and networking for members. Provides opportunities for competition, professional recognition and access to educational forums with other culinarians at local, regional, national and international events. **Affiliated With:** American Culinary Federation.

6798 ■ Veteran Motor Car Club of America - Brass and Gas Chapter
c/o Leo Parnagian, Pres.
16191 32 Mile Rd.
Armada, MI 48005
Ph: (586)752-6662
URL: National Affiliate–www.vmcca.org
Contact: Leo Parnagian, Pres.
Local. Affiliated With: Veteran Motor Car Club of America.

Ashley

6799 ■ Ashley Lions Club
c/o Brent Beracy, Pres.
PO Box 261
Ashley, MI 48806-0261
Ph: (989)847-2803
E-mail: bigbear@bearnet.net
URL: http://www.district11c2.org
Contact: Brent Beracy, Pres.
Local. Affiliated With: Lions Clubs International.

Athens

6800 ■ Friends of the St. Joe River Association (FOTSJR)
c/o Al Smith, Exec.Dir./Founder
PO Box 354
Athens, MI 49011
Ph: (269)729-5174
Fax: (269)729-5045
E-mail: fotsjr01@sbcglobal.net
URL: http://www.fotsjr.org
Contact: Al Smith, Exec.Dir./Founder
Founded: 1994. **Members:** 74. **Membership Dues:** individual, family, $25 (annual) • senior, $15 (annual)

• contributor, $100 (annual) • friend, $50-$99 (annual) • business sustaining, $500-$999 (annual) • business contributor, $100-$499 (annual) • life, $300 • business benefactor, $1,000 (annual). **Budget:** $20,000. **Local**. Supports the issues which concern the welfare of the St. Joseph River, the conservation of the water supply in the river and it's watersheds, the maintenance of the water quality of the river, evaluation of hydrological data of the river and its tributaries so that decisions and actions of the corporation may be conducive to the betterment of the river, and operate exclusively for educational, historical, charitable, and scientific purposes. **Conventions/Meetings:** monthly board meeting.

Atlanta

6801 ■ American Legion, Atlanta Post 201
PO Box 481
Atlanta, MI 49709
Ph: (517)371-4720
Fax: (517)371-2401
URL: National Affiliate–www.legion.org
Local. **Affiliated With:** American Legion.

6802 ■ Atlanta Area Chamber of Commerce
PO Box 410
Atlanta, MI 49709
Ph: (989)785-3400
Fax: (989)785-3400
E-mail: chamber_office@atlantamichigan.com
URL: http://www.atlantamichigan.com
Contact: Betty Comoford, Pres.
Founded: 1986. **Membership Dues:** business, $75 (annual) • associate, $50 (annual) • individual, $15 (annual). **Local**. Promotes business and community development in Atlanta, MI.

6803 ■ Great Lakes Curling Association - Lewiston Curling Club
c/o Van Beaureagard
16361 Harwood Rd.
Atlanta, MI 49709
Ph: (989)785-2142
URL: http://www.usacurl.org/basics/U.S.%20clubs/glakes.html
Contact: Larry Mathias, Contact
Local. **Affiliated With:** United States Curling Association.

6804 ■ Michigan National Wild Turkey Federation, Elk Country Gobblers
6115 N M33
Atlanta, MI 49709
Ph: (517)785-4041
URL: http://www.mi-nwtf.org/Elkcountry.htm
Contact: Bud Klein, Pres.
Local.

Au Gres

6805 ■ Au Gres Chamber of Commerce
PO Box 455
Au Gres, MI 48703
Ph: (989)876-6688
Contact: Eric Forton, Pres.
Local.

6806 ■ Michigan National Wild Turkey Federation, Arenac County
2032 W Jodway Rd.
Au Gres, MI 48703
Ph: (989)876-8446
URL: http://www.mi-nwtf.org/arenac_co_.htm
Contact: Jeff Hayes, Contact
Local.

Auburn

6807 ■ Auburn Area Chamber of Commerce
PO Box 215
Auburn, MI 48611
Ph: (989)662-4001
E-mail: cornfest@auburnchambermi.com
URL: http://www.auburnchambermi.com
Contact: Dave Hill, Pres.
Local. Promotes business and community development in the Auburn, MI area. **Conventions/Meetings:** semimonthly meeting - every 2nd and 4th Thursday in Auburn, MI.

6808 ■ Auburn Lions Club - Michigan
c/o Robert McCloy, Sec.
306 Noble St.
Auburn, MI 48611
Ph: (989)450-6268
URL: http://www.geocities.com/dist11d1
Contact: Lynn Keeley, Pres.
Local. **Affiliated With:** Lions Clubs International.

6809 ■ National Active and Retired Federal Employees Association - Manley 1705
1763 W Beaver Rd. R1
Auburn, MI 48611-9790
Ph: (517)662-4633
URL: National Affiliate–www.narfe.org
Contact: Martin O. Kohn, Contact
Local. Protects the retirement future of employees through education. Informs members on issues affecting the retirement. **Affiliated With:** National Association of Retired Federal Employees.

6810 ■ Sweet Adelines International, Tri-City Chapter
Western High School
500 W Midland Rd.
Auburn, MI 48611-9300
Ph: (989)686-5255
URL: National Affiliate–www.sweetadelineintl.org
Contact: Janelle Snyder, Contact
Local. Advances the musical art form of barbershop harmony through education and performances. Provides education, training and coaching in the development of women's four-part barbershop harmony. **Affiliated With:** Sweet Adelines International.

Auburn Hills

6811 ■ American Association for Clinical Chemistry, Michigan Section
c/o Elena Dvorin, MD, Chair
Quest Diagnostics
Admin.
4444 Giddings Rd.
Auburn Hills, MI 48326
Ph: (248)364-1244
Fax: (248)364-1030
URL: National Affiliate–www.aacc.org
Contact: Elena Dvorin MD, Chair
State. Represents the interests of clinical laboratory professionals, physicians, research scientists and other individuals involved with clinical chemistry and other clinical laboratory science-related disciplines. Seeks to improve the practice of clinical chemistry. Establishes standards for education and training in the field. **Affiliated With:** American Association for Clinical Chemistry.

6812 ■ American Legion, Hill-Gazette Post 143
96 Churchill Rd.
Auburn Hills, MI 48326
Ph: (517)371-4720
Fax: (517)371-2401
URL: National Affiliate–www.legion.org
Local. **Affiliated With:** American Legion.

6813 ■ Detroit Society for Coatings Technology (DSCT)
c/o Ms. Bernadette M. Colonna, Pres.
Bayer MaterialScience
2401 Walton Blvd.
Auburn Hills, MI 48326-1957
Ph: (248)475-7708
Fax: (248)475-7701
E-mail: bernadette.colonna@bayermaterialscience.com
URL: http://www.dsct.org
Contact: Ms. Bernadette M. Colonna, Pres.
Local. Represents chemists, chemical engineers, technologists and supervisory production personnel in the decorative and protective coatings industry and allied industries. Works to gather and disseminate practical and technical facts, data and standards fundamental to the manufacturing and use of paints, varnishes, lacquers, related protective coatings and printing inks. **Affiliated With:** Federation of Societies for Coatings Technology.

6814 ■ International Visitors Council of Metropolitan Detroit
2601 Cambridge Ct., Ste.500
Auburn Hills, MI 48326
Ph: (248)375-7300
Fax: (248)375-7101
E-mail: mail@ivcdetroit.org
URL: http://www.ivcdetroit.org
Contact: Ms. Julie Oldani, Exec.Dir.
Founded: 1972. **Members:** 500. **Membership Dues:** individual, $75 (annual). **Local**. **Publications:** Newsletter, quarterly. **Conventions/Meetings:** quarterly board meeting.

6815 ■ Phi Theta Kappa, Alpha Omicron Rho Chapter - Oakland Community College
c/o Michelle Casanova
Auburn Hills Campus
2900 Featherstone Rd.
Auburn Hills, MI 48326
Ph: (248)232-4511
E-mail: mrcasano@occ.cc.mi.us
URL: http://www.ptk.org/directories/chapters/MI/6790-1.htm
Contact: Michelle Casanova, Advisor
Local.

6816 ■ Society of Manufacturing Engineers - Baker College U159
1500 Univ. Dr.
Auburn Hills, MI 48326
Ph: (248)340-0600
E-mail: jpawlina@ati-us.com
URL: National Affiliate–www.sme.org
Local. Advances manufacturing knowledge to gain competitive advantage. Improves skills and manufacturing solutions for the growth of economy. Provides resources and opportunities for manufacturing professionals. **Affiliated With:** Society for Mining, Metallurgy, and Exploration.

6817 ■ Society of Manufacturing Engineers - Oakland County Community College S144
2900 Featherstone
Auburn Hills, MI 48326-2817
Ph: (248)232-4193
Fax: (248)232-4190
E-mail: pdcrocke@oaklandcc.edu
URL: National Affiliate–www.sme.org
Contact: Phillip Crockett, Contact
Local. Advances manufacturing knowledge to gain competitive advantage. Improves skills and manufacturing solutions for the growth of economy. Provides resources and opportunities for manufacturing professionals. **Affiliated With:** National Association for Interpretation.

Augusta

6818 ■ Southwest MMBA
PO Box 23
Augusta, MI 49012

Ph: (269)731-4078
E-mail: southwest@mmba.org
URL: http://www.mmba.org
Local. Affiliated With: International Mountain Bicycling Association.

Bad Axe

6819 ■ American Legion, Bad Axe Post 318
3365 Sand Beach Rd.
Bad Axe, MI 48413
Ph: (517)371-4720
Fax: (517)371-2401
URL: National Affiliate–www.legion.org
Local. Affiliated With: American Legion.

6820 ■ Bad Axe Chamber of Commerce
PO Box 87
Bad Axe, MI 48413
Ph: (989)269-6936
Fax: (989)269-2611
Free: (800)469-5146
E-mail: badaxemi@yahoo.com
Contact: Charlene Kramer, Sec.-Treas.
Local.

6821 ■ Greater Huron County United Way
PO Box 212
Bad Axe, MI 48413-0212
Ph: (989)551-2833
URL: National Affiliate–national.unitedway.org
Local. Affiliated With: United Way of America.

Baldwin

6822 ■ American Legion, Michigan Post 133
c/o Charles Dobry
PO Box 284
Baldwin, MI 49304
Ph: (517)371-4720
Fax: (517)371-2401
URL: National Affiliate–www.legion.org
Contact: Charles Dobry, Contact
Local. Affiliated With: American Legion.

6823 ■ Baldwin Lions Club - Michigan
c/o William Downey, Pres.
PO Box 1320
Baldwin, MI 49304
Ph: (231)745-8014
E-mail: bilmar1955@yahoo.com
URL: http://lions.silverthorn.biz/11-e1
Contact: William Downey, Pres.
Local. Affiliated With: Lions Clubs International.

Bancroft

6824 ■ Bancroft Lions Club
c/o Tracy Temple, Pres.
PO Box 2
Bancroft, MI 48414-0002
Ph: (989)634-9740
URL: http://www.district11c2.org
Contact: Tracy Temple, Pres.
Local. Affiliated With: Lions Clubs International.

6825 ■ MS Connection
c/o Donna S. Domby, Pres.
6214 Lemon Rd.
Bancroft, MI 48414-9483
Ph: (989)634-9434 (810)635-8816
E-mail: msconnection@comcast.net
URL: http://msconnect.org
Contact: Donna S. Domby, Pres.
Founded: 1998. **Members:** 8. **Budget:** $100. **State Groups:** 1. **Local.** Works to improve the lives of people with multiple sclerosis by supporting and disseminating research based on describable, observable and replicable data. **Computer Services:** Online services, information on non-traditional health options for those living with multiple sclerosis.

Bangor

6826 ■ American Legion, Wilcox-Eastman-Salinas Post 160
19 N Center St.
Bangor, MI 49013
Ph: (517)371-4720
Fax: (517)371-2401
URL: National Affiliate–www.legion.org
Local. Affiliated With: American Legion.

6827 ■ Bangor Lions Club
PO Box 13
Bangor, MI 49013
E-mail: crigozzigriffioen@yahoo.com
URL: http://milions11b2.org
Local. Affiliated With: Lions Clubs International.

6828 ■ Michigan National Wild Turkey Federation, Vanburen Longbeards
53467 M-43
Bangor, MI 49013
Ph: (616)427-6015
URL: http://www.mi-nwtf.org/vanburenlongbeards.htm
Contact: Dan Hogmire, Pres.
Local.

Baraga

6829 ■ American Legion, Foucault-Funke Post 444
505 Superior Ave.
Baraga, MI 49908
Ph: (517)371-4720
Fax: (517)371-2401
URL: National Affiliate–www.legion.org
Local. Affiliated With: American Legion.

Bark River

6830 ■ American Legion, John-Rheaume-Fred-Knauf Post 438
PO Box 164
Bark River, MI 49807
Ph: (517)371-4720
Fax: (517)371-2401
URL: National Affiliate–www.legion.org
Local. Affiliated With: American Legion.

Baroda

6831 ■ American Legion, Baroda Community Post 345
PO Box 217
Baroda, MI 49101
Ph: (517)371-4720
Fax: (517)371-2401
URL: National Affiliate–www.legion.org
Local. Affiliated With: American Legion.

6832 ■ Baroda Lions Club
PO Box 85
Baroda, MI 49101
E-mail: jwilk@ndfcu.org
URL: http://milions11b2.org
Local. Affiliated With: Lions Clubs International.

Barryton

6833 ■ American Legion, Gerald Pitts Post 473
PO Box 151
Barryton, MI 49305
Ph: (517)371-4720
Fax: (517)371-2401
URL: National Affiliate–www.legion.org
Local. Affiliated With: American Legion.

Bath

6834 ■ American Legion, Michigan Post 412
c/o Ray Barker
5480 Clark Rd.
Bath, MI 48808
Ph: (517)371-4720
Fax: (517)371-2401
URL: National Affiliate–www.legion.org
Contact: Ray Barker, Contact
Local. Affiliated With: American Legion.

6835 ■ Bath Township Lions Club
c/o Ken Robertson, Sec.
12425 Center Rd.
Bath, MI 48808
Ph: (517)641-4269
E-mail: bathlion@yahoo.com
URL: http://www.district11c2.org
Contact: Ken Robertson, Sec.
Local. Affiliated With: Lions Clubs International.

6836 ■ Earth Share of Michigan
PO Box 363
Bath, MI 48808-0363
Ph: (517)641-7200
Fax: (517)641-7877
Free: (800)386-3326
E-mail: info@earthsharemichigan.org
URL: http://www.earthsharemichigan.org
Contact: Vanessa Martin, Exec.Dir.
State. Affiliated With: Earth Share.

6837 ■ Independent Accountants Association of Michigan (IAAM)
c/o Jon A. Hayes, Exec.Dir.
PO Box 370
Bath, MI 48808
Ph: (517)641-7505
Fax: (517)641-4402
E-mail: staff@iaam.net
URL: http://www.iaam.net
Contact: Jon A. Hayes, Exec.Dir.
State.

6838 ■ Michigan Society for Clinical Laboratory Science (MSCLS)
5653 Drumheller Rd.
Bath, MI 48808
Ph: (231)591-2327
E-mail: deregnid@ferris.edu
URL: http://www.mscls.org
Contact: John Landis, Pres.
Founded: 1946. **Members:** 750. **State.** Certified medical technologists and clinical laboratory scientists. Promotes continuing education of members. Disseminates information to the public on the role of laboratory scientists in health care. **Affiliated With:** American Society for Clinical Laboratory Science. **Formerly:** Michigan Society for Medical Technology. **Publications:** *MSCLS Newslinks*, bimonthly. Newsletter. **Conventions/Meetings:** annual meeting (exhibits) - always spring.

6839 ■ Michigan Wildlife Conservancy
PO Box 393
6380 Drumheller Rd.
Bath, MI 48808
Ph: (517)641-7677
Fax: (517)641-7877
E-mail: wildlife@miwildlife.org
URL: http://www.miwildlife.org
Contact: Dennis Fijalkowski, Exec.Dir.
State. Works to preserve wildlife habitats on private lands such as wetlands, prairies, rivers and streams. **Formerly:** (2003) Michigan Wildlife Habitat Foundation.

Battle Creek

6840 ■ ACF of Kalamazoo/Battle Creek
c/o Steven E. Deal
16 Sunnyside Dr.
Battle Creek, MI 49015
Ph: (616)962-0935
E-mail: chefdeal@aol.com
URL: National Affiliate–www.acfchefs.org
Contact: Steven E. Deal, Pres.
Local. Promotes the culinary profession. Provides on-going educational training and networking for members. Provides opportunities for competition, professional recognition and access to educational forums with other culinarians at local, regional, national and international events. **Affiliated With:** American Culinary Federation.

6841 ■ American Federation of Government Employees, AFL-CIO - DOD Local Union 1626
74 N Washington Ave.
Battle Creek, MI 49017
Ph: (269)961-5471
E-mail: webmaster@afge1626.com
URL: http://www.afge1626.com
Contact: Susan Buckley, Pres.
Members: 460. **Local**. Federal employees including food inspectors, nurses, printers, cartographers, lawyers, police officers, census workers, OSHA inspectors, janitors, truck drivers, secretaries, artists, plumbers, immigration inspectors, scientists, doctors, cowboys, botanists, park rangers, computer programmers, foreign service workers, airplane mechanics, environmentalists, and writers. Seeks to provide good government services, while ensuring that government workers are treated fairly and with dignity. **Affiliated With:** American Federation of Government Employees.

6842 ■ American Federation of Government Employees, AFL-CIO - Veterans' Affairs Local Union 1629
5500 Armstrong Rd.
Battle Creek, MI 49015
Ph: (269)966-5600
Fax: (269)963-0694
E-mail: afge1629@mei.net
URL: http://www.afge1629.org
Contact: Mark Bissot, Pres.
Members: 487. **Local**. Federal employees including food inspectors, nurses, printers, cartographers, lawyers, police officers, census workers, OSHA inspectors, janitors, truck drivers, secretaries, artists, plumbers, immigration inspectors, scientists, doctors, cowboys, botanists, park rangers, computer programmers, foreign service workers, airplane mechanics, environmentalists, and writers. Seeks to help provide good government services, while ensuring that government workers are treated fairly and with dignity. **Affiliated With:** American Federation of Government Employees.

6843 ■ American Legion, Fort Custer Post 257
1995 Ensign Ave.
Battle Creek, MI 49015
Ph: (517)371-4720
Fax: (517)371-2401
URL: National Affiliate–www.legion.org
Local. **Affiliated With:** American Legion.

6844 ■ American Legion, Legion Villa Post 210
107 Evergreen Rd.
Battle Creek, MI 49015
Ph: (517)371-4720
Fax: (517)371-2401
URL: National Affiliate–www.legion.org
Local. **Affiliated With:** American Legion.

6845 ■ American Legion, Michigan Post 54
c/o Gen. George A. Custer
1125 Columbia Ave. E
Battle Creek, MI 49014
Ph: (517)371-4720
Fax: (517)371-2401
URL: National Affiliate–www.legion.org
Contact: Gen. George A. Custer, Contact
Local. **Affiliated With:** American Legion.

6846 ■ American Legion, Michigan Post 298
c/o Capt. Oscar Brady
228 20th St. N
Battle Creek, MI 49015
Ph: (517)371-4720
Fax: (517)371-2401
URL: National Affiliate–www.legion.org
Contact: Capt. Oscar Brady, Contact
Local. **Affiliated With:** American Legion.

6847 ■ American Red Cross, Calhoun County Chapter
615 Cliff St.
Battle Creek, MI 49014
Ph: (269)962-7528
Free: (888)919-1011
URL: http://calhounbranchmi.redcross.org
Local.

6848 ■ Association of the United States Army, Southwestern Michigan
c/o LTC John Anderson
203 Chestnut St.
Battle Creek, MI 49017-3771
Ph: (269)962-7754
E-mail: painters4@triton.net
URL: National Affiliate–www.ausa.org
Contact: LTC John Anderson, Contact
Local. Represents the interests and concerns of American Soldiers. Fosters public support of the Army's role in national security. Provides professional education and information programs.

6849 ■ Audio Engineering Society, West Michigan Section
c/o John Loser
16 Shellenberger Ave.
Battle Creek, MI 49017
Ph: (616)528-9850
Fax: (616)538-4311
URL: National Affiliate–www.aes.org
Contact: John Loser, Sec.
Local. Represents the interests of engineers, administrators and technicians for radio, television and motion picture operation. Operates educational and research foundation. **Affiliated With:** Audio Engineering Society.

6850 ■ Battle Creek Area Association of Realtors (BCAAR)
214 Capital Ave. NE
Battle Creek, MI 49017
Ph: (269)962-5193
Fax: (269)962-5404
E-mail: bcaar@jasnetworks.net
URL: http://www.bcaar.com
Contact: Kathy A. Perrett, CEO
Members: 290. **Staff:** 3. **Local**. Licensed real estate brokers, salespersons, and appraisers. Works to advance the industry. **Committees:** Grievance and Professional Standards; Multi-Listing Service; Technology. **Affiliated With:** National Association of Realtors. **Publications:** *Billboard*, biweekly. Newsletter. **Price:** included in membership dues • *Roster*, periodic. Directory.

6851 ■ Battle Creek Area Chamber of Commerce (BCACC)
77 E Michigan Ave., Ste.80
Commerce Pointe
Battle Creek, MI 49017
Ph: (269)962-4076
Fax: (269)962-6309
E-mail: kmechem@battlecreek.org
URL: http://www.battlecreek.org
Contact: Kathleen L. Mechem, Pres./CEO
Founded: 1913. **Members:** 900. **Local**. Promotes business and community development in the Battle Creek, MI area. **Awards:** Athena Award. **Frequency:** annual. **Type:** recognition • Harley Simmons Award. **Frequency:** annual. **Type:** recognition. **Recipient:** for an individual who has significantly contributed to the safety and security of citizens in the Battle Creek area. **Committees:** Ambassadors; Public Policy. **Publications:** *Insight*, monthly. Newsletter • Membership Directory, annual. **Conventions/Meetings:** annual retreat.

6852 ■ Battle Creek Area Habitat for Humanity (BCAHFH)
551 W Michigan Ave.
Battle Creek, MI 49017
Ph: (269)966-2502
Fax: (269)966-2568
E-mail: habitatbc@ctsmail.net
URL: http://www.habitatbc.org
Local. **Affiliated With:** Habitat for Humanity International.

6853 ■ Battle Creek Host Lions Club
c/o Frank E. Hendrickson, Pres.
112 Minges Forest Rd.
Battle Creek, MI 49015
Ph: (269)968-0019 (269)968-1018
E-mail: frank@waterfield.com
URL: http://www.lionsdistrict11b1.org/lc_battle_creek_host.htm
Contact: Frank E. Hendrickson, Pres.
Local. **Affiliated With:** Lions Clubs International.

6854 ■ Battle Creek Lakeview Lions Club
c/o Chris Craft, Pres.
616 Linn Ave.
Battle Creek, MI 49015
Ph: (269)964-4634
URL: http://www.lionsdistrict11b1.org/lc_battle_creek_lakeview.htm
Contact: Chris Craft, Pres.
Local. **Affiliated With:** Lions Clubs International.

6855 ■ BMW Of Battle Creek No. 14
c/o John Blackmore
53 Grandview Ct.
Battle Creek, MI 49015
Ph: (269)965-1673
E-mail: njkimble@comcast.net
URL: http://www.geocities.com/bcbmwclub
Contact: John Blackmore, Contact
Local. BMW motorcycle owners organized for pleasure, recreation, safety, and dissemination of information concerning BMW motorcycles. **Affiliated With:** BMW Motorcycle Owners of America.

6856 ■ Calhoun County Medical Society - Michigan
PO Box 278
Battle Creek, MI 49016-0278
Ph: (269)660-0893
E-mail: calhouncms@yahoo.com
URL: http://www.msms.org
Contact: Diane Cummins, Exec.Dir.
Local. Advances the art and science of medicine. Promotes patient care and the betterment of public health. **Affiliated With:** Michigan State Medical Society.

6857 ■ Cereal City Lions Club
PO Box 790
Battle Creek, MI 49016
E-mail: admin@cerealcitylionsclub.org
URL: http://www.cerealcitylionsclub.org
Contact: Paul Helm, Pres.
Local. **Affiliated With:** Lions Clubs International.

6858 ■ Employee Stock Ownership Plan Association, Michigan
c/o Mr. James Treadwell, Pres.
Kendall Elec., Inc.
131 Grand Truck Ave.
Battle Creek, MI 49015-2225

Ph: (269)963-5585 (269)565-2371
E-mail: jtreadwell@kendallgroup.com
URL: National Affiliate–www.esopassociation.org
Contact: Mr. James Treadwell, Pres.
State. Affiliated With: ESOP Association.

6859 ■ International Association of Machinists and Aerospace Workers, AFL-CIO, CLC - Local Lodge 46
120 Blueberry Ln.
Battle Creek, MI 49017-1258
E-mail: msims88763@aol.com
URL: http://ll46.goiam.org
Contact: Harold Hagan, Pres.
Members: 277. **Local. Affiliated With:** International Association of Machinists and Aerospace Workers.

6860 ■ Junior Achievement, South Central Michigan
34 W Jackson St., Ste.3B
Battle Creek, MI 49017
Ph: (269)968-9188
Fax: (269)660-6635
E-mail: bkaufmann@jaswmi.org
URL: http://battlecreek.ja.org
Contact: Brad Kaufmann, Pres.
Local. Teaches workforce readiness skills with hands-on activities. **Affiliated With:** Junior Achievement.

6861 ■ Laborers AFL-CIO, LU 355
1500 E Columbia Ave.
Battle Creek, MI 49014-5137
Ph: (269)962-8010
Fax: (269)962-1431
Free: (877)616-9845
E-mail: l.local355@comcast.net
URL: http://local355.org
Contact: Alex Zurek, Business Mgr.
Founded: 1903. **Members:** 1,300. **Staff:** 7. **Local. Affiliated With:** AFL-CIO.

6862 ■ National Association of Miniature Enthusiasts - Mini-Fingers of Kalamazoo
c/o Robin Peterson
34 W Territorial Rd.
Battle Creek, MI 49015
Ph: (269)968-9348
E-mail: mininutrsp@aol.com
URL: http://www.miniatures.org/states/MI.html
Contact: Robin Peterson, Contact
Local. Affiliated With: National Association of Miniature Enthusiasts.

6863 ■ National Association of Miniature Enthusiasts - One More Time
c/o Robin Peterson
163 N 21st St.
Battle Creek, MI 49015-1704
Ph: (269)964-7311
E-mail: mininutrsp@aol.com
URL: http://www.miniatures.org/states/MI.html
Contact: Robin Peterson, Contact
Local. Affiliated With: National Association of Miniature Enthusiasts.

6864 ■ National Novelty Salt and Pepper Shakers Club - Michigan
581 Joy Rd.
Battle Creek, MI 49014
E-mail: itburg@comcast.net
URL: National Affiliate–www.saltandpepperclub.com
Contact: Irene Thornburg, Pres.
Membership Dues: single person or two people residing in the same household, $5 (annual). **Regional.** Assists members in learning more about the collecting of novelty salt and pepper shakers. **Computer Services:** Mailing lists. **Also Known As:** (1989) Michigan Chapter of the Novelty Salt and Pepper Shakers Club.

6865 ■ National Technical Honor Society - Calhoun Area Technology Center Michigan (CATC)
475 E Roosevelt Ave.
Battle Creek, MI 49017
Ph: (269)968-2271
Fax: (269)968-4344
E-mail: vogelj@calhounareatech.com
URL: http://www.calhounareatech.com
Contact: Jan Vogel, Contact
Local.

6866 ■ Pennfield Lions Club
c/o Tim R. Beuchler, Sec.
312 Overlook Ln.
Battle Creek, MI 49017
Ph: (269)968-8181 (269)962-7387
Fax: (269)968-6960
E-mail: tbeek13@comcast.net
URL: http://www.lionsdistrict11b1.org/lc_pennfield.htm
Contact: Tim R. Beuchler, Sec.
Local. Affiliated With: Lions Clubs International.

6867 ■ Pennfield Parent Teacher and Student Organization
Pennfield School District
8587 Q Dr. N
Battle Creek, MI 49017
Ph: (269)961-9781
Fax: (269)961-9799
E-mail: margy_everett@yahoo.com
URL: http://www.pennfield.k12.mi.us/PPTSO
Local.

6868 ■ Phi Theta Kappa, Alpha Nu Eta Chapter - Kellogg Community College
c/o Terah Zaremba
450 North Ave.
Battle Creek, MI 49016
Ph: (269)965-3931
E-mail: zarembat@kellogg.edu
URL: http://www.ptk.org/directories/chapters/MI/2058-1.htm
Contact: Terah Zaremba, Advisor
Local.

6869 ■ Southwestern District Dental Society, Michigan
1774 Monroe Beach
Battle Creek, MI 49014
Ph: (269)964-4330
Fax: (269)964-4330
E-mail: vm4bauer@earthlink.net
URL: National Affiliate–www.ada.org
Contact: Ms. Victoria Bauer, Exec.Sec.
Local. Represents the interests of dentists committed to the public's oral health, ethics and professional development. Encourages the improvement of the public's oral health and promotes the art and science of dentistry. **Affiliated With:** American Dental Association; Michigan Dental Association.

6870 ■ Southwestern Michigan Urban League
172 W Van Buren
Battle Creek, MI 49017
Ph: (269)962-5553
URL: National Affiliate–www.nul.org
Local. Affiliated With: National Urban League.

6871 ■ Sweet Adelines International, Battle Creek Chapter
Kellogg Community Coll.
450 North Ave.
Battle Creek, MI 49017-3306
Ph: (269)979-5451
E-mail: swtadelinda@juno.com
URL: National Affiliate–www.sweetadelineintl.org
Contact: Linda Sheldon, Contact
Local. Advances the musical art form of barbershop harmony through education and performances. Provides education, training and coaching in the development of women's four-part barbershop harmony. **Affiliated With:** Sweet Adelines International.

6872 ■ U.S. Naval Sea Cadet Corps, Windward Division
c/o William H. Larson
101 Base Ave.
Battle Creek, MI 49015-1242
Ph: (269)968-9216
Contact: Leiutenant Jerry Works, Commanding Officer
Local.

6873 ■ United Way of Greater Battle Creek
PO Box 137
Battle Creek, MI 49016-0137
Ph: (269)962-9538
Fax: (269)962-0074
E-mail: info@uwgbc.org
URL: http://www.uwgbc.org
Contact: Michael J. Larson, Pres./CPO
Local. Affiliated With: United Way of America.

6874 ■ Veteran Motor Car Club of America - Battle Creek Chapter
c/o Chris Craft, Pres.
616 Linn Ave.
Battle Creek, MI 49015
Ph: (616)964-4634
URL: National Affiliate–www.vmcca.org
Contact: Chris Craft, Pres.
Local. Affiliated With: Veteran Motor Car Club of America.

Bay City

6875 ■ American Legion, Harding-Olk-Craidge Post 18
700 Adams St.
Bay City, MI 48708
Ph: (517)371-4720
Fax: (517)371-2401
URL: National Affiliate–www.legion.org
Local. Affiliated With: American Legion.

6876 ■ American Red Cross, East Shoreline Chapter
228 Washington Ave.
Bay City, MI 48708
Ph: (989)892-1541
Fax: (989)892-2811
Free: (800)472-6225
URL: http://www.eastshorelinearc.org
Local.

6877 ■ American Society of Women Accountants, Saginaw/Midland/Bay Chapter No. 034
c/o Marilyn Eichinger, Pres.
Lutheran Child and Family Ser. of Michigan
1505 Woodmere Pl.
Bay City, MI 48708-5542
Ph: (989)686-7650 (989)894-4629
Fax: (989)686-7688
E-mail: meiching@lcfsmi.org
URL: National Affiliate–www.aswa.org
Contact: Marilyn Eichinger, Pres.
Local. Affiliated With: American Society of Women Accountants.

6878 ■ Ancient Order of Hibernians of Bay County - Robert Shea Division
c/o Mike Campau
1204 Long St.
Bay City, MI 48706
Ph: (989)686-1225
E-mail: pscampau@yahoo.com
URL: http://www.michiganaoh.com
Contact: Mike Campau, Contact
Local. Affiliated With: Ancient Order of Hibernians in America.

6879 ■ Association of Women's Health, Obstetric and Neonatal Nurses - Michigan Section
c/o Patti Krenz, RN
3060 E Riverview Dr.
Bay City, MI 48706
Ph: (989)686-3664
E-mail: patticake@chartermi.net
URL: National Affiliate–www.awhonn.org
Contact: Carol Wilson, Chair
State. Represents registered nurses and other health care providers who specialize in obstetric, women's health, and neonatal nursing. Advances the nursing profession by providing nurses with information and support to help them deliver quality care for women and newborns. **Affiliated With:** Association of Women's Health, Obstetric and Neonatal Nurses.

6880 ■ Bat/Arenac Alliance for the Mentally Ill
c/o Larry Stahl, Pres.
3520 Bangor Rd.
Bay City, MI 48706
Ph: (517)686-6709
URL: http://mi.nami.org/bat.html
Contact: Larry Stahl, Pres.
Local. Strives to improve the quality of life of children and adults with severe mental illness through support, education, research and advocacy. **Affiliated With:** National Alliance for the Mentally Ill.

6881 ■ Bay Area Chamber of Commerce (BACC)
901 Saginaw St.
Bay City, MI 48708
Ph: (989)893-4567
Fax: (989)995-5594
E-mail: chamber@baycityarea.com
URL: http://www.baycityarea.com
Contact: Michael D. Seward CCE, Pres./CEO
Local. Promotes business and community development in the Bay City, MI area. **Awards:** Athena Award. **Frequency:** annual. **Type:** recognition. **Recipient:** for women who have attained and personified the highest level of professional excellence in business • Leadership Alumni Community Service Award. **Frequency:** annual. **Type:** recognition. **Recipient:** for individuals who exemplify the principles of community leadership. **Affiliated With:** U.S. Chamber of Commerce. **Publications:** *Bay Area Business Journal*, bimonthly. **Price:** free • *Bay Area Chamber Handbook*. Membership Directory. **Conventions/Meetings:** annual meeting - always spring.

6882 ■ Bay Area Convention and Visitors Bureau
901 Saginaw St.
Bay City, MI 48708
Ph: (989)893-1222
Free: (888)BAY-TOWN
E-mail: info@tourbaycitymi.org
URL: http://www.tourbaycitymi.org
Contact: Shirley Roberts, Exec.Dir.
Local. Promotes convention business and tourism in area. **Publications:** *Welcome to the Bay Area*, annual. Booklet. **Price:** free.

6883 ■ Bay Arts Council (BAC)
915 Washington Ave.
Bay City, MI 48708
Ph: (989)893-0343
Fax: (989)893-6443
E-mail: director@bayartscouncil.org
URL: http://www.BayArtsCouncil.org
Contact: Ms. Joy Butler, Exec.Dir.
Founded: 1978. **Members:** 620. **Membership Dues:** individual, $25 (annual) • contributor, $50 (annual) • benefactor, $75 (annual) • patron, $100 (annual) • sustainer, $200 (annual) • senior, $20 (annual). **Staff:** 2. **Budget:** $120,000. **Local**. Individuals interested in promoting the arts. Awards dance scholarship. **Committees:** Masonic Temple Renovation; Nominating; Programming. **Publications:** *Participation*, quarterly. Newsletter.

6884 ■ Bay City Lions Club
c/o Darlene Trigg, Past Pres.
2930 W Ohio Rd.
Bay City, MI 48706
Ph: (989)671-3333
E-mail: dartrigg@yahoo.com
URL: http://www.geocities.com/dist11d1
Contact: Earl Bovia, Pres.
Local. Affiliated With: Lions Clubs International.

6885 ■ Bay City Yacht Club (BCYC)
PO Box 872
Bay City, MI 48707-0872
Ph: (517)686-1130
URL: http://www.baycityyachtclub.com
Contact: Don Noble, Commodore
Local.

6886 ■ Bay County Genealogical Society of Michigan (BCGS)
c/o Norma Campbell, Pres.
PO Box 1366
Bay City, MI 48706-0366
E-mail: campy712@tm.net
Contact: Rose Moldenhauer, Treas.
Founded: 1968. **Members:** 97. **Membership Dues:** single, $15 (annual) • family, $20 (annual). **State Groups:** 1. **Local Groups:** 1. **Local**. Individuals interested in the study of genealogy. **Libraries: Type:** by appointment only. **Holdings:** 240; archival material, books, periodicals. **Subjects:** genealogy. **Publications:** *Clarion*, bimonthly. Newsletter. **Price:** free for members. **Circulation:** 97. **Conventions/Meetings:** monthly meeting, publications from library (exhibits) - always 2nd Wednesday in Bay City, MI; except July, August, and December.

6887 ■ Bay County REACT
PO Box 1702
Bay City, MI 48706
Ph: (989)686-4929
E-mail: oslunds@chartermi.net
URL: http://www.reactintl.org/teaminfo/usa_teams/teams-usmi.htm
Local. Trained communication experts and professional volunteers. Provides volunteer public service and emergency communications through the use of radios (Citizen Band, General Mobile Radio Service, UHF and HAM). Coordinates with radio industries and government on safety communication matters and supports charitable activities and community organizations.

6888 ■ Bay County Realtor Association, Michigan
PO Box 860
Bay City, MI 48707
Ph: (989)892-8541
Fax: (989)892-8585
E-mail: bobadamowski@chartermi.net
URL: National Affiliate–www.realtor.org
Contact: Robert J. Adamowski, Exec. Officer
Local. Strives to develop real estate business practices. Advocates the right to own, use and transfer real property. Provides a facility for professional development, research and exchange of information among members. **Affiliated With:** National Association of Realtors.

6889 ■ Home Builders Association of Bay County
c/o Kelly Duhaime
2939 Skill Center Dr.
Bay City, MI 48708-5832
Ph: (989)684-3560
Fax: (989)684-2040
E-mail: bayhba@inetmail.att.net
URL: http://www.baycountyhba.org
Single and multifamily home builders, commercial builders, and others associated with the building industry. **Affiliated With:** National Association of Home Builders.

6890 ■ MACU Association Group
PO Box 1400
Bay City, MI 48706
Ph: (989)922-0095
Fax: (989)922-0093
Free: (800)572-4597
E-mail: macu@voyager.net
URL: http://www.macuonline.net
Founded: 1960. **Members:** 125. **Staff:** 5. **Budget:** $550,000. **Regional Groups:** 3. **State**. Represents credit unions and businesses that offer products or services to other credit unions. Provides education, legal services, and legislative advocacy. **Telecommunication Services:** electronic mail, email@macuassocgp.org. **Publications:** *Associate*, bimonthly. Newsletter. Contains management and regulatory information for CEO's and directors. **Circulation:** 85. **Advertising:** accepted • *1995-96 C U Service Provider Directory*, annual. **Conventions/Meetings:** annual Fall Development Conference and Exposition (exhibits) • annual Leadership Conference and Meeting.

6891 ■ Michigan Mosquito Control Association (MMCA)
PO Box 366
Bay City, MI 48707
Ph: (989)894-4555
Fax: (989)894-0526
E-mail: info@mimosq.org
URL: http://www.mimosq.org
Contact: Randy Knepper, Pres.
Founded: 1986. **Members:** 90. **Membership Dues:** regular, $10 (annual) • sustaining, $50 (annual) • student, $7 (annual). **State**. Advocates for management of mosquito populations through scientifically and ecologically sound methods. **Libraries: Type:** reference. **Holdings:** books, periodicals, video recordings. **Subjects:** mosquito control, insect transmitted disease. **Awards:** MMCA Annual Scholarship. **Frequency:** annual. **Type:** scholarship. **Recipient:** to a science major, undergraduate student. **Publications:** *Skeeter Scanner*, quarterly. Newsletter. **Price:** included in membership dues. **Advertising:** accepted. **Conventions/Meetings:** annual conference (exhibits) - first week of February.

6892 ■ National Active and Retired Federal Employees Association - Bay City 165
3615 State St. Rd.
Bay City, MI 48706-2114
Ph: (989)684-3500
URL: National Affiliate–www.narfe.org
Contact: Louis F. Lewandowski, Contact
Local. Protects the retirement future of employees through education. Informs members on issues affecting the retirement. **Affiliated With:** National Association of Retired Federal Employees.

6893 ■ PFLAG Bay City/Saginaw/Midland
PO Box 834
Bay City, MI 48707
Ph: (989)893-2475
E-mail: questions@pflag-mbs.org
URL: National Affiliate–www.pflag.org
Local. Affiliated With: Parents, Families, and Friends of Lesbians and Gays.

6894 ■ RSVP of Bay County
c/o Cathy McFarland, Dir.
PO Box 602
Bay City, MI 48707
Ph: (989)893-6060
Fax: (989)893-0087
E-mail: cathy@unitedwaybaycounty.org
URL: http://www.seniorcorps.gov/about/programs/rsvp_state.asp?usestateabbr=mi&Search4.x=0&Search4.y=0
Contact: Cathy McFarland, Dir.
Local. Affiliated With: Retired and Senior Volunteer Program.

6895 ■ Saginaw Bay Resource Conservation and Development Council
4044 S Three Mile
Bay City, MI 48706-9206
Ph: (989)684-5650
Fax: (989)684-5896
E-mail: james.hergott@mi.usda.gov
URL: National Affiliate–www.rcdnet.org
Contact: Ames Hergott, Coor.
Local. Affiliated With: National Association of Resource Conservation and Development Councils.

6896 ■ Sk8 Bay Figure Skating Club
Bay County Civic Arena
4231 Shrestha Dr.
Bay City, MI 48706
Ph: (989)671-1000
E-mail: sk8bay@yahoo.com
URL: http://sk8bayfigureskating.tripod.com
Contact: Deanna Ledesma, Contact
Local. Provides programs to encourage participation and achievement in the sport of figure skating on ice. Defines and maintains uniform standards of skating proficiency. Organizes and sponsors competitions and exhibitions for the purpose of stimulating interest in figure skating. **Affiliated With:** United States Figure Skating Association.

6897 ■ United Way of Bay County
PO Box 602
Bay City, MI 48707-0602
Ph: (989)893-7508
Fax: (989)893-0087
E-mail: george@unitedwaybaycounty.org
URL: http://www.unitedwaybaycounty.org
Contact: George Heron, Exec.Dir.
Local. Affiliated With: United Way of America.

6898 ■ Women's Outdoor Sports Association
c/o Cindy Plant
PO Box 1815
Bay City, MI 48706
Ph: (989)797-4169 (989)662-4248
Contact: Cindy A. Plant, Pres.
Founded: 1998. **Membership Dues:** $12 (annual). **Regional Groups:** 1. **State Groups:** 1. **Local Groups:** 1. **Local. Awards:** Women's Outdoor Sports Association Scholarship Fund. **Frequency:** annual. **Type:** scholarship. **Publications:** *The Compass*, quarterly. Newsletter. **Advertising:** not accepted. **Conventions/Meetings:** annual Shooting Sports Outdoor Challenge - 2nd weekend in July, Hemlock, MI; Avg. Attendance: 150.

Bay Port

6899 ■ American Legion, Steele-Lambert Post 533
PO Box 217
Bay Port, MI 48720
Ph: (517)371-4720
Fax: (517)371-2401
URL: National Affiliate–www.legion.org
Local. Affiliated With: American Legion.

Bear Lake

6900 ■ Bear Lake Lions Club
PO Box 405
Bear Lake, MI 49614
Ph: (231)864-3957
E-mail: trichard@bearlake-net.com
URL: http://bearlakemi.lionwap.org
Contact: Bruce Grosso, Pres.
Local. Affiliated With: Lions Clubs International.

Beaverton

6901 ■ Infusion Nurses Society, Mid-Michigan
2333 River Rd.
Beaverton, MI 48612
Ph: (989)435-9928
E-mail: jedtad@yahoo.com
URL: National Affiliate–www.ins1.org
Contact: Judy Doyle, Pres.
Local. Represents the interests of healthcare professionals who are involved with the practice of infusion therapy. Seeks to advance the delivery of quality therapy to patients. Promotes research and education in the practice of infusion nursing. **Affiliated With:** Infusion Nurses Society.

Belding

6902 ■ American Legion, Hugo Fales Post 203
121 S Broas St.
Belding, MI 48809
Ph: (517)371-4720
Fax: (517)371-2401
URL: National Affiliate–www.legion.org
Local. Affiliated With: American Legion.

Bellaire

6903 ■ American Legion, Bellaire Post 247
PO Box 425
Bellaire, MI 49615
Ph: (616)377-7057
Fax: (517)371-2401
URL: National Affiliate–www.legion.org
Local. Affiliated With: American Legion.

6904 ■ Bellaire Area Chamber of Commerce
PO Box 205
Bellaire, MI 49615
Ph: (231)533-6023
Fax: (231)533-6023
E-mail: info@bellairemichigan.com
URL: http://www.bellairemichigan.com
Contact: Pat DuBois, Exec.Dir.
Local. Promotes business and community development in the Bellaire, MI area. **Computer Services:** Information services, member directory. **Publications:** Newsletter, bimonthly. **Conventions/Meetings:** monthly meeting - every 2nd Tuesday in Bellaire, MI.

6905 ■ Grass River Natural Area (GRNA)
c/o Mark Randolph, Exec.Dir.
PO Box 231
Bellaire, MI 49615
Ph: (231)533-8314
E-mail: info@grassriver.org
URL: http://www.grassriver.org
Contact: Mark Randolph, Exec.Dir.
Local. Works to manage and protect the Grass River and its watershed; conducts educational activities that increase understanding and appreciation of the natural environment.

Belleville

6906 ■ Ann Arbor Dueling Society
c/o Bill Emerson
49450 Cross St.
Belleville, MI 48111-1003
E-mail: themanicscribe@gmail.com
URL: http://www.msu.edu/user/emerson1/aads.html
Contact: Bill Emerson, Contact
Local. Amateur fencers. **Affiliated With:** United States Fencing Association.

6907 ■ Antique Automobile Club of America, Wolverine State Region (AACA-WSR)
c/o Robert Scheffler
19963 Sumpter Rd.
Belleville, MI 48111
Ph: (734)699-1177
E-mail: bpaxton@peoplepc.com
URL: http://clubs.hemmings.com/frameset.cfm?club=wolverinestateregionaaca
Contact: Robert Scheffler, Pres.
Local. Collectors, hobbyists, and others interested in the preservation, maintenance, and restoration of automobiles and in automotive history. **Affiliated With:** Antique Automobile Club of America.

6908 ■ Belleville Area Chamber of Commerce (BCC)
248 Main St.
Belleville, MI 48111
Ph: (734)697-7151
Fax: (734)697-1415
E-mail: bellechamber@sbcglobal.net
URL: http://www.bellevillech.org
Contact: Janet Millard, Exec.Dir.
Founded: 1963. **Members:** 230. **Membership Dues:** business (depends on the number of employees), $140-$1,250 (annual) • associate, club, organization, $95 (annual). **Local.** Promotes business and community development in the Belleville, MI area. Participates in annual Strawberry Festival. Holds monthly board meeting. **Computer Services:** database, of members • information services, fact about Belleville, MI. **Affiliated With:** U.S. Chamber of Commerce. **Publications:** *Calendar with Directory*, annual. Lists members categorically. Includes current facts and figures on the area. • *Tri-Community Commentator*, monthly. Newsletter. Alternate Formats: online. **Conventions/Meetings:** annual meeting • quarterly meeting.

6909 ■ Chinese Shar-Pei Rescue of Michigan
c/o Amy Cox
13700 Hoeft
Belleville, MI 48111-3401
Ph: (734)697-1137 (810)635-7490
E-mail: peisaver@comcast.net
URL: http://www.petfinder.org/mi88.htm
Contact: Amy Cox, Pres.
Founded: 1992. **State.** Works to find homes for unwanted, abused and stray Shar Pei; educates people about the breed.

6910 ■ Michigan Toy Fox Terrier Association
c/o Julie Slauterbeck, Pres.
22481 Bohn Rd.
Belleville, MI 48111
Ph: (734)699-7179
E-mail: preludetfts@aol.com
URL: National Affiliate–www.ntfta.netfirms.com
Contact: Julie Slauterbeck, Pres.
State. Affiliated With: National Toy Fox Terrier Association.

Bellevue

6911 ■ American Legion, Bellevue Post 280
7805 Wildt Hwy.
Bellevue, MI 49021
Ph: (517)371-4720
Fax: (517)371-2401
URL: National Affiliate–www.legion.org
Local. Affiliated With: American Legion.

6912 ■ Bellevue Lions Club - Michigan
c/o James E. Louis, Sec.
10197 Battle Creek Hwy.
Bellevue, MI 49021
Ph: (269)763-3136
E-mail: jjjlouis@aol.com
URL: http://www.district11c2.org
Contact: James E. Louis, Sec.
Local. Affiliated With: Lions Clubs International.

6913 ■ Michigan Draft Horse Breeders Association
6871 S Ionia Rd.
Bellevue, MI 49021

Ph: (269)763-3839
E-mail: belleviewperch@aol.com
URL: National Affiliate–www.nasdha.net/RegionalAssoc.htm
Contact: Renee Dingman, Sec.-Treas.
State.

Belmont

6914 ■ American Association of Critical Care Nurses, West Michigan Chapter
c/o Deb Ryan
6242 Middale Dr. NE
Belmont, MI 49306
Ph: (616)391-1263
E-mail: wmc.info@aacn.org
URL: http://www.aacn.org/chapters/wmc.nsf/other/homepage?opendocument
Contact: Linda Spoelma, Pres.
Founded: 1988. **Local**. Represents the interests of professional critical care nurses. Provides education programs for nurses specializing in critical care and develops standards of nursing care of critically ill patients. **Affiliated With:** American Association of Critical-Care Nurses.

6915 ■ Trout Unlimited - West Michigan Chapter
2961 Gold Dust
Belmont, MI 49306
Ph: (616)447-0946
URL: http://www.tu.org
Contact: Scott Steiner, Pres.

Benton Harbor

6916 ■ American Legion, Benton Harbor Post 105
1645 Paw Paw Ave.
Benton Harbor, MI 49022
Ph: (517)371-4720
Fax: (517)371-2401
URL: National Affiliate–www.legion.org
Local. Affiliated With: American Legion.

6917 ■ American Legion, Michigan Post 410
c/o Dorie Miller
1884 Farmer Ave.
Benton Harbor, MI 49022
Ph: (517)371-4720
Fax: (517)371-2401
URL: National Affiliate–www.legion.org
Contact: Dorie Miller, Contact
Local. Affiliated With: American Legion.

6918 ■ American Red Cross, Berrien County Chapter
303 Riverview Dr.
Benton Harbor, MI 49022
Ph: (269)927-2288
Fax: (269)927-1208
E-mail: redcross@berrienredcross.org
URL: http://www.berrienredcross.org
Local.

6919 ■ Harbor Habitat for Humanity
785 E Main St.
Benton Harbor, MI 49022
Ph: (269)925-9635
Fax: (269)926-4051
E-mail: info@harborhabitat.org
URL: http://www.harborhabitat.org
Contact: Michael Green, Exec.Dir.
Local. Affiliated With: Habitat for Humanity International.

6920 ■ Lake Michigan College Education Association
c/o Cole Lovett
2756 E Napier
Benton Harbor, MI 49022-1881
Ph: (269)927-3571 (269)927-8100
Fax: (269)927-8164
Free: (800)252-1562
URL: http://www.lakemichigancollege.edu
Contact: Anne Erdman, VP Admin. Services
Local.

6921 ■ Phi Theta Kappa, Mu Nu Chapter - Lake Michigan College
c/o Eddie Anderson
2755 E Napier Ave.
Benton Harbor, MI 49022
Ph: (269)927-8100
E-mail: andersoe@lakemichigancollege.edu
URL: http://www.ptk.org/directories/chapters/MI/249-1.htm
Contact: Eddie Anderson, Advisor
Local.

6922 ■ Southwestern Michigan Tourist Council
2300 Pipestone Rd.
Benton Harbor, MI 49022
Ph: (269)925-6301
Fax: (269)925-7540
E-mail: info@swmichigan.org
URL: http://www.swmichigan.org
Contact: Millicent Huminsky, Exec.Dir.
Founded: 1982. **Members:** 250. **Membership Dues:** non-profit, $110 (annual) • business, $165 (annual). **Staff:** 8. **Budget:** $400,000. **Regional**. Promotes convention business and tourism in the area.

6923 ■ United Way of Southwest Michigan
PO Box 807
Benton Harbor, MI 49023-0807
Ph: (269)925-7772
Fax: (269)925-1590
E-mail: info@uwsm.org
URL: http://www.uwsm.org
Contact: Martin S. Golob III, Pres.
Regional. Affiliated With: United Way of America. **Formerly:** Blossomland Chapter of the United Way.

6924 ■ We Can Make a Difference
c/o Neldine Edwards
PO Box 8824
Benton Harbor, MI 49023-8824
Ph: (269)934-9740
E-mail: wcmdparenting@aol.com
Contact: Neldine Edwards, Exec.Dir.
Founded: 2001. **Staff:** 3. **Budget:** $120,000. Provides parent education program and children's program for southwest Michigan area. Also conducts parenting workshops and seminars. **Awards:** Parenting Class Certificates. **Type:** recognition.

Benzonia

6925 ■ Benzie County Chamber of Commerce (BCCC)
826 Michigan Ave.
PO Box 204
Benzonia, MI 49616
Ph: (231)882-5801
Fax: (231)882-9249
Free: (800)882-5801
E-mail: chamberinfo@benzie.org
URL: http://www.benzie.org
Contact: Carol Davidson, Exec.Dir.
Founded: 1981. **Members:** 320. **Staff:** 2. **Budget:** $60,000. **Local**. Promotes business, tourism, and community development in Benzie County, MI. Sponsors festivals, including Winterfest; Home & Garden Show; Benzonia Days; Beulah Art Fair; Port City Run; Cherry Field Day; Frankfort Art Fair; and National Coho Festival. **Computer Services:** database, list of members. **Telecommunication Services:** electronic mail, chamber@benzie.org • electronic mail, cdavidson@benzie.org. **Affiliated With:** U.S. Chamber of Commerce. **Publications:** *Moving Up*, quarterly. Newsletter • Directory, annual. **Price:** $5.00 /year for nonmembers; free for members. **Circulation:** 15,000. **Advertising:** accepted • Newsletter, quarterly. **Conventions/Meetings:** annual dinner - always October • monthly luncheon, with educational program.

Bergland

6926 ■ American Legion, Desrosier-Windnagle Post 562
PO Box 411
Bergland, MI 49910
Ph: (517)371-4720
Fax: (517)371-2401
URL: National Affiliate–www.legion.org
Local. Affiliated With: American Legion.

6927 ■ Lake Gogebic Area Chamber of Commerce
PO Box 114
Bergland, MI 49910-0114
Ph: (906)842-3611
Fax: (906)842-3653
Free: (888)464-3242
E-mail: info@lakegogebicarea.com
URL: http://www.lakegogebicarea.com
Contact: Carol Peterson, Sec.
Local. Promotes business and community development in Lake Gogebic, MI area. **Additional Websites:** http://michiganupperpeninsula.com/up_chamber_offices.html.

6928 ■ Michigan National Wild Turkey Federation, Western U.P. Tommy Knockers Chapter
PO Box 151
Bergland, MI 49910
Ph: (906)575-3345
URL: http://www.mi-nwtf.org/WesternUP.htm
Contact: Ron Gross, Pres.
Local.

Berkley

6929 ■ American Legion, Berkley Post 374
2079 W 12 Mile Rd.
Berkley, MI 48072
Ph: (517)371-4720
Fax: (517)371-2401
URL: National Affiliate–www.legion.org
Local. Affiliated With: American Legion.

6930 ■ Greater Berkley Chamber of Commerce
PO Box 72-1253
Berkley, MI 48072
Ph: (248)414-9157
URL: http://www.berkleybusiness.com
Contact: Ross Leonard CLU, Pres.
Local. Promotes and encourages business in Berkley. Creates favorable commercial climate within the City. Acts as a unified voice and liaison between businesses and others. Assists businesses in the City.

6931 ■ Michigan Greyhound Connection
c/o Susan Bilsky, Pres.
PO Box 725384
Berkley, MI 48072
Free: (800)398-4364
E-mail: sbilsky@s4online.com
URL: http://www.michgreys.org
Contact: Susan Bilsky, Pres.
Founded: 1989. **Members:** 1,300. **State**. Committed to rescuing and finding suitable homes for retired racing greyhound dogs. Sponsors educational programs and events to promote the rescue and adoption of retired racing greyhound dogs; also educates the public regarding the retired race dog's plight at the hands of the greyhound racing industry.

6932 ■ Mid-Michigan Pug Club
c/o Diane Rismann
3643 Prairie
Berkley, MI 48072
Ph: (248)398-3791
E-mail: shaynapugs@comcast.net
URL: http://midmichiganpugclub.com
Contact: Diane Rismann, Contact
Founded: 1978. **Membership Dues:** active, $12 (annual) • associate, $10 (annual) • newsletter, $11 (annual). **State**. Promotes the Pug breed through education, shows, breeding, pets, and rescue. **Programs:** For the Love of Pugs Rescue. **Publications:** *Michigan Pugs*. Newsletter. **Price:** $11.00/year. **Advertising:** accepted.

6933 ■ Theosophical Society in Detroit
27745 Woodward Ave.
Berkley, MI 48072-0906
Ph: (248)545-1961
URL: http://www.tsdetroit.org
Local. Affiliated With: Theosophical Society in America.

Berrien Springs

6934 ■ American Legion, E.J. Stover and A.D. Wagner Post 85
112 N Bluff St.
Berrien Springs, MI 49103
Ph: (517)371-4720
Fax: (517)371-2401
URL: National Affiliate–www.legion.org
Local. Affiliated With: American Legion.

6935 ■ Berrien Library Consortium
Andrews Univ.
Berrien Springs, MI 49104
Ph: (269)471-3283
Fax: (269)471-6166
E-mail: helmsc@andrews.edu
URL: http://server.remc11.k12.mi.us/bclibcon
Contact: Cynthia Mae Helms, Treas.
Founded: 1957. **Members:** 8. **Membership Dues:** library, $350 (annual). **Budget:** $3,500. **Local.** Libraries. Provides forum for discussion and resource sharing. **Conventions/Meetings:** quarterly Business Meetings.

6936 ■ Psi Chi, National Honor Society in Psychology - Andrews University
c/o Dept. of Psychology
123 Nethery Hall
100 N US Hwy. 31
Berrien Springs, MI 49104-0030
Ph: (269)471-3152 (269)471-3153
Fax: (269)471-3108
E-mail: berecz@andrews.edu
URL: http://www.psichi.org/chapters/info.asp?chapter_id=433
Contact: John Berecz PhD, Advisor
Local.

Bessemer

6937 ■ American Legion, Peter-Gedda-Francis-Cychosz Post 27
209 N Moore St.
Bessemer, MI 49911
Ph: (517)371-4720
Fax: (517)371-2401
URL: National Affiliate–www.legion.org
Local. Affiliated With: American Legion.

Beverly Hills

6938 ■ Oakland County Dental Society
16205 W 14 Mile Rd., Ste.201
Beverly Hills, MI 48025-3325
Ph: (248)540-9333
Fax: (248)540-2016
E-mail: ocdsdental@aol.com
URL: http://www.oaklandcountydentalsociety.com
Contact: Ms. Brigitte Boyungs, Exec.Dir.
Local. Represents the interests of dentists committed to the public's oral health, ethics and professional development. Encourages the improvement of the public's oral health and promotes the art and science of dentistry. **Affiliated With:** American Dental Association; Michigan Dental Association.

Big Rapids

6939 ■ American Legion, Michigan Post 98
c/o Harry K. Kunzie
PO Box 323
Big Rapids, MI 49307
Ph: (517)371-4720
Fax: (517)371-2401
URL: National Affiliate–www.legion.org
Contact: Harry K. Kunzie, Contact
Local. Affiliated With: American Legion.

6940 ■ AMVETS, Big Rapids
320 S 4th St.
Big Rapids, MI 49307
Ph: (231)796-6998
URL: http://geocities.com/amvets1941
Contact: C. Bill Buck, Commander
Local. Affiliated With: AMVETS - American Veterans.

6941 ■ Big Rapids Lions Club
PO Box 807
Big Rapids, MI 49307
E-mail: perrinr@hotmail.com
URL: http://bigrapidsmi.lionwap.org
Contact: Dick Perrin, Pres.
Local. Affiliated With: Lions Clubs International.

6942 ■ Big Rapids - Wyldlife
PO Box 334
Big Rapids, MI 49307
Ph: (231)592-1390
URL: http://sites.younglife.org/_layouts/ylext/default.aspx?ID=C-1126
Local. Affiliated With: Young Life.

6943 ■ Big Rapids - Young Life
PO Box 334
Big Rapids, MI 49307
Ph: (231)592-1390
URL: http://sites.younglife.org/_layouts/ylext/default.aspx?ID=C-1127
Local. Affiliated With: Young Life.

6944 ■ County of Mecosta Development Corporation
c/o Jonathan Scott, Exec.Dir.
246 N State St.
Big Rapids, MI 49307-1445
Ph: (231)592-3403
Fax: (231)592-4085
Free: (866)632-6782
E-mail: mecostaedc@yahoo.com
URL: http://www.mecostaedc.com
Contact: Jonathan Scott, Exec.Dir.
Founded: 1996. **Members:** 46. **Staff:** 1. **Budget:** $90,000. **Local.** All communities in Mecosta County. Promotes economic development. Offers recreational and business opportunities. Provides services in job training, industrial operations, infrastructure improvements and other business assistance.

6945 ■ Greater Michigan MSCA Student Chapter
c/o Mike Feutz, Dept. Chm.
Ferris State Univ.
605 S Warren Ave.
Big Rapids, MI 49307-2287
Ph: (231)591-2351
Fax: (231)591-2492
E-mail: feutzm@ferris.edu
URL: National Affiliate–www.mcaa.org
Contact: Mike Feutz, Contact
Local. Affiliated With: Mechanical Contractors Association of America.

6946 ■ Home Builders Association of Mecosta County
c/o Tony Caputo
PO Box 1062
Big Rapids, MI 49307
Ph: (231)796-6855
Fax: (231)769-2003
E-mail: mecostahba@hotmail.com
URL: http://www.hbamc.com
Contact: Mr. Tony Caputo, Exec.Off.
Members: 90. **Membership Dues:** builders and associates, $305 (annual). **Staff:** 1. **Budget:** $80,000. **Local.** Represents professionals in a broad spectrum of housing related businesses, from builders and remodelers to banks and water conditioning companies. Serves the citizens of Mecosta County and bordering communities located in Osceola, Newaygo, and Montcalm Counties in Michigan. **Libraries: Type:** not open to the public. **Holdings:** 30; papers. **Subjects:** various documentation on building trades. **Awards:** Scholarship to high school graduating students. **Frequency:** annual. **Type:** scholarship. **Recipient:** for students in the building trades who have shown academic, leadership and community achievement. **Computer Services:** database • information services • mailing lists • online services. **Committees:** Home Show. **Affiliated With:** National Association of Home Builders. **Publications:** *HBAMC Newsletter*, monthly. Contains current information of membership interest. **Price:** free to members. **Circulation:** 105. **Advertising:** accepted. **Conventions/Meetings:** monthly General Membership Meeting, with dinner, social and presentations (exhibits) • annual Home Show, exhibitor displays (exhibits).

6947 ■ Mecosta County Area Chamber of Commerce (MCACC)
246 N State St.
Big Rapids, MI 49307
Ph: (231)796-7649
Fax: (231)796-1625
E-mail: mcacc@mecostacounty.com
URL: http://www.mecostacounty.com
Contact: Anja J. Wing, Exec.Dir.
Founded: 1937. **Members:** 450. **Membership Dues:** base, $197 (annual) • associate, $95 (annual) • financial institution, $15 (annual) • accountant, legal, medical, $80 (annual) • manufacturing, governmental institution, not-for-profit hospital, $3 (annual). **Staff:** 3. **Budget:** $155,000. **Local.** Promotes business and community development in the Mecosta County, MI area. **Councils:** Business Advancement; Ferris State University/Community; Golf Outing; Governmental Affairs; Holiday Gala; Labor Day Arts and Crafts; Membership Development. **Affiliated With:** U.S. Chamber of Commerce. **Formerly:** (1982) Big Rapids Chamber of Commerce. **Publications:** *Chamber News*, monthly. Newsletter • Directory, periodic. **Conventions/Meetings:** annual Labor Day Arts and Crafts - festival (exhibits) • monthly meeting.

6948 ■ Mecosta County Convention and Visitors Bureau
247 N State St.
Big Rapids, MI 49307
Ph: (231)796-7640
Fax: (231)796-0832
Free: (888)229-4FUN
URL: http://www.bigrapids.org
Contact: Connie Kopke, Exec.Dir.
Founded: 1989. **Members:** 6. **Staff:** 3. **Budget:** $100,000. **State Groups:** 1. **Local.** Promotes convention business and tourism in area. **Publications:** *Calendar of Events*. Brochure • *Mecosta County Visitors Guide*, annual. Directory. **Circulation:** 30,000. **Advertising:** accepted.

6949 ■ Mecosta County Support Group (MCSG)
1724 N State
Big Rapids, MI 49307-9073
Ph: (231)796-4637
Fax: (231)796-4637
E-mail: trund@nov.com
URL: http://www.nov.com
Contact: Thomas J. Rundquist, Pres.
Founded: 2001. **Members:** 5. **Staff:** 3. **Budget:** $150. **Local.** Works as a bipolar support group.

6950 ■ Mecosta-Osceola United Way
315 Ives Ave.
Big Rapids, MI 49307-2001
Ph: (231)592-4144
URL: National Affiliate–national.unitedway.org
Local. Affiliated With: United Way of America.

6951 ■ RSVP Mecosta/Lake/Osceola
c/o Sandy Dalrymple, Dir.
14485 Northland Dr.
Big Rapids, MI 49307-2368
Ph: (231)796-4848
Fax: (231)796-7864
E-mail: rsvp@tucker-usa.com
URL: http://www.seniorcorps.gov/about/programs/rsvp_state.asp?usestateabbr=mi&Search4.x=0&Search4.y=0
Contact: Sandy Dalrymple, Dir.
Founded: 1969. **Members:** 322. **Staff:** 2. **Local. Affiliated With:** Retired and Senior Volunteer Program.

6952 ■ Society of Manufacturing Engineers - Ferris State University S129
Swan 107, Ferris State Univ.
915 Campus Dr.
Big Rapids, MI 49307
Ph: (231)592-3591
E-mail: wistj@ferris.edu
URL: National Affiliate–www.sme.org
Contact: Joe Wist, Contact
Local. Advances manufacturing knowledge to gain competitive advantage. Improves skills and manufacturing solutions for the growth of economy. Provides resources and opportunities for manufacturing professionals. **Affiliated With:** Society of Motion Picture and Television Engineers.

6953 ■ Stanwood Lions Club
c/o Gerald Tossey, Pres.
10700 Riverview Dr.
Big Rapids, MI 49307
Ph: (231)796-9374
E-mail: thanestout@hotmail.com
URL: http://lions.silverthorn.biz/11-e1
Contact: Gerald Tossey, Pres.
Local. Affiliated With: Lions Clubs International.

6954 ■ Young Life North Central Michigan
PO Box 334
Big Rapids, MI 49307
Ph: (231)592-1390
Fax: (231)592-1393
URL: http://sites.younglife.org/sites/ylncm/default.aspx
Local. Affiliated With: Young Life.

Bingham Farms

6955 ■ Michigan Green Industry Association
30600 Telegraph Rd., Ste.3360
Bingham Farms, MI 48025
Ph: (248)646-4992
Fax: (248)646-4994
Free: (800)354-6352
E-mail: dandrews@landscape.org
URL: http://www.landscape.org
Contact: Diane Andrews, Exec.Dir.
Founded: 1960. **Members:** 700. **Membership Dues:** business, $185 (annual). **State.** Represents landscape, lawn maintenance, irrigation, snow removal and tree care workers. **Affiliated With:** American Nursery and Landscape Association. **Formerly:** (2002) Metropolitan Detroit Landscaping Association. **Publications:** *The Landsculptor Magazine.* **Conventions/Meetings:** annual trade show.

Birch Run

6956 ■ American Legion, Birch Run Post 125
PO Box 305
Birch Run, MI 48415
Ph: (517)371-4720
Fax: (517)371-2401
URL: National Affiliate–www.legion.org
Local. Affiliated With: American Legion.

6957 ■ American Legion, Brown and Vernon Post 312
2318 E Curtis Rd.
Birch Run, MI 48415
Ph: (517)371-4720
Fax: (517)371-2401
URL: National Affiliate–www.legion.org
Local. Affiliated With: American Legion.

6958 ■ Birch Run Area Chamber of Commerce
PO Box 153
Birch Run, MI 48415
Ph: (989)624-9193
Fax: (989)624-5337
Free: (888)624-9193
E-mail: info@birchrunchamber.com
URL: http://www.birchrunchamber.com
Contact: Tammey S. Inman, Exec.Dir.
Staff: 2. **Local.**

6959 ■ Birch Run Lions Club
c/o Deborah McConnell, Pres.
11856 Silver Creek Dr.
Birch Run, MI 48415
Ph: (989)624-2656
URL: http://www.geocities.com/dist11d1
Contact: Deborah McConnell, Pres.
Local. Affiliated With: Lions Clubs International.

6960 ■ Flint Rock and Gem Club
c/o Suzette Millard, Pres.
10595 Lange Rd.
Birch Run, MI 48415
E-mail: suzettem@usol.com
URL: National Affiliate–www.amfed.org
Contact: Susan Selves, Sec.
Local. Aims to further the study of Earth Sciences and the practice of lapidary arts and mineralogy. **Affiliated With:** American Federation of Mineralogical Societies.

Birmingham

6961 ■ American Rose Society, Great Lakes District
c/o Mrs. Diane Schrift, District Dir.
2419 Yorkshire
Birmingham, MI 48009
Ph: (248)649-6161
E-mail: schrifts@tir.com
URL: http://www.greatlakesdistrict.info
Contact: Mrs. Diane Schrift, District Dir.
Regional. Affiliated With: American Rose Society.

6962 ■ Birmingham-Bloomfield Chamber of Commerce (BBCC)
124 W Maple Rd.
Birmingham, MI 48009-3322
Ph: (248)644-1700
Fax: (248)644-0286
E-mail: thechamber@bbcc.com
URL: http://www.bbcc.com
Contact: Pamela Iacobelli, Pres.
Founded: 1948. **Members:** 750. **Membership Dues:** business (based on number of employees), $280-$850 (annual). **Staff:** 4. **Local.** Promotes business and community development in Beverly Hills, Bingham Farms, Birmingham, Bloomfield Hills, and Bloomfield Township, MI. **Computer Services:** database, listing of members • information services, facts about local communities. **Telecommunication Services:** electronic mail, deidrec@bbcc.com. **Committees:** Ambassadors; Leading Entrepreneurs Advocate Progress; Public Policy Steering. **Publications:** *Business Insight E-News*, monthly. Newsletter. **Price:** free. **Advertising:** accepted. Alternate Formats: online • *IMAGES of Birmingham Bloomfield*, annual. Magazine. Contains community information and visitors guide. **Price:** free for members. **Advertising:** accepted. Alternate Formats: online • *Insight*, monthly. Magazine. **Advertising:** accepted • Membership Directory, annual.

6963 ■ Birmingham Bloomfield Families in Action (BBFA)
PO Box 1088
Birmingham, MI 48012-1088
Ph: (248)341-6340
E-mail: bbfa01@hotmail.com
URL: http://www.bbfaprevention.org
Contact: Dennis Rozema, Pres.
Founded: 1981. **Membership Dues:** family, $25 (annual) • contributing, $26-$99 (annual) • supporting, $100-$499 (annual) • patron, $500-$999 (annual) • school, $100 (annual). **Local. Publications:** *Connections.* Newsletter. Alternate Formats: online.

6964 ■ Michigan Photographic Historical Society (MiPHS)
PO Box 2278
Birmingham, MI 48012-2278
Ph: (248)549-6026
E-mail: motz48073@yahoo.com
URL: http://www.miphs.org
Contact: Cynthia Motzenbecker, Pres.
Founded: 1972. **Members:** 210. **Membership Dues:** anyone interested in the history of photography, $20 (annual) • student (with ID), $10 (annual). **Budget:** $2,500. **State.** Individuals united to promote the collection and study of vintage images, cameras, equipment and literature, especially as it relates to Michigan and its history. Disseminates information about the history of photography through meetings and the newsletter The Photogram. **Affiliated With:** The Photographic Historical Society. **Publications:** *Photogram*, quarterly. Newsletter. Research and various articles about historical photography, hardware and images. **Price:** included in membership dues. ISSN: 1082-6874. **Circulation:** 250. **Advertising:** accepted • Directory, 3-4 years. **Conventions/Meetings:** annual dinner (exhibits) • meeting - 3/year • annual trade show.

6965 ■ National Organization of Circumcision Information Resource Centers of Michigan
c/o Lori Hanna
PO Box 333
Birmingham, MI 48012-0333
Ph: (248)642-5703 (248)361-1422
Fax: (248)642-9528
E-mail: lori@nocircofmi.org
URL: http://www.NoCircofMI.org
Contact: Mr Norman Cohen, Dir.
Founded: 1995. **Local.** Seeks to educate professionals and the public in MI about routine infant male circumcision and proper care. **Additional Websites:** http://www.NoCirc.org. **Affiliated With:** National Organization of Circumcision Information Resource Centers. **Also Known As:** (1989) National Organization of Circumcision Information Resource Centers (NoCirc) Michigan Chapter. **Publications:** *The Informant*, quarterly.

6966 ■ NOCIRC of Michigan
c/o Norm Cohen
PO Box 333
Birmingham, MI 48012
Ph: (248)642-5703 (248)361-1422
Fax: (248)642-9528
E-mail: normcohen@nocircofmi.org
URL: http://www.NOCIRCofMI.org
Contact: Lori Hanna, Educ.Coor.
State. Provides circumcision information; seeks to educate about circumcision, the benefit of intact genitals, and proper care instructions.

6967 ■ Oakland County Medical Society (OCMS)
346 Park St.
Birmingham, MI 48009
Ph: (248)646-4700
Fax: (248)646-9467
E-mail: dlagosh@msms.org
URL: http://www.ocms-mi.org
Contact: Donna LaGosh, Dir.
Local. Advances the art and science of medicine. Promotes patient care and the betterment of public health. **Affiliated With:** Michigan State Medical Society.

6968 ■ Swedish American Chamber of Commerce - Detroit Chapter
c/o Melissa Mark
PO Box 0396
Birmingham, MI 48012-0396
Ph: (248)644-8170
E-mail: sacc-detroit@atsprodigy.net
Contact: Melissa Mark, Exec.Dir
Founded: 1988. **Members:** 105. **Staff:** 1. **Regional Groups:** 18. **Languages:** English, Swedish. **Local**.

Blanchard

6969 ■ American Legion, Guy Stanton Post 240
PO Box 14
Blanchard, MI 49310
Ph: (517)371-4720
Fax: (517)371-2401
URL: National Affiliate–www.legion.org
Local. **Affiliated With:** American Legion.

6970 ■ Edmore Lions Club
c/o Rich Adgate, Pres.
155 Taylor
Blanchard, MI 49310
Ph: (989)427-5448
E-mail: rich@eaglerealtymi.com
URL: http://lions.silverthorn.biz/11-e1
Contact: Rich Adgate, Pres.
Local. **Affiliated With:** Lions Clubs International.

6971 ■ Michigan Alliance of Cooperatives
4771 Rolland Rd.
Blanchard, MI 49310-9753
Ph: (517)561-5037
Fax: (517)561-5193
E-mail: mslagh@northeastcoop.com
URL: National Affiliate–www.ncba.org
Contact: Mark Slagh, Exec.Dir.
Founded: 1981. **Members:** 60. **Staff:** 4. **Budget:** $150,000. **Local Groups:** 7. **State**. Promotes cooperative economic development. Conducts research, consultation, training, and technical assistance aimed at encouraging cooperative growth. Encourages cooperation among cooperatives. Trains co-op leaders. **Libraries: Type:** reference. **Holdings:** 250; books, periodicals, reports. **Subjects:** cooperatives, economics, social issues. **Affiliated With:** National Cooperative Business Association. **Publications:** *Cooperative Action*, quarterly. Newsletter. **Price:** included in membership dues. **Circulation:** 2,000. **Advertising:** accepted. **Conventions/Meetings:** annual Membership Meeting - workshop, educational (exhibits) - October.

Blissfield

6972 ■ American Legion, Robert Meachen Post 325
PO Box 142
Blissfield, MI 49228
Ph: (517)371-4720
Fax: (517)371-2401
URL: National Affiliate–www.legion.org
Local. **Affiliated With:** American Legion.

6973 ■ Blissfield Area Chamber of Commerce
PO Box 25
Blissfield, MI 49228-0025
Ph: (517)486-3642
Fax: (517)486-4328
E-mail: info@blissfieldchamber.org
URL: http://www.blissfield.net
Contact: Beth Borchardt, Pres.
Membership Dues: area church, $50 • home based business, non-profit service/charitable organization, $75 • business (based on number of employees), $110-$500. **Local**. Promotes business and community development in Blissfield, MI area. **Committees:** Administration, Finance and Budget; Community Interaction and Community Development; Retail, Promotions and Tourism. **Conventions/Meetings:** monthly board meeting - every 1st Thursday • bimonthly Breakfast Club - meeting - every 2nd Friday • monthly Food For Thought - meeting - every 3rd Thursday.

6974 ■ Blissfield Area Lions Club
c/o Doug Hickman, Pres.
332 Cherry St.
Blissfield, MI 49228
Ph: (517)486-4713
E-mail: hodgepodgehouse@yahoo.com
URL: http://www.lionsdistrict11b1.org/lc_blissfield_area.htm
Contact: Doug Hickman, Pres.
Local. **Affiliated With:** Lions Clubs International.

6975 ■ Michigan National Wild Turkey Federation, Lenawee Limbhangers
9702 E Mulberry Rd.
Blissfield, MI 49228
Ph: (517)486-3966
URL: http://www.mi-nwtf.org/Lenewee.htm
Contact: Ron Bateson, Pres.
Local.

Bloomfield

6976 ■ Ancient Order of Hibernians of Oakland County - James O. Flynn Division
c/o Gerry Fitzgerald, Sec.
2831 Acorn Rd.
Bloomfield, MI 48302
Ph: (248)338-4806
E-mail: fitzgerfitz@hotmail.com
URL: http://www.aohflynn.com
Contact: Gerry Fitzgerald, Sec.
Local. **Affiliated With:** Ancient Order of Hibernians in America.

6977 ■ Detroit Telugu Literary Club (DTLC)
c/o Krishnarao Maddipati
1659 Squirrel Valley Dr.
Bloomfield, MI 48304-1175
E-mail: detroittelugu@comcast.net
URL: http://groups.yahoo.com/group/DTLCgroup
Contact: Krishnarao Maddipati PhD, Pres.
Founded: 1998. **Members:** 80. **Staff:** 4. **Budget:** $1,000. **Languages:** English, Telugu. **Local**. Strives to promote Telugu literature through reading, discussing and publishing. Conducts Telugu literary conferences. **Libraries: Type:** not open to the public. **Holdings:** 100; books. **Subjects:** novel, stories, history, drama, literary criticism.

Bloomfield Hills

6978 ■ Birmingham Athletic Club (BAC)
c/o James A. Taylor, Jr.
4033 W Maple Rd.
Bloomfield Hills, MI 48301
Ph: (248)646-5050
E-mail: info@mail.birminghamathleticclub.com
URL: http://www.birminghamathleticclub.com
Contact: Tim Gardella, General Mgr.
Local.

6979 ■ Children's Rights Council of Michigan
6632 Telegraph Rd.
Bloomfield Hills, MI 48301
Ph: (248)376-2102
E-mail: crcmichiganed@yahoo.com
URL: http://www.crcofmichigan.org
State. **Affiliated With:** Children's Rights Council.

6980 ■ Community Associations Institute, Michigan Chapter
6632 Telegraph Rd., Ste.347
Bloomfield Hills, MI 48301
Ph: (248)681-6017
Fax: (248)682-2161
E-mail: agruzin@comcast.net
URL: http://www.caimichigan.org
Contact: Amanda Gruzin, Exec.Dir.
Membership Dues: volunteer leader (based on number of individuals), $85-$470 (annual) • community manager, $95 (annual) • management company, $350 (annual) • business partner, $495 (annual) • multi-chapter (base), $245 (annual) • national corporate, $7,500 (annual). **State**. Represents the common interests of communities, property management companies and related service professionals and providers; provides resources, education and related services. **Affiliated With:** Community Associations Institute.

6981 ■ Construction Association of Michigan
PO Box 3204
Bloomfield Hills, MI 48302
Ph: (248)972-1000
Fax: (248)972-1001
E-mail: marketing@cam-online.com
URL: http://www.cam-online.com
Contact: Stephen R. Dailey, Chm.
State. Represents general contractors, subcontractors, suppliers, manufacturers' representatives and individual firms related to the construction industry. Provides information on construction and building procedures. **Affiliated With:** International Builders Exchange Executives.

6982 ■ Cranbrook Peace Foundation (CPF)
470 Church Rd.
Bloomfield Hills, MI 48304
Ph: (248)345-3475
Fax: (248)548-1119
E-mail: postmaster@cranbrookpeace.org
URL: http://www.cranbrookpeace.org
Contact: Felix J. Rogers, Pres.
Founded: 1987. **Members:** 600. **Membership Dues:** public, non-voting, $35 (annual). **Staff:** 1. **Budget:** $50,000. **Local**. Promotes non-violent conflict resolution and supports peacemaking organizations in southeastern Michigan. **Awards:** Cranbrook Peace Foundation Grants. **Frequency:** semiannual. **Type:** monetary. **Recipient:** for projects that propagate peace, focus on school or local community • Peace Award. **Frequency:** annual. **Type:** recognition. **Publications:** Newsletter, quarterly. **Price:** included in membership dues. **Circulation:** 1,200. **Conventions/Meetings:** annual Peace Lecture and Peace Award - fall.

6983 ■ Detroit Jewish Coalition for Literacy (DJCL)
c/o Ms. Phyllis Jarvis, Project Coor.
6735 Telegraph Rd., Ste.205
Bloomfield Hills, MI 48301
Ph: (248)642-5393
Fax: (248)642-6469
E-mail: jarvis@jfmd.org
Contact: Ms. Phyllis Jarvis, Project Coor.
Local. Works to increase the Jewish community's involvement in the fight against illiteracy by mobilizing, training and placing volunteer readers, tutors and book drive organizers.

6984 ■ East Michigan Environmental Action Council (EMEAC)
21220 W 14 Mile Rd.
Bloomfield Hills, MI 48301-4000

Ph: (248)258-5188
Fax: (248)731-0040
E-mail: emeac@aol.com
URL: http://www.emeac.org
Contact: Elizabeth Harris, Exec.Dir.
Founded: 1970. **Membership Dues:** basic, $20 (annual). **Staff:** 1. **Local**. Individuals, organizations, and governmental units in southeastern Michigan with an interest in environmental quality. Promotes environmental education and public interest. Holds annual lecture. **Telecommunication Services:** electronic mail, rachelemeac@aol.com. **Publications:** *Target Earth*, 10/year. Newsletter • Brochures, periodic.

6985 ■ Hospitality Financial and Technology Professionals - Greater Detroit Chapter
c/o Cheryl Brennan, CHAE, Pres.
Bloomfield Hills Country Club
350 W Long Lake Rd.
Bloomfield Hills, MI 48304-2624
Ph: (248)644-6262
Fax: (248)644-6756
E-mail: cbrennan@bloomfieldhillscc.org
URL: National Affiliate–www.hftp.org
Contact: Cheryl Brennan, Pres.
Local. Provides opportunities to members through professional and educational development. **Affiliated With:** Hospitality Financial and Technology Professionals. **Conventions/Meetings:** meeting, networking - 8/year.

6986 ■ Jewish Federation of Metropolitan Detroit
PO Box 2030
Bloomfield Hills, MI 48303-2030
Ph: (248)642-4260
URL: http://www.thisisfederation.org
Contact: Robert Aronson, CEO
Local.

6987 ■ Michigan Orchid Society
c/o Glenda Lask
5526 Westwood Ln.
Bloomfield Hills, MI 48301
Ph: (248)851-3835
E-mail: glendalask_568@msn.com
Contact: Glenda Lafk, Contact
Local. Professional growers, botanists, hobbyists, and others interested in extending the knowledge, production, use, and appreciation of orchids. **Affiliated With:** American Orchid Society.

6988 ■ Motor City Viper Owners (MCVO)
c/o Jim Bielenda, Pres.
PO Box 311
Bloomfield Hills, MI 48303
Ph: (248)616-0610
E-mail: viper@mcvo.net
URL: http://www.mcvo.net
Local.

6989 ■ National Association of Industrial and Office Properties, Michigan Chapter
c/o Sanford Aaron
PO Box 3000
Bloomfield Hills, MI 48302-3000
Ph: (248)758-1316
E-mail: sjaaron@gmail.com
URL: National Affiliate–www.naiop.org
Contact: Sanford Aaron, Pres.
State. Represents the interests of developers and owners of industrial, office and related commercial estate. Provides communication, networking, business opportunities and a forum to its members. Promotes effective public policy to create, protect and enhance property values. **Affiliated With:** National Association of Industrial and Office Properties.

6990 ■ Oakland County Bar Association (OCBA)
1760 S Telegraph Rd., Ste.100
Bloomfield Hills, MI 48302
Ph: (248)334-3400
Fax: (248)334-7757
E-mail: lstadig@ocba.org
URL: http://www.ocba.org
Contact: Lisa Stadig Elliot, Exec.Dir.
Founded: 1933. **Members:** 3,500. **Staff:** 11. **Budget:** $1,200,000. **Local**. Promotes the legal profession in Oakland County, MI. Conducts legal education and provides legal referral and court mediation services. Sponsors community service projects. **Publications:** *Laches*, monthly. Journal. **Price:** free for members. **Circulation:** 3,500. **Advertising:** accepted. **Conventions/Meetings:** annual meeting - always in Oakland County, MI.

6991 ■ Southeastern Michigan Computer Organization (SEMCO)
PO Box 707
Bloomfield Hills, MI 48303-0707
Ph: (248)398-7560
E-mail: semco@semco.org
URL: http://www.semco.org
Contact: Gary DeNise, Pres.
Local. Promotes and encourages an interest in computers and in computer use as an art and science. **Publications:** Newsletter, monthly. **Conventions/Meetings:** monthly meeting.

6992 ■ Town and Country African Violet Club
c/o Lynn Allen
1195 Fairfax Ave.
Bloomfield Hills, MI 48301
E-mail: lynn.allen@takata.com
URL: National Affiliate–www.avsa.org
Contact: Lynn Allen, Contact
Local. Affiliated With: African Violet Society of America.

6993 ■ Trout Unlimited, Challenge Chapter
c/o Don Silsbe, State Council Representative
PO Box 63
Bloomfield Hills, MI 48303
Ph: (248)792-2197
Fax: (313)493-1194
E-mail: bwrthor@yahoo.com
URL: http://challengechapter.org
Contact: Bill Thorsted, Pres.
Local. Affiliated With: Trout Unlimited.

Bloomingdale

6994 ■ Bloomingdale/Gobles (KalHaven Trail) Lions Club
PO Box 418
Bloomingdale, MI 49026
E-mail: fergeson2@juno.com
URL: http://milions11b2.org
Local. Affiliated With: Lions Clubs International.

Boyne City

6995 ■ American Legion, Michigan Post 228
c/o Ernest Peterson
302 S Lake St.
Boyne City, MI 49712
Ph: (517)371-4720
Fax: (517)371-2401
URL: National Affiliate–www.legion.org
Contact: Ernest Peterson, Contact
Local. Affiliated With: American Legion.

6996 ■ Boyne Area City Chamber of Commerce
28 S Lake St.
Boyne City, MI 49712
Ph: (231)582-6222 (231)582-5855
Fax: (231)582-6963
E-mail: boynechamber@boynechamber.com
URL: http://www.boynecity.com
Contact: Scott MacKenzie, Exec.Dir.
Membership Dues: general (base), $195 • individual, $100. **Local**. Works to enhance the economic, industrial, professional, cultural, and civic welfare of the Boyne City Area. **Telecommunication Services:** electronic mail, info@boynechamber.com. **Committees:** Ambassador.

6997 ■ Junior Achievement of the Michigan Great Lakes, Northern Service Office
04575 Fontenoy E
Boyne City, MI 49712
Ph: (231)582-4660
Fax: (231)582-4661
E-mail: jansom@race2000.com
URL: http://westmichigan.ja.org
Contact: Mike Ogden, District Mgr.
Founded: 1956. **Local. Affiliated With:** Junior Achievement.

Boyne Falls

6998 ■ Ruffed Grouse Society, Michigan Chapter
c/o Doug Doherty
03695 Cobb Rd.
Boyne Falls, MI 49713
Ph: (231)549-5063
URL: National Affiliate–www.ruffedgrousesociety.org
Contact: Doug Doherty, Contact
State. Affiliated With: Ruffed Grouse Society.

6999 ■ Ruffed Grouse Society, Roy W. Strickland Chapter
c/o Doug Doherty
03695 Cobb Rd.
Boyne Falls, MI 49713
Ph: (810)392-3827
URL: National Affiliate–www.ruffedgrousesociety.org
Contact: Doug Doherty, Contact
Local. Affiliated With: Ruffed Grouse Society.

Breckenridge

7000 ■ American Legion, Wolverton-Sawvel-Falor Post 295
PO Box 541
Breckenridge, MI 48615
Ph: (517)371-4720
Fax: (517)371-2401
URL: National Affiliate–www.legion.org
Local. Affiliated With: American Legion.

Bridgeport

7001 ■ American Society of Heating, Refrigerating and Air-Conditioning Engineers Eastern Michigan
c/o Brad Notter, Pres.
R.L. Deppmann
6200 Baron Dr.
Bridgeport, MI 48722
Ph: (989)652-3049
Fax: (989)652-3324
E-mail: bnotter@deppmann.com
URL: http://www.emichashrae.org
Contact: Brad Notter, Pres.
Local. Advances the arts and sciences of heating, ventilation, air-conditioning and refrigeration. Provides a source of technical and educational information, standards and guidelines. Conducts seminars for professional growth. **Affiliated With:** American Society of Heating, Refrigerating and Air-Conditioning Engineers.

Bridgman

7002 ■ American Legion, Bridgman Post 331
PO Box 67
Bridgman, MI 49106
Ph: (517)371-4720
Fax: (517)371-2401
URL: National Affiliate–www.legion.org
Local. Affiliated With: American Legion.

7003 ■ Bridgman Lions Club
9163 N Gast Rd.
Bridgman, MI 49106
Ph: (616)465-4428 (616)465-5699
E-mail: ehanover@aol.com
URL: http://bridgmanmi.lionwap.org
Contact: Bill Miller, Pres.
Local. Affiliated With: Lions Clubs International.

Brighton

7004 ■ AAA Michigan
8350 W Grand River Ave.
Brighton, MI 48116
Ph: (810)229-7100
State.

7005 ■ ACF Ann Arbor Culinary Association
c/o Frank Luzietti, Pres.
28 Pike St.
Brighton, MI 48116
Ph: (810)227-4443
URL: National Affiliate–www.acfchefs.org
Contact: Frank T. Luzietti, Pres.
Local. Promotes the culinary profession. Provides on-going educational training and networking for members. Provides opportunities for competition, professional recognition and access to educational forums with other culinarians at local, regional, national and international events. **Affiliated With:** American Culinary Federation.

7006 ■ American Cancer Society, Livingston County
7208 W Grand River
Brighton, MI 48114
Ph: (810)225-8590
URL: http://www.cancer.org
Contact: Laura Seyfried, Project Coor.
Local. Affiliated With: American Cancer Society.

7007 ■ American Legion, Michigan Post 235
c/o Jesse B. Cooley
10590 E Grand River
Brighton, MI 48116
Ph: (517)371-4720
Fax: (517)371-2401
URL: National Affiliate–www.legion.org
Contact: Jesse B. Cooley, Contact
Local. Affiliated With: American Legion.

7008 ■ Association for Psychological Type - Detroit
c/o Julianna Taylor
11336 Shadywood Dr.
Brighton, MI 48114
Ph: (810)227-9662
E-mail: julianna@liveyourvision.com
URL: National Affiliate–www.aptinternational.org
Contact: Julianna Taylor, Contact
Local. Promotes the practical application and ethical use of psychological type. Provides members with opportunities for continuous learning, sharing experiences and creating understanding and knowledge through research. **Affiliated With:** Association for Psychological Type.

7009 ■ Brain Injury Association of Michigan
c/o Michael Dabbs, Pres.
8619 W Grand River, Ste.I
Brighton, MI 48116-2334
Ph: (810)229-5880
Fax: (810)229-8947
Free: (800)772-4323
E-mail: info@biami.org
URL: http://www.biami.org
Membership Dues: supporting, $6 (annual) • contributing, $38 (annual) • sustaining, $100 (annual) • corporate, $250 (annual). **State.** Works to enhance the lives of those affected by brain injury through education, advocacy, research and local support groups; and to reduce the incidence of brain injury through prevention. **Affiliated With:** Brain Injury Association of America.

7010 ■ Brighton Art Guild
c/o Norma Gray
PO Box 65
Brighton, MI 48116
Ph: (810)220-9091
E-mail: randgra@chartermi.net
URL: http://www.brightonartguild.com
Contact: Norma Gray, Pres.
Founded: 1999. **Members:** 75. **Membership Dues:** $25 (annual). **Local. Publications:** *Brighton Art Guild*, monthly. Newsletter. Contains news of interest to members. **Price:** included in membership dues. **Circulation:** 75.

7011 ■ Brighton Lions Club
c/o Geene Smith, Sec.
555 Foxboro Sq.
Brighton, MI 48116
Ph: (586)575-3954 (810)227-1968
Fax: (810)227-2644
E-mail: imgsmith@aol.com
URL: http://www.district11c2.org
Contact: Geene Smith, Sec.
Local. Affiliated With: Lions Clubs International.

7012 ■ Greater Brighton Area Chamber of Commerce (GBACC)
131 Hyne St.
Brighton, MI 48116
Ph: (810)227-5086
Fax: (810)227-5940
E-mail: info@brightoncoc.org
URL: http://www.brightoncoc.org
Contact: Pam McConeghy, Exec.Dir.
Founded: 1972. **Members:** 875. **Membership Dues:** business (based on number of employees), $250-$890 (annual) • professional, $265 (annual) • bank/savings and loans, $595 (annual) • associate, $150 (annual) • retiree, $100 (annual) • nonprofit club and organization, $150 (annual). **Budget:** $500,000. **Local.** Promotes business and community development in the Brighton, MI area. Participates in the Great American Folk Art Festival. **Publications:** *Update Magazine*, monthly. **Conventions/Meetings:** annual Livingston Business and Trade Expo - trade show.

7013 ■ Home Builders Association of Livingston County
c/o Carol Kull, CAE, BIAE
132 E Grand River Ave.
Brighton, MI 48116-1510
Ph: (810)227-6210
Fax: (810)227-1840
E-mail: kate@hbalc.com
URL: http://www.hbalc.com
Contact: Kate Stepanva, Admin.Asst.
Local. Single and multifamily home builders, commercial builders, and others associated with the building industry. **Affiliated With:** National Association of Home Builders.

7014 ■ International Facility Management Association, Southeastern Michigan Chapter
c/o Ms. Susan Eagle, Chapter Administrator
11695 Brandywine Dr.
Brighton, MI 48114
Ph: (810)229-8973
Fax: (810)227-2826
E-mail: susaneagle@comcast.net
URL: http://www.ifmasemichigan.org
Contact: Mr. Robert N. Beuter, Pres.
Local. Spots trends, conducts research, provides educational programs, and assists corporate and organizational facility managers in developing strategies to manage human, facility and real estate resources. Holds monthly programs of interest for diverse membership. **Affiliated With:** International Facility Management Association.

7015 ■ Livingston County Habitat for Humanity (LCHFH)
1175 Rickett Rd., Ste.3
Brighton, MI 48116
Ph: (810)220-9986
Fax: (810)220-5351
E-mail: ichfh@sbcglobal.net
URL: http://www.livingstonhabitat.org
Contact: Kevin Dowd, Exec.Dir.
Local. Affiliated With: Habitat for Humanity International.

7016 ■ Michigan Association of Woodturners (MAW)
c/o Tim Morris, Treas.
1673 Woodlake Cir.
Brighton, MI 48116
Ph: (810)229-7156
E-mail: information@michiganwoodturner.org
URL: http://www.michiganwoodturner.org
Contact: Tom Mogford, Pres.
Membership Dues: individual, $95 (annual). **State. Affiliated With:** American Association of Woodturners.

7017 ■ Michigan Council of Chapters of the MOAA
c/o Cdr. Roy Yaple
4704 Mt. Brighton Dr.
Brighton, MI 48116-9409
Ph: (810)225-8657
E-mail: yapler@comcast.net
URL: National Affiliate–www.moaa.org
Contact: Cdr. Roy Yaple, Contact
State. Affiliated With: Military Officers Association of America.

7018 ■ Michigan Elks Association
c/o Louis J. Roos, Sec.
PO Box 668
Brighton, MI 48116
Ph: (810)694-5540
E-mail: jpopoff@tir.com
URL: http://mielks.org
Contact: Chad V. High, Pres.
State. Promotes the principles of charity, justice, brotherhood and loyalty among members. Fosters the spirit of American Patriotism. Seeks to stimulate pride and respect toward patriotism. **Affiliated With:** Benevolent and Protective Order of Elks.

7019 ■ National Association of Miniature Enthusiasts - Little Gems
c/o Tobie S. Pesmark
101 Brookside Ln.
Brighton, MI 48116
Ph: (810)220-8251
E-mail: topez@ismi.net
URL: http://www.miniatures.org/states/MI.html
Contact: Tobie S. Pesmark, Contact
Local. Affiliated With: National Association of Miniature Enthusiasts.

7020 ■ National Organization for Women - Livingston County
c/o Johanna Yuhas
PO Box 974
Brighton, MI 48116
Ph: (810)227-3314
E-mail: jmydjk@tir.com
URL: http://www.michnow.org
Contact: Johanna Yuhas, Contact
Local. Affiliated With: National Organization for Women.

7021 ■ Siberian Husky Club of Greater Detroit (SHCGD)
c/o Sharon Young
1355 Maxfield Rd.
Brighton, MI 48114
E-mail: yukonwind@earthlink.net
URL: http://members.aol.com/shclubgd/shcgd.htm
Contact: Brian Palmer, Pres.
Local.

7022 ■ Sierra Club - Mackinac Chapter - Crossroads Group
c/o Rick Pearsall, Chm.
PO Box 306
Brighton, MI 48116
Ph: (810)227-6298
E-mail: rick.pearsall@michigan.sierraclub.org
URL: http://michigan.sierraclub.org/crossroads/index.html
Contact: Rick Pearsall, Chm.
Local.

7023 ■ State Guard Association of the United States, Michigan
c/o Robert A. Hagan, Col.
139 Forno Dr., Rt. 2
Brighton, MI 48116-9620
Ph: (810)229-4173
E-mail: bobhagan@msn.com
URL: National Affiliate–www.sgaus.org
Contact: Col. Robert A. Hagan, Contact
State. Affiliated With: State Guard Association of the United States.

7024 ■ United Way of Livingston County
2980 Dorr Rd.
Brighton, MI 48116
Ph: (810)494-3000 (810)494-3003
Fax: (810)494-3004
E-mail: nrosso@lcunitedway.org
URL: http://www.lcunitedway.org
Contact: Nancy Rosso, Exec.Dir.
Founded: 1980. **Staff:** 5. **Local. Affiliated With:** United Way of America.

Britton

7025 ■ American Legion, Michigan Post 155
c/o Glen H. Daykin
133 E Chicago Blvd.
Britton, MI 49229
Ph: (517)371-4720
Fax: (517)371-2401
URL: National Affiliate–www.legion.org
Contact: Glen H. Daykin, Contact
Local. Affiliated With: American Legion.

7026 ■ Ridgeway Township Firefighters Association
c/o Gary Judkins
PO Box 222
Britton, MI 49229-0222
Ph: (517)451-8264
Local.

Bronson

7027 ■ American Legion, Alderman-Luce Post 259
131 York St.
Bronson, MI 49028
Ph: (517)371-4720
Fax: (517)371-2401
URL: National Affiliate–www.legion.org
Local. Affiliated With: American Legion.

7028 ■ Michigan National Wild Turkey Federation, Branch County Longbeards
275 N Parham Rd.
Bronson, MI 49028
Ph: (517)369-1349
URL: http://www.mi-nwtf.org/branchco.htm
Contact: Tom Leister, Pres.
Local.

Brooklyn

7029 ■ American Legion, Wilber-Bartlett Post 315
211 Chicago St.
Brooklyn, MI 49230
Ph: (517)371-4720
Fax: (517)371-2401
URL: National Affiliate–www.legion.org
Local. Affiliated With: American Legion.

7030 ■ Brooklyn - Irish Hills Chamber of Commerce
221 N Main St.
Brooklyn, MI 49230-8999
Ph: (517)592-8907
Fax: (517)592-8907
E-mail: bihcc@frontiernet.net
URL: http://www.brooklynmi.com
Contact: Linda Reynolds, Exec.Dir.
Local. Business owners and professional men and women who invest their time and money in a development program for the entire community. Works to improve the economic, social, cultural, commercial, industrial and civic welfare of the Brooklyn-Irish Hills area. **Committees:** Area Promotion; Economic Development; Legislative; Tourist; Various Activities. **Task Forces:** Education. **Publications:** Newsletters, monthly.

Brownstown

7031 ■ American Legion, Huron Valley Post 231
23887 Ada St.
Brownstown, MI 48183
Ph: (517)371-4720
Fax: (517)371-2401
URL: National Affiliate–www.legion.org
Local. Affiliated With: American Legion.

7032 ■ Brownstown Lions Club
c/o Luisito Vitug, Jr., Pres.
20039 Syracuse Ave.
Brownstown, MI 48183
Ph: (734)479-2886
E-mail: rubenormac@aol.com
URL: http://www.metrodetroitlions.org
Contact: Luisito Vitug Jr., Pres.
Local. Affiliated With: Lions Clubs International.

Bruce Crossing

7033 ■ Ottawa Back Country Horsemen, Michigan
16591 N Paynesville Rd.
Bruce Crossing, MI 49912-8782
Ph: (906)250-3016
E-mail: sheena@america.hm
URL: National Affiliate–www.backcountryhorse.com
Local. Affiliated With: Back Country Horsemen of America.

Buchanan

7034 ■ American Legion, Ralph Rumbaugh Post 51
403 E Front St.
Buchanan, MI 49107
Ph: (517)371-4720
Fax: (517)371-2401
URL: National Affiliate–www.legion.org
Local. Affiliated With: American Legion.

7035 ■ Buchanan Area Chamber of Commerce (BACC)
103 W Front St.
Buchanan, MI 49107-1410
Ph: (269)695-3291
Fax: (269)695-3813
E-mail: bacc@buchanan.mi.us
URL: http://www.buchanan.mi.us
Contact: Michelle Klarich, Exec.Dir.
Founded: 1956. **Members:** 110. **Membership Dues:** regular business, $150 (annual) • non-profit, $75 (annual) • family citizen supporter, $25 (annual). **Staff:** 1. **Budget:** $37,000. **Local.** Businesses and individuals promoting economic and community development in the Buchanan, MI area. Conducts annual dinner, area wide promotions, special events and business-related workshops. **Computer Services:** database, lists of local businesses and institutions • information services, facts about Buchanan. **Publications:** *News & Views*, monthly. Newsletter • *Redbud Area Directory*, quarterly. Contains list of area businesses, services and contact persons. **Price:** $4.00 • *Redbud Area News*, monthly.

Burton

7036 ■ Bedrock Jeepers
2069 E Williamson Ave.
Burton, MI 48529-2443
Fax: (509)757-5024
E-mail: scramblerkid@hotmail.com
URL: http://www.geocities.com/bedrockjeeps
Family-oriented Jeep and off-roading club. **Affiliated With:** United Four-Wheel Drive Associations.

7037 ■ Great Lakes Swing Dance Club (GLSDC)
PO Box 190085
Burton, MI 48519-0085
Ph: (810)664-7894
E-mail: bpranger@intouchmi.com
URL: http://greatlakesswingdance.com
Contact: Betty Ranger, Pres.
Regional. Promotes and preserves bop, swing, shag and jitterbug dance styles and the heritage of those styles of music that center on the beat and rhythm. Strives to enhance communication and promotional coordination of activities throughout the membership.

Byron

7038 ■ Byron Area Lions Club
c/o David R. Keys, Pres.
11751 Britton Rd.
Byron, MI 48418
Ph: (810)266-5589
E-mail: davidrkeys@earthlink.net
URL: http://www.district11c2.org
Contact: David R. Keys, Pres.
Local. Affiliated With: Lions Clubs International.

7039 ■ Michigan Association of Agriscience Educators
c/o Tate Forbush, Pres.
312 W Maple Ave.
Byron, MI 48418
Ph: (810)266-4620
Fax: (810)266-5010
E-mail: forbush@byron.k12.mi.us
URL: http://www.teachanr.com
Contact: Tate Forbush, Pres.
State. Seeks to advance agricultural education and promotes the professional interests and growth of agriculture teachers. Provides agricultural education through visionary leadership, advocacy and service. **Affiliated With:** National Association of Agricultural Educators.

Byron Center

7040 ■ American Legion, Byron Center Post 292
4445 88th St.
Byron Center, MI 49315
Ph: (517)371-4720
Fax: (517)371-2401
URL: National Affiliate–www.legion.org
Local. Affiliated With: American Legion.

7041 ■ Michigan National Barrel Horse Association
1950 64th St.
Byron Center, MI 49315
Ph: (616)532-2150
URL: National Affiliate–www.nbha.com
State. Promotes the sport of barrel horse racing. Conducts barrel racing competitions. Establishes standard rules for the sport. **Affiliated With:** National Barrel Horse Association.

Cadillac

7042 ■ American Legion, Michigan Post 94
c/o Ray E. Bostick
422 N Mitchell St.
Cadillac, MI 49601
Ph: (517)371-4720
Fax: (517)371-2401
URL: National Affiliate–www.legion.org
Contact: Ray E. Bostick, Contact
Local. Affiliated With: American Legion.

7043 ■ AMVETS, Cadillac Post 110
127 W Cass St.
Cadillac, MI 49601
Ph: (231)775-7433
URL: http://netonecom.net/~nanny/A110.html
Contact: Howard R. Karcher, Contact
Local. Affiliated With: AMVETS - American Veterans.

7044 ■ Cadillac Area Chamber of Commerce (CACC)
222 Lake St.
Cadillac, MI 49601-1874
Ph: (231)775-9776
Fax: (231)775-1440
E-mail: info@cadillac.org
URL: http://www.cadillac.org
Contact: Bill Tencza, Pres.
Founded: 1933. **Membership Dues:** business (plus $1.75 per employee over 101), $210-$905 (annual) • individual senior citizen, $95 (annual) • bank (plus $20 per million in assets), $210 (annual) • utility, $709 (annual) • hotel/motel/resort (plus $7 per room), $210 (annual) • insurance, $95 (annual). **Local**. Promotes business and community development in the Cadillac, MI area. **Publications:** *Cadillac Area Business Magazine*, bimonthly. Alternate Formats: online • Newsletter, bimonthly • Membership Directory, periodic.

7045 ■ Cadillac Area Visitors Bureau
222 Lake St.
Cadillac, MI 49601
Ph: (231)775-0657
Fax: (231)775-1440
Free: (800)22-LAKES
E-mail: visit@cadillacmichigan.com
URL: http://www.cadillacmichigan.com
Contact: Carol Potter, Contact
Founded: 1986. **Members:** 45. **Staff:** 2. **Budget:** $150,000. **Local**. Promotes convention business and tourism in the area.

7046 ■ Cadillac Lions Club
10797 Pine Shores Dr.
Cadillac, MI 49601-8257
Ph: (231)779-5502 (231)775-2939
E-mail: liontim@scantek.com
URL: http://cadillacmi.lionwap.org
Contact: Timothy Anderson, Pres.
Local. Affiliated With: Lions Clubs International.

7047 ■ Michigan Association of Conservation Districts (MACD)
c/o Marilyn Shy, Exec.Dir.
201 N Mitchell St., Ste.203
Cadillac, MI 49601
Ph: (231)876-0328
Fax: (231)876-0372
E-mail: macd@macd.org
URL: http://macd.org
Contact: Tom Middleton, Pres.
Founded: 1941. **Members:** 82. **Membership Dues:** regular, $25-$100 (annual) • life, $250. **Staff:** 6. **Budget:** $300,000. **Regional Groups:** 10. **State Groups:** 1. **Local Groups:** 82. **State**. Conservation districts. Promotes the wise and safe use of soil, water, and related resources. **Publications:** *Earth Steward*, quarterly. Newsletter. **Advertising:** accepted • *Friday Letter*, monthly. Newsletter. **Price:** included in membership dues. **Conventions/Meetings:** annual conference (exhibits).

7048 ■ Paul Bunyan Board of Realtors
9052 E 13th St., Ste.D
Cadillac, MI 49601
Ph: (231)775-2660
Fax: (231)775-0462
E-mail: info@pbbr.com
URL: http://www.pbbr.com
Contact: Ken Carlson, Pres.
Local. Strives to develop real estate business practices. Advocates the right to own, use and transfer real property. Provides a facility for professional development, research and exchange of information among members. **Affiliated With:** National Association of Realtors.

7049 ■ SCORE Cadillac
222 N Lake St.
Cadillac, MI 49601
Ph: (231)775-9776
Fax: (231)775-1440
E-mail: score@cadillac.org
URL: http://www.score.org
Local. Affiliated With: SCORE.

7050 ■ United Way of Wexford County
PO Box 177
Cadillac, MI 49601
Ph: (231)775-3753
Fax: (231)775-0169
E-mail: info@unitedwaywexford.org
URL: http://unitedwaywexford.org
Contact: Diane Dykstra, Exec.Dir.
Local. Affiliated With: United Way of America.

7051 ■ Wexford County Habitat for Humanity
PO Box 828
Cadillac, MI 49601
Ph: (231)775-7561 (231)824-3043
Fax: (231)775-7561
E-mail: wexfordhabitat@netonecom.net
URL: http://users.netonecom.net/~wexfordhabitat
Local. Affiliated With: Habitat for Humanity International.

7052 ■ Wexford County Historical Society and Museum
c/o Richard Harvey
PO Box 124
Cadillac, MI 49601
Ph: (231)775-1717

Caledonia

7053 ■ American Legion, Caledonia Memorial Post 305
9548 Cherry Valley Ave. SE
Caledonia, MI 49316
Ph: (517)371-4720
Fax: (517)371-2401
URL: National Affiliate–www.legion.org
Local. Affiliated With: American Legion.

7054 ■ Horseless Carriage Club of America, Grand Rapids
c/o Bob Palmer
5031 108th Dr.
Caledonia, MI 49316-9445
Ph: (616)891-2205
URL: http://geocities.com/grandrapidshcca
Contact: Bob Palmer, Contact
Local. Affiliated With: Horseless Carriage Club of America.

7055 ■ Michigan Muskie Alliance
PO Box 512
Caledonia, MI 49316
Ph: (616)447-1688
E-mail: w.schultz@comcast.net
URL: http://www.michiganmuskiealliance.org
Contact: Will Schultz, Pres.
State.

Calumet

7056 ■ Great Lakes Curling Association - Copper Country Curling Club
PO Box 264
Calumet, MI 49913
Ph: (906)482-6788
E-mail: gmaclean@starband.net
URL: http://www.coppercountrycurlingclub.com
Contact: Gordon Maclean, Contact
Local. Affiliated With: United States Curling Association.

Cannonsburg

7057 ■ Michigan Chapter of IARP (MIARP)
c/o Ms. Karen Starr, Pres.
Starr & Associates
PO Box 870
Cannonsburg, MI 49317
Ph: (616)874-5642
Fax: (616)874-1408
E-mail: kstarr@starrandassociates.net
Contact: Ms. Karen Starr, Pres.
Founded: 1985. **Members:** 100. **Regional Groups:** 1. **State**. Represents medical and vocational case managers that work with individuals receiving benefits for workers' compensation, LTD/STD and auto no-fault. **Affiliated With:** International Association of Rehabilitation Professionals. **Conventions/Meetings:** conference, ethics (exhibits).

Canton

7058 ■ American Legion, Belleville Post 58
c/o Gary Weckerly
2211 Woodmont Dr. W
Canton, MI 48188
Ph: (517)371-4720
Fax: (517)371-2401
URL: National Affiliate–www.legion.org
Contact: Gary Weckerly, Contact
Local. Affiliated With: American Legion.

7059 ■ American Legion, Canton Post 188
2211 Woodmont Dr.
Canton, MI 48188
Ph: (517)371-4720
Fax: (517)371-2401
URL: National Affiliate–www.legion.org
Local. Affiliated With: American Legion.

7060 ■ Arctic Figure Skating Club (AFSC)
46615 Michigan Ave.
Canton, MI 48188
Ph: (734)487-7777
E-mail: nancyelaine@yahoo.com
URL: http://arcticfsc.com
Local. Provides programs to encourage participation and achievement in the sport of figure skating on ice. Defines and maintains uniform standards of skating proficiency. Organizes and sponsors competitions and exhibitions for the purpose of stimulating interest in figure skating. **Affiliated With:** United States Figure Skating Association.

7061 ■ Canton Chamber of Commerce (CCC)
45525 Hanford Rd.
Canton, MI 48187
Ph: (734)453-4040
Fax: (734)453-4503
E-mail: info@cantonchamber.com
URL: http://www.cantonchamber.com
Contact: Dianne Cojei, Pres.
Founded: 1972. **Membership Dues:** home based business (self-employed), $137 (annual) • business (based on number of employees), $212-$482 (annual) • associate, realtor associate, church, organization, $107 (annual). **Staff:** 6. **Local**. Promotes business and community development in Canton, Michigan. **Telecommunication Services:** electronic mail, diannec@cantonchamber.com. **Committees:** Ambassadors Club; Auction; Communications; Education; Golf; Government Relations; Grub Crawl; Technology. **Publications:** *Networker*, monthly. Newsletter. Includes information about business in the chamber and the community. **Advertising:** accepted. Alternate Formats: online • Membership Directory, annual. **Advertising:** accepted. Alternate Formats: online.

7062 ■ Canton Lions Club - Michigan
c/o Charles Mott, Pres.
3800 Herbey St.
Canton, MI 48188
Ph: (734)397-5495
E-mail: motski@earthlink.com
URL: http://www.metrodetroitlions.org
Contact: Charles Mott, Pres.
Local. Affiliated With: Lions Clubs International.

7063 ■ Dancing Cuckoos, Metropolitan Detroit Tent of the International Sons of the Desert (DCMDTISD)
c/o Rose Lahiff, Grand Shiek
220 Edington Cir.
Canton, MI 48187
Ph: (734)981-2798
E-mail: rozlaf@aol.com
URL: http://www.sotd.org/oasis2.htm
Contact: Rose Lahiff, Grand Sheik
Founded: 1965. **Members:** 100. **Membership Dues:** $20 (annual). **Local**. Fans of the films of Stan Laurel and Oliver Hardy. **Awards:** The Fine Mess Award. **Frequency:** annual. **Type:** recognition. **Recipient:** to the person or group who in the past year most exemplifies Ollie's famous comment to Stan, "Here's another fine mess you've gotten me into" • Virtuous Cuckoo Award. **Frequency:** periodic. **Type:** recognition. **Recipient:** for those who revere and respect all things funny in the tradition of Stan Laurel and Oliver Hardy. **Affiliated With:** Sons of the Desert. **Publications:** *Cuckoo Chronicle*, 5/year. Newsletter • *Intra-Tent Journal*, quarterly. **Conventions/Meetings:** biennial International Convention.

7064 ■ IEEE Electromagnetic Compatibility Society, Southeastern Michigan
c/o Scott Lytle, NCE, EMC Laboratory Mgr.
Yazaki Testing Ctr.
6800 N Haggerty Rd.
Canton, MI 48187-3577
Ph: (734)983-6012 (734)397-8215
Fax: (734)983-6013
E-mail: s.r.lytle@ieee.org
URL: http://www.emcsociety.org
Founded: 1989. **Local. Affiliated With:** IEEE Electromagnetic Compatibility Society.

7065 ■ International Union, United Automobile, Aerospace and Agricultural Implement Workers of America, AFL-CIO - Local Union 735
48055 Michigan Ave.
Canton, MI 48188
Ph: (734)482-5620 (734)595-3636
Fax: (734)482-0089
E-mail: treasurer@local735uaw.org
URL: http://www.local735uaw.org
Contact: Alice Britz, Financial Sec.-Treas.
Members: 4,188. **Local**. AFL-CIO. **Affiliated With:** International Union, United Automobile, Aerospace and Agricultural Implement Workers of America.

7066 ■ International Union, United Automobile, Aerospace and Agricultural Implement Workers of America, AFL-CIO - Local Union 845
8770 N Canton Center Rd.
Canton, MI 48187
Ph: (734)453-1240
Fax: (734)453-3809
URL: http://www.uaw845.org
Contact: Paul Haver, Pres.
Members: 1,594. **Local**. AFL-CIO. **Affiliated With:** International Union, United Automobile, Aerospace and Agricultural Implement Workers of America.

7067 ■ Michigan Association of Alcoholism and Drug Abuse Counselors (MAADAC)
c/o Junnie Morrow, Office Mgr.
7755 Ridge Rd., Ste.200
Canton, MI 48187-1121
Ph: (734)254-9333
Fax: (734)453-8365
E-mail: jmorrow@maadac.com
State. Affiliated With: NAADAC The Association for Addiction Professionals.

7068 ■ Michigan State Numismatic Society
c/o Joe H. LeBlanc
PO Box 87931
Canton, MI 48187
Ph: (734)453-0504
E-mail: jhl@michsoft.com
URL: http://www.michigancoinclub.org
Contact: Joe H. LeBlanc, Contact
State. Affiliated With: American Numismatic Association.

7069 ■ National Association of Miniature Enthusiasts - People with Unfinished Projects
c/o Rosanne Jacobs
1401 Whittier Dr.
Canton, MI 48187
Ph: (734)981-6073
E-mail: varj@provide.net
URL: http://www.miniatures.org/states/MI.html
Contact: Rosanne Jacobs, Contact
Local. Affiliated With: National Association of Miniature Enthusiasts.

7070 ■ National Association of Watch and Clock Collectors, Great Lakes Chapter 6
c/o Gordon Webb
6663 Sturbridge
Canton, MI 48187
E-mail: gordonwebb1@yahoo.com
URL: http://www.nawcc6.org
Contact: Robert Arnold, Pres.
Founded: 1972. **Membership Dues:** local chapter, $5. **Regional.**

7071 ■ National Technical Honor Society - ITT Technical Institute - Canton Michigan
1905 S Haggerty Rd.
Canton, MI 48188-2025
Ph: (734)397-7800
Free: (800)247-4477
URL: http://www.itt-tech.edu
Local.

7072 ■ Ruffed Grouse Society, Ann Arbor Chapter
c/o Todd Alexander
43587 Proctor Rd.
Canton, MI 48188
Ph: (734)398-9783
E-mail: brdhunter@peoplepc.com
URL: National Affiliate–www.ruffedgrousesociety.org
Contact: Todd Alexander, Contact
Local. Affiliated With: Ruffed Grouse Society.

7073 ■ Society for Nonprofit Organizations
c/o Katie Burnham Laverty
5820 Canton Center Rd., Ste.165
Canton, MI 48187
Ph: (734)451-3582
Fax: (734)451-5935
E-mail: kburnham@snpo.org
URL: http://www.snpo.org
Contact: Katie Burnham Laverty, Contact
Local. Promotes a vigorous nonprofit sector through education, collaboration, and research in order to advance healthy and participatory communities. Publishes a management and leadership magazine, "Nonprofit World"; a monthly funding information e-newsletter, "Funding Alert"; and produces educational programs, including a certificate program. Also produces a job listing site; maintains an archive of over 500 management and leadership articles on the Web, free to members.

Capac

7074 ■ American Legion, Michigan Post 142
c/o Albert A. Glassford
115 N Main St.
Capac, MI 48014
Ph: (517)371-4720
Fax: (517)371-2401
URL: National Affiliate–www.legion.org
Contact: Albert A. Glassford, Contact
Local. Affiliated With: American Legion.

7075 ■ Capac Area Chamber of Commerce
PO Box 520
Capac, MI 48014
Ph: (810)395-4359
Contact: Rosy Cousins, Contact
Local.

7076 ■ Capac Community Historical Society
c/o Daniel Bell
401 E. Kempf Court
Capac, MI 48014
Ph: (810)395-2859

Carleton

7077 ■ American Legion, Carleton Post 66
PO Box 294
Carleton, MI 48117
Ph: (517)371-4720
Fax: (517)371-2401
URL: National Affiliate–www.legion.org
Local. Affiliated With: American Legion.

Carney

7078 ■ American Legion, Carney-Nadeau Post 487
222 US 41
Carney, MI 49812
Ph: (517)371-4720
Fax: (517)371-2401
URL: National Affiliate–www.legion.org
Local. Affiliated With: American Legion.

7079 ■ Michigan National Wild Turkey Federation, Menominee Strutting Chapter
13162 N County Rd.
Carney, MI 49812
Ph: (906)639-2217
URL: http://www.mi-nwtf.org/menomine.htm
Contact: Scott Mack, Pres.
Local.

Caro

7080 ■ American Legion, Michigan Post 7
c/o Theron W. Atwood, Sr.
110 W Frank St.
Caro, MI 48723

Ph: (517)371-4720
Fax: (517)371-2401
URL: National Affiliate–www.legion.org
Contact: Theron W. Atwood Sr., Contact
Local. Affiliated With: American Legion.

7081 ■ Bay Area Music Teachers Association (BAMTA)
c/o Diana Spitnale Miller
208 W Burnside St.
Caro, MI 48723-1501
Ph: (989)673-4355
E-mail: ddmiller@centurytel.net
URL: http://www.mi-mtna.org/bamta.html
Contact: Diana Spitnale Miller, Contact
Local. Professional society of music teachers committed to furthering the art of music through programs that encourage and support teaching, performance, composition, and scholarly research. **Affiliated With:** Music Teachers National Association.

7082 ■ Caro Chamber of Commerce
157 N State St.
Caro, MI 48723
Ph: (989)673-5211
Fax: (989)672-4098
E-mail: executivedirector@carochamber.org
URL: http://www.carochamber.org
Contact: Susan Steinhoff, Exec.Dir.
Founded: 1922. **Members:** 200. **Membership Dues:** business (depends on the number of employees), $150-$350 (annual) • individual, $100 (annual) • associate (outside Caro), $75 (annual) • non-profit, $150 (annual). **Budget:** $55,000. **State Groups:** 2. **Local.** Promotes business and community development in the Caro, MI area. Sponsors Cars and Crafts Weekend. **Awards:** Chamber Business. **Frequency:** annual. **Type:** recognition • Chamber Member. **Frequency:** annual. **Type:** recognition • Chamber Merit. **Frequency:** annual. **Type:** recognition • Citizen of Year. **Frequency:** annual. **Type:** recognition. **Computer Services:** database, list of members • information services, profile of Caro. **Affiliated With:** U.S. Chamber of Commerce. **Publications:** *Action*, monthly. Newsletter. **Price:** free. **Circulation:** 285. **Advertising:** accepted. Alternate Formats: online • Membership Directory, annual. **Conventions/Meetings:** monthly board meeting - every 3rd Wednesday.

7083 ■ Caro Lions Club
c/o Scott Wood, Pres.
1549 E Deckerville Rd.
Caro, MI 48723
Ph: (989)450-6161
E-mail: scottwood@centurytel.net
URL: http://www.geocities.com/dist11d1
Contact: Scott Wood, Pres.
Local. Affiliated With: Lions Clubs International.

7084 ■ Humane Society of Tuscola County (HSTC)
c/o Judy Murphy, Pres.
PO Box 245
Caro, MI 48723
Ph: (989)672-7387
E-mail: judy@humanesocietytusco.org
URL: http://www.humanesocietytusco.org
Contact: Judy Murphy, Pres.
Founded: 1986. **Members:** 245. **Membership Dues:** individual, $15 (annual) • family, $25 (annual) • student, $5 (annual). **Staff:** 8. **Budget:** $20,000. **Local.** Citizens interested in the prevention of cruelty to animals, relief of suffering animals, and humane education to children and the public. Reunites lost animals with their owners. **Publications:** Newsletter, monthly. **Price:** available to members only. **Circulation:** 245. Alternate Formats: CD-ROM. **Conventions/Meetings:** monthly board meeting • quarterly meeting.

7085 ■ National Technical Honor Society - Tuscola Technology Center - Michigan (TTC)
1401 Cleaver Rd.
Caro, MI 48723
Ph: (989)673-5300
Fax: (989)673-4228
E-mail: sley@tisd.k12.mi.us
URL: http://www.tisd.k12.mi.us
Contact: Stephen Ley, Contact
Local.

7086 ■ Thumb Area RSVP
c/o Julia DeGuise, Dir.
429 Montague Ave.
Caro, MI 48723-1997
Ph: (989)673-4121
Fax: (989)673-2031
E-mail: juliad@hdc-caro.org
URL: http://www.seniorcorps.gov
Contact: Julia DeGuise, Dir.
Local. Affiliated With: Retired and Senior Volunteer Program.

7087 ■ Watrousville-Caro Area Historical Society
PO Box 15
Caro, MI 48723-0015
Ph: (989)823-3638
E-mail: grayjoann@hotmail.com
URL: http://www.hsmichigan.org/caro/
Contact: JoAnn Gray, Treas.
Local.

Carson City

7088 ■ American Legion, Carson City Post 380
121 N Mercantile St.
Carson City, MI 48811
Ph: (517)371-4720
Fax: (517)371-2401
URL: National Affiliate–www.legion.org
Local. Affiliated With: American Legion.

7089 ■ Carson City Lions Club
10002 E Carson City Rd.
Carson City, MI 48811
Ph: (989)584-3422
E-mail: carsoncitylions@pathwaynet.com
URL: http://carsoncitymi.lionwap.org
Contact: Lainie Niemi, Sec.
Local. Affiliated With: Lions Clubs International.

7090 ■ Lagos Grandes Peruvian Horse Club (LGPHC)
c/o Connie Hydel, Pres.
Wendy Moncada
11079 E Boyer
Carson City, MI 48811
Ph: (517)584-3275
E-mail: info@lgphc.org
URL: http://www.lgphc.org
Contact: Connie Hydel, Pres.
Local. Affiliated With: North American Peruvian Horse Association.

Caseville

7091 ■ American Legion, Jean Post 543
PO Box 1044
Caseville, MI 48725
Ph: (517)371-4720
Fax: (517)371-2401
URL: National Affiliate–www.legion.org
Local. Affiliated With: American Legion.

Caspian

7092 ■ Iron County Historical and Museum Society (ICHMS)
PO Box 272
Caspian, MI 49915
Ph: (906)265-2617
E-mail: icmuseum@up.net
URL: http://ironcountymuseum.com
Founded: 1962. **Members:** 200. **Membership Dues:** supporter, $24 (annual) • patron, $50 (annual) • benefactor, $100 (annual) • life (accumulative), $1,000 • Sr. Citizen, $5 (annual). **Budget:** $60,000. **Local.** Individuals seeking to record and preserve the history of Iron County, MI. Offers educational programs for grades 1-7, and cultural activities for people of all ages. Maintains a 22-building museum. Sponsors ethnic festivals, art festivals, and competitions. Conducts charitable activities. **Libraries: Type:** by appointment only. **Holdings:** 300. **Subjects:** occupations, ethnic groups, mining, logging, pioneer, school. **Affiliated With:** American Association for State and Local History; Historical Society of Michigan. **Publications:** *Barns, Farms, and Yarns*. Book • *Past-Present Prints*, semiannual. Newsletter. **Price:** free.

Cass City

7093 ■ Cass City Chamber of Commerce
6506 Main St.
Cass City, MI 48726-1524
Ph: (989)872-4618
Fax: (989)872-4855
Free: (866)266-3822
E-mail: chamber@cass-city.net
URL: http://www.casscity.org
Contact: Kay Warner, Administrator
Founded: 1951. **Members:** 196. **Local.** Promotes business and community development in Cass City, MI. **Conventions/Meetings:** monthly board meeting - every 2nd Wednesday.

7094 ■ Cass City Lions Club
c/o Gary Jones, Sec.
6809 Herron Dr.
Cass City, MI 48726
Ph: (989)872-2639
E-mail: gdjones@avci.net
URL: http://www.geocities.com/dist11d1
Contact: Gary Jones, Sec.
Local. Affiliated With: Lions Clubs International.

7095 ■ Northern Thumb District Dental Society
6240 Hill St.
Cass City, MI 48726
Ph: (989)872-3870
Fax: (989)872-4582
URL: National Affiliate–www.ada.org
Contact: Dr. James Thomas, Pres.
Local. Represents the interests of dentists committed to the public's oral health, ethics and professional development. Encourages the improvement of the public's oral health and promotes the art and science of dentistry. **Affiliated With:** American Dental Association; Michigan Dental Association.

7096 ■ United Way of Tuscola County
PO Box 51
Cass City, MI 48726-0051
Ph: (989)635-7679
URL: National Affiliate–national.unitedway.org
Local. Affiliated With: United Way of America.

Cassopolis

7097 ■ American Legion, Diamond Island Post 335
21290 Carlton Dr.
Cassopolis, MI 49031
Ph: (517)371-4720
Fax: (517)371-2401
URL: National Affiliate–www.legion.org
Local. Affiliated With: American Legion.

7098 ■ American Legion, Efton James Post 206
131 S Broadway
Cassopolis, MI 49031
Ph: (517)371-4720
Fax: (517)371-2401
URL: National Affiliate–www.legion.org
Local. Affiliated With: American Legion.

7099 ■ Boys and Girls Club of Cass County
c/o Mary McFarland, Pres.
60405 Decatur Rd.
Cassopolis, MI 49031-0456
Ph: (269)445-1601
E-mail: boysandgirlsclub@beanstalk.net
URL: http://users.beanstalk.net/boysandgirlsclub
Contact: Mary McFarland, Pres.
Local.

7100 ■ Cassopolis (Central Cass) Lions Club
PO Box 9
Cassopolis, MI 49031
E-mail: jmbollweg@beanstalk.net
URL: http://milions11b2.org
Local. Affiliated With: Lions Clubs International.

7101 ■ National Active and Retired Federal Employees Association - Three Rivers 1521
25637 Hosp. St.
Cassopolis, MI 49031-9642
Ph: (616)445-8394
URL: National Affiliate–www.narfe.org
Contact: Marshall E. Redmond, Contact
Local. Protects the retirement future of employees through education. Informs members on issues affecting the retirement. **Affiliated With:** National Association of Retired Federal Employees.

Cedar

7102 ■ Michigan Parents of Blind Children
c/o Sharon Darga
8941 E Hoxsie Rd.
Cedar, MI 49621-9776
Ph: (231)947-3972
E-mail: bossclaw@aol.com
URL: National Affiliate–www.nfb.org
Contact: Sharon Darga, Contact
State. Provides information and support to parents of blind children. Develops and expands resources available to parents and their children. Aims to eliminate discrimination and prejudice against the blind. **Affiliated With:** National Organization of Parents of Blind Children.

7103 ■ Plumbing-Heating-Cooling Contractors Association, Northwestern Michigan
c/o Larry Wichern, Pres.
3432 E Hohnke Rd.
Cedar, MI 49621-9736
Ph: (231)228-5784
URL: National Affiliate–www.phccweb.org
Contact: Larry Wichern, Pres.
Local. Represents the plumbing, heating and cooling contractors. Promotes the construction industry. Protects the environment, health, safety and comfort of society. **Affiliated With:** Plumbing-Heating-Cooling Contractors Association.

Cedar Springs

7104 ■ American Legion, Glen Hill Post 287
91 First St.
Cedar Springs, MI 49319
Ph: (517)371-4720
Fax: (517)371-2401
URL: National Affiliate–www.legion.org
Local. Affiliated With: American Legion.

Center Line

7105 ■ Michigan Association of Blood Banks (MABB)
c/o Janet Silvestri, Exec. Administrator
PO Box 3605
Center Line, MI 48015-0605
Ph: (586)573-2500
Fax: (586)573-7058
E-mail: janet@hfcc.net
URL: http://www.mabb.org
Contact: Ms. Janet Silvestri, Exec. Administrator
Founded: 1955. **Members:** 450. **Membership Dues:** individual, $30 (annual) • physician, $60 (annual) • institutional, $75 (annual) • corporate, $350 (annual). **Staff:** 1. **State Groups:** 1. **State.** Blood banks and individuals involved in health care. Seeks to further the interests of individuals involved in providing blood to be used for transfusions. **Awards:** Emanuel Hackel Scholarship. **Frequency:** annual. **Type:** scholarship • Vi Williams. **Frequency:** annual. **Type:** scholarship. **Computer Services:** database • mailing lists • online services. **Committees:** Education; Publications. **Affiliated With:** American Association of Blood Banks. **Publications:** *In a Different Vein*, quarterly. Newsletter. **Advertising:** accepted. **Conventions/Meetings:** annual meeting, related to blood banking (exhibits) - usually September • annual Spring Workshop - May.

7106 ■ Michigan-Ontario Identification Association (MOIA)
PO Box 3809
Center Line, MI 48015
E-mail: webmaster@moia.org
URL: http://www.moia.org
Contact: John Satawa, Sec.-Treas.
Regional. Organizes people in the profession of forensic identification, investigation and scientific examination of physical evidence, through education, training and research. Advances the scientific techniques of forensic identification and crime detection.

Central Lake

7107 ■ Central Lake Chamber of Commerce
2587 N M-88 Hwy.
Central Lake, MI 49622
Ph: (231)544-3322
E-mail: clcc@torchlake.com
URL: http://www.central-lake.com
Contact: Jackie White, Pres.
Local. Promotes business and community development in Central Lake, MI area. **Conventions/Meetings:** monthly meeting - every 4th Tuesday.

Centreville

7108 ■ Centreville Lions Club - Michigan
PO Box 441
Centreville, MI 49032
E-mail: bcooley@net-link.net
URL: http://milions11b2.org
Local. Affiliated With: Lions Clubs International.

7109 ■ Phi Theta Kappa, Alpha Delta Omega Chapter - Glen Oaks Community College
c/o Kevin Gave
62249 Shimmel Rd.
Centreville, MI 49032
Ph: (269)467-9945
E-mail: gavekj@net-link.net
URL: http://www.ptk.org/directories/chapters/MI/256-1.htm
Contact: Kevin Gave, Advisor
Local.

7110 ■ St. Joseph County Association of Realtors
PO Box 340
Centreville, MI 49032-0340
Ph: (269)467-6261
Fax: (269)467-7232
E-mail: mjmyers@sjcarhomes.com
URL: http://www.sjcarhomes.com
Contact: Martha Myers, Exec.VP
Local. Strives to develop real estate business practices. Advocates the right to own, use and transfer real property. Provides a facility for professional development, research and exchange of information among members. **Affiliated With:** National Association of Realtors.

7111 ■ St. Joseph County United Way, Michigan
PO Box 577
Centreville, MI 49032
Ph: (269)467-9099
Fax: (269)467-7119
E-mail: info@sjcuf.com
URL: http://www.sjcuf.com
Contact: Kelly Hostetler, Dir.
Local. Affiliated With: United Way of America.

Champion

7112 ■ Ishpeming Beagle Club
c/o Sherry Solka
PO Box 274
Champion, MI 49814-0274
URL: National Affiliate–clubs.akc.org
Contact: Sherry Solka, Contact
Local.

Charlevoix

7113 ■ American Legion, Michigan Post 226
c/o Leslie T. Shapton
106 E Garfield
Charlevoix, MI 49720
Ph: (517)371-4720
Fax: (517)371-2401
URL: National Affiliate–www.legion.org
Contact: Leslie T. Shapton, Contact
Local. Affiliated With: American Legion.

7114 ■ CharEm United Way
PO Box 22
Charlevoix, MI 49720
Ph: (231)237-9551
URL: National Affiliate–national.unitedway.org
Local. Affiliated With: United Way of America.

7115 ■ Charlevoix Area Chamber of Commerce
408 Bridge St.
PO Box 358
Charlevoix, MI 49720-1417
Ph: (231)547-2101
Fax: (231)547-6633
Free: (800)951-2101
E-mail: info@charlevoix.org
URL: http://www.charlevoix.org
Contact: Jacqueline Merta, Pres.
Regional. Acts as the energizing and vitalizing force in the community. Aims to unite all individuals, retail, and industrial types of business, for the promotion of commerce and the betterment of the community. Helps businesses to prosper and grow; to increase job opportunities; to encourage an orderly expansion and development of all segments of the community; to contribute to the overall economic stability of the community; to encourage and promote the nation's private enterprise system of competitive marketing.

7116 ■ Charlevoix Rod and Gun Club
U.S. 31 N
PO Box 112
Charlevoix, MI 49720-0000
Ph: (231)547-2785
E-mail: rbyar@freeway.net
URL: http://charlevoixrodandgun.com
Contact: Mr. Ron Svoboda, Pres.
Founded: 1946. **Members:** 364. **Membership Dues:** $50 • senior, $35 (annual). **Staff:** 2. **Budget:** $75,000. **Local.** Offers shooting facilities, including rifle and pistol ranges, skeet, trap, sporting clays, and 5-stand. **Computer Services:** Mailing lists. **Affiliated With:** Michigan United Conservation Clubs. **Publications:** Newsletter, quarterly. **Circulation:** 364. **Conventions/Meetings:** monthly Membership Meeting, with informal dinner - 1st Thursday.

Charlotte

7117 ■ American Legion, Greenawalt-Flaherty Post 42
PO Box 741
Charlotte, MI 48813
Ph: (517)371-4720
Fax: (517)371-2401
URL: National Affiliate–www.legion.org
Local. Affiliated With: American Legion.

7118 ■ American Society for Quality, Lansing-Jackson Section 1008
c/o Grace Looney
1856 Glass Dr.
Charlotte, MI 48813-8726
Ph: (517)282-8961
E-mail: looneycqe@aol.com
URL: http://groups.asq.org/1008
Contact: Grace Looney, Contact
Local. Advances learning, quality improvement and knowledge exchange to improve business results and to create better workplaces and communities worldwide. Provides a forum for information exchange, professional development and continuous learning in the science of quality. **Affiliated With:** American Society for Quality.

7119 ■ Charlotte Chamber of Commerce
PO Box 356
Charlotte, MI 48813
Ph: (517)543-0400
Fax: (517)543-9638
E-mail: charlotte@ia4u.net
Contact: Ann Garvey, Dir.
Local.

7120 ■ Charlotte Lions Club
c/o Louise Bradley, Pres.
524 Emerald Dr.
Charlotte, MI 48813
Ph: (517)543-7833 (517)543-6683
E-mail: bradleylions@ia4u.net
URL: http://www.district11c2.org
Contact: Louise Bradley, Pres.
Local. Affiliated With: Lions Clubs International.

7121 ■ Eaton County Genealogical Society
PO Box 337
Charlotte, MI 48813-0337
Ph: (517)543-8792
Fax: (517)543-6999
E-mail: ecgsoc@juno.com
URL: http://www.rootsweb.com/~miecgs
Contact: Drouscella Halsey, Corr.Sec.
Founded: 1988. **Members:** 140. **Membership Dues:** single, $5 (annual) • single w/quarterly, $15 (annual) • family w/quarterly, $17 (annual). **State Groups:** 1. **Local.** Seeks to aid the general public in the pursuit of their ancestry and learning about the history of Eaton County. **Libraries: Type:** open to the public. **Holdings:** 3,000; articles, books, periodicals, photographs. **Subjects:** history - genealogy, court records, probate records. **Publications:** *Eaton County Quest*, quarterly. Magazine. Contains historical and genealogical information. **Price:** $15.00. ISSN: 1075-881. **Conventions/Meetings:** monthly general assembly - always third Wednesday of the month; none in June, July, August, and December • periodic workshop.

7122 ■ Eaton County United Way
PO Box 14
Charlotte, MI 48813
Ph: (517)543-5402
Fax: (517)543-5651
E-mail: ecuw@ecuw.org
URL: http://www.eatoncountyunitedway.org
Contact: Ms. Joni Risner, Exec.Dir.
Founded: 1971. **Members:** 50. **Staff:** 2. **Budget:** $80,000. **Local. Affiliated With:** United Way of America. **Formerly:** United Way of the Charlotte-Potterville Area; (2005) Eaton Rapids United Way.

7123 ■ Great Lakes Area Show Series Educational Dressage (GLASS-ED)
c/o Julie Hume
1396 W Kinsel Hwy.
Charlotte, MI 48813
Ph: (517)543-3358
E-mail: odie@cablespeed.com
URL: http://www.glass-ed.org
Contact: Julie Hume, Contact
Regional. Affiliated With: United States Dressage Federation.

7124 ■ Michigan National Wild Turkey Federation, Sycamore Creek Chapter
PO Box 387
Charlotte, MI 48813
Ph: (616)781-0071
URL: http://www.mi-nwtf.org/Sycamore.htm
Contact: Rob Whitaker, Pres.
Local.

7125 ■ Michigan Sheep Breeders Association (MSBA)
c/o Duane Tirrell, Exec.Sec.
700 Tirrell Rd.
Charlotte, MI 48813
Ph: (517)543-7395
E-mail: info@misheep.org
URL: http://www.misheep.org
Contact: Duane Tirrell, Exec.Sec.
State.

7126 ■ Police and Firemen's Insurance Association - Inghamn County Sheriff
c/o Harvey J. Clark
2935 Tubbs Rd.
Charlotte, MI 48813
Ph: (517)541-0386
URL: National Affiliate–www.pfia.net
Contact: Harvey J. Clark, Contact
Local. Affiliated With: Police and Firemen's Insurance Association.

Chassell

7127 ■ American Legion, Michigan Post 218
c/o Leo M. Leggett
RR 1, Box 434a
Chassell, MI 49916
Ph: (517)371-4720
Fax: (517)371-2401
URL: National Affiliate–www.legion.org
Contact: Leo M. Leggett, Contact
Local. Affiliated With: American Legion.

7128 ■ American Legion, Sauvola Post 265
19916 Schultz Rd.
Chassell, MI 49916
Ph: (517)371-4720
Fax: (517)371-2401
URL: National Affiliate–www.legion.org
Local. Affiliated With: American Legion.

Cheboygan

7129 ■ American Legion, Michigan Post 95
c/o Francis A. Barlow
PO Box 437
Cheboygan, MI 49721
Ph: (517)371-4720
Fax: (517)371-2401
URL: National Affiliate–www.legion.org
Contact: Francis A. Barlow, Contact
Local. Affiliated With: American Legion.

7130 ■ Black Lake Chapter of Sturgeon for Tomorrow
1604 N Black River Rd.
Cheboygan, MI 49721
Ph: (231)625-2776
Fax: (231)625-2775
Free: (888)603-2776
URL: http://www.sturgeonfortomorrow.org
Contact: Brenda Archambo, Pres.
Membership Dues: regular, $10 (annual). **Local.** Assists in the rehabilitation of Lake Sturgeon; works to advance education to further other charitable, educational and scientific research; and to engage in and facilitate scientific research furtherance of such purposes.

7131 ■ Cheboygan Area Chamber of Commerce (CACC)
124 N Main St.
PO Box 69
Cheboygan, MI 49721
Ph: (231)627-7183
Fax: (231)627-2770
Free: (800)968-3302
E-mail: mgrisdale@cheboygan.com
URL: http://www.cheboygan.com
Contact: Michael Grisdale, Exec.Dir.
Founded: 1943. **Members:** 416. **Staff:** 3. **Budget:** $200,000. **Local.** Promotes business and community development in the Cheboygan, MI area. Sponsors Home Show, Parades, Riverfest, AutumnFest and Buffalo Bash. **Publications:** *Cheboygan Area Chamber of Commerce Membership Directory and Buying Guide*, annual • *Executive Report*, monthly. Newsletter.

7132 ■ Cheboygan County Genealogical Society (CCGS)
PO Box 51
Cheboygan, MI 49721
Ph: (231)238-7611
E-mail: nhastie@voyager.net
URL: http://www.rootsweb.com/~miccgs/CCGSmainx.html
Contact: Nancy Hastie, Pres.
Founded: 1979. **Members:** 95. **Membership Dues:** individual, $10 (annual). **Local Groups:** 1. **Local.** Individuals interested in the genealogy, particularly but not limited to, Cheboygan County, MI. **Libraries: Type:** not open to the public; lending. **Holdings:** 100; books, periodicals. **Subjects:** genealogy. **Working Groups:** Computer Users. **Publications:** *Cheboygan Rivertown Roots*, quarterly. Newsletter. **Price:** included in membership dues. **Conventions/Meetings:** monthly meeting, business discussion; with speaker and workshop - always 2nd Wednesday in Cheboygan, MI • monthly meeting - always 3rd Tuesday in Cheboygan, MI.

7133 ■ Cheboygan County United Way
224 N Main St., Ste.A
Cheboygan, MI 49721-1640
Ph: (231)627-2288
URL: National Affiliate–national.unitedway.org
Local. Affiliated With: United Way of America.

7134 ■ Habitat for Humanity Cheboygan County
PO Box 309
Cheboygan, MI 49721-1802
Ph: (231)597-4663
Fax: (231)597-0496
E-mail: hfhcc@nmo.net
URL: http://www.geocities.com/hfhcheboyganco
Local. Affiliated With: Habitat for Humanity International.

7135 ■ North Star Figure Skating Association
PO Box 5278
Cheboygan, MI 49721
E-mail: howardscleaningd@hotmail.com
URL: National Affiliate–www.usfigureskating.org
Local. Provides programs to encourage participation and achievement in the sport of figure skating on ice. Defines and maintains uniform standards of skating

proficiency. Organizes and sponsors competitions and exhibitions for the purpose of stimulating interest in figure skating. **Affiliated With:** United States Figure Skating Association.

7136 ■ Straits Area Home Builders Association
c/o Gregory Elliott
PO Box 5203
Cheboygan, MI 49721-5203
Ph: (231)627-4725
Fax: (231)627-7871
E-mail: gelliott@chesaba.com
URL: National Affiliate–www.nahb.org
Contact: Greg Elliott, Exec. Officer
Local. Single and multifamily home builders, commercial builders, and others associated with the building industry. **Affiliated With:** National Association of Home Builders.

Chelsea

7137 ■ American Legion, Michigan Post 31
c/o Herbert J. Mc Kune
1700 Ridge Rd.
Chelsea, MI 48118
Ph: (517)371-4720
Fax: (517)371-2401
URL: National Affiliate–www.legion.org
Contact: Herbert J. Mc Kune, Contact
Local. Affiliated With: American Legion.

7138 ■ Ann Arbor Host Lions Club
c/o Harold Link, Sec.
4718 Cottonwood Ln.
Chelsea, MI 48118
Ph: (734)997-4681 (734)475-1602
E-mail: 2link@chartermi.net
URL: http://www.lionsdistrict11b1.org/lc_ann_arbor_host.htm
Contact: Harold Link, Sec.
Local. Affiliated With: Lions Clubs International.

7139 ■ Chelsea Area Chamber of Commerce
522 N Main St.
Chelsea, MI 48118
Ph: (734)475-1145
Fax: (734)475-6102
E-mail: info@chelseamichamber.org
URL: http://www.chelseamichamber.org
Contact: Bob Pierce, Exec.Dir.
Membership Dues: owner (including spouse), $150 • business (based on number of employees), $275-$550 • friend of chamber, $50 • non-profit organization, government taxing authority and elected official, $100. **Staff:** 3. **Local**. Promotes business and community development in Chelsea, MI area. **Telecommunication Services:** electronic mail, bpierce@chelseamichamber.org. **Publications:** Newsletter.

7140 ■ Chelsea Hockey Association
509 Coliseum Dr.
Chelsea, MI 48118
Ph: (734)433-9665
E-mail: info@chelseahockey.org
URL: http://www.chelseahockey.org
Contact: EJ Gilbert, Pres.
Founded: 2000. **Members:** 500. **Staff:** 10. **Local Groups:** 1. **Local**. Promotes youth hockey.

7141 ■ Chelsea Lions Club
c/o Paul Weber, Pres.
19990 Ivey Rd.
Chelsea, MI 48118
Ph: (734)475-2741
E-mail: weber2542@aol.com
URL: http://www.lionsdistrict11b1.org/lc_chelsea.htm
Contact: Paul Weber, Pres.
Local. Affiliated With: Lions Clubs International.

7142 ■ Chelsea United Way
PO Box 176
Chelsea, MI 48118-0176
Ph: (734)475-0020
URL: National Affiliate–national.unitedway.org
Local. Affiliated With: United Way of America.

7143 ■ National Speleological Society, Detroit Urban Grotto (DUG)
204 Washington St.
Chelsea, MI 48118
Ph: (313)522-0599
E-mail: beanl@michigan.gov
URL: http://home.comcast.net/~fisher-ridger
Contact: Larry Bean, Chm.
Local. Seeks to study, explore and conserve cave and karst resources. Protects access to caves and promotes responsible caving. Encourages responsible management of caves and their unique environments. **Affiliated With:** National Speleological Society.

Chesaning

7144 ■ American Legion, Chesaning Post 212
15053 Mckeighan Rd.
Chesaning, MI 48616
Ph: (517)371-4720
Fax: (517)371-2401
URL: National Affiliate–www.legion.org
Local. Affiliated With: American Legion.

7145 ■ Chesaning Chamber of Commerce (CCC)
218 N Front St.
PO Box 83
Chesaning, MI 48616
Ph: (989)845-3055
Fax: (989)845-6006
Free: (800)255-3055
E-mail: info@chesaningchamber.org
URL: http://www.chesaningchamber.org
Contact: Sandi Richardson, Exec.Dir.
Founded: 1926. **Members:** 150. **Staff:** 1. **Local**. Promotes business and community development in Chesaning, MI. **Libraries: Type:** open to the public. **Conventions/Meetings:** monthly board meeting - always second Monday.

7146 ■ Chesaning Lions Club
c/o Mary Vogelaar, Sec.
8344 Volkmer Rd.
Chesaning, MI 48616
Ph: (989)845-7302
E-mail: matyvolgelaar@aol.com
URL: http://www.geocities.com/dist11d1
Contact: Mary Vogelaar, Sec.
Local. Affiliated With: Lions Clubs International.

7147 ■ Kiwanis Club of Chesaning, Michigan
PO Box 138
Chesaning, MI 48616
E-mail: shparker@centurytel.net
URL: http://www.chesaningkiwanis.org
Contact: Kenn Bueche, Pres.
Local.

7148 ■ Michigan National Wild Turkey Federation, Shiawasse River Strutters Chapter
7150 W Ditch Rd.
Chesaning, MI 48616
Ph: (517)845-3166
URL: http://www.mi-nwtf.org/Shiawassee.htm
Contact: Cliff Smith, Pres.
Local.

7149 ■ Saginaw Alliance for the Mentally Ill
c/o Ray Albert, Pres.
11106 Baldwin Rd.
Chesaning, MI 48616
Ph: (517)845-2598
URL: http://mi.nami.org/sag.html
Contact: Ray Albert, Pres.
Local. Strives to improve the quality of life of children and adults with severe mental illness through support, education, research and advocacy. **Affiliated With:** National Alliance for the Mentally Ill.

Chesterfield

7150 ■ Macomb Dental Society (MDS)
27322 23 Mile Rd., Ste.1
Chesterfield, MI 48051
Ph: (586)677-9178
Fax: (586)677-2914
E-mail: macdent@tir.com
URL: http://www.macombdental.org
Contact: Dr. David Borlas, Exec.Dir.
Local. Represents the interests of dentists committed to the public's oral health, ethics and professional development. Encourages the improvement of the public's oral health and promotes the art and science of dentistry. **Affiliated With:** American Dental Association; Michigan Dental Association.

7151 ■ Michigan Organization of Diabetes Educators (MODE)
c/o Patricia Ripari, Treas.
53462 Spurry Ln.
Chesterfield, MI 48051
E-mail: pripari@comcast.net
URL: http://www.modeonline.org
Contact: Patricia Ripari, Treas.
State. Promotes the development of quality diabetes education for the diabetic consumer. Fosters communication and cooperation among individuals and organizations involved in diabetes patient education. Provides educational opportunities for the professional growth and development of members. **Affiliated With:** American Association of Diabetes Educators.

China

7152 ■ East China Consolidated Parent Teacher Organization
c/o Michele L. Defever
3575 King Rd.
China, MI 48054-2009
Local.

Clare

7153 ■ Clare Area Chamber of Commerce
429 N McEwan St.
Clare, MI 48617
Ph: (989)386-2442
Fax: (989)386-3173
Free: (888)ATC-LARE
E-mail: chamberoffice@claremichigan.com
URL: http://www.claremichigan.com
Contact: Ann Doherty, Pres.
Members: 235. **Staff:** 2. **Local**. Businesses seeking to promote economic and community development in the Clare, MI area. Sponsors Irish Festival and Summerfest. **Formerly:** Greater Clare Area Chamber of Commerce. **Publications:** *The Voice*, monthly. Newsletter. Alternate Formats: online. **Conventions/Meetings:** annual Crafts in the Park - trade show • bimonthly meeting.

7154 ■ Clare County Visitor and Convention Bureau
PO Box 226
Clare, MI 48617-0226
Ph: (989)386-6400
Free: (800)715-3550
E-mail: clareco@c-zone.net
URL: http://www.clarecounty.com
Contact: Lori Schuh, Exec.Dir.
Founded: 1997. **Members:** 15. **Staff:** 1. **Local. Publications:** *Visitor's Guide*, annual. **Price:** free. **Circulation:** 20,000. **Advertising:** accepted.

7155 ■ United Way and Volunteer Center of Clare County
PO Box 116
Clare, MI 48617-0116
Ph: (989)386-6015
Fax: (989)386-6548
E-mail: info@unitedwayclare.org
URL: http://www.unitedwayclare.org
Contact: Sandina Hages, Exec.Dir.
Local. Affiliated With: United Way of America.

Clarklake

7156 ■ Clark Lake Foundation
c/o Michael R. McKay
PO Box 224
Clarklake, MI 49234
Ph: (517)536-4300 (517)529-9331
Fax: (517)536-4211
Contact: Michael R. McKay, Pres.
Founded: 1997. **Members:** 10. **Budget:** $83,000. **Local. Committees:** Clark Lake Historical District.

7157 ■ Clarklake Lions Club
c/o Dorrol Ford, Sec.
3501 Reed Rd.
Clarklake, MI 49234
Ph: (517)529-4388
URL: http://www.lionsdistrict11b1.org/lc_clarklake.htm
Contact: Dorrol Ford, Sec.
Local. Affiliated With: Lions Clubs International.

Clarkston

7158 ■ American Legion, Campbell-Richmond Post 63
8047 Ortonville Rd.
Clarkston, MI 48348
Ph: (248)625-9912
Fax: (517)371-2401
URL: National Affiliate–www.legion.org
Local. Affiliated With: American Legion.

7159 ■ American Maltese Association (AMA)
c/o Richard Glenn
10175 Reese Rd.
Clarkston, MI 48348
URL: http://www.americanmaltese.org
Contact: Richard Glenn, Delegate
State. Affiliated With: American Kennel Club.

7160 ■ American Vaulting Association - Blue Moon Vaulters
c/o Karen Rach, Coach
10460 Allen Rd.
Clarkston, MI 48348
Ph: (248)625-2618
E-mail: sinbad5646@aol.com
URL: National Affiliate–www.americanvaulting.org
Contact: Karen Rach, Coach
Local. Affiliated With: American Vaulting Association.

7161 ■ American Vaulting Association - MSU Vaulters
c/o Karen Rach, Coach
10460 Allen Rd.
Clarkston, MI 48348
Ph: (248)625-2618
E-mail: metzge26@msu.edu
URL: National Affiliate–www.americanvaulting.org
Contact: Karen Rach, Coach
Local. Affiliated With: American Vaulting Association.

7162 ■ Clarkston Area Chamber of Commerce
5856 S Main
Clarkston, MI 48346
Ph: (248)625-8055
Fax: (248)625-8041
E-mail: info@clarkston.org
URL: http://www.clarkston.org
Contact: Penny Shanks, Exec.Dir.
Members: 500. **Local.**

7163 ■ Greater Detroit Romance Writers of America (GDRWA)
c/o Patti Shenberger, Pres.
6019 Mary Sue
Clarkston, MI 48346-3262
E-mail: president@gdrwa.org
URL: http://www.gdrwa.org
Contact: Patti Shenberger, Pres.
Local. Works to provide networking and support to individuals seriously pursuing a career in romance fiction. Helps writers become published and established in their writing field. **Affiliated With:** Romance Writers of America.

7164 ■ National Technical Honor Society - Oakland Schools Tech Campus Northwest - Michigan
8211 Big Lake Rd.
Clarkston, MI 48346
Ph: (248)922-5800
E-mail: chuck.locklear@oakland.k12.mi.us
URL: http://www.oakland.k12.mi.us
Contact: Chuck Locklear, Contact
Local.

7165 ■ Puppeteers of America - Detroit Puppeteers Guild
5248 Sashabaw Rd.
Clarkston, MI 48346
Ph: (248)623-0393
E-mail: thatpuppetguy@aol.com
URL: http://www.puppet-detroit.us
Contact: Brad Lowe, Pres.
Local.

Clawson

7166 ■ American Legion, Michigan Post 167
c/o David E. Cleary
655 S Main St.
Clawson, MI 48017
Ph: (517)371-4720
Fax: (517)371-2401
URL: National Affiliate–www.legion.org
Contact: David E. Cleary, Contact
Local. Affiliated With: American Legion.

7167 ■ Association for Professionals in Infection Control and Epidemiology, Greater Detroit
c/o Joan M. Wideman, CIC
208 Hendrickson Blvd.
Clawson, MI 48017-1688
Ph: (248)588-4467
Fax: (248)588-4467
E-mail: jmoody@botsford.org
URL: http://www.apicgd.org
Contact: Janet Moody, Pres.-Elect
Local. Works to influence, support and improve the quality of healthcare through the development of educational programs and standards. Promotes quality research and standardization of practices and procedures. **Affiliated With:** Association for Professionals in Infection Control and Epidemiology.

7168 ■ STARFLEET: USS Valkyrie
c/o Dwayne Sklar
705 W Elmwood Ave.
Clawson, MI 48017
E-mail: ussvalkyrie@region13.org
URL: http://valkyrie.region13.org
Contact: Dwayne Sklar, Contact
Local. Affiliated With: STARFLEET.

Climax

7169 ■ American Legion, Climaxscotts Post 465
PO Box 186
Climax, MI 49034
Ph: (517)371-4720
Fax: (517)371-2401
URL: National Affiliate–www.legion.org
Local. Affiliated With: American Legion.

Clinton

7170 ■ American Legion, Pieper-Hull-Sparks Post 176
204 Jackson St.
Clinton, MI 49236
Ph: (517)371-4720
Fax: (517)371-2401
URL: National Affiliate–www.legion.org
Local. Affiliated With: American Legion.

7171 ■ Southern Michigan Beagle Club
c/o Joanne MacRae
11890 N Adrian Hwy.
Clinton, MI 49236-9723
URL: National Affiliate–clubs.akc.org
Contact: Joanne MacRae, Contact
Local.

Clinton Township

7172 ■ American Legion, Detroit Police Post 161
PO Box 380416
Clinton Township, MI 48038
Ph: (517)371-4720
Fax: (517)371-2401
URL: National Affiliate–www.legion.org
Local. Affiliated With: American Legion.

7173 ■ ARC Services of Macomb
44050 Gratiot Ave.
Clinton Township, MI 48036-1308
Ph: (586)469-1600
Fax: (586)469-2527
E-mail: arcservices@arcservices.org
URL: http://www.arcservices.org
Contact: Lisa Piercey-Lepine, Contact
Founded: 1953. **Membership Dues:** individual, family, $25 (annual) • consumer, $15 (annual) • business, benefactor, $35 (annual). **Local.** People with disabilities, parents, friends, and professionals. Provides an array of services for people with disabilities in Macomb County. **Affiliated With:** Arc of the United States.

7174 ■ Clean Water Action of Clinton Township
38875 Harper
Clinton Township, MI 48036
Ph: (586)783-8900
Fax: (586)783-4033
E-mail: metrodetroit@cleanwater.org
Local.

7175 ■ Detroit Model Yacht Club No. 88
c/o Ralph Templin
23431 Donalson
Clinton Township, MI 48035
Ph: (810)791-6773
URL: http://www.orgsites.com/mi/dmyc
Contact: Ralph Templin, Contact
Local.

7176 ■ Girl Scouts of Macomb County - Otsikita Council
42804 Garfield
Clinton Township, MI 48038
Ph: (586)263-0220
Fax: (586)263-6320
Free: (866)575-0220
E-mail: dnikolas@girlscouts-macomb.org
URL: http://www.girlscouts-macomb.org
Local. Young girls and adult volunteers, corporate, government and individual supporters. Strives to develop potential and leadership skills among its members. Conducts trainings, educational programs and outdoor activities.

7177 ■ Habitat for Humanity Macomb County
42627 Garfield, Ste.217
Clinton Township, MI 48038
Ph: (586)263-1540
Fax: (586)263-9425
E-mail: info@macombhabitat.org
URL: http://www.macombhabitat.org
Contact: Daniel Wiiki, Exec.Dir
Local. Affiliated With: Habitat for Humanity International.

7178 ■ Kiwanis Club of Clinton Township, Michigan
c/o Bill Lakin, Pres.
44260 Boulder Dr.
Clinton Township, MI 48038
Ph: (586)286-3498
E-mail: lakin25@comcast.net
URL: http://clintontownshipkiwanis.org
Contact: Bill Lakin, Pres.
Local.

7179 ■ Macomb County Medical Society
36359 Harper, Ste.B
Clinton Township, MI 48035
Ph: (586)790-3090
Fax: (586)790-4950
E-mail: mcms@msms.org
URL: http://www.msms.org
Contact: Shirley Montagne, Exec.Dir.
Local. Advances the art and science of medicine. Promotes patient care and the betterment of public health. **Affiliated With:** Michigan State Medical Society.

7180 ■ Macomb Literacy Partners (MLP)
c/o Marsha DeVergilio, Interim Dir.
Macomb County Lib.
16480 Hall Rd.
Clinton Township, MI 48038-1132
Ph: (586)286-2750
Fax: (586)286-4023
Free: (800)544-1340
E-mail: read@macombliteracy.org
URL: http://www.macombliteracy.org
Contact: Sue Javid, Pres.
Founded: 1984. **Membership Dues:** sponsoring partner, $25 (annual) • contributing partner, $50 (annual) • sustaining partner, $100 (annual). **Budget:** $230,000. **Local.** Strives to eradicate adult illiteracy in Macomb County by training volunteer tutors to work one-on-one with adults who read below a level of functional literacy. **Affiliated With:** ProLiteracy Worldwide. **Also Known As:** Macomb Reading Partners. **Formerly:** Macomb Literacy Project. **Publications:** *Read On*, quarterly. Newsletter. **Conventions/Meetings:** annual seminar - always September.

7181 ■ Michigan Association of Commercial Dental Laboratories (MACDL)
c/o Irene Leidich, Exec.Sec./Program Coor.
22800 Stair Dr.
Clinton Township, MI 48036-2747
Ph: (586)469-1121
Fax: (586)469-1147
E-mail: irene@macdl.org
URL: http://www.macdl.org
Contact: Irene Leidich, Exec.Sec./Program Coor.
State.

7182 ■ Michigan Association for Education Data Systems (MAEDS)
c/o Butch Murray, Treas.
44001 Garfield Rd.
Clinton Township, MI 48038-1100
E-mail: bmurray@misd.net
URL: http://www.maeds.org
Contact: Butch Murray, Treas.
State. Seeks to improve the quality of education through the innovative use of technology. Facilitates the exchange of information and resources between policy makers and professional organizations. Encourages research and evaluation relating to the use of technology in education. **Affiliated With:** International Society for Technology in Education.

7183 ■ Michigan Wrestling Federation (MWF)
39045 Bramblebush Ct.
Clinton Township, MI 48038
Ph: (586)286-3733 (586)723-2402
Free: (877)297-4950
E-mail: mail@mwfonline.org
URL: http://www.mwfonline.org
Contact: Al Kastl, State Dir.
State. Affiliated With: U.S.A. Wrestling.

7184 ■ Mount Clemens - Macomb County Gem and Lapidary Society
44314 Macomb Indus. Dr.
Clinton Township, MI 48036
Ph: (586)468-2939
E-mail: club-info@sbcglobal.net
URL: http://www.orgsites.commimichigan-clubindex.html
Contact: Bobbie Kranner, Sec.
Local. Aims to further the study of Earth Sciences and the practice of lapidary arts and mineralogy. **Affiliated With:** American Federation of Mineralogical Societies.

7185 ■ National Technical Honor Society - Pankow Vocational Technical Center Michigan
24600 F. V. Pankow Blvd.
Clinton Township, MI 48036
Ph: (586)783-6570
Fax: (586)783-6577
E-mail: hopege@lc-ps.org
URL: http://www.lc-ps.org
Contact: Gerry Hope, Contact
Local.

7186 ■ Phi Theta Kappa, Beta Lambda Kappa Chapter - Macomb Community College
c/o Diane Wisnewski
44575 Garfield Rd.
Clinton Township, MI 48038
Ph: (586)286-2000
E-mail: wisnewskid@macomb.edu
URL: http://www.ptk.org/directories/chapters/MI/10855-2.htm
Contact: Diane Wisnewski, Advisor
Local.

7187 ■ RSVP of Macomb
c/o Suzanne White, Dir.
16931 19 Mile Rd., Ste.140
Clinton Township, MI 48038
Ph: (586)412-8054
Fax: (586)412-8084
E-mail: csmseniors@hotmail.com
URL: http://www.csmacomb.org
Contact: Suzanne White, Dir.
Local. Affiliated With: Retired and Senior Volunteer Program.

Clio

7188 ■ American Legion, Neeley La Bar Post 158
3400 W Vienna Rd.
Clio, MI 48420
Ph: (517)371-4720
Fax: (517)371-2401
URL: National Affiliate–www.legion.org
Local. Affiliated With: American Legion.

7189 ■ Clio Lions Club
c/o Richard Taylor, Pres.
545 Allen St.
Clio, MI 48420
Ph: (810)686-2136
URL: http://www.geocities.com/dist11d1
Contact: Richard Taylor, Pres.
Local. Affiliated With: Lions Clubs International.

7190 ■ Friends of the Trolley Line Trail
c/o Sandra Bisson
PO Box 543
Clio, MI 48420-0543
Ph: (810)639-4547 (810)686-4480
Fax: (810)687-7777
Contact: Sandy Bisson, Contact
Founded: 1998. **Members:** 35. **Membership Dues:** $25 (annual). **Local.**

7191 ■ Genesee County Alliance for the Mentally Ill
c/o Erma Barber, Acting Pres.
8444 Webster
Clio, MI 48420
Ph: (810)686-1358 (810)232-6498
URL: http://mi.nami.org/gen.html
Contact: Erma Barber, Acting Pres.
Local. Strives to improve the quality of life of children and adults with severe mental illness through support, education, research and advocacy. **Affiliated With:** National Alliance for the Mentally Ill.

7192 ■ Michigan Society of Radiologic Technologists
c/o Todd E. Williams, Pres.
13090 N Linden Rd.
Clio, MI 48420-8206
Ph: (810)687-1719 (810)235-9311
Fax: (810)235-9318
E-mail: twilliams0013@msn.com
URL: National Affiliate–www.asrt.org
State. Represents the interests of professionals working in the field of radiologic technology. Advances the science of radiologic technology through education, research and advocacy. Strengthens professional standards.

7193 ■ National Association of Miniature Enthusiasts - Pinocchio's Mini Makers
c/o Brenda Ellingson
3251 W Willard Rd.
Clio, MI 48420
Ph: (810)686-2175
E-mail: belling@comcast.net
URL: http://www.miniatures.org/states/MI.html
Contact: Brenda Ellingson, Contact
Local. Affiliated With: National Association of Miniature Enthusiasts.

7194 ■ Ruffed Grouse Society, Keith Davis Chapter
c/o Roger Moore
1278 E Farrand Rd.
Clio, MI 48420
Ph: (810)687-2347
E-mail: rmoore6888@aol.com
URL: National Affiliate–www.ruffedgrousesociety.org
Contact: Roger Moore, Contact
Local. Affiliated With: Ruffed Grouse Society.

Coldwater

7195 ■ American Legion, Coldwater Post 52
84 W Chicago St.
Coldwater, MI 49036
Ph: (517)371-4720
Fax: (517)371-2401
URL: National Affiliate–www.legion.org
Local. Affiliated With: American Legion.

7196 ■ Branch County Area Chamber of Commerce
20 Div. St.
Coldwater, MI 49036-1966
Ph: (517)278-5985
Fax: (517)278-8369
E-mail: info@branch-county.com
URL: http://www.branch-county.com
Contact: Hillary Eley, Pres.
Founded: 1943. **Members:** 557. **Staff:** 3. **Local**. Promotes business and community development in the Branch County, MI area. **Awards:** Business of the Year. **Frequency:** annual. **Type:** recognition • Citizen of the Year. **Frequency:** annual. **Type:** recognition • Community Organization of the Year. **Frequency:** annual. **Type:** recognition • Teacher of the Year. **Frequency:** annual. **Type:** recognition. **Formerly:** (2006) Coldwater - Branch County Chamber of Commerce. **Publications:** *The Connection*, monthly. Newsletter • Directory, annual. **Price:** $5.00 for nonmembers; free for members.

7197 ■ Branch County Association of Realtors
28 W Chicago St., Ste.3E
Coldwater, MI 49036
Ph: (517)278-3192
Fax: (517)278-4164
E-mail: info@bcarealtors.com
URL: National Affiliate–www.realtor.org
Contact: Darlene Harmon, Exec. Officer
Local. Strives to develop real estate business practices. Advocates the right to own, use and transfer real property. Provides a facility for professional development, research and exchange of information among members. **Affiliated With:** National Association of Realtors.

7198 ■ Branch County Literacy Council
10 E Chicago St.
Coldwater, MI 49036-1615
Ph: (517)279-9833
Fax: (517)279-7134
E-mail: brcolitco@cbpu.com
URL: National Affiliate–www.proliteracy.org
Contact: Ms. Ruth Vanderpool-Omlor, Dir.
Membership Dues: individual, $15 (annual). **Local**. Strives to provide opportunities and supports to local residents who wish to increase their reading skills. Provides one-to-one tutor for adults. **Libraries: Type:** lending. **Holdings:** books. **Affiliated With:** ProLiteracy Worldwide.

7199 ■ Branch County Tourism Bureau
20 Div. St.
Coldwater, MI 49036
Ph: (517)278-0241
Fax: (517)278-8369
Free: (800)968-9333
E-mail: dyee@discover-michigan.com
URL: http://www.discover-michigan.com
Contact: Debra Yee, Exec.Dir.
Founded: 1994. **Local**. Promotes Branch County, MI as a tourist destination.

7200 ■ Branch County United Way
PO Box 312
Coldwater, MI 49036-0312
Ph: (517)279-7129
URL: National Affiliate–national.unitedway.org
Local. **Affiliated With:** United Way of America.

7201 ■ Sweet Adelines International, Sauk Trail Sound Chapter
H&C Burnside Senior Ctr.
65 Grahl Dr.
Coldwater, MI 49036-1572
Ph: (517)849-9758
URL: National Affiliate–www.sweetadelineintl.org
Contact: Patricia Morgan, Contact
Local. Advances the musical art form of barbershop harmony through education and performances. Provides education, training and coaching in the development of women's four-part barbershop harmony. **Affiliated With:** Sweet Adelines International.

Coleman

7202 ■ Coleman Lions Club
c/o Albert Roeseler, Pres.
3972 Harsh Dr.
Coleman, MI 48618
Ph: (989)465-6060 (989)465-6482
Fax: (989)465-1099
E-mail: abroeseler@dmci.net
URL: http://lions.silverthorn.biz/11-e1
Contact: Albert Roeseler, Pres.
Local. **Affiliated With:** Lions Clubs International.

7203 ■ Saginaw Valley Orchid Society
c/o Annette Sobolewski
5695 Wade Rd.
Coleman, MI 48618
Ph: (989)465-1534
E-mail: annastas@tir.com
URL: National Affiliate–www.orchidweb.org
Contact: Annette Sobolewski, Contact
Local. Professional growers, botanists, hobbyists, and others interested in extending the knowledge, production, use, and appreciation of orchids. **Affiliated With:** American Orchid Society.

Coloma

7204 ■ American Legion, Coloma Post 362
PO Box 103
Coloma, MI 49038
Ph: (517)371-4720
Fax: (517)371-2401
URL: National Affiliate–www.legion.org
Local. **Affiliated With:** American Legion.

7205 ■ Berrien County Chapter of Pheasants Forever
4385 Schumhl Rd.
Coloma, MI 49038
Ph: (269)849-3035
E-mail: roblskinner@hotmail.com
URL: http://www.berriencountypf.com
Contact: Rob Skinner, Sec.
Local. **Affiliated With:** Pheasants Forever.

7206 ■ Coloma Lions Club
PO Box 698
Coloma, MI 49038
Ph: (269)468-3959 (269)468-6526
E-mail: dhafer@juno.com
URL: http://colomami.lionwap.org
Contact: Don Hafer, Sec.
Local. **Affiliated With:** Lions Clubs International.

7207 ■ Coloma-Watervliet Area Chamber of Commerce (CWACC)
PO Box 418
Coloma, MI 49038
Ph: (269)468-9160
Fax: (269)468-7088
E-mail: info@coloma-watervliet.org
URL: http://www.coloma-watervliet.org
Contact: Sandy Kraemer, Pres.
Membership Dues: full, $75. **Local**. Promotes businesses in the Coloma-Watervliet area. Organizes Business After Hours, Welcome Baskets to new businesses, ribbon cuttings, ground breakings and offers quarterly newsletters and listing on the website to members. **Formerly:** (2005) Coloma Area Chamber of Commerce.

7208 ■ Driftskippers Snowmobile Club
PO Box 279
Coloma, MI 49038
Ph: (269)468-6093
URL: http://www.driftskippers.com
Membership Dues: single, $12 • family, $20. **Local**.

7209 ■ Lakeland Valley District Dental Society
4770 Bundy Rd.
Coloma, MI 49038-9470
Ph: (269)468-7625
Fax: (269)468-7721
URL: National Affiliate–www.ada.org
Contact: Ms. Wendy Gire, Exec.Dir.
Local. Represents the interests of dentists committed to the public's oral health, ethics and professional development. Encourages the improvement of the public's oral health and promotes the art and science of dentistry. **Affiliated With:** American Dental Association; Michigan Dental Association.

Colon

7210 ■ American Legion, Snyder-Lewis-Welty Post 454
PO Box 251
Colon, MI 49040
Ph: (517)371-4720
Fax: (517)371-2401
URL: National Affiliate–www.legion.org
Local. **Affiliated With:** American Legion.

Columbiaville

7211 ■ Lapeer County Alliance for the Mentally Ill
c/o Dottie Arms, Pres.
3366 Kalm Dr.
Columbiaville, MI 48421
Ph: (810)982-9230
URL: http://mi.nami.org/lap.html
Contact: Dottie Arms, Pres.
Local. Strives to improve the quality of life of children and adults with severe mental illness through support, education, research and advocacy. **Affiliated With:** National Alliance for the Mentally Ill.

Columbus

7212 ■ American Legion, Department of Street Railways Post 394
2144 Arlington Rd.
Columbus, MI 48063
Ph: (517)371-4720
Fax: (517)371-2401
URL: National Affiliate–www.legion.org
Local. **Affiliated With:** American Legion.

Commerce Township

7213 ■ American Association for Medical Transcription, Southeast Michigan Chapter
c/o Laurie Umlauf, Pres.
486 Charlevoix St.
Commerce Township, MI 48382
E-mail: laurieumlauf@aol.com
URL: http://www.aamt.org/ca/smc
Contact: Laurie Umlauf, Pres.
Local. Works to represent and advance the profession of medical transcription and its practitioners. **Affiliated With:** American Association for Medical Transcription.

Comstock Park

7214 ■ American Legion, Louis Teistler Post 47
3811 W River Dr.
Comstock Park, MI 49321
Ph: (517)371-4720
Fax: (517)371-2401
URL: National Affiliate–www.legion.org
Local. **Affiliated With:** American Legion.

7215 ■ Timberland Resource Conservation and Development Council
6655 Alpine Ave. NW
Comstock Park, MI 49321
Ph: (616)784-1090
Fax: (616)784-1268
E-mail: steven.law@mi.usda.gov
URL: http://www.natureandpeople.org
Contact: Steven V. Law, Coor.
Local. Affiliated With: National Association of Resource Conservation and Development Councils.

Concord

7216 ■ American Legion, Concord-Pulaski-Memorial Post 81
310 Homer St.
Concord, MI 49237
Ph: (517)371-4720
Fax: (517)371-2401
URL: National Affiliate–www.legion.org
Local. Affiliated With: American Legion.

7217 ■ Concord Lions Club - Michigan
c/o Albert E. Aldrich, Sec.
PO Box 73
Concord, MI 49237
Ph: (517)524-8490
URL: http://www.lionsdistrict11b1.org/lc_concord.htm
Contact: Albert E. Aldrich, Sec.
Local. Affiliated With: Lions Clubs International.

Conklin

7218 ■ American Legion, Michigan Post 537
c/o Reinhard W. Roman
19340a 32nd Ave.
Conklin, MI 49403
Ph: (517)371-4720
Fax: (517)371-2401
URL: National Affiliate–www.legion.org
Contact: Reinhard W. Roman, Contact
Local. Affiliated With: American Legion.

Constantine

7219 ■ American Legion, Michigan Post 223
c/o Arthur E. Stears
65079 US 131 N
Constantine, MI 49042
Ph: (517)371-4720
Fax: (517)371-2401
URL: National Affiliate–www.legion.org
Contact: Arthur E. Stears, Contact
Local. Affiliated With: American Legion.

7220 ■ Western Michigan Appaloosa Horse Club
c/o Terry Shelhamer, Pres.
13775 Riverside Dr.
Constantine, MI 49042
Ph: (269)435-7276
Fax: (269)445-8202
E-mail: bestfarms@triton.com
URL: http://www.wmarapp.com
Contact: Terry Shelhamer, Pres.
Local. Affiliated With: Appaloosa Horse Club.

Conway

7221 ■ Northwoods Area of Narcotics Anonymous
PO Box 71
Conway, MI 49722
Ph: (231)348-1866
E-mail: northwoodsarea@michigan-na.org
URL: http://michigan-na.org/northwoods/index.htm
Local. Affiliated With: Narcotics Anonymous.

Cooks

7222 ■ American Legion, Manistique Post 83
687 N Peterson Rd.
Cooks, MI 49817
Ph: (517)371-4720
Fax: (517)371-2401
URL: National Affiliate–www.legion.org
Local. Affiliated With: American Legion.

Coopersville

7223 ■ Coopersville Area Chamber of Commerce
289 Danforth St.
Coopersville, MI 49404-0135
Ph: (616)997-9731 (616)997-5164
Fax: (616)997-6679
E-mail: jrichardson@cityofcoopersville.com
URL: http://www.coopersville.com
Contact: Mrs. Jan Richardson, Exec.Dir
Members: 240. **Membership Dues:** business with under 25 employees, $150 (annual) • business with 26-100 employees, $250 (annual) • business with 101-250 employees, $375 (annual). **Staff:** 2. **For-Profit. Local. Telecommunication Services:** electronic mail, ctimmerman@cityofcoopersville.com. **Publications:** Newsletter. **Advertising:** accepted • Directory. **Advertising:** accepted.

7224 ■ International Union, United Automobile, Aerospace and Agricultural Implement Workers of America, AFL-CIO - Local Union 2151
140 N 64th Ave.
Coopersville, MI 49404
Ph: (616)837-9339
Fax: (616)837-5876
E-mail: spowers@uaw2151.org
URL: http://www.uaw2151.org
Contact: John Blomeling, Contact
Members: 628. **Local.** AFL-CIO. **Affiliated With:** International Union, United Automobile, Aerospace and Agricultural Implement Workers of America.

Copemish

7225 ■ American Legion, Read-Osborne Post 531
18483 Cadillac Hwy.
Copemish, MI 49625
Ph: (517)371-4720
Fax: (517)371-2401
URL: National Affiliate–www.legion.org
Local. Affiliated With: American Legion.

Corunna

7226 ■ Friends of the Corunna Historical Village of Shiawassee County
c/o Judy Horton
402 N. Shiawassee St.
Corunna, MI 48817-1036
Local.

Covert

7227 ■ Covert Township Lions Club
PO Box 208
Covert, MI 49043
Ph: (269)764-8106
E-mail: rllorej@aol.com
URL: http://coverttwpmi.lionwap.org
Contact: Cecilia Seabury, Pres.
Local. Affiliated With: Lions Clubs International.

Croswell

7228 ■ American Legion, Cecil Service Post 255
97 W Harrington Rd.
Croswell, MI 48422
Ph: (517)371-4720
Fax: (517)371-2401
URL: National Affiliate–www.legion.org
Local. Affiliated With: American Legion.

Croton

7229 ■ American Legion, Michigan Post 381
c/o Walter F. Howarth
6580 Croton Hardy Dr.
Croton, MI 49337
Ph: (231)652-7776
Fax: (517)371-2401
URL: National Affiliate–www.legion.org
Contact: Walter F. Howarth, Contact
Local. Affiliated With: American Legion.

Crystal

7230 ■ Crystal Lions Club - Michigan
c/o Deborah Wilson, Pres.
300 S Main St.
Crystal, MI 48818
Ph: (989)824-0692 (989)235-5223
E-mail: borntofish@cmsinter.net
URL: http://crystalmi.lionwap.org
Contact: Tom Crites, Sec.
Local. Affiliated With: Lions Clubs International.

Crystal Falls

7231 ■ American Legion, Michigan Post 87
c/o Louis Bowman
203 Lind Rd.
Crystal Falls, MI 49920
Ph: (517)371-4720
Fax: (517)371-2401
URL: National Affiliate–www.legion.org
Contact: Louis Bowman, Contact
Local. Affiliated With: American Legion.

Curtis

7232 ■ Michigan National Wild Turkey Federation, U.P. Snow Gobblers
W 17545 Whispering Pine Rd., Apt. 30
Curtis, MI 49820
URL: http://www.mi-nwtf.org/UPsnow.htm
Contact: Roger Shoemaker, Pres.
Local.

Davisburg

7233 ■ Border Beagle Club
c/o Charles P. Green
11655 Eagle Rd.
Davisburg, MI 48350-1416
URL: National Affiliate–clubs.akc.org
Contact: Charles P. Green, Contact
Local.

Davison

7234 ■ American Legion, Burton Post 130
719 E Chelsea Cir.
Davison, MI 48423
Ph: (517)371-4720
Fax: (517)371-2401
URL: National Affiliate–www.legion.org
Local. Affiliated With: American Legion.

7235 ■ American Legion, Michigan Post 267
c/o Charles N. Skellenger
10309 E Davison Rd.
Davison, MI 48423
Ph: (517)371-4720
Fax: (517)371-2401
URL: National Affiliate–www.legion.org
Contact: Charles N. Skellenger, Contact
Local. Affiliated With: American Legion.

7236 ■ Davison Area Chamber of Commerce (DACC)
105 E 2nd St., Ste.7
Davison, MI 48423
Ph: (810)653-6266
Fax: (810)653-0669
E-mail: dcofcomm@yahoo.com
Contact: Phil Becker, Exec.Dir.
Founded: 1951. **Members:** 250. **Membership Dues:** $150 (annual). **Staff:** 1. **Local.** Promotes business and community development in the Davison, MI area. Sponsors annual Miss Davison Pageant. **Awards:** Davison Chamber of Commerce Service Scholarship. **Frequency:** annual. **Type:** scholarship. **Recipient:** for volunteer service in community. **Publications:** *Chamber Review*, quarterly. Newspaper. Quarterly business spotlight section of weekly town paper. **Price:** free. **Circulation:** 10,000. **Advertising:** accepted. **Conventions/Meetings:** annual Candlewalk - meeting • annual Fall Pumpkinfest - festival • monthly general assembly - second Wednesday.

7237 ■ Davison Athletic Club
G-2140 Fairway Dr.
Davison, MI 48423
Ph: (810)658-8153 (810)653-9602
URL: http://www.usatt.org/clubs
Contact: Jon Bosika, Contact
Local. Affiliated With: U.S.A. Table Tennis.

7238 ■ Goodrich Lions Club
c/o Stephen Hill, Sec.
5385 Stimson Rd.
Davison, MI 48423
Ph: (810)636-2623
E-mail: hillsfarm@centrytel.net
URL: http://www.geocities.com/dist11d1
Contact: Stephen Hill, Sec.
Local. Affiliated With: Lions Clubs International.

7239 ■ Song of the Lakes Sweet Adelines Chorus
Davison Senior Ctr.
10135 Lapeer Rd.
Davison, MI 48423-8171
Ph: (810)742-0977
E-mail: sasongofthelakes@webtv.net
URL: http://songofthelakeschorus.com
Contact: Kelli Kelly, Dir.
Local. Advances the musical art form of barbershop harmony through education and performances. Provides education, training and coaching in the development of women's four-part barbershop harmony. **Affiliated With:** Sweet Adelines International.

De Tour Village

7240 ■ Eastern Upper Peninsula Fine Arts Council
c/o W. R. Wytiaz
PO Box 202
De Tour Village, MI 49725
Ph: (906)297-8103
E-mail: info@eupfac.org
URL: http://www.eupfac.org
Local.

7241 ■ Forgotten Eagles
c/o Terrence Nelson, Pres.
PO Box 151
De Tour Village, MI 49725-0151
Ph: (906)297-2141
E-mail: diligaf@lighthouse.net
URL: http://www.forgotteneagles.org
Contact: Terrence Nelson, Pres.
Local.

Dearborn

7242 ■ AAA Michigan
18800 Hubbard Dr., No. 100
Dearborn, MI 48126
Ph: (313)336-0990
Free: (800)222-4304
URL: http://www.aaamichigan.com
State.

7243 ■ Allen Park Lions Club
c/o Lester Worth, Pres.
3731 Gertrude St.
Dearborn, MI 48124
Ph: (313)389-4286 (313)562-4728
URL: http://www.metrodetroitlions.org
Contact: Lester Worth, Pres.
Local. Affiliated With: Lions Clubs International.

7244 ■ American Legion, Armenian Vartan Post 307
St. Sarkis Armenian Church
19300 Ford Rd.
Dearborn, MI 48128
Ph: (517)371-4720
Fax: (517)371-2401
URL: National Affiliate–www.legion.org
Local. Affiliated With: American Legion.

7245 ■ American Legion, Ford Motor Company Post 173
4211 Maple St.
Dearborn, MI 48126
Ph: (517)371-4720
Fax: (517)371-2401
URL: National Affiliate–www.legion.org
Local. Affiliated With: American Legion.

7246 ■ American Legion, Fort Dearborn Post 364
3001 S Telegraph Rd.
Dearborn, MI 48124
Ph: (517)371-4720
Fax: (517)371-2401
URL: National Affiliate–www.legion.org
Local. Affiliated With: American Legion.

7247 ■ American Legion, Michigan Post 555
c/o William S. Knudsen
23615 Oak St.
Dearborn, MI 48128
Ph: (517)371-4720
Fax: (517)371-2401
URL: National Affiliate–www.legion.org
Contact: William S. Knudsen, Contact
Local. Affiliated With: American Legion.

7248 ■ Arab-American Alliance for the Mentally Ill
c/o Agnes Hagopian, Pres.
7739 Hartwell
Dearborn, MI 48126
Ph: (313)581-3583
URL: http://mi.nami.org/ara.html
Contact: Agnes Hagopian, Pres.
Local. Strives to improve the quality of life of children and adults with severe mental illness through support, education, research and advocacy. **Affiliated With:** National Alliance for the Mentally Ill.

7249 ■ Association for Computing Machinery, University of Michigan-Dearborn
4901 Evergreen Rd.
Dearborn, MI 48128
Ph: (313)436-9145
Fax: (313)593-9967
E-mail: boss@umich.edu
URL: http://www.engin.umd.umich.edu/~acm
Contact: Nathan Whitehead, Chm.
Founded: 1947. **Local.** Works to advance the art, science, engineering and application of information technology. Serves professional and public interests through open interchange of information, and promotes professional and ethical standards. **Affiliated With:** Association for Computing Machinery.

7250 ■ Church and Synagogue Library Association, Metro Detroit Chapter (CSLA-MDC)
413 Robindale Ave.
Dearborn, MI 48128-1590
Ph: (313)278-3689
Fax: (313)977-3734
Free: (800)LIB-CSLA
E-mail: getwag@aol.com
Contact: Gail Waggoner, Pres.
Founded: 1986. **Members:** 35. **Membership Dues:** individual, $37 (annual) • church or synagogue, $67 (annual) • affiliate group, $105 (annual) • institution, $125 (annual). **State Groups:** 4. **Local.** Church and synagogue librarians and interested individuals in southeastern Michigan. Aids in establishing and maintaining congregational libraries. Provides a forum for the exchange of information on library maintenance. **Affiliated With:** Church and Synagogue Library Association. **Publications:** *Church and Synagogue Library Guides*, bimonthly. **Price:** included in membership dues • *Tracts*, bimonthly • Bibliographies, bimonthly • Video, bimonthly. **Conventions/Meetings:** annual meeting (exhibits).

7251 ■ Dearborn Area Alliance for the Mentally Ill
c/o Alfred H. Chapman, Pres.
461 Ft. Dearborn St.
Dearborn, MI 48124
Ph: (313)563-1245
URL: http://mi.nami.org/dbr.html
Contact: Alfred H. Chapman, Pres.
Local. Strives to improve the quality of life of children and adults with severe mental illness through support, education, research and advocacy. **Affiliated With:** National Alliance for the Mentally Ill.

7252 ■ Dearborn Area Board of Realtors (DABOR)
2350 Monroe Blvd.
Dearborn, MI 48124
Ph: (313)278-2220
E-mail: support@dabor.com
URL: http://www.dabor.com
Contact: Kathy Viculis, Exec. Officer
Founded: 1926. **Local.** Promotes education, high professional standards, and modern techniques in specialized real estate work.

7253 ■ Dearborn Chamber of Commerce
15544 Michigan Ave.
Dearborn, MI 48126
Ph: (313)584-6100
Fax: (313)584-9818
E-mail: info@dearbornchamber.org
URL: http://www.dearbornchamber.org
Members: 630. **Membership Dues:** between 1-10 employees, $185 (annual). **Staff:** 4. **Local.** Aims to promote Dearborn and to help its members to succeed. Promotes business in Dearborn by listing their businesses on the website and on printed directory. Organizes event for networking between members. **Publications:** *Dearborn Business Journal*, monthly. Magazine. Includes news about local businesses and information about chamber events and activities. **Advertising:** accepted • *Newsbyte*, biweekly. Newsletter. Contains upcoming events and

deadlines. **Advertising:** accepted. Alternate Formats: online • Membership Directory, annual. **Advertising:** accepted.

7254 ■ Dearborn Community Arts Council (DCAC)
c/o Timothy M. Briody, Exec.Dir.
15801 Michigan Ave.
Dearborn, MI 48126
Ph: (313)943-3095
Fax: (313)943-2368
E-mail: tbriody@ci.dearborn.mi.us
URL: http://www.dcacarts.org
Contact: Timothy M. Briody, Exec.Dir.
Founded: 1969. **Local**. Works to facilitate, encourage, and support the arts.

7255 ■ Dearborn Figure Skating Club (DFSC)
PO Box 5581
Dearborn, MI 48128
Ph: (313)943-4098
Fax: (313)584-4549
E-mail: dfscsk8rs@aol.com
URL: http://www.dfsc.ws
Contact: Shannon Iatzko, Pres.
Local. Provides programs to encourage participation and achievement in the sport of figure skating on ice. Defines and maintains uniform standards of skating proficiency. Organizes and sponsors competitions and exhibitions for the purpose of stimulating interest in figure skating. **Affiliated With:** United States Figure Skating Association.

7256 ■ Dearborn Lions Club
c/o Ronald Haining, Pres.
3355 Monroe St.
Dearborn, MI 48124
Ph: (313)561-8681
E-mail: mexican@peoplepc.com
URL: http://www.metrodetroitlions.org
Contact: Ronald Haining, Pres.
Local. Affiliated With: Lions Clubs International.

7257 ■ Dearborn Soccer Club
c/o Marvin Purdy, Pres
PO Box 741
Dearborn, MI 48121-0741
Ph: (313)565-4433
E-mail: mpurdy@dearbornsoccer.org
URL: http://www.dearbornsoccer.org
Local.

7258 ■ Detroit Chinese Business Association
PO Box 2769
Dearborn, MI 48123
E-mail: info@dcba.com
URL: http://www.dcba.com
Contact: Mr. Raymond Xu, Pres.
Founded: 1995. **Members:** 1,500. **Languages:** Chichewa, English. **Local**. Fosters beneficial business relationship between Chinese and American business. Serves as a catalyst to promote entrepreneurship within the Chinese American community. **Publications:** *DCBA Online*, monthly. Newsletter. Contains reports of DCBA activities. **Circulation:** 1,500. **Advertising:** accepted. Alternate Formats: online.

7259 ■ Detroit Hispanic Lions Club
c/o Jesse Anaya, Pres.
1416 Nowlin St.
Dearborn, MI 48124
Ph: (313)278-3552
URL: http://www.metrodetroitlions.org
Contact: Jesse Anaya, Pres.
Local. Affiliated With: Lions Clubs International.

7260 ■ Haigh PTA
601 N Silvery Ln.
Dearborn, MI 48128
Ph: (313)827-6200
URL: http://familyeducation.com/MI/haighpta
Contact: Jamie Bettinger, Pres.
Local. Parents, teachers, students, and others interested in uniting the forces of home, school, and community. Promotes the welfare of children and youth.

7261 ■ Hugh O'Brian Youth Leadership of Michigan (MIHOBY)
PO Box 2441
Dearborn, MI 48123-2441
Ph: (313)595-3032
E-mail: mihoby@comcast.net
URL: http://www.mihoby.org
Contact: Yvette Shockey, Pres.
State. Encourages and aids young people in their struggle for self-identification and self-development. Serves as a liaison among young potential leaders and recognized leaders in business, education, government, science and the professions. **Affiliated With:** Hugh O'Brian Youth Leadership.

7262 ■ International Union, United Automobile, Aerospace and Agricultural Implement Workers of America, AFL-CIO - Local Union 245
1226 Monroe
Dearborn, MI 48124
Ph: (313)561-7500
Fax: (313)561-4901
Free: (800)525-8243
E-mail: local245@uawlocal245.org
URL: http://www.uawlocal245.org
Contact: Bob MacDonald, Financial Sec.-Treas.
Members: 1,485. **Local**. AFL-CIO. **Affiliated With:** International Union, United Automobile, Aerospace and Agricultural Implement Workers of America.

7263 ■ Michigan Society of Healthcare Risk Management (MSHRM)
PO Box 1923
Dearborn, MI 48121-1923
Ph: (810)606-6638
Fax: (810)606-6668
E-mail: info@mshrm.org
URL: http://www.mshrm.org
Contact: Greg Knuth, Pres.
State. Affiliated With: American Society for Healthcare Risk Management.

7264 ■ Midwest Mineralogical and Lapidary Society
PO Box 368
Dearborn, MI 48121
E-mail: mmls57@aol.com
URL: National Affiliate–www.amfed.org
Contact: Russell Ranker, Sec.
Regional. Aims to further the study of Earth Sciences and the practice of lapidary arts and mineralogy. **Affiliated With:** American Federation of Mineralogical Societies.

7265 ■ National Association of Miniature Enthusiasts - My Mini Friends
c/o Shirley Fox
23950 Princeton St.
Dearborn, MI 48124
Ph: (313)561-5935
URL: http://www.miniatures.org/states/MI.html
Contact: Shirley Fox, Contact
Local. Affiliated With: National Association of Miniature Enthusiasts.

7266 ■ Phi Theta Kappa, Alpha Xi Mu Chapter - Henry Ford Community College
c/o Nabeel Abraham
5101 Evergreen Rd.
Dearborn, MI 48128
Ph: (313)845-6460
E-mail: nabraham@hfcc.net
URL: http://www.ptk.org/directories/chapters/MI/4627-1.htm
Contact: Nabeel Abraham, Advisor
Local.

7267 ■ Psi Chi, National Honor Society in Psychology - University of Michigan-Dearborn
c/o Behavioral Sciences Dept.
4901 Evergreen Rd.
Dearborn, MI 48128-1491
Ph: (313)593-5520 (313)593-5163
Fax: (313)593-5552
E-mail: rhymes@umich.edu
URL: National Affiliate–www.psichi.org
Local. Affiliated With: Psi Chi, National Honor Society in Psychology.

7268 ■ Redford Township Lions Club
c/o Alan R. Gaiefsky, Pres.
22751 Lawrence St.
Dearborn, MI 48128
Ph: (313)278-3221
URL: http://www.metrodetroitlions.org
Contact: Alan R. Gaiefsky, Pres.
Local. Affiliated With: Lions Clubs International.

7269 ■ Society of Automotive Engineers - University of Michigan-Dearborn
4901 Evergreen Rd.
Dearborn, MI 48128-1491
E-mail: tshim@umich.edu
URL: National Affiliate–www.sae.org
Contact: Taehyun Shim PhD, Contact
Local. Advances the engineering mobility systems. Provides technical information and expertise used in designing, building, maintaining and operating self-propelled vehicles, whether land, sea, air or space based. Collects and disseminates information on cars, trucks, aircraft, space vehicles, off-highway vehicles, marine equipment and engine of all types. Fosters information exchange among the worldwide automotive and aerospace communities. **Affiliated With:** SAE International - Society of Automotive Engineers.

7270 ■ Society of Manufacturing Engineers, Henry Ford Community College Student Chapter S-331
c/o Gerald Klein, Faculty Advisor
5101 Evergreen Rd.
Dearborn, MI 48128
Ph: (313)845-6424 (313)845-9600
Fax: (313)845-9872
Free: (800)585-4322
E-mail: gklein@hfcc.edu
URL: http://www.hfcc.edu
Contact: Gerald Klein, Faculty Advisor
Founded: 2000. **Members:** 32. **Membership Dues:** student, $20 (annual). **Local**. Aims to serve its members and the manufacturing community through the advancement of professionalism, knowledge, and learning. **Affiliated With:** Society of Manufacturing Engineers. **Conventions/Meetings:** monthly meeting.

7271 ■ Society of Manufacturing Engineers - University of Michigan - Dearborn S326
4901 Evergreen Rd.
Dearborn, MI 48128
Ph: (313)593-5581
Fax: (313)593-5386
E-mail: orady@umich.edu
URL: National Affiliate–www.sme.org
Contact: Prof. Elsayed A. Orady, Contact
Local. Advances manufacturing knowledge to gain competitive advantage. Improves skills and manufacturing solutions for the growth of economy. Provides resources and opportunities for manufacturing professionals. **Affiliated With:** Natural Science for Youth Foundation.

7272 ■ University of Michigan-Dearborn - Student Environmental Association
4901 Evergreen Rd.
Dearborn, MI 48128
Ph: (313)593-5000
E-mail: greenw@umd.umich.edu
Contact: Kelly Greenwald, Pres.
Local.

7273 ■ Utility Workers Union of America, AFL-CIO - Buildings and Properties Division Local Union 223
7041 Schaefer Rd.
Dearborn, MI 48126-1891
Ph: (313)846-3040
Fax: (313)846-6707
E-mail: jimharrison@local223uwua.org
URL: http://www.local223uwua.org/
Contact: Jim Harrison, Pres.
Members: 70. **Local. Affiliated With:** Utility Workers Union of America, AFL-CIO.

7274 ■ Utility Workers Union of America, AFL-CIO - Meter Reading-Detroit Division Local Union 223
c/o Jim Harrison
7041 Schaefer Rd.
Dearborn, MI 48126-1891
Ph: (313)846-3040
Fax: (313)846-6707
E-mail: jimharrison@local223uwua.org
URL: http://www.local223uwua.org/
Contact: Jim Harrison, Pres.
Members: 11. **Local. Affiliated With:** Utility Workers Union of America, AFL-CIO.

7275 ■ Utility Workers Union of America, AFL-CIO - Office, Professional and Technical Division Local Union 223
c/o Alan Grayewski, Chm.
7041 Schaefer Rd.
Dearborn, MI 48126
Ph: (313)846-0335
Fax: (313)846-2574
E-mail: alangrayewski@local223uwua.org
URL: http://www.local223uwua.org/
Contact: Jean Calvert, Treas.
Members: 990. **Local. Affiliated With:** Utility Workers Union of America, AFL-CIO.

7276 ■ Utility Workers Union of America, AFL-CIO - Substation Division Local Union 223
c/o Jack Jaskowski, Chm.
7041 Schaefer Rd.
Dearborn, MI 48126-1891
Ph: (313)581-8944
E-mail: jaskowski@dteenergy.com
URL: http://www.local223uwua.org/
Contact: Jack Jaskowski, Chm.
Members: 465. **Local. Affiliated With:** Utility Workers Union of America, AFL-CIO.

7277 ■ Vietnam Veterans of America, Chapter 267
c/o James L. Huard
3001 S Telegraph Rd.
Dearborn, MI 48128
Ph: (313)562-9090
E-mail: post364@sbcglobal.net
URL: http://www.vvachapter267.org
Contact: James L. Huard, Contact
Local. Affiliated With: Vietnam Veterans of America.

7278 ■ Wayne-Westland Alliance for the Mentally Ill
c/o Clarence Porter, Pres.
22213 Tenny St.
Dearborn, MI 48124-2784
Ph: (313)562-8498 (313)292-9015
E-mail: docandjimmie@aol.com
URL: http://mi.nami.org/wwl.html
Contact: Clarence Porter, Pres.
Local. Strives to improve the quality of life of children and adults with severe mental illness through support, education, research and advocacy. **Affiliated With:** National Alliance for the Mentally Ill.

Dearborn Heights

7279 ■ American Legion, Detroit News Post 519
5983 N Waverly St.
Dearborn Heights, MI 48127
Ph: (517)371-4720
Fax: (517)371-2401
URL: National Affiliate–www.legion.org
Local. Affiliated With: American Legion.

7280 ■ American Legion, Michigan Post 86
c/o Frederick M. Alger
4417 Acad. St.
Dearborn Heights, MI 48125
Ph: (517)371-4720
Fax: (517)371-2401
URL: National Affiliate–www.legion.org
Contact: Frederick M. Alger, Contact
Local. Affiliated With: American Legion.

7281 ■ American Legion, Michigan Post 232
c/o Carl E. Stitt
23850 Military Rd.
Dearborn Heights, MI 48127
Ph: (517)371-4720
Fax: (517)371-2401
URL: National Affiliate–www.legion.org
Contact: Carl E. Stitt, Contact
Local. Affiliated With: American Legion.

7282 ■ Dearborn Heights Lions Club
c/o Jerri Allen, Pres.
6101 Ardmore Park Cir.
Dearborn Heights, MI 48127
Ph: (313)278-2993
E-mail: jj@dhol.org
URL: http://www.metrodetroitlions.org
Contact: Jerri Allen, Pres.
Local. Affiliated With: Lions Clubs International.

7283 ■ Eastern Michigan Chapter of American Society of Plumbing Engineers
c/o Esteban Cabello, PE, Pres.
JRED Engg., Inc.
5608 N Charlesworth St.
Dearborn Heights, MI 48127
Ph: (313)565-5580
E-mail: jredengineering@comcast.net
URL: http://www.aspe.org/Eastern_Michigan
Contact: Esteban Cabello PE, Pres.
Local. Represents the interests of individuals dedicated to the advancement of the science of plumbing engineering. Seeks to resolve professional problems in plumbing engineering. Advocates greater cooperation among members and plumbing officials, contractors, laborers and the public. **Affiliated With:** American Society of Plumbing Engineers.

Decatur

7284 ■ American Legion, Phoenix Post 309
560 N Phelps St.
Decatur, MI 49045
Ph: (517)371-4720
Fax: (517)371-2401
URL: National Affiliate–www.legion.org
Local. Affiliated With: American Legion.

7285 ■ Greater Decatur Chamber of Commerce
PO Box 211
Decatur, MI 49045
Ph: (269)423-2411
E-mail: info@decaturmi.org
URL: http://www.decaturmi.org
Contact: Dave Moormann, Pres.
Local. Promotes business and community development in Greater Decatur, MI area. **Telecommunication Services:** electronic mail, villageofdecatur@comcast.net.

7286 ■ Michiana Dressage Club (MDC)
c/o Kitty Pielemeier, Pres.
84063 56th St.
Decatur, MI 49045
Ph: (269)782-3409
E-mail: flimflamfarms@aol.com
URL: http://www.michianadressageclub.org
Contact: Kitty Pielemeier, Pres.
Local. Affiliated With: United States Dressage Federation.

7287 ■ Van Buren Regional Genealogical Society (VBRGS)
PO Box 143
Decatur, MI 49045
Ph: (269)423-4771
E-mail: tbenson@vbdl.org
URL: http://www.rootsweb.com/~mivbrgs/vbrgs.htm
Contact: Toni I. Benson, Librarian
Founded: 1987. **Members:** 150. **Membership Dues:** single, $14 (annual) • student, $11 (annual) • family, $17 (annual) • sponsor, $25 (annual) • life, $250. **Regional.** Seeks to preserve family/local history for the Michigan counties of Allegan, Berrien, Cass, Kalamazoo and Van Buren. **Libraries: Type:** open to the public. **Holdings:** 3,000; archival material, books, maps, photographs, video recordings. **Subjects:** Allegan, Berrien, Cass, Kalamazoo, St Joseph and Van Buren Counties, Michigan; General Michigan; New England and Midwestern States. **Computer Services:** database, vital records and other record compilations • online services, website. **Publications:** *Van Buren Echoes*, quarterly. Journal.

Deckerville

7288 ■ American Legion, Sickles-Arnold Post 516
2941 Mills Rd.
Deckerville, MI 48427
Ph: (517)371-4720
Fax: (517)371-2401
URL: National Affiliate–www.legion.org
Local. Affiliated With: American Legion.

Deerfield

7289 ■ American Legion, Deerfield Post 392
105 W River St.
Deerfield, MI 49238
Ph: (517)371-4720
Fax: (517)371-2401
URL: National Affiliate–www.legion.org
Local. Affiliated With: American Legion.

Delton

7290 ■ Kalamazoo Kennel Club (KKC)
c/o Cheryl Shea, Obedience Chair
4998 Lindsey Rd.
Delton, MI 49046
Ph: (269)795-9551 (269)345-5677
E-mail: kkc@iserv.net
URL: http://www.kalamazookennelclub.com
Contact: Cheryl Shea, Obedience Chair
Local. Affiliated With: American Kennel Club.

Detroit

7291 ■ 100 Black Men of Greater Detroit
PO Box 231361
Detroit, MI 48223
Fax: (248)670-4110
Free: (866)670-4110
E-mail: info@100bmdetroit.com
URL: http://www.100bmdetroit.org
Local. Affiliated With: 100 Black Men of America.

7292 ■ Accounting Aid Society
18145 Mack Ave.
Detroit, MI 48224
Ph: (313)647-9628
Fax: (313)647-9628
Contact: Marshall Hunt, Interim Pres.
Founded: 1972. **Members:** 500. **Staff:** 8. **Budget:** $500,000. **Local**. Accountants, business professionals, nonprofit organizations, and students. Helps strengthen the management of nonprofit organizations through the application of appropriate business skills. Coordinates income tax services for low income families. Conducts 100 seminars/year. **Awards:** Jeanne Vost Celebration of Leadership. **Frequency:** annual. **Type:** recognition. **Recipient:** for leadership in nonprofit management. **Affiliated With:** Accountants for the Public Interest; Alliance for Nonprofit Management. **Publications:** *Getting Started-A Guide to Starting A Tax Exempt Nonprofit Organization in the State of Michigan*. **Price:** $10.00 • *Michigan Nonprofit Management Manual, 3rd Ed.*. **Price:** $79.00 nonprofit members • Newsletter, quarterly. **Price:** included in membership dues. **Advertising:** accepted. **Conventions/Meetings:** weekly seminar.

7293 ■ Adcraft Club of Detroit
3011 W Grand Blvd., Ste.1715
Detroit, MI 48202-3000
Ph: (313)872-7850
Fax: (313)872-7858
E-mail: adcraft@adcraft.org
URL: http://www.adcraft.org
Contact: Robert Guerrini, Exec.Dir.
Founded: 1905. **Members:** 2,600. **Membership Dues:** personal, $75 (annual). **Staff:** 4. **Local**. Individuals in the metropolitan Detroit, MI area who are employed in advertising. Promotes networking and exchange of information about the industry. **Affiliated With:** Michigan Advertising Industry Alliance. **Publications:** *The Adcrafter*, biweekly. Magazine. **Price:** $35.00/year. **Conventions/Meetings:** weekly banquet.

7294 ■ Adopt-A-Child-Size and Support Services
c/o Teresa D. Moore, Exec.Dir.
PO Box 42187
Detroit, MI 48242
Ph: (734)722-4025
Fax: (734)722-3903
E-mail: info@adopt-a-child-size.org
URL: http://www.adopt-a-child-size.org
Contact: Teresa Moore, Exec.Dir.
Founded: 1986. **Local**. Provides new winter clothing to disadvantaged children in Wayne County and Eastern Washtenaw County. Provides non-financial services to families and individuals. Provides toys and bicycles on limited basis.

7295 ■ AIDS Partnership Michigan (APM)
2751 E Jefferson Ave., Ste.301
Detroit, MI 48207
Ph: (313)446-9800
Fax: (313)446-9839
Free: (800)872-2437
E-mail: info@aidspartnership.org
URL: http://www.aidspartnership.org
Founded: 1996. **State**. Services include case management, behavioral health services, AIDS Interfaith Network, Linda's Home Delivered Meals, Project Med-Line, transportation, Michigan AIDS Hotline, Teen link HIV/STD Hotline, speaker's bureau, and HIV counseling and testing.

7296 ■ Alcoholics Anonymous World Services, Detroit and Wayne County Office
3208 Gratiot Ave.
Detroit, MI 48207
Ph: (313)921-1967 (313)921-1942
E-mail: dwcioaa@earthlink.com
URL: http://www.alcoholics-anonymous.org
Contact: Ernest Lee, Chair
Local. Individuals recovering from alcoholism. AA maintains that members can solve their common problem and help others achieve sobriety through a twelve step program that includes sharing their experience, strength, and hope with each other. **Affiliated With:** Alcoholics Anonymous World Services.

7297 ■ Alliance for the Mentally Ill - Downtown Detroit
c/o Betty Harris, Pres.
2939 E Learned
Detroit, MI 48207
Ph: (313)567-4777
URL: http://mi.nami.org/dtd.html
Contact: Betty Harris, Pres.
Local. Strives to improve the quality of life of children and adults with severe mental illness through support, education, research and advocacy. **Affiliated With:** National Alliance for the Mentally Ill.

7298 ■ American Association of Collegiate Registrars and Admissions Officers, Michigan (MACRAO)
c/o Diane Praet
Univ. of Detroit Mercy
4001 W McNichols Rd.
Detroit, MI 48221-3038
Ph: (313)993-3313
Fax: (313)993-3317
E-mail: praetdm@udmercy.edu
URL: http://www.macrao.org
Contact: Diane Praet, Contact
State. **Affiliated With:** American Association of Collegiate Registrars and Admissions Officers.

7299 ■ American Chemical Society, Detroit Section
c/o Mark Antony Benvenuto, Chm.
PO Box 19900
Detroit, MI 48219-0900
Ph: (313)993-1184
Fax: (313)993-1144
E-mail: benvenma@udmercy.edu
URL: National Affiliate–acswebcontent.acs.org
Contact: Mark Antony Benvenuto, Chm.
Local. Represents the interests of individuals dedicated to the advancement of chemistry in all its branches. Provides opportunities for peer interaction and career development. **Affiliated With:** American Chemical Society.

7300 ■ American Civil Liberties Union of Michigan
c/o Kary Moss, Esq., Exec.Dir.
60 W Hancock
Detroit, MI 48201-1343
Ph: (313)578-6800
Fax: (313)578-6811
E-mail: aclu@aclumich.org
URL: http://www.aclumich.org
Contact: Ms. Kary Moss Esq., Exec.Dir.
Founded: 1961. **Members:** 15,000. **Membership Dues:** basic, $20 (annual) • joint, $30 (annual) • student, $5 (annual) • contributing, $35 (annual) • supporting, $50 (annual) • sustaining, $75 (annual). **Staff:** 10. **Local Groups:** 9. **State**. Champions the rights set forth in the Bill of Rights of the U.S. Constitution: freedom of speech, press, assembly, and religion; due process of law and fair trial; equality before the law regardless of race, color, sexual orientation, national origin, political opinion, or religious belief. Activities include litigation, advocacy, and public education. **Affiliated With:** American Civil Liberties Union.

7301 ■ American Guild of Organists, Ann Arbor (531)
c/o Dr. Edward Maki-Schramm
587 E Grand Blvd.
Detroit, MI 48207
E-mail: eschramm@umich.edu
URL: http://www.annarborago.org
Contact: Dr. Edward Maki-Schramm, Contact
Local. Promotes the organ in its historic and evolving roles, encourages excellence in the performance of organ and choral music, provides a forum for mutual support, inspiration, education, and certification of Guild members. **Affiliated With:** American Guild of Organists.

7302 ■ American Institute of Architects, Michigan (AIAMI)
c/o Mike Mosley
553 E Jefferson Ave.
Detroit, MI 48226
Ph: (313)965-4100
Fax: (313)965-1501
E-mail: aiami@aiami.com
URL: http://aiami.com
Contact: Rae Dumke, Exec.Dir.
Founded: 1887. **Members:** 1,700. **Staff:** 5. **Budget:** $650,000. **Local Groups:** 10. **State**. Architects. Promotes high professional standards and continuing education. **Awards:** AIA College Of Fellows. **Frequency:** annual. **Type:** fellowship. **Recipient:** for members who have made contributions of national significance to the profession • Building Award. **Frequency:** annual. **Type:** recognition. **Recipient:** to a single or related group of buildings • Gold Medal. **Frequency:** annual. **Type:** recognition. **Recipient:** for an architect who has clearly demonstrated distinguished leadership • Hastings Award. **Frequency:** annual. **Type:** recognition. **Recipient:** for architects who made significant contributions to the improvement of architecture • Interior Architecture Award. **Frequency:** annual. **Type:** recognition. **Recipient:** for excellence and diversity of interiors projects designed by members of the organization itself • Low Budget/Small Project Award. **Frequency:** annual. **Type:** recognition. **Recipient:** for design excellence within the constraints of small budget, scale and size • President's Award. **Frequency:** annual. **Type:** recognition. **Recipient:** for architects in the education and corporate field • 25 Year Award. **Frequency:** annual. **Type:** recognition. **Recipient:** for distinguished projects designed by an AIA member and used for at least 25 years • Young Architect. **Frequency:** annual. **Type:** recognition. **Recipient:** for a member of minimum of three years and is 40 years old or younger. **Affiliated With:** American Institute of Architects. **Publications:** *Place Magazine*, quarterly • Newsletter, monthly • Directory, annual. **Conventions/Meetings:** periodic competition • annual conference - always August • annual meeting - always February.

7303 ■ American Legion, Dorchester Chaplains Post 387
1731 Parker
Detroit, MI 48201
Ph: (517)371-4720
Fax: (517)371-2401
URL: National Affiliate–www.legion.org
Local. **Affiliated With:** American Legion.

7304 ■ American Legion, Grosse Pointe Post 303
4810 E Outer Dr.
Detroit, MI 48234
Ph: (517)371-4720
Fax: (517)371-2401
URL: National Affiliate–www.legion.org
Local. **Affiliated With:** American Legion.

7305 ■ American Legion, Jeep Gabrys Post 388
212 S Dupont St.
Detroit, MI 48209
Ph: (517)371-4720
Fax: (517)371-2401
URL: National Affiliate–www.legion.org
Local. **Affiliated With:** American Legion.

7306 ■ American Legion, Mexican-American Post 505
8083 Longworth St.
Detroit, MI 48209
Ph: (517)371-4720
Fax: (517)371-2401
URL: National Affiliate–www.legion.org
Local. **Affiliated With:** American Legion.

7307 ■ American Legion, Michigan Post 56
c/o Woodbridge N. Ferris
18463 Muirland St.
Detroit, MI 48221
Ph: (517)371-4720
Fax: (517)371-2401
URL: National Affiliate–www.legion.org
Contact: Woodbridge N. Ferris, Contact
Local. Affiliated With: American Legion.

7308 ■ American Legion, Michigan Post 77
c/o Charles Young
PO Box 8146
Detroit, MI 48208
Ph: (517)371-4720
Fax: (517)371-2401
URL: National Affiliate–www.legion.org
Contact: Charles Young, Contact
Local. Affiliated With: American Legion.

7309 ■ American Legion, Michigan Post 126
c/o Fred W. Beaudry
12775 Harper Ave.
Detroit, MI 48213
Ph: (517)371-4720
Fax: (517)371-2401
URL: National Affiliate–www.legion.org
Contact: Fred W. Beaudry, Contact
Local. Affiliated With: American Legion.

7310 ■ American Legion, Michigan Post 128
c/o Garfield Heath, Sr.
1244 S Liebold St.
Detroit, MI 48217
Ph: (517)371-4720
Fax: (517)371-2401
URL: National Affiliate–www.legion.org
Contact: Garfield Heath Sr., Contact
Local. Affiliated With: American Legion.

7311 ■ American Legion, Michigan Post 184
c/o Tom Phillips
10235 Gratiot Ave.
Detroit, MI 48213
Ph: (517)371-4720
Fax: (517)371-2401
URL: National Affiliate–www.legion.org
Contact: Tom Phillips, Contact
Local. Affiliated With: American Legion.

7312 ■ American Legion, Michigan Post 202
c/o Coleman A. Young
14000 Puritan St.
Detroit, MI 48227
Ph: (517)371-4720
Fax: (517)371-2401
URL: National Affiliate–www.legion.org
Contact: Coleman A. Young, Contact
Local. Affiliated With: American Legion.

7313 ■ American Legion, Michigan Post 214
c/o John C. Carter
19720 Conant
Detroit, MI 48234
Ph: (517)371-4720
Fax: (517)371-2401
URL: National Affiliate–www.legion.org
Contact: John C. Carter, Contact
Local. Affiliated With: American Legion.

7314 ■ American Legion, Michigan Post 375
c/o Joe Louis
19486 Sherwood
Detroit, MI 48234
Ph: (517)371-4720
Fax: (517)371-2401
URL: National Affiliate–www.legion.org
Contact: Joe Louis, Contact
Local. Affiliated With: American Legion.

7315 ■ American Legion, Northwest Detroit Post 302
PO Box 38848
Detroit, MI 48238
Ph: (517)371-4720
Fax: (517)371-2401
URL: National Affiliate–www.legion.org
Local. Affiliated With: American Legion.

7316 ■ American Legion, Security Post 284
7631 Plainview Ave.
Detroit, MI 48228
Ph: (517)371-4720
Fax: (517)371-2401
URL: National Affiliate–www.legion.org
Local. Affiliated With: American Legion.

7317 ■ American Library Association, Wayne State University (ALAWSU)
Lib. and Info. Sci. Prog.
106 Kresge Lib.
Wayne State Univ.
Detroit, MI 48202-3939
E-mail: at6126@wayne.edu
URL: http://www.lisp.wayne.edu/ala
Contact: Kevin Delecki, Pres.
Local. Affiliated With: American Library Association.

7318 ■ American Red Cross Southeastern Michigan Blood Region
PO Box 33351
Detroit, MI 48232-5351
Ph: (313)833-4440
URL: http://www.semredcross.org
Regional.

7319 ■ American Red Cross, Southeastern Michigan Chapter
PO Box 44110
Detroit, MI 48244-0110
Ph: (313)883-4440
Fax: (313)831-1504
Free: (800)774-6066
E-mail: info@semredcross.org
URL: http://www.semredcross.org
Contact: Neil G. Bristol, Chm.
Founded: 1909. **Staff:** 100. **Local.** Provides a variety of services to help people prevent, prepare for and cope with emergencies. Serves members of the armed forces, veterans and their families; assists disaster victims; supports other community services. Conducts first aid, CPR, and AED training; makes available health care, promotion, and HIV/AID education services. Trains and places youth volunteers with community service projects. **Affiliated With:** American Red Cross National Headquarters. **Conventions/Meetings:** annual meeting - June.

7320 ■ American Society of Heating, Refrigerating and Air-Conditioning Engineers Detroit
c/o Filza H. Walters, Pres.
Wayne State Univ.
5454 Cass Ave.
Detroit, MI 48202
Ph: (313)577-1970
Fax: (313)577-1817
E-mail: f.walters@wayne.edu
URL: http://www.detroitashrae.org
Contact: Filza H. Walters, Pres.
Local. Advances the arts and sciences of heating, ventilation, air-conditioning and refrigeration. Provides a source of technical and educational information, standards and guidelines. Conducts seminars for professional growth. **Affiliated With:** American Society of Heating, Refrigerating and Air-Conditioning Engineers.

7321 ■ American Society for Microbiology - Michigan Branch
c/o Judith Whittum-Hudson
374 Lande-Immunology
550 E Canfield Ave.
Detroit, MI 48201
Ph: (313)577-5501
Fax: (313)577-5559
E-mail: jhudson@med.wayne.edu
URL: National Affiliate–www.asm.org
Contact: Judith Whittum-Hudson, Contact
State. Advances the knowledge in the field of microbiology. Improves educational programs and encourages fundamental and applied research in microbiological sciences. Supports training and public information. **Affiliated With:** American Society for Microbiology.

7322 ■ American Society of Sanitary Engineering, Michigan Chapter
c/o John R. Nussbaum, Sec.
14801 W 8 Mile Rd.
Detroit, MI 48235
E-mail: jnussbaum@pmcdetroit.com
URL: National Affiliate–www.asse-plumbing.org
Contact: John R. Nussbaum, Sec.
State. Represents plumbing officials, sanitary engineers, plumbers, plumbing contractors, building officials, architects, engineers, designing engineers, physicians, and others interested in health. Conducts research on plumbing and sanitation and develops performance standards for components of the plumbing system. Sponsors disease research programs and other studies of water-borne epidemics. **Affiliated With:** American Society of Sanitary Engineering.

7323 ■ American Theatre Organ Society, Motor City Chapter
c/o Elaine Mundt, Sec.
16889 W Riverdale Dr.
Detroit, MI 48219-3774
Ph: (313)531-4407
E-mail: midnight66@juno.com
URL: National Affiliate–www.atos.org
Contact: Elaine Mundt, Sec.
Local. Aims to restore, preserve and promote the theatre pipe organ and its music. Encourages the youth to learn the instrument. Operates a committee that gathers history and old music from silent film days and information on theatre organists, theaters and organ installations of the silent film era. **Affiliated With:** American Theatre Organ Society.

7324 ■ Asian American Bar Association of Michigan
471 Palmer St.
Detroit, MI 48202
Ph: (313)577-3951
Fax: (313)577-6000
E-mail: ricardo.villarosa@wayne.edu
URL: http://mapaba.org
Contact: Lawrence G. Almeda, Pres.-Elect
State. Represents the interests of Asian Pacific American attorneys and their communities. Promotes justice, equity and opportunity for Asian Pacific Americans. Fosters professional development, legal scholarship, advocacy and community development. **Affiliated With:** National Asian Pacific American Bar Association.

7325 ■ Association of Community Organizations for Reform Now, Detroit
1249 Washington Blvd., Ste.1303
Detroit, MI 48226
Ph: (313)963-1840
Fax: (313)963-4268
E-mail: miacorn@acorn.org
URL: National Affiliate–www.acorn.org
Local. Affiliated With: Association of Community Organizations for Reform Now.

7326 ■ Association for Computing Machinery, Wayne State University
c/o Prof. Weisong Shi
Cmpt. Sci. Dept.
431 State Hall
5143 Cass Ave.
Detroit, MI 48202

Ph: (313)577-2477
Fax: (313)577-6868
E-mail: eford@wayne.edu
URL: http://acm.cs.wayne.edu
Contact: Bin Peng, Pres.
Local. Biological, medical, behavioral, and computer scientists; hospital administrators; programmers and others interested in application of computer methods to biological, behavioral, and medical problems. Stimulates understanding of the use and potential of computers in the Biosciences. **Affiliated With:** Association for Computing Machinery.

7327 ■ Association of Medical School Microbiology and Immunology Chairs (AMSMIC)
c/o Dr. Paul C. Montgomery, Sec.-Treas.
Dept. of Immunology/Microbiology
Wayne State Univ. School of Medicine
540 E Canfield Ave.
Detroit, MI 48201-1928
Ph: (313)577-1591
Fax: (313)577-1155
E-mail: pmontgo@med.wayne.edu
URL: http://www.amsmic.org
Contact: Dr. Paul C. Montgomery, Sec.-Treas.
Founded: 1972. **Members:** 125. **Membership Dues:** full, $100 (annual). **Local**. Seeks to promote, advance, and support the educational and scientific purposes of the field of microbiology and immunology and to provide a forum for communication among chairpersons of Departments of Microbiology and Immunology or equivalent organizational units responsible for teaching medical students. Aids in the education and training of medical students and physicians; explores means, methods, agencies, and funds by which such microbiological and immunological and other scientific research and education may be furthered; and assists in the dissemination of related information. **Affiliated With:** Association of American Medical Colleges. **Publications:** Membership Directory, annual. **Price:** free.

7328 ■ Bayview Yacht Club
100 Clairpointe
Detroit, MI 48215
Ph: (313)822-1853
Fax: (313)822-8020
E-mail: kerrie@byc.com
URL: http://www.byc.com
Contact: Kerrie Barno, Administrator
Local.

7329 ■ Black Data Processing Associates - Detroit Chapter
c/o Eatonia Acoff, Pres.
65 Cadillac Sq., Ste.2200
Detroit, MI 48226
Ph: (313)965-0193
E-mail: detpres@bdpa-detroit.org
URL: http://www.bdpa-detroit.org
Local.

7330 ■ Booker T. Washington Business Association (BTWBA)
2886 E Grand Blvd.
Detroit, MI 48202
Ph: (313)875-4250
Fax: (313)875-4887
E-mail: bross@btwba.org
URL: http://www.btwba.org
Contact: W.R. Ross, Pres./CEO
Founded: 1930. **Local**.

7331 ■ Boys Hope Girls Hope of Detroit
c/o Darlene Thomas, Exec.Dir.
PO Box 21085
Detroit, MI 48221
Ph: (313)862-0707
Fax: (313)862-0716
E-mail: detroit@bhgh.org
URL: http://www.boyshopegirlshope.org/locations/detroit/home.html
Contact: Darlene Thomas, Exec.Dir.
Local. Affiliated With: Boys Hope Girls Hope.

7332 ■ Casino Management Association (CMA)
PO Box 14610
Detroit, MI 48214
Ph: (313)965-9038
Fax: (313)961-1651
E-mail: info@cmaweb.org
URL: http://www.casinovendors.com/VendorPage.cfm/79968.html
Contact: Debra Kent, Sec.
Founded: 1994. **Members:** 650. **Membership Dues:** company, $400 (annual) • individual, $100 (annual). **Staff:** 1. **Budget:** $125,000. **Local**. Professional trade association of and for casino professionals. Prepares and drafts professional standards for the casino industry. **Awards:** CMA Scholarship. **Frequency:** annual. **Type:** scholarship. **Recipient:** for a casino management major; must have 3.4 GPA. **Publications:** *Casino Management News*, monthly. Newsletter. Includes 4 pages of upcoming CMA and industrial events. **Price:** free. **Circulation:** 2,500. **Conventions/Meetings:** monthly meeting - except June, July, December.

7333 ■ Central City Alliance (CCA)
c/o Laura Howard
3040 E Grand Blvd., 2nd Fl.
Detroit, MI 48202
Ph: (313)433-8262
Fax: (313)392-6061
E-mail: ccalliance@netscape.net
URL: http://www.neighborhoodlink.com/detroit/ccalliance
Contact: Laura Howard, Contact
Local.

7334 ■ Citizens for Better Care (CBC)
c/o Nancy Jackson, Exec.Dir.
4750 Woodward Ave., Ste.410
Detroit, MI 48201
Ph: (313)832-6387
Fax: (313)832-7407
Free: (800)833-9548
E-mail: info@cbcmi.org
URL: http://www.cbcmi.org
Contact: Nancy Jackson, Exec.Dir.
Founded: 1969. **Members:** 2,500. **Staff:** 30. **Budget:** $1,200,000. **Local Groups:** 5. **Local**. Senior citizens, citizens' groups, and interested professionals. Works to improve the quality of long-term care; disseminates information about nursing homes, homes for the aged, and long-term care programs or services; helps in linking or directing the family with other continuing care resources; provides information about nursing home and adult foster care law and other regulations in long-term care facilities; assists in planning care for frail, elderly, and disabled adults. Sponsors speakers bureau. **Affiliated With:** National Citizens Coalition for Nursing Home Reform. **Formed by Merger of:** (1981) Citizens for Better Care in Nursing Homes for the Aged; Citizens for Better Care Institute. **Publications:** *Directory of Nursing Homes*, periodic • *Rising Standard*, 3/year. Newsletter. **Price:** free to members & donors. **Conventions/Meetings:** periodic meeting.

7335 ■ City Connect Detroit
163 Madison St., 3rd Fl.
Detroit, MI 48226
Ph: (313)963-9722
Fax: (313)963-9723
E-mail: info@cityconnectdetroit.org
URL: http://www.cityconnectdetroit.org
Contact: Geneva J. Williams, Pres./CEO
Founded: 1998. **Membership Dues:** basic (based on budget level), $150-$900 (annual) • premium (based on budget level), $250-$1,000 (annual). **Local**. Aims to attract a greater share of federal government and national foundation dollars to Detroit and the State of Michigan to help solve community problems.

7336 ■ City Year Detroit
c/o Penelope Bailer, Exec.Dir.
1 Ford Pl.
Detroit, MI 48202
Ph: (313)874-6825
Fax: (313)874-6865
E-mail: pbailer@cityyear.org
URL: http://www.cityyear.org
Local. Works as a fulltime AmericCorps program that brings together a group of idealistic, enthusiastic 17-24 year olds for a year of fulltime community service, civic engagement, and leadership development. Members work with children and youth while gaining valuable skills and earning a weekly stipend, health benefits, and a scholarship for higher education.

7337 ■ College of Art and Design Student Association for Computing Machinery SIGGRAPH Center for Creative Studies
201 E Kirby
Detroit, MI 48202-4034
E-mail: bbrock@campus.ccscad.edu
URL: http://www.ccscad.siggraph.org
Contact: Damian Fulmer, Chair
Local. Biological, medical, behavioral, and computer scientists; hospital administrators; programmers and others interested in application of computer methods to biological, behavioral, and medical problems. Stimulates understanding of the use and potential of computers in the Biosciences. **Affiliated With:** Association for Computing Machinery.

7338 ■ Depression and Bipolar Support Alliance Metropolitan Detroit (MDDA)
PO Box 32531
Detroit, MI 48232-0531
Ph: (734)284-5563
Fax: (734)324-7056
E-mail: dbsadetroit@yahoo.com
Contact: Mary Ann Bozenski, Pres.
Founded: 1983. **Members:** 1,200. **Membership Dues:** individual, $18 (annual) • family, $28 (annual) • professional, $40 (annual) • institutional, $100 (annual). **Local Groups:** 25. **Local**. Psychiatrists, psychologists, social workers, and mental health patients and their family and friends. Provides support to persons who are manic depressive and depressive; conducts educational programs. Mainly, it is a self-help support group organization. **Boards:** Fund Raising. **Committees:** Public Relations. **Subgroups:** By Laws; Group Development; MDDA of Metro Detroit; Membership; Volunteer. **Affiliated With:** Depression and Bipolar Support Alliance. **Publications:** *Life in Balance*, monthly. Newsletter. Contains educational and informational news. **Price:** included in membership dues. **Circulation:** 1,200. **Advertising:** accepted. **Conventions/Meetings:** annual conference (exhibits).

7339 ■ Detroit ACORN
c/o Alliea Groupp
1249 Washington Blvd., Ste.1303
Detroit, MI 48226
Ph: (313)963-1840
Fax: (313)963-4268
E-mail: miacornde@acorn.org
URL: http://www.acorn.org
State. Also Known As: (2005) Michigan ACORN.

7340 ■ Detroit Association of Realtors
2111 Woodard Ave., Ste.509
Detroit, MI 48201
Ph: (313)962-1313
Fax: (313)962-0844
E-mail: detroitassociation@sbcglobal.net
URL: National Affiliate–www.realtor.org
Contact: Darralyn C. Bowers, Exec. Officer
Local. Strives to develop real estate business practices. Advocates the right to own, use and transfer real property. Provides a facility for professional development, research and exchange of information among members. **Affiliated With:** National Association of Realtors.

7341 ■ Detroit Black Chamber of Commerce
3011 W Grand Blvd., Ste.1200
Detroit, MI 48202-3013
Ph: (313)664-2000 (313)887-1377
E-mail: info@detroitblackchamber.com
Contact: Kathi Dones-Carson, Pres.
Local.

7342 ■ Detroit District Dental Society
3011 W Grand Blvd., Ste.460
Detroit, MI 48202-3045
Ph: (313)871-3500
Fax: (313)871-3503
E-mail: teeth@provide.net
URL: http://www.detroitdentalsociety.com
Contact: Ms. Sherri Doig, Exec.Dir.
Local. Represents the interests of dentists committed to the public's oral health, ethics and professional development. Encourages the improvement of the public's oral health and promotes the art and science of dentistry. **Affiliated With:** American Dental Association; Michigan Dental Association.

7343 ■ Detroit Downtown (DDI)
535 Griswold St., Ste.220
Detroit, MI 48226-3602
Ph: (313)961-1403
Fax: (313)961-9547
Contact: Linda M. Bade, Pres.
Founded: 1922. **Members:** 250. **Staff:** 10. **Budget:** $400,000. **Local**. Nonprofit, membership association of businesses, backed by a professional staff, dedicated to the continued revitalization of the Downtown Detroit area. Seeks to develop and support initiatives to make the downtown area a clean, safe, beautiful, and inviting environment in which to live, work, play, visit, invest, and conduct business. Attention is placed on maintenance, security, business attraction, transportation, retailing, culture, and entertainment. **Publications:** *Detroit Downtown, Inc. Annual Report*, annual. **Price:** for members; $10.00/nonmember. **Circulation:** 1,000. **Advertising:** accepted. Alternate Formats: CD-ROM; online; magnetic tape • *The Insider*, monthly. Newsletter. **Conventions/Meetings:** monthly breakfast - always second Wednesday of the month except July and August. Detroit, MI • annual Membership Luncheon Meeting - always in April. Detroit, MI.

7344 ■ Detroit Downtown Lions Club
c/o Karen Douglas, Pres.
2901 Oakman Blvd.
Detroit, MI 48238
Ph: (313)224-4452 (313)834-4127
E-mail: kdchefatwork@aol.com
URL: http://www.metrodetroitlions.org
Contact: Karen Douglas, Pres.
Local. Affiliated With: Lions Clubs International.

7345 ■ Detroit East Area Narcotics Anonymous
13560 E McNichols
Detroit, MI 48205-3426
E-mail: metrodetroitregion@comcast.net
URL: http://michigan-na.org/detroit_east
Local. Affiliated With: Narcotics Anonymous.

7346 ■ Detroit Economic Club (DEC)
211 W Fort St., Ste.505
Detroit, MI 48226-3286
Ph: (313)963-8547
Fax: (313)963-7399
E-mail: info@econclub.org
URL: http://www.econclub.org
Contact: Beth Chappell, Pres./CEO
Founded: 1934. **Membership Dues:** sustaining, $350 (annual) • regular, $150 (annual) • associate/nonresident, $120 (annual) • junior executive, $75 (annual). **Local**.

7347 ■ Detroit Historical Society (DHS)
5401 Woodward Ave.
Detroit, MI 48202
Ph: (313)833-7935
Fax: (313)833-5342
E-mail: dhswebmaster@hist.ci.detroit.mi.us
URL: http://www.detroithistorical.org
Contact: Robert Bury, Exec.Dir.
Founded: 1921. **Members:** 2,200. **Membership Dues:** individual, $35-$40 (annual) • student, teacher, $15-$30 (annual) • family, $60 (annual) • patron, $150 (annual) • donor, $300 (annual) • historian, sponsor, $500-$1,000 (annual). **Staff:** 10. **Budget:** $1,350,000. **Local**. Corporations, foundations, government agencies, and individuals in southeastern Michigan. Promotes interest in the history of the Detroit, MI area through support of education and preservation programs of the Society and the City of Detroit Historical Department's museums. **Publications:** *Calendar of Events*, quarterly • *Making History*, quarterly. Newsletter. **Conventions/Meetings:** annual meeting.

7348 ■ Detroit Institute of Arts (DIA)
5200 Woodward Ave.
Detroit, MI 48202
Ph: (313)833-7900
URL: http://www.dia.org
Contact: Graham W. J. Beal, Dir.
Local. Formerly: (2005) Detroit Institute of Arts Volunteer Committee.

7349 ■ Detroit Kiwanis Club No. 1, Michigan
PO Box 21621
Detroit, MI 48221-0621
E-mail: bwiggie@yahoo.com
URL: http://comnet.org/kiwanis1
Contact: Beverly L. Wiggins, Pres.
Local.

7350 ■ Detroit Metro Convention and Visitors Bureau
211 W Fort St., Ste.1000
Detroit, MI 48226
Ph: (313)202-1800
Fax: (313)202-1808
Free: (800)338-7648
E-mail: vic@visitdetroit.com
URL: http://www.visitdetroit.com
Contact: Larry Alexander, Pres./CEO
Founded: 1896. **Staff:** 65. **Budget:** $13,370,048. **Local**. Promotes convention business and tourism in area.

7351 ■ Detroit Michigan of the Association of Occupational Health Nurses
c/o Pat Savino, RN, Pres.
Detroit Receiving Hosp.
4201 St. Antoine
Detroit, MI 48201
Ph: (313)966-7110
Fax: (313)745-7200
E-mail: psavino@dmc.org
URL: http://www.michaohn.org
Contact: Pat Savino RN, Pres.
Local. Advances the profession of occupational and environmental health nursing. Promotes public awareness of occupational health nursing. **Affiliated With:** American Association of Occupational Health Nurses.

7352 ■ Detroit New Center Lions Club
c/o Janice Howell, Pres.
1010 Trevor Pl.
Detroit, MI 48207
Ph: (313)567-3610
E-mail: jbhowell@talkamerica.net
URL: http://www.metrodetroitlions.org
Contact: Janice Howell, Pres.
Local. Affiliated With: Lions Clubs International.

7353 ■ Detroit Northwest Lions Club
c/o Gail McEntee, Pres.
16625 Grand River Ave.
Detroit, MI 48227
Ph: (313)272-3900
E-mail: mcentee@gdabvi.com
URL: http://www.metrodetroitlions.org
Contact: Gail McEntee, Pres.
Local. Affiliated With: Lions Clubs International.

7354 ■ Detroit Regional Chamber (DRC)
PO Box 33840
Detroit, MI 48232-0840
Fax: (313)964-0183
Free: (866)MBR-LINE
E-mail: members@detroitchamber.com
URL: http://www.detroitchamber.com
Contact: Richard E. Blouse Jr., Pres./CEO
Founded: 1903. **Members:** 11,000. **Membership Dues:** business builder level, $525 (annual) • bronze level, $1,075 (annual) • silver level, $2,650 (annual) • gold level, $6,000 (annual). **Staff:** 125. **Budget:** $10,000,000. **Local**. Promotes business and community development in the southeastern Michigan counties of Lapeer, Livingston, Macomb, Monroe, Oakland, St. Clair, Washtenaw, and Wayne. **Formerly:** Detroit Board of Commerce; (1999) Greater Detroit Chamber of Commerce. **Publications:** *Buyers' Guide*, annual. Directory. **Price:** $35.00. **Advertising:** accepted • *Detroiter*, monthly. Magazine. **Price:** $18.00 /year for nonmembers. **Advertising:** accepted. Alternate Formats: online • *Greater Detroit Fact Book* • *Greater Detroit Major Employers Directory* • *Greater Detroit Manufacturers Directory* • *Greater Detroit Relocation Package* • *Passport to International Detroit*, annual • Annual Report, annual. Alternate Formats: online. **Conventions/Meetings:** annual conference (exhibits).

7355 ■ Detroit Regional Economic Partnership
c/o Detroit Regional Chamber
1 Woodward, Ste.1900
PO Box 33840
Detroit, MI 48232-0840
Ph: (313)596-0463
Fax: (313)964-0183
Free: (888)MBM-LINE
E-mail: jcarroll@detroitchamber.com
URL: http://www.detroitchamber.com
Contact: Mr. John W. Carroll, Exec.Dir.
Founded: 1997. **Members:** 75. **Staff:** 15. **Budget:** $2,500,000. **Local**. Helps businesses to expand customer base, increase product line and to be globally competitive.

7356 ■ Detroit Renaissance Lions Club
c/o Sylia McLeod, Pres.
16162 Praire St.
Detroit, MI 48221
Ph: (313)341-1893
URL: http://www.metrodetroitlions.org
Contact: Sylia McLeod, Pres.
Local. Affiliated With: Lions Clubs International.

7357 ■ Detroit Urban League
208 Mack Ave.
Detroit, MI 48201
Ph: (313)832-4600
Fax: (313)832-3222
E-mail: webmaster@deturbanleague.org
URL: http://www.detroiturbanleague.org
Contact: N. Charles Anderson, Pres./CEO
Founded: 1916. **Membership Dues:** regular, $50 (annual). **Staff:** 70. **Budget:** $5,500,000. **Local**. Works to enable African-Americans, and other minorities, to reach their full potential. Programs and services focus on the areas of employment, health and substance abuse, male and female responsibility, nutritional education, senior citizen development, and education. **Affiliated With:** National Urban League. **Publications:** Newsletter, 3/year.

7358 ■ Detroit Urban - Young Life
PO Box 27797
Detroit, MI 48227
Ph: (313)850-8002
URL: http://sites.younglife.org/_layouts/ylext/default.aspx?ID=C-1075
Local. Affiliated With: Young Life.

7359 ■ Detroit Youth for Christ
PO Box 40801
Detroit, MI 48240
Ph: (313)535-3800
Fax: (313)535-3800
URL: http://www.yfcdetroit.com
Local. Affiliated With: Youth for Christ/U.S.A.

7360 ■ Disabled American Veterans, Detroit
477 Michigan Ave., No. 1200
Detroit, MI 48226
Ph: (313)964-6595
URL: National Affiliate–www.dav.org
Local. Affiliated With: Disabled American Veterans.

7361 ■ Executive Women International, Detroit-Windsor Chapter
c/o Jo Ann Nyquist
Wayne County Community Coll. District
801 W Ft. St.
Detroit, MI 48226
Ph: (313)943-4055
Fax: (313)943-4025
E-mail: sstone@bcbsm.com
URL: http://www.ewidetroitwindsor.org
Contact: Sharon Stone, Pres.

Founded: 1968. **Members:** 62. **Local**. Works to promote member firms and improve their communities. Provides opportunities for business and personal growth. **Committees:** Budget; Bylaws; Courtesy; Historian/Photographer; Hospitality; Literacy/Reading Rally; Mentoring/Orientation; Nominating. **Affiliated With:** Executive Women International. **Publications:** *Pulse*, monthly. Newsletter. **Advertising:** accepted. Alternate Formats: online.

7362 ■ Federalist Society for Law and Public Policy Studies - Michigan Chapter (Detroit)
c/o Robert J. Curtis
Timmis & Inman PLLC
300 Talon Ctre.
Detroit, MI 48207
Ph: (313)396-4200
Fax: (313)396-4228
E-mail: rcurtis@timmis-inman.com
URL: National Affiliate–www.fed-soc.org
Contact: Robert J. Curtis, Contact

State. Seeks to bring about a reordering of priorities within the U.S. legal system that will emphasize individual liberty, traditional values, and the rule of law. **Affiliated With:** Federalist Society for Law and Public Policy Studies.

7363 ■ Focus: HOPE
1355 Oakman Blvd.
Detroit, MI 48238
Ph: (313)494-5500 (313)494-4423
Fax: (313)494-4571
E-mail: admissions@focushope.edu
URL: http://www.focushope.edu
Contact: Eleanor Josaitis, CEO/Co-founder

Founded: 1968. **Members:** 47,000. **Staff:** 750. **Budget:** $78,700,000. **State Groups:** 1. **Languages:** Arabic, English, Spanish. **Local**. Civil and human rights organization serving the Detroit, MI tri-county area. Sponsors food program for the elderly, and mothers and their children. Operates Fast Track job training program, Machinist Training Institute and Center for Advanced Technologies. Maintains children's center. **Publications:** *Hope in Focus*, 3/year. Newsletter. Contains information on the activities of Focus Hope and related news items. **Price:** free.

7364 ■ Foster Parents Mission Club
17330 Quincy St.
Detroit, MI 48221
Ph: (313)342-4066
Fax: (313)342-6816
E-mail: info@pimeusa.org
URL: http://www.pimeusa.org
Contact: Fr. Ken Mazur, Superior Dir.

Local.

7365 ■ Gift of Reading
600 W Fort St.
Detroit, MI 48226
Ph: (313)222-6429 (313)222-6595
Fax: (313)222-8874
Free: (800)678-6400
URL: http://www.freep.com/charities
Contact: J. G. Teagan, Treas.

Founded: 1987. **Members:** 2. **Local**. Provides storybooks and other literacy services to disadvantaged youngsters, birth to seven years, during the holiday season.

7366 ■ Government Administrators Association (GAA)
c/o Patricia Pena, Adm.Off.
2625 Cadillac Tower
Detroit, MI 48226-2822
Ph: (313)224-5076
Fax: (313)224-0064
Contact: Lawrence Verbiest, Association Exec.

Founded: 1968. **Members:** 840. **Local**. Administrators, executives, managers, supervisors, and professional employees working for Wayne County, MI or Wayne County Courts. Represents membership in labor relations and enhances the image of career public servants. **Libraries: Type:** reference. **Holdings:** video recordings. **Subjects:** education, personal development. **Awards:** GAA Member of the Year. **Frequency:** annual. **Type:** recognition • Service Award. **Frequency:** annual. **Type:** recognition • Special Achievement Award. **Frequency:** annual. **Type:** recognition. **Publications:** *Gazette*, bimonthly. Newsletter. **Conventions/Meetings:** annual Leadership Conference - fall.

7367 ■ Great Lakes Fabricators and Erectors Association (GLFEA)
c/o D. James Walker, Jr., Exec.Dir.
1001 Woodward Ave., Ste.1101
Detroit, MI 48226-1904
Ph: (313)309-2000
Fax: (313)309-2004
E-mail: execdir@glfea.org
URL: http://www.glfea.org
Contact: D. James Walker Jr., Exec.Dir.

Founded: 1938. **Members:** 70. **Local**.

7368 ■ Greater Detroit Chapter Chief Petty Officers Association
c/o USCG Group
110 Mt. Elliott St.
Detroit, MI 48207-4380
Ph: (313)568-9528
E-mail: mbogue@grudetroit.uscg.mil
URL: http://www.uscgcpoa.org/1-cpoa/1-cpoa_index.htm
Contact: Paul Orlando, Pres.

Local. **Affiliated With:** United States Coast Guard Chief Petty Officers Association.

7369 ■ Greater Detroit Michigan Chapter of Concerned Black Men
19401 W McNichols Rd.
Detroit, MI 48219
Ph: (313)537-8202
E-mail: info@cbmdetroit.org
URL: http://www.cbmdetroit.org

Local.

7370 ■ Greening of Detroit
1418 Michigan Ave.
Detroit, MI 48216
Ph: (313)237-8733
Fax: (313)237-8737
E-mail: info@greeningofdetroit.com
URL: http://www.greeningofdetroit.com
Contact: Janet Ortiz, Office Mgr.

Founded: 1989. **Local**.

7371 ■ Habitat for Humanity Detroit
14325 Jane St.
Detroit, MI 48205
Ph: (313)521-6691
Fax: (313)371-3400
E-mail: execdir@habitatdetroit.org
URL: http://www.habitatdetroit.org
Contact: Robert Dewaelsche, Exec.Dir.

Founded: 1986. **Staff:** 10. **Budget:** $1,500,000. **Local**. Commits in building low-cost housing for low-income families. **Publications:** *Habitat Herald*, periodic. Newsletter.

7372 ■ Hampton Elementary PTA
3901 Magareta St.
Detroit, MI 48221
Ph: (313)494-7307
URL: http://familyeducation.com/MI/Hampton_Elementary
Contact: Linda Coles, Pres.

Local. Parents, teachers, students, and others interested in uniting the forces of home, school, and community. Promotes the welfare of children and youth.

7373 ■ Harvest Community Development Corporation
17346 Six Mile
Detroit, MI 48235-3323
Ph: (313)273-9655 (313)592-0102
Fax: (313)273-9137
Contact: Patricia Benson, Dir.

Founded: 1999. **Members:** 30. **Staff:** 6. **Local**. Development programs in the areas of youth, teenage pregnancy, addiction, and homelessness.

7374 ■ Heidelberg Project
PO Box 19377
Detroit, MI 48219
Ph: (313)537-8037
Fax: (313)537-8037
E-mail: jwhitfield@heidelberg.org
URL: http://www.heidelberg.org
Contact: Jenenne Whitfield, Exec.Dir.

Founded: 1986. **Staff:** 3. **Budget:** $250,000. **Local**. Works to develop awareness and appreciation of the arts in the heart of an urban community. Activities include Art and Education, Community Development and Tourism, and Cultural Diversity. **Libraries: Type:** by appointment only. **Holdings:** 75; articles, books, periodicals, video recordings. **Subjects:** art, community development, art environments. **Affiliated With:** ArtServe Michigan. **Formerly:** Detroit Heidelberg Community Street Art.

7375 ■ Indian Village Historical Collections
PO Box 14340
Detroit, MI 48214-0340
Ph: (313)331-7917
Fax: (313)822-2300
E-mail: damartin48@comcast.net
URL: http://www.neighborhoodlink.com/detroit/ivil
Contact: Dorothea A. Martin, Sec.

Local. Seeks to collect and preserve the history of the homes and residents of Indian Village.

7376 ■ Industrial Workers of the World - Detroit
PO Box 08161
Detroit, MI 48208
E-mail: detroit@iww.org
URL: National Affiliate–www.iww.org

Local. **Affiliated With:** Industrial Workers of the World.

7377 ■ Inforum
3663 Woodward Ave., Ste.4-1610
Detroit, MI 48201-2403
Ph: (313)578-3230
Fax: (313)578-3245
E-mail: info@inforummichigan.org
URL: http://www.inforummichigan.org
Contact: Terry A. Barclay, Pres./CEO

Founded: 1962. **Members:** 2,000. **Membership Dues:** transitional, $75 (annual) • executive, $500 (annual) • regular, $150 (annual). **Staff:** 7. **Budget:** $700,000. **State**. Women's professional organization. Provides a speaker's luncheon forum for the presentation of current local and national issues; offers support and networking opportunities. Conducts seminars. **Awards: Type:** recognition. **Programs:** Inforum Ctr. for Leadership. **Formerly:** (2005) Women's Economic Club. **Publications:** *Inside Inforum*, quarterly. Newsletter. Contains events, articles. **Price:** included in membership dues. **Circulation:** 2,000. **Conventions/Meetings:** monthly luncheon.

7378 ■ International Association for Healthcare Security and Safety - Michigan Chapter
c/o John Weigle
Henry Ford Hosp.
2799 W Grand Blvd.
Detroit, MI 48202
Ph: (313)876-1122
URL: National Affiliate–www.iahss.org
Contact: John Weigle, Contact
State. Works to advance security and safety within the healthcare institution. Develops educational and credentialing programs. **Affiliated With:** International Association for Healthcare Security and Safety.

7379 ■ International Association of Ministers Wives and Ministers Widows, Michigan
4501 W Outer St.
Detroit, MI 48235
Ph: (313)393-0477
URL: National Affiliate–www.iamwmw.org
Contact: Mrs. Cynthia Gallard, Pres.
State. **Affiliated With:** International Association of Ministers Wives and Ministers Widows.

7380 ■ International Union of Operating Engineers, Local 547
24270 W Seven Mile Rd.
Detroit, MI 48219
Ph: (313)532-2022
Fax: (313)532-7306
Free: (800)253-2316
E-mail: iuoe547@iuoelocal547.com
URL: http://www.iuoelocal547.com
Contact: Philip Schloop, Business Mgr.
Local. Works to bring economic justice to the workplace and to improve the lives of working families. **Affiliated With:** International Union of Operating Engineers.

7381 ■ International Union, United Automobile, Aerospace and Agricultural Implement Workers of America, AFL-CIO - Local Union 22
4300 Michigan Ave.
Detroit, MI 48210-3292
Ph: (313)897-8850
Fax: (313)897-6220
E-mail: localuaw22@mail.unionsamerica.com
URL: http://www.localuaw22.org
Contact: Craig A. Nothnagel, Pres.
Members: 3,997. **Local**. AFL-CIO. **Affiliated With:** International Union, United Automobile, Aerospace and Agricultural Implement Workers of America.

7382 ■ Jackets for Jobs Michigan WORKS
c/o Alison Vaughn, Exec.Dir.
5555 Conner, Ste.2097
Detroit, MI 48213
Ph: (313)579-9160
Fax: (313)579-9180
URL: http://www.jacketsforjobs.org
Contact: Alison Vaughn, Exec.Dir.
Founded: 2000. **Staff:** 3. **Budget:** $108,000. **Local**. Helps women make the transition from welfare to work by providing clothing and employment skills. **Formerly:** (2005) Jackets for Jobs.

7383 ■ Jim Dandy Ski Club
PO Box 32706
Detroit, MI 48232
Ph: (313)345-8997
E-mail: cgeorgeehair@yahoo.com
URL: http://jimdandyskiclub.com
Contact: Christina A. George, Membership Chair
Local. **Affiliated With:** National Brotherhood of Skiers.

7384 ■ Joy-Southfield Community Development Corporation
18700 Joy Rd.
Detroit, MI 48228-3156
Ph: (313)493-9767
Fax: (313)493-4045
Contact: Joseph Ellison, Chm.
Local.

7385 ■ Junior Achievement, Southeastern Michigan
c/o Lynn A. Feldhouse, Pres.
577 E Larned St., Ste.100
Detroit, MI 48226
Ph: (313)962-2550
Fax: (313)964-8884
Free: (877)479-7012
E-mail: mail@jamichigan.org
URL: http://www.jamichigan.org
Contact: Cindy Bazner, SVP/COO
Founded: 1949. **Members:** 50,000. **Staff:** 7. **Budget:** $1,500,000. **For-Profit**. **Local**. Educates and inspires young people to value free enterprise, business, and economics to improve the quality of their lives. **Affiliated With:** Junior Achievement.

7386 ■ Labor Council for Latin American Advancement - Oakland County Chapter
8000 E Jefferson
Detroit, MI 48214
E-mail: lrivera@uaw.net
URL: National Affiliate–www.lclaa.org
Contact: Lorenzo Rivera, Pres.
Local. **Affiliated With:** American Dog Owner's Association.

7387 ■ Literacy Volunteers of America-Detroit
Fisher Bldg.
3011 W Grand Blvd., Ste.215
Detroit, MI 48202
Ph: (313)872-1333
E-mail: lvadetroit@aol.com
URL: http://www.volunteersolutions.org/uwcs/org/220400.html
Contact: Margaret Thorpe-Williamson, Exec.Dir.
Local. Recruits and trains volunteers to provide free literacy services to adults aged sixteen and older, and their families. **Affiliated With:** Laubach Literacy International.

7388 ■ Maltese-American Benevolent Society (MABS)
1832 Michigan Ave.
Detroit, MI 48216
Ph: (313)961-8393
Fax: (313)961-2050
Contact: Carmen Nino, Pres.
Founded: 1929. **Members:** 300. **Membership Dues:** individual, $25 (annual). **Staff:** 8. **Budget:** $1,200,000. Serves social and patriotic needs of Detroit's Maltese population, estimated to be 66,000 and believed to be the largest in the U.S. Supports children's services. Offers activities for members and their families. **Libraries:** **Type:** reference. **Holdings:** books, video recordings. **Subjects:** U.S. history, Maltese folklore. **Awards:** Gentleman of the Year Award. **Frequency:** annual. **Type:** recognition. **Recipient:** outstanding service to Maltese Community or community in general • George Zammit Award. **Frequency:** annual. **Type:** recognition. **Recipient:** For outstanding citizenship displayed by an individual of Maltese descent • Maltese American Scholarship Award. **Frequency:** annual. **Type:** scholarship. **Recipient:** for an outstanding Maltese student. **Committees:** Activities; Benevolent; Educational; Ethnic Studies; Travel; Urban Renewal. **Councils:** Maltese Organizations. **Publications:** *Meetings and Conventions*, quarterly. Newsletter. **Price:** free. **Circulation:** 180. **Advertising:** not accepted • *Times of Malta*, daily. **Conventions/Meetings:** quarterly general assembly • monthly Ladies Auxiliary - meeting.

7389 ■ Metropolitan Detroit Science Teachers Association (MDSTA)
c/o Christine Brownfield, Pres.
Off. of Sci. Educ.
Albert Kahn Bldg., 3rd Fl.
7430 Second Ave.
Detroit, MI 48202
E-mail: mdsta_brownfield@yahoo.com
URL: http://www.mdsta.org
Contact: Christine Brownfield, Pres.
Local. Promotes excellence and innovation in science teaching and learning for all. Serves as the voice for excellence and innovation in science teaching and learning, curriculum and instruction, and assessment. Promotes interest and support for science education. **Affiliated With:** National Science Teachers Association.

7390 ■ Mexicantown Community Development Corporation
2810 W Vernor
Detroit, MI 48216
Ph: (313)967-9898
Fax: (313)967-9903
E-mail: info@mexicantown.org
URL: http://www.mexicantown.org
Local.

7391 ■ Michigan Advertising Industry Alliance (MAIA)
3011 W Grand Blvd., Ste.1715
Detroit, MI 48202-3000
Ph: (313)872-7850
Fax: (313)872-7858
E-mail: bguerrini@adcraft.org
URL: http://www.adcraft.org/i4a/pages/index.cfm?pageid=35
Contact: Jan Starr, Pres.
Founded: 1972. **Members:** 65. **Membership Dues:** corporate, $300 (annual). **Staff:** 2. **State**. Advertising firms united for legislative action on issues affecting the industry. **Publications:** Newsletter, periodic. **Conventions/Meetings:** annual meeting.

7392 ■ Michigan Architectural Foundation (MAF)
553 E Jefferson
Detroit, MI 48226
Ph: (313)965-4100
Fax: (313)965-1501
E-mail: mikaaia@mb-architects.com
URL: http://aiami.com/maf_home.htm
Contact: Mike Marshburn, Pres.
Founded: 1957. **Members:** 9. **Staff:** 5. **Local**. Architects united to promote the industry. Conducts public awareness programs. **Libraries:** **Type:** not open to the public. **Awards:** **Type:** grant • **Type:** scholarship. **Conventions/Meetings:** periodic Educational Facilities - conference • periodic Health Facilities - conference.

7393 ■ Michigan Association for Evaluation (MAE)
c/o Center for Urban Studies
Wayne State Univ.
3073 Faculty Admin. Bldg.
656 W Kirby St.
Detroit, MI 48202
Ph: (313)841-7442 (313)577-9918
E-mail: bdates@swcds.org
URL: http://www.maeeval.org
Contact: Neva Nahan, Pres.
State. Seeks to improve evaluation practices and methods. Provides a forum for professional development, networking and exchange of practical, methodological and theoretical knowledge in the field of evaluation. Promotes evaluation as a profession. **Affiliated With:** American Evaluation Association.

7394 ■ Michigan Association of Neurological Surgeons
c/o Dr. Guthikonda
4160 John R Rd., Ste.930
Detroit, MI 48201-2017
Ph: (313)993-8600
URL: National Affiliate–www.aans.org
Contact: Dr. Guthikonda, Contact
State. Represents neurological surgeons united to promote excellence in neurological surgery and its related sciences. Provides funding to foster research in the neurosciences. **Affiliated With:** American Association of Neurological Surgeons.

7395 ■ Michigan Disabled American Veterans
Virginia Regional Off. McNamara Fed. Bldg.
477 Michigan Ave., Rm. 1200
Detroit, MI 48226

Ph: (313)964-6595
URL: National Affiliate–www.dav.org
State. **Affiliated With:** Disabled American Veterans.

7396 ■ Michigan Federation of Teachers and School Related Personnel (MFT&SRP)
c/o David Hecker, Pres.
2661 E Jefferson
Detroit, MI 48207
Ph: (313)393-2200
Fax: (313)393-2236
Free: (800)638-8868
E-mail: dhecker@mftsrp.org
URL: http://www.mftsrp.org
State.

7397 ■ Michigan Minority Business Development Council (MMBDC)
c/o Dr. E. Delbert Gray, PhD, Pres./CEO
3011 W Grand Blvd., No. 230
Detroit, MI 48202-3011
Ph: (313)873-3200
Fax: (313)873-4783
E-mail: mail@mmbdc.com
URL: http://www.mmbdc.com
Contact: Dr. E. Delbert Gray PhD, Pres./CEO
Founded: 1978. **Members:** 2,000. **Staff:** 14. **Budget:** $1,000,000. **State**. Seeks to promote the minority business community by providing corporate members with qualified minority suppliers. Sponsors annual dinner and golf outing. **Publications:** *Impact News*. Newsletter • *Michigan Business Network*, quarterly. Magazine. **Conventions/Meetings:** annual Michigan Minority Procurement Conference - workshop (exhibits).

7398 ■ Michigan National Lawyers Guild
PO Box 311458
Detroit, MI 48231-1458
Ph: (313)963-0843
Fax: (866)337-4937
E-mail: nlgdetroit@wideopenwest.com
URL: http://www.michigannlg.org
Contact: Tom Schram, Ed.
State. Lawyers, legal workers and law students who want to work for justice, to the end that human rights shall be regarded as more sacred than property rights. **Affiliated With:** National Lawyers Guild. **Formerly:** (2005) National Lawyers Guild - Detroit Chapter.

7399 ■ Michigan Parking Association
c/o Jon Frederick, Pres.
Wayne State Univ.
6050 Cass Ave.
Detroit, MI 48202
Ph: (313)577-4349
Fax: (313)577-6992
E-mail: ah9818@wayne.edu
URL: http://www.michiganparkingassociation.org
Contact: Jon Frederick, Pres.
Founded: 1981. **Members:** 110. **Membership Dues:** individual and corporate, $75 (annual). **State**. Seeks to promote the mutual interests of the membership in the provision and operation of adequate, efficient, convenient, and economical public and private parking as a proper and necessary function for the economic and social well being of the membership and industry. Organize and act as a unified force for the state of Michigan, to promote the legislation of state and local laws, ordinance and regulations relating to parking that will aid and benefit the association membership and the industry; and t o assist and aid association members in fostering up-to-date understanding of parking principles, practices and the interaction with transportation objectives. **Committees:** By-laws. **Affiliated With:** International Parking Institute; National Parking Association. **Publications:** *Parking Spaces*, quarterly. Newsletters. Contains information related to the parking industry and events sponsored by the Michigan Parking Association. **Price:** included in membership dues. **Circulation:** 100. Alternate Formats: online. **Conventions/Meetings:** annual MPA Fall Conference, variety speakers presenting on topics and trends in the parking industry (exhibits).

7400 ■ Michigan Supreme Court Historical Society
c/o Philip J. Kessler, Chm.
150 W Jefferson, Ste.900
Detroit, MI 48226-4450
Ph: (313)225-7000
Fax: (313)225-7080
E-mail: kessler@butzel.com
URL: National Affiliate–www.supremecourthistory.org
Contact: Philip J. Kessler, Chm.
State. Collects and preserves the history of the Supreme Court of the United States. Conducts educational programs and supports historical research. Collects antiques and artifacts related to the Court's history. Increases public awareness of the Court's contributions to the nation's constitutional heritage. **Affiliated With:** Supreme Court Historical Society.

7401 ■ Moslem Shriners
c/o Albert J. Koury
434 Temple Ave.
Detroit, MI 48201
Ph: (313)831-7600
Fax: (313)832-4727
URL: http://www.beeoneinc.com/moslem
Contact: Albert J. Koury, Contact
Local. **Affiliated With:** Imperial Council of the Ancient Arabic Order of the Nobles of the Mystic Shrine for North America.

7402 ■ Motor City Theatre Organ Society (MCTOS)
c/o Elaine Mundt, Sec.
16889 W Riverdale Dr.
Detroit, MI 48219-3774
Ph: (313)531-4407
E-mail: midnight66@juno.com
URL: http://redfordtheatre.com/mctos
Contact: Thomas Hurst, Pres.
Local. **Affiliated With:** American Theatre Organ Society.

7403 ■ Motown Association for Computing Machinery SIGGRAPH
c/o Ed McDonald, Chair
Coll. for Creative Stud.
201 E Kirby
Detroit, MI 48202-4034
Ph: (313)664-7699
Fax: (313)664-7880
URL: http://www.ccscad.edu
Contact: Ed McDonald, Chair
Local. Biological, medical, behavioral, and computer scientists; hospital administrators; programmers and others interested in application of computer methods to biological, behavioral, and medical problems. Stimulates understanding of the use and potential of computers in the Biosciences. **Affiliated With:** Association for Computing Machinery.

7404 ■ National Active and Retired Federal Employees Association - Detroit 89
19280 Greydale
Detroit, MI 48219-1839
Ph: (313)531-8006
URL: National Affiliate–www.narfe.org
Contact: David Adams, Contact
Local. Protects the retirement future of employees through education. Informs members on issues affecting the retirement. **Affiliated With:** National Association of Retired Federal Employees.

7405 ■ National Active and Retired Federal Employees Association - Tarcom 1593
14072 Clover Lawn
Detroit, MI 48238-2479
Ph: (313)491-7664
URL: National Affiliate–www.narfe.org
Contact: Mamie Cokley, Contact
Local. Protects the retirement future of employees through education. Informs members on issues affecting the retirement. **Affiliated With:** National Association of Retired Federal Employees.

7406 ■ National Association for the Advancement of Colored People-Detroit Branch
2900 E Grand Blvd.
Detroit, MI 48202
Ph: (313)871-2087
Fax: (313)871-7745
E-mail: info@detroitnaacp.org
URL: http://www.detroitnaacp.org
Contact: Rev. Wendell Anthony, Pres.
Founded: 1919. **Members:** 50,000. **Membership Dues:** adult (21 and over), $30 (annual) • young adult (ages 18-21), $15 (annual) • youth (up to 18 years old), $10 (annual) • life (junior), $100 • life (bronze), $400 • life (silver), $750 • life (golden), $1,500 • life (diamond), $2,500 • corporate, $5,000 (annual). **Local**. Works to ensure the political, educational, social and economic equality of all persons and to eradicate racial hatred and racial discrimination. **Affiliated With:** National Association for the Advancement of Colored People.

7407 ■ National Association of Black Journalists - Detroit Chapter
PO Box 31-1609
Detroit, MI 48231
Ph: (313)561-8146
Fax: (313)223-4884
E-mail: dnichols@detnews.com
URL: National Affiliate–www.nabj.org
Contact: Darren Nichols, Pres.
Local. Advocates the rights of black journalists. Provides informational and training services and professional development to black journalists and to the general public. **Affiliated With:** National Association of Black Journalists.

7408 ■ National Association of Women Business Owners, Greater Detroit Chapter (NAWBO)
c/o Amy S. Marshall, Exec.Dir.
660 Woodward Ave., Ste.1166
Detroit, MI 48226-3507
Ph: (313)961-4748
Fax: (313)961-5434
E-mail: info@nawbogdc.org
URL: http://www.nawbogdc.org
Contact: Amy S. Marshall, Exec.Dir.
Founded: 1980. **Members:** 420. **Membership Dues:** established business owner (2 years or longer in business), $200 (annual) • corporate partner base, $3,500 (annual) • emerging business owner (in business less than 2 years), $150 (annual). **Budget:** $370,000. **Local**. Women business owners and corporate partners seeking networking opportunities, educational seminars, political and economic influence through organization with a national presence. **Libraries: Type:** reference. **Holdings:** audio recordings, books. **Awards:** Salute to Women in the Automotive Industry. **Type:** trophy. **Recipient:** for women with outstanding leadership, contributions and influential impact • Top 10 Michigan Business Womens Award. **Frequency:** annual. **Type:** trophy. **Recipient:** for prominent and outstanding women business owners in Michigan. **Computer Services:** Mailing lists, of members. **Affiliated With:** National Association of Women Business Owners. **Publications:** *Vision*, bimonthly. Newsletter. **Conventions/Meetings:** monthly board meeting • periodic luncheon • annual meeting • monthly meeting • periodic Salute to African American Women Business Owners - meeting.

7409 ■ National Black MBA Association, Detroit Chapter
PO Box 02398
Detroit, MI 48202
Ph: (313)972-4832
E-mail: nbmbaa_detroit@ameritech.net
URL: http://www.detblackmba.org
Contact: Ms. Corrie Patton, Pres.
Founded: 1976. **Membership Dues:** full, associate, $125 (annual) • student, $60 (annual) • life, $1,000. **Local**. **Affiliated With:** National Black MBA Association.

7410 ■ National Black United Front, Detroit Chapter
10100 Harper Ave.
Detroit, MI 48213
Ph: (313)921-9422
Fax: (313)921-9214
E-mail: alkebu@aol.com
URL: http://www.nbufront.org/html/Chapters/NBUF-Detroit.html
Local. Affiliated With: National Black United Front.

7411 ■ National Council on Alcoholism and Drug Dependence, Greater Detroit Area (NCADD-GDA)
16647 Wyoming Ave.
Detroit, MI 48221
Fax: (313)861-0413
Free: (800)388-9891
E-mail: customerhelp@ncadd-detroit.org
URL: http://www.ncadd-detroit.org
Founded: 1947. **Members:** 10. **Membership Dues:** general, $25 (annual). **Staff:** 16. **Budget:** $825,000. **Local**. Supports individuals with substance abuse problem to resolve their addiction. Sponsors forums. **Libraries: Type:** open to the public. **Holdings:** articles, books, video recordings. **Subjects:** drugs, alcohol, recovery. **Awards:** Lamplighter of the Year. **Frequency:** annual. **Type:** recognition. **Recipient:** for outstanding accomplishments in combatting substance abuse • Recovery is Possible Award. **Frequency:** annual. **Type:** recognition. **Recipient:** for individuals who have maintained more than 5 years of sobriety and help others to recover from addiction. **Affiliated With:** National Council on Alcoholism and Drug Dependence. **Publications:** *The Lamplighter*, quarterly. Newsletter. **Circulation:** 1,100. **Conventions/Meetings:** annual conference (exhibits).

7412 ■ National Management Association, Blue Cross and Blue Shield of Michigan
c/o Ms. Tammy Conway, Pres.
Blue Cross & Blue Shield of Mich.
600 Lafayette, MC: 1630
Detroit, MI 48226
Ph: (313)225-9546
E-mail: tconway@bcbsm.com
URL: National Affiliate–www.nma1.org
Contact: Ms. Tammy Conway, Pres.
Local. Business and industrial management personnel; membership comes from supervisory level, with the remainder from middle management and above. Seeks to develop and recognize management as a profession and to promote the free enterprise system. **Affiliated With:** National Management Association.

7413 ■ National Organization for Women - Detroit
c/o Sandy Hardwick
PO Box 21446
Detroit, MI 48221
Ph: (313)273-7400
E-mail: jsh34sp@sbcglobal.net
URL: http://www.michnow.org
Contact: Sandy Hardwick, Contact
Local. Affiliated With: National Organization for Women.

7414 ■ National Society of Black Engineers - Detroit Alumni Extension
PO Box 441531
Detroit, MI 48244-1531
Ph: (313)927-3232
URL: http://www.nsbe-dae.org
Contact: Randall Cobb, Chm.
Local. Strives to increase the number of culturally responsible Black engineers who excel academically, succeed professionally and positively impact the community. **Affiliated With:** National Society of Black Engineers.

7415 ■ National Writers Union, Southeast Michigan
c/o Amy Rose
PO Box 10407
Detroit, MI 48210
Ph: (313)438-1829
E-mail: nwu@nwu-sem.org
URL: http://www.nwu-sem.org
Local. Affiliated With: National Writers Union.

7416 ■ Outdoor Advertising Association of Michigan (OAAM)
c/o Lynda Brynalfson, Legislative Dir.
88 Custer Ave.
Detroit, MI 48202
Ph: (313)872-6030
Fax: (313)872-8066
URL: http://www.oaam.org
Founded: 1875. **State**.

7417 ■ PFLAG Family Reunion: People Of Color Chapter
131 W Parkhurst Pl.
Detroit, MI 48203
Ph: (313)585-5656
E-mail: ajlocks@yahoo.com
URL: http://www.pflag.org/Michigan.216.0.html
Local. Affiliated With: Parents, Families, and Friends of Lesbians and Gays.

7418 ■ Phi Theta Kappa, Alpha Upsilon Zeta Chapter - Wayne County Community College
c/o Liz Chamberlain
Downtown Campus
1001 W Fort St.
Detroit, MI 48226
Ph: (734)374-3220
E-mail: lchambe1@wcccd.edu
URL: http://www.ptk.org/directories/chapters/MI/18136-1.htm
Contact: Liz Chamberlain, Advisor
Local.

7419 ■ Plumbing-Heating-Cooling Contractors Association, Southeastern Michigan
c/o Carl M. Evans, Exec.Mgr.
14801 W 8 Mile Rd.
Detroit, MI 48235-1623
Ph: (313)341-7661
Fax: (313)341-1007
URL: National Affiliate–www.phccweb.org
Contact: Carl M. Evans, Exec.Mgr.
Local. Represents the plumbing, heating and cooling contractors. Promotes the construction industry. Protects the environment, health, safety and comfort of society. **Affiliated With:** Plumbing-Heating-Cooling Contractors Association.

7420 ■ Plumbing and Mechanical Contractors of Detroit (PMC)
14801 W 8 Mile Rd.
Detroit, MI 48235
Ph: (313)341-7661
Fax: (313)341-1007
E-mail: cevans@pmcdetroit.com
URL: http://www.pmcdetroit.com
Contact: Carl M. Evans, Pres.
Members: 50. **Staff:** 3. **Budget:** $300,000. **Local**. Represents plumbing and mechanical contractors in Huron, Macomb, Oakland, St. Clair, Sanilac, and Wayne counties, MI. Works to standardize materials and methods used in the industry. Promotes educational programs, legislative activities, and negotiations. **Libraries: Type:** not open to the public. **Holdings:** 75; audio recordings. **Subjects:** construction. **Affiliated With:** Mechanical Contractors Association of America; Plumbing-Heating-Cooling Contractors Association. **Formerly:** (2006) Metropolitan Detroit Plumbing and Mechanical Contractors Association. **Publications:** Journal • Magazine • Newsletter. **Conventions/Meetings:** annual workshop - 3/year.

7421 ■ Police and Firemen's Insurance Association - Detroit Police Department
c/o Joanna Graves
19969 Sorrento St.
Detroit, MI 48235
Ph: (313)861-7893
URL: National Affiliate–www.pfia.net
Contact: Joanna Graves, Contact
Local. Affiliated With: Police and Firemen's Insurance Association.

7422 ■ Preservation Wayne
c/o Board of Directors, VP
4735 Cass Ave.
Detroit, MI 48202
Ph: (313)577-3559
Fax: (313)577-7666
E-mail: preswayne@aol.com
URL: http://preservationwayne.org
Contact: Karen Nagher, Board VP
Local. Works to preserve, promote, and protect the districts, neighborhoods, and structures that define the heritage and future of Detroit.

7423 ■ Prevailing Community Development Corp.
c/o Rev. Claude O. Cline
6136 Hazlett
Detroit, MI 48210
Ph: (313)896-4070
Fax: (313)896-1026
E-mail: pcdc@aol.com
URL: National Affiliate–www.cdadonline.org/index.html
Contact: Rev. Claude O. Cline, Contact
Local.

7424 ■ Psi Chi, National Honor Society in Psychology - Marygrove College
c/o Dept. of Psychology
8425 W McNichols Rd.
Detroit, MI 48221-2599
Ph: (313)927-1325
Fax: (313)927-1345
E-mail: ktracy@marygrove.edu
URL: http://www.psichi.org/chapters/info.asp?chapter_id=804
Contact: Karen Tracy PhD, Advisor
Local.

7425 ■ Psi Chi, National Honor Society in Psychology - Wayne State University
c/o Dept. of Psychology
5057 Woodward Ave., 7th Fl.
Detroit, MI 48202
Ph: (313)577-2800 (313)577-2879
Fax: (313)577-7636
E-mail: dbarnett@sun.science.wayne.edu
URL: National Affiliate–www.psichi.org
Local. Affiliated With: Psi Chi, National Honor Society in Psychology.

7426 ■ RSVP Wayne County
c/o Essie Mahaffy, Dir.
9851 Hamilton Ave.
Detroit, MI 48202-2389
Ph: (313)883-7764
Fax: (313)883-0601
E-mail: emahaffy@csswayne.org
URL: http://www.csswayne.org
Contact: Essie Mahaffy, Dir.
Local. Affiliated With: Retired and Senior Volunteer Program.

7427 ■ Sacred Heart-St. Elizabeth Community Development Corp.
c/o Jacqueline Kamuyu
4141 Mitchell
Detroit, MI 48207-2004
Ph: (313)921-2090
Fax: (313)921-2093
E-mail: shsecdc@yahoo.com
Contact: Jacqueline Kamuyu, Exec.Dir.
Founded: 1999. **Members:** 15. **Staff:** 1. **Local**. Affordable housing for low and moderate income people.

7428 ■ St. Paul African Methodist Episcopal Church
c/o E. Anne Henning Byfield, Pastor
2260 Hunt St.
Detroit, MI 48207
Ph: (313)567-9643 (313)567-3373
Fax: (313)567-7144
E-mail: stpaul@stpaulame.org
URL: http://stpaulame.org
Contact: Rev. E. Anne Henning Byfield, Pres.
Founded: 2000. **Members:** 15. **Staff:** 4. **Budget:** $300,000. **Local. Formerly:** (2005) St. Paul Community Development Corp.

7429 ■ Scarab Club (SC)
217 Farnsworth
Detroit, MI 48202
Ph: (313)831-1250
Fax: (313)831-6815
E-mail: scarabclub@aol.com
URL: http://scarabclub.org
Contact: Ms. Christine Renner, Exec.Dir.
Founded: 1907. **Members:** 300. **Membership Dues:** active, $260 (annual). **Staff:** 3. **Budget:** $100,000. **Regional.** Artists, collectors, and patrons of the arts united to advance appreciation and knowledge of the arts in the Detroit, MI area. Sponsors educational programs and exhibits. **Libraries: Type:** not open to the public. **Holdings:** archival material, articles. **Subjects:** club history. **Awards:** Gold Medal Annual. **Frequency:** annual. **Type:** recognition. **Recipient:** for artistic excellence • Silver Medal. **Frequency:** annual. **Type:** recognition. **Recipient:** for artistic excellence. **Formerly:** The Hopkins Painters. **Publications:** *Exhibition and Auction Catalogs* • *The Scarab Buzz*, monthly. Newsletter. **Price:** included in membership dues. **Circulation:** 300. **Advertising:** accepted. Alternate Formats: CD-ROM. **Conventions/Meetings:** monthly conference (exhibits).

7430 ■ SCORE Detroit
c/o Emily Olivero, CHR
477 Michigan Ave., Rm. 515-SBA
Detroit, MI 48226
Ph: (313)226-7947
Fax: (313)226-3448
E-mail: detscore@sbcglobal.net
URL: http://scoredetroit.org
Contact: Ms. Emily Olivero, Chair
Founded: 1964. **Members:** 98. **Staff:** 2. **Languages:** English, Spanish. **State.** Seeks to provide counseling for new and small business. **Libraries: Type:** reference. **Subjects:** business plans. **Awards:** Client of the Year. **Frequency:** annual. **Type:** recognition. **Affiliated With:** SCORE. **Publications:** *SCORE Scribblings*, quarterly. Newsletter. **Advertising:** accepted.

7431 ■ SER - Jobs for Progress, Metro Detroit
c/o Eva Dewaelsche, Pres./CEO
9301 Michigan Ave.
Detroit, MI 48210
Ph: (313)846-2240
Fax: (313)846-2247
E-mail: edewaelsche@sermetro.org
URL: http://www.sermetro.org
Contact: Eva Dewaelsche, Pres./CEO
Local. Affiliated With: SER - Jobs for Progress National.

7432 ■ Sickle Cell Disease Association of America - Michigan
18516 James Couzens
Detroit, MI 48235
Ph: (313)864-4406
Fax: (313)864-6669
Free: (800)842-0973
E-mail: hollanddeborah@yahoo.com
URL: National Affiliate–www.sicklecelldisease.org
Contact: Deborah Holland, Exec.Dir.
State. Aims to create awareness of the negative impact of sickle cell disease on the health, economic, social and educational well being of the individual and his or her family. Encourages support for research activities leading to improved treatment and cure. **Affiliated With:** Sickle Cell Disease Association of America.

7433 ■ Society of American Military Engineers, Detroit Post
PO Box 3026
Detroit, MI 48231
Ph: (313)226-6753
Fax: (313)226-2013
E-mail: charles.a.uhlarik@usace.army.mil
URL: http://posts.same.org/detroit
Contact: Charlie Uhlarik, Contact
Local. Works to advance the science of military engineering. Promotes and facilitates engineering support for national security. Develops and enhances relationships and competencies among uniformed services, public and private sector engineers and related professionals.

7434 ■ Society for Applied Spectroscopy, Detroit
c/o Paul M. Beckwith, Chm.
The Detroit Edison Co.
6100 W Warren
Detroit, MI 48210
Ph: (313)897-1417
E-mail: rcarter@ford.com
URL: National Affiliate–www.s-a-s.org
Contact: Paul M. Beckwith, Chm.
Local. Affiliated With: Society for Applied Spectroscopy.

7435 ■ Society of Manufacturing Engineers - Focus-Hope Center for Advanced Technologies S279
1400 Oakman Blvd. - H Bldg.
Detroit, MI 48238
Ph: (313)494-4461
Fax: (313)494-4428
E-mail: zhengl@focushope.edu
URL: National Affiliate–www.sme.org
Contact: Lixin Zheng, Contact
Local. Advances manufacturing knowledge to gain competitive advantage. Improves skills and manufacturing solutions for the growth of economy. Provides resources and opportunities for manufacturing professionals. **Affiliated With:** Mycological Society of America.

7436 ■ Society of Manufacturing Engineers - University of Detroit - Mercy S081
Univ. of Detroit - Mercy, Mech. Engg. Dept.
PO Box 19900
Detroit, MI 48219-0900
Ph: (313)993-1656
E-mail: mostafme@udmercy.edu
URL: National Affiliate–www.sme.org
Contact: Mostafa Mehrabi, Contact
Local. Advances manufacturing knowledge to gain competitive advantage. Improves skills and manufacturing solutions for the growth of economy. Provides resources and opportunities for manufacturing professionals. **Affiliated With:** John Burroughs Association.

7437 ■ Southeast Michigan Council of Governments (SEMCOG)
535 Griswold St., Ste.300
Detroit, MI 48226-3602
Ph: (313)961-4266
Fax: (313)961-4869
E-mail: infoservices@semcog.org
URL: http://www.semcog.org
Contact: Paul E. Tait, Exec.Dir.
Founded: 1967. **Members:** 140. **Staff:** 77. **Budget:** $8,200,000. **Local.** Regional planning and association of local governments in Livingston, Macomb, Monroe, Oakland, St. Clair, Washtenaw, and Wayne counties in Michigan. **Libraries: Type:** open to the public. **Holdings:** 20,000; periodicals. **Subjects:** economic development, environment, transportation, land use, demographics, intergovernmental cooperation. **Affiliated With:** National Association of Regional Councils. **Publications:** *Semscope*, quarterly. Newsletter. **Price:** free. ISSN: 0361-1310. **Circulation:** 8,500. Alternate Formats: online. **Conventions/Meetings:** periodic executive committee meeting • periodic general assembly.

7438 ■ Southeast Michigan Jobs with Justice
600 W Lafayette, 2nd Fl.
Detroit, MI 48226
Ph: (313)961-0800
Fax: (313)961-9776
E-mail: jwjsem@gmail.com
URL: National Affiliate–www.jwj.org
Local. Aims to improve the social status of workers. Seeks to fight for job security and protect workers' right. **Affiliated With:** Jobs with Justice.

7439 ■ Southwest Detroit Business Association (SDBA)
c/o Kathleen Wendler, Pres.
7752 W. Vernor Hwy.
Detroit, MI 48209
Ph: (313)842-0986
Fax: (313)842-6350
E-mail: kathyw@southwestdetroit.com
URL: http://www.southwestdetroit.com
Founded: 1957. **Members:** 250. **Staff:** 18. **Languages:** English, Spanish. **For-Profit. Local.** Promotes community based economic development in Southwest Detroit. **Awards:** Community Investment. **Frequency:** annual. **Type:** recognition. **Recipient:** for committee review. **Publications:** *SDBA Community News* (in English and Spanish), quarterly. Newspaper. **Price:** free. **Circulation:** 23,000. **Advertising:** accepted. Alternate Formats: CD-ROM; online.

7440 ■ Southwest Detroit Environmental Vision (SDEV)
c/o Billie Hickey
PO Box 9400
Detroit, MI 48209
Ph: (313)842-1961
Fax: (313)842-1961
E-mail: swdev@flash.net
URL: http://www.comnet.org/sdev
Local.

7441 ■ Teamsters for a Democratic Union (TDU)
PO Box 10128
Detroit, MI 48210
Ph: (313)842-2600
Fax: (313)842-0227
E-mail: webmaster@tdu.org
URL: http://www.tdu.org
Local.

7442 ■ Transition of Prisoners (TOP)
c/o Joseph Williams
40 Hague
Detroit, MI 48202-2119
Ph: (313)875-3883
Fax: (313)875-3886
E-mail: dettopinc@msn.com
URL: http://www.topinc.net
Contact: Joseph Williams, CEO
Founded: 2000. **Staff:** 10. **Budget:** $1,000,000. **Local. Publications:** *On Top*, quarterly. Newsletter. **Price:** free. **Circulation:** 2,500.

7443 ■ Transportation Riders United
c/o Karen Kendrick-Hands
500 Griswold, Ste.1650
Detroit, MI 48226-1978
Ph: (313)963-8872
URL: http://www.detroittransit.org
Contact: Paulette Chaplin, Exec.Dir.
Local.

7444 ■ Triangle Foundation
c/o Jeffrey Montgomery, Exec.Dir.
19641 W Seven Mile Rd.
Detroit, MI 48219-2721

Ph: (313)537-3323
Fax: (313)537-3379
Free: (877)787-4264
E-mail: info@tri.org
URL: http://www.tri.org
Contact: Jeffrey Montgomery, Exec.Dir.
State. Michigan's statewide civil rights, advocacy and anti-violence organization for gay, lesbian, bisexual and transgender persons.

7445 ■ United Brotherhood of Carpenters and Joiners of America, Michigan Regional Council of Carpenters and Millwrights
3800 Woodward Ave., Ste.1200
Detroit, MI 48201
Ph: (313)832-3887
Fax: (313)832-1578
Free: (888)HAMMER-9
E-mail: info@hammer9.com
URL: http://www.hammer9.com
Contact: Walter R. Marby, Exec.Sec.-Treas.
Regional. **Affiliated With:** United Brotherhood of Carpenters and Joiners of America. **Formerly:** (2005) United Brotherhood of Carpenters and Joiners of America, Michigan Regional Council 4085.

7446 ■ United States Naval Sea Cadet Corps - James M. Hannan Division
Redford Presbyterian Church
22122 W McNichols
Detroit, MI 48219
E-mail: hannandivision@hotmail.com
URL: http://www.geocities.com/hannandivision
Local. Works to instill good citizenship and patriotism in youth. Encourages qualities such as personal neatness, loyalty, obedience, dependability, and responsibility to others. Offers courses in physical fitness and military drill, first aid, water safety, basic seamanship, and naval history and traditions. **Affiliated With:** Naval Sea Cadet Corps.

7447 ■ United Way for Southeastern Michigan
1212 Griswold St.
Detroit, MI 48226
Ph: (313)226-9200
Free: (800)552-1183
URL: http://www.uwsem.org
Contact: Michael J. Brennan, Pres./CEO
Local. **Affiliated With:** United Way of America.

7448 ■ University of Detroit-Mercy Association for Computing Machinery
c/o Matthew Perkowski, Chm.
Dept. of Math and Cmpt. Sci.
4001 W. NcNichols Rd.
PO Box 19900
Detroit, MI 48219-0900
Ph: (313)993-1057
Fax: (313)993-1163
E-mail: al-ahmas@udmercy.edu
URL: National Affiliate–www.acm.org
Contact: Mr. Saer Al-ahmar, Prof.Chm.
Local. University students enrolled in computer-related courses. **Affiliated With:** Association for Computing Machinery. **Formerly:** (2001) Association for +Computing +Machinery, University of Detroit-Mercy.

7449 ■ Urban Solutions Training and Development Corporation
3544 Algonquin
Detroit, MI 48215-2484
Ph: (313)331-4929 (313)579-0655
Contact: Sharon Dumas-Pugh, Exec.Dir.
Founded: 2001. **Members:** 25. **Staff:** 2. **Local**.

7450 ■ U.S.A. Track and Field, Michigan
c/o Jacqueline DeVose, Pres./Membership Chair
3521 Oakman Blvd.
Detroit, MI 48204
Ph: (313)934-0126
Fax: (313)934-0126
E-mail: jdevose@aol.com
URL: http://michigan.usatf.org
Contact: Jacqueline DeVose, Pres./Membership Chair
Founded: 1992. **Members:** 1,562. **Membership Dues:** youth, $12 (annual) • adult, $20 (annual) • club (from November 1 - April 30), $55 (annual) • club (after May 1), $100 (annual). **Budget:** $15,000. **State**. Works to train athletes from the grass roots to the Olympics in the sport of track and field, racewalking and long distance running. **Awards:** Best Athletes of the Year. **Frequency:** annual. **Type:** recognition. **Recipient:** to athletes who exhibit outstanding sportsmanship and athletic ability. **Affiliated With:** U.S.A. Track and Field. **Formerly:** (2005) U.S.A. Track and Field, Michigan Top.

7451 ■ Vietnam Veterans of America-State of Michigan Council
477 Michigan Ave.
Detroit, MI 48226
Ph: (313)961-9568
URL: National Affiliate–www.vva.org
Contact: Phil Smith, Dir.
State. **Affiliated With:** Vietnam Veterans of America.

7452 ■ VSA Arts of Michigan
c/o Lora Frankel, Exec.Dir.
51 W Hancock
Detroit, MI 48201-1382
Ph: (313)832-3303
Fax: (313)832-3387
E-mail: info@vsami.org
URL: http://www.vsami.org
Contact: Lora Frankel, Exec.Dir.
Founded: 1977. **Members:** 15. **Budget:** $180,000. **State**. Provides access and opportunities for children and adults with disabilities to grow through the arts; offers classes, conferences, professional development for educators, art exhibitions, performances and technical assistance. **Affiliated With:** VSA arts. **Publications:** *Expressions*, semiannual. Newsletter. **Conventions/Meetings:** annual Arts Strand at the Michigan Council for Exceptional Children Convention • annual retreat, for VSA providers.

7453 ■ Warren West Resident Council
c/o Hubert M. Reaves
4100 W Warren, Ste.908
Detroit, MI 48210-1478
Contact: Charles H. Williams, Pres.
Local.

7454 ■ Wayne County Medical Society of Southeast Michigan (WCMSSM)
3031 W Grand Blvd., Ste.645
Detroit, MI 48202
Ph: (313)874-1360
Fax: (313)874-1366
E-mail: info@wcmssm.org
URL: http://www.wcmssm.org
Contact: Adam R. Jablonowski MPA, Exec.Dir.
Local. Advances the art and science of medicine. Promotes patient care and the betterment of public health. **Affiliated With:** Michigan State Medical Society.

7455 ■ Wolverine Bar Association
645 Griswold, Ste.961
Detroit, MI 48226
Ph: (313)962-0250
Fax: (313)962-5906
E-mail: wbaoffice@ameritech.net
URL: http://www.michbar.org/localbars/wolverine/web.html
Contact: Lionel C. Sims Jr., Pres.
Local. **Affiliated With:** National Bar Association.

7456 ■ Women in Community Service, Midwest Region
5555 Conner Ave., Ste.3218
Detroit, MI 48213
Ph: (313)267-0593
Fax: (313)267-0629
Free: (800)992-WICS
E-mail: kgarrett@wics.org
URL: National Affiliate–www.wics.org
Contact: Karen D. Garrett, Dir.
Regional. Works to reduce the number of women and youth living in poverty by promoting self-reliance and economic independence. Provides a support network for those transitioning into the community and workplace; assists women and youth interested in having extra support as they enter the workforce, advanced training or education. Helps identify needs and implement strategies for success. **Affiliated With:** Women in Community Service.

7457 ■ Young Audiences of Michigan
c/o Colette S. Gilewicz, Exec.Dir.
231 Eastlawn
Detroit, MI 48215
Ph: (313)871-2936
Fax: (313)871-6016
E-mail: cgyami@aol.com
URL: http://www.youngaudiencesofmichigan.com
Contact: Colette S. Gilewicz, Contact
State. Provides arts education activities, primarily conducted in schools, libraries and community centers. **Affiliated With:** Young Audiences. **Publications:** *Ready, Set, Go!*. Manual. Guide for pre-school arts education activities. **Price:** $15.00.

7458 ■ Young Life Detroit
PO Box 27797
Detroit, MI 48227
Ph: (313)850-8002
Fax: (313)273-2134
URL: http://sites.younglife.org/sites/detroiturban/default.aspx
Local. **Affiliated With:** Young Life.

7459 ■ Zeitgeist Detroit
c/o Troy Richard
2661 Michigan Ave.
Detroit, MI 48216
Ph: (313)965-9192
E-mail: gallery@zeitgeistdetroit.org
URL: http://www.zeitgeistdetroit.org
Contact: Troy Richard, Contact
Local.

DeWitt

7460 ■ American Legion, De Witt Post 379
PO Box 137
DeWitt, MI 48820
Ph: (517)371-4720
Fax: (517)371-2401
URL: National Affiliate–www.legion.org
Local. **Affiliated With:** American Legion.

7461 ■ DeWitt Host Lions Club
c/o George Walter, Sec.
4230 Driftwood Dr.
DeWitt, MI 48820
Ph: (517)669-5688
URL: http://www.district11c2.org
Contact: George Walter, Sec.
Local. **Affiliated With:** Lions Clubs International.

7462 ■ Michigan Apple Committee (MAC)
13105 Schavey Rd., Ste.2
DeWitt, MI 48820
Ph: (517)669-8353
Fax: (517)669-9506
Free: (800)456-2753
E-mail: staff@michiganapples.com
URL: http://www.michiganapples.com
Contact: Denise Yockey, Exec.Dir.
Founded: 1965. **Members:** 1,500. **Staff:** 6. Marketing commodity association for Michigan apples and

apple products. Offers seminars; sponsors competitions; compiles statistics. Conducts research programs. **Publications:** *Directory of Apple Fresh and Processed*, periodic • *Michigan Apple News*, bimonthly. Newsletter. Includes marketing updates, public relations activities, and research updates. **Circulation:** 1,900 • Also publishes point-of-sale materials and recipes.

7463 ■ Michigan Corn Growers Association
12800 Escanaba Dr., Ste.B
DeWitt, MI 48820
Ph: (517)668-2676
Fax: (517)323-6601
Free: (888)323-6601
URL: http://www.micorn.org
Contact: Jody E. Pollok, Exec.Dir.
Membership Dues: $50 (annual). **State.**

7464 ■ Michigan Potato Industry Commission (MPIC)
c/o Ben Kudwa, Exec.Dir.
13109 Schavey Rd., Ste.No. 7
DeWitt, MI 48820
Ph: (517)669-8377
Fax: (517)669-1121
E-mail: info@mipotato.com
URL: http://www.mipotato.com
Contact: Ben Kudwa, Exec.Dir.
State.

7465 ■ Opticians Association of Michigan (OAM)
1940 Theresa Ave.
DeWitt, MI 48820
Ph: (231)726-4337 (517)249-1029
Fax: (231)722-1982
Free: (800)297-1668
E-mail: theoam@theoam.org
URL: http://www.theoam.org
Contact: Roxanne Slancik, Pres.
State.

7466 ■ Police and Firemen's Insurance Association - Lansing Fire Department
c/o Eric Weber
9711 S Francis Rd.
DeWitt, MI 48820
Ph: (517)272-2991
URL: National Affiliate–www.pfia.net
Contact: Eric Weber, Contact
Local. Affiliated With: Police and Firemen's Insurance Association.

7467 ■ Tasters Guild International - Lansing, Chapter No. 039
11733 Silverspring Dr.
DeWitt, MI 48820
Ph: (517)669-9580
E-mail: vandertuukmike@hotmail.com
URL: National Affiliate–www.tastersguild.com
Contact: Connie Van Der Tuuk, Contact
Local. Aims to educate consumers and spread the word of responsible wine and food consumption. Provides opportunity to encounter the best in wine and culinary delights. **Affiliated With:** Tasters Guild International.

7468 ■ Trout Unlimited - Lansing Chapter
c/o Gregory S. Bovee
4250 W Cutler Rd.
DeWitt, MI 48820
Ph: (517)669-8166 (517)323-2382
Fax: (517)323-0459
E-mail: hlllc632@aol.com
URL: http://www.tu.org
Contact: Gregory S. Bovee, Pres.
Local. Seeks to conserve, protect and restore cold water fisheries and their watersheds by activities in legislative, education, fund raising and work project agendas.

7469 ■ Wacousta Lions Club
c/o Barb Addison, Pres.
12201 Francis Rd.
DeWitt, MI 48820
Ph: (517)669-2316
URL: http://www.district11c2.org
Contact: Barb Addison, Pres.
Local. Affiliated With: Lions Clubs International.

Dexter

7470 ■ American Legion, Dexter Post 557
8225 Dexter Chelsea Rd.
Dexter, MI 48130
Ph: (517)371-4720
Fax: (517)371-2401
URL: National Affiliate–www.legion.org
Local. Affiliated With: American Legion.

7471 ■ West Highland White Terrier Club of Southeastern Michigan (WHWTCSEM)
c/o Michelle Bogart
6463 Meadow Ridge Ct.
Dexter, MI 48130
Ph: (734)424-2886
E-mail: chellester7@charter.net
URL: http://www.westieclubamerica.com/regclubs/whwtcsm.html
Contact: Janet Lindgren, Pres.
Local.

Dimondale

7472 ■ Dimondale Lions Club
c/o Laurence Jones, Sec.
10140 Lafayette Ln.
Dimondale, MI 48821-9548
Ph: (517)646-9104
E-mail: larkayjones@aol.com
URL: http://www.district11c2.org
Contact: Laurence Jones, Sec.
Local. Affiliated With: Lions Clubs International.

7473 ■ Great Lakes Renewable Energy Association (GLREA)
PO Box 346
Dimondale, MI 48821
Ph: (517)646-6269
Fax: (517)646-8584
Free: (800)434-9788
E-mail: info@glrea.org
URL: http://www.glrea.org
Contact: Mr. Brendan Schauffler, Program Coor.
Founded: 1991. **Membership Dues:** individual, $30 (annual) • family, $45 (annual) • small business, $100 (annual). **Staff:** 4. **Regional.** Serves as a venue for citizens, business members, energy professionals, industry leaders, and energy educators to promote the mainstream use of renewable energy technology and sustainable energy practices. Offers renewable energy education, organizes an annual alternative energy conference, and participates in programs to advance the state of renewable energy. **Libraries: Type:** reference. **Holdings:** 250; books, periodicals, video recordings. **Subjects:** renewable energy, energy efficiency, green building, sustainable living, energy policy. **Affiliated With:** American Solar Energy Society. **Publications:** *Energy Times*, quarterly. Newsletter. Features updates on renewable energy developments affecting the Great Lakes Region. **Price:** included in membership dues. **Advertising:** accepted.

7474 ■ Huntington's Disease Society of America, Michigan Chapter
c/o Dave Stickles, Pres.
Dimondale Ctr.
4000 N Michigan Rd.
Dimondale, MI 48821-9744
Fax: (517)646-0885
Free: (800)909-0073
E-mail: hdsamich@iserv.net
URL: http://www.hdsami.org
Contact: Dave Stickles, Pres.
Founded: 1976. **Members:** 2,000. **Membership Dues:** individual, $5 (annual) • family, $25 (annual). **Staff:** 2. **Budget:** $150,000. **State.** Individuals and groups of volunteers concerned with Huntington's disease, an inherited and terminal neurological condition causing progressive brain and nerve deterioration. Goals are to: identify HD families; educate the public and professionals, with emphasis on increasing consumer awareness of HD; promote and support basic and clinical research into the causes and cure of HD; to assist families in meeting the social, economic, and emotional problems resulting from HD. Is working to change the attitude of the working community toward the HD patient, enhance the HD patient's lifestyle, and promote better health care and treatment, both in the community and in facilities. **Libraries: Type:** not open to the public. **Holdings:** books, video recordings. **Subjects:** Huntington's disease. **Affiliated With:** Huntington's Disease Society of America. **Publications:** *HDSA Michigan - Bridges of Hope*, quarterly. Newsletter. **Price:** free. **Circulation:** 1,700. Alternate Formats: online. **Conventions/Meetings:** monthly board meeting • annual convention - always April • weekly People with HD - meeting • monthly support group meeting.

Dorr

7475 ■ American Legion, Michigan Post 127
c/o George Wagner
PO Box 68
Dorr, MI 49323
Ph: (517)371-4720
Fax: (517)371-2401
URL: National Affiliate–www.legion.org
Contact: George Wagner, Contact
Local. Affiliated With: American Legion.

7476 ■ Michigan National Wild Turkey Federation, Rabbit River Chapter
1795 142 Ave.
Dorr, MI 49323
Ph: (616)681-0601
URL: http://www.mi-nwtf.org/rabbit_river.htm
Contact: Bob Bottrall, Pres.
Local.

Dowagiac

7477 ■ American Legion, Doe-Wah-Jack Post 563
806 N Orchard St.
Dowagiac, MI 49047
Ph: (517)371-4720
Fax: (517)371-2401
URL: National Affiliate–www.legion.org
Local. Affiliated With: American Legion.

7478 ■ Cass County United Way, Michigan
205 S Front St.
Dowagiac, MI 49047-1738
Ph: (616)782-5659
URL: National Affiliate–national.unitedway.org
Local. Affiliated With: United Way of America.

7479 ■ Dowagiac Conservation Club
c/o Mel Lyons
225 E Prairie Ronde St.
Dowagiac, MI 49047
URL: National Affiliate–www.shootata.com
Contact: Mel Lyons, Contact
Local.

7480 ■ Dowagiac Lions Club
PO Box 415
Dowagiac, MI 49047
E-mail: lindayauchstetter@hotmail.com
URL: http://milions11b2.org
Local. Affiliated With: Lions Clubs International.

7481 ■ Greater Dowagiac Area Chamber of Commerce
200 Depot Dr.
Dowagiac, MI 49047
Ph: (269)782-8212
Fax: (269)782-6701
E-mail: vickie@dowagiacchamber.com
URL: http://www.dowagiacchamber.com
Contact: Vickie Phillipson, Program Dir.

Founded: 1964. **Members:** 180. **Membership Dues:** business (based on number of employees), $145-$505 (annual) • associate or retired, $45 (annual) • nonprofit group, $120 (annual) • professional, $145 (annual) • financial institution, $385 (annual) • utility, $505 (annual). **Staff:** 1. **Local**. Promotes business and community development in the Dowagiac, MI area. **Publications:** *Dowagiac Event and Festival*, annual. Brochure • *Dowagiac Tourist Guide*, annual. Newsletter. **Price:** free • *Looking to the Future*, monthly. Directory. **Price:** free • *Newcomers Guide and Membership Directory*, annual. **Price:** $10.00.

7482 ■ Phi Theta Kappa, Sigma Psi Chapter - Southwestern Michigan College
c/o Brenda Pavolka
58900 Cherry Grove Rd.
Dowagiac, MI 49047
Ph: (269)782-1311
E-mail: bpavolka@swmich.edu
URL: http://www.ptk.org/directories/chapters/MI/250-1.htm
Contact: Brenda Pavolka, Advisor

Local.

Dowling

7483 ■ Bedford Lions Club
c/o Jack Wykoff, Sec.
11045 S M-37 Hwy.
Dowling, MI 49050
Ph: (269)721-8181
E-mail: jwykoff@aol.com
URL: http://www.geocities.com/lionsofbedford
Contact: Jack Wykoff, Sec.

Local. **Affiliated With:** Lions Clubs International.

Drummond Island

7484 ■ ACF Upper Michigan Chapter
c/o Nathan Mileski
33494 S Maxton Rd.
Drummond Island, MI 49726
Ph: (906)493-1014 (906)493-1013
E-mail: chefnathanmileski@hotmail.com
URL: National Affiliate–www.acfchefs.org
Contact: Chef Nathan Mileski, Chm. of the Board

Local. Promotes the culinary profession and provides on-going educational training and networking for members. Provides opportunities for competition, professional recognition, and access to educational forums with other culinarians at local, regional, national, and international events. **Affiliated With:** American Culinary Federation.

7485 ■ DeTour Reef Light Preservation Society (DRLPS)
PO Box 307
Drummond Island, MI 49726
Ph: (906)493-6609
E-mail: drlps@lighthouse.net
URL: http://www.drlps.com
Contact: Jeri Baron Feltner, Sec.

Founded: 1998. **Members:** 555. **Membership Dues:** individual, $20 (annual) • family, $30 (annual) • patron, $50 (annual) • keeper, $100 (annual) • life, $500 • grand keeper, $1,000 (annual). **Staff:** 8. **Local**. Interested in the restoration and preservation of the DeTour Reef Lighthouse in the Detour Village, MI area.

Dryden

7486 ■ Commemorative Bucks of Michigan (CBM)
PO Box 518
Dryden, MI 48428
Ph: (810)796-2825
Free: (800)298-BUCK
E-mail: tira@buckfax.com
URL: http://www.buckfax.com
Contact: Tira O'Brien, Contact

Founded: 1981. **Members:** 3,800. **Membership Dues:** regular, $25 (annual). **Budget:** $150,000. **State**. Promotes the sport of deer hunting. **Publications:** *Buck Fax*, bimonthly. Magazine. Contains Michigan hunter information by Michigan hunters. **Price:** included in membership dues.

7487 ■ For the Love of Rotts, The Michigan Connection
c/o Linda J. St. Jean, Pres.
4124 Lake George Rd.
Dryden, MI 48428-9712
Ph: (810)796-9434
E-mail: rescue@fortheloveofrotts.org
URL: http://www.fortheloveofrotts.org
Contact: Linda J. St. Jean, Pres.

Founded: 2000. **State**. Focuses on the rescue and placement of Rottweiler dogs. Dogs are evaluated, spayed, neutered, microchipped, vaccinated, and treated for any medical conditions prior to placement.

Dundee

7488 ■ American Legion, Michigan Post 72
c/o Harry W. Bamm
418 Dunham St.
Dundee, MI 48131
Ph: (517)371-4720
Fax: (517)371-2401
URL: National Affiliate–www.legion.org
Contact: Harry W. Bamm, Contact

Local. **Affiliated With:** American Legion.

Durand

7489 ■ American Legion, Durand Post 124
6381 Exchange Rd.
Durand, MI 48429
Ph: (517)371-4720
Fax: (517)371-2401
URL: National Affiliate–www.legion.org

Local. **Affiliated With:** American Legion.

7490 ■ Durand Area Chamber of Commerce (DACC)
100 W Clinton St.
Durand, MI 48429
Ph: (989)288-3715
Fax: (989)288-5177
E-mail: office@durandchamber.com
URL: http://www.durandchamber.com
Contact: Candalee Rathbun, Exec.Sec.

Founded: 1960. **Members:** 123. **Staff:** 1. **Local**. Businesses, service groups, industries, and merchants united to promote commerce in the Durand, MI area. Sponsors festival. **Formerly:** (1999) Greater Durand Area Chamber of Commerce. **Publications:** *Railnet*, quarterly. Newsletter • Directory, periodic.

7491 ■ Durand Lions Club
c/o William Amidon, Pres.
4146 Durand Rd.
Durand, MI 48429
Ph: (989)288-2987
URL: http://www.district11c2.org
Contact: William Amidon, Pres.

Local. **Affiliated With:** Lions Clubs International.

7492 ■ National Speleological Society, Pinckney Area Grotto
c/o Gary R. Casady, Chm.
7806 Goodall Rd.
Durand, MI 48429-9780
Ph: (810)955-9808
E-mail: grcasady@hotmail.com
URL: http://groups.yahoo.com/group/PinckneyAreaGrotto
Contact: Gary Casady, Chm.

Local. Seeks to study, explore and conserve cave and karst resources. Protects access to caves and promotes responsible caving. Encourages responsible management of caves and their unique environments. **Affiliated With:** National Speleological Society.

Eagle Harbor

7493 ■ Keweenaw County Historical Society (KCHS)
670 Lighthouse Rd.
Eagle Harbor, MI 49950
Ph: (906)289-4990 (906)296-2561
Contact: David Thomas, Pres.

Founded: 1980. **Members:** 752. **Membership Dues:** life, $500 (annual). **Budget:** $45,000. **Local**. Membership is concentrated in Keweenaw and Houghton counties, MI, but extends to anyone. Seeks to preserve the history of Keweenaw County. **Libraries: Type:** not open to the public. **Awards:** Lauri W. Leskinen Memorial Award. **Frequency:** annual. **Type:** recognition. **Recipient:** for historic preservation in Keweenaw County. **Supersedes:** Keweenaw Historical Society. **Publications:** *Superior Signal*, quarterly. Newsletter. **Price:** free to members. **Circulation:** 600. **Conventions/Meetings:** annual meeting - always 3rd Saturday in January • monthly meeting - always the 2nd Thursday of the month.

East Grand Rapids

7494 ■ Phoenix Society for Burn Survivors
2153 Wealthy St. SE No. 215
East Grand Rapids, MI 49506
Ph: (616)458-2773
Fax: (616)458-2831
Free: (800)888-BURN
E-mail: info@phoenix-society.org
URL: http://www.phoenix-society.org
Contact: Amy Acton, Exec.Dir.

Founded: 1977. **Members:** 8,000. **Membership Dues:** burn member, $25 (annual) • associate member, $50 (annual) • professional member, $100 (annual). **Staff:** 2. **Budget:** $200,000. **Regional**. Self-help group for burn survivors and their families. Provides psychological and social support to recent burn victims and their families. **Libraries: Type:** open to the public. **Holdings:** 30. **Subjects:** burn injuries, psychological healing. **Affiliated With:** Phoenix Society for Burn Survivors. **Publications:** *Phoenix Society Newsletter*, quarterly. **Price:** free to burn survivors. **Circulation:** 8,000. Alternate Formats: online • Directory, periodic. **Conventions/Meetings:** annual World Burn Congress - conference, medical, cosmetologists, information (exhibits).

East Jordan

7495 ■ American Legion, Rebec-Hosler-Sweet Post 227
PO Box 456
East Jordan, MI 49727
Ph: (517)371-4720
Fax: (517)371-2401
URL: National Affiliate–www.legion.org

Local. **Affiliated With:** American Legion.

7496 ■ East Jordan Area Chamber of Commerce (EJACC)
PO Box 137
100 Main St., Ste.B
East Jordan, MI 49727
Ph: (231)536-7351
Fax: (231)536-0966
E-mail: info@ejchamber.org
URL: http://www.ejchamber.org
Contact: Mary H. Faculak, Exec.Dir.
Founded: 1961. **Members:** 175. **Membership Dues:** hotel/motel/bed and breakfast (based on number of units or rooms), $195-$260 (annual) • professional (plus $55 per additional associate/partner), $205 (annual) • financial institution (plus $20 per million assets minimum investment), $365 (annual) • business (based on number of employees), $165-$770 (annual) • individual, $45 (annual) • non-profit organization, $50 (annual). **Local.** Businesses, churches, service groups, and individuals interested in promoting business and tourism in the East Jordan, MI area. **Awards:** Ambassador of the Year. **Frequency:** annual. **Type:** recognition • Citizen of the Year. **Frequency:** annual. **Type:** recognition • President's Award. **Frequency:** annual. **Type:** recognition. **Publications:** *Business and Visitors Guide*, annual. Directory. **Circulation:** 25,000 • *News Capsule*, quarterly. Newsletter. **Conventions/Meetings:** monthly board meeting - every 3rd Tuesday.

East Lansing

7497 ■ ACF Capitol Area Professional Chefs and Cooks Association
c/o Rajeev Patgaonkar, Pres.
2166 Rolling Brook Ln.
East Lansing, MI 48823
Ph: (517)336-7031 (517)432-4000
Fax: (517)353-1872
E-mail: chefrajeevpatgaonkar@yahoo.com
URL: National Affiliate–www.acfchefs.org
Contact: Rajeev Patgaonkar CEC, Pres.
Local. Promotes the culinary profession. Provides on-going educational training and networking for members. Provides opportunities for competition, professional recognition and access to educational forums with other culinarians at local, regional, national and international events. **Affiliated With:** American Culinary Federation.

7498 ■ American Association of Blacks in Energy, Michigan State University
c/o Eric Beda
Michigan State Univ.
1528 C Spartan Village
East Lansing, MI 48823
Ph: (517)355-2858
E-mail: bedaeric@msu.edu
URL: National Affiliate–www.aabe.org
Contact: Eric Beda, Contact
Local. Affiliated With: American Association of Blacks in Energy.

7499 ■ American Baptist Churches of Michigan
c/o Dr. Michael A. Williams, Exec. Minister
4578 S Hagadorn Rd.
East Lansing, MI 48823
Ph: (517)332-3594
Fax: (517)332-3186
Free: (800)632-2953
E-mail: mawilliams@abc-mi.org
URL: http://www.abc-mi.org
Contact: Dr. Michael A. Williams, Exec. Minister
State. Seeks to assist American Baptists congregations in realizing the individual's kingdom potential and in advocating church mission. **Affiliated With:** ABW Ministries.

7500 ■ American Cancer Society, Capital Area Service Center
1755 Abbey Rd.
East Lansing, MI 48823
Ph: (517)332-3300
Fax: (517)641-1491
URL: http://www.cancer.org
Local. Affiliated With: American Cancer Society.

7501 ■ American Chemical Society, Michigan State University Section
c/o Dr. Christina Chan, Sec.
Michigan State Univ.
Chem. Eng. Material Sci. Dept.
2527 Engg.
East Lansing, MI 48824
Ph: (517)432-4530
Fax: (517)432-1105
E-mail: krischan@egr.msu.edu
URL: National Affiliate–acswebcontent.acs.org
Contact: Dr. Christina Chan, Sec.
Local. Represents the interests of individuals dedicated to the advancement of chemistry in all its branches. Provides opportunities for peer interaction and career development. **Affiliated With:** American Chemical Society.

7502 ■ American College of Surgeons - Michigan Chapter
c/o F.B. "Tom" Plasman, Administrator
120 W Saginaw
East Lansing, MI 48823
Ph: (517)336-7586
Fax: (517)337-2590
E-mail: tplasman@msms.org
URL: http://www.facs.org/chapters/michigan/index.html
Contact: F.B. "Tom" Plasman, Adminisrator
State. Affiliated With: American College of Surgeons.

7503 ■ American Dairy Science Association - Michigan State University Dairy Science Club
Michigan State Univ.
Dept. of Animal Sci.
1272 Anthony Hall
East Lansing, MI 48824
E-mail: jurosjai@pilot.msu.edu
URL: National Affiliate–www.adsa.org
Local. Affiliated With: American Dairy Science Association.

7504 ■ American Legion, Oldsmobile Post 237
2368 Lake Lansing Rd.
East Lansing, MI 48823
Ph: (517)371-4720
Fax: (517)371-2401
URL: National Affiliate–www.legion.org
Local. Affiliated With: American Legion.

7505 ■ American Society of Addiction Medicine, Michigan
c/o Cathy Pisano, Communication Dir.
PO Box 6554
East Lansing, MI 48823
Ph: (517)648-2290
E-mail: weirca@msu.edu
URL: http://www.misam.info
Contact: Cathy Pisano, Communication Dir.
State. Affiliated With: American Society of Addiction Medicine.

7506 ■ American Welding Society, Central Michigan
c/o Roy Bailiff, Chm.
MSU-Coll. of Engr.
A113A Engg. Bldg.
East Lansing, MI 48824
Ph: (517)355-5151
Fax: (517)353-1750
E-mail: bailiff@eng.msu.edu
URL: National Affiliate–www.aws.org
Contact: Roy Bailiff, Chm.
Local. Affiliated With: American Welding Society.

7507 ■ ASIS International, Lansing Chapter 120
c/o Robyn R. Mace, PhD, Chm.
School of Criminal Justice
446 Baker Hall
East Lansing, MI 48824
Ph: (517)432-4232
Fax: (517)432-1787
E-mail: robyn.mace@gmail.com
URL: http://www.lansingasis.org
Contact: Robyn R. Mace PhD, Chm.
Local. Seeks to increase the effectiveness and productivity of security practices by developing educational programs and materials that address security concerns. **Affiliated With:** ASIS International.

7508 ■ Associated Landscape Contractors of America, Michigan State University Horticulture Club
c/o Brad Rowe, Faculty Advisor
A288 Plant and Soil Sci. Bldg.
East Lansing, MI 48824
Ph: (517)432-3946
Fax: (517)353-0890
URL: National Affiliate–www.alca.org
Contact: Brad Rowe, Faculty Advisor
Local. Affiliated With: Professional Landcare Network.

7509 ■ Association of Community Organizations for Reform Now, Lansing
2875 Northwind Dr., Ste.130
East Lansing, MI 48823
Ph: (517)664-2620
E-mail: miacornlaro@acorn.org
URL: National Affiliate–www.acorn.org
Local. Affiliated With: Association of Community Organizations for Reform Now.

7510 ■ Association for Computing Machinery, Michigan State University
Dept. of Cmpt. Sci.
3115 Engg. Bldg.
East Lansing, MI 48824
Ph: (517)355-3148
Fax: (517)432-1061
E-mail: acm@acm.msu.edu
URL: http://acm.msu.edu
Contact: James Pita, Pres.
Founded: 1964. **Members:** 60. **Membership Dues:** full, $10 (annual). **Budget:** $1,000,000. **Local Groups:** 1. **Local.** Seeks to advance the understanding and use of computing technology in Michigan State Campus. Prepares tomorrow's computing professionals for their position in the computing industry. **Affiliated With:** Association for Computing Machinery.

7511 ■ Association of Eritreans and their Friends in Michigan (AEFM)
PO Box 293
East Lansing, MI 48826-0293
E-mail: aefm@eritrean-aefm.org
URL: http://www.eritrean-aefm.org
Founded: 1998. **State.** Works to promote social, cultural and educational interactions between the people of Eritrea and the United States.

7512 ■ Bay County Medical Society
120 W Saginaw St.
East Lansing, MI 48823
Ph: (517)324-2505
Fax: (517)337-2590
E-mail: dzannoth@msms.org
URL: http://www.msms.org
Contact: Deborah L. Zannoth, Exec.Dir.
Local. Advances the art and science of medicine. Promotes patient care and the betterment of public health. **Affiliated With:** Michigan State Medical Society.

7513 ■ Capital Area United Way
1111 Michigan Ave., Ste.300
East Lansing, MI 48823
Ph: (517)203-5000
Fax: (517)203-5001
E-mail: s.eman@capitalareaunitedway.org
URL: http://www.capitalareaunitedway.org
Contact: Michael Brown, Pres.
Local.

7514 ■ Community Volunteers for International Programs (CVIP)
12C Intl. Ctr.
Michigan State Univ.
East Lansing, MI 48824
Ph: (517)353-1735
Fax: (517)355-4657
E-mail: cvip@msu.edu
URL: http://www.isp.msu.edu/cvip
Contact: Stacey Bieler, Pres.
Regional. Seeks to increase international understanding between foreign visitors, scholars, students and their families, and members of the American community by participation in mutually enriching educational and cross-cultural activities.

7515 ■ East Lansing Aikikai
Mac-2900 Hannah Blvd.
East Lansing, MI 48823
Ph: (516)333-4621
URL: http://www.usaikifed.com
Contact: Merry Jo Hill, Instructor
Local. **Affiliated With:** United States Aikido Federation.

7516 ■ East Lansing Police Athletic League
c/o James O. Campbell, Jr.
409 Park Ln.
East Lansing, MI 48823-3340
Ph: (517)351-4220
URL: http://www.cityofeastlansing.com
Contact: Kevin Daley, Contact
Local.

7517 ■ East Lansing - Young Life
1518 River Terr.
East Lansing, MI 48823
Ph: (517)324-3294 (517)712-6519
E-mail: jasonkat@msu.edu
URL: http://sites.younglife.org/sites/EastLansing/default.aspx
Contact: Katie Jason, Contact
Local. **Affiliated With:** Young Life.

7518 ■ Eaton Rapids - Young Life
1518 River Terr.
East Lansing, MI 48823
Ph: (517)324-3294 (517)881-1429
E-mail: brownm52@msu.edu
URL: http://sites.younglife.org/sites/EatonRapids/default.aspx
Contact: Mark Brown, Contact
Local. **Affiliated With:** Young Life.

7519 ■ FarmHouse Fraternity - Michigan State FarmHouse
151 Bogue St.
East Lansing, MI 48823
Ph: (517)332-8635
E-mail: thielkev@msu.edu
URL: http://www.msu.edu/user/farmhous
Contact: Kevin Robert Thiel, Pres.
State. Promotes good fellowship and studiousness. Encourages members to seek the best in their chosen lines of study as well as in life. Works for the intellectual, spiritual, social, moral and physical development of members. **Affiliated With:** Farmhouse.

7520 ■ FFA - Michigan Association
c/o Michigan State University
108 Natural Resources
East Lansing, MI 48824-1222
Ph: (517)353-9221
Fax: (517)432-5632
E-mail: association@michiganffa.com
URL: http://www.michiganffa.com
Contact: Dave Wyrick, State Project Consultant
State.

7521 ■ Financial Planning Association of Greater Michigan
c/o Susan D. Elder
PO Box 4824
East Lansing, MI 48826-0824
Ph: (517)347-7157
Fax: (517)347-7157
E-mail: fpa@danamgt.com
URL: http://www.fpanet.org/chapters/GreaterMichigan
Contact: Susan D. Elder, Chapter Exec.
Local. Supports the financial planning process in order to help people achieve their goals and dreams. Promotes the value of the financial planning process and advances the financial planning profession. **Affiliated With:** Financial Planning Association.

7522 ■ Historical Society of Michigan (HSM)
1305 Abbott Rd.
East Lansing, MI 48823
Ph: (517)324-1828
Fax: (517)324-4370
Free: (800)692-1828
E-mail: hsm@hsmichigan.org
URL: http://www.hsmichigan.org
Contact: Larry J. Wagenaar, Exec.Dir.
Founded: 1828. **Members:** 2,800. **Membership Dues:** basic; includes HSM Chronicle magazine, $25 (annual) • regular; includes HSM Chronicle and Michigan Historical Review, $35 (annual) • enhanced; includes HSM Chronicle, Michigan Historical Review, and Michigan History Magazine, $50 (annual) • joint, $45 (annual) • educator, $60 (annual) • supporting, $65 (annual) • contributing, $85 (annual) • sustaining, $125 (annual) • life, $2,000 • historical/genealogical society, $50 (annual) • library/museum, $65 (annual) • business, $100 (annual) • patron, $500 (annual). **Staff:** 4. **Budget:** $205,000. **State**. Individuals and historical organizations interested in Michigan history. Promotes interest in Michigan history through the dissemination of information. Sponsors Michigan History Day competition (part of National History Day), State History Conference, Upper Peninsula History Conference, curriculum development, and teacher workshops and material. Publishes the Chronicle and newsletter four times per year. **Libraries: Type:** open to the public. **Holdings:** 1,500; books, periodicals. **Subjects:** Michigan history. **Awards:** Awards of Merit. **Frequency:** annual. **Type:** recognition. **Recipient:** historic preservation, publications media, special programs/events, distinguished service, institutions, education, local societies, business • Charles Follo UP History Award. **Frequency:** annual. **Type:** recognition. **Recipient:** historic preservation, publications media, special programs/events, distinguished service, institutions, education, local societies, business • Milestone Awards. **Frequency:** annual. **Type:** recognition. **Recipient:** historic preservation, publications media, special programs/events, distinguished service, institutions, education, local societies, business. **Additional Websites:** http://hsofmich.org. **Publications:** *Directory of Historical Societies, Agencies, and Historic District Commissions in Michigan*, biennial. Lists historical societies, agencies, and historic commissions within the state of MI. **Price:** $19.95/each • *Historical Society of Michigan Chronicle*, quarterly. Magazine • *Michigan Historical Review*, semiannual. Journal • *Michigan History Magazine*, bimonthly • *The Michigan Teacher*, 3/year. Newsletter. **Conventions/Meetings:** annual Mulling Over Michigan - conference, for teachers (exhibits) • annual State History Conference, focuses on Michigan history topics, tours, workshops, and other opportunities (exhibits) • annual Upper Peninsula History Conference, focuses on the history of Michigan's Upper Peninsula.

7523 ■ Ingham County Medical Society
120 W Saginaw
East Lansing, MI 48823
Ph: (517)336-9019
Fax: (517)337-2590
E-mail: dzannoth@msms.org
URL: http://www.msms.org
Contact: Deborah Zannoth, CEO
Local. Advances the art and science of medicine. Promotes patient care and the betterment of public health. **Affiliated With:** Michigan State Medical Society.

7524 ■ International Association of Psychosocial Rehabilitation Services, Michigan Chapter
c/o Steve Szilvagyi, CPRP, Treas.
227 Clarendon Rd.
East Lansing, MI 48823
Ph: (517)351-0323
E-mail: szilvagy@umich.edu
URL: http://www.miapsrs.org
Contact: Steve Szilvagyi CPRP, Treas.
Founded: 1990. **Members:** 120. **Membership Dues:** individual, $90 (annual) • associate, $30 (annual). **Budget:** $5,000. **State**. Promotes, supports, and strengthens community-oriented rehabilitation services and resources for individuals with psychiatric disorders. **Awards:** Phyllie Levine Legislative Advocacy Award. **Frequency:** annual. **Type:** trophy. **Recipient:** for legislative advocacy on behalf of people with psychiatric disabilities. **Affiliated With:** United States Psychiatric Rehabilitation Association. **Publications:** *Michigan Dispatch*, quarterly. Newsletter. **Conventions/Meetings:** Annual Psychological Rehabilitation Service - rally (exhibits) • annual conference (exhibits) • annual meeting • annual picnic (exhibits).

7525 ■ Kiwanis Club of East Lansing
PO Box 6593
East Lansing, MI 48826-6593
E-mail: kiwanisatmsu@netscape.net
URL: http://www.msu.edu/user/kiwanis
Local.

7526 ■ Lansing Skating Club
Suburban Ice East Lansing
2810 Hannah Blvd.
East Lansing, MI 48823
Ph: (517)336-4272
URL: http://www.lansingsc.com
Contact: Steve Davis, Pres.
Local. Provides programs to encourage participation and achievement in the sport of figure skating on ice. Defines and maintains uniform standards of skating proficiency. Organizes and sponsors competitions and exhibitions for the purpose of stimulating interest in figure skating. **Affiliated With:** United States Figure Skating Association.

7527 ■ Mason Middle School - Wyldlife
1518 River Terr.
East Lansing, MI 48823
Ph: (517)324-3294 (517)676-5961
E-mail: kburley@msu.edu
URL: http://sites.younglife.org/sites/Masonwyld/default.aspx
Contact: Katie Burley, Contact
Local. **Affiliated With:** Young Life.

7528 ■ Mason - Young Life
1518 River Terr.
East Lansing, MI 48823
Ph: (517)324-3294 (248)756-6004
E-mail: ananmere@msu.edu
URL: http://sites.younglife.org/sites/ylMason/default.aspx
Contact: Meredith Anan, Contact
Local. **Affiliated With:** Young Life.

7529 ■ Medical Ethics Resource Network of Michigan (MERN)
c/o Center for Ethics and Humanities in the Life Sciences
C-208 E Fee Hall
Michigan State Univ.
East Lansing, MI 48824-1316
Ph: (517)355-7550
E-mail: mern@msu.edu
URL: http://www.mern.org
Contact: Cheryl Allen SSJ, Sec.
Founded: 1988. **Members:** 253. **Membership Dues:** student, $15 (annual) • individual, $30 (annual) • non-hospital, $100 (annual). **State Groups:** 1. **State.** Promotes the study of, and interest in, medical ethics. Also promotes closer collaboration between members who work in hospital or other health care settings and those who work in academic settings. **Publications:** *Ethics-In-Formation*, periodic. Newsletter. **Price:** included in membership dues. **Conventions/Meetings:** annual conference - always April or May and June.

7530 ■ Michigan Academy of Physician Assistants (MAPA)
c/o Michael DeGrow, Exec.Dir.
120 W Saginaw St.
East Lansing, MI 48823-2605
Ph: (517)336-1498
Fax: (517)337-2490
Free: (887)937-6272
E-mail: mapa@michiganpa.org
URL: http://www.michiganpa.org
Contact: Michael DeGrow, Exec.Dir.
State. Physician assistants who have graduated from an accredited program and/or are certified by the National Commission on Certification of Physician Assistants; individuals who are enrolled in an accredited PA educational program. Purposes are to: enhance public access to quality, cost-effective health care, educate the public about the physician assistant profession; represent physician assistants' interests before Congress, government agencies, and health-related organizations; assure the competence of physician assistants through development of educational curricula and accreditation programs; provide services for members. **Affiliated With:** American Academy of Physician Assistants.

7531 ■ Michigan Agri Business Association
c/o James Byrum, Pres./Sec.-Treas.
1501 N Shore Dr.
East Lansing, MI 48823
Ph: (517)336-0223
Fax: (517)336-0227
E-mail: jim@miagbiz.org
URL: http://www.miagbiz.org
Contact: James Byrum, Pres./Sec.-Treas.
Founded: 1933. **Members:** 550. **Staff:** 2. **Budget:** $275,000. **State.** Businesses producing grain, feed, seed, fertilizer chemicals, and other agricultural products. Conducts legislative, public relations, educational, and member service activities. **Awards: Type:** scholarship. **Affiliated With:** National Grain and Feed Association. **Formerly:** (1986) Michigan Grain and Agri-Dealers Association; (1990) Michigan Agri-Dealers Association. **Publications:** *Membership Ag Fax*, bimonthly. Bulletin. **Price:** for members • *State Industry Directory*, annual. **Conventions/Meetings:** annual convention (exhibits) - always January.

7532 ■ Michigan Applied Systems User Group
c/o Hacker-King-Sherry
2205 Abbott Rd.
East Lansing, MI 48823-1468
Ph: (517)337-6000
Fax: (517)337-0982
E-mail: mthomas@hackerkingsherry.com
URL: National Affiliate–www.ascnet.org
Contact: Mindy Thomas, Pres.
State. Represents insurance agents and brokers using the Agency Manager software. Promotes successful automation and business practices through communication, education, and advocacy. **Affiliated With:** Applied Systems Client Network.

7533 ■ Michigan Association of Community Bankers (MACB)
c/o Ms. Judith Sullivan, CEO
3505 Coolidge Rd., Ste.200
East Lansing, MI 48823
Ph: (517)336-4430
Fax: (517)336-7833
E-mail: info@macb.org
URL: http://www.macb.org
Contact: Ms. Judith Sullivan, CEO
Founded: 1974. **State.** Members are defined as national and state chartered banks as well as federal and state savings and loan associations and state savings banks which subscribe to the independent community banking philosophy. Advocates for community banking in Michigan; Develops and provide quality services specifically to community banks; Supports programs that encourage the profitability and autonomy of community banks; Provides quality educational opportunities for and facilitate interaction between community bankers; and represents community banks when necessary with legislators and bank regulators.

7534 ■ Michigan Association for the Education of Young Children (MiAEYC)
Beacon Pl.
4572 S Hagadorn Rd., Ste.1-D
East Lansing, MI 48823-5385
Ph: (517)336-9700
Fax: (517)336-9790
Free: (800)336-6424
E-mail: miaeyc@miaeyc.org
URL: http://www.miaeyc.org
Contact: Keith Myers, Exec.Dir.
Founded: 1974. **Members:** 3,800. **Membership Dues:** regular, $50 (annual) • student, $45 (annual) • comprehensive, $85 (annual). **Staff:** 6. **Budget:** $1,000,000. **Local Groups:** 20. **State.** Teachers and administrators of day care centers and preschools; teachers and administrators of elementary schools; college faculty and social service workers; head start teachers and administrators. Promotes high standards for the care and education of young children and advocates on their behalf. Promotes continued study of the development of young children. Works to ensure the welfare of young children and their families. **Awards:** Betty Garlick Lifetime Achievement Award. **Frequency:** annual. **Type:** recognition. **Recipient:** for lifelong commitment to Michigan's children. **Computer Services:** Information services, news page for information related to early childhood. **Committees:** Communications; Nominating; Professional Development; Programs; Public Policy. **Subcommittees:** Michigan Wolf Trap Program; Public Relations. **Task Forces:** Michigan Child Care. **Affiliated With:** National Association for the Education of Young Children. **Also Known As:** Michigan AEYC, MIAEYC. **Publications:** *Appropriate Assessment of Young Children*. Paper. Alternate Formats: online • *Basic Qualifications, Training and Education*. Paper. Alternate Formats: online • *Bats on Parade*. Book • *Beacon*, 3/year. Newsletter. Contains news, events, legislation, and people around the state. **Circulation:** 4,500. **Advertising:** accepted. Alternate Formats: online • *Young Children*. Journal. Provides information about innovative classroom practices, issues in early childhood education, research, and reviews. **Conventions/Meetings:** Annual Early Childhood Conference (exhibits) - always in Grand Rapids, MI.

7535 ■ Michigan Association of Substance Abuse Coordinating Agencies (MASACA)
c/o Robin Reynolds, Exec.Dir.
2875 Northwind Dr., Ste.215
East Lansing, MI 48823-5035
Ph: (517)337-4406
Fax: (517)337-8578
URL: http://www.mssac.com
Contact: Ms. Robin Reynolds, Exec.Dir.
Founded: 1978. **Members:** 15. **State.** Agencies which coordinate substance abuse services. Promotes public awareness and prevention of substance abuse. **Formerly:** Michigan Association of Substance Abuse Coordinators. **Conventions/Meetings:** annual meeting.

7536 ■ Michigan Automobile Dealers Association (MADA)
PO Box 2525
East Lansing, MI 48826-2525
Ph: (517)351-7800
Fax: (517)351-3120
E-mail: mada@voyager.net
URL: http://www.michiganada.org
Contact: Mr. Terry Burns, Exec.VP
Founded: 1921. **Members:** 850. **Staff:** 20. **State.** Represents the trade association of franchised automobile dealerships. **Publications:** *MADA Bulletin*, bimonthly. **Conventions/Meetings:** annual convention - always July.

7537 ■ Michigan Consumer Federation (MCF)
4990 Northwind Dr., Ste.225
East Lansing, MI 48823
Ph: (517)324-9930
Fax: (517)324-9942
E-mail: mcf@acd.net
URL: http://www.michiganconsumer.org
State.

7538 ■ Michigan Disability Sports Alliance
c/o J.J. Lewis, Exec.Dir.
211 IM Sports West
Michigan State Univ.
East Lansing, MI 48824-1026
Ph: (517)404-6990
Fax: (801)730-9866
E-mail: midsa@midsa.org
URL: http://www.MiDSA.org
Contact: J.J. Lewis, Exec.Dir.
State. Sports organization for athletes with various physical disabilities. Works to assist the athletes with training and to provide them with competitive opportunities.

7539 ■ Michigan Education Association (MEA)
c/o Lu Battaglieri, Exec.Dir.
PO Box 2573
East Lansing, MI 48826-2573
Ph: (517)332-6551
Fax: (517)337-5587
Free: (800)292-1934
E-mail: lbattaglieri@mea.org
URL: http://www.mea.org
Contact: Lu Battaglieri, Exec.Dir.
State.

7540 ■ Michigan High School Athletic Association (MHSAA)
1661 Ramblewood Dr.
East Lansing, MI 48823-7392
Ph: (517)332-5046
Fax: (517)332-4071
URL: http://www.mhsaa.com
Contact: John E. Roberts, Exec.Dir.
State. Affiliated With: National Federation of State High School Associations.

7541 ■ Michigan Licensed Beverage Association (MLBA)
c/o Lou Adado, CEO
PO Box 4067
East Lansing, MI 48826-4067
Ph: (517)374-9611
Fax: (517)374-1165
Free: (877)292-2896
E-mail: info@mlba.org
URL: http://www.mlba.org
Contact: Cathy Pavick, Exec.Dir.
Founded: 1939. **Membership Dues:** business, $250 (annual). **State.** Represents businesses in the hospitality industry. **Publications:** *Michigan Beverage Journal*, monthly. Magazine. **Price:** $52.00/year. **Conventions/Meetings:** monthly board meeting.

7542 ■ Michigan Medical Group Management Association (MMGMA)
c/o Sherry Barnhart, Exec.Sec.
PO Box 950
East Lansing, MI 48826-0950

Ph: (517)336-5786
Fax: (517)337-2490
E-mail: sbarnhart@michmgma.org
URL: http://www.michmgma.org
Contact: Sherry Barnhart, Exec.Sec.

Members: 700. **State Groups:** 1. **State**. Promotes effective medical practices in the state and delivering quality patient care. Represents over 700 business managers and administrators statewide. **Committees:** Aging; Assist Impaired Physicians; Bioethics; CME Accreditation; CME Programming; Communications and Professional Relations; Maternal and Perinatal Health. **Task Forces:** AIDS Education. **Affiliated With:** Medical Group Management Association. **Publications:** *Practice Focus*, quarterly. Newsletter. Contains medical news and legislative updates. Alternate Formats: online. **Conventions/Meetings:** semiannual conference (exhibits) - always spring and fall.

7543 ■ Michigan Ophthalmological Society (MOS)
120 W Saginaw
East Lansing, MI 48823
Ph: (517)333-6739
Fax: (517)336-5797
E-mail: penglerth@msms.org
URL: http://www.mieyemd.org
Contact: Penny Englerth, Exec.Dir.

Members: 330. **Membership Dues:** active, practicing, $550 (annual) • 2nd year practicing, $300 (annual) • 1st year practicing, $250 (annual). **Staff:** 2. **State**. Continuing education, community service, and advocacy. **Subgroups:** Young Ophthalmologists Section. **Publications:** *Eye on Michigan*, monthly. Newsletter. Contains news of interest to Michigan ophthalmologists. **Price:** free for members. **Circulation:** 330. **Advertising:** accepted. **Conventions/Meetings:** annual conference (exhibits) - always summer.

7544 ■ Michigan Psychiatric Society
c/o Kathleen Gross, Exec.Dir.
271 Woodland Pass, Ste.125
East Lansing, MI 48823
Ph: (517)333-0838
Fax: (517)333-0220
E-mail: kgross@mpsonline.org
URL: http://www.mpsonline.org
Contact: Kathleen Gross, Exec.Dir.
State.

7545 ■ Michigan Public Health Association (MPHA)
c/o Monty Fakhouri, Pres.
PO Box 1564
East Lansing, MI 48826-1564
E-mail: montyf@arabacc.org
URL: http://www.mipha.org/
Contact: Mr. Monty Fakhouri, Pres.

Founded: 1921. **Membership Dues:** active, $50 (annual) • retiree, $20 (annual) • student, $15 (annual) • associate (health agency), $75 (annual) • supporting (corporate), $200 (annual). **State**. Promotes public health in Michigan, conducts and sponsors research in public health and disseminates information concerning developments in public health. **Affiliated With:** American Public Health Association.

7546 ■ Michigan Public Transit Association (MPTA)
c/o Clark Harder, Exec.Dir.
2875 Northwind Dr., Ste.120
East Lansing, MI 48823
Ph: (517)324-0858
Fax: (517)324-7034
E-mail: charder@mptaonline.org
URL: http://www.mptaonline.org
Contact: Cindy Zolkowski, Dir. of Admin. Services

Founded: 1974. **Members:** 85. **Membership Dues:** associate, $100 (annual). **Staff:** 2. **State**. Transit authorities. Represents the interests of members. **Publications:** *In-Transit*, quarterly. Newsletter. **Conventions/Meetings:** monthly board meeting • annual conference, legislative issues - always February • annual meeting - always August.

7547 ■ Michigan Rural Health Association (MRHA)
PO Box 845
East Lansing, MI 48826
Fax: (517)381-8008
Free: (800)487-8566
E-mail: mindyketels@charter.net
URL: http://www.miruralhealth.org
Contact: Anne Rosewarne, Pres.

Founded: 1997. **Membership Dues:** individual, $25 (annual) • student, $10 (annual) • organization, $100 (annual). **State**. Advocates for policies and funding to improved the quality of life and health of Michigan's rural communities. **Affiliated With:** National Rural Health Association. **Publications:** *The Rural Implication of Emergency Preparedness Planning*. Paper. Alternate Formats: online.

7548 ■ Michigan Society of Association Executives (MSAE)
c/o Bruce Aldrich, CAE, Chm.
1350 Haslett Rd.
East Lansing, MI 48823
Ph: (517)332-6723
Fax: (517)332-6724
E-mail: info@msae.org
URL: http://www.msae.org
Contact: Bruce Aldrich CAE, Chm.

State. Affiliated With: American Society of Association Executives.

7549 ■ Michigan Speech-Language-Hearing Association (MSHA)
790 W Lake Lansing Rd., Ste.500-A
East Lansing, MI 48823
Ph: (517)332-5691
Fax: (517)332-5870
E-mail: mainoffice@michiganspeechhearing.org
URL: http://www.michiganspeechhearing.org
Contact: Ms. Dawn Kutney, Admin. Consultant

Founded: 1939. **Members:** 1,200. **Membership Dues:** student, $35 (annual) • active, $70 (annual) • advocate, affiliate, $15 (annual) • associate, $60 (annual). **Staff:** 2. **Budget:** $140,000. **Regional Groups:** 8. **State Groups:** 1. **State**. Speech pathologists, audiologists, and teachers of the hearing-impaired. Promotes professional development among those working in the speech, language, and hearing field. **Libraries: Type:** not open to the public. **Holdings:** 75; articles, books, periodicals. **Subjects:** hearing impairment. **Awards:** Clinical Service Award. **Frequency:** annual. **Type:** recognition. **Recipient:** for outstanding clinical speech, language, and hearing programs in the state of Michigan as well as those persons responsible for their development and implementation • Distinguished Service Award. **Frequency:** annual. **Type:** recognition. **Recipient:** for individuals who have provided specific acts or contributions serving the communicatively impaired • Honors of the Association. **Frequency:** annual. **Type:** recognition. **Recipient:** for sustained, outstanding accomplishments in the profession of speech, language, and hearing • Public School Program of the Year Award. **Frequency:** annual. **Type:** recognition. **Recipient:** for outstanding speech, language, and hearing programs in the public schools of Michigan and to those persons responsible for their development and implementation • Student Scholarship Award. **Frequency:** annual. **Type:** recognition. **Recipient:** for outstanding student. **Computer Services:** Information services, job placement service • mailing lists. **Affiliated With:** American Speech-Language-Hearing Association. **Publications:** *Et Cetera*, quarterly. Newsletter. **Price:** free. **Circulation:** 1,300. **Advertising:** accepted • Directory, biennial. **Conventions/Meetings:** biennial CCC Review - lecture, help students prepare for the national exam • annual conference - usually March • biennial Continuing Professional Development Workshop.

7550 ■ Michigan State Medical Society (MSMS)
PO Box 950
120 W Saginaw St.
East Lansing, MI 48823
Ph: (517)337-1351
Fax: (517)337-2490
E-mail: msms@msms.org
URL: http://www.msms.org
Contact: Kevin A. Madigan, Exec.Dir.

Founded: 1866. **Members:** 14,400. **Membership Dues:** individual physician, $540 (annual) • student, $88 (quadrennial) • resident, $20 (annual). **Staff:** 85. **State**. Represents physicians in Michigan. **Computer Services:** database, physician locator, staff directory. **Committees:** Advisory Committee on Medical Economics; Aging; Bioethics; CME Accreditation; CME Programming; Concerns of Women Physicians; Federal Legislation; Hospice Medical Directors. **Affiliated With:** American Medical Association. **Publications:** *Medigram*, weekly. Newsletter. Features headlines and relevant information for physicians. • *Michigan Medicine*, 6/year. Magazine. Features analysis of health care environment, regulations, profiles of policymakers and physicians. **Conventions/Meetings:** annual conference - always late October • annual meeting, continuing medical education (exhibits) - always May.

7551 ■ Michigan State Police Troopers Association (MSPTA)
1715 Abbey Rd., Ste.B
East Lansing, MI 48823
Ph: (517)336-7782
Fax: (517)336-8997
E-mail: wbecker@mspta.net
URL: http://www.mspta.net
Contact: Wilda Becker, Office Mgr.

Founded: 1962. **Members:** 1,850. **Staff:** 6. **State**. Police troopers. Represents members before the executive branch of the state government, civil service commission, Department of State Police, and the legislature. **Publications:** *Trooper*, bimonthly. Magazine. **Conventions/Meetings:** quarterly meeting.

7552 ■ Michigan State University Extension 4-H Youth Programs
Michigan State Univ.
160 Agriculture Hall
East Lansing, MI 48824-1039
Ph: (517)432-7575
Fax: (517)355-6748
E-mail: msue4h@msu.edu
URL: http://www.msue.msu.edu/msue/cyf/youth/index.html
Contact: Dr. Cheryl N. Booth PhD, State Leader

Founded: 1914. **Members:** 204,472. **Local Groups:** 10,539. **State**. Youths (204,472) and volunteer leaders (25,026). Provides educational activities designed to promote development of good citizenship, leadership, and self-sufficiency. Sponsors charitable activities for public foundation. **Formerly:** (1996) Michigan 4-H Youth Programs. **Publications:** *Michigan 4-H Today Leader Magazine*, 3/year. **Price:** free.

7553 ■ Michigan State University Figure Skating Club
205 IM W
East Lansing, MI 48824
Ph: (248)321-4272
E-mail: msufigureskating@hotmail.com
URL: http://www.msufigureskating.com

Local. Provides programs to encourage participation and achievement in the sport of figure skating on ice. Defines and maintains uniform standards of skating proficiency. Organizes and sponsors competitions and exhibitions for the purpose of stimulating interest in figure skating. **Affiliated With:** United States Figure Skating Association.

7554 ■ Mid-Michigan Aikikai
Orchard St. "Pump House"
Community Center
368 Orchard St.
East Lansing, MI 48823

Ph: (517)652-4759
E-mail: mmaiki@comcast.net
URL: http://mmaiki.home.comcast.net
Contact: Frank A. Apodaca Jr., Instructor
Local. Affiliated With: United States Aikido Federation.

7555 ■ Muslim Students' Association of Michigan State University (MSA MSU)
c/o Kashif Saleem, Pres.
920 S Harrison Rd.
East Lansing, MI 48823
Ph: (517)353-5735
E-mail: saleemka@msu.edu
URL: http://www.msu.edu/~msa
Contact: Kashif Saleem, Pres.
Local. Muslim students in North America. Seeks to advance the interests of members; works to enable members to practice Islam as a complete way of life. **Affiliated With:** Muslim Students Association of the United States and Canada.

7556 ■ National Active and Retired Federal Employees Association - Lansing Area 289
1952 Pinecrest Dr.
East Lansing, MI 48823-1350
Ph: (517)332-5780
URL: National Affiliate–www.narfe.org
Contact: Ed Essler, Contact
Local. Protects the retirement future of employees through education. Informs members on issues affecting the retirement. **Affiliated With:** National Association of Retired Federal Employees.

7557 ■ National Council of Teachers of English Student Affiliate of Michigan State University
c/o Janet Swensson, Faculty Advisor
MSU Writing Ctr.
500 Bessey Hall
East Lansing, MI 48824
Ph: (517)432-3610
URL: National Affiliate–www.ncte.org
Contact: Janet Swensson, Faculty Advisor
Local. Works to increase the effectiveness of instruction in English language and literature. **Affiliated With:** National Council of Teachers of English.

7558 ■ National Organization for Women - Lansing
c/o Shanna Strouse, Co-Pres.
PO Box 1392
East Lansing, MI 48826
Ph: (517)485-8648
E-mail: lanow@hotmail.com
URL: http://www.michnow.org
Contact: Shanna Strouse, Co-Pres.
Local. Affiliated With: National Organization for Women.

7559 ■ National Organization for Women - Michigan
PO Box 860
East Lansing, MI 48826
Ph: (517)485-9687
E-mail: pres@michnow.org
URL: http://www.michnow.org
State. Affiliated With: National Organization for Women.

7560 ■ National Society of Black Engineers - Michigan State University Chapter
1108 Engg. Bldg.
East Lansing, MI 48824
Ph: (517)355-8310
E-mail: nsbe@egr.msu.edu
URL: http://www.egr.msu.edu/nsbe
Contact: Robyn Badon, Pres.
Local. Strives to increase the number of culturally responsible Black engineers who excel academically, succeed professionally and positively impact the community. **Affiliated With:** National Society of Black Engineers.

7561 ■ National Technical Honor Society - Career Quest Computer Learning Center and Staffing Service - Michigan
5000 Northwind Dr., Ste.120
East Lansing, MI 48823
Ph: (517)318-3330
Fax: (517)318-3331
Free: (888)810-6080
E-mail: tbrewer@careerquest1.com
URL: http://www.careerquest1.com
Contact: Todd Brewer, Dir.
Local.

7562 ■ North Lansing Lions Club
c/o Brian R. Sheehan, Sec.
613 Spartan Ave.
East Lansing, MI 48823
Ph: (517)332-5202
E-mail: brs2@prodigy.net
URL: http://www.district11c2.org
Contact: Brian R. Sheehan, Sec.
Local. Affiliated With: Lions Clubs International.

7563 ■ Pine Lake Small Craft Association
c/o Sandy Bryson, Sec.
333 Whitehills Dr.
East Lansing, MI 48823
Ph: (517)351-5976
E-mail: sbryson@msu.edu
URL: National Affiliate–www.tsca.net
Contact: Sandy Bryson, Sec.
Local.

7564 ■ Professional Golfers Association of America - Michigan Section
PO Box 4399
East Lansing, MI 48826-4399
Ph: (517)641-7421
Fax: (517)641-7830
E-mail: khelm@michiganpga.com
URL: http://michigan.pga.com
Contact: Kevin Helm, Exec.Dir.
Founded: 1916. **State.**

7565 ■ Psi Chi, National Honor Society in Psychology - Michigan State University
c/o Dept. of Psychology
100 Psychology Bldg.
East Lansing, MI 48824-1118
Ph: (517)355-9561 (517)353-0753
Fax: (517)355-5139
E-mail: grady@msu.edu
URL: http://www.psichi.org/chapters/info.asp?chapter_id=203
Contact: Sally M. Grady PhD, Advisor
Local.

7566 ■ Religious Coalition for Reproductive Choice - Michigan Chapter
PO Box 739
East Lansing, MI 48826
E-mail: bfrede8223@aol.com
URL: National Affiliate–www.rcrc.org
State. Affiliated With: Religious Coalition for Reproductive Choice.

7567 ■ Society of Manufacturing Engineers - Michigan State University S329
3524 Engg. Bldg.
East Lansing, MI 48824-1226
Ph: (517)432-5260
Fax: (517)353-9842
E-mail: chalou@egr.msu.edu
URL: National Affiliate–www.sme.org
Contact: Robert A. Chalou, Contact
Local. Advances manufacturing knowledge to gain competitive advantage. Improves skills and manufacturing solutions for the growth of economy. Provides resources and opportunities for manufacturing professionals. **Affiliated With:** American Quaternary Association.

7568 ■ USA Weightlifting - Cougars
c/o David Peterson
5452 Amber Dr.
East Lansing, MI 48823
Ph: (517)627-3816 (517)332-3450
Fax: (517)332-3450
E-mail: frostie397@aol.com
URL: National Affiliate–www.usaweightlifting.org
Contact: Frank Tuma, Sec.
Local. Affiliated With: USA Weightlifting.

7569 ■ Williamston Middle School - Wyldlife
1518 River Terr.
East Lansing, MI 48823
Ph: (517)324-3294 (517)896-3658
E-mail: faustk@msu.edu
URL: http://sites.younglife.org/sites/WillWyld/default.aspx
Contact: Kurt Faust, Contact
Local. Affiliated With: Young Life.

7570 ■ Williamston - Young Life
1518 River Terr.
East Lansing, MI 48823
Ph: (517)324-3294 (517)614-3190
E-mail: backusm3@msu.edu
URL: http://sites.younglife.org/sites/Williamston/default.aspx
Contact: Mark Backus, Contact
Local. Affiliated With: Young Life.

7571 ■ Young Life Greater Lansing
1518 River Terr.
East Lansing, MI 48823
Ph: (517)324-3294
Fax: (517)324-3281
URL: http://sites.younglife.org/sites/Lansing/default.aspx
Local. Affiliated With: Young Life.

East Leroy

7572 ■ Great Lakes German Shorthaired Pointer Club and Rescue
c/o Billie Jo Weeks
8775 1 1/2 Mile Rd.
East Leroy, MI 49051-8746
Ph: (269)979-7931
E-mail: billiejo@greatlakesgsprescue.org
URL: http://www.greatlakesgsprescue.org
Contact: Billie Jo Weeks, Pres./Treas.
Founded: 2000. **Members:** 5. **Membership Dues:** $15 (annual). **Regional. Formerly:** (2005) Great Lakes GSP Rescue. **Publications:** *Bone Talk*, semiannual. Newsletter. Features dog stories, medical information for dog owners, and dogs available for adoption. **Price:** free. **Advertising:** accepted.

East Tawas

7573 ■ American Legion, Audie Johnson Post 211
900 E Lincoln St.
East Tawas, MI 48730
Ph: (517)371-4720
Fax: (517)371-2401
URL: National Affiliate–www.legion.org
Local. Affiliated With: American Legion.

Eastpointe

7574 ■ American Legion, Michigan Post 386
c/o Frank J. Calcaterra
21555 Gratiot Ave.
Eastpointe, MI 48021
Ph: (517)371-4720
Fax: (517)371-2401
URL: National Affiliate–www.legion.org
Contact: Frank J. Calcaterra, Contact
Local. Affiliated With: American Legion.

7575 ■ East Detroit Historical Society (EDHS)
PO Box 110
Eastpointe, MI 48021-0110
Ph: (586)775-1414 (586)218-4875
E-mail: pix41@aol.com
Contact: Ms. Suzanne Pixley, Pres.

Founded: 1975. **Members:** 60. **Membership Dues:** individual, $10 (annual) • family, $15 (annual) • business, $25 (annual) • Life, $100. **Budget:** $4,000. **Local Groups:** 1. **Local**. Works for the restoration and maintenance of a historic (1872) schoolhouse; conducts research and places historic markers; collects and distributes historical data; publishes local history. The Halfway Schoolhouse open to the public on the second Sunday of every month from 2-4 p.m; other events include a historical festival in July and a home tour in September. **Libraries: Type:** open to the public. **Subjects:** old textbook, local history. **Awards:** National Landmark. **Type:** recognition. **Committees:** Fire Truck Restoration Book. **Publications:** *East Detroit Historical Society*, bimonthly. Newsletter. **Price:** free for members. **Circulation:** 120 • *Images of America*. Book. **Conventions/Meetings:** quarterly meeting, with speakers - February, April, October, December, 2nd Thursday.

7576 ■ Eastpointe Chamber of Commerce (EACC)
23801 Gratiot Ave.
PO Box 24
Eastpointe, MI 48021-0024
Ph: (586)776-5520
Fax: (586)776-7808
URL: http://www.epchamber.com
Contact: Catherine Green, Exec.Dir.

Founded: 1944. **Membership Dues:** business (base), $150 (annual) • associate, $50 (annual). **Local**. Promotes business and community development in Eastpointe, MI. **Publications:** *Newsline*, monthly. Newsletter. **Advertising:** accepted. Alternate Formats: online.

Eaton Rapids

7577 ■ American College of Cardiology - Michigan Chapter
c/o Alice H. Betz, Exec.Sec.
11793 VFW Rd.
Eaton Rapids, MI 48827-9708
Ph: (517)663-6622
Fax: (517)663-6655
URL: http://www.accmi.org
Contact: Alice H. Betz, Exec.Sec.

State. **Affiliated With:** American College of Cardiology.

7578 ■ American Legion, Michigan Post 15
c/o Harold Teeter
416 Dutton St.
Eaton Rapids, MI 48827
Ph: (517)371-4720
Fax: (517)371-2401
URL: National Affiliate–www.legion.org
Contact: Harold Teeter, Contact

Local. Affiliated With: American Legion.

7579 ■ APICS, The Association for Operations Management - Mid Michigan Chapter
c/o Mike Foley, Pres.
2224 S Canal
Eaton Rapids, MI 48827
Ph: (517)663-7750
E-mail: foley.m@att.net
URL: http://www.apics-mdmi.org
Contact: Mike Foley, Pres.

Local. Provides information and services in production and inventory management and related areas to enable members, enterprises and individuals to add value to their business performance. **Affiliated With:** APICS - The Association for Operations Management.

7580 ■ Capital Area Astronomy Club
2955 N Gunnell Rd.
Eaton Rapids, MI 48827
E-mail: dbatch@msu.edu
URL: http://www.pa.msu.edu/abrams/AstronomyClub
Contact: Steve Stanicki, Contact

Local. Promotes the science of astronomy. Works to encourage and coordinate activities of amateur astronomical societies. Fosters observational and computational work and craftsmanship in various fields of astronomy. **Affiliated With:** Astronomical League.

7581 ■ Eaton Rapids Lions Club
c/o Dale Nyquist, Pres.
442 Plains St.
Eaton Rapids, MI 48827
Ph: (517)663-8499
URL: http://www.district11c2.org
Contact: Dale Nyquist, Pres.

Local. **Affiliated With:** Lions Clubs International.

7582 ■ Great Lakes Sword Club (GLSC)
c/o Kim Rahl
5839 Ferris Rd.
Eaton Rapids, MI 48827-9616
Ph: (517)663-5032
Fax: (517)663-0351
E-mail: kim@glswords.com
URL: http://www.glswords.com/
Contact: Kim Rahl, Contact

Local. Amateur fencers. **Affiliated With:** United States Fencing Association.

7583 ■ Ruffed Grouse Society, South Central Michigan Chapter
c/o Donald Robertson
325 S Waverly Rd.
Eaton Rapids, MI 48827
Ph: (517)663-7830
URL: National Affiliate–www.ruffedgrousesociety.org
Contact: Donald Robertson, Contact

Local. **Affiliated With:** Ruffed Grouse Society.

7584 ■ Wooden Canoe Heritage Association, Michigan
c/o Russ Hicks, Pres.
7900 Columbia Hwy.
Eaton Rapids, MI 48827-9321
Ph: (517)663-3882
URL: National Affiliate–www.wcha.org
Contact: Russ Hicks, Pres.

State. **Affiliated With:** Wooden Canoe Heritage Association.

Eau Claire

7585 ■ American Legion, Eau Claire Post 353
PO Box 285
Eau Claire, MI 49111
Ph: (517)371-4720
Fax: (517)371-2401
URL: National Affiliate–www.legion.org

Local. **Affiliated With:** American Legion.

7586 ■ American Vaulting Association - Agape Vaulters
c/o Jane Egger, Coach
5329 Old Pipestone Rd.
Eau Claire, MI 49111
Ph: (269)782-3206
E-mail: jegger@remc11.k12.mi.us
URL: National Affiliate–www.americanvaulting.org
Contact: Jane Egger, Coach

Local. **Affiliated With:** American Vaulting Association.

7587 ■ Eau Claire Lions Club
PO Box 574
Eau Claire, MI 49111-0574
E-mail: sandrablckbrn@aol.com
URL: http://milions11b2.org

Local. **Affiliated With:** Lions Clubs International.

Ecorse

7588 ■ American Legion, Ecorse-Roy-B.-Salliotte Post 319
31 Elton
Ecorse, MI 48229
Ph: (517)371-4720
Fax: (517)371-2401
URL: National Affiliate–www.legion.org

Local. Affiliated With: American Legion.

Edwardsburg

7589 ■ American Legion, Edwardsburg Post 365
25995 US Hwy. 12
Edwardsburg, MI 49112
Ph: (517)371-4720
Fax: (517)371-2401
URL: National Affiliate–www.legion.org

Local. Affiliated With: American Legion.

7590 ■ Edwardsburg Area Chamber of Commerce
PO Box 575
Edwardsburg, MI 49112
Ph: (269)663-6344
Fax: (269)663-5344
Free: (800)942-8413
Contact: Karen Sinkiewicz, Exec.Sec.

Local.

7591 ■ Edwardsburg Museum Group
c/o Jo-Ann Beopple
PO Box 694
Edwardsburg, MI 49112
E-mail: jobeopple@aol.com
URL: http://www.hsmichigan.org/edwardsburg/

Founded: 1999. **Members:** 150. **Membership Dues:** $5 (annual). **Budget:** $2,000. **Local**. Preservation of historical artifacts of the area.

7592 ■ Elkhart County Beagle Club
c/o Larry Ackels
70089 Lakeview Dr.
Edwardsburg, MI 49112
URL: National Affiliate–www.akc.org
Contact: Larry Ackels, Contact

Local.

7593 ■ Michiana Beagle Club
c/o Richard Ward
71090 Ridgewood
Edwardsburg, MI 49112
URL: National Affiliate–clubs.akc.org
Contact: Richard Ward, Contact

Local.

Elk Rapids

7594 ■ Antrim County Habitat for Humanity
133 Ames St., Ste.2
Elk Rapids, MI 49629
Ph: (231)264-0022
Fax: (231)264-0033
E-mail: achfh@torchlake.com
URL: http://www.torchlake.com/achfh

Local. **Affiliated With:** Habitat for Humanity International.

7595 ■ Elk Rapids Area Chamber of Commerce (ERACC)
305 U.S. 31 N
PO Box 854
Elk Rapids, MI 49629-0854

Ph: (231)264-8202
Fax: (231)264-6591
Free: (800)626-7328
E-mail: info@elkrapidschamber.org
URL: http://www.elkrapidschamber,org
Contact: Terri Crandall-Kimble, Exec.Dir.
Founded: 1965. **Members:** 325. **Membership Dues:** regular, $175 (annual). **Regional Groups:** 3. **State Groups:** 3. **Local Groups:** 15. **Local**. Promotes business and community development in Antrim County, MI. **Libraries: Type:** open to the public; lending. **Computer Services:** Electronic publishing • information services • mailing lists • online services. **Formerly:** (2004) Elk Rapids Chamber of Commerce. **Publications:** *Antrim County Visitors Guide and Membership Directory*. **Advertising:** accepted. Alternate Formats: online. **Conventions/Meetings:** monthly meeting.

7596 ■ Elk Rapids Sportsman's Club
PO Box 536
Elk Rapids, MI 49629
Ph: (231)264-5250
E-mail: chrryjce@charter.net
URL: http://www.ersc.org
Local. **Affiliated With:** National Skeet Shooting Association.

Ellsworth

7597 ■ American Legion, Jansen-Richardson Post 488
PO Box 72
Ellsworth, MI 49729
Ph: (517)371-4720
Fax: (517)371-2401
URL: National Affiliate–www.legion.org
Local. **Affiliated With:** American Legion.

Elsie

7598 ■ American Legion, Huffman-Hammond-Rando Post 502
PO Box 282
Elsie, MI 48831
Ph: (517)371-4720
Fax: (517)371-2401
URL: National Affiliate–www.legion.org
Local. **Affiliated With:** American Legion.

7599 ■ Elsie Lions Club
c/o Joseph B. Thering, PDG, Sec.
9044 E Maple Rapids Rd.
Elsie, MI 48831
Ph: (989)862-5319
E-mail: rmthering@yahoo.com
URL: http://www.district11c2.org
Contact: Joseph B. Thering PDG, Sec.
Local. **Affiliated With:** Lions Clubs International.

Elwell

7600 ■ West Michigan Beagle Club
c/o Jim Stone
9920 Monroe Rd.
Elwell, MI 48832-9788
URL: National Affiliate–www.akc.org
Contact: Jim Stone, Contact
Local. **Affiliated With:** American Kennel Club.

Emmett

7601 ■ Blue Water Beagle Club
c/o Jim Stephens
5010 Gleason Rd.
Emmett, MI 48022-1908
URL: National Affiliate–clubs.akc.org
Contact: Jim Stephens, Contact
Local.

Empire

7602 ■ American Legion, Leelanau County Post 199
8558 W Stormer Rd.
Empire, MI 49630
Ph: (517)371-4720
Fax: (517)371-2401
URL: National Affiliate–www.legion.org
Local. **Affiliated With:** American Legion.

7603 ■ Empire Lions Club
PO Box 239
Empire, MI 49630
Ph: (231)326-5682
E-mail: denmates2@centurytel.net
URL: http://empiremi.lionwap.org
Contact: Ronald Fornowski, Pres.
Local. **Affiliated With:** Lions Clubs International.

7604 ■ Preserve Historic Sleeping Bear (PHSB)
PO Box 453
Empire, MI 49630
Ph: (231)334-6103
E-mail: phsb@leelanau.com
URL: http://www.PHSB.org
Contact: Mr. Lanny Sterling, Chm.
Founded: 1998. **Staff:** 1. **Local Groups:** 1. **Local**. Works to preserve the historic structures and cultural landscapes within the Sleeping Bear Dunes National Lakeshore through raising private donations, writing grants, sponsoring work projects, and providing educational awareness through presentations and programs. **Committees:** Development; Events; PR; Stabilization. **Publications:** *The Clapboard*, semiannual. Newsletter. **Price:** free. **Circulation:** 1,000.

Engadine

7605 ■ American Legion, Feneley-Mcneil-Nesbit Post 290
PO Box 86
Engadine, MI 49827
Ph: (517)371-4720
Fax: (517)371-2401
URL: National Affiliate–www.legion.org
Local. **Affiliated With:** American Legion.

Erie

7606 ■ Michigan Vegetable Council
PO Box 277
Erie, MI 48133
Ph: (734)848-8899
Contact: David Smith, Exec.Sec.
Founded: 1964. **Members:** 2,800. **Membership Dues:** $35 (annual). **Staff:** 1. **Budget:** $35,000. **Regional Groups:** 1. **Regional**. **Awards:** Associate Master Vegetable Farmer. **Frequency:** annual. **Type:** recognition. **Recipient:** chosen from nominations • Master Vegetable Farmer of the Year. **Frequency:** annual. **Type:** recognition. **Committees:** Council Organization and Nominating; Legislative; Michigan State University Coordinating. **Publications:** *Vegetable Growers News*, monthly. Newspaper. **Circulation:** 14,000. **Advertising:** accepted. **Conventions/Meetings:** annual Great Lakes Vegetable Growers Convention and Farm Market Show (exhibits).

Escanaba

7607 ■ American Legion, Cloverland Post 82
928 N Lincoln
Escanaba, MI 49829
Ph: (517)371-4720
Fax: (517)371-2401
URL: National Affiliate–www.legion.org
Local. **Affiliated With:** American Legion.

7608 ■ Bay de Noc Kiwanis Golden K of Escanaba
PO Box 61
Escanaba, MI 49829
E-mail: ladee_bugg_@hotmail.com
URL: http://community-2.webtv.net/snowscoop/KiwanisGoldenK
Contact: Harold Ogren, Pres.
Local.

7609 ■ Central Upper Peninsula Planning and Development Regional Commission
2415 14th Ave. S
Escanaba, MI 49829
Ph: (906)786-9234
Fax: (906)786-4442
Contact: David Gillis, Exec.Dir.
Regional.

7610 ■ Cloverland District Dental Society
1830 Ludington St.
Escanaba, MI 49829
Ph: (906)786-3936
URL: National Affiliate–www.ada.org
Contact: Dr. Eric Knudsen, Pres.
Local. Represents the interests of dentists committed to the public's oral health, ethics and professional development. Encourages the improvement of the public's oral health and promotes the art and science of dentistry. **Affiliated With:** American Dental Association; Michigan Dental Association.

7611 ■ Delta County Area Chamber of Commerce
230 Ludington St.
Escanaba, MI 49829
Ph: (906)786-2192
Fax: (906)786-8830
Free: (800)DEL-TAMI
E-mail: info@deltami.org
URL: http://www.deltami.org
Contact: Vickie Micheau, Exec.Dir.
Founded: 1921. **Members:** 650. **Membership Dues:** business (plus $8.50/full-time equivalent employee up to 500 employees, $4/full-time with over 500 employees), $190 (annual) • professional (plus $35/professional partner), $190 (annual) • non-profit civic organization/agency, $190 (annual) • financial institution (per million in Delta County deposits, $190 minimum), $25 (annual) • associate (non-voting), $65 (annual) • additional business (same owner), $65 (annual) • manufacturing (base), $190 (annual) • seasonal business, $95 (annual). **Staff:** 4. **Local**. Promotes business and community development in Delta County, MI. **Publications:** *Communicator*, monthly. Newsletter. **Price:** $12.00/year. **Conventions/Meetings:** monthly party, informal get-together - every last Wednesday.

7612 ■ Delta County Genealogical Society (DCGS)
c/o Marguerite Larson
PO Box 442
Escanaba, MI 49829-0442
E-mail: tazgal1@charter.net
URL: http://www.grandmastree.com/society
Contact: Marguerite Larson, Contact
Founded: 1981. **Members:** 75. **Membership Dues:** single, $7 (annual) • family, $10 (annual). **Staff:** 6. **Regional**. Assists in genealogical research and the compilation of local records. **Libraries: Type:** open to the public. **Holdings:** 1,500; articles, books, films, periodicals. **Subjects:** genealogy, local history. **Publications:** *Delta Pedigree Press*, quarterly. Newsletter. **Price:** included in membership dues. ISSN: 1071-4146. **Conventions/Meetings:** monthly meeting - except May, June, July & August.

7613 ■ Escanaba Areas Figure Skating Club (EAFSC)
PO Box 164
Escanaba, MI 49829
Ph: (906)428-4192
URL: http://www.eafsc.org
Contact: Annelise Aschbacher, Contact
Local. Provides programs to encourage participation and achievement in the sport of figure skating on ice.

Defines and maintains uniform standards of skating proficiency. Organizes and sponsors competitions and exhibitions for the purpose of stimulating interest in figure skating. **Affiliated With:** United States Figure Skating Association.

7614 ■ Escanaba Kiwanis Club
PO Box 264
Escanaba, MI 49829
E-mail: info@escanabakiwanis.org
URL: http://www.escanabakiwanis.org
Contact: Julie Mallard, Pres.
Local.

7615 ■ Michigan National Wild Turkey Federation, Bay De Noc Gobblers
4912 12th Rd.
Escanaba, MI 49829
Ph: (906)786-0183
URL: http://www.mi-nwtf.org/Baydenoc.htm
Contact: Ken Buchholtz, Contact
Local.

7616 ■ National Active and Retired Federal Employees Association - Escanaba 1389
515 S 10th St.
Escanaba, MI 49829-3330
Ph: (906)786-1268
URL: National Affiliate–www.narfe.org
Contact: David Koski, Contact
Local. Protects the retirement future of employees through education. Informs members on issues affecting the retirement. **Affiliated With:** National Association of Retired Federal Employees.

7617 ■ Phi Theta Kappa, Alpha Xi Delta Chapter - Bay de Noc Community College
c/o Joseph Shaw
2001 N Lincoln Rd.
Escanaba, MI 49829
Ph: (906)786-5802
E-mail: shawj@baycollege.edu
URL: http://www.ptk.org/directories/chapters/MI/3487-1.htm
Contact: Joseph Shaw, Advisor
Local.

7618 ■ RSVP Menominee/Delta/Schoolcraft
c/o Theresa Nelson, Dir.
507 1st Ave. N
Escanaba, MI 49829-3998
Ph: (906)786-7080
Fax: (906)786-9423
E-mail: tnelson@mdscaa.org
URL: http://www.seniorcorps.gov/about/programs/rsvp_state.asp?usestateabbr=mi&Search4.x=0&Search4.y=0
Contact: Theresa Nelson, Dir.
Local. Affiliated With: Retired and Senior Volunteer Program.

7619 ■ Ruffed Grouse Society, Central Upper Peninsula Chapter
c/o Keith Mattson
6773 M Rd.
Escanaba, MI 49829
Ph: (906)786-0322
URL: National Affiliate–www.ruffedgrousesociety.org
Contact: Keith Mattson, Contact
Local. Affiliated With: Ruffed Grouse Society.

7620 ■ United Way of Delta County
1100 Ludington St., Ste.300
Escanaba, MI 49829
Ph: (906)786-3736
URL: National Affiliate–national.unitedway.org
Local. Affiliated With: United Way of America.

Essexville

7621 ■ American Cancer Society, Bay Area Service Center
1481 W Center Rd., Ste.1
Essexville, MI 48732
Ph: (989)895-1730
Fax: (989)895-1745
URL: National Affiliate–www.cancer.org
Contact: Sue Wendt, Area Exec.Dir.
Local. Affiliated With: American Cancer Society.

7622 ■ American Cancer Society, Gladwin County
1480 W Center Rd., Ste.1
Essexville, MI 48732
Ph: (989)895-1730
Fax: (989)895-1745
Free: (800)728-2323
E-mail: stacy.king@cancer.org
URL: http://www.cancer.org
Contact: Stacy King, Contact
Local. Works to eliminate cancer as a major health problem through research, education, advocacy and service. **Affiliated With:** American Cancer Society.

7623 ■ American Legion, Essexville-Hampton Post 249
820 N Jones Rd.
Essexville, MI 48732
Ph: (517)371-4720
Fax: (517)371-2401
URL: National Affiliate–www.legion.org
Local. Affiliated With: American Legion.

7624 ■ Catholics United for the Faith - Immaculate Heart of Mary Chapter
1193 Orchard Rd.
Essexville, MI 48732
Ph: (989)892-3638
E-mail: sal2@chartermi.net
URL: National Affiliate–www.cuf.org
Contact: Sally Havercamp, Contact
Local.

7625 ■ Essexville-Hampton Lions Club
c/o Robert Davision, Pres.
303 Main St.
Essexville, MI 48732
Ph: (989)892-1368
E-mail: rdavid303@yahoo.com
URL: http://www.geocities.com/dist11d1
Contact: Robert Davision, Pres.
Local. Affiliated With: Lions Clubs International.

7626 ■ Trout Unlimited - Arnold J. Copeland Chapter
316 Birney St.
Essexville, MI 48732-1673
Ph: (517)892-7074
URL: National Affiliate–www.tu.org
Contact: Mark DeSanto, Pres.
Local.

Evart

7627 ■ American Legion, Michigan Post 236
c/o Joseph W. Guyton
520 N Hemlock St.
Evart, MI 49631
Ph: (517)371-4720
Fax: (517)371-2401
URL: National Affiliate–www.legion.org
Contact: Joseph W. Guyton, Contact
Local. Affiliated With: American Legion.

7628 ■ Evart Area Chamber of Commerce (EACC)
PO Box 688
Evart, MI 49631-0688
Ph: (231)734-6119 (231)734-2181
Fax: (231)734-2055
E-mail: chamber@evart.org
URL: http://www.evart.org
Contact: Roger Elkins, Pres.
Founded: 1924. **Members:** 115. **Membership Dues:** regular, $50 (annual) • retired, $25 (annual). **Local.** Promotes business and community development in Evart, MI. Sponsors social and promotional events. **Awards:** Business Person of the Year. **Frequency:** annual. **Type:** recognition. **Recipient:** for 5 years successfully in business, community involvement and promotion. **Computer Services:** Information services, informative about city and area. **Formerly:** (1999) Evart Chamber of Commerce. **Publications:** Newsletter, monthly. **Price:** included in membership dues. **Conventions/Meetings:** monthly meeting, general membership meeting - 2nd Wednesday.

7629 ■ Evart Lions Club
327 S Main St.
Evart, MI 49631
E-mail: landg@netonecom.net
URL: http://evartmi.lionwap.org
Contact: James Whitten, Pres.
Local. Affiliated With: Lions Clubs International.

Ewen

7630 ■ American Legion, Ewen Post 41
PO Box 212
Ewen, MI 49925
Ph: (517)371-4720
Fax: (517)371-2401
URL: National Affiliate–www.legion.org
Local. Affiliated With: American Legion.

7631 ■ Just Kidding 4-H Dairy Goat Club
c/o Jean Trudgeon
Rte. 1, Box 7
Ewen, MI 49925
Ph: (906)988-2533
URL: National Affiliate–adga.org
Contact: Jean Trudgeon, Contact
Local. Affiliated With: American Dairy Goat Association.

7632 ■ Northern Lights Goat Association
c/o Jean Trudgeon
Rte. 1, Box 7
Ewen, MI 49925
Ph: (906)988-2533
URL: National Affiliate–adga.org
Contact: Jean Trudgeon, Contact
Local. Affiliated With: American Dairy Goat Association.

Fairgrove

7633 ■ Fairgrove Lions Club
c/o Jesse Ruiz, Pres.
PO Box 360
Fairgrove, MI 48733
Ph: (989)693-6680
URL: http://www.geocities.com/dist11d1
Contact: Jesse Ruiz, Pres.
Local. Affiliated With: Lions Clubs International.

Farmington

7634 ■ American Legion, George Washington Post 88
36864 Blanchard Blvd., No. 204
Farmington, MI 48335
Ph: (517)371-4720
Fax: (517)371-2401
URL: National Affiliate–www.legion.org
Local. Affiliated With: American Legion.

7635 ■ American Legion, Groves-Walker Post 346
31775 Grand River Ave.
Farmington, MI 48336
Ph: (517)371-4720
Fax: (517)371-2401
URL: National Affiliate–www.legion.org
Local. Affiliated With: American Legion.

7636 ■ American Legion, Michigan Post 483
c/o Joseph Carano
33253 Kirby St.
Farmington, MI 48336
Ph: (517)371-4720
Fax: (517)371-2401
URL: National Affiliate–www.legion.org
Contact: Joseph Carano, Contact
Local. Affiliated With: American Legion.

7637 ■ American Society for Training and Development - Greater Detroit Chapter
32425 Grand River Ave.
Farmington, MI 48336
Ph: (248)471-7187
Fax: (248)478-6437
E-mail: tonih@ameritech.net
URL: http://www.detroitastd.org
Contact: Pat Ball, Pres.
Local. Promotes workplace learning and the improvement of skills of workplace professionals. Provides resource and professional development to individuals in the field of learning and development. Recognizes and sets standards for learning and performance professionals. **Affiliated With:** American Society for Training and Development.

7638 ■ Association of Fundraising Professionals - Greater Detroit (AFP)
c/o Toni Holmes, Administrator
32425 Grand River Ave.
Farmington, MI 48336
Ph: (248)478-6401
Fax: (248)478-6437
E-mail: tonih@ameritech.net
URL: http://www.afpdetroit.org
Contact: Toni Holmes, Administrator
Local. Affiliated With: Association of Fundraising Professionals. **Formerly:** (2005) National Society of Fund Raising Executives - Greater Detroit Chapter.

7639 ■ Direct Marketing Association of Detroit
32425 Grand River Ave.
Farmington, MI 48336
Ph: (248)478-4888
Fax: (248)478-6437
Contact: Ann Dixon, Pres.
Founded: 1959. **Members:** 675. **Membership Dues:** $90 (annual). **Staff:** 1. **Local.** Promotes excellence in the direct marketing industry in Michigan. Facilitates networking; provides referrals. **Libraries: Type:** reference. **Awards:** Target Award. **Frequency:** annual. **Type:** recognition. **Recipient:** individual or company developing best direct mail or direct response program during preceding calendar year. **Affiliated With:** Direct Marketing Association. **Formerly:** Direct Mail Club of Detroit. **Publications:** *Response*, monthly. Newsletter • Membership Directory, annual. **Price:** members only. **Conventions/Meetings:** annual Automotive Direct Marketing Day - seminar (exhibits) • monthly luncheon - except July and August; always 1st Thursday of the month.

7640 ■ Farmington Area Jaycees
c/o Sarah Griffiths, Pres.
PO Box 33
Farmington, MI 48332
Ph: (248)477-5227
E-mail: info@fajc.org
URL: http://fajc.org
Contact: Sarah Griffiths, Pres.
Founded: 1946. **Local.**

7641 ■ Farmington Hills Figure Skating Club (FHFSC)
35500 Eight Mile Rd.
Farmington, MI 48335
Ph: (734)953-6777
E-mail: fhfsc4t@yahoo.com
URL: http://fhfsc.4t.com
Contact: AnneMarie Messineo, Pres.
Local. Provides programs to encourage participation and achievement in the sport of figure skating on ice. Defines and maintains uniform standards of skating proficiency. Organizes and sponsors competitions and exhibitions for the purpose of stimulating interest in figure skating. **Affiliated With:** United States Figure Skating Association.

7642 ■ Farmington Wyldlife
PO Box 798
Farmington, MI 48332
Ph: (248)427-0912 (248)426-6755
URL: http://sites.younglife.org/sites/FarmWyldlife/default.aspx
Contact: Corky Erickson, Contact
Local. Affiliated With: Young Life.

7643 ■ Farmington Young Life
PO Box 798
Farmington, MI 48332
Ph: (248)427-0912 (248)346-5149
Fax: (248)427-0913
E-mail: emeryeriksen@yahoo.com
URL: http://sites.younglife.org/sites/Farmington/default.aspx
Contact: Emery Eriksen, Contact
Local. Affiliated With: Young Life.

7644 ■ Human Resource Association of Greater Detroit (HRAGD)
32425 Grand River Ave.
Farmington, MI 48336
Ph: (248)478-6498
Fax: (248)478-6569
E-mail: hragd@ameritech.net
URL: http://www.hragd.org
Contact: Nancy Davies, Pres.
Local. Represents the interests of human resource and industrial relations professionals and executives. Promotes the advancement of human resource management.

7645 ■ Institute of Real Estate Management - Michigan Chapter No. 5
24125 Drake Rd.
Farmington, MI 48335
Ph: (248)615-3885
Fax: (248)615-3888
E-mail: info@iremmi5.org
URL: http://www.iremmi5.org
Contact: Bea King, Exec.Dir.
State. Represents real property and asset management professionals. Works to promote professional ethics and standards in the field of property management. Strives to keep its members informed on the latest legislative activities and current industry trends. Provides classroom training, continuing education seminars, job referral service and candidate assistance services to enhance the effectiveness and professionalism of its members. **Affiliated With:** Institute of Real Estate Management.

7646 ■ Michigan Ontario Compensation Association (MOCA)
3245 Grand River Ave.
Farmington, MI 48336
Ph: (248)478-6401
Fax: (248)478-6437
E-mail: lpriebe@cooperstandard.com
URL: http://www.mocaonline.com
Contact: Larissa Priebe, Treas.
Founded: 1987. **Members:** 200. **Membership Dues:** individual, $50 (annual) • student, $25 (annual). **Local.** Comprises of managerial, professional, and executive level professionals in business, industry, and government who are responsible for the design, establishment, execution, administration, or application of total compensation practices (including benefits) and policies in there organizations. Furthers the development of compensation and benefits professionals by providing a forum to share current practices, trends and research in the area of total rewards. **Affiliated With:** WorldatWork. **Publications:** *Moca Monitor*, quarterly. Newsletter.

7647 ■ National Speakers Association/Michigan
c/o Amy Jones, Chapter Administrator
33039 Tall Oaks St.
Farmington, MI 48336
Ph: (248)476-2134
Fax: (248)473-8487
Free: (800)990-7726
E-mail: info@nsamichigan.org
URL: http://www.nsamichigan.org
Contact: Peggy Kline, Pres.
State. Affiliated With: National Speakers Association.

7648 ■ Pastways
c/o Brian M. Golden, Exec.Dir.
PO Box 551
Farmington, MI 48332
Ph: (248)701-8112
E-mail: bgolden@pastways.info
URL: http://pastways.info/index.html
Local.

7649 ■ Western Wayne Oakland County Association of Realtors
24125 Drake Rd.
Farmington, MI 48335
Ph: (248)478-1700
Fax: (248)478-3150
URL: http://www.wwocar.com
Contact: Dale Smith, Exec. Officer
Local. Strives to develop real estate business practices. Advocates the right to own, use and transfer real property. Provides a facility for professional development, research and exchange of information among members. **Affiliated With:** National Association of Realtors.

Farmington Hills

7650 ■ ACI Greater Michigan Chapter (ACI GMC)
PO Box 3384
Farmington Hills, MI 48333-3384
Ph: (313)429-2429
Fax: (313)429-2448
E-mail: meetings@acigmc.org
URL: http://www.acigmc.org
Contact: Tony Johnson, Pres.
Founded: 1960. **Members:** 180. **Membership Dues:** ACI international, $25 (annual) • affiliate, $30 (annual). **Local.** Comprises of engineers, architects, contractors, educators, and others interested in improving techniques of design construction and maintenance of concrete products and structures. **Affiliated With:** American Concrete Institute. **Conventions/Meetings:** bimonthly dinner.

7651 ■ American Legion, Warren Post 490
31535 Kingston Ct.
Farmington Hills, MI 48336
Ph: (517)371-4720
Fax: (517)371-2401
URL: National Affiliate–www.legion.org
Local. Affiliated With: American Legion.

7652 ■ American Society of Mechanical Engineers, Metro Detroit Section
PO Box 2534
Farmington Hills, MI 48333
Ph: (248)506-7125
E-mail: alversonk@asme.org
URL: http://www.asmedetroit.com
Contact: Kent Alverson, Chm.
Local. Promotes the art, science and practice of Mechanical Engineering and allied arts and sciences.

Encourages original research and fosters engineering education. Promotes the technical and societal contribution of engineers. **Affiliated With:** American Society of Mechanical Engineers.

7653 ■ Apartment Association of Michigan (AAM)
c/o Irvin H. Yackness, Contact
30375 Northwestern Hwy., Ste.100
Farmington Hills, MI 48334
Ph: (248)737-4477
Fax: (248)538-4078
E-mail: 76176.2035@compuserve.com
State. Publications: *Building Business and Apartment Management.* **Conventions/Meetings:** quarterly meeting.

7654 ■ Associated Food Dealers of Michigan
30415 W Thirteen Mile Rd.
Farmington Hills, MI 48334
Ph: (248)671-9600
Fax: (248)671-9610
Free: (800)666-6233
E-mail: info@afdom.org
URL: http://www.afdom.org
Contact: Jane Shallal, Pres.
Members: 3,000. **State**. Represents nearly 3,000 food and beverage retailers, wholesalers, distributors and manufacturers throughout the state. Focuses on the exchange of business ideas, fair legislative representation, financial benefits, educational opportunities, and positive promotion of the industry.

7655 ■ BMW Car Club of America, Motor City Chapter
c/o Helene Weissberg, Activity Dir.
PO Box 2174
Farmington Hills, MI 48333-2174
Ph: (248)357-2871
E-mail: meredi5@comcast.net
URL: http://www.motorcitybmwcca.org
Contact: Helene Weissberg, Activity Dir.
Local. Affiliated With: BMW Car Club of America.

7656 ■ Building Industry Association of Southeastern Michigan
c/o Irvin Yackness
30375 Northwestern Hwy., Ste.100
Farmington Hills, MI 48334-3233
Ph: (248)737-4477
Fax: (248)862-1012
E-mail: bia@builders.org
URL: National Affiliate–www.nahb.org
Contact: Susan Adler Shanteau, Communications Dir.
Founded: 1928. **Members:** 2,200. **Membership Dues:** all, $560 (annual). **Staff:** 20. **Local**. Single and multifamily home builders, commercial builders, and others associated with the building industry. **Affiliated With:** Michigan Association of Home Builders; National Association of Home Builders; National Association of Home Builders. **Publications:** *Building Business and Apartment Management*, monthly. Magazine. **Price:** $48.00 per year. **Circulation:** 5,500. **Advertising:** accepted.

7657 ■ Building Owners and Managers Association of Metropolitan Detroit
c/o Janet Langlois-Resto, Exec.Dir.
38800 Country Club Dr.
Farmington Hills, MI 48331
Ph: (248)848-3714
Fax: (248)848-3744
E-mail: info@bomadet.org
URL: http://www.bomadet.org
Contact: Janet Langlois-Resto, Exec.Dir.
Founded: 1908. **Members:** 400. **Membership Dues:** principal, $875 (annual) • associate principal (2 or more members), $350-$430 (annual) • principal allied, $925 (annual) • associate allied (2 or more members), $350-$485 (annual) • non-profit group, $620 (annual) • student, $50 (annual). **Staff:** 3. **Budget:** $75,000. **Local**. Owners and managers of commercial real estate and representatives from organizations that furnish services and supplies to the commercial real estate industry. Facilitates exchange information and promotes the industry. **Libraries: Type:** not open to the public. **Subjects:** office building. **Awards:** The Office Building of the Year. **Frequency:** annual. **Type:** trophy. **Recipient:** for excellence in office building management. **Committees:** Award; Education; Golf; Government Affairs; Speaker; Supplier. **Affiliated With:** Building Owners and Managers Association International. **Publications:** *BOMA Visions*, bimonthly. **Price:** included in membership dues. **Circulation:** 700. **Advertising:** accepted. Alternate Formats: CD-ROM; magnetic tape; online • *Books Formats.* Alternate Formats: online • Membership Directory. **Advertising:** accepted. Alternate Formats: magnetic tape. **Conventions/Meetings:** annual convention • monthly meeting (exhibits).

7658 ■ Crohn's and Colitis Foundation of America, Michigan Chapter
31313 Northwestern Hwy., Ste.209
Farmington Hills, MI 48334
Ph: (248)737-0900
Fax: (248)737-0904
E-mail: michigan@ccfa.org
URL: National Affiliate–www.ccfa.org
Contact: Bernard L. Riker, Exec.Dir.
Membership Dues: regular, $25 (annual). **Staff:** 3. **Regional Groups:** 1. **Regional**. Raises funds for research and education. **Affiliated With:** Crohn's and Colitis Foundation of America. **Publications:** Newsletter, quarterly. **Conventions/Meetings:** annual conference, teaches coping skills to members • monthly meeting, to give support to its members.

7659 ■ Farmington - Farmington Hills Chamber of Commerce
c/o Marcotte Dental Bldg.
30903 W Ten Mile Rd., Ste.B
Farmington Hills, MI 48336
Ph: (248)474-3440
Fax: (248)474-9235
E-mail: atopouzian@ffhchamber.com
URL: http://ffhchamber.com
Contact: Ara Topouzian, Pres./CEO
Founded: 1963. **Members:** 865. **Membership Dues:** business (based on number of full-time employees), $225-$1,500 (annual). **Local**. Strives to enhance the economy and business environment in the greater Farmington-Farmington Hills area. **Computer Services:** Information services, business directory. **Committees:** Ambassadors. **Divisions:** Government Affairs. **Publications:** *The Voice of Business*, bimonthly. Newsletter. **Advertising:** accepted.

7660 ■ Finnish Center Association (FCA)
c/o Eva Koskimaki, Sec.Gen.
35200 W 8 Mile Rd.
Farmington Hills, MI 48335-5108
Ph: (248)478-6939
Fax: (248)478-5671
E-mail: fcafinn@juno.com
URL: http://home.socal.rr.com/emrozek/fca
Contact: Norbert Leppanen, Chm.
Local.

7661 ■ Golf Association of Michigan (GAM)
24116 Res. Dr.
Farmington Hills, MI 48335
Ph: (248)478-9242
Fax: (248)478-5536
E-mail: dgraham@gam.org
URL: http://www.gam.org
Contact: David Graham, Exec.Dir.
Founded: 1919. **State.**

7662 ■ Institute of Internal Auditors, Detroit Chapter
c/o Suzanne McCormick
30032 Fink Ave.
Farmington Hills, MI 48336
Ph: (248)471-3075
E-mail: harrisj@ci.detroit.mi.us
URL: National Affiliate–www.theiia.org
Contact: Joe Harris, Pres.
Membership Dues: regular, $115 (annual) • educator, $65 (annual) • student, retired, $30 (annual) • life, $2,100 • sustainer (government auditors only), $50 (annual) • organization ($65 per staff member over 5; $50 per staff member over 100), $425-$6,600 (annual). **Local**. Serves as an advocate for the internal audit profession. Provides certification, education, research, and technological guidance for the profession. **Affiliated With:** Institute of Internal Auditors.

7663 ■ Institute of Real Estate Management - West Michigan Chapter No. 62
c/o Bea King
24125 Drake Rd.
Farmington Hills, MI 48335
Ph: (248)615-3885
Fax: (248)615-3888
E-mail: mzzbea22@aol.com
URL: National Affiliate–www.irem.org
Contact: Bea King, Contact
Local. Represents real property and asset management professionals. Works to promote professional ethics and standards in the field of property management. Strives to keep its members informed on the latest legislative activities and current industry trends. Provides classroom training, continuing education seminars, job referral service and candidate assistance services to enhance the effectiveness and professionalism of its members. **Affiliated With:** Institute of Real Estate Management.

7664 ■ Metro Airport Lions Club
c/o Ben Yelco, Pres.
21200 Parker St.
Farmington Hills, MI 48334
Ph: (248)471-2600 (248)426-6507
URL: http://www.metrodetroitlions.org
Contact: Ben Yelco, Pres.
Local. Affiliated With: Lions Clubs International.

7665 ■ Michigan Association of Professional Psychologists
27650 Farmington Rd., Ste.B-2
Farmington Hills, MI 48334-3380
Ph: (248)324-0100
Fax: (248)324-1750
E-mail: miapp@flash.net

7666 ■ Michigan Boxer club
c/o Jennifer Walker, Sec.
28423 Kendallwood Dr.
Farmington Hills, MI 48334
Ph: (248)489-1963
E-mail: info@michiganboxerclub.com
URL: http://www.michiganboxerclub.com
Contact: Joan Johnson, Pres.
Local.

7667 ■ Michigan Chefs de Cuisine Association (MCCA)
c/o Kevin Enright, CEC, Apprentice Coor.
Oakland Community Coll.
27055 Orchard Lake Rd.
Farmington Hills, MI 48334
Ph: (248)522-3710
Fax: (248)522-3706
E-mail: kmenrigh@oaklandcc.edu
URL: http://www.mccachefs.org
Contact: Kevin Enright CEC, Apprentice Coor.
Founded: 1970. **Members:** 350. **State**. Promotes the culinary profession. Provides on-going educational training and networking for members. Provides opportunities for competition, professional recognition and access to educational forums with other culinarians at local, regional, national and international events. **Affiliated With:** American Culinary Federation. **Publications:** *The Michigan Chefs*, monthly. Newsletter. Alternate Formats: online.

7668 ■ Michigan Health Information Management Association, Southeast
c/o Michelle Mercieca, RHIT, Pres.
24136 Locust St.
Farmington Hills, MI 48335
Ph: (248)858-3182 (248)426-9602
E-mail: merciecm@trinity-health.org
URL: http://www.mhima.org
Contact: Michelle Mercieca RHIT, Pres.

Local. Represents the interests of individuals dedicated to the effective management of personal health information needed to deliver quality healthcare to the public. Provides career, professional development and practice resources. Sets standards for education and certification. Advocates public policy that advances Health Information Management (HIM) practice. **Affiliated With:** American Health Information Management Association; Michigan Health Information Management Association.

7669 ■ Michigan Psychoanalytic Society
32841 Middlebelt Rd., Ste.411
Farmington Hills, MI 48334
Ph: (248)851-3380
Fax: (248)851-1806
URL: National Affiliate–www.apsa.org
Contact: Steve Nickoloff MD, Pres.-Elect

State. Educates and promotes public awareness and interest in the science and art of psychoanalysis. Establishes and maintains standards for the training of psychoanalysts and for the practice of psychoanalysis. **Affiliated With:** American Psychoanalytic Association.

7670 ■ Michigan Society of Clinical Hypnosis
28952 Orchard Lake Rd., Ste.301
Farmington Hills, MI 48334
Ph: (248)626-8151
Fax: (248)626-7277
E-mail: carolyndaitch@comcast.net
URL: National Affiliate–www.asch.net
Contact: Carolyn Daitch PhD, Contact

State. Represents health and mental health care professionals using clinical hypnosis. Provides and encourages education programs to further the knowledge, understanding and application of hypnosis in health care. Works for the recognition and acceptance of hypnosis as an important tool in clinical health care. **Affiliated With:** American Society of Clinical Hypnosis.

7671 ■ Michigan Tooling Association (MTA)
PO Box 9151
Farmington Hills, MI 48333-9151
Ph: (248)488-0300
Fax: (248)488-0500
Free: (800)969-9MTA
E-mail: rob@mtaonline.com
URL: http://www.mtaonline.com
Contact: Robert J. Dumont, Managing Dir.

Founded: 1933. **Members:** 730. **Membership Dues:** corporation (1 to over 400 employees), $75-$690 (quarterly). **Staff:** 8. **Budget:** $1,200,000. **For-Profit**. Manufacturers of dies, jigs, fixtures, molds, gages, tools, special machinery, and related products; suppliers of die tryout, machining, and experimental and designing service. **Formerly:** (1990) Detroit Tooling Association. **Publications:** *Tool Talk*, monthly. Newsletter. **Price:** included in membership dues. **Circulation:** 1,250. Alternate Formats: online.

7672 ■ Oldsmobile Club of America, Motor City Rockets
28954 Glenarden St.
Farmington Hills, MI 48334
E-mail: info@motorcityrockets.com
URL: http://www.motorcityrockets.com
Contact: Steve Apking, Pres.

Membership Dues: individual, $20 (annual) • individual, $35 (biennial). **Local**. **Affiliated With:** Oldsmobile Club of America.

7673 ■ Phi Theta Kappa, Alpha Omicron Xi Chapter - Oakland Community College
c/o Richard Trombley
Orchard Ridge Campus
27055 Orchard Lake Rd.
Farmington Hills, MI 48334
Ph: (248)522-3400
E-mail: rjtrombl@oaklandcc.edu
URL: http://www.ptk.org/directories/chapters/MI/6603-1.htm
Contact: Richard Trombley, Advisor

Local.

7674 ■ Sweet Adelines International, Spirit of Detroit Chapter
Bethlehem Ev. Lutheran Church
35300 W 8 Mile Rd.
Farmington Hills, MI 48335
E-mail: webmaster@spiritofdetroit.org
URL: http://www.spiritofdetroitchorus.org
Contact: LeAnn K. Hazlett, Dir.

Local. Advances the musical art form of barbershop harmony through education and performances. Provides education, training and coaching in the development of women's four-part barbershop harmony. **Affiliated With:** Sweet Adelines International.

7675 ■ Tasters Guild International - Oakland County, Chapter No. 040
c/o Oakland Community College, Orchard Ridge Campus
27055 Orchard Lake Rd.
Farmington Hills, MI 48334
Ph: (248)522-3703
URL: National Affiliate–www.tastersguild.com
Contact: Darlene Levinson, Contact

Local. Aims to educate consumers and spread the word of responsible wine and food consumption. Provides opportunity to encounter the best in wine and culinary delights. **Affiliated With:** Tasters Guild International.

7676 ■ Turkish American Cultural Association of Michigan (TACAM)
PO Box 3445
Farmington Hills, MI 48333-3445
Ph: (248)763-9544
Fax: (248)626-8279
E-mail: email@tacam.org
URL: http://www.tacam.org
Contact: Mehtap Aksoy, Pres.

Founded: 1972. **Members:** 300. **Membership Dues:** family, $100 (annual) • adult, $50 (annual) • student, $25 (annual). **Budget:** $25,000. **State**. Follows the philosophy of Mustafa Kemal Ataturk, founder of the Turkish Republic, which encompasses the nation's creative legacy as well as the best values of world civilization. Emphasis is placed on personal and universal humanism. Seeks to promote cultural independence; to provide social function gatherings; to provide educational workshops in the community; and to provide political awareness. Sponsors cultural events that educate the MI community. **Affiliated With:** Assembly of Turkish American Associations.

7677 ■ United Association of Journeymen and Apprentices of the Plumbing and Pipe Fitting Industry of the United States and Canada - Local Union 636
30100 Northwestern Hwy.
Farmington Hills, MI 48334
Ph: (248)538-6636
Fax: (248)538-7060
E-mail: tdevlin636@msn.com
URL: http://www.pipefitters636.org
Contact: Tom Devlin, Business Mgr.

Members: 2,400. **Local**. **Affiliated With:** United Association of Journeymen and Apprentices of the Plumbing, Pipe Fitting, Sprinkler Fitting Industry of the U.S. and Canada.

Farwell

7678 ■ American Legion, Clare-Farwell Post 558
PO Box 361
Farwell, MI 48622
Ph: (517)371-4720
Fax: (517)371-2401
URL: National Affiliate–www.legion.org
Local. **Affiliated With:** American Legion.

7679 ■ Farwell Area Chamber of Commerce (FACC)
c/o Tom Pirnstill
PO Box 771
Farwell, MI 48622-0771
Ph: (989)588-0580
Fax: (989)588-0580
E-mail: facc@farewellareachamber.com
URL: http://www.farwellareachamber.com
Contact: Wanda L. Agle, Office Mgr.

Members: 80. **Membership Dues:** business, $125 (annual) • individual, $25 (annual). **Staff:** 1. **Local**. **Publications:** Newsletter. **Price:** free. **Conventions/Meetings:** monthly meeting, general business.

Fennville

7680 ■ American Legion, Fennville Post 434
2380 62nd St.
Fennville, MI 49408
Ph: (517)371-4720
Fax: (517)371-2401
URL: National Affiliate–www.legion.org
Local. **Affiliated With:** American Legion.

Fenton

7681 ■ American Legion, James De Witt Post 38
PO Box 4
Fenton, MI 48430
Ph: (517)371-4720
Fax: (517)371-2401
URL: National Affiliate–www.legion.org
Local. **Affiliated With:** American Legion.

7682 ■ Cairn Terrier Club of Greater Detroit
c/o Patricia Holmes, Corresponding Sec.
8070 Sheraton Park
Fenton, MI 48430
Ph: (810)629-2889
E-mail: kirkshire@chartermi.net
URL: http://cairnmichigan.com
Contact: Peggy McIlwaine, Pres.

Local.

7683 ■ Fenton Area Chamber of Commerce
114 N Leroy St.
Fenton, MI 48430
Ph: (810)629-5447
Fax: (810)629-6608
E-mail: info@fentonchamber.com
URL: http://www.fentonchamber.com
Contact: Mrs. Shelly Day, Pres.

Founded: 1929. **Local**. Advocates for member businesses through services and resources, while encouraging a prosperous Fenton Area. **Publications:** *Business Perspective*, monthly. Newsletter.

7684 ■ Fenton Lions Club
c/o Betsy Morath, Pres.
13336 Wenwood Dr.
Fenton, MI 48430
Ph: (810)750-9372
E-mail: prixstg@yahoo.com
URL: http://www.geocities.com/dist11d1
Contact: Betsy Morath, Pres.

Local. **Affiliated With:** Lions Clubs International.

7685 ■ Flint Flying Eagle Coin Club
c/o Raymond W. Dillard
PO Box 161
Fenton, MI 48430
Ph: (810)629-3041
URL: National Affiliate–www.money.org
Contact: Raymond W. Dillard, Contact
Local. Affiliated With: American Numismatic Association.

7686 ■ Livingston Gem and Mineral Society
c/o Sue McEwen, Pres.
16397 Oakhill Dr.
Fenton, MI 48430
E-mail: lgms@gwise.hartland.k12.mi.us
URL: National Affiliate–www.amfed.org
Contact: Isla Mitchell, Sec.
Local. Aims to further the study of Earth Sciences and the practice of lapidary arts and mineralogy. **Affiliated With:** American Federation of Mineralogical Societies.

7687 ■ Michigan Justin Morgan Horse Association (MJMHA)
c/o Cyndi Mortensen
6333 Hartland Rd.
Fenton, MI 48430
Ph: (810)750-6315
E-mail: ckm@daimlerchrysler.com
URL: http://www.mjmha.com
Contact: Cyndi Mortensen, Contact
Membership Dues: single, family, $30-$40 (annual). **State.** Promotes the Morgan Horse and Horse Shows in Michigan. **Affiliated With:** American Morgan Horse Association.

7688 ■ National Active and Retired Federal Employees Association - Flint 285
404 Main St.
Fenton, MI 48430-2134
Ph: (810)629-6604
URL: National Affiliate–www.narfe.org
Contact: Melvin J. Tormey, Contact
Local. Protects the retirement future of employees through education. Informs members on issues affecting the retirement. **Affiliated With:** National Association of Retired Federal Employees.

7689 ■ National Association of Professional Organizers, Michigan Chapter
12434 Orchardwood Dr.
Fenton, MI 48430
Ph: (810)348-1772
URL: National Affiliate–www.napo.net
State. Promotes the profession of professional organizing. Educates the public about the field of professional organizing. Supports, educates, and provides a networking forum for members.

7690 ■ National Softball Association - Michigan
c/o Bill Horton, Dir.
PO Box 187
Fenton, MI 48430
Ph: (810)629-9551
E-mail: nsareg5@aol.com
URL: National Affiliate–www.playnsa.com
Contact: Bill Horton, Dir.
State. Affiliated With: National Softball Association.

7691 ■ Sweet Adelines International, Fenton Lakes Chorus
A.J. Schmidt Middle School
Donaldson Dr.
Fenton, MI 48430
Ph: (810)953-0805
E-mail: mmhson01@earthlink.com
URL: http://www.fentonlakeschorus.com
Contact: Mary Harrison, Team Leader
Local. Advances the musical art form of barbershop harmony through education and performances. Provides education, training and coaching in the development of women's four-part barbershop harmony. **Affiliated With:** Sweet Adelines International.

Ferndale

7692 ■ American Legion, Michigan Post 330
c/o George W. Danuk
1741 Livernois St.
Ferndale, MI 48220
Ph: (248)544-9676
Fax: (517)371-2401
URL: National Affiliate–www.legion.org
Contact: George W. Danuk, Contact
Local. Affiliated With: American Legion.

7693 ■ American Subcontractors Association of SE Michigan (ASA)
c/o Rose Szwed
22934 Woodward Ave., Studio S
Ferndale, MI 48220
Ph: (248)542-7314
Fax: (248)542-7305
E-mail: asaofsemichigan@aol.com
State. Affiliated With: American Subcontractors Association.

7694 ■ Great Lakes Curling Association - Detroit Curling Club
1615 E Lewiston
Ferndale, MI 48220
E-mail: president@detroitcurlingclub.com
URL: http://www.detroitcurlingclub.com/index.php
Local. Affiliated With: United States Curling Association.

7695 ■ Holly Flint MMBA
1576 W Troy St.
Ferndale, MI 48220-1664
Ph: (248)398-1032
E-mail: hollyflint@mmba.org
URL: http://www.mmba.org
Local. Affiliated With: International Mountain Bicycling Association.

7696 ■ Midwest AIDS Prevention Project (MAPP)
429 Livernois
Ferndale, MI 48220
Ph: (248)545-1435
Fax: (248)545-3313
Free: (888)A-CONDOM
E-mail: info@aidsprevention.org
URL: http://www.aidsprevention.org
Contact: Craig Covey, CEO
State. Strives to prevent HIV transmission through AIDS education and safer sex information. Offers behavior-based workshops, outreach projects and education programs for a wide variety of populations and locations.

7697 ■ NAMES Project Michigan
427 Livernois Ave.
Ferndale, MI 48220
Ph: (248)691-1122
E-mail: contactus@namesproject-michigan.org
URL: http://www.namesproject-michigan.org
Contact: David Agius, Co-Chm.
State. Affiliated With: Names Project Foundation - AIDS Memorial Quilt.

7698 ■ National Association of Women in Construction, Detroit Chapter
PO Box 20755
Ferndale, MI 48220-0775
Ph: (248)542-4141
E-mail: info@nawicdetroit.com
URL: http://www.nawicdetroit.com
Contact: Myrt Hagood, Pres.
Founded: 1971. **Local.** Serves as the voice of women in the construction industry. Contributes to the development of the industry. Encourages women to pursue and establish career in construction. Promotes cooperation, fellowship and understanding among members of the association. **Affiliated With:** National Association of Women in Construction.

Fife Lake

7699 ■ American Legion, Fife Lake Post 219
10283 M-186
Fife Lake, MI 49633
Ph: (517)371-4720
Fax: (517)371-2401
URL: National Affiliate–www.legion.org
Local. Affiliated With: American Legion.

7700 ■ American Welding Society, Northern Michigan Section 158
c/o William Neil, Chm.
309 Oak Hill Rd.
Fife Lake, MI 49633
Ph: (231)369-4142
Fax: (231)369-4246
URL: National Affiliate–www.aws.org
Contact: William Neil, Chm.
Local. Promotes the interests of professional engineering society in the field of welding. **Affiliated With:** American Welding Society.

Filion

7701 ■ Michigan National Wild Turkey Federation, Upper Thumb Gobblers
3797 Carpender Rd.
Filion, MI 48432
Ph: (517)874-2020
Contact: Rodney Jimkowski, Pres.
Local.

Flat Rock

7702 ■ American Legion, Mittlestat-Smith Post 337
PO Box 97
Flat Rock, MI 48134
Ph: (517)371-4720
Fax: (517)371-2401
URL: National Affiliate–www.legion.org
Local. Affiliated With: American Legion.

7703 ■ Flat Rock Kiwanis
PO Box 94
Flat Rock, MI 48134
E-mail: thammar@juno.com
URL: http://mywebpage.netscape.com/frkiwanis
Contact: Tim Hammar, Pres.
Local.

7704 ■ International Union, United Automobile, Aerospace and Agricultural Implement Workers of America, AFL-CIO - Local Union 387
24250 Telegraph Rd.
Flat Rock, MI 48134
Ph: (734)782-2771 (734)671-7096
E-mail: president@local387.org
URL: http://www.local387.com
Contact: Kevin B. Madigan, Pres.
Members: 2,345. **Local.** Seeks for the dignity and equality of the workers. Strives to provide contractors with well-trained, productive employees. **Affiliated With:** International Union, United Automobile, Aerospace and Agricultural Implement Workers of America.

7705 ■ Michigan National Wild Turkey Federation, Flat Rock Longbeards
14867 Monroe St.
Flat Rock, MI 48134
Ph: (734)782-0482
URL: http://www.mi-nwtf.org/flat_rock.htm
Contact: Gary Scheffer, Pres.
Local.

7706 ■ Rockwood Lions Club
c/o John Miller, Pres.
26793 Hawthorne Blvd.
Flat Rock, MI 48134-1858

Ph: (734)779-0690 (734)782-3922
URL: http://www.metrodetroitlions.org
Contact: John Miller, Pres.
Local. Affiliated With: Lions Clubs International.

Flint

7707 ■ American Cancer Society, East Michigan Area Service Center
2413 S Linden Rd., Ste.A
Flint, MI 48532
Ph: (810)733-3702
Fax: (810)733-1480
URL: http://www.cancer.org
Contact: Amy Woodworth, Admin.Asst.
Local. Affiliated With: American Cancer Society.

7708 ■ American Legion, A.C. of Flint Post 366
G4314 W Carpenter Rd.
Flint, MI 48504
Ph: (517)371-4720
Fax: (517)371-2401
URL: National Affiliate–www.legion.org
Local. Affiliated With: American Legion.

7709 ■ American Legion, Federal Employees Post 496
G4314 W Carpenter Rd.
Flint, MI 48504
Ph: (517)371-4720
Fax: (517)371-2401
URL: National Affiliate–www.legion.org
Local. Affiliated With: American Legion.

7710 ■ American Legion, Fisher Body Post 342
4314g W Carpenter Rd.
Flint, MI 48504
Ph: (517)371-4720
Fax: (517)371-2401
URL: National Affiliate–www.legion.org
Local. Affiliated With: American Legion.

7711 ■ American Legion, Michigan Post 151
c/o William G. Haan Red Arrow
G4314 W Carpenter Rd.
Flint, MI 48504
Ph: (517)371-4720
Fax: (517)371-2401
URL: National Affiliate–www.legion.org
Contact: William G. Haan Red Arrow, Contact
Local. Affiliated With: American Legion.

7712 ■ American Legion, Michigan Post 306
c/o Dorie Miller
PO Box 1128
Flint, MI 48501
Ph: (517)371-4720
Fax: (517)371-2401
URL: National Affiliate–www.legion.org
Contact: Dorie Miller, Contact
Local. Affiliated With: American Legion.

7713 ■ American Legion, Oakley Traynor Post 64
G-4314 W Carpenter Rd.
Flint, MI 48504
Ph: (517)371-4720
Fax: (517)371-2401
URL: National Affiliate–www.legion.org
Local. Affiliated With: American Legion.

7714 ■ American Red Cross - Genesee/Lapeer Chapter
1401 S Grand Traverse
Flint, MI 48503
Ph: (810)232-1401
Fax: (810)232-8670
Free: (800)608-4272
E-mail: redcross@geneseelapeer-redcross.org
URL: http://www.geneseelapeer-redcross.org
Contact: Ken Vavra, Exec.Dir.
Local.

7715 ■ American Society of Women Accountants, Flint Chapter No. 054
c/o Teena Uhrig, Pres.
Lewis & Knopf, CPA's
5206 Gateway Ctre., Ste.100
Flint, MI 48507
Ph: (810)238-4617 (810)230-7286
Fax: (810)238-5083
E-mail: tuhrig@lewis-knopf.com
URL: National Affiliate–www.aswa.org
Contact: Teena Uhrig, Pres.
Local. Affiliated With: American Society of Women Accountants.

7716 ■ Association of Community Organizations for Reform Now, Flint
436 S Saginaw St., Ste.400
Flint, MI 48502
Ph: (810)424-6547
Fax: (810)424-6629
E-mail: miacornflro@acorn.org
URL: National Affiliate–www.acorn.org
Local. Affiliated With: Association of Community Organizations for Reform Now.

7717 ■ Association for Computing Machinery, University of Michigan/Flint
c/o Juli Spielman, Chm.
375 UCEN
303 E. Kearsley St.
Flint, MI 48502-2186
Ph: (810)762-3182
Fax: (810)762-3469
URL: National Affiliate–www.acm.org
Biological, medical, behavioral, and computer scientists; hospital administrators; programmers and others interested in application of computer methods to biological, behavioral, and medical problems. Stimulates understanding of the use and potential of computers in the Biosciences. **Affiliated With:** Association for Computing Machinery.

7718 ■ Career Paths of Flint
c/o Flint Genesee Job Corps Ctr.
2400 N. Saginaw St.
Flint, MI 48505-4442
Local.

7719 ■ Companion Dog Training Club of Flint, Michigan
4126 Holiday Dr.
Flint, MI 48506
E-mail: cdtcofflint@hotmail.com
URL: http://www.companiondogtrainingclub.com
Contact: David Tucker, Pres.
State. Affiliated With: American Kennel Club. **Formerly:** (2005) Companion Dog Training Club of Flint.

7720 ■ Compassionate Friends - Flint, Michigan Chapter
PO Box 7192
Flint, MI 48507-7192
Ph: (810)235-5600
E-mail: flinttcf@yahoo.com
URL: http://www.geocities.com/flinttcf
Contact: Connie Ayres, Chapter Leader
Local.

7721 ■ The Disability Network (TDN)
c/o Mike Zelley, Pres./CEO
3600 S Dort Hwy., Ste.54
Flint, MI 48507
Ph: (810)742-1800
Fax: (810)742-2400
E-mail: tdn@disnetwork.org
URL: http://www.disnetwork.org
Contact: Mike Zelley, Pres./CEO
Local. Aims to realize consumer empowerment, self determination, full inclusion and participation of all people in different communities through independent living philosophy and the unequivocal implementation of the Americans with Disabilities Act (ADA).

7722 ■ Dress for Success Flint
711 N Saginaw St.
Flint, MI 48503
Ph: (810)233-4380
Fax: (810)760-9332
E-mail: flint@dressforsuccess.org
URL: National Affiliate–www.dressforsuccess.org
Local.

7723 ■ East Flint Lions Club
c/o Floyd Illeg, Pres.
3601 N Term St.
Flint, MI 48506
Ph: (810)736-2170
URL: http://www.geocities.com/dist11d1
Contact: Floyd Illeg, Pres.
Local. Affiliated With: Lions Clubs International.

7724 ■ Easter Seals Genesee County, Michigan
1420 W Third Ave.
Flint, MI 48504-4897
Ph: (810)238-0475
Fax: (810)238-9270
E-mail: jcocciolone@essmichigan.org
URL: http://easterseaisgenco.com
Contact: Mr. John Cocciolone, Pres./CEO
Local. Works to help individuals with disabilities and special needs, and their families. Conducts programs to assist people of all ages with disabilities. Provides outpatient medical rehabilitation services. Advocates for the passage of legislation to help people with disabilities achieve independence, including the Americans with Disabilities Act (ADA). **Affiliated With:** Easter Seals.

7725 ■ Flint Area Association of Realtors
G-4428 Fenton Rd.
Flint, MI 48507
Ph: (810)767-6330
Fax: (810)234-9767
E-mail: info@flinthomes.net
URL: http://www.flinthomes.net
Contact: Susan Yeotis, Exec. Officer
Local. Strives to develop real estate business practices. Advocates the right to own, use and transfer real property. Provides a facility for professional development, research and exchange of information among members. **Affiliated With:** National Association of Realtors.

7726 ■ Flint Area Chamber of Commerce (FACC)
519 S Saginaw St., Ste.200
Flint, MI 48502-1802
Ph: (810)232-7101
Fax: (810)233-7437
E-mail: flintchamber@flint.org
URL: http://flintchamber.org
Contact: Larry Ford, Pres.
Founded: 1906. **Members:** 1,760. **Staff:** 9. **Budget:** $650,000. **Local.** Business and professional organizations that promote business and community development in the Flint, MI area. Maintains Career Guidance Institute. Sponsors 60-80 seminars per year; holds annual Trade Fair. **Awards:** Athena Award. **Frequency:** annual. **Type:** recognition • Citizen of the Year Award. **Frequency:** annual. **Type:** recognition. **Affiliated With:** U.S. Chamber of Commerce. **Publications:** *Business to Business*, monthly. Newsletter. **Price:** free • Membership Directory, annual. **Conventions/Meetings:** periodic convention.

7727 ■ Flint Area Convention and Visitors Bureau (FACVB)
316 Water St.
Flint, MI 48503
Ph: (810)232-8900
Fax: (810)232-1515
Free: (800)25-FLINT
E-mail: dsharp@flint.org
URL: http://www.flint.org
Contact: Dawn Stableford, Tourism Dir.
Local.

7728 ■ Flint Area Narcotics Anonymous
PO Box 747
Flint, MI 48501-0747
Ph: (810)238-3636
E-mail: fascna@michigan-na.org
URL: http://www.michigan-na.org/flint
Local. Affiliated With: Narcotics Anonymous.

7729 ■ Flint Corvette Club (FCC)
PO Box 984
Flint, MI 48501
Ph: (810)686-7212
E-mail: widams1@aol.com
URL: http://www.flintcorvetteclub.com
Contact: Wilburn Adams, Pres.
Local. Affiliated With: National Council of Corvette Clubs.

7730 ■ Flint Inner City Lions Club
c/o Melzon Williams, Pres.
4064 Kimberly Woods Dr.
Flint, MI 48504
Ph: (810)789-1866
E-mail: delh1318@aol.com
URL: http://www.geocities.com/dist11d1
Contact: Melzon Williams, Pres.
Local. Affiliated With: Lions Clubs International.

7731 ■ Flint Jewish Federation (FJF)
c/o Gary S. Alter, Exec.Dir.
619 Wallenberg St.
Flint, MI 48502
Ph: (810)767-5922
Fax: (810)767-9024
E-mail: fjf@tm.net
URL: http://users.tm.net/flint
Local.

7732 ■ Flint Lawn Bowling Club
Pierce Community Ctr.
2302 Brookside
Flint, MI 48502
Ph: (810)766-7425
E-mail: retiredron@aol.com
URL: http://www.members.aol.com/uslbacentral/index.htm
Local. Affiliated With: United States Lawn Bowls Association.

7733 ■ Flint - North Central Weed and Seed
c/o Joyce Thomas
2712 N Saginaw St., Ste.115
Flint, MI 48505-4480
Ph: (810)235-5555 (810)237-5012
Local.

7734 ■ Flint Snowbirds SkiClub
PO Box 261
Flint, MI 48501
E-mail: carla.pansil-collins@gm.com
URL: National Affiliate–www.nbs.org
Contact: Charles Collins, Pres.
Local. Affiliated With: National Brotherhood of Skiers.

7735 ■ Flint Table Tennis Club (FTTC)
Sobey Elementary School
3701 N Averill Ave.
Flint, MI 48506
Ph: (810)629-7324
E-mail: g.naugle@worldnet.att.net
URL: http://webpages.charter.net/backhandloop
Contact: Gerry Naugle, Contact
Local. Affiliated With: U.S.A. Table Tennis.

7736 ■ Genesee County Bar Association
315 E Court St.
Flint, MI 48502
Ph: (810)232-6012
Fax: (810)232-8310
E-mail: gcba@gcbalaw.org
URL: http://www.gcbalaw.org
Contact: Ramona Sain, Exec.Dir.
Founded: 1897. **Members:** 550. **Membership Dues:** sustaining, $260 (annual) • regular, $150 (annual) • young lawyer, $80 (annual). **Staff:** 4. **Budget:** $200,000. **Local.** Attorneys in good standing. Seeks to improve the administration of civil and criminal justice, and the availability of legal services to the public. Provides membership benefits package and lawyers referral service. Sponsors continuing legal education seminars, speaker's bureau. **Publications:** *Bar Beat Magazine*, bimonthly. **Price:** included in membership dues. **Conventions/Meetings:** monthly luncheon, with programs • annual meeting.

7737 ■ Genesee County Medical Society (GCMS)
c/o PPI Communications
4438 Oak Bridge Dr., Ste.B
Flint, MI 48532
Ph: (810)733-6260
Fax: (810)230-3737
E-mail: info@gcms.org
URL: http://www.ppicom.com/gcms.html
Contact: Peter A. Levine, Exec.Dir.
Local. Advances the art and science of medicine. Promotes patient care and the betterment of public health. **Affiliated With:** Michigan State Medical Society.

7738 ■ Genesee District Dental Society
G3269 Beecher Rd.
Flint, MI 48503-4631
Ph: (810)733-7120
Fax: (810)733-7721
E-mail: jwerschky@aol.com
URL: National Affiliate–www.ada.org
Contact: Dr. Jay Werschky, Exec.Dir.
Local. Represents the interests of dentists committed to the public's oral health, ethics and professional development. Encourages the improvement of the public's oral health and promotes the art and science of dentistry. **Affiliated With:** American Dental Association; Michigan Dental Association.

7739 ■ Girl Scouts Fair Winds Council
2300 Austin Pkwy.
Flint, MI 48507
Ph: (810)230-0244
Fax: (810)230-0955
Free: (800)482-6734
E-mail: dreha@gsfwc.org
URL: http://www.fwgsc.org
Contact: Dawn Reha, CEO
Local. Young girls and adult volunteers, corporate, government and individual supporters. Strives to develop potential and leadership skills among its members. Conducts trainings, educational programs and outdoor activities.

7740 ■ Habitat for Humanity of Genesee County
PO Box 13066
Flint, MI 48503
Ph: (810)238-1366
Fax: (810)238-5497
E-mail: office@geneseehabitat.org
URL: http://www.geneseehabitat.org
Contact: Judy Hibbett, Office Mgr.
Local. Maintains responsibility for construction decisions and the raising of funds to build houses in Flint and Genesee County. **Affiliated With:** Habitat for Humanity International.

7741 ■ Heart of Michigan English Cocker Spaniel
c/o Judy Priestley
3805 Lorraine Ave.
Flint, MI 48506
Ph: (810)742-3320
E-mail: carillonec@comcast.net
URL: http://mywebpages.comcast.net
Contact: Lora Richards, Pres.
Local.

7742 ■ International Institute of Flint
515 Stevens St.
Flint, MI 48502-1719
Ph: (810)767-0720
Fax: (810)767-0724
URL: http://www.gfn.org/~iif
Contact: Deborah Pascoe, Exec.Dir.
Founded: 1922. **Members:** 540. **Membership Dues:** student, $15 (annual) • individual, $35 (annual) • family, $55 (annual) • donor, $100 (annual) • silver/ethnic or cultural group, $250 (annual) • gold/non-profit organization, $500 (annual) • corporate, $1,000 (annual). **Staff:** 6. **Budget:** $300,000. **Local.** Associations and individuals interested in helping foreign-born residents and their descendants. Assists foreign-born individuals with their integration into the community. Works to educate the community about other cultures. Facilitates international exchange; makes available translation and language instruction services. **Libraries: Type:** open to the public. **Awards:** Parmalee Scholarship. **Frequency:** annual. **Type:** scholarship. **Recipient:** for undergraduate students majoring in foreign languages, ethnic areas, or international studies. **Affiliated With:** United Way of Genesee County. **Publications:** *Interpreter*, bimonthly. Newsletter. **Circulation:** 550. **Advertising:** accepted. **Conventions/Meetings:** annual meeting - always second Tuesday of October in Flint, MI.

7743 ■ International Union, United Automobile, Aerospace and Agricultural Implement Workers of America, AFL-CIO - Local Union 598
G-3293 Van Slyke Rd.
Flint, MI 48507
Ph: (810)238-4605
E-mail: webmaster@uawlocal598.org
URL: http://www.uawlocal598.org
Contact: Ben Mata, Pres.
Members: 3,071. **Local.** Seeks for the dignity and equality of the workers. Strives to provide contractors with well-trained, productive employees. **Affiliated With:** International Union, United Automobile, Aerospace and Agricultural Implement Workers of America.

7744 ■ Junior Achievement of Greater Genesee Valley
c/o Yvette Flippen, Exec.Dir.
503 Saginaw St., Ste.510
Flint, MI 48502
Ph: (810)235-3571
Fax: (810)235-3572
E-mail: yflippen@jamichigan.org
URL: http://www.ja.org
Contact: Yvette Flippen, Contact
Local. Seeks to educate and inspire young people to value free enterprise, business, and economics to improve the quality or their lives. Curricula address business and economic concepts and workforce skills that build in intensity from kindergarten through grade 12. **Affiliated With:** Junior Achievement.

7745 ■ Michigan Association of Professional Court Reporters
c/o Zo Turner
Ripka, Boroski & Associates
PO Box 1206
Flint, MI 48501
Ph: (810)234-7785
URL: National Affiliate–www.ncraonline.org
State. Affiliated With: National Court Reporters Association.

7746 ■ Michigan Educational Research Association (MERA)
c/o Leonard Bianchi, PhD, Pres.
923 E Kearsley St.
Flint, MI 48503-1974
Ph: (810)760-1883
Fax: (810)760-6878
E-mail: lbianchi@flintschools.org
URL: http://www.mera.net
Contact: Leonard Bianchi PhD, Pres.
Founded: 1971. **Members:** 100. **Membership Dues:** individual, $15 (annual). **State Groups:** 1. **State.**

Represents K-12 and ISD research, evaluation and assessment professionals, and university researchers. Holds two conferences annually. **Publications:** *Mera Memo*, semiannual. Newsletter. Provides information on conferences. **Price:** included in membership dues. **Circulation:** 100. **Conventions/Meetings:** semiannual conference, with presentations and seminars - always June and November.

7747 ■ Michigan National Wild Turkey Federation, Flint River Chapter
441 Catalpa Ct.
Flint, MI 48506
Ph: (810)736-1570
E-mail: jmturkey@aol.com
URL: http://www.mi-nwtf.org/Flintriver.htm
Contact: Jim Miller, Pres.
Local.

7748 ■ Muscular Dystrophy Association
c/o Amy Gach, District Dir.
G-6054 Fenton Rd.
Flint, MI 48507
Ph: (810)232-3190
Fax: (810)232-5844
E-mail: flintdistrict@mdausa.org
URL: http://www.mdausa.org
Local.

7749 ■ National Council on Alcoholism and Addictions-Greater Flint Area
3600 S Dort Hwy., Ste.46
Flint, MI 48507
Ph: (810)767-0350
Fax: (810)767-4031
URL: http://www.ncaaflint.com
Contact: Ron Winters, Pres.
Local. Works to reduce the incidence and prevalence of alcoholism and other drug addiction diseases and their related problems. **Affiliated With:** National Council on Alcoholism and Drug Dependence.

7750 ■ Phi Theta Kappa, Alpha Omicron Iota Chapter - Mott Community College
c/o Brenda Zicha
1401 E Court St.
Flint, MI 48503
Ph: (810)232-8021
E-mail: bzicha@mcc.edu
URL: http://www.ptk.org/directories/chapters/MI/6128-1.htm
Contact: Brenda Zicha, Advisor
Local.

7751 ■ Police and Firemen's Insurance Association - Flint Police Department
c/o Michael P. Sullivan
3418 Comanche Ave.
Flint, MI 48507
Ph: (810)232-8781
URL: National Affiliate–www.pfia.net
Contact: Michael P. Sullivan, Contact
Local. Affiliated With: Police and Firemen's Insurance Association.

7752 ■ Police and Firemen's Insurance Association - Oakland County Sheriff
c/o Robert L. Negri
1358 Fieldcrest Ct.
Flint, MI 48507
Ph: (810)239-4597
URL: National Affiliate–www.pfia.net
Contact: Robert L. Negri, Contact
Local. Affiliated With: Police and Firemen's Insurance Association.

7753 ■ Priority Children
c/o Gail Stimson, Pres./Interim Dir.
806 Tuuri Pl.
Flint, MI 48503
Ph: (810)234-5007
Fax: (810)234-5017
E-mail: kids@prioritychildren.org
URL: http://www.prioritychildren.org
Contact: Gail Stimson, Pres./Interim Dir.
Local. Affiliated With: Voices for America's Children.

7754 ■ Psi Chi, National Honor Society in Psychology - University of Michigan-Flint
c/o Dept. of Psychology
411 William R. Murchie Sci. Bldg.
Flint, MI 48502
Ph: (810)762-3424
Fax: (810)762-3426
E-mail: jashelto@umflint.edu
URL: http://www.umflint.edu/departments/psychology/psichi/index.php
Local. Affiliated With: Psi Chi, National Honor Society in Psychology.

7755 ■ Rotaract Club of Flint, Michigan
PO Box 13212
Flint, MI 48501
Ph: (810)233-5726
E-mail: flint@rotaract.org
Group of 18-30 students or young professionals who meet to perform service activities that better the Flint metro area.

7756 ■ RSVP of Genesee and Shiawassee Counties
c/o Karen Reid, Dir.
2421 Corunna Rd., Rm. 118
Flint, MI 48503-3358
Ph: (810)760-1092
Fax: (810)760-5388
E-mail: rsvpfnt@aol.com
URL: http://www.seniorcorps.gov/about/programs/rsvp.asp
Contact: Karen Reid, Dir.
Local. Affiliated With: Retired and Senior Volunteer Program.

7757 ■ Society of Manufacturing Engineers - Kettering University S041
Kettering Univ., IMED Dept.
1700 W 3rd Ave.
Flint, MI 48504
Ph: (810)762-7974
Fax: (810)762-9924
E-mail: wschelle@kettering.edu
URL: National Affiliate–www.sme.org
Contact: Dr. William Scheller, Contact
Local. Advances manufacturing knowledge to gain competitive advantage. Improves skills and manufacturing solutions for the growth of economy. Provides resources and opportunities for manufacturing professionals. **Affiliated With:** North American Mycological Association.

7758 ■ Theta Xi Fraternity, Kappa Sigma Chapter
2829 Sunset Dr.
Flint, MI 48503
Ph: (810)234-4625
E-mail: superfultron@hotmail.com
URL: http://www.gmi.edu/~thetaxi/asec
Contact: Andrew Fulton, A-Section Sec.
Local. Affiliated With: Theta Xi.

7759 ■ United Auto Workers Local No. 599 Environmental Committee
812 Leith St.
Flint, MI 48505
Ph: (810)238-1616 (810)732-0565
Fax: (810)238-3378
Contact: Dan Emerton, Contact
Local.

7760 ■ United Way of Genesee County
PO Box 949
Flint, MI 48501
Ph: (810)232-8121 (810)767-0500
Fax: (810)232-2898
E-mail: ameister@unitedwaygenesee.org
URL: http://www.unitedwaygenesee.org
Contact: Ronald J. Butler, Exec.Dir.
Founded: 1922. **Staff:** 25. **Budget:** $7,002,000. **Local. Affiliated With:** United Way of America. **Formerly:** (2001) United Way of Genesee and Lapeer Counties.

7761 ■ Urban League of Flint
c/o Paul Newman, Interim Pres.
5005 Cloverlawn Dr.
Flint, MI 48504
Ph: (810)789-7611
E-mail: ulflint@aol.com
Contact: Paul Newman, Interim Pres.
Local. Affiliated With: National Urban League.

Flushing

7762 ■ American Legion, Flushing American Legion Post 283
PO Box 125
Flushing, MI 48433
Ph: (517)371-4720
Fax: (517)371-2401
URL: National Affiliate–www.legion.org
Local. Affiliated With: American Legion.

7763 ■ American Saddlebred Horse Association of Michigan
c/o Dave Bedell
3119 N Seymour Rd.
Flushing, MI 48433
Ph: (248)628-2926
URL: http://www.asham.org/phpx/index.php
Contact: Nancy Spindler, Pres.
State. Affiliated With: American Saddlebred Horse Association.

7764 ■ Flint Township Lions Club
c/o Lisa Rice, Sec.
135 Brookside Dr.
Flushing, MI 48433
Ph: (810)487-7373
E-mail: greganlisarice@aol.com
URL: http://www.geocities.com/dist11d1
Contact: Lisa Rice, Sec.
Local. Affiliated With: Lions Clubs International.

7765 ■ Flushing Area Chamber of Commerce
133 E Main St.
PO Box 44
Flushing, MI 48433
Ph: (810)659-4141
Fax: (810)659-6964
E-mail: flushingchamber@sbcglobal.net
URL: http://www.flushingchamber.com
Contact: Susan Little, Exec.Dir.
Membership Dues: regular, $150 (annual) • deluxe, $230 (annual) • church/club/service organization, $75 (annual). **Local.** Promotes business and community development in the Flushing, MI area.

7766 ■ Flushing Area Historical Society
431 W Main St.
Flushing, MI 48433
Ph: (810)659-3980
URL: http://www.flushinghistorical.org
Contact: Mary Wilson, Pres.
Local.

7767 ■ Flushing Lions Club
c/o Steve Kozel, Pres.
8346 Gallant Fox Trail
Flushing, MI 48433

Ph: (810)659-3474
E-mail: stepenkozel@yahoo.com
URL: http://www.geocities.com/dist11d1
Contact: Steve Kozel, Pres.
Local. Affiliated With: Lions Clubs International.

7768 ■ Genesee Sportsman's Club
8208 N Seymour Rd.
Flushing, MI 48433
Ph: (810)639-5100
URL: National Affiliate–www.mynssa.com
Local. Affiliated With: National Skeet Shooting Association.

7769 ■ Michigan Environmental Balancing Bureau
3419 Pierson Pl.
Flushing, MI 48433
Ph: (810)230-6202
Fax: (810)230-6208
E-mail: atorrence@power-net.net
URL: National Affiliate–www.nebb.org
Contact: Aneta Torrence, Chapter Coor.
State. Works to help architects, engineers, building owners, and contractors produce buildings with HVAC systems. Establishes and maintains industry standards, procedures, and specifications for testing, adjusting, and balancing work. **Affiliated With:** National Environmental Balancing Bureau.

7770 ■ PFLAG Flint/Genesee County
8285 N Seymour Rd.
Flushing, MI 48433
Ph: (810)639-3595
E-mail: onesmith@centurytel.net
URL: http://www.pflaggcflint.org
Local. Affiliated With: Parents, Families, and Friends of Lesbians and Gays.

7771 ■ Plumbers and Pipefitters Union, Local 370
5500 W Pierson Rd.
Flushing, MI 48433-2331
Ph: (810)720-5243 (810)720-5244
Fax: (810)732-3805
E-mail: ualocal370@boyager.net
Contact: Mark A. Johnson, Business Mgr.
Founded: 1907. **Members:** 420. **Staff:** 1. **Budget:** $150,000. **State Groups:** 1. **Local.** Journeymen and apprentice plumbers and pipefitters in Genesee, Lapeer, and Shiawassee counties, MI. Trains and supplies skilled manpower for the piping industry. **Awards:** Years of Service. **Frequency:** annual. **Type:** recognition. **Recipient:** son/daughter, member/owner. **Affiliated With:** AFL-CIO; United Association of Journeymen and Apprentices of the Plumbing, Pipe Fitting, Sprinkler Fitting Industry of the U.S. and Canada. **Formerly:** U.A. Local 370. **Publications:** Journal, monthly • Newsletter, biweekly. **Conventions/Meetings:** monthly meeting - always first Tuesday of the month.

7772 ■ United Association of Journeymen and Apprentices of the Plumbing and Pipe Fitting Industry of the United States and Canada - Local Union 370
G-5500 W Pierson Rd.
Flushing, MI 48433
Ph: (810)720-5243
Fax: (810)732-3805
E-mail: ualocal370@comcast.net
URL: http://www.ualocal370.org
Contact: Mark A. Johnson, Business Mgr.
Members: 467. **Local. Affiliated With:** United Association of Journeymen and Apprentices of the Plumbing, Pipe Fitting, Sprinkler Fitting Industry of the U.S. and Canada.

Fort Gratiot

7773 ■ National Active and Retired Federal Employees Association - Port Huron 12
4333 24th Ave., Lot 149
Fort Gratiot, MI 48059-3879
Ph: (810)385-2984
URL: National Affiliate–www.narfe.org
Contact: Charles W. Nurnberg, Contact
Local. Protects the retirement future of employees through education. Informs members on issues affecting the retirement. **Affiliated With:** National Association of Retired Federal Employees.

7774 ■ Port Huron Northern High School Skating Club
3415 Birchgrove Tr.
Fort Gratiot, MI 48059
Ph: (810)385-4280
E-mail: seelyrajnay@aol.com
URL: National Affiliate–www.usfigureskating.org
Contact: Steven Rajnay, Contact
Local. Provides programs to encourage participation and achievement in the sport of figure skating on ice. Defines and maintains uniform standards of skating proficiency. Organizes and sponsors competitions and exhibitions for the purpose of stimulating interest in figure skating. **Affiliated With:** United States Figure Skating Association.

7775 ■ STARFLEET Region 13
c/o Michael Dugas, Regional Coor.
3735 Teeple Ave.
Fort Gratiot, MI 48059
E-mail: rc@region13.org
URL: http://www.region13.org
Contact: Michael Dugas, Regional Coor.
Regional. Affiliated With: STARFLEET.

7776 ■ STARFLEET: USS White Star
c/o Laura Dugas, Commanding Officer
3735 Teeple Ave.
Fort Gratiot, MI 48059
E-mail: usswhitestar@region13.org
URL: http://www.region13.org
Contact: Laura Dugas, Commanding Officer
Local. Affiliated With: STARFLEET.

Fowlerville

7777 ■ American Legion, Michigan Post 215
c/o Orson A. Rose
PO Box 518
Fowlerville, MI 48836
Ph: (517)371-4720
Fax: (517)371-2401
URL: National Affiliate–www.legion.org
Contact: Orson A. Rose, Contact
Local. Affiliated With: American Legion.

Frankenmuth

7778 ■ American Legion, Frankenmuth Post 150
990 Flint St.
Frankenmuth, MI 48734
Ph: (517)371-4720
Fax: (517)371-2401
URL: National Affiliate–www.legion.org
Local. Affiliated With: American Legion.

7779 ■ Frankenmuth Chamber of Commerce and Convention and Visitors Bureau
635 S Main St.
Frankenmuth, MI 48734
Fax: (989)652-3841
Free: (800)FUN-TOWN
E-mail: ceo@frankenmuth.org
URL: http://www.frankenmuth.org
Contact: Jennifer Tebedo CAE, Pres./CEO
Founded: 1902. **Members:** 490. **Staff:** 2. **Budget:** $450,000. **Languages:** English, German. **Local.** Promotes business and community development in Frankenmuth, MI. **Formerly:** (2005) Frankenmuth Chamber of Commerce. **Publications:** *Handleskammer*, periodic. Newsletter • Membership Directory, periodic. **Conventions/Meetings:** annual meeting - always in January.

7780 ■ Frankenmuth Lions Club
PO Box 298
Frankenmuth, MI 48734
E-mail: admin@frankenmuthlionsclub.org
URL: http://www.frankenmuthlionsclub.org
Contact: Chuck Bellsky, Pres.
Local. Affiliated With: Lions Clubs International.

7781 ■ Michigan Soybean Association (MSA)
PO Box 287
Frankenmuth, MI 48734-0287
Ph: (989)652-3294
Fax: (989)652-3296
E-mail: soyinfo@michigansoybean.org
URL: http://www.michigansoybean.org
Contact: Kathy Maurer, Contact
State. Affiliated With: American Soybean Association.

7782 ■ Ruffed Grouse Society, Saginaw Valley Chapter
c/o Dr. Brian Seefeldt
754 Zehnder Dr.
Frankenmuth, MI 48734
Ph: (989)652-4780
E-mail: jucbas@peoplepc.com
URL: National Affiliate–www.ruffedgrousesociety.org
Contact: Dr. Brian Seefeldt, Contact
Local. Affiliated With: Ruffed Grouse Society.

Frankfort

7783 ■ ACF of Northwestern Michigan
c/o Lucille A. House, Pres.
6285 Swamp Rd.
Frankfort, MI 49635
Ph: (231)995-7196
Fax: (231)995-1134
E-mail: lhouse@nmc.edu
URL: National Affiliate–www.acfchefs.org
Contact: Lucille A. House CEC, Pres.
Local. Promotes the culinary profession. Provides on-going educational training and networking for members. Provides opportunities for competition, professional recognition and access to educational forums with other culinarians at local, regional, national and international events. **Affiliated With:** American Culinary Federation.

7784 ■ American Legion, Michigan Post 221
c/o John A. Mortenson
PO Box 433
Frankfort, MI 49635
Ph: (517)371-4720
Fax: (517)371-2401
URL: National Affiliate–www.legion.org
Contact: John A. Mortenson, Contact
Local. Affiliated With: American Legion.

7785 ■ Frankfort - Elberta Area Chamber of Commerce
PO Box 566
Frankfort, MI 49635
Ph: (231)352-7251
Fax: (231)352-6750
E-mail: fcofc@frankfort-elberta.com
URL: http://www.frankfort-elberta.com
Contact: Alice Fewins, Exec.Dir.
Local. Formerly: (1999) Frankfort Area Chamber of Commerce.

7786 ■ Frankfort Lions Club
c/o John Maier, Pres.
PO Box 1006
Frankfort, MI 49635
Ph: (231)352-6628
E-mail: knight01@charter.net
URL: http://lions.silverthorn.biz/11-e1
Contact: John Maier, Pres.
Local. Affiliated With: Lions Clubs International.

Fraser

7787 ■ Detroit Medical Center Lions Club
c/o Karen Arendall, Pres.
15461 Sherwood Ln.
Fraser, MI 48026
Ph: (313)745-4510
E-mail: arendall@dmc.org
URL: http://www.metrodetroitlions.org
Contact: Karen Arendall, Pres.
Local. Affiliated With: Lions Clubs International.

7788 ■ First Catholic Slovak Ladies Association - Detroit Junior Branch 327
32489 Crestwood Ln.
Fraser, MI 48026-2176
Ph: (810)293-3323
URL: National Affiliate–www.fcsla.com
Local. Affiliated With: First Catholic Slovak Ladies Association.

7789 ■ First Catholic Slovak Ladies Association - Detroit Senior Branch 403
32489 Crestwood Ln.
Fraser, MI 48026-2176
Ph: (810)293-3323
URL: National Affiliate–www.fcsla.com
Local. Affiliated With: First Catholic Slovak Ladies Association.

7790 ■ Fraser Figure Skating Club (FFSC)
34400 Utica Rd.
Fraser, MI 48026
Ph: (586)294-4132
Fax: (586)294-6076
E-mail: fraserfsc@aol.com
URL: http://www.fraserfsc.com
Contact: Nick Benedetti, Chm.
Local. Provides programs to encourage participation and achievement in the sport of figure skating on ice. Defines and maintains uniform standards of skating proficiency. Organizes and sponsors competitions and exhibitions for the purpose of stimulating interest in figure skating. **Affiliated With:** United States Figure Skating Association.

7791 ■ Michigan Pest Control Association
c/o Christine Arnold, Exec.Sec.
PO Box 26546
Fraser, MI 48026
Ph: (586)296-9580
Fax: (586)296-9581
E-mail: mipca@aol.com
Membership Dues: joint membership with National Pest Management Association, $320 (annual). **State.**

7792 ■ Society for the Advancement of Material and Process Engineering, Michigan Chapter
c/o Michael T. Wilson, Dir.
Coll. Park Indus.
17505 Helro Dr.
Fraser, MI 48026
Ph: (586)294-7950
Fax: (586)294-0067
E-mail: mwilson@college-park.com
URL: National Affiliate–www.sampe.org
Contact: Michael T. Wilson, Dir.
State. Represents individuals engaged in the development of advanced materials and processing technology in airframe, missile, aerospace, propulsion, electronics, life sciences, management, and related industries. Provides scholarships for science students seeking financial assistance. Provides placement services for members. **Affiliated With:** Society for the Advancement of Material and Process Engineering.

Freeland

7793 ■ Public Relations Society of America, White Pine
c/o Barbara J. Muessig, APR
Muessig Enterprises
10630 Webster Rd.
Freeland, MI 48623
Ph: (517)695-9310
Fax: (517)692-0302
E-mail: barb.muessig@voyager.net
URL: http://www.ecd.prsa.org
Affiliated With: Public Relations Society of America.

Fremont

7794 ■ American Legion, C.C. Upton Post 91
PO Box 91
Fremont, MI 49412
Ph: (517)371-4720
Fax: (517)371-2401
URL: National Affiliate–www.legion.org
Local. Affiliated With: American Legion.

7795 ■ The Arc/Newaygo County
PO Box 147
Fremont, MI 49412
Ph: (231)924-5840
E-mail: arc@ncats.net
URL: National Affiliate–www.TheArc.org
Contact: Maggie Kolk, Pres./Bd.
Founded: 1966. **Members:** 120. **Membership Dues:** self-advocate, $18 (annual) • individual, $25 (annual) • senior, $18 (annual) • family, $35 (annual) • company/organization, $35 (annual). **Budget:** $400,000. **Local.** Seeks acceptance for persons with developmental disabilities as full citizens with the right to live, work and play in the community and to an education in the least restrictive environment. **Affiliated With:** Arc of the United States. **Publications:** *Horizon*, monthly. Newsletter. **Conventions/Meetings:** monthly board meeting • annual meeting.

7796 ■ Fremont Area Chamber of Commerce (FACC)
7 E Main St.
Fremont, MI 49412
Ph: (231)924-0770
Fax: (231)924-9248
E-mail: fchamber@ncats.net
URL: http://www.fremontcommerce.com
Contact: Ron Vliem, Exec.Dir.
Founded: 1903. **Members:** 190. **Staff:** 2. **Local.** Promotes business and community development in Fremont, MI. Issues periodic publication. **Convention/Meeting:** none. **Computer Services:** Information services, business directory. **Formerly:** (2005) Fremont Chamber of Commerce. **Publications:** *Community Profile and Business Directory*, annual. Includes listing of member businesses and contacts. **Price:** $15.00.

7797 ■ Fremont Lions Club - Michigan
PO Box 115
Fremont, MI 49412
Ph: (231)924-0126
E-mail: rgibson@wolvermemutual.com
URL: http://www.lions.lighthouseseeker.com
Contact: Ron Gibson, Pres.
Local. Affiliated With: Lions Clubs International.

7798 ■ Michigan National Wild Turkey Federation, Freemont Area Chapter
4148 S Stone Rd.
Fremont, MI 49412
URL: http://www.mi-nwtf.org/freemont.htm
Contact: Jeremiah Cook, Pres.
Local.

7799 ■ Michigan Rural Health Clinics Organization
c/o Ronald Nelson
2 E Main
Fremont, MI 49412-1244
Ph: (231)924-9200
Fax: (231)924-4882
URL: http://www.hsagroup.net
Contact: Ron Nelson, Pres.
State.

7800 ■ Newaygo County Habitat for Humanity
509 E Maple St.
Fremont, MI 49412
Ph: (231)924-0350
E-mail: habnew@ncats.net
URL: http://www.newaygohabitat.org
Contact: Janet Fisher, Pres.
Local. Affiliated With: Habitat for Humanity International.

7801 ■ United Way of Newaygo County
PO Box B
4424 W 48th St.
Fremont, MI 49412
Ph: (231)924-7613
Fax: (231)924-5391
E-mail: unitedway@tfacf.org
URL: http://www.uwmich.org/public/luw/luwdefault.asp?uworgid=57
Contact: Joseph Frendo, Pres.
Founded: 1945. **Staff:** 1. **Local.**

Gaastra

7802 ■ Michigan National Wild Turkey Federation, Northern Snow Shoe Toms Chapter
118 Youngs Ln.
Gaastra, MI 49927
Ph: (906)265-6843
URL: http://www.mi-nwtf.org/NorthernSnowShoe.htm
Contact: George Polich, Pres.
Local.

Gaines

7803 ■ Flint Antique Bottle and Collectibles Club
c/o Bill Heatley, Pres.
11353 W Cook Rd.
Gaines, MI 48436-9742
Ph: (989)271-9193
E-mail: tbuda@shianet.org
URL: National Affiliate–www.fohbc.com
Contact: Bill Heatley, Pres.
Local. Affiliated With: Federation of Historical Bottle Collectors.

7804 ■ Gaines Area Lions Club
c/o John Crandel, Pres.
10081 Ray Rd.
Gaines, MI 48436
Ph: (989)271-8547
URL: http://www.geocities.com/dist11d1
Contact: John Crandel, Pres.
Local. Affiliated With: Lions Clubs International.

Galesburg

7805 ■ National Active and Retired Federal Employees Association - Battle Creek 123
PO Box 574
Galesburg, MI 49053-0574
Ph: (269)665-7940
URL: National Affiliate–www.narfe.org
Contact: June Cupples Jones, Contact
Local. Protects the retirement future of employees through education. Informs members on issues affecting the retirement. **Affiliated With:** National Association of Retired Federal Employees.

7806 ■ National Space Society Southwest Michigan Chapter
13613 E L. Ave.
Galesburg, MI 49053
Ph: (616)746-5268
E-mail: louann.grover@wmich.edu
URL: National Affiliate–www.nss.org
Contact: Lon Grover, Contact
Local. Works for the creation of a spacefaring civilization. Encourages the establishment of self-

sustaining human settlements in space. Promotes large-scale industrialization and private enterprise in space.

Galien

7807 ■ American Legion, Michigan Post 344
c/o Roy Chilson
PO Box 206
Galien, MI 49113
Ph: (517)371-4720
Fax: (517)371-2401
URL: National Affiliate–www.legion.org
Contact: Roy Chilson, Contact
Local. Affiliated With: American Legion.

Garden

7808 ■ American Legion, Garden Post 545
PO Box 198
Garden, MI 49835
Ph: (517)371-4720
Fax: (517)371-2401
URL: National Affiliate–www.legion.org
Local. Affiliated With: American Legion.

Garden City

7809 ■ American Legion, Michigan Post 396
c/o Otto Miller, Jr.
6860 Middlebelt Rd.
Garden City, MI 48135
Ph: (517)371-4720
Fax: (517)371-2401
URL: National Affiliate–www.legion.org
Contact: Otto Miller Jr., Contact
Local. Affiliated With: American Legion.

7810 ■ American Legion, Redford-Township-Tansey-Weil Post 271
31171 Elmwood
Garden City, MI 48135
Ph: (517)371-4720
Fax: (517)371-2401
URL: National Affiliate–www.legion.org
Local. Affiliated With: American Legion.

7811 ■ Garden City Chamber of Commerce (GCCC)
30120 Ford Rd., Ste.D
Garden City, MI 48135
Ph: (734)422-4448
Fax: (734)422-1601
URL: http://www.gardencity.org
Contact: Amelia J. Oliverio, Exec.Dir.
Founded: 1957. **Members:** 225. **Membership Dues:** business (based on number of employees), $125-$295 (annual) • associate, $100 (annual) • club/organization, $100 (annual). **Staff:** 2. **Budget:** $35,000. **Local.** Promotes business and community development in Garden City, MI. Participates in community festival. **Awards:** Business Person of the Year. **Frequency:** annual. **Type:** recognition • Firefighter of the Year. **Frequency:** annual. **Type:** recognition • First Citizen Award. **Type:** recognition • Police Officer of the Year. **Frequency:** annual. **Type:** recognition. **Publications:** Newsletter, monthly. **Price:** included in membership dues • Directory, annual. **Conventions/Meetings:** monthly luncheon - every 1st Tuesday.

7812 ■ Garden City Lions Club - Michigan
c/o Victoria Kowalik, Pres.
28437 Dawson St.
Garden City, MI 48135
Ph: (734)524-1330
E-mail: zicky48135@aol.com
URL: http://www.metrodetroitlions.org
Contact: Victoria Kowalik, Pres.
Local. Affiliated With: Lions Clubs International.

7813 ■ Lathers Elementary School PTA
c/o Beth Collins, Pres.
28458 Marquette
Garden City, MI 48135
Ph: (734)522-3887
E-mail: lac826@wideopenwest.com
URL: http://familyeducation.com/MI/LathersPTA
Contact: Beth Collins, Pres.
Local. Parents, teachers, students, and others interested in uniting the forces of home, school, and community. Promotes the welfare of children and youth.

7814 ■ Michigan National Wild Turkey Federation, Huron Valley Chapter
32124 Rosslyn St.
Garden City, MI 48135
Ph: (734)421-2593
URL: http://www.mi-nwtf.org/Huron.htm
Contact: Ken Humphrey, Pres.
Local.

Gaylord

7815 ■ American Legion, Michigan Post 458
c/o John N. Cottrell
PO Box 2034
Gaylord, MI 49734
Ph: (517)371-4720
Fax: (517)371-2401
URL: National Affiliate–www.legion.org
Contact: John N. Cottrell, Contact
Local. Affiliated With: American Legion.

7816 ■ Ancient Order of Hibernians of Otsego County - Hogan Division
c/o William O'Neill
2977 E Dixon Lake Rd.
Gaylord, MI 49735
Ph: (989)731-4329
E-mail: oneill@state.mi.com
URL: http://www.michiganaoh.com
Contact: William O'Neill, Contact
Local. Affiliated With: Ancient Order of Hibernians in America.

7817 ■ Associated Builders and Contractors Northern Michigan Chapter (ABC)
126 E Main St.
Gaylord, MI 49735
Ph: (989)732-6211
Fax: (989)732-8206
E-mail: abcnmc@voyager.net
URL: http://www.abc.org/nmichigan
Contact: Linda Wiseley, Exec.Dir.
Local. Promotes merit-based rewards for workers. **Affiliated With:** Associated Builders and Contractors.

7818 ■ Gaylord Area Convention and Tourism Bureau
101 W Main St.
Gaylord, MI 49735
Ph: (989)732-4000
Fax: (989)732-7990
Free: (800)345-8621
E-mail: info@gaylordmichigan.net
URL: http://www.gaylordmichigan.net
Local. Promotes convention, business and tourism in the area.

7819 ■ Gaylord - Otsego County Chamber of Commerce (GOCCC)
101 W Main St.
PO Box 513
Gaylord, MI 49734
Ph: (989)732-6333
Fax: (989)732-7990
Free: (800)345-8621
E-mail: info@gaylordchamber.com
URL: http://www.gaylordchamber.com
Contact: Bob Kasprzak, Exec.Dir.
Founded: 1948. **Membership Dues:** general business (based on number of employees), $250-$810 (annual) • insurance/real estate broker/professional (plus $38 per associate), $250 (annual) • lodging (based on number of units), $250-$549 (annual) • recreation, $250 (annual) • associate (for profit), $250 (annual) • nonprofit (religious, social/fraternal, education, hospital), $150 (annual) • retired, $125 (annual). **Local.** Promotes business and community development in Otsego County, MI. Sponsors annual Alpenfest. **Affiliated With:** U.S. Chamber of Commerce. **Publications:** *Business to Business Journal*, quarterly. Newsletter. **Circulation:** 1,000. **Advertising:** accepted • *Gaylord/Otsego County Chamber of Commerce Membership Directory and Community Profile*, annual. **Advertising:** accepted. **Conventions/Meetings:** annual Alpenfest - festival • annual Chamber Golf Outing - tour.

7820 ■ National Active and Retired Federal Employees Association - Grayling 2305
829 Lancewood St.
Gaylord, MI 49735-9443
Ph: (989)732-7819
URL: National Affiliate–www.narfe.org
Contact: Richard F. Barber, Contact
Local. Protects the retirement future of employees through education. Informs members on issues affecting the retirement. **Affiliated With:** National Association of Retired Federal Employees.

7821 ■ Otsego County Fair Association
PO Box 500
895 N. Center
Gaylord, MI 49734-0500
Ph: (989)732-3811
Fax: (989)732-0541
E-mail: otsegofair@dunnsonline.com
Contact: Dawn Ellison, Pres.
Members: 15. **Membership Dues:** associate, $5 (annual). **Local.**

7822 ■ Otsego County United Way
116 E 5th St.
Gaylord, MI 49735-1270
Ph: (989)732-8929
URL: National Affiliate–national.unitedway.org
Local. Affiliated With: United Way of America.

7823 ■ RSVP of Otsego County
c/o Tami Phillips, Dir.
PO Box 1025
Gaylord, MI 49735-1253
Ph: (989)732-6232
Fax: (989)732-8080
E-mail: rsvp@freeway.net
URL: http://www.otsego.org/rsvp/rsvp.htm
Contact: Tami Phillips, Dir.
Local. Affiliated With: Retired and Senior Volunteer Program.

7824 ■ Sweet Adelines International, Michigan Northern Lights Chapter
Trinity Lutheran Church
1354 S Otsego Ave.
Gaylord, MI 49735-7711
Ph: (989)939-8211
E-mail: jkelsey@gaylordhospital.org
URL: National Affiliate–www.sweetadelineintl.org
Contact: Jeanie Kelsey, Contact
Local. Advances the musical art form of barbershop harmony through education and performances. Provides education, training and coaching in the development of women's four-part barbershop harmony. **Affiliated With:** Sweet Adelines International.

7825 ■ Water Wonderland Board of Realtors
122 S Otsego Ave.
Gaylord, MI 49735
Ph: (989)732-8226
Fax: (989)732-8231
E-mail: board@waterwonderlandboard.com
URL: http://www.waterwonderlandboard.com
Contact: Larry Curriston, Pres.
Local. Strives to develop real estate business practices. Advocates the right to own, use and transfer real property. Provides a facility for profes-

sional development, research and exchange of information among members. **Affiliated With:** National Association of Realtors.

Genesee

7826 ■ Genesee Lions Club
c/o Charles Oliver, Jr., Pres.
7168 Russell St.
Genesee, MI 48437
Ph: (810)640-1427
URL: http://www.geocities.com/dist11d1
Contact: Charles Oliver Jr., Pres.
Local. Affiliated With: Lions Clubs International.

Gladstone

7827 ■ Alliance for the Mentally Ill of Delta County
c/o Barb Lehouiller, Pres.
3 Park Ave.
Gladstone, MI 49837
Ph: (906)786-1752
URL: http://mi.nami.org/del.html
Contact: Barb Lehouiller, Pres.
Local. Strives to improve the quality of life of children and adults with severe mental illness through support, education, research and advocacy. **Affiliated With:** National Alliance for the Mentally Ill.

7828 ■ American Legion, August Mattson Post 71
802 Delta Ave.
Gladstone, MI 49837
Ph: (517)371-4720
Fax: (517)371-2401
URL: National Affiliate–www.legion.org
Local. Affiliated With: American Legion.

7829 ■ American Legion, Escanaba River Post 115
7597 County 426 M5 Rd.
Gladstone, MI 49837
Ph: (517)371-4720
Fax: (517)371-2401
URL: National Affiliate–www.legion.org
Local. Affiliated With: American Legion.

7830 ■ Great Lakes Curling Association - Delta Rocks Curling Club
Arena Ice
6 Aspen Ln.
Gladstone, MI 49837
Ph: (906)786-8107 (906)428-1337
E-mail: john37@charter.net
URL: http://www.deltarocks.com
Contact: John Viau, Pres.
Local. Affiliated With: United States Curling Association.

7831 ■ National Organization for Women - Lake-to-Lake
PO Box 204
Gladstone, MI 49837
URL: http://www.michnow.org
Local. Affiliated With: National Organization for Women.

Gladwin

7832 ■ American Legion, Gladwin County Post 171
PO Box 15
Gladwin, MI 48624
Ph: (517)371-4720
Fax: (517)371-2401
URL: National Affiliate–www.legion.org
Local. Affiliated With: American Legion.

7833 ■ Clare Gladwin Board of Realtors
298 Birwood St.
Gladwin, MI 48624
Ph: (989)246-0714
Fax: (989)246-0715
E-mail: cgboard@glccomputers.com
URL: National Affiliate–www.realtor.org
Contact: Kim Hatchew, Exec. Officer
Local. Strives to develop real estate business practices. Advocates the right to own, use and transfer real property. Provides a facility for professional development, research and exchange of information among members. **Affiliated With:** National Association of Realtors.

7834 ■ Gladwin Area Hockey Association
PO Box 181
Gladwin, MI 48624-0181
Local.

7835 ■ Gladwin County Chamber of Commerce (GCCC)
608 W. Cedar Ave.
Gladwin, MI 48624-2028
Ph: (989)426-5451
Fax: (989)426-1074
Free: (800)789-4812
E-mail: chamber@ejourney.com
URL: National Affiliate–www.uschamber.com
Contact: Tom Tucholski, Exec.Dir.
Founded: 1938. **Members:** 249. **Staff:** 2. **Budget:** $60,000. **Local.** Businesses, professionals and individuals working together to make Gladwin County a better place for everyone to live and work. **Libraries: Type:** open to the public. **Awards:** Business/Industry of the Year. **Frequency:** annual. **Type:** recognition • Citizen of the Year. **Frequency:** annual. **Type:** recognition. **Affiliated With:** U.S. Chamber of Commerce. **Publications:** *Chamber Directory*, annual • *Chamber Newsletter*, monthly. **Price:** free. **Circulation:** 270. **Advertising:** accepted. **Conventions/Meetings:** biweekly board meeting - always second and fourth Thursday of each month • annual dinner.

7836 ■ Michigan State Bowling Association (MSBA)
4343 Hamilton Way
Gladwin, MI 48624-8634
Ph: (989)426-8403
E-mail: fpeters@mistatebowl.com
URL: http://www.mistatebowl.com
Contact: Frank Peters, Exec.Dir.
Founded: 1928. **Members:** 270,000. **State.** Bowlers and bowling organizations. Conducts state championship bowling tournament. **Publications:** none. **Awards:** Scholarships. **Frequency:** semiannual. **Type:** scholarship. **Recipient:** for graduating high school senior boy. **Affiliated With:** United States Bowling Congress. **Conventions/Meetings:** annual conference - always first weekend after Labor Day (September) • annual convention - always fourth Sunday in June.

7837 ■ United Way of Gladwin County
PO Box 620
Gladwin, MI 48624
Ph: (989)426-9225
E-mail: uwgc@ejourney.com
URL: http://www.unitedwaygladwinco.org
Contact: Tami Jenkinson, Exec.Dir.
Local. Affiliated With: United Way of America.

Glen Arbor

7838 ■ Sleeping Bear Area Chamber of Commerce
PO Box 217
Glen Arbor, MI 49636
Ph: (231)334-3238
Fax: (231)334-3238
E-mail: gullinglen@aol.com
URL: http://www.sleepingbeararea.com
Contact: Bill Thompson, Pres.
Local. Formerly: (2000) Glen Lake Chamber of Commerce; (2005) Glen Lake/Sleeping Bear Area Chamber of Commerce.

Goodrich

7839 ■ Grand Blanc Huntsman's Club
PO Box 303
Goodrich, MI 48438
Ph: (810)636-7261
E-mail: info@gbhuntsmans.org
URL: http://www.gbhuntsmans.com
Local. Affiliated With: National Skeet Shooting Association.

Grand Blanc

7840 ■ ACF Great Lakes Thumb Chapter
c/o Mitchell L. Plant
8313 Perry Rd.
Grand Blanc, MI 48439
Ph: (810)636-2929
E-mail: letscook55@hotmail.com
URL: National Affiliate–www.acfchefs.org
Contact: Mitchell L. Plant, Pres.
Local. Promotes the culinary profession. Provides on-going educational training and networking for members. Provides opportunities for competition, professional recognition and access to educational forums with other culinarians at local, regional, national and international events. **Affiliated With:** American Culinary Federation.

7841 ■ American Legion, Grand Blanc Post 413
375 E Grand Blanc Rd.
Grand Blanc, MI 48439
Ph: (517)371-4720
Fax: (517)371-2401
URL: National Affiliate–www.legion.org
Local. Affiliated With: American Legion.

7842 ■ Automotive Recyclers of Michigan (ARM)
c/o Barbara Utter, Exec.Dir.
G-8469 S Saginaw Rd.
Grand Blanc, MI 48439
Ph: (810)695-6760
Fax: (810)695-6762
Free: (800)831-2519
E-mail: arm@automotiverecyclers.org
URL: http://www.automotiverecyclers.org
Contact: Barbara Utter, Exec.Dir.
State.

7843 ■ Genesee Fencing Club
c/o Ron Shrank
8303 Parkside Dr.
Grand Blanc, MI 48439-7436
Ph: (810)694-5674
E-mail: gfcfencing@att.net
URL: http://home.att.net/~r.shrank/wsb
Contact: Ron Shrank, Contact
Local. Amateur fencers. **Affiliated With:** United States Fencing Association.

7844 ■ Grand Blanc Chamber of Commerce (GBCC)
512 E Grand Blanc Rd.
Grand Blanc, MI 48439
Ph: (810)695-4222
Fax: (810)695-0053
E-mail: jet@grandblancchamber.org
URL: http://www.grandblancchamber.org
Contact: Jet Kilmer, Pres.
Founded: 1977. **Members:** 400. **Membership Dues:** retiree/individual, $125 (annual) • business (based on average number of employees), $199-$435 (annual) • community service organization, $125 (annual) • additional principal (associate member), $90 (annual). **Budget:** $103,000. **Local.** Businesses and organizations dedicated to advancing the commercial, agricultural, industrial, and civic interests of the community. Offers group health insurance and discounts on charge cards; conducts charitable activities, summer festival and golf outing. **Awards: Type:** scholarship. **Publications:** *The Business Index*, monthly. Newslet-

ter • *Chamber Buzz*, monthly. Newsletter • *Grand Blanc Community Directory and Buyer's Guide*. **Conventions/Meetings:** monthly Ambassadors Meeting • monthly board meeting • monthly Chamber Breakfast • weekly Issues Committee Meeting.

7845 ■ Home Builders Association of Metro Flint
c/o Barry Simon
PO Box 940
Grand Blanc, MI 48439-0940
Ph: (810)603-2200
Fax: (810)603-2225
E-mail: barry@bamfhome.com
URL: http://www.bamfhome.com

Single and multifamily home builders, commercial builders, and others associated with the building industry. **Affiliated With:** National Association of Home Builders.

7846 ■ International Personnel Management Association, Michigan
c/o Diane Guzak, Personnel Dir., City of Grand Blanc
203 E Grand Blanc Rd.
Grand Blanc, MI 48439
Ph: (810)694-1118
Fax: (810)694-9517
URL: National Affiliate–www.ipma-hr.org

Founded: 1972. **Members:** 280. **Membership Dues:** single, $7 (annual) • family, $10 (annual) • student, $1 (annual) • life, $100. **State**. Individuals interested in the history of the region. Provides help with genealogical research; transcribes letters, diaries, and ledgers. Maintains museum; sponsors marker program and May open house. **Libraries: Type:** reference. **Holdings:** books, maps, photographs. **Awards:** Heritage Award. **Type:** recognition. **Affiliated With:** International Public Management Association for Human Resources. **Publications:** *Footsteps Thru the Great White Country*. Book. **Price:** $7.00 • *Grand Blanc Heritage Directory*, annual. Membership Directory • *More Secrets from Grand Blanc Cupboards*, 5/year. Newsletter. **Price:** $5.00. **Conventions/Meetings:** semiannual meeting - always spring and fall.

7847 ■ International Union, United Automobile, Aerospace and Agricultural Implement Workers of America, AFL-CIO - Local Union 1292
6153 S Dort Hwy.
Grand Blanc, MI 48439
Ph: (810)694-4151
Fax: (810)694-9739
E-mail: uawl292@sbcglobal.net
URL: http://www.uawlocal1292.org
Contact: Brian Kosbar, Pres.

Members: 3,459. **Local**. AFL-CIO. **Affiliated With:** International Union, United Automobile, Aerospace and Agricultural Implement Workers of America.

7848 ■ InventorEd
c/o Ronald J. Riley, Dir.
1323 W Cook Rd.
Grand Blanc, MI 48439
Ph: (810)936-4356
E-mail: help@inved.org
URL: http://www.inventored.org
Contact: Ronald J. Riley, Dir.

Local. Provides information on history of invention, inventing, inventors, obtaining a patent, and enforcement of patent rights for both adults and children. **Affiliated With:** United Inventors Association of the U.S.A.

7849 ■ Izaak Walton League of America - Fenton (IWLA)
c/o Dent Green
4227 E Cook Rd.
Grand Blanc, MI 48439-8346
Ph: (810)694-4792
URL: http://www.iwla.org
Contact: Dent Green, Contact

Local. Educates the public to conserve, maintain, protect, and restore the soil, forest, water, and other natural resources of the U.S. Promotes the utilization of these resources. Sponsors environmental programs.

7850 ■ Rankin Lions Club - Michigan
c/o Richard Brugger, IPDG, Sec.
7388 Rory St.
Grand Blanc, MI 48439
Ph: (810)655-4261
E-mail: dbru909530@aol.com
URL: http://www.geocities.com/dist11d1
Contact: Richard Brugger IPDG, Sec.
Local. **Affiliated With:** Lions Clubs International.

Grand Haven

7851 ■ Alliance for the Great Lakes
700 Washington Ave., Ste.150
Grand Haven, MI 49417
Ph: (616)850-0745
Fax: (616)850-0765
E-mail: michigan@greatlakes.org
URL: http://www.lakemichigan.org
Contact: Dale Bryson, Pres.
Founded: 1970. **State**. **Formerly:** (2006) Lake Michigan Federation.

7852 ■ American Legion, Michigan Post 28
c/o Charles A. Conklin
PO Box 439
Grand Haven, MI 49417
Ph: (517)371-4720
Fax: (517)371-2401
URL: National Affiliate–www.legion.org
Contact: Charles A. Conklin, Contact
Local. **Affiliated With:** American Legion.

7853 ■ American Truck Historical Society, West Michigan Chapter
c/o James Miel
622 Fulton
Grand Haven, MI 49417
Ph: (616)846-1584
URL: National Affiliate–www.aths.org
Contact: James Miel, Contact
Local.

7854 ■ American Welding Society, Western Michigan
c/o Kevin Foster, Chm.
Shape Corp.
1835 Hayes
Grand Haven, MI 49417
Ph: (616)844-3477
Fax: (616)530-8953
E-mail: fosterk@shape-corp.com
URL: National Affiliate–www.aws.org
Contact: Kevin Foster, Chm.
Local. Professional engineering society in the field of welding. **Affiliated With:** American Welding Society.

7855 ■ The Chamber - Grand Haven, Spring Lake, Ferrysburg
PO Box 509
1 S Harbor Dr.
Grand Haven, MI 49417-0509
Ph: (616)842-4910
Fax: (616)842-0379
E-mail: areainfo@grandhavenchamber.org
URL: http://www.grandhavenchamber.org
Contact: Joy A. Gaasch, Pres.

Members: 625. **Membership Dues:** retail, service, professional, industrial, construction, government (plus $3 per employee over 131 employees), $211-$1,298 (annual) • bank/financial institution (plus $28 per million in deposits), $211 (annual) • accommodation (plus $6 per room), $211 (annual) • nonprofit, seasonal attraction, educational institution, $211 (annual) • associate, individual, $119 (annual) • seasonal agricultural business (plus $3 per full-time employee over 5 employees), $211 (annual). **Local**. Works to serve the interests of the local business community. **Computer Services:** Mailing lists, membership listings. **Formerly:** (2002) Association of Commerce and Industry. **Publications:** *Business Beacon*. Brochure. **Price:** included in membership dues • *Clubs and Organizations Directory*. **Price:** included in membership dues; $5.00 for nonmembers • *Industrial Directory*. **Price:** $5.00 for members; $15.00 for nonmembers • *Relocation Guide*. Directory. **Price:** $5.00 • Membership Directory. **Price:** $5.00 for members.

7856 ■ Council of Michigan Foundations (CMF)
PO Box 599
Grand Haven, MI 49417
Ph: (616)842-7080
Fax: (616)842-1760
E-mail: cmf@cmif.org
URL: http://www.cmif.org
Contact: Robert Collier, Pres.

Founded: 1973. **Members:** 481. **Staff:** 23. **Budget:** $3,000,000. **Regional**. Community, corporate, and private foundations. Provides a forum for exchanging experiences, expertise, ideas, and information among grantmakers. **Libraries: Type:** reference. **Holdings:** 5,000; audio recordings, books, periodicals, video recordings. **Subjects:** philanthropy, foundation administration, boards and governance, nonprofit leadership. **Publications:** *The Michigan Foundation Directory*, biennial. **Price:** $50.00. **Circulation:** 2,500. **Conventions/Meetings:** annual conference, regional gathering of grantmakers in the country (exhibits).

7857 ■ GHHS PTSA
17001 Ferris St.
Grand Haven, MI 49417
Ph: (616)850-6000
E-mail: ghhs@ptamail.com
URL: http://familyeducation.com/MI/GHHS_PTSA
Contact: Cindy Rosso, Pres.

Local. Parents, teachers, students, and others interested in uniting the forces of home, school, and community. Promotes the welfare of children and youth.

7858 ■ Grand Haven-Spring Lake Convention and Visitors Bureau
1 S. Harbor Dr.
Grand Haven, MI 49417
Ph: (616)842-4910
Fax: (616)842-0379
Free: (800)303-4096
E-mail: mcisneros@grandhavenchamber.org
URL: http://www.visitgrandhaven.com
Contact: Marci Cisneros, Exec.Dir.

Founded: 1986. **Members:** 19. **Staff:** 2. **Budget:** $150,000. **State Groups:** 1. **Local Groups:** 1. **Local**. Promotes convention business and tourism in area. **Libraries: Type:** not open to the public. **Holdings:** 1,500; photographs. **Subjects:** tourism photos. **Awards:** Tourism Employee Excellence Award. **Frequency:** monthly. **Type:** recognition. **Recipient:** for excellent customer service. **Committees:** Business Development; Marketing; Public Relations. **Councils:** Ottawa County Tourism. **Publications:** *Grand Haven, Spring Lake, Ferrysburg Visitor's Guide*, annual. Newsletter. Includes information on tourism. **Price:** free. **Advertising:** accepted. Alternate Formats: online. **Conventions/Meetings:** annual meeting (exhibits); Avg. Attendance: 25.

7859 ■ Grand Haven - Young Life
PO Box 473
Grand Haven, MI 49417
Ph: (616)844-1977
URL: http://sites.younglife.org/sites/grandhaven/default.aspx
Local. **Affiliated With:** Young Life.

7860 ■ Great Lakes Booksellers Association (GLBA)
PO Box 901
208 Franklin St.
Grand Haven, MI 49417
Ph: (616)847-2460
Fax: (616)842-0051
Free: (800)745-2460
E-mail: info@books-glba.org
URL: http://www.books-glba.org
Contact: Jim Dana, Exec.Dir.

Founded: 1989. **Members:** 575. **Membership Dues:** retail bookseller, business, $75 (annual) • affiliate (wholesaler, publisher, rep, librarian, author), $75 (annual) • individual, $30 (annual). **Staff:** 3. **Budget:** $450,000. Booksellers. Supports bookstores and promotes excellence in publishing, distribution, promotion, and selling of books. Provides a forum for information exchange; fosters a sense of community among booksellers; provides information and services for the advancement of members; promotes literacy; and supports the First Amendment rights of members. **Awards:** Great Lakes Book Awards. **Frequency:** annual. **Type:** recognition. **Computer Services:** Mailing lists, labels. **Publications:** *Books for Holiday Giving*, annual. Catalog • *Directory and Handbook*, annual. Lists member bookstores and representatives, wholesalers and publishers in the Great Lakes region, and monitors regional First Amendment challenges. **Price:** $10.00/for members; $25.00/for nonmembers. **Circulation:** 700. **Advertising:** accepted • *Great Lakes Bookseller*, bimonthly. Newsletter. Covers association news, member news, trade shows, and important dates. **Conventions/Meetings:** annual convention and trade show, includes presentations from sales representatives on lead books, readings and autographs from authors, workshops on the practical aspects of bookselling, and a silent auction (exhibits).

7861 ■ Junior Achievement West Michigan Lakeshore
201 N 3rd St.
Grand Haven, MI 49417
Ph: (616)844-0800
Fax: (616)844-0622
E-mail: etomaras@jalakeshore.org
URL: http://www.jalakeshore.org
Contact: Eileen Tomaras, Office Mgr.

Regional.

7862 ■ Michigan Association of Educational Representatives (M.A.E.R.)
c/o Lisa A. Roossien, Exec.Sec.
214 S Beacon Blvd.
Grand Haven, MI 49417
Ph: (616)846-7730
Fax: (616)846-7732
E-mail: lisaabs@tds.net
URL: http://www.miedreps.com
Contact: Lisa A. Roossien, Exec.Sec.

Founded: 1931. **Members:** 170. **Regional**. An association created for the purpose of fostering professional relationships between educational representatives and Michigan schools and libraries. **Formerly:** Michigan Bookmen's Club. **Publications:** *M.A.E.R. Messenger*, bimonthly. Newsletter. Lists exhibits, MAER business activities. **Advertising:** accepted. Also Cited As: *printed.* **Conventions/Meetings:** annual meeting - always held in June.

7863 ■ National Association of Miniature Enthusiasts - Harbor Mini Crafters
c/o Joan Cook
12556 Lakeshore Dr.
Grand Haven, MI 49417
Ph: (616)846-8924
E-mail: jimjo@novagate.com
URL: http://www.miniatures.org/states/MI.html
Contact: Joan Cook, Contact

Local. **Affiliated With:** National Association of Miniature Enthusiasts.

7864 ■ North Ottawa Rod and Gun Club
PO Box 683
Grand Haven, MI 49417
E-mail: info@norgc.com
URL: http://norgc.com

Local. **Affiliated With:** National Skeet Shooting Association.

7865 ■ Professional Photographers of Western Michigan
c/o Dallas Stalzer
13063 Acacia Dr.
Grand Haven, MI 49417
Ph: (616)846-1827
E-mail: dmcst@novagate.com
URL: http://www.ppwm.org
Contact: Dallas Stalzer, Membership Chair

Local.

7866 ■ Spring Lake - Young Life
PO Box 473
Grand Haven, MI 49417
Ph: (616)844-1977
URL: http://sites.younglife.org/sites/SpringLake/default.aspx

Local. **Affiliated With:** Young Life.

7867 ■ West Michigan Lakeshore Association of Realtors
12916 168th Ave.
Grand Haven, MI 49417
Ph: (616)846-6240
Fax: (616)846-5155
Free: (800)611-7300
E-mail: info@wmlar.com
URL: http://www.wmlar.com
Contact: Tom Speet, Pres.

Local. Strives to develop real estate business practices. Advocates the right to own, use and transfer real property. Provides a facility for professional development, research and exchange of information among members. **Affiliated With:** National Association of Realtors.

7868 ■ West Shore Chorus of Sweet Adelines International
Second Reformed Church
1000 Waverly Ave.
Grand Haven, MI 49417-2249
Ph: (616)842-2374
E-mail: bluetaurus@webtv.net
URL: http://www.westshorechorus.com
Contact: Michael Oonk, Dir.

Local. Advances the musical art form of barbershop harmony through education and performances. Provides education, training and coaching in the development of women's four-part barbershop harmony. **Affiliated With:** Sweet Adelines International.

7869 ■ Young Life Lakeshore - Grand Haven
PO Box 473
Grand Haven, MI 49417
Ph: (616)844-1977
Fax: (616)844-1977
URL: http://sites.younglife.org/sites/lakeshore/default.aspx

Local. **Affiliated With:** Young Life.

Grand Ledge

7870 ■ American Legion, Cole-Briggs Post 48
731 N Clinton St.
Grand Ledge, MI 48837
Ph: (517)371-4720
Fax: (517)371-2401
URL: National Affiliate–www.legion.org

Local. **Affiliated With:** American Legion.

7871 ■ Grand Ledge Area Chamber of Commerce (GLACC)
121 S Bridge St.
Grand Ledge, MI 48837
Ph: (517)627-2383
Fax: (517)627-5006
E-mail: glacc@grandledgemi.com
URL: http://www.grandledgemi.com
Contact: Norman Snyder, Exec.Dir.

Founded: 1970. **Members:** 182. **Membership Dues:** business (based on number of employees), $220-$552 (annual) • nonprofit organization/service club/church, $135 (annual) • president's circle, $750 (annual) • friend, $70 (annual). **Staff:** 1. **Local**. Promotes business and community development in Eaton County, MI. Holds monthly board meeting. **Awards:** Athena and Businessman of the Year. **Frequency:** annual. **Type:** recognition. **Computer Services:** Information services, membership directory. **Publications:** Newsletter, monthly. Alternate Formats: online. **Conventions/Meetings:** monthly board meeting - every 3rd Tuesday, 11:30 A.M. in Grand Ledge, MI.

7872 ■ Grand Ledge Lions Club
c/o Clive Peabody, Sec.
629 W Jefferson St.
Grand Ledge, MI 48837
Ph: (517)627-6145
Fax: (517)627-3241
E-mail: cspeabod2000@yahoo.com
URL: http://www.district11c2.org
Contact: Clive Peabody, Sec.

Local. **Affiliated With:** Lions Clubs International.

7873 ■ Holbrook Elementary School PTA
615 Jones St.
Grand Ledge, MI 48837
Ph: (517)627-6830
Fax: (517)622-1801
E-mail: jaquettefamily@comcast.net
Contact: Ruthann Jaquette, Pres.

Local. Parents, teachers, students and others interested in uniting the forces of home, school and community. Promotes the welfare of children and youth.

7874 ■ Military Officers Association of America, Capitol Area Chapter
c/o Col. George Noirot
5985 Austin Way
Grand Ledge, MI 48837-9118
Ph: (517)877-5770
E-mail: redleg6@comcast.net
URL: National Affiliate–www.moaa.org
Contact: Col. George Noirot, Contact

Local. **Affiliated With:** Military Officers Association of America.

7875 ■ National Association of Miniature Enthusiasts - Magic of Miniatures
c/o Vicki L. Dukes
314 Mineral St.
Grand Ledge, MI 48837
Ph: (517)627-8089
E-mail: dukesvid@peoplepc.com
URL: http://www.miniatures.org/states/MI.html
Contact: Vicki L. Dukes, Contact

Local. **Affiliated With:** National Association of Miniature Enthusiasts.

7876 ■ Willow Ridge Elementary PTA
12840 Nixon Rd.
Grand Ledge, MI 48837
Ph: (517)627-4888
E-mail: willowridgepta@ptamail.com
URL: http://familyeducation.com/MI/william_ford_pta
Contact: Amy O'Keefe, Pres.

Local. Parents, teachers, students, and others interested in uniting the forces of home, school, and community. Promotes the welfare of children and youth. **Additional Websites:** http://familyeducation.com/MI/Willow_Ridge_Elementary_PTA.

Grand Rapids

7877 ■ AAA Michigan
4650 Plainfield NE
Grand Rapids, MI 49525
Ph: (616)364-6111
Free: (800)442-8304
URL: http://www.aaamich.com
Contact: Jack Peet, Contact
State.

7878 ■ ACF Greater Grand Rapids Chefs Association
c/o Timothy L. England
649 Union Ave. SE
Grand Rapids, MI 49503
Ph: (616)526-6686
Fax: (616)526-6533
E-mail: tengland@calvin.edu
URL: National Affiliate–www.acfchefs.org
Contact: Timothy England CEC, Pres.
Local. Promotes the culinary profession. Provides on-going educational training and networking for members. Provides opportunities for competition, professional recognition and access to educational forums with other culinarians at local, regional, national and international events. **Affiliated With:** American Culinary Federation.

7879 ■ Adoptive Family Support Network
233 E Fulton, Ste.108
Grand Rapids, MI 49503
Ph: (616)458-7945
URL: http://www.afsn.org
Contact: Janice Fonger, Dir.
Local.

7880 ■ Alcoholics Anonymous, Kent County Central Office
1404 Plainfield Ave. NE
Grand Rapids, MI 49505
Ph: (616)913-9149 (616)913-9216
E-mail: graaweb@iserv.net
URL: http://www.grandrapidsaa.org
Local. Individuals recovering from alcoholism. Maintains that members can solve their common problem and help others achieve sobriety through a twelve step program that includes sharing their experience, strength, and hope with each other. **Affiliated With:** Alcoholics Anonymous World Services.

7881 ■ Alliance for Health
c/o Lodewyk P. Zwarensteyn, Pres.
1011 40th St. SE, Ste.100
Grand Rapids, MI 49508
Ph: (616)248-3820
Fax: (616)248-9170
E-mail: alliance@afh.org
URL: http://www.afh.org
Contact: Lodewyk P. Zwarensteyn, Pres.
Founded: 1948. **Members:** 250. **Staff:** 3. **Regional Groups:** 1. **For-Profit**. **Regional**. Seeks to promote health care service by providing resource planning, health education and health delivery system of information sharing. **Libraries: Type:** open to the public; reference. **Holdings:** articles, periodicals, video recordings. **Subjects:** health care, health care system.

7882 ■ Alliance for the Mentally Ill - Share of Grand Rapids
c/o Betty Walker, Pres.
7391 Shadowbrook SE
Grand Rapids, MI 49546
Ph: (616)956-6141
URL: http://mi.nami.org/sgr.html
Contact: Betty Walker, Pres.
Local. Strives to improve the quality of life of children and adults with severe mental illness through support, education, research and advocacy. **Affiliated With:** National Alliance for the Mentally Ill.

7883 ■ ALS Association, West Michigan Chapter (ALSA)
731 Front St. NW
Grand Rapids, MI 49504-5342
Ph: (616)459-1900
Free: (800)387-7121
E-mail: mail@alsa-westmichigan.org
URL: http://www.alsa-westmichigan.org
Contact: Tom Farley, Exec.Dir.
Founded: 1985. **Members:** 400. **Membership Dues:** individual, $25 (annual). **Staff:** 3. **Budget:** $100,000. **State Groups:** 2. **Local Groups:** 3. **State**. Provides support and services to families with ALS, creating awareness and understanding within the community while contributing to the discovery of the cure for ALS. **Libraries: Type:** open to the public. **Holdings:** 50; articles, books, periodicals, video recordings. **Subjects:** amyotrophic lateral sclerosis. **Awards:** Caregiver Appreciation Certificate. **Frequency:** annual. **Type:** recognition. **Recipient:** for an individual who demonstrates compassionate care of a family member with ALS. **Also Known As:** Amyotrophic Lateral Sclerosis Association, West Michigan Chapter. **Publications:** *Connections*, quarterly. Newsletter. Includes fundraising information and other news. **Price:** free. **Circulation:** 4,000. Alternate Formats: online. **Conventions/Meetings:** annual Advocacy Day - conference, includes leadership and clinical conference (exhibits) - always May.

7884 ■ American Association of Airport Executives, Michigan
c/o Phillip E. Johnson, AAE
Gerald R. Ford Intl. Airport
5500 44th St. SE
Grand Rapids, MI 49512
Ph: (616)233-6000
Fax: (616)233-6025
E-mail: pjohnson@grr.org
URL: http://www.glcaaae.org
Contact: Phillip E. Johnson AAE, Contact
State. Represents airport management personnel at public airports. Promotes professionalism and financial stability in the administration of airports. Furthers airport safety and operational efficiency. Seeks to develop a systematic exchange of information and experience in the development, maintenance and operation of airports. **Affiliated With:** American Association of Airport Executives.

7885 ■ American Association of University Women, Grand Rapids Branch
c/o Rosemary E. Johnsen
1042 Lakeside Dr. SE
Grand Rapids, MI 49506
Ph: (616)554-7034 (616)248-5425
E-mail: karenamos1@comcast.net
URL: http://www.aauw-michigan.org
Contact: Karen Amos, Membership VP
Founded: 1941. **Members:** 60. **Membership Dues:** man and woman, $64 (annual). **Staff:** 12. **Local**. Graduates of accredited four-year colleges and universities. Works to promote equity for all women and girls, lifelong education and positive societal change. Sponsors fundraisers, works on community committees affecting equity, co-sponsors "Science is for Girls" event and organizes study groups. **Awards: Type:** grant • **Type:** scholarship. **Subgroups:** Book Study. **Affiliated With:** American Association of University Women; International Federation of University Women - Switzerland. **Publications:** *News Brief*, monthly. Newsletter. **Price:** free. Alternate Formats: online • Directory, annual. **Price:** for members only. **Conventions/Meetings:** annual convention - always first Saturday in May • monthly meeting, with interesting speakers - every 1st Wednesday.

7886 ■ American Board of Trial Advocates - Michigan
330 E Fulton
Grand Rapids, MI 49503
Ph: (616)458-6111
Fax: (616)458-6446
E-mail: gary@mcbowen.com
Contact: Gary J. McInerney, Pres.
Local. Improves the ethical and technical standards of practice in the field of advocacy. Elevates the standards of integrity, honor and courtesy in the legal profession. Promotes the efficient administration of justice and improvement of the law. **Affiliated With:** American Board of Trial Advocates.

7887 ■ American Camp Association Michigan
c/o Theresa Moore, Exec.
PO Box 6177
Grand Rapids, MI 49516
Ph: (616)245-5255
Fax: (616)245-5259
Free: (888)ACA-MICH
E-mail: executive@aca-michigan.org
URL: http://www.aca-michigan.org
Contact: Theresa Moore, Exec.
State. Represents the organized camping industry and all segments of the camp profession, including agencies serving youth and adults, independent camps, religious and fraternal organizations and public/municipal agencies. Serves as a knowledge center for the camping industry, educating camp owners and directors in the administration of camp operations, particularly program quality, health and safety, and assisting parents, families and caregivers nationwide in selecting camps that meet industry-accepted and government recognized standards.

7888 ■ American Cancer Society, West Michigan Area Service Center
400 Ann St. NW, Ste.202
Grand Rapids, MI 49504
Ph: (616)364-6121
Fax: (616)364-6451
Free: (866)364-6284
E-mail: joan.kulesa@cancer.org
URL: http://www.cancer.org
Contact: Joan Kulesa, Exec.Dir.
Local. **Affiliated With:** American Cancer Society.

7889 ■ American Choral Directors Association - Michigan Chapter
c/o Pearl Shangkuan, Pres.
Calvin Coll., Music Dept.
3201 Burton St., SE
Grand Rapids, MI 49546
Ph: (616)248-3494 (616)526-6519
E-mail: pshangku@calvin.edu
URL: http://www.acdami.org
Contact: Paul Krasnovsky, Pres.
Membership Dues: associate/active, $75 (annual) • student, $30 (annual) • life, $2,000. **State**. Promotes excellence in choral music through performance, composition, publication, research and teaching. Elevates choral music's position in American society. **Additional Websites:** http://www.acdaonline.org/Central/. **Subgroups:** Repertoire and Standards; Technology. **Affiliated With:** American Choral Directors Association. **Publications:** *Bella Voce*. Newsletter. Alternate Formats: online. **Conventions/Meetings:** annual convention.

7890 ■ American Diabetes Association
c/o Nicole Pascaru, Program Dir.
648 Monroe Ave. NW, Ste.004
Grand Rapids, MI 49503
Ph: (616)458-9341
Fax: (616)458-0317
E-mail: npascaru@diabetes.org
URL: http://www.diabetes.org
Local.

7891 ■ American Legion, Daniel Waters Cassard Post 208
133 44th St. SE
Grand Rapids, MI 49548
Ph: (517)371-4720
Fax: (517)371-2401
URL: National Affiliate–www.legion.org
Local. **Affiliated With:** American Legion.

7892 ■ American Legion, Furniture City Post 258
401 N Park St. NE
Grand Rapids, MI 49505
Ph: (517)371-4720
Fax: (517)371-2401
URL: National Affiliate–www.legion.org
Local. Affiliated With: American Legion.

7893 ■ American Legion, Mc-Donald-Osmer Post 451
3390 Thornapple River Dr. SE
Grand Rapids, MI 49546
Ph: (517)371-4720
Fax: (517)371-2401
URL: National Affiliate–www.legion.org
Local. Affiliated With: American Legion.

7894 ■ American Legion, Michigan Post 2
c/o Carl A. Johnson
401 N Park NE
Grand Rapids, MI 49525
Ph: (517)371-4720
Fax: (517)371-2401
URL: National Affiliate–www.legion.org
Contact: Carl A. Johnson, Contact
Local. Affiliated With: American Legion.

7895 ■ American Legion, Michigan Post 179
c/o Neal E. Fonger
2327 Wilson Ave. SW
Grand Rapids, MI 49544
Ph: (517)371-4720
Fax: (517)371-2401
URL: National Affiliate–www.legion.org
Contact: Neal E. Fonger, Contact
Local. Affiliated With: American Legion.

7896 ■ American Legion, Michigan Post 430
c/o Chester F. Mikulski
600 Douglas St. NW
Grand Rapids, MI 49504
Ph: (517)371-4720
Fax: (517)371-2401
URL: National Affiliate–www.legion.org
Contact: Chester F. Mikulski, Contact
Local. Affiliated With: American Legion.

7897 ■ American Legion, North Eastern Post 459
658 Michigan St. NE
Grand Rapids, MI 49503
Ph: (517)371-4720
Fax: (517)371-2401
URL: National Affiliate–www.legion.org
Local. Affiliated With: American Legion.

7898 ■ American Legion, Valley City Post 356
401 N Park St. NE
Grand Rapids, MI 49525
Ph: (517)371-4720
Fax: (517)371-2401
URL: National Affiliate–www.legion.org
Local. Affiliated With: American Legion.

7899 ■ American Legion, Walter Durkee Post 311
2824 E Beltline Ln.
Grand Rapids, MI 49525
Ph: (517)371-4720
Fax: (517)371-2401
URL: National Affiliate–www.legion.org
Local. Affiliated With: American Legion.

7900 ■ American Red Cross of West Central Michigan
1050 Fuller NE
Grand Rapids, MI 49503
Ph: (616)456-8661
Fax: (616)235-2355
URL: http://www.redcrosswcm.org
Regional.

7901 ■ American Society of Appraisers, Greater Michigan Chapter
c/o Paul H. Taylor, Pres.
Plante & Moran, PLLC
333 Bridge St. NW, Ste.600
Grand Rapids, MI 49504
Ph: (616)774-8221
Fax: (616)774-0702
E-mail: paul.taylor@plantemoran.com
URL: http://www.appraisers.org/michigan
Contact: Paul H. Taylor, Pres.
State. Serves as a professional appraisal educator, testing and accrediting society. Sponsors mandatory recertification program for all members. Offers consumer information service to the public. **Affiliated With:** American Society of Appraisers.

7902 ■ American Society of Heating, Refrigerating and Air-Conditioning Engineers - West Michigan Chapter
c/o Dave Shugars, Pres.
R.L. Deppmann
4121 Brockton Dr. SE
Grand Rapids, MI 49512
Ph: (616)656-0821
Fax: (616)656-0830
E-mail: dshugars@deppmann.com
URL: http://www.ashraewestmi.org
Contact: Dave Shugars, Pres.
Local. Advances the arts and sciences of heating, ventilation, air-conditioning and refrigeration. Provides a source of technical and educational information, standards and guidelines. Conducts seminars for professional growth. **Affiliated With:** American Society of Heating, Refrigerating and Air-Conditioning Engineers.

7903 ■ American Society of Women Accountants, Grand Rapids Chapter No. 010
c/o Emily Irish, CPA, Pres.
BDO Seidman, LLP
99 Monroe Ave. NW, No. 800
Grand Rapids, MI 49503
Ph: (616)774-7000 (616)891-8462
Fax: (616)776-3680
E-mail: eirish@bdo.com
URL: National Affiliate–www.aswa.org
Contact: Emily Irish CPA, Pres.
Local. Affiliated With: American Society of Women Accountants.

7904 ■ American Women in Radio and Television Western Michigan
c/o Suzin Vandercook Claver, Pres.
Comcast Media Sers.
3500 Patterson
Grand Rapids, MI 49512
Ph: (616)247-3600
Fax: (616)940-9505
E-mail: suzin_claver@cable.comcast.com
URL: National Affiliate–www.awrt.org
Contact: Suzin Vandercook Claver, Pres.
Regional. Affiliated With: American Women in Radio and Television.

7905 ■ Ancient Order of Hibernians of Kent County - Fr. John Whalen McGee Division
c/o Billy Quinn, Pres.
PO Box 6002
Grand Rapids, MI 49516
Ph: (616)453-7803
E-mail: liamgr@comcast.net
URL: http://www.geocities.com/shipfittermetal
Contact: Billy Quinn, Pres.
Local. Affiliated With: Ancient Order of Hibernians in America.

7906 ■ APICS, The Association for Operations Management - Grand Rapids Chapter
PO Box 230256
Grand Rapids, MI 49523-0256
Ph: (616)248-8900 (616)394-6611
E-mail: apicswestmi@aol.com
URL: http://www.apics-gr.org
Contact: Jon Karel, Pres.
Local. Provides information and services in production and inventory management and related areas to enable members, enterprises and individuals to add value to their business performance. **Affiliated With:** APICS - The Association for Operations Management.

7907 ■ Arc Kent County
1331 Lake Dr. SE No. 2
Grand Rapids, MI 49506
Ph: (616)459-3339
Fax: (616)459-5299
E-mail: thearc@iserv.net
URL: National Affiliate–www.TheArc.org
Contact: Ms. Rachel S. Urquhart J.D., Exec.Dir.
Founded: 1950. **Members:** 100. **Membership Dues:** consumer, $15 (annual) • friend/family, $25 (annual) • group home and day program service provider, $10 (annual). **Staff:** 3. **Budget:** $170,000. **Local. Affiliated With:** Arc of the United States.

7908 ■ ARMA, Western Michigan Chapter
c/o Todd Baareman, Pres.
PO Box 1967
Grand Rapids, MI 49501-1967
Ph: (616)246-9581
Fax: (616)475-2193
E-mail: tbaarema@steelcase.com
URL: http://www.wmiarma.org
Contact: Todd Baareman, Pres.
Local. Provides education, research, and networking opportunities to information professionals, enabling them to use their skills and experience to leverage the value of records, information and knowledge as corporate assets and as contributors to organizational success. **Affiliated With:** ARMA International - The Association of Information Management Professionals.

7909 ■ Art's Council of Greater Grand Rapids
PO Box 2265
Grand Rapids, MI 49501-2265
Ph: (616)459-2787
URL: http://www.artsggr.org
Contact: Iliana Ordaz-Jeffries, Exec.Dir.
Local.

7910 ■ Associated Builders and Contractors, Western Michigan Chapter (ABC)
c/o John Doherty, Jr., Exec.VP
580 Cascade W Pkwy.
Grand Rapids, MI 49546
Ph: (616)942-9960
Fax: (616)942-5901
E-mail: jdoherty@abcwmc.org
URL: http://www.abcwmc.org
Contact: John Doherty Jr., Exec.VP
Local. Promotes merit-based rewards for workers. **Affiliated With:** Associated Builders and Contractors.

7911 ■ Association for Corporate Growth, Western Michigan Chapter
c/o David Brenner, Pres.
169 Monroe NW, Ste.320
Grand Rapids, MI 49503
Ph: (616)454-4033
Fax: (616)454-4474
E-mail: amy.pakiela@abnamro.com
Affiliated With: Association for Corporate Growth.

7912 ■ Association of Energy Engineers, West Michigan Chapter (WMAEE)
c/o Mark Zoeteman
Fisherbeck, Thompson, Carr & Huber, Inc.
1515 Arboretum Dr. SE
Grand Rapids, MI 49546-6494
Ph: (616)575-3824
Fax: (616)464-3999
E-mail: mrzoeteman@ftch.com
URL: National Affiliate–www.aeecenter.org
Contact: Mark Zoeteman, Contact
State. Affiliated With: Association of Energy Engineers.

7913 ■ Better Business Bureau of Western Michigan (BBB WMI)
354 Trust Bldg.
40 Pearl St. NW, Ste.354
Grand Rapids, MI 49503
Ph: (616)774-8236
Fax: (616)774-2014
Free: (800)684-3222
E-mail: bbbinfo@iserv.net
URL: http://www.grandrapids.bbb.org
Contact: Kenneth J. Vander Meeden, Pres./CEO
Founded: 1937. **Members:** 2,000. **Membership Dues:** company (1-10 employees), $235 (annual) • company (11-25 employees), $260 (annual) • company (26-50 employees), $280 (annual) • company (51-100 employees), $350 (annual) • company (101-500 employees), $400 (annual) • company (501-1000 employees), $500 (annual) • company (1001-2000 employees), $750 (annual) • company (2001-5000 employees), $1,000 (annual) • company (more than 5000 employees), $1,500 (annual) • company (optional BBB online dues schedule for 1-10 employees), $100 (annual) • company (optional BBB online dues schedule for more than 11 employees), $200 (annual). **Staff:** 12. **Budget:** $450,000. **Local.** Promotes through self-regulation, the highest standards of business ethics, and to instill public confidence in business through programs of education and action that inform, protect and assist. **Libraries: Type:** open to the public. **Holdings:** 18,500. **Subjects:** company and charity reliability reports. **Awards:** Best in Business Award. **Frequency:** annual. **Type:** recognition. **Recipient:** for integrity and involvement in advertising, customer service and community service. **Publications:** *Factfinder*, monthly. Newsletter. **Price:** included in membership dues. **Circulation:** 3,000. **Advertising:** accepted.

7914 ■ Builders Exchange of Grand Rapids
PO Box 2031
Grand Rapids, MI 49501
Ph: (616)949-8650
Fax: (616)949-6831
URL: http://www.grbx.com
Contact: Kraig Kloostra, Pres.
Founded: 1911. **Membership Dues:** $440 (annual). **Staff:** 7. **Local.** Represents general contractors, subcontractors, suppliers, manufacturers' representatives and individual firms related to the construction industry. Provides information on construction and building procedures. **Affiliated With:** International Builders Exchange Executives. **Publications:** Bulletin, weekly.

7915 ■ Caledonia - Young Life
3347 E Beltline
Grand Rapids, MI 49525
Ph: (616)559-2624
URL: http://sites.younglife.org/_layouts/ylext/default.aspx?ID=C-1069
Local. Affiliated With: Young Life.

7916 ■ Camp Fire USA West Michigan Council
Waters Cir.
1257 E Beltline NE
Grand Rapids, MI 49525
Ph: (616)949-2500
Fax: (616)949-7081
E-mail: info@campfireusawmc.org
URL: http://www.campfireusawmc.org
Contact: Gayle Orange, Exec.Dir.
Local. Offers after-school and summer day camp programs in inner city Grand Rapids by providing activities, teaching personal safety and enriching personal development. **Affiliated With:** Camp Fire USA.

7917 ■ Catholics United for the Faith - Mary, Seat of Wisdom Chapter
c/o Joseph Scholten
1436 Johnston St. SE
Grand Rapids, MI 49507
Ph: (616)245-7661
URL: National Affiliate–www.cuf.org
Contact: Joseph Scholten, Contact
Local.

7918 ■ City High School - Young Life
PO Box 68206
Grand Rapids, MI 49516
Ph: (616)988-4794
URL: http://sites.younglife.org/sites/CityHigh/default.aspx
Local. Affiliated With: Young Life.

7919 ■ Clean Water Action of Michigan
c/o Cyndi Roper
959 Wealthy St. SE, Ste.2
Grand Rapids, MI 49506
Ph: (616)742-4084
Fax: (616)742-4072
E-mail: grandrapids@cleanwater.org
URL: http://cleanwateraction.org
Local.

7920 ■ Coalition of Reef Lovers (CORL)
c/o Michael R King
2124 Plainfield Ave. NE
Grand Rapids, MI 49505
Ph: (616)363-6991
Fax: (616)363-6991
E-mail: mike@corl.org
URL: http://www.corl.org
Contact: Michael R King, Contact
Local.

7921 ■ Connecting Business Men to Christ - Grand Rapids
4079 Park E Ct. SE, Ste.2
Grand Rapids, MI 49546-6296
Ph: (616)942-0044
E-mail: grcbmc@cs.com
URL: http://www.cbmc.com/gr
Local.

7922 ■ Creative Arts Repertoire Ensemble (CARE)
PO Box 6307
Grand Rapids, MI 49546
Ph: (616)464-3682
E-mail: careballet@comcast.net
URL: http://www.careballet.org
Contact: Judy Genson, Artistic Dir.
Founded: 1992. **Members:** 15. **Staff:** 3. **Budget:** $50,000. **Local.** Presents three public ballet performances per year at St. Cecilia Music Society. Provides tours to schools in West Michigan. **Conventions/Meetings:** show.

7923 ■ Down Syndrome Association of West Michigan (DSAWM)
PO Box 8804
Grand Rapids, MI 49518-8703
Ph: (616)956-3488
Fax: (616)974-9612
Free: (866)665-7451
E-mail: dsawm@iserv.net
URL: http://www.dsawm.org
Founded: 1985. **Members:** 250. **Membership Dues:** family, $15 (annual). **Local.** Associations, medical and social agency personnel, and families of persons with Down Syndrome. Serves as a support group. Addresses social and educational issues. Promotes growth and development of people with Down Syndrome. Acts as an information resource. Provides speakers. Conducts workshops. **Libraries: Type:** lending; not open to the public. **Holdings:** 150; books, video recordings. **Subjects:** Down Syndrome, people with special needs. **Affiliated With:** National Association for Down Syndrome; National Down Syndrome Congress; National Down Syndrome Society. **Publications:** *DSA Press*, monthly. Newsletter • Directory, annual • Brochures. **Conventions/Meetings:** semiannual conference, various topics relevant to Down Syndrome.

7924 ■ East Grand Rapids High - Young Life
PO Box 68206
Grand Rapids, MI 49516
Ph: (616)988-4794
URL: http://sites.younglife.org/sites/egrhs/default.aspx
Local. Affiliated With: Young Life.

7925 ■ East Grand Rapids Middle School - Wyldlife
PO Box 68206
Grand Rapids, MI 49516
Ph: (616)988-4794 (616)822-2963
E-mail: led2@calvin.edu
URL: http://sites.younglife.org/sites/egrms/default.aspx
Contact: Lauren DeWitt, Sr. Leader
Local. Affiliated With: Young Life.

7926 ■ Eaton Rapids Middle School - Wyldlife
PO Box 68206
Grand Rapids, MI 49516
Ph: (616)988-4794 (616)822-2963
E-mail: led2@calvin.edu
URL: http://sites.younglife.org/sites/egrms/default.aspx
Contact: Lauren DeWitt, Sr. Leader
Local. Affiliated With: Young Life.

7927 ■ Educators for Social Responsibility, Grand Rapids Chapter (ESRGR)
1850 Whirlaway Ct. SE
Grand Rapids, MI 49546
Ph: (616)956-0521
E-mail: mfranz2@netzero.com
URL: http://www.esr.org
Contact: Michael Franz, Pres.
Founded: 1983. **Members:** 12. **Membership Dues:** educator, $35 (annual). **Staff:** 1. **Local.** Educators, clergy, and individuals dedicated to expanding students' knowledge concerning conflict resolution, peace, multi-cultural and global education. Creates educational programs and provides in-service training for teachers in the Grand Rapids area. **Awards:** Dr. Phillip Sigal Peace and Justice Scholarship. **Frequency:** annual. **Type:** scholarship. **Recipient:** for community involvement in peace and justice areas. **Affiliated With:** Educators for Social Responsibility. **Publications:** *Grand Rapids Global Resources Newsletter and Calendar*, quarterly. Contains teaching ideas for conflict resolution in the classroom. **Price:** $10.00/year. **Circulation:** 250. **Conventions/Meetings:** annual Community Peace Art Exhibit and Program - meeting (exhibits) - usually in February • annual Week of Peace Education - meeting (exhibits) - usually in January.

7928 ■ The Employers' Association (TEA)
c/o David J. Smith, CAE, Pres./CEO
5570 Executive Pkwy., SE
Grand Rapids, MI 49512
Ph: (616)698-1167
Fax: (616)698-6624
Free: (888)807-9020
E-mail: tea@teagr.org
URL: http://www.teagr.org
Contact: David J. Smith CAE, Pres./CEO
Founded: 1939. **Members:** 530. **Membership Dues:** association (based on number of employees), $300-$3,000 (annual). **Staff:** 11. **Budget:** $1,500,000. **Local.** Consists of registered businesses seeking to enhance employee relations and promote excellence in the management of people. **Affiliated With:** Employers Association. **Publications:** *Executive Update*. Newsletter. **Price:** included in membership dues. Alternate Formats: online.

7929 ■ Federal Bar Association, Western Michigan 869/06
c/o John W. Allen, Pres.
161 Ottawa NW, Ste.203-B
Grand Rapids, MI 49503

Ph: (269)553-3501
E-mail: lbeatty@garanlucow.com
URL: http://www.wdfba.org
Contact: John W. Allen, Pres.
Membership Dues: individual, $25 (annual). **Local**. **Affiliated With:** Federal Bar Association.

7930 ■ Federalist Society for Law and Public Policy Studies - Grand Rapids Chapter
c/o Mr. Robert A. Buchanan, Pres.
Law, Weathers & Richardson, PC
333 Bridge St. NW, Ste.800
Grand Rapids, MI 49504
Ph: (616)732-1743
Fax: (616)913-1243
E-mail: bobbuchanan@lwr.com
URL: National Affiliate–www.fed-soc.org
Contact: Mr. Robert A. Buchanan, Pres.
Local. Seeks to bring about a reordering of priorities within the U.S. legal system that will emphasize individual liberty, traditional values, and the rule of law. **Affiliated With:** Federalist Society for Law and Public Policy Studies.

7931 ■ Financial Executives International, Western Michigan Chapter
c/o Ms. Lisa Hern, Administrator
PO Box 230342
Grand Rapids, MI 49523-0342
Ph: (616)308-5433
E-mail: a_little_exec_asst@ameritech.net
URL: http://www.fei.org/eWeb/startpage.aspx?site=ch_miw
Contact: Mr. Thomas Bush, Pres. Elect
Local. Promotes personal and professional development of financial executives. Provides peer networking opportunities and advocacy services. **Committees:** Career Services. **Affiliated With:** Financial Executives International.

7932 ■ Forest Hills Central High School - Young Life
3347 E Beltline
Grand Rapids, MI 49525
Ph: (616)447-1090
URL: http://sites.younglife.org/_layouts/ylext/default.aspx?ID=C-1147
Local. **Affiliated With:** Young Life.

7933 ■ Forest Hills Central Middle School - Wyldlife
3347 E Beltline
Grand Rapids, MI 49525
Ph: (616)447-1090
URL: http://sites.younglife.org/_layouts/ylext/default.aspx?ID=C-1150
Local. **Affiliated With:** Young Life.

7934 ■ Forest Hills Eastern High School - Young Life
3347 E Beltline
Grand Rapids, MI 49525
Ph: (616)447-1090
URL: http://sites.younglife.org/_layouts/ylext/default.aspx?ID=C-3876
Local. **Affiliated With:** Young Life.

7935 ■ Forest Hills Eastern Middle School - Wyldlife
3347 E Beltline
Grand Rapids, MI 49525
Ph: (616)447-1090
URL: http://sites.younglife.org/_layouts/ylext/default.aspx?ID=C-4044
Local. **Affiliated With:** Young Life.

7936 ■ Forest Hills Northern High School - Young Life
3347 E Beltline
Grand Rapids, MI 49525
Ph: (616)447-1090
URL: http://sites.younglife.org/_layouts/ylext/default.aspx?ID=C-1149
Local. **Affiliated With:** Young Life.

7937 ■ Forest Hills Northern Middle School - Wyldlife
3347 E Beltline
Grand Rapids, MI 49525
Ph: (616)447-1090
URL: http://sites.younglife.org/_layouts/ylext/default.aspx?ID=C-1148
Local. **Affiliated With:** Young Life.

7938 ■ Gerald R. Ford Foundation
c/o Diane VanAllsburg, Admin.Asst.
303 Pearl St. NW
Grand Rapids, MI 49504
Ph: (616)254-0396
E-mail: geraldfordfoundation@nara.gov
URL: http://www.geraldrfordfoundation.org
Contact: Martin J. Allen Jr., Chm.
Local. Focuses on museum exhibits, conferences, community affairs, educational programs, research grants and special projects to enhance citizen interest and understanding of the challenges that confront government, particularly the presidency.

7939 ■ Gerontology Network
500 Cherry St. SE
Grand Rapids, MI 49503
Ph: (616)456-6135
Fax: (616)771-9771
E-mail: bcoleman@michiganseniors.org
URL: http://www.gerontologynetwork.org
Contact: Barb Coleman, Dir. of Development
Local.

7940 ■ Gilda's Club Grand Rapids
c/o Leann D. Arkema, Exec.Dir.
1806 Bridge St. NW
Grand Rapids, MI 49504
Ph: (616)453-8300
Fax: (616)453-8355
Free: (800)426-1419
E-mail: info@gildasclubgr.org
URL: http://www.gildasclubgr.org
Contact: Leann D. Arkema, Exec.Dir.
Founded: 1997. **Members:** 1,200. **Membership Dues:** donor, $100 (annual). **Staff:** 4. **Budget:** $500,000. **Regional Groups:** 20. **Local**. Provides a free, non-residential place where men, women, and children with cancer and their families and friends join together to build social and emotional support. **Awards: Frequency:** periodic. **Type:** recognition.

7941 ■ Girl Scouts of Michigan Trails
3275 Walker Ave. NW
Grand Rapids, MI 49544
Ph: (616)784-3341
Fax: (616)784-8187
Free: (800)442-1401
E-mail: service.center@gsmt.org
URL: http://www.gsmt.org
State. **Telecommunication Services:** teletype, (616) 784-5605.

7942 ■ Golden K Kiwanis Club of Grand Rapids, Michigan
c/o Clark Grant
2307 Whimbrel Ct. NE
Grand Rapids, MI 49505-7157
Ph: (616)365-2558
Contact: Clark Grant, Contact
Local.

7943 ■ Grand Rapids Area Chamber of Commerce (GRACC)
111 Pearl St. NW
Grand Rapids, MI 49503-2831
Ph: (616)771-0300
Fax: (616)771-0318
E-mail: info@grandrapids.org
URL: http://grandrapids.org
Contact: Ms. Jeanne Englehart, Pres./CEO
Founded: 1887. **Members:** 2,800. **Local**. Creates opportunities for business success in the Grand Rapids, MI area. **Publications:** *Business Directory*, annual. **Price:** free to members; $25.00 non-members. **Advertising:** accepted • *Chamber News*, periodic. Newsletter.

7944 ■ Grand Rapids Association of Realtors
660 Kenmoor Ave. SE
Grand Rapids, MI 49546
Ph: (616)940-8200
Fax: (616)940-8216
Free: (888)940-GRAR
E-mail: bobschautz@grar.com
URL: http://www.grar.com
Contact: Bob Schautz, Pres.
Local. Strives to develop real estate business practices. Advocates the right to own, use and transfer real property. Provides a facility for professional development, research and exchange of information among members. **Affiliated With:** National Association of Realtors.

7945 ■ Grand Rapids Bar Association (GRBA)
161 Ottawa NW, Ste.203-B
Grand Rapids, MI 49503
Ph: (616)454-5550
Fax: (616)454-7707
E-mail: rjdugan@grlaw.com
URL: http://www.grbar.org
Contact: Paul T. Sorensen, Pres.
Founded: 1886. **Members:** 1,400. **Local**. Seeks to improve the administration of civil and criminal justice, and the availability of legal services to the public. Provides continuing education; maintains private law library. **Affiliated With:** American Bar Association. **Publications:** *GR News*, monthly. Newsletter. **Price:** included in membership dues • Membership Directory, annual. **Price:** $20.00.

7946 ■ Grand Rapids Chorus of Sweet Adelines International
PO Box 2984
Grand Rapids, MI 49501
Ph: (616)452-4542
E-mail: info@grsa.net
URL: http://www.grandrapidssweetadelines.com
Contact: Ann Jarchow, Dir.
Local. Advances the musical art form of barbershop harmony through education and performances. Provides education, training and coaching in the development of women's four-part barbershop harmony. **Affiliated With:** Sweet Adelines International.

7947 ■ Grand Rapids Christian High - Young Life
PO Box 68206
Grand Rapids, MI 49516
Ph: (616)988-4794
URL: http://sites.younglife.org/sites/grchs/default.aspx
Local. **Affiliated With:** Young Life.

7948 ■ Grand Rapids Christian Middle School - Wyldlife
PO Box 68206
Grand Rapids, MI 49516
Ph: (616)988-4794
URL: http://sites.younglife.org/sites/grcms/default.aspx
Local. **Affiliated With:** Young Life.

7949 ■ Grand Rapids Federation of Musicians - Local 56, American Federation of Musicians
800 Monroe NW, Ste.230
Grand Rapids, MI 49503
Ph: (616)451-4374
Fax: (616)451-2403
Free: (800)637-0498
E-mail: grfm@livemusicgr.org
URL: http://www.livemusicgr.org
Contact: Eric VanderStel, Pres.
Local. AFL-CIO. Musicians. Seeks to improve the wages and working conditions of professional musicians. **Affiliated With:** American Federation of Musicians of the United States and Canada.

7950 ■ Grand Rapids/Kent County Convention and Visitors Bureau
171 Monroe Ave. NW, Ste.700
Grand Rapids, MI 49503
Ph: (616)459-8287
Fax: (616)459-7291
Free: (800)678-9859
E-mail: mailbox@visitgrandrapids.org
URL: http://www.visitgrandrapids.org
Contact: Steve Wilson, Pres.

Founded: 1927. **Members:** 250. **Staff:** 8. **Budget:** $725,000. **Local**. Businesses, government groups, and individuals united to promote visitor and convention activity in Grand Rapids, MI. **Affiliated With:** International Association of Convention and Visitor Bureaus. **Formerly:** Greater Grand Rapids Convention Bureau. **Publications:** *Convention Calendar*, annual • *Convention News*, bimonthly. **Conventions/Meetings:** meeting - 8/year.

7951 ■ Grand Rapids Opportunities for Women (GROW)
25 Sheldon SE, Ste.210
Grand Rapids, MI 49503
Ph: (616)458-3404
Fax: (616)458-6557
URL: http://www.growbusiness.org
Contact: Rita VanderVen, Exec.Dir.

Founded: 1989. **Local**. **Publications:** *Destinations*. Newsletter. Alternate Formats: online.

7952 ■ Grand Rapids Urban League
c/o Walter M. Brame, Ed.D., Pres.
745 Eastern Ave. SE
Grand Rapids, MI 49503
Ph: (616)245-2207
E-mail: ceogrul@aol.com
URL: National Affiliate–www.nul.org
Contact: Walter M. Brame Ed.D., Pres.

Local. **Affiliated With:** National Urban League.

7953 ■ Grand Rapids Women's Chorus (GRWC)
c/o Lori C. Tennenhouse
PO Box 68486
Grand Rapids, MI 49516
Ph: (616)459-2655
E-mail: info@grwc.org
URL: http://www.grwc.org
Contact: Lori C. Tennenhouse, Contact

Founded: 1996. **Members:** 44. **Budget:** $18,000. **Regional Groups:** 1. **State Groups:** 1. **Local Groups:** 1. **Local**. Sings culturally diverse music that promotes appreciation of women composers and arrangers. Establishes for the education, enjoyment, and enrichment of its members and its audience, the organization seeks to create and inspire meaningful experience through musical expression. **Subgroups:** GRWC Small Ensemble.

7954 ■ Grand River Fly Tyers
c/o Wolf M. Schrey, Pres.
2141 Deer Hollow Dr. SE
Grand Rapids, MI 49508
E-mail: president@grandriverflytyers.org
URL: http://www.grandriverflytyers.org
Contact: Wolf M. Schrey, Pres.

Local. **Affiliated With:** Federation of Fly Fishers.

7955 ■ Grand River Folk Arts Society
c/o Glenn Warners
2520 Russit Dr. NE
Grand Rapids, MI 49525
Ph: (616)361-9219
E-mail: gjwarners@juno.com
URL: http://www.grfolkarts.org
Contact: Glenn Warners, Contact

Local. **Affiliated With:** Country Dance and Song Society.

7956 ■ Great Lakes Chapter of the American College of Healthcare Executives
PO Box 68013
Grand Rapids, MI 49516-8013
Ph: (616)456-8013 (616)486-2411
Fax: (616)451-3108
E-mail: stephanie.hearn@spectrum-health.org
URL: http://Greatlakes.ache.org
Contact: Stephanie A. Hearn FACHE, Pres.

Local. Works to improve the health status of society by advancing healthcare leadership and management excellence. Conducts research, career development and public policy programs. **Affiliated With:** American College of Healthcare Executives.

7957 ■ Great Lakes Pastel Society
PO Box 1386
Grand Rapids, MI 49501-1386
E-mail: breckonab@aol.com
URL: http://www.glps.org
Contact: Ann Breckon, Pres.

Membership Dues: general, $25 (annual). **Regional**. Promotes the use of pastel in fine arts. Increases public awareness of pastel painting as a fine art medium. **Publications:** *Purely Pastel*, bimonthly. Newsletter. Contains information on society members, achievement and opportunities. **Conventions/Meetings:** board meeting - 5/year.

7958 ■ Greater Grand Rapids Association for Human Resource Management
PO Box 2064
Grand Rapids, MI 49501
E-mail: proch@blackmer.com
URL: http://www.ahrm.net
Contact: Judy Proch, Pres.

Local. Represents the interests of human resource and industrial relations professionals and executives. Promotes the advancement of human resource management.

7959 ■ Greater Grand Rapids Figure Skating Club (GGRFSC)
2250 Patterson SE
Grand Rapids, MI 49546
Ph: (616)942-4814
E-mail: beckyharps@comcast.net
URL: http://www.ggrfsc.org
Contact: Becky Somsel, Pres.

Local. Provides programs to encourage participation and achievement in the sport of figure skating on ice. Defines and maintains uniform standards of skating proficiency. Organizes and sponsors competitions and exhibitions for the purpose of stimulating interest in figure skating. **Affiliated With:** United States Figure Skating Association.

7960 ■ Habitat for Humanity of Kent County
539 New St. SW
Grand Rapids, MI 49503
Ph: (616)774-2431
Fax: (616)774-4120
E-mail: pdotynation@habitatkent.org
URL: http://www.habitatkent.org
Contact: Pam Doty-Nation, Exec.Dir.

Local. **Affiliated With:** Habitat for Humanity International.

7961 ■ Healthcare Financial Management Association, Western Michigan Chapter
c/o Oliver A. Jurkovic, Pres.-Elect
Plante & Moran, PLLC
333 Bridge St. NW, Ste.600
Grand Rapids, MI 49504-5365
Ph: (616)643-4046
Fax: (248)233-8976
E-mail: oliver.jurkovic@plantemoran.com
URL: http://www.wmihfma.org
Contact: Oliver A. Jurkovic, Pres.-Elect

Local. Provides education, analysis and guidance to healthcare finance professionals. Helps members and other individuals in advancing the financial management of health care and in improving the business performance of organizations serving the healthcare field. **Affiliated With:** Healthcare Financial Management Association.

7962 ■ Heart of West Michigan United Way
118 Commerce Ave. SW
Grand Rapids, MI 49503-4106
Ph: (616)459-6281
Fax: (616)459-8460
URL: http://www.unitedwaycares.com
Contact: Robert G. Haight, Pres.

Local. **Affiliated With:** United Way of America.

7963 ■ Heritage Hill Association (HHA)
126 Coll. SE
Grand Rapids, MI 49503
Ph: (616)459-8950
Fax: (616)459-2409
E-mail: heritage@heritagehillweb.org
URL: http://www.heritagehillweb.org
Contact: James Karsen, Pres.

Local. Seeks to provide neighbors a way of collectively building a healthy, historically-preserved community in which people can live and work in a secure and stable environment. Organizes block clubs. Hosts' annual home tour.

7964 ■ Humane Society of Kent County
3077 Wilson Dr. NW
Grand Rapids, MI 49544-7565
Ph: (616)453-8900
Fax: (616)453-5752
E-mail: humane@hskc.com
URL: http://www.kent-humane.org
Contact: Karen Terpstra, Exec.Dir.

Founded: 1883. **Staff:** 15. **Budget:** $800,000. **Local**. Dedicated to the protection and care of all animals. **Formerly:** Kent County Humane Society. **Publications:** *Animal Advocate*, quarterly. Newsletter. **Circulation:** 10,000. **Conventions/Meetings:** monthly board meeting - always third Wednesday • annual meeting - always May.

7965 ■ Industrial Workers of the World - Grand Rapids
PO Box 6629
Grand Rapids, MI 49516
Ph: (616)881-5263
E-mail: griww@earthlink.net
URL: National Affiliate–www.iww.org

Local. **Affiliated With:** Industrial Workers of the World.

7966 ■ Inner City Christian Federation (ICCF)
816 Madison Ave. SE
Grand Rapids, MI 49507
Ph: (616)336-9333
Fax: (616)243-9911
URL: http://www.iccf.org
Contact: Jonathan Bradford, CEO

Budget: $4,806,053. **Local**. **Publications:** *Blueprints*. Newsletter. Alternate Formats: online.

7967 ■ Institute of Internal Auditors, Western Michigan Chapter
c/o Thomas Siegfried, CPA, CIA
Jefferson Wells Intl.
2680 Horizon Dr. SE, Ste.F1
Grand Rapids, MI 49546
Ph: (616)862-7315
E-mail: thomas_siegfried@jeffersonwells.com
URL: National Affiliate–www.theiia.org

Founded: 1975. **Members:** 156. **Membership Dues:** regular, $115 (annual) • educator, $65 (annual) • student, retired, $30 (annual) • life, $2,100 • sustainer (government auditors only), $50 (annual) • organization ($65 per staff member over 5; $50 per staff member over 100), $425-$6,600 (annual). **Local**. Serves as an advocate for the internal audit profession. Provides certification, education, research, and technological guidance for the profession. **Committees:** Academic Relations; Certifications; Chapter Anniversary Celebration; Communication. **Affiliated With:** Institute of Internal Auditors. **Publications:** Newsletter, monthly. Alternate Formats: online.

7968 ■ International Facility Management Association, Ferris State University
1286 Kenowa SW
Grand Rapids, MI 49544
Ph: (616)530-0023
E-mail: rozg1@fsuimail.ferris.edu
URL: National Affiliate–www.ifma.org
Contact: Kimberly J. Rozga, Pres.
Local. Works to enhance the professional goals of persons involved in the field of facility management. Conducts educational and research programs. Cultivates cooperation, understanding and interest among individuals, firms and associations.

7969 ■ International Union, United Automobile, Aerospace and Agricultural Implement Workers of America, AFL-CIO - Local Union 730
3852 Buchanan Ave. SW
Grand Rapids, MI 49548
Ph: (616)532-7613
URL: http://www.uawlocal730.com
Contact: Larry S. Palmer, Financial Sec.
Members: 2,234. **Local**. AFL-CIO. **Affiliated With:** International Union, United Automobile, Aerospace and Agricultural Implement Workers of America.

7970 ■ Junior Achievement of the Michigan Great Lakes
3665 28th St. SE, Ste.C
Grand Rapids, MI 49512
Ph: (616)575-9080
Fax: (616)575-9028
E-mail: bcoderre@iserv.net
URL: http://westmichigan.ja.org
Contact: Bill Coderre, Pres.
Founded: 1955. **State**. Educates and inspires young people to value free enterprise, business, and economics to improve the quality of their lives.

7971 ■ Junior League of Grand Rapids (JLGR)
25 Sheldon Blvd. SE, Ste.127
Grand Rapids, MI 49503
Ph: (616)451-0452
Fax: (616)451-1936
E-mail: jrleague@iserv.net
URL: http://www.juniorleaguegr.com
Contact: Ms. Kathy Gill, Office Mgr.
Founded: 1924. **Members:** 550. **Membership Dues:** individual, $76 (annual). **Staff:** 2. **Budget:** $200,000. **Local**. Works to meet community needs by developing leadership among women and promoting volunteerism. **Publications:** *Happenings*, monthly. Newsletter.

7972 ■ Kent County Literacy Council
c/o Susan Ledy, MA, Exec.Dir.
111 Lib. St. NE
Grand Rapids, MI 49504
Ph: (616)459-5151
Fax: (616)245-8069
E-mail: info@kentliteracy.org
URL: http://www.kentliteracy.org
Contact: Susan Ledy MA, Exec.Dir.
Founded: 1986. **Local**. Seeks to reduce adult illiteracy. Motivates and supports teaching of illiterate adults and older youths to a level of listening, speaking, reading, writing, and basic computational skills enabling them to solve their daily problems. **Affiliated With:** Laubach Literacy International.

7973 ■ Kentwood - Young Life
3347 E Beltline
Grand Rapids, MI 49525
Ph: (616)559-2624
URL: http://sites.younglife.org/_layouts/ylext/default.aspx?ID=C-1070
Local. **Affiliated With:** Young Life.

7974 ■ Land Conservancy of West Michigan (LCWM)
c/o April Scholtz, Dir.
1345 Monroe Ave. NW, Ste.324
Grand Rapids, MI 49505
Ph: (616)451-9476
Fax: (616)451-1874
E-mail: lcwm@naturenearby.org
URL: http://www.naturenearby.org/index.cfm
Contact: Julie Stoneman, Exec.Dir.
Founded: 1976. **Local**. Regional land trust serving 5 1/2 counties in Central West Michigan.

7975 ■ Local 132C, Chemical Workers Council of the UFCW
2123 Diamond Ave.
Grand Rapids, MI 49505
Ph: (616)632-2615
URL: National Affiliate–www.ufcw.org
Local. **Affiliated With:** United Food and Commercial Workers International Union.

7976 ■ Make-A-Wish Foundation of Michigan, Grand Rapids Office
Metro Grand Rapids office
2900 E Beltline NE, Ste.E
Grand Rapids, MI 49525
Ph: (616)363-4607
Fax: (616)363-5415
Free: (877)631-9474
E-mail: wish@wishmich.org
URL: http://www.wishmich.org
Contact: Susan Fenters Lerch, Pres./CEO
Local. Grants wishes of children with life-threatening medical conditions and enriches the human experience with hope, strength, and joy. **Affiliated With:** Make-A-Wish Foundation of America.

7977 ■ Media Communications Association International, Mid Michigan
c/o Mike Silverstein
1125 Alger SE
Grand Rapids, MI 49507
Ph: (616)261-7956
Fax: (616)261-7684
E-mail: smartin@gfs.com
URL: http://www.mcai-midmichigan.org
Contact: Steve Martin, Pres.
Local. Provides networking and education opportunities to media communications professionals. Facilitates effective communication using new technology and with sound communication principles. **Affiliated With:** Chemical Coaters Association International. **Publications:** *Slate*. Newsletter.

7978 ■ Michigan Alliance for Gifted Education (MAGE)
5355 Northland Dr. NE, Ste.C188
Grand Rapids, MI 49525
Ph: (616)365-8230
E-mail: migiftedchild@migiftedchild.org
URL: http://www.migiftedchild.org
Membership Dues: affiliate, $20 (annual) • individual, $30 (annual) • institutional, $100 (annual). **State**. Advances interest in programs for the gifted. Seeks to further education of the gifted and enhances their potential creativity. Unites to address the unique needs of children and youth with demonstrated gifts and talents as well as those children who may be able to develop their talent potentials with appropriate educational experiences. Encourages and responds to the diverse expressions of gifts and talents in children and youth from all cultures, racial and ethnic backgrounds, and socioeconomic groups. **Affiliated With:** National Association for Gifted Children.

7979 ■ Michigan Council Trout Unlimited (MCTU)
c/o Richard Bowman, Exec.Dir.
7 Trowbridge NE
Grand Rapids, MI 49503
Ph: (616)460-0477
Fax: (775)542-7572
E-mail: rbowman@mctu.org
URL: http://www.mctu.org
Contact: Richard Bowman, Exec.Dir.
Founded: 1959. **Members:** 6,100. **State**. Aims to conserve, protect, and restore Michigan's watersheds that support wild trout and salmon. **Affiliated With:** Trout Unlimited. **Publications:** *Michigan Trout*, quarterly. Magazine. **Advertising:** accepted.

7980 ■ Michigan Medical Directors Association
c/o Iris Boettcher, MD
4500 Breton Rd. SE
Grand Rapids, MI 49508
Ph: (616)486-2401
E-mail: iris.boettcher@spectrum-health.org
URL: http://www.amda.com/chapters/states/mi.htm
Contact: Suresh Gupta MD, Pres.
State. Represents medical directors and physicians practicing in the long term care continuum. Provides education, member advocacy and professional development. **Affiliated With:** American Medical Directors Association.

7981 ■ Michigan Organization of Nurse Executives - District 3
c/o Jane Renwick, Dir.
Saint Mary's Healthcare
200 Jefferson St. SE
Grand Rapids, MI 49503
Ph: (616)752-6944
Fax: (616)732-8905
E-mail: renwickj@trinity-health.org
URL: http://www.mone.org
Contact: Jane Renwick, Dir.
Local. Represents nurse leaders who improve healthcare. Provides leadership, professional development, advocacy and research. Advances the nursing administration practice and patient care. **Affiliated With:** American Organization of Nurse Executives.

7982 ■ Michigan Reading Association
668 Three Mile Rd. NW, Ste.C
Grand Rapids, MI 49544
Ph: (616)647-9310
Fax: (616)647-9378
Free: (800)MRA-READ
E-mail: mra@michiganreading.org
Contact: Mr. Gary Gillissie, Exec.Dir.
Founded: 1956. **Members:** 5,000. **Membership Dues:** $35 (annual). **Staff:** 3. **Budget:** $250,000. **Regional Groups:** 10. **State**. Reading specialists, university faculty, administrators, parents, and teachers promoting reading. Seeks to improve the quality of reading instruction at all educational levels. Sponsors annual reading conference and works with the Michigan Department of Education to improve literacy. **Affiliated With:** International Reading Association. **Publications:** *Michigan Journal of Reading*, 3/year. **Price:** $4.00 • *MRA News and Views*, quarterly. Newsletter • Directory, annual. **Conventions/Meetings:** annual Reading Conference (exhibits) - always March.

7983 ■ Michigan Snowmobile Association (MSA)
4336 Plainfield Ave. NE, Ste.F
Grand Rapids, MI 49525
Ph: (616)361-2285
Fax: (616)363-0661
Free: (800)246-0260
E-mail: office@msasnow.com
URL: http://www.msasnow.org
Contact: Rick Brown, Pres.
Founded: 1982. **State**. Includes individuals, clubs/councils, and businesses. Develops a common appreciation, understanding and knowledge of the sport of snowmobiling in Michigan. Conducts annual conventions, general membership meetings, and snow shows.

7984 ■ Michigan State Auctioneers Association (MSAA)
c/o Tricia D. Wiltjer, Exec.Dir.
4529 Gibbs NW
Grand Rapids, MI 49544

Ph: (616)785-8288
Fax: (616)785-8506
E-mail: info@msaa.org
URL: http://www.msaa.org
Contact: Tricia D. Wiltjer, Exec.Dir.
Founded: 1951. **Members:** 416. **Membership Dues:** general, $100 (annual). **State. Publications:** *Michigan Auction Gavel*, quarterly. Magazine. **Advertising:** accepted. **Conventions/Meetings:** annual convention, education, election, auctioneer championship, awards and President's banquet (exhibits).

7985 ■ Moms Club
3145 Crisfield NE
Grand Rapids, MI 49525
Local.

7986 ■ Mothers Against Drunk Driving, Kent County Chapter
1011 40th St. SE, Ste.100
Grand Rapids, MI 49508
Ph: (616)456-6233
Fax: (616)475-5785
URL: National Affiliate–www.madd.org
Founded: 1982. **Members:** 150. **Membership Dues:** individual, $20 (annual). **Staff:** 1. **Budget:** $45,000. **State Groups:** 1. **Local Groups:** 23. **Local.** Men and women dedicated to supporting victims of drunk driving. Advocates for tougher legislation and penalties for drunk driving. Promotes community awareness. **Affiliated With:** Mothers Against Drunk Driving. **Publications:** *Local Newsletter*, semiannual. **Price:** included in membership dues. **Conventions/Meetings:** annual Candlelight Vigil - meeting - always December.

7987 ■ Myasthenia Gravis Foundation, Great Lakes Chapter (MGF)
2680 Horizon Dr. SE, No. C9
Grand Rapids, MI 49546
Ph: (616)956-0622
Fax: (616)956-9234
E-mail: greatlakesmgf@msn.com
Contact: Esther M. Land, Founder and Trustee
Founded: 1976. **Members:** 650. **Membership Dues:** $20 (annual). **Staff:** 1. **State.** Individuals suffering from the autoimmune neuromuscular disease myasthenia gravis, their families and friends, and other interested persons. Seeks to educate the public about the disease. Offers services and support to patients. Funds medical research. **Affiliated With:** Myasthenia Gravis Foundation of America. **Publications:** *MG Communicator*, quarterly. Newsletter. Contains news about local chapter and national foundation activities and medical reports, and tips on living with disease. **Price:** free to members. **Conventions/Meetings:** annual meeting • periodic Patient Support Meeting - support group meeting.

7988 ■ National Active and Retired Federal Employees Association - Grand Rapids 234
PO Box 1262
Grand Rapids, MI 49501-1262
Ph: (616)534-4617
URL: National Affiliate–www.narfe.org
Contact: John W Kibler, Contact
Local. Protects the retirement future of employees through education. Informs members on issues affecting the retirement. **Affiliated With:** National Association of Retired Federal Employees.

7989 ■ National Association of Home Builders of the U.S., Home and Building Association of Greater Grand Rapids
c/o Judy Barnes, CAE
Local No. 2336
2021 44th St. SE
Grand Rapids, MI 49508-5009
Ph: (616)281-2021
Fax: (616)281-4500
Free: (800)305-2021
E-mail: jbarnes@hbaggr.com
URL: National Affiliate–www.nahb.org
Contact: Judy Barnes, Exec.VP/CEO
Local. Home builders, remodelers, commercial builders and all related industries belong to this organization, whose jurisdiction includes Kent and Ottawa Counties. **Affiliated With:** National Association of Home Builders.

7990 ■ National Association of Investors Corporation, Western Michigan Chapter
7314 Cascade Rd. SE
Grand Rapids, MI 49546
Ph: (616)949-7869
E-mail: jgehling@comcast.net
URL: http://better-investing.org/chapter/westmich
Contact: Madge Gehling, Dir.
Local. Teaches individuals how to become successful strategic long-term investors. Provides highly focused learning resources and investment tools that empower individuals to become better investors. **Affiliated With:** National Association of Investors Corporation.

7991 ■ National Association of Legal Investigators, Mid-Eastern Region
c/o Thomas P. Cole, CLI
Cole & Co.
247 Lafayette Ave. NE
Grand Rapids, MI 49503-3306
Ph: (405)721-4231
Fax: (405)721-4289
E-mail: tangocharlie8@hotmail.com
URL: National Affiliate–www.nalionline.org
Contact: Thomas P. Cole CLI, Contact
Regional. Affiliated With: National Association of Legal Investigators.

7992 ■ National Association of Women in Construction, Grand Rapids Chapter
650 - 44th St. SE
Grand Rapids, MI 49548
Ph: (616)532-8181 (616)532-8191
Fax: (616)532-8193
E-mail: wicfaye@aol.com
URL: http://www.nawic194.org
Contact: Faye Staskewicz, Pres.
Local. Serves as the voice of women in the construction industry. Contributes to the development of the industry. Encourages women to pursue and establish career in construction. Promotes cooperation, fellowship and understanding among members of the association. **Affiliated With:** National Association of Women in Construction. **Publications:** *NAWIC Ink*, monthly. Newsletter. **Advertising:** accepted. Alternate Formats: online. **Conventions/Meetings:** monthly meeting - every 2nd Wednesday of the month.

7993 ■ National Technical Honor Society - ITT Technical Institute - Grand Rapids - Michigan
4020 Sparks Dr. SE
Grand Rapids, MI 49546-6192
Ph: (616)956-1060
Free: (800)632-4676
URL: http://www.itt-tech.edu
Local.

7994 ■ North American Die Casting Association West Michigan Chapter 3
c/o Ron Holland
3400 Wentworth Dr. SW
Grand Rapids, MI 49509
Ph: (517)204-6430
E-mail: bob@worthycompany.com
URL: National Affiliate–www.diecasting.org
Contact: Bob Worthy, Treas.
Local. Develops product standards; compiles trade statistics on metal consumption trends; conducts promotional activities; provides information on chemistry, mechanics, engineering, and other arts and sciences related to die casting. Provides training materials and short, intensive courses in die casting. Maintains speakers' bureau. **Affiliated With:** North American Die Casting Association.

7995 ■ Northeast Grand Rapids Young Life
3347 E Beltline
Grand Rapids, MI 49525
Ph: (616)447-1090
Fax: (616)954-6855
URL: http://sites.younglife.org/sites/northeastgrandrapids/default.aspx
Local. Affiliated With: Young Life.

7996 ■ PFLAG Grand Rapids
PO Box 6226
Grand Rapids, MI 49506
Ph: (616)336-1382
E-mail: info@pflaggrandrapids.org
URL: http://www.pflaggrandrapids.org
Local. Affiliated With: Parents, Families, and Friends of Lesbians and Gays.

7997 ■ Phi Theta Kappa, Alpha Upsilon Kappa Chapter - Grand Rapids Community College
c/o Eric Mullen
143 Bostwick Ave. NE
Grand Rapids, MI 49503
Ph: (616)234-4164
E-mail: emullen@grcc.edu
URL: http://www.ptk.org/directories/chapters/MI/20496-1.htm
Contact: Eric Mullen, Advisor
Local.

7998 ■ Pinewood Middle - Wyldlife
3347 E Beltline
Grand Rapids, MI 49525
Ph: (616)559-2624
URL: http://sites.younglife.org/_layouts/ylext/default.aspx?ID=C-3870
Local. Affiliated With: Young Life.

7999 ■ Project Management Institute, Western Michigan Chapter
PO Box 150335
Grand Rapids, MI 49515-0335
Ph: (616)954-9556
Fax: (616)246-4424
E-mail: president@westmichpmi.org
URL: http://www.westmichpmi.org
Contact: Mr. Mark A. Moore PMP, Pres.
Founded: 1993. **Members:** 540. **Membership Dues:** regular, $20 (annual). **Local.** Corporations and individuals engaged in the practice of project management; project management students and educators. Seeks to advance the study, teaching, and practice of project management. **Affiliated With:** Project Management Institute. **Publications:** *On Target*, bimonthly. Newsletter. Contains articles on project management and other information concerning the local chapters. **Price:** free. **Advertising:** accepted. Alternate Formats: online. **Conventions/Meetings:** monthly dinner, networking opportunity and educational presentation related to project management - except in June, July, August, December.

8000 ■ Psi Chi, National Honor Society in Psychology - Aquinas College
c/o Dept. of Psychology
1607 Robinson Rd. SE
Grand Rapids, MI 49506-1799
Ph: (616)459-8281
E-mail: ozarobur@aquinas.edu
URL: http://www.psichi.org/chapters/info.asp?chapter_id=509
Contact: Burt Ozarow PhD, Advisor
Local.

8001 ■ Psi Chi, National Honor Society in Psychology - Calvin College
c/o Dept. of Psychology
3201 Burton St. SE, SB 361
Grand Rapids, MI 49546-4388

Ph: (616)526-6216 (616)526-6745
Fax: (616)526-8551
E-mail: dtelling@calvin.edu
URL: http://www.psichi.org/chapters/info.asp?chapter_id=900
Contact: Don Tellinghuisen PhD, Advisor
Local.

8002 ■ Public Museum of Grand Rapids
272 Pearl St. NW
Grand Rapids, MI 49504-5371
Ph: (616)456-3724
Fax: (616)456-3873
E-mail: inquiries@ci.grand-rapids.mi.us
URL: http://www.grmuseum.org
Contact: Timothy Chester, Museum Dir.
Local. Promotes the community's interest and involvement in the Museum.

8003 ■ Public Relations Society of America, West Michigan Chapter (WMPRSA)
c/o Sue Ann Clark, Administrator
PO Box 68124
Grand Rapids, MI 49516-8124
Ph: (616)336-0678
Fax: (616)451-3108
E-mail: admin@wmprsa.org
URL: http://www.wmprsa.org
Contact: Sue Ann Clark, Administrator
Local. Affiliated With: Public Relations Society of America. **Formerly:** (2005) Public Relations Society of America, West Michigan.

8004 ■ Racquetball Association of Michigan
111 Pearl St., NW
Grand Rapids, MI 49503
Ph: (616)771-0312
URL: http://www.michiganracquetball.net
Contact: Twayne Howard, Contact
State. Affiliated With: United States Racquetball Association.

8005 ■ Right to Life of Michigan (RLM)
PO Box 901
Grand Rapids, MI 49519-0901
Ph: (616)532-2300
Fax: (616)532-3461
E-mail: info@rtl.org
URL: http://www.rtl.org
Contact: Barbara Listing, Pres.
State. Promotes the rights of the unborn and those threatened by euthanasia. **Libraries: Type:** open to the public. **Holdings:** 2,000; articles, audio recordings, books, video recordings. **Subjects:** abortion, euthanasia, fetal development, adoption, assisted suicide. **Awards:** Oratory Award. **Type:** monetary. **Recipient:** for teen pro-life activity • Outstanding Pro-life Youth Awards. **Type:** monetary. **Recipient:** for high school senior students. **Affiliated With:** National Right to Life Committee. **Publications:** *Adoption Focus*, quarterly. Newsletter. **Price:** free • *One Share in Life Campaign*. Brochure • *Right to Life of Michigan News*, bimonthly. Newspaper. **Price:** included in membership dues. **Conventions/Meetings:** annual conference - always late September, early October.

8006 ■ Ruffed Grouse Society, Grand Rapids, Michigan Chapter
c/o Jason Marvin
2474 Grand River Dr.
Grand Rapids, MI 49525
Ph: (616)447-8317
E-mail: tom.otto@yellowcorp.com
URL: National Affiliate–www.ruffedgrousesociety.org
Contact: Jason Marvin, Contact
Local. Affiliated With: Ruffed Grouse Society.

8007 ■ Saladin Shriners
c/o Richard T. Higgins, P.P.
4200 Saladin Dr. SE
Grand Rapids, MI 49546
Ph: (616)942-1570
Fax: (616)942-6374
E-mail: saladinrecorder@tds.net
URL: http://www.saladinshrine.com
Contact: Richard T. Higgins P.P., Recorder
Local. Affiliated With: Imperial Council of the Ancient Arabic Order of the Nobles of the Mystic Shrine for North America.

8008 ■ Schrems West Michigan Trout Unlimited (WMTU)
PO Box 230094
Grand Rapids, MI 49523
Ph: (616)752-8596
E-mail: wmtu@wmtu.org
URL: http://www.wmtu.org
Contact: Eric Starck, Pres.
Local. Affiliated With: Trout Unlimited.

8009 ■ SCORE Grand Rapids
c/o Judith K. Thome, Chair
111 Pearl St. NW
Grand Rapids, MI 49503
Ph: (616)771-0305
Fax: (616)771-0328
E-mail: score@grandrapids.org
URL: http://scoregr.org
Contact: Judith K. Thome, Chapter Chair
Local. Dedicated to entrepreneur education and the formation, growth and success of small businesses nationwide. **Affiliated With:** SCORE.

8010 ■ Society of Manufacturing Engineers - Grand Valley State University S283
Grand Valley State Univ., Padnos School of Engg.
301 W Fulton, Ste.No. 718, Eberhard Center
Grand Rapids, MI 49504-6495
Ph: (616)331-6845
Fax: (616)336-7215
E-mail: choudhuri@gvsu.edu
URL: National Affiliate–www.sme.org
Contact: Shabbir Choudhuri, Contact
Local. Advances manufacturing knowledge to gain competitive advantage. Improves skills and manufacturing solutions for the growth of economy. Provides resources and opportunities for manufacturing professionals.

8011 ■ Society of Otorhinolaryngology and Head/Neck Nurses - Grand Rapids Chapter
330 Lafayette NE
Grand Rapids, MI 49503
Ph: (616)391-1510
Fax: (616)391-1251
E-mail: rosemary.buzzelli@spectrum-health.org
URL: National Affiliate–www.sohnnurse.com
Contact: Rosemary Buzzeli RS, Contact
Local. Advances the professional growth and development of nurses dedicated to the specialty of Otorhinolaryngology nursing through education and research. Promotes innovations in practice, research and healthcare policy initiatives. **Affiliated With:** Society of Otorhinolaryngology and Head/Neck Nurses.

8012 ■ South Christian - Young Life
3347 E Beltline
Grand Rapids, MI 49525
Ph: (616)559-2624
URL: http://sites.younglife.org/_layouts/ylext/default.aspx?ID=C-1072
Local. Affiliated With: Young Life.

8013 ■ Tammy's Loyal Companions
c/o Tammy Lafay
2223 Darwin
Grand Rapids, MI 49507
Ph: (616)243-1201
Fax: (616)245-7135
E-mail: tlc892@cs.com
URL: http://www.petfinder.org/shelters/MI84.html
Contact: Tammy Lafay, Contact
Local.

8014 ■ Tasters Guild International - Grand Rapids, Chapter No. 007
3853 Crystal Waters Ln. NE
Grand Rapids, MI 49525
E-mail: joeb@tastersguild.com
URL: National Affiliate–www.tastersguild.com
Contact: Joe Borrello, Contact
Local. Aims to educate consumers and spread the word of responsible wine and food consumption. Provides opportunity to encounter the best in wine and culinary delights. **Affiliated With:** Tasters Guild International.

8015 ■ Toastmasters International-District 62
c/o Beverly Sue Wall, DTM, PID, Lt. Gov Education and Training
3207 Shadyside NE
Grand Rapids, MI 49505
Ph: (616)285-0005 (269)923-7481
Fax: (616)363-2293
Free: (800)96-TOAST
E-mail: bevwall@aol.com
URL: http://www.62toast.com/
Contact: Patricia A. Brown-May, District Governor
Local. Affiliated With: Toastmasters International.

8016 ■ United Food and Commercial Workers AFL-CIO, Local 951
3270 Evergreen Dr. NE
Grand Rapids, MI 49525
Ph: (616)361-7683
Fax: (616)447-1000
Free: (800)999-0951
E-mail: information@ufcw951.com
URL: http://www.ufcw951.com
Contact: Robert Potter, Pres.
Founded: 1951. **Members:** 33,000. **Staff:** 50. **State.** Works in partnership with its members, employers, and communities. **Affiliated With:** AFL-CIO. **Publications:** *Local 951 Journal*, quarterly. Magazine. Includes membership information. **Price:** free. **Circulation:** 35,000 • *Local 951 Leadership Update*, monthly. Newsletter. Contains unit leader's information. **Price:** free. **Circulation:** 1,200.

8017 ■ Visiting Nurse Association of West Michigan
c/o Georgiann Greemann, Volunteer Coor.
1401 Cedar NE
Grand Rapids, MI 49503
Ph: (616)235-5341
Fax: (616)774-7017
Free: (800)774-2702
E-mail: georgiann.greemann@spectrum-health.org

8018 ■ Wedgwood - Other
3347 E Beltline
Grand Rapids, MI 49525
Ph: (616)559-2624
URL: http://sites.younglife.org/_layouts/ylext/default.aspx?ID=C-1073
Local. Affiliated With: Young Life.

8019 ■ West Michigan Cochlear Implant Club
c/o Maria Davis
2401 Breton Rd. SE
Grand Rapids, MI 49546
Ph: (616)956-5533
URL: National Affiliate–www.cici.org
Contact: Maria Davis, Contact
Local. Educates and supports cochlear implant recipients and their families. Works to secure the rights of people with hearing loss. Aims to improve public and private financial support for individuals receiving cochlear implants. **Affiliated With:** Cochlear Implant Association, Inc.

8020 ■ West Michigan District Dental Society (WMDDS)
161 Ottawa Ave. NW
511-F Waters Bldg.
Grand Rapids, MI 49503-2701

Ph: (616)234-5605
Fax: (616)454-6549
E-mail: contact@wmdds.org
URL: http://www.wmdds.org
Contact: Ms. Elaine Fleming, Exec.Dir.

Local. Represents the interests of dentists committed to the public's oral health, ethics and professional development. Encourages the improvement of the public's oral health and promotes the art and science of dentistry. **Affiliated With:** American Dental Association; Michigan Dental Association.

8021 ■ West Michigan Environmental Action Council (WMEAC)
c/o Tom Leonard
1514 Wealthy SE, Ste.280
Grand Rapids, MI 49506
Ph: (616)451-3051
Fax: (616)451-3054
E-mail: info@wmeac.org
URL: http://www.wmeac.org
Contact: Lisa Locke, Admin.Coor.

Local. Grassroots environmental organizations working to preserve and protect the natural and human environment in West Michigan and help people translate their concerns into positive action.

8022 ■ West Michigan Regional Planning Commission (WMRPC)
820 Monroe NW, Ste.214
Grand Rapids, MI 49503-1478
Ph: (616)774-8400
Fax: (616)774-0808
E-mail: info@wmrpc.org
URL: http://www.wmrpc.org
Contact: Dave Bee, Dir.

Local.

8023 ■ West Michigan Society for Healthcare Engineering (WMSHE)
c/o Mary Wiersma, Pres.
Pine Rest Christian Mental Hea. Services
300 68th St.
Grand Rapids, MI 49501-0165
Ph: (616)281-6363
Fax: (616)493-6005
E-mail: mary.wiersma@pinerest.org
URL: National Affiliate–www.ashe.org
Contact: Mary Wiersma, Pres.

Local. Promotes better patient care by encouraging members to develop their knowledge and increase their competence in the field of facilities management. Cooperates with hospitals and allied associations in matters pertaining to facilities management. **Affiliated With:** American Society for Healthcare Engineering of the American Hospital Association.

8024 ■ West Michigan Tourist Association (WMTA)
3665 28th St. SE, Ste.B
Grand Rapids, MI 49512
Ph: (616)245-2217
Fax: (616)954-3924
Free: (800)442-2084
E-mail: travel@wmta.org
URL: http://www.wmta.org
Contact: Mr. Rick Hert, Exec.Dir.

Founded: 1917. **Members:** 800. **Membership Dues:** business, $250 (annual). **Staff:** 7. **Budget:** $800,000. **State.** Promotes tourism in western MI. **Awards:** Hospitality. **Frequency:** annual. **Type:** recognition. **Recipient:** for outstanding service/contribution to industry. **Publications:** *Lake Michigan Circle Tour and Lighthouse Guide*, annual. Magazine. Contains guide to Lake Michigan's shoreline. **Price:** free. **Circulation:** 75,000. **Advertising:** accepted. Alternate Formats: CD-ROM; online • *West Michigan: Carefree Travel*, annual. Magazine. Contains 50 word descriptions of all members by area and category with ads. **Price:** free. **Circulation:** 150,000. **Advertising:** accepted. Alternate Formats: CD-ROM; online.

8025 ■ West Walker Sportsman's Club
PO Box 141104
Grand Rapids, MI 49544
Ph: (616)453-5081
E-mail: info@wwsc.org
URL: http://www.wwsc.org

Local. Affiliated With: National Skeet Shooting Association.

8026 ■ Western Michigan Chapter of American Society of Plumbing Engineers
PO Box 140341
Grand Rapids, MI 49514-0314
Ph: (296)664-5766
E-mail: glberridge@earthlink.net
URL: http://www.aspe.org/Western_Michigan/index.html
Contact: Gordon Berridge, Pres.

Local. Represents the interests of individuals dedicated to the advancement of the science of plumbing engineering. Seeks to resolve professional problems in plumbing engineering. Advocates greater cooperation among members and plumbing officials, contractors, laborers and the public. **Affiliated With:** American Society of Plumbing Engineers.

8027 ■ Western Michigan Estate Planning Council (WMEPC)
c/o Deb Perin
6534 Clay SW
Grand Rapids, MI 49548-7832
Ph: (616)698-7787
Fax: (616)698-2603
E-mail: assoc@altoprecision.com
URL: National Affiliate–councils.naepc.org
Contact: Richard J. Puhek, Pres.

State. Promotes cooperative efforts in the field of estate planning among the professions and businesses represented by the members. Fosters an understanding of the relationships and functions in the field of estate planning field. Assists its members in keeping abreast of laws and other developments in the field of estate planning to render better service to clients and to the community in Western Michigan. **Affiliated With:** National Association of Estate Planners and Councils.

8028 ■ Western Michigan Genealogical Society (WMGS)
c/o Mrs. Mindy Koole, Pres.
Grand Rapids Public Lib.
111 Lib. St. NE
Grand Rapids, MI 49503-3268
Ph: (616)691-7986
E-mail: wmgs@wmgs.org
URL: http://www.wmgs.org
Contact: Mrs. Mindy Koole, Pres.

Regional. Works to preserve and make available for genealogical research the records of ancestors, while encouraging and assisting members in genealogical research and promoting the exchange of knowledge.

8029 ■ Western Michigan Mortgage Lenders Association (WMMLA)
John A. Meyer Appraisal Co.
1676 View Pond SE, No. 100A
Grand Rapids, MI 49508
Ph: (616)281-2022
Fax: (616)281-1811
E-mail: dianalmeyer@aol.com
URL: http://www.mmla.net/wmmla/index.htm
Contact: Diana Meyer, Pres.

Local. Promotes fair and ethical lending practices and fosters professional excellence among real estate finance employees. Seeks to create an environment that enables members to invest in communities and achieve their business objectives. **Affiliated With:** Mortgage Bankers Association.

8030 ■ Young Life Central Grand Rapids
PO Box 68206
Grand Rapids, MI 49516
Ph: (616)988-4794
Fax: (616)988-4795
URL: http://sites.younglife.org/sites/CentralGrandRapids/default.aspx

Local. Affiliated With: Young Life.

8031 ■ Young Life Grand Rapids Urban
PO Box 68206
Grand Rapids, MI 49516
Ph: (616)988-4797
Fax: (616)954-0517
URL: http://sites.younglife.org/_layouts/ylext/default.aspx?ID=A-MI30

Local. Affiliated With: Young Life.

8032 ■ Young Life South Grand Rapids
3347 E Beltline
Grand Rapids, MI 49525
Ph: (616)559-2624
Fax: (616)954-0517
URL: http://sites.younglife.org/sites/southgrandrapids/default.aspx

Local. Affiliated With: Young Life.

8033 ■ Young Life Western Great Lakes Region
3347 E Beltline
Grand Rapids, MI 49525
Ph: (616)954-6740
Fax: (616)954-0517
URL: http://sites.younglife.org/sites/WesternGreatLakes/default.aspx

Regional. Affiliated With: Young Life.

8034 ■ YWCA of Grand Rapids
25 Sheldon Blvd. SE
Grand Rapids, MI 49503
Ph: (616)459-4681
Fax: (616)459-5423
E-mail: info@gr-ywca.org
URL: http://www.ywca.org/grandrapids
Contact: Bridget White, Chair

Founded: 1900. **Local. Affiliated With:** Girls Inc.

Grandville

8035 ■ Calvin Christian High School - Young Life
PO Box 503
Grandville, MI 49468-0503
Ph: (616)538-4372
URL: http://sites.younglife.org/sites/CCHS/default.aspx
Contact: Jake Weilhouwer, Contact

Local. Affiliated With: Young Life.

8036 ■ Calvin Christian Middle School - Wyldlife
PO Box 503
Grandville, MI 49468-0503
Ph: (616)538-4372
URL: http://sites.younglife.org/sites/CCMS/default.aspx

Local. Affiliated With: Young Life.

8037 ■ Grand Valley Corvette Association (GVCA)
0-65 Ravenswood Dr.
Grandville, MI 49418-2151
Ph: (616)866-6458
E-mail: wdelo@comcast.net
URL: http://www.grandvalleycorvette.org
Contact: Bill Delo, Pres.

Local. Affiliated With: National Council of Corvette Clubs.

8038 ■ Grandville Chamber of Commerce
2905 Wilson Ave., Ste.202-A
Grandville, MI 49418
Ph: (616)531-8890
Fax: (616)531-8896
E-mail: gcc@grandvillechamber.org
URL: http://www.grandvillechamber.org
Contact: Chris Konyndyk, Exec.Dir.

Membership Dues: business (based on number of employees), $150-$225. **Local.** Promotes and stimulates long-term, well-planned economic growth, educational opportunities and community resources of Grandville. **Computer Services:** Information services, business directory.

8039 ■ Grandville High School - Young Life
PO Box 503
Grandville, MI 49468-0503
Ph: (616)538-4372 (989)430-3680
E-mail: secondedition@yahoo.com
URL: http://sites.younglife.org/sites/Grandvillehighschool/default.aspx
Contact: Carson Brown, Contact
Local. Affiliated With: Young Life.

8040 ■ Grandville Middle School - Wyldlife
PO Box 503
Grandville, MI 49468-0503
Ph: (616)538-4372 (734)216-7575
E-mail: storeye@student.gvsu.edu
URL: http://sites.younglife.org/sites/GMS/default.aspx
Contact: Erin Storey, Contact
Local. Affiliated With: Young Life.

8041 ■ Kenowa Hills High School - Young Life
PO Box 503
Grandville, MI 49468-0503
Ph: (616)538-4372
E-mail: khyounglife@yahoo.com
URL: http://sites.younglife.org/sites/KHHS/default.aspx
Contact: Dawn Braat, Contact
Local. Affiliated With: Young Life.

8042 ■ Lee High School - Young Life
PO Box 503
Grandville, MI 49468-0503
Ph: (616)538-4372 (616)901-5113
E-mail: lee.younglife@gmail.com
URL: http://www.xanga.com/lee_younglife
Contact: Heather Hamby, Contact
Local. Affiliated With: Young Life.

8043 ■ Michigan National Wild Turkey Federation, Grand Valley Chapter
2856 Tansy Trail
Grandville, MI 49418
Ph: (616)538-4934
URL: http://www.mi-nwtf.org/Grandvalley.htm
Contact: Gary Salmon, Pres.
Local.

8044 ■ National Spa and Pool Institute Region VI
c/o John L Spoelstra, Pres.
3420 Chicago Dr. SW
Grandville, MI 49418-1094
Ph: (616)538-0805
Fax: (616)538-0699
Regional. Affiliated With: Association of Pool and Spa Professionals.

8045 ■ Plumbing-Heating-Cooling Contractors Association, West Michigan
c/o Bob Ayers, Pres.
PO Box 38
Grandville, MI 49468-0038
Ph: (616)457-5660
Fax: (616)457-5515
URL: National Affiliate–www.phccweb.org
Contact: Bob Ayers, Pres.
Local. Represents the plumbing, heating and cooling contractors. Promotes the construction industry. Protects the environment, health, safety and comfort of society. **Affiliated With:** Plumbing-Heating-Cooling Contractors Association.

8046 ■ Reformed Free Publishing Association (RFPA)
c/o Mr. Timothy Pipe, Business Mgr.
4949 Ivanrest SW
Grandville, MI 49418-9709
Ph: (616)224-1518 (616)531-1490
Fax: (616)224-1517
E-mail: mail@rfpa.org
URL: http://www.rfpa.org
Contact: Mr. Timothy Pipe, Business Mgr.
Founded: 1924. **Members:** 170. **Staff:** 7. **Local Groups:** 1. **Regional.** Reformed publishing association. **Committees:** Book Publishing; Finance; Membership and Advertising. **Publications:** *The Standard Bearer*, semimonthly. Magazine. Contains religious reading material. **Price:** $17.50 in U.S.; $20.00 outside U.S. ISSN: 0362-4692. **Circulation:** 2,700. Alternate Formats: online; magnetic tape; microform. **Conventions/Meetings:** annual meeting - last Thursday in September.

8047 ■ Variety of Western Michigan
4165 Spartan Ind. Dr.
Grandville, MI 49418
Ph: (616)531-8600
Fax: (616)531-7555
E-mail: varietywestmich@usvariety.org
URL: National Affiliate–www.usvariety.org
Local. Affiliated With: Variety International - The Children's Charity.

8048 ■ Western Michigan Thunderbird Club
3526 Canal SW
Grandville, MI 49418
Ph: (616)538-7226
URL: National Affiliate–www.vintagethunderbirdclub.org
Local. Affiliated With: Vintage Thunderbird Club International.

8049 ■ Western MMBA
2879 Elwood
Grandville, MI 49418
Ph: (616)318-2390
E-mail: western@mmba.org
URL: http://www.mmba.org
Local. Affiliated With: International Mountain Bicycling Association.

8050 ■ Young Life Grand Rapids West
PO Box 503
Grandville, MI 49468-0503
Ph: (616)538-4372
Fax: (616)538-5681
URL: http://sites.younglife.org/sites/grwest/default.aspx
Local. Affiliated With: Young Life.

Grant

8051 ■ Grant Lions Club
c/o Roger Hilbrand, Pres.
13194 Elder Ave. SE
Grant, MI 49327
Ph: (231)834-5144
E-mail: mhilbrand@ncats.net
URL: http://www.grantps.net/grant_lions_club_grant.htm
Contact: Roger Hilbrand, Pres.
Local. Affiliated With: Lions Clubs International.

8052 ■ Michigan National Wild Turkey Federation, Grant Gobblers
678 E 128th St.
Grant, MI 49327
Ph: (231)834-7246
URL: http://www.mi-nwtf.org/grant_gobblers.htm
Contact: Ken Longstreet, Pres.
Local.

Grass Lake

8053 ■ American Legion, Michigan Post 252
c/o Anthony Steble
PO Box 523
Grass Lake, MI 49240
Ph: (517)371-4720
Fax: (517)371-2401
URL: National Affiliate–www.legion.org
Contact: Anthony Steble, Contact
Local. Affiliated With: American Legion.

8054 ■ German Wirehaired Pointer Club of America
c/o Barbara Tucker
PO Box 677
Grass Lake, MI 49240
E-mail: jedsgwp@msn.com
URL: http://www.gwpca.com
Contact: Barbara Tucker, Contact
Regional.

8055 ■ Grass Lake Lions Club
c/o William Anderson, Sec.
226 Clark St.
Grass Lake, MI 49240
Ph: (517)522-4563
E-mail: gllions@aol.com
URL: http://www.lionsdistrict11b1.org/lc_grass_lake.htm
Contact: William Anderson, Sec.
Local. Affiliated With: Lions Clubs International.

8056 ■ Michigan National Wild Turkey Federation, Waterloo Longbeards
6580 Wild Turkey Dr.
Grass Lake, MI 49240
Ph: (517)522-4292
URL: http://www.mi-nwtf.org/Waterloo.htm
Contact: Gerald Tisch, Pres.
Local.

Grayling

8057 ■ American Legion, Grayling Post 106
106 S James Ave.
Grayling, MI 49738
Ph: (517)371-4720
Fax: (517)371-2401
URL: National Affiliate–www.legion.org
Local. Affiliated With: American Legion.

8058 ■ Anglers of the Au Sable
c/o Calvin H. Gates, Jr., Pres.
403 Black Bear Dr.
Grayling, MI 49738
Ph: (989)348-8462
Fax: (989)348-2541
E-mail: gator@gateslodge.com
URL: http://www.ausableanglers.org
Contact: Calvin H. Gates Jr., Pres.
Local.

8059 ■ Crawford County United Way, Michigan
PO Box 171
Grayling, MI 49738-0171
Ph: (989)344-9300
URL: National Affiliate–national.unitedway.org
Local. Affiliated With: United Way of America.

8060 ■ Grayling Area Visitors Council
PO Box 217
Grayling, MI 49738
Ph: (989)348-4945
Fax: (989)348-9168
Free: (800)937-8837
E-mail: visitor@grayling-mi.com
URL: http://www.grayling-mi.com
Contact: Ilene Geiss-Wilson, Exec.Dir.
Founded: 1986. **Members:** 20. **Staff:** 1. **Local.** Promotes convention business and tourism in area.

8061 ■ Grayling Regional Chamber of Commerce (GRCC)
213 N James St.
PO Box 406
Grayling, MI 49738
Ph: (989)348-2921
Fax: (989)348-7315
Free: (800)937-8837
E-mail: director@graylingchamber.com
URL: http://www.grayling-mi.com
Contact: Timothy E. Zigila, Exec.Dir.
Founded: 1955. **Members:** 310. **Membership Dues:** business, $200-$830 (annual) • business associate,

$27 (annual) • individual/nonprofit, $55 (annual) • utility/education/government, $300 (annual). **Staff:** 2. **Budget:** $170,000. **Local.** Promotes business and community development in Crawford County, MI. Sponsors AuSable River Festival and Canoe Marathon and Grayling's Winter-Fest. **Additional Websites:** http://www.graylingchamber.com. **Affiliated With:** U.S. Chamber of Commerce. **Publications:** *Chamber Update*, monthly. Newsletter • *Grayling Community Guide and Membership Directory*, periodic. **Conventions/Meetings:** annual meeting.

8062 ■ Grayling Sportsmen's Club
PO Box 682
Grayling, MI 49738
Ph: (989)348-8899
URL: National Affiliate–www.mynssa.com
Local. Affiliated With: National Skeet Shooting Association.

8063 ■ Huron Pines Resource Conservation and Development Council
501 Norway St.
Grayling, MI 49738-1719
Ph: (989)348-9319
Fax: (989)348-7945
E-mail: kathleen.ryan@mi.usda.gov
URL: http://www.huronpines.org
Contact: Kathleen Ryan, Coor.
Local. Affiliated With: National Association of Resource Conservation and Development Councils.

8064 ■ Northern Michigan Appaloosa Horse Club
c/o Susan Phillips
2150 Shaw Park Rd.
Grayling, MI 49738
Ph: (989)348-8424
E-mail: taffyappy@hotmail.com
URL: National Affiliate–www.appaloosa.com
Contact: Susan Phillips, Contact
Local. Affiliated With: Appaloosa Horse Club.

Greenville

8065 ■ American Legion, Michigan Post 101
c/o Ray I. Booth
1320 W Washington St.
Greenville, MI 48838
Ph: (517)371-4720
Fax: (517)371-2401
URL: National Affiliate–www.legion.org
Contact: Ray I. Booth, Contact
Local. Affiliated With: American Legion.

8066 ■ Flat River Historical Society and Museums
PO Box 188
Greenville, MI 48838
Ph: (616)754-5296 (616)754-4838
Fax: (616)794-7911
E-mail: frhs@iserv.net
URL: http://www.flatriverhistoricalsociety.org
Contact: Sandra Brown, Pres.
Founded: 1967. **Members:** 85. **Membership Dues:** single, $10 (annual) • couple, $18 (annual) • life, $250 (annual). **Staff:** 1. **Budget:** $15,000. **Local.** Individuals interested in preserving the history of Montcalm County, MI. Maintains museum, artifacts, and genealogical data. Conducts monthly educational programs. **Libraries: Type:** by appointment only. **Subjects:** local history and genealogy. **Computer Services:** Online services, iserv. **Publications:** *Logmark*, quarterly. Newsletter. Contains information on past and coming activities. **Price:** included in membership dues. **Circulation:** 220. **Conventions/Meetings:** monthly meeting, for public - always third Wednesday of the month. Greenville, MI • annual Danish Festival, dedicated to celebrating the Danish Heritage of Greenville - third weekend of August. Greenville, MI.

8067 ■ Greenville Area Chamber of Commerce (GACC)
108 N Lafayette St., Ste.C
Greenville, MI 48838
Ph: (616)754-5697
Fax: (616)754-4710
E-mail: info@greenvillechamber.net
URL: http://www.greenvillechamber.net
Contact: Jeff Cook, Chm.
Founded: 1947. **Members:** 275. **Membership Dues:** business (varies with the number of employees), $183-$566 • industry/manufacture/agriculture (varies with the number of employees), $206-$678 • professional (varies with the number of employees), $255-$399 • retiree/service organization, $50 • nonprofit, $45 • individual, $75. **Staff:** 3. **Local.** Promotes business and community development in the Greenville, MI area. **Committees:** Danish Festival; Farmer's Market; Marketing; Stan Kemp Action. **Affiliated With:** Michigan Chamber of Commerce; U.S. Chamber of Commerce. **Publications:** *Business Beat*, monthly. Newsletter. **Price:** free for members • *Greater Greenville*. Newsletter. Alternate Formats: online.

8068 ■ Greenville Lions Club - Michigan
c/o Michael Blanding, Pres.
11225 W Harlow Rd.
Greenville, MI 48838
Ph: (616)754-2698
E-mail: myagent@charter.net
URL: http://www.glions.org
Contact: Michael Blanding, Pres.
Local. Affiliated With: Lions Clubs International.

8069 ■ Michigan Quarter Horse Association (MQHA)
PO Box 278
Greenville, MI 48838
Ph: (616)225-8211
Fax: (616)225-8313
E-mail: mqha@hotmail.com
URL: http://www.miquarterhorse.com
State. Affiliated With: American Quarter Horse Association.

8070 ■ Montcalm County Association of Realtors
309 1/2 S Lafayette, Ste.206
Greenville, MI 48838
Ph: (616)754-8896
E-mail: bill@billslating.com
URL: http://www.montcalm-realtors.com
Contact: Bill Slating, Pres.
Local. Strives to develop real estate business practices. Advocates the right to own, use and transfer real property. Provides a facility for professional development, research and exchange of information among members. **Affiliated With:** National Association of Realtors.

8071 ■ United Way of Montcalm County
PO Box 128
Greenville, MI 48838-0128
Ph: (616)225-1082
URL: National Affiliate–national.unitedway.org
Local. Affiliated With: United Way of America.

8072 ■ West Michigan Bonsai Club
c/o Mollie Hollar, Pres.
520 S St.
Greenville, MI 48838-2258
E-mail: mollie_hollar@wmbonsai.org
URL: http://www.wmbonsai.org
Local.

Grosse Ile

8073 ■ American Legion, Grosse Ile Post 75
7974 Siding Ct.
Grosse Ile, MI 48138
Ph: (517)371-4720
Fax: (517)371-2401
URL: National Affiliate–www.legion.org
Local. Affiliated With: American Legion.

8074 ■ Grosse Ile Lions Club
c/o Doug Kujala, Pres.
24566 Hally Crescent Dr.
Grosse Ile, MI 48138
Ph: (734)692-2737
E-mail: kujala8@comcast.net
URL: http://www.metrodetroitlions.org
Contact: Doug Kujala, Pres.
Local. Affiliated With: Lions Clubs International.

8075 ■ International Brotherhood of Magicians, Ring 210 - Duke Stern
c/o George Honer, Pres.
26050 Yorkshire
Grosse Ile, MI 48138
Ph: (734)675-3055
E-mail: magicbygeorge@hotmail.com
URL: http://www.aamagic.org
Contact: George Honer, Pres.
Local. Professional and semiprofessional magicians; suppliers, assistants, agents, and others interested in magic. Seeks to advance the art of magic in the field of amusement, entertainment, and culture. Promotes proper means of discouraging false or misleading advertising of effects, tricks, literature, merchandise, or actions appertaining to the magical arts; opposes exposures of principles of the art of magic, except in books on magic and magazines devoted to such art for the exclusive use of magicians and devotees of the art; encourages humane treatment and care of live animals whenever employed in magical performances. **Affiliated With:** International Brotherhood of Magicians.

8076 ■ Michigan Organization of Nurse Executives - District 1
c/o Josephine Wahl, Dir.
MedSeek
8063 Ferry Rd.
Grosse Ile, MI 48138
Ph: (734)676-0651
E-mail: jo.wahl@medseek.com
URL: http://www.mone.org
Contact: Josephine Wahl, Dir.
Local. Represents nurse leaders who improve healthcare. Provides leadership, professional development, advocacy and research. Advances the nursing administration practice and patient care. **Affiliated With:** American Organization of Nurse Executives.

8077 ■ National Organization for Women - Downriver
c/o Irene Z. Will
17689 Parke Ln.
Grosse Ile, MI 48138
Ph: (313)671-1230
E-mail: izwill@comcast.net
URL: http://www.michnow.org
Contact: Irene Z. Will, Contact
Local. Affiliated With: National Organization for Women.

8078 ■ Road Runners Club of America - Island Road Runners
9924 Lakewood
Grosse Ile, MI 48138
Ph: (734)240-4524 (734)755-6850
Fax: (734)240-4535
E-mail: mjackel@comcast.net
Contact: Mr. James Jackel, Treas.
Founded: 1981. **Members:** 65. **Membership Dues:** $10 (annual). **Budget:** $5,000. **Local. Affiliated With:** Road Runners Club of America.

Grosse Pointe

8079 ■ American Legion, Mike-Militello-Joseph Post 570
16919 St. Paul St.
Grosse Pointe, MI 48230
Ph: (517)371-4720
Fax: (517)371-2401
URL: National Affiliate–www.legion.org
Local. Affiliated With: American Legion.

8080 ■ Detroit Women's Rowing Association (DWRA)
c/o Renee Adams Schulte, Pres.
765 Lakeland
Grosse Pointe, MI 48230-1272
Ph: (313)881-2931
E-mail: info@dwra.org
URL: http://www.dwra.org
Contact: Renee Adams Schulte, Pres.
Local.

8081 ■ Gardeners of America/Men's Garden Clubs of America - Men's Garden Club of Grosse Pointe
c/o Rodney J. Girolami, Pres.
770 Univ. Pl.
Grosse Pointe, MI 48236
Ph: (313)881-3161
E-mail: rgiro@earthlink.net
URL: National Affiliate–www.tgoa-mgca.org
Contact: Rodney J. Girolami, Pres.
Local.

8082 ■ Grosse Pointe Board of Realtors
710 Notre Dame St.
Grosse Pointe, MI 48230
Ph: (313)882-8000
Fax: (313)882-6062
E-mail: gpbr@gpbr.com
URL: http://www.gpbr.com
Contact: Kay Agney, Pres.
Local. Strives to develop real estate business practices. Advocates the right to own, use and transfer real property. Provides a facility for professional development, research and exchange of information among members. **Affiliated With:** National Association of Realtors.

8083 ■ Grosse Pointe Lions Club
c/o John Moran, Pres.
984 Lincoln Rd.
Grosse Pointe, MI 48230
Ph: (313)881-4399
E-mail: gplions99@aol.com
URL: http://www.metrodetroitlions.org
Contact: John Moran, Pres.
Local. Affiliated With: Lions Clubs International.

8084 ■ Southeastern Michigan Mortgage Lenders Association (SEMMLA)
Washington Mutual - Correspondent Lending
715 Fisher Rd.
Grosse Pointe, MI 48230
Ph: (313)886-3234
Fax: (313)731-0572
E-mail: molly.gross@wamu.net
URL: http://www.mmla.net/semmla.htm
Contact: Molly Gross, Pres.
Local. Promotes fair and ethical lending practices and fosters professional excellence among real estate finance employees. Seeks to create an environment that enables members to invest in communities and achieve their business objectives. **Affiliated With:** Mortgage Bankers Association.

8085 ■ Wayne County Council for Arts, History, and Humanities (WCCAHH)
c/o Robert Maniscalco
17728 Mack Ave.
Grosse Pointe, MI 48230
E-mail: robert@maniscalcogallery.com
URL: http://www.waynearts.org
Contact: Robert Maniscalco, Pres.
Founded: 1987. **Members:** 24. **Budget:** $50,000. **Local. Awards: Frequency:** annual. **Type:** recognition. **Publications:** *Call for Entries*, annual. **Advertising:** accepted. **Conventions/Meetings:** monthly meeting.

8086 ■ Young Life Grosse Pointe
21 Kercheval, Ste.265
Grosse Pointe, MI 48236
Ph: (313)640-1761
Fax: (313)640-7925
URL: http://sites.younglife.org/sites/grossepointe/default.aspx
Contact: Anthony Grosso, Contact
Local. Affiliated With: Young Life.

Grosse Pointe Farms

8087 ■ Doublehanded Sailing Association
PO Box 36149
Grosse Pointe Farms, MI 48236
E-mail: rlrabine@voyager.net
URL: http://www.sailwith2.org
Contact: Ron Rabine, Commodore
Local.

8088 ■ Grosse Pointe Historical Society
381 Kercheval Ave.
Grosse Pointe Farms, MI 48236
Ph: (313)884-7010
Fax: (313)884-7699
E-mail: info@gphistorical.org
URL: http://www.gphistorical.org
Contact: Linda Johnson, Administrator
Local.

8089 ■ Grosse Pointe Lacrosse Association
PO Box 36043
Grosse Pointe Farms, MI 48236
URL: http://www.eteamz.com/grossepointe
Founded: 1994. **Local.**

8090 ■ Junior League of Detroit (JLD)
32 Lake Shore Rd.
Grosse Pointe Farms, MI 48236
Ph: (313)881-0040
Fax: (313)881-9813
E-mail: jldoffice@ameritech.net
URL: http://www.jldetroit.org
Contact: Ms. Nancy Orr, Pres.
Founded: 1914. **Members:** 675. **Membership Dues:** $135 (annual). **Staff:** 1. **Budget:** $280,000. **Local.** Women's organization that promotes volunteerism and trains volunteers for community service. Sponsors social events and fundraisers. **Awards:** Community Assistance. **Frequency:** quarterly. **Type:** grant • CorPLUS. **Frequency:** annual. **Type:** grant. **Recipient:** for retired individual volunteering service focused in the city of Detroit. **Publications:** *Connections*, monthly. Newsletter. **Advertising:** accepted • Report, annual. **Conventions/Meetings:** annual Association of Junior Leagues International - convention • General Membership - meeting - 6-7/year.

Grosse Pointe Woods

8091 ■ AAA Michigan
19299 Mack Ave.
Grosse Pointe Woods, MI 48236
Ph: (313)343-6000
Contact: Marsha Woods, Mgr.
State.

8092 ■ American Legion, Cadillac Post 333
51 Radner Cir.
Grosse Pointe Woods, MI 48236
Ph: (517)371-4720
Fax: (517)371-2401
URL: National Affiliate–www.legion.org
Local. Affiliated With: American Legion.

8093 ■ American Legion, Red Arrow 32nd Division Post 361
1572 Cook Rd.
Grosse Pointe Woods, MI 48236
Ph: (517)371-4720
Fax: (517)371-2401
URL: National Affiliate–www.legion.org
Local. Affiliated With: American Legion.

Gwinn

8094 ■ Lakeshore Pembroke Welsh Corgi Club (LPWCC)
c/o Kathi Charpie
75 Blueberry St.
Gwinn, MI 49841
Ph: (906)346-5580
E-mail: corgizotto@ncn.net
URL: http://www.lakeshorecorgi.com
Contact: Pati Wiedel, Pres.
Local. Affiliated With: Pembroke Welsh Corgi Club of America.

8095 ■ Mid-up Shooters
541 N County Rd. 557
Gwinn, MI 49841
Ph: (906)475-4957
URL: National Affiliate–www.mynssa.com
Local. Affiliated With: National Skeet Shooting Association.

8096 ■ United States Naval Sea Cadet Corps - Darter-Dace Division
Naval Reserve Center Marquette
402 3rd St.
Gwinn, MI 49841
E-mail: rllayne118@hotmail.com
URL: http://dolphin.seacadets.org/US_units/UnitDetails.asp?UnitID=092DDD
Contact: LTJG Russell C. Layne, Commanding Officer
Local. Works to instill good citizenship and patriotism in youth. Encourages qualities such as personal neatness, loyalty, obedience, dependability, and responsibility to others. Offers courses in physical fitness and military drill, first aid, water safety, basic seamanship, and naval history and traditions. **Affiliated With:** Naval Sea Cadet Corps.

Hale

8097 ■ American Legion, Michigan Post 422
c/o Glenn Staley
PO Box 255
Hale, MI 48739
Ph: (517)371-4720
Fax: (517)371-2401
URL: National Affiliate–www.legion.org
Contact: Glenn Staley, Contact
Local. Affiliated With: American Legion.

8098 ■ Northeastern Michigan Board of Realtors
PO Box 332
Hale, MI 48739
Ph: (989)728-5165
Fax: (989)728-5873
E-mail: neboard@m33access.com
URL: National Affiliate–www.realtor.org
Contact: Kristi Benedict, Exec. Officer
Local. Strives to develop real estate business practices. Advocates the right to own, use and transfer real property. Provides a facility for professional development, research and exchange of information among members. **Affiliated With:** National Association of Realtors.

8099 ■ Vietnam Veterans of America, Chapter No. 882
PO Box 2
Hale, MI 48739-0002
Ph: (989)728-8820
E-mail: davenelsey@m33access.com
URL: http://www.halemichigan.net/vva/vva.html
Local. Affiliated With: Vietnam Veterans of America.

Hamburg

8100 ■ American Legion, Whitmore Lake Post 359
8891 Spicer Rd.
Hamburg, MI 48139
Ph: (517)371-4720
Fax: (517)371-2401
URL: National Affiliate–www.legion.org
Local. Affiliated With: American Legion.

8101 ■ National Association of Rocketry - Huron Valley Rocket Society (HUVARS)
c/o Jim Fackert
Box 430
Hamburg, MI 48139
Ph: (248)349-9079
E-mail: huvars@umich.edu
URL: http://www.huvars.org
Local.

Hamilton

8102 ■ International Facility Management Association, West Michigan
c/o David Kuiper, CFM, Pres.
3266 Oakridge Cir.
Hamilton, MI 49419
Ph: (616)531-6047
Fax: (616)654-7586
E-mail: dave_kuiper@hermanmiller.com
URL: National Affiliate–www.ifma.org
Facility managers representing all types of organizations including banks, insurance companies, hospitals, colleges and universities, utility companies, electronic equipment manufacturers, petroleum companies, museums, auditoriums, and federal, state, provincial, and local governments. Works to enhance the professional goals of persons involved or interested in the field of facility management (the planning, designing, and managing of workplaces). **Affiliated With:** International Facility Management Association.

Hamtramck

8103 ■ American Legion, Chrysler A.B.D. Post 242
2955 Roosevelt St.
Hamtramck, MI 48212
Ph: (517)371-4720
Fax: (517)371-2401
URL: National Affiliate–www.legion.org
Local. Affiliated With: American Legion.

8104 ■ American Legion, Hamtramck Falcon Post 455
2401 Zinow St.
Hamtramck, MI 48212
Ph: (517)371-4720
Fax: (517)371-2401
URL: National Affiliate–www.legion.org
Local. Affiliated With: American Legion.

8105 ■ Call to Action of Michigan
PO Box 12161
Hamtramck, MI 48212
E-mail: cta-mi@comcast.net
URL: http://www.cta-mi.org
State. Affiliated With: Call For Action.

Hancock

8106 ■ American Legion, Michigan Post 186
c/o Alfred Erickson
1308 Quincy St.
Hancock, MI 49930
Ph: (517)371-4720
Fax: (517)371-2401
URL: National Affiliate–www.legion.org
Contact: Alfred Erickson, Contact
Local. Affiliated With: American Legion.

8107 ■ Copper Country Community Arts Council (CCCAC)
126 Quincy St.
Hancock, MI 49930
Ph: (906)482-2333
E-mail: ccarts@chartermi.net
URL: http://www.pasty.com/~ccarts
Contact: Ray Sharp, Pres.
Founded: 1972. **Members:** 250. **Membership Dues:** individual, $25 (annual) • family, $50 (annual) • donor, $100 (annual). **Staff:** 4. **Budget:** $110,000. **Local.** Serves Michigan counties of Baraga, Houghton, Ontonagon, and Keweenaw. Works to promote the appreciation of visual and performing arts. Sponsors sales and competitions; owns and operates the Community Arts Center which consists of 3 galleries, classrooms, studios, and a performance space. **Special Interest Groups:** Artists Market Sales Gallery. **Also Known As:** Community Arts Center. **Publications:** *Arts Calendar*, quarterly. Contains calendar of art events. **Price:** included in membership dues. **Circulation:** 2,000 • *CCCAC News*, quarterly. Newsletter. **Price:** free to members & visitors to CAC. **Circulation:** 250. **Conventions/Meetings:** monthly board meeting - first Monday.

8108 ■ Copper Country Rock and Mineral Club (CCRMC)
c/o Marge Rohrer, Pres.
1002 Second St.
Hancock, MI 49930
E-mail: swhelan@up.net
URL: http://www.ccrmc.info
Contact: Carol Wiitanen, Sec.
Local. Aims to further the study of Earth Sciences and the practice of lapidary arts and mineralogy. **Affiliated With:** American Federation of Mineralogical Societies.

8109 ■ Copper County District Dental Society
1550 W Quincy St.
Hancock, MI 49930
Ph: (906)482-3621
Fax: (906)482-3676
URL: National Affiliate–www.ada.org
Contact: Dr. Anthony Sarazin, Pres.
Local. Represents the interests of dentists committed to the public's oral health, ethics and professional development. Encourages the improvement of the public's oral health and promotes the art and science of dentistry. **Affiliated With:** American Dental Association; Michigan Dental Association.

8110 ■ George Wright Society (GWS)
PO Box 65
Hancock, MI 49930-0065
Ph: (906)487-9722
Fax: (906)487-9405
E-mail: info@georgewright.org
URL: http://www.georgewright.org
Contact: David Harmon, Exec.Dir.
Founded: 1980. **Local.**

8111 ■ Trout Unlimited - Copper County Chapter
708 Hecla
Hancock, MI 49930
Ph: (906)482-2615
E-mail: salbee@up.net
URL: http://www.tu.org
Contact: Bill Deephouse, Pres.
Local.

8112 ■ Western Upper Peninsula RSVP
c/o Barbara Maronen, Dir.
540 Depot St.
Hancock, MI 49930
Ph: (906)482-7382
E-mail: bmaronen@hline.org
URL: http://www.seniorcorps.gov
Contact: Barbara Maronen, Dir.
Local. Affiliated With: Retired and Senior Volunteer Program.

Hanover

8113 ■ American Legion, Hanover-Horton Post 270
321 Railroad St.
Hanover, MI 49241
Ph: (517)371-4720
Fax: (517)371-2401
URL: National Affiliate–www.legion.org
Local. Affiliated With: American Legion.

Harbor Beach

8114 ■ American Legion, Burhans-Hagedon Post 197
PO Box 9
Harbor Beach, MI 48441
Ph: (517)371-4720
Fax: (517)371-2401
URL: National Affiliate–www.legion.org
Local. Affiliated With: American Legion.

8115 ■ Harbor Beach Chamber of Commerce
PO Box 113
Harbor Beach, MI 48441
Ph: (989)479-6477
Fax: (989)479-6477
Free: (800)HBM-ICH5
E-mail: visitor@harborbeachchamber.com
URL: http://www.harborbeachchamber.com
Contact: Bill Duerr, Exec.Sec.
Local. Works to advance businesses within Harbor Beach and the surrounding areas.

Harbor Springs

8116 ■ American Legion, Smith-Hoover Post 281
PO Box 436
Harbor Springs, MI 49740
Ph: (517)371-4720
Fax: (517)371-2401
URL: National Affiliate–www.legion.org
Local. Affiliated With: American Legion.

8117 ■ American Meteorological Society, University of Michigan - Ann Arbor
c/o Doug Boyer
PO Box 733
Harbor Springs, MI 49740
URL: National Affiliate–www.ametsoc.org/AMS
Contact: Doug Boyer, Contact
Local. Affiliated With: American Meteorological Society.

8118 ■ Harbor Springs Chamber of Commerce (HSCC)
368 E Main St.
Harbor Springs, MI 49740-0037
Ph: (231)526-7999
Fax: (231)526-5593
Free: (866)526-7999
E-mail: info@harborspringschamber.com
URL: http://www.harborspringschamber.com
Contact: Kathy Lott, Exec.Dir.
Members: 280. **Membership Dues:** business (based on number of employees), $200-$575 (annual) • insurance/real estate (plus $10/associate), $200 (annual) • professional (plus $10/associate), $200 (annual) • lodging (plus $3/room or unit), $200-$295 (annual) • restaurant/tavern/lounge (plus $3/seat), $200-$295 (annual) • associate, $200 (annual) • financial (plus $10/million dollar in assets), $200 (annual) • resort (year round), $1,140 (annual) • resort (sea-

sonal), $575 (annual). **Local**. Strives to promote, enhance, and contribute to the well-being of the business community, while preserving the character and traditions of Harbor Springs. **Computer Services:** Information services, business directory. **Affiliated With:** American Chamber of Commerce Executives; U.S. Chamber of Commerce. **Publications:** *Back to Business*, monthly. Newsletter. **Advertising:** accepted. Alternate Formats: online • *Community Connection*, bimonthly. Newsletter. **Advertising:** accepted. Alternate Formats: online • *Visitors Guide*, annual. Handbook. **Advertising:** accepted • Directory, annual. **Advertising:** accepted • Brochure. **Advertising:** accepted.

8119 ■ Tasters Guild International - Harbor Springs/Petoskey, Chapter No. 096
PO Box 4609
Harbor Springs, MI 49740
Ph: (231)526-9665
URL: National Affiliate–www.tastersguild.com
Contact: Dr. Eugene W. Mauch, Contact
Local. Aims to educate consumers and spread the word of responsible wine and food consumption. Provides opportunity to encounter the best in wine and culinary delights. **Affiliated With:** Tasters Guild International.

Harper Woods

8120 ■ American Legion, Harper Woods Post 99
19919 Fleetwood Dr.
Harper Woods, MI 48225
Ph: (517)371-4720
Fax: (517)371-2401
URL: National Affiliate–www.legion.org
Local. Affiliated With: American Legion.

8121 ■ American Legion, National-Guard-Iron-Fist Post 70
20243 Van Antwerp
Harper Woods, MI 48225
Ph: (517)371-4720
Fax: (517)371-2401
URL: National Affiliate–www.legion.org
Local. Affiliated With: American Legion.

8122 ■ Michigan National Wild Turkey Federation, Macomb Lost Gobblers
20400 Woodside
Harper Woods, MI 48225
URL: http://www.mi-nwtf.org/Macomb%20Lost%20Gobblers.htm
Contact: Brian Bunch, Pres.
Local.

Harrietta

8123 ■ National Active and Retired Federal Employees Association - Cadillac Area 1946
5690 W 28 1/2 Michigan Rd.
Harrietta, MI 49638
Ph: (231)389-2597
URL: National Affiliate–www.narfe.org
Contact: L. Maxine Lazar, Contact
Local. Protects the retirement future of employees through education. Informs members on issues affecting the retirement. **Affiliated With:** National Association of Retired Federal Employees.

Harris

8124 ■ American Legion, Hannahville Potawatomi Post 116
PO Box 103
Harris, MI 49845
Ph: (517)371-4720
Fax: (517)371-2401
URL: National Affiliate–www.legion.org
Local. Affiliated With: American Legion.

Harrison

8125 ■ American Legion, Harrison Post 404
1267 W M-61
Harrison, MI 48625
Ph: (517)371-4720
Fax: (517)371-2401
URL: National Affiliate–www.legion.org
Local. Affiliated With: American Legion.

8126 ■ Harrison Chamber of Commerce
809 N 1st St.
PO Box 682
Harrison, MI 48625-0682
Ph: (989)539-6011
Fax: (989)539-6099
E-mail: harrisonchamber@sbcglobal.net
URL: http://www.harrisonchamber.com
Contact: Debbie Gadberry, Pres.
Members: 153. **Membership Dues:** general, $150 (annual) • silver, $300 (annual) • gold, $500 (annual). **Staff:** 1. **Local**. Promotes businesses in Harrison area. **Computer Services:** Information services, membership directory. **Formerly:** (2005) Harrison Area Chamber of Commerce. **Publications:** Newsletter, quarterly. Contains upcoming events and latest Chamber news.

8127 ■ Harrison Lions Club - Michigan
PO Box 232
Harrison, MI 48625
Ph: (989)539-1010 (989)539-7260
E-mail: kbrandt@sbcglobal.net
URL: http://harrisonmi.lionwap.org
Contact: Pat Stachowiak, Pres.
Local. Affiliated With: Lions Clubs International.

8128 ■ Michigan Lake to Lake Bed and Breakfast Association
c/o Angela Carrier, Exec.Dir.
PO Box 863
Harrison, MI 48625
Ph: (989)539-7935
E-mail: innfo@laketolake.com
URL: http://www.laketolake.com
Contact: Angela Carrier, Exec.Dir.
Founded: 1986. **Members:** 215. **Staff:** 1. **Budget:** $100,000. **State. Formerly:** (1999) Lake to Lake Bed and Breakfast Association. **Publications:** *Looking Out*, bimonthly. Newsletter. **Price:** free. **Circulation:** 500. **Advertising:** accepted.

8129 ■ Michigan Rural Water Association (MRWA)
c/o Tim Neumann, Office Mgr./CFO
PO Box 960
Harrison, MI 48625
Ph: (989)539-4111
Fax: (989)539-4055
E-mail: mrwa@chartermi.net
URL: http://www.mrwa.net
Contact: Tim Neumann, Office Mgr./CFO
State.

8130 ■ Phi Theta Kappa, Alpha Omicron Omicron Chapter - Mid Michigan Community College
c/o Niky Bean
1375 S Clare Ave.
Harrison, MI 48625
Ph: (989)386-6634
E-mail: nbean@midmich.edu
URL: http://www.ptk.org/directories/chapters/MI/6778-1.htm
Contact: Niky Bean, Advisor
Local.

Harrison Township

8131 ■ National Active and Retired Federal Employees Association - Macomb 1474
26941 Beamer St.
Harrison Township, MI 48045-2523
Ph: (586)463-9228
URL: National Affiliate–www.narfe.org
Contact: Donald A. Brandenburg, Contact
Local. Protects the retirement future of employees through education. Informs members on issues affecting the retirement. **Affiliated With:** National Association of Retired Federal Employees.

8132 ■ Southeastern Michigan Chapter, MOAA
c/o Cdr. Roy Yaple
PO Box 450037
Harrison Township, MI 48045-0037
Ph: (810)225-8657
E-mail: yapler@comcast.net
URL: National Affiliate–www.moaa.org
Contact: Cdr. Roy Yaple, Contact
Local. Affiliated With: Military Officers Association of America.

Harrisville

8133 ■ Huron Shores Chamber of Commerce
PO Box 581
Harrisville, MI 48740
Ph: (989)724-5107
Fax: (989)724-5107
Free: (800)432-2823
E-mail: info@huronshoreschamber.com
URL: http://www.huronshoreschamber.com
Contact: Cheryl Peterson, Pres.
Membership Dues: business (depends upon the benefits), $20-$75. **Local**. Promotes Alcona County and its communities.

Harsens Island

8134 ■ Middle Channel Improvement Association
c/o Perry Dubay
8296 Middle Channel
Harsens Island, MI 48028-9578
Founded: 2000. **Members:** 49. **Local**.

Hart

8135 ■ American Legion, Fred-W.-Strong-Donald-W.-Wolf Post 234
PO Box 163
Hart, MI 49420
Ph: (517)371-4720
Fax: (517)371-2401
URL: National Affiliate–www.legion.org
Local. Affiliated With: American Legion.

8136 ■ Hart Lions Club
c/o Terry Dykema, Pres.
5550 N Oceana Dr.
Hart, MI 49420
Ph: (231)873-5136
E-mail: shchapman@earthlink.net
URL: http://lions.silverthorn.biz/11-e1
Contact: Terry Dykema, Pres.
Local. Affiliated With: Lions Clubs International.

8137 ■ Hart - Silver Lake Mears Chamber of Commerce
2388 N Comfort Dr.
Hart, MI 49420
Ph: (231)873-2247
Fax: (231)873-1683
Free: (800)870-9786
E-mail: info@hartsilverlakemears.com
URL: http://www.hartsilverlakemears.com
Contact: Tom Rickhoff, Pres.
Membership Dues: primary business, $200 (annual) • secondary business, $100 (annual) • associate, $50 (annual). **Local**. Progressive business people and citizens. Strives to promote the business community and to improve the general welfare and development of Hart, Mears and Silver Lake areas. **Computer**

Services: Information services, membership directory. **Committees:** Ambassador; Christmas; Fundraising; Special Events; Volunteer; Web Site and Marketing. **Publications:** Newsletter, quarterly. **Price:** included in membership dues. Alternate Formats: online.

Hartford

8138 ■ American Legion, Stoddard Post 93
66297 Red Arrow Hwy.
Hartford, MI 49057
Ph: (517)371-4720
Fax: (517)371-2401
URL: National Affiliate–www.legion.org
Local. Affiliated With: American Legion.

8139 ■ Hartford Lions Club - Michigan
68328 CR 372
Hartford, MI 49057
E-mail: walls7@hotmail.com
URL: http://milions11b2.org
Local. Affiliated With: Lions Clubs International.

8140 ■ Michigan State Horticultural Society (MSHS)
63806 90th Ave.
Hartford, MI 49057
Ph: (269)424-3990
Fax: (269)424-3096
E-mail: mihortsociety@aol.com
URL: http://www.mihortsociety.org
Contact: Mike Wittenbach, Pres.
Founded: 1870. **Members:** 1,400. **Membership Dues:** $65 (annual). **Regional.** Individuals interested in promoting Michigan's fruit industry. **Libraries: Type:** reference. **Subjects:** fruit culture. **Awards:** Distinguished Service Award. **Frequency:** annual. **Type:** recognition. **Recipient:** for research in fruit industry • Michigan Apple Cider Award. **Frequency:** annual. **Type:** recognition • Student Scholarship. **Frequency:** annual. **Type:** scholarship. **Additional Websites:** http://www.glexpo.com. **Publications:** Annual Report, annual. Contains information related to fruit culture and marketing. ISSN: 0096-7688. **Circulation:** 1,500. **Conventions/Meetings:** annual Great Lakes Expo - meeting, topics include fruit production, marketing, handling, supplies and services (exhibits) - always December.

Hartland

8141 ■ American Legion, Austin-Moore Post 415
PO Box 212
Hartland, MI 48353
Ph: (517)371-4720
Fax: (517)371-2401
URL: National Affiliate–www.legion.org
Local. Affiliated With: American Legion.

8142 ■ American Legion, Waterford Post 24
1700 Helena Ave.
Hartland, MI 48353
Ph: (517)371-4720
Fax: (517)371-2401
URL: National Affiliate–www.legion.org
Local. Affiliated With: American Legion.

8143 ■ Hartland Lions Club
c/o Bud Kimball, Pres.
4288 Fenton Rd.
Hartland, MI 48353
Ph: (248)887-5827
URL: http://www.district11c2.org
Contact: Bud Kimball, Pres.
Local. Affiliated With: Lions Clubs International.

Haslett

8144 ■ American Association for Medical Transcription, Red Cedar Chapter
c/o Ava Marie George, Pres.
452 Haslett Rd.
Haslett, MI 48840
E-mail: avageorge@hotmail.com
URL: http://www.aamt.org/ca/redcedar
Contact: Ava Marie George, Pres.
Local. Works to represent and advance the profession of medical transcription and its practitioners. **Affiliated With:** American Association for Medical Transcription.

8145 ■ American Legion, Chief Okemos Post 269
PO Box 245
Haslett, MI 48840
Ph: (517)371-4720
Fax: (517)371-2401
URL: National Affiliate–www.legion.org
Local. Affiliated With: American Legion.

8146 ■ Citizens Against Repressive Zoning (CARZ)
c/o Jack Downs, Pres.
PO Box 536
Haslett, MI 48840-0536
Ph: (517)351-6751
Fax: (517)339-4926
E-mail: malzoning@earthlink.net
URL: http://clubs.hemmings.com/clubsites/fightcityhall/index.htm
Contact: Jack Downs PhD, Pres.
Founded: 1978. **Members:** 250. **Membership Dues:** $15 (annual). **Staff:** 5. **Regional.**

8147 ■ Infusion Nurses Society, Capital
5729 Ridgeway Dr., Apt. 10
Haslett, MI 48840
Ph: (517)575-0316
E-mail: lmgallobsn89@aol.com
URL: National Affiliate–www.ins1.org
Contact: Linda Gallo, Pres.
Local. Represents the interests of healthcare professionals who are involved with the practice of infusion therapy. Seeks to advance the delivery of quality therapy to patients. Promotes research and education in the practice of infusion nursing. **Affiliated With:** Infusion Nurses Society.

8148 ■ Michigan Chapter - Sheet Metal and Air Conditioning Contractors' National Association
c/o Richard C. Northrup
PO Box 220
Haslett, MI 48840-0220
Ph: (517)339-1123
Fax: (517)339-3372
E-mail: smacna@comcast.net
URL: National Affiliate–www.smacna.org
Contact: Richard C. Northrup, Contact
State. Affiliated With: Sheet Metal and Air Conditioning Contractors' National Association.

8149 ■ Michigan Floral Association (MFA)
c/o Rod Crittenden, Exec.VP/CEO
1152 Haslett Rd.
PO Box 67
Haslett, MI 48840
Ph: (517)575-0110
Fax: (517)575-0115
E-mail: rod@michiganfloral.org
URL: http://www.michiganfloral.org
Contact: Rod Crittenden, Exec.VP
State.

8150 ■ Michigan State Grange (MG)
c/o Jeffrey A. Swainston, Pres.
1730 Chamberlain
Haslett, MI 48840
Ph: (517)339-2171
Fax: (517)339-3636
Free: (800)337-1502
E-mail: msgrange@voyager.net
URL: http://www.michigangrange.org
Contact: Jeffrey A. Swainston, Pres.
Founded: 1873. **Members:** 3,000. **Membership Dues:** $20 (annual). **Staff:** 2. **Regional Groups:** 14. **State Groups:** 1. **Local Groups:** 61. **State.** Agricultural workers, education professionals, community service organizations, and families. Seeks to educate and elevate the position of the American farmer and to serve the rural community. Sponsors Grange Deaf Activities. **Affiliated With:** National Grange. **Publications:** *Michigan Grange News*, monthly. Newsletter. **Price:** free to members. **Conventions/Meetings:** annual Michigan State Grange Convention, crafts, photography, art (exhibits).

8151 ■ Military Order of the Purple Heart - Capital City Chapter 37
c/o Mack M. Bates
1433 Franklin St.
Haslett, MI 48840-8402
Ph: (517)339-8922
E-mail: mackmccoy82@aol.com
URL: National Affiliate–www.purpleheart.org
Contact: Mack M. Bates, Contact
Local. Affiliated With: Military Order of the Purple Heart of the United States of America.

8152 ■ National Nutritional Foods Association-Southwest
1068 Haslett Rd.
Haslett, MI 48840
Ph: (517)575-0520
Fax: (517)339-4129
Free: (888)663-2791
E-mail: info@nnfasw.org
URL: http://www.nnfasw.org
Contact: Dale Power-Wells, Exec.Dir.
Regional. Affiliated With: National Nutritional Foods Association.

Hastings

8153 ■ American Legion, Michigan Post 45
c/o Lawrence J. Bauer
2160 S M37 Hwy.
Hastings, MI 49058
Ph: (517)371-4720
Fax: (517)371-2401
URL: National Affiliate–www.legion.org
Contact: Lawrence J. Bauer, Contact
Local. Affiliated With: American Legion.

8154 ■ American Youth Soccer Organization, Region 1196
877 E Cloverdale Rd.
Hastings, MI 49058
Ph: (269)721-3739
E-mail: kvaughan@mei.net
URL: http://www.hastingsayso.com
Local. Affiliated With: American Youth Soccer Organization.

8155 ■ Barry County Area Chamber of Commerce (BACC)
221 W State St.
Hastings, MI 49058
Ph: (269)945-2454
Fax: (269)945-3839
Free: (800)510-2922
E-mail: barrychamber@sbcglobal.net
URL: http://www.barrychamber.com
Contact: Julie DeBoer, Exec.Dir.
Staff: 1. **Budget:** $60,000. **State Groups:** 1. **Local.** Promotes business and community development in the Hastings, MI area. **Computer Services:** Online services, message board. **Committees:** Barry Quality Initiative; Chamber Ways and Means; Economic and Community Development; Education and Government; Festivals, Clubs and Events; Membership. **Publications:** *Chamber Directory*, annual • *Chamber*

Newsletter, bimonthly. **Conventions/Meetings:** annual conference - always February • monthly luncheon - 4th Thursday.

8156 ■ Barry County United Way
PO Box 644
Hastings, MI 49058
Ph: (269)945-4010
Fax: (269)945-4536
E-mail: bcuw@sbcglobal.com
URL: http://www.bcunitedway.org
Contact: Lani Forbes, Exec.Dir.
Local. Affiliated With: United Way of America.

8157 ■ Habitat for Humanity Barry County
1135 Enterprise Dr.
PO Box 234
Hastings, MI 49058
Ph: (269)948-9939
Fax: (269)948-9939
E-mail: barryhfh@triton.net
URL: National Affiliate–www.habitat.org
Local. Affiliated With: Habitat for Humanity International.

8158 ■ Wolverine Beagle Club
c/o Paul S. Gonzales
4700 Hammond Rd.
Hastings, MI 49058-8528
URL: National Affiliate–www.akc.org
Contact: Paul S. Gonzales, Contact
Founded: 1919. **Members:** 15. **Membership Dues:** stockholder, $50 (annual). **Staff:** 9. **Budget:** $5,700. **Regional Groups:** 4. **State Groups:** 13. **Regional.** Promotes pure-bred beagles in Brace Field Trial competition. **Publications:** none. **Libraries: Type:** open to the public. **Awards:** American Kennel Club. **Frequency:** monthly. **Type:** trophy. **Affiliated With:** American Kennel Club. **Conventions/Meetings:** annual meeting - always first Tuesday in October.

Hawks

8159 ■ Michigan National Wild Turkey Federation, Black Mountain Chapter
9011 W 638 Hwy.
Hawks, MI 49743
Ph: (517)734-4688
URL: http://www.mi-nwtf.org/Blackmountain.htm
Contact: Mark Schuler, Pres.
Local.

Hazel Park

8160 ■ Adoption Identity Movement of Michigan (AIM)
PO Box 812
Hazel Park, MI 48030
Ph: (248)548-6291
E-mail: dgeorgew@aol.com
URL: National Affiliate–www.americanadoptioncongress.org/
Contact: Tina Caudill, Founder
Founded: 1972. **Members:** 250. **Membership Dues:** search assistance required, support or professional, $30 (annual). **State.** Search and support group for adult adoptees, birthparents, and adoptive parents; members of related organizations devoted to leadership in adoption reform. Works to disseminate information about adoption and related social-psychological issues. Maintains speakers' bureau. Provides search assistance to members and education to the community. **Affiliated With:** American Adoption Congress. **Publications:** *AIM Newsletter*, semiannual. **Price:** included in membership. **Circulation:** 300. **Conventions/Meetings:** monthly meeting - always 3rd Wednesday of September through June. Hazel Park, MI - Avg. Attendance: 40.

8161 ■ World Future Society, Detroit
c/o Edward Klobucher
585 E Shevlin
Hazel Park, MI 48030
Ph: (248)542-5539
E-mail: eklobucher@aol.com
URL: National Affiliate–www.wfs.org
Contact: Edward Klobucher, Contact
Local. Affiliated With: World Future Society.

Hemlock

8162 ■ Hemlock Lions Club
c/o Margie Curtis, Pres.
949 N Fordney Rd.
Hemlock, MI 48626
Ph: (989)642-2387
URL: http://www.geocities.com/dist11d1
Contact: Margie Curtis, Pres.
Local. Affiliated With: Lions Clubs International.

Hermansville

8163 ■ American Legion, Floriano-Stecker Post 340
PO Box 144
Hermansville, MI 49847
Ph: (517)371-4720
Fax: (517)371-2401
URL: National Affiliate–www.legion.org
Local. Affiliated With: American Legion.

Hersey

8164 ■ National Active and Retired Federal Employees Association - Muskegon River 1921
327 S Main St.
Hersey, MI 49639-9701
Ph: (231)832-9203
URL: National Affiliate–www.narfe.org
Contact: Charlene M. Ferguson, Contact
Local. Protects the retirement future of employees through education. Informs members on issues affecting the retirement. **Affiliated With:** National Association of Retired Federal Employees.

Hesperia

8165 ■ American Legion, Michigan Post 411
c/o Thomas Richard Annis
4075 S 198th Ave.
Hesperia, MI 49421
Ph: (517)371-4720
Fax: (517)371-2401
URL: National Affiliate–www.legion.org
Contact: Thomas Richard Annis, Contact
Local. Affiliated With: American Legion.

8166 ■ Hesperia Lions Club
c/o Scott Kroepel, Pres.
PO Box 87
Hesperia, MI 49421
Ph: (231)854-5915
E-mail: dlheaven@yahoo.com
URL: http://lions.silverthorn.biz/11-e1
Contact: Scott Kroepel, Pres.
Local. Affiliated With: Lions Clubs International.

8167 ■ Michigan Midwives Association (MMA)
c/o Patrice Bobier
4220 Loop Rd.
Hesperia, MI 49421
Ph: (231)861-2234 (231)929-3563
Fax: (231)861-2924
Free: (877)BIRTH-4-U
E-mail: pbobier@voyager.net
URL: http://www.michiganmidwives.org
Contact: Patrice Bobier, Treas.
Founded: 1979. **Members:** 75. **Membership Dues:** student, $30 (annual) • professional, $50 (annual). **Budget:** $10,000. **State.** Midwives, midwives-in-training, birth educators, and interested individuals. Seeks to better inform the public regarding midwifery and childbirth. Responds to legal needs and encourages further relations between the profession and other health care professions. Facilitates communication among members; encourages the education of midwives. Sponsors Healthy Mothers/Healthy Babies Coalition. Holds public information sessions. **Affiliated With:** Midwives Alliance of North America. **Publications:** *Annual Statistics*, annual • Directory, biennial • Newsletter, quarterly. **Conventions/Meetings:** quarterly conference (exhibits) - always January, May, July, and October.

Hessel

8168 ■ Friends of Les Cheneaux Community Library
c/o Betty J. Lindberg
PO Box 332
Hessel, MI 49745-0332
Ph: (906)484-3866 (772)545-1156
Fax: (906)484-6509
E-mail: martiharness@cedarville.com
Contact: Betty Lindberg, Pres.
Founded: 2001. **Nonmembership. Local.** Works to build and maintain a building which will house the Branch of Bayless Public Library, Sault Ste. Marie, Michigan. **Libraries: Type:** open to the public. **Holdings:** 5,000.

Hickory Corners

8169 ■ American Legion, Simmonds-Williams Post 484
PO Box 41
Hickory Corners, MI 49060
Ph: (517)371-4720
Fax: (517)371-2401
URL: National Affiliate–www.legion.org
Local. Affiliated With: American Legion.

Highland Park

8170 ■ American Legion, Michigan Post 132
c/o Benjamin O. Davis, Sr.
55 Victor St.
Highland Park, MI 48203
Ph: (517)371-4720
Fax: (517)371-2401
URL: National Affiliate–www.legion.org
Contact: Benjamin O. Davis Sr., Contact
Local. Affiliated With: American Legion.

8171 ■ Dress for Success Detroit
1200 E McNichols
Highland Park, MI 48203
Ph: (313)957-2277
Fax: (313)823-4118
E-mail: detroit@dressforsuccess.org
URL: National Affiliate–www.dressforsuccess.org
Contact: Jo-Ann Lucas, Exec.Dir.
Local.

8172 ■ Highland Park Lions Club - Michigan
c/o Alvin Peterson, Pres.
110 California St.
Highland Park, MI 48203

Ph: (313)865-5102
E-mail: margaretlewis@mainspring.com
URL: http://www.metrodetroitlions.org
Contact: Alvin Peterson, Pres.
Local. Affiliated With: Lions Clubs International.

Hillman

8173 ■ Hillman Area Chamber of Commerce
PO Box 506
Hillman, MI 49746
Ph: (989)742-3739
Fax: (989)742-3739
Contact: Ms. Margaret Kirby, Pres.
Local.

Hillsdale

8174 ■ American Legion, Michigan Post 53
c/o Leighr A. Wright
PO Box 157
Hillsdale, MI 49242
Ph: (517)371-4720
Fax: (517)371-2401
URL: National Affiliate–www.legion.org
Contact: Leighr A. Wright, Contact
Local. Affiliated With: American Legion.

8175 ■ Hillsdale County Board of Realtors
PO Box 253
Hillsdale, MI 49242
Ph: (517)439-1770
Fax: (517)437-6910
E-mail: hcboard@yahoo.com
URL: National Affiliate–www.realtor.org
Contact: Shirley Smith, Exec. Officer
Local. Strives to develop real estate business practices. Advocates the right to own, use and transfer real property. Provides a facility for professional development, research and exchange of information among members. **Affiliated With:** National Association of Realtors.

8176 ■ Hillsdale County Chamber of Commerce
22 N Manning St.
Hillsdale, MI 49242
Ph: (517)437-6401
Fax: (517)437-6408
E-mail: info@hillsdalecountychamber.com
URL: http://www.hillsdalecountychamber.com
Contact: Karri Doty, Exec.Dir./Pres.
Local. Strives to enhance the economy of Hillsdale County by providing services in identifying local sources for products and services. **Computer Services:** Information services, membership directory. **Committees:** Annual Business Exposition/Culinary Row; Annual Car Show; Annual Holiday Bazaar. **Programs:** Ambassador; Member to Member Advantage Discount. **Publications:** *Commerce Connection*. Newsletter. **Advertising:** accepted. **Conventions/Meetings:** annual Holiday Bazaar - trade show (exhibits) - 2006 Nov. 27, Hillsdale, MI.

8177 ■ Hillsdale County United Way
PO Box 203
Hillsdale, MI 49242
Ph: (517)439-5050
Fax: (517)439-5058
E-mail: hcuw@frontiernet.net
URL: http://www.hillsdalecountyunitedway.org
Contact: Pia Seebach-York, Exec.Dir.
Local. Affiliated With: United Way of America.

8178 ■ Hillsdale Lions Club
c/o Lisa M. Begley, Pres.
16 Goodrich St.
Hillsdale, MI 49242
Ph: (517)437-5164 (517)439-1154
E-mail: lmbegley@comsast.com
URL: http://www.lionsdistrict11b1.org/lc_hillsdale.htm
Contact: Lisa M. Begley, Pres.
Local. Affiliated With: Lions Clubs International.

8179 ■ Hillsdale - Wyldlife
212 N Manning
Hillsdale, MI 49242
Ph: (517)437-5943
URL: http://sites.younglife.org/_layouts/ylext/default.aspx?ID=C-1134
Local. Affiliated With: Young Life.

8180 ■ Hillsdale - Young Life
212 N Manning
Hillsdale, MI 49242
Ph: (517)437-5943
URL: http://sites.younglife.org/_layouts/ylext/default.aspx?ID=C-1133
Local. Affiliated With: Young Life.

8181 ■ Jelly Jammers
c/o Janet Lee, Pres.
4300 W Bacon Rd.
Hillsdale, MI 49242-8205
E-mail: dequiltbear@aol.com
URL: National Affiliate–www.fohbc.com
Contact: Janet Lee, Pres.
Local. Affiliated With: Federation of Historical Bottle Collectors.

8182 ■ Jonesville Wyld Life - Wyldlife
212 N Manning
Hillsdale, MI 49242
Ph: (517)437-5943
URL: http://sites.younglife.org/_layouts/ylext/default.aspx?ID=C-4326
Local. Affiliated With: Young Life.

8183 ■ Michigan Coin Laundry Association (MICLA)
c/o Cameron Mitchell
164 Lewis St.
Hillsdale, MI 49242
Ph: (517)437-2789
E-mail: cjmitchell@earthlink.net
URL: National Affiliate–www.coinlaundry.org
Contact: Cameron Mitchell, Contact
State. Affiliated With: Coin Laundry Association.

8184 ■ Psi Chi, National Honor Society in Psychology - Hillsdale College
c/o Dept. of Psychology
33 E Coll. St.
Hillsdale, MI 49242-1298
Ph: (517)437-7341
E-mail: fritz.tsao@hillsdale.edu
URL: http://www.psichi.org/chapters/info.asp?chapter_id=429
Contact: Frederick Tsao PhD, Advisor
Local.

8185 ■ Young Life Hillsdale
212 N Manning
Hillsdale, MI 49242
Ph: (517)437-5943
URL: http://sites.younglife.org/sites/Hillsdale/default.aspx
Local. Affiliated With: Young Life.

Holland

8186 ■ AAA Michigan
587 E 8th St.
Holland, MI 49423
Ph: (616)392-5171
Contact: Barbra Burgess, Contact
State.

8187 ■ Alzheimer's Association, West Michigan
225 W. 30th St.
Holland, MI 49423
Ph: (616)392-8365
Fax: (616)392-1712
Free: (800)893-8365
E-mail: janet.magennis@alz.org
Family members of sufferers of Alzheimer's disease. Combats Alzheimer's disease and related disorders. (Alzheimer's disease is a progressive, degenerative brain disease in which changes occur in the central nervous system and outer region of the brain causing memory loss and other changes in thought, personality, and behavior.) Promotes research to find the cause, treatment, and cure for the disease. **Affiliated With:** Alzheimer's Association.

8188 ■ American Cancer Society, Lakeshore Area Service Center
854 S Washington Ave., Ste.410
Holland, MI 49423
Ph: (616)396-5576
Fax: (616)396-2673
E-mail: angela.luedke@cancer.org
URL: http://www.cancer.org
Contact: Angela Luedke, Contact
Local. Works to eliminate cancer as a major health problem through research, education, advocacy and service. **Affiliated With:** American Cancer Society.

8189 ■ American Guild of Organists, Holland Area C556
c/o Elizabeth Claar, CAGO, Dean
274 E 12th St.
Holland, MI 49423
Ph: (616)355-2297
E-mail: eclaar@musician.org
URL: http://www.agohq.org/chapters/hollandarea
Contact: Elizabeth Claar CAGO, Dean
Founded: 1985. **Members:** 40. **Local.** Promotes organ and choral music. **Affiliated With:** American Guild of Organists. **Also Known As:** Holland Area AGO. **Publications:** *Holland Area Ago News*, monthly. Newsletter. **Price:** included in membership dues.

8190 ■ American Institute of Aeronautics and Astronautics, Michigan
c/o Andrew Santangelo
Michigan Technic Corp.
376 Howard Ave.
Holland, MI 49424
E-mail: andrew_santangelo@mac.com
URL: National Affiliate–www.aiaa.org/
Contact: Andrew Santangelo, Contact
State. Affiliated With: American Institute of Aeronautics and Astronautics.

8191 ■ American Legion, Michigan Post 6
c/o Willard G. Leenhouts
PO Box 1463
Holland, MI 49422
Ph: (517)371-4720
Fax: (517)371-2401
URL: National Affiliate–www.legion.org
Contact: Willard G. Leenhouts, Contact
Local. Affiliated With: American Legion.

8192 ■ American Red Cross of Ottawa County
270 James St.
Holland, MI 49424
Ph: (616)396-6545
Fax: (616)396-3921
E-mail: arcinfo@ottawaredcross.org
URL: http://ottawaredcross.org
Contact: Sindee Maxwell, Exec.Dir.
Founded: 1909. **Members:** 509. **Staff:** 6. **Local.** Provides relief to victims of disasters and helps people prevent, prepare for, and respond to emergencies. **Departments:** Armed Forces Emergency Services; Disaster Preparedness and Relief; Health and Safety Services; Volunteer. **Publications:** *Red Cross Winds*, quarterly. Newsletter.

8193 ■ Association for Computing Machinery, Hope College
c/o Chris Johnson, Chair
Dept. of Cmpt. Sci.
27 Graves Pl.
Holland, MI 49422-9000

Ph: (616)395-7508
Fax: (616)395-7123
E-mail: dershem@cs.hope.edu
URL: National Affiliate–www.acm.org
Contact: Chris Johnson, Chair
Local. Biological, medical, behavioral, and computer scientists; hospital administrators; programmers and others interested in application of computer methods to biological, behavioral, and medical problems. Stimulates understanding of the use and potential of computers in the Biosciences. **Affiliated With:** Association for Computing Machinery.

8194 ■ Boys and Girls Club of Greater Holland
435 VanRaalte
Holland, MI 49423-3941
Ph: (616)392-4102
URL: http://www.bgch.org
Contact: Andy Page, Exec.Dir.
Local.

8195 ■ Children's Resource Network 4-C (CRN)
710 Chicago Dr., No. 250
Holland, MI 49423
Ph: (616)396-8151
Fax: (616)396-4349
Free: (800)332-5049
E-mail: crn@crn.nu
URL: http://www.crn.nu
Contact: Jim Welsh, Exec.Dir.
Founded: 1971. **Local**.

8196 ■ Grand Valley Orchid Society (GVOS)
c/o Judi Manning, Ed.
17012 Lakeview Dr.
Holland, MI 49424
E-mail: gvos@macatawa.org
URL: http://www.macatawa.org/~gvos
Contact: Judi Manning, Ed.
Local. Aims to promote, carry on, and aid in every possible way the development, improvement and preservation of orchids of all kinds. **Affiliated With:** American Orchid Society.

8197 ■ Great Lakes SAAB Club
c/o Jim Laman
617 Beechwood
Holland, MI 49423
Ph: (616)335-5215
E-mail: lamanjim@juno.com
URL: National Affiliate–www.saabclub.com
Contact: Jim Laman, Contact
Founded: 1984. **Members:** 125. **Regional**. Seeks to promote the enjoyment and preservation of Saab automobiles and to meet others who share this common interest. **Affiliated With:** Saab Club of North America.

8198 ■ Greater Ottawa County United Way
PO Box 1349
Holland, MI 49422-1349
Ph: (616)842-7130 (616)396-7811
Free: (800)VOLUNTEER
E-mail: info@gouwvc.org
URL: http://www.gouwvc.org
Contact: Sylvia Geisler, Pres.
Local. Affiliated With: United Way of America.

8199 ■ Hamilton - Young Life
680 Washington, Ste.3
Holland, MI 49423
Ph: (616)392-6555
URL: http://sites.younglife.org/sites/hamiltonhigh/default.aspx
Local. Affiliated With: Young Life.

8200 ■ Holland Area Chamber of Commerce (HACC)
272 E 8th St.
Holland, MI 49423
Ph: (616)392-2389
Fax: (616)392-7379
E-mail: info@hollandchamber.org
URL: http://www.hollandchamber.org
Contact: Jane Clark, Pres.
Founded: 1914. **Members:** 1,400. **Membership Dues:** basic, $260. **Staff:** 12. **Local**. Promotes business and community development in the Holland, MI area. **Computer Services:** Mailing lists, mailing lists of members. **Telecommunication Services:** 24-hour hotline, lived-answered customer care and easy to read invoices. **Committees:** Ambassadors; Environment and Infrastructure; Governmental Affairs; Health Workforce; Meetings; Small Business; Technology. **Publications:** *Chamber Newsletter*, monthly • Membership Directory, annual.

8201 ■ Holland Christian - Young Life
680 Washington, Ste.3
Holland, MI 49423
Ph: (616)392-6555 (616)540-4172
E-mail: joegrahamyl@gmail.com
URL: http://sites.younglife.org/sites/HollandChristian/default.aspx
Contact: Joe Graham, Contact
Local. Affiliated With: Young Life.

8202 ■ Holland Convention and Visitor's Bureau
76 E Eighth St.
Holland, MI 49423
Ph: (616)394-0000
Fax: (616)394-0122
Free: (800)506-1299
E-mail: info@holland.org
URL: http://www.holland.org
Contact: Sally Laukitis, Contact
Founded: 1985. **Staff:** 5. **Budget:** $373,000. **Regional Groups:** 1. **State Groups:** 1. **Nonmembership**. **Local**. Promotes convention business and tourism in area. **Formerly:** (2005) Holland Area +Convention and +Visitors Bureau. **Publications:** *Holland Area Visitor Guide*, periodic. **Circulation:** 500,000. **Advertising:** accepted • Brochures, periodic. **Conventions/Meetings:** periodic convention • periodic meeting.

8203 ■ Holland High - Young Life
680 Washington, Ste.3
Holland, MI 49423
Ph: (616)392-6555
URL: http://sites.younglife.org/sites/Hollanddutch/default.aspx
Local. Affiliated With: Young Life.

8204 ■ Holland - Wyldlife
680 Washington, Ste.3
Holland, MI 49423
Ph: (616)392-6555
URL: http://sites.younglife.org/sites/hollandwyldLife/default.aspx
Local. Affiliated With: Young Life.

8205 ■ Hopkins - Young Life
680 Washington, Ste.3
Holland, MI 49423
Ph: (616)392-6555
URL: http://sites.younglife.org/_layouts/ylext/default.aspx?ID=C-1098
Local. Affiliated With: Young Life.

8206 ■ Lakeshore Human Resources Management Association
PO Box 1242
Holland, MI 49422
E-mail: bmitchell@hollandhospice.org
URL: http://lhrma.org
Contact: Bridget Mitchell, Contact
Local. Represents the interests of human resource and industrial relations professionals and executives. Promotes the advancement of human resource management.

8207 ■ Local 705, RWDSU District Council of the UFCW
412 W 24th St.
Holland, MI 49423
Ph: (616)396-6953
URL: National Affiliate–www.ufcw.org
Local. Affiliated With: United Food and Commercial Workers International Union.

8208 ■ Local 822, RWDSU District Council of the UFCW
412 W 24th St.
Holland, MI 49423
Ph: (616)392-3822
URL: National Affiliate–www.ufcw.org
Local. Affiliated With: United Food and Commercial Workers International Union.

8209 ■ Macatawa Greenway Partnership
c/o Ken Freestone
112 E 7th St.
Holland, MI 49423-3503
Ph: (616)396-2353 (616)396-4253
Fax: (616)392-8879
Contact: Ken Freestone, Exec.Dir.
Founded: 1996. **Members:** 7. **Staff:** 1. **Budget:** $100,000. **Local Groups:** 1. **Local**. Committed to preserve and connect natural habitats, waterways, and open lands for people and wildlife in the greater Macatawa area. Helping to create the Macatawa Greenway Network. **Libraries: Type:** by appointment only. **Holdings:** articles, books, periodicals, reports. **Subjects:** greenways, land use. **Committees:** Action.

8210 ■ Michigan Communities In Schools (MCIS)
11172 Adams St.
Holland, MI 49423
Ph: (616)396-7566
Fax: (616)396-6893
E-mail: mail@lifeservicessystem.org
Contact: Deanna DePree, Dir.
Founded: 1994. **State. Affiliated With:** Communities in Schools.

8211 ■ Michigan Health Information Management Association, Southwest
c/o Lynn Helms, RHIA, Pres.
Zeeland Community
529 Douglas Ave., Apt. 13
Holland, MI 49424
Ph: (616)772-7561 (616)392-3372
Fax: (616)772-5760
E-mail: lhelms@zch.org
URL: http://www.mhima.org
Contact: Lynn Helms RHIA, Pres.
Local. Represents the interests of individuals dedicated to the effective management of personal health information needed to deliver quality healthcare to the public. Provides career, professional development and practice resources. Sets standards for education and certification. Advocates public policy that advances Health Information Management (HIM) practice. **Affiliated With:** American Health Information Management Association; Michigan Health Information Management Association.

8212 ■ National Association of Rocketry - US Aerospace Challenge
c/o Steve Redmond
1121 Ottawa Beach Rd.
Holland, MI 49424
Ph: (616)399-4045
E-mail: sredmond@chartermi.net
URL: National Affiliate–www.nar.org
Contact: Steve Redmond, Contact
Regional.

8213 ■ National Association of Student Personnel Administrators, Michigan
c/o Richard Frost, Coor.
Hope Coll.
100 E 8th St., Ste.210
Holland, MI 49423
Ph: (616)395-7940
Fax: (616)395-7183
E-mail: frost@hope.edu
URL: National Affiliate–www.naspa.org
Contact: Richard Frost, Coor.
State. Provides professional development and advocacy for student affairs educators and administrators. Seeks to promote, assess and support student learning through leadership. **Affiliated**

With: National Association of Student Personnel Administrators.

8214 ■ Ottawa and Allegan Counties Youth for Christ
PO Box 2121
Holland, MI 49422
Ph: (616)392-1479
Fax: (616)392-1988
URL: http://www.ghyfc.org
Local. Affiliated With: Youth for Christ/U.S.A.

8215 ■ Ottawa County Medical Society
59 Forest Hills Dr.
Holland, MI 49424
Ph: (616)738-6094
E-mail: hare@wmol.com
URL: http://www.msms.org
Contact: Harriet VanHeest, Admin.Asst.
Local. Advances the art and science of medicine. Promotes patient care and the betterment of public health. **Affiliated With:** Michigan State Medical Society.

8216 ■ PFLAG Holland/Lakeshore
PO Box 1246
Holland, MI 49422
Ph: (616)494-0765
Fax: (616)399-2161
E-mail: pflaghols@juno.com
URL: http://www.pflag.org/Michigan.216.0.html
Local. Affiliated With: Parents, Families, and Friends of Lesbians and Gays.

8217 ■ Phi Beta Kappa, Hope College
c/o Kelly T. Osborne
PO Box 9000
Holland, MI 49422-9000
Ph: (616)395-7761
URL: http://www.hope.edu
Contact: Prof. Kelly T. Osborne, Sec.-Treas.
Local. Affiliated With: Phi Betá Kappa.

8218 ■ Psi Chi, National Honor Society in Psychology - Hope College
c/o Dept. of Psychology
Sci. Ctr.
35 E 12th St.
Holland, MI 49422-9000
Ph: (616)395-7730
Fax: (616)395-7121
E-mail: psych@hope.edu
URL: http://www.hope.edu/academic/psychology/info/psichi.htm
Local. Affiliated With: Psi Chi, National Honor Society in Psychology.

8219 ■ Saugatuck - Young Life
680 Washington, Ste.3
Holland, MI 49423
Ph: (616)392-6555
URL: http://sites.younglife.org/_layouts/ylext/default.aspx?ID=C-1099
Local. Affiliated With: Young Life.

8220 ■ Shoreline Amateur Astronomy Association (SAAA)
c/o Mark Logsdon, VP and Chm.
183 E 28th St.
Holland, MI 49423
Ph: (616)399-3448
E-mail: mlogsdon@triton.net
Contact: Mark Logsdon, VP and Chm.
Local. Affiliated With: Astronomical League.

8221 ■ Skaters Edge of West Michigan
4444 N Holland Ave.
Holland, MI 49424
Ph: (616)738-0733
E-mail: kjhall28@hotmail.com
URL: http://www.skatersedgewmi.com
Local. Provides programs to encourage participation and achievement in the sport of figure skating on ice. Defines and maintains uniform standards of skating proficiency. Organizes and sponsors competitions and exhibitions for the purpose of stimulating interest in figure skating. **Affiliated With:** United States Figure Skating Association.

8222 ■ Vietnam Veterans of America, Chapter No. 73
c/o Bob Erickson
PO Box 1705
Holland, MI 49423-1705
Ph: (616)755-1029
E-mail: reric66139@cs.com
URL: http://www.vvoachapters.org/Chapter73
Contact: Bob Erickson, Contact
Local. Affiliated With: Vietnam Veterans of America.

8223 ■ West Michigan Chapter of the APA
c/o USF Holland Inc.
750 E 40th St.
Holland, MI 49423
Ph: (616)395-5044
E-mail: jim.bolek@usfc.com
URL: http://www.apawestmichigan.org
Contact: Jim Bolek, Pres.
Local. Aims to increase the Payroll Professional's skill level through education and mutual support. Represents the Payroll Professional before legislative bodies. Administers the certified payroll professional program of recognition. Provides public service education on payroll and employment issues. **Affiliated With:** American Payroll Association.

8224 ■ West Michigan District of Precision Metalforming Association
c/o Barb Bott, Administrator
Trans-Matic Mfg. Co., Inc.
300 E 48th St.
Holland, MI 49423-5301
Ph: (616)820-2457
Fax: (616)820-2464
E-mail: bbott@transmatic.com
URL: http://wmichigan.pma.org
Contact: Barb Bott, Administrator
Local. Promotes and safeguards the interests of the metalforming industry. Conducts technical and educational programs. Provides legislative and regulatory assistance to members. **Affiliated With:** Precision Metalforming Association.

8225 ■ West Ottawa - Wyldlife
680 Washington, Ste.3
Holland, MI 49423
Ph: (616)392-6555
URL: http://sites.younglife.org/_layouts/ylext/default.aspx?ID=C-2847
Local. Affiliated With: Young Life.

8226 ■ West Ottawa Young Life
680 Washington, Ste.3
Holland, MI 49423
Ph: (616)392-6555
E-mail: meredithcb@juno.com
URL: http://sites.younglife.org/sites/WestOttawa/default.aspx
Contact: Meredith Bulkeley, Contact
Local. Affiliated With: Young Life.

8227 ■ Western Michigan Planned Giving Group (WMPGG)
c/o Kathi Bates
Holland Christian Schools
956 Ottawa Ave.
Holland, MI 49423
Ph: (616)820-2805
Fax: (616)820-2810
E-mail: kbates@hollandchristian.org
URL: http://www.wmpgg.org
Contact: Kathi Bates, Dir.
Membership Dues: local chapter, $40 (annual) • national group, $140 (annual) • local and national, $140 (annual). **Local. Affiliated With:** National Committee on Planned Giving.

8228 ■ Young Life Holland
680 Washington, Ste.3
Holland, MI 49423
Ph: (616)392-6555
Fax: (616)392-6588
URL: http://sites.younglife.org/sites/Holland/default.aspx
Local. Affiliated With: Young Life.

8229 ■ Young Life West Ottawa-Zeeland
680 Washington, Ste.3
Holland, MI 49423
Ph: (616)392-6555
Fax: (616)392-6588
URL: http://sites.younglife.org/sites/WOZ/default.aspx
Contact: Tony DiLaura, Contact
Local. Affiliated With: Young Life.

8230 ■ Zeeland - Wyldlife
680 Washington, Ste.3
Holland, MI 49423
Ph: (616)392-6555
URL: http://sites.younglife.org/_layouts/ylext/default.aspx?ID=C-2846
Local. Affiliated With: Young Life.

8231 ■ Zeeland - Young Life
680 Washington, Ste.3
Holland, MI 49423
Ph: (616)392-6555
URL: http://sites.younglife.org/sites/Zeeland/default.aspx
Contact: Tony DiLaura, Area Dir.
Local. Affiliated With: Young Life.

Holly

8232 ■ American Association for Medical Transcription, Mid-Michigan Chapter
c/o Ellyn G. Serra, CMT, FAAMT, Pres.
18105 Ottieway Ct.
Holly, MI 48442
E-mail: egserra@speed2u.net
URL: http://www.aamt.org/ca/mmc
Contact: Ellyn G. Serra CMT, Pres.
Local. Works to represent and advance the profession of medical transcription and its practitioners. **Affiliated With:** American Association for Medical Transcription.

8233 ■ American Legion, Michigan Post 149
c/o Amel Schwartz
408 S Saginaw St.
Holly, MI 48442
Ph: (517)371-4720
Fax: (517)371-2401
URL: National Affiliate–www.legion.org
Contact: Amel Schwartz, Contact
Local. Affiliated With: American Legion.

8234 ■ Four Seasons Bonsai Club of Michigan
7480 E Holly Rd.
Holly, MI 48442-9603
E-mail: jimantique@aol.com
URL: http://www.fourseasonsbonsai.org
Contact: Jimmy WhiteLey, Pres.
Local. Affiliated With: Bonsai Clubs International.

8235 ■ Groveland Township Firefighters and Dive Team Association
14645 Dixie Hwy.
Holly, MI 48442-9631
Ph: (248)634-7722 (248)627-9955
Fax: (248)634-0600
URL: http://www.grovelandfire.org
Contact: Chief Steve McGee, Head
Members: 48. **Local.** Provides advanced life support treatment and transportation service to the people of Groveland Township. Protects over 7 miles of Interstate 75.

8236 ■ Holly Area Chamber of Commerce
PO Box 214
Holly, MI 48442
Ph: (248)634-1900
Fax: (248)634-1049
E-mail: staff@hollymi.com
Contact: Thomas McKenney, Pres.
Membership Dues: business (based on number of employees), $175-$300 (annual) • concerned citizen, $75 (annual) • nonprofit, church, $100 (annual) • school, government, $275 (annual). **Local**. Strives to facilitate new business networking, promote communication among existing business and support the development of the community.

8237 ■ Michigan Chapter of National Association of Tax Practitioners
3404 Mitchell Rd
Holly, MI 48442
Ph: (248)634-2100
Fax: (248)634-2106
E-mail: tcglenmitchell@yahoo.com
URL: National Affiliate–www.natptax.com
Contact: Glen Mitchell, Pres.
Local. Affiliated With: National Association of Tax Professionals.

8238 ■ Michigan National Wild Turkey Federation, North Oakland Gobblers
7328 Groveland Rd.
Holly, MI 48442
Ph: (248)240-5996
E-mail: jmkubiak@aol.com
URL: http://www.mi-nwtf.org/north_oakland.htm
Contact: Marei Kubiak, Pres.
Local.

Holt

8239 ■ American Legion, Buck-Reasoner Post 238
4294 Veterans Dr.
Holt, MI 48842
Ph: (517)371-4720
Fax: (517)371-2401
URL: National Affiliate–www.legion.org
Local. Affiliated With: American Legion.

8240 ■ Holt Lions Club
c/o Kevin Storberg, Pres.
2287 Rolling Ridge Ln.
Holt, MI 48842-8720
Ph: (517)694-6394
E-mail: k.storbert@comcast.net
URL: http://www.district11c2.org
Contact: Kevin Storberg, Pres.
Local. Affiliated With: Lions Clubs International.

8241 ■ Michigan Association for Computer Users in Learning (MACUL)
PO Box 518
Holt, MI 48842-0518
Ph: (517)694-9756
Fax: (517)694-9773
E-mail: macul@macul.org
URL: http://www.macul.org
Contact: Mr. Ric Wiltse, Exec.Dir.
Founded: 1975. **Members:** 5,000. **Membership Dues:** $40 (annual). **Staff:** 4. **Budget:** $1,000,000. **State**. Technology using educators. Provides for the sharing of best practices of technology to enhance teaching and learning. Sponsors local and state conferences, awards, and grants, and implements other programs to promote effective use of educational technology. **Awards:** Technology Using-Educator of the Year. **Frequency:** annual. **Type:** grant. **Special Interest Groups:** Computer Science; Elementary Education; Logo; Multi-Media; Special Education; Technicians; Technology Coordinator; Telecommunications. **Affiliated With:** International Society for Technology in Education. **Publications:** *MACUL Newsletter*, bimonthly. Features columns related to educational computing and information about local and national events of interest to computer-using educators. **Price:** included in membership dues. **Advertising:** accepted. Alternate Formats: online. **Conventions/Meetings:** annual conference, with educational uses of computers and technology, featured speakers, workshops (exhibits) - always March.

8242 ■ Michigan Capitol Girl Scout Council
1974 Cedar St.
Holt, MI 48842
Ph: (517)699-9400
Fax: (517)699-9405
URL: http://www.gsmcc.net
Contact: Pam Sievers, Pres.
State.

8243 ■ Military Order of the Loyal Legion of the United States, Michigan Commandery (MI - MOLLUS)
c/o Mr. Keith G. Harrison, Past Commander
4209 Santa Clara Dr.
Holt, MI 48842-1868
Ph: (517)694-9394
E-mail: pcinc@prodigy.net
URL: http://suvcw.org/mollus/mi/mollus.html
Contact: Mr. Keith G. Harrison, Past Commander
Founded: 1885. **Membership Dues:** all, $25 (annual). **Budget:** $25. **State Groups:** 1. **State.** Seeks to foster military and naval science, promote allegiance to the United States government; to perpetuate the memory of those who fought to preserve the union; and to honor the memory and promote the ideals of President Abraham Lincoln. **Awards:** MOLLUS ROTC Award. **Frequency:** annual. **Type:** medal. **Recipient:** one Army, Air Force, and Navy ROTC Cadet per university (University of Michigan, Eastern Michigan University and Michigan State University); for scholarly excellence. **Computer Services:** Information services, Union Officer Military Records. **Affiliated With:** Military Order of the Loyal Legion of the United States. **Publications:** *Historical Journal of the Loyal Legion*, quarterly. Published by the National Organization of the Military Order of the Loyal Legion of the United States.

8244 ■ Summit Skating Club of Michigan
5175 Beaumaris Cir.
Holt, MI 48842
E-mail: juliehaubert@hotmail.com
URL: http://www.angelfire.com/sports/summitskatingclub
Local. Provides programs to encourage participation and achievement in the sport of figure skating on ice. Defines and maintains uniform standards of skating proficiency. Organizes and sponsors competitions and exhibitions for the purpose of stimulating interest in figure skating. **Affiliated With:** United States Figure Skating Association.

Holton

8245 ■ American Legion, Cobb-Trygstad-Anderson Post 397
9150 Holton Rd.
Holton, MI 49425
Ph: (517)371-4720
Fax: (517)371-2401
URL: National Affiliate–www.legion.org
Local. Affiliated With: American Legion.

Homer

8246 ■ Homer Lions Club - Michigan
c/o Alan E. Nelson, Pres.
26441 J Dr. S
Homer, MI 49245
Ph: (517)568-4034
URL: http://www.lionsdistrict11b1.org/lc_homer.htm
Contact: Alan E. Nelson, Pres.
Local. Affiliated With: Lions Clubs International.

Honor

8247 ■ Honor Lions Club
PO Box 142
Honor, MI 49640
Ph: (231)882-7042
E-mail: bettyc@chartermi.net
URL: http://lions.silverthorn.biz/11-e1
Contact: James Mallison, Pres.
Local. Affiliated With: Lions Clubs International.

Houghton

8248 ■ American Chemical Society, Upper Peninsula Section
c/o Sarah A. Green, Chair
Michigan Technological Univ., Chemistry Dept.
1400 Townsend Dr.
Houghton, MI 49931-1200
Ph: (906)487-3419
Fax: (906)487-2061
E-mail: sgreen@mtu.edu
URL: National Affiliate–acswebcontent.acs.org
Contact: Sarah A. Green, Chair
Local. Represents the interests of individuals dedicated to the advancement of chemistry in all its branches. Provides opportunities for peer interaction and career development. **Affiliated With:** American Chemical Society.

8249 ■ Association for Computing Machinery, Michigan Technological University
1400 Townsend Dr.
Houghton, MI 49931-1295
Ph: (906)487-2209
Fax: (906)487-2283
E-mail: pop@mtu.edu
URL: http://www.sos.mtu.edu/acm
Contact: Nick Young, Sec.-Treas.
Local. Biological, medical, behavioral, and computer scientists; hospital administrators; programmers and others interested in application of computer methods to biological, behavioral, and medical problems. Stimulates understanding of the use and potential of computers in the biosciences. **Affiliated With:** Association for Computing Machinery.

8250 ■ Copper Country Cycling Club (C4)
106 Memorial Union Bldg.
1400 Townsend Dr.
Houghton, MI 49931
Ph: (906)370-4301
E-mail: cycling@mtu.edu
Contact: Jen Weber, Pres.
Membership Dues: general, $5 (annual). **Local. Affiliated With:** International Mountain Bicycling Association.

8251 ■ Copper Country Habitat for Humanity
PO Box 231
Houghton, MI 49931
Ph: (906)482-5376
E-mail: cchfh@pasty.com
URL: http://www.coppercountryh4h.org
Local. Affiliated With: Habitat for Humanity International.

8252 ■ Copper Country United Way
PO Box 104
Houghton, MI 49931
Ph: (906)482-3276
URL: National Affiliate–national.unitedway.org
Contact: Jan Woodbeck, Sec.
Founded: 1956. **Members:** 27. **Staff:** 1. **Local.** Works to assist in fundraising by conducting residential and company-wide employee campaigns and by encouraging corporate contributions. **Conventions/Meetings:** monthly board meeting.

8253 ■ Houghton-Portage Township Highschool Skating Club
1524 Brookside Dr.
Houghton, MI 49931
Ph: (906)482-1365
E-mail: csrichar@mtu.edu
URL: National Affiliate–www.usfigureskating.org
Contact: Carrie Richards, Contact

Local. Provides programs to encourage participation and achievement in the sport of figure skating on ice. Defines and maintains uniform standards of skating proficiency. Organizes and sponsors competitions and exhibitions for the purpose of stimulating interest in figure skating. **Affiliated With:** United States Figure Skating Association.

8254 ■ Isle Royale Natural History Association (IRNHA)
800 E Lakeshore Dr.
Houghton, MI 49931
Ph: (906)482-7860
Free: (800)678-6925
E-mail: irnha@irnha.org
URL: http://www.irnha.org
Contact: Jill Burkland, Exec.Dir.

Founded: 1957. **Members:** 1,000. **Staff:** 3. **Regional. Publications:** *Greenstone*. Newspaper • *Wolf's Eye*. Newsletter.

8255 ■ Keweenaw Peninsula Chamber of Commerce
902 Coll. Ave.
PO Box 336
Houghton, MI 49931-0336
Ph: (906)482-5240
Fax: (906)482-5241
Free: (866)304-5722
E-mail: info@keweenaw.org
URL: http://www.keweenaw.org
Contact: Mr. Richard L. Baker, Exec.Dir.

Founded: 1959. **Members:** 600. **Membership Dues:** general (additional $8 1-20 employees, $2 21-80 employees, $1 81 employees and up), $165 (annual) • financial (in deposits to $20000000, $25000000 in deposits to $21000000-$4000000, $10000000 in deposits to above 40000000), $35,000,000 (annual) • hotel-motel (plus $5 over 10 units), $165 (annual) • insurance, real state (plus $30 licensed sales employee, $8 non licensed), $165 (annual) • professional (plus $50 licensed professional partner, $8 non-licensed), $165 (annual) • utility ($80-1000 connected costumers), $165 (annual) • associate (individual), $55 (annual). **Staff:** 4. **Budget:** $140,000. **Local**. Promotes business and community development in Houghton and Keweenaw counties, MI. Promotes tourism. Sponsors Strassenfest. **Awards:** Honorary. **Frequency:** annual. **Type:** recognition • Person of the Year. **Frequency:** annual. **Type:** recognition • Sparkplug. **Frequency:** annual. **Type:** recognition. **Publications:** *Chamber Update*, monthly. Newsletter. Six-page newsletter for members. **Price:** part of membership benefits. **Circulation:** 650 • *Keweenaw Peninsula Chamber of Commerce Membership Directory*, annual. **Conventions/Meetings:** Business After Hours Forum - meeting - 10/year • annual meeting.

8256 ■ Michigan Technological University National Organization for the Reform of Marijuana Laws
c/o Joshua Luther
106 Memorial Union Bldg.
1400 Townsend Dr.
Houghton, MI 49931-1295
E-mail: norml-l@mtu.edu
URL: National Affiliate–www.norml.org

Local. Seeks a more reasonable treatment for marijuana consumers in federal, state, and local laws and policies. Provides speakers for interested groups. Collects and disseminates educational materials. **Affiliated With:** National Organization for the Reform of Marijuana Laws.

8257 ■ Michigan Technological University Synchronized Skating Club (MTUSSC)
106 Memorial Bldg.
1400 Townsend Dr.
Houghton, MI 49931
Ph: (906)487-2994
E-mail: mtuskating@hotmail.com
URL: http://www.sos.mtu.edu/skate
Contact: Kristin Susens, Pres.

Local. Provides programs to encourage participation and achievement in the sport of figure skating on ice. Defines and maintains uniform standards of skating proficiency. Organizes and sponsors competitions and exhibitions for the purpose of stimulating interest in figure skating. **Affiliated With:** United States Figure Skating Association.

8258 ■ MTU Fencing Club
c/o Jon Jelsma
187 Dhh 1700 Townsend Dr.
Houghton, MI 49931
E-mail: jgjelsma@mtu.edu
URL: http://www.sos.mtu.edu/fencing

Local. Amateur fencers. **Affiliated With:** United States Fencing Association.

8259 ■ National Active and Retired Federal Employees Association - Lake Superior 1254
604 4th St.
Houghton, MI 49931-2311
Ph: (906)482-4674
URL: National Affiliate–www.narfe.org
Contact: Janice A. Anderson, Contact

Local. Protects the retirement future of employees through education. Informs members on issues affecting the retirement. **Affiliated With:** National Association of Retired Federal Employees.

8260 ■ PFLAG Keweenaw
22229 Royalewood Rd.
Houghton, MI 49931
Ph: (906)482-4357
E-mail: keweenawpflag@yahoo.com
URL: http://www.pflag.org/Michigan.216.0.html

Local. Affiliated With: Parents, Families, and Friends of Lesbians and Gays.

8261 ■ Society for Industrial Archeology (SIA)
c/o Dr. Patrick Martin, Exec.Sec.
Dept. of Social Sciences
Michigan Technological Univ.
1400 Townsend Dr.
Houghton, MI 49931
Ph: (906)487-1889 (906)487-2070
Fax: (906)487-2468
E-mail: pem-194@mtu.edu
URL: http://www.sia-web.org
Contact: Dr. Patrick Martin, Exec.Sec.

Founded: 1971. **Members:** 1,800. **Membership Dues:** individual, $35 (annual). **Staff:** 3. **Budget:** $100,000. **Regional Groups:** 6. **Regional**. Encourages the study, interpretation and preservation of historically significant industrial sites, structures, artifacts, and technology through publications, conferences, tours, and projects. Promotes the study and preservation of the physical survivals of technological and industrial development and change. Conducts a forum for the discussion and exchange of information. Advances an awareness and appreciation of the value of preserving the industrial heritage. Seeks to raise awareness among communities, public agencies, and property owners about the advantages of preserving the landscapes, structures, and equipment of significance in the history of technology, engineering, and industry, through continued or adaptive reuse. **Awards:** General Tools Award. **Frequency:** annual. **Type:** trophy. **Recipient:** for contributions to the field other than publication. **Computer Services:** Online services, publication sales, registration for meetings and events and publications. **Special Interest Groups:** Roebling Chapter in NY and NJ. **Publications:** *IA, Journal of the Society for Industrial Archeology*, biennial. Contains articles, book reviews and editorials. **Price:** $35.00. ISSN: 01601040. **Circulation:** 2,000. **Advertising:** accepted • *SIA Newsletter*, quarterly. Newsletters. Contains news regarding industrial heritage: events, schedule, exhibitions and others. **Price:** $35.00 included in membership benefits. **Circulation:** 2,000. **Conventions/Meetings:** annual conference and meeting, includes scholarly papers as well as tours of area, industrial heritage sites and active industries (exhibits) • annual Fall Tour, tour of industrial heritage sites and active industries.

8262 ■ Society of Manufacturing Engineers - Michigan Technological Univ. S077
815 R.L. Smith Bldg., 1400 Townsend Dr.
Houghton, MI 49931
Ph: (906)487-1850
Fax: (906)487-2822
E-mail: gparker@mtu.edu
URL: National Affiliate–www.sme.org
Contact: Gordon Parker, Contact

Local. Advances manufacturing knowledge to gain competitive advantage. Improves skills and manufacturing solutions for the growth of economy. Provides resources and opportunities for manufacturing professionals. **Affiliated With:** American Society of Naturalists.

8263 ■ Upper Peninsula Environmental Coalition (UPEC)
PO Box 673
Houghton, MI 49931
Ph: (906)524-7899
E-mail: srasch@up.net
URL: http://www.upenvironment.org
Contact: Ms. Susan Rasch, Bus.Mgr./Newsletter Ed.

Founded: 1972. **Members:** 375. **Membership Dues:** regular, $20 (annual) • supporting, $50 (annual) • student/low-income, $15 (annual). **Staff:** 1. **Local**.

Houghton Lake

8264 ■ Houghton Lake Chamber of Commerce (HLCC)
1625 W Houghton Lake Dr.
Houghton Lake, MI 48629
Ph: (989)366-5644
Fax: (989)366-9472
Free: (800)248-5253
E-mail: hlcc@houghtonlakemichigan.net
URL: http://www.houghtonlakechamber.org
Contact: Georgetta Garner, Contact

Local. Promotes business and community development in Houghton Lake, MI area. **Computer Services:** Information services, membership directory.

8265 ■ Michigan National Wild Turkey Federation, Houghton Lake Longbeards
4395 W Nestel
Houghton Lake, MI 48629
Ph: (517)366-4606
URL: http://www.mi-nwtf.org/HoughtonLakeLongbeards.htm
Contact: Mike Ignat, Pres.

Local.

Howard City

8266 ■ Howard City Lions Club
c/o Richard Stevens, Pres.
311 S Alder St.
Howard City, MI 49329
Ph: (231)937-4303 (231)937-7444
E-mail: mirhw@pathwaynet.com
URL: http://lions.silverthorn.biz/11-e1
Contact: Richard Stevens, Pres.

Local. Affiliated With: Lions Clubs International.

8267 ■ Police and Firemen's Insurance Association - Grand Rapids Fire Department
c/o Kathleen Thompson
8912 W Suwanee Trail
Howard City, MI 49329

Ph: (231)937-6009
URL: National Affiliate–www.pfia.net
Contact: Kathleen Thompson, Contact
Local. Affiliated With: Police and Firemen's Insurance Association.

8268 ■ Six Lakes Lions Club
c/o William Roscoe, Pres.
8191 Jones Rd.
Howard City, MI 49329
Ph: (231)937-5267
E-mail: billboy7@verizon.net
URL: http://lions.silverthorn.biz/11-e1
Contact: William Roscoe, Pres.
Local. Affiliated With: Lions Clubs International.

Howell

8269 ■ American Legion, Devereaux Post 141
3265 W Grand River Ave.
Howell, MI 48855
Ph: (517)371-4720
Fax: (517)371-2401
URL: National Affiliate–www.legion.org
Local. Affiliated With: American Legion.

8270 ■ American Red Cross of Livingston County
1372 W Grand River Ave.
Howell, MI 48843
Ph: (517)546-0326
Fax: (517)546-0886
URL: http://www.liv-redcross.org
Local.

8271 ■ APMI Michigan
c/o Richard L. Forbes
3849 W Marr Rd.
Howell, MI 48855-8719
Ph: (517)552-4901
Fax: (517)552-4901
E-mail: bulldogrealty@ameritech.net
URL: National Affiliate–www.mpif.org
Contact: Richard L. Forbes, Treas.
State. Maintains speakers' bureau and placement service. Serves the technical and informational needs of individuals interested or involved in the science and art of powder metallurgy. Provides the best source of information about the most up-to-date developments and advances in this dynamic, expanding technology through its publications, conferences and local section activities. **Affiliated With:** APMI International.

8272 ■ Arc Livingston
1004 Pinckney Rd., Ste.201
Howell, MI 48843
Ph: (517)546-1228
E-mail: sboyd@arclivingston.org
URL: http://www.arclivingston.org
Contact: Sherri L. Boyd, Contact
Founded: 1954. **Local.** Seeks to ensure the rights of people with disabilities and build quality community life for them and their families. **Affiliated With:** Arc of the United States.

8273 ■ Big Brothers Big Sisters of Livingston County
1004 Pinckney Rd., Ste.203
Howell, MI 48843
Ph: (517)546-1140
Fax: (517)546-0092
E-mail: bbbslc@sbcglobal.net
URL: http://www.bbbslc.net
Contact: Shari Davis-Schoech, Exec.Dir.
Local. Works to provide quality-mentoring relationships between children and qualified adults and promote their development into competent, confident and caring individuals. **Affiliated With:** Big Brothers Big Sisters of America.

8274 ■ Detroit, Eastern Michigan and Northern Ohio Chapter, Pennsylvania Railroad Technical and Historical Society
c/o Mr. Floyd E. Foust, Sec.-Treas.
1174 Catherine's Way
Howell, MI 48843-7172
E-mail: floydefoust@aol.com
URL: National Affiliate–www.prrths.com
Contact: Mr. Floyd E. Foust, Sec.-Treas.
Regional. Brings together people who are interested in the history of the Pennsylvania Railroad. Promotes the preservation and recording of all information regarding the organization, operation, facilities and equipment of the Pennsylvania Railroad. **Affiliated With:** Pennsylvania Railroad Technical and Historical Society.

8275 ■ Howell Area Chamber of Commerce
123 E Washington St.
Howell, MI 48843
Ph: (517)546-3920
Fax: (517)546-4115
E-mail: pconvery@howell.org
URL: http://www.howell.org
Contact: Ms. Pat Convery, Pres.
Members: 900. **Membership Dues:** business (based on number of employees), $250-$895 (annual) • associate, $125 (annual) • organization, $150 (annual) • second business, $200 (annual). **Local.** Works to improve the business community through various programs and services. **Publications:** *Business Views*. Newsletter. Includes issues and events affecting business.

8276 ■ Howell Lions Club
c/o Kenneth Ridalls, Pres.
3083 Beattie Rd.
Howell, MI 48843-7401
Ph: (517)338-0254 (517)548-4082
E-mail: cridalls@htdconnect.com
URL: http://www.district11c2.org
Contact: Kenneth Ridalls, Pres.
Local. Affiliated With: Lions Clubs International.

8277 ■ Huron Valley Beagle Club
c/o Jeff Sikora
790 N Latson Rd.
Howell, MI 48843-8595
URL: National Affiliate–clubs.akc.org
Contact: Jeff Sikora, Contact
Local.

8278 ■ Livingston Association of Realtors
5380 E Grand River
Howell, MI 48843-9101
Ph: (517)546-8300
E-mail: carol@griffithrealty.com
URL: http://www.lar-michigan.com
Contact: Carol Griffith, Pres.
Local.

8279 ■ Livingston County Association of Realtors
5380 E Grand River
Howell, MI 48843
Ph: (517)546-8300
E-mail: brussell@michigangroup.com
URL: http://www.lar-michigan.com
Contact: William Russell, Pres.
Local. Strives to develop real estate business practices. Advocates the right to own, use and transfer real property. Provides a facility for professional development, research and exchange of information among members. **Affiliated With:** National Association of Realtors.

8280 ■ Livingston County Convention and Visitors Bureau
123 E Washington St.
Howell, MI 48843
Ph: (517)548-1795
Fax: (517)546-4115
Free: (800)686-8474
E-mail: info@lccvb.org
URL: http://www.lccvb.org
Contact: Barbara J. Barden, Exec.Dir.
Founded: 1991. **Members:** 20. **Staff:** 2. **Budget:** $80,000. **Local.** Promotes convention business and tourism in area. Provides free planning assistance for visitors, events, motorcoach tours and conventions. **Formerly:** (1998) Livingston County Visitors Bureau. **Publications:** *Golf Guide*, annual. Magazine. **Circulation:** 20,000 • *Visitors Guide*, annual. Magazine. **Price:** free. **Advertising:** accepted.

8281 ■ Livingston County Pheasants Forever
c/o Jim Witt
3635 Crandall Rd.
Howell, MI 48855
Ph: (517)546-8542
E-mail: lcpheasantsforever@earthlink.net
Contact: Ray Green, Contact
Local. Affiliated With: Pheasants Forever.

8282 ■ Michigan Christmas Tree Association (MCTA)
c/o Marsha Gray, Exec.Dir./Ed.
PO Box 377
Howell, MI 48844-0377
Fax: (517)545-4501
Free: (800)589-8733
E-mail: marsha@mcta.org
URL: http://www.mcta.org
Contact: Marsha Gray, Exec.Dir./Ed.
State. Affiliated With: National Christmas Tree Association. **Formerly:** (2005) National Christmas Tree Association, Michigan.

8283 ■ Michigan Medical Device Association (MMDA)
PO Box 170
Howell, MI 48844
Fax: (517)546-3356
Free: (800)930-5698
E-mail: info@mmda.org
URL: http://www.mmda.org
Contact: Mike Tanner, Pres.
Founded: 1993. **Members:** 50. **Membership Dues:** corporate, affiliate, $500 (annual). **Staff:** 1. **Budget:** $25,000. **State.** Aims to promote and support the medical device industry in Michigan. Conducts government relations' activities, training workshops, networking/speaker luncheons and education. **Committees:** Government Relations; Programs. **Affiliated With:** Advanced Medical Technology Association; Medical Device Manufacturers Association. **Formerly:** (1999) Michigan Medical Device Manufacturers and Suppliers Association. **Publications:** Newsletter, quarterly. Provides information on association and industry in Michigan. **Price:** free. **Circulation:** 500. **Advertising:** accepted. **Conventions/Meetings:** annual Michigan Medical Device Expo - trade show (exhibits) - always May in Lansing, MI • monthly workshop (exhibits).

8284 ■ Michigan National Wild Turkey Federation, Livingston Longbeards
1948 N Hacker
Howell, MI 48843
Ph: (517)552-8521
URL: http://www.mi-nwtf.org/Livingston.htm
Contact: Paul Camilleri, Pres.
Local.

8285 ■ USA Weightlifting - Atomic Athletic Club
c/o Roger LaPointe
PO Box 183
Howell, MI 48844
Ph: (517)766-2223
URL: National Affiliate–www.usaweightlifting.org
Contact: Roger LaPointe, Contact
Local. Affiliated With: USA Weightlifting.

Hubbardston

8286 ■ American Legion, Michigan Post 182
c/o Walter T. Roach
PO Box 182
Hubbardston, MI 48845

Ph: (517)371-4720
Fax: (517)371-2401
URL: National Affiliate–www.legion.org
Contact: Walter T. Roach, Contact
Local. Affiliated With: American Legion.

Hubbell

8287 ■ American Legion, Rheault-Cavis-Moilanen Post 291
52290 Duncan Ave.
Hubbell, MI 49934
Ph: (517)371-4720
Fax: (517)371-2401
URL: National Affiliate–www.legion.org
Local. Affiliated With: American Legion.

Hudson

8288 ■ American Legion, Hannan-Colvin Post 180
16113 Cadmus Rd.
Hudson, MI 49247
Ph: (517)371-4720
Fax: (517)371-2401
URL: National Affiliate–www.legion.org
Local. Affiliated With: American Legion.

8289 ■ Hudson Area Chamber of Commerce
300 W Main St.
Hudson, MI 49247
Ph: (517)448-6666
URL: http://www.hudsonmich.com
Contact: Brian Golden, Pres.
Local. Supports Hudson Business District.

Hudsonville

8290 ■ Hudsonville Area Chamber of Commerce (HACC)
PO Box 216
Hudsonville, MI 49426
Ph: (616)662-0900
Fax: (616)662-4557
E-mail: hcc@netpenny.net
Contact: Laurie Van Haitsma, Dir.
Founded: 1979. **Members:** 110. **Membership Dues:** $115 (annual). **Staff:** 2. **Local.** Businesses and individuals seeking to promote economic and community development in the Hudsonville, MI area. **Convention/Meeting:** none. **Publications:** *Hudsonville Area Chamber of Commerce Profile*, periodic. Directory. **Advertising:** accepted • *Progress Report*, bimonthly.

8291 ■ Mercedes-Benz Club of America of the Western Michigan Section
5489 32nd Ave.
Hudsonville, MI 49426
Ph: (616)662-7473
E-mail: risesales@aol.com
URL: http://www.wmmbca.org/index.html
Contact: Jim Luikens, Pres.
Local. Affiliated With: Mercedes-Benz Club of America.

8292 ■ Michigan Celery Promotion Cooperative (MCPC)
c/o Duane Frens, Gen.Mgr.
PO Box 306
Hudsonville, MI 49426
Ph: (616)669-1250
Fax: (616)669-2890
URL: http://www.michigancelery.com
Founded: 1951. **State.**

8293 ■ Ottawa County Beagle Club
c/o Phil Hoezee
4004 48th Ave.
Hudsonville, MI 49426-9408
URL: National Affiliate–clubs.akc.org
Contact: Phil Hoezee, Contact
Local.

Hulbert

8294 ■ American Legion, Barrus-Mc-Culligh-Stewart Post 393
PO Box 21
Hulbert, MI 49748
Ph: (517)371-4720
Fax: (517)371-2401
URL: National Affiliate–www.legion.org
Local. Affiliated With: American Legion.

Huntington Woods

8295 ■ Detroit University/New Gratiot Lions Club
c/o Robert Beggs, Pres.
10554 Elgin Ave.
Huntington Woods, MI 48070
Ph: (248)546-4183
URL: http://www.metrodetroitlions.org
Contact: Robert Beggs, Pres.
Local. Affiliated With: Lions Clubs International.

8296 ■ Motor City Striders
c/o Edward H. Kozloff, Dr.
10144 Lincoln
Huntington Woods, MI 48070
Ph: (248)544-9099
E-mail: run@motorcitystriders.com
URL: http://www.motorcitystriders.com
Contact: Dr. Edward H. Kozloff, Contact
Founded: 1959. **Members:** 1,100. **Membership Dues:** individual, $15 (annual). **Local.** Promotes health, fitness and helps raise money for a dozen different charities in Southeastern Michigan. **Publications:** *Racebreak*, quarterly. Newsletter.

8297 ■ National Association of Miniature Enthusiasts - Dollhouse Divas
c/o Amy Shapiro
10834 Talbot Ave.
Huntington Woods, MI 48070
E-mail: ashapiro@shaareyzedek.org
URL: http://www.miniatures.org/states/MI.html
Contact: Amy Shapiro, Contact
Local. Affiliated With: National Association of Miniature Enthusiasts.

Ida

8298 ■ American Legion, Michigan Post 514
c/o Lynn C. Weeman
PO Box 141
Ida, MI 48140
Ph: (517)371-4720
Fax: (517)371-2401
URL: National Affiliate–www.legion.org
Contact: Lynn C. Weeman, Contact
Local. Affiliated With: American Legion.

8299 ■ Bedford - Young Life
PO Box 94
Ida, MI 48140-0094
Ph: (734)777-8133
URL: http://sites.younglife.org/_layouts/ylext/default.aspx?ID=C-1142
Local. Affiliated With: Young Life.

8300 ■ Erie Mason - Young Life
PO Box 94
Ida, MI 48140-0094
Ph: (734)777-8133
URL: http://sites.younglife.org/_layouts/ylext/default.aspx?ID=C-3401
Local. Affiliated With: Young Life.

8301 ■ Ida - Young Life
PO Box 94
Ida, MI 48140-0094
Ph: (734)777-8133
URL: http://sites.younglife.org/_layouts/ylext/default.aspx?ID=C-1143
Local. Affiliated With: Young Life.

8302 ■ Monroe County Young Life
PO Box 94
Ida, MI 48140-0094
Ph: (734)777-8133
Fax: (734)269-6263
URL: http://sites.younglife.org/sites/monroecounty/default.aspx
Local. Affiliated With: Young Life.

8303 ■ Monroe - Young Life
PO Box 94
Ida, MI 48140-0094
Ph: (734)777-8133
URL: http://sites.younglife.org/_layouts/ylext/default.aspx?ID=C-1145
Local. Affiliated With: Young Life.

Idlewild

8304 ■ American Legion, Idlewild American Legion Post 263
PO Box 289
Idlewild, MI 49642
Ph: (517)371-4720
Fax: (517)371-2401
URL: National Affiliate–www.legion.org
Local. Affiliated With: American Legion.

8305 ■ Lake County Merry Makers
PO Box 221
Idlewild, MI 49642
Ph: (231)745-2233
E-mail: rfwmabel@carrinter.net
URL: http://www.historicidlewild.com/index.html
Contact: Freddie Mitchell, Pres.
Founded: 1991. **Members:** 12. **Membership Dues:** $30 (annual). **Local.** Persons subscribing to the objectives of the organization, actively participating in activities, submitting desire to become a member and being voted in by the membership. Works in conjunction with the Lake County Enterprise Community Board and Fivecap, Inc. to establish an Idlewild historic and cultural center to display and build on the Afro-American cultural traditions of the area, and to encourage and provide affordable cultural enrichment for the community that will foster appreciation for Afro-American contributions to society. Activities include sponsoring "Friends of Historic Idlewild", a fund-raising arm of the center; operating the future home of the historic and cultural center; and sponsoring the Idlewild drill team. The center is also part of the economic development strategic plan to create an end destination resort to attract and encourage tourism in the area.

Imlay City

8306 ■ American Legion, Michigan Post 135
c/o Harry F. Hovey
212 E 3rd St.
Imlay City, MI 48444
Ph: (517)371-4720
Fax: (517)371-2401
URL: National Affiliate–www.legion.org
Contact: Harry F. Hovey, Contact
Local. Affiliated With: American Legion.

8307 ■ Michigan National Wild Turkey Federation, Blue Water Chapter
c/o Jeff Weingartz, VP
6490 Bowers Rd.
Imlay City, MI 48444
Ph: (810)724-0119
URL: http://www.mi-nwtf.org/bluewater.htm
Contact: Bill Bevins, Pres.
Local.

Indian River

8308 ■ Indian River Resort Region Chamber of Commerce
3435 S Straits Hwy.
PO Box 57
Indian River, MI 49749-0057
Ph: (231)238-9325
Fax: (231)238-0949
Free: (800)EXIT-310
E-mail: info@irchamber.com
URL: http://www.irchamber.com
Contact: Jeff Comps, Pres.
Members: 204. **Membership Dues:** full, $225 • dual, $75 • associate, $50. **Local**. Promotes business and community development in Indian River, MI. **Awards:** Beautification. **Frequency:** annual. **Type:** recognition. **Recipient:** for a business that has made a significant contribution for the beautification of the Indian River area • Citizen of the Year. **Frequency:** annual. **Type:** recognition. **Recipient:** for an individual who exemplifies excellence in community leadership • Lifetime Achievement. **Frequency:** annual. **Type:** recognition. **Recipient:** for an individual who contributes to the quality of life of the community • Member of the Year. **Frequency:** annual. **Type:** recognition. **Recipient:** for a member with volunteer excellence • Organization of the Year. **Frequency:** annual. **Type:** recognition. **Recipient:** for a member community service organization. **Computer Services:** Information services, membership directory. **Additional Websites:** http://www.irmi.org. **Publications:** Membership Directory • Newsletter, bimonthly. **Advertising:** accepted.

8309 ■ National Active and Retired Federal Employees Association - Little Traverse Bay Area 1483
6858 Chippewa Trail
Indian River, MI 49749-8702
Ph: (231)238-4840
URL: National Affiliate–www.narfe.org
Contact: Cheryl L. Perkette, Contact
Local. Protects the retirement future of employees through education. Informs members on issues affecting the retirement. **Affiliated With:** National Association of Retired Federal Employees.

Inkster

8310 ■ American Legion, Bivens-Bonner Post 285
PO Box 975
Inkster, MI 48141
Ph: (517)371-4720
Fax: (517)371-2401
URL: National Affiliate–www.legion.org
Local. **Affiliated With:** American Legion.

8311 ■ Inkster Chamber of Commerce
c/o Inkster Weed and Seed
29150 Carlysle St.
Inkster, MI 48141-2807
Ph: (734)722-5146 (734)552-1391
Contact: Ernestine Williams, Pres.
Local.

8312 ■ Inkster Housing and Redevelopment Commission
4500 Inkster Rd.
Inkster, MI 48141-3068
Ph: (313)561-2600
Fax: (313)561-2893
Contact: Tony Love, Exec.Dir.
Local.

Interlochen

8313 ■ Interlochen Area Chamber of Commerce
PO Box 13
Interlochen, MI 49643
Ph: (231)276-7141
E-mail: interlochenchamber@juno.com
URL: http://www.interlochenchamber.org
Contact: Laura M. Franke, Dir.
Local. Promotes business and community development in Interlochen, MI area.

Ionia

8314 ■ American Legion, Girard-Horrocks Post 37
PO Box 137
Ionia, MI 48846
Ph: (517)371-4720
Fax: (517)371-2401
URL: National Affiliate–www.legion.org
Local. **Affiliated With:** American Legion.

8315 ■ Ionia Area Chamber of Commerce (IACC)
434 W Main St.
Ionia, MI 48846
Ph: (616)527-2560
Fax: (616)527-0894
E-mail: info@ioniachamber.net
URL: http://www.ioniachamber.com
Contact: Dawn Ketchum, Exec.Dir.
Founded: 1937. **Members:** 190. **Staff:** 2. **Budget:** $83,000. **Local**. Promotes business and community development in the Ionia, MI area. Sponsors festival. **Libraries: Type:** open to the public. **Publications:** *Chamber News*, monthly. Newsletter. **Price:** free. **Circulation:** 30.

8316 ■ Ionia County Board of Realtors
1009 W Lincoln Ave.
Ionia, MI 48846
Ph: (616)527-9101
Fax: (616)527-4265
E-mail: vschmi26@grar.com
URL: National Affiliate–www.realtor.org
Contact: Valerie Schmitz, Exec. Officer
Local. Strives to develop real estate business practices. Advocates the right to own, use and transfer real property. Provides a facility for professional development, research and exchange of information among members. **Affiliated With:** National Association of Realtors.

8317 ■ Pheasants Forever Ionia County Chapter 161
c/o Holly Ingvartsen
2054 Kellogg Rd.
Ionia, MI 48846
Ph: (616)527-9521
E-mail: muffy092353@yahoo.com
URL: http://www.ioniapheasantsforever.com
Contact: Pat Maurer, Pres.
Local. **Affiliated With:** Pheasants Forever.

8318 ■ United Way of Ionia County
PO Box 95
Ionia, MI 48846-0095
Ph: (616)522-0339
URL: National Affiliate–national.unitedway.org
Local. **Affiliated With:** United Way of America.

Iron Mountain

8319 ■ American Legion, Uren-Cooper-Johnson Post 50
916 River St.
Iron Mountain, MI 49801
Ph: (906)774-5797
Fax: (517)371-2401
URL: National Affiliate–www.legion.org
Local. **Affiliated With:** American Legion.

8320 ■ Big Brothers Big Sisters of Dickinson County and Surrounding Areas
427 S Stephenson Ave., Ste.L 108
PO Box 157
Iron Mountain, MI 49801-0157
Ph: (906)774-2180
Fax: (906)774-9396
URL: National Affiliate–www.bbbsa.org
Contact: Ann Malwitz, Exec.Dir.
Founded: 1968. **Members:** 100. **Staff:** 3. **Budget:** $56,000. **State Groups:** 1. **Local**. Individuals from Dickinson County, MI, and Florence and northern Marinett counties, WI. Works to provide quality volunteer and professional services for youths at risk. Assists youths in working to achieve their potential. Enhances self-confidence. Works to change behavior. **Affiliated With:** Big Brothers Big Sisters of America. **Publications:** Newsletter, monthly. **Conventions/Meetings:** annual convention (exhibits) - always June • monthly meeting.

8321 ■ Dickinson Area Bocce Association (DABA)
1 Columbus Dr.
Iron Mountain, MI 49801
Ph: (906)779-1832
URL: National Affiliate–www.bocce.com
Local. **Affiliated With:** United States Bocce Federation.

8322 ■ Dickinson Area Partnership
600 S Stephenson Ave.
Iron Mountain, MI 49801
Ph: (906)774-2002
Fax: (906)774-2004
Free: (800)236-2447
E-mail: info@ironmountain.org
URL: http://www.ironmountain.org
Contact: Bruce Orttenburger, Pres.
Founded: 1987. **Members:** 16. **Staff:** 2. **Local**. Promotes convention business and tourism in the area. **Affiliated With:** Upper Peninsula Travel and Recreation Association. **Publications:** *Color Guide*, periodic • *County Lure Piece*, periodic • *Fishing Guide*, periodic • *Snowmobile Map*, periodic • *Trail Map*, periodic • *Visitor Guide*, periodic.

8323 ■ GFWC Upper Peninsula District No. 5
N3782 Moon Lake Dr.
Iron Mountain, MI 49801
URL: http://www.exploringthenorth.com/gfwc/gfwc.html
Contact: Alice Smith, Pres.
Local.

8324 ■ RSVP of Iron and Dickinson Counties
c/o Kristin Sommerfeld, Dir.
800 Crystal Lake Blvd., Ste.104
Iron Mountain, MI 49801
Ph: (906)774-2256
Fax: (906)774-2257
E-mail: rsvp@chartermi.net
URL: http://www.seniorcorps.gov/about/programs/rsvp.asp
Contact: Kristin Sommerfeld, Dir.
Local. **Affiliated With:** Retired and Senior Volunteer Program.

8325 ■ Sportsmen Off-Road Vehicle Association
c/o Albert W. Heidenreich
PO Box 174
Iron Mountain, MI 49801-0174
Local.

8326 ■ Spring Lake Animal Shelter
W 8459 Shelter Dr.
Iron Mountain, MI 49801
Ph: (906)774-1005
E-mail: springlake@uplogon.com
URL: http://www.petfinder.org/shelters/MI293.html
Contact: Diane Luczak, Mgr.
Founded: 1972. **Staff:** 4. **Budget:** $80,000. **Local**. Private non-profit organization that houses unwanted pets and strays. Facilitates adoption of pets. **For-**

merly: (2004) Spring Lake Humane Society. **Publications:** Newsletter, semiannual. **Conventions/Meetings:** monthly meeting.

8327 ■ United Way of Dickinson County
N3307 Woodland Dr.
Iron Mountain, MI 49801-9433
Ph: (906)774-3089
URL: National Affiliate–national.unitedway.org
Local. Affiliated With: United Way of America.

8328 ■ Upper Peninsula Travel and Recreation Association (UPTRA)
PO Box 400
Iron Mountain, MI 49801
Ph: (906)774-5480
Fax: (906)774-5190
Free: (800)562-7134
E-mail: info@uptravel.com
URL: http://www.uptravel.com
Contact: Tom Nemacheck, Exec.Dir.
Founded: 1911. **Members:** 800. **Staff:** 5. **Budget:** $700,000. **Regional.** Businesses and government organizations united to promote tourism in the Upper Peninsula of Michigan. **Formerly:** (1956) Upper Peninsula Development Bureau; (1970) Upper Michigan Tourist Association. **Publications:** *Michigan Upper Peninsula Four Season Travel Planner.* Magazine • *Travel Planner.* Magazine. **Price:** free. **Circulation:** 300,000 • *Upper Peninsula Travel Planner*, annual. Magazine. **Conventions/Meetings:** annual meeting.

8329 ■ Veterans Affairs Physician Assistant Association (VAPAA)
PO Box 128
Iron Mountain, MI 49801
Fax: (906)774-1839
Free: (866)828-2722
E-mail: vapaa@vapaa.org
URL: http://www.vapaa.org
Contact: John Fields PA-C, Pres.
Founded: 1984. **Members:** 291. **Membership Dues:** individual, $75 (annual). **Local.** Physician assistants who have graduated from an accredited program and/or are certified by the National Commission on Certification of Physician Assistants; individuals who are enrolled in an accredited PA educational program. Purposes are to: enhance public access to quality, cost-effective health care; educate the public about the physician assistant profession; represent physician assistants' interests before Congress, government agencies, and health-related organizations; assure the competence of physician assistants through development of educational curricula and accreditation programs; provide services for members. **Affiliated With:** American Academy of Physician Assistants. **Publications:** *The Voice*, quarterly. Newsletter. **Conventions/Meetings:** annual conference.

Iron River

8330 ■ American Legion, Michigan Post 17
c/o Alfred Branchini
326 N 1st Ave.
Iron River, MI 49935
Ph: (517)371-4720
Fax: (517)371-2401
URL: National Affiliate–www.legion.org
Contact: Alfred Branchini, Contact
Local. Affiliated With: American Legion.

8331 ■ American Legion, Reino Post 21
212 Washington Ave.
Iron River, MI 49935
Ph: (517)371-4720
Fax: (517)371-2401
URL: National Affiliate–www.legion.org
Local. Affiliated With: American Legion.

8332 ■ Iron County Chamber of Commerce
50 E Genesee St.
Iron River, MI 49935
Ph: (906)265-3822
Fax: (906)265-5605
Free: (888)TRY-IRON
E-mail: info@iron.org
URL: http://www.tryiron.org
Contact: Gayle Dae, Exec.Dir.
Founded: 1955. **Members:** 225. **Staff:** 2. **Budget:** $40,000. **Local.** Industries, retail and wholesale businesses, civic organizations, and individuals organized to promote business and community development in Iron County, MI. Strives to cooperate with units of government, businesses and industries, potential businesses, residents and visitors and to promote the economic development of Iron County in a spirit of unity. Works in the tourism trade in the area by assisting other organizations in their activities and holding annual events, such as the Home and Recreation Show and highway pickups. **Publications:** *Chamber Report*, quarterly. Newsletter.

8333 ■ Michigan Organization of Nurse Executives - District 7
c/o Michelle Sand, Dir.
Iron County Community Hosp.
1400 W Ice Rd.
Iron River, MI 49935
Ph: (906)265-0446
Fax: (906)265-2033
E-mail: msand@icch.org
URL: http://www.mone.org
Contact: Michelle Sand, Dir.
Local. Represents nurse leaders who improve healthcare. Provides leadership, professional development, advocacy and research. Advances the nursing administration practice and patient care. **Affiliated With:** American Organization of Nurse Executives.

8334 ■ Trout Unlimited - Menominee Range Chapter
c/o Dave Tiller, Pres.
231 E Brule Lake Rd.
Iron River, MI 49935-8299
Ph: (906)822-7373
E-mail: dtiller@up.net
URL: http://www.tu.org
Contact: Dave Tiller, Pres.
Local.

Ironwood

8335 ■ American Legion, Ironwood Post 5
PO Box 284
Ironwood, MI 49938
Ph: (517)371-4720
Fax: (517)371-2401
URL: National Affiliate–www.legion.org
Local. Affiliated With: American Legion.

8336 ■ Gogebic Range Beagle Club
c/o Don Saari
N8490 Van Buskirk Rd.
Ironwood, MI 49938-9350
URL: National Affiliate–clubs.akc.org
Contact: Don Saari, Contact
Local.

8337 ■ Gogebic Range Genealogy Society
c/o Gary Harrington, Pres.
PO Box 23
Ironwood, MI 49938
E-mail: info@gogebicroots.com
URL: http://www.gogebicroots.com
Contact: Gary Harrington, Pres.
Local.

8338 ■ Gogebic Range United Way
PO Box 248
Ironwood, MI 49938-0248
Ph: (906)932-2420
URL: National Affiliate–national.unitedway.org
Local. Affiliated With: United Way of America.

8339 ■ Ironwood Area Chamber of Commerce (IACC)
PO Box 45
Ironwood, MI 49938
Ph: (906)932-1122
Fax: (906)932-2756
E-mail: chamber@ironwoodmi.org
URL: http://www.ironwoodmi.org
Contact: Kim Kolesar, Exec.Dir.
Founded: 1912. **Members:** 280. **Membership Dues:** individual/club/group (with no paid employees), $50 (annual) • nonprofit business (varies with the number of employees), $75-$150 (annual) • for profit (varies with the number of employees), $175-$225 (annual) • gold, $500 (annual) • privately owned rental home, $175 (annual). **Staff:** 2. **Local.** Businesses and professionals. Promotes business and community development and tourism in the Ironwood, MI area. Conducts annual Jack Frost festival of Lights parade. **Publications:** *Chamber Chat*, monthly. Newsletter. Features business of the month and articles from members. • *Ironwood - Best of Michigan*, annual. **Conventions/Meetings:** annual meeting • monthly meeting.

8340 ■ Phi Theta Kappa, Alpha Rho Chi Chapter - Gogebic Community College
c/o Amanda Delich
4946 Jackson Rd.
Ironwood, MI 49938
Ph: (906)932-4231
E-mail: amanda.delich@gogebic.edu
URL: http://www.ptk.org/directories/chapters/MI/9838-1.htm
Contact: Amanda Delich, Advisor
Local.

8341 ■ Ruffed Grouse Society, Superior Chapter
c/o David Johnson
1300 E Cloverland Dr.
Ironwood, MI 49938
Ph: (906)932-1323
URL: National Affiliate–www.ruffedgrousesociety.org
Contact: David Johnson, Contact
Local. Affiliated With: Ruffed Grouse Society.

8342 ■ Trout Unlimited - Ottawa Chapter (TU)
c/o Roy Minkin
726 Hill St.
Ironwood, MI 49938-2306
Ph: (906)932-4751 (906)932-2701
Fax: (906)932-9915
E-mail: rminkin@goisd.k12.mi.us
URL: http://www.tu.org
Contact: Ron T Minkin, Pres.
Local.

8343 ■ Western U.P. Convention and Visitors Bureau
PO Box 706
Ironwood, MI 49938-0706
Ph: (906)932-4850
Fax: (906)932-3455
Free: (800)522-5657
E-mail: bigsnow@westernup.com
URL: http://www.westernup.com
Contact: Dee Gee Pawlicki, Dir.
Founded: 1985. **Members:** 125. **Staff:** 3. **Local.** Promotes convention business and tourism in the area. **Publications:** *Big Snow Country Guide*, annual. **Circulation:** 100,000 • *Clearly Superior.*

Ishpeming

8344 ■ American Legion, Ishpemingnegaunee Post 136
PO Box 339
Ishpeming, MI 49849
Ph: (517)371-4720
Fax: (517)371-2401
URL: National Affiliate–www.legion.org
Local. Affiliated With: American Legion.

8345 ■ American Legion, Michigan Post 114
c/o Lillian Larson
3050 County Rd. 496
Ishpeming, MI 49849
Ph: (517)371-4720
Fax: (517)371-2401
URL: National Affiliate–www.legion.org
Contact: Lillian Larson, Contact
Local. Affiliated With: American Legion.

8346 ■ Ishpeming Office of Lake Superior Community Partnership
610 Palms Ave.
Ishpeming, MI 49849
Ph: (906)486-4841
Fax: (906)486-4850
Free: (888)57-UNITY
E-mail: mqtinfo@marquette.org
URL: http://www.marquette.org
Contact: Amy Clickner, Dir. of Chamber Operations
Founded: 1951. **Members:** 375. **Membership Dues:** general business (plus $9.45 per employee), $189 (annual) • nonprofit (based on operating budget), $142-$284 (annual) • educational institution ($2.26 per employee), $100 (annual) • health care organization (plus $3.36 per employee), $189 (annual) • apartment (plus $1.11 per unit), $189 (annual) • individual, $116 (annual) • student, $58 (annual) • financial institution (based on amount of per million deposits), $557-$1,118 (annual) • industrial/manufacturing (based on number of employees), $284-$557 (annual) • shopping mall (plus $7.35 per full-time employee), $189 (annual) • multiple business/location ($95 second business, $47 for each additional business), $189 (annual) • hotel/motel (plus $4.47 per unit), $189 (annual) • organization/association, $116-$284 (annual). **Staff:** 3. **Budget:** $80,000. **Local.** Individuals and commercial, industrial, and professional organizations. Promotes business and community development in the Ishpeming-Negaunee, MI areas. **Awards:** Miss Ishpeming. **Frequency:** annual. **Type:** scholarship • Miss Negaunee. **Frequency:** annual. **Type:** scholarship. **Committees:** Chamber of Commerce; Economic Development; Lake Superior Partners in Education; Tourism and Recreation. **Affiliated With:** U.S. Chamber of Commerce. **Publications:** *The Voice of Business*, monthly. Newsletter. **Price:** free for members. **Advertising:** accepted. Alternate Formats: online • Directory, annual. **Price:** included in membership dues • Annual Report, annual. Alternate Formats: online. **Conventions/Meetings:** semimonthly Business After Hours - meeting - every 1st Monday and 3rd Wednesday.

8347 ■ Ishpeming Rock and Mineral Club
PO Box 102
Ishpeming, MI 49849
E-mail: lynn-egghead@yahoo.com
URL: National Affiliate–www.amfed.org
Contact: John Crady, Sec.
Local. Aims to further the study of Earth Sciences and the practice of lapidary arts and mineralogy. **Affiliated With:** American Federation of Mineralogical Societies.

8348 ■ Marquette Beagle Club
c/o John Pruett
295 Marble St.
Ishpeming, MI 49849-2618
URL: National Affiliate–clubs.akc.org
Contact: John Pruett, Contact
Local.

8349 ■ Michigan Health Information Management Association, Upper Peninsula
c/o Beverly Achatz, RHIT, Pres.
PO Box 402
Ishpeming, MI 49849-0402
Ph: (906)485-2150
Fax: (906)485-2116
E-mail: bachatz@bellmemorial.org
URL: http://www.mhima.org
Contact: Beverly Achatz RHIT, Pres.
Local. Represents the interests of individuals dedicated to the effective management of personal health information needed to deliver quality healthcare to the public. Provides career, professional development and practice resources. Sets standards for education and certification. Advocates public policy that advances Health Information Management (HIM) practice. **Affiliated With:** American Health Information Management Association; Michigan Health Information Management Association.

8350 ■ Spina Bifida Association of the Upper Peninsula of Michigan
1220 N 3rd St.
Ishpeming, MI 49849
Ph: (906)485-5127
E-mail: cbengson@nmu.edu
URL: http://www.sba-up.8m.com
Contact: Lois Ann Bengson, Pres.
Founded: 1971. **Members:** 14. **Membership Dues:** regular, $25 (annual). **Regional Groups:** 1. **State Groups:** 4. **Local Groups:** 1. **Local.** Provides support and assistance to children with spina bifida and their parents. Gathers and disseminates information. **Libraries: Type:** reference. **Holdings:** books, periodicals. **Subjects:** spina bifida. **Conventions/Meetings:** annual convention - mid-June • meeting - 4-5/year.

Ithaca

8351 ■ American Legion, Ithaca Post 334
515 S Pine River St.
Ithaca, MI 48847
Ph: (517)371-4720
Fax: (517)371-2401
URL: National Affiliate–www.legion.org
Local. Affiliated With: American Legion.

8352 ■ Ithaca Lions Club - Michigan
c/o Bill Dilts, Sec.
667 N Grafton Rd.
Ithaca, MI 48847
Ph: (989)875-5101 (989)875-4262
URL: http://www.district11c2.org
Contact: Bill Dilts, Sec.
Local. Affiliated With: Lions Clubs International.

Jackson

8353 ■ AAA Michigan
1201 S West Ave.
Jackson, MI 49203
Ph: (517)787-7300
State.

8354 ■ Alliance for the Mentally Ill of Jackson/Hillsdale Counties
c/o Marlene Henderson, Pres.
810 W Franklin St.
Jackson, MI 49203
Ph: (517)787-2853
URL: http://mi.nami.org/jh.html
Contact: Marlene Henderson, Pres.
Local. Strives to improve the quality of life of children and adults with severe mental illness through support, education, research and advocacy. **Affiliated With:** National Alliance for the Mentally Ill.

8355 ■ Amateur Astronomers of Jackson
910 Edgewood St.
Jackson, MI 49202
Ph: (517)784-9061
E-mail: bfrybarger@ameritech.net
URL: http://aaoj.homestead.com/files/current.htm
Contact: Bob Frybarger, Contact
Local. Promotes the science of astronomy. Works to encourage and coordinate activities of amateur astronomical societies. Fosters observational and computational work and craftsmanship in various fields of astronomy. **Affiliated With:** Astronomical League.

8356 ■ American Association of Blacks in Energy, Michigan
c/o Eugene Hurd, Supervisor
Consumers Energy
1945 W Parnell
Jackson, MI 49201
Ph: (517)788-2296
E-mail: ehurd@cmsenergy.com
URL: http://aabe.org
Contact: Eugene Hurd, Supervisor
State. Represents the interests of African Americans and other minorities in the discussions and developments of energy policies and related fields. **Affiliated With:** American Association of Blacks in Energy.

8357 ■ American Legion, Michigan Post 29
c/o Richard F. Smith
3200 Lansing Ave.
Jackson, MI 49202
Ph: (517)371-4720
Fax: (517)371-2401
URL: National Affiliate–www.legion.org
Contact: Richard F. Smith, Contact
Local. Affiliated With: American Legion.

8358 ■ American Legion, Rose City Post 324
1190 Falahee Rd.
Jackson, MI 49203
Ph: (517)371-4720
Fax: (517)371-2401
URL: National Affiliate–www.legion.org
Local. Affiliated With: American Legion.

8359 ■ American Legion, Sauk Trail Post 246
439 E Prospect St.
Jackson, MI 49203
Ph: (517)371-4720
Fax: (517)371-2401
URL: National Affiliate–www.legion.org
Local. Affiliated With: American Legion.

8360 ■ American Legion, Vandercook Lake Post 166
PO Box 4229
Jackson, MI 49203
Ph: (517)371-4720
Fax: (517)371-2401
URL: National Affiliate–www.legion.org
Local. Affiliated With: American Legion.

8361 ■ American Red Cross, South Central Michigan Chapter
729 W Michigan Ave.
Jackson, MI 49201
Ph: (517)782-9486
Free: (888)782-9322
URL: http://www.redcross-scmichigan.org
Regional.

8362 ■ Downtown Kiwanis Club of Jackson, Michigan
c/o Joseph Wolfe
The Protection Ctr.
1203 First St.
Jackson, MI 49203
E-mail: info@jacksonkiwanis.com
URL: http://www.jacksonkiwanis.com
Contact: Pat Kiessling, Pres.
Local.

8363 ■ East Jackson Lions Club
c/o Bert Smith, Pres.
2947 Whitlock Rd.
Jackson, MI 49202
Ph: (517)812-5215
URL: http://www.lionsdistrict11b1.org/lc_east_jackson.htm
Contact: Bert Smith, Pres.
Local. Affiliated With: Lions Clubs International.

8364 ■ Girl Scouts - Irish Hills Council
209 E Washington Ave., Ste.No. 355
Jackson, MI 49201
Ph: (517)784-8543
Fax: (517)784-9553
Free: (800)322-1209
E-mail: dtrusty@girlscoutsihc.org
URL: http://www.girlscoutsihc.org
Contact: Jean Ann Hughes, CEO
Local. Young girls and adult volunteers, corporate, government and individual supporters. Strives to develop potential and leadership skills among its members. Conducts trainings, educational programs and outdoor activities.

8365 ■ Great Lakes Military Vehicle Preservation Association
c/o John McEntire, Pres.
7002 Ann Arbor Rd.
Jackson, MI 49201
Ph: (517)522-8684
E-mail: mcentjb@modempool.com
URL: National Affiliate–www.mvpa.org
Contact: John McEntire, Pres.
Regional. Affiliated With: Military Vehicle Preservation Association.

8366 ■ Greater Jackson Chamber of Commerce (GJCC)
One Jackson Sq., 11th Fl.
PO Box 80
Jackson, MI 49204-0080
Ph: (517)782-8221
Fax: (517)782-0061
E-mail: smilhoan@enterprisegroup.org
URL: http://www.gjcc.org
Contact: Susan L. Milhoan, Pres.
Founded: 1909. **Members:** 858. **Membership Dues:** business, professional, $240 (annual) • individual, $100 (annual) • diversified, $380 (annual). **Staff:** 4. **Local.** Promotes business and community development in the Jackson County, MI area.

8367 ■ Hanover-Horton Lions Club
c/o Brian McClain, Pres.
617 6th St.
Jackson, MI 49203
Ph: (517)563-8540
E-mail: mcclain617@cs.com
URL: http://www.lionsdistrict11b1.org/lc_hanover_horton.htm
Contact: Brian McClain, Pres.
Local. Affiliated With: Lions Clubs International.

8368 ■ Inter-Lakes Lions Club
c/o Vicki Lautzenheiser, Pres.
PO Box 6581
Jackson, MI 49204
Ph: (517)569-2677
E-mail: lautzevl@modempool.com
URL: http://www.lionsdistrict11b1.org/lc_interlakes.htm
Contact: Vicki Lautzenheiser, Pres.
Local. Affiliated With: Lions Clubs International.

8369 ■ Jackson Affordable Housing Corporation (JAHC)
161 W Michigan Ave., 7th Fl.
Jackson, MI 49201
Ph: (517)788-4626
Contact: Sharon Pedersen, Exec.Dir.
Founded: 1990. **Staff:** 4. **Budget:** $1,000,000. **Local Groups:** 1. **Nonmembership. Local.** Assists low and moderate income people to become homeowners in Jackson County, MI. Provides down payment and closing cost financial assistance, education and training on the home buying process, and rehabilitation of vacant and sub-standard dwellings.

8370 ■ Jackson Area Association of Realtors
505 S Jackson St.
Jackson, MI 49203
Ph: (517)787-6175
Fax: (517)787-2223
E-mail: mtee@voyager.net
URL: http://www.jacksonmihomes.com
Contact: Melissa Tee, Exec.VP
Local. Strives to develop real estate business practices. Advocates the right to own, use and transfer real property. Provides a facility for professional development, research and exchange of information among members. **Affiliated With:** National Association of Realtors.

8371 ■ Jackson Audubon Society
PO Box 6453
Jackson, MI 49204
Ph: (517)529-9031
E-mail: bflylady27@netzero.net
URL: http://www.jacksonaudubon.org
Contact: Connie Spotts, Pres.
Local. Works to conserve and restore natural ecosystems, focusing on birds and other wildlife for the benefit of humanity and the earth's biological diversity. **Affiliated With:** National Audubon Society.

8372 ■ Jackson Cascades Lions Club
c/o Winfred Mandody, Pres.
323 Grinnell St.
Jackson, MI 49202-4211
Ph: (734)913-7417 (517)782-1914
E-mail: mandodw@nsk-corp.com
URL: http://www.lionsdistrict11b1.org/lc_jackson_cascades.htm
Contact: Winfred Mandody, Pres.
Local. Affiliated With: Lions Clubs International.

8373 ■ Jackson Convention and Tourist Bureau
PO Box 80
Jackson, MI 49204
Ph: (517)764-4440
Fax: (517)764-4480
Free: (800)245-5282
E-mail: jcvb@voyager.net
URL: http://www.jackson-mich.org
Contact: Susan Milhoan, Exec.Dir.
Founded: 1990. **Staff:** 3. **Local.** Promotes convention business and tourism in area.

8374 ■ Jackson Corvette Club
PO Box 6363
Jackson, MI 49201
E-mail: k.minteer@comcast.net
URL: http://www.michcom.net/~arterio
Contact: Keith Minteer, Pres.
Local. Affiliated With: National Council of Corvette Clubs.

8375 ■ Jackson County Genealogical Society
c/o Jackson District Library
244 W Michigan Ave.
Jackson, MI 49201-2275
Ph: (517)784-8038
E-mail: sshiley@acd.net
URL: http://www.rootsweb.com/~mijackso/jcgs.htm
Contact: Steve Shiley, Pres.
Founded: 1977. **Members:** 140. **Membership Dues:** individual, $15 (annual). **Local.** Seeks to preserve and make available the genealogical records of Jackson County, MI. Encourages the study of family history. **Libraries: Type:** open to the public. **Holdings:** articles, books, periodicals. **Subjects:** genealogy and history of Jackson County. **Publications:** *Lexicon*, quarterly. Journal • Newsletter, bimonthly, September through May. **Price:** free for members. Alternate Formats: online. **Conventions/Meetings:** monthly meeting - always first Tuesday, from September through May.

8376 ■ Jackson County Medical Society - Michigan
PO Box 1325
Jackson, MI 49204-1325
Ph: (517)787-6470
Fax: (517)787-8636
E-mail: richardambs@voyager.net
URL: http://www.msms.org
Contact: Richard L. Ambs, Exec.Dir.
Local. Advances the art and science of medicine. Promotes patient care and the betterment of public health. **Affiliated With:** Michigan State Medical Society.

8377 ■ Jackson County Wolverine REACT
1500 Lansing Ave., Apt. 1
Jackson, MI 49202-2132
Ph: (517)768-9610
E-mail: n8rdp@arrl.net
URL: http://www.reactintl.org/teaminfo/usa_teams/teams-usmi.htm
Local. Trained communication experts and professional volunteers. Provides volunteer public service and emergency communications through the use of radios (Citizen Band, General Mobile Radio Service, UHF and HAM). Coordinates with radio industries and government on safety communication matters and supports charitable activities and community organizations.

8378 ■ Jackson District Dental Society
2691 Springport Rd.
Jackson, MI 49202
Ph: (517)787-4712
Fax: (517)787-2724
URL: National Affiliate–www.ada.org
Contact: Dr. Robert Rando, Exec.Dir.
Local. Represents the interests of dentists committed to the public's oral health, ethics and professional development. Encourages the improvement of the public's oral health and promotes the art and science of dentistry. **Affiliated With:** American Dental Association; Michigan Dental Association.

8379 ■ Jackson Eye Openers Lions Club
c/o Roberta Sexton, Pres.
4246 Jane Dr.
Jackson, MI 49201
E-mail: rsexton89@aol.com
URL: http://www.lionsdistrict11b1.org/lc_jackson_eyeopeners.htm
Contact: Roberta Sexton, Pres.
Local. Affiliated With: Lions Clubs International.

8380 ■ Jackson Host Lions Club
c/o Denny Vass, Pres.
1742 Lochmoor Dr.
Jackson, MI 49201
Ph: (517)768-0043 (517)787-2451
E-mail: denny.vass@countynationalbank.com
URL: http://www.lionsdistrict11b1.org/lc_jackson_host.htm
Contact: Denny Vass, Pres.
Local. Affiliated With: Lions Clubs International.

8381 ■ Jackson Model Rocketry Club
c/o Roger Sadowsky, VP/Co-Founder
4788 Moon Lake Rd.
Jackson, MI 49201-8584
Ph: (517)764-7514
E-mail: info@jmrconline.org
URL: http://jmrconline.org
Contact: Roger Sadowsky, VP/Co-Founder
Founded: 2001. **Members:** 50. **Membership Dues:** adult, $30 (annual) • kid, $10 (annual). **Staff:** 6. **Budget:** $3,000. **Local.** Educates kids and public through hands-on activities with model and high-powered rocketry. **Libraries: Type:** by appointment only. **Subjects:** space history, rocketry. **Affiliated With:** National Association of Rocketry.

8382 ■ Jackson - Young Life
3522 Scheele Dr.
Jackson, MI 49202
Ph: (517)789-7578
URL: http://sites.younglife.org/sites/Jackson1/default.aspx
Local. Affiliated With: Young Life.

8383 ■ Junior Achievement, Michigan Edge
209 E Washington, Ste.180
Jackson, MI 49201
Ph: (517)782-7822 (517)266-8281
Fax: (517)780-0385
Free: (866)782-7828
E-mail: cpoisson@jamichiganedge.com
URL: http://www.jamichiganedge.com
Contact: Mrs. Connie Poisson, Pres.
Founded: 1952. **Staff:** 4. **State Groups:** 12. **Local Groups:** 1. **Nonmembership. Local. Affiliated With:** Junior Achievement.

8384 ■ Michigan Bluebird Society
PO Box 6103
Jackson, MI 49204
Ph: (517)750-4085 (810)736-7060
E-mail: mibluebird@excite.com
URL: http://mibluebirdsociety.tripod.com
State. Affiliated With: North American Bluebird Society.

8385 ■ Michigan Coalition of Essential Schools
2545 Spring Arbor Rd., Ste.104
Jackson, MI 49203
Ph: (517)780-9814
Fax: (517)780-4079
E-mail: walters@michigances.org
URL: http://www.michigances.org
Contact: Teresa Walters, Contact
State.

8386 ■ Michigan Women's Bowling Association (MWBA)
PO Box 1348
Jackson, MI 49204-1348
Ph: (517)841-6846
Fax: (517)841-6847
Contact: Mary Jones, Exec.Sec.
Members: 140,458. **State.** Women bowlers and women's bowling organizations. Conducts state bowling tournament. **Publications:** *Ten Pin Topics*, quarterly. Newsletter. **Conventions/Meetings:** board meeting - 3/year • annual convention - always 1st week of June.

8387 ■ Mid State MMBA
308 Bates St.
Jackson, MI 49202
Ph: (517)783-0143
E-mail: midstate@mmba.org
URL: http://www.mmba.org
Local. Affiliated With: International Mountain Bicycling Association.

8388 ■ Napoleon Lions Club
c/o Gary Morrill, Sec.
4674 Moon Lake Rd.
Jackson, MI 49201
Ph: (517)764-5791
E-mail: gcmorrill@modempool.com
URL: http://www.lionsdistrict11b1.org/lc_napoleon.htm
Contact: Gary Morrill, Sec.
Local. Affiliated With: Lions Clubs International.

8389 ■ National Active and Retired Federal Employees Association - Jackson 25
1644 Foye Dr.
Jackson, MI 49203-5409
Ph: (517)782-7022
URL: National Affiliate–www.narfe.org
Contact: Robert E. Richardson, Contact
Local. Protects the retirement future of employees through education. Informs members on issues affecting the retirement. **Affiliated With:** National Association of Retired Federal Employees.

8390 ■ National Association of Rocketry - Jackson Model Rocketry Club (JMRC)
c/o Roger Sadowsky
4788 Moon Lake Rd.
Jackson, MI 49201
Ph: (517)764-7514
E-mail: info@jmrconline.org
URL: http://www.jmrconline.org
Contact: Roger Sadowsky, Contact
Local.

8391 ■ National Technical Honor Society - Jackson Area Career Center - Michigan
6800 Browns Lake Rd.
Jackson, MI 49203
Ph: (517)768-5200
E-mail: denise.belt@jcisd.org
URL: http://www.jacc-mi.net
Contact: Denise Belt, Contact
Local.

8392 ■ North Jackson Lions Club
c/o Verne Cappell, Pres.
4738 Birch Haven Rd.
Jackson, MI 49201
Ph: (517)789-7117
E-mail: vccappel@cmsenergy.com
URL: http://www.lionsdistrict11b1.org/lc_north_jackson.htm
Contact: Verne Cappell, Pres.
Local. Affiliated With: Lions Clubs International.

8393 ■ Phi Theta Kappa, Alpha Rho Lambda Chapter - Jackson Community College
c/o Mark Ott
2111 Emmons Rd.
Jackson, MI 49201
Ph: (517)796-8574
E-mail: mark_ott@jccmi.edu
URL: http://www.ptk.org/directories/chapters/MI/9337-1.htm
Contact: Mark Ott, Advisor
Local.

8394 ■ Polish Falcons of America, Nest 336
1423 Joy Ave.
Jackson, MI 49203
Ph: (517)789-6321
URL: http://www.polishfalcons.org/nest/336/index.html
Contact: Dennis R. Zaski, Pres.
Local. Affiliated With: Polish Falcons of America.

8395 ■ Region 2 Planning Commission
120 W Michigan Ave., 16th Fl.
Jackson, MI 49201
Ph: (517)788-4426
Fax: (517)788-4635
E-mail: creisdor@co.jackson.mi.us
Contact: Charles Reisdorf, Exec.Dir.
Regional.

8396 ■ RSVP of Jackson County
c/o Pamela McCrum, Dir.
407 S Mechanic St.
Jackson, MI 49201-2331
Ph: (517)782-4616
Fax: (517)782-2693
E-mail: rsvpcss@dmci.net
URL: http://www.seniorcorps.gov/about/programs/rsvp.asp
Contact: Pamela McCrum, Dir.
Local. Affiliated With: Retired and Senior Volunteer Program.

8397 ■ Ruffed Grouse Society, Andy Ammann Chapter
c/o Michael J. Le Masters
7160 Jones Rd.
Jackson, MI 49201-8116
Ph: (517)784-6449
E-mail: settersrest@aol.com
URL: National Affiliate–www.ruffedgrousesociety.org
Contact: Michael J. Le Masters, Contact
Local. Affiliated With: Ruffed Grouse Society.

8398 ■ South Central Human Resources Management Association (SCHRMA)
c/o Chris Bristow
PO Box 5974
Jackson, MI 49204-5974
Ph: (517)782-0559
E-mail: christina.bristow@adeccona.com
URL: http://www.schrma.org
Local.

8399 ■ United Way of Jackson County
729 W Michigan Ave.
Jackson, MI 49201
Ph: (517)784-0511
Fax: (517)784-2430
E-mail: rjewell@uwjackson.org
URL: http://www.uwjackson.org
Contact: Rita Jewell, Office Mgr.
Founded: 1924. **Members:** 87. **Staff:** 4. **Budget:** $1,300,000. **Local.** Works to improve lives by mobilizing the caring power of Jackson County communities. **Affiliated With:** United Way of America.

8400 ■ Vandercook Lake Lions Club
c/o James Sexton, Sec.
209 Park Dr.
Jackson, MI 49203
Ph: (517)782-0185
E-mail: jnjsexton@acd.net
URL: http://www.lionsdistrict11b1.org/lc_east_jackson.htm
Contact: James Sexton, Sec.
Local. Affiliated With: Lions Clubs International.

Jeddo

8401 ■ Michigan Horseshoer's Association No. 4
c/o Timothy A. Quinn, Pres.
8290 Rolling Meadows
Jeddo, MI 48032
Ph: (810)327-0361
E-mail: katedvm@hotmail.com
URL: National Affiliate–www.americanfarriers.org
Contact: Timothy A. Quinn, Pres.
State. Affiliated With: American Farrier's Association.

Jenison

8402 ■ American Legion, Hudsonville Post 329
PO Box 347
Jenison, MI 49429
Ph: (517)371-4720
Fax: (517)371-2401
URL: National Affiliate–www.legion.org
Local. Affiliated With: American Legion.

8403 ■ Army and Navy Club of Grand Rapids
c/o Capt. Paul Ryan
2210 Tyler St.
Jenison, MI 49428-7771
Ph: (616)653-5213
E-mail: paul.ryan@53.com
URL: National Affiliate–www.moaa.org
Contact: Capt. Paul Ryan, Contact
Local. Affiliated With: Military Officers Association of America.

8404 ■ Grand Rapids Area Youth for Christ
PO Box 379
Jenison, MI 49429-0379
Ph: (616)831-7900
Fax: (616)831-7889
URL: http://www.gryfc.org
Local. Affiliated With: Youth for Christ/U.S.A.

8405 ■ Michigan FCA
c/o Rock Campbell
PO Box 894
Jenison, MI 49429-0894
Ph: (616)669-4598
E-mail: rcampbell@fca.org
URL: http://www.michiganfca.org
Contact: Rock Campbell, Dir.
State.

8406 ■ Western Michigan Model Yacht Assn No. 103
c/o Dick Carter
8259 Hearthway
Jenison, MI 49428
Ph: (616)457-3604
URL: http://wmmya.center-of-effort.com
Contact: Dick Carter, Contact
Local.

Jones

8407 ■ American Legion, Hutton-Avery-Sherry Post 262
12112 Spatterdock Lk
Jones, MI 49061
Ph: (517)371-4720
Fax: (517)371-2401
URL: National Affiliate–www.legion.org
Local. Affiliated With: American Legion.

8408 ■ Christian Camp and Conference Association, Great Lakes Region
c/o Bob Tissot, Representative
12500 Prang St.
Jones, MI 49061
Ph: (269)244-5193
Fax: (269)244-5016
URL: National Affiliate–www.ccca-us.org
Contact: Bob Tissot, Representative
Regional. Affiliated With: Christian Camping International/U.S.A.

Jonesville

8409 ■ American Legion, Boyce-Carpenter-Bunce Post 195
440 Evans St.
Jonesville, MI 49250
Ph: (517)371-4720
Fax: (517)371-2401
URL: National Affiliate–www.legion.org
Local. Affiliated With: American Legion.

8410 ■ Jonesville Lions Club
c/o Keith Brown, Pres.
7020 Brown Rd.
Jonesville, MI 49250
Ph: (517)849-2368
E-mail: keith@horseandcarriagebandb.com
URL: http://www.lionsdistrict11b1.org/lc_jonesville.htm
Contact: Keith Brown, Pres.
Local. Affiliated With: Lions Clubs International.

Kalamazoo

8411 ■ Advocacy Services for Kids (ASK)
321 W South St.
Kalamazoo, MI 49007
Ph: (269)343-5896
Fax: (269)344-4645
E-mail: webmaster@askforkids.org
URL: http://www.askforkids.org
Contact: Sandra Roethler, Contact
Local. Affiliated With: Federation of Families for Children's Mental Health.

8412 ■ Alzheimer's Association, Michigan Great Lakes Chapter, Southwest Region
530 Whites Rd., Ste.1
Kalamazoo, MI 49008-3055
Ph: (269)342-1482
Fax: (269)342-1489
E-mail: kathleen.hoekstra@alz.org
URL: http://www.alzmigreatlakes.org
Contact: Kathleen Hoekstra, Program/Operations Mgr.
Local. Offers information and support to persons with Alzheimer's disease, or other progressive dementias, and their caregivers. Services include support groups, a help line, educational programs, quarterly newsletters and a resource center. **Affiliated With:** Alzheimer's Association.

8413 ■ American Chemical Society, Kalamazoo Section
c/o Michael Lawrence Kiella, Chm.
7000 Portage Rd.
Kalamazoo, MI 49001-0102
Ph: (616)833-9863
E-mail: michael.l.kiella@pfizer.com
URL: National Affiliate–acswebcontent.acs.org
Contact: Michael Lawrence Kiella, Chm.
Local. Represents the interests of individuals dedicated to the advancement of chemistry in all its branches. Provides opportunities for peer interaction and career development. **Affiliated With:** American Chemical Society.

8414 ■ American Legion, Kalamazoo Post 134
2233 N Burdick St.
Kalamazoo, MI 49007
Ph: (517)371-4720
Fax: (517)371-2401
URL: National Affiliate–www.legion.org
Local. Affiliated With: American Legion.

8415 ■ American Legion, Michigan Post 36
c/o Joseph B. Westnedge
730 Lake St.
Kalamazoo, MI 49001
Ph: (517)371-4720
Fax: (517)371-2401
URL: National Affiliate–www.legion.org
Contact: Joseph B. Westnedge, Contact
Local. Affiliated With: American Legion.

8416 ■ American Legion, Michigan Post 260
c/o Lt. John R. Fox
924 N Rose St.
Kalamazoo, MI 49007
Ph: (517)371-4720
Fax: (517)371-2401
URL: National Affiliate–www.legion.org
Contact: Lt. John R. Fox, Contact
Local. Affiliated With: American Legion.

8417 ■ American Red Cross, Greater Kalamazoo Area Chapter
5640 Venture Ct.
Kalamazoo, MI 49009
Ph: (269)353-6180
Fax: (269)353-8657
E-mail: mail@greaterkzooredcross.org
URL: http://www.greaterkzooredcross.org
Local.

8418 ■ American Society for Quality, Battle Creek-Kalamazoo Section 1003
c/o Murali Krishnan
PO Box 4070
Kalamazoo, MI 49003-4070
E-mail: murali.krishnan@mpiresearch.com
URL: http://groups.asq.org/1003
Contact: Murali Krishnan, Contact
Local. Advances learning, quality improvement and knowledge exchange to improve business results and to create better workplaces and communities worldwide. Provides a forum for information exchange, professional development and continuous learning in the science of quality. **Affiliated With:** American Society for Quality.

8419 ■ American Statistical Association, Southwest Michigan Chapter
c/o Gerald L. Sievers, Pres.
Western Michigan Univ.
Dept. of Statistics
Kalamazoo, MI 49008
Ph: (616)387-4510
E-mail: sievers@wmich.edu
URL: National Affiliate–www.amstat.org
Contact: Gerald L. Sievers, Pres.
Local. Promotes statistical practice, applications and research. Works for the improvement of statistical education at all levels. Seeks opportunities to advance the statistics profession. **Affiliated With:** American Statistical Association.

8420 ■ American Theatre Organ Society, Southwest Michigan Chapter
c/o Dayton Maynard, Pres.
1823 Royce Ave.
Kalamazoo, MI 49001
Ph: (616)342-9600
URL: National Affiliate–www.atos.org
Contact: Dayton Maynard, Pres.
Local. Aims to restore, preserve and promote the theatre pipe organ and its music. Encourages the youth to learn the instrument. Operates a committee that gathers history and old music from silent film days and information on theatre organists, theaters and organ installations of the silent film era. **Affiliated With:** American Theatre Organ Society.

8421 ■ Barbershop Harmony Society - Pioneer District
c/o Raleigh Bloch, Pres.
2033 Wild Cherry Ln.
Kalamazoo, MI 49009
E-mail: rbloch@compuserve.com
URL: http://www.harmonize.com/Pioneer/pio.htm
Contact: Raleigh Bloch, Pres.
Local. Encourages and preserves barbershop harmony through the support of vocal music education. Serves members by sharing fellowship, performance skills and leadership development. **Affiliated With:** Society for the Preservation and Encouragement of Barber Shop Quartet Singing in America.

8422 ■ Big Brothers Big Sisters, A Community of Caring
605 Howard St.
Kalamazoo, MI 49008-1919
Ph: (269)382-6800
Fax: (269)382-4108
Free: (888)898-3001
E-mail: petertripp@bbbscommunity.org
URL: http://www.bbbscommunity.org
Contact: Peter Tripp, Exec.Dir.
Local. Serves children in Kalamazoo, Calhoun, Barry, Allegan, and Van Buren Counties in Michigan by creating and nurturing quality relationships between children and mentors to help children become caring, socially competent and responsible adults. **Affiliated With:** Big Brothers Big Sisters of America.

8423 ■ Christians Golfers' Association - Kalamazoo
c/o Richard Bird, Pres.
10141 Portage Rd.
Kalamazoo, MI 49002

Ph: (269)327-1637
E-mail: tigerbird@charter.net
URL: National Affiliate–www.christiangolfer.org
Contact: Richard Bird, Pres.
Local.

8424 ■ Community AIDS Resource and Education Services of Southwest Michigan (CARES)
629 Pioneer St.
Kalamazoo, MI 49008-1801
Ph: (269)381-2437
Fax: (269)381-4050
Free: (800)944-2437
E-mail: info@caresswm.org
URL: http://www.caresswm.org
Contact: Dave Kirby, Interim Exec.Dir.
Founded: 1985. **Staff:** 12. **Budget:** $880,000. **Languages:** English, Spanish. **Regional.** Seeks to minimize further transmission of HIV and maximize the quality of life of persons affected by HIV in southwest Michigan. Offers a buddy program, support groups, care coordination, prevention education, speakers, transportation assistance, and free HIV counseling and testing. **Formerly:** (1998) Kalamazoo AIDS Resource and Education Services. **Publications:** *HIV Lifeline*, monthly. Newsletter.

8425 ■ Country Dancing in Kalamazoo (CDK)
c/o Mike Clark
3618 Woodcliff Dr.
Kalamazoo, MI 49008
Ph: (269)372-7613
E-mail: michael.clark@wmich.edu
URL: http://www.albion.edu/math/ram/cdk
Contact: Mike Clark, Treas.
Membership Dues: individual, $12 (annual) • household, $18 (annual). **Local.** Promotes traditional dancing by sponsoring contra, square, swing, and English Country dances. **Affiliated With:** Country Dance and Song Society.

8426 ■ Forest Products Society, Great Lakes Section
c/o Bill Adams, Chm.
Select Millwork Co.
383 E D. Ave.
Kalamazoo, MI 49009
Ph: (269)349-7841
Fax: (269)349-5190
E-mail: selectmillwork@selectmillwork.com
URL: National Affiliate–www.forestprod.org
Contact: Bill Adams, Chm.
Regional. Strives to foster innovation and research in the environmentally sound processing and use of wood and fiber resources by disseminating information and providing forums for networking and the exchange of knowledge. **Affiliated With:** Forest Products Society.

8427 ■ Girl Scouts of Glowing Embers Council
1011 W Maple
Kalamazoo, MI 49048
Ph: (269)343-1516
Free: (800)788-4919
E-mail: bgiesen@core.com
URL: http://www.gsgec.org
Contact: Janet Barker, CEO
Local. Young girls and adult volunteers, corporate, government and individual supporters. Strives to develop potential and leadership skills among its members. Conducts trainings, educational programs and outdoor activities.

8428 ■ Greater Kalamazoo Association of Realtors (GKAR)
5830 Venture Park Dr.
Kalamazoo, MI 49009
Ph: (269)382-1597
Fax: (269)382-3462
E-mail: micheles@gkar.com
URL: http://gkar.com
Contact: Michele Smith, Staff Asst.
Founded: 1911. **Members:** 950. **Staff:** 10. **Budget:** $1,000,000. **Local.** Professional organization of real estate brokers and salespeople in Kalamazoo, Van Buren, and Allegan counties, MI. **Affiliated With:** National Association of Realtors. **Publications:** *Bearings*, weekly. Newsletter • *Exchange*, monthly. Newsletter. **Conventions/Meetings:** periodic meeting.

8429 ■ Greater Kalamazoo United Way
709 S Westnedge Ave.
Kalamazoo, MI 49007-6003
Ph: (269)343-2524
Fax: (269)344-7250
E-mail: information@kalamazoounitedway.org
URL: http://www.kalamazoounitedway.org
Local. Affiliated With: United Way of America.

8430 ■ IEEE West Michigan Section
c/o Dept. of Electrical and Computer Engineering
Western Michigan Univ.
Kalamazoo, MI 49008
Ph: (616)387-4057
Fax: (616)387-4096
URL: http://ewh.ieee.org/r4/west_michigan
Contact: Ron Fredricks, Chair
Local. Engineers and scientists in electrical engineering, electronics, and allied fields. Promotes creating, developing, integrating, sharing, and applying knowledge about electro and information technologies and sciences for the benefit of humanity and the profession. Conducts lectures on current engineering and scientific topics.

8431 ■ Institute of Packaging Professionals, West Michigan Chapter
c/o Stu Smith, Pres.
3000 Covington Rd.
Kalamazoo, MI 49001
Ph: (269)381-7130
Fax: (269)381-6344
E-mail: ssmith@shippac.com
URL: National Affiliate–www.iopp.org
Contact: Stu Smith, Pres.
Founded: 1970. **Members:** 200. **Membership Dues:** individual or business, $150 (annual). **Local.** Packaging professionals from among the leading companies in western MI. Works to promote packaging and support the next generation of packaging professionals through scholarships and mentoring programs with Michigan State University's School of Packaging students. Benefits include professional enhancement through monthly tours/meetings of local industries and staying connected within the industry professional network. **Affiliated With:** Institute of Packaging Professionals. **Publications:** *West Michigan IOPP Chapter Newsletter*, monthly. **Conventions/Meetings:** annual Technical Conference.

8432 ■ Junior Achievement of Kalamazoo and Van Buren Counties
350 E Michigan Ave., Ste.115
Kalamazoo, MI 49007
Ph: (269)343-0860
Fax: (269)343-3506
E-mail: jakalamazoo@ameritech.net
URL: http://kalamazoo.ja.org
Local.

8433 ■ Kalamazoo Animal Liberation League (KALL)
PO Box 20131
Kalamazoo, MI 49019-1131
Ph: (616)383-4656 (616)344-8763
E-mail: mike@kallnet.org
URL: http://www.kallnet.org
Contact: Mike Schuur, Event Coor.
Founded: 1989. **Members:** 200. **Membership Dues:** $25 (annual). **State.** Animal advocates dedicated to public education about animals and animal rights issues. Works to investigate, expose, and challenge all forms of animal exploitation and abuse. **Publications:** *KALL To Action*, monthly. Newsletter. Reports on association activities; covers regional, national, and international developments in animal rights and advocacy. **Price:** included in membership dues. **Circulation:** 200. **Advertising:** accepted. Alternate Formats: online. **Conventions/Meetings:** monthly meeting - Kalamazoo, MI.

8434 ■ Kalamazoo Area Youth for Christ
122 W Crosstown Pkwy.
Kalamazoo, MI 49001
Ph: (269)388-3888
Fax: (269)388-9374
URL: http://www.kalamazooyfc.org
Local. Affiliated With: Youth for Christ/U.S.A.

8435 ■ Kalamazoo Astronomical Society
c/o KAMSC
600 W Vine, Ste.400
Kalamazoo, MI 49008
Ph: (269)375-4867
E-mail: ngcphile@sbcglobal.net
URL: http://www.kasonline.org
Contact: Roger G. Williams, Contact
Local. Promotes the science of astronomy. Works to encourage and coordinate activities of amateur astronomical societies. Fosters observational and computational work and craftsmanship in various fields of astronomy. **Affiliated With:** Astronomical League.

8436 ■ Kalamazoo Builders Exchange
3431 E Kilgore Rd.
Kalamazoo, MI 49001-5513
Ph: (269)349-2507
Fax: (269)349-9306
E-mail: kim@builder-exchange.com
URL: http://www.buildersexchange.com/coprofile.htm
Contact: Craig Valentine, Pres.
Founded: 1960. **Members:** 300. **Local.** Represents general contractors, subcontractors, suppliers, manufacturers' representatives and individual firms related to the construction industry. Provides information on construction and building procedures. **Affiliated With:** International Builders Exchange Executives. **Publications:** Bulletin.

8437 ■ Kalamazoo Christian - Young Life
3319 Donnegal
Kalamazoo, MI 49006
Ph: (269)353-0919 (269)303-5493
E-mail: gretchenlemmer@yahoo.com
URL: http://sites.younglife.org/sites/kchristian/default.aspx
Contact: Gretchen Lemmer, Contact
Local. Affiliated With: Young Life.

8438 ■ Kalamazoo Corvette Club (KCC)
PO Box 2773
Kalamazoo, MI 49003
E-mail: glennrussell@thurstonwoods.org
URL: http://www.kzoovette.org
Contact: Glenn Russell, Pres.
Local. Affiliated With: National Council of Corvette Clubs.

8439 ■ Kalamazoo Dog Training Club (KDTC)
c/o Grace Stevens
1223 Bretton Dr.
Kalamazoo, MI 49006-2115
Fax: (269)344-3474
E-mail: graceace@aol.com
URL: http://www.kdtc.org
Local.

8440 ■ Kalamazoo Downtown Lions Club
PO Box 50494
Kalamazoo, MI 49005
E-mail: deluw@aol.com
URL: http://milions11b2.org
Local. Affiliated With: Lions Clubs International.

8441 ■ Kalamazoo Figure Skating Club (KFSC)
Twin Star Ice Arena
5076 Sports Dr.
Kalamazoo, MI 49009

Ph: (269)978-0118
E-mail: kalamazoofsc@yahoo.com
URL: http://kalamazoofsc.tripod.com
Local. Provides programs to encourage participation and achievement in the sport of figure skating on ice. Defines and maintains uniform standards of skating proficiency. Organizes and sponsors competitions and exhibitions for the purpose of stimulating interest in figure skating. **Affiliated With:** United States Figure Skating Association.

8442 ■ Kalamazoo Gay-Lesbian Resource Center (KGLRC)
c/o Sharon Roepke, Exec.Dir.
629 Pioneer St.
Kalamazoo, MI 49008
Ph: (269)349-4234
Free: (888)377-7271
E-mail: kglrc1@hotmail.com
URL: http://www.kglrc.org
Contact: Sharon Roepke, Exec.Dir.
Founded: 1987. **Members:** 100. **Membership Dues:** student, $20 (annual) • single, basic, $35 (annual) • family, $56 (annual). **Staff:** 2. **Budget:** $80,000. **Local.** Provides support and resources to lesbian, gay, bisexual, and transgender individuals. Runs a community center and lending library; handles youth group, resource line, diversity training and speaking panels. **Libraries: Type:** open to the public. **Holdings:** 500. **Subjects:** lesbian, gay issues, history, political issues. **Affiliated With:** Lesbian Resource Center. **Publications:** *Resource Center News*, quarterly. Newsletter. Contains news and resources for lesbian and gay people in South West Michigan. **Price:** $20.00/year. **Circulation:** 700. **Advertising:** accepted.

8443 ■ Kalamazoo Regional Chamber of Commerce (KRCC)
346 W Michigan Ave.
Kalamazoo, MI 49007
Ph: (269)381-4000
Fax: (269)343-0430
E-mail: info@kazoochamber.com
URL: http://www.kazoochamber.com
Contact: David P. Sanford, Interim Pres./CEO
Founded: 1904. **Members:** 3,000. **Local.** Companies (1200) representing 2000 individuals. Promotes business and community development in Kalamazoo County, MI. Conducts community affairs. Sponsors festival. **Divisions:** Business Advocacy and Communications; Business and Community Development; Conventions Visitors Bureau; Economic Development; Financial/Administration; Membership and Events; Tourism; Website. **Affiliated With:** U.S. Chamber of Commerce. **Publications:** *Enterprise*, monthly. Magazine. Alternate Formats: online • *Kalamazoo County*. Book. Relocation guide about Kalamazoo. **Price:** free for non-residents; $5.00 for members; $7.00 for nonmembers • *Kalamazoo County Connection*, annual. Directory. **Conventions/Meetings:** annual Business Expo - meeting - always May, Kalamazoo, MI.

8444 ■ Kalamazoo Valley District Dental Society (KVDDS)
1900 Whites Rd.
Kalamazoo, MI 49008
E-mail: info@kvdds.com
URL: http://www.kvdds.com
Contact: Dr. John Spurr, Pres.-Elect
Local. Represents the interests of dentists committed to the public's oral health, ethics and professional development. Encourages the improvement of the public's oral health and promotes the art and science of dentistry. **Affiliated With:** American Dental Association; Michigan Dental Association.

8445 ■ Kalamazoo Valley Habitat for Humanity (KVHH)
c/o Brent Hepp
525 E Kalamazoo Ave.
Kalamazoo, MI 49007
Ph: (269)344-2443
Fax: (269)344-2252
E-mail: mailbox@habitatkalamazoo.org
URL: http://www.habitatkalamazoo.org
Local.

8446 ■ Kalamazoo Valley Landscape and Nursery Association (KVLNA)
3520 S 28th St.
Kalamazoo, MI 49048
Ph: (269)226-4340
Fax: (269)226-4340
E-mail: kvlna2000@yahoo.com
URL: http://kvlna.org
Contact: Caryn Mortimore, Exec.Sec.
Founded: 1952. **Members:** 65. **Membership Dues:** business, family, individual, $115 (annual). **Staff:** 1. **Budget:** $9,500. **Local.** Group of Green industry professionals dedicated to the promotion of horticulture, specializing in growing and planting nursery stock, grounds maintenance, and landscape design. **Affiliated With:** American Nursery and Landscape Association; Michigan Nursery and Landscape Association. **Publications:** *Update*, monthly. Newsletter. **Circulation:** 68. **Advertising:** accepted. **Conventions/Meetings:** monthly meeting - from September to April • annual Michigan Mid-Winter Conference.

8447 ■ Mattawan - Young Life
3319 Donnegal
Kalamazoo, MI 49006
Ph: (269)353-0919
URL: http://sites.younglife.org/sites/mattawan/default.aspx
Local. Affiliated With: Young Life.

8448 ■ Michigan Citizen Action (MCA)
729 Acad. St.
Kalamazoo, MI 49007
Ph: (269)349-9170
Fax: (269)349-9271
E-mail: info@michcitizenaction.org
URL: http://www.michcitizenaction.org
Contact: Linda Teeter, Exec.Dir.
State.

8449 ■ Michigan Dark-Sky Association
122 Sydelle Ave.
Kalamazoo, MI 49006
URL: http://www.net-link.net/~memiller
Contact: Mark Miller, Contact
State. Astronomical societies, lighting and engineering groups, professional astronomers. Seeks to inform about the effects of nighttime lighting. Builds awareness about the problems that have effects on astronomy. Presents examples of good lighting design. Conducts speaker's bureau. Documents on good and bad lighting through photos and videos.

8450 ■ Michigan Organization of Nurse Executives - District 2
c/o Brad Gordon, Dir.
Borgess Medical Ctr.
1521 Gull Rd.
Kalamazoo, MI 49048-1640
Ph: (269)226-8143
Fax: (269)226-5988
E-mail: bradgordon@borgess.com
URL: http://www.mone.org
Contact: Brad Gordon, Dir.
Local. Represents nurse leaders who improve healthcare. Provides leadership, professional development, advocacy and research. Advances the nursing administration practice and patient care. **Affiliated With:** American Organization of Nurse Executives.

8451 ■ Mid-Michigan Chapter of Romance Writers of America (MMRWA)
PO Box 2725
Kalamazoo, MI 49003-2725
E-mail: bartleyd@chartermi.net
URL: http://midmichiganrwa.org
Local. Works to provide networking and support to individuals seriously pursuing a career in romance fiction. Helps writers become published and established in their writing field. **Affiliated With:** Romance Writers of America.

8452 ■ Minority Business Alliance of Southwest Michigan
c/o Orman Gordan
225 Parsons St.
Kalamazoo, MI 49007
Ph: (269)341-4456 (269)873-0563
E-mail: ermagordonmba@yahoo.com
Contact: Orman E. Gordon, Exec.Dir.
Founded: 2000. **Members:** 30. **Membership Dues:** non voting, $120 (annual). **Staff:** 2. **Budget:** $30,000. **Local.** Works to assist start-up minority and women owned businesses in the SW Michigan area. Provides educational programs and subsidized below market office rental opportunities and business support services.

8453 ■ NALS of Michigan
c/o Elisa M. Hooper, Pres.
900 Comerica Bldg.
151 S Rose St.
Kalamazoo, MI 49007-4719
Ph: (269)381-8844
E-mail: para14_2000@yahoo.com
URL: http://www.nalsofmichigan.org
Contact: Elisa M. Hooper, Pres.
State. Committed to providing quality legal services through continuing education to members of the association (legal support professionals).

8454 ■ National Active and Retired Federal Employees Association - Southwest Michigan 173
1208 Piccadilly Rd.
Kalamazoo, MI 49006-2623
Ph: (269)344-5681
URL: National Affiliate–www.narfe.org
Contact: Vernon L. Curran, Contact
Local. Protects the retirement future of employees through education. Informs members on issues affecting the retirement. **Affiliated With:** National Association of Retired Federal Employees.

8455 ■ National Alliance for the Mentally Ill of Kalamazoo
PO Box 51693
Kalamazoo, MI 49005-1693
Ph: (616)343-6952
E-mail: tunabase@chartermi.net
URL: http://mi.nami.org/kal.html
Contact: Michael D. Kenny, Pres.
Local. Strives to improve the quality of life of children and adults with severe mental illness through support, education, research and advocacy. **Affiliated With:** National Alliance for the Mentally Ill.

8456 ■ National Association for the Advancement of Colored People, Western Michigan University Chapter
1903 W Michigan Ave.
Kalamazoo, MI 49008-5201
E-mail: naacp_wmu@hotmail.com
URL: http://www.rso.wmich.edu/naacp
Contact: Quan Lateef, Pres.
Local.

8457 ■ National Association of Catholic Family Life Ministers, Region VI
c/o Joe Schmitt, Region Representative
Off. of Marriage & Family
215 N Westnedge Ave.
Kalamazoo, MI 49007-3760
Ph: (269)349-8714
Fax: (269)349-6440
E-mail: jschmitt@dioceseofkalamazoo.org
URL: National Affiliate–www.nacflm.org
Contact: Joe Schmitt, Region Representative
Regional. Affiliated With: National Association of Catholic Family Life Ministers.

8458 ■ National Organization for Women - Greater Kalamazoo Area
c/o April Woodward-Slack, Pres.
2611 Portage St.
Kalamazoo, MI 49001
Ph: (269)720-0795
E-mail: kalamazoonow@michnow.org
URL: http://www.michnow.org
Contact: April Woodward-Slack, Pres.
Local. Affiliated With: National Organization for Women.

8459 ■ New Latino Visions (NLV)
c/o John Fraire, Exec.Dir. and Founder
PO Box 2168
Kalamazoo, MI 49003-2168
Ph: (269)384-0859
URL: http://www.newlatinovisions.org
Contact: John Fraire, Exec.Dir. and Founder
Local.

8460 ■ Phi Theta Kappa, Alpha Rho Nu Chapter - Kalamazoo Valley Community College
c/o Lynne Morrison
6767 West O Ave.
Kalamazoo, MI 49009
Ph: (269)488-4164
E-mail: lmorrison@kvcc.edu
URL: http://www.ptk.org/directories/chapters/MI/9633-1.htm
Contact: Lynne Morrison, Advisor
Local.

8461 ■ Points of Light Foundation - Volunteer Center Of Greater Kalamazoo
709 S Westnedge Ave., Ste.A
Kalamazoo, MI 49007-6003
Ph: (269)382-8350
Fax: (269)382-8362
E-mail: jhuth@volunteerkalamazoo.org
URL: National Affiliate–www.pointsoflight.org
Contact: Ms. Judy Huth, Exec.Dir.
Local. Affiliated With: Points of Light Foundation. **Publications:** *Volunteer Center Newsletter*, quarterly. Features best practices in volunteerism. **Circulation:** 1,500. Alternate Formats: online • *Volunteer Guidebook*, annual. Catalog. Listing of on-going volunteer opportunities within the community. **Circulation:** 4,500. Alternate Formats: online.

8462 ■ Portage - Young Life
3319 Donnegal
Kalamazoo, MI 49006
Ph: (269)353-0919 (231)580-6016
E-mail: looneymooney757@hotmail.com
URL: http://sites.younglife.org/sites/portage/default.aspx
Contact: Pat Shea, Contact
Local. Affiliated With: Young Life.

8463 ■ Psi Chi, National Honor Society in Psychology - Western Michigan University
c/o Dept. of Psychology
3700 Wood Hall
Kalamazoo, MI 49008
E-mail: rso_pc@wmich.edu
URL: http://www.rso.wmich.edu/psichi
Local. Affiliated With: Psi Chi, National Honor Society in Psychology.

8464 ■ RSVP Kalamazoo County
c/o Tracie Wheeler, Dir.
918 Jasper St.
Kalamazoo, MI 49001-2853
Ph: (269)382-0515
Fax: (269)382-3189
E-mail: twheeler@seniorservices1.org
URL: http://www.seniorcorps.gov/about/programs/rsvp_state.asp?usestateabbr=mi&Search4.x=0&Search4.y=0
Contact: Tracie Wheeler, Dir.
Local. Additional Websites: http://www.seniorservices1.org. **Affiliated With:** Retired and Senior Volunteer Program.

8465 ■ Safety Council for West Michigan
c/o Jeannine Hemry
437 W. Crosstown Pkwy.
Kalamazoo, MI 49001
Ph: (616)344-6189
Fax: (269)344-3103
Free: (800)704-7676
E-mail: council@scwmi.org
Affiliated With: National Safety Council.

8466 ■ Sauk Trails Resource Conservation and Development Council
5360 Holiday Terr.
Kalamazoo, MI 49009-2126
Ph: (616)372-8947
Fax: (616)372-8986
E-mail: robert.baetsen@mi.usda.gov
URL: National Affiliate–www.rcdnet.org
Contact: Robert Baetsen, Coor.
Local. Affiliated With: National Association of Resource Conservation and Development Councils.

8467 ■ Sigma Gamma Epsilon, Zeta Sigma Chapter, Western Michigan University
Dept. of Geology
1187 Rood Hall
1903 W Michigan Ave.
Kalamazoo, MI 49008-5150
URL: http://www.wmich.edu/geology/sge.html
Contact: Dr. Alan Kehew, Advisor
Local.

8468 ■ Sons of Norway, Askeladden Lodge 5-610
c/o Orlin K. Loen, Pres.
1615 Royce Ave.
Kalamazoo, MI 49001-5107
Ph: (269)342-4142
E-mail: okloen@net-link.net
URL: National Affiliate–www.sofn.com
Contact: Orlin K. Loen, Pres.
Local. Affiliated With: Sons of Norway.

8469 ■ Southern Michigan Gun Club
809 E Crosstown Pkwy.
Kalamazoo, MI 49001
Ph: (269)382-2238
URL: http://www.southernmichigangunclub.com
Local. Affiliated With: National Skeet Shooting Association.

8470 ■ Vicksburg - Young Life
3319 Donnegal
Kalamazoo, MI 49006
Ph: (269)353-0919
URL: http://sites.younglife.org/sites/vicksburg/default.aspx
Contact: Christopher Sell, Contact
Local. Affiliated With: Young Life.

8471 ■ Western Michigan University Skating Club
Lawson Ice Arena
1903 W Michigan Ave.
Kalamazoo, MI 49008-5335
E-mail: bronco_skating@hotmail.com
URL: http://www.rso.wmich.edu/skating
Contact: Leslie Graham, Pres.
Local. Provides programs to encourage participation and achievement in the sport of figure skating on ice. Defines and maintains uniform standards of skating proficiency. Organizes and sponsors competitions and exhibitions for the purpose of stimulating interest in figure skating. **Affiliated With:** United States Figure Skating Association.

8472 ■ Young Life Kalamazoo
3319 Donnegal
Kalamazoo, MI 49006
Ph: (269)353-0919 (269)998-4960
Fax: (269)353-0919
E-mail: ryan@kalamazoo.younglife.org
URL: http://sites.younglife.org/sites/Kalamazoo/default.aspx
Contact: Ryan Nienhuis, Contact
Local. Affiliated With: Young Life.

8473 ■ Young Women's Christian Association of Kalamazoo
353 E Michigan Ave.
Kalamazoo, MI 49007
Ph: (269)345-5595
Fax: (269)345-8230
E-mail: info@ywcakalamazoo.org
URL: http://www.ywca.org/site/pp.asp?c=bpLJJTOvHmE&b=420737
Contact: Jennifer A. Shoub, CEO
Founded: 1885. **Members:** 475. **Membership Dues:** regular, $40 (annual). **Budget:** $1,800,000. **Local.** Strives toward the empowerment of women and girls and the elimination of racism. Draws together members who strive to create opportunities for women's growth, leadership and power in order to create a common vision: peace, justice, freedom and dignity for all people. Services include: providing quality, affordable child care for children 6 weeks up to kindergarten; providing education, recognition and self-enrichment program for members and the community as well as advocacy and public awareness on mission and program-related issues; providing counseling, crisis line, support groups and shelter for victims of domestic assault and their families; providing comfortable fitness programming for women and men as well as programming related to women's health issues; providing mentoring for economic and personal self-sufficiency for adult and teen women; and providing counseling, crisis line, support groups and advocacy for victims and survivors of sexual assault and their friends and families. **Awards:** YMCA Women of Achievement Award. **Frequency:** annual. **Type:** recognition. **Affiliated With:** Young Women's Christian Association of the United States of America YWCA of the U.S.A. **Publications:** *The Leading Edge*, quarterly. Newsletter.

Kaleva

8474 ■ Kaleva Lions Club
14361 9 Mile Rd.
Kaleva, MI 49645-9347
Ph: (231)362-3174 (231)362-2812
E-mail: jpmak@kaltelnet.net
URL: http://kalevami.lionwap.org
Contact: Ken Kuuttila, Pres.
Local. Affiliated With: Lions Clubs International.

Kalkaska

8475 ■ American Legion, Michigan Post 480
c/o Robert E. Beebe
406 Hyde St.
Kalkaska, MI 49646
Ph: (517)371-4720
Fax: (517)371-2401
URL: National Affiliate–www.legion.org
Contact: Robert E. Beebe, Contact
Local. Affiliated With: American Legion.

8476 ■ Kalkaska Area Chamber of Commerce
353 S Cedar St.
PO Box 291
Kalkaska, MI 49646
Ph: (231)258-9103
Fax: (231)258-6155
Free: (800)487-6880
E-mail: chamber@kalkaskami.com
URL: http://www.kalkaskami.com
Contact: Sharon Coppock, Office Mgr.
Local. Strives to improve the community by promoting the economic, civic, commercial, cultural, industrial, and educational interests of the Kalkaska area. **Publications:** Newsletters, monthly. **Conventions/Meetings:** annual meeting - 2007 Mar. 3, Kalkaska, MI.

8477 ■ Michigan National Wild Turkey Federation, Kalkaska Gobblers
0517 Lake Dr. NE
Kalkaska, MI 49646

Ph: (231)258-5549
URL: http://www.mi-nwtf.org/kalkaska.htm
Contact: David Asch, Sec.
Local.

8478 ■ Northwestern Michigan Orchid Society (NMOS)
c/o Richard Asmus
PO Box 885
Kalkaska, MI 49646
Ph: (231)258-5126
E-mail: asmo34@hotmail.com
URL: National Affiliate–www.orchidweb.org
Contact: Richard Asmus, Contact
Local. Professional growers, botanists, hobbyists, and others interested in extending the knowledge, production, use, and appreciation of orchids. **Affiliated With:** American Orchid Society.

8479 ■ Wolverine Morgan Horse Association (WMHA)
PO Box 392
Kalkaska, MI 49646
Ph: (231)331-6615
E-mail: trbmorgans@triton.net
URL: http://www.wmhaclub.com
Contact: Jayne Cook, Contact
Local. Affiliated With: American Morgan Horse Association.

Kawkawlin

8480 ■ American Society of Farm Managers and Rural Appraisers Michigan Chapter
c/o Tracy Koch, Sec.-Treas.
Greenstone FCS
PO Box 175
Kawkawlin, MI 48631
Ph: (989)686-5100
Fax: (989)686-6972
E-mail: tkoch@greenstonefcs.com
URL: National Affiliate–www.asfmra.org
Contact: Tracy Koch, Sec.-Treas.
State. Affiliated With: American Society of Farm Managers and Rural Appraisers.

8481 ■ Folk Music Society of Midland
c/o Margaret Loper
1508 Fraser Rd.
Kawkawlin, MI 48631
Ph: (989)684-1499
E-mail: fmsm@dulcimers.com
URL: http://www.dulcimers.com/fmsm
Contact: Margaret Loper, Contact
Local. Affiliated With: Country Dance and Song Society.

Keego Harbor

8482 ■ Michigan Adaptive Sports (MAS)
PO Box 569
Keego Harbor, MI 48320
Ph: (248)988-0156
Fax: (248)363-1941
URL: http://www.michiganadaptivesports.org
Contact: Carol Roubal, Sec.
Founded: 1983. **Members:** 125. **Membership Dues:** $25 (annual). **Budget:** $25,000. **State.** Adaptive snow and water skiing, kayaking, and handcycling for individuals with disabilities. **Affiliated With:** Disabled Sports USA. **Formerly:** (1997) Michigan Handicapped Sports and Recreation Association. **Publications:** Newsletter, semiannual. **Price:** free.

8483 ■ Oakland County Child Care Council
2111 Cass Lake Rd., Ste.104
Keego Harbor, MI 48320
Ph: (248)681-9192
Fax: (248)738-6230
Free: (866)424-4532
E-mail: info@oaklandchildcare.org
URL: http://www.oaklandchildcare.org
Contact: Susan Ray Allen, Exec.Dir.
Local.

Kent City

8484 ■ American Legion, Evans-Swanson Post 123
14111 Ball Creek Rd. NW
Kent City, MI 49330
Ph: (517)371-4720
Fax: (517)371-2401
URL: National Affiliate–www.legion.org
Local. Affiliated With: American Legion.

Kentwood

8485 ■ AAA Michigan
2560 E Paris Ave. SE
Kentwood, MI 49546
Ph: (616)957-4455
Free: (800)222-3103
URL: http://www.aaamich.com
Contact: Carol Jachim, Contact
State.

8486 ■ American Legion, Crispus Attucks Post 59
PO Box 88023
Kentwood, MI 49518
Ph: (517)371-4720
Fax: (517)371-2401
URL: National Affiliate–www.legion.org
Local. Affiliated With: American Legion.

8487 ■ Michigan Mutual UFO Network
PO Box 8532
Kentwood, MI 49518-8532
Ph: (231)582-7097 (248)515-9568
E-mail: wjk@mimufon.org
URL: http://www.mimufon.org
Contact: Bill Konkolesky, Dir.
State. Promotes the scientific and systematic collection and analysis of UFO/Abduction data with the ultimate goal of learning the origin, nature and purpose of the UFO/Abduction phenomenon and share it with the people of Michigan, other MUFON organizations, and the general public. **Affiliated With:** Mutual UFO Network.

8488 ■ Military Order of the Loyal Legion of the United States Michigan Commandery (MOLLUS)
c/o Commander Bruce B. Butgereit
1691 Summerfield St. SE
Kentwood, MI 49508-6499
Ph: (616)827-3369
Fax: (616)827-3366
E-mail: civil-war@comcast.net
URL: http://suvcw.org/mollus/mi/mollus.html
Contact: Commander Bruce B. Butgereit, Contact
Founded: 1865. **Members:** 18. **Membership Dues:** individual, $25 (annual). **State.** Descendants of Union officers in U.S. Civil War 1861-1865. **Affiliated With:** Military Order of the Loyal Legion of the United States. **Publications:** *The Journal*, quarterly. **Conventions/Meetings:** semiannual meeting.

8489 ■ Professional Photographers of Western Michigan (PPWM)
c/o Michael Simmons, Pres.
4425 Morningside Dr. SE
Kentwood, MI 49512
Ph: (616)698-8444
E-mail: simmonsphoto@juno.com
URL: http://www.ppwm.org
Contact: Michael Simmons, Pres.
State. Affiliated With: Professional Photographers of America.

8490 ■ Two Trackers Four Wheel Drive Club
c/o Frank Ringewold
PO Box 88063
Kentwood, MI 49518-9998
Ph: (616)878-1653
E-mail: twotrackers@hotmail.com
URL: http://www.twotrackers.org
Contact: Frank Ringewold, Contact
Local. 4x4 Trail Riding Club with forest clean up and other charitable contributions. **Affiliated With:** United Four-Wheel Drive Associations.

Kimball

8491 ■ Friends of the Airport
c/o Theresa Orzel
250 N. Airport Dr.
Kimball, MI 48074-4408
Local.

Kingsford

8492 ■ American Legion, Carpenter-Clash Post 363
1227 W Breen Ave.
Kingsford, MI 49802
Ph: (517)371-4720
Fax: (517)371-2401
URL: National Affiliate–www.legion.org
Local. Affiliated With: American Legion.

8493 ■ National Active and Retired Federal Employees Association Michigan-Wisconsin Border 1673
107 Ford St.
Kingsford, MI 49802-5825
Ph: (906)774-1321
URL: National Affiliate–www.narfe.org
Contact: Agnes A. Lindstrom, Contact
Local. Protects the retirement future of employees through education. Informs members on issues affecting the retirement. **Affiliated With:** National Association of Retired Federal Employees.

Kingsley

8494 ■ American Legion, Paradise Valley Post 436
PO Box 81
Kingsley, MI 49649
Ph: (517)371-4720
Fax: (517)371-2401
URL: National Affiliate–www.legion.org
Local. Affiliated With: American Legion.

Kingston

8495 ■ Kingston Lions Club - Michigan
c/o Alice Zajac, PDG, Pres.
6545 Legg Rd.
Kingston, MI 48741
Ph: (989)683-2497
URL: http://www.geocities.com/dist11d1
Contact: Alice Zajac PDG, Pres.
Local. Affiliated With: Lions Clubs International.

Laingsburg

8496 ■ American Legion, Clare Burt Post 248
PO Box 322
Laingsburg, MI 48848
Ph: (517)371-4720
Fax: (517)371-2401
URL: National Affiliate–www.legion.org
Local. Affiliated With: American Legion.

8497 ■ Laingsburg Lions Club
c/o Jack Dast, Sec.
6021 Twin Oaks Dr.
Laingsburg, MI 48848

Ph: (517)651-6080
E-mail: jpdast@aol.com
URL: http://www.district11c2.org
Contact: Jack Dast, Sec.
Local. Affiliated With: Lions Clubs International.

8498 ■ Laingsburg Pioneer Cheerleaders
c/o Cindy Malone
PO Box 166
Laingsburg, MI 48848-0166
Local.

8499 ■ Rolling Readers USA Mid-Michigan Chapter
c/o Maxie Patel, Chapter Leader
Laingsburg Elementary School
117 Prospect
Laingsburg, MI 48848
Ph: (517)651-5067
Fax: (517)651-2615
E-mail: monna@voyager.net
URL: http://www.rollingreaders.org
Contact: Maxie Patel, Contact
Local. Serves 1,400 children and their families in rural Mid-Michigan. Programs offer one-on-one reading tutoring, motivation and skill-building; provides free books to school children that help foster a lifelong love of reading.

Lake

8500 ■ Barryton Lions Club
c/o James Dague, Pres.
11024 W Battle Rd.
Lake, MI 48632
Ph: (989)382-7012
E-mail: ndague@rural-net.com
URL: http://lions.silverthorn.biz/11-e1
Contact: James Dague, Pres.
Local. Affiliated With: Lions Clubs International.

8501 ■ Citizens for Alternatives to Chemical Contamination (CACC)
8735 Maple Grove Rd.
Lake, MI 48632-9511
Ph: (989)544-3318 (989)892-6174
Fax: (989)544-3318
E-mail: info@caccmi.org
URL: http://www.caccmi.org
Contact: John Witucki, Chair
Founded: 1978. **Members:** 500. **Membership Dues:** individual, $15 (annual) • family, $20 • organization, $25. **Staff:** 1. **Budget:** $75,000. **Local Groups:** 4. Grassroots environmental education and advocacy organization dedicated to the principles of social justice, pollution prevention, empowerment, and the protection of the Great Lakes human and natural ecosystem. Works to increase public awareness of toxic chemical threats to the environment. Conducts research and educational programs; offers children's services. **Libraries: Type:** lending; reference; not open to the public. **Holdings:** 500; archival material, audiovisuals, books, clippings, monographs, periodicals. **Subjects:** environment. **Awards: Frequency:** annual. **Type:** recognition. **Recipient:** for outstanding work for environmental equity and social justice, especially from grassroots. **Publications:** *CACC Clearinghouse*, monthly. Newsletter. **Price:** included in membership dues. **Circulation:** 750. **Advertising:** accepted. **Conventions/Meetings:** annual Backyard Eco Conference (exhibits) - always May/June in Central Michigan, MI.

Lake Ann

8502 ■ Lake Ann Lions Club
c/o Kelly Beauchamp, Pres.
PO Box 312
Lake Ann, MI 49650
Ph: (231)275-5502
E-mail: doturich@earthlink.net
URL: http://lions.silverthorn.biz/11-e1
Contact: Kelly Beauchamp, Pres.
Local. Affiliated With: Lions Clubs International.

Lake City

8503 ■ American Legion, Jackson-Koster-Gray Post 300
114 N Main St.
Lake City, MI 49651
Ph: (517)371-4720
Fax: (517)371-2401
URL: National Affiliate–www.legion.org
Local. Affiliated With: American Legion.

8504 ■ Cadillac - Young Life
PO Box 366
Lake City, MI 49651
Ph: (231)779-0171
URL: http://sites.younglife.org/_layouts/ylext/default.aspx?ID=C-1074
Local. Affiliated With: Young Life.

8505 ■ Green Point Flyers Association
10603 W Kelly Rd.
Lake City, MI 49651
Ph: (231)779-0246
E-mail: isaiah4031@bignetnorth.net
URL: National Affiliate–www.ushga.org
Local. Affiliated With: U.S. Hang Gliding Association.

8506 ■ Lake City Area Chamber of Commerce
PO Drawer H
Lake City, MI 49651
Ph: (231)839-4969
Fax: (231)839-5991
E-mail: info@lakecitymich.com
URL: http://www.lakecitymich.com
Contact: Kim Mosher, Admin.Asst.
Founded: 1953. **Members:** 200. **Membership Dues:** business, $100 (annual) • organization, $50 (annual) • individual, $25 (annual) • senior, $15 (annual). **Staff:** 10. **Local.** Promotes commerce in the Lake City area. **Computer Services:** Information services, membership directory. **Publications:** *Lake City Chamber Corner*, weekly • Directory, periodic.

8507 ■ Young Life Clearwater Cove Development
PO Box 688
Lake City, MI 49651
Ph: (231)839-7552
URL: http://sites.younglife.org/_layouts/ylext/default.aspx?ID=A-8490
Local. Affiliated With: Young Life.

8508 ■ Young Life Northern Lakes
PO Box 366
Lake City, MI 49651
Ph: (231)779-0171
URL: http://sites.younglife.org/_layouts/ylext/default.aspx?ID=A-MI230
Local. Affiliated With: Young Life.

8509 ■ Young Life Timber Wolf Lake
4909 N Morey Rd.
Lake City, MI 49651
Ph: (231)839-7552
Fax: (231)839-7544
URL: http://sites.younglife.org/camps/TimberWolf/default.aspx
Local. Affiliated With: Young Life.

Lake Linden

8510 ■ American Legion, Williams-Giroux Post 90
452 4th St.
Lake Linden, MI 49945
Ph: (517)371-4720
Fax: (517)371-2401
URL: National Affiliate–www.legion.org
Local. Affiliated With: American Legion.

8511 ■ Houghton County Historical Museum Society
c/o Leo W. Chaput, Curator
PO Box 127
Lake Linden, MI 49945
Ph: (906)296-4121
E-mail: info@houghtonhistory.org
URL: http://www.houghtonhistory.org
Contact: Leo W. Chaput, Curator
Local. Telecommunication Services: electronic mail, dmkorman@houghtonhistory.org.

8512 ■ National Alliance for the Mentally Ill - Ba-Ho-Ke-On
c/o Lawrence W. Evers, Pres.
PO Box 152
Lake Linden, MI 49945
Ph: (906)296-0601
E-mail: lcevers@portup.com
URL: http://mi.nami.org/ba.html
Contact: Lawrence W. Evers, Pres.
Local. Strives to improve the quality of life of children and adults with severe mental illness through support, education, research and advocacy. **Affiliated With:** National Alliance for the Mentally Ill.

8513 ■ Upper Peninsula Publishers and Authors Association (UPPAA)
c/o Walt Shiel, Ed.
28151 Quarry Lake Rd.
Lake Linden, MI 49945
E-mail: wshiel@slipdownmountain.com
URL: http://www.findingmichigan.com/uppaa.html
Contact: Walt Shiel, Ed.
Local. Serves individuals and corporate groups involved in book, audio and video publishing. Advances the professional interests of independent publishers. Aims to provide training programs and cooperative marketing assistance within the publishing industry. **Affiliated With:** PMA - Independent Book Publishers Association.

Lake Odessa

8514 ■ American Rabbit Breeders Association, Michigan
c/o George Carpenter, Pres.
14436 Goddard Rd.
Lake Odessa, MI 48849
Ph: (616)374-3021
E-mail: anoldcrab@hotmail.com
URL: http://www.arba.net/district/8/michigan.htm
Contact: George Carpenter, Pres.
State. Affiliated With: American Rabbit Breeders Association.

Lake Orion

8515 ■ American Legion, Charlton-Polan Post 233
164 S Broadway
Lake Orion, MI 48361
Ph: (517)371-4720
Fax: (517)371-2401
URL: National Affiliate–www.legion.org
Local. Affiliated With: American Legion.

8516 ■ Oakland Astronomy Club
503 Forest Lake Blvd.
Lake Orion, MI 48362
Ph: (248)652-1496
E-mail: oac@surmount.com
URL: http://www.surmount.com/oac/
Contact: Jim Saoud, Pres.
Local.

8517 ■ Orion Area Chamber of Commerce
PO Box 484
Lake Orion, MI 48361
Ph: (248)693-6300
Fax: (248)693-9227
E-mail: oacc@msn.com
URL: http://www.orion.lib.mi.us/orion
Contact: Donna Heyniger, Managing Dir.
Founded: 1950. **Members:** 210. **Membership Dues:** business, $125-$500 (annual) • nonprofit and community group, $75 (annual) • school, government, individual, $100 (annual). **Staff:** 1. **Local**. Promotes business and community development in the Lake Orion, MI area. **Libraries: Type:** reference. **Holdings:** 20. **Subjects:** starting a business, marketing, resources. **Awards:** Business Scholarship. **Frequency:** annual. **Type:** scholarship. **Recipient:** for academic course of study. **Computer Services:** Mailing lists, of members. **Committees:** Budget and Finance; Business and Professional Development; Communications and Marketing; Community Business Partnership; Membership Development; Organization; Women of the Chamber. **Publications:** *Chamber Report*, monthly. Newsletter. **Price:** free. **Circulation:** 12,000. **Advertising:** accepted. Alternate Formats: CD-ROM; online • *Community Profile and Business Directory*, annual. **Price:** free. **Circulation:** 12,000. **Advertising:** accepted. Alternate Formats: online • Newspaper, monthly • Pamphlets. **Price:** free. **Circulation:** 12,000. **Advertising:** accepted. **Conventions/Meetings:** Annual Community Business Expo - festival (exhibits) • monthly breakfast - fourth Tuesday • monthly Membership Meeting - luncheon, with informative presentations and update of chamber activity - always first Thursday • monthly Women of the Chamber - meeting - fourth Tuesday.

Lakeview

8518 ■ Lakeview Area Chamber of Commerce (LACC)
PO Box 57
Lakeview, MI 48850
Ph: (989)352-1200
E-mail: fssinc@pathwaynet.com
URL: http://www.lakeviewmi.org
Contact: April Finup, Sec.
Members: 59. **Local**. Promotes business and community development in the Lakeview, MI area. **Formerly:** (2005) Lakeview Chamber of Commerce.

8519 ■ Lakeview Lions Club - Michigan
c/o Richard Goedge, Pres.
8923 E Tamarack Rd.
Lakeview, MI 48850
Ph: (989)352-7052
E-mail: rgoedge@yahoo.com
URL: http://lions.silverthorn.biz/11-e1
Contact: Richard Goedge, Pres.
Local. **Affiliated With:** Lions Clubs International.

8520 ■ Michigan National Wild Turkey Federation, Tamarock Toms Chapter
7875 Tamarack Rd.
Lakeview, MI 48850
Ph: (517)352-7707
URL: http://www.mi-nwtf.org/Tamaracktoms.htm
Contact: Daryl Johnson, Pres.
Local.

Lakeville

8521 ■ Plumbing-Heating-Cooling Contractors Association, South Macomb
c/o Dan Israel, Exec.Mgr.
PO Box 458
Lakeville, MI 48366-0458
Ph: (248)693-7790
Fax: (248)693-7738
URL: National Affiliate–www.phccweb.org
Contact: Dan Israel, Exec.Mgr.
Local. Represents the plumbing, heating and cooling contractors. Promotes the construction industry. Protects the environment, health, safety and comfort of society. **Affiliated With:** Plumbing-Heating-Cooling Contractors Association.

8522 ■ South Macomb Association of Plumbing Contractors
c/o Dan Israel, Exec.Mgr.
PO Box 458
Lakeville, MI 48366-0458
Ph: (248)693-7790
Fax: (248)693-7738
URL: National Affiliate–www.phccweb.org
Contact: Dan Israel, Exec.Mgr.
Local.

Lambertville

8523 ■ Bedford Township Lions Club
c/o Gregory W. Stewart, Pres.
7350 Kenilworth Dr.
Lambertville, MI 48144
Ph: (734)856-4105
URL: http://www.metrodetroitlions.org
Contact: Gregory W. Stewart, Pres.
Local. **Affiliated With:** Lions Clubs International.

Lanse

8524 ■ American Legion, Michigan Post 144
c/o William S. Mc Glue
115 N Front St.
Lanse, MI 49946
Ph: (517)371-4720
Fax: (517)371-2401
URL: National Affiliate–www.legion.org
Contact: William S. Mc Glue, Contact
Local. **Affiliated With:** American Legion.

Lansing

8525 ■ AAA Michigan
2830 E Grand River Ave.
Lansing, MI 48912
Ph: (517)487-6171
State.

8526 ■ AARP Michigan
309 N Washington Sq., Ste.100
Lansing, MI 48933
Fax: (517)482-2794
Free: (866)227-7448
E-mail: miaarp@aarp.org
URL: National Affiliate–www.aarp.org
Contact: George Rowan PhD, Pres.
State. Seeks to improve every aspect of living for older people. Addresses the needs and interests of older people, working or retired. Promotes positive social change and delivers value to members through information, advocacy and service. **Affiliated With:** American Association of Retired Persons.

8527 ■ Alcoholics Anonymous World Services, Lansing Central Office
1500 E Michigan Ave.
Lansing, MI 48912
Ph: (517)377-1444
Fax: (517)377-1446
E-mail: aalansing@ameritech.net
URL: http://www.aalansingmi.org
Contact: Vickie Vandenbossche, Office Mgr.
Local. Individuals recovering from alcoholism. AA maintains that members can solve their common problem and help others achieve sobriety through a twelve step program that includes sharing their experience, strength, and hope with each other. **Affiliated With:** Alcoholics Anonymous World Services.

8528 ■ American Alcohol and Drug Information Foundation (AADIF)
PO Box 10212
Lansing, MI 48901-0212
Ph: (517)485-9900
Fax: (517)485-1928
E-mail: alcoholresearch@ameritech.net
Contact: Robert Hammond, VP
Founded: 1955. **Staff:** 3. **Budget:** $174,000. **Nonmembership**. **Regional**. Promotes a program of alcohol and drug education. Works to increase focus on prevention, education, and curriculum needs. **Libraries: Type:** open to the public. **Holdings:** 45. **Formerly:** (1993) Michigan Alcohol and Drug Information. **Publications:** *Hurrah! He's Sober*. Pamphlet • *I Can't Be an Alcoholic Because.*. Pamphlet. ISSN: 0090-1482 • *Journal of Alcohol and Drug Education*, quarterly. ISSN: 0090-1482. **Conventions/Meetings:** annual board meeting • annual conference.

8529 ■ American Association of Retired Persons, Michigan
310 N Washington Sq., Ste.110
Lansing, MI 48933
Ph: (517)482-2772
Fax: (517)482-2794
Free: (866)227-7448
E-mail: miaarp@aarp.org
URL: http://www.aarp.org
Contact: Stephen Gools, State Dir.
State. Persons 50 years of age or older, working or retired. Seeks to improve every aspect of living for older people. **Affiliated With:** American Association of Retired Persons.

8530 ■ American Council of Engineering Companies of Michigan
PO Box 19189
Lansing, MI 48901-9189
Ph: (517)332-2066
Fax: (517)332-4333
E-mail: mail@acec-mi.org
URL: http://www.acec-mi.org
Contact: Mr. Ronald W. Brenke PE, Exec.Dir.
Members: 120. **State**. Strives to promote the business interests of engineering companies by providing legislative advocacy and business services. **Affiliated With:** American Council of Engineering Companies. **Formerly:** Consulting Engineers Council of Michigan; (2004) American Consulting Engineers Council of Michigan.

8531 ■ American Federation of State, County and Municipal Employees, AFL-CIO - Michigan Council 25
1034 N Washington Ave.
Lansing, MI 48906
Ph: (517)487-5081
Fax: (517)487-3970
Free: (800)AFSCME25
E-mail: webmaster@miafscme.org
URL: http://www.miafscme.org
Contact: Albert Garrett, Pres.
Members: 58,792. **Local**. Represents the interests of workers coming from different areas of government, health, education and other services, both public and private. **Affiliated With:** American Federation of State, County and Municipal Employees.

8532 ■ American Legion Auxiliary of Michigan
c/o Judy Gregory, Pres.
212 N Verlinden Ave.
Lansing, MI 48915
Ph: (517)371-4720
Fax: (517)371-2401
E-mail: michalaux@voyager.net
URL: http://www.michalaux.org
Contact: Judy Gregory, Pres.
State. Affiliated With: American Legion Auxiliary.

8533 ■ American Legion, Business and Professional Post 530
PO Box 20165
Lansing, MI 48901
Ph: (517)371-4720
Fax: (517)371-2401
URL: National Affiliate–www.legion.org
Local. Affiliated With: American Legion.

8534 ■ American Legion, Capital City Post 12
PO Box 18013
Lansing, MI 48901
Ph: (517)371-4720
Fax: (517)371-2401
URL: National Affiliate–www.legion.org
Local. Affiliated With: American Legion.

8535 ■ American Legion, Fisher Body Lansing Post 183
PO Box 10146
Lansing, MI 48901
Ph: (517)371-4720
Fax: (517)371-2401
URL: National Affiliate–www.legion.org
Local. Affiliated With: American Legion.

8536 ■ American Legion, Lansing Post 336
2400 Hall St.
Lansing, MI 48906
Ph: (517)371-4720
Fax: (517)371-2401
URL: National Affiliate–www.legion.org
Local. Affiliated With: American Legion.

8537 ■ American Legion-Michigan Department
c/o Patrick W Lafferty, Adj.
212 N Verlinden Ave.
Lansing, MI 48915
Ph: (517)371-4720
Fax: (517)371-2401
E-mail: info@michiganlegion.org
URL: http://www.michiganlegion.org
Contact: John H. Skinner, Commander
State. Affiliated With: American Legion.

8538 ■ American Legion, Michigan Post 178
c/o James H. Mc Clain
2518 Gary St.
Lansing, MI 48906
Ph: (517)371-4720
Fax: (517)371-2401
URL: National Affiliate–www.legion.org
Contact: James H. Mc Clain, Contact
Local. Affiliated With: American Legion.

8539 ■ American Legion, Michigan Post 225
212 N Verlinden Ave.
Lansing, MI 48915
Ph: (517)371-4720
Fax: (517)371-2401
URL: National Affiliate–www.legion.org
Local. Affiliated With: American Legion.

8540 ■ American Legion, Mount Moriah Post 460
2130 W Holmes Rd.
Lansing, MI 48910
Ph: (517)371-4720
Fax: (517)371-2401
URL: National Affiliate–www.legion.org
Local. Affiliated With: American Legion.

8541 ■ American Legion, Raymond Rankins Post 308
212 N Verlinden Ave.
Lansing, MI 48915
Ph: (517)371-4720
Fax: (517)371-2401
URL: National Affiliate–www.legion.org
Local. Affiliated With: American Legion.

8542 ■ American Legion, Southfield Post 328
212 N Verlinden Ave.
Lansing, MI 48915
Ph: (517)371-4720
Fax: (517)371-2401
URL: National Affiliate–www.legion.org
Local. Affiliated With: American Legion.

8543 ■ American Legion, Temple Post 273
212 N Verlinden Ave.
Lansing, MI 48915
Ph: (517)371-4720
Fax: (517)371-2401
URL: National Affiliate–www.legion.org
Local. Affiliated With: American Legion.

8544 ■ American Legion, William Riker Johnson Post 205
112 S Howard St.
Lansing, MI 48912
Ph: (517)371-4720
Fax: (517)371-2401
URL: National Affiliate–www.legion.org
Local. Affiliated With: American Legion.

8545 ■ American Red Cross - Mid-Michigan Chapter
c/o John H. Cauley, Jr., Exec.Dir.
PO Box 30101
1800 E Grand River
Lansing, MI 48909
Ph: (517)484-7461
Fax: (517)484-3799
Free: (800)TAP-HELP
E-mail: jcauley@midmichiganredcross.org
Contact: John H. Cauley Jr., Exec.Dir.
Provides relief to victims of disaster as well as works to help people prevent, prepare for and respond to emergencies. **Affiliated With:** American Red Cross National Headquarters.

8546 ■ American Society for Training and Development - South Central Michigan (ASTD-SCMC)
PO Box 22211
Lansing, MI 48909
Ph: (517)333-1299
URL: http://www.astd-scmc.org
Contact: Deborah Myrand, Pres.
Local. Promotes workplace learning and the improvement of skills of workplace professionals. Provides resource and professional development to individuals in the field of learning and development. Recognizes and sets standards for learning and performance professionals. **Affiliated With:** American Society for Training and Development.

8547 ■ American Water Resources Association, Michigan State Section
c/o Stephanie M. Smith
PO Box 27173
Lansing, MI 48909-7173
E-mail: fluker@msu.edu
URL: http://www.mi-awra.org
Contact: Stephanie M. Smith, Contact
State. Seeks to advance water resources research, planning, development, and management. Collects, organizes and disseminates ideas and information in the field of water resources science and technology. **Affiliated With:** American Water Resources Association.

8548 ■ Area Agencies on Aging Association of Michigan (AAAAM)
c/o Mary Ablan, Dir.
6105 W St. Joseph Hwy., Ste.209
Lansing, MI 48917
Ph: (517)886-1029
Fax: (517)886-1305
E-mail: ablan@iserv.net
URL: http://www.mi-seniors.org
Contact: Mary Ablan, Dir.
Founded: 1973. **State.** Represents 16 regional Area Agencies on Aging located statewide. Advocates for programs and policies that benefit older adults.

8549 ■ Associated Builders and Contractors, Central Michigan Chapter
1501 Rensen St., Ste.C
Lansing, MI 48910
Ph: (517)394-4481
Fax: (517)394-6275
E-mail: bonnie@abccmc.org
URL: http://www.abccmc.org
Contact: Douglas C. Kelsey CAE, Exec.Dir.
Founded: 1962. **Members:** 160. **Budget:** $350,000. **Local.** Promotes the concept of free enterprise and the right of individuals to competitively bid regardless of affiliation. **Affiliated With:** Associated Builders and Contractors. **Publications:** *Friday Facts*, weekly. Newsletter. **Conventions/Meetings:** monthly meeting.

8550 ■ Associated Builders and Contractors of Michigan
115 W Allegan, 10B
Lansing, MI 48933-1812
Ph: (517)485-8020
E-mail: abcmi@coast.net
URL: National Affiliate–www.abc.org
Contact: Andy Anuzis, Exec.VP
State. Affiliated With: Associated Builders and Contractors.

8551 ■ Associated General Contractors of America - Michigan Chapter
c/o Bart O. Carrigan, Exec.VP
PO Box 27005
Lansing, MI 48909
Ph: (517)371-1550
Fax: (517)371-1131
E-mail: bartc@mi.agc.org
URL: http://www.mi.agc.org
Contact: Bart O. Carrigan, Exec.VP
State. Affiliated With: Associated General Contractors of America.

8552 ■ Association for Children's Mental Health (ACMH)
100 W Washtenaw St., Ste.4
Lansing, MI 48933-2129
Ph: (517)372-4016
Fax: (517)372-4032
Free: (888)226-4543
E-mail: ajwinans@aol.com
URL: http://www.acmh-mi.org
Contact: Amy Winans, Exec.Dir.
State. Affiliated With: Federation of Families for Children's Mental Health.

8553 ■ Autism Society of Michigan (ASM)
6035 Executive Dr., Ste.109
Lansing, MI 48911
Ph: (517)882-2800
Fax: (517)882-2816
Free: (800)223-6722
E-mail: autism@autism-mi.org
URL: http://www.autism-mi.org
Contact: Sally Burton-Hoyle EdD, Exec.Dir.
Founded: 1976. **Members:** 800. **Membership Dues:** individual parent, $20 (annual) • professional, $30 (annual) • family, $25 (annual) • full-time student, $10 (annual) • agency affiliation, $175 (annual). **State.** Parents, professionals, educators, and interested individuals organized to increase public awareness of autism. Provides information, referral services, and advocacy for individuals who have autism. Works to

assure full participation and self determination in every aspect of life for each individual. On site library and mail order bookstore. **Libraries: Type:** open to the public. **Holdings:** 600; books. **Subjects:** autism, developmental disabilities. **Affiliated With:** Autism Society of America. **Publications:** *Horizons*, quarterly. Newsletter. Contains current literature and research regarding autism as well as book reviews written by a woman with autism. **Circulation:** 800 • Annual Report, annual. Alternate Formats: online. **Conventions/Meetings:** semiannual conference, highlights current treatments, medical research and educational strategies - always spring.

8554 ■ Boys and Girls Club of Lansing
4315 Pleasant Grove Rd.
Lansing, MI 48910-4257
Ph: (517)394-0455
URL: http://www.bgclansing.org
Contact: Carmen Turner, Pres.
Local.

8555 ■ Bretton Woods Lions Club
c/o Graig Mestemaker, Pres.
924 Alexandria Dr.
Lansing, MI 48917-3990
Ph: (517)323-1130
E-mail: mestemakerc@hotmail.com
URL: http://www.district11c2.org
Contact: Graig Mestemaker, Pres.
Local. Affiliated With: Lions Clubs International.

8556 ■ Builders Exchange of Lansing and Central Michigan
c/o Michael A. Nystrom, Exec.Dir./Mgr.
1240 E Saginaw St.
Lansing, MI 48906
Ph: (517)372-8930
Fax: (517)372-5022
E-mail: planroom@bxlansing.com
URL: http://www.bxlansing.com
Contact: Michael A. Nystrom, Exec.Dir./Mgr.
Founded: 1945. **Members:** 800. **Local.**

8557 ■ Capital Area Literacy Coalition (CALC)
c/o Dr. Lois Bader, Exec.Dir.
1028 E Saginaw
Lansing, MI 48906
Ph: (517)485-4949
Fax: (517)485-1924
E-mail: mail@thereadingpeople.org
URL: http://www.thereadingpeople.org
Contact: Dr. Lois Bader, Exec.Dir.
Founded: 1986. **Members:** 1,000. **Staff:** 20. **Budget:** $400,000. **Local.** Trains and aids individuals and organizations to tutor adults in basic reading and conversational English. **Affiliated With:** ProLiteracy Worldwide.

8558 ■ Capital City Corvette Club (CCCC)
PO Box 27295
Lansing, MI 48909
E-mail: president@cccorvette.org
URL: http://www.cccorvette.org
Contact: Dave Kuempel, Pres.
Local. Affiliated With: National Council of Corvette Clubs.

8559 ■ Central District Dental Society, Michigan
5001 W St. Joseph
Lansing, MI 48917
Ph: (517)321-2358
Fax: (517)321-7757
URL: National Affiliate–www.ada.org
Contact: Dr. Julia Gudmundsen, Exec.Dir.
Local. Represents the interests of dentists committed to the public's oral health, ethics and professional development. Encourages the improvement of the public's oral health and promotes the art and science of dentistry. **Affiliated With:** American Dental Association; Michigan Dental Association.

8560 ■ Cherry Marketing Institute (CMI)
c/o Philip J. Korson, II, Pres./Managing Dir.
PO Box 30285
Lansing, MI 48909-7785
Ph: (517)669-4264
Fax: (517)669-3354
URL: http://www.cherrymkt.org
Contact: Philip J. Korson II, Pres./Managing Dir.
Founded: 1988. **State.**

8561 ■ Common Cause of Michigan (CC/MI)
109 E Oakland Ave., 2nd Fl.
Lansing, MI 48906
Ph: (734)763-0689
Fax: (734)763-9181
E-mail: johnch@umich.edu
URL: http://www.commoncause.org
Contact: John Chamberlin, Chm.
Founded: 1973. **Members:** 7,500. **Staff:** 1. **Budget:** $79,000. **State.** Individuals working for an ethical, open, and accountable government. Promotes campaign finance reform, voter registration, and open legislative meetings. **Affiliated With:** Common Cause. **Publications:** *Legislative Update*, 3/year. Newsletter • *Links*, 3/year. Newsletter.

8562 ■ Community Economic Development Association of Michigan (CEDAM)
c/o Tony Lentych, Dir.
100 S Washington Ave., Ste.101
Lansing, MI 48912-1647
Ph: (517)485-3588
Fax: (517)484-1560
E-mail: staff@cedam.info
URL: http://www.cedam.info/about_us.html
Contact: Tony Lentych, Dir.
State. Affiliated With: National Congress for Community Economic Development.

8563 ■ County Road Association of Michigan (CRAM)
417 Seymour, Ste.1
PO Box 12067
Lansing, MI 48901-2067
Ph: (517)482-1189
Fax: (517)482-1253
E-mail: info@micountyroads.org
URL: http://www.micountyroads.org
Contact: John D. Niemela, Dir.
State. Represents the interests and concerns of the county road agencies in Michigan. Promotes efficiency in the operation of Michigan county road systems through the cooperative efforts of its members.

8564 ■ DeWitt Breakfast Lions Club
c/o Doug Vaughan, Pres.
3776 Wynbrooke Dr.
Lansing, MI 48906-9211
Ph: (517)669-8817 (517)886-2057
E-mail: jodug@hotmail.com
URL: http://www.district11c2.org
Contact: Doug Vaughan, Pres.
Local. Affiliated With: Lions Clubs International.

8565 ■ Dispute Resolution Association of Michigan (DRAM)
c/o Craig Pappas
2929 Covington Ct., Ste.201
Lansing, MI 48912
Ph: (517)485-2274
Fax: (517)485-1183
E-mail: resolve@tds.net
URL: http://www.michiganresolution.org
Contact: Craig Pappas, Pres.
State.

8566 ■ End Violent Encounters (EVE)
PO Box 14149
Lansing, MI 48901
Ph: (517)372-5976 (517)372-3382
URL: http://www.msu.edu/~cdaadmin
Contact: Staci Garcia, Volunteer Coor.
Founded: 1977. **Membership Dues:** regular, $25 (annual). **Budget:** $700,000. **Local.** Seeks to provide shelter and support services to the victims of domestic violence and their children while seeking to end domestic violence through public awareness and community education. **Telecommunication Services:** hotline, crisis hotline, (517)372-5572. **Formerly:** (2002) Council Against Domestic Assault; (2005) EVE-End Violent Encounters. **Publications:** Newsletter, quarterly. **Conventions/Meetings:** monthly board meeting.

8567 ■ Frank Bob Perrin - Lansing, Michigan Chapter of Trout Unlimited
c/o Robert Flickinger, Treas.
6603 Windsong Way
Lansing, MI 48917
Ph: (517)323-9572
E-mail: info@lansing-tu.org
URL: http://www.lansing-tu.org
Contact: Robert Flickinger, Treas.
Local. Affiliated With: Trout Unlimited. **Formerly:** (2003) Trout Unlimited, Lansing.

8568 ■ Fraternal Order of Police, Michigan State Lodge
124 W Allegan St., Ste.No. 636
Lansing, MI 48933
Ph: (517)367-8000
Fax: (517)367-8262
Free: (888)367-6424
E-mail: mifop@aol.com
URL: http://mifop.com
Contact: John Buczek, Exec.Dir.
State. Works to encourage fraternal, educational, charitable and social activities among law enforcement officers; to support the improvement of the standard of living and working conditions of the law enforcement profession. **Affiliated With:** Fraternal Order of Police, Grand Lodge.

8569 ■ Friends of Ingham County Animal Shelter (FICAS)
PO Box 11115
Lansing, MI 48901
Ph: (517)676-8370
E-mail: hollyls@sbcglobal.net
URL: http://www.petfinder.com/shelters/ficas.html
Contact: Holly Strobel, Pres.
Founded: 2000. **Members:** 5. **Local.**

8570 ■ Great Lakes Petroleum Retailers and Allied Trades Association
c/o Ron Milburn, Dir. of Membership Services
611 S Capitol Ave.
Lansing, MI 48933
Ph: (517)484-4096
Fax: (517)484-5705
Free: (800)748-0060
E-mail: oprralm@aol.com
URL: http://www.oprra.com
Contact: Ron Milburn, Dir. of Membership Services
Regional. Formed by Merger of: (2004) Ohio Petroleum Retailers and Repair Association and Service Station Dealers Association of Michigan.

8571 ■ Greater Detroit Golf Course Superintendents Association (GDGCSA)
PO Box 80212
Lansing, MI 48908
Ph: (517)327-3333
Fax: (517)321-5822
E-mail: gdgcsa@comcast.net
URL: http://www.gdgcsa.org
Contact: Dan T. Billette, Pres.
Local. Represents the interests of golf course superintendents. Advances members' profession for career success. Enhances the enjoyment, growth and vitality in the game of golf. Educates members concerning efficient and economical management of golf courses. **Affiliated With:** Golf Course Superintendents Association of America.

8572 ■ Greater Lansing Association of Realtors
3350 N Grand River Ave.
Lansing, MI 48906-2750
Ph: (517)323-4090
Fax: (517)323-0586
E-mail: info@lansing-realestate.com
URL: http://www.lansing-realestate.com
Contact: Elaine B. West CAE, CEO
Founded: 1907. **Members:** 1,385. **Membership Dues:** individual, $173 (annual). **Staff:** 15. **Budget:** $1,700,000. **State Groups:** 1. **Local Groups:** 1. **Local**. Promotes education, high professional standards, and modern techniques in specialized real estate work. **Awards:** Award of Professionalism. **Frequency:** annual. **Type:** recognition • Chair of the Year. **Frequency:** annual. **Type:** recognition • Circle of Excellence. **Frequency:** annual. **Type:** recognition • Realtor of the Year. **Frequency:** annual. **Type:** recognition. **Affiliated With:** National Association of Realtors. **Formerly:** (1994) GR Lans Assn. of Realtors. **Publications:** *Time Out!*, weekly. Newsletter. **Price:** included in membership dues. **Circulation:** 1,385. **Advertising:** accepted. Alternate Formats: online. **Conventions/Meetings:** General Membership Meeting - always January, May, and September • annual meeting • monthly meeting • Planning Session - meeting.

8573 ■ Greater Lansing Convention and Visitors Bureau (GLCVB)
1223 Turner St., Ste.100
Lansing, MI 48906
Ph: (517)487-6800
Fax: (517)487-5151
Free: (888)LAN-SING
E-mail: glcvb-info@lansing.org
URL: http://www.lansing.org
Contact: W. Lee Hladki, Pres.
Founded: 1960. **Members:** 630. **Staff:** 18. **Budget:** $2,300,000. **Local**. Promotes convention, business and tourism in the area. **Publications:** *Destination Planner*, annual. Alternate Formats: CD-ROM • *Fun Guide Calendar of Events*, semiannual • *Visitor's Guide*, annual.

8574 ■ Greater Lansing Home Builders Association
c/o Douglas Carr
6240 W Mt. Hope
Lansing, MI 48917-2467
Ph: (517)323-3254
Fax: (517)323-0390
E-mail: dcarr@glhba.org
URL: National Affiliate–www.nahb.org
Local. Single and multifamily home builders, commercial builders, and others associated with the building industry. **Affiliated With:** National Association of Home Builders.

8575 ■ Habitat for Humanity of Michigan (HFHM)
c/o Dr. Ken Bensen, Pres.
1000 S Washington
Lansing, MI 48910
Ph: (517)485-1006
Fax: (517)485-1509
Free: (800)467-5430
E-mail: kbensen@habitatmichigan.org
URL: http://www.habitatmichigan.org
Contact: Dr. Ken Bensen, Pres.
Founded: 1992. **Staff:** 4. **Budget:** $500,000. **State Groups:** 1. **Local Groups:** 84. **Nonmembership**. **State**. Individuals interested in providing affordable housing for people in need. **Affiliated With:** Habitat for Humanity International. **Conventions/Meetings:** annual conference.

8576 ■ Human Resource Management Association of Mid-Michigan (HRMAMM)
PO Box 19122
Lansing, MI 48901
E-mail: slewis@hrmamm.com
URL: http://www.hrmamm.com
Contact: Shana M. Lewis, Pres.
Local. Represents the interests of human resource and industrial relations professionals and executives. Promotes the advancement of human resource management.

8577 ■ Institute of Internal Auditors, Lansing Chapter
c/o Craig Murray
PO Box 11029
Lansing, MI 48901-1029
Ph: (517)334-8060
Fax: (517)334-8079
E-mail: murrayc@michigan.gov
URL: National Affiliate–www.theiia.org
Contact: Mark Stypinski CPA, Pres.
Founded: 1979. **Members:** 85. **Membership Dues:** regular, $115 (annual) • educator, $65 (annual) • student, retired, $30 (annual) • life, $2,100 • sustainer (government auditors only), $50 (annual) • organization ($65 per staff member over 5; $50 per staff member over 100), $425-$6,600 (annual). **Local**. Serves as an advocate for the internal audit profession. Provides certification, education, research, and technological guidance for the profession. **Awards: Frequency:** annual. **Type:** scholarship. **Recipient:** for undergraduate student pursuing business degree in internal auditing field. **Committees:** Academic Relations; Audit; Awards; Government Relations; Meeting Arrangements; Newsletter; Promotion; Research. **Affiliated With:** Institute of Internal Auditors. **Publications:** *Courier*, monthly. Newsletter. Alternate Formats: online.

8578 ■ Insurance Institute of Michigan (IIM)
334 Townsend St.
Lansing, MI 48933
Ph: (517)371-2880
Fax: (517)371-2882
E-mail: iiofmichigan@aol.com
URL: http://www.iiminfo.org
Contact: Peter Kuhnmuench, Exec.Dir.
Founded: 1981. **Members:** 35. **Staff:** 4. **Budget:** $650,000. **State**. Government affairs association of property-casualty insurance companies doing business in MI. **Formerly:** (2005) Michigan Insurance Federation. **Publications:** *MIF Notes*, monthly. Newsletters. **Conventions/Meetings:** annual conference.

8579 ■ International Brotherhood of Teamsters, Chauffeurs, Warehousemen and Helpers of America, AFL-CIO - Local Union 580
PO Box 25096
5800 Exec. Dr.
Lansing, MI 48911
Ph: (517)887-2944
E-mail: information@teamsterslocal580.com
URL: http://www.teamsterslocal580.com
Members: 2,120. **State**. **Affiliated With:** International Brotherhood of Teamsters.

8580 ■ International Union of Bricklayers and Allied Craftworkers, AFL-CIO-CLC Local Union 9
3321 Remy Dr.
Lansing, MI 48906
Ph: (517)886-2221 (517)886-9781
Fax: (517)886-5450
E-mail: nmcmath@bac9mich.org
URL: http://www.bac9mich.org
Contact: Nelson McMath, Pres.
Members: 2,529. **Local**. **Affiliated With:** International Union of Bricklayers and Allied Craftworkers.

8581 ■ International Union, United Automobile, Aerospace and Agricultural Implement Workers of America, AFL-CIO - Local Union 652
426 Clare St.
Lansing, MI 48917
Ph: (517)372-7581
Fax: (517)372-3839
URL: http://www.uawlocal652.org
Contact: Mike Belsito, Financial Sec.
Members: 6,034. **Local**. AFL-CIO. **Affiliated With:** International Union, United Automobile, Aerospace and Agricultural Implement Workers of America.

8582 ■ IPMA-HR Michigan Chapter
c/o Harold Hailey, Pres.
5303 S Cedar, Ste.2102
Lansing, MI 48911-3800
Ph: (571)887-4327
Fax: (571)887-4396
E-mail: hhailey@ingham.org
URL: National Affiliate–www.ipma-hr.org
Contact: Harold Hailey, Pres.
Local. Seeks to improve human resource practices in government through provision of testing services, advisory service, conferences, professional development programs, research and publications. Sponsors seminars, conferences and workshops on various phases of public personnel administration.

8583 ■ Joseph Watts Philanthropic Golden Gloves Boxing Group
PO Box 11099
Lansing, MI 48901

8584 ■ Justice In Mental Health Organization (JIMHO)
c/o Brenda Wellwood, Dir.
421 Seymour St.
Lansing, MI 48933
Ph: (517)371-2266 (517)371-2221
Fax: (517)371-5770
Free: (800)831-8035
E-mail: brwellwood@aol.com
URL: http://jimho.net
Founded: 1980. **Local**.

8585 ■ Labor and Employment Relations Association, Mid - Michigan
c/o Kathryn Van Dagens, Pres.
PO Box 27383
Lansing, MI 48909
Ph: (517)381-1390
E-mail: lera@lir.msu.edu
URL: http://www.lera.uiuc.edu/chapters/Profiles/MI-MidMichigan.html
Contact: Janet Roe-Darden, Pres.
Local.

8586 ■ Labor Management Partnership of Mid-Michigan (LMPMM)
c/o Cynthia Corbin, LMPMM Coor.
PO Box 22025
Lansing, MI 48909-2025
Ph: (517)887-4374
E-mail: ccorbin@ingham.org
URL: http://www.mlma.org/MidMichigan
Contact: Cynthia Corbin, LMPMM Coor.
Local.

8587 ■ Lansing Area AIDS Network (LAAN)
913 W Holmes Rd., Ste.115
Lansing, MI 48910
Ph: (517)394-3560
Fax: (517)394-1298
E-mail: laancontact@lansingareaaidsnetwork.org
URL: http://www.myne.com/501C/LAAN
Contact: Jacob Distel, Exec.Dir.
Founded: 1985. **Local**. Provides programs and services designed to assist people living with HIV/AIDS in mid-Michigan. Services include direct client care through comprehensive case management, prevention, education and outreach programs, and anonymous HIV antibody testing throughout the area. Programs include buddy support, transportation, food pantry, support groups, client education, and social activities.

8588 ■ Lansing Black Lawyers Association
c/o R. Vincent Green, Pres.
1300 N Waverly Rd., Ste.7
Lansing, MI 48917
Ph: (517)323-9305
E-mail: rvincentgreenpc@aol.com
URL: National Affiliate–www.nationalbar.org
Contact: R. Vincent Green, Pres.
Local. **Affiliated With:** National Bar Association.

8589 ■ Lansing Delta Lions Club
c/o Alvin Whitfield, Pres.
1241 Runaway Bay Dr., C-3
Lansing, MI 48917
Ph: (517)703-9666
E-mail: alwhit@worldnet.att.net
URL: http://www.district11c2.org
Contact: Alvin Whitfield, Pres.
Local. Affiliated With: Lions Clubs International.

8590 ■ Lansing Host Lions Club
c/o Marion Contompasis, Pres.
2810 Tulane Dr.
Lansing, MI 48912
Ph: (517)485-8116 (517)372-4199
Fax: (517)485-8125
E-mail: contompasis@impression5.org
URL: http://www.district11c2.org
Contact: Marion Contompasis, Pres.
Local. Affiliated With: Lions Clubs International.

8591 ■ Lansing Neighborhood Council
c/o Cheryl A. Risner, Dir.
Partington Educ. Center
500 W Lenawee, No. 319
Lansing, MI 48933
Ph: (517)372-6290
Fax: (517)372-5011
E-mail: lansingneighborhoodcouncil@yahoo.com
Contact: Cheryl Risner, Contact
Local. Helps organize neighborhood organizations. Addresses issues and concerns of Lansing citizens which affect their daily lives. Provides forums for the exchange of ideas between neighborhoods and organizations that represent them. **Awards:** Bea Christy. **Type:** recognition. **Recipient:** community volunteer. **Publications:** *Lansing Neighborhood Council Newsletter*, 3/year. **Price:** free. **Conventions/Meetings:** monthly board meeting.

8592 ■ Lansing REACT
PO Box 80121
Lansing, MI 48908-0121
Ph: (517)394-3359
URL: http://www.reactintl.org/teaminfo/usa_teams/teams-usmi.htm
Local. Trained communication experts and professional volunteers. Provides volunteer public service and emergency communications through the use of radios (Citizen Band, General Mobile Radio Service, UHF and HAM). Coordinates with radio industries and government on safety communication matters and supports charitable activities and community organizations.

8593 ■ Lansing Regional Chamber of Commerce
PO Box 14030
Lansing, MI 48901
Ph: (517)487-6340
Fax: (517)484-6910
E-mail: klane@lansingchamber.org
URL: http://www.lansingchamber.org
Contact: Bill Sepic, Pres.
Members: 2,000. **Staff:** 15. **Regional.** Works to facilitate economic development through the support of existing business and the attraction of new businesses for providing business advocacy and offering membership services. **Awards:** ATHENA Award. **Frequency:** annual. **Type:** recognition. **Recipient:** to individuals who strive toward the highest levels of professional accomplishment, men and women who excel in their chosen field, have devoted time and energy to their community, and who open paths so that others may follow • Community Service Award. **Frequency:** annual. **Type:** recognition. **Recipient:** for outstanding individuals of sound moral character who give their time and expertise to make Lansing a better community; act as an inspiration to the community and a credit to their business or profession • Outstanding Small Business Advocate Award. **Frequency:** annual. **Type:** recognition. **Recipient:** to a local individual who has successfully and voluntarily advocated for at least 3 years, partnered with organizations serving small businesses and has demonstrated a commitment to diversity • Outstanding Small Business Award. **Frequency:** annual. **Type:** recognition. **Recipient:** for a local business that has demonstrated stability, innovation, perseverance, and a commitment to diversity and community • Outstanding Small Business Person Award. **Frequency:** annual. **Type:** recognition. **Recipient:** to the owner of a local business that has demonstrated business stability, innovation, perseverance, and a commitment to diversity and community. **Committees:** Ambassadors; Economic Club; Events Advisory; Legislative Analysis; Membership Conference. **Councils:** Small Business Advisory. **Publications:** *Focus*, monthly. Newsletter. Alternate Formats: online • *Regional Vision*, bimonthly. Magazine. Alternate Formats: online • Annual Report, annual. Contains the development and information about the organization. Alternate Formats: online. **Conventions/Meetings:** quarterly Business Lunch Training Seminar Series - luncheon, informative seminars that focus on professional development and relevant topics and issues facing small business today • annual conference, 30-minute keynote address kicks off the conference and is followed by two 90-minute seminars, one in the morning and one in the afternoon (exhibits) - every September in Lansing, MI • annual dinner, program includes the Chamber's incoming and outgoing Board Chair, presentation of the prestigious ATHENA, Community Service and Small Business Awards, followed by a nationally recognized speaker - late February or early March • annual Lansing Open - competition, golf tournament, played in a scramble format with First Place gross winners at each course awarded a trophy and prize package • monthly Member Mixers - meeting, hosted by various Chamber members; strictly networking, there is no speaker or presentation - every second Tuesday.

8594 ■ Lansing Youth for Christ
PO Box 80555
Lansing, MI 48908
Ph: (517)322-2091
Fax: (517)322-4932
URL: http://www.lansingyfc.org
Local. Affiliated With: Youth for Christ/U.S.A.

8595 ■ League of Michigan Bicyclists (LMB)
PO Box 16201
Lansing, MI 48901
Ph: (517)334-9100
Fax: (517)334-9111
Free: (888)MI-BIKES
E-mail: office@lmb.org
URL: http://www.lmb.org
Contact: Rick Oberle, Interim Exec.Dir.
Founded: 1981. **Members:** 2,000. **Membership Dues:** family and individual, $20 (annual) • organization/club/shop, $50 (annual) • sustaining, $60 (annual) • supporting, $120 (annual) • life, $400 • life (organization), $1,000. **Staff:** 2. **Budget:** $150,000. **State.** Strives to promote biking for transportation and recreation. Educates motorists and bicyclists on safe sharing of the roadways by partnering with public and private agencies. Promotes bicycle tours and events and conducts charitable activities. Sponsors educational programs on bicycle safety and enjoyment. **Libraries: Type:** reference; open to the public; by appointment only. **Holdings:** 3,000; audio recordings, books, business records, clippings, video recordings. **Subjects:** bicycle safety, pedestrian safety, transit, land use, urban planning, tourism and economic development. **Awards:** Cyclist of the Year. **Frequency:** annual. **Type:** recognition. **Recipient:** for contributions in advancing cycling in Michigan • Herman Hoffer Memorial Award. **Frequency:** annual. **Type:** recognition • Volunteer of the Year. **Frequency:** annual. **Type:** recognition. **Affiliated With:** League of American Bicyclists. **Publications:** *Michigan Bicyclist*, quarterly. Magazine. Features international bicycling topics. **Price:** included in membership dues. **Circulation:** 3,000. **Advertising:** accepted. Alternate Formats: online. **Conventions/Meetings:** annual Shoreline Bicycle Tour.

8596 ■ League of Women Voters of the Lansing Area (LWVLA)
200 Museum Dr., Ste.104
Lansing, MI 48933-1997
Ph: (517)484-5383
Fax: (517)484-3086
E-mail: lwvmi@voyager.net
URL: National Affiliate–www.lwv.org
Contact: Anne Magoun, Contact
Membership Dues: individual, $45 (annual). **Local.** Aims to promote political responsibility through informed and active participation of citizens in government and to act on selected governmental issues. **Affiliated With:** League of Women Voters of Michigan; League of Women Voters of the United States. **Formerly:** League of Women Voters, Lansing Area. **Publications:** *Capital Voter*, periodic. Newsletter.

8597 ■ League of Women Voters of Michigan (LWVMI)
200 Museum Dr.
Lansing, MI 48933-1997
Ph: (517)484-5383
Fax: (517)484-3086
E-mail: info@lwvmi.org
URL: http://www.lwvmi.org
Contact: Patricia Donath, Dir.-at-Large
Founded: 1920. **Members:** 2,135. **Membership Dues:** regular, $50 (annual) • household, $75 (annual) • student, $25 (annual). **Staff:** 1. **Local Groups:** 27. **State.** Citizens 18 years old or older. Promotes political responsibility through informed and active participation of all citizens. **Affiliated With:** League of Women Voters of the United States. **Publications:** *Keeping This Land Ours: Taking an Active Role in the Decision-Making Process*. Booklet • *Michigan Voter*, bimonthly. Book • *The State We're In*. Book • *This Land is Ours: An Introduction to the Planning Process*. Booklet. **Conventions/Meetings:** semiannual meeting.

8598 ■ Learning Disabilities Association of Michigan
200 Museum Dr., Ste.101
Lansing, MI 48933-1914
Ph: (517)485-8160
Fax: (517)485-8462
Free: (888)597-7809
E-mail: ldami@aol.com
URL: http://www.ldaofmichigan.org
Contact: Nannette Clatterbuck, Pres.
Founded: 1965. **Members:** 1,300. **Membership Dues:** individual, $35 (annual). **Local.** Seeks to enhance the quality of life for all individuals with learning disabilities and their families; to alleviate the restricting effects of learning disabilities; and to support endeavors to determine the causes of learning disabilities. Addresses its missions through advocacy, education, research, service and collaborative efforts. **Telecommunication Services:** electronic mail, info@ldaofmichigan.org. **Affiliated With:** Learning Disabilities Association of America. **Publications:** *Outlook*, bimonthly. Newsletter. **Conventions/Meetings:** annual conference.

8599 ■ Libertarian Party of Michigan
c/o Michael Donahue, Chair
PO Box 27065
Lansing, MI 48924-7065
Free: (888)373-3669
E-mail: chair@lpmich.org
URL: http://www.mi.lp.org/
State. Affiliated With: Libertarian National Committee.

8600 ■ Life Insurance Association of Michigan
c/o Lawrence J. Kish, Pres.
230 N. Washington Sq., Ste.306
Lansing, MI 48933
Ph: (517)482-7058
Fax: (517)482-5405
E-mail: liam@voyager.net
State.

8601 ■ MARAL Pro-Choice Michigan
4515 W Saginaw Hwy., Ste.201
Lansing, MI 48917
Ph: (517)327-4707
Fax: (517)327-4710
E-mail: maral@prochoicemichigan.org
URL: http://www.prochoicemichigan.org
Contact: Kelly Hamilton, Contact
Founded: 1979. **State**. Works to develop a pro-choice political constituency in order to maintain the right to legal abortion for all women. Initiates and coordinates political action of individuals and groups concerned with maintaining the 1973 Supreme Court abortion decision affirming the choice of abortion as a constitutional right. **Affiliated With:** NARAL Pro-Choice America. **Also Known As:** (2005) Michigan Abortion and Reproductive Rights Action League.

8602 ■ MARO Employment and Training Association
PO Box 16218
Lansing, MI 48901
Ph: (517)484-5588
Fax: (517)484-5411
E-mail: dprice@maro.org
URL: http://www.maro.org
Contact: David J. Price, Exec.Dir.
Founded: 1974. **Members:** 65. **Staff:** 5. **Budget:** $450,000. **State**. Creates opportunities for people with barriers to employment and community access. **Formerly:** (1998) Michigan Association of Rehabilitation Organizations. **Publications:** *MARO Update*, periodic. Newsletter. **Conventions/Meetings:** annual Michigan Rehabilitation Conference (exhibits).

8603 ■ Massachusetts Thoracic Society
c/o Steve Springer, Administrator
403 Seymour Ave.
Lansing, MI 48933-1179
Ph: (517)484-4541
E-mail: sspringer@alam.org
URL: National Affiliate–www.thoracic.org
Contact: Kevin M. Chan MD, Pres.
State. Aims to improve the study and practice of thoracic surgery and related disciplines. Seeks to prevent and fight respiratory diseases through research, education and patient advocacy. **Affiliated With:** American Thoracic Society.

8604 ■ Michigan Asphalt Paving Association
c/o A. John Becsey, Managing Dir.
6639 Centurion Dr., Ste.120
Lansing, MI 48917
Ph: (517)323-7800
Fax: (517)323-6505
Free: (800)292-5959
E-mail: jbecsey@mi-asphalt.org
URL: http://www.hotmix.org/view_article.php?ID=64
Contact: A. John Becsey, Managing Dir.
State.

8605 ■ Michigan Association of Ambulance Services (MAAS)
412 W Ottawa
Lansing, MI 48933-1518
Ph: (517)485-3376
E-mail: execdir@miambulance.org
URL: http://www.miambulance.org
Contact: Brian P. Lovellette CAE, Exec.Dir.
State. Represents the interests of Michigan's pre-hospital care providers. Provides information, education and legislative and regulatory representation.

8606 ■ Michigan Association of Broadcasters (MAB)
c/o Karole L. White, Pres./CEO
819 N Washington Ave.
Lansing, MI 48906
Ph: (517)484-7444
Fax: (517)484-5810
Free: (800)YOUR-MAB
E-mail: mab@michmab.com
URL: http://www.michmab.com
Contact: Karole L. White, Pres./CEO
Founded: 1948. **Members:** 262. **Staff:** 8. **Budget:** $1,300,000. **State**. Radio stations (231) and television stations (31). Conducts educational and legislative activities. Holds congressional dinner. Sponsors public service advertising. Conducts charitable activities. **Awards:** MAB Award for Broadcast Excellence. **Frequency:** annual. **Type:** recognition. **Recipient:** for outstanding achievement in broadcasting by Michigan radio and television stations • Station of the Year. **Frequency:** annual. **Type:** recognition. **Recipient:** to the most number of points scored by the station. **Affiliated With:** National Association of Broadcasters. **Publications:** *The MAB Broadcaster*, bimonthly. Newsletter. **Conventions/Meetings:** annual conference, focuses on regulatory and management issues (exhibits).

8607 ■ Michigan Association of Cherry Producers (MACP)
c/o Cherry Marketing Institute
PO Box 30285
Lansing, MI 48909-7785
Ph: (517)669-4264
Fax: (517)669-3354
E-mail: info@usacherries.com
URL: http://www.usacherries.com
Contact: Philip J. Korson II, Pres./Managing Dir./Exec.Dir.
Founded: 1938. **Members:** 2,000. **Staff:** 5. Carries out educational and promotional work for Michigan tart and sweet cherry growers. **Conventions/Meetings:** annual meeting - always late December.

8608 ■ Michigan Association of Community and Adult Education (MACAE)
6500 Centurion Dr., Ste.265
Lansing, MI 48917
Ph: (517)321-2395
Fax: (517)321-2397
Free: (888)214-0131
E-mail: macae@macae.org
URL: http://www.macae.org
Contact: Ken Walsh, Exec.Dir.
Membership Dues: individual active, $369 (annual) • associate, $129 (annual) • emeritus, $50 (annual) • vendor, $250 (annual). **State**. Works to enhance member effectiveness by providing the highest quality of information services, professional training, and legislative support to make possible the delivery of comprehensive community education services for all.

8609 ■ Michigan Association of Community Arts Agencies (MACAA)
c/o Deborah E. Mikula, Exec.Dir.
1310 Turner St., Ste.B
Lansing, MI 48906
Ph: (517)371-1720
Fax: (517)371-1743
Free: (800)203-9633
E-mail: macaa@macaa.com
URL: http://www.macaa.com
Contact: Deborah E. Mikula, Exec.Dir.
Founded: 1977. **State**.

8610 ■ Michigan Association of Community Mental Health Boards (MACMHB)
c/o Mr. David Lalumia, Exec.Dir.
426 S Walnut
Lansing, MI 48933
Ph: (517)374-6848
Fax: (517)374-1053
E-mail: dlalumia@macmhb.org
URL: http://www.macmhb.org
Contact: Mr. David Lalumia, Exec.Dir.
State.

8611 ■ Michigan Association of Convenience Stores
c/o Mark A. Griffin, Pres.
7521 Wetshire Dr., Ste.200
Lansing, MI 48917
Ph: (517)622-3530
Fax: (517)622-3420
E-mail: mpamacs@mpamacs.org
URL: http://mpamacs.org
State.

8612 ■ Michigan Association for Deaf, Hearing and Speech Services (MADHS)
c/o John D. Berchtold, Exec.Dir.
2929 Covington Ct., Ste.200
Lansing, MI 48912-4939
Ph: (517)487-0066 (517)487-0202
Fax: (517)480-2586
Free: (800)YOU-REAR
E-mail: john@madhs.org
URL: http://www.madhs.org
Contact: John D. Berchtold, Exec.Dir.
Founded: 1931. **Members:** 635. **Membership Dues:** individual, family, $25 (annual) • professional, organization, $50 (annual) • advocate, $100 (annual) • other, $50 (annual). **Budget:** $450,000. **State**. Provides deaf and hard of hearing programs including camping, leadership education, employment opportunities, and substance abuse prevention. Sponsors advocacy; directs coalition for deaf and hard of hearing individuals; public education; and service coordination. Offers equipment distribution for deaf and hard of hearing people. **Publications:** *The Communique*, quarterly. Newsletter. **Conventions/Meetings:** quarterly board meeting • semiannual Consortium for Universal Newborn Hearing Screening • quarterly meeting.

8613 ■ Michigan Association of Emergency Medical Technicians (MAEMT)
412 W Ottawa St.
Lansing, MI 48933-1518
Ph: (517)372-7391
Fax: (517)372-1731
E-mail: execdir@maemt.org
URL: http://www.maemt.org
Contact: Brian P. Lovellette CAE, Exec.Dir.
Founded: 1974. **Members:** 750. **Membership Dues:** individual, $25 (annual). **State**. **Publications:** *Vital Signs*, quarterly. Newsletter. **Conventions/Meetings:** monthly board meeting.

8614 ■ Michigan Association of Fairs and Exhibitions (MAFE)
c/o E.J. Brown, Exec.Dir.
124 W Allegan St., Ste.1100
Lansing, MI 48933
Ph: (517)371-2000
Fax: (989)659-2911
E-mail: mifairs@yahoo.com
URL: http://www.michiganfairs.org
Contact: E.J. Brown, Exec.Dir.
Founded: 1885. **State**. Promotes the development of agricultural and related industries, coordinates the objectives of fairs and exhibition. Informs and educates its members across the state through meetings and annual convention and encourages the participation of youth in these endeavors.

8615 ■ Michigan Association of Fire Chiefs (MAFC)
3315 S Pennsylvania Ave.
Lansing, MI 48910
Ph: (517)394-4398
Fax: (517)394-1117
E-mail: info@michiefs.org
URL: http://www.michiefs.org
Contact: Suzy Carter, Exec.Dir.
State.

8616 ■ Michigan Association of Governmental Employees (MAGE)
c/o John De Tizio, Dir. of Labor Relations
6920 S Cedar, Ste.4
Lansing, MI 48911
Ph: (517)694-3123
Fax: (517)694-8250
Free: (800)477-MAGE
E-mail: mage@tir.com
URL: http://mage.org
Contact: Ann Sanders, Admin.Asst. to Pres.
Founded: 1980. **State**.

8617 ■ Michigan Association of Health Plans (MAHP)
c/o Richard B. Murdock, Exec.Dir.
327 Seymour
Lansing, MI 48933
Ph: (517)371-3181
Fax: (517)482-8866
E-mail: mahpadmin@mahp.org
URL: http://mahp.org
Contact: Richard B. Murdock, Exec.Dir.
Founded: 1979. **Members:** 71. **Membership Dues:** limited service, $2,700 (annual) • business affiliate, $1,620 (annual). **Staff:** 7. **State**. Strives to provide leadership for the promotion and advocacy of high quality, affordable, accessible health care for the citizens of Michigan. **Computer Services:** database • mailing lists. **Committees:** Executive; Government Programs; Legislative; Medical Directors; Public Relations; Summer Conference. **Formerly:** (1997) Association of HMOs in Michigan. **Publications:** *MAHP Insights*, bimonthly. Newsletter. **Advertising:** accepted. **Conventions/Meetings:** annual conference (exhibits).

8618 ■ Michigan Association of Home Builders
c/o Lynn Egbert
1628 S Creyts Rd.
Lansing, MI 48917
Ph: (517)322-0224
Fax: (517)322-0504
Free: (800)748-0432
E-mail: egbert.lynn@mahb.com
URL: National Affiliate–www.nahb.org
Contact: Cindy Riegsecker, Contact
State. Single and multifamily home builders, commercial builders, and others associated with the building industry. **Affiliated With:** National Association of Home Builders.

8619 ■ Michigan Association of Insurance Agents (MAIA)
PO Box 80620
Lansing, MI 48908-0620
Ph: (517)323-9473
Fax: (517)323-1629
Free: (800)589-6501
E-mail: rpierce@michagent.org
URL: http://www.michagent.org
Contact: Robert D. Pierce CAE, CEO
Founded: 1992. **State**.

8620 ■ Michigan Association for Local Public Health (MALPH)
PO Box 13276
Lansing, MI 48901-3276
Ph: (517)485-0660
Fax: (517)485-6412
E-mail: mbertler@malph.org
URL: http://www.malph.org
Contact: Mark J. Bertler CAE, Exec.Dir.
Founded: 1985. **Members:** 45. **Membership Dues:** associate, $25 (annual). **Staff:** 5. **Budget:** $500,000. **State**. Local health departments. Provides statewide advocacy, policy review and development, and professional development and representation. **Awards:** Friend of Local Public Health. **Frequency:** annual. **Type:** recognition • Public Health Partnership. **Frequency:** annual. **Type:** recognition. **Publications:** *Local Health Department Directory*, annual. **Conventions/Meetings:** annual conference (exhibits) - always August.

8621 ■ Michigan Association of Non-Public Schools (MANS)
501 S Capitol Ave.
Lansing, MI 48933
Ph: (517)372-0003
Fax: (517)334-5526
URL: National Affiliate–www.capenet.org
Contact: Glen Walstra, Exec.Dir.
Founded: 1972. **Members:** 510. **Staff:** 3. **Local Groups:** 510. **State**. Private schools dedicated to providing a framework for communication among public and non-public educators and government agencies at local, state, and federal levels. Promotes diversity and choice in education. **Awards:** MANS Educator Achievement Award. **Frequency:** triennial. **Type:** recognition. **Affiliated With:** Council for American Private Education; National Catholic Educational Association. **Publications:** *MANS Notes*, bimonthly. Newsletter. **Price:** included in membership dues. **Conventions/Meetings:** triennial Educational Conference, for school leaders and teachers (exhibits).

8622 ■ Michigan Association of Occupational Health Nurses (MAOHN)
PO Box 80332
Lansing, MI 48908-0134
Ph: (313)966-7110
Fax: (313)745-3263
E-mail: sheryl.ebaugh@gm.com
URL: http://www.michaohn.org
Contact: Sheryl Ebaugh, Pres.
State. Advances the profession of occupational and environmental health nursing. Promotes public awareness of occupational health nursing. **Affiliated With:** American Association of Occupational Health Nurses.

8623 ■ Michigan Association of Professional Landmen (MAPL)
PO Box 21068
Lansing, MI 48909
Ph: (231)941-0073
E-mail: rabbott@auroraenergy.com
URL: National Affiliate–www.landman.org
Contact: Rebecca L. Abbott CPL, Pres.
State. Promotes the highest standards of performance for all land professionals. Encourages sound stewardship of energy and mineral resources.

8624 ■ Michigan Association for Pupil Transportation (MAPT)
6250 W Michigan Ave., Ste.A
Lansing, MI 48917-2454
Ph: (517)886-0881
Fax: (517)886-0882
E-mail: klosch@mapt.org
URL: http://www.mapt.org
Contact: Karen Losch, Exec.Dir.
State.

8625 ■ Michigan Association of Realtors (MAR)
PO Box 40725
Lansing, MI 48901-7925
Ph: (517)372-8890
Fax: (517)334-5568
Free: (800)454-7842
URL: http://www.mirealtors.com
Contact: Bill Martin RCE, CEO
Members: 24,000. **State**. Real estate professionals united to provide members with programs, products, and services to enhance their businesses. Advocates and promotes the preservation and advancement of property rights. **Affiliated With:** National Association of Realtors. **Publications:** *Michigan Realtor*, 10/year. Magazine. **Conventions/Meetings:** annual conference - always October • annual meeting - always January.

8626 ■ Michigan Association of School Administrators (MASA)
1001 Centennial Way, Ste.300
Lansing, MI 48917-9279
Ph: (517)327-5910
Fax: (517)327-0771
E-mail: jscofield@gomasa.org
URL: http://www.gomasa.org
Contact: William H. Mayes, Exec.Dir.
Founded: 1948. **Members:** 850. **Membership Dues:** professional, $325 (annual). **Staff:** 10. **Budget:** $1,100,000. **Regional Groups:** 10. **State**. Superintendents and first line assistants. Seeks to improve public education; promotes the advancement of the profession of school administrators. **Publications:** *Fortnighter*, biweekly. Newsletter. **Conventions/Meetings:** annual conference - always in autumn • annual conference - held during January • annual Political Action - conference - held during the spring.

8627 ■ Michigan Association of School Boards (MASB)
c/o Justin P. King, Exec.Dir.
1001 Centennial Way, Ste.400
Lansing, MI 48917
Ph: (517)327-5900
Fax: (517)327-0775
E-mail: jking@masb.org
URL: http://www.masb.org
Contact: Justin P. King, Exec.Dir.
State.

8628 ■ Michigan Association of Secondary School Principals (MASSP)
1001 Centennial Way, Ste.100
Lansing, MI 48917
Ph: (517)327-5315
Fax: (517)327-5360
E-mail: jimb@michiganprincipals.org
URL: http://www.michiganprincipals.org
Contact: Mark Thomas, Pres.
Founded: 1911. **Members:** 1,800. **Membership Dues:** professional, $340 (annual) • retired, $65 (annual) • educator, $140 (annual). **Staff:** 5. **Budget:** $1,000,000. **State**. Represents the interests of secondary school principals. Unites to uphold a commitment to secondary education. **Awards:** Principals of the Year. **Frequency:** annual. **Type:** recognition. **Affiliated With:** National Association of Secondary School Principals. **Publications:** *MASSP Bulletin*, 10/year. **Price:** included in membership dues. **Circulation:** 2,300 • *Secondary Education Today*, quarterly. Journal. **Conventions/Meetings:** annual Principal Fall Conference (exhibits) • annual Summer Retreat.

8629 ■ Michigan Association for Supervision and Curriculum Development (ASCD)
c/o Olga Moir
1001 Centennial Way, Ste.300
Lansing, MI 48917-9279
Ph: (517)327-5910 (517)327-9269
Fax: (517)327-0771
E-mail: mascd@admin.melg.org
URL: http://www.michiganascd.org
Contact: Olga Moir, Exec.Dir.
Members: 1,400. **Membership Dues:** regular, $75 (annual) • student, $20 (annual). **Staff:** 2. **Budget:** $100,000. **Regional Groups:** 8. **State Groups:** 1. **For-Profit**. **State**. Organization of diverse educators committed to excellence in teaching and learning. Seeks to lead the educational community by initiating, influencing, and advocating equity and success for all students. **Libraries:** **Type:** reference. **Holdings:** 200; books, periodicals, video recordings. **Subjects:** education. **Computer Services:** database • electronic publishing • information services • online services. **Affiliated With:** Association for Supervision and Curriculum Development. **Publications:** Newsletter, bimonthly. **Price:** free to members. **Circulation:** 1,400. **Advertising:** accepted. Alternate Formats: online.

8630 ■ Michigan Association of Timbermen (MAT)
c/o Timothy Karasek
409 W Ionia St.
Lansing, MI 48933
Ph: (517)364-8733
Fax: (517)364-8736
E-mail: karasek@timbermen.org
URL: http://www.timbermen.org
Founded: 1972. **State**.

8631 ■ Michigan Association of United Ways
1627 Lake Lansing Rd., Ste.B
Lansing, MI 48912
Ph: (517)371-4360
Fax: (517)371-1801
E-mail: cnelson@uwmich.org
URL: http://www.uwmich.org
Contact: Christopher L. Nelson, Pres./CEO
State. **Affiliated With:** United Way of America.

8632 ■ Michigan Audubon Society (MAS)
6011 W St. Joseph Hwy., Ste.403
Lansing, MI 48917
Ph: (517)886-9144
Fax: (517)886-9466
E-mail: mas@michiganaudubon.org
URL: http://www.michiganaudubon.org
Founded: 1904. **Members:** 9,500. **Membership Dues:** $20 (annual). **Staff:** 4. **State Groups:** 1. **Local Groups:** 43. **State**. Promotes protection of wildlife and habitat of the upper Great Lakes Region. Educates public; supports ecological research; maintains sanctuaries. **Affiliated With:** National Audubon Society. **Publications:** *Jack Pine Warbler*, bimonthly. Newsletter • *Michigan Birds and Natural History*, quarterly. Journal.

8633 ■ Michigan Bankers Association (MBA)
507 S Grand Ave.
Lansing, MI 48933
Ph: (517)485-3600
Fax: (517)485-3672
E-mail: dkoons@mibankers.com
URL: http://www.mibankers.com
Contact: Dennis R. Koons CAE, Pres./CEO
Founded: 1887. **State**.

8634 ■ Michigan Basin Geological Society
PO Box 18074
Lansing, MI 48901-8074
Ph: (517)241-3769
E-mail: info@mbgs.org
URL: http://www.mbgs.org
Contact: Dr. Robb Gillespie, Pres.
State. Fosters scientific research and advances the science of geology. Promotes technology and inspires high professional conduct. **Affiliated With:** American Association of Petroleum Geologists.

8635 ■ Michigan Beer and Wine Wholesalers Association (MB&WWA)
c/o Michael J. Lashbrook, Pres.
332 Townsend St.
Lansing, MI 48933-2071
Ph: (517)482-5555
Fax: (517)482-1532
E-mail: info@mbwwa.org
URL: http://www.mbwwa.org
Contact: Michael J. Lashbrook, Pres.
State.

8636 ■ Michigan Black Independent Publishers Association
PO Box 14304
Lansing, MI 48901-4304
Ph: (517)204-4197
E-mail: mbipa_mi@hotmail.com
URL: National Affiliate–www.pma-online.com
Contact: Tanya Bates, Pres.
State. Serves individuals and corporate groups involved in book, audio and video publishing. Advances the professional interests of independent publishers. Aims to provide training programs and cooperative marketing assistance within the publishing industry. **Affiliated With:** PMA - Independent Book Publishers Association.

8637 ■ Michigan Board of Optometry
Bur. of Hea. Professions
PO Box 30670
Lansing, MI 48909
Ph: (517)335-0918
Fax: (517)373-2179
E-mail: bhpinfo@michigan.gov
URL: http://www.michigan.gov/healthlicense
State. **Affiliated With:** Association of Regulatory Boards of Optometry.

8638 ■ Michigan Campaign Finance Network
200 Museum Dr.
Lansing, MI 48933
Ph: (517)482-7198
E-mail: mcfn@mcfn.org
URL: http://www.mcfn.org
Contact: Richard Robinson, Exec.Dir.
State.

8639 ■ Michigan Chamber of Commerce
600 S Walnut St.
Lansing, MI 48933
Ph: (517)371-2100
Fax: (517)371-7224
Free: (800)748-0266
E-mail: info@michamber.com
URL: http://www.michamber.com
Contact: Jim Barrett, Pres./CEO
Founded: 1959. **Members:** 6,300. **State**. Works to represent employer interests in promoting economic development in Michigan. **Publications:** *Michigan Forward*, bimonthly. Magazine. Includes legislative briefings, business news and information about chamber activities. **Advertising:** accepted.

8640 ■ Michigan Chapter of the American Society of Landscape Architects (MASLA)
1000 W St. Joseph Hwy., Ste.200
Lansing, MI 48915
Ph: (517)485-7711
E-mail: manager@michiganasla.org
URL: http://www.michiganasla.org
Contact: Timothy Britain, Pres.
State. Promotes the growth of the landscape architecture profession. Fosters high standards of quality in design, planning, development, and conservation in the field. Promotes the exchange of technical information and supports scientific research in all aspects of landscape architecture. **Telecommunication Services:** electronic mail, president@michiganasla.org. **Affiliated With:** American Society of Landscape Architects.

8641 ■ Michigan Chemical Council (MCC)
c/o Andrew J. Such, CAE, Exec.Dir.
Capitol Corners
326 W Ottawa
Lansing, MI 48933-1530
Ph: (517)372-8898
Fax: (517)372-9020
E-mail: suchmcc@voyager.net
URL: http://www.michiganchemistry.com
Contact: Andrew J. Such CAE, Exec.Dir.
Founded: 1967. **Members:** 75. **Staff:** 4. **Budget:** $350,000. **State**. **Conventions/Meetings:** annual meeting (exhibits) - always May in Lansing, MI.

8642 ■ Michigan Chiropractic Society (MCS)
416 W Ionia
Lansing, MI 48933
Ph: (517)367-2225
Fax: (517)367-2228
Free: (800)949-1401
E-mail: info@chiromini.com
URL: http://www.chiromi.com
Contact: Kristine Dowell, Exec.Dir.
Founded: 1988. **Members:** 1,060. **Membership Dues:** 2nd full fiscal year licensed, $200 (annual) • 3rd full fiscal year licensed, $400 (annual) • 4th year and beyond licensed, $600 (annual) • century club, $1,200 (annual) • vendors/out of state DC's, $200 (annual) • retired DC's, $75 (annual) • semi-retired DC's, $200 (annual). **State**. Commits to professional excellence within the state of MI. Protects and serves the chiropractic profession by presenting a united front to the public, media, and public policy makers, and by mobilizing doctors to advocate for chiropractic issues. **Publications:** *The Society*, 10/year. Newsletter. **Conventions/Meetings:** semiannual convention - spring and fall.

8643 ■ Michigan Clothiers Association (MCA)
c/o James P. Hallan, Pres.
603 S Washington Ave.
Lansing, MI 48933
Ph: (517)372-5656
Fax: (517)372-1303
Free: (800)366-3699
E-mail: jhallan@retailers.com
URL: http://www.retailers.com
State.

8644 ■ Michigan College of Emergency Physicians (MCEP)
6647 W St. Joseph Hwy.
Lansing, MI 48917
Ph: (517)327-5700
Fax: (517)327-7530
E-mail: mcep@mcep.org
URL: http://www.mcep.org
Contact: Diane Kay Bollman, Exec.Dir.
Founded: 1969. **Members:** 1,300. **Staff:** 3. **Budget:** $525,000. **State**. Emergency medicine physicians. Provides a unifying direction of purpose to physicians specializing in emergency medicine. **Awards:** Emergency Physician of the Year. **Frequency:** annual. **Type:** recognition. **Recipient:** for outstanding community service • Krome Meritorious Service Award. **Frequency:** annual. **Type:** recognition. **Recipient:** for outstanding leadership. **Affiliated With:** American College of Emergency Physicians. **Formerly:** American College of Emergency Physicians Michigan Chapter. **Publications:** *News and Views*, monthly. Newsletter. **Circulation:** 1,500. **Advertising:** accepted. **Conventions/Meetings:** annual Michigan Emergency Medicine Assembly - meeting, with educational presentation (exhibits).

8645 ■ Michigan Community Action Agency Association (MCAAA)
516 S Creyts Rd., Ste.A
Lansing, MI 48917
Ph: (517)321-7500
Fax: (517)321-7504
E-mail: contact@mcaaa.org
URL: http://www.mcaaa.org
Contact: Doreen K. Woodward, Exec.Dir.
State.

8646 ■ Michigan Community College Association (MCCA)
c/o Thomas M. Bernthal, Pres.
222 N Chestnut St.
Lansing, MI 48933-1000
Ph: (517)372-4350
Fax: (517)372-0905
E-mail: mcca@mcca.org
URL: http://www.mcca.org
Contact: Thomas M. Bernthal, Pres.
Founded: 1970. **Members:** 28. **Staff:** 3. **State**. Promotes and represents the interests of community colleges. **Publications:** *Annual Directory*, annual • Newsletter, quarterly. **Conventions/Meetings:** annual meeting.

8647 ■ Michigan Community Coordinated Child Care Association
c/o J. Mark Sullivan, Exec.Dir.
839 Centennial Way
Lansing, MI 48917
Ph: (517)351-4171
Fax: (517)351-0157
Free: (800)950-4171
E-mail: mi4c@mi4c.org
URL: http://www.mi4c.org
Contact: J. Mark Sullivan, Exec.Dir.
State. Local Regional 4C agencies dedicated to the optimal care and development of Michigan's children and families.

8648 ■ Michigan Concrete Association (MCA)
3130 Pine Tree Rd.
Lansing, MI 48911
Ph: (517)393-1711
Fax: (517)393-1791
Free: (800)678-9622
E-mail: miconcreteassn@voyager.net
URL: http://www.miconcrete.org
Contact: Shel Wheatley, Chair
Founded: 1952. **State**.

8649 ■ Michigan Conference of the American Association of University Professors (MIAAUP)
115 W Allegan St., Ste.320
Lansing, MI 48933

Ph: (517)482-2775
Fax: (517)482-6115
E-mail: miaaup@aol.com
URL: http://www.miaaup.org
Contact: Robert C. Grosvenor, Exec.Dir.

Founded: 1953. **Members:** 3,300. **Membership Dues:** student, $10 (annual) • full, $179 (annual) • entrant, part-time, $113 (annual). **Staff:** 2. **Budget:** $100,000. **State**. College and university faculty, librarians, counselors, and advisors working to promote the profession. Seeks to inform members and public policymakers. **Awards:** Legislator of the Year. **Frequency:** annual. **Type:** recognition • President's Award. **Frequency:** annual. **Type:** recognition. **Recipient:** for outstanding member. **Affiliated With:** American Association of University Professors. **Publications:** Newsletter, quarterly. **Price:** included in membership dues. **Circulation:** 4,000. **Conventions/Meetings:** annual meeting - usually May.

8650 ■ Michigan Congress of Parents, Teachers and Students
1011 N Washington Ave.
Lansing, MI 48906
Ph: (517)485-4345
Fax: (517)485-4345
E-mail: communications@michiganpta.org
URL: http://www.michiganpta.org
Contact: Donna Oser, Admin.Dir.

Founded: 1918. **Members:** 90,000. **Membership Dues:** individual, $3 (annual) • business, $50 (annual). **State**. **Libraries: Type:** not open to the public. **Holdings:** articles, books, video recordings. **Subjects:** parenting, education, child advocacy. **Computer Services:** Electronic publishing • mailing lists • online services. **Publications:** *Michigan PTSA Bulletin*, monthly. Newsletter. Includes articles on parents, teachers and children relationships.

8651 ■ Michigan Corrections Organization (MCO)
c/o Mel Grieshaber, Exec.Dir.
421 W Kalamazoo St.
Lansing, MI 48933
Ph: (517)485-3310
Fax: (517)485-3319
Free: (800)451-4878
E-mail: mail@mco-seiu.org
URL: http://www.mco-seiu.org
Contact: Mel Grieshaber, Exec.Dir.

State.

8652 ■ Michigan Council on Crime and Delinquency (MCCD)
1115 S Pennsylvania Ave., Ste.201
Lansing, MI 48912
Ph: (517)482-4161
Fax: (517)482-0020
E-mail: mail@miccd.org
Contact: Elizabeth Arnovits, Exec.Dir.

Founded: 1956. **Members:** 450. **Membership Dues:** organizational, $20 (annual). **Staff:** 8. **Budget:** $500,000. **Local**. Seeks to reduce delinquency and crime through research, technical assistance and advocacy. **Publications:** *Council Bulletin*, 3/year. Newsletter. **Price:** $20.00/year. **Conventions/Meetings:** annual meeting - always October or November.

8653 ■ Michigan Counseling Association (MCA)
530 W Ionia St., Ste.C
Lansing, MI 48933
Ph: (248)865-6768
Fax: (517)371-1170
Free: (800)444-2014
E-mail: lark.t@gcsionline.com
URL: http://www.wccnet.edu/orgs/mca
Contact: Charles Jennings, Pres.

Founded: 1965. **Members:** 2,200. **Membership Dues:** regular/associate, $75 • student/emeritus, $37. **State**. Counselors. Promotes interests of personnel and guidance services. **Libraries: Type:** open to the public. **Formerly:** Michigan Personnel and Guidance Association. **Publications:** *Michigan Journal of Counseling and Development*, semiannual • *Quest*, bimonthly. Newsletter • Directory, annual. **Conventions/Meetings:** annual conference (exhibits).

8654 ■ Michigan County Social Service Association (MCSSA)
c/o Ellen Speckman-Randall, Exec.Dir.
935 N Washington Ave.
Lansing, MI 48906-5156
Ph: (517)371-5303
Fax: (517)371-5310
E-mail: ellen@mcssa.com
URL: http://www.mcssa.com
Contact: Jay Bortz, Pres.

Founded: 1939. **Members:** 400. **Staff:** 2. **Budget:** $250,000. **Local Groups:** 6. **State**. Social service officials working to promote humane and equitable social service policy and legislation. Seeks to educate members, professionals, and the public on social service issues and needs. **Publications:** Bulletin, 9/year. **Conventions/Meetings:** semiannual conference.

8655 ■ Michigan Crop Improvement Association
c/o Randel H. Judd, Mgr.
PO Box 21008
Lansing, MI 48909
Ph: (517)332-3546
Fax: (517)332-9301
E-mail: juddr@michcrop.com
URL: http://www.michcrop.com
Contact: Randel H. Judd, Mgr.

State.

8656 ■ Michigan Democratic Party
c/o Mr. Mark Brewer, Chm.
606 Townsend St.
Lansing, MI 48933
Ph: (517)371-5410
Fax: (517)371-2056
E-mail: midemparty@mi-democrats.com
URL: http://www.mi-democrats.com
Contact: Mr. Mark Brewer, Chm.

Members: 15,000. **Membership Dues:** $15 (annual). **Staff:** 12. **Local Groups:** 200. **State**. **Subgroups:** Club; Congressional District; County. **Affiliated With:** Democratic National Committee. **Publications:** Newsletter, 3/year. **Price:** free for members. **Circulation:** 40,000. Also Cited As: *Gearing Up*.

8657 ■ Michigan Dental Association (MDA)
c/o Ms. Geraldine M. Cherney, CAE, Exec.Dir.
230 N Washington Sq., Ste.208
Lansing, MI 48933-1392
Ph: (517)372-9070
Fax: (517)372-0008
E-mail: mda@michigandental.org
URL: http://www.smilemichigan.com
Contact: Ms. Geraldine M. Cherney CAE, Exec.Dir.

Founded: 1856. **Members:** 5,824. **Membership Dues:** full, active, $831 (annual). **Staff:** 32. **Local Groups:** 26. **State**. Works to provide continuing education, peer review, journals, and others concerning dentistry and dental care. **Computer Services:** Mailing lists, of members. **Conventions/Meetings:** annual convention, includes exhibit, social event, and continuing education (exhibits).

8658 ■ Michigan Developmental Disabilities Council
c/o Vendella Collins
Lewis Cass Bldg.
Lansing, MI 48913
Ph: (517)334-6123
Fax: (517)334-7353
E-mail: collinsve@michigan.gov

State. Strives to support people with developmental disabilities to achieve life dreams. **Affiliated With:** National Association of Councils on Developmental Disabilities.

8659 ■ Michigan Distributors and Vendors Association (MDVA)
523 W Ionia St.
Lansing, MI 48933
Ph: (517)372-2323
Fax: (517)372-4404
E-mail: mdva@mdva.org
URL: http://www.mdva.org
Contact: Polly Reber, Pres.

Founded: 1947. **Members:** 110. **Staff:** 2. **Budget:** $400,000. **State**. Wholesale distributors of candy, tobacco, grocery products, vending and food service operations. **Publications:** Yearbook, annual • Newsletter, quarterly. **Conventions/Meetings:** annual convention (exhibits).

8660 ■ Michigan Electric and Gas Association (MEGA)
c/o James Ault, Pres.
110 W Michigan Ave., Ste.1000 B
Lansing, MI 48933
Ph: (517)484-7730
Fax: (517)484-5020
E-mail: jaault@voyager.net
URL: http://www.gomega.org

Founded: 1983. **Members:** 14. **Staff:** 2. **State**. Electric and gas companies. Represents the interests of investor-owned gas and electric companies. Conducts seminars and conferences. **Publications:** *Megabits*, quarterly. Newsletter. **Conventions/Meetings:** annual conference - always September.

8661 ■ Michigan Environmental Council (MEC)
119 Pere Marquette Dr., Ste.2A
Lansing, MI 48912
Ph: (517)487-9539
Fax: (517)487-9541
E-mail: mec@voyager.net
URL: http://www.mecprotects.org
Contact: Lana Pollack, Pres.

Founded: 1980. **Local**.

8662 ■ Michigan Environmental Health Association (MEHA)
PO Box 13276
Lansing, MI 48901
Ph: (517)485-9033
Fax: (517)485-6412
E-mail: questions@meha.net
URL: http://www.meha.net
Contact: Alan Hauck, Pres.

State. Advances the environmental health and protection profession. Provides educational and training opportunities for members. Works to establish standards of competence and ethics for the profession. **Affiliated With:** National Environmental Health Association.

8663 ■ Michigan Family Forum (MFF)
PO Box 15216
Lansing, MI 48901-5216
Ph: (517)374-1171
Fax: (517)374-6112
E-mail: info@michiganfamily.org
URL: http://www.michiganfamily.org
Contact: Brad Snavely, Exec.Dir.

State. Research and education organization that focuses on family issues in the Michigan Legislature.

8664 ■ Michigan Farm Bureau (MFB)
c/o John Vander Molen
7373 W Saginaw Hwy.
PO Box 30960
Lansing, MI 48909-8460
Ph: (517)323-7000
Fax: (517)323-6793
Free: (800)292-2680
URL: http://www.michiganfarmbureau.com
Contact: John Vander Molen, COO

Founded: 1919. **Members:** 155,000. **Membership Dues:** regular, associate, $45 (annual). **Staff:** 70. **Budget:** $161,000. **Local Groups:** 68. **State**. Farmer advocacy organization. Provides buyer services and insurance. **Affiliated With:** American Farm Bureau

Federation. **Publications:** *Mich Farm News*, bimonthly. Newspapers • *Rural Living*, quarterly. Magazine. **Conventions/Meetings:** annual meeting.

8665 ■ Michigan Federation for Children and Families
309 N Washington Sq., Ste.011
Lansing, MI 48933
Ph: (517)485-8552
Fax: (517)485-6680
E-mail: lansing@michfed.org
URL: http://www.michfed.org
Contact: Elizabeth Carey, Exec.Dir.
Founded: 1969. **Members:** 63. **Staff:** 4. **Budget:** $509,000. **State**. Private child and family welfare agencies. Promotes the social welfare of children and families. Holds annual special recognition luncheon for members and periodic workshop. **Formerly:** (2005) Michigan Federation of Private Child and Family Agencies. **Publications:** *Anthem*, quarterly. Newsletter • *Michigan Adoption Fact Book*, biennial. Brochure. Contains information related to adoption in Michigan. **Price:** $5.00 for members; $6.00 for nonmembers • Membership Directory, annual. Contains information about member agencies. **Price:** $10.00 each. **Conventions/Meetings:** annual Special Recognition Awards - luncheon - always May.

8666 ■ Michigan Forest Resource Alliance (MFRA)
600 S Walnut St.
Lansing, MI 48933
Ph: (906)822-7393
Fax: (906)822-7397
Free: (800)474-1718
E-mail: mfralor@up.net
URL: http://www.mfra.org
Contact: Lorraine Wirtanen, Office Mgr.
Founded: 1989. **Members:** 165. **Staff:** 2. **State**. Loggers, landowners, corporations, and individuals. Provides education and public relations for the forest community. Holds exhibits at fairs and expos. **Programs:** Tree. **Publications:** *MFRA TreeFarm Newsletter*, quarterly. Contains forest information for land owners and the general public. **Price:** free. Alternate Formats: online.

8667 ■ Michigan Fraternal Order of Police
c/o John Buczek, Exec.Dir.
124 W Allegan St., Ste.636
Lansing, MI 48933
Ph: (517)367-8000
Fax: (517)367-8262
Free: (888)367-6424
E-mail: info@mifop.com
URL: http://www.mifop.com
Contact: John Buczek, Exec.Dir.
Founded: 1939. **State**.

8668 ■ Michigan Glass Association (MGA)
530 W Iona, Ste.C
Lansing, MI 48933
Ph: (517)374-6488
Fax: (517)371-1170
E-mail: schnetzler.c@gcsionline.com
URL: http://www.mgaglass.org
Contact: Steve Green, Contact
State. **Affiliated With:** National Glass Association.

8669 ■ Michigan Golf Course Owners Association
226 W Washtenaw St.
Lansing, MI 48933
Ph: (517)482-4312
Contact: Kate Moore, Exec.Dir.
State.

8670 ■ Michigan Grocers Association (MGA)
221 N Walnut St.
Lansing, MI 48933-8102
Ph: (517)372-6800
Fax: (517)372-3002
Free: (800)947-6237
E-mail: contact@michigangrocers.org
URL: http://www.michigangrocers.org
Contact: Linda Gobler, Pres.
Founded: 1917. **Members:** 1,200. **Membership Dues:** retail, $145 (annual) • supplier, $325 (annual). **Staff:** 8. **State**. Wholesale and retail grocers and suppliers. Provides governmental representation; offers educational programs. **Publications:** *Michigan Food News*, monthly. Newspaper. **Price:** $25.00/year for nonmembers. **Advertising:** accepted. **Conventions/Meetings:** annual trade show (exhibits).

8671 ■ Michigan Health and Hospital Association (MHA)
c/o Spencer C. Johnson, Pres.
6215 W St. Joseph Hwy.
Lansing, MI 48917
Ph: (517)323-3443
Fax: (517)323-0946
E-mail: sjohnson@lans.mha.org
URL: http://www.mha.org
State.

8672 ■ Michigan Historic Preservation Network (MHPN)
107 E Grand River Ave.
Lansing, MI 48906
Ph: (517)371-8080
Fax: (517)371-9090
E-mail: info@mhpn.org
URL: http://www.mhpn.org
Contact: Nancy M. Finegood, Exec.Dir.
State. Provides education and advocacy on behalf of historic homes, barns, lighthouses, and commercial buildings. Promotes a preservation/rehabilitation tax credit. **Publications:** *Construction Trades Directory*, periodic. **Conventions/Meetings:** periodic conference • periodic workshop.

8673 ■ Michigan Hospice and Palliative Care Organization (MHPCO)
5123 W St. Joseph Hwy., Ste.204
Lansing, MI 48917
Ph: (517)886-6667
Fax: (517)886-6737
Free: (800)536-6300
E-mail: mihospice@mihospice.org
URL: http://mihospice.org
Contact: Jeff Towns, Pres./CEO
Founded: 1979. **Members:** 300. **Budget:** $500,000. **State**. Administers Michigan partnership for the advancement of end of life care and other hospice grant programs. Programs include advocacy, education, public information, referrals, technical assistance to hospice programs and liaison with Medicare and Medicaid. **Affiliated With:** National Association for Home Care and Hospice. **Formerly:** (2000) Michigan Hospice Organization. **Publications:** *Hospice Guide for Consumers* • *Physician's Guide to Hospice Care* • Newsletter, quarterly.

8674 ■ Michigan Hotel, Motel and Resort Association (MHMRA)
3815 West St., Joseph Hwy., Ste.A200
Lansing, MI 48917
Ph: (517)267-8989
Fax: (517)267-8990
E-mail: hotels@michiganhotels.org
URL: http://www.michiganhotels.org
Contact: Steve Yencich, Pres./CEO
Members: 500. **State**. Promotes and educates Michigan's lodging industry. **Affiliated With:** American Hotel and Lodging Association. **Publications:** *Michigan Lodging*, monthly. Newsletter. Alternate Formats: online • *Michigan Lodging and Tourism*, annual. Directory. **Circulation:** 100,000.

8675 ■ Michigan Humanities Council (MHC)
119 Pere Marquette, Ste.3B
Lansing, MI 48912
Ph: (517)372-7770
Fax: (517)372-0027
E-mail: contact@mihumanities.org
URL: http://michiganhumanities.org
Contact: Scott Hirko, Public Relations Officer
State. Provides grants to nonprofit organizations for public humanities programs; conducts public humanities programming.

8676 ■ Michigan Industrial Sand Association
c/o Knight Consulting
115 W Allegan, Ste.200
Lansing, MI 48933
Ph: (517)484-6917
Fax: (517)484-7037
Contact: Joe Fodo, Pres.
State. Represents members' interests; conducts lobbying activities. Holds seminars and workshops.

8677 ■ Michigan Institute of Laundering and Drycleaning (MILD)
3225 W St. Joseph
Lansing, MI 48917
Ph: (517)327-9207
Fax: (517)321-0495
E-mail: info@mildmi.org
URL: http://www.mildmi.org
Contact: Dave Dupuis, Chm.
Founded: 1913. **State**.

8678 ■ Michigan Jaycees
c/o Jay Simon, Exec.Dir.
535 S Walnut
Lansing, MI 48933
Ph: (517)487-6077
Fax: (517)487-6078
URL: http://www.mijaycees.org
Contact: Jay Simon, Exec.Dir.
State. **Computer Services:** Online services, message board/document library. **Conventions/Meetings:** convention.

8679 ■ Michigan Land Title Association (MLTA)
PO Box 15339
Lansing, MI 48901-5339
Ph: (517)374-2728
Fax: (517)485-9408
E-mail: mlta@kindsvatterassociates.com
URL: http://www.milta.org
Contact: Christian H. Kindsvatter, Exec.Dir.
State. Represents the interests of abstracters, title insurance companies and attorneys specializing in real property law. Improves the skills and knowledge of providers in real property transactions.

8680 ■ Michigan Lawyers Auxiliary
Michael Franck Bldg.
306 Townsend St.
Lansing, MI 48933-2083
E-mail: fmaunique@aol.com
Contact: Ms. Sharon Wilson, Pres.
Founded: 1919. **Members:** 31. **Budget:** $6,000. **Local Groups:** 5. **State**. **Affiliated With:** American Bar Association Center on Children and the Law; American Bar Association Center for Professional Responsibility; American Bar Association Commission on Homelessness and Poverty; American Bar Association Criminal Justice Section; American Bar Association Section of Dispute Resolution; American Bar Association Section of International Law and Practice; American Bar Association Section of International Law and Practice; American Bar Association Young Lawyers Division. **Publications:** Newsletter, periodic.

8681 ■ Michigan League for Human Services
c/o Ann Marston, Pres./CEO
1115 S Pennsylvania, Ste.202
Lansing, MI 48912
Ph: (517)487-5436
Fax: (517)371-4546
E-mail: amarston@mlan.net
URL: http://www.milhs.org
Contact: Ann Marston, Pres./CEO
Founded: 1912. **Members:** 1,900. **Membership Dues:** individual, $35 (annual) • organizational, $125 (annual). **Staff:** 15. **Budget:** $875,000. **State**. Statewide membership organization helping all MI residents through research, planning, information dissemination, advocacy, and technical services to charitable organizations. Focuses on poverty and children in need. **Affiliated With:** National Council of Nonprofit Associations. **Publications:** *Helping Handbook*, periodic • *Human Services Connection Bulletin*

Series, periodic. Newsletter • *Kids Count in Michigan Data Book*, annual • *Legislative Bulletin*, 3/year. **Conventions/Meetings:** annual conference - always October or November.

8682 ■ Michigan Library Association
c/o Stephen Kershner, Exec.Dir.
1407 Rensen St., Ste.2
Lansing, MI 48910
Ph: (517)394-2774
Fax: (517)394-2675
E-mail: mla@mlc.lib.mi.us
Founded: 1965. **Members:** 2,300. **Staff:** 5. **Budget:** $500,000. Institutions and individuals promoting continuing professional education for librarians and public familiarity with library practices. **Affiliated With:** American Library Association. **Publications:** *Michigan Librarian*, 10/year. Newsletter. **Price:** $40. 00. **Conventions/Meetings:** annual conference (exhibits) - always late fall.

8683 ■ Michigan Licensed Practical Nurses Association (MLPNA)
c/o Doris J. Nedry, Pres.
5900 Executive Dr.
Lansing, MI 48911-5390
Ph: (517)882-6657
Fax: (517)882-6004
Free: (888)280-6576
E-mail: info@mlpna.org
URL: http://www.mlpna.org
Contact: Linda Wheeler, Office Mgr.
Founded: 1944. **Members:** 700. **Membership Dues:** student, $20 (annual) • retiree (65 and over), $30 (annual) • regular, $80 (annual) • associate, $65 (annual) • health care facility/school, $150 (annual) • new graduate (within one year of licensure), $40 (annual). **Staff:** 2. **Budget:** $75,000. **Local Groups:** 13. **State**. Promotes and supports licensed practical nursing in Michigan. Offers membership to LPNs, practical nurse students, health care facilities, schools, and non-licensed individuals. Sponsors annual convention, student practical nurse day, and educational seminars. **Affiliated With:** National Association for Practical Nurse Education and Service. **Publications:** *Practical Nursing News*, quarterly. Newsletter. **Price:** included in membership dues. **Advertising:** accepted. **Conventions/Meetings:** annual convention, with education speakers (exhibits) • annual Student Practical Nurse Day Program.

8684 ■ Michigan Lumber and Building Materials Association (MLBMA)
5815 Executive Dr., Ste.A
Lansing, MI 48911
Ph: (517)394-5225
Fax: (517)394-5228
E-mail: assn@mlbma.org
URL: http://www.mlbma.org
Founded: 1889. **Staff:** 7. **State**. Provides services to retail lumberyards and home centers. **Publications:** *Framework*, bimonthly. Newsletter. **Conventions/Meetings:** annual trade show.

8685 ■ Michigan Manufacturers Association (MMA)
PO Box 14247
Lansing, MI 48901-4247
Ph: (517)372-5900
Fax: (517)372-3322
Free: (800)253-9039
E-mail: ask@mma-net.org
URL: http://www.mma-net.org
Contact: John W. MacIlroy, Pres./CEO
Founded: 1902. **Members:** 3,100. **Membership Dues:** $285 (annual). **Staff:** 26. **Budget:** $5,000,000. **State**. Companies united to promote the interests of manufacturers in MI. **Libraries: Type:** open to the public. **Holdings:** articles. **Subjects:** manufacturing efficiency, legal issues, human resources, governmental developments and other general manufacturing issues. **Awards:** Michigan Advocate of the Year. **Frequency:** annual. **Type:** recognition. **Recipient:** varies • Michigan Legislator of the Year. **Frequency:** annual. **Type:** recognition. **Recipient:** varies • Michigan Manufacturer of the Year. **Frequency:** annual. **Type:** recognition. **Recipient:** varies. **Publications:** *Enterprise*, monthly. Magazine. **Circulation:** 6,000 • *Environmental Report*. Newsletter. Contains report on manufacturing subjects and issues. **Price:** free to members. Alternate Formats: online • *HR Report*. Newsletter. Contains report on manufacturing subjects and issues. **Price:** free to members. Alternate Formats: online • *MMA/NAM Washington Update*. Newsletter. Contains report on manufacturing subjects and issues. **Price:** free to members. Alternate Formats: online • *Weekly Report*. Newsletter. Contains report on manufacturing subjects and issues. **Price:** free to members. Alternate Formats: online. **Conventions/Meetings:** annual Michigan Manufacturing Week - meeting, series of events to celebrate the importance of manufacturing to Michigan.

8686 ■ Michigan Motorcycle Dealers Association (MMDA)
3225 W St. Joseph
Lansing, MI 48917
Ph: (517)323-8323
Fax: (517)321-0495
E-mail: info@michmda.org
URL: http://www.michmda.org
State.

8687 ■ Michigan Movers Association (MMA)
c/o Donnelly K. Eurich, CAE, Exec.Dir.
3225 W St. Joseph St.
Lansing, MI 48917-3600
Ph: (517)327-9207
Fax: (517)321-0495
E-mail: donnad@eurich.com
URL: http://www.mimovers.org
Contact: Donnelly K. Eurich CAE, Exec.Dir.
State. **Formerly:** (2005) Michigan Movers and Warehousemen's Association.

8688 ■ Michigan Municipal Electric Association (MMEA)
c/o Gary Zimmerman, Exec.VP
809 Centennial Way
Lansing, MI 48917-9277
Ph: (517)323-8346
Fax: (517)323-8373
E-mail: mmea@mpower.org
State.

8689 ■ Michigan Museums Association (MMA)
c/o Teresa M. Goforth, Dir.
PO Box 10067
Lansing, MI 48901-0067
Ph: (517)482-4055
Fax: (517)482-7997
E-mail: goforth@michiganmuseums.org
URL: http://www.michiganmuseums.org
Contact: Teresa M. Goforth, Dir.
State.

8690 ■ Michigan Nonprofit Association (MNA)
1048 Pierpont Dr., Ste.3
Lansing, MI 48911
Ph: (517)492-2400
Fax: (517)492-2410
Free: (888)242-7075
E-mail: mnaweb@action.mnaonline.org
URL: http://www.mnaonline.org
Contact: Sam Singh, Pres./CEO
Founded: 1990. **Members:** 585. **Budget:** $964,000. **State**. Promotes the awareness and effectiveness of Michigan's nonprofit sector, and to advance the cause of volunteerism and philanthropy in the state. **Affiliated With:** National Council of Nonprofit Associations. **Publications:** *Association and Nonprofit Compensation and Benefit Survey*, biennial • *Michigan in Brief*, biennial. Book • *MNA Links*, monthly. Newsletter • *Nonprofit Resource and Networking Directory*, annual. **Conventions/Meetings:** biennial Grantmakers-Grantseekers Conference • biennial Volunteerism Super Conference.

8691 ■ Michigan Occupational Therapy Association (MiOTA)
124 W Allegan, Ste.500
Lansing, MI 48933
Ph: (517)267-3918
Fax: (517)484-4442
E-mail: office@mi-ota.com
URL: http://www.mi-ota.com
Contact: Cheryl Chapko, Contact
Founded: 1919. **Members:** 1,400. **Membership Dues:** associate, $95 (annual) • OTR, $89 (annual) • COTA, $79 (annual) • student, $39 (annual) • retired OTR, $44 • retired COTA, $39. **Staff:** 1. **State**. Occupational therapists, certified occupational therapy assistants, and occupational therapy students. **Affiliated With:** American Occupational Therapy Association. **Publications:** *Medicare Resources*, quarterly. Article • *The MiOTA Newsletter*, quarterly. Informs the members regarding issues arising in MI. **Advertising:** accepted • Directory, annual. **Conventions/Meetings:** annual conference (exhibits) - always fall.

8692 ■ Michigan Optometric Association (MOA)
530 W Ionia St., Ste.A
Lansing, MI 48933-1062
Ph: (517)482-0616
Fax: (517)482-1611
E-mail: mioptoassn@aol.com
URL: http://www.themoa.org
Contact: William D. Dansby CAE, Exec.VP
Founded: 1896. **Members:** 849. **Membership Dues:** individual, $1,336 (annual). **Staff:** 3. **Budget:** $648,000. **Regional Groups:** 8. **State**. Optometrists. Seeks to improve eye care and to promote the optometry profession. **Affiliated With:** American Foundation for Vision Awareness; American Optometric Association; American Optometric Foundation. **Publications:** *Michigan Optometrist*, monthly. Magazine. Keeps members informed about the state association news, issues and activities. • Membership Directory, annual. **Circulation:** 833. **Advertising:** accepted • Newsletter, semimonthly. **Conventions/Meetings:** annual conference (exhibits).

8693 ■ Michigan Oral History Association
5580 W State Rd.
Lansing, MI 48906
Ph: (517)321-1746
URL: http://www.h-net.org/~oralhist/moha
Contact: Geoffrey Reynolds, Pres.
State. Represents individuals interested in oral history as a way of collecting and interpreting human memories. Encourages standards of excellence in the collection, preservation, dissemination and uses of oral testimony. Offers advice and guidelines to individuals concerned in oral documentation. **Affiliated With:** Oral History Association.

8694 ■ Michigan Organization of Nurse Executives - District 4
c/o Deb LeBlanc, Dir.
Ingham Regional Medical Ctr.
401 W Greenlawn Ave.
Lansing, MI 48910-2819
Ph: (517)334-2349
Fax: (517)334-2462
E-mail: deborah.leblanc@irmc.org
URL: http://www.mone.org
Contact: Deb LeBlanc, Dir.
Local. Represents nurse leaders who improve healthcare. Provides leadership, professional development, advocacy and research. Advances the nursing administration practice and patient care. **Affiliated With:** American Organization of Nurse Executives.

8695 ■ Michigan Petroleum Association (MPA)
7521 Westshire Dr., Ste.200
Lansing, MI 48917

Ph: (517)622-3530
Fax: (517)622-3420
E-mail: mpamacs@mpamacs.org
URL: http://www.mpamacs.org
Contact: Tom Barron, Chm.

Founded: 1934. **Members:** 600. **Staff:** 5. **State.** Represents the interests of Independent petroleum marketers; petroleum product suppliers. Promotes petroleum marketing. **Publications:** *Marketing Directory*, annual • *MPA/MACS Marketer*, quarterly • *MPA/MACS Newsletter*, monthly. **Conventions/Meetings:** annual convention (exhibits) - always spring • annual meeting - always fall.

8696 ■ Michigan Pharmacists Association
815 N Washington Ave.
Lansing, MI 48906
Ph: (517)484-1466
Fax: (517)484-4893
E-mail: mpa@michiganpharmacists.org
URL: http://www.michiganpharmacists.org
Contact: Larry D. Wagenknecht, CEO

Founded: 1883. **Members:** 3,200. **Staff:** 13. **Local Groups:** 19. **State.** Supports and promotes the professional interests of member pharmacists and seeks to better the industry. **Awards:** Innovative Pharmacist of the Year. **Frequency:** annual. **Type:** recognition. **Recipient:** for individual who has demonstrated an innovative pharmacy practice program, resulting in improved patient care • MPA Bowl Of Hygeia Award. **Frequency:** annual. **Type:** recognition. **Recipient:** for individual who has compiled an outstanding record of community service which apart from his/her specific identification as a pharmacist • MPA Distinguished Young Pharmacist Award. **Frequency:** annual. **Type:** recognition. **Recipient:** for pharmacist licensed to practice for nine years or fewer licensed to practice in the state of Michigan • MPA Fred W. Arnold Public Relations Award. **Frequency:** annual. **Type:** recognition. **Recipient:** for member of the Michigan pharmacists association who has shown in the previous year outstanding achievement and dedication to the pharmacy profession through community education with an emphasis on public speaking and/or presentations • MPA Pharmacists of the Year. **Frequency:** annual. **Type:** recognition. **Recipient:** to a member of the Michigan pharmacists association, for professional excellence and exemplary service to the profession in advancing public health. **Publications:** *Michigan Pharmacist*, bimonthly. Journal. **Price:** free to members. **Advertising:** accepted. **Conventions/Meetings:** annual convention - always August.

8697 ■ Michigan Podiatric Medical Association (MPMA)
112 E Allegan, Ste.500
Lansing, MI 48933
Ph: (517)484-MPMA
Fax: (517)484-1930
Free: (800)YOU-MPMA
E-mail: emccloud@mpma.org
URL: http://www.mpma.org
Contact: Mark Dickens, Exec.Dir.

Founded: 1914. **State.** Serves and protects the public's Podiatric Health and maintains ethical conduct among its members. **Affiliated With:** American Podiatric Medical Association.

8698 ■ Michigan Press Association (MPA)
c/o Michael MacLaren, Exec.Dir.
827 N Washington Ave.
Lansing, MI 48906-5135
Ph: (517)372-2424
Fax: (517)372-2429
E-mail: mpa@michiganpress.org
URL: http://www.michiganpress.org
Contact: Michael MacLaren, Exec.Dir.

Founded: 1868. **State.**

8699 ■ Michigan Propane Gas Association
PO Box 15339
Lansing, MI 48901
Ph: (517)487-2021
Fax: (517)485-9408
E-mail: mpga@kindsvatterassociates.com
URL: http://www.mipga.org
Contact: Christian H. Kindsvatter, Exec.Dir.

State. Represents the interests of propane marketers in Michigan. **Publications:** *The Gas Log.* **Conventions/Meetings:** semiannual meeting.

8700 ■ Michigan Protection and Advocacy Service (MPAS)
4095 Legacy Pkwy., Ste.500
Lansing, MI 48911-4263
Ph: (517)487-1755
Fax: (517)487-0827
Free: (800)288-5923
E-mail: molson@mpas.org
URL: http://www.mpas.org
Contact: Elmer L. Cerano, Exec.Dir.

Founded: 1981. **Members:** 11. **Staff:** 65. **Budget:** $3,775,000. **State.** Works to protect the rights of persons with developmental, mental, and other disabilities and advocates on their behalf through information and referral, law reform, legislation, and litigation. **Affiliated With:** National Disability Rights Network. **Publications:** *Exchange*, quarterly. Newsletter.

8701 ■ Michigan Racing Association
121 W Allegan St.
Lansing, MI 48933
Ph: (517)482-5028
Fax: (517)482-9934
Contact: Joseph A. Garcia, VP, Gen. Coun.

Founded: 1970. **Members:** 7. **Staff:** 3. **Budget:** $120,000. Seeks to represent the legitimate interests of Michigan's horse race track owners and meet operators before the Michigan legislature and agencies of state government. **Publications:** Newsletter.

8702 ■ Michigan Railroads Association (MRA)
120 N Washington Sq., Ste.601
Lansing, MI 48933
Ph: (517)482-9413
Fax: (517)482-9225
E-mail: mra@michiganrailroadsassociation.com
URL: http://www.michiganrailroadsassociation.com
Contact: Robert J. Chaprnka, Pres.

Membership Dues: associate (non-voting), $1,000 (annual). **State.** Reviews and proposes legislation that affect the rail industry. Supports activities of Michigan's Operation Lifesaver. Aims to prevent railroad connected accidents through engineering, enforcement and education. **Publications:** *Michigan Rail Update*, semiannual. Newsletter. Alternate Formats: online.

8703 ■ Michigan Recycling Coalition (MRC)
3225 W St. Joseph
Lansing, MI 48917
Ph: (517)327-9207
Fax: (517)321-0495
E-mail: info@michiganrecycles.org
URL: http://www.michiganrecycles.org
Contact: Nancy Hawkins, Exec.Dir.

Founded: 1983. **Members:** 250. **Membership Dues:** supporter, $10 (annual) • individual, $75 (annual) • non-profit, $110 (annual) • government, $145 (annual) • business, $165 (annual) • sustaining, $305 (annual). **Staff:** 4. **Budget:** $200,000. **State Groups:** 1. **State.** Works to foster environmental conservation in Michigan by promoting sustainable resource use and recovery. **Libraries: Type:** open to the public. **Holdings:** 300; articles, books, periodicals. **Subjects:** recycling, composting, waste reduction, solid waste. **Awards:** Recycler of the Year. **Frequency:** annual. **Type:** recognition. **Councils:** Compost; Paper. **Affiliated With:** National Recycling Coalition. **Publications:** *MRC Update*, quarterly. Newsletter. Contains field articles and recycling information. **Price:** included in membership dues. **Circulation:** 280. **Advertising:** accepted. **Conventions/Meetings:** annual conference (exhibits) • quarterly workshop.

8704 ■ Michigan Resource Center for Health and Safety (MRCHS)
111 W Edgewood Blvd.
Lansing, MI 48911
Ph: (517)318-3787
Fax: (517)318-0527
Free: (800)487-6709
E-mail: lori@michiganresourcecenter.org
URL: http://www.tsamichigan.org
Contact: Cynthia Agle, Exec.Dir.

Founded: 1941. **Members:** 60. **Staff:** 2. **Budget:** $200,000. **State.** Automotive, banking, insurance, and public utility corporations interested in promoting traffic safety. Sponsors public information campaigns and corporate workshops. **Libraries: Type:** open to the public. **Holdings:** articles, books, video recordings. **Subjects:** traffic safety, free loan. **Awards:** Recognition Awards. **Frequency:** annual. **Type:** recognition. **Recipient:** achievement. **Formerly:** (2005) Traffic Safety Association of Michigan. **Publications:** *TSA Newsletter*, periodic • Brochures. **Price:** free. **Conventions/Meetings:** annual Recognition Luncheon.

8705 ■ Michigan Restaurant Association (MRA)
c/o Robert A. Gifford, Exec.Dir.
225 W Washtenaw St.
Lansing, MI 48933-1506
Ph: (517)482-5244
Fax: (517)482-7663
Free: (800)968-9668
E-mail: rgifford@mramail.org
URL: http://www.michiganrestaurant.org
Contact: Robert A. Gifford, Exec.Dir.

Founded: 1921. **State.**

8706 ■ Michigan Retail Hardware Association (MRHA)
PO Box 30085
4414 S Pennsylvania Ave.
Lansing, MI 48909-7585
Ph: (517)394-1710
Fax: (517)394-1782
E-mail: info@mirha.com
URL: http://www.mirha.com
Contact: Tom Ruedisueli, Pres./CEO

Founded: 1895. **State.**

8707 ■ Michigan Retailers Association (MRA)
c/o Larry L. Meyer, CAE, Chm./CEO
603 S Washington Ave.
Lansing, MI 48933
Ph: (517)372-5656
Fax: (517)372-1303
Free: (800)366-3699
E-mail: mra@retailers.com
URL: http://www.retailers.com
Contact: Larry Meyer CAE, Chm./CEO

Founded: 1940. **Members:** 4,900. **Staff:** 35. **Budget:** $10,000,000. **State Groups:** 1. **For-Profit. State.** Retail stores and outlets. Promotes the interests of members through legislative and educational activities. **Publications:** *Michigan Retailer*, monthly. Newspaper. **Circulation:** 6,000. **Advertising:** accepted. **Conventions/Meetings:** periodic meeting.

8708 ■ Michigan Road Builders Association (MRBA)
c/o Anthony Milo, Exec.VP
924 Centennial Way, Ste.460
Lansing, MI 48917
Ph: (517)886-9000
Fax: (517)886-8960
E-mail: mrba@mrba.com
URL: http://www.mrba.com

State. Affiliated With: American Road and Transportation Builders Association.

8709 ■ Michigan School Business Officials (MSBO)
1001 Centennial Way, Ste.200
Lansing, MI 48917-9279

Ph: (517)372-5920
Fax: (517)327-0768
E-mail: msbo@msbo.org
URL: http://www.msbo.org
Contact: Thomas E. White PhD, Exec.Dir.
Founded: 1937. **Members:** 1,085. **Staff:** 7. **Budget:** $603,000. **Regional Groups:** 12. **State**. Represents school business officials and supervisory staff; vendors of school service supplies; and students interested in school business management. Seeks to enhance school business management. Provides professional in-service programs; studies environmental and management issues. **Affiliated With:** Association of School Business Officials International. **Publications:** Newsletter, 9/year. Alternate Formats: online • Brochures • Handbooks. **Conventions/Meetings:** annual meeting - always April. 2007 Apr. 24-27, Grand Rapids, MI; 2008 Apr. 29-May 2, Grand Rapids, MI.

8710 ■ Michigan School Investment Association (MSIA)
4710 W Saginaw Hwy., Ste.1
Lansing, MI 48917-2697
Ph: (517)323-7868
Fax: (517)321-8866
E-mail: mguastella@mischoolinvest.com
URL: http://www.mischoolinvest.com
Contact: S. Mark Guastella, Exec.Dir.
Founded: 1976. **Members:** 40. **Staff:** 2. **Budget:** $138,000. **State**. Public school districts united to study cash management and analyze cash flow. Provides investment and borrowing counseling and workshops on related topics to its membership. **Publications:** *Money Market Outlook*, every 6-8 weeks. Newsletter. Summarizes investment rates available and feature items. **Price:** free. **Circulation:** 120. **Conventions/Meetings:** annual meeting, membership - always May in Lansing, MI.

8711 ■ Michigan School Public Relations Association (MSPRA)
c/o Dianne Branch
1001 Centennial Way, Ste.300
Lansing, MI 48917
Ph: (517)327-9266
Fax: (517)327-0771
E-mail: dbranch@gomasa.org
URL: http://www.mspra.org
Contact: Dianne Branch, Contact
Membership Dues: professional, $65 (annual) • student, $20 (annual) • retired/associate, $20 (annual) • business/vendor, $65 (annual). **State**. Provide communications and community relations for Michigan's public schools. **Committees:** Awards and Recognition; Issues Management; Outreach; Professional Growth. **Affiliated With:** National School Public Relations Association. **Formerly:** (2005) National School Public Relations Association, Michigan. **Publications:** *MEMO*, quarterly. Newsletters. **Circulation:** 300. Alternate Formats: online.

8712 ■ Michigan Sheriffs' Association (MSA)
515 N Capitol Ave.
Lansing, MI 48933-1209
Ph: (517)485-3135
Fax: (517)485-1013
E-mail: dcarmichael@michigansheriff.com
URL: http://www.michigansheriff.com
Contact: Terrence L. Jugel, Exec.Dir.
Founded: 1877. **Members:** 25,000. **Membership Dues:** citizen associate, professional associate, $25 (annual) • citizen silver star, professional silver star, $50 (annual) • citizen gold star, professional gold star, $100 (annual) • citizen bronze star, professional bronze star, $250 (annual) • citizen honorary sheriff, professional honorary sheriff, $500 (annual) • business associate, $50 (annual) • business silver star, $65 (annual) • business gold star, $125 (annual) • business bronze star, $285 (annual) • business honorary sheriff, $550 (annual). **Staff:** 4. **Budget:** $1,100,000. **State**. Provides assistance to and works in conjunction with businesses and the general public to assist local departments. Offers training in law enforcement, victim witness, and marine safety. Serves as a liaison between legislature and sheriff's office. **Awards:** Bud Grysen Scholarship. **Frequency:** annual. **Type:** scholarship. **Recipient:** by nomination. **Affiliated With:** National Sheriffs' Association. **Formerly:** (2004) Michigan Sheriffs' Association Educational Services. **Publications:** *Criminal Law and Procedure* • *MSA Sheriff's Star*, quarterly. Journal • *Sheriffs' Journal*, quarterly • *Traffic Law and Procedure*. **Conventions/Meetings:** annual conference • semiannual Training Conference (exhibits) - always July and October.

8713 ■ Michigan Sierra Club
109 E Grand River Ave.
Lansing, MI 48906
Ph: (517)484-2372
Fax: (517)484-3108
E-mail: mackinac.chapter@sierraclub.org
URL: http://michigan.sierraclub.org
Contact: Anne Woiwode, Dir.
State. Affiliated With: Sierra Club.

8714 ■ Michigan Society of Anesthesiologists (MSA)
530 W Ionia, Ste.C
Lansing, MI 48933
Ph: (517)346-5088
Fax: (517)371-1170
E-mail: admin@mianesthesiologist.org
URL: http://www.mianesthesiologist.org
Contact: Robert Snyder DO, Sec.-Treas.
State.

8715 ■ Michigan Society of Health-System Pharmacists (MSHP)
815 N Washington Ave.
Lansing, MI 48906
Ph: (517)484-1466
E-mail: mpa@michiganpharmacists.org
URL: http://www.michiganpharmacists.org/pharm_prof/mshppub.html
Contact: Fred Schmidt, Pres.
State. Advances and supports the professional practice of pharmacists in hospitals and health systems. Serves as the collective voice on issues related to medication use and public health. **Affiliated With:** American Society of Health System Pharmacists.

8716 ■ Michigan Society of Professional Engineers (MSPE)
c/o Maura Nessan, Exec.Mgr.
PO Box 15276
Lansing, MI 48901-5276
Ph: (517)487-9388
Fax: (517)487-0635
E-mail: mspe@voyager.net
URL: http://www.michiganspe.org
Contact: Maura Nessan PE, Exec.Mgr.
Founded: 1946. **Members:** 3,000. **Membership Dues:** professional engineer, engineer in training, associate, engineering student, $158 (annual). **Staff:** 3. **Budget:** $290,800. **Regional Groups:** 19. **Local Groups:** 19. **State**. Engineers organized to advance the engineering profession. Sponsors Mathcounts competition for seventh and eighth graders. Sponsors scholarships. **Awards:** Engineer of the Year. **Frequency:** annual. **Type:** recognition • Engineering and Surveying Excellence Awards. **Frequency:** annual. **Type:** recognition. **Affiliated With:** National Society of Professional Engineers. **Publications:** *The Michigan Professional Engineer*, annual. Directory. **Price:** $35.00. **Circulation:** 250. **Advertising:** accepted • *Michigan Professional Engineer*, 9/year. Journal. **Conventions/Meetings:** annual conference (exhibits) - always in May.

8717 ■ Michigan Society of Professional Surveyors (MSPS)
c/o Roland Self, Exec.Dir.
220 S Museum Dr.
Lansing, MI 48933-1905
Ph: (517)484-2413
Fax: (517)484-3711
E-mail: mich_survey@misocprofsurveyors.org
URL: http://www.misocprofsurveyors.org
Contact: Michael J. Bartolo PS, Pres.
Founded: 1941. **Membership Dues:** licensed professional surveyor, $250 (annual) • associate, affiliate, $75 (annual) • firm, $40 (annual) • sustaining, $375 (annual). **State. Awards:** Country Road Association Awards. **Frequency:** annual. **Type:** recognition • Member of the Year. **Frequency:** annual. **Type:** recognition. **Recipient:** for members who give of themselves in a special way to advance the Society • Michigan Land Surveyors of the Past. **Frequency:** annual. **Type:** recognition. **Recipient:** for local land surveyors • Ralph Moore Berry Education Awards. **Frequency:** annual. **Type:** recognition. **Committees:** ACSM/NSPS; Continuing Education; County Surveyors-County Representatives; Geodetic Control-Geographic Information System; Legislative; Past Presidents; Proprietors; Scholarship. **Affiliated With:** National Society of Professional Surveyors. **Publications:** *Professional Surveyor*, bimonthly. Newsletter. Alternate Formats: online. **Conventions/Meetings:** annual meeting (exhibits) - 2007 Feb. 20-23, Mount Pleasant, MI; 2008 Feb. 19-22, Sault Ste. Marie, MI.

8718 ■ Michigan Soft Drink Association (MSDA)
Boji Tower, Ste.634
124 W Allegan
Lansing, MI 48933-1707
Ph: (517)371-4499
Fax: (517)371-1113
E-mail: msta@boyager.net
URL: National Affiliate–www.nsda.org
Contact: William Lobenherz, Pres.
Founded: 1911. **Members:** 4. **Staff:** 2. **State**. Soft drink producers. Promotes the soft drink industry. Provides information on industry activity and pertinent legislation. **Affiliated With:** American Beverage Association. **Publications:** *Update*, periodic. Bulletin • Newsletter, quarterly. **Conventions/Meetings:** annual meeting - always August.

8719 ■ Michigan State AFL-CIO
419 S Washington Sq., Ste.200
Lansing, MI 48933
Ph: (517)487-5966
Fax: (517)487-5213
E-mail: miaflcio@miaflcio.org
URL: http://www.miaflcio.org
Contact: Mark P. Gaffney, Pres.
Founded: 1958. **State. Affiliated With:** AFL-CIO.

8720 ■ Michigan State Building and Construction Trades Council
436 Washington Sq., S
Lansing, MI 48933
Ph: (517)484-8427
Fax: (517)484-1038
Free: (800)642-2897
Contact: Mary Bechtor, Admin.Asst.
State.

8721 ■ Michigan State Employees Association (MSEA)
6035 Executive Dr., Ste.204
Lansing, MI 48910
Ph: (517)394-5900
Fax: (517)394-4060
Free: (800)228-5901
E-mail: msea@msea.org
URL: http://www.msea.org
Contact: Jack Yoak, Pres.
Founded: 1950. **Members:** 3,500. **Staff:** 11. **Regional Groups:** 10. **State**. Labor union for individuals working for the state of Michigan and various counties as well as university employees. **Libraries: Type:** not open to the public. **Affiliated With:** American Federation of State, County and Municipal Employees. **Publications:** *MSEA News*, monthly. Newsletter. **Circulation:** 3,500. **Conventions/Meetings:** biennial general assembly - July or August.

8722 ■ Michigan Townships Association (MTA)
c/o Larry Merrill, Exec.Dir.
512 Westshire Dr.
Lansing, MI 48917
Ph: (517)321-6467
Fax: (517)321-8908
E-mail: larry@michigantownships.org
URL: http://www.michigantownships.org
Contact: Larry Merrill, Exec.Dir.
Founded: 1953. **Members:** 6,500. **Staff:** 18. **Budget:** $2,000,000. **Local Groups:** 65. **State**. Elected township officials. Seeks to further township interest through its involvement with state agencies, the legislature, and the judicial system. **Awards:** Robinson Memorial Scholarship Fund. **Frequency:** annual. **Type:** monetary. **Affiliated With:** National Association of Towns and Townships. **Publications:** *Capitol Currents*, monthly. Newsletter • *Michigan Township News*, monthly. Journal • Directory, quadrennial. **Conventions/Meetings:** annual conference - always January in Detroit, MI.

8723 ■ Michigan Trial Lawyers Association (MTLA)
504 S Creyts Rd., Ste.B
Lansing, MI 48917
Ph: (517)321-3073
Fax: (517)321-4694
E-mail: info@mtla.net
URL: http://www.mtla.net
Contact: Jane R. Bailey, Exec.Dir.
Founded: 1945. **Members:** 2,000. **Membership Dues:** regular (based on number of years in service), $60-$300 (annual) • sustaining individual, $600 (annual). **Staff:** 9. **State**. Legal education association. Works to promote safety for all Michigan citizens by standing up for accountability and responsibility. **Publications:** *Advance Sheet*, 8/year. Newsletter. **Price:** included in membership dues • *MTLA Quarterly*. Newsletter. **Price:** included in membership dues. **Conventions/Meetings:** Various Topics - lecture, legal education (exhibits) - every ten years.

8724 ■ Michigan Truck Stop Operators Association
535 N Capital Ave.
Lansing, MI 48933
Ph: (517)485-5536
Fax: (517)485-2550
E-mail: steve@scosesconsulting.com
Contact: Steve Scoses, CEO
State.

8725 ■ Michigan Trucking Association (MTA)
1131 Centennial Way
Lansing, MI 48917
Ph: (517)321-1951
Fax: (517)321-0884
E-mail: wheinritzi@mitrucking.org
URL: http://www.mitrucking.org
Contact: Walter Heinritzi, Exec.Dir.
Founded: 1934. **Members:** 1,000. **Staff:** 6. **State**. Carrier companies and trucking-related businesses. Serves as a voice for members and represents the trucking industry before state government. **Publications:** *Legislative Report*, periodic • *Michigan Trucking Today*, monthly. Newsletter. **Conventions/Meetings:** annual convention - always September.

8726 ■ Michigan United Conservation Clubs (MUCC)
PO Box 30235
Lansing, MI 48909-7735
Ph: (517)371-1041
Fax: (517)371-1505
E-mail: breich@mucc.org
URL: http://www.mucc.org
Contact: Sam Washington, Exec.Dir.
Founded: 1937. **Members:** 100,000. **Membership Dues:** bronze, $25 (annual) • silver, $30 (annual) • gold, $50 (annual) • sustaining, $100 (annual) • life, $500. **Budget:** $5,000,000. **State**. Unites citizens to conserve Michigan's natural resources and protect the state's outdoor heritage. Promotes the wise and scientific use of resources through education, legislative, and advocacy efforts. **Publications:** *Michigan Out-of-Doors*, monthly. Magazine. **Conventions/Meetings:** annual convention - always in June • annual Outdoor Expo - show, 3-day outdoor sport and travel show - 4th weekend in June • annual Outdoorama - show, 10-day sport and travel show - starts last weekend in February.

8727 ■ Michigan Women's Commission
110 W Michigan Ave., Ste.800
Lansing, MI 48933
Ph: (517)373-2884
Fax: (517)335-1649
E-mail: mdcr-womenscomm@michigan.gov
URL: http://www.michigan.gov/mdcr
Contact: Judy Karandjeff, Exec.Dir.
Founded: 1968. **Members:** 34. **Staff:** 2. **State Groups:** 1. **State**. Works to improve the quality of life for Michigan women, as outlined by PA 1 of 1968. **Computer Services:** Information services, services and topics of interests to women • online services, commission publications on website • record retrieval services, women resource directory. **Affiliated With:** National Association of Commissions for Women. **Publications:** *Club Drugs: What you and your kids should know*. Brochure • *Domestic Violence Mirror Cling*. Brochure • *Ecstasy: It's a No-Brainer*. Brochure • *GHB: A Vicious Scam. A Proven Killer*. Brochure • *Michigan Women*, quarterly. Newsletter. Contains issues of interest to Michigan women, proposed legislation, state programs and events. **Price:** free. **Circulation:** 16,000. Alternate Formats: online. **Conventions/Meetings:** quarterly Commission Meetings, formal meeting of the commission to conduct business.

8728 ■ Michigan Women's Studies Association (MWSA)
213 W Main St.
Lansing, MI 48933
Ph: (517)484-1880
Fax: (517)372-0170
E-mail: mail@michiganwomenshalloffame.org
URL: http://www.michiganwomenshalloffame.org
Contact: Gladys Beckwith PhD, Pres.
Founded: 1973. **Members:** 1,800. **Membership Dues:** basic, $15 (annual). **Staff:** 5. **Budget:** $180,000. **Local Groups:** 1. **State**. Educators, education institutions, and others interested in promoting women's studies in schools and universities. Works to promote information on American women. Aims to eliminate bias against and stereotyping of women. Promotes nonracist and nonsexist education in schools; encourages research by, for, and about women. Maintains Women's Hall of Fame and Women's Historical Center. Holds annual picnic. **Affiliated With:** National Women's Studies Association. **Publications:** *House Handbill*, quarterly. Newsletter • *Michigan Women: Firsts and Founders, Vol. I & Vol. II*. Booklets • Membership Directory, periodic • Newsletter, quarterly. **Conventions/Meetings:** annual conference - always April • annual Hall of Fame Induction Dinner - always October • annual symposium.

8729 ■ Michigan's Children
428 W Lenawee
Lansing, MI 48933-2240
Ph: (517)485-3500
Fax: (517)485-3650
Free: (800)330-8674
E-mail: info@michiganschildren.org
URL: http://www.michiganschildren.org
Contact: Sharon Claytor Peters, Pres./CEO
State. Represents the needs of children and the views of a broad network of "friends" and donors to the organization. **Affiliated With:** Voices for America's Children.

8730 ■ Mid-Michigan Environmental Action Council
417 S Cedar St., Ste.C
Lansing, MI 48912
Ph: (517)485-9001
Local.

8731 ■ Mid-Michigan Genealogical Society
PO Box 16033
Lansing, MI 48901-6033
Ph: (517)627-5763
URL: http://www.rootsweb.com/~mimmgs
Contact: Jack Worthington, Pres.
Founded: 1966. **Members:** 250. **Membership Dues:** individual, $15 (annual). **Local**. Encourages and assists in the study of family history. Promotes the exchange of knowledge and the deposit of genealogical records. **Publications:** Newsletter, 3/year. **Price:** included in membership dues.

8732 ■ Mid-Michigan Mechanical Contractors Association (3MCA)
c/o Michael H. West, Exec.Dir.
700 N Washington Ave.
Lansing, MI 48906-5133
Ph: (517)485-7990
Fax: (517)485-4129
E-mail: mwest@mid-michiganmca.org
URL: http://www.mid-michiganmca.org
Contact: Michael H. West, Exec.Dir.
Membership Dues: regular, $350 (annual). **Staff:** 3. **Local**. Contractors who furnish, install, and service piping and mechanical systems and related equipment for heating, cooling, refrigeration, ventilating, fire sprinkler, temperature control, and air conditioning systems. **Affiliated With:** Mechanical Contractors Association of America; National Certified Pipe Welding Bureau.

8733 ■ Mothers Against Drunk Driving, Michigan State
PO Box 21157
Lansing, MI 48909
Ph: (517)487-6233
Fax: (517)702-0185
Free: (800)323-6233
E-mail: maddmi@tds.net
URL: http://www.madd.org/mi
Contact: Homer Smith, Exec.Dir.
Founded: 1981. **State**. Seeks to stop drunk driving, supports the victims of this violent crime, and prevents underage drinking. Offers services to individuals and families who have been affected by a drunk driving crash. Conducts programs and training for individuals and groups working with young people in order to prevent underage drinking. Conducts annual community awareness and advocates for public policy initiatives that affect its mission. **Affiliated With:** Mothers Against Drunk Driving.

8734 ■ National Alliance for the Mentally Ill of Michigan
921 N Washington
Lansing, MI 48906
Ph: (517)485-4049
Fax: (517)485-2333
Free: (800)331-4264
E-mail: namimichigan@acd.net
URL: http://mi.nami.org
Contact: Kristina Zwick, Contact
State. **Affiliated With:** National Alliance for the Mentally Ill.

8735 ■ National Association for the Advancement of Colored People, Lansing Branch
LeJon Bldg.
1801 W Main
Lansing, MI 48915
Ph: (517)484-9171
Fax: (517)484-5051
URL: http://www.naacplansing.org
Contact: James R. Gill Jr., Pres.
Local.

8736 ■ National Association of Investors Corporation, Capital Area Chapter
c/o Fonda Williams
PO Box 80391
Lansing, MI 48909-0391

Ph: (517)393-6897
E-mail: kadickenson@comcast.net
URL: http://better-investing.org/chapter/capcity
Contact: Kathy Dickenson, Pres.
Local. Teaches individuals how to become successful strategic long-term investors. Provides highly focused learning resources and investment tools that empower individuals to become better investors. **Affiliated With:** National Association of Investors Corporation.

8737 ■ National Association of Social Workers - Michigan Chapter
741 N Cedar St., Ste.100
Lansing, MI 48906
Ph: (517)487-1548
Fax: (517)487-0675
Free: (800)292-7871
E-mail: office@nasw-michigan.org
URL: http://www.nasw-michigan.org
Contact: Maxine Thome PhD, Exec.Dir.
State. Affiliated With: National Association of Social Workers.

8738 ■ National Association of State Foresters, Michigan
c/o Lynne M. Boyd
PO Box 30452
Lansing, MI 48909-7952
Ph: (517)373-1056
E-mail: boydlm@michigan.gov
URL: National Affiliate–www.stateforesters.org
Contact: Lynne M. Boyd, Contact
State. Affiliated With: National Association of State Foresters.

8739 ■ National Council on Alcoholism and Drug Dependence of Michigan (NCADD)
913 W Holmes Rd., Ste.111
Lansing, MI 48910-0411
Ph: (517)394-1252
Fax: (517)394-1518
Free: (800)344-3400
E-mail: advocacy@ncaddm.org
Contact: Randy O'Brien, Exec.Dir.
Founded: 1973. **Members:** 100. **Membership Dues:** individual, $35 (annual) • associate, $100 (annual). **Staff:** 5. **Budget:** $161,500. **State.** Works for the prevention and control of alcoholism through programs of public and professional education, community service, and the promotion of alcoholism research. Advocates for members of addiction recovery community to reduce stigma associated with addiction and to improve treatment availability. **Affiliated With:** National Council on Alcoholism and Drug Dependence. **Publications:** Newsletter, quarterly. **Price:** free. **Circulation:** 1,200. **Advertising:** accepted • Pamphlet. **Conventions/Meetings:** workshop (exhibits) - 3 per year; Avg. Attendance: 200.

8740 ■ National Council on Alcoholism/Lansing Regional Area (NCA/LRA)
3400 S Cedar St., Ste.200
Lansing, MI 48910
Ph: (517)887-0226
Fax: (517)887-8121
Free: (800)337-2310
E-mail: info@ncalra.com
URL: http://www.ncalra.com
Contact: Rod Macdonald, Exec.Dir.
Founded: 1960. **Staff:** 40. **Budget:** $1,500,000. **Local.** Dedicated to identifying and meeting the needs of individuals and families experiencing problems with alcohol and other drugs through a full range of AOD treatment and education services. **Subgroups:** Glass House; Holden House. **Affiliated With:** National Council on Alcoholism and Drug Dependence. **Publications:** *Recovery Review*, quarterly. Newsletter. **Price:** free for members.

8741 ■ National Electrical Contractors Association, Michigan Chapter (NECA)
1026 N Washington Ave.
Lansing, MI 48906
Ph: (517)372-3080
Fax: (517)372-4313
E-mail: ejr@necanet.org
URL: http://www.electrical-contractors.org
Contact: Emilio J. Rouco, Public Relations Dir.
Founded: 1944. **Local.** Electrical contractors erecting, installing, repairing, servicing and maintaining electrical wiring and appliances. **Affiliated With:** National Electrical Contractors Association.

8742 ■ National Federation of the Blind of Michigan
c/o Fred Wurtzel, Pres.
1212 N Foster
Lansing, MI 48912
Ph: (517)372-8700
E-mail: nfbm@comcast.net
URL: http://www.nfbmi.org
Contact: Fred Wurtzel, Pres.
State. Works to help blind persons achieve self-confidence and self-respect. Acts as a vehicle for collective self-expression by the blind. Provides education, information and referral services, scholarships, literature, and publications about blindness.

8743 ■ National Federation of Independent Business - Michigan
c/o Charles Owens, State Dir.
115 W Allegan St., Ste.310
Lansing, MI 48933
Ph: (517)485-3409
Fax: (517)485-2155
E-mail: Charles.Owens@NFIB.org
State. Affiliated With: National Federation of Independent Business.

8744 ■ National Guard Association of Michigan (NGAM)
300 Elvin Ct.
Lansing, MI 48913-5103
Ph: (517)484-1644
Fax: (517)484-1680
Free: (800)477-1644
E-mail: ngam@voyager.net
URL: http://www.ngam.org
Contact: Ret. Brigadier Gen. Roger Allen, Exec.Dir.
Founded: 1956. **State. Affiliated With:** Enlisted Association of National Guard of the United States.

8745 ■ National Management Association, The Blues
c/o Robert Davis
Blue Cross Blue Shield of MI
1405 S Creyts Rd.
Lansing, MI 48917
E-mail: rdavis@bcbsm.com
URL: National Affiliate–www.nma1.org
Contact: Robert Davis, Contact
Local. Business and industrial management personnel; membership comes from supervisory level, with the remainder from middle management and above. Seeks to develop and recognize management as a profession and to promote the free enterprise system. **Affiliated With:** National Management Association.

8746 ■ Nature Conservancy Michigan Chapter, Ives Rd. Fen Preserve
c/o Laurel Malvitz
101 E Grand River Ave.
Lansing, MI 48906
Ph: (517)316-0300
E-mail: michigan@tnc.org
URL: http://nature.org/michigan
State.

8747 ■ Nature Conservancy, Michigan Chapter Office
101 E. Grand River
Lansing, MI 48906
Ph: (517)316-0300
Fax: (517)332-8382
E-mail: michigan@tnc.org
URL: http://nature.org/michigan
Contact: Helen Taylor, State Dir.
Founded: 1980. **Members:** 28,000. **Membership Dues:** $25 (annual). **Staff:** 36. **State.** Dedicated to the preservation of ecological diversity through the protection of natural areas. **Affiliated With:** Nature Conservancy. **Publications:** *The Michigan Conservancy*, quarterly. Newsletter. Contains new nature preserve projects, field trip and work day schedules. **Price:** included in membership dues. **Conventions/Meetings:** annual meeting - always summer.

8748 ■ Office and Professional Employees International Union, AFL-CIO, CLC - Local Union 512
PO Box 80475
Lansing, MI 48908
Ph: (517)323-4541
Free: (800)852-0565
E-mail: opeiu@voyager.net
URL: http://my.voyager.net/%7Eopeiu/index.html
Contact: Tom Katona, VP
Members: 1,080. **Local. Affiliated With:** Office and Professional Employees International Union.

8749 ■ Operation Lifesaver, Michigan
111 W Edgewood Blvd.
Lansing, MI 48911
Ph: (419)661-3049 (517)318-3787
Fax: (517)318-0527
E-mail: aeb1277@aol.com
URL: National Affiliate–www.oli.org
Contact: Al Bard, State Coor.
State. Affiliated With: Operation Lifesaver.

8750 ■ Phi Theta Kappa, Mu Tau Chapter - Lansing Community College
c/o Jennifer Lock
PO Box 40010
Lansing, MI 48933
Ph: (517)483-5263
E-mail: jlock@lcc.edu
URL: http://www.ptk.org/directories/chapters/MI/251-1.htm
Contact: Jennifer Lock, Advisor
Local.

8751 ■ Polish Falcons of America, Nest 652
1030 W Mt. Hope Ave.
Lansing, MI 48910
Ph: (517)374-0419
URL: http://www.polishfalcons.org/nest/652/index.html
Contact: Patricia A. Krawczynski, Pres.
Local. Affiliated With: Polish Falcons of America.

8752 ■ Professors Fund for Educational Issues
c/o Robert C. Grosvenor, Exec.Dir.
115 W Allegan, Ste.320
Lansing, MI 48933-1712
Ph: (517)482-2775
Fax: (517)482-6115
E-mail: miaaup@aol.com
URL: http://www.miaaup.org
Contact: Robert C. Grosvenor, Exec.Dir.
Founded: 1990. **Membership Dues:** voluntary, $25 (annual). **State.** Fosters effective cooperation among teachers, scholars, and other academic professionals in universities, colleges, and professional schools of similar grade. Promotes the interest of higher education and research. **Awards: Type:** grant. **Publications:** Brochure. **Conventions/Meetings:** annual meeting - usually May.

8753 ■ Project Management Institute, Michigan Capital Area Chapter (PMI-MCAC)
c/o Michigan Department of Information Technology
Proj. Mgt. Rsrc. Ctr.
Romney Bldg., 4th Fl. SE
111 S Capital Ave.
Lansing, MI 48913
Ph: (517)335-5099
Fax: (517)706-5503
E-mail: president@pmi-mcac.org
URL: http://www.pmi-mcac.org
Contact: Stanley Samuel MBA, Pres.
Local. Corporations and individuals engaged in the practice of project management; project management

students and educators. Seeks to advance the study, teaching, and practice of project management. **Affiliated With:** Project Management Institute. **Formerly:** (2005) Project Management Institute, Michigan Capitol Area.

8754 ■ Property Management Association of Mid-Michigan (PMAMM)
PO Box 27011
Lansing, MI 48909
Ph: (517)281-0815
Fax: (517)484-1753
E-mail: darlj@pmamm.com
URL: http://www.pmamm.com
Contact: Darlene Littlejohn, Association Exec.

Local. Affiliated With: National Apartment Association.

8755 ■ Prosecuting Attorneys Coordinating Council (PACC)
c/o Thomas Robertson, Exec.Sec.
116 W Ottawa St., Ste.200
Lansing, MI 48913-1600
Ph: (517)334-6060
Fax: (517)334-6351
URL: http://www.ag.state.mi.us/pacc

State. Additional Websites: http://www.michiganprosecutor.org. **Formerly:** (2005) Prosecuting Attorneys Association of Michigan.

8756 ■ RSVP-Ingham/Eaton/Clinton County
c/o Janet Clark, Dir.
6545 Mercantile Way, Ste.1A-1
Lansing, MI 48911
Ph: (517)887-6116
Fax: (517)887-7313
E-mail: rsvplansing@voyager.net
URL: http://www.joinseniorservice.org
Contact: Janet Clark, Dir.

Local. Affiliated With: Retired and Senior Volunteer Program.

8757 ■ St. Stephan's Community Lions Club
c/o Bennie Boyd, Pres.
3662 Delta River Dr.
Lansing, MI 48906
Ph: (517)321-3858
E-mail: bennieboydrenee@aol.com
URL: http://www.district11c2.org
Contact: Bennie Boyd, Pres.

Local. Affiliated With: Lions Clubs International.

8758 ■ Service Station Dealers Association of Michigan (SSDA)
611 S Capitol
Lansing, MI 48933
Ph: (517)484-4096
Fax: (517)484-5705
E-mail: membership@ssdami.com
URL: http://www.ssdami.com

State.

8759 ■ Sierra Club - Mackinac Chapter
c/o Alison Horton
109 E Grand River
Lansing, MI 48906
Ph: (517)484-2372
Fax: (517)484-3108
E-mail: mackinac.chapter@sierraclub.org
URL: http://www.sierraclub.org/chapters/mi
Contact: Alison Horton, Contact

Local. Affiliated With: Sierra Club.

8760 ■ Small Business Association of Michigan (SBAM)
222 N Washington Sq., Ste.100
PO Box 16158
Lansing, MI 48901-6158
Ph: (517)482-8788
Fax: (517)482-4205
Free: (800)362-5461
E-mail: sbam@sbam.org
URL: http://www.sbam.org
Contact: Robert D. Fowler, Pres./CEO

Founded: 1969. **Members:** 8,000. **Membership Dues:** general, $185 (annual). **Staff:** 13. **Budget:** $2,000,000. **State.** Aims to promote free enterprise and the interests of Michigan's small businesses through leadership and advocacy. **Awards:** Innovation Awards. **Frequency:** annual. **Type:** trophy. **Affiliated With:** National Small Business Association. **Publications:** *Journal of Small Business*, bimonthly • *Small Business Barometer*, quarterly. Contains surveys of Michigan business owners and reports on their economic outlook. • Directory, annual. **Conventions/Meetings:** annual meeting.

8761 ■ Sons of Norway, Sonja Henie Lodge 5-490
c/o Steven R. Munkvold, Pres.
300 E Willard Ave.
Lansing, MI 48910-3050
Ph: (517)393-3632
E-mail: steve.munkvold@sparrow.org
URL: National Affiliate–www.sofn.com
Contact: Steven R. Munkvold, Pres.

Local. Affiliated With: Sons of Norway.

8762 ■ State Bar of Michigan
c/o John T. Berry, Exec.Dir.
306 Townsend St.
Lansing, MI 48933-2083
Ph: (517)346-6300
Fax: (517)482-6248
Free: (800)968-1442
E-mail: jberry@mail.michbar.org
URL: http://www.michbar.org
Contact: John T. Berry, Exec.Dir.

Founded: 1935. **Members:** 24,900. **Staff:** 38. **Budget:** $3,990,000. **State.** Practicing attorneys and judges who promote: improvements in the administration of justice and relations between the legal profession and the public; the interests of the legal profession in the state. **Supersedes:** Michigan State Bar Association. **Publications:** *Michigan Bar Journal*, monthly. **Conventions/Meetings:** annual seminar.

8763 ■ Telecommunications Association of Michigan (TAM)
c/o Scott Stevenson, Pres.
124 W Allegan, Ste.1400
Lansing, MI 48933
Ph: (517)482-4166
Fax: (517)482-3548
E-mail: stevenson.scott@telecommich.org
URL: http://www.telecommich.org
Contact: Scott Stevenson, Pres.

Founded: 1935. **Members:** 37. **Membership Dues:** local exchange carrier, $2,000 (annual) • telecommunication service provider, $1,000 (annual) • consultant/supplier, $400 (annual). **Staff:** 4. **Budget:** $950,000. **State.** Enhances the overall statewide business environment in which member firms and corporations operate in compliance with applicable laws and regulations. Pursues its mission by collecting and disseminating information relative to the telecommunications industry by providing a forum for discussion and revolution of industry issues, and by providing leadership and communication on such issues among members and the public. **Conventions/Meetings:** annual convention, educational, legislative, and regulatory speakers (exhibits).

8764 ■ Tomorrow's Child/Michigan Sudden Infant Death Syndrome
824 N Capitol Ave.
Lansing, MI 48906
Ph: (517)485-7437
Free: (800)331-7437
E-mail: info@tomorrowschildmi.org
URL: http://www.tomorrowschildmi.org
Contact: Sandra Frank, Exec.Dir.

State. Formerly: (2006) Tomorrow's Child/Michigan SIDS Alliance.

8765 ■ Tri-County Community Advocates for People with Developmental Disabilities
922 N Washington Ave.
Lansing, MI 48906-5137
Ph: (517)484-3068
URL: National Affiliate–www.TheArc.org
Contact: Jan Gormely, Exec.Dir.

Local. Parents, professional workers, and others interested in individuals with mental retardation. Works to promote services, research, public understanding, and legislation for people with mental retardation and their families. **Affiliated With:** Arc of the United States.

8766 ■ UAW Local 602
2510 W Michigan Ave.
Lansing, MI 48917
Ph: (517)372-4626
E-mail: djg602@aol.com
URL: http://www.local602.org
Contact: Art Luna, Pres.

Founded: 1939. **Members:** 3,243. **Local.** Serves as a collective bargaining agent for members. **Affiliated With:** International Union, United Automobile, Aerospace and Agricultural Implement Workers of America.

8767 ■ United Cerebral Palsy Association, Michigan
3401 E Saginaw, Ste.216
Lansing, MI 48912
Ph: (517)203-1200
Fax: (517)203-1203
Free: (800)828-2714
E-mail: ucp@ucpmichigan.org
URL: http://www.ucpmichigan.org
Contact: Linda Potter, Exec.Dir.

State. Assists persons with cerebral palsy and other disabilities, and their families. Goals are to enhance productivity, independence and full citizenship of people with cerebral palsy and other disabilities. Specific emphasis on assistive technology, public policy, transportation, and return-to-work benefits. **Affiliated With:** United Cerebral Palsy Associations.

8768 ■ United States Naval Sea Cadet Corps - United States Division
NMCRC Lansing
1620 E Saginaw St.
Lansing, MI 48912
E-mail: stevev@zeelandlumber.com
URL: http://dolphin.seacadets.org/US_units/UnitDetails.asp?UnitID=094USA
Contact: Lt. Stephen D. Van Antwerpen, Commanding Officer

Local. Works to instill good citizenship and patriotism in youth. Encourages qualities such as personal neatness, loyalty, obedience, dependability, and responsibility to others. Offers courses in physical fitness and military drill, first aid, water safety, basic seamanship, and naval history and traditions. **Affiliated With:** Naval Sea Cadet Corps.

8769 ■ USA Dance - Central Michigan Chapter No. 2037
c/o Diane West, Sec./Membership Chair
2111 Stirling Ave.
Lansing, MI 48910
Ph: (517)484-3340
E-mail: westdance@juno.com
URL: http://usadance2037.org
Contact: Diane West, Sec./Membership Chair

Local. Encourages and promotes the physical, mental and social benefits of partner dancing. Organizes and supports programs for the recreational enjoyment of ballroom dancing. Creates opportunities for the general public to participate in ballroom dancing and DanceSport.

8770 ■ Voice of the Retarded, Michigan
2215 Wellington Rd.
Lansing, MI 48910
Ph: (517)485-6425
E-mail: joranko@aol.com
URL: National Affiliate–www.vor.net
Contact: Joyce Joranko, Dir.

State. Affiliated With: Voice of the Retarded.

8771 ■ Young Entomologists' Society (Y.E.S.)
6907 W Grand River Ave.
Lansing, MI 48906-9158
Ph: (517)886-0630
Fax: (517)886-0630
E-mail: yesbugs@aol.com
URL: http://members.aol.com/YESbugs/bugclub.html
Contact: Dianna K. Dunn, Exec.Dir.
Founded: 1965. **Local.**

8772 ■ Young Life Eastern Great Lakes Region
1000 Long Blvd., Ste.8
Lansing, MI 48911
Ph: (517)694-3580
Fax: (517)694-5942
URL: http://sites.younglife.org/sites/eglregion/default.aspx
Regional. Affiliated With: Young Life.

8773 ■ Youth Development Corporation (YDC)
c/o Jaime Hutchinson, Dir.
806 N Capitol Ave.
Lansing, MI 48906
Ph: (517)482-2081
Fax: (517)482-2022
E-mail: ydc@iserv.net
URL: http://www.theydc.org
Contact: Jaime Hutchinson, Dir.
Local.

Lapeer

8774 ■ American Legion, Lapeer Post 16
1701 W Genesee St.
Lapeer, MI 48446
Ph: (517)371-4720
Fax: (517)371-2401
URL: National Affiliate–www.legion.org
Local. Affiliated With: American Legion.

8775 ■ Big Brothers Big Sisters of America of Lapeer County
55 W Nepessing St.
Lapeer, MI 48446
Ph: (810)667-9368
URL: http://lapeer.org/serviceorg/bigbbigs
Local. Helps children reach their potential through professionally supported, one-to-one relationships with measurable impact. Serves as a mentor for relationships for all children who need and want them, contributing to better schools, brighter futures, and stronger communities for all. **Affiliated With:** Big Brothers Big Sisters of America.

8776 ■ Lapeer Area Chamber of Commerce (LACC)
108 W Park St.
Lapeer, MI 48446
Ph: (810)664-6641
Fax: (810)664-4349
E-mail: staff@lapeerareachamber.org
URL: http://www.lapeerareachamber.org
Contact: Diana Faught, Exec.Dir.
Local. Works to promote and foster the business community and enhance the quality of life in the area. **Computer Services:** Information services, membership directory. **Publications:** *Business Connections*, monthly. Newsletter. Provides information about the community and local businesses. **Advertising:** accepted.

8777 ■ Lapeer Area Citizens Against Domestic Assault
PO Box 356
Lapeer, MI 48446
Ph: (810)667-4175
Fax: (810)667-4743
URL: http://www.lacada.com
Contact: Tracey Walker, Exec. Co-Dir.
Founded: 1991. **Staff:** 10. **Budget:** $200,000. **Local.** Works to prevent and report domestic assault. Provides shelter and services to victims of domestic assault. Maintains 24-hour crisis hotline. **Publications:** none.

8778 ■ Lapeer County Community Mental Health Services
1570 Suncrest Dr.
Lapeer, MI 48446
Ph: (810)667-0500
Contact: Mike Bizena, Dir.
Founded: 1971. **Members:** 2,000. **Staff:** 120. **Budget:** $12,000,000. **Regional Groups:** 1. **State Groups:** 1. **Local Groups:** 1. **Languages:** English, Spanish. **Local.** Promotes mental health. **Libraries: Type:** open to the public. **Holdings:** 400. **Subjects:** Mental Health. **Boards:** Advisory; Directors. **Publications:** Annual Report, annual. **Circulation:** 500. **Advertising:** accepted. **Conventions/Meetings:** annual seminar, with accreditation.

8779 ■ Lapeer Development Corporation (LDC)
449 McCormick Dr.
Lapeer, MI 48446
Ph: (810)667-0080
Fax: (810)667-3541
E-mail: info@lapeerdevelopment.com
URL: http://www.lapeerdevelopment.com
Contact: Jay Schwedler, Exec.Dir.
Founded: 1981. **Members:** 175. **Staff:** 2. **Budget:** $180,000. **Local.** Individuals dedicated to the economic growth of Lapeer County, MI. Coordinates local, state, and federal efforts concerning expansion or relocation within Lapeer County. Assists businesses in obtaining financial incentives, site selection, job training, and business planning. **Convention/Meeting:** none. **Publications:** *Development Dialogue*, periodic. Newsletter • *Lapeer County Industrial Directory*, annual • *Lapeer County Profile*, annual • *Lapeer County Wage and Benefit Survey*, annual.

8780 ■ Lapeer and Upper Thumb Association of Realtors
309 S Court St.
Lapeer, MI 48446
Ph: (810)664-0271
Fax: (810)664-6750
E-mail: sharon@mithumb.com
URL: http://www.mithumb.com
Contact: Sharon Buckner, Exec. Officer
Local. Strives to develop real estate business practices. Advocates the right to own, use and transfer real property. Provides a facility for professional development, research and exchange of information among members. **Affiliated With:** National Association of Realtors.

8781 ■ Michigan National Wild Turkey Federation, Lapeer Longbeards
2410 Roods Lake Rd.
Lapeer, MI 48446
Ph: (810)664-1570
URL: http://www.mi-nwtf.org/lapeer.htm
Contact: Dan Borgacz, Pres.
Local.

8782 ■ National Association of Miniature Enthusiasts - Mini Biddies
c/o Elvina P. Atwood
PO Box 175
Lapeer, MI 48446
Ph: (810)664-6082
URL: http://www.miniatures.org/states/MI.html
Contact: Elvina P. Atwood, Contact
Local. Affiliated With: National Association of Miniature Enthusiasts.

8783 ■ Tasters Guild International - Lapeer, Chapter No. 076
605 Rolling Hills Ln.
Lapeer, MI 48446
Ph: (810)664-0442
E-mail: dethridge@chartermi.net
URL: National Affiliate–www.tastersguild.com
Contact: David Ethridge, Contact
Local. Aims to educate consumers and spread the word of responsible wine and food consumption. Provides opportunity to encounter the best in wine and culinary delights. **Affiliated With:** Tasters Guild International.

8784 ■ Vintage Chevrolet Club of America, Lower Michigan Region No. 7
c/o Bruce Granger, Dir.
1690 Newark Rd.
Lapeer, MI 48446
Ph: (810)667-0144
URL: National Affiliate–www.vcca.org
Contact: Bruce Granger, Dir.
Local. Affiliated With: Vintage Chevrolet Club of America.

Lasalle

8785 ■ North Cape Yacht Club
11850 Toledo Beach Rd.
Lasalle, MI 48145
Ph: (734)242-5081
Fax: (734)242-1496
E-mail: clubmanager@ncyc.net
URL: http://www.ncyc.net
Local.

Lathrup Village

8786 ■ American Society for Quality, Greater Detroit Section 1000
c/o Rita Ita, Sec.
27350 Southfield Rd., Ste.102
Lathrup Village, MI 48076
Ph: (313)218-5407
E-mail: ir522@aol.com
URL: http://asqdetroit.org
Contact: Rita Ita, Sec.
Local. Advances learning, quality improvement and knowledge exchange to improve business results and to create better workplaces and communities worldwide. Provides a forum for information exchange, professional development and continuous learning in the science of quality. **Affiliated With:** American Society for Quality.

8787 ■ APICS, The Association for Operations Management - The Greater Detroit Chapter
27350 Southfield Rd., PMB 111
Lathrup Village, MI 48076
Ph: (248)443-9630
E-mail: info@apicsdet.org
URL: http://www.apicsdet.org
Contact: Kendall Scheer, Pres.
Local. Provides information and services in production and inventory management and related areas to enable members, enterprises and individuals to add value to their business performance. **Affiliated With:** APICS - The Association for Operations Management.

8788 ■ Detroit Mid-City Lions Club
c/o Fred Shorter, Pres.
2672 Lathrup Blvd.
Lathrup Village, MI 48076
Ph: (248)559-4775
E-mail: marijune99@yahoo.com
URL: http://www.metrodetroitlions.org
Contact: Fred Shorter, Pres.
Local. Affiliated With: Lions Clubs International.

8789 ■ Rosenwald Harlanites
c/o Victor Payne, Pres.
17536 Roseland Blvd.
Lathrup Village, MI 48076
E-mail: webmaster@rosenwaldharlanites.org
URL: http://www.rosenwaldharlanites.org
Contact: Victor Payne, Pres.
Local.

Laurium

8790 ■ American Legion, Michigan Post 61
c/o Ira Penberthy
PO Box 661
Laurium, MI 49913
Ph: (517)371-4720
Fax: (517)371-2401
URL: National Affiliate–www.legion.org
Contact: Ira Penberthy, Contact
Local. Affiliated With: American Legion.

Lawrence

8791 ■ American Legion, Hess-Eastman Post 174
PO Box 174
Lawrence, MI 49064
Ph: (517)371-4720
Fax: (517)371-2401
URL: National Affiliate–www.legion.org
Local. Affiliated With: American Legion.

Lawton

8792 ■ American Legion, Waters-Hackenberg Post 220
PO Box 253
Lawton, MI 49065
Ph: (517)371-4720
Fax: (517)371-2401
URL: National Affiliate–www.legion.org
Local. Affiliated With: American Legion.

8793 ■ Lawton Lions Club
PO Box 192
Lawton, MI 49065
E-mail: don@s-m-l-a.com
URL: http://milions11b2.org
Local. Affiliated With: Lions Clubs International.

8794 ■ Local 825, RWDSU District Council of the UFCW
PO Box 133
Lawton, MI 49065-0133
Ph: (616)347-0302
URL: National Affiliate–www.ufcw.org
Local. Affiliated With: United Food and Commercial Workers International Union.

Leland

8795 ■ Leelanau Conservancy
PO Box 1007
Leland, MI 49654
Ph: (231)256-9665
E-mail: conservancy@leelanau.com
URL: http://www.theconservancy.com
Contact: Brian R Price, Exec.Dir.
Local.

8796 ■ Leelanau Historical Society and Museum (LHS)
203 E Cedar St.
PO Box 246
Leland, MI 49654
Ph: (231)256-7475
Fax: (231)256-7650
E-mail: info@leelanauhistory.org
URL: http://www.leelanauhistory.org
Contact: John Mitchell, Dir.
Founded: 1957. **Members:** 560. **Membership Dues:** steward, $25-$49 (annual) • guardian, $50-$99 (annual) • collector, $100-$199 (annual) • historian, $200-$499 (annual) • founder, $500 (annual) • visionary, $1,000 (annual). **Staff:** 4. **Budget:** $160,000. **For-Profit. Local.** Permanent and seasonal residents of Leelanau County, MI seeking to preserve the history and promote the cultural heritage of the area. Operates Leelanau Historical Museum; sponsors educational programs, exhibits, documentation projects. **Libraries: Type:** open to the public; by appointment only. **Holdings:** 500; articles, audio recordings, books, periodicals, video recordings. **Subjects:** Leelanau County history, Lake Michigan maritime. **Awards:** Edmund F. Ball Fellowship. **Frequency:** periodic. **Type:** fellowship. **Publications:** *LEEMUSE Newsletter*, semiannual. **Price:** included in membership dues. **Circulation:** 1,000. **Advertising:** accepted. **Conventions/Meetings:** annual Ice Cream Social - meeting • quarterly meeting • quarterly Membership Meeting - general assembly, business agenda and program - last Monday in August, Leland MI.

Lennon

8797 ■ Inventors Council of Mid-Michigan (ICMM)
PO Box 232
Lennon, MI 48449-0232
Ph: (810)232-7909
E-mail: icmm@inventorscouncil.com
URL: http://inventorscouncil.org
Contact: Jim White, Pres.
State. Helps inventors pursue their dreams of bringing new and innovative products to market. Provides education and business networking among fellow inventors. **Affiliated With:** United Inventors Association of the U.S.A.

8798 ■ Lennon Lions Club
c/o Robert Sturgis, PDG, Pres.
255 Raleigh Pl.
Lennon, MI 48449
Ph: (810)621-3285
URL: http://www.geocities.com/dist11d1
Contact: Robert Sturgis PDG, Pres.
Local. Affiliated With: Lions Clubs International.

Lenox

8799 ■ Bluewater Area Woodturners
37840 29 Mile Rd.
Lenox, MI 48048
Ph: (586)291-5027
E-mail: billandbon@aiis.net
URL: http://www.home.comcast.net./~bluewaterareawoodturners
Contact: Bill Youngblood, Pres.
Local. Amateur and professional woodturners, gallery owners, wood and equipment suppliers, and collectors. Provides educational and organizational leadership in the art of woodturning. **Affiliated With:** American Association of Woodturners.

Leslie

8800 ■ American Legion, Michigan Post 491
c/o Lyle Edwards
422 Woodworth St.
Leslie, MI 49251
Ph: (517)371-4720
Fax: (517)371-2401
URL: National Affiliate–www.legion.org
Contact: Lyle Edwards, Contact
Local. Affiliated With: American Legion.

8801 ■ Celtic Corner Miniature Club
c/o Lori D. Raymond
307 Washington St.
Leslie, MI 49251
Ph: (517)589-9820
E-mail: celticcornerminiatures@msn.com
URL: http://www.miniatures.org/states/MI.html
Contact: Lori D. Raymond, Contact
Local. Affiliated With: National Association of Miniature Enthusiasts.

8802 ■ Leslie Lions Club
c/o David Allard, Pres.
11520 Dutch Rd.
Leslie, MI 49251
Ph: (517)589-9810
URL: http://www.district11c2.org
Contact: David Allard, Pres.
Local. Affiliated With: Lions Clubs International.

Lewiston

8803 ■ American Fisheries Society, Michigan Chapter President
c/o Todd C. Wills, Pres.
Michigan Dept. of Natural Resources
Hunt Creek Fisheries Res. Sta.
1581 Halberg Rd.
Lewiston, MI 49756
Ph: (989)786-2613
E-mail: willst@michigan.gov
URL: http://www.fisheries.org/miafs
Contact: Todd C. Wills, Pres.
Local. Affiliated With: American Fisheries Society.

8804 ■ American Legion, Lewiston Post 198
PO Box 623
Lewiston, MI 49756
Ph: (517)371-4720
Fax: (517)371-2401
URL: National Affiliate–www.legion.org
Local. Affiliated With: American Legion.

8805 ■ Lewiston Area Chamber of Commerce (LACC)
2946 Kneeland St.
PO Box 656
Lewiston, MI 49756
Ph: (989)786-2293
Fax: (989)786-4515
E-mail: lewistonchamber@i2k.net
URL: http://lewistonchamber.com
Founded: 1958. **Members:** 140. **Membership Dues:** club, $135 (annual). **Staff:** 1. **Budget:** $55,000. **Local.** Promotes business and community development and tourism in the Lewiston, MI area. Sponsors annual Morel Mushroom and Timberfest events, Car Show, and Arts and Crafts Fairs. **Publications:** *Communicator*, monthly. Newsletter. **Conventions/Meetings:** monthly Ambassadors Formation - board meeting • annual Governors Tourism - conference • annual MCCE - meeting • Sunrise Association - meeting.

8806 ■ Montmorency County Habitat for Humanity
PO Box 911
Lewiston, MI 49756
Ph: (989)786-3385 (989)786-4908
Fax: (989)786-3385
URL: http://www.nemichigan.com
Local. Affiliated With: Habitat for Humanity International.

8807 ■ Ruffed Grouse Society, Jim Foote Chapter
c/o James Johnson
PO Box 241
Lewiston, MI 49756-0241
E-mail: michael@ura2000.com
URL: National Affiliate–www.ruffedgrousesociety.org
Contact: James Johnson, Contact
Local. Affiliated With: Ruffed Grouse Society.

Lexington

8808 ■ Greater Croswell - Lexington Chamber of Commerce
PO Box 142
Lexington, MI 48450
Ph: (810)359-2262
E-mail: croslex@greatlakes.net
URL: http://www.cros-lex-chamber.com
Contact: Marleen Reynolds, Pres.
Membership Dues: business and industry, $75 (annual) • local unit of government, $60 (annual) • sole

proprietor, $40 (annual) • non-profit organization, $35 (annual) • friend of chamber, $15 (annual). **Local**. Promotes business and community development in Greater Croswell-Lexington, MI.

8809 ■ United Way of Sanilac County
PO Box 245
Lexington, MI 48450-0245
Ph: (810)359-7300
Fax: (810)359-7318
E-mail: uwsc@greatlakes.net
URL: http://www.kjpassociates.com/unitedway
Contact: Kent France, Exec.Dir.
Local. Affiliated With: United Way of America.

Lincoln

8810 ■ Alcona County Habitat for Humanity
PO Box 429
Lincoln, MI 48742-0429
Ph: (989)848-5617 (989)735-2981
E-mail: bobem@centurytel.net
Contact: Mr. Ray Brimm, Pres.
Founded: 1995. **Local**. Provide simple decent housing to families in need. **Affiliated With:** Habitat for Humanity International; Habitat for Humanity of Michigan. **Also Known As:** (2005) Alcona Habitat.

Lincoln Park

8811 ■ American Legion, Michigan Post 67
c/o Robert A. De Mars
1430 Southfield
Lincoln Park, MI 48146
Ph: (517)371-4720
Fax: (517)371-2401
URL: National Affiliate–www.legion.org
Contact: Robert A. De Mars, Contact
Local. Affiliated With: American Legion.

8812 ■ Downriver Genealogical Society (DRGS)
PO Box 476
Lincoln Park, MI 48146
Ph: (313)381-0507
E-mail: sherry@localonline.net
URL: http://www.rootsweb.com/~midrgs/drgs.htm
Contact: Sherry Huntington, Pres.
Founded: 1980. **Members:** 360. **Membership Dues:** $10 (annual). **Local**. Individuals interested in researching and preserving the history and genealogy of their ancestors. Objectives are: to encourage and assist members in genealogical research; to compile and preserve history; to sponsor educational courses and activities in genealogy and history. **Libraries: Type:** open to the public. **Holdings:** 1,000; books. **Subjects:** local history, Downriver area, Michigan, various states, Ontario and Quebec, passenger list books, periodicals, city directories, French-Canadian research. **Awards:** Descendant of Downriver. **Type:** recognition. **Affiliated With:** Federation of Genealogical Societies; National Genealogical Society. **Publications:** *Ancestor Charts II*. Book. **Price:** $20.00 add $3.50 for shipping/handling • *Bloomdale Cemetery*. **Price:** $9.00 add $2.50 for shipping/handling • *Downriver Seeker*, quarterly. Newsletter • *The First Twenty Years of Woodmere Cemetery 1868-1888*. Book. **Price:** $26.00 add $3.50 for shipping and handling • *Indexlist of Landowners from the 1876 Illustrated and Historical Atlas of Wayne County, Michigan*. Book. **Price:** $26.00 add $3.50 for shipping and handling. **Conventions/Meetings:** monthly meeting - except July, August, and December; always 3rd Wednesday.

8813 ■ Lincoln Park Chamber of Commerce
1335 Southfield Rd.
PO Box 382
Lincoln Park, MI 48146
Ph: (313)386-0140
Fax: (313)386-0140
E-mail: lpchamberofcommerce@juno.com
Contact: Karen Maniaci, Exec.Dir.
Local.

8814 ■ Lincoln Park Lions Club - Michigan
c/o Joseph Griggs, Pres.
PO Box 826
Lincoln Park, MI 48146
Ph: (313)682-8283
E-mail: just4urose@aol.com
URL: http://www.metrodetroitlions.org
Contact: Joseph Griggs, Pres.
Local. Affiliated With: Lions Clubs International.

8815 ■ Riverview Lions Club
c/o John Dlugopolski, Pres.
1011 Ford Blvd.
Lincoln Park, MI 48146
Ph: (313)282-4444 (313)388-9599
E-mail: jk801g@home.com
URL: http://www.metrodetroitlions.org
Contact: John Dlugopolski, Pres.
Local. Affiliated With: Lions Clubs International.

Linden

8816 ■ American Legion, Linden Post 119
PO Box 514
Linden, MI 48451
Ph: (517)371-4720
Fax: (517)371-2401
URL: National Affiliate–www.legion.org
Local. Affiliated With: American Legion.

8817 ■ Byron Area Athletic Association
c/o Board of Directors
9438 Lakeview Dr.
Linden, MI 48451
Local.

8818 ■ Fenton/Flint Table Tennis Club
Fenton Intermediate School
4179 E Rolston Rd.
Linden, MI 48451
Ph: (810)735-7352 (248)676-1311
E-mail: bay_tt@yahoo.com
URL: http://www.fentontabletennisclub.bravehost.com
Contact: Jerry Sagady, Contact
Local. Affiliated With: U.S.A. Table Tennis.

8819 ■ Linden Argentine Chamber of Commerce
PO Box 219
Linden, MI 48451-0128
Ph: (810)735-1277
Fax: (810)735-7738
E-mail: info@lindenchamber.com
URL: http://www.lindenchamber.com
Contact: Brian E. Chidsey, Pres.
Membership Dues: non-profit, $50 (annual) • business, $125-$225 (annual). **Local**. Promotes business and community development in Linden, MI area. **Computer Services:** Information services, membership directory. **Telecommunication Services:** electronic mail, jrsloan@lindenchamber.com. **Committees:** Communication; Events; Marketing; Public Affairs.

8820 ■ Linden Lions Club - Michigan
c/o William Wyckoff, Pres.
9376 Evergreen Dr.
Linden, MI 48451-8748
Ph: (810)735-6588
URL: http://www.geocities.com/dist11d1
Contact: William Wyckoff, Pres.
Local. Affiliated With: Lions Clubs International.

Linwood

8821 ■ American Legion, Michigan Post 239
c/o John K. Fowler
557 N Garfield Rd.
Linwood, MI 48634
Ph: (517)371-4720
Fax: (517)371-2401
URL: National Affiliate–www.legion.org
Contact: John K. Fowler, Contact
Local. Affiliated With: American Legion.

8822 ■ Bay County Conservation Club
860 N Rogers Rd.
Linwood, MI 48634
Ph: (989)631-9944
E-mail: jaglynn@msn.com
URL: National Affiliate–www.mynssa.com
Local. Affiliated With: National Skeet Shooting Association.

Litchfield

8823 ■ American Legion, Michigan Post 279
c/o Harry S. Kelly
PO Box 32
Litchfield, MI 49252
Ph: (517)371-4720
Fax: (517)371-2401
URL: National Affiliate–www.legion.org
Contact: Harry S. Kelly, Contact
Local. Affiliated With: American Legion.

8824 ■ Litchfield Chamber of Commerce
PO Box 343
Litchfield, MI 49252
Ph: (517)542-2921
Fax: (517)542-2491
E-mail: litchcity@chartermi.net
URL: http://www.ci.litchfield.mi.us
Contact: Marge Delaney, Pres.
Founded: 1967. **Members:** 50. **Membership Dues:** business, $50 (annual). **Local**. Promotes business and community development in Litchfield, MI. **Libraries: Type:** open to the public. **Conventions/Meetings:** monthly General - meeting.

Little Lake

8825 ■ American Legion, Morton-Guntley Post 349
PO Box 335
Little Lake, MI 49833
Ph: (517)371-4720
Fax: (517)371-2401
URL: National Affiliate–www.legion.org
Local. Affiliated With: American Legion.

Livonia

8826 ■ Alliance for the Mentally Ill of Suburban West
c/o Art Adaline, Pres.
33089 Curtis St.
Livonia, MI 48152-3211
Ph: (734)427-1435
URL: http://mi.nami.org/sw.html
Contact: Art Adaline, Pres.
Local. Strives to improve the quality of life of children and adults with severe mental illness through support, education, research and advocacy. **Affiliated With:** National Alliance for the Mentally Ill.

8827 ■ American Association of Legal Nurse Consultants, Greater Detroit Chapter (GDC-AALNC)
14397 Norman St.
Livonia, MI 48154
Ph: (586)776-0117
Fax: (586)776-0118
E-mail: laconklin2000@yahoo.com
URL: http://www.gdc-aalnc.org
Contact: Laura Conklin RN, Pres.
Founded: 1990. **Local. Affiliated With:** American Association of Legal Nurse Consultants.

8828 ■ American Legion, Ex-Cell-O Post 440
16633 Riverside Dr.
Livonia, MI 48154
Ph: (517)371-4720
Fax: (517)371-2401
URL: National Affiliate–www.legion.org
Local. Affiliated With: American Legion.

8829 ■ American Legion, Michigan Post 32
c/o Myron H. Beals
9318 Newburgh Rd.
Livonia, MI 48150
Ph: (517)371-4720
Fax: (517)371-2401
URL: National Affiliate–www.legion.org
Contact: Myron H. Beals, Contact
Local. Affiliated With: American Legion.

8830 ■ American Public Works Association, Michigan Chapter
c/o Mr. Evan N. Pratt, PE, Pres.
34000 Plymouth Rd.
Livonia, MI 48150-1512
Fax: (734)522-6427
Free: (888)522-6711
E-mail: evan.pratt@ohm-eng.com
URL: http://michigan.apwa.net
Contact: Mr. Evan N. Pratt PE, Pres.
State. Promotes professional excellence and public awareness through education, advocacy and the exchange of knowledge. **Affiliated With:** American Public Works Association.

8831 ■ Association of the United States Army, Detroit
c/o Donald W. Kolhoff
14066 Mayfield
Livonia, MI 48154
Ph: (734)522-0721
E-mail: dkol14066@aol.com
URL: National Affiliate–www.ausa.org
Local. Represents the interests and concerns of American Soldiers. Fosters public support of the Army's role in national security. Provides professional education and information programs.

8832 ■ Big Family of Michigan
c/o Jeanne Fowler
PO Box 530194
Livonia, MI 48153
Ph: (248)615-0327
E-mail: helpkids@bigfamilyofmichigan.com
URL: http://www.bigfamilyofmichigan.org
Contact: Jeanne Fowler, Contact
Local.

8833 ■ Center for Military Readiness (CMR)
PO Box 51600
Livonia, MI 48151
Ph: (202)347-5333
E-mail: info@cmrlink.org
URL: http://www.cmrlink.org
Contact: Elaine Donnelly, Pres.
Founded: 1993. **Members:** 6,500. **Membership Dues:** regular, $25 (annual). **Staff:** 2. **Budget:** $235,000. **Local.** Military (active and retired) and civilians. Works to research and distribute information regarding military personnel policies. **Publications:** *CMR Notes*, 10/year. Newsletter • Report. **Conventions/Meetings:** annual convention.

8834 ■ Christian Association for Psychological Studies, Midwest
c/o Mary Clark, EdD, Dir.
Alpha Psychological Services
39209 W 6 Mile Rd., No. 207
Livonia, MI 48152-3957
E-mail: alpha@ameritech.net
URL: National Affiliate–www.caps.net
Contact: Mary Clark EdD, Dir.
Regional. Encourages understanding of the relationship between Christianity and the behavioral sciences at both the clinical/counseling and the theoretical/research levels. Aims to help members explore the fields of psychology, pastoring and psychotherapy for a better insight into personality and interpersonal relations. **Affiliated With:** Christian Association for Psychological Studies.

8835 ■ Churchill High School PTSA
8900 Newburgh
Livonia, MI 48150
Ph: (734)744-2650
E-mail: churchill_ptsa@mailsnare.net
URL: http://www.livonia.k12.mi.us/schools/high/churchill/PTSA/index.htm
Contact: Barbara Stoner, Pres.
Local. Parents, teachers, students, and others interested in uniting the forces of home, school, and community. Promotes the welfare of children and youth.

8836 ■ Citizens Research Council of Michigan
38777 W 6 Mile Rd., Ste.208
Livonia, MI 48152-2660
Ph: (734)542-8001
Fax: (734)542-8004
E-mail: crcmich@crcmich.org
URL: http://www.crcmich.org
Contact: Earl M. Ryan, Pres.
Founded: 1916. **Members:** 140. **Staff:** 8. **Budget:** $670,000. **State.** Leading Michigan citizens. Provides tools citizens need to secure good government. Conducts in-depth studies of major public policy issues; evaluates the structure and organization of government; analyzes state and local tax and spending issues; promotes efficiency and effectiveness in governmental operations. Sponsors speakers; conducts presentations. **Awards:** The Lent D. Upson-Loren B. Miller Fellowship. **Frequency:** annual. **Type:** fellowship. **Recipient:** to an individual pursuing a master's degree in public administration or a similar field. **Publications:** *Memorandums*, 5/year. Report • Reports, periodic. **Conventions/Meetings:** annual meeting - always September.

8837 ■ Educational Teleconsortium of Michigan (ETOM)
c/o Colette Perugia, Business Mgr.
Schoolcraft Coll.
18600 Haggerty Rd.
Livonia, MI 48152
Ph: (734)462-4570
Fax: (734)462-4589
E-mail: cperugia@schoolcraft.cc.mi.us
URL: http://www.etom.org
Contact: Colette Perugia, Business Mgr.
Founded: 1980. **Local.**

8838 ■ Friends of Michigan Libraries (FOML)
c/o Harriet Larson
Livonia Civic Ctr. Lib.
32777 Five Mile Rd.
Livonia, MI 48154
E-mail: fomlquestion@gmail.com
URL: http://www.foml.org
Contact: Carol Perrin, Pres.
State. Works to provide training, consultation and resources to further the development of support for libraries. **Affiliated With:** Friends of Libraries U.S.A.

8839 ■ Great Lakes Chapter of the American Association of Physicists in Medicine (GLC-AAPM)
c/o Misbah Gulam, Sec.
St. Mary Mercy Hosp., Radiation Oncology
36475 Five Mile Rd.
Livonia, MI 48154
E-mail: gulamm@trinity-health.org
URL: http://www.freewebs.com/greatlakeschapter
Contact: Iris Ouyang, Pres.
Regional. Advances the practice of physics in medicine and biology through research and development and scientific and technical information. Fosters the education and professional development of medical physicists. Promotes the highest quality medical services for patients. **Affiliated With:** American Association of Physicists in Medicine.

8840 ■ Hostelling International, Michigan Council
PO Box 510228
Livonia, MI 48151-6228
Ph: (248)545-0511
Fax: (248)545-0514
E-mail: info@hi-michigan.org
URL: http://www.hi-michigan.org
Contact: Deb Bell, Pres.
State. Affiliated With: Hostelling International-American Youth Hostels.

8841 ■ International Union of Operating Engineers, Local 324
37450 Schoolcraft Rd., Ste.110
Livonia, MI 48150
Ph: (734)462-3660
Fax: (734)462-4830
Free: (888)324-3315
E-mail: info@iuoe324.org
URL: http://www.iuoe324.org
Contact: Michael Bartholomew, Contact
Local. Works to bring economic justice to the workplace and to improve the lives of working families. **Affiliated With:** International Union of Operating Engineers.

8842 ■ Livonia Chamber of Commerce (LCC)
33233 Five Mile Rd.
Livonia, MI 48154
Ph: (734)427-2122
Fax: (734)427-6055
E-mail: chamber@livonia.org
URL: http://www.livonia.org
Contact: Wes Graff, Pres.
Founded: 1954. **Members:** 800. **Membership Dues:** business (1-999 employees), $250-$1,345 • business (plus $3/employee over 1000), $1,345 • volunteer club, $125. **Local.** Business association that promotes economic and community development in the city of Livonia, MI. **Publications:** *Communicator*, monthly. Newsletter. **Advertising:** accepted. Alternate Formats: online • *Industrial Directory*, periodic • *Livonia Business Directory*, annual • *Manufacturer's Directory*, annual. Contains listing of manufacturers, processors, and other industrial firms in Livonia. **Conventions/Meetings:** monthly meeting.

8843 ■ Livonia Hi-Nooners Lions Club
c/o Arthur Blom, Pres.
29832 Orangelawn St.
Livonia, MI 48150
Ph: (734)525-3883
URL: http://www.metrodetroitlions.org
Contact: Arthur Blom, Pres.
Local. Affiliated With: Lions Clubs International.

8844 ■ Make-A-Wish Foundation of Michigan, Livonia Office
37727 Professional Center Dr., Ste.135D
Livonia, MI 48154
Ph: (734)953-0040
Fax: (734)432-9799
Free: (888)857-9474
E-mail: ostimpson@wishmich.org
URL: http://www.wishmich.org
Contact: Laura Stimpson, Office Mgr.
Local. Affiliated With: Make-A-Wish Foundation of America.

8845 ■ Mason Contractors Association (MCA)
12870 Farmington Rd., Ste.B
Livonia, MI 48150
Ph: (734)522-7350
Fax: (734)522-7435
URL: http://www.mcamichigan.org
Contact: Brad Leidal, Pres.
Founded: 1903. **Members:** 87. **Staff:** 2. **State.** Aims to create and maintain a good standard in the Mason Contracting business in the State of Michigan. **Publications:** *On the Level*. Newsletter. Alternate Formats: online.

8846 ■ Masonry Institute of Michigan (MIM)
12870 Farmington Rd., Ste.A
Livonia, MI 48150
Ph: (734)458-8544
Fax: (734)458-8545
E-mail: dan@mim-online.org
URL: http://www.mim-online.org
Contact: Daniel S. Zechmeister, Exec.Dir.
Founded: 1958. **State**. Dedicated to the promotion and advancement of the masonry industry.

8847 ■ Michigan Assisted Living Association (MALA)
15441 Middlebelt Rd.
Livonia, MI 48154
Ph: (734)525-0831
Fax: (734)525-2453
Free: (800)482-0118
E-mail: mala@miassistedliving.org
URL: http://www.miassistedliving.org
Contact: Robert Stein, Gen. Counsel
Founded: 1967. **Members:** 3,500. **Staff:** 12. **State**. Residential care and assisted living facilities. Promotes quality community residential services for mentally ill, developmentally disabled, and elderly persons. Provides information concerning legislation, rules, and policies. Conducts liaison and lobbying activities. Administers a Political Action Committee. Offers various group insurance programs. Provides legal consultation to members. Sponsors seminars and legislative meetings. **Affiliated With:** Assisted Living Federation of America. **Publications:** *Budget Updates*, periodic • *MALA Newsletter*, bimonthly • *Special Reports*, periodic • Bulletin, periodic. **Conventions/Meetings:** annual Provider Conference (exhibits) - always Lansing, MI.

8848 ■ Michigan Association of Physicians of Indian Origin
c/o Chandrika Joshi, MD, Pres.
PO Box 531840
Livonia, MI 48153-1840
Ph: (248)426-9292
Fax: (248)426-9292
E-mail: mapi@mapiusa.com
URL: http://www.mapiusa.com
Contact: Chandrika Joshi MD, Pres.
State. Represents Indian American physicians. Promotes excellence in patient care, teaching and research. Serves as a forum for scientific, educational and social interaction among members and other medical scientists of Indian heritage. Fosters the availability of medical assistance to indigent people in the United States. **Affiliated With:** American Association of Physicians of Indian Origin.

8849 ■ Michigan Boating Industries Association (MBIA)
32398 Five Mile Rd.
Livonia, MI 48154-6109
Ph: (734)261-0123
Fax: (734)261-0880
Free: (800)932-2628
E-mail: boatmichigan@mbia.org
URL: http://www.mbia.org
Contact: Mr. Van W. Snider Jr., Pres.
Founded: 1958. **Members:** 380. **Membership Dues:** regular, $265 (annual) • associate, $290 (annual). **Staff:** 6. **Budget:** $2,700,000. **State Groups:** 3. **State**. Represents the recreational marine industry. Educates, promotes, and protects the boating industry in Michigan. Produces the Detroit Boat Show and Spring Boating Expo. **Libraries: Type:** open to the public. **Holdings:** 1. **Subjects:** boating. **Awards:** Administrator of the Recreational Boating Industries Educational Foundation. **Frequency:** annual. **Type:** scholarship. **Recipient:** for participation in the boating industry. **Affiliated With:** National Marine Manufacturers Association. **Publications:** *Marine Trade News*, monthly. Newsletter. Contains issues affecting the boating industry. **Price:** included in membership dues. **Circulation:** 600. Alternate Formats: online • *Michigan Boating Annual*, annual. Magazine. **Conventions/Meetings:** monthly board meeting • annual conference, with educational seminars (exhibits) • annual show.

8850 ■ Michigan Carpentry Contractors Association
c/o Darin Baydoun, Exec.Dir.
32190 Schoolcraft
Livonia, MI 48150
Ph: (734)421-8232
Fax: (734)421-8283
Founded: 1954. **Members:** 40. **Staff:** 2. **State. Conventions/Meetings:** monthly meeting - 2nd Tuesday of every month. Farmington Hills, MI - Avg. Attendance: 25.

8851 ■ Michigan Interscholastic Athletic Administrators Association (MIAAA)
35445 Hathaway
Livonia, MI 48150-2513
Ph: (734)422-3569
Fax: (734)762-9957
E-mail: jakdoljohn@aol.com
URL: http://www.miaaa.com
Contact: Mr. Jack Johnson, Conference Chm.
Founded: 1962. **Members:** 700. **Membership Dues:** regular, $35 (annual). **Staff:** 2. **State Groups:** 1. **State**. Middle school/high school athletic directors and administrators. Promotes and supports interscholastic athletics in Michigan public and private schools. Activities include leadership training classes and scholarships. **Awards:** Athletic Director of Year (State). **Frequency:** annual. **Type:** recognition • Jack Johnson Distinguished Service Award. **Frequency:** annual. **Type:** recognition • MIAAA Scholarship. **Frequency:** annual. **Type:** scholarship. **Recipient:** son or daughter of member with high academic achievement and sports participation. **Affiliated With:** National Interscholastic Athletic Administrators Association. **Publications:** *Michigan Athletic Director*, quarterly. Newsletter. **Price:** free. **Circulation:** 2,000. **Advertising:** accepted. **Conventions/Meetings:** annual conference (exhibits) • annual convention, for exhibitors; with seminars (exhibits) • annual workshop.

8852 ■ Michigan Mineralogical Society
c/o John Vitkay, Membership Chm.
29125 Perth
Livonia, MI 48154
E-mail: president@michmin.org
URL: http://www.michmin.org
Contact: Stan Woolans, Pres.
State. Aims to further the study of Earth Sciences and the practice of lapidary arts and mineralogy. **Affiliated With:** American Federation of Mineralogical Societies.

8853 ■ Phi Theta Kappa, Omicron Iota Chapter - Schoolcraft College
c/o Sherry Springer
18600 Haggerty Rd.
Livonia, MI 48152
Ph: (734)462-4422
E-mail: sspringe@schoolcraft.edu
URL: http://www.ptk.org/directories/chapters/MI/248-1.htm
Contact: Sherry Springer, Advisor
Local.

8854 ■ Plumbing-Heating-Cooling Contractors Association, Michigan
c/o Mr. Anthony D'Ascenzo, Pres.
34400 Glendale St.
Livonia, MI 48150-1302
Ph: (734)513-9550 (517)484-5225
Fax: (734)513-9513
E-mail: tonyd@guardianplumbing.com
URL: National Affiliate–www.phccweb.org
Contact: Mr. Anthony D'Ascenzo, Pres.
State. Represents the plumbing, heating and cooling contractors. Promotes the construction industry. Protects the environment, health, safety and comfort of society. **Affiliated With:** Plumbing-Heating-Cooling Contractors Association.

8855 ■ Psi Chi, National Honor Society in Psychology - Madonna University
c/o Dept. of Psychology
36600 Schoolcraft Rd.
Livonia, MI 48150-1173
Ph: (734)432-5530 (734)432-5734
Fax: (734)432-5393
E-mail: joneill@madonna.edu
URL: http://www.psichi.org/chapters/info.asp?chapter_id=770
Contact: Jim O'Neill PhD, Advisor
Local.

8856 ■ Right to Life - Lifespan
29200 Vassar St., Ste.545
Livonia, MI 48152-2193
Ph: (248)478-8878 (734)422-6230
Fax: (248)478-8854
E-mail: mainoffice@rtl-lifespan.org
URL: http://www.ring.com/nprofit/lifespan
Contact: Diane Fagelman, Pres.
Founded: 1970. **Members:** 10,000. **Membership Dues:** ordinary, $20 (annual) • senior/student, $10 (annual). **Staff:** 9. **Local**. Individuals in Southeastern Michigan opposed to abortion, infanticide, and euthanasia. Seeks an end to abortion and the prevention of infanticide and euthanasia by working toward the passage of a Human Life Amendment to the U.S. Constitution for protecting all stages of human life. Supports pregnancy service groups and post-abortion healing groups. Maintains speaker's bureau. Sponsors competitions; compiles statistics. Provide clothing, diapers, baby food and formula for infants on an emergency basis. **Libraries: Type:** open to the public. **Holdings:** 500. **Subjects:** abortion, euthanasia, infanticide. **Awards:** Mother of the Year. **Frequency:** annual. **Type:** recognition. **Recipient:** for residents of tri-county area (Wayne, Oakland, Macomb); by nomination • Student Essay Awards. **Type:** recognition. **Recipient:** to winning high school students who write papers on abortion, infanticide or euthanasia. **Affiliated With:** National Right to Life Committee. **Formerly:** (1972) People Taking Action Against Abortion; (2005) Right-to-Life Lifespan of Metro Detroit. **Publications:** *Lifespan News*, monthly. Newsletter • *Resource Book*, annual. Journal. Contains current educational and legislative information. **Price:** free upon request. **Conventions/Meetings:** annual Legislative Breakfast - fall • annual Mother's Day Dinner, with awards - always May.

8857 ■ Southeast Michigan Air Conditioning Contractors of America (SEMIACCA)
33504 Five Mile Rd.
Livonia, MI 48154
Ph: (734)266-5475
Fax: (734)261-5479
E-mail: cjones@semiacca.org
URL: http://www.semiacca.org
Contact: Craig Jones, Pres.
Local. Works to represent contractors involved in installation and service of heating, air conditioning, and refrigeration systems. **Affiliated With:** Air Conditioning Contractors of America. **Conventions/Meetings:** monthly meeting - every 1st Wednesday.

8858 ■ STARFLEET: USS Parallax
c/o Capt. Samuel Cummings, Commanding Officer
9993 S Arcola Dr.
Livonia, MI 48150-3203
E-mail: ussparallax@region13.org
URL: http://www.region13.org
Contact: Capt. Samuel Cummings, Commanding Officer
Local. Affiliated With: STARFLEET.

8859 ■ USA Weightlifting - Dynamic Fitness
c/o Bud Charniga
30242 Buckingham St.
Livonia, MI 48154-2866
Ph: (734)425-2862
URL: National Affiliate–www.usaweightlifting.org
Contact: Bud Charniga, Contact
Local. Affiliated With: USA Weightlifting.

Lowell

8860 ■ American Hiking Society - North Country Trail Association
229 E Main St.
Lowell, MI 49331
Ph: (616)897-5987
Fax: (616)897-6605
URL: http://www.NorthCountryTrail.org
Local.

8861 ■ American Legion, Clark-Ellis Post 152
3116 Alden Nash SE
Lowell, MI 49331
Ph: (517)371-4720
Fax: (517)371-2401
URL: National Affiliate–www.legion.org
Local. Affiliated With: American Legion.

8862 ■ American Society for Quality, Grand Rapids Section 1001
c/o Kurt Roudabush
10766 Peck Lake Rd.
Lowell, MI 49331
Ph: (616)913-5993
URL: http://www.asq1001.org
Contact: Kurt Roudabush, Contact
Local. Advances learning, quality improvement and knowledge exchange to improve business results and to create better workplaces and communities worldwide. Provides a forum for information exchange, professional development and continuous learning in the science of quality. **Affiliated With:** American Society for Quality.

8863 ■ Lowell Area Chamber of Commerce (LACC)
113 Riverwalk Plz.
PO Box 224
Lowell, MI 49331
Ph: (616)897-9161
Fax: (616)897-9101
E-mail: info@lowellchamber.org
URL: http://www.lowellchamber.org
Contact: Liz Baker, Exec.Dir.
Founded: 1966. **Members:** 122. **Membership Dues:** industrial (based on number of employees), $110-$300 (annual) • service (based on number of employees), $85-$300 (annual) • professional, $140 (annual) • church, $60 (annual) • nonprofit, $60 (annual). **Local.** Promotes business and community development in the Lowell, MI area. Sponsors semiannual sidewalk sales. Sponsors Riverwalk Arts and Crafts. Christmas festivities, and a golf outing. **Awards:** Person of the Year. **Frequency:** annual. **Type:** recognition. **Computer Services:** Information services, member listing. **Publications:** Directory, annual • Newsletter, quarterly. **Conventions/Meetings:** monthly board meeting - always second Wednesday • quarterly meeting.

8864 ■ North Country Trail Association (NCTA)
229 E Main St.
Lowell, MI 49331-1711
Ph: (616)897-5987
Fax: (616)897-6605
Free: (866)HIK-ENCT
E-mail: hq@northcountrytrail.org
URL: http://northcountrytrail.org
Contact: Rob Corbett, Exec.Dir.
Founded: 1981. **Members:** 2,800. **Membership Dues:** regular, $30 • student, $10 • sponsored, $18 • organization, $45 • trail leader, $50 • pathfinder, $100 • business, $150 • patron, $250 • life, $1,000. **Staff:** 8. **Budget:** $400,000. **Regional Groups:** 25. **State Groups:** 7. Promotes, constructs and maintains a nonmotorized connected footpath, to be called the North Country National Scenic Trail; preserves and restores the natural environment of the trail. Acts as a clearinghouse for information on the trail. Promotes cooperation and coordination among individuals and groups using the trail and encourages active volunteer participation in its construction, repair, and cleanup. Stresses trail education for safe and enjoyable use. Sponsors hikes. **Libraries: Type:** reference. **Holdings:** archival material, audiovisuals, books, business records, clippings, periodicals. **Subjects:** national trail system and its parts. **Awards:** Communicator of the Year Award. **Frequency:** annual. **Type:** recognition. **Recipient:** to a volunteer for exemplary work in promoting the organization • Distinguished Service Award. **Type:** recognition. **Recipient:** for significant commitment and accomplishment over three or more years • Leadership Award. **Frequency:** annual. **Type:** recognition. **Recipient:** to a volunteer demonstrating exceptional leadership • Lifetime Achievement Award. **Frequency:** annual. **Type:** recognition. **Recipient:** for significant commitment and accomplishment over ten or more years • Outreach Award. **Frequency:** annual. **Type:** recognition. **Recipient:** to a volunteer contributing to ongoing success of organization • Rising Star Award. **Frequency:** annual. **Type:** recognition. **Recipient:** to a volunteer, ages 8-18 • Sweep Award. **Frequency:** annual. **Type:** recognition. **Recipient:** to a volunteer, for work and achievement behind the scenes on behalf of the organization • Trail Builder of the Year. **Frequency:** annual. **Type:** recognition. **Recipient:** to a volunteer for outstanding development of new trail or facility over the past year • Trail Maintainer of the Year. **Frequency:** annual. **Type:** recognition. **Recipient:** to a volunteer demonstrating exceptional dedication or achievement over the past year • Trailblazer Award. **Type:** recognition. **Recipient:** for a business or foundation's far sighted vision and support • Vanguard Award. **Type:** recognition. **Recipient:** for a legislator or public servant. **Telecommunication Services:** electronic mail, robcorbett@northcountrytrail.org. **Affiliated With:** American Hiking Society; Buckeye Trail Association; Kekekabic Trail Club; Superior Hiking Trail Association. **Publications:** *Guide to the North Country Trail—Chippewa National Forest*. Book. **Price:** $1.25 • *Michigan Mapsets* • *NCT Trail Map Sets*. **Price:** prices vary/map • *Newsletter of the North Country Trail Association - North Star*, quarterly • *North Star*, quarterly. Magazine • Annual Report. **Conventions/Meetings:** annual conference - usually in August, travels from state to state.

8865 ■ Prader-Willi Michigan Association
c/o Jim Loker, Co-Pres.
10756 Woodbushe
Lowell, MI 49331
Ph: (616)664-3379
E-mail: carolynloker@yahoo.com
URL: National Affiliate–www.pwsausa.org
Contact: Jim Loker, Co-Pres.
Members: 120. **Local. Affiliated With:** Prader-Willi Syndrome Association (U.S.A.). **Conventions/Meetings:** bimonthly meeting, with support and advocacy issues discussed - except summer.

8866 ■ School of Missionary Aviation Technology
730 Lincoln Lake Rd.
Lowell, MI 49331
Ph: (616)897-5785
Fax: (616)897-4827
E-mail: info@smat-aviation.org
URL: http://www.smat-aviation.org
Contact: Marvin C. Tyler, Pres.
Founded: 1971. **Staff:** 4. **Local Groups:** 1. **Regional. Formerly:** (1998) Cornerstone Aviation Services.

8867 ■ West Michigan Angus Association
c/o Joe Merriman, Pres.
5214 Bancroft
Lowell, MI 49331
Ph: (616)868-9948
URL: National Affiliate–www.angus.org
Contact: Joe Merriman, Pres.
Regional. Affiliated With: American Angus Association.

8868 ■ Western Michigan Compensation Association
c/o Tom Powell, VP Human Resources
Attwood Corp.
1016 N Monroe
Lowell, MI 49331
Ph: (616)897-2237
Fax: (616)897-2376
E-mail: tpowell@steelcase.com
URL: National Affiliate–www.worldatwork.org
Contact: Tom Powell, VP Human Resources
Local. Affiliated With: WorldatWork.

Ludington

8869 ■ American Legion, Michigan Post 76
c/o Edwin H. Ewing
318 N James St.
Ludington, MI 49431
Ph: (616)845-7094
Fax: (517)371-2401
URL: National Affiliate–www.legion.org
Contact: Edwin H. Ewing, Contact
Local. Affiliated With: American Legion.

8870 ■ Habitat for Humanity of Mason County, Michigan
PO Box 322
Ludington, MI 49431-0322
Ph: (231)843-7888
Fax: (231)845-0990
E-mail: hfhmason@verizon.net
URL: National Affiliate–www.habitat.org
Local. Affiliated With: Habitat for Humanity International.

8871 ■ Ludington Area Chamber of Commerce (LACC)
5300 W U.S. 10
Ludington, MI 49431
Ph: (231)845-0324
Fax: (231)845-6857
E-mail: ludington@ludington.org
URL: http://www.ludington.org
Contact: Alberta L. Muzzin, Pres./CEO
Founded: 1929. **Members:** 515. **Membership Dues:** individual, $125 (annual) • nonprofit, $135 (annual) • professional office, $230 (annual) • financial institution, $500 (annual) • business (based on number of employees), $230-$500 (annual) • sole proprietorship, $200 (annual) • food and beverage facility/accommodation, $230-$300 (annual). **Staff:** 3. **Budget:** $300,000. **Local.** Businesses and individuals interested in promoting business and community development in Ludington area and Mason County, MI. Sponsors Ludington Carferry Festival; Gus Macker 3-on-3 Charity Basketball Tournament; Harbor Festival; Gold Coast Arts and Crafts and Spirit of the Season Parade. **Awards:** Business Leader of the Year. **Frequency:** annual. **Type:** recognition • Citizen of the Year. **Frequency:** annual. **Type:** recognition. **Computer Services:** Mailing lists, of members. **Affiliated With:** U.S. Chamber of Commerce. **Publications:** *Area Map*, annual • *Business to Business*, monthly. Newsletter. **Advertising:** accepted • *Menu Guide*, annual • *Visitors Guide*, annual • Membership Directory, annual. **Circulation:** 3,500. **Conventions/Meetings:** monthly board meeting • periodic executive committee meeting • quarterly Human Resources Meeting • annual meeting.

8872 ■ Ludington Area Convention and Visitors Bureau
5300 W U.S. 10
Ludington, MI 49431
Ph: (616)845-1747
Fax: (616)845-6857
Free: (877)420-6618
URL: http://www.ludingtoncvb.com
Contact: Sue Brillhart, Exec.VP
Founded: 1987. **Members:** 90. **Membership Dues:** associate, $150 (annual). **Budget:** $140,000. **Local.** Promotes Ludington, MI as a convention and tourism location. **Publications:** *Ludington and Mason Co*, annual. Brochure. **Price:** free. **Circulation:** 70,000 • *Ludington Area Visitor's Guide*, annual. Booklet. **Price:** free.

8873 ■ Ludington Coin Club
c/o Marvyn Kelsey
PO Box 502
Ludington, MI 49431
Ph: (231)757-3944
E-mail: heglund@t-one.net
URL: National Affiliate–www.money.org
Contact: Marvyn Kelsey, Contact
Local. Affiliated With: American Numismatic Association.

8874 ■ Ludington Lions Club
c/o Frank Longmore, Pres.
305 N Robert St.
Ludington, MI 49431
Ph: (231)843-6800
E-mail: ludingtonlions@frankencutters.com
URL: http://lions.silverthorn.biz/11-e1
Contact: Frank Longmore, Pres.
Local. Affiliated With: Lions Clubs International.

8875 ■ Mason-Oceana-Manistree Board of Realtors
239 N Jebavy Dr.
Ludington, MI 49431
Ph: (231)845-1896
Fax: (231)845-1897
E-mail: realtors@momboard.com
URL: http://www.momboard.com
Contact: Teresa Vander Wall, Association Exec.
Local. Strives to develop real estate business practices. Advocates the right to own, use and transfer real property. Provides a facility for professional development, research and exchange of information among members. **Affiliated With:** National Association of Realtors.

8876 ■ United Way of Mason County
5816 W US Hwy. 10, Ste.A
Ludington, MI 49431-2496
Ph: (231)843-8593
Fax: (231)843-2670
E-mail: larussell@jackpine.com
URL: National Affiliate–national.unitedway.org
Contact: Lynne Russell, Exec.Dir.
Staff: 1. **Local. Affiliated With:** United Way of America.

8877 ■ West Michigan Mycological Society (WMMS)
115 N Emily St.
Ludington, MI 49431
Ph: (231)845-8055
Fax: (231)845-1465
URL: http://dancingmac.com/wmms
Contact: Gene Campbell, Pres.
Regional. Affiliated With: North American Mycological Association.

8878 ■ West Shore Rock and Mineral Club
c/o George Ruby, Pres.
5626 N Peterson Rd.
Ludington, MI 49431
E-mail: drrock@mich.com
URL: National Affiliate–www.amfed.org
Contact: Brenda Freeman, Sec.
Local. Aims to further the study of Earth Sciences and the practice of lapidary arts and mineralogy. **Affiliated With:** American Federation of Mineralogical Societies.

8879 ■ West Shore Youth for Christ
PO Box 515
Ludington, MI 49431-0515
Ph: (231)843-1323
Fax: (231)843-9405
URL: National Affiliate–www.yfc.net
Local. Affiliated With: Youth for Christ/U.S.A.

Luna Pier

8880 ■ American Legion, Michigan Post 193
c/o James E. Yenor
11045 Harold Dr.
Luna Pier, MI 48157
Ph: (517)371-4720
Fax: (517)371-2401
URL: National Affiliate–www.legion.org
Contact: James E. Yenor, Contact
Local. Affiliated With: American Legion.

Luther

8881 ■ Luther Lions Club
c/o Allan Armstrong, Pres.
9809 E 7 Mile Rd.
Luther, MI 49656
Ph: (231)829-3969
E-mail: barmstrong@michweb.net
URL: http://lions.silverthorn.biz/11-e1
Contact: Allan Armstrong, Pres.
Local. Affiliated With: Lions Clubs International.

Luzerne

8882 ■ American Legion, Wally Bartley Post 162
PO Box 186
Luzerne, MI 48636
Ph: (517)371-4720
Fax: (517)371-2401
URL: National Affiliate–www.legion.org
Local. Affiliated With: American Legion.

Lyons

8883 ■ Michigan Dairy Goat Society
c/o Linda Coon
4855 E Riverside Dr.
Lyons, MI 48851
Ph: (989)855-3896
URL: http://www.mdgs.org
Contact: Linda Coon, Contact
State. Affiliated With: American Dairy Goat Association.

Macatawa

8884 ■ Kiwanis Club of Holland
PO Box 12
Macatawa, MI 49434
URL: http://www.hollandkiwanis.org
Local.

Mackinac Island

8885 ■ American Legion, Mackinac Island Post 299
PO Box 1518
Mackinac Island, MI 49757
Ph: (517)371-4720
Fax: (517)371-2401
URL: National Affiliate–www.legion.org
Local. Affiliated With: American Legion.

8886 ■ Mackinac Island Tourism Bureau
PO Box 451
Mackinac Island, MI 49757
Ph: (906)847-6418 (906)847-6419
Fax: (906)847-3571
Free: (800)454-5227
E-mail: info@mackinacisland.org
URL: http://www.mackinacisland.org
Contact: Mrs. Mary McGuire Slevin, Exec.Dir.
Local. Promotes business and community development on Mackinac Island, MI. Provides tourism and visitor information. **Additional Websites:** http://www.mackinacislandlilacfestival.com, http://www.mackinacislanddogandponyclub.com. **Formerly:** (2005) Mackinac Island Chamber of Commerce. **Publications:** *Discover Mackinac Island Guide Book*, annual. Contains historic tourist attractions and island profiles. **Price:** $2.00 plus shipping and handling. **Conventions/Meetings:** monthly board meeting.

Mackinaw City

8887 ■ American Legion, Clayton Murray Post 159
PO Box 940
Mackinaw City, MI 49701
Ph: (517)371-4720
Fax: (517)371-2401
URL: National Affiliate–www.legion.org
Local. Affiliated With: American Legion.

8888 ■ Great Lakes Lighthouse Keepers Association (GLLKA)
4901 Evergreen Rd.
PO Box 219
Mackinaw City, MI 49701-0219
Ph: (231)436-5580
Fax: (231)436-5466
E-mail: info@gllka.com
URL: http://www.gllka.com
Contact: Richard L. Moehl, Pres.
Founded: 1982. **Members:** 3,500. **Membership Dues:** individual, $35 (annual) • individual, $60 (biennial) • family, $50 (annual) • family, $85 (biennial) • life, $1,500 • keeper, $120 (annual) • keeper, $200 (biennial) • inspector, $250 (annual) • inspector, $400 (biennial) • superintendent, beacon, $500 (annual) • superintendent, beacon, $900 (biennial) • corporate, $2,000 (annual) • corporate, $3,000 (biennial) • small business, $75 (annual) • small business, $140 (biennial). **Staff:** 2. Anyone interested in the historic preservation and restoration of lighthouses on the Great Lakes; those seeking contact with the descendants of lighthouse keepers on the Great Lakes. Conducts teacher workshops & supplies education materials for those wishing to teach students about Great Lakes maritime heritage. Acts as a clearinghouse of information concerning restoration projects; sponsors seminars; conducts research programs; compiles statistics. Holds annual conferences and cruises. **Formerly:** (1983) Lighthouse Keepers Association. **Publications:** *The Beacon*, quarterly. Newsletter. Provides a forum for the exchange of information on the history of Great Lakes lighthouses, lighthouse keepers, and historic preservation activities. **Price:** included in membership dues. **Circulation:** 3,500 • *Curriculum Guide, A Workbook for Teachers* • *Index to the GLLKA Oral History Tape Collection*, periodic. Catalog. Contains oral history tape collection listing interviews conducted with former keepers and their families. **Price:** free. **Circulation:** 500 • Brochure. Describes the purpose and activities of the association. Includes membership information. • Also publishes calendars and reprints of historical books. **Conventions/Meetings:** Great Lakes Conference and Workshop, on each of the Great Lakes (exhibits) - 5/year • annual Maritime Heritage Educator - workshop.

8889 ■ Mackinaw City Chamber of Commerce (MCCC)
216 E Central Ave.
PO Box 856
Mackinaw City, MI 49701
Ph: (231)436-5574
Free: (888)455-8100
E-mail: dedwards@mackinawchamber.com
URL: http://www.mackinawchamber.com
Contact: Dawn Edwards, Exec.Dir.
Founded: 1955. **Members:** 191. **Membership Dues:** friend, $50 (annual) • apartment/condominium/hotel/cabin/motel/cottage (based on number of units), $150 (annual) • barber/beauty salon/massage, $200 (annual) • campground (based on number of sites), $150 (annual) • carriage tour, $353 (annual) • casino, $150

(annual) • charter boat/service station, $150 (annual) • contractor (industrial), $500 (annual) • contractor (small), $300 (annual) • farm/flower market, $167 (annual) • ferry, $205 (annual) • financial institution, $510 (annual) • fishery/dairy/meat processor, $350 (annual) • golf course (based on number of holes and restaurant seats), $200-$321 (annual) • media (graphics/signs/photography/print/radio), $300 (annual) • professional (based on number of associate and staff), $150 (annual) • miscellaneous entertainment, $321 (annual) • nonprofit, $100 (annual) • information technology, $250 (annual) • restaurant/bar (plus $3.35 per seat), $150 (annual) • retail (based on the size of sales area), $150 (annual) • service station (plus $38.20 per island), $150 (annual) • state/county/city park, $1,000 (annual) • storage (based on size per sq. ft.), $150 (annual) • taxi/bus (plus $40 per vehicle), $150 (annual) • theater/entertainment complex, $500 (annual) • unclassified, $200 (annual) • utility ($5 per staff), $150 (annual). **Staff:** 2. **Budget:** $90,000. **Local**. Promotes business and community development and tourism in the Mackinaw City, MI area. Works to "create an inviting community dedicated to economic growth and excellence in customer satisfaction.". **Formerly:** (1999) Greater Mackinaw Area Chamber of Commerce. **Publications:** *Community Profile and Membership Directory*, annual. **Price:** included in membership dues • *Fall/Winter/Spring Guide*, annual. Directory • *The Greater Mackinaw Area Chamber of Commerce*. Newsletter. **Price:** included in membership dues • *Mackinaw Area Travel Planner*, annual. Magazine. **Price:** free • *Summer Visitor's Guide*, annual. Directory. **Conventions/Meetings:** biweekly board meeting - always first and third Thursday of each month.

Madison Heights

8890 ■ American Legion, Christopher Columbus Post 354
630 E 11 Mile Rd.
Madison Heights, MI 48071
Ph: (313)526-0690
Fax: (517)371-2401
URL: National Affiliate–www.legion.org
Local. Affiliated With: American Legion.

8891 ■ Animal Welfare Society of Southeastern Michigan (AWS)
29081 Dequindre Rd., Ste.E
Madison Heights, MI 48071
Ph: (248)548-1150 (248)548-1183
E-mail: animalwelfaresociety@yahoo.com
URL: http://www.animalwelfaresociety.net
Contact: Pete Siska, Dir.
Founded: 1982. **Local**.

8892 ■ Associated Builders and Contractors-Southeastern Michigan Chapter
25229 Dequindre Rd.
Madison Heights, MI 48071
Ph: (248)399-6460
Fax: (248)399-9413
E-mail: abcsemi@cs.com
URL: http://www.abcsemi.com
Contact: Mark Sawyer, Pres.
Founded: 1982. **Members:** 231. **Staff:** 6. **State Groups:** 1. **Local**. Promotes merit-based rewards for workers. **Councils:** Electrical Contractors. **Affiliated With:** Associated Builders and Contractors. **Publications:** *Contractor's Choice*, monthly. Newsletter. **Price:** $25.00 /year for nonmembers. **Advertising:** accepted. **Conventions/Meetings:** periodic Apprenticeship Training - workshop.

8893 ■ Associated Concrete Contractors of Michigan (ACCM)
30555 Dequindre
Madison Heights, MI 48071-2245
Ph: (248)588-5528
Fax: (248)588-2327
Contact: Marino Censoni, Pres.
Founded: 1965. **Members:** 200. **Budget:** $75,000. **State**. Commercial and residential flat work concrete contractors. **Publications:** *ACCM Newsletter*, monthly. **Conventions/Meetings:** quarterly meeting.

8894 ■ International Association of Business Communicators, Detroit Chapter
c/o Nancy Skidmore
1824 Greig
Madison Heights, MI 48071
Ph: (248)546-5490
URL: http://www.iabcdetroit.com
Contact: Ms. Nancy Skidmore, Exec.Sec.
Local. Represents the interests of communication managers, public relations directors, writers, editors and audiovisual specialists. Encourages establishment of college-level programs in organizational communication. Conducts surveys on employee communication effectiveness and media trends. Conducts research in the field of communication. **Affiliated With:** International Association of Business Communicators.

8895 ■ Leukemia and Lymphoma Society, Michigan Chapter
1421 E 12 Mile Rd., Bldg. A
Madison Heights, MI 48071
Ph: (248)582-2900
Fax: (248)582-2925
Free: (800)456-5413
E-mail: slaughterj@lls.org
URL: http://www.leukemia-lymphoma.org
Contact: Jim Slaughter, Exec.Dir.
State. Committed to finding a cure for leukemia, lymphoma, Hodgkin's Disease, and myeloma. Supports patient aid, public/professional education, and community service programs. **Affiliated With:** Leukemia and Lymphoma Society. **Formerly:** (2000) Leukemia Society of America - Michigan Chapter.

8896 ■ Madison Heights - Hazel Park Chamber of Commerce (MHHPCC)
724 W 11 Mile Rd.
Madison Heights, MI 48071
Ph: (248)542-5010
Fax: (248)542-6821
E-mail: info@madisonheights.org
URL: http://www.madisonheightschamber.org
Contact: Mary Lou Sames, Exec.Dir.
Founded: 1968. **Members:** 500. **Membership Dues:** business (varies with the number of employees), $100-$400 (annual) • non-profit, $75 (annual). **Budget:** $10,075. **Local**. Promotes business and community development in Madison Heights, MI. Sponsors annual Bowl-A-Thon and auction. **Affiliated With:** U.S. Chamber of Commerce. **Formerly:** (1999) Madison Heights +Chamber of Commerce. **Publications:** *Business to Business*, periodic. Directory • *Chamber Communique*, monthly. Newsletter • *Community Profile*, annual. **Conventions/Meetings:** annual Business Expo - trade show - always spring • monthly meeting.

8897 ■ Michigan Chapter of the Association of Rehabilitation Nurses (MI-ARN)
1525 W 13 Mile Rd.
Madison Heights, MI 48071
Ph: (248)588-4499
E-mail: margnnora@msn.com
URL: http://www.miarn.org
Contact: Lynn Lariviere RN, Pres.
State. Works to advance the quality of rehabilitation nursing practice. Provides educational opportunities and facilitates the exchange of ideas among members. **Affiliated With:** Association of Rehabilitation Nurses.

8898 ■ National Association of Credit Management Great Lakes (NACM)
c/o Elizabeth Hedke, CCE, Pres.
28157 Dequindre Rd.
PO Box 71049
Madison Heights, MI 48071
Ph: (248)547-0300
Fax: (248)547-0308
E-mail: liz@nacmgreatlakes.com
URL: http://www.nacmgreatlakes.com
Contact: Elizabeth Hedke CCE, Pres.
Local. Affiliated With: National Association of Credit Management. **Formerly:** (2005) National Association of Credit Managers Great Lakes.

8899 ■ Public Relations Society of America, Detroit Chapter (PRSA)
c/o Nancy Skidmore, Exec.Sec.
1824 Greig
Madison Heights, MI 48071
Ph: (248)545-6499
Fax: (248)545-4944
E-mail: info@prsadetroit.org
URL: http://www.prsadetroit.org
Local. Affiliated With: Public Relations Society of America.

8900 ■ Renaissance Fencing Club
31171 Stephenson Hwy.
Madison Heights, MI 48071
Ph: (248)616-0960
Fax: (248)616-0969
E-mail: refencing@earthlink.net
URL: http://www.renaissancefencing.net
Local. Amateur fencers. **Affiliated With:** United States Fencing Association.

8901 ■ United Food and Commercial Workers, Local 876, Central Region
876 Horace Brown Dr.
Madison Heights, MI 48071-1890
Ph: (248)585-9671
URL: http://www.ufcw876.org
Local. Affiliated With: United Food and Commercial Workers International Union.

8902 ■ Veggies in Motion (VIM)
c/o Mr. James Corcoran, Pres.
PO Box 71311
Madison Heights, MI 48071-0311
Ph: (248)616-9676
Fax: (248)616-9676
E-mail: vim@veggiesinmotion.org
URL: http://www.veggiesinmotion.org
Contact: Mr. James Corcoran, Pres.
Founded: 1999. **Members:** 83. **Membership Dues:** regular, $25 (annual). **Regional**. Promotes the awareness of the health, ecological and ethical consequences of food choices. Provides support to members while reaching out to educate the public about the many benefits of shifting towards a plant-based lifestyle. **Affiliated With:** American Vegan Society; North American Vegetarian Society. **Formerly:** (2005) Vegans in Motion. **Publications:** *News For Life*, monthly. Newsletter.

Mancelona

8903 ■ Alliance for the Mentally Ill of Antrim/Kalkaska Counties
c/o Jack Meeder, Pres.
402 Parkside St.
Mancelona, MI 49659
Ph: (616)587-5562
URL: http://mi.nami.org/akc.html
Contact: Jack Meeder, Pres.
Local. Strives to improve the quality of life of children and adults with severe mental illness through support, education, research and advocacy. **Affiliated With:** National Alliance for the Mentally Ill.

8904 ■ American Legion, George Puckett Post 264
PO Box 646
Mancelona, MI 49659
Ph: (517)371-4720
Fax: (517)371-2401
URL: National Affiliate–www.legion.org
Local. Affiliated With: American Legion.

8905 ■ Mancelona Area Chamber of Commerce
PO Box 558
Mancelona, MI 49659
Ph: (231)587-5500
Fax: (231)587-5500
E-mail: info@mancelonachamber.org
URL: http://www.mancelonachamber.org
Local. Promotes business and community development in Mancelona, MI.

8906 ■ National Association of Rocketry - Kalkaska Aerospace Club
c/o Doug Anger
7535 Cunningham Rd.
Mancelona, MI 49659
Ph: (231)587-5025
E-mail: douganger@mac.com
URL: http://nar.org
Contact: Doug Anger, Contact
Local.

Manchester

8907 ■ American Legion, Emil Jacob Post 117
PO Box 144
Manchester, MI 48158
Ph: (517)371-4720
Fax: (517)371-2401
URL: National Affiliate–www.legion.org
Local. Affiliated With: American Legion.

8908 ■ Manchester Area Chamber of Commerce (MACC)
PO Box 521
Manchester, MI 48158
Ph: (734)428-6222 (734)476-4565
E-mail: president@manchestermi.org
URL: http://www.manchestermi.org
Contact: Bill Chizmar, Pres.
Founded: 1984. **Members:** 100. **Local.** Businesses and individuals organized to promote economic and community development in the Manchester, MI area. **Publications:** *Community Resource Guide*, annual. Directory. Contains local telephone and yellow pages. **Price:** free. **Circulation:** 4,000. **Advertising:** accepted • *MAC Connections*, bimonthly. Newsletter. **Conventions/Meetings:** monthly meeting (exhibits).

8909 ■ Michigan Ground Water Association (MGWA)
c/o Mr. John E. Schmitt, Exec.Dir.
10475 Noggles Rd.
Manchester, MI 48158-9658
Ph: (734)428-0020
Fax: (734)428-0088
E-mail: michiganwater@aol.com
URL: http://www.michigangroundwater.com
Contact: Mr. John E. Schmitt CWD/PI, Exec.Dir.
Founded: 1928. **Members:** 600. **Membership Dues:** active contractor, $205 (annual) • manufacturer, supplier, technical, $110 (annual) • female, $25 (annual). **Staff:** 2. **Regional Groups:** 18. **State.** Promotes the theory and practice of water well drilling and water pump installation and repair. **Awards:** Distinguished Service Award. **Frequency:** annual. **Type:** recognition • Well Driller of the Year. **Frequency:** annual. **Type:** recognition. **Recipient:** for a person who is good at his trade. **Telecommunication Services:** phone referral service, only normal business hour phone. **Affiliated With:** National Ground Water Association. **Formerly:** (1995) Michigan Well Drillers Association. **Publications:** Newsletter, quarterly. Contains lists of upcoming events and industry news. **Price:** free for members. **Circulation:** 600. **Advertising:** accepted. Alternate Formats: diskette; online. **Conventions/Meetings:** annual convention - 2007 Mar. 20-21, Grand Rapids, MI; 2008 Mar. 17-18, Lansing, MI; 2009 Mar. 16-17, Lansing, MI.

8910 ■ Michigan National Wild Turkey Federation, Washtenaw County Chapter
18321 Lehman Rd.
Manchester, MI 48158
Ph: (734)475-7602
URL: http://www.mi-nwtf.org/washtenaw.htm
Contact: Mike Rose, Pres.
Local.

Manistee

8911 ■ American Legion, Manistee Post 10
10 Mason St.
Manistee, MI 49660
Ph: (517)371-4720
Fax: (517)371-2401
URL: National Affiliate–www.legion.org
Local. Affiliated With: American Legion.

8912 ■ Manistee Area Chamber of Commerce (MACC)
11 Cypress St.
Manistee, MI 49660
Ph: (231)723-2575
Fax: (231)723-1515
Free: (800)288-2286
E-mail: chamber@manistee.com
URL: http://www.manisteecountychamber.com
Contact: Dave Yarnell, Exec.Dir.
Founded: 1916. **Members:** 412. **Membership Dues:** individual/church/service club/civic, $100 (annual) • business (varies with the number of employees), $230-$700 (annual) • professional, $230 (annual) • educational institution/government agency, $300 (annual) • financial institution, $350 (annual) • gold, $500 (annual). **Staff:** 3. **Local.** Promotes business and community development in Manistee County, MI. Promotes tourism. **Awards:** Citizen of the Year. **Frequency:** annual. **Type:** recognition • Community Action Award. **Frequency:** annual. **Type:** recognition • Corporate Citizen of the Year. **Frequency:** annual. **Type:** recognition • President's Award. **Frequency:** annual. **Type:** recognition • Volunteer Award. **Frequency:** annual. **Type:** recognition. **Divisions:** Chamber of Commerce; Economic Development. **Formerly:** Manistee County Chamber of Commerce. **Publications:** Newsletter, monthly • Membership Directory.

8913 ■ Manistee Lions Club
PO Box 224
Manistee, MI 49660
Ph: (231)723-9067
E-mail: manisteelions@silverthorn.biz
URL: http://lions.silverthorn.biz/manistee
Contact: Lorraine Conway, Pres.
Local. Affiliated With: Lions Clubs International.

8914 ■ Manistee-Mason District Dental Society
1400 E Parkdale Ave., Ste.2
Manistee, MI 49660
Ph: (231)723-6512
E-mail: dsmiller@alumni.indiana.edu
URL: National Affiliate–www.ada.org
Contact: Dr. Donald Miller, Pres.
Local. Represents the interests of dentists committed to the public's oral health, ethics and professional development. Encourages the improvement of the public's oral health and promotes the art and science of dentistry. **Affiliated With:** American Dental Association; Michigan Dental Association.

8915 ■ Michigan Organization of Nurse Executives - District 6
c/o Suzanne Cleere, Dir.
West Shore Medical Ctr.
1465 E Parkdale Ave.
Manistee, MI 49660-9709
Ph: (231)398-1103
Fax: (231)398-1516
E-mail: scleere@westshoremedcenter.org
URL: http://www.mone.org
Contact: Suzanne Cleere, Dir.
Local. Represents nurse leaders who improve healthcare. Provides leadership, professional development, advocacy and research. Advances the nursing administration practice and patient care. **Affiliated With:** American Organization of Nurse Executives.

8916 ■ United Way of Manistee County
30 Jones St.
Manistee, MI 49660-1436
Ph: (231)723-2331
URL: National Affiliate–national.unitedway.org
Local. Affiliated With: United Way of America.

Manistique

8917 ■ Humane Society of Schoolcraft County (HSSC)
6091 W US-2
Manistique, MI 49854
Ph: (906)341-1000
E-mail: hssc@reiters.net
URL: http://www.thehssc.com
Contact: Char Crosby, Pres.
Founded: 1997. **Members:** 90. **Membership Dues:** business, $50 (annual) • family, $15 (annual) • individual, $12 (annual) • senior, $7 (annual) • student, $3 (annual). **Staff:** 1. **Budget:** $36,000. **Local.** Individuals in the Schoolcraft County, MI area who care about the welfare of animals. Promotes the prevention of cruelty to animals, the relief of suffering animals, and the education of the public on humane treatment of animals. Provides humane care and treatment for homeless animals. **Affiliated With:** American Humane Association.

8918 ■ Manistique Area Kiwanis Club
PO Box 73
Manistique, MI 49854
E-mail: kiwanis@chartermi.net
URL: http://kiwanis.centralup.com/home.htm
Contact: Robyn Loviska, Pres.
Local.

8919 ■ Schoolcraft County Chamber of Commerce (SCCC)
1000 W Lakeshore Dr.
Manistique, MI 49854
Ph: (906)341-5010
Fax: (906)341-1549
E-mail: chamber@upmail.com
URL: http://www.manistique.com
Contact: Ms. Lenore Heminger, Exec.Dir.
Local. Promotes business and community development in Schoolcraft County, MI. **Publications:** Directory, periodic • Newsletter, periodic.

Manton

8920 ■ Korean War Veterans Association, Dale H. Williams Post No. 1996 Chapter
c/o George S. Blossingham
6501 N 35th Rd.
Manton, MI 49663-9756
Ph: (231)824-6611
E-mail: g1k2bloss@voyager.net
URL: National Affiliate–www.kwva.org
Contact: George S. Blossingham, Contact
Local. Affiliated With: Korean War Veterans Association.

Maple City

8921 ■ Cedar-Maple City Lions Club
100 E Bellinger Rd.
Maple City, MI 49664
E-mail: tftriebes@earthlink.net
URL: http://cedar-maplecitymi.lionwap.org
Contact: Tom Triebes, Sec.
Local. Affiliated With: Lions Clubs International.

8922 ■ National Active and Retired Federal Employees Association - Grand Traverse Bay Area 1215
7420 S Bohemian Rd.
Maple City, MI 49664-8731
Ph: (231)228-5257
URL: National Affiliate–www.narfe.org
Contact: Patrick M. Hobbins, Contact
Local. Protects the retirement future of employees through education. Informs members on issues affecting the retirement. **Affiliated With:** National Association of Retired Federal Employees.

Marcellus

8923 ■ American Legion, Wood-Hill Post 39
PO Box 623
Marcellus, MI 49067
Ph: (517)371-4720
Fax: (517)371-2401
URL: National Affiliate–www.legion.org
Local. **Affiliated With:** American Legion.

Marenisco

8924 ■ American Legion, Carleton Mc Nicholas Post 523
PO Box 216
Marenisco, MI 49947
Ph: (517)371-4720
Fax: (517)371-2401
URL: National Affiliate–www.legion.org
Local. **Affiliated With:** American Legion.

Marine City

8925 ■ Marine City Chamber of Commerce
PO Box 38
Marine City, MI 48039
Ph: (810)765-4501
Fax: (810)765-4501
E-mail: cheryl@marinecitychamber.org
Contact: Cheryl Zech, Pres.
Local.

Marion

8926 ■ Marion Area Chamber of Commerce
PO Box 294
Marion, MI 49665
Ph: (231)743-2461
Fax: (231)743-2461
E-mail: rebeccainmarion@hotmail.com
Contact: Rebecca Martinson, VP
Local.

Marlette

8927 ■ Michigan National Wild Turkey Federation, Cass River Chapter
8100 Howard Rd.
Marlette, MI 48453
Ph: (517)635-3752
URL: http://www.mi-nwtf.org/Cassriver.htm
Contact: Harold Howard, Pres.
Local.

Marne

8928 ■ American Legion, Marne Post 376
PO Box 225
Marne, MI 49435
Ph: (517)371-4720
Fax: (517)371-2401
URL: National Affiliate–www.legion.org
Local. **Affiliated With:** American Legion.

Marquette

8929 ■ AAA Michigan
3020 US 41 W, Ste.1213
Marquette, MI 49855
Ph: (906)225-6750
Free: (800)526-4241
Contact: Karla Weaver, Contact
State.

8930 ■ Ahmed Shriners
c/o R. Thomas Peters, Jr.
128 W Washington St.
Marquette, MI 49855-4320
Ph: (906)225-1157
Fax: (906)225-1152
E-mail: office@ahmedshrine.org
URL: http://marquette.lodges.gl-mi.org/ahmed
Contact: R. Thomas Peters Jr., Contact
Local. **Affiliated With:** Imperial Council of the Ancient Arabic Order of the Nobles of the Mystic Shrine for North America.

8931 ■ Alzheimer's Association, Greater Michigan Chapter, Upper Peninsula Region
710 Chippewa Sq., Ste.201
Marquette, MI 49855
Ph: (906)228-3910
Fax: (906)228-2455
Free: (800)272-3900
E-mail: alzgmc.upregion@alz.org
URL: http://www.alzgmc.org
Contact: Beverly Bartlett, Dir.
Local. Strives to enhance the quality of life for all persons affected by Alzheimer's disease and related disorders through comprehensive educational programs, compassionate services, access to resources and support for research. **Affiliated With:** Alzheimer's Association.

8932 ■ American Legion, Michigan Post 44
c/o Richard M. Jopling
700 W Bluff St.
Marquette, MI 49855
Ph: (517)371-4720
Fax: (517)371-2401
URL: National Affiliate–www.legion.org
Contact: Richard M. Jopling, Contact
Local. **Affiliated With:** American Legion.

8933 ■ Association for Computing Machinery, Northern Michigan University
c/o Randy Appleton
Math & Cmpt. Sci. Dept.
161 W Sci.
Marquette, MI 49855
Ph: (906)227-1000
E-mail: acm@nmu.edu
URL: http://acm.nmu.edu
State. **Affiliated With:** Association for Computing Machinery.

8934 ■ Central Lake Superior Watershed Partnership (CLSWP)
c/o Larry Gould
1030 Wright St.
Marquette, MI 49855-1834
Ph: (906)226-9460
Fax: (906)228-4484
E-mail: info@superiorwatersheds.org
URL: http://www.superiorwatersheds.org
Contact: Carl Lindquist, Dir.
Local. Strives to protect and improve the natural resources of the Upper Peninsula of Michigan.

8935 ■ Great Lakes Athletic Trainers Association (GLATA)
c/o Julie Rochester, Pres.-Elect
Northern Michigan Univ.
1401 Presque Isle Ave.
Marquette, MI 49855-5305
Ph: (906)227-2026
Fax: (906)227-2181
URL: http://www.glata.org
Contact: Julie Rochester, Pres.-Elect
Regional. **Affiliated With:** National Athletic Trainers' Association.

8936 ■ March of Dimes Birth Defects Foundation, Marquette Division
1021 W Baraga Ave.
Marquette, MI 49855
Ph: (906)228-6942
Fax: (906)228-8659
Free: (800)906-DIME
E-mail: mi630@marchofdimes.com
URL: http://www.modimes.com
Contact: Stacy L. Van Buren, Division Dir.
Staff: 2. **Local**. Works for the prevention of birth defects, infant mortality, low birth weight, and prematurity. **Libraries: Type:** lending. **Holdings:** video recordings. **Subjects:** preventing birth defects, pregnancy. **Awards: Frequency:** biennial. **Type:** grant. **Recipient:** qualified applicants. **Affiliated With:** March of Dimes Birth Defects Foundation. **Formerly:** (2005) March of Dimes Birth Defects Foundation, Upper Peninsula Division. **Publications:** Brochures. Contains prenatal health information. **Price:** free.

8937 ■ Marquette-Alger County Medical Society (MACMS)
PO Box 68
Marquette, MI 49855
Ph: (906)226-6200
Fax: (906)226-2600
E-mail: mary@mtazone.com
URL: http://www.superiormed.org
Contact: Mary E. Tavernini, Exec.Dir.
Local. Advances the art and science of medicine. Promotes patient care and the betterment of public health. **Affiliated With:** Michigan State Medical Society.

8938 ■ Marquette Area Chamber of Commerce- Lake Superior Community Partnership
501 S Front St.
Marquette, MI 49855
Ph: (906)226-6591
Fax: (906)226-2099
Free: (888)57U-NITY
E-mail: mqtinfo@marquette.org
URL: http://www.marquette.org
Contact: Amy Clickner, Exec.Dir.
Founded: 1930. **Members:** 740. **Membership Dues:** general business, $189 (annual) • nonprofit (depends on the amount of budget), $142-$284 (annual) • individual, $116 (annual) • student, $58 (annual) • association/organization (depends on the number of members), $116-$284 (annual) • bank/financial institution (depends on the amount of deposit), $557-$1,118 (annual) • health care organization, hotel, motel, apartment, $189 (annual) • industrial/manufacturing (based on number of employees), $284-$557 (annual). **Budget:** $153,500. **Local**. Promotes business, tourism, and community development in the Marquette County, MI area. **Committees:** Chamber of Commerce; Economic Development; Lake Superior Partners in Education; Tourism and Recreation. **Formerly:** (1999) Marquette Area Chamber of Commerce; (2001) Marquette Area Chamber of Commerce - Lake Superior Community Partnership. **Publications:** *Directory and Planning Calendar*, annual. Includes membership listing and planning calendar. • *Superior Newsletter*, monthly. **Conventions/Meetings:** annual dinner - always January • monthly meeting.

8939 ■ Marquette Astronomical Society
Shiras Planetarium
1201 W Fair Ave.
Marquette, MI 49855

Ph: (906)228-6636
E-mail: speters@nmu.edu
URL: http://www.geocities.com/sstobbelaar/mqtastro.html
Contact: Stephen H. Peters, Contact
Local. Promotes the science of astronomy. Works to encourage and coordinate activities of amateur astronomical societies. Fosters observational and computational work and craftsmanship in various fields of astronomy. **Affiliated With:** Astronomical League.

8940 ■ Marquette County Convention and Visitors Bureau
337 W Washington St.
Marquette, MI 49855
Ph: (906)228-7749
Free: (800)544-4321
E-mail: frontdesk@marquettecountry.org
URL: http://www.marquettecountry.org
Local. Promotes convention business and tourism in area.

8941 ■ Marquette County Exchange Club
PO Box 395
Marquette, MI 49855
Ph: (906)249-1476 (906)228-7189
E-mail: pjm@superiorlink.com
URL: http://www.marquetteexchangeclub.com
Contact: Dave Martiin, Pres.
Local.

8942 ■ Marquette County Genealogical Society
217 N Front St.
Marquette, MI 49855
Ph: (906)228-7078
E-mail: sherryew@aol.com
URL: http://members.aol.com/MQTCGS/MCGS/mcgs.html
Contact: Midge Waters, Pres.
Founded: 1988. **Members:** 100. **Membership Dues:** regular, $12 (annual). **Local**. Gathers, restores, preserves, and disseminates historic genealogical information. **Libraries: Type:** reference; open to the public. **Holdings:** 1,000; archival material, archival material, audio recordings, books, films, video recordings. **Subjects:** genealogy, local history. **Computer Services:** database. **Publications:** *Lake Superior Roots*, 3/year. Newsletter. **Price:** included in membership dues. **Advertising:** accepted. **Conventions/Meetings:** monthly meeting - always third Wednesday in Marquette, MI.

8943 ■ Marquette County Habitat for Humanity
c/o Laurie Schmit, Volunteer Coor.
1027 N Third St.
PO Box 213
Marquette, MI 49855
Ph: (906)228-3578
Fax: (906)228-2314
E-mail: info@mqthabitat.org
URL: http://www.geocities.com/Eureka/Suite/2571
Contact: Laurie Schmit, Volunteer Coor.
Founded: 1992. **Local**. Aims to eliminate inadequate housing and to make decent shelters.

8944 ■ Marquette County History Museum
213 N Front St.
Marquette, MI 49855
Ph: (906)226-3571
Fax: (906)226-0919
E-mail: khiebel@up.net
URL: http://www.marquettecohistory.org
Contact: Kaye Hiebel, Exec.Dir.
Founded: 1918. **Members:** 800. **Membership Dues:** basic individual, $25 (annual) • supporting individual, basic family, $40 (annual) • supporting family, $65 (annual) • life individual, $1,000 • nonprofit, $50 (annual) • business, corporation (based on number of employees), $50-$375 (annual). **Staff:** 6. **Budget:** $165,000. **Local**. Individuals interested in the history of Marquette County. Conducts changing and permanent exhibits, educational and entertaining programs, and fund raising events. **Libraries: Type:** reference. **Holdings:** 15,000; archival material, books, maps, photographs. **Subjects:** Upper Great Lakes history. **Awards:** Helen Longyear Paul Memorial Award. **Frequency:** annual. **Type:** recognition. **Recipient:** for contributions to study, research and preservation of local history • Peter White Memorial Award. **Frequency:** annual. **Type:** recognition. **Recipient:** for contributions to study, research and preservation of local history. **Publications:** *Harlow's Wooden Man*, quarterly. Journal.

8945 ■ Marquette County RSVP
c/o Kathy Herrala, Dir.
200 W Spring St.
Marquette, MI 49855
Ph: (906)226-4180
Fax: (906)226-4188
E-mail: kherrala@mqtcty.org
URL: http://www.seniorcorps.gov/about/programs/rsvp_state.asp?usestateabbr=mi&Search4.x=0&Search4.y=0
Contact: Kathy Herrala, Dir.
Local. **Affiliated With:** Retired and Senior Volunteer Program.

8946 ■ Marquette Figure Skating Club (MFSC)
Lakeview Arena
300 W Baraga Ave.
Marquette, MI 49855
Ph: (906)226-3441
E-mail: danlanders@marquettefigureskating.org
URL: http://www.marquettefigureskating.org
Contact: Dan Landers, Pres.
Local. Provides programs to encourage participation and achievement in the sport of figure skating on ice. Defines and maintains uniform standards of skating proficiency. Organizes and sponsors competitions and exhibitions for the purpose of stimulating interest in figure skating. **Affiliated With:** United States Figure Skating Association.

8947 ■ Marquette Junior Hockey
PO Box 992
Marquette, MI 49855
Ph: (906)228-9193
Fax: (906)228-5277
E-mail: wcatgoal@mqthockey.org
URL: http://www.mqthockey.org
Contact: Tim McIntosh, Dir.
Founded: 1957. **Members:** 600. **Staff:** 1. **Budget:** $500,000. **Regional Groups:** 1. **State Groups:** 1. **Local**. Amateur hockey teams. Promotes the sport of hockey. **Affiliated With:** USA Hockey.

8948 ■ Marquette Professional Police Officers Association
300 W Baraga Ave.
Marquette, MI 49855-4712
Ph: (906)228-0400
Fax: (906)228-0446
E-mail: ssnowaert@mqtcty.org
Contact: Eve Snowaert, Pres.
Founded: 1996. **Members:** 38. **Staff:** 5. **Local**.

8949 ■ Michigan Association of College Stores (MACS)
c/o Michael Kuzak, CCR, Pres.-Elect
Northern Michigan Univ. Bookstore
1401 Presque Isle
Marquette, MI 49855-5389
Ph: (906)227-1126
Fax: (906)227-1344
E-mail: mkuzak@nmu.edu
URL: http://www.michigancollegestores.org
Contact: Michael Kuzak CCR, Pres.-Elect
State. Promotes the collegiate retailing industry. Enhances the college store industry through service, education and research. Promotes high standards of business practices and ethics within the industry. **Affiliated With:** National Association of College Stores.

8950 ■ Michigan Association for Institutional Research (MI/AIR)
c/o Paul B. Duby, Treas.
Northern Michigan Univ.
506 Cohodas Admin. Ctr.
Marquette, MI 49855
Ph: (906)227-2670
Fax: (906)227-2965
E-mail: pduby@nmu.edu
URL: http://www.miair.wayne.edu
Contact: Paul B. Duby, Treas.
State. Represents individuals interested in institutional research. Fosters research leading to improved understanding, planning, and operation of institutions of postsecondary education. **Affiliated With:** Association for Institutional Research.

8951 ■ Michigan National Wild Turkey Federation, Superior Turkey Trackers Chapter
22 Tracie Ln.
Marquette, MI 49855
Ph: (906)249-3902
E-mail: hendu89@aol.com
URL: http://www.mi-nwtf.org/Superior.htm
Contact: Scott Hendrickson, Pres.
Local.

8952 ■ National Active and Retired Federal Employees Association - North Central U.P. 1900
1530 W Ridge St. Apt. 39
Marquette, MI 49855-5706
Ph: (906)225-0824
URL: National Affiliate–www.narfe.org
Contact: John Erm, Contact
Local. Protects the retirement future of employees through education. Informs members on issues affecting the retirement. **Affiliated With:** National Association of Retired Federal Employees.

8953 ■ National Alliance for the Mentally Ill - Alger-Marquette County
c/o Jane Ryan, Chair
2 E Nicolet
Marquette, MI 49855
Ph: (906)226-8551
E-mail: ryanrj@chartermi.net
URL: http://mi.nami.org/alg.html
Contact: Jane Ryan, Chair
Local. Strives to improve the quality of life of children and adults with severe mental illness through support, education, research and advocacy. **Affiliated With:** National Alliance for the Mentally Ill.

8954 ■ National Association of Home Builders of the U.S., Home Builders Association of the Upper Penninsula (UPBA)
Local No. 2361
914 W Baraga Ave., Ste.A
Marquette, MI 49855-0999
Ph: (906)228-2312
Fax: (906)228-8252
E-mail: upbamqt@yahoo.com
URL: http://www.upbuildersassociation.com
Contact: Brian White, Exec.Dir.
Regional. Single and multifamily home builders, commercial builders, and others associated with the building industry. **Affiliated With:** National Association of Home Builders.

8955 ■ Northern Michigan University Figure Skating Club
PO Box 34
Marquette, MI 49855
E-mail: nmufsc_wildcats@hotmail.com
URL: http://nmufsc.tripod.com
Local. Provides programs to encourage participation and achievement in the sport of figure skating on ice. Defines and maintains uniform standards of skating proficiency. Organizes and sponsors competitions and exhibitions for the purpose of stimulating interest in figure skating. **Affiliated With:** United States Figure Skating Association.

8956 ■ Parents Anonymous of Marquette, Michigan
1000 Silver Creek Rd.
Marquette, MI 49855
Ph: (906)249-5437
Fax: (906)249-5438
E-mail: chris.myers@teachingfamilyhomes.com
URL: http://www.teachingfamilyhomes.com
Contact: Christine Myers, CEO
Local.

8957 ■ Psi Chi, National Honor Society in Psychology - Northern Michigan University
c/o Dept. of Psychology
1401 Presque Isle Ave.
Marquette, MI 49855
Ph: (906)227-2935 (906)227-2944
Fax: (906)227-2954
E-mail: fquinnel@nmu.edu
URL: National Affiliate–www.psichi.org
Local. Affiliated With: Psi Chi, National Honor Society in Psychology.

8958 ■ Ruffed Grouse Society, Mid Up Chapter
c/o F. Gregory Murphy
424 E Michigan St.
Marquette, MI 49855
Ph: (231)549-5063
E-mail: rgsdrd@hotmail.com
URL: National Affiliate–www.ruffedgrousesociety.org
Contact: F. Gregory Murphy, Contact
Local. Affiliated With: Ruffed Grouse Society.

8959 ■ Superior District Dental Society
101 S Front St.
Marquette, MI 49855
Ph: (906)228-6830
Fax: (906)228-6842
URL: National Affiliate–www.ada.org
Contact: Dr. George Peter Kelly, Pres.
Local. Represents the interests of dentists committed to the public's oral health, ethics and professional development. Encourages the improvement of the public's oral health and promotes the art and science of dentistry. **Affiliated With:** American Dental Association; Michigan Dental Association.

8960 ■ United Way of Marquette County
PO Box 73
Marquette, MI 49855
Ph: (906)226-8171
Fax: (906)226-7050
E-mail: unitedway@uwmqt.org
URL: http://www.uwmqt.org
Contact: Barbara Meyer, Dir. of Operations
Founded: 1943. **Members:** 45. **Staff:** 3. **State Groups:** 1. **Local. Affiliated With:** United Way of America.

8961 ■ Upper Peninsula Association of Realtors
1014 N Third St.
Marquette, MI 49855
Ph: (906)228-4870
Fax: (906)228-4877
E-mail: upar@chartermi.net
URL: National Affiliate–www.realtor.org
Contact: Cynthia J. Spafford, Exec. Officer
Local. Strives to develop real estate business practices. Advocates the right to own, use and transfer real property. Provides a facility for professional development, research and exchange of information among members. **Affiliated With:** National Association of Realtors.

8962 ■ Upper Peninsula Mountain Bike Club
514 N 3rd St.
Marquette, MI 49855
Ph: (906)226-9290
E-mail: gear@downwindsports.com
URL: http://www.downwindsports.com
Local. Affiliated With: International Mountain Bicycling Association.

8963 ■ Upper Peninsula Resource Conservation and Development Council (UP RC&D)
201 Rublein St.
Marquette, MI 49855-4094
Ph: (906)226-7487
Fax: (906)226-7040
E-mail: randy.wilkinson@mi.usda.gov
URL: http://www.uprcd.org
Contact: Randy Wilkinson, Coor.
Local. Affiliated With: National Association of Resource Conservation and Development Councils.

8964 ■ Upper Peninsula Youth for Christ
1111 Lincoln Ave.
Marquette, MI 49855
Ph: (906)228-4932
Fax: (906)228-5610
URL: http://www.upyfc.org
Local. Affiliated With: Youth for Christ/U.S.A.

Marshall

8965 ■ American Legion, Michigan Post 79
c/o Stanley E. Lamb
15380 C Dr. S
Marshall, MI 49068
Ph: (517)371-4720
Fax: (517)371-2401
URL: National Affiliate–www.legion.org
Contact: Stanley E. Lamb, Contact
Local. Affiliated With: American Legion.

8966 ■ Calhoun County Genealogical Society
PO Box 879
Marshall, MI 49068-0879
E-mail: michigancalhoungene@yahoo.com
URL: http://www.rootsweb.com/~micalhou/ccgs.htm
Contact: Anita C. Stuever, Pres.
Founded: 1988. **Members:** 220. **Membership Dues:** $12 (annual). **Local.** Gathers and preserves information of genealogical value; encourages the deposit of such information in suitable depositories; aids individuals studying family history through knowledge exchange; publishes and promotes genealogical materials, particularly materials about Calhoun County. Members need not live in Calhoun County. **Libraries: Type:** reference. **Holdings:** archival material. **Committees:** Cemetery Transcription. **Publications:** *Cemeteries of Clarence Twp., Calhoun Co., MI* • *Cemeteries of Clarendon Twp., Calhoun Co., MI* • *Cemeteries of Convis Twp., Calhoun Co., MI* • *Cemeteries of Eckford Twp., Calhoun Co., MI* • *Cemeteries of Lee Twp., Calhoun Co., MI* • *Cemeteries of Tekonsha Twp.* • *Generations*, semimonthly. Newsletter • *Marriage Records of Calhoun County, MI 1836-1890* • *1877 History of Calhoun County, MI*. **Conventions/Meetings:** monthly board meeting • monthly general assembly - always fourth Tuesday of the month. Marshall, MI.

8967 ■ Calhoun County Michigan Chapter of Pheasants Forever
c/o Ben Lark
10300-17 Mile Rd.
Marshall, MI 49068
Ph: (616)781-6044
E-mail: blarkpf@aol.com
URL: http://www.pfchapter.com/mi-calhoun
Contact: Ben Lark, Contact
Local. Affiliated With: Pheasants Forever.

8968 ■ Marshall Area Chamber of Commerce (MACC)
424 E Michigan Ave.
Marshall, MI 49068
Ph: (269)781-5163
Free: (800)877-5163
E-mail: chamber@marshallmi.org
URL: http://www.marshallmi.org
Contact: Monica Anderson, Pres.
Founded: 1947. **Members:** 300. **Membership Dues:** base, $185 • individual/nonprofit/civic group, $93 • retiree, $36 • hotel/motel/apartment/financial institution/residential care facility, $185 • public utility, $370 • retailer (based on square footage of selling space), $185-$495. **Local.** Promotes business and community development in the Marshall, MI area. **Awards:** Athena Award Program. **Frequency:** annual. **Type:** recognition. **Recipient:** for an outstanding professional and businesswoman. **Computer Services:** Mailing lists, of members. **Telecommunication Services:** electronic mail, mcoc@voyager.net. **Committees:** Ambassador; Athena Award; Chicken Barbecue; Christmas; Dream Dollar; Golf Outing; Michigan Week. **Councils:** Tourism Advisory. **Divisions:** Retail/Small Business. **Roundtables:** Diversity; Human Resource. **Affiliated With:** U.S. Chamber of Commerce. **Publications:** *Buyers Guide*, annual. Directory • *Chamber News*, bimonthly. Newsletter. Highlights issues about business, the chamber, and community activities.

8969 ■ Marshall United Way, Michigan
PO Box 190
Marshall, MI 49068-0190
Ph: (616)781-3325
URL: National Affiliate–national.unitedway.org
Local. Affiliated With: United Way of America.

8970 ■ Michigan Federation of Business and Professional Women's Clubs (BPW/MI)
132 Eastman Ct.
Marshall, MI 49068
E-mail: bpwmichigan@yahoo.com
URL: http://www.bpw-michigan.org
Contact: Trish Knight, Pres.
Founded: 1919. **Members:** 700. **Membership Dues:** member-at-large, $105 (annual). **Budget:** $75,000. **State Groups:** 53. **Local Groups:** 48. **State.** Achieves equity for all women in the workplace through advocacy, education and information. **Awards:** Harriet A. Myer Achievement Award. **Frequency:** annual. **Type:** trophy. **Recipient:** to a woman who has been an active member, and who is recognized for her outstanding achievement in her profession or in a service to her community • Hastings Journalism/Media Award. **Frequency:** annual. **Type:** monetary. **Recipient:** to a BPW local organization that has the best newsletter/publication printed and/or original news and press releases related to the organization for the preceding year • Plymouth BPW Political Service Award. **Frequency:** annual. **Type:** recognition. **Recipient:** for individual who has been an example of advocacy through community service, and who holds an elected or appointed post in government • Southwest District Advocates Against Domestic Violence Award. **Frequency:** annual. **Type:** monetary. **Recipient:** to a BPW local individual member who has exhibited outstanding support for domestic violence shelters, programs, victims and/or establishes a program to work with the victims of domestic violence • Three Rivers We Care For Kids Award. **Frequency:** annual. **Type:** recognition. **Recipient:** to a local organization who has demonstrated outstanding work with youth by furthering the BPW objectives and mission • Woman of Achievement. **Frequency:** annual. **Type:** recognition. **Recipient:** to a woman within a BPW local who is an active member, has been recognized for many achievements, displays an outstanding dedication of BPW and helping other women, and has made contributions to her community • Woman of the Year. **Frequency:** annual. **Type:** recognition. **Recipient:** to a woman within a community who has given of herself to improve the community and its families through volunteerism and/or financial contributions. **Conventions/Meetings:** annual conference, meeting and educational opportunities for state membership (exhibits).

8971 ■ Michigan Rifle and Pistol Association (MRPA)
c/o Charles Hayes, Sec.-Treas.
PO Box 71
Marshall, MI 49068-0071
Ph: (269)781-1223
Free: (888)655-MRPA
E-mail: cfhayes@voyager.net
URL: http://www.michrpa.com
Contact: Charles Hayes, Sec.-Treas.
Membership Dues: regular/club, $20 (annual) • junior, $10 (annual). **State. Affiliated With:** National Rifle Association of America.

8972 ■ Potawatomi Resource Conservation and Development Council
315 W Green St.
Clahoun Co. Bldg.
Marshall, MI 49068-1518
Ph: (616)789-2354
Fax: (616)789-2357
E-mail: james.coury@mi.usda.gov
URL: National Affiliate–www.rcdnet.org
Contact: James Coury, Coor.
Local. Affiliated With: National Association of Resource Conservation and Development Councils.

Marysville

8973 ■ American Legion, Marysville Post 449
299 Huron Blvd.
Marysville, MI 48040
Ph: (517)371-4720
Fax: (517)371-2401
URL: National Affiliate–www.legion.org
Local. Affiliated With: American Legion.

8974 ■ Marysville Chamber of Commerce
2055 Gratiot Blvd., Ste.D
Marysville, MI 48040
Ph: (810)364-6180
Fax: (810)364-9388
E-mail: chamber@marysvillechamber.com
URL: http://www.marysvillechamber.com
Contact: Laura J. Crawford, Exec.Dir.
Founded: 1987. **Members:** 110. **Membership Dues:** sole proprietor to large manufacturer, $110-$565 (annual). **Staff:** 1. **Local.** Consists of sole proprietors to large manufacturers. Serves as a voice for the business community, offering programs and activities to foster the continued success of the members. Through specific members services and community events, the Chamber strives to meet its goals. These include: developing and enhancing the marketing of the Marysville area, and recognizing and promoting excellence in education to ensure a sound foundation of human resources for a healthy local economy. **Awards:** Business of the Year Award. **Frequency:** annual. **Type:** recognition • Citizen of the Year Award. **Frequency:** annual. **Type:** recognition. **Publications:** *Bi-Annual Member Directory*, semiannual. Membership Directory. Contains map/shopping guide. **Circulation:** 1,000 • Newsletter, quarterly. **Circulation:** 500. **Advertising:** accepted.

8975 ■ Mothers Against Drunk Driving, St. Clair/Sanilac Counties
108 Huron Blvd.
Marysville, MI 48040
Ph: (810)364-9919
Fax: (810)364-9921
Free: (800)GET-MADD
URL: http://www.stclairmadd.org
Contact: Cricket Gwisdala, Program Coor.
Local. Victims of drunk driving crashes; concerned citizens. Encourages citizen participation in working towards reform of the drunk driving problem and the prevention of underage drinking. Acts as the voice of victims of drunk driving crashes by speaking on their behalf to communities, businesses, and educational groups. **Affiliated With:** Mothers Against Drunk Driving.

Mason

8976 ■ American Legion, Browne-Cavender Post 148
PO Box 361
Mason, MI 48854
Ph: (517)371-4720
Fax: (517)371-2401
URL: National Affiliate–www.legion.org
Local. Affiliated With: American Legion.

8977 ■ American Legion, Nuwarine Post 535
2296 Tomlinson Rd.
Mason, MI 48854
Ph: (517)371-4720
Fax: (517)371-2401
URL: National Affiliate–www.legion.org
Local. Affiliated With: American Legion.

8978 ■ Mason Area Chamber of Commerce (MACC)
148 E Ash St.
Mason, MI 48854-1646
Ph: (517)676-1046
Fax: (517)676-8504
E-mail: masonchamber@masonchamber.org
URL: http://www.masonchamber.org
Contact: Mr. Douglas Klein APR, Exec.Dir.
Founded: 1972. **Members:** 150. **Membership Dues:** individual, $50 • nonprofit, $85 • home based business, $85 • school, $250 • financial institution, $400 • government department, $85 • business (based on number of employees), $200-$500 • second business, $50. **Local.** Promotes business and community development in the Mason, MI area. **Awards:** MACC Presidents Award. **Frequency:** annual. **Type:** recognition • Mason Citizen of the Year. **Frequency:** annual. **Type:** recognition • Mason Educator of the Year. **Frequency:** annual. **Type:** recognition. **Computer Services:** Information services, member listing. **Publications:** *Mason in Motion*, monthly. Newsletter. Alternate Formats: online. **Conventions/Meetings:** monthly meeting.

8979 ■ Mason Lions Club - Michigan
c/o Karen G. Routson, CS, Sec.
2576 Tuttle Rd.
Mason, MI 48854
Ph: (517)244-9515
E-mail: routsonkg@aol.com
URL: http://www.district11c2.org
Contact: Karen G. Routson CS, Sec.
Local. Affiliated With: Lions Clubs International.

8980 ■ Michigan District of Kiwanis International (MDKI)
PO Box 231
Mason, MI 48854-0231
Ph: (517)676-3837
Fax: (517)676-6600
Free: (877)645-4926
E-mail: mikiwanis@sbcglobal.net
URL: http://www.michigankiwanis.org
Contact: Alan Dailey, Exec.Dir.
Founded: 1915. **Members:** 7,300. **Staff:** 2. **Local Groups:** 220. **State.** Federation of business and professional civic service clubs. Encourages member clubs to perform community service with a special concentration on youth and the disadvantaged. **Affiliated With:** Kiwanis International. **Publications:** *Michigan Builder*, monthly. **Conventions/Meetings:** annual convention (exhibits) • quarterly meeting.

8981 ■ Michigan Elementary and Middle School Principals Association (MEMSPA)
c/o Joanne Welihan, Exec.Dir.
1980 N Coll. Rd.
Mason, MI 48854
Ph: (517)694-8955
Fax: (517)694-8945
Free: (800)227-0824
E-mail: info@memspa.org
URL: http://www.memspa.org
Contact: Joanne Welihan, Exec.Dir.
Members: 1,625. **State.**

8982 ■ National Sojourners, John S. Bersey No. 316
c/o Capt. Bruce F. Archer
409 E Maple St.
Mason, MI 48854-1751
Ph: (517)676-9370
E-mail: brucearcher@juno.com
URL: National Affiliate–www.nationalsojourners.org
Contact: Capt. Bruce F. Archer, Contact
Local.

8983 ■ Public Relations Society of America, Central Michigan Chapter
c/o Douglas Klein, APR
Star Associates
617 Randolph St.
Mason, MI 48854-1328
Ph: (517)676-3933 (517)525-1402
E-mail: dougklein@usa.net
URL: http://www.cmprsa.org
Local. A local chapter of the Public Relations Society of America. **Awards:** PACE Awards. **Frequency:** annual. **Type:** trophy. **Affiliated With:** Public Relations Society of America.

8984 ■ Veteran Motor Car Club of America - Lansing Chapter
c/o Tom Wellman, Sec.
721 Wolverine Rd.
Mason, MI 48854
Ph: (517)676-6647
URL: National Affiliate–www.vmcca.org
Contact: Tom Wellman, Sec.
Local. Affiliated With: Veteran Motor Car Club of America.

Mass City

8985 ■ American Legion, Houghton Post 80
109 VFW Rd.
Mass City, MI 49948
Ph: (517)371-4720
Fax: (517)371-2401
URL: National Affiliate–www.legion.org
Local. Affiliated With: American Legion.

Mattawan

8986 ■ Five Cities Association of Michigan
c/o Marvin R. Followell
49886 Jasmine Way
Mattawan, MI 49071-9725
Ph: (269)668-7090
Fax: (269)668-8201
E-mail: smacna@net-link.net
URL: National Affiliate–www.smacna.org
Contact: Marvin R. Followell, Contact
Local. Affiliated With: Sheet Metal and Air Conditioning Contractors' National Association.

8987 ■ Mattawan Lions Club
PO Box 62
Mattawan, MI 49071-0062
Ph: (269)668-3116
E-mail: lionsholm@peoplepc.com
URL: http://mattawanmi.lionwap.org
Contact: Harvey Holm, Sec.
Local. Affiliated With: Lions Clubs International.

Mayville

8988 ■ American Legion, Morrison-Mead Post 181
PO Box 39
Mayville, MI 48744
Ph: (517)371-4720
Fax: (517)371-2401
URL: National Affiliate–www.legion.org
Local. Affiliated With: American Legion.

8989 ■ Mayville Lions Club
c/o Henry Wymore, Pres.
1885 W Blackmore Rd.
Mayville, MI 48744
Ph: (989)843-6092
URL: http://www.geocities.com/dist11d1
Contact: Henry Wymore, Pres.
Local. Affiliated With: Lions Clubs International.

8990 ■ National Association of Miniature Enthusiasts - Mail-A-Mini Swappers
c/o Katie MacNeil
5100 Chambers Rd.
Mayville, MI 48744
Ph: (989)843-6996
E-mail: ktmacneil@tds.net
URL: http://www.miniatures.org/states/MI.html
Contact: Katie MacNeil, Contact
Local. Affiliated With: National Association of Miniature Enthusiasts.

McBain

8991 ■ McBain Area Chamber of Commerce
PO Box 203
McBain, MI 49657-0203
Ph: (231)825-2893
Fax: (231)825-8008
E-mail: info@mcbainmichigan.com
URL: http://www.mcbainmichigan.com
Contact: Paula Dykhouse, Pres.
Membership Dues: business, individual, $75 (annual). **Local**. Promotes business and community development in McBain, MI area. **Telecommunication Services:** electronic mail, president@mcbainmichigan.com.

8992 ■ Michigan National Wild Turkey Federation, Clam River Gobblers
2990 W Falmouth Rd.
McBain, MI 49657
URL: http://www.mi-nwtf.org/Clamriver.htm
Contact: Melvin Quist, Pres.
Local.

Mears

8993 ■ Michigan High School Coaches Association (MHSCA)
c/o Richard Tompkins, Exec.Dir.
9 S Lighthouse Dr.
Mears, MI 49436
Ph: (231)873-4498
Fax: (231)873-5203
E-mail: rtompkins420@txbi.net
URL: http://www.mhsca.org
Contact: Richard Tompkins, Exec.Dir.
Founded: 1955. **Members:** 6,500. **Membership Dues:** $15 (annual). **Staff:** 2. **State Groups:** 1. **Local Groups:** 16. **State**. High school and junior high school athletic coaches and athletic directors. Promotes high school sports. Offers coaches clinic; honors coaches of the year. Sponsors Michigan High School Coaches Hall of Fame. Holds semiannual board meeting. **Awards:** Coach of the Year. **Frequency:** annual. **Type:** recognition. **Recipient:** for individuals with years of coaching and good coaching record • Coach Service Awards. **Frequency:** annual. **Type:** recognition • Hall of Fame. **Type:** recognition. **Recipient:** for individuals with 25 years in coaching and service to school and community. **Affiliated With:** National High School Athletic Coaches Association. **Publications:** *Michigan Coach*, 3/year. Newsletter. **Circulation:** 6,500. **Advertising:** accepted. **Conventions/Meetings:** annual Individual Sports Association - meeting, clinics.

8994 ■ Silver Lake Sand Dunes Area Chamber of Commerce
c/o Ernest D. Schwarz
1951 N 24th Ave.
Mears, MI 49436-9687
Ph: (231)873-2778
Local.

Mecosta

8995 ■ Alliance for the Mentally Ill of Mecosta County
c/o Ruth Sheldon, Pres.
8832 5 Mile Rd.
Mecosta, MI 49332
Ph: (616)972-7889
URL: http://mi.nami.org/mc.html
Contact: Ruth Sheldon, Pres.
Local. Strives to improve the quality of life of children and adults with severe mental illness through support, education, research and advocacy. **Affiliated With:** National Alliance for the Mentally Ill.

8996 ■ Mecosta Lions Club
c/o Leon Thomas, Pres.
8900 90th Ave.
Mecosta, MI 49332
Ph: (231)972-7214
E-mail: towood@finaltel.net
URL: http://lions.silverthorn.biz/11-e1
Contact: Leon Thomas, Pres.
Local. Affiliated With: Lions Clubs International.

Melvindale

8997 ■ American Legion, Melvindale Post 472
17011 Raupp Rd.
Melvindale, MI 48122
Ph: (517)371-4720
Fax: (517)371-2401
URL: National Affiliate–www.legion.org
Local. Affiliated With: American Legion.

8998 ■ Melvindale Figure Skating Club
Melvindale Kessey Arena
4300 S Dearborn St.
Melvindale, MI 48122
E-mail: alena@melvindale.org
URL: National Affiliate–www.usfigureskating.org
Local. Provides programs to encourage participation and achievement in the sport of figure skating on ice. Defines and maintains uniform standards of skating proficiency. Organizes and sponsors competitions and exhibitions for the purpose of stimulating interest in figure skating. **Affiliated With:** United States Figure Skating Association.

Memphis

8999 ■ American Legion, Merrick Potter Post 566
PO Box 502
Memphis, MI 48041
Ph: (517)371-4720
Fax: (517)371-2401
URL: National Affiliate–www.legion.org
Local. Affiliated With: American Legion.

9000 ■ Memphis Chamber of Commerce
PO Box 41006
Memphis, MI 48041
Ph: (810)392-2394 (810)392-2385
Fax: (810)392-3600
Contact: Nina Powers, Pres.
Local.

Menominee

9001 ■ American Legion, Menominee Post 146
818 1st St.
Menominee, MI 49858
Ph: (517)371-4720
Fax: (517)371-2401
URL: National Affiliate–www.legion.org
Local. Affiliated With: American Legion.

9002 ■ National Active and Retired Federal Employees Association - Menominee 2246
N418 West Dr. S
Menominee, MI 49858-9781
Ph: (301)681-9062
URL: National Affiliate–www.narfe.org
Contact: Mark Scully, Contact
Local. Protects the retirement future of employees through education. Informs members on issues affecting the retirement. **Affiliated With:** National Association of Retired Federal Employees.

9003 ■ National Alliance for the Mentally Ill - Marinette and Menominee
c/o Don Butman, Pres.
N2177 M-35
Menominee, MI 49858
Ph: (906)863-8947
URL: http://mi.nami.org/m&m.html
Contact: Don Butman, Pres.
Local. Strives to improve the quality of life of children and adults with severe mental illness through support, education, research and advocacy. **Affiliated With:** National Alliance for the Mentally Ill.

9004 ■ River Cities Regional Chamber of Commerce
PO Box 427
Menominee, MI 49858
Ph: (906)863-2679
Fax: (906)863-3288
E-mail: info@rivercities.net
Contact: Sylvia Nelson, Pres.
Local. Promotes business and community development in Menominee City and County. **Formerly:** (2003) Menominee Area Chamber of Commerce. **Publications:** Newsletter, quarterly.

9005 ■ Sweet Adelines International, Menominee River Chapter
Bethel Evangelical Lutheran Church
1309 14th Ave.
Menominee, MI 49858-2747
Ph: (906)864-0179
E-mail: ewanderc@yahoo.com
URL: National Affiliate–www.sweetadelineintl.org
Contact: Edwina Wandersee, Contact
Local. Advances the musical art form of barbershop harmony through education and performances. Provides education, training and coaching in the development of women's four-part barbershop harmony. **Affiliated With:** Sweet Adelines International.

Merrill

9006 ■ Merrill Lions Club
c/o Brooks Hale, Pres.
23000 O'Hara Rd.
Merrill, MI 48637
Ph: (989)643-5692
E-mail: brolinhale@triton.net
URL: http://www.geocities.com/dist11d1
Contact: Brooks Hale, Pres.
Local. Affiliated With: Lions Clubs International.

9007 ■ Michigan National Wild Turkey Federation, Tri-Valley Gobblers
20576 Dice Rd.
Merrill, MI 48637
Ph: (989)643-7613
URL: http://www.mi-nwtf.org/tri_valley.htm
Contact: David Dohning, Pres.
Local.

Mesick

9008 ■ American Association for Medical Transcription, West Michigan Chapter
c/o Colleen M. Runyon, Pres.
8340 W 6 Rd.
Mesick, MI 49668-9110
E-mail: cmrunyon@acegroup.cc
URL: http://www.aamt.org/ca/wmc
Contact: Colleen M. Runyon, Pres.
Local. Works to represent and advance the profession of medical transcription and its practitioners. **Affiliated With:** American Association for Medical Transcription.

9009 ■ Mesick Area Chamber of Commerce
PO Box 548
Mesick, MI 49668
Ph: (231)885-3200
Fax: (231)885-2650
E-mail: jkjellens@netscape.net
URL: http://www.mesick-michigan.org
Contact: Jeff Ellens, Pres.
Membership Dues: general, $35 • individual, $25. **Local.** Aims to bring community and surrounding businesses together in pursuit of economic growth for all, while maintaining the integrity of the natural resources. **Conventions/Meetings:** monthly meeting - every 1st Thursday in Mesick Area Chamber office in MI.

9010 ■ Mesick Lions Club
PO Box 456
Mesick, MI 49668
Ph: (231)885-2679 (231)885-1043
E-mail: lhughes@acegroup.cc
URL: http://mesickmi.lionwap.org
Contact: Andrew Wuotila, Pres.
Local. Affiliated With: Lions Clubs International.

Metamora

9011 ■ Project Management Institute, Michigan Thumb
c/o Thomas Bartholomew
3848 Casey Rd.
Metamora, MI 48455
Ph: (248)753-3798
E-mail: bart@intouchmi.com.com
Contact: Thomas Bartholomew, Contact
Corporations and individuals engaged in the practice of project management; project management students and educators. Seeks to advance the study, teaching, and practice of project management. **Affiliated With:** Project Management Institute.

Michigan Center

9012 ■ American Cancer Society, South Central Michigan Service Center
4400 Page Ave.
Michigan Center, MI 49254
Ph: (517)787-0382
Fax: (517)787-1613
URL: National Affiliate–www.cancer.org
Local. Affiliated With: American Cancer Society.

9013 ■ Michigan Bass Chapter Federation (MBCF)
c/o Dewey W. Graves, Jr.
310 Broad St.
Michigan Center, MI 49254
Ph: (517)764-2483 (586)286-3523
E-mail: dgraves@michiganbass.net
URL: http://www.michiganbass.net
Contact: Dennis Beltz, Pres.
State.

9014 ■ Michigan Center Lions Club
c/o Howard Waite, Pres.
594 5th St.
Michigan Center, MI 49254
E-mail: howdydoody@modempool.com
URL: http://www.lionsdistrict11b1.org/lc_michigan_center_lions.htm
Contact: Howard Waite, Pres.
Local. Affiliated With: Lions Clubs International.

Middleville

9015 ■ American Legion, Middleville Post 140
2085 N M-37 Hwy.
Middleville, MI 49333
Ph: (517)371-4720
Fax: (517)371-2401
URL: National Affiliate–www.legion.org
Local. Affiliated With: American Legion.

9016 ■ American Sewing Guild, Grand Rapids Chapter
c/o Mary Sisko-Smith
7255 Boulman Dr.
Middleville, MI 49333
Ph: (269)795-7181
E-mail: sisko-prolynx@voyager.net
URL: http://www.grasg.org
Contact: Mary Sisko-Smith, Contact
Local. Affiliated With: American Sewing Guild.

Midland

9017 ■ Affordable Housing Alliance
c/o Jeff Ratcliffe
220 W Main St.
Midland, MI 48640
Ph: (989)633-9910
URL: National Affiliate–www.apartmentfinderz.com
Contact: Jeff Ratcliffe, Contact
Local.

9018 ■ Alcoholics Anonymous World Services, Midland Area Unity Council Intergroup
PO Box 523
Midland, MI 48640
Ph: (989)695-2975
URL: http://www.midlandaa.org
Local. Individuals recovering from alcoholism. AA maintains that members can solve their common problem and help others achieve sobriety through a twelve step program that includes sharing their experience, strength, and hope with each other. **Affiliated With:** Alcoholics Anonymous World Services.

9019 ■ American Chemical Society, Midland Section
c/o Dr. Deidre Strand, Chm.-Elect
2716 Whitewood Dr.
Midland, MI 48642-3939
Ph: (989)636-5056
E-mail: strandda@dow.com
URL: National Affiliate–acswebcontent.acs.org
Contact: Dr. Deidre Strand, Chm.-Elect
Local. Represents the interests of individuals dedicated to the advancement of chemistry in all its branches. Provides opportunities for peer interaction and career development. **Affiliated With:** American Chemical Society.

9020 ■ American Family Association of Michigan
c/o Gary Glenn
PO Box 1904
Midland, MI 48641-1904
Ph: (989)835-7978
Fax: (810)222-5109
E-mail: garyglenn@afamichigan.org
URL: http://www.afamichigan.org
State.

9021 ■ American Legion, Berryhill Post 165
5111 Hedgewood Dr.
Midland, MI 48640
Ph: (517)371-4720
Fax: (517)371-2401
URL: National Affiliate–www.legion.org
Local. Affiliated With: American Legion.

9022 ■ American Red Cross, Midland/Gladwin Chapter
220 W Main St., Ste.104
Midland, MI 48640
Ph: (989)631-3262
Fax: (989)631-8997
URL: http://midland-gladwin.redcross.org
Local.

9023 ■ Associated Builders and Contractors, Saginaw Valley Chapter
4520 E Ashman Rd., Ste.G
Midland, MI 48642
Ph: (989)832-8879
Fax: (989)832-6412
E-mail: abcsvc@chartermi.net
URL: http://www.abcsvac.org
Contact: Jim Bockelman CAE, Pres. and CEO
Local. Works to achieve and maintain a position of authority and leadership in of the construction and business community. Promotes the merit shop philosophy free enterprise. Conducts educational and training programs. **Affiliated With:** Associated Builders and Contractors. **Publications:** *Transit*, monthly. Newsletter. **Price:** included in membership dues. **Conventions/Meetings:** monthly meeting.

9024 ■ Dow/Midland - Young Life
1310 Ashman
Midland, MI 48640
Ph: (989)631-8585
URL: http://sites.younglife.org/_layouts/ylext/default.aspx?ID=C-1116
Local. Affiliated With: Young Life.

9025 ■ Great Lakes Curling Association - Midland Curling Club
PO Box 1122
Midland, MI 48641-1122
Ph: (989)496-2390
E-mail: info@midlandcurls.org
URL: http://www.midlandcurls.org
Contact: Izzy Castellon, Contact
Local. Affiliated With: United States Curling Association.

9026 ■ Great Lakes Four Wheel Drive Association (GLFWDA)
2960 E Ashby Rd.
Midland, MI 48640
Ph: (989)823-7538
Fax: (888)705-8683
Free: (888)705-8683
E-mail: info@glfwda.org
URL: http://www.glfwda.org
Contact: Pat Kinne, Pres.
Founded: 1969. **Members:** 300. **Membership Dues:** club, $30 (annual) • individual, $35 (annual). **State Groups:** 20. **State. Awards:** AL Ransom. **Type:** recognition. **Recipient:** for history of dedication and volunteering within the association • PUH Caverly. **Type:** recognition. **Recipient:** for history of dedication and volunteering within the association. **Computer Services:** Information services • mailing lists • online services, calendar of events/web forums. **Affiliated With:** United Four-Wheel Drive Associations. **Publications:** *Boondocker*, quarterly. Newsletter. **Price:** included in membership dues. **Circulation:** 500. **Advertising:** accepted. Alternate Formats: online; CD-ROM. **Conventions/Meetings:** quarterly meeting - second Sunday of January, April, July and October, in Midland, MI.

9027 ■ International Facility Management Association, Mid-Michigan (IFMA)
c/o Sheri L. Wolford, Pres.
Design RSVP Inc.
2520 E Wheeler St.
Midland, MI 48642-3178
Ph: (989)430-5995 (989)832-3711
Fax: (989)832-3216
E-mail: sheri@ifmamichigan.org
URL: http://www.ifmamichigan.org
Contact: Sheri L. Wolford, Pres.
Regional. Provides support to facility management professionals through programs of career development, education, and research. **Affiliated With:** International Facility Management Association.

9028 ■ Literacy Council of Midland County
220 W Main St., Ste.206
Midland, MI 48640

Ph: (989)839-0540
Fax: (989)839-4393
E-mail: info@literacymidland.org
URL: http://www.literacymidland.org
Contact: Allen Richard, Exec.Dir.
Founded: 1986. **Local**. Works to assist people achieve personal goals through literacy. **Affiliated With:** ProLiteracy Worldwide.

9029 ■ Michigan Amateur Softball Association (MASA)
c/o Jerry Hanson, Commissioner
3316 Isabella St.
Midland, MI 48640
Ph: (989)835-5821
Fax: (989)835-1276
E-mail: jerryhanson@masasoftball.org
URL: http://www.masasoftball.org
Contact: Jerry Hanson, Commissioner
State. Promotes amateur softball for all persons regardless of age, sex, race, religion, national origin or ancestry. **Affiliated With:** Amateur Softball Association of America. **Formerly:** (2005) Amateur Softball Association of America, Michigan.

9030 ■ Michigan Chapter of National Emergency Number Association
c/o Suzan B. Hensel, ENP, Pres.
Midland County Central Dispatch
2727 Rodd St.
Midland, MI 48640
Ph: (989)839-6464
Fax: (989)839-6476
E-mail: shensel@midland911.org
URL: http://www.michigannena.org
Contact: Suzan B. Hensel ENP, Pres.
State. Promotes the technical advancement, availability, and implementation of a universal emergency telephone number system. **Affiliated With:** National Emergency Number Association.

9031 ■ Mid-Michigan USA Dance
PO Box 2702
Midland, MI 48641-2702
Ph: (989)777-2687
E-mail: djohncole@aol.com
URL: http://home.att.net./~kubinjd3/usadance/index.htm
Contact: John Cole, Pres.
Local. Encourages and promotes the physical, mental and social benefits of partner dancing. Organizes and supports programs for the recreational enjoyment of ballroom dancing. Creates opportunities for the general public to participate in ballroom dancing and DanceSport.

9032 ■ Midland Alliance for the Mentally Ill
c/o Duane S. Lehman, Pres.
704 Lenwood Dr.
Midland, MI 48640
Ph: (989)835-9578
URL: http://mi.nami.org/mid.html
Contact: Duane S. Lehman, Pres.
Local. Strives to improve the quality of life of children and adults with severe mental illness through support, education, research and advocacy. **Affiliated With:** National Alliance for the Mentally Ill.

9033 ■ Midland Area Chamber of Commerce (MACC)
300 Rodd St., Ste.101
Midland, MI 48640
Ph: (989)839-9901
Fax: (989)835-3701
E-mail: chamber@macc.org
URL: http://www.macc.org
Contact: Mr. Sid Allen, Pres./CEO
Local. Promotes, develop, and support its membership in order to foster a sustainable, prosperous business environment and a high quality, livable community. Supports the vision that Midland can be the best place to work, invest, raise a family and live, in all stages of life. **Awards:** Athena Award. **Frequency:** annual. **Type:** recognition. **Recipient:** for individuals who strive to toward an outstanding professional accomplishment • J. Kermit Campbell Partnership Award. **Frequency:** annual. **Type:** recognition. **Recipient:** for business person or business organization that shows interest in business/education partnerships. **Publications:** Directory, annual.

9034 ■ Midland Area Youth Football League (MAYFL)
717 E Haley
Midland, MI 48640-5671
Ph: (989)839-9797
E-mail: president@mayfl.org
URL: http://www.mayfl.org
Contact: Terry Hanley, Pres.
Local.

9035 ■ Midland Board of Realtors
2514 Louanna St.
Midland, MI 48640
Ph: (989)631-6350
E-mail: info@midland-realtors.com
URL: http://www.midland-realtors.com
Contact: Patty Young, Contact
Local. Strives to develop real estate business practices. Advocates the right to own, use and transfer real property. Provides a facility for professional development, research and exchange of information among members. **Affiliated With:** National Association of Realtors.

9036 ■ Midland County Medical Society
4005 Orchard Dr.
Midland, MI 48670
Ph: (989)839-3166
Fax: (989)839-1970
URL: http://www.msms.org
Contact: Beverly Wackerle, Exec.Dir.
Local. Advances the art and science of medicine. Promotes patient care and the betterment of public health. **Affiliated With:** Michigan State Medical Society.

9037 ■ Midland Figure Skating Club (MFSC)
PO Box 1371
Midland, MI 48641
Ph: (989)835-5616
E-mail: contactus@midlandfigureskatingclub.org
URL: http://www.midlandfigureskatingclub.org
Local. Provides programs to encourage participation and achievement in the sport of figure skating on ice. Defines and maintains uniform standards of skating proficiency. Organizes and sponsors competitions and exhibitions for the purpose of stimulating interest in figure skating. **Affiliated With:** United States Figure Skating Association.

9038 ■ Northeast MMBA
4016 E St. Andrew
Midland, MI 48642
Ph: (989)832-1973
E-mail: northeast@mmba.org
URL: http://www.mmba.org
Local. **Affiliated With:** International Mountain Bicycling Association.

9039 ■ Pheasants Forever Bay/Midland Chapter of Michigan
PO Box 23
Midland, MI 48640
Ph: (989)280-2013
E-mail: ernielafave@baymidlandpf.org
URL: http://www.baymidlandpf.org
Contact: Ernie LaFave, Pres.
Local. **Affiliated With:** Pheasants Forever.

9040 ■ School Nutrition Association of Michigan (SNAM)
c/o Mary J. Hardy
884 E Isabella Rd.
Midland, MI 48640
Ph: (989)631-3663 (989)631-5202
Fax: (989)631-4541
Free: (800)677-8955
E-mail: snam@michigansna.org
URL: http://www.michigansna.org
Contact: Paul Yettaw, Pres.
Members: 1,800. **State**. Promotes school food nutrition. **Awards:** 100 Certification Award. **Type:** recognition • 100 Membership Award. **Type:** recognition • **Type:** scholarship • Super Owl Awards. **Type:** recognition • 25-Year Award. **Type:** recognition. **Affiliated With:** School Nutrition Association. **Also Known As:** (2005) American School Food Service Association - Mideast Regional Chapter. **Formerly:** (2005) Michigan School Food Service Association. **Publications:** *First Hand News*, quarterly. Journal. Contains association and industry news. **Price:** included in membership dues. **Conventions/Meetings:** annual convention (exhibits) - always spring.

9041 ■ Society for Applied Spectroscopy, Mid-Michigan
c/o Gary E. Kozerski, Chm.
Dow Corning Corp.
2200 W Salzburd Rd., M/S AUB1007
PO Box 994
Midland, MI 48642
Ph: (517)496-6788
E-mail: gary.kozerski@dowcorning.com
URL: National Affiliate–www.s-a-s.org
Contact: Gary E. Kozerski, Chm.
Local. **Affiliated With:** Society for Applied Spectroscopy.

9042 ■ Trout Unlimited - Leon P. Martuch Chapter
2401 Louanna
Midland, MI 48640
Ph: (517)631-3079
Contact: Tom Monto, Pres.

9043 ■ United Way of Midland County
220 W Main St., Ste.100
Midland, MI 48640
Ph: (989)631-3670
Fax: (989)832-5524
E-mail: answers@unitedwaymidland.org
URL: http://www.unitedwaymidland.org
Contact: John Zimmerman, Exec.Dir.
Local. **Affiliated With:** United Way of America.

9044 ■ Young Life Midland
1310 Ashman
Midland, MI 48640
Ph: (989)631-8585
Fax: (989)835-6770
URL: http://sites.younglife.org/sites/midlandyl/default.aspx
Local. **Affiliated With:** Young Life.

Mikado

9045 ■ American Legion, Mikado Post 254
2205 Alger St.
Mikado, MI 48745
Ph: (517)371-4720
Fax: (517)371-2401
URL: National Affiliate–www.legion.org
Local. **Affiliated With:** American Legion.

Milan

9046 ■ American Federation of Government Employees, AFL-CIO - DOJ Local Union 1741
PO Box 9999
Milan, MI 48160-9999
E-mail: president@1741.com
URL: http://www.1741.com
Contact: Glenn Belcher, Pres.
Members: 113. **Local**. Federal employees including food inspectors, nurses, printers, cartographers, lawyers, police officers, census workers, OSHA

inspectors, janitors, truck drivers, secretaries, artists, plumbers, immigration inspectors, scientists, doctors, cowboys, botanists, park rangers, computer programmers, foreign service workers, airplane mechanics, environmentalists, and writers. Seeks to help provide good government services, while ensuring that government workers are treated fairly and with dignity. **Affiliated With:** American Federation of Government Employees.

9047 ■ American Legion, Earl Gladfelter Post 268
44 Wabash St.
Milan, MI 48160
Ph: (517)371-4720
Fax: (517)371-2401
URL: National Affiliate–www.legion.org
Local. Affiliated With: American Legion.

9048 ■ Milan Area Chamber of Commerce
PO Box 164
Milan, MI 48160-0164
Ph: (734)439-7932
Fax: (734)241-3520
E-mail: info@milanchamber.org
URL: http://www.milanchamber.org
Contact: Jean Wilson, Pres.
Local.

Milford

9049 ■ American Legion, Michigan Post 216
c/o Ernest F. Oldenburg
510 W Commerce Rd.
Milford, MI 48381
Ph: (517)371-4720
Fax: (517)371-2401
URL: National Affiliate–www.legion.org
Contact: Ernest F. Oldenburg, Contact
Local. Affiliated With: American Legion.

9050 ■ Huron Valley Chamber of Commerce (HVCC)
317 Union St., Ste.F
Milford, MI 48381
Ph: (248)685-7129
Fax: (248)685-9047
E-mail: info@huronvcc.com
URL: http://www.huronvcc.com
Contact: Susan Happel, Exec.Dir.
Membership Dues: business (based on number of employees), $200-$460 (annual) • associate, $70 (annual) • additional business, $65 (annual). **Local.** Promotes business and community development in the Huron Valley, MI area. **Awards:** Barbara Gavitt Memorial Scholarship Fund. **Type:** scholarship • Business Improvement Award. **Type:** recognition • Business of the Year. **Frequency:** annual. **Type:** recognition • Citizen of the Year. **Frequency:** annual. **Type:** recognition. **Computer Services:** Information services, member directory. **Formerly:** (1999) Huron Valley Area Chamber of Commerce. **Publications:** *Business Directory and Buying Guide*, annual. Contains community profiles of Huron Valley and member listing. **Circulation:** 30,000. **Advertising:** accepted • *Chamber News*, monthly. Newsletter. **Circulation:** 750. **Advertising:** accepted. Alternate Formats: online.

9051 ■ Michigan Atheists
c/o Bradley Sampeer, Literature Coor.
PO Box 314
Milford, MI 48381-0314
E-mail: darwinsnerdman@hotmail.com
URL: http://www.michiganatheists.org
Contact: Bradley Sampeer, Literature Coor.
State. Affiliated With: American Atheists.

9052 ■ Milford Historical Society (MHS)
124 E Commerce St.
Milford, MI 48381
Ph: (248)685-7308
E-mail: mildfordhistory@yahoo.com
URL: http://www.milfordhistory.org
Contact: Dave Chase, Pres.
Founded: 1973. **Members:** 200. **Membership Dues:** individual, $15 (annual) • family, $25 (annual) • life, $250 • student, $5 (annual) • senior, $10 (annual) • small business, $50 (annual) • silver, gold, platinum, $250-$1,000 (annual). **Local Groups:** 1. **Local.** Individuals interested in the history of Milford, MI. Maintains museum. **Committees:** Pettibone Creek Hydroelectric Plant Restoration. **Publications:** *The Milford Historian*. Newsletter • *Ten Minutes Ahead of the Rest of the World*. Book. **Price:** $30.00.

Millersburg

9053 ■ Glawe School Committee
c/o Joyce Foster
14610 Pomranke Hwy.
Millersburg, MI 49759-9732
Founded: 2000. **Local.**

Millington

9054 ■ American Legion, Conrad-Wager-Keene Post 164
5397 Millington Rd.
Millington, MI 48746
Ph: (517)371-4720
Fax: (517)371-2401
URL: National Affiliate–www.legion.org
Local. Affiliated With: American Legion.

9055 ■ Millington Lions Club - Michigan
c/o Todd Ostrander, Pres.
7653 Osborne Rd.
Millington, MI 48746
Ph: (989)871-3432
URL: http://www.geocities.com/dist11d1
Contact: Todd Ostrander, Pres.
Local. Affiliated With: Lions Clubs International.

Mio

9056 ■ American Legion, Michigan Post 348
c/o Arthur Randall
945 E 8th St.
Mio, MI 48647
Ph: (517)826-2359
Fax: (517)371-2401
URL: National Affiliate–www.legion.org
Contact: Arthur Randall, Contact
Local. Affiliated With: American Legion.

Mohawk

9057 ■ American Legion, Clyde Johnston Post 230
122 Stanton Ave.
Mohawk, MI 49950
Ph: (517)371-4720
Fax: (517)371-2401
URL: National Affiliate–www.legion.org
Local. Affiliated With: American Legion.

Monroe

9058 ■ American Legion, Matt Urban Post 40
PO Box 663
Monroe, MI 48161
Ph: (517)371-4720
Fax: (517)371-2401
URL: National Affiliate–www.legion.org
Local. Affiliated With: American Legion.

9059 ■ American Legion, Michigan Post 60
c/o Carl F. Payson
101 W 1st St.
Monroe, MI 48161
Ph: (313)241-7039
Fax: (517)371-2401
URL: National Affiliate–www.legion.org
Contact: Carl F. Payson, Contact
Local. Affiliated With: American Legion.

9060 ■ American Legion, Michigan Post 217
c/o Edward C. Headman
PO Box 2001
Monroe, MI 48161
Ph: (517)371-4720
Fax: (517)371-2401
URL: National Affiliate–www.legion.org
Contact: Edward C. Headman, Contact
Local. Affiliated With: American Legion.

9061 ■ American Red Cross of Monroe County
PO Box 1338
Monroe, MI 48161
Ph: (734)289-1481
Fax: (734)289-1730
Free: (800)391-8668
URL: http://www.arc-monroe.org
Local.

9062 ■ Arc of Monroe County
753 S Monroe St., Ste.B
Monroe, MI 48161
Ph: (734)241-5881
Fax: (734)241-3694
E-mail: arcmonroe@foxberry.net
Contact: Cynthia A. Harden, Exec.Dir.
Local. Parents, clients, professionals, and persons in Monroe County, MI interested in the developmentally disabled and their concerns and issues. Provides advocacy services for these individuals.

9063 ■ Concerned Parents for Literacy
c/o Kellie Vining, Chair/Exec.Dir.
1437 Peters
Monroe, MI 48161-1054
E-mail: cpfl1@netzero.com
URL: http://www.cpfl.netfirms.com
Contact: Kellie Vining, Chair/Exec.Dir.
Local.

9064 ■ Floral City Stamp Club
c/o Adele Rottenbucher, Sec.
3785 Heiss Rd.
Monroe, MI 48162
URL: National Affiliate–www.stamps.org
Contact: Adele Rottenbucher, Sec.
Founded: 1974. **Members:** 32. **Membership Dues:** adult, $8 (annual) • child under 12, $2 (annual). **Budget:** $300. **Local.** Promotes the hobby of stamp collecting. Holds monthly meetings with a small auction, APS sales booklets, annual picnic with balloon/cachet launch, and Christmas party. **Affiliated With:** American Philatelic Society. **Publications:** *Mint Sheet*, monthly. Newsletter. Features club news and minutes. **Price:** $8.00 for members only.

9065 ■ Model A Restorers Club, Floral City A Region
c/o Terry Bennett, Pres.
152 Doty Rd.
Monroe, MI 48162
Ph: (734)323-8176 (734)241-0164
URL: http://www.geocities.com/floralcitya
Contact: Terry Bennett, Pres.
Local. Affiliated With: Model "A" Restorers Club. **Publications:** Newsletter. Alternate Formats: online.

9066 ■ Monroe Alliance for the Mentally Ill
c/o Tom Acton, Pres.
5572 Raven Pkwy.
Monroe, MI 48161
Ph: (313)242-0604
URL: http://mi.nami.org/mon.html
Contact: Tom Acton, Pres.
Local. Strives to improve the quality of life of children and adults with severe mental illness through support, education, research and advocacy. **Affiliated With:** National Alliance for the Mentally Ill.

9067 ■ Monroe County Association of Realtors
14930 Laplaisance Rd., Ste.109
Monroe, MI 48161
Ph: (734)242-6866
Fax: (734)242-1729
E-mail: staff@mcar.ws
URL: http://www.mcar.ws
Contact: Kim Nissen, Pres.
Local. Helps members become more successful and profitable in their businesses. Strives to develop real estate business practices. Provides information about the real estate industry. **Affiliated With:** National Association of Realtors.

9068 ■ Monroe County Chamber of Commerce (MCCC)
1122 W Front St.
Monroe, MI 48161
Ph: (734)242-3366
Fax: (734)242-7253
E-mail: chamber@monroecountychamber.com
URL: http://www.monroecountychamber.com
Contact: Michelle S. Nisley, Pres.
Founded: 1957. **Local.** Promotes business and community development in Monroe County, MI. **Awards:** Athena Award. **Frequency:** annual. **Type:** recognition. **Recipient:** for demonstrating service to women • Small Business Person of the Year. **Frequency:** annual. **Type:** recognition. **Recipient:** for demonstrating consistent growth, community service, and leadership. **Committees:** Political Action.

9069 ■ Monroe County Planning Commission
106 E 1st St.
Monroe, MI 48161
Ph: (734)240-7375
Fax: (734)240-7385
Free: (888)354-5500
E-mail: peggy_tyniw@monroemi.org
URL: http://www.co.monroe.mi.us
Contact: Royce R. Maniko, Dir.
Founded: 1968. **Members:** 11. **Staff:** 9. **Local.** Individuals from labor, agriculture, education, and government sectors. Prepares and adopts a comprehensive plan for the development of Monroe County. Coordinates planning activities. Provides demographic information mapping service. **Libraries: Type:** open to the public. **Holdings:** books, periodicals. **Subjects:** planning, zoning, land use. **Publications:** *Mobile Home Park Study*. Report • *Monroe County Annual Building Activities*. Report • *Monroe County Comprehensive Plan Update*. Report. **Conventions/Meetings:** monthly meeting.

9070 ■ Monroe Figure Skating Club (MFSC)
PO Box 811
Monroe, MI 48161-0811
Ph: (734)242-1300
E-mail: monroefsc@hotmail.com
URL: http://www.monroefsc.org
Local. Provides programs to encourage participation and achievement in the sport of figure skating on ice. Defines and maintains uniform standards of skating proficiency. Organizes and sponsors competitions and exhibitions for the purpose of stimulating interest in figure skating. **Affiliated With:** United States Figure Skating Association.

9071 ■ Monroe Golden Lions Club
c/o David N. Hasley, Sec.
5126 Evergreen Dr.
Monroe, MI 48161
Ph: (734)242-6065
URL: http://www.metrodetroitlions.org
Contact: David N. Hasley, Sec.
Local. Affiliated With: Lions Clubs International.

9072 ■ National Active and Retired Federal Employees Association - Ann Arbor 304
754 Westwood Blvd.
Monroe, MI 48161-1858
Ph: (734)241-7567
URL: National Affiliate–www.narfe.org
Contact: Kraig Hayner, Contact
Local. Protects the retirement future of employees through education. Informs members on issues affecting the retirement. **Affiliated With:** National Association of Retired Federal Employees.

9073 ■ Phi Theta Kappa, Tau Omicron Chapter - Monroe County Community College
c/o Cheryl Kehrer
1555 S Raisinville Rd.
Monroe, MI 48161
Ph: (734)384-4106
E-mail: ckehrer@mail.monroeccc.edu
URL: http://www.ptk.org/directories/chapters/MI/252-1.htm
Contact: Cheryl Kehrer, Advisor
Local.

9074 ■ Vietnam Veterans of America, Monroe County - Chapter 142
PO Box 1407
Monroe, MI 48161
Ph: (734)457-4838
URL: http://www.vietnamveterans142.org
Local. Affiliated With: Vietnam Veterans of America.

Montgomery

9075 ■ American Legion, Stout-Nesbit Post 156
PO Box 148
Montgomery, MI 49255
Ph: (517)296-4308
Fax: (517)371-2401
URL: National Affiliate–www.legion.org
Local. Affiliated With: American Legion.

9076 ■ Michigan National Wild Turkey Federation, Hillsdale Chapter
9020 W Territorial Rd.
Montgomery, MI 49255
Ph: (517)368-5965
URL: http://www.mi-nwtf.org/Hillsdale.htm
Contact: Phillip Quist, Pres.
Local.

Montrose

9077 ■ American Legion, Michigan Post 367
c/o Harry Baker
PO Box 317
Montrose, MI 48457
Ph: (517)371-4720
Fax: (517)371-2401
URL: National Affiliate–www.legion.org
Contact: Harry Baker, Contact
Local. Affiliated With: American Legion.

9078 ■ Michigan Competing Band Association (MCBA)
10237 N Seymour Rd.
Montrose, MI 48457-9014
Ph: (810)639-2442
Fax: (810)639-3786
E-mail: greenb@huronvalley.k12.mi.us
URL: http://www.michcompband.org
Contact: Robert Green, Pres.
Founded: 1992. **Members:** 85. **Membership Dues:** unit, $150 (annual) • associate, $40 (annual). **Staff:** 2. **Budget:** $130,000. **State.** Michigan high school bands. Promotes instrumental music education in Michigan through the sponsoring of marching band contests, music clinics for instructors and students, and the offering of college scholarships. **Awards:** MCBA Scholarship. **Frequency:** annual. **Type:** scholarship. **Recipient:** for a Michigan high school senior majoring in music at a college/university in the following year; based on honors, awards, proficiency scores on state exams, and recommendation. **Conventions/Meetings:** meeting - 3/year.

9079 ■ Montrose Lions Club - Michigan
c/o Linda Lewellyn, Sec.
150 Erean St.
Montrose, MI 48457
Ph: (810)639-7196
E-mail: llslim@yahoo.com
URL: http://www.geocities.com/dist11d1
Contact: Linda Lewellyn, Sec.
Local. Affiliated With: Lions Clubs International.

Moran

9080 ■ National Alliance for the Mentally Ill of Mackinac
c/o Carol Jenkins
PO Box 16
Moran, MI 49760
Ph: (906)643-1514
URL: http://mi.nami.org/eup.html
Contact: Carol Jenkins, Contact
Local. Strives to improve the quality of life of children and adults with severe mental illness through support, education, research and advocacy. **Affiliated With:** National Alliance for the Mentally Ill.

9081 ■ Strait's of Mackinac Beagle Club
c/o Neva Johnson
PO Box 130
Moran, MI 49760-0130
URL: National Affiliate–clubs.akc.org
Contact: Neva Johnson, Contact
Local.

Morenci

9082 ■ American Legion, Morenci Post 368
9010 Morenci Rd.
Morenci, MI 49256
Ph: (517)371-4720
Fax: (517)371-2401
URL: National Affiliate–www.legion.org
Local. Affiliated With: American Legion.

Morley

9083 ■ American Legion, Knox-Helms Post 554
2560 Northland Dr.
Morley, MI 49336
Ph: (517)371-4720
Fax: (517)371-2401
URL: National Affiliate–www.legion.org
Local. Affiliated With: American Legion.

Morrice

9084 ■ Morrice Lions Club
c/o James Fike, Pres.
211 E Lansing Rd.
Morrice, MI 48857
Ph: (517)625-7250
URL: http://www.district11c2.org
Contact: James Fike, Pres.
Local. Affiliated With: Lions Clubs International.

Mount Clemens

9085 ■ American Legion, Michigan Post 4
c/o Harry Ollrich
401 N Groesbeck Hwy.
Mount Clemens, MI 48043
Ph: (517)371-4720
Fax: (517)371-2401
URL: National Affiliate–www.legion.org
Contact: Harry Ollrich, Contact
Local. Affiliated With: American Legion.

9086 ■ Central Macomb County Chamber of Commerce (CMCCC)
49 Macomb Pl.
Mount Clemens, MI 48043
Ph: (586)493-7600
Fax: (586)493-7602
E-mail: info@central-macomb.com
URL: http://www.central-macomb.com
Contact: Grace M. Shore, Pres.
Founded: 1903. **Members:** 525. **Staff:** 8. **Budget:** $315,000. **Local**. Brings together businesses united to promote economic development and improve the quality of life in Macomb County, MI. Lobbies on economic issues. Participates in annual Farm City Festival. **Convention/Meeting:** none. **Computer Services:** database, member directory • mailing lists, of members. **Committees:** Ambassadors; Community Development; Economic Development; Operations; Programs and Services; Public Policy/ Legislative Affairs. **Publications:** *Membership and Community Directory*, annual. Contains complete listing of chamber members and the services they offer. **Price:** $15.00 for nonmembers; free for members. **Circulation:** 6,000 • Newsletter, monthly. Alternate Formats: online • Book, monthly. Contains upcoming events the chamber is planning.

9087 ■ Macomb County Bar Association (MCBA)
40 N Main St., Ste.435
Mount Clemens, MI 48043
Ph: (586)468-2940 (586)468-8300
Fax: (586)468-6926
E-mail: rtroy@macombbar.org
URL: http://www.macombbar.org
Contact: Rick R. Troy, Exec.Dir.
Founded: 1906. **Members:** 1,354. **Staff:** 5. **Budget:** $310,000. **Local**. Local bar association with approx. 1400 volunteer members. Public service projects include Lawyer Referral Service, Law Day celebration, Pro Bono service, Law in the Schools, Legally Speaking television program, and Community Dispute Resolution Center. **Publications:** *Bar Briefs*, monthly. Magazine. Includes timely legal articles. **Price:** included in membership dues; $35.00 /year for nonmembers. **Circulation:** 1,400. **Advertising:** accepted • *Macomb County Court Directory*, annual. **Conventions/Meetings:** quarterly meeting - always February, April, October, and December in Macomb County, MI.

9088 ■ Macomb County Deputies and Dispatchers Association
c/o Patric Maceroni
PO Box 182
Mount Clemens, MI 48046-0182
Contact: Charles Gudneau, Pres.
Founded: 2002. **Members:** 195. **Membership Dues:** voluntary, $20. **Staff:** 8. **Budget:** $14,500. **Local**. Includes deputies and dispatchers of the Macomb County Sheriff Department. **Formerly:** (2004) Macomb County Professional Deputy Association. **Conventions/Meetings:** meeting, union meetings only.

9089 ■ Macomb County Genealogy Group
c/o Mt. Clemens Public Library
150 Cass Ave.
Mount Clemens, MI 48043
Ph: (586)469-6200
Fax: (586)469-6668
Contact: Ann Faulkner, Exec. Officer
Founded: 1973. **Members:** 60. **Local**. Acts as a forum for persons interested in genealogy to exchange information. **Publications:** none. **Conventions/Meetings:** biennial meeting.

9090 ■ Michigan Healthcare Resource and Materials Management
c/o Janis Klos, Purchasing Asst.
Mt. Clemens Gen. Hosp.
1000 Harrington St.
Mount Clemens, MI 48043-2920
Ph: (586)493-2816
Fax: (586)493-8709
E-mail: jklos@mcgh.org
URL: National Affiliate–www.ahrmm.org
Contact: Janis Klos, Purchasing Asst.
State. Represents purchasing agents and materials managers active in the field of purchasing, inventory, distribution and materials management as performed in hospitals, related patient care institutions and government and voluntary health organizations. Provides networking and educational opportunities for members. Develops new business ventures that ensure the financial stability of members. **Affiliated With:** Association for Healthcare Resource and Materials Management.

9091 ■ Mothers Against Drunk Driving, Macomb County
59 N Walnut, No. 206
Mount Clemens, MI 48043
Ph: (586)463-3611
Fax: (586)463-5048
E-mail: maddmacomb@aol.com
URL: http://www.madd.org/mi/macomb
Contact: Alice Stacy, Exec.Dir.
Founded: 1993. **Local**. Supports victims of drunk driving by offering emotional support, help with the justice system and other areas as needed. Works to stop drunk driving and prevent under age drinking through public awareness and educational programs at community events, educational institutions and businesses. **Affiliated With:** Mothers Against Drunk Driving.

9092 ■ National Organization for Women - Macomb County
c/o Diane Russel
PO Box 1174
Mount Clemens, MI 48046
Ph: (586)997-7270
E-mail: russell89@sbcglobal.net
URL: http://www.michnow.org
Contact: Diane Russel, Contact
Local. **Affiliated With:** National Organization for Women.

Mount Morris

9093 ■ Ancient Order of Hibernians of Genesee County - Sullivan and O'Sullivan Division
c/o John Roach
4155 W 50th St.
Mount Morris, MI 48458
Ph: (810)686-6784
E-mail: irishalley@sbcglobal.net
URL: http://www.michiganaoh.com
Contact: John Roach, Contact
Local. **Affiliated With:** Ancient Order of Hibernians in America.

9094 ■ Mt. Morris Lions Club
c/o Cindy Reynolds, Pres.
1028 Haven St.
Mount Morris, MI 48458
Ph: (810)687-2949
URL: http://www.geocities.com/dist11d1
Contact: Cindy Reynolds, Pres.
Local. **Affiliated With:** Lions Clubs International.

9095 ■ National Association of Investors Corporation, Mid-Michigan Chapter
7076 Birchwood Dr.
Mount Morris, MI 48458
Ph: (810)640-2231
E-mail: kkavula1@comcast.net
URL: http://better-investing.org/chapter/midmich
Contact: Ken Kavula, Pres.
Local. Teaches individuals how to become successful strategic long-term investors. Provides highly focused learning resources and investment tools that empower individuals to become better investors. **Affiliated With:** National Association of Investors Corporation.

Mount Pleasant

9096 ■ American Legion, Owen Barrett Post 110
209 S Oak St.
Mount Pleasant, MI 48858
Ph: (517)371-4720
Fax: (517)371-2401
URL: National Affiliate–www.legion.org
Local. **Affiliated With:** American Legion.

9097 ■ American Meteorological Society, Central Michigan University
c/o Christina L. Bennett, Pres.
296A Dow Sci. Bldg.
Mount Pleasant, MI 48859
E-mail: midnytesky@hotmail.com
URL: http://www.cst.cmich.edu/org/cmuscams
Contact: Christina L. Bennett, Pres.
Regional. Professional meteorologists, oceanographers, and hydrologists; interested students and nonprofessionals. **Affiliated With:** American Meteorological Society.

9098 ■ American Orff-Schulwerk Association, West Michigan Chapter No. 32 (WMOC)
c/o Joan Sampson, Membership Representative
408 S Brown St.
Mount Pleasant, MI 48858
E-mail: westmichiganorff@hotmail.com
URL: http://wmoc.tripod.com
Contact: Joan Sampson, Membership Representative
Local. Provides a forum for the continued growth and development of Orff Schulwerk. Promotes the value and use of Orff Schulwerk.

9099 ■ American Red Cross, Central Michigan Chapter
215 E Broadway
Mount Pleasant, MI 48858-2313
Ph: (989)773-3615
URL: http://centralmichigan.redcross.org
Regional.

9100 ■ Association for Computing Machinery, Central Michigan University
Pearce 413
Dept. of Cmpt. Sci.
Mount Pleasant, MI 48858
Ph: (989)277-1465
E-mail: acmatcmu@hotmail.com
URL: National Affiliate–www.acm.org
Contact: David K. Wenzlick, Pres.
Regional. Biological, medical, behavioral, and computer scientists; hospital administrators; programmers and others interested in application of computer methods to biological, behavioral, and medical problems. Stimulates understanding of the use and potential of computers in the Biosciences. **Affiliated With:** Association for Computing Machinery.

9101 ■ Big Brothers Big Sisters of Isabella County
304 W Michigan, Ste.7
Mount Pleasant, MI 48858
Ph: (989)772-5232
E-mail: bbbsic@power-net.net
URL: http://www.bbbsic.org
Contact: Angela Stanton, Exec.Dir.
Local. Works to provide quality-mentoring relationships between children and qualified adults and promote their development into competent, confident and caring individuals. **Affiliated With:** Big Brothers Big Sisters of America.

9102 ■ Central Michigan Association of Realtors (CMAR)
111 S Lansing St.
Mount Pleasant, MI 48858
Ph: (989)773-2564
Fax: (989)773-0193
E-mail: candy@cmiar.com
URL: http://www.cmiar.com
Contact: Candy Meyers, Exec. Officer
Local. Strives to develop real estate business practices. Advocates the right to own, use and

transfer real property. Provides a facility for professional development, research and exchange of information among members. **Affiliated With:** National Association of Realtors.

9103 ■ Designers Without Borders
c/o David Stairs
PO Box 2063
Mount Pleasant, MI 48804
Ph: (989)773-2119
Fax: (989)774-2278
E-mail: mackay-stairs@designerswithoutborders.org
URL: http://www.designerswithoutborders.org
Contact: David Stairs, Exec.Dir.
Founded: 2000. **Local**. Assists under resourced institutions of the developing world with communication design needs.

9104 ■ Friends of the Broadway
c/o Samuel W. Staples
PO Box 823
Mount Pleasant, MI 48804-0823
Ph: (517)772-2075
Fax: (989)775-9900
E-mail: us@friendsofthebroadway.org
URL: http://www.friendsofthebroadway.com
Contact: Sam Staples, Pres.
Founded: 2000. **Members:** 13. **Budget:** $100,000. **Local Groups:** 1. **For-Profit**. **Local**. Presentation of Broadway theater with various shows, plays, concerts, etc. **Subgroups:** Broadway Players; Community Players. **Conventions/Meetings:** monthly board meeting.

9105 ■ Great Lakes Humanist Society (GLHS)
PO Box 1183
Mount Pleasant, MI 48804-1183
E-mail: info@glhumanist.org
URL: http://glhumanist.org
Contact: John Scalise, Pres.
Founded: 1998. **Members:** 50. **Local**. **Affiliated With:** American Humanist Association.

9106 ■ Home Builders Association of Central Michigan
226 Independence
Mount Pleasant, MI 48858-1517
Ph: (989)775-7747
Fax: (989)775-7748
Free: (800)775-7747
E-mail: hbacentralmi@journey.com
URL: http://www.hbacm.com
Contact: Carmelina Crisci, Exec. Officer
Local. Single and multifamily home builders, commercial builders, and others associated with the building industry. **Affiliated With:** National Association of Home Builders.

9107 ■ Michigan Art Education Association (MAEA)
c/o Cindy Smith
3750 Greenacres Dr.
Mount Pleasant, MI 48858-9503
E-mail: rguimond@eup.k12.mi.us
URL: http://www.miarted.org
Contact: Richard A Guimond, Pres.
State. Promotes art education through professional development, service, advancement of knowledge, and leadership.

9108 ■ Michigan Association of Collegiate Registrars and Admissions Officers (MACRAO)
c/o Dorene Root, Historian
Central Michigan Univ.
Warriner Hall 212
Mount Pleasant, MI 48859
Ph: (989)774-4000
Fax: (989)774-3783
E-mail: mulseth@hfcc.net
URL: http://www.macrao.org
Contact: Dorene Root, Historian
Founded: 1910. **Members:** 900. **Membership Dues:** institutional, $150 (annual). **Budget:** $60,000. **State**. Provides for the exchange of information concerning problems of interest to its members and contributes to the advancement of educators in Michigan. **Committees:** Articulation; College Day/Night; Data and Technology; Enrollment Management; Equal Education Opportunity; Graduate and Professional Studies; Professional Development; Registrar's Practices; Secondary School Relations; Standing. **Publications:** Newsletter, semiannual. **Price:** included in membership dues. Alternate Formats: online. **Conventions/Meetings:** annual conference (exhibits) - always November.

9109 ■ Michigan Council for the Social Studies
c/o Dr. Renay Scott, Pres.
Central Michigan Univ.
223 Ronan
Mount Pleasant, MI 48859
Ph: (989)774-3976
Fax: (989)774-3152
E-mail: scott1rm@cmich.edu
URL: http://www.michcouncilss.org
Contact: Dr. Renay Scott, Pres.
State. Represents teachers of elementary and secondary social studies, including instructors of civics, geography, history, law, economics, political science, psychology, sociology, and anthropology. Promotes the teaching of social studies. Provides members with opportunities to share strategies, have access to new material, and keep abreast of the national education scene. **Affiliated With:** National Council for the Social Studies.

9110 ■ Michigan National Wild Turkey Federation, Mecosta County Strutters Chapter
2410 S Coldwater
Mount Pleasant, MI 48858
Ph: (313)640-5939
URL: http://www.mi-nwtf.org/Mecosta.htm
Contact: Nick Giuliani, Pres.
Local.

9111 ■ Michigan National Wild Turkey Federation, Mountain Top Gobblers
1696 E Deerfield
Mount Pleasant, MI 48858
Ph: (517)773-5721
URL: http://www.mi-nwtf.org/Moutaintop.htm
Contact: Kip Cosan, Pres.
Local.

9112 ■ MiCTA
1500 W High St.
Mount Pleasant, MI 48858
Fax: (989)772-3239
Free: (888)870-8677
E-mail: info@micta.org
URL: http://www.micta.org
Contact: Kim Ellertson, CEO
Local.

9113 ■ Mid Michigan Human Resource Association
PO Box 0917
Mount Pleasant, MI 48804
E-mail: vicki.a.graczyk@cmich.edu
URL: http://www.mmhra.org
Contact: Vicki Graczyk, Pres.
Local. Represents the interests of human resource and industrial relations professionals and executives. Promotes the advancement of human resource management.

9114 ■ Mid-Michigan Professional Photographers Association
c/o Daniel Pulver
302 Chippewa St.
Mount Pleasant, MI 48858
Ph: (517)772-2167
E-mail: dpulvie@aol.com
URL: National Affiliate–ppa.com
Contact: Daniel Pulver, Contact
State. **Affiliated With:** Professional Photographers of America.

9115 ■ Mount Pleasant Area Chamber of Commerce (MPACC)
114 E Broadway
Mount Pleasant, MI 48858
Ph: (989)772-2396
Fax: (989)773-2656
E-mail: jkostrava@mt-pleasant.net
URL: http://www.mt-pleasant.net
Contact: James E. Kostrava CAE, Pres./CEO
Founded: 1938. **Membership Dues:** individual, $77 (annual) • basic (based on number of employees), $216-$551 (annual) • chairman's circle (based on number of employees), $324-$827 (annual). **Local**. Promotes business and community development in the Mt. Pleasant, MI area. Participates in area festivals. **Awards:** Citizen of the Year. **Frequency:** annual. **Type:** recognition. **Recipient:** for the most outstanding community leader • Eagle Award. **Frequency:** annual. **Type:** recognition. **Recipient:** for the most outstanding volunteers and local organizations. **Computer Services:** Mailing lists, of members. **Telecommunication Services:** electronic mail, aosburn@mt-pleasant.net • electronic mail, bcataldo@mt-pleasant.net. **Committees:** Golf Outing. **Publications:** *Business News*, monthly. Newsletter. Informs about business updates, special events, announcements and chamber happenings. **Circulation:** 900. **Advertising:** accepted. Alternate Formats: online.

9116 ■ Mt. Pleasant Figure Skating Club
PO Box 975
Mount Pleasant, MI 48804-0975
Ph: (989)779-0690
E-mail: mtpleasantfsc@yahoo.com
URL: http://www.geocities.com/mtpleasantfsc
Local. Provides programs to encourage participation and achievement in the sport of figure skating on ice. Defines and maintains uniform standards of skating proficiency. Organizes and sponsors competitions and exhibitions for the purpose of stimulating interest in figure skating. **Affiliated With:** United States Figure Skating Association.

9117 ■ Mount Pleasant Lions Club - Michigan
PO Box 744
Mount Pleasant, MI 48804-0744
E-mail: ml3153@power-net.net
URL: http://www.mplions.com
Contact: John Schimmelmann, Pres.
Local. **Affiliated With:** Lions Clubs International.

9118 ■ NACE International, Detroit Section
c/o Keith Brian Boswell, Chm.
BGL Asset Services, LLC
1611 S Isabella Rd.
Mount Pleasant, MI 48858
Ph: (989)772-8888
Fax: (989)772-7778
E-mail: keithb@bglas.com
URL: National Affiliate–www.nace.org
Contact: Keith Brian Boswell, Chm.
Local. Promotes public safety by advancing the knowledge of corrosion engineering and science. Works to raise awareness of corrosion control and prevention technology among government agencies and legislators, businesses, professional societies and the general public. **Affiliated With:** NACE International: The Corrosion Society.

9119 ■ National Organization for Women - Mount Pleasant
c/o Linda Mason
414 E Grand Ave.
Mount Pleasant, MI 48858
Ph: (989)772-5334
E-mail: masontree@aol.com
URL: http://www.michnow.org
Contact: Linda Mason, Contact
Local. **Affiliated With:** National Organization for Women.

9120 ■ National Technical Honor Society - Mt. Pleasant Area Technical Center Michigan (MPATC)
1155 S Elizabeth St.
Mount Pleasant, MI 48858
Ph: (989)775-2210
Free: (888)GO-MPATC
E-mail: mpung@mtpleasant.edzone.net
URL: http://www.mpatc.com
Contact: Michael Pung, Dir.
Local.

9121 ■ Ninth District Dental Society, MIC
305 E Broadway St.
Mount Pleasant, MI 48858
Ph: (989)779-8747
E-mail: judytoothdoctor@hotmail.com
URL: National Affiliate–www.ada.org
Contact: Dr. Judith Wybenga, Pres.
Local. Represents the interests of dentists committed to the public's oral health, ethics and professional development. Encourages the improvement of the public's oral health and promotes the art and science of dentistry. **Affiliated With:** American Dental Association; Michigan Dental Association.

9122 ■ PFLAG Mt. Pleasant
1802 Morning Mist Ln.
Mount Pleasant, MI 48858
Ph: (989)775-6447
E-mail: jacob1s@cmich.edu
URL: http://www.pflag.org/Michigan.216.0.html
Local. Affiliated With: Parents, Families, and Friends of Lesbians and Gays.

9123 ■ Psi Chi, National Honor Society in Psychology - Central Michigan University
c/o Dept. of Psychology
101 Sloan Hall
Mount Pleasant, MI 48858
Ph: (989)774-3001
Fax: (989)774-2553
E-mail: psy@cmich.edu
URL: http://www.chsbs.cmich.edu/Psychology
Local. Affiliated With: Psi Chi, National Honor Society in Psychology.

9124 ■ Special Olympics Michigan (SOMI)
Central Michigan Univ.
Mount Pleasant, MI 48859
Ph: (989)774-3911
Fax: (989)774-3034
Free: (800)644-6404
E-mail: somi@somi.org
URL: http://www.somi.org
Contact: Lois Arnold, Pres./CEO
State. Promotes physical fitness, sports training, and athletic competition for children and adults with mental retardation. Seeks to contribute to the physical, social, and psychological development of persons with mental retardation. Participants range in age from 8 years to adult and compete in track and field, swimming, gymnastics, bowling, ice skating, basketball, and other sports. **Affiliated With:** Special Olympics.

9125 ■ United States Naval Sea Cadet Corps - Chosin Division
Central Michigan Univ.
Finch Field House
Mount Pleasant, MI 48858-9137
E-mail: nscc-chosin@home.com
URL: http://dolphin.seacadets.org/US_units/UnitDetails.asp?UnitID=092CHO
Contact: LCDR John W. Smith, Commanding Officer
Local. Works to instill good citizenship and patriotism in youth. Encourages qualities such as personal neatness, loyalty, obedience, dependability, and responsibility to others. Offers courses in physical fitness and military drill, first aid, water safety, basic seamanship, and naval history and traditions. **Affiliated With:** Naval Sea Cadet Corps.

9126 ■ United Way of Isabella County
402 S Univ.
Mount Pleasant, MI 48858
Ph: (989)773-9863
Fax: (989)772-8152
E-mail: nbliss@unitedwayisaco.org
URL: http://www.unitedwayisaco.org
Contact: Nichole Bliss, Exec.Dir.
Local. Affiliated With: United Way of America.

Mulliken

9127 ■ Mulliken Lions Club
c/o Donald H. Leik, Pres.
PO Box 125
Mulliken, MI 48861-0125
Ph: (517)649-8920
URL: http://www.district11c2.org
Contact: Donald H. Leik, Pres.
Local. Affiliated With: Lions Clubs International.

Munger

9128 ■ Bereaved Parents of the USA, Saginaw Chapter
c/o Cherie Gotham
PO Box 13
Munger, MI 48747
Ph: (989)892-8980
E-mail: cheriegotham@hotmail.com
URL: National Affiliate–www.bereavedparentsusa.org
Contact: Cherie Gotham, Contact
Local.

Munising

9129 ■ Alger Chamber of Commerce
PO Box 405
Munising, MI 49862
Ph: (906)387-2138
Fax: (906)387-1858
E-mail: chamber@algercounty.org
URL: http://www.algercounty.org
Contact: Kay LeVeque, Dir.
Local. Promotes convention business and tourism in the area. **Computer Services:** Information services, member directory. **Formerly:** Munising Visitors Bureau. **Conventions/Meetings:** annual dinner - always fourth Saturday of January.

9130 ■ American Legion, Roderick Prato Post 131
610 W Munising Ave.
Munising, MI 49862
Ph: (906)387-2697
Fax: (517)371-2401
URL: National Affiliate–www.legion.org
Local. Affiliated With: American Legion.

9131 ■ Vietnam Veterans of America, Chapter 237
PO Box 608
Munising, MI 49862
Ph: (906)378-3837
Fax: (906)378-3837
E-mail: namvet@up.net
URL: http://vva_chapter_237.tripod.com
Local. Affiliated With: Vietnam Veterans of America.

Munith

9132 ■ American Legion, Michigan Post 526
c/o Richard H. Reno, Jr.
PO Box 141
Munith, MI 49259
Ph: (517)371-4720
Fax: (517)371-2401
URL: National Affiliate–www.legion.org
Contact: Richard H. Reno Jr., Contact
Local. Affiliated With: American Legion.

9133 ■ Munith Lions Club
c/o Alan Hager, Pres.
416 S Main St.
Munith, MI 49259
Ph: (517)596-2763
E-mail: aljane@ameritech.net
URL: http://www.lionsdistrict11b1.org/lc_munith.htm
Contact: Alan Hager, Pres.
Local. Affiliated With: Lions Clubs International.

Muskegon

9134 ■ ACF West Michigan Lakeshore Chapter
c/o Robb White, Pres.
1903 Marquette Ave.
Muskegon, MI 49442
Ph: (231)777-5321
E-mail: robb.white@baker.edu
URL: National Affiliate–www.acfchefs.org
Contact: Robert J. White CEC, Pres.
Local. Promotes the culinary profession. Provides on-going educational training and networking for members. Provides opportunities for competition, professional recognition and access to educational forums with other culinarians at local, regional, national and international events. **Affiliated With:** American Culinary Federation.

9135 ■ American Chemical Society, Western Michigan Section
c/o Francis Regis Kearney, Chm.
PO Box 448
Muskegon, MI 49443-0448
Ph: (231)727-6405
Fax: (231)727-6452
E-mail: fkearney@escocompany.com
URL: National Affiliate–acswebcontent.acs.org
Contact: Francis Regis Kearney, Chm.
Local. Represents the interests of individuals dedicated to the advancement of chemistry in all its branches. Provides opportunities for peer interaction and career development. **Affiliated With:** American Chemical Society.

9136 ■ American Guild of Organists, Muskegon-Lakeshore (538)
c/o Eileen R. Hoogterp
2929 McCracken Ave.
Muskegon, MI 49441
Ph: (231)755-1953
Fax: (231)759-7074
E-mail: sfnorton@iserv.net
URL: National Affiliate–www.agohq.org
Local. Affiliated With: American Guild of Organists.

9137 ■ American Legion, Merritt Lamb Post 9
2575 Friendship Ln.
PMB 191
Muskegon, MI 49442
Ph: (616)744-6411
Fax: (517)371-2401
URL: National Affiliate–www.legion.org
Local. Affiliated With: American Legion.

9138 ■ American Legion, Michigan Post 185
c/o David O. Kamp
6285 Apple Ave.
Muskegon, MI 49442
Ph: (517)371-4720
Fax: (517)371-2401
URL: National Affiliate–www.legion.org
Contact: David O. Kamp, Contact
Local. Affiliated With: American Legion.

9139 ■ American Red Cross, Muskegon - Oceana Chapter
313 W Webster Ave.
Muskegon, MI 49440
Ph: (231)726-3555
Fax: (231)722-4126
Free: (800)813-8111
E-mail: info@arcmon.org
URL: http://www.arcmon.org
Local.

9140 ■ Arc/Muskegon
1146 E Wesley Ave.
Muskegon, MI 49442-2197
Ph: (231)777-2006
Fax: (231)777-3507
URL: http://www.arcmuskegon.org
Contact: Margaret O'Toole, Exec.Dir.
Founded: 1952. **Members:** 109. **Membership Dues:** individual/family, $25 (annual) • professional, $75 (annual) • Agnes Potuznik Honor Roll, $125 (annual). **Local**. Persons interested in the welfare of people with developmental disabilities. **Affiliated With:** Arc of the United States. **Publications:** *ARC/Muskegon News*, quarterly. Newsletter. **Conventions/Meetings:** monthly board meeting • conference - 2-3/year • annual meeting.

9141 ■ Big Brothers Big Sisters of the Lakeshore
c/o Brian Obits, CEO
1358 Terrace St.
Muskegon, MI 49442
Ph: (231)728-2447
Fax: (231)728-2448
Free: (888)499-BIGS
E-mail: bigs@bbbslakeshore.org
URL: http://www.bbbslakeshore.org
Contact: Brian Obits, CEO
Founded: 1969. **Local**.

9142 ■ Creative Network of West Michigan
530 E Giles Rd.
Muskegon, MI 49445
Free: (866)719-1290
E-mail: orvilles@comcast.net
URL: National Affiliate–www.uiausa.org
Contact: Orville Crain, Contact
Local. Represents inventors' organizations and providers of services to inventors. Seeks to facilitate the development of innovation conceived by independent inventors. Provides leadership and support services to inventors and inventors' organizations. **Affiliated With:** United Inventors Association of the U.S.A.

9143 ■ First Priority of Muskegon
c/o M. James Keck
PO Box 5314
Muskegon, MI 49445-0314
Ph: (231)744-8973 (231)206-1990
E-mail: jimfirstprioritymuskegon@juno.com
URL: http://www.fpoa.org
Contact: Rev. M. James Keck, Dir.
Founded: 2001. **Staff:** 1. **Budget:** $40,000. **Nonmembership**. **Local**. Committed to assisting Christian students in reaching friends at school with the good news of eternal life through Jesus Christ. Helps Christian students establish clubs on school campus so they can become better acquainted, equipped and mobilized for this purpose.

9144 ■ Golden Years Alaskan Malamute Rescue
c/o Shirley E. Thomas
2430 Lorenson
Muskegon, MI 49445-9382
Ph: (231)766-2170
E-mail: shirleye@gte.net
URL: http://www.goldenyearsamr.org
Contact: Shirley Thomas, Pres.
Founded: 2000. **Budget:** $25,000. **Local**. Provides homes for abandoned and homeless Malamutes. Encourages breeding programs and public awareness advocacy for the dogs. **Formerly:** (2004) Golden Years AMR.

9145 ■ Lakeshore Lung Society
c/o Stella Burns, President
1147 3rd St.
Muskegon, MI 49441
Ph: (231)722-2361
Fax: (231)725-2611
E-mail: lungsociety@mail.com

9146 ■ Lakeshore Youth for Christ
PO Box 711
Muskegon, MI 49443-0711
Ph: (231)739-3117
Fax: (231)739-3127
URL: National Affiliate–www.yfc.net
Local. **Affiliated With:** Youth for Christ/U.S.A.

9147 ■ Local 530, RWDSU District Council of the UFCW
526 Brooks Rd.
Muskegon, MI 49442
Ph: (616)924-6280
URL: National Affiliate–www.ufcw.org
Local. **Affiliated With:** United Food and Commercial Workers International Union.

9148 ■ Michigan Health Information Management Association (MHIMA)
c/o Marsha Allen
3311 David Bee St.
Muskegon, MI 49444
Ph: (231)767-9717
Fax: (231)767-2557
E-mail: marsha@mhima.org
URL: http://www.mhima.org
Contact: Marsha Allen RHIA, Office Coor.
Founded: 1929. **Members:** 1,600. **Budget:** $125,000. **State**. Strives to increase the accuracy, use and availability of healthcare information for healthcare professionals, consumers and providers so that the quality of healthcare delivered in Michigan will be improved. **Affiliated With:** American Health Information Management Association. **Publications:** *Focus*. **Conventions/Meetings:** bimonthly board meeting • annual meeting - May.

9149 ■ Michigan Health Information Management Association, Northwest
c/o Mari Dulin, RHIT, Pres.
1733 Jarman St.
Muskegon, MI 49442
Ph: (231)739-9492
E-mail: mari@westshoreurology.com
URL: http://www.mhima.org
Contact: Mari Dulin RHIT, Pres.
Local. Represents the interests of individuals dedicated to the effective management of personal health information needed to deliver quality healthcare to the public. Provides career, professional development and practice resources. Sets standards for education and certification. Advocates public policy that advances Health Information Management (HIM) practice. **Affiliated With:** American Health Information Management Association; Michigan Health Information Management Association.

9150 ■ Muskegon Area Chamber of Commerce (MEGA)
900 Third St., Ste.200
Muskegon, MI 49440
Ph: (231)722-3751
Fax: (231)728-7251
E-mail: macc@muskegon.org
URL: http://www.muskegon.org
Contact: Cindy Larsen, Pres.
Founded: 1989. **Members:** 1,270. **Staff:** 7. **Budget:** $700,000. **Local**. Strives to provide the voice of business, promotes the business community, specifically the members; and to use combined resources to provide high quality benefits at the lowest possible price. **Committees:** Ambassador League; Benefits; Community Development; Golf; Health; White Pine. **Councils:** Entrepreneur Advisory; Manufacturer's Council. **Affiliated With:** U.S. Chamber of Commerce. **Publications:** *Business Directory*, annual • *Industrial Directory*, annual • Newsletter, monthly.

9151 ■ Muskegon Co REACT
PO Box 295
Muskegon, MI 49443
Ph: (231)798-2665
E-mail: jeanhentschel1@aol.com
URL: http://www.reactintl.org/teaminfo/usa_teams/teams-usmi.htm
Local. Trained communication experts and professional volunteers. Provides volunteer public service and emergency communications through the use of radios (Citizen Band, General Mobile Radio Service, UHF and HAM). Coordinates with radio industries and government on safety communication matters and supports charitable activities and community organizations.

9152 ■ Muskegon County Convention and Visitors Bureau
610 W Western Ave.
Muskegon, MI 49440
Ph: (231)724-3100
Fax: (231)724-1398
Free: (800)250-WAVE
E-mail: visitmuskegon@co.muskegon.mi.us
URL: http://www.visitmuskegon.org
Contact: Sam Wendling, Community Development Dir.
Staff: 5. **Local**. Promotes convention business and tourism in the area. **Publications:** *The Waters Edge*, quarterly. Magazine. Provides updates on events, calendars, and other information. **Price:** free. **Advertising:** accepted.

9153 ■ Muskegon County Medical Society
2574 Morton Ave.
Muskegon, MI 49441
Ph: (231)759-9000
Fax: (231)759-9000
E-mail: sgreen1043@aol.com
URL: http://www.msms.org
Contact: Shirley M. Green, Exec.Dir.
Local. Advances the art and science of medicine. Promotes patient care and the betterment of public health. **Affiliated With:** Michigan State Medical Society.

9154 ■ Muskegon District Dental Society
427 Seminole Rd., Ste.209
Muskegon, MI 49444-3747
Ph: (231)733-1105
Fax: (231)733-2841
E-mail: c.verhagen@comcast.net
URL: National Affiliate–www.ada.org
Contact: Dr. Connie M. Verhagen, Exec.Dir.
Local. Represents the interests of dentists committed to the public's oral health, ethics and professional development. Encourages the improvement of the public's oral health and promotes the art and science of dentistry. **Affiliated With:** American Dental Association; Michigan Dental Association.

9155 ■ Muskegon Lakeshore Figure Skating Club
4470 Airline Rd.
Muskegon, MI 49444
Ph: (231)737-5283
Fax: (231)737-5283
E-mail: bpat@i2k.com
URL: http://www.muskegonlakeshorefsc.org
Contact: Paula Beck, Pres.
Local. Provides programs to encourage participation and achievement in the sport of figure skating on ice. Defines and maintains uniform standards of skating proficiency. Organizes and sponsors competitions and exhibitions for the purpose of stimulating interest in figure skating. **Affiliated With:** United States Figure Skating Association.

9156 ■ National Active and Retired Federal Employees Association - Muskegon 309
1040 Green St.
Muskegon, MI 49442-4145
Ph: (231)773-1914
URL: National Affiliate–www.narfe.org
Contact: George Halverson, Contact
Local. Protects the retirement future of employees through education. Informs members on issues affecting the retirement. **Affiliated With:** National Association of Retired Federal Employees.

9157 ■ Police and Firemen's Insurance Association - Muskegon Fire Department
c/o David A. Slagh
6387 Martin Rd.
Muskegon, MI 49444-8715
Ph: (231)206-5445
URL: National Affiliate–www.pfia.net
Contact: David A. Slagh, Contact
Local. **Affiliated With:** Police and Firemen's Insurance Association.

9158 ■ Polish Falcons of America, Nest 276
1014 Hackley Ave.
Muskegon, MI 49441
Ph: (616)755-1451
URL: http://www.polishfalcons.org/nest/276/index.html
Contact: James A. Wentzloff, Pres.
Local. **Affiliated With:** Polish Falcons of America.

9159 ■ Port City Beagle Club
c/o Gene Paulson
5776 Lake Harbor Rd.
Muskegon, MI 49441-5859
URL: National Affiliate–clubs.akc.org
Contact: Gene Paulson, Contact
Local.

9160 ■ SCORE Muskegon
c/o Muskegon Area C of C
900 Third St., Ste.200
Muskegon, MI 49443-1087
Ph: (231)722-3751
Fax: (231)728-7251
E-mail: score@muskegon.org
URL: http://www.score.org
Local. **Affiliated With:** SCORE.

9161 ■ Seaway Gun Club
3400 W Bard Rd.
Muskegon, MI 49445
Ph: (231)766-3428
E-mail: seawaygunclub@aol.com
URL: National Affiliate–www.mynssa.com
Local. **Affiliated With:** National Skeet Shooting Association.

9162 ■ Sons of Norway, Sognefjord Lodge 5-523
c/o Gordon M. Gutowski, Pres.
5130 Davis Rd.
Muskegon, MI 49441-5802
Ph: (231)798-4888
E-mail: gmgutowski@hotmail.com
URL: National Affiliate–www.sofn.com
Contact: Gordon M. Gutowski, Pres.
Local. **Affiliated With:** Sons of Norway.

9163 ■ United States Naval Sea Cadet Corps - West Michigan Division
PO Box 1692
Muskegon, MI 49443
E-mail: jbenchich@hotmail.com
URL: http://dolphin.seacadets.org/US_units/UnitDetails.asp?UnitID=094WMI
Contact: Lt. Kevin D. Buckley, Commanding Officer
Local. Works to instill good citizenship and patriotism in youth. Encourages qualities such as personal neatness, loyalty, obedience, dependability, and responsibility to others. Offers courses in physical fitness and military drill, first aid, water safety, basic seamanship, and naval history and traditions. **Affiliated With:** Naval Sea Cadet Corps.

9164 ■ United Way of Muskegon County
PO Box 207
Muskegon, MI 49443
Ph: (231)722-3134
Fax: (231)722-3137
URL: http://www.uwmusk.org
Contact: Christine Robere, Pres.
Local. **Affiliated With:** United Way of America.

9165 ■ Urban League of Greater Muskegon
c/o Rodney Brown, Pres.
425 Catawaba Ave.
Muskegon, MI 49442-5140
Ph: (231)726-6019
E-mail: rbceoulgm@aol.com
URL: National Affiliate–www.nul.org
Contact: Rodney Brown, Pres.
Local. **Affiliated With:** National Urban League.

9166 ■ Volunteer Muskegon RSVP
c/o Ms. Kerri Roberts, Dir.
880 Jefferson, Ste.A
Muskegon, MI 49440
Ph: (231)722-6600
Fax: (231)722-6611
E-mail: rsvp@volunteermuskegon.org
URL: http://www.seniorcorps.gov
Contact: Ms. Kerri Roberts, Dir.
Local. **Affiliated With:** Retired and Senior Volunteer Program.

9167 ■ West Michigan Artificial Reef Society
c/o Heather Bloom
2516 Glade St.
Muskegon, MI 49444-1318
Ph: (231)733-4200
Local.

9168 ■ West Michigan Shoreline Regional Development Commission (WMSRDC)
316 Morris Ave., Ste.340
PO Box 387
Muskegon, MI 49443-0387
Ph: (231)722-7878
Fax: (231)722-9362
E-mail: wmsrdc@wmsrdc.org
URL: http://www.wmsrdc.org
Contact: Sandeep Dey, Exec.Dir.
Founded: 1970. **Members:** 120. **Staff:** 15. **Budget:** $1,175,068. **Local**. County and local governments of Muskegon, Oceana, Lake Mason, and Newago counties, MI. Works to improve economic, environmental, governmental, housing, and transportation programs through regional cooperation. **Publications:** *Commission Communications*, bimonthly. Newsletter • Annual Report, annual. **Circulation:** 550 • Directory, annual. **Conventions/Meetings:** bimonthly meeting.

9169 ■ Western Michigan Association of Insurance and Financial Advisors
c/o Eugene J. Kendra, Sec.
2124 Carter Dr.
Muskegon, MI 49441-4419
Ph: (231)780-2329
Fax: (231)476-6547
E-mail: genekendra@aol.com
URL: http://naifa-ne.org
Contact: Eugene J. Kendra, Sec.
Founded: 1943. **Members:** 30. **Membership Dues:** $281 (annual). **State Groups:** 1. **Local**.

Muskegon Heights

9170 ■ First Catholic Slovak Ladies Association - Muskegon Heights Senior Branch 445
3033 Hoyt St.
Muskegon Heights, MI 49444
Ph: (231)733-4961
URL: National Affiliate–www.fcsla.com
Local. **Affiliated With:** First Catholic Slovak Ladies Association.

9171 ■ First Catholic Slovak Ladies Association - Muskegon Junior Branch 357
3033 Hoyt St.
Muskegon Heights, MI 49444
Ph: (231)733-4961
URL: National Affiliate–www.fcsla.com
Local. **Affiliated With:** First Catholic Slovak Ladies Association.

9172 ■ National Organization for Women - Muskegon-Ottawa
c/o Rosemary Kowalski
PO Box 4243
Muskegon Heights, MI 49444
Ph: (231)744-6665
E-mail: nowrose@comcast.net
URL: http://www.michnow.org
Contact: Rosemary Kowalski, Contact
Local. **Affiliated With:** National Organization for Women.

Nashville

9173 ■ Michigan National Wild Turkey Federation, Thornapple Valley Chapter
8845 Thornapple Lake Rd.
Nashville, MI 49073
Ph: (517)852-2551
URL: http://www.mi-nwtf.org/Thornapple.htm
Contact: Adamm Brumm, Pres.
Local.

National City

9174 ■ Discover Golf on Michigan's Sunrise Side
1361 Fletcher St.
National City, MI 48748-9666
Ph: (989)469-4544
E-mail: misunriseside@centurytel.net
URL: http://www.misunriseside.com
Contact: Tom Ferguson, Exec.Dir.
Founded: 1989. **Members:** 25. **Staff:** 1. **Budget:** $250,000. **State**. Promotes the sport of golf. **Publications:** Directory, periodic. Lists golf courses for the northeast Lower Peninsula area of Michigan. **Price:** free. **Circulation:** 750,000.

9175 ■ Michigan's Sunrise Side Travel Association
1361 Fletcher St.
National City, MI 48748-9666
Ph: (989)469-4544
Fax: (989)469-4232
E-mail: misunriseside@centurytel.net
URL: http://www.misunriseside.com
Contact: Tom Ferguson, Exec.Dir.
Founded: 1988. **Members:** 325. **Staff:** 3. **Budget:** $225,000. **State**. Promotes convention business and tourism in the northeastern Lower Peninsula area of MI. **Publications:** *Northeast Michigan Vacation Travel Planner*, annual. Magazine. **Price:** free. **Circulation:** 200,000. **Advertising:** accepted. Also Cited As: *Zip or Sy Quest*. **Conventions/Meetings:** annual meeting (exhibits) - always September; Avg. Attendance: 100.

Negaunee

9176 ■ American Association of Critical-Care Nurses, Lake Superior Chapter (AACNLSC)
c/o Janet Penhale, Pres.
323 Cherry St.
Negaunee, MI 49866
Ph: (906)228-3736
Free: (800)809-CARE
URL: http://www.aacn.org
Contact: Janet Penhale, Pres.
Members: 15. **Membership Dues:** national, $78 (annual) • local, $5 (annual). **Local**. Professional critical care nurses united to provide continuing education

for nurses specializing in critical care and develop standards of nursing care of critically ill patients. **Affiliated With:** American Association of Critical-Care Nurses. **Publications:** Newsletter, periodic. **Conventions/Meetings:** bimonthly meeting, informational and educational meetings.

9177 ■ Big Brothers Big Sisters of Marquette County
101 S Pioneer Ave.
Negaunee, MI 49866
Ph: (906)475-7801
Fax: (906)475-7443
URL: http://www.uproc.lib.mi.us/bbbs
Contact: Jayne Letts, Exec.Dir.
Local. Provides programs that enhance the life experiences of children and their families. **Affiliated With:** Big Brothers Big Sisters of America. **Formerly:** (2005) Big Brothers Big Sisters of America of Marquette County.

9178 ■ Marquette County Humane Society
84 Snowfield Rd.
Negaunee, MI 49866
Ph: (906)475-6661
Fax: (906)475-6669
E-mail: infor@upaws.org
URL: http://www.upaws.org
Local.

9179 ■ Vietnam Veterans of America, Chapter 380
173 US 41 E
Negaunee, MI 49866
Ph: (906)475-6435
E-mail: vva380@chartermi.net
URL: http://www.vva380.org
Local. Affiliated With: Vietnam Veterans of America.

New Baltimore

9180 ■ Anchor Bay Chamber of Commerce (ABCC)
35054 23 Mile Rd., Ste.110
New Baltimore, MI 48047
Ph: (586)725-5148
Fax: (586)725-5369
E-mail: info@anchorbaychamber.com
URL: http://www.anchorbaychamber.com
Contact: Lisa Edwards, Exec.Dir.
Founded: 1991. **Members:** 150. **Membership Dues:** $110 (annual). **Staff:** 2. **Local.** Promotes business and community development in Anchor Bay area of MI. **Libraries: Type:** not open to the public. **Subjects:** business topics. **Awards:** Gold Medal Award. **Frequency:** annual. **Type:** recognition. **Recipient:** to a chamber member demonstrating commitment to the community. **Computer Services:** Information services, member's directory. **Committees:** Activities; Ambassadors; Educational and Economic Development; Executives; Finances; Governmental Affairs. **Publications:** *ABCC Newsletter*, monthly. Contains business and member information. **Price:** available to members only. **Advertising:** accepted • *Community Profile and Membership Directory*, annual. **Price:** free. **Circulation:** 40,000. **Advertising:** accepted. **Conventions/Meetings:** monthly Educational Program - workshop, business format • periodic Meet the Candidates - meeting.

9181 ■ Institute of Packaging Professionals, Michigan Chapter
c/o Joseph C. Shippell, Pres.
Anchor Bay Package Corp.
30905 23 Mile Rd.
New Baltimore, MI 48047
Ph: (810)949-4040
Fax: (810)949-9997
E-mail: jshippel@anchorbaypackaging.com
URL: National Affiliate–www.iopp.org
Contact: Joseph C. Shippell, Design Engr.
State. Affiliated With: Institute of Packaging Professionals.

9182 ■ Michigan Industrial Hygiene Society (MIHS)
PO Box 128
New Baltimore, MI 48047
Ph: (313)805-7996
Fax: (313)594-9692
E-mail: info@mihsweb.org
URL: http://www.mihsweb.org
Contact: Sharkey Mingela CIH, Pres.
State. Promotes the study and control of environmental factors affecting the health and well being of workers. Sponsors continuing education courses in industrial hygiene, government affairs, and public relations. Conducts educational and research programs. **Affiliated With:** American Industrial Hygiene Association.

9183 ■ New Baltimore Historical Society (NBHS)
51065 Washington
New Baltimore, MI 48047
Ph: (586)725-4755
E-mail: ejllanne@cs.com
URL: http://www.newbaltimorehistoricalsociety.org
Contact: Richard Gonyeau, Pres.
Founded: 1975. **Members:** 270. **Membership Dues:** family, $15 (annual). **Local Groups:** 1. **Local.** Individuals interested in the history of New Baltimore, MI. Offers workshops for children and adults. Hosts the annual History Fair. Sponsors fundraisers. Maintains Grand Pacific House Museum. **Libraries: Type:** open to the public. **Holdings:** 100. **Subjects:** New Baltimore and Anchor Bay history. **Awards:** Award of Appreciation. **Frequency:** annual. **Type:** recognition. **Recipient:** to a member who exemplifies outstanding service to the society • Award of Merit. **Frequency:** annual. **Type:** recognition. **Recipient:** to a member, organization, or business that promotes/supports local history. **Affiliated With:** Historical Society of Michigan. **Publications:** *New Baltimore Historical Society Newsletter*, bimonthly. **Price:** free. **Circulation:** 240. **Conventions/Meetings:** monthly board meeting - always first Thursday • monthly meeting, with speakers - always third Thursday.

New Boston

9184 ■ Huron Township Chamber of Commerce (HTC of C)
19132 Huron River Dr.
PO Box 247
New Boston, MI 48164
Ph: (734)753-4220
Fax: (734)753-4602
E-mail: township@provide.net
URL: http://www.members.tripod.com/htcc48164
Contact: Teresa Trosin, Exec. Office Sec.-Treas.
Founded: 1983. **Members:** 80. **Membership Dues:** regular (profit company), $125 (annual) • associate (nonprofit individual/company), $75 (annual). **Staff:** 1. **Local.** Strives to bring community and business together. Promotes business and community development within Huron Township, MI. Sponsors annual Chamber Barn Dance, Scholarship Golf Outing (for local H.S.). Participates in the Huron Toys for Tots & Teens program. Holds monthly board meetings. **Libraries: Type:** open to the public. **Awards:** 4/$500.00 Scholarships. **Frequency:** annual. **Type:** scholarship. **Recipient:** for local H.S. seniors that are going on to college. **Computer Services:** Information services, member mailing list, local business info • online services, website. **Telecommunication Services:** information service, member phone/fax listing. **Committees:** Barn Dance; Christmas Decoration Contest; Golf Outing; Historical Days; Huron Toys for Tots & Teens; Scholarships; 25th Anniversary. **Publications:** *Chamber Chips*, monthly. Newsletter. Contains member information. **Circulation:** 80. **Advertising:** accepted • Directory, semiannual. **Conventions/Meetings:** quarterly meeting.

New Buffalo

9185 ■ American Legion, Michigan Post 169
c/o Edward C. Sexton
19139 W US 12
New Buffalo, MI 49117
Ph: (517)371-4720
Fax: (517)371-2401
URL: National Affiliate–www.legion.org
Contact: Edward C. Sexton, Contact
Local. Affiliated With: American Legion.

9186 ■ Harbor Country Chamber of Commerce
530 S Whittaker, Ste.F
New Buffalo, MI 49117
Ph: (269)469-5409
Fax: (269)469-2257
E-mail: info@harborcounty.org
URL: http://www.harborcountry.org
Contact: Karen Gear, Pres.
Founded: 1980. **Members:** 310. **Membership Dues:** general, $180 (annual) • additional business, $90 (annual) • full, $240 (annual) • associate business, $42 (annual) • financial institution, $240 (annual). **Staff:** 3. **Local.** Promotes convention business and tourism in area. **Publications:** *Connection*, monthly. Newsletter. Alternate Formats: online • *Harbor County Guide*, annual. Magazine. Covers eight communities. **Circulation:** 70,000.

New Haven

9187 ■ Air and Waste Management Association - East Michigan Chapter
PO Box 480435
New Haven, MI 48048-0435
Ph: (313)845-1920
URL: http://www.emawma.org
Local. Affiliated With: Air and Waste Management Association.

9188 ■ Great Lakes Rottweiler Club of Southeast Michigan
c/o Richard Lawless, Pres.
57600 Wederman
New Haven, MI 48048
Ph: (586)749-5370
E-mail: touchelowchen@msn.com
URL: http://www.geocities.com/glrottweiler
Contact: Richard Lawless, Pres.
Local.

New Hudson

9189 ■ Pontiac MMBA
382 Grayling
New Hudson, MI 48165
Ph: (248)231-7212
E-mail: pontiaclake@mmba.org
URL: http://www.mmba.org
Local. Affiliated With: International Mountain Bicycling Association.

New Lothrop

9190 ■ New Lothrop Lions Club
c/o Fred Barrigar, Sec.
PO Box 92
New Lothrop, MI 48460-0092
Ph: (810)610-0167 (810)638-3012
E-mail: cen08353@centurytel.net
URL: http://www.district11c2.org
Contact: Fred Barrigar, Sec.
Local. Affiliated With: Lions Clubs International.

New Troy

9191 ■ American Legion, Wee-Chick Post 518
PO Box 89
New Troy, MI 49119
Ph: (517)371-4720
Fax: (517)371-2401
URL: National Affiliate–www.legion.org
Local. Affiliated With: American Legion.

Newaygo

9192 ■ Air Conditioning Contractors of America, West Michigan Chapter
c/o Jan Anderson, Exec.Sec.
9115 E 36th St.
Newaygo, MI 49337
Ph: (231)856-0006
Fax: (231)856-0006
E-mail: wmiacca@triton.net
URL: National Affiliate–www.acca.org
Contact: Jan Anderson, Exec.Sec.
Local. Works to represent contractors involved in installation and service of heating, air conditioning, and refrigeration systems. **Affiliated With:** Air Conditioning Contractors of America.

9193 ■ National Alliance for the Mentally Ill - Newaygo
c/o John Fries
PO Box 323
Newaygo, MI 49337
Ph: (616)942-1287
URL: http://mi.nami.org/ne.html
Contact: John Fries, Contact
Local. Strives to improve the quality of life of children and adults with severe mental illness through support, education, research and advocacy. **Affiliated With:** National Alliance for the Mentally Ill.

9194 ■ Newaygo Lions Club
c/o Steve Barber, Pres.
6101 Barberry Ave.
Newaygo, MI 49337
Ph: (231)652-7488
E-mail: davesue@charter.net
URL: http://lions.silverthorn.biz/11-e1
Contact: Steve Barber, Pres.
Local. Affiliated With: Lions Clubs International.

Newberry

9195 ■ American Legion, Hugh Allen Mc Innes Post 74
1101 S Newberry Ave.
7964 St. Hwy. M 123
Newberry, MI 49868
Ph: (517)371-4720
Fax: (517)371-2401
URL: National Affiliate–www.legion.org
Local. Affiliated With: American Legion.

9196 ■ Eastern Upper Peninsula Search and Rescue
c/o Luce Co. Sheriff Dept.
411 W. Harrie St.
Newberry, MI 49868-1208
Local.

9197 ■ Michigan Association of Timbermen (MAT)
c/o Douglas A. Lee, Exec.Dir.
7350 M-123
Newberry, MI 49868
Fax: (906)293-5444
Free: (800)682-4979
E-mail: timbermn@up.net
URL: http://www.timbermen.org
Contact: Douglas A. Lee, Exec.Dir.
Founded: 1972. **State**.

9198 ■ Newberry Area Chamber of Commerce (NACC)
4947 E County Rd., No. 460
PO Box 308
Newberry, MI 49868
Ph: (906)293-5562
Fax: (906)293-5739
Free: (800)831-7292
E-mail: newberry@sault.com
Contact: Melissa Ronquist, Exec.Dir.
Local. Promotes business and community development in the Newberry, MI area. Sponsors Fourth of July and Christmas activities. **Publications:** Directory, annual • Newsletter, bimonthly.

9199 ■ Newberry Area Tourism Association
PO Box 308
Newberry, MI 49868
Ph: (906)293-5562
Free: (800)831-7292
E-mail: newberry@sault.com
URL: http://www.visitnewberrymi.org
Contact: Sharon Schultz, Exec.Dir.
Local. Promotes convention business and tourism in the area.

9200 ■ Newberry High School Key Club
700 Newberry Ave.
Newberry, MI 49868
Fax: (906)420-3701
E-mail: newberryhighkeyclub@yahoogroups.com
URL: http://www.keyclub.org/club/newberry
Contact: Julia Diem, Pres.
Local.

9201 ■ Trout Unlimited - Two Heart Chapter
c/o James Diem
209 W Truman Blvd.
Newberry, MI 49868
Ph: (906)293-3537
URL: National Affiliate–www.tu.org
Contact: James Diem, Member
Local. Affiliated With: Trout Unlimited.

Niles

9202 ■ American Chemical Society, St. Joseph Valley Section
c/o Matt Guisbert, Chm.
Qa Metallurgical Services
1795 Found. Dr.
Niles, MI 49120-8987
E-mail: guisbert@msu.edu
URL: National Affiliate–acswebcontent.acs.org
Contact: Matt Guisbert, Chm.
Local. Represents the interests of individuals dedicated to the advancement of chemistry in all its branches. Provides opportunities for peer interaction and career development. **Affiliated With:** American Chemical Society.

9203 ■ American Legion, Kalamazoo Post 332
745 Colony Ct., No. 3
Niles, MI 49120
Ph: (517)371-4720
Fax: (517)371-2401
URL: National Affiliate–www.legion.org
Local. Affiliated With: American Legion.

9204 ■ American Legion, Larue Messenger Post 26
1707 Miller Dr.
Niles, MI 49120
Ph: (517)371-4720
Fax: (517)371-2401
URL: National Affiliate–www.legion.org
Local. Affiliated With: American Legion.

9205 ■ Edwardsburg Lions Club
421 Brush Rd.
Niles, MI 49120
E-mail: kdloder1@aol.com
URL: http://milions11b2.org
Local. Affiliated With: Lions Clubs International.

9206 ■ Four Flags Area Chamber of Commerce (FFACC)
321 E Main St.
Niles, MI 49120-0010
Ph: (269)683-3720
Fax: (269)683-3722
E-mail: nileschamber@qtm.net
URL: http://www.nilesmi.com
Contact: Ronald J. Sather, Pres./CEO
Founded: 1927. **Members:** 300. **Staff:** 3. **Budget:** $150,000. **Regional Groups:** 1. **State Groups:** 1. **Local**. Promotes business and community development in the Niles County, MI area. **Awards:** Chamber Scholarship. **Frequency:** annual. **Type:** scholarship. **Recipient:** for selected high school seniors. **Computer Services:** database, membership directory. **Affiliated With:** American Chamber of Commerce Executives; U.S. Chamber of Commerce. **Also Known As:** Niles Society. **Publications:** *Clubs and Civic Organizations*, periodic. Directory • *Manufacturer's Guide*, periodic. Newsletter • *Niles Renaissance*, annual. Annual Report • Membership Directory, annual. **Conventions/Meetings:** periodic meeting.

9207 ■ Four Flags Area Council on Tourism
321 E Main St.
PO Box 1300
Niles, MI 49120
Ph: (269)684-7444
Fax: (269)683-3722
E-mail: info@fourflagsarea.org
URL: http://www.fourflagsarea.org
Contact: Barb Williams, Dir.
Founded: 1982. **Members:** 400. **Membership Dues:** individual, $25 (annual) • non-profit, $50 (annual) • for profit business, $100 (annual). **Staff:** 1. **Regional Groups:** 1. **State Groups:** 1. **Local**. Promotes convention business and tourism for Berrien Springs, Buchanan, Eau Claire, and Niles, MI. **Publications:** *Calendar of Events*, annual. Brochure. Promotes tourism, lists festivals and events in area. **Price:** free • *Fishing the St. Joseph River*. Brochure. Lists places to stay and has map of St. Joseph River. • *Key to Fun Four Flags*. Booklet. An overview of area and attractions. • *Museums and Historic Sites*. Brochure. Lists sites and hours of operation.

9208 ■ Habitat for Humanity of Niles-Buchanan Area
PO Box 305
Niles, MI 49120-0305
Ph: (269)689-1672
E-mail: punkinjoan@aol.com
URL: National Affiliate–www.habitat.org
Contact: Ms. Joan Schmidt, Pres.
Local. Builds decent, affordable houses for people in need. **Affiliated With:** Habitat for Humanity International.

9209 ■ Michiana Figure Skating Club (MFSC)
233 Carter Ave.
Niles, MI 49120
E-mail: mfsc792@cs.com
URL: http://www.michianafsc.org
Contact: Sharon Rajski, Contact
Local. Provides programs to encourage participation and achievement in the sport of figure skating on ice. Defines and maintains uniform standards of skating proficiency. Organizes and sponsors competitions and exhibitions for the purpose of stimulating interest in figure skating. **Affiliated With:** United States Figure Skating Association.

9210 ■ Michigan National Wild Turkey Federation, Dowagiac River Chapter
2256 Bell Rd.
Niles, MI 49120
Ph: (616)684-6227
URL: http://www.mi-nwtf.org/Dowagiac.htm
Contact: Richard Krassow, Pres.
Local.

9211 ■ National Association of Miniature Enthusiasts - Quality Dreamers
c/o Colleen Chute
751 Oak St.
Niles, MI 49120
Ph: (269)683-4766
URL: http://www.miniatures.org/states/MI.html
Contact: Colleen Chute, Contact
Local. Affiliated With: National Association of Miniature Enthusiasts.

9212 ■ Niles Lions Club - Michigan
PO Box 223
Niles, MI 49120
E-mail: morriesmanor@aol.com
URL: http://milions11b2.org
Local. Affiliated With: Lions Clubs International.

9213 ■ United Way of Greater Niles
210 E Main St.
Niles, MI 49120
Ph: (269)683-1011
E-mail: john.stauffer@unitedway.org
URL: http://www.unitedwayniles.com
Contact: John Stauffer, Exec.Dir.
Local. Affiliated With: United Way of America.

North Adams

9214 ■ North Adams Lions Club
c/o George Cook, Pres.
445 W Main St.
North Adams, MI 49262-9753
Ph: (517)287-5769
URL: http://www.lionsdistrict11b1.org/lc_north_adams.htm
Contact: George Cook, Pres.
Local. Affiliated With: Lions Clubs International.

North Branch

9215 ■ American Legion, North Branch Post 457
PO Box 159
North Branch, MI 48461
Ph: (517)371-4720
Fax: (517)371-2401
URL: National Affiliate–www.legion.org
Local. Affiliated With: American Legion.

North Muskegon

9216 ■ Tasters Guild International - Michigan Lakeshore, Chapter No. 057
1709 Ruddiman Dr.
North Muskegon, MI 49445
Ph: (231)744-3013
URL: National Affiliate–www.tastersguild.com
Contact: Ruth Long, Contact
Local. Aims to educate consumers and spread the word of responsible wine and food consumption. Provides opportunity to encounter the best in wine and culinary delights. **Affiliated With:** Tasters Guild International.

9217 ■ Trout Unlimited - Muskegon White River Chapter
c/o Pete Blackburn
1817 Ruddiman Ave.
North Muskegon, MI 49445
Ph: (231)865-6335
E-mail: psblackbrn@aol.com
URL: http://www.tu.org
Contact: Pete Blackburn, Contact
Local.

Northport

9218 ■ Northport Lions Club
Box 550
Northport, MI 49670
Ph: (231)386-7746
E-mail: a_mops_520@chartermi.net
URL: http://lions.silverthorn.biz/11-e1
Contact: Dorothy Young, Pres.
Local. Affiliated With: Lions Clubs International.

9219 ■ Sons of Norway, Christian Radich Lodge 5-568
c/o Suzanne E. Wollenweber, Sec.
9332 N Manitou Trail
Northport, MI 49670-9407
Ph: (231)386-5443
E-mail: wollenwebers@hotmail.com
URL: National Affiliate–www.sofn.com
Contact: Suzanne E. Wollenweber, Sec.
Local. Affiliated With: Sons of Norway.

Northville

9220 ■ American Legion, Michigan Post 147
c/o Lloyd H. Green
100 W Dunlap St.
Northville, MI 48167
Ph: (517)371-4720
Fax: (517)371-2401
URL: National Affiliate–www.legion.org
Contact: Lloyd H. Green, Contact
Local. Affiliated With: American Legion.

9221 ■ American Legion, Michigan Post 343
c/o Gen. George Pomutz
39480 Edgewater Dr.
Northville, MI 48167
Ph: (517)371-4720
Fax: (517)371-2401
URL: National Affiliate–www.legion.org
Contact: Gen. George Pomutz, Contact
Local. Affiliated With: American Legion.

9222 ■ American Vaulting Association - Sunshine Vaulters
c/o Loretta Scheel, Coach
9807 Currie Rd.
Northville, MI 48167
Ph: (248)348-5041
E-mail: sunshinefarm@charter.net
URL: National Affiliate–www.americanvaulting.org
Contact: Loretta Scheel, Coach
Local. Affiliated With: American Vaulting Association.

9223 ■ Ancient Order of Hibernians of Wayne County - Patrick Ryan Division
c/o Tim Higgins
PO Box 29
Northville, MI 48167
Ph: (248)449-6570
E-mail: irishtim80@aol.com
URL: http://www.michiganaoh.com
Contact: Tim Higgins, Contact
Local. Affiliated With: Ancient Order of Hibernians in America.

9224 ■ Ann Arbor Model Yacht Club No. 138
c/o Russ Bergendahl
7841 Oak Knoll
Northville, MI 48168
Ph: (248)486-9676
URL: http://www.amya.org
Contact: Russ Bergendahl, Contact
Local.

9225 ■ Michigan Towing Association (MTA)
PO Box 220
Northville, MI 48167-0220
Ph: (248)348-4433
Fax: (248)348-7364
E-mail: jasoffice@jeromeaustin.com
URL: http://www.michtow.org
Contact: David E. Jerome, Exec.Sec.
Founded: 1941. **Members:** 150. **Membership Dues:** regular, $200 (annual). **State.** Towing companies; distributors and service companies related to the towing industry. Seeks to upgrade and promote the industry through education and legislative reform. Sponsors annual towing rodeo. **Awards:** William Dendinger Driver of the Year. **Frequency:** annual. **Type:** recognition. **Recipient:** for driving competition. **Publications:** Newsletter, monthly. **Conventions/Meetings:** monthly meeting - every 2nd Wednesday • annual meeting, rodeo (exhibits) - August.

9226 ■ Northville Chamber of Commerce
195 S Main St.
Northville, MI 48167
Ph: (248)349-7640
Fax: (248)349-8730
E-mail: chamber@northville.org
URL: http://www.northville.org
Contact: Jody Humphries, Pres.
Founded: 1964. **Members:** 320. **Membership Dues:** business (varies with the number of employees), $225-$575 (annual) • non-business, $150 (annual) • individual, $100 (annual). **Staff:** 5. **Budget:** $140,000. **Local.** Promotes business and community development in the Northville, MI area. **Computer Services:** Mailing lists, of members. **Publications:** Newsletter, monthly. **Conventions/Meetings:** annual Art in the Sun - show (exhibits) - weekend of June 19th and 20th.

9227 ■ Northville Historical Society (NHS)
PO Box 71
Northville, MI 48167-0071
Ph: (248)348-1845
Fax: (248)348-0056
URL: http://northville.lib.mi.us/community/groups/history
Contact: Juliet Culp, Office Mgr.
Founded: 1964. **Members:** 300. **Membership Dues:** individual, $15 (annual) • family, $20 (annual) • senior, $10 (annual). **Staff:** 2. **State Groups:** 1. **Local Groups:** 1. **Local.** Individuals interested in local history. Administers Mill Race Historical Village, which consists of a church, gazebo, school, general store, wooden bridge, blacksmith shop, and several homes built prior to 1900. Sponsors classes and family events. **Libraries: Type:** open to the public. **Holdings:** 5,000; archival material. **Subjects:** Northville community history, local businesses and families. **Committees:** Archives; Finance; Stone Gang (Maintenance); Tivoli Fair; Victorian Festival. **Publications:** *Mill Race Quarterly*. Newsletter. Includes articles on community history and organizational news. **Price:** included in membership dues. ISSN: 0894-7341. **Circulation:** 300. **Advertising:** accepted.

9228 ■ Northville Lions Club
c/o Phyllis Heckemeyer, Pres.
630 Potomac St.
Northville, MI 48167
Ph: (248)349-0282
E-mail: heckemeyer@comcast.net
URL: http://www.metrodetroitlions.org
Contact: Phyllis Heckemeyer, Pres.
Local. Affiliated With: Lions Clubs International.

9229 ■ South Eastern Michigan Bromeliad Society
c/o Penrith B. Goff, Pres.
20051 Caldwell St.
Northville, MI 48167-1331
Ph: (248)380-7359
E-mail: pgoff@wideopenwest.com
Contact: Penrith Goff, Pres.
Local. Affiliated With: Bromeliad Society International.

Norway

9230 ■ American Legion, Hall-Dewinter Post 145
PO Box 61
Norway, MI 49870
Ph: (517)371-4720
Fax: (517)371-2401
URL: National Affiliate–www.legion.org
Local. Affiliated With: American Legion.

Novi

9231 ■ American Legion, Novi Post 19
PO Box 259
Novi, MI 48376
Ph: (517)371-4720
Fax: (517)371-2401
URL: National Affiliate–www.legion.org
Local. Affiliated With: American Legion.

9232 ■ ArtBridge
c/o Steven D. Myers, Pres.
PO Box 1244
Novi, MI 48376-1244
Fax: (248)344-0092
E-mail: inquiries@artbridge.org
URL: http://www.artbridge.org
Contact: Steven D. Myers, Pres.
Founded: 2001. **Staff:** 4. **Languages:** English, Japanese. **Nonmembership. Regional.**

9233 ■ Crossroads Donkey Rescue
c/o Sharon Windsor
40445 14 Mile Rd.
Novi, MI 48377
Ph: (248)669-1971
E-mail: donkeygirl13@hotmail.com
URL: http://www.donkeyrescue.org/crossroads
Contact: Sharon Windsor, Contact
Local.

9234 ■ Eastern Michigan Mortgage Lenders Association (EMMLA)
AIG United Guaranty
39500 Orchard Hill Pl. Dr., Ste.310
Novi, MI 48375
Ph: (586)457-3619
Fax: (248)344-0126
E-mail: karen.bondar@ugcorp.com
URL: http://www.mmla.net/emmla.htm
Contact: Karen Bondar, Chair
Local. Promotes fair and ethical lending practices and fosters professional excellence among real estate finance employees. Seeks to create an environment that enables members to invest in communities and achieve their business objectives. **Affiliated With:** Mortgage Bankers Association.

9235 ■ Essex County Stamp Club
c/o Joan Seeley
22513 Cranbrooke Dr.
Novi, MI 48375
E-mail: lacumo@cogeco.ca
URL: http://ec-sc.tripod.com
Contact: Joan Seeley, Contact
Local. Affiliated With: American Philatelic Society.

9236 ■ Friends of Novi Parks
c/o LuAnne Kozma, Sec.
PO Box 123
Novi, MI 48376-0123
E-mail: info@friendsofnoviparks.org
URL: http://www.friendsofnoviparks.org
Contact: Bob Shaw, Pres.
Local.

9237 ■ MBCA - International Stars Section
c/o Michael Salemi, Pres
21129 Chase Dr.
Novi, MI 48375
Ph: (248)380-6332
E-mail: mdsalemi@covad.net
URL: http://www.internationalstars.org
Contact: Michael Salemi, Pres.
Local. Affiliated With: Mercedes-Benz Club of America.

9238 ■ Michigan Chess Association
c/o Tim Sawmiller
43422 W Oaks Dr.
PMB 296
Novi, MI 48377
Ph: (248)344-4269
Free: (888)MIC-HESS
E-mail: tsawmiller@mailcity.com
URL: http://www.michess.org
Contact: Tim Sawmiller, Membership Sec.
Founded: 1931. **Members:** 1,500. **Membership Dues:** adult, $20 (annual) • junior, $10 (annual) • senior, $10 (annual). **Budget:** $25,000. **State Groups:** 1. **State.** Promotes interest and enjoyment in chess through educational programs, tournaments, matches, and other activities. **Awards:** Hall of Fame Membership. **Frequency:** biennial. **Type:** recognition. **Affiliated With:** United States Chess Federation. **Publications:** *Michigan Chess*, bimonthly. Magazine. Contains news and articles on chess. **Price:** $3.00. **Circulation:** 1,100. **Advertising:** accepted. Alternate Formats: CD-ROM. **Conventions/Meetings:** annual meeting, in conjunction with the Michigan Open - Labor Day weekend.

9239 ■ Michigan Milk Producers Association (MMPA)
PO Box 8002
Novi, MI 48376-8002
Ph: (248)474-6672
Fax: (248)474-0924
E-mail: kirkpatrick@mimilk.com
URL: http://www.mimilk.com
Contact: Elwood Kirkpatrick, Pres.
Founded: 1916. **State.**

9240 ■ Michigan Translators/Interpreters Network (MITIN)
c/o Kenneth Widd, Pres.
PO Box 852
Novi, MI 48376-0852
Ph: (586)778-7304
Fax: (248)344-0092
E-mail: info@mitinweb.org
URL: http://www.mitinweb.org
Contact: Kenneth Widd, Pres.
Founded: 1995. **State. Affiliated With:** American Translators Association. **Publications:** Newsletter, monthly. Alternate Formats: online.

9241 ■ Novi Chamber of Commerce (NCC)
47601 Grand River Ave., Ste.A 208
Novi, MI 48374
Ph: (248)349-3743
Fax: (248)349-4523
E-mail: info@novichamber.com
URL: http://www.novichamber.com
Contact: Nora Champion, Pres.
Founded: 1960. **Members:** 400. **Membership Dues:** business (depends on the number of employees), $195-$235 (annual) • charitable, $95 (annual). **Staff:** 2. **Budget:** $200,000. **Local.** Businesses, organizations, and individuals interested in promoting business and community development in Novi, MI. Sponsors 50's Festival in July and Art festival in August. **Computer Services:** Mailing lists, of members. **Committees:** Novi Convention and Visitors Bureau. **Affiliated With:** U.S. Chamber of Commerce. **Publications:** *Member Business & Community Directory*, annual. Includes member business listing. **Price:** $5.00. **Circulation:** 13,000. **Advertising:** accepted • *Novi Chamber of Commerce Newsletter*, monthly. **Conventions/Meetings:** monthly meeting, with luncheon - 3rd Tuesday at Noon.

9242 ■ Novi High School Skating Club
21022 Chase Dr.
Novi, MI 48375
E-mail: nharbin@msn.com
URL: National Affiliate–www.usfigureskating.org
Contact: Nancy Harbin, Contact
Local. Provides programs to encourage participation and achievement in the sport of figure skating on ice. Defines and maintains uniform standards of skating proficiency. Organizes and sponsors competitions and exhibitions for the purpose of stimulating interest in figure skating. **Affiliated With:** United States Figure Skating Association.

9243 ■ Oakland County Kennel Club
c/o Dr. Barry Wyerman, Corresponding Sec.
45895 Willingham Dr.
Novi, MI 48374-3665
E-mail: wyerbr@aol.com
URL: National Affiliate–www.akc.org
Contact: Dr. Barry Wyerman, Corresponding Sec.
Founded: 1934. **Local. Affiliated With:** American Kennel Club.

9244 ■ Paralyzed Veterans of America, Michigan Chapter
40550 Grand River Ave.
Novi, MI 48375
Ph: (248)476-9000
Fax: (248)476-9545
Free: (800)638-MPVA
E-mail: chapterhq@michiganpva.org
URL: http://www.comnet.org/mpva
Contact: Maurice Jordan, Exec.Dir.
Founded: 1961. **Members:** 600. **Staff:** 7. **Budget:** $500,000. **State.** Veterans who have incurred an injury or disease affecting the spinal cord and causing paralysis. **Affiliated With:** Paralyzed Veterans of America.

9245 ■ Teens Aiding the Cancer Community (TACC)
PO Box 360
Novi, MI 48376-0360
Ph: (248)344-1494
E-mail: tacc@taccinc.org
URL: http://www.taccinc.org
Contact: Bryan Hornacek, Pres.
Founded: 2001. **Members:** 80. **Staff:** 8. **Budget:** $15,000. **Regional Groups:** 2. **State Groups:** 1. **Local Groups:** 1. **State.** Assembles and delivers toy-filled backpacks for children affected by cancer. Backpacks are also delivered to Michigan medical centers, focus groups, cancer camps, and children's homes.

9246 ■ WyldLife Northville
41160 W Ten Mile Rd.
Novi, MI 48375-3470
Ph: (248)888-0166
URL: http://sites.younglife.org/sites/wyldlifenorthville/default.aspx
Local. Affiliated With: Young Life.

9247 ■ WyldLife Novi
41160 W Ten Mile Rd.
Novi, MI 48375-3470
Ph: (248)888-0166
URL: http://sites.younglife.org/sites/wyldlifenovi/default.aspx
Local. Affiliated With: Young Life.

9248 ■ Wyldlife South Lyon
41160 W Ten Mile Rd.
Novi, MI 48375-3470
Ph: (248)888-0166
URL: http://sites.younglife.org/sites/wyldlifesouthlyon/default.aspx
Local. Affiliated With: Young Life.

9249 ■ WyldLife Walled Lake
41160 W Ten Mile Rd.
Novi, MI 48375-3470
Ph: (248)888-0166
URL: http://sites.younglife.org/sites/wyldlifewalledlake/default.aspx
Local. Affiliated With: Young Life.

9250 ■ Young Life Northville
41160 W 10 Mile Rd.
Novi, MI 48375-3470
Ph: (248)888-0166
URL: http://sites.younglife.org/sites/northville/default.aspx
Local. Affiliated With: Young Life.

9251 ■ Young Life Novi
41160 W 10 Mile Rd.
Novi, MI 48375-3470
Ph: (248)888-0166
URL: http://sites.younglife.org/sites/novi/default.aspx
Local. Affiliated With: Young Life.

9252 ■ Young Life NW Suburban Detroit
41160 W 10 Mile Rd.
Novi, MI 48375-3470
Ph: (248)888-0166
Fax: (248)888-0177
E-mail: dave@nwsub.younglife.org
URL: http://sites.younglife.org/sites/nwsub/default.aspx
Contact: Dave Koone, Area Dir.
Local. Affiliated With: Young Life.

9253 ■ Young Life South Lyon
41160 W 10 Mile Rd.
Novi, MI 48375-3470
Ph: (248)888-0166
URL: http://sites.younglife.org/sites/southlyon/default.aspx
Local. Affiliated With: Young Life.

9254 ■ Young Life Walled Lake
41160 W 10 Mile Rd.
Novi, MI 48375-3470
Ph: (248)888-0166
URL: http://sites.younglife.org/sites/walledlake/default.aspx
Local. Affiliated With: Young Life.

Oak Park

9255 ■ American Lung Association of Michigan (ALAM)
25900 Greenfield Rd., Ste.401
Oak Park, MI 48237
Ph: (248)784-2000
Fax: (248)784-2008
Free: (800)543-5864
E-mail: alam@alam.org
URL: http://alam.org
Contact: Rose Adams, CEO
Founded: 1904. **Budget:** $5,300,000. **State**. Works to prevent lung disease. Promotes lung health through education, advocacy and research. **Affiliated With:** American Lung Association. **Publications:** *Advocate*, quarterly. Newsletter • *Inside ALAM*, monthly. Newsletter • *Pathways*, 3/year. Newsletter. **Conventions/Meetings:** board meeting - 3/year • executive committee meeting - 4-5/year.

9256 ■ Association of Energy Engineers, Michigan/East Michigan
c/o Keith Willis
23409 Oneida
Oak Park, MI 48237-2241
Ph: (734)523-0224
Fax: (734)523-0569
E-mail: doctorwillis@aol.com
URL: National Affiliate–www.aeecenter.org
Contact: Keith Willis, Pres.
Local. Affiliated With: Association of Energy Engineers.

9257 ■ Gray Panthers, Metro Detroit
c/o Randy Block
PO Box 37033
Oak Park, MI 48237
Ph: (248)549-5170 (248)669-6343
E-mail: beelock47@comcast.net
URL: National Affiliate–www.graypanthers.org
Contact: Randy Block, Contact
Membership Dues: individual, $20 (annual) • family, $35 (annual) • organization, $50 (annual). **Local**. Works on issues which affect people of all ages: universal health care, peace, strengthening Social Security and Medicare, challenging discrimination, education reform, economic justice, fair labor practices and campaign finance reform. **Affiliated With:** Gray Panthers.

9258 ■ Michigan Equipment Distributors
c/o Todd A. Moilanen, Pres.
Cloverdale Equip. Co.
13133 Cloverdale
Oak Park, MI 48237-3272
Ph: (248)399-6600
Fax: (248)399-7730
URL: National Affiliate–www.aednet.org
Contact: Todd A. Moilanen, Pres.
State. Represents the interests of companies that sell, rent and service equipment used in construction, mining, forestry, power generation and industrial applications. Helps members enhance their success through networking, industry knowledge and education. **Affiliated With:** Associated Equipment Distributors.

9259 ■ National Active and Retired Federal Employees Association - Livonia Area 1163
23111 Avon
Oak Park, MI 48237-2457
Ph: (248)968-7497
URL: National Affiliate–www.narfe.org
Contact: Marvin L. Green, Contact
Local. Protects the retirement future of employees through education. Informs members on issues affecting the retirement. **Affiliated With:** National Association of Retired Federal Employees.

9260 ■ Southeastern Michigan Society of Health-System Pharmacists (SMSHP)
c/o Ken Gaynor
14670 Labelle
Oak Park, MI 48237
Ph: (313)745-5272
E-mail: kgaynor@dmc.org
URL: http://www.smshp.org
Contact: Dave Ruta RPh, Pres.
Local. Advances and supports the professional practice of pharmacists in hospitals and health systems. Serves as the collective voice on issues related to medication use and public health. **Affiliated With:** American Society of Health System Pharmacists.

Oakland

9261 ■ American Truck Historical Society, Motor City Chapter
c/o John Papsdorf
222 Letts Rd.
Oakland, MI 48363
Ph: (586)752-7514
URL: National Affiliate–www.aths.org
Contact: John Papsdorf, Contact
Local.

Okemos

9262 ■ American Sewing Guild, Lansing Chapter
c/o Beverly Pollok
4541 Hawthorne
Okemos, MI 48864-1916
Ph: (517)337-7707
E-mail: sew4fun234@aol.com
URL: http://www.geocities.com/lansingclippers
Contact: Beverly Pollok, Contact
Local. Affiliated With: American Sewing Guild.

9263 ■ American Society of Interior Designers, Ohio North Chapter
Administrative Off.
1950 Penobscot Dr.
Okemos, MI 48864-2732
Fax: (877)214-5632
Free: (877)214-2743
E-mail: asidohn@comcast.net
URL: http://www.asidohnchapter.org
Contact: Lisa Eldridge ASID, Pres.
Local. Represents practicing professional interior designers, students and industry partners. Strives to advance the interior design profession. Aims to demonstrate and celebrate the power of design to positively change people's lives. **Affiliated With:** American Society of Interior Designers.

9264 ■ Associated Underground Contractors-West Michigan Region (AUC)
c/o Robert A. Patzer, Exec.Dir.
PO Box 1640
Okemos, MI 48805-1640
Ph: (517)347-8336
Fax: (517)347-8344
Free: (800)878-2821
E-mail: patzer.bob@aucmi.org
URL: http://www.aucmi.org
State.

9265 ■ Association for Accounting Administration, Michigan Chapter
c/o Robin Cook, Pres.
2121 Univ. Park, Ste.150
Okemos, MI 48864
Ph: (517)347-5000
Fax: (517)347-5007
E-mail: cookr@mcco-cpa.com
URL: National Affiliate–www.cpaadmin.org
Contact: Robin Cook, Pres.
State. Fosters the professional skills needed as firm administrators. Promotes accounting administration profession. Provides education to enhance the professional and personal competencies of accounting administration. **Affiliated With:** Association for Accounting Administration.

9266 ■ Connecting Business Men to Christ - Mid Michigan
4708 Okemos Rd., Ste.2
Okemos, MI 48864
Ph: (517)321-4523
Fax: (517)321-4363
E-mail: mwinter@cbmc.com
URL: http://www.lansing.cbmc.com
Contact: Mike Winter, Dir.
Local.

9267 ■ Dairy Council of Michigan
c/o United Dairy Industry of Michigan
2163 Jolly Rd.
Okemos, MI 48864-3961
Ph: (517)349-8923
Fax: (517)349-6218
Free: (800)241-MILK
E-mail: udim@udim.org
URL: http://www.udim.org
Contact: Nick Bellows, Contact
State.

9268 ■ East Lansing-Meridian Lions Club
c/o Ray Kley, Pres.
4162 Mariner Ln.
Okemos, MI 48864
Ph: (517)347-1112
E-mail: ray_kley@hotmail.com
URL: http://www.district11c2.org
Contact: Ray Kley, Pres.
Local. Affiliated With: Lions Clubs International.

9269 ■ Greater Lansing Orchid Society (GLOS)
c/o Marilyn J. Lee, Membership Chair, AOS Rep.
3926 E Sunwind Dr.
Okemos, MI 48864
Ph: (517)351-0915 (517)484-3406
E-mail: lee@msu.edu
URL: http://homepage.mac.com/dotbarnett/glos/index.html
Contact: Marilyn J. Lee, Membership Chair, AOS Rep.
Founded: 1977. **Members:** 125. **Membership Dues:** regular/individual ($4 for individual in same household), $8 (annual) • life, $80. **Budget:** $5,000. **Local**. Hobbyists, professional growers, botanists, and others interested in extending the growing knowledge, use, and appreciation of orchids. Holds regular meetings with programs. Sponsors annual orchid show

and post show lectures. **Awards: Frequency:** annual. **Type:** recognition. **Recipient:** for service • **Frequency:** annual. **Type:** trophy. **Recipient:** to exhibitors. **Affiliated With:** American Orchid Society; Mid-America Orchid Congress. **Publications:** *Calypso*. Newsletter. Includes announcements, events, meetings, committee reports, articles of interest, minutes of meetings, and mid-America orchid congress news. **Price:** included in membership dues. **Circulation:** 125. **Advertising:** accepted.

9270 ■ Metro Detroit Amateur Softball Association (MDASA)
c/o Michigan Recreation and Park Association
2465 Woodlake Cir., Ste.180
Okemos, MI 48864-6008
Ph: (517)485-9888 (248)981-5655
Fax: (517)485-7932
E-mail: tim@etdred.com
URL: http://www.metrodetroitasa.com
Contact: Tim Doyle, Commissioner
Local. Promotes amateur softball for all persons regardless of age, sex, race, religion, national origin or ancestry. **Affiliated With:** Amateur Softball Association of America.

9271 ■ Michigan Academy of Family Physicians (MAFP)
c/o Janice Klos, CAE, CEO
2164 Commons Pkwy.
Okemos, MI 48864
Ph: (517)347-0098
Fax: (517)347-1289
Free: (800)833-5151
E-mail: info@mafp.com
URL: http://www.mafp.com
Contact: Janice Klos CAE, CEO
State. Acts as an advocate for patients; provides continuing medical education to members; monitors and responds to legislative issues impacting patients and the specialty of family practice. Serves to promote the specialty of family practice to medical students as a viable career choice and to the general public. **Publications:** *Michigan Family Practice*. **Conventions/Meetings:** annual meeting.

9272 ■ Michigan Association of Chiefs of Police (MACP)
2133 Univ. Park Dr., Ste.200
Okemos, MI 48864-3975
Ph: (517)349-9420
Fax: (517)349-5823
E-mail: info@michiganpolicechiefs.org
URL: http://www.michiganpolicechiefs.org
Contact: Thomas A. Hendrickson, Exec.Dir.
Founded: 1924. **Members:** 1,000. **Membership Dues:** associate, active voting, $100 (annual) • active, $85 (annual) • retired, unemployed, $35 (annual) • sustaining, $500 (annual). **Staff:** 2. **Budget:** $200,000. **State.** Professional association of law enforcement executives. Sponsors training program. **Awards:** Community Policing. **Frequency:** annual. **Type:** recognition • Officer Awards. **Frequency:** annual. **Type:** recognition • Traffic Safety. **Frequency:** annual. **Type:** recognition • Youth Scholarship. **Frequency:** annual. **Type:** scholarship. **Affiliated With:** International Association of Chiefs of Police. **Publications:** *Michigan Police Chiefs Newsletter*, monthly. **Circulation:** 1,300. **Conventions/Meetings:** conference (exhibits) - 3-6/year.

9273 ■ Michigan Association of Recreational Vehicles and Campgrounds (MARVAC)
2222 Assn. Dr.
Okemos, MI 48864-5978
Ph: (517)349-8881
Fax: (517)349-3543
E-mail: marvac@marvac.org
URL: http://www.marvac.org
Contact: Timothy J. DeWitt CAE, Exec.Dir.
Founded: 1941. **Members:** 295. **Membership Dues:** campground, $175-$265 (annual) • dealer (with additional fee for each additional location), $265 (annual) • honorary, $65 (annual) • lender, special service, $360 (annual) • manufacturer, $310 (annual) • servicer, supplier (with additional fee for each additional location), $250 (annual). **Staff:** 8. **State.** Manufacturers, retailers, insurance companies, campgrounds, financial personnel, brokers/appraisers, accountants, engineers, consultants, architectural services, campground developers, legal counsel, suppliers, and servicers involved in the recreational vehicle and campground industries. **Publications:** *Communicator*, monthly. Newsletter. **Price:** included in membership dues • *Marvac's RV and Campsite Directory*, annual. **Price:** included in membership dues. **Conventions/Meetings:** annual meeting - always September in Frankenmuth, MI.

9274 ■ Michigan Beef Industry Commission (MBIC)
c/o Kathleen Hawkins, Exec.Dir.
2145 Univ. Park Dr., Ste.300
Okemos, MI 48864
Ph: (517)347-0911
Fax: (517)347-0919
E-mail: mibeef@aol.com
URL: http://www.mibeef.org
Contact: Kathleen Hawkins, Exec.Dir.
Founded: 1972. **State.**

9275 ■ Michigan Coalition Against Domestic and Sexual Violence (MCADSV)
3893 Okemos Rd., No. B-2
Okemos, MI 48864
Ph: (517)347-7000 (517)381-8470
Fax: (517)347-1377
E-mail: general@mcadsv.org
URL: http://www.mcadsv.org
Contact: Mary Keefe, Exec.Dir.
Founded: 1978. **Members:** 70. **State.** Represents the interests of agencies, business, and individuals dedicated to the empowerment of all the state's survivors of domestic and sexual violence. Seeks to develop and promote efforts aimed at the elimination of all domestic and sexual violence in MI. Provides leadership, analysis, and advocacy in the legislative and public policy arena on all of the emerging policy issues relevant to survivors of domestic and sexual violence and the programs which serve them, both at the state and national level. Provides training and technical assistance opportunities through consultations, conferences, and regional meetings. **Publications:** *The Coalition Connection*, monthly. Newsletter • *MCADSV Review*, semiannual. Newsletter • *Public Policy Update*, semiannual. Newsletter. **Conventions/Meetings:** annual conference • annual New Executive Director Training - meeting • quarterly New Service Provider Training - workshop • periodic Training Session to Domestic and Sexual Violence Service Providers - workshop - throughout the year.

9276 ■ Michigan Concrete Paving Association
2111 Univ. Park Dr., Ste.550
Okemos, MI 48864
Ph: (517)347-7720
Fax: (517)347-7740
Free: (877)517-6272
URL: http://www.durableroads.com
Contact: Robert J. Risser Jr., Exec.Dir.
Founded: 1967. **Members:** 51. **Membership Dues:** contractor, $1,000 (annual) • associated company, $600-$700 (annual). **Staff:** 2. **Budget:** $950,000. **State.** Represents the concrete paving industry. Works to promote the use of concrete paving for roads, streets, airfields, and other public improvements. **Libraries: Type:** reference; not open to the public. **Subjects:** concrete pavement. **Awards:** Concrete Paving Awards. **Frequency:** annual. **Type:** recognition. **Recipient:** for job done in previous construction season. **Affiliated With:** American Concrete Pavement Association. **Publications:** *Concrete Solutions*, quarterly. Newsletter. Contains industry information. **Price:** free. **Circulation:** 2,700. **Conventions/Meetings:** annual workshop, with sessions on concrete pavement topics (exhibits) - every February or March.

9277 ■ Michigan Dental Hygienists' Association
c/o Karlene Belyea
2310 Jolly Oaks Rd.
Okemos, MI 48864
Ph: (517)381-8557
Fax: (517)549-5818
URL: National Affiliate–www.adha.org
Founded: 1923. **Members:** 1,300. **Staff:** 2. **Budget:** $150,000. **Local Groups:** 19. **State.** Registered dental hygienists organized to provide professional education and communication. **Affiliated With:** American Dental Hygienists' Association. **Publications:** *The Advisor*, annual. Newsletter • *The Bulletin of MDHA*, 3/year. Journal. Professional journal of MI dental hygienists. **Conventions/Meetings:** annual Scientific Session - conference - always spring; Avg. Attendance: 400.

9278 ■ Michigan Funeral Directors Association (MFDA)
c/o Phil Douma, Exec.Dir.
2420 Sci. Pkwy.
Okemos, MI 48864
Ph: (517)349-9565
Fax: (517)349-9819
E-mail: pdouma@mfda.org
URL: http://mfda.org
Contact: Phil Douma, Exec.Dir.
State.

9279 ■ Michigan Harness Horsemen's Association (MHHA)
c/o Nancy Corrion, Gen.Mgr.
PO Box 349
Okemos, MI 48805
Ph: (517)349-2920
Fax: (517)349-4983
Free: (888)898-6442
E-mail: nancycorrion@mhha-online.com
URL: http://www.ambersystems.com/mhha
Contact: Nancy Corrion, Gen.Mgr.
Founded: 1947. **State.**

9280 ■ Michigan Health Council (MHC)
c/o Anne W. Rosewarne, Pres.
2410 Woodlake Dr.
Okemos, MI 48864-3997
Ph: (517)347-3332
Fax: (517)347-4096
E-mail: mhc@mhc.org
URL: http://www.mhc.org
Contact: Anne W. Rosewarne, Pres.
Founded: 1943. **State.**

9281 ■ Michigan Home Health Association (MHHA)
c/o Harvey Zuckerberg, Exec.Dir.
2140 Univ. Park Dr., Ste.220
Okemos, MI 48864
Ph: (517)349-8089
Fax: (517)349-8090
URL: http://www.mhha.org
Contact: Chris Chesny, Pres.
Founded: 1981. **Members:** 300. **Staff:** 5. **Budget:** $500,000. **State.** State trade association representing individuals from the home care industry. The primary provider of home health education in MI. Supports and promotes cost savings projects and industry research. Also promotes understanding, cooperation, and communication among home health care providers and serves as a liaison with other organizations at local, state, and national levels. Educates federal and state legislators and regulatory bodies on the merits of home care and how it can be used most efficiently. **Conventions/Meetings:** annual conference • periodic seminar • periodic workshop.

9282 ■ Michigan HOSA
2410 Woodlake Dr.
Okemos, MI 48864
Ph: (517)347-8088
Fax: (517)347-4096
E-mail: hosa@mhc.org
URL: http://www.michiganhosa.org
Contact: Itika Williams, Pres.
State. Represents secondary and postsecondary students enrolled in health occupations education

programs. Works to improve the quality of healthcare for all Americans by urging members to develop self-improvement skills. Encourages members to develop understanding of current healthcare issues, environmental concerns, and survival needs. Conducts programs to help individuals improve their occupational skills and leadership qualities. **Affiliated With:** Health Occupations Students of America.

9283 ■ Michigan Infrastructure and Transportation Association (MITA)
PO Box 1640
Okemos, MI 48805-1640
Ph: (517)347-8336
Fax: (517)347-8344
Free: (800)878-8336
E-mail: bobpatzer@mi-ita.com
URL: http://www.mi-ita.com
Contact: Bob Patzer, Exec.VP

Founded: 2005. **Staff:** 12. **State**. Represents contractors, suppliers, and manufacturers involved in water, sewer, gas, electric, telecommunications, site work, and other segments of the industry across the US. Provides safety training and education for all underground utility construction professionals. Unites and strengthens construction markets. Improves the business environment for the utility construction community through dedicated involvement in legislative action, networking and communication. **Affiliated With:** National Utility Contractors Association.

9284 ■ Michigan Literacy (MLI)
PO Box 1036
Okemos, MI 48805
Ph: (517)349-7511
Fax: (517)349-6667
E-mail: mli@voyager.net
URL: http://www.michiganliteracy.org
Contact: Levona Whitaker, Exec.Dir.

Founded: 1969. **Members:** 200. **Membership Dues:** individual, organizational, $40 (annual). **Staff:** 3. **Budget:** $175,000. **Local Groups:** 135. **State**. Volunteer literacy tutors, educators, and public library personnel. Seeks to reduce adult illiteracy through organization, maintenance, and support of local volunteer literacy programs. Provides services to local agencies dedicated to reducing illiteracy. Works with local chapters, Adult Basic Education programs, and public libraries to provide promotion, recruitment, and program management; coordinates training of volunteers and support training methods. Acts as a resource center for programs, providing a consultation network, cross-program referrals, data collection materials, and program evaluation tools. **Affiliated With:** ProLiteracy Worldwide. **Publications:** *LIT-Flash*, quarterly. Newsletter • *LITSTART*. Book • *Michigan's Volunteer Literacy Organizations Directory*, periodic • *Tutor Trainer Directory*, periodic • *Tutoring Made Easy (peer tutoring manual for youth)*. **Conventions/Meetings:** annual State Literacy Conference, book, software, multi-media vendors (exhibits) - every September.

9285 ■ Michigan Manufactured Housing Association (MMHA)
2222 Assn. Dr.
Okemos, MI 48864-5978
Ph: (517)349-3300
Fax: (517)349-3543
Free: (800)422-6478
E-mail: michhome@michhome.org
URL: http://www.michhome.org
Contact: Timothy J. DeWitt CAE, Exec.Dir.

Founded: 1941. **Members:** 1,253. **Staff:** 7. **State**. Individuals and companies involved in the manufactured housing industry. Represents the interest of members. **Affiliated With:** Manufactured Housing Institute. **Formerly:** Michigan Manufactured Housing Institute. **Publications:** *Communicator*, monthly. Newsletter. **Advertising:** accepted • *Michigan Home Magazine*, annual. **Price:** free. **Advertising:** accepted. **Conventions/Meetings:** annual conference - usually the end of July.

9286 ■ Michigan Nursery and Landscape Association (MNLA)
c/o Amy Frankmann, Exec.Dir.
2149 Commons Pkwy.
Okemos, MI 48864
Ph: (517)381-0437
Fax: (517)381-0638
Free: (800)879-6652
E-mail: amyf@mnla.org
URL: http://www.mnla.org
Contact: Amy Frankmann, Exec.Dir.

Founded: 1922. **Membership Dues:** key employee, student/educator, retired, $50 (annual) • non-resident, $190 (annual). **State**. **Affiliated With:** Professional Landcare Network. **Publications:** *Michigan Landscape*, bimonthly. Magazine. **Price:** $52.95 /year for members; $77.95 /year for nonmembers.

9287 ■ Michigan Nurses Association (MNA)
c/o Tom Renkes, RN, CEO
2310 Jolly Oak Rd.
Okemos, MI 48864
Ph: (517)349-5640
Fax: (517)349-5818
Free: (800)MI-NURSE
E-mail: minurses@minurses.org
URL: http://www.minurses.org
Contact: Tom Renkes RN, CEO

Founded: 1904. **Members:** 9,395. **Membership Dues:** full, $444 (annual) • reduced, $222 (annual) • special, $111 (annual). **Local Groups:** 8. **State**. Serves to represent, promote and advocate for registered professional nurses, nursing practice and quality patient outcomes. **Awards:** Excellence in Nursing Practice. **Frequency:** annual. **Type:** recognition. **Recipient:** for professional practice and achievements that exemplify excellence in nursing. **Affiliated With:** American Nurses Association. **Publications:** Articles, periodic. Alternate Formats: online.

9288 ■ Michigan Osteopathic Association (MOA)
c/o Dennis M. Paradis, Exec.Dir.
2445 Woodlake Cir.
Okemos, MI 48864
Ph: (517)347-1555
Fax: (517)347-1566
Free: (800)657-1556
E-mail: moa@mi-osteopathic.org
URL: http://www.mi-osteopathic.org
Contact: Dennis M. Paradis, Exec.Dir.

Founded: 1898. **Members:** 3,200. **Staff:** 12. **Budget:** $1,600,000. **Regional Groups:** 5. **State Groups:** 1. **Local Groups:** 20. **State**. **Formerly:** (1998) Michigan Association of Osteopathic Physicians and Surgeons.

9289 ■ Michigan Psychological Association
c/o Judith Kovach, PhD, Exec.Dir.
2105 Univ. Park Dr., Ste.C-1
Okemos, MI 48864
Ph: (517)347-1885
Fax: (517)347-1896
E-mail: mpa@acd.net
URL: http://www.michpsych.org
Contact: Judith Kovach PhD, Exec.Dir.

Founded: 1935. **Members:** 1,000. **State**. Professional organization for psychologists. **Affiliated With:** American Psychological Association. **Publications:** *The Michigan Psychologist*, bimonthly. Newsletter. **Conventions/Meetings:** semiannual conference - always April and October.

9290 ■ Michigan Recreation and Park Association (MRPA)
c/o Michael J. Maisner, Exec.Dir.
2465 Woodlake Cir., Ste.180
Okemos, MI 48864
Ph: (517)485-9888
Fax: (517)485-7932
E-mail: info@mrpaonline.org
URL: http://www.mrpaonline.org
Contact: Michael J. Maisner, Exec.Dir.

Founded: 1935. **Members:** 1,900. **Staff:** 6. **State**. Recreation and park professionals. **Publications:** *Leisure Focus*, monthly. Newsletter • *MRPA Newsletter*, monthly. **Conventions/Meetings:** annual meeting - always first week in February.

9291 ■ Michigan School Band and Orchestra Association (MSBOA)
3965 Okemos Rd., Ste.A3
Okemos, MI 48864-4206
Ph: (517)347-7321
Fax: (517)347-7325
Free: (800)9MS-BOA9
E-mail: stanifer@umich.edu
URL: http://www.msboa.org
Contact: Paul E. Stanifer, Exec.Dir.

Founded: 1934. **Members:** 2,100. **Membership Dues:** school, $340 (annual) • sustaining, $150 (annual) • non-teaching, $50 (annual). **Staff:** 3. **Regional Groups:** 16. **State**. Schools that encourage interest in instrumental music. Sponsors student activities and teacher in-service programs. **Publications:** *MSBOA Bulletin*, 3/year. Newsletter • Book, annual • Journal, semiannual, 2 per school year • Directory • Yearbook, annual. Contains festival rules, information, applications, and required music list. **Conventions/Meetings:** annual meeting • Michigan Music Conference - 3/year.

9292 ■ Michigan Veal Committee (MVC)
c/o Kathleen Hawkins, Exec.Dir.
2145 Univ. Park Dr., Ste.300
Okemos, MI 48864
Ph: (517)347-0911
Fax: (517)347-0919
E-mail: mibeef@aol.com
URL: http://www.miveal.org
Contact: Robert Kamp, Pres.

Founded: 1984. **State**. Assists consumers, foodservice operators and retailers in making an informed choice through promotion, information programs and research on veal.

9293 ■ Michigan Veterinary Medical Association (MVMA)
2144 Commons Pkwy.
Okemos, MI 48864-3986
Ph: (517)347-4710
Fax: (517)347-4666
E-mail: belyea@michvma.org
URL: http://www.michvma.org
Contact: Karlene Belyea, Exec.Dir.

State. **Affiliated With:** American Veterinary Medical Association.

9294 ■ Michigan's Heavy Construction Association
c/o Robert Patzer, Exec.Dir.
PO Box 1640
Okemos, MI 48805-1640
Ph: (517)347-8336
Fax: (517)347-8344
E-mail: patzer.bob@aucmi.org
URL: http://www.aucmi.org
Contact: Robert A. Patzer, Exec.Dir.

State. **Affiliated With:** American Road and Transportation Builders Association.

9295 ■ Mid-Michigan Mortgage Lenders Association (MMMLA)
Countrywide Home Loans
5100 N Marsh Rd., No. H2
Okemos, MI 48864
Ph: (517)349-3456
Fax: (517)349-6944
E-mail: lydia_burtraw@countrywide.com
URL: http://www.mmla.net/mmmla.htm
Contact: Lydia Burtraw, Pres.

Local. Promotes fair and ethical lending practices and fosters professional excellence among real estate finance employees. Seeks to create an environment that enables members to invest in communities and achieve their business objectives. **Affiliated With:** Mortgage Bankers Association.

9296 ■ Middle Cities Education Association (MCEA)
2199 Jolly Rd., Ste.100
Okemos, MI 48864-3968
Ph: (517)347-0292
Fax: (517)347-0383
E-mail: palderman@middlecities.org
Contact: Raymond S. Telman, Exec.Dir.
Founded: 1972. **Members:** 26. **Staff:** 12. **State**. Urban school districts in Michigan. Works to promote a better understanding of the needs of school districts located in cities. Supports the needs of children who are economically and educationally disadvantaged. **Awards:** Robert and Patricia Muth Excellence in Leadership Award. **Frequency:** annual. **Type:** monetary. **Publications:** *Newsbrief*, monthly. Newsletter.

9297 ■ National Alliance for the Mentally Ill - Lansing
PO Box 648
Okemos, MI 48805-0648
Ph: (517)484-3404 (517)641-4709
E-mail: namilansin@aol.com
URL: http://mi.nami.org/gl.html
Contact: Judy R. Wells, Pres.
Local. Strives to improve the quality of life of children and adults with severe mental illness through support, education, research and advocacy. **Affiliated With:** National Alliance for the Mentally Ill.

9298 ■ National Association of Black Accountants, Lansing
c/o Tommie Benson
4599 Mistywood Dr.
Okemos, MI 48864-0316
Ph: (517)349-6423 (517)862-8383
E-mail: bensonth@state.mi.us
URL: National Affiliate–www.nabainc.org
Contact: Lesley Benson, Contact
Local. **Affiliated With:** National Association of Black Accountants.

9299 ■ PFLAG Lansing
PO Box 35
Okemos, MI 48805
Ph: (517)332-4550
Fax: (517)349-3612
E-mail: pflaglansing@yahoo.com
URL: http://www.geocities.com/pflaglansing
Local. **Affiliated With:** Parents, Families, and Friends of Lesbians and Gays.

Old Mission

9300 ■ American Legion, Garland-Tompkins Post 399
PO Box 39
Old Mission, MI 49673
Ph: (517)371-4720
Fax: (517)371-2401
URL: National Affiliate–www.legion.org
Local. **Affiliated With:** American Legion.

Olivet

9301 ■ Association for Computing Machinery, Olivet College
c/o Kit Nip, Sponsor
320 S Main St.
Olivet, MI 49076
Ph: (269)749-7663
E-mail: knip@olivetcollege.edu
URL: National Affiliate–www.acm.org
Contact: Marcus M. Darden, Chair
Local. Biological, medical, behavioral, and computer scientists; hospital administrators; programmers and others interested in application of computer methods to biological, behavioral, and medical problems. Stimulates understanding of the use and potential of computers in the Biosciences. **Affiliated With:** Association for Computing Machinery.

9302 ■ Olivet Lions Club
c/o Sharon Powell, Pres.
PO Box 492
Olivet, MI 49076-0492
Ph: (269)749-9486
E-mail: sharonpowell@peoplepc.com
URL: http://www.district11c2.org
Contact: Sharon Powell, Pres.
Local. **Affiliated With:** Lions Clubs International.

9303 ■ Psi Chi, National Honor Society in Psychology - Olivet College
c/o Dept. of Psychology
320 S Main St.
Olivet, MI 49076-9406
Ph: (269)749-7275 (269)749-7603
E-mail: cgraessle@olivetcollege.edu
URL: http://www.psichi.org/chapters/info.asp?chapter_id=454
Contact: Charles Graessle PhD, Advisor
Local.

Onaway

9304 ■ American Legion, Michigan Post 317
c/o Forest Preston, Jr.
19415 M 68 E
Onaway, MI 49765
Ph: (517)371-4720
Fax: (517)371-2401
URL: National Affiliate–www.legion.org
Contact: Forest Preston Jr., Contact
Local. **Affiliated With:** American Legion.

Onekama

9305 ■ Onekama Lions Club
PO Box 321
Onekama, MI 49675
Ph: (231)889-4179
E-mail: rmaue@jackpine.net
URL: http://onekamami.lionwap.org
Contact: Rose Ann Maue, Pres.
Local. **Affiliated With:** Lions Clubs International.

Onondaga

9306 ■ Highfields - Helping People Grow in Michigan
c/o Dorene Craig
5123 Old Plank Rd.
PO Box 98
Onondaga, MI 49264
Ph: (517)628-2287
Fax: (517)628-3421
E-mail: dcraig@highfields.org
URL: http://www.highfields.org/
State.

Onsted

9307 ■ American Legion, Durkee-Seager Post 550
PO Box 234
Onsted, MI 49265
Ph: (517)371-4720
Fax: (517)371-2401
URL: National Affiliate–www.legion.org
Local. **Affiliated With:** American Legion.

Ontonagon

9308 ■ American Legion, Ontonagon Post 288
PO Box 33
Ontonagon, MI 49953
Ph: (517)371-4720
Fax: (517)371-2401
URL: National Affiliate–www.legion.org
Local. **Affiliated With:** American Legion.

9309 ■ Northern Lights Sams
c/o Garnet Maki
215 Old Norwich Trail
Ontonagon, MI 49953-9607
Local.

9310 ■ Ontonagon Area High School Skating Club
PO Box 214
Ontonagon, MI 49953
Ph: (906)884-4456
E-mail: annmariecleary@hotmail.com
URL: National Affiliate–www.usfigureskating.org
Contact: Ann Cleary, Contact
Local. Provides programs to encourage participation and achievement in the sport of figure skating on ice. Defines and maintains uniform standards of skating proficiency. Organizes and sponsors competitions and exhibitions for the purpose of stimulating interest in figure skating. **Affiliated With:** United States Figure Skating Association.

9311 ■ Ontonagon County Chamber of Commerce
PO Box 266
Ontonagon, MI 49953
Ph: (906)884-4735
E-mail: ontcofc@up.net
URL: http://www.ontonagonmi.com
Contact: Edith Basile, Corresponding Sec.
Founded: 1961. **Members:** 140. **Membership Dues:** individual, small and large business, $25-$300 (annual). **Budget:** $12,000. **Local**. Promotes the county and helps local businesses prosper. **Libraries: Type:** open to the public. **Holdings:** business records, clippings, maps, photographs, reports. **Subjects:** tourism information. **Awards:** Ambassador Outside the County. **Frequency:** annual. **Type:** recognition. **Recipient:** for resident of Ontonagon county who promotes the area to the outside world • Ontonagon County Action Award. **Frequency:** annual. **Type:** recognition. **Recipient:** for resident of the county who works overtime for the good of the county. **Computer Services:** Information services, responding to information requests. **Formerly:** (2002) Ontonagon County Chamber of Commerce and Tourism Association.

Orchard Lake

9312 ■ St. Mary's Preparatory Moms and Dads Club
c/o Molly Hittinger, Admin.Asst.
3535 Indian Trail
Orchard Lake, MI 48324-1623
Ph: (248)683-0532 (248)683-0530
Fax: (248)683-1740
E-mail: mhittinger@stmarysprep.com
URL: http://www.stmarysprep.com
Contact: Molly Hittinger, Admin.Asst.
Local.

9313 ■ Veteran Motor Car Club of America - Huron Valley Chapter
c/o Carl Dawes, Pres.
3209 Erie Dr.
Orchard Lake, MI 48324
Ph: (248)682-1197
E-mail: snotop@juno.com
URL: National Affiliate–www.vmcca.org
Contact: Carl Dawes, Pres.
Local. **Affiliated With:** Veteran Motor Car Club of America.

Ortonville

9314 ■ Fort Detroit Golden Retriever Club
c/o Lynn Knape
2195 Hadley
Ortonville, MI 48462

Ph: (248)627-5987
E-mail: kurtcmacauley@aol.com
URL: http://www.fdgrc.org
Contact: Kurt Macauley, Pres.
Local. **Affiliated With:** Golden Retriever Club of America.

Oscoda

9315 ■ American Legion, Loud Merkel La Plante Post 274
349 S State St.
Oscoda, MI 48750
Ph: (517)371-4720
Fax: (517)371-2401
URL: National Affiliate–www.legion.org
Local. **Affiliated With:** American Legion.

9316 ■ National Active and Retired Federal Employees Association - Oscoda 1955
4056 W River Rd.
Oscoda, MI 48750
Ph: (989)739-9693
URL: National Affiliate–www.narfe.org
Contact: Roy E. Silvers, Contact
Local. Protects the retirement future of employees through education. Informs members on issues affecting the retirement. **Affiliated With:** National Association of Retired Federal Employees.

9317 ■ Oscoda Area United Way
5671 N Skeel Ave., Ste.32
Oscoda, MI 48750-1535
Ph: (517)739-2849
URL: National Affiliate–national.unitedway.org
Local. **Affiliated With:** United Way of America.

Oshtemo

9318 ■ Kalamazoo West Side Lions Club
PO Box 621
Oshtemo, MI 49077
Ph: (269)649-3130
E-mail: willbe1944@aol.com
URL: http://kalamazoomi.lionwap.org
Contact: Bill Bennett, Pres.
Local. **Affiliated With:** Lions Clubs International.

9319 ■ Southwest Michigan Associates of Health Underwriters
PO Box 1
Oshtemo, MI 49077-0001
Ph: (269)353-8686
Fax: (269)353-8899
Free: (800)343-3200
E-mail: oshtemotpa@aol.com
URL: National Affiliate–www.nahu.org
Contact: William F. Hamilton, Treas.
Founded: 1993. **Members:** 50. **Membership Dues:** agents, $185 (annual). **Budget:** $10,000. **State Groups:** 1. **Local**. Health insurance professionals. **Awards:** William F. Hamilton Distinguished Service Award. **Frequency:** annual. **Type:** recognition. **Affiliated With:** National Association of Health Underwriters. **Formerly:** (1998) Kalamazoo Regional Associates of Health Underwriters. **Publications:** *SMAHU Newsletter*, monthly. **Price:** free. **Circulation:** 50. **Advertising:** not accepted. Alternate Formats: online. **Conventions/Meetings:** monthly meeting, general membership - 2nd Wednesday of the month from Sept.-May. Kalamazoo, MI - Avg. Attendance: 30.

Osseo

9320 ■ Pittsford Area Lions Club
c/o Leslie Moosew, Pres.
6886 Shannon Dr.
Osseo, MI 49266
Ph: (517)523-2325
URL: http://www.lionsdistrict11b1.org/lc_pittsford_area.htm
Contact: Leslie Moosew, Pres.
Local. **Affiliated With:** Lions Clubs International.

Otisville

9321 ■ Beecher Lions Club
c/o Marie E. Estes, Sec.
8311 E Frances Rd.
Otisville, MI 48463
Ph: (810)631-6690
E-mail: estesmenaph@aol.com
URL: http://www.geocities.com/dist11d1
Contact: Marie E. Estes, Sec.
Local. **Affiliated With:** Lions Clubs International.

9322 ■ Otisville Lions Club
c/o Robinette Chandler, Pres.
PO Box 251
Otisville, MI 48463
Ph: (810)631-6313
URL: http://www.geocities.com/dist11d1
Contact: Robinette Chandler, Pres.
Local. **Affiliated With:** Lions Clubs International.

9323 ■ Westwood Heights Lions Club
c/o Howard Davis, Pres.
9235 N Gale Rd.
Otisville, MI 48463
Ph: (810)631-2727
E-mail: grammajudie@yahoo.com
URL: http://www.geocities.com/dist11d1
Contact: Howard Davis, Pres.
Local. **Affiliated With:** Lions Clubs International.

Otsego

9324 ■ American Legion, Otsego Post 84
PO Box 116
Otsego, MI 49078
Ph: (517)371-4720
Fax: (517)371-2401
URL: National Affiliate–www.legion.org
Local. **Affiliated With:** American Legion.

9325 ■ Otsego Area Chamber of Commerce
135 E Allegan St.
Otsego, MI 49078
Ph: (269)694-6880
E-mail: chamber@mei.net
URL: http://otsegochamber.org
Contact: Tracy Allard, Exec.Dir.
Membership Dues: business (varies with the number of employees), $125-$225 (annual) • nonprofit, $50 (annual) • retired/non-business individual, $25 (annual). **Local**. Promotes business and community development in the Otsego, MI area.

9326 ■ Otsego Area Historical Society
c/o Sam Simpson, Trustee
218 N Farmer St.
Otsego, MI 49078
Ph: (269)692-3775
E-mail: oahs@otsegohistory.org
URL: http://www.otsegohistory.org
Contact: Ryan Wieber, Chm.
Local.

Ottawa Lake

9327 ■ American Legion, Lambertville Post 191
4120 Piehl Rd.
Ottawa Lake, MI 49267
Ph: (517)371-4720
Fax: (517)371-2401
URL: National Affiliate–www.legion.org
Local. **Affiliated With:** American Legion.

9328 ■ Glass City Miniatures Guild
c/o Sharon Larrow
8240 Whiteford Ctr.
Ottawa Lake, MI 49267
Ph: (734)854-6652
E-mail: vicladymin@aol.com
URL: http://www.miniatures.org/states/MI.html
Contact: Sharon Larrow, Contact
Local. **Affiliated With:** National Association of Miniature Enthusiasts.

Otter Lake

9329 ■ American Legion, Heminger-Jones Post 504
PO Box 155
Otter Lake, MI 48464
Ph: (517)371-4720
Fax: (517)371-2401
URL: National Affiliate–www.legion.org
Local. **Affiliated With:** American Legion.

Ovid

9330 ■ Goat Lovers of Michigan
c/o Linda A. Kast
4901 S Meridian Rd.
Ovid, MI 48866
Ph: (517)834-5871
URL: National Affiliate–adga.org
Contact: Linda A. Kast, Contact
State. **Affiliated With:** American Dairy Goat Association.

9331 ■ Ovid Lions Club
c/o Carol Garlock, Sec.
331 W Williams St.
Ovid, MI 48866
Ph: (989)834-5617
E-mail: glgarlock@juno.com
URL: http://www.district11c2.org
Contact: Carol Garlock, Sec.
Local. **Affiliated With:** Lions Clubs International.

Owosso

9332 ■ American Legion, Patterson-Dawson Post 57
PO Box 575
Owosso, MI 48867
Ph: (517)371-4720
Fax: (517)371-2401
URL: National Affiliate–www.legion.org
Local. **Affiliated With:** American Legion.

9333 ■ Michigan Society of EAs
c/o Robert Hemenway
602 W Main St.
Owosso, MI 48867
Ph: (989)723-5977
Fax: (989)725-8372
E-mail: bob@hbstax.com
URL: http://www.naea.org/MemberPortal/StateAffiliates/Listing
Contact: Robert Hemenway EA, Contact
State. **Affiliated With:** National Association of Enrolled Agents.

9334 ■ Owosso/Corunna Lions Club
c/o Mike Calhaun, Pres.
2491 N Lexington St.
Owosso, MI 48867
Ph: (989)725-6429
E-mail: mjkrcalhaun@juno.com
URL: http://www.district11c2.org
Contact: Mike Calhaun, Pres.
Local. **Affiliated With:** Lions Clubs International.

9335 ■ Shiawassee Family and Friends Alliance for the Mentally Ill
c/o Pauline Hills, Pres.
415 Clinton St.
Owosso, MI 48867
Ph: (517)723-3769
URL: http://mi.nami.org/sff.html
Contact: Pauline Hills, Pres.
Local. Strives to improve the quality of life of children and adults with severe mental illness through support, education, research and advocacy. **Affiliated With:** National Alliance for the Mentally Ill.

9336 ■ Shiawassee Regional Board of Realtors
217 N Washington St., Ste.No. 102
Owosso, MI 48867
Ph: (989)723-4672
Fax: (989)723-5959
E-mail: shiboard@michonline.net
URL: http://www.shiboard.com
Contact: Jim Civille, Pres.
Local. Strives to develop real estate business practices. Advocates the right to own, use and transfer real property. Provides a facility for professional development, research and exchange of information among members. **Affiliated With:** National Association of Realtors.

9337 ■ Shiawassee Regional Chamber of Commerce (SRCC)
215 N Water St.
Owosso, MI 48867-2875
Ph: (989)723-5149
Fax: (989)723-8353
E-mail: customerservice@shiawasseechamber.org
URL: http://www.shiawasseechamber.org
Contact: Marsha Lyttle, Interim Pres.
Founded: 1908. **Members:** 600. **Membership Dues:** individual, $75 (annual) • sole proprietor, $234 (annual) • business (based on number of employees), $243-$698 (annual). **Staff:** 12. **Budget:** $900,000. **Regional**. Strives to energize the economic growth of the county through leadership actions. **Awards:** ATHENA Award. **Frequency:** annual. **Type:** recognition • Citizen of the Year. **Frequency:** annual. **Type:** recognition • Mission Award. **Frequency:** annual. **Type:** recognition • Outstanding Small, Medium and Large Business. **Frequency:** annual. **Type:** recognition. **Computer Services:** Information services • mailing lists • online services. **Affiliated With:** Michigan Chamber of Commerce; U.S. Chamber of Commerce. **Formerly:** (2003) Owosso-Corunna Area Chamber of Commerce. **Publications:** *Business Directory*, annual. Contains information about Shiawassee county. **Price:** $25.00. **Circulation:** 18,000. **Advertising:** accepted • *Shiawassee Business Monthly*. Newsletter. **Conventions/Meetings:** annual dinner, with awards presentation (exhibits) - usually February.

9338 ■ Shiawassee United Way
PO Box 664
Owosso, MI 48867-0664
Ph: (989)723-4987
URL: National Affiliate–national.unitedway.org
Local. Affiliated With: United Way of America.

Oxford

9339 ■ American Legion, Walter Fraser Post 108
130 E Drahner Rd.
Oxford, MI 48371
Ph: (517)371-4720
Fax: (517)371-2401
URL: National Affiliate–www.legion.org
Local. Affiliated With: American Legion.

9340 ■ Oxford Area Chamber of Commerce (OACC)
PO Box 142
Oxford, MI 48371-0142
Ph: (248)628-0410
Fax: (248)628-0430
E-mail: info@oxfordchamber.com
URL: http://oxfordchamber.com
Contact: Jennifer Duncan, Exec.Dir.
Founded: 1950. **Members:** 250. **Membership Dues:** business, $150 (annual) • individual, nonprofit, government, $75 (annual). **Staff:** 1. **For-Profit. Local**. Promotes business and community development in the Oxford, MI area. Conducts business promotions, monthly program, annual golf outing, community awards, and Christmas parade. **Awards:** Community Awards. **Frequency:** annual. **Type:** recognition. **Recipient:** for contribution to the community. **Computer Services:** Information services, promotion of Chamber members. **Absorbed:** (1986) Oxford Merchant Association. **Publications:** *Oxford News*, monthly. Newsletter. **Price:** free. **Advertising:** accepted • Brochure, annual. **Conventions/Meetings:** monthly General Membership Meeting, with speakers and demonstrations - usually third Thursday.

9341 ■ Paper Money Collectors of Michigan
c/o Dr. Wallace Lee
102 Conda Ln.
Oxford, MI 48371-4621
E-mail: doclee99@aaahawk.com
URL: National Affiliate–www.money.org
Contact: Dr. Wallace Lee, Contact
State. Affiliated With: American Numismatic Association.

9342 ■ Trout Unlimited - Challenge Chapter
c/o Bill Thorsted
206 Oxford Lake Dr.
Oxford, MI 48371
Ph: (248)628-6373 (248)293-7587
Fax: (248)293-5917
E-mail: bwrthor@yahoo.com
URL: http://www.challengechapter.org
Contact: Nancy Spence, Pres.
Local.

9343 ■ USA Weightlifting - Power X-Treme
c/o Christopher Brocco
944 Wise Ave.
Oxford, MI 48371
Ph: (248)628-8195
URL: National Affiliate–www.usaweightlifting.org
Contact: Christopher Brocco, Contact
Local. Affiliated With: USA Weightlifting.

Parma

9344 ■ Parma-Spring Arbor Lions Club
c/o Theresa Datte, Sec.
3620 N Dearing Rd.
Parma, MI 49269
Ph: (517)817-2314
E-mail: kdatte@sbcglobal.net
URL: http://www.lionsdistrict11b1.org/lc_parma_springarbor.htm
Contact: Theresa Datte, Sec.
Local. Affiliated With: Lions Clubs International.

Paw Paw

9345 ■ American Legion, Mc-Gowan-Johnson Post 68
PO Box 19
Paw Paw, MI 49079
Ph: (517)371-4720
Fax: (517)371-2401
URL: National Affiliate–www.legion.org
Local. Affiliated With: American Legion.

9346 ■ Greater Paw Paw Chamber of Commerce
804 S Kalamazoo St., Ste.4
PO Box 105
Paw Paw, MI 49079
Ph: (269)657-5395
Fax: (269)655-8755
E-mail: mary@pawpawchamber.com
URL: http://www.pawpawmi.com
Contact: Mary Springer, Community Relations Representative
Local. Works to promote business interests in the greater Paw Paw area through advocacy and leadership in education, local economic, governmental and community issues. **Computer Services:** Information services, member index. **Telecommunication Services:** electronic mail, jerry@hostingmi.com. **Committees:** Education; Marketing; Retail, Service and Business; Special Events; Website; Wine and Harvest Festival. **Formerly:** (1999) Paw Paw Chamber of Commerce. **Publications:** Directory, annual • Newsletter, monthly.

9347 ■ Paw Paw Lions Club
PO Box 92
Paw Paw, MI 49079-0092
E-mail: fjdoubleu@aol.com
URL: http://milions11b2.org
Local. Affiliated With: Lions Clubs International.

9348 ■ Van Buren County United Way
181 W Michigan Ave., Ste.4
Paw Paw, MI 49079-1432
Ph: (269)657-2410
URL: National Affiliate–national.unitedway.org
Contact: Edgar T. Britton, Exec.Dir.
Local. Works to assist in fundraising by conducting company-wide employee campaigns and by encouraging corporate contributions. **Affiliated With:** United Way of America.

Peck

9349 ■ American Legion, Peck Post 489
5894 Cass Rd.
Peck, MI 48466
Ph: (517)371-4720
Fax: (517)371-2401
URL: National Affiliate–www.legion.org
Local. Affiliated With: American Legion.

Pentwater

9350 ■ American Legion, Pentwater Post 327
PO Box 210
Pentwater, MI 49449
Ph: (517)371-4720
Fax: (517)371-2401
URL: National Affiliate–www.legion.org
Local. Affiliated With: American Legion.

9351 ■ Catholics United for the Faith - Our Daily Bread Chapter
c/o Roberta Williams
PO Box 1050
Pentwater, MI 49449
Ph: (231)869-8141
URL: National Affiliate–www.cuf.org
Contact: Roberta Williams, Contact
Local.

9352 ■ Pentwater Chamber of Commerce
PO Box 614
Pentwater, MI 49449
Ph: (231)869-4150
Fax: (231)869-5286
E-mail: travelinfo@pentwater.org
URL: http://www.pentwater.org
Contact: Julie Shaw, Exec.Dir.
Membership Dues: general, $150 (annual). **Local**. Promotes business and community development in Pentwater, MI area. **Formerly:** (2005) Pentwater Area Chamber of Commerce.

Perkins

9353 ■ American Legion, Perkins Post 540
PO Box 5
Perkins, MI 49872
Ph: (517)371-4720
Fax: (517)371-2401
URL: National Affiliate–www.legion.org
Local. Affiliated With: American Legion.

Perrinton

9354 ■ Maple Valley Lions Club
c/o Bill A. Burnham, Sec.
10255 Hill Run
Perrinton, MI 48871
Ph: (989)236-5102 (989)682-4654
E-mail: elebel14@hotmail.com
URL: http://www.district11c2.org
Contact: Bill A. Burnham, Sec.
Local. Affiliated With: Lions Clubs International.

Perry

9355 ■ Michigan National Wild Turkey Federation, Timber Ghost Gobblers
406 NE St.
Perry, MI 48872
Ph: (517)625-6787
URL: http://www.mi-nwtf.org/timber_ghost.htm
Contact: Eric Fischer, Pres.
Local.

9356 ■ Perry-Morrice Jr. Football Association
c/o Tracey C. Hammond
9650 S. Ruess Rd.
Perry, MI 48872-9757
Ph: (517)625-9109
Fax: (517)625-5480
Contact: Ryan D. Hammond, Pres.
Founded: 2000. **Members:** 125. **Membership Dues:** $100 (annual). **Local Groups:** 1. **Local.** Works to allow community children entering 4th through 8th grades to have the opportunity to participate in football and cheerleading.

Petersburg

9357 ■ Michigan National Wild Turkey Federation, Whiteford Valley Chapter
5300 School Rd.
Petersburg, MI 49270
Ph: (734)856-2386
URL: http://www.mi-nwtf.org/Whiteford.htm
Contact: Jerry Long, Pres.
Local.

9358 ■ Petersburg-Summerfield Lions Club
c/o Mike Goodin, Pres.
181 Vesey St.
Petersburg, MI 49270
Ph: (734)279-2672
E-mail: goodin@cass.net
URL: http://www.metrodetroitlions.org
Contact: Mike Goodin, Pres.
Local. Affiliated With: Lions Clubs International.

Petoskey

9359 ■ AAA Michigan
1321 Springs St.
Petoskey, MI 49770
Ph: (231)347-8284
Fax: (231)347-1081
Free: (800)294-6503
State.

9360 ■ Alliance for the Mentally Ill of Northern Lower Michigan
c/o Joe Hebel
1 MacDonald Dr., Ste.C
Petoskey, MI 49770
Ph: (616)347-0740
URL: http://mi.nami.org/nlm.html
Contact: Albert Quaal, Pres.
Local. Strives to improve the quality of life of children and adults with severe mental illness through support, education, research and advocacy. **Affiliated With:** National Alliance for the Mentally Ill.

9361 ■ American Legion, Michigan Post 194
c/o Carl O. Weaver
PO Box 253
Petoskey, MI 49770
Ph: (517)371-4720
Fax: (517)371-2401
URL: National Affiliate–www.legion.org
Contact: Carl O. Weaver, Contact
Local. Affiliated With: American Legion.

9362 ■ American Red Cross, Northern Lower Michigan Chapter
PO Box 2478
Petoskey, MI 49770
Ph: (231)348-7666
Fax: (231)348-7661
URL: http://northernlowermichigan.redcross.org
Regional.

9363 ■ Emmet Association of Realtors
616 Petoskey St., Ste.310
Petoskey, MI 49770
Ph: (231)347-0700
Fax: (231)347-8710
E-mail: info@emmetrealtors.com
URL: National Affiliate–www.realtor.org
Contact: Cynthia F. Zumbaugh, Exec. Officer
Local. Strives to develop real estate business practices. Advocates the right to own, use and transfer real property. Provides a facility for professional development, research and exchange of information among members. **Affiliated With:** National Association of Realtors.

9364 ■ Little Traverse Figure Skating Club
609 Bay St.
Petoskey, MI 49770
E-mail: britishlanding@chartermi.net
URL: National Affiliate–www.usfigureskating.org
Contact: Anne Murray, Contact
Local. Provides programs to encourage participation and achievement in the sport of figure skating on ice. Defines and maintains uniform standards of skating proficiency. Organizes and sponsors competitions and exhibitions for the purpose of stimulating interest in figure skating. **Affiliated With:** United States Figure Skating Association.

9365 ■ Michigan Hemingway Society
PO Box 922
Petoskey, MI 49770
Ph: (231)347-0117
E-mail: mhs@freeway.net
URL: http://www.northquest.com/hemingway
Contact: Nancy A. Nicholson, Membership Chm.
Founded: 1993. **Members:** 100. **Membership Dues:** individual, $10 (annual). **Budget:** $6,000. **State.** Seeks to encourage the study of Ernest Hemingway's relationship to Michigan in his life and work; to support and publish interpretation and criticism of Hemingway's work by scholars and researchers; and to collect, interpret and preserve artifacts and memorabilia connected with Hemingway. **Libraries: Type:** reference. **Holdings:** archival material, books, papers, periodicals, photographs, video recordings. **Subjects:** Ernest Hemingway. **Conventions/Meetings:** annual Up in Michigan, A Hemingway Weekend - conference, lectures, readings, author discussions, tours (exhibits) - last weekend in October usually.

9366 ■ Michigan National Wild Turkey Federation, Little Traverse Bay Gobbler Chapter
1237 Hoag Rd.
Petoskey, MI 49770
Ph: (231)348-7662
URL: http://www.mi-nwtf.org/lil%20traverse.htm
Contact: Brian Gutowski, Pres.
Local.

9367 ■ Petoskey-Harbor Springs-Boyne Country Visitors Bureau
401 E Mitchell St.
Petoskey, MI 49770
Ph: (231)348-2755
Fax: (231)348-1810
Free: (800)845-2828
E-mail: info@boynecountry.com
URL: http://www.boynecountry.com
Contact: Peter Fitzsimons, Contact
Founded: 1985. **Members:** 49. **Staff:** 2. **Local.** Promotes convention business and tourism in area. **Formerly:** (2001) Boyne Country Convention and Visitors Bureau. **Publications:** Brochure. **Price:** free.

9368 ■ Petoskey Regional Chamber of Commerce (PRCC)
401 E Mitchell St.
Petoskey, MI 49770-2623
Ph: (231)347-4150
Fax: (231)348-1810
E-mail: chamber@petoskey.com
URL: http://www.petoskey.com
Contact: Carlin Smith, Exec.Dir.
Founded: 1920. **Members:** 650. **Membership Dues:** general business, retail (based on number of employees), $233-$327 (annual) • resort, $669-$1,273 (annual) • non profit, $233 (annual). **Staff:** 4. **Budget:** $250,000. **Local.** Promotes business, tourism, and community development in the Petoskey, MI area. **Awards:** Mission Award. **Frequency:** annual. **Type:** recognition. **Recipient:** for individuals, businesses or organizations that contribute significantly to the Chamber • Service Excellence Award. **Frequency:** annual. **Type:** recognition. **Recipient:** for individuals, businesses or organizations demonstrating superior, unique and unequaled service to the public. **Committees:** Air Service Task Force; Ambassador; Downtown; Government Affairs; Housing; Leadership Little Traverse; Membership; Workforce Development. **Affiliated With:** U.S. Chamber of Commerce. **Publications:** *Back to Business*, monthly. Newsletter. Alternate Formats: online • *Community Profile and Business Directory*, annual. **Price:** free for members • *Petoskey Harbor Springs Community Profile*, annual. Directory. Contains a list of all members. **Circulation:** 5,000. **Conventions/Meetings:** annual Art in the Park - show (exhibits) - always 3rd Saturday of July.

9369 ■ Phi Theta Kappa, Alpha Omicron Upsilon Chapter - North Central Michigan College
c/o Gary Kersting
1515 Howard St.
Petoskey, MI 49770
Ph: (231)348-6646
E-mail: gkers@sunny.ncmc.cc.mi.us
URL: http://www.ptk.org/directories/chapters/MI/6876-1.htm
Contact: Gary Kersting, Advisor
Local.

9370 ■ Ruffed Grouse Society, Al Litzenburger Chapter
c/o Mike Harrington
PO Box 180
Petoskey, MI 49770
Ph: (815)943-7790
E-mail: printim@aol.com
URL: National Affiliate–www.ruffedgrousesociety.org
Contact: Mike Harrington, Contact
Local. Affiliated With: Ruffed Grouse Society.

9371 ■ Scenic Michigan
445 E Mitchell St.
Petoskey, MI 49770
Ph: (231)347-1171
Fax: (231)347-1185
E-mail: info@scenicmichigan.org
URL: http://www.scenicmichigan.org
Contact: Debbie Rohe, Pres.
Founded: 1995. **Members:** 600. **State**. Seeks to preserve, protect, and enhance the scenic character of MI communities and roadsides. Has promoted conservation of city gateways, encouraged community control over billboards and sign construction, and assisted in the creation of management plans for scenic transportation corridors. **Conventions/Meetings:** quarterly board meeting • annual meeting.

9372 ■ SCORE Petoskey
401 E Mitchell
Petoskey, MI 49770
Ph: (231)347-4150
Fax: (231)348-1810
E-mail: chamber@petoskey.com
URL: http://www.score.org
Local. Affiliated With: SCORE.

9373 ■ Tip of the Mitt Watershed Council
426 Bay St.
Petoskey, MI 49770
Ph: (231)347-1181
Fax: (231)347-5928
E-mail: info@watershedcouncil.org
URL: http://www.watershedcouncil.org
Contact: Gail Gruenwald, Exec.Dir.
Local.

9374 ■ Vacationland District Dental Society
2115 M 119 Hwy.
Petoskey, MI 49770
Ph: (231)347-2518
Fax: (231)347-8530
URL: National Affiliate–www.ada.org
Contact: Dr. Michael Doctor, Pres.
Local. Represents the interests of dentists committed to the public's oral health, ethics and professional development. Encourages the improvement of the public's oral health and promotes the art and science of dentistry. **Affiliated With:** American Dental Association; Michigan Dental Association.

Pickford

9375 ■ American Legion, Pickford Post 323
PO Box 563
Pickford, MI 49774
Ph: (517)371-4720
Fax: (517)371-2401
URL: National Affiliate–www.legion.org
Local. Affiliated With: American Legion.

Pigeon

9376 ■ Bluewater Thumb Youth for Christ
PO Box 447
Pigeon, MI 48755-0447
Ph: (989)453-3239
Fax: (989)453-2906
URL: National Affiliate–www.yfc.net
Local. Affiliated With: Youth for Christ/U.S.A.

9377 ■ Cass City Gun Club
263 S Main St.
Pigeon, MI 48755
Ph: (989)872-5395
URL: National Affiliate–www.mynssa.com
Local. Affiliated With: National Skeet Shooting Association.

9378 ■ Pigeon Chamber of Commerce
PO Box 618
Pigeon, MI 48755
Ph: (989)453-7400
E-mail: pgncofc@avci.net
URL: http://www.pigeonchamber.com
Contact: Bill Esch, Pres.
Founded: 1903. **Members:** 80. **Membership Dues:** platinum, $500 • gold, $300 • silver, $200 • bronze, $100 • church, civic, $50 • individual, $25. **Local**. Promotes business and community development in Pigeon, MI area. **Computer Services:** Information services, membership directory. **Committees:** Farmers' Festival.

9379 ■ Plumbing-Heating-Cooling Contractors Association, Thumb Area
c/o Mr. Durward H. Miller, Pres.
7641 Pigeon Rd.
Pigeon, MI 48755-9701
Ph: (989)453-3931
URL: National Affiliate–www.phccweb.org
Contact: Mr. Durward H. Miller, Pres.
Local. Represents the plumbing, heating and cooling contractors. Promotes the construction industry. Protects the environment, health, safety and comfort of society. **Affiliated With:** Plumbing-Heating-Cooling Contractors Association.

Pinckney

9380 ■ American Legion, Pinckney Memorial Post 419
9807 Whitewood Rd.
Pinckney, MI 48169
Ph: (517)371-4720
Fax: (517)371-2401
URL: National Affiliate–www.legion.org
Local. Affiliated With: American Legion.

9381 ■ Michigan Association of Professional Court Reporters (MAPCR)
PO Box 366
Pinckney, MI 48169
Ph: (734)498-2627
Fax: (734)498-8415
E-mail: cfarmer@tvli.net
URL: http://www.mapcr.org
Contact: Cheryl Anne Farmer, Exec.Dir.
State. Affiliated With: National Court Reporters Association.

9382 ■ Pinckney Lions Club
c/o Shirley A. Marshall, Pres.
PO Box 165
Pinckney, MI 48169-0165
Ph: (734)761-4511 (734)887-0588
E-mail: lionshirley@charter.net
URL: http://www.district11c2.org
Contact: Shirley A. Marshall, Pres.
Local. Affiliated With: Lions Clubs International.

Pinconning

9383 ■ Pinconning Area Chamber of Commerce
PO Box 628
Pinconning, MI 48650
Ph: (989)879-2816 (989)879-2360
Contact: Tina Bergeron, Pres.
Founded: 1965. **Members:** 35. **Local**. Promotes business and community development in Pinconning, MI. Conducts charitable activities. **Formerly:** (1999) Pinconning Chamber of Commerce. **Publications:** Newsletter, quarterly.

9384 ■ Pinconning Lions Club
c/o Harold Schmann, Pres.
3205 Frasier Rd.
Pinconning, MI 48650
Ph: (989)879-4511
URL: http://www.geocities.com/dist11d1
Contact: Harold Schmann, Pres.
Local. Affiliated With: Lions Clubs International.

Plainwell

9385 ■ American Legion, Michigan Post 250
c/o Walter Miller
PO Box 233
Plainwell, MI 49080
Ph: (517)371-4720
Fax: (517)371-2401
URL: National Affiliate–www.legion.org
Contact: Walter Miller, Contact
Local. Affiliated With: American Legion.

9386 ■ Gun River Skeet and Trap
Box 151
Plainwell, MI 49080
Ph: (616)685-5280
URL: National Affiliate–www.mynssa.com
Local. Affiliated With: National Skeet Shooting Association.

9387 ■ Michigan National Wild Turkey Federation, Highbanks Chapter
10641 Douglas Ave.
Plainwell, MI 49080
Ph: (616)685-6432
URL: http://www.mi-nwtf.org/Highbanks.htm
Contact: Bert Vanderweele, Pres.
Local.

9388 ■ Plainwell Chamber of Commerce (PCC)
131 S Main St., Ste.A
Plainwell, MI 49080-1684
Ph: (269)685-8877
Fax: (269)685-1844
E-mail: plchcom@aol.com
URL: http://www.michamber.com
Contact: Lori Sanyder, Exec.Dir.
Founded: 1989. **Members:** 110. **Staff:** 2. **Budget:** $37,000. **Local**. Promotes business and community development in Plainwell, MI. Sponsors community festival. **Affiliated With:** U.S. Chamber of Commerce. **Publications:** Newsletter, monthly • Directory, annual.

Pleasant Ridge

9389 ■ American Legion, Business and Professional Mens Post 372
35 Norwich Rd.
Pleasant Ridge, MI 48069
Ph: (517)371-4720
Fax: (517)371-2401
URL: National Affiliate–www.legion.org
Local. Affiliated With: American Legion.

Plymouth

9390 ■ American Legion, Beasley-Zalesny Post 112
14116 Meadow Hill Ln.
Plymouth, MI 48170
Ph: (517)371-4720
Fax: (517)371-2401
URL: National Affiliate–www.legion.org
Local. Affiliated With: American Legion.

9391 ■ American Legion, Passage-Gayde Post 391
190 Hamilton St.
Plymouth, MI 48170
Ph: (517)371-4720
Fax: (517)371-2401
URL: National Affiliate–www.legion.org
Local. Affiliated With: American Legion.

9392 ■ American Legion, Westland Post 251
9223 Westbury Ave.
Plymouth, MI 48170
Ph: (517)371-4720
Fax: (517)371-2401
URL: National Affiliate–www.legion.org
Local. Affiliated With: American Legion.

9393 ■ Ancient Order of Hibernians of Wayne County - Thomas Dunleavy Division
c/o Brian Dunleavy
12282 Deercreek Cir.
Plymouth, MI 48170
Ph: (313)274-8856 (313)382-4545
URL: http://www.michiganaoh.com
Contact: Brian Dunleavy, Contact
Local. Affiliated With: Ancient Order of Hibernians in America.

9394 ■ Astronomical Society of Michigan
11422 Waverly Dr.
Plymouth, MI 48170-4360
E-mail: starmikebest@aol.com
URL: http://members.aol.com/StarMikeBest
Contact: Mike Best, Contact
State. Promotes the science of astronomy. Works to encourage and coordinate activities of amateur astronomical societies. Fosters observational and computational work and craftsmanship in various fields of astronomy. **Affiliated With:** Astronomical League.

9395 ■ Automotive Service Councils of Michigan (ASC)
c/o Ron Meyer, Pres.
744 Wing St.
Plymouth, MI 48170-1735
Ph: (734)354-9250
Fax: (734)354-9255
Free: (800)451-2726
E-mail: info@ascmich.com
URL: http://www.ascmich.com
State.

9396 ■ Canton/Plymouth/Salem - Young Life
PO Box 6187
Plymouth, MI 48170
Ph: (734)558-5978
URL: http://sites.younglife.org/sites/PC/default.aspx
Local. Affiliated With: Young Life.

9397 ■ Clarenceville - Young Life
PO Box 6187
Plymouth, MI 48170
Ph: (734)558-5978
URL: http://sites.younglife.org/sites/Clarenceville/default.aspx
Local. Affiliated With: Young Life.

9398 ■ Great Dane Rescue
c/o S. Suarez
PO Box 5543
Plymouth, MI 48170
Ph: (734)454-3683
E-mail: danelair@comcast.net
URL: http://www.greatdanerescueinc.com
Contact: Sandra Suarez, Dir.
Founded: 1995. **Members:** 20. **Budget:** $3,000. **State Groups:** 5. **Regional.** Dedicated to finding permanent, safe and loving homes for unwanted/neglected Great Danes. **Publications:** *Great Dane Rescue Report*, quarterly. Newsletter. **Conventions/Meetings:** monthly board meeting.

9399 ■ Greater Detroit Frozen Food Association
Crossmark Sales & Marketing
PO Box 8032
Plymouth, MI 48170-8032
Ph: (734)207-7900 (734)207-9454
Fax: (734)207-0443
E-mail: joe.yurasek@crossmark.com
Contact: Joe Yurasek Jr., Chm.
Founded: 1975. **Members:** 18. **Local.** Frozen food industry executives. Works to promote the sales and consumption of frozen foods through education, training, research, sales planning, and by providing a forum for industry dialogues. **Awards:** Golden & Silver Penguin Awards. **Frequency:** annual. **Type:** recognition. **Recipient:** sales and merchandising excellence. **Conventions/Meetings:** annual convention, with frozen food products, merchandising tools and equipment (exhibits) - October; Avg. Attendance: 500.

9400 ■ Habitat for Humanity Western Wayne County
638 Starkweather
Plymouth, MI 48170
Ph: (734)459-7744
Fax: (734)459-7750
E-mail: homes@habitatwwc.org
URL: http://www.habitatwwc.org
Contact: Alice Dent, Exec.Dir.
Local. Affiliated With: Habitat for Humanity International.

9401 ■ IEEE Communications Society, Southeastern Michigan Chapter
c/o Robert G. Desoff
685 Ross
Plymouth, MI 48170
Ph: (734)455-0338
E-mail: r.desoff@ieee.org
URL: National Affiliate–www.comsoc.org
Contact: Robert G. Desoff, Contact
Local. Affiliated With: IEEE Communications Society.

9402 ■ Michigan Credit Union League
c/o David Adams, Pres./CEO
15800 N Haggerty Rd.
Plymouth, MI 48170
Ph: (734)420-1530
Fax: (734)420-1540
Free: (800)262-6285
E-mail: dave.adams@mcul.org
URL: http://www.mcul.org
Contact: David Adams, Pres./CEO
State.

9403 ■ PC - WyldLife
PO Box 6187
Plymouth, MI 48170
Ph: (734)558-5978
URL: http://sites.younglife.org/sites/PCWyldLife/default.aspx
Local. Affiliated With: Young Life.

9404 ■ Plymouth Community Arts Council (PCAC)
774 N Sheldon Rd.
Plymouth, MI 48170-1047
Ph: (734)416-4278
Fax: (734)416-4267
E-mail: info@plymoutharts.com
URL: http://www.plymoutharts.com
Contact: Stella Greene, Exec.Dir.
Founded: 1969. **Members:** 200. **Membership Dues:** student, $25 (annual) • individual, $50 (annual) • family, $75 (annual) • contributing, $150 (annual) • business, $100 (annual) • patron, $500 (annual). **Staff:** 4. **Budget:** $175,000. **State.** Community Arts Council providing arts and humanities programming for all ages. Includes children's theatre, class/workshop, Music in the Park, art exhibit, outreach Art Volunteer Program, and the Art Rental Gallery. **Awards:** Student Scholarship. **Frequency:** annual. **Type:** monetary. **Recipient:** artistic or musical ability • Teacher Aid Grants. **Frequency:** annual. **Type:** monetary. **Recipient:** for arts or humanities program. **Programs:** ARTReach. **Publications:** *ArtBeat*, quarterly. Newsletter. **Price:** free. **Circulation:** 4,000. **Advertising:** accepted.

9405 ■ Plymouth Community Chamber of Commerce (PCCC)
850 W Ann Arbor Trail
Plymouth, MI 48170
Ph: (734)453-1540
Fax: (734)453-1724
E-mail: chamber@plymouthmi.org
URL: http://www.plymouthchamber.org
Contact: Fran Toney, Exec.Dir.
Founded: 1950. **Members:** 700. **Membership Dues:** base, $185 (annual). **Staff:** 4. **Budget:** $400,000. **Local.** Promotes business and community development in the Plymouth, MI area. **Affiliated With:** Michigan Chamber of Commerce. **Publications:** *News Views*, monthly. Newsletter. **Circulation:** 800. **Advertising:** accepted.

9406 ■ Plymouth Community United Way
960 W Ann Arbor Trl., Ste.No. 2
Plymouth, MI 48170
Ph: (734)453-6879
E-mail: plymouthunitedway@ameritech.net
URL: http://www.plymouthunitedway.org
Local. Affiliated With: United Way of America.

9407 ■ Plymouth Historical Society (PHS)
155 S Main St.
Plymouth, MI 48170
Ph: (734)455-8940
Fax: (734)455-7797
E-mail: director@plymouthhistory.org
URL: http://www.plymouthhistory.org
Contact: Beth Stewart, Exec.Dir.
Founded: 1948. **Members:** 750. **Staff:** 2. **Budget:** $75,000. **Languages:** English, German, Spanish. **Regional.** Artifacts, exhibits and archival materials relating to Plymouth history, Michigan history, Civil War history, including new acquisition of 5,000 pieces of material relating to the life and presidency of Abraham Lincoln from the Weldon Petz Abraham Lincoln Collection. **Libraries: Type:** open to the public. **Holdings:** 2,500. **Subjects:** Michigan history, civil war, Lincoln, Plymouth. **Computer Services:** Bibliographic search • database • electronic publishing • information services • mailing lists • online services • record retrieval services. **Projects:** Phoenix Mill Women's History. **Roundtables:** Abraham Lincoln. **Special Interest Groups:** KC8SWR Plymouth Museum Radio Club. **Working Groups:** 17th Michigan Reenactment Group. **Affiliated With:** West Suburban Stamp Club. **Also Known As:** (2005) Plymouth Historical Museum. **Publications:** *Plymouth's First Century: Innovators and Industry*. Book • *Postcards of Plymouth*. Book • *The Story of Plymouth*. Book • Newsletter, monthly. **Conventions/Meetings:** monthly Plymouth Museum Programs - meeting, with speakers - always second Thursday.

9408 ■ Plymouth Lions Club - Michigan
c/o James Meadows, Pres.
41037 Russet Ln.
Plymouth, MI 48170
Ph: (734)453-9450 (734)420-8104
E-mail: jkmeadows@comcast.net
URL: http://www.metrodetroitlions.org
Contact: James Meadows, Pres.
Local. Affiliated With: Lions Clubs International.

9409 ■ Police and Firemen's Insurance Association - Wayne County Sheriff
c/o Michael L. Duffey
784 York St.
Plymouth, MI 48170
Ph: (734)416-5041
E-mail: sgt.duffey@aol.com
URL: National Affiliate–www.pfia.net
Contact: Michael L. Duffey, Contact
Local. Affiliated With: Police and Firemen's Insurance Association.

9410 ■ Police and Firemen's Insurance Association - Western Wayne County Fire Department
c/o Guy F. Balok
50348 Benjamin Ct.
Plymouth, MI 48170

Ph: (734)564-3176
URL: National Affiliate–www.pfia.net
Contact: Guy F. Balok, Contact
Local. Affiliated With: Police and Firemen's Insurance Association.

9411 ■ Southeast MMBA
15095 Northville Rd.
Plymouth, MI 48170
Ph: (248)735-0119
E-mail: southeast@mmba.org
URL: http://www.trails-edge.com
Local. Affiliated With: International Mountain Bicycling Association.

9412 ■ West Suburban Stamp Club (WSSC)
c/o Joe Picard, Sec.
PO Box 700049
Plymouth, MI 48170
E-mail: wssc@comcast.net
URL: http://mywebpages.comcast.net/wssc/wssc.htm
Contact: Joe Picard, Sec.
Regional. Affiliated With: American Philatelic Society.

9413 ■ Young Life Plymouth-Canton and Clarenceville
PO Box 6187
Plymouth, MI 48170
Ph: (734)558-5978
Fax: (734)453-8143
URL: http://sites.younglife.org/sites/YLPC/default.aspx
Local. Affiliated With: Young Life.

Pontiac

9414 ■ American Legion, Chief Pontiac Post 377
PO Box 430004
Pontiac, MI 48343
Ph: (517)371-4720
Fax: (517)371-2401
URL: National Affiliate–www.legion.org
Local. Affiliated With: American Legion.

9415 ■ American Legion, Cook-Nelson Post 20
206 Auburn Ave.
Pontiac, MI 48342
Ph: (517)371-4720
Fax: (517)371-2401
URL: National Affiliate–www.legion.org
Local. Affiliated With: American Legion.

9416 ■ Friends of the Pontiac Public Library
c/o Dr. Doris Burks Taylor, PhD
314 Nelson St.
Pontiac, MI 48342-1543
Ph: (248)334-1508 (248)753-6009
Fax: (248)334-6904
E-mail: drdoris2@aol.com
Founded: 2001. **Members:** 10. **Staff:** 4. **Local.**

9417 ■ Habitat for Humanity of Oakland County
14 Judson St.
Pontiac, MI 48342-2205
Ph: (248)338-1843
Fax: (248)338-1361
E-mail: office@habitatoaklandmi.org
URL: http://habitat-oakland-mi.org
Contact: Steve Campbell, Exec.Dir.
Local. Telecommunication Services: electronic mail, ed@habitat-oakland-mi.org. **Affiliated With:** Habitat for Humanity International.

9418 ■ Help Against Violent Encounters Now (HAVEN)
PO Box 431045
Pontiac, MI 48343
Ph: (248)334-1284 (248)334-1274
Free: (877)922-1274
E-mail: help@haven-oakland.org
URL: http://www.haven-oakland.org
Contact: Lynne E. Deitch, Chair
Founded: 1975. **Staff:** 85. **Budget:** $3,000,000. **Local.** Provides services to victims of domestic violence, sexual assault, and child abuse. Offers shelter, counseling, prevention education, advocacy, and supervised parenting time.

9419 ■ International Union, United Automobile, Aerospace and Agricultural Implement Workers of America, AFL-CIO - Local Union 594
525 Martin Luther King Jr. Blvd. S
Pontiac, MI 48341
Ph: (248)334-2557
E-mail: autoworker@prodigy.net
Contact: Gloria J. Morgan, Pres.
Members: 6,404. **Local.** Seeks for the dignity and equality of the workers. Strives to provide contractors with well-trained, productive employees. **Affiliated With:** International Union, United Automobile, Aerospace and Agricultural Implement Workers of America.

9420 ■ International Union, United Automobile, Aerospace and Agricultural Implement Workers of America, AFL-CIO - Pontiac Local Local Union 653
670 E Walton
Pontiac, MI 48340
Ph: (248)373-7774
E-mail: ctiedeman@uawlocal653.org
URL: http://www.uawlocal653.org
Contact: Charles E. Tiedeman, Pres.
Members: 4,711. **Local.** AFL-CIO. **Affiliated With:** International Union, United Automobile, Aerospace and Agricultural Implement Workers of America.

9421 ■ National Technical Honor Society - Oakland Schools Tech Campus Northeast - Michigan
1371 N Perry Rd.
Pontiac, MI 48340
Ph: (248)451-2700
E-mail: roosevelt.daniel@oakland.k12.mi.us
URL: http://www.oakland.k12.mi.us
Contact: Roosevelt Daniel, Contact
Local.

9422 ■ Oakland County Pioneer and Historical Society (OCPHS)
405 Cesar E. Chavez Ave.
Pontiac, MI 48342
Ph: (248)338-6732
Fax: (248)338-6731
E-mail: ocphs@wwnet.net
Contact: Michael Willis, Pres.
Founded: 1874. **Members:** 600. **Membership Dues:** student, senior (65 and over), $15 (annual) • individual, non-profit organization, $20 (annual) • couple, $35 (annual) • family (parents and children), patron, $50-$75 (annual) • benefactor, $150 (annual) • corporate sponsor, $500 (annual). **Staff:** 1. **Local.** Historians, researchers, genealogists, archaeologists, students, and educators. Collects, preserves, and interprets the history of Oakland County, Michigan. **Libraries: Type:** open to the public. **Holdings:** 11,000; books, photographs. **Subjects:** history of Oakland County, civil war. **Publications:** *Oakland Gazette*, biennial. Newsletter. **Price:** included in membership dues. **Circulation:** 500. **Conventions/Meetings:** annual dinner - October in Pontiac, MI • annual meeting - January in Pontiac, MI.

9423 ■ Pontiac Regional Chamber
402 N Telegraph Rd.
Pontiac, MI 48341
Ph: (248)335-9600
Fax: (248)335-9601
E-mail: info@pontiacchamber.com
URL: http://www.pontiacchamber.com
Contact: Rosemary Gallardo, Pres.
Membership Dues: business, $150-$1,250 • government agency, utility, hospital, $600 • nonprofit service organization and charity, $150. **Local.** Promotes growth and development of the business community while contributing to a safe, stable, and prosperous environment. **Computer Services:** Information services, membership directory. **Formerly:** (2006) Greater Pontiac Area Chamber of Commerce. **Publications:** *Inside Business*, monthly. Magazine. Contains practical strategies to assist the chamber members in managing their businesses. **Circulation:** 15,000. **Advertising:** accepted.

9424 ■ Pontiac Yacht Club (PYC)
PO Box 430594
Pontiac, MI 48343
Ph: (248)682-8020
E-mail: bjsailing@aol.org
URL: http://www.lightningclass.org/fleet54
Local.

Port Austin

9425 ■ American Legion, Frank Horetski Post 499
PO Box 6871
Port Austin, MI 48467
Ph: (517)371-4720
Fax: (517)371-2401
URL: National Affiliate–www.legion.org
Local. Affiliated With: American Legion.

9426 ■ Port Austin Reeflight Association
c/o Louis M. Schillinger
8265 N Van Dyke
Port Austin, MI 48467-9521
Ph: (989)738-6555
Contact: Louis M. Schillinger, Pres.
Local.

Port Huron

9427 ■ AAA Michigan
933 Lapeer
Port Huron, MI 48060
Ph: (810)987-4800
Free: (800)462-9968
Contact: Rose Harvey, Contact
State.

9428 ■ American Legion, Michigan Post 8
c/o Charles A. Hammond
1026 6th St.
Port Huron, MI 48060
Ph: (517)371-4720
Fax: (517)371-2401
URL: National Affiliate–www.legion.org
Contact: Charles A. Hammond, Contact
Local. Affiliated With: American Legion.

9429 ■ American Red Cross, St. Clair County Chapter
615 Pine St.
Port Huron, MI 48060
Ph: (810)985-7117
Fax: (810)985-9612
URL: http://www.sccrc.org
Local.

9430 ■ Blue Water Area Convention and Visitors Bureau
520 Thomas Edison Pkwy.
Port Huron, MI 48060
Ph: (810)987-8687
Free: (800)852-4242
E-mail: bluewater@bluewater.org
URL: http://www.bluewater.org
Contact: Marci Fogal, Pres.
Local.

9431 ■ Blue Water Habitat for Humanity
PO Box 611867
Port Huron, MI 48061-1867
Ph: (810)985-9080
Fax: (810)985-4798
E-mail: info@bwhabitat.org
URL: http://www.bwhabitat.org
Contact: Jim Faulkner, Exec.Dir.
Local. Telecommunication Services: electronic mail, jim@bwhabitat.org. **Affiliated With:** Habitat for Humanity International.

9432 ■ Eastern Thumb Association of Realtors
2443 10th Ave.
Port Huron, MI 48060
Ph: (810)982-0155
Fax: (810)982-6889
E-mail: etar@easternthumb.com
URL: http://www.easternthumbhomes.com
Contact: Mike Basey, Pres.
Local. Strives to develop real estate business practices. Advocates the right to own, use and transfer real property. Provides a facility for professional development, research and exchange of information among members. **Affiliated With:** National Association of Realtors.

9433 ■ Epsilon Sigma Phi, NC Alpha PSI - Michigan
c/o Katherine Hale, Pres.-Elect
200 Grand River Ave., Ste.102
Port Huron, MI 48060
Ph: (810)989-6935
Fax: (810)985-3557
E-mail: halek@msu.edu
URL: http://web1.msue.msu.edu/esp
Contact: Katherine Hale, Pres.-Elect
State. Affiliated With: Epsilon Sigma Phi.

9434 ■ Greater Port Huron Area Chamber of Commerce
920 Pine Grove Ave.
Port Huron, MI 48060
Ph: (810)985-7101
Fax: (810)985-7311
Free: (800)361-0526
E-mail: info@porthuron-chamber.org
URL: http://www.porthuron-chamber.org
Contact: Lisa Hatch, Exec.Dir.
Founded: 1917. **Members:** 450. **Membership Dues:** base (motels, hotels, apartments, assisted living, nursing homes), $200 (annual) • business (based on number of employees), $190-$850 (annual). **Local.** Retailers, service providers, manufacturers and community organizations. Strives to improve the business community and to enhance the quality of life in greater Port Huron area. **Committees:** Education; Planning and Events; Public Affairs. **Publications:** Directory, annual. **Circulation:** 2,000. **Advertising:** accepted • Newsletter, monthly. **Circulation:** 550. **Advertising:** accepted. Alternate Formats: online.

9435 ■ Michigan Council of the Blind and Visually Impaired
c/o Michael Geno, Pres.
2028 St. Clair St.
Port Huron, MI 48060
E-mail: mcbvi@sbcglobal.net
URL: National Affiliate–www.acb.org
Contact: Michael Geno, Pres.
State. Strives to improve the well-being of all blind and visually impaired individuals. Seeks to elevate the social, economic and cultural levels of blind people. Improves educational and rehabilitation facilities and opportunities for the visually impaired. **Affiliated With:** American Council of the Blind.

9436 ■ PFLAG Port Huron/Sarnia-Bluewater
PO Box 611866
Port Huron, MI 48061
Ph: (810)987-4342
E-mail: sbwpflag@aol.com
URL: http://www.pflag.org/Michigan.216.0.html
Local. Affiliated With: Parents, Families, and Friends of Lesbians and Gays.

9437 ■ Phi Theta Kappa, Lambda Mu Chapter - St. Clair County Community College
c/o Thomas Obee
323 Erie St.
Port Huron, MI 48061
Ph: (810)989-5587
E-mail: tom.obee@ptk.org
URL: http://www.ptk.org/directories/chapters/MI/247-1.htm
Contact: Thomas Obee, Advisor
Local.

9438 ■ Port Huron Minor Hockey Association
701 McMorran Blvd.
PO Box 610251
Port Huron, MI 48061-0251
Ph: (810)982-0242
Fax: (810)982-7475
URL: http://www.phhockey.com
Contact: Erik Parker, Pres.
Amateur hockey teams. Promotes the sport of hockey.

9439 ■ St. Clair County Convention and Visitors Bureau
520 Thomas Edison Pkwy.
Port Huron, MI 48060
Ph: (810)987-8687
Fax: (810)987-1441
Free: (800)852-4242
E-mail: bluewater@bluewater.org
URL: http://www.bluewater.org
Contact: Nancy-Sharon Bland, Pres. & CEO
Promotes convention business and tourism in area. **Formerly:** (1995) Blue Water Area Tourist Bureau. **Publications:** *Blue Water Area*, annual. Brochure. Contains information on St. Clair County. **Price:** free. **Advertising:** accepted.

9440 ■ St. Clair County Medical Society - Michigan (SCCMS)
2925 Riverside Dr.
Port Huron, MI 48060-1897
Ph: (810)985-9502
Fax: (810)987-1375
E-mail: bonnie@sccms.org
URL: http://www.sccms.org
Contact: Bonnie Jean Campbell MSLS, Exec.Dir.
Local. Advances the art and science of medicine. Promotes patient care and the betterment of public health. **Affiliated With:** Michigan State Medical Society.

9441 ■ St. Clair County Youth for Christ
PO Box 610533
Port Huron, MI 48061-0533
Ph: (810)982-9551
Fax: (810)982-9552
URL: http://www.yfcscc.org
Local. Affiliated With: Youth for Christ/U.S.A.

9442 ■ United Way of St. Clair County
1723 Military St.
Port Huron, MI 48060
Ph: (810)985-8169
Fax: (810)982-7202
URL: http://uwsccmi.org
Contact: Lonnie Stevens, Exec.Dir.
Local. Affiliated With: United Way of America.

9443 ■ Veteran Motor Car Club of America - Blue Water Chapter
c/o Bart Dickey, Pres.
2528 Riverwood Dr.
Port Huron, MI 48060
Ph: (810)982-9512
URL: National Affiliate–www.vmcca.org
Contact: Bart Dickey, Pres.
Local. Affiliated With: Veteran Motor Car Club of America.

Portage

9444 ■ American Legion, Portage Post 207
8845 Sprinkle Rd.
Portage, MI 49002
Ph: (269)323-9088
Fax: (517)371-2401
URL: National Affiliate–www.legion.org
Local. Affiliated With: American Legion.

9445 ■ BMW Car Club of America, Michiana Chapter
c/o Matt Napieralski, VP
PO Box 2523
Portage, MI 49081-2523
Ph: (574)289-1220
E-mail: matt@bendermold.com
URL: http://www.michiana-bmwcca.com
Contact: Matt Napieralski, VP
Local. Affiliated With: BMW Car Club of America.

9446 ■ Kalamazoo Antique Bottle Club
c/o Charles H. Parker, Jr., Pres.
607 Crocket Ave.
Portage, MI 49024
Ph: (616)329-0853
E-mail: prostock@net-link.net
URL: National Affiliate–www.fohbc.com
Contact: Charles H. Parker Jr., Pres.
Local. Affiliated With: Federation of Historical Bottle Collectors.

9447 ■ Kalamazoo Human Resources Management Association
PO Box 1444
Portage, MI 49081
Ph: (269)488-3653
E-mail: oliphant@hinmancompany.com
URL: http://www.khrma.org
Contact: Mary-Frances Oliphant, Pres.
Local. Represents the interests of human resource and industrial relations professionals and executives. Promotes the advancement of human resource management.

9448 ■ Kalamazoo Michigan Bocce Club
716 Barberry Ave.
Portage, MI 49002
Ph: (269)327-4958
E-mail: billvandermay@aol.com
URL: National Affiliate–www.bocce.com
Local. Affiliated With: United States Bocce Federation.

9449 ■ Kalamazoo Numismatic Club
c/o Russell F. Barr
PO Box 462
Portage, MI 49081-0876
E-mail: russell_9@sbcglobal.net
URL: National Affiliate–www.money.org
Contact: Russell F. Barr, Contact
Local. Affiliated With: American Numismatic Association.

9450 ■ Long Lake Association
c/o David Steffens, Pres.
5019 S Long Lake Dr.
Portage, MI 49002
E-mail: dsteffens@wsc-mi.com
URL: http://www.longlakeassoc.com
Contact: David Steffens, Pres.
Local.

9451 ■ Michigan Association of Acupuncture and Oriental Medicine (MAAOM)
4855 W Centre Ave., Ste.B
Portage, MI 49024-4686
Ph: (269)353-3520
Fax: (269)353-3038
E-mail: staff@michiganacupuncture.org
URL: http://www.michiganacupuncture.org
Contact: Beverly Yee, Pres.
State. Affiliated With: American Association of Oriental Medicine.

9452 ■ PFLAG Kalamazoo/Southwest Michigan
PO Box 1201
Portage, MI 49081
Ph: (269)664-6892
Fax: (269)968-2960
E-mail: pflagswm@yahoo.com
URL: http://www.geocities.com/pflagswm
Local. Affiliated With: Parents, Families, and Friends of Lesbians and Gays.

9453 ■ Portage Lions Club - Michigan
PO Box 134
Portage, MI 49081
E-mail: lgb5025@charter.net
URL: http://milions11b2.org
Local. Affiliated With: Lions Clubs International.

9454 ■ Southwest Michigan Skating Club
PO Box 1722
Portage, MI 49081-1722
Ph: (269)345-5777
E-mail: bonnie.blair@boiseoffice.com
URL: http://www.swmichskatingclub.org
Local. Provides programs to encourage participation and achievement in the sport of figure skating on ice. Defines and maintains uniform standards of skating proficiency. Organizes and sponsors competitions and exhibitions for the purpose of stimulating interest in figure skating. **Affiliated With:** United States Figure Skating Association.

9455 ■ USA Weightlifting - Husky Power Training
c/o Dave Laing
1000 Idaho
Portage, MI 49024
Ph: (616)329-7371 (616)323-5581
Fax: (616)323-5581
URL: National Affiliate–www.usaweightlifting.org
Contact: Dave Laing, Contact
Local. Affiliated With: USA Weightlifting.

Portland

9456 ■ American Legion, Michigan Post 129
c/o Dale E. Hyland
PO Box 291
Portland, MI 48875
Ph: (517)371-4720
Fax: (517)371-2401
URL: National Affiliate–www.legion.org
Contact: Dale E. Hyland, Contact
Local. Affiliated With: American Legion.

9457 ■ Portland Area Chamber of Commerce (PACC)
PO Box 303
Portland, MI 48875
Ph: (517)647-2100
Fax: (517)647-2100
E-mail: portlandmichamber@yahoo.com
Contact: Terry Schrauben, Pres.
Founded: 1952. **Members:** 60. **Local.** Promotes business and community development in the Portland, MI area. **Publications:** none. **Conventions/Meetings:** monthly meeting.

Potterville

9458 ■ American Legion, Dimondale Potterville Post 272
PO Box 152
Potterville, MI 48876
Ph: (517)371-4720
Fax: (517)371-2401
URL: National Affiliate–www.legion.org
Local. Affiliated With: American Legion.

9459 ■ Capital Area Astronomy Association
c/o Michael Rogers, Sec./Program Dir.
3979 E Gresham Hwy.
Potterville, MI 48876
Ph: (517)645-6666
E-mail: miker@foxobservatory.org
URL: http://www.foxobservatory.org
Contact: Michael Rogers, Sec./Program Dir.
Local. Amateur astronomers of all interest and experience levels.

9460 ■ Potterville Lions Club
c/o Chuck Brien, Pres.
201 Pinetree Rd.
Potterville, MI 48876
Ph: (517)645-2532
URL: http://www.district11c2.org
Contact: Chuck Brien, Pres.
Local. Affiliated With: Lions Clubs International.

Powers

9461 ■ American Legion, Tony Rivord Post 244
PO Box 344
Powers, MI 49874
Ph: (517)371-4720
Fax: (517)371-2401
URL: National Affiliate–www.legion.org
Local. Affiliated With: American Legion.

Prescott

9462 ■ American Legion, Schuster-Stahl Post 370
PO Box 4028
Prescott, MI 48756
Ph: (517)836-2660
Fax: (517)371-2401
URL: National Affiliate–www.legion.org
Local. Affiliated With: American Legion.

Prudenville

9463 ■ American Legion, Houghton-Higgins-Lake Post 245
3565 S Reserve Rd.
Prudenville, MI 48651
Ph: (517)371-4720
Fax: (517)371-2401
URL: National Affiliate–www.legion.org
Local. Affiliated With: American Legion.

Quincy

9464 ■ American Legion, Sherman-Rice-Demorest Post 157
104 E Chicago St.
Quincy, MI 49082
Ph: (517)371-4720
Fax: (517)371-2401
URL: National Affiliate–www.legion.org
Local. Affiliated With: American Legion.

9465 ■ Humane Society of Branch County
969 W Wildwood Rd.
Quincy, MI 49082-9508
Ph: (517)639-4426 (517)639-5415
E-mail: humanesociety@cbpu.com
URL: http://www.cbpu.com
Contact: John Fyfe, Pres.
Founded: 1973. **Members:** 85. **Membership Dues:** family, $10 (annual). **Staff:** 7. **Local. Conventions/Meetings:** monthly meeting - 1st Tuesday.

9466 ■ Michigan Youth in Government (MYIG)
c/o Brent Veysey, Dir.
PO Box 65
Quincy, MI 49082
Ph: (517)639-4480
Fax: (517)639-3525
E-mail: myig@charter.net
URL: http://www.myig.org
Contact: Brent Veysey, Dir.
State.

9467 ■ Quincy Chamber of Commerce
PO Box 132
Quincy, MI 49082
Ph: (517)639-8369
Fax: (517)639-5757
Contact: Kim Hemker, Pres.
Local.

9468 ■ Quincy Lions Club - Michigan
c/o Richard Marowelli, Sec.
109 E Jefferson St.
Quincy, MI 49082
Ph: (517)639-3022 (517)639-8056
Fax: (517)639-3078
E-mail: kamacct@yahoo.com
URL: http://www.lionsdistrict11b1.org/lc_quincy.asp
Contact: Richard Marowelli, Sec.
Local. Affiliated With: Lions Clubs International.

Rapid River

9469 ■ American Legion, Michigan Post 301
c/o Walter W. Cole
PO Box 301
Rapid River, MI 49878
Ph: (517)371-4720
Fax: (517)371-2401
URL: National Affiliate–www.legion.org
Contact: Walter W. Cole, Contact
Local. Affiliated With: American Legion.

9470 ■ Bay De Noc Gem and Mineral Club (BDNGMC)
c/o Rob Wolfe, Pres.
12239 Church P, 1 Rd.
Rapid River, MI 49878
E-mail: bdngmc@yahoo.com
URL: http://www.geocities.com/bdngmc
Contact: Sarah Norman, Sec.
Local. Aims to further the study of Earth Sciences and the practice of lapidary arts and mineralogy. **Affiliated With:** American Federation of Mineralogical Societies.

Ravenna

9471 ■ American Legion, Michigan Post 297
c/o Sherman Moore
PO Box 302
Ravenna, MI 49451
Ph: (517)371-4720
Fax: (517)371-2401
URL: National Affiliate–www.legion.org
Contact: Sherman Moore, Contact
Local. Affiliated With: American Legion.

9472 ■ West Michigan Corvair Club
255 John Kent Dr.
Ravenna, MI 49451
E-mail: wmcc@corvair.org
URL: http://www.corvair.org/chapters/chapter495
Contact: Steve Ridderman, Pres.
Membership Dues: regular, $18 (annual). **Local.** Enthusiasts of the Corvair automobile united for technical assistance and parts availability. **Affiliated With:** Corvair Society of America.

Reading

9473 ■ American Legion, Wolverine Post 360
PO Box 13
Reading, MI 49274
Ph: (517)371-4720
Fax: (517)371-2401
URL: National Affiliate–www.legion.org
Local. Affiliated With: American Legion.

Redford

9474 ■ Al-Anon Family Groups of Metro Detroit
26150 Five Mile Rd., Ste.19
Redford, MI 48239
Ph: (313)242-0300
Fax: (313)242-0303
Free: (800)813-3105
E-mail: info@metrodetroitafg.org
URL: http://www.metrodetroitafg.org
Contact: Thomas Coffey, Exec.Sec.
Founded: 1951. **Staff:** 2. **Local Groups:** 200. **Local.** Works to aid families and friends of problem drinkers. **Formerly:** (2005) Al-Anon Family Groups of the Detroit Area. **Publications:** *What's the Buzz*, monthly. Newsletter. Contains news and upcoming events. **Circulation:** 375 • *Where to find Al-Anon, Alateen and Al-Anon Adult Children in S.E. Michigan*, semiannual. Directory. **Price:** $1.25 each. **Conventions/Meetings:** monthly Detroit Area Al-Anon Council - meeting, meeting of representatives from each group.

9475 ■ American Legion, Rosedale Park Post 390
12879 Leverne
Redford, MI 48239
Ph: (313)387-1615
Fax: (517)371-2401
URL: National Affiliate–www.legion.org
Local. Affiliated With: American Legion.

9476 ■ Cadillac Squares
PO Box 40487
Redford, MI 48240-0487
Ph: (313)837-7966
E-mail: johnandj@ameritech.net
URL: http://www.cadillacsquares.com
Contact: Mr. Jay Steffka, Treas.
Local. Affiliated With: International Association of Gay Square Dance Clubs.

9477 ■ Livonia Lamplighter Lions Club
c/o Arne Syversen, Pres.
14417 Seminole
Redford, MI 48239
Ph: (734)421-0523
URL: http://www.metrodetroitlions.org
Contact: Arne Syversen, Pres.
Local. Affiliated With: Lions Clubs International.

9478 ■ Michigan Norml
c/o George Sherfield
25017 Curtis
Redford, MI 48240
Ph: (313)533-6108
E-mail: minorml@sbcglobal.net
URL: National Affiliate–www.norml.org
State. Affiliated With: National Organization for the Reform of Marijuana Laws.

9479 ■ Redford Township Chamber of Commerce (RTCC)
26050 5 Mile Rd.
Redford, MI 48239-3289
Ph: (313)535-0960
Fax: (313)535-6356
E-mail: rtcc@htdconnect.com
URL: http://redfordchamber.org
Contact: Dan Lis, Pres.
Founded: 1950. **Membership Dues:** basic, $180 (annual). **Local.** Promotes business and community development in Redford Township, MI. **Publications:** *Redford Township Directory*, annual • Newsletter, monthly. **Conventions/Meetings:** monthly luncheon - 3rd Wednesday.

Reed City

9480 ■ American Legion, Michigan Post 78
c/o Gilbert A. Samis
500 N Park St.
Reed City, MI 49677
Ph: (517)371-4720
Fax: (517)371-2401
URL: National Affiliate–www.legion.org
Contact: Gilbert A. Samis, Contact
Local. Affiliated With: American Legion.

9481 ■ National Speleological Society, West Michigan Grotto
c/o Patty Fasbender
6767 Lakola Rd.
Reed City, MI 49677
Ph: (231)832-1531
E-mail: ronpatty@tm.net
URL: National Affiliate–www.caves.org
Contact: Patty Fasbender, Contact
Local. Seeks to study, explore and conserve cave and karst resources. Protects access to caves and promotes responsible caving. Encourages responsible management of caves and their unique environments. **Affiliated With:** National Speleological Society.

9482 ■ Osceola Economic Alliance (OEA)
c/o Dan Massy
301 W Upton
Reed City, MI 49677
Ph: (231)832-7397
Fax: (231)832-6197
E-mail: massyd@msu.edu
URL: http://www.osceola-alliance.org
Contact: Dan Massy, Community and Economic Developer
Founded: 1985. **Staff:** 1. **Local.** Individuals, businesses, and local units of government interested in improving community and economic development opportunities in Osceola County, MI. **Formerly:** (1998) Osceola Economic Development Corp. **Publications:** *Osceola County Manufacturers/Industrial Business Directory*, annual. Book. Contains data on all Osceola County based manufacturers. **Price:** $30.00. **Conventions/Meetings:** semimonthly board meeting.

9483 ■ Reed City Area Chamber of Commerce (RCACC)
PO Box 27
Reed City, MI 49677
Ph: (231)832-5431
Fax: (231)832-5431
Free: (877)832-7332
E-mail: sally.rccc@charter.net
URL: http://www.reedcitycrossroads.com
Contact: Mr. David Langworthy, Pres.
Local. Helps the business, industry and tourism of Reed City Area to prosper.

9484 ■ Reed City Lions Club
c/o Norm VanArsdale, Pres.
9714 210th Ave.
Reed City, MI 49677
Ph: (231)832-4629
E-mail: thatchroof@charter.net
URL: http://lions.silverthorn.biz/11-e1
Contact: Norm VanArsdale, Pres.
Local. Affiliated With: Lions Clubs International.

Reese

9485 ■ American Legion, Reese Post 139
PO Box 396
Reese, MI 48757
Ph: (517)371-4720
Fax: (517)371-2401
URL: National Affiliate–www.legion.org
Local. Affiliated With: American Legion.

9486 ■ Reese Chamber of Commerce
PO Box 113
Reese, MI 48757
Ph: (989)868-9810
Contact: Rick Keyser, Pres.
Members: 50. **Local. Formerly:** (2005) Reese Area Chamber of Commerce.

Richland

9487 ■ Hospitality Financial and Technology Professionals - West Michigan Chapter
c/o Dale Shockley
9725 W Gull Lake Dr.
Richland, MI 49083-9541
Ph: (269)629-9714
Fax: (269)629-5045
E-mail: dshockley@gullakecc.com
URL: National Affiliate–www.hftp.org
Contact: Dale Shockley, Pres.
Local. Provides opportunities to members through professional and educational development. **Affiliated With:** Hospitality Financial and Technology Professionals. **Conventions/Meetings:** monthly luncheon - every third Thursday of each month.

Richmond

9488 ■ Pheasants Forever, Macomb County
26877 Dayton Rd.
Richmond, MI 48062
E-mail: pfchapter549@aol.com
URL: http://www.geocities.com/macombphez4ever
Local. Affiliated With: Pheasants Forever.

9489 ■ Richmond Area Chamber of Commerce
68371 Oak St.
Richmond, MI 48062
Ph: (586)727-3266
Fax: (586)727-3635
E-mail: kim@racc-online.org
URL: http://www.racc-online.org
Contact: Kim Galante, Exec.Dir.
Local. Promotes economic growth and development of Richmond, MI.

9490 ■ Ruffed Grouse Society, Robert J. Lytle Chapter
c/o John Pomante, Jr.
31162 Bordman Rd.
Richmond, MI 48062
Ph: (810)392-3827
E-mail: jpomante@massnet1.net
URL: National Affiliate–www.ruffedgrousesociety.org
Contact: John Pomante Jr., Contact
Local. Affiliated With: Ruffed Grouse Society.

Richville

9491 ■ American Legion, Michigan Post 400
c/o Alvin F. Miller
PO Box 161
Richville, MI 48758

Ph: (517)371-4720
Fax: (517)371-2401
URL: National Affiliate–www.legion.org
Contact: Alvin F. Miller, Contact
Local. **Affiliated With:** American Legion.

River Rouge

9492 ■ Ecorse-River Rouge Lions Club
c/o Robert Wilson, Pres.
345 Beechwood St.
River Rouge, MI 48218
Ph: (313)553-3005
E-mail: ai2831@wayne.edu
URL: http://www.metrodetroitlions.org
Contact: Robert Wilson, Pres.
Local. Affiliated With: Lions Clubs International.

Riverside

9493 ■ Preserve the Dunes
c/o Charles Davis
PO Box 581
Riverside, MI 49084
E-mail: sosdunes@daac.com
URL: http://www.daac.com/sosdunes
Local.

Riverview

9494 ■ American Legion, Clough-Lambrix Post 389
17116 Quarry St.
Riverview, MI 48192
Ph: (517)371-4720
Fax: (517)371-2401
URL: National Affiliate–www.legion.org
Local. Affiliated With: American Legion.

9495 ■ Barefoot Connections
c/o Linda J. LeMonde, Pres.
PO Box 2065
Riverview, MI 48192-1065
Fax: (206)888-2094
E-mail: senior-staff@nativenewsonline.org
URL: http://www.nativenewsonline.org/mission.htm
Contact: Linda J. LeMonde, Pres.
Local.

Rives Junction

9496 ■ Cycle Conservation Club of Michigan (CCC)
10504 Broughwell Rd.
Rives Junction, MI 49277-9653
Ph: (517)569-9999
Fax: (517)569-9979
E-mail: cccboard@cycleconservationclub.org
URL: http://www.cycleconservationclub.org
Contact: Ron Mollitor, Pres.
Founded: 1968. **Members:** 4,000. **Membership Dues:** active, $30 (annual) • family, $37 (annual) • sustaining, $50-$500 (annual). **Staff:** 2. **Budget:** $200,000. **State Groups:** 15. **State**. Promotes off-road trail riding as a family activity. Works to preserve and expand trail network in MI. Conducts recreational activities; operates summer camp; sponsors charitable activities, rider education program and trail maintenance grant program. **Publications:** *Great Lakes Trail Rider*, monthly. Magazine. Covers club activities; provides trail riding information and legislative and land use issues. **Price:** included in membership dues. **Circulation:** 5,300. **Advertising:** accepted • *Michigan ORV Trail System*. Includes map of off-road trails in Michigan. **Price:** included in membership dues. **Conventions/Meetings:** quarterly board meeting - always third Wednesday • periodic Land Use Workshop • annual meeting - always first weekend of May.

Rochester

9497 ■ American Association of Physics Teachers, Michigan Section
c/o Alan M. Gibson, Representative
Connect2Science
3200 W Tienken Rd.
Rochester, MI 48306
Ph: (248)651-1726
E-mail: fziksman@yahoo.com
URL: http://www.miaapt.org
Contact: Alan M. Gibson, Representative
State. Seeks to enhance the understanding and appreciation of physics through teaching. Aims to improve the pedagogical skills and physics knowledge of teachers at all levels. **Affiliated With:** American Association of Physics Teachers.

9498 ■ American Association of Physics Teachers, Puerto Rico Section
c/o Alan M. Gibson
3200 W Tienken Rd.
Rochester, MI 48306
Ph: (248)651-1726
E-mail: fziksman@yahoo.com
URL: National Affiliate–www.aapt.org
Contact: Alan M. Gibson, Contact
State. Seeks to enhance the understanding and appreciation of physics through teaching. Aims to improve the pedagogical skills and physics knowledge of teachers at all levels. **Affiliated With:** American Association of Physics Teachers.

9499 ■ American Legion, Homer Wing Post 172
234 Walnut Blvd.
Rochester, MI 48307
Ph: (517)371-4720
Fax: (517)371-2401
URL: National Affiliate–www.legion.org
Local. Affiliated With: American Legion.

9500 ■ American Statistical Association, Detroit Chapter
c/o Robert Kushler, Treas.
Oakland Univ.
Dept. of Mathematics and Statistics
Rochester, MI 48309
Ph: (248)370-3445
E-mail: kushler@oakland.edu
URL: National Affiliate–www.amstat.org
Contact: Robert Kushler, Treas.
Local. Promotes statistical practice, applications and research. Works for the improvement of statistical education at all levels. Seeks opportunities to advance the statistics profession. **Affiliated With:** American Statistical Association.

9501 ■ Clinton Valley Trout Unlimited
c/o Carlton Crook, Bd. Member
3742 Mildred
Rochester, MI 48309
Ph: (248)852-0639
E-mail: miflyfish@netzero.net
URL: http://www.clintonvalleytu.com/
Contact: Ed Roden, Pres.
Local. Affiliated With: Trout Unlimited.

9502 ■ Detroit Rugby Football Club of Metropolitan Detroit (DRFC)
c/o Gareth Davies
1017 Inglewood
Rochester, MI 48307
Ph: (248)650-9283
E-mail: drfc@detroitrugby.org
URL: http://www.detroitrugby.org
Contact: Gareth Davies, Pres.
Founded: 1968. **Members:** 200. **Local**. Promotes the sport of rugby at all age levels, within the Detroit Metropolitan area, including youth (boys and girls ages 11-18), men and women (18) and senior men (35); programs include coaching, refereeing and program development. Introductory "Fun Days" are also held for children under age 11.

9503 ■ Hugger Elementary PTA
5050 Shelton Rd.
Rochester, MI 48306
Ph: (248)601-1402
E-mail: markandkonni@aol.com
URL: http://familyeducation.com/MI/Huggerschool
Contact: Konni Behounek, Pres.
Local. Parents, teachers, students, and others interested in uniting the forces of home, school, and community. Promotes the welfare of children and youth.

9504 ■ IEEE Computer Society, Southeastern Michigan Chapter
c/o Subramanian Ganesan
Oakland Univ.
2200 N Squirrel Hill Rd.
Rochester, MI 48309-4401
Ph: (248)370-2206
E-mail: ganesan@oakland.edu
URL: National Affiliate–www.computer.org
Contact: Subramanian Ganesan, Contact
Local. Affiliated With: IEEE Computer Society.

9505 ■ Michigan Council of Teachers of English (MCTE)
c/o Ray H. Lawson, Treas.
PO Box 81152
Rochester, MI 48308-1152
E-mail: treasurer@mienglishteacher.org
URL: http://www.mienglishteacher.org
Contact: Ray H. Lawson, Treas.
Founded: 1924. **State.**

9506 ■ Michigan Mental Health Counselors Association (MMHCA)
PO Box 80036
Rochester, MI 48308
Ph: (248)420-8010
Free: (800)98M-MHCA
E-mail: dbaker@mmhca.org
URL: http://www.mmhca.org
Contact: Diane Baker, Pres.
Members: 2. **Membership Dues:** clinical, $75 (annual) • student, $50 (annual). **Staff:** 1. **State Groups:** 1. **State**. **Awards:** Distinguished Service Award. **Frequency:** annual. **Type:** recognition • President's Award. **Frequency:** annual. **Type:** recognition. **Committees:** Conference; Marketing; Membership. **Publications:** *Michigan Mental Health Counselors Register*, annual. Lists counselors in the area. **Price:** free. **Conventions/Meetings:** annual conference • periodic workshop.

9507 ■ Michigan Senior Olympics
650 Letica Dr.
Rochester, MI 48307
Ph: (248)608-0250
Fax: (248)656-3153
URL: http://www.michiganseniorolympics.org
Contact: Ann Brewer, Office Mgr.
State.

9508 ■ Paint a Miracle
c/o Yolanda E. Propson
302B W Univ.
Rochester, MI 48309
Ph: (248)652-3346
E-mail: shelly@paintamiracle.org
URL: http://www.paintamiracle.org
Local.

9509 ■ Psi Chi, National Honor Society in Psychology - Oakland University
c/o Dept. of Psychology
111 Pryale Hall
Rochester, MI 48309
Ph: (248)370-2300
Fax: (248)370-4612
E-mail: stewart@oakland.edu
URL: http://www2.oakland.edu/psych/psychstudent
Local. Affiliated With: Psi Chi, National Honor Society in Psychology.

9510 ■ Rochester Junior Woman's Club (RJWC)
PO Box 80743
Rochester, MI 48308-0743
Ph: (248)652-2765
E-mail: lmo102967@aol.com
Contact: Lynn Marie Oates, Pres.
Local.

9511 ■ Society of Automotive Engineers - Northern Michigan University
School of Engg.
155 Dodge Hall
Rochester, MI 48309-4478
E-mail: tmeravi@nmu.edu
URL: National Affiliate–www.sae.org
Contact: Jeff Hoffman, Contact
Local. Advances the engineering mobility systems. Provides technical information and expertise used in designing, building, maintaining and operating self-propelled vehicles, whether land, sea, air or space based. Collects and disseminates information on cars, trucks, aircraft, space vehicles, off-highway vehicles, marine equipment and engine of all types. Fosters information exchange among the worldwide automotive and aerospace communities. **Affiliated With:** SAE International - Society of Automotive Engineers.

Rochester Hills

9512 ■ Assistance League of Southeastern Michigan
3128 Walton Blvd.
PMB 247
Rochester Hills, MI 48309-1232
Ph: (248)656-0414
Fax: (248)656-0341
E-mail: semichal@hotmail.com
URL: http://semich.assistanceleague.org
Local. Affiliated With: Assistance League.

9513 ■ Corvette Club of Michigan (CCM)
603 Parkland Dr.
Rochester Hills, MI 48307-3453
E-mail: brickpaver@peoplepc.com
URL: http://www.corvetteclubmi.com
Contact: Mary Wentzel, Pres.
Local. Affiliated With: National Council of Corvette Clubs.

9514 ■ Flint Downtown Host Lions Club
c/o Raymond Percival, Sec.
3250 Walton Blvd., Apt. 222
Rochester Hills, MI 48309-1281
Ph: (248)375-0543
E-mail: raymondpercival@comcast.net
URL: http://www.geocities.com/dist11d1
Contact: Raymond Percival, Sec.
Local. Affiliated With: Lions Clubs International.

9515 ■ National Association of Miniature Enthusiasts - Wee Bee's of Birmingham
c/o Mary Rosenbusch
476 W Maryknoll Rd.
Rochester Hills, MI 48309
Ph: (248)375-0892
URL: http://www.miniatures.org/states/MI.html
Contact: Mary Rosenbusch, Contact
Local. Affiliated With: National Association of Miniature Enthusiasts.

9516 ■ Paint Creek Foklore Society
c/o University Presbyterian Church
1385 S Adams Rd.
Rochester Hills, MI 48306
Ph: (586)778-9643
E-mail: denisestein@hotmail.com
URL: http://www.Paintcreekfolkloresociety.org
Contact: Ms. Denise Marie Stein, VP
Founded: 1974. **Members:** 100. **Membership Dues:** single, $35 (annual) • family, $50 (annual) • visitor, $7 (annual). **Local Groups:** 1. **Local**. Participatory folk music group designed to share talents and knowledge among members and the greater community. **Affiliated With:** Country Dance and Song Society. **Publications:** *Keeping Tabs*, monthly. Newsletter. Covers current events, upcoming events and folk calendar. **Price:** $15.00/yr.; free with membership. Alternate Formats: online.

9517 ■ Psi Chi, National Honor Society in Psychology - Rochester College
c/o Dept. of Psychology
800 W Avon Rd.
Rochester Hills, MI 48307-2764
Ph: (248)218-2122
Fax: (248)218-2235
E-mail: gmackinnon@rc.edu
URL: http://www.psichi.org/chapters/info.asp?chapter_id=920
Contact: Gordon MacKinnon PhD, Advisor
Local.

9518 ■ Rochester High School PTSA (RHS PTSA)
180 S Livernois
Rochester Hills, MI 48307
Ph: (248)652-7067
E-mail: ddbstrickr@aol.com
URL: http://familyeducation.com/MI/RHSPTSA
Contact: Diane Stricker, Pres.
Local. Parents, teachers, students, and others interested in uniting the forces of home, school, and community. Promotes the welfare of children and youth.

9519 ■ SE Michigan TSCA
c/o John VanSlembrouck
Stoney Creek Wooden Boat Shop
1058 E Tienken Rd.
Rochester Hills, MI 48306
E-mail: stoneycreek@stoneycreekboatshop.com
URL: National Affiliate–www.tsca.net
Contact: John VanSlembrouck, Contact
State.

9520 ■ Southern Michigan Obedience Training Club (SMOTC)
390 Lehigh
Rochester Hills, MI 48307
Ph: (248)546-2727
Free: (800)798-9992
E-mail: dawgmom@mindspring.com
URL: http://www.smotc.com
Contact: Carol Vollick, Contact
Founded: 1948. **State**. Provides training for dogs through education, shows, breeding, pets, and rescue.

Rock

9521 ■ American Legion, Rock Post 559
14454 M-35
Rock, MI 49880
Ph: (517)371-4720
Fax: (517)371-2401
URL: National Affiliate–www.legion.org
Local. Affiliated With: American Legion.

Rockford

9522 ■ Algoma Township Historical Society
10531 Algoma Ave.
Rockford, MI 49341-9136
Ph: (616)866-1583
Fax: (616)866-3832
E-mail: info@algomatwp.org
URL: http://www.algomatwp.org
Contact: Julie Sjogren, Admin.Asst.
Founded: 1987. **Members:** 222. **Membership Dues:** regular, $10 (annual). **Local**. Individuals interested in preserving the history of Algoma Township, MI. Maintains showcases of artifacts and pictures of the area. Restores landmarks. **Publications:** Newsletter, quarterly. **Conventions/Meetings:** quarterly meeting, with special speakers and annual picnic - always April, July, and October • quarterly meeting, with speakers.

9523 ■ American Legion, Merritt Lamb Post 102
122 Courtland
Rockford, MI 49341
Ph: (517)371-4720
Fax: (517)371-2401
URL: National Affiliate–www.legion.org
Local. Affiliated With: American Legion.

9524 ■ Hospice Patients Alliance (HPA)
c/o Ronald R. Panzer, Pres.
PO Box 744
Rockford, MI 49341-7899
Ph: (616)866-9127
E-mail: patientadvocates@hospicepatients.org
URL: http://www.hospicepatients.org
Contact: Ronald R. Panzer, Pres.
Founded: 1998. **Regional**. Promotes quality end of life care. **Publications:** *Guide to Hospice Care*. Book • *The Heart of End-of-Life Care*. Book. Alternate Formats: online.

9525 ■ Izaak Walton League of America, Dwight Lydell Chapter
5285 Windmill Dr. NE
Rockford, MI 49341-9311
Ph: (616)866-4769
E-mail: rstegmier@ameritech.net
URL: http://www.michiganikes.org
Contact: Robert Stegmier, Membership Chm.
Founded: 1924. **Members:** 270. **Membership Dues:** individual, $50 (annual) • family, $68 (annual) • student, $24 (annual) • youth, $13 (annual). **Local**. Promotes grassroots conservation work, including the protection of soil, air, woods, waters and wildlife. **Libraries: Type:** not open to the public. **Holdings:** 150. **Subjects:** environmental, conservation, natural resources. **Affiliated With:** Izaak Walton League of America.

9526 ■ Izaak Walton League of America, Michigan Division
c/o E. John Trimberger
6260 Blythfield NE
Rockford, MI 49341
Ph: (616)866-8475
E-mail: jtrimber@earthlink.net
URL: National Affiliate–www.iwla.org
Affiliated With: Izaak Walton League of America.

9527 ■ Michigan National Wild Turkey Federation, North Kent Chapter
7911 Blakely Rd.
Rockford, MI 49341
Ph: (616)866-3691
URL: http://www.mi-nwtf.org/NorthKent.htm
Contact: John Stevenson, Pres.
Local.

9528 ■ Rockford Area Chamber of Commerce (RACC)
PO Box 520
12 Squires St.
Rockford, MI 49341
Ph: (616)866-2000
Fax: (616)866-2141
E-mail: info@rockfordmichamber.com
URL: http://www.rockfordmichamber.com
Contact: Brenda Davis, Exec.Dir.
Founded: 1943. **Members:** 210. **Membership Dues:** general, $300 (annual). **Staff:** 3. **Local**. Promotes business and community development in the Rockford, MI area. Sponsors annual Start of Summer Celebration and annual Harvest Festival. **Publications:** *How Your Chamber Works For You!*, annual. Brochure. **Price:** free • *Rockford Living Magazine* • *Update*, bimonthly. Newsletter. **Advertising:** accepted.

9529 ■ Rockford Sportsman's Club
PO Box 624
Rockford, MI 49341
Ph: (616)866-4273
E-mail: mdroche@comcast.net
URL: http://www.vision2.net/rsc
Contact: George Mayhak, Pres.
Local. Affiliated With: National Skeet Shooting Association.

9530 ■ SkillsUSA Michigan
PO Box 793
Rockford, MI 49341
Ph: (616)866-0474
Fax: (616)866-0802
E-mail: miskillsusa@charter.net
URL: http://www.miskillsusa.org
Contact: Dan Cleveland, Dir.
State. Affiliated With: Skills USA - VICA. **Formerly:** (2006) Skills USA-VICA, Michigan.

9531 ■ Society for the Preservation of Old Mills, Great Lakes Chapter
c/o Dick Sulin, VP
111 S Main St.
Rockford, MI 49341-1221
Ph: (616)866-0609
URL: National Affiliate–www.spoom.org
Contact: Dick Sulin, VP
Regional. Promotes interest in old mills of all types. Helps in the preservation and reconstruction of such structures. Honors individuals whose work and ideas made these mills possible. Acts as a clearinghouse on mill information. **Affiliated With:** Society for the Preservation of Old Mills.

9532 ■ USA Diving - Rock Solid Diving
9008 Loveless Dr. NE
Rockford, MI 49341
Ph: (616)874-5800
E-mail: jstwrigt@hotmail.com
URL: National Affiliate–www.usdiving.org
Contact: Ann Wright, Contact
Local. Affiliated With: USA Diving.

9533 ■ West Michigan Golf Course Superintendents Association (WMGCSA)
c/o Keith Paterson
8585 Winterforest
Rockford, MI 49341
Ph: (616)363-1262
E-mail: info@wmgcsa.org
URL: http://www.wmgcsa.org
Contact: Joseph C. Hancock, Pres.
Founded: 1963. **Members:** 286. **Membership Dues:** class A, $70 (annual) • class B, $60 (annual) • class C, $50 (annual) • affiliate, $75 (annual) • student, $10 (annual). **Local**. Represents the interests of golf course superintendents. Advances members' profession for career success. Enhances the enjoyment, growth and vitality in the game of golf. Educates members concerning efficient and economical management of golf courses. **Affiliated With:** Golf Course Superintendents Association of America.

Rockland

9534 ■ American Legion, Michigan Post 92
c/o Milton G. Preiss
PO Box 342
Rockland, MI 49960
Ph: (517)371-4720
Fax: (517)371-2401
URL: National Affiliate–www.legion.org
Contact: Milton G. Preiss, Contact
Local. Affiliated With: American Legion.

Rockwood

9535 ■ American Legion, Rockwood Post 441
PO Box 332
Rockwood, MI 48173
Ph: (517)371-4720
Fax: (517)371-2401
URL: National Affiliate–www.legion.org
Local. Affiliated With: American Legion.

Rodney

9536 ■ Chippewa Lake Lions Club
12195 Arthur Rd.
Rodney, MI 49342
Ph: (231)796-4564 (231)972-8885
E-mail: kroebuck@greenridge.com
URL: http://chippewalakemi.lionwap.org
Contact: Karla Roebuck, Pres.
Local. Affiliated With: Lions Clubs International.

9537 ■ Christian Camp and Conference Association, Michigan
c/o Scott Barger, Sr., Pres.
Cran-Hill Ranch
14444 17 Mile Rd.
Rodney, MI 49342
Ph: (231)796-7669
URL: National Affiliate–www.ccca-us.org
Contact: Scott Barger Sr., Pres.
State. Affiliated With: Christian Camping International/U.S.A.

Rogers City

9538 ■ Alliance for the Mentally Ill of Northeast Michigan
c/o Laura Gray, Pres.
336 W Erie
Rogers City, MI 49779
Ph: (517)734-0046 (517)471-2577
E-mail: dmacconn@freeway.net
URL: http://mi.nami.org/nem.html
Contact: Laura Gray, Pres.
Local. Strives to improve the quality of life of children and adults with severe mental illness through support, education, research and advocacy. **Affiliated With:** National Alliance for the Mentally Ill.

9539 ■ American Legion, Michigan Post 121
c/o Harold L. Young
538 Stone Ln.
Rogers City, MI 49779
Ph: (517)371-4720
Fax: (517)371-2401
URL: National Affiliate–www.legion.org
Contact: Harold L. Young, Contact
Local. Affiliated With: American Legion.

9540 ■ Catholics United for the Faith - St. John Vianney Chapter
c/o Kathy Hollabaugh
1186 Cedar St.
Rogers City, MI 49779
Ph: (989)734-4165
URL: National Affiliate–www.cuf.org
Contact: Kathy Hollabaugh, Contact
Local.

9541 ■ Habitat for Humanity of Presque Isle County
PO Box 137
Rogers City, MI 49779-0137
Ph: (989)734-7359
Fax: (989)734-7359
E-mail: kjhouk@i2k.net
URL: National Affiliate–www.habitat.org
Local. Provides housing and construction projects for families at Presque Isle County. **Affiliated With:** Habitat for Humanity International.

9542 ■ Michigan National Wild Turkey Federation, Presque Isle Longbeards
298 Wenonah Dr.
Rogers City, MI 49779
Ph: (517)734-2141
URL: http://www.mi-nwtf.org/PresqueIsleLongbeards.htm
Contact: Bill Hansen, Pres.
Local.

9543 ■ Rogers City Chamber of Commerce
PO Box 55
Rogers City, MI 49779
Ph: (989)734-2535
Fax: (989)734-7767
Free: (800)622-4148
E-mail: rcchamber@lhi.net
URL: http://www.rogerscitychamber.com
Contact: William Hanchett, Exec.Dir.
Local. Promotes and develops a vital business environment, considering the needs of the community and preserving the unique identity of the Rogers City, MI area.

Romeo

9544 ■ Main Street Romeo
c/o Michael L. Nudi
410 S Main St., Ste.203
Romeo, MI 48065-4617
Ph: (586)752-7701
E-mail: info@mainstreetromeo.org
Contact: Michael L. Nudi, Contact
Founded: 1985. **Members:** 23. **Membership Dues:** company, $100 (annual) • individual, $35 (annual). **Staff:** 5. **Budget:** $11,000. **Local**. Dedicated to promoting the Romeo Community.

9545 ■ Michigan Association of PeriAnesthesia Nurses (MAPAN)
3675 29 Mile Rd.
Romeo, MI 48065
E-mail: direland@crittenton.com
URL: http://www.mapan.org
Contact: Dolly Ireland, Co-Chair
State. Promotes quality and cost effective care for patients, their families and the community through public and professional education, research and standards of practice. **Affiliated With:** American Society of PeriAnesthesia Nurses.

9546 ■ Romeo-Washington Chamber of Commerce (RWCC)
228 N Main, Ste.D
PO Box 175
Romeo, MI 48065-0175
Ph: (586)752-4436
Fax: (586)752-2835
E-mail: joyce@rwchamber.com
URL: http://www.rwchamber.com
Contact: Joyce E. Dych, Exec.Dir.
Founded: 1975. **Members:** 236. **Membership Dues:** small business, $150 • business builder, $180 • bronze, $250 • silver, $400 • gold, $600 • individual, $100 • friend of the chamber, $75 • hospital, $330 • school, $330. **Staff:** 1. **Local**. Promotes business and community development in Macomb County, MI. Sponsors competitions and festival. Conducts charitable activities. **Awards:** Ambassador of the Year. **Frequency:** annual. **Type:** recognition • The Brick Award. **Frequency:** annual. **Type:** recognition • Lifetime Achievement Award. **Frequency:** annual. **Type:** recognition • Member of the Month. **Frequency:** monthly. **Type:** recognition • Senior Volunteer of the Year. **Frequency:** annual. **Type:** recognition • Young Female Entrepreneur of the Year. **Frequency:** annual. **Type:** recognition. **Computer Services:** Information services, membership directory. **Publications:** *Business Directory*, periodic • *Cornerstone*, bimonthly. Newsletter. **Advertising:** accepted. Alternate Formats: online • Membership Directory, periodic. **Conventions/Meetings:** quarterly luncheon, with speaker.

9547 ■ Trout Unlimited, Vanguard
c/o Todd Randall, Pres.
131 Minot St.
Romeo, MI 48065-4628
Ph: (586)336-0995 (586)697-1233
Fax: (586)781-0888
E-mail: trandall@tir.com
URL: http://www.mctu.org
Contact: Todd Randall, Pres.
Founded: 1980. **Members:** 222. **Membership Dues:** regular, $35 (annual) • family/contributor, $50 (an-

nual) • sponsor, $100 (annual). **Budget:** $10,000. **State Groups:** 20. **Local Groups:** 3. **Local**. Works to conserve, protect, and restore Michigan's watersheds that support wild trout and salmon. **Awards:** Chapter of the Year. **Frequency:** annual. **Type:** recognition. **Recipient:** for outstanding resource work and chapter involvement. **Affiliated With:** Trout Unlimited. **Publications:** *Trout Times*, quarterly. Newsletter. **Circulation:** 200. **Advertising:** accepted. **Conventions/Meetings:** monthly Membership Meeting - always second Wednesday in Rochester Hills, MI.

Romulus

9548 ■ American Wine Society - Metropolitan Detroit
c/o Frank Carson, Co-Chm.
17450 Beech Daly
Romulus, MI 48174
Ph: (734)941-8747
E-mail: fcarson@peoplepc.com
URL: National Affiliate–www.americanwinesociety.org
Contact: Frank Carson, Co-Chm.
Local. Affiliated With: American Wine Society.

9549 ■ Greater Romulus Chamber of Commerce
c/o Best Western Hotel
9191 Wickham
Romulus, MI 48174
Ph: (734)326-4290
Fax: (734)326-3489
E-mail: info@romuluschamber.org
URL: http://www.romuluschamber.org
Contact: David B. Goodwin, Pres.
Membership Dues: business (based on number of employees), $110-$550 (annual) • non-resident business, $75 (annual) • individual supporting, $35 (annual) • non-profit organization, $50 (annual). **Local**. Small businesses interested in fostering and creating a healthy environment to do business. Works to improve business community by providing various promotional and profitable opportunities.

9550 ■ Michigan Charter Boat Association (MCBA)
c/o Ron Dubsky, Sec.
38000 Castle Dr.
Romulus, MI 48174
Ph: (734)941-4106
Fax: (734)941-9435
Free: (800)622-2971
E-mail: captron@icebreaker2.com
URL: http://www.micharterboats.com
Contact: Dick Stafford, Pres.
Founded: 1971. **Members:** 500. **Membership Dues:** regular, $75 (annual). **Staff:** 1. **State**. Promotes fishing, diving, duck hunting, cruises, and excursions in the state of Michigan. **Awards: Frequency:** annual. **Type:** recognition. **Publications:** Directory, periodic. Lists boat charters in Michigan. **Price:** free. **Advertising:** accepted. **Conventions/Meetings:** annual general assembly (exhibits).

9551 ■ Midwest Association of Housing Cooperatives (MAHC)
c/o Carolyn Jackson, Office Mgr.
37140 Goddard
Romulus, MI 48174
Ph: (734)955-9516
Fax: (734)955-9518
E-mail: carolynmahc@aol.com
URL: http://www.mahc.coop
Contact: Carolyn Jackson, Office Mgr.
Local. Affiliated With: National Association of Housing Cooperatives.

9552 ■ Transport Workers Union of America, AFL-CIO - Local Union 521
36518 Goddard Rd.
Romulus, MI 48174
Ph: (734)941-2880
Fax: (734)941-7160
URL: http://local521.twuatd.org
Contact: Jon W. Madish, Pres.
Members: 223. **Local. Affiliated With:** Transport Workers Union of America.

Roscommon

9553 ■ American Legion, Roscommon Post 96
219 Terence Dr.
Roscommon, MI 48653
Ph: (517)371-4720
Fax: (517)371-2401
URL: National Affiliate–www.legion.org
Local. Affiliated With: American Legion.

9554 ■ Michigan National Wild Turkey Federation, Beaver Creek Chapter
215 Pioneer Rd.
Roscommon, MI 48653
Ph: (517)275-4113
URL: http://www.mi-nwtf.org/Beavercreek.htm
Contact: Brian Mc-Phail, Contact
Local.

9555 ■ Mikenauk Rock and Gem Club
c/o Robert Anderson, Pres.
11701 Lancewood Dr.
Roscommon, MI 48653
E-mail: amcherven@i2k.com
URL: National Affiliate–www.amfed.org
Contact: Gwen Anderson, Sec.
Local. Aims to further the study of Earth Sciences and the practice of lapidary arts and mineralogy. **Affiliated With:** American Federation of Mineralogical Societies.

9556 ■ Phi Theta Kappa, Alpha Omicron Gamma Chapter - Kirtland Community College
c/o Kathy Koch
10775 N Saint Helen Rd.
Roscommon, MI 48653
Ph: (989)275-5000
E-mail: kochk@kirtland.cc.mi.us
URL: http://www.ptk.org/directories/chapters/MI/5557-1.htm
Contact: Kathy Koch, Advisor
Local.

9557 ■ Roscommon County United Way
PO Box 324
Roscommon, MI 48653-0324
Ph: (989)275-2067
URL: National Affiliate–national.unitedway.org
Local. Affiliated With: United Way of America.

9558 ■ Tri-Lakes Home Builders Association
PO Box 25
Roscommon, MI 48653
Ph: (989)275-4759
Fax: (989)275-4759
E-mail: trilakes@charter.net
URL: http://www.tl-hba.org
Contact: Wilma E. Barber, Exec. Officer
Founded: 1986. **Members:** 126. **Membership Dues:** regular, $300 (annual). **Staff:** 1. **State Groups:** 1. **Local. Publications:** Newsletter, monthly. **Circulation:** 126. **Advertising:** accepted. **Conventions/Meetings:** annual Home Show - meeting (exhibits).

Rosebush

9559 ■ American Legion, Varga-Fall Post 383
3963 E Denver Rd.
Rosebush, MI 48878
Ph: (517)371-4720
Fax: (517)371-2401
URL: National Affiliate–www.legion.org
Local. Affiliated With: American Legion.

9560 ■ OCIA Michigan, Chapter 2
3654 E Weidman
Rosebush, MI 48878-9715
Ph: (989)433-0197
Contact: Pat Graham, Admin.
Members: 90. **Staff:** 1. **State Groups:** 3. **Local**. Provides organic certification and education.

9561 ■ Organic Crop Improvement Association, Michigan- Chapter 2
c/o Pat Graham
3654 E Weidman Rd.
Rosebush, MI 48878
Ph: (989)433-0197
Fax: (989)433-2196
E-mail: graham@glccomputers.com
URL: National Affiliate–www.ocia.org
Contact: Pat Graham, Contact
Local. Affiliated With: Organic Crop Improvement Association.

Roseville

9562 ■ 101st Airborne Division Association, Michigan Chapter
c/o Paul Rosenbaum, Pres.
19789 Macel St.
Roseville, MI 48066-1129
Ph: (586)296-0485
E-mail: rosey1582000@yahoo.com
URL: National Affiliate–www.screamingeagle.org
Contact: Paul Rosenbaum, Pres.
State. Affiliated With: 101st Airborne Division Association.

9563 ■ American Legion, East Detroit Roseville Post 261
28444 Utica Rd.
Roseville, MI 48066
Ph: (517)371-4720
Fax: (517)371-2401
URL: National Affiliate–www.legion.org
Local. Affiliated With: American Legion.

9564 ■ American Legion, Hudson Motor Post 357
17871 Elizabeth St.
Roseville, MI 48066
Ph: (517)371-4720
Fax: (517)371-2401
URL: National Affiliate–www.legion.org
Local. Affiliated With: American Legion.

9565 ■ Michigan Amateur Athletic Union
c/o Michelle Young, Registrar
29217 Commonwealth
Roseville, MI 48066
Ph: (586)774-3779
Fax: (586)772-3753
E-mail: miaauregistrar@aol.com
URL: National Affiliate–aausports.org
Contact: Michelle Young, Registrar
State. Affiliated With: Amateur Athletic Union.

9566 ■ NORML of Macomb County
c/o Charles David Frakes
25195 Ronald St.
Roseville, MI 48066-4926
Ph: (586)873-5084
E-mail: mcnorml@netzero.net
URL: http://www.mcnorml.org
Contact: Charles David Frakes, Founder/Pres.
Founded: 2000. **Local. Affiliated With:** National Organization for the Reform of Marijuana Laws.

9567 ■ Shorewood Kiwanis Club (SKC)
21055 12 Mile Rd.
Roseville, MI 48066
Ph: (586)772-0100
Contact: Dr. Carl Papa, Contact
Founded: 1959. **Members:** 50. **Budget:** $30,000. **Local**. Service organization for business and profes-

sional men and women. **Affiliated With:** Kiwanis International. **Publications:** *Shorewood News*, weekly.

9568 ■ Vietnam Veterans of America, Chapter 154
16945 Twelve Mile Rd.
Roseville, MI 48066-2479
Ph: (586)776-9810
E-mail: piofficer@vva154.com
URL: http://www.vva154.com
Local. Affiliated With: Vietnam Veterans of America.

Royal Oak

9569 ■ Alliance of Construction Management Professionals, Detroit Area Chapter
c/o Annie Noce
609 S West St.
Royal Oak, MI 48067
E-mail: annienoce@alum.dartmouth.org
Founded: 2000. **Members:** 65. **Local. Libraries: Type:** reference. **Publications:** Newsletter, monthly. **Conventions/Meetings:** annual convention.

9570 ■ American Legion, Calvary Post 276
3415 Benjamin Ave., No. 104
Royal Oak, MI 48073
Ph: (517)371-4720
Fax: (517)371-2401
URL: National Affiliate–www.legion.org
Local. Affiliated With: American Legion.

9571 ■ American Legion, Michigan Post 25
c/o William H. Campbell
PO Box 1874
Royal Oak, MI 48068
Ph: (517)371-4720
Fax: (517)371-2401
URL: National Affiliate–www.legion.org
Contact: William H. Campbell, Contact
Local. Affiliated With: American Legion.

9572 ■ American Legion, Michigan Post 187
c/o Thomas A. Edison
209 Charlotte
2000 2nd Ave.
Royal Oak, MI 48073
Ph: (517)371-4720
Fax: (517)371-2401
URL: National Affiliate–www.legion.org
Contact: Thomas A. Edison, Contact
Local. Affiliated With: American Legion.

9573 ■ American Legion, Michigan Post 253
c/o Frank Wendtland
1505 N Main St.
Royal Oak, MI 48068
Ph: (517)371-4720
Fax: (517)371-2401
URL: National Affiliate–www.legion.org
Contact: Frank Wendtland, Contact
Local. Affiliated With: American Legion.

9574 ■ Ancient Order of Hibernians of Oakland County - Norman O'Brien, Division 1
c/o Timothy Clarey
PO Box 1530
Royal Oak, MI 48068-1530
Ph: (248)842-0390
E-mail: ubslimbo@hotmail.com
URL: http://www.michiganaoh.com
Contact: Timothy Clarey, Contact
Local. Affiliated With: Ancient Order of Hibernians in America.

9575 ■ Ancient Order of Hibernians of Wayne County - O' Brian Division
c/o Timothy Clarey
PO Box 1530
Royal Oak, MI 48068
Ph: (248)842-0390
URL: http://www.michiganaoh.com
Contact: Timothy Clarey, Contact
Local. Affiliated With: Ancient Order of Hibernians in America.

9576 ■ Bluewater Michigan Chapter, National Railway Historical Society (NRHS)
PO Box 296
Royal Oak, MI 48068-0296
Ph: (248)541-1000
URL: http://bluewaternrhs.com
Contact: Sigrid Moore, Sec.
Founded: 1982. **Members:** 900. **Membership Dues:** active, $32 (annual). **Staff:** 15. **Budget:** $750,000. **Local.** Individuals who collect, preserve, and disseminate artifacts and data relating to railroad history. Maintains museum, archives, and reference library. Restores and operates railroad passenger cars. Operates extensive schedule of railroad excursions. **Libraries: Type:** reference. **Holdings:** 3,000. **Subjects:** railroads. **Awards:** Member of the Year. **Frequency:** annual. **Type:** recognition. **Recipient:** for outstanding service to the chapter • President's Appreciation Award. **Frequency:** annual. **Type:** recognition. **Recipient:** for outstanding service to the chapter. **Affiliated With:** National Railway Historical Society. **Publications:** *Bluewater Sentinel*, quarterly. Newsletter. Contains information on railroad history and current events. **Price:** included in membership dues. **Circulation:** 900. **Conventions/Meetings:** monthly meeting, movies, slides, videos (exhibits) - second Thursday.

9577 ■ Boys and Girls Club of South Oakland County
c/o Brett Tillander, Exec.Dir.
1545 E Lincoln
Royal Oak, MI 48067
Ph: (248)544-4166
Fax: (248)545-7668
E-mail: bgc@boysandgirlsclub.us
URL: http://www.boysandgirlsclub.us
Contact: Brett Tillander, Exec.Dir.
Founded: 1958. **Regional.**

9578 ■ Detroit Area Council of Teachers of Mathematics
c/o Mary F. Zeppelin, Pres.
PO Box 1877
Royal Oak, MI 48068-1877
E-mail: zeppelin@oakland.edu
URL: http://www.dactm.org
Contact: Mary F. Zeppelin, Pres.
Local. Aims to improve the teaching and learning of mathematics. Provides vision, leadership and professional development to support teachers in ensuring mathematics learning of the highest quality for all students. **Affiliated With:** National Council of Teachers of Mathematics.

9579 ■ Detroit Audubon Society (DAS)
1320 N Campbell Rd.
Royal Oak, MI 48067
Ph: (248)545-2929
Fax: (248)545-2860
E-mail: detas@bignet.net
URL: http://detroitaudubon.expage.com/home
Contact: Rochelle Breitenbach, Pres.
Founded: 1939. **Members:** 5,500. **Membership Dues:** joint (National Audubon Society in association with Detroit Audubon), $20 (annual) • chapter, $15 (annual). **Staff:** 1. **State.** Strives to promote awareness of the environment through education and participation. **Libraries: Type:** open to the public; lending; reference. **Holdings:** 1,000; books, periodicals, video recordings. **Subjects:** nature, birds, environment. **Awards:** Conservation Organization of the year. **Frequency:** annual. **Type:** medal. **Recipient:** for outstanding contribution to the conservation of natural resources • Conservationist of the Year. **Frequency:** annual. **Type:** medal. **Recipient:** for outstanding contribution to the conservation of natural resources. **Affiliated With:** National Audubon Society; National Audubon Society. **Publications:** *Flyway*, bimonthly. Newsletter. Includes field trip and shared story. **Price:** included in membership dues. **Circulation:** 5,500. **Advertising:** accepted. Alternate Formats: online. **Conventions/Meetings:** monthly Membership Meetings (exhibits) - every 2nd Thursday in Wyandotte; every 3rd Thursday in Southfield.

9580 ■ Esperanto Society of Michigan
PO Box 1274
Royal Oak, MI 48068-1274
E-mail: sylvanz@aol.com
URL: National Affiliate–www.esperanto-usa.org
Contact: Sylvan J. Zaft PhD, Dir.
Founded: 1984. **Members:** 55. **Membership Dues:** individual, $12 (annual). **Languages:** English, Esperanto. **State.** Promotes the use of Esperanto. Works to help and encourage those interested in learning the language and to provide opportunities to use the language. **Libraries: Type:** lending; reference; by appointment only. **Holdings:** 200; books, periodicals, video recordings. **Subjects:** Esperanto. **Affiliated With:** Esperanto League for North America. **Conventions/Meetings:** weekly Conversational Meeting, members and guests converse in Esperanto.

9581 ■ Flygirls of Michigan
c/o Jennifer Nelson, Pres.
731 S Altadena Ave.
Royal Oak, MI 48067
E-mail: president@flygirls.ws
URL: http://www.flygirls.ws
Contact: Jennifer Nelson, Pres.
State. Affiliated With: Federation of Fly Fishers.

9582 ■ Greater Royal Oak Chamber of Commerce
200 S Washington Ave.
Royal Oak, MI 48067-3821
Ph: (248)547-4000
Fax: (248)547-0504
E-mail: coc@virtualroyaloak.com
URL: http://www.virtualroyaloak.com
Contact: Mrs. Liz Tillander, Exec.Dir.
Founded: 1936. **Members:** 625. **Staff:** 4. **Budget:** $330,000. **Local.** Aims to bring business leaders, civic groups and citizens together to improve and enhance the community.

9583 ■ ISPI Michigan Chapter
PO Box 189
Royal Oak, MI 48068
Ph: (248)526-1166
Fax: (248)625-2020
E-mail: president@ispimi.org
URL: http://www.ispimi.org
Contact: Patricia O'Brien, Pres.
State. Performance technologists, training directors, human resource managers, instructional designers, human factors practitioners, and organizational development consultants who work in a variety of industries such as automotive, communications and telecommunications, computer, financial services, government agencies, health services, manufacturing, the military, travel/hospitality, and education. Dedicated to improving productivity and performance in the workplace through the application of performance and instructional technologies.

9584 ■ Jane Addams Middle School PTA
2222 W Webster
Royal Oak, MI 48073
Ph: (248)288-3100
E-mail: addams.pta@ptamail.com
URL: http://familyeducation.com/MI/Addams_PTA
Contact: Cindy Murphy, Pres.
Local. Parents, teachers, students, and others interested in uniting the forces of home, school, and community. Promotes the welfare of children and youth.

9585 ■ Lambda Car Club, Detroit Region (LCC)
PO Box 446
Royal Oak, MI 48068
E-mail: info@lccdetroit.org
URL: http://lccdetroit.org
Contact: Bob Anderson, Pres.
Founded: 1985. **Members:** 100. **Membership Dues:** local/national, $48-$58 (annual). **Staff:** 8. **Budget:**

$2,400. **Regional Groups:** 1. **Local**. Old and special interest car club for gay men in the Detroit/Southeastern Michigan area. Strives for enjoyment and exchange of information on old and special interest motor vehicles, combined with social fellowship by gay men and lesbians. **Publications:** *The Headliner*, 11/year. Newsletter. **Price:** included in membership dues. **Circulation:** 140. **Conventions/Meetings:** annual show, 23 different events planned per year.

9586 ■ National Active and Retired Federal Employees Association - Royal Oak 1532
811 N Vermont
Royal Oak, MI 48067-2023
Ph: (248)542-8849
URL: National Affiliate–www.narfe.org
Contact: Juanita L. Tucker, Contact
Local. Protects the retirement future of employees through education. Informs members on issues affecting the retirement. **Affiliated With:** National Association of Retired Federal Employees.

9587 ■ National Organization for Women - Oakland County
c/o Gerrie Barclay
PO Box 1381
Royal Oak, MI 48068
Ph: (248)681-3805
E-mail: jburg2000@comcast.net
URL: http://www.michnow.org
Contact: Gerrie Barclay, Contact
Local. Affiliated With: National Organization for Women.

9588 ■ Oakland Highlanders Rugby Football Club
902 Whitcomb
Royal Oak, MI 48073-2048
E-mail: swede@comcast.net
URL: http://www.oaklandrugby.8m.com
Contact: Jacob Schell, Pres.
Local.

9589 ■ PFLAG Detroit
PO Box 1169
Royal Oak, MI 48068
Ph: (248)656-2875
E-mail: genoffice@pflagdetroit.org
URL: http://www.pflagdetroit.org
Local. Affiliated With: Parents, Families, and Friends of Lesbians and Gays.

9590 ■ Resolve of Michigan
PO Box 1108
Royal Oak, MI 48068-1108
Ph: (248)975-8866
E-mail: foxtaillily57@yahoo.com
URL: http://www.resolveofmichigan.homestead.com
Contact: Kathy Rollinger, Pres.
Membership Dues: basic, $55 (annual) • contributing, $65 (annual) • supporting, $75 (annual) • circle of friend, $100 (annual) • professional, $150 (annual). **State. Affiliated With:** Resolve, The National Infertility Association.

9591 ■ Royal Oak Coin Club
c/o Ken Rama
PO Box 445
Royal Oak, MI 48068-0445
E-mail: r.o.c.c.@usa.com
URL: National Affiliate–www.money.org
Contact: Ken Rama, Contact
Local. Affiliated With: American Numismatic Association.

9592 ■ Sweet Adelines International, Shoreline Sound Chapter
Royal Oak Church of Christ
115 S Campbell
Royal Oak, MI 48067
Ph: (313)884-4310
E-mail: jkramer91@comcast.net
URL: http://www.shorelinesound.org
Contact: JoAnn Kramer, Pres.
Local. Advances the musical art form of barbershop harmony through education and performances. Provides education, training and coaching in the development of women's four-part barbershop harmony. **Affiliated With:** Sweet Adelines International.

9593 ■ Tip Toppers Club of Detroit
PO Box 1838
Royal Oak, MI 48068
Ph: (734)458-7887
E-mail: detroit@tall.org
URL: http://www.tall.org/clubs/mi/detroit
Local. Affiliated With: Tall Clubs International.

9594 ■ Troy Soldiers Miniatures Club
c/o Saundra Wells
5015 Crooks Rd., Condo No. 29
Royal Oak, MI 48073
Ph: (248)288-6069
E-mail: dwells00@ameritech.net
URL: http://www.miniatures.org/states/MI.html
Contact: Saundra Wells, Contact
Local. Affiliated With: National Association of Miniature Enthusiasts.

Saginaw

9595 ■ American Association for Medical Transcription, Bay Area Chapter
c/o Dianna Faye Hall, CMT, FAAMT, Pres.
5705 Hacienda Ct.
Saginaw, MI 48603
E-mail: dhall@chs-mi.com
URL: http://www.aamt.org/ca/bac
Contact: Dianna Faye Hall CMT, Pres.
Local. Works to represent and advance the profession of medical transcription and its practitioners. **Affiliated With:** American Association for Medical Transcription.

9596 ■ American Historical Society of Germans from Russia, Saginaw Valley Chapter
c/o Mrs. Carol L. Niederquell, Pres.
6910 Trowbridge Cir.
Saginaw, MI 48603-8637
Ph: (989)799-4266
E-mail: clniederusa@netscape.net
URL: http://www.ahsgr.org/saginaw_valley_chapter.htm
Contact: Mrs. Carol L. Niederquell, Pres.
Founded: 1972. **Members:** 100. **Membership Dues:** individual (local), $5 (annual) • family - husband and wife (local), $7 (annual) • individual (international), $50 (annual). **State Groups:** 3. **Local Groups:** 1. **Local**. Individuals who are of Russian German ancestry; researchers, historians, libraries, genealogical societies, and historical societies. Works to record the history of Germans from Russia, encourage research, and assist with genealogical research. **Libraries: Type:** not open to the public; by appointment only; lending. **Holdings:** 100; articles, books, periodicals, video recordings. **Subjects:** Germans from Russia, research and family history. **Affiliated With:** American Historical Society of Germans From Russia. **Publications:** Newsletter, semiannual. **Price:** included in membership dues. **Circulation:** 100. **Conventions/Meetings:** general assembly, open to public (exhibits) - 4th Tuesday of February, April, August, October; 1st Sunday of December.

9597 ■ American Legion, Blumfield Post 229
PO Box 14445
Saginaw, MI 48601
Ph: (517)371-4720
Fax: (517)371-2401
URL: National Affiliate–www.legion.org
Local. Affiliated With: American Legion.

9598 ■ American Legion, Jastrzemski-Lelo Post 439
5190 Weiss St.
Saginaw, MI 48603
Ph: (517)371-4720
Fax: (517)371-2401
URL: National Affiliate–www.legion.org
Local. Affiliated With: American Legion.

9599 ■ American Legion, Martinez-Garcia-Nerio-Reyes Post 500
PO Box 2124
Saginaw, MI 48605
Ph: (517)771-9395
Fax: (517)371-2401
URL: National Affiliate–www.legion.org
Local. Affiliated With: American Legion.

9600 ■ American Legion, Phillips-Elliott-Hodges Post 22
2200 S Niagara St.
Saginaw, MI 48602
Ph: (517)371-4720
Fax: (517)371-2401
URL: National Affiliate–www.legion.org
Local. Affiliated With: American Legion.

9601 ■ American Legion, Shields Post 314
7870 Gratiot Rd.
Saginaw, MI 48609
Ph: (517)371-4720
Fax: (517)371-2401
URL: National Affiliate–www.legion.org
Local. Affiliated With: American Legion.

9602 ■ American Red Cross, Saginaw County Chapter
1231 N Michigan Ave.
Saginaw, MI 48602
Ph: (989)754-8181
Fax: (989)754-8333
E-mail: arc@redcross-saginaw.org
URL: http://www.redcross-saginaw.org
Local.

9603 ■ American Society for Quality, Saginaw Valley Section 1004
c/o Rudy Salinger, Sec.
PO Box 14947
Saginaw, MI 48601-0947
E-mail: qualityrudy@yahoo.com
URL: http://www.asq1004.org
Contact: Rudy Salinger, Sec.
Local. Advances learning, quality improvement and knowledge exchange to improve business results and to create better workplaces and communities worldwide. Provides a forum for information exchange, professional development and continuous learning in the science of quality. **Affiliated With:** American Society for Quality.

9604 ■ Bridgeport Lions Club - Michigan
c/o Charles D. Wedding, PRC, Pres.
4312 Williamson St.
Saginaw, MI 48601
Ph: (989)777-2656
URL: http://www.geocities.com/dist11d1
Contact: Charles D. Wedding PRC, Pres.
Local. Affiliated With: Lions Clubs International.

9605 ■ Buena Vista Lions Club - Michigan
c/o Willie Underwood, Pres.
1684 Joy Rd.
Saginaw, MI 48601
Ph: (989)752-2857
URL: http://www.geocities.com/dist11d1
Contact: Willie Underwood, Pres.
Local. Affiliated With: Lions Clubs International.

9606 ■ Carrollton Lions Club - Michigan
c/o Joan Douglas, Pres.
1828 Kelly Dr.
Saginaw, MI 48604

Ph: (989)753-7261
E-mail: douglasj@e-hps.net
URL: http://www.geocities.com/dist11d1
Contact: Joan Douglas, Pres.
Local. Affiliated With: Lions Clubs International.

9607 ■ Cystic Fibrosis Foundation, Greater Michigan Chapter - Eastern Region
3064 Boardwalk Dr.
Saginaw, MI 48603-2324
Ph: (989)790-2233
Fax: (989)790-1050
Free: (800)968-7169
E-mail: saginaw-mi@cff.org
URL: http://www.cff.org
Contact: Patti Saunders, Exec.Dir.
Founded: 1955. **Members:** 1,500. **Staff:** 20. **Local.** Cystic fibrosis patients, their families, and interested individuals. Provides patient care and educational programs; conducts research. **Affiliated With:** Cystic Fibrosis Foundation.

9608 ■ Elf Khurafeh Shriners
c/o Ronald W. Downing
PO Box 3261
Saginaw, MI 48605-3261
Ph: (810)686-2641
Fax: (810)686-2782
URL: National Affiliate–www.shrinershq.org
Contact: Ronald W. Downing, Contact
Local. Affiliated With: Imperial Council of the Ancient Arabic Order of the Nobles of the Mystic Shrine for North America.

9609 ■ Home Builders Association of Saginaw (HBAS)
3165 Cabaret Trail S
Saginaw, MI 48603
Ph: (989)793-1120
Fax: (989)793-0459
E-mail: hbas@chartermi.net
URL: http://www.hbas.org
Contact: Carole Hemminger, Exec.Dir.
Founded: 1955. **Members:** 514. **Membership Dues:** builder/associate, $390 (annual). **Staff:** 4. **Local.** Residential builders, contractors, and individuals in related industries in the Saginaw, MI area. Promotes the home building industry. Conducts charitable activities through local agencies. **Committees:** Christmas Party; Golf Outing; In-Keepers; Member Expo; Silent Auction. **Affiliated With:** National Association of Home Builders. **Publications:** *Housing Industry Reporter*, monthly. Newsletter. **Price:** included in membership dues • Directory. **Price:** available to members only. **Conventions/Meetings:** monthly meeting - always third Monday; except June, July and August.

9610 ■ International Brotherhood of Electrical Workers, AFL-CIO, CFL - Local Union 557
7303 Gratiot Rd.
Saginaw, MI 48609
Ph: (989)781-0516
Fax: (989)781-0563
E-mail: ibew557@worldnet.att.net
URL: http://www.ibew557.org
Contact: Charles Gricar, Pres.
Members: 196. **Local.** Works to elevate the moral, intellectual and social conditions of workers. **Affiliated With:** International Brotherhood of Electrical Workers.

9611 ■ International Union, United Automobile, Aerospace and Agricultural Implement Workers of America, AFL-CIO - Local Union 699
1911 Bagley St.
Saginaw, MI 48601
Ph: (989)755-0569
E-mail: uaw699@sbcglobal.net
URL: http://www.uaw699.com
Contact: Al Coven, Pres.
Members: 4,496. **Local.** AFL-CIO. **Affiliated With:** International Union, United Automobile, Aerospace and Agricultural Implement Workers of America.

9612 ■ Kochville Lions Club
c/o Allan Bader, Pres.
6727 Davis Rd.
Saginaw, MI 48604
Ph: (989)754-1565
URL: http://www.geocities.com/dist11d1
Contact: Allan Bader, Pres.
Local. Affiliated With: Lions Clubs International.

9613 ■ Korean War Veterans Association, Saginaw/Frankenmuth Chapter
c/o Major G. Leckie
1 Slatestone Dr.
Saginaw, MI 48603
Ph: (989)799-9246
E-mail: voyageurmp@bigplanet.com
URL: National Affiliate–www.kwva.org
Contact: Major G. Leckie, Contact
Local. Affiliated With: Korean War Veterans Association.

9614 ■ Michigan Association of Middle School Educators (MAMSE)
PO Box 6304
Saginaw, MI 48608-6304
Ph: (989)249-0831
Fax: (989)793-5947
E-mail: charpike@yahoo.com
URL: http://www.mamse.org
Contact: Dr. Thomas N. Barris, Exec.Dir.
Founded: 1973. **Members:** 1,000. **Membership Dues:** individual, $30 (annual). **Staff:** 1. **Regional Groups:** 14. **State.** Works to instruct individuals and groups of educators for the improvement or development of their understanding in middle level schools, and to instruct the public on what a middle level school is through group discussions, forums, panels, lecturers, and print materials. **Awards:** Administrator of the Year. **Frequency:** annual. **Type:** recognition • Collegiate Educator of the Year. **Frequency:** annual. **Type:** recognition • Educator of the Year. **Frequency:** annual. **Type:** recognition • Hall of Fame Award. **Frequency:** annual. **Type:** recognition. **Recipient:** to honor a parent, teacher, administrator, college professor or lay person who has contributed most to the middle school movement • Louis G. Romano Scholarship. **Frequency:** annual. **Type:** scholarship. **Recipient:** for academic performance, leadership, citizenship, community service and participation in co-curricular activities • Parent of the Year. **Frequency:** annual. **Type:** recognition • Teaching Team of the Year. **Frequency:** annual. **Type:** recognition. **Affiliated With:** Michigan Association of Secondary School Principals; National Middle School Association. **Publications:** *Michigan Middle School Journal*, semiannual. Reports current best practices and issues concerning middle level education. **Price:** included in membership dues. **Circulation:** 1,000. **Advertising:** accepted.

9615 ■ Michigan Model Sailing Club No. 70
c/o Wayne Westendorf
3401 Christy Way N
Saginaw, MI 48603
Ph: (517)793-8025
URL: National Affiliate–www.amya.org
Contact: Wayne Westendorf, Contact
Local.

9616 ■ Michigan Organization of Nurse Executives - District 5
c/o Marc Augsburger, Dir.
Covenant HealthCare
900 Cooper Ave.
Saginaw, MI 48603
Ph: (989)583-6259
Fax: (989)583-7181
E-mail: maugsburger@chs-mi.com
URL: http://www.mone.org
Contact: Marc Augsburger, Dir.
Local. Represents nurse leaders who improve healthcare. Provides leadership, professional development, advocacy and research. Advances the nursing administration practice and patient care. **Affiliated With:** American Organization of Nurse Executives.

9617 ■ Michigan Sports Unlimited (MSU)
c/o Brian Sheridan, OTR/L, Chm.
1915 Fordney St.
Saginaw, MI 48601
Ph: (989)771-5530
URL: http://www.misportsunlimited.com
Contact: Brian Sheridan OTR/L, Chm.
State.

9618 ■ Midwest Dressage Association
c/o Melanie Walchak
706 Shepard St.
Saginaw, MI 48604
Ph: (989)684-8158
E-mail: cvancise@chartermi.net
URL: http://www.midwestdressage.org
Contact: Carolyn Van Cise, Pres.
Regional. Affiliated With: United States Dressage Federation.

9619 ■ National Active and Retired Federal Employees Association - Saginaw 376
4886 W Michigan Rd.
Saginaw, MI 48603-6312
Ph: (517)792-1597
URL: National Affiliate–www.narfe.org
Contact: Lois Borden, Contact
Local. Protects the retirement future of employees through education. Informs members on issues affecting the retirement. **Affiliated With:** National Association of Retired Federal Employees.

9620 ■ National Association of Miniature Enthusiasts - Tri City Miniature Makers
c/o Betty Claus
4690 Hemmeter Ct., Apt. 9
Saginaw, MI 48603
Ph: (989)792-2551
URL: http://www.miniatures.org/states/MI.html
Contact: Betty Claus, Contact
Local. Affiliated With: National Association of Miniature Enthusiasts.

9621 ■ National Association of Miniature Enthusiasts - Whole Fam Damily
c/o Chandra Pansing
2631 Starlite Dr.
Saginaw, MI 48603
Ph: (989)799-2916
E-mail: cpansing@chartermi.net
URL: http://www.miniatures.org/states/MI.html
Contact: Chandra Pansing, Contact
Local. Affiliated With: National Association of Miniature Enthusiasts.

9622 ■ Newcomers Club of Saginaw
PO Box 6473
Saginaw, MI 48608-6473
Ph: (989)776-5375
E-mail: webmaster@newcomersclubofsaginaw.org
URL: http://www.newcomersclubofsaginaw.org
Members: 100. **Membership Dues:** $12 (monthly). **Budget:** $3,000. **Local.** Committed to welcoming new people to the community; provides social group for those already living in the community.

9623 ■ Northeastern Michigan Estate Planning Council
c/o Mary Ann Jahnke, Admin.Asst.
PO Box 5848
Saginaw, MI 48603-0848
Ph: (989)792-6259
Fax: (989)792-6259
E-mail: admin@nmepc.org
URL: National Affiliate–councils.naepc.org
Contact: Gary R. Apsey PhD, Pres.
Local. Promotes the coordination of professional services necessary to proper estate planning. Improves the understanding, knowledge and skill of professional groups engaged in estate planning with the purpose of rendering better service to clients. Encourages cooperation among members comprised of attorneys, CPAs, chartered life underwriters, bank trust officers, and financial planners. **Affiliated With:** National Association of Estate Planners and Councils.

9624 ■ Plumbing-Heating-Cooling Contractors Association, Saginaw Valley
c/o Merle Grover, Exec.Mgr.
6285 Wild Oak Dr.
Saginaw, MI 48603-4208
Ph: (989)792-0212
Fax: (989)792-8621
URL: National Affiliate–www.phccweb.org
Contact: Merle Grover, Exec.Mgr.
Local. Represents the plumbing, heating and cooling contractors. Promotes the construction industry. Protects the environment, health, safety and comfort of society. **Affiliated With:** Plumbing-Heating-Cooling Contractors Association.

9625 ■ Police and Firemen's Insurance Association - Saginaw County Police Department
c/o Dennis Ray Martin
2309 State St.
Saginaw, MI 48602
Ph: (517)793-5319
URL: National Affiliate–www.pfia.net
Contact: Dennis Ray Martin, Contact
Local. Affiliated With: Police and Firemen's Insurance Association.

9626 ■ Polish Falcons of America, Nest 124
5940 Swan Creek Rd.
Saginaw, MI 48609
Ph: (517)781-4030
URL: http://www.polishfalcons.org/nest/124/index.html
Contact: Bernard Wolny, Pres.
Local. Affiliated With: Polish Falcons of America.

9627 ■ Public Relations Society of America, White Pine
c/o Karen Stiffler, APR, Pres.
St. Mary's Found.
800 S Washington Ave.
Saginaw, MI 48601
Ph: (989)776-8300
Fax: (989)776-8141
E-mail: kstiffle@saintmarys-saginaw.org
URL: http://www.ecd.prsa.org
Contact: Karen Stiffler APR, Pres.
Members: 30. **Local.** Professional association for individuals in the public relations field who want to have access to continuing educational opportunities through programs, professional development, universal accreditation in public relations (APR). **Computer Services:** Online services, offers searchable fields including media type, city and distribution, quick link to media sources. **Affiliated With:** Public Relations Society of America. **Publications:** *The Pine Cone*, annual. Newsletter. Includes upcoming events, chapter news and personnel announcements.

9628 ■ Saginaw Area IDA Collaborative
c/o Bettie Brown
1 Tuscola, MSSU Ext.
Saginaw, MI 48607-1287
Local.

9629 ■ Saginaw Board of Realtors
902 Court St.
Saginaw, MI 48602
E-mail: saginawbd@sbcglobal.net
URL: http://www.homesofsaginaw.com
Contact: Jerry Meyers, Pres.
Local. Strives to develop real estate business practices. Advocates the right to own, use and transfer real property. Provides a facility for professional development, research and exchange of information among members. **Affiliated With:** National Association of Realtors.

9630 ■ Saginaw County Chamber of Commerce
515 N Washington Ave., 2nd Fl.
Saginaw, MI 48607-1370
Ph: (989)752-7161
Fax: (989)752-9055
E-mail: info@saginawchamber.org
URL: http://www.saginawchamber.org
Contact: Bob Van Deventer, Pres./CEO
Members: 1,000. **Local.** Manufacturers, agricultural producers, retail stores, service companies and organizations that share a common vision for the community. Strives to develop the business community in Saginaw County. **Councils:** Commodore. **Publications:** *Business Advocate*, monthly. Magazine • Annual Report, annual.

9631 ■ Saginaw County Convention and Visitors Bureau
515 N Washington Ave., 3rd Fl.
Saginaw, MI 48607
Ph: (989)752-7164
Fax: (989)752-6642
Free: (800)444-9979
E-mail: info@visitsaginawcounty.com
URL: http://www.visitsaginawcounty.com
Contact: Wendy Scott, Dir.
Local. Works to increase the economic impact of tourism on the local hospitality community, most significantly, the lodging industry. **Also Known As:** (2005) Saginaw Valley Convention and Visitors Bureau.

9632 ■ Saginaw County Medical Society (SCMS)
350 St. Andrews Rd., Ste.242
Saginaw, MI 48638-5988
Ph: (989)790-3590
Fax: (989)790-3640
E-mail: scms@msms.org
URL: http://www.saginawmedicalsociety.org
Contact: Diane P. Schutt, Exec.Dir.
Local. Advances the art and science of medicine. Promotes patient care and the betterment of public health. **Affiliated With:** Michigan State Medical Society.

9633 ■ Saginaw Future
c/o JoAnn Crary, CEO/Pres.
515 N Washington Ave., 3rd Fl.
Saginaw, MI 48607
Ph: (989)754-8222
Fax: (989)754-1715
E-mail: info@saginawfuture.com
URL: http://www.saginawfuture.com
Contact: JoAnn Crary, CEO/Pres.
Founded: 1992. **Staff:** 7. **Budget:** $750,000. **Local.** Works to increase economic opportunity for all people of the Saginaw region and to ensure continuing long-term growth and prosperity. **Publications:** *Business and Beyond*, quarterly. Newsletter • *Saginaw County Manufacturers Directory*, semiannual. Book. Covers manufacturers in Saginaw County including address, phone, fax, contact, nature of business, community, numbers of employees.

9634 ■ Saginaw Gun Club
PO Box 6054
Saginaw, MI 48603
Ph: (989)781-2260
URL: National Affiliate–www.mynssa.com
Local. Affiliated With: National Skeet Shooting Association.

9635 ■ Saginaw Habitat for Humanity
316 S Jefferson Ave.
Saginaw, MI 48607-1126
Ph: (989)753-5200
E-mail: paulwarriner@saginawhfh.org
URL: http://www.saginawhfh.org
Contact: Paul Warriner, Exec.Dir.
Local. Affiliated With: Habitat for Humanity International.

9636 ■ Saginaw Valley District Dental Society
3456 Shattuck
Saginaw, MI 48603
Ph: (989)792-8400
URL: National Affiliate–www.ada.org
Contact: Dr. Joseph Zolinski, Pres.
Local. Represents the interests of dentists committed to the public's oral health, ethics and professional development. Encourages the improvement of the public's oral health and promotes the art and science of dentistry. **Affiliated With:** American Dental Association; Michigan Dental Association.

9637 ■ Saginaw Valley Railroad Historical Society (SVRHS)
900 Maple St.
Saginaw, MI 48602-1175
Ph: (517)790-7994
Fax: (517)791-3504
URL: http://www.rypn.org/svrhs
Contact: James Trier, Chm.
Founded: 1980. **Members:** 56. **Membership Dues:** individual, $15 (annual) • family, $25 (annual) • supporting, $45 (annual) • brass hat, $50 (annual) • sustaining, $75 (annual) • champion, $100 (annual). **Staff:** 4. **Budget:** $15,000. **Local.** Strives to preserve and enhance the railroad lore and technology through railway museum. **Libraries: Type:** open to the public. **Holdings:** 600. **Subjects:** railroad history, practice and technology. **Computer Services:** database, off line and for local use only. **Publications:** *The Semaphore*, 3/year. Newsletter. **Price:** included in membership dues. **Circulation:** 56.

9638 ■ Saginaw West Lions Club
c/o Albert Premo, Sec.
2624 Darwin Ln.
Saginaw, MI 48603
Ph: (989)792-2226
E-mail: albertpremo@msn.com
URL: http://www.geocities.com/dist11d1
Contact: Albert Premo, Sec.
Local. Affiliated With: Lions Clubs International.

9639 ■ Shields Lions Club
c/o Tim Ader, Pres.
947 Lutzke Rd.
Saginaw, MI 48609
Ph: (989)781-4999
URL: http://www.geocities.com/dist11d1
Contact: Tim Ader, Pres.
Local. Affiliated With: Lions Clubs International.

9640 ■ Tri-Cities Dog Training Club of Saginaw Michigan
c/o Linda Lemmer, Pres.
1311 Williams St.
Saginaw, MI 48602-2443
Ph: (989)791-4743
E-mail: tervtuvok@msn.com
Contact: Linda Lemmer, Pres.
Founded: 1972. **Members:** 50. **Membership Dues:** single, $20 (annual) • family, $30 (annual) • junior (10-17 years old), $5 (annual). **State.** Seeks to train the general public and members to train their dogs. **Publications:** *The Recall*, monthly. Newsletter. **Conventions/Meetings:** monthly Membership - meeting.

9641 ■ Tri-County Youth for Christ
PO Box 5420
Saginaw, MI 48603
Ph: (989)865-8011
Fax: (989)797-2380
URL: National Affiliate–www.yfc.net
Local. Affiliated With: Youth for Christ/U.S.A.

9642 ■ Trout Unlimited - William B. Mershon Chapter
PO Box 1555
Saginaw, MI 48605-1555
Ph: (989)249-6420 (989)799-5000
Fax: (989)799-8982
E-mail: rad8jd4@hotmail.com
URL: http://www.tu.org
Contact: Chris Radke, Pres.
Members: 310. **Local.**

9643 ■ Umoja Ski Club
PO Box 14776
Saginaw, MI 48601
Ph: (989)777-9171 (989)754-1102
E-mail: charpar1@aol.com
URL: National Affiliate–www.nbs.org
Contact: Charles S. Parker, Pres.
Local. Affiliated With: National Brotherhood of Skiers.

9644 ■ United States Naval Sea Cadet Corps - HR Doud Division
AFTC Saginaw
3500 Douglass
Saginaw, MI 48601
E-mail: priddy@navy.mil
URL: http://dolphin.seacadets.org/US_units/UnitDetails.asp?UnitID=092HRD
Contact: ENS Linda J. Priddy, Commanding Officer
Local. Works to instill good citizenship and patriotism in youth. Encourages qualities such as personal neatness, loyalty, obedience, dependability, and responsibility to others. Offers courses in physical fitness and military drill, first aid, water safety, basic seamanship, and naval history and traditions. **Affiliated With:** Naval Sea Cadet Corps.

9645 ■ United Way of Saginaw County
100 S Jefferson Ave.
Saginaw, MI 48607
Ph: (989)755-0505
E-mail: info@unitedwaysaginaw.org
URL: http://www.unitedwaysaginaw.org
Local. Affiliated With: United Way of America.

9646 ■ Valley Society for Human Resource Management
PO Box 5448
Saginaw, MI 48603
E-mail: mtucker@xo.com
URL: http://vshrm.org
Contact: Mary Tucker, Pres.
Local. Represents the interests of human resource and industrial relations professionals and executives. Promotes the advancement of human resource management.

9647 ■ Wood Truss Council of Michigan (WTCM)
c/o Mr. Dennis Metiva, Pres.
Delta Truss Inc.
PO Box 6007
Saginaw, MI 48608
Ph: (989)792-6800
Fax: (989)792-4110
E-mail: dmetiva@deltatruss.com
URL: http://www.wtcmich.com
Contact: Mr. Dennis Metiva, Pres.
State. Affiliated With: Wood Truss Council of America.

9648 ■ Zilwaukee Lions Club
c/o Bert Rivette, Sec.
883 Waukee Ln.
Saginaw, MI 48604
Ph: (989)753-5603
E-mail: bdr754j@charter.net
URL: http://www.geocities.com/dist11d1
Contact: Bert Rivette, Sec.
Local. Affiliated With: Lions Clubs International.

St. Charles

9649 ■ American Legion, St. Charles Post 468
11005 Spencer Rd.
St. Charles, MI 48655
Ph: (517)371-4720
Fax: (517)371-2401
URL: National Affiliate–www.legion.org
Local. Affiliated With: American Legion.

9650 ■ St. Charles Lions Club - Michigan
c/o James Slick, Pres.
8120 Fordney Rd.
St. Charles, MI 48655-9762
Ph: (989)865-6818
URL: http://www.geocities.com/dist11d1
Contact: James Slick, Pres.
Local. Affiliated With: Lions Clubs International.

St. Clair

9651 ■ American Legion, Michigan Post 382
c/o Charles J. Fulton
1322 Clinton Ave.
St. Clair, MI 48079
Ph: (517)371-4720
Fax: (517)371-2401
URL: National Affiliate–www.legion.org
Contact: Charles J. Fulton, Contact
Local. Affiliated With: American Legion.

St. Clair Shores

9652 ■ American Legion, Arnold-B.-Moll-John-W.-Hazard Post 385
PO Box 80808
St. Clair Shores, MI 48080
Ph: (517)371-4720
Fax: (517)371-2401
URL: National Affiliate–www.legion.org
Local. Affiliated With: American Legion.

9653 ■ American Legion, Weatherford-Vander-Hoeven Post 552
21704 13th Mile Rd.
St. Clair Shores, MI 48082
Ph: (517)371-4720
Fax: (517)371-2401
URL: National Affiliate–www.legion.org
Local. Affiliated With: American Legion.

9654 ■ Ancient Order of Hibernians of Macomb County - Fr. Solanus Casey Division
c/o Tom Hannon
22625 Revere St.
St. Clair Shores, MI 48080-2883
E-mail: hannons3@aol.com
URL: http://www.michiganaoh.com
Contact: Tom Hannon, Contact
Local. Affiliated With: Ancient Order of Hibernians in America.

9655 ■ Detroit Triumph Sportscar Club (DTSC)
c/o Dave Jonker, Membership Chm.
22609 Carolina St.
St. Clair Shores, MI 48080
E-mail: membership@detroittriumph.org
URL: http://www.detroittriumph.org
Contact: Dave Jonker, Membership Chm.
Local. Affiliated With: Vintage Triumph Register.

9656 ■ Great Lakes Yacht Club (GLYC)
23900 Jefferson Ave.
St. Clair Shores, MI 48080
Ph: (586)778-9510
Fax: (586)778-0698
E-mail: glyc@aol.com
URL: http://www.greatlakesyc.com
Contact: David Parkes, Commodore
Regional.

9657 ■ Greater Detroit Bowling Association (GDBA)
22601 Greater Mack Ave.
PO Box C
St. Clair Shores, MI 48080
Ph: (586)773-6350
Fax: (586)773-6271
Free: (888)753-6350
E-mail: info@gdba.com
URL: http://www.gdba.com
Contact: Mark A. Martin, Exec.Dir.
Founded: 1913. **Members:** 72,000. **Staff:** 6. **Local Groups:** 6. **Local.** Adult male bowlers in metropolitan Detroit, MI area organized to promote bowling and aid bowling leagues. Honors all-city teams; holds annual Masters tournament; maintains Hall of Fame. **Awards:** Bowlers' Man of the Year. **Frequency:** annual. **Type:** recognition. **Affiliated With:** United States Bowling Congress. **Publications:** Yearbook, annual. **Price:** $5.00. **Conventions/Meetings:** semiannual meeting.

9658 ■ Harper Woods Lions Club
c/o Martin Malone, Pres.
28208 Gladstone St.
St. Clair Shores, MI 48081
Ph: (586)773-0746
URL: http://www.metrodetroitlions.org
Contact: Martin Malone, Pres.
Local. Affiliated With: Lions Clubs International.

9659 ■ Inventors Association of Metropolitan Detroit
c/o Frank Wales
749 Clairepointe Cir.
St. Clair Shores, MI 48081
E-mail: unclefj@yahoo.com
URL: National Affiliate–www.uiausa.org
Contact: Frank Wales, Contact
Local. Affiliated With: United Inventors Association of the U.S.A. **Conventions/Meetings:** monthly meeting, with speakers - every 3rd Thursday of the month from September through May.

9660 ■ Lake Shore Sail Club (LSSC)
PO Box 806219
St. Clair Shores, MI 48080
Ph: (313)417-0278
URL: http://www.lakeshoresailclub.org
Contact: Tom Boyce, Commodore
Local.

9661 ■ Lupus Alliance of America, Michigan/Indiana Affiliate
26507 Harper Ave.
St. Clair Shores, MI 48081
Ph: (586)775-8310
Fax: (586)775-8494
Free: (800)705-6677
E-mail: info@milupus.org
URL: http://www.milupus.org
Contact: Mr. Thomas G. Roberts, Exec.Dir.
Founded: 1975. **Members:** 3,000. **Membership Dues:** regular, $25 (annual). **Staff:** 5. **Budget:** $300,000. **Regional Groups:** 5. **State Groups:** 1. **Local Groups:** 10. **Languages:** English, Spanish. **Regional.** Lupus patients, their families, and friends. Educates patients and promotes public awareness and research. **Libraries: Type:** open to the public. **Subjects:** symptoms, treatments, lupus information. **Affiliated With:** Lupus Foundation of America. **Absorbed:** (1998) Lupus Foundation of America, Northeast Indiana Chapter. **Formerly:** (2003) Michigan/Northeast Indiana Lupus Foundation. **Publications:** *Lupus News Link*, bimonthly. Newsletter. Contains research information about various lupus topics. **Price:** free. **Circulation:** 3,500. **Advertising:** accepted. **Conventions/Meetings:** annual meeting (exhibits) - first Sunday in May • periodic Patient Education Workshop.

9662 ■ Metro East Chamber of Commerce (MECC)
27601 Jefferson Ave.
St. Clair Shores, MI 48081-2053
Ph: (586)777-2741
Fax: (586)777-4811
Free: (810)777-2741
E-mail: metroeastcc@aol.com
URL: National Affiliate–www.uschamber.com
Contact: Mary Jane Amicarelli, Exec.Dir.
Founded: 1946. **Members:** 650. **Staff:** 4. **Local.** Businesses and individuals. Seeks to promote the

growth of the business community in Fraser, the Grosse Pointes, Harper Woods, Roseville, and St. Clair Shores, MI. Monitors legislation; holds annual Chamber Cruise and Golf Outing. **Affiliated With:** U.S. Chamber of Commerce. **Publications:** *Business Guide*, annual. Membership Directory. **Price:** free • *The Focus*, monthly. Newsletter.

9663 ■ Michigan Dietetic Association (MDA)
c/o Susanne Consiglio, RD, Exec.Dir.
23100 E Jefferson, Ste.B
St. Clair Shores, MI 48080
Ph: (586)774-7447
Fax: (586)778-3004
E-mail: mda.execdir@sbcglobal.net
URL: http://www.eatrightmich.org
Contact: Susanne Consiglio RD, Exec.Dir.
State. Promotes optimal nutrition and well being for all people by advocating for its members. **Affiliated With:** American Dietetic Association. **Conventions/ Meetings:** annual lecture, lectures and nutrition/food service product exhibits (exhibits).

9664 ■ Michigan Healthcare Executive Group and Associates (MHEGA)
22732 Alger St., Ste.200
St. Clair Shores, MI 48080
Ph: (248)937-3375
Fax: (586)776-1069
E-mail: dkellis@wideopenwest.com
URL: http://mhega.ache.org
Contact: Robert J. Yellan, Pres.
State. Works to improve the health status of society by advancing healthcare leadership and management excellence. Conducts research, career development and public policy programs. **Affiliated With:** American College of Healthcare Executives.

9665 ■ St. Clair Shores Figure Skating Club (SCSFSC)
20000 Stephens Dr.
St. Clair Shores, MI 48080
Ph: (586)774-7530
Fax: (586)774-3272
E-mail: roberneil@aol.com
URL: http://www.scsfsc.org
Contact: Lisa Fisk, Pres.
Local. Provides programs to encourage participation and achievement in the sport of figure skating on ice. Defines and maintains uniform standards of skating proficiency. Organizes and sponsors competitions and exhibitions for the purpose of stimulating interest in figure skating. **Affiliated With:** United States Figure Skating Association.

9666 ■ Veteran Motor Car Club of America - Lakeshore Chapter
c/o Pat Gough, Pres.
23345 Elaine St.
St. Clair Shores, MI 48080
Ph: (586)778-2667
URL: National Affiliate–www.vmcca.org
Contact: Pat Gough, Pres.
Local. Affiliated With: Veteran Motor Car Club of America.

St. Helen

9667 ■ American Legion, St. Helen Post 416
10062 Ford Dr.
St. Helen, MI 48656
Ph: (517)371-4720
Fax: (517)371-2401
URL: National Affiliate–www.legion.org
Local. Affiliated With: American Legion.

St. Ignace

9668 ■ American Legion, Michigan Post 62
c/o Thomas F. Grant
PO Box 211
St. Ignace, MI 49781
Ph: (517)371-4720
Fax: (517)371-2401
URL: National Affiliate–www.legion.org
Contact: Thomas F. Grant, Contact
Local. Affiliated With: American Legion.

9669 ■ Michigan Underwater Preserves Council (MUPC)
560 N State St.
St. Ignace, MI 49781
Ph: (906)643-8717
Fax: (906)643-9380
Free: (800)338-6660
E-mail: sicc@up.net
URL: http://www.michiganpreserves.org
Contact: Janet Peterson, Treas.
Founded: 1987. **Members:** 11. **Budget:** $2,000. **State**. Promotes sport diving in the State of Michigan. Educates and informs divers. **Publications:** *Dive Michigan Underwater Preserves*, annual. Booklet. Describes diving in Michigan ULW Preserves. **Price:** free. **Advertising:** accepted.

9670 ■ Ruffed Grouse Society, Eastern Up Chapter
c/o Bill Borst
36 Prospect St.
St. Ignace, MI 49781-1435
Ph: (906)847-6483
URL: National Affiliate–www.ruffedgrousesociety.org
Contact: Bill Borst, Contact
Local. Affiliated With: Ruffed Grouse Society.

9671 ■ St. Ignace Area Convention and Visitors Bureau
560 N State St.
St. Ignace, MI 49781
Free: (800)338-6660
E-mail: info@stignace.com
URL: http://www.stignace.com
Local. Promotes convention business and tourism in area.

9672 ■ St. Ignace Chamber of Commerce
560 N State St.
St. Ignace, MI 49781-1429
Ph: (906)643-8717 (906)643-6950
Fax: (906)643-9380
Free: (800)970-8717
E-mail: info@stignace.com
URL: http://www.stignace.com
Contact: Janet Peterson, Exec.Dir.
Members: 200. **Membership Dues:** advertising media, service, retail, restaurant, $265 (annual) • amusement, $292 (annual) • lodging, $237 (annual) • boat line, $306 (annual). **Staff:** 1. **Local**. Encourages businesses by building coalitions to promote the St. Ignace area as a great place to live, work, visit and do business. **Awards:** Citizen of the Year. **Frequency:** annual. **Type:** trophy. **Recipient:** for citizen with the biggest contribution to the community. **Publications:** *St. Ignace - Mackinac Area's Premier Vacation Guide*. Handbook. **Conventions/Meetings:** monthly board meeting - every 3rd Wednesday.

St. Johns

9673 ■ American Legion, Michigan Post 153
c/o Edwin T. Stiles
PO Box 265
St. Johns, MI 48879
Ph: (517)371-4720
Fax: (517)371-2401
URL: National Affiliate–www.legion.org
Contact: Edwin T. Stiles, Contact
Local. Affiliated With: American Legion.

9674 ■ Catholics United for the Faith - Incarnate Word Chapter
c/o Mariann Niznak
1200 Sunview Dr., No. 4
St. Johns, MI 48879
Ph: (989)227-8581
URL: National Affiliate–www.cuf.org
Contact: Mariann Niznak, Contact
Local.

9675 ■ Fowler Lions Club
c/o Terry Schneider, Pres.
3375 S Williams Rd.
St. Johns, MI 48879
Ph: (989)224-1647
E-mail: tschneider@copper.net
URL: http://www.district11c2.org
Contact: Terry Schneider, Pres.
Local. Affiliated With: Lions Clubs International.

9676 ■ Michigan Bean Commission
c/o Robert Green, Exec.Dir.
1031 S U.S. 27
St. Johns, MI 48879
Ph: (989)224-1361
Fax: (989)224-6374
E-mail: mbc@mutualdata.com
URL: http://www.michiganbean.org
Contact: Robert Green, Exec.Dir.
Founded: 1966. **State.**

9677 ■ Relief after Violent Encounter, Ionia-Montcalm (RAVE)
c/o Beth L. Morrison
PO Box 472
St. Johns, MI 48879-0472
Local.

9678 ■ St. Johns Area Chamber of Commerce (SJACC)
1013 S US 27
PO Box 61
St. Johns, MI 48879
Ph: (989)224-7248
Fax: (989)224-7667
E-mail: ccchamber@power-net.net
URL: http://www.stjohnschamber.org
Contact: Brenda Terpening, Exec.Dir.
Members: 300. **Membership Dues:** regular, $120 (annual) • associate, $50 (annual). **Local**. Promotes business and community development in the St. Johns, MI area. Sponsors St. Johns Mint Festival, annual Christmas House Decorating Contest and Parade. **Awards:** St. Johns Area Chamber of Commerce/Mint Festival Scholarship. **Frequency:** annual. **Type:** scholarship. **Recipient:** for education in business. **Committees:** Mint Festival Steering. **Also Known As:** (2005) Clinton County Chamber of Commerce. **Publications:** *Chamber News*, monthly. Newsletter. Alternate Formats: online. **Conventions/ Meetings:** annual festival • monthly Membership Luncheon, luncheon with agenda - every 3rd Thursday.

9679 ■ St. Johns Lions Club
c/o George Ayoub, Pres.
6252 W Walker Rd.
St. Johns, MI 48879
Ph: (989)463-3141 (989)224-2608
URL: http://www.district11c2.org
Contact: George Ayoub, Pres.
Local. Affiliated With: Lions Clubs International.

St. Joseph

9680 ■ American Society for Quality, St. Joseph-Benton Harbor Section 1007
c/o Michael Duke, Sec.
PO Box 616
St. Joseph, MI 49085-0616
E-mail: contact@asq1007.org
URL: http://www.asq1007.org
Contact: Michael Duke, Sec.
Local. Advances learning, quality improvement and knowledge exchange to improve business results and to create better workplaces and communities worldwide. Provides a forum for information exchange, professional development and continuous

learning in the science of quality. **Affiliated With:** American Society for Quality.

9681 ■ Berrien County Medical Society
PO Box 145
St. Joseph, MI 49085-0145
Ph: (269)983-7501
Fax: (269)983-6975
E-mail: berriencountymed@sbcglobal.net
URL: http://www.msms.org
Contact: Cheryl J. Schulte, Exec.Dir.
Local. Advances the art and science of medicine. Promotes patient care and the betterment of public health. **Affiliated With:** Michigan State Medical Society.

9682 ■ Bridgman - Young Life
2627 Niles Ave.
St. Joseph, MI 49085
Ph: (269)983-4741
URL: http://sites.younglife.org/_layouts/ylext/default.aspx?ID=C-1086
Local. Affiliated With: Young Life.

9683 ■ Lakeshore - Young Life
2627 Niles Ave.
St. Joseph, MI 49085
Ph: (269)983-4741
URL: http://sites.younglife.org/_layouts/ylext/default.aspx?ID=C-1087
Local. Affiliated With: Young Life.

9684 ■ Michigan Chapter of NALMS (MCNALMS)
620 Broad St., Ste.100
St. Joseph, MI 49085
E-mail: astamand@phycotech.com
URL: http://www.nalms.org/mcnalms
Contact: Ann St. Amand, Contact
State. Affiliated With: North American Lake Management Society.

9685 ■ Michigan National Wild Turkey Federation, Berrien County
3280 W Valley View Driver St.
St. Joseph, MI 49085
URL: http://www.mi-nwtf.org/berrian_co_.htm
Contact: Roger Seely, Pres.
Local.

9686 ■ National Active and Retired Federal Employees Association - South West Michigan 572
2894 Sandra Terr.
St. Joseph, MI 49085-3126
Ph: (269)428-0667
URL: National Affiliate–www.narfe.org
Contact: Richard D. Peterson, Contact
Local. Protects the retirement future of employees through education. Informs members on issues affecting the retirement. **Affiliated With:** National Association of Retired Federal Employees.

9687 ■ National Association of Pastoral Musicians, Kalamazoo
c/o Mr. Mike Kiebel
St. Joseph Church
211 Church St.
St. Joseph, MI 49085-1128
Ph: (269)983-9671
E-mail: liturgyandmusic@hotmail.com
URL: National Affiliate–www.npm.org
Contact: Mr. Mike Kiebel, Contact
Local. Affiliated With: National Association of Pastoral Musicians.

9688 ■ PFLAG St. Joseph/Berrien County
4340 Lincoln Ave.
St. Joseph, MI 49085
Ph: (269)429-6160
E-mail: pflagberriencounty@yahoo.com
URL: http://www.pflag.org/Michigan.216.0.html
Local. Affiliated With: Parents, Families, and Friends of Lesbians and Gays.

9689 ■ St. Joe - Young Life
2627 Niles Ave.
St. Joseph, MI 49085
Ph: (269)983-4741
URL: http://sites.younglife.org/_layouts/ylext/default.aspx?ID=C-1088
Local. Affiliated With: Young Life.

9690 ■ St. Joseph Lions Club
PO Box 353
St. Joseph, MI 49085
E-mail: gary.teske@chemicalbankmi.com
URL: http://milions11b2.org
Local. Affiliated With: Lions Clubs International.

9691 ■ Saint Joseph, Michigan Kiwanis Club
2975 McLin Rd.
St. Joseph, MI 49085
Ph: (616)429-2025
E-mail: emeny@sbcglobal.net
URL: http://sjkiwanis.org
Contact: Dick Peterson, Pres.
Local.

9692 ■ Southwestern Michigan Association of Realtors
3123 Lake Shore Dr.
St. Joseph, MI 49085-2625
Ph: (269)983-6375
Fax: (269)983-5206
E-mail: gwalter@swmar.org
URL: National Affiliate–www.realtor.org
Contact: Gary Walter, Exec. Officer
Local. Strives to develop real estate business practices. Advocates the right to own, use and transfer real property. Provides a facility for professional development, research and exchange of information among members. **Affiliated With:** National Association of Realtors.

9693 ■ Southwestern Michigan Estate Planning Council
c/o Nanette Keiser, Treas.
2900 S State St., Ste.2E
St. Joseph, MI 49085
Ph: (269)983-3486
Fax: (269)983-4439
E-mail: nkeiser@qtm.net
URL: National Affiliate–councils.naepc.org
Contact: William E. Westerbeke CPA, Pres.
Local. Fosters understanding of the proper relationship between the functions of professionals in the estate planning field. Provides forum for estate planning professionals in Southwestern Michigan. Encourages cooperation among members. **Affiliated With:** National Association of Estate Planners and Councils.

9694 ■ SWM - Wyldlife
2627 Niles Ave.
St. Joseph, MI 49085
Ph: (269)983-4741
URL: http://sites.younglife.org/_layouts/ylext/default.aspx?ID=C-1089
Local. Affiliated With: Young Life.

9695 ■ Young Life Southwest Michigan
2627 Niles Ave.
St. Joseph, MI 49085
Ph: (269)983-4741
Fax: (269)983-2614
URL: http://sites.younglife.org/sites/SouthwestMichigan/default.aspx
Contact: Mike Bredeweg, Area Dir.
Local. Affiliated With: Young Life.

St. Louis

9696 ■ American Legion, Fields-Myers-Smith-Dittenber Post 256
PO Box 194
St. Louis, MI 48880
Ph: (517)371-4720
Fax: (517)371-2401
URL: National Affiliate–www.legion.org
Local. Affiliated With: American Legion.

9697 ■ St. Louis Lions Club
c/o Donna L. Kelley, Sec.
336 N Clinton St.
St. Louis, MI 48880-1801
Ph: (989)681-2549
E-mail: dkelly@edzone.net
URL: http://www.district11c2.org
Contact: Donna L. Kelley, Sec.
Local. Affiliated With: Lions Clubs International.

Saline

9698 ■ American Legion, Michigan Post 322
c/o William B. Lutz
PO Box 226
Saline, MI 48176
Ph: (517)371-4720
Fax: (517)371-2401
URL: National Affiliate–www.legion.org
Contact: William B. Lutz, Contact
Local. Affiliated With: American Legion.

9699 ■ Community Economic Development and Information Technology
c/o Kenneth Russell Brown, PhD
833 Hatfield Cir.
Saline, MI 48176-9247
Ph: (734)429-9202
Local.

9700 ■ International Union, United Automobile, Aerospace and Agricultural Implement Workers of America, AFL-CIO - Local Union 892
601 Woodland Dr.
Saline, MI 48176-1297
Ph: (734)429-5140
Fax: (734)429-3600
E-mail: caruso@uaw892.org
URL: http://www.uaw892.org
Contact: Mark Caruso, Pres.
Members: 2,178. **Local**. Seeks for the dignity and equality of the workers. Strives to provide contractors with well-trained, productive employees. **Affiliated With:** International Union, United Automobile, Aerospace and Agricultural Implement Workers of America.

9701 ■ Michigan Angus Association
c/o Steve Thelen, Pres.
7821 Weber Rd.
Saline, MI 48176
Ph: (734)944-6262
E-mail: sthelen22@aol.com
URL: National Affiliate–www.angus.org
Contact: Steve Thelen, Pres.
State. Affiliated With: American Angus Association.

9702 ■ Project Management Institute, Michigan Huron Valley Chapter (PMI-HVC)
c/o Dale A. Inder, Pres.
892 Berkshire Dr.
Saline, MI 48176
E-mail: pmihvcpres@pmi-hvc.org
URL: http://www.pmi-hvc.org
Local. Affiliated With: Project Management Institute.

9703 ■ Saline Area Chamber of Commerce
141 E Michigan Ave.
PO Box 198
Saline, MI 48176-0198
Ph: (734)429-4494
Fax: (734)944-6835
E-mail: salinechamber@aol.com
URL: http://www.salinechamber.com
Contact: Mr. Larry Osterling, Exec.Dir.
Founded: 1980. **Members:** 437. **Membership Dues:** business, $165-$925 (annual) • governmental, $100 (annual) • non-profit or individual, $80 (annual). **Staff:** 3. **Local**. Works to increase the community's economic progress while preserving the high quality of life that makes Saline so unique through its various community events and projects, members services and activities. **Libraries: Type:** open to the public;

reference. **Holdings:** articles, periodicals. **Subjects:** city, townships, area organizations, area committees, government, state, county, local issues, consumer protection, identity theft, internet fraud, small business, merchant information, insurance, mortgages, real estate information, resumes, area events, activities, projects. **Awards:** Business Enterprise Award. **Frequency:** annual. **Type:** recognition. **Recipient:** for outstanding businesses with high ethical practices and customer service and an ongoing commitment to the betterment of the Saline area community • Citizen of the Year. **Frequency:** annual. **Type:** recognition • George A. Anderson Vision Award. **Frequency:** annual. **Type:** recognition • Lifetime Achievement. **Frequency:** annual. **Type:** recognition. **Committees:** Destination Saline. **Affiliated With:** American Cancer Society, Little Rock; Ann Arbor Area Convention and Visitors Bureau. **Publications:** *Saline Business Advocate*, monthly. Newsletter. **Price:** $25.00 /year for nonmembers; free to members. **Advertising:** accepted.

9704 ■ Saline Area Lions Club
c/o Earl Laughrey, Sec.
291 Tower Dr.
Saline, MI 48176
Ph: (734)429-4468
E-mail: elaughrey@hotmail.com
URL: http://www.lionsdistrict11b1.org/lc_saline.htm
Contact: Earl Laughrey, Sec.
Local. Affiliated With: Lions Clubs International.

9705 ■ Southeastern Michigan Angus Association
c/o Steve Thelen, Pres.
7821 Weber Rd.
Saline, MI 48176
Ph: (734)944-6262
E-mail: sthelen22@aol.com
URL: National Affiliate–www.angus.org
Contact: Steve Thelen, Pres.
Regional. Affiliated With: American Angus Association.

Sand Lake

9706 ■ Sand Lake Lions Club
c/o Karen Hayden, Pres.
11933 Butternut Ave.
Sand Lake, MI 49343
Ph: (616)636-5425
E-mail: haydengk@wmis.net
URL: http://lions.silverthorn.biz/11-e1
Contact: Karen Hayden, Pres.
Local. Affiliated With: Lions Clubs International.

Sandusky

9707 ■ American Legion, Michigan Post 369
c/o Russell Wakefield
695 W Wedge Rd.
Sandusky, MI 48471
Ph: (517)371-4720
Fax: (517)371-2401
URL: National Affiliate–www.legion.org
Contact: Russell Wakefield, Contact
Local. Affiliated With: American Legion.

Sanford

9708 ■ American Legion, Thomas-Daniels-Hand Post 443
2080 N Meridian Rd., No. 11
Sanford, MI 48657
Ph: (517)371-4720
Fax: (517)371-2401
URL: National Affiliate–www.legion.org
Local. Affiliated With: American Legion.

9709 ■ Michigan National Wild Turkey Federation, Gateway Gobblers
c/o Chad Stearns, Pres.
W Love Rd.
Sanford, MI 48657
Ph: (989)386-3475
URL: http://www.mi-nwtf.org/Gateway.htm
Contact: Jim Bailer, VP
Local.

9710 ■ Midland Lions Club
c/o Jim Dunlap, Pres.
4402 N Francis Shores Dr.
Sanford, MI 48657
Ph: (989)687-9698
E-mail: jjdunlap@aol.com
URL: http://lions.silverthorn.biz/11-e1
Contact: Jim Dunlap, Pres.
Local. Affiliated With: Lions Clubs International.

9711 ■ Midland Michigan Kennel Club (MMKC)
24 E Saginaw Rd.
Sanford, MI 48657
Ph: (989)687-2590
E-mail: brehaven@rural-net.com
URL: http://www.mmkc.org
Contact: Brenda Landers, Pres.
State.

9712 ■ Sanford Lions Club - Michigan
PO Box 231
Sanford, MI 48657
Ph: (989)859-1219 (989)687-6100
Fax: (989)687-9497
E-mail: burnison@tds.net
URL: http://sanfordmi.lionwap.org
Contact: Robert Burnison, Pres.
Local. Affiliated With: Lions Clubs International.

Saranac

9713 ■ American Legion, Michigan Post 175
c/o Leroy L. Dausman
PO Box 273
Saranac, MI 48881
Ph: (517)371-4720
Fax: (517)371-2401
URL: National Affiliate–www.legion.org
Contact: Leroy L. Dausman, Contact
Local. Affiliated With: American Legion.

Saugatuck

9714 ■ American Legion, Bruner-Frehse Post 137
248 Mason St.
Saugatuck, MI 49453
Ph: (517)371-4720
Fax: (517)371-2401
URL: National Affiliate–www.legion.org
Local. Affiliated With: American Legion.

9715 ■ Puppeteers of America - West Michigan Puppetry Guild
c/o Dodie Vander Vere
PO Box 114
Saugatuck, MI 49453
E-mail: dcv@datawise.net
URL: National Affiliate–www.puppeteers.org
Contact: Dodie Vander Vere, Contact
Local.

9716 ■ Saugatuck-Douglas Art Club
c/o James D. Suerth
PO Box 176
Saugatuck, MI 49453-0176
Local.

Sault Ste. Marie

9717 ■ American Legion, Michigan Post 3
c/o Ira D. Mac Lachlan
PO Box 336
Sault Ste. Marie, MI 49783
Ph: (517)371-4720
Fax: (517)371-2401
URL: National Affiliate–www.legion.org
Contact: Ira D. Mac Lachlan, Contact
Local. Affiliated With: American Legion.

9718 ■ Eastern Upper Peninsula Board of Realtors
2006 Ashmun St.
Sault Ste. Marie, MI 49783
Ph: (906)632-7336
Fax: (906)632-3033
E-mail: eupboard@sbcglobal.net
URL: National Affiliate–www.realtor.org
Contact: Jan Bourque, Exec. Officer
Local. Strives to develop real estate business practices. Advocates the right to own, use and transfer real property. Provides a facility for professional development, research and exchange of information among members. **Affiliated With:** National Association of Realtors.

9719 ■ Inter-Tribal Council of Michigan
c/o Sharon L. Teeple, Exec.Dir.
2956 Ashmun St.
Sault Ste. Marie, MI 49783
Ph: (906)632-6896
Fax: (906)632-1810
Free: (800)562-4957
E-mail: knystrom@itcmi.org
URL: http://www.itcmi.org
Contact: Kim Nystrom, Admin. Services Mgr.
Local.

9720 ■ Izaak Walton League of America, Lock City Chapter
1012 Johnson St.
Sault Ste. Marie, MI 49783-3326
Ph: (906)632-8170
URL: National Affiliate–www.iwla.org
Local. Works to educate the public to conserve, maintain, protect, and restore the soil, forest, water, and other natural resources of the U.S; promotes the enjoyment and wholesome utilization of these resources. **Affiliated With:** Izaak Walton League of America.

9721 ■ Local 799C, Chemical Workers Council of the UFCW
110 Dawson St.
Sault Ste. Marie, MI 49783
Ph: (906)632-8386
E-mail: local799@voyager.net
URL: National Affiliate–www.ufcw.org
Local. Affiliated With: United Food and Commercial Workers International Union.

9722 ■ National Active and Retired Federal Employees Association - Lock City 477
1012 Johnstone
Sault Ste. Marie, MI 49783-3326
Ph: (906)632-8170
URL: National Affiliate–www.narfe.org
Contact: Colin J. Edward, Contact
Local. Protects the retirement future of employees through education. Informs members on issues affecting the retirement. **Affiliated With:** National Association of Retired Federal Employees.

9723 ■ North Star Habitat for Humanity
PO Box 122
Sault Ste. Marie, MI 49783
Ph: (906)632-6245
URL: http://www.geocities.com/northstar49783
Founded: 1993. **Local. Affiliated With:** Habitat for Humanity International.

9724 ■ Sault Area Arts Council (SAAC)
217 Ferris St.
Sault Ste. Marie, MI 49783
Ph: (906)635-1312
E-mail: saac@saultarts.org
URL: http://www.saultarts.org
Contact: David Bigelow, Chm.

Founded: 1969. **Members:** 550. **Membership Dues:** individual, $15. **Staff:** 3. **Regional Groups:** 3. **State Groups:** 1. **Local Groups:** 1. **Local.** Individuals interested in promoting the arts. Conducts charitable activities. Hosts competitions and exhibitions. Produces area festival each summer, art gallery, and art center. Conducts fundraising events and arts auction. **Libraries: Type:** not open to the public. **Subjects:** art-related. **Awards:** Aarve Lahti Award. **Frequency:** periodic. **Type:** monetary • Best of Show. **Frequency:** annual. **Type:** monetary • Exhibition Award. **Frequency:** periodic. **Type:** monetary. **Boards:** Olive Craig Gallery. **Publications:** *Alberta House News*, monthly. Newsletter. Includes calendar of events. **Price:** $5.00 in U.S.; $6.00 in Canada. **Circulation:** 800. **Advertising:** accepted. **Conventions/Meetings:** monthly board meeting, includes exhibits each month except January (exhibits) - always third Tuesday • annual Sault Summer Arts Festival - always first Tuesday in August.

9725 ■ Sault Area Chamber of Commerce (SACC)
2581 I-75 Bus. Spur
Sault Ste. Marie, MI 49783
Ph: (906)632-3301
Fax: (906)632-2331
E-mail: info@saultstemarie.org
URL: http://www.saultstemarie.org
Contact: Virginia R. Zinser, Exec.Dir.

Founded: 1889. **Members:** 460. **Membership Dues:** base, $195 (annual). **Staff:** 3. **Budget:** $160,000. **Local.** Business persons, professionals, and individuals interested in promoting business and community development in the Sault Ste. Marie, MI area. Sponsors charitable activities, festivals, and other special events. **Libraries: Type:** reference. **Subjects:** business. **Affiliated With:** U.S. Chamber of Commerce. **Publications:** *Sault Area Business Directory*, annual. Includes scope of member activities. **Circulation:** 1,500. **Advertising:** accepted • Newsletter, monthly.

9726 ■ Sault Ste. Marie Convention and Visitors Bureau
536 Ashmun St.
Sault Ste. Marie, MI 49783
Ph: (906)632-3366
Free: (800)MI-SAULT
E-mail: info@saultstemarie.com
URL: http://www.saultstemarie.com
Contact: David McCord, Contact

Founded: 1984. **Members:** 40. **Staff:** 4. **Local.** Promotes convention business and tourism in area. **Also Known As:** (1993) Sault Convention and Visitors Bureau.

9727 ■ Sault Ste. Marie District Dental Society
709 Johnston St.
Sault Ste. Marie, MI 49783
Ph: (906)635-6020
Fax: (906)635-7687
URL: National Affiliate–www.ada.org
Contact: Dr. Clayton C. Shunk, Pres.

Local. Represents the interests of dentists committed to the public's oral health, ethics and professional development. Encourages the improvement of the public's oral health and promotes the art and science of dentistry. **Affiliated With:** American Dental Association; Michigan Dental Association.

9728 ■ Society of Manufacturing Engineers - Lake Superior State University S082
Lake Superior State Univ., Engg. Dept.
650 W Easterday Ave.
Sault Ste. Marie, MI 49783
Ph: (906)635-2131
Fax: (906)635-6663
E-mail: jdevaprasad@lssu.edu
URL: National Affiliate–www.sme.org
Contact: James Devaprasad, Contact

Local. Advances manufacturing knowledge to gain competitive advantage. Improves skills and manufacturing solutions for the growth of economy. Provides resources and opportunities for manufacturing professionals. **Affiliated With:** Academy of Natural Sciences.

9729 ■ United States Naval Sea Cadet Corps - Michigan Sea Tigers Division
1437th Multi Role Bridge Co.
1179 E Portage Ave.
Sault Ste. Marie, MI 49783
E-mail: monica.r.williams@navy.mil
URL: http://dolphin.seacadets.org/US_units/UnitDetails.asp?UnitID=092STD
Contact: LTJG Monica R. Williams, Commanding Officer

Local. Works to instill good citizenship and patriotism in youth. Encourages qualities such as personal neatness, loyalty, obedience, dependability, and responsibility to others. Offers courses in physical fitness and military drill, first aid, water safety, basic seamanship, and naval history and traditions. **Affiliated With:** Naval Sea Cadet Corps.

9730 ■ United Way of Chippewa County
PO Box 451
Sault Ste. Marie, MI 49783-0451
Ph: (432)685-7700
Fax: (906)632-3190
E-mail: unitedwaycc@30below.com
URL: National Affiliate–national.unitedway.org
Contact: Molly M. Paquin, Exec.Dir.

Founded: 1956. **Members:** 21. **Staff:** 3. **State Groups:** 22. **Local Groups:** 15. **Local. Affiliated With:** United Way of America.

Schoolcraft

9731 ■ AMBUCS - Alive After Five
c/o Donna A. Whitcomb, Pres.
6348 W S Ave.
Schoolcraft, MI 49087
Ph: (269)372-3581 (269)372-0174
Fax: (269)372-0174
E-mail: dwhit831@aol.com
URL: National Affiliate–www.ambucs.com
Contact: Donna A. Whitcomb, Pres.

Local. Seeks to create mobility and independence for people with disabilities. Performs community service. Provides therapeutic tricycles to children with disabilities. Provides scholarships to therapists. **Affiliated With:** National AMBUCS.

9732 ■ American Legion, Wileykoon Post 475
425 E Clay St.
Schoolcraft, MI 49087
Ph: (517)371-4720
Fax: (517)371-2401
URL: National Affiliate–www.legion.org

Local. Affiliated With: American Legion.

9733 ■ Clumber Spaniel Fanciers of Michigan (CSFM)
c/o James Fankhauser
15545 S 2nd St.
Schoolcraft, MI 49087-9728
Ph: (269)679-5095
E-mail: carol.sanford@hstna.com
URL: http://www.clumberfanciersofmi.org
Contact: Carol Sanford, Sec.

State.

Scotts

9734 ■ Climax - Scotts PTA
PO Box 66
Scotts, MI 49088
URL: http://familyeducation.com/MI/Climax_Scotts_PTA

Local. Parents, teachers, students, and others interested in uniting the forces of home, school, and community. Promotes the welfare of children and youth.

Scottville

9735 ■ Phi Theta Kappa, Alpha Phi Phi Chapter - West Shore Community College
c/o Sean Henne
2000 N Stiles Rd.
Scottville, MI 49454
Ph: (231)845-6211
E-mail: swhenne@westshore.edu
URL: http://www.ptk.org/directories/chapters/MI/20532-1.htm
Contact: Sean Henne, Contact

Local.

9736 ■ Scottville Area Chamber of Commerce
140 S Main St.
PO Box 224
Scottville, MI 49454-0224
Ph: (231)757-4304
Fax: (231)757-4341
E-mail: chamber@scottville.org
URL: http://www.scottville.org
Contact: Albert Muzzin, Exec.Dir.

Members: 134. **Local.** Promotes business and community development in Mason County, MI. Participates in annual Harvest Festival. Conducts annual Rubber Duck Race in Pere Marquette River, annual Chicken BBQ. **Publications:** none.

Sebewaing

9737 ■ American Legion, Stamnitz-Lindeman Post 293
8255 Unionville Rd.
Sebewaing, MI 48759
Ph: (517)371-4720
Fax: (517)371-2401
URL: National Affiliate–www.legion.org

Local. Affiliated With: American Legion.

9738 ■ Michigan National Wild Turkey Federation, Sebawaing Gobblers
10440 Haist Rd.
Sebewaing, MI 48759
Ph: (517)883-2124
E-mail: beachcom@avci.net
URL: http://www.mi-nwtf.org/Sebewaig.htm
Contact: Herbert Lorentz, Pres.

Local.

9739 ■ Michigan National Wild Turkey Federation, Tuscola Longbeards
2705 Unionville Rd.
Sebewaing, MI 48759
Ph: (517)883-2823
URL: http://www.mi-nwtf.org/Tuscola.htm
Contact: Paula Doerr, Pres.

Local.

9740 ■ Sebewaing Chamber of Commerce
PO Box 622
Sebewaing, MI 48759
Ph: (989)883-2150
Fax: (989)883-9367
Contact: Dave Burrows, Pres.

Local.

Selfridge

9741 ■ United States Naval Sea Cadet Corps - Tomcat Squadron
NARC Selfridge
41130 Castle Ave.
Selfridge, MI 48045
URL: http://dolphin.seacadets.org/US_units/UnitDetails.asp?UnitID=093TCT
Contact: LTJG Joseph G. Faucher, Commanding Officer
Local. Works to instill good citizenship and patriotism in youth. Encourages qualities such as personal neatness, loyalty, obedience, dependability, and responsibility to others. Offers courses in physical fitness and military drill, first aid, water safety, basic seamanship, and naval history and traditions. **Affiliated With:** Naval Sea Cadet Corps.

Shelby

9742 ■ American Legion, Michigan Post 30
c/o Gordon Bates
122 Ferry St.
Shelby, MI 49455
Ph: (517)371-4720
Fax: (517)371-2401
URL: National Affiliate–www.legion.org
Contact: Gordon Bates, Contact
Local. Affiliated With: American Legion.

Shelby Township

9743 ■ American Legion, Fraser Post 243
8897 Shelby Woods Dr.
Shelby Township, MI 48317
Ph: (517)371-4720
Fax: (517)371-2401
URL: National Affiliate–www.legion.org
Local. Affiliated With: American Legion.

9744 ■ American Legion, Hellenic Post 100
48844 Keystone Ct.
Shelby Township, MI 48315
Ph: (517)371-4720
Fax: (517)371-2401
URL: National Affiliate–www.legion.org
Local. Affiliated With: American Legion.

9745 ■ Colored Pencil Society of America, Detroit Chapter No. 104
54349 Horizon
Shelby Township, MI 48316
Ph: (586)781-6903
E-mail: rradtke01@comcast.net
URL: http://cpsadetroit.com
Contact: Diane Radtke, Pres.
Founded: 1990. **Members:** 72. **Membership Dues:** chapter, $15 (annual). **For-Profit. Local.** Weekend pleasure painters, professional artists and artists who love using colored pencils. Strives to promote colored pencil art. **Publications:** *Drawing Together*, 4-6/yr. Newsletter. Contains information on meetings, minutes, and articles of interest. Alternate Formats: online. **Conventions/Meetings:** bimonthly meeting, with lectures, demonstrations, and workshops.

9746 ■ Michigan Catalysis Society (MCS)
c/o Galen B. Fisher
Delphi Res. Labs
51786 Shelby Pkwy.
Shelby Township, MI 48315-1786
Ph: (586)323-4141
Fax: (586)323-9898
E-mail: galen.b.fisher@delphi.com
URL: http://www.nacatsoc.org
Contact: Galen B. Fisher, Contact
State. Aims to promote and encourage the growth and development of the science of catalysis and those scientific disciplines; and to provide educational services to members and other interested individuals. **Affiliated With:** North American Catalysis Society.

9747 ■ Professional Photographers of Michigan (PPM)
12219 24 Mile Rd.
Shelby Township, MI 48315
Ph: (248)318-5182
E-mail: edir@ppm.org
URL: http://www.ppm.org
Contact: Scott Green, Exec.Dir.
Founded: 1940. **Members:** 400. **Membership Dues:** active, out of state, $275 (annual) • associate, $175 (annual) • allied, $300 (annual) • student, corporate, $100 (annual) • retired, $125 (annual). **Staff:** 1. **Budget:** $150,000. **Local Groups:** 5. **State.** Photographers; individuals working in the photography industry. Promotes the industry. Sponsors social events. **Awards:** Photographer of the Year. **Frequency:** annual. **Type:** recognition. **Affiliated With:** Professional Photographers of America. **Publications:** *Michigan Photographer*, bimonthly. Newsletter. Includes information to keep members up to date with information within the industry. **Circulation:** 500. **Advertising:** accepted. **Conventions/Meetings:** annual convention (exhibits).

9748 ■ STARFLEET: USS Empress
c/o Richard Smith, Commanding Officer
49997 Downing Ct.
Shelby Township, MI 48315
E-mail: ussempress@region13.org
URL: http://www.region13.org
Contact: Richard Smith, Commanding Officer
Local. Affiliated With: STARFLEET.

Shepherd

9749 ■ Michigan Loon Preservation Association/Michigan Loonwatch (MLPA/MLW)
c/o Joanne C. Williams, Coor.
PO Box 294
Shepherd, MI 48883
Ph: (989)828-6019
E-mail: michiganloons@yahoo.com
URL: http://www.michiganloons.org
Contact: Joanne C. Williams, Coor.
Founded: 1987. **Members:** 600. **Membership Dues:** individual, $20 (annual) • senior, student, $15 (annual) • contributing, organization, $50 (annual) • supporting, $100 (annual) • benefactor, $500 (annual) • life, $450. **Budget:** $20,000. **State.** Strives to conserve and enhance the Common Loon population through research, habitat protection and restoration, species protection, and public awareness and involvement. **Publications:** *Loon Echoes*, quarterly. Newsletter. **Conventions/Meetings:** quarterly board meeting • annual conference - spring.

9750 ■ Shepherd Lions Club
c/o Kent Roth, Pres.
PO Box 427
Shepherd, MI 48883
Ph: (989)828-5434 (989)828-6029
E-mail: gotobar@charter.net
URL: http://lions.silverthorn.biz/11-e1
Contact: Kent Roth, Pres.
Local. Affiliated With: Lions Clubs International.

9751 ■ Sweet Adelines International, Heart of Michigan Chapter
Shepherd School Choral Rm.
100 E Hall St.
Shepherd, MI 48883-9004
Ph: (989)828-5778
E-mail: lrbush46@yahoo.com
URL: National Affiliate–www.sweetadelineintl.org
Contact: Lida Bush, Contact
Local. Advances the musical art form of barbershop harmony through education and performances. Provides education, training and coaching in the development of women's four-part barbershop harmony. **Affiliated With:** Sweet Adelines International.

Sheridan

9752 ■ Sheridan Lions Club - Michigan
c/o Randall Hansen, Pres.
PO Box 250
Sheridan, MI 48884
Ph: (989)352-5919
E-mail: nassif@auis.net
URL: http://lions.silverthorn.biz/11-e1
Contact: Randall Hansen, Pres.
Local. Affiliated With: Lions Clubs International.

Sherwood

9753 ■ Michigan American Eskimo Dog Association
c/o Karla A. Cole
720 Locke Rd.
Sherwood, MI 49089
Ph: (517)741-3754
URL: National Affiliate–www.eskie.com/naeda
Contact: Karla A. Cole, Contact
State.

Sidney

9754 ■ Phi Theta Kappa, Alpha Tau Alpha Chapter - Montcalm Community College
c/o Debra Alexander
PO Box 300
Sidney, MI 48885
Ph: (989)328-1243
E-mail: dalexander@montcalm.edu
URL: http://www.ptk.org/directories/chapters/MI/12332-1.htm
Contact: Debra Alexander, Advisor
Local.

Smiths Creek

9755 ■ American Legion, Smiths Creek Post 525
PO Box 86
Smiths Creek, MI 48074
Ph: (517)371-4720
Fax: (517)371-2401
URL: National Affiliate–www.legion.org
Local. Affiliated With: American Legion.

Sodus

9756 ■ American Legion, St. Joseph Post 163
3998 Dohm Rd.
Sodus, MI 49126
Ph: (517)371-4720
Fax: (517)371-2401
URL: National Affiliate–www.legion.org
Local. Affiliated With: American Legion.

9757 ■ Berrien County Alliance for the Mentally Ill
c/o Margaret Prillwitz, Pres.
3180 Hillside
Sodus, MI 49126
Ph: (616)944-5449
URL: http://mi.nami.org/ber.html
Contact: Margaret Prillwitz, Pres.
Local. Strives to improve the quality of life of children and adults with severe mental illness through support, education, research and advocacy. **Affiliated With:** National Alliance for the Mentally Ill.

9758 ■ Log Cabin Society of Michigan
c/o Ms. Virginia M. Handy
3503 Rock Edwards Dr.
Sodus, MI 49126-8700

Ph: (269)925-3836
Fax: (269)925-3836
E-mail: logcabincrafts@qtm.net
URL: http://www.qtm.net/logcabincrafts
Contact: Ms. Virginia M. Handy, Contact

Founded: 1988. **Members:** 350. **Membership Dues:** individual, $25 (annual) • society, $35 (annual) • library, $10 (annual) • senior (ages 60 or over), $20 (annual) • life, $100. **Budget:** $5,000. **State Groups:** 1. **State**. Individuals interested in the discovery, preservation, and promotion of log cabins. Sponsors statewide Log Cabin Day, Lenehan Log Cabin Photography Competition, and Michigan Log Cabin Survey. **Libraries: Type:** reference. **Holdings:** 1,400; articles, books, clippings, photographs, video recordings. **Subjects:** log cabin history. **Awards:** Lenehan Log Cabin Photography Competition. **Frequency:** annual. **Type:** monetary. **Recipient:** for high quality photos of log cabins suitable for publication in state and national periodicals and books, and for calendars. **Computer Services:** Online services, web site listing log cabins and links. **Publications:** *Log Cabin News*, quarterly. Newsletters. Contains events and news pertaining to log cabins. **Price:** $1.00 for members; $10.00 /year for libraries. ISSN: 1061-5857. **Circulation:** 500. **Advertising:** accepted. **Conventions/Meetings:** annual meeting, with tour of the log cabin site (exhibits) - always third Sunday of October.

South Boardman

9759 ■ American Legion, Gardnerneihardt Post 463
PO Box 1
South Boardman, MI 49680
Ph: (517)371-4720
Fax: (517)371-2401
URL: National Affiliate–www.legion.org
Local. Affiliated With: American Legion.

South Branch

9760 ■ Michigan State Spiritualists Association
7140 N Chain Lake Dr.
South Branch, MI 48761
URL: National Affiliate–www.nsac.org

Founded: 1892. **Members:** 98. **Staff:** 9. **State Groups:** 1. **Local Groups:** 7. **State**. Individuals promoting the philosophy, religion, and science of modern spiritualism. **Libraries: Type:** open to the public. **Holdings:** books. **Subjects:** religious. **Affiliated With:** National Spiritualist Association of Churches. **Publications:** *Michigan Spiritualists Newsletter*, monthly. **Price:** for members. **Circulation:** 150 • *National Spiritualist Summit - Spotlight (Children)*, monthly. Features religious articles. **Conventions/Meetings:** annual Michigan State Spiritualist Association of Churches - convention, books on spiritualism - 3rd weekend in May.

South Haven

9761 ■ American Legion, Brown-Webb Post 209
812 Kalamazoo St.
South Haven, MI 49090
Ph: (517)371-4720
Fax: (517)371-2401
URL: National Affiliate–www.legion.org
Local. Affiliated With: American Legion.

9762 ■ American Legion, Michigan Post 49
c/o Edward W. Thompson
129 Michigan Ave.
South Haven, MI 49090
Ph: (517)371-4720
Fax: (517)371-2401
URL: National Affiliate–www.legion.org
Contact: Edward W. Thompson, Contact
Local. Affiliated With: American Legion.

9763 ■ Greater South Haven Area Chamber of Commerce (GSHACC)
606 Phillips St.
South Haven, MI 49090
Ph: (616)637-5171
Fax: (616)639-1570
E-mail: cofc@southhavenmi.com
URL: http://www.southhavenmi.com

Founded: 1932. **Members:** 350. **Staff:** 2. **Budget:** $85,000. **Local**. Retail, commercial, industrial, and professional organizations in the South Haven, MI area organized to promote economic and community development. Holds board meetings, luncheons, and annual dinner. **Computer Services:** Mailing lists, of members. **Publications:** *Chamber Connection*, quarterly. Newsletter. Includes business statistics and other related information. • Annual Report, annual. **Conventions/Meetings:** annual meeting - always spring.

9764 ■ Pheasants Forever Lake Michigan Chapter 75
c/o Mike Seroke
714 Chambers St.
South Haven, MI 49090
Ph: (269)637-2048
E-mail: rwlinderman@yahoo.com
URL: http://www.frictionpoint.com/pheasantsforever
Contact: Bob Linderman, Contact
Local. Affiliated With: Pheasants Forever.

9765 ■ South Haven - Black River Lions Club
PO Box 691
South Haven, MI 49090
Ph: (269)637-6891
E-mail: lionlindabosma@verizon.net
URL: http://southhavenblackriverlionsmi.lionwap.org
Contact: Linda Bosma, Pres.
Local. Affiliated With: Lions Clubs International.

9766 ■ South Haven Visitors Bureau
546 Phoenix St.
South Haven, MI 49090
Ph: (269)637-5252
Fax: (269)637-8710
Free: (800)SO-HAVEN
E-mail: relax@southhaven.org
URL: http://www.southhaven.org
Contact: Bruce Barker, Exec.Dir.

Founded: 1987. **Staff:** 2. **Regional**. Promotes convention business and tourism in area. **Awards:** Business of the Year. **Frequency:** annual. **Type:** recognition. **Recipient:** for person or business active in tourism. **Formerly:** (1998) Lakeshore Convention and Visitors Bureau. **Conventions/Meetings:** convention.

South Lyon

9767 ■ AAA Michigan
558 N Lafayette
South Lyon, MI 48178
Ph: (248)437-1729
Free: (800)783-1729
State.

9768 ■ American Legion, South Lyon Post 338
61257 Heritage Blvd.
South Lyon, MI 48178
Ph: (517)371-4720
Fax: (517)371-2401
URL: National Affiliate–www.legion.org
Local. Affiliated With: American Legion.

9769 ■ American Society of Media Photographers, Michigan
c/o Cris Burkhalter, VP
Creative Photography of the Constructed Env.
PO Box 501
South Lyon, MI 48178
Ph: (313)407-3693
Fax: (248)446-3197
E-mail: crisb@cbphoto.com
URL: http://www.asmpmichigan.org
Contact: Rosh Sillars, Pres.
State. Affiliated With: American Society of Media Photographers.

9770 ■ Detroit Club Managers Association
PO Box 838
South Lyon, MI 48178
Ph: (248)446-8172
Fax: (248)446-0234
E-mail: dcmajan@peoplepc.com
URL: http://www.dcma.cc
Contact: John G. Paul CCM, Pres.
Local. Promotes and advances friendly relations between and among persons connected with the management of clubs. Encourages the education and advancement of members in the field of club management. **Affiliated With:** Club Managers Association of America.

9771 ■ Financial Planning Association of Michigan (FPAMI)
PO Box 476
South Lyon, MI 48178-0476
Ph: (248)446-8909
Fax: (248)446-8939
E-mail: admin@fpami.com
URL: http://www.fpami.com
Contact: Alan J. Ferrara JD, Pres.
State. Supports the financial planning process in order to help people achieve their goals and dreams. Promotes the value of the financial planning process and advances the financial planning profession. Promotes its members in reaching their highest potential for serving the needs of their clients. **Affiliated With:** Financial Planning Association.

9772 ■ Michigan Appaloosa Horse Association (MApHA)
c/o Judy Biber, Treas.
28328 Dixboro Rd.
South Lyon, MI 48178
Ph: (248)486-0695
URL: http://www.michappclub.com
Contact: Judy Biber, Treas.
State. Affiliated With: Appaloosa Horse Club.

9773 ■ Penn State Alumni Association, Michigan
c/o Steve Porter, Pres.
61440 Richfield Rd.
South Lyon, MI 48178
Ph: (248)214-6778
E-mail: psuofmich@yahoo.com
URL: http://www.psualum.com/chapter/Michigan
Contact: Steve Porter, Pres.
State. Aims to connect Penn State alumni. Supports the university's mission of teaching, research and service. **Awards:** Academic/Scholarship Awards. **Frequency:** annual. **Type:** scholarship. **Recipient:** to students for outstanding academics and extra curricular activities.

9774 ■ South Lyon Area Chamber of Commerce
125 N Lafayette (Pontiac Trail)
South Lyon, MI 48178
Ph: (248)437-3257
Fax: (248)437-4116
E-mail: greeter@southlyonchamber.com
URL: http://www.southlyonchamber.com
Contact: Michele Tucholke, Co-Exec.Dir.

Founded: 1965. **Members:** 300. **Staff:** 1. **Regional Groups:** 1. **State Groups:** 1. **Local**. Promotes business and community development in South Lyon, Lyon Township, Green Oak, and Salem, MI. Conducts annual Taste of South Lyon. **Awards:** Community Appreciation Awards. **Type:** recognition. **Computer Services:** Information services, member directory. **Telecommunication Services:** electronic mail, laura@southlyonchamber.com. **Subgroups:** Women's Forum. **Publications:** Directory, annual • Newsletter, monthly. **Conventions/Meetings:** annual Golf Outing - competition • annual Taste of South Lyon - festival.

South Range

9775 ■ American Legion, Michigan Post 304
c/o Elmer J. Perkins
PO Box 11
South Range, MI 49963
Ph: (517)371-4720
Fax: (517)371-2401
URL: National Affiliate–www.legion.org
Contact: Elmer J. Perkins, Contact
Local. Affiliated With: American Legion.

South Rockwood

9776 ■ American Vaulting Association - Victory Vaulters
c/o Katie Ferraro, Coach
11312 Haggerman Rd.
South Rockwood, MI 48179
Ph: (734)379-1341
E-mail: ferrarofamily4@comcast.net
URL: National Affiliate–www.americanvaulting.org
Contact: Katie Ferraro, Coach
Local. Affiliated With: American Vaulting Association.

Southfield

9777 ■ Alzheimer's Association, Greater Michigan Chapter
20300 Civic Center Dr., Ste.100
Southfield, MI 48076
Ph: (248)351-0280
Fax: (248)351-0417
Free: (800)272-3900
E-mail: dian.wilkins@alz.org
URL: http://www.alzgmc.org
Contact: Dian Wilkins, Pres.
Founded: 1981. **Members:** 4,000. **Staff:** 60. **Budget:** $3,900,000. **Local.** Individuals in Southeastern Michigan working to find the cause and cure to Alzheimer's Disease. Provides services and education for Alzheimer's patients and their families: Adult day care, in-home care, telephone helpline, family counseling, care management, support groups, "safe return" wanderers program, caregiver training and training for professionals. **Libraries: Type:** open to the public. **Holdings:** 30; articles, books, periodicals, video recordings. **Subjects:** Alzheimer's disease/ dementia, support groups, education programs. **Affiliated With:** Alzheimer's Association. **Formerly:** Alzheimer's Disease and Related Disorders Association, Southfield Chapter; (2002) Alzheimer's Association, Detroit Area Chapter. **Publications:** Newsletter, quarterly • Brochures. Covers many areas and topics associated with Alzheimer's Disease. **Conventions/ Meetings:** periodic Community Education to Caregiver - workshop, with speaker presentations.

9778 ■ American Arbitration Association, Michigan
c/o Janice Holdinski, VP
27777 Franklin Rd., Ste.1150, 11th Fl.
Southfield, MI 48034
Ph: (248)352-5500
Fax: (248)352-3147
E-mail: holdinskij@adr.org
URL: http://www.adr.org
Contact: Ms. Janice Holdinski, VP
State. Works to the development and use of prompt, effective and economical methods of dispute resolution. Offers a broad range of dispute resolution services to business executives, attorneys, individuals, trade associations, unions, management, consumers, families, communities and all levels of government. **Affiliated With:** American Arbitration Association. **Also Known As:** (2005) International Center for Dispute Resolution (ICDR).

9779 ■ American Cancer Society, Metro Detroit Area Service Center
18505 W 12 Mile Rd.
Southfield, MI 48076
Ph: (248)557-5353
Fax: (248)557-6128
Free: (800)227-2345
URL: http://www.cancer.org
Founded: 1913. **Staff:** 36. **Local.** Volunteers supporting education and research in cancer prevention, education, detection, and treatment. **Affiliated With:** American Cancer Society. **Formerly:** American Cancer Society, Macomb County Unit; (2006) American Cancer Society, Southeast Michigan Resource Center. **Publications:** *Voices*, quarterly. Newsletter. **Price:** free.

9780 ■ American Heart Association, Midwest Affiliate
24445 Northwestern Hwy., Ste.100
Southfield, MI 48075
Ph: (248)827-4214
Fax: (248)827-4234
Free: (800)968-1793
URL: http://www.americanheart.org
Contact: Almarie Wagner, Exec.VP
State. Seeks to reduce disability and death from cardiovascular diseases and stroke. **Affiliated With:** American Heart Association. **Formerly:** (1998) American Heart Association, Michigan Affiliate.

9781 ■ American Society of Employers (ASE)
23815 Northwestern Hwy.
Southfield, MI 48075-7713
Ph: (248)353-4500
Fax: (248)353-1224
E-mail: mcorrado@aseonline.org
URL: http://www.aseonline.org
Contact: Ms. Mary Corrado, Pres./CEO
Founded: 1902. **Members:** 1,000. **Staff:** 45. **State.** Provides prompt, high-quality service to member organizations as the state of Michigan's preeminent authority on human resource management issues.

9782 ■ American Society of Safety Engineers, Greater Detroit Chapter
21700 Northwestern Hwy., Ste.110
Southfield, MI 48075
Ph: (248)557-7010
E-mail: info@greaterdetroitasse.org
URL: http://www.greaterdetroitasse.org
Contact: Dr. Charles W. McGlothlin Jr., Pres.
Local. Enhances the advancement of the safety profession and the safety professional. Promotes the technical, societal and economic well-being of safety practitioners. **Affiliated With:** American Society of Safety Engineers.

9783 ■ Amyotrophic Lateral Sclerosis of Michigan
21311 Civic Ctr. Dr., No. 200
Southfield, MI 48076
Ph: (248)354-6100
Fax: (248)354-6440
Free: (800)882-5764
E-mail: alsofmi@alsofmi.org
URL: http://www.alsofmi.org
Contact: Joanne Berry, Dir. of Development
Founded: 1986. **Staff:** 8. **Budget:** $850,000. **Nonmembership. State.** Provides services to people with ALS (pALS), their families and caregivers to help them live with ALS. Supports research into the causes and possible cure of ALS. **Libraries: Type:** lending; open to the public; reference. **Holdings:** articles, audio recordings, books, films, periodicals, software. **Subjects:** hospice, caring for a person with ALS, ALS, caregiving. **Computer Services:** Information services, patient resource manual can be downloaded in format, as well as the newsletter online • online services, resource manual. **Programs:** Augmentative and Assistive Communication Services; Children's Programs about ALS; Equipment Loan Closet; Respite Care; Support Groups; Workshops and Seminars. **Affiliated With:** Amyotrophic Lateral Sclerosis Association. **Also Known As:** (2005) ALS of Michigan. **Formerly:** Amyotrophic Lateral Sclerosis of Michigan, Inc. **Publications:** *ALS Informer*, quarterly. Newsletter. **Price:** free. **Circulation:** 12,000. **Conventions/Meetings:** annual ALS Advocacy Day - conference, opportunity to bring issues of importance related to ALS to legislators - May.

9784 ■ ArtServe Michigan
17515 W 9 Mile Rd., Ste.1025
Southfield, MI 48075
Ph: (248)557-8288
Fax: (248)557-8581
Free: (888)WE-ENDOW
E-mail: bkratchman@artservemichigan.org
URL: http://www.artservemichigan.org
Contact: Barbara Kratchman, Pres./CEO
Founded: 1997. **State.** Builds support for the arts, artists, and cultural activities among citizens of Michigan through advocacy, education, and services.

9785 ■ ASIS International, Detroit Chapter
PO Box 4071
Southfield, MI 48037-4071
Ph: (248)849-3080
E-mail: haywooda@usa.redcross.org
URL: http://www.asisdetroit.com
Contact: Albert Lee Haywood Jr., Chm.
Local. Seeks to increase the effectiveness and productivity of security practices by developing educational programs and materials that address security concerns. **Affiliated With:** ASIS International.

9786 ■ Associated General Contractors of America, Greater Detroit Chapter (AGC)
20300 Civic Center Dr., Ste.408
Southfield, MI 48076
Ph: (248)948-7000
Fax: (248)948-7008
E-mail: msmith@agcdetriot.com
URL: http://www.detroit.agc.org
Contact: Michael P. Smith, Pres./CEO
Founded: 1916. **Members:** 250. **Staff:** 7. **Budget:** $1,000,000. **Local.** Provides quality service to members and innovative leadership for the construction industry. **Affiliated With:** Associated General Contractors of America.

9787 ■ Association of Colombians of Michigan (ACM)
PO Box 2436
Southfield, MI 48037-2436
URL: http://www.geocities.com/asocolmichigan
Contact: Mauricio Arbelaez, Sec.
Founded: 1985. **Members:** 350. **Languages:** English, Spanish. **State. Publications:** *CARTA Colombiana*, quarterly. Newsletter. **Circulation:** 400. **Advertising:** accepted.

9788 ■ Association for Computing Machinery, Lawrence Technological University (LTU ACM)
c/o Chan-Jin Chung, PhD, Faculty Advisor
Mathematics and Cmpt. Sci. Dept.
21000 W Ten Mile Rd.
Sci. Bldg., Rm. 112
Southfield, MI 48075
Ph: (248)204-3504 (248)204-3560
Fax: (248)204-3518
E-mail: chung@ltu.edu
URL: http://www.ltu.edu
Contact: Chan-Jin Chung, Faculty Advisor
Local. Stimulates understanding of the use and potential of computers in the biosciences. **Additional Websites:** http://ltu164.ltu.edu/acm. **Affiliated With:** Association for Computing Machinery.

9789 ■ Asthma and Allergy Foundation of America Michigan State Chapter
17520 W 12 Mile Rd., No. 102
Southfield, MI 48076-1943
Ph: (248)557-8050
Fax: (248)557-8768
Free: (888)444-0333
E-mail: aafamich@sbcglobal.net
URL: National Affiliate–www.aafa.org
Contact: Kathleen Slonager, Exec.Dir.

State. Seeks to improve the quality of life for those with asthma or allergic diseases through education, research and advocacy. **Affiliated With:** Asthma and Allergy Foundation of America.

9790 ■ Audio Engineering Society, Detroit Section
c/o Tom Conlin
Panasonic Automotive Syss. Co.
26455 Amer. Dr.
Southfield, MI 48034
Ph: (313)399-3705
URL: National Affiliate–www.aes.org
Contact: Tom Conlin, Contact

Local. Represents the interests of engineers, administrators and technicians for radio, television and motion picture operation. Operates educational and research foundation. **Affiliated With:** Audio Engineering Society.

9791 ■ Better Business Bureau of Detroit and Eastern Michigan
30555 Southfield Rd., Ste.200
Southfield, MI 48076-7751
Ph: (248)644-9100
Fax: (248)644-5026
E-mail: info@easternmichiganbbb.org
URL: http://www.easternmichiganbbb.org
Contact: Fred Hoffecker, Pres.

Founded: 1917. **Local**. Seeks to promote and foster ethical relationship between businesses and the public through voluntary self-regulation, consumer and business education, and service excellence. Provides information to help consumers and businesses make informed purchasing decisions and avoid costly scams and frauds; settles consumer complaints through arbitration and other means. **Additional Websites:** http://www.detroitbbb.org, http://www.bbbup.org. **Affiliated With:** BBB Wise Giving Alliance.

9792 ■ Big Brothers and Big Sisters of Metropolitan Detroit
23077 Greenfield Rd., Ste.430
Southfield, MI 48075
Ph: (248)569-0600
Fax: (248)569-7322
E-mail: info@bbbs-detroit.com
URL: http://www.bbbsdetroit.org
Contact: Michele A. Samuels, Chair

Founded: 1974. **Staff:** 35. **Budget:** $1,700,000. **State Groups:** 27. **Local Groups:** 500. **Nonmembership**. **Regional**. Strives to strengthen children in need through one-to-one relationships with volunteer mentors. **Libraries: Type:** reference. **Holdings:** 220. **Subjects:** mentoring. **Conventions/Meetings:** monthly Mentoring Institute - workshop, discussion on a variety of mentoring issues (exhibits).

9793 ■ BMW Touring Club of Detroit No. 1 (BMWTCD)
PO Box 2653
Southfield, MI 48037
Ph: (810)229-2843
E-mail: president1@bmwtcd.org
URL: http://www.bmwtcd.org
Contact: Ken Hugelier, Pres.

Local. Represents BMW motorcycle owners organized for pleasure, recreation, safety, and dissemination of information concerning BMW motorcycles. **Affiliated With:** BMW Motorcycle Owners of America.

9794 ■ Camp Fire USA Wathana Council
16250 Northland Dr., Ste.301
Southfield, MI 48075
Ph: (248)559-5840
Fax: (248)559-4307
E-mail: campfireusa@wathana.org
URL: http://www.comnet.org/campfirewathana
Contact: Linda Tarjeft, Exec.Dir.

Regional. Works to provide programs that empower youth from diverse backgrounds and communities to realize their full potential and to function effectively as caring, self-directed individuals responsible to themselves and others. **Affiliated With:** Camp Fire USA.

9795 ■ Children's Leukemia Foundation of Michigan
29777 Telegraph Rd., Ste.1651
Southfield, MI 48034
Ph: (248)353-8222
Fax: (248)353-0157
Free: (800)825-2536
E-mail: info@leukemiamichigan.org
URL: http://www.leukemiamichigan.org
State.

9796 ■ Connecting Business Men to Christ - Southeast Michigan
26776 W 12 Mile Rd., Ste.202
Southfield, MI 48034
Ph: (248)552-8358
Fax: (248)552-8691
URL: http://www.detroit.cbmc.com
Local.

9797 ■ Detroit Federation of Musicians - Local 5, American Federation of Musicians
c/o Gordon E. Stump, Pres.
20833 Southfield Rd.
Southfield, MI 48075
Ph: (248)569-5400
Fax: (248)569-1393
E-mail: local5@afm.org
URL: http://www.detroitmusicians.net
Contact: Gordon E. Stump, Pres.

Founded: 1897. **Members:** 1,400. **Membership Dues:** regular, $35 (quarterly). **Local**. AFL-CIO. Musicians. Seeks to improve the wages and working conditions of professional musicians. **Awards:** David Kaplan Memorial Scholarship. **Frequency:** annual. **Type:** scholarship. **Recipient:** for Music Major at Wayne State University. **Boards:** Executive Board of Directors. **Committees:** Advanced Programs Development; Detroit Symphony Orchestra; Law; Michigan Opera Theatre; Scale; Theater. **Affiliated With:** American Federation of Musicians of the United States and Canada; Jobs with Justice. **Formerly:** (2004) Federation of Musicians - Local 5, American Federation of Musicians. **Publications:** *Keynote*, quarterly. Newsletter. **Price:** not for sale. **Advertising:** accepted.

9798 ■ Detroit North Central Lions Club
c/o Charles Wilson, Pres.
29145 Murray Crescent Dr.
Southfield, MI 48076
Ph: (313)961-2748 (248)352-2645
E-mail: attywilson@hotmail.com
URL: http://www.metrodetroitlions.org
Contact: Charles Wilson, Pres.
Local. **Affiliated With:** Lions Clubs International.

9799 ■ Epilepsy Foundation of Michigan
20300 Civic Center Dr., Ste.250
Southfield, MI 48076-4128
Ph: (248)351-7979
Fax: (248)351-2101
Free: (800)377-6226
E-mail: letters@epilepsymichigan.org
URL: http://www.epilepsyfoundation.org/michigan
Contact: Dennis Egan, Chm.

Founded: 1948. **Staff:** 16. **Budget:** $1,300,000. **Nonmembership**. **For-Profit**. **State**. Seeks to provide and improve the diagnosis and treatment of epilepsy. Educates and informs the public about epilepsy; makes available referral, counseling, family support and psychological testing services. Also provides services to people with mobility impairments. **Libraries: Type:** open to the public; reference. **Holdings:** books, video recordings. **Subjects:** epilepsy. **Telecommunication Services:** electronic mail, vtarnas@epilepsymichigan.org. **Affiliated With:** Epilepsy Foundation. **Formed by Merger of:** (1957) Michigan Epilepsy Center; Michigan Association for Epilepsy. **Formerly:** (1957) Michigan Epilepsy Center and Association; (1971) Epilepsy Center of Michigan. **Publications:** *Epilepsy: First Aid for Seizures*. Brochure • *Headline*, quarterly. Newsletter • *Women with Epilepsy*. Handbook. Alternate Formats: online. **Conventions/Meetings:** monthly Accessible Transit Coalition - meeting - every 2nd Monday at 1:00-3:00 PM in Southfield, MI • annual Epilepsy Today Conference - October • annual meeting - October.

9800 ■ Fathers For Equal Rights of America, Michigan
Box 2272
Southfield, MI 48037-2272
Ph: (248)354-3080
URL: National Affiliate–www.fathers4kids.org/html/fathers.htm
Contact: Alan Z. Lebow, Exec. Officer

Founded: 1975. **Membership Dues:** individual, $50 (annual). **Staff:** 2. **Budget:** $1,200. **Regional Groups:** 1. **State Groups:** 1. **Local Groups:** 1. **Local**. Works to help fathers and grandparents acquire custody or visitation rights to their children in divorce, separation, and unwed fatherhood, to teach them to survive in the legal system, and to help children survive the aforementioned situations and systems. Also provides phone crisis intervention. **Libraries: Type:** open to the public. **Subjects:** separation, divorce, custody issues, divorce mediation, visitation/parenting time, false accusations, child support. **Affiliated With:** Fathers for Equal Rights. **Formerly:** Equal Rights for Fathers. **Conventions/Meetings:** monthly General Meeting - general assembly (exhibits) - third Wednesday of the month. Oak Park, MI - Avg. Attendance: 20.

9801 ■ International Interior Design Association, Michigan Chapter
c/o Christie Johnson, Pres.
PO Box 2514
Southfield, MI 48037-2514
Ph: (248)737-0180
Fax: (248)926-8264
E-mail: michiganiida@aol.com
URL: http://www.iida.org

State. Networking and educational association of more than 10,000 members in eight specialty forums, nine regions, and more than 30 chapters around the world committed to enhancing the quality of life through excellence in interior design and advancing interior design through knowledge. **Affiliated With:** International Interior Design Association.

9802 ■ Juvenile Diabetes Research Foundation, Metropolitan Detroit and Southeast Michigan Chapter
24359 Northwestern Hwy., Ste.225
Southfield, MI 48075
Ph: (248)355-1133
Fax: (248)355-1188
E-mail: metrodetroit@jdrf.org
URL: http://www.jdrfdetroit.org
Contact: Karen M. Breen, Exec.Dir.

Founded: 1970. **Members:** 5,000. **Membership Dues:** $25 (annual). **Staff:** 4. **Budget:** $2,000,000. **Local**. Diabetics, their parents and families, and the corporate community. Supports research to find the cause, prevention, and cure of diabetes. Sponsors fundraising activities. Holds research conferences. **Libraries: Type:** open to the public. **Holdings:** 25. **Committees:** Golf Classic; Major Gifts/Planned Giving; Promise Ball; Walk to Cure Diabetes. **Affiliated With:** Juvenile Diabetes Research Foundation International. **Formerly:** (2000) Juvenile Diabetes Foundation, Metropolitan Detroit Chapter. **Publications:** *Countdown*, quarterly. Magazine • *Update*, quarterly. Newsletter. **Conventions/Meetings:** quarterly board meeting • semiannual conference • quarterly executive committee meeting.

9803 ■ March of Dimes/Michigan
c/o Thomas Riopelle, Exec.Dir.
27600 Northwestern Hwy., No. 150
Southfield, MI 48034
Ph: (248)359-1550
Fax: (248)213-4923
Free: (800)244-9255
E-mail: mi630@marchofdimes.com
URL: http://www.marchofdimes.com/michigan
Contact: Thomas Riopelle, State Dir.
Nonmembership. **State**. Committed to improving the health of babies by preventing birth defects, premature birth and infant mortality. Provides programs including research, community services, education and advocacy. **Affiliated With:** March of Dimes Birth Defects Foundation.

9804 ■ Mathematical Association of America, Lawrence Technology University Student Chapter
c/o Prof. Ruth Favro, Advisor
21000 W Ten Mile Rd.
Southfield, MI 48075-1058
E-mail: favro@ltu.edu
URL: http://ltu164.ltu.edu/maa
Contact: Prof. Ruth Favro, Advisor
Local. Promotes the general understanding and appreciation of mathematics. Advances and improves the education in the mathematical sciences at the collegiate level. Provides resources and activities that foster scholarship, professional growth and cooperation among teachers, other professionals and students. **Affiliated With:** Mathematical Association of America.

9805 ■ Mental Health Association in Michigan (MHAM)
c/o Mark Reinstein, PhD, Pres.
30233 Southfield Rd., Ste.220
Southfield, MI 48076
Ph: (248)647-1711
Fax: (248)647-1732
E-mail: msrmha@aol.com
URL: http://www.mha-mi.org
Contact: Mark Reinstein PhD, Pres.
Founded: 1937. **Membership Dues:** student, senior citizen, mental health consumer, $10 (annual) • active, $50 (annual) • professional, $75 (annual) • organization, $300 (annual) • patron, $500 (annual) • sustaining, $1,000 (annual). **Budget:** $500,000. **State**. Promotes mental wellness and the prevention of mental illness. Advocates for the improvement of care and treatment in the state of MI. **Publications:** *Advocate*, 3/year. Newsletter. **Conventions/Meetings:** annual meeting - always spring.

9806 ■ Michigan Colleges Foundation (MCF)
26555 Evergreen Rd., Ste.870
Southfield, MI 48076-4239
Ph: (248)356-3114
Fax: (248)356-3241
E-mail: webmaster@michigancolleges.org
URL: http://www.michigancolleges.org
Contact: William H. Liebold II, Pres.
Founded: 1949. **Members:** 14. **Staff:** 4. **Budget:** $400,000. **State**. Dedicated to providing students the opportunity for a values-based, high quality education at member liberal arts colleges by securing financial resources from the private sector. **Publications:** Report, annual. Alternate Formats: online.

9807 ■ Michigan Humane Society (MHS)
26711 Northwestern Hwy., Ste.175
Southfield, MI 48034
Ph: (248)799-7400
Fax: (248)355-4123
E-mail: mail@michiganhumane.org
URL: http://www.michiganhumane.org
Contact: Cal Morgan, Exec.Dir.
State.

9808 ■ Michigan Parkinson Foundation (MPF)
30161 Southfield Rd., Ste.119
Southfield, MI 48076
Ph: (248)433-1011
Fax: (248)433-1150
Free: (800)852-9781
E-mail: mpfdir@aol.com
URL: http://www.parkinsonsmi.org
Contact: Deborah Orloff-Davidson, CEO
Founded: 1983. **Members:** 21,000. **Staff:** 4. **Budget:** $550,000. **Regional Groups:** 36. **Local Groups:** 36. **State**. Dedicated to assisting people with Parkinson's disease and their families through support and education. Services include information and referral, medication assistance, adult day care, multidisciplinary second opinion Parkinson's clinics, health care professional training, and educational programs for consumers. Sponsors 38 support groups in MI. Maintains a resource file on issues about the disease and will provide information to callers. Promotes research by awarding student fellowships. **Libraries: Type:** open to the public. **Awards:** Raymond B. Bauer Research. **Frequency:** semiannual. **Type:** grant • Student Fellowship Program. **Frequency:** annual. **Type:** grant. **Affiliated With:** Parkinson's Disease Foundation. **Publications:** *The Michigan Parkinson Foundation Messenger*, quarterly. Newsletter. **Price:** free. **Circulation:** 16,000. Alternate Formats: online. Also Cited As: *Messenger*. **Conventions/Meetings:** quarterly meeting.

9809 ■ Michigan State Association of Parliamentarians (MSAP)
c/o Rosa L. Williams, PRP, Pres.
23145 Orleans Pl., Apt. 324
Southfield, MI 48034-3372
Ph: (313)433-4666
E-mail: rosa.williams02@detroitk12.org
URL: http://www.misap.org
Contact: Rosa L. Williams PRP, Pres.
State. Aims to study, teach, promote and disseminate the democratic principles of parliamentary law and procedure. **Affiliated With:** National Association of Parliamentarians.

9810 ■ Myasthenia Gravis Association (MGA)
17117 W 9 Mile, Ste.No. 1409
Southfield, MI 48075
Ph: (248)423-9700
Fax: (248)423-9705
E-mail: mgadetroit1@sbcglobal.net
URL: http://www.mgadetroit.org
Local. **Affiliated With:** Myasthenia Gravis Foundation of America. **Formerly:** (2005) Detroit Chapter of Myasthenia Gravis Foundation of America.

9811 ■ National Association for the Advancement of Colored People, Southern Oakland County
PO Box 4205
Southfield, MI 48037-4205
Ph: (248)552-8913
Fax: (248)552-9814
E-mail: socnaacp@aol.com
URL: http://www.naacp.org
Contact: G. Whitney McRipley Esq., Pres.
Local.

9812 ■ National Association of Professional Mortgage Women - Southeastern Michigan
c/o Zan Phelps, Pres.
20455 Westland Dr.
Southfield, MI 48075
Ph: (248)353-1325
Fax: (248)353-1345
E-mail: zano@comcast.net
URL: National Affiliate–www.napmw.org
Contact: Zan Phelps, Pres.
Local. Encourages women to pursue careers in mortgage banking. Aims to maintain high standards of professional conduct. Works for equal recognition and professional opportunities for women. **Affiliated With:** National Association of Professional Mortgage Women.

9813 ■ National Association of Telecommunications Officers and Advisors, Michigan
c/o Kathy Sherman, Pres.
26000 Evergreen Rd.
Southfield, MI 48076
Ph: (248)351-1301
E-mail: k_sherman@cityofsouthfield.com
URL: http://www.mi-natoa.org
Contact: Leslie Helwig, Sec.
State. Represents cable television and telecommunications administrators, staff personnel from local governments and public interest groups. Seeks to establish an information-sharing network among local telecommunications regulators and users in the public sector. Provides education and training for local government officials to enhance their capacity to deal with cable and telecommunications issues. Provides technical and policy development assistance to members. Maintains speakers' bureau. **Affiliated With:** National Association of Telecommunications Officers and Advisors.

9814 ■ National Multiple Sclerosis Society, Michigan Chapter
21311 Civic Center Dr.
Southfield, MI 48076
Ph: (248)350-0020
Fax: (248)353-3850
Free: (800)243-5767
E-mail: info@mig.nmss.org
URL: http://www.nmssmi.org
Contact: Jean Wroblewski, Admin.Asst.
Local. **Affiliated With:** National Multiple Sclerosis Society.

9815 ■ Oakland County RSVP
c/o Herschell T. Masten, Dir.
18310 W 12 Mile Rd.
Southfield, MI 48076
Ph: (248)559-1147
Fax: (248)559-2309
E-mail: mastenh@cssoc.org
URL: http://www.seniorcorps.gov/about/programs/rsvp_state.asp?usestateabbr=mi&Search4.x=0&Search4.y=0
Contact: Herschell T. Masten, Dir.
Local. **Affiliated With:** Retired and Senior Volunteer Program.

9816 ■ Phi Theta Kappa, Alpha Omicron Psi Chapter - Oakland Community College
c/o Jan Akehurst
Royal Oak/Southfield Campus
22322 Rutland Ave.
Southfield, MI 48075
Ph: (248)246-2611
E-mail: jlakehur@oaklandcc.edu
URL: http://www.ptk.org/directories/chapters/MI/6972-1.htm
Contact: Jan Akehurst, Advisor
Local.

9817 ■ Printing Industries of Michigan (PIM)
23815 Northwestern Hwy., Ste.2700
Southfield, MI 48075
Ph: (248)354-9200
Fax: (248)354-1711
Free: (800)482-1355
E-mail: info@print.org
URL: http://www.print.org
Contact: Nick Wagner, Pres./Gen.Mgr.
Founded: 1888. **State**. Commercial printing firms and allied companies in the graphic arts field. **Additional Websites:** http://www.printinmich.org. **Affiliated With:** Printing Industries of America. **Publications:** *Graphic News*, monthly. Newsletter • *P.I.M. Member Directory and Buyers Guide*, annual. Membership Directory • Bulletin, periodic. Contains issues on human resources. **Conventions/Meetings:** semiannual conference.

9818 ■ Safety Council for Southeast Michigan
21700 Northwestern Hwy., Ste.110
Southfield, MI 48075-4901
Ph: (248)557-7010
Fax: (248)557-1281
Free: (800)263-7130
E-mail: safetycouncilse@earthlink.net
URL: http://www.safetycouncilsemi.org
Contact: Edward G. Ratzenberger CSP, Pres./CEO
Founded: 1913. **Members:** 275. **Membership Dues:** regular (minimum), $215 • regular (maximum), $15,000. **Staff:** 2. **Budget:** $280,000. **Local**. Individuals, businesses, organizations, and agencies working to promote health protection and accident prevention education for the work and home. Offers safety and health training, driver improvement classes and first aid/CPR classes and sells safety and health training materials. **Libraries: Type:** open to the public. **Holdings:** 1,200; articles, books, periodicals. **Subjects:** safety, health environment. **Awards:** President's Award. **Frequency:** annual. **Type:** recognition. **Recipient:** for accomplishments in safety • Safety Hall of Fame. **Frequency:** annual. **Type:** recognition. **Affiliated With:** National Safety Council. **Publications:** *Speaking of Safety*, monthly. Newsletter. Contains safety and health information, program and training announcements, and ads for materials. **Price:** free. **Circulation:** 1,600. **Advertising:** accepted. **Conventions/Meetings:** annual Safety Conference for Southeast Michigan, sessions on safety, health and environmental issues at work, home and on the road (exhibits).

9819 ■ Sheet Metal Workers AFL-CIO, LU 80
17100 W 12 Mile Rd., 2nd Fl.
Southfield, MI 48076-2115
Ph: (248)557-7575
Fax: (248)557-4660
E-mail: staff@sheet80.org
URL: http://www.benesysinc.com/benefit/sheet80.asp
Contact: Harold T. Ingalls, Contact
Founded: 1964. **Members:** 2,303. **Staff:** 10. **Local**. Ensures that members will earn a good standard of living, along with a comfortable retirement. **Affiliated With:** Sheet Metal Workers' International Association.

9820 ■ Society of Manufacturing Engineers - Lawrence Technological University S011
21000 W 10 Mile Rd.
Southfield, MI 48075
Ph: (248)204-2580
E-mail: alwerfalli@ltu.edu
URL: National Affiliate–www.sme.org
Contact: Dr. D. Alwerfalli, Contact
Local. Advances manufacturing knowledge to gain competitive advantage. Improves skills and manufacturing solutions for the growth of economy. Provides resources and opportunities for manufacturing professionals. **Affiliated With:** American Museum of Natural History.

9821 ■ Society for Marketing Professional Services/Michigan
c/o Donna Jakubowicz, CPSM
26500 Amer. Dr.
Southfield, MI 48034
Ph: (248)436-5502
Fax: (248)436-5503
E-mail: donna.jakubowicz@bartonmalow.com
URL: http://www.smps-mi.org
Contact: Donna Jakubowicz CPSM, Pres.
State. Strives to be the premier marketing advocate for the built environment through marketing efforts directed to the general business community, and to enhance the professional marketer's career by improving their skills and educating the built environment on the value of marketing. **Affiliated With:** Society for Marketing Professional Services.

9822 ■ Society of Tribologists and Lubrication Engineers - Detroit Section
c/o Mr. Richard Kuhlman, Chm.
Afton Chem.
2000 Town Ctr., Ste.1750
Southfield, MI 48075
Ph: (248)350-0640
Fax: (248)350-0025
E-mail: dick.kuhlman@aftonchemical.com
URL: National Affiliate–www.stle.org
Contact: Mr. Richard Kuhlman, Chm.
Local. Promotes the advancement of tribology and the practice of lubrication engineering. Stimulates the study and development of lubrication tribology techniques. Promotes higher standards in the field. **Affiliated With:** Society of Tribologists and Lubrication Engineers.

9823 ■ Southeast Michigan Census Council
28300 Franklin Rd.
Southfield, MI 48034-1657
Ph: (248)354-6520
Fax: (248)354-6645
E-mail: info@semcc.org
URL: http://www.semcc.org
Contact: Ms. Patricia C. Becker, Exec.Dir.
Founded: 1946. **Members:** 100. **Membership Dues:** organizational, $120 (annual) • non-Michigan resident, $50 (annual). **Staff:** 1. **Budget:** $30,000. **Regional Groups:** 1. **Local**. Organizations and agencies in Michigan using census and/or other demographic and related data regularly. Represents state interests to Census Bureau and provides information and education to the public. **Libraries: Type:** reference. **Holdings:** 1,000; reports. **Subjects:** census. **Computer Services:** accessing census data for applications, assistance in linking local administrative files with census data. **Formerly:** Detroit Regional Census Advisory Committee; Detroit Regional Census Advisory Council. **Publications:** *Census Tract Coding Guides (6 volumes)*, periodic. Book. Provides a way to look up an address and assign it to the correct census tract. • *Empowerment Zone Coding Guide*, periodic. Book. **Price:** $15.00 • *SEMCC News*, 10/year. Newsletter • *2000 Census Community Profiles*, periodic, every 10 years. Report. Contains 2000 census data for communities in 7 county southeast Michigan area and for subcommunities in the City of Detroit. **Price:** $20.00 subcommunities in the City of Detroit; $30.00; $60.00 subscribers outside Michigan. **Conventions/Meetings:** annual conference • Lunch and Learn - luncheon, with speaker - 5/year.

9824 ■ Southeastern Michigan Chapter, National Electrical Contractors Association
PO Box 385
Southfield, MI 48037-0385
Ph: (248)355-3500
Fax: (248)355-3868
E-mail: dan@smsneca.org
URL: http://www.smcneca.org
Contact: Mr. Jerry Dancey, Pres.
Local. Aims to promote and advance the interests of the electrical contracting industry. **Affiliated With:** National Electrical Contractors Association.

9825 ■ Southfield Area Chamber of Commerce
17515 W 9 Mile Rd., Ste.750
Southfield, MI 48075
Ph: (248)557-6661
Fax: (248)557-3931
E-mail: southfieldchamber@yahoo.com
URL: http://www.southfieldchamber.com
Contact: Ed Powers, Exec.Dir.
Local. Promotes business and community development in the Southfield, MI area. **Formerly:** (2005) Southfield Chamber of Commerce.

9826 ■ Substance Abuse Prevention Coalition of Southeast Michigan (PREVCO)
c/o Ann Comiskey
PO Box 2970
Southfield, MI 48037
Ph: (586)296-9890
Fax: (586)296-0446
E-mail: theprevco@aol.com
Founded: 1990. **Members:** 4,020. **Staff:** 2. **Budget:** $200,000. **Local**. Seeks to promote alcohol, tobacco and other drug abuse prevention messages through media strategies that support a healthy southeast Michigan.

9827 ■ Suspender Wearers Association of America
c/o Judee Herman
21421 Hilltop St., Ste.16
Southfield, MI 48034
Ph: (248)386-0252
Fax: (248)352-1185
Free: (800)700-4515

9828 ■ United Cerebral Palsy Association of Metropolitan Detroit
23077 Greenfield, Ste.205
Southfield, MI 48075-3745
Ph: (248)557-5070
Fax: (248)557-4456
Free: (800)827-4843
E-mail: main@ucpdetroit.org
URL: http://www.ucpdetroit.org
Contact: Leslynn Angel, Pres./CEO
Founded: 1949. **Staff:** 21. **Budget:** $1,500,000. **Languages:** English, French. **Local**. Advances the independence, productivity, and full citizenship of individuals with cerebral palsy and similar disabilities. **Awards:** Empowerment. **Frequency:** annual. **Type:** monetary. **Recipient:** to eligible individuals by random drawing. **Committees:** Advisory. **Affiliated With:** United Cerebral Palsy Associations. **Publications:** *Turning Obstacles into Opportunities*, quarterly. Newsletter. **Price:** free for members. **Conventions/Meetings:** weekly workshop, advocacy training.

9829 ■ Variety of Detroit
30161 Southfield Rd., Ste.301
Southfield, MI 48076
Ph: (248)258-5511
Fax: (248)258-5575
E-mail: variety5@msn.com
URL: http://www.variety-detroit.com
Local. **Affiliated With:** Variety International - The Children's Charity.

9830 ■ Volunteers of America Michigan
21415 Civic Center Dr., Ste.100
Southfield, MI 48076
Ph: (248)945-0101
Fax: (248)945-0202
E-mail: info@voami.org
URL: http://www.voami.org
Contact: Alex Brodrick, Pres./CEO
State. **Affiliated With:** Volunteers of America.

9831 ■ Wayne Oakland Region of Interlibrary Cooperation
c/o Helen L. DeRoy Medical Library
Providence Hosp. and Medical Centers
16001 W 9 Mile Rd.
Southfield, MI 48075
Ph: (248)849-3294 (248)849-3000
E-mail: deroy.library@providence-hospital.org
URL: http://www.stjohn.org/Providence/Library
Founded: 1949. **Staff:** 3. **Budget:** $199,000. **Local**. Provides information to medical and nursing staffs, allied health employees, administration, and residents of Providence Hospital. **Libraries: Type:** not open to the public. **Holdings:** 20,000; books, periodicals. **Subjects:** medicine. **Additional Websites:** http://www.realmedicine.org/Providence/Library.

9832 ■ Women's Action for New Directions, Michigan
PO Box 2577
Southfield, MI 48037
E-mail: wandmichigan@comcast.net
URL: National Affiliate–www.wand.org
Contact: Clare Mead Rosen, Pres.
State. **Affiliated With:** Women's Action for New Directions.

Southgate

9833 ■ American Legion, Lamond-Frank Post 478
16200 Dix Toledo Rd.
Southgate, MI 48195

Ph: (517)371-4720
Fax: (517)371-2401
URL: National Affiliate–www.legion.org
Local. Affiliated With: American Legion.

9834 ■ Detroit Motorcity Chapter Electric Auto Association
c/o Richard Sands, Pres.
13162 Fordline
Southgate, MI 48195
Ph: (734)281-4087
E-mail: rsands01@comcast.net
URL: http://geocities.com/detroit_eaa
Contact: Richard Sands, Pres.
Local. Affiliated With: Electric Auto Association. **Formerly:** (2005) Detroit Motorcity Chapter DMC-Electric Auto Association.

9835 ■ Humanists of Southeast Michigan
c/o Thelma Murrell
12792 Elaine Dr.
Southgate, MI 48195-2339
Ph: (734)284-1890
E-mail: humanists-semichigan@usa.net
URL: National Affiliate–www.americanhumanist.org
Contact: Thelma Murrell, Contact
Local. Affiliated With: American Humanist Association.

9836 ■ International Association of Administrative Professionals, River Park Chapter
Holiday Inn Heritage Center
Southgate, MI 48195
Ph: (248)646-7106
Fax: (248)540-9645
E-mail: service@iaap-hg.org
URL: http://www.iaap-hq.org
Contact: Jodie Cooper, Pres.
Founded: 1954. **Members:** 32. **Membership Dues:** student, professional, or merited, $87 (annual). **Budget:** $3,000. **Regional Groups:** 1. **State Groups:** 1. **Local.** Professional organization of administrative professionals. **Awards:** River Park Chapter Scholarship. **Frequency:** annual. **Type:** scholarship. **Affiliated With:** International Association of Administrative Professionals. **Formerly:** (1998) Professional Secretaries International - River Park Chapter. **Publications:** *IAAP River Park Chapter News Flash*, monthly. Newsletter. Brief notes on chapter news. **Price:** free to members. **Conventions/Meetings:** monthly meeting - always third Thursday of the month, September - June; Avg. Attendance: 20.

9837 ■ Michigan Association for Infant Mental Health (MAIMH)
The Guidance Center
Inst. for Children, Youth, and Families
13101 Allen Rd., Unit 200
Southgate, MI 48195
Ph: (734)785-7700
Fax: (734)287-1680
E-mail: dkahraman@guidance-center.org
URL: http://www.mi-aimh.msu.edu
Contact: Deborah Weatherston PhD, Exec.Dir.
Founded: 1977. **Members:** 350. **Membership Dues:** regular (without journal), $60 (annual) • student (without journal), $30 (annual) • student (with journal), $75 (annual) • regular, in U.S. (with journal), $105 (annual) • sustaining, $125 (annual) • organization, $500 (annual) • regular, in Canada, $108 (annual) • retiree, $30 (annual). **Staff:** 1. **Regional Groups:** 13. **State.** Nurses, doctors, social workers, psychologists, educators, and others interested in infant care. Promotes the optimal development of infants and their families. Sponsors workshops. **Awards:** Fraiberg Award. **Frequency:** annual. **Type:** recognition. **Recipient:** for special service to infants and families • Tableman Award. **Frequency:** annual. **Type:** recognition. **Recipient:** for special service to infants and families. **Publications:** *Infant Crier*, quarterly. Newsletter • *Infant Mental Health Journal*, quarterly. **Price:** included in membership dues. **Conventions/Meetings:** annual conference, with speakers (exhibits) - usually the end of April in Ann Arbor, MI.

9838 ■ Michigan State African Violet Society
c/o Steve Turner
14965 Overbrook Dr., Apt. 107
Southgate, MI 48195
Ph: (734)285-5560
E-mail: kayakman@wowway.com
URL: National Affiliate–www.avsa.org
Contact: Steve Turner, Contact
State. Affiliated With: African Violet Society of America.

9839 ■ National Active and Retired Federal Employees Association - Dearborn Area 1515
15011 California Cir.
Southgate, MI 48195-2112
Ph: (734)284-8432
URL: National Affiliate–www.narfe.org
Contact: Thomas F. Flynn, Contact
Local. Protects the retirement future of employees through education. Informs members on issues affecting the retirement. **Affiliated With:** National Association of Retired Federal Employees.

9840 ■ PFLAG Downriver
PO Box 1797
Southgate, MI 48195
Ph: (734)783-2950
E-mail: info@pflagdownriver.org
URL: http://www.pflagdownriver.org
Local. Affiliated With: Parents, Families, and Friends of Lesbians and Gays.

9841 ■ Polish Falcons of America, Nest 79
14063 Dix-Toledo Rd.
Southgate, MI 48195
Ph: (313)283-2229
URL: http://www.polishfalcons.org/nest/79/index.html
Contact: Helen Pett, Pres.
Local. Affiliated With: Polish Falcons of America.

9842 ■ South Metro Shores Figure Skating Club
13383 Kerr St.
Southgate, MI 48195
Ph: (734)285-1552
E-mail: jbehm8502@wideopenwest.com
URL: National Affiliate–www.usfigureskating.org
Contact: Debra Nelson, Contact
Local. Provides programs to encourage participation and achievement in the sport of figure skating on ice. Defines and maintains uniform standards of skating proficiency. Organizes and sponsors competitions and exhibitions for the purpose of stimulating interest in figure skating. **Affiliated With:** United States Figure Skating Association.

9843 ■ Southgate Lions Club
c/o James Edwards, Pres.
15132 Cook St.
Southgate, MI 48195
Ph: (734)285-0778
URL: http://www.metrodetroitlions.org
Contact: James Edwards, Pres.
Local. Affiliated With: Lions Clubs International.

9844 ■ Wyandotte Lions Club - Michigan
c/o Sonja Gardner, Pres.
15148 McCann St.
Southgate, MI 48195
E-mail: jsimmsm@aol.com
URL: http://www.metrodetroitlions.org
Contact: Sonja Gardner, Pres.
Local. Affiliated With: Lions Clubs International.

Sparta

9845 ■ American Legion, Lekstrum-Burnett Post 107
75 N Union St.
Sparta, MI 49345
Ph: (517)371-4720
Fax: (517)371-2401
URL: National Affiliate–www.legion.org
Local. Affiliated With: American Legion.

9846 ■ National Farmers Union, Michigan
3280 9 Mile Rd.
Sparta, MI 49345
Ph: (616)887-1370
E-mail: cowsmonaut@aol.com
URL: National Affiliate–www.nfu.org
Contact: Marilynn Momber, Pres.
State. Affiliated With: National Farmers Union.

Spring Arbor

9847 ■ Psi Chi, National Honor Society in Psychology - Spring Arbor University
c/o Dept. of Psychology
106 E Main St.
Spring Arbor, MI 49283-9799
Ph: (517)750-6314 (517)750-6319
Fax: (517)750-6662
E-mail: candym@arbor.edu
URL: National Affiliate–www.psichi.org
Contact: Prof. Candy McCorkle MS, Advisor
Local.

Spring Lake

9848 ■ Studebakers Driver's Club, Crossroads Zone
c/o Terry Judd
16215 Pine Hollow Ave.
Spring Lake, MI 49456
E-mail: terryjudd@i2k.com
URL: National Affiliate–www.studebakerdriversclub.com
Contact: Terry Judd, Contact
Regional. Owners of Studebaker automobiles and trucks. Attempts to aid in the restoration of, procure parts for, and reproduce old instruction manuals of the Studebaker car. **Affiliated With:** Studebaker Driver's Club.

9849 ■ Tri-Cities Strikers Soccer Club
c/o Dave Redman, Admin.
18500 Shawnee Dr.
Spring Lake, MI 49456
E-mail: redman@chartermi.net
URL: http://www.tricitiesstrikers.com
Contact: Dave Redman, Admin.
Local.

Springport

9850 ■ American Legion, Bernheisel and Riley Post 313
230 Mechanic St.
Springport, MI 49284
Ph: (517)371-4720
Fax: (517)371-2401
URL: National Affiliate–www.legion.org
Local. Affiliated With: American Legion.

9851 ■ Springport Lions Club
c/o Joyce Betz, Sec.
1589 Peters Rd.
Springport, MI 49284
Ph: (517)788-4099 (517)857-4018
E-mail: betz@scns.sps.k12.mi.us
URL: http://www.lionsdistrict11b1.org/lc_springport.htm
Contact: Joyce Betz, Sec.
Local. Affiliated With: Lions Clubs International.

Standish

9852 ■ American Legion, Johnson Day Post 104
PO Box 523
Standish, MI 48658
Ph: (517)371-4720
Fax: (517)371-2401
URL: National Affiliate–www.legion.org
Local. Affiliated With: American Legion.

9853 ■ Michigan Boer Goat Association
c/o Lisa Hemmer
1032 Stover Rd.
Standish, MI 48658
E-mail: remmeh65@hotmail.com
URL: National Affiliate–usbga.org
Contact: Lisa Hemmer, Contact
State.

Stanton

9854 ■ American Legion, Stanton Post 452
PO Box 442
Stanton, MI 48888
Ph: (517)371-4720
Fax: (517)371-2401
URL: National Affiliate–www.legion.org
Local. Affiliated With: American Legion.

9855 ■ National Active and Retired Federal Employees Association - Greenville 2227
612 Woodland Dr.
Stanton, MI 48888-9227
Ph: (517)831-4076
URL: National Affiliate–www.narfe.org
Contact: Lillian D. Hansen, Contact
Local. Protects the retirement future of employees through education. Informs members on issues affecting the retirement. **Affiliated With:** National Association of Retired Federal Employees.

9856 ■ Stanton Lions Club - Michigan
c/o Thomas Wall, Pres.
891 Clifford Lake Dr.
Stanton, MI 48888
Ph: (989)831-8314 (989)831-4943
E-mail: twallburrco@yahoo.com
URL: http://lions.silverthorn.biz/11-e1
Contact: Thomas Wall, Pres.
Local. Affiliated With: Lions Clubs International.

Stanwood

9857 ■ Michigan National Wild Turkey Federation, Newaygo Valley Gobblers
5875 Northland Dr.
Stanwood, MI 49346
Ph: (231)823-2954
URL: http://www.mi-nwtf.org/Newaygo.htm
Contact: Scott Kosaski, Pres.
Local.

9858 ■ Remus Lions Club
c/o Jim Leszczynski, Pres.
11171 E Royal Rd.
Stanwood, MI 49346
Ph: (231)972-4608
E-mail: a24mivol@chartermi.net
URL: http://lions.silverthorn.biz/11-e1
Contact: Jim Leszczynski, Pres.
Local. Affiliated With: Lions Clubs International.

Stephenson

9859 ■ American Legion, Godfrey Anderson Post 43
W 5554 River Rd.
Stephenson, MI 49887
Ph: (517)371-4720
Fax: (517)371-2401
URL: National Affiliate–www.legion.org
Local. Affiliated With: American Legion.

Sterling

9860 ■ Sturgeon Creek Beagle Club
c/o Dennis J. Haut
842 Klein Rd.
Sterling, MI 48659-9709
URL: National Affiliate–clubs.akc.org
Contact: Dennis J. Haut, Contact
Local.

Sterling Heights

9861 ■ American Legion, Michigan Post 326
c/o Robert L. Poxon
39505 Mound Rd.
Sterling Heights, MI 48310
Ph: (517)371-4720
Fax: (517)371-2401
URL: National Affiliate–www.legion.org
Contact: Robert L. Poxon, Contact
Local. Affiliated With: American Legion.

9862 ■ American Legion, Roose-Vanker Post 286
3543 Veronica Dr.
Sterling Heights, MI 48310
Ph: (517)371-4720
Fax: (517)371-2401
URL: National Affiliate–www.legion.org
Local. Affiliated With: American Legion.

9863 ■ American Welding Society, Detroit Section 011
c/o John McKenzie, Chm.
3010 Barton Dr.
Sterling Heights, MI 48310
Ph: (586)979-4447
Fax: (313)755-0226
E-mail: jdmckenzie@msn.com
URL: National Affiliate–www.aws.org
Local. Professional engineering society in the field of welding. **Affiliated With:** American Welding Society.

9864 ■ American Youth Soccer Organization, Region 190
42376 Parkdale Ct.
Sterling Heights, MI 48314
Ph: (586)932-6285
E-mail: jcoulter@umich.edu
URL: http://www.ayso190.org
Local. Affiliated With: American Youth Soccer Organization.

9865 ■ Detroit Eastside-Friendship Lions Club
c/o Arnold Beller, Pres.
11988 Burtley Dr.
Sterling Heights, MI 48313
Ph: (586)978-1935 (586)731-2866
E-mail: arnieb2@yahoo.com
URL: http://www.metrodetroitlions.org
Contact: Arnold Beller, Pres.
Local. Affiliated With: Lions Clubs International.

9866 ■ International Union, United Automobile, Aerospace and Agricultural Implement Workers of America, AFL-CIO - Local Union 228
39209 Mound Rd.
Sterling Heights, MI 48310
Ph: (586)264-5100
Fax: (586)264-1429
URL: http://www.uaw-228.com
Contact: Bob Rebecca, Pres.
Members: 6,811. **Local.** AFL-CIO. **Affiliated With:** International Union, United Automobile, Aerospace and Agricultural Implement Workers of America.

9867 ■ Michigan National Wild Turkey Federation, Beards and Spurs Chapter
38302 Lincolndale
Sterling Heights, MI 48310
Ph: (586)979-9128
URL: http://www.mi-nwtf.org/Beard-spurs.htm
Contact: Ted Hundich, Contact
Local.

9868 ■ Michigan Pathfinders
c/o Don Vartanian
2810 Burningbush Dr.
Sterling Heights, MI 48314-1886
Ph: (317)842-1072
E-mail: donvart@yahoo.com
URL: National Affiliate–www.ava.org
Contact: Don Vartanian, Contact
State.

9869 ■ Michigan Whirlybirds
34836 Moravian Dr., Apt. 204
Sterling Heights, MI 48312-5478
URL: http://www.michbirds.addr.com
Contact: John Kermizian, Contact
Local.

9870 ■ Sterling Heights Area Chamber of Commerce (SHACC)
12900 Hall Rd., Ste.190
Sterling Heights, MI 48313
Ph: (586)731-5400
Fax: (586)731-3521
E-mail: ladams@suscc.com
URL: http://www.suscc.com
Contact: Lil Adams, Exec.Dir.
Founded: 1961. **Members:** 1,850. **Membership Dues:** business (depends on classification), $250-$550 (annual) • individual, $320 (annual). **Local.** Promotes business and community development in the Sterling Heights, Utica, and Shelby Township, MI area. Sponsors Down Home Days and community ball. **Committees:** Ambassadors. **Subgroups:** Business Resource Alliance Group. **Affiliated With:** U.S. Chamber of Commerce. **Formerly:** (1986) Northwest Macomb Chamber of Commerce. **Publications:** *Business Advisor*, monthly. Newsletter. Provides updates on legislative issues and chamber events. **Advertising:** accepted • *Community Directory*, annual • *Impact*, monthly. **Conventions/Meetings:** semiannual Business Expo - meeting • annual dinner • monthly luncheon • quarterly seminar.

9871 ■ Sterling Heights Computer Club
PO Box 385
Sterling Heights, MI 48311-0385
Ph: (586)731-9232
E-mail: info@sterlingheightscomputerclub.org
URL: http://www.SterlingHeightsComputerClub.org
Contact: Don VanSyckel, Pres.
Founded: 1987. **Members:** 120. **Membership Dues:** individual, family, $25 (annual). **Local.** Seeks to educate members about PC hardware and software. **Publications:** *The Wysiwyg*, monthly, except July and August. Newsletter. **Conventions/Meetings:** monthly meeting.

9872 ■ Sweet Adelines International, Great Lakes Chorus
St. Thomas Lutheran Church
8771 15 Mile Rd.
Sterling Heights, MI 48312-3605
Ph: (586)731-2834
E-mail: jrbuiteweg@comcast.net
URL: http://www.glcsing.org
Contact: JoAnne Buiteweg, Contact
Local. Advances the musical art form of barbershop harmony through education and performances. Provides education, training and coaching in the development of women's four-part barbershop harmony. **Affiliated With:** Sweet Adelines International.

9873 ■ Veteran Motor Car Club of America - Detroit Chapter
c/o Ed Syrocki, Pres.
39159 Casimira Ave.
Sterling Heights, MI 48313
Ph: (586)566-8413
URL: National Affiliate–www.vmcca.org
Contact: Ed Syrocki, Pres.
Local. Affiliated With: Veteran Motor Car Club of America.

Stevensville

9874 ■ American Legion, Stevensville Post 568
3093 Johnson Rd.
Stevensville, MI 49127
Ph: (517)371-4720
Fax: (517)371-2401
URL: National Affiliate–www.legion.org
Local. Affiliated With: American Legion.

9875 ■ Lakeshore Chamber of Commerce
PO Box 93
Stevensville, MI 49127-0093
Ph: (269)429-1170
Fax: (269)429-8882
E-mail: information@lakeshorechamber.org
URL: http://www.lakeshorechamber.org
Contact: Susan Hardy, Sec.
Membership Dues: full, $65 (annual). **Local.** Works to advance the commercial, industrial, civic and cultural opportunities in the Lakeshore community and surrounding areas. **Computer Services:** database, membership. **Publications:** Newsletter. Alternate Formats: online.

Stockbridge

9876 ■ American Legion, Mackinder-Glenn Post 510
830 S Clinton St.
Stockbridge, MI 49285
Ph: (517)371-4720
Fax: (517)371-2401
URL: National Affiliate–www.legion.org
Local. Affiliated With: American Legion.

9877 ■ Michigan Trail Riders Association (MTRA)
3010 N M-52
Stockbridge, MI 49285-9764
Ph: (517)851-7554
Contact: Judy Chanter, Contact
Founded: 1963. **Members:** 1,500. **Membership Dues:** new member, $30 (annual) • renewal, $20 (annual). **Staff:** 1. **Regional.** Individuals interested in hiking, horseback riding, and cross-country skiing on the shore-to-shore trail and the North-South trail. Builds and maintains trail and camps. **Publications:** Newsletter, quarterly. **Price:** included in membership dues. **Conventions/Meetings:** annual convention - always March; Avg. Attendance: 400.

9878 ■ Stockbridge Lions Club
c/o John Ocwieja, Pres.
4155 Brogan Rd.
Stockbridge, MI 49285
Ph: (517)780-5152 (517)851-4376
URL: http://www.district11c2.org
Contact: John Ocwieja, Pres.
Local. Affiliated With: Lions Clubs International.

Sturgis

9879 ■ American Legion, Neuman-Wenzel Post 73
500 W Chicago Rd.
Sturgis, MI 49091
Ph: (517)371-4720
Fax: (517)371-2401
URL: National Affiliate–www.legion.org
Local. Affiliated With: American Legion.

9880 ■ River Country Tourism Bureau
65984 M66
Sturgis, MI 49091
Ph: (269)659-8811
Fax: (269)651-4342
Free: (800)447-2821
URL: http://www.rivercountry.com
Contact: Laura Culver, Exec.Dir.
Founded: 1988. **Members:** 100. **Regional Groups:** 4. **Local.** Promotes convention business and tourism in area. **Publications:** *Treasure Hunt in River Country*, annual. Magazine. **Price:** free. **Circulation:** 50,000.

9881 ■ Saint Joseph County Conservation
28760 Fawn River Rd.
Sturgis, MI 49091
Ph: (269)467-7128
URL: National Affiliate–www.mynssa.com
Local. Affiliated With: National Skeet Shooting Association.

9882 ■ Southwest Michigan Youth for Christ (SWMYFC)
c/o Ken Mills
PO Box 382
Sturgis, MI 49091
Ph: (616)651-1669
Fax: (616)651-1669
Free: (800)316-7268
E-mail: swmiyfc@voyager.net
Contact: Ken Mills, Contact
Founded: 1986. **Staff:** 6. **Budget:** $100,000. **Local.** Interdenominational organization promoting the evangelization of teenagers. Conducts charitable activities for youths. **Affiliated With:** Youth for Christ/U.S.A. **Publications:** *YFC Ministry News*, monthly. Newsletter. Contains supporter information. **Circulation:** 900. **Advertising:** accepted. **Conventions/Meetings:** periodic meeting - varies throughout the year; during school year - weekly.

9883 ■ Sturgis Area Chamber of Commerce (SACC)
200 W Main
PO Box 189
Sturgis, MI 49091-0189
Ph: (269)651-5758
Fax: (269)651-4124
E-mail: sturgischamber@charter.net
URL: http://www.sturgischamber.com
Contact: Cathi Garn, Exec.Dir.
Founded: 1941. **Members:** 350. **Staff:** 3. **Local.** Promotes business and community development in Sturgis, MI. Sponsors Michigan Week Festival and 4th of July celebration. Also sponsors the Sturgis area Business/Education Alliance. **Affiliated With:** U.S. Chamber of Commerce. **Publications:** *Chamber Calling*, monthly. Newsletter • Article, annual. **Conventions/Meetings:** monthly board meeting.

Sunfield

9884 ■ Sunfield Lions Club
c/o William Teller, Sec.
PO Box 23
Sunfield, MI 48890-0023
Ph: (517)566-8964
E-mail: wmteller@cablespeed.com
URL: http://www.district11c2.org
Contact: William Teller, Sec.
Local. Affiliated With: Lions Clubs International.

Suttons Bay

9885 ■ American Legion, Eagletown Post 120
2605 NW Bay Shore Dr.
Suttons Bay, MI 49682
Ph: (517)371-4720
Fax: (517)371-2401
URL: National Affiliate–www.legion.org
Local. Affiliated With: American Legion.

9886 ■ Inland Seas Education Association (ISEA)
100 Dame St.
Suttons Bay, MI 49682
Ph: (231)271-3077
Fax: (231)271-3088
E-mail: isea@greatlakeseducation.org
URL: http://www.greatlakeseducation.org
Contact: Colleen Masterson, Education Dir.
Founded: 1989. **Members:** 500. **Membership Dues:** patron, $1,000 (annual) • sustaining, $500 (annual) • contributing, $100 (annual) • family, $40 (annual) • supporting, $60 (annual) • individual, $25 (annual). **Staff:** 12. Individuals concerned with the stewardship of the Great Lakes. Develops leadership, understanding, and commitment needed for long-term stewardship of the Great Lakes. Provides shipboard educational programs where people of all ages can gain first-hand training and experience in the Great Lakes ecosystem. Offers aquatic science, environmental awareness, and sail training classes. **Computer Services:** database • mailing lists • online services. **Telecommunication Services:** phone referral service. **Programs:** Schoolship; Volunteer Instructor Training. **Publications:** *Schoolship Log*, quarterly. Newsletter. **Price:** free to members. **Circulation:** 1,400 • Also publishes schoolship instructor's manual, program manuals.

9887 ■ Leelanau Peninsula Chamber of Commerce
5046 SW Bayshore Dr., Ste.G
Suttons Bay, MI 49682
Ph: (231)271-9895
Fax: (231)271-9896
Free: (800)980-9895
E-mail: info@leelanauchamber.com
URL: http://www.leelanauchamber.com
Contact: Richard Stearns, Pres.
Founded: 1960. **Members:** 293. **Membership Dues:** general, $175 • associate, $125 • individual, $75 • qualified non-profit/service organization, $25. **Local.** Promotes business and community development and tourism in Leelanau County, MI. **Formerly:** (1999) Leelanau County Chamber of Commerce. **Publications:** Newsletter, monthly.

9888 ■ Michigan Food Processors Association
c/o K. Terry Morrison, Exec.Dir.
4747 S. Elm Valley Rd.
Suttons Bay, MI 49682-9427
Ph: (231)271-5752
Fax: (231)271-5753

9889 ■ Suttons Bay Chamber of Commerce
PO Box 46
Suttons Bay, MI 49682-0046
Ph: (231)271-5077
URL: http://www.suttonsbayarea.com
Contact: Piper Goldson, Pres.
Local. Represents the interests of business and organizations in Suttons Bay.

Swartz Creek

9890 ■ ACF Flint/Saginaw Valley Chapter
c/o Grant E. Short, CEC, Chm.
4444 Grand Blanc Rd.
Swartz Creek, MI 48473
Ph: (810)655-2269
Fax: (810)743-9440
E-mail: chefs@acf-flint-saginaw.org
URL: http://www.acf-flint-saginaw.org
Contact: Grant E. Short CEC, Chm.
Local. Promotes the culinary profession. Provides on-going educational training and networking for members. Provides opportunities for competition, professional recognition and access to educational forums with other culinarians at local, regional, national and international events. **Affiliated With:** American Culinary Federation.

9891 ■ American Legion, Bernard A. Bendle Post 294
3440 N Morrish Rd.
Swartz Creek, MI 48473
Ph: (517)371-4720
Fax: (517)371-2401
URL: National Affiliate–www.legion.org
Local. Affiliated With: American Legion.

9892 ■ American Legion, Buick Liberty Motor Post 310
1358 Houston Dr.
Swartz Creek, MI 48473
Ph: (517)371-4720
Fax: (517)371-2401
URL: National Affiliate–www.legion.org
Local. Affiliated With: American Legion.

9893 ■ Detroit Area Corvair Club (DACC)
5498 Duffield Rd.
Swartz Creek, MI 48473-8587
E-mail: corvairkid1963@aol.com
URL: http://dacc.provide.net
Contact: Clark Hartzel, Contact
Local. Affiliated With: Corvair Society of America.

9894 ■ Flint 4 Seasons Figure Skating Club
5438 Seymour Rd.
Swartz Creek, MI 48473
Ph: (810)635-3581
URL: National Affiliate–www.usfigureskating.org
Contact: David Clark, Contact
Local. Provides programs to encourage participation and achievement in the sport of figure skating on ice. Defines and maintains uniform standards of skating proficiency. Organizes and sponsors competitions and exhibitions for the purpose of stimulating interest in figure skating. **Affiliated With:** United States Figure Skating Association.

9895 ■ Michigan State Firemen's Association (MSFA)
9001 Miller Rd., Ste.10
PO Box 405
Swartz Creek, MI 48473
Ph: (810)635-9513
Fax: (810)635-2858
Free: (800)445-3844
E-mail: msfassoc@aol.com
URL: http://www.angelfire.com/mi/michiganstatefiremen
Contact: Joseph J. Edgerton, Sec.-Treas.
Founded: 1875. **Members:** 7,000. **Membership Dues:** individual, retired, associate, $30 (annual) • organized fire department/brigade, $75 (annual). **Staff:** 2. **Budget:** $194,700. **State.** Firefighters. Offers education to firefighters and the public on fire prevention. **Awards:** Max Brandt Memorial. **Frequency:** annual. **Type:** scholarship. **Recipient:** for higher education of members or their families. **Affiliated With:** National Volunteer Fire Council. **Publications:** *Fireplug*, periodic. Journal. **Advertising:** accepted. **Conventions/Meetings:** annual conference (exhibits) - always 3rd weekend in June.

9896 ■ Swartz Creek Lions Club
c/o Wilfred Morgan, Pres.
5388 Greenleaf Dr.
Swartz Creek, MI 48473
Ph: (810)635-3467
E-mail: wwm5388@aol.com
URL: http://www.geocities.com/dist11d1
Contact: Wilfred Morgan, Pres.
Local. Affiliated With: Lions Clubs International.

Sylvan Lake

9897 ■ Sylvan Lake Bocce Club
2276 Garland Blvd.
Sylvan Lake, MI 48320
Ph: (248)505-4744
E-mail: boccemg@msn.com
URL: National Affiliate–www.bocce.com
Local. Affiliated With: United States Bocce Federation.

Tawas City

9898 ■ Tawas Area Chamber of Commerce
402 E Lake St.
PO Box 608
Tawas City, MI 48764-0608
Ph: (989)362-8643
Fax: (989)362-7880
Free: (800)55T-AWAS
E-mail: info@tawas.com
URL: http://www.tawas.com
Contact: Jamie Gentry, Exec.Dir.
Membership Dues: apartment and lodging (based on number of units), $125-$1,050 • automobile dealer (all classes), $400 • campground, trailer park, marina (public or private), $190-$750 • general (based on number of employees), $180-$425 • church, organization, crafter, artisan, $75 • individual (all classes), $40. **Local.** Strives to promote a healthy business climate and build a strong community. **Publications:** *Executive Report*, monthly. Newsletter. **Circulation:** 400 • Membership Directory.

Taylor

9899 ■ American Legion, Taylor Post 200
11800 Michael St.
Taylor, MI 48180
Ph: (517)371-4720
Fax: (517)371-2401
URL: National Affiliate–www.legion.org
Local. Affiliated With: American Legion.

9900 ■ Down River Association of Realtors
20300 Superior Rd., Ste.No. 140
Taylor, MI 48180
Ph: (734)287-8060
Fax: (734)287-4230
E-mail: elaine@drar.com
URL: http://www.drar.com
Contact: Elaine Adkins, CEO
Local. Strives to develop real estate business practices. Advocates the right to own, use and transfer real property. Provides a facility for professional development, research and exchange of information among members. **Affiliated With:** National Association of Realtors.

9901 ■ Downriver Council for the Arts (DCA)
c/o Martine Mac Donald, Gallery Dir.
20904 Northline Rd.
Taylor, MI 48180
Ph: (734)287-6103
Fax: (734)287-6151
E-mail: dc4arts@cs-net.net
URL: http://www.downriverarts.org
Contact: Martine Mac Donald, Gallery Dir.
Founded: 1978. **Regional.** Strives to enrich the quality of life in the downriver communities by advocating and promoting the arts and providing opportunities for involvement and participation in arts and cultural activities.

9902 ■ Infusion Nurses Society, Great Lakes
25314 Haskell St.
Taylor, MI 48180
Ph: (313)291-6316
E-mail: llenihan1@hfhs.org
URL: National Affiliate–www.ins1.org
Contact: Laura Lenihan, Pres.
Regional. Represents the interests of healthcare professionals who are involved with the practice of infusion therapy. Seeks to advance the delivery of quality therapy to patients. Promotes research and education in the practice of infusion nursing. **Affiliated With:** Infusion Nurses Society.

9903 ■ International Association of Heat and Frost Insulators and Asbestos Workers, Asbestos Abatement Workers Regional Local 207
26465 Northline Rd.
Taylor, MI 48180
Ph: (734)947-1745
Fax: (734)947-1753
Free: (800)207-5622
E-mail: local207@mycomcast.com
URL: http://www.local207.org
Local.

9904 ■ National Sojourners, Detroit No. 1
c/o MML1/C Raymond E. King
15159 Beech Daly Rd.
Taylor, MI 48180-5042
Ph: (734)941-4986
E-mail: rking15159@aol.com
URL: National Affiliate–www.nationalsojourners.org
Contact: MML1/C Raymond E. King, Contact
Local.

9905 ■ Southern Wayne County Regional Chamber (SWCRC)
20600 Eureka Rd., Ste.315
Taylor, MI 48180-5306
Ph: (734)284-6000
Fax: (734)284-0198
E-mail: info@swccc.org
URL: http://www.swccc.org
Contact: James Williams, Chm.
Founded: 1966. **Members:** 1,000. **Membership Dues:** business (0-600 employees), $160-$909 • business (601-1400 employees), $1,020-$1,686. **Staff:** 12. **Budget:** $350,000. **Local.** Promotes business and community development in southern Wayne County, MI. Conducts business seminars and legislative forums. Maintains numerous committees. **Affiliated With:** U.S. Chamber of Commerce. **Formerly:** (2005) Southern Wayne County Chamber of Commerce. **Publications:** *Business Connection*, monthly. Magazine. Includes upcoming events, legislative, educational small business updates, and lists of new members. **Price:** included in membership dues. **Advertising:** accepted. Alternate Formats: online • *Buyer's Guide*, annual. Book. Contains membership roster, government and city information, and district maps. **Price:** $5.00 for members (additional copy); $25.00 for nonmembers. **Advertising:** accepted • *Membership Roster*, annual. Newsletter • Newsletter, monthly. **Conventions/Meetings:** monthly luncheon - always first Monday.

Tecumseh

9906 ■ American Legion, Underwood-Orr Post 34
101 W Pottawatamie St.
Tecumseh, MI 49286
Ph: (517)371-4720
Fax: (517)371-2401
URL: National Affiliate–www.legion.org
Local. Affiliated With: American Legion.

9907 ■ Lenawee County Medical Society
PO Box 146
Tecumseh, MI 49286
Ph: (517)263-7118
Fax: (517)263-6781
E-mail: lencomed@hotmail.com
URL: http://www.msms.org
Contact: Melinda S. Ahleman, Exec.Sec.
Local. Advances the art and science of medicine. Promotes patient care and the betterment of public health. **Affiliated With:** Michigan State Medical Society.

9908 ■ Michigan National Wild Turkey Federation, River Raisin Chapter
312 E Chicago Blvd.
Tecumseh, MI 49286
Ph: (517)424-5602
URL: http://www.mi-nwtf.org/RiverRaisin.htm
Contact: Dwaine Knouse, Pres.
Local.

Tekonsha

9909 ■ Tekonsha Lions Club
c/o Lorraine Lindsey, Sec.
1279 Klink Rd.
Tekonsha, MI 49092

Ph: (517)767-4623 (517)767-3222
Fax: (517)767-4537
E-mail: lal3222@yahoo.com
URL: http://www.lionsdistrict11b1.org/lc_tekonsha.htm
Contact: Lorraine Lindsey, Sec.
Local. Affiliated With: Lions Clubs International.

Temperance

9910 ■ American Legion, Michigan Post 192
c/o Sherman H. Osborne
620 W Temperance Rd.
Temperance, MI 48182
Ph: (517)371-4720
Fax: (517)371-2401
URL: National Affiliate–www.legion.org
Contact: Sherman H. Osborne, Contact
Local. Affiliated With: American Legion.

9911 ■ RSVP Monroe County
c/o Deb Briscol, Dir.
1623 W Sterns Rd.
Temperance, MI 48182
Ph: (734)850-6044
Fax: (734)850-6099
E-mail: briscold@bedford.k12.mi.us
URL: http://www.seniorcorps.gov/about/programs/rsvp_state.asp?usestateabbr=mi&Search4.x=17&Search4.y=0
Contact: Deb Briscol, Dir.
Local. Affiliated With: Retired and Senior Volunteer Program.

Three Oaks

9912 ■ American Legion, Randall Couchman Post 204
PO Box 141
Three Oaks, MI 49128
Ph: (517)371-4720
Fax: (517)371-2401
URL: National Affiliate–www.legion.org
Local. Affiliated With: American Legion.

Three Rivers

9913 ■ American Legion, Hice-Shutes Post 170
59990 S Main St.
Three Rivers, MI 49093
Ph: (517)371-4720
Fax: (517)371-2401
URL: National Affiliate–www.legion.org
Local. Affiliated With: American Legion.

9914 ■ American Vaulting Association - Diamond E Vaulters
c/o Cindy Mehaney, Coach
10481 Camp Eberhart Rd.
Three Rivers, MI 49093
Ph: (269)273-2667
E-mail: vaultingmomde@peoplepc.com
URL: National Affiliate–www.americanvaulting.org
Contact: Cindy Mehaney, Coach
Local. Affiliated With: American Vaulting Association.

9915 ■ International Union, United Automobile, Aerospace and Agricultural Implement Workers of America, AFL-CIO - Local Union 2093
15802 Hoffman
Three Rivers, MI 49093
Ph: (269)279-5201
Fax: (269)279-6308
URL: http://my.voyager.net/~uaw
Contact: Erv Heidbrink, Pres.
Members: 1,153. **Local.** AFL-CIO. **Affiliated With:** International Union, United Automobile, Aerospace and Agricultural Implement Workers of America.

9916 ■ Michigan Lake and Stream Associations (ML&SA)
c/o Donald E. Winne, Exec.Dir.
PO Box 249
Three Rivers, MI 49093
Ph: (269)273-8200
Fax: (269)273-2919
E-mail: info@mlswa.org
URL: http://www.mlswa.org
Contact: Donald E. Winne, Exec.Dir.
Founded: 1961. **State.**

9917 ■ Michigan National Wild Turkey Federation, St. Joe Valley Limbhangers
222 N Douglas Ave.
Three Rivers, MI 49093
Ph: (616)273-1863
E-mail: dgtmjohnson@aol.com
URL: http://www.mi-nwtf.org/StJoeValley.htm
Contact: Kyle Foster, VP
Local.

9918 ■ Three Rivers Area Chamber of Commerce
57 N Main St.
Three Rivers, MI 49093
Ph: (616)278-8193
Fax: (616)273-1751
E-mail: info@trchamber.com
URL: http://www.trchamber.com
Contact: Bruce Snook, Gen.Mgr.
Local. Works to improve business community and industrial opportunity to enhance the quality of life in the Three River area. **Councils:** Tourism. **Affiliated With:** Michigan Chamber of Commerce; U.S. Chamber of Commerce. **Publications:** *Chamber News*, monthly. Newsletter. Highlights area business activities, upcoming seminars, workshops and other events of interests to the business community. • Membership Directory.

9919 ■ Three Rivers Lions Club
PO Box 134
Three Rivers, MI 49093
E-mail: thespian49093@yahoo.com
URL: http://milions11b2.org
Local. Affiliated With: Lions Clubs International.

Traverse City

9920 ■ Alcoholics Anonymous World Services, District 11 Central Office
124 N Div.
Traverse City, MI 49684
Ph: (231)946-8823
URL: National Affiliate–www.aa.org
Local. Individuals recovering from alcoholism. AA maintains that members can solve their common problem and help others achieve sobriety through a twelve step program that includes sharing their experience, strength, and hope with each other. **Affiliated With:** Alcoholics Anonymous World Services.

9921 ■ American Legion, Bowen-Holliday Post 35
PO Box 123
Traverse City, MI 49685
Ph: (517)371-4720
Fax: (517)371-2401
URL: National Affiliate–www.legion.org
Local. Affiliated With: American Legion.

9922 ■ American Red Cross, Northwest Michigan Chapter
735 S Garfield Ave., Ste.B100
Traverse City, MI 49686
Ph: (231)947-7286
Fax: (231)947-1767
URL: http://www.northwestmichigan.redcross.org
Regional.

9923 ■ Ancient Order of Hibernians of Grand Traverse County - Bun Brady Division
c/o Howard E. Byrne
15591 Upper Birch Dr.
Traverse City, MI 49686-8337
Ph: (231)223-4193
E-mail: mecb@pentel.net
URL: http://www.michiganaoh.com
Contact: Howard E. Byrne, Contact
Local. Affiliated With: Ancient Order of Hibernians in America.

9924 ■ Antique Automobile Club of America, Northwestern Michigan Region
c/o Ervin Irish
838 Floresta St.
Traverse City, MI 49686
URL: National Affiliate–www.aaca.org
Contact: Ervin Irish, Contact
Members: 42. **Membership Dues:** regular, $10 (annual). **Local.** Automobile collectors and hobbyists. **Awards:** Ed Grace Memorial. **Frequency:** annual. **Type:** recognition. **Recipient:** for leadership activity. **Affiliated With:** Antique Automobile Club of America. **Publications:** *Antique Automobile*, bimonthly. Magazine. **Price:** $26.00. **Advertising:** accepted. **Conventions/Meetings:** monthly meeting • tour.

9925 ■ Between the Bays Dance Camps
c/o Henry Morgenstein
255 E 10th St.
Traverse City, MI 49684
Ph: (231)946-4782
E-mail: hmorgenstein@mbx.nmc.edu
URL: http://www.nmc.edu/~hmorgenstein/
Contact: Henry Morgenstein, Contact
Local. Affiliated With: Country Dance and Song Society.

9926 ■ Conservation Resource Alliance (CRA)
Grandview Plz.
10850 Traverse Hwy.
Traverse City, MI 49684-1363
Ph: (231)946-6817
Fax: (231)947-5441
E-mail: james.haveman@mi.usda.gov
URL: http://www.rivercare.org
Contact: James Haveman, Coor.
Local. Affiliated With: National Association of Resource Conservation and Development Councils.

9927 ■ Easter Seals Michigan
c/o Northwestern Region
109 S Union, Ste.209
Traverse City, MI 49684
Ph: (231)941-1271
Fax: (231)941-1990
E-mail: essofmich@aol.com
URL: http://www.mi-ws.easter-seals.org
Contact: Liz Hughes, Dir.
Regional. Affiliated With: Easter Seals.

9928 ■ Eastern Upper Peninsula Beagle Club
c/o Jim Scrivener
5918 Beverly Dr.
Traverse City, MI 49684-8516
URL: National Affiliate–clubs.akc.org
Contact: Jim Scrivener, Contact
Local.

9929 ■ For Animals
PO Box 6324
Traverse City, MI 49696-6324
Ph: (231)922-6083
E-mail: tcforanimals@coslink.net
URL: http://www.foranimalstc.org
Contact: Ms. Michele Lonoconus, Pres.
Founded: 1989. **Members:** 70. **Membership Dues:** family, $15 (annual) • student, $5 (annual). **Local.** Individuals interested in preventing abuse and exploitation of animals and the environment through education and the promotion of a compassionate lifestyle. **Publications:** *Yearly Report*, annual.

Newsletter. **Conventions/Meetings:** monthly general assembly - always second Tuesday, Traverse City, MI.

9930 ■ Girl Scouts of Crooked Tree
1820 Oak Hollow Dr.
Traverse City, MI 49686
Ph: (231)947-7354
Free: (800)968-5030
E-mail: servicecenter@girlscoutscrookedtree.org
URL: http://www.girlscoutscrookedtree.org
Local. Young girls and adult volunteers, corporate, government and individual supporters. Strives to develop potential and leadership skills among its members. Conducts trainings, educational programs and outdoor activities.

9931 ■ Grand Traverse Area Genealogical Society (GTAGS)
PO Box 2015
Traverse City, MI 49685-2015
E-mail: maryrose@chartermi.net
URL: http://www.rootsweb.com/~migtags/gtag.htm
Contact: Mary Rose, Pres.
Founded: 1979. **Members:** 75. **Membership Dues:** individual, $15 (annual) • family, $20 (annual). **Budget:** $1,275. **For-Profit**. **Local**. Sponsors genealogy research programs and publications of cemetery information on area cemeteries. **Libraries: Type:** open to the public. **Holdings:** 1,600; books, films, periodicals. **Subjects:** genealogy. **Computer Services:** Online services, website with links to area resources. **Publications:** *Kinship Tales*, quarterly. Newsletter. **Price:** $3.00. ISSN: 1043-9342. **Circulation:** 150. **Advertising:** accepted. Alternate Formats: online. **Conventions/Meetings:** annual seminar.

9932 ■ Grand Traverse Chorus of Sweet Adelines International
Grand Traverse Heritage Ctr.
322 6th St.
Traverse City, MI 49684-2414
Ph: (231)533-8532
E-mail: pres@grandtraversechorus.org
URL: http://grandtraversechorus.org
Contact: Cam Lacy, Pres.
Local. Advances the musical art form of barbershop harmony through education and performances. Provides education, training and coaching in the development of women's four-part barbershop harmony. **Affiliated With:** Sweet Adelines International.

9933 ■ Home Builders Association of the Grand Traverse Area
3040 Sunset Ln.
Traverse City, MI 49684-4672
Ph: (231)946-2305
Fax: (231)946-1051
Free: (800)422-5166
E-mail: mailbox@hbagta.com
URL: http://www.hbagta.com
Contact: Kris Guyot, Contact
Founded: 1970. **Local**. Single and multifamily home builders, commercial builders, and others associated with the building industry. **Affiliated With:** National Association of Home Builders.

9934 ■ Kiwanis Club of Traverse City
PO Box 864
Traverse City, MI 49685
E-mail: tckiwanis@aol.com
URL: http://www.tckiwanis.homestead.com
Contact: Bill Siler, Pres.
Local.

9935 ■ Korean War Veterans Association, Northwest Michigan Chapter
c/o Albert C. Ockert
356 W River Rd.
Traverse City, MI 49684
Ph: (231)946-4698
URL: National Affiliate–www.kwva.org
Contact: Albert C. Ockert, Contact
Local. **Affiliated With:** Korean War Veterans Association.

9936 ■ Land Information Access Association (LIAA)
324 Munson Ave.
Traverse City, MI 49686
Ph: (231)929-3696
Fax: (231)929-3771
E-mail: jvander@liaa.org
URL: http://www.liaa.org
Contact: Joe VanderMeulen, Exec.Dir.
Local. **Publications:** *Beyond Borders*. Newsletter. Alternate Formats: online • *Building a Sense of Place*. Booklet. Alternate Formats: online.

9937 ■ Michigan Association of School Psychologists (MASP)
c/o Nancy Korbel
2205 Kewaunee
Traverse City, MI 49686
E-mail: djrogg@aol.com
URL: http://www.masponline.org
Contact: Jayanne Roggenbaum, CEO
State. Represents and supports school psychology through leadership. Enhances the mental health and educational competence of children. Informs the public on the services and practice of school psychology. **Affiliated With:** National Association of School Psychologists.

9938 ■ Michigan Audubon Society - Grand Traverse Audubon Club
c/o Leonard Graf, Treas.
7429 E Fouch Rd.
Traverse City, MI 49684
E-mail: gtac@grandtraverseaudubon.org
URL: http://www.grandtraverseaudubon.org
Contact: Kay Beerthuis, Ed.
State. Activities include meetings, field trips, service projects and environmental action related to birding.

9939 ■ Michigan Infectious Diseases Society (MIDS)
c/o Cathie L. Martin, Exec.Dir.
13937 Morgan Hill Rd.
Traverse City, MI 49684
Ph: (231)947-2772
Fax: (231)947-3195
E-mail: earlymart@charter.net
URL: http://www.midsociety.org
Contact: Cathie L. Martin, Exec.Dir.
Founded: 1985. **Members:** 100. **State**. Aims to improve the health of individuals, communities and society. Promotes education and research relating to infectious diseases. **Computer Services:** Online services, infectious diseases image collection • online services, message board. **Affiliated With:** Infectious Diseases Society of America. **Publications:** Newsletter, quarterly. Features articles from the president, editor and members. Alternate Formats: online.

9940 ■ Mississippi Association for Psychology in the Schools (MAPS)
c/o Nancy Korbel
2205 Kewaunee
Traverse City, MI 49686
E-mail: djrogg@aol.com
URL: http://www.masponline.org
Contact: Jayanne Roggenbaum, CEO
State. Represents and supports school psychology through leadership. Enhances the mental health and educational competence of children. Informs the public on the services and practice of school psychology. **Affiliated With:** National Association of School Psychologists.

9941 ■ National Alliance for the Mentally Ill of Northwest Michigan
c/o Maxine Rideout, Pres.
2164 Hammond Pl.
Traverse City, MI 49686
Ph: (231)922-2665
E-mail: info@nami-nwmi.org
URL: http://mi.nami.org/gtl.html
Contact: Maxine Rideout, Pres.
Local. Strives to improve the quality of life of children and adults with severe mental illness through support, education, research and advocacy. **Affiliated With:** National Alliance for the Mentally Ill.

9942 ■ National Organization for Women - Grand Traverse
PO Box 6835
Traverse City, MI 49686
Ph: (231)941-9158
E-mail: danmaura@hotmail.com
URL: http://www.michnow.org
Local. **Affiliated With:** National Organization for Women.

9943 ■ Northwest Michigan Council of Governments (NWMCOG)
Univ. Center Campus
2194 Dendrinos Dr.
Traverse City, MI 49684
Ph: (231)929-5000
Free: (800)692-7774
E-mail: bshipste@nwm.cog.mi.us
URL: http://www.nwm.cog.mi.us
Contact: Bud Shipstead, Dir.
Founded: 1973. **Local**.

9944 ■ PetSafe Rescue Alliance
c/o Doris Schenck
PO Box 2328
Traverse City, MI 49685-2328
Ph: (231)392-3125
E-mail: petsafe@petsaferescue.com
URL: http://www.petsafe.petfinder.org
Local.

9945 ■ PFLAG Traverse City
c/o Third Level Center
1022 E Front St.
Traverse City, MI 49686
Ph: (231)922-4800
Free: (800)442-7315
E-mail: joanpw@coslink.net
URL: http://www.pflag.org/Michigan.216.0.html
Local. **Affiliated With:** Parents, Families, and Friends of Lesbians and Gays.

9946 ■ Phi Theta Kappa, Alpha Rho Pi Chapter - Northwestern Michigan College
c/o Kari Kahler
1701 E Front St.
Traverse City, MI 49686
Ph: (231)995-1228
E-mail: kkahler@nmc.edu
URL: http://www.ptk.org/directories/chapters/MI/9714-1.htm
Contact: Kari Kahler, Advisor
Local.

9947 ■ Police and Firemen's Insurance Association - Grand Traverse County Fire and Police Department
c/o Karyl L. Moore
12857 Roseland Dr.
Traverse City, MI 49684
Ph: (231)947-1758
URL: National Affiliate–www.pfia.net
Contact: Karyl L. Moore, Contact
Local. **Affiliated With:** Police and Firemen's Insurance Association.

9948 ■ Resort District Dental Society
876 E Front St.
Traverse City, MI 49686
Ph: (231)947-6880
E-mail: cote49@aol.com
URL: http://www.rdds.org
Contact: Dr. Daniel Cote, Pres.
Local. Represents the interests of dentists committed to the public's oral health, ethics and professional development. Encourages the improvement of the public's oral health and promotes the art and science of dentistry. **Affiliated With:** American Dental Association; Michigan Dental Association.

9949 ■ Robot Club of Traverse City, Michigan (RCTC)
1892 Pinewood Ave.
Traverse City, MI 49684
Ph: (231)946-0187
E-mail: pgrayson@traverse.net
URL: http://groups.yahoo.com/group/robotclubof traversecitymi
Contact: Engr. Paul F. Grayson, Founder
Founded: 1999. **Members:** 472. **Membership Dues:** family, $20 (annual). **Staff:** 1. **Budget:** $1,000. **State**. United to meet other people with similar interests. **Libraries: Type:** by appointment only; reference; open to the public. **Holdings:** 7,000; articles, artwork, books, clippings, films, periodicals. **Subjects:** robots, salesmanship, business management, engineering. **Awards:** Science Fair Prize. **Frequency:** annual. **Type:** recognition. **Recipient:** for outstanding presentation of math, science or engineering project at a science fair. **Computer Services:** Bibliographic search • database • information services • mailing lists • online services. **Projects:** American Industrial Magic, LLC-Aim Racing; Autonomous Vehicle Racing. **Publications:** *Update*, biweekly. Newsletter. **Circulation:** 410. **Advertising:** accepted. Alternate Formats: online. **Conventions/Meetings:** monthly workshop, members exhibits, news items, robot videos (exhibits).

9950 ■ RSVP of Northwest Michigan
c/o Susan McQuade, Dir.
PO Box 694
Traverse City, MI 49685
Ph: (231)947-3200
Fax: (231)947-3201
E-mail: susan@unitedway.tcnet.org
URL: http://www.unitedway.tcnet.org/rsvp.html
Contact: Susan McQuade, Dir.
Local. Affiliated With: Retired and Senior Volunteer Program.

9951 ■ Ruffed Grouse Society, Le Grand Traverse Chapter
c/o George Clayton
775 Munson Ave.
Traverse City, MI 49686
Ph: (231)922-2231
URL: National Affiliate–www.ruffedgrousesociety.org
Contact: George Clayton, Contact
Local. Affiliated With: Ruffed Grouse Society.

9952 ■ SCORE Traverse City
c/o Pat Hobson
202 E Grandview Pkwy.
Traverse City, MI 49684
Ph: (231)947-5075
Fax: (231)946-2565
E-mail: score@tcchamber.org
URL: http://www.score-traversecity.org
Contact: Pat Hobson, Contact
Local. Provides entrepreneurs with free, confidential, face-to-face and email business counseling. **Affiliated With:** SCORE.

9953 ■ Table Tennis/Traverse City
Grand Traverse Bay YMCA
3000 Racquet Club Dr.
Traverse City, MI 49684
Ph: (231)929-2721
Free: (800)424-3663
URL: http://www.usatt.org/clubs
Contact: Kevin H. Johnson, Contact
Local. Affiliated With: U.S.A. Table Tennis.

9954 ■ Tasters Guild International - Grand Traverse, Chapter No. 018
c/o Folgarelli's Import Market
424 W Front St.
Traverse City, MI 49684
E-mail: darric@folgarellis.com
URL: National Affiliate–www.tastersguild.com
Contact: Darric Newman, Contact
Local. Aims to educate consumers and spread the word of responsible wine and food consumption. Provides opportunity to encounter the best in wine and culinary delights. **Affiliated With:** Tasters Guild International.

9955 ■ Traverse Area Association of Realtors
852 S Garfield Ave.
Traverse City, MI 49686
Ph: (231)947-2050
Fax: (231)947-1910
E-mail: stan@stantornga.com
URL: http://taar.com
Contact: Stan Tornga, Pres.
Local. Strives to develop real estate business practices. Advocates the right to own, use and transfer real property. Provides a facility for professional development, research and exchange of information among members. **Affiliated With:** National Association of Realtors.

9956 ■ Traverse Area Human Resources Association
1050 Bus. Park Dr.
Traverse City, MI 49686
E-mail: pwilliam@brownlumber.net
URL: http://tahratc.org
Contact: Patricia Williams, Pres.
Local. Represents the interests of human resource and industrial relations professionals and executives. Promotes the advancement of human resource management.

9957 ■ Traverse Bay Area Central Labor Council (TBACLC)
PO Box 5547
Traverse City, MI 49696-5547
Ph: (231)943-3537
Fax: (231)943-3537
E-mail: tbaclc@workingfamilies.com
URL: http://www.tbaclc.org
Contact: John Toth, Pres.
Founded: 1976. **Members:** 3,750. **Membership Dues:** affiliation (per member), $1 (monthly). **State Groups:** 1. **Local**. Members of organized labor from Antrim, Benzie, Grand Traverse, also counties of Charlevoix, Emmet, Missaukee, Wexford, Kalkaska, and Leelanau counties, MI. Sponsors Northwest Michigan United Labor Food Bank. **Awards:** Bob Felzke Community Service. **Frequency:** annual. **Type:** recognition. **Affiliated With:** AFL-CIO. **Publications:** *Northwest Michigan Labor News*, monthly. Newsletter. **Price:** free. **Circulation:** 500. Alternate Formats: online. **Conventions/Meetings:** monthly meeting (exhibits) - 2nd Thursday • quarterly meeting.

9958 ■ Traverse City Area Chamber of Commerce
202 E Grandview Pkwy.
PO Box 387
Traverse City, MI 49685-0387
Ph: (231)947-5075
E-mail: info@tcchamber.org
URL: http://www.tcchamber.org
Contact: Douglas R. Luciani, Pres.
Members: 2,700. **Membership Dues:** general, $220-$570 (annual) • retiree, $110 (annual) • bank, financial institution, accommodation, $220 (annual) • non-profit organization (depends upon the annual revenue), $110-$220 (annual). **Local**. Strives to develop business community by creating collaborations with community vital partners. **Councils:** Small Business. **Programs:** Ambassador. **Publications:** *Your Chamber News*, monthly. Newsletter. Contains information about chamber activities and programs and health care legislative issues. **Circulation:** 3,000 • Membership Directory. Identifies local sources for products and services. **Circulation:** 2,700.

9959 ■ Traverse City At-Risk Boxing
c/o William Bustance, Pres.
1777A S Garfield
Traverse City, MI 49686
Ph: (231)933-7050
E-mail: rbustance@aol.com
URL: http://www.TriggerBoxing.com
Contact: William Bustance, Pres.
Founded: 2001. **Members:** 100. **Staff:** 2. **Budget:** $7,000. **Local**. Works with the Probate Court and Charitable groups to identify at-risk-young people and mark their progression in boxing program. Provides an after school environment that is open to all area youth.

9960 ■ Traverse City Lions Club
Box 101
Traverse City, MI 49685
Ph: (231)943-0340
E-mail: zeke1944@aol.com
URL: http://traversecitymi.lionwap.org
Contact: Victor Rioux, Pres.
Local. Affiliated With: Lions Clubs International.

9961 ■ Trout Unlimited - Adams Chapter
Box 2129
Traverse City, MI 49685-2129
Ph: (231)941-7102
E-mail: wlf@traverse.com
URL: http://www.tu.org
Contact: Bill Fernandez, Pres.
Local.

9962 ■ Twin Bays Skating Club (TBSC)
1600 Chartwell Dr.
Traverse City, MI 49686
Ph: (231)933-7465 (231)922-4893
URL: http://www.twinbays.org
Local. Provides programs to encourage participation and achievement in the sport of figure skating on ice. Defines and maintains uniform standards of skating proficiency. Organizes and sponsors competitions and exhibitions for the purpose of stimulating interest in figure skating. **Affiliated With:** United States Figure Skating Association.

9963 ■ United Way of Northwest Michigan
c/o Becky Beauchamp, Exec.Dir.
521 S Union St.
PO Box 694
Traverse City, MI 49685
Ph: (806)669-1001
Fax: (231)947-3201
E-mail: becky@unitedway.tcnet.org
URL: http://www.unitedway.tcnet.org
Contact: Becky Beauchamp, Exec.Dir.
Local.

9964 ■ We Are Traverse City
PO Box 9
Traverse City, MI 49685
E-mail: mail@wearetraversecity.com
URL: http://www.wearetraversecity.com
Contact: Ms. M'Lynn Hartwell, Pres.
Founded: 2000. **Staff:** 1. **Regional Groups:** 1. **Nonmembership. Regional. Libraries: Type:** reference; not open to the public. **Holdings:** books, video recordings. **Computer Services:** Information services • online services. **Additional Websites:** http://www.wearemichigan.com.

Trenton

9965 ■ American Legion, Michigan Post 426
c/o Harold J. Chatell
2423 W Jefferson Ave.
Trenton, MI 48183

Ph: (517)371-4720
Fax: (517)371-2401
URL: National Affiliate–www.legion.org
Contact: Harold J. Chatell, Contact
Local. Affiliated With: American Legion.

9966 ■ Michigan Professional Fire Fighters Union (MPFFU)
c/o Paul Hufnagel, Pres.
1651 Kingsway Ct., Ste.E
Trenton, MI 48183
Ph: (734)675-0206
Fax: (734)675-6083
Free: (800)886-7338
E-mail: phufnagel@mpffu.org
URL: http://www.mpffu.org
Contact: Paul Hufnagel, Pres.
Founded: 1934. **State.**

9967 ■ Trenton Lions Club - Michigan
c/o Walt Zellman, Pres.
2611 Edgemont Rd.
Trenton, MI 48183
Ph: (734)675-0073
URL: http://www.metrodetroitlions.org
Contact: Walt Zellman, Pres.
Local. Affiliated With: Lions Clubs International.

Trout Creek

9968 ■ American Legion, Trombley-Polkas Post 494
RR 1, Box 39
Trout Creek, MI 49967
Ph: (517)371-4720
Fax: (517)371-2401
URL: National Affiliate–www.legion.org
Local. Affiliated With: American Legion.

Troy

9969 ■ American Legion, Michigan Post 14
c/o Charles Edwards
1340 W Maple Rd.
Troy, MI 48084
Ph: (517)371-4720
Fax: (517)371-2401
URL: National Affiliate–www.legion.org
Contact: Charles Edwards, Contact
Local. Affiliated With: American Legion.

9970 ■ American Sewing Guild, Detroit Chapter
c/o Marianne Balogh
5541 Shale
Troy, MI 48098-3953
Ph: (248)828-3079
E-mail: mbalogh@wideopenwest.com
URL: http://www.detroitasg.com
Contact: Marianne Balogh, Contact
Local. Affiliated With: American Sewing Guild.

9971 ■ American Society of Appraisers, Detroit Chapter
c/o Michael N. Kahaian, Pres.
Doeren Mayhew
755 W Big Beaver Rd., Ste.2300
Troy, MI 48084
Ph: (248)244-3217
Fax: (248)273-6817
E-mail: kahaian@doeren.com
URL: http://www.appraisers.org/detroit
Contact: Michael N. Kahaian, Pres.
Local. Works to enhance professional deportment of valuation expertise. Provides immediate and long lasting value-added amenities. **Affiliated With:** American Society of Appraisers.

9972 ■ American Society of Interior Designers - Michigan Chapter (ASID)
1700 Stutz Dr., Ste.No. 79
Troy, MI 48084-4502
Ph: (248)649-6770
Fax: (248)649-2007
E-mail: admin@asidmi.org
URL: http://www.asidmi.org
Contact: Xandra Coles, Administrator
Founded: 1975. **Members:** 900. **State.** Dedicated to the profession of interior design. Promotes the advancement of design excellence, education and communication, professional membership, and the pursuit of the right to practice. **Affiliated With:** American Society of Interior Designers. **Publications:** *Visions*, bimonthly. Newsletter. Alternate Formats: online. **Conventions/Meetings:** monthly board meeting • annual convention.

9973 ■ Arc of Oakland County
1641 W Big Beaver Rd.
Troy, MI 48084
Ph: (248)816-1900
E-mail: tfk@thearcoakland.org
Contact: Thomas Kendziorski, Exec.Dir.
Founded: 1967. **Local.** Works through education, research and advocacy to improve the quality of life for children and adults with mental retardation and their families; and works to prevent both the causes and effects of mental retardation. **Affiliated With:** Arc of the United States.

9974 ■ Arthritis Foundation, Michigan Chapter
1050 Wilshire Dr., Ste.302
Troy, MI 48084-1564
Ph: (248)649-2891
Fax: (248)649-2895
Free: (800)968-3030
E-mail: info.mi@arthritis.org
URL: http://www.arthritis.org/communities/Chapters/Chapter.asp?chapid=29
Contact: Jo Swaney, Exec.Asst.
Founded: 1948. **Members:** 16,000. **Membership Dues:** individual, $25 (annual). **Staff:** 16. **Budget:** $3,160,928. **State.** Works to improve lives through leadership in the prevention, control, and cure of arthritis and related diseases. **Affiliated With:** Arthritis Foundation. **Publications:** *Arthritis Today*, bimonthly. Magazine. **Price:** included in membership dues; $12.95 /year for nonmembers. **Advertising:** accepted. Alternate Formats: online • *Spectrum*, quarterly. Newsletter. **Conventions/Meetings:** bimonthly board meeting • annual meeting.

9975 ■ Association of Certified Fraud Examiners, Southeast Michigan Area Chapter, No. 37 (SEMCACFE)
PO Box 4336
Troy, MI 48099-4336
Ph: (248)895-8434
E-mail: membership@semcacfe.org
URL: http://www.semcacfe.org
Contact: Dan Murdock, Pres.
Members: 230. **Membership Dues:** certified, $50 (annual) • associate, $55 (annual) • affiliate, $55 (annual) • student, $25 (annual) • retiree/government employee, $35 (annual). **Local Groups:** 90. **Local.** Auditors, accountants, fraud investigators, loss prevention specialists, law enforcement officers, attorneys, educators, criminologists, document examiners. Strives to fight white-collar crime throughout the world. Seeks to educate and train qualified individuals in the highly specialized aspects of detecting, investigating and deterring fraud. **Libraries: Type:** reference. **Holdings:** books, reports, video recordings. **Subjects:** fraud issues, investigation. **Affiliated With:** Association of Certified Fraud Examiners. **Publications:** *The Examiner*. Newsletter. **Advertising:** accepted. Alternate Formats: online. **Conventions/Meetings:** monthly meeting, with speakers - September through June.

9976 ■ Association for Computing Machinery, Walsh College
c/o Don Gottwald
PO Box 7006
3838 Livernois Rd.
Troy, MI 48007-7006
Ph: (810)689-8282
Fax: (810)689-6178
Free: (800)925-7401
E-mail: tmlahuis@yahoo.com
URL: http://www.walshcollege.edu
Local. Affiliated With: Association for Computing Machinery.

9977 ■ Barnard Elementary School Parent Teacher Organization
3601 Forge Dr.
Troy, MI 48083
Ph: (248)823-4300
URL: http://barnard.troy.k12.mi.us/web/index.html
Contact: Vera Rettberg, Pres.
Membership Dues: $10 (annual). **Local.**

9978 ■ Boys and Girls Club of Troy
4571 John R
Troy, MI 48085
Ph: (248)689-1687
URL: http://www.bgctroy.org
Contact: Steven Toth, Exec.Dir.
Local.

9979 ■ Business Marketing Association, Detroit Chapter
c/o Roland R. Kracoe, Pres.
Kracoe, Szykula & Townsend
2950 W Square Lake Rd., Ste.207
Troy, MI 48098
Ph: (248)641-7500
Fax: (248)641-4779
URL: National Affiliate–www.marketing.org
Contact: Roland R. Kracoe, Pres.
Membership Dues: $40. **Local.** Promotes the development of business-to-business marketing and communications professionals through education, training and networking. **Affiliated With:** Business Marketing Association. **Conventions/Meetings:** monthly meeting - every 3rd Thursday of the month.

9980 ■ D. Augustus Straker Bar Association
c/o Erika Akinyemi, Pres.
PO Box 1898
Troy, MI 48099-1898
Ph: (248)351-3000
E-mail: gardnerjr5@aol.com
URL: http://www.michbar.org/localbars/straker
Contact: Erika Akinyemi, Pres.
Founded: 1990. **Membership Dues:** regular, $50 (annual) • associate, $15 (annual) • continuing, $75 (annual). **Local. Affiliated With:** National Bar Association.

9981 ■ DAMA-Michigan Chapter
c/o John Mieczkowski, EDS
5555 New King St.
MS 4A
Troy, MI 48098
E-mail: info@dama-michigan.org
URL: http://www.dama-michigan.org
Contact: Sidney L. Stoffer, Contact
Founded: 2001. **Members:** 150. **State. Publications:** *DAMA Michigan Bits & Bytes*, quarterly. Newsletter. Contains articles and announcements.

9982 ■ Detroit Auto Dealers Association
c/o Rod Alberts, Exec.Dir.
1900 W Big Beaver Rd.
Troy, MI 48084
Ph: (248)643-0250
Fax: (248)643-8788
E-mail: info@dada.org
URL: http://www.dada.org
Contact: Rod Alberts, Exec.Dir.
Founded: 1908. **Members:** 240. **Local.** Automobile dealers. Represents members' interests before legislative and industrial bodies; conducts educational

programs; facilitates communication among members. **Affiliated With:** National Automobile Dealers Association. **Also Known As:** (1999) North American International Auto Show. **Publications:** *Show Talk*, September through February. Newsletter. **Conventions/Meetings:** annual International Auto Show.

9983 ■ Detroit Chapter of the Society of Financial Service Professionals
c/o Kristine M. Wolfe, Exec.Dir.
3331 W Big Beaver Rd., Ste.104
Troy, MI 48084
Ph: (248)643-9313
Fax: (248)643-9313
E-mail: gdalu@globalbiz.net
URL: http://www.sfsp.net/Detroit
Contact: Kristine M. Wolfe, Exec.Dir.
Local. Represents the interests of financial advisers. Fosters the development of professional responsibility. Helps clients achieve their personal and business-related financial goals. **Affiliated With:** Society of Financial Service Professionals.

9984 ■ Detroit Guild of the Catholic Medical Association (DGCMA)
PO Box 1932
Troy, MI 48099
Ph: (248)879-8166
E-mail: dgcma@attglobal.net
URL: http://www.dgcma.org
Contact: John Damiani DO, Pres.
Local. Seeks to uphold the principles of the Catholic faith in the science and practice of medicine. **Affiliated With:** Catholic Medical Association.

9985 ■ Detroit Organization Network
c/o Dennis Roblee
671 E Big Beaver Rd., Ste.207
Troy, MI 48083-1422
Ph: (248)740-2280
Fax: (248)740-2779
E-mail: manoni@metadynamics.biz
URL: http://www.metadynamics.biz
Contact: Michelle Manoni, Office Mgr.
Local. Affiliated With: Organization Development Network.

9986 ■ East Central Michigan Society for Healthcare Engineering (ECMSHE)
c/o Louis M. Poineau, CHFM, Pres.
Beaumont Services Co., L.L.C.
850 Stephenson Hwy., Ste.615
Troy, MI 48083
Ph: (248)837-1634
Fax: (248)733-1568
E-mail: lpoineau@bsc.rscservices.com
URL: National Affiliate–www.ashe.org
Contact: Louis M. Poineau CHFM, Pres.
Local. Promotes better patient care by encouraging members to develop their knowledge and increase their competence in the field of facilities management. Cooperates with hospitals and allied associations in matters pertaining to facilities management. **Affiliated With:** American Society for Healthcare Engineering of the American Hospital Association.

9987 ■ East Michigan District of Precision Metalforming Association
c/o Judy Major, Administrator
Dallas Indus., Inc.
103 Park St.
Troy, MI 48083
Ph: (248)583-9400
Fax: (248)583-9402
E-mail: judym@dallasindustries.com
URL: http://emichigan.pma.org
Contact: Judy Major, Administrator
Local. Promotes and safeguards the interests of the metalforming industry. Conducts technical and educational programs. Provides legislative and regulatory assistance to members. **Affiliated With:** Precision Metalforming Association.

9988 ■ Exchange Club of Detroit
c/o Leo Brennan
2359 Livernois
Troy, MI 48083
Ph: (248)362-3131
Fax: (248)362-2355
E-mail: info@exchangedetroit.org
URL: http://www.exchangedetroit.org
Contact: John Schober, Pres.
Local.

9989 ■ Financial and Estate Planning Council of Metro Detroit
c/o Kristine M. Wolfe, Administrator
3331 W Big Beaver Rd., Ste.104
Troy, MI 48084
Ph: (248)643-9313
Fax: (248)643-0455
E-mail: admin@metrodetroitfepc.org
URL: National Affiliate–councils.naepc.org
Contact: Thomas H. Bergh JD, Pres.
Local. Promotes cooperative efforts among various professionals engaged in the business of financial and estate planning. Engages in study, discussions, meetings and other activities with the purpose of rendering better service to clients. Fosters an understanding of the roles and relationships among the professions having to do with estate planning. Promotes an understanding of financial and estate planning matters with the public. **Affiliated With:** National Association of Estate Planners and Councils.

9990 ■ Greater Ann Arbor Society for Human Resource Management (GAASHRM)
c/o Lexington Computer Services
1786 Lexington Dr.
Troy, MI 48084
E-mail: robin@mrannarbor.com
URL: http://www.gaashrm.org
Contact: Robin Baun, Pres.
Local. Represents the interests of human resource and industrial relations professionals and executives. Promotes the advancement of human resource management.

9991 ■ Hearing Loss Association of America, Michigan
c/o Janet Haines, Pres.
PO Box 4808
Troy, MI 48099-4808
E-mail: jhaines@mi-shhh.org
URL: National Affiliate–www.hearingloss.org
Contact: Janet Haines, Pres.
State. Promotes understanding of the nature, causes, complications and remedies of hearing loss. Raises public awareness of the special needs of people who are hard of hearing through information, education, advocacy and support. **Affiliated With:** Hearing Loss Association of America.

9992 ■ Information Systems Audit and Control Association, Detroit Chapter
PO Box 1317
Troy, MI 48099-1317
Ph: (248)447-2600
E-mail: patricia.earl-cole@lafarge-na.com
URL: http://www.isaca-det.org
Contact: Patti Earl-Cole, Pres.
Local. Affiliated With: Information Systems Audit and Control Association and Foundation.

9993 ■ Master Insulation Association of Greater Detroit
c/o Joe Wilson
1360 Wrenwood Dr.
Troy, MI 48084
Ph: (248)644-7774
Fax: (248)644-6578
URL: National Affiliate–www.insulation.org
Contact: Joe Wilson, Treas.
Local. Affiliated With: National Insulation Association.

9994 ■ Metropolitan Consolidated Association of Realtors
2125 Butterfield Rd., Ste.100
Troy, MI 48084
Ph: (248)879-5730
Fax: (248)879-8280
E-mail: walt@mcar.com
URL: http://www.mcaronline.com
Contact: Walt Baczkowski Jr., CEO
Local. Strives to develop real estate business practices. Advocates the right to own, use and transfer real property. Provides a facility for professional development, research and exchange of information among members. **Affiliated With:** National Association of Realtors.

9995 ■ Metropolitan Detroit Antique Bottle Club
c/o Bruce Heckman, VP
2725 Creek Bend Rd.
Troy, MI 48098
Ph: (586)219-9980
E-mail: bottlemike@wowway.com
URL: National Affiliate–www.fohbc.com
Contact: Michael Brodzik, Pres.
Local. Affiliated With: Federation of Historical Bottle Collectors.

9996 ■ Michigan Association of Certified Public Accountants (MACPA)
PO Box 5068
Troy, MI 48007-5068
Ph: (248)267-3700
Fax: (248)267-3737
Free: (888)877-4CPE
E-mail: macpa@michcpa.org
URL: http://www.michcpa.org
Contact: Peggy A. Dzierzawski CAE, Pres./CEO
State.

9997 ■ Michigan Detroit Area Woodturners
c/o Greg Smith, Pres.
3232 Essex Dr.
Troy, MI 48084
Ph: (248)649-3565
E-mail: info@detroitareawoodturners.org
URL: http://www.detroitareawoodturners.org
Contact: Greg Smith, Pres.
Membership Dues: individual, $20 (annual) • family, $25 (annual). **Local. Affiliated With:** American Association of Woodturners.

9998 ■ Michigan Metro Girl Scout Council
575 E Big Beaver Rd.
Troy, MI 48083-1398
Ph: (248)619-0395
Fax: (248)619-0396
E-mail: info@hypertek.net
URL: http://www.hypertek.net/design/portfolio/mmgsc/
Contact: Arlene M. Robinson, Exec.Dir.
State. Provides leadership and cultural opportunities for more than 39,000 girls in most of Wayne and Oakland Counties in MI. Helps cultivate values, social conscience, and self-esteem in young girls, while also teaching them critical life skills that will enable them to succeed as adults. Girls discover fun, friendship, and power of girls together.

9999 ■ Michigan Speech Coaches
c/o Bette Kashi
480 Serenity Ct.
Troy, MI 48098-1775
Ph: (248)879-8998 (517)663-0970
Fax: (248)828-0655
URL: http://www.mscionline.org/index.php
Contact: Bette Kashi, Contact
Members: 8. **Membership Dues:** regular, $10 (annual) • retiree and student, $5 (annual). **State Groups:** 1. **State.** Current or retired speech coaches interested in promoting better speech activities in MI. **Awards:** Debate Grant. **Frequency:** annual. **Type:** monetary. **Recipient:** based on need and skill by individual who wishes to study at the summer debate institute. **Affiliated With:** Michigan Interscholastic

Forensic Association. **Publications:** *EKOTA Journal*, annual. **Price:** $3.00/members; available to members only. **Circulation:** 200. **Advertising:** accepted. Alternate Formats: CD-ROM. **Conventions/Meetings:** annual Mackinac Spring Conference - Mackinac Island, MI • annual meeting.

10000 ■ Michigan Wheelchair Athletic Association (MWAA)
c/o Diane Winterstein, Games Dir.
PO Box 1455
Troy, MI 48099
Ph: (586)979-8253
E-mail: dianecrash@yahoo.com
URL: http://www.miwheelchairathleticassociation.org
Contact: Diane Winterstein, Games Dir.

State. **Affiliated With:** Wheelchair Sports, USA.

10001 ■ NAIFA Southeast Michigan
3331 W. Big Beaver S-104
Troy, MI 48084
Ph: (248)643-9313
Fax: (248)643-0455
E-mail: gdalu@globalbiz.net
Contact: Eileen Penn, Exec.Dir.

Formerly: (2003) Greater Detroit Association of Life Underwriters.

10002 ■ National Association of Fleet Administrators, Michigan Chapter
c/o Mr. John Rhaesa, Chm.
Bio-Serv Corp.
PO Box 309
Troy, MI 48099-0309
Ph: (248)588-1005
Fax: (248)585-5518
E-mail: jarhaesa@roseexterminator.com
URL: National Affiliate–www.nafa.org
Contact: Mr. John Rhaesa, Chm.

State. Promotes the professional management of vehicles through education, government and industry relations and services to members. **Affiliated With:** National Association of Fleet Administrators.

10003 ■ National Society of Professional Insurance Investigators, Michigan Chapter
c/o Kurt D. Meyer, Pres.
Gregory & Meyer, P.C.
340 E Big Beaver Rd., Ste.520
Troy, MI 48083
Ph: (248)689-3920
Fax: (248)689-4560
URL: National Affiliate–www.nspii.com
Contact: Kurt D. Meyer, Pres.

State.

10004 ■ National Spa and Pool Institute Michigan Chapter
Professional Pool Care
1117 Badder Dr.
Troy, MI 48083-2861
Ph: (248)585-2656
Fax: (248)585-9624
URL: National Affiliate–www.nspi.org
Contact: Jim Norman, Contact

State. **Affiliated With:** Association of Pool and Spa Professionals.

10005 ■ Payments Authority
1301 W Long Lake Rd., Ste.360
Troy, MI 48098
Ph: (248)952-5800
Fax: (248)952-5820
E-mail: info@thepaymentauthority.org
URL: http://www.thepaymentsauthority.org
Contact: Amy Smith, Pres./CEO

Local. Promotes the development of electronic solutions to improve payments systems. **Affiliated With:** NACHA: The Electronic Payments Association.

10006 ■ Project Management Institute, Great Lakes Chapter (PMIGLC)
PO Box 35
Troy, MI 48099-0035
Ph: (313)621-4805
E-mail: president@pmiglc.org
URL: http://www.pmiglc.org
Contact: Suketu Nagrecha PMP, Pres.

Local. Aims to advance the methods of project management. Supports this objective by: fostering recognition by its members of the need for professionalism in project management; providing a forum for the free exchange of project management issues, problems, solutions and applications; developing and disseminating common PM terminology and techniques; providing an interface between users and suppliers of PM related hardware, software and service; providing guidelines and instructions leading to PMP Certification and career opportunities in project management; and promoting and facilitating business relationships with regional industries and centers of education. **Affiliated With:** Project Management Institute.

10007 ■ Right to Life-Lifespan - Oakland Chapter
1637 W Big Beaver, Ste.G
Troy, MI 48084-3540
Ph: (248)816-1546
Fax: (248)816-9066
E-mail: oakmac@rtl-lifespan.org
URL: http://www.ring.com/nprofit/lifespan
Contact: Irene Tharp, Dir.

Local.

10008 ■ Risk and Insurance Management Society, Detroit Chapter
c/o Michael E. Thoits
Kemp, Klein, Umphrey and Endelman
201 W Big Beaver, Ste.600
Troy, MI 48084
Ph: (248)740-5678
Fax: (248)528-5129
E-mail: me.thoits@kkue.com
URL: http://detroit.rims.org
Contact: Michael E. Thoits, Contact

Local. Seeks to promote the discipline of risk management and enhance the image of professional risk managers. Fosters the educational and professional development of risk managers and others involved in the risk management and insurance industry. **Affiliated With:** Risk and Insurance Management Society.

10009 ■ Sheet Metal and Air Conditioning Contractors National Association Metropolitan Detroit Chapter
3221 W Big Beaver Rd., Ste.305
Troy, MI 48084-2896
Ph: (248)649-5450
Fax: (248)649-2024
E-mail: smacnad@bignet.net
URL: http://www.smacna.org/detroit

Local. Ventilating, air handling, warm air heating, architectural and industrial sheet metal, kitchen equipment, testing and balancing, siding, and decking and specialty fabrication contractors. **Affiliated With:** Sheet Metal and Air Conditioning Contractors' National Association.

10010 ■ Society of Consumer Affairs Professionals in Business, Great Lakes Chapter
c/o Judy Degenfelder
The Dako Gp.
2966 Indus. Row
Troy, MI 48084
Ph: (248)655-0100
Fax: (248)655-0101
E-mail: greatlakes@socap.org
URL: http://www.socapgreatlakes.org
Contact: Ms. Judy Degenfender, Pres.

Members: 98. **Membership Dues:** regular, $295 (annual). **For-Profit**. **Regional**. **Awards:** Esther K. Shapiro Award. **Frequency:** annual. **Type:** recognition. **Recipient:** for contributions to consumer affairs within Great Lakes region. **Affiliated With:** Society of Consumer Affairs Professionals in Business.

10011 ■ Trout Unlimited - Paul H. Young Chapter
c/o Bob Thorsen, Pres.
840 W Long Lake Rd., Ste.200
Troy, MI 48098
Ph: (248)267-3277
E-mail: bthorsen@paulyoungtu.org
URL: http://www.paulyoungtu.org
Contact: Bob Thorsen, Pres.

Founded: 1959. **Local**.

10012 ■ Troy Chamber of Commerce
4555 Investment Dr., 3rd Fl., Ste.300
Troy, MI 48098-6338
Ph: (248)641-8151
Fax: (248)641-0545
E-mail: theteam@troychamber.com
URL: http://www.troychamber.com
Contact: Michele Hodges, Pres.

Membership Dues: Troy-based (exclusive, elite, enhanced, essential), $265-$2,440 (annual) • non-Troy (exclusive, elite, enhanced, essential), $350-$2,440 (annual). **Local**. **Committees:** Ambassadors; Best of Troy; Economic Development; FUNraisers; Hotel; Internettroy; Networking/Referrals. **Roundtables:** Building Owners and Managers. **Publications:** *Connection*. Newsletter.

10013 ■ Troy Community Foundation
1120 E Long Lake, Ste.250
Troy, MI 48085
Ph: (248)740-7600
E-mail: tomkaszubski@hotmail.com
URL: http://www.communityfoundationoftroy.org
Contact: Thomas Kaszubski, Pres.

Founded: 1995. **Local**.

10014 ■ Troy Special Services Parent Teacher Organization (TSS-PTO)
4420 Livernois
Troy, MI 48098
Ph: (248)823-4000
E-mail: members@tss-pto.org
URL: http://www.tss-pto.org
Contact: Natalie Luyckx, Pres.

Founded: 2001. **Members:** 100. **Budget:** $3,000. **Local**. Parents, teachers and students who have or are receiving special education in the Troy School District. Promotes the welfare of students with special needs and encourages public involvement. **Libraries:** **Type:** lending. **Publications:** *TSS-PTO Times*, monthly. Newsletter. **Price:** free. **Circulation:** 1,200. **Conventions/Meetings:** quarterly meeting.

Trufant

10015 ■ Trufant Area Chamber of Commerce
PO Box 129
Trufant, MI 49347-0129
Ph: (616)984-2555 (616)984-2543
Fax: (616)984-6311
Contact: Dean Jensen, Pres.

Founded: 1978. **Members:** 75. **Membership Dues:** $10. **For-Profit**. **Local**. Promotes community development.

Tustin

10016 ■ American Chesapeake Club, Michigan
c/o Carole Bomberger
14775 23 Mile Rd.
Tustin, MI 49688-8589

Ph: (616)775-6083
E-mail: baydame@netonecom.net
URL: National Affiliate–www.amchessieclub.org
Contact: Carole Bomberger, Contact
State. Affiliated With: American Chesapeake Club.

10017 ■ Michigan National Wild Turkey Federation, Three Corners Habitat Chapter
20811 21 Mile Rd.
Tustin, MI 49688
Ph: (231)829-3047
URL: http://www.mi-nwtf.org/three_corners.htm
Contact: Dean Molner, Pres.
Local.

10018 ■ Trout Unlimited - Pine River Chapter
c/o Patrick Kochanny
23297 Mackinaw Trl.
Tustin, MI 49688
Ph: (231)775-9717
E-mail: pkochanny@netonecom.net
URL: http://www.tu.org
Contact: Patrick Kochanny, Pres.
Local.

Union City

10019 ■ American Legion, Union City Post 196
1392 Cherokee Dr.
Union City, MI 49094
Ph: (517)371-4720
Fax: (517)371-2401
URL: National Affiliate–www.legion.org
Local. Affiliated With: American Legion.

10020 ■ Athens-Union City Lions Club
c/o Ronna Steel, Pres.
422 St. Joseph St.
Union City, MI 49094
Ph: (517)741-5331 (517)741-7432
URL: http://www.lionsdistrict11b1.org/lc_athens_union_city.htm
Contact: Ronna Steel, Pres.
Local. Affiliated With: Lions Clubs International.

Union Lake

10021 ■ National Speleological Society, Michigan Interlakes Grotto (MIG)
PO Box 218
Union Lake, MI 48387
Ph: (616)560-7955
E-mail: devriesj@aol.com
URL: http://www.caves.org/grotto/mig
Contact: Jean DeVries, Contact
Local. Seeks to study, explore and conserve cave and karst resources. Protects access to caves and promotes responsible caving. Encourages responsible management of caves and their unique environments. **Affiliated With:** National Speleological Society.

Union Pier

10022 ■ New Buffalo Lions Club
PO Box 332
Union Pier, MI 49129
E-mail: brycor@myvine.com
URL: http://www.newbuffalolions.org
Local. Affiliated With: Lions Clubs International.

Unionville

10023 ■ American Legion, Gateway Post 421
2690 Cass St.
Unionville, MI 48767
Ph: (517)371-4720
Fax: (517)371-2401
URL: National Affiliate–www.legion.org
Local. Affiliated With: American Legion.

10024 ■ Fish Point Wildlife Association
c/o Stephen G. Karas
7750 Ringle Rd.
Unionville, MI 48767-9488
Ph: (989)674-2511
Local.

10025 ■ Gateway Sportsmen's Club
4126 Bay City
Unionville, MI 48767
Ph: (989)823-0126
E-mail: johnandmomma@tps.net
URL: National Affiliate–www.mynssa.com
Local. Affiliated With: National Skeet Shooting Association.

University Center

10026 ■ Association for Computing Machinery, Saginaw Valley State University (SVSU ACM)
c/o Prof. Moe Bidgoli
Cmpt. Sci. and Info. Systems Dept.
Coll. of Sci., Engg. and Tech.
7400 Bay Rd.
University Center, MI 48710
Ph: (989)964-4097
Fax: (989)964-4097
E-mail: acm-officers@acm.svsu.edu
URL: http://acm.svsu.edu
Contact: Mathew Slack, Pres.
Members: 35. **Membership Dues:** full, $10 (annual). **Local.** Biological, medical, behavioral, and computer scientists; hospital administrators; programmers and others interested in application of computer methods to biological, behavioral, and medical problems. Stimulates understanding of the use and potential of computers in the biosciences. **Affiliated With:** Association for Computing Machinery.

10027 ■ Michigan Association of Campus Law Enforcement Administrators
c/o Craig T. Maxwell, Pres.
Saginaw Valley State Univ.
7400 Bay Rd.
University Center, MI 48710
Ph: (989)964-4141
Fax: (989)790-0046
E-mail: maxwell@svsu.edu
URL: National Affiliate–www.iaclea.org
Contact: Craig T. Maxwell, Pres.
State. Affiliated With: International Association of Campus Law Enforcement Administrators.

10028 ■ Michigan Mathematical Association of Two-Year Colleges (MichMATYC)
c/o Phoebe Lutz, Pres.
1961 Delta Rd., G205
University Center, MI 48710
Ph: (989)686-9761
E-mail: pglutz@delta.edu
URL: http://www.michmatyc.org
Contact: Phoebe Lutz, Pres.
State. Promotes and increases awareness of the role of two-year colleges in mathematics education. Provides a forum for the improvement of mathematics instruction in the first two years of college. Provides professional development opportunities for educators interested in the first two years of collegiate mathematics instruction. **Affiliated With:** American Mathematical Association of Two-Year Colleges.

10029 ■ Michigan Student Financial Aid Association (MSFAA)
c/o Kim Donat, Pres.
Delta Coll.
1961 Delta Rd.
University Center, MI 48710
Ph: (989)686-9302
E-mail: kimdonat@delta.edu
URL: http://www.msfaa.org
Contact: Kim Donat, Pres.
State. Represents the interests and needs of students, faculties and other persons involved in student financial aid. Promotes student aid legislation, regulatory analysis and professional development of financial aid legislators. Seeks to improve activities relating to the quality and improvement of student financial assistance in Higher Education institutions. **Affiliated With:** National Association of Student Financial Aid Administrators.

10030 ■ Phi Theta Kappa, Xi Delta Chapter - Delta College
c/o David Baskind
1961 Delta Dr.
University Center, MI 48710
Ph: (989)686-9000
E-mail: debaskin@alpha.delta.edu
URL: http://www.ptk.org/directories/chapters/MI/255-1.htm
Contact: David Baskind, Advisor
Local.

10031 ■ Psi Chi, National Honor Society in Psychology - Saginaw Valley State University
c/o Dept. of Psychology
7400 Bay Rd.
University Center, MI 48710-0001
Ph: (989)964-4492 (989)964-4351
Fax: (989)964-7656
E-mail: jslynch@svsu.edu
URL: http://www.psichi.org/chapters/info.asp?chapter_id=578
Contact: Julie Lynch PhD, Advisor
Local.

10032 ■ Society of Manufacturing Engineers - Delta College U185
1961 Delta Rd.
University Center, MI 48710
Ph: (989)686-9271
E-mail: rlmuelle@delta.edu
URL: National Affiliate–www.sme.org
Contact: Rodney Mueller, Contact
Local. Advances manufacturing knowledge to gain competitive advantage. Improves skills and manufacturing solutions for the growth of economy. Provides resources and opportunities for manufacturing professionals.

Utica

10033 ■ American Legion, Michigan Post 351
c/o Victor I. Rieck
46146 Cass Ave.
Utica, MI 48317
Ph: (517)371-4720
Fax: (517)371-2401
URL: National Affiliate–www.legion.org
Contact: Victor I. Rieck, Contact
Local. Affiliated With: American Legion.

10034 ■ American Legion, Romeo Post 109
7021 Greeley St.
Utica, MI 48317
Ph: (517)371-4720
Fax: (517)371-2401
URL: National Affiliate–www.legion.org
Local. Affiliated With: American Legion.

10035 ■ International Union, United Automobile, Aerospace and Agricultural Implement Workers of America, AFL-CIO - Local Union 2280
45116 Cass Ave.
Utica, MI 48317
Ph: (586)731-0010
Fax: (586)731-1835
URL: http://www.uaw2280.com
Contact: Frank Turoski, Pres.
Members: 2,171. **Local.** AFL-CIO. **Affiliated With:** International Union, United Automobile, Aerospace and Agricultural Implement Workers of America.

10036 ■ International Union, United Automobile, Aerospace and Agricultural Implement Workers of America, AFL-CIO - Mt. Clemens-Highland Park Local Union 400
50595 Mound Rd.
Utica, MI 48317-1319
Ph: (586)731-6270
URL: http://www.uawlocal400.com
Contact: Anthony Pinelli, Pres.
Members: 6,903. **Local.** AFL-CIO. **Affiliated With:** International Union, United Automobile, Aerospace and Agricultural Implement Workers of America.

10037 ■ National Active and Retired Federal Employees Association - Rochester 2179
45662 Custer
Utica, MI 48317-5708
Ph: (810)739-3746
URL: National Affiliate–www.narfe.org
Contact: Edward B. Leland, Contact
Local. Protects the retirement future of employees through education. Informs members on issues affecting the retirement. **Affiliated With:** National Association of Retired Federal Employees.

10038 ■ Utica Police Officers Association
c/o Douglas Julien
7550 Auburn Rd.
Utica, MI 48317-5216
Ph: (586)731-2345
Fax: (586)731-2530
URL: http://www.cityofutica.org
Local.

Vanderbilt

10039 ■ Trout Unlimited - Headwaters Chapter (TU)
c/o John Walters, Pres.
6269 Mt. Vernon Hills Dr.
Vanderbilt, MI 49795-9785
Ph: (989)983-4404
E-mail: john.walters@weyerhaeuser.com
URL: http://www.headwaterstu.org
Contact: John Walters, Pres.
Local.

Vassar

10040 ■ Cass River Habitat for Humanity (CRHFH)
PO Box 86
Vassar, MI 48768
Ph: (989)823-8711
Fax: (989)823-3733
URL: http://www.geocities.com/picketfence/garden/4005
Founded: 1995. **Local. Affiliated With:** Habitat for Humanity International.

10041 ■ Korean War Veterans Association, Mid-Michigan Chapter
c/o Clarence E. Millikin
911 Waterman Rd.
Vassar, MI 48768-9456
Ph: (989)823-7048
URL: National Affiliate–www.kwva.org
Contact: Clarence E. Millikin, Contact
Local. Affiliated With: Korean War Veterans Association.

10042 ■ Michigan Skeet Association
397 Div. St.
Vassar, MI 48768
Ph: (989)823-8397
E-mail: khwarner@charter.net
URL: National Affiliate–www.mynssa.com
State. Affiliated With: National Skeet Shooting Association.

10043 ■ Vassar Lions Club
c/o Charles Partridge, Sec.
7579 Bray Rd.
Vassar, MI 48768
Ph: (989)577-2806
E-mail: cpartridge@speednetllc.com
URL: http://www.geocities.com/dist11d1
Contact: Charles Partridge, Sec.
Local. Affiliated With: Lions Clubs International.

Vermontville

10044 ■ American Legion, Childs-Demeray Post 222
PO Box 188
Vermontville, MI 49096
Ph: (517)371-4720
Fax: (517)371-2401
URL: National Affiliate–www.legion.org
Local. Affiliated With: American Legion.

10045 ■ Michigan National Wild Turkey Federation, Grand River Longbeards
8228 W Mt. Hope Hwy.
Vermontville, MI 49096
Ph: (517)566-4007
URL: http://www.mi-nwtf.org/grand_river.htm
Contact: Joe Vaillancourt, Pres.
Local.

10046 ■ Vermontville Lions Club
c/o Bill Martin, Pres.
9914 Valley Hwy.
Vermontville, MI 49096-9509
Ph: (517)726-1254
URL: http://www.district11c2.org
Contact: Bill Martin, Pres.
Local. Affiliated With: Lions Clubs International.

Vestaburg

10047 ■ Vestaburg Lions Club
Box 179
Vestaburg, MI 48891
E-mail: sandye@firstbank-corp.com
URL: http://lions.silverthorn.biz/11-e1
Contact: Ken Nixon, Pres.
Local. Affiliated With: Lions Clubs International.

Vicksburg

10048 ■ American Legion, Roy Canavan Post 213
PO Box 21
Vicksburg, MI 49097
Ph: (517)371-4720
Fax: (517)371-2401
URL: National Affiliate–www.legion.org
Local. Affiliated With: American Legion.

10049 ■ Dunes-Kalamazoo Orchid Society
c/o John G. Talpa
11437 S 34th St.
Vicksburg, MI 49097-9523
Ph: (269)649-4340
E-mail: jtcompany@bizloop.com
Local. Professional growers, botanists, hobbyists, and others interested in extending the knowledge, production, use, and appreciation of orchids. **Affiliated With:** American Orchid Society.

10050 ■ Michigan National Wild Turkey Federation, Southwestern Michigan Chapter
16431 S 24th St.
Vicksburg, MI 49097
Ph: (616)649-0384
URL: http://www.mi-nwtf.org/Southwest.htm
Contact: Gary Vandyke, Pres.
Local.

10051 ■ Tasters Guild International - Kalamazoo, Chapter No. 038
11898 Highview Shores
Vicksburg, MI 49097-8349
Ph: (269)649-0616
E-mail: tastersguildkzoo@aol.com
URL: National Affiliate–www.tastersguild.com
Contact: John Wilks, Contact
Local. Aims to educate consumers and spread the word of responsible wine and food consumption. Provides opportunity to encounter the best in wine and culinary delights. **Affiliated With:** Tasters Guild International.

Wakefield

10052 ■ American Legion, Geroux Post 11
605 River St.
Wakefield, MI 49968
Ph: (517)371-4720
Fax: (517)371-2401
URL: National Affiliate–www.legion.org
Local. Affiliated With: American Legion.

Walker

10053 ■ National Association of Rocketry - Southwest Michigan Association of Spacemodeling Hobbyists (SMASH)
c/o Kelo Waivio
1797 Awixa NW
Walker, MI 49544
Ph: (616)735-4045
E-mail: kelo9@comcast.net
URL: http://www.homestead.com/smashNAR500
Contact: Kelo Waivio, Contact
Local.

Walled Lake

10054 ■ Compassionate Friends - Lakes Area Chapter
1601 High Pointe Dr.
Walled Lake, MI 48390
Ph: (248)960-0792
E-mail: gregoryk@bignet.net
URL: http://www.lakesareatcf.org
Contact: Dorothy Gregory, Chapter Leader
Local.

10055 ■ Detroit Gun Club
2775 Oakley Park Rd.
Walled Lake, MI 48390
Ph: (248)624-9647
Fax: (248)624-2995
E-mail: scottdgc@msn.com
URL: National Affiliate–www.mynssa.com
Local. Affiliated With: National Skeet Shooting Association.

10056 ■ Lakes Area Chamber of Commerce (LACC)
305 N Pontiac Trail, Ste.B
Walled Lake, MI 48390-3479
Ph: (248)624-2826
Fax: (248)624-2892
E-mail: info@lakesareachamber.com
URL: http://www.lakesareachamber.com
Contact: Jo Louise Alley, Exec.Dir.
Founded: 1962. **Members:** 387. **Staff:** 2. **Budget:** $105,000. **Local.** Promotes business and community development in the townships of Commerce, Waterford, and White Lake, cities of Walled Lake and Wixom, and village of Wolverine, MI. Sponsors golf and bowling tournaments. **Awards:** Lakes Area Chamber of Commerce Scholarship. **Frequency:** annual. **Type:** scholarship. **Recipient:** for local high school students. **Affiliated With:** U.S. Chamber of Commerce. **Formerly:** (1962) Walled Lake Chamber of Commerce. **Publications:** *Lakes Area Chamber of Commerce Membership Directory*, annual • *Today's*

Business Choice, monthly. Newsletter. **Circulation:** 475. **Advertising:** accepted. **Conventions/Meetings:** annual Taste of the Lakes - meeting (exhibits) - always November.

Warren

10057 ■ Alliance for the Mentally Ill of Macomb County
c/o Fred Bristol, Pres.
28304 Aline Dr.
Warren, MI 48093
Ph: (810)574-0124
URL: http://mi.nami.org/mac.html
Contact: Fred Bristol, Pres.
Local. Strives to improve the quality of life of children and adults with severe mental illness through support, education, research and advocacy. **Affiliated With:** National Alliance for the Mentally Ill.

10058 ■ American Federation of Government Employees, AFL-CIO - DOD Local Union 1658
c/o Dan Martin, Pres.
6501 E 11 Mile Rd., Bldg. 230, Rm. 136W
Warren, MI 48397-5000
Ph: (586)574-6102
E-mail: martind@tacom.army.mil
URL: http://home.comcast.net/~afge1658
Contact: Dan Martin, Pres.
Members: 1,461. **Local**. Federal employees including food inspectors, nurses, printers, cartographers, lawyers, police officers, census workers, OSHA inspectors, janitors, truck drivers, secretaries, artists, plumbers, immigration inspectors, scientists, doctors, cowboys, botanists, park rangers, computer programmers, foreign service workers, airplane mechanics, environmentalists, and writers. Seeks to provide good government services, while ensuring that government workers are treated fairly and with dignity. **Affiliated With:** American Federation of Government Employees.

10059 ■ American Guild of Organists, Detroit Chapter (AGO)
5405 Ten Mile Rd.
Warren, MI 48091-1587
E-mail: secretary@detroitago.org
URL: http://detroitago.org
Contact: Glenn Burdette, Sec.
Founded: 1910. **Members:** 350. **Membership Dues:** individual, $70 (annual). **Regional Groups:** 9. **State Groups:** 11. **Local Groups:** 1. **Local**. Church musicians, choir directors, organists, and lovers of organ music in metropolitan Detroit, MI. Advances the cause of organ and sacred music; enhances the professionalism and collegiality among members; and provides educational opportunities for members and the community. Conducts youth and student competitions. Sponsors concerts and choirs. **Awards: Frequency:** annual. **Type:** scholarship. **Recipient:** to 5 students who are proficient in minimum keyboard skills. **Committees:** Educational Concerns Placement; Professional Concerns; Programs. **Affiliated With:** American Guild of Organists. **Publications:** *AGO Detroit*, annual. Directory. Contains member listing of the local guild. **Price:** included in membership dues. **Circulation:** 350. **Advertising:** accepted • *The American Organist*, monthly. Journal. Contains information for organists. **Price:** $42.00 /year for nonmembers; included in membership dues. **Circulation:** 23,000. **Advertising:** accepted • *The Bombarde*, monthly. Newsletter • *The Employment of Musicians in Churches and Synagogues*. Booklet. **Price:** $5.00. **Conventions/Meetings:** biennial National Convention, includes music and organ related education (exhibits) - always even-numbered years in late June or early July • biennial Regional Convention - always odd-numbered years in late June or early July.

10060 ■ American Legion, Michigan Post 1
c/o Charles A. Learned
PO Box 92356
Warren, MI 48092
Ph: (313)883-4389
Fax: (517)371-2401
URL: National Affiliate–www.legion.org
Contact: Charles A. Learned, Contact
Local. **Affiliated With:** American Legion.

10061 ■ American Legion, Woodrow Wilson Post 347
5247 Lyons Circle S
Warren, MI 48092
Ph: (517)371-4720
Fax: (517)371-2401
URL: National Affiliate–www.legion.org
Local. **Affiliated With:** American Legion.

10062 ■ ASM International - Detroit Chapter
c/o Caryn L. Ruzich, Administrator
PO Box 1398
Warren, MI 48090-1398
Ph: (586)573-0700
Fax: (586)573-0720
E-mail: admin@asm-detroit.org
URL: http://www.asm-detroit.org
Contact: Caryn L. Ruzich, Administrator
Local. Works to advance scientific engineering, and technical knowledge, particularly with respect to the manufacture, processing, characterization, selection, understanding, use, and life cycle of metals and other engineering materials. Accomplishes through education, research and the compilation and dissemination of information that serves technical and professional needs and interest, thereby benefiting the general public. **Affiliated With:** ASM International.

10063 ■ Eastern Market Merchants Association
c/o Edward Deeb
Administrative Offices
27700 Hoover Rd., Ste.100
Warren, MI 48093
Ph: (586)393-8800
Fax: (586)393-8810
Contact: Ed Deeb, Chm.
Regional. Seeks to foster the vitality of the Eastern Market and the members by providing various programs, services, workshops, communications, benefits, promotions and public relations. Enhances the member ability to meet the needs of their customers and the area.

10064 ■ International Union of Bricklayers and Allied Craftworkers, AFL-CIO-CLC Michigan Local Union 1
21031 Ryan Rd.
Warren, MI 48091
Ph: (586)754-0888
Fax: (586)754-5889
E-mail: information@bricklayers.org
URL: http://www.bricklayers.org
Contact: Raymond Chapman, Pres./Business Mgr.
Members: 2,513. **Local**. **Affiliated With:** International Union of Bricklayers and Allied Craftworkers.

10065 ■ International Union, United Automobile, Aerospace and Agricultural Implement Workers of America, AFL-CIO - Local Union 160
28504 Lorna
Warren, MI 48092
Ph: (586)751-4474
Fax: (586)751-8496
E-mail: daryl@uawlocal160.org
URL: http://www.uawlocal160.org
Contact: Daryl L. Henson, Financial Sec.-Treas.
Members: 2,250. **Local**. Seeks for the dignity and equality of the workers. Strives to provide contractors with well-trained, productive employees. **Affiliated With:** International Union, United Automobile, Aerospace and Agricultural Implement Workers of America.

10066 ■ International Union, United Automobile, Aerospace and Agricultural Implement Workers of America, AFL-CIO - Local Union 412
2005 Tobsal Ct.
Warren, MI 48091
Ph: (586)754-2450
Fax: (586)754-1277
E-mail: bob@local412.org
URL: http://www.uawlocal412.org
Contact: Paul J. Carr, Pres.
Members: 4,464. **Local**. AFL-CIO. **Affiliated With:** International Union, United Automobile, Aerospace and Agricultural Implement Workers of America.

10067 ■ International Union, United Automobile, Aerospace and Agricultural Implement Workers of America, AFL-CIO - Local Union 909
5587 Stephens
Warren, MI 48091-5600
Ph: (586)759-4320
Fax: (586)759-5210
E-mail: ajbenchich@aol.com
URL: http://www.uawlocal909.org
Contact: Al Benchich, Pres.
Members: 1,648. **Local**. AFL-CIO. **Affiliated With:** International Union, United Automobile, Aerospace and Agricultural Implement Workers of America.

10068 ■ Macomb Chamber
31201 Chicago Rd., Ste.C-102
Chicago Plz.
Warren, MI 48093
Ph: (586)268-6430
Fax: (586)268-6397
E-mail: info@macombchamber.com
URL: http://www.macombchamber.com
Contact: Melanie D. Davis, Pres.
Local. Works to encourage the economic development of local businesses by providing information, education, and advocacy and member benefits while making partnerships and investments throughout Macomb County. **Committees:** ATHENA Awards; Executive; Golf Outing; Macomb Hall of Fame; Marketing; Nominating; Public Policy; Technology Advisory. **Formerly:** (2004) Warren - Center Line - Sterling Heights Chamber of Commerce.

10069 ■ Michigan Business and Professional Association (MBPA)
c/o Edward Deeb, Pres./CEO
27700 Hoover Rd., Ste.100
Warren, MI 48093
Ph: (586)393-8800
Fax: (586)393-8810
E-mail: info@michbusiness.org
URL: http://www.michbusiness.org
Contact: Edward Deeb, Pres./CEO
Founded: 1990. **Members:** 14,200. **Staff:** 11. **Budget:** $500,000. **State**. **Awards:** Distinguished Service Awards. **Frequency:** annual. **Type:** recognition • Outstanding Women Leadership Awards. **Frequency:** annual. **Type:** recognition. **Boards:** Minority Advisory. **Publications:** *Association Spotlight*, quarterly. Magazine. **Circulation:** 16,000. **Advertising:** accepted. **Conventions/Meetings:** annual Women's Conference - meeting.

10070 ■ Michigan Food and Beverage Association
c/o Edward Deeb, Pres.
27700 Hoover Rd., Ste.100
Warren, MI 48093
Ph: (586)393-8800
Fax: (586)393-8810
Free: (888)277-6464
E-mail: info@michbusiness.org
URL: http://www.michbusiness.org
Founded: 1987. **Members:** 3,200. **Staff:** 9. **State**. Serves as a liaison between food and beverage companies. Seeks to enhance industry communications. **Awards:** Distinguished Service Award. **Frequency:** annual. **Type:** recognition. **Formerly:** Michigan Food Council; (1984) Michigan Food

Trade Council. **Publications:** *Associations Spotlight*, quarterly. Magazine. **Circulation:** 16,000. **Advertising:** accepted • *Food-and-Beverage Newsgram*, quarterly. Newsletter • *Position Papers*, periodic. **Conventions/Meetings:** annual meeting.

10071 ■ Michigan Roofing Contractors Association (MIRCA)
3560 E 9 Mile Rd.
Warren, MI 48091
Ph: (586)759-2140
Fax: (586)759-0528
E-mail: karen.colver@smrca.org
URL: http://www.mirca.org
Contact: Karen Colver, Exec.Dir.
Founded: 1958. **Members:** 134. **Membership Dues:** contractor, $80 (annual) • associate, $200 (annual). **Staff:** 3. **Budget:** $350,000. **State**. Roofing, sheet metal and waterproofing contractors in Michigan. Represents members' interests. **Libraries: Type:** by appointment only. **Holdings:** books, periodicals, video recordings. **Affiliated With:** National Roofing Contractors Association. **Formerly:** (1995) Roofing Industry Promotion Fund. **Publications:** *Michigan Roofer*, semiannual, spring and fall. Newsletter • *MRCA Directory*, annual. **Price:** free. **Conventions/Meetings:** annual convention - always July or August.

10072 ■ Old Village Business Alliance (OVBA)
31376 Pagels
Warren, MI 48092
Ph: (586)795-3956
Contact: Kenneth DeGrandchamp, Pres.
Founded: 1994. **Local**. Businesses in the Old Village District of Warren, MI. Represents members' interests before local government.

10073 ■ Society of Manufacturing Engineers - Macomb Community College S071
Macomb Community Coll., Design Tech. R-124
Div. of Career and Tech. Educ.
14500 E Twelve Mile Rd.
Warren, MI 48093
Ph: (586)698-8903
E-mail: buhalish@macomb.edu
URL: National Affiliate–www.sme.org
Contact: Dr. Harry J. Buhalis, Professor SME Faculty Advisor Consultant
Local. Advances manufacturing knowledge to gain competitive advantage. Improves skills and manufacturing solutions for the growth of economy. Provides resources and opportunities for manufacturing professionals. **Affiliated With:** American Nature Study Society.

10074 ■ Warren Astronomical Society
PO Box 1505
Warren, MI 48090-1505
Ph: (810)447-2424
E-mail: astroblain@aol.com
URL: http://www.boonhill.net/was
Contact: Blaine McCullough, Contact
Local. Promotes the science of astronomy. Works to encourage and coordinate activities of amateur astronomical societies. Fosters observational and computational work and craftsmanship in various fields of astronomy. **Affiliated With:** Astronomical League.

10075 ■ Warren Jaycees
c/o Sharon Linsday, Pres.
PO Box 1784
Warren, MI 48090-1784
Ph: (586)704-0055
E-mail: info@warrenjaycees.org
URL: http://www.warrenjaycees.net
Contact: Sharon Linsday, Pres.
Local. Promotes leadership training through community service. Activities include a monthly general membership meeting, community Easter egg hunt, park cleanup, fund raising, partnering with city groups, zoo outings, and much more.

Washington

10076 ■ Healthcare Financial Management Association, Eastern Michigan Chapter (HFMA EMC)
c/o Susan Stokes
13064 Burningwood Dr.
Washington, MI 48094
Ph: (586)786-9532
Fax: (586)786-7396
E-mail: susan-stokes@hfmaemc.org
URL: http://www.hfmaemc.org
Contact: Susan Stokes, Contact
Regional. **Affiliated With:** Healthcare Financial Management Association.

10077 ■ National Corvette Restorers Society, Michigan Chapter (NCRS)
c/o Mr. John P. Hinckley, Chm.
68347 Copperwood Dr.
Washington, MI 48095
Ph: (586)336-9650
E-mail: snake488@aol.com
URL: http://www.michiganncrs.org
Contact: Mr. John P. Hinckley, Chm.
Founded: 1982. **Members:** 180. **Membership Dues:** $20 (annual). **Budget:** $10,000. **State Groups:** 1. **State**. Dedicated to the enjoyment, restoration, and preservation of 1953-1987 Chevrolet Corvettes. **Libraries: Type:** not open to the public. **Holdings:** 50. **Subjects:** Chevrolet Corvette. **Awards:** Top Flight. **Frequency:** annual. **Type:** recognition. **Recipient:** for originality and condition of restored or unrestored original Corvettes. **Affiliated With:** National Corvette Restorers Society. **Publications:** *Vette Signal*, quarterly. Newsletter. Includes chapter news, events and technical articles. **Price:** included in membership dues. **Circulation:** 200. **Advertising:** accepted.

10078 ■ North Macomb Sportsman Club
3231 Inwood Rd.
Washington, MI 48095
Ph: (586)752-2450
E-mail: webmaster@northmacomb.org
URL: National Affiliate–www.mynssa.com
Local. **Affiliated With:** National Skeet Shooting Association.

Waterford

10079 ■ Al-Anon/Alateen of Central Oakland County
3720 Elizabeth Lake Rd.
Waterford, MI 48328-3014
Ph: (248)706-1020
E-mail: information@oaklandafg.org
URL: http://www.oaklandafg.org
Contact: Ms. Susan Stapleton, Treas.
Founded: 1997. **Members:** 100. **Budget:** $7,500. **Languages:** English, French, German, Russian, Swedish. **Local**. For over 50 years, Al-Anon (which includes Alateen for younger members) has been offering hope and help to families and friends of alcoholics. It is estimated that each alcoholic affects the lives of at least four other people. alcoholism is truly a family disease. No matter what relationship you have with an alcoholic, whether they are still drinking or not, all who have been affected by someone else's drinking can find solutions that lead to serenity in the Al-Anon/Alateen fellowship. **Libraries: Type:** by appointment only. **Holdings:** 25; audio recordings, books. **Affiliated With:** Alateen.

10080 ■ Camp Fire USA North Oakland Council
4450 Walton Blvd., Ste.C
Waterford, MI 48329
Ph: (248)618-9050
Fax: (248)618-9052
E-mail: campfireusano@aol.com
URL: http://www.comnet.org/campfirenoc
Contact: Margie J. Williams, Exec.Dir.
Founded: 1910. **Members:** 3,000. **Membership Dues:** basic, $10 (annual). **Staff:** 3. **Budget:** $195,700. **Local**. Works to develop leadership and responsibility in youth through informal education and recreational programs. Promotes environmental awareness. **Affiliated With:** Camp Fire USA. **Formerly:** (1995) Camp Fire-North Oakland Council. **Conventions/Meetings:** annual Summer Day Camp, with outdoor education program.

10081 ■ Easter Seals Michigan
1105 N Telegraph Rd.
Waterford, MI 48328
Ph: (248)451-2900
Fax: (248)338-0095
Free: (800)75-SEALS
E-mail: esofmi@aol.com
URL: http://www.mi.easter-seals.org
Contact: Ms. Julie Dorcey, Regional Dir.
State. Works to help individuals with disabilities and special needs, and their families. Conducts programs to assist people of all ages with disabilities. Provides outpatient medical rehabilitation services. Advocates for the passage of legislation to help people with disabilities achieve independence, including the Americans with Disabilities Act (ADA). **Affiliated With:** Easter Seals.

10082 ■ Fraternal Order of Eagles, Waterford No. 2887
4761 Highland Rd.
Waterford, MI 48328
Ph: (248)673-9980 (248)673-5841
Fax: (248)673-7729
E-mail: foe2887@comcast.net
URL: http://www.foe.com/2887
Contact: Phil Myers, Pres.
Local. **Affiliated With:** Grand Aerie, Fraternal Order of Eagles.

10083 ■ Friends of Pontiac Lake Recreation Area
c/o Eldon Montross
7800 Gale Rd.
Waterford, MI 48327-1058
Ph: (248)666-1020
Local.

10084 ■ Huron Valley Bottle and Insulator Club (HVBIC)
c/o Shaun Kotlarsky
2475 W Walton Blvd.
Waterford, MI 48329-4435
Ph: (248)673-1650
E-mail: hvbic@clubs.insulators.com
URL: http://www.insulators.com/clubs/hvbic.htm
Contact: Shaun Kotlarsky, Contact
State. **Affiliated With:** National Insulator Association.

10085 ■ Korean War Veterans Association, Oakland, Macomb, Wayne Chapter
2884 Beacham Dr.
Waterford, MI 48329-4500
Ph: (248)334-6917
E-mail: mike_adragna@comcast.net
URL: National Affiliate–www.kwva.org
Contact: Robert C. Sharrard, Contact
Local. **Affiliated With:** Korean War Veterans Association.

10086 ■ Michigan Chapter of Association for Career and Technical Education
c/o William DiGiulio, Exec.Dir.
Oakland Schools
2111 Pontiac Lake Rd.
Waterford, MI 48328
Ph: (248)209-2020
Fax: (248)209-2024
E-mail: william.digiulio@oakland.k12.mi.us
URL: http://www.acteonline.org/about/states/MI.cfm
Contact: William DiGiulio, Exec.Dir.
State. Works to advance vocational technical education. **Affiliated With:** Association for Career and Technical Education.

10087 ■ Michigan Mountain Bike Association (MMBA)
5119 Highland Rd.
PMB 268
Waterford, MI 48327
Ph: (248)288-3753
E-mail: info@mmba.org
URL: http://www.mmba.org
Contact: Todd Scott, Exec.Dir.
State. Affiliated With: International Mountain Bicycling Association.

10088 ■ Mothers Against Drunk Driving, Oakland County
3525 Elizabeth Lake Rd., Ste.B
Waterford, MI 48328
Ph: (248)682-2220
Fax: (248)682-6392
E-mail: maddoakland@ameritech.net
URL: National Affiliate–www.madd.org
Contact: Michele Compton, Exec.Dir.
Founded: 1982. **Members:** 428. **Staff:** 5. **Budget:** $150,000. **Languages:** English, Spanish. **Local.** Victims of drunk driving crash and concerned citizens. Encourages citizen participation in working towards reform of the drunk driving problem and the prevention of underage drinking. Acts as the voice of victims of drunk driving crashes by speaking on their behalf to communities, businesses, and educational groups. **Affiliated With:** Mothers Against Drunk Driving.

10089 ■ Mudchuggers Four Wheel Drive Club
c/o Jim Salo
PO Box 300391
Waterford, MI 48330
Ph: (248)393-6198
E-mail: snoblind@mudchuggers.org
URL: http://www.mudchuggers.org
Contact: Jim Salo, Contact
Local. Affiliated With: United Four-Wheel Drive Associations.

10090 ■ North Oakland County Board of Realtors
4400 W Walton Blvd.
Waterford, MI 48329
Ph: (248)674-4080
Fax: (248)674-8112
URL: http://nocbor.com
Contact: Donald Bartus, Pres.
Local. Strives to develop real estate business practices. Advocates the right to own, use and transfer real property. Provides a facility for professional development, research and exchange of information among members. **Affiliated With:** National Association of Realtors.

10091 ■ Phi Theta Kappa, Alpha Omicron Kappa Chapter - Oakland Community College
c/o Bryan Dubin
Highland Lakes Campus
7350 Cooley Lake Rd.
Waterford, MI 48327
Ph: (248)942-3152
E-mail: bmdubin@oaklandcc.edu
URL: http://www.ptk.org/directories/chapters/MI/6493-1.htm
Contact: Bryan Dubin, Advisor
Local.

10092 ■ Pontiac-Oakland Club International, Michigan WideTrackers
c/o Kendra Klein, Membership Coor.
7065 Howell Ave.
Waterford, MI 48327
E-mail: bobnkendra@comcast.net
URL: http://www.widetrackers.com
Contact: Kendra Klein, Membership Coor.
Membership Dues: family, $18 (annual). **Local. Affiliated With:** Pontiac-Oakland Club International.

10093 ■ Saint Bernard Club of Greater Detroit
4840 Cass Elizabeth Rd.
Waterford, MI 48327-3209
Ph: (248)682-9628
E-mail: ambersandsaints@aol.com
Contact: Mr. Nick Little, Pres.
Local. Provides education and support of owners and would-be owners of Saint Bernard pure-bred dogs throughout Michigan and surrounding area. **Affiliated With:** Saint Bernard Club of America.

10094 ■ Sons of Norway, Samhold Lodge 5-473
c/o Eugene E. Steensma, Pres.
2941 Golfhill Dr.
Waterford, MI 48329-4514
Ph: (248)332-9647
E-mail: genesteensma@aol.com
URL: http://www.gloriadei.cc/son
Contact: Eugene E. Steensma, Pres.
Local. Affiliated With: Sons of Norway.

10095 ■ STARFLEET: USS Sinclair
c/o Capt. Joseph A. Sare, III, Commanding Officer
2716 Sinclair Ave.
Waterford, MI 48328
E-mail: usssinclair@region13.org
URL: http://sinclair.region13.org
Contact: Capt. Joseph A. Sare III, Commanding Officer
Local. Affiliated With: STARFLEET.

10096 ■ Waterford Township Historical Society
PO Box 300491
Waterford, MI 48330-0491
Ph: (248)623-2449
E-mail: dancerjoy@sbcglobal.net
URL: http://www.waterfordhistoricalsociety.org
Contact: Joy Smith, Pres.
Founded: 1977. **Members:** 180. **Membership Dues:** $10 (annual) • life, $75 • couple (life), $100. **Budget:** $12,000. **Local.** Waterford residents who are interested in collecting and preserving the history of Waterford for generations to come. **Libraries: Type:** open to the public. **Subjects:** history of Waterford and Oakland County. **Publications:** *Waterford Township Historical Society Newsbill*, monthly. Newsletter. Describes upcoming events, meetings, and activities. **Price:** included in membership dues. **Circulation:** 200 • Brochure, periodic. Handout that contains the history of various buildings in the area. **Conventions/Meetings:** monthly meeting - always 3rd Thursday.

Wayland

10097 ■ American Legion, Forrest Lewis Post 266
312 Plum St.
Wayland, MI 49348
Ph: (517)371-4720
Fax: (517)371-2401
URL: National Affiliate–www.legion.org
Local. Affiliated With: American Legion.

10098 ■ Paws with a Cause NH Chapter
4646 S Div.
Wayland, MI 49348
Ph: (616)877-7297
Free: (800)253-7297
URL: http://www.pawswithacause.org
Local.

Wayne

10099 ■ American Legion, Wayne Post 111
4422 S Wayne Rd.
Wayne, MI 48184
Ph: (517)371-4720
Fax: (517)371-2401
URL: National Affiliate–www.legion.org
Local. Affiliated With: American Legion.

10100 ■ Independent Order of Odd Fellows, Nankin Lodge No. 396
32975 Glenwood Rd.
Wayne, MI 48184
E-mail: nankin396@ioofmichigan.org
URL: http://www.ioofmichigan.org/lodges/396/index.html
Contact: Terry Cope, Vice Grand
Local.

10101 ■ The Senior Alliance (Area Agency on Aging 1-C in Michigan) (TSA)
3850 Second St., Ste.No. 201
Wayne, MI 48184-1755
Ph: (734)722-2830
Fax: (734)722-2836
Free: (800)815-1112
E-mail: info@tsalink.org
URL: http://www.aaa1c.org
Local.

10102 ■ Wayne Chamber of Commerce (WCC)
35122 W Michigan Ave.
Wayne, MI 48184
Ph: (734)721-0100
Fax: (734)721-3070
E-mail: gayle@waynechamber.net
URL: http://www.waynechamber.net
Contact: Gayle Rediske, Dir.
Founded: 1939. **Members:** 220. **Local.** Promotes business and community development in Wayne, MI. **Affiliated With:** U.S. Chamber of Commerce. **Publications:** Directory, annual • Newsletter, monthly. **Conventions/Meetings:** monthly luncheon.

10103 ■ Wayne County Sportsman's Club
4124 Filbert
Wayne, MI 48184
Ph: (313)941-9688
URL: National Affiliate–www.mynssa.com
Local. Affiliated With: National Skeet Shooting Association.

10104 ■ Wayne Lions Club
c/o William Depetro, Pres.
33510 Clinton St.
Wayne, MI 48184
Ph: (734)390-1970 (734)721-1947
URL: http://www.metrodetroitlions.org
Contact: William Depetro, Pres.
Local. Affiliated With: Lions Clubs International.

Webberville

10105 ■ Arabian Horse Association of Michigan (AHAM)
c/o Clara Burns
185 S Kane Rd.
Webberville, MI 48892
Ph: (517)521-3026
E-mail: scburns@arq.net
URL: http://www.miarabhorse.com
Contact: Tom Connelly, Pres.
State. Works to promote, encourage and stimulate interest in the many uses of the Arabian Horse.

10106 ■ Webberville Lions Club
c/o Norm Nack, Pres.
4791 E Columbia Rd.
Webberville, MI 48892-9220
Ph: (517)521-4838
URL: http://www.district11c2.org
Contact: Norm Nack, Pres.
Local. Affiliated With: Lions Clubs International.

Weidman

10107 ■ Humane Animal Treatment Society (HATS)
c/o Deborah Dorn
6600 W Shore Dr.
Weidman, MI 48893-8778
E-mail: hatscommittee@hatsweb.org
URL: http://www.hatsweb.org
Contact: Deborah Dorn, Contact
Local.

10108 ■ National Active and Retired Federal Employees Association - Mid-Michigan 2103
1009 N Littlefield Rd.
Weidman, MI 48893-8789
Ph: (517)644-2403
URL: National Affiliate–www.narfe.org
Contact: Robert J. Armbrustmacher, Contact
Local. Protects the retirement future of employees through education. Informs members on issues affecting the retirement. **Affiliated With:** National Association of Retired Federal Employees.

10109 ■ Weidman Lions Club
c/o Bruce Cotter, Pres.
6680 W Shore Dr.
Weidman, MI 48893
Ph: (989)644-3133
E-mail: harlonsandy@aol.com
URL: http://lions.silverthorn.biz/11-e1
Contact: Bruce Cotter, Pres.
Local. Affiliated With: Lions Clubs International.

West Bloomfield

10110 ■ Alpha Kappa Alpha, Theta Lambda Omega
7081 S Oak Ct. E
West Bloomfield, MI 48323
E-mail: webmaster@aka-thetalambdaomega.org
URL: http://aka-thetalambdaomega.org
Contact: Gwendolyn Bynum, Pres.
Founded: 1965. **Local**. Provides community services. **Affiliated With:** Alpha Kappa Alpha.

10111 ■ American String Teachers Association, Michigan Chapter (MASTA)
5670 Commerce Rd.
West Bloomfield, MI 48324
Ph: (248)645-4645
Fax: (248)645-4629
URL: National Affiliate–www.astaweb.com
Contact: David Reed, Pres.
Founded: 1946. **Members:** 405. **Membership Dues:** active individual, $54 (annual). **State Groups:** 50. **State**. Works to encourage, develop, and support the performance of string music in solo, ensemble, and orchestra, at all levels of achievement. **Awards:** Administrator of the Year. **Frequency:** annual. **Type:** recognition • String Teacher of the Year. **Frequency:** annual. **Type:** recognition. **Affiliated With:** American String Teachers Association. **Publications:** *Michigan ASTA Journal*, quarterly. **Circulation:** 450. **Advertising:** accepted. **Conventions/Meetings:** annual Midwestern Conference on School Instrumental & Vocal Music (exhibits) - every January. Ann Arbor, MI - Avg. Attendance: 1300.

10112 ■ Chaldean Americans Reaching and Encouraging (C.A.R.E.)
c/o Ed Babbie
6346 Orchard Lake Rd., Ste.22
West Bloomfield, MI 48322
Ph: (248)737-4369
E-mail: info@voicesthatcare.com
URL: http://www.voicesthatcare.org
Local.

10113 ■ Friendship Circle
c/o Levi Shemtov
6891 W Maple Rd.
West Bloomfield, MI 48322-3032
Ph: (248)788-7878
Fax: (248)788-7854
URL: http://www.friendshipcircle.org
Contact: Levi Shemtov, Dir.
Local.

10114 ■ Greater West Bloomfield Chamber of Commerce (WBCC)
6668 Orchard Lake Rd., Ste.207
West Bloomfield, MI 48322
Ph: (248)626-3636
Fax: (248)626-4218
E-mail: wbcc@sbcglobal.net
URL: http://www.westbloomfieldchamber.com
Contact: Maureen Malone, Exec.Dir.
Founded: 1973. **Members:** 200. **Membership Dues:** business (1-20 employees), $225 (annual) • business (21-75 employees), $255 (annual) • business (75 plus employees), $325 (annual) • home-based, $200 (annual) • nonprofit, $210 (annual) • supporting, $250 (annual) • sustaining, $275 (annual). **Staff:** 2. **Budget:** $108,185. **Local**. Promotes business and community development in West Bloomfield, MI. Sponsors West Bloomfield Artfest, Business Person of the Year, Business Beautification Awards, Taste of West Bloomfield, and 6th Annual Golf Classic; conducts charitable activities. **Awards:** Business Beautification. **Frequency:** annual. **Type:** recognition • Business Person of the Year. **Type:** recognition. **Computer Services:** Mailing lists, of members. **Affiliated With:** U.S. Chamber of Commerce. **Formerly:** (2005) West Bloomfield Chamber of Commerce. **Publications:** *West Bloomfield Community Directory*, annual • *West Bloomfield Update*, monthly. Newsletter. Alternate Formats: online. **Conventions/Meetings:** periodic Art Fest - festival.

10115 ■ International Brotherhood of Magicians, Ring 22
c/o Fred Apel
4958 Countryside Dr.
West Bloomfield, MI 48323
Ph: (248)738-0491
E-mail: fredapel@usa.net
URL: http://www.ibmring22.com
Contact: Fred Apel, Contact
Founded: 1928. **Members:** 40. **Membership Dues:** regular, $25 (annual) • junior, $15 (annual). **Local**. Professional and semiprofessional magicians; suppliers, assistants, agents, and others interested in magic. Seeks to advance the art of magic in the field of amusement, entertainment, and culture. Promotes proper means of discouraging false or misleading advertising of effects, tricks, literature, merchandise, or actions appertaining to the magical arts; opposes exposures of principles of the art of magic, except in books on magic and magazines devoted to such art for the exclusive use of magicians and devotees of the art; encourages humane treatment and care of live animals whenever employed in magical performances. **Affiliated With:** International Brotherhood of Magicians.

10116 ■ Jewish Historical Society of Michigan (JHSM)
6600 W Maple Rd.
West Bloomfield, MI 48322-3003
Ph: (248)432-5600 (248)661-1000
E-mail: jhsofmichigan@msn.com
URL: http://www.michjewishhistory.org
Contact: Aimee Ergas, Exec. Administrator
Founded: 1959. **Members:** 750. **Membership Dues:** regular, $36 (annual) • life, $360 • organization (journal subscription only), $20 (annual). **Staff:** 2. **State**. Synagogues, temples, Jewish libraries, and individuals interested in Jewish history. Preserves records in libraries of Jewish activities in Michigan. Establishes plaques and memorials; conducts tours; and sponsors exhibits. Publishes annual journal, Michigan Jewish History. **Awards:** Leonard N. Simons History Award. **Frequency:** annual. **Type:** recognition. **Recipient:** for preservation and dissemination of Michigan Jewish history. **Affiliated With:** American Jewish Historical Society. **Publications:** *Michigan Jewish History*, annual. Journal. ISSN: 0543-9833. **Circulation:** 600. **Conventions/Meetings:** annual luncheon - always June.

10117 ■ Michigan Association of Art Therapy (MAAT)
4517 Kevin Ct.
West Bloomfield, MI 48322
Ph: (248)868-6355
E-mail: kschurgin@comcast.net
URL: http://www.micharttherapy.org
Contact: Sarah Campbell, Pres.-Elect
Founded: 1977. **Members:** 83. **Membership Dues:** professional, $35 (annual) • associate, $25 (annual) • student, $15 (annual) • patron, $40 (annual) • retired, $10 (annual). **State**. Represents professionals using art as a creative process in healing and life enhancement. Supports the progressive development of the therapeutic uses of art, advancement in its research, and improvements in the standards of practice. **Libraries: Type:** not open to the public. **Holdings:** archival material, audio recordings, audiovisuals, books, business records, video recordings. **Computer Services:** Electronic publishing. **Boards:** Executive. **Committees:** Archivist; Constitution; Ethics; Membership; Publications. **Subcommittees:** Graduate/Student Liaison. **Subgroups:** Mandala Art. **Affiliated With:** American Art Therapy Association. **Publications:** *MOSAIC*, quarterly. Newsletters. **Advertising:** accepted. Alternate Formats: online.

10118 ■ Michigan Association for Healthcare Quality (MAHQ)
c/o Collen Cieszkowski, MA
2981 Bloomfield Park Dr.
West Bloomfield, MI 48323-3508
Ph: (248)465-7309
Fax: (248)489-5266
E-mail: ccieszko@mpro.com
URL: National Affiliate–www.nahq.org
Contact: Colleen Cieszkowski MA, Contact
State. Represents expertise from quality management, medical records, case management, managed care, information systems, infection control, and other areas of health care. Increases the quality of care through education, best practice implementation, and teamwork. **Affiliated With:** National Association for Healthcare Quality.

10119 ■ Michigan Cactus and Succulent Society
c/o Louis Kilbert, Pres.
5601 Coomer Rd.
West Bloomfield, MI 48324-1110
Ph: (248)681-4791
E-mail: cuzenlouie37@yahoo.com
URL: http://www.cactus-mall.com/clubs/michigan.html
Contact: Louis Kilbert, Pres.
Founded: 1946. **Members:** 50. **Membership Dues:** individual, $12 (annual) • partnership, $15 (annual). **State**. United to study, propagate, and cultivate cacti and other succulents. Programs include slide shows, field trips, lectures, workshops, plant shows, and sales. **Publications:** *Spinal Column*, monthly. Newsletter. **Conventions/Meetings:** monthly meeting - always second Sunday.

10120 ■ National Academy of Television Arts and Sciences, Michigan Chapter
c/o Stacia N. Mottley, Administrator
PO Box 251937
West Bloomfield, MI 48325
Ph: (248)592-0086
Fax: (248)592-0087
Free: (888)430-3669
E-mail: smottley@comcast.net
URL: http://www.mi-nta.org
Contact: Stacia N. Mottley, Administrator
State. Promotes excellence in broadcasting. Inspires the next generation of broadcast journalists. Educates television viewers. **Affiliated With:** National Academy of Television Arts and Sciences.

10121 ■ National Association of Investors Corporation, Southeastern Michigan Chapter
PO Box 251832
West Bloomfield, MI 48325-1832
Ph: (248)626-7041
E-mail: dianeamendt@flash.net
URL: http://better-investing.org/chapter/semich
Contact: Diane Amendt, Pres.
Local. Teaches individuals how to become successful strategic long-term investors. Provides highly focused learning resources and investment tools that empower individuals to become better investors. **Affiliated With:** National Association of Investors Corporation.

10122 ■ Oakland County Traditional Dance Society (OCTDS)
c/o Robin Kaufman
5846 Red Coat Ln.
West Bloomfield, MI 48322
Ph: (248)968-3565 (248)967-1055
E-mail: octds@comcast.net
URL: http://web.mac.com/sgold/iWeb/OCTDS
Contact: Robin Kaufman, Contact
Founded: 1990. **Local**. Sponsors contra-dance activities. Holds dances on fourth Saturdays of the month. **Conventions/Meetings:** monthly meeting.

10123 ■ Red River Valley Fighter Pilot Association - Michigan
6702 Blue Spruce St.
West Bloomfield, MI 48324
E-mail: prfvsh@aol.com
URL: National Affiliate–www.river-rats.org
Contact: Richard Fisher, Contact
State. Affiliated With: Red River Valley Fighter Pilots Association.

10124 ■ Society of Reliability Engineer, Southeastern Michigan Chapter
c/o Dr. Gary Wasserman, VP
4556 Pine Village Dr.
West Bloomfield, MI 48323
Ph: (248)737-0876
E-mail: gwasserm@comcast.net
URL: National Affiliate–www.sre.org
Contact: Dr. Gary Wasserman, VP
Local. Seeks to develop and advance the techniques effective in the application of reliability principles. Promotes reliability programs through the education fund. **Affiliated With:** Society of Reliability Engineers.

10125 ■ Volunteer Impact
6960 Orchard Lake Rd., Ste.204
West Bloomfield, MI 48322
Ph: (248)559-4950 (248)932-2580
Fax: (248)932-2581
E-mail: volunteer_impact@yahoo.com
URL: http://www.volunteerimpact.org
Contact: Nancy Welber Barr, Pres.
Founded: 1990. **Local**. Aims to improve the Detroit Metropolitan community through hands-on volunteerism.

10126 ■ West Bloomfield School District Parent Communications Network
5810 Commerce Rd.
West Bloomfield, MI 48324
Ph: (248)865-6420
Fax: (248)865-6421
E-mail: wasko@westbloomfield.k12.mi.us
URL: http://www.westbloomfield.k12.mi.us
Contact: Steve Wasko, Asst. Superintendent
Founded: 1987. **Members:** 18. **Local**. Parents, teachers, students, principals, administrators, and others interested in uniting the forces of home, school, and community in behalf of children and youth enrolled in the school district. Sponsors school-related events. **Publications:** none. **Formerly:** (1998) West Bloomfield School District Communications Governance Committee. **Conventions/Meetings:** monthly general assembly • periodic Parenting Conference.

West Branch

10127 ■ American Legion, Ogemaw Post 103
403 S 1st St.
West Branch, MI 48661
Ph: (517)371-4720
Fax: (517)371-2401
URL: National Affiliate–www.legion.org
Local. Affiliated With: American Legion.

10128 ■ Cherryland Beagle Club
c/o Marlene Byers
1887 Indianwood Trail
West Branch, MI 48661-9731
URL: National Affiliate–www.akc.org
Contact: Marlene Byers, Contact
Membership Dues: $25 (annual). **Local**. Sponsors AKC field trials and trains beagles. **Affiliated With:** American Kennel Club.

10129 ■ Michigan Health Information Management Association, North Central
c/o Bonnie Owens, RHIT, Pres.
Standish Community Hosp.
1100 Brick Rd.
West Branch, MI 48661
Ph: (989)846-3452 (989)345-3445
Fax: (989)846-2020
E-mail: bonnieo@stmarys-standish.org
URL: http://www.mhima.org
Contact: Bonnie Owens RHIT, Pres.
Local. Represents the interests of individuals dedicated to the effective management of personal health information needed to deliver quality healthcare to the public. Provides career, professional development and practice resources. Sets standards for education and certification. Advocates public policy that advances Health Information Management (HIM) practice. **Affiliated With:** American Health Information Management Association; Michigan Health Information Management Association.

10130 ■ Michigan National Wild Turkey Federation, Ogemaw Hills Chapter
c/o Karen Dillon
4700 Boutell Ranch Rd.
West Branch, MI 48661
Ph: (989)345-7180
E-mail: kdillon56@msn.com
URL: http://www.mi-nwtf.org/ogemaw.htm
Contact: Renee Rickel, VP
Local.

10131 ■ North Eastern Michigan Industrial Association (NEMIA)
c/o Michael Pangborn, Administrator
PO Box 23
West Branch, MI 48661
Ph: (989)362-6407
Fax: (989)362-6538
E-mail: mpangborn@mishworks4u.org
URL: http://www.nemia.org
Contact: Michael Pangborn, Administrator
Founded: 1997. **Members:** 30. **Membership Dues:** associate, $75 (annual) • general, $100 (annual). **Regional**. Provides a continuous improvement of network designed to strengthen the growth and success of area manufacturers. **Conventions/Meetings:** bimonthly Educational Workshops.

10132 ■ Ogemaw County Friends of Casa
c/o Ogemaw County Casa
806 W Houghton Ave., Ste.203
West Branch, MI 48661-1215
Ph: (989)345-5920
Fax: (989)345-5901
E-mail: ogemawcasa@voyager.net
Local. Trained volunteers advocating for children involved in neglect/abuse cases in Ogemaw County Family Court.

10133 ■ Ogemaw County United Way
PO Box 588
West Branch, MI 48661-0588
Ph: (989)345-5532
URL: National Affiliate–national.unitedway.org
Local. Affiliated With: United Way of America.

10134 ■ Stittsville Beagle Club
c/o Marlene Byers
1887 Indianwood Trail
West Branch, MI 48661-9731
URL: National Affiliate–www.akc.org
Contact: Marlene Byers, Contact
Founded: 1990. **Members:** 25. **Membership Dues:** $25 (annual). **Staff:** 5. **Local**. Promotes the training of hunting beagles for competition in AKC licensed trials. **Affiliated With:** American Kennel Club. **Conventions/Meetings:** semiannual Trial - specialty show.

10135 ■ West Branch Area Chamber of Commerce (WBACC)
422 W Houghton Ave.
West Branch, MI 48661
Ph: (989)345-2821
Free: (800)755-9091
E-mail: chamber@westbranch.com
URL: http://www.wbacc.com
Contact: Steven G. Leonard, Exec.Dir.
Founded: 1948. **Members:** 260. **Staff:** 2. **Local**. Promotes business and community development in West Branch, MI. Sponsors festivals. **Publications:** Directory, annual.

10136 ■ West Branch-Ogemaw County Travel and Visitors Bureau
422 W Houghton Ave.
West Branch, MI 48661
Ph: (989)345-2821
Fax: (989)345-9075
Free: (800)755-9091
E-mail: info@wboctvb.com
URL: http://wboctvb.com
Contact: Steven G. Leonard, Exec.Dir.
Founded: 1989. **Members:** 8. **Staff:** 2. **Local**. Promotes convention business and tourism in area. **Publications:** Brochures. **Price:** free. **Conventions/Meetings:** monthly board meeting - always third Wednesday.

Westland

10137 ■ Arc of Western Wayne County
2257 S Wayne Rd.
Westland, MI 48186
Ph: (734)729-9100
Fax: (734)729-9695
E-mail: info@thearcww.org
URL: http://www.thearcww.org
Contact: Cheryl S. Polite, Exec.Dir.
Founded: 1954. **Local**. Parents, professional workers, and others interested in individuals with mental retardation. Works to promote services, research, public understanding, and legislation for people with mental retardation and their families. **Affiliated With:** Arc of the United States.

10138 ■ Compassionate Friends - Livonia, Michigan Chapter
c/o Pat O'Donnell
37758 Marquette
Westland, MI 48185
Ph: (734)778-0800
E-mail: billyodee@comcast.net
URL: http://www.tcflivonia.org
Contact: Pat O'Donnell, Chapter Leader
Local.

10139 ■ Michigan Humane Society - Westland
900 N Newburgh Rd.
Westland, MI 48185
Ph: (734)721-7300
E-mail: mail@michiganhumane.org
URL: http://www.michiganhumane.org
Local.

10140 ■ Mothers Against Drunk Driving, Wayne County
PO Box 85570
Westland, MI 48185-0570
Ph: (734)721-8181
Fax: (734)721-6595
E-mail: maddwayneco@wwnet.net
URL: http://www.madd.org/mi/wayne
Victims of drunk driving crashes; concerned citizens. Encourages citizen participation in working towards reform of the drunk driving problem and the prevention of underage drinking. Acts as the voice of victims

of drunk driving crashes by speaking on their behalf to communities, businesses, and educational groups. **Affiliated With:** Mothers Against Drunk Driving.

10141 ■ Plumbing-Heating-Cooling Contractors Association, Western Wayne County
c/o Dorothy Carr, Exec.Mgr.
33850 Tawas Trail
Westland, MI 48185-6932
Ph: (734)427-7106
URL: National Affiliate–www.phccweb.org
Contact: Dorothy Carr, Exec.Mgr.
Local. Represents the plumbing, heating and cooling contractors. Promotes the construction industry. Protects the environment, health, safety and comfort of society. **Affiliated With:** Plumbing-Heating-Cooling Contractors Association.

10142 ■ Taylor Lions Club - Michigan
c/o Linda Garrick, Pres.
1288 Surrey Heights
Westland, MI 48186
Ph: (734)728-5933
URL: http://www.metrodetroitlions.org
Contact: Linda Garrick, Pres.
Local. Affiliated With: Lions Clubs International.

10143 ■ Westland Breakfast Lions Club
c/o Edna Parker, Pres.
4946 Julius Blvd.
Westland, MI 48186
Ph: (734)722-2868
URL: http://www.metrodetroitlions.org
Contact: Edna Parker, Pres.
Local. Affiliated With: Lions Clubs International.

10144 ■ Westland Chamber of Commerce
36900 Ford Rd.
Westland, MI 48185-2231
Ph: (734)326-7222
Fax: (734)326-6040
E-mail: info@westlandchamber.com
URL: http://www.westlandchamber.com
Contact: Lori Brist, Pres./CEO
Members: 310. **Membership Dues:** business (varies with the number of employees), $145-$465 (annual) • non-business, $105 (annual). **Local**. Promotes business and community development in Westland, MI. **Computer Services:** database, list of members. **Publications:** *Commerce Commentary*, monthly. Newsletter. Alternate Formats: online.

10145 ■ Westland Figure Skating Club
Mike Modano Ice Arena
6210 N Wildwood
Westland, MI 48185
E-mail: aaamom@aol.com
URL: http://www.westlandfsc.com
Local. Provides programs to encourage participation and achievement in the sport of figure skating on ice. Defines and maintains uniform standards of skating proficiency. Organizes and sponsors competitions and exhibitions for the purpose of stimulating interest in figure skating. **Affiliated With:** United States Figure Skating Association.

10146 ■ Westland Fire Fighters Public Awareness Committee
37201 Marquette
Westland, MI 48185-3253
Ph: (734)467-3201 (734)467-3260
Contact: Chris Szpara, Fire Marshall
Local.

10147 ■ Westland Host Lions Club
c/o William Acton, Pres.
32227 Hazelwood St.
Westland, MI 48186
Ph: (734)326-2607
E-mail: williamacton@aol.com
URL: http://www.metrodetroitlions.org
Contact: William Acton, Pres.
Local. Affiliated With: Lions Clubs International.

10148 ■ Westland Lawn Bowling Club
c/o Bill Davidson
8021 Coventry
Westland, MI 48185
Ph: (734)425-4804
URL: National Affiliate–www.bowlsamerica.org
Contact: Bill Davidson, Contact
Local. Affiliated With: United States Lawn Bowls Association.

10149 ■ Wheelmen, Michigan
38236 N Rickham Ct.
Westland, MI 48186
Ph: (734)729-3496
E-mail: bswheels@comcast.net
URL: National Affiliate–www.thewheelmen.org
State.

10150 ■ Women of Westland (WOW)
c/o Joy Ebel
5719 N Berry
Westland, MI 48185
Ph: (734)467-9113
E-mail: info@womenofwestland.com
URL: http://www.womenofwestland.com
Local.

10151 ■ Women's National Book Association, Detroit Chapter
c/o Ms. Cynthia Dooley, Pres.
PO Box 85523
Westland, MI 48185
E-mail: cjpdooley@yahoo.com
URL: http://www.wnba-books.org
Contact: Ms. Cynthia Dooley, Chapter Pres.
Founded: 1966. **Members:** 35. **Membership Dues:** regular, $30 (annual) • patron, $75 (annual) • friend, $50 (annual) • benefactor, $100 (annual). **Budget:** $1,300. **Regional Groups:** 9. **Local Groups:** 1. **Local**. Promotes reading and supports the role of women in the community of books. Brings together women and men in the world of books; educates the public about the need to create, produce, distribute, and use books; provides information about books and supports projects to disseminate such information; serves as a catalyst for those in the book community who wish to work together; recognizes women's achievements in the book industry. Contributes to local organizations that share the value of literacy and support the growth of women. **Awards:** The Eastman Grant. **Frequency:** annual. **Type:** grant. **Recipient:** for librarians • The Pannell Award. **Frequency:** annual. **Type:** monetary. **Recipient:** for booksellers • The WNBA Award. **Frequency:** annual. **Type:** recognition. **Recipient:** to "a living American woman who derives part or all of her income from books and allied arts, and who has done meritorious work in the world of books beyond the duties or responsibilities of her profession or occupation". **Affiliated With:** Women's National Book Association.

White Cloud

10152 ■ Michigan National Wild Turkey Federation, White River Longbeards
575 N Walnut
White Cloud, MI 49349
Ph: (231)689-6260
URL: http://www.mi-nwtf.org/whiteriv.htm
Contact: Chuck Trapp, Pres.
Local.

10153 ■ White Cloud Area Chamber of Commerce
12 N Charles
White Cloud, MI 49349
Ph: (231)689-6607
E-mail: ladams@gtlakes.net
URL: http://www.whitecloudchamber.org
Contact: Ms. Sherry Adams, Sec.
Membership Dues: individual, business (less than 5 employees), $60 (annual) • business (with 5 or more employees), $85 (annual). **Local**. Promotes business and community development in White Cloud, MI.

10154 ■ White Cloud Lions Club
Box 116
White Cloud, MI 49349
Ph: (231)689-6410
E-mail: janalee@riverview.net
URL: http://whiteclouddmi.lionwap.org
Contact: Russell Lucas, Pres.
Local. Affiliated With: Lions Clubs International.

White Lake

10155 ■ American Legion, Sylvester Lyczynski Post 420
321 Union Lake Rd.
White Lake, MI 48386
Ph: (517)371-4720
Fax: (517)371-2401
URL: National Affiliate–www.legion.org
Local. Affiliated With: American Legion.

10156 ■ Jayco Jafari International Travel Club, Flight 117 Lake Jayco Jypsies
c/o Richard Dunham, Pres.
9845 Mandon St.
White Lake, MI 48386
E-mail: onebigtrk@sbclgobal.net
URL: National Affiliate–www.jaycorvclub.com
Contact: Richard Dunham, Pres.
Local. Affiliated With: Jayco Travel Club.

10157 ■ Michigan Fox Trotter Association (MFTA)
c/o Bryon Quinlan, Pres.
7660 Pontiac Lake Rd.
White Lake, MI 48386
Ph: (248)666-9015
E-mail: punchandrodeo@aol.com
URL: http://www.geocities.com/henryw5809
Contact: Bryon Quinlan, Pres.
Membership Dues: single, $15 (annual) • family, $20 (annual). **State. Affiliated With:** Missouri Fox Trotting Horse Breed Association.

10158 ■ Pontiac Lake Horsemans Association (PLHA)
c/o James L. Pickard
4450 Jozwik Ln.
White Lake, MI 48383-1369
E-mail: plhanews@aol.com
URL: http://plha.info
Contact: James L. Pickard, Sec.
Founded: 2000. **Members:** 42. **Membership Dues:** $20 (annual). **Local**.

White Pigeon

10159 ■ American Legion, Swartz-Van-Fleet Post 138
PO Box 293
White Pigeon, MI 49099
Ph: (517)371-4720
Fax: (517)371-2401
URL: National Affiliate–www.legion.org
Local. Affiliated With: American Legion.

10160 ■ White Pigeon Lions Club
PO Box 363
White Pigeon, MI 49099
E-mail: jackijo@net-link.net
URL: http://milions11b2.org
Local. Affiliated With: Lions Clubs International.

White Pine

10161 ■ American Legion, Nonesuch Post 462
62 Hemlock St.
White Pine, MI 49971
Ph: (517)371-4720
Fax: (517)371-2401
URL: National Affiliate–www.legion.org
Local. Affiliated With: American Legion.

Whitehall

10162 ■ American Legion, Algot Johnson Post 69
803 E Colby St.
Whitehall, MI 49461
Ph: (517)371-4720
Fax: (517)371-2401
URL: National Affiliate–www.legion.org
Local. Affiliated With: American Legion.

10163 ■ Local 70C, Chemical Workers Council of the UFCW
3570 Michillinda Rd.
Whitehall, MI 49461
Ph: (616)893-6701
URL: National Affiliate–www.ufcw.org
Local. Affiliated With: United Food and Commercial Workers International Union.

10164 ■ Michigan National Wild Turkey Federation, Dune Drummers Chapter
3391 Orshal Rd.
Whitehall, MI 49461
Ph: (231)766-3820
URL: http://www.mi-nwtf.org/Dunedrum.htm
Contact: Mike Parrish, Pres.
Local.

10165 ■ White Lake Area Chamber of Commerce
124 W Hanson St.
Whitehall, MI 49461
Ph: (231)893-4585
Fax: (231)893-0914
Free: (800)879-9702
E-mail: info@whitelake.org
URL: http://www.whitelake.org
Contact: Carol Wood, Exec.Dir.
Founded: 1971. **Members:** 265. **Local.** Promotes business and community development in Muskegon County, MI. Sponsors festival. **Awards:** Athena Award. **Type:** recognition • El Award. **Type:** recognition. **Recipient:** for excellence in business and community service. **Computer Services:** database, local businesses • information services, facts about White Lake, MI. **Committees:** Fundraising; Industrial; Membership Development; Retail; Tourism; 2000 Plus; White Lake Area Pride. **Affiliated With:** U.S. Chamber of Commerce. **Publications:** *On the Right Track*, monthly. Newsletter. **Conventions/Meetings:** monthly Membership Meeting - always first Monday.

Whitmore Lake

10166 ■ Dexter Lions Club
7108 Ryan Rd.
Whitmore Lake, MI 48189
E-mail: lff_409@yahoo.com
URL: http://www.dexterlions.org
Contact: Larry France, Pres.
Local. Affiliated With: Lions Clubs International.

Williamsburg

10167 ■ American Legion, Deal-Ridgeway Post 289
PO Box 32
Williamsburg, MI 49690
Ph: (517)371-4720
Fax: (517)371-2401
URL: National Affiliate–www.legion.org
Local. Affiliated With: American Legion.

10168 ■ American Theatre Organ Society, Northern Michigan Chapter
c/o Andy Struble, Pres.
7377 US 31 N
Williamsburg, MI 49690
Ph: (231)938-9301
E-mail: musicmachines@juno.com
URL: National Affiliate–www.atos.org
Contact: Andy Struble, Pres.
Local. Aims to restore, preserve and promote the theatre pipe organ and its music. Encourages the youth to learn the instrument. Operates a committee that gathers history and old music from silent film days and information on theatre organists, theaters and organ installations of the silent film era. **Affiliated With:** American Theatre Organ Society.

10169 ■ Michigan National Wild Turkey Federation, Kalamazoo Chapter
5128 Meadowlark Ln.
Williamsburg, MI 49690
URL: http://www.mi-nwtf.org/Kalamazoo.htm
Contact: Dan Doherty, Pres.
Local.

10170 ■ National Association of Investors Corporation, Northern Michigan Chapter
c/o Ruth Williams
10978 Lakeshore Rd.
Williamsburg, MI 49690
Ph: (231)943-9040 (231)947-9286
E-mail: hlemcool@chmaint.com
URL: http://better-investing.org/chapter/nmich
Contact: Herbert Lemcool Jr., Pres.
Local. Teaches individuals how to become successful strategic long-term investors. Provides highly focused learning resources and investment tools that empower individuals to become better investors. **Affiliated With:** National Association of Investors Corporation.

Williamston

10171 ■ American Legion, Wycoff Post 296
PO Box 125
Williamston, MI 48895
Ph: (517)371-4720
Fax: (517)371-2401
URL: National Affiliate–www.legion.org
Local. Affiliated With: American Legion.

10172 ■ Jaxon Kennel Club
c/o Claudia Shimmin, Corresponding Sec.
4151 Meadowdale Dr.
Williamston, MI 48895-0000
E-mail: yorkey@voyager.net
URL: National Affiliate–www.akc.org
Local.

10173 ■ Michigan Health Information Management Association, Mid-Michigan
c/o Julia Harshbarger, RHIA, Pres.
SoftMed Systems, Inc.
316 S Cedar St.
Williamston, MI 48895
Free: (800)234-0422
E-mail: jharshba@softmed.com
URL: http://www.mhima.org
Contact: Julia Harshbarger RHIA, Pres.
Local. Represents the interests of individuals dedicated to the effective management of personal health information needed to deliver quality healthcare to the public. Provides career, professional development and practice resources. Sets standards for education and certification. Advocates public policy that advances Health Information Management (HIM) practice. **Affiliated With:** American Health Information Management Association; Michigan Health Information Management Association.

10174 ■ Red Cedar Beagle Club
c/o Jon Kazsuk
5400 Zimmer Rd.
Williamston, MI 48895-9181
URL: National Affiliate–clubs.akc.org
Contact: Jon Kazsuk, Contact
Local.

10175 ■ Williamston Area Chamber of Commerce
PO Box 53
369 W Grand River
Williamston, MI 48895
Ph: (517)655-1549
Fax: (517)655-8859
E-mail: info@williamston.org
URL: http://www.williamston.org
Contact: Ms. Barbara Burke, Exec.Dir.
Local. Promotes business and community development in Williamston, MI area.

10176 ■ Williamston Lions Club - Michigan
c/o Janet Dorn, Sec.
219 Wallace St.
Williamston, MI 48895
Ph: (517)655-3738
E-mail: ddorn39703@aol.com
URL: http://www.district11c2.org
Contact: Janet Dorn, Sec.
Local. Affiliated With: Lions Clubs International.

Wilson

10177 ■ Superiorland Chapter of Human Resource Professionals
c/o Jeannette Lockman, Pres.
Hannahville Indian Community
N14911 Hannahville B - 1 Rd.
Wilson, MI 49896
Ph: (906)466-0306
Fax: (906)466-0307
E-mail: jhelgeson@hvl.bia.edu
URL: http://jobsearch.nmu.edu/schrp/index.php
Contact: Jeannette Lockman, Pres.
Local. Represents the interests of human resource and industrial relations professionals and executives. Promotes the advancement of human resource management.

Wixom

10178 ■ American Legion, Constitution Post 224
2652 Loon Lake Rd.
Wixom, MI 48393
Ph: (248)624-9742
Fax: (517)371-2401
URL: National Affiliate–www.legion.org
Local. Affiliated With: American Legion.

10179 ■ International Union, United Automobile, Aerospace and Agricultural Implement Workers of America, AFL-CIO - Local Union 36
28930 S Wixom Rd.
Wixom, MI 48393
Ph: (248)349-2448
Free: (888)249-0036
E-mail: local36@uawlocal36.com
URL: http://www.uawlocal36.com
Contact: Dave Berry, Pres.
Members: 2,599. **Local.** AFL-CIO. **Affiliated With:** International Union, United Automobile, Aerospace and Agricultural Implement Workers of America.

10180 ■ National Technical Honor Society - Oakland Schools Tech Campus Soutwest - Michigan
1000 Beck Rd.
Wixom, MI 48393
Ph: (248)668-5600
Fax: (248)668-5670
E-mail: allen.becker@oakland.k12.mi.us
URL: http://www.oakland.k12.mi.us
Contact: Allen Becker, Contact
Local.

Wolverine

10181 ■ American Legion, Michigan Post 122
c/o Robert Vroman
12900 Straits Hwy.
Wolverine, MI 49799
Ph: (517)371-4720
Fax: (517)371-2401
URL: National Affiliate–www.legion.org
Contact: Robert Vroman, Contact
Local. Affiliated With: American Legion.

Wolverine Lake

10182 ■ Ancient Order of Hibernians of Wayne County - Stephen Walsh Division
c/o Richard McNichol
2277 Darnell St.
Wolverine Lake, MI 48390
Ph: (248)669-4530
E-mail: rmcnich@aol.com
URL: http://www.michiganaoh.com
Contact: Richard McNichol, Contact
Local. Affiliated With: Ancient Order of Hibernians in America.

Wyandotte

10183 ■ American Legion, Ford Wagar Memorial Post 447
PO Box 389
Wyandotte, MI 48192
Ph: (517)371-4720
Fax: (517)371-2401
URL: National Affiliate–www.legion.org
Local. Affiliated With: American Legion.

10184 ■ Female Alumni Athletic Boosters (FAAB)
c/o Thomas Wilson
4045 23rd St.
Wyandotte, MI 48192-6902
Ph: (313)235-2168
E-mail: tomwilson@mi-gender-equity.com
URL: http://mi-gender-equity.com/Boosters3.doc
Contact: Tom Wilson, Pres.
Founded: 1999. **Local Groups:** 1. **Local.** Provides financial support to students, particularly female athletes at Theodore Roosevelt High School in Wyandotte, MI; sponsors fundraising activities and solicits funds to finance support and encourage education-related organizations to comply with the equal treatment requirements of the Federal Title IX and Michigan Elliot Larson laws. **Awards:** Scholarships. **Type:** scholarship. **Recipient:** to students attending Roosevelt High School, Wyandotte, MI.

10185 ■ Monroe Coin Club
c/o Bill Summerell
3105 21st St.
Wyandotte, MI 48192
E-mail: monroecoinclub@coinfan.net
URL: National Affiliate–www.money.org
Contact: Bill Summerell, Contact
Local. Affiliated With: American Numismatic Association.

10186 ■ Skate Company Skating Club
3669 16th St.
Wyandotte, MI 48192
Ph: (734)285-1855
E-mail: placinski@wyan.org
URL: National Affiliate–www.usfigureskating.org
Contact: Bonnie Placinski, Contact
Local. Provides programs to encourage participation and achievement in the sport of figure skating on ice. Defines and maintains uniform standards of skating proficiency. Organizes and sponsors competitions and exhibitions for the purpose of stimulating interest in figure skating. **Affiliated With:** United States Figure Skating Association.

Wyoming

10187 ■ American Legion, North Park Post 401
1281 Blanchard SW
Wyoming, MI 49509
Ph: (517)371-4720
Fax: (517)371-2401
URL: National Affiliate–www.legion.org
Local. Affiliated With: American Legion.

10188 ■ American Legion, Roger B. Chaffee Post 154
2327 Byron Center Ave. SW
Wyoming, MI 49519
Ph: (517)371-4720
Fax: (517)371-2401
URL: National Affiliate–www.legion.org
Local. Affiliated With: American Legion.

10189 ■ Indian Mounds Rock and Mineral Club (IMRMC)
c/o Gordon Spalenka, Pres.
2119 Waldron St.
Wyoming, MI 49509
E-mail: edben@prodigy.net
URL: http://tomaszewski.net/~IMRMC/Index.shtml
Contact: Joyce Potter, Sec.
Local. Aims to further the study of Earth Sciences and the practice of lapidary arts and mineralogy. **Affiliated With:** American Federation of Mineralogical Societies.

10190 ■ International Brotherhood of Magicians, Ring 211 - John DeVries Magic Club
c/o Michele Parkes
4339 Illinois Ave. SW
Wyoming, MI 49509
Ph: (616)534-1997 (616)742-3898
E-mail: sales@hippityhop.com
URL: http://ring211.tripod.com
Contact: Michele Parkes, Contact
Local. Professional and semi-professional magicians; suppliers, assistants, agents, and others interested in magic. Seeks to advance the art of magic in the field of amusement, entertainment, and culture. Promotes proper means of discouraging false or misleading advertising of effects, tricks, literature, merchandise, or actions appertaining to the magical arts; opposes exposures of principles of the art of magic, except in books on magic and magazines devoted to such art for the exclusive use of magicians and devotees of the art; encourages humane treatment and care of live animals whenever employed in magical performances. **Affiliated With:** International Brotherhood of Magicians.

10191 ■ National Association of Credit Management - Western Michigan (NACM-WM)
3959 Clay Ave. SW
Wyoming, MI 49548-3014
Ph: (616)257-0617
Fax: (616)257-0626
E-mail: info@nacmwm.org
URL: http://www.nacmwm.org
Contact: Michael A. Doubek, Pres.
Founded: 1901. **Members:** 361. **Membership Dues:** full, $245 (annual). **Staff:** 13. **Budget:** $750,000. **Regional Groups:** 1. **Local Groups:** 12. **Regional.** Credit and financial executives representing manufacturers, wholesalers, financial institutions, insurance companies, utilities, and other businesses interested in business credit. **Affiliated With:** National Association of Credit Management. **Publications:** Newsletter, periodic. Alternate Formats: online.

10192 ■ Property Management Association of West Michigan (PMAWM)
2757 44th St. SW, Ste.306
Wyoming, MI 49519
Ph: (616)531-5243
Fax: (616)257-0398
Free: (866)989-9800
E-mail: pma970@aol.com
URL: http://www.pmawm.com
Contact: Kathy Vallie, Exec.Dir.
Founded: 1994. **Membership Dues:** management company, $160 (annual) • business partner (vendor), $285 (annual) • apartment community (per unit/additional $30 property fee), $125 (annual). **Staff:** 2. **Local. Awards:** GLAStar Award. **Frequency:** annual. **Type:** trophy. **Recipient:** for community members as well as business partners relating to the apartment industry. **Computer Services:** Information services, market surveys • mailing lists, member directory • online services, online training. **Affiliated With:** National Apartment Association. **Publications:** *Directions*, monthly. Newsletter. Contains ads, articles, and inserts (education and event registrations). **Price:** $25.00 /year for individuals. **Circulation:** 360. **Advertising:** accepted. Alternate Formats: online. **Conventions/Meetings:** annual trade show - each February.

10193 ■ Society of Antique Modelers - Michigan 4
4690 Burlingame SW
Wyoming, MI 49509
Ph: (616)538-3077
URL: National Affiliate–www.antiquemodeler.org
Local. Affiliated With: Society of Antique Modelers.

10194 ■ Wyoming Kentwood Area Chamber of Commerce (WKACC)
590-32nd St. SE
Wyoming, MI 49548-2345
Ph: (616)531-5990
Fax: (616)531-0252
E-mail: john@southkent.org
URL: http://www.southkent.org
Contact: John J. Crawford, Pres./CEO
Founded: 1980. **Members:** 700. **Membership Dues:** regular, $199 (annual). **Staff:** 5. **Budget:** $290,000. **Local.** Promotes business and community development in Wyoming, MI. **Awards:** Business of the Year. **Frequency:** annual. **Type:** scholarship. **Affiliated With:** U.S. Chamber of Commerce. **Publications:** *Manufacturer Directory*, annual • *Metro Guide*, annual. Directory • *My Business Advocate*, monthly. Newsletter. **Price:** included in membership dues. **Circulation:** 1,000. **Advertising:** accepted • *Organization Directory*, annual. **Conventions/Meetings:** annual meeting.

Yale

10195 ■ American Legion, Memorial Post 320
105 S Main St.
Yale, MI 48097
Ph: (517)371-4720
Fax: (517)371-2401
URL: National Affiliate–www.legion.org
Local. Affiliated With: American Legion.

Ypsilanti

10196 ■ American Association for Laboratory Animal Science - Michigan (MI-AALAS)
c/o Kathleen Burke, Treas.
PO Box 971793
Ypsilanti, MI 48197
Ph: (734)763-0980 (734)622-7686
E-mail: kalohr@med.umich.edu
URL: http://www.mi.d5aalas.org
Contact: Kathleen Burke, Treas.
State. Serves as a clearinghouse for the collection and exchange of information and expertise in the

care and use of laboratory animals. Promotes and encourages the highest level of ethics within the profession of laboratory animal science. Provides educational and training programs for members and others who are professionally engaged in the production, care, use and study of laboratory animals. **Affiliated With:** American Association for Laboratory Animal Science.

10197 ■ American Legion, Ypsilanti Post 282
117 S Huron St.
Ypsilanti, MI 48197
Ph: (517)371-4720
Fax: (517)371-2401
URL: National Affiliate–www.legion.org
Local. Affiliated With: American Legion.

10198 ■ Association for Computing Machinery, Eastern Michigan University
c/o Kevin Lee Knaus, Chm.
511 F Pray-Harrold
Ypsilanti, MI 48197
Ph: (734)487-7081
E-mail: kknaus@emich.edu
Contact: Kevin Lee Knaus, Chm.
Regional. Biological, medical, behavioral, and computer scientists; hospital administrators; programmers and others interested in application of computer methods to biological, behavioral, and medical problems. Stimulates understanding of the use and potential of computers in the Biosciences. **Affiliated With:** Association for Computing Machinery.

10199 ■ Behavior Analysis Association of Michigan (BAAM)
c/o James T. Todd
Dept. of Psychology
Eastern Michigan Univ.
Ypsilanti, MI 48197
Ph: (734)487-0376
E-mail: baam@emich.edu
URL: http://www.baam.emich.edu
Contact: James T. Todd, Contact
Membership Dues: full, $10 (annual) • student, $5 (annual). **State. Affiliated With:** Association for Behavior Analysis.

10200 ■ Beta Gamma Sigma, Eastern Michigan University Chapter
c/o Dr. Badie N. Farah
Eastern Michigan Univ.
Dept. of Cmpt. Info. Systems
Ypsilanti, MI 48197
Ph: (734)487-2454 (734)487-1098
Fax: (734)487-1941
E-mail: badie.farah@emich.edu
URL: National Affiliate–www.betagammasigma.org
Contact: Dr. Badie N. Farah, Contact
Members: 250. **Regional.** Honor society for business students in the top 10% of their class. Encourages and rewards scholarship; promotes advancement in business; fosters integrity in the field. **Affiliated With:** Beta Gamma Sigma.

10201 ■ Business Professionals of America, Michigan Association
c/o Maurice S. Henderson, Dir.
Eastern Michigan Univ.
202 Welch Hall
Ypsilanti, MI 48197
Ph: (734)487-1700
Fax: (734)487-4329
E-mail: maurice.henderson@emich.edu
URL: http://www.michiganbpa.org
Contact: Maurice S. Henderson, Dir.
Founded: 1972. **Members:** 4,800. **Membership Dues:** individual, $8 (annual). **State.** Prepares high school and college students for careers in business by providing them with leadership development conferences. **Affiliated With:** Business Professionals of America. **Publications:** *News and Notes*, bimonthly. Newsletter. **Conventions/Meetings:** annual conference.

10202 ■ Creative Change Educational Solutions
c/o Susan Marie Santone, Exec.Dir.
229 Miles St.
Ypsilanti, MI 48198-4017
Ph: (734)482-0924
Fax: (734)482-5250
E-mail: info@creativechange.net
URL: http://www.creativechange.net
Contact: Susan Marie Santone, Exec.Dir.
Local.

10203 ■ Dress for Success Michigan
3075 Clark Rd., Ste.108
Ypsilanti, MI 48197
Ph: (734)712-0517
Fax: (734)712-3608
E-mail: michigan@dressforsuccess.org
URL: National Affiliate–www.dressforsuccess.org
Contact: Cathleen Taylor, Exec.Dir.
State.

10204 ■ Family, Career and Community Leaders of America, Michigan
c/o Dave Wait
B-18 -A Goodard Hall
Ypsilanti, MI 48197-0000
Ph: (734)487-3322
Fax: (734)487-4329
E-mail: dave.wait@emich.edu
State. Young men and women studying family and consumer sciences and related occupational courses in public and private schools through grade 12. Youth assume social roles in areas of personal growth, family life, vocational preparation, and community involvement. **Affiliated With:** Family, Career and Community Leaders of America.

10205 ■ Forty and Eight: Voiture 957
c/o Jim Farmer
1273 Fall River Rd.
Ypsilanti, MI 48198
Ph: (734)941-1958
URL: http://www.post282.org/40%268.htm
Contact: Jim Farmer, Contact
Local. Affiliated With: Forty and Eight.

10206 ■ Hemophilia Foundation of Michigan (HFM)
1921 W Michigan Ave.
Ypsilanti, MI 48197
Ph: (734)544-0015
Fax: (734)544-0095
Free: (800)482-3041
E-mail: hfm@hfmich.org
URL: http://www.hfmich.org
Contact: Colleen Joiner MSW, Contact
Members: 2,500. **Staff:** 8. **State.** Support services for people with hemophilia and other hereditary bleeding disorders including complications with HIV/AIDS. Coordinates hemophilia treatment centers, conducts counseling, facilitates support groups, provides youth camping programs, and educational activities. Supports research for finding a cure. **Awards:** Academic Assistance Award. **Frequency:** annual. **Type:** scholarship. **Recipient:** for people affected by bleeding disorder, Michigan resident. **Affiliated With:** National Hemophilia Foundation. **Publications:** *Artery Newsletter*, periodic. **Price:** free • *HFM Information Update*, monthly. Newsletter. Contains news and information relevant to the bleeding disorder community. • *In Focus*, semiannual. Newsletter. Single topic educational booklet. **Conventions/Meetings:** annual Spring Fest - conference (exhibits).

10207 ■ Huron Valley Area Intergroup
31 South Huron st.
Ypsilanti, MI 48197
Ph: (734)482-0707
E-mail: office@hvai.org
URL: http://www.hvai.org
Contact: Linda Koffron, Office Mgr.
Founded: 1984. **Staff:** 1. **Local Groups:** 270. **Languages:** English, French, Spanish. **Nonmembership. Local.** Individuals interested in information about alcoholism or recovering from alcoholism. Help achieve sobriety through a twelve-step program that includes sharing their experience, strength, and hope with each other. **Libraries: Type:** open to the public. **Holdings:** books. **Subjects:** alcoholic anonymous literature. **Telecommunication Services:** 24-hour hotline. **Committees:** Corrections; Public Information; Treatment. **Affiliated With:** Alcoholics Anonymous World Services. **Formerly:** (2003) Huron Valley Intergroup; (2004) Alcoholics Anonymous World Services, Huron Valley Intergroup. **Publications:** *Local Meeting Directory* • Newsletter. **Price:** free.

10208 ■ Huron Valley Sunrise Lions Club
c/o Gary Moss, Pres.
4729 Merritt St.
Ypsilanti, MI 48197
Ph: (734)434-7755
E-mail: gmoss5152@aol.com
URL: http://www.lionsdistrict11b1.org/lc_huron_valley_sunrise.htm
Contact: Gary Moss, Pres.
Local. Affiliated With: Lions Clubs International.

10209 ■ International Union, United Automobile, Aerospace and Agricultural Implement Workers of America, AFL-CIO - Local Union 898
8975 Textile
Ypsilanti, MI 48197-7067
Ph: (734)482-8320
Free: (800)521-7152
E-mail: local898@provide.net
URL: http://www.uawlocal898.org
Contact: Ralph Mayer, Pres.
Members: 2,267. **Local.** AFL-CIO. **Affiliated With:** International Union, United Automobile, Aerospace and Agricultural Implement Workers of America.

10210 ■ Michigan DECA
Eastern Michigan Univ.
Ypsilanti, MI 48197
Ph: (734)487-3322
Fax: (734)487-4329
E-mail: dave.wait@emich.edu
URL: http://mideca.org
Contact: David Wait, Dir.
Founded: 1947. **Members:** 7,500. **Membership Dues:** $17 (annual). **Staff:** 9. **Budget:** $900,000. **Regional Groups:** 8. **State Groups:** 1. **Local Groups:** 165. **State.** Students studying marketing, merchandising, management, and entrepreneurship. Conducts 22 leadership and competitive event conferences. **Publications:** *Spotlight on DECA*, quarterly. Newsletter. **Price:** included in membership dues. **Circulation:** 7,000. **Advertising:** accepted. **Conventions/Meetings:** annual Career Development Conference (exhibits).

10211 ■ National Council of Teachers of English Student Affiliate at Eastern Michigan State University
c/o Heidi Estrem, Faculty Co-Advisor
Eastern Michigan Univ.
601 Pray Harrold
Ypsilanti, MI 48197
Ph: (734)482-9603
URL: National Affiliate–www.ncte.org
Contact: Heidi Estrem, Faculty Co-Advisor
Local. Works to increase the effectiveness of instruction in English language and literature. **Affiliated With:** National Council of Teachers of English.

10212 ■ National Organization for Women - Ann Arbor/Washtenaw County
c/o Bev Fish
1406 W Cross
Ypsilanti, MI 48197

Ph: (734)484-1897
E-mail: beverly.fish@comcast.net
URL: http://www.michnow.org
Contact: Bev Fish, Contact
Local. **Affiliated With:** National Organization for Women.

10213 ■ Psi Chi, National Honor Society in Psychology - Eastern Michigan University
c/o Dept. of Psychology
537 Mark Jefferson Hall
Ypsilanti, MI 48197-2207
Ph: (734)487-1155 (734)487-0189
Fax: (734)487-6553
E-mail: ellen.koch@emich.edu
URL: http://www.psichi.org/chapters/info.asp?chapter_id=448
Contact: Ellen I. Koch PhD, Advisor
Local.

10214 ■ Raisin River Aikikai
432 N Hewitt
Ypsilanti, MI 48197
Ph: (737)777-6376
URL: http://www.raisinriveraikikai.com
Local. **Affiliated With:** United States Aikido Federation.

10215 ■ Society of Manufacturing Engineers - Eastern Michigan University S111
Eastern Michigan Univ., Indus. Tech. Dept.
118 Sill Hall
Ypsilanti, MI 48197-2243
Ph: (734)487-2040
Fax: (734)487-8755
E-mail: philip.rufe@emich.edu
URL: National Affiliate–www.sme.org
Contact: Philip Rufe, Contact
Local. Advances manufacturing knowledge to gain competitive advantage. Improves skills and manufacturing solutions for the growth of economy. Provides resources and opportunities for manufacturing professionals.

10216 ■ Sweet Adelines International, County Connection Chorus
PO Box 970597
Ypsilanti, MI 48197
Ph: (734)480-8843
E-mail: chorus@countyconnectionchorus.org
URL: http://www.sweetadelines.org
Contact: Paula Reading, Events Coor.
Local. Advances the musical art form of barbershop harmony through education and performances. Provides education, training and coaching in the development of women's four-part barbershop harmony. **Affiliated With:** Sweet Adelines International.

10217 ■ Veterans For Peace - Chapter 93
c/o Bob Krzewinski
706 Dwight St.
Ypsilanti, MI 48198
Ph: (734)487-9058
E-mail: wolverbob@cs.com
URL: http://www.vfpwc.org
Contact: Bob Krzewinski, Contact
Local. **Affiliated With:** Veterans for Peace.

10218 ■ Washtenaw Literacy
5577 Whittaker Rd.
Ypsilanti, MI 48197
Ph: (734)879-1320 (734)769-0099
Fax: (734)879-1319
E-mail: info@washtenawliteracy.org
URL: http://www.washtenawliteracy.org
Contact: Chris Roberts, Exec.Dir.
Founded: 1971. **Staff:** 6. **Budget:** $229,726. **Local**. Seeks to reduce illiteracy in Washtenaw County, MI. Recruits and trains volunteer tutors and matches them with low-literate adults for one-on-one or small group instruction in basic reading skills or English as a Second Language. **Libraries:** **Type:** open to the public. **Holdings:** 2,000; books. **Subjects:** literacy, basic reading, ESL. **Awards:** Washtenaw Literacy Scholar Award. **Frequency:** annual. **Type:** recognition. **Recipient:** for outstanding performance as literacy student. **Affiliated With:** Michigan Literacy; ProLiteracy Worldwide. **Publications:** *Washtenaw Literacy News, STARS*, periodic. Newsletter • *Washtenaw Literacy Stars Learner Newsletter*, periodic, 3-4 times per year. **Conventions/Meetings:** annual Appreciation Day - meeting (exhibits) - always May • annual World Literacy Day - meeting - every September 8.

10219 ■ Young Life Ypsilanti
300 N Washington
Ypsilanti, MI 48197
Ph: (734)482-1525
URL: http://sites.younglife.org/sites/Ypsilanti/default.aspx
Contact: Heide Geib, Contact
Local. **Affiliated With:** Young Life.

10220 ■ Ypsilanti Area Chamber of Commerce
301 W Michigan Ave., Ste.101
Ypsilanti, MI 48197-5450
Ph: (734)482-4920
Fax: (734)482-2021
E-mail: keith@ypsichamber.org
URL: http://www.ypsichamber.org
Contact: Keith Peters, Pres.
Founded: 1918. **Members:** 650. **Membership Dues:** business (depends on the number of employees), $225-$800 (annual) • nonprofit, $225 (annual) • individual, $100 (annual) • retired individual, $50 (annual) • in-home sole proprietor, $170 (annual). **Staff:** 5. **Budget:** $400,000. **Local**. Promotes business and community development in the Ypsilanti, MI area. **Awards:** Athena Award. **Frequency:** annual. **Type:** recognition. **Recipient:** for contribution to women • Distinguished Service Award. **Frequency:** annual. **Type:** recognition. **Recipient:** for contribution to the community • E3 Award. **Frequency:** annual. **Type:** recognition. **Recipient:** for contribution in K-12 education • Small Business Person of the Year Award. **Frequency:** annual. **Type:** recognition. **Computer Services:** database, of members • information services, facts about Ypsilanti. **Councils:** Women. **Divisions:** Community Development; Education; Public Policy. **Subcommittees:** Central Business Community. **Publications:** *Business Talk*, monthly. Newsletter. **Circulation:** 100. **Advertising:** accepted. Alternate Formats: online • *Membership and Business*, annual. Directory. **Price:** $50.00. Alternate Formats: diskette. **Conventions/Meetings:** monthly Brown Bag - roundtable - every second Friday excluding July and August.

10221 ■ Ypsilanti Convention and Visitors Bureau
106 W Michigan Ave.
Ypsilanti, MI 48197
Ph: (734)483-4444
E-mail: info@ypsilanti.org
URL: http://www.ypsilanti.org
Local. Promotes convention business and tourism in area. **Publications:** *Conference Planner's Guide - Business Resource Guide*, annual. Contains resource guide. **Price:** free • *Ypsilanti Visitors' Guide*, annual. Contains information for visitors. **Price:** free.

10222 ■ Ypsilanti Lions Club
c/o Doris Walker, Sec.
2235 McKinley St.
Ypsilanti, MI 48197
Ph: (734)434-1122
E-mail: djwalk@webtv.net
URL: http://www.lionsdistrict11b1.org/lc_ypsilanti.htm
Contact: Doris Walker, Sec.
Local. **Affiliated With:** Lions Clubs International.

Zeeland

10223 ■ American Legion, Michigan Post 33
c/o Gilbert D. Karsten
1668 Lakeview Dr.
Zeeland, MI 49464
Ph: (517)371-4720
Fax: (517)371-2401
URL: National Affiliate–www.legion.org
Contact: Gilbert D. Karsten, Contact
Local. **Affiliated With:** American Legion.

10224 ■ Chemical Coaters Association International, West Michigan
c/o Rich Saddler, Pres.
PO Box 302
Zeeland, MI 49464
Ph: (616)654-3329
Fax: (616)654-6037
E-mail: rich_saddler@hermanmiller.com
URL: National Affiliate–www.ccaiweb.com
Contact: Rich Saddler, Pres.
Local. Provides information and training on surface coating technologies. Raises the standards of finishing operations through educational meetings and seminars, training manuals, certification programs, and outreach programs with colleges and universities. **Affiliated With:** Chemical Coaters Association International.

10225 ■ Grand Rapids and Indiana Chapter, Pennsylvania Railroad Technical and Historical Society
c/o Robert Krikke, Sec.-Treas.
4099 80th Ave.
Zeeland, MI 49464
E-mail: krikkelan@charter.net
URL: National Affiliate–www.prrths.com
Contact: Robert Krikke, Sec.-Treas.
Regional. Brings together people who are interested in the history of the Pennsylvania Railroad. Promotes the preservation and recording of all information regarding the organization, operation, facilities and equipment of the Pennsylvania Railroad. **Affiliated With:** Pennsylvania Railroad Technical and Historical Society.

10226 ■ Holland Piano Teachers Forum (HPTF)
c/o Sheryl Iott Richardson
6421 Byron Rd.
Zeeland, MI 49464
Ph: (616)772-6815
E-mail: richa385@msu.edu
URL: http://www.geocities.com/hollandpianoteachersforum
Contact: Sheryl Iott Richardson, Pres.
Members: 35. **Membership Dues:** all, $25 (annual). **Local**. Professional society of music teachers committed to furthering the art of music through programs that encourage and support teaching, performance, composition, and scholarly research. **Libraries:** **Type:** lending. **Holdings:** archival material, audio recordings, books, periodicals, software, video recordings. **Subjects:** music history, piano pedagogy, western art music styles. **Awards:** Bolhuis-VanderKuy Scholarship Award. **Frequency:** annual. **Type:** scholarship. **Recipient:** scholarship award by drawing to student to attend interlochen arts camp or blue lake fine arts camp • Trethewy Scholarship Award. **Frequency:** annual. **Type:** scholarship. **Recipient:** scholarship by drawing to first-time students of blue lake arts camp. **Programs:** Holland Piano Clubs; Macatawa Musikanten - National Federation of Music club. **Affiliated With:** Music Teachers National Association.

10227 ■ Lakeshore Corvette Club (LCC)
c/o Brady Guidry, Pres.
10425 Chicago Dr.
Zeeland, MI 49464

Ph: (616)540-6417
E-mail: bradyg@chartermi.net
URL: http://lakeshorecorvetteclub.8m.com
Contact: Brady Guidry, Pres.
Local. Affiliated With: National Council of Corvette Clubs.

10228 ■ Michigan National Wild Turkey Federation, North Ottawa Toms Chapter
6220 84th Ave.
Zeeland, MI 49464
Ph: (616)875-7935
URL: http://www.mi-nwtf.org/NorthOttawaToms.htm
Contact: Craig Steves, Pres.
Local.

10229 ■ National Active and Retired Federal Employees Association - Holland 1243
10629 Brookview Dr.
Zeeland, MI 49464-6823
Ph: (616)772-4367
URL: National Affiliate–www.narfe.org
Contact: James Sterken, Contact
Local. Protects the retirement future of employees through education. Informs members on issues affecting the retirement. **Affiliated With:** National Association of Retired Federal Employees.

10230 ■ Pontiac-Oakland Club International, West Michigan Chapter (WMPOCI)
c/o Wendell Miller
8830 Taylor St.
Zeeland, MI 49464
E-mail: ensingts@iserv.net
URL: http://hometown.aol.com/michres/westmichiganpontiacclub.html
Contact: Wendell Miller, Contact
Membership Dues: individual, $15 (annual). **Local. Affiliated With:** Pontiac-Oakland Club International.

10231 ■ Product Development and Management Association, Great Lakes
c/o Brian Green, Pres.
Herman Miller, Inc.
855 E Main Ave.
Mail Stop 443
Zeeland, MI 49464
Ph: (616)654-3116
Fax: (616)654-7586
E-mail: bgreen@pdma.org
URL: National Affiliate–www.pdma.org
Contact: Brian Green, Pres.
Regional. Affiliated With: Product Development and Management Association.

10232 ■ Zeeland Chamber of Commerce (ZCC)
149 Main Pl.
Zeeland, MI 49464-1735
Ph: (616)772-2494
Fax: (616)772-0065
E-mail: zchamber@zeelandcofc.org
URL: http://www.zeelandcofc.org
Contact: Ann L. Query, Pres.
Founded: 1937. **Members:** 350. **Local.** Promotes business and community development in Zeeland, MI. **Publications:** *The Zeelander*, 10/year. Newsletter • Directory, annual.

10233 ■ Zeeland Volk's Corporation
c/o Nancy Tuls
21 S Elm St.
Zeeland, MI 49464-0000
Ph: (616)396-4217
URL: National Affiliate–www.ava.org
Contact: Nancy Tuls, Contact
Local.

Ada

10234 ■ Ada Chamber of Commerce
PO Box 1
Ada, MN 56510-0001
Ph: (218)784-3542
Fax: (218)784-2108
E-mail: leeannko@loretel.net
URL: http://www.ci.ada.mn.us
Contact: Lee Ann Konkin, Sec.
Local.

10235 ■ Ada Lions Club - Minnesota
c/o Kim Peters, Pres.
PO Box 263
Ada, MN 56510
Ph: (218)784-5110 (218)784-7118
Fax: (218)784-2706
E-mail: kpeters@loretel.net
URL: http://lions5m11.org/sys-tmpl/adawebpage
Contact: Kim Peters, Pres.
Local. **Affiliated With:** Lions Clubs International.

10236 ■ American Legion, Simonson Betcher Post 26
PO Box 244
Ada, MN 56510
Ph: (651)291-1800
Fax: (651)291-1057
URL: National Affiliate–www.legion.org
Local. **Affiliated With:** American Legion.

10237 ■ Borup Lions Club
c/o Arnold G. Schick, Sec.
PO Box 48
Ada, MN 56510
Ph: (218)784-7407
Fax: (218)784-4112
E-mail: cschick@loretel.net
URL: http://lions5m11.org/sys-tmpl/door
Contact: Arnold G. Schick, Sec.
Local. **Affiliated With:** Lions Clubs International.

Adams

10238 ■ Adams Lions Club
c/o Nathan Augustine, Sec.
Box 32
Adams, MN 55909
Ph: (507)582-1002
E-mail: august11@myclearwave.net
URL: http://www.lions5m1.org/adams
Contact: Nathan Augustine, Sec.
Local. **Affiliated With:** Lions Clubs International.

10239 ■ American Legion, Adams Post 146
PO Box 181
Adams, MN 55909
Ph: (651)291-1800
Fax: (651)291-1057
URL: National Affiliate–www.legion.org
Local. **Affiliated With:** American Legion.

10240 ■ American Legion, Big Red One Post 1111
68127 150th St.
Adams, MN 55909
Ph: (651)291-1800
Fax: (651)291-1057
URL: National Affiliate–www.legion.org
Local. **Affiliated With:** American Legion.

Adrian

10241 ■ American Legion, Argonne Post 32
PO Box 175
Adrian, MN 56110
Ph: (651)291-1800
Fax: (651)291-1057
URL: National Affiliate–www.legion.org
Local. **Affiliated With:** American Legion.

Afton

10242 ■ St. Croix Valley Kennel Club
4490 Neal Ave. S
Afton, MN 55001-9501
Ph: (651)407-7054
Fax: (651)407-7980
E-mail: tcslats@aol.com
URL: http://www.scvkc.org
Contact: Sue Stoterau, Dir.
Founded: 1969. **Members:** 60. **Membership Dues:** individual, $10 (annual). **Local**. Promotes purebred dogs. **Affiliated With:** American Kennel Club. **Publications:** *The St. Croix Scoop*, monthly. Newsletter. **Conventions/Meetings:** monthly meeting - always 1st Tuesday • show - 2 every August.

Aitkin

10243 ■ Aitkin Area Chamber of Commerce (AACC)
PO Box 127
Aitkin, MN 56431-0127
Ph: (218)927-2316
Fax: (218)927-4494
Free: (800)526-8342
E-mail: upnorth@aitkin.com
URL: http://www.aitkin.com
Contact: Carroll Kukowski, Exec.Dir.
Founded: 1945. **Local**. Promotes business and community development in the Aitkin, MN area. Sponsors Riverboat Heritage Days and Festival of Adventures. **Convention/Meeting:** none. **Computer Services:** Online services, membership directory. **Publications:** Directory, periodic • Newsletter, quarterly.

10244 ■ American Legion, Aitkin-Lee Post 86
20 1st Ave. NE
Aitkin, MN 56431
Ph: (651)291-1800
Fax: (651)291-1057
URL: National Affiliate–www.legion.org
Local. **Affiliated With:** American Legion.

10245 ■ Cuyuna Rock, Gem and Mineral Society
c/o Mavis McGuire, Pres.
29203 410th Pl.
Aitkin, MN 56431
E-mail: katmoose@emilv.net
URL: National Affiliate–www.amfed.org
Contact: Kat Thomas, Sec.
Local. Aims to further the study of Earth Sciences and the practice of lapidary arts and mineralogy. **Affiliated With:** American Federation of Mineralogical Societies.

10246 ■ Ruffed Grouse Society, Aikit Area Chapter
c/o James Mac Donald
HC 7 Box 8
Aitkin, MN 56431
Ph: (218)927-2669
URL: National Affiliate–www.ruffedgrousesociety.org
Contact: James Mac Donald, Contact
Local. **Affiliated With:** Ruffed Grouse Society.

10247 ■ Wealthwood Rod and Gun Club
23573 420th Pl.
Aitkin, MN 56431
Ph: (218)678-2281
Free: (888)691-6883
E-mail: wrgc@mlecmn.net
URL: http://www.wealthwoodrodandgunclub.com
Local. **Affiliated With:** National Skeet Shooting Association.

Akeley

10248 ■ American Legion, Minnesota Post 363
c/o Neal Todd
PO Box 182
Akeley, MN 56433
Ph: (651)291-1800
Fax: (651)291-1057
URL: National Affiliate–www.legion.org
Contact: Neal Todd, Contact
Local. **Affiliated With:** American Legion.

Albany

10249 ■ Albany Chamber of Commerce (ACC)
PO Box 634
Albany, MN 56307-0634

Ph: (320)845-7777
Fax: (320)845-2346
E-mail: albanycc@albanytel.com
URL: http://www.albanymnchamber.org
Contact: Berleen Hollenkamp, Sec.
Members: 100. **Local**. Promotes business and community development in Albany, MN. Sponsors annual Albany Heritage Day. **Publications:** none. **Awards: Frequency:** annual. **Type:** scholarship. **Publications:** *Chamber Membership Directory*, annual • Newsletter, monthly.

10250 ■ Albany Sportsmen's Club
PO Box 385
Albany, MN 56307
Ph: (612)845-4271
URL: National Affiliate–www.mynssa.com
Local. **Affiliated With:** National Skeet Shooting Association.

10251 ■ American Legion, Al Besemann Post 482
PO Box 507
Albany, MN 56307
Ph: (651)291-1800
Fax: (651)291-1057
URL: National Affiliate–www.legion.org
Local. **Affiliated With:** American Legion.

Albert Lea

10252 ■ Albert Lea Convention and Visitors Bureau
c/o Jill Slette, Exec.Dir.
2566 N Bridge Ave.
Albert Lea, MN 56007
Fax: (507)373-2316
Free: (800)345-8414
E-mail: alcvb@smig.net
URL: http://www.albertleatourism.org
Contact: Jill Slette, Exec.Dir.
Staff: 2. **Budget:** $110,000. **Nonmembership**. **Local**. Aims to bring in more visitors and tourists in Albert Lea through promotional and informational efforts.

10253 ■ Albert Lea Figure Skating Club
PO Box 368
Albert Lea, MN 56007
E-mail: alljlmlpl@deskmedia.com
URL: National Affiliate–www.usfigureskating.org
Local. Provides programs to encourage participation and achievement in the sport of figure skating on ice. Defines and maintains uniform standards of skating proficiency. Organizes and sponsors competitions and exhibitions for the purpose of stimulating interest in figure skating. **Affiliated With:** United States Figure Skating Association.

10254 ■ Albert Lea - Freeborn County Chamber of Commerce (ALFCCOC)
701 Marshall St.
Albert Lea, MN 56007
Ph: (507)373-3938
Fax: (507)373-0344
E-mail: susiep@albertlea.org
URL: http://www.albertlea.org
Local. **Publications:** *Business Monthly*. Newsletters. **Advertising:** accepted • *E-Biz*, weekly. Newsletter. Alternate Formats: online.

10255 ■ American Legion, Leo Carey Post 56
PO Box 1056
Albert Lea, MN 56007
Ph: (651)291-1800
Fax: (651)291-1057
URL: National Affiliate–www.legion.org
Local. **Affiliated With:** American Legion.

10256 ■ American Truck Historical Society, Hiawathaland Chapter
c/o Joe Becker
2401 Becker Dr.
Albert Lea, MN 56007
Ph: (507)373-8598 (507)373-8513
URL: National Affiliate–www.aths.org
Contact: Joe Becker, Contact
Local.

10257 ■ Freeborn County Genealogical Society (FCGS)
1033 Bridge Ave.
Albert Lea, MN 56007-2205
Ph: (507)373-9269
E-mail: jmjohns@smig.net
URL: http://www.fcgs.org
Contact: Sonja Johnson, Pres.
Founded: 1979. **Members:** 75. **Membership Dues:** $12 (annual). **Local**. Individuals interested in the genealogy of Freeborn County, MN. **Affiliated With:** Freeborn County Historical Society. **Publications:** *Freeborn County Tracer*, quarterly. Newsletter. **Price:** $1.00 plus tax. **Conventions/Meetings:** monthly meeting - always 2nd Monday except December.

10258 ■ Freeborn County Historical Society (FCHS)
1031 Bridge Ave.
Albert Lea, MN 56007
Ph: (507)373-8003
E-mail: bjackso@smig.net
URL: http://www.smig.net/fchm
Contact: Beverly J. Jackson, Exec.Dir.
Founded: 1959. **Members:** 1,050. **Membership Dues:** $20 (annual). **Staff:** 6. **Budget:** $90,000. **Regional**. Individuals interested in collecting, preserving, and interpreting the history of Freeborn County, MN. Freeborn County, Historical Museum. Sponsors Autumn in the Village, summer camps, tours, Eddie Cochran Weekend, Christmas Open House, and various year-round history related events. **Libraries: Type:** open to the public. **Holdings:** 2,000; articles, audiovisuals, books, papers, periodicals, photographs. **Subjects:** Freeborn County and surrounding area history - genealogy and historical research. **Also Known As:** Freeborn County Museum and Historical Village. **Publications:** *Freeborn County Minnesota*. Book. Part of the Images of America series from Arcadia Publishing. **Price:** $18.99 • *The Hollandale Story: 1918-1950*. Book. **Price:** $2.00 • *Reprint of the 1882 History of Freeborn County*. Book. **Price:** $36.95 • *Walking Tour Brochure of Albert Lea* • Newsletter, quarterly.

10259 ■ Lake Chapeau Habitat Committee
2734 Campus Ln.
Albert Lea, MN 56007-4358
Ph: (507)373-8927
Contact: Thomas Tubbs, Pres.
Founded: 1999. **Members:** 100. **Local Groups:** 1. **Local**. Dedicated to improving the environment and habitat in and around Lake Chapeau, located in Freeborn County, MN. **Publications:** Newsletter, 2-3/year. **Price:** free. **Conventions/Meetings:** periodic meeting.

10260 ■ National Active and Retired Federal Employees Association - Albert Lea-Austin 469
210 E Second St.
Albert Lea, MN 56007-3002
Ph: (507)373-8113
URL: National Affiliate–www.narfe.org
Contact: Jonathon J. Green, Contact
Local. Protects the retirement future of employees through education. Informs members on issues affecting the retirement. **Affiliated With:** National Association of Retired Federal Employees.

10261 ■ Skills USA, Albert Lea High School
2000 Tiger Ln.
Albert Lea, MN 56007
Ph: (507)379-5411
Fax: (507)379-5498
E-mail: wwebb@albertlea.k12.mn.us
URL: http://www.mnskillsusa.org
Contact: William Webb, Contact
Local. Serves high school and college students enrolled in technical, skilled, and service and health occupations. Provides quality education experiences for students in leadership, teamwork, citizenship and character development. Builds and reinforces self-confidence, work attitudes and communication skills. Emphasizes total quality at work, high ethical standards, superior work skills, and life-long education. Promotes understanding of the free enterprise system and involvement in community service. **Affiliated With:** Skills USA - VICA.

10262 ■ So. Mn. Albert Lea REACT
PO Box 305
Albert Lea, MN 56007
Ph: (507)874-3422
E-mail: christch@smig.net
URL: http://www.reactintl.org/teaminfo/usa_teams/teams-usmn.htm
Local. Trained communication experts and professional volunteers. Provides volunteer public service and emergency communications through the use of radios (Citizen Band, General Mobile Radio Service, UHF and HAM). Coordinates with radio industries and government on safety communication matters and supports charitable activities and community organizations.

10263 ■ Sons of Norway, Normanna Lodge 1-52
c/o Robert D. Field, Pres.
316 Fairview Dr.
Albert Lea, MN 56007-2222
Ph: (507)373-9007
E-mail: rdfield@smig.net
URL: National Affiliate–www.sofn.com
Contact: Robert D. Field, Pres.
Local. **Affiliated With:** Sons of Norway.

10264 ■ South Central Minnesota Youth for Christ
116 W Clark St.
Albert Lea, MN 56007
Ph: (507)373-1015
Fax: (507)373-1007
URL: http://www.yfctherock.com
Local. **Affiliated With:** Youth for Christ/U.S.A.

10265 ■ Southern Tri-County RSVP
c/o Beth Spande, Dir.
1659 1/2 W Main St.
Albert Lea, MN 56007-4500
Ph: (507)377-2377
Fax: (507)377-2879
E-mail: bspande.volunteer@charterinternet.net
URL: http://www.seniorcorps.gov
Contact: Beth Spande, Dir.
Local. **Affiliated With:** Retired and Senior Volunteer Program.

10266 ■ Sustainable Farming Association of Minnesota - South Central
c/o Julie Ackland, Coor.
26154 State Hwy. 13
Albert Lea, MN 56007
Ph: (507)826-3358
E-mail: southcentralsfa@hotmail.com
URL: http://www.sfa-mn.org
Contact: Julie Ackland, Coor.
Regional.

10267 ■ United Food and Commercial Workers International Union, AFL-CIO, CLC - Local Union 6
404 E Main St.
Albert Lea, MN 56007-2934
Ph: (507)373-0649
Free: (800)300-0649
E-mail: local6@smig.net
URL: http://spider.smig.net/users/local6/index.htm
Contact: Patrick Neilon, Pres.
Members: 1,541. **Local**. **Affiliated With:** United Food and Commercial Workers International Union.

10268 ■ United Way of Freeborn County
341 S Broadway Ave.
Albert Lea, MN 56007-4502
Ph: (507)373-8670
Fax: (507)377-0851
E-mail: uwfc@smig.net
URL: National Affiliate–national.unitedway.org
Contact: Jean Eaton, Exec.Dir.
Founded: 1947. **Members:** 25. **Staff:** 2. **Local. Affiliated With:** United Way of America.

Albertville

10269 ■ Albertville Lions Club
PO Box 82
Albertville, MN 55301
Ph: (763)497-6031
E-mail: lionstevebrown@charter.net
URL: http://albertvillemn.lionwap.org
Contact: Steve Brown, 1st VP
Local. Affiliated With: Lions Clubs International.

Alden

10270 ■ American Legion, Alden Post 404
151 N Broadway
Alden, MN 56009
Ph: (651)291-1800
Fax: (651)291-1057
URL: National Affiliate–www.legion.org
Local. Affiliated With: American Legion.

Alexandria

10271 ■ Alexandria Lakes Area Chamber of Commerce (AACC)
206 Broadway
Alexandria, MN 56308
Ph: (320)763-3161
Fax: (320)763-6857
Free: (800)235-9441
E-mail: alexrecr@rea-alp.com
URL: http://www.alexandriamn.org
Contact: Coni McKay, Exec.Dir.
Founded: 1907. **Local.** Promotes business and community development in the Alexandria, MN area. **Publications:** *Alexandria Lakes Area Visitor Guide*, annual. Magazine. Contains information on lodging and attractions in Douglas county area. **Price:** free • *Runeskriber*, monthly. Newsletter. Includes organization and community news. **Price:** free to members; $15.00/year for non-members.

10272 ■ American Legion, Alexandria Post 87
PO Box 1243
Alexandria, MN 56308
Ph: (612)763-4313
Fax: (651)291-1057
URL: National Affiliate–www.legion.org
Local. Affiliated With: American Legion.

10273 ■ American Legion, Inspiration Peak Post 527
804 Shady Ln. SW
Alexandria, MN 56308
Ph: (651)291-1800
Fax: (651)291-1057
URL: National Affiliate–www.legion.org
Local. Affiliated With: American Legion.

10274 ■ Carlos Lions Club
c/o Dave Schnieder, Sec.
6273 Maple Ln. NE
Alexandria, MN 56308
Ph: (320)852-7913
E-mail: schneids@midwestinfo.net
URL: http://www.5m4lions.org
Contact: Dave Schnieder, Sec.
Local. Affiliated With: Lions Clubs International.

10275 ■ Douglas County Historical Society
c/o Rachel Barduson, Dir.
1219 Nokomis St.
Alexandria, MN 56308
Ph: (320)762-0382
E-mail: historic@rea-alp.com
Contact: Rachel Barduson, Dir.
Membership Dues: $15 (annual). **Local.**

10276 ■ Forada Lions Club
c/o Travis Lay, Sec.
5202 Rockwood Rd. SW
Alexandria, MN 56308
Ph: (320)763-8503
E-mail: afl@rea-alp.com
URL: http://www.5m4lions.org
Contact: Travis Lay, Sec.
Local. Affiliated With: Lions Clubs International.

10277 ■ Glacial Ridge AIFA
c/o Pat Hacker
107 5th Ave. W
Alexandria, MN 56308
Ph: (320)763-3151
Fax: (320)763-0874
E-mail: phacker@rea-alp.com
URL: National Affiliate–naifa.org
Contact: Pat Hacker, Contact
Local. Represents the interests of insurance and financial advisors. Advocates for a positive legislative and regulatory environment. Enhances business and professional skills of members. **Affiliated With:** National Association of Insurance and Financial Advisors.

10278 ■ Greater Alexandria Area Association of Realtors
409 Nokomis St.
Alexandria, MN 56308
Ph: (320)762-2022
Fax: (320)762-9021
Free: (866)281-9786
E-mail: info@alexandriamnrealtors.com
URL: http://www.alexandriamnrealtors.com
Contact: Mike Munson, Pres.
Local. Strives to develop real estate business practices. Advocates the right to own, use and transfer real property. Provides a facility for professional development, research and exchange of information among members. **Affiliated With:** National Association of Realtors.

10279 ■ Heart of Lakes Chapter of the United Way
PO Box 1148
Alexandria, MN 56308
Ph: (320)763-4840
Fax: (320)763-4840
E-mail: unitedw@rea-alp.com
URL: http://www.alexweb.net/unitedway
Contact: Linda Roles, Exec.Dir.
Founded: 1950. **Staff:** 2. **Budget:** $482,750. **Nonmembership. Local.** Promotes community building, working for donors, raising and distributing funds for agencies providing health and human services to residents of Douglas County. **Affiliated With:** United Way of America.

10280 ■ Miltona Lions Club
c/o Frank Timmins, Pres.
12935 Miltona Bay Rd. NE
Alexandria, MN 56308
Ph: (320)852-7320
E-mail: miltonaskipp@yahoo.com
URL: http://www.5m4lions.org
Contact: Frank Timmins, Pres.
Local. Affiliated With: Lions Clubs International.

10281 ■ Minnesota Ambulance Association, West Central
c/o Rick Wagner, Dir.
PO Box 818
Alexandria, MN 56308
Ph: (320)763-6160
Fax: (320)763-5589
E-mail: rick.wagner@northmemorial.com
URL: http://www.mnems.org
Contact: Rick Wagner, Dir.
Local. Seeks to maintain the financial viability of the EMS industry by advocating education, legislation and regulatory change. **Affiliated With:** Minnesota Ambulance Association.

10282 ■ Minnesota Pharmacists Association, Central District
c/o Jeff Lindoo, Chm.
Thrifty White Drug Stores, Inc.
2107 Ridgewood Dr. NW
Alexandria, MN 56308
Ph: (763)513-4362
E-mail: jlindoo@thriftywhite.com
URL: http://www.mpha.org
Contact: Jeff Lindoo, Chm.
Local. Works to provide leadership for the pharmacy profession. Seeks to protect and enhance public health. Enhances the knowledge, ethics and skills of pharmacists through advocacy, education, research and the development of standards. **Affiliated With:** Minnesota Pharmacists Association.

10283 ■ National Active and Retired Federal Employees Association - Vikingland 2213
2812 County Rd. 82 NW
Alexandria, MN 56308-8145
Ph: (320)763-5933
URL: National Affiliate–www.narfe.org
Contact: Ward J. Aas, Contact
Local. Protects the retirement future of employees through education. Informs members on issues affecting the retirement. **Affiliated With:** National Association of Retired Federal Employees.

10284 ■ Phi Theta Kappa, Alpha Pi Phi Chapter - Alexandria Technical College
c/o Cherryl Grammentz
1601 Jefferson St.
Alexandria, MN 56308
Ph: (320)762-4542
E-mail: cherylg@alextech.edu
URL: http://www.ptk.org/directories/chapters/MN/8553-1.htm
Contact: Cheryl Grammentz, Advisor
Local.

10285 ■ Sons of Norway, Runic Vennskap Lodge 1-530
c/o Lars Nelson, Pres.
300 Fingal Dr.
Alexandria, MN 56308-2115
Ph: (320)763-1723
E-mail: larsjoan@rea-alp.com
URL: National Affiliate–www.sofn.com
Contact: Lars Nelson, Pres.
Local. Affiliated With: Sons of Norway.

10286 ■ Sweet Adelines International, Alexienne Chapter
First Lutheran Church
822 Douglas
Alexandria, MN 56308
Ph: (320)834-4661
E-mail: fynboh@direcway.com
URL: National Affiliate–www.sweetadelineintl.org
Contact: Kathy Fynboh, Contact
Local. Advances the musical art form of barbershop harmony through education and performances. Provides education, training and coaching in the development of women's four-part barbershop harmony. **Affiliated With:** Sweet Adelines International.

10287 ■ WesMin Resource Conservation and Development Council
900 Robert St., Ste.No. 104
Alexandria, MN 56308

Ph: (320)763-3191
Fax: (320)762-5502
E-mail: sheila.barsness@rcdnet.net
URL: http://www.wesminrcd.org
Contact: Sheila Barsness, Exec.Dir.
Local. Affiliated With: National Association of Resource Conservation and Development Councils.

Altura

10288 ■ Altura Lions Club
c/o Yvonne Ruhoff, Sec.
PO Box 26
Altura, MN 55910
Ph: (507)796-6731
E-mail: ruhoff.yvonne@mayo.edu
URL: http://www.lions5m1.org/altura
Contact: Yvonne Ruhoff, Sec.
Local. Affiliated With: Lions Clubs International.

Alvarado

10289 ■ Alvarado Lions Club
c/o Matthew Edman, Sec.
44734 240th St. NW
Alvarado, MN 56710
Ph: (218)965-4854
E-mail: matlos@wiktel.com
URL: http://lions5m11.org/sys-tmpl/door
Contact: Matthew Edman, Sec.
Local. Affiliated With: Lions Clubs International.

10290 ■ American Legion, Minnesota Post 35
c/o Art Yanish
105 6th St.
Alvarado, MN 56710
Ph: (651)291-1800
Fax: (651)291-1057
URL: National Affiliate–www.legion.org
Contact: Art Yanish, Contact
Local. Affiliated With: American Legion.

Amboy

10291 ■ American Legion, Jennings Post 276
PO Box 275
Amboy, MN 56010
Ph: (651)291-1800
Fax: (651)291-1057
URL: National Affiliate–www.legion.org
Local. Affiliated With: American Legion.

10292 ■ American Legion, Minnesota Post 616
c/o Robert H. Stratton
12817 542nd Ave.
Amboy, MN 56010
Ph: (651)291-1800
Fax: (651)291-1057
URL: National Affiliate–www.legion.org
Contact: Robert H. Stratton, Contact
Local. Affiliated With: American Legion.

10293 ■ Minnesota Quarter Horse Association, District 2
c/o Todd Flatness
51422 State Hwy. 30
Amboy, MN 56010
Ph: (507)674-3911
URL: http://www.mnqha.com/index_main.htm
Contact: Todd Flatness, Contact
Local. Affiliated With: American Quarter Horse Association.

Andover

10294 ■ American Legion, Ham Lake Post 2000
14750 Palm St. NW
Andover, MN 55304
Ph: (651)291-1800
Fax: (651)291-1057
URL: National Affiliate–www.legion.org
Local. Affiliated With: American Legion.

10295 ■ Andover Lions Club
16185 Verdin Ave.
Andover, MN 55304
Ph: (763)434-2417 (763)434-8464
E-mail: tboshart@terix.com
URL: http://andovermn.lionwap.org
Contact: Tom Boshart, Treas.
Local. Affiliated With: Lions Clubs International.

10296 ■ Minnesota Pharmacists Association, West Metro District
c/o Scott M. Benson, Chm.
Goodrich Pharmacy
15245 Bluebird St. NW
Andover, MN 55304
Ph: (763)434-1901
E-mail: 6bensons@comcast.net
URL: http://www.mpha.org
Contact: Scott M. Benson, Chm.
Local. Works to provide leadership for the pharmacy profession. Seeks to protect and enhance public health. Enhances the knowledge, ethics and skills of pharmacists through advocacy, education, research and the development of standards. **Affiliated With:** Minnesota Pharmacists Association.

10297 ■ Minnesota Woodturners Association
c/o Ron Meilahn, Treas.
13968 Alder St. NW
Andover, MN 55304-4251
E-mail: jim.w.zangl@healthpartners.com
URL: http://mnwoodturners.com
Contact: Jim Zangl, Pres.
Members: 204. **Membership Dues:** general, $25 (annual). **State.** Represents amateur and professional woodturners, gallery owners, wood and equipment suppliers, and collectors. **Libraries: Type:** not open to the public; lending. **Holdings:** video recordings. **Subjects:** woodturning. **Affiliated With:** American Association of Woodturners.

10298 ■ Sons of Norway, Nidaros Lodge 1-1
c/o Carolyn J. Townsend, Pres.
1268 146th Ave. NW
Andover, MN 55304-7712
Ph: (763)434-5650
E-mail: cjtownsen@comcast.net
URL: http://www.nidaros1.org
Contact: Carolyn J. Townsend, Pres.
Local. Affiliated With: Sons of Norway.

Annandale

10299 ■ American Legion, Annandale Post 176
271 Myrtle Dr. S
Annandale, MN 55302
Ph: (612)274-8427
Fax: (651)291-1057
URL: National Affiliate–www.legion.org
Local. Affiliated With: American Legion.

10300 ■ Friendship Ventures
c/o Catherine
10509 108th St. NW
Annandale, MN 55302
Ph: (952)852-0101
Fax: (952)852-0123
Free: (800)450-8376
E-mail: fv@friendshipventures.org
URL: http://www.friendshipventures.org
Local.

Anoka

10301 ■ American Legion, Minnesota Post 102
c/o Edward B. Cutter
400 W Main St.
Anoka, MN 55303
Ph: (651)291-1800
Fax: (651)291-1057
URL: National Affiliate–www.legion.org
Contact: Edward B. Cutter, Contact
Local. Affiliated With: American Legion.

10302 ■ American Subcontractors Association of Minnesota
c/o Rocci Lueck
16112 Wake St. NE
Anoka, MN 55304
Ph: (763)413-0669
Fax: (763)413-1131
E-mail: asamn@msn.com
URL: National Affiliate–www.asaonline.com
Contact: Ms. Rocci Lueck, Exec.Dir.
Founded: 1990. **Members:** 50. **Membership Dues:** all, $595 (annual). **Staff:** 1. **State Groups:** 1. **Local Groups:** 1. **State.** Works to educate subcontractors and suppliers in the construction industry. **Awards:** TOPS Award. **Frequency:** annual. **Type:** trophy. **Affiliated With:** American Subcontractors Association. **Publications:** *Sub-News*, quarterly. Newsletter. **Price:** included in membership dues. **Circulation:** 50. **Advertising:** accepted.

10303 ■ Anoka Area Chamber of Commerce (AACC)
12 Bridge Sq.
Anoka, MN 55303
Ph: (763)421-7130
Fax: (763)421-0577
E-mail: mail@anokaareachamber.com
URL: http://www.anokaareachamber.com
Contact: Peter Turok, Pres.
Founded: 1952. **Members:** 460. **Local.** Promotes business and community development in Andover, Anoka, Champlin, Dayton, and Ramsey, MN. **Publications:** *Directory and Map*, annual • Newsletter, monthly.

10304 ■ Anoka County Historical Society
2135 3rd Ave. N
Anoka, MN 55303
Ph: (763)421-0600
Fax: (763)323-0218
URL: http://www.ac-hs.org
Contact: Bunny McDonald, Exec.Dir.
Local.

10305 ■ Anoka County RSVP
c/o Diane Pokorney, Dir.
Govt. Center
2100 3rd Ave.
Anoka, MN 55303-2264
Ph: (763)422-7090
Fax: (763)422-6987
E-mail: diane.pokorney@co.anoka.mn.us
URL: http://www.seniorcorps.gov/about/programs/rsvp_state.asp?usestateabbr=mn&Search4.x=14&Search4.y=13
Contact: Diane Pokorney, Dir.
Local. Affiliated With: Retired and Senior Volunteer Program.

10306 ■ Minnesota Environmental Health Association (MEHA)
PO Box 441
Anoka, MN 55303
Ph: (763)531-1144
Fax: (763)531-1188
E-mail: info@mehaonline.org
URL: http://www.mehaonline.org
Contact: Chris Forslund, Pres.
State. Advances the environmental health and protection profession. Provides educational and training opportunities for members. Works to establish standards of competence and ethics for the

profession. **Affiliated With:** National Environmental Health Association.

10307 ■ Minnesota Women of Today (MN WT)
c/o Nancy Dvoracek, Exec.Dir.
PO Box 232
Anoka, MN 55303
Ph: (763)421-4718
Fax: (763)421-4718
E-mail: csc@mnwt.org
URL: http://www.mnwt.org
Contact: Nancy Dvoracek, Exec.Dir.
Founded: 1950. **Members:** 2,200. **Membership Dues:** $35 (annual). **Staff:** 1. **Local Groups:** 112. **State**. Seeks to help women improve their own lives and the lives of the communities around them. Young women are actively encouraged to become involved and hold positions of leadership. Members are encouraged to contribute to their communities by raising funds for worthy causes and by providing services or education to benefit community members. They are encouraged to develop and to foster skills and talents related to becoming successful individuals, interacting well with other people and becoming capable leaders. Members also learn to develop friendships and to find personal support within the organization. **Awards:** Key Women. **Frequency:** quarterly. **Type:** recognition. **Recipient:** for member for accomplishments in organization lifetime achievement award • Outstanding Woman in Government. **Frequency:** annual. **Type:** recognition. **Recipient:** for women involved in governmental positions; elected or volunteer can be local, state or national level nominated by local chapters • Outstanding Young Adult. **Frequency:** annual. **Type:** scholarship. **Recipient:** to youth involved in community service nominated by local chapters • Outstanding Young Woman. **Frequency:** annual. **Type:** recognition. **Recipient:** for young women under the age of 40 involved in community service nominated by local chapters. **Computer Services:** Information services, of chapters and members on programming area and organizational materials • mailing lists, of members. **Conventions/Meetings:** annual Summer Awards - convention, statewide meeting offering programming training for chapters (exhibits).

10308 ■ Minnetonka Game and Fish Club
PO Box 276
Anoka, MN 55303
Ph: (763)545-9331
E-mail: contact@mgfc-mrc.org
URL: http://mgfc.org
Local. Affiliated With: National Skeet Shooting Association.

10309 ■ North Star African Violet Council (NSAVC)
c/o Carol Samrau
2912 9th Ave. N
Anoka, MN 55303
Ph: (763)421-0242
E-mail: gail.podany@lindjensen.com
URL: http://nsavc.home.comcast.net
Contact: Carol Samrau, Contact
Local. Affiliated With: African Violet Society of America.

10310 ■ Phi Theta Kappa, Beta Nu Omicron Chapter - Anoka Technical College
c/o Julie Lundquist
1355 W Hwy. 10
Anoka, MN 55303
Ph: (763)576-4812
E-mail: jlundquist@ank.tec.mn.us
URL: http://www.ptk.org/directories/chapters/MN/22271-1.htm
Contact: Julie Lundquist, Advisor
Local.

10311 ■ Skills USA, Anoka-Hennepin Technical College
1355 W Hwy. 10
Anoka, MN 55303
Ph: (763)576-4977
E-mail: dszabla@ank.tec.mn.us
URL: http://www.mnskillsusa.org
Contact: Dale Szabla, Contact
Local. Serves high school and college students enrolled in technical, skilled, and service and health occupations. Provides quality education experiences for students in leadership, teamwork, citizenship and character development. Builds and reinforces self-confidence, work attitudes and communication skills. Emphasizes total quality at work, high ethical standards, superior work skills, and life-long education. Promotes understanding of the free enterprise system and involvement in community service. **Affiliated With:** Skills USA - VICA.

10312 ■ Skills USA, Anoka High School
3939 7th Ave. N
Anoka, MN 55303
Ph: (763)506-6394
Fax: (763)506-6203
E-mail: keith.packer@anoka.k12.mn.us
URL: http://www.mnskillsusa.org
Contact: Keith Packer, Contact
Local. Serves high school and college students enrolled in technical, skilled, and service and health occupations. Provides quality education experiences for students in leadership, teamwork, citizenship and character development. Builds and reinforces self-confidence, work attitudes and communication skills. Emphasizes total quality at work, high ethical standards, superior work skills, and life-long education. Promotes understanding of the free enterprise system and involvement in community service. **Affiliated With:** Skills USA - VICA.

10313 ■ Skills USA, S.T.E.P. - Secondary Technical Education Program
1353 W Hwy. 10
Anoka, MN 55303
Ph: (763)433-4001
Fax: (763)433-4003
URL: http://www.mnskillsusa.org/secondaryChapters.htm
Contact: Ginny Karboski, Dir.
Local. Serves high school and college students enrolled in technical, skilled, and service and health occupations. Provides quality education experiences for students in leadership, teamwork, citizenship and character development. Builds and reinforces self-confidence, work attitudes and communication skills. Emphasizes total quality at work, high ethical standards, superior work skills, and life-long education. Promotes understanding of the free enterprise system and involvement in community service. **Affiliated With:** Skills USA - VICA.

Apple Valley

10314 ■ American Legion, Apple Valley Post 1776
14521 Granada Dr.
Apple Valley, MN 55124
Ph: (651)291-1800
Fax: (651)291-1057
URL: National Affiliate–www.legion.org
Local. Affiliated With: American Legion.

10315 ■ American Rose Society, North Central District
c/o Norma Booty
7412 Upper 136th St. W
Apple Valley, MN 55124-7633
Ph: (952)432-4313
E-mail: applerose44@hotmail.com
URL: http://www.northcentralrose.org
Contact: Norma Booty, Dir.
Local. Affiliated With: American Rose Society.

10316 ■ Apple Valley Chamber of Commerce
14800 Galaxie Ave. W, Ste.301
Apple Valley, MN 55124
Ph: (952)432-8422
Fax: (952)432-7964
Free: (800)301-9435
E-mail: info@applevalleychamber.com
URL: http://www.applevalleychamber.com
Contact: Edward Kearney, Pres.
Members: 320. **Membership Dues:** business (based on number of full time employees), $220-$1,085 • apartment, mobile home park, non-profit organization, $220 • financial institution, utility, $750 • hospital, health care facility, $645 • industrial park, land developer, office building, shopping center, $345 • hotel, motel (base), $240 • individual (non-voting and non-business owner), $105. **Local**. Businesses interested in prospering and creating a healthy, positive environment in which to conduct business. Strives to enhance the business environment and to build a better community by uniting businesses and professional firms. **Publications:** *Newsline*, monthly. Newsletter. Alternate Formats: online • Annual Report.

10317 ■ Apple Valley Lions Club
c/o Don Johnson, Sec.
6580 134th St. W
Apple Valley, MN 55124
Ph: (952)432-8294
E-mail: applevalleylions@yahoo.com
URL: http://www.geocities.com/applevalleylions
Contact: Don Johnson, Sec.
Local. Affiliated With: Lions Clubs International.

10318 ■ Cosmos Cricket Club
8749 134th St.
Apple Valley, MN 55124
URL: http://www.usaca.org/Clubs.htm
Local.

10319 ■ Eagan-Heights Figure Skating Club
7215 121st St. W
Apple Valley, MN 55124
Ph: (651)675-5590
E-mail: eaganheightsfsc@aol.com
URL: http://www.geocities.com/eaganheightsfsc
Local. Provides programs to encourage participation and achievement in the sport of figure skating on ice. Defines and maintains uniform standards of skating proficiency. Organizes and sponsors competitions and exhibitions for the purpose of stimulating interest in figure skating. **Affiliated With:** United States Figure Skating Association.

10320 ■ Minnesota Career Development Association (MCDA)
c/o Shelia Cunningham-McComb, Pres.
14985 Glazier Ave., Ste.550
Apple Valley, MN 55124
E-mail: peter@careerplanningresources.com
URL: http://www.mcda.net
Contact: Shelia Cunningham-McComb, Pres.
Members: 275. **Membership Dues:** individual, $30 (annual) • graduate student enrolled half time or more, $15 (annual). **Budget:** $40,000. **State**. Career counselors, coaches, educators, training and development professionals, human resource professionals, outplacement consultants, psychologists and career planning and placement professionals. Aims to provide professional development and opportunities to impact the field of career development. Holds an annual spring conference, a fall professional development event and a winter seminar. **Awards:** Jules Kerlan Outstanding Achievement Award. **Frequency:** annual. **Type:** recognition • Marty Dockman. **Frequency:** annual. **Type:** recognition • Sunny Hansen Graduate Student Award. **Frequency:** annual. **Type:** monetary. **Computer Services:** database. **Affiliated With:** National Career Development Association. **Publications:** *The Communique*, quarterly. Newsletter. **Circulation:** 275. **Conventions/Meetings:** annual conference, with notable keynote speakers (exhibits).

10321 ■ Moms Club of Apple Valley
13693 Findlay Ave.
Apple Valley, MN 55124-8145
E-mail: avmomsclub@yahoo.com
URL: http://www.shoutmusic.com/MOMSClub/
Founded: 1996. **Members:** 35. **Local. Conventions/Meetings:** monthly meeting - every 3rd Thursday of the month.

10322 ■ Northland Chapter of Falcon Club of America
PO Box 241382
Apple Valley, MN 55124
E-mail: falcon1964@frontiernet.net
URL: http://www.northland-falcons.com
Regional.

10323 ■ Ring Around the Arts
PO Box 240243
Apple Valley, MN 55124-0243
Ph: (952)985-3463
Fax: (952)891-4250
E-mail: info@ringaroundthearts.com
URL: http://www.ringaroundthearts.com
Contact: Regina Mulder, Contact
Founded: 1992. **Staff:** 1. **Budget:** $30,000. **Local.** Promotes public awareness and appreciation of the arts in Apple Valley, MN. Annual outdoor arts festival. **Conventions/Meetings:** annual festival.

10324 ■ Seniors Learning Together
PO Box 240773
Apple Valley, MN 55124-0773
Local. Provides seminars for senior adults.

10325 ■ Turkish American Association of Minnesota (TAAM)
PO Box 240394
Apple Valley, MN 55124
E-mail: taam@taam.org
URL: http://www.taam.org
Contact: Serpil Metin, Pres.
Founded: 1989. **Members:** 128. **Membership Dues:** family, $25 (annual) • individual, $15 (annual) • student, $7 (annual). **Budget:** $5,500. **Languages:** English, Turkish. **State.** Fosters awareness in the community of the richness of Turkish heritage and the contributions of the people of Turkey and their families to American life and to the cultures of the world and seeks to keep Turkish culture alive among the people of Turkey and their families who are residing in the state of MN. Organizes social, educational, recreational, and other functions to promote better understanding and friendship both among the members of this corporation and among individuals and organizations within MN who share an interest in Turkish culture; activities include social events, concerts, student welcome nights, film shows, and slide shows. Attends the International Festival in MN to represent Turkey and its culture. **Affiliated With:** Assembly of Turkish American Associations. **Publications:** *SOHBET* (in English and Turkish), quarterly. Newsletter. **Price:** included in membership dues. **Advertising:** accepted. Alternate Formats: online. **Conventions/Meetings:** monthly board meeting • annual meeting, membership.

10326 ■ Twin Cities Human Resource Association
14985 Glazier Ave., Ste.550
Apple Valley, MN 55124
Ph: (952)432-7755
E-mail: dstachowski@stuartco.com
URL: http://www.tchra.org
Contact: Deb Stachowski, Pres.
Local. Represents the interests of human resource and industrial relations professionals and executives. Promotes the advancement of human resource management.

10327 ■ Twin Cities Vizsla Club (TCVC)
c/o Lance Huston
200 Ridgeview Dr.
Apple Valley, MN 55124
E-mail: tcvc@yahoo.com
URL: http://www.tcvc.org
Contact: George Noren, Pres.
Local.

Appleton

10328 ■ American Legion, Prairie Post 1998
PO Box 500
Appleton, MN 56208
Ph: (651)291-1800
Fax: (651)291-1057
URL: National Affiliate–www.legion.org
Local. Affiliated With: American Legion.

10329 ■ American Legion, Russell Johnson Post 72
35 N Miles St.
Appleton, MN 56208
Ph: (651)291-1800
Fax: (651)291-1057
URL: National Affiliate–www.legion.org
Local. Affiliated With: American Legion.

10330 ■ Appleton Lions Club
c/o Dan Enke, Pres.
324 S Hering St.
Appleton, MN 56208
Ph: (320)289-1724
E-mail: denke@info-link.net
URL: http://www.5m4lions.org
Contact: Dan Enke, Pres.
Local. Affiliated With: Lions Clubs International.

Arden Hills

10331 ■ American Meteorological Society, Twin Cities
c/o Kurt Scholz, Newsletter Ed.
3233 Snelling Ave. N
Arden Hills, MN 55112
Ph: (651)631-1248
E-mail: k9scholz@stthomas.edu
Contact: Kurt Scholz, Newsletter Ed.
Local. Affiliated With: American Meteorological Society.

10332 ■ Studebakers Driver's Club, North Star Chapter
c/o Jerry Pearson, Pres.
1121 Amble Dr.
Arden Hills, MN 55112
Ph: (651)635-0161
E-mail: stude.one@usfamily.net
URL: http://www.northstarwheel.com
Contact: Jerry Pearson, Pres.
Local. Owners of Studebaker automobiles and trucks. Attempts to aid in the restoration of, procure parts for, and reproduce old instruction manuals of the Studebaker car. **Affiliated With:** Studebaker Driver's Club.

Argyle

10333 ■ American Legion, Hogberg-Gerszewski Post 353
106 E 3rd St.
Argyle, MN 56713
Ph: (651)291-1800
Fax: (651)291-1057
URL: National Affiliate–www.legion.org
Local. Affiliated With: American Legion.

10334 ■ Argyle Lions Club
PO Box 91
Argyle, MN 56713
Ph: (218)745-8502 (218)965-4992
Fax: (218)745-6014
E-mail: dad417@yahoo.com
URL: http://lions5m11.org/sys-tmpl/door
Contact: David Durand, Sec.
Local. Affiliated With: Lions Clubs International.

10335 ■ Red River Valley Angus Association
c/o Arnold Donarski, Pres.
29339 440th Ave. NW
Argyle, MN 56713
Ph: (218)437-8224
URL: National Affiliate–www.angus.org
Contact: Arnold Donarski, Pres.
Local. Affiliated With: American Angus Association.

Arlington

10336 ■ American Legion, Scharmer-Berger Post 250
PO Box 451
Arlington, MN 55307
Ph: (651)291-1800
Fax: (651)291-1057
URL: National Affiliate–www.legion.org
Local. Affiliated With: American Legion.

10337 ■ Arlington Area Chamber of Commerce (AACC)
PO Box 650
Arlington, MN 55307
Ph: (507)964-2256
Fax: (507)964-5550
E-mail: trisha_rosenfield@hotmail.com
Contact: Trisha Rosenfield, Pres.
Local. Promotes business and community development in the Arlington, MN area. **Conventions/Meetings:** monthly meeting.

10338 ■ Arlington Lions Club - Minnesota
147 W Main St.
Arlington, MN 55307
E-mail: liondan@mchsi.com
URL: http://home.mchsi.com/~liondan/wsb/html/view.cgi-home.html-.html
Local. Affiliated With: Lions Clubs International.

10339 ■ Minnesota Angus Association
c/o Jim Scharpe, Sec.-Treas.
20573 401st Ave.
Arlington, MN 55307
Ph: (507)964-5756
E-mail: scharpe8@frontiernet.net
URL: http://www.mn-angus.com
Contact: Jim Scharpe, Sec.-Treas.
Membership Dues: $30 (annual). **State. Affiliated With:** American Angus Association.

10340 ■ Sibley County Pheasants Forever
24539 431st Ave.
Arlington, MN 55307
Ph: (952)873-4564
URL: http://www.sibleycountypf.com
Contact: Bruce Ponath, Pres.
Local. Affiliated With: Pheasants Forever.

Ashby

10341 ■ American Legion, Pederson-Tripp Post 357
100 Larson St.
Ashby, MN 56309
Ph: (651)291-1800
Fax: (651)291-1057
URL: National Affiliate–www.legion.org
Local. Affiliated With: American Legion.

10342 ■ Ashby Lions Club
c/o Donna Grover, Sec.
PO Box 81
Ashby, MN 56309
Ph: (218)747-2205
E-mail: donnafay@prtel.net
URL: http://www.5m4lions.org
Contact: Donna Grover, Sec.
Local. Affiliated With: Lions Clubs International.

Askov

10343 ■ American Legion, Minnesota Post 243
c/o Jens H. Jensen
PO Box 134
Askov, MN 55704
Ph: (651)291-1800
Fax: (651)291-1057
URL: National Affiliate–www.legion.org
Contact: Jens H. Jensen, Contact
Local. Affiliated With: American Legion.

Atwater

10344 ■ American Legion, Samstad-Jensen Post 375
PO Box 85
Atwater, MN 56209
Ph: (651)291-1800
Fax: (651)291-1057
URL: National Affiliate–www.legion.org
Local. Affiliated With: American Legion.

10345 ■ Atwater Lions Club
c/o Blanche West, Sec.
PO Box 267
Atwater, MN 56209
Ph: (320)974-8935
URL: http://www.5m4lions.org
Contact: Blanche West, Sec.
Local. Affiliated With: Lions Clubs International.

Audubon

10346 ■ American Legion, Audubon American Legion Post 339
15529 Maple Ridge Rd.
Audubon, MN 56511
Ph: (651)291-1800
Fax: (651)291-1057
URL: National Affiliate–www.legion.org
Local. Affiliated With: American Legion.

Aurora

10347 ■ American Legion, Quayle-Shuster-Truman-Muhich Post 241
PO Box 117
Aurora, MN 55705
Ph: (651)291-1800
Fax: (651)291-1057
URL: National Affiliate–www.legion.org
Local. Affiliated With: American Legion.

10348 ■ Aurora Lions Club
c/o Marie Brierley, Sec.
313 S 2nd St. E
Aurora, MN 55705
Ph: (218)229-2145
E-mail: nanook446@msn.com
URL: http://lions5m10.org
Contact: Marie Brierley, Sec.
Local. Affiliated With: Lions Clubs International.

Austin

10349 ■ Albert Lea-Austin AIFA
c/o Paul Wahlstrom
2110 SW 7th Ave.
Austin, MN 55912
Ph: (507)433-7890
Fax: (507)433-7998
E-mail: pswahlstrom@charter.net
URL: National Affiliate–naifa.org
Contact: Paul Wahlstrom, Contact
Local. Represents the interests of insurance and financial advisors. Advocates for a positive legislative and regulatory environment. Enhances business and professional skills of members. **Affiliated With:** National Association of Insurance and Financial Advisors.

10350 ■ American Legion, Austin Post 91
809 12th St. SW
Austin, MN 55912
Ph: (507)437-1151
Fax: (651)291-1057
URL: National Affiliate–www.legion.org
Local. Affiliated With: American Legion.

10351 ■ American Legion, Spam Post 570
2000a Burr Oak Dr.
Austin, MN 55912
Ph: (651)291-1800
Fax: (651)291-1057
URL: National Affiliate–www.legion.org
Local. Affiliated With: American Legion.

10352 ■ American Red Cross, Mower County Chapter
305 NW 4th Ave.
Austin, MN 55912
Ph: (507)437-4589
Fax: (507)437-9121
URL: http://mowercounty.redcross.org
Local.

10353 ■ Austin Area Chamber of Commerce (AACC)
329 N Main St., Ste.102
Austin, MN 55912
Ph: (507)437-4561
Fax: (507)437-4869
Free: (888)319-5655
E-mail: execdir@austincoc.com
URL: http://www.austincoc.com
Contact: Sandy Forstner, Exec.Dir.
Founded: 1940. **Members:** 420. **Membership Dues:** professional, business (rate based on number of full time employees), $250 (annual) • out of area firm, $260 (annual) • non-profit organization, $125 (annual). **Staff:** 6. **Budget:** $230,000. **Local.** Promotes business and community development in the Austin, MN area. **Awards:** Business of the Year Awards. **Frequency:** annual. **Type:** recognition. **Computer Services:** Online services, business directory. **Committees:** Agri-Business; Ambassadors; Business Development; Business Education; Christmas in the City; Government Affairs; Ladies Night Out; 100-Club. **Publications:** *Someplace Special.* Magazine. **Price:** included in membership dues • *Welcome to Austin.* Brochure • Membership Directory, annual • Newsletter, monthly. Highlights on Chamber programs, members, and business-related news. **Conventions/Meetings:** annual AMIGO Day - competition - always September • annual Ladies Night Out - dinner, for women in business, with entertainment and prizes - always October • annual meeting, election of officers - always October.

10354 ■ Austin Lions Club
PO Box 866
Austin, MN 55912
Ph: (507)433-3473
E-mail: jwolesky@fawver.com
URL: http://www.austinlionsclub.org
Contact: Jerry Wolesky, Pres.
Local. Affiliated With: Lions Clubs International.

10355 ■ Izaak Walton League of America, Austin Chapter
c/o Al Layman
PO Box 595
Austin, MN 55912-0595
Ph: (507)437-1297
E-mail: atlayman@smig.net
URL: National Affiliate–www.iwla.org
Local. Works to educate the public to conserve, maintain, protect, and restore the soil, forest, water, and other natural resources of the U.S; promotes the enjoyment and wholesome utilization of these resources. **Affiliated With:** Izaak Walton League of America.

10356 ■ Minnesota Pharmacists Association, Southeast District
c/o Tim Gallagher, Chm.
Astrup Drug Inc.
905 N Main St.
Austin, MN 55912
Ph: (507)434-7428
E-mail: timg@astrupdrug.com
URL: http://www.mpha.org
Contact: Tim Gallagher, Chm.
Local. Works to provide leadership for the pharmacy profession. Seeks to protect and enhance public health. Enhances the knowledge, ethics and skills of pharmacists through advocacy, education, research and the development of standards. **Affiliated With:** Minnesota Pharmacists Association.

10357 ■ Phi Theta Kappa, Zeta Eta Chapter - Riverland Community College
c/o Todd Johnson
1900 8th Ave. NW
Austin, MN 55912
Ph: (507)319-0481
E-mail: tjohnson@riverland.edu
URL: http://www.ptk.org/directories/chapters/MN/259-1.htm
Contact: Todd Johnson, Advisor
Local.

10358 ■ Skills USA, Austin High School
301 3rd St. NW
Austin, MN 55912
Ph: (507)433-0497
Fax: (507)433-0403
E-mail: cknippel@austin.k12.mn.us
URL: http://www.mnskillsusa.org
Contact: Craig Knippel, Contact
Local. Serves high school and college students enrolled in technical, skilled, and service and health occupations. Provides quality education experiences for students in leadership, teamwork, citizenship and character development. Builds and reinforces self-confidence, work attitudes and communication skills. Emphasizes total quality at work, high ethical standards, superior work skills, and life-long education. Promotes understanding of the free enterprise system and involvement in community service. **Affiliated With:** Skills USA - VICA.

10359 ■ Society of Manufacturing Engineers - Riverland Community College U164
1900 8th Ave. NW
Austin, MN 55912
Ph: (507)433-0647
E-mail: mrand@river.cc.mn.us
URL: National Affiliate–www.sme.org
Contact: Michael Rand, Contact
Local. Advances manufacturing knowledge to gain competitive advantage. Improves skills and manufacturing solutions for the growth of economy. Provides resources and opportunities for manufacturing professionals. **Affiliated With:** American Society of Naval Engineers.

10360 ■ Sons of Norway, Storting Lodge 1-519
c/o Ramona E. Swenson, Pres.
301 16th St. NW
Austin, MN 55912-1429
Ph: (507)437-3701
E-mail: gramma_lefse@yahoo.com
URL: National Affiliate–www.sofn.com
Contact: Ramona E. Swenson, Pres.
Local. Affiliated With: Sons of Norway.

10361 ■ Southeastern District Dental Society, Minnesota
c/o Dr. Travis Schmitt, Sec.-Treas.
204 4th St. SW, Ste.144
Austin, MN 55912

Ph: (507)437-2023
E-mail: tschmitt@smig.net
URL: http://southeastern.mndental.org
Contact: Dr. Travis Schmitt, Sec.-Treas.
Local. Represents the interests of dentists committed to the public's oral health, ethics and professional development. Encourages the improvement of the public's oral health and promotes the art and science of dentistry. **Affiliated With:** American Dental Association; Minnesota Dental Association.

10362 ■ United Food and Commercial Workers International Union, AFL-CIO, CLC -Local Union 9 (UFCW)
Austin Labor Ctr.
316 NE 4th Ave.
Austin, MN 55912
Ph: (507)437-8647
E-mail: ufcwlocal9@smig.net
URL: National Affiliate–www.ufcw.org
Members: 2,708. **Local**. **Affiliated With:** United Food and Commercial Workers International Union.

10363 ■ United Way of Mower County
301 N Main St.
PO Box 605
Austin, MN 55912
Ph: (507)437-2313
E-mail: uwmarketing@smig.net
URL: http://www.uwmower.org
Contact: Amy J. Baskin, Exec.Dir.
Founded: 1958. **Members:** 23. **Staff:** 2. **Local**. **Affiliated With:** United Way of America. **Formerly:** (1998) United Way of Austin.

Avoca

10364 ■ American Legion, Dovray Post 632
2641 121st St.
Avoca, MN 56114
Ph: (651)291-1800
Fax: (651)291-1057
URL: National Affiliate–www.legion.org
Local. **Affiliated With:** American Legion.

10365 ■ American Legion, Minnesota Post 576
c/o Donald E. Ewy, Membership Chm.
PO Box 151
Avoca, MN 56114
Ph: (651)291-1800
Fax: (651)291-1057
URL: National Affiliate–www.legion.org
Contact: Donald E. Ewy, Membership Chm.
Local. **Affiliated With:** American Legion.

Avon

10366 ■ American Legion, Avon Post 538
PO Box 183
Avon, MN 56310
Ph: (651)291-1800
Fax: (651)291-1057
URL: National Affiliate–www.legion.org
Local. **Affiliated With:** American Legion.

Babbitt

10367 ■ American Legion, Maki-Pinola Post 535
PO Box 323
Babbitt, MN 55706
Ph: (651)291-1800
Fax: (651)291-1057
URL: National Affiliate–www.legion.org
Local. **Affiliated With:** American Legion.

10368 ■ Babbit Lions Club
c/o Val Sherman, Pres.
28 Balsam Cir.
Babbitt, MN 55706
Ph: (218)827-2369
URL: http://lions5m10.org
Contact: Val Sherman, Pres.
Local. **Affiliated With:** Lions Clubs International.

10369 ■ Babbitt Figure Skating Club
PO Box 248
Babbitt, MN 55706
E-mail: rykken@timberbay.com
URL: National Affiliate–www.usfigureskating.org
Contact: Beth Rykken, Contact
Local. Provides programs to encourage participation and achievement in the sport of figure skating on ice. Defines and maintains uniform standards of skating proficiency. Organizes and sponsors competitions and exhibitions for the purpose of stimulating interest in figure skating. **Affiliated With:** United States Figure Skating Association.

Backus

10370 ■ American Legion, Maxson-Van-Eps Post 368
PO Box 3
Backus, MN 56435
Ph: (651)291-1800
Fax: (651)291-1057
URL: National Affiliate–www.legion.org
Local. **Affiliated With:** American Legion.

10371 ■ Ruffed Grouse Society, Deep Portage Chapter
c/o David Sheley
437 48th Ave. SW
Backus, MN 56435
Ph: (218)947-3113
URL: National Affiliate–www.ruffedgrousesociety.org
Contact: David Sheley, Contact
Local. **Affiliated With:** Ruffed Grouse Society.

Bagley

10372 ■ American Legion, Irvin Blix Post 16
PO Box 159
Bagley, MN 56621
Ph: (651)291-1800
Fax: (651)291-1057
URL: National Affiliate–www.legion.org
Local. **Affiliated With:** American Legion.

10373 ■ Bagley Lions Club
Rte. 1, Box 525
Bagley, MN 56621
Ph: (218)694-4078
E-mail: vsmith_on@hotmail.com
URL: http://lions5m11.org/sys-tmpl/bagleywebpage
Contact: Val Smith, Sec.
Local. **Affiliated With:** Lions Clubs International.

10374 ■ Clearwater County Historical Society
PO Box 241
Bagley, MN 56621
Ph: (218)785-2000
Fax: (218)785-2440
E-mail: cchshist@gvtel.com
Contact: Tamara Edevold, Exec.Dir.
Founded: 1968. **Members:** 800. **Membership Dues:** $25 (annual). **Staff:** 3. **Budget:** $50,000. **Local**. Disseminates information on the history of Clearwater County and relates it to the History of Minnesota and the United States. **Libraries: Type:** open to the public. **Also Known As:** The History Center. **Publications:** *Clearwater History News*, 6 times annual. Newsletter. Contains news and events of county's past, plus activities of Society. **Price:** free to members. **Circulation:** 500. **Conventions/Meetings:** monthly meeting.

10375 ■ Headwaters AIFA
c/o Lisa Haberman
22 Clearwater Ave.
Bagley, MN 56621
Ph: (218)694-6137
Fax: (218)694-3301
E-mail: rsandbo@amfam.com
URL: National Affiliate–naifa.org
Contact: Lisa Haberman, Contact
Local. Represents the interests of insurance and financial advisors. Advocates for a positive legislative and regulatory environment. Enhances business and professional skills of members. **Affiliated With:** National Association of Insurance and Financial Advisors.

Balaton

10376 ■ American Legion, Stone Groeneweg Post 237
142 3rd St.
Balaton, MN 56115
Ph: (651)291-1800
Fax: (651)291-1057
URL: National Affiliate–www.legion.org
Local. **Affiliated With:** American Legion.

Barnesville

10377 ■ American Legion, Minnesota Post 153
c/o Maurice E. Masterson
101 2nd St. SE
Barnesville, MN 56514
Ph: (651)291-1800
Fax: (651)291-1057
URL: National Affiliate–www.legion.org
Contact: Maurice E. Masterson, Contact
Local. **Affiliated With:** American Legion.

10378 ■ Barnesville Lions Club
PO Box 101
Barnesville, MN 56514
Ph: (218)354-7679
E-mail: jfeigum@rrt.net
URL: http://lions5m11.org/sys-tmpl/door
Contact: Jerry Feigum, Pres.
Local. **Affiliated With:** Lions Clubs International.

10379 ■ Barnesville Thursday Nite Lions Club
c/o Julie Johnson, Pres.
PO Box 333
Barnesville, MN 56514
Ph: (218)354-7648
URL: http://lions5m11.org/sys-tmpl/barnesvillethursdaynite
Contact: Julie Johnson, Pres.
Local. **Affiliated With:** Lions Clubs International.

Barnum

10380 ■ American Legion, Peterson-Westerberg Post 415
3907 Deer Park Rd.
Barnum, MN 55707
Ph: (651)291-1800
Fax: (651)291-1057
URL: National Affiliate–www.legion.org
Local. **Affiliated With:** American Legion.

10381 ■ Carlton Lions Club
c/o Joel Soukkala, Pres.
2411 Sunset Ln.
Barnum, MN 55707-8838
Ph: (218)389-3198
E-mail: woodfrey@juno.com
URL: http://lions5m10.org
Contact: Ron Haupt, Sec.
Local. **Affiliated With:** Lions Clubs International.

Barrett

10382 ■ American Legion, Sandberg-Carlson Post 351
PO Box 277
Barrett, MN 56311
Ph: (651)291-1800
Fax: (651)291-1057
URL: National Affiliate–www.legion.org
Local. Affiliated With: American Legion.

Battle Lake

10383 ■ American Legion, Minnesota Post 289
c/o Paul Putnam
PO Box 242
Battle Lake, MN 56515
Ph: (651)291-1800
Fax: (651)291-1057
URL: National Affiliate–www.legion.org
Contact: Paul Putnam, Contact
Local. Affiliated With: American Legion.

10384 ■ Battle Lake Lions Club
PO Box 131
Battle Lake, MN 56515
E-mail: bllions@hotmail.com
URL: http://www.battlelakelions.org
Contact: Steve Bailey, Pres.
Local. Affiliated With: Lions Clubs International.

Baudette

10385 ■ American Legion, Linwood Laughy Post 217
PO Box 619
Baudette, MN 56623
Ph: (651)291-1800
Fax: (651)291-1057
URL: National Affiliate–www.legion.org
Local. Affiliated With: American Legion.

10386 ■ Baudette-Lake of the Woods Chamber of Commerce
PO Box 659
Baudette, MN 56623-0659
Ph: (218)634-1174
Fax: (218)634-2915
Free: (800)382-3474
E-mail: lakwoods@wiktel.com
URL: http://www.lakeofthewoodsmn.com
Contact: Jane Sindelir, Office Mgr.
Founded: 1973. **Members:** 96. **Membership Dues:** general business ($5/employee; maximum of $300), $150 (annual) • new business (1st year), $75 (annual) • financial institution, $300 (annual) • out of town vendor, $100 (annual) • manufacturing (plus $5/ employee; maximum of $600), $150 (annual) • associate, $35 (annual). **Local.** Promotes business and community development in Lake of the Woods County, MN. **Publications:** *Minnesota's Lake of the Woods Area Vacation Guide*, annual. **Price:** free. **Conventions/Meetings:** monthly meeting - always 2nd Thursday.

10387 ■ Lake of the Woods Tourism
PO Box 518
Baudette, MN 56623
Ph: (218)634-1174
Fax: (218)634-2915
Free: (800)382-3474
E-mail: lakwoods@wiktel.com
URL: http://www.lakeofthewoodsmn.com
Contact: Jane Sindelir, Exec.Dir.
Local. Maintains a year-round tourist information center containing a variety of information about the area.

Baxter

10388 ■ Greater Lakes Association of Realtors
15344 Pearl Dr.
Baxter, MN 56425
Ph: (218)828-4567
Fax: (218)829-8178
E-mail: office@greaterlakesrealtors.com
URL: National Affiliate–www.realtor.org
Contact: Janie M. Weston, Exec. Officer
Local. Strives to develop real estate business practices. Advocates the right to own, use and transfer real property. Provides a facility for professional development, research and exchange of information among members. **Affiliated With:** National Association of Realtors.

10389 ■ Paul Bunyan ALU
PO Box 2775
Baxter, MN 56425-2775
Ph: (218)825-9550
Fax: (218)825-4976
URL: National Affiliate–www.naifa.org
Local. Represents the interest of insurance and financial advisors. Advocates for a positive legislative and regulatory environment. Enhances business and professional skills of members. **Affiliated With:** National Association of Insurance and Financial Advisors.

10390 ■ PFLAG Brainerd Lakes
PO Box 2503
Baxter, MN 56425
Ph: (218)824-0209
URL: http://www.pflag.org/Minnesota.217.0.html
Local. Affiliated With: Parents, Families, and Friends of Lesbians and Gays.

Bayport

10391 ■ American Legion, Hesley Jensen Post 491
PO Box 187
Bayport, MN 55003
Ph: (651)439-5463
Fax: (651)291-1057
URL: National Affiliate–www.legion.org
Local. Affiliated With: American Legion.

10392 ■ American Red Cross, St. Croix Valley Chapter
342 Fifth Ave. N
Bayport, MN 55003
Ph: (651)439-0031
Fax: (651)439-6431
URL: http://www.stcroixvalleyarc.org
Local.

10393 ■ National Association of Fleet Administrators, North Central Chapter
c/o Ms. Rita Knoll, Chair
Andersen Windows, Inc.
100 4th Ave. N
Bayport, MN 55003
Ph: (651)264-5469
Fax: (651)351-3556
E-mail: rknoll@andersencorp.com
URL: National Affiliate–www.nafa.org
Contact: Ms. Rita Knoll, Chair
Regional. Promotes the professional management of vehicles through education, government and industry relations and services to members. **Affiliated With:** National Association of Fleet Administrators.

Beardsley

10394 ■ American Legion, August Altheide Post 302
PO Box 187
Beardsley, MN 56211
Ph: (651)291-1800
Fax: (651)291-1057
URL: National Affiliate–www.legion.org
Local. Affiliated With: American Legion.

Becker

10395 ■ American Legion, Minnesota Post 193
c/o Oscar Peterson
PO Box 322
Becker, MN 55308
Ph: (651)291-1800
Fax: (651)291-1057
URL: National Affiliate–www.legion.org
Contact: Oscar Peterson, Contact
Local. Affiliated With: American Legion.

10396 ■ Santiago Lions Club
14628 57th St.
Becker, MN 55308
Ph: (763)441-7271 (763)856-4370
E-mail: bambam@usfamily.net
URL: http://www.lionwap.org/SantiagoMN
Contact: Barbara McKinley, 1st VP
Local. Affiliated With: Lions Clubs International.

10397 ■ Sherburne County Historical Society (SCHS)
13122 1st St.
Becker, MN 55308
Ph: (763)261-4433
Fax: (763)261-4437
E-mail: bgscott@sherbtel.net
URL: http://www.rootsweb.com/~mnschs
Contact: Kurt Kragness, Exec.Dir.
Founded: 1972. **Members:** 500. **Membership Dues:** individual, $20 (annual) • ox cart, $500 (annual) • patron, $150 (annual) • booster, $50 (annual) • family, $30 (annual) • senior, $12 (annual) • student, $7 (annual). **Staff:** 4. **Budget:** $152,000. **Local.** Individuals interested in preserving the history of Sherburne County, MN. Provides exhibits and educational programs. **Libraries: Type:** reference. **Holdings:** books. **Affiliated With:** American Association of Museums; American Association for State and Local History. **Publications:** *Historically Speaking*, quarterly. Newsletter. Contains history articles. **Price:** included in membership dues. **Conventions/Meetings:** annual meeting - always third Monday of October • quarterly meeting - always third Monday.

Bellchester

10398 ■ American Legion, Bellechester Post 598
601 Main St.
Bellchester, MN 55027
Ph: (651)291-1800
Fax: (651)291-1057
URL: National Affiliate–www.legion.org
Local. Affiliated With: American Legion.

Belle Plaine

10399 ■ American Legion, Minnesota Post 144
c/o Leo B. Neubeiser
221 N Meridian St.
Belle Plaine, MN 56011
Ph: (651)291-1800
Fax: (651)291-1057
URL: National Affiliate–www.legion.org
Contact: Leo B. Neubeiser, Contact
Local. Affiliated With: American Legion.

Bellingham

10400 ■ American Legion, Kanthak-Matthies Post 441
PO Box 335
Bellingham, MN 56212
Ph: (651)291-1800
Fax: (651)291-1057
URL: National Affiliate–www.legion.org
Local. Affiliated With: American Legion.

Beltrami

10401 ■ American Legion, Minnesota Post 626
c/o Sigwald Anderson
HCR 1, Box 123
Beltrami, MN 56517
Ph: (651)291-1800
Fax: (651)291-1057
URL: National Affiliate–www.legion.org
Contact: Sigwald Anderson, Contact
Local. Affiliated With: American Legion.

Belview

10402 ■ American Legion, August Donner Post 309
PO Box 151
Belview, MN 56214
Ph: (651)291-1800
Fax: (651)291-1057
URL: National Affiliate–www.legion.org
Local. Affiliated With: American Legion.

Bemidji

10403 ■ American Legion, Ralph Gracie Post 14
217 Minnesota Ave.
Bemidji, MN 56601
Ph: (651)291-1800
Fax: (651)291-1057
URL: National Affiliate–www.legion.org
Local. Affiliated With: American Legion.

10404 ■ Bemidji Area Chamber of Commerce (BACC)
300 Bemidji Ave.
PO Box 850
Bemidji, MN 56601
Ph: (218)444-3541
Fax: (218)444-4276
Free: (800)458-2223
E-mail: chamber@paulbunyan.net
URL: http://www.bemidji.org
Contact: Lori Paris, Exec.Dir.
Founded: 1907. **Membership Dues:** motel/hotel/resort (rate based on number of bedrooms; plus $70 for restaurant, bar, and health club), $230 (annual) • campground (plus $2 for each additional site), $230 (annual) • second business/same owner, $125 (annual) • associate (representative with firm not located in the Bemidji area), $230 (annual) • individual, $55 (annual) • financial depository ($13 per million with $100 million or under in deposits and $10 per million with over $100 million), $13 (annual). **Local.** Promotes business and community development in the Bemidji, MN area. **Computer Services:** Online services, business directory. **Committees:** Public Affairs. **Publications:** *Chamber Report*, monthly. Newsletter • Membership Directory, annual.

10405 ■ Bemidji Area Youth for Christ
522 Beltrami Ave. NW
Bemidji, MN 56601
Ph: (218)444-1382
URL: National Affiliate–www.yfc.net
Local. Affiliated With: Youth for Christ/U.S.A.

10406 ■ Bemidji/Cass Lake Chapter of Muskies
115 Misty Meadows Rd. SW
Bemidji, MN 56601
Ph: (218)694-4076
E-mail: kwillberg@yahoo.com
URL: http://www.muskiesinc.org/chapters/46
Contact: Kirk Willberg, Pres.
Local.

10407 ■ Bemidji Curling Club
1230 23rd St. NW
PO Box 101
Bemidji, MN 56601
Ph: (218)751-1123 (218)444-4813
E-mail: curlbem@paulbunyan.net
URL: http://www.bemidjicurling.org
Contact: Peter Bahr, Pres.
Local. Affiliated With: United States Curling Association.

10408 ■ Bemidji Figure Skating Club
PO Box 24
Bemidji, MN 56619
Ph: (218)444-9355
E-mail: sk8@paulbunyan.net
URL: http://www.paulbunyan.net/users/bfsc
Local. Provides programs to encourage participation and achievement in the sport of figure skating on ice. Defines and maintains uniform standards of skating proficiency. Organizes and sponsors competitions and exhibitions for the purpose of stimulating interest in figure skating. **Affiliated With:** United States Figure Skating Association.

10409 ■ Bemidji First City Lions Club
c/o Flavia Sagedahl, Pres.
2613 Bemidji Ave. N
Bemidji, MN 56601
Ph: (218)444-6694
E-mail: flavia@paulbunyan.net
URL: http://lions5m10.org
Contact: Flavia Sagedahl, Pres.
Local. Affiliated With: Lions Clubs International.

10410 ■ Bemidji Jaycees
PO Box 293
Bemidji, MN 56619
Ph: (218)444-4401
E-mail: zimzoe@paulbunyan.net
URL: http://www.bemidjijaycees.com
Contact: Char Blashill, Pres.
Local.

10411 ■ Bemidji Lions Club
c/o Ronald Porter, Pres.
6615 Tall Pines Rd.
Bemidji, MN 56601
Ph: (218)751-6596
E-mail: rporter@paulbunyan.net
URL: http://lions5m10.org
Contact: Ronald Porter, Pres.
Local. Affiliated With: Lions Clubs International.

10412 ■ Bemidji Trap and Skeet Club
PO Box 1052
Bemidji, MN 56619
Ph: (218)751-8806
URL: National Affiliate–www.mynssa.com
Local. Affiliated With: National Skeet Shooting Association.

10413 ■ Bemidji Visitors and Convention Bureau
c/o Gayle Quistgard, Exec.Dir.
PO Box 66
Bemidji, MN 56619
Ph: (218)759-0164
Fax: (218)759-0810
Free: (800)458-2223
E-mail: gayle@visitbemidji.com
URL: http://www.visitbemidji.com
Contact: Gayle Quistgard, Exec.Dir.
Founded: 1987. **Staff:** 2. **Local.** Works to advertise the Bemidji area to potential visitors, meetings and conventions planners and tour group planners.

10414 ■ Elks Lodge
116 4th St. NW
Bemidji, MN 56601
Ph: (218)751-1052

10415 ■ Fraternal Order of Eagles, Bemidji No. 351
PO Box 1385
Bemidji, MN 56619
Ph: (218)751-9985
Fax: (218)444-9351
URL: http://www.foe.com
Contact: Bina Silverthorn, Bar Mgr.
Local. Affiliated With: Grand Aerie, Fraternal Order of Eagles.

10416 ■ Giziibii Resource Conservation and Development Council
3217 Bemidji Ave. N, Ste.4
Bemidji, MN 56601-4328
Ph: (218)751-1942
Fax: (218)751-9531
E-mail: colleen.oestrich@mn.usda.gov
URL: National Affiliate–www.rcdnet.org
Contact: Colleen Oestrich, Coor.
Local. Affiliated With: National Association of Resource Conservation and Development Councils.

10417 ■ Minnesota Nurses Association - District 11
1619 Bixby Ave. NE
Bemidji, MN 56601
Ph: (218)444-4210
E-mail: becky@paulbunyan.net
URL: http://www.mnnurses.org
Contact: Rebecca Koehnen, Contact
Local. Works to advance the nursing profession. Seeks to meet the needs of nurses and health care consumers. Fosters high standards of nursing practice. Promotes the economic and general welfare of nurses in the workplace. **Affiliated With:** American Nurses Association; Minnesota Nurses Association.

10418 ■ Minnesota Pharmacists Association, Northwest District
c/o Karla P. Eischens, Sec.-Treas.
Progressive Hea. Care
401 Beltrami Ave., Ste.A
Bemidji, MN 56601
Ph: (218)444-6876
E-mail: karla@phcofbemidji.com
URL: http://www.mpha.org
Contact: Karla P. Eischens, Sec.-Treas.
Local. Works to provide leadership for the pharmacy profession. Seeks to protect and enhance public health. Enhances the knowledge, ethics and skills of pharmacists through advocacy, education, research and the development of standards. **Affiliated With:** Minnesota Pharmacists Association.

10419 ■ Minnesota Quarter Horse Association, District 9
c/o Kathy Baumgartner
1201 Julia Way NW
Bemidji, MN 56601
Ph: (218)243-2042
URL: http://www.mnqha.com/index_main.htm
Contact: Kathy Baumgartner, Contact
Local. Affiliated With: American Quarter Horse Association.

10420 ■ Mississippi Headwaters Audubon Society
PO Box 193
Bemidji, MN 56601
E-mail: nell@paulbunyan.net
URL: http://www.audubon.org/chapter/mn/index.html
Contact: Alan Goldberg, Pres.
Local. Formerly: (2005) National Audubon Society - Mississippi Headwaters.

10421 ■ National Active and Retired Federal Employees Association - Bemidji 1049
402 Rako St. SW
Bemidji, MN 56601
Ph: (218)444-9492
URL: National Affiliate–www.narfe.org
Contact: Jack D. Hunt, Contact
Local. Protects the retirement future of employees through education. Informs members on issues af-

fecting the retirement. **Affiliated With:** National Association of Retired Federal Employees.

10422 ■ National Association of Home Builders of the U.S., Headwaters Builders Association
c/o Lisa Knutson
Local No. 2480
11247 Misty Meadows Rd., SW
Bemidji, MN 56601
Ph: (218)751-7410
Fax: (218)751-7410
E-mail: hbalisa@paulbunyan.net
URL: National Affiliate–www.nahb.org
Contact: Lisa Knutson, Contact
Local. Single and multifamily home builders, commercial builders, and others associated with the building industry. **Affiliated With:** National Association of Home Builders.

10423 ■ PFLAG Bemidji
12459 Power Dam Rd. NE
Bemidji, MN 56601
Ph: (218)759-2556
Fax: (218)755-4011
E-mail: wpeck@paulbunyan.net
URL: http://www.pflag.org/Minnesota.217.0.html
Local. Affiliated With: Parents, Families, and Friends of Lesbians and Gays.

10424 ■ Phi Theta Kappa, Beta Nu Tau Chapter - Northwest Technical College
c/o Deborah Grovum
905 Grant Ave. SE
Bemidji, MN 56601
Ph: (218)755-4270
E-mail: debbie.grovum@ntcmn.edu
URL: http://www.ptk.org/directories/chapters/MN/21423-1.htm
Contact: Deborah Grovum, Advisor
Local.

10425 ■ Ruffed Grouse Society, Northcentral Minnesota Chapter
c/o Clyde A. Horlick
3503 Cedar Ln. NW
Bemidji, MN 56601
Ph: (218)387-1923
URL: National Affiliate–www.ruffedgrousesociety.org
Contact: Clyde A. Horlick, Contact
Local. Affiliated With: Ruffed Grouse Society.

10426 ■ Society of Manufacturing Engineers - Bemidji State University S182
Bemidji State Univ., 230 Bridgeman Hall
PO Box 34
Bemidji, MN 56601
Ph: (218)755-2995
Fax: (218)755-4011
E-mail: lnelson@bemidjistate.edu
URL: National Affiliate–www.sme.org
Contact: Dr. Leon Nelson, Contact
Local. Advances manufacturing knowledge to gain competitive advantage. Improves skills and manufacturing solutions for the growth of economy. Provides resources and opportunities for manufacturing professionals. **Affiliated With:** Western Society of Naturalists.

10427 ■ Sons of Norway, Bemidji Lodge 1-500
c/o Lois J. Egelhof, Pres.
6879 Beltrami Line Rd. SW
Bemidji, MN 56601
Ph: (218)586-8712
E-mail: jvaulter@paulbunyan.net
URL: National Affiliate–www.sofn.com
Contact: Lois J. Egelhof, Pres.
Local. Affiliated With: Sons of Norway.

10428 ■ Trout Unlimited - Headwaters Chapter
c/o Kirby Harmon
19970 Lake Julia Dr. NW
Bemidji, MN 56601
Ph: (218)243-2257
E-mail: kilihar@paulbunyan.net
URL: http://www.tu.org
Contact: Kirby Harmon, Contact
Local.

10429 ■ United Federation of Doll Clubs - Region 5
5827 Balsam Rd. NW
Bemidji, MN 56601
E-mail: barco37@mchsi.com
URL: http://www.ufdc.org/ufdcregion5.htm
Contact: Sharon Geisen, Dir.
Regional. Affiliated With: United Federation of Doll Clubs.

10430 ■ United Way of Bemidji Area
PO Box 27
Bemidji, MN 56619-0027
Ph: (218)444-8929
Fax: (218)444-8928
E-mail: bjiuw@paulbunyan.net
URL: http://www.unitedwaybemidji.org
Contact: Penny Echternach, Exec.Dir.
Founded: 1986. **Staff:** 1. **Budget:** $300,000. **Local. Awards:** Venture Grants. **Frequency:** annual. **Type:** grant. **Recipient:** new project/enhancement program, non-profit in Bemidji Area. **Affiliated With:** United Way of America.

Bena

10431 ■ American Legion, Leech Lake Post 2001
PO Box 25
Bena, MN 56626
Ph: (651)291-1800
Fax: (651)291-1057
URL: National Affiliate–www.legion.org
Local. Affiliated With: American Legion.

Benson

10432 ■ American Legion, Benson Post 62
410 13th St. S
Benson, MN 56215
Ph: (651)291-1800
Fax: (651)291-1057
URL: National Affiliate–www.legion.org
Local. Affiliated With: American Legion.

10433 ■ Benson Lions Club
c/o Donald Edwards, Pres.
1530 Utah Ave.
Benson, MN 56215
Ph: (320)843-2222
E-mail: jndedwards@earthlink.net
URL: http://www.5m4lions.org
Contact: Donald Edwards, Pres.
Local. Affiliated With: Lions Clubs International.

10434 ■ Humane Society of Swift County
c/o Robin W. Finke
114 14th St. N
Benson, MN 56215
Ph: (320)843-2134
Fax: (320)843-2348
E-mail: hsscol@hotmail.com
URL: http://petfinder.com
Contact: Liz Bouta, Contact
Founded: 2001. **Membership Dues:** $5 (annual). **Local Groups:** 1. **Local. Conventions/Meetings:** monthly board meeting.

10435 ■ Sons of Norway, Bjorgvin Lodge 1-10
c/o Myrtle L. Holzheimer, Sec.
1716 Atlantic Ave.
Benson, MN 56215-1132
Ph: (320)843-3441
E-mail: myrtle@willmar.com
URL: National Affiliate–www.sofn.com
Contact: Myrtle L. Holzheimer, Sec.
Local. Affiliated With: Sons of Norway.

Bertha

10436 ■ American Legion, Minnesota Post 366
c/o Harold Goepferd
PO Box 335
Bertha, MN 56437
Ph: (651)291-1800
Fax: (651)291-1057
URL: National Affiliate–www.legion.org
Contact: Harold Goepferd, Contact
Local. Affiliated With: American Legion.

Big Falls

10437 ■ American Legion, Johnson-Olson Post 494
PO Box 1
Big Falls, MN 56627
Ph: (651)291-1800
Fax: (651)291-1057
URL: National Affiliate–www.legion.org
Local. Affiliated With: American Legion.

10438 ■ Big Falls Lions Club
c/o Karen Baird, Pres.
Box 192
Big Falls, MN 56627
Ph: (218)276-2501
E-mail: kptbone@citilink.net
URL: http://lions5m10.org
Contact: Karen Baird, Pres.
Local. Affiliated With: Lions Clubs International.

10439 ■ Sons of Norway, Vinland Lodge 1-193
c/o Donald W. Robertson, Pres.
PO Box 406
Big Falls, MN 56627-0406
Ph: (218)276-2408
E-mail: donrob@pocketmail.com
URL: National Affiliate–www.sofn.com
Contact: Donald W. Robertson, Pres.
Local. Affiliated With: Sons of Norway.

Big Lake

10440 ■ American Legion, Minnesota Post 147
c/o Arthur Embretson
19943 County Rd. 43
Big Lake, MN 55309
Ph: (651)291-1800
Fax: (651)291-1057
URL: National Affiliate–www.legion.org
Contact: Arthur Embretson, Contact
Local. Affiliated With: American Legion.

Bigelow

10441 ■ American Legion, Haack-Good Post 496
PO Box 82
Bigelow, MN 56117
Ph: (651)291-1800
Fax: (651)291-1057
URL: National Affiliate–www.legion.org
Local. Affiliated With: American Legion.

Bird Island

10442 ■ American Legion, Thomas-Devaney-Collier Post 430
PO Box 4
Bird Island, MN 55310
Ph: (651)291-1800
Fax: (651)291-1057
URL: National Affiliate–www.legion.org
Local. Affiliated With: American Legion.

10443 ■ Bird Island Lions Club
c/o Craig Brenner, Pres.
PO Box 97
Bird Island, MN 55310
Ph: (320)365-4613
E-mail: cbrenner@gsl.k12.mn.us
URL: http://www.5m4lions.org
Contact: Craig Brenner, Pres.
Local. Affiliated With: Lions Clubs International.

Biwabik

10444 ■ American Legion, Peterson-Lofquist-Bronczyk Post 160
PO Box 648
Biwabik, MN 55708
Ph: (651)291-1800
Fax: (651)291-1057
URL: National Affiliate–www.legion.org
Local. Affiliated With: American Legion.

Blackduck

10445 ■ American Legion, Blackduck Post 372
PO Box 57
Blackduck, MN 56630
Ph: (651)291-1800
Fax: (651)291-1057
URL: National Affiliate–www.legion.org
Local. Affiliated With: American Legion.

10446 ■ Blackduck Lions Club
c/o Dwight Warden, Pres.
PO Box 445
Blackduck, MN 56630
Ph: (218)835-4269
E-mail: dlwarden@blackduck.net
URL: http://lions5m10.org
Contact: Dwight Warden, Pres.
Local. Affiliated With: Lions Clubs International.

10447 ■ Ruffed Grouse Society, Blackduck Chapter
c/o Kurt Benson
22383 Nebish Rd. NE
Blackduck, MN 56630
Ph: (218)835-5863
URL: National Affiliate–www.ruffedgrousesociety.org
Contact: Kurt Benson, Contact
Local. Affiliated With: Ruffed Grouse Society.

Blaine

10448 ■ Blaine Jaycees
PO Box 49014
Blaine, MN 55449
Ph: (763)785-0691
URL: http://www.blainejaycees.org
Contact: Chad Hobot, Pres.
Local.

10449 ■ MetroNorth Chamber of Commerce
21st Century Bank Bldg.
9380 Central Ave. NE, Ste.210
Blaine, MN 55434
Ph: (763)783-3553
Fax: (763)783-3557
E-mail: chamber@metronorthchamber.org
URL: http://www.metronorthchamber.org
Contact: Thomas Snell, Exec.Dir.
Founded: 1982. **Members:** 825. **Membership Dues:** in-home business, $150 (annual) • general business, $260-$1,515 (annual). **Staff:** 4. **Local.** Promotes business and community development in Anoka County, MN. **Committees:** Ambassadors; Business Education Partnership; Communications/Marketing; Government and Public Affairs. **Formerly:** (2005) MetroNorth Chamber of Commerce - Serving Anoka County and Surrounding Areas. **Publications:** *Community Resource Guide*, annual. Directory • Membership Directory. **Advertising:** accepted. Alternate Formats: online • Newsletter, monthly. Contains the latest news on Chamber's events and programs. **Circulation:** 1,200. Alternate Formats: online. **Conventions/Meetings:** annual Com-Mark Computer and Marketing Expo - trade show (exhibits).

10450 ■ NAIFA-North Metro
c/o Jason Moehring, Pres.
11990 Eberoaddeen St. NE, Ste.4
Blaine, MN 55449
Ph: (763)862-2885
Fax: (763)862-4903
E-mail: jason.moehring@thrivent.com
URL: National Affiliate–naifa.org
Contact: Jason Moehring, Pres.
Local. Represents the interests of insurance and financial advisors. Advocates for a positive legislative and regulatory environment. Enhances business and professional skills of members. **Affiliated With:** National Association of Insurance and Financial Advisors.

10451 ■ Northern Blades Figure Skating Club
c/o National Sports Center
1700-105th Ave. NE
Blaine, MN 55449
E-mail: president@northernblades.org
URL: http://www.northernblades.org
Contact: Sharon Christensen, Pres.
Local. Provides programs to encourage participation and achievement in the sport of figure skating on ice. Defines and maintains uniform standards of skating proficiency. Organizes and sponsors competitions and exhibitions for the purpose of stimulating interest in figure skating. **Affiliated With:** United States Figure Skating Association.

10452 ■ Skills USA, Blaine High School
12555 Univ. Ave.
Blaine, MN 55434
Ph: (763)506-6543
Fax: (763)506-6503
E-mail: uthe@anoka.k12.mn.us
URL: http://www.mnskillsusa.org
Contact: Gary Uthe, Contact
Local. Serves high school and college students enrolled in technical, skilled, and service and health occupations. Provides quality education experiences for students in leadership, teamwork, citizenship and character development. Builds and reinforces self-confidence, work attitudes and communication skills. Emphasizes total quality at work, high ethical standards, superior work skills, and life-long education. Promotes understanding of the free enterprise system and involvement in community service. **Affiliated With:** Skills USA - VICA.

10453 ■ University Avenue Parent Teacher Organization
c/o Rachel Durfee
9901 University Ave. NE
Blaine, MN 55434-8012
Ph: (763)506-4514
Local.

Blomkest

10454 ■ Willmar Diamond Edge Figure Skating Club
1800 127th Ave. SE
Blomkest, MN 56216
E-mail: wachter@kanditech.com
URL: National Affiliate–www.usfigureskating.org
Contact: David Peterson, Contact
Local. Provides programs to encourage participation and achievement in the sport of figure skating on ice. Defines and maintains uniform standards of skating proficiency. Organizes and sponsors competitions and exhibitions for the purpose of stimulating interest in figure skating. **Affiliated With:** United States Figure Skating Association.

Blooming Prairie

10455 ■ American Legion, Otto T. Lund Post 52
PO Box 211
Blooming Prairie, MN 55917
Ph: (651)291-1800
Fax: (651)291-1057
URL: National Affiliate–www.legion.org
Local. Affiliated With: American Legion.

10456 ■ Blooming Prairie Chamber of Commerce (BPCC)
138 Hwy. 218 S
PO Box 805
Blooming Prairie, MN 55917
Ph: (507)583-4472
Fax: (507)583-4520
E-mail: bpcofc@smig.net
Contact: Becky Noble, Exec.Dir.
Members: 95. **Local.** Promotes business and community development in Blooming Prairie, MN. Sponsors Old Fashioned 4th of July festival.

Bloomington

10457 ■ AAA Minneapolis
9868 Lyndale Ave. S
Bloomington, MN 55420
Ph: (952)888-4232
Fax: (952)927-2578
Contact: Roe Henrienta, Mgr.
Local.

10458 ■ American Federation of Government Employees, District 8
c/o Jane Nygaard, Natl.VP
2950 Metro Dr., Ste.315
Bloomington, MN 55425
Ph: (952)854-3216
E-mail: jnygaard@afge.org
URL: http://www.afgedist8.org
Contact: Jane Nygaard, Natl.VP
Regional. Affiliated With: American Federation of Government Employees.

10459 ■ American Legion, Minnesota Post 550
9320 Lyndale Ave. S
Bloomington, MN 55420
Ph: (651)291-1800
Fax: (651)291-1057
URL: National Affiliate–www.legion.org
Local. Affiliated With: American Legion.

10460 ■ American Legion, Viking Post 493
PO Box 201124
Bloomington, MN 55420
Ph: (651)291-1800
Fax: (651)291-1057
URL: National Affiliate–www.legion.org
Local. Affiliated With: American Legion.

10461 ■ American Rabbit Breeders Association, Minnesota
c/o Ross Becker, Pres.
9908 Stevens Ave. S
Bloomington, MN 55420
Ph: (952)884-0632
E-mail: beck0485@tc.umn.edu
Contact: Ross Becker, Pres.
State. **Affiliated With:** American Rabbit Breeders Association.

10462 ■ American Society of Sanitary Engineering, Region No. 2 - North Central
c/o Robert Aagaard, Dir.
1800 W Old Shakopee Rd.
Bloomington, MN 55431
Ph: (952)563-8956
URL: National Affiliate–www.asse-plumbing.org
Contact: Robert Aagaard, Dir.
Regional. Represents plumbing officials, sanitary engineers, plumbers, plumbing contractors, building officials, architects, engineers, designing engineers, physicians, and others interested in health. Conducts research on plumbing and sanitation and develops performance standards for components of the plumbing system. Sponsors disease research programs and other studies of water-borne epidemics. **Affiliated With:** American Society of Sanitary Engineering.

10463 ■ APICS, The Association for Operations Management - Twin Cities Chapter
10313 Virginia Rd.
Bloomington, MN 55438-2023
Ph: (952)941-7305
Fax: (952)941-8668
E-mail: dreddan@apicstc.org
URL: http://www.apicstc.org
Contact: Jim Ogren CIRM, Pres.
Local. Provides information and services in production and inventory management and related areas to enable members, enterprises and individuals to add value to their business performance. **Affiliated With:** APICS - The Association for Operations Management.

10464 ■ ARMA International - The Information Management Professionals, Twin Cities Chapter
c/o Tammy Price
PO Box 202035
Bloomington, MN 55420
Ph: (612)376-7707
E-mail: tprice@briggs.com
URL: http://www.twincities.arma.barr.com
Contact: Lynette Downing CRM, Pres.
Members: 222. **Membership Dues:** $200 (annual). **Local**. Works to provide education, research, and networking opportunities to information professionals, to enable them to use their skills and experience to leverage the value of records, information and knowledge as corporate assets and as contributors to organizational success. **Affiliated With:** ARMA International - The Association of Information Management Professionals. **Publications:** *Metro Record*, 10/year, September through June. Newsletter. **Price:** free. **Advertising:** accepted. **Conventions/Meetings:** meeting, with speakers talking about current information management issues, includes vendor exhibits every April (exhibits) - every 2nd Tuesday of the month from September to May.

10465 ■ Bloomington Convention and Visitors Bureau (BCVB)
7900 Intl. Dr., Ste.990
Bloomington, MN 55425
Ph: (952)858-8500
Fax: (952)858-8854
Free: (800)346-4289
E-mail: info@bloomingtonmn.org
URL: http://www.bloomingtonmn.org
Contact: Bonnie L. Carlson, Pres./CEO
Founded: 1975. **Staff:** 16. **Budget:** $1,800,000. **Nonmembership**. **Regional**. Promotes convention business and tourism in Bloomington, MN. **Awards:** Bloomington Diamond Service Awards. **Frequency:** annual. **Type:** recognition. **Recipient:** for service. **Affiliated With:** International Association of Convention and Visitor Bureaus. **Publications:** *Bloomington Convention and Visitors Bureau Quarterly*. Newsletter. **Price:** free • *Bloomington Roomers*, quarterly. Newsletter. **Price:** free.

10466 ■ Bloomington Obedience Training Club (BOTC)
8127 Pleasant Ave. S
Bloomington, MN 55420
Ph: (952)888-4998
E-mail: desk@botcmn.org
URL: http://www.botcmn.org
Contact: Diane Porotko, Pres.
Local.

10467 ■ Figure Skating Club of Bloomington
PO Box 201632
Bloomington, MN 55420
Ph: (952)563-8842 (952)832-0228
URL: http://www.fscbloomington.org
Local. Provides programs to encourage participation and achievement in the sport of figure skating on ice. Defines and maintains uniform standards of skating proficiency. Organizes and sponsors competitions and exhibitions for the purpose of stimulating interest in figure skating. **Affiliated With:** United States Figure Skating Association.

10468 ■ Institute of Internal Auditors, Twin Cities Chapter (TCIIA)
363 E 97 1/2 St.
Bloomington, MN 55420
Ph: (952)884-9032
Fax: (952)884-8970
E-mail: iiatc@isd.net
URL: National Affiliate–www.theiia.org
Contact: Grant Ostler, Contact
Membership Dues: regular, $115 (annual) • educator, $65 (annual) • student, retired, $30 (annual) • life, $2,100 • sustainer (government auditors only), $50 (annual) • organization ($65 per staff member over 5; $50 per staff member over 100), $425-$6,600 (annual). **Local**. Serves as an advocate for the internal audit profession. Provides certification, education, research, and technological guidance for the profession. **Committees:** Academic Relations; Certification; Communications; Long Range Planning; Nominations; Volunteers. **Affiliated With:** Institute of Internal Auditors.

10469 ■ Izaak Walton League of America, Minneapolis Chapter
c/o Tom Harris, Pres.
6601 Auto Club Rd.
Bloomington, MN 55438
Ph: (952)944-1423
E-mail: tom.harris@colder.com
URL: National Affiliate–www.iwla.org
Contact: Ned Winters, Contact
Founded: 1923. **Members:** 55. **Membership Dues:** student under 18, $15 (annual) • student 18 and over, $30 (annual) • individual, $50 (annual) • family, $70 (annual). **Budget:** $12,000. **State**. Offers walking access to the Minnesota River Valley Biking/Hiking Trail system and supports DNR evaluations of erosion prevention. Supports a Trout pond which overflows to a protected marsh environment, both are fed by natural ground springs year round. **Awards:** Minnesota Environmental Camp Scholarships. **Frequency:** annual. **Type:** scholarship. **Recipient:** for promising students ages 11-16. **Affiliated With:** Izaak Walton League of America. **Publications:** Newsletter, 8-10/year, August through May. **Conventions/Meetings:** monthly meeting - second Sunday, September through May. Bloomington, MN - Avg. Attendance: 30.

10470 ■ Judges Council of Minnesota
c/o Sandy Officer
8920 Southwood Dr.
Bloomington, MN 55420
Ph: (952)835-8603
URL: National Affiliate–www.avsa.org
Contact: Sandy Officer, Contact
State. **Affiliated With:** African Violet Society of America.

10471 ■ Juvenile Diabetes Research Foundation International, Minnesota Chapter
2626 E 82nd St., Ste.225
Bloomington, MN 55425
Ph: (952)851-0770
Fax: (952)851-0766
Free: (800)663-1860
E-mail: minnesota@jdrf.org
URL: http://www.jdrf.org/minnesota
Contact: Jackie Casey, Exec.Dir.
Founded: 1980. **Staff:** 5. **State**. Strives to find a cure for diabetes and its complications through research. **Affiliated With:** Juvenile Diabetes Research Foundation International.

10472 ■ Labrador Retriever Club of the Twin Cities (LRCTC)
c/o Wendy McCance, Sec.
6925 W 83rd St.
Bloomington, MN 55438
E-mail: wendy.mccance@so.mnscu.edu
URL: http://lrctc.com
Contact: Wendy McCance, Sec.
Local.

10473 ■ Lupus Foundation of Minnesota
The Atrium, Ste.135
2626 E 82nd St.
Bloomington, MN 55425
Ph: (952)746-5151
Free: (800)645-1131
E-mail: info@lupusmn.org
URL: http://www.lupusmn.org
Contact: Bill Jenison, Pres.
Founded: 1978. **Members:** 1,350. **Membership Dues:** regular, $25 (annual). **Staff:** 7. **Budget:** $400,000. **Languages:** English, Spanish. **State**. Provides educational materials, offers a source of hope, strength, empowerment and comfort and supports research focused on finding the cause of and cure for lupus. **Libraries: Type:** open to the public. **Awards:** Research. **Frequency:** annual. **Type:** monetary. **Recipient:** for research in lupus. **Publications:** *Minnesota Lupus News*, bimonthly. Newsletter. Contains information on foundation and research. **Price:** included in membership dues. **Circulation:** 2,000. Alternate Formats: CD-ROM.

10474 ■ Minnesota Association on Higher Education and Disability (MN AHEAD)
c/o Debbie Tillman, Treas.
Off. for Students with Disabilities
Normandale Community Coll.
9700 France Ave. S
Bloomington, MN 55431-4399
Ph: (952)487-7035
Fax: (952)487-7031
E-mail: debbie.tillman@normandale.edu
URL: http://www.ahead.org/about/regional_affiliates/minnesota/minnesota.htm
Contact: Debbie Tillman, Treas.
State. Represents individuals interested in promoting the equal rights and opportunities of disabled postsecondary students, staff, faculty and graduates. Provides educational and professional development opportunities for persons with disabilities in postsecondary education. Encourages and supports legislation for the benefit of disabled students. **Affiliated With:** Association on Higher Education and Disability.

10475 ■ Minnesota Athletic Trainers' Association (MATA)
Dupont Ctr., Ste.250
9801 Dupont Ave.
Bloomington, MN 55431

Ph: (952)886-3317
Fax: (952)884-9836
E-mail: cgebeck@smdc.org
URL: http://www.mnata.com
Contact: Chris Gebeck, Pres.-Elect
State. Affiliated With: National Athletic Trainers' Association.

10476 ■ Minnesota Cricket Club
8315 11th Ave. S
Bloomington, MN 55420
URL: http://www.usaca.org/Clubs.htm
Contact: Syed Abbas, Contact
Local.

10477 ■ Minnesota Dental Hygienists' Association
7800 Metro Pkwy., Ste.300
Bloomington, MN 55425
Ph: (952)876-0187
Fax: (952)876-0187
E-mail: ask@mndha.com
URL: http://www.mndha.com
Contact: Patti Peterson, Pres.
State. Aims to advance the art and science of dental hygiene. Maintains the highest standards of dental hygiene practice. Represents and protects the interests of the dental hygiene profession. Improves the professional competence of the dental hygienist. **Affiliated With:** American Dental Hygienists' Association.

10478 ■ Minnesota Multi Housing Association (MHA)
1650 W 82nd St., Ste.250
Bloomington, MN 55431
Ph: (952)854-8500
Fax: (952)854-3810
E-mail: mha@mmha.com
URL: http://www.mmha.com
Contact: Mary M. Rippe, Pres.
State.

10479 ■ Minnesota River Valley Audubon Chapter
c/o Anne Hanley, Pres.
PO Box 20400
Bloomington, MN 55420
E-mail: anne_hanley90@hotmail.com
URL: http://home.comcast.net/~mrvac
Contact: Anne Hanley, Pres.
Local. Works to conserve and restore natural ecosystems, focusing on birds and other wildlife for the benefit of humanity and the earth's biological diversity. **Affiliated With:** National Audubon Society.

10480 ■ Minnesota Section of Optical Society of America (MSOSA)
c/o David Vaughnn, Pres.
Rudolf Technologies
4900 W 78th St.
Bloomington, MN 55435
Ph: (952)259-1752
E-mail: david.vaughnn@rudolphtech.com
URL: http://www.osa.org/localsections/minnesota/index.html
Contact: David Vaughnn, Pres.
State. Persons interested in any branch of optics: research, instruction, optical applications, manufacture, distribution of optical equipment, and physiological optics. **Affiliated With:** Optical Society of America.

10481 ■ Minnesota Shopping Center Association (MSCA)
8120 Penn Ave. S, Ste.114
Bloomington, MN 55431
Ph: (952)888-3491
Fax: (952)888-0000
E-mail: info@msca-online.com
URL: http://www.msca-online.com
Contact: Karla Keller Torp, Exec.Dir.
Founded: 1988. **Members:** 530. **Membership Dues:** general, $295 (annual) • affiliate, non-resident, $130 (annual). **Staff:** 2. **State.** Represents the interests of developers, shopping center owners, brokers, property managers, retailers, attorneys, architects, appraisers, contractors and all professionals serving the Minnesota real estate industry. Offers educational and networking opportunities to members; distributes information about market research and trends; participates in governmental affairs.

10482 ■ Minnesota Society of Certified Public Accountants (MNCPA)
c/o Betsy Adrian, Pres.
1650 W 82nd St., Ste.600
Bloomington, MN 55431
Ph: (952)831-2707
Fax: (952)831-7875
Free: (800)331-4288
E-mail: info@mncpa.org
URL: http://www.mncpa.org
Contact: Betsy Adrian, Pres.
Founded: 1904. **State.**

10483 ■ National Audubon Society - Minnesota River Valley Audubon Chapter (MRVAC)
PO Box 20400
Bloomington, MN 55420
E-mail: anne_hanley90@hotmail.com
URL: http://www.MRVAC.org
Contact: Anne Hanley, Pres.
Founded: 1969. **Members:** 1,000. **Membership Dues:** national, $20 (annual) • local, $15 (annual). **Local.** Fosters a community to preserve and enhance the natural environment through education and advocacy. Focuses on birds, wildlife and their habitat, emphasizing the species of the Minnesota River Valley. Supports environmental education for children through various types of scholarships and grants. Sponsors field trips and lectures on natural and environmental topics. **Libraries: Type:** not open to the public. **Subjects:** birds. **Awards: Frequency:** annual. **Type:** scholarship. **Recipient:** student or teacher nature training. **Formerly:** (2004) National Audubon Society - Minnesota River Valley Club. **Publications:** *Trumpeter*, 9/year. Newsletter. **Price:** $15.00 /year for members. **Circulation:** 1,000. Alternate Formats: online.

10484 ■ North Central Electric League (NCEL)
c/o Dale G. Yohnke, Exec.Dir.
2901 Metro Dr., Ste.203
Bloomington, MN 55425
Ph: (952)854-4405
Fax: (952)854-7076
Free: (800)925-4985
E-mail: dale@ncel.org
URL: http://www.ncel.org
Contact: Dale G. Yohnke, Exec.Dir.
Regional.

10485 ■ Phi Theta Kappa, Alpha Kappa Alpha Chapter - Normandale Community College
c/o Linda Tetzlaff
9700 France Ave. S
Bloomington, MN 55431
Ph: (952)487-7163
E-mail: linda.tetzlaff@ptk.org
URL: http://www.ptk.org/directories/chapters/MN/271-1.htm
Contact: Linda Tetzlaff, Advisor
Local.

10486 ■ Samoyed Association of Minneapolis-St. Paul (SAMS)
c/o Lori Sorenson
8825 Stevens Ave. S
Bloomington, MN 55420
E-mail: gsorenson@mn.rr.com
URL: http://www.samsmn.org
Contact: Ann Musker, Pres.
Local.

10487 ■ Scam Victims United
c/o Shawn Mosch
PO Box 20611
Bloomington, MN 55420
E-mail: info@scamvictimsunited.com
URL: http://www.ScamVictimsUnited.com
Local.

10488 ■ Skills USA, John F. Kennedy High School
9701 Nicollet Ave. S
Bloomington, MN 55420
Ph: (952)681-5218
E-mail: kchederquist943@earthlink.net
URL: http://www.mnskillsusa.org
Contact: Kevin Chederquist, Contact
Local. Serves high school and college students enrolled in technical, skilled, and service and health occupations. Provides quality education experiences for students in leadership, teamwork, citizenship and character development. Builds and reinforces self-confidence, work attitudes and communication skills. Emphasizes total quality at work, high ethical standards, superior work skills, and life-long education. Promotes understanding of the free enterprise system and involvement in community service. **Affiliated With:** Skills USA - VICA.

10489 ■ Table Tennis Minnesota - Bloomington
Northwest Athletic Club - Bloomington
1001 W 98th St.
Bloomington, MN 55431
Ph: (952)892-7078
E-mail: ttminn@aol.com
URL: http://www.tabletennismn.com
Contact: Mitchell Seidenfeld, Contact
Local. Affiliated With: U.S.A. Table Tennis.

10490 ■ Transport Workers Union of America, AFL-CIO - Local Union 543
8009 34th Ave. S, Ste.130
Bloomington, MN 55425-1766
Ph: (952)854-5838
Fax: (952)854-5838
E-mail: twulocal543@aol.com
URL: http://local543.twuatd.org
Contact: Perry Sprague, Pres.
Members: 224. **Local. Affiliated With:** Transport Workers Union of America.

10491 ■ Trout Unlimited, Minnesota
c/o Elliott Olson - Council Chm.
4801 W 81st St., Ste.105
Bloomington, MN 55437-1111
Ph: (952)835-4505
Fax: (952)835-4461
E-mail: e.olson@dakotaww.com
URL: http://www.mntu.org/
State. Affiliated With: Trout Unlimited.

10492 ■ Trout Unlimited - Paul Bunyan Chapter
5415 Mt. Normandale Curve
Bloomington, MN 55437-1019
Ph: (612)310-7000
E-mail: bob@lawyerbob.com
URL: http://www.tu.org
Contact: Mickey O Johnson, Pres.
Local.

10493 ■ Twin Cities Association for Computing Machinery SIGAda
c/o Paul Stachour, Chm.
9532 First Ave. S
Bloomington, MN 55420-4401
Ph: (952)884-5977
E-mail: pstachour@acm.org
Contact: Paul Stachour, Chm.
Founded: 1983. **Members:** 25. **Local.** United as a forum for exploring the ways in which software engineers create reliable and maintainable software. Seeks to promote the open exchange of experiences and ideas related to how to produce quality software. Strives to help sustain commitment and enhance

software engineering skills through an active program of networking and mutual support and to serve as a source of educational and experiential information for its members, other organizations and the general community of software professionals. **Affiliated With:** Association for Computing Machinery.

10494 ■ Twin Cities Volkssport
c/o Jane Kempf
8236 Upton Ave. S
Bloomington, MN 55431
Ph: (952)472-6958
E-mail: mistycat13@msn.com
URL: http://www.geocities.com/tcvwalking
Contact: Jane Kempf, Contact
Local. Affiliated With: American Volkssport Association.

Blue Earth

10495 ■ American Legion, Blue Earth Post 89
115 W 6th St.
Blue Earth, MN 56013
Ph: (651)291-1800
Fax: (651)291-1057
URL: National Affiliate–www.legion.org
Local. Affiliated With: American Legion.

10496 ■ Blue Earth Area Chamber of Commerce (BEACC)
118 E 6th St.
Blue Earth, MN 56013-2002
Ph: (507)526-2916
Fax: (507)526-2244
E-mail: chamber@bevcomm.net
Contact: Shelly Greimann, Dir.
Founded: 1941. **Members:** 200. **Staff:** 2. **Regional Groups:** 1. **State Groups:** 1. **Local.** Promotes business and community development in the Blue Earth, MN area. Sponsors promotional and community events. **Libraries: Type:** open to the public. **Holdings:** 200; articles, books. **Subjects:** tourism, political, business, educational. **Computer Services:** Online services, member listings. **Publications:** *Chamber Focus*, weekly. Newsletter. **Circulation:** 35. **Advertising:** accepted • *Community Directory*, annual. Newsletter • *Update*, bimonthly.

10497 ■ Blue Earth Area Mentors (BEAM)
c/o Tamara Armstrong
216 E 9th St.
Blue Earth, MN 56013
Ph: (507)526-5219
E-mail: beam@bevcomm.net
Contact: Tamara Armstrong, Contact
Founded: 1997. **Members:** 25. **Staff:** 1. **Budget:** $20,000. **Local Groups:** 1. **Local.** Local mentor group that matches youth with adults in order that the adults may be an extra friend in the child's life. Mentor and child meets once a week and participate in planned activities.

Bovey

10498 ■ American Legion, Hurlbut-Ziemer Post 476
36501 County Rd. 336
Bovey, MN 55709
Ph: (651)291-1800
Fax: (651)291-1057
URL: National Affiliate–www.legion.org
Local. Affiliated With: American Legion.

10499 ■ Greenway Lions Club
c/o Bob Berghammer, Sec.
PO Box 50
Bovey, MN 55709
Ph: (218)885-2576
URL: http://lions5m10.org
Contact: Del Halling, Pres.
Local. Affiliated With: Lions Clubs International.

Bowlus

10500 ■ American Legion, Minnesota Post 642
c/o Carl Raymond Masog
PO Box 73
Bowlus, MN 56314
Ph: (651)291-1800
Fax: (651)291-1057
URL: National Affiliate–www.legion.org
Contact: Carl Raymond Masog, Contact
Local. Affiliated With: American Legion.

Boy River

10501 ■ American Legion, Minnesota Post 458
c/o William H. Robbins
127 City Rd. 4
Boy River, MN 56672
Ph: (651)291-1800
Fax: (651)291-1057
URL: National Affiliate–www.legion.org
Contact: William H. Robbins, Contact
Local. Affiliated With: American Legion.

Boyd

10502 ■ American Legion, Minnesota Post 169
c/o J. Ben Johnson
3755 260th Ave.
Boyd, MN 56218
Ph: (651)291-1800
Fax: (651)291-1057
URL: National Affiliate–www.legion.org
Contact: J. Ben Johnson, Contact
Local. Affiliated With: American Legion.

10503 ■ American Legion, Oien-Horgen Post 198
PO Box 246
Boyd, MN 56218
Ph: (651)291-1800
Fax: (651)291-1057
URL: National Affiliate–www.legion.org
Local. Affiliated With: American Legion.

Brainerd

10504 ■ American Cancer Society, Brainerd
17 Washington St., Ste.2
Brainerd, MN 56401
Ph: (218)829-6212
Fax: (218)829-6258
Free: (877)381-8787
URL: http://www.cancer.org
Contact: Marcie Larsen, Admin. Support
Local. Affiliated With: American Cancer Society.

10505 ■ American Legion, Minnesota Post 255
c/o Gaylord Zelinske
708 Front St.
Brainerd, MN 56401
Ph: (651)291-1800
Fax: (651)291-1057
URL: National Affiliate–www.legion.org
Contact: Gaylord Zelinske, Contact
Local. Affiliated With: American Legion.

10506 ■ Brainerd Area Sertoma Club
PO Box 9
Brainerd, MN 56401
URL: http://sertoma.brainerd.com
Contact: Rory Coit, Pres.
Local.

10507 ■ Brainerd Lakes Area Audubon Society
c/o Sandy Holm, Pres.
PO Box 521
Brainerd, MN 56401
E-mail: blaas@eudoramail.com
URL: National Affiliate–www.audubon.org
Contact: Sandy Holm, Pres.
Local. Affiliated With: National Audubon Society.

10508 ■ Brainerd Lakes Area Chambers of Commerce
124 N 6th St.
PO Box 356
Brainerd, MN 56401-0356
Ph: (218)829-2838
Fax: (218)829-8199
Free: (800)450-2838
E-mail: info@explorebrainerdlakes.com
URL: http://www.explorebrainerdlakes.com
Contact: Lisa Paxton, CEO
Founded: 1882. **Members:** 780. **Membership Dues:** professional, $185 (annual) • retired, $50 (annual) • business (based on number of employees), $285-$2,040 (annual) • association, organization, $135 (annual) • government representative, $170 (annual) • second business (same category), $140 (annual) • second business (different category), $210 (annual) • lodging, $450-$645 (annual). **Staff:** 7. **Local.** Promotes business and community development in the Brainerd, MN area. Sponsors Brainerd Lakes Woods and Irons. **Computer Services:** Mailing lists, of members. **Committees:** Commerce and Industry Show; Crosslake Retail; Forestry Affairs; Manufacturing Alliance; Pequot Lakes/Breezy Point Advisory; Welcome Center Advisory; Winter Auction. **Task Forces:** Air Transportation. **Affiliated With:** Minnesota Festivals and Events Association; Minnesota State Chamber of Commerce; U.S. Council of Better Business Bureaus. **Formerly:** (1999) Brainerd Lakes Area Chamber of Commerce and Convention and Visitors Bureau; (2005) Brainerd Lakes Area Chamber of Commerce and Convention/Visitors Bureau. **Publications:** *Chamber Connection*, monthly. Newsletter. **Circulation:** 1,500. **Advertising:** accepted. Alternate Formats: online • *Chamber E-Newsletter*, weekly, every Monday afternoon. Contains current issues, new members, marketing opportunities, and upcoming events. **Price:** free for members. **Advertising:** accepted. Alternate Formats: online • *Indoor/Outdoor Activity and Restaurant Guide*, annual. Directory. Features attractions, shopping, dining, golf course, and fishing information. **Price:** free. **Circulation:** 20,000. **Advertising:** accepted. Also Cited As: *Brainerd Lakes Area Vacation Planner* • *Relocation and Buyer's Guide*. Handbook. Includes membership directory. **Advertising:** accepted • *Vacation Planning Guide*, annual. Directory. Contains lodging information. **Price:** free. **Conventions/Meetings:** monthly board meeting - every 3rd Thursday in Brainerd, MN • annual Commerce and Industry Show, area businesses (exhibits) - April.

10509 ■ Brainerd Lakes Area Development Corporation (BLADC)
c/o Sheila Wasnie Haverkamp, Exec.Dir.
124 N Sixth St.
Brainerd, MN 56401
Ph: (218)828-0096
Fax: (218)829-8199
Free: (888)322-5232
E-mail: info@bladc.org
URL: http://www.bladc.org
Contact: Sheila Wasnie Haverkamp, Exec.Dir.
Founded: 1985. **Members:** 150. **Membership Dues:** individual, $100 (annual) • business, $250 (annual) • life, $5,000. **Staff:** 2. **Budget:** $140,000. **Local.** Supports the mission of job creation and economic diversification of the Brainerd Lakes Area.

10510 ■ Crow Wing County Genealogical Society
2103 Graydon Ave.
Brainerd, MN 56401

Ph: (218)829-9738
E-mail: lkirk@brainerd.net
URL: http://www.rootsweb.com/~mncwcghs
Contact: Lucille Kirkeby, Treas.
Founded: 1977. **Members:** 42. **Membership Dues:** single, $10 (annual) • family, $12 (annual). **Local**. Individuals interested in preserving the history of central Minnesota and its people. Conducts genealogical research. **Libraries: Type:** open to the public; reference. **Holdings:** 200; books, periodicals. **Formerly:** Brainerd Genealogical Society. **Publications:** *Heir Mail*, quarterly. Newsletter. **Price:** included in membership dues. **Conventions/Meetings:** quarterly meeting, with speaker in between months; features research, special projects or socialization - except December, June, July, and August.

10511 ■ Crow Wing County United Way
PO Box 381
Brainerd, MN 56401
Ph: (218)829-2619
URL: http://www.unitedwaynow.org
Contact: Heidi Funk, Exec.Dir.
Founded: 1969. **Local**. **Affiliated With:** United Way of America.

10512 ■ Lake Area Habitat for Humanity (LAHFH)
PO Box 234
Brainerd, MN 56401
Ph: (218)828-8517
Fax: (218)825-4867
E-mail: hab4hum@uslink.net
URL: http://www.lakesareahabitat.org
Local. **Affiliated With:** Habitat for Humanity International.

10513 ■ Mid-Minnesota Home Builders Association (MMBA)
c/o Colleen M. Faacks
17068 Commercial Park Rd.
Brainerd, MN 56401
Ph: (218)829-4982
Fax: (218)828-3739
E-mail: mmba@brainerd.net
URL: http://www.midmnba.org
Founded: 1980. **Members:** 270. **Local**. Single and multifamily home builders, commercial builders, and others associated with the building industry. **Telecommunication Services:** voicemail, email and website. **Committees:** Home and Patio Show; Lakes Area Home Tour. **Affiliated With:** National Association of Home Builders. **Publications:** Newsletter, monthly. **Circulation:** 300. **Advertising:** accepted. **Conventions/Meetings:** monthly General Membership - meeting, networking of members (exhibits) - every 4th Tuesday of the month; Avg. Attendance: 90.

10514 ■ Minnesota Lakes Association (MLA)
17021 Commercial Park Dr., Ste.No. 4
Brainerd, MN 56401
Ph: (218)824-5565
Fax: (218)824-5566
Free: (800)515-5253
E-mail: lakes@mnlakes.org
URL: http://www.mnlakes.org
Contact: Paula West, Exec.Dir.
Membership Dues: individual, $20 (annual) • business and government affiliate, $100 (annual). **State**. Dedicated to the protection and enhancement of Minnesota lakes through education, legislation, and coalition building. **Affiliated With:** North American Lake Management Society. **Publications:** *Reporter*, quarterly. Newsletter. **Conventions/Meetings:** annual conference - always in the spring.

10515 ■ Minnesota North District, The Lutheran Church-Missouri Synod
PO Box 604
Brainerd, MN 56401-0604
Ph: (218)829-1781
Fax: (218)829-0037
E-mail: mnndist@mnnlcms.org
URL: http://www.mnn.lcms.org
Contact: Rev. Donald Fondow, Pres.
Local.

10516 ■ Minnesota Senior Federation, Heartland Region
803 Kingwood St.
Brainerd, MN 56401
Ph: (218)828-8457
URL: http://mnseniors.org
Local.

10517 ■ Muskies Brainerd Lakes Chapter
9143 Lone Pine Rd.
Brainerd, MN 56401
Ph: (218)764-2580
E-mail: jyoung@brainerd.net
URL: http://www.brainerdmuskies.com
Contact: Jeff Young, Pres.
Local.

10518 ■ Phi Theta Kappa, Upsilon Omega Chapter - Central Lakes College
c/o Nancy Smith
501 W Coll. Dr.
Brainerd, MN 56401
Ph: (218)855-8174
E-mail: nsmith@clcmn.edu
URL: http://www.ptk.org/directories/chapters/MN/264-1.htm
Contact: Nancy Smith, Advisor
Local.

10519 ■ RSVP Volunteer Services
c/o Mike Koecheler, Dir.
312 Front St.
Brainerd, MN 56401-3522
Ph: (218)824-1345
Fax: (218)824-1346
E-mail: rsvp@co.crow-wing.mn.us
URL: http://www.co.crow-wing.mn.us/social_services/volunteers_-_rsvp
Contact: Mike Koecheler, Dir.
Local. **Affiliated With:** Retired and Senior Volunteer Program.

10520 ■ Ruffed Grouse Society, Drumming Log Chapter
c/o Mark Haglin
14752 Three Mile Rd.
Brainerd, MN 56401
Ph: (218)829-2631
E-mail: mark@pineshadows.com
URL: National Affiliate–www.ruffedgrousesociety.org
Contact: Mark Haglin, Contact
Local. **Affiliated With:** Ruffed Grouse Society.

10521 ■ Sons of Norway, Sagatun Lodge 1-18
c/o Janet M. Almquist, Pres.
1531 S 6th St.
Brainerd, MN 56401-4349
Ph: (218)828-6363
URL: National Affiliate–www.sofn.com
Contact: Janet M. Almquist, Pres.
Local. **Affiliated With:** Sons of Norway.

10522 ■ Vacationland Figure Skating Club (VFSC)
PO Box 173
Brainerd, MN 56401
Ph: (218)829-9023
Free: (800)450-VFSC
E-mail: vacationland@skating.brainerd.com
URL: http://www.skating.brainerd.com
Local. Provides programs to encourage participation and achievement in the sport of figure skating on ice. Defines and maintains uniform standards of skating proficiency. Organizes and sponsors competitions and exhibitions for the purpose of stimulating interest in figure skating. **Affiliated With:** United States Figure Skating Association.

10523 ■ West Central District Dental Society, Minnesota
c/o Dr. Roland Kehr, Ed.
524 Kingwood St.
Brainerd, MN 56401
Ph: (218)829-0365
E-mail: docs@brainerd.net
URL: http://westcentral.mndental.org
Contact: Dr. Roland Kehr, Ed.
Local. Represents the interests of dentists committed to the public's oral health, ethics and professional development. Encourages the improvement of the public's oral health and promotes the art and science of dentistry. **Affiliated With:** American Dental Association; Minnesota Dental Association.

Brandon

10524 ■ American Legion, Argonne Forest Post 278
12973 Tanglewood Rd. NW
Brandon, MN 56315
Ph: (651)291-1800
Fax: (651)291-1057
URL: National Affiliate–www.legion.org
Local. **Affiliated With:** American Legion.

10525 ■ Brandon Lions Club - Minnesota
c/o Michael Ranweiler, Pres.
PO Box 217
Brandon, MN 56315
Ph: (320)524-2679
E-mail: lakesare@gctel.net
URL: http://www.5m4lions.org
Contact: Michael Ranweiler, Pres.
Local. **Affiliated With:** Lions Clubs International.

Breckenridge

10526 ■ American Legion, Minnesota Post 53
c/o Otto T. Lund
PO Box 124
Breckenridge, MN 56520
Ph: (651)291-1800
Fax: (651)291-1057
URL: National Affiliate–www.legion.org
Contact: Otto T. Lund, Contact
Local. **Affiliated With:** American Legion.

10527 ■ Wilkin County Agricultural Society
c/o Mary Ann Conrad
120 8th St.
Breckenridge, MN 56520-0000
Ph: (218)643-6561 (218)643-9117
URL: http://www.breckenridgemn.net
Contact: Mary Ann Conrad, Gen.Mgr.
Founded: 1890. **Members:** 40. **Staff:** 8. **Budget:** $50,000. **Local Groups:** 1. **Local**. Members are interested individuals and 4-H representatives participating or associated with fair activities. **Publications:** *Wilkin County Fair (Premium Book)*, annual. Magazine. Features listing of events, information, items accepted at the fair to be judged, etc. **Price:** free. **Advertising:** accepted. **Conventions/Meetings:** meeting - 3/year.

10528 ■ Wilkin County Historical Society (WCHS)
704 Nebraska Ave.
Breckenridge, MN 56520-1547
Ph: (218)643-1303
Contact: Gordon Martinson, Exec. Officer
Members: 520. **Membership Dues:** individual, $3 (annual). **Staff:** 2. **Local**. Individuals interested in preserving the history of Wilken County, MN. Participates in local community activities. **Publications:** none. **Conventions/Meetings:** annual meet - tenth month of each year; Avg. Attendance: 75.

Breezy Point

10529 ■ Minnesota Chapter of Myasthenia Gravis Foundation of America
29234 Piney Way
Breezy Point, MN 56472

Ph: (218)562-4594
E-mail: mgcorn@uslink.net
Contact: B.J. Corner, State Chair
State. Affiliated With: Myasthenia Gravis Foundation of America.

Brewster

10530 ■ American Legion, Brewster Post 464
PO Box 356
Brewster, MN 56119
Ph: (651)291-1800
Fax: (651)291-1057
URL: National Affiliate–www.legion.org
Local. Affiliated With: American Legion.

Bricelyn

10531 ■ American Legion, Nels Lee Post 165
PO Box 97
Bricelyn, MN 56014
Ph: (651)291-1800
Fax: (651)291-1057
URL: National Affiliate–www.legion.org
Local. Affiliated With: American Legion.

Brook Park

10532 ■ Minnesota Quarter Horse Association, District 8
c/o Randy Isham
23524 Sunny Hill Rd.
Brook Park, MN 55007
Ph: (320)629-7226
URL: http://www.mnqha.com/index_main.htm
Contact: Randy Isham, Contact
Local. Affiliated With: American Quarter Horse Association.

Brooklyn Center

10533 ■ American Legion, Bainbridge Post 355
PO Box 290016
Brooklyn Center, MN 55429
Ph: (651)291-1800
Fax: (651)291-1057
URL: National Affiliate–www.legion.org
Local. Affiliated With: American Legion.

10534 ■ American Legion, Duoos Brothers Post 630
6110 Brooklyn Blvd.
Brooklyn Center, MN 55429
Ph: (651)291-1800
Fax: (651)291-1057
URL: National Affiliate–www.legion.org
Local. Affiliated With: American Legion.

10535 ■ Anaconda Cricket Club
1507 Woodbine Ln.
Brooklyn Center, MN 55430
URL: http://www.usaca.org/Clubs.htm
Contact: Floyd Campbell, Contact
Local.

10536 ■ Girl Scout Council of Greater Minneapolis
c/o Human Resources
5601 Brooklyn Blvd.
Brooklyn Center, MN 55429
Ph: (763)535-4602
Fax: (763)535-7524
Free: (800)548-5250
E-mail: hr@girlscoutsmpls.org
URL: http://www.girlscoutsmpls.org
Local.

10537 ■ International Personnel Management Association, Minnesota
c/o Kelli Wick, Pres.
63301 Shingle Creek Pkwy.
Brooklyn Center, MN 55430
Ph: (612)569-3302
Fax: (612)569-3493
E-mail: kwick@ci.brooklyn-center.mn.us
URL: National Affiliate–www.ipma-hr.org
Contact: Kelli Wick, Pres.
Local. Affiliated With: International Public Management Association for Human Resources.

10538 ■ IPMA-HR Minnesota Chapter
c/o Kelli Wick, Pres.
63301 Shingle Creek Pkwy.
Brooklyn Center, MN 55430
Ph: (612)569-3302
Fax: (612)569-3493
E-mail: kwick@ci.brooklyn-center.mn.us
URL: National Affiliate–www.ipma-hr.org
Contact: Kelli Wick, Pres.
Local. Seeks to improve human resource practices in government through provision of testing services, advisory service, conferences, professional development programs, research and publications. Sponsors seminars, conferences and workshops on various phases of public personnel administration.

10539 ■ Minnesota Association of Plumbing-Heating-Cooling Contractors (MAPHCC)
6300 Shingle Creek Pkwy., Ste.320
Brooklyn Center, MN 55430
Ph: (763)569-0891
Fax: (763)569-0893
Free: (800)646-6742
E-mail: jory@minnesotaphcc.org
URL: http://www.minnesotaphcc.org
Contact: Jory L. Isakson, Exec.Dir.
State. Represents the plumbing, heating and cooling contractors. Promotes the construction industry. Protects the environment, health, safety and comfort of society. **Affiliated With:** Plumbing-Heating-Cooling Contractors Association. **Publications:** Newsletter, monthly.

10540 ■ Minnesota Music Educators Association (MMEA)
c/o Ms. Mary Schaefle, Exec.Dir.
6680 Shingle Creek Pkwy., Ste.103
Brooklyn Center, MN 55430
Ph: (763)566-1460
Fax: (763)566-1578
Free: (888)678-6632
E-mail: info@mmea.org
URL: http://www.mmea.org
Contact: Ms. Mary Schaefle, Exec.Dir.
Local. Affiliated With: MENC: The National Association for Music Education.

10541 ■ Plumbing-Heating-Cooling Contractors Association, Metro
c/o Jory Isakson, Exec.Mgr.
6300 Shingle Creek Pkwy., Ste.320
Brooklyn Center, MN 55430
Ph: (763)569-0891
Fax: (763)569-0893
E-mail: jory@minnesotaphcc.org
URL: National Affiliate–www.phccweb.org
Contact: Jory Isakson, Exec.Mgr.
Local. Represents the plumbing, heating and cooling contractors. Promotes the construction industry. Protects the environment, health, safety and comfort of society. **Affiliated With:** Plumbing-Heating-Cooling Contractors Association.

10542 ■ Qwest Pioneers Minnesota Chapter 8
c/o LuAnn Chambliss
6300 Shingle Creek Pkwy., 4th Fl.
Brooklyn Center, MN 55430
Ph: (763)585-3406
E-mail: luann.chambliss@qwest.com
URL: http://www.mnpioneers.com
Contact: Phyllis Johnson, Sec.
State. Affiliated With: TelecomPioneers.

10543 ■ Sales and Marketing Executives, Minneapolis/St. Paul (SME)
2781 Freeway Blvd., Ste.100
Brooklyn Center, MN 55430
Ph: (763)746-3400
Fax: (763)746-3401
E-mail: info@smemn.org
URL: http://www.smemn.org
Contact: Drenda G. Wendell, Exec.Dir.
Membership Dues: individual, $240 (annual) • initiation fee, $75. **Local.**

Brooklyn Park

10544 ■ American Legion, Business and Professional Mens Post 450
9013 Glen Edin Ln.
Brooklyn Park, MN 55443
Ph: (651)291-1800
Fax: (651)291-1057
URL: National Affiliate–www.legion.org
Local. Affiliated With: American Legion.

10545 ■ Antique Automobile Club of America, Minnesota Region - Capitol City Chapter
c/o Priscilla Johansen
4008 Brookdale Dr.
Brooklyn Park, MN 55443
Ph: (763)784-7698
E-mail: elfrisk@usfamily.net
URL: http://local.aaca.org/ccc
Contact: Joan Frisk, Pres.
Founded: 1964. **Membership Dues:** individual, $15 (annual). **Local.** Collectors, hobbyists, and others interested in the preservation, maintenance, and restoration of automobiles and in automotive history. **Affiliated With:** Antique Automobile Club of America.

10546 ■ Brooklyn Center Lions Club
c/o David Holmes, Pres.
4000 Hollyhook Cir.
Brooklyn Park, MN 55443
Ph: (763)424-4724
URL: http://www.5m5.org
Contact: David Holmes, Pres.
Local. Affiliated With: Lions Clubs International.

10547 ■ Brooklyn Park Figure Skating Club (BPFSC)
5600 85th Ave. N
Brooklyn Park, MN 55443
E-mail: mike@itzin.com
URL: http://www.bpfsc.com
Contact: Mike Itzin, Contact
Local. Provides programs to encourage participation and achievement in the sport of figure skating on ice. Defines and maintains uniform standards of skating proficiency. Organizes and sponsors competitions and exhibitions for the purpose of stimulating interest in figure skating. **Affiliated With:** United States Figure Skating Association.

10548 ■ Brooklyn Park Lady Lions Club
c/o Jan Christofferson, Pres.
9161 Cambridge Ave. N
Brooklyn Park, MN 55443
Ph: (763)493-8578
URL: http://www.5m5.org
Contact: Jan Christofferson, Pres.
Local. Affiliated With: Lions Clubs International.

10549 ■ Brooklyn Park Lions Club
c/o Brenda Reeves, Sec.
3916 Sunset Rd. N
Brooklyn Park, MN 55445

Ph: (763)427-2507 (612)625-5319
URL: http://www.5m5.org
Contact: Brenda Reeves, Sec.
Local. Affiliated With: Lions Clubs International.

10550 ■ IEEE Engineering Management Society - Twin Cities Section
c/o Phyllis L. Brown
8437 W River Rd.
Brooklyn Park, MN 55444-1429
Ph: (763)786-2405
Fax: (763)786-5778
E-mail: brown@jged.com
URL: National Affiliate–www.ewh.ieee.org/soc/ems
Contact: Phyllis L. Brown, Contact
Local. Promotes the practice of engineering and technology management as a profession. Encourages theoretical and conceptual developments for the management of organizations. Provides learning and development opportunities for its members. **Affiliated With:** IEEE Engineering Management Society.

10551 ■ Minneapolis Riverview Lions Club
c/o Grant Hendrickson, Pres.
9025 Telford Crossing
Brooklyn Park, MN 55443
Ph: (763)391-7628 (612)721-1696
URL: http://www.5m5.org
Contact: Grant Hendrickson, Pres.
Local. Affiliated With: Lions Clubs International.

10552 ■ Minnesota Chapter of Associated Locksmiths of America
c/o Alan J. Morgan, Jr., Chm.
Speedy Lock & Key
8005 W River Rd.
Brooklyn Park, MN 55444
Ph: (612)566-2637
Fax: (612)566-6465
E-mail: almorgan@aol.com
URL: http://www.aloa.org
Contact: Alan J. Morgan Jr., Chm.
Membership Dues: regular, $75 (annual) • associate, $125 (annual) • apprentice, $25 (annual). **State. Affiliated With:** Associated Locksmiths of America.

10553 ■ Minnesota International Cricket Club
300 75th Ave. N
Brooklyn Park, MN 55444
URL: http://www.usaca.org/Clubs.htm
Contact: Charles Peterson, Contact
Local.

10554 ■ Minnesota United Snowmobilers Association (MnUSA)
7040 Lakeland Ave. N, Ste.212
Brooklyn Park, MN 55428
Ph: (763)577-0185
Fax: (763)577-0186
E-mail: website@mnsnowmobiler.org
URL: http://www.snowmobile-mnusa.org
Contact: Curtis Berg, Pres.
Founded: 1978. **Members:** 20,000. **Membership Dues:** individual, family, $20 (annual) • business, $50 (annual). **Staff:** 2. **Regional Groups:** 9. **State Groups:** 1. **Local Groups:** 295. **State.** Promotes the sport of snowmobiling in Minnesota; coordinates with community leaders, businesses, and legislators. **Awards:** Dealer of the Year. **Frequency:** annual. **Type:** recognition • Snowmobiler of the Year. **Frequency:** annual. **Type:** recognition. **Publications:** *Minnesota Snowmobiling*, 8/year. Magazine. **Price:** $2.95/copy; $15.00/year. **Circulation:** 30,000. **Advertising:** accepted. **Conventions/Meetings:** quarterly board meeting (exhibits) • annual convention (exhibits).

10555 ■ North Metro I-35W Corridor Coalition
8525 Edinbrook Xing, Ste.5
Brooklyn Park, MN 55443-1966
Ph: (763)493-5115
Fax: (763)424-1174
URL: http://www.I35w.org
Contact: Joseph Strauss, Exec.Dir.
Local.

10556 ■ Phi Theta Kappa, Beta Kappa Xi Chapter - Hennepin Technical College
c/o Michelle Zeig
9000 Brooklyn Blvd.
Brooklyn Park, MN 55445
Ph: (952)995-1561
E-mail: michelle.zeig@hennepintech.edu
URL: http://www.ptk.org/directories/chapters/MN/21209-1.htm
Contact: Michelle Zeig, Advisor
Local.

10557 ■ Phi Theta Kappa, Phi Xi Chapter - North Hennepin Community College
c/o Peggy LePage
7411 85th Ave. N
Brooklyn Park, MN 55445
Ph: (763)424-0874
E-mail: peggy.lepage@nhcc.mnscu.edu
URL: http://www.ptk.org/directories/chapters/MN/266-1.htm
Contact: Peggy LePage, Advisor
Local.

10558 ■ St. Louis Park Lions Club
c/o Sonjia Wagner, Sec.
9823 Greenspruce Ave. N
Brooklyn Park, MN 55443
Ph: (763)425-5434 (763)533-3070
E-mail: bnjamin55@aol.com
URL: http://www.5m5.org
Contact: Sonjia Wagner, Sec.
Local. Affiliated With: Lions Clubs International.

10559 ■ Skills USA, Hennepin Technical College
9000 Brooklyn Blvd.
Brooklyn Park, MN 55445
Ph: (952)995-1300
Fax: (763)488-2951
E-mail: dale.boyenga@hennepintech.edu
URL: http://www.mnskillsusa.org
Contact: Dale Boyenga, Contact
Local. Serves high school and college students enrolled in technical, skilled, and service and health occupations. Provides quality education experiences for students in leadership, teamwork, citizenship and character development. Builds and reinforces self-confidence, work attitudes and communication skills. Emphasizes total quality at work, high ethical standards, superior work skills, and life-long education. Promotes understanding of the free enterprise system and involvement in community service. **Affiliated With:** Skills USA - VICA.

10560 ■ Upper Midwest ACH Association (UMACHA)
7100 Northland Cir., Ste.212
Brooklyn Park, MN 55428
Ph: (763)549-7000
Fax: (763)549-7004
Free: (800)348-3692
E-mail: fredl@umacha.org
URL: http://www.umacha.org
Contact: Mr. Fred Laing II, Pres.
Regional. Promotes the development of electronic solutions to improve payments systems. **Affiliated With:** NACHA: The Electronic Payments Association.

10561 ■ Upper Midwest Automated Clearing House Association (UMACHA)
7100 Northland Cir., No. 212
Brooklyn Park, MN 55428
Ph: (763)549-7000
Fax: (763)549-7004
Free: (800)348-3692
E-mail: fredl@umacha.org
URL: http://umacha.org
Contact: Fred Laing II, Pres.
Founded: 1973. **Members:** 850. **Budget:** $625,000. **Local. Publications:** *ACH Corporate User Guide*, annual • *ACH Update*, semimonthly. Newsletter.

Brookston

10562 ■ American Legion, Tester-Niemi Post 562
PO Box 351
Brookston, MN 55711
Ph: (651)291-1800
Fax: (651)291-1057
URL: National Affiliate–www.legion.org
Local. Affiliated With: American Legion.

Brooten

10563 ■ American Legion, Ranten-Sundflot Post 288
PO Box 9
Brooten, MN 56316
Ph: (651)291-1800
Fax: (651)291-1057
URL: National Affiliate–www.legion.org
Local. Affiliated With: American Legion.

Browerville

10564 ■ American Legion, Browerville Post 293
E 7th St.
Browerville, MN 56438
Ph: (651)291-1800
Fax: (651)291-1057
URL: National Affiliate–www.legion.org
Local. Affiliated With: American Legion.

Browns Valley

10565 ■ American Legion, William Krensing Post 58
PO Box 58
Browns Valley, MN 56219
Ph: (651)291-1800
Fax: (651)291-1057
URL: National Affiliate–www.legion.org
Local. Affiliated With: American Legion.

Brownsville

10566 ■ Brownsville Lions Club
c/o Rick Denstad, Pres.
807 Ramsey St.
Brownsville, MN 55919
Ph: (507)482-6890
URL: http://www.lions5m1.org/brownsville
Contact: Rick Denstad, Pres.
Local. Affiliated With: Lions Clubs International.

Brownton

10567 ■ American Legion, Minnesota Post 143
c/o Edward Ewald
PO Box 397
Brownton, MN 55312
Ph: (651)291-1800
Fax: (651)291-1057
URL: National Affiliate–www.legion.org
Contact: Edward Ewald, Contact
Local. Affiliated With: American Legion.

Bruno

10568 ■ American Legion, Minnesota Post 563
c/o Douglas Nelson
HC 1
Bruno, MN 55712

Ph: (651)291-1800
Fax: (651)291-1057
URL: National Affiliate–www.legion.org
Contact: Douglas Nelson, Contact
Local. Affiliated With: American Legion.

10569 ■ Minnesota Trappers Association (MTA)
c/o Gary Meis, Pres.
69555 One Mile Rd.
Bruno, MN 55712
Ph: (320)838-1570
E-mail: trappergabby@hotmail.com
URL: http://www.mntrappers.com
Contact: Gary Meis, Pres.
State. Affiliated With: National Trappers Association.

Buffalo

10570 ■ American Legion, Buffalo Post 270
304 10th Ave. S
Buffalo, MN 55313
Ph: (651)291-1800
Fax: (651)291-1057
URL: National Affiliate–www.legion.org
Local. Affiliated With: American Legion.

10571 ■ Broiler and Egg Association of Minnesota
100 Marty Dr.
Buffalo, MN 55313
Ph: (763)682-2171
Fax: (763)682-5546
E-mail: memberservices@minnesotaturkeys.com
Contact: Nicole Jones, Exec.Sec.
Staff: 5. **State. Publications:** *Focus on Feathers*, quarterly. Newsletter. **Price:** free for members only. **Conventions/Meetings:** quarterly board meeting • annual meeting.

10572 ■ Buffalo Area Chamber of Commerce (BACC)
9 Central Ave.
Buffalo, MN 55313
Ph: (763)682-4902
Fax: (763)682-5677
E-mail: info@buffalochamber.org
URL: http://www.buffalochamber.org
Contact: Sally Custer, Pres.
Founded: 1969. **Members:** 280. **Staff:** 2. **Budget:** $115,000. **Local.** Promotes business and community development in the Buffalo, MN area. Holds annual Buffalo Days, Sidewalk Art and Craft Festival, and Buffalo P.R.C.A. Rodeo. **Affiliated With:** Minnesota State Chamber of Commerce. **Publications:** Directory, periodic • Newsletter, monthly. **Conventions/Meetings:** periodic meeting.

10573 ■ Crystal Lions Club
c/o Craig Tomseth, Sec.
335 Halsey Ave. NE
Buffalo, MN 55313-8858
Ph: (763)477-4845 (612)616-4089
URL: http://www.5m5.org
Contact: Craig Tomseth, Sec.
Local. Affiliated With: Lions Clubs International.

10574 ■ Midwest Poultry Federation (MPF)
c/o Steve Olson, Exec.Dir.
108 Marty Dr.
Buffalo, MN 55313
Ph: (763)682-2171
Fax: (763)682-5546
E-mail: lara@midwestpoultry.com
URL: http://www.midwestpoultry.com
Contact: Steve Olson, Exec.Dir.
Founded: 1971. **Members:** 17. **Staff:** 4. **Budget:** $225,000. **Regional.** Hosts annual convention for the federation administrators. **Awards: Frequency:** annual. **Type:** scholarship. **Recipient:** for high school senior or college student pursuing career in poultry industry. **Conventions/Meetings:** annual trade show, annual regional convention emphasizing on farm poultry production (exhibits).

10575 ■ Minnesota Dairy Herd Improvement Association
c/o Bruce Dokkebakken, Gen.Mgr.
307 Brighton Ave. S
Buffalo, MN 55313-2304
Ph: (763)682-1091
Fax: (763)682-1117
Free: (800)827-3442
E-mail: admin@mndhia.org
URL: http://www.mndhia.org
Contact: Bruce Dokkebakken, Gen.Mgr.
State.

10576 ■ Minnesota Turkey Growers Association (MTGA)
c/o Steve Olson, Exec.Dir.
108 Marty Dr.
Buffalo, MN 55313
Ph: (763)682-2171
Fax: (763)682-5546
E-mail: info@minnesotaturkey.com
URL: http://www.minnesotaturkeys.com
Contact: Steve Olson, Exec.Dir.
Founded: 1939. **Members:** 400. **Staff:** 5. **State.** Turkey growers, hatchers, and processors. **Publications:** *Gobbles*, monthly. Newsletter. **Price:** $25.00/year. **Circulation:** 1,000. **Advertising:** accepted.

10577 ■ Minnesota Turkey Research and Promotion Council (MTRPC)
108 Marty Dr.
Buffalo, MN 55313
Ph: (763)682-2171
Fax: (763)682-5546
E-mail: info@minnesotaturkey.com
URL: http://www.minnesotaturkeys.com
Contact: Steve Olson, Exec.Dir.
State.

10578 ■ Skills USA, Wright Technical Center
1400 N Hwy. 25, Box 239
Buffalo, MN 55313
Ph: (763)684-2242
Fax: (763)682-4113
E-mail: bunnie.craddock@wtc.k12.mn.us
URL: http://www.mnskillsusa.org
Contact: Bunnie Craddock, Contact
Local. Serves high school and college students enrolled in technical, skilled, and service and health occupations. Provides quality education experiences for students in leadership, teamwork, citizenship and character development. Builds and reinforces self-confidence, work attitudes and communication skills. Emphasizes total quality at work, high ethical standards, superior work skills, and life-long education. Promotes understanding of the free enterprise system and involvement in community service. **Affiliated With:** Skills USA - VICA.

10579 ■ Vintage Chevrolet Club of America, Viking Region No. 4
c/o Roger James, Dir.
1620 60th St. NE
Buffalo, MN 55313
Ph: (763)682-3111
URL: National Affiliate–www.vcca.org
Contact: Roger James, Dir.
Local. Affiliated With: Vintage Chevrolet Club of America.

10580 ■ Wright County Chapter, American Red Cross
PO Box 142
Buffalo, MN 55313
Ph: (763)684-0068
Free: (800)560-7641
E-mail: arcwright@qwest.net
URL: http://www.wrightctyarc.org
Contact: Jenny Vergin, Mgr.
Local. Serves members of the armed forces and veterans and their families and aids disaster victims. Other activities include: blood services; community services; service opportunities for youth. **Affiliated With:** American Red Cross National Headquarters. **Publications:** Newsletter. Alternate Formats: online.

Buffalo Lake

10581 ■ American Legion, Minnesota Post 469
c/o Marvin Michelson, Adj.
PO Box 143
Buffalo Lake, MN 55314
Ph: (651)291-1800
Fax: (651)291-1057
URL: National Affiliate–www.legion.org
Contact: Marvin Michelson, Adj.
Local. Affiliated With: American Legion.

10582 ■ Buffalo Lake Lions Club
c/o Brian Ryberg, Sec.
16659 667th Ave.
Buffalo Lake, MN 55314
Ph: (320)833-2062
E-mail: bsr0715@earthlink.net
URL: http://www.5m4lions.org
Contact: Brian Ryberg, Sec.
Local. Affiliated With: Lions Clubs International.

Burnsville

10583 ■ AAA Minnesota/Iowa
600 W Travelers Trail
Burnsville, MN 55337-2518
Ph: (952)707-4200
Fax: (952)707-4270
Free: (800)222-1333
URL: http://www.aaa.com
Contact: Sheryl Andersen, Mgr.
Local.

10584 ■ Aggregate Ready Mix Association of Minnesota (ARM)
c/o Mr. Fred Corrigan, Exec.Dir.
12300 Dupont Ave. S
Burnsville, MN 55337
Ph: (952)707-1250
Fax: (952)707-1251
Free: (888)733-4649
E-mail: fcorrigan@armofmn.com
URL: http://www.armofmn.com
Contact: Mr. Fred Corrigan, Exec.Dir.
Founded: 1950. **Staff:** 6. **State.** Commits to the aggregate and ready mix industries through promotion, education, environment, and government issues. **Libraries: Type:** reference. **Holdings:** articles, books, clippings, papers, periodicals, reports. **Awards:** ARM Lifetime Achievement Awards. **Frequency:** annual. **Type:** recognition. **Recipient:** for nonmember who has demonstrated a commitment to the industries through a lifetime of effort professionally and as a volunteer • ARM Members Scholarship. **Frequency:** annual. **Type:** scholarship • ARM Promoter of the Year Award. **Frequency:** annual. **Type:** recognition. **Recipient:** for member who has gone above and beyond to promote the aggregate and/or ready mix industries • Building Excellence Awards. **Frequency:** annual. **Type:** recognition. **Recipient:** for member companies for the outstanding efforts made in the course of their business related to the aggregate and ready mix concrete industries. **Additional Websites:** http://www.chooseconcrete.com. **Committees:** Aggregate; Insulating Concrete Form; Marketing; Parking Lot/Local Roads; Technical. **Affiliated With:** Builders Association of the Twin Cities, National Association of Home Building; National Association of Home Builders of the U.S., Central Minnesota Builders Association; National Ready Mixed Concrete Association; National Stone, Sand and Gravel Association; Portland Cement Association. **Publications:** Membership Directory • Newsletters.

10585 ■ American Legion, Minnesota Post 1700
c/o Patrick Kopp
PO Box 1834
Burnsville, MN 55337

Ph: (651)291-1800
Fax: (651)291-1057
URL: National Affiliate–www.legion.org
Contact: Patrick Kopp, Contact
Local. Affiliated With: American Legion.

10586 ■ Apple Valley - Young Life
14300 Nicollet Ct., Ste.207
Burnsville, MN 55306
Ph: (952)892-3722
URL: http://sites.younglife.org/_layouts/ylext/default.aspx?ID=C-1188
Local. Affiliated With: Young Life.

10587 ■ Burnsville Chamber of Commerce (BCC)
101 W Bursnville Pkwy., Ste.150
Burnsville, MN 55337-2571
Ph: (952)435-6000
Fax: (952)435-6972
E-mail: chamber@burnsvillechamber.com
URL: http://www.burnsvillechamber.com
Contact: Daron Van Helden, Pres.
Founded: 1965. **Members:** 600. **Local.** Promotes business and community development in Burnsville, MN. **Computer Services:** Online services, membership directory. **Publications:** *At Work*, monthly. Newsletter • *Chamber Membership Directory*, annual.

10588 ■ Burnsville Convention and Visitors Bureau
101 W Burnsville Pkwy., Ste.150B
Burnsville, MN 55337
Ph: (952)898-5646
Fax: (952)487-1777
Free: (800)521-6055
E-mail: info@burnsvillemn.com
URL: http://www.burnsvillemn.com
Contact: Melissa Flach-Saurer, Exec.Dir.
Founded: 1987. **Staff:** 3. **Local.** A destination marketing business. **Awards:** Hospitality Award. **Frequency:** annual. **Type:** recognition. **Recipient:** to employees who demonstrate outstanding customer service and team spirit at local tourism related businesses. **Affiliated With:** American Bus Association; Midwest Society of Association Executives; National Tour Association.

10589 ■ Burnsville-Minnesota Valley Figure Skating Club (BMVFSC)
PO Box 994
Burnsville, MN 55337
E-mail: webmaster@bmvfsc.org
URL: http://www.bmvfsc.org
Local. Provides programs to encourage participation and achievement in the sport of figure skating on ice. Defines and maintains uniform standards of skating proficiency. Organizes and sponsors competitions and exhibitions for the purpose of stimulating interest in figure skating. **Affiliated With:** United States Figure Skating Association.

10590 ■ Burnsville Young Life
14300 Nicollet Ct., Ste.207
Burnsville, MN 55306
Ph: (952)892-3722
URL: http://sites.younglife.org/sites/burnsville/default.aspx
Local. Affiliated With: Young Life.

10591 ■ Farmington Wyldlife
14300 Nicollet Ct., Ste.207
Burnsville, MN 55306
Ph: (952)892-3722
URL: http://sites.younglife.org/sites/farmingtonwyldlife/default.aspx
Local. Affiliated With: Young Life.

10592 ■ Infusion Nurses Society, Upper Midwest
14416 Portland Ave. S
Burnsville, MN 55337
Ph: (952)432-7148
E-mail: patrice.bennetts@allina.com
URL: National Affiliate–www.ins1.org
Contact: Patrice Bennetts, Pres.
Regional. Represents the interests of healthcare professionals who are involved with the practice of infusion therapy. Seeks to advance the delivery of quality therapy to patients. Promotes research and education in the practice of infusion nursing. **Affiliated With:** Infusion Nurses Society.

10593 ■ Lakeville HS - Young Life
14300 Nicollet Ct., Ste.207
Burnsville, MN 55306
Ph: (952)892-3722
URL: http://sites.younglife.org/_layouts/ylext/default.aspx?ID=C-3477
Local. Affiliated With: Young Life.

10594 ■ Minneapolis Southwest Lions Club
c/o Doug Mehr, Sec.
13812 Scott St.
Burnsville, MN 55337
Ph: (952)894-9036 (952)240-9138
URL: http://www.5m5.org
Contact: Doug Mehr, Sec.
Local. Affiliated With: Lions Clubs International.

10595 ■ Minnesota Chapter, MOAA
c/o Col. John Abrahamson
3302 Red Oak Cir. N
Burnsville, MN 55337-3308
Ph: (651)777-7301
E-mail: jabecol@aol.com
URL: National Affiliate–www.moaa.org
Contact: Col. John Abrahamson, Contact
State. Affiliated With: Military Officers Association of America.

10596 ■ Minnesota Chiropractic Association (MCA)
12445 River Ridge Blvd., Ste.100
Burnsville, MN 55337
Ph: (952)882-9411
Fax: (952)882-9397
Free: (800)864-3769
E-mail: mnchiro@mnchiro.com
URL: http://www.mnchiro.com
Contact: Howard Fidler DC, Contact
State.

10597 ■ Minnesota Concrete Masonry Association (MCMA)
c/o Mike Johnsrud, Exec.Dir.
12300 Dupont Ave. S
Burnsville, MN 55337
Ph: (952)707-1976
Fax: (952)707-1251
E-mail: mjohnsrud@mcma.net
URL: http://www.mcma.net
Contact: Mike Johnsrud, Exec.Dir.
Founded: 1953. **Members:** 80. **Staff:** 3. **Budget:** $300,000. **State.** Manufacturers of concrete blocks, segmental retaining walls, concrete products and their suppliers in Minnesota and surrounding areas. Conducts promotion, education and case activities for the industry. **Libraries: Type:** open to the public. **Holdings:** books, periodicals, video recordings. **Subjects:** concrete, concrete masonry, aggregate. **Awards:** Minnesota Masonry Project Awards. **Frequency:** annual. **Type:** recognition. **Recipient:** for outstanding concrete masonry projects. **Affiliated With:** National Concrete Masonry Association. **Conventions/Meetings:** annual Concrete Con-Expo - meeting (exhibits).

10598 ■ Minnesota Jaycees
2101 W Hwy. 13
Burnsville, MN 55337
Ph: (952)890-8000
Fax: (952)890-8029
Free: (800)862-5242
E-mail: executivedirector@mnjaycees.org
URL: http://www.mnjaycees.org
Contact: Josh Bohmbach, Pres.
State. Contributes to the advancement of Minnesota communities by providing the opportunity for young individuals to develop their skills, social responsibility, entrepreneurship and fellowship.

10599 ■ Minnesota Off-Road Cyclists (MORC)
1905 Woods Ln.
Burnsville, MN 55337
Ph: (612)722-5299
E-mail: president@morcmtb.org
URL: http://www.morcmtb.org
Contact: Scott Thayer, Pres.
State. Comprises of biking enthusiasts in MN dedicated to gaining and maintaining mountain bike trails within the state. **Affiliated With:** International Mountain Bicycling Association.

10600 ■ Minnesota Saddlebred Horse Association
c/o Alice Lear
14750 Burnsville Pkwy., No. 138
Burnsville, MN 55306
Ph: (952)447-8464
E-mail: info@msha.org
URL: http://www.msha.org
Contact: Sally Snyder Tesch, Pres.
State. Affiliated With: American Saddlebred Horse Association.

10601 ■ Minnesota Society of Professional Surveyors (MSPS)
c/o Steven A. Jobe, Pres.
201 W Travelers Trail, Ste.18
Burnsville, MN 55337
Ph: (952)224-9999
Fax: (952)224-9998
Free: (800)890-LAND
E-mail: melissag@integra.net
URL: http://www.mnsurveyor.com
Contact: Melissa K. Zupon, Exec.Dir.
Founded: 1953. **Members:** 600. **Membership Dues:** licensed, $150 (annual) • training, $75 (annual) • associate, $70 (annual) • technical, $65 (annual) • student, $35 (annual) • sustaining, $280 (annual) • firm, $140-$680 (annual). **Budget:** $240,000. **State.** Licensed land surveyors and those in related fields. Seeks to unite all licensed land surveyors; elevate standards; and establish basic minimum requirements. Sponsors educational programs, legislation, and scholarships. **Awards: Frequency:** annual. **Type:** scholarship. **Recipient:** for college and technical school students in Minnesota. **Affiliated With:** National Society of Professional Surveyors. **Publications:** *Minnesota Surveyor*, quarterly. Magazine. **Conventions/Meetings:** bimonthly board meeting • annual meeting - 2007 Jan. 31-Feb. 2; 2008 Jan. 30-Feb. 1 • semiannual workshop - always April and December.

10602 ■ Minnesota South District, The Lutheran Church-Missouri Synod
14301 Grand Ave. S
Burnsville, MN 55306-5790
Ph: (952)435-2550
Fax: (952)435-2581
E-mail: information@mnsdistrict.org
URL: http://mns.lcms.org
Contact: Dr. Lane Seitz, Pres.
Local.

10603 ■ Minnesota Valley Young Life
14300 Nicollet Ct., Ste.207
Burnsville, MN 55306
Ph: (952)892-3722
URL: http://sites.younglife.org/sites/mnvalley/default.aspx
Local. Affiliated With: Young Life.

10604 ■ National Association of Rocketry - Minnesota Amateur Spacemodelers Association (MASA)
c/o David Whitaker
2900 Sunnyside Cir.
Burnsville, MN 55306
Ph: (320)764-9303
E-mail: masa@mn-rocketry.net
URL: http://www.mn-rocketry.net/masa
Contact: Mike Erpelding, Pres.
State.

10605 ■ National Model Railroad Association, Thousand Lakes Region
c/o Bruce Selb, Pres.
PO Box 1113
Burnsville, MN 55337
Ph: (612)382-7347
E-mail: tlrprez@hq.nmra.org
URL: http://www.thousandlakesregion.org
Contact: Bruce Selb, Pres.
Founded: 1982. **Members:** 300. **Membership Dues:** member, $8 (annual). **Regional Groups:** 9. **Regional. Affiliated With:** National Model Railroad Association. **Publications:** Newsletter, quarterly. Contains information that serves as communications vehicle for membership. **Advertising:** accepted. **Conventions/Meetings:** annual convention, 3 or 4 day event (exhibits).

10606 ■ Red River Valley Fighter Pilot Association - Minnesota
76 Garden Dr.
Burnsville, MN 55337
E-mail: riverrat@mninter.net
URL: National Affiliate–www.river-rats.org
Contact: Robert Jasperson, Contact
State. Affiliated With: Red River Valley Fighter Pilots Association.

10607 ■ Savage Wyldlife
14300 Nicollet Ct., Ste.207
Burnsville, MN 55306
Ph: (952)892-3722
URL: http://sites.younglife.org/_layouts/ylext/default.aspx?ID=C-3782
Local. Affiliated With: Young Life.

10608 ■ SCORE South Metro
c/o Steven Saefke, Chm.
101 W Burnsville Pkwy., Ste.152
Burnsville, MN 55337
Ph: (952)890-7020
Fax: (952)890-7019
E-mail: southmetro@scoreminn.org
URL: National Affiliate–www.score.org
Contact: Steven Saefke, Chm.
Local. Affiliated With: SCORE.

10609 ■ Sons of Norway, Norumbega Lodge 1-217
c/o Arlen I. Erdahl, Pres.
13413 Nicollet Ln.
Burnsville, MN 55337-2775
Ph: (952)890-5273
URL: National Affiliate–www.sofn.com
Contact: Arlen I. Erdahl, Pres.
Local. Affiliated With: Sons of Norway.

10610 ■ Sweet Adelines International, Twin Cities Show Chorus
904 Crystal Lake Rd.
Burnsville, MN 55306
Ph: (952)435-7740
E-mail: rose@realtyneeds.net
URL: http://www.regionsix.org/chorus/twin_cities.htm
Contact: Rose Berglund, Pres.
Local. Advances the musical art form of barbershop harmony through education and performances. Provides education, training and coaching in the development of women's four-part barbershop harmony. **Affiliated With:** Sweet Adelines International.

10611 ■ TROA Council of MN Chapters - Military Officers Association of America
3302 Red Oak Cir. S
Burnsville, MN 55337
Ph: (952)894-1857
E-mail: engr549@msn.com
URL: National Affiliate–www.moaa.org
Local. Affiliated With: Military Officers Association of America.

10612 ■ USA Weightlifting - Rosemount Weightlifting Club
c/o Jed Smith
3313 Selkirk Dr.
Burnsville, MN 55337
Ph: (952)894-6455
URL: National Affiliate–www.usaweightlifting.org
Contact: Jed Smith, Contact
Local. Affiliated With: USA Weightlifting.

Byron

10613 ■ American Legion, Minnesota Post 119
c/o Sumner R. Hair
PO Box 687
Byron, MN 55920
Ph: (651)291-1800
Fax: (651)291-1057
URL: National Affiliate–www.legion.org
Contact: Sumner R. Hair, Contact
Local. Affiliated With: American Legion.

10614 ■ Izaak Walton League of America, Rochester Chapter
c/o Chad Jorgensen
309 9th St. NW
Byron, MN 55920-1368
Ph: (507)775-2814
E-mail: safgrenjorgensen@charter.net
URL: National Affiliate–www.iwla.org
Contact: Chad Jorgensen, Dues Sec.
Founded: 1923. **Members:** 70. **Membership Dues:** individual, $42 (annual) • family, $58 (annual) • student, $27 (annual) • youth, $8 (annual). **State Groups:** 1. **Local Groups:** 1. **Local.** Works to promote conservation of natural resources, clean water; improve fish and wildlife habitat; establish and protect public parks, forests, lakeshores, and refuges. **Awards: Frequency:** annual. **Type:** scholarship. **Recipient:** for students who are interested in conservation • Science Award. **Frequency:** annual. **Type:** monetary. **Recipient:** for best science exhibits. **Affiliated With:** Izaak Walton League of America. **Publications:** Newsletter. **Conventions/Meetings:** monthly meeting - always first Tuesday of the month. Rochester, MN - Avg. Attendance: 25.

10615 ■ Minnesota State Grange
8249 Country Club Rd.
Byron, MN 55920-4201
Ph: (507)775-6825
E-mail: rhfield@frontiernet.net
URL: National Affiliate–www.nationalgrange.org
Contact: Richard Field, Master
State. Rural family service organization with a special interest in agriculture. Promotes mission and goals through legislative, social, educational, community service, youth, and member services programs. **Affiliated With:** National Grange.

Caledonia

10616 ■ American Legion, Loveless-Eikens Post 191
PO Box 326
Caledonia, MN 55921
Ph: (651)291-1800
Fax: (651)291-1057
URL: National Affiliate–www.legion.org
Local. Affiliated With: American Legion.

Cambridge

10617 ■ American Legion, Minnesota Post 290
c/o Howard Mc Carty
200 2nd Ave. SE
Cambridge, MN 55008
Ph: (651)291-1800
Fax: (651)291-1057
URL: National Affiliate–www.legion.org
Contact: Howard Mc Carty, Contact
Local. Affiliated With: American Legion.

10618 ■ Cambridge Area Chamber of Commerce
PO Box 343
Cambridge, MN 55008
Ph: (763)689-2505
Fax: (763)552-2505
E-mail: cambchbr@sherbtel.net
URL: http://www.cambridge-chamber.com
Contact: Kathi Schaff, Exec.Dir.
Founded: 1940. **Members:** 200. **Membership Dues:** general (depends upon the number of employees), $228-$1,766 (annual). **Local.** Promotes business and community development in the Cambridge, MN area. **Telecommunication Services:** electronic mail, chamber2@sherbtel.net. **Committees:** Ambassadors; Economic Development, Industry and Technology; Education; Fund Raising; Leadership Initiatives; Legal; Marketing and Value Added Benefits; Programs. **Publications:** *Chamber News Page*, monthly. Newsletter. **Circulation:** 14,000. **Advertising:** accepted. Alternate Formats: online • *Friday Facts*, weekly. Newsletter. **Circulation:** 300. Alternate Formats: online. **Conventions/Meetings:** monthly meeting.

10619 ■ Cambridge-Isanti - Young Life
PO Box 389
Cambridge, MN 55008
Ph: (763)689-3823
URL: http://sites.younglife.org/sites/Cambridge-IsantiYL/default.aspx
Local. Affiliated With: Young Life.

10620 ■ East Central Minnesota Habitat for Humanity
218 Ashland St. S
Cambridge, MN 55008
Ph: (763)689-0288
Fax: (763)689-0288
Free: (866)600-0288
E-mail: chabitat@ecenet.com
URL: http://www.ecmhabitat.com
Contact: Wayne Eller, Exec.Dir.
Local. Affiliated With: Habitat for Humanity International.

10621 ■ East Central Minnesota Young Life
PO Box 389
Cambridge, MN 55008
Ph: (763)689-3823
Fax: (763)552-3823
URL: http://sites.younglife.org/sites/EastCentralMinnesota/default.aspx
Local. Affiliated With: Young Life.

10622 ■ East Central Wyldlife
PO Box 389
Cambridge, MN 55008
Ph: (763)689-3823
URL: http://sites.younglife.org/sites/WyldLife1/default.aspx
Local. Affiliated With: Young Life.

10623 ■ Isanti County Historical Society (ICHS)
PO Box 525
Cambridge, MN 55008
Ph: (763)689-4229
Fax: (763)552-0740
E-mail: ichs@izoom.net
URL: http://www.ICHS.ws
Contact: Kathy McCully, Exec.Dir.
Founded: 1965. **Members:** 450. **Membership Dues:** individual, $15 (annual) • family, $25 (annual) • sustaining, $35 (annual) • patron (bronze-platinum), $100-$500 (annual). **Staff:** 2. **Budget:** $75,000. **Regional Groups:** 1. **State Groups:** 2. **Local Groups:** 1. **Languages:** English, German, Swedish. **For-Profit. Local.** Works to promote the history of the

County by funding research, programming, outreach, edification and displays. **Libraries: Type:** open to the public. **Holdings:** 2,500; articles, biographical archives, books, maps, periodicals, photographs. **Subjects:** immigration, agriculture, social and customs, transportation, people. **Publications:** *Isanti Cuttings* (in English and Swedish), quarterly. Newsletter. **Price:** $15.00. **Circulation:** 2,500. **Advertising:** accepted • Reprint (in English and Swedish), annual. **Conventions/Meetings:** annual Swedish Language Camp for Children - workshop, summer camp for children to introduce them to the language and customs of Swedish immigrants to the county - last week in August.

10624 ■ Minnesota Nurses Association - District 12
2052 352nd Ave. NE
Cambridge, MN 55008
Ph: (763)552-0469
E-mail: kellismith120@hotmail.com
URL: http://www.mnnurses.org
Contact: Kelli Smith, Pres.
Local. Works to advance the nursing profession. Seeks to meet the needs of nurses and health care consumers. Fosters high standards of nursing practice. Promotes the economic and general welfare of nurses in the workplace. **Affiliated With:** American Nurses Association; Minnesota Nurses Association.

10625 ■ Phi Theta Kappa, Alpha Delta Upsilon Chapter - Anoka-Ramsey Community College - Cambridge
c/o Kathleen Hoffman
300 Polk St. S
Cambridge, MN 55008
Ph: (763)689-7000
E-mail: kathleen.hoffman@anokaramsey.edu
URL: http://www.ptk.org/directories/chapters/MN/272-1.htm
Contact: Kathleen Hoffman, Advisor
Local.

10626 ■ Skills USA, Cambridge High School
430 NW 8th Ave.
Cambridge, MN 55008
Ph: (763)689-2020
Fax: (763)689-6060
E-mail: burns@cambridge.k12.mn.us
URL: http://www.mnskillsusa.org
Contact: Ed Burns, Contact
Local. Serves high school and college students enrolled in technical, skilled, and service and health occupations. Provides quality education experiences for students in leadership, teamwork, citizenship and character development. Builds and reinforces self-confidence, work attitudes and communication skills. Emphasizes total quality at work, high ethical standards, superior work skills, and life-long education. Promotes understanding of the free enterprise system and involvement in community service. **Affiliated With:** Skills USA - VICA.

Canby

10627 ■ Canby Area Chamber of Commerce
123 1st St. E
Canby, MN 56220
Ph: (507)223-7775 (507)223-7295
E-mail: josh@prairiehub.net
URL: http://canbychamber.com
Contact: Pat Stanley, Pres.
Local. Provides information on tourist attractions and outdoor activities in the Canby area.

10628 ■ Minnesota Pharmacists Association, Southwest District
c/o Mark Whittier, Chm.
Canby Drug & Gifts
130 St. Olaf Ave. N
Canby, MN 56220
Ph: (507)223-5955
E-mail: canbyrx@frontiernet.net
URL: http://www.mpha.org
Contact: Mark Whittier, Chm.
Local. Works to provide leadership for the pharmacy profession. Seeks to protect and enhance public health. Enhances the knowledge, ethics and skills of pharmacists through advocacy, education, research and the development of standards. **Affiliated With:** Minnesota Pharmacists Association.

10629 ■ Sons of Norway, Vennskap Lodge 1-554
c/o Irene B. Madsen, Sec.
507 Oscar Ave. N
Canby, MN 56220-1110
Ph: (507)223-7770
E-mail: imadsen@mycidco.com
URL: National Affiliate–www.sofn.com
Contact: Irene B. Madsen, Sec.
Local. Affiliated With: Sons of Norway.

Cannon Falls

10630 ■ American Legion, Kraft-Ostrom-American-Legion Post 142
218 4th St. N
Cannon Falls, MN 55009
Ph: (651)291-1800
Fax: (651)291-1057
URL: National Affiliate–www.legion.org
Local. Affiliated With: American Legion.

10631 ■ Cannon Falls Area Chamber of Commerce (CFACC)
PO Box 2
Cannon Falls, MN 55009
Ph: (507)263-2289
Fax: (507)263-2785
E-mail: tourism@cannonfalls.org
URL: http://www.cannonfalls.org
Contact: Patricia A. Anderson, Pres.
Founded: 1979. **Local.** Promotes business and community development in the Cannon Falls, MN area. **Publications:** *Discover Cannon Falls*, annual. Magazine. Contains an overview and promotion of Cannon Falls. **Price:** free.

10632 ■ Minnesota Quarter Horse Association
c/o Linda Henderson, Pres.
PO Box 433
Cannon Falls, MN 55009-0433
Ph: (507)263-2056
E-mail: ihnh64@reconnect.com
URL: http://www.mnqha.com/index_main.htm
Contact: Linda Henderson, Pres.
State. Affiliated With: American Quarter Horse Association.

10633 ■ National Active and Retired Federal Employees Association - Red Wing 1661
35139 Wagner Hill Way
Cannon Falls, MN 55009-5213
Ph: (507)263-3227
URL: National Affiliate–www.narfe.org
Contact: Oscar J. Quittem, Contact
Local. Protects the retirement future of employees through education. Informs members on issues affecting the retirement. **Affiliated With:** National Association of Retired Federal Employees.

10634 ■ USA Weightlifting - Team Cannon Weightlifting
c/o Aaron Kurtz
820 E Minnesota St.
Cannon Falls, MN 55009
Ph: (507)263-4177
Fax: (507)263-4177
URL: National Affiliate–www.usaweightlifting.org
Contact: Aaron Kurtz, Contact
Local. Affiliated With: USA Weightlifting.

Canton

10635 ■ American Legion, Paul Blagen Post 400
PO Box 1
Canton, MN 55922
Ph: (651)291-1800
Fax: (651)291-1057
URL: National Affiliate–www.legion.org
Local. Affiliated With: American Legion.

10636 ■ Mabel Lions Club
c/o Ross Duckett, Sec.
Box 186
Canton, MN 55922
Ph: (507)743-8333 (507)743-8435
E-mail: rcducket@acegroup.cc
URL: http://www.lions5m1.org/mabel
Contact: Ross Duckett, Sec.
Local. Affiliated With: Lions Clubs International.

Cass Lake

10637 ■ American Legion, Minnesota Post 284
c/o Jack Kimball
PO Box 126
Cass Lake, MN 56633
Ph: (651)291-1800
Fax: (651)291-1057
URL: National Affiliate–www.legion.org
Contact: Jack Kimball, Contact
Local. Affiliated With: American Legion.

Center City

10638 ■ Wild River Audubon Society
31450 Oasis Rd.
Center City, MN 55012
Ph: (651)674-7922 (651)257-6044
E-mail: kblomquist@sherbetel.net
URL: http://www.audubon.org/chapter/mn/index.html
Contact: Kathy Blomquist, Contact
Local. Formerly: (2005) National Audubon Society - Wild River.

Centerville

10639 ■ Centerville Lions Club - Minnesota
7155 Brian Dr.
Centerville, MN 55038
Ph: (612)221-9122 (651)653-1833
E-mail: greg.kieselhorst@comcast.net
URL: http://www.lionwap.org/CentervilleMN
Contact: Greg Kieselhorst, Sec.
Local. Affiliated With: Lions Clubs International.

Ceylon

10640 ■ American Legion, Nassen-Detert Post 529
PO Box 352
Ceylon, MN 56121
Ph: (651)291-1800
Fax: (651)291-1057
URL: National Affiliate–www.legion.org
Local. Affiliated With: American Legion.

Champlin

10641 ■ American Legion, Champlin Post 600
12450 Bus. Park Blvd. N
Champlin, MN 55316
Ph: (612)427-6870
Fax: (651)291-1057
URL: National Affiliate–www.legion.org
Local. Affiliated With: American Legion.

10642 ■ Champlin Lions Club
c/o Chuck Fortman, Pres.
13056 Saratoga Ln.
Champlin, MN 55316
Ph: (763)427-1277 (612)598-6712
URL: http://www.5m5.org
Contact: Chuck Fortman, Pres.
Local. Affiliated With: Lions Clubs International.

10643 ■ Metro Marines
c/o James Herzog
PO Box 402
Champlin, MN 55316-0402
Ph: (763)420-9516 (763)561-4648
Fax: (763)420-9516
E-mail: mndskinc2@attbi.com
Contact: James Herzog, Contact
Founded: 1993. **Members:** 175. **Membership Dues:** $17 (annual). **Budget:** $25,000. **Local Groups:** 3. **Local.** U.S. Marines, active duty, retired, reserve, honorably discharged and released from active duty, including U.S. Navy Corpsmen who served with Fleet Marine Force (FMF); activities include assisting with High School Enlistment Poolee Program; retired veteran contacts; works with Marine Reserve on Toys for Tots Program. **Publications:** *Beachhead*, monthly, September through May. Newsletter. **Circulation:** 20. **Advertising:** accepted. Alternate Formats: online.

10644 ■ Skills USA, Champlin Park High School
6025 109th Ave. N
Champlin, MN 55316
Ph: (763)506-6837
Fax: (763)506-6803
E-mail: nelsonjj@anoka.k12.mn.us
URL: http://www.mnskillsusa.org
Contact: Joe Nelson, Contact
Local. Serves high school and college students enrolled in technical, skilled, and service and health occupations. Provides quality education experiences for students in leadership, teamwork, citizenship and character development. Builds and reinforces self-confidence, work attitudes and communication skills. Emphasizes total quality at work, high ethical standards, superior work skills, and life-long education. Promotes understanding of the free enterprise system and involvement in community service. **Affiliated With:** Skills USA - VICA.

Chanhassen

10645 ■ American Legion, Chanhassen Post 580
290 Lake Dr. E
Chanhassen, MN 55317
Ph: (651)291-1800
Fax: (651)291-1057
URL: National Affiliate–www.legion.org
Local. Affiliated With: American Legion.

10646 ■ Chanhassen Lions Club
PO Box 484
Chanhassen, MN 55317
Ph: (952)361-5447
E-mail: tdrewiske@k-a-c.com
URL: http://www.chanhassenlions.org
Contact: Thomas Drewiske, Pres.
Local. Affiliated With: Lions Clubs International.

10647 ■ Minnesota American Legion Baseball
c/o Darwin Berg, Dir.
7159 Derby Dr.
Chanhassen, MN 55317
Ph: (952)975-9742
E-mail: darwbe@aol.com
URL: http://www.mnlegion.org/baseball
Contact: Darwin Berg, Dir.
State.

10648 ■ Minnesota HOSA
8553 Chanhassen Hills Dr. S
Chanhassen, MN 55317
Ph: (952)995-1510
E-mail: josaysgodisgood@yahoo.com
URL: http://www.uscusers.com/mnhosa/index.htm
Contact: Sara Jo Larson, Pres.
State. Represents secondary and postsecondary students enrolled in health occupations education programs. Works to improve the quality of healthcare for all Americans by urging members to develop self-improvement skills. Encourages members to develop understanding of current healthcare issues, environmental concerns, and survival needs. Conducts programs to help individuals improve their occupational skills and leadership qualities. **Affiliated With:** Health Occupations Students of America.

Chaska

10649 ■ American Legion, Minnesota Post 57
c/o Leo Carey
102 W 4th St.
Chaska, MN 55318
Ph: (651)291-1800
Fax: (651)291-1057
URL: National Affiliate–www.legion.org
Contact: Leo Carey, Contact
Local. Affiliated With: American Legion.

10650 ■ Audio Engineering Society, Upper Midwest Section
c/o John Nygren
888 Bavaria Hills Terr.
Chaska, MN 55318
Ph: (763)591-2154
URL: National Affiliate–www.aes.org
Contact: John Nygren, Contact
Regional. Represents the interests of engineers, administrators and technicians for radio, television and motion picture operation. Operates educational and research foundation. **Affiliated With:** Audio Engineering Society.

10651 ■ Chaska Area Jaycees
PO Box 285
Chaska, MN 55318
Ph: (612)418-7621
E-mail: chaskajaycees@aol.com
URL: http://www.chaskajaycees.com
Contact: Bryan Heise, Contact
Founded: 1972. **Local.**

10652 ■ Chaska Lions Club
PO Box 93
Chaska, MN 55318
Ph: (763)755-3439
E-mail: billb763@msn.com
URL: http://www.chaskalions.com
Contact: Bill Bultinck, Pres.
Local. Affiliated With: Lions Clubs International.

10653 ■ North Country Region USA Volleyball
c/o Sarah Storms
325 Engler Blvd., No. 109
Chaska, MN 55318
Ph: (952)831-9150
Fax: (952)942-5584
Free: (800)657-6967
E-mail: judy@ncrusav.org
URL: http://www.ncrusav.org
Contact: Judy Praska, Exec.Dir.
Regional. Adults and juniors who are interested in the sport of volleyball. Acts as official representative of USA volleyball for the region. Fosters and conducts regional and national amateur volleyball competition. Teaches the sport of volleyball to adults and youth through clinics conducted by qualified instructors. Provides lectures, seminars, and clinics through which trainees may be schooled in competitive coaching, playing, and officiating. Selects and trains candidates in the sport of volleyball in national and international competition, thereby improving the caliber of candidates representing the U.S. in Olympic and international competitions. **Affiliated With:** United States Volleyball Association/United States Volleyball Association.

10654 ■ Skills USA, Carver-Scott Educational Cooperative
401 E 4th St.
Chaska, MN 55318
Ph: (952)368-8800
Fax: (952)368-8858
E-mail: cwalters@cseced.org
URL: http://www.mnskillsusa.org
Contact: Cindy Walters, Contact
Local. Serves high school and college students enrolled in technical, skilled, and service and health occupations. Provides quality education experiences for students in leadership, teamwork, citizenship and character development. Builds and reinforces self-confidence, work attitudes and communication skills. Emphasizes total quality at work, high ethical standards, superior work skills, and life-long education. Promotes understanding of the free enterprise system and involvement in community service. **Affiliated With:** Skills USA - VICA.

Chatfield

10655 ■ American Legion, Bailey-Kinnear Post 197
PO Box 414
Chatfield, MN 55923
Ph: (651)291-1800
Fax: (651)291-1057
URL: National Affiliate–www.legion.org
Local. Affiliated With: American Legion.

10656 ■ Chatfield Lions Club
c/o John Martinka, Pres.
14 Fillmore St. NE
Chatfield, MN 55923
Ph: (507)867-3530
E-mail: copperheads@earthlink.net
URL: http://www.lions5m1.org/chatfield
Contact: John Martinka, Pres.
Local. Affiliated With: Lions Clubs International.

10657 ■ Minnesota Ambulance Association, Southeast
c/o Sue Kester, Dir.
Chatfield Ambulance
21 2nd St. SE
Chatfield, MN 55923
Ph: (507)867-1512
Fax: (507)867-9093
E-mail: skester@ci.chatfield.mn.us
URL: http://www.mnems.org
Contact: Sue Kester, Dir.
Local. Seeks to maintain the financial viability of the EMS industry by advocating education, legislation and regulatory change. **Affiliated With:** Minnesota Ambulance Association.

Chisago City

10658 ■ American Legion, Chisago City Post 272
PO Box 209
Chisago City, MN 55013
Ph: (651)291-1800
Fax: (651)291-1057
URL: National Affiliate–www.legion.org
Local. Affiliated With: American Legion.

Chisholm

10659 ■ American Legion, Press-Lloyd Post 247
319 W Lake St.
Chisholm, MN 55719
Ph: (651)291-1800
Fax: (651)291-1057
URL: National Affiliate–www.legion.org
Local. Affiliated With: American Legion.

10660 ■ Chisholm Area Chamber of Commerce (CACC)
10 NW 2nd Ave.
Chisholm, MN 55719
Ph: (218)254-7930
Fax: (218)254-7932
Free: (800)422-0806
E-mail: chisholm@cpinternet.com
URL: http://www.chisholmchamber.com
Contact: Shannon Kishel Roche, Exec.Dir.
Founded: 1933. **Members:** 130. **Local.** Promotes business and community development in the Chisholm, MN area. Sponsors Christmas lighting competition, annual Polar Bear Days, annual Firedays, and All Class Grand Reunion. **Computer Services:** Online services, business directory. **Publications:** Newsletter, quarterly.

10661 ■ United Way of Northeastern Minnesota
229 W Lake St.
Chisholm, MN 55719
Ph: (218)254-3329
E-mail: info@unitedwaynemn.org
URL: http://www.unitedwaynemn.org
Contact: Shelley Renner, Exec.Dir.
Local. Affiliated With: United Way of America.

Circle Pines

10662 ■ American Camp Association Northland
4132 88th Ln. NE
Circle Pines, MN 55014
Ph: (612)784-5400
Fax: (612)784-5400
Free: (800)842-0308
E-mail: acanorthland@qwest.net
URL: http://www.acanorthland.org
Contact: Karon Albright, Exec.Sec.
Founded: 1909. **Members:** 188. **Membership Dues:** associate, $50-$100 (annual) • professional, $150-$400 (annual). **Staff:** 1. **Budget:** $45,000. **For-Profit. Regional.** Camp professionals dedicated to enriching the lives of children and adults through the camp experience. Conducts camp standards. **Affiliated With:** Boy Scouts of America; Girl Scouts of the U.S.A.; YMCA of the United States of America; Young Women's Christian Association of the United States of America YWCA of the U.S.A. **Publications:** *Camping Magazine*, bimonthly. **Advertising:** accepted. **Conventions/Meetings:** monthly meeting, with educational topics - from October to May.

10663 ■ Circle Pines - Lexington Lions Club
PO Box 13
Circle Pines, MN 55014
Ph: (763)786-3474
E-mail: jrsorte@comcast.net
URL: http://circlelexmn.lionwap.org
Contact: Ginny Hestekind, Pres.
Local. Affiliated With: Lions Clubs International.

10664 ■ German Shepherd Dog Club of Minneapolis and St. Paul
c/o Mada Parnell, Corresponding Sec.
106 Twinkle Ter.
Circle Pines, MN 55014
E-mail: wildfanz@comcast.net
URL: http://www.gsdcmsp.org
Contact: Lindsay Wallace III, Pres.
Local.

10665 ■ North Central Mountain Bike Patrol (NCMBP)
PO Box 212
Circle Pines, MN 55014
Ph: (612)770-6162
E-mail: mtnbikemedic1@juno.com
URL: http://www.ncmbp.org
Contact: Hans Erdman, Reg. Patrol Coor.
Local. Provides medical standby at races and community events; patrols trails in a number of local and state parks and the three National Forests in the service area. **Affiliated With:** International Mountain Bicycling Association.

10666 ■ Parents of Murdered Children Minnesota Hope Chapter
PO Box 516
Circle Pines, MN 55014
Ph: (651)484-0336
E-mail: pomcmn@isd.net
URL: http://www.pomc.com/minnesota
Contact: Jim Lym, Co-Leader
Local. Affiliated With: Parents of Murdered Children.

10667 ■ Portuguese Water Dog Club of the Twin Cities (PWDCTC)
c/o Stacey Runkle
8706 Xebec St. NE
Circle Pines, MN 55014-4081
E-mail: srunkle@dragonpwd.com
URL: http://www.pwdctc.org
Contact: Signe Pagel, Pres.
Local.

Clara City

10668 ■ American Legion, Clara City Post 485
PO Box 238
Clara City, MN 56222
Ph: (651)291-1800
Fax: (651)291-1057
URL: National Affiliate–www.legion.org
Local. Affiliated With: American Legion.

10669 ■ Clara City Lions Club
c/o Annette Rosen, Pres.
PO Box 508
Clara City, MN 56222
Ph: (320)847-3219 (320)847-3355
URL: http://www.5m4lions.org
Contact: Annette Rosen, Pres.
Local. Affiliated With: Lions Clubs International.

10670 ■ Friesen Historical Society
c/o Marvin Bohlsen
PO Box 611
4075 140th Ave. SE
Clara City, MN 56222-0611
Local.

Claremont

10671 ■ American Legion, Albert Dennis Connell Post 422
220 W Front St.
Claremont, MN 55924
Ph: (651)291-1800
Fax: (651)291-1057
URL: National Affiliate–www.legion.org
Local. Affiliated With: American Legion.

Clarissa

10672 ■ American Legion, Clarissa Post 213
PO Box 306
Clarissa, MN 56440
Ph: (651)291-1800
Fax: (651)291-1057
URL: National Affiliate–www.legion.org
Local. Affiliated With: American Legion.

Clarkfield

10673 ■ Sons of Norway, Elvidal Lodge 1-509
c/o Larry D. Stensrud, Pres.
3972 230th Ave.
Clarkfield, MN 56223-3031
Ph: (320)669-7134
E-mail: stensrud@maxminn.com
URL: National Affiliate–www.sofn.com
Contact: Larry D. Stensrud, Pres.
Local. Affiliated With: Sons of Norway.

Clear Lake

10674 ■ American Legion, Eiffert-Kirchenbauer Post 354
PO Box 233
Clear Lake, MN 55319
Ph: (651)291-1800
Fax: (651)291-1057
URL: National Affiliate–www.legion.org
Local. Affiliated With: American Legion.

10675 ■ Siberian Husky Club of the Twin Cities
c/o Brenda Hinkemeyer
9841 - 58th Ave.
Clear Lake, MN 55319
Ph: (320)743-3631
E-mail: brenda@nikosha.net
URL: http://www.shctc.org
Founded: 1972. **Local.**

Clearbrook

10676 ■ American Legion, Minnesota Post 256
c/o Melvin Johnson
PO Box 32
Clearbrook, MN 56634
Ph: (651)291-1800
Fax: (651)291-1057
URL: National Affiliate–www.legion.org
Contact: Melvin Johnson, Contact
Local. Affiliated With: American Legion.

Clearwater

10677 ■ American Legion, Beatty-Humphries Post 323
PO Box 102
Clearwater, MN 55320
Ph: (651)291-1800
Fax: (651)291-1057
URL: National Affiliate–www.legion.org
Local. Affiliated With: American Legion.

10678 ■ Minnesota Society of Enrolled Agents
935 Clearwater Ctr.
PO Box 104
Clearwater, MN 55320-0104
Ph: (320)558-6800
Fax: (320)558-6019
E-mail: rkohls@usinternet.com
URL: http://mnsea.org
Contact: Ronald Kohls, Treas.
State.

Clements

10679 ■ American Legion, Minnesota Post 519
c/o Robert Seikora
PO Box 44
Clements, MN 56224
Ph: (651)291-1800
Fax: (651)291-1057
URL: National Affiliate–www.legion.org
Contact: Robert Seikora, Contact
Local. Affiliated With: American Legion.

Cleveland

10680 ■ American Legion, Ray Keenan Post 207
PO Box 354
Cleveland, MN 56017
Ph: (651)291-1800
Fax: (651)291-1057
URL: National Affiliate–www.legion.org
Local. Affiliated With: American Legion.

Climax

10681 ■ American Mothers - Minnesota Chapter
c/o Janet Gerla, Pres.
37049 State Hwy. 220 SW
Climax, MN 56523
Ph: (218)857-3305
E-mail: janeteg@rrv.net
URL: National Affiliate–www.americanmothers.org
Contact: Janet Gerla, Pres.
State. Affiliated With: American Mothers, Inc.

Clinton

10682 ■ American Legion, Campbell-Williams Post 258
PO Box 261
Clinton, MN 56225
Ph: (651)291-1800
Fax: (651)291-1057
URL: National Affiliate–www.legion.org
Local. Affiliated With: American Legion.

Clitherall

10683 ■ Christian Camp and Conference Association, North Central Region
c/o Greg Anderson, Representative
13207 Inspiration Trail
Clitherall, MN 56524-9556
Ph: (218)864-5379
URL: National Affiliate–www.ccca-us.org
Contact: Greg Anderson, Representative
Regional. Affiliated With: Christian Camping International/U.S.A.

10684 ■ Minnesota Nurses Association - District 7
18905 Quartz Rd.
Clitherall, MN 56524
Ph: (218)864-8179
E-mail: ruthp@prtel.com
URL: http://www.mnnurses.org
Contact: Ruth Pallansch, Pres.
Local. Works to advance the nursing profession. Seeks to meet the needs of nurses and health care consumers. Fosters high standards of nursing practice. Promotes the economic and general welfare of nurses in the workplace. **Affiliated With:** American Nurses Association; Minnesota Nurses Association.

Cloquet

10685 ■ Aitkin-Carlton County RSVP
c/o Jill Hatfield, Dir.
1003 Cloquet Ave., Ste.102
Cloquet, MN 55720-1694
Ph: (218)879-9238
Fax: (218)879-1196
E-mail: jhatfield@monetbroadband.net
URL: http://www.seniorcorps.gov/about/programs/rsvp_state.asp?usestateabbr=mn&Search4.x=26&Search4.y=7
Contact: Jill Hatfield, Dir.
Local. Affiliated With: Retired and Senior Volunteer Program.

10686 ■ American Fisheries Society, Minnesota Chapter President
c/o Brian Borkholder
Fond du Lac Reservation
1720 Big Lake Rd.
Cloquet, MN 55720
Ph: (218)878-8004
E-mail: brianborkholder@fdlrez.com
URL: http://www.mnafs.org
State. Affiliated With: American Fisheries Society.

10687 ■ American Legion, Minnesota Post 262
c/o Carl Anderson
1216 Cloquet Ave.
Cloquet, MN 55720
Ph: (651)291-1800
Fax: (651)291-1057
URL: National Affiliate–www.legion.org
Contact: Carl Anderson, Contact
Local. Affiliated With: American Legion.

10688 ■ Carlton County Gem and Mineral Club
c/o Ben Anderson, Pres.
46 2nd St.
Cloquet, MN 55720
E-mail: 9c.risdon@juno.com
URL: National Affiliate–www.amfed.org
Contact: Mary Johnson, Sec.
Local. Aims to further the study of Earth Sciences and the practice of lapidary arts and mineralogy. **Affiliated With:** American Federation of Mineralogical Societies.

10689 ■ Carlton County Historical Society (CCHS)
406 Cloquet Ave.
Cloquet, MN 55720
Ph: (218)879-1938
Fax: (218)879-1938
E-mail: director@carltoncountyhs.org
URL: http://www.carltoncountyhs.org
Contact: Ellen Bassett, Sec.
Founded: 1949. **Members:** 800. **Membership Dues:** individual, $15 (annual) • family, $25 (annual) • patron, $100 (annual) • friend, $50 (annual) • sponsor, $75 (annual). **Staff:** 4. **Local.** Individuals interested in preserving the history of Carlton County, MN. **Libraries: Type:** open to the public. **Holdings:** 400; articles, audio recordings, books. **Subjects:** local history, lumber and paper industries, Native Americans. **Publications:** *A Hometown Album: Cloquet's Centennial Story*. Book. **Price:** $20.00 • *Brief History of the Pioneers of the Cromwell, Minnesota Area*. Book. **Price:** $15.00 • *Carlton County Historical Society News*, quarterly. Newsletter. Contains current society events. **Price:** included in membership dues. **Circulation:** 650 • *Crossroads in Time: A History of Carlton County*. Book. **Price:** $16.00 • *Fire Storm: The Great Fires of 1918*. Book. **Price:** $18.00 • *Fury of the Flames: A Pictorial History of the Great Forest Fires of Northern Minnesota, October 12-15, 1918*. Book. **Price:** $4.98 • *History of the Thomson Farming Area*. Book. **Price:** $15.00 • *Reflections of Our Past: A Pictorial History of Carlton County*. Book. **Price:** $24.95. **Conventions/Meetings:** quarterly meeting, with educational programs (exhibits) - always first Monday of March, June, September, and December.

10690 ■ Cloquet Carlton Area Chamber of Commerce
225 Sunnyside Dr.
Cloquet, MN 55720-1149
Ph: (218)879-1551
Fax: (218)878-0223
Free: (800)554-4350
E-mail: chamber@cloquet.com
URL: http://www.cloquet.com
Contact: Della D. Schmidt, Pres.
Founded: 1952. **Members:** 275. **Staff:** 2. **Budget:** $250,000. **Local.** Promotes business and community development in the Cloquet, MN area. Provides business consulting and business plan preparation. **Libraries: Type:** not open to the public. **Holdings:** audio recordings, books, video recordings. **Subjects:** business. **Awards:** Business of the Year. **Frequency:** annual. **Type:** recognition • Volunteer of the Year. **Frequency:** annual. **Type:** recognition. **Computer Services:** Online services, business directory. **Committees:** Business Enhancement Team; Forestry Affairs; Legislative Affairs; Tourism. **Subgroups:** Ambassador Club. **Publications:** *Chamber Review*, monthly. Newsletter. **Price:** free with membership. **Circulation:** 25. Alternate Formats: diskette • *Membership Directory and Buyers Guide*, annual • *Who's Who in Carlton County*. **Conventions/Meetings:** annual dinner, with auction and dance (exhibits) - always third Saturday in April.

10691 ■ Muskies Lake Superior
2031 Hwy. 33 S
Cloquet, MN 55720
Ph: (218)879-2712
E-mail: muskie2031@mchsi.com
URL: National Affiliate–www.muskiesinc.org
Contact: Terry De Menge, Pres.
Local.

10692 ■ Phi Theta Kappa, Alpha Phi Upsilon Chapter - Hennepin Technical College
c/o Marla Ahlgren
2101 14th St.
Cloquet, MN 55720
Ph: (218)879-0800
E-mail: mahlgren@fdltcc.edu
URL: http://www.ptk.org/directories/chapters/MN/20531-1.htm
Contact: Marla Ahlgren, Advisor
Local.

10693 ■ United Way of Carlton County
PO Box 250
202 Avenue C
Cloquet, MN 55720-0250
Ph: (218)879-8404
URL: National Affiliate–national.unitedway.org
Contact: Carol Longseth, Exec.Dir.
Staff: 2. **Local. Affiliated With:** United Way of America. **Formerly:** United Way of North East Carlton County.

10694 ■ Western Lake Superior Flying and Hiking Society
1005 Wilson Ave.
Cloquet, MN 55720
Ph: (218)879-2629
URL: National Affiliate–www.antiquemodeler.org
Local. Affiliated With: Society of Antique Modelers.

Cokato

10695 ■ American Legion, Cokato Post 209
PO Box 43
Cokato, MN 55321
Ph: (651)291-1800
Fax: (651)291-1057
URL: National Affiliate–www.legion.org
Local. Affiliated With: American Legion.

10696 ■ Cokato Chamber of Commerce (CCC)
255 Broadway Ave.
PO Box 819
Cokato, MN 55321
Ph: (320)286-5505
Fax: (320)286-5876
E-mail: depclerk@cokato.mn.us
URL: http://www.cokato.mn.us
Contact: Louann Worden, Sec.
Local. Promotes business and community development in Cokato, MN.

10697 ■ Cokato Lions Club
PO Box 691
Cokato, MN 55321
Ph: (320)286-6244
E-mail: abe.abrahamson@co.wright.mn.us
URL: http://www.lionwap.org/cokatomn
Contact: Abe Abrahamson, Sec.
Local. Affiliated With: Lions Clubs International.

Cold Spring

10698 ■ American Legion, Frank Kray Post 455
209 Main St.
Cold Spring, MN 56320
Ph: (651)291-1800
Fax: (651)291-1057
URL: National Affiliate–www.legion.org
Local. Affiliated With: American Legion.

10699 ■ Cold Spring Area Chamber of Commerce (CSACC)
312 1st St. N
PO Box 328
Cold Spring, MN 56320-0328
Ph: (320)685-4186
Fax: (320)685-4186
E-mail: scacc@netlinkcom.com
Contact: David Olson, Exec.Dir.
Founded: 1963. **Members:** 100. **Staff:** 2. **Local.** Promotes business and community development in the Cold Spring, MN area. **Publications:** *Chamber News*, monthly. Newsletter.

10700 ■ Cold Spring Home Pride Lions Club
15433 241st St.
Cold Spring, MN 56320
Ph: (320)685-7748
E-mail: dibellmont@yahoo.com
URL: http://www.lionwap.org/coldspringhomepridelionsmn
Contact: Diann Bellmont, Sec.
Local. Affiliated With: Lions Clubs International.

Coleraine

10701 ■ Muskies St. Cloud Chapter
PO Box 516
Coleraine, MN 55722
E-mail: jmustar@auslink.net
URL: National Affiliate–www.muskiesinc.org
Contact: Joe Mustar, Pres.
Local.

Collegeville

10702 ■ College of St. Benedict and St. John's University Students In Free Enterprise
PO Box 2000
Collegeville, MN 56321
E-mail: sife@csbsju.edu
URL: http://www.csbsju.edu/sife
Contact: Michael Kubovec, Pres.
Local.

10703 ■ Psi Chi, National Honor Society in Psychology - Saint John's University
c/o Dept. of Psychology
Gen. Delivery
Collegeville, MN 56321-9999
Ph: (320)363-3131
URL: http://www.psichi.org/chapters/info.asp?chapter_id=335
Local.

Comfrey

10704 ■ Minnesota State Cattlemen's Association
26296 620th Ave.
Comfrey, MN 56019
Ph: (507)877-5003
Fax: (507)877-5003
Contact: Ron Lindeen, Service Coor.
Membership Dues: dues, $30 (annual). **State. Formerly:** Minnesota Cattlemen's Association. **Publications:** *Minnesota Cattleman Newsletter*, monthly. **Advertising:** accepted. **Conventions/Meetings:** annual Leadership Conference - convention (exhibits) - always 1st Friday and Saturday in December; Avg. Attendance: 300.

Cook

10705 ■ Cook Area Chamber of Commerce
PO Box 296
Cook, MN 55723
Ph: (218)666-5850
Fax: (218)666-0022
Free: (800)648-5897
E-mail: info@cookminnesota.com
URL: http://www.cookminnesota.com
Contact: Lee Phillips, Pres.
Membership Dues: business, $100 (annual). **Local.** Works to increase awareness of the area, support events, tourism promotion, support economic and community development and business affairs that will benefit the entire community. **Computer Services:** Information services, membership directory.

10706 ■ Cook Lions Club
c/o Mark Eyre, Sec.
2672 W Vermilion Shores Rd.
Cook, MN 55723
Ph: (218)666-5542
E-mail: mp@cpinternet.com
URL: http://lions5m10.org
Contact: Mark Eyre, Sec.
Local. Affiliated With: Lions Clubs International.

Coon Rapids

10707 ■ American Legion, Coon Rapids Post No. 334 Social Club
11640 Crooked Lake Blvd. NW
Coon Rapids, MN 55433
Ph: (763)421-6260
URL: National Affiliate–www.legion.org
Contact: Al Michels, Commander
Members: 1,200. **Membership Dues:** veteran, $22 (annual). **Local. Affiliated With:** American Legion. **Publications:** *Coon Tales*, monthly. Newsletter. **Price:** $15.00. **Circulation:** 1,600. **Advertising:** accepted. **Conventions/Meetings:** monthly Post Meeting - third Thursday.

10708 ■ Coon Rapids Cardinal Lions Club
PO Box 48954
Coon Rapids, MN 55448
Ph: (763)856-4925
E-mail: mikeanddenise@peoplepc.com
URL: http://www.crclions.org
Contact: Mike Stack, Pres.
Local. Affiliated With: Lions Clubs International.

10709 ■ Coon Rapids Lions Club
PO Box 48176
Coon Rapids, MN 55448-0176
E-mail: lionjohnl@coonrapidslions.org
URL: http://www.coonrapidslions.org
Contact: John Leggate, Pres.
Local. Affiliated With: Lions Clubs International.

10710 ■ Minnesota Brittany Club
c/o Diane Hedstrome, Sec.
10415 Osage St. NW
Coon Rapids, MN 55433
Ph: (763)755-1784
E-mail: minnesotabrittanyclub@earthlink.net
URL: http://home.earthlink.net/~minnesotabrittanyclub
Contact: Harold Revoir, Pres.
State.

10711 ■ Minnesota Brittany Club
10415 Osage St. NW
Coon Rapids, MN 55433
Ph: (763)755-1784
E-mail: minnesotabrittanyclub@earthlink.net
URL: http://home.earthlink.net/~minnesotabrittanyclub
Contact: Diane Hedstrom, Sec.-Treas.
Founded: 1960. **State. Affiliated With:** American Brittany Club.

10712 ■ Minnesota Council of Teachers of English (MCTE)
PO Box 480122
Coon Rapids, MN 55448
E-mail: jzb@burtness.com
URL: http://www.mcte.org
Contact: JeanMarie Burtness, Exec.Sec.
Founded: 1960. **Members:** 450. **Membership Dues:** individual, regular, $30 (annual). **State.** Teachers of English and language arts. Works to improve the teaching of English; encourages research; represents members' interests. Provides information about activities and events of value to teachers of English/language arts. Sponsors workshops and conferences. **Affiliated With:** National Council of Teachers of English. **Publications:** *MCTE News*, periodic. Newsletter. Alternate Formats: online • *Minnesota English Journal*, annual, fall. Alternate Formats: online • *Minnesota English Journal - Student Writing Issue*, annual, summer. Alternate Formats: online. **Conventions/Meetings:** semiannual conference - always spring and fall • annual conference - spring • annual workshop - fall.

10713 ■ Minnesota Section PGA of America (MNPGA)
c/o Jon Tollette, Exec.Dir.
Bunker Hills Golf Club
12800 Bunker Prairie Rd.
Coon Rapids, MN 55448
Ph: (763)754-0820 (763)754-6641
Fax: (763)754-6682
E-mail: info@minnesotapga.com
URL: http://www.minnesotapga.com
Contact: Jon Tollette, Exec.Dir.
State. Formerly: (2005) Professional Golfers Association of America - Minnesota Section.

10714 ■ North Metro Realtors Association
11450 Robinson Dr. NW
Coon Rapids, MN 55433-7402
Ph: (763)757-7230
Fax: (763)757-7296
E-mail: tracey@northmetro.com
URL: National Affiliate–www.realtor.org
Contact: Tracey Mae Jean Douglas, Exec. Officer
Local. Strives to develop real estate business practices. Advocates the right to own, use and transfer real property. Provides a facility for professional development, research and exchange of information among members. **Affiliated With:** National Association of Realtors.

10715 ■ Park River Estates Resident Council Foundation
c/o Vicki Petersen, Pres./Activity Dir.
9899 Avocet St. NW
Coon Rapids, MN 55433-6413
Ph: (763)757-2320
Fax: (763)757-6946
E-mail: vpetersen@parkriverestates.com
Contact: Vicki Petersen, Pres./Activity Dir.
Local. Enhances the lives of the residents of Park River Estates Care Center by purchasing items or sponsoring events for that purpose. Consists of Board of Directors who meet quarterly throughout the year.

10716 ■ Phi Theta Kappa, Alpha Delta Alpha Chapter - Anoka-Ramsey Community College
c/o Gordy Wax
11200 Mississippi Blvd. NW
Coon Rapids, MN 55433
Ph: (763)422-3514
E-mail: gordy.wax@anokaramsey.edu
URL: http://www.ar.cc.mn.us/ptk
Contact: Gordy Wax, Contact
Local.

10717 ■ Skills USA, Coon Rapids High School
2340 Ndale Blvd.
Coon Rapids, MN 55433
Ph: (763)506-7133
Fax: (763)506-7103
E-mail: voigt@anoka.k12.mn.us
URL: http://www.mnskillsusa.org
Contact: Bill Voigt, Contact
Local. Serves high school and college students enrolled in technical, skilled, and service and health occupations. Provides quality education experiences for students in leadership, teamwork, citizenship and character development. Builds and reinforces self-confidence, work attitudes and communication skills. Emphasizes total quality at work, high ethical standards, superior work skills, and life-long education. Promotes understanding of the free enterprise system and involvement in community service. **Affiliated With:** Skills USA - VICA.

10718 ■ Society of Minnesota Inventors
13055 Riverdale Dr., Ste.500-236
Coon Rapids, MN 55448
Ph: (763)753-2766
E-mail: pgpent@yahoo.com
URL: National Affiliate–www.uiausa.org
Contact: Paul Paris, Contact
State. Represents inventors' organizations and providers of services to inventors. Seeks to facilitate the development of innovation conceived by independent inventors. Provides leadership and support services to inventors and inventors' organizations. **Affiliated With:** United Inventors Association of the U.S.A.

10719 ■ Sons of Norway, Vennekretsen Lodge 1-559
c/o Rodney H. Halvorson, Pres.
9939 Redwood St. NW
Coon Rapids, MN 55433-8219
Ph: (763)767-4807
E-mail: rhh@midwestlsce.com
URL: National Affiliate–www.sofn.com
Contact: Rodney H. Halvorson, Pres.
Local. Affiliated With: Sons of Norway.

Corcoran

10720 ■ Corcoran Lions Club
c/o Tim Holmquist, Pres.
21030 County Rd. 50
Corcoran, MN 55340
Ph: (763)494-3962 (763)420-8733
URL: http://www.5m5.org
Contact: Tim Holmquist, Pres.
Local. Affiliated With: Lions Clubs International.

10721 ■ Northwest Suburban Chamber of Commerce
c/o Barbara Lantsberger, Exec.Dir.
8200 County Rd. 116, Ste.100
Corcoran, MN 55340-9303
Ph: (763)420-3242
Fax: (763)420-5964
E-mail: info@nwschamber.com
URL: http://www.nwschamber.com
Contact: Barbara Lantsberger, Exec.Dir.
Founded: 1957. **Membership Dues:** individual (retirees, individuals not affiliated with a business or organization), $75 (annual) • business (based on number of employees), $190-$860 (annual) • associate/non-profit organization (based on number of employees), $190-$250 (annual). **Local**. Represents civic and business people. Works to promote business, economic and civic environment of Northwest communities. **Committees:** Administration; Ambassador; Communication/Promotions; Community Relations; Programs and Special Events. **Publications:** *News*, monthly. Newsletter. **Advertising:** accepted.

Cosmos

10722 ■ American Legion, Beack-Thompson Post 126
PO Box 296
Cosmos, MN 56228
Ph: (651)291-1800
Fax: (651)291-1057
URL: National Affiliate–www.legion.org
Local. Affiliated With: American Legion.

Cottage Grove

10723 ■ Anoka County Gem and Mineral Club
c/o Martha Miss, Pres.
8445 Grange Blvd.
Cottage Grove, MN 55016
E-mail: jnewcomb@tias2.net
URL: National Affiliate–www.amfed.org
Contact: Lynn Rood, Sec.
Local. Aims to further the study of Earth Sciences and the practice of lapidary arts and mineralogy. **Affiliated With:** American Federation of Mineralogical Societies.

10724 ■ Bhakta Cricket Club
7125 S 80th St.
Cottage Grove, MN 55016
URL: http://www.usaca.org/Clubs.htm
Contact: Kirit Bhakta, Contact
Local.

10725 ■ Buick Club of America - Gopher State Chapter
c/o Mike Long
8438 Foothill Rd. S
Cottage Grove, MN 55016
Ph: (651)459-8765
E-mail: membership@gopherstatebuick.org
URL: http://www.gopherstatebuick.org
Contact: Mike Long, Contact
State. Represents individuals who are interested in Buick automobiles. Promotes the development, publication and interchange of technical, historical, and other information among members. Encourages the maintenance, restoration, and preservation of Buick automobiles. **Affiliated With:** Buick Club of America.

10726 ■ Cottage Grove Area Chamber of Commerce
PO Box 16
Cottage Grove, MN 55016-0016
Ph: (651)458-8334
Fax: (651)458-8383
E-mail: cgchambr@rconnect.com
URL: http://www.cottagegrovechamber.org
Contact: Mary Slusser, Pres.
Founded: 1968. **Local**. Businesses in Cottage Grove, Newport, and St. Paul Park, in South Washington County, Minnesota. Strives to promote economic development and business growth within the Chamber area; develop a strong business-education partnership and identify legislative issues affecting private enterprise.

10727 ■ Heart of America Scottish Terrier Club (HASTC)
c/o Susan Jacobsen
7088 Irish Ave.
Cottage Grove, MN 55016
E-mail: scottyjake@aol.com
URL: http://www.hastc.net
Contact: Earle Teegarden, Pres.
Local.

10728 ■ Minnesota Hunting Spaniel Association (MHSA)
c/o Leanne Schmitz, Corresponding Sec.
9674 Hale Ave. S
Cottage Grove, MN 55016-3893
E-mail: lschmitz@comcast.net
URL: http://www.mnhuntingspaniel.org
Contact: Leanne Schmitz, Corresponding Sec.
Founded: 1995. **Members:** 150. **Membership Dues:** family, $35 (annual). **Local**. Dog owners working to provide information and education for members and the public on care, breeding, training and ability testing for purebred flushing spaniels. Conducts training programs, hunting tests, working trials and related events to promote breeds' abilities. **Awards:** Glenhurst Versatility Award. **Frequency:** annual. **Type:** recognition. **Recipient:** to an individual who received titles in three AKC venues • MHSA Recognition Certificates. **Frequency:** annual. **Type:** recognition. **Recipient:** to qualifying scores, titles and placements received for the year • Whistlestop Puppy Achievement Award. **Frequency:** annual. **Type:** recognition. **Recipient:** to a club member with the most field trial puppy points for the year.

10729 ■ Minnesota National Guard Enlisted Association
c/o Paul Cocchiarella, SGT
PO Box 253
Cottage Grove, MN 55016
Ph: (651)768-8914
E-mail: pjcooch@comcast.net
URL: http://www.mngea.org
Contact: Paul Cocchiarella, Exec.Sec.
State. Affiliated With: Enlisted Association of National Guard of the United States.

Cottonwood

10730 ■ American Legion, Cottonwood Post 503
PO Box 424
Cottonwood, MN 56229
Ph: (651)291-1800
Fax: (651)291-1057
URL: National Affiliate–www.legion.org
Local. Affiliated With: American Legion.

10731 ■ Minnesota Ambulance Association, Southwest
c/o Dane Meyer, Dir.
PO Box 137
Cottonwood, MN 56229
Ph: (507)829-5054
Fax: (507)637-5717
E-mail: meyerdane@hotmail.com
URL: http://www.mnems.org
Contact: Dane Meyer, Dir.
Local. Seeks to maintain the financial viability of the EMS industry by advocating education, legislation and regulatory change. **Affiliated With:** Minnesota Ambulance Association.

Crookston

10732 ■ American Legion, Minnesota Post 20
c/o Nels T. Wold
102 S Ash St.
Crookston, MN 56716
Ph: (651)291-1800
Fax: (651)291-1057
URL: National Affiliate–www.legion.org
Contact: Nels T. Wold, Contact
Local. Affiliated With: American Legion.

10733 ■ Crookston Convention and Visitors Bureau
118 Fletcher St.
Crookston, MN 56716

Ph: (218)281-4320
Fax: (218)281-4349
Free: (800)809-5997
E-mail: crookstoncvb@rrv.net
URL: http://www.visitcrookston.com
Contact: Jeannine Windels, CEO/Pres.
Local. Promotes business and community development in Crookston, MN area. **Formerly:** (2005) Crookston Area Chamber of Commerce.

10734 ■ Crookston Dawn To Dusk Lions Club
c/o Karen L. Marx, Sec.
401 Jefferson Ave.
Crookston, MN 56716
Ph: (218)281-1823 (218)281-5359
E-mail: kmarx003@hotmail.com
URL: http://lions5m11.org/sys-tmpl/door
Contact: Karen L. Marx, Sec.
Local. Affiliated With: Lions Clubs International.

10735 ■ Crookston Figure Skating Club
PO Box 145
Crookston, MN 56716
E-mail: jtwareken@gra.midco.net
URL: National Affiliate–www.usfigureskating.org
Contact: Donna Larson, Contact
Local. Provides programs to encourage participation and achievement in the sport of figure skating on ice. Defines and maintains uniform standards of skating proficiency. Organizes and sponsors competitions and exhibitions for the purpose of stimulating interest in figure skating. **Affiliated With:** United States Figure Skating Association.

10736 ■ Crookston Lions Club
c/o Kari Thompson, Pres.
510 County Rd. 71, Ste.No. 1
Crookston, MN 56716
Ph: (218)281-8054 (218)281-7406
E-mail: kthompso@mail.crk.umn.edu
URL: http://lions5m11.org/sys-tmpl/door
Contact: Kari Thompson, Pres.
Local. Affiliated With: Lions Clubs International.

10737 ■ Minnesota Ambulance Association, Northwest
c/o Brian Holmer, Dir.
PO Box 26
Crookston, MN 56716
Ph: (218)281-4302
Fax: (218)281-3232
E-mail: bholmer@greatplainsems.com
URL: http://www.mnems.org
Contact: Brian Holmer, Dir.
Local. Seeks to maintain the financial viability of the EMS industry by advocating education, legislation and regulatory change. **Affiliated With:** Minnesota Ambulance Association.

10738 ■ RSVP of Red River Valley
c/o Deanna Patenaude, Dir.
Univ. of Minnesota
2900 Univ. Ave.
Crookston, MN 56716-5001
Ph: (218)281-8288
Fax: (218)281-8250
E-mail: dpatenau@mail.crk.umn.edu
URL: http://www.umcrookston.edu/people/services/RSVP/index.htm
Contact: Deanna Patenaude, Dir.
Local. Additional Websites: http://www.crk.umn.edu/people/services/RSVP/index.htm. **Affiliated With:** Retired and Senior Volunteer Program.

10739 ■ Sons of Norway, Morgensol Lodge 1-458
c/o Janet Solheim, Pres.
17600 350th St. SW
Crookston, MN 56716-8744
Ph: (218)281-2182
E-mail: jsolheim@mail.crk.umn.edu
URL: National Affiliate–www.sofn.com
Contact: Janet Solheim, Pres.
Local. Affiliated With: Sons of Norway.

10740 ■ United Way of Crookston
PO Box 218
Crookston, MN 56716-0218
Ph: (218)281-4547
URL: National Affiliate–national.unitedway.org
Local. Affiliated With: United Way of America.

Crosslake

10741 ■ American Legion, Potz Heartland Post 500
PO Box 362
Crosslake, MN 56442
Ph: (651)291-1800
Fax: (651)291-1057
URL: National Affiliate–www.legion.org
Local. Affiliated With: American Legion.

10742 ■ Crosslake-Ideal Lions Club
PO Box 4
Crosslake, MN 56442
Ph: (218)692-3331
E-mail: roetreat@crosslake.net
URL: http://crosslakeideallions.lionwap.org
Contact: Steve Roe, Sec.
Local. Affiliated With: Lions Clubs International.

10743 ■ Whitefish Area Lions Club
PO Box 276
Crosslake, MN 56442
E-mail: bear01@crosslake.net
URL: http://www.whitefishareallions.org
Local. Affiliated With: Lions Clubs International.

Crystal

10744 ■ National Active and Retired Federal Employees Association - North West Suburbia-Twin Cities 2243
5025 N 52nd Ave.
Crystal, MN 55429-3202
Ph: (763)537-9289
URL: National Affiliate–www.narfe.org
Contact: Homer L. Hanson, Contact
Local. Protects the retirement future of employees through education. Informs members on issues affecting the retirement. **Affiliated With:** National Association of Retired Federal Employees.

10745 ■ Robbinsdale Lions Club
c/o Dan Enna, Sec.
4239 Louisiana Ave. N
Crystal, MN 55428
Ph: (763)531-0285 (763)442-8327
URL: http://www.5m5.org
Contact: Dan Enna, Sec.
Local. Affiliated With: Lions Clubs International.

Currie

10746 ■ American Legion, Lionel Boudreau Post 322
PO Box 56
Currie, MN 56123
Ph: (651)291-1800
Fax: (651)291-1057
URL: National Affiliate–www.legion.org
Local. Affiliated With: American Legion.

Dalton

10747 ■ American Legion, Haug-Hammer Post 508
PO Box 266
Dalton, MN 56324
Ph: (651)291-1800
Fax: (651)291-1057
URL: National Affiliate–www.legion.org
Local. Affiliated With: American Legion.

Danube

10748 ■ American Legion, Minnesota Post 227
c/o Clarence W. Lueck
PO Box 301
Danube, MN 56230
Ph: (651)291-1800
Fax: (651)291-1057
URL: National Affiliate–www.legion.org
Contact: Clarence W. Lueck, Contact
Local. Affiliated With: American Legion.

10749 ■ Danube Lions Club
c/o Rod Black, Sec.
PO Box 33
Danube, MN 56230
Ph: (320)826-2274
E-mail: rodblack@tds.net
URL: http://www.5m4lions.org
Contact: Rod Black, Sec.
Local. Affiliated With: Lions Clubs International.

Darfur

10750 ■ American Legion, Norman Schulte Post 549
PO Box 142
Darfur, MN 56022
Ph: (651)291-1800
Fax: (651)291-1057
URL: National Affiliate–www.legion.org
Local. Affiliated With: American Legion.

Darwin

10751 ■ Darwin Lions Club
c/o Daryl Johnson, Pres.
67292 CSAH 33
Darwin, MN 55324
Ph: (320)275-2669
URL: http://www.5m4lions.org
Contact: Daryl Johnson, Pres.
Local. Affiliated With: Lions Clubs International.

Dassel

10752 ■ American Legion, Johnson-Kelly Post 483
72150 Csah 27
Dassel, MN 55325
Ph: (651)291-1800
Fax: (651)291-1057
URL: National Affiliate–www.legion.org
Local. Affiliated With: American Legion.

10753 ■ American Legion, Paul F. Dille Post 364
PO Box 423
Dassel, MN 55325
Ph: (651)291-1800
Fax: (651)291-1057
URL: National Affiliate–www.legion.org
Local. Affiliated With: American Legion.

10754 ■ Kingston Lions Club - Minnesota
30896 722nd Ave.
Dassel, MN 55325
Ph: (320)275-3169
E-mail: dazhdmhl@lakedalelink.net
URL: http://lkdllink.net/~dazhdmhl/index.html
Contact: Joann Strand, Sec.
Local. Affiliated With: Lions Clubs International.

Dawson

10755 ■ American Legion, Oscar Lee Post 177
PO Box 507
Dawson, MN 56232
Ph: (651)291-1800
Fax: (651)291-1057
URL: National Affiliate–www.legion.org
Local. Affiliated With: American Legion.

10756 ■ Dawson Lions Club
c/o Clyde Dessonville, Pres.
RR 2, Box 36
Dawson, MN 56232
E-mail: mwins@frontiernet.com
URL: http://www.5m4lions.org
Contact: Clyde Dessonville, Pres.
Local. Affiliated With: Lions Clubs International.

Dayton

10757 ■ American Legion, Dayton Rogers Post 531
PO Box 61
Dayton, MN 55327
Ph: (651)291-1800
Fax: (651)291-1057
URL: National Affiliate–www.legion.org
Local. Affiliated With: American Legion.

10758 ■ American Legion, Daytons Bluff Post 515
PO Box 172
Dayton, MN 55327
Ph: (651)291-1800
Fax: (651)291-1057
URL: National Affiliate–www.legion.org
Local. Affiliated With: American Legion.

10759 ■ Dayton Lions Club
c/o Greg Giese, Pres.
13901 Balsam Ln. N
Dayton, MN 55327
Ph: (763)422-9028 (763)323-3024
URL: http://www.5m5.org
Contact: Greg Giese, Pres.
Local. Affiliated With: Lions Clubs International.

De Graff

10760 ■ American Legion, Hughes-Mc-Cormick Post 362
304 3rd St. S
De Graff, MN 56271
Ph: (651)291-1800
Fax: (651)291-1057
URL: National Affiliate–www.legion.org
Local. Affiliated With: American Legion.

Deephaven

10761 ■ Bob Speltz Land O' Lakes Chapter of the Antique and Classic Boat Society (BSLOL ACBS)
c/o Peggy Merjanian, Ed.
18275 Hummingbird Rd.
Deephaven, MN 55391-3226
Ph: (952)473-6601 (952)473-4936
Fax: (952)475-1384
Free: (877)636-3111
E-mail: pmerjanian@st-barts.org
URL: http://www.acbs-bslol.com
Contact: Peggy Merjanian, Ed.
Members: 425. **Membership Dues:** local, $25 (annual) • national, $35 (annual). **Staff:** 19. **Budget:** $100,000. **Regional Groups:** 44. **Local Groups:** 1. **Local.** Promotes the preservation, restoration, and education of all antique and classic boats both wood and fiberglass. **Libraries: Type:** reference. **Holdings:** video recordings. **Subjects:** restoration, boats, motors, events. **Committees:** Advertising; Education; Events; Scholarship. **Affiliated With:** Antique and Classic Boat Society. **Publications:** *The Boathouse*, bimonthly. Magazine. Contains articles and information on history, restoration, and events. **Price:** included in membership dues. **Circulation:** 500. **Advertising:** accepted. **Conventions/Meetings:** Restoration Workshop - 3/year • semiannual show (exhibits) - always winter and summer.

Deer Creek

10762 ■ American Legion, Minnesota Post 283
c/o Edward Carlson
PO Box 158
Deer Creek, MN 56527
Ph: (651)291-1800
Fax: (651)291-1057
URL: National Affiliate–www.legion.org
Contact: Edward Carlson, Contact
Local. Affiliated With: American Legion.

Deer River

10763 ■ American Legion, Minnesota Post 122
c/o Louis A. Lequier
PO Box 176
Deer River, MN 56636
Ph: (651)291-1800
Fax: (651)291-1057
URL: National Affiliate–www.legion.org
Contact: Louis A. Lequier, Contact
Local. Affiliated With: American Legion.

10764 ■ Deer River Avenue of Pines Lions Club
c/o Audrey Moede, Sec.
42890 Chase Lake Rd.
Deer River, MN 56636
Ph: (218)246-8428
E-mail: ramo@paulbunyan.net
URL: http://lions5m10.org
Contact: Audrey Moede, Sec.
Local. Affiliated With: Lions Clubs International.

10765 ■ Deer River Golden Age Club
PO Box 643
Deer River, MN 56636-0643
Local.

10766 ■ Deer River Lions Club
c/o Victor Williams, Pres.
44871 Chase Lake Rd.
Deer River, MN 56636-3153
Ph: (218)246-2697
E-mail: drpd263@paulbunyan.net
URL: http://lions5m10.org
Contact: Victor Williams, Pres.
Local. Affiliated With: Lions Clubs International.

Deerwood

10767 ■ American Legion, Walter Scott Erickson Post 557
PO Box 55
Deerwood, MN 56444
Ph: (651)291-1800
Fax: (651)291-1057
URL: National Affiliate–www.legion.org
Local. Affiliated With: American Legion.

Delano

10768 ■ American Legion, Delano Post 377
PO Box E
Delano, MN 55328
Ph: (651)291-1800
Fax: (651)291-1057
URL: National Affiliate–www.legion.org
Local. Affiliated With: American Legion.

10769 ■ Delano Area Chamber of Commerce
PO Box 27
Delano, MN 55328-0027
Ph: (763)972-6756
Fax: (763)972-9326
E-mail: info@delanochamber.com
URL: http://www.delanochamber.com
Contact: Lisa Blodgett, Exec.Dir.
Membership Dues: church, associate, non-profit organization, $105 • business (based on number of employees), $180-$550 • city/public utility, $550. **Local.** Works to improve the business community of Delano area. **Programs:** Mentor. **Subgroups:** Business Development; Economic Development; Public Affairs. **Publications:** *Access*, monthly. Newsletter. **Advertising:** accepted. Alternate Formats: online. **Conventions/Meetings:** monthly Membership Meeting - every 3rd Thursday.

10770 ■ Delano Loretto Area United Way
PO Box 578
Delano, MN 55328-0578
Ph: (763)972-2935
URL: National Affiliate–national.unitedway.org
Local. Affiliated With: United Way of America.

Delavan

10771 ■ American Legion, Minnesota Post 486
c/o Edward Holt
101 N Main St.
Delavan, MN 56023
Ph: (651)291-1800
Fax: (651)291-1057
URL: National Affiliate–www.legion.org
Contact: Edward Holt, Contact
Local. Affiliated With: American Legion.

Detroit Lakes

10772 ■ American Legion, John Bridges Post 15
810 W Lake Dr.
Detroit Lakes, MN 56501
Ph: (651)291-1800
Fax: (651)291-1057
URL: National Affiliate–www.legion.org
Local. Affiliated With: American Legion.

10773 ■ Detroit Lakes Regional Chamber of Commerce (DLRCC)
700 Washington Ave.
PO Box 348
Detroit Lakes, MN 56502-0348
Ph: (218)847-9202
Fax: (218)847-9082
Free: (800)542-3992
E-mail: dlchamber@lakesnet.net
URL: http://www.visitdetroitlakes.com
Contact: David E. Hochhalter, Pres.
Members: 550. **Membership Dues:** individual, $200 (annual). **Staff:** 4. **Local.** Promotes business and community development in the Detroit Lakes, MN area. **Computer Services:** Online services, business directory. **Committees:** Agri-Business; Ambassadors; Arts and Crafts in the Park; Beautification; Festival of Birds; Legislative Affairs. **Task Forces:** Annual Meeting; Chamber Building. **Publications:** *The Chamber*, monthly. Newsletter. **Advertising:** accepted. Alternate Formats: online • *Membership Directory/Buyers Guide*. **Advertising:** accepted.

10774 ■ Lakes Area Builders Association (LABA)
PO Box 145
Detroit Lakes, MN 56502
Ph: (218)844-4332
Fax: (218)844-5941
E-mail: builders@lakesnet.net
URL: National Affiliate–www.nahb.org
Contact: Carrie Johnston, Contact
Founded: 1984. **Members:** 60. **Membership Dues:** builder or associate, $265 (annual). **Staff:** 1. **Local.**

Licensed builders, contractors and businesses that offer support to the building industry in the Detroit Lakes, MN area. Sponsors annual Home and Interior Showcase. Supports area vocational schools and local high school's Youthbuild Program; conducts community service projects. **Affiliated With:** National Association of Home Builders. **Publications:** *Catalog of Home Products and Services*, annual • *Lakes Area Builders are on the Level*, monthly • Directory, annual. **Conventions/Meetings:** annual Builders' Show (exhibits) • monthly meeting.

10775 ■ Lakes Area Young Life
PO Box 970
Detroit Lakes, MN 56502
Ph: (218)847-3567
Fax: (218)847-3567
URL: http://sites.younglife.org/sites/lakesarea/default.aspx
Local. Affiliated With: Young Life.

10776 ■ Lakes Country Association of Realtors
PO Box 203
Detroit Lakes, MN 56502
Ph: (218)847-1950
Fax: (218)844-1054
E-mail: dlprbd@tekstar.com
URL: National Affiliate–www.realtor.org
Contact: Jill M. Barnby, Exec. Officer
Local. Strives to develop real estate business practices. Advocates the right to own, use and transfer real property. Provides a facility for professional development, research and exchange of information among members. **Affiliated With:** National Association of Realtors.

10777 ■ Lakes Curling Club
PO Box 5
Hwy. 59 N
Detroit Lakes, MN 56502
Ph: (218)847-8186
E-mail: lakescurling@lakescurling.com
URL: http://www.lakescurling.com
Contact: Tom Spry, Pres.
Local. Affiliated With: United States Curling Association.

10778 ■ Mahube RSVP
c/o John Haack, Dir.
PO Box 747
Detroit Lakes, MN 56502
Ph: (218)847-1385
Fax: (218)847-1388
E-mail: jhaack@mahube.org
URL: http://www.seniorcorps.gov/about/programs/rsvp_state.asp?usestateabbr=mn&Search4.x=17&Search4.y=5
Contact: John Haack, Dir.
Local. Affiliated With: Retired and Senior Volunteer Program.

10779 ■ Minnesota State High School Coaches Association (MSHSCA)
c/o John Erickson, Exec.Dir.
PO Box 519
Detroit Lakes, MN 56502
Ph: (218)847-6796
Fax: (218)847-5493
E-mail: jomar@lakesnet.net
URL: http://www.mshsca.org
Contact: John Erickson, Exec.Dir.
Founded: 1936. **Members:** 5,989. **Staff:** 2. **State.**

10780 ■ Mothers Against Drunk Driving, Becker County
1000 Hwy. 10 W
Detroit Lakes, MN 56501
Free: (800)487-6233
URL: National Affiliate–www.madd.org
Local. Victims of drunk driving crashes; concerned citizens. Encourages citizen participation in working towards reform of the drunk driving problem and the prevention of underage drinking. Acts as the voice of victims of drunk driving crashes by speaking on their behalf to communities, businesses, and educational groups. **Affiliated With:** Mothers Against Drunk Driving.

10781 ■ National Active and Retired Federal Employees Association - Detroit Lakes 1842
324 Maple Dr.
Detroit Lakes, MN 56501
Ph: (218)847-4785
URL: National Affiliate–www.narfe.org
Contact: Francis Boelter, Contact
Local. Protects the retirement future of employees through education. Informs members on issues affecting the retirement. **Affiliated With:** National Association of Retired Federal Employees.

10782 ■ Northern Lights Library Network (NLLN)
103 Graystone Plz.
Detroit Lakes, MN 56501
Ph: (218)847-2825
Fax: (218)847-4161
Free: (800)450-1032
E-mail: nloffice@nlln.org
URL: http://www.nlln.org
Contact: Ruth Solie, Dir.
Founded: 1980. **Members:** 243. **Staff:** 2. **Budget:** $151,000. **State.** Public, school, academic, and special libraries in Northwestern Minnesota. Promotes cooperation among member libraries in areas such as database development, continuing education, and resource sharing, and long range planning. **Publications:** Newsletter, 9/year. Alternate Formats: online. **Conventions/Meetings:** annual conference, invited vendors (exhibits) - always April in Detroit Lakes, MN.

10783 ■ Ruffed Grouse Society, Benay of the Lakes Chapter
c/o Earl Johnson
25170 Almquist Rd.
Detroit Lakes, MN 56501
Ph: (218)847-3529
E-mail: earl.johnson@dnr.state.mn.us
URL: National Affiliate–www.ruffedgrousesociety.org
Contact: Earl Johnson, Contact
Local. Affiliated With: Ruffed Grouse Society.

10784 ■ Sons of Norway, Vikingland Lodge 1-495
c/o Mary L. Sletmoe, Pres.
13232 Fairhaven Ln.
Detroit Lakes, MN 56501-7141
Ph: (218)847-5659
URL: National Affiliate–www.sofn.com
Contact: Mary L. Sletmoe, Pres.
Local. Affiliated With: Sons of Norway.

10785 ■ United Way of Becker County
PO Box 348
Detroit Lakes, MN 56502-0348
Ph: (218)846-7400
Fax: (218)846-7404
Free: (800)492-4804
E-mail: lporter@wfc.des.state.mn.us
URL: National Affiliate–national.unitedway.org
Contact: LuAnn Porter, Exec.Dir.
Founded: 1986. **Staff:** 2. **Budget:** $125,000. **Local.** Serve the human needs of the people in Becker County. **Affiliated With:** United Way of America. **Formerly:** (1986) Detroit Lakes United Fund; (2001) United Way of the Detroit Lakes Area.

Dilworth

10786 ■ American Legion, Green-Hill Post 397
PO Box 397
Dilworth, MN 56529
Ph: (651)291-1800
Fax: (651)291-1057
URL: National Affiliate–www.legion.org
Local. Affiliated With: American Legion.

10787 ■ Dilworth Lions Club
PO Box 116
Dilworth, MN 56529
Ph: (218)287-2855 (218)236-6173
Fax: (218)238-0050
URL: http://lions5m11.org/sys-tmpl/door
Contact: Donald M. Vogel, Pres.
Local. Affiliated With: Lions Clubs International.

10788 ■ Education Minnesota, Dilworth
1675 Center Ave. W, Ste.A
Dilworth, MN 56529
Ph: (218)233-1347
Fax: (218)233-9336
Free: (800)622-4981
URL: http://www.educationminnesota.org
Contact: Rhonda Hopkins, Support Staff
Local. Affiliated With: American Federation of Teachers.

Dodge Center

10789 ■ American Legion, Wells-Peterson Post 384
401 Hwy. St. W, No. 692
Dodge Center, MN 55927
Ph: (651)291-1800
Fax: (651)291-1057
URL: National Affiliate–www.legion.org
Local. Affiliated With: American Legion.

10790 ■ Dodge Center Lions Club
c/o Jim Jenson, Pres.
15 Central Ave. N
Dodge Center, MN 55927
Ph: (507)633-2749
E-mail: jjjensen308@yahoo.com
URL: http://www.lions5m1.org/dodgecenter
Contact: Jim Jenson, Pres.
Local. Affiliated With: Lions Clubs International.

10791 ■ United Way of Dodge County, Minnesota
PO Box 718
Dodge Center, MN 55927-0718
Ph: (507)634-7048
URL: National Affiliate–national.unitedway.org
Local. Affiliated With: United Way of America.

Doran

10792 ■ Sons of Norway, Henrik Ibsen Lodge 4-565
c/o Kay E. Jacobson, Pres.
4161 340th Ave.
Doran, MN 56522-9034
Ph: (218)630-5517
E-mail: amicamagna@yahoo.com
URL: National Affiliate–www.sofn.com
Contact: Kay E. Jacobson, Pres.
Local. Affiliated With: Sons of Norway.

Duluth

10793 ■ AAA Minnesota/Iowa
2216 Mountain Shadow Dr.
Duluth, MN 55811-5607
Ph: (218)723-8055
URL: http://www.aaa.com
Contact: Renee Crassweller, Mgr.
Local.

10794 ■ ACF Arrowhead Professional Chefs Association
PO Box 16486
Duluth, MN 55816
Ph: (218)391-7762
E-mail: dmf52@mchsi.com
URL: http://www.acfarrowheadchefs.com
Contact: Dan M. Flesch CEC, Pres.
Local. Promotes the culinary profession. Provides on-going educational training and networking for

members. Provides opportunities for competition, professional recognition and access to educational forums with other culinarians at local, regional, national and international events. **Affiliated With:** American Culinary Federation.

10795 ■ Alcoholics Anonymous World Services, Twin Ports Area Intergroup
331 E 1St St.
Duluth, MN 55805
Ph: (218)727-8117
URL: National Affiliate–www.aa.org
Local. Individuals recovering from alcoholism. AA maintains that members can solve their common problem and help others achieve sobriety through a twelve step program that includes sharing their experience, strength, and hope with each other. **Affiliated With:** Alcoholics Anonymous World Services.

10796 ■ Alzheimer's Association-Duluth Center
c/o Mary Alice Carlson, Center Dir.
202 Ordean Bldg.
424 W Superior St.
Duluth, MN 55802
Ph: (218)726-4819
Fax: (218)726-4849
E-mail: mary.carlson@alz.org
URL: http://www.alzmndak.org
Contact: Mary Alice Carlson, Center Dir.
Local.

10797 ■ American Legion, David-Wisted-Zenith-City Post 28
PO Box 161353
Duluth, MN 55816
Ph: (651)291-1800
Fax: (651)291-1057
URL: National Affiliate–www.legion.org
Local. Affiliated With: American Legion.

10798 ■ American Legion, Lakeview Post 342
PO Box 3166
Duluth, MN 55803
Ph: (651)291-1800
Fax: (651)291-1057
URL: National Affiliate–www.legion.org
Local. Affiliated With: American Legion.

10799 ■ American Legion, Lakewood Post 571
PO Box 3408
Duluth, MN 55803
Ph: (651)291-1800
Fax: (651)291-1057
URL: National Affiliate–www.legion.org
Local. Affiliated With: American Legion.

10800 ■ American Legion, Minnesota Post 71
c/o Ivan V. Sarff
5814 Grand Ave.
Duluth, MN 55807
Ph: (651)291-1800
Fax: (651)291-1057
URL: National Affiliate–www.legion.org
Contact: Ivan V. Sarff, Contact
Local. Affiliated With: American Legion.

10801 ■ American Legion, Minnesota Post 558
c/o Don Johnson, Finance Officer
815 N 40th Ave. E
Duluth, MN 55804
Ph: (651)291-1800
Fax: (651)291-1057
URL: National Affiliate–www.legion.org
Contact: Don Johnson, Finance Officer
Local. Affiliated With: American Legion.

10802 ■ American Red Cross, Northland Chapter
2524 Maple Grove Rd.
Duluth, MN 55811
Ph: (218)722-0071
Fax: (218)722-0992
Free: (800)950-4275
E-mail: redcross@redcrossnorthland.org
URL: http://www.redcrossnorthland.org
Local.

10803 ■ American Society for Training and Development - Lake Superior Chapter
PO Box 7
Duluth, MN 55801
E-mail: kboedigheimer@fdlrez.com
URL: http://www.astd-duluth.org
Contact: Kelly Boedigheimer, Pres.
Regional. Promotes workplace learning and the improvement of skills of workplace professionals. Provides resource and professional development to individuals in the field of learning and development. Recognizes and sets standards for learning and performance professionals. **Affiliated With:** American Society for Training and Development.

10804 ■ Animal Allies Humane Society of Duluth, Minnesota
407 1/2 W Michigan St.
Duluth, MN 55802
Ph: (218)722-5341
E-mail: animalalliesduluth@yahoo.com
URL: http://www.animalallies.net
Local.

10805 ■ Arrowhead Health Care Engineers Association (AHCEA)
c/o Ron Daigle, Pres.
SMDC Hea. Sys.
400 E 3rd St.
Duluth, MN 55805
Ph: (218)786-4167
Fax: (218)786-4840
E-mail: rdaigle@smdc.org
URL: National Affiliate–www.ashe.org
Contact: Ron Daigle, Pres.
Local. Promotes better patient care by encouraging members to develop their knowledge and increase their competence in the field of facilities management. Cooperates with hospitals and allied associations in matters pertaining to facilities management. **Affiliated With:** American Society for Healthcare Engineering of the American Hospital Association.

10806 ■ Arrowhead Regional Development Commission (ARDC)
221 W 1st St.
Duluth, MN 55802
Ph: (218)722-5545
Fax: (218)529-7592
Free: (800)232-0707
E-mail: info@ardc.org
URL: http://www.ardc.org
Contact: Henry Hanka, Exec.Dir.
Local. Serves the counties of Aitkin, Carlton, Cook, Itasca, Koochiching, Lake and St. Louis in Northeastern Minnesota. Works towards community and economic development.

10807 ■ Association for Computing Machinery, University of Minnesota/Duluth
Dept. of Cmpt. Sci.
Univ. of Minnesota Duluth
320 Heller Hall
1114 Kirby Dr.
Duluth, MN 55812-2496
Ph: (218)726-7607
Fax: (218)726-8240
E-mail: cs@d.umn.edu
URL: http://www.d.umn.edu/cs
Contact: Mr. Steven Holtz, Faculty Advisor
Local. Aims to foster interest in the fields of computer science and information technology, to prepare members for the professional world and to facilitate communication between students and professors. **Affiliated With:** Association for Computing Machinery.

10808 ■ Bridge Syndicate
PO Box 215
Duluth, MN 55801
Ph: (218)724-4184
E-mail: info@bridgesydnicate.org
Contact: Shane Maki, Chair
Founded: 2000. **Members:** 500. **Local Groups:** 1. **Local**. Aims to increase civic, cultural and economic opportunities in the Twin Ports (Duluth, MN and Superior, WI) area. **Awards:** Bridgie Awards. **Frequency:** annual. **Type:** recognition. **Recipient:** to individual with commitment to improving the Twin Ports area. **Committees:** PR/Marketing; Welcoming. **Conventions/Meetings:** annual Birthday Celebration & Bridge Awards Banquet - party.

10809 ■ College of St. Scholastica Figure Skating Club
CSS Box 1887
Duluth, MN 55811
E-mail: ewalin@css.edu
URL: National Affiliate–www.usfigureskating.org
Local. Provides programs to encourage participation and achievement in the sport of figure skating on ice. Defines and maintains uniform standards of skating proficiency. Organizes and sponsors competitions and exhibitions for the purpose of stimulating interest in figure skating. **Affiliated With:** United States Figure Skating Association.

10810 ■ Community Health Information Collaborative
c/o Cheryl Stephens
404 W Superior St., Ste.No. 250
Duluth, MN 55802
Ph: (218)625-5515
Fax: (218)625-5518
Free: (877)411-CHIC
URL: http://www.medinfosystems.org
Contact: Katheleen Howard, Admin.Asst.
Local.

10811 ■ Cyclists of Gitchee Gumee Shores (COGGS)
PO Box 161261
Duluth, MN 55806
Ph: (715)395-6343
E-mail: chair@coggs.com
URL: http://www.coggs.com
Contact: Ross Fraboni, Chm.
Founded: 1994. **Local. Affiliated With:** International Mountain Bicycling Association.

10812 ■ Duluth Area Association of Realtors
4031 Grand Ave.
Duluth, MN 55807
Ph: (218)728-5676
Fax: (218)728-1534
E-mail: tracy@daar.com
URL: http://www.daar.com
Contact: Tracy Huotari, CEO
Local. Strives to develop real estate business practices. Advocates the right to own, use and transfer real property. Provides a facility for professional development, research and exchange of information among members. **Affiliated With:** National Association of Realtors.

10813 ■ Duluth Area Chamber of Commerce (DACC)
5 W First St.
Duluth, MN 55802
Ph: (218)722-5501
Fax: (218)722-3223
E-mail: inquiry@duluthchamber.com
URL: http://www.duluthchamber.com
Contact: David M. Ross, Pres. & CEO
Founded: 1870. **Members:** 1,100. **Staff:** 12. **Local**. Promotes business and community development in Duluth, MN. **Programs:** Leadership Duluth; Let's Do Lunch, Duluth; Professional Development Series. **Subgroups:** Ambassadors; Harborview

Toastmasters. **Formerly:** (1999) Duluth +Chamber of Commerce. **Publications:** *Xpress*. Newsletter • Magazine. **Conventions/Meetings:** monthly Business After Hours - meeting - every 3rd Thursday • monthly First Fridays - meeting, networking opportunities - every 1st Friday.

10814 ■ Duluth Audubon Society
PO Box 3091
Duluth, MN 55803-3901
E-mail: info@duluthaudubon.org
URL: http://www.duluthaudubon.org

Local. Works to conserve and restore natural ecosystems, focusing on birds and other wildlife for the benefit of humanity and the earth's biological diversity. **Affiliated With:** National Audubon Society. **Publications:** *Call Notes*, September through May. Newsletter. Contains information of interest to members of the Society.

10815 ■ Duluth Builders Exchange (DBE)
802 Garfield Ave.
Duluth, MN 55802
Ph: (218)722-2836
Fax: (218)722-2626
E-mail: info@duluthbx.com
URL: http://www.duluthbx.com
Contact: Jim Schwerdt, Exec.Dir.

Founded: 1902. **Members:** 430. **Local**. Represents general contractors, subcontractors, suppliers, manufacturers' representatives and individual firms related to the construction industry. Provides information on construction and building procedures. **Affiliated With:** International Builders Exchange Executives.

10816 ■ Duluth Convention and Visitors Bureau (DCVB)
21 W Superior St., Ste.100
Duluth, MN 55802-2326
Ph: (218)722-4011
Fax: (218)722-1322
Free: (800)438-5884
E-mail: cvb@visitduluth.com
URL: http://www.visitduluth.com
Local.

10817 ■ Duluth Curling Club
327 Harbor Dr.
Duluth, MN 55802
Ph: (218)727-1851
Fax: (218)727-6326
E-mail: office@duluthcurlingclub.org
URL: http://www.duluthcurlingclub.org
Contact: Kevin Kemp, Pres.

Local. **Affiliated With:** United States Curling Association.

10818 ■ Duluth Figure Skating Club (DFSC)
PO Box 161032
Duluth, MN 55816-1032
E-mail: oberstars@charter.net
URL: http://www.duluthfsc.org
Contact: David Oberstar, Pres.

Local. Provides programs to encourage participation and achievement in the sport of figure skating on ice. Defines and maintains uniform standards of skating proficiency. Organizes and sponsors competitions and exhibitions for the purpose of stimulating interest in figure skating. **Affiliated With:** United States Figure Skating Association.

10819 ■ Duluth Lions Club
c/o Joel Manns, Pres.
210 W Anoka St.
Duluth, MN 55803
Ph: (218)728-2633
E-mail: jmanns@cpinternet.com
URL: http://lions5m10.org
Contact: Joel Manns, Pres.
Local. **Affiliated With:** Lions Clubs International.

10820 ■ Duluth Saddle Club
c/o Susan C. Carter, Pres.
2662 E. Lismore Rd.
Duluth, MN 55804-9679
Local.

10821 ■ Duluth Spirit Valley Lions Club
c/o Keith Bischoff, Sec.
626 N 46th Ave. W
Duluth, MN 55807
Ph: (218)628-1469
E-mail: keithb.dlh@juno.com
URL: http://lions5m10.org
Contact: Keith Bischoff, Sec.
Local. **Affiliated With:** Lions Clubs International.

10822 ■ Environmental Association for Great Lakes Education (EAGLE)
394 Lake Ave. S, Ste.222
Duluth, MN 55802
Ph: (218)726-1828
Fax: (218)726-1828
E-mail: contact@eagle-ecosource.org
URL: http://eagle-ecosource.org
Contact: Jan Conley, Founder/Pres.
Local.

10823 ■ Esko Lions Club
c/o Donald Olson, Pres.
4715 Morris Thomas Rd.
Duluth, MN 55811
Ph: (218)723-2339
URL: http://lions5m10.org
Contact: Donald Olson, Pres.
Local. **Affiliated With:** Lions Clubs International.

10824 ■ Head of the Lakes Youth for Christ
PO Box 16111
Duluth, MN 55816
Ph: (218)722-9820
Fax: (218)723-8753
URL: http://www.encounteryfc.com
Local. **Affiliated With:** Youth for Christ/U.S.A.

10825 ■ Hotel Employees and Restaurant Employees International Union, Local 99 Duluth
c/o Todd Erickson, Pres./CEO
2027 W Superior St.
Duluth, MN 55806
Ph: (218)728-6861
Fax: (218)728-1720
Free: (877)728-6861
E-mail: staff@unitehere99.com
URL: http://www.unitehere99.com
Contact: Todd Erickson, Pres./CEO
Local. **Affiliated With:** UNITE HERE.

10826 ■ Institute of Internal Auditors, Lake Superior Chapter (LSIIA)
c/o Doug Welnetz
ALLETE-Internal Audit
30 W Superior St.
Duluth, MN 55802
URL: National Affiliate–www.theiia.org
Contact: Kathy Sanders, Pres.

Membership Dues: regular, $115 (annual) • educator, $65 (annual) • student, retired, $30 (annual) • life, $2,100 • sustainer (government auditors only), $50 (annual) • organization ($65 per staff member over 5; $50 per staff member over 100), $425-$6,600 (annual). **Local**. Serves as an advocate for the internal audit profession. Provides certification, education, research, and technological guidance for the profession. **Affiliated With:** Institute of Internal Auditors. **Publications:** *Auditwire*, bimonthly. Newsletter. **Advertising:** accepted. Alternate Formats: online • *IIA Educator*, 3/year. Newsletter. Alternate Formats: online.

10827 ■ Institute of Management Accountants, Lake Superior Chapter
c/o Thomas M. Samson, Pres.
227 W First St., Ste.700
Duluth, MN 55802
Ph: (218)336-3155
E-mail: tom.samson@rsmi.com
URL: http://www.ima-northernlights.imanet.org
Contact: Thomas M. Samson, Pres.

Local. Promotes professional and ethical standards. Equips members and students with knowledge and training required for the accounting profession. **Councils:** Northern Lights Council. **Affiliated With:** Institute of Management Accountants.

10828 ■ Iron Mining Association of Minnesota
11 E Superior St., Ste.514
Duluth, MN 55802
Ph: (218)722-7724
Fax: (218)720-6707
E-mail: info@tacnoite.org
URL: http://www.taconite.org
Contact: Frank Ongaro, Pres.
State.

10829 ■ Izaak Walton League of America, W. J. McCabe Chapter
2116 Columbus Ave.
Duluth, MN 55803-2221
Ph: (218)834-9800
E-mail: zentner@cpinternet.com
URL: National Affiliate–www.iwla.org
Contact: Terry Frank, Pres.

Local. Works to educate the public to conserve, maintain, protect, and restore the soil, forest, water, and other natural resources of the U.S; promotes the enjoyment and wholesome utilization of these resources. **Affiliated With:** Izaak Walton League of America.

10830 ■ Lake Superior AIFA
c/o Robert Zimmerman
302 W Superior St., No. 400
Duluth, MN 55802
Ph: (218)722-7443
Fax: (218)722-0158
E-mail: tusadk@mchsi.com
URL: National Affiliate–naifa.org
Contact: Robert Zimmerman, Contact

Local. Represents the interests of insurance and financial advisors. Advocates for a positive legislative and regulatory environment. Enhances business and professional skills of members. **Affiliated With:** National Association of Insurance and Financial Advisors.

10831 ■ Lake Superior Medical Society
Alworth Bldg., Ste.804
306 W Superior St.
Duluth, MN 55802
Ph: (218)727-3325
Fax: (218)727-6976
E-mail: medsoc@lsmedsoc.org
URL: http://www.mnmed.org/lsms
Contact: Jane Abrams, Exec.Dir.

Local. Represents the interests of physicians, residents and medical students. Promotes excellence in health care. Ensures a healthy practice environment. Preserves the professionalism of medicine. **Affiliated With:** Minnesota Medical Association.

10832 ■ Laurentian Resource Conservation and Development Council
4850 Miller Trunk Hwy.
Duluth, MN 55811
Ph: (218)720-5225
Fax: (218)720-3129
E-mail: steven.kluess@mn.usda.gov
URL: http://www.lrcd.org
Contact: Steven Kluess, Coor.

Local. **Affiliated With:** National Association of Resource Conservation and Development Councils.

10833 ■ Military Officers Association of America, Head O'The Lakes Chapter
504 Colby Ave.
Duluth, MN 55804-2603
Ph: (218)727-6483
E-mail: acwillman@yahoo.com
URL: http://www.moaa.org/Chapters/CustomChapter.asp?ChaptCode=MN01
Contact: 1Lt. Allen C. Willman, Contact
Local. Affiliated With: Military Officers Association of America.

10834 ■ Minnesota Board of Water and Soil Resources
394 S. Lake Ave., Ste.403
Duluth, MN 55802
Ph: (218)723-4752
Fax: (218)723-4794
E-mail: mark.nelson@bwsr.state.mn.us
Contact: Mark Nelson, Board Conservationist

10835 ■ Minnesota Dachshund Club (MDC)
c/o Kathy Johnson, Treas.
221 W Heard St.
Duluth, MN 55808
Ph: (763)389-4622
E-mail: beestee@aol.com
URL: http://members.tripod.com/mdcdachshund
Contact: Marlies Noll, Pres.
Founded: 1945. **State.**

10836 ■ Minnesota Forest Industries (MFI)
903 Medical Arts Bldg.
324 W Superior St.
Duluth, MN 55802
Ph: (218)722-5013
E-mail: minntrees@aol.com
URL: http://www.minnesotaforests.org
State.

10837 ■ Minnesota Nurses Association - District 2
27 Deerwood St.
Duluth, MN 55811
Ph: (218)726-1510
E-mail: ruthju42@hotmail.com
URL: http://www.mnnurses.org
Contact: Ruth Juntune, Pres.
Local. Works to advance the nursing profession. Seeks to meet the needs of nurses and health care consumers. Fosters high standards of nursing practice. Promotes the economic and general welfare of nurses in the workplace. **Affiliated With:** American Nurses Association; Minnesota Nurses Association.

10838 ■ Minnesota Pharmacists Association, Northeast District
c/o Gregory M. Eaton, Chm.
K-Mart Pharmacy
215 Central Ave. N
Duluth, MN 55807
Ph: (218)624-9305
E-mail: nemn60@yahoo.com
URL: http://www.mpha.org
Contact: Gregory M. Eaton, Chm.
Local. Works to provide leadership for the pharmacy profession. Seeks to protect and enhance public health. Enhances the knowledge, ethics and skills of pharmacists through advocacy, education, research and the development of standards. **Affiliated With:** Minnesota Pharmacists Association.

10839 ■ Minnesota Timber Producers Association
c/o Mr. Wayne E. Brandt, Exec.VP
903 Medical Arts Bldg.
324 W Superior St.
Duluth, MN 55802
Ph: (218)722-5013
Fax: (218)722-2065
E-mail: wbrandt11@aol.com
URL: http://www.forestresources.org/ALLIES/state-assoc.html
Contact: Mr. Wayne E. Brandt, Exec.VP
State.

10840 ■ Minnesotans for Responsible Recreation
PO Box 111
Duluth, MN 55801-0111
Ph: (218)740-3175
Fax: (218)740-3179
URL: http://www.mnresponsiblerec.org
Contact: Jeff Brown, Exec.Dir.
State.

10841 ■ National Active and Retired Federal Employees Association - Arrowhead 106
617 N 11th Ave. E
Duluth, MN 55805-2239
Ph: (218)728-2068
URL: National Affiliate–www.narfe.org
Contact: John M. Rust, Contact
Local. Protects the retirement future of employees through education. Informs members on issues affecting the retirement. **Affiliated With:** National Association of Retired Federal Employees.

10842 ■ National Association of Home Builders, Arrowhead Builders Association
c/o Tamilee Depre
802 Garfield Ave.
Duluth, MN 55802-2640
Ph: (218)722-5707
Fax: (218)722-1448
E-mail: aba@abamn.org
URL: http://www.abamn.org
Contact: Tamilee Taylor-Depre, Exec. Officer
Local. Single and multifamily home builders, commercial builders, and others associated with the building industry. **Affiliated With:** National Association of Home Builders.

10843 ■ Nettleton Magnet School PTA
c/o Nettleton Magnet Elementary School
108 E Sixth St.
Duluth, MN 55805
E-mail: upnorth38@aol.com
URL: http://familyeducation.com/MN/NettletonPTA
Contact: Jonie Langdon-Larson, Contact
Local. Parents, teachers, students, and others interested in uniting the forces of home, school, and community. Promotes the welfare of children and youth.

10844 ■ North American Butterfly Association-Northern Crescents Chapter (NABANC)
c/o Pat Thomas, Pres.
6219 E Superior St.
Duluth, MN 55804
Ph: (218)525-1656
E-mail: pthomas55804@yahoo.com
URL: http://www.naba.org/chapters/nabanc
Contact: Pat Thomas, Pres.
Founded: 2002. **Membership Dues:** regular, $30 (annual) • family, $40 (annual) • regular outside North America, $60 (annual). **Local. Affiliated With:** North American Butterfly Association. **Formerly:** (2002) North American Butterfly Association-Duluth.

10845 ■ Northeastern District Dental Society, Minnesota
c/o Dr. Steve L'Abbe, Sec.-Treas.
1432 London Rd.
Duluth, MN 55805-2425
Ph: (218)728-5095
Fax: (218)728-9164
E-mail: stevelabbe@charter.net
URL: http://northeast.mndental.org
Contact: Dr. Steve L'Abbe, Sec.-Treas.
Local. Represents the interests of dentists committed to the public's oral health, ethics and professional development. Encourages the improvement of the public's oral health and promotes the art and science of dentistry. **Affiliated With:** American Dental Association; Minnesota Dental Association.

10846 ■ Northland Human Resource Association
PO Box 16336
Duluth, MN 55816
E-mail: info@northlandhra.org
URL: http://www.northlandhra.org
Contact: Denise Frankki, Pres.
Local. Represents the interests of human resource and industrial relations professionals and executives. Promotes the advancement of human resource management.

10847 ■ Northland Senior Games
c/o Erin Wenneson, State Coor.
12 E 4th St.
Duluth, MN 55805
Ph: (218)723-3724 (218)626-4521
Fax: (218)723-3634
E-mail: ewenneson@ci.duluth.mn.us
URL: National Affiliate–www.nsga.com
Contact: Erin Wenneson, State Coor.
Regional. Affiliated With: National Senior Games Association.

10848 ■ PFLAG Duluth
2310 E 4th St.
Duluth, MN 55812
Ph: (218)728-4405
E-mail: pilgrimdlh@aol.com
URL: http://www.pflag.org/Minnesota.217.0.html
Local. Affiliated With: Parents, Families, and Friends of Lesbians and Gays.

10849 ■ Phi Theta Kappa, Alpha Upsilon Gamma Chapter - Lake Superior College
c/o Ms. Brenda Koneczny, Faculty Staff
2101 Trinity Rd.
Duluth, MN 55811
Ph: (218)733-7609
E-mail: b.koneczny@lsc.mnscu.edu
URL: http://www.ptk.org/directories/chapters/MN/17413-1.htm
Contact: Ms. Brenda Koneczny, Faculty Staff
Local.

10850 ■ Psi Chi, National Honor Society in Psychology - University of Minnesota, Duluth
c/o Dept. of Psychology
330 Bohannon Hall
10 Univ. Dr.
Duluth, MN 55812-2496
Ph: (218)726-7116 (218)726-7860
Fax: (218)726-7073
E-mail: rlloyd@d.umn.edu
URL: National Affiliate–www.psichi.org
Contact: Dr. Robert Lloyd PhD, Advisor
Local.

10851 ■ Rolling Readers of Duluth
c/o Susan Henke, Chapter Leader
2632 E. 5th St.
Duluth, MN 55812
Ph: (218)782-5508
E-mail: shenke@computerpro.com
Contact: Susan Henke, Chap.Leader

10852 ■ St. Louis River Citizens Action Committee (SLRCAC)
394 Lake Ave. S, Rm. 303B
Duluth, MN 55802
Ph: (218)733-9520
Fax: (218)723-4794
E-mail: slrcac@stlouisriver.org
URL: http://www.StLouisRiver.org
Contact: Diane Thompson, Sec.
Local.

10853 ■ Skills USA, Duluth Secondary Technical Center
730 E Central Entrance
Duluth, MN 55811
Ph: (218)733-2066
Fax: (218)722-9196
E-mail: blampi@duluth.k12.mn.us
URL: http://www.mnskillsusa.org/secondaryChapters.htm
Contact: Barry Lampi, Contact
Local. Serves high school and college students enrolled in technical, skilled, and service and health

occupations. Provides quality education experiences for students in leadership, teamwork, citizenship and character development. Builds and reinforces self-confidence, work attitudes and communication skills. Emphasizes total quality at work, high ethical standards, superior work skills, and life-long education. Promotes understanding of the free enterprise system and involvement in community service. **Affiliated With:** Skills USA - VICA.

10854 ■ Society of American Registered Architects - Minnesota Council
c/o Melissa Graftaas, Pres.
Architecture Advantage
4085 E Calvary Rd.
Duluth, MN 55803
Ph: (218)728-4293
Fax: (218)724-5589
E-mail: melissa@architecureadvantage.com
URL: National Affiliate–www.sara-national.org
Contact: Melissa Graftaas, Pres.
State. Seeks to provide a link between the architect and the user of architectural services. Supports the concept of profitable professionalism for all members. **Affiliated With:** Society of American Registered Architects.

10855 ■ Sons of Norway, Nortun Lodge 1-16
c/o Lynne L. Erickson, Sec.
105 Vassar St.
Duluth, MN 55803-1542
Ph: (218)724-5393
E-mail: lericks5@d.umn.edu
URL: National Affiliate–www.sofn.com
Contact: Lynne L. Erickson, Sec.
Local. Affiliated With: Sons of Norway.

10856 ■ Sweetwater Alliance
c/o Jill Jacoby
PO Box 3100
Duluth, MN 55803-3100
Ph: (218)728-5392
E-mail: info@sweetwateralliance.org
URL: http://www.sweetwateralliance.org
Contact: Jill Jacoby, Exec.Dir.
Founded: 2002. **Staff:** 1. **Budget:** $25,000. **Regional.** Strives to fuse ecological restoration, art and community education to restore and improve water quality. **Publications:** *Sweetwater*, annual. Newsletter. Contains updates on projects & progress. **Price:** free. **Circulation:** 1,000. Alternate Formats: online.

10857 ■ Twin Ports-Arrowhead Chapter National Electrical Contractors Association
c/o Blair Mahan, Pres.
802 Garfield Ave., No. 102
Duluth, MN 55802
Ph: (218)722-8115
Fax: (218)722-6816
E-mail: necanet@charterinternet.com
URL: National Affiliate–www.necanet.org
Contact: Mr. Blair Mahan, Pres.
Local. Affiliated With: National Electrical Contractors Association.

10858 ■ United Food and Commercial Workers, Local 12A, Northcentral Region
2002 London Rd., Ste.208
Duluth, MN 55812
Ph: (218)724-4986
URL: National Affiliate–www.ufcw.org
Local. Affiliated With: United Food and Commercial Workers International Union.

10859 ■ United Food and Commercial Workers, Local 1116, Northcentral Region
PO Box 16388
Duluth, MN 55816-0388
Ph: (218)728-5174
URL: http://www.ufcw1116.org
Local. Affiliated With: United Food and Commercial Workers International Union.

10860 ■ United Way of Greater Duluth
424 W Superior St., Ste.402
Duluth, MN 55802
Ph: (218)726-4770
Fax: (218)726-4778
E-mail: info@unitedwayduluth.org
URL: http://unitedwayduluth.org
Contact: Paula Reed, Pres./CEO
Local. Affiliated With: United Way of America.

10861 ■ University of Minnesota-Duluth Literary Guild
10 Univ. Dr., Hmt. 410
Duluth, MN 55812-2403
E-mail: literaryguild@d.umn.edu
URL: http://www.d.umn.edu/~litguild
Local. Publications: *The Roaring Muse*, semiannual. Magazine. Contains poetry, prose, short stories, and artwork. **Price:** $3.00. **Advertising:** accepted.

Dundee

10862 ■ American Legion, Minnesota Post 386
c/o Joseph Suding
221 N Main St.
Dundee, MN 56131
Ph: (651)291-1800
Fax: (651)291-1057
URL: National Affiliate–www.legion.org
Contact: Joseph Suding, Contact
Local. Affiliated With: American Legion.

Eagan

10863 ■ American Legion, Eagan Post 594
PO Box 21013
Eagan, MN 55121
Ph: (651)291-1800
Fax: (651)291-1057
URL: National Affiliate–www.legion.org
Local. Affiliated With: American Legion.

10864 ■ American Postal Workers Union, AFL-CIO - Twin Cities Postal Data Center Local Union 7019
2825 Lone Oak Pkwy.
Eagan, MN 55121-9100
Ph: (651)406-2592
E-mail: apwu7019@aol.com
URL: http://www.twincitiesapwu.org
Contact: Steve Brooks, Pres.
Members: 324. **Local.** AFL-CIO. **Affiliated With:** American Postal Workers Union.

10865 ■ City of Lakes Sweet Adelines Chorus
4452 Hamilton Dr.
Eagan, MN 55123-1974
Ph: (952)945-0337
E-mail: info@cityoflakes.org
URL: http://www.cityoflakes.org
Contact: Brent Graham, Dir.
Local. Advances the musical art form of barbershop harmony through education and performances. Provides education, training and coaching in the development of women's four-part barbershop harmony. **Affiliated With:** Sweet Adelines International.

10866 ■ Dakotas Children Auxiliary
680 Oneill Dr.
Eagan, MN 55121-1535
Ph: (651)688-8808
Fax: (651)688-8892
URL: http://www.dakotacommunities.org
Contact: Paula Hart, Pres.
Local.

10867 ■ Independent Community Bankers of Minnesota (ICBM)
2600 Eagan Woods Dr., Ste.200
Eagan, MN 55121
Ph: (651)687-9080
Fax: (651)687-9387
E-mail: icbm@communitybanks.org
URL: http://www.communitybanks.org
Contact: Will Haddeland, Pres./CEO
State.

10868 ■ Minnesota Gymkhana Cricket Club
1518 Clemson Dr.
Eagan, MN 55122
URL: http://www.usaca.org/Clubs.htm
Contact: Srinivas Avvari, Contact
Local.

10869 ■ Minnesota Lakers Cricket Club
1027 Northview Park Rd.
Eagan, MN 55123
URL: http://www.usaca.org/Clubs.htm
Contact: Sheilash Bhakta, Contact
Local.

10870 ■ National Association of Housing and Redevelopment Officials, Minnesota Chapter (MNNAHRO)
c/o Patricia Gustafson, Exec.Dir.
1228 Town Ctre. Dr.
Eagan, MN 55123
Ph: (651)675-4490
Fax: (651)675-4405
Free: (800)242-6804
E-mail: mnnahro@qwest.net
URL: http://www.housingcenter.com/public/hosted_sites/minn/minn_frm.html
Contact: Patricia Gustafson, Exec.Dir.
State. Individuals and public agencies engaged in community rebuilding by community development, public housing, large-scale private or cooperative housing rehabilitation, and conservation of existing neighborhoods through housing code enforcement, voluntary citizen action, and government action. **Affiliated With:** National Association of Housing and Redevelopment Officials.

10871 ■ National Association of Housing and Redevelopment Officials, North Central Regional Council (NAHRO-NCRC)
c/o Michael Hagemeyer, Pres.
1228 Town Cte. Dr.
Eagan, MN 55123
Ph: (651)675-4490
Fax: (651)675-4405
Free: (800)818-9327
E-mail: ncrcnahro@qwest.net
URL: http://www.housingcenter.com/public/hosted_sites/ncrc/ncrc_frm.html
Founded: 1942. **Regional. Affiliated With:** National Association of Housing and Redevelopment Officials.

10872 ■ Northern Dakota County Chamber of Commerce
1121 Town Center Dr., Ste.102
Eagan, MN 55123
Ph: (651)452-9872
Fax: (651)452-8978
E-mail: info@ndcchambers.com
URL: http://www.ndcchambers.com
Contact: Ruthe Batulis, Pres.
Founded: 1957. **Membership Dues:** business (based on number of employees), $273-$2,114. **Local.** Works to unite and strengthen the business community by providing networking, supporting educational opportunities, encouraging business and community development and determining public policy. **Committees:** Ambassadors; Big Fun Event; Communications and Marketing; Golf; Government Affairs; Programs; Steering. **Subgroups:** ChamberNet. **Publications:** Newsletter, bimonthly. Alternate Formats: online.

10873 ■ Sons of Norway, Vonheim Lodge 1-108
c/o David T. Kompelien, Pres.
1726 Kyllo Ln.
Eagan, MN 55122-1131
Ph: (651)454-7019
E-mail: dtck1@msn.com
URL: http://www.vonheimlodge.homestead.com
Contact: David T. Kompelien, Pres.
Local. Affiliated With: Sons of Norway.

10874 ■ Southern Twin Cities Association of Realtors
4490 Erin Dr.
Eagan, MN 55122
Ph: (651)452-6611
Fax: (651)452-2911
E-mail: rcovert@stcar.com
URL: http://www.stcar.com
Contact: Ron Covert, CEO
Local. Strives to develop real estate business practices. Advocates the right to own, use and transfer real property. Provides a facility for professional development, research and exchange of information among members. **Affiliated With:** National Association of Realtors.

10875 ■ Twin Cities German Wirehair Pointer Club (TCGWPC)
c/o Deb Finstad, Treas.
701 Bradford Pl.
Eagan, MN 55123
Ph: (651)405-9308
E-mail: finst004@umn.edu
URL: http://www.tcgwpc.com
Contact: Deb Finstad, Treas.
Local.

10876 ■ Young Life Northern Dakota County
4399 Hamilton Dr.
Eagan, MN 55123
Fax: (651)688-3018
URL: http://sites.younglife.org/_layouts/ylext/default.aspx?ID=A-MN76
Local. Affiliated With: Young Life.

Eagle Bend

10877 ■ American Legion, Minnesota Post 280
c/o Frederick E. Cossentine
PO Box 7
Eagle Bend, MN 56446
Ph: (651)291-1800
Fax: (651)291-1057
URL: National Affiliate–www.legion.org
Contact: Frederick E. Cossentine, Contact
Local. Affiliated With: American Legion.

Eagle Lake

10878 ■ American Legion, Eagle Lake Post 617
PO Box 96
Eagle Lake, MN 56024
Ph: (651)291-1800
Fax: (651)291-1057
URL: National Affiliate–www.legion.org
Local. Affiliated With: American Legion.

10879 ■ National Active and Retired Federal Employees Association - Mankato 282
PO Box 353
Eagle Lake, MN 56024-0353
Ph: (507)257-3594
URL: National Affiliate–www.narfe.org
Contact: Roger A. Mayer, Contact
Local. Protects the retirement future of employees through education. Informs members on issues affecting the retirement. **Affiliated With:** National Association of Retired Federal Employees.

East Bethel

10880 ■ Association for Corporate Growth, Minnesota Chapter (ACGMN)
c/o Nicole Vincent, Administrator
18461 Lakeview Point Dr. NE
East Bethel, MN 55092-9518
Ph: (612)305-5076 (612)590-1041
Fax: (763)413-7328
E-mail: acgminnesota@acg.org
URL: http://www.acg.org/minnesota
Contact: Nicole Vincent, Administrator
State. Affiliated With: Association for Corporate Growth.

East Grand Forks

10881 ■ American Legion, East Grand Forks Post 157
1009 Central Ave. NW
East Grand Forks, MN 56721
Ph: (651)291-1800
Fax: (651)291-1057
URL: National Affiliate–www.legion.org
Local. Affiliated With: American Legion.

10882 ■ East Grand Forks Chamber of Commerce (EGFCC)
218 4th St. NW
East Grand Forks, MN 56721
Ph: (218)773-7481
Fax: (218)773-7482
E-mail: info@eastgrandforkschamber.com
Contact: Diane Blair, Pres.
Members: 247. **Staff:** 2. **Local**. Promotes business and community development in East Grand Forks, MN. **Committees:** Agribusiness; Beautification Task Force; Campground; Captains Club; Catfish Day and Tournament; Cats Incredible; Legislative; Marketing Advisory Group; Military Affairs; Steppin Out Ball. **Publications:** *Advocate*, monthly. Newsletter. **Price:** free. **Circulation:** 45. **Advertising:** accepted.

10883 ■ East Grand Forks Lions Club
PO Box 60
East Grand Forks, MN 56721
Ph: (218)773-7933 (218)773-8304
E-mail: c_kbuckalew@hotmail.com
URL: http://lions5m11.org/sys-tmpl/door
Contact: Craig Buckalew, Pres.
Local. Affiliated With: Lions Clubs International.

10884 ■ Phi Theta Kappa, Beta Nu Kappa Chapter - Northland Community and Technical College
c/o Kelli Hallsten
East Grand Forks Campus
2022 Central Ave. NE
East Grand Forks, MN 56721
Ph: (218)773-3441
E-mail: kelli.hallsten@northlandcollege.edu
URL: http://www.ptk.org/directories/chapters/MN/22267-1.htm
Contact: Kelli Hallsten, Advisor
Local.

10885 ■ Skills USA, East Grand Forks High School
1420 4th Ave. NW
East Grand Forks, MN 56721
Ph: (218)773-2405
Fax: (218)773-3070
E-mail: dpelarski@egf.k12.mn.us
URL: http://www.mnskillsusa.org/secondaryChapters.htm
Contact: David Pelarski, Contact
Local. Serves high school and college students enrolled in technical, skilled, and service and health occupations. Provides quality education experiences for students in leadership, teamwork, citizenship and character development. Builds and reinforces self-confidence, work attitudes and communication skills. Emphasizes total quality at work, high ethical standards, superior work skills, and life-long education. Promotes understanding of the free enterprise system and involvement in community service. **Affiliated With:** Skills USA - VICA.

Easton

10886 ■ American Legion, Easton Post 569
48260 225th St.
Easton, MN 56025
Ph: (651)291-1800
Fax: (651)291-1057
URL: National Affiliate–www.legion.org
Local. Affiliated With: American Legion.

Echo

10887 ■ American Legion, Edward Gill Post 204
PO Box 75
Echo, MN 56237
Ph: (651)291-1800
Fax: (651)291-1057
URL: National Affiliate–www.legion.org
Local. Affiliated With: American Legion.

Eden Prairie

10888 ■ Agile Alliance
c/o Robert C. Martin
7666 Carnelian Ln.
Eden Prairie, MN 55346
E-mail: aanponotify@agilealliance.org
URL: http://www.agilealliance.org
Contact: Robert C. Martin, Contact
Local.

10889 ■ Associated Builders and Contractors Minnesota Chapter
c/o Robert T. Heise, CAE, Pres.
10193 Crosstown Cir.
Eden Prairie, MN 55344
Ph: (952)941-8693
Fax: (952)941-8698
E-mail: rheise@mnabc.com
URL: http://www.mnabc.com
Contact: Robert T. Heise CAE, Pres.
Founded: 1976. **Members:** 400. **Staff:** 7. **Budget:** $1,000,000. **Regional Groups:** 2. **State Groups:** 1. **Local**. Promotes merit-based rewards for workers. **Affiliated With:** Associated Builders and Contractors.

10890 ■ Eden Prairie Chamber of Commerce
11455 Viking Dr., Ste.No. 270
Eden Prairie, MN 55344
Ph: (952)944-2830
Fax: (952)944-0229
E-mail: pat.mulqueeny@epchamber.org
URL: http://www.epchamber.org
Contact: Pat MulQueeny, Pres.
Local. Provides their members opportunities for community leadership. Acts as an advocate for commerce. Promotes community growth and development.

10891 ■ Eden Prairie Council for the Gifted and Talented (EPCGT)
17532 Alcove Cir.
Eden Prairie, MN 55347
E-mail: jennifer_urbanski@att.net
URL: http://www.epcgt.org
Contact: Jennifer Urbanski, Pres.
Founded: 1995. **Members:** 100. **Membership Dues:** family, $30. **Local**. Advances interest in programs for the gifted. Seeks to further education of the gifted and enhances their potential creativity. Unites to address the unique needs of children and youth with demonstrated gifts and talents as well as those children who may be able to develop their talent potentials with appropriate educational experiences. Encourages and responds to the diverse expressions

of gifts and talents in children and youth from all cultures, racial and ethnic backgrounds, and socio-economic groups. **Affiliated With:** National Association for Gifted Children.

10892 ■ Eden Prairie Figure Skating Club (EPFSC)
16526 W 78th St.
Eden Prairie, MN 55346
E-mail: president@edenprairiefsc.org
URL: http://www.edenprairiefsc.org
Contact: Paul Hannan, Pres.
Local. Provides programs to encourage participation and achievement in the sport of figure skating on ice. Defines and maintains uniform standards of skating proficiency. Organizes and sponsors competitions and exhibitions for the purpose of stimulating interest in figure skating. **Affiliated With:** United States Figure Skating Association.

10893 ■ Eden Prairie Lions Club
c/o Boyd Wasson, Pres.
7264 Sunshine Dr.
Eden Prairie, MN 55346
Ph: (952)937-7070
E-mail: eplions@mn.rr.com
URL: http://www.eplions.org
Contact: Boyd Wasson, Pres.
Local. Affiliated With: Lions Clubs International.

10894 ■ Minnesota Association of Orthopaedic Technologists
16269 Mayfield Dr.
Eden Prairie, MN 55347
Ph: (612)974-2885 (952)285-5175
Fax: (952)848-0646
E-mail: coopersky@aol.com
URL: National Affiliate–naot.org
Contact: Cheryl Cooper OTC, Contact
State. Promotes continued professional education for members and other orthopedic health care providers. Administers certification examinations. Seeks to enhance public understanding of orthopedics. **Affiliated With:** National Association of Orthopaedic Technologists.

10895 ■ Minnesota Crop Production Retailers (MCPR)
7500 Flying Cloud Dr., Ste.900
Eden Prairie, MN 55344
Ph: (952)253-6244
Fax: (952)835-4774
E-mail: office@mcpr-cca.org
URL: http://www.mcpr-cca.org
Contact: Bill Bond, Exec.Dir.
State.

10896 ■ Minnesota Glass Association (MGA)
7500 Flying Cloud Dr., No. 900
Eden Prairie, MN 55344
Ph: (651)633-8300
Fax: (651)633-8844
E-mail: info@mnglass.org
URL: http://www.mnglass.org
Contact: Rod Ellison, Pres.
State. Affiliated With: National Glass Association.

10897 ■ Minnesota Independent Insurance Agents and Brokers (MIIAB)
c/o Dan Riley, Exec.VP/Acting CEO
7500 Flying Cloud Dr., Ste.900
Eden Prairie, MN 55344
Ph: (952)835-4180
Fax: (952)835-4774
Free: (800)864-3846
E-mail: miia@miia.org
URL: http://www.iiaba.net/mn/default?ContentPreference=MN
Contact: Owen O. Peterson, Pres.
Members: 4,600. **Staff:** 10. **State.** Provides their member agents with products and services; offers professional education courses for independent agency system. **Awards:** Agency of the Year. **Frequency:** annual. **Type:** recognition • Agent of the Year. **Frequency:** annual. **Type:** recognition • Company Award of Excellence. **Type:** recognition • Company Representative of the Year. **Frequency:** annual. **Type:** recognition • Executive Vice President's Award. **Frequency:** annual. **Type:** recognition • Insurance Company Executive of the Year. **Frequency:** annual. **Type:** recognition • President's Award. **Type:** recognition • Retiring Director. **Type:** recognition • Young Agent of the Year. **Frequency:** annual. **Type:** recognition. **Affiliated With:** Insurance Information Institute. **Formerly:** (2004) Minnesota Independent Insurance Agents. **Publications:** *Minnesota Agent*. Newspaper. Features news on insurance industry, education, legislation and state meetings. **Price:** included in membership dues.

10898 ■ Mothers Connection PTA
6813 Woodland Dr.
Eden Prairie, MN 55346
E-mail: themothersconnection@hotmail.com
URL: http://myschoolonline.com/mn/themothersconnection
Contact: Becky Evans, Membership VP
Local. Parents, teachers, students, and others interested in uniting the forces of home, school, and community. Promotes the welfare of children and youth.

10899 ■ North Central Morgan Horse Association
c/o Terry Sanborn, VP
18231 Warbler Ln.
Eden Prairie, MN 55346
Ph: (952)934-5261
E-mail: tshorse@mn.rr.com
URL: http://www.northcentralmorgan.com
Contact: Terry Sanborn, VP
Local. Affiliated With: American Morgan Horse Association.

10900 ■ Prader-Willi Syndrome Association of Minnesota (PWSA-MN)
c/o Denise Westenfield, Pres.
6400 Craig Dr.
Eden Prairie, MN 55346
Ph: (952)949-3631
E-mail: dwestenfield@datalink.com
URL: http://www.pwsausa.org/MN
Contact: Denise Westenfield, Pres.
Membership Dues: $20 (annual). **State.** Dedicated to improving the lives of people affected by Prader-Willi (PWS)Syndrome in the U.S. PWS is a complex genetic disorder that typically causes low muscle tone, short stature, incomplete sexual development, cognitive disabilities, problem behaviors, and a chronic feeling of hunger that can lead to excessive eating and life-threatening obesity. Represents people with PWS, their families, friends, and caregivers in Minnesota. Seeks to offer information and support to one another and to foster public awareness of this syndrome. **Affiliated With:** Prader-Willi Syndrome Association (U.S.A.).

10901 ■ Skills USA, Independent District 287
13100 Coll. View Dr.
Eden Prairie, MN 55347
Ph: (952)995-1300
Fax: (952)995-1382
E-mail: tod.hoaby@hennepintech.edu
URL: http://www.mnskillsusa.org
Contact: Tod Hoaby, Contact
Local. Serves high school and college students enrolled in technical, skilled, and service and health occupations. Provides quality education experiences for students in leadership, teamwork, citizenship and character development. Builds and reinforces self-confidence, work attitudes and communication skills. Emphasizes total quality at work, high ethical standards, superior work skills, and life-long education. Promotes understanding of the free enterprise system and involvement in community service. **Affiliated With:** Skills USA - VICA.

10902 ■ Starlight Ice Dance Club
11731 Shannon Ct., No. 1113
Eden Prairie, MN 55344
E-mail: schacko@mn.rr.com
URL: http://www.geocities.com/starlighticedance
Contact: Susan Chacko, Contact
Local. Provides programs to encourage participation and achievement in the sport of figure skating on ice. Defines and maintains uniform standards of skating proficiency. Organizes and sponsors competitions and exhibitions for the purpose of stimulating interest in figure skating. **Affiliated With:** United States Figure Skating Association.

Eden Valley

10903 ■ American Legion, Eden Valley Post 381
PO Box 337
Eden Valley, MN 55329
Ph: (651)291-1800
Fax: (651)291-1057
URL: National Affiliate–www.legion.org
Local. Affiliated With: American Legion.

10904 ■ Eden Valley Lions Club
746 State St. S
Eden Valley, MN 55329-1111
Ph: (320)453-8193
E-mail: peggyb@meltel.net
URL: http://www.lionwap.org/edenvalleylionsmn
Contact: Harold Bethel, Sec.
Local. Affiliated With: Lions Clubs International.

Edgerton

10905 ■ Sons of Norway, Stenlandet Lodge 1-640
c/o Ethelyn C. Fey, Sec.
2454 160th Ave.
Edgerton, MN 56128
Ph: (507)442-8822
E-mail: efey@frontiernet.net
URL: National Affiliate–www.sofn.com
Contact: Ethelyn C. Fey, Sec.
Local. Affiliated With: Sons of Norway.

Edina

10906 ■ ACF Minneapolis Chapter
c/o Christopher J. Dwyer, CEC, Pres.
405 Adams Ave. S
Edina, MN 55343
Ph: (612)659-6030
Fax: (612)659-6825
E-mail: chefgadget@aol.com
URL: National Affiliate–www.acfchefs.org
Contact: Christopher J. Dwyer CEC, Pres.
Local. Promotes the culinary profession. Provides on-going educational training and networking for members. Provides opportunities for competition, professional recognition and access to educational forums with other culinarians at local, regional, national and international events. **Affiliated With:** American Culinary Federation.

10907 ■ Braemar-City of Lakes Figure Skating Club
7501 Ikola Way
Edina, MN 55439
Ph: (952)941-2082
E-mail: info@braemarfsc.org
URL: http://www.braemarfsc.org
Local. Provides programs to encourage participation and achievement in the sport of figure skating on ice. Defines and maintains uniform standards of skating proficiency. Organizes and sponsors competitions and exhibitions for the purpose of stimulating interest in figure skating. **Affiliated With:** United States Figure Skating Association.

10908 ■ Centennial Lakes Lawn Bowling Club
7499 France Ave.
Edina, MN 55435-4702
Ph: (612)893-9890
E-mail: ron@tseg.com
URL: National Affiliate–www.bowlsamerica.org
Local. Affiliated With: United States Lawn Bowls Association.

10909 ■ Edina Lions Club
c/o Jerry Johnson, Pres.
4620 Valley View Rd.
Edina, MN 55424
Ph: (952)925-6118
URL: http://www.5m5.org
Contact: Jerry Johnson, Pres.
Local. Affiliated With: Lions Clubs International.

10910 ■ Greater Metropolitan Automobile Dealers Association of Minnesota (GMADA)
7300 Metro Blvd., Ste.540
Edina, MN 55439
Ph: (952)831-8019
Fax: (952)831-7687
E-mail: staff@gmada.com
URL: http://www.gmada.com
Contact: Mr. William E. Abraham, Pres.
State.

10911 ■ Hiawatha Valley Sail and Power Squadron (HVSPS)
c/o Lt. Bobbie Moesle, Ed.
4509 Claremore Ct.
Edina, MN 55435
E-mail: moesealong@aol.com
URL: http://www.hiawathavalleyps.org
Contact: Lt. Bobbie Moesle, Ed.
Local. Affiliated With: United States Power Squadrons.

10912 ■ In His Presence
c/o Pam Loffhagen
5801 Jeff Pl.
Edina, MN 55436-1937
Local.

10913 ■ Job Transition Support Group
c/o Colonial Church of Edina
6200 Colonial Way
Edina, MN 55436
Ph: (952)925-2711
Fax: (952)925-1591
E-mail: pberry@colonialchurch.org
URL: http://www.colonialchurch.org
Contact: Paula Berry, Ministry Asst.
Founded: 1978. **Members:** 25. **Local Groups:** 1. **Local.** Unemployed and underemployed in Minneapolis/St. Paul, Minnesota area. Provides support, encouragement, and resources. **Conventions/Meetings:** weekly support group meeting.

10914 ■ Legislative Efforts for Animal Protection
c/o Cristy Gaffney Kruse
PMB 102, 5021 Vernon Ave.
Edina, MN 55436
Ph: (952)903-4999
E-mail: leap@leap-mn.org

10915 ■ March of Dimes Minnesota Chapter
c/o Michele Clarke, Exec.Dir.
Pakwa Bus. Park
5233 Edina Indus. Blvd.
Edina, MN 55439
Ph: (952)835-3033
Fax: (952)835-8661
E-mail: mn631@marchofdimes.com
URL: http://www.modimesmn.org
Contact: Michele Clarke, Exec.Dir.
State. Voluntary health organization that has as its mission the prevention of birth defects and infant mortality through research, advocacy, community service, and educational programs.

10916 ■ Minneapolis Area Association of Realtors
5750 Lincoln Dr.
Edina, MN 55436
Ph: (952)933-9020
Fax: (952)933-9021
URL: http://www.mplsrealtor.com
Contact: Mark Allen, CEO
Local. Strives to develop real estate business practices. Advocates the right to own, use and transfer real property. Provides a facility for professional development, research and exchange of information among members. **Affiliated With:** National Association of Realtors.

10917 ■ Minnesota Association of Mortgage Brokers (MAMB)
c/o Patrick Martyn, Exec.Dir.
5200 Willson Rd., Ste.300
Edina, MN 55424
Ph: (952)345-3240
Fax: (952)920-1533
E-mail: martyninc@aol.com
URL: http://www.mnamb.org
Contact: Patrick Martyn, Exec.Dir.
State.

10918 ■ Minnesota Association of Realtors (MNAR)
5750 Lincoln Dr.
Edina, MN 55436
Ph: (952)935-8313
Fax: (952)935-3815
Free: (800)862-6097
E-mail: info@mnrealtor.com
URL: http://www.mnrealtor.com
Contact: Glenn Dorfman CAE, COO
State.

10919 ■ Minnesota Association for Supervision and Curriculum Development
c/o Lori Sandvig, Exec.Sec.
5033 W 56th St.
Edina, MN 55436
Ph: (952)920-9123
Fax: (952)920-9123
E-mail: lori@isarep.com
URL: http://www.mnascd.org
Contact: Lori Sandvig, Exec.Sec.
State. Advocates policies and practices that positively influence learning, teaching and leadership in education. Provides programs, services and professional development for effective teaching and learning. **Affiliated With:** Association for Supervision and Curriculum Development.

10920 ■ Minnesota Bankers Association (MBA)
c/o Joe Witt, Pres./CEO
7601 France Ave. S, Ste.200
Edina, MN 55435
Ph: (952)835-3900
Fax: (952)896-1100
Free: (866)835-3900
E-mail: mba@minnbankers.com
URL: http://www.minnbankers.com
Contact: Joe Witt, Pres./CEO
Founded: 1889. **State.**

10921 ■ Minnesota Council for the Gifted and Talented (MCGT)
5701 Normandale Rd., Ste.315
Edina, MN 55424
Ph: (952)848-4906
E-mail: jamie.thorp@mcgt.net
URL: http://www.mcgt.net
Contact: Jamie Thorp, Sec.
Membership Dues: regular / family, $30. **State.** Advances interest in programs for the gifted. Seeks to further education of the gifted and enhances their potential creativity. Unites to address the unique needs of children and youth with demonstrated gifts and talents as well as those children who may be able to develop their talent potentials with appropriate educational experiences. Encourages and responds to the diverse expressions of gifts and talents in children and youth from all cultures, racial and ethnic backgrounds, and socioeconomic groups. **Affiliated With:** National Association for Gifted Children.

10922 ■ Minnesota Golf Association (MGA)
6550 York Ave. S, Ste.211
Edina, MN 55435
Ph: (952)927-4643 (952)345-3971
Fax: (952)927-9642
Free: (800)642-4405
E-mail: info@mngolf.org
URL: http://www.mngolf.org
Contact: Tom Ryan, Exec.Dir./COO
Founded: 1901. **State.**

10923 ■ Minnesota Nurses Association - District 3
4445 W 77th St., Ste.121
Edina, MN 55435
Ph: (952)920-9860
Fax: (952)920-8689
E-mail: info@nursesce.com
URL: http://www.nursesce.com
Contact: Cheryl Ernst, Pres.
Local. Works to advance the nursing profession. Seeks to meet the needs of nurses and health care consumers. Fosters high standards of nursing practice. Promotes the economic and general welfare of nurses in the workplace. **Affiliated With:** American Nurses Association; Minnesota Nurses Association.

10924 ■ Minnesota Workers' Compensation Insurers Association (MWCIA)
c/o Bruce Tollefson, Pres.
7701 France Ave. S, Ste.450
Edina, MN 55435
Ph: (952)897-1737
Fax: (952)897-6495
E-mail: info@mwcia.org
URL: http://www.mwcia.org
Contact: Bruce Tollefson, Pres.
State.

10925 ■ Pontiac-Oakland Club International, Tomahawk Chapter 13
c/o Jim Felker, Treas.
5500 Merritt Cir.
Edina, MN 55436
E-mail: tomahawk13@sprynet.com
URL: http://www.tomahawkpontiacclub.org
Contact: Jim Felker, Treas.
Membership Dues: individual, $20 (annual). **Local. Affiliated With:** Pontiac-Oakland Club International.

10926 ■ Resolve of Minnesota
7455 France Ave., Ste.267
Edina, MN 55435
Ph: (651)659-0333
Free: (888)959-0333
E-mail: info@resolvemn.org
URL: http://www.resolvemn.org
Membership Dues: basic, $55 (annual) • contributing, $65 (annual) • supporting, $75 (annual) • circle of friend, $100 (annual) • professional, $150 (annual). **State. Affiliated With:** Resolve, The National Infertility Association. **Formerly:** (2005) Resolve of Minnesota, Minnesota.

10927 ■ Tango Society of Minnesota
c/o Lois Donnay
PO Box 24044
Edina, MN 55424
Ph: (763)576-3349
E-mail: tsom@mntango.org
URL: http://www.mntango.org
Contact: John MacFarlane, Pres.
Founded: 1998. **Members:** 135. **Membership Dues:** $20 (annual). **Languages:** English, Spanish. **State.** Promotes Argentine Tango in Minnesota. **Publications:** *TSOM Newsletter*, bimonthly. **Price:** free. **Circulation:** 200. **Advertising:** accepted.

10928 ■ Twin City Healthcare Engineering Association (TCHEA)
c/o Dave Fashant, Pres.
Fairview Southdale Hosp.
6401 France Ave. S
Edina, MN 55435
Ph: (952)924-5015
Fax: (951)924-1501
E-mail: dfashan1@fairview.org
URL: National Affiliate–www.ashe.org
Contact: Dave Fashant, Pres.
Local. Promotes better patient care by encouraging members to develop their knowledge and increase their competence in the field of facilities management. Cooperates with hospitals and allied associations in matters pertaining to facilities management. **Affiliated With:** American Society for Healthcare Engineering of the American Hospital Association.

10929 ■ Windians Cricket Club
5520 Interlachen Blvd., Apt. 2
Edina, MN 55436
URL: http://www.usaca.org/Clubs.htm
Contact: Remy Ramadhar, Contact
Local.

Effie

10930 ■ American Legion, Waldron-Flaat Post 182
PO Box 83
Effie, MN 56639
Ph: (651)291-1800
Fax: (651)291-1057
URL: National Affiliate–www.legion.org
Local. Affiliated With: American Legion.

10931 ■ Big Fork Lions Club
c/o Bill Hastings, Pres.
PO Box 68
Effie, MN 56639-0068
Ph: (218)743-3870
URL: http://lions5m10.org
Contact: Bill Hastings, Pres.
Local. Affiliated With: Lions Clubs International.

10932 ■ Society of American Foresters, Minnesota
PO Box 95
Effie, MN 56639-0095
Ph: (218)743-3694
Fax: (218)743-1942
E-mail: admin@mnsaf.org
URL: http://www.mnsaf.org
Contact: Greg Russell, Chair
State. Affiliated With: Society of American Foresters.

Eitzen

10933 ■ Eitzen Lions Club
c/o Leon Feil, Sec.
Box 476
Eitzen, MN 55931
Ph: (507)495-3197
E-mail: lfeil@acegroup.cc
URL: http://www.lions5m1.org/eitzen
Contact: Leon Feil, Sec.
Local. Affiliated With: Lions Clubs International.

Elbow Lake

10934 ■ American Legion, Minnesota Post 321
c/o Carl A. Hanson
PO Box 418
Elbow Lake, MN 56531
Ph: (651)291-1800
Fax: (651)291-1057
URL: National Affiliate–www.legion.org
Contact: Carl A. Hanson, Contact
Local. Affiliated With: American Legion.

10935 ■ Elbow Lake Lions Club
c/o Carlin Berg, Pres.
PO Box 382
Elbow Lake, MN 56531
Ph: (218)685-4901
E-mail: bbcb@runestone.net
URL: http://www.5m4lions.org
Contact: Carlin Berg, Pres.
Local. Affiliated With: Lions Clubs International.

10936 ■ Grant County Historical Society
PO Box 1002
115 2nd Ave. NE
Elbow Lake, MN 56531
Ph: (218)685-4864
E-mail: gcmnhist@runestone.net
URL: http://www.rootsweb.com/~mngrant/hist.htm
Contact: Patricia Benson, Curator
Founded: 1944. **Members:** 140. **Membership Dues:** individual, $15 (annual) • family, $25 (annual). **Staff:** 1. **Budget:** $24,000. **Local.** Collects and preserves the history of Grant County, Minnesota. Genealogical Resource also available. **Libraries: Type:** open to the public. **Holdings:** 500; books, photographs. **Subjects:** local history, genealogy. **Also Known As:** Grant County Museum.

10937 ■ Midwest Manufacturers' Association
PO Box 150
Elbow Lake, MN 56531
Ph: (218)685-5356
Fax: (218)685-5397
Free: (800)654-5773
E-mail: midwest@runestone.net
Contact: Sandy Kashmark, Exec.Dir.
Founded: 1989. **Members:** 204. **Membership Dues:** regular, $125-$350 (annual). **Staff:** 1. **Regional.** Promotes the growth and success of manufacturers throughout the Upper Midwest region. Seeks to foster the creation, growth, and success of manufacturers' association or trade groups that share in this mission. **Formerly:** (2003) Tri-State Manufacturers' Association. **Publications:** *The Network News*, monthly. Newsletter. **Price:** free. **Advertising:** accepted. **Conventions/Meetings:** monthly meeting - always first Tuesday.

10938 ■ Minnesota Rural Water Association (MRWA)
217 12th Ave. SE
Elbow Lake, MN 56531
Ph: (218)685-5197
Fax: (218)685-5272
E-mail: mrwa@mrwa.com
URL: http://www.mrwa.com
Contact: Ruth Hubbard, Administrator
State.

10939 ■ West Central Minnesota RSVP
c/o Karen Alvstad, Dir.
411 Indus. Park Blvd.
Elbow Lake, MN 56531
Ph: (218)685-4486
Fax: (218)685-6741
E-mail: rsvp@co.grant.mn.us
URL: http://www.seniorcorps.gov
Contact: Karen Alvstad, Dir.
Local. Additional Websites: http://www.wcmca.org. **Affiliated With:** Retired and Senior Volunteer Program.

Elgin

10940 ■ American Legion, Elgin Post 573
PO Box 144
Elgin, MN 55932
Ph: (651)291-1800
Fax: (651)291-1057
URL: National Affiliate–www.legion.org
Local. Affiliated With: American Legion.

10941 ■ Elgin Lions Club
c/o Henry Schroeder, Pres.
Box 134
Elgin, MN 55932
Ph: (507)876-2209
URL: http://www.lions5m1.org/elgin
Contact: Henry Schroeder, Pres.
Local. Affiliated With: Lions Clubs International.

Elk River

10942 ■ Air and Waste Management Association - Upper Midwest Section
c/o Mark Strohfus
PO Box 800
Elk River, MN 55330-0800
Ph: (763)241-2491
Fax: (763)241-6033
E-mail: mstrohfus@grenergy.com
URL: http://www.awma-ums.org
Contact: Mark Strohfus, Contact
Regional. Affiliated With: Air and Waste Management Association.

10943 ■ American Legion, Davis-Darrow-Meyer Post 112
PO Box 26
Elk River, MN 55330
Ph: (651)291-1800
Fax: (651)291-1057
URL: National Affiliate–www.legion.org
Local. Affiliated With: American Legion.

10944 ■ Caring Rivers United Way
PO Box 36
Elk River, MN 55330
Ph: (763)633-5886
E-mail: margaret.ostman@unitedway.org
URL: http://www.caringrivers.org
Local. Affiliated With: United Way of America.

10945 ■ Elk River Area Chamber of Commerce (ERACC)
509 Hwy. 10
Elk River, MN 55330-1415
Ph: (763)441-3110
Fax: (763)441-3409
E-mail: eracc@elkriverchamber.org
URL: http://www.elkriverchamber.org
Contact: Jeffrey A. Gongoll, Pres.
Founded: 1968. **Members:** 380. **Membership Dues:** business, $215-$1,150 (annual) • financial institution (minimum; $15 per million in total assets), $300 (annual) • associate, $110 (annual). **Local.** Promotes business and community development in the Elk River, MN area. **Computer Services:** Online services, members directory. **Committees:** Ambassadors; Economic Development; Education; Government Action; Marketing and Public Relations; Membership and Retention; Programs; Special Events. **Publications:** *City Map*. Directory. **Circulation:** 10,000. **Advertising:** accepted • Membership Directory. **Circulation:** 1,000 • Directory, annual • Newsletter, monthly. **Circulation:** 600. **Conventions/Meetings:** monthly meeting, with speakers - third Tuesday, except July and August.

10946 ■ Elk River Lions Club
PO Box 736
Elk River, MN 55330
E-mail: info@elkriverlions.org
URL: http://www.elkriverlions.org
Contact: Tony Mikols, Pres.
Local. Affiliated With: Lions Clubs International.

10947 ■ Greater Twin Cities St. Bernard Club
9033 194th Ln. NW
Elk River, MN 55330
Ph: (763)441-2204 (763)576-1415
E-mail: debbie@gentleinc.com
URL: National Affiliate–www.saintbernardclub.org
Contact: Rob-Lyn Hiltz, Chm.
Local.

10948 ■ Hopkins Noontime Lions Club
c/o Colleen DeMars, Pres.
526 Roosevelt Cir.
Elk River, MN 55330
Ph: (763)441-8009
URL: http://www.5m5.org
Contact: Colleen DeMars, Pres.
Local. Affiliated With: Lions Clubs International.

10949 ■ Suburban Northwest Builders Association (SNBA)
c/o Sharon Kampa, Exec.Dir.
19365 Zumbro Ct.
Elk River, MN 55330
Ph: (763)241-9536
Fax: (763)241-8454
E-mail: skampa@snbaonline.com
URL: http://www.snbaonline.com
Contact: Sharon Kampa, Exec.Dir.
Membership Dues: general, $475 (annual). **Local.** Single and multifamily home builders, commercial builders, and others associated with the building industry. **Committees:** Energy House; Golf Tournament; Home and Landscape Show; New Home Tour. **Affiliated With:** National Association of Home Builders. **Publications:** Magazine • Membership Directory • Newsletter.

Ellendale

10950 ■ American Legion, Fidelity Post 296
PO Box 275
Ellendale, MN 56026
Ph: (651)291-1800
Fax: (651)291-1057
URL: National Affiliate–www.legion.org
Local. Affiliated With: American Legion.

Ellsworth

10951 ■ American Legion, Minnesota Post 196
c/o Gilbert Larson
30053 Ahlers Ave.
Ellsworth, MN 56129
Ph: (651)291-1800
Fax: (651)291-1057
URL: National Affiliate–www.legion.org
Contact: Gilbert Larson, Contact
Local. Affiliated With: American Legion.

Elmore

10952 ■ American Legion, Sanford Post 192
PO Box 42
Elmore, MN 56027
Ph: (651)291-1800
Fax: (651)291-1057
URL: National Affiliate–www.legion.org
Local. Affiliated With: American Legion.

Ely

10953 ■ American Legion, Lozar-Mrace-Loushin Post 248
30 S 1st Ave. E, No. 10
Ely, MN 55731
Ph: (651)291-1800
Fax: (651)291-1057
URL: National Affiliate–www.legion.org
Local. Affiliated With: American Legion.

10954 ■ Ely Chamber of Commerce (ECC)
1600 E Sheridan St.
Ely, MN 55731
Ph: (218)365-6123
Fax: (218)365-5929
Free: (800)777-7281
E-mail: fun@ely.org
URL: http://www.ely.org
Contact: Linda Fryer, Admin.Dir.
Founded: 1908. **Members:** 170. **Membership Dues:** regular, $100-$550 (annual). **Staff:** 6. **For-Profit. Local.** Promotes business and tourism in Ely, MN. Sponsors Blueberry Art Festival and Fall Harvest Moon Festival. **Publications:** *Vacation Guide*, annual. Directory. **Price:** free.

10955 ■ Ely Lions Club
c/o Patrick Koschak, Pres.
1125 E Camp St.
Ely, MN 55731
Ph: (218)365-5786
URL: http://lions5m10.org
Contact: Patrick Koschak, Pres.
Local. Affiliated With: Lions Clubs International.

10956 ■ National Active and Retired Federal Employees Association - Vermilion 1725
745 E Camp St.
Ely, MN 55731-1605
Ph: (218)365-3091
URL: National Affiliate–www.narfe.org
Contact: Donald E. Church, Contact
Local. Protects the retirement future of employees through education. Informs members on issues affecting the retirement. **Affiliated With:** National Association of Retired Federal Employees.

10957 ■ Ruffed Grouse Society, Crazy Flight Chapter
c/o John Schiltz
101 W Sheridan
Ely, MN 55731
Ph: (218)365-6084
E-mail: wyatt@rangenet.com
URL: National Affiliate–www.ruffedgrousesociety.org
Contact: John Schiltz, Contact
Local. Affiliated With: Ruffed Grouse Society.

10958 ■ Society of American Foresters, Vermilion Community College Student Chapter
c/o Lori Schmidt, Chair
1900 E Camp St.
Ely, MN 55731
Ph: (218)365-7242
E-mail: l.schmidt@vcc.edu
URL: http://www.mnsaf.org
Contact: Lori Schmidt, Chair
Local. Affiliated With: Society of American Foresters.

10959 ■ Tower-Soudan Lions Club
c/o Rogr Lamppa, Pres.
1272 Walsh Rd.
Ely, MN 55731
Ph: (218)365-5452
URL: http://lions5m10.org
Contact: Rogr Lamppa, Pres.
Local. Affiliated With: Lions Clubs International.

10960 ■ Young Life Ely
34 S 2nd Ave. E, Ste.204
Ely, MN 55731
Ph: (218)365-7472
E-mail: rbhunte@juno.com
URL: http://sites.younglife.org/sites/ElyYL/default.aspx
Contact: Ryan Hunter, Area Dir.
Local. Affiliated With: Young Life.

Elysian

10961 ■ American Legion, C.-Adams-R-Stierlen Post 311
104 E Main St.
Elysian, MN 56028
Ph: (651)291-1800
Fax: (651)291-1057
URL: National Affiliate–www.legion.org
Local. Affiliated With: American Legion.

Emmons

10962 ■ American Legion, Louis Tveite Post 317
PO Box 81
Emmons, MN 56029
Ph: (651)291-1800
Fax: (651)291-1057
URL: National Affiliate–www.legion.org
Local. Affiliated With: American Legion.

Erskine

10963 ■ American Legion, Bailey-Throne Post 596
PO Box 63
Erskine, MN 56535
Ph: (651)291-1800
Fax: (651)291-1057
URL: National Affiliate–www.legion.org
Local. Affiliated With: American Legion.

10964 ■ Erskine Lions Club
c/o Lisa Stuhaug, Pres.
PO Box 86
Erskine, MN 56535
Ph: (218)687-2289
URL: http://lions5m11.org/sys-tmpl/door
Contact: Lisa Stuhaug, Pres.
Local. Affiliated With: Lions Clubs International.

Esko

10965 ■ Sons of Norway, Heimsyn Lodge 1-15
c/o Nancy E. Brekke, Pres.
96 W Palkie Rd.
Esko, MN 55733-9718
Ph: (218)879-6511
E-mail: albrekke@juno.com
URL: National Affiliate–www.sofn.com
Contact: Nancy E. Brekke, Pres.
Local. Affiliated With: Sons of Norway.

Euclid

10966 ■ American Legion, Euclid Post 539
23861 130th St. SW
Euclid, MN 56722
Ph: (651)291-1800
Fax: (651)291-1057
URL: National Affiliate–www.legion.org
Local. Affiliated With: American Legion.

Evansville

10967 ■ American Legion, West Douglas County Post 188
PO Box 416
Evansville, MN 56326
Ph: (651)291-1800
Fax: (651)291-1057
URL: National Affiliate–www.legion.org
Local. Affiliated With: American Legion.

Eveleth

10968 ■ Eveleth Lions Club
c/o Kelly Klander, Pres.
304 Monroe St.
Eveleth, MN 55734
Ph: (218)744-0711
E-mail: kklander@grecorp.com
URL: http://lions5m10.org
Contact: Kelly Klander, Pres.
Local. Affiliated With: Lions Clubs International.

Excelsior

10969 ■ Edina Model Yacht Club No. 192
c/o Tony Johnson
80 Florence Dr.
Excelsior, MN 55331
Ph: (952)470-8818
URL: http://www.emyc.org
Contact: Tony Johnson, Contact
Local.

10970 ■ Freshwater Society
c/o Donald Brauer
2500 Shadywood Rd.
Excelsior, MN 55331
Ph: (952)471-9773
Fax: (952)471-7685
Free: (888)471-9773
E-mail: dbrauer@freshwater.org
URL: http://www.freshwater.org
Contact: Donald Brauer, Exec.Dir.
Local.

10971 ■ South Shore Lions Club
c/o Marvin TenClay
19655 Vine St.
Excelsior, MN 55331
Ph: (952)474-3924
URL: http://www.5m5.org
Contact: Marvin TenClay, Contact
Local. Affiliated With: Lions Clubs International.

Eyota

10972 ■ American Legion, Eyota Post 551
11 Madison SW
Eyota, MN 55934
Ph: (651)291-1800
Fax: (651)291-1057
URL: National Affiliate–www.legion.org
Local. Affiliated With: American Legion.

Fairfax

10973 ■ American Legion, Buehler-Bruggeman-Mantel Post 205
PO Box 517
Fairfax, MN 55332
Ph: (651)291-1800
Fax: (651)291-1057
URL: National Affiliate–www.legion.org
Local. Affiliated With: American Legion.

10974 ■ Fairfax Lions Club
c/o Dennis Schweiss, Pres.
RR 1, Box 1A
Fairfax, MN 55332
Ph: (507)426-7010
URL: http://www.5m4lions.org
Contact: Dennis Schweiss, Pres.
Local. Affiliated With: Lions Clubs International.

Fairmont

10975 ■ Alcoholics Anonymous
1131 N North Ave.
Fairmont, MN 56031
Ph: (507)238-2114
Local.

10976 ■ American Legion, Lee C. Prentice Post 36
106 E 1st St.
Fairmont, MN 56031
Ph: (651)291-1800
Fax: (651)291-1057
URL: National Affiliate–www.legion.org
Local. Affiliated With: American Legion.

10977 ■ Fairmont Area Chamber of Commerce (FACC)
206 N State St.
PO Box 826
Fairmont, MN 56031-0826
Ph: (507)235-5547
Fax: (507)235-8411
E-mail: chamber@fairmont.org
URL: http://www.fairmont.org
Contact: Bob Wallace, Pres.
Founded: 1947. **Members:** 400. **Membership Dues:** general business, professional, health care facility, non-profit municipal organization with paid employee (minimum), $232 (annual) • individual, agriculture, out of town business, $232 (annual) • hotel and motel (plus $14 per unit over 10), $232 (annual) • non-profit organization without paid employees, $118 (annual) • retired, $72 (annual) • bank (minimum; per million in deposits), $40 (annual). **Local.** Promotes business and community development in the Fairmont, MN area. **Computer Services:** Online services, business listings. **Committees:** Agri-Business; Ambassadors; Bureau 14; Business/Education Partnership; Glows; Governmental Affairs; Retail; Tourism. **Affiliated With:** U.S. Chamber of Commerce. **Publications:** *Chamber Update*, monthly. Newsletter. **Price:** free. **Conventions/Meetings:** annual banquet.

10978 ■ Fairmont Convention and Visitors Bureau
1201 Torgerson Dr.
Fairmont, MN 56031
Ph: (507)235-8585
E-mail: director@fairmontcvb.com
URL: http://www.fairmontcvb.com
Contact: Kathy Silverthorn, Exec. Officer
Founded: 1991. **Members:** 6. **Staff:** 2. **Budget:** $70,000. **State Groups:** 1. **Local.** Promotes tourism and conventions in Fairmont, MN.

10979 ■ Martin County Historical Society (MCHS)
304 E Blue Earth Ave.
Fairmont, MN 56031
Ph: (507)235-5178
Fax: (507)235-5179
E-mail: mch@frontiernet.net
URL: http://www.co.martin.mn.us/mchs
Contact: Lenny Tvedten, Exec.Dir.
Founded: 1929. **Members:** 1,008. **Membership Dues:** individual, family, corporation, $25-$1,000 (annual). **Staff:** 4. **Budget:** $81,500. **Local.** Preserves and interpret local history in a meaningful and articulate manner. Members are located locally, throughout the United States, Canada, and England. Activities include genealogy, research, tours, and power point presentations both on and off site. **Libraries: Type:** open to the public; reference. **Holdings:** audio recordings, biographical archives, business records, maps, photographs, video recordings. **Subjects:** picture files, history files, city and telephone directories dating back to the early 1900's, antique furniture and furnishings, historic clothing and signs, historic transportation including buggies, cars, trucks, and fire engines, microfilmed county newspapers dating back to 1874, obituaries, family and church histories, antique musical instruments, toys and carpenter tools, and school records. **Publications:** *Martin County Historical Society Newsletter*, 3/year. **Conventions/Meetings:** annual meeting - always September.

10980 ■ Minnesota Professional Photographers Association (MPPA)
c/o Pam Carlson, Exec.Sec.
525 Tilden St.
Fairmont, MN 56031
Fax: (507)238-2969
Free: (800)362-5855
E-mail: info@mnppa.com
URL: http://www.mnppa.com
Contact: Pam Carlson, Exec.Sec.
State. Professional society of portrait, wedding, commercial, and industrial, and specialized photographers. **Affiliated With:** Professional Photographers of America.

10981 ■ United Way of Fairmont
PO Box 102
Fairmont, MN 56031-0102
Ph: (507)235-9342
URL: National Affiliate–national.unitedway.org
Local. Affiliated With: United Way of America.

Faribault

10982 ■ American Legion, Minnesota Post 43
c/o Kenneth F. Kingsley
112 5th St. NE
Faribault, MN 55021
Ph: (651)291-1800
Fax: (651)291-1057
URL: National Affiliate–www.legion.org
Contact: Kenneth F. Kingsley, Contact
Local. Affiliated With: American Legion.

10983 ■ American Red Cross, Rice-LeSueur Counties Chapter
421 Central Ave.
Faribault, MN 55021
Ph: (507)334-8471
Fax: (507)334-8541
URL: http://www.rlsredcross.org
Local.

10984 ■ Catholics United for the Faith - St. Peter the Rock Chapter
c/o Daniel Milbert
22425 Dahle Ave.
Faribault, MN 55021
Ph: (507)334-7526
URL: National Affiliate–www.cuf.org
Contact: Daniel Milbert, Contact
Local.

10985 ■ Faribault Area Chamber of Commerce (FACC)
530 Wilson Ave.
PO Box 434
Faribault, MN 55021-0434
Ph: (507)334-4381
Fax: (507)334-1003
Free: (800)658-2354
E-mail: chamber@faribaultmn.org
URL: http://www.faribaultmn.org
Contact: Kymn Anderson, Pres.
Founded: 1920. **Members:** 450. **Staff:** 4. **Budget:** $195,000. **Local.** Promotes agricultural, business, and community development in the Faribault, MN area. Promotes tourism. Holds annual Heritage Days festival and Balloon Rally. Business Expo - yearly. **Awards:** Business of the Year Award. **Frequency:** annual. **Type:** recognition • Partnership in Education Award. **Frequency:** annual. **Type:** recognition. **Computer Services:** Online services, member listings. **Committees:** Agribusiness; Ambassadors; Downtown; Education; Expo; Faribault's Future; Government Affairs; Job Service Employers. **Affiliated With:** American Chamber of Commerce Executives; U.S. Chamber of Commerce. **Publications:** *Chamber Members Directory*, periodic. **Price:** $100.00 • *Manufacturers Directory*, periodic • *Organizational Directory*, periodic • *Products and Services Directory*, annual • Newsletter, monthly. **Advertising:** accepted. **Conventions/Meetings:** annual Business Farm Luncheon • annual Golf Social - competition • annual Taste of Faribault - festival.

10986 ■ Phi Theta Kappa, Beta Nu Beta Chapter - South Central Technical College
c/o Alan Bronnenberg
1225 3rd St. SW
Faribault, MN 55021
Ph: (507)332-5849
E-mail: al.bronnenberg@southcentral.edu
URL: http://www.ptk.org/directories/chapters/MN/22254-1.htm
Contact: Alan Bronnenberg, Advisor
Local.

10987 ■ Sons of Norway, Nordmarka Lodge 1-585
c/o Carol M. Quail, Sec.
728 Colonial Cir.
Faribault, MN 55021-5724
Ph: (507)334-7113
URL: National Affiliate–www.sofn.com
Contact: Carol M. Quail, Sec.
Local. Affiliated With: Sons of Norway.

10988 ■ United Way of Faribault
303 1st Ave. NE, Ste.No. 370
Faribault, MN 55021-0644
Ph: (507)334-0660
URL: National Affiliate–national.unitedway.org
Local. Affiliated With: United Way of America.

Farmington

10989 ■ American Legion, Minnesota Post 189
c/o Clifford Larson
PO Box 186
Farmington, MN 55024
Ph: (651)291-1800
Fax: (651)291-1057
URL: National Affiliate–www.legion.org
Contact: Clifford Larson, Contact
Local. Affiliated With: American Legion.

10990 ■ Farmington Area Chamber of Commerce
PO Box 252
Farmington, MN 55024
Ph: (651)460-6444
Fax: (651)460-2434
E-mail: fgtncham@frontiernet.net
Contact: Marg Van Dale, Co-Chm.
Members: 90. **For-Profit. Local.** Promotes business and community development in Farmington, MN. **Awards:** Business Person of the Year. **Frequency:** annual. **Type:** recognition. **Recipient:** community nomination • Citizen of the Year. **Frequency:** annual. **Type:** recognition. **Recipient:** community nomination. **Boards:** Directors. **Publications:** *Chamber Update*, monthly. Newsletter. **Conventions/Meetings:** monthly board meeting.

10991 ■ Tri-County Figure Skating Club (TCFSA)
114 W Spruce St.
Farmington, MN 55024
Ph: (651)463-2510
E-mail: suppes@integraonline.com
URL: http://tricountyfsc.org
Contact: Matt Piller, Contact
Local. Provides programs to encourage participation and achievement in the sport of figure skating on ice. Defines and maintains uniform standards of skating proficiency. Organizes and sponsors competitions and exhibitions for the purpose of stimulating interest in figure skating. **Affiliated With:** United States Figure Skating Association.

10992 ■ USA Weightlifting - Farmington
c/o Scott Meier
800 Denmark Ave.
Farmington, MN 55024
Ph: (651)460-1919
E-mail: smeier@farmington.k12.mn.us
URL: National Affiliate–www.usaweightlifting.org
Contact: Scott Meier, Contact
Local. Affiliated With: USA Weightlifting.

Fergus Falls

10993 ■ Alzheimer's Association-Fergus Falls Center
c/o Darlene Akerman, Center Dir.
210 N Cascade St.
Fergus Falls, MN 56537
Ph: (218)739-2760
Fax: (218)998-9178
E-mail: darlene.akerman@alz.org
URL: http://www.alzmndak.org
Contact: Darlene Akerman, Center Dir.
Local.

10994 ■ American Legion, Adamson-Norman Post 30
2010 S Pebble Lake Rd.
Fergus Falls, MN 56537
Ph: (651)291-1800
Fax: (651)291-1057
URL: National Affiliate–www.legion.org
Local. Affiliated With: American Legion.

10995 ■ American Theatre Organ Society, Central Minnesota Chapter
c/o Richard C. Baker, MD, Pres.
22630 N Swan Lake Rd.
Fergus Falls, MN 56537
Ph: (218)736-3006
E-mail: rbaksr@prtel.com
URL: National Affiliate–www.atos.org
Contact: Richard C. Baker MD, Pres.
Local. Aims to restore, preserve and promote the theatre pipe organ and its music. Encourages the youth to learn the instrument. Operates a committee that gathers history and old music from silent film days and information on theatre organists, theaters and organ installations of the silent film era. **Affiliated With:** American Theatre Organ Society.

10996 ■ Fergus Falls Area Chamber of Commerce (FFACC)
202 S Court St.
Fergus Falls, MN 56537
Ph: (218)736-6951
Fax: (218)736-6952
E-mail: chamber@prtel.com
URL: http://www.fergusfalls.com
Contact: Stephanie Hoff, Exec.Dir.
Founded: 1886. **Members:** 300. **Local.** Promotes business and community development in the Fergus Falls, MN area. Holds annual Scandinavian and Frostbite Festivals. **Awards:** Champion Citizens. **Frequency:** annual. **Type:** recognition. **Computer Services:** Online services, membership directory. **Affiliated With:** U.S. Chamber of Commerce. **Publications:** *Chamber Update*, monthly. Newsletter. **Circulation:** 850. **Advertising:** accepted. **Conventions/Meetings:** annual banquet, for members - always October • annual Golf Tournament - competition.

10997 ■ Fergus Falls Convention and Visitors Bureau (CVB)
112 Washington Ave.
Fergus Falls, MN 56537
Ph: (218)739-0125
Free: (800)726-8959
E-mail: info@visitfergusfalls.com
URL: http://www.visitfergusfalls.com
Contact: Jean Bowman, Exec.Dir.
Local. Works to attract convention business, visitors and overnight travelers to the Fergus Falls area.

10998 ■ Lake Region Association of Realtors
210 W Lincoln
Fergus Falls, MN 56537
Ph: (218)739-0595
Fax: (218)736-0989
E-mail: lrar@qwest.net
Contact: Vicki Junge, Exec. Officer
Members: 130. **Staff:** 1. **Local.**

10999 ■ Midwest Minnesota Chapter, American Red Cross
221 W Cavour
Fergus Falls, MN 56537
Ph: (218)736-3481
Fax: (218)739-2389
E-mail: rogero@prtel.com
URL: National Affiliate–www.redcross.org
Contact: Roger Ophus, Exec.Dir.
Founded: 1917. **Local.** Serves members of the armed forces, veterans, and their families and aids disaster victims. Other activities include: blood services; community services; service opportunities for youth. **Affiliated With:** American Red Cross National Headquarters.

11000 ■ National Active and Retired Federal Employees Association - Lake Region 1207
1408 Somerset Rd.
Fergus Falls, MN 56537-1704
Ph: (218)736-2988
URL: National Affiliate–www.narfe.org
Contact: Kenneth R. Rose, Contact
Local. Protects the retirement future of employees through education. Informs members on issues affecting the retirement. **Affiliated With:** National Association of Retired Federal Employees.

11001 ■ Ottertail County - Young Life
PO Box 36
Fergus Falls, MN 56538
Ph: (218)998-5433
URL: http://sites.younglife.org/_layouts/ylext/default.aspx?ID=C-1165
Local. Affiliated With: Young Life.

11002 ■ Phi Theta Kappa, Omicron Omicron Chapter - Minnesota State Community and Technical College
c/o Steve Lindgren
1414 Coll. Way
Fergus Falls, MN 56537
Ph: (218)736-1536
E-mail: steve.lindgren@minnesota.edu
URL: http://www.ptk.org/directories/chapters/MN/258-1.htm
Contact: Steve Lindgren, Advisor
Local.

11003 ■ Skills USA, Fergus Falls High School
502 Friberg Ave. N
Fergus Falls, MN 56537
Ph: (218)998-0544
Fax: (218)998-3946
E-mail: rgronner@fergusfalls.k12.mn.us
URL: http://www.mnskillsusa.org
Contact: Rick Gronner, Contact
Local. Serves high school and college students enrolled in technical, skilled, and service and health occupations. Provides quality education experiences for students in leadership, teamwork, citizenship and character development. Builds and reinforces self-confidence, work attitudes and communication skills. Emphasizes total quality at work, high ethical standards, superior work skills, and life-long education. Promotes understanding of the free enterprise system and involvement in community service. **Affiliated With:** Skills USA - VICA.

11004 ■ Sons of Norway, Heimskringla Lodge 1-12
c/o Gerald E. Ziesemer, Pres.
934 W Linden St.
Fergus Falls, MN 56537-1048
Ph: (218)739-4190
E-mail: ziesemer@hotmail.com
URL: National Affiliate–www.sofn.com
Contact: Gerald E. Ziesemer, Pres.
Local. Affiliated With: Sons of Norway.

11005 ■ United Way of Otter Tail County
PO Box 54
Fergus Falls, MN 56537
Ph: (218)736-5147
Fax: (218)736-3727
Free: (877)457-2185
E-mail: uwotc@prtel.com
URL: http://www.uwotc.com
Contact: Lynne Olson, Exec.Dir.
Local. Affiliated With: United Way of America.

11006 ■ Young Life Ottertail County
PO Box 36
Fergus Falls, MN 56538
Ph: (218)998-5433
Fax: (218)998-3322
URL: http://sites.younglife.org/_layouts/ylext/default.aspx?ID=A-MN22
Local. Affiliated With: Young Life.

Fertile

11007 ■ American Legion, Fertile Post 238
PO Box 144
Fertile, MN 56540
Ph: (651)291-1800
Fax: (651)291-1057
URL: National Affiliate–www.legion.org
Local. Affiliated With: American Legion.

11008 ■ Fertile Lions Club
c/o Stephen Taylor, Sec.
RR 1, Box 71
Fertile, MN 56540
Ph: (218)945-6552
URL: http://lions5m11.org/sys-tmpl/door
Contact: Stephen Taylor, Sec.
Local. Affiliated With: Lions Clubs International.

Fisher

11009 ■ American Legion, Theodore Stalemo Post 242
PO Box 142
Fisher, MN 56723
Ph: (651)291-1800
Fax: (651)291-1057
URL: National Affiliate–www.legion.org
Local. Affiliated With: American Legion.

Flensburg

11010 ■ American Legion, Minnesota Post 136
c/o Stephen Jendro
PO Box 21
Flensburg, MN 56328
Ph: (651)291-1800
Fax: (651)291-1057
URL: National Affiliate–www.legion.org
Contact: Stephen Jendro, Contact
Local. Affiliated With: American Legion.

Floodwood

11011 ■ Floodwood Area Lions Club
c/o Marilyn Arro, Pres.
11647 Parantala Rd.
Floodwood, MN 55736
Ph: (218)476-2640
URL: http://lions5m10.org
Contact: Marilyn Arro, Pres.
Local. Affiliated With: Lions Clubs International.

Foley

11012 ■ American Legion, Earl James Howe Post 298
131 4th Ave.
Foley, MN 56329
Ph: (651)291-1800
Fax: (651)291-1057
URL: National Affiliate–www.legion.org
Local. Affiliated With: American Legion.

Forest Lake

11013 ■ American Institute of Chemical Engineers - Upper Midwest Section
c/o Nathan C. Johnson, Membership Sec.
8500 177th Ln.
Forest Lake, MN 55025
Ph: (651)733-8799
E-mail: doc_curtis@rocketmail.com
URL: http://www.aichelocal.org/tc
Contact: Nathan C. Johnson, Membership Sec.
Regional. Represents the interests of chemical engineering professionals. Aims to contribute to the improvement of chemical engineering curricula offered in universities. Seeks to enhance the lifelong career development and financial security of chemical engineers through products, services, networking and advocacy. **Affiliated With:** American Institute of Chemical Engineers.

11014 ■ American Legion, Forest Lake Post 225
PO Box 520
Forest Lake, MN 55025
Ph: (651)291-1800
Fax: (651)291-1057
URL: National Affiliate–www.legion.org
Local. Affiliated With: American Legion.

11015 ■ American Statistical Association, Twin Cities Minnesota Chapter
c/o John R. Fieberg, Pres.
Minnesota Dept. of Natural Resources
5463 - C W Broadway
Forest Lake, MN 55025-8824
Ph: (651)296-2704
E-mail: john.fieberg@dnr.state.mn.us
URL: National Affiliate–www.amstat.org
Contact: John R. Fieberg, Pres.
Local. Promotes statistical practice, applications and research. Works for the improvement of statistical education at all levels. Seeks opportunities to advance the statistics profession. **Affiliated With:** American Statistical Association.

11016 ■ Columbus Parent Teacher Organization
c/o Columbus Elementary School
17345 Notre Dame St.
Forest Lake, MN 55025-8872
Local.

11017 ■ Forest Lake Area Chamber of Commerce (FLACC)
56 E Broadway Ave.
PO Box 474
Forest Lake, MN 55025-0474
Ph: (651)464-3200
Fax: (651)464-3201
E-mail: chamber@flacc.org
URL: http://www.flacc.org
Contact: Deborah Feist, Pres.
Founded: 1963. **Members:** 200. **Local.** Promotes business and community development in the Forest Lake, MN area. Sponsors Fun in the Forest festival. **Convention/Meeting:** none. **Computer Services:** Online services, business directory. **Affiliated With:** U.S. Chamber of Commerce. **Publications:** *Chamber Connection*, monthly. Newsletter. **Advertising:** accepted. Alternate Formats: online • Directory, annual.

11018 ■ Minnesota Field Trial Association
c/o Nancy Dooley
6907 W Broadway Ave.
Forest Lake, MN 55025-8441
Ph: (651)464-0885
E-mail: nadool2002@aol.com
URL: http://www.mfta.8m.com
Contact: Jim Dresen, Pres.
State. Affiliated With: American Kennel Club.

11019 ■ Northwoods Humane Society
7153 Lake Blvd.
PO Box 513
Forest Lake, MN 55025
Ph: (651)982-0240
E-mail: info@northwoodshs.org
URL: http://www.northwoodshs.org
Contact: Jack Felix, Pres.
Local.

Foreston

11020 ■ Minnesota Boer Goat Association
c/o Dan Davison
14050 185th Ave. NE
Foreston, MN 56330
E-mail: sdavison@ecenet.com
URL: National Affiliate–usbga.org
Contact: Dan Davison, Contact
State.

Fort Benedict

11021 ■ Sons of Norway, Skogvannet Lodge 1-658
c/o Warren L. Broughton, Pres.
PO Box 75
Fort Benedict, MN 56436-0075
Ph: (218)224-3832
E-mail: kbrought@paulbunyan.net
URL: National Affiliate–www.sofn.com
Contact: Warren L. Broughton, Pres.
Local. Affiliated With: Sons of Norway.

Fosston

11022 ■ American Legion, Tangen-Walstrom Post 114
PO Box 595
Fosston, MN 56542
Ph: (651)291-1800
Fax: (651)291-1057
URL: National Affiliate–www.legion.org
Local. Affiliated With: American Legion.

11023 ■ Fosston-Lengby Lions Club
RR 3, Box 110
Fosston, MN 56542
Ph: (218)435-1677
E-mail: opmalwit@grtel.com
URL: http://lions5m11.org/sys-tmpl/door
Contact: William Malwitz, Sec.
Local. Affiliated With: Lions Clubs International.

11024 ■ Northwestern District Dental Society, Minnesota
c/o Dr. Roger Sjulson, Sec.-Treas.
109 N Johnson Ave.
Fosston, MN 56542
Ph: (218)435-1599
Fax: (218)435-6568
E-mail: rwsdds@gvtel.com
URL: http://northwestern.mndental.org
Contact: Dr. Roger Sjulson, Sec.-Treas.
Local. Represents the interests of dentists committed to the public's oral health, ethics and professional development. Encourages the improvement of the public's oral health and promotes the art and science of dentistry. **Affiliated With:** American Dental Association; Minnesota Dental Association.

Fountain

11025 ■ American Legion, Romsos-Malia Post 492
PO Box 104
Fountain, MN 55935
Ph: (651)291-1800
Fax: (651)291-1057
URL: National Affiliate–www.legion.org
Local. Affiliated With: American Legion.

Franklin

11026 ■ American Legion, Martin-Jensen Post 308
PO Box 298
Franklin, MN 55333
Ph: (651)291-1800
Fax: (651)291-1057
URL: National Affiliate–www.legion.org
Local. Affiliated With: American Legion.

11027 ■ Franklin Lions Club - Minnesota
c/o Tom Zeman, Pres.
38730 670th Ave.
Franklin, MN 55333
Ph: (507)557-2776 (507)557-2233
URL: http://www.5m4lions.org
Contact: Tom Zeman, Pres.
Local. Affiliated With: Lions Clubs International.

11028 ■ Indianhead Appaloosa Horse Club
c/o Sandy Rebstock
37035 State Hwy. 19
Franklin, MN 55333
Ph: (507)557-8211
URL: National Affiliate–www.appaloosa.com
Contact: Sandy Rebstock, Contact
Local. Affiliated With: Appaloosa Horse Club.

Frazee

11029 ■ Northarvest Bean Growers Association (NBGA)
c/o Timothy Courneya, Exec.VP
50072 E Lake Seven Rd.
Frazee, MN 56544
Ph: (218)334-6351
Fax: (218)334-6360
E-mail: nhbean@loretel.net
URL: http://www.northarvestbean.org
Contact: Timothy Courneya, Exec.VP
Founded: 1976. **Members:** 4,000. **Budget:** $926,000. **Local.** Seeks to provide promotion, research, development, and communications on the subject of dry beans. **Publications:** *Northarvest Bean Grower Magazine*, bimonthly. **Conventions/Meetings:** periodic board meeting - 4-6 times/year • annual convention - in January.

Freeborn

11030 ■ American Legion, Gilmore-Stensrud Post 552
202 5th Ave.
Freeborn, MN 56032
Ph: (651)291-1800
Fax: (651)291-1057
URL: National Affiliate–www.legion.org
Local. Affiliated With: American Legion.

Fridley

11031 ■ African Violet Society of Minnesota (AVSM)
c/o Ruth Bann
680 Marigold Terr.
Fridley, MN 55421
Ph: (763)571-6703
E-mail: rebels@mninter.net
URL: National Affiliate–www.avsa.org
Contact: Ruth Bann, Contact
State. Affiliated With: African Violet Society of America.

11032 ■ American Legion, Shaddrick and La Beau Post 303
7365 Central Ave. NE
Fridley, MN 55432
Ph: (651)291-1800
Fax: (651)291-1057
URL: National Affiliate–www.legion.org
Local. Affiliated With: American Legion.

11033 ■ Fridley Lions Club
PO Box 32815
Fridley, MN 55432
E-mail: slinder71@aol.com
URL: http://www.geocities.com/fridleylions
Contact: Bud Dauphin, Pres.
Local. Affiliated With: Lions Clubs International.

11034 ■ Greater Minneapolis St. Paul Basset Hound Club
c/o Barb Sorensen
1455 N Danube Rd. NE
Fridley, MN 55432
Ph: (763)571-2436
E-mail: info@mnbasset.org
URL: http://www.mnbasset.org
Contact: Casey Wilda, Pres.
Local.

11035 ■ Minnesota Recreation and Park Association (MRPA)
c/o Michelle Snider, Exec.Dir.
200 Charles St. NE
Fridley, MN 55432
Ph: (763)571-1305
Fax: (763)571-5204
Free: (800)862-3659
E-mail: snider@mnrecpark.org
URL: http://www.mnrpa.org
Contact: Michelle Snider, Exec.Dir.
Founded: 1937. **Members:** 1,500. **Staff:** 6. **Budget:** $850,000. **State.** Recreational professionals, citizen board members, and students. Seeks to broaden the understanding and visibility of the park and recreation movement. Promotes continuing education, cooperation with other organizations, and the professional status of its members. Sponsors workshops; is developing intercommunity recreational sports program. **Affiliated With:** Minnesota Recreation and Park Association. **Also Known As:** MRPA. **Publications:** *Keeping Up*, monthly. Newsletter. **Circulation:** 1,500. **Advertising:** accepted. **Conventions/Meetings:** annual conference (exhibits) - October or November.

11036 ■ Table Tennis Minnesota - Fridley
Northwest Athletic Club - Fridley
1200 E Moore Lake Dr.
Fridley, MN 55432
Ph: (952)892-7078
E-mail: ttminn@aol.com
URL: http://www.tabletennismn.com
Contact: Mitchell Seidenfeld, Contact
Local. Affiliated With: U.S.A. Table Tennis.

Fulda

11037 ■ American Legion, Emil King Post 318
PO Box 305
Fulda, MN 56131
Ph: (651)291-1800
Fax: (651)291-1057
URL: National Affiliate–www.legion.org
Local. Affiliated With: American Legion.

Garvin

11038 ■ American Legion, Minnesota Post 273
c/o Victor Hegge
2294 US Hwy. 59
Garvin, MN 56132
Ph: (651)291-1800
Fax: (651)291-1057
URL: National Affiliate–www.legion.org
Contact: Victor Hegge, Contact
Local. Affiliated With: American Legion.

Gary

11039 ■ American Legion, Gary Post 505
PO Box 84
Gary, MN 56545
Ph: (651)291-1800
Fax: (651)291-1057
URL: National Affiliate–www.legion.org
Local. Affiliated With: American Legion.

11040 ■ Gary Lions Club
c/o Merlyn Meyer, Sec.
PO Box 125
Gary, MN 56545
Ph: (218)435-1705 (218)356-8717
URL: http://lions5m11.org/sys-tmpl/door
Contact: Ray Larson, Pres.
Local. Affiliated With: Lions Clubs International.

Gaylord

11041 ■ American Legion, Manthey-Asmus Post 433
PO Box 502
Gaylord, MN 55334
Ph: (651)291-1800
Fax: (651)291-1057
URL: National Affiliate–www.legion.org
Local. Affiliated With: American Legion.

Ghent

11042 ■ American Legion, Engels-Wilson Post 564
PO Box 11
Ghent, MN 56239
Ph: (651)291-1800
Fax: (651)291-1057
URL: National Affiliate–www.legion.org
Local. Affiliated With: American Legion.

Gibbon

11043 ■ American Legion, Loftness-Bandow Post 226
31824 633rd Ave.
Gibbon, MN 55335
Ph: (651)291-1800
Fax: (651)291-1057
URL: National Affiliate–www.legion.org
Local. Affiliated With: American Legion.

11044 ■ National Active and Retired Federal Employees Association - New Ulm 1444
PO Box 84
Gibbon, MN 55335-0084
Ph: (507)834-6188
URL: National Affiliate–www.narfe.org
Contact: Luverne S. Kent, Contact
Local. Protects the retirement future of employees through education. Informs members on issues affecting the retirement. **Affiliated With:** National Association of Retired Federal Employees.

Gilbert

11045 ■ American Legion, Moe-Indihar Post 138
PO Box 383
Gilbert, MN 55741
Ph: (651)291-1800
Fax: (651)291-1057
URL: National Affiliate–www.legion.org
Local. Affiliated With: American Legion.

11046 ■ St. Louis County Promotional Bureau
c/o Walter Hautala
5088 Maple Dr.
Gilbert, MN 55741-8352
Ph: (218)865-4247
Fax: (218)865-4247
E-mail: stlouiscountypromo@rangenet.com
URL: http://www.stlouisctymnmap-guide.com
Contact: Walter Hautala, Exec.Sec.
Members: 12. **Local**.

Glencoe

11047 ■ American Legion, Glencoe Post 95
PO Box 145
Glencoe, MN 55336
Ph: (651)291-1800
Fax: (651)291-1057
URL: National Affiliate–www.legion.org
Local. Affiliated With: American Legion.

11048 ■ Glencoe Area Chamber of Commerce
630 E 10th St.
Glencoe, MN 55336
Ph: (320)864-3650
Fax: (320)864-6405
E-mail: chamber@glencoechamber.com
URL: http://www.glencoechamber.com
Contact: Larry Anderson, Pres.
Members: 120. **Membership Dues:** standard business (based on number of individuals), $175-$1,075 • civic group/church/public official, $100 • retired professional, $50 • hospital/municipal service/financial institution, $1,400 • school district/utility, $500. **Local**. Strives to create, promote, and enhance the business environment and improve the quality of life in the Glencoe area. **Committees:** Ambassadors; Auto, Agricultural and Manufacturing; Economic Development; Greeter/Website; Professional and Retail. **Publications:** *Connection*. Newsletter. **Circulation:** 340. Alternate Formats: online.

11049 ■ USA Weightlifting - Glencoe
c/o Richard Smith
Panther Fieldhouse
1621 16th St. E
Glencoe, MN 55336
Ph: (320)327-3039 (320)864-2418
Fax: (320)864-2418
URL: National Affiliate–www.usaweightlifting.org
Contact: Richard Smith, Contact
Local. Affiliated With: USA Weightlifting.

Glenville

11050 ■ American Legion, Glenville Post 264
PO Box 56
Glenville, MN 56036
Ph: (651)291-1800
Fax: (651)291-1057
URL: National Affiliate–www.legion.org
Local. Affiliated With: American Legion.

Glenwood

11051 ■ American Legion, Johnson-Roll-Dougherty Post 187
PO Box 115
Glenwood, MN 56334
Ph: (651)291-1800
Fax: (651)291-1057
URL: National Affiliate–www.legion.org
Local. Affiliated With: American Legion.

11052 ■ Glenwood Area Chamber of Commerce (GACC)
202 N Franklin St.
Glenwood, MN 56334
Ph: (320)634-3636
Fax: (320)634-3637
Free: (866)634-3636
E-mail: glenstar@akeva.com
URL: http://www.glenwood-starbuck.org
Contact: Brenda Baumler, Office Mgr.
Members: 169. **Local**. Promotes business and community development in Glenwood, MN. Sponsors Waterama festival, Lake Minnewaska Ice Fishing Contest and Physically Limited Golfers Association National Tournament. **Computer Services:** Information services • mailing lists, of members. **Telecommunication Services:** information service. **Formerly:** (1999) Glenwood Chamber of Commerce. **Publications:** *Glenwood Chamber of Commerce Newsletter*, monthly • Directory, annual. **Price:** $25.00 for nonmembers.

11053 ■ Glenwood Lions Club - Minnesota
c/o Wayne Anderson, Pres.
25404 190th St.
Glenwood, MN 56334
Ph: (320)239-4557 (320)634-5729
E-mail: wayne.anderson@co.pope.mn.us
URL: http://www.5m4lions.org
Contact: Wayne Anderson, Pres.
Local. Affiliated With: Lions Clubs International.

11054 ■ Habitat for Humanity of Prairie Lakes (HFHPL)
PO Box 122
Glenwood, MN 56334
Ph: (320)634-0355
E-mail: tarnis@habitatprairielakes.org
URL: http://www.habitatprairielakes.org
Contact: Curt Larson, Pres.
Local. Telecommunication Services: electronic mail, curtl@habitatprairielakes.org. **Affiliated With:** Habitat for Humanity International.

11055 ■ Sons of Norway, Mjosen Lodge 1-175
c/o Gloria C. Danter, Sec.
18722 Whitemore Ln.
Glenwood, MN 56334-5045
Ph: (320)634-4802
E-mail: ddanter@runestone.net
URL: National Affiliate–www.sofn.com
Contact: Gloria C. Danter, Sec.
Local. Affiliated With: Sons of Norway.

Glyndon

11056 ■ American Theater Organ Society, Red River
c/o Faye Crume, Pres.
131 130th St. S
Glyndon, MN 56547-9551
Ph: (218)498-2874
E-mail: prodietpet@cs.com
URL: National Affiliate–www.atos.org
Contact: Faye Crume, Pres.
Local. Affiliated With: American Theatre Organ Society.

11057 ■ Glyndon Lions Club
PO Box 311
Glyndon, MN 56547
Ph: (218)498-2949
URL: http://lions5m11.org/sys-tmpl/door
Contact: Locki Carlson, Pres.
Local. Affiliated With: Lions Clubs International.

Golden Valley

11058 ■ American Legion, Chester Bird Post 523
200 Lilac Dr. N
Golden Valley, MN 55422
Ph: (651)291-1800
Fax: (651)291-1057
URL: National Affiliate–www.legion.org
Local. Affiliated With: American Legion.

11059 ■ American Public Works Association, Minnesota Chapter
c/o Mr. Thomas L. Klatt, Pres.
7800 Golden Valley Rd.
Golden Valley, MN 55427-4508
Ph: (763)593-3981
Fax: (763)593-3988
E-mail: tklatt@ci.golden-valley.mn.us
URL: http://minnesota.apwa.net
Contact: Mr. Thomas L. Klatt, Pres.
State. Promotes professional excellence and public awareness through education, advocacy and the exchange of knowledge. **Affiliated With:** American Public Works Association.

11060 ■ Fraternal Order of Police, Minnesota State Lodge
c/o Gary Cayo, Pres.
PO Box 270026
Golden Valley, MN 55427
Ph: (952)895-0405
Fax: (952)736-3378
E-mail: gcayo@eminnetonka.com
URL: http://www.mnfop.com
Contact: Gary Cayo, Pres.
State. Affiliated With: Fraternal Order of Police, Grand Lodge.

11061 ■ Minnesota Association of Rehabilitation Providers (MARP)
c/o James Stubbe, Pres.
PO Box 27262
Golden Valley, MN 55427
Ph: (952)470-4907
E-mail: jstubbe@stubbe.com
URL: http://www.rehabpro.org
Contact: Kaylene Kickhafer, Pres.
Founded: 1980. **Members:** 280. **State**. Professionals with degrees and/or certification in rehabilitation counseling, psychology, nursing, occupational therapy, psychology and divinity. Provide services to injured workers. **Affiliated With:** International Association of Rehabilitation Professionals. **Conventions/Meetings:** quadrennial conference - spring, summer, and fall.

11062 ■ Minnesota Genealogical Society (MGS)
c/o David Eugene Cross
5768 Olson Memorial Hwy.
Golden Valley, MN 55422
Ph: (763)595-9347
E-mail: dcross@davidecross.com
URL: http://mngs.org/
State.

11063 ■ Minnesota Self Storage Association (MSSA)
1724 Douglas Dr. N
Golden Valley, MN 55422
Ph: (612)991-4880
Fax: (763)512-7723
E-mail: info@mnmssa.com
URL: http://www.mnmssa.com
Contact: Ellis Gottlieb, Pres.
State. Represents owners and operators of self storage facilities. Works to improve the quality of management, customer service and facilities. Promotes public awareness of the self storage industry. Conducts educational meetings on management, marketing, security, and related topics. Lobbies for state legislation protecting and recognizing self storage owners and operators. **Affiliated With:** Self Storage Association.

11064 ■ North Central Wheelchair Athletic Association
c/o Sharon Van Winkle
Courage Center
3915 Golden Valley Rd.
Golden Valley, MN 55422

Ph: (763)520-0537
Fax: (763)520-0577
E-mail: sports@courage.org
URL: http://www.courage.org
Contact: Sharon Van Winkle, Contact
Local. Provides wheelchair sports to individuals with permanent physical disabilities in Golden Valley. Improves the physical condition and quality of life of the disabled through participation in sports. **Additional Websites:** http://www.ncpad.org/organizations/index-title.php?id=534&letter=N&PHPSESSID. **Affiliated With:** Wheelchair Sports, USA.

11065 ■ NPPA Region 5
c/o Ron Stover, Dir.
3055 Scott Ave. N
Golden Valley, MN 55422
Ph: (763)797-7215 (612)685-0907
E-mail: ronstover@comcast.net
URL: http://www.nppa5.org
Contact: Ron Stover, Dir.
Local. Promotes the advancement of photojournalism, creation, editing and distribution in all news media. Encourages photojournalists to reflect high standards of quality of performance and personal code of ethics. Provides continuing educational programs and fraternalism.

11066 ■ Volunteers of America-Minnesota
c/o Bonnie Kratzke
5905 Golden Valley Rd., Ste.110
Golden Valley, MN 55422
Ph: (763)546-3242
Fax: (763)546-2774
E-mail: bkratzke@voamn.org
URL: http://www.voamn.org
State.

Gonvick

11067 ■ American Legion, Gonvick Post 304
184 Elm St.
Gonvick, MN 56644
Ph: (651)291-1800
Fax: (651)291-1057
URL: National Affiliate–www.legion.org
Local. Affiliated With: American Legion.

Goodhue

11068 ■ Goodhue Lions Club
c/o Curt Schrimpf, Pres.
20555 360th St.
Goodhue, MN 55027
Ph: (651)923-4821
E-mail: jes@hotmail.com
URL: http://www.lions5m1.org/goodhue
Contact: Curt Schrimpf, Pres.
Local. Affiliated With: Lions Clubs International.

Goodland

11069 ■ American Legion, Pletcher-Chutich-Skrbich Post 575
HC 1, Box 64
Goodland, MN 55742
Ph: (651)291-1800
Fax: (651)291-1057
URL: National Affiliate–www.legion.org
Local. Affiliated With: American Legion.

Goodridge

11070 ■ Goodridge Lion Tamers Club
c/o Cindi Kotrba, Pres.
15249 370th Ave. NE
Goodridge, MN 56725
Ph: (218)378-4324
E-mail: mck5star@gvtel.com
URL: http://lions5m11.org/sys-tmpl/door
Contact: Cindi Kotrba, Pres.
Local. Affiliated With: Lions Clubs International.

Goodview

11071 ■ Winona AIFA
1220 49th Ave.
Goodview, MN 55987
Ph: (507)689-4289
URL: National Affiliate–www.naifa.org
Local. Represents the interest of insurance and financial advisors. Advocates for a positive legislative and regulatory environment. Enhances business and professional skills of members. **Affiliated With:** National Association of Insurance and Financial Advisors.

Granada

11072 ■ American Legion, Granada Post 319
125 S Main St.
Granada, MN 56039
Ph: (651)291-1800
Fax: (651)291-1057
URL: National Affiliate–www.legion.org
Local. Affiliated With: American Legion.

Grand Marais

11073 ■ American Legion, Grand Marais Post 413
PO Box 721
Grand Marais, MN 55604
Ph: (651)291-1800
Fax: (651)291-1057
URL: National Affiliate–www.legion.org
Local. Affiliated With: American Legion.

11074 ■ Grand Marais Aikikai
HC 86 Box 787B
Grand Marais, MN 55604
Ph: (218)387-1983
URL: http://www.usaikifed.com
Contact: Craig Waver, Instructor
Local. Affiliated With: United States Aikido Federation.

11075 ■ Grand Marais Chamber of Commerce
PO Box 805
Grand Marais, MN 55604-0805
Ph: (218)387-9112
E-mail: gmcc@boreal.org
URL: http://www.grandmaraismn.com
Contact: Bev Wolke, Exec.Dir.
Local. Supports member businesses, economic growth, and community events in the Grand Marais Area.

11076 ■ Grand Marais Lions Club
c/o Mark Sandbo, Pres.
PO Box 745
Grand Marais, MN 55604
Ph: (218)387-9384
E-mail: mjsandbo@boreal.org
URL: http://lions5m10.org
Contact: Mark Sandbo, Pres.
Local. Affiliated With: Lions Clubs International.

11077 ■ Minnesota Ambulance Association, Northeast
c/o Lisa Bolen, Dir.
PO Box 1292
Grand Marais, MN 55604
Ph: (218)387-9343
E-mail: bolen@boreal.org
URL: http://www.mnems.org
Contact: Lisa Bolen, Dir.
Local. Seeks to maintain the financial viability of the EMS industry by advocating education, legislation and regulatory change. **Affiliated With:** Minnesota Ambulance Association.

11078 ■ Ruffed Grouse Society, North Shore Chapter
c/o Scott Puch
PO Box 83
Grand Marais, MN 55604
Ph: (715)336-2523
URL: National Affiliate–www.ruffedgrousesociety.org
Contact: Scott Puch, Contact
Local. Affiliated With: Ruffed Grouse Society.

Grand Meadow

11079 ■ American Legion, Minnesota Post 140
c/o Harry T. Anderson
PO Box 592
Grand Meadow, MN 55936
Ph: (651)291-1800
Fax: (651)291-1057
URL: National Affiliate–www.legion.org
Contact: Harry T. Anderson, Contact
Local. Affiliated With: American Legion.

Grand Rapids

11080 ■ AAA Minnesota/Iowa
1279 S Pokegama Ave.
Grand Rapids, MN 55744-4208
Ph: (218)326-8531
Contact: Diane Skelly, Sr. Travel Agent
Regional.

11081 ■ American Legion, Mc-Veigh-Dunn Post 60
9 NW 2nd St.
Grand Rapids, MN 55744
Ph: (651)291-1800
Fax: (651)291-1057
URL: National Affiliate–www.legion.org
Local. Affiliated With: American Legion.

11082 ■ Animal Love and Loss Network (ALLN)
PO Box 132
Grand Rapids, MN 55744
Ph: (218)327-0135
E-mail: info@alln.org
URL: http://www.alln.org
Local.

11083 ■ Eldercircle RSVP
c/o Valerie Jensen, Dir.
ElderCircle, Inc.
10 NW 5th St.
Grand Rapids, MN 55744
Ph: (218)326-3175
Fax: (218)326-7965
E-mail: donna@eldercircle.org
URL: http://www.seniorcorps.gov/about/programs/rsvp_state.asp?usestateabbr=mn&Search4.x=17&Search4.y=8
Contact: Valerie Jensen, Dir.
Local. Affiliated With: Retired and Senior Volunteer Program.

11084 ■ Grand Rapids Area Chamber of Commerce (GRACC)
1 NW 3rd St.
Grand Rapids, MN 55744-2718
Ph: (218)326-6619
Fax: (218)326-4825
Free: (800)GRA-NDMN
E-mail: answers@grandmn.com
URL: http://www.grandmn.com
Contact: Bud Stone, Pres.
Founded: 1902. **Members:** 623. **Staff:** 7. **Budget:** $326,000. **Local**. Promotes business and community

development in the Grand Rapids, MN area. **Computer Services:** Online services, member directory. **Committees:** Ambassadors; Area Business; Forestry Affairs; Government; Program; Tourism; Transportation; Workforce Development. **Publications:** *The Chamber Network*, monthly. Newsletter • Report, annual • Directory, annual. **Conventions/Meetings:** annual Golf Outing - competition, sponsorship opportunity - always July • monthly luncheon - last Monday of each month except July.

11085 ■ Grand Rapids Gun Club
PO Box 911
Grand Rapids, MN 55744
Ph: (218)326-3348
URL: National Affiliate–www.mynssa.com
Local. Affiliated With: National Skeet Shooting Association.

11086 ■ Grand Rapids Star of the North Lions Club
c/o Dennis Roy, Pres.
PO Box 324
Grand Rapids, MN 55744
Ph: (218)326-5408
E-mail: dwroy@paulbunyan.net
URL: http://lions5m10.org
Contact: Dennis Roy, Pres.
Local. Affiliated With: Lions Clubs International.

11087 ■ Itasca County Board of Realtors
807 NE 4th St.
Grand Rapids, MN 55744
Ph: (218)326-4533
Fax: (218)326-4542
E-mail: itabdpcs@grandnet.com
URL: National Affiliate–www.realtor.org
Contact: Phyllis C. Scherf, Exec. Officer
Local. Strives to develop real estate business practices. Advocates the right to own, use and transfer real property. Provides a facility for professional development, research and exchange of information among members. **Affiliated With:** National Association of Realtors.

11088 ■ Itasca County Habitat for Humanity
PO Box 81
Grand Rapids, MN 55744-0081
Ph: (218)326-6185
Fax: (218)326-3659
E-mail: shannon@itascahabitat.org
URL: National Affiliate–www.habitat.org
Local. Affiliated With: Habitat for Humanity International.

11089 ■ Itasca Curling Club
902 Hale Lake Pointe
PO Box 863
Grand Rapids, MN 55744
Ph: (218)327-1847
E-mail: kimmarie214@hotmail.com
URL: http://www.itascacurlingclub.com
Contact: John Hanson, Pres.
Local. Affiliated With: United States Curling Association.

11090 ■ Itasca Youth for Christ
PO Box 209
Grand Rapids, MN 55744
Ph: (218)326-9079
Fax: (218)327-0344
URL: National Affiliate–www.yfc.net
Local. Affiliated With: Youth for Christ/U.S.A.

11091 ■ Minnesota Forestry Association (MFA)
PO Box 496
Grand Rapids, MN 55744
Ph: (612)823-2618
Free: (800)821-8733
E-mail: information@mnforest.com
URL: http://www.mnforest.com
Contact: Culver Adams, Pres.
State. Promotes active management and stewardship of non-industrial private forest resources in Minnesota. Members are primarily non-industrial private forest landowners but land ownership is not limited to forest ownership.

11092 ■ PFLAG Grand Rapids/Itasca
PO Box 524
Grand Rapids, MN 55744
Free: (800)800-0350
E-mail: itasca-glbt-alliance@yahoo.com
URL: http://www.pflag.org/Minnesota.217.0.html
Local. Affiliated With: Parents, Families, and Friends of Lesbians and Gays.

11093 ■ Trout Unlimited, Waybinahbe 650
c/o Wayne Hoshal
18867 Adair Rd.
Grand Rapids, MN 55744-4570
Ph: (218)327-2390
E-mail: whoshal@hotmail.com
URL: National Affiliate–www.tu.org/
Contact: Wayne Hoshal, Contact
Local. Affiliated With: Trout Unlimited.

11094 ■ United Way of 1000 Lakes
201 NW 4th St., Ste.111
Grand Rapids, MN 55744
Ph: (218)327-8859
Fax: (218)327-8856
E-mail: uway@2z.net
URL: http://www.unitedwayof1000lakes.org
Local. Affiliated With: United Way of America.

Granite Falls

11095 ■ American Legion, Minnesota Post 69
c/o Everett H. Hale
60 6th Ave.
Granite Falls, MN 56241
Ph: (612)564-2537
Fax: (651)291-1057
URL: National Affiliate–www.legion.org
Contact: Everett H. Hale, Contact
Local. Affiliated With: American Legion.

11096 ■ Granite Falls Area Chamber of Commerce (GFACC)
PO Box 220
Granite Falls, MN 56241
Ph: (320)564-4039
Fax: (320)564-3210
E-mail: gfchamber@kilowatt.net
URL: http://www.granitefalls.com
Contact: Rita L. Knutson, Exec.Dir.
Members: 145. **Local.** Promotes business and community development in the Granite Falls, MN area. **Computer Services:** Online services, business directory. **Committees:** Education; Government Affairs; Personnel; Professional/Service; Retail; Royalty; Tourism; Western Fest. **Affiliated With:** U.S. Chamber of Commerce. **Formerly:** (2005) Granite Falls Area Chamber of Commerce - Convention and Visitors Bureau. **Publications:** Newsletter, monthly. **Circulation:** 150.

Green Isle

11097 ■ American Legion, Green Isle Post 408
37597 180th St.
Green Isle, MN 55338
Ph: (651)291-1800
Fax: (651)291-1057
URL: National Affiliate–www.legion.org
Local. Affiliated With: American Legion.

Greenbush

11098 ■ American Legion, Moen-Zimek Post 88
PO Box 81
Greenbush, MN 56726
Ph: (651)291-1800
Fax: (651)291-1057
URL: National Affiliate–www.legion.org
Local. Affiliated With: American Legion.

11099 ■ Greenbush Lions Club
c/o Peter C. Duncan, Pres.
924 Old Ridge Rd.
Greenbush, MN 56726
Ph: (218)782-2457
URL: http://lions5m11.org/sys-tmpl/door
Contact: Peter C. Duncan, Pres.
Local. Affiliated With: Lions Clubs International.

Grey Eagle

11100 ■ American Legion, Southern Todd County Post 547
PO Box 115
Grey Eagle, MN 56336
Ph: (651)291-1800
Fax: (651)291-1057
URL: National Affiliate–www.legion.org
Local. Affiliated With: American Legion.

Grove City

11101 ■ Grove City Lions Club
c/o Sandra Danielson, Sec.
PO Box 161
Grove City, MN 56243
Ph: (320)857-2771
E-mail: sandradanielson@hotmail.com
URL: http://www.5m4lions.org
Contact: Sandra Danielson, Sec.
Local. Affiliated With: Lions Clubs International.

Grygla

11102 ■ American Legion, Holte-Grygla-Fourtown Post 162
PO Box 45
Grygla, MN 56727
Ph: (651)291-1800
Fax: (651)291-1057
URL: National Affiliate–www.legion.org
Local. Affiliated With: American Legion.

11103 ■ Grygla Lions Club
c/o Wayne Warne, Sec.
28144 390th Ave. NE
Grygla, MN 56727
Ph: (218)459-3316
URL: http://lions5m11.org/sys-tmpl/door
Contact: Steve Sparby, Pres.
Local. Affiliated With: Lions Clubs International.

Gully

11104 ■ American Legion, Gully Post 603
PO Box 84
Gully, MN 56646
Ph: (651)291-1800
Fax: (651)291-1057
URL: National Affiliate–www.legion.org
Local. Affiliated With: American Legion.

11105 ■ Sons of Norway, Granlund Lodge 1-240
c/o Helen G. Sordahl, Pres.
20425 400th Ave. SE
Gully, MN 56646
Ph: (218)268-4465
E-mail: hsordahl@gvtel.com
URL: National Affiliate–www.sofn.com
Contact: Helen G. Sordahl, Pres.
Local. Affiliated With: Sons of Norway.

Hackensack

11106 ■ American Legion, Hackensack Post 202
PO Box 325
Hackensack, MN 56452
Ph: (651)291-1800
Fax: (651)291-1057
URL: National Affiliate–www.legion.org
Local. Affiliated With: American Legion.

Hallock

11107 ■ American Legion, G.A. Leonard Norberg Post 63
PO Box 243
Hallock, MN 56728
Ph: (651)291-1800
Fax: (651)291-1057
URL: National Affiliate–www.legion.org
Local. Affiliated With: American Legion.

11108 ■ Hallock Lions Club
PO Box 851
Hallock, MN 56728
Ph: (218)843-2451
E-mail: dmklein@wiktel.com
URL: http://lions5m11.org/sys-tmpl/door
Contact: David Klein, Pres.
Local. Affiliated With: Lions Clubs International.

Halstad

11109 ■ American Legion, Minnesota Post 402
c/o Carlson Hillerud
PO Box 402
Halstad, MN 56548
Ph: (651)291-1800
Fax: (651)291-1057
URL: National Affiliate–www.legion.org
Contact: Carlson Hillerud, Contact
Local. Affiliated With: American Legion.

11110 ■ Halstad Lions Club
c/o Ronald W. Laqua, Sec.
PO Box 191
Halstad, MN 56548
Ph: (218)456-2125 (218)456-2300
Fax: (218)456-2196
E-mail: rlaqua@rrv.net
URL: http://lions5m11.org/sys-tmpl/door
Contact: Ronald W. Laqua, Sec.
Local. Affiliated With: Lions Clubs International.

11111 ■ Sons of Norway, Tordenskjold Lodge 1-55
c/o Bardulf Ueland, Pres.
PO Box 298
Halstad, MN 56548-0298
Ph: (218)456-2574
E-mail: bueland@rrv.net
URL: National Affiliate–www.sofn.com
Contact: Bardulf Ueland, Pres.
Local. Affiliated With: Sons of Norway.

Ham Lake

11112 ■ Minnesota Fruit and Vegetable Growers Association (MFVGA)
15125 W Vermillion Cir. NE
Ham Lake, MN 55304
Ph: (763)434-0400
Fax: (763)413-9585
E-mail: info@mfvga.org
URL: http://www.mfvga.org
Contact: Marilyn Nysetvold Johnson, Exec.Coor.
State.

Hamel

11113 ■ American Legion, Minnesota Post 394
c/o John Pohlker
PO Box 96
Hamel, MN 55340
Ph: (651)291-1800
Fax: (651)291-1057
URL: National Affiliate–www.legion.org
Contact: John Pohlker, Contact
Local. Affiliated With: American Legion.

11114 ■ Hamel Lions Club
PO Box 301
Hamel, MN 55340
Ph: (763)473-0664
URL: http://www.hamellions.org
Contact: Marlene Roberts, Contact
Local. Affiliated With: Lions Clubs International.

Hancock

11115 ■ Hancock Lions Club
c/o Dennis Schroeder, Pres.
375 Hancock Ave.
Hancock, MN 56244
Ph: (320)392-5989
E-mail: gasmands@yahoo.com
URL: http://www.5m4lions.org
Contact: Dennis Schroeder, Pres.
Local. Affiliated With: Lions Clubs International.

Hanska

11116 ■ American Legion, Minnesota Post 365
c/o Oscar O. Haugen
PO Box 163
Hanska, MN 56041
Ph: (651)291-1800
Fax: (651)291-1057
URL: National Affiliate–www.legion.org
Contact: Oscar O. Haugen, Contact
Local. Affiliated With: American Legion.

Hardwick

11117 ■ American Legion, Minnesota Post 478
c/o Arthur Moeller
PO Box 111
Hardwick, MN 56134
Ph: (651)291-1800
Fax: (651)291-1057
URL: National Affiliate–www.legion.org
Contact: Arthur Moeller, Contact
Local. Affiliated With: American Legion.

Harmony

11118 ■ American Legion, Gustav Berg Post 81
PO Box 512
Harmony, MN 55939
Ph: (651)291-1800
Fax: (651)291-1057
URL: National Affiliate–www.legion.org
Local. Affiliated With: American Legion.

11119 ■ Harmony Lions Club
c/o David Laechel, Sec.
Box 536
Harmony, MN 55939
Ph: (507)886-4148
E-mail: dleachel@means.net
URL: http://www.lions5m1.org/harmony
Contact: David Laechel, Sec.
Local. Affiliated With: Lions Clubs International.

11120 ■ Southeastern Minnesota Historic Bluff Country
15 2nd St. NW
Box 609
Harmony, MN 55939-0609
Ph: (507)886-2230 (507)886-2241
Fax: (507)886-2934
Free: (800)428-2030
E-mail: hbc@means.net
URL: http://www.bluffcountry.com
Contact: Sylvia C. Leitzen, Admin,Dir.
Founded: 1985. **Members:** 150. **Membership Dues:** business, $150. **Staff:** 2. **Budget:** $80,000. **Regional.** Promotes Southeastern Minnesota as a desirable vacation destination, emphasizing the natural beauty of the area, recreational trails, river activities, caves, Amish tours, arts, unique shopping, and variety of lodging facilities. **Libraries: Type:** open to the public. **Holdings:** 2. **Subjects:** tourism. **Publications:** *Back Roads Visitor Guide*, annual • *Bike Trail Map & Directory - Root River & Harmony-Preston State Trails*, annual. Brochure • *Historic Bluff Country National Scenic Byway Map*, annual. Brochure. **Conventions/Meetings:** annual Artist Studio Tour - always last weekend in April • annual Birding Festival - always third weekend in May.

Harris

11121 ■ American Legion, Harris Post 139
43563 Giner Ave.
Harris, MN 55032
Ph: (651)291-1800
Fax: (651)291-1057
URL: National Affiliate–www.legion.org
Local. Affiliated With: American Legion.

Hartland

11122 ■ American Legion, Lundberg-Lee Post 266
PO Box 45
Hartland, MN 56042
Ph: (651)291-1800
Fax: (651)291-1057
URL: National Affiliate–www.legion.org
Local. Affiliated With: American Legion.

11123 ■ Mothers Against Drunk Driving, Freeborn County
66274 318 St.
Hartland, MN 56042
Ph: (507)863-2161
E-mail: kowskies@cvtel.net
URL: National Affiliate–www.madd.org
Contact: Mary Malakowsky, Coor.
Local. Victims of drunk driving crashes; concerned citizens. Encourages citizen participation in working towards reform of the drunk driving problem and the prevention of underage drinking. Acts as the voice of victims of drunk driving crashes by speaking on their behalf to communities, businesses, and educational groups. **Affiliated With:** Mothers Against Drunk Driving.

Hastings

11124 ■ American Legion, Minnesota Post 47
c/o Richard Howard Ferrell
50 Sibley St.
Hastings, MN 55033
Ph: (651)291-1800
Fax: (651)291-1057
URL: National Affiliate–www.legion.org
Contact: Richard Howard Ferrell, Contact
Local. Affiliated With: American Legion.

11125 ■ Hastings Area Chamber of Commerce and Tourism Bureau
111 E 3rd St.
Hastings, MN 55033-1211
Ph: (651)437-6775
Fax: (651)437-2697
Free: (888)612-6122
E-mail: info@hastingsmn.org
URL: http://www.hastingsmn.org
Contact: Michelle Jacobs, Pres.
Local.

11126 ■ High Technology Crime Investigation Association - Minnesota
PO Box 247
Hastings, MN 55033
Ph: (952)949-6256
E-mail: mgustad@edenprairie.org
URL: http://www.mn-htcia.org
Contact: Mark Gustad, Pres.
State. Promotes the voluntary interchange of data, information, experience, ideas and knowledge about methods, processes, and techniques relating to investigations and security in advanced technologies. **Affiliated With:** High Technology Crime Investigation Association International.

11127 ■ Minnesota Land Title Association (MLTA)
PO Box 456
Hastings, MN 55033
Ph: (651)304-3501
Fax: (651)437-6937
E-mail: richard@dcatitle.com
URL: http://www.mlta.org
Contact: Richard Welshons, Sec.-Treas.
State. Represents the interests of abstracters, title insurance companies and attorneys specializing in real property law. Improves the skills and knowledge of providers in real property transactions.

11128 ■ Orchid Society of Minnesota (OSM)
c/o Patricia Hartmann
17525 203rd St. E
Hastings, MN 55033
Ph: (651)438-2299
E-mail: rick@tjbhomes.com
URL: http://www.orchidsocietyofminnesota.com
Contact: Rick Budzynski, Pres.
State. Professional growers, botanists, hobbyists, and others interested in extending the knowledge, production, use, and appreciation of orchids. **Affiliated With:** American Orchid Society.

11129 ■ Ruffed Grouse Society, Missa-Croix Chapter
c/o Mike Brown
1945 Highland Dr.
Hastings, MN 55033
Ph: (651)437-2214
E-mail: mike.brown@nmcco.com
URL: National Affiliate–www.ruffedgrousesociety.org
Contact: Mike Brown, Contact
Local. Affiliated With: Ruffed Grouse Society.

11130 ■ Sons of Norway, Hjemkomst Lodge 1-599
c/o Duane R. Davick, Pres.
1217 Maple St.
Hastings, MN 55033-2615
Ph: (651)438-3738
E-mail: phddrd@aol.com
URL: National Affiliate–www.sofn.com
Contact: Duane R. Davick, Pres.
Local. Affiliated With: Sons of Norway.

11131 ■ TROA Council of MN Chapters
c/o Capt. Anthony Stauber
221 8th St. W
Hastings, MN 55033-2010
Ph: (218)525-5059
URL: National Affiliate–www.moaa.org
Contact: Capt. Anthony Stauber, Contact
State. Affiliated With: Military Officers Association of America.

11132 ■ United Way of Hastings, Minnesota
PO Box 353
Hastings, MN 55033-0353
Ph: (651)438-3337
URL: National Affiliate–national.unitedway.org
Local. Affiliated With: United Way of America.

Hawley

11133 ■ American Legion, Johnson Post 382
PO Box 70
Hawley, MN 56549
Ph: (651)291-1800
Fax: (651)291-1057
URL: National Affiliate–www.legion.org
Local. Affiliated With: American Legion.

11134 ■ Dress for Success, Northwest Minnesota
PO Box 237
Hawley, MN 56549-0237
Ph: (218)483-3145
Fax: (218)483-3149
E-mail: nwminnesota@dressforsuccess.org
URL: http://www.dressforsuccess.org
Contact: Laurie Albright, Board Chm.
Founded: 1998. **Budget:** $69,000. **Nonmembership. Local.** Provides free interview suit, confidence boost and career development to low-income women transitioning into the workforce. **Subgroups:** Professional Women's Group. **Publications:** *Professional Women's Group Newsletter*, monthly. **Price:** free for members. **Circulation:** 200. **Advertising:** not accepted.

11135 ■ Hawley Lions Club
c/o Robert T. Olson, Pres.
367 220th St. S
Hawley, MN 56549
Ph: (218)483-4815
URL: http://lions5m11.org/sys-tmpl/door
Contact: Robert T. Olson, Pres.
Local. Affiliated With: Lions Clubs International.

Hayfield

11136 ■ American Legion, Rothie Post 330
PO Box 448
Hayfield, MN 55940
Ph: (651)291-1800
Fax: (651)291-1057
URL: National Affiliate–www.legion.org
Local. Affiliated With: American Legion.

11137 ■ Hayfield Lions Club
c/o Harry Roberts, Sec.
73830 170th Ave.
Hayfield, MN 55940
Ph: (507)447-3212
E-mail: bandsroberts@pctc.net
URL: http://www.lions5m1.org/hayfield
Contact: Harry Roberts, Sec.
Local. Affiliated With: Lions Clubs International.

Hazel Run

11138 ■ American Legion, Anderson-Tongen Post 559
500 1st St.
Hazel Run, MN 56241
Ph: (651)291-1800
Fax: (651)291-1057
URL: National Affiliate–www.legion.org
Local. Affiliated With: American Legion.

Hector

11139 ■ American Legion, Minnesota Post 135
c/o Carl O. Potter
PO Box 223
Hector, MN 55342
Ph: (651)291-1800
Fax: (651)291-1057
URL: National Affiliate–www.legion.org
Contact: Carl O. Potter, Contact
Local. Affiliated With: American Legion.

11140 ■ Hector Lions Club - Minnesota
c/o Steve Wolff, Sec.
Box 66
Hector, MN 55342
Ph: (320)848-6514 (320)848-2233
E-mail: swolff@blh.k12.mn.us
URL: http://www.5m4lions.org
Contact: Steve Wolff, Sec.
Local. Affiliated With: Lions Clubs International.

Henderson

11141 ■ American Legion, Minnesota Post 74
c/o Russell Johnson
PO Box 306
Henderson, MN 56044
Ph: (651)291-1800
Fax: (651)291-1057
URL: National Affiliate–www.legion.org
Contact: Russell Johnson, Contact
Local. Affiliated With: American Legion.

Hendricks

11142 ■ American Legion, Minnesota Post 195
c/o Reuben Hansen
210 W Lincoln St.
Hendricks, MN 56136
Ph: (651)291-1800
Fax: (651)291-1057
URL: National Affiliate–www.legion.org
Contact: Reuben Hansen, Contact
Local. Affiliated With: American Legion.

Hendrum

11143 ■ American Legion, Holland-Swenson Post 434
PO Box 171
Hendrum, MN 56550
Ph: (651)291-1800
Fax: (651)291-1057
URL: National Affiliate–www.legion.org
Local. Affiliated With: American Legion.

Henning

11144 ■ American Legion, Buseth-Tusow Post 18
24734 490th Ave.
Henning, MN 56551
Ph: (651)291-1800
Fax: (651)291-1057
URL: National Affiliate–www.legion.org
Local. Affiliated With: American Legion.

Herman

11145 ■ American Legion, C. Walter Larson Post 378
PO Box 116
Herman, MN 56248
Ph: (651)291-1800
Fax: (651)291-1057
URL: National Affiliate–www.legion.org
Local. Affiliated With: American Legion.

11146 ■ American Legion, Hillestad-Borgeson Post 410
PO Box 247
Herman, MN 56248
Ph: (651)291-1800
Fax: (651)291-1057
URL: National Affiliate–www.legion.org
Local. Affiliated With: American Legion.

11147 ■ Hoffman Lions Club
c/o Theodore Anderson, Pres.
19310 140th St.
Herman, MN 56248
Ph: (320)986-2722
E-mail: tedmarse@runestone.net
URL: http://www.5m4lions.org
Contact: Theodore Anderson, Pres.
Local. Affiliated With: Lions Clubs International.

Hermantown

11148 ■ Aad Shriners
c/o Gordy Granmoe, Office Mgr.
5152 Miller Trunk Hwy.
Hermantown, MN 55811
Ph: (218)722-7488
Fax: (218)723-8162
Free: (888)863-1079
E-mail: shrineoffice@qwest.net
URL: http://www.aadshrine.org
Contact: Gordy Granmoe, Office Mgr.
Local. Affiliated With: Imperial Council of the Ancient Arabic Order of the Nobles of the Mystic Shrine for North America.

11149 ■ Hermantown Arena Board
c/o Cheryl Borndal
4309 Ugstad Rd.
Hermantown, MN 55811-1335
Ph: (218)729-5493
Fax: (218)729-9374
E-mail: hawkdome@hermantown.k12.mn.us
Contact: Lisa Paczynski, Office Mgr.
Local.

11150 ■ Hermantown Chamber of Commerce
4940 Lightning Dr.
Hermantown, MN 55811-1447
Ph: (218)729-6843
Fax: (218)729-7132
E-mail: hermcham@uslink.net
URL: http://www.hermantownchamber.com
Contact: Kay Knight, Exec.Dir.
Local. Promotes business and community development in the Hermantown, MN area. Provides leadership for the community, promotes local resources, enhances local programs, and coordinates development efforts.

11151 ■ Trout Unlimited - Gitche Gumee Chapter
3717 Keene Creek Ln.
Hermantown, MN 55811
Ph: (218)722-1972
Fax: (218)723-8233
E-mail: benoit23@peoplepc.com
URL: http://www.tu.org
Contact: Kenneth Benoit, Pres.
Local.

Heron Lake

11152 ■ American Legion, Herbert K. Kellam Post 224
312 10th St.
Heron Lake, MN 56137
Ph: (651)291-1800
Fax: (651)291-1057
URL: National Affiliate–www.legion.org
Local. Affiliated With: American Legion.

11153 ■ Sons of Norway, Stavanger Lodge 1-538
c/o Bonnie F. Frederickson, Pres.
42990 900th St.
Heron Lake, MN 56137-3152
Ph: (507)831-5091
E-mail: bonnie.frederickson@co.jackson.mn.us
URL: National Affiliate–www.sofn.com
Contact: Bonnie F. Frederickson, Pres.
Local. Affiliated With: Sons of Norway.

Hibbing

11154 ■ American Chesapeake Club, Minnesota
c/o Gary Sorenson
3875 Berg Rd.
Hibbing, MN 55746
Ph: (218)262-0721
E-mail: gdsorens@uslink.net
URL: National Affiliate–www.amchessieclub.org
Contact: Gary Sorenson, Contact
State. Affiliated With: American Chesapeake Club.

11155 ■ American Legion, Cobb-Williams-Nehiba Post 222
PO Box 592
Hibbing, MN 55746
Ph: (651)291-1800
Fax: (651)291-1057
URL: National Affiliate–www.legion.org
Local. Affiliated With: American Legion.

11156 ■ Church and Synagogue Library Association, Hibbing Church Library Network
c/o J. Terry Moore, Library Dir.
2020 E 5th Ave.
Hibbing, MN 55746
Ph: (218)262-1038
Fax: (218)262-5407
E-mail: hibbingpl@arrowhead.lib.mn.us
URL: http://www.hibbing.lib.mn.us
Contact: J. Terry Moore, Library Dir.
Founded: 1990. **Members:** 7. **Local.** Seeks to share library resources among the church libraries and the public library. **Libraries: Type:** reference. **Holdings:** 5,000. **Affiliated With:** Church and Synagogue Library Association.

11157 ■ Hibbing Area Chamber of Commerce
211 E Howard St.
PO Box 727
Hibbing, MN 55746-1763
Ph: (218)262-3895
Fax: (218)262-3897
E-mail: hibbcofc@hibbing.org
URL: http://www.hibbing.org
Contact: Lory Fedo, Pres./CEO
Founded: 1905. **Members:** 500. **Membership Dues:** business, $182-$1,264 (annual) • professional, $182 (annual) • associate, $75 (annual) • lodging, $196 (annual) • insurance/real estate, $182 (annual). **Staff:** 4. **Local.** Promotes business and community development in Hibbing, MN. **Committees:** Ambassadors; Government Affairs; Membership Enhancement; Mines and Pines Jubilee; Special Events. **Subgroups:** Business and Education Partnership; Community and Business Partnerships. **Affiliated With:** Downtown Merchants Association; Iron Mining Association of Minnesota; Junior Achievement. **Formerly:** (1999) Hibbing Chamber of Commerce.

11158 ■ Hibbing Figure Skating Club
726 E 25th St.
Hibbing, MN 55746
Ph: (218)263-3407
E-mail: rms@the-bridge.net
URL: National Affiliate–www.usfigureskating.org
Contact: Suzie Novak, Contact
Local. Provides programs to encourage participation and achievement in the sport of figure skating on ice. Defines and maintains uniform standards of skating proficiency. Organizes and sponsors competitions and exhibitions for the purpose of stimulating interest in figure skating. **Affiliated With:** United States Figure Skating Association.

11159 ■ Hibbing Historical Society
c/o Richard K. Sellman
400 23rd St. & 5th Ave. E
Hibbing, MN 55746
Ph: (218)263-8522
E-mail: hibbhist@uslink.net
Founded: 1976. **Members:** 100. **Membership Dues:** individual, $15 (annual) • senior citizen, $10 (annual) • life, $200. **Staff:** 1. **Local. Libraries: Type:** reference; open to the public. **Holdings:** 400; books, maps. **Subjects:** hibbing, location, mining, logging. **Publications:** *Frank's Place*. Newsletter. **Price:** free for members.

11160 ■ Hibbing Lions Club
c/o Michael Bresnahan, Pres.
2017 E 36th St.
Hibbing, MN 55746
Ph: (218)885-2727
URL: http://lions5m10.org
Contact: Michael Bresnahan, Pres.
Local. Affiliated With: Lions Clubs International.

11161 ■ Phi Theta Kappa, Theta Kappa Chapter - Hibbing Community College
c/o Roberta Morrow, Advisor
Hibbing Campus
1515 E 25th St.
Hibbing, MN 55746
Ph: (218)262-7270
E-mail: robertamorrow@hibbing.edu
URL: http://www.ptk.org/directories/chapters/MN/263-1.htm
Contact: Roberta Morrow, Advisor
Local.

11162 ■ The Retired Enlisted Association Chapter 96 (TREA)
c/o Ted Polacec, Pres.
PO Box 466
Hibbing, MN 55746-0466
Ph: (218)744-2647
E-mail: skyfire@uslink.net
URL: National Affiliate–www.trea.org
Contact: Ted Polacec, Pres.
Local. Affiliated With: The Retired Enlisted Association.

11163 ■ United Way of Hibbing
2142 1st Ave.
Hibbing, MN 55746-1805
Ph: (218)262-1313
URL: National Affiliate–national.unitedway.org
Local. Affiliated With: United Way of America.

Hill City

11164 ■ American Legion, Minnesota Post 340
c/o James Kobernat
PO Box 183
Hill City, MN 55748
Ph: (651)291-1800
Fax: (651)291-1057
URL: National Affiliate–www.legion.org
Contact: James Kobernat, Contact
Local. Affiliated With: American Legion.

Hillman

11165 ■ American Legion, Wojciak-Talberg Post 602
37285 167th St.
Hillman, MN 56338
Ph: (651)291-1800
Fax: (651)291-1057
URL: National Affiliate–www.legion.org
Local. Affiliated With: American Legion.

11166 ■ Hillman Adult Leisure Club
c/o Mary Grunwald
24901 Peavey Lake Dr.
Hillman, MN 56338-2358
Ph: (320)277-3841
Founded: 1978. **Members:** 36. **Local**.

11167 ■ Memorial Rifle Squad, Minnesota State Veterans Cemetery
c/o Mel Buesseler
37253 173rd St.
Hillman, MN 56338-2217
Ph: (320)277-3304
E-mail: melnetty@littlefalls.net
Contact: Mel Buesseler, Committee Chm.
Founded: 2001. **State**.

Hills

11168 ■ American Legion, Hills Post 399
PO Box 95
Hills, MN 56138
Ph: (651)291-1800
Fax: (651)291-1057
URL: National Affiliate–www.legion.org
Local. Affiliated With: American Legion.

Hinckley

11169 ■ American Legion, Minnesota Post 347
c/o William O. Machart
34001 Hinckley Rd.
Hinckley, MN 55037
Ph: (651)291-1800
Fax: (651)291-1057
URL: National Affiliate–www.legion.org
Contact: William O. Machart, Contact
Local. Affiliated With: American Legion.

11170 ■ American Legion, Stenmark-Farnsworth Post 388
PO Box 181
Hinckley, MN 55037
Ph: (651)291-1800
Fax: (651)291-1057
URL: National Affiliate–www.legion.org
Local. Affiliated With: American Legion.

Hitterdal

11171 ■ American Legion, Minnesota Post 13
c/o Floyd N. Knudtson
6409 Hwy. 32 N
Hitterdal, MN 56552
Ph: (651)291-1800
Fax: (651)291-1057
URL: National Affiliate–www.legion.org
Contact: Floyd N. Knudtson, Contact
Local. Affiliated With: American Legion.

11172 ■ Hitterdal Lions Club
c/o Russell McDougall, Sec.
310 W Front St.
Hitterdal, MN 56552-0125
Ph: (218)962-3433
E-mail: rgrjdoug@feltontel.net
URL: http://lions5m11.org/sys-tmpl/door
Contact: Russell McDougall, Sec.
Local. Affiliated With: Lions Clubs International.

Hoffman

11173 ■ American Legion, Hoffman Post 393
127 Main Ave.
Hoffman, MN 56339
Ph: (651)291-1800
Fax: (651)291-1057
URL: National Affiliate–www.legion.org
Local. Affiliated With: American Legion.

Hokah

11174 ■ American Legion, Hokah Post 498
PO Box 188
Hokah, MN 55941
Ph: (651)291-1800
Fax: (651)291-1057
URL: National Affiliate–www.legion.org
Local. Affiliated With: American Legion.

Holdingford

11175 ■ American Legion, Frank Feia Post 211
PO Box 263
Holdingford, MN 56340
Ph: (651)291-1800
Fax: (651)291-1057
URL: National Affiliate–www.legion.org
Local. Affiliated With: American Legion.

Holland

11176 ■ American Legion, Minnesota Post 534
c/o Earl Gruis
RR 1, Box 223
Holland, MN 56139
Ph: (651)291-1800
Fax: (651)291-1057
URL: National Affiliate–www.legion.org
Contact: Earl Gruis, Contact
Local. Affiliated With: American Legion.

Hopkins

11177 ■ American Legion, Eagle Post 509
10 12th Ave. S
Hopkins, MN 55343
Ph: (651)291-1800
Fax: (651)291-1057
URL: National Affiliate–www.legion.org
Local. Affiliated With: American Legion.

11178 ■ American Legion, Edina Post 471
10 12th Ave. S
Hopkins, MN 55343
Ph: (651)291-1800
Fax: (651)291-1057
URL: National Affiliate–www.legion.org
Local. Affiliated With: American Legion.

11179 ■ American Legion, Minnesota Post 320
c/o John Wilbur Moore
PO Box 554
Hopkins, MN 55343
Ph: (651)291-1800
Fax: (651)291-1057
URL: National Affiliate–www.legion.org
Contact: John Wilbur Moore, Contact
Local. Affiliated With: American Legion.

11180 ■ Bloomington Wyldlife
175 Jackson Ave. N, Ste.429
Hopkins, MN 55343
Ph: (952)922-8338
URL: http://sites.younglife.org/sites/BloomingtonWyldLife/default.aspx
Local. Affiliated With: Young Life.

11181 ■ Bloomington Young Life
175 Jackson Ave. N, Ste.429
Hopkins, MN 55343
Ph: (952)922-8338
URL: http://sites.younglife.org/sites/Bloomington/default.aspx
Local. Affiliated With: Young Life.

11182 ■ Eden Prairie - Young Life
175 Jackson Ave. N, Ste.429
Hopkins, MN 55343
Ph: (952)922-8338
URL: http://sites.younglife.org/sites/EPYL/default.aspx
Local. Affiliated With: Young Life.

11183 ■ Edina - Young Life
175 Jackson Ave. N, Ste.429
Hopkins, MN 55343
Ph: (952)922-8338
E-mail: ylrobin@hotmail.com
URL: http://sites.younglife.org/sites/Edina/default.aspx
Local. Affiliated With: Young Life.

11184 ■ Hopkins Area Jaycees
6 6th Ave. N
Hopkins, MN 55343
Ph: (952)931-0132
E-mail: mickey1928us@yahoo.com
URL: http://www.hopkinsjaycees.com
Contact: Monica Sage, Pres.
Founded: 1950. **Local**.

11185 ■ Hopkins Young Life
175 Jackson Ave. N, Ste.429
Hopkins, MN 55343
Ph: (952)922-8338
E-mail: nickabel@hotmail.com
URL: http://sites.younglife.org/sites/Hopkins/default.aspx
Contact: Nick Abel, Contact
Local. Affiliated With: Young Life.

11186 ■ Minneapolis South Young Life
175 Jackson Ave. N, Ste.429
Hopkins, MN 55343
Ph: (952)922-8338
Fax: (952)922-8263
URL: http://sites.younglife.org/sites/MinneapolisSouth/default.aspx
Local. Affiliated With: Young Life.

11187 ■ Minnehaha Academy - Wyldlife
175 Jackson Ave. N, Ste.429
Hopkins, MN 55343
Ph: (952)922-8338
URL: http://sites.younglife.org/sites/MA/default.aspx
Local. Affiliated With: Young Life.

11188 ■ Minnesota Amateur Athletic Union
c/o Dave Peller, Treas.
Eisenhower Recreation Ctr.
1001 Hwy. 7
Hopkins, MN 55305
Ph: (612)865-9781
E-mail: davidpreller@comcast.net
URL: http://www.minnesotaaau.org
Contact: Dave Peller, Treas.
State. Affiliated With: Amateur Athletic Union.

11189 ■ Minnesotans Against Terrorism
c/o Amy Rotenberg
PO Box 368
Hopkins, MN 55343-0368
Ph: (612)677-3268
Fax: (612)677-3839
E-mail: webcontact@matmn.org
URL: http://www.matmn.org
Contact: Amy Rotenberg, Media Contact
State.

11190 ■ Minnetonka South Lions Club
c/o Tom Heinecke, Pres.
PO Box 4233
Hopkins, MN 55343
Ph: (952)945-9583 (952)939-4180
URL: http://www.5m5.org
Contact: Tom Heinecke, Pres.
Local. Affiliated With: Lions Clubs International.

11191 ■ Private School B - Young Life
175 Jackson Ave. N, Ste.429
Hopkins, MN 55343
Ph: (952)922-8338
URL: http://sites.younglife.org/sites/privateschool/default.aspx
Local. Affiliated With: Young Life.

11192 ■ Richfield - Young Life
175 Jackson Ave. N, Ste.429
Hopkins, MN 55343
Ph: (952)922-8338
URL: http://sites.younglife.org/sites/Richfield/default.aspx
Contact: Patricia Kelley, Contact
Local. Affiliated With: Young Life.

11193 ■ Sons of Norway, Vestland Lodge 1-601
c/o W. Pitt Rolfe, Pres.
302 Burnes Dr.
Hopkins, MN 55343-9202
Ph: (952)938-2920
E-mail: pittrolfe@mn.rr.com
URL: National Affiliate–www.sofn.com
Contact: W. Pitt Rolfe, Pres.
Local. Affiliated With: Sons of Norway.

11194 ■ Twin Cities Professional Photographers of America
c/o Dave Johnson
319 Sweet Briar Ln.
Hopkins, MN 55343
Ph: (612)759-3921
E-mail: davej@silverimages.com
URL: National Affiliate–ppa.com
Contact: Dave Johnson, Contact
Local. Affiliated With: Professional Photographers of America.

11195 ■ Young Life Northern States Region
750 2nd St. NE, Ste.140
Hopkins, MN 55343
Ph: (952)927-6928
Fax: (952)927-6968
URL: http://sites.younglife.org/sites/NorthernStatesRegion/default.aspx
Regional. Affiliated With: Young Life.

11196 ■ Young Life Urban Growth Project
750 2nd St. NE, Ste.140
Hopkins, MN 55343
Ph: (952)927-6928
Fax: (952)922-8263
URL: http://sites.younglife.org/_layouts/ylext/default.aspx?ID=A-AG210
Local. Affiliated With: Young Life.

Houston

11197 ■ American Legion, Arnet-Sheldon Post 423
PO Box 146
Houston, MN 55943
Ph: (651)291-1800
Fax: (651)291-1057
URL: National Affiliate–www.legion.org
Local. Affiliated With: American Legion.

11198 ■ Houston Lions Club - Minnesota
c/o Larry Jerviss, Sec.
Box 292
Houston, MN 55943
Ph: (507)896-2144
E-mail: ljerv@acegroup.cc
URL: http://www.lions5m1.org/houston
Contact: Larry Jerviss, Sec.
Local. Affiliated With: Lions Clubs International.

Howard Lake

11199 ■ American Legion, Howard Post 145
PO Box 33
Howard Lake, MN 55349
Ph: (651)291-1800
Fax: (651)291-1057
URL: National Affiliate–www.legion.org
Local. Affiliated With: American Legion.

11200 ■ Minnesota Quarter Horse Association, District 5
c/o Deb Seppelt
9520 10th St. SW
Howard Lake, MN 55349
Ph: (320)543-2292
URL: http://www.mnqha.com/index_main.htm
Contact: Deb Seppelt, Contact
Local. Affiliated With: American Quarter Horse Association.

Hoyt Lakes

11201 ■ Hoyt Lakes Lions Club
c/o Michael Patchin, Pres.
332 Hampshire Dr.
Hoyt Lakes, MN 55750-1228
Ph: (218)225-2205
URL: http://lions5m10.org
Contact: Michael Patchin, Pres.
Local. Affiliated With: Lions Clubs International.

Hugo

11202 ■ American Legion, Hugo Post 620
5383 140th St. N
Hugo, MN 55038
Ph: (651)291-1800
Fax: (651)291-1057
URL: National Affiliate–www.legion.org
Local. Affiliated With: American Legion.

Hutchinson

11203 ■ American Legion, Hutchinson Post 96
35 3rd Ave. SE
Hutchinson, MN 55350
Ph: (651)291-1800
Fax: (651)291-1057
URL: National Affiliate–www.legion.org
Local. Affiliated With: American Legion.

11204 ■ Audio Engineering Society, Ridgewater College, Hutchinson Campus Section
c/o Dave Igl
Ridgewater Coll.
Hutchinson Campus
2 Century Ave. SE
Hutchinson, MN 55350
Ph: (320)587-0223
URL: National Affiliate–www.aes.org
Contact: Dave Igl, Contact
Local. Represents the interests of engineers, administrators and technicians for radio, television and motion picture operation. Operates educational and research foundation. **Affiliated With:** Audio Engineering Society.

11205 ■ Cedar Mills Lions Club
c/o Corrinne Schlueter, Sec.
23157 215th St.
Hutchinson, MN 55350
Ph: (320)587-6471 (320)234-4753
E-mail: cschluter@hahc-hm.com
URL: http://www.5m4lions.org
Contact: Corrinne Schlueter, Sec.
Local. Affiliated With: Lions Clubs International.

11206 ■ Crow River Habitat for Humanity (CRHFH)
The Hope Center
305 Main St. S, Ste.107
Hutchinson, MN 55350
Ph: (320)587-8868
Fax: (320)234-9581
E-mail: crhfh@crhfh.org
URL: http://www.crhfh.org
Contact: Judy Dinger, Exec.Dir.
Local. Affiliated With: Habitat for Humanity International.

11207 ■ Hutchinson Area Chamber of Commerce (HACCCVB)
2 Main St. S
Hutchinson, MN 55350
Ph: (320)587-5252
Fax: (320)587-4752
Free: (800)572-6689
E-mail: info@explorehutchinson.com
URL: http://www.explorehutchinson.com
Founded: 1948. **Members:** 335. **Membership Dues:** general business (plus $1 for each additional employee), $209-$898 (annual) • bank (minimum; per million in deposits), $48 (annual) • home business, $105 (annual) • individual, $84 (annual) • organization and association, $84 (annual) • retired business person, $50 (annual). **Local.** Promotes business and community development in the Hutchinson, MN area. **Councils:** Crow River Area Quality. **Subgroups:** Hutchinson Ambassadors. **Task Forces:** Agri-Business; Arts and Craft; Business Development; Leadership Development; Music in the Park; Public Relations. **Publications:** *Hometown Happenings*, monthly. Newsletter. **Advertising:** accepted.

11208 ■ Hutchinson Area Convention and Visitors Bureau
12 Main St. S
Hutchinson, MN 55350
Ph: (320)587-5252
Fax: (320)587-4752
Free: (800)572-6689
E-mail: info@hutchinsonchamber.com
URL: http://hutchinsonchamber.com
Contact: Keith Enstad, Contact
Local. Seeks to promote city of Hutchinson, MN as a place for conventions and business gatherings.

11209 ■ Hutchinson Jaycees
PO Box 624
Hutchinson, MN 55350
E-mail: info@hutchinsonjaycees.org
URL: http://users.hutchtel.net/~jaycees
Contact: Lonnie Krueger, Pres.
Local.

11210 ■ Midwest Regional Gas Task Force Association
c/o John Webster
225 Michigan
Hutchinson, MN 55350-1905
Ph: (320)587-4746
Fax: (320)587-4721
E-mail: jwebster@ci.hutchinson.mn.us
Contact: William Bombich, Pres.
Members: 18. **Regional.**

11211 ■ Minnesota Elks Association
c/o Dennis Schroeder, Sec.
1074 Prairie View SW
Hutchinson, MN 55350
Ph: (320)587-3660
E-mail: elks@mnelks.org
URL: http://www.mnelks.org
Contact: Joe Syvrud, Pres.
State. Promotes the principles of charity, justice, brotherhood and loyalty among members. Fosters the spirit of American Patriotism. Seeks to stimulate pride and respect toward patriotism. **Affiliated With:** Benevolent and Protective Order of Elks.

11212 ■ Phi Theta Kappa, Beta Eta Chi Chapter - Ridgewater College
c/o Kathy Steffen
Hutchinson Campus
2 Century Ave.
Hutchinson, MN 55350
Ph: (320)234-0328
URL: http://www.ptk.org/directories/chapters/MN/21605-1.htm
Contact: Kathy Steffen, Advisor
Local.

11213 ■ United Way of the Hutchinson Area
12 Main St. S
Hutchinson, MN 55350
Ph: (320)587-5252
Fax: (320)587-4752
E-mail: info@hutchinsonchamber.com
URL: National Affiliate–national.unitedway.org
Contact: Joy Schmitz, Pres.
Founded: 1962. **Members:** 26. **Budget:** $178,800. **Local**. **Affiliated With:** United Way of America.

International Falls

11214 ■ American Legion, William Robideau Post 66
2707 Crescent Dr.
International Falls, MN 56649
Ph: (651)291-1800
Fax: (651)291-1057
URL: National Affiliate–www.legion.org
Local. **Affiliated With:** American Legion.

11215 ■ Friends of Voyageurs National Park
3131 Hwy. 53
International Falls, MN 56649-0945
Ph: (218)283-9821
Contact: Jo Kallemeyn, Pres.
Founded: 1995. **Members:** 90. **Regional**. Sponsors outreach that supports natural, historical, and educational activities available at Voyageurs National Park. **Conventions/Meetings:** monthly meeting - International Falls, MN.

11216 ■ International Falls Area Chamber of Commerce (IFACC)
301 2nd Ave.
International Falls, MN 56649
Ph: (218)283-9400
Fax: (218)283-3572
Free: (800)FAL-LSMN
E-mail: intlfall@intlfalls.org
URL: http://www.internationalfallsmn.us
Contact: Kallie L. Briggs, Exec.Dir.
Local. Promotes business and community development in the International Falls, MN area. **Computer Services:** Online services, business directory. **Formerly:** (1999) Greater International Falls +Chamber of Commerce.

11217 ■ International Falls Lions Club
c/o Dick Briese, Pres.
3563 County Rd. 21
International Falls, MN 56649
Ph: (218)286-2070
E-mail: iceboxdick@charter.net
URL: http://lions5m10.org
Contact: Dick Briese, Pres.
Local. **Affiliated With:** Lions Clubs International.

11218 ■ Phi Theta Kappa, Alpha Rho Alpha Chapter - Rainy River Community College
c/o Sue Olson
1501 Hwy. 71
International Falls, MN 56649
Ph: (218)285-2279
E-mail: solson@rrcc.mnscu.edu
URL: http://www.ptk.org/directories/chapters/MN/8742-1.htm
Contact: Sue Olson, Advisor
Local.

11219 ■ Ruffed Grouse Society, Voyageur Chapter
c/o Pete Schultz
510 11th Ave.
International Falls, MN 56649
Ph: (218)283-9765
URL: National Affiliate–www.ruffedgrousesociety.org
Contact: Pete Schultz, Contact
Local. **Affiliated With:** Ruffed Grouse Society.

11220 ■ Society of American Foresters, Headwaters Chapter
c/o Kara Dunning, Chair
400 3rd Ave. E
International Falls, MN 56649
Ph: (218)285-5449
E-mail: karadunning@boisepaper.com
URL: http://www.mnsaf.org
Contact: Kara Dunning, Chair
Local. **Affiliated With:** Society of American Foresters.

Inver Grove

11221 ■ Minnesota Mathematical Association of Two-Year Colleges (MinnMATYC)
c/o Keven Dockter, Pres.
2500 80th St. E
Inver Grove, MN 55076
Ph: (651)450-8662
E-mail: kdockte@inverhills.mnscu.edu
URL: http://www.minnmatyc.org
Contact: Keven Dockter, Pres.
State. Promotes and increases awareness of the role of two-year colleges in mathematics education. Provides a forum for the improvement of mathematics instruction in the first two years of college. Provides professional development opportunities for educators interested in the first two years of collegiate mathematics instruction. **Affiliated With:** American Mathematical Association of Two-Year Colleges.

Inver Grove Heights

11222 ■ American Legion, Inver Grove Heights Post 424
PO Box 2064
Inver Grove Heights, MN 55076
Ph: (651)291-1800
Fax: (651)291-1057
URL: National Affiliate–www.legion.org
Local. **Affiliated With:** American Legion.

11223 ■ Institute of Management Accountants, Saint Paul
c/o Jason R. Golde, Pres.
5925 Candace Ave.
Inver Grove Heights, MN 55076
Ph: (952)984-3160
E-mail: igolde@hotmail.com
URL: http://www.stpaul.imanet.org
Contact: Jason R. Golde, Pres.
Local. Promotes professional and ethical standards. Equips members and students with knowledge and training required for the accounting profession. **Additional Websites:** http://www.ima-northernlights.imanet.org. **Councils:** Northern Lights. **Affiliated With:** Institute of Management Accountants. **Publications:** *The Bottom Line*, monthly. Newsletter. Alternate Formats: online.

11224 ■ Northstar Weimaraner Club
c/o Marianne Burns, Pres.
1170 E 90th St.
Inver Grove Heights, MN 55077
Ph: (651)457-4817
E-mail: aranar@iphouse.com
URL: http://www.northstarweim.com
Contact: Marianne Burns, Pres.
Local.

11225 ■ Phi Theta Kappa, Alpha Omicron Beta Chapter - Inver Hills Community College
c/o Elizabeth Evensen
2500 80th St. E
Inver Grove Heights, MN 55076
Ph: (651)554-3714
E-mail: liz.evensen@ptk.org
URL: http://www.ptk.org/directories/chapters/MN/5427-1.htm
Contact: Elizabeth Evensen, Advisor
Local.

11226 ■ Puppeteers of America - Twin Cities Puppeteers
c/o Karen Backes
7500 Babcock Trail
Inver Grove Heights, MN 55077
URL: http://tcpuppet.org
Contact: Karen Backes, Contact
Membership Dues: individual, $20 (annual) • couple, $30 (annual). **Local**.

11227 ■ River Heights Chamber of Commerce (RHCC)
5782 Blackhire Path
Inver Grove Heights, MN 55076
Ph: (651)451-2266
Fax: (651)451-0846
E-mail: info@riverheights.com
URL: http://www.riverheights.com
Contact: Jennifer Gale, Pres.
Founded: 1903. **Members:** 400. **Membership Dues:** business, $278-$2,340 (annual) • utility, $824 (annual) • financial institution, $785 (annual) • civic organization and association, $278 (annual) • associate, $139 (annual). **Staff:** 5. **Budget:** $300,000. **Local**. Promotes business and community development in South St. Paul-Inver Grove Heights, MN. **Awards:** Business of the Year. **Frequency:** annual. **Type:** recognition • Small Business of the Year. **Frequency:** annual. **Type:** recognition • Visions of Excellence. **Type:** recognition. **Recipient:** for outstanding entrepreneurs. **Computer Services:** Online services, membership directory. **Boards:** Leadership Advisory. **Committees:** Ambassador; Cahill Corridor; Concord Business; Legislative Action; Personal Business Mentor. **Task Forces:** Golf Tournament; Holiday Gala. **Affiliated With:** U.S. Chamber of Commerce. **Formerly:** (1999) South St. Paul-Inver Grove Heights Chamber of Commerce. **Publications:** *Business Perspective*, monthly. Newsletter. **Circulation:** 725. **Advertising:** accepted. Alternate Formats: online • Newsletter, weekly. Alternate Formats: online • Membership Directory, annual. **Conventions/Meetings:** annual Leadership Conference - always October in South St. Paul, MN • annual meeting • annual Small Business Luncheon (exhibits) - always April.

Iron

11228 ■ Mountain Iron Lions Club
c/o Anthony Nigro, Pres.
4084 Hartman Rd.
Iron, MN 55751
Ph: (218)262-4769
URL: http://lions5m10.org
Contact: Anthony Nigro, Pres.
Local. **Affiliated With:** Lions Clubs International.

Ironton

11229 ■ American Legion, Myrin-James Post 443
PO Box 37
Ironton, MN 56455
Ph: (651)291-1800
Fax: (651)291-1057
URL: National Affiliate–www.legion.org
Local. **Affiliated With:** American Legion.

Isanti

11230 ■ Ruffed Grouse Society, Rum River Chapter
c/o Kevin Domogalla
25225 Davenport St. NE
Isanti, MN 55040
Ph: (763)444-6535
E-mail: krdram85@aol.com
URL: National Affiliate–www.ruffedgrousesociety.org
Contact: Kevin Domogalla, Contact
Local. Affiliated With: Ruffed Grouse Society.

Isle

11231 ■ Sons of Norway, Tusenvann Lodge 1-659
c/o Robert W. Skogman, Pres.
18639 327th Ave.
Isle, MN 56342-4784
Ph: (320)684-2078
E-mail: a1level@mlec2.net
URL: National Affiliate–www.sofn.com
Contact: Robert W. Skogman, Pres.
Local. Affiliated With: Sons of Norway.

Ivanhoe

11232 ■ American Legion, Minnesota Post 194
c/o Stanley Dastych
PO Box 86
Ivanhoe, MN 56142
Ph: (651)291-1800
Fax: (651)291-1057
URL: National Affiliate–www.legion.org
Contact: Stanley Dastych, Contact
Local. Affiliated With: American Legion.

Jackson

11233 ■ American Legion, Jackson Liberty Post 130
411 1st St.
Jackson, MN 56143
Ph: (651)291-1800
Fax: (651)291-1057
URL: National Affiliate–www.legion.org
Local. Affiliated With: American Legion.

11234 ■ Jackson Area Chamber of Commerce (JACC)
82 W Ashley St.
Jackson, MN 56143-1669
Ph: (507)847-3867
Fax: (507)847-3869
E-mail: chamber@cityofjacksonmn.com
URL: http://jacksonmn.com
Contact: Cari Boell, Exec.Dir.
Members: 150. **Local.** Promotes business and community development in Jackson, MN. Holds annual Town and Country Day Celebration, Agriculture Day, Craft, Antique, and Toy show. **Computer Services:** Online services, member listings. **Publications:** *Chamber Chatter*, quarterly. Newsletter • *Experience the Jackson Area*. Booklet.

Janesville

11235 ■ American Legion, Janesville Post 281
PO Box 335
Janesville, MN 56048
Ph: (651)291-1800
Fax: (651)291-1057
URL: National Affiliate–www.legion.org
Local. Affiliated With: American Legion.

Jasper

11236 ■ American Legion, Oscar Iverson Post 133
PO Box 148
Jasper, MN 56144
Ph: (651)291-1800
Fax: (651)291-1057
URL: National Affiliate–www.legion.org
Local. Affiliated With: American Legion.

Jeffers

11237 ■ American Legion, Odegaard-Quade Post 401
PO Box 41
Jeffers, MN 56145
Ph: (651)291-1800
Fax: (651)291-1057
URL: National Affiliate–www.legion.org
Local. Affiliated With: American Legion.

Johnson

11238 ■ American Legion, Jesse Poole Post 297
105 4th Ave.
Johnson, MN 56236
Ph: (651)291-1800
Fax: (651)291-1057
URL: National Affiliate–www.legion.org
Local. Affiliated With: American Legion.

Jordan

11239 ■ American Legion, Robert Patterson Post 3
259 Valley Green Park
Jordan, MN 55352
Ph: (651)291-1800
Fax: (651)291-1057
URL: National Affiliate–www.legion.org
Local. Affiliated With: American Legion.

Karlstad

11240 ■ American Legion, Elwood Monroe Swenson Post 445
PO Box 43
Karlstad, MN 56732
Ph: (651)291-1800
Fax: (651)291-1057
URL: National Affiliate–www.legion.org
Local. Affiliated With: American Legion.

11241 ■ Karlstad Lions Club
c/o Gary Cook, Pres.
PO Box 35
Karlstad, MN 56732
Ph: (218)436-2414
URL: http://lions5m11.org/sys-tmpl/door
Contact: Gary Cook, Pres.
Local. Affiliated With: Lions Clubs International.

Kasota

11242 ■ American Legion, Kasota Post 348
PO Box 187
Kasota, MN 56050
Ph: (651)291-1800
Fax: (651)291-1057
URL: National Affiliate–www.legion.org
Local. Affiliated With: American Legion.

Kasson

11243 ■ American Legion, Adolph Oiseth Post 333
212 W Main St.
Kasson, MN 55944
Ph: (651)291-1800
Fax: (651)291-1057
URL: National Affiliate–www.legion.org
Local. Affiliated With: American Legion.

11244 ■ Faith in Action in Dodge County
PO Box 246
Kasson, MN 55944
Ph: (507)634-3654
E-mail: fiadodge@kmtel.com
URL: http://www.fiadodgecounty.org
Local.

11245 ■ Kasson-Mantorville Lions Club
PO Box 121
Kasson, MN 55944
E-mail: rcnorton@charter.net
URL: http://www.crosswinds.net/%7Ekmlions
Contact: Ron Norton, Contact
Local. Affiliated With: Lions Clubs International.

11246 ■ Minnesota Quarter Horse Association, District 3
c/o Jim Schultze
65576 230th Ave.
Kasson, MN 55944
Ph: (507)634-6540
URL: http://www.mnqha.com/index_main.htm
Contact: Jim Schultze, Contact
Local. Affiliated With: American Quarter Horse Association.

Keewatin

11247 ■ American Legion, Venier-Molea Post 452
PO Box 6
Keewatin, MN 55753
Ph: (651)291-1800
Fax: (651)291-1057
URL: National Affiliate–www.legion.org
Local. Affiliated With: American Legion.

Kelliher

11248 ■ American Legion, Ahlberg-Weigelt Post 470
PO Box 217
Kelliher, MN 56650
Ph: (651)291-1800
Fax: (651)291-1057
URL: National Affiliate–www.legion.org
Local. Affiliated With: American Legion.

Kellogg

11249 ■ American Legion, Kellogg Post 546
PO Box 54
Kellogg, MN 55945
Ph: (651)291-1800
Fax: (651)291-1057
URL: National Affiliate–www.legion.org
Local. Affiliated With: American Legion.

11250 ■ Kellogg Lions Club
c/o Joe Feils, Pres.
Box 211
Kellogg, MN 55945
Ph: (507)767-3287
E-mail: jbfeils@lakes.com
URL: http://www.lions5m1.org/kellogg
Contact: Joe Feils, Pres.
Local. Affiliated With: Lions Clubs International.

Kensington

11251 ■ American Legion, Ogmar Post 268
PO Box 143
Kensington, MN 56343
Ph: (651)291-1800
Fax: (651)291-1057
URL: National Affiliate–www.legion.org
Local. Affiliated With: American Legion.

11252 ■ Kensington Lions Club
c/o Dale Rau, Pres.
23 Grand Ave. N
Kensington, MN 56343
Ph: (320)965-2293
URL: http://www.5m4lions.org
Contact: Dale Rau, Pres.
Local. Affiliated With: Lions Clubs International.

Kenyon

11253 ■ American Legion, Joseph A. Gates Post 78
PO Box 64
Kenyon, MN 55946
Ph: (651)291-1800
Fax: (651)291-1057
URL: National Affiliate–www.legion.org
Local. Affiliated With: American Legion.

11254 ■ Kenyon Lions Club
c/o Dennis Monroe, Sec.
49543 County 59 Blvd.
Kenyon, MN 55946
Ph: (507)789-6399
E-mail: monroed@clear.lakes.com
URL: http://www.lions5m1.org/kenyon
Contact: Dennis Monroe, Sec.
Local. Affiliated With: Lions Clubs International.

11255 ■ Sons of Norway, Kenyon Viking Lodge 1-487
c/o Carol J.G. Lozon, Pres.
418 1st St.
Kenyon, MN 55946-1103
Ph: (507)789-6497
E-mail: clozon@mchsi.com
URL: National Affiliate–www.sofn.com
Contact: Carol J.G. Lozon, Pres.
Local. Affiliated With: Sons of Norway.

11256 ■ Sustainable Farming Association of Minnesota - Cannon River
c/o Kathy Zeman, Coor.
11539 E 200th St.
Kenyon, MN 55946
Ph: (507)789-6375
E-mail: wrens@rconnect.com
URL: http://www.sfa-mn.org
Contact: Kathy Zeman, Coor.
Local.

Kerkhoven

11257 ■ American Legion, Brenden-Johnson Post 223
PO Box 314
Kerkhoven, MN 56252
Ph: (651)291-1800
Fax: (651)291-1057
URL: National Affiliate–www.legion.org
Local. Affiliated With: American Legion.

11258 ■ Kerkhoven Lions Club
c/o Erv Kallstrom, Pres.
309 N 8th St.
Kerkhoven, MN 56252
Ph: (320)264-1307
URL: http://www.5m4lions.org
Contact: Erv Kallstrom, Pres.
Local. Affiliated With: Lions Clubs International.

Kettle River

11259 ■ American Legion, Kettle River Post 360
Veterans Bldg., 3960 Main St.
Kettle River, MN 55757
Ph: (651)291-1800
Fax: (651)291-1057
URL: National Affiliate–www.legion.org
Local. Affiliated With: American Legion.

Kiester

11260 ■ American Legion, Kiester Post 454
PO Box 327
Kiester, MN 56051
Ph: (651)291-1800
Fax: (651)291-1057
URL: National Affiliate–www.legion.org
Local. Affiliated With: American Legion.

Kimball

11261 ■ American Legion, Minnesota Post 261
c/o Frederick A. Metcalf
PO Box 193
Kimball, MN 55353
Ph: (651)291-1800
Fax: (651)291-1057
URL: National Affiliate–www.legion.org
Contact: Frederick A. Metcalf, Contact
Local. Affiliated With: American Legion.

La Crescent

11262 ■ American Legion, Gittens-Leidel Post 595
PO Box 162
La Crescent, MN 55947
Ph: (651)291-1800
Fax: (651)291-1057
URL: National Affiliate–www.legion.org
Local. Affiliated With: American Legion.

11263 ■ Coulee Kennel Club
c/o Janet Veit, Corresponding Sec.
129 Janell Ave.
La Crescent, MN 55947
E-mail: becky@couleekennelclub.com
URL: http://www.couleekennelclub.com
Contact: Becky Pomeroy, Pres.
Local.

11264 ■ Coulee Rock Club Of Lacrosse
c/o Allison Conrad, Pres.
88 Janell Ave.
La Crescent, MN 55947
E-mail: alliebob@acegroup.cc
URL: National Affiliate–www.amfed.org
Contact: Sally Frisby, Sec.
Local. Aims to further the study of Earth Sciences and the practice of lapidary arts and mineralogy. **Affiliated With:** American Federation of Mineralogical Societies.

11265 ■ Hokah Lions Club
c/o Steve Eisenhouth, Pres.
PO Box 177
La Crescent, MN 55947
Ph: (507)894-4672
URL: http://www.lions5m1.org/hokah
Contact: Steve Eisenhouth, Pres.
Local. Affiliated With: Lions Clubs International.

11266 ■ La Crescent Chamber of Commerce (LCCC)
PO Box 132
La Crescent, MN 55947
Ph: (507)895-2800
Fax: (507)895-2619
Free: (800)926-9480
E-mail: lacrescent.chamber@acegroup.com
URL: http://www.lacrescent.com
Contact: Beverly Jiardina, Exec.Sec.
Founded: 1975. **Members:** 100. **Local.** Promotes business, community development, and tourism in La Crescent, MN. **Computer Services:** Online services, member listings.

11267 ■ LaCrescent Lions Club
c/o Dean Bergstrom, Pres.
160 Crescent Ave.
La Crescent, MN 55947
Ph: (507)895-2084
E-mail: deanb701@aol.com
URL: http://www.lions5m1.org/lacrescent
Contact: Dean Bergstrom, Pres.
Local. Affiliated With: Lions Clubs International.

Lafayette

11268 ■ American Legion, Lafayette Post 300
PO Box 2
Lafayette, MN 56054
Ph: (651)291-1800
Fax: (651)291-1057
URL: National Affiliate–www.legion.org
Local. Affiliated With: American Legion.

Lake Benton

11269 ■ American Legion, Henry Sollie Post 10
PO Box 114
Lake Benton, MN 56149
Ph: (651)291-1800
Fax: (651)291-1057
URL: National Affiliate–www.legion.org
Local. Affiliated With: American Legion.

11270 ■ Lake Benton Area Chamber of Commerce and Convention and Visitors Bureau
110 S Center St.
PO Box 205
Lake Benton, MN 56149
Ph: (507)368-9577
Fax: (507)368-9577
E-mail: lbenton@itctel.com
URL: http://www.itctel.com/lbenton
Contact: Ms. Heather Ulrich, Exec.Dir.
Members: 50. **Membership Dues:** chamber, $80 (annual). **Staff:** 1. **Budget:** $8,000. **Local.** Provides information about business opportunities in Lake Benton.

Lake Bronson

11271 ■ American Legion, Olaf Locken Post 315
PO Box 57
Lake Bronson, MN 56734
Ph: (651)291-1800
Fax: (651)291-1057
URL: National Affiliate–www.legion.org
Local. Affiliated With: American Legion.

11272 ■ Lake Bronson Lions Club
c/o Ronald Johnson, Pres.
RR 2, Box 96
Lake Bronson, MN 56734
Ph: (218)843-2601 (218)754-2481
URL: http://lions5m11.org/sys-tmpl/door
Contact: Ronald Johnson, Pres.
Local. Affiliated With: Lions Clubs International.

Lake City

11273 ■ American Legion, Minnesota Post 110
c/o Louis Mc Cahill
224 Washington St. S
Lake City, MN 55041
Ph: (651)291-1800
Fax: (651)291-1057
URL: National Affiliate–www.legion.org
Contact: Louis Mc Cahill, Contact
Local. Affiliated With: American Legion.

11274 ■ International Dark-Sky Association - Minnesota
RR 4, Box 82 B
Lake City, MN 55041
URL: http://www.darksky.org/aboutida/sections
Contact: Tine Thevenin, Contact
State. Astronomical societies, lighting and engineering groups, professional astronomers. Seeks to inform about the effects of nighttime lighting. Builds awareness about the problems that have effects on astronomy. Presents examples of good lighting design. Conducts speaker's bureau. Documents on good and bad lighting through photos and videos.

11275 ■ Lake City Area Chamber of Commerce (LCACC)
101 W Center St.
Lake City, MN 55041
Ph: (651)345-4123
Fax: (651)345-4195
Free: (800)369-4123
E-mail: lcchamber@earthlink.net
URL: http://www.lakecity.org
Contact: Mary Huselid, Exec.Dir.
Founded: 1935. **Members:** 200. **Staff:** 1. **Local.** Promotes business and community development in the Lake City, MN area. Sponsors 3 community festivals per year. **Publications:** none. **Awards:** Water Ski Days Queen. **Frequency:** annual. **Type:** scholarship. **Recipient:** for person skiing as Lake City Youth Ambassador. **Computer Services:** Online services, member listings. **Committees:** Business; Government/Public Affairs; Johnny Appleseed Days; Thursday Night Street Market; Water Ski Days. **Task Forces:** Technologies/Utilities; Tourism; Workplace. **Affiliated With:** U.S. Chamber of Commerce. **Publications:** Newsletter, quarterly. Includes updates on Chamber's activities, business-related news items and community issues affecting business. **Circulation:** 300 • Membership Directory. **Price:** included in membership dues. **Conventions/Meetings:** monthly board meeting - every 1st Monday • annual Johnny Appleseed Days - festival - 1st full weekend of October.

11276 ■ Lake City Lions Club
c/o Richard Ulland, Sec.
36410 Hwy. 61 Blvd.
Lake City, MN 55041
Ph: (651)345-2747
E-mail: wfish@mchsi.com
URL: http://www.lions5m1.org/lakecity
Contact: Richard Ulland, Sec.
Local. Affiliated With: Lions Clubs International.

Lake Crystal

11277 ■ American Legion, J.W. Roth Post 294
PO Box 935
Lake Crystal, MN 56055
Ph: (651)291-1800
Fax: (651)291-1057
URL: National Affiliate–www.legion.org
Local. Affiliated With: American Legion.

11278 ■ Lake Crystal Area Chamber of Commerce
PO Box 27
Lake Crystal, MN 56055
Ph: (507)726-6088
Fax: (507)726-2045
E-mail: lcchambr@hickorytech.net
URL: http://www.lakecrystalchamber.com
Contact: Sara Nilson, Exec.Coor.
Local. Promotes business and community development in Lake Crystal Area, MN.

Lake Elmo

11279 ■ Foster and Adoptive Care Association of Minnesota (FACAM)
c/o Judy Howell
2119 Lake Elmo Ave.
Lake Elmo, MN 55042-8455
Ph: (651)770-1247
Fax: (651)770-7571
E-mail: mfcapres@aol.com
URL: http://www.facam.org
Contact: Judy Howell, Pres.
State. Seeks to identify and advocate the needs of children in foster care and those who care for them. Works to improve the foster parenting image nationwide and educate the courts, legislators, and the public to the needs of children in the foster care system. Informs foster parents of their legal rights; encourages mandatory parenting skills training and a minimum requirement of pre-service training for all foster parents. Maintains speakers' bureau. **Affiliated With:** National Foster Parent Association.

11280 ■ Frontenac Flyer Association
4375 Kimbro Ave. N
Lake Elmo, MN 55042
Ph: (651)736-2401
URL: National Affiliate–www.ushga.org
Local. Affiliated With: U.S. Hang Gliding Association.

11281 ■ Lake Elmo Jaycees
PO Box 198
Lake Elmo, MN 55042
Ph: (651)340-5815
E-mail: president@lakeelmojaycees.org
URL: http://www.lakeelmojaycees.org
Contact: Jesse Henning, Pres.
Local.

11282 ■ Lake Elmo Minnesota Lions Club
PO Box 50
Lake Elmo, MN 55042
Ph: (651)777-8365
E-mail: lakeelmolions@comcast.net
URL: http://lakeelmolionsmn.lionwap.org
Contact: Steve Madsen, Sec.
Local. Affiliated With: Lions Clubs International.

11283 ■ Product Development and Management Association, Minnesota (PDMA)
c/o Gary Jader, VP Communications
Ideas on the Wall
974 Jasmine Ave. N
Lake Elmo, MN 55042
Ph: (651)702-6476
E-mail: sburke@mmm.com
URL: http://www.pdmamn.org
Contact: Sean Burke, Pres.
Founded: 1976. **State.** Strives to advance the art and science of product development. Works to improve the effectiveness of people engaged in all aspects of developing and managing new products—both new manufactured goods and new services. **Affiliated With:** Product Development and Management Association.

Lake Lillian

11284 ■ American Legion, Bomsta-Johnson Post 615
PO Box 103
Lake Lillian, MN 56253
Ph: (651)291-1800
Fax: (651)291-1057
URL: National Affiliate–www.legion.org
Local. Affiliated With: American Legion.

Lake Park

11285 ■ American Legion, Minnesota Post 181
c/o Gustav L. Handegard
PO Box 31
Lake Park, MN 56554
Ph: (651)291-1800
Fax: (651)291-1057
URL: National Affiliate–www.legion.org
Contact: Gustav L. Handegard, Contact
Local. Affiliated With: American Legion.

Lake Wilson

11286 ■ American Legion, Ezra Barrows Post 338
772 30th Ave.
Lake Wilson, MN 56151
Ph: (651)291-1800
Fax: (651)291-1057
URL: National Affiliate–www.legion.org
Local. Affiliated With: American Legion.

11287 ■ American Legion, Minnesota Post 285
c/o Herbert Holtke
PO Box 71
Lake Wilson, MN 56151
Ph: (651)291-1800
Fax: (651)291-1057
URL: National Affiliate–www.legion.org
Contact: Herbert Holtke, Contact
Local. Affiliated With: American Legion.

Lakefield

11288 ■ American Legion, Sioux Valley Post 614
PO Box 58
Lakefield, MN 56150
Ph: (651)291-1800
Fax: (651)291-1057
URL: National Affiliate–www.legion.org
Local. Affiliated With: American Legion.

11289 ■ American Legion, Swen Rasmussen Post 4
PO Box 942
Lakefield, MN 56150
Ph: (651)291-1800
Fax: (651)291-1057
URL: National Affiliate–www.legion.org
Local. Affiliated With: American Legion.

11290 ■ Jackson County Historical Society (JCHS)
PO Box 238
Lakefield, MN 56150-0238
Ph: (507)662-5505
Contact: Judy Nelson, Museum Mgr.
Founded: 1931. **Members:** 187. **Membership Dues:** single, $20 • family, $30 • business or organization, $50. **Staff:** 3. **Budget:** $35,000. **Regional Groups:** 1. **State Groups:** 1. **Local.** Individuals interested in preserving the history of Jackson County, MN. Collects genealogical data, artifacts, and manuscripts. Conducts oral histories. **Libraries: Type:** open to the public. **Subjects:** local and state history, genealogy.

Publications: *JCHS Jottings*, 3/year. Newsletter. Contains society/museum news, local interest, oral histories. **Price:** free with membership; $2.00 per issue. **Circulation:** 250. **Conventions/Meetings:** annual meeting, with elections (exhibits).

Lakeland

11291 ■ Minnesota Osteopathic Medical Society
c/o Colleen Jensen, Exec.Dir.
PO Box 314
Lakeland, MN 55043-0314
Ph: (612)623-3268
Fax: (612)677-3200
E-mail: info@mndo.org
URL: http://www.mndo.org
Contact: Colleen Jensen, Exec.Dir.
State. Affiliated With: American Osteopathic Association.

11292 ■ Minnesota Urological Society (MUS)
PO Box 314
Lakeland, MN 55043
Ph: (612)670-7810
Fax: (612)677-3200
E-mail: colleenjensen@pressenter.com
URL: http://www.mnus.org
Contact: Colleen Jensen, Exec.Dir.
State. Stimulates interest in the science and practice of urology. Promotes understanding of socioeconomic and political affairs affecting medical practice. Formulates healthcare policies for urologists.

Lakeville

11293 ■ American Legion, John Vessey Post 44
PO Box 111
Lakeville, MN 55044
Ph: (651)291-1800
Fax: (651)291-1057
URL: National Affiliate–www.legion.org
Local. Affiliated With: American Legion.

11294 ■ Community Action Council (CAC)
c/o Jeannie Hill, Volunteer Coor., Violence Prevention & Intervention
20730 Holyoke Ave.
PO Box 1256
Lakeville, MN 55044
Ph: (952)985-5300
Fax: (952)985-4015
E-mail: jhill@communityactioncouncil.org
URL: http://www.communityactioncouncil.org
Local. Provides support to people and communities to prevent violence, ensure school success and promote long-term self-sufficiency.

11295 ■ Minnesota Table Tennis Federation
16255 Jatos Cir.
Lakeville, MN 55044
Ph: (952)892-7078
E-mail: ttminn@aol.com
URL: http://www.tabletennismn.com
Contact: Mitchell Seidenfeld, Contact
State. Affiliated With: U.S.A. Table Tennis.

11296 ■ Skills USA, Lakeville High School
19600 Ipavia Ave. W
Lakeville, MN 55044
Ph: (952)469-7350
Fax: (952)469-3367
URL: http://www.mnskillsusa.org/secondaryChapters.htm
Contact: Christine Parker, Contact
Local. Serves high school and college students enrolled in technical, skilled, and service and health occupations. Provides quality education experiences for students in leadership, teamwork, citizenship and character development. Builds and reinforces self-confidence, work attitudes and communication skills. Emphasizes total quality at work, high ethical standards, superior work skills, and life-long education. Promotes understanding of the free enterprise system and involvement in community service. **Affiliated With:** Skills USA - VICA.

11297 ■ USA Weightlifting - Lakeville
c/o Chris Rousemiller
19600 Ipava Ave.
Lakeville, MN 55044
Ph: (952)469-7166
E-mail: cirousemiller@isd194.k12.mn.us
URL: National Affiliate–www.usaweightlifting.org
Contact: Chris Rousemiller, Contact
Local. Affiliated With: USA Weightlifting.

Lamberton

11298 ■ American Legion, Minnesota Post 41
c/o Henry M. Guttormson
19664 Hunter Ave.
Lamberton, MN 56152
Ph: (651)291-1800
Fax: (651)291-1057
URL: National Affiliate–www.legion.org
Contact: Henry M. Guttormson, Contact
Local. Affiliated With: American Legion.

Lancaster

11299 ■ American Legion, Minnesota Post 214
c/o Olof A. Bergquist
112 Hawaii Ave.
Lancaster, MN 56735
Ph: (651)291-1800
Fax: (651)291-1057
URL: National Affiliate–www.legion.org
Contact: Olof A. Bergquist, Contact
Local. Affiliated With: American Legion.

11300 ■ Lancaster Lions Club - Minnesota
c/o Barbara Peterson, Pres.
1006 2nd St. W
Lancaster, MN 56735
Ph: (218)762-5400 (218)762-6661
URL: http://lions5m11.org/sys-tmpl/door
Contact: Barbara Peterson, Pres.
Local. Affiliated With: Lions Clubs International.

Lanesboro

11301 ■ American Legion, Henry M. Guttormson Post 40
PO Box 285
Lanesboro, MN 55949
Ph: (651)291-1800
Fax: (651)291-1057
URL: National Affiliate–www.legion.org
Local. Affiliated With: American Legion.

11302 ■ Lanesboro Lions Club
c/o Tom Manion, Pres.
RR 1, Box 90
Lanesboro, MN 55949
Ph: (507)268-4224
E-mail: tmanion@acegroup.cc
URL: http://www.lions5m1.org/lanesboro
Contact: Tom Manion, Pres.
Local. Affiliated With: Lions Clubs International.

11303 ■ Sons of Norway, Heimbygda Lodge 1-376
c/o Audrey J. Overland, Sec.
RR 2, Box 109
Lanesboro, MN 55949-9641
Ph: (507)467-3726
E-mail: adover@acegroup.cc
URL: National Affiliate–www.sofn.com
Contact: Audrey J. Overland, Sec.
Local. Affiliated With: Sons of Norway.

Laporte

11304 ■ American Legion, Anderson-Black Post 462
30246 354th St.
Laporte, MN 56461
Ph: (651)291-1800
Fax: (651)291-1057
URL: National Affiliate–www.legion.org
Local. Affiliated With: American Legion.

Le Center

11305 ■ American Legion, Le Center Post 108
PO Box 102
Le Center, MN 56057
Ph: (651)291-1800
Fax: (651)291-1057
URL: National Affiliate–www.legion.org
Local. Affiliated With: American Legion.

11306 ■ Minnesota Ambulance Association, South Central
c/o Stanley Stocker, Dir.
Le Center Ambulance
344 E Minnesota St.
Le Center, MN 56057
Ph: (507)357-4448
E-mail: stockcon@frontiernet.net
URL: http://www.mnems.org
Contact: Stanley Stocker, Dir.
Local. Seeks to maintain the financial viability of the EMS industry by advocating education, legislation and regulatory change. **Affiliated With:** Minnesota Ambulance Association.

11307 ■ Southern District Dental Society, Minnesota
c/o Dr. Ron Leach
PO Box 97
Le Center, MN 56057
Ph: (507)357-2280
Fax: (507)357-2287
E-mail: sdds@frontiernet.net
URL: http://southern.mndental.org
Contact: Dr. Ron Leach, Contact
Local. Represents the interests of dentists committed to the public's oral health, ethics and professional development. Encourages the improvement of the public's oral health and promotes the art and science of dentistry. **Affiliated With:** American Dental Association; Minnesota Dental Association.

Le Roy

11308 ■ American Legion, Meighen-Thompson Post 161
PO Box 46
Le Roy, MN 55951
Ph: (651)291-1800
Fax: (651)291-1057
URL: National Affiliate–www.legion.org
Local. Affiliated With: American Legion.

Le Sueur

11309 ■ American Legion, Minnesota Post 55
c/o Leo C. Peterson
PO Box 15
Le Sueur, MN 56058
Ph: (651)291-1800
Fax: (651)291-1057
URL: National Affiliate–www.legion.org
Contact: Leo C. Peterson, Contact
Local. Affiliated With: American Legion.

11310 ■ Le Sueur Area Chamber of Commerce (LSACC)
500 N Main St.
Le Sueur, MN 56058
Ph: (507)665-2501
Fax: (507)665-4372
E-mail: info@lesueurchamber.org
URL: http://www.lesueurchamber.org
Contact: Julie Boyland, Exec.Dir.
Founded: 1951. **Members:** 135. **Membership Dues:** associate, $50 (annual) • individual, $55 (annual) • professional, $115 (annual) • retail base, $169 (annual). **Staff:** 2. **Budget:** $53,850. **Local.** Promotes business and community development in the Le Sueur, MN area. Sponsors Legislative Day at the Capitol, garage sales, Farm and Home Show, Giant Celebration, Agriculture Appreciation Affair and Manufacture Expo. **Computer Services:** Online services, business directory. **Telecommunication Services:** electronic mail, julie@lesueurchamber.org. **Committees:** Agriculture; Ambassadors; Farm and Home Show; Giant Celebration; Legislative; Retail Trade; Technical Services; Tourism. **Publications:** *Voice of Le Sueur Newsletter*, quarterly. Alternate Formats: online • Brochure. **Circulation:** 10,000 • Membership Directory. **Conventions/Meetings:** annual Farm and Home Show - always first Thursday and Friday in April.

11311 ■ Le Sueur Area United Way
PO Box 82
Le Sueur, MN 56058-0082
Ph: (507)665-2501
URL: National Affiliate–national.unitedway.org
Local. Affiliated With: United Way of America.

Lester Prairie

11312 ■ American Legion, Ray Kirkpatrick Post 463
PO Box 3
Lester Prairie, MN 55354
Ph: (651)291-1800
Fax: (651)291-1057
URL: National Affiliate–www.legion.org
Local. Affiliated With: American Legion.

Lewiston

11313 ■ American Legion, Jackson-O-Meara Post 90
PO Box 296
Lewiston, MN 55952
Ph: (651)291-1800
Fax: (651)291-1057
URL: National Affiliate–www.legion.org
Local. Affiliated With: American Legion.

11314 ■ Minnesota Official Measures
c/o Craig Pierce
Box 82
Lewiston, MN 55952-0082
Ph: (320)762-7253 (218)845-2109
E-mail: dc240nt@rea-alp.com
Contact: Craig Pierce, Contact
Founded: 1995. **Members:** 73. **Membership Dues:** general, $10 (annual). **Staff:** 10. **Budget:** $2,500. **State Groups:** 1. **State. Publications:** *MOM Newsletter*, quarterly. Contains rule updates, meeting and show schedules, activities and news. **Price:** included in membership dues. **Circulation:** 80. **Conventions/Meetings:** meeting - 3/year.

Lewisville

11315 ■ American Legion, Lewisville Post 561
121 W Lewis St.
Lewisville, MN 56060
Ph: (651)291-1800
Fax: (651)291-1057
URL: National Affiliate–www.legion.org
Local. Affiliated With: American Legion.

Lindstrom

11316 ■ American Legion, Lindstrom Post 83
PO Box 41
Lindstrom, MN 55045
Ph: (651)291-1800
Fax: (651)291-1057
URL: National Affiliate–www.legion.org
Local. Affiliated With: American Legion.

11317 ■ Skills USA, Chisago Lakes High School
29400 Olinda Trail
Lindstrom, MN 55045
Ph: (651)213-2500
Fax: (651)213-2550
URL: http://www.mnskillsusa.org/secondaryChapters.htm
Contact: Mark Plumley, Contact
Local. Serves high school and college students enrolled in technical, skilled, and service and health occupations. Provides quality education experiences for students in leadership, teamwork, citizenship and character development. Builds and reinforces self-confidence, work attitudes and communication skills. Emphasizes total quality at work, high ethical standards, superior work skills, and life-long education. Promotes understanding of the free enterprise system and involvement in community service. **Affiliated With:** Skills USA - VICA.

11318 ■ Sons of Norway, Vennelag Lodge 1-546
c/o Donna M. Johnson, Pres.
11385 335th St.
Lindstrom, MN 55045-9035
Ph: (651)257-3314
E-mail: dwdmjohn@cornernet.com
URL: National Affiliate–www.sofn.com
Contact: Donna M. Johnson, Pres.
Local. Affiliated With: Sons of Norway.

Lino Lakes

11319 ■ American Legion, Lino Lakes Post 566
7731 Lake Dr.
Lino Lakes, MN 55014
Ph: (651)291-1800
Fax: (651)291-1057
URL: National Affiliate–www.legion.org
Local. Affiliated With: American Legion.

11320 ■ Anoka County Chapter of Pheasants Forever
6327 W Shadow Lake Dr.
Lino Lakes, MN 55014
Ph: (651)766-8415
E-mail: jnewpower@msn.com
URL: http://www.anokapf.org
Contact: John Newpower, Pres.
Local. Affiliated With: Pheasants Forever.

11321 ■ Computer Measurement Group, Minneapolis-St. Paul
161 Woodridge Ln.
Lino Lakes, MN 55014
Ph: (612)348-6230
E-mail: bill.feeney@co.hennepin.mn.us
URL: http://regions.cmg.org/regions/mspcmg/index.html
Contact: Bill Feeney, Advisor
Founded: 1983. **Members:** 100. **Regional.** Committed to the measurement and management of computer systems. Concerned with performance evaluation of existing systems to maximize performance and with capacity management, where planned enhancements to existing systems or the design of new systems are evaluated to find the necessary resources required to provide adequate performance at a reasonable cost. **Affiliated With:** Computer Measurement Group. **Publications:** *Journal of Computer Resource Management*, quarterly. **Conventions/Meetings:** annual conference • annual meeting - every December.

11322 ■ Minneapolis-St. Paul Computer Measurement Group
c/o Thomas Becchetti
161 Woodridge Ln.
Lino Lakes, MN 55014
Ph: (952)591-3937
Fax: (952)591-3918
E-mail: mspcmg@cmg.org
URL: National Affiliate–www.cmg.org
Contact: Mr. Tom Becchetti, Chm.
Founded: 1980. **Members:** 150. **Regional Groups:** 1. **Regional.** Strives to promote the sharing information on computer performance topics. **Affiliated With:** Computer Measurement Group.

11323 ■ Minnesota Oldsmobile Club
c/o Gail Pinola
1045 Crystal Ct.
Lino Lakes, MN 55014
E-mail: pinola@comcast.net
URL: http://www.mnoldsclub.org
Contact: Steve McKenzie, Pres.
Founded: 1979. **Membership Dues:** individual, $20 (annual). **Local.** Unites owners of vehicles built by Oldsmobile in order to promote the restoration and preservation of them for future generations through activities involving the club, community, and family participation. **Affiliated With:** Oldsmobile Club of America.

Lismore

11324 ■ American Legion, Schaap-Galagan Post 636
PO Box 12
Lismore, MN 56155
Ph: (651)291-1800
Fax: (651)291-1057
URL: National Affiliate–www.legion.org
Local. Affiliated With: American Legion.

Litchfield

11325 ■ American Legion, Nelsan-Horton Post 104
PO Box 638
Litchfield, MN 55355
Ph: (651)291-1800
Fax: (651)291-1057
URL: National Affiliate–www.legion.org
Local. Affiliated With: American Legion.

11326 ■ Cosmos Lions Club
c/o Harold Weseloh, Sec.
19084 610th Ave.
Litchfield, MN 55355
Ph: (320)693-9518
E-mail: weseloh@hotmail.com
URL: http://www.5m4lions.org
Contact: Harold Weseloh, Sec.
Local. Affiliated With: Lions Clubs International.

11327 ■ Crow River Area Youth for Christ
PO Box 906
Litchfield, MN 55355
Ph: (320)693-7426
Fax: (320)693-9311
URL: http://www.crowriveryfc.org
Local. Affiliated With: Youth for Christ/U.S.A.

11328 ■ Litchfield Chamber of Commerce (LCC)
219 N Sibley Ave.
PO Box 820
Litchfield, MN 55355-0820

Ph: (320)693-8184
Fax: (320)593-8184
E-mail: litch@litch.com
URL: http://www.litch.com
Contact: Christian Lenz, Exec.Dir.
Local. Promotes business and community development in Litchfield, MN.

11329 ■ Litchfield Lions Club
c/o Troy Atkinson, Pres.
308 S Litchfield Ave.
Litchfield, MN 55355
Ph: (320)693-2073 (320)693-6115
E-mail: troyat20@hotmail.com
URL: http://www.5m4lions.org
Contact: Troy Atkinson, Pres.
Local. Affiliated With: Lions Clubs International.

11330 ■ National Active and Retired Federal Employees Association - Crow River 2019
62162 200th St.
Litchfield, MN 55355-6410
Ph: (320)282-1527
URL: National Affiliate–www.narfe.org
Contact: Otto W. Anderberg, Contact
Local. Protects the retirement future of employees through education. Informs members on issues affecting the retirement. **Affiliated With:** National Association of Retired Federal Employees.

11331 ■ Navy Club of USS Meeker County - Ship No. 222
306 Miller Ave. N
Litchfield, MN 55355
Ph: (320)593-6230
URL: National Affiliate–www.navyclubusa.org
Contact: Richard C. Holtz, Commander
Local. Represents individuals who are, or have been, in the active service of the U.S. Navy, Naval Reserve, Marine Corps, Marine Corps Reserve, and Coast Guard. Promotes and encourages further public interest in the U.S. Navy and its history. Upholds the spirit and ideals of the U.S. Navy. Acts as a public forum for members' views on national defense. Assists the Navy Recruiting Command whenever and wherever possible. Conducts charitable activities. **Affiliated With:** Navy Club of the United States of America.

Little Canada

11332 ■ International Union of Elevator Constructors, Local 9 - Minneapolis, Minnesota
433 E Little Canada Rd.
Little Canada, MN 55117
Ph: (651)287-0819
URL: http://www.local9.com
Contact: Doug Stanger, Pres.
Members: 445. **Local. Affiliated With:** International Union of Elevator Constructors.

Little Falls

11333 ■ American Legion, Minnesota Post 46
c/o Charles Borak
108 1st St. NE
Little Falls, MN 56345
Ph: (651)291-1800
Fax: (651)291-1057
URL: National Affiliate–www.legion.org
Contact: Charles Borak, Contact
Local. Affiliated With: American Legion.

11334 ■ Habitat for Humanity of Morrison County
PO Box 321
Little Falls, MN 56345-0321
Ph: (320)616-2084
Fax: (320)632-2335
E-mail: hfhmc@fallsnet.com
URL: National Affiliate–www.habitat.org
Local. Affiliated With: Habitat for Humanity International.

11335 ■ Little Falls Area Chamber of Commerce (LFACC)
200 NW 1st St.
Little Falls, MN 56345-1365
Ph: (320)632-5155
Fax: (320)632-2122
E-mail: assistance@littlefallsmnchamber.com
URL: http://littlefallsmnchamber.com
Contact: Debora K. Boelz, Pres./CEO
Founded: 1888. **Members:** 376. **Local.** Promotes business and community development in the Little Falls, MN area. Holds arts and crafts fair. **Divisions:** Communications; Community Partnerships; Development Services; Little Falls Pride; Membership Services. **Affiliated With:** U.S. Chamber of Commerce. **Publications:** *Program of Work*, annual. Directory • Annual Report, annual • Newsletter, monthly • Newsletter, annual. Alternate Formats: online. **Conventions/Meetings:** annual Little Falls Arts and Crafts Fair - festival (exhibits).

11336 ■ Little Falls Taekwondo
47 E Broadway
Little Falls, MN 56345
Ph: (320)632-6556
Fax: (320)632-6550
E-mail: info@littlefallstkd.com
URL: http://www.littlefallstkd.com
Contact: Bryan Schoenberger, Instructor
Local. Affiliated With: U.S. Taekwondo Union.

11337 ■ Morrison County United Way
107 2nd St. SE, Apt. 104
Little Falls, MN 56345-3075
Ph: (320)632-5102
URL: National Affiliate–national.unitedway.org
Local. Affiliated With: United Way of America.

11338 ■ Rice Creek Hunting Dog Club
c/o Margaret Grondahl, Sec.
PO Box 503
Little Falls, MN 56345
E-mail: info@rchdc.com
URL: http://www.rchdc.com/?
Contact: Margaret Grondahl, Sec.
Local. Affiliated With: American Kennel Club.

11339 ■ Sons of Norway, Trollheim Lodge 1-511
c/o Marlene A. Williams, Sec.
1025 3rd Ave. NE
Little Falls, MN 56345-2918
Ph: (320)632-4290
E-mail: misskitty12@juno.com
URL: National Affiliate–www.sofn.com
Contact: Marlene A. Williams, Sec.
Local. Affiliated With: Sons of Norway.

Little Marais

11340 ■ Organic Consumers Association (OCA)
6101 Cliff Estate Rd.
Little Marais, MN 55614
Ph: (218)226-4164
Fax: (218)353-7652
Free: (888)403-1007
E-mail: information@organicconsumers.org
URL: http://www.organicconsumers.org
Contact: Loranda McLeete, Contact
Local.

Littlefork

11341 ■ American Legion, Littlefork Post 490
PO Box 391
Littlefork, MN 56653
Ph: (651)291-1800
Fax: (651)291-1057
URL: National Affiliate–www.legion.org
Local. Affiliated With: American Legion.

11342 ■ Little Fork Lions Club
c/o Truman Lindvall, Pres.
1204 5th Ave.
Littlefork, MN 56653
Ph: (218)278-6752
URL: http://lions5m10.org
Contact: Truman Lindvall, Pres.
Local. Affiliated With: Lions Clubs International.

Long Lake

11343 ■ National Corvette Restorers Society, North Central Chapter
c/o Jim Fenske
765 Dickey Lake Dr.
Long Lake, MN 55356
Ph: (952)476-4051
E-mail: info@northcentralncrs.org
URL: http://www.northcentralncrs.org
Contact: Denny Adams, Pres.
Membership Dues: individual, $25 (annual). **Local. Affiliated With:** National Corvette Restorers Society.

11344 ■ Orono District Lions Club
c/o Donny Chillstrom, Pres.
267 Charles St.
Long Lake, MN 55356
Ph: (952)476-1254 (612)710-0569
URL: http://www.5m5.org
Contact: Donny Chillstrom, Pres.
Local. Affiliated With: Lions Clubs International.

Long Prairie

11345 ■ American Legion, Minnesota Post 12
c/o William T. Lewis
714 Commerce Rd.
Long Prairie, MN 56347
Ph: (651)291-1800
Fax: (651)291-1057
URL: National Affiliate–www.legion.org
Contact: William T. Lewis, Contact
Local. Affiliated With: American Legion.

11346 ■ Long Prairie Area Chamber of Commerce (LPACC)
9 Central Ave., Ste.3
Long Prairie, MN 56347
Ph: (320)732-2514
Fax: (320)732-2514
E-mail: lpchambr@rea-alp.com
URL: http://www.longprairie.org
Contact: Toni Tebben, Pres.
Founded: 1961. **Members:** 135. **Local.** Promotes business and community development in the Long Prairie, MN area. Sponsors Prairie Days Festival. **Computer Services:** Online services, member directory. **Publications:** *The Voice of Commerce*, monthly. Newsletter. Alternate Formats: online. **Conventions/Meetings:** monthly board meeting - always first Thursday.

Longville

11347 ■ Longville Lakes Area Snowmobile Club
c/o Muriel Reid
PO Box 321
Longville, MN 56655-0321
Local.

Lonsdale

11348 ■ American Legion, Lonsdale Post 586
PO Box 66
Lonsdale, MN 55046
Ph: (651)291-1800
Fax: (651)291-1057
URL: National Affiliate–www.legion.org
Local. Affiliated With: American Legion.

Loretto

11349 ■ Loretto Lions Club
c/o Patrick Y. Thomas, Sec.
430 Edgewood Dr.
Loretto, MN 55357
Ph: (763)479-2479 (763)370-7374
URL: http://www.5m5.org
Contact: Patrick Y. Thomas, Sec.
Local. Affiliated With: Lions Clubs International.

Lowry

11350 ■ American Legion, Minnesota Post 253
c/o Gust F. Holden
PO Box 103
Lowry, MN 56349
Ph: (651)291-1800
Fax: (651)291-1057
URL: National Affiliate–www.legion.org
Contact: Gust F. Holden, Contact
Local. Affiliated With: American Legion.

11351 ■ Lowry Lions Club
c/o Curt Larson, Pres.
PO Box 195
Lowry, MN 56349
Ph: (320)283-5422
E-mail: clars@runestone.net
URL: http://www.5m4lions.org
Contact: Curt Larson, Pres.
Local. Affiliated With: Lions Clubs International.

Lucan

11352 ■ American Legion, Minnesota Post 467
c/o Arthur Kramer
PO Box 26
Lucan, MN 56255
Ph: (651)291-1800
Fax: (651)291-1057
URL: National Affiliate–www.legion.org
Contact: Arthur Kramer, Contact
Local. Affiliated With: American Legion.

Lutsen

11353 ■ Minnesota Maple Syrup Producers (MMSPA)
c/o Sonja Helland, Sec.-Treas.
PO Box 101
Lutsen, MN 55612
Ph: (218)663-7841
E-mail: sonja@boreal.org
Contact: Sonja Helland, Sec.-Treas.
Founded: 1966. **Members:** 55. **Membership Dues:** $15 (annual). **State.** Individuals or firms engaged in any phase of producing, processing, and/or marketing maple syrup. Seeks to produce the best possible maple syrup. **Publications:** *Minnesota Maple News*, semiannual. Newsletter. **Price:** $3.00 for members. **Circulation:** 55. **Advertising:** accepted. **Conventions/Meetings:** North American Maple Syrup Council - convention - every 12-15 years.

Luverne

11354 ■ American Legion, Dell-Hogan Post 123
124 W Main
Luverne, MN 56156
Ph: (651)291-1800
Fax: (651)291-1057
URL: National Affiliate–www.legion.org
Local. Affiliated With: American Legion.

11355 ■ Luverne Area Chamber of Commerce (LCC)
211 E Main St.
Luverne, MN 56156
Ph: (507)283-4061
Fax: (507)283-4061
Free: (888)283-4061
E-mail: info@luvernemn.com
URL: http://www.luvernemn.com
Contact: Dave Smith, Exec.Dir.
Founded: 1917. **Members:** 190. **Local.** Promotes business and community development in Rock County, MN. Holds Tri-State Band Festival and Buffalo Days Celebration. **Computer Services:** Online services, member listings. **Committees:** Agriculture; Brandenburg Gallery; Business Education; Community Development; Convention and Visitors Bureau; Fund Raising; Legislative; Retail; Special Events. **Affiliated With:** U.S. Chamber of Commerce. **Publications:** Newsletter, monthly. **Conventions/Meetings:** monthly board meeting - always second Wednesday.

11356 ■ Southwestern Minnesota AIFA
c/o Jason W. Vote, Pres.
222 E Main, No. 104
Luverne, MN 56156
Ph: (507)283-9586
Fax: (507)449-9586
E-mail: jason.vote.jys3@statefarm.com
URL: National Affiliate–naifa.org
Contact: Jason W. Vote, Pres.
Local. Represents the interests of insurance and financial advisors. Advocates for a positive legislative and regulatory environment. Enhances business and professional skills of members. **Affiliated With:** National Association of Insurance and Financial Advisors.

Lyle

11357 ■ American Legion, Lyle Post 105
112 Grove St.
Lyle, MN 55953
Ph: (507)325-4134
Fax: (651)291-1057
URL: National Affiliate–www.legion.org
Local. Affiliated With: American Legion.

11358 ■ Lyle Lions Club
c/o Wayne Helgeson, Sec.
Box 104
Lyle, MN 55953
Ph: (507)325-4515
E-mail: whelgeson@mchsi.com
URL: http://www.lions5m1.org/lyle
Contact: Wayne Helgeson, Sec.
Local. Affiliated With: Lions Clubs International.

11359 ■ North American Horse and Mule Loggers Association
RR 1 Box 114
Lyle, MN 55953
E-mail: tecarrol@smig.net
URL: National Affiliate–www.nasdha.net/RegionalAssoc.htm
Contact: Tim Carroll, Pres.
Regional.

Mabel

11360 ■ American Legion, Minnesota Post 299
c/o Joseph B. Lund
PO Box 221
Mabel, MN 55954
Ph: (651)291-1800
Fax: (651)291-1057
URL: National Affiliate–www.legion.org
Contact: Joseph B. Lund, Contact
Local. Affiliated With: American Legion.

11361 ■ Caledonia Lions Club
c/o Lloyd Swalve, Sec.
Rte. 1, Box 35
Mabel, MN 55954
E-mail: lswalve@acegroup.cc
URL: http://www.lions5m1.org/caledonia
Contact: Lloyd Swalve, Sec.
Local. Affiliated With: Lions Clubs International.

11362 ■ Northeast Iowa Angus Breeders Association
c/o Larry Miller, Pres.
R.R. 1, Box 61
Mabel, MN 55954
Ph: (507)743-8370
URL: National Affiliate–www.angus.org
Contact: Larry Miller, Pres.
Local. Affiliated With: American Angus Association.

Madelia

11363 ■ American Legion, Madelia Post 19
PO Box 125
Madelia, MN 56062
Ph: (651)291-1800
Fax: (651)291-1057
URL: National Affiliate–www.legion.org
Local. Affiliated With: American Legion.

11364 ■ Madelia Area Chamber of Commerce (MACC)
PO Box 171
Madelia, MN 56062
Ph: (507)642-8822
Fax: (507)642-8556
Free: (888)941-7283
E-mail: mchamber@madeliamn.com
URL: http://www.madeliamn.com/chamber.htm
Contact: Tara Mueller, Exec.Dir.
Members: 98. **Membership Dues:** church organization, $51 (annual) • individual, retired, $61 (annual) • daycare provider, $77 (annual) • business with 1-3 employees, $154 (annual) • business with 4-7 employees, $257 (annual) • business with 8-49 employees, $453 (annual) • business with more than 50 employees, $772 (annual). **Local.** Promotes business and community development in the Madelia, MN area. **Computer Services:** Online services, membership directory. **Committees:** Ag; Madelia Marketing and Tourism; Retail and Business; Special Events; Tourism. **Publications:** *Business Directory* • Newsletter, monthly. Alternate Formats: online. **Conventions/Meetings:** monthly dinner • monthly meeting - every 2nd Tuesday.

Madison

11365 ■ American Legion, Lac Qui Parle Post 158
PO Box 142
Madison, MN 56256
Ph: (651)291-1800
Fax: (651)291-1057
URL: National Affiliate–www.legion.org
Local. Affiliated With: American Legion.

11366 ■ Madison Area Chamber of Commerce (MACC)
623 W 3rd St.
PO Box 70
Madison, MN 56256-0070
Ph: (320)598-7301
Fax: (320)598-7955
E-mail: loutfisk@yahoo.com
URL: http://www.madisonmn.info
Contact: Maynard R. Meyer, Coor.
Founded: 1952. **Members:** 110. **Staff:** 2. **Budget:** $30,000. **Regional Groups:** 1. **State Groups:** 1. **Local.** Promotes business and community development in the Madison, MN area. **Conventions/Meetings:** annual MN at Your Service - workshop.

11367 ■ Madison Lions Club - Minnesota
c/o Rhoda Schuller, Sec.
2425 201st Ave.
Madison, MN 56256
Ph: (320)598-7648
E-mail: rgs@frontiernet.net
URL: http://www.5m4lions.org
Contact: Rhoda Schuller, Sec.
Local. Affiliated With: Lions Clubs International.

11368 ■ Sons of Norway, Nornen Lodge 1-41
c/o Bernice L. Oellien, Pres.
2570 280th St.
Madison, MN 56256-3013
Ph: (320)752-4757
E-mail: oelmal@farmerstel.net
URL: National Affiliate–www.sofn.com
Contact: Bernice L. Oellien, Pres.
Local. Affiliated With: Sons of Norway.

Madison Lake

11369 ■ American Legion, Madison Lake Post 269
PO Box 269
Madison Lake, MN 56063
Ph: (651)291-1800
Fax: (651)291-1057
URL: National Affiliate–www.legion.org
Local. Affiliated With: American Legion.

Mahnomen

11370 ■ American Legion, Isaacson-Bjorge Post 31
PO Box 461
Mahnomen, MN 56557
Ph: (651)291-1800
Fax: (651)291-1057
URL: National Affiliate–www.legion.org
Local. Affiliated With: American Legion.

11371 ■ Mahnomen Lions Club
c/o David Tilleraas, Sec.
2289 154th Ave.
Mahnomen, MN 56557
Ph: (218)935-2638
Fax: (218)935-2231
URL: http://lions5m11.org/sys-tmpl/door
Contact: David Tilleraas, Sec.
Local. Affiliated With: Lions Clubs International.

Mankato

11372 ■ AAA Minnesota/Iowa
1217 Caledonia St.
Mankato, MN 56001-4329
Ph: (507)345-4609
Regional.

11373 ■ American Legion, Lorentz Post 11
222 E Walnut St.
Mankato, MN 56001
Ph: (651)291-1800
Fax: (651)291-1057
URL: National Affiliate–www.legion.org
Local. Affiliated With: American Legion.

11374 ■ American Red Cross, South Central Minnesota Chapter
105 Homestead Dr.
Mankato, MN 56001
Ph: (507)387-6664
Fax: (507)345-7079
URL: http://www.southcentralmn.redcross.org
Regional.

11375 ■ Association for Computing Machinery, Minnesota State University, Mankato
c/o Christopher Veltsos, Faculty Advisor
273 Wissink Hall
Mankato, MN 56001
Ph: (507)389-1412
Fax: (507)389-6376
E-mail: christophe.veltsos@mnsu.edu
URL: http://acm.cs.mnsu.edu
Contact: Christopher Veltsos, Faculty Advisor
Local. Biological, medical, behavioral, and computer scientists; hospital administrators; programmers and others interested in application of computer methods to biological, behavioral, and medical problems. Stimulates understanding of the use and potential of computers in the biosciences. **Additional Websites:** http://cset.mnsu.edu/cis. **Affiliated With:** Association for Computing Machinery. **Formerly:** (2005) Association for Computing Machinery, Minnesota State University.

11376 ■ Blue Earth County Chapter of Pheasants Forever
c/o C. Stedman
56352 202nd St.
Mankato, MN 56001
URL: http://blueearthcountypf.homestead.com
Contact: John Reeves, Pres.
Local. Affiliated With: Pheasants Forever.

11377 ■ Greater Mankato Area United Way
101 N 2nd St., No. 202
Mankato, MN 56001
Ph: (507)345-4551
Fax: (507)345-3724
E-mail: mankatouw@mankatounitedway.org
URL: http://www.mankatounitedway.org
Contact: Ron Volden, Pres.
Local. Affiliated With: United Way of America.

11378 ■ Greater Mankato Chamber of Commerce
112 S Riverfront Dr.
PO Box 999
Mankato, MN 56002-1269
Ph: (507)345-4519
Fax: (507)345-4451
Free: (800)657-4733
E-mail: info@greatermankato.com
URL: http://www.greatermankato.com
Contact: Mike King, Chm.
Founded: 1983. **Members:** 240. **Membership Dues:** general business, $310 • financial institution, $700 • professional, $310 • small to large charitable non-profit, $200-$400 • associate (individuals, elected officials, retired), $145. **Staff:** 3. **Local.** Aids new industrial/business retention and recruitment, financial and technical support. Assists with expansion needs, and facilitates creation of new business ventures. **Awards:** Brian Fazio Business Education Partnership. **Frequency:** annual. **Type:** recognition. **Recipient:** for partnerships that promote educational opportunities in the community • Hap Halligan Leadership Award. **Frequency:** annual. **Type:** recognition. **Recipient:** for individual whose participation in the Leadership Institute of Greater Mankato program has helped to provide an impetus for outstanding contributions to the community. **Formerly:** (2005) Valley Industrial Development Corp. **Publications:** *Greater Mankato Today*, monthly. Newsletter. Contains chamber news and updates. Alternate Formats: online.

11379 ■ Habitat for Humanity of South Central Minnesota
512 Mulberry St.
Mankato, MN 56001
Ph: (507)388-2081
Fax: (507)388-1618
E-mail: hfhmkto@hickorytech.net
URL: http://www.gotocrystal.net/~hfhscmn
Contact: Julie Schmillen, Exec.Dir.
Founded: 1989. **Local.** Aims to build simple, decent, and affordable housing with and for families in need.

11380 ■ Institute of Management Accountants, South Central Minnesota
c/o Robert J. Butterfield, Pres.
Bolton and Menk, Inc.
133 Marabou Dr.
Mankato, MN 56001-5533
Ph: (507)625-4171
Fax: (507)625-4177
E-mail: bobbu@bolton-menk.com
URL: http://www.scmn.imanet.org
Contact: Robert J. Butterfield, Pres.
Local. Promotes professional and ethical standards. Equips members and students with knowledge and training required for the accounting profession. **Awards:** South Central IMA Member of the Year Award. **Frequency:** annual. **Type:** recognition. **Recipient:** for chapter member. **Additional Websites:** http://www.ima-northernlights.imanet.org. **Councils:** Northern Lights. **Affiliated With:** Institute of Management Accountants.

11381 ■ Junior Achievement, Mankato Area
210 Lime St.
Mankato, MN 56001
Ph: (507)387-9609
Fax: (507)387-9604
E-mail: tami@jaum.org
URL: http://www.jaum.org
Contact: Tami Reuter, VP-District Operations
Local. Affiliated With: Junior Achievement.

11382 ■ Katoland Chapter IAAP
PO Box 773
Mankato, MN 56002-0773
E-mail: bobbin@ofc-clinic.com
URL: http://www.katolandiaap.freeservers.com
Contact: Bobbi Nawrocki, Pres.
Local. Professionals, corporations, academic institutions and students. Develops research and educational projects for administrative professionals. Provides training, seminars, conferences and educational programs.

11383 ■ Korean War Veterans Association, Frozen Chosin Chapter
c/o William A. Maher
217 Viola St.
Mankato, MN 56001-4576
Ph: (507)388-5577
E-mail: tjohnson@hickorytech.net
URL: National Affiliate–www.kwva.org
Contact: William A. Maher, Contact
Local. Affiliated With: Korean War Veterans Association.

11384 ■ Mankato Area Environmentalists (MAE)
c/o Sister Gladys Schmitz
1411 Pohl Rd.
Mankato, MN 56001-5751
Ph: (507)345-4494
Fax: (507)345-6679
E-mail: enviros@hickorytech.net
URL: http://www.hickorytech.net/~enviros
Contact: Katy Wortel, Contact
Founded: 1987. **Members:** 30. **Membership Dues:** regular, $15 (annual). **Local.** Strives to be an ongoing voice for environmental quality, a resource for other groups, and a source of action to shape environmental policies and practices in the Minnesota River Valley-Bend of the River area. **Awards:** Earth Keeper of the Year. **Frequency:** periodic. **Type:** recognition. **Recipient:** for service above and beyond the call of duty for the good of the environment. **Telecommunication Services:** electronic mail, gladysssnd@juno.com. **Publications:** *Mankato Area Environmental News*, annual. Newsletter.

11385 ■ Mankato Figure Skating Club (MFSC)
PO Box 4312
Mankato, MN 56001
Ph: (507)345-8958
E-mail: dlh1@hickorytech.net
URL: http://www.mankatofsc.org
Contact: Deanna Hofmeister, Pres.
Local. Provides programs to encourage participation and achievement in the sport of figure skating on ice.

Defines and maintains uniform standards of skating proficiency. Organizes and sponsors competitions and exhibitions for the purpose of stimulating interest in figure skating. **Affiliated With:** United States Figure Skating Association.

11386 ■ Minnesota College Personnel Association (MCPA)
c/o Jennifer Guyer-Wood, Pres.
Minnesota State Univ., Mankato
Career Development Ctr., MSU
209 Wigley Admin.
Mankato, MN 56001
Ph: (507)389-6061
Fax: (507)389-5114
E-mail: jennifer.guyer-wood@mnsu.edu
URL: http://www.myacpa.org/sid/mn
Contact: Jennifer Guyer-Wood, Pres.
State. Provides outreach, advocacy, research and professional development to foster college student learning. **Affiliated With:** American College Personnel Association.

11387 ■ Minnesota Nurses Association - District 5
57201 238th St.
Mankato, MN 56001
Ph: (507)345-1487
E-mail: rossow.linda@mayo.edu
URL: http://www.mnnurses.org
Contact: Linda Rossow, Pres.
Local. Works to advance the nursing profession. Seeks to meet the needs of nurses and health care consumers. Fosters high standards of nursing practice. Promotes the economic and general welfare of nurses in the workplace. **Affiliated With:** American Nurses Association; Minnesota Nurses Association.

11388 ■ Minnesota Rural Health Association (MRHA)
102 Wiecking Ctr.
Mankato, MN 56001
Ph: (507)389-3262
Fax: (507)389-2411
E-mail: office@mnruralhealth.org
URL: http://www.mnruralhealth.org
Contact: Maddy Forsberg, Pres.
Membership Dues: individual, $50 (annual) • student, $10 (annual) • organization, $300 (annual). **State**. Works for the preservation and enhancement of health in rural communities in Minnesota. **Affiliated With:** National Rural Health Association. **Publications:** *MRHA Weekly*, biweekly. Newsletter. Alternate Formats: online.

11389 ■ Minnesota Senior Federation, South Central Region
Gus Johnson Plz.
413 N 4th St., Ste.200
Mankato, MN 56001
Ph: (507)345-7814
Fax: (507)345-6980
E-mail: sfsocent@hickorytech.net
URL: http://mnseniors.org
Local.

11390 ■ Minnesota State Curling Association - Caledonian Curling Club
PO Box 75
Mankato, MN 56002-0075
Ph: (507)388-3335
E-mail: mankatocurling@hotmail.com
URL: http://www.mankatocurling.org
Contact: Kevin Birr, Pres.
Local. **Affiliated With:** United States Curling Association.

11391 ■ Minnesota Valley Action Council (MVAC)
464 Raintree Rd.
Mankato, MN 56001
Ph: (507)345-6822
Free: (800)767-7139
E-mail: lynn@mvac.mankato.mn.us
URL: http://www.mnvac.org
Contact: Charles Woehler, Pres.
Founded: 1966. **Staff:** 180. **Budget:** $15,725,280. **Local**. Aims to empower the people to find solutions to their economic problems and to offer opportunities to create a future that reflects their self-reliance. **Publications:** *Community Connections*, quarterly. Newsletter.

11392 ■ NAIFA-Southern Minnesota
c/o Mary McClure
PO Box 1969
Mankato, MN 56002
Ph: (507)345-4747
Fax: (507)345-7061
URL: National Affiliate–www.naifa.org
Local. Represents the interest of insurance and financial advisors. Advocates for a positive legislative and regulatory environment. Enhances business and professional skills of members. **Affiliated With:** National Association of Insurance and Financial Advisors.

11393 ■ National Association of Home Builders, Minnesota River Building Authority
c/o Steve Meister
1821 Bassett Dr., Ste.102
Mankato, MN 56001-6203
Ph: (507)625-4084
Fax: (507)625-5766
E-mail: slm6056@hickorytech.net
URL: http://www.mnrba.com
Contact: Steve Meister, Treas.
Local. Single and multifamily home builders, commercial builders, and others associated with the building industry. **Affiliated With:** National Association of Home Builders.

11394 ■ National Association of Miniature Enthusiasts - Tiny Treasure Makers
c/o Vivian Siemer
10 Ruth Ct.
Mankato, MN 56001
Ph: (507)387-4906
E-mail: 103404.1015@compuserve.com
URL: http://www.miniatures.org/states/MN.html
Contact: Vivian Siemer, Contact
Local. **Affiliated With:** National Association of Miniature Enthusiasts.

11395 ■ Northwest Agri-Dealers Association
c/o Thomas E. Cashman, Exec.VP
PO Box 698
303 Lundin Blvd.
Mankato, MN 56002
Ph: (507)387-4464
Fax: (507)387-7234
E-mail: nwada@gotocrystal.net
URL: National Affiliate–www.ngfa.org
Contact: Tom Cashman, Exec.VP
Regional. **Affiliated With:** National Grain and Feed Association.

11396 ■ Partners for Affordable Housing
512 E Mulberry
Mankato, MN 56001
Ph: (507)387-2115
Fax: (507)387-1321
E-mail: pah@hickorytech.net
URL: http://www.p4ah.org
Contact: Keith Luebke, Exec.Dir.
Founded: 1984. **Local**. Provides housing and supportive services to low income families and individuals.

11397 ■ Pony of the Americas Club, Minnesota
c/o Jack Geller, Pres.
129 Ironwood Ct.
Mankato, MN 56001
Ph: (507)385-0837
E-mail: gellerfam@chartermi.net
URL: National Affiliate–www.poac.org
State. **Affiliated With:** Pony of the Americas Club.

11398 ■ Retired and Senior Volunteer Program of South Central Minnesota
c/o Nadene C. Ruthenbeck, Dir.
518 S 5th
Mankato, MN 56001
Ph: (507)345-7787
Fax: (507)345-3668
E-mail: rsvp@hickorytech.net
URL: http://www.seniorcorps.gov/about/programs/rsvp_state.asp?usestateabbr=mn&Search4.x=27&Search4.y=6
Contact: Nadene C. Ruthenbeck, Dir.
Local. **Additional Websites:** http://www.hickorytech.net/~rsvp. **Affiliated With:** Retired and Senior Volunteer Program.

11399 ■ Skills USA, Mankato West High School
PO Box 8763
Mankato, MN 56001
Ph: (507)387-3461
Fax: (507)345-1502
E-mail: djeske1@mail.isd77.k12.mn.us
URL: http://www.mnskillsusa.org/secondaryChapters.htm
Contact: Dennis Jeske, Contact
Local. Serves high school and college students enrolled in technical, skilled, and service and health occupations. Provides quality education experiences for students in leadership, teamwork, citizenship and character development. Builds and reinforces self-confidence, work attitudes and communication skills. Emphasizes total quality at work, high ethical standards, superior work skills, and life-long education. Promotes understanding of the free enterprise system and involvement in community service. **Affiliated With:** Skills USA - VICA.

11400 ■ Sons of Norway, Elvesvingen Lodge 1-582
PO Box 1091
Mankato, MN 56002
Ph: (507)387-2223
E-mail: almorken@yahoo.com
URL: http://www.sonsofnorwaymankato.org
Contact: Audrey L. Morken, Pres.
Local. **Affiliated With:** Sons of Norway.

11401 ■ Sons of Norway, Lin-Hans-Rud Lodge 1-479
c/o Joel Botten, Pres.
410 W 9th St.
Mankato, MN 56001-2225
Ph: (507)388-1995
E-mail: jbottenjr@yahoo.com
URL: National Affiliate–www.sofn.com
Contact: Joel Botten, Pres.
Local. **Affiliated With:** Sons of Norway.

11402 ■ Southern Minnesota Area Human Resource Association
c/o Krista Amos
PO Box 3368
Mankato, MN 56002
E-mail: krista@smahra.org
URL: http://www.smahra.org
Contact: Krista Amos, Chair
Local. Represents the interests of human resource and industrial relations professionals and executives. Promotes the advancement of human resource management.

11403 ■ Sweet Adelines International, Minnesota Valley Chapter
Mankato East High School
2600 Hoffman Rd.
Mankato, MN 56001-5805
Ph: (507)549-3320
E-mail: demt@hickorytech.net
URL: National Affiliate–www.sweetadelineintl.org
Contact: Diane Mountain, Contact
Local. Advances the musical art form of barbershop harmony through education and performances. Provides education, training and coaching in the

development of women's four-part barbershop harmony. **Affiliated With:** Sweet Adelines International.

11404 ■ Technology Plus of Mankato
1961 Premier Dr.
Mankato, MN 56001-5901
Ph: (507)385-3200
Fax: (507)385-3202
URL: http://www.mankatotechplus.com
Contact: Amanda Schwabe, Economic Developer
Local.

11405 ■ United Brotherhood of Carpenters and Joiners of America, Mankato Local Union No. 464
310 McKenzie St.
Mankato, MN 56001
Ph: (507)388-6031
Fax: (507)388-1226
E-mail: 464kato@hickorytech.net
URL: http://www.mncarpenter.org
Local. Affiliated With: United Brotherhood of Carpenters and Joiners of America.

Mantorville

11406 ■ Dodge County Historical Society (DCHS)
616 N Main St.
Mantorville, MN 55955-0456
Ph: (507)635-5508
Contact: Idella Conwell, Contact
Founded: 1876. **Members:** 250. **Membership Dues:** $10 (annual). **Staff:** 1. **Local.** Individuals interested in preserving the history of Dodge County, MN. Operates museum and 1883 Schoolhouse and maintains 1858 school building and Civil War Recruiting Station. **Publications:** none. **Conventions/Meetings:** annual meeting.

Maple Grove

11407 ■ ASIS International, Minnesota Chapter No. 25
PO Box 2165
Maple Grove, MN 55311
Ph: (612)961-8879
Fax: (952)423-4993
E-mail: michael.brady@securitasinc.com
URL: http://www.asismn.org
Contact: Michael Brady CPP, Chm.
State. Seeks to increase the effectiveness and productivity of security practices by developing educational programs and materials that address security concerns. **Affiliated With:** ASIS International.

11408 ■ Bloomington Lions Club - Minnesota
c/o Wade Grantham, Pres.
9233 Merrimac Ln. N
Maple Grove, MN 55311-4425
Ph: (763)416-1935 (651)778-3676
URL: http://www.5m5.org
Contact: Wade Grantham, Pres.
Local. Affiliated With: Lions Clubs International.

11409 ■ Continental Cricket Club
9249 Shenandoah Ln.
Maple Grove, MN 55369
URL: http://www.usaca.org/Clubs.htm
Contact: Sandeep Hirekerur, Contact
Local.

11410 ■ Education Minnesota, Osseo (EM-O)
10200 73rd Ave. N, Ste.126
Maple Grove, MN 55369
Ph: (763)315-3416
Fax: (763)315-3417
E-mail: drainville@educationminnesota.org
URL: http://www.edmnosseo.com
Contact: Dick Rainville, Pres.
Local. Affiliated With: American Federation of Teachers.

11411 ■ Jobs for Minnesota's Graduates
c/o Scott Redd, Coor.
11275 96th Ave. N
Maple Grove, MN 55369
Ph: (763)416-3086
Fax: (763)420-4653
E-mail: sdredd@nws.k12.mn.us
URL: http://www.jag.org/minnesota
Contact: Scott Redd, Coor.
Founded: 2001. **State. Affiliated With:** Jobs for America's Graduates.

11412 ■ Maple Grove Dande Lions Club
c/o Joan Dindorf, Pres.
12623 73rd Ave. N
Maple Grove, MN 55369
Ph: (763)425-5287
URL: http://www.5m5.org
Contact: Joan Dindorf, Pres.
Local. Affiliated With: Lions Clubs International.

11413 ■ Maple Grove Lions Club
c/o Richard Kentzelman, Pres.
9928 95th Ave. N
Maple Grove, MN 55369
Ph: (763)425-5225
URL: http://www.5m5.org
Contact: Richard Kentzelman, Pres.
Local. Affiliated With: Lions Clubs International.

Maple Lake

11414 ■ American Legion, Maple Lake Post 131
PO Box 264
Maple Lake, MN 55358
Ph: (651)291-1800
Fax: (651)291-1057
URL: National Affiliate–www.legion.org
Local. Affiliated With: American Legion.

Maple Plain

11415 ■ American Legion, Minnesota Post 514
c/o Paul Stinson
PO Box 222
Maple Plain, MN 55359
Ph: (651)291-1800
Fax: (651)291-1057
URL: National Affiliate–www.legion.org
Contact: Paul Stinson, Contact
Local. Affiliated With: American Legion.

11416 ■ Maple Plain Lions Club
c/o Richard Golfis, Pres.
5995 W Main St.
Maple Plain, MN 55359
Ph: (763)479-6135
URL: http://www.5m5.org
Contact: Richard Golfis, Pres.
Local. Affiliated With: Lions Clubs International.

Maplewood

11417 ■ American Legion, Public Safety Post 449
1907 Phalen Pl.
Maplewood, MN 55109
Ph: (651)291-1800
Fax: (651)291-1057
URL: National Affiliate–www.legion.org
Local. Affiliated With: American Legion.

11418 ■ Bowling Proprietors Association of Minnesota (BPAM)
235 Roselawn Ave. E, Ste.17
Maplewood, MN 55117
Ph: (651)487-2141
Free: (800)622-7769
E-mail: bpam300@hotmail.com
URL: http://www.bpam.org
Contact: Kenn Rockler, Exec.Dir.
State. Seeks to increase the value of its members investment by promoting and improving the image of bowlers. Strives to strengthen the professionalism of its members and provide resources to increase the profitability of their operations.

11419 ■ Junior Achievement of the Upper Midwest
c/o Gina Blayney, Pres.
1800 White Bear Ave. N
Maplewood, MN 55109
Ph: (651)255-0055
Fax: (651)255-0460
E-mail: administrator@jaum.org
URL: http://www.jaum.org
Contact: Gina Blayney, Pres.
Founded: 1949. **Local.** Educates and inspires young people to value free enterprise, business, and economics to improve the quality of their lives.

11420 ■ Minnesota Association for Volunteer Administration (MAVA)
1800 White Bear Ave. N
Maplewood, MN 55109-3704
Ph: (651)255-0469
Fax: (651)255-0460
E-mail: office@mavanetwork.org
URL: http://www.mavanetwork.org
Contact: Renee Cardarelle, Pres.
Local. Seeks to advance the profession of the management of volunteers through leadership, advocacy, and education; envisions environments that integrate managers, volunteers, programs and services to build strong communities. **Affiliated With:** Association for Volunteer Administration.

11421 ■ St. Paul East Parks Lions Club
1821 Myrtle St.
Maplewood, MN 55109
Ph: (651)777-6514
E-mail: foxxx012@tc.umn.edu
URL: http://stpauleastparksmn.lionwap.org
Contact: Joseph L. Fox, Sec.
Local. Affiliated With: Lions Clubs International.

11422 ■ St. Paul Sail and Power Squadron
2487 Oak Cir. E
Maplewood, MN 55119-7177
Ph: (952)472-9300
E-mail: roboat.mn@netzero.net
URL: http://www.usps.org/localusps/stpaul
Contact: Ron Bakken, Commander
Local. Affiliated With: United States Power Squadrons.

11423 ■ Sheet Metal Workers' International Association, AFL-CIO, CFL - Local Union 10
1681 E Cope Ave.
Maplewood, MN 55109
Ph: (651)770-2388
Fax: (651)770-8539
E-mail: rleitschuh@smw10.org
URL: http://www.smw10.com
Contact: Richard Leitschuh, Financial Sec.-Treas.
Members: 5,299. **Local. Affiliated With:** Sheet Metal Workers' International Association.

11424 ■ Society for Applied Spectroscopy, Minnesota
c/o Delony Langer, Chm.
3M Ctr., Bldg. 201-2S-13
Maplewood, MN 55144-1000

Ph: (651)733-7206
E-mail: dllanger@mmm.com
URL: National Affiliate–www.s-a-s.org
Contact: Delony Langer, Chm.
Local. Affiliated With: Society for Applied Spectroscopy.

11425 ■ Solid Waste Association of North America, Minnesota Land of Lakes Chapter
c/o Michael Reed
Ramsey County Enval. Hea.
1670 Beam Ave., Ste.A
Maplewood, MN 55109-1176
Ph: (651)773-4443
Fax: (651)773-4454
E-mail: michael.reed@co.ramsey.mn.us
URL: National Affiliate–www.swana.org
Affiliated With: Solid Waste Association of North America.

Marble

11426 ■ American Legion, Poppe-Smuk-Appelget Post 327
PO Box 384
Marble, MN 55764
Ph: (651)291-1800
Fax: (651)291-1057
URL: National Affiliate–www.legion.org
Local. Affiliated With: American Legion.

Marcell

11427 ■ Grand Rapids Cap Baker Lions Club
c/o Cordell Bennett, Pres.
43515 Spider Shores Rd.
Marcell, MN 56657
Ph: (218)326-5865
E-mail: cabnntt@aol.com
URL: http://lions5m10.org
Contact: Cordell Bennett, Pres.
Local. Affiliated With: Lions Clubs International.

11428 ■ Sons of Norway, Nordstjernen Lodge 1-563
c/o Ivan S. Brattelid, Pres.
37573 E Little Deadhorse Rd.
Marcell, MN 56657-2084
Ph: (218)832-3290
E-mail: pineloft@bigfork.net
URL: National Affiliate–www.sofn.com
Contact: Ivan S. Brattelid, Pres.
Local. Affiliated With: Sons of Norway.

Marietta

11429 ■ American Legion, Minnesota Post 156
c/o Duane Kruse
PO Box 133
Marietta, MN 56257
Ph: (651)291-1800
Fax: (651)291-1057
URL: National Affiliate–www.legion.org
Contact: Duane Kruse, Contact
Local. Affiliated With: American Legion.

Marine on St. Croix

11430 ■ Norwegian Elkhound Association of Minnesota
c/o Karen Elvin
14465 St. Croix Trail N
Marine on St. Croix, MN 55047
Ph: (651)433-4666 (651)435-2066
Fax: (651)433-4666
E-mail: sangrud@earthlink.net
URL: http://www.neaa.net
Contact: Karen Elvin, Sec.
Founded: 1947. **Languages:** English, Norwegian. **State.** Promotes and protects the Norwegian Elkhound dogs. Sponsors dog shows, obedience trials and ability trials. Provides information and assistance to owners and fanciers of Norwegian Elkhounds. **Affiliated With:** American Kennel Club. **Publications:** *Elkhound Tales*, quarterly. Newsletter. Alternate Formats: online.

Marshall

11431 ■ American Legion, Minnesota Post 113
PO Box 284
Marshall, MN 56258
Ph: (651)291-1800
Fax: (651)291-1057
URL: National Affiliate–www.legion.org
Local. Affiliated With: American Legion.

11432 ■ American Society of Farm Managers and Rural Appraisers Minnesota Chapter
c/o Donald L. Kinker, AFM, Pres.
Farmers Natl. Company
PO Box 707
Marshall, MN 56258
Ph: (507)537-1335
Fax: (507)537-1335
E-mail: dkinker@farmers-national.com
URL: National Affiliate–www.asfmra.org
Contact: Donald L. Kinker AFM, Pres.
State. Affiliated With: American Society of Farm Managers and Rural Appraisers.

11433 ■ Habitat for Humanity of Lyon County, Minnesota
PO Box 584
Marshall, MN 56258-0584
Ph: (507)929-0371
E-mail: cmchorne@southwestmsu.edu
URL: National Affiliate–www.habitat.org
Contact: Mr. Chris McHorney, Pres.
Local. Affiliated With: Habitat for Humanity International.

11434 ■ Marshall Area Chamber of Commerce (MACC)
317 W Main St.
PO Box 352B
Marshall, MN 56258
Ph: (507)532-4484
Fax: (507)532-4485
E-mail: chamber@starpoint.net
URL: http://www.marshall-mn.org
Contact: Tracy Veglahn, Pres./CEO
Founded: 1932. **Members:** 430. **Staff:** 3. **Local.** Promotes business and community development in the Marshall, MN area. **Computer Services:** Information services, facts about business and community. **Committees:** Ambassadors; Education; Government Affairs; Industrial Development; Marshall Leadership Academy; Sounds of Summer Planning. **Councils:** Downtown. **Publications:** *Chamber Perspectives*, monthly. Newsletter. **Circulation:** 500. **Advertising:** accepted. Alternate Formats: online • Newspaper, annual. **Circulation:** 25,000. **Advertising:** accepted • Magazine. **Circulation:** 25,000. **Advertising:** accepted. **Conventions/Meetings:** monthly Business After Hours - meeting - every 3rd Monday.

11435 ■ Marshall Convention and Visitors Bureau
317 W Main St.
Marshall, MN 56258
Ph: (507)537-1865
Fax: (507)532-4485
E-mail: mshlcvb@starpoint.net
URL: http://www.marshall-mn.org
Local.

11436 ■ Minnesota Association of Financial Aid Administrators (MAFAA)
c/o Marcia Hubner, Treas.-Elect
Off. of Financial Aid
SW Minnesota State
1501 State St.
Marshall, MN 56258
Ph: (507)933-7530
E-mail: rhelgeso@gustavus.edu
URL: http://www.mafaa.org
Contact: Robert Helgeson, Pres.-Elect
State. Represents the interests and needs of students, faculties and other persons involved in student financial aid. Promotes student aid legislation, regulatory analysis and professional development of financial aid legislators. Seeks to improve activities relating to the quality and improvement of student financial assistance in Higher Education institutions. **Affiliated With:** National Association of Student Financial Aid Administrators.

11437 ■ Minnesota Association of Verbatim Reporters and Captioners (MAVRC)
PO Box 375
Marshall, MN 56258
Ph: (612)371-9383
E-mail: rite2jackie@aol.com
URL: http://www.mavrc.org
Contact: Jackie Young, Pres.
State. Affiliated With: National Court Reporters Association.

11438 ■ Minnesota Quarter Horse Association, District 1
c/o Bob Richards
2235 250th St.
Marshall, MN 56258
Ph: (507)537-0856
URL: http://www.mnqha.com/index_main.htm
Contact: Bob Richards, Contact
Local. Affiliated With: American Quarter Horse Association.

11439 ■ PFLAG Marshall/Buffalo Ridge
506 Thomas Ave.
Marshall, MN 56258
Ph: (507)532-0231
Fax: (507)929-0583
E-mail: rkwyatt1@juno.com
URL: http://www.pflag.org/Minnesota.217.0.html
Local. Affiliated With: Parents, Families, and Friends of Lesbians and Gays.

11440 ■ Society of Physics Students - Southwest Minnesota State University Chapter No. 6666
1501 State St.
Marshall, MN 56258
Ph: (507)537-6173
Fax: (507)537-6151
E-mail: kmurphy@southwestmsu.edu
URL: National Affiliate–www.spsnational.org
Local. Offers opportunities for the students to enrich their experiences and skills about physics. Helps students to become professional in the field of physics. **Affiliated With:** Society of Physics Students.

11441 ■ Southwest Minnesota State University Students In Free Enterprise (SMSU SIFE)
1501 State St., CH 105
Marshall, MN 56258
Ph: (507)537-7095
Fax: (507)537-6569
E-mail: sife@southwestmsu.edu
URL: http://www.smsusife.org
Local.

11442 ■ United Way of Southwest Minnesota
109 S 5th St.
PO Box 41
Marshall, MN 56258

Ph: (507)929-2273
Fax: (507)929-2274
E-mail: unitedwaylc@iw.net
URL: http://www.gomarshall.net/unitedwayofswmn.html
Contact: Ruth Ascher, Exec.Dir.
Founded: 1962. **Members:** 26. **Staff:** 1. **Budget:** $150,000. **Local**. Raises and distributes funds to charitable or non-profit organizations and agencies serving people in Lyon County, Minnesota. **Affiliated With:** United Way of America. **Formerly:** United Way of Marshall; (2005) United Way of Lyon County.

Maynard

11443 ■ American Legion, Holien-Thompson Post 252
PO Box 202
Maynard, MN 56260
Ph: (651)291-1800
Fax: (651)291-1057
URL: National Affiliate–www.legion.org
Local. Affiliated With: American Legion.

11444 ■ Maynard Lions Club
c/o Marian Bloomquist, Sec.
10463 Chip Renville St. SE
Maynard, MN 56260
Ph: (320)367-2815
E-mail: bbloom@maxminn.com
URL: http://www.5m4lions.org
Contact: Marian Bloomquist, Sec.
Local. Affiliated With: Lions Clubs International.

Mazeppa

11445 ■ American Legion, Mazeppa Post 588
PO Box 337
Mazeppa, MN 55956
Ph: (651)291-1800
Fax: (651)291-1057
URL: National Affiliate–www.legion.org
Local. Affiliated With: American Legion.

11446 ■ Mazeppa Lions Club
c/o Jon Liffrig, Pres.
RR 1, Box 1971
Mazeppa, MN 55956
Ph: (507)843-5234
E-mail: liffrig.jon@mayo.edu
URL: http://www.lions5m1.org/mazeppa
Contact: Jon Liffrig, Pres.
Local. Affiliated With: Lions Clubs International.

Mcgregor

11447 ■ American Legion, Minnesota Post 23
c/o Dale A. Wayrynen
PO Box 117
Mcgregor, MN 55760
Ph: (651)291-1800
Fax: (651)291-1057
URL: National Affiliate–www.legion.org
Contact: Dale A. Wayrynen, Contact
Local. Affiliated With: American Legion.

Medicine Lake

11448 ■ Association for Psychological Type - Twin Cities
c/o Gary Fleishacker
169 Peninsula Rd.
Medicine Lake, MN 55441
Ph: (763)525-1005 (763)544-4167
Fax: (763)525-1093
E-mail: garyfleishacker@aol.com
URL: National Affiliate–www.aptinternational.org
Contact: Gary Fleishacker, Contact
Local. Promotes the practical application and ethical use of psychological type. Provides members with opportunities for continuous learning, sharing experiences and creating understanding and knowledge through research. **Affiliated With:** Association for Psychological Type.

Medina

11449 ■ American Society of Appraisers, Twin Cities Chapter
c/o John H. Heidebrecht, Pres.
Berning & Berning Ltd.
809 Meander Ct.
Medina, MN 55340
Ph: (952)544-1212
Fax: (952)767-0112
E-mail: john@berningcpa.com
URL: http://www.appraisers.org/twin_cities
Contact: John H. Heidebrecht, Pres.
Local. Serves as a professional appraisal educator, testing and accrediting society. Sponsors mandatory recertification program for all members. Offers consumer information service to the public. **Affiliated With:** American Society of Appraisers.

Melrose

11450 ■ American Legion, Melrose Post 101
PO Box 152
Melrose, MN 56352
Ph: (651)291-1800
Fax: (651)291-1057
URL: National Affiliate–www.legion.org
Local. Affiliated With: American Legion.

11451 ■ American Legion, Othmar Braun Post 612
29658 325th Ave.
Melrose, MN 56352
Ph: (651)291-1800
Fax: (651)291-1057
URL: National Affiliate–www.legion.org
Local. Affiliated With: American Legion.

11452 ■ Melrose Chamber of Commerce
407 E Main St.
PO Box 214
Melrose, MN 56352
Ph: (320)256-7174
Fax: (320)256-7177
E-mail: chamber@meltel.net
URL: http://www.melrosemn.org
Contact: Kelly Neu, Exec.Dir.
Founded: 1928. **Members:** 131. **Local**. Promotes business and community development in Melrose, MN. Sponsors festival and beauty pageant. **Publications:** Newsletter, monthly.

Menahga

11453 ■ American Legion, Pine Tree Post 448
14220 Stocking Lake Rd.
Menahga, MN 56464
Ph: (651)291-1800
Fax: (651)291-1057
URL: National Affiliate–www.legion.org
Local. Affiliated With: American Legion.

Mendota

11454 ■ Mendota Mdewakanton Dakota Community
PO Box 50835
Mendota, MN 55150
Ph: (651)452-4141
Fax: (651)452-4232
E-mail: kangi42159@aol.com
URL: http://www.mendotadakota.org
Contact: Michael Scott, Chm.
Members: 250. **Local**. Seeks to protect and preserve Dakota culture.

11455 ■ Parents Television Council - Minnesota Chapter
c/o Phyllis Plum, Dir.
PO Box 50807
Mendota, MN 55150-0807
Ph: (651)389-2840
Free: (888)221-0328
E-mail: minnesotachapter@parentstv.org
URL: National Affiliate–www.parentstv.org
Contact: Phyllis Plum, Dir.
State.

Mendota Heights

11456 ■ ACF St. Paul Chefs Association
c/o William Niemer, Membership Chm.
1440 Northland Dr.
Mendota Heights, MN 55120
Ph: (651)675-4756
Fax: (651)675-4775
E-mail: wniemer@browncollege.edu
URL: http://www.saintpaulchefs.org
Contact: Lawrence A. Fischer CEC, Pres.
Local. Promotes the culinary profession. Provides on-going educational training and networking for members. Provides opportunities for competition, professional recognition and access to educational forums with other culinarians at local, regional, national and international events. **Affiliated With:** American Culinary Federation.

11457 ■ Hemophilia Foundation of Minnesota/Dakotas (HFMD)
750 S Plaza Dr., Ste.207
Mendota Heights, MN 55120
Ph: (651)406-8655
Fax: (651)406-8656
E-mail: hemophiliafound@visi.com
URL: http://www.hfmd.org
Contact: Jim Paist, Exec.Dir.
Local. Works to meet the needs and to enhance the quality of life for persons who live with hemophilia related genetic bleeding disorders, and their complications. Services include financial support for research, camps for children, emergency assistance funds, financial assistance for post-high school education, quarterly newsletter, support workshops, retreats for couples and families, educational presentations and materials. **Affiliated With:** National Hemophilia Foundation.

11458 ■ Henry Sibley High School PTA
c/o Henry Sibley High School
1897 Delaware Ave.
Mendota Heights, MN 55118
Ph: (651)681-2350
E-mail: sue.schway@thomson.com
URL: http://www.rschooltoday.com/henrysibleyhigh/PTA
Contact: Sue Schway, Pres.
Local. Parents, teachers, students, and others interested in uniting the forces of home, school, and community. Promotes the welfare of children and youth.

11459 ■ International Association of Machinists and Aerospace Workers, AFL-CIO, CLC - District Lodge 143
2510 Lexington Ave. S
Mendota Heights, MN 55120
Ph: (651)688-2640
Fax: (651)688-7229
E-mail: iamaw143@aol.com
URL: http://www.iam143.org
Contact: Robert B. De Pace, Pres./Directing Gen. Chm.
Members: 21,701. **Regional. Affiliated With:** International Association of Machinists and Aerospace Workers.

11460 ■ National Sojourners, Minnesota No. 25
c/o 1Lt. Donald A. Wurden
623 Watersedge Terr.
Mendota Heights, MN 55120-1931
Ph: (651)688-8150
E-mail: webmaster@zuhrah.org
URL: National Affiliate–www.nationalsojourners.org
Contact: 1Lt. Donald A. Wurden, Contact
Local.

Mentor

11461 ■ American Legion, Vanderwaal-Lusty Post 421
RR 2, Box 70
Mentor, MN 56736
Ph: (651)291-1800
Fax: (651)291-1057
URL: National Affiliate–www.legion.org
Local. Affiliated With: American Legion.

11462 ■ Northwest Minnesota Multi-County Housing and Redevelopment Authority
PO Box 128
Mentor, MN 56736-0000
Ph: (218)637-2431
Fax: (218)637-2433
E-mail: stacy@nwmnhra.org
URL: http://www.nwmnhra.org
Contact: Lee Meier, Exec.Dir.
Founded: 1975. **Budget:** $5,000,000. **Regional. Formerly:** (2005) Northwest Minnesota Community Housing Development Organization.

Middle River

11463 ■ American Legion, Minnesota Post 444
c/o Hans E. Lian
PO Box 66
Middle River, MN 56737
Ph: (651)291-1800
Fax: (651)291-1057
URL: National Affiliate–www.legion.org
Contact: Hans E. Lian, Contact
Local. Affiliated With: American Legion.

Milaca

11464 ■ American Legion, Hansen-Hayes Post 178
PO Box 41
Milaca, MN 56353
Ph: (651)291-1800
Fax: (651)291-1057
URL: National Affiliate–www.legion.org
Local. Affiliated With: American Legion.

11465 ■ Central Mille Lacs United Way
PO Box 73
Milaca, MN 56353-0073
Ph: (320)983-1348
URL: National Affiliate–national.unitedway.org
Local. Affiliated With: United Way of America.

11466 ■ Milaca Chamber of Commerce
PO Box 155
255 1st St. SE
Milaca, MN 56353
Ph: (320)983-3140
Fax: (320)983-3142
E-mail: chamber@milacacity.com
URL: http://www.cityofmilaca.org
Contact: Heather Jones, Pres.
Membership Dues: retail, media, manufacturing (plus $5 per employee number 11-60 and $1 per employee number 61 and up), $175 (annual) • financial institution ($45 per million deposits), $45 (annual) • public utility ($0.60 per in-city customer), $0 (annual) • hospital and nursing home (plus $1 per bed), $175 (annual) • professional, $50-$175 (annual) • associate, $50 (annual) • seasonal business, $90 (annual). **Local.** Works to create, protect and enhance the healthy business environment for the benefit of the area. **Publications:** Newsletter. Alternate Formats: online.

Milan

11467 ■ American Legion, Milan Post 359
PO Box 166
Milan, MN 56262
Ph: (651)291-1800
Fax: (651)291-1057
URL: National Affiliate–www.legion.org
Local. Affiliated With: American Legion.

11468 ■ Milan Lions Club - Minnesota
c/o Joel A. Lund, Sec.
PO Box 122
Milan, MN 56262
Ph: (320)734-4729
E-mail: joellund@fedtel.net
URL: http://www.5m4lions.org
Contact: Joel A. Lund, Sec.
Local. Affiliated With: Lions Clubs International.

Millville

11469 ■ American Legion, Millville Valley Post 579
PO Box 23
Millville, MN 55957
Ph: (651)291-1800
Fax: (651)291-1057
URL: National Affiliate–www.legion.org
Local. Affiliated With: American Legion.

Milroy

11470 ■ American Legion, Minnesota Post 274
c/o Earl Christopherson
PO Box 116
Milroy, MN 56263
Ph: (507)336-2384
Fax: (651)291-1057
URL: National Affiliate–www.legion.org
Contact: Earl Christopherson, Contact
Local. Affiliated With: American Legion.

Miltona

11471 ■ American Legion, Olson-Stitzel Post 219
PO Box 97
Miltona, MN 56354
Ph: (651)291-1800
Fax: (651)291-1057
URL: National Affiliate–www.legion.org
Local. Affiliated With: American Legion.

11472 ■ PFLAG Alexandria
12256 E Lake Miltona Dr. NE
Miltona, MN 56354
Ph: (218)943-1431
E-mail: esphult@midwestinfo.net
URL: http://www.pflag.org/Minnesota.217.0.html
Local. Affiliated With: Parents, Families, and Friends of Lesbians and Gays.

Minneapolis

11473 ■ AAA Minneapolis
733 Marquette Ave.
Minneapolis, MN 55402-1605
Ph: (612)338-8432
Local.

11474 ■ Alcoholics Anonymous-Alano Society of Minneapolis
2218 1st Ave. S.
Minneapolis, MN 55404
Ph: (612)871-2218
Contact: Tim Koland, Ofc.Mgr.
Founded: 1942. **Members:** 300. **Membership Dues:** donation, $12 (monthly). **Staff:** 9. **Budget:** $150,000. **State.** Provides clubhouse for recovering alcoholics to share their experience to the alcoholic who still suffers. **Publications:** *Alanotes*, monthly. Newsletter. **Price:** free. **Conventions/Meetings:** annual Founders Day Weekend - convention, A.A. roundup with speakers, meetings, and fellowship.

11475 ■ Aliveness Project (AP)
730 E 38th St.
Minneapolis, MN 55407
Ph: (612)822-7946
Fax: (612)822-9668
E-mail: aliveness@aliveness.org
URL: http://www.aliveness.org
Contact: Joseph A. Larson, Exec.Dir
Founded: 1985. **Members:** 1,200. **Staff:** 6. **Budget:** $300,000. **Local.** Persons with HIV/AIDS and their families and friends in Minnesota. Provides on-site meals, food shelf, complementary therapies (acupuncture, massage, chiropractic treatment, etc.), advocacy, and educational services. **Libraries: Type:** open to the public. **Holdings:** 100; books, periodicals. **Subjects:** aids, wellness, nutrition. **Telecommunication Services:** electronic mail, executive@aliveness.org. **Affiliated With:** National Association of People With AIDS. **Publications:** *The Aliveline*, bimonthly. Newsletter. **Price:** free to members. Alternate Formats: online.

11476 ■ Alliance of Automotive Service Providers of Minnesota (AASP-MN)
c/o Judell Anderson, CAE, Exec.Dir.
2520 Broadway St. NE, Ste.202
Minneapolis, MN 55413
Ph: (612)623-1110
Fax: (612)623-1122
Free: (800)852-9071
E-mail: aaspmn@qwest.net
URL: http://aaspmn.org
Contact: Judell Anderson CAE, Exec.Dir.
Founded: 1955. **Members:** 700. **Membership Dues:** associate, $245 (annual) • educational, $100 (annual). **Staff:** 2. **State.** Dedicated to improve the state's automotive service industry and the success of its members. Advances excellence, professionalism, and integrity by providing education and member benefit programs; serves as a resource and advocates on issues affecting the industry; and promotes the code of ethics. **Formerly:** (1999) Automotive Service Association of Minnesota; (2000) Automotive Service Professionals of Minnesota. **Publications:** *AASP News*, monthly. Newsletter. **Circulation:** 3,500. **Advertising:** accepted • Membership Directory, semiannual. **Price:** free for associate members. **Conventions/Meetings:** annual convention.

11477 ■ Alliance of Early Childhood Professionals (AECP)
2438 18th Ave. S
Minneapolis, MN 55404
Ph: (612)721-4246
Fax: (612)721-2428
E-mail: allecp@aol.com
URL: http://earlychildpro.org
Contact: Margaret C. Boyer, Founder/Exec.Dir.
Founded: 1979. **Members:** 550. **Membership Dues:** individual, $18 (annual) • organizational (5-20 employees), $25 (annual) • organizational (20 and above employees), $50 (annual). **Staff:** 5. **Budget:** $500,000. **State.** Seeks to improve the quality of care that children receive through better training, increased wages, better working conditions, and improved benefits for early childhood and out-of-school time workforce. Works on public policy issues and advocacy. **Formerly:** (1996) Child Care Workers Alliance. **Publications:** *A Primer: Understanding the Child Care Trilemma from an Economic Perspective* • *The Action Plan for Early Care and Education in Min-*

nesota • *Circle Time*, quarterly. Newsletter • *The Cost of Expanding Coverage To Child Care in Minnesota* • *Economic Retreat: Looking For Solutions to the Child Care Trilemma* • *Eliminating Sex-based Wage Disparities: Pay Equity and Minnesota's Child Care and Education Employees* • *The First Step: Looking at Your Working Conditions* • *Learning Between Systems: Higher Education as a Model for Financing Early Care and Education.* **Conventions/Meetings:** quarterly meeting.

11478 ■ Alliance of the Street
330 E 22nd St.
Minneapolis, MN 55404-2664
Ph: (612)870-0529
Local.

11479 ■ Alliance for Sustainability - International Alliance for Sustainable Agriculture
Hillel Center, Univ. of Minnesota
1521 Univ. Ave. SE
Minneapolis, MN 55414
Ph: (612)331-1099
Fax: (612)379-1527
E-mail: iasa@mtn.org
URL: http://allianceforsustainability.net
Contact: Krista Leraas, Office Mgr.
Local.

11480 ■ ALS Association, Minnesota Chapter
333 N Washington Ave., Ste.105
Minneapolis, MN 55401
Ph: (612)672-0484
Fax: (612)672-9110
Free: (888)672-0484
E-mail: info@alsmn.org
URL: http://www.alsmn.org
Contact: Sue Spalding, Exec.Dir.
Founded: 1993. **Staff:** 7. **Budget:** $1,500,000. **State.** Provides services for people with ALS (Lou Gehrig's disease) and their families; respite program, communication program, support groups, an equipment loan closet, family consultation, support and education. **Libraries: Type:** lending. **Holdings:** books, periodicals, video recordings. **Subjects:** caregiving, death and dying, stories for children. **Affiliated With:** Amyotrophic Lateral Sclerosis Association.

11481 ■ Alzheimer's Association, Minnesota Lakes
4550 W 77th St., Ste.200
Minneapolis, MN 55435
Ph: (952)830-0512
Fax: (952)830-0513
Free: (800)232-0851
E-mail: marsha.berry@alz.org
URL: http://www.alzmndak.org
Contact: Marsha Berry, Education Mgr.
Local. Family members of sufferers of Alzheimer's disease. Combats Alzheimer's disease and related disorders. (Alzheimer's disease is a progressive, degenerative brain disease in which changes occur in the central nervous system and outer region of the brain causing memory loss and other changes in thought, personality, and behavior.) Promotes research to find the cause, treatment, and cure for the disease. **Affiliated With:** Alzheimer's Association.

11482 ■ American Accounting Association, Midwest Region
c/o Jane Saly, Pres.-Elect
Mail No. MPL343
Univ. of St. Thomas
1000 LaSalle Ave.
Minneapolis, MN 55403-2005
Ph: (651)962-4254
Fax: (651)962-4710
E-mail: pjsaly@stthomas.edu
URL: http://aaahq.org/midwest/midwest.htm
Contact: Jane Saly, Pres.-Elect
Regional. Promotes excellence in accounting education, research and practice. Advances accounting instruction and encourages qualified individuals to enter careers in the teaching of accounting. Promotes the development and uses of accounting for internal management purposes. **Affiliated With:** American Accounting Association.

11483 ■ American Arbitration Association, Minnesota
c/o Romack Franklin, VP
200 S Sixth St.
Minneapolis, MN 55402-1092
Ph: (612)332-6545
Fax: (612)342-2334
E-mail: franklinr@adr.org
URL: National Affiliate–www.adr.org
Contact: Romack Franklin, VP
State. Affiliated With: American Arbitration Association.

11484 ■ American Board of Trial Advocates - Minnesota
800 LaSalle Ave., No. 2800
Minneapolis, MN 55402
Ph: (612)349-8500
Fax: (612)339-4181
E-mail: kfpeterson@rkmc.com
Contact: Kathleen Flynn Peterson, Pres.
State. Improves the ethical and technical standards of practice in the field of advocacy. Elevates the standards of integrity, honor and courtesy in the legal profession. Promotes the efficient administration of justice and improvement of the law. **Affiliated With:** American Board of Trial Advocates.

11485 ■ American College of Emergency Physicians - Minnesota Chapter
c/o Shari Augustin, Exec.Dir.
Hennepin County Medical Center ED
701 Park Ave.
Minneapolis, MN 55415-1623
Ph: (612)873-5645
Fax: (612)904-4241
E-mail: mn.chapter@acep.org
URL: http://www.acep.org
Contact: Shari Augustin, Exec.Dir.
State. Affiliated With: American College of Emergency Physicians.

11486 ■ American College of Obstetricians and Gynecologists-Minnesota
c/o Colleen Jensen
3433 Broadway St. NE, Ste.300
Minneapolis, MN 55413-1761
Ph: (612)362-3737
Fax: (612)378-3875
E-mail: colleenjensen@pressenter.com
URL: http://www.acog.org
Contact: Colleen Jensen, Exec.Dir.
State. Affiliated With: American College of Obstetricians and Gynecologists.

11487 ■ American Council of the Blind of Minnesota (ACB-M)
PO Box 7341
Minneapolis, MN 55407
Ph: (612)236-4115
E-mail: kgr@isd.net
URL: http://www.acb.org/minnesota
Contact: Ken Rodgers, Pres.
State. Strives to improve the well-being of all blind and visually impaired individuals. Seeks to elevate the social, economic and cultural levels of blind people. Improves educational and rehabilitation facilities and opportunities for the visually impaired. **Affiliated With:** American Council of the Blind.

11488 ■ American Heart Association
c/o Maureen McGinnis, Marketing Mgr.
4701 W 77th St.
Minneapolis, MN 55435
Ph: (952)835-3300
Fax: (952)835-5828
URL: http://www.americanheart.org
Contact: Maureen McGinnis, Marketing Mgr.
Local. Represents the interests of physicians, scientists and laypersons. Supports research, education and community service programs with the objective of reducing premature death and disability from cardiovascular diseases and stroke.

11489 ■ American Hiking Society - Kekekabic Trail Club
309 Cedar Ave. S
Minneapolis, MN 55454-1030
Free: (800)818-4455
E-mail: info@kek.org
URL: http://www.kek.org
Local.

11490 ■ American Institute of Aeronautics and Astronautics, Twin Cities
c/o Rodney Reeve
Phoenix Solutions Co.
3324 Winpark Dr.
Minneapolis, MN 55427
E-mail: rodney@phoenixsolutionsco.com
URL: National Affiliate–www.aiaa.org/
Contact: Rodney Reeve, Contact
Local. Affiliated With: American Institute of Aeronautics and Astronautics.

11491 ■ American Institute of Architects - Minnesota
275 Market St., Ste.54
Minneapolis, MN 55405
Ph: (612)338-6763
Fax: (612)338-7981
E-mail: hauschild@aia-mn.org
URL: http://www.aia-mn.org
Contact: Beverly Hauschild-Baron, Exec.VP
Staff: 9. **Local Groups:** 3. **State.** Strives to represent and advocate the Minnesota architect as the collaborative leader in shaping the built environment for the public good. **Affiliated With:** American Institute of Architects. **Publications:** *Architecture Minnesota*, bimonthly. Magazine. **Advertising:** accepted. Alternate Formats: online • *Working With An Architect.* Brochure. Contains information on how to hire and work with an architect and what to expect in the building process. Alternate Formats: online.

11492 ■ American Legion, Arthur and Leonard Falldin Post 555
2201 40th Ave. NE
Minneapolis, MN 55421
Ph: (651)291-1800
Fax: (651)291-1057
URL: National Affiliate–www.legion.org
Local. Affiliated With: American Legion.

11493 ■ American Legion, Business and Professional Mens Post 332
PO Box 29615
Minneapolis, MN 55429
Ph: (651)291-1800
Fax: (651)291-1057
URL: National Affiliate–www.legion.org
Local. Affiliated With: American Legion.

11494 ■ American Legion, Calhoun Post 231
2916 Lyndale S
Minneapolis, MN 55408
Ph: (651)291-1800
Fax: (651)291-1057
URL: National Affiliate–www.legion.org
Local. Affiliated With: American Legion.

11495 ■ American Legion, Courthouse Post 310
PO Box 80078
Minneapolis, MN 55408
Ph: (651)291-1800
Fax: (651)291-1057
URL: National Affiliate–www.legion.org
Local. Affiliated With: American Legion.

11496 ■ American Legion, Gopher Post 440
PO Box 6167
Minneapolis, MN 55406
Ph: (651)291-1800
Fax: (651)291-1057
URL: National Affiliate–www.legion.org
Local. Affiliated With: American Legion.

11497 ■ American Legion, Hellenic Post 129
2727 26th Ave. S
Minneapolis, MN 55406
Ph: (651)291-1800
Fax: (651)291-1057
URL: National Affiliate–www.legion.org
Local. Affiliated With: American Legion.

11498 ■ American Legion, Longton Post 618
3444 Mc Kinley St.
Minneapolis, MN 55418
Ph: (612)823-9511
Fax: (651)291-1057
URL: National Affiliate–www.legion.org
Local. Affiliated With: American Legion.

11499 ■ American Legion, Mark Hamilton Post 232
PO Box 8717
Minneapolis, MN 55408
Ph: (651)291-1800
Fax: (651)291-1057
URL: National Affiliate–www.legion.org
Local. Affiliated With: American Legion.

11500 ■ American Legion, Minneapolis Fire and Police Post 396
4636 Xerxes Ave. S
Minneapolis, MN 55410
Ph: (612)433-4085
Fax: (651)291-1057
URL: National Affiliate–www.legion.org
Local. Affiliated With: American Legion.

11501 ■ American Legion, Minneapolis Post 1
PO Box 6630
Minneapolis, MN 55406
Ph: (651)291-1800
Fax: (651)291-1057
URL: National Affiliate–www.legion.org
Local. Affiliated With: American Legion.

11502 ■ American Legion, Minnesota Post 99
c/o Richard Dingle
5600 34th Ave. S
Minneapolis, MN 55417
Ph: (651)291-1800
Fax: (651)291-1057
URL: National Affiliate–www.legion.org
Contact: Richard Dingle, Contact
Local. Affiliated With: American Legion.

11503 ■ American Legion, Minnesota Post 234
c/o Vincent L. Giantvalley
3751 Minnehaha Ave.
Minneapolis, MN 55406
Ph: (651)291-1800
Fax: (651)291-1057
URL: National Affiliate–www.legion.org
Contact: Vincent L. Giantvalley, Contact
Local. Affiliated With: American Legion.

11504 ■ American Legion, Minnesota Post 291
c/o Johnnie Baker
3010 4th Ave. S
Minneapolis, MN 55408
Ph: (651)291-1800
Fax: (651)291-1057
URL: National Affiliate–www.legion.org
Contact: Johnnie Baker, Contact
Local. Affiliated With: American Legion.

11505 ■ American Legion, Minnesota Post 437
c/o Robert White
806 Sheridan Ave. N
Minneapolis, MN 55411
Ph: (651)291-1800
Fax: (651)291-1057
URL: National Affiliate–www.legion.org
Contact: Robert White, Contact
Local. Affiliated With: American Legion.

11506 ■ American Legion, Minnesota Post 468
c/o Joe Smith
3444 Mckinley St. NE
Minneapolis, MN 55418
Ph: (651)291-1800
Fax: (651)291-1057
URL: National Affiliate–www.legion.org
Contact: Joe Smith, Contact
Local. Affiliated With: American Legion.

11507 ■ American Legion, Minnesota Post 511
c/o Richard D. Berg
3641 Morgan Ave. N
Minneapolis, MN 55412
Ph: (651)291-1800
Fax: (651)291-1057
URL: National Affiliate–www.legion.org
Contact: Richard D. Berg, Contact
Local. Affiliated With: American Legion.

11508 ■ American Legion, Minnesota Veterans Home Post 581
5101 Minnehaha Ave.
Minneapolis, MN 55417
Ph: (612)721-0600
Fax: (651)291-1057
URL: National Affiliate–www.legion.org
Local. Affiliated With: American Legion.

11509 ■ American Legion, North Side Post 230
PO Box 11531
Minneapolis, MN 55411
Ph: (651)291-1800
Fax: (651)291-1057
URL: National Affiliate–www.legion.org
Local. Affiliated With: American Legion.

11510 ■ American Legion, Twin City Ford Post 439
4346 Longfellow Ave.
Minneapolis, MN 55407
Ph: (651)291-1800
Fax: (651)291-1057
URL: National Affiliate–www.legion.org
Local. Affiliated With: American Legion.

11511 ■ American Ostrich Association, Minnesota
c/o Patricia Lovelette
PO Box 6354
Minneapolis, MN 55406-0354
E-mail: patlovelette@starbirdhq.com
URL: National Affiliate–www.ostriches.org
Contact: Patricia Lovelette, Contact
State. Aims to promote the ostrich industry, educate the public on the benefits of ostriches and ostrich products, and to produce quality ostrich products such as the meat, leather products and feathers. **Affiliated With:** American Ostrich Association.

11512 ■ American Parkinson Disease Association Minnesota Chapter
c/o Susan Knight, Pres.
800 E 28th St.
Minneapolis, MN 55407
Ph: (651)863-5850
E-mail: sknight@gillettechildrens.com
URL: National Affiliate–www.apdaparkinson.org
Contact: Susan Knight, Pres.
State. Works to find the cure for Parkinson's disease and to alleviate the suffering of its victims. **Affiliated With:** American Parkinson Disease Association.

11513 ■ American Postal Workers Union, AFL-CIO - Minneapolis Area Local Union 125
1234 4th St. NE
Minneapolis, MN 55413
Ph: (612)623-0677 (612)623-0665
Fax: (612)623-3214
E-mail: unionbull@aol.com
URL: http://www.minneapolisapwu.org
Contact: Jerry Sirois, Pres.
Members: 2,329. **Local.** AFL-CIO. **Affiliated With:** American Postal Workers Union.

11514 ■ American Red Cross - Minneapolis Area Chapter
c/o Rose L.
1201 W River Pkwy.
Minneapolis, MN 55454-2020
Ph: (612)871-7676
Fax: (612)872-3200
E-mail: mplsinformation@mplsredcross.org
URL: http://www.mplsredcross.org
Local.

11515 ■ American Sewing Guild, Minneapolis/St. Paul Chapter
c/o Joan Zandlo
PO Box 21214
Minneapolis, MN 55421-0214
Ph: (763)788-4966
E-mail: joandave4022@hotmail.com
URL: http://www.asg-mpls-stpaul.org
Contact: Joanna Zandlo, Contact
Local. Affiliated With: American Sewing Guild.

11516 ■ American Society of Business Publication Editors - Twin Cities Chapter
c/o Karen McMahon, Sec.
Primedia Bus. Info.
7900 Intl. Dr., Ste.300
Minneapolis, MN 55425
Ph: (952)851-4680
Fax: (952)851-4601
E-mail: kmcmahon@primediabusiness.com
URL: National Affiliate–www.asbpe.org
Contact: Lisa Jo Lupo, Pres.
Local. Promotes the public and professional understanding of business publication. Serves to enhance editorial standards and quality and to raise the level of publication management skills of its members. **Affiliated With:** American Society of Business Publication Editors.

11517 ■ American Society for Healthcare Food Service Administrators, Central Minnesota Chapter
c/o Peggy Kearns, Pres.
Minneapolis VA Medical Ctr.
1 Veterans Dr.
Minneapolis, MN 55417
Ph: (612)725-2004
Fax: (612)727-5997
E-mail: mjca@sttheresenh.org
URL: National Affiliate–www.ashfsa.org
Contact: Peggy Kearns, Pres.
Local. Advances healthcare foodservice leadership through education, networking and advocacy. **Affiliated With:** American Society for Healthcare Food Service Administrators.

11518 ■ American Society of Interior Designers, Minnesota Chapter
275 Market St., No. 160
Minneapolis, MN 55405

Ph: (612)339-6003
Fax: (612)339-8691
E-mail: info@asidmn.org
URL: http://www.asidmn.org
Contact: Carol Arnold, Administrator
State. **Affiliated With:** American Society of Interior Designers. **Formerly:** (2005) American Society of Interior Designers, Minnesota.

11519 ■ American Society of Sanitary Engineering, Minnesota Chapter
c/o Craig Bing, Pres.
5013 France Ave. S
Minneapolis, MN 55410
E-mail: bingplumbing@yahoo.com
URL: National Affiliate–www.asse-plumbing.org
Contact: Craig Bing, Pres.
State. Represents plumbing officials, sanitary engineers, plumbers, plumbing contractors, building officials, architects, engineers, designing engineers, physicians, and others interested in health. Conducts research on plumbing and sanitation and develops performance standards for components of the plumbing system. Sponsors disease research programs and other studies of water-borne epidemics. **Affiliated With:** American Society of Sanitary Engineering.

11520 ■ ARC, Hennepin-Carver
Diamond Hill Center
4301 Hwy. 7, Ste.140
Minneapolis, MN 55416
Ph: (952)920-0855
Fax: (952)920-1480
E-mail: mail@archennepin.org
URL: http://www.archennepincarver.org
Contact: Kim Keprios, Exec.Dir.
Founded: 1940. **Local**. Works to secure opportunities for people with mental retardation and related developmental disabilities and their families to live, learn, and play as they choose.

11521 ■ Art Libraries Society of North America - Twin Cities Chapter
c/o Kay Streng, Sec.-Treas.
Minneapolis Coll. of Art & Design Lib.
2501 Stevens Ave. S
Minneapolis, MN 55404
E-mail: kheuer@cva.edu
URL: http://www.arthist.umn.edu/slides/ARLIS
Contact: Kathryn Heuer, Chair
Local. Aims to address the needs of art libraries and other professionals. Serves as a means of communication between art librarians and other notable groups and individuals in the industry. Strives to assist in the publishing of articles on art. Advocates art appreciation. **Affiliated With:** Art Libraries Society/North America.

11522 ■ Arts Midwest
2908 Hennepin Ave., Ste.200
Minneapolis, MN 55408-1987
Ph: (612)341-0755
Fax: (612)341-0902
E-mail: general@artsmidwest.org
URL: http://www.artsmidwest.org
Contact: David J. Fraher, Exec.Dir.
Founded: 1985. **Staff:** 10. **Budget:** $2,200,000. **Nonmembership**. **Regional**. Aims to connect the arts to audiences throughout the nine-state region of IN, IA, MI, MN, ND, OH, SD, and WI. Seeks to enable individuals and families throughout America's heartland to share in and to enjoy the arts and cultures of the region and the world. Sponsors cultural programs, theater and dance performances, music ensembles, arts educational activities, exhibitions, and conferences. **Awards:** Performing Arts Fund. **Frequency:** annual. **Type:** grant. **Recipient:** to support presenters such as performing arts centers, councils, or colleges and universities. **Telecommunication Services:** teletype, emergency number, (612)822-2956. **Publications:** *Arts Midwest News*, annual. Annual Report. **Price:** free. **Conventions/Meetings:** annual Midwest Arts Conference - convention (exhibits) - September.

11523 ■ Assistance League of Minneapolis/St. Paul
PO Box 27154
Minneapolis, MN 55427-0154
Ph: (612)729-0495
E-mail: assistanceleague@mn.rr.com
URL: http://msp.assistanceleague.org
Local. **Affiliated With:** Assistance League.

11524 ■ Association for the Advancement of Hmong Women in Minnesota
c/o Shannon Cahill
1518 E Lake St.
Minneapolis, MN 55407
Ph: (612)724-3066
Fax: (612)724-3098
E-mail: shannoncahill@aahwm.org
URL: http://www.aahwm.org
State.

11525 ■ Association of Certified Fraud Examiners, Twin Cities Chapter No. 47
c/o David G. Kiwus, CFE, CPA, CMA
Schechter, Dokken, Kanter, Andrews, & Selcer, Ltd.
100 Washington Ave. S, Ste.1600
Minneapolis, MN 55401
Ph: (612)332-5500 (612)332-9339
Fax: (612)332-1529
E-mail: dkiwus@sdkcpa.com
URL: National Affiliate–www.cfenet.com
Contact: David G. Kiwus, Contact
Founded: 1993. **Members:** 100. **Membership Dues:** individual, $25 (annual). **Local**. Corporate managers, executives, auditors, trainers, security directors, and others employed in financial institutions; business, law enforcement, and social science professionals. Works to classify and examine financial crimes such as white-collar embezzlement, forgery, and fraud as well as their frequency and methodology to develop effective preventive plans and policies for businesses. **Affiliated With:** Association of Certified Fraud Examiners.

11526 ■ Association for Computing Machinery, University of Minnesota Student Chapter
4-192 EE/CS Bldg.
200 Union St. SE
Minneapolis, MN 55455
Ph: (612)626-1535
E-mail: officers@acm.cs.umn.edu
URL: http://acm.cs.umn.edu
Contact: James Greene, Pres.
Members: 100. **Local**. Biological, medical, behavioral, and computer scientists; hospital administrators; programmers and others interested in application of computer methods to biological, behavioral, and medical problems. Stimulates understanding of the use and potential of computers in the biosciences. **Affiliated With:** Association for Computing Machinery. **Formerly:** (2005) Association for Computing Machinery, University of Minnesota/Minneapolis. **Conventions/Meetings:** monthly meeting.

11527 ■ Association of Energy Engineers, Minnesota/Twin Cities Chapter
c/o Mr. Wade Wiken
800 Lasalle Ave., Ste.2230
Minneapolis, MN 55402-2033
Ph: (612)321-4693
Fax: (612)321-5081
Free: (800)495-9880
E-mail: wade.wiken@centerpointenergy.com
URL: http://www.aeecenter.org
Contact: Mr. Wade Wiken, Pres.
Founded: 2003. **Members:** 75. **Membership Dues:** regular, $160 (annual) • student, $15 (annual) • retired, $15 (annual). **Regional**. Assists local energy professionals to meet with peers and discuss latest happenings in their industries. **Awards:** National Scholarship. **Type:** scholarship. **Affiliated With:** Association of Energy Engineers. **Conventions/Meetings:** monthly meeting, tours of presentations - every first Wednesday.

11528 ■ Association of Independent Commercial Producers/Minnesota
c/o Kirk Hokanson, Pres.
728 E Hennepin Ave.
Minneapolis, MN 55414
Ph: (612)617-0000
Fax: (612)617-9999
E-mail: aicp_minnesota@yahoo.com
URL: National Affiliate–www.aicp.com
Contact: Kirk Hokanson, Pres.
State. **Affiliated With:** Association of Independent Commercial Producers.

11529 ■ Audubon Chapter of Minneapolis
c/o Jerry Bahls, Pres.
PO Box 3801
Minneapolis, MN 55403
E-mail: bahls001@tc.umn.edu
URL: http://www.geocities.com/RainForest/5835
Contact: Jerry Bahls, Pres.
Local. Works to conserve and restore natural ecosystems, focusing on birds and other wildlife for the benefit of humanity and the earth's biological diversity. **Affiliated With:** National Audubon Society.

11530 ■ Ballet Arts Minnesota
528 Hennepin Ave., Ste.203
Hennepin Ctr. for Arts
Minneapolis, MN 55403
Ph: (612)340-1071
Fax: (612)335-9266
E-mail: info@balletartsminnesota.org
URL: http://www.balletartsminnesota.org
Contact: Marcia Chapman, Contact
Founded: 1989. **Staff:** 12. **Budget:** $500,000. **Local**. Supports and promotes the arts, particularly ballet, in Minnesota. Conducts 2-3 performances per year. Offers pre-professional dance training. **Publications:** Newsletter, quarterly. **Conventions/Meetings:** periodic Workshops and Dance Classes - always September through May and Summer: June through August.

11531 ■ BKS Iyengar Yoga Association Minnesota (IYAMN)
c/o Julie Kaminski
PO Box 582381
Minneapolis, MN 55458
E-mail: iyamn@iynaus.org
URL: National Affiliate–www.iynaus.org
Contact: Julie Kaminski, Contact
State. **Affiliated With:** B.K.S. Iyengar Yoga National Association of the U.S.

11532 ■ Blaisdell YMCA
3335 Blaisdell Ave. S
Minneapolis, MN 55408
Ph: (612)827-5401
Fax: (612)827-5406
URL: http://www.ymcatwincities.org
Local.

11533 ■ BMW Car Club of America, North Star Chapter
PO Box 2774
Minneapolis, MN 55402-0774
Ph: (952)472-8622 (952)918-3508
E-mail: president@northstarbmw.org
URL: http://northstarbmw.org
Contact: Duane Thompson, Pres.
Members: 685. **Membership Dues:** general, $35 (annual). **Staff:** 10. **State**. Owners of BMW (Bavarian Motor Works) automobiles and other interested persons. Promotes interest in BMW automobiles through technical, social, and driving events; encourages the exchange of information among members. **Affiliated With:** BMW Car Club of America. **Publications:** *Northstar Bavarian*, quarterly. Newsletter. **Price:** free. **Circulation:** 700. **Advertising:** accepted. Alternate Formats: CD-ROM; online.

11534 ■ Brain Injury Association of Minnesota
34 13th Ave. NE, Ste.B001
Minneapolis, MN 55413
Ph: (612)378-2742
Fax: (612)378-2789
Free: (800)669-6442
E-mail: info@braininjurymn.org
URL: http://www.braininjurymn.org
Contact: Sharon Rolenc, Public Awareness Dir.

Founded: 1983. **Members:** 350. **Staff:** 14. **Budget:** $680,000. **Local Groups:** 35. **Languages:** English, Spanish. **State**. Strives to create a better future for people of Minnesota who live with disability due to brain injury through brain injury prevention, research, education and advocacy. **Libraries: Type:** open to the public. **Holdings:** articles, video recordings. **Subjects:** brain injury, rehabilitation. **Telecommunication Services:** electronic mail, sharon@braininjurymn.org. **Programs:** Education; Individual Assistance; Information and Resources; Multicultural Outreach; Public Awareness and Prevention Activities; Public Policy Advocacy; Resource Facilitation. **Affiliated With:** Brain Injury Association of America. **Publications:** *Headlines*, quarterly. Newsletter. **Circulation:** 8,000. **Advertising:** accepted. Alternate Formats: online. **Conventions/Meetings:** annual Statewide Conference on Brain Injury (exhibits).

11535 ■ Brick Distributors of Minnesota
c/o Olene Bigelow, Marketing Dir.
275 Market St., Ste.511
Minneapolis, MN 55405-1625
Ph: (612)332-1545
Fax: (612)332-1621
E-mail: brickdistofmn@qwest.net

Members: 25. Brick distributors and related suppliers. Promotes quality design and construction using brick masonry. **Publications:** Newsletter, quarterly.

11536 ■ Brotherhood of Locomotive Engineers and Trainmen, AFL-CIO - Division 333 (BLET)
742 Tyler St. NE
Minneapolis, MN 55413
E-mail: rbehne@mninter.net
URL: National Affiliate–www.ble.org
Contact: Ryan Behne, Pres.

Members: 42. **Local**. **Affiliated With:** Brotherhood of Locomotive Engineers and Trainmen, A Division of the Rail Conference of the International Brotherhood of Teamsters. **Formerly:** (2005) International Brotherhood of Locomotive Engineers, AFL-CIO - Division 333.

11537 ■ Camden Lions Club
c/o Craig Johnson, Sec.
4640 Lyndale Ave. N
Minneapolis, MN 55412
Ph: (612)521-1903
URL: http://www.5m5.org
Contact: James Cain, Pres.

Local. **Affiliated With:** Lions Clubs International.

11538 ■ Campus Atheists and Secular Humanists (CASH)
Univ. of Minnesota
300 Washington Ave. SE, No. 126
Minneapolis, MN 55455
E-mail: cash@cashumn.org
URL: http://www.cashumn.org

Local. **Affiliated With:** American Atheists.

11539 ■ Catholic Single Adults Club of the Twin Cities (CSAC)
PO Box 581321
Minneapolis, MN 55458-1321
Ph: (612)338-1288
E-mail: tedtri@aol.com
URL: http://www.caci.org/cac/tccac.html
Contact: Carl Bergstrom, Pres.

Local. **Affiliated With:** Catholic Alumni Clubs, International.

11540 ■ Cedar Lake Park Association (CLPA)
2000 Aldrich Ave. S
Minneapolis, MN 55405
Ph: (612)377-9522
E-mail: info@cedarlakepark.org
URL: http://www.cedarlakepark.org
Contact: Keith Prussing, Pres.

Founded: 1989. **Members:** 3,000. **Budget:** $30,000. **Local Groups:** 1. **Regional**. Citizens group established to preserve the woodlands and meadows surrounding the north end of Cedar Lake in Minneapolis and St. Louis Park for use as a nature and environmental education area. Seeks to connect neighborhoods and communities with each other and the parklands via walking and non motorized commuter trails. Seeks to develop Cedar Lake Park, 170 acres of water and 170 acres of land, through native landscape restoration, into a world-class urban nature park. Also provides advocacy work and educational activities. **Also Known As:** Save Cedar Lake Park. **Formerly:** (2005) Cedar Lake Park Preservation and Development Association. **Publications:** *Cedar Lake Park Update*, quarterly. Newsletter. **Circulation:** 4,000. **Conventions/Meetings:** monthly Steering Committee Meeting - always 2nd Monday in Minneapolis, MN.

11541 ■ Childcare Works
c/o Ann Kaner-Roth, Exec.Dir.
212 2nd St. SE, Ste.116
Minneapolis, MN 55414
Ph: (612)455-1055
Fax: (612)455-1056
E-mail: info@childcareworks.nonprofitoffice.com
URL: http://www.childcareworks.org
Contact: Ann Kaner-Roth, Exec.Dir.

Founded: 1981. **Members:** 10,000. **Membership Dues:** individual, $25 (annual) • organization, $200 (annual). **Staff:** 1. **Budget:** $100,000. **State**. Statewide coalition of organizations and individuals working through public education and advocacy for quality care and education for all children in MN and their families. **Committees:** Advocacy; Development; Issues Advisory; Public Relations. **Formerly:** (2001) Childcare Works-Education Division. **Publications:** *In the Works*, semiannual. Newsletter. **Price:** free for members. **Circulation:** 10,000. **Advertising:** accepted. **Conventions/Meetings:** biennial convention.

11542 ■ Children of Lesbians and Gays Everywhere Minneapolis
c/o Abigail Garner, Teen Group
1730 New Brighton Blvd., No. 175
Minneapolis, MN 55413
Ph: (612)362-3389
Free: (866)245-4281
E-mail: familieslikemine@yahoo.com
URL: http://www.familieslikemine.com

Local. **Affiliated With:** COLAGE.

11543 ■ Christian Athletes United for Spiritual Empowerment
3400 Park Ave.
Minneapolis, MN 55407-2020
Ph: (612)822-6866 (612)822-2113
E-mail: karen@christianathlete.com
URL: http://www.christianathlete.com
Contact: Karen Baynard, Admin.Coor.

Local.

11544 ■ Christians for Biblical Equality (CBE)
c/o Mary Seltzer
122 W Franklin Ave., Ste.218
Minneapolis, MN 55404-2451
Ph: (612)872-6898
Fax: (612)872-6891
E-mail: cbe@cbeinternational.org
URL: http://www.cbeinternational.org

Local.

11545 ■ Church World Service/CROP, Minn-Kota Region
122 W Franklin, Ste.622
Minneapolis, MN 55404-2447
Ph: (612)230-3277
Fax: (612)230-3269
Free: (888)297-2767
E-mail: pgraham@churchworldservice.org
URL: http://cwscrop.org/minnkota
Contact: Ms. Perri Graham, Dir.

Founded: 1946. **Members:** 35. **Staff:** 2. **Regional Groups:** 23. **Local Groups:** 80. **Local**. Works on behalf of 36 member denominations in the areas of self-help development, disaster relief, and aid to refugees. Provides educational resources and information about the programs of CWS in Minnesota and the Dakotas. **Libraries: Type:** reference. **Holdings:** video recordings. **Subjects:** hunger, development, disaster relief, refugees. **Affiliated With:** National Council of Churches of Christ in the U.S.A. **Also Known As:** Crop. **Publications:** *Cropwalker*, biennial. Newsletters • *Service Illustrated-News From the Pews*, biennial. Newsletters • Annual Report, annual.

11546 ■ Classical Association of Northern Plains Region
Univ. of Minnesota
Dept. of Classical & N.E. Stud.
245 Nicholson Hall
216 Pillsbury Dr. SE
Minneapolis, MN 55455
Ph: (612)625-3326
E-mail: gasheets@umn.edu
URL: http://www.camws.org
Contact: George A. Sheets, VP

Regional. Represents university, college, secondary and elementary teachers of Latin, Greek and all other studies which focus on the world of classical antiquity. Supports and promotes the study of classical languages.

11547 ■ Clinical Laboratory Management Association, Minnesota Chapter
c/o Edrie Murphy
Fairview Hea. Services
Rehabilitation Bldg., R300D
2512 7th St. S
Minneapolis, MN 55454
Ph: (612)672-4185
E-mail: emurphy2@fairview.org
URL: http://www.mnclma.com
Contact: Edrie Murphy, Contact

State. Provides clinical laboratory leaders with resources to balance science and technology with the art of management. Promotes efficient, productive, and high quality operations. Enhances the professional, managerial and leadership skills of members. **Affiliated With:** Clinical Laboratory Management Association.

11548 ■ Compassionate Action for Animals (CAA)
c/o David Rolsky, Sec.
PO Box 13149
Minneapolis, MN 55414
Ph: (612)626-5785
Fax: (612)822-8466
E-mail: info@ca4a.org
URL: http://www.ca4a.org
Contact: David Rolsky, Sec.

Founded: 1996. **Members:** 1,800. **Budget:** $40,000. **Local Groups:** 2. **Local**. Works to create a nonviolent and just society for all beings. Focuses on exposing the violence of animal agriculture and promoting a compassionate, healthy, and environmental-friendly vegan diet. **Libraries: Type:** by appointment only. **Holdings:** 200; books, periodicals. **Subjects:** animal rights, animal welfare, animal treatment. **Working Groups:** Team Veg; VegGuide.Org. **Formerly:** (1999) Animal Liberation League.

11549 ■ Compassionate Friends - Minneapolis Chapter
7520 Golden Valley Rd.
Minneapolis, MN 55427-4506
Ph: (952)475-1350 (952)975-3627
E-mail: srudenick@prodigy.net
URL: http://www.thecompassionatefriendsmpls.org
Contact: Steve Rudenick, Contact
Local.

11550 ■ Corporation for National and Community Service - Missouri
c/o Robert Jackson
431 S 7th St., Rm. 2480
Minneapolis, MN 55415-1854
Ph: (612)334-4083
Fax: (612)334-4084
E-mail: mn@cns.gov
URL: http://www.nationalservice.gov/about/role_impact/state_profiles_detail.asp?tbl_profiles_state=MO
Contact: Robert Jackson, Contact
State.

11551 ■ Council on Crime and Justice
822 S 3rd St., Ste.100
Minneapolis, MN 55415
Ph: (612)348-7874
Fax: (612)348-9272
E-mail: johnsont@crimeandjustice.org
URL: http://www.crimeandjustice.org
Contact: Tom Johnson, Pres.
Local.

11552 ■ Counselors of Real Estate, Minnesota Chapter
c/o Bettina L. Hoye, CRE, Chair
Nelson, Tietz & Hoye, Inc.
81 S 9th St., Ste.330
Minneapolis, MN 55402
Ph: (612)359-3203
Fax: (612)344-1540
E-mail: thoye@nth-inc.com
URL: National Affiliate–www.cre.org
Contact: Bettina L. Hoye CRE, Chair
State. **Affiliated With:** Counselors of Real Estate.

11553 ■ Design-Build Institute of America - Upper Midwest Chapter
c/o David J. Galey, P.E.
701 Washington Ave. N
Minneapolis, MN 55401-1180
Ph: (612)758-4348
Fax: (612)758-4199
E-mail: dgaley@hga.com
URL: National Affiliate–www.dbia.org
Contact: David J. Galey P.E., Pres.
Regional. Works to advocate and advance single source project delivery within the design and construction community. Promotes the use of innovative design-build teams on non-residential building, civil infrastructure and process industry projects. **Affiliated With:** Design-Build Institute of America.

11554 ■ Dignity - Twin Cities
PO Box 583402
Minneapolis, MN 55458-3402
Ph: (612)827-3103
E-mail: dignitytwincities@hotmail.com
URL: http://www.dignitytwincities.org
Contact: Brian McNeill, Pres.
Local.

11555 ■ Downtown Minneapolis Transportation Management Organization (TMO)
220 S 6th St., Ste.230
Minneapolis, MN 55402
Ph: (612)370-3987
Fax: (612)339-1412
E-mail: teresa@mplstmo.org
Contact: Teresa Wernecke, Exec.Dir.
Founded: 1991. **Members:** 11. **Staff:** 5. **Local**. Promotes congestion mitigation strategies and advocates for environmentally sound transportation policies to assure the continuous and orderly growth of Downtown Minneapolis and the region. **Conventions/Meetings:** monthly executive committee meeting.

11556 ■ Earthsave International, Minnesota
5025 Morgan Ave. S
Minneapolis, MN 55419
Ph: (952)930-1205
E-mail: twincities@earthsave.org
URL: http://twincities.earthsave.org
State. **Affiliated With:** EarthSave International.

11557 ■ EarthSave, Twin Cities
5025 Morgan Ave. S
Minneapolis, MN 55419
Ph: (952)930-1205
E-mail: twincities@earthsave.org
URL: http://twincities.earthsave.org
Local. **Affiliated With:** EarthSave International.

11558 ■ ESOP Association, Minnesota Chapter
c/o Sue Crockett, Exec.Dir.
5724 Beard Ave. S
Minneapolis, MN 55410
Ph: (952)922-9672
Fax: (952)922-4230
E-mail: scrockett@mnesop.org
URL: http://www.mnesop.org
Contact: Sue Crockett, Exec.Dir.
State. **Affiliated With:** ESOP Association.

11559 ■ Figure Skating Club of Minneapolis
5115 Excelsior Blvd., No. 244
Minneapolis, MN 55416
Ph: (612)926-2220
E-mail: jeff@jeffminsurance.com
URL: http://www.geocities.com/~fsc_mpls
Contact: Jeff Meyer, Pres.
Local. Provides programs to encourage participation and achievement in the sport of figure skating on ice. Defines and maintains uniform standards of skating proficiency. Organizes and sponsors competitions and exhibitions for the purpose of stimulating interest in figure skating. **Affiliated With:** United States Figure Skating Association.

11560 ■ Financial Executives International, Twin Cities Chapter
c/o Ms. Lyn Schroeder, Administrator
PO Box 24555
Minneapolis, MN 55424-0555
Ph: (952)829-5937
Fax: (952)829-5891
E-mail: feitwincities@aol.com
URL: http://fei.org/chapter/twincities
Contact: Ms. Leota Pearson, Pres.
Members: 360. **Local**. Promotes personal and professional development of financial executives. Provides peer networking opportunities and advocacy services. **Committees:** Academic Relations; Career Services; Communications; Government Issues Coordination; Professional Development; Programs; Retires Members; Strategic Partners. **Affiliated With:** Financial Executives International. **Publications:** Newsletter. Alternate Formats: online.

11561 ■ Financial Planning Association of Greater Hudson Valley
3900 Main St., NE
Minneapolis, MN 55421
Ph: (203)956-3248
Free: (877)817-8400
E-mail: rdrew@hitachicapitalamerica.com
URL: http://www.fpaghv.org
Contact: Richard J. Drew CFP, Pres.
Regional. Supports the financial planning process in order to help people achieve their goals and dreams. Promotes the legislative, regulatory and professional interests of the financial service industry. Fosters the value of financial planning and advances the financial planning profession. **Affiliated With:** Financial Planning Association.

11562 ■ Financial Planning Association of Minnesota (FPA MN)
3900 Main St. NE
Minneapolis, MN 55421
Ph: (763)781-1212
E-mail: office@fpamn.org
URL: http://www.fpamn.org
Contact: Janet Stanzak CFP, Pres.
State. Supports the financial planning process in order to help people achieve their goals and dreams. Promotes the value of the financial planning process and advances the financial planning profession. Fosters stewardship the development of recognized knowledge and competence. **Affiliated With:** Financial Planning Association.

11563 ■ Free Arts for Abused Children of Minnesota
c/o Michelle Silverman, Exec.Dir.
112 N 3rd St., Ste.201
Minneapolis, MN 55401
Ph: (612)824-2787 (612)824-2394
Fax: (612)338-5060
E-mail: faacmn@mninter.net
URL: http://www.freeartsmn.org
Founded: 1997. **Staff:** 3. **Budget:** $250,000. **State**.

11564 ■ Friends of the Boundary Waters Wilderness
401 N 3rd St., Ste.290
Minneapolis, MN 55401-1475
Ph: (612)332-9630
Fax: (612)332-9624
E-mail: info@friends.bwca.org
URL: http://www.friends-bwca.org
Contact: John Roth, Exec.Dir.
Founded: 1976. **Local**.

11565 ■ Friends of the Minneapolis Public Library
c/o Janet Urbanowicz, Asst.Dir./Volunteer Coor.
300 Nicollet Mall
Minneapolis, MN 55401
Ph: (612)630-6170 (612)630-6173
Fax: (612)630-6180
E-mail: friends@mplib.org
URL: http://friendsofmpl.org
Contact: Janet Urbanowicz, Asst.Dir./Volunteer Coor.
Local.

11566 ■ Friends of the Minnesota Sinfonia
901 N 3rd St., Ste.112
Minneapolis, MN 55401
Ph: (612)871-1701
Fax: (612)871-1701
E-mail: mnsinfonia@aol.com
URL: http://www.mnsinfonia.org
Contact: Jay Fishman, Exec.Dir.
Founded: 1989. **Staff:** 2. **State**. Provides quality musical and educational opportunities to communities of Minnesota. Conducts Young Artist Competition for students 21 and under. Events are free to public. **Awards:** YACW. **Type:** recognition. **Recipient:** for young artist competition winner.

11567 ■ Gaia Collective
c/o Malia Long
2538 Garfield St. NE
Minneapolis, MN 55418
Ph: (612)210-6834
URL: http://www.exploreminnesota.com/listing/index.cfm?id=9093
Local.

11568 ■ Gelende Ski Club
PO Box 580655
Minneapolis, MN 55458-0655
E-mail: gelendeskiclub@yahoo.com
URL: http://www.nbs.org/clubs/clubsbystate.php
Contact: Wendy Reno, Pres.
Local. **Affiliated With:** National Brotherhood of Skiers.

11569 ■ Gray Panthers, Twin Cities
c/o Sally Brown
3249 Hennepin Ave. S, No. 220
Minneapolis, MN 55408
Ph: (612)822-1011
E-mail: seeljh@esns.org
URL: National Affiliate–www.graypanthers.org
Contact: Jane Hanger Seeley, Co-Convener
Affiliated With: Gray Panthers.

11570 ■ Greater Minneapolis Convention and Visitors Association (GMCVA)
250 Marquette Ave. S, Ste.1300
Minneapolis, MN 55401
Ph: (612)767-8000
Free: (888)676-6757
E-mail: peterh@minneapolis.org
URL: http://www.minneapolis.org
Founded: 1933. **Members:** 800. **Budget:** $6,500,000. **Local.** Assists with the sales and marketing efforts for the Minneapolis Convention Center for meetings and conventions. **Publications:** *Japanese Visitor's Guide*, annual • *Meeting Planner's Guide*, annual • *Official Visitor's Guide*, semiannual.

11571 ■ Greater Twin Cities United Way
404 S 8th St.
Minneapolis, MN 55404-1084
Ph: (612)340-7400
Fax: (612)340-7675
E-mail: info@unitedwaytwincities.org
URL: http://www.unitedwaytwincities.org
Contact: Lauren A. Segal, Pres./CEO
Local.

11572 ■ Green Party of Minnesota (GPMN)
621 W Lake St., No. 205
Minneapolis, MN 55408
Ph: (612)871-4585
E-mail: info@mngreens.org
URL: http://www.mngreens.org
State.

11573 ■ Habitat for Humanity of Minnesota (HFH-MN)
c/o Jan Plimpton, Exec.Dir.
113 27th Ave. NE, Ste.T
Minneapolis, MN 55418
Ph: (612)331-4439
Fax: (612)789-0846
Free: (877)804-3466
E-mail: jan@hfhmn.org
URL: http://www.hfhmn.org
Contact: Jan Plimpton, Exec.Dir.
Local. Aims to eliminate housing poverty in Minnesota.

11574 ■ Health Partners
PO Box 1309
Minneapolis, MN 55440-1309
Ph: (952)883-6000
URL: http://www.healthpartners.com
Contact: Mary Brainerd, Pres./CEO
Local.

11575 ■ Healthcare Financial Management Association, Minnesota Chapter
PO Box 24732
Minneapolis, MN 55402-0732
Ph: (612)397-4408
E-mail: sgilman@deloitte.com
URL: http://www.mnhfma.org
Contact: Stephanie D. Gilman CPA, Pres.-Elect
State. Provides education, analysis and guidance to healthcare finance professionals. Helps members and other individuals in advancing the financial management of health care and in improving the business performance of organizations serving the healthcare field. **Affiliated With:** Healthcare Financial Management Association.

11576 ■ Hennepin Medical Society (HMS)
1300 Godward St. NE, Ste.2000
Minneapolis, MN 55413
Ph: (612)623-2885
Fax: (612)623-2888
URL: http://www.metrodoctors.com
Contact: James A. Rohde MD, Chm.
Local. Represents the interests of physicians, residents and medical students. Promotes excellence in health care. Ensures a healthy practice environment. Preserves the professionalism of medicine. **Affiliated With:** Minnesota Medical Association.

11577 ■ Hiawatha Bicycling Club (HBC)
c/o Wilbur Thomas, Pres.
PO Box 24920
Minneapolis, MN 55424-0920
Ph: (952)935-1672
Fax: (651)659-0207
E-mail: wthomas3@worldnet.att.net
URL: http://www.hiawathabike.org
Contact: Bruce L. Beck, LAB Liaison
Local. Affiliated With: American Hiking Society.

11578 ■ Hispanic Chamber of Commerce of Minnesota
3000 N 2nd St.
Minneapolis, MN 55411
Ph: (612)312-1692
Fax: (612)312-1693
E-mail: info@hispanicmn.org
URL: http://www.hispanicmn.org
State.

11579 ■ Hotel Employees and Restaurant Employees International Union Local 17
312 Central Ave., No. 444
Minneapolis, MN 55414
Ph: (612)379-4730
Fax: (612)379-8698
E-mail: info@here17.org
URL: http://www.here17.org
State. Affiliated With: UNITE HERE.

11580 ■ Howard Pulleys Pro-Am Basketball League
c/o Rene Pulley
605 Harry Davis Ln.
Minneapolis, MN 55411-3440
Ph: (612)770-0309
Fax: (612)522-7399
E-mail: howardpulleypanphers@yahoo.com
URL: http://www.howardpulleybasketball.com
Contact: Rene Pulley, Exec.Dir.
Local.

11581 ■ Humanists of Minnesota
PO Box 582997
Minneapolis, MN 55458-2997
Ph: (651)335-3800
E-mail: president@humanistviews.org
URL: http://www.humanistviews.org
Contact: Ron Scribner, Pres.
Founded: 1984. **Members:** 172. **Membership Dues:** individual and couple, $35 (annual). **Budget:** $14,000. **Local.** Promotes "responsible, rational living" through adherence to the ethical and moral tenets of humanism, which are based on the human strengths of reason and critical intelligence as opposed to faith or higher authority. **Affiliated With:** American Humanist Association. **Formerly:** (1999) Humanist Association of Minneapolis-Saint Paul. **Publications:** *Humanist News & Views*, monthly. Newsletter. **Price:** $20.00/year. ISSN: 1054-9633. **Circulation:** 450. **Advertising:** accepted. **Conventions/Meetings:** monthly meeting (exhibits) - always third Thursday of the month.

11582 ■ IEEE Communications Society, Twin Cities Chapter
c/o Ahmed H. Tewfik
Univ. of Minnesota - Dept. of Elecl. Engg.
4-174 EE/CSCI Bldg.
200 Union St., SE
Minneapolis, MN 55455
Ph: (612)625-6024
Fax: (612)625-4583
E-mail: tewfik@ece.umn.edu
URL: National Affiliate–www.comsoc.org
Contact: Ahmed H. Tewfik, Contact
Local. Affiliated With: IEEE Communications Society.

11583 ■ IEEE Computer Society, Twin Cities Chapter
c/o David E Farmer
Univ. of Minnesota
2218 Univ. Ave. SE
Minneapolis, MN 55414-3029
Ph: (612)812-9952
E-mail: farmer@umn.edu
Affiliated With: IEEE Computer Society.

11584 ■ IEEE Electromagnetic Compatibility Society - Twin Cities Chapter
c/o Joel Peltier, Chm.
Medtronic
7000 Central Ave. NE
Minneapolis, MN 55432
Ph: (763)514-4377
Fax: (763)514-8126
E-mail: joel.peltier@medtronic.com
URL: http://www.tc-ieee-emc.org
Contact: Joel Peltier, Chm.
Local. Provides a forum for educational, professional, and social affiliation of engineers, technicians, and scientists involved in electromagnetic compatibility. **Affiliated With:** IEEE Electromagnetic Compatibility Society.

11585 ■ Industrial Workers of the World - Twin Cities
PO Box 14111
Minneapolis, MN 55414
Ph: (612)339-4418
E-mail: jpila@iww.org
URL: National Affiliate–www.iww.org
Local. Affiliated With: Industrial Workers of the World.

11586 ■ Institute of Real Estate Management - Minnesota Chapter No. 45
c/o Gretchen Huetteman
4248 Park Glen Rd.
Minneapolis, MN 55416
Ph: (952)928-4664
Fax: (952)929-1318
E-mail: ghuetteman@harringtoncompany.com
URL: National Affiliate–www.irem.org
Contact: Gretchen Huetteman, Contact
State. Represents real property and asset management professionals. Works to promote professional ethics and standards in the field of property management. Strives to keep its members informed on the latest legislative activities and current industry trends. Provides classroom training, continuing education seminars, job referral service and candidate assistance services to enhance the effectiveness and professionalism of its members. **Affiliated With:** Institute of Real Estate Management.

11587 ■ International Alliance of Theatrical Stage Employees, Moving Picture Technicians, Artists, S 13
United Labor Center
312 Central Ave. SE, Rm. 398
Minneapolis, MN 55414

Ph: (612)379-7564
Fax: (612)379-1402
E-mail: info@iatse.org
URL: http://www.iatse13.org
Contact: Royce Jackson, Financial Sec.

Members: 296. **Local. Affiliated With:** International Alliance of Theatrical Stage Employees, Moving Picture Technicians, Artists and Allied Crafts of the United States, Its Territories and Canada.

11588 ■ International Association of Gay/Lesbian Country Western Dance Clubs, Northern Lights
3010 Hennepin Ave. S, No. 125
Minneapolis, MN 55408
Ph: (651)255-6955
URL: http://www.northernlightsdance.org
Contact: Michael McGee, Chm.

Regional. Affiliated With: International Association of Gay/Lesbian Country Western Dance Clubs.

11589 ■ International Masonry Institute, Minneapolis
c/o Olene Bigelow, Area Dir., Market Development
275 Market St., Ste.511
Minneapolis, MN 55405-1625
Ph: (612)332-2214
Fax: (612)332-1621
E-mail: obigelow@imiweb.org
URL: http://www.imiweb.org
Contact: Olene Bigelow, Area Dir.

State. Affiliated With: International Masonry Institute.

11590 ■ International Union of Operating Engineers, Local 049
2829 Anthony Ln. S
Minneapolis, MN 55418
Ph: (612)788-9441
Fax: (612)788-1936
Free: (866)788-9441
URL: http://www.local49.org
Contact: Glen Johnson, Business Mgr.

Local. Represents operating engineers, who work as heavy equipment operators, mechanics, and surveyors in the construction industry, and stationary engineers, who work in operations and maintenance in building and industrial complexes, and in the service industries. **Affiliated With:** International Union of Operating Engineers.

11591 ■ Izaak Walton League of America, Bush Lake Chapter
7515 Izaak Walton Rd.
Minneapolis, MN 55438
Ph: (952)941-7047
E-mail: andersonkj@earthlink.net
URL: National Affiliate–www.iwla.org

Local. Works to educate the public to conserve, maintain, protect, and restore the soil, forest, water, and other natural resources of the U.S; promotes the enjoyment and wholesome utilization of these resources. **Affiliated With:** Izaak Walton League of America.

11592 ■ Joint Religious Legislative Coalition (JRLC)
122 Franklin Ave. W, Ste.315
Minneapolis, MN 55404
Ph: (612)870-3670
Fax: (612)870-3671
Free: (888)870-1402
E-mail: info@jrlc.org
URL: http://www.jrlc.org
Contact: Brian A. Rusche, Exec.Dir.

Local. Furthers the cause of social justice in Minnesota by proposing and promoting responsible legislation, assisting congregations in the task of discerning and teaching God's vision of justice, and calling communities of faith to prophetic and unified action.

11593 ■ Kekekabic Trail Club
309 Cedar Ave. S
Minneapolis, MN 55454
Free: (800)818-4453
E-mail: info@kek.org
URL: http://www.kek.org

Local. Affiliated With: American Hiking Society.

11594 ■ KFAI Fresh Air of Minnesota (KFAI)
c/o Pam Hill Kroyer, Coor.
1808 Riverside Ave.
Minneapolis, MN 55454
Ph: (612)341-3144
Fax: (612)341-4281
E-mail: phill@kfai.org
URL: http://www.kfai.org
Contact: Pam Hill Kroyer, Coor.

State. Exists to broadcast information, arts and entertainment programming for a Twin Cities audience of diverse racial, social and economic backgrounds.

11595 ■ Kids for Saving Earth Worldwide (KSE)
PO Box 421118
Minneapolis, MN 55442
Ph: (763)559-1234
Fax: (763)559-6980
E-mail: kseww@aol.com
URL: http://www.kidsforsavingearth.org
Contact: Tessa Hill, Pres.

Local. Provides free educational material to members.

11596 ■ League of Women Voters of Minneapolis (LWVMPLS)
81 S Ninth St., Ste.335
Minneapolis, MN 55402
Ph: (612)333-6319
Fax: (612)333-6310
E-mail: vote@lwvmpls.org
URL: http://www.lwvmpls.org
Contact: Carol Green, Office Mgr.

Founded: 1920. **Local.** Aims to encourage informed and active participation in community and government and to influence public policy through education and advocacy.

11597 ■ Little Brothers Friends of the Elderly, Minneapolis/St. Paul, Minnesota (LBFE)
c/o Therese Cain, Exec.Dir.
Twin Cities Off.
1845 E Lake St.
Minneapolis, MN 55407
Ph: (612)721-6215
Fax: (612)721-5848
E-mail: twincities@littlebrothers.org
URL: http://www.littlebrothers.org/twincities/

Local.

11598 ■ Mail Systems Management Association, Minnesota Chapter
c/o IKON Management Services
2740 W 80th St.
Minneapolis, MN 55431-1203
Ph: (612)885-3644
Fax: (612)888-7640
URL: National Affiliate–www.msmanational.org
Contact: Sara Mathies, Pres.

Local. Provide a forum for people involved in the management, supervision and support of mail systems in business, industry, government and institutions. Raises the level of management prestige and esteem for managers employed in mail management.

11599 ■ Make-A-Wish Foundation of Minnesota
615 First Ave. NE, No. 415
Minneapolis, MN 55413
Ph: (612)767-9474
Fax: (612)767-2768
E-mail: info@wishmn.org
URL: http://www.wishmn.org
Contact: Tom McKinney, Exec.Dir.

Founded: 1982. **State.** Grants wishes to children with life-threatening illnesses, thereby providing these children and their families with special memories and a welcome respite from the daily stress of their situation. **Affiliated With:** Make-A-Wish Foundation of America. **Publications:** *The Wishing Well*, semiannual. Newsletter. **Conventions/Meetings:** monthly board meeting.

11600 ■ Media Communications Association International, Minnesota (MCAI-MN)
PO Box 582862
Minneapolis, MN 55458-2862
Ph: (952)927-8747
E-mail: webmaster@mcai-mn.org
URL: http://www.mcai-mn.org
Contact: Ms. Bethany Goss, Administrator

State. Provides networking and education opportunities to media communications professionals. Facilitates effective communication using new technology and with sound communication principles. **Affiliated With:** Chemical Coaters Association International.

11601 ■ Mentoring Partnership of Minnesota (MPM)
81 S Ninth St., Ste.200
Minneapolis, MN 55402
Ph: (612)370-9180
Fax: (612)370-9195
E-mail: mentor@mentoringworks.org
URL: http://www.mentoringworks.org
Contact: Joellen Gonder-Spacek, Exec.Dir.

Founded: 1994. **Staff:** 5. **Local.** Recruits adults to teach young people; provides training, technical assistance, information and referrals on mentoring; educates people of how important mentoring is. **Conventions/Meetings:** annual Mentor Conference.

11602 ■ Metro Meals on Wheels
PO Box 18232
Minneapolis, MN 55418
Ph: (612)789-5007 (612)623-3363
Fax: (612)331-9401
E-mail: rebecca@meals-on-wheels.com
URL: http://www.meals-on-wheels.com
Contact: Rebecca Becker, Admin.Asst.

Local. Affiliated With: Meals on Wheels Association of America.

11603 ■ Metrokids
c/o Elizabeth Coldren, Exec.Dir.
810 S 7th St.
Minneapolis, MN 55415
URL: http://www.metrokids.org

Local.

11604 ■ Midwest Direct Marketing Association (MDMA)
c/o Amy Sellheim, Exec.Dir.
4248 Park Glen Rd.
Minneapolis, MN 55416
Ph: (952)928-4643
Fax: (952)929-1318
E-mail: mdma@mdma.org
URL: http://www.mdma.org
Contact: Amy Sellheim, Exec.Dir.

Founded: 1960. **Membership Dues:** corporate (first 5, $30 for additional member), $350 (annual) • supplier, $125 (annual) • direct marketer, $95 (annual). **Regional.** Dedicated to the advancement of professional and ethical practice of direct response marketing by members throughout the Upper Midwest. **Awards:** ARC Award. **Frequency:** annual. **Type:** recognition. **Recipient:** for outstanding creative work that generated outstanding results • Direct Marketer of the Year Award. **Frequency:** annual. **Type:** recognition. **Recipient:** for an organization that demonstrates innovation and/or industry growth • William Holes Long Term Achievement Award. **Frequency:** annual. **Type:** recognition. **Recipient:** for an individual recognized for his/her industry leadership, innovation, and integrity. **Affiliated With:** Direct Marketing Association.

11605 ■ Midwest Fiction Writers (MFW)
PO Box 24107
Minneapolis, MN 55424
E-mail: president@midpestfiction.com
URL: http://www.midwestfiction.com
Contact: Jane Lindstrom, Pres.
Regional. Works to provide networking and support to individuals seriously pursuing a career in romance fiction. Helps writers become published and established in their writing field. **Affiliated With:** Romance Writers of America.

11606 ■ Midwest Independent Publishers Association (MIPA)
PO Box 581432
Minneapolis, MN 55458-1432
Ph: (651)917-0021
E-mail: parmorris@comcast.net
URL: http://www.mipa.org
Contact: Pat Morris, Pres.
Regional. Serves individuals and corporate groups involved in book, audio and video publishing. Advances the professional interests of independent publishers. Aims to provide training programs and cooperative marketing assistance within the publishing industry. **Affiliated With:** PMA - Independent Book Publishers Association.

11607 ■ Minneapolis AIFA
c/o Whitley P. Mott, Pres.
1405 Lilac Dr. N, No. 121
Minneapolis, MN 55422
Ph: (763)544-8087
Fax: (763)544-1631
E-mail: todd@naifa-mn.org
URL: National Affiliate–naifa.org
Contact: Whitley P. Mott, Pres.
Local. Represents the interests of insurance and financial advisors. Advocates for a positive legislative and regulatory environment. Enhances business and professional skills of members. **Affiliated With:** National Association of Insurance and Financial Advisors.

11608 ■ Minneapolis Amateur Softball Association
c/o Scott Gagnon, Commissioner
2117 W River Rd.
Minneapolis, MN 55411-2227
Ph: (612)230-6487
Fax: (612)230-6507
E-mail: sgagnon@minneapolisparks.org
URL: National Affiliate–www.asasoftball.com
Contact: Scott Gagnon, Commissioner
Local. **Affiliated With:** Amateur Softball Association of America.

11609 ■ Minneapolis Ambassadores Lions Club
c/o Jennifer Marshall, Sec.
MMC 493-420 Delaware St. SE
Minneapolis, MN 55455
Ph: (651)699-4714 (612)626-6081
URL: http://www.5m5.org
Contact: Jennifer Marshall, Sec.
Local. **Affiliated With:** Lions Clubs International.

11610 ■ Minneapolis Builders Exchange
1123 Glenwood Ave.
Minneapolis, MN 55405
Ph: (612)381-2620
Fax: (612)381-2621
URL: http://www.mbex.org
Contact: David L. Fritz, Exec.Dir.
Founded: 1888. **Membership Dues:** active, $360 (annual). **Local**. Represents general contractors, subcontractors, suppliers, manufacturers' representatives and individual firms related to the construction industry. Provides information on construction and building procedures. **Affiliated With:** International Builders Exchange Executives.

11611 ■ Minneapolis Chapter of International Association of Administrative Professionals
Berkley Risk Administrators Co., LLC
222 S Ninth St.
Minneapolis, MN 55402-3332
Ph: (612)766-3345
Fax: (612)766-3397
E-mail: metiaap@yahoo.com
URL: http://www.iaap-minneapolis.org
Contact: Mary Ellen Tieche, Pres.
Local. Professionals, corporations, academic institutions and students. Develops research and educational projects for administrative professionals. Provides training, seminars, conferences and educational programs.

11612 ■ Minneapolis Chapter National Electrical Contractors Association
5100 Gamble Dr., No. 365
Minneapolis, MN 55416
Ph: (952)591-1800
Fax: (952)591-1930
E-mail: johman@mplsneca.org
URL: National Affiliate–www.necanet.org
Contact: Mr. Joel Moryn, Pres.
Local. **Affiliated With:** National Electrical Contractors Association.

11613 ■ Minneapolis Consortium of Community Developers
3137 Chicago Ave.
Minneapolis, MN 55407
Ph: (612)789-7337
Fax: (612)822-1489
E-mail: jroth@cando.org
URL: http://www.mccdmn.org
Contact: Jim Roth, Exec.Dir.
State. **Formerly:** (2005) Minnesota Consortium of Community Developers.

11614 ■ Minneapolis Hiawatha Lions Club
c/o James Letson, Sec.
4116 Columbus Ave. S
Minneapolis, MN 55407
Ph: (612)822-2273
URL: http://www.5m5.org
Contact: James Letson, Sec.
Local. **Affiliated With:** Lions Clubs International.

11615 ■ Minneapolis Metro North Convention and Visitors Bureau
6200 Shingle Creek Pkwy., Ste.248
Minneapolis, MN 55430
Ph: (763)566-7722
Fax: (763)566-6526
Free: (800)541-4364
E-mail: info@justaskmn.com
Contact: John Connelly, Exec.Dir.
Founded: 1986. **Members:** 15. **Staff:** 5. **Budget:** $500,000. **Local**. Hotels and motels interested in promoting the northern suburbs of Minneapolis, MN and surrounding areas as a convention and tourism site. Issues publications. **Formerly:** Northern Metro Convention and Tourism Bureau.

11616 ■ Minneapolis North Lions Club
c/o Mary Britts, Pres.
1711 W Broadway Ave.
Minneapolis, MN 55411
Ph: (612)302-7261
URL: http://www.5m5.org
Contact: Mary Britts, Pres.
Local. **Affiliated With:** Lions Clubs International.

11617 ■ Minneapolis Northeast Lions Club
c/o Stephen Peterson, Pres.
3423 Maplewood Dr.
Minneapolis, MN 55418
Ph: (612)781-7611
URL: http://www.5m5.org
Contact: Stephen Peterson, Pres.
Local. **Affiliated With:** Lions Clubs International.

11618 ■ Minneapolis Regional Chamber of Commerce
81 S 9th St., Ste.200
Minneapolis, MN 55402-3223
Ph: (612)370-9100
Fax: (612)370-9195
E-mail: info@minneapolischamber.org
URL: http://www.minneapolischamber.org
Contact: Todd Klingel, Pres./CEO
Members: 6,000. **Local**. Promotes business and community development in the Minneapolis, MN area. **Awards:** Quality of Life Awards. **Frequency:** annual. **Type:** recognition. **Computer Services:** Online services, membership directory. **Committees:** Ambassadors; Bloomington Governmental Forum; Diplomats; Emerging Leaders; Event; Membership Advisory; Public Policy. **Publications:** *BusinessBriefing*. Magazine. **Circulation:** 6,000. **Advertising:** accepted • *Connections*. Newsletter. **Circulation:** 5,000. **Advertising:** accepted. Alternate Formats: online • Membership Directory. **Price:** free for members. **Advertising:** accepted. **Conventions/Meetings:** monthly Seminar Luncheons, with speakers - every 4th Tuesday.

11619 ■ Minnesota 1st Antique Bottle Club
c/o Steve Ketcham, Pres.
5001 Queen Ave. N
Minneapolis, MN 55430
Ph: (512)521-9874
URL: National Affiliate–www.fohbc.com
Contact: Steve Ketcham, Pres.
State. **Affiliated With:** Federation of Historical Bottle Collectors.

11620 ■ Minnesota Academy of Physician Assistants (MAPA)
4248 Park Glen Rd.
Minneapolis, MN 55416-4758
Ph: (952)928-7472
Fax: (952)929-1318
E-mail: office@mnacadpa.org
URL: http://www.mnacadpa.org
Contact: Lisa Larson, Pres.-Elect
Founded: 1977. **Members:** 350. **Membership Dues:** fellow/sustaining/associate, $125 (annual) • affiliate, $100 (annual) • student, $15 (annual). **Staff:** 1. **State**. Physician assistants in Minnesota. Fosters education and programs, monitors issues of regulation and reimbursement, and promotes PA services throughout the health care community. **Awards:** PA of the Year. **Frequency:** annual. **Type:** recognition. **Publications:** *imPAct*, bimonthly. Newsletter • Membership Directory, annual. **Conventions/Meetings:** semiannual Continuing Education Seminar (exhibits) - fall and spring.

11621 ■ Minnesota Advocates for Human Rights (MAHR)
650 3rd Ave. S, No. 550
Minneapolis, MN 55402-1940
Ph: (612)341-3302 (612)341-9845
Fax: (612)341-2971
E-mail: hrights@mnadvocates.org
URL: http://www.mnadvocates.org
Contact: Robin Phillips, Exec.Dir.
Founded: 1983. **Members:** 35,000. **Membership Dues:** student, individual, family, $25 (annual). **Staff:** 17. **Budget:** $900,000. **Local**. Works locally, nationally, and internationally to implement international human rights standards, to develop civil society and reinforce the rule of law by building broad-based constituencies and by involving volunteers in research, education and advocacy. **Libraries:** **Type:** reference. **Holdings:** 1,000. **Subjects:** international human rights. **Awards:** Volunteer Recognition Award. **Frequency:** annual. **Type:** recognition. **Projects:** Asylum; Battered Immigrant Women's Program; Building Immigrant Awareness and Support Education; Child Labor/Children Soldiers; Conflict Prevention/Crisis Response; Death Penalty Abolition; Domestic Violence in the Balkan States; General Women's Rights; Global Child Survival - Uganda, Mexico, U.S.; Mexico; Partners in Human Rights Education. **Formerly:** Minnesota Lawyers International Human Rights Committee. **Publications:**

Albania: Violations of the Right to Freedom of Thought, Conscience and Religion. Book • *Another Violence Against Women: The Lack of Accountability in Haiti.* Book • *Children's Rights in Haiti.* Book • *Oakdale Detention Centers: The First Year of Operation.* Book • *The Observer,* 3/year. Newsletter. **Circulation:** 1,400. **Conventions/Meetings:** annual Human Rights Awards Dinner.

11622 ■ Minnesota Ambulance Association, Metro
c/o Martin Van Buren, Dir.
HCMC EMS
701 Park Ave. S
Minneapolis, MN 55415
Ph: (612)873-2172
Fax: (612)904-4605
E-mail: martin.vanburen@co.hennepin.mn.us
URL: http://www.mnems.org
Contact: Martin Van Buren, Dir.
Local. Seeks to maintain the financial viability of the EMS industry by advocating education, legislation and regulatory change. **Affiliated With:** Minnesota Ambulance Association.

11623 ■ Minnesota American Indian Chamber of Commerce
c/o Joan Anderson
1508 E Franklin Ave., Ste.100
Minneapolis, MN 55404
Ph: (612)870-4533
Fax: (612)870-1060
E-mail: info@maicc.org
URL: http://www.maicc.org
Founded: 1989. **State.**

11624 ■ Minnesota Association of Black Lawyers (MABL)
c/o Jerry Blackwell, Pres.
PO Box 582892
Minneapolis, MN 55458-2892
Ph: (952)646-0400
E-mail: president@mabl.org
URL: http://www.mabl.org
Contact: Jerry Blackwell, Pres.
Membership Dues: attorney (private practice), $125 (annual) • attorney (public sector), $95 (annual) • retired or inactive attorney/judge, $75 (annual) • student, $25 (annual). **State.** Promotes and supports the professional development of Black lawyers, judges, and law students in Minnesota. Represents the interests of Black citizens and their community in the legal profession and in the judicial system throughout the state. **Affiliated With:** National Bar Association.

11625 ■ Minnesota Association of Black Physicians (MABP)
c/o Henry T. Smith, MD, Pres.
825 S 8th St., Ste.206
Minneapolis, MN 55404-1214
Ph: (612)347-7535
URL: http://www.mnmed.org/MABP
Contact: Henry T. Smith MD, Pres.
Membership Dues: physician, $125 (annual). **State.** Association of medical professionals and interested community members. **Affiliated With:** National Medical Association. **Conventions/Meetings:** quarterly meeting.

11626 ■ Minnesota Association for Developmental Education (MNADE)
2435-34th Ave. S
Minneapolis, MN 55406
Ph: (651)999-5948
E-mail: kathy.wellington@metrostate.edu
URL: National Affiliate–www.nade.net
Contact: Katherine Wellington, Pres.
State. Seeks to improve the theory and practice of developmental education. Enhances the professional capabilities of development educators. Supports student learning and provides public leadership. **Affiliated With:** National Association for Developmental Education.

11627 ■ Minnesota Association of Scholars (MAS)
c/o Jim van Houten, Pres.
Univ. of Minnesota
Carlson School of Bus.
Minneapolis, MN 55410
Ph: (612)863-0120
E-mail: jvanhouten01@msn.com
URL: http://www.mnscholars.org
Contact: Jim Van Houten, Pres.
State. Works to enrich the substance and to strengthen the integrity of scholarship and teaching. Provides a forum for the discussion of curricular issues and trends in higher education.

11628 ■ Minnesota Atheists
c/o August Berkshire, Pres.
PO Box 6261
Minneapolis, MN 55406-0261
Ph: (612)588-7031
E-mail: info@mnatheists.org
URL: http://www.mnatheists.org
Contact: August Berkshire, Pres.
State.

11629 ■ Minnesota Beef Council
c/o Ronald F. Eustice, Exec.Dir.
2950 Metro Dr., Ste.102
Minneapolis, MN 55425
Ph: (952)854-6980
Fax: (952)854-6906
E-mail: info@mnbeef.org
URL: http://www.mnbeef.org
Contact: Ronald F. Eustice, Exec.Dir.
State.

11630 ■ Minnesota Beer Wholesalers Association (MBWA)
701 4th Ave. S, Ste.1710
Minneapolis, MN 55415
Ph: (612)604-4400 (612)604-2588
Fax: (612)604-2598
E-mail: email@mnbwa.com
URL: http://www.mnbwa.com
Contact: Michael D. Madigan, Pres.
Founded: 1945. **Members:** 42. **Staff:** 4. Representatives of state beer wholesale associations. Promotes the welfare of beer association executives and beer wholesalers. Provides speakers; sponsors legislative conferences; compiles statistics. Bestows annual awards. **Telecommunication Services:** electronic mail, madigan@mnbwa.com. **Formerly:** Beer Distributors Secretaries of America; State Beer Wholesalers Secretaries; (1946) National Association of State Beer Association Secretaries; (1977) State Beer Association of Executives of America; (2000) Wholesale Beer Association Executives of America. **Publications:** *Exectic Exhortations,* bimonthly • *MBWA Directory,* annual • *WBAE Directory,* annual. **Conventions/Meetings:** semiannual conference.

11631 ■ Minnesota Bonsai Society (MBS)
PO Box 32901
Minneapolis, MN 55432
E-mail: admin@minnesotabonsai.com
URL: http://www.minnesotabonsai.com
Contact: Bob Hampel, Pres.
Founded: 1971. **Members:** 250. **Membership Dues:** individual, $35 (annual) • dual (same household), $40 (annual). **State.** Promotes and educates the public about the art of bonsai. **Affiliated With:** American Bonsai Society. **Publications:** *Minnesota Bonsai,* monthly. Newsletter. Alternate Formats: online. **Conventions/Meetings:** monthly meeting - except January.

11632 ■ Minnesota Book Publishers Roundtable (MBPR)
c/o Susan Doerr, Pres.
111 Third Ave. S, Ste.290
Minneapolis, MN 55401
Ph: (612)627-1967
Fax: (612)627-1980
E-mail: doer0012@umn.edu
URL: http://www.publishersroundtable.org
Contact: Susan Doerr, Pres.
Founded: 1960. **Members:** 78. **Membership Dues:** organization, $50 (annual) • individual, $35 (annual). **Budget:** $9,000. **State.** Works to establish a means by which those engaged in book publishing may assist one another through exchange of ideas and experience; to promote spirit of good fellowships and friendly cooperation among members; to promote highest standards of craftsmanship and integrity in book publishing; to promote further understanding between all related professions and trades concerned with the book publishing industry.

11633 ■ Minnesota Boston Terrier Club (MBTC)
c/o Barbara Bartholomew
4032 - 10th Ave. S
Minneapolis, MN 55407
Ph: (651)254-9874
E-mail: barbarasbostons@yahoo.com
URL: http://www.petfinder.com/shelters/MN125.html
State.

11634 ■ Minnesota Broadcasters Association (MBA)
3033 Excelsior Blvd., Ste.301
Minneapolis, MN 55416
Ph: (612)926-8123
Fax: (612)926-9761
Free: (800)245-5838
E-mail: jdubois@minnesotabroadcasters.com
URL: http://www.minnesotabroadcasters.com
Contact: James du Bois, Pres./CEO
State.

11635 ■ Minnesota Chapter of the American Society of Landscape Architects (MASLA)
Intl. Market Sq.
275 Market St., Ste.54
Minneapolis, MN 55405
Ph: (612)339-0797
Fax: (612)338-7981
E-mail: johnslack@dsuplan.com
URL: http://www.masla.org
Contact: Jack Slack, Pres.
State. Promotes the growth of the landscape architecture profession. Fosters high standards of quality in design, planning, development, and conservation in the field. Promotes the exchange of technical information and supports scientific research in all aspects of landscape architecture. **Affiliated With:** American Society of Landscape Architects.

11636 ■ Minnesota Chapter of the International Society for Performance Improvement (MNISPI)
1730 New Brighton Blvd., No. 104-308
Minneapolis, MN 55413-1661
Ph: (651)338-8787
E-mail: benjohnson@safeaccess.com
URL: http://www.mnispi.org
Contact: Ben Johnson, Pres.
State. Represents the interests of performance technologists, training directors, human resource managers, instructional designers, human factors practitioners, and organizational development consultants who work in a variety of industries such as automotive, communications and telecommunications, computer, financial services, government agencies, health services, manufacturing, the military, travel/hospitality, and education. Commits in improving productivity and performance in the workplace through the application of performance and instructional technologies.

11637 ■ Minnesota Chapter of the National Association of Corporate Directors (NACD-MN)
c/o Mr. John H. Stout, Chm.
200 S Sixth St., Ste.4000
Minneapolis, MN 55402-1425

Ph: (612)492-7012 (612)492-7518
Fax: (612)492-7077
E-mail: jstout@fredlaw.com
URL: http://NACD-MN.org
Contact: Mr. John Stout, Chm.
State. Improves corporate boards performance through effective corporate governance. Offers educational programs and information on board governance issues and practices, and access to NACD's research, symposia, and in boardroom educational services. **Awards:** Annual Outstanding Directors Awards (TM). **Frequency:** annual. **Type:** recognition. **Recipient:** for outside corporate directors who have made outstanding contributions to the companies they served during the past year. **Affiliated With:** National Association of Corporate Directors.

11638 ■ Minnesota Chapter of the Society of Architectural Historians
275 Market St., Ste.54
Minneapolis, MN 55405
Ph: (651)659-9932
E-mail: lock.bounds@thomson.com
URL: http://www.mnsah.org
Contact: Lock Bounds, Pres.
State. Promotes the preservation of buildings of historical and aesthetic significance. Encourages scholarly research in the field of architectural history. **Affiliated With:** Society of Architectural Historians.

11639 ■ Minnesota Chronic Fatigue Syndrome/Fibromyalgia Association
12527 Central Ave. NE, Ste.335
Minneapolis, MN 55434
Ph: (651)644-4975
E-mail: cfsmn@visi.com
URL: http://www.cfsmn.org
Contact: Barbara Tuccitto Warren, Exec.Dir.
Founded: 1986. **Members:** 350. **Membership Dues:** individual, $25 (annual) • family, $30 (annual) • corporate, $200 (annual) • professional, $100 (annual) • allied health/non-profit, $50 (annual). **Budget:** $28,000. **State**. Chronic Fatigue Syndrome patients, families, and friends working to raise awareness, support patients, and fund research via publications, referral lists, support groups, CFS resource materials, and grants for research. **Publications:** *Energy Crisis: The Impact of Chronic Fatigue Syndrome*. Booklet. **Price:** $3.00 • *Info and Update*, quarterly. Newsletter. **Price:** included in membership dues. **Circulation:** 700 • *Life Stories: Coping with Chronic Fatigue Syndrome*. Booklet. **Price:** $3.00 • *Long Night's Journey: Coping with Chronic Fatigue Syndrome*. Booklet. **Price:** $3.00 • *Referral Lists (Physician, Allied Health, Attorneys)*, periodic. **Conventions/Meetings:** annual conference • monthly support group meeting • bimonthly support group meeting.

11640 ■ Minnesota Citizens Concerned for Life (MCCL)
4249 Nicollet Ave.
Minneapolis, MN 55409
Ph: (612)825-6831
Fax: (612)825-5527
E-mail: information@mccl.org
URL: http://www.mccl.org
Contact: Leo LaLonde, Pres.
State. **Affiliated With:** National Right to Life Committee.

11641 ■ Minnesota Coalition for the Homeless
122 W Franklin Ave., Ste.306
Minneapolis, MN 55404
Ph: (612)870-7073
Fax: (612)870-9085
E-mail: info@mnhomelesscoalition.org
URL: http://www.mnhomelesscoalition.org
Contact: Deborah Mitchell, Pres.
Founded: 1984. **Members:** 130. **Membership Dues:** friend, $25 (annual) • regular, $50 (annual) • sustaining, $100 (annual) • vanguard, $250 (annual). **Staff:** 2. **Budget:** $140,000. **State**. Aims to generate policies, community support, and local resources for housing and services to end homelessness in Minnesota. **Awards:** Distinguished Service Awards. **Type:** recognition. **Recipient:** for deserving individuals and organizations. **Publications:** *The Homeless Report*, quarterly. Newsletter. Contains local, state, national news on homelessness, policy changes. **Price:** free. **Circulation:** 4,000. Alternate Formats: online. **Conventions/Meetings:** annual conference (exhibits).

11642 ■ Minnesota Commercial Association of Realtors
c/o Judy Puhl
5750 Lincoln Dr. No. 210
Minneapolis, MN 55436-1663
Ph: (952)908-1780
Fax: (952)908-1799
E-mail: aimee@mncar.org
URL: http://www.mncar.org
Contact: Ms. Judy Puhl, Exec.Dir.
State.

11643 ■ Minnesota Construction Association (MCA)
c/o Ms. Stephanie Atwell, Exec.Dir.
4248 Park Glen Rd.
Minneapolis, MN 55416
Ph: (952)928-4646
Fax: (952)929-1318
E-mail: satwell@harringtoncompany.com
URL: http://www.cmaanet.org
Contact: Ms. Stephanie Atwell, Exec.Dir.
State. Represents the interests of construction professionals of all types. **Formerly:** (2001) Minnesota Construction Management Association.

11644 ■ Minnesota Council on Foundations
c/o Bill King, Pres.
100 Portland Ave. S, Ste.225
Minneapolis, MN 55401-2575
Ph: (612)338-1989
Fax: (612)337-5089
E-mail: info@mcf.org
URL: http://www.mcf.org
Contact: Bill King, Pres.
State. Works to improve the vitality and health of communities; committed to strengthening and expanding philanthropy. **Affiliated With:** Council on Foundations.

11645 ■ Minnesota Electrical Association (MEA)
3100 Humboldt Ave. S
Minneapolis, MN 55408
Ph: (612)827-6117
Fax: (612)827-0920
Free: (800)829-6117
E-mail: mea@electricalassociation.com
URL: http://www.electricalassociation.com
Contact: Judith A. Rubin, Pres.
Founded: 1928. **State**. **Publications:** *Minnesota Electrical Association News*, bimonthly. Newsletter. Contains information on electrical industries. **Price:** included in membership dues. **Circulation:** 3,200. **Advertising:** accepted.

11646 ■ Minnesota Environmental Initiative (MEI)
219 N 2nd St., Ste.201
Minneapolis, MN 55401
Ph: (612)334-3388
Fax: (612)334-3093
E-mail: mharley@mn-ei.org
URL: http://mn-ei.org
Contact: Mike Harley, Exec.Dir.
Founded: 1991. **Members:** 650. **Membership Dues:** individual, $95 (annual) • corporate, $550 (annual) • corporate (non-profit, small business, government), $295 (annual) • patron, $2,000-$3,499 (annual) • patron (non-profit, small business, government), $1,000 (annual) • sponsor, $3,500-$4,999 (annual) • guarantor, $5,000-$7,999 (annual) • benefactor (maximum), $8,000 (annual). **Staff:** 10. **Budget:** $500,000. **State**. Seeks to foster improved public policy that benefits Minnesota's environment and economy. Promotes constituency cooperation through programs and events. **Awards:** Environmental Initiative Awards. **Frequency:** annual. **Type:** recognition. **Recipient:** for projects that have achieved extraordinary environmental outcomes. **Publications:** *Environmental Initiative Update*, monthly. Newsletter. **Price:** included in membership dues • Brochures. **Conventions/Meetings:** quarterly conference • periodic convention • monthly workshop.

11647 ■ Minnesota Evaluation Association (MNEA)
3010 Hennepin Ave. S
PMB 191
Minneapolis, MN 55408
Ph: (612)824-0724
E-mail: bcohen@mtn.org
URL: http://www.mneval.org
Contact: Barry Cohen, Pres.
State. Seeks to improve evaluation practices and methods. Provides a forum for professional development, networking and exchange of practical, methodological and theoretical knowledge in the field of evaluation. Promotes evaluation as a profession. **Affiliated With:** American Evaluation Association.

11648 ■ Minnesota Falcons Cricket Club
2600 California St. NE
Minneapolis, MN 55418
URL: http://www.usaca.org/Clubs.htm
Contact: Lochan Samkaran, Contact
Local.

11649 ■ Minnesota Grain and Feed Association
c/o Bob Zelenka, Exec.Dir.
400 S 4th St., 852 Grain Exchange
Minneapolis, MN 55415
Ph: (612)339-5043
Fax: (612)339-5673
E-mail: mgfa@usinternet.com
URL: http://www.mgfa.org
Contact: Bob Zelenka, Exec.Dir.
State. **Affiliated With:** National Grain and Feed Association. **Formerly:** (2000) Farmers Elevator Association of Minnesota.

11650 ■ Minnesota Heartland Tall Society
PO Box 580832
Minneapolis, MN 55458-0832
Ph: (952)881-8916
E-mail: st.paul@tall.org
URL: http://clubs.tall.org/mn/heartland
State. **Affiliated With:** Tall Clubs International.

11651 ■ Minnesota Herpetological Society (MHS)
Bell Museum of Natural History
10 Church St. SE
Minneapolis, MN 55455-0104
Ph: (612)624-7065
Fax: (612)647-5118
E-mail: zzzbuzzi@aol.com
URL: http://www.mnherpsoc.org
Contact: Barb Buzicky, Recording Sec.
Founded: 1981. **Membership Dues:** active (basic), $15 (annual) • active (contributing), $30 (annual) • active (sustaining), $60 (annual) • commercial, $25 (annual). **State**. Aims to promote the conservation and preservation of reptiles and amphibians. Educates the public to the value of reptiles and amphibians. Educates its members as to the proper care of reptiles and amphibians and the importance of maintaining natural populations of reptiles and amphibians. Promotes an atmosphere for open discussion of reptiles and amphibians among its members. **Libraries:** **Type:** reference. **Holdings:** books, periodicals. **Additional Websites:** http://www.bellmuseum.org/herpetology/Main.html. **Publications:** Newsletter, monthly. Contains information about MHS business and general meeting happenings; upcoming events and special articles. **Advertising:** accepted. Alternate Formats: online.

11652 ■ Minnesota Jung Association
c/o Laraine Kurisko, PhD., LP
PO Box 14726
Minneapolis, MN 55414
Ph: (651)644-4284
E-mail: mnjung75@hotmail.com
URL: http://www.minnesotajung.org
Contact: Dr. Laraine Patricia Kurisko PhD., Pres.
Founded: 1972. **Members:** 200. **Membership Dues:** regular, $45 (annual) • reside outside Twin Cities, senior, student, second member of household, $35 (annual) • patron, $75 (annual) • life (patron), $1,500. **Regional Groups:** 1. **State Groups:** 1. **Local Groups:** 1. **Regional**. **Libraries: Type:** not open to the public. **Holdings:** 1,400; articles, books, periodicals, video recordings. **Subjects:** Psychology of CG Jung, psychology. **Publications:** *Elements*, quarterly. Newsletter. Contains articles, information of events, and notices. **Price:** included in membership dues. **Advertising:** accepted.

11653 ■ Minnesota Kite Society (MKS)
PO Box 580016
Minneapolis, MN 55458-0016
Ph: (763)536-8552
E-mail: membership@mnkites.org
URL: http://www.mnkites.org
Contact: Ken Wilkowski, Pres.
Founded: 1985. **Members:** 120. **Membership Dues:** individual, $15 (annual). **Budget:** $2,500. **State**. Organizes meetings and events for MN kite fliers. Promotes kite flying with the region and serves as a liaison between local kite fliers and other kiting organizations. Events include Fun Fly, Frosty Fingers Kite Fly in the winter, the Kiwanis Kite Fly in the spring, and the Flying Colors Kite Fly in the summer. **Affiliated With:** American Kitefliers Association. **Publications:** *Minnesota Kite Society News*, bimonthly. Newsletter. **Conventions/Meetings:** monthly board meeting • annual Business Meeting and Auction.

11654 ■ Minnesota Legal Administrators Association (MLAA)
c/o Susan L. Melrose
Dorsey & Whitney LLP
50 S 6th St., Ste.1500
Minneapolis, MN 55402
Ph: (952)896-3217
E-mail: mbrauch@lhdl.com
URL: http://www.mlaa-ala.org
Contact: Mark A. Brauch, Contact
State. Affiliated With: Association of Legal Administrators.

11655 ■ Minnesota Medical Association (MMA)
1300 Godward St. NE, Ste.2500
Minneapolis, MN 55413
Ph: (612)378-1875
Fax: (612)378-3875
E-mail: mma@mnmed.org
URL: http://www.mnmed.org
Contact: Robert K. Meiches MD, CEO
State.

11656 ■ Minnesota Medical Directors Association
c/o Minnesota Medical Association
1300 Godward St. NE, Ste.2500
Minneapolis, MN 55413
Ph: (612)362-3736
Fax: (612)378-3875
E-mail: rclampright@mnmed.org
URL: http://www.amda.com
Contact: Robyn Lampright, Exec.Dir.
State.

11657 ■ Minnesota Municipal Beverage Association (MMBA)
c/o Paul Kaspszak, Exec.Dir.
PO Box 32966
Minneapolis, MN 55432
Ph: (763)572-0222
Fax: (763)572-8163
Free: (800)848-4912
E-mail: kaspszak@visi.com
URL: http://www.municipalbev.com
Contact: Paul Kaspszak, Exec.Dir.
State.

11658 ■ Minnesota Neuropathy Association
2221 Minneapolis Ave.
Minneapolis, MN 55406-1432
Ph: (612)338-1995
Fax: (612)338-2556
E-mail: neuropathy-minn@usjet.net
URL: http://www.neuropathy.org
Contact: A.R. Porte, Pres.
Founded: 1996. **Members:** 124. **Membership Dues:** all, $25 (annual). **Regional Groups:** 178. **State Groups:** 178. **For-Profit. State**. Provides patient and family support and education. Promotes research into the causes and cures of neuropathy. Stimulates awareness of and knowledge of little known disease among doctors and other health care professionals. Applies for funding to create and broadcast educational material to medical facilities, patients, families of patients, and neurology clinics. Holds monthly programs for sufferers where neurologists and other healthcare professionals speak, focusing on neuropathy and to answer patient's questions. **Publications:** *Neuropathy News*, 3/year. Newsletter. **Price:** including with national membership. **Conventions/Meetings:** annual convention.

11659 ■ Minnesota News Council (MNC)
c/o Mr. Gary Gilson, Exec.Dir.
12 S 6th St., Ste.927
Minneapolis, MN 55402
Ph: (612)341-9357
Fax: (612)341-9358
Free: (877)OUR-NEWS
E-mail: info@news-council.org
URL: http://www.news-council.org
Contact: Mr. Gary Gilson, Exec.Dir.
Founded: 1970. **Members:** 24. **Staff:** 3. **Budget:** $225,000. **State**. Strives to promote fair, vigorous and trusted journalism by engaging the public and news outlets in public conversations about standards of fairness, and by helping the public hold news outlets accountable. **Awards:** Accountability Award. **Frequency:** annual. **Type:** trophy. **Recipient:** for newspapers that demonstrated exceptional openness. **Computer Services:** Bibliographic search, archives of case determinations from 1971 to present • electronic publishing, archives of Newsworthy magazines (publication of the News Council); articles by executive director published as op ed pieces in local newspapers • online services, web site with complaint procedures and forms • record retrieval services, mock hearing curriculum for high schools and colleges; news media ethics codes. **Publications:** *Newsworthy*, semiannual. Magazine. Features discussion of ethics issues in the news media. **Price:** free. **Circulation:** 6,000.

11660 ■ Minnesota Newspaper Association (MNA)
c/o Linda I. Falkman, Exec.Dir.
12 S 6th St., Ste.1120
Minneapolis, MN 55402-1502
Ph: (612)332-8844
Fax: (612)342-2958
Free: (800)279-2979
E-mail: mna@mna.org
URL: http://www.mnnewspapernet.org
Contact: Linda I. Falkman, Exec.Dir.
Founded: 1867. **Members:** 375. **Staff:** 14. **State**. Trade association of the newspaper industry. Represents and promotes the industry. Services provided to newspapers and to the public include placement of newspaper advertising in Minnesota and nationwide. **Committees:** Advertising; Daily; Environment; Journalism Education; Legislative; Nominating; Past Presidents; Technology. **Affiliated With:** National Newspaper Association. **Publications:** *MNA Bulletin*, weekly. **Price:** included in membership dues. **Advertising:** accepted. Alternate Formats: CD-ROM; diskette. **Conventions/Meetings:** annual convention (exhibits) - January.

11661 ■ Minnesota Operators of Music and Amusement (MOMA)
c/o Hy Sandler
4805 Zenith Ave. S
Minneapolis, MN 55410-1824
Ph: (612)927-6662
Fax: (612)927-6662
E-mail: moma-ops@juno.com
URL: http://www.moma-ops.org
Contact: Hy Sandler, Contact
State. Aims to further the interests of those engaged in the sales, marketing, distribution and manufacturing of coin operated equipment. Fosters and promotes goodwill, mutual respect and fair dealing among those engaged in the business of coin-operated amusement devices. **Affiliated With:** Amusement and Music Operators Association.

11662 ■ Minnesota Optometric Association (MOA)
c/o Jim Meffert-Nelson, Exec.Dir.
3601 Minnesota Dr., Ste.800
Minneapolis, MN 55435
Ph: (952)841-1122
Fax: (952)921-5801
Free: (800)678-8232
E-mail: jim@mneyedocs.org
URL: http://www.mneyedocs.org
Contact: Jim Meffert-Nelson, Exec.Dir.
Founded: 1900. **Membership Dues:** first year after graduation from OD school, $170 (annual) • second year after graduation from OD school, $340 (annual) • third year after graduation from OD school, $851 (annual) • fourth year after graduation from OD school, $1,277 (annual) • fifth year after graduation from OD school, $1,703 (annual) • retired, $170 (annual). **State**. Provides optometrists a place where they could come together to further their professional knowledge and, advance and improve the primary eye care that patients receive throughout Minnesota. **Libraries: Type:** by appointment only. **Holdings:** 7; video recordings. **Subjects:** topic about the eyes. **Affiliated With:** American Optometric Association.

11663 ■ Minnesota Orienteering Club (MNOC)
c/o Ian Harding
PO Box 580030
Minneapolis, MN 55458
Ph: (651)779-6143
E-mail: maps@mnoc.org
URL: http://www.mnoc.org
Contact: Ian Harding, Contact
Regional. Affiliated With: United States Orienteering Federation.

11664 ■ Minnesota Ornithologists' Union (MOU)
J.F. Bell Museum of Natural History
10 Church St. SE
Minneapolis, MN 55455-0104
Ph: (763)780-8890 (218)728-5030
Free: (800)657-3700
E-mail: mou@moumn.org
URL: http://moumn.org
Contact: Mark Alt, Pres.
Founded: 1964. **State**.

11665 ■ Minnesota Parents of Blind Children
c/o Carrie Gilmer, Pres.
1152 106th Ln. NE
Minneapolis, MN 55434-3723
Ph: (612)872-0100
E-mail: cgilmer@blindinc.org
URL: National Affiliate–www.nfb.org
Contact: Carrie Gilmer, Pres.
State. Provides information and support to parents of blind children. Develops and expands resources available to parents and their children. Aims to eliminate discrimination and prejudice against the blind. **Affiliated With:** National Organization of Parents of Blind Children.

11666 ■ Minnesota Polygraph Association
5200 W 73rd St.
Minneapolis, MN 55439
Ph: (612)897-6500
URL: National Affiliate–www.polygraph.org
Contact: Charles L. Yeschke, Contact
State. Represents individuals dedicated to providing a valid and reliable means to verify the truth and establish the highest standards of moral, ethical, and professional conduct in the polygraph field. Establishes standards of ethical practices, techniques, instrumentation, research, advanced training and continuing educational programs. Provides a forum for the presentation and exchange of information derived from such research, training and education. **Affiliated With:** American Polygraph Association.

11667 ■ Minnesota Psychoanalytic Society
c/o Steven E. Clarke, MD, Pres.
1550 Foshay Tower
821 Marqueete Ave.
Minneapolis, MN 55402-2934
Ph: (612)332-9110
URL: National Affiliate–www.apsa.org
Contact: Steven E. Clarke MD, Pres.
State. Educates and promotes public awareness and interest in the science and art of psychoanalysis. Establishes and maintains standards for the training of psychoanalysts and for the practice of psychoanalysis. **Affiliated With:** American Psychoanalytic Association.

11668 ■ Minnesota Public Health Association (MPHA)
c/o Deb Burns, Co-Pres.
PO Box 14709
Minneapolis, MN 55414
E-mail: info@mpha.net
URL: http://www.mpha.net
Founded: 1907. **Members:** 400. **State**. **Affiliated With:** American Public Health Association.

11669 ■ Minnesota Public Interest Research Group (MPIRG)
1313 Fifth St. SE
Minneapolis, MN 55414
Ph: (612)627-4035
Fax: (612)627-4050
E-mail: info@mpirg.org
URL: http://www.mpirg.org
Contact: Rachel Bartleson, Exec.Dir.
Founded: 1971. **Members:** 20,000. **Local Groups:** 8. **State**. Seeks to train and empower students to work for public interests of the state. **Publications:** *Statewatch*, once each semester. Newsletter. Contains MIRG campaigns, events, campus activities and staff. **Advertising:** accepted.

11670 ■ Minnesota Quilters
3000 Univ. Ave. SE, Ste.120
Minneapolis, MN 55414
Ph: (612)436-0449
E-mail: quilter@mnquilt.org
URL: http://www.mnquilt.org
State.

11671 ■ Minnesota Region of Narcotics Anonymous
310 38th St.
Minneapolis, MN 55409
Ph: (612)882-9472
Fax: (612)882-8212
E-mail: umsiinfo@naminnesota.org
URL: http://www.naminnesota.org
State. **Affiliated With:** Narcotics Anonymous.

11672 ■ Minnesota Renewable Energy Society (MRES)
2928 5th Ave. S
Minneapolis, MN 55408
Ph: (612)308-4757
E-mail: volunteers@mres-solar.org
URL: http://www.mres-solar.org
Contact: David Boyce, Contact
Founded: 1978. **State**. Helps to develop awareness and to promote the use of renewable energy resources. Sponsors activities that include conference on the use of solar energy in Minneapolis area. **Affiliated With:** American Solar Energy Society.

11673 ■ Minnesota Space Frontier Society
3331 Cedar Ave. So. No. 2
Minneapolis, MN 55407
Ph: (612)721-4772
E-mail: mnsfs@freemars.org
URL: http://www.mnsfs.org
Contact: David Buth, Contact
State. Works for the creation of a spacefaring civilization. Encourages the establishment of self-sustaining human settlements in space. Promotes large-scale industrialization and private enterprise in space.

11674 ■ Minnesota State Bar Association (MSBA)
c/o Timothy Groshens, Exec.Dir.
600 Nicollet Mall, No. 380
Minneapolis, MN 55402
Ph: (612)333-1183
Fax: (612)333-4927
Free: (800)882-6722
E-mail: tgroshen@statebar.gen.mn.us
State.

11675 ■ Minnesota Supreme Court Historical Society
c/o Daniel R. Shulman, Esq., Chm.
500 IDS Ctr., 80 S Eighth St.
Minneapolis, MN 55402
Ph: (612)632-3000
Fax: (612)632-4444
URL: National Affiliate–www.supremecourthistory.org
Contact: Daniel R. Shulman Esq., Chm.
State. Collects and preserves the history of the Supreme Court of the United States. Conducts educational programs and supports historical research. Collects antiques and artifacts related to the Court's history. Increases public awareness of the Court's contributions to the nation's constitutional heritage. **Affiliated With:** Supreme Court Historical Society.

11676 ■ Minnesota Sword Club
c/o Alina Benford
4744 Chicago Ave. S
Minneapolis, MN 55407-3515
Ph: (612)825-9935
URL: http://mnsword.com
Contact: Alina Benford, Contact
Founded: 1940. **Members:** 200. **Staff:** 5. **Regional Groups:** 1. **State Groups:** 1. **Local Groups:** 1. **Local**. **Formerly:** (2005) Minneapolis-St. Cloud Fencers Association.

11677 ■ Minnesota Trial Lawyers Association (MTLA)
c/o Richard E. Martin, Exec.Dir.
706 Second Ave. S
140 Baker Bldg.
Minneapolis, MN 55402
Ph: (612)375-1707
Fax: (612)334-3142
Free: (800)898-MTLA
E-mail: mtla@mntla.com
URL: http://www.mntla.com
Contact: Richard E. Martin, Exec.Dir.
State.

11678 ■ Minnesota Triumphs
PO Box 11116
Minneapolis, MN 55411
E-mail: president@mntriumphs.org
URL: http://www.mntriumphs.org
Contact: Chal Setala, Pres.
Local. **Affiliated With:** Vintage Triumph Register.

11679 ■ Minnesota USA Wrestling
1422 Emerson Ave. N
Minneapolis, MN 55411
Ph: (612)822-2298 (612)822-1030
E-mail: mnusaw@citilink.com
URL: http://www.mnusawrestling.org
Contact: Bill Hinchley, State Dir.
State. **Affiliated With:** U.S.A. Wrestling.

11680 ■ Minnesota Users Group of Applied Systems
c/o Truck Writers Inc.
8970 W 35W Ser. Dr.
Minneapolis, MN 55449
Ph: (763)785-0500
Fax: (763)785-9360
E-mail: lisab@truckwriters.com
URL: National Affiliate–www.ascnet.org
Contact: Lisa Burnside, Pres.
State. Represents insurance agents and brokers using the Agency Manager software. Promotes successful automation and business practices through communication, education, and advocacy. **Affiliated With:** Applied Systems Client Network.

11681 ■ Minnesota Veterans for Peace - Chapter 27
2123 Clinton Ave. S
Minneapolis, MN 55404
Ph: (612)821-9141
E-mail: vfpchapter27@hotmail.com
URL: http://www.twincitiesvfp.org
State. **Affiliated With:** Veterans for Peace.

11682 ■ Minnesota Volkssport Association
c/o Donna Seline
3951 Russell Ave. N
Minneapolis, MN 55412
Ph: (612)529-0552
E-mail: dseline@mn.rr.com
URL: http://www.winternet.com/~stachour
Contact: Donna Seline, Contact
Founded: 1985. **Membership Dues:** club, $25 (annual). **Staff:** 4. **State**. Non-competitive sports enthusiasts. Conducts 10k walks, 25k bicycle events, and 300 meter swim events. **Awards:** MV Volunteer Award. **Type:** recognition. **Recipient:** for twelve hours on event preparation per year. **Affiliated With:** American Volkssport Association. **Formerly:** (1998) Minnesota State Volkssport Association. **Conventions/Meetings:** quarterly meeting.

11683 ■ Minnesota Women Lawyers (MWL)
600 Nicollet Mall, Ste.390B
Minneapolis, MN 55403
Ph: (612)338-3205
Fax: (612)338-1507
E-mail: mwl@mwlawyers.org
URL: http://www.mwlawyers.org
Contact: Daniel'la Deering, Pres.
Founded: 1972. **State**. Works to secure the full and equal participation of women in the legal profession.

11684 ■ Minnesotans Against the Death Penalty (MNADP)
529 S Seventh St., Ste.636
Minneapolis, MN 55415
Ph: (651)649-4618
E-mail: mnadp_web@yahoo.com
URL: http://www.mnadp.org
State. **Affiliated With:** National Coalition to Abolish the Death Penalty.

11685 ■ Mississippi Corridor Neighborhood Coalition (MCNC)
PO Box 18748
Minneapolis, MN 55418-0748
Ph: (612)331-4738
Fax: (612)331-4738
E-mail: info@mcnc-mpls.org
URL: http://www.mcnc-mpls.org
Contact: Randy Kouri, Pres.
State.

11686 ■ Moms Club of Brooklyn Center/North Minneapolis
c/o Laurel Hove Tausend
4651 Colfax Ave. N.
Minneapolis, MN 55412-1323
Ph: (612)522-1954
E-mail: laurelsings@mn.rr.com
URL: National Affiliate–www.momsclub.org
Contact: Laurel Hove Tausend, Pres.

Founded: 1999. **Members:** 15. **Membership Dues:** general, $25 (annual). **Local Groups:** 1. **Local**. Stay-at-home moms support group. **Affiliated With:** International MOMS Club. **Publications:** Newsletter, monthly. Contains member information. **Price:** $25.00/year. **Circulation:** 15. **Advertising:** accepted. **Conventions/Meetings:** monthly meeting - 3rd Friday; Avg. Attendance: 10.

11687 ■ Muslim Student Association, University of Minnesota
300 Washington Ave. SE, No. 126
Minneapolis, MN 55455
Ph: (612)229-0724
E-mail: muslimsa@tc.umn.edu
Contact: Mus'ab Husaini, Pres.

Local. Muslim students in North America. Seeks to advance the interests of members; works to enable members to practice Islam as a complete way of life. **Affiliated With:** Muslim Students Association of the United States and Canada.

11688 ■ NACM North Central
PO Box 59149
Minneapolis, MN 55459-0149
Ph: (612)341-9600
Fax: (612)341-9648
Free: (800)279-6226
E-mail: info@nacmnc.com
URL: http://www.nacmnc.com
Contact: Don Mosher CAE, Pres.

Founded: 1896. **Members:** 1,300. **Staff:** 30. **Regional Groups:** 6. **Local Groups:** 18. Credit executives and owners of distribution and manufacturing companies. Seeks promotion of mutually beneficial ideas on credit techniques and methods. Provides forum to exchange credit information. **Computer Services:** Online services, commercial credit information. **Also Known As:** National Association of Credit Management North Central. **Formerly:** National Radiator Manufacturing Credit Association; (1986) National Radiator Core Manufacturing Credit Association. **Conventions/Meetings:** semiannual conference.

11689 ■ NAIFA-Minnesota
c/o Roger I. Grumdahl, Pres.
1405 N Lilac Dr., Ste.121
Minneapolis, MN 55422
Ph: (763)544-8087
Fax: (763)544-1631
Free: (800)896-5143
E-mail: naifa@naifa-mn.org
URL: http://www.naifa-mn.org
Contact: Roger I. Grumdahl, Pres.

State. Represents the interests of insurance and financial advisors. Advocates for a positive legislative and regulatory environment. Enhances business and professional skills of members. **Affiliated With:** National Association of Insurance and Financial Advisors.

11690 ■ NAIFA-St. Paul
c/o Naifa Minnesota
1405 Lilac Dr. N, No. 121
Minneapolis, MN 55422-4528
Ph: (763)544-8087
Fax: (763)544-1631
URL: National Affiliate–www.naifa.org

Local. Represents the interest of insurance and financial advisors. Advocates for a positive legislative and regulatory environment. Enhances business and professional skills of members. **Affiliated With:** National Association of Insurance and Financial Advisors.

11691 ■ National Asian Pacific American Bar Association - Minnesota Chapter
2221 Univ. Ave. SE, Ste.425
Minneapolis, MN 55414
Ph: (612)627-6980
Fax: (612)627-5419
E-mail: ngoc.nguyen@state.mn.us
URL: http://www.napabamn.org
Contact: Ngoc Nguyen, Pres.

State. Represents the interests of Asian Pacific American attorneys and their communities. Promotes justice, equity and opportunity for Asian Pacific Americans. Fosters professional development, legal scholarship, advocacy and community development. **Affiliated With:** National Asian Pacific American Bar Association.

11692 ■ National Association for the Advancement of Colored People, Minneapolis Branch
2000 Plymouth Ave.
Minneapolis, MN 55411
Ph: (612)522-4461
Fax: (612)522-4476
URL: http://www.naacp.org
Contact: Brett Buckner, Pres.

Local.

11693 ■ National Association of Asian American Professionals, Minnesota Chapter
PO Box 3435
Minneapolis, MN 55403
Ph: (612)210-8256
E-mail: info@naaap-mn.org
URL: http://naaap-mn.org
Contact: Ann Phi-Wendt, Pres.

State. Enhances the leadership and professional development of Asian Americans in their careers and in the community. Raises awareness of Asian Americans in corporate America. Seeks to ensure that Asian Americans are included in diversity programs. **Affiliated With:** National Association of Asian American Professionals.

11694 ■ National Association of Industrial and Office Properties Minnesota Chapter
c/o Anthony R. LeClerc
4248 Park Glen Rd.
Minneapolis, MN 55416
Ph: (952)928-4647
Fax: (952)929-1318
E-mail: info@naiopmn.org
URL: http://www.naiopmn.org
Contact: Anthony R. LeClerc, Contact

Founded: 1974. **Members:** 780. **Membership Dues:** principal, associate (first member in the chapter from any given company), $745 (annual) • principal affiliate, associate affiliate (second member in the same chapter from any given company), $365 (annual) • chapter-based corporate (four or more individuals within the same company and chapter; $185 per additional individual), $1,660 (annual). **Staff:** 5. **State Groups:** 49. **State**. **Awards:** Awards of Excellence. **Frequency:** annual. **Type:** recognition. **Recipient:** for excellence in specific commercial real estate categories, judged by a panel of members working in the field. **Committees:** Community Enhancement; Golf; Long Range Planning; National Board Representatives; Program; Public Policy; Special Events; Sponsorship. **Affiliated With:** National Association of Industrial and Office Properties. **Publications:** *City Survey*, periodic. **Price:** included in membership dues • *Comparative Tax Study*, periodic. Report. **Price:** included in membership dues • *Industrial and Office Market Updates*, annual. Overviews of the current commercial real estate market. **Price:** $10.00. Alternate Formats: CD-ROM • *TaxWatch*, quarterly. Newsletter. Includes information about Minnesota taxes that affect the members. **Price:** included in membership dues. Alternate Formats: online • *Universe*, bimonthly. Newsletter. Contains information about the members and the activities of the association. **Price:** included in membership dues. **Circulation:** 800. **Advertising:** accepted. Alternate Formats: online • *Your Property Taxes*, periodic. Paper. **Price:** included in membership dues. Alternate Formats: online.

11695 ■ National Association of Minority Contractors of Upper Midwest (NAMC-UM)
c/o Bobby Champion, Exec.Dir.
1404 14th Ave. N
Minneapolis, MN 55411
Ph: (612)521-3366
Fax: (612)521-3405
E-mail: michellerogers30@msn.com
URL: http://www.namc-um.org/
Contact: Bobby Champion, Exec.Dir.

Members: 77. **Membership Dues:** $400 (annual). **Staff:** 1. **Regional**.

11696 ■ National Association of the Remodeling Industry of Minnesota
275 Market St., C-13
Minneapolis, MN 55405
Ph: (612)332-6274
Fax: (612)332-7854
E-mail: info@narimn.org
URL: http://www.narimn.org
Contact: Dave Klun, Pres.

Founded: 1982. **Members:** 300. **State**. Provides information, education and mentoring to its members and the community. Works to promote the professional image of members. Provides an annual directory of members, holds monthly meetings for members to learn and network and sponsors an annual golf outing. **Affiliated With:** National Association of the Remodeling Industry.

11697 ■ National Ataxia Foundation, Mark A. Newell
2600 Fernbrook Ln., Ste.119
Minneapolis, MN 55447
Ph: (763)553-0020
Fax: (763)553-0167
E-mail: naf@ataxia.org
URL: http://www.alaska.net/~mnewell

Local. Support organization for individuals suffering from ataxia (a genetic disease characterized by the degeneration of the nerves of the spinal cord and the cerebellum, causing a loss of coordination and disturbance in gait and related conditions such as peroneal muscular atrophy, hereditary spastic paraplegia, hereditary tremor, and ataxia telangiectasia.). **Affiliated With:** National Ataxia Foundation.

11698 ■ National Ataxia Foundation, Minneapolis, Minnesota Support Group
c/o Ginny & Joe Cain
2600 Fernbrook Ln., Ste.119
Minneapolis, MN 55447-4752
Ph: (763)553-0020
Fax: (763)553-0167
E-mail: naf@ataxia.org
URL: http://www.geocities.com/twincitiesataxia

Local. **Affiliated With:** National Ataxia Foundation.

11699 ■ National Black MBA Association, Twin Cities
PO Box 2709
Minneapolis, MN 55402
Ph: (651)223-7373
E-mail: info@nbmbaatc.org
URL: http://www.nbmbaatc.org
Contact: Linda Sloan, Pres.

Local. **Affiliated With:** National Black MBA Association.

11700 ■ National Coalition of Free Men (NCFM)
c/o Joe Hill
PO Box 582023
Minneapolis, MN 55458

Ph: (516)482-6378
Free: (888)223-1280
E-mail: ncfm@ncfm.org
URL: http://www.ncfm.org
Contact: Joe Hill, Admin.

Local. Committed to studying the ways sex discrimination affects men and boys; Publishes Transitions: Journal of Men's Perspectives; sponsors chapters and events.

11701 ■ National Kidney Foundation of Minnesota
920 S 7th St.
Minneapolis, MN 55415
Ph: (612)337-7300
Fax: (612)904-4268
E-mail: nkf@nkfmn.org
URL: National Affiliate–www.kidney.org

State. Aims to prevent kidney and urinary tract diseases; to improve the health and well-being of individuals and families affected by these diseases; and to increase the availability of all organs for transplantation. **Awards: Type:** recognition. **Affiliated With:** National Kidney Foundation.

11702 ■ National Multiple Sclerosis Society, Minnesota Chapter
c/o William T. Mac Nally, Chm.
200 12th Ave. S
Minneapolis, MN 55415
Ph: (612)335-7900
Fax: (612)335-7997
Free: (800)582-5296
E-mail: info@mssociety.org
URL: http://www.mssociety.com
Contact: William T. Mac Nally, Chm.

Founded: 1955. **Staff:** 4. **State**. Works to help people and families suffering with Multiple Sclerosis.

11703 ■ National Organization for Women - Twin Cities
PO Box 582058
Minneapolis, MN 55458
Ph: (612)338-7472
E-mail: info@tcnow.org
URL: http://www.tcnow.org

Local. Affiliated With: National Organization for Women.

11704 ■ National Stroke Association, Minnesota Chapter (NSA)
c/o Kathleen Miller, Exec.Dir.
13705 26th Ave. N, Ste.106
Minneapolis, MN 55441
Ph: (763)553-0088
Free: (800)647-4123
E-mail: mnstroke@covad.net
URL: http://www.strokemn.org
Contact: Kathleen Miller, Exec.Dir.

Founded: 1992. **Members:** 1,000. **Staff:** 1. **Budget:** $90,000. **State**. Works to reduce the incidence and impact of stroke in Minnesota through collaborative community partnerships. Programs and services are focused on stroke prevention education and community rehabilitation programs and survivor and family education and resources. **Libraries: Type:** open to the public. **Holdings:** books, video recordings. **Subjects:** stroke prevention, treatment, rehabilitation. **Awards:** Sister Kenny Institute International Art Show for Artists with Disabilities. **Frequency:** annual. **Type:** monetary. **Recipient:** for artwork by Minnesota stroke survivor. **Boards:** Survivor Advisory. **Committees:** Public Education and Awareness; Strides for Stroke. **Affiliated With:** Community Health Charities. **Publications:** *Minnesota Stroke Association Update*, semiannual. Newsletter. Provides information on past and upcoming chapter activities and educational opportunities. **Price:** included in membership dues. **Conventions/Meetings:** annual Strike Out Stroke Day at the Dome - meeting - always May • annual Stroke Survivor Workshop, workshop for stroke survivors and their families.

11705 ■ National Writers Union, Twin Cities Chapter (NWU-TC)
PO Box 50367
Minneapolis, MN 55403
Ph: (612)879-5572
E-mail: info@nwu-tc.org
URL: http://www.nwu-tc.org

Founded: 1987. **Members:** 125. **Membership Dues:** individual (based on income from writing), $260 (annual). **Local Groups:** 1. **State**. Supports writers in all genres, including book authors, journalists, literary writers, business and technical writers. Works to improve working conditions for writers. Provides contract advice and grievance assistance to members. **Special Interest Groups:** Writers 4 Change. **Affiliated With:** National Writers Union; National Writers Union, UAW Local 1981, AFL-CIO.

11706 ■ Nature Conservancy of Minnesota (TNC)
1101 W River Pkwy., Ste.200
Minneapolis, MN 55415-1291
Ph: (612)331-0750
E-mail: minnesota@tnc.org
URL: http://www.tnc.org
Contact: Rob McKim, Divisional & State Dir.

Founded: 1951. **Members:** 22,500. **Membership Dues:** individual, $25 (annual). **Staff:** 30. **Budget:** $1,900,000. **Regional Groups:** 11. **State Groups:** 50. **Local Groups:** 200. **State**. Preserves plants, animals and natural communities that represent the diversity of life on earth by protecting the lands and waters they need to survive. **Awards:** Katherine Ordway Stewardship Award. **Frequency:** semiannual. **Type:** grant. **Recipient:** for research and stewardship of biological diversity. **Additional Websites:** http://www.tnc.org/minnesota. **Affiliated With:** Nature Conservancy. **Formerly:** The Nature Conservancy, Minnesota Field Office. **Publications:** *Minnesota Chapter News*, quarterly. Brochure. Contains stories on land protection and science. Lists of donors. **Price:** for members. **Circulation:** 19,600. Alternate Formats: online. **Conventions/Meetings:** annual meeting, keynote speaker and presentations on ecological topics (exhibits) - usually April. St. Paul, MN - Avg. Attendance: 250.

11707 ■ Neurofibromatosis - Minnesota
PO Box 18246
Minneapolis, MN 55418
Ph: (651)225-1720
E-mail: johne@cipmn.org
URL: http://www.nfincmn.org
Contact: John Everett, Pres.

Membership Dues: individual, $25 (annual) • family, $35 (annual) • professional, $50 (annual). **State**. Provides information, support and referrals to anyone interested in neurofibromatosis. **Affiliated With:** Neurofibromatosis.

11708 ■ NORML at the University of Minnesota
c/o Jason Samuels
126 Coffman Memorial Union
300 Washington Ave. SE
Minneapolis, MN 55455
Ph: (612)889-3168
E-mail: norml@umn.edu

Local. Exists to educate students about the benefits and risks of cannabis for recreational, medicinal, and industrial use; also disseminates information, works to raise awareness of issues and bring about changes in the current drug laws. **Affiliated With:** National Organization for the Reform of Marijuana Laws.

11709 ■ North Central Business Travel Association (NCBTA)
PO Box 2629
Minneapolis, MN 55402
Ph: (952)403-1477
E-mail: kari.schroeder@atsaceworldwide.com
URL: http://www.northcentralbta.org
Contact: Kari Schroeder, Pres.

Regional. Represents travel managers and providers. Promotes the value of the travel manager in meeting corporate travel needs and financial goals. Cultivates a positive public image of the corporate travel industry. Protects the interests of members and their corporations in legislative and regulatory matters. Promotes safety, security, efficiency and quality travel. Provides a forum for the exchange of information and ideas among members. **Affiliated With:** National Business Travel Association.

11710 ■ North Central Chapter of the American Association of Physicists in Medicine (NCCAAPM)
c/o Parham Alaei, PhD, Sec.-Treas.
Dept. of Therapeutic Radiology
Mayo Mail Code 494
420 Delaware St. SE
Minneapolis, MN 55455
Ph: (612)626-6505
Fax: (612)626-7060
E-mail: alaei001@umn.edu
URL: http://chapter.aapm.org/nccaapm
Contact: Walter L. Tang, Pres.

Regional. Advances the practice of physics in medicine and biology through research and development and scientific and technical information. Fosters the education and professional development of medical physicists. Promotes the highest quality medical services for patients. **Affiliated With:** American Association of Physicists in Medicine.

11711 ■ North Central Environmental Balancing Bureau
c/o SMARCA, Inc.
1405 Lilac Dr. N, No. 100
Minneapolis, MN 55422-4598
Ph: (763)593-0941
Fax: (763)593-0944
E-mail: carol@smarca.com
URL: National Affiliate–www.nebb.org
Contact: Carol Daniels, Coor.

Regional. Works to help architects, engineers, building owners, and contractors produce buildings with HVAC systems. Establishes and maintains industry standards, procedures, and specifications for testing, adjusting, and balancing work. **Affiliated With:** National Environmental Balancing Bureau.

11712 ■ North Central Region Health Ministries Network
6939 Grives Ave. N
Minneapolis, MN 55428
Ph: (763)236-4342
E-mail: info@healthministries.info
URL: http://www.healthministries.info
Contact: Lyla Pagels, Pres.

Regional.

11713 ■ North Star Historical Bottle Association
c/o Doug Shilson, Pres.
3308 32nd Ave. S
Minneapolis, MN 55406-2015
Ph: (612)721-4165
E-mail: bittersdug@aol.com
URL: National Affiliate–www.fohbc.com
Contact: Doug Shilson, Pres.

Local. Affiliated With: Federation of Historical Bottle Collectors.

11714 ■ NorthStar Trail Travelers (NSTT)
c/o Donna Seline
3951 Russell Ave. N
Minneapolis, MN 55412
Ph: (612)529-0552
E-mail: info@nstt.org
URL: http://www.nstt.org
Contact: Donna Seline, Contact

Local. Affiliated With: American Volkssport Association.

11715 ■ Northwest Coin Club
c/o Pete Smith
PO Box 18053
Minneapolis, MN 55418
E-mail: beiers@hotmail.com
URL: National Affiliate–www.money.org
Contact: Pete Smith, Contact
Local. Affiliated With: American Numismatic Association.

11716 ■ Northwestern Lumber Association (NLA)
1405 Lilac Dr. N, Ste.130
Minneapolis, MN 55422
Ph: (763)544-6822
Fax: (763)595-4060
Free: (800)331-0193
E-mail: nlassn@nlassn.org
URL: http://www.nlassn.org
Contact: Paula Siewert, Exec.Dir.
Founded: 1890. **Members:** 250. **Staff:** 1. **Regional Groups:** 22. **State Groups:** 1. **Regional. Libraries: Type:** not open to the public. **Subjects:** law, antitrust. **Committees:** Legislative. **Affiliated With:** National Lumber and Building Material Dealers Association. **Formerly:** (2003) Iowa Lumber Association. **Publications:** *Building Products Connection*, bimonthly. Magazine. **Advertising:** accepted. **Conventions/Meetings:** annual convention, with education programs, product displays, and legislative meetings (exhibits).

11717 ■ Optical Society of America, Minnesota
c/o Joseph J. Talghader
Dept. of Elect. and Cmpt. Engg.
Univ. of Minnesota EE/CSCI 5-165
200 Union St. SE
Minneapolis, MN 55455
Ph: (612)625-4524
E-mail: joey@umn.edu
URL: National Affiliate–www.osa.org
Contact: Joseph J. Talghader, Contact
Affiliated With: Optical Society of America.

11718 ■ Order of the Eastern Star Minnesota Grand Chapter
6121 Excelsior Blvd., Ste.210
Minneapolis, MN 55416-2772
Ph: (952)926-9384
Contact: Glen Carlson, Grand Sec.
State. Fraternal organization of men and women. Provides charitable and social services. **Conventions/Meetings:** annual meeting - always May.

11719 ■ PACER Center
8161 Normandale Blvd.
Minneapolis, MN 55437-1044
Ph: (952)838-9000
Fax: (952)838-0199
Free: (888)248-0822
E-mail: alliance@taalliance.org
URL: http://www.taalliance.org
Contact: Paula Goldberg, Exec.Dir.
Founded: 1977. **Staff:** 73. **Languages:** English, Somali, Spanish. **Regional.** Offers parents of children and adults with disabilities one-to-one assistance, publications, and free workshops. Strives to improve and expand opportunities that enhance the quality of life of children and adults with disabilities. **Libraries: Type:** not open to the public. **Holdings:** 1,000. **Subjects:** disability, non-profit management. **Awards:** Volunteer of the Year-Norma Hepter Award. **Frequency:** annual. **Type:** recognition. **Additional Websites:** http://www.fape.org. **Publications:** *Pacesetter*, 3/year. Newsletter. Provides information on legislation policy, disability-specific issues and other information related to special education. **Circulation:** 98,000. **Conventions/Meetings:** Basic Rights in Special Education - workshop, information for parents and professionals - several times a month • Getting to Work - convention, information for parents and professionals - several times a year • IEP - convention, information for parents and professionals - several times a year.

11720 ■ Peace Corps-Minneapolis
330 2nd Ave. S., Ste.420
Minneapolis, MN 55401
Fax: (612)348-1474
Free: (800)424-8580
E-mail: minneapolis@peacecorps.gov
URL: http://www.peacecorps.gov

11721 ■ People Who Care Booster Club
c/o Ameliah Jihad
PO Box 50346
Minneapolis, MN 55405-0346
Ph: (612)521-6686 (612)529-4378
Local. Subgroups: Mpls Hustlers Basketball.

11722 ■ PFLAG St. Paul/Minneapolis
PO Box 19290
Minneapolis, MN 55419
Ph: (612)825-1660
E-mail: admin@pflagtc.org
URL: http://www.pflagtc.org
Local. Affiliated With: Parents, Families, and Friends of Lesbians and Gays.

11723 ■ Phi Theta Kappa, Alpha Epsilon Sigma Chapter - Minneapolis Community and Technical College
c/o Jon Westby
1501 Hennepin Ave.
Minneapolis, MN 55403
Ph: (612)341-7031
E-mail: jon.westby@minneapolis.edu
URL: http://www.ptk.org/directories/chapters/MN/273-1.htm
Contact: Jon Westby, Advisor
Local.

11724 ■ Phi Theta Kappa, Beta Lambda Xi Chapter - Dunwood College of Technology
c/o Todd Kreuscher
818 Dunwoody Blvd.
Minneapolis, MN 55403
Ph: (612)381-3333
E-mail: tkreuscher@dunwoody.edu
URL: http://www.ptk.org/directories/chapters/MN/21140-1.htm
Contact: Todd Kreuscher, Advisor
Local.

11725 ■ Points of Light Foundation - Volunteer Resource Center
2021 E Hennepin Ave., Ste.420
Minneapolis, MN 55413-1868
Ph: (612)379-4900
Fax: (612)379-3104
E-mail: mark@volunteertwincities.org
URL: National Affiliate–www.pointsoflight.org
Contact: Mark Hiemenz, Contact
Local. Affiliated With: Points of Light Foundation.

11726 ■ Printing Industry of Minnesota (PIM)
c/o David Radziej, Pres.
2829 Univ. Ave. SE, Ste.750
Minneapolis, MN 55414
Ph: (612)379-3360
Fax: (612)379-6030
E-mail: davidr@pimn.org
URL: http://www.pimn.org
Contact: David Radziej, Pres.
State. Commercial printing firms (lithography, letterpress, gravure, platemakers, typographic houses); allied firms in the graphic arts. Offers education, networking, and government affairs. **Affiliated With:** Printing Industries of America.

11727 ■ Professional Risk Managers International Association (PRMIA)
c/o Dorsey and Whitney, LLP
50 S 6th St.
Minneapolis, MN 55402-1540
E-mail: support@prmia.org
URL: http://www.prmia.org
Local.

11728 ■ Psi Chi, National Honor Society in Psychology - North Central University
c/o Dept. of Psychology
910 Elliot Ave. S
Minneapolis, MN 55404-1391
Ph: (612)343-4787
Fax: (612)343-8066
E-mail: daniel.nelson@northcentral.edu
URL: http://www.psichi.org/chapters/info.asp?chapter_id=968
Contact: Daniel R. Nelson PhD, Advisor
Local.

11729 ■ Rainbow Families
711 W Lake St., Ste.210
Minneapolis, MN 55408
Ph: (612)827-7731
Fax: (612)822-2759
E-mail: connect@rainbowfamilies.org
URL: http://www.rainbowfamilies.org
Contact: Laura Smidzik, Exec.Dir.
Founded: 1995. **Members:** 1,200. **Membership Dues:** household, $45 (annual) • limited income household, $20 (annual) • household, $105 (triennial). **Staff:** 4. **Budget:** $350,000. **Regional.** Provides support, information, and advocacy for lesbian, gay, bisexual, and transgender parents and their children in the Upper Midwest, currently serving more than 2000 families. **Affiliated With:** COLAGE.

11730 ■ Rams Cricket Club
3827 30th Ave. S
Minneapolis, MN 55406
URL: http://www.usaca.org/Clubs.htm
Contact: Gansham Ramnarine, Contact
Local.

11731 ■ Religious Coalition for Reproductive Choice - Minnesota Chapter
122 W Franklin Ave., Ste.303
Minneapolis, MN 55404
Ph: (612)870-0974
E-mail: nadean@mnrcrc.org
URL: http://www.mnrcrc.org
State. Affiliated With: Religious Coalition for Reproductive Choice.

11732 ■ Risk and Insurance Management Society, Minnesota Chapter
c/o Carmen Ferguson
222 S 9th St., Ste.2300
Minneapolis, MN 55402-4099
Ph: (612)376-3085
Fax: (612)376-3180
E-mail: cmferguson@bemis.com
URL: http://minnesota.rims.org
Contact: Barry Glaser, Delegate
Local. Seeks to promote the discipline of risk management and enhance the image of professional risk managers. Fosters the educational and professional development of risk managers and others involved in the risk management and insurance industry. **Affiliated With:** Risk and Insurance Management Society.

11733 ■ SCORE Minneapolis
Bremer Bank Bldg., Ste.103
8800 Hwy. 7
Minneapolis, MN 55426
Ph: (952)938-4570
Fax: (952)938-2651
E-mail: minneapolis@scoreminn.org
URL: http://www.scoreminn.org
Local. Affiliated With: SCORE.

11734 ■ Sheet Metal and Air Conditioning Contractors' National Association of Minnesota
c/o James E. Bigham
1405 Lilac Dr. N., Ste.100
Minneapolis, MN 55422-4528

Ph: (763)593-0941
Fax: (763)593-0944
E-mail: jim@smarca.com
URL: National Affiliate–www.smacna.org
Contact: James E. Bigham, Contact
State. Affiliated With: Sheet Metal and Air Conditioning Contractors' National Association.

11735 ■ Sheridan Neighborhood Organization (SNO)
c/o Maureen Rath
1226 2nd St. NE
Minneapolis, MN 55413
Ph: (612)379-0728
E-mail: sno@sheridanneighborhood.org
URL: http://www.sheridanneighborhood.org
Contact: Jenny Fortman, Board Member
Local.

11736 ■ Single Volunteers of Twin Cities (SVTC)
c/o Richard Gerth, Pres.
PO Box 201357
Minneapolis, MN 55420
Ph: (612)203-6436
E-mail: pres@svtconline.org
URL: http://www.svtconline.org
Local.

11737 ■ Skills USA, Edison High School
700 22nd Ave. NE
Minneapolis, MN 55418
Ph: (612)668-1336
Fax: (612)668-1320
E-mail: spoelstr@mpls.k12.mn.us
URL: http://www.mnskillsusa.org
Contact: Shirley Poelstra, Contact
Local. Serves high school and college students enrolled in technical, skilled, and service and health occupations. Provides quality education experiences for students in leadership, teamwork, citizenship and character development. Builds and reinforces self-confidence, work attitudes and communication skills. Emphasizes total quality at work, high ethical standards, superior work skills, and life-long education. Promotes understanding of the free enterprise system and involvement in community service. **Affiliated With:** Skills USA - VICA.

11738 ■ Skills USA, Minneapolis Public Schools
1006 W Lake St.
Minneapolis, MN 55408
Ph: (612)668-3962
E-mail: wendie.palazzo@mpls.k12.mn.us
URL: http://www.mnskillsusa.org
Contact: Wendy Palazzo, Contact
Local. Serves high school and college students enrolled in technical, skilled, and service and health occupations. Provides quality education experiences for students in leadership, teamwork, citizenship and character development. Builds and reinforces self-confidence, work attitudes and communication skills. Emphasizes total quality at work, high ethical standards, superior work skills, and life-long education. Promotes understanding of the free enterprise system and involvement in community service. **Affiliated With:** Skills USA - VICA.

11739 ■ Skills USA, North Community High School
1500 James Ave. N
Minneapolis, MN 55413
Ph: (612)668-1704
E-mail: ethanlaubach@mpls.k12.mn.us
URL: http://www.mnskillsusa.org
Contact: Ethan Laubach, Contact
Local. Serves high school and college students enrolled in technical, skilled, and service and health occupations. Provides quality education experiences for students in leadership, teamwork, citizenship and character development. Builds and reinforces self-confidence, work attitudes and communication skills. Emphasizes total quality at work, high ethical standards, superior work skills, and life-long education. Promotes understanding of the free enterprise system and involvement in community service. **Affiliated With:** Skills USA - VICA.

11740 ■ Skills USA, Patrick Henry High School
4320 Newton Ave. N
Minneapolis, MN 55412
Ph: (612)668-2000
E-mail: patricia.prouse@mpls.k12.mn.us
URL: http://www.mnskillsusa.org
Contact: Trish Prouse, Work Coor.
Local. Serves high school and college students enrolled in technical, skilled, and service and health occupations. Provides quality education experiences for students in leadership, teamwork, citizenship and character development. Builds and reinforces self-confidence, work attitudes and communication skills. Emphasizes total quality at work, high ethical standards, superior work skills, and life-long education. Promotes understanding of the free enterprise system and involvement in community service. **Affiliated With:** Skills USA - VICA.

11741 ■ Skills USA, Roosevelt High School
4029 S 28th Ave.
Minneapolis, MN 55406
Ph: (612)668-4879
Fax: (612)668-4810
E-mail: sally.rothberg@mpls.k12.mn.us
URL: http://www.mnskillsusa.org
Contact: Sally Rothenberg, Work Coor.
Local. Serves high school and college students enrolled in technical, skilled, and service and health occupations. Provides quality education experiences for students in leadership, teamwork, citizenship and character development. Builds and reinforces self-confidence, work attitudes and communication skills. Emphasizes total quality at work, high ethical standards, superior work skills, and life-long education. Promotes understanding of the free enterprise system and involvement in community service. **Affiliated With:** Skills USA - VICA.

11742 ■ Skills USA, South High School
3131 19th St.
Minneapolis, MN 55407
Ph: (612)668-4322
E-mail: gregory.hendricks@mpls.k12.mn.us
URL: http://www.mnskillsusa.org
Contact: Gregory Hendricks, Work Coor.
Local. Serves high school and college students enrolled in technical, skilled, and service and health occupations. Provides quality education experiences for students in leadership, teamwork, citizenship and character development. Builds and reinforces self-confidence, work attitudes and communication skills. Emphasizes total quality at work, high ethical standards, superior work skills, and life-long education. Promotes understanding of the free enterprise system and involvement in community service. **Affiliated With:** Skills USA - VICA.

11743 ■ Skills USA, Southwest High School
3414 W 47th St.
Minneapolis, MN 55407
Ph: (612)817-4511
E-mail: ktsimon4426@cs.com
URL: http://www.mnskillsusa.org
Contact: Katie Simonson, Work Coor.
Local. Serves high school and college students enrolled in technical, skilled, and service and health occupations. Provides quality education experiences for students in leadership, teamwork, citizenship and character development. Builds and reinforces self-confidence, work attitudes and communication skills. Emphasizes total quality at work, high ethical standards, superior work skills, and life-long education. Promotes understanding of the free enterprise system and involvement in community service. **Affiliated With:** Skills USA - VICA.

11744 ■ Skills USA, Washburn High School
201 W 49th St.
Minneapolis, MN 55409
Ph: (612)688-3400
E-mail: godfrey.edaferierhi@mpls.k12.mn.us
URL: http://www.mnskillsusa.org
Contact: Godfrey Edaferierhi, Work Coor.
Local. Serves high school and college students enrolled in technical, skilled, and service and health occupations. Provides quality education experiences for students in leadership, teamwork, citizenship and character development. Builds and reinforces self-confidence, work attitudes and communication skills. Emphasizes total quality at work, high ethical standards, superior work skills, and life-long education. Promotes understanding of the free enterprise system and involvement in community service. **Affiliated With:** Skills USA - VICA.

11745 ■ Skills USA, Work Opportunity Center
1006 W Lake St.
Minneapolis, MN 55408
Ph: (612)668-3970
URL: http://www.mnskillsusa.org/secondaryChapters.htm
Contact: Barb Huebl, Work Coor.
Local. Serves high school and college students enrolled in technical, skilled, and service and health occupations. Provides quality education experiences for students in leadership, teamwork, citizenship and character development. Builds and reinforces self-confidence, work attitudes and communication skills. Emphasizes total quality at work, high ethical standards, superior work skills, and life-long education. Promotes understanding of the free enterprise system and involvement in community service. **Affiliated With:** Skills USA - VICA.

11746 ■ SkillsUSA Minnesota
PO Box 29286
Minneapolis, MN 55429
Ph: (763)560-1932
Fax: (763)560-1936
E-mail: skillsusaminnesota@comcast.net
URL: http://www.mnskillsusa.org
Contact: Jennifer Polz, Exec.Dir.
State. Represents high school and college students enrolled in training programs in technical, skilled, service and health occupations. Teaches the importance of developing leadership skills, positive attitudes and pride in workmanship. Promotes understanding of the free enterprise system and involvement in community service activities. **Affiliated With:** Skills USA - VICA.

11747 ■ Society of Consumer Affairs Professionals in Business, Minnesota Chapter (SOCAP MN)
c/o Jan Foster
10625 32nd Ave. N
Minneapolis, MN 55441
Ph: (612)720-1825
E-mail: minnesota@socap.org
URL: National Affiliate–www.socap.org
State. Individuals engaged in the management of consumer affairs/customer service divisions of businesses. Aims to provide the tools needed; to reach maximum customer loyalty, excellent customer service and value-added innovations. **Affiliated With:** Society of Consumer Affairs Professionals in Business.

11748 ■ Society for Marketing Professional Services/Twin Cities Chapter
c/o Tanya M. Pierce, Pres.
6701 W 23rd St.
Minneapolis, MN 55426
Ph: (952)525-2314
Fax: (952)525-2333
E-mail: info@smps-tc.org
URL: http://www.smps-tc.org
Contact: Tanya M. Pierce, Pres.
Founded: 1981. **Local.** Strives to be the primary resource for education, team building and strategic and marketing information for SMPS members and others involved in the built environment. Offers each

member a variety of ways to gain new contacts and relationships and further their professional development. **Affiliated With:** Society for Marketing Professional Services.

11749 ■ Society for Protective Coatings, North Central
c/o Patrick J. Skodje, Chair
Swanson & Youngdale, Inc.
6565 W 23rd St.
PO Box 26070
Minneapolis, MN 55426
Ph: (952)545-2541
Fax: (952)591-2548
E-mail: pskodje@swansonyoungdale.com
URL: National Affiliate–www.sspc.org
Contact: Mr. Patrick J. Skodje, Chair
Regional. Affiliated With: SSPC: The Society for Protective Coatings.

11750 ■ Sons of Norway, Oslo Lodge 1-2
c/o Louise E. Bakken, Pres.
1711 Winnetka Ave. N
Minneapolis, MN 55427-3922
Ph: (763)545-4827
E-mail: furballs66@comcast.net
URL: National Affiliate–www.sofn.com
Contact: Louise E. Bakken, Pres.
Local. Affiliated With: Sons of Norway.

11751 ■ Special Libraries Association, Minnesota Chapter
c/o Karen Stauber, Pres.-Elect
Property Development Target
1000 Nicollet Mall TPN-10C
Minneapolis, MN 55403
Ph: (612)761-7194
E-mail: karen.stauber@target.com
URL: http://www.sla.org/chapter/cmn/index.html
Contact: Karen Stauber, Pres.-Elect
State. Seeks to advance the leadership role of special librarians. Promotes and strengthens members through learning, advocacy and networking initiatives. **Affiliated With:** Special Libraries Association.

11752 ■ Special Olympics Minnesota
100 Washington Ave. S, Ste.550
Minneapolis, MN 55401
Ph: (612)333-0999
Fax: (612)333-8782
Free: (800)783-7732
E-mail: somn@somn.org
URL: http://www.specialolympicsminnesota.org
Contact: David Dorn, Pres.
Founded: 1973. **Members:** 6,000. **State.** Provides a year-round program of sports training and competition in 20 Olympic-type sports for the benefit of individuals with mental disabilities. Individuals are eligible for participation at the age of 8, being diagnosed by a medical professional as having a mental disability or cognitive delay. **Affiliated With:** Special Olympics. **Publications:** *Forerunner*, quarterly. Newsletter. **Conventions/Meetings:** competition - 8/year.

11753 ■ Suicide Awareness Voices of Education (SAVE)
9001 E Bloomington Fwy., Ste.150
Minneapolis, MN 55420
Ph: (952)946-7998
Fax: (952)829-0841
E-mail: save@save.org
URL: http://www.save.org
Contact: Patty Johnson, Program Dir.
Founded: 1989. **Staff:** 5. **Budget:** $500,000. **State.** Provides educational services aimed at suicide prevention and also supports suicide survivors. **Publications:** *Suicide: A Survivor's Guide*. Book • *Suicide: Why*. Book • *Voices*, quarterly. Newsletter. Contains educational information on suicide prevention efforts. **Price:** free. Alternate Formats: online.

11754 ■ Tapestry Folkdance Center
3748 Minnehaha Ave.
Minneapolis, MN 55406-2668
Ph: (612)722-2914
E-mail: staff@tapestryfolkdance.org
URL: http://www.tapestryfolkdance.org
Contact: Mr. Palmer Van Beest, Exec.Dir.
Founded: 1983. **Members:** 540. **Membership Dues:** basic individual, $40 (annual) • basic household, $65 (annual). **Staff:** 3. **Budget:** $270,000. **Regional. Libraries: Type:** not open to the public. **Subjects:** organizational management for nonprofits, folkdancing. **Computer Services:** Information services • online services, website, personal answers to e-mail, list-serve updates, online membership processing. **Committees:** Board Resources Committee; Community Outreach Committee; Fundraising Committee. **Affiliated With:** Country Dance and Song Society. **Publications:** *Tapestry Calendar*, bimonthly. Directory. Lists of upcoming events and activities. **Circulation:** 1,500. Alternate Formats: online.

11755 ■ Turn Off the Violence
c/o Sheila Miller, Exec.Dir.
PO Box 27321
Minneapolis, MN 55427
E-mail: info@turnofftheviolence.org
URL: http://www.turnofftheviolence.org
Contact: Sheila Miller, Exec.Dir.
Local.

11756 ■ Twin Cities Black Journalists
c/o Shannon Gibney, Pres.
3040 17th Ave. S
Minneapolis, MN 55407
Ph: (612)210-8049
E-mail: shannongibney@gmail.com
URL: National Affiliate–www.nabj.org
Contact: Shannon Gibney, Pres.
Local. Advocates the rights of black journalists. Provides informational and training services and professional development to black journalists and to the general public. **Affiliated With:** National Association of Black Journalists.

11757 ■ Twin Cities Chapter of Muskies
5704 Wentworth Ave. S
Minneapolis, MN 55419
Ph: (952)380-1218
E-mail: windgods@msn.com
URL: http://www.twincitiesmuskiesinc.org
Contact: Shawn Kellett, Pres.
Local.

11758 ■ Twin Cities Habitat for Humanity
c/o Susan Haigh, Exec.Dir.
3001 4th St. SE
Minneapolis, MN 55414
Ph: (612)331-4090
Fax: (612)331-1540
E-mail: info@tchabitat.org
URL: http://www.tchabitat.org
Local.

11759 ■ Twin Cities Musicians Union, Local 30-73
Itasca Bldg.
708 First St. N, Ste.243
Minneapolis, MN 55401-1145
Ph: (612)338-5013
Fax: (612)338-5018
E-mail: tcmu@mn.rr.com
URL: http://www.tcmu.com
Contact: Thomas W. Baskerville, Sec.-Treas.
Founded: 1897. **Members:** 1,487. **Membership Dues:** regular, $154 (annual). **Staff:** 4. **Budget:** $500,000. **Local.** Seeks to unite musicians for the better protection of their interests in general, the establishment of a minimum rate of prices to be charged by members for their professional services and the enforcement of good faith and fair dealings among members. **Awards:** Amy L. Bloom Memorial Scholarship Fund. **Frequency:** annual. **Type:** scholarship. **Recipient:** less than college age music students who are recommended by music teachers and who have been accepted to summer music camp programs. **Affiliated With:** American Federation of Musicians of the United States and Canada. **Publications:** *Duet*, bimonthly. Newsletter. **Price:** for members. **Circulation:** 2,000. **Advertising:** accepted. **Conventions/Meetings:** biweekly board meeting - meet on alternate Monday yearly • quarterly General Membership - meeting.

11760 ■ Twin Cities Obedience Training Club (TCOTC)
2101 Broadway NE
Minneapolis, MN 55413
Ph: (612)379-1332
E-mail: tcotc@mac.com
URL: http://www.tcotc.com
Contact: Nanette Malcomson, Pres.
Local.

11761 ■ Twin Cities Poodle Club (TCPC)
c/o Holly Corbett
5748 27th Ave. S
Minneapolis, MN 55417
Ph: (612)722-8736
E-mail: hollyc31681@webtv.net
URL: http://www.geocities.com/tcpoodleclub
Contact: Kay Reilly, Pres.
Local.

11762 ■ Twin Cities Quorum
c/o Ronald E. Brunk
3010 Hennepin Ave. S, No. 179
Minneapolis, MN 55408
URL: http://www.twincitiesquorum.com
Local.

11763 ■ Twin Cities Tall Club
c/o Coral Rose
PO Box 581091
Minneapolis, MN 55458-1091
Ph: (952)953-7665
E-mail: minneapolis@tall.org
URL: National Affiliate–www.tall.org
Contact: Coral Rose, Contact
Local. Affiliated With: Tall Clubs International.

11764 ■ United Association of Journeymen and Apprentices of the Plumbing and Pipe Fitting Industry of the United States and Canada - Local Union 15
708 S 10th St.
Minneapolis, MN 55404
Ph: (612)333-8601
Fax: (612)341-0958
Free: (888)333-8965
E-mail: bobpul15@qwest.net
URL: http://www.plumberslocal15.org
Contact: Bob Hansen, Business Mgr.
Members: 1,871. **Local. Affiliated With:** United Association of Journeymen and Apprentices of the Plumbing, Pipe Fitting, Sprinkler Fitting Industry of the U.S. and Canada.

11765 ■ U.S. Electric Wheelchair Hockey Association
c/o Craig McClellan, Pres. and Exec.Dir.
7216 39th Ave. N
Minneapolis, MN 55427
Ph: (763)535-4736
E-mail: info@powerhockey.com
URL: http://www.powerhockey.com
Regional. Affiliated With: Disabled Sports USA.

11766 ■ United States Psychiatric Rehabilitation Association - Minnesota
c/o CIP
1600 Broadway St. NE
Minneapolis, MN 55413
Ph: (612)362-4449
Fax: (612)362-4479
E-mail: ellies@cipmn.org
URL: National Affiliate–www.uspra.org
Contact: Ellie Skelton, Pres.
State. Promotes the advancement of the role, scope, and quality of service designed to facilitate the

readjustment into the community of adults with psychiatric disabilities. Provides a forum for the exchange of ideas, experiences, and contributions to the field. Encourages the development of improved concepts and methodologies in the field of psychiatry. **Affiliated With:** United States Psychiatric Rehabilitation Association.

11767 ■ United Synagogue of Conservative Judaism, Mid-Continent Region
4820 Minnetonka Blvd., Ste.410
Minneapolis, MN 55416-2263
Ph: (952)920-7068
Fax: (952)920-7183
E-mail: mid-continent@uscj.org
URL: http://www.uscj.org/mid-continent
Contact: Rabbi Paul S. Drazen, Exec.Dir.
Regional. Affiliated With: United Synagogue of Conservative Judaism.

11768 ■ United Union Roofers, Waterproofers and Allied Workers, 96
c/o Ray Waldron, Pres.
312 Central Ave., Rm. 456
Minneapolis, MN 55414
Ph: (612)379-2918
Free: (800)223-4815
URL: http://www.rooferslocal.com
Contact: Ray Waldron, Pres.
Local. Affiliated With: United Union of Roofers, Waterproofers and Allied Workers.

11769 ■ University of Minnesota - Civil Engineering Department - Environmental Engineering Society
500 Pillsbury Dr. SE
Minneapolis, MN 55455-0116
Ph: (612)625-5522
Fax: (612)626-7750
E-mail: cive@umn.edu
URL: http://www1.umn.edu/tc/
Contact: TorOve Leiknes, Pres.
Local.

11770 ■ Upper Midwest Booksellers Association (UMBA)
c/o Susan Walker, Exec.Dir.
3407 W 44th St.
Minneapolis, MN 55410
Ph: (612)926-5868
Fax: (612)926-6657
Free: (800)784-7522
E-mail: umbaoffice@aol.com
URL: http://www.abookaday.com
Regional. Publications: *Holiday Catalog* • Membership Directory • Newsletter.

11771 ■ Upper Midwest Chapter of the Acoustical Society of America (UMCASA)
c/o Tom Horner, Treas.
2753 Dean Pkwy.
Minneapolis, MN 55416
Ph: (612)824-2654
E-mail: janhorner@aol.com
URL: http://home.comcast.net/~rwgerdes/umcasa.html
Contact: Tom Horner, Treas.
Regional. Increases knowledge of acoustics and promotes its practical applications. Provides an opportunity for the exchange of knowledge and point of views on matters relevant to acoustics. **Affiliated With:** Acoustical Society of America.

11772 ■ Upper Midwest Translators and Interpreters Association (UMTIA)
c/o Dr. Laurence H. Bogoslaw, Pres.
Minnesota Translation Lab
Univ. of Minnesota
218 Nolte Ctr.
Minneapolis, MN 55455
Ph: (612)625-3096
Fax: (612)624-4579
E-mail: mtl@tc.umn.edu
URL: http://www.umtia.com
Contact: Dr. Laurence H. Bogoslaw, Pres.
Local. Affiliated With: American Translators Association.

11773 ■ Voice of the Retarded, Minnesota
5208 Logan Ave. S
Minneapolis, MN 55419-1022
Ph: (612)928-0636 (612)928-8920
Fax: (612)928-0759
E-mail: mary@dreblow.com
URL: National Affiliate–www.vor.net
Contact: Mary Joppru, Dir.
State. Affiliated With: Voice of the Retarded.

11774 ■ Volunteers of America of Minnesota
5905 Golden Valley Rd., Ste.110
Minneapolis, MN 55422
Ph: (763)546-3242
Fax: (763)546-2774
URL: http://www.voamn.org
State. Provides local human service programs and opportunities for individual and community involvement. **Affiliated With:** Volunteers of America.

11775 ■ Voyageurs National Park Association (VNPA)
126 N 3rd St., Ste.400
Minneapolis, MN 55401
Ph: (612)333-5424
Fax: (612)339-4731
E-mail: vnpa@voyageurs.org
URL: http://www.voyageurs.org
Contact: Ms. Cory MacNulty, Exec.Dir.
Founded: 1965. **State.** Protects and promotes the natural, recreational, and historic resources of Voyageurs National Park. Aims for an ecologically and historically significant Park where people can enjoy scenic, education, scientific and recreational treasures in a natural setting and in balance with the natural resources and uses of the Park, leaving it unimpaired for future generations.

11776 ■ VSA arts of Minnesota
528 Hennepin Ave., Ste.305
Minneapolis, MN 55403
Ph: (612)332-3888
Fax: (612)305-0132
Free: (800)801-3883
E-mail: craig.vsarts@bcmn.com
URL: http://mn.vsarts.org/
Contact: Mr. Craig Dunn, Exec.Dir.
Founded: 1986. **Staff:** 3. **Budget:** $245,000. **Nonmembership. State.** Dedicated to promoting quality, accessible arts experiences for people with disabilities. Offers granting programs, artists-in-residence, gallery showings, access training and awards, networking for ASL-interpreted or audio-described performances and other opportunities for artists with disabilities. **Awards:** Artist Recognition Grant. **Frequency:** annual. **Type:** monetary. **Recipient:** for excellence and merit or work in performing arts • Arts Access Awards. **Frequency:** annual. **Type:** trophy. **Recipient:** for forwarding efforts of making the arts accessible to people with disabilities or organizational level. **Affiliated With:** VSA arts. **Publications:** *Artists' Pipeline*, biweekly. Alternate Formats: online • *Arts Access*, quarterly. Newsletter. **Conventions/Meetings:** bimonthly board meeting.

11777 ■ Warehouse District Business Association
c/o Dario Anselmo
322 1st Ave. N
Minneapolis, MN 55401-1618
Ph: (612)334-3131
Local.

11778 ■ Wheelmen, Minnesota
2322 Johnson St. NE
Minneapolis, MN 55418-3938
Ph: (612)781-9954
E-mail: jon.sharratt@mts.com
URL: National Affiliate–www.thewheelmen.org
State.

11779 ■ World Future Society, Minneapolis-St. Paul
c/o Earl Joseph
Anticipatory Scis., Inc.
825 Summit Ave., Apt. 307
Minneapolis, MN 55403
Ph: (651)290-2846
E-mail: ejoseph@waldenu.edu
URL: National Affiliate–www.wfs.org
Contact: Earl Joseph, Contact
Local. Affiliated With: World Future Society.

11780 ■ YWCA of Minneapolis
c/o Kimberly Reeve, Dir. of Development
1130 Nicollet Mall
Minneapolis, MN 55403
Ph: (612)332-0501
E-mail: ywca@ywca-minneapolis.org
URL: http://www.ywcampls.org
Contact: Kimberly Reeve, Dir. of Development
Local. Seeks to empower women and girls and eliminate racism. Serves over 25,000 individuals in the Minneapolis, MN area through programs associated with health and fitness, early childhood education, public policy, and wellness for girls, youth, and women.

11781 ■ Zuhrah Shriners
c/o Donald M. Goetzman, P.P.
2540 Park Ave.
Minneapolis, MN 55404
Ph: (612)871-3555
Fax: (612)871-2632
URL: http://www.zuhrah.org
Contact: Donald M. Goetzman P.P., Contact
Local. Affiliated With: Imperial Council of the Ancient Arabic Order of the Nobles of the Mystic Shrine for North America.

Minneota

11782 ■ American Legion, Minneota Post 199
208 N Jefferson St.
Minneota, MN 56264
Ph: (651)291-1800
Fax: (651)291-1057
URL: National Affiliate–www.legion.org
Local. Affiliated With: American Legion.

Minnesota Lake

11783 ■ American Legion, Minnesota Post 287
c/o Fred K. Werner
14 N Main St.
Minnesota Lake, MN 56068
Ph: (651)291-1800
Fax: (651)291-1057
URL: National Affiliate–www.legion.org
Contact: Fred K. Werner, Contact
Local. Affiliated With: American Legion.

Minnetonka

11784 ■ American Council of Engineering Companies of Minnesota (ACEC/MN)
10201 Wayzata Blvd., Ste.240
Minnetonka, MN 55305
Ph: (952)593-5533
Fax: (952)593-5552
E-mail: mail@acecmn.org
URL: http://www.acecmn.org
Contact: David E. Oxley, Exec.Dir.
State. Affiliated With: American Council of Engineering Companies. **Formerly:** (2004) Consulting Engineers Council of Minnesota.

11785 ■ Association for Accounting Administration, Minn Dak Chapter
c/o Laurie Simonson, Pres.
301 Carlson Pkwy., Ste.350
Minnetonka, MN 55305
Ph: (952)473-2002
Fax: (952)473-2766
E-mail: lsimonson@baunedosen.com
URL: National Affiliate–www.cpaadmin.org
Contact: Laurie Simonson, Pres.
Local. Promotes the accounting administration profession. Educates the public accounting profession on the advantages of hiring professional administrators. **Affiliated With:** Association for Accounting Administration.

11786 ■ College Reading and Learning Association, Minnesota/North Dakota/South Dakota
c/o Linda Russell
Minneapolis Community & Tech. Coll.
5423 Maple Ridge Ct.
Minnetonka, MN 55343
Ph: (612)359-1512
Fax: (612)359-1357
E-mail: linda.russell@minneapolis.edu
URL: National Affiliate–www.crla.net
Contact: Linda Russell, Contact
Regional. Represents student-oriented professionals active in the fields of reading, learning assistance, developmental education and tutorial services at the college/adult level. Provides a forum for the interchange of ideas, methods and information to improve student learning and to facilitate the professional growth of members. **Affiliated With:** College Reading and Learning Association.

11787 ■ Hopkins Evening Lions Club
c/o Wayne Harkness, Sec.
5216 Birch Rd.
Minnetonka, MN 55345
Ph: (952)974-9283 (763)550-9056
URL: http://www.5m5.org
Contact: Wayne Harkness, Sec.
Local. Affiliated With: Lions Clubs International.

11788 ■ Institute of Management Accountants, Minneapolis Chapter
c/o Lance Elston, Pres.
10641 Smetana Rd., No. 109
Minnetonka, MN 55343
Ph: (651)205-1165
Fax: (651)205-3001
E-mail: lance.elston@usbank.com
URL: http://www.imaminneapolis.org
Contact: Lance Elston, Pres.
Local. Promotes professional and ethical standards. Equips members and students with knowledge and training required for the accounting profession. **Computer Services:** Online services, registration. **Additional Websites:** http://www.ima-northernlights.imanet.org. **Councils:** Northern Lights. **Affiliated With:** Institute of Management Accountants.

11789 ■ Midwest Energy Association (MEA)
6012 Blue Circle Dr.
Minnetonka, MN 55343-9104
Ph: (952)832-9915
Fax: (952)832-9308
E-mail: update@midwestenergy.org
URL: http://www.midwestenergy.org
Contact: Richard Hinkie, Pres.
Regional. **Formerly:** (2001) Midwest Gas Association.

11790 ■ Minneapolis Jewish Federation
c/o Sue Freeman, Marketing Dir.
13100 Wayzata Blvd., Ste.200
Minnetonka, MN 55305
Ph: (952)593-2600
Fax: (952)593-2544
E-mail: sfreeman@mplsfed.org
URL: http://www.jewishminnesota.org
Contact: Sue Freeman, Marketing Dir.
State. Seeks to build the community, care for the welfare of Jews everywhere, and maximize participation in Jewish life by planning, developing and allocating financial aid and human resources in partnership with Jewish institutions, locally, and overseas.

11791 ■ Minnesota Association of Occupational Health Nurses
c/o Bonnie Schultz, Admin. Support
14909 Lake St. Extension
Minnetonka, MN 55345
E-mail: maohn@maohn.org
URL: http://www.maohn.org
Contact: Bonnie Schultz, Admin. Support
State. Advances the profession of occupational and environmental health nursing. Promotes public awareness of occupational health nursing. **Affiliated With:** American Association of Occupational Health Nurses.

11792 ■ Minnesota Golf Course Superintendents Association
11900 Wayzata Blvd., Ste.130
Minnetonka, MN 55305-2018
Ph: (952)473-0557
Fax: (952)546-1652
Free: (800)642-7227
E-mail: scott@mgcsa.org
URL: http://www.mgcsa.org
Contact: Robert Panuska, Pres.
State. Represents the interests of golf course superintendents. Advances members' profession for career success. Enhances the enjoyment, growth and vitality in the game of golf. Educates members concerning efficient and economical management of golf courses. **Affiliated With:** Golf Course Superintendents Association of America.

11793 ■ Minnesota Northstar Cricket Club
5628 Pompano Dr.
Minnetonka, MN 55343
URL: http://www.usaca.org/Clubs.htm
Contact: Kanwal Kumar, Contact
Local.

11794 ■ Minnesota Rifle and Revolver Association (MRRA)
c/o Mark Rohmann
15800 Lexington Ave.
Minnetonka, MN 55345
E-mail: mike123066@hotmail.com
URL: http://www.mrra.org
Contact: Mark Rohmann, Contact
State.

11795 ■ Minnesota Society of Health-System Pharmacists (MSHP)
13911 Ridgedale Dr., Ste.260
Minnetonka, MN 55305
Ph: (952)541-9499
Fax: (952)541-9684
Free: (800)906-MSHP
E-mail: smartin@mnshp.org
URL: http://www.mnshp.org
Contact: Scott Martin, Exec.Dir.
State.

11796 ■ Skills USA, Hopkins High School
2400 Lindergh Dr.
Minnetonka, MN 55305
Ph: (952)988-4668
Fax: (952)988-4663
E-mail: jean_zimmerman@hokins.k12.mn.us
URL: http://www.mnskillsusa.org
Contact: Jean Zimmerman, Contact
Local. Serves high school and college students enrolled in technical, skilled, and service and health occupations. Provides quality education experiences for students in leadership, teamwork, citizenship and character development. Builds and reinforces self-confidence, work attitudes and communication skills. Emphasizes total quality at work, high ethical standards, superior work skills, and life-long education. Promotes understanding of the free enterprise system and involvement in community service. **Affiliated With:** Skills USA - VICA.

11797 ■ Tourette Syndrome Association of Minnesota Chapter
10249 Yellow Circle Dr., Ste.103
Minnetonka, MN 55343
Ph: (952)918-0350
E-mail: director@tsa-mn.org
URL: http://www.tsa-mn.org
Contact: Maureen Kenney, Exec.Dir.
State. Works to identify the cause of, find the cure for and control the effects of Tourette Syndrome (TS). Offers resources and referrals to help people and their families cope with the problems that occur with TS. Raises public awareness and counter media stereotypes about TS. **Affiliated With:** Tourette Syndrome Association.

11798 ■ TwinWest Chamber of Commerce
10550 Wayzata Blvd.
Minnetonka, MN 55305-5504
Ph: (952)540-0234
Fax: (952)540-0237
E-mail: info@twinwest.com
URL: http://www.twinwest.com
Contact: Barbara Obershaw, Pres.
Members: 943. **Staff:** 7. **Local**. Promotes business and community development in the areas of Brooklyn Center, Brooklyn Park, Crystal, Golden Valley, Hopkins, Medicine Lake, Minnetonka, New Hope, Plymouth, and St. Louis Park. **Awards:** TwinWest Foundation Scholarships. **Frequency:** annual. **Type:** scholarship. **Recipient:** for local high school seniors and adults continuing education. **Publications:** *TwinWest Directions*, monthly. Newsletter • *TwinWest Membership Directory and Business Resource Guide*, annual.

Montevideo

11799 ■ American Legion, Minnesota Post 59
c/o William Krensing
613 N Legion Dr.
Montevideo, MN 56265
Ph: (651)291-1800
Fax: (651)291-1057
URL: National Affiliate–www.legion.org
Contact: William Krensing, Contact
Local. Affiliated With: American Legion.

11800 ■ Chippewa County Historical Society
c/o June Lynne
Junction Hwy. 7 and 59
Montevideo, MN 56265
Ph: (320)269-7636
Fax: (320)269-7636
E-mail: cchs.june@juno.com
URL: http://www.montechamber.com/cchs/cchshp.htm
Contact: June Lynne, Exec.Dir.
Founded: 1936. **Members:** 385. **Staff:** 1. **Budget:** $61,000. **Local**. People interested in preservation of their local history. **Libraries: Type:** not open to the public. **Awards:** Hall of Fame Induction. **Frequency:** annual. **Type:** recognition. **Recipient:** member. **Publications:** *Pioneer Crier*, monthly. Newsletter. **Price:** for members. **Circulation:** 403.

11801 ■ Montevideo Area Chamber of Commerce
110 N 1st St.
Montevideo, MN 56265
Ph: (320)269-5527
Fax: (320)269-5586
Free: (800)269-5527
E-mail: generalinfo@montechamber.com
URL: http://www.montechamber.com
Contact: Lori Evenstad, Exec.Dir.
Founded: 1905. **Members:** 200. **Staff:** 1. **Budget:** $75,000. **Local**. Promotes business and community

development in the Montevideo, MN area. Administers Convention and Visitors' Bureau. **Computer Services:** database, membership directory. **Telecommunication Services:** electronic mail, lori@montechamber.com. **Committees:** Admirals; Agricultural; Crime Prevention; Government Affairs; Health and Wellness Coalition; Retail/Commercial Development; Special Events. **Divisions:** Convention and Visitors Bureau. **Publications:** Newsletter, monthly. Contains information on current events and programs. **Circulation:** 250.

11802 ■ Montevideo Area United Way
PO Box 2
Montevideo, MN 56265-0002
Ph: (320)269-7644
URL: National Affiliate–national.unitedway.org
Local. Affiliated With: United Way of America.

11803 ■ Montevideo Lions Club
c/o Leon Johnson, Pres.
4027 55th Ave. SW
Montevideo, MN 56265
Ph: (320)269-7913 (320)269-6528
E-mail: leon.johnson@mn.usda.gov
URL: http://www.5m4lions.org
Contact: Leon Johnson, Pres.
Local. Affiliated With: Lions Clubs International.

11804 ■ NAIFA-Sioux Valley
c/o Ivan Anderson, Pres.
PO Box 86
4080 Hwy. 7 SW
Montevideo, MN 56265
Ph: (320)269-2131
Fax: (320)269-2132
E-mail: jthompson@fbfs.com
URL: National Affiliate–naifa.org
Contact: Ivan Anderson, Pres.
Local. Represents the interests of insurance and financial advisors. Advocates for a positive legislative and regulatory environment. Enhances business and professional skills of members. **Affiliated With:** National Association of Insurance and Financial Advisors.

11805 ■ Sons of Norway, Jaabaek Lodge 1-264
c/o Barbara J. Oleson, Pres.
2012 54th St. SW
Montevideo, MN 56265-4044
Ph: (320)269-9130
URL: National Affiliate–www.sofn.com
Contact: Barbara J. Oleson, Pres.
Local. Affiliated With: Sons of Norway.

Montgomery

11806 ■ ACF Southeastern Minnesota Culinarian Chapter
c/o Robert Foix, Pres.
PO Box 61
Montgomery, MN 56069
Ph: (952)758-1220
Fax: (952)758-1299
E-mail: harly1chef@aol.com
URL: National Affiliate–www.acfchefs.org
Contact: Robert Foix CEC, Pres.
Local. Promotes the culinary profession. Provides on-going educational training and networking for members. Provides opportunities for competition, professional recognition and access to educational forums with other culinarians at local, regional, national and international events. **Affiliated With:** American Culinary Federation.

11807 ■ American Legion, Minnesota Post 79
c/o Joseph A. Gates
102 Elm Ave. W
Montgomery, MN 56069
Ph: (651)291-1800
Fax: (651)291-1057
URL: National Affiliate–www.legion.org
Contact: Joseph A. Gates, Contact
Local. Affiliated With: American Legion.

11808 ■ Mobilize Montgomery
206 1st St. S
Montgomery, MN 56069
Ph: (507)364-5577
Fax: (507)364-5230
E-mail: mobilize@frontiernet.net
URL: http://www.montgomerymn.org
Contact: Troy Domine, Dir.
Founded: 1992. **Local.** Works to promote community development in Montgomery, MN.

Monticello

11809 ■ American Legion, Monticello Post 260
PO Box 806
Monticello, MN 55362
Ph: (651)291-1800
Fax: (651)291-1057
URL: National Affiliate–www.legion.org
Local. Affiliated With: American Legion.

11810 ■ Central Minnesota Chapter 115, The Retired Enlisted Association
c/o Richard Habeck, Pres.
2459 155th St.
Monticello, MN 55362-6222
Ph: (763)878-2934
Fax: (763)878-2558
E-mail: habeckrh@aol.com
URL: National Affiliate–www.trea.org
Local. Affiliated With: The Retired Enlisted Association.

11811 ■ Monticello Area Chamber of Commerce
PO Box 192
Monticello, MN 55362
Ph: (763)295-2700
Fax: (763)295-2705
E-mail: info@monticellochamber.com
URL: http://www.monticellochamber.com
Contact: Dr. Susie Wojchouski, Dir.
Membership Dues: business (based on number of employees), $150-$550 (annual) • non-profit, $100 (annual) • manufacturer, $250-$500 (annual). **Local.** Promotes business and community development in Monticello, MN. **Awards:** Business of the Year. **Frequency:** annual. **Type:** recognition. **Recipient:** for a business member and has operated at least 5 years • **Type:** scholarship. **Recipient:** for high school graduates. **Computer Services:** Information services, membership directory. **Committees:** Home for the Holidays; Monticello Showcase; Riverside Art in the Park/Taste o Monticello. **Formerly:** (1999) Monticello Chamber of Commerce. **Publications:** Newsletter, monthly. **Conventions/Meetings:** monthly board meeting - every 2nd Wednesday at 7:30 AM in Monticello, MN.

11812 ■ Wright County Area United Way
PO Box 243
Monticello, MN 55362
Ph: (763)271-0420
URL: National Affiliate–national.unitedway.org
Local. Affiliated With: United Way of America.

11813 ■ Wright County Minnesota Kennel Club
c/o Beverly Capstick
8615 Haug Ave. NE
Monticello, MN 55362-3091
Ph: (763)295-6206
E-mail: bcapstick@tds.net
URL: National Affiliate–www.akc.org
Contact: Beverly Capstick, Contact
Founded: 1976. **Members:** 50. **Membership Dues:** individual, $8 (annual) • family, $12 (annual). **Staff:** 11. **Local Groups:** 1. **Local. Affiliated With:** American Kennel Club. **Conventions/Meetings:** monthly meeting - always second Thursday in Buffalo, MN.

Montrose

11814 ■ Minnesota Truss Manufacturers Association (MTMA)
c/o Jim Scheible, Pres.
Automated Building Components
100 Zephyr Ave. S
Montrose, MN 55363
Ph: (763)675-7376
Fax: (763)675-3522
E-mail: jim_scheible@trussabc.com
URL: National Affiliate–www.sbcindustry.com
Contact: Jim Scheible, Pres.
State. Represents manufacturers and suppliers of structural wood components. Protects and advances the interests of members, manufacturers and suppliers of related products. Encourages the use of structural wood components. Supports research, development and testing of wood trusses. **Affiliated With:** Wood Truss Council of America.

Moorhead

11815 ■ American Association of Physics Teachers, Minnesota Section
c/o Linda Irene Winkler, Pres.
Minnesota State Univ. - Moorhead
Dept. of Physics and Astronomy
1104 7th Ave. S
Moorhead, MN 56563
Ph: (218)236-2290
E-mail: winklerl@mnstate.edu
URL: http://www.maapt.org
Contact: Linda Irene Winkler, Pres.
State. Seeks to enhance the understanding and appreciation of physics through teaching. Aims to improve the pedagogical skills and physics knowledge of teachers at all levels. **Affiliated With:** American Association of Physics Teachers.

11816 ■ American Cancer Society, Moorhead
1001 Center Ave., Ste.K
Moorhead, MN 56560
Ph: (218)233-6114
Fax: (218)236-6307
Free: (800)225-0289
URL: http://www.cancer.org
Local. Affiliated With: American Cancer Society.

11817 ■ American Chemical Society, Red River Valley Section
c/o Gary Martin Edvenson, Sec.
Minnesota State Univ. Moorhead, Dept. of Chemistry
1104 7th Ave. S
Moorhead, MN 56563-0001
Ph: (218)236-2232
E-mail: edvenson@mnstate.edu
URL: National Affiliate–acswebcontent.acs.org
Contact: Gary Martin Edvenson, Sec.
Local. Represents the interests of individuals dedicated to the advancement of chemistry in all its branches. Provides opportunities for peer interaction and career development. **Affiliated With:** American Chemical Society.

11818 ■ American Legion, Minnesota Post 21
c/o Melvin E. Hearl
303 30th St. N
Moorhead, MN 56560
Ph: (651)291-1800
Fax: (651)291-1057
URL: National Affiliate–www.legion.org
Contact: Melvin E. Hearl, Contact
Local. Affiliated With: American Legion.

11819 ■ Association for Computing Machinery, Concordia College
c/o Dan Thureen, Sponsor
901 8th St. S
Moorhead, MN 56562
Ph: (218)299-4151
Fax: (218)299-4308
E-mail: hcc@gloria.cord.edu
Contact: Brady Brodsho, Contact
Biological, medical, behavioral, and computer scientists; hospital administrators; programmers and others interested in application of computer methods to biological, behavioral, and medical problems. Stimulates understanding of the use and potential of computers in the Biosciences. **Affiliated With:** Association for Computing Machinery.

11820 ■ Association for Computing Machinery, Minnesota State University/Moorhead
c/o Roland E. Barden, PhD, Pres.
Bridges Hall 160
1104 7th Ave. S
Moorhead, MN 56563
Ph: (218)477-2243
E-mail: msuacm@mnstate.edu
URL: http://acm.mnstate.edu
Contact: Mr. Andy David Vig, Chm.
State. Biological, medical, behavioral, and computer scientists; hospital administrators; programmers and others interested in application of computer methods to biological, behavioral, and medical problems. Stimulates understanding of the use and potential of computers in the biosciences. **Additional Websites:** http://www.mnstate.edu/comcis. **Affiliated With:** Association for Computing Machinery.

11821 ■ Camp Fire USA Northern Star Council (CFNSC)
725 Center Ave., No. 16
Moorhead, MN 56560-1966
Ph: (218)236-1090
Fax: (218)236-1094
E-mail: campfireusans@juno.com
Contact: Myrna Johnson, Exec.Dir.
Founded: 1927. **Members:** 1,000. **Membership Dues:** individual/family, $15 (annual). **Staff:** 4. **Budget:** $198,000. **Regional**. Youth from five through 21 years of age and adult volunteers in northwestern Minnesota and eastern North Dakota. Provides informal educational opportunities for boys and girls and leadership opportunities for adults through club, response, and camping programs. **Affiliated With:** Camp Fire USA. **Formerly:** (2000) Northern Star Camp Fire Council. **Publications:** *Crossed Logs*, bimonthly. Newsletter. **Price:** free. **Conventions/Meetings:** annual meeting (exhibits) - April.

11822 ■ Chamber of Commerce of Fargo Moorhead (CCFM)
202 1st Ave. N
Moorhead, MN 56560
Ph: (218)233-1100
Fax: (218)233-1200
E-mail: info@fmchamber.com
URL: http://www.fmchamber.com
Contact: David K. Martin, Pres.
Founded: 1998. **Members:** 1,800. **Regional**. Promotes business and community development in the Fargo, ND and Moorhead, MN regional area. **Awards:** Business of the Year. **Frequency:** annual. **Type:** recognition • Chamber Ambassador of the Year. **Frequency:** annual. **Type:** recognition • Entrepreneurial Business of the Year. **Frequency:** annual. **Type:** recognition • Small Business of the Year. **Frequency:** annual. **Type:** recognition. **Computer Services:** Online services, membership directory. **Committees:** Ambassadors; Business-Education Partnership; Business Training; Fargo Moorhead Leadership; Public Affairs; Regional Economy Partnership; Young Professionals Network; Youth Leadership. **Formerly:** (1999) Moorhead Area Chamber of Commerce. **Publications:** *The Bridge*, monthly. Newsletter. **Circulation:** 3,000. **Advertising:** accepted • *Membership Directory and Community Profile*. **Advertising:** accepted. **Conventions/Meetings:** annual Chamber Golf Outing and Social - competition, networking opportunities • annual dinner.

11823 ■ Clay County Historical Society
PO Box 501
Moorhead, MN 56561-0501
Ph: (218)299-5520
Fax: (218)299-5525
E-mail: mark.peihl@ci.moorhead.mn.us
URL: http://www.info.co.clay.mn.us/history
Contact: Lisa Vedaa, Dir.
Founded: 1932. **Members:** 550. **Membership Dues:** individual, $20 (annual) • family, $35 (annual) • business, $50 (annual). **Staff:** 3. **Budget:** $137,000. **Local**. Works to collect, preserve and disseminate the history of Clay County. Maintains a museum, archives. **Libraries: Type:** open to the public. **Holdings:** 200. **Subjects:** Clay County Minnesota history, 1860-present. **Publications:** *Clay County Historical Society*, bimonthly. Newsletter. Contains articles of historical interest with professional research. **Price:** for members. ISSN: 1086-2307. **Circulation:** 700. **Conventions/Meetings:** monthly board meeting.

11824 ■ Fargo-Moorhead Audubon Society
c/o Robert O'Connor, Pres.
Biology Dept.
Concordia Coll.
Moorhead, MN 56560
E-mail: robert.oconnor@ndsu.nodak.edu
URL: National Affiliate–www.audubon.org
Contact: Robert O'Connor, Pres.
Local. Works to conserve and restore natural ecosystems, focusing on birds and other wildlife for the benefit of humanity and the earth's biological diversity. **Affiliated With:** National Audubon Society.

11825 ■ Minn-Dak Woodturners
c/o Ron Williams, Pres.
1011 10th St. S
Moorhead, MN 56560
Ph: (218)236-9140
E-mail: info@minndakwoodturners.com
URL: http://www.minndakwoodturners.com
Contact: Ron Williams, Pres.
Local. Represents amateur and professional woodturners, gallery owners, wood and equipment suppliers, and collectors. **Affiliated With:** American Association of Woodturners.

11826 ■ Moorhead Midday-Central Lions Club
c/o Jeff Dangerfield, Pres.
518 Appletree Ln.
Moorhead, MN 56560
Ph: (218)233-8681 (218)233-7665
Fax: (218)291-1784
E-mail: jeffd@bertsonline.com
URL: http://lions5m11.org/sys-tmpl/door
Contact: Jeff Dangerfield, Pres.
Local. Affiliated With: Lions Clubs International.

11827 ■ Psi Chi, National Honor Society in Psychology - Concordia College
c/o Dept. of Psychology
901 8th St. S
Moorhead, MN 56562-0001
Ph: (218)299-4030 (218)299-3299
Fax: (218)299-4308
E-mail: ibrahim@cord.edu
URL: http://www.psichi.org/chapters/info.asp?chapter_id=998
Contact: Dr. Mona Ibrahim, Advisor
Local.

11828 ■ Society of Manufacturing Engineers - Minnesota State University Moorhead S189
1104-7th Ave. S
Moorhead, MN 56563
Ph: (218)236-2465
Fax: (218)299-5958
E-mail: kian@mnstate.edu
URL: National Affiliate–www.sme.org
Contact: Aziz Kian, Contact
Local. Advances manufacturing knowledge to gain competitive advantage. Improves skills and manufacturing solutions for the growth of economy. Provides resources and opportunities for manufacturing professionals. **Affiliated With:** Yosemite Association.

Moose Lake

11829 ■ American Legion, Pedersen Maunula Post 379
PO Box 867
Moose Lake, MN 55767
Ph: (651)291-1800
Fax: (651)291-1057
URL: National Affiliate–www.legion.org
Local. Affiliated With: American Legion.

11830 ■ Moose Lake Area Chamber of Commerce
PO Box 110
Moose Lake, MN 55767
Ph: (218)485-4145
Free: (800)635-3680
E-mail: mlchamber@moose-tec.com
URL: http://www.mooselake-mn.com
Contact: Dean Paulson, Exec.Dir.
Local. Publications: Newsletter.

Mora

11831 ■ American Legion, Lee Goldsmith Post 201
118 Railroad Ave. NE
Mora, MN 55051
Ph: (651)291-1800
Fax: (651)291-1057
URL: National Affiliate–www.legion.org
Local. Affiliated With: American Legion.

11832 ■ East Central Minnesota RSVP
c/o Monique Mendyke, Dir.
105 S Union St.
Mora, MN 55051
Ph: (320)679-1080
Fax: (320)679-9036
E-mail: mmendyke@voamn.org
URL: http://www.seniorcorps.gov/about/programs/rsvp_state.asp?usestateabbr=mn&Search4.x=29&Search4.y=7
Contact: Monique Mendyke, Dir.
Local. Affiliated With: Retired and Senior Volunteer Program.

11833 ■ Kanabec Area Chamber of Commerce (KACC)
805 W Forest
Mora, MN 55051
Ph: (320)679-5792
Free: (800)291-5792
E-mail: macc@ncis.com
URL: http://www.moramn.com
Contact: Madolyn Amundson, Pres.
Members: 110. **Membership Dues:** business (base), $235 (annual). **Staff:** 1. **Budget:** $63,000. **Local**. Promotes business and community development in the Mora, MN area. Conducts East Central Home and Leisure Show. **Committees:** Community Events Sign; Downtown Revitalization; Economic Development; Events; Government Affairs; Tourism. **Formerly:** (2003) Mora Area Chamber of Commerce. **Publications:** *Progress*, monthly. Newsletter. **Conventions/Meetings:** monthly board meeting - 3rd Wednesday.

11834 ■ Mora Lions Club
400 E Fair Ave.
Mora, MN 55051-1808
Ph: (320)679-2523
E-mail: stevewal@youbetnet.net
URL: http://www.moralionsmn.lionwap.org
Contact: Steven Walbridge, Contact
Local. Affiliated With: Lions Clubs International.

11835 ■ Onanegozie-Land Resource Conservation and Development Council
119 S Lake St.
Mora, MN 55051-1526
Ph: (320)679-4604
Fax: (320)679-2215
E-mail: lmn@mn.nrcs.usda.gov
URL: National Affiliate–www.rcdnet.org
Contact: Larry Nelson, Coor.
Local. Affiliated With: National Association of Resource Conservation and Development Councils.

Morris

11836 ■ American Legion, Walter Tripp Post 29
507 Pacific Ave.
Morris, MN 56267
Ph: (651)291-1800
Fax: (651)291-1057
URL: National Affiliate–www.legion.org
Local. Affiliated With: American Legion.

11837 ■ Association for Computing Machinery, University of Minnesota/Morris (ACM)
c/o Michael C. Maurer, Chm.
Div. of Sci. and Math
600 E 4th St.
Morris, MN 56267
Ph: (320)589-6328
E-mail: csclub@cda.mrs.umn.edu
URL: http://csci.morris.umn.edu/UMMCSciWiki/bin/view/ACMCSClub
Contact: Michael Maurer, Pres.
Local. Biological, medical, behavioral, and computer scientists; hospital administrators; programmers and others interested in application of computer methods to biological, behavioral, and medical problems. Stimulates understanding of the use and potential of computers in the Biosciences. **Affiliated With:** Association for Computing Machinery.

11838 ■ Morris Area Chamber of Commerce and Agriculture
507 Atlantic Ave.
Morris, MN 56267
Ph: (320)589-1242
Fax: (320)585-4814
E-mail: mchamber@info-link.net
URL: http://www.morrismnchamber.org
Contact: Carolyn Peterson, Exec.Dir.
Founded: 1940. **Local.** Promotes business and community development in the Morris, MN area. Sponsors Prairie Pioneer Days. **Computer Services:** database, list of businesses • information services, facts about the local community. **Publications:** *Chamber Connection*, monthly. Newsletter. **Conventions/Meetings:** annual Grand Parade of Lights - festival • annual Prairie Pioneer Days - festival.

11839 ■ Morris Lions Club
c/o Dale Livingston, Pres.
10 Ridge Rd.
Morris, MN 56267
Ph: (320)589-1970 (320)589-6106
URL: http://www.5m4lions.org
Contact: Dale Livingston, Pres.
Local. Affiliated With: Lions Clubs International.

11840 ■ Prairie Renaissance Cultural Alliance
630 Atlantic Ave.
Morris, MN 56267-0101
Ph: (320)585-5037
E-mail: prca@prairierenaissance.org
URL: http://www.geocities.com/prcamorris
Contact: Athena Kildegaard, Exec.Dir.
Founded: 2002. **Members:** 200. **Membership Dues:** basic, $20 (annual) • family/contributor, $50 (annual) • sustaining, $100 (annual). **Staff:** 1. **Budget:** $55,000. **Local. Publications:** *The Prairie Muse*, quarterly. Newsletter. Contains membership information. **Circulation:** 200.

11841 ■ Psi Chi, National Honor Society in Psychology - University of Minnesota, Morris
c/o Dept. of Psychology
109 Camden Hall
600 E 4th St.
Morris, MN 56267-2134
Ph: (320)589-6200 (320)589-6196
Fax: (320)589-6117
E-mail: stewartd@mrs.umn.edu
URL: http://www.psichi.org/chapters/info.asp?chapter_id=592
Contact: Dennis S. Stewart PhD, Advisor
Local.

11842 ■ Sons of Norway, Norskfodt Lodge 1-590
c/o Leroy G. Aker, Pres.
3 N Court St.
Morris, MN 56267-1611
Ph: (320)589-3451
E-mail: leroyaker@hometownsolutions.net
URL: National Affiliate–www.sofn.com
Contact: Leroy G. Aker, Pres.
Local. Affiliated With: Sons of Norway.

Morristown

11843 ■ American Legion, Minnesota Post 149
c/o Roy Leider
PO Box 62
Morristown, MN 55052
Ph: (651)291-1800
Fax: (651)291-1057
URL: National Affiliate–www.legion.org
Contact: Roy Leider, Contact
Local. Affiliated With: American Legion.

Morton

11844 ■ American Legion, Oscar Wellnitz Post 344
PO Box 190
Morton, MN 56270
Ph: (651)291-1800
Fax: (651)291-1057
URL: National Affiliate–www.legion.org
Local. Affiliated With: American Legion.

11845 ■ Morton Lions Club
c/o Richard Gewerth, Pres.
31113 Porter Ave.
Morton, MN 56270
Ph: (320)697-6183
E-mail: satch-56270@yahoo.com
URL: http://www.5m4lions.org
Contact: Richard Gewerth, Pres.
Local. Affiliated With: Lions Clubs International.

Motley

11846 ■ American Legion, Tri-County Post 124
11312 79th Ave. SW
Motley, MN 56466
Ph: (651)291-1800
Fax: (651)291-1057
URL: National Affiliate–www.legion.org
Local. Affiliated With: American Legion.

Mound

11847 ■ American Legion, Minnetonka Post 398
2333 Wilshire Blvd.
Mound, MN 55364
Ph: (651)291-1800
Fax: (651)291-1057
URL: National Affiliate–www.legion.org
Local. Affiliated With: American Legion.

Mounds View

11848 ■ Twin Cities North Chamber of Commerce
5394 Edgewood Dr., Ste.100
Mounds View, MN 55112
Ph: (763)571-9781
Fax: (763)572-7950
E-mail: info@twincitiesnorth.org
URL: http://www.twincitiesnorth.org
Contact: Shannon Meyer, Pres./CEO
Founded: 1958. **Members:** 500. **Local.** Promotes business and community development in the northern Twin Cities suburbs, specifically Arden Hills, Blaine, Columbia Heights, Fridley, Mounds View, New Brighton, Shoreview and Spring Lake Park. **Formerly:** (1999) Fridley Chamber of Commerce; (2003) Southern Anoka County Chamber of Commerce. **Publications:** Directory, annual • Newsletter, monthly.

11849 ■ Upper Midwest Dairy Industry Association
5205 Quincy St.
Mounds View, MN 55112-1438
Ph: (763)785-0484
E-mail: paul@dqci.com
URL: National Affiliate–www.foodprotection.org
Contact: Paul Nierman, Contact
Regional. Provides food safety professionals with a forum to exchange information on protecting the food supply. Promotes sanitary methods and procedures for the development, production, processing, distribution, preparation and serving of food. **Affiliated With:** International Association for Food Protection.

11850 ■ Wooden Canoe Heritage Association, Minnesota
c/o Dan Lindberg, Pres.
7188 Knollwood Dr.
Mounds View, MN 55112
E-mail: dan.lindberg@udlp.com
URL: National Affiliate–www.wcha.org
Contact: Dan Lindberg, Pres.
State. Affiliated With: Wooden Canoe Heritage Association.

Mountain Iron

11851 ■ American Legion, Yoki-Bergman Post 220
PO Box 361
Mountain Iron, MN 55768
Ph: (651)291-1800
Fax: (651)291-1057
URL: National Affiliate–www.legion.org
Local. Affiliated With: American Legion.

11852 ■ North Country Library Cooperative (NCLC)
5528 Emerald Ave., Rm. 116
Mountain Iron, MN 55768
Ph: (218)741-1907
Fax: (218)741-1908
Free: (800)950-4401
E-mail: lwadman@arrowhead.lib.mn.us
URL: http://www.nclcmn.org
Contact: Linda J. Wadman, Dir.
Founded: 1979. **Members:** 173. **Staff:** 2. **Budget:** $120,000. **Regional Groups:** 1. **State Groups:** 3. **Local.** Libraries in northeastern Minnesota. Provides opportunities for resource sharing, communication, common database development, and continuing education. **Affiliated With:** American Library Association. **Publications:** *Cooperative Connection*, quarterly. Newsletter. **Circulation:** 200 • Membership Directory, annual. **Conventions/Meetings:** annual meeting.

Mountain Lake

11853 ■ American Legion, Albin Johnson Post 244
39498 County Rd. 47
Mountain Lake, MN 56159
Ph: (651)291-1800
Fax: (651)291-1057
URL: National Affiliate–www.legion.org
Local. Affiliated With: American Legion.

11854 ■ American Legion, Mountain Lake Post 389
PO Box 366
Mountain Lake, MN 56159
Ph: (651)291-1800
Fax: (651)291-1057
URL: National Affiliate–www.legion.org
Local. Affiliated With: American Legion.

11855 ■ Minnesota Dietary Managers Association
c/o Collette Johnson, CDM, Pres.
745 Basinger Memorial Dr.
Mountain Lake, MN 56159
Ph: (507)427-2464
E-mail: cjohnson@good-sam.com
URL: http://www.dmaonline.org/MN
Contact: Collette Johnson CDM, Pres.
State. Represents dietary managers. Maintains a high level of competency and quality in dietary departments through continuing education. Provides optimum nutritional care through foodservice management. **Affiliated With:** Dietary Managers Association.

Nashwauk

11856 ■ American Legion, Walter Riley Post 307
301 Central Ave.
Nashwauk, MN 55769
Ph: (651)291-1800
Fax: (651)291-1057
URL: National Affiliate–www.legion.org
Local. Affiliated With: American Legion.

Nassau

11857 ■ American Legion, Meyer-Thompson Post 536
PO Box 207
Nassau, MN 56257
Ph: (651)291-1800
Fax: (651)291-1057
URL: National Affiliate–www.legion.org
Local. Affiliated With: American Legion.

Navarre

11858 ■ Lake Minnetonka Chamber of Commerce
c/o Patsy Kiesow, Exec.Dir.
3600 Shoreline Dr.
PO Box 115
Navarre, MN 55392
Ph: (952)471-0768
Fax: (952)471-0577
E-mail: chamber@lakeminnetonkachamber.com
URL: http://www.lakeminnetonkachamber.com
Contact: Patsy Kiesow, Exec.Dir.
Membership Dues: business with 1-2 employees, $204 (annual) • business with 3-6 employees, $274 (annual) • business with 7-10 employees, $344 (annual) • business with 11-15 employees, $391 (annual) • business with 16-30 employees, $437 (annual) • business with 31-50 employees, $474 (annual) • business with 50 or more employees, $572 (annual) • school or government, $232 (annual) • individual community member or charitable organization, $129 (annual) • associate (employee, partner, or officers of businesses that are Lake Minnetonka members), $129 (annual) • 2nd business listing, $204 (annual) • one time, $25. **Staff:** 2. **Local.** Promotes business and community development in the Lake Minnetonka area.

Nerstrand

11859 ■ Dennison Lions Club
c/o Rene D. Koester, Sec.
9536 135th St. E
Nerstrand, MN 55053
Ph: (507)645-8914
E-mail: rkoester@rconnect.com
URL: http://www.lions5m1.org/dennison
Contact: Rene D. Koester, Sec.
Local. Affiliated With: Lions Clubs International.

New Brighton

11860 ■ American Legion, Tri-City Post 513
400 Old Hwy. 8 NW
New Brighton, MN 55112
Ph: (651)291-1800
Fax: (651)291-1057
URL: National Affiliate–www.legion.org
Local. Affiliated With: American Legion.

11861 ■ Minneapolis District Dental Society (MDDS)
2475 15th St. NW, Ste.C
New Brighton, MN 55112-5606
Ph: (651)631-9845
Fax: (651)631-9846
E-mail: mdds@mplsdds.org
URL: http://mplsdds.org
Contact: Michelle M. Quade, Exec.Dir.
Founded: 1925. **Members:** 1,110. **Staff:** 2. **Local.** Promotes the art and science of dentistry. Encourages public awareness of the importance of good oral hygiene. **Publications:** Newsletter, monthly. **Conventions/Meetings:** quarterly meeting.

11862 ■ Minnesota Asphalt Pavement Association
c/o Richard O. Wolters, Exec.Dir.
900 Long Lake Rd., Ste.100
New Brighton, MN 55112
Ph: (651)636-4666
Fax: (651)636-4790
E-mail: rwolters@mnapa.org
URL: http://www.asphaltisbest.com
Contact: Richard O. Wolters, Exec.Dir.
Founded: 1942. **Members:** 46. **Staff:** 4. **State.**

11863 ■ Minnesota Council of Teachers of Mathematics (MCTM)
c/o Arnie Cutler, Exec.Dir.
PO Box 120418
New Brighton, MN 55112
Ph: (651)631-2136
E-mail: cutler@umn.edu
URL: http://www.mctm.org
Contact: Arnie Cutler, Exec.Dir.
Founded: 1948. **Members:** 1,200. **Membership Dues:** professional, $25 (annual) • student, retired, $12 (annual). **Budget:** $95,000. **State.** Mathematics teachers' K-16 promoting mathematics education. **Publications:** *Math Bits*, monthly. Newsletter • *Math Times*, semiannual. Journal. **Conventions/Meetings:** semiannual conference (exhibits) - always October and March/April.

11864 ■ Minnesota SAAB Club
c/o Dean Nelson
1420 15 Terr. NW
New Brighton, MN 55112
Ph: (651)636-3771
E-mail: chrisluick@prodigy.net
URL: http://www.mnsaabclub.org
Contact: Dean Nelson, Contact
State. Affiliated With: Saab Club of North America.

New Germany

11865 ■ American Legion, Lowell Stender Post 601
PO Box 86
New Germany, MN 55367
Ph: (651)291-1800
Fax: (651)291-1057
URL: National Affiliate–www.legion.org
Local. Affiliated With: American Legion.

New Hope

11866 ■ American Society of Heating, Refrigerating and Air-Conditioning Engineers - Minnesota Chapter
c/o Curt Ratajczak, Pres.
TMS Johnson Inc.
2908 Nevada Ave. N
New Hope, MN 55427
Ph: (763)544-5442
Fax: (763)544-5569
E-mail: curtr@tmsj.com
URL: http://www.mnashrae.org
Contact: Curt Ratajczak, Pres.
State. Advances the arts and sciences of heating, ventilation, air-conditioning and refrigeration. Provides a source of technical and educational information, standards and guidelines. Conducts seminars for professional growth. **Affiliated With:** American Society of Heating, Refrigerating and Air-Conditioning Engineers.

11867 ■ BMW Motorcycle Owners Club of Minnesota No. 49 (BMWMOCM)
c/o Donald Sidler
2901 Flag Ave. N
New Hope, MN 55427
Ph: (763)542-1499
E-mail: dsid@comcast.net
URL: http://www.bmwmocm.com
Contact: Jeff Martin, Pres.
Membership Dues: household, $20 (annual). **State. Affiliated With:** BMW Motorcycle Owners of America.

11868 ■ Golden Valley Lions Club
c/o Gerry Gries, Sec.
3525 Yukon Ave. N
New Hope, MN 55427
Ph: (763)593-1258 (763)595-7315
URL: http://www.5m5.org
Contact: Gerry Gries, Sec.
Local. Affiliated With: Lions Clubs International.

11869 ■ Minnesota Microscopy Society (MMS)
4763 Decatur Ave. N
New Hope, MN 55428
Ph: (763)514-4678
E-mail: sue.okerstrom@medtronic.com
URL: http://www.mnmicroscopy.org
Contact: Bede Willenbring, Treas.
State. Affiliated With: Microscopy Society of America.

11870 ■ New Hope Lions Club
c/o Dave Whitney, Pres.
5967 Hillsboro Ave. N
New Hope, MN 55428
Ph: (763)533-9361
URL: http://www.5m5.org
Contact: Dave Whitney, Pres.
Local. Affiliated With: Lions Clubs International.

New London

11871 ■ American Legion, Robert Ihlang Post 537
PO Box 154
New London, MN 56273
Ph: (651)291-1800
Fax: (651)291-1057
URL: National Affiliate–www.legion.org
Local. Affiliated With: American Legion.

11872 ■ Izaak Walton League of America, New London Chapter
3176 19th Ave. NE
New London, MN 56273
Ph: (320)354-5279
E-mail: housewren@tds.net
URL: National Affiliate–www.iwla.org
Local. Works to educate the public to conserve, maintain, protect, and restore the soil, forest, water, and other natural resources of the U.S; promotes the enjoyment and wholesome utilization of these resources. **Affiliated With:** Izaak Walton League of America.

11873 ■ New London Lions Club
c/o Dawn Weber, Sec.
9755 240th Ave. NE
New London, MN 56273
Ph: (320)354-0306 (320)235-1902
E-mail: attorneydawnweber@yahoo.com
URL: http://www.5m4lions.org
Contact: Dawn Weber, Sec.
Local. Affiliated With: Lions Clubs International.

11874 ■ West Central Antique Power Collectors
c/o Kent Medalen
2840 Co. Rd. 40 NE
New London, MN 56273-9552
Ph: (320)354-4571 (320)214-3714
E-mail: kmedalen@tds.net
URL: http://www.geocities.com/wcapc_1
Contact: Chuck Molitor, Pres.
Founded: 1996. **Members:** 50. **Membership Dues:** $6 (annual). **Local Groups:** 1. **Local. Conventions/Meetings:** monthly general assembly - 3rd Tuesday.

11875 ■ West Central Builders Association
c/o Nancy Lohn, Exec. Officer
PO Box 447
New London, MN 56273
Ph: (320)354-7373
Fax: (320)354-7304
E-mail: westcentralbuilders@tds.net
URL: http://www.westcentralbuilders.com
Contact: Nancy Lohn, Exec. Officer
Founded: 1992. **Members:** 80. **Membership Dues:** builder/associate, $295 (annual). **Staff:** 1. **State Groups:** 1. **Local.** Promotes the construction industry. **Conventions/Meetings:** monthly meeting.

New Prague

11876 ■ American Legion, Minnesota Post 45
c/o John Vessey
PO Box 113
New Prague, MN 56071
Ph: (651)291-1800
Fax: (651)291-1057
URL: National Affiliate–www.legion.org
Contact: John Vessey, Contact
Local. Affiliated With: American Legion.

11877 ■ Minnesota Lamb and Wool Producers Association
c/o Jeremy Geske, Pres.
1507 7th St. NE
New Prague, MN 56071
Ph: (952)758-7938
URL: http://www.mlwp.org
Contact: Jeremy Geske, Pres.
State. Affiliated With: American Sheep Industry Association.

11878 ■ New Prague Chamber of Commerce (NPCC)
101 E Main St.
PO Box 191
New Prague, MN 56071
Ph: (952)758-4360
Fax: (952)758-5396
E-mail: npcofc@bevcomm.net
URL: http://www.newprague.com
Contact: Kim Gassner, Exec.Dir.
Members: 170. **Staff:** 2. **Local.** Promotes business and community development in New Prague, MN. Conducts charitable activities. Holds annual arts and crafts show, New Prague Half-Marathon, Dozinky Czechoslovakian Harvest Festival, garage and sidewalk sales, and Christmas programs. **Committees:** Charitable Gambling; Member Services; Retail; Sponsorship; Tourism. **Publications:** Directory, annual • Newsletter, monthly • Brochures, periodic. **Conventions/Meetings:** annual Dozinky Czechoslovakian Harvest - festival - every 3rd Saturday of September • annual meeting.

11879 ■ New Prague Figure Skating Club (NPAFSC)
167 Penny Ln. SW
New Prague, MN 56071
E-mail: pliepold@bevcomm.net
URL: http://www.npafsc.org
Contact: Paula Liepold, Pres.
Local. Provides programs to encourage participation and achievement in the sport of figure skating on ice. Defines and maintains uniform standards of skating proficiency. Organizes and sponsors competitions and exhibitions for the purpose of stimulating interest in figure skating. **Affiliated With:** United States Figure Skating Association.

New Richland

11880 ■ American Legion, Andrew Borgen Post 75
PO Box 483
New Richland, MN 56072
Ph: (651)291-1800
Fax: (651)291-1057
URL: National Affiliate–www.legion.org
Local. Affiliated With: American Legion.

New Ulm

11881 ■ American Legion, Evans Post 329
RR 4, Box 54a
New Ulm, MN 56073
Ph: (651)291-1800
Fax: (651)291-1057
URL: National Affiliate–www.legion.org
Local. Affiliated With: American Legion.

11882 ■ American Legion, Seifert-Bianchi Post 132
PO Box 471
New Ulm, MN 56073
Ph: (507)354-4016
Fax: (651)291-1057
URL: National Affiliate–www.legion.org
Local. Affiliated With: American Legion.

11883 ■ Brown County Historical Society
2 N Broadway
New Ulm, MN 56073-1714
Ph: (507)233-2616
Fax: (507)354-1068
E-mail: bchs@newulmtel.net
URL: http://browncountyhistoryMNUSA.org
Contact: Bob Burgess, Dir.
Founded: 1930. **Members:** 489. **Membership Dues:** household, $20 (annual). **Staff:** 6. **Budget:** $130,000. **Regional Groups:** 2. **State Groups:** 1. **Local Groups:** 1. **Local.** County Historical museum offers exhibits on 3 floors. Educational programming and research library. **Libraries: Type:** open to the public. **Holdings:** 2,000. **Subjects:** local and regional history. **Publications:** *News Notes*, quarterly. Newsletter. Membership Newsletter. **Price:** $2.00 • Book, periodic. **Conventions/Meetings:** annual meeting - November.

11884 ■ Minnesota Festivals and Events Association
c/o Leo H. Berg, Exec.Dir.
PO Box 461
New Ulm, MN 56073-0461
Ph: (507)359-3378
Fax: (507)354-8853
E-mail: mfea@newulmtel.net
URL: http://www.mfea.eventwebsitebuilder.com/page/page/481055.htm
Founded: 1990. **Members:** 275. **Staff:** 2. **Budget:** $30,000. **State. Awards:** Certified Festival Manager. **Frequency:** annual. **Type:** scholarship. **Publications:** *Festive Talk*, quarterly. Newsletter. **Circulation:** 600. **Advertising:** accepted • *Guide to Minnesota Festivals & Events*. **Circulation:** 180,000. **Conventions/Meetings:** annual conference, with vendors (exhibits).

11885 ■ New Ulm Area Chamber of Commerce
1 N Minnesota St.
PO Box 384
New Ulm, MN 56073
Ph: (507)233-4300
Fax: (507)354-1504
Free: (888)463-9856
E-mail: nuchamber@newulmtel.net
URL: http://www.newulm.com
Contact: Sharon Weinkauf, Pres./CEO
Founded: 1940. **Members:** 340. **Staff:** 6. **Local.** Promotes business and community development in the New Ulm, MN area. Conducts annual Oktoberfest. **Computer Services:** database, list of members • information services, facts about the local community. **Telecommunication Services:** electronic mail, eberg@newulmtel.net • electronic mail, jeckstein@newulmtel.net. **Committees:** Activating Community Horizons; Business Action Team; Network New Ulm; Tourism; Willkommen. **Subgroups:** Convention and Visitors' Bureau. **Publications:** *NU Business Trends*, monthly. Newsletter • *Program of Work*, annual. Directory • Booklet.

11886 ■ New Ulm Figure Skating Club (NUFSC)
PO Box 2
New Ulm, MN 56073
Ph: (507)354-7469
URL: http://www.geocities.com/nufsc
Contact: Shelly Keune, Pres.
Local. Provides programs to encourage participation and achievement in the sport of figure skating on ice. Defines and maintains uniform standards of skating proficiency. Organizes and sponsors competitions and exhibitions for the purpose of stimulating interest in figure skating. **Affiliated With:** United States Figure Skating Association.

11887 ■ SCORE New Ulm Area
c/o William J. Fenske, Ch.
1 N Minnesota St.
PO Box 384
New Ulm, MN 56073
Ph: (507)233-4300
E-mail: newulm@scoreminn.org
URL: http://www.score.org
Affiliated With: SCORE.

11888 ■ United Way of New Ulm
PO Box 476
New Ulm, MN 56073
Ph: (507)354-6512
Fax: (507)354-9712
E-mail: unitedway@newulmtel.net
URL: http://www.unitedwaynewulm.com
Contact: Ms. Anne G. Makepeace, Exec.Dir.
Local. Affiliated With: United Way of America.

New York Mills

11889 ■ American Legion, Stinar-Sturdevant-Stoltz Post 116
PO Box 68
New York Mills, MN 56567
Ph: (651)291-1800
Fax: (651)291-1057
URL: National Affiliate–www.legion.org
Local. Affiliated With: American Legion.

11890 ■ GFWC of Minnesota
51656 Cty. Hwy. 14
New York Mills, MN 56567-9122
Ph: (218)385-3596
URL: http://gfwcmn.org
Local.

11891 ■ RSVP Todd/Wadena/Otter Tail/Wilkin
c/o Kathryn Quittschreiber, Dir.
PO Box L
New York Mills, MN 56567
Ph: (218)385-2900
Fax: (218)385-4544
E-mail: katieq@otwcac.org
URL: http://www.otwcac.org/RSVP/RSVP_index.htm
Contact: Kathryn Quittschreiber, Dir.
Local. Affiliated With: Retired and Senior Volunteer Program.

Newfolden

11892 ■ American Legion, Otto Knutson Post 427
PO Box 284
Newfolden, MN 56738
Ph: (651)291-1800
Fax: (651)291-1057
URL: National Affiliate–www.legion.org
Local. Affiliated With: American Legion.

11893 ■ Newfolden Lions Club
c/o John Bjorsness, Pres.
13298 290th St. NW
Newfolden, MN 56738
Ph: (218)874-4801
URL: http://lions5m11.org/sys-tmpl/door
Contact: John Bjorsness, Pres.
Local. Affiliated With: Lions Clubs International.

Nicollet

11894 ■ American Legion, Nicollet Post 510
PO Box 253
Nicollet, MN 56074
Ph: (651)291-1800
Fax: (651)291-1057
URL: National Affiliate–www.legion.org
Local. Affiliated With: American Legion.

Nielsville

11895 ■ American Legion, Hubbard Post 336
PO Box 114
Nielsville, MN 56568
Ph: (651)291-1800
Fax: (651)291-1057
URL: National Affiliate–www.legion.org
Local. Affiliated With: American Legion.

Nisswa

11896 ■ American Legion, Minnesota Post 627
c/o Billie Brown
PO Box 427
Nisswa, MN 56468
Ph: (651)291-1800
Fax: (651)291-1057
URL: National Affiliate–www.legion.org
Contact: Billie Brown, Contact
Local. Affiliated With: American Legion.

11897 ■ Gull Area Lakes Association (GALA)
Box 102
Nisswa, MN 56468
Ph: (218)963-2229
E-mail: cathy@gala.org
URL: http://www.gala.org
Contact: Cathy Taylor, Exec.Sec.-Treas.
Founded: 1971. **Members:** 650. **Membership Dues:** regular, $25 (annual). **Staff:** 1. **Local.** Maintains and improves water quality and safety in Gull Lake area. **Formerly:** Gull Lake Area Property Owners Association. **Publications:** Newsletter, quarterly. **Conventions/Meetings:** annual meeting - always July in East Gull Lake, MN.

11898 ■ Nisswa Chamber of Commerce (NCC)
25532 Main St.
PO Box 185
Nisswa, MN 56468
Ph: (218)963-2620
Fax: (218)963-1420
Free: (800)950-9610
E-mail: requests@nisswa.com
URL: http://www.nisswa.com
Contact: Susan Mezzenga, Exec.Dir.
Founded: 1946. **Members:** 160. **Staff:** 3. **Budget:** $50,000. **Local.** Promotes business and community development in Nisswa, MN. Sponsors arts and crafts festival. **Awards:** Nisswa Citizen of the Year Award. **Frequency:** annual. **Type:** recognition. **Publications:** *Nisswa Newspaper*, annual • Newsletter, monthly • Membership Directory, annual. **Price:** free for members.

North Branch

11899 ■ American Legion, North Branch Post 85
PO Box 87
North Branch, MN 55056
Ph: (651)291-1800
Fax: (651)291-1057
URL: National Affiliate–www.legion.org
Local. Affiliated With: American Legion.

11900 ■ North Branch Area Chamber of Commerce
PO Box 577
6372 Main St.
North Branch, MN 55056
Ph: (651)674-4077
Fax: (651)674-2600
E-mail: nbchamber@sherbtel.net
URL: http://www.northbranchchamber.com
Contact: Kathy Lindo, Coor.
Founded: 1990. **Members:** 250. **Staff:** 3. **Local.** Promotes local business and organizations. Activities include networking opportunities, publication, community celebrations and festivals. **Conventions/Meetings:** annual Community Connection - meeting (exhibits); Avg. Attendance: 1000.

11901 ■ North Branch Lions Club
PO Box 172
North Branch, MN 55056
Ph: (651)674-0168
E-mail: mankidd1@nsatel.net
URL: http://northbranchmn.lionwap.org
Contact: David Danielson, Pres.
Local. Affiliated With: Lions Clubs International.

North Mankato

11902 ■ American Legion, North Mankato Post 518
PO Box 2233
North Mankato, MN 56002
Ph: (651)291-1800
Fax: (651)291-1057
URL: National Affiliate–www.legion.org
Local. Affiliated With: American Legion.

11903 ■ International Association of Machinists and Aerospace Workers, AFL-CIO, CLC - Local Lodge 924
836 Lyndale St.
North Mankato, MN 56003
Fax: (507)243-4548
E-mail: iam924@hickorytech.net
URL: http://ll924.goiam.org/
Contact: Dennis Partika, Pres.
Members: 198. **Local. Affiliated With:** International Association of Machinists and Aerospace Workers.

11904 ■ Loyola Booster Club
c/o Daniel C. Rotchadl
1901 Lee Blvd.
North Mankato, MN 56003-2506
Ph: (507)387-1107
Fax: (507)387-1068
Contact: Daniel C. Rotchadl, Pres.
Founded: 2001. **Local.** Provides support for extracurricular activites.

11905 ■ Minnesota Pork Producers Association
c/o David Preisler, Exec.Dir.
360 Pierce Ave., Ste.106
North Mankato, MN 56003
Ph: (507)345-8814
Fax: (507)345-8681
E-mail: porkmn@hickorytech.net
URL: http://www.mnpork.com
State.

11906 ■ Minnesota Soybean Growers Association (MSGA)
c/o Jim Palmer, Exec.Dir.
360 Pierce Ave., Ste.110
North Mankato, MN 56003
Ph: (507)388-1635
Free: (888)896-9678
URL: http://www.mnsoybean.org/MSGA/Index.cfm
Contact: Jim Palmer, Exec.Dir.
Founded: 1963. **Members:** 3,580. **Membership Dues:** regular, $90 (annual) • regular, $250 (triennial). **Staff:** 7. **State.** Soybean farmers and persons in the agricultural business. Promotes the industry in the best interests of soybean producers. Informs and educates soybean growers on important issues facing the industry. **Affiliated With:** American Soybean Association. **Publications:** Newsletter, monthly. **Conventions/Meetings:** annual meeting.

11907 ■ Phi Theta Kappa, Beta Mu Eta Chapter - South Central Technical College
c/o Gail Burgess
1920 Lee Blvd.
North Mankato, MN 56003
Ph: (507)389-7200
E-mail: gailb@sctc.mnscu.edu
URL: http://www.ptk.org/directories/chapters/MN/21521-1.htm
Contact: Gail Burgess, Advisor
Local.

11908 ■ Riverbend Striders Volksmarch Club
c/o Earl Von Holt
1709 Linda Ln.
North Mankato, MN 56003-1938
Ph: (507)625-5375
E-mail: eavonholt@charter.net
Contact: Earl Von Holt, Contact
Founded: 1983. **Members:** 8. **Membership Dues:** individual, $7 (annual) • family, $10 (annual). **State Groups:** 1. **Local.** Non-competitive sports

enthusiasts. Usually 10k walks, biking and swimming. **Affiliated With:** American Volkssport Association. **Publications:** *The American Wanderer*, bimonthly. Newspaper. Publication of the American Volkssport Association. **Conventions/Meetings:** quarterly meeting.

North St. Paul

11909 ■ American Legion, Minnesota Post 39
c/o Melvin Daskam
2678 7th Ave. E
North St. Paul, MN 55109
Ph: (651)291-1800
Fax: (651)291-1057
URL: National Affiliate–www.legion.org
Contact: Melvin Daskam, Contact
Local. Affiliated With: American Legion.

Northfield

11910 ■ American Choral Directors Association - Minnesota Chapter
c/o Wayne Kivell, Exec.Sec.
1003 Maple St.
Northfield, MN 55057
E-mail: execu-sec@acda-mn.org
URL: http://www.acda-mn.org
Contact: Mary Kay Getson, Pres.
Members: 800. **Membership Dues:** active, $75 (annual) • student, $30 (annual) • life, $2,000 • retired, $25 (annual) • industry, $125 (annual) • institutional, $100 (annual) • associate, $65 (annual). **State**. Promotes the understanding of choral music as an important medium of contemporary artistic impression. Fosters the organization and development of choral societies in cities and communities. Disseminates professional news and information on choral music. **Awards:** F. Melius Christiansen Lifetime Achievement Award. **Frequency:** annual. **Type:** recognition. **Recipient:** for outstanding contribution and distinguished service to ICDA • Minnesota Choral Director of the Year. **Frequency:** annual. **Type:** recognition. **Recipient:** for establishing high performance and literature standards in choral music • Outstanding Young Choral Director of the Year. **Frequency:** annual. **Type:** recognition. **Recipient:** for establishing high performance and literature standards in choral music. **Computer Services:** Mailing lists, of members • online services, discussion forum. **Subgroups:** Repertoire and Standards. **Affiliated With:** American Choral Directors Association. **Publications:** *The Star of the North*, quarterly. Newsletter. **Advertising:** accepted. **Conventions/Meetings:** annual convention, with student symposium • annual Men's and Women's Choir - festival.

11911 ■ American Legion, Northfield Post 84
1055 Hwy. 3 N
Northfield, MN 55057
Ph: (651)291-1800
Fax: (651)291-1057
URL: National Affiliate–www.legion.org
Local. Affiliated With: American Legion.

11912 ■ Association for Computing Machinery, Carleton College
c/o Amy Csizmar Dalal, Sponsor
300 N Coll. St.
Dept. of Math and Comp. Sci.
Northfield, MN 55057
Ph: (507)646-5632
Fax: (507)646-4312
E-mail: adalal@carleton.edu
URL: National Affiliate–www.acm.org
Contact: Samuel Patterson, Chair
Local. Biological, medical, behavioral, and computer scientists; hospital administrators; programmers and others interested in application of computer methods to biological, behavioral, and medical problems. Stimulates understanding of the use and potential of computers in the Biosciences. **Affiliated With:** Association for Computing Machinery.

11913 ■ Classical Association of the Middle West and South (CAMWS)
St. Olaf Coll.
Dept. of Classics
1520 St. Olaf Ave.
Northfield, MN 55057-1098
Ph: (507)646-3238
Fax: (507)646-3732
E-mail: newlands@stolaf.edu
URL: http://www.camws.org
Contact: Anne H. Groton, Sec.-Treas.
Regional. Represents university, college, secondary and elementary teachers of Latin, Greek and all other studies which focus on the world of classical antiquity. Supports and promotes the study of classical languages.

11914 ■ Girl Scout Council of Cannon Valley
PO Box 61
Northfield, MN 55057
Ph: (507)645-6603
Free: (800)344-4757
E-mail: secretary@gsccv.org
URL: http://www.gsccv.org
Local. Young girls and adult volunteers, corporate, government and individual supporters. Strives to develop potential and leadership skills among its members. Conducts trainings, educational programs and outdoor activities.

11915 ■ NAFSA: Association of International Educators, Region IV
c/o Petra E. Crosby, Chair
Carleton Coll.
1 N Coll. St.
Northfield, MN 55057
Ph: (507)646-5937
Fax: (507)646-7551
E-mail: pcrosby@acs.carleton.edu
URL: http://www.region4.nafsa.org
Contact: Petra E. Crosby, Chair
Regional. Advocates for increased awareness and support of international education and exchange on campuses, in government and in communities. Provides training, professional development and networking opportunities to individuals in the field of international education. **Affiliated With:** NAFSA/ Association of International Educators.

11916 ■ Northfield Area Chamber of Commerce
205 3rd St. W, Ste.A
PO Box 198
Northfield, MN 55057-0198
Ph: (507)645-5604
Fax: (507)663-7782
Free: (800)658-2548
E-mail: info@northfieldchamber.com
URL: http://www.northfieldchamber.com
Contact: Kathy Feldbrugge, Exec.Dir.
Membership Dues: general, $275-$3,000 (annual) • retiree, $100 (annual). **Staff:** 3. **Local**. Promotes business and community development in the Northfield, MN area. **Awards:** Business of the Year. **Frequency:** annual. **Type:** recognition. **Recipient:** for outstanding contribution to the community • Business Person of the Year. **Frequency:** annual. **Type:** recognition. **Recipient:** for outstanding contribution to the community. **Computer Services:** database, membership directory • information services, facts about the local community. **Boards:** Convention and Visitors Bureau Advisory. **Committees:** Ambassador; Creative Professionals; Economic Development Forum; Government Affairs; Leadership; Retail. **Task Forces:** Business Education/Training; Marketing. **Publications:** Newsletter, monthly.

11917 ■ Northfield Area United Way
PO Box 56
Northfield, MN 55057-0056
Ph: (507)664-3510
URL: National Affiliate–national.unitedway.org
Local. Affiliated With: United Way of America.

11918 ■ PFLAG Northfield
1208 Nevada St.
Northfield, MN 55057
Ph: (507)645-4609
URL: http://www.pflag.org/Minnesota.217.0.html
Local. Affiliated With: Parents, Families, and Friends of Lesbians and Gays.

11919 ■ Psi Chi, National Honor Society in Psychology - St. Olaf College
c/o Dept. of Psychology
309 Holland Hall
1520 St. Olaf Ave.
Northfield, MN 55057-1098
Ph: (507)646-3142 (507)646-3147
Fax: (507)646-3774
E-mail: dickinss@stolaf.edu
URL: http://www.psichi.org/chapters/info.asp?chapter_id=314
Contact: Shelly D. Dickinson PhD, Advisor
Local.

11920 ■ USA Weightlifting - Northfield
c/o Scott Sahli
1400 Divs. St.
Northfield, MN 55057
Ph: (507)663-0632 (952)440-4178
Fax: (952)645-3417
E-mail: scott_sahli@ufld.k12.mn.us
URL: National Affiliate–www.usaweightlifting.org
Contact: Scott Sahli, Contact
Local. Affiliated With: USA Weightlifting.

Northome

11921 ■ American Legion, Dahlgren-Ettestad Post 499
PO Box 51
Northome, MN 56661
Ph: (651)291-1800
Fax: (651)291-1057
URL: National Affiliate–www.legion.org
Local. Affiliated With: American Legion.

Northrop

11922 ■ American Legion, Schwieger Kahler Post 522
PO Box 32
Northrop, MN 56075
Ph: (651)291-1800
Fax: (651)291-1057
URL: National Affiliate–www.legion.org
Local. Affiliated With: American Legion.

Norwood

11923 ■ American Legion, Edward Born Post 343
PO Box 343
Norwood, MN 55368
Ph: (651)291-1800
Fax: (651)291-1057
URL: National Affiliate–www.legion.org
Local. Affiliated With: American Legion.

Norwood Young America

11924 ■ Carver County Chapter, American Red Cross
315 W. Elm.
Box 686
Norwood Young America, MN 55368

Ph: (952)467-4449
Fax: (952)467-4448
E-mail: carverco@crossnet.org
URL: National Affiliate–www.redcross.org
Contact: Lavonne Kroells, Chapter Exec.
Founded: 1917. **Members:** 500. **Staff:** 1. **Local**. Serves members of the armed forces, veterans, and their families and aids disaster victims. Other activities include: blood services; community services; service opportunities for youth. **Affiliated With:** American Red Cross National Headquarters.

Oakdale

11925 ■ 3M Trap and Skeet Club
848 Henslow Ave. N
Oakdale, MN 55128
Ph: (651)459-8240
E-mail: rcraths@isd.net
URL: National Affiliate–www.mynssa.com
Local. Affiliated With: National Skeet Shooting Association.

11926 ■ Autonomy Party
c/o Andrew Bushard
6282 12th St. N, Apt. 105
Oakdale, MN 55128
Ph: (507)385-0470
E-mail: autonomy_party@wowmail.com
URL: http://www.freewebs.com/autonomyparty
Contact: Andrew Bushard, Ldr.
Local. Promotes a third political party.

11927 ■ Maplewood Figure Skating Club (MFSC)
6192 49th St. N
Oakdale, MN 55128
E-mail: mligday@aol.com
URL: http://www.mfscskate.org
Contact: Mike Ligday, Contact
Local. Provides programs to encourage participation and achievement in the sport of figure skating on ice. Defines and maintains uniform standards of skating proficiency. Organizes and sponsors competitions and exhibitions for the purpose of stimulating interest in figure skating. **Affiliated With:** United States Figure Skating Association.

11928 ■ Maplewood-Oakdale Lions Club
PO Box 28366
Oakdale, MN 55128
E-mail: maplewoodoakdalelions@comcast.net
URL: http://home.comcast.net/~maplewoodoakdalelions
Contact: Greg Lennartson, Pres.
Local. Affiliated With: Lions Clubs International.

11929 ■ Skills USA, Tartan High School
828 Greenway Ave.
Oakdale, MN 55128
Ph: (651)702-8683
Fax: (651)702-8691
E-mail: jaydt@era.k12.mn.us
URL: http://www.mnskillsusa.org
Contact: Jim Aydt, Contact
Local. Serves high school and college students enrolled in technical, skilled, and service and health occupations. Provides quality education experiences for students in leadership, teamwork, citizenship and character development. Builds and reinforces self-confidence, work attitudes and communication skills. Emphasizes total quality at work, high ethical standards, superior work skills, and life-long education. Promotes understanding of the free enterprise system and involvement in community service. **Affiliated With:** Skills USA - VICA.

Odessa

11930 ■ American Legion, Odessa Post 520
117 Bloomington Ave. N
Odessa, MN 56276
Ph: (651)291-1800
Fax: (651)291-1057
URL: National Affiliate–www.legion.org
Local. Affiliated With: American Legion.

Ogema

11931 ■ American Legion, White Earth Indian Nation Post 625
PO Box 13
Ogema, MN 56569
Ph: (651)291-1800
Fax: (651)291-1057
URL: National Affiliate–www.legion.org
Local. Affiliated With: American Legion.

Ogilvie

11932 ■ American Legion, Ogilvie Post 640
PO Box 215
Ogilvie, MN 56358
Ph: (651)291-1800
Fax: (651)291-1057
URL: National Affiliate–www.legion.org
Local. Affiliated With: American Legion.

Okabena

11933 ■ American Legion, Sievert-Peterson Post 608
PO Box 73
Okabena, MN 56161
Ph: (651)291-1800
Fax: (651)291-1057
URL: National Affiliate–www.legion.org
Local. Affiliated With: American Legion.

Oklee

11934 ■ American Legion, Frank Lund Post 159
PO Box 85
Oklee, MN 56742
Ph: (651)291-1800
Fax: (651)291-1057
URL: National Affiliate–www.legion.org
Local. Affiliated With: American Legion.

Olivia

11935 ■ American Legion, Erickson-Strom Post 186
2450 W Lincoln Ave.
Olivia, MN 56277
Ph: (651)291-1800
Fax: (651)291-1057
URL: National Affiliate–www.legion.org
Local. Affiliated With: American Legion.

11936 ■ Olivia Area Chamber of Commerce (OACC)
PO Box 37
Olivia, MN 56277-0037
Ph: (320)523-1350
Fax: (320)523-1827
Free: (888)265-CORN
E-mail: oliviachamber@tds.net
URL: http://www.olivia.mn.us
Contact: Libby Revier, Exec.Dir.
Local. Works to create, promote and enhance a healthy business environment and image of the Olivia area. **Computer Services:** database, list of members. **Publications:** *Chamber Update*, monthly. Newsletter.

11937 ■ Olivia Lions Club
c/o Charles Hunt, Pres.
PO Box 58
Olivia, MN 56277
Ph: (320)523-2666
E-mail: chunt2@mchsi.com
URL: http://5m4lions.org/olivialions
Contact: Charles Hunt, Pres.
Local. Affiliated With: Lions Clubs International.

11938 ■ Renville/Redwood Chapter, American Red Cross
2510 W Lincoln
Olivia, MN 56277
Ph: (320)523-1342 (320)522-0690
E-mail: rcarc@redred.com
Contact: Barb Billmeier, Chapter Mgr.
Founded: 1917. **Local**. Serves members of the armed forces and their families and aids disaster victims in Renville and Redwood Counties. Other activities include: blood services; community services; and service opportunities for youth. **Affiliated With:** American Red Cross National Headquarters. **Publications:** Newsletter, annual.

Onamia

11939 ■ American Legion, Prudent Van Risseghem Post 395
38692 US Hwy. 169
Onamia, MN 56359
Ph: (320)532-3134
Fax: (651)291-1057
URL: National Affiliate–www.legion.org
Local. Affiliated With: American Legion.

11940 ■ Red Bull Historic Military Vehicle Association
c/o John A. Varner, Pres./Newsletter Ed.
32342 125th Ave.
Onamia, MN 56359
Ph: (320)532-9009
E-mail: jvarner@onamia.k12.mn.us
URL: National Affiliate–www.mvpa.org
Contact: John A. Varner, Pres./Newsletter Ed.
Local. Affiliated With: Military Vehicle Preservation Association.

Orr

11941 ■ American Bear Association - Minnesota
c/o Klari Lea, Pres.
PO Box 77
Orr, MN 55771
Ph: (218)757-0172
E-mail: bears@rangenet.com
URL: http://www.americanbear.org
Regional.

11942 ■ American Legion, Orr Post 480
4543 Hwy. 53
Orr, MN 55771
Ph: (651)291-1800
Fax: (651)291-1057
URL: National Affiliate–www.legion.org
Local. Affiliated With: American Legion.

11943 ■ Orr Lions Club
c/o Jeremy Scofield, Pres.
PO Box 61
Orr, MN 55771-0061
Ph: (218)757-3408
URL: http://lions5m10.org
Contact: Jeremy Scofield, Pres.
Local. Affiliated With: Lions Clubs International.

Ortonville

11944 ■ American Legion, Spink-Dobak Post 97
547 Minnesota St. N
Ortonville, MN 56278
Ph: (651)291-1800
Fax: (651)291-1057
URL: National Affiliate–www.legion.org
Local. Affiliated With: American Legion.

11945 ■ Big Stone Lake Area Chamber of Commerce (BSLACC)
987 U.S. Hwy. 12
Ortonville, MN 56278
Ph: (320)839-3284
Fax: (320)839-2621
Free: (800)568-5722
E-mail: chamber@bigstonelake.com
URL: http://www.bigstonelake.com

Membership Dues: retail, lodging, restaurant (minimum; plus fee for FTE employees), $137 (annual). **Local**. Promotes tourism and economic development in the Big Stone Lake Area. **Formerly:** (1999) Ortonville Area Chamber of Commerce. **Conventions/ Meetings:** biweekly board meeting - always second and fourth Thursday.

11946 ■ Ortonville Lions Club
c/o Orlou Mittlestaedt, Sec.
51 McCloud St.
Ortonville, MN 56278
Ph: (320)839-4238 (320)839-3284
E-mail: orlou@wat.midco.net
URL: http://www.5m4lions.org
Contact: Orlou Mittlestaedt, Sec.

Local. **Affiliated With:** Lions Clubs International.

11947 ■ RSVP Volunteers United
c/o Karin Mack, Dir.
127 NW 2nd St.
Ortonville, MN 56278-1408
Ph: (320)839-2111
Fax: (320)839-2373
E-mail: rsvpvu@maxminn.com
URL: http://www.bigstonecounty.org/RetiredSeniorVolunteerProgram.html
Contact: Karin Mack, Dir.

Local. **Affiliated With:** Retired and Senior Volunteer Program.

Osakis

11948 ■ American Legion, Minnesota Post 111
c/o Franklin J. Lyons
PO Box 517
Osakis, MN 56360
Ph: (651)291-1800
Fax: (651)291-1057
URL: National Affiliate–www.legion.org
Contact: Franklin J. Lyons, Contact

Local. **Affiliated With:** American Legion.

11949 ■ Osakis Lions Club
c/o Richard Hoff, Sec.
PO Box 236
Osakis, MN 56360
Ph: (320)859-4663
E-mail: rnhoff@midwestinfo.net
URL: http://www.5m4lions.org
Contact: Richard Hoff, Sec.

Local. **Affiliated With:** Lions Clubs International.

Oslo

11950 ■ American Legion, Minnesota Post 331
c/o Rita Havis
309 Main St.
Oslo, MN 56744
Ph: (651)291-1800
Fax: (651)291-1057
URL: National Affiliate–www.legion.org
Contact: Rita Havis, Contact

Local. **Affiliated With:** American Legion.

11951 ■ Oslo Lions Club
PO Box 151
Oslo, MN 56744
Ph: (218)965-4887 (218)965-4655
URL: http://lions5m11.org/sys-tmpl/door
Contact: Dave Lind, Pres.

Local. **Affiliated With:** Lions Clubs International.

Osseo

11952 ■ American Legion, Rudolph Priebe Post 172
260 4th Ave. SE
Osseo, MN 55369
Ph: (651)291-1800
Fax: (651)291-1057
URL: National Affiliate–www.legion.org

Local. **Affiliated With:** American Legion.

11953 ■ North Hennepin Area Chamber of Commerce
229 1st Ave. NE
Osseo, MN 55369-1201
Ph: (763)424-6744
Fax: (763)424-6927
E-mail: info@nhachamber.com
URL: http://www.nhachamber.com
Contact: David Looby, Pres./CEO

Local. Serves members and their communities through identification and advocacy of business issues and the promotion of economic, civic, and educational interests. **Awards:** Career Change Scholarship. **Type:** monetary • Student Scholarship. **Type:** monetary. **Committees:** Ambassador; Business Education Partnership; Government Affairs; Wide Open Golf Tournament; Winter Gala/Silent Auction. **Subgroups:** Chamber Networking. **Affiliated With:** American Chamber of Commerce Executives; Better Business Bureau; Minneapolis Metro North Convention and Visitors Bureau; Minnesota State Chamber of Commerce; U.S. Chamber of Commerce. **Publications:** Newsletter, monthly.

Ostrander

11954 ■ American Legion, Hanson-Hatlestad Post 544
PO Box 182
Ostrander, MN 55961
Ph: (651)291-1800
Fax: (651)291-1057
URL: National Affiliate–www.legion.org

Local. **Affiliated With:** American Legion.

11955 ■ Ostrander Lions Club
c/o Margaret Wierson, Sec.
RR 1, Box 43A
Ostrander, MN 55961
Ph: (507)657-2384
E-mail: mjpenny@acegroup.cc
URL: http://www.lions5m1.org/ostrander
Contact: Margaret Wierson, Sec.

Local. **Affiliated With:** Lions Clubs International.

Owatonna

11956 ■ American Legion, Minnesota Post 77
c/o Wallace S. Chute
137 W Broadway St.
Owatonna, MN 55060
Ph: (651)291-1800
Fax: (651)291-1057
URL: National Affiliate–www.legion.org
Contact: Wallace S. Chute, Contact

Local. **Affiliated With:** American Legion.

11957 ■ American Red Cross, Steele County Chapter
302 N Cedar
Owatonna, MN 55060
Ph: (507)451-2777
Fax: (507)444-9155
E-mail: steelarc@ic.owatonna.mn.us
URL: http://steelecounty.redcross.org

Local.

11958 ■ APICS, The Association for Operations Management - Southern Minnesota Chapter
Box 122
Owatonna, MN 55060
Ph: (507)253-5693
E-mail: sorochab@us.ibm.com
URL: http://www.apicssomn.org
Contact: Barb Sorochak, Pres.

Local. Provides information and services in production and inventory management and related areas to enable members, enterprises and individuals to add value to their business performance. **Affiliated With:** APICS - The Association for Operations Management.

11959 ■ Minnesota Nurses Association - District 13
803 20th St. NE
Owatonna, MN 55060
Ph: (507)451-0371
E-mail: bribusho@mnic.net
URL: http://www.mnnurses.org
Contact: Stephanie Busho, Sec.

Local. Works to advance the nursing profession. Seeks to meet the needs of nurses and health care consumers. Fosters high standards of nursing practice. Promotes the economic and general welfare of nurses in the workplace. **Affiliated With:** American Nurses Association; Minnesota Nurses Association.

11960 ■ Minnesota-South Dakota Equipment Dealers Association
121 E Park Sq.
Owatonna, MN 55060
Ph: (507)455-5318
Fax: (507)455-5909
E-mail: office@msdeda.com
URL: http://www.msdeda.com
Contact: Richard Strom, Exec.VP

Regional. Retail farm, industrial and outdoor power equipment dealers. **Formerly:** (2006) Farm Equipment Association of Minnesota and South Dakota.

11961 ■ National Active and Retired Federal Employees Association - Owatonna 1975
2030 N E 3rd Ave.
Owatonna, MN 55060-1329
Ph: (507)451-0856
URL: National Affiliate–www.narfe.org
Contact: Ben G. Hiniker, Contact

Local. Protects the retirement future of employees through education. Informs members on issues affecting the retirement. **Affiliated With:** National Association of Retired Federal Employees.

11962 ■ Owatonna Area Chamber of Commerce and Tourism (OACCT)
320 Hoffman Dr.
Owatonna, MN 55060
Ph: (507)451-7970
Fax: (507)451-7972
Free: (800)423-6466
E-mail: oacct@owatonna.org
URL: http://www.owatonna.org
Contact: Brad Meier, Pres./CEO

Founded: 1924. **Members:** 480. **Staff:** 7. **Budget:** $230,000. **Local**. Seeks to be the leading partner of the regional center, dedicated to the continuance of its economic prosperity while maintaining community values and pride. Activities include membership, legislative advocacy, communications, information brokering, leadership development, facilitation, networking, cooperative marketing, economic development and tourism promotion. **Committees:** Ambassadors; Economic Development; Mainstreet Owatonna; Marketing; Public Policy; Tourism. **Affiliated With:** U.S. Chamber of Commerce. **Formerly:** (1999) Owatonna Area Chamber of Commerce. **Publications:** *Business Brief*, monthly. Newsletter. Contains information regarding membership, tourism, economic development, and OACCT happenings. **Advertising:** accepted. Alternate Formats: online • *Chamber Reporter*, monthly. Newsletter. **Conventions/Meetings:** monthly Business After Hours - meeting - 4th Tuesday • monthly Good Morning Owatonna - meeting - 2nd Wednesday.

11963 ■ Owatonna Arts Center
c/o Silvan Durban
PO Box 134
Owatonna, MN 55060
Ph: (507)451-0533
Fax: (507)451-4601
URL: http://www.owatonnaartscenter.org
Contact: Silvan Durban, Dir.
Local. Formerly: (2005) Owatonna Arts Council.

11964 ■ Owatonna Business Incubator
1065 SW 24th Ave.
PO Box 505
Owatonna, MN 55060
Ph: (507)451-0517
Fax: (507)455-2788
E-mail: obi@owatonnaincubator.com
URL: http://www.owatonnaincubator.com
Founded: 1988. **Staff:** 2. **Local.** Seeks to promote initial small business growth, create jobs, and foster an environment conducive to entrepreneurial business success within the Owatonna area. Conducts business-related seminars. **Formerly:** (2000) Owatonna Incubator. **Publications:** Newsletter, quarterly.

11965 ■ Owatonna Figure Skating Club
PO Box 733
Owatonna, MN 55060
E-mail: mllaramee@juno.com
URL: http://www.owatonnafsc.org
Local. Provides programs to encourage participation and achievement in the sport of figure skating on ice. Defines and maintains uniform standards of skating proficiency. Organizes and sponsors competitions and exhibitions for the purpose of stimulating interest in figure skating. **Affiliated With:** United States Figure Skating Association.

11966 ■ Owatonna Wyldlife
202 1/2 N Cedar
Owatonna, MN 55060
Ph: (507)451-9401
URL: http://sites.younglife.org/sites/OwatonnaWL/default.aspx
Local. Affiliated With: Young Life.

11967 ■ Owatonna Young Life
202 1/2 N Cedar
Owatonna, MN 55060
Ph: (507)451-9401
URL: http://sites.younglife.org/sites/OwatonnaYL/default.aspx
Local. Affiliated With: Young Life.

11968 ■ Skills USA, Owatonna High School
333 E School St.
Owatonna, MN 55060
Ph: (507)359-1957
E-mail: jmiller@owatonna.k12.mn.us
URL: http://www.mnskillsusa.org
Contact: Jeff Miller, Contact
Local. Serves high school and college students enrolled in technical, skilled, and service and health occupations. Provides quality education experiences for students in leadership, teamwork, citizenship and character development. Builds and reinforces self-confidence, work attitudes and communication skills. Emphasizes total quality at work, high ethical standards, superior work skills, and life-long education. Promotes understanding of the free enterprise system and involvement in community service. **Affiliated With:** Skills USA - VICA.

11969 ■ Southern Minnesota Hunting Retriever Association (SMHRA)
c/o Mike Kingland, Sec.-Treas.
8431 County Rd. 45 S
Owatonna, MN 55060
Ph: (507)455-9661
E-mail: mksk1993@bevcomm.net
URL: http://www.geocities.com/Heartland/Plains/2998
Contact: Dan Drugg, Pres.
Local.

11970 ■ Steele County Astronomical Society
809 Robinswood Pl. NE
Owatonna, MN 55060
Ph: (507)451-2239
E-mail: ntryhus@charter.net
URL: http://minnesotasky.tripod.com
Contact: Neil Tryhus, Contact
Local. Promotes the science of astronomy. Works to encourage and coordinate activities of amateur astronomical societies. Fosters observational and computational work and craftsmanship in various fields of astronomy. **Affiliated With:** Astronomical League.

11971 ■ Tri County AIFA
c/o Paul Proft, Sec.
660 W Bridge St., Ste.200
Owatonna, MN 55060
Fax: (507)455-1160
Free: (800)592-7322
E-mail: paul_proft@thrivent.com
URL: National Affiliate–naifa.org
Contact: Paul Proft, Sec.
Local. Represents the interests of insurance and financial advisors. Advocates for a positive legislative and regulatory environment. Enhances business and professional skills of members. **Affiliated With:** National Association of Insurance and Financial Advisors.

11972 ■ United Way of Steele County
PO Box 32
Owatonna, MN 55060-0032
Ph: (507)455-1180
Fax: (507)444-0718
E-mail: unitedway@unitedwaysteelecounty.org
URL: http://unitedwaysteelecounty.org
Contact: Evelina Giobbe, Exec.Dir.
Local. Affiliated With: United Way of America.

11973 ■ Young Life Owatonna
202 1/2 N Cedar
Owatonna, MN 55060
Ph: (507)451-9401
Fax: (507)444-6236
URL: http://sites.younglife.org/sites/Owatonna/default.aspx
Local. Affiliated With: Young Life.

Park Rapids

11974 ■ American Association of Healthcare Administrative Management, Gopher Chapter
c/o Eileen Froelich, CPAM, Pres.
St. Joseph's Area Hea. Services
600 Pleasant Ave.
Park Rapids, MN 56470
Ph: (218)237-5504
Fax: (218)237-5585
E-mail: eileenfroelich@catholichealth.net
URL: National Affiliate–www.aaham.org
Contact: Eileen Froelich CPAM, Pres.
Local. Represents the interests of healthcare administrative management professionals. Seeks proper recognition for the financial aspect of hospital and clinic management. Provides member services and leadership in the areas of education, communication, representation, professional standards and certification. **Affiliated With:** American Association of Healthcare Administrative Management.

11975 ■ American Ex-Prisoners of War, Lakes Region Chapter
c/o Glenys Hotzler
400 Washington Ave.
Park Rapids, MN 56470
Ph: (218)732-4398
URL: National Affiliate–www.axpow.org
Regional. Affiliated With: American Ex-Prisoners of War.

11976 ■ American Legion, Otto Hendrickson Post 212
900 1st St. E
Park Rapids, MN 56470
Ph: (651)291-1800
Fax: (651)291-1057
URL: National Affiliate–www.legion.org
Local. Affiliated With: American Legion.

11977 ■ Mid-Western Health Care Engineering Association (MWHCEA)
c/o James M. Limmer, Pres.
600 Pleasant Ave. S
Park Rapids, MN 56470-1432
Ph: (218)732-3311
Fax: (218)732-1368
URL: National Affiliate–www.ashe.org
Contact: James M. Limmer, Pres.
Regional. Promotes better patient care by encouraging members to develop their knowledge and increase their competence in the field of facilities management. Cooperates with hospitals and allied associations in matters pertaining to facilities management. **Affiliated With:** American Society for Healthcare Engineering of the American Hospital Association.

11978 ■ Park Rapids Area Chamber of Commerce (PRACC)
1204 S Park, Hwy. 71 S
PO Box 249
Park Rapids, MN 56470-0249
Ph: (218)732-4111
Fax: (218)732-4112
Free: (800)247-0054
E-mail: chamber@parkrapids.com
URL: http://www.parkrapids.com
Contact: Katherine Magozzi, Exec.Dir.
Members: 375. **Membership Dues:** business (base), $270 (annual) • associate (outside Park Rapids), $135 (annual) • nonprofit, individual, $115 (annual) • retiree, $50 (annual) • owner-operated, $175 (annual). **Staff:** 5. **Local.** Promotes business and community development in the Park Rapids, MN area. **Computer Services:** Information services, facts about the community. **Committees:** Advertising/Marketing and Internet; Ambassadors; Economic Development; Legislative; Retail Development. **Task Forces:** Loon Capital. **Publications:** *Vacation Guide*. Directory. **Price:** free • Directory, annual.

11979 ■ PFLAG Park Rapids
16939 Dogwood Rd.
Park Rapids, MN 56470
Ph: (218)732-0954
E-mail: spitfire2322@yahoo.com
URL: http://www.pflag.org/Minnesota.217.0.html
Local. Affiliated With: Parents, Families, and Friends of Lesbians and Gays.

11980 ■ Sons of Norway, Nordskogen Lodge 1-626
c/o Paul T. Dove, Pres.
11700 Island Lake Dr.
Park Rapids, MN 56470-4638
Ph: (218)732-7096
E-mail: pd5@evansville.edu
URL: National Affiliate–www.sofn.com
Contact: Paul T. Dove, Pres.
Local. Affiliated With: Sons of Norway.

Parkers Prairie

11981 ■ Muskies Vikingland Chapter
609 S Otter Ave.
Parkers Prairie, MN 56361
Ph: (218)338-5441
E-mail: koepbait@midwestinfo.net
URL: National Affiliate–www.muskiesinc.org
Contact: Bruce Lamar, Pres.
Local.

Paynesville

11982 ■ American Legion, Minnesota Post 271
c/o Kenneth Lee Olson
PO Box 211
Paynesville, MN 56362
Ph: (651)291-1800
Fax: (651)291-1057
URL: National Affiliate–www.legion.org
Contact: Kenneth Lee Olson, Contact
Local. Affiliated With: American Legion.

11983 ■ Paynesville Area Chamber of Commerce (PACC)
PO Box 4
Paynesville, MN 56362-0004
Ph: (320)243-3233
Contact: Kay Spooner, Sec.
Members: 125. **Staff:** 1. **Local.** Promotes business and community development in the Paynesville, MN area.

Pel Rapids

11984 ■ American Legion, Cornell-Syverson Post 17
PO Box 209
Pel Rapids, MN 56572
Ph: (651)291-1800
Fax: (651)291-1057
URL: National Affiliate–www.legion.org
Local. Affiliated With: American Legion.

Pelican Rapids

11985 ■ Northern Lights Ballroom Dance Club
c/o Robyne Williams, Treas.
41820 Bagley Bay Ln.
Pelican Rapids, MN 56572
Ph: (218)863-3686
E-mail: robyne.williams@ndsu.nodak.edu
URL: http://northernlightsballroom.org
Contact: Robyne Williams, Treas.
Local. Encourages and promotes the physical, mental and social benefits of partner dancing. Organizes and supports programs for the recreational enjoyment of ballroom dancing. Creates opportunities for the general public to participate in ballroom dancing and DanceSport.

11986 ■ Pelican Rapids Area Chamber of Commerce (PRCC)
PO Box 206
Pelican Rapids, MN 56572-0206
Ph: (218)863-1221
Fax: (218)863-2662
Free: (800)545-3711
E-mail: tourism@loretel.net
URL: http://www.pelicanrapidschamber.com
Contact: Jane Aschnewitz, Exec.Dir.
Local. Promotes business and community development in Pelican Rapids, MN. **Computer Services:** Online services, member listings. **Formerly:** (2005) Pelican Rapids Chamber of Commerce. **Conventions/Meetings:** annual Octoberfest - festival • annual Pelican Rapids Turkey Festival - always in July.

11987 ■ Pelican Rapids CC Walking Club
c/o Joseph Hilber
PO Box 501
Pelican Rapids, MN 56572
Ph: (218)863-1075
E-mail: hilber@att.net
URL: National Affiliate–www.ava.org
Contact: Joseph Hilber, Contact
Local.

Pengilly

11988 ■ Sons of Norway, Midnatsolen Lodge 1-58
c/o Peggy R. Mattson, Sec.
29022 W Shore Ln.
Pengilly, MN 55775-2222
Ph: (218)885-2358
E-mail: cygnuslp@scicable.com
URL: National Affiliate–www.sofn.com
Contact: Peggy R. Mattson, Sec.
Local. Affiliated With: Sons of Norway.

Pennock

11989 ■ Pennock Lions Club
c/o Charles Diederich, Pres.
401 Dakota Ave. NW
Pennock, MN 56279
Ph: (320)599-4152 (320)599-4787
E-mail: cldied@tds.net
URL: http://www.5m4lions.org
Contact: Charles Diederich, Pres.
Local. Affiliated With: Lions Clubs International.

Pequot Lakes

11990 ■ American Legion, Ben Krueger Post 49
PO Box 238
Pequot Lakes, MN 56472
Ph: (651)291-1800
Fax: (651)291-1057
URL: National Affiliate–www.legion.org
Local. Affiliated With: American Legion.

Perham

11991 ■ American Legion, Burelbach Post 61
PO Box 223
Perham, MN 56573
Ph: (651)291-1800
Fax: (651)291-1057
URL: National Affiliate–www.legion.org
Local. Affiliated With: American Legion.

11992 ■ Fort Thunder PSC
43391 Ft. Thunder Rd.
Perham, MN 56573
Ph: (218)346-6083
URL: National Affiliate–www.mynssa.com
Local. Affiliated With: National Skeet Shooting Association.

11993 ■ Minnesota Dry Edible Bean Research and Promotion Council
c/o Mark Dombeck, Chm.
45898 County Rd. 60
Perham, MN 56573
Ph: (218)346-5952
E-mail: dombeckm@yahoo.com
URL: http://www.northarvestbean.org
Contact: Mark Dombeck, Chm.
Founded: 1979. **Members:** 1,000. **Budget:** $200,000. **State.** Dry bean farmers. Promotes the consumption of dry beans and develops growing beans and helps with disease problems. Offers informational services and networking. **Publications:** Magazine, bimonthly. **Conventions/Meetings:** board meeting - 4-6/year • annual convention - always January.

11994 ■ Perham Area Chamber of Commerce (PACC)
135 E Main St.
Perham, MN 56573
Ph: (218)346-7710
Fax: (218)346-7712
Free: (800)634-6112
E-mail: chamber@perham.com
URL: http://www.perham.com
Contact: Sue Huebsch, Pres.
Founded: 1985. **Local.** Promotes business and community development in the Perham, MN area. Sponsors festival. **Committees:** Agri-Business; Beautification; Legislative. **Publications:** Journal, periodic • Directory, periodic • Newsletter, monthly.

11995 ■ Plumbing-Heating-Cooling Contractors Association, Lakes Area
c/o Robin Hanson, Pres.
PO Box 301
Perham, MN 56573-0301
Ph: (218)346-3226
Fax: (218)346-2418
E-mail: rhanson@eot.com
URL: National Affiliate–www.phccweb.org
Contact: Robin Hanson, Pres.
Local. Represents the plumbing, heating and cooling contractors. Promotes the construction industry. Protects the environment, health, safety and comfort of society. **Affiliated With:** Plumbing-Heating-Cooling Contractors Association.

Peterson

11996 ■ American Legion, Gilbertson-Rude Post 526
PO Box 7
Peterson, MN 55962
Ph: (651)291-1800
Fax: (651)291-1057
URL: National Affiliate–www.legion.org
Local. Affiliated With: American Legion.

Pierz

11997 ■ American Legion, Rich Prairie Post 341
PO Box 371
Pierz, MN 56364
Ph: (651)291-1800
Fax: (651)291-1057
URL: National Affiliate–www.legion.org
Local. Affiliated With: American Legion.

11998 ■ Pierz Lions Club
PO Box 220
Pierz, MN 56364
Ph: (320)468-6451
E-mail: brebischke@horizonhealthservices.com
URL: http://www.lionwap.org/pierzlionsmn
Contact: Barb Rebischke, Pres.
Local. Affiliated With: Lions Clubs International.

Pillager

11999 ■ American Legion, Pillager Post 100
PO Box 86
Pillager, MN 56473
Ph: (651)291-1800
Fax: (651)291-1057
URL: National Affiliate–www.legion.org
Local. Affiliated With: American Legion.

12000 ■ Baxter Snowmobile Club
c/o John Laufersweiler
Rte. 2, Box 1500
Pillager, MN 56473-9548

Ph: (218)829-4155
URL: http://mnsnowmobiler.org
Local.

Pine City

12001 ■ American Legion, Heath-Perkins Post 51
525 Main St. N
Pine City, MN 55063
Ph: (651)291-1800
Fax: (651)291-1057
URL: National Affiliate–www.legion.org
Local. **Affiliated With:** American Legion.

12002 ■ Phi Theta Kappa, Beta Kappa Rho Chapter - Northwest Technical College
c/o Kathryn Krier
900 4th St. SE
Pine City, MN 55063
Ph: (320)629-4513
E-mail: krierk@pinetech.edu
URL: http://www.ptk.org/directories/chapters/MN/21462-1.htm
Contact: Kathryn Krier, Advisor
Local.

12003 ■ Pine City Area Chamber of Commerce
610 2nd Ave. SW
Pine City, MN 55063
Ph: (320)629-3861
Fax: (320)629-3861
E-mail: info@pinecitychamber.com
URL: http://www.pinecitychamber.com
Contact: Bonnie Garrett, Exec.Sec.
Staff: 1. **Local**.

Pine Island

12004 ■ American Legion, Minnesota Post 184
c/o Charles Cowden
PO Box 255
Pine Island, MN 55963
Ph: (651)291-1800
Fax: (651)291-1057
URL: National Affiliate–www.legion.org
Contact: Charles Cowden, Contact
Local. **Affiliated With:** American Legion.

12005 ■ Pine Island Lions Club
PO Box 458
Pine Island, MN 55963
Ph: (507)356-8975
E-mail: lionsinfo@pineislandlions.org
URL: http://www.pineislandlions.org
Contact: Wes Moreland, Pres.
Local. **Affiliated With:** Lions Clubs International.

Pine River

12006 ■ American Legion, Fraser-Nelson Post 613
PO Box 264
Pine River, MN 56474
Ph: (651)291-1800
Fax: (651)291-1057
URL: National Affiliate–www.legion.org
Local. **Affiliated With:** American Legion.

12007 ■ Christian Camp and Conference Association, Minn-E-Dakotas Section
c/o James Rock, Pres.
Trout Lake Camp
10173 Trout Lake Dr.
Pine River, MN 56474-2555
Ph: (218)543-4565
URL: http://minnedakotas.ccca-us.org
Contact: James Rock, Pres.
Regional. **Affiliated With:** Christian Camping International/U.S.A.

Pinewood

12008 ■ American Legion, Minnesota Post 438
c/o Harold Kolstad
24141 Debs Rd. NW
Pinewood, MN 56676
Ph: (651)291-1800
Fax: (651)291-1057
URL: National Affiliate–www.legion.org
Contact: Harold Kolstad, Contact
Local. **Affiliated With:** American Legion.

Pipestone

12009 ■ American Legion, Michael-Boock Post 6
PO Box 233
Pipestone, MN 56164
Ph: (651)291-1800
Fax: (507)825-1057
URL: National Affiliate–www.legion.org
Local. **Affiliated With:** American Legion.

12010 ■ Pipestone Area Chamber of Commerce (PACC)
117 8th Ave. SE
PO Box 8
Pipestone, MN 56164
Ph: (507)825-3316
Fax: (507)825-3317
E-mail: pipecham@pipestoneminnesota.com
URL: http://www.pipestoneminnesota.com
Contact: Mick Myers, Exec.Dir.
Founded: 1939. **Members:** 175. **Membership Dues:** regular, $145-$2,085 (annual) • individual/retired/farmer, $50 (annual). **Local**. Promotes business and community development in Pipestone County, MN. **Publications:** none. **Computer Services:** Online services, member directory. **Committees:** Ag; Ambassadors; Pipestone Planning; Rodeo; Watertower. **Affiliated With:** U.S. Chamber of Commerce. **Formerly:** (1999) Pipestone +Chamber of Commerce.

12011 ■ Pipestone County Historical Society
113 S. Hiawatha Ave.
Pipestone, MN 56164
Ph: (507)825-2563
Fax: (507)825-2563
Free: (866)747-3687
E-mail: pipctymu@rconnect.com
URL: http://www.pipestoneminnesota.com/museum
Contact: Susan Hoskins, Dir.
Founded: 1880. **Members:** 450. **Membership Dues:** adult, $15 (annual) • senior, $10 (annual) • family, $25 (annual) • student, $3 (annual) • life, $100 • patron, $250 • benefactor, life, $500. **Staff:** 4. **Local**. Seeks to discover, preserve, and disseminate knowledge about the history of Pipestone County. Maintains a history museum, one-room schoolhouse, materials and facilities, for both history and genealogy research. Provides programming for local and area schools, community groups, and other interested parties. **Libraries: Type:** reference; open to the public. **Subjects:** local and state history. **Publications:** *Couteau Journal*, periodic. Features local history topics, articles, photos, etc. **Price:** $5.00. **Circulation:** 2,500 • *The Prairie Traveler*, quarterly. Newsletter.

12012 ■ United Way - Pipestone, Ihlen, Woodstock, Holland, Ruthton
PO Box 35
Pipestone, MN 56164-0035
Ph: (507)825-6745
URL: National Affiliate–national.unitedway.org
Local. **Affiliated With:** United Way of America.

Plainview

12013 ■ American Legion, William Allen Post 179
215 3rd St. SW
Plainview, MN 55964
Ph: (651)291-1800
Fax: (651)291-1057
URL: National Affiliate–www.legion.org
Local. **Affiliated With:** American Legion.

12014 ■ Plainview Lions Club
PO Box 504
Plainview, MN 55964
Ph: (507)534-2578
E-mail: dennyranta@hotmail.com
URL: http://www.plainviewlions.org
Contact: Denny Ranta, Pres.
Local. **Affiliated With:** Lions Clubs International.

12015 ■ Southeast Minnesota Agriculture Alliance
c/o Bill Rowekamp, VP
PO Box 533
Plainview, MN 55964
Ph: (507)534-1313
E-mail: agalliancesemn@earthlink.net
URL: http://www.semnagalliance.org
Contact: Bill Rowekamp, VP
Local.

Plato

12016 ■ American Legion, Plato Post 641
PO Box 164
Plato, MN 55370
Ph: (651)291-1800
Fax: (651)291-1057
URL: National Affiliate–www.legion.org
Local. **Affiliated With:** American Legion.

Plummer

12017 ■ American Legion, Plummer Post 623
PO Box 4
Plummer, MN 56748
Ph: (651)291-1800
Fax: (651)291-1057
URL: National Affiliate–www.legion.org
Local. **Affiliated With:** American Legion.

12018 ■ Plummer Lions Club
c/o Jim Duchamp, Pres.
PO Box 14
Plummer, MN 56748
Ph: (218)465-4239
URL: http://lions5m11.org/sys-tmpl/door
Contact: Jim Duchamp, Pres.
Local. **Affiliated With:** Lions Clubs International.

12019 ■ Plummers Lions Too Club
c/o Lynn Gallant, Pres.
PO Box 164
Plummer, MN 56748
Ph: (218)465-4373
Free: (800)279-2281
E-mail: lgallant@articcatinc.com
URL: http://lions5m11.org/sys-tmpl/door
Contact: Lynn Gallant, Pres.
Local. **Affiliated With:** Lions Clubs International.

Plymouth

12020 ■ American Women in Radio and Television, Twin Cities Media Network
c/o Barb Gehlen, Pres.
PO Box 47954
Plymouth, MN 55447

Ph: (952)417-3040
Fax: (952)417-3035
E-mail: barbgehlen@clearchannel.com
URL: National Affiliate–www.awrt.org
Contact: Barb Gehlen, Pres.

Founded: 1951. **Members:** 125. **Membership Dues:** individual/business, $120 (annual). **Local**. Advances the impact of women in the electronic media and allied fields, by educating, advocating, and acting as a resource to members and the industry. Works to improve the quality of the electronic media, to promote the entry, development, and advancement of women in the electronic media and allied fields, to serve as a medium of communication and idea exchange, and to become involved in community concerns. **Affiliated With:** American Women in Radio and Television. **Publications:** *Newsletter of the Twin Cities Chapter of AWRT*, monthly. **Conventions/Meetings:** monthly board meeting • monthly luncheon.

12021 ■ Children's Literature Network
c/o Vicki Palmquist
PO Box 46163
Plymouth, MN 55446-0163
E-mail: info@childrensliteraturenetwork.org
URL: http://www.childrensliteraturenetwork.org

Founded: 2002. **Members:** 300. **Membership Dues:** $40 (annual). **Staff:** 6. **Regional Groups:** 1. **Local**. Teachers, librarians, writers, illustrators, and publishers striving to encourage young people to read. Activities include website, conference, workshops, book festivals, and research. **Publications:** *eMagine*, bimonthly. Magazine. Includes "provocative" articles about childrens literature. **Price:** included in membership dues. Alternate Formats: online. **Conventions/Meetings:** annual Movers and Shakers in Children's Literature - conference, featuring the founders and future of the books for childrens.

12022 ■ Employers Association, Plymouth
c/o Thomas A. Ebert, Pres./CEO
9805 45th Ave. N
Plymouth, MN 55442
Ph: (763)253-9100
Fax: (763)253-9737
Free: (888)242-1359
E-mail: info@employersinc.com
URL: http://www.employersinc.com
Contact: Thomas A. Ebert, Pres./CEO

Local. **Affiliated With:** Employers Association.

12023 ■ International Facilities Management Association - Minneapolis/St. Paul Chapter
c/o Jaime Nolan
3131 Fernbrook Ln., Ste.111
Plymouth, MN 55447
Ph: (763)566-6098
Fax: (763)566-5780
E-mail: management@msp-ifma.org
URL: http://www.msp-ifma.org
Contact: Jaime Nolan, Contact

Local.

12024 ■ International Facility Management Association, Minneapolis/St. Paul
3131 Fernbrook Ln., Ste.111
Plymouth, MN 55447
Ph: (763)566-6098
Fax: (763)566-5780
E-mail: management@msp-ifma.org
URL: http://www.msp-ifma.org
Contact: Kristine Fisher CFM, Pres.

Local. Promotes excellence in the management of facilities through research, trends, educational programs; and assists corporate and organizational facility managers in developing strategies to manage human, facility and real estate resources. Hosts monthly informational meetings, spring and fall seminars, and a variety of networking opportunities. **Affiliated With:** International Facility Management Association.

12025 ■ Minnesota Funeral Directors Association (MFDA)
10800 County Rd. 15
Plymouth, MN 55441
Ph: (763)398-0115
Fax: (763)398-0118
E-mail: info@mnfuneral.org
URL: http://www.mnfuneral.org
Contact: Mr. Kelly F. Guncheon CAE, Exec.Dir.

Founded: 1890. **Members:** 565. **Membership Dues:** licensed funeral director, $260 (annual) • associate, $60 (annual) • sponsor, $100 (annual). **Staff:** 4. **Budget:** $415,000. **State Groups:** 11. **Local Groups:** 2. **State**. Licensed funeral directors. Conducts educational, legislative, and public relations activities. **Awards:** Robert C. Slater. **Frequency:** annual. **Type:** scholarship. **Recipient:** for residents enrolled in mortuary science. **Affiliated With:** National Funeral Directors Association. **Publications:** *MFDA Bulletin*, monthly. Newsletter. Update on activities and issues affecting Minnesota funeral service. **Price:** included in membership dues; $35.00 /year for nonmembers. **Circulation:** 500. **Advertising:** accepted. **Conventions/Meetings:** annual convention, two-and-a-half day meeting that educates and informs funeral directors about issues affecting how they serve families (exhibits) - usually May.

12026 ■ Minnesota Municipal Utilities Association (MMUA)
3025 Harbor Ln. N, Ste.400
Plymouth, MN 55447-5142
Ph: (763)551-1230
Fax: (763)551-0459
E-mail: jkegel@mmua.org
URL: http://www.mmua.org
Contact: Jack Kegel, Exec.Dir.

Founded: 1931. **Members:** 170. **Staff:** 25. **Budget:** $2,800,000. **State**. Serves as a common voice for municipal utilities by lobbying concerns of community to government, establishing technical training for utility operations and other related activities that involves municipal utilities improvement. **Affiliated With:** American Public Gas Association; American Public Power Association; League of Minnesota Cities. **Publications:** *The Resource*, monthly. Newsletter • Membership Directory, annual.

12027 ■ Minnesota Precision Manufacturing Association (MPMA)
c/o Charles Arnold, Exec.Dir.
3131 Fernbrook Ln. N, Ste.111
Plymouth, MN 55447
Ph: (763)566-5696
Fax: (763)566-5780
E-mail: luann@mpma.com
URL: http://www.mpma.com
Contact: Charles Arnold, Exec.Dir.

Founded: 1955. **Members:** 295. **Staff:** 4. **Budget:** $1,000,000. **State Groups:** 1. **State**. Minnesota to be recognized as the world leader in contract precision machining and related technologies. Help relieve the workforce shortage of qualified workers. **Formerly:** (1995) Minnesota Tooling and Machining Association. **Publications:** *Minnesota Precision Manufacturing Journal*, 8/year. Contains industry focused articles and ads. **Price:** free. **Circulation:** 10,000. **Advertising:** accepted • *Scratchpad*.

12028 ■ Minnesota Racquetball Association
4580 Ranier Ct.
Plymouth, MN 55446
Ph: (763)208-2531
E-mail: scott.p.nelson@comcast.net
URL: http://www.mnrball.com
Contact: Scott Nelson, Contact

State. **Affiliated With:** United States Racquetball Association.

12029 ■ National Association of Professional Organizers, Minnesota Chapter
3500 Vicksburg Ln. N, Ste.168
Plymouth, MN 55447-1333
Ph: (612)339-1331
URL: http://www.mnnapo.org
Contact: Lisa Wendt, Contact

State. Works in a cooperative manner to: educate the public about organizing as a profession; promote the benefits of organizing services; and provide support, education, and a networking forum for its members. **Affiliated With:** National Association of Professional Organizers.

12030 ■ National Speakers Association - Minnesota Chapter
c/o Liz Kuntz
3131 Fernbrook Ln. N, Ste.111
Plymouth, MN 55447
Ph: (763)398-0818
Fax: (763)566-5780
E-mail: administrator@nsaminesota.com
URL: http://www.nsaminnesota.com
Contact: Ms. Liz Kuntz, Chapter Administrator

Founded: 1982. **Members:** 103. **Membership Dues:** professional - new member, $275 (annual) • professional - renewal, $250 (annual) • vendor partner - new, $295 (annual) • vendor partner - renewal, $250 (annual). **Staff:** 2. **State**. Provides growth, learning, support and connecting opportunities for NSA-MN members and related professionals. Dedicated to advancing the art and value of experts who speak professionally by: enhancing platform excellence; facilitating business development opportunities; fostering community; increasing NSA's brand identity; and developing strategic partnerships. **Affiliated With:** National Speakers Association. **Formerly:** (2001) NSA-Minnesota Chapter. **Publications:** *Minnesota Speaks!*, monthly. Newsletter. Alternate Formats: online.

12031 ■ North Metro Muskies
PO Box 41216
Plymouth, MN 55441-0216
Ph: (763)537-0781
E-mail: info@northmetromuskies.com
URL: http://www.northmetromuskies.com
Contact: Chris Cochran, Pres.

Local.

12032 ■ Osseo Lions Club
c/o Peter Kelzenberg, Pres.
14735 39th Ave. N
Plymouth, MN 55446-3337
Ph: (763)694-9330
URL: http://www.5m5.org
Contact: Peter Kelzenberg, Pres.

Local. **Affiliated With:** Lions Clubs International.

12033 ■ Plymouth Lions Club - Minnesota
c/o Merv Bjerke, Sec.
15925 4th Ave. N
Plymouth, MN 55447
Ph: (763)473-1946
URL: http://www.5m5.org
Contact: Merv Bjerke, Sec.

Local. **Affiliated With:** Lions Clubs International.

12034 ■ Professional Insurance Agents of Minnesota
c/o Gregory E. Sather, AIC, Exec.VP
3600 Holly Ln. N, Ste.90
Plymouth, MN 55447
Ph: (763)694-7070
Fax: (763)694-9955
Free: (866)694-7070
E-mail: gsather@piamn.com
URL: http://www.piamn.com
Contact: Gregory E. Sather AIC, Exec.VP

Founded: 1994. **Members:** 250. **Membership Dues:** agency, $355 (annual) • associate, $195 (annual). **Staff:** 4. **Budget:** $500,000. **State**. Serves as an advocate for independent insurance agents and their employers who sell and service all types of insurance, primarily those specializing in property and casualty insurance. Serves the needs of its members by providing information and education and representing the interests of members before various governmental, regulatory and public bodies. **Affiliated With:** National Association of Professional Insurance Agents. **Publications:** *Agent Focus*, quarterly. Newsletter. **Circulation:** 1,850. **Advertising:** accepted. **Conventions/Meetings:** annual Education Day - convention, continuing education, company exhibits, networking opportunities.

12035 ■ Skills USA, Wayzata High School
4955 Peony Ln. N
Plymouth, MN 55446-1600
Ph: (763)745-6600
Fax: (763)745-6691
URL: http://www.wayzata.k12.mn.us
Contact: Dr. Craig Paul, Principal

Local. Serves high school and college students enrolled in technical, skilled, and service and health occupations. Provides quality education experiences for students in leadership, teamwork, citizenship and character development. Builds and reinforces self-confidence, work attitudes and communication skills. Emphasizes total quality at work, high ethical standards, superior work skills, and life-long education. Promotes understanding of the free enterprise system and involvement in community service. **Affiliated With:** Skills USA - VICA.

12036 ■ Society of Fire Protection Engineers - Minnesota
c/o Paul Watercott, Sec.
SimplexGrinell
5400 Nathan Ln.
Plymouth, MN 55442
E-mail: secretary@mnsfpe.org
URL: http://www.mnsfpe.org
Contact: Ed Meijer, Pres.

State. Advances the science and practice of fire protection engineering. Aims to maintain high professional and ethical standards among members. Fosters fire protection engineering education. **Affiliated With:** Society of Fire Protection Engineers.

12037 ■ Table Tennis Minnesota - Plymouth
Plymouth Middle School
10011 36th Ave. N
Plymouth, MN 55441
Ph: (952)892-7078
E-mail: ttminn@aol.com
URL: http://www.tabletennismn.com
Contact: Mitchell Seidenfeld, Contact

Local. Affiliated With: U.S.A. Table Tennis.

12038 ■ Thunderbird Midwest
5915 Norwood Ln. N
Plymouth, MN 55442
Ph: (763)694-0644
URL: http://www.thunderbirdmidwest.org

Regional. Affiliated With: Vintage Thunderbird Club International.

12039 ■ The Trumpeter Swan Society (TTSS)
12615 County Rd. 9, Ste.100
Plymouth, MN 55441-1248
Ph: (763)694-7851
Fax: (763)557-4943
E-mail: ttss@threeriversparkdistrict.org
URL: http://www.trumpeterswansociety.org
Contact: Ruth E. Shea, Exec.Dir.

Founded: 1968. **Members:** 450. **Membership Dues:** student, retired, $15 (annual) • regular, $25 (annual) • family, $30 (annual) • organization, $50 (annual) • supporting, $100 (annual) • life, $500. **Staff:** 2. **Regional. Publications:** *North American Swans*, annual. Bulletin • *Trumpetings*. Newsletter.

12040 ■ United Food and Commercial Workers, Local 653, Northcentral Region
505 N Hwy. 169, Ste.755
Plymouth, MN 55441
Ph: (763)525-1500
URL: National Affiliate–www.ufcw.org

Local. Affiliated With: United Food and Commercial Workers International Union.

12041 ■ USA Weightlifting - Armstrong Falcons
c/o Ted Meikle
10900 38th Ave. N
Plymouth, MN 55441
Ph: (612)375-1887
E-mail: ted@meikle.org
URL: National Affiliate–www.usaweightlifting.org
Contact: Ted Meikle, Contact

Local. Affiliated With: USA Weightlifting.

Porter

12042 ■ American Legion, Porter Post 457
PO Box 68
Porter, MN 56280
Ph: (651)291-1800
Fax: (651)291-1057
URL: National Affiliate–www.legion.org

Local. Affiliated With: American Legion.

Preston

12043 ■ American Legion, Viall Post 166
PO Box 253
Preston, MN 55965
Ph: (651)291-1800
Fax: (651)291-1057
URL: National Affiliate–www.legion.org

Local. Affiliated With: American Legion.

Princeton

12044 ■ American Legion, Woodcock-Herbst Post 216
202 Rum River Dr.
Princeton, MN 55371
Ph: (612)389-2122
Fax: (651)291-1057
URL: National Affiliate–www.legion.org

Local. Affiliated With: American Legion.

12045 ■ Kinship Youth Mentoring of Princeton
c/o Jeanne Bromberg
604 S 3rd St., No. 151
Princeton, MN 55371-1502
Ph: (763)631-5967
E-mail: kinship@sherbtel.net
Contact: Jeanne Bromberg, Dir.

Founded: 2001. **Members:** 24. **Staff:** 1. **Budget:** $40,000. **Local.** Offers one-to-one, adult-to-youth mentoring, for 4-10 month period. Strives to provide a safe, quality, mentoring relationship to improve the lives of youth in the community.

12046 ■ Princeton Area Chamber of Commerce (PACC)
705 N 2nd St.
Princeton, MN 55371-1550
Ph: (763)389-1764
E-mail: pacc@sherbtel.net
URL: http://www.princetonmnchamber.org
Contact: Nancy Campbell, Pres.

Members: 120. **Staff:** 1. **Local.** Promotes business and community development in Princeton, MN. Sponsors Rum River Festival. **Computer Services:** Online services, membership directory. **Telecommunication Services:** electronic mail, ncampbell@princetonmn.org. **Formerly:** (1999) Princeton Area +Chamber of Commerce. **Publications:** Newsletter, monthly. **Conventions/Meetings:** monthly meeting - always second Tuesday.

12047 ■ Rum River Cycling Team
706 First St.
Princeton, MN 55371
Fax: (763)389-9142
E-mail: tim.dalton@princeton.k12.mn.us
URL: http://www.rumrivercycling.com

Local. Affiliated With: International Mountain Bicycling Association.

Prior Lake

12048 ■ American Legion, Prior Lake Post 447
PO Box 552
Prior Lake, MN 55372
Ph: (651)291-1800
Fax: (651)291-1057
URL: National Affiliate–www.legion.org

Local. Affiliated With: American Legion.

12049 ■ Independent Computer Consultants Association, Minnesota
6782 Hillcrest St. SE
Prior Lake, MN 55372-2949
Ph: (612)245-6222
E-mail: wjm@usfamily.net
URL: http://www.icca-mn.org
Contact: Bill Middlecamp, Pres.

State. Affiliated With: Independent Computer Consultants Association.

12050 ■ Lake Country Retriever Club (LCRC)
PO Box 417
Prior Lake, MN 55372
E-mail: comet@isd.net
URL: http://www.lcretrieverclub.org
Contact: Bill Howland, Pres.

Founded: 1986. **Members:** 200. **Membership Dues:** regular, $35 (annual). **Local.** Individuals in the Prior Lake, MN area interested in the retriever breed of dog. **Affiliated With:** American Kennel Club. **Publications:** Newsletter, monthly. **Price:** free. **Circulation:** 200. Alternate Formats: online. **Conventions/Meetings:** monthly meeting.

12051 ■ Midwest Sunbeam Registry (MSR)
20700 Huntington Way
Prior Lake, MN 55372-9725
Ph: (952)440-6300
E-mail: wbjennings@integraonline.com
Contact: William B. Jennings, Bd.Chm.

Founded: 1981. **Members:** 120. Collectors and enthusiasts of Sunbeam Alpine and Tiger sports cars throughout the U.S. who preserve and restore Sunbeam Alpine and Tiger sports cars manufactured in England. Promotes good fellowship among members through car-related activities. Conducts technical training sessions. Compiles statistics. **Libraries: Type:** reference. **Holdings:** artwork, books, periodicals. **Subjects:** British sports cars. **Computer Services:** National Sunbeam Owners Registry. **Publications:** *Midwest Sunbeam Registry—Membership Roster*, annual. Membership Directory • *Sunbeam Sentinel*, monthly. Newsletter.

12052 ■ Minneapolis Gun Club
20006 Judicial Rd.
Prior Lake, MN 55372
Ph: (952)469-4386
Fax: (952)469-8347
URL: http://www.mplsgunclub.com

Local. Affiliated With: National Skeet Shooting Association.

12053 ■ Moms Club
c/o Melissa Werner
9281 195th St. E
Prior Lake, MN 55372
Contact: Melissa Werner, Co-Pres.

Founded: 1999. **Members:** 41. **Membership Dues:** single, $25 (annual). **Local.** Moms offering moms support, educational, information, recreational and social activities. **Conventions/Meetings:** monthly meeting.

12054 ■ Prior Lake Area Chamber of Commerce
PO Box 114
Prior Lake, MN 55372
Ph: (952)440-1000
Fax: (952)440-1611
E-mail: priorlakechamber@integraonline.com
URL: http://www.priorlakechamber.org
Contact: Sandi Fleck, Exec.Dir.

Members: 140. **Membership Dues:** home based business, associate, $175 • non-profit organization,

$250 • business (based on number of employees), $250-$500. **Local**. Strives to foster business development to enhance the quality of life of the community. **Committees:** Ambassadors; Communication/ Technology; Golf Classic; Program. **Publications:** *Chamber News*, monthly. Newsletter. **Advertising:** accepted.

12055 ■ Prior Lake Association (PLA)
PO Box 88
Prior Lake, MN 55372
Ph: (952)447-0600
E-mail: info@priorlakeassociation.org
URL: http://www.priorlakeassociation.org
Contact: Loren Jones, Pres.
Membership Dues: general, $20 (annual) • senior citizen, $15 (annual). **Local**. Provides leadership and assistance to preserve and protect the natural resources.

12056 ■ Prior Lake Lions Club
16228 Main Ave., Ste.110
Prior Lake, MN 55372
Ph: (952)447-7277
E-mail: pllions@integra.com
URL: http://www.priorlake.5m2lions.org
Local. **Affiliated With:** Lions Clubs International.

Proctor

12057 ■ American Legion, Lind-Gordon-Berg Post 106
3 6th St.
Proctor, MN 55810
Ph: (651)291-1800
Fax: (651)291-1057
URL: National Affiliate–www.legion.org
Local. **Affiliated With:** American Legion.

12058 ■ Proctor Lions Club
c/o Jake Benson, Pres.
215 5th St.
Proctor, MN 55810-1686
Ph: (218)624-3344 (218)628-2770
E-mail: jake@proctormn.com
URL: http://lions5m10.org
Contact: Jake Benson, Pres.
Local. **Affiliated With:** Lions Clubs International.

12059 ■ Skills USA, Proctor High School
131 9th Ave.
Proctor, MN 55810
Ph: (218)628-4926
Fax: (218)628-1931
E-mail: mkoppy@proctor.k12.mn.us
URL: http://www.mnskillsusa.org
Contact: Mike Koppy, Contact
Local. Serves high school and college students enrolled in technical, skilled, and service and health occupations. Provides quality education experiences for students in leadership, teamwork, citizenship and character development. Builds and reinforces self-confidence, work attitudes and communication skills. Emphasizes total quality at work, high ethical standards, superior work skills, and life-long education. Promotes understanding of the free enterprise system and involvement in community service. **Affiliated With:** Skills USA - VICA.

12060 ■ Wildlife Society - Minnesota Chapter
c/o Martha Minchak
9439 Westgate Blvd.
Proctor, MN 55810
E-mail: mark.hanson@dnr.state.mn.us
URL: http://www.crk.umn.edu/tws/MN/index.htm
Contact: Mark Hanson, Pres.-Elect
Founded: 1944. **State**. **Affiliated With:** The Wildlife Society.

Racine

12061 ■ Racine Lions Club
c/o Paul Thompson, Pres.
PO Box 37
Racine, MN 55967
Ph: (507)378-2121 (507)378-4551
URL: http://www.lions5m1.org/racine
Contact: Paul Thompson, Pres.
Local. **Affiliated With:** Lions Clubs International.

Ramsey

12062 ■ International Brotherhood of Magicians, Ring 19
c/o Tod Erickson, Sec.
6921 137th Ave. NW
Ramsey, MN 55303
Ph: (763)323-8315
E-mail: info@ring19.org
URL: http://www.ring19.org
Contact: Tod Erickson, Sec.
Local. Professional and semiprofessional magicians; suppliers, assistants, agents, and others interested in magic. Seeks to advance the art of magic in the field of amusement, entertainment, and culture. Promotes proper means of discouraging false or misleading advertising of effects, tricks, literature, merchandise, or actions appertaining to the magical arts; opposes exposures of principles of the art of magic, except in books on magic and magazines devoted to such art for the exclusive use of magicians and devotees of the art; encourages humane treatment and care of live animals whenever employed in magical performances. **Affiliated With:** International Brotherhood of Magicians.

12063 ■ Ramsey Lions Club
PO Box 771
Ramsey, MN 55303
Ph: (763)439-2695
E-mail: president@ramseylions.org
URL: http://www.ramseylions.org
Local. **Affiliated With:** Lions Clubs International.

12064 ■ School Nurse Organization of Minnesota (SNOM)
c/o Lillian Levine, Membership Chair
5810 169th Ave. NW
Ramsey, MN 55303
Ph: (763)753-7099 (763)753-5895
E-mail: cynthia.hiltz@anoka.k12.mn.us
URL: http://www.minnesotaschoolnurses.org
Contact: Cindy Hiltz, Pres.
State. Advances the delivery of professional school health services. Increases the awareness of students on the necessity of health and learning. Improves the health of children by developing school nursing practices. **Affiliated With:** National Association of School Nurses.

Randall

12065 ■ Licensed Family Child Care Association of Morrison County
c/o Patricia Ann Orth
4883 170th St.
Randall, MN 56475-2911
Local.

Randolph

12066 ■ Minnesota National Barrel Horse Association
7552 280th St. E
Randolph, MN 55065
Ph: (507)263-8326
URL: National Affiliate–www.nbha.com
Contact: Margy Vagt, Dir.
State. Promotes the sport of barrel horse racing. Conducts barrel racing competitions. Establishes standard rules for the sport. **Affiliated With:** National Barrel Horse Association.

Ray

12067 ■ National Active and Retired Federal Employees Association International Falls 1582
2570 County Rd. 99
Ray, MN 56669-9043
Ph: (218)875-2032
URL: National Affiliate–www.narfe.org
Contact: Einar R. Sundin, Contact
Local. Protects the retirement future of employees through education. Informs members on issues affecting the retirement. **Affiliated With:** National Association of Retired Federal Employees.

Raymond

12068 ■ American Legion, Peter Leuze Post 420
16085 50th St. NE
Raymond, MN 56282
Ph: (651)291-1800
Fax: (651)291-1057
URL: National Affiliate–www.legion.org
Local. **Affiliated With:** American Legion.

12069 ■ Raymond Lions Club - Minnesota
c/o Darrell Vick, Pres.
10250 75th Ave. SW
Raymond, MN 56282
Ph: (320)967-4680
URL: http://www.5m4lions.org
Contact: Darrell Vick, Pres.
Local. **Affiliated With:** Lions Clubs International.

Red Lake Falls

12070 ■ American Legion, Gunder Austad Post 22
PO Box 178
Red Lake Falls, MN 56750
Ph: (651)291-1800
Fax: (651)291-1057
URL: National Affiliate–www.legion.org
Local. **Affiliated With:** American Legion.

12071 ■ Minnesota Association of Wheat Growers (MAWG)
2600 Wheat Dr.
Red Lake Falls, MN 56750
Ph: (218)253-4311
Fax: (218)253-4320
E-mail: mnwheat@gvtel.com
URL: http://www.smallgrains.org
Contact: David Torgerson, Exec.Dir.
State.

12072 ■ Organic Crop Improvement Association, Minnesota
c/o Lorri Ann Hartel
2609 Wheat Dr.
Red Lake Falls, MN 56750
Ph: (218)253-4907
Fax: (218)253-4320
E-mail: lhartel@prairieagcomm.com
URL: National Affiliate–www.ocia.org
Contact: Lorri Ann Hartel, Contact
State. **Affiliated With:** Organic Crop Improvement Association.

12073 ■ Pembina Trail Resource Conservation and Development Council
2605 Wheat Dr.
Red Lake Falls, MN 56750-4800
Ph: (218)253-2181
Fax: (218)253-4112
E-mail: john.schmidt@mn.usda.gov
URL: National Affiliate–www.rcdnet.org
Contact: John Schmidt, Coor.
Local. **Affiliated With:** National Association of Resource Conservation and Development Councils.

12074 ■ Red Lake Falls Lions Club
c/o Douglas Purath, Pres.
PO Box 51
Red Lake Falls, MN 56750
E-mail: dkpx2@msn.com
URL: http://lions5m11.org/sys-tmpl/door
Contact: Douglas Purath, Pres.
Local. Affiliated With: Lions Clubs International.

Red Wing

12075 ■ American Association of University Women - Minnesota State
c/o Pat Sween, State Pres.
2524 Oriole Cir.
Red Wing, MN 55066
Ph: (651)385-8951
E-mail: pasween@redwing.net
URL: http://www1.minn.net/~aauwmn
Contact: Pat Sween, Pres.
State. Promotes equity for all women and girls, lifelong education and positive societal change. Activities include providing funds for education, research and self-development, and support for women seeking judicial redress for sex discrimination. **Affiliated With:** American Association of University Women.

12076 ■ American Legion, Minnesota Post 54
c/o Alfred Lockman
218 W 4th St.
Red Wing, MN 55066
Ph: (651)291-1800
Fax: (651)291-1057
URL: National Affiliate–www.legion.org
Contact: Alfred Lockman, Contact
Local. Affiliated With: American Legion.

12077 ■ American Red Cross, Goodhue County Chapter
PO Box 29
Red Wing, MN 55066
Ph: (651)388-9166
Fax: (651)267-0619
E-mail: gcarc@charterinternet.com
URL: http://www.goodhueredcross.org
Local.

12078 ■ Goodhue County Habitat for Humanity
480 W 8th St.
Red Wing, MN 55066
Ph: (651)388-9360
Fax: (651)388-9178
E-mail: goodhuecountyhfh@charterinternet.com
URL: http://www.geocities.com/goodhuecountyhfh
Local. Affiliated With: Habitat for Humanity International.

12079 ■ Goodhue County Historical Society
1166 Oak St.
Red Wing, MN 55066
Ph: (651)388-6024
Fax: (651)388-3577
E-mail: goodhuecountyhis@qwest.net
URL: http://www.goodhuehistory.mus.mn.us
Contact: Char Henn, Dir.
Founded: 1869. **Members:** 600. **Membership Dues:** family, $50 (annual) • sustaining, $250 (annual) • business/individual, $500 (annual) • life, $1,000 • basic, $35 (annual). **Staff:** 6. **Budget:** $250,000. **Local.** Collects, protects, preserves, and interprets the pre-history and history of Goodhue County. **Libraries: Type:** open to the public. **Holdings:** 7,500; books, photographs. **Subjects:** genealogy, local history. **Publications:** *Goodhue County Historical News*, quarterly. Newsletter. Contains new topics of county history. **Price:** included in membership dues.

12080 ■ PFLAG Red Wing
1821 Bohmbach Dr.
Red Wing, MN 55066
Ph: (651)388-9610
E-mail: dsguida@charter.net
URL: http://www.pflag.org/Minnesota.217.0.html
Local. Affiliated With: Parents, Families, and Friends of Lesbians and Gays.

12081 ■ Red Wing Area Chamber of Commerce (RWACC)
439 Main St.
Red Wing, MN 55066
Ph: (651)388-4719
Fax: (651)388-6991
Free: (800)762-9516
E-mail: chamber@redwingchamber.com
URL: http://www.redwingchamber.com
Contact: Arne Skyberg, Pres.
Local. Promotes business and community development in the Red Wing, MN area. **Computer Services:** Mailing lists, of members. **Telecommunication Services:** electronic mail, arne@redwingchamber.com. **Committees:** Ambassadors; Golf Outing; Government Affairs; Potter's Picnic; Red Wing 2020; River City Days. **Publications:** *Chamber Forum*, bimonthly. Newsletter. **Circulation:** 1,200.

12082 ■ Red Wing Area United Way
PO Box 319
Red Wing, MN 55066-0319
Ph: (651)388-6309
Fax: (651)385-8104
E-mail: rwauw@redwing.net
URL: National Affiliate–national.unitedway.org
Contact: Mary B. Plein, Exec.Dir.
Founded: 1958. **Staff:** 2. **Budget:** $450,000. **State Groups:** 1. **Local.** Works to increase the organized capacity of people to care for one another in the community. **Awards: Frequency:** annual. **Type:** grant. **Affiliated With:** United Way of America.

12083 ■ Red Wing High School - Young Life
PO Box 374
Red Wing, MN 55066
Ph: (651)388-8100
URL: http://sites.younglife.org/_layouts/ylext/default.aspx?ID=C-2951
Local. Affiliated With: Young Life.

12084 ■ Red Wing Visitors and Convention Bureau (VCB)
420 Levee St.
Red Wing, MN 55066
Ph: (651)385-5934
Fax: (651)388-3900
Free: (800)498-3444
E-mail: info@redwing.org
URL: http://www.redwing.org
Contact: Bob Musil, Dir.
Founded: 1994. **Members:** 75. **Staff:** 2. **State Groups:** 1. **Local.** Promotes Red Wing, MN as a tourist destination. **Telecommunication Services:** electronic mail, visitorscenter@redwing.org.

12085 ■ Skills USA, Red Wing Central High School
2451 Eagle Ridge Dr.
Red Wing, MN 55066
Ph: (651)385-4652
Fax: (651)385-4610
E-mail: mjohanse@redwingl.k12.mn.us
URL: http://www.mnskillsusa.org/secondaryChapters.htm
Contact: Mark Johansen, Contact
Local. Serves high school and college students enrolled in technical, skilled, and service and health occupations. Provides quality education experiences for students in leadership, teamwork, citizenship and character development. Builds and reinforces self-confidence, work attitudes and communication skills. Emphasizes total quality at work, high ethical standards, superior work skills, and life-long education. Promotes understanding of the free enterprise system and involvement in community service. **Affiliated With:** Skills USA - VICA.

12086 ■ Sons of Norway, Lauris Norstad Lodge 1-558
c/o Paul H. Christenson, Pres.
1620 Woodcrest Ct.
Red Wing, MN 55066-2943
Ph: (651)388-1244
E-mail: bestefar@pressenter.com
URL: http://www.laurisnorstadlodge.com
Contact: Paul H. Christenson, Pres.
Local. Affiliated With: Sons of Norway.

12087 ■ Trout Unlimited - Wa Hue Chapter
1604 Old W Main St.
Red Wing, MN 55066
Ph: (651)267-4133
E-mail: leakywaders@stewartfishingco.com
URL: http://www.tu.org
Contact: Bill Schad, Pres.
Local.

12088 ■ Twin Bluff - Wyldlife
PO Box 374
Red Wing, MN 55066
Ph: (651)388-8100
URL: http://sites.younglife.org/_layouts/ylext/default.aspx?ID=C-1179
Local. Affiliated With: Young Life.

12089 ■ United Food and Commercial Workers, Local 335, Northcentral Region
319 1/2 W 3rd St.
Red Wing, MN 55066
Ph: (651)388-6904
URL: National Affiliate–www.ufcw.org
Local. Affiliated With: United Food and Commercial Workers International Union.

12090 ■ United Food and Commercial Workers, Local 527, Northcentral Region
319 W 3rd St.
Red Wing, MN 55066
Ph: (651)388-3785
URL: National Affiliate–www.ufcw.org
Local. Affiliated With: United Food and Commercial Workers International Union.

12091 ■ USA Weightlifting - Red Wing
c/o John Drewes
528 15th St.
Red Wing, MN 55066
Ph: (651)388-7314
URL: National Affiliate–www.usaweightlifting.org
Contact: John Drewes, Contact
Local. Affiliated With: USA Weightlifting.

12092 ■ Young Life Red Wing
PO Box 374
Red Wing, MN 55066
Ph: (651)388-8100
Fax: (651)388-8100
URL: http://sites.younglife.org/_layouts/ylext/default.aspx?ID=A-MN28
Local. Affiliated With: Young Life.

Redwood Falls

12093 ■ American Legion, Minnesota Post 38
c/o William R. Witty
PO Box 354
Redwood Falls, MN 56283
Ph: (651)291-1800
Fax: (651)291-1057
URL: National Affiliate–www.legion.org
Contact: William R. Witty, Contact
Local. Affiliated With: American Legion.

12094 ■ Girl Scouts Peacepipe Council
809 E Bridge St.
Redwood Falls, MN 56283
Ph: (507)637-3569
Fax: (507)627-2138
Free: (800)332-4475
E-mail: info@girlscoutsppc.org
URL: http://www.girlscoutsppc.org
Contact: Teresa Albu, Contact
Local. Young girls and adult volunteers, corporate, government and individual supporters. Strives to develop potential and leadership skills among its members. Conducts trainings, educational programs and outdoor activities.

12095 ■ Minnesota Inventors Congress (MIC)
PO Box 71
Redwood Falls, MN 56283-0071
Ph: (507)637-2344
Fax: (507)637-4082
Free: (800)468-3681
E-mail: mic@inventhelper.org
URL: http://www.inventhelper.org
Contact: Deb Hess, Exec.Dir.
Founded: 1958. **Staff:** 1. **State**. Provides resources to help inventors/entrepreneurs with the development of their new product idea. Hosts an Expo the second weekend in June, which provides a forum for the inventor/entrepreneur to bring their working model/prototype for test marketing. **Affiliated With:** United Inventors Association of the U.S.A.

12096 ■ National Active and Retired Federal Employees Association - Marshall 1580
400 E 5th St. No. 114
Redwood Falls, MN 56283-1788
Ph: (507)637-3663
URL: National Affiliate–www.narfe.org
Contact: Rosemary P. March, Contact
Local. Protects the retirement future of employees through education. Informs members on issues affecting the retirement. **Affiliated With:** National Association of Retired Federal Employees.

12097 ■ Redwood Area Chamber and Tourism (RACT)
200 S Mill St.
PO Box 21
Redwood Falls, MN 56283
Ph: (507)637-2828
Fax: (507)637-5202
Free: (800)657-7070
E-mail: chamber@redwoodfalls.org
URL: http://www.redwoodfalls.org
Contact: Beth Anderson, Exec.Dir.
Local. Promotes business and community development in the Redwood Falls, MN area. **Awards:** First Dollar. **Type:** recognition • Progress. **Frequency:** periodic. **Type:** recognition. **Computer Services:** database • information services • mailing lists. **Telecommunication Services:** information service. **Formerly:** (1999) Redwood Falls Area Chamber of Commerce.

12098 ■ Redwood Area United Way
PO Box 455
Redwood Falls, MN 56283-0455
Ph: (507)627-3184
URL: National Affiliate–national.unitedway.org
Local. **Affiliated With:** United Way of America.

Remer

12099 ■ American Legion, Eugene Wilson Post 346
PO Box 133
Remer, MN 56672
Ph: (651)291-1800
Fax: (651)291-1057
URL: National Affiliate–www.legion.org
Local. **Affiliated With:** American Legion.

Renville

12100 ■ American Legion, Adwell-Garvey Post 180
PO Box 456
Renville, MN 56284
Ph: (651)291-1800
Fax: (651)291-1057
URL: National Affiliate–www.legion.org
Local. **Affiliated With:** American Legion.

12101 ■ Minnesota Nurses Association - District 8
Box 504
Renville, MN 56284
Ph: (320)231-4301
URL: http://www.mnnurses.org
Contact: Carol Thompson, Pres.
Local. Works to advance the nursing profession. Seeks to meet the needs of nurses and health care consumers. Fosters high standards of nursing practice. Promotes the economic and general welfare of nurses in the workplace. **Affiliated With:** American Nurses Association; Minnesota Nurses Association.

12102 ■ Renville Lions Club
c/o Glenn Hannah, Pres.
PO Box 506
Renville, MN 56284
Ph: (320)329-3322
URL: http://www.5m4lions.org
Contact: Glenn Hannah, Pres.
Local. **Affiliated With:** Lions Clubs International.

Revere

12103 ■ American Legion, Minnesota Post 582
c/o Francis Harnack
S Main St.
Revere, MN 56166
Ph: (651)291-1800
Fax: (651)291-1057
URL: National Affiliate–www.legion.org
Contact: Francis Harnack, Contact
Local. **Affiliated With:** American Legion.

Rice

12104 ■ American Legion, Hassel Briese Post 473
PO Box 277
Rice, MN 56367
Ph: (651)291-1800
Fax: (651)291-1057
URL: National Affiliate–www.legion.org
Local. **Affiliated With:** American Legion.

12105 ■ Police and Firemen's Insurance Association - St. Cloud Fire and Police Department
c/o Dave Bentrud
9765 Oak Ct. NE
Rice, MN 56367
Ph: (320)393-3174
E-mail: dbtrud@msn.com
URL: National Affiliate–www.pfia.net
Contact: Dave Bentrud, Contact
Local. **Affiliated With:** Police and Firemen's Insurance Association.

Richfield

12106 ■ American Legion, Bearcat Post 504
PO Box 23049
Richfield, MN 55423
Ph: (651)291-1800
Fax: (651)291-1057
URL: National Affiliate–www.legion.org
Local. **Affiliated With:** American Legion.

12107 ■ American Legion, Minneapolis Post office Post 540
PO Box 23467
Richfield, MN 55423
Ph: (651)291-1800
Fax: (651)291-1057
URL: National Affiliate–www.legion.org
Local. **Affiliated With:** American Legion.

12108 ■ American Legion, Minneapolis-Richfield Post 435
6501 Portland Ave.
Richfield, MN 55423
Ph: (651)291-1800
Fax: (651)291-1057
URL: National Affiliate–www.legion.org
Local. **Affiliated With:** American Legion.

12109 ■ Information Systems Security Association, Minnesota Chapter
PO Box 23900
Richfield, MN 55423-0900
E-mail: rick.ensenbach@shavlik.com
URL: http://www.mn-issa.org
Contact: Rick Ensenbach, Pres.
State. Represents information security professionals and practitioners. Enhances the knowledge, skill and professional growth of members. Provides educational forums and peer interaction opportunities. **Affiliated With:** Information Systems Security Association.

12110 ■ Lions Cricket Club
6701 Vincent Ave. S
Richfield, MN 55423
URL: http://www.usaca.org/Clubs.htm
Contact: Sena Abeygunawardena, Contact
Local.

12111 ■ Minnesota State Patrol Troopers Association (MSPTA)
c/o Tim Jensen, Pres.
7538 15th Ave. S
Richfield, MN 55423
Ph: (218)729-0152
Free: (800)255-5610
E-mail: tjensen@mspta.com
URL: http://www.mspta.com
Contact: Tim Jensen, Pres.
State.

12112 ■ National Active and Retired Federal Employees Association - Minneapolis 150
6600 Lyndale Ave. S Apt. 805
Richfield, MN 55423-2312
Ph: (612)236-1301
URL: National Affiliate–www.narfe.org
Contact: Walter Couillard, Contact
Local. Protects the retirement future of employees through education. Informs members on issues affecting the retirement. **Affiliated With:** National Association of Retired Federal Employees.

12113 ■ Richfield Chamber of Commerce
6601 Lyndale Ave. S, Ste.106
Richfield, MN 55423
Ph: (612)866-5100
Fax: (612)861-8302
E-mail: info@richfieldchambercvb.org
Contact: Steven Lindgren, Pres.
Membership Dues: business (based on number of employees), $125-$725 • non-profit organization, $180. **Local**.

12114 ■ STARFLEET: USS Czar'ak
PO Box 23352
Richfield, MN 55423-0352
E-mail: davidk50@skypoint.com
URL: http://www.geocities.com/czarak_ncc_1798a
Contact: Cynthia Henry, Exec. Officer
Local. **Affiliated With:** STARFLEET.

Richmond

12115 ■ American Legion, Richmond Post 292
PO Box 431
Richmond, MN 56368
Ph: (651)291-1800
Fax: (651)291-1057
URL: National Affiliate–www.legion.org
Local. Affiliated With: American Legion.

Robbinsdale

12116 ■ American Legion, Westphal Post 251
3600 France Ave. N
Robbinsdale, MN 55422
Ph: (651)291-1800
Fax: (651)291-1057
URL: National Affiliate–www.legion.org
Local. Affiliated With: American Legion.

12117 ■ Central Minnesota Self-Help for Hard of Hearing
3836 Hubbard Ave. N
Robbinsdale, MN 55422
Ph: (320)255-3502
Fax: (320)654-5157
E-mail: rich.diedrichsen@state.mn.us
Contact: Rich Diedrichsen, Contact
Founded: 1982. **Members:** 23. **Membership Dues:** $10 (annual). **State Groups:** 2. **Local Groups:** 2. **Regional**. Assists people with hearing losses who choose to communicate using their remaining hearing and voice; shares information, resources and personal experiences to help others find ways to cope with everyday challenges related to their hearing loss. Conducts support meetings. **Conventions/Meetings:** annual convention, with workshops and research symposium (exhibits).

12118 ■ Creative Housing Alternative of Minnesota (CHAIN of MN)
c/o Charlotte Williams, Dir.
PO Box 22393
Robbinsdale, MN 55422
Ph: (612)588-7567 (763)971-0377
Fax: (612)588-7567
E-mail: info@chainofmn.org
URL: http://www.chainofmn.org
Contact: Charlotte Williams, Dir.
Founded: 1996. **Budget:** $250,000. **Local**. Strives to connect landlords who have available rental housing with families and individuals in search of available affordable rental housing. Provides a free online rental classified databases. **Formerly:** (2002) Pride-N-Living Housing Development Corp.

12119 ■ Or Emet Congregation, Humanistic Jews of Minnesota
c/o Michael Persellin
Box 22513
Robbinsdale, MN 55422
Ph: (763)535-2226
E-mail: mperse@spacestar.net
URL: http://www.oremet.org
Contact: Michael Persellin, Contact
Founded: 1985. **Members:** 40. **Membership Dues:** individual, $125 • family, $300. **Staff:** 1. **Budget:** $7,000. **Local**. Congregation and children's school. Seeks to promote Humanistic Judaism. **Affiliated With:** Society for Humanistic Judaism. **Publications:** Newsletter, quarterly, 4 issues between September and May. **Circulation:** 250. **Advertising:** accepted. Alternate Formats: online. **Conventions/Meetings:** annual meeting, membership - May.

12120 ■ Robbinsdale Chamber of Commerce
PO Box 22646
Robbinsdale, MN 55422-0646
Ph: (763)531-1279 (763)537-2471
Contact: Kathy Murphy, Pres.
Local.

Rochester

12121 ■ AAA Minnesota/Iowa
1535 Greenview Dr. SW
Rochester, MN 55902-1095
Ph: (507)289-1851
Free: (800)648-6718
E-mail: janice.gates@mn-ia.aaa.com
URL: http://www.aaa.com
Contact: Janice Gates, Acting Office Mgr.
Regional.

12122 ■ Alzheimer's Association-Rochester Center
c/o Jamie Pennington, Center Dir.
Assissi Heights
1001 - 14th St. NW
Rochester, MN 55901
Ph: (507)289-3950
Fax: (507)289-4666
E-mail: jamie.pennington@alz.org
URL: http://www.alzmndak.org
Contact: Jamie Pennington, Center Dir.
Local.

12123 ■ American Cancer Society, Rochester
882 7th St. NW
Rochester, MN 55901
Ph: (507)287-2044
Fax: (507)287-2178
Free: (888)535-4227
URL: http://www.cancer.org
Local. Affiliated With: American Cancer Society.

12124 ■ American Legion, Rochester Post 446
2002 2nd St. SW
Rochester, MN 55902
Ph: (651)291-1800
Fax: (651)291-1057
URL: National Affiliate–www.legion.org
Local. Affiliated With: American Legion.

12125 ■ American Legion, William T. Mc Coy Post 92
315 1st Ave. NW
Rochester, MN 55901
Ph: (651)291-1800
Fax: (651)291-1057
URL: National Affiliate–www.legion.org
Local. Affiliated With: American Legion.

12126 ■ American Red Cross, Southeast Minnesota Chapter
310 14th St. SE
Rochester, MN 55904
Ph: (507)287-2200
Fax: (507)287-2688
E-mail: chapter@redcross-semn.org
URL: http://www.redcross-semn.org
Regional.

12127 ■ Antique Automobile Club of America, Minnesota Region - Hiawatha Chapter
c/o Ken Stiles, Newsletter Ed.
714 NE 21st St.
Rochester, MN 55906
E-mail: hiawathachapter@yahoo.com
URL: http://local.aaca.org/hiawatha
Contact: Shirley Lind, Pres.
Founded: 1961. **Membership Dues:** individual, $10 (annual). **Local**. Collectors, hobbyists, and others interested in the preservation, maintenance, and restoration of automobiles and in automotive history. **Affiliated With:** Antique Automobile Club of America.

12128 ■ Appraisal Institute, Metro/Minnesota Chapter
c/o Robert Springer, Pres.
Springer Appraisal Assoc., Inc.
208 4th St. SE
Rochester, MN 55904
Ph: (507)282-8630
Fax: (507)282-1202
E-mail: cspringer@springerappraisal.com
URL: http://www.metromn.org
Contact: Robert Springer, Pres.
Local. Affiliated With: Appraisal Institute.

12129 ■ Arc Southeastern Minnesota
2200 2nd St. SW, Ste.101
Rochester, MN 55902
Ph: (507)287-2032
Free: (888)732-8520
E-mail: bhennessey@arcse-mn.org
URL: http://arcse-mn.org
Contact: Buff Hennessey, Exec.Dir.
Founded: 1955. **Local**. Persons with developmental disabilities; their friends and families; medical professionals; interested others. Provides support, information, and quality of life improvement services. Provides parent to parent support group. Offers advocacy and support for people with developmental disabilities and their families. Also offers newborn and community support. Educates the public about developmental disabilities. Conducts charitable activities. **Libraries: Type:** reference. **Holdings:** 1,500; articles. **Subjects:** all developmental disabilities (Autism, Down Syndrome, Cerebral Palsy, Mental Retardation, Spina Bifida, Epilepsy). **Formerly:** (1999) Arc Olmsted County.

12130 ■ Boy Scouts of America, Gamehaven Council
1124 11 1/2 St. SE
Rochester, MN 55904-4097
Ph: (507)287-1410
Fax: (507)287-1413
Free: (800)524-3907
E-mail: scouts@gamehavencouncil.org
URL: http://www.gamehavenbsa.org
Contact: Richard W. Good, Scout Exec.
Founded: 1916. **Members:** 12,800. **Membership Dues:** regular, $7 (annual). **Staff:** 6. **Budget:** $770,000. **Local Groups:** 183. **Local**. Supports and promotes the teaching of leadership, citizenship, and self-reliance to young boys grades 1-12 and young ladies ages 14-20. Sponsors various programs and provides adult leadership. **Affiliated With:** Boy Scouts of America. **Publications:** *Trails*, monthly. Newsletter. **Circulation:** 2,000. **Advertising:** accepted. **Conventions/Meetings:** annual Business and Recognition Banquet - first Saturday of March.

12131 ■ Builders Exchange of Rochester
108 Elton Hills Ln.
Rochester, MN 55901
Ph: (507)282-6531
Fax: (507)282-6351
E-mail: planroom@bexroch.com
URL: http://www.bexroch.com/contact.html
Contact: Sandy Friend, Exec. Officer
Founded: 1987. **Local**. Represents general contractors, subcontractors, suppliers, manufacturers' representatives and individual firms related to the construction industry. Provides information on construction and building procedures. **Affiliated With:** International Builders Exchange Executives. **Publications:** Bulletin, weekly.

12132 ■ Children's Rights Council of Minnesota
5905 Chateau Rd. NW
Rochester, MN 55901-0137
Ph: (507)289-5745
E-mail: bk@mncrc.org
URL: http://www.mncrc.org
State. Affiliated With: Children's Rights Council.

12133 ■ Classical Association of Minnesota
Mayo High School
1420 11th Ave. SE
Rochester, MN 55904

Ph: (507)281-6296
E-mail: elsassenberg@rochester.k12.mn.us
URL: http://www.camws.org
Contact: Ellen D. Sassenberg, VP
State. Represents university, college, secondary and elementary teachers of Latin, Greek and all other studies which focus on the world of classical antiquity. Supports and promotes the study of classical languages.

12134 ■ Cornbelt Professional Photographers Association
c/o Don Anderson
1403 Glendale Hills Dr. NE
Rochester, MN 55906
Ph: (507)280-8840
E-mail: aphotodga@aol.com
URL: National Affiliate–ppa.com
Local. Represents the interests of professional society of portrait, wedding, commercial, industrial and specialized photographers. **Affiliated With:** Professional Photographers of America.

12135 ■ Dyslexia Institute of Minnesota
847 NW 5th St.
Rochester, MN 55901
Ph: (507)288-5271
Fax: (507)288-6424
E-mail: read@thereadingcenter.org
URL: http://thereadingcenter.org
Contact: Nancy Sears, Exec.Dir.
Founded: 1951. **Staff:** 4. **Budget:** $400,000. **Nonmembership**. **State**. Provides information and assistance to individuals who experience unexpected difficulty with reading. Offers teacher training and tutoring. Sponsors parents support group. **Libraries: Type:** reference. **Holdings:** 500. **Subjects:** dyslexia, learning disabilities, attention deficit disorder, teaching materials. **Doing business as:** The Reading Center. **Publications:** *Client Newsletter*, monthly. **Price:** free. **Circulation:** 175. Alternate Formats: online. **Conventions/Meetings:** quarterly meeting, parent support group.

12136 ■ Easter Seals Minnesota - Rochester
660 37th St. NW
Rochester, MN 55901
Ph: (507)281-9651
Fax: (507)281-3749
URL: http://www.goodwilleasterseals.org
Contact: Ms. Char Tewalt, Equipment Loan Coor.
Local. Works to help individuals with disabilities and special needs, and their families. Conducts programs to assist people of all ages with disabilities. Provides outpatient medical rehabilitation services. Advocates for the passage of legislation to help people with disabilities achieve independence, including the Americans with Disabilities Act (ADA). **Affiliated With:** Easter Seals.

12137 ■ Elder Network
c/o Mary Doucette, Exec.Dir.
1130 1/2 Seventh St. NW, Ste.205
Rochester, MN 55901-1732
Ph: (507)285-5272
Fax: (507)285-0884
E-mail: eldernetwork@elder-network.org
URL: http://www.elder-network.org
Contact: Mary Doucette, Exec.Dir.
Local. Aims to build a functional broad-based network of mental health support services for older adults by utilizing the services of peer volunteers.

12138 ■ Evangelical Pastors Fellowship of Rochester
c/o First Baptist Church
415 16th St. SW
Rochester, MN 55902
Ph: (507)288-8880
E-mail: firstb@firstb.org
URL: http://www.firstb.org
Contact: C. John Steer, Sr. Pastor
Members: 50. **Membership Dues:** $10 (annual). **Budget:** $5,000. **Local**. Religious organization for pastors and leaders of Evangelical churches. **Conventions/Meetings:** monthly meeting - always 3rd Thursday of the month at the Rochester Athletic Club; Avg. Attendance: 35.

12139 ■ Executive Women International, Rochester Chapter
c/o Jill Mickelson
Short Elliott Hendrickson, Inc.
3240 E River Rd., NE
Rochester, MN 55906
Ph: (507)529-7214
Fax: (507)529-7201
E-mail: jmickelson@sehinc.com
URL: http://www.executivewomenmn.org/rochester.html
Contact: Jill Mickelson, Pres.
Founded: 1997. **Members:** 18. **Local**. Works to promote member firms and improve their communities. Provides opportunities for business and personal growth. **Affiliated With:** Executive Women International. **Publications:** *Pulse*, monthly. Newsletter. **Advertising:** accepted. Alternate Formats: online. **Conventions/Meetings:** monthly meeting - 2nd Thursday of each month.

12140 ■ Family Service Rochester
1110 6th St. NW
Rochester, MN 55901
Ph: (507)287-2010
Fax: (507)287-7805
E-mail: office@familyservicerochester.org
URL: http://familyservicerochester.org
Contact: Brad J. Lohrbach, Exec.Dir.
Staff: 5. **Local**. Provides counseling in the areas of child safety, family stability, and well-being. **Conventions/Meetings:** meeting - 4-5/year.

12141 ■ Figure Skating Club of Rochester (RFSC)
21 Elton Hills Dr. NW
Rochester, MN 55901
Ph: (507)288-7536
Fax: (507)288-7536
E-mail: rfsc@charterinternet.net
URL: http://www.web-site.com/rfsc
Contact: Lynne Hemann, Pres.
Local. Promotes the sport of figure skating in the Rochester, MN area. Offers year-round lessons to children and adults. **Affiliated With:** United States Figure Skating Association. **Conventions/Meetings:** monthly meeting - always 3rd Wednesday of the month.

12142 ■ Gay/Lesbian Community Services of Rochester
PO Box 454
1500 First Ave. NE
Rochester, MN 55903-0454
Ph: (507)281-3265
E-mail: info@glcsmn.org
URL: http://www.glcsmn.org
Founded: 1980. **Members:** 150. **Local**. Provides a focal point for support and communication for gay, lesbian and bisexual persons. **Libraries: Type:** open to the public. **Holdings:** 200. **Subjects:** sexual orientation, gay, lesbian, bisexual, transgender. **Telecommunication Services:** hotline, AIDS hotline, (800)752-4281. **Publications:** *Rochester Gayzette*, monthly. Newsletter. **Price:** $18.00/year. **Conventions/Meetings:** monthly Business Meeting - always 2nd Wednesday.

12143 ■ Girl Scout Council of River Trails
4228 8th St. SW
Rochester, MN 55903
Ph: (507)288-4703
Free: (800)598-5516
E-mail: pwinters@rivertrails.org
URL: http://www.rivertrails.org
Contact: Peg Winters, Exec.Dir.
Local. Young girls and adult volunteers, corporate, government and individual supporters. Strives to develop potential and leadership skills among its members. Conducts trainings, educational programs and outdoor activities.

12144 ■ Hiawatha Valley Resource Conservation and Development Council
1485 Indus. Dr. NW
Rochester, MN 55901
Ph: (507)281-1959
Fax: (507)536-0176
E-mail: roger.lenzmeier@mn.usda.gov
URL: National Affiliate–www.rcdnet.org
Contact: Roger Lenzmeier, Coor.
Local. Affiliated With: National Association of Resource Conservation and Development Councils.

12145 ■ Hotel Employees and Restaurant Employees International Union, AFL-CIO, CLC - Local Union 21
105 N Broadway
Rochester, MN 55906
Ph: (507)288-2021
Fax: (507)288-0755
E-mail: dave@local21.com
URL: http://www.local21.com
Contact: Rod Pierce, Pres.
Members: 2,326. **Local. Affiliated With:** UNITE HERE.

12146 ■ Hotel Employees and Restaurant Employees International Union, AFL-CIO, CLC - Minnesota State Council
PO Box 847
Rochester, MN 55903
Ph: (507)288-2021
Fax: (507)288-0755
E-mail: dave@local21.com
URL: http://www.local21.com
Contact: David Blanchard, Pres.
Members: 5,947. **State. Affiliated With:** UNITE HERE.

12147 ■ Human Rights Commission of Olmsted County
151 4th St., SE
Rochester, MN 55904
Ph: (507)287-1347
Fax: (507)287-1610
E-mail: vettel.marcia@co.olmsted.mn.us
URL: http://www.olmstedcounty.com
Contact: Jacob Malwitz, Chm.
Members: 13. **Budget:** $8,000. **Local**. Strives to resolve complaints of age, sex, race, and religious discrimination within Olmsted County. **Formerly:** (2000) Human Rights Commission of Rochester. **Conventions/Meetings:** monthly meeting - always third Tuesday.

12148 ■ IEEE Communications Society, Southern Minnesota Chapter
c/o Scott S. Dahl
2701 Maywood Ln. SW
Rochester, MN 55902-1097
Ph: (507)253-0428
Fax: (507)253-2870
E-mail: ssdahl@us.ibm.com
URL: National Affiliate–www.comsoc.org
Contact: Scott S. Dahl, Contact
Local. Industry professionals with a common interest in advancing all communications technologies. Seeks to foster original work in all aspects of communications science, engineering, and technology and encourages the development of applications that use signals to transfer voice, data, image, and/or video information between locations. Promotes the theory and use of systems involving all types of terminals, computers, and information processors; all pertinent systems and operations that facilitate transfer; all transmission media; switched and unswitched networks; and network layout, protocols, architectures, and implementations. **Affiliated With:** IEEE Communications Society.

12149 ■ IEEE Computer Society, Southern Minnesota Chapter
c/o Ron Jensen, Chair
12431 White Bridge Ln.
Rochester, MN 55901-8252

Ph: (507)253-3887
E-mail: d.j.wenzel@ieee.org
URL: National Affiliate–www.computer.org
Contact: Ron Jensen, Chair

Local. **Affiliated With:** IEEE Computer Society.

12150 ■ IEEE Southern Minnesota Section
6751 Country Club Rd. SW
Rochester, MN 55902-8740
Ph: (507)253-2369
E-mail: j.clegg@ieee.org
URL: http://ewh.ieee.org/r4/southern_minnesota
Contact: Jason Clegg, Chair

Local. Engineers and scientists in electrical engineering, electronics, and allied fields. Promotes creating, developing, integrating, sharing, and applying knowledge about electro and information technologies and sciences for the benefit of humanity and the profession. Conducts lectures on current engineering and scientific topics.

12151 ■ Institute of Management Accountants, Southern Minnesota
c/o Nancy A. Richardson, Pres.
1850 Terracewood Dr. NW
Rochester, MN 55901-2437
Ph: (507)288-5408
E-mail: namzr@hotmail.com
URL: http://www.ima-northernlights.imanet.org
Contact: Nancy A. Richardson, Pres.

Local. Promotes professional and ethical standards. Equips members and students with knowledge and training required for the accounting profession. **Councils:** Northern Lights. **Affiliated With:** Institute of Management Accountants.

12152 ■ Junior Achievement, Rochester Area
c/o Kim Norton, District Mgr.
Educational Services Bldg.
334 16th St. SE, Ste.132
Rochester, MN 55904
Ph: (507)281-6156
Fax: (507)285-8606
E-mail: kim@jaum.org
URL: http://www.jarochester.com
Contact: Kim Norton, District Mgr.

Local. Affiliated With: Junior Achievement.

12153 ■ March of Dimes Birth Defects Foundation, Southeast Minnesota Division
32 Woodlake Dr. SE
Rochester, MN 55904
Ph: (507)282-0649
Fax: (507)282-9673
E-mail: mn631@marchofdimes.com
URL: http://www.modimes.org
Contact: Kelly Watercott, Community Dir.

Founded: 1938. **Staff:** 3. **Regional Groups:** 1. **State Groups:** 1. **Local Groups:** 1. **Local**. Promotes healthy childbirth and the prevention of birth defects. Sponsors research and education programs. **Libraries: Type:** open to the public. **Holdings:** 125; video recordings. **Subjects:** how to have a healthy baby. **Awards: Frequency:** annual. **Type:** grant. **Affiliated With:** March of Dimes Birth Defects Foundation. **Formerly:** (1996) March of Dimes Birth Defects Foundation, Rochester Chapter; (2005) March of Dimes Birth Defects Foundation, Southeastern Minnesota Division.

12154 ■ Mayo School of Health-Related Sciences Alumni Association
c/o Karen Skiba
200 1st St. SW
Rochester, MN 55905-0001
Ph: (507)284-2511 (507)284-2317
Fax: (507)538-7442
URL: http://www.mayo.edu

Local.

12155 ■ Meals on Wheels of Rochester
1110 6th St. NW
Rochester, MN 55901
Ph: (507)287-2010
Fax: (507)287-7805
E-mail: office@familyservicerochester.org
URL: http://www.familyservicerochester.org
Contact: Brad Lohrbach MSW, Exec.Dir.

Local. Delivers meals to the needy.

12156 ■ Mid-America Orthopaedic Association
Kahler Mezzanine Level
20 Second Ave. SW
Rochester, MN 55902-3013
Ph: (507)281-3431
Fax: (507)281-0291
E-mail: maoa@rconnect.com
URL: http://www.maoa.org
Contact: Ham Peterson MD, Managing Dir.

Founded: 1982. **Regional**.

12157 ■ Minnesota Association of Law Enforcement Firearms Instructors
c/o Mark Erickson
101 4th St. SE
Rochester, MN 55904-3761
Ph: (507)285-8300
Contact: Mark Erickson, Contact

Members: 76. **State Groups:** 1. **State**.

12158 ■ Minnesota Chapter of National Association of Tax Practitioners
c/o JoAnn Schoen, EA, Pres.
1700 N Broadway, No. 106
Rochester, MN 55906-4144
Ph: (507)281-5128
Fax: (507)281-9631
E-mail: accounttax@aol.com
URL: National Affiliate–www.natptax.com
Contact: JoAnn Schoen EA, Pres.

State. **Affiliated With:** National Association of Tax Professionals.

12159 ■ Minnesota Chapter of National Association of Tax Professionals
c/o JoAnn Schoen, EA, Pres.
1700 N. Broadway No. 106
Rochester, MN 55906-4144
Ph: (507)281-5128
Fax: (507)281-9631
E-mail: accounttax@aol.com
URL: National Affiliate–www.natptax.com
Contact: JoAnn Schoen EA, Pres. of the State Board

Founded: 1986. **Members:** 500. **Membership Dues:** full membership to National automatically gives state Chapter membership, $99 (annual). **Budget:** $13,000. **State**. **Affiliated With:** National Association of Tax Professionals. **Conventions/Meetings:** annual conference, with education and networking (exhibits).

12160 ■ Minnesota Council for Exceptional Children
c/o Melissa Schaller
2293 Boulder Ridge Dr. NW
Rochester, MN 55901
Ph: (507)433-0957
Fax: (507)433-0958
E-mail: mschaller@austin.k12.mn.us
URL: http://www.cec.sped.org/ab/federati.html
Contact: Melissa Schaller, Contact

State. **Additional Websites:** http://www.mo-cec.org.

12161 ■ Minnesota Nurses Association - District 6
2767 Charles Ct. NW
Rochester, MN 55901
Ph: (507)266-7499
E-mail: snyder.barbara@mayo.edu
URL: http://www.mnnurses.org
Contact: Barbara Snyder, Pres.

Local. Works to advance the nursing profession. Seeks to meet the needs of nurses and health care consumers. Fosters high standards of nursing practice. Promotes the economic and general welfare of nurses in the workplace. **Affiliated With:** American Nurses Association; Minnesota Nurses Association.

12162 ■ NAIFA-Rochester
c/o Pat Schwartzhoff, Exec.
6010 Hillsboro Ln. NW
Rochester, MN 55901
Ph: (507)252-8696
Fax: (507)280-9519
E-mail: patschwartzhoff@charter.net
URL: National Affiliate–naifa.org
Contact: Pat Schwartzhoff, Exec.

Local. Represents the interests of insurance and financial advisors. Advocates for a positive legislative and regulatory environment. Enhances business and professional skills of members. **Affiliated With:** National Association of Insurance and Financial Advisors.

12163 ■ NAMI Olmsted County
903 W Center St., Ste.200
Rochester, MN 55902
Ph: (507)287-1692
Fax: (507)529-4824
E-mail: office@namiolmstedco.org
URL: http://www.namiolmstedco.org
Contact: Anne Kamin, Dir.

Founded: 1986. **Members:** 215. **Membership Dues:** individual, family, business, organization, $30 (annual). **Staff:** 3. **Budget:** $47,000. **Local**. Persons with mental illnesses; their families and friends, professionals, interested citizens. Seeks improved quality of life and public awareness for persons with mental illness. Offers support, educational, and assistance services. **Libraries: Type:** open to the public. **Subjects:** mental illness. **Formerly:** (1998) Alliance for the Mentally Ill, Rochester Area. **Publications:** *Olmstead County*, bimonthly. Newsletter. **Conventions/Meetings:** periodic Special Event - meeting • semimonthly support group meeting.

12164 ■ National Association for the Advancement of Colored People, Rochester Branch 507
PO Box 6472
Rochester, MN 55903-6472
Fax: (507)288-5300
E-mail: president@rochesternaacp.org
URL: http://www.rochesternaacp.org
Contact: W.C. Jordan Jr., Pres.

Local.

12165 ■ Olmsted County Government Center
151 4th St. SE
Rochester, MN 55904
Ph: (507)285-8115
Fax: (507)287-2693
E-mail: adminweb@co.olmsted.mn.us

Local.

12166 ■ Olmsted County Historical Society
1195 W Circle Dr. SW
Rochester, MN 55902-6619
Ph: (507)282-9447
E-mail: ochs@olmstedhistory.com
URL: http://olmstedhistory.com
Contact: John Hunziker, Exec.Dir.

Founded: 1926. **Members:** 500. **Membership Dues:** individual, $30 (annual) • family, $40 (annual) • corporate, $100 (annual). **Staff:** 30. **Budget:** $400,000. **Regional**. Collects and preserves the history of Olmsted County, Minnesota. Tours are conducted through the museum and historic sites. Extensive research and genealogical materials are found in the library and archives. **Libraries: Type:** open to the public. **Holdings:** 12,000; articles, books, papers, periodicals, photographs, video recordings. **Subjects:** historical information. **Computer Services:** database, searchable databases on the web • online services, online ordering of research services, resources can be searched by computer. **Formerly:** Historical Society of Olmsted County. **Publications:** *Olmsted Historican*, quarterly. Newsletter. **Price:** free to members. **Advertising:** accepted.

12167 ■ Parents are Important in Rochester (PAIIR)
c/o Northrop Education Center
201 8th St. NW
Rochester, MN 55901
Ph: (507)285-8033
Fax: (507)529-4625
E-mail: colord@rochester.k12.mn.us
URL: http://www.rochester.k12.mn.us/school86
Contact: Courtney Lord, Outreach Coor.
Founded: 1974. **Staff:** 27. **Local.** Administers early childhood and family education program. Offers early childhood education, parent education, parent-child interaction, single parents, and Dad 'n Me programs. **Libraries: Type:** lending. **Holdings:** books, video recordings. **Conventions/Meetings:** periodic meeting, classes for parents with preschool children.

12168 ■ PFLAG Rochester/Southern Minnesota
PO Box 6302
Rochester, MN 55903-6302
Ph: (507)282-8874
E-mail: pflagsomn@charter.net
URL: National Affiliate–www.pflag.org
Contact: Joseph Nix, Chapter Pres.
Founded: 1989. **Members:** 60. **Membership Dues:** single, $20 (annual) • family, $30 (annual). **Local.** Support group for families and friends of lesbians, gays, bisexuals, and transgenders. **Libraries: Type:** open to the public. **Holdings:** 100; books, video recordings. **Subjects:** homosexual issues. **Formerly:** (2005) PFLAG-Rochester. **Publications:** Newsletter, monthly. **Price:** $10.00/year. **Circulation:** 65.

12169 ■ Phi Theta Kappa, Omicron Chapter - Rochester Community and Technical College
c/o Barbara Mollberg
851 30th Ave. SE
Rochester, MN 55904
Ph: (507)285-7111
E-mail: barb.mollberg@roch.edu
URL: http://www.ptk.org/directories/chapters/MN/257-1.htm
Contact: Barbara Mollberg, Advisor
Local.

12170 ■ Plumbing-Heating-Cooling Contractors Association, Rochester
c/o Mr. Craig Curley, Pres.
1244 60th Ave. NW
Rochester, MN 55901-2933
Ph: (507)289-0229
Fax: (507)289-8360
URL: National Affiliate–www.phccweb.org
Contact: Mr. Craig Curley, Pres.
Local. Represents the plumbing, heating and cooling contractors. Promotes the construction industry. Protects the environment, health, safety and comfort of society. **Affiliated With:** Plumbing-Heating-Cooling Contractors Association.

12171 ■ Rochester Area Chamber of Commerce (RACC)
220 S Broadway, Ste.100
Rochester, MN 55904-6517
Ph: (507)288-1122
Fax: (507)282-8960
E-mail: chamber@rochestermnchamber.com
URL: http://www.rochestermnchamber.com
Contact: John Wade, Pres.
Founded: 1866. **Members:** 1,150. **Staff:** 8. **Local.** Promotes business and community development in the Rochester, MN area. **Awards:** Athena. **Frequency:** annual. **Type:** recognition • Lamp of Knowledge Awards. **Frequency:** annual. **Type:** recognition • Small Business of the Year. **Frequency:** annual. **Type:** recognition • Volunteer of the Year. **Frequency:** annual. **Type:** recognition. **Computer Services:** Online services, membership directory. **Committees:** Agri-Business; Ambassadors; Business Solutions; Chamber Toastmasters; Diversity Awareness; Government Affairs; Government Forums; Preparing Workforce. **Publications:** *Advantage*, monthly. Newsletter • *Business Reference Guide and Membership Directory*, annual. Contains Chamber information, community profile, directory of elected officials, and Chamber membership. **Price:** $35.00. **Circulation:** 2,500.

12172 ■ Rochester Area Disabled Athletics and Recreation (RADAR)
539 N Broadway, No. 117
Rochester, MN 55906
Ph: (507)280-6995
Fax: (507)292-8798
E-mail: radarsports@aol.com
Contact: Loretta Verbout, Exec.Dir.
Founded: 1985. **Members:** 1,000. **Staff:** 2. **Budget:** $100,000. **Local.** Provides sports and recreation for individuals with all types of disabilities. **Publications:** *Doings and Dates*, bimonthly. Contains listing and information about upcoming activities. **Price:** free. **Circulation:** 950.

12173 ■ Rochester Astronomy Club
1407 Weatherhill Ridge Ct. SW
Rochester, MN 55902
Ph: (507)288-5660
E-mail: mcallahan@mayo.edu
URL: http://www.rochesterskies.org
Contact: Mark Callahan, Contact
Local. Promotes the science of astronomy. Works to encourage and coordinate activities of amateur astronomical societies. Fosters observational and computational work and craftsmanship in various fields of astronomy. **Affiliated With:** Astronomical League.

12174 ■ Rochester Boychoir
PO Box 823
Rochester, MN 55903-0823
Ph: (507)282-1618
E-mail: info@rochesterboychoir.org
URL: http://www.rochesterboychoir.org
Contact: Sue Foster, Pres.
Founded: 1963. **Members:** 2,000. **Staff:** 2. **Local.** 5000. **Libraries: Type:** reference. **Subjects:** music.

12175 ■ Rochester Coin and Stamp Club
c/o Jay Darby
3628 6th St. NW.
Rochester, MN 55901
E-mail: maomt@aol.com
URL: National Affiliate–www.money.org
Contact: Jay Darby, Contact
Local. Affiliated With: American Numismatic Association.

12176 ■ Rochester Convention and Visitors Bureau (RCVB)
111 S Broadway Ste.301
Centerplace Galleria
Rochester, MN 55904
Ph: (507)288-4331
Fax: (507)288-9144
Free: (800)634-8277
E-mail: info@rochestercvb.org
URL: http://www.visitrochestermn.com
Contact: Mr. Brad Jones, Exec.Dir.
Founded: 1989. **Staff:** 8. **Budget:** $1,200,000. **Nonmembership. Local.** Promotes Rochester, Minnesota as a destination for conventions, tourism and sports events. Provides free convention and visitors services and planning assistance. **Affiliated With:** International Association of Convention and Visitor Bureaus.

12177 ■ Rochester Dog Obedience Club (RDOC)
200 E River Ln. NE
Rochester, MN 55906
E-mail: rdocmn@yahoo.com
URL: http://www.rdocmn.org
Local.

12178 ■ Rochester Host Lions Club
PO Box 134
Rochester, MN 55906
E-mail: staver.randy@mayo.edu
URL: http://www2.isl.net/lions
Contact: Randy Staver, Pres.
Local. Affiliated With: Lions Clubs International.

12179 ■ Rochester Human Resources Association
PO Box 6662
Rochester, MN 55903
URL: http://www.rhra.org
Contact: Kelly Spaulding, Pres.
Local. Represents the interests of human resource and industrial relations professionals and executives. Promotes the advancement of human resource management.

12180 ■ Rochester Minnesota Kennel Club (RMKC)
c/o Marie Christiansen, Corresponding Sec.
319 11th St. SE
Rochester, MN 55904-7445
URL: http://rmkc.8m.com
Local.

12181 ■ Rochester Police Athletic Activities League
c/o Fred Fanning
101 4th St. SE
Rochester, MN 55904-3761
Contact: Fred Fanning, Contact
Local. Sworn officers participating in athletic and educational activities with children between the ages 5-18 in the Rochester area; seeks to enhance relationships as well as providing role models for youth.

12182 ■ Rochester Table Tennis Club
Univ. Center Rochester
851 30th Ave. SE
Rochester, MN 55904
Ph: (507)252-8492
E-mail: info@rttc-mn.org
Contact: Chi Lam, Pres.
Local. Affiliated With: U.S.A. Table Tennis.

12183 ■ SCORE Counselors to America's Small Business (SCORE)
220 S Broadway, Ste.100
Rochester, MN 55904
Ph: (507)288-8103
Fax: (507)282-8960
E-mail: rochester@scoremn.org
URL: http://SCOREmn.org
Contact: Charmaine Flen, Chair
Members: 139. **Staff:** 1. **Local.** Volunteer businessmen and women. Provides free small business management assistance to individuals in the Rochester, MN area. Sponsors workshops. **Conventions/Meetings:** weekly meeting - always Tuesday.

12184 ■ Sertoma 700 Club Of Rochester
PO Box 721
Rochester, MN 55903
Ph: (507)424-2807
E-mail: info@sertoma700.com
URL: http://www.sertoma700.com
Contact: Scott Heck, Pres.
Local.

12185 ■ Skills USA, Century High School
2525 Viola Dr. NE
Rochester, MN 55906
Ph: (507)287-7997
Fax: (507)285-8595
E-mail: kastellpflug@rochester.k12.mn.us
URL: http://www.mnskillsusa.org
Contact: Kari Stellpflug, Contact
Local. Serves high school and college students enrolled in technical, skilled, and service and health occupations. Provides quality education experiences for students in leadership, teamwork, citizenship and character development. Builds and reinforces self-

confidence, work attitudes and communication skills. Emphasizes total quality at work, high ethical standards, superior work skills, and life-long education. Promotes understanding of the free enterprise system and involvement in community service. **Affiliated With:** Skills USA - VICA.

12186 ■ Skills USA, John Marshall High School
1510 14th St. NW
Rochester, MN 55901
Ph: (507)287-1456
E-mail: riswenson@rochester.k12.mn.us
URL: http://www.mnskillsusa.org
Contact: Richard Swenson, Contact
Local. Serves high school and college students enrolled in technical, skilled, and service and health occupations. Provides quality education experiences for students in leadership, teamwork, citizenship and character development. Builds and reinforces self-confidence, work attitudes and communication skills. Emphasizes total quality at work, high ethical standards, superior work skills, and life-long education. Promotes understanding of the free enterprise system and involvement in community service. **Affiliated With:** Skills USA - VICA.

12187 ■ Skills USA, Mayo High School
1420 SE 11th Ave.
Rochester, MN 55904
Ph: (507)281-6296
Fax: (507)285-8792
E-mail: gakomaniecki@rochester.k12.mn.us
URL: http://www.mnskillsusa.org
Contact: Gary Komaniecki, Contact
Local. Serves high school and college students enrolled in technical, skilled, and service and health occupations. Provides quality education experiences for students in leadership, teamwork, citizenship and character development. Builds and reinforces self-confidence, work attitudes and communication skills. Emphasizes total quality at work, high ethical standards, superior work skills, and life-long education. Promotes understanding of the free enterprise system and involvement in community service. **Affiliated With:** Skills USA - VICA.

12188 ■ Society of American Foresters, Southern Chapter
c/o Lance Sorenson, Chair
2300 Silver Creek Rd. NE
Rochester, MN 55906
Ph: (507)280-5369
E-mail: lance.sorenson@dnr.state.mn.us
URL: http://www.mnsaf.org
Contact: Lance Sorenson, Chair
Local. Affiliated With: Society of American Foresters.

12189 ■ Society for Neuroscience, Southern Minnesota Chapter
c/o Allan J. Bieber, PhD
Mayo Clinic and Found.
Dept. of Neurology, Guggenheim 428
200 First St. SW
Rochester, MN 55905
Ph: (507)284-8729
Fax: (507)284-1637
E-mail: bieber.allan@mayo.edu
URL: http://web.sfn.org/content/programs/chapters2/Addresses1
Contact: Allan J. Bieber PhD, Contact
Local. Affiliated With: Society for Neuroscience.

12190 ■ Sons of Norway, Kristiania Lodge 1-47
c/o Byron D. Stadsvold, Pres.
3732 Valleyridge Ct. NE
Rochester, MN 55906-6278
Ph: (507)288-1409
E-mail: bdstadsvold@msn.com
URL: National Affiliate–www.sofn.com
Contact: Byron D. Stadsvold, Pres.
Local. Affiliated With: Sons of Norway.

12191 ■ Southeast Minnesota Association of Realtors (SEMAR)
3400 E River Rd. NE
Rochester, MN 55906
Ph: (507)285-9833
Fax: (507)282-2450
Free: (877)885-4635
E-mail: kas@semnrealtors.com
URL: http://www.semnrealtors.com
Contact: Kathleen A. Schwartz, CEO
Founded: 1961. **Members:** 700. **Staff:** 3. **State Groups:** 1. **Local**. Real estate trade association of realtors and others interested in real estate. **Additional Websites:** http://www.cyberhomes.com, http://www.realtor.com. **Formerly:** (1999) Rochester Area Realtors Association. **Publications:** *The Realtor Seminar*, monthly. Newsletter. Alternate Formats: online.

12192 ■ Southeastern Minnesota Flying Club (SEMFC)
PO Box 6664
Rochester, MN 55903-6664
Ph: (507)288-2676
E-mail: rochester@flyingclub.com
URL: http://www.flyingclub.com/rochester
Contact: Joe Fishburn, VP
Founded: 1958. **Members:** 100. **Regional**. Individuals in the Rochester, MN area interested in aviation. Provides low-cost flying opportunities. **Conventions/Meetings:** monthly meeting - always 2nd Wednesday in Rochester, MN.

12193 ■ Southern Minnesota Healthcare Engineers Association (SMHCEA)
c/o Larry Udstuen, Pres.
Olmsted Medical Ctr.
1650 4th St. SE
Rochester, MN 55904-4717
Ph: (507)285-8485
Fax: (507)285-8504
E-mail: ludstuen@olmmed.org
URL: National Affiliate–www.ashe.org
Contact: Larry Udstuen, Pres.
Local. Promotes better patient care by encouraging members to develop their knowledge and increase their competence in the field of facilities management. Cooperates with hospitals and allied associations in matters pertaining to facilities management. **Affiliated With:** American Society for Healthcare Engineering of the American Hospital Association.

12194 ■ Sweet Adelines International, Zumbro Valley Chorus
Trinity Luthern Church
222 6th Ave. SW
Rochester, MN 55902
E-mail: carolfern4@aol.com
URL: http://www.regionsix.org/chorus/zumbro_valley.htm
Contact: Carol Sorenson, Asst.Dir.
Local. Advances the musical art form of barbershop harmony through education and performances. Provides education, training and coaching in the development of women's four-part barbershop harmony. **Affiliated With:** Sweet Adelines International.

12195 ■ Trout Unlimited - Hiawatha Chapter
2222 21st Ave. SE
Rochester, MN 55904
Ph: (507)288-5313
URL: http://www.millcomm.com/~andyd/

12196 ■ United Way of Olmsted County
903 W Ctr. St.
Rochester, MN 55902
Ph: (507)287-2000
E-mail: uwoc@uwolmsted.org
URL: http://www.unitedway.org
Contact: Karen Erlenbusch, Pres.
Local. Affiliated With: United Way of America.

12197 ■ USA Dance - Southern Minnesota Chapter No. 2017
PO Box 7354
Rochester, MN 55903-7354
E-mail: info@somnusabda.org
URL: http://somnusabda.org
Contact: Sally Moorhead, Contact
Local. Encourages and promotes the physical, mental and social benefits of partner dancing. Organizes and supports programs for the recreational enjoyment of ballroom dancing. Creates opportunities for the general public to participate in ballroom dancing and DanceSport.

12198 ■ Women's Shelter
PO Box 457
Rochester, MN 55901
Ph: (507)285-1010 (507)285-1938
Fax: (507)281-8224
Free: (800)438-6439
E-mail: wsi5@ll.net
URL: http://www.womens-shelter.org
Contact: Judy Miller, Exec.Dir.
Founded: 1976. **Staff:** 32. **Budget:** $1,350,000. **Languages:** English, Laotian, Spanish, Vietnamese. **Regional**. Provides support for battered women. Offers free child care. **Conventions/Meetings:** weekly support group meeting - always Thursday • weekly Women's Group - meeting - always Tuesday.

12199 ■ Zumbro Valley Audubon Society (ZVAS)
PO Box 6244
Rochester, MN 55903-6244
Ph: (507)289-9030
E-mail: chrisb@fullcircleimage.com
URL: http://www.audubon.org/chapter/mn/zumbro
Contact: Chris Benson, Pres.
Local. Offers programs and field trips relating to nature. Provides protection and sanctuary to birds in Olmstead County and Southeastern Minnesota. **Formerly:** (2005) National Audubon Society - Zumbro Valley.

12200 ■ Zumbro Valley Medical Society
200 1st St. SW
Rochester, MN 55905
Ph: (507)284-3180
Fax: (507)284-0964
E-mail: frank.jane@mayo.edu
Contact: Dr. F. T. Nobrega, Exec. Officer
Local. Medical doctors. Promotes the art and science of medicine and quality patient care. **Conventions/Meetings:** annual meeting, with individual committee meetings.

Rockford

12201 ■ American Legion, Minnesota Post 628
c/o Larry A. Roush
105 Edgewater Dr.
Rockford, MN 55373
Ph: (651)291-1800
Fax: (651)291-1057
URL: National Affiliate–www.legion.org
Contact: Larry A. Roush, Contact
Local. Affiliated With: American Legion.

Rockville

12202 ■ Rockville Lions Club
PO Box 406
Rockville, MN 56369-0406
Ph: (320)203-0803
URL: http://www.lionwap.org/rockvillelionsmn
Contact: Mike Hoffman, Pres.
Local. Affiliated With: Lions Clubs International.

Rogers

12203 ■ I-94 West Chamber of Commerce
21370 John Milless Dr.
PO Box 95
Rogers, MN 55374-0095
Ph: (763)428-2921
Fax: (763)428-9068
E-mail: requests@i94westchamber.org
URL: http://www.i94westchamber.org
Contact: Kathleen Poate, Pres.
Founded: 1988. **Members:** 330. **Local**. Promotes business and community development in Dayton, MN. **Formerly:** (1999) Rogers-Dayton Chamber of Commerce; (2002) Rogers Area Chamber of Commerce.

12204 ■ Rogers Area Lions Club - Minnesota
PO Box 112
Rogers, MN 55374
Ph: (763)428-9053 (763)428-9083
URL: http://www.rogersmnlions.org
Contact: Dean Eggert, Pres.
Local. **Affiliated With:** Lions Clubs International.

12205 ■ Rogers Area Youth Basketball Association (RAYBA)
PO Box 298
Rogers, MN 55374
Ph: (763)425-5700
E-mail: info@rayba.org
URL: http://www.rayba.org
Contact: Steve Molander, Board Member
Local.

Rollingstone

12206 ■ Rollingstone Area Jaycees
PO Box 24
Rollingstone, MN 55969
E-mail: info@rollingstonejaycees.org
URL: http://www.rollingstonejaycees.org
Contact: Fran Hengel, Contact
Founded: 1977. **Local**.

Roosevelt

12207 ■ American Legion, Goldstrand-Beadle Post 371
PO Box 157
Roosevelt, MN 56673
Ph: (651)291-1800
Fax: (651)291-1057
URL: National Affiliate–www.legion.org
Local. **Affiliated With:** American Legion.

Roseau

12208 ■ American Legion, Minnesota Post 24
c/o Kaleb E. Lindquist
321 Main Ave. N
Roseau, MN 56751
Ph: (651)291-1800
Fax: (651)291-1057
URL: National Affiliate–www.legion.org
Contact: Kaleb E. Lindquist, Contact
Local. **Affiliated With:** American Legion.

12209 ■ Roseau County Historical Society (RCHS)
110 2nd Ave. NE
Roseau, MN 56751
Ph: (218)463-1918
E-mail: rchsroseau@mncable.net
URL: http://www.roseaucohistoricalsociety.org
Contact: Charleen A. Haugen, Dir.
Founded: 1927. **Members:** 295. **Membership Dues:** single, $10 (annual) • family, $15 (annual) • sponsor, $25 (annual) • sustaining, $100 (annual). **Staff:** 3. **Budget:** $58,000. **Local**. Works to collect and preserve the history of Roseau County and relate it to the history of the state of Minnesota. **Libraries: Type:** open to the public. **Holdings:** 15,000; articles, books. **Subjects:** genealogy, county, state and local history. **Boards:** Roseau County Historical Society Board of Directors. **Publications:** *Minnesota's Historic Great Northwest*, semiannual. Newsletter. **Conventions/Meetings:** annual meeting, museum artifacts (exhibits) - March or April; Avg. Attendance: 65.

12210 ■ Roseau Lions Club
c/o Edward C. Turn, Sec.
618 Etta Ct.
Roseau, MN 56751
Ph: (218)463-0780 (218)463-0475
E-mail: ed.turn@borderstatebank.com
URL: http://lions5m11.org/sys-tmpl/door
Contact: Edward C. Turn, Sec.
Local. **Affiliated With:** Lions Clubs International.

12211 ■ Skills USA, Roseau High School
509 3rd St. NE
Roseau, MN 56751
Ph: (218)463-2770
Fax: (218)463-3658
E-mail: nick_gerulli@roseau.k12.mn.us
URL: http://www.mnskillsusa.org
Contact: Nick Gerulli, Contact
Local. Serves high school and college students enrolled in technical, skilled, and service and health occupations. Provides quality education experiences for students in leadership, teamwork, citizenship and character development. Builds and reinforces self-confidence, work attitudes and communication skills. Emphasizes total quality at work, high ethical standards, superior work skills, and life-long education. Promotes understanding of the free enterprise system and involvement in community service. **Affiliated With:** Skills USA - VICA.

12212 ■ Wannaska Lions Club
c/o Robert L. Ruud, Sec.
21136 State Hwy. 89
Roseau, MN 56751
Ph: (218)463-2821 (218)425-7728
Fax: (218)463-1515
E-mail: robert.ruud@dot.state.mn.us
URL: http://lions5m11.org/sys-tmpl/door
Contact: Robert L. Ruud, Sec.
Local. **Affiliated With:** Lions Clubs International.

Rosemount

12213 ■ American Legion, Rosemount Post 65
PO Box 284
Rosemount, MN 55068
Ph: (651)291-1800
Fax: (651)291-1057
URL: National Affiliate–www.legion.org
Local. **Affiliated With:** American Legion.

12214 ■ Associated Landscape Contractors of America, Dakota County Technical College
c/o Edward Plaster, Faculty Advisor
1300 E 145th St.
Rosemount, MN 55068
Ph: (651)423-8498
Fax: (651)423-7028
E-mail: edward.plaster@dctc.mnscu.edu
URL: National Affiliate–www.alca.org
Contact: Edward Plaster, Faculty Advisor
Local. **Affiliated With:** Professional Landcare Network.

12215 ■ Minnesota Natural Health Coalition (MNHC)
c/o Victoria G. Welch, Exec.Dir.
PO Box 315
Rosemount, MN 55068
Ph: (651)322-4542 (612)721-3305
E-mail: mnhc@charter.net
URL: http://www.minnesotanaturalhealth.org
Contact: Victoria G. Welch, Exec.Dir.
Founded: 1997. **Members:** 2,000. **Membership Dues:** regular, $35 (annual). **Staff:** 1. **Budget:** $10,000. **State Groups:** 1. **State**. Provides research and education in regards of complementary and alternative health care. Sponsors educational activities and disseminates information. **Libraries: Type:** open to the public. **Holdings:** 200; books. **Subjects:** alternative health care treatment methods, health freedom issues. **Publications:** Newsletter, periodic. **Price:** free or donation. **Circulation:** 7,000. **Conventions/Meetings:** periodic Public Meeting, with guest speakers.

12216 ■ Phi Theta Kappa, Beta Theta Tau Chapter - Dakota County Technical College
c/o Diana Sullivan
1300 E 145th St.
Rosemount, MN 55068
Ph: (651)423-8483
E-mail: diana.sullivan@dctc.mnscu.edu
URL: http://www.ptk.org/directories/chapters/MN/21614-1.htm
Contact: Diana Sullivan, Advisor
Local.

12217 ■ Skills USA, Dakota County Technical Center
1300 145th St. E
Rosemount, MN 55068
Ph: (651)423-8458
Fax: (651)423-8760
E-mail: russell.anthony@isd917.k12.mn.us
URL: http://www.isd917.k12.mn.us
Contact: Russ Anthony, Contact
Local. Serves high school and college students enrolled in technical, skilled, and service and health occupations. Provides quality education experiences for students in leadership, teamwork, citizenship and character development. Builds and reinforces self-confidence, work attitudes and communication skills. Emphasizes total quality at work, high ethical standards, superior work skills, and life-long education. Promotes understanding of the free enterprise system and involvement in community service. **Affiliated With:** Skills USA - VICA.

Roseville

12218 ■ American Legion, Fifteen Grand Post 583
2325 Prior Ave. N
Roseville, MN 55113
Ph: (651)291-1800
Fax: (651)291-1057
URL: National Affiliate–www.legion.org
Local. **Affiliated With:** American Legion.

12219 ■ American Legion, Rosetown Memorial Post 542
700 County Rd. C W
Roseville, MN 55113
Ph: (651)291-1800
Fax: (651)291-1057
URL: National Affiliate–www.legion.org
Local. **Affiliated With:** American Legion.

12220 ■ American Physical Therapy Association, Minnesota Chapter (MNAPTA)
1711 W County Rd. B, Ste.102-S
Roseville, MN 55113-4036
Ph: (651)635-0902
Fax: (651)635-0903
Free: (800)999-2782
E-mail: info@mnapta.org
URL: http://www.mnapta.org
Contact: Joan C. Purrington PT, Pres.
Founded: 1927. **Members:** 1,500. **Staff:** 4. **Budget:** $550,000. **Regional Groups:** 1. **State**. Physical therapists and assistants, and student physical therapists and assistants. Works to meet physical

therapy needs through research, education, and practice. Sponsors Physical Therapy Month (October). **Committees:** Bylaws; Communication; Education; Ethics; Fundraising; Government Affairs; Human Resources. **Special Interest Groups:** Affiliate. **Affiliated With:** American Physical Therapy Association. **Publications:** *Soundwaves*, bimonthly • Directory, annual. **Advertising:** accepted. **Conventions/Meetings:** semiannual conference (exhibits) - always spring and fall.

12221 ■ American Theatre Organ Society, Land O' Lakes
c/o Terry Kleven, Pres.
1173 W Sandhurst Dr.
Roseville, MN 55113
Ph: (651)489-2074
E-mail: century@mninter.net
URL: National Affiliate–www.atos.org
Contact: Terry Kleven, Pres.
Local. Affiliated With: American Theatre Organ Society.

12222 ■ Association for Women in Computing - Twin Cities Chapter
PO Box 131022
Roseville, MN 55113
E-mail: president@awctc.org
URL: http://www.awctc.org
Contact: Heike Peters, Pres.
Local. Furthers the interests of women in the computing fields, in business, industry, science, education, government and military. Promotes the education, professional development and advancement of women in computing. Provides opportunities for professional growth through networking and programs on technical and career-oriented topics. **Affiliated With:** Association for Women in Computing.

12223 ■ Builders Association of the Twin Cities, National Association of Home Building
2960 Ctre. Pointe Dr.
Roseville, MN 55113
Ph: (651)697-1954
Fax: (651)697-7599
E-mail: diann@batc.org
URL: http://www.batconline.org
Contact: Bob Hanson, Exec.VP
Founded: 1948. **Staff:** 15. **Local.** Residential home builders, remodelers, and others associated with the building industry. **Affiliated With:** National Association of Home Builders.

12224 ■ Chippewa Wyldlife
3116 Fairview Ave. N
Roseville, MN 55113
Ph: (651)484-5234
URL: http://sites.younglife.org/sites/Chippewa/default.aspx
Local. Affiliated With: Young Life.

12225 ■ Concerns of Police Survivors, Minnesota Chapter
c/o Mr. Paul Gertsen, Pres.
PO Box 131382
Roseville, MN 55113
Ph: (651)489-8080
E-mail: paulgertsen8080@aol.com
URL: National Affiliate–www.nationalcops.org
Contact: Mr. Paul Gertsen, Pres.
State.

12226 ■ Falcon Heights-Lauderdale Lions Club
1796 Skillman Ave. W
Roseville, MN 55113
Ph: (651)633-3271
E-mail: crea@umn.edu
URL: http://falconhtslauderdalemn.lionwap.org
Contact: Ken Crea, Sec.
Local. Affiliated With: Lions Clubs International.

12227 ■ Friends of Lexington Area Parks
PO Box 131846
Roseville, MN 55113
E-mail: mbakeman@scc.net
Contact: Mary Bakeman, Contact
Nonmembership. Local. Supports the development of Lexington Park through sweat equity and financial means.

12228 ■ Greater Twin Cities Whippet Club
c/o Gail Wieberdink, Sec.
569 Woodhill Dr.
Roseville, MN 55113
URL: National Affiliate–www.americanwhippetclub.net
Contact: Gail Wieberdink, Sec.
Founded: 1977. **Members:** 70. **Membership Dues:** single, $12 (annual) • couple, $17 (annual). **Local.** Individuals in the Minneapolis and St. Paul, MN area interested in promoting the whippet as a race and show dog. Sponsors matches, schooling races, and programs dealing with all phases of health and maintenance of whippet dogs. **Affiliated With:** American Whippet Club. **Publications:** *GTCWC Newsletter*, bimonthly. **Price:** $10.00/year. **Advertising:** accepted. **Conventions/Meetings:** annual meeting - always February • monthly meeting - except December.

12229 ■ Highview Wyldlife
3116 Fairview Ave. N
Roseville, MN 55113
Ph: (651)484-5234
URL: http://sites.younglife.org/sites/highview/default.aspx
Contact: Cesar Castillejos, Contact
Local. Affiliated With: Young Life.

12230 ■ Information Systems Audit and Control Association and Foundation, Minnesota Chapter
1711 W County Rd. B, Ste.300 N
Roseville, MN 55113
Ph: (612)667-8075
Fax: (612)667-9683
E-mail: travis.e.finstad@wellsfargo.com
URL: http://www.mnisaca.org
Contact: Travis Finstad, Pres.
Founded: 1975. **Members:** 550. **Local. Affiliated With:** Information Systems Audit and Control Association and Foundation. **Publications:** *ISACA Chapter*, annual. Report. Alternate Formats: online.

12231 ■ Irondale Young Life
3116 Fairview Ave. N
Roseville, MN 55113
Ph: (651)484-5234
URL: http://sites.younglife.org/sites/Irondale/default.aspx
Local. Affiliated With: Young Life.

12232 ■ Land O' Lakes Theatre Organ Society
c/o Terry Kleven, Pres.
1173 W Sandhurst Dr.
Roseville, MN 55113
Ph: (651)489-2074
E-mail: century@mninter.net
URL: http://www.loltos.org
Contact: Terry Kleven, Pres.
Local. Aims to restore, preserve and promote the theatre pipe organ and its music. Encourages the youth to learn the instrument. Operates a committee that gathers history and old music from silent film days and information on theatre organists, theaters and organ installations of the silent film era. **Affiliated With:** American Theatre Organ Society.

12233 ■ Minnesota Association for Career and Technical Education
c/o Marlys J. Bucher, Pres.
1500 Hwy. 36 W
Roseville, MN 55113-4035
Ph: (651)582-8315
Fax: (651)582-8492
E-mail: marlys.bucher@state.mn.us
URL: National Affiliate–www.acteonline.org
Contact: Marlys J. Bucher, Pres.
State. Affiliated With: Association for Career and Technical Education.

12234 ■ Minnesota Association of Community Telecommunications Administrators
Rosewood Off. Plaza
1711 W County Rd. B, Ste.300N
Roseville, MN 55113
Ph: (651)635-0306
Fax: (651)635-0307
E-mail: jlueders@ci.lakeville.mn.us
URL: http://www.mactamn.org
Contact: Jeff Lueders, Cable Administrator
State. Provides education and training for local government officials. Improves the administration of cable television franchises in the state of Minnesota. Promotes local government interests in the use, development, and regulation of cable television and telecommunications systems at the local, state and federal levels. **Affiliated With:** National Association of Telecommunications Officers and Advisors.

12235 ■ Minnesota Association of Public Accountants (MAPA)
1711 W County Rd. B, Ste.300N
Roseville, MN 55113
Ph: (651)635-0706
Fax: (651)635-0307
Free: (800)501-4521
E-mail: admin@mapa-mn.com
URL: http://www.mapa-mn.com
Contact: Bonnie Young, Mgr./Conference Coor.
State.

12236 ■ Minnesota Council for the Social Studies (MCSS)
c/o Michael Foster, Recording Sec.
Minnesota Dept. of Educ.
1500 Hwy. 36 W
Roseville, MN 55113
Ph: (651)582-8286
E-mail: michael.foster@state.mn.us
URL: http://www.mcss.org
Contact: Michael Foster, Recording Sec.
State. Represents teachers of elementary and secondary social studies, including instructors of civics, geography, history, law, economics, political science, psychology, sociology, and anthropology. Promotes the teaching of social studies. Provides members with opportunities to share strategies, have access to new material, and keep abreast of the national education scene. **Affiliated With:** National Council for the Social Studies.

12237 ■ Minnesota Dietetic Association (MDA)
1910 W County Rd., B, Rm. 212
Roseville, MN 55113
Ph: (651)628-9250
Fax: (651)628-0023
E-mail: mda@eatrightmn.org
URL: http://www.mndietetics.org
Contact: D'Ann Brosnahan, Exec.Dir.
State. Affiliated With: American Dietetic Association.

12238 ■ Minnesota Educational Media Organization (MEMO)
PO Box 130555
Roseville, MN 55113-0005
Ph: (651)771-8672
Fax: (651)771-8672
E-mail: dsylte@tcq.net
URL: http://www.memoweb.org
Contact: Laurie Conzemius, Co-Pres.
State. Provides leadership in educational communications and technology by linking professionals holding a common interest in the use of educational technology and its application of the learning process.

12239 ■ Minnesota Farrier's Association No. 14
c/o David C. Kleinendorst, Pres.
1965 Roselawn Ave. W
Roseville, MN 55113
Ph: (651)645-1008
E-mail: dkleinendorst@attbi.com
URL: National Affiliate–www.americanfarriers.org
Contact: David C. Kleinendorst, Pres.
State. Affiliated With: American Farrier's Association.

12240 ■ Minnesota Pharmacists Association (MPhA)
1935 W County Rd. B-2, Ste.165
Roseville, MN 55113
Ph: (651)697-1771
Fax: (651)697-1776
Free: (800)451-8349
E-mail: julie@mpha.org
URL: http://www.mpha.org
Contact: Julie K. Johnson RPh, Exec.VP
State.

12241 ■ Minnesota Quarter Horse Association, District 4
c/o Sandra Jagger
2621 N Fisk St.
Roseville, MN 55113
Ph: (651)582-4934
URL: http://www.mnqha.com/index_main.htm
Contact: Sandra Jagger, Contact
Local. Affiliated With: American Quarter Horse Association.

12242 ■ Minnesota School Public Relations Association (MinnSPRA)
c/o Ann Kvaal, Admin. Services Coor.
1027 W Roselawn Ave.
Roseville, MN 55113
Ph: (651)489-1321
Fax: (651)489-1322
E-mail: minnspra@comcast.net
URL: http://www.minnspra.org
Contact: Beth Johnson, Pres.
Members: 150. **Membership Dues:** individual, $55 (annual). **State.** Public relations leadership advocating public education. **Affiliated With:** National School Public Relations Association. **Formerly:** (2005) National School Public Relations Association, Minnesota. **Conventions/Meetings:** monthly board meeting • semiannual conference.

12243 ■ Minnesota Service Station Association (MSSA)
c/o Barb Blunt, Exec.Dir.
1705 Marion St.
Roseville, MN 55113
Ph: (651)487-1983
Fax: (651)487-2447
Free: (800)752-4884
E-mail: barbblunt@mnssa.com
Founded: 1966. **State. Formerly:** (2005) Minnesota Service Station and Convenience Store Association.

12244 ■ Minnesota Trucking Association (MTA)
2277 Hwy. 36 W, No. 302
Roseville, MN 55113
Ph: (651)646-7351
Fax: (651)641-8995
E-mail: mta@mntruck.org
URL: http://www.mntruck.org
State. Promotes increased efficiency, productivity, and competitiveness in the trucking industries. **Councils:** Maintenance, Safety, Registration & Tax. **Affiliated With:** American Trucking Associations.

12245 ■ Moundsview - Young Life
3116 Fairview Ave. N
Roseville, MN 55113
Ph: (651)484-5234
URL: http://sites.younglife.org/sites/moundsview/default.aspx
Local. Affiliated With: Young Life.

12246 ■ Roseville Figure Skating Club
PO Box 131042
Roseville, MN 55113
Ph: (651)635-0693
URL: http://www.rosevillefsc.org
Local. Provides programs to encourage participation and achievement in the sport of figure skating on ice. Defines and maintains uniform standards of skating proficiency. Organizes and sponsors competitions and exhibitions for the purpose of stimulating interest in figure skating. **Affiliated With:** United States Figure Skating Association.

12247 ■ Roseville - Young Life
3116 Fairview Ave. N
Roseville, MN 55113
Ph: (651)484-5234
URL: http://sites.younglife.org/sites/rahs/default.aspx
Local. Affiliated With: Young Life.

12248 ■ St. Anthony Wyldlife
3116 Fairview Ave. N
Roseville, MN 55113
Ph: (651)484-5234
URL: http://sites.younglife.org/sites/stanthony/default.aspx
Local. Affiliated With: Young Life.

12249 ■ USA Weightlifting - Twin City Barbell
c/o Roger Sadecki
667 County Rd. C
Roseville, MN 55113-2137
Ph: (612)490-0310
URL: National Affiliate–www.usaweightlifting.org
Contact: Roger Sadecki, Contact
Local. Affiliated With: USA Weightlifting.

12250 ■ YoungLife Northern Twin Cities
3116 Fairview Ave. N
Roseville, MN 55113
Ph: (651)484-5234
Fax: (651)636-3366
URL: http://sites.younglife.org/sites/ntc/default.aspx
Local. Affiliated With: Young Life.

Rothsay

12251 ■ American Legion, Ellingson-Brenden Post 376
PO Box 36
Rothsay, MN 56579
Ph: (651)291-1800
Fax: (651)291-1057
URL: National Affiliate–www.legion.org
Local. Affiliated With: American Legion.

Round Lake

12252 ■ American Legion, Minnesota Post 461
c/o Charles Flentje
409 2nd Ave.
Round Lake, MN 56167
Ph: (651)291-1800
Fax: (651)291-1057
URL: National Affiliate–www.legion.org
Contact: Charles Flentje, Contact
Local. Affiliated With: American Legion.

Royalton

12253 ■ American Legion, Minnesota Post 137
c/o Osmer J. Leigh
PO Box 217
Royalton, MN 56373
Ph: (651)291-1800
Fax: (651)291-1057
URL: National Affiliate–www.legion.org
Contact: Osmer J. Leigh, Contact
Local. Affiliated With: American Legion.

Rush City

12254 ■ American Legion, Minnesota Post 93
c/o William T. Mc Coy
PO Box 358
Rush City, MN 55069
Ph: (651)291-1800
Fax: (651)291-1057
URL: National Affiliate–www.legion.org
Contact: William T. Mc Coy, Contact
Local. Affiliated With: American Legion.

Rushford

12255 ■ American Legion, Murphy-Johnson Post 94
PO Box 246
Rushford, MN 55971
Ph: (651)291-1800
Fax: (651)291-1057
URL: National Affiliate–www.legion.org
Local. Affiliated With: American Legion.

12256 ■ Hardwood Country Sportsman's Club
c/o Nate Vitse
23224 Lapman Dr.
Rushford, MN 55971-0000
E-mail: hcsc_inc@hotmail.com
Contact: Butch Johnson, Treas.
Founded: 2002. **Members:** 188. **Membership Dues:** regular, $20 (annual). **Staff:** 11. **Budget:** $25,000. **Local Groups:** 1. **Local.** Provides a shooting and recreational facility for the local community.

12257 ■ Rushford Lions Club
PO Box 101
Rushford, MN 55971
E-mail: johnp@acegroup.cc
URL: http://www.angelfire.com/mn2/Rushford/lions.html
Contact: John Petersen, Pres.
Local. Affiliated With: Lions Clubs International.

12258 ■ Semcac RSVP
c/o Sharon Rustad, Dir.
PO Box 549
Rushford, MN 55971-0549
Ph: (507)864-7741
Fax: (507)864-2440
E-mail: sharon.rustad@semcac.org
URL: http://www.seniorcorps.gov
Contact: Sharon Rustad, Dir.
Local. Additional Websites: http://www.semcac.org. **Affiliated With:** Retired and Senior Volunteer Program.

Russell

12259 ■ American Legion, Minnesota Post 460
c/o George C. Johnson
PO Box 321
Russell, MN 56169
Ph: (651)291-1800
Fax: (651)291-1057
URL: National Affiliate–www.legion.org
Contact: George C. Johnson, Contact
Local. Affiliated With: American Legion.

Ruthton

12260 ■ American Legion, Woodrow Wilson Post 506
PO Box 41
Ruthton, MN 56170
Ph: (651)291-1800
Fax: (651)291-1057
URL: National Affiliate–www.legion.org
Local. Affiliated With: American Legion.

Sabin

12261 ■ Sabin Lions Club
c/o Rodney Schmidt, Sec.
9099 70th St. S
Sabin, MN 56580
Ph: (218)789-7133
E-mail: seedpotato@prodigy.net
URL: http://lions5m11.org/sys-tmpl/door
Contact: Rodney Schmidt, Sec.
Local. Affiliated With: Lions Clubs International.

Sacred Heart

12262 ■ American Legion, Joseph Viken Post 229
PO Box 284
Sacred Heart, MN 56285
Ph: (651)291-1800
Fax: (651)291-1057
URL: National Affiliate–www.legion.org
Local. Affiliated With: American Legion.

12263 ■ Sacred Heart Lions Club
c/o Orlynn Hegna, Pres.
83436 County Rd. 10
Sacred Heart, MN 56285
Ph: (320)765-2969
URL: http://www.5m4lions.org
Contact: Orlynn Hegna, Pres.
Local. Affiliated With: Lions Clubs International.

St. Bonifacius

12264 ■ American Legion, Minnesota Post 597
c/o James Weiland
PO Box 26
St. Bonifacius, MN 55375
Ph: (651)291-1800
Fax: (651)291-1057
URL: National Affiliate–www.legion.org
Contact: James Weiland, Contact
Local. Affiliated With: American Legion.

12265 ■ St. Bonifacius Lions Club
c/o Steve Peterka, Pres.
PO Box 831
St. Bonifacius, MN 55375
Ph: (952)446-1239
URL: http://www.5m5.org
Contact: Steve Peterka, Pres.
Local. Affiliated With: Lions Clubs International.

St. Charles

12266 ■ American Legion, Hugh Watson Post 190
1148 Whitewater Ave.
St. Charles, MN 55972
Ph: (651)291-1800
Fax: (651)291-1057
URL: National Affiliate–www.legion.org
Local. Affiliated With: American Legion.

12267 ■ St. Charles Lions Club
c/o Patrica Schlickenmeyer, Pres.
1242 Morse Ave.
St. Charles, MN 55972-1616
Ph: (507)932-5838
E-mail: joepatsc@hbcsc.net
URL: http://www.lions5m1.org/stcharles
Contact: Patrica Schlickenmeyer, Pres.
Local. Affiliated With: Lions Clubs International.

St. Clair

12268 ■ American Legion, W.-Grams-R-Schmidt Post 475
117 E Main St.
St. Clair, MN 56080
Ph: (651)291-1800
Fax: (651)291-1057
URL: National Affiliate–www.legion.org
Local. Affiliated With: American Legion.

St. Cloud

12269 ■ Acacia, St. Cloud State Chapter
398 3rd Ave. S
St. Cloud, MN 56301
Ph: (320)251-2380
URL: National Affiliate–www.acacia.org
Contact: Jacob Sundquist, Venerable Dean
Local. Affiliated With: Acacia.

12270 ■ American Cancer Society, St. Cloud
3721 23rd St. S., Ste.102
St. Cloud, MN 56301
Ph: (320)255-0220
Fax: (320)255-5517
Free: (800)239-7028
URL: http://www.cancer.org
Local. Affiliated With: American Cancer Society.

12271 ■ American Legion, Minnesota Post 76
c/o Andrew Borgen
1307 Lincoln Ave. SE
St. Cloud, MN 56304
Ph: (651)291-1800
Fax: (651)291-1057
URL: National Affiliate–www.legion.org
Contact: Andrew Borgen, Contact
Local. Affiliated With: American Legion.

12272 ■ American Legion, St. Augusta Post 621
1894 247th St.
St. Cloud, MN 56301
Ph: (651)291-1800
Fax: (651)291-1057
URL: National Affiliate–www.legion.org
Local. Affiliated With: American Legion.

12273 ■ APICS, The Association for Operations Management - Central Minnesota Chapter
PO Box 457
St. Cloud, MN 56302
Ph: (320)203-7600
E-mail: preeth@ventureallies.com
URL: http://www.cemnapics.org
Contact: Preeth John, Pres.
Local. Provides information and services in production and inventory management and related areas to enable members, enterprises and individuals to add value to their business performance. **Affiliated With:** APICS - The Association for Operations Management.

12274 ■ Arc St. Cloud
PO Box 251
St. Cloud, MN 56302
Ph: (320)251-7272
E-mail: cowen@arcmidstate.org
URL: http://www.arcmidstate.org
Contact: Cindy Owen, Dir.
Local. Parents, professional workers, and others interested in individuals with mental retardation. Works to promote services, research, public understanding, and legislation for people with mental retardation and their families. **Affiliated With:** Arc of the United States.

12275 ■ Association for Computing Machinery, St. Cloud State University
c/o Jamie Overholt, Pres.
720 4th Ave. S.
ECC 139
St. Cloud, MN 56301
Ph: (320)255-0120
Fax: (320)255-4269
E-mail: acm@eeyore.stcloudstate.edu
Contact: Jamie Overholt, Pres.
Students pursuing a computer science degree. Seeks to futher educate computer science students through speakers, tours and activities. Provides resume books and other means to find internships and careers for members. **Affiliated With:** Association for Computing Machinery.

12276 ■ Big Brothers Big Sisters of Central Minnesota
c/o Perry Rollings, Associate Dir.
15 6th Ave. N
St. Cloud, MN 56303
Ph: (320)253-1616
Fax: (320)253-1702
E-mail: sharren@bbbscentralmn.org
URL: http://www.bbbscentralmn.org
Contact: Troy Fritz, Exec.Dir.
Regional.

12277 ■ Centracare Health Foundation
c/o Mark Larkin, Exec.Dir.
1406 6th Ave. N
St. Cloud, MN 56303
Ph: (320)240-2810
Fax: (320)656-7115
E-mail: foundation@centracare.com
URL: http://www.centracare.com
Contact: Mark Larkin, Exec.Dir.
Founded: 1996. **Staff:** 5. **Budget:** $425,417. **Local.** Engages the philanthropic community in partnership to improve health and health care. **Awards:** Spirit of Caring Award. **Frequency:** annual. **Type:** monetary. **Recipient:** for collaborative effort to improve health in service area. **Formerly:** (1999) Centracare Foundation.

12278 ■ Central Minnesota Area Chapter of the American Association of Critical Care Nurses (CMAC/AACN)
c/o Karla Koenig, Pres.
PO Box 274
St. Cloud, MN 56302
Ph: (320)251-3887
E-mail: cmac.info@aacn.org
URL: http://www.aacn.org/chapters/cmac.nsf/other/homepage?opendocument
Contact: Karla Koenig, Pres.
Founded: 1989. **Members:** 35. **Membership Dues:** regular, $15 (annual). **Staff:** 20. **Budget:** $3,500. **Regional Groups:** 1. **State Groups:** 3. **Local Groups:** 1. **State.** Critical nurses, predominately hospital employed. Conducts community education concerning health care. **Awards:** Critical Care Nurse of the Year. **Frequency:** annual. **Type:** monetary. **Recipient:** for members of CMAC. **Affiliated With:** American Association of Critical-Care Nurses. **Publications:** Newsletter, monthly. **Price:** free. **Conventions/Meetings:** monthly meeting - every 1st Thursday • semiannual seminar • annual workshop - always spring.

12279 ■ Central Minnesota Audubon Society (CMAS)
12299 Sauk River Rd.
St. Cloud, MN 56301
URL: http://www.cloudnet.com/~audubon
Contact: Linda Peck, Pres.
Founded: 1980. **Local. Formerly:** (2005) National Audubon Society - Central Minnesota.

12280 ■ Central Minnesota Council on Aging
2700 1st St. N, Ste.307
St. Cloud, MN 56301

Ph: (320)253-9349
Fax: (320)253-9576
Free: (800)333-2433
E-mail: nicole@cmcoa.org
URL: http://www.cmcoa.org
Local. Aims to maintain the highest level of independence with older people by developing and coordinating community care, reducing isolation, and improving access to services.

12281 ■ Central Minnesota Libraries Exchange (CMLE)
c/o St. Cloud State University
Miller Center 130-D
St. Cloud, MN 56301-4498
Ph: (320)308-2950
Fax: (320)308-5131
Free: (800)657-3796
E-mail: cmle@stcloudstate.edu
URL: http://www.cmle.org
Contact: Patricia A. Post, Dir.
Founded: 1979. **Members:** 282. **Staff:** 4. **Budget:** $119,000. **State**. Libraries and media centers in central Minnesota. Works to encourage, develop, and facilitate resource sharing and improve services. Holds workshops. **Publications:** *Exchanger*, quarterly. Newsletter. Contains information on local, regional and national trends and upcoming events in the library/media field. **Price:** free to members. **Conventions/Meetings:** annual meeting - fall.

12282 ■ Central Minnesota Society for Human Resource Management
PO Box 824
St. Cloud, MN 56302
E-mail: presidentelect@cmshrm.org
URL: http://www.cmshrm.org
Contact: Jill Magelssen, Pres.
Local. Represents the interests of human resource and industrial relations professionals and executives. Promotes the advancement of human resource management.

12283 ■ Central Minnesota Youth for Christ
PO Box 375
St. Cloud, MN 56302
Ph: (320)251-8711
Fax: (320)251-1643
URL: http://www.cmyfc.org
Local. **Affiliated With:** Youth for Christ/U.S.A.

12284 ■ Del-Tone/Luth Gun Club
3322 12th St. SE
St. Cloud, MN 56304
Ph: (320)251-9873
E-mail: pbraun@netlinkcom.com
URL: http://www.del-tone-luth.com
Local. **Affiliated With:** National Skeet Shooting Association.

12285 ■ First Call for Help (FCFH)
c/o Tonya Hauschild
PO Box 542
St. Cloud, MN 56302
Ph: (320)252-3474
Free: (800)543-7709
E-mail: firstcall@cloudnet.com
URL: http://www.fcfh.org
Contact: Tonya Hauschild, Contact
Founded: 1970. **Staff:** 2. **Regional Groups:** 1. **State Groups:** 11. **Local**. Information and referral agency. **Formerly:** (2002) Information and Referral Coalition.

12286 ■ Greater Saint Cloud RSVP
c/o Lisa Braun, Dir.
400 2nd St. S
St. Cloud, MN 56301
Ph: (320)255-7295
Fax: (320)650-3461
E-mail: lbraun@ci.stcloud.mn.us
URL: http://www.seniorcorps.gov/about/programs/rsvp_state.asp?usestateabbr=mn&Search4.x=27&Search4.y=12
Contact: Lisa Braun, Dir.
Local. **Affiliated With:** Retired and Senior Volunteer Program.

12287 ■ Institute of Management Accountants, Central Minnesota
c/o Gary S. Owen, Pres.
Meyer Associates, Inc.
14 7th Ave. N
St. Cloud, MN 56303-4753
Ph: (320)656-4145 (320)255-1746
Fax: (320)259-4044
E-mail: gowen@callmeyer.com
URL: http://www.ima-northernlights.imanet.org
Contact: Gary S. Owen, Pres.
Local. Promotes professional and ethical standards. Equips members and students with knowledge and training required for the accounting profession. **Councils:** Northern Lights. **Affiliated With:** Institute of Management Accountants.

12288 ■ International Association of Machinists and Aerospace Workers, District Lodge 165
1903 4th St. N
St. Cloud, MN 56303
Ph: (320)252-4654
Fax: (320)252-4659
E-mail: lneumanjr@qwest.net
URL: http://www.iamdl165.org
Contact: Lewis Neuman Jr., Directing Business Representative
Members: 3,402. **Local**. Represents workers. Strives to provide contractors with well-trained and productive employees. **Affiliated With:** International Association of Machinists and Aerospace Workers.

12289 ■ Lac Qui Parle County Service Unit, American Red Cross
c/o Central Minnesota Chapter
1301 W St. Germain St.
St. Cloud, MN 56301
Ph: (320)251-7641
Fax: (320)251-6400
Free: (800)560-7641
E-mail: beth@cenmnredcross.org
URL: http://www.cenmnredcross.org
Contact: Cheryl Knoll, Local Representative
Members: 20. **State Groups:** 50. **Local Groups:** 1. **Local**. Serves members of the armed forces and veterans and their families and aids disaster victims. Other activities include: blood services; community services; service opportunities for youth. **Affiliated With:** American Red Cross National Headquarters.

12290 ■ Minnesota Ambulance Association (MAA)
PO Box 823
St. Cloud, MN 56302-0823
Ph: (320)654-1767
Fax: (320)251-8154
Free: (800)852-2776
E-mail: office@mnems.org
URL: http://www.mnems.org
Contact: Buck McAlpin, Pres.
Members: 306. **Membership Dues:** ambulance service single base (over 5000 runs), $3,500 (annual) • ambulance service multiple base (over 5000 runs), $5,500 (annual) • associate vendor/individual, $200 (annual) • ambulance service (1 - 5000 runs), $150-$1,700 (annual) • individual, $15 (annual) • responder, $75 (annual). **Staff:** 1. **Local**. Seeks to maintain the financial viability of the EMS industry through advocacy, education, legislation, and regulatory change. **Publications:** Newsletter.

12291 ■ Minnesota Jewelers Association (MJA)
c/o Nancy Fischer, Exec.Dir.
PO Box 6192
St. Cloud, MN 56302-6192
Ph: (320)654-6775
Fax: (320)253-3324
Free: (800)544-6416
E-mail: info@minnesotajewelers.org
URL: http://www.mnndjewelers.org
State. Trade association for retail jewelers in Minnesota and North Dakota.

12292 ■ NAIFA-Central Minnesota
c/o Thomas Bernartz
549 25th Ave. N
St. Cloud, MN 56303
Ph: (320)259-9427
Fax: (320)257-8127
E-mail: thomasbernatz@thrivent.com
URL: National Affiliate–naifa.org
Contact: Thomas Bernartz, Contact
Local. Represents the interests of insurance and financial advisors. Advocates for a positive legislative and regulatory environment. Enhances business and professional skills of members. **Affiliated With:** National Association of Insurance and Financial Advisors.

12293 ■ National Association of Catholic Family Life Ministers, Region No. 8 (NACFLM)
c/o Christine Codden, Region Representative
Family Life & Respect Life Off.
305 N 7th Ave., Ste.100
St. Cloud, MN 56303-3633
Ph: (320)252-4721
Fax: (320)258-7658
E-mail: ccodden@gw.stcdio.org
URL: http://www.nacflm.org
Contact: Christine Codden, Region Representative
Regional. **Affiliated With:** National Association of Catholic Family Life Ministers.

12294 ■ National Association of Home Builders of the U.S., Central Minnesota Builders Association (CMBA)
c/o Bonnie Moeller, Exec.Dir.
Local No. 2410
1124 W St. Germain St.
St. Cloud, MN 56301-3403
Ph: (320)251-4382
Fax: (320)251-3754
E-mail: info@cmbaonline.org
URL: http://www.cmbaonline.org
Contact: Bonnie Moeller, Exec.Dir.
Founded: 1971. **Local**. Single and multifamily home builders, commercial builders, and others associated with the building industry. **Affiliated With:** National Association of Home Builders.

12295 ■ PFLAG St. Cloud/Central Minnesota
PO Box 7641
St. Cloud, MN 56302
Ph: (320)251-4966
Fax: (320)252-5189
E-mail: bradbury@astound.net
URL: http://www.pflag.org/Minnesota.217.0.html
Local. **Affiliated With:** Parents, Families, and Friends of Lesbians and Gays.

12296 ■ The Retired Enlisted Association, Chapter, 115
c/o Tony R. Nathe, Pres.
PO Box 313
St. Cloud, MN 56302-0313
Ph: (320)255-1492
Fax: (320)255-1492
E-mail: trea115@aol.com
URL: National Affiliate–www.trea.org
Affiliated With: The Retired Enlisted Association.

12297 ■ Ruffed Grouse Society, West Central Minnesota Chapter
c/o Larry Brutger
100 4th Ave. S
St. Cloud, MN 56302
Ph: (320)252-6262
E-mail: lbrutger@brutgerequities.com
URL: National Affiliate–www.ruffedgrousesociety.org
Contact: Larry Brutger, Contact
Local. **Affiliated With:** Ruffed Grouse Society.

12298 ■ St. Cloud Area Chamber of Commerce (SCACC)
110 S 6th Ave.
PO Box 487
St. Cloud, MN 56302-0487

Ph: (320)251-2940
Fax: (320)251-0081
E-mail: information@stcloudareachamber.com
URL: http://www.stcloudareachamber.com
Contact: Teresa Bohnen, Pres.
Founded: 1869. **Members:** 1,200. **Local**. Promotes business and community development in the St. Cloud, MN area. **Computer Services:** Mailing lists, of members • online services, business directory. **Divisions:** Workforce Development. **Publications:** *The Bottom Line*, monthly. Newsletter. **Price:** $15.00. **Circulation:** 2,200. Alternate Formats: online • *Business Central*, bimonthly. Magazine. Contains feature stories, business tips, and news from throughout Central Minnesota. **Circulation:** 6,000. **Advertising:** accepted • *Chamber Edge*, monthly. Newsletter. Alternate Formats: online • *Chamber News*, monthly. Newsletter. **Price:** $15.00 • Directory, annual. **Circulation:** 1,500. **Conventions/Meetings:** weekly Chamber Connection - meeting, includes networking and a continental breakfast - every Friday • annual Chamber Golf Open - competition, with sponsors - every August • annual show (exhibits) - every February.

12299 ■ St. Cloud Area Planning Organization (APO)
c/o William G. Hansen, Exec.Dir.
1040 County Rd. 4
St. Cloud, MN 56303-0643
Ph: (320)252-7568
Fax: (320)252-6557
E-mail: hansen@stcloudapo.org
URL: http://www.stcloudapo.org
Contact: William G. Hansen, Exec.Dir.
Local. Members include the cities of St. Cloud, Sartell, Sauk Rapids, St. Joseph, St. Augusta and Waite Park; Stearns County; Sherburne County; Benton County; Haven Township; St. Joseph Township; and Lesauk Township. Offers long-range transportation planning preparation, planning, and coordination.

12300 ■ St. Cloud Builders Exchange
PO Box 746
St. Cloud, MN 56302-0746
Ph: (320)252-5832
URL: http://www.stcloudbuildersexchange.com
Contact: Jeff Bechtold, Contact
Membership Dues: $175 (annual). **Local**. Represents general contractors, subcontractors, suppliers, manufacturers' representatives and individual firms related to the construction industry. Provides information on construction and building procedures. **Affiliated With:** International Builders Exchange Executives.

12301 ■ St. Cloud Extraordinary Pseudoscience Teaching Investigations and Community Service (SKEPTICS)
c/o Jerry Mertens, Coord.
Psychology Dept.
St. Cloud State Univ.
St. Cloud, MN 56301
Ph: (320)308-2138 (320)251-3134
E-mail: gmertens@stcloudstate.edu
Contact: Jerry Mertens, Coord.
Founded: 1977. **Local Groups:** 1. **Local**. Provides an alternate look at supposed extraordinary claims and pseudoscience. **Committees:** St Cloud ESP Teaching Investigation Committee. **Formerly:** (2001) St. Kloud ESP Teaching Investigation Committee. **Publications:** *Skeptical Newsletter*. **Conventions/Meetings:** Speakers/Psychology Tour Class/Investigation/Presentations/Fake Psychic Demos - meeting; Avg. Attendance: 70.

12302 ■ St. Cloud Figure Skating Club
PO Box 1401
St. Cloud, MN 56302-1401
Ph: (320)253-1355
E-mail: dmmehr@astound.net
URL: http://www.stcloudfsc.com
Local. Provides programs to encourage participation and achievement in the sport of figure skating on ice. Defines and maintains uniform standards of skating proficiency. Organizes and sponsors competitions and exhibitions for the purpose of stimulating interest in figure skating. **Affiliated With:** United States Figure Skating Association.

12303 ■ Saint Cloud Jaycees
PO Box 773
St. Cloud, MN 56302
E-mail: president@stcjaycees.org
URL: http://www.stcjaycees.org
Contact: Chad Groetsch, Pres.
Local.

12304 ■ St. Cloud Lions Club
PO Box 384
St. Cloud, MN 56302
Ph: (320)285-5300
E-mail: stcloudlions@aol.com
URL: http://www.lionwap.org/stcloudlionsmn
Contact: Mike Evans, 1st VP
Local. **Affiliated With:** Lions Clubs International.

12305 ■ St. Cloud State University National Organization for the Reform of Marijuana Laws
c/o Amie Stockholm
AMC 117-E
720 Fourth Ave. S
St. Cloud, MN 56301
Ph: (320)493-0546
E-mail: scsunorml@yahoo.com
URL: http://www.scsunorml.org
Contact: Amie Stockholm, Pres.
Works to raise awareness of the need to reform or remove laws prohibiting marijuana; advocates decriminalization of the use of marijuana for medicinal, religious, and responsible recreational use by adults. Supports the legalization of industrial hemp for farming and commercial uses in the U.S. **Affiliated With:** National Organization for the Reform of Marijuana Laws.

12306 ■ St. Cloud - Young Life
725 N 27th Ave.
St. Cloud, MN 56303
Ph: (320)267-9310
URL: http://sites.younglife.org/_layouts/ylext/default.aspx?ID=C-3599
Local. **Affiliated With:** Young Life.

12307 ■ SCORE Central Area (St. Cloud)
c/o Mr. John Wertz, Chm.
616 Roosevelt Rd., Ste.100
St. Cloud, MN 56301-1332
Ph: (320)240-1332
E-mail: stcloud@scoreminn.org
URL: http://www.stcloudscore.org
Contact: Mr. John Wertz, Chm.
Local. Provides one-on-one confidential business consultation, at no cost. Offers low-cost workshops to current and potential entrepreneurs on business planning, finance, marketing, and similar topics. **Affiliated With:** SCORE.

12308 ■ Skills USA, Technical High School
233 12th Ave. S
St. Cloud, MN 56301
Ph: (320)252-2231
Fax: (320)252-0257
URL: http://www.mnskillsusa.org/secondaryChapters.htm
Contact: Bill Garceau, Contact
Local. Serves high school and college students enrolled in technical, skilled, and service and health occupations. Provides quality education experiences for students in leadership, teamwork, citizenship and character development. Builds and reinforces self-confidence, work attitudes and communication skills. Emphasizes total quality at work, high ethical standards, superior work skills, and life-long education. Promotes understanding of the free enterprise system and involvement in community service. **Affiliated With:** Skills USA - VICA.

12309 ■ Society of Manufacturing Engineers - St. Cloud State University - S225
St. Cloud State Univ., Dept. of Mech. and Mfg. Engg.
720 Fourth Ave. S
St. Cloud, MN 56301-4498
Ph: (320)225-3843
Fax: (320)229-5653
E-mail: baliga@stcloudstate.edu
URL: National Affiliate–www.sme.org
Contact: Dr. Bantwal Baliga, Contact
Local. Advances manufacturing knowledge to gain competitive advantage. Improves skills and manufacturing solutions for the growth of economy. Provides resources and opportunities for manufacturing professionals. **Affiliated With:** Association of Scientists and Engineers of the Naval Sea Systems Command.

12310 ■ Society of Physics Students - St. Cloud State University Chapter No. 6122
720 4th Ave. S
St. Cloud, MN 56301-4498
Ph: (320)308-2011
Fax: (320)308-4728
E-mail: haglin@stcloudstate.edu
Contact: Juan Cabanela, Faculty Advisor
Budget: $1,000. **Local**. Offers opportunities for the students to enrich their experiences and skills about physics. Helps students to become professional in the field of physics. **Libraries: Type:** not open to the public. **Holdings:** books, films, monographs, video recordings. **Affiliated With:** Society of Physics Students.

12311 ■ St Cloud REACT
2311 10th Ave. S
St. Cloud, MN 56301-5840
Ph: (320)251-7844
E-mail: kbopxt@juno.com
URL: http://www.reactintl.org/teaminfo/usa_teams/teams-usmn.htm
Local. Trained communication experts and professional volunteers. Provides volunteer public service and emergency communications through the use of radios (Citizen Band, General Mobile Radio Service, UHF and HAM). Coordinates with radio industries and government on safety communication matters and supports charitable activities and community organizations.

12312 ■ Stearns-Benton County Medical Society
56 S 33rd Ave.
Box 244
St. Cloud, MN 56301
Ph: (320)252-8550
Fax: (612)378-3875
E-mail: sbcms@mnmed.org
URL: http://www.mnmed.org
Contact: Susan Sweezo, Exec.Dir.
Local. Represents the interests of physicians, residents and medical students. Promotes excellence in health care. Ensures a healthy practice environment. Preserves the professionalism of medicine. **Affiliated With:** Minnesota Medical Association.

12313 ■ Stearns History Museum
235 33rd Ave. S
St. Cloud, MN 56301
Ph: (320)253-8424
Fax: (320)253-2172
Free: (866)253-8424
E-mail: info@stearns-museum.org
URL: http://www.stearns-museum.org
Contact: David Ebnet, Exec.Dir.
Founded: 1936. **Members:** 1,000. **Membership Dues:** individual, $25 (annual) • family, $40 (annual) • family plus, $50 (annual) • discovery, $125 (annual) • heritage, $500 (annual) • patron's circle, $1,000 (annual). **Staff:** 13. **Budget:** $800,000. **Local**. Strives to nurture knowledge of and an appreciation for the history of Stearns County and Minnesota and cultivate in people the awareness and appreciation of local history. **Libraries: Type:** open to the public. **Hold-**

ings: 2,200; archival material, audio recordings, photographs. **Subjects:** Stearns County and Minnesota. **Formerly:** (1998) Stearns County Historical Society; (1999) Stearns County History Museum. **Publications:** *Crossings*, bimonthly. Magazine. Publishes local and regional history. **Circulation:** 1,250. **Conventions/Meetings:** monthly meeting.

12314 ■ Sweet Adelines International, Granite City Sound Chapter
First Presbyterian Church
373 4th Ave. S
St. Cloud, MN 56301-4452
E-mail: granitecitysound@yahoo.com
URL: http://www.geocities.com/granitecitysound
Contact: Joan Lowe, Dir.
Local. Advances the musical art form of barbershop harmony through education and performances. Provides education, training and coaching in the development of women's four-part barbershop harmony. **Affiliated With:** Sweet Adelines International.

12315 ■ United Cerebral Palsy Association of Central Minnesota (UCP-CM)
510 25th Ave. N
St. Cloud, MN 56303
Ph: (320)253-0765
Fax: (320)253-6753
Free: (888)616-3726
E-mail: info@ucpcentralmn.org
URL: http://www.ucpcentralmn.org
Contact: Ms. Judy Moening, Exec.Dir.
Founded: 1954. **Staff:** 3. **Budget:** $170,000. **State Groups:** 1. **Local Groups:** 1. **Nonmembership. Local.** Strives to advance the independence, productivity and full citizenship of people with cerebral palsy and other disabilities. Programs and services include information and referral; public education; scholarships; financial assistance for equipment purchase for persons with cerebral palsy; and Computers Go Round, a program to recycle donated computers to persons with any type of disability. **Libraries: Type:** open to the public. **Holdings:** articles, books, video recordings. **Subjects:** cerebral palsy. **Awards:** Post-Secondary Scholarship. **Frequency:** annual. **Type:** scholarship. **Recipient:** for persons diagnosed with cerebral palsy; resident of Benton, Sherburne, or Stearns counties; for post secondary education. **Affiliated With:** United Cerebral Palsy Associations. **Publications:** *United Cerebral Palsy Newsletter*, quarterly. **Price:** free. **Circulation:** 1,300. **Advertising:** accepted. **Conventions/Meetings:** monthly board meeting - 2nd Wednesday.

12316 ■ United Way of Central Minnesota
2700 1st St. N, Ste.300
St. Cloud, MN 56303
Ph: (320)252-0227
Fax: (320)252-6213
E-mail: info@unitedwayhelps.org
URL: http://www.unitedwayhelps.org
Contact: Noreen J. Dunnells, CPO
Founded: 1967. **Members:** 40. **Staff:** 10. **Budget:** $2,976,552. **Regional Groups:** 2. **State Groups:** 1. **Local. Awards:** Response Fund. **Frequency:** annual. **Type:** grant. **Recipient:** fit into pre-approved emphasis areas. **Affiliated With:** United Way of America. **Formerly:** United Way of the St. Cloud Area.

12317 ■ Vietnam Veterans of America, Central Minnesota - Chapter 290
PO Box 7004
St. Cloud, MN 56302
E-mail: smithj@vvachapter290mn.org
URL: http://www.vvachapter290mn.org
Local. Affiliated With: Vietnam Veterans of America.

12318 ■ Young Life St. Cloud
725 N 27th Ave.
St. Cloud, MN 56303
Ph: (320)267-9310
URL: http://sites.younglife.org/sites/stcloud/default.aspx
Local. Affiliated With: Young Life.

St. Francis

12319 ■ American Legion, Minnesota Post 622
c/o John Colline
PO Box 727
St. Francis, MN 55070
Ph: (651)291-1800
Fax: (651)291-1057
URL: National Affiliate–www.legion.org
Contact: John Colline, Contact
Local. Affiliated With: American Legion.

12320 ■ St. Francis Lions Club
PO Box 173
St. Francis, MN 55070
Ph: (763)753-0820
E-mail: lions@stfrancismn.com
URL: http://stfrancismn.lionwap.org
Contact: John Hane, Pres.
Local. Affiliated With: Lions Clubs International.

12321 ■ Skills USA, St. Francis High School
3325 Bridge St.
St. Francis, MN 55070
Ph: (763)753-7000
Fax: (763)753-4917
E-mail: chrnei@stfrancis.k12.mn.us
URL: http://www.mnskillsusa.org
Contact: Chris Neises, Contact
Local. Serves high school and college students enrolled in technical, skilled, and service and health occupations. Provides quality education experiences for students in leadership, teamwork, citizenship and character development. Builds and reinforces self-confidence, work attitudes and communication skills. Emphasizes total quality at work, high ethical standards, superior work skills, and life-long education. Promotes understanding of the free enterprise system and involvement in community service. **Affiliated With:** Skills USA - VICA.

St. James

12322 ■ American Legion, St. James Post 33
PO Box 408
St. James, MN 56081
Ph: (651)291-1800
Fax: (651)291-1057
URL: National Affiliate–www.legion.org
Local. Affiliated With: American Legion.

12323 ■ Watonwan County Humane Society
PO Box 346
St. James, MN 56081-0346
Ph: (507)956-2613 (507)375-1113
Fax: (507)956-2613
E-mail: petcompany@hotmail.com
URL: http://www.petcompany.petfinder.org
Contact: Cheryl Bjoin, Pres.
Founded: 1997. **Members:** 27. **Membership Dues:** $10 (annual). **Budget:** $23,000. **Local.** Adopts out spayed and neutered cats and dogs. Promotes the education of the public regarding animal welfare. Supports the humane treatment of animals.

St. Joseph

12324 ■ American Legion, Minnesota Post 328
c/o John Kuebelbeck
PO Box 381
St. Joseph, MN 56374
Ph: (651)291-1800
Fax: (651)291-1057
URL: National Affiliate–www.legion.org
Contact: John Kuebelbeck, Contact
Local. Affiliated With: American Legion.

12325 ■ American Legion, St. Stephen Post 221
PO Box 882
St. Joseph, MN 56374
Ph: (651)291-1800
Fax: (651)291-1057
URL: National Affiliate–www.legion.org
Local. Affiliated With: American Legion.

12326 ■ Minnesota Association of Farm Mutual Insurance Companies (MAFMIC)
c/o Keith M. Anderson, Pres.
PO Box 880
St. Joseph, MN 56374
Ph: (320)271-0909
Fax: (320)271-0912
E-mail: info@mafmic.org
URL: http://www.mafmic.org
Founded: 1895. **Members:** 132. **Budget:** $500,000. **State.** Seeks to promote the township mutual insurance industry in Minnesota. **Publications:** *MAFMIC Newsbulletin*, 10/year. Newsletter. **Conventions/Meetings:** quarterly board meeting • annual convention • periodic seminar.

12327 ■ St. Joseph Chamber of Commerce (SJCC)
PO Box 696
St. Joseph, MN 56374
Ph: (320)363-7575 (320)363-7233
URL: National Affiliate–www.uschamber.com
Contact: Ken Jacobson, Pres.
Members: 1,500. **Local.** Promotes business and community development in the eastern and northern suburbs of St. Paul, MN. **Convention/Meeting:** none. **Affiliated With:** U.S. Chamber of Commerce.

St. Leo

12328 ■ American Legion, St. Leo Post 524
301 Main St. N
St. Leo, MN 56264
Ph: (651)291-1800
Fax: (651)291-1057
URL: National Affiliate–www.legion.org
Local. Affiliated With: American Legion.

St. Louis Park

12329 ■ Alcoholics Anonymous, Intergroup Association of Minneapolis and Suburban Area
7204 W 27th St., Ste.113
St. Louis Park, MN 55426-3112
Ph: (952)922-0880
Fax: (952)922-1061
E-mail: info@aaminneapolis.org
URL: http://www.aaminneapolis.org
Contact: Chuck Rice, Office Mgr.
Founded: 1940. **Local.** Assists problem drinkers in finding meetings of Alcoholics Anonymous in Greater Minneapolis. Acts as a local service office for the AA Groups in the seven county metropolitan areas. **Affiliated With:** Alcoholics Anonymous World Services.

12330 ■ American Legion, Minnesota Post 282
c/o Frank H. Lundberg
5605 36th St.
St. Louis Park, MN 55416
Ph: (651)291-1800
Fax: (651)291-1057
URL: National Affiliate–www.legion.org
Contact: Frank H. Lundberg, Contact
Local. Affiliated With: American Legion.

12331 ■ American Society of Media Photographers, Minneapolis/St. Paul (ASMP-MSP)
3724 Oregon Ave. S
St. Louis Park, MN 55426
E-mail: info@asmp-msp.org
URL: http://www.asmp-msp.org
Contact: Joel Butkowski, Co-Pres.
Regional. Affiliated With: American Society of Media Photographers.

12332 ■ Corvair Minnesota
3370 Lib. Ln.
St. Louis Park, MN 55426-4224
Ph: (952)929-9174
E-mail: schmfran@juno.com
URL: http://clubs.hemmings.com/clubsites/cmi
Contact: Fran Schmit, Contact
Founded: 1973. **Members:** 120. **Membership Dues:** regular, $15 (annual). **State.** Enthusiasts of Corvair automobiles. **Affiliated With:** Corvair Society of America. **Publications:** *Leeky Seel*, monthly. Newsletter. Contains Prez's Page, meeting minutes, technical and trip reports. **Price:** included in membership dues. **Conventions/Meetings:** monthly meeting - always second Tuesday.

12333 ■ Hopkins Royals Boys Basketball Association (HRBBA)
c/o Kim Rossow, Pres.
1618 Melrose Ave. S
St. Louis Park, MN 55426-1846
Ph: (952)545-6224
E-mail: kimrossow@aol.com
URL: http://www.hrbbabasketball.net
Local.

12334 ■ Minneapolis Fort Snelling Lions Club
c/o Marilyn Kunde, Pres.
2908 Brunswick Ave. S
St. Louis Park, MN 55416
Ph: (952)929-3565 (952)829-9601
URL: http://www.5m5.org
Contact: Marilyn Kunde, Pres.
Local. Affiliated With: Lions Clubs International.

12335 ■ Minneapolis Lyn Lake Lions Club
c/o Rod Jenkins, Pres.
4301 Park Glen Rd., No. 119
St. Louis Park, MN 55416
Ph: (952)922-3178
URL: http://www.5m5.org
Contact: Rod Jenkins, Pres.
Local. Affiliated With: Lions Clubs International.

12336 ■ Minnesota Academy of Family Physicians (MAFP)
c/o Virginia Barzan, CAE, Exec.VP
600 S Hwy. 169, Ste.1680
St. Louis Park, MN 55426
Ph: (952)542-0130
Fax: (952)542-0135
Free: (800)999-8198
E-mail: office@mafp.org
URL: http://www.mafp.org
Contact: Virginia Barzan CAE, Exec.VP
State.

12337 ■ Minnesota Speech-Language-Hearing Association (MSHA)
c/o Frances J. Laven, Mgr.
PO Box 26115
St. Louis Park, MN 55426
Ph: (952)920-0787
Fax: (952)920-6098
Free: (800)344-8808
E-mail: msha@incnet.com
URL: http://www.msha.net
Contact: Leslie Glaze, Pres.
Founded: 1936. **Members:** 800. **Membership Dues:** student, $20 (annual) • professional, $80 (annual) • associate, $70 (annual) • affiliate, $40 (annual) • life (associate; member for at least ten years), $20. **Staff:** 1. **Budget:** $130,000. **State.** Persons concerned with communication disorders. Disseminates information about legislation, continuing education programs, and research involving communication disorders. **Libraries: Type:** lending. **Holdings:** audio recordings, video recordings. **Subjects:** auditory disorders. **Awards:** Distinguished Service Award. **Frequency:** annual. **Type:** recognition • Honors of the Association. **Frequency:** annual. **Type:** recognition. **Computer Services:** database • mailing lists. **Publications:** Newsletter, bimonthly. **Price:** $25.00. **Advertising:** accepted. **Conventions/Meetings:** semiannual convention (exhibits) - always April and October.

12338 ■ National Show Horse Association of Minnesota
c/o Cindy Backlund, Pres.
3313 Huntington Ave. S
St. Louis Park, MN 55416
Ph: (952)215-5169
E-mail: zoikers@mn.rr.com
URL: National Affiliate–www.nshregistry.org
Contact: Cindy Backlund, Pres.
State. Affiliated With: National Show Horse Registry.

12339 ■ USABDA Minnesota Chapter
c/o Carol Post, Membership Dir.
3600 France Ave. S
St. Louis Park, MN 55416
Ph: (651)483-5467
E-mail: cpost949@msn.com
URL: http://usabda-mn.org
Contact: Carol Post, Membership Dir.
State. Encourages and promotes the physical, mental and social benefits of partner dancing. Organizes and supports programs for the recreational enjoyment of ballroom dancing. Creates opportunities for the general public to participate in ballroom dancing and DanceSport.

St. Michael

12340 ■ American Legion, St. Michael Post 567
PO Box 97
St. Michael, MN 55376
Ph: (651)291-1800
Fax: (651)291-1057
URL: National Affiliate–www.legion.org
Local. Affiliated With: American Legion.

12341 ■ Minnesota Association of Townships (MAT)
Edgewood Professional Bldg.
PO Box 267
St. Michael, MN 55376
Ph: (763)497-2330
Fax: (763)497-3361
Free: (800)228-0296
E-mail: info@mntownships.org
URL: http://www.mntownships.org
Contact: David A. Fricke, Exec.Dir.
Founded: 1933. **Members:** 1,786. **Staff:** 10. **Budget:** $2,000,000. **Regional Groups:** 13. **Local Groups:** 85. **State.** Townships. Educational, advisory, promotional, and developmental organization for local governments. Operates insurance agency. Sponsors seminars and workshops. **Awards:** Township Leader of the Year. **Frequency:** annual. **Type:** recognition. **Recipient:** for Minnesota township officer. **Publications:** *Directory of Minnesota Township Officers*, annual. Features a list of all Minnesota Township officers. **Price:** $60.00 plus tax • *Minnesota Township News*, bimonthly. Newsletter. **Conventions/Meetings:** monthly board meeting • annual conference - always November.

St. Paul

12342 ■ 3-M Stamp Club
c/o Ms. Judy Koza
3-M Center, Bldg. 220-7E-06
St. Paul, MN 55144-1000
E-mail: jlkoza3@mmm.com
URL: National Affiliate–www.stamps.org
Contact: Ms. Judy Koza, Contact
Local. Affiliated With: American Philatelic Society.

12343 ■ AARP Minnesota
30 E Seventh St., Ste.1200
St. Paul, MN 55101
Fax: (651)221-2636
Free: (866)554-5381
E-mail: aarpmn@aarp.org
URL: National Affiliate–www.aarp.org
Contact: Skip Humphrey, Pres.
State. Seeks to improve every aspect of living for older people. Addresses the needs and interests of older people, working or retired. Promotes positive social change and delivers value to members through information, advocacy and service. **Affiliated With:** American Association of Retired Persons.

12344 ■ Advertising Federation of Minnesota
1821 Univ. Ave. W, Ste.S256
St. Paul, MN 55104
Ph: (651)917-6251
Fax: (651)917-1835
E-mail: office@adfed.org
URL: http://www.adfed.org
Contact: Gabe Castaneda, Pres.
Founded: 1907. **Members:** 500. **Membership Dues:** individual, $175 (annual) • associate, $80 (annual) • retired, $55 (annual) • student, graduate, $25 (annual) • corporate, $150-$640 (annual). **Budget:** $300,000. **State.** Advertising, marketing/communications, creative and production professionals. Offers monthly programs, professional development seminars, special events and networking opportunities. Strives to advance public understanding and respect for advertising; to encourage professional growth and development of its members; to promote participation in public service advertising by its members; to encourage high standards of advertising practices; and to represent the advertising industry in working with government at the federal, state and local levels in areas of mutual concern. **Awards:** Paul Foss Award. **Type:** recognition. **Recipient:** for achievement within the advertising industry • Silver Medal Award. **Type:** medal. **Recipient:** for achievement within Ad Fed. **Conventions/Meetings:** monthly board meeting.

12345 ■ Advocates for Colorectal Education (ACE)
c/o Jane Ellen Nielsen, Pres.
PO Box 14266
St. Paul, MN 55114
Ph: (651)312-1556
Fax: (651)312-1595
E-mail: janenielsen@earthlink.net
URL: http://www.acemn.org
Contact: Jane Ellen Nielsen, Pres.
Local.

12346 ■ African-American Adoption Agency (AAAA)
c/o Marquita Stephens, Pres./CEO
2356 Univ. Ave. W, Ste.220
St. Paul, MN 55104
Ph: (651)659-0460
Fax: (651)644-5306
Free: (888)840-4084
E-mail: afadopt@afadopt.org
URL: http://www.afadopt.org
Contact: Marquita Stephens, Pres./CEO
Founded: 1998. **Staff:** 13. **Budget:** $1,000,000. **Local.** Interested in decreasing the number of children in the state of MN waiting for adoption. Focuses on promoting permanency for children by recruiting and preparing families to adopt or provide foster homes.

12347 ■ Air Force Association, General E.W. Rawlings Chapter
PO Box 11802
St. Paul, MN 55111
E-mail: glennshull@yahoo.com
URL: http://www.rawlings-afa.org
Contact: Glenn Shull, Pres.
Local. Promotes public understanding of aerospace power and the role it plays in the security of the nation. Sponsors symposia and disseminates infor-

mation through outreach programs. **Affiliated With:** Air Force Association.

12348 ■ All Stars Cricket Club
218 Kipling St., Apt. No. 207
St. Paul, MN 55119
URL: http://www.usaca.org/Clubs.htm
Contact: Sudir Muthevi, Contact
Local.

12349 ■ American Academy of Pediatrics, Minnesota Chapter (MNAAP)
1493 Idaho Ave. W
St. Paul, MN 55108
Ph: (651)402-2056
Fax: (952)831-0312
E-mail: ann.ricketts@mnaap.org
URL: http://www.mnaap.org
Contact: Ann Ricketts, Exec.Dir.
Founded: 1948. **Members:** 932. **Membership Dues:** fellow, $110 (annual) • candidate fellow, $50 (annual). **Staff:** 1. **Budget:** $50,000. **Languages:** English, Spanish. **State**. Strives to attain optimal physical, mental, and social health and well-being for all infants, children, adolescents, and young adults. **Libraries: Type:** not open to the public. **Awards:** Child Advocate Award. **Frequency:** annual. **Type:** recognition. **Recipient:** for a person who advocates a child healthcare access • Distinguished Service Award. **Frequency:** annual. **Type:** recognition. **Recipient:** for a member who works for the betterment of pediatrics within Minnesota. **Subgroups:** Children with Disabilities; Communication; Environmental Health; Public Policy. **Affiliated With:** American Academy of Pediatrics. **Publications:** *Minnesota Pediatrician*, quarterly. Newsletter. **Price:** free for members. **Circulation:** 1,000. **Advertising:** accepted. Alternate Formats: online. **Conventions/Meetings:** annual general assembly, dinner, awards, lecture (exhibits).

12350 ■ American Association for Laboratory Animal Science - Minnesota (MN AALAS)
c/o Jim Kadera, Treas.
4100 Hamline Ave. N
St. Paul, MN 55112
E-mail: jim.kadera@guidant.com
URL: http://www.ahc.umn.edu/rar/MNAALAS
Contact: Jim Kadera, Treas.
State. Serves as a clearinghouse for the collection and exchange of information and expertise in the care and use of laboratory animals. Promotes and encourages the highest level of ethics within the profession of laboratory animal science. Provides educational and training programs for members and others who are professionally engaged in the production, care, use and study of laboratory animals. **Affiliated With:** American Association for Laboratory Animal Science.

12351 ■ American Association of Teachers of German - Minnesota Chapter
c/o David Rutledge
1409 Fairmount Ave.
St. Paul, MN 55105
Ph: (651)702-8879
E-mail: ammianus@usfamily.net
URL: http://courseweb.stthomas.edu/paschons/language_http/German/MNAATG.html
Contact: David Rutledge, Contact
State. Represents teachers of German at all levels of instruction and all those interested in the teaching of German. Advances and improves the teaching of the language, literatures and cultures of the German-speaking countries. Provides members with educational and professional services. **Affiliated With:** American Association of Teachers of German.

12352 ■ American Cancer Society, East Metro Unit
c/o Judy Ireland, Cancer Control Specialist
1096 Raymond Ave.
St. Paul, MN 55108
Ph: (651)644-1224
Fax: (651)644-2819
URL: http://www.cancer.org/
Affiliated With: American Cancer Society.

12353 ■ American Civil Liberties Union of Minnesota (ACLU-MN)
c/o Charles Samuelson, Exec.Dir.
450 N Syndicate St., Ste.230
St. Paul, MN 55104
Ph: (651)645-4097
Fax: (651)647-5948
E-mail: support@aclu-mn.org
Contact: Charles Samuelson, Exec.Dir.
Founded: 1952. **Staff:** 7. **State**. Champions the rights set forth in the Bill of Rights of the U.S. Constitution: freedom of speech, press, assembly, and religion; due process of law and fair trial; equality before the law regardless of race, color, sexual orientation, national origin, political opinion, or religious belief. Activities include litigation, advocacy, and public education. **Affiliated With:** American Civil Liberties Union.

12354 ■ American Hiking Society - Parks and Trails Council of Minnesota
275 Fourth St. E, No. 642
St. Paul, MN 55101
Ph: (651)726-2457
Fax: (651)726-2458
E-mail: dgrilley@parkandtrails.org
URL: http://www.parksandtrails.org
Contact: Dorian Grilley, Exec.Dir.
Local.

12355 ■ American Industrial Hygiene Association - Upper Midwest Section
PO Box 131224
St. Paul, MN 55113-0011
Ph: (651)490-0316
E-mail: rebeccag@usfamily.net
URL: http://www.aiha.org/LocalSections/html/umw/umwhome.htm
Contact: Rebecca Cornwall, Pres.-Elect
Regional. Represents the interests of occupational and environmental health professionals practicing in industry, government, labor and academic institutions and independent organizations. Promotes the certification of industrial hygienists. Administers educational programs for environmental health and safety professionals. **Affiliated With:** American Industrial Hygiene Association.

12356 ■ American Legion, 3 M Post 599
1737 E Fourth St.
St. Paul, MN 55106
Ph: (651)291-1800
Fax: (651)291-1057
URL: National Affiliate–www.legion.org
Local. Affiliated With: American Legion.

12357 ■ American Legion, And-Quist Post 218
20 W 12st, Rm. 300-A
St. Paul, MN 55155
Ph: (651)291-1800
Fax: (651)291-1057
URL: National Affiliate–www.legion.org
Local. Affiliated With: American Legion.

12358 ■ American Legion, Arcade-Phalen Post 577
1129 Arcade St.
St. Paul, MN 55106
Ph: (651)291-1800
Fax: (651)291-1057
URL: National Affiliate–www.legion.org
Local. Affiliated With: American Legion.

12359 ■ American Legion, Attucks-Brooks Post 606
976 Concordia Ave.
St. Paul, MN 55104
Ph: (651)291-1800
Fax: (651)291-1057
URL: National Affiliate–www.legion.org
Local. Affiliated With: American Legion.

12360 ■ American Legion, Christie-De-Parcq Post 406
PO Box 75541
St. Paul, MN 55175
Ph: (651)291-1800
Fax: (651)291-1057
URL: National Affiliate–www.legion.org
Local. Affiliated With: American Legion.

12361 ■ American Legion, Hamline Post 418
1309 Prior Ave. S
St. Paul, MN 55116
Ph: (651)291-1800
Fax: (651)291-1057
URL: National Affiliate–www.legion.org
Local. Affiliated With: American Legion.

12362 ■ American Legion, Lester Tjernlund Post 451
1671 E Nevada Ave.
St. Paul, MN 55106
Ph: (651)291-1800
Fax: (651)291-1057
URL: National Affiliate–www.legion.org
Local. Affiliated With: American Legion.

12363 ■ American Legion of Minnesota
c/o Lyle R. Foltz, Adj.
20 W 12th St. Rm. 300-A
St. Paul, MN 55155-2000
Ph: (651)291-1800
Fax: (651)291-1057
E-mail: department@mnlegion.org
URL: http://www.mnlegion.org
Contact: Calvin Vanhorn, Commander
State. Affiliated With: American Legion.

12364 ■ American Legion, Minnesota At Large Post 1982
20 W 12th St., Rm. 300-a
St. Paul, MN 55155
Ph: (651)291-1800
Fax: (651)291-1057
URL: National Affiliate–www.legion.org
Local. Affiliated With: American Legion.

12365 ■ American Legion, Minnesota Post 484
c/o Raymond J. Sperl
835 Lafond Ave.
St. Paul, MN 55104
Ph: (651)291-1800
Fax: (651)291-1057
URL: National Affiliate–www.legion.org
Contact: Raymond J. Sperl, Contact
Local. Affiliated With: American Legion.

12366 ■ American Legion, Minnesota Post 572
c/o George Grui
St. Marys Church Hall
189 Atwater St.
St. Paul, MN 55117
Ph: (651)291-1800
Fax: (651)291-1057
URL: National Affiliate–www.legion.org
Contact: George Grui, Contact
Local. Affiliated With: American Legion.

12367 ■ American Legion, Minnesota Post 634
c/o Norm Horton, Sr.
1030 Manvel St.
St. Paul, MN 55114

Ph: (651)291-1800
Fax: (651)291-1057
URL: National Affiliate–www.legion.org
Contact: Norm Horton Sr., Contact
Local. Affiliated With: American Legion.

12368 ■ American Legion, Minnesota Post 4444
c/o Reginald Burt
435 E Univ. Ave.
St. Paul, MN 55101
Ph: (612)228-9318
Fax: (651)291-1057
URL: National Affiliate–www.legion.org
Contact: Reginald Burt, Contact
Local. Affiliated With: American Legion.

12369 ■ American Legion, North End Post 474
72 Ivy Ave. W
St. Paul, MN 55117
Ph: (651)291-1800
Fax: (651)291-1057
URL: National Affiliate–www.legion.org
Local. Affiliated With: American Legion.

12370 ■ American Legion, Railroad Post 416
1573 Osceola Ave.
St. Paul, MN 55105
Ph: (651)291-1800
Fax: (651)291-1057
URL: National Affiliate–www.legion.org
Local. Affiliated With: American Legion.

12371 ■ American Legion, St. Paul Memorial Post 533
1053 Flandrau St.
St. Paul, MN 55106
Ph: (651)291-1800
Fax: (651)291-1057
URL: National Affiliate–www.legion.org
Local. Affiliated With: American Legion.

12372 ■ American Legion, St. Paul Post 8
PO Box 75450
St. Paul, MN 55175
Ph: (651)291-1800
Fax: (651)291-1057
URL: National Affiliate–www.legion.org
Local. Affiliated With: American Legion.

12373 ■ American Legion, Triple Six Post 666
20 W 12th St., Rm. 300-a
St. Paul, MN 55155
Ph: (651)291-1800
Fax: (651)291-1057
URL: National Affiliate–www.legion.org
Local. Affiliated With: American Legion.

12374 ■ American Legion, Twin Cities American Indian Post 419
940 Albemarle St.
St. Paul, MN 55117
Ph: (651)291-1800
Fax: (651)291-1057
URL: National Affiliate–www.legion.org
Local. Affiliated With: American Legion.

12375 ■ American Legion, University of Minnesota Post 548
334 Cherokee Ave., Apt. 412
St. Paul, MN 55107
Ph: (651)291-1800
Fax: (651)291-1057
URL: National Affiliate–www.legion.org
Local. Affiliated With: American Legion.

12376 ■ American Lung Association of Minnesota
c/o Robert Moffitt, Communications Dir.
490 Concordia Ave.
St. Paul, MN 55103-2441
Ph: (651)227-8014
Fax: (651)227-5459
Free: (800)642-LUNG
E-mail: info@alamn.org
URL: http://www.alamn.org
Contact: Robert Moffitt, Communications Dir.
State. Physicians, nurses, and laymen interested in the prevention and control of lung disease. Conducts patient education, advocacy, and research; major areas of focus are asthma, tobacco control, and environmental health. **Affiliated With:** American Lung Association.

12377 ■ American Marketing Association - Minnesota Chapter
1821 Univ. Ave. W, Ste.S256
St. Paul, MN 55104
Ph: (651)917-6241
Free: (800)262-1150
URL: http://www.mnama.org
Contact: Lisa M. France, Pres.
State. Affiliated With: American Marketing Association.

12378 ■ American Payroll Association, Northstar Chapter
PO Box 131412
St. Paul, MN 55113-0012
E-mail: communications@apanorthstar.org
URL: http://www.apanorthstar.org
Contact: Karen Klein CPP, Pres.
Local. Aims to increase the Payroll Professional's skill level through education and mutual support. Represents the Payroll Professional before legislative bodies. Administers the certified payroll professional program of recognition. Provides public service education on payroll and employment issues. **Affiliated With:** American Payroll Association.

12379 ■ American Red Cross North Central Blood Services Region
100 S Robert St.
St. Paul, MN 55107
Ph: (651)291-4600
URL: http://www.yourbloodcenter.org
Regional.

12380 ■ American Red Cross of the St. Paul Area
176 S Robert St.
St. Paul, MN 55107
Ph: (651)291-6789
Fax: (651)290-8993
E-mail: redcross@arcstp.org
URL: http://stpaulredcross.org
Contact: David J. Therkelsen, CEO
Founded: 1917. **Local.** Serves members of the armed forces and veterans and their families and aids disaster victims. Other activities include: blood services; community services; service opportunities for youth. **Programs:** Red Cross Emergency Social Services. **Affiliated With:** American Red Cross National Headquarters. **Publications:** *Neighbors*, 3/year. Newsletter. Contains information about the St. Paul area Red Cross. Alternate Formats: online.

12381 ■ American Society for Quality, Minnesota Section 1203
PO Box 9370
St. Paul, MN 55109-0370
Ph: (651)779-9820
Fax: (651)779-0244
E-mail: mnasq@aol.com
URL: http://www.mnasq.org
Contact: William Stevenson, Sec.
State. Advances learning, quality improvement and knowledge exchange to improve business results and to create better workplaces and communities worldwide. Provides a forum for information exchange, professional development and continuous learning in the science of quality. **Affiliated With:** American Society for Quality.

12382 ■ American Society for Training and Development, Twin Cities Chapter (ASTD-TCC)
1000 Westgate Dr., Ste.252
St. Paul, MN 55114
Ph: (651)290-6262
Fax: (651)290-2266
E-mail: info@astd-tcc.org
URL: http://www.astd-tcc.org
Contact: Kathie Pugaczewski, Exec.Dir.
Members: 900. **Membership Dues:** professional, $85 (annual) • corporate, $400-$975 (annual) • student, $40 (annual). **Local.** Represents individuals engaged in the training and development of business, industry, education, and government employees. **Affiliated With:** ASTD. **Formerly:** (2002) American Society for Training and Development, Southern Minnesota Chapter.

12383 ■ Arc Minnesota
770 Transfer Rd., Ste.26
St. Paul, MN 55114
Ph: (651)523-0823
Fax: (651)523-0829
Free: (800)582-5256
E-mail: mail@arcminnesota.com
URL: http://www.arcminnesota.com
Contact: Steve Larson, Exec.Dir.
Founded: 1955. **Members:** 6,300. **Membership Dues:** individual, $30 (annual) • family, $40 (annual) • organization, $150 (annual). **Staff:** 15. **Budget:** $840,000. **Local Groups:** 37. **State.** Provides advocacy and support for people with developmental disabilities and their families. **Libraries: Type:** lending; open to the public; reference. **Holdings:** articles, books, periodicals, video recordings. **Subjects:** advocacy, cooking and nutrition, integration, general works on disabilities. **Affiliated With:** Arc of the United States. **Formerly:** Association for Retarded Citizens, Minnesota Office; Minnesota Association for Retarded Citizens. **Publications:** *FOCUS*, 3/year. Newspaper. Covers legislative issues affecting people with developmental disabilities and their families. **Price:** included in membership dues. **Conventions/Meetings:** annual convention, for persons with developmental disabilities; members and people working in the disability field (exhibits) - always fall.

12384 ■ Arthritis Foundation, North Central Chapter
1902 Minnehaha Ave. W
St. Paul, MN 55104
Ph: (651)644-4108
Fax: (651)644-4219
Free: (800)333-1380
E-mail: info.mn@arthritis.org
URL: National Affiliate–www.arthritis.org
Contact: Deborah Sales Maysack, Pres./CEO
Founded: 1955. **Membership Dues:** $20 (annual). **Staff:** 14. **Budget:** $2,000,000. **State Groups:** 1. **State.** Strives to improve lives through leadership in the prevention, control, and cure of arthritis and related diseases. **Affiliated With:** Arthritis Foundation. **Formerly:** (2001) Arthritis Foundation, Minnesota Chapter. **Publications:** *Jottings*, periodic. Newsletter. **Circulation:** 1,000 • *Tipsheet*, periodic. Newsletter. **Circulation:** 15,000. **Conventions/Meetings:** annual Care Conference - workshop, health education conference (exhibits).

12385 ■ Asian Women United of Minnesota (AWUM)
1954 Univ. Ave., Ste.4
St. Paul, MN 55104
Ph: (651)646-2118
Fax: (651)646-2284
E-mail: awum@awum.org
URL: http://www.awum.org
Contact: Sinuon Sin, Exec.Dir.
State. Committed to ending violence against Asian women and children, empowering Asian women and girls, and building stronger and safer communities. **Telecommunication Services:** 24-hour hotline, crisis line, (612)724-8823.

12386 ■ Associated General Contractors of Minnesota
Capitol Off. Bldg.
525 Park St., Ste.110
St. Paul, MN 55103-2186
Ph: (651)632-8929
Fax: (651)632-8928
E-mail: info@agcmn.org
URL: http://www.agcmn.org
Contact: David C. Semerad, CEO
State. Represents general contractors, specialty contractors and affiliated suppliers involved in the construction of buildings, highways, heavy-industrial and municipal-utility projects. Creates programs that support the construction industry, the active involvement of member firms, and its stature in the economic-political-business community. Strives to promote the legislative and economic strength and image of Minnesota's construction industry.

12387 ■ Association of Community Organizations for Reform Now, Minnesota
757 Raymond Ave.
St. Paul, MN 55114
Ph: (651)642-9639
Fax: (651)642-0060
E-mail: mnacorn@acorn.org
URL: National Affiliate–www.acorn.org
State. Affiliated With: Association of Community Organizations for Reform Now.

12388 ■ Association for Computing Machinery, Macalester College
c/o Azamat Sagatov, Chair
1600 Grand Ave.
Math/Cmpt. Sci. Dept.
St. Paul, MN 55105
Ph: (651)696-6287
Fax: (651)696-6518
E-mail: fox@macalester.edu
URL: National Affiliate–www.acm.org
Contact: Azamat Savatov, Chair
Local. Affiliated With: Association for Computing Machinery.

12389 ■ Association of Minnesota Counties (AMC)
c/o James A. Mulder, Exec.Dir.
125 Charles Ave.
St. Paul, MN 55103-2108
Ph: (651)224-3344
Fax: (651)224-6540
E-mail: jmulder@mncounties.org
URL: http://www.mncounties.org
Contact: James A. Mulder, Exec.Dir.
State. Affiliated With: National Association of Counties.

12390 ■ Association for Professionals in Infection Control and Epidemiology, Minnesota Chapter
c/o Cheri Talsness, VP
United Hosp.
333 Smith Ave.
St. Paul, MN 55102
Ph: (651)241-8403
Fax: (651)241-7244
E-mail: cheri.talsness@allina.com
URL: http://www.apicmn.org
Contact: Cheri Talsness, VP
State. Works to influence, support and improve the quality of healthcare through the development of educational programs and standards. Promotes quality research and standardization of practices and procedures. **Affiliated With:** Association for Professionals in Infection Control and Epidemiology.

12391 ■ Audio Engineering Society, Music Tech College Section
c/o David Barto
MusicTech Coll. of Music and Recording Arts
19 Echange St. E
St. Paul, MN 55101
Ph: (651)291-0177
Fax: (651)291-0366
URL: National Affiliate–www.aes.org
Contact: David Barto, Contact
Local. Represents the interests of engineers, administrators and technicians for radio, television and motion picture operation. Operates educational and research foundation. **Affiliated With:** Audio Engineering Society.

12392 ■ Better Business Bureau Serving Minnesota and North Dakota
2706 Gannon Rd.
St. Paul, MN 55116-2600
Ph: (612)699-1111
Fax: (612)699-7665
Free: (800)646-6222
E-mail: ask@mnd.bbb.org
URL: http://www.mnd.bbb.org
Contact: Jane Driggs, Pres.
Founded: 1912. **Staff:** 40. **State.** Provides programs and services to assist consumers and businesses. **Awards:** Better Business Bureau Integrity Awards. **Frequency:** annual. **Type:** recognition. **Recipient:** for companies that display outstanding ethics in dealings with customers, employees, vendors and the community. **Formerly:** (1995) Better Business Bureau of St. Paul. **Publications:** *BBB Connections*, quarterly. Newsletter. Contains tips on business and money. **Price:** included in membership dues • *Better Pages*, annual. Membership Directory. Contains information on BBB services and membership benefits. **Conventions/Meetings:** annual meeting.

12393 ■ Big Brothers Big Sisters of the Greater Twin Cities
2550 Univ. Ave., Ste.410N
St. Paul, MN 55114
Ph: (651)789-2400
Fax: (651)789-2499
E-mail: bbbs@bigstwincities.org
URL: http://www.bigstwincities.org
Contact: Gloria C. Lewis, Pres./CEO
Founded: 1920. **Staff:** 55. **Budget:** $3,400,000. **Nonmembership. Local.** Seeks to enrich young people's lives through one-to-one relationships with young people between ages 7 and 13. **Affiliated With:** Big Brothers Big Sisters of America.

12394 ■ Bikers Against Child Abuse, Minnesota Chapter
PO Box 14472
St. Paul, MN 55114
Ph: (651)497-1618
URL: National Affiliate–www.bacausa.com
State.

12395 ■ Builders Exchange of St. Paul (BXSP)
445 Farrington St.
St. Paul, MN 55103
Ph: (651)224-7545
Fax: (651)224-7549
E-mail: info@bxsp.org
URL: http://www.bxsp.org
Founded: 1900. **Members:** 635. **Membership Dues:** company, $365 (annual). **Staff:** 4. **Budget:** $400,000. **Local.** Construction and construction related firms in the Minneapolis and St. Paul, MN area. Operates as clearinghouse for construction bid project information. Operates plan room for project bidding. **Affiliated With:** International Builders Exchange Executives. **Publications:** *Building Newsletter*, weekly • *Membership Roster and Buying Guide*, annual. **Conventions/Meetings:** annual meeting - always second Tuesday of December.

12396 ■ Camp Fire USA Minnesota Council
2610 Univ. Ave. W
St. Paul, MN 55114-1090
Ph: (651)647-4407 (651)647-1090
Fax: (651)647-5717
Free: (888)335-8778
E-mail: info@campfireusa-mn.org
Contact: Andrea Platt Dwyer, CEO
Founded: 1910. **Members:** 650,000. **Membership Dues:** adult and youth, $10 (annual). **Staff:** 23. **Budget:** $1,300,000. **State.** Provides all-inclusive, coeducational programs such as youth leadership, self-reliance, after school groups, camping and environmental education, and child care. **Awards:** Youth Leadership Awards. **Frequency:** annual. **Type:** recognition. **Recipient:** for community leadership on youth issues. **Subcommittees:** Classic Clubs; Community Family Club; School Age Child Care Clubs; Youth Empowerment Leadership and Learning. **Affiliated With:** American Camping Association; Camp Fire USA. **Formerly:** (1995) Camp Fire Boys & Girls, Minnesota Lakes Council; (2001) Camp Fire Boys & Girls, Minnesota Council. **Publications:** *Camp Fire News*, quarterly. **Conventions/Meetings:** annual meeting.

12397 ■ Casa De Esperanza
PO Box 75177
St. Paul, MN 55175
Ph: (651)646-5553
Fax: (651)646-5999
E-mail: info@casadeesperanza.org
URL: http://www.casadeesperanza.org
Contact: Lupe R. Serrano, Exec.Dir.
Founded: 1982. **Staff:** 24. **Languages:** English, Spanish. **Local.** Mobilizes Latina and Latino communities to end domestic violence.

12398 ■ Chemical Coaters Association International, Twin Cities
2570 Dianne St.
St. Paul, MN 55109
Fax: (612)779-9707
Free: (800)526-4473
E-mail: doug.vanduyne@chemetall.com
URL: http://www.ccatc.com
Contact: Doug Van Duyne, Pres.
Local. Provides information and training on surface coating technologies. Raises the standards of finishing operations through educational meetings and seminars, training manuals, certification programs, and outreach programs with colleges and universities. **Affiliated With:** Chemical Coaters Association International.

12399 ■ Chicanos Latinos Unidos En Servicio (CLUES)
797 E 7th St.
St. Paul, MN 55106
Ph: (651)379-4200
Fax: (651)292-0347
URL: http://www.clues.org
Contact: Jesse Bethke Gomez MMA, Pres.
State.

12400 ■ Children's Defense Fund, Minnesota (CDF-MN)
200 Univ. Ave. W, Ste.210
St. Paul, MN 55103
Ph: (651)227-6121
Fax: (651)227-2553
E-mail: cdf-mn@cdf-mn.org
URL: http://www.cdf-mn.org
Contact: Jim Koppel, Dir.
Founded: 1985. **State. Affiliated With:** Children's Defense Fund.

12401 ■ Children's Home Society and Family Services (CHSFS)
c/o Jerry Jackson, VP of Development
1605 Eustis St.
St. Paul, MN 55108-1219
Ph: (651)646-7771
Fax: (651)646-8676
E-mail: volunteer@chsm.com
URL: http://www.chsm.com
Contact: Jerry Jackson, VP of Development
Local. Committed to helping children thrive; to build and sustain safe, loving families and to provide opportunities for individual growth. **Formerly:** (2005) Children's Home Society of Minnesota.

12402 ■ Citizens League
555 N Wabasha St., Ste.240
St. Paul, MN 55102
Ph: (651)293-0575
Fax: (651)293-0576
E-mail: skershaw@citizensleague.net
URL: http://www.citizensleague.net
Contact: Sean Kershaw, Exec.Dir.
Founded: 1952. **Members:** 1,300. **Membership Dues:** individual, $70 (annual) • household, $90 (annual) • student, $25 (annual). **Staff:** 4. **Budget:** $350,000. **State**. Focuses on public policy issues at the local, metropolitan and state level. **Publications:** *Minnesota Journal*, monthly. Contains information concerning public policy issues. **Circulation:** 1,300. Alternate Formats: online.

12403 ■ Cochlear Implant Club Minnesota
c/o Jack Maddio, Pres.
1231 McAfee St.
St. Paul, MN 55106
Ph: (651)776-0697
E-mail: jjmaddio@ix.netcom.com
URL: National Affiliate–www.cici.org
Contact: Jack Maddio, Pres.
State. Educates and supports cochlear implant recipients and their families. Works to secure the rights of people with hearing loss. Aims to improve public and private financial support for individuals receiving cochlear implants. **Affiliated With:** Cochlear Implant Association, Inc.

12404 ■ College Democrats of Minnesota
c/o Chris Montana, Pres.
255 E Plato Blvd.
St. Paul, MN 55107
Ph: (651)251-6366
Free: (800)999-7457
E-mail: info@mncollegedems.org
URL: http://www.mncollegedems.org
Local.

12405 ■ Common Hope
c/o Sue Wheeler, U.S. Dir.
PO Box 14298
St. Paul, MN 55114
Ph: (651)917-0917
Fax: (651)917-7458
E-mail: info@mn.commonhope.org
URL: http://www.commonhope.org
Contact: Sue Wheeler, U.S. Dir.
Local. Promotes hope and opportunity in Guatemala, encourages children, families and communities participate in a process of development to improve their lives through education, health care, and housing. Practices a comprehensive approach to human development by working simultaneously in these areas: education, health care, housing, economic development, and family and community development. Offers diverse programs within these areas for the whole family that help both children and parents develop the tools for realizing their dreams.

12406 ■ Community Associations Institute - Minnesota Chapter (CAI-MN)
1000 Westgate Dr., Ste.252
St. Paul, MN 55114
Ph: (651)203-7250
Fax: (651)290-2266
E-mail: dgh@hjlawfirm.com
URL: http://www.cai-mn.com
Contact: David Hellmuth, Pres.
Founded: 1973. **Members:** 550. **Staff:** 4. **State**. Aims to provide leadership for successful development and operation of community associations through information, research, and education. **Affiliated With:** Community Associations Institute. **Publications:** *CA Eye*. Newsletter • Journal.

12407 ■ Democratic Socialists of America, Twin Cities
c/o Dan Frankot
695 Ottawa Ave.
St. Paul, MN 55107
Ph: (651)224-8262
E-mail: info@twincitiesdsa.org
URL: http://www.twincitiesdsa.org
Contact: Dan Frankot, Contact
Local. **Affiliated With:** Democratic Socialists of America.

12408 ■ Education Minnesota
41 Sherburn Ave.
St. Paul, MN 55103-2196
Ph: (651)227-9541
Fax: (651)292-4802
Free: (800)652-9073
E-mail: judy.schaubach@educationminnesota.org
URL: http://www.educationminnesota.org
Contact: Judy Schaubach, Pres.
State.

12409 ■ Epilepsy Foundation of Minnesota
1600 Univ. Ave. W, Ste.205
St. Paul, MN 55104
Ph: (651)287-2300 (651)287-2303
Fax: (651)287-2325
Free: (800)779-0777
E-mail: jthompson@efmn.org
URL: http://www.efmn.org
Contact: Vicki Kopplin, Associate Exec.
State. Enhances the quality of life of those affected by epilepsy. Provides Epilepsy Awareness Programs, Information and Referral, Advocacy and Support and Youth and Family Programs, including Camp Oz for kids and teens with epilepsy. **Libraries: Type:** open to the public. **Holdings:** 180; books, video recordings. **Subjects:** epilepsy. **Affiliated With:** Epilepsy Foundation. **Conventions/Meetings:** monthly meeting - always 2nd Tuesday of the month.

12410 ■ Executive Women International, Minneapolis Chapter (EWI)
c/o Ms. Janet Tschida, Membership Dir.
S&T Off. Products
1000 Kristen Ct.
St. Paul, MN 55110
Ph: (651)486-1291
Fax: (651)483-0550
E-mail: jtschida@stoffice.com
URL: http://www.executivewomenmn.org
Contact: Ms. Janet Tschida, Membership Dir.
Founded: 1960. **Members:** 52. **State Groups:** 3. **Local**. Dedicated to addressing the business professional's quest for personal achievement and drive for professional development. Works to promote member firms and improve their communities. Offers a number of benefits to both the representative and the company. **Awards:** Adult Students in Scholastic Transition Award. **Frequency:** annual. **Type:** scholarship. **Committees:** Membership; Mentoring/Retention; Philanthropy; Program/Hospitality; Publication; Ways and Means. **Affiliated With:** Executive Women International. **Publications:** *Pulse*, monthly. Newsletter. **Advertising:** accepted. Alternate Formats: online.

12411 ■ Executive Women International, Saint Paul Chapter
c/o Michelle Maltby
Mairs & Power, Inc.
W-1420 First Natl. Bank Bldg.
332 Minnesota St.
St. Paul, MN 55101-1363
Ph: (651)222-8478
Fax: (651)222-8470
E-mail: mmaltby@mairsandpower.com
URL: http://www.executivewomenmn.org
Contact: Michelle Maltby, Pres.
Founded: 1976. **Members:** 27. **Local**. Works to promote member firms and improve their communities. Provides opportunities for business and personal growth. **Affiliated With:** Executive Women International. **Publications:** *Pulse*, monthly. Newsletter. Alternate Formats: online. **Conventions/Meetings:** monthly meeting - 1st Tuesday of each month.

12412 ■ FarmHouse Fraternity - Minnesota FarmHouse
1505 N Cleveland Ave.
St. Paul, MN 55108
Ph: (651)646-3196
E-mail: schm1347@umn.edu
URL: http://www.tc.umn.edu/~farmhous/index.htm
Contact: Tony Dahlman, Pres.
State. Promotes good fellowship and studiousness. Encourages members to seek the best in their chosen lines of study as well as in life. Works for the intellectual, spiritual, social, moral and physical development of members. **Affiliated With:** Farmhouse.

12413 ■ Filipino-American Women's Network, Minnesota
c/o Kim Paray, Co-Chair
PO Box 16533
St. Paul, MN 55116-0533
Ph: (763)560-5858
E-mail: info@fawnmn.org
Contact: Kim Paray, Co-Chair
Works to empower Filipino Americans through education about culture, leadership development, and dialogue with the greater community to promote better understanding of Asian-Americans in contemporary society.

12414 ■ Friends of the Mississippi River (FMR)
360 N Robert St.
St. Paul, MN 55101
Ph: (651)222-2193
Fax: (651)222-6005
E-mail: info@fmr.org
URL: http://www.fmr.org
Contact: Whitney Clark, Exec.Dir.
Local.

12415 ■ Friends for a Non-Violent World (FNVW)
1050 Selby Ave.
St. Paul, MN 55104
Ph: (651)917-0383
Fax: (651)917-0379
E-mail: info@fnvw.org
URL: http://www.fnvw.org
Regional.

12416 ■ Geospatial Information and Technology Association Minnesota Regional Chapter
c/o Rick Person, Scholarship Coor.
City of St. Paul
St. Paul, MN 55102
Ph: (651)266-6122
Fax: (651)298-4559
E-mail: rick.person@ci.stpaul.mn.us
URL: National Affiliate–www.gita.org
Contact: Mark Kill, Pres.
State. Works to provide a forum for technology information exchange in the areas and regions they represent. Sponsors education sesssions and meetings that attract interested people from specific geographical areas who otherwise might not be able to participate in the activities of the association. **Affiliated With:** Geospatial Information and Technology Association.

12417 ■ Girl Scout Council of St. Croix Valley
c/o Lisa Hiebert, Dir. of Marketing and Communications
400 Robert St. S
St. Paul, MN 55107
Ph: (651)227-8835
Fax: (651)227-7533
Free: (800)845-0787
E-mail: girlscouts@girlscoutscv.org
URL: http://www.girlscoutscv.org
Contact: Lisa Hiebert, Dir. of Marketing and Communications
Regional. Helps more than 18,600 girls grow strong with the help of 6,900 adult volunteers in 11 counties of eastern Minnesota and western Wisconsin. Dedi-

cated solely to girls aged 5-17 to build character and skills for success in the real world.

12418 ■ Global Citizens Network
c/o Eden Rock, Exec.Dir.
130 N Howell St.
St. Paul, MN 55104
Ph: (651)644-0960
Free: (800)644-9292
E-mail: eden@globalcitizens.org
URL: http://www.globalcitizens.org
Contact: Ms. Eden Rock, Exec.Dir.

Founded: 1992. **Staff:** 1. **Budget:** $100,000. **Nonmembership. Regional.** Sends small teams of volunteers to rural communities around the world to immerse themselves in the daily life of the local culture for one to three weeks. The teams work on community projects initiated by the local people, such as planting trees, digging irrigation trenches, setting up a schoolroom, or teaching commercial skills. Current sites include Arizona, Washington, New Mexico, Guatemala, Mexico, Kenya, and Nepal. **Affiliated With:** International Volunteer Programs Association; Minnesota Council of Nonprofits. **Publications:** *Harambee*, 3/year. Newsletter.

12419 ■ Global Volunteers
375 E Little Canada Rd.
St. Paul, MN 55117
Fax: (651)482-0915
Free: (800)487-1074
E-mail: email@globalvolunteers.org
URL: http://www.globalvolunteers.org
Contact: Barbara DeGroot, Media Relation Mgr.

Founded: 1984. **Staff:** 40. **Regional.** Offers short-term service opportunities on human and economic development projects in 19 countries around the world. The goals is to build intercultural understanding and enhance world peace by bringing together people of diverse backgrounds to work together on these vital community improvement endeavors. **Publications:** *Global Volunteers Adventure in Service*, annual. Catalog • *The Link*, monthly. Newsletter. Alternate Formats: online.

12420 ■ Goodwill Industries/Easter Seals - Minnesota
553 Fairview Ave. N
St. Paul, MN 55104
Ph: (651)379-5800
Fax: (651)379-5803
Free: (800)669-6719
URL: http://mnges.easter-seals.org
Contact: Michael Wirth-Davis, Pres./CEO

Founded: 1919. **Staff:** 300. **Budget:** $15,000,000. **Nonmembership. State.** Provides education, job training, and employment services for people with disabilities or disadvantages. **Affiliated With:** Easter Seals; Goodwill Industries International. **Formerly:** (1999) Goodwill Industries/Easter Seals Society of Minnesota. **Publications:** *Partners*, quarterly. Newsletter • *Solutions*, quarterly. Newsletter. Alternate Formats: online.

12421 ■ Great River Greening
c/o Adam Zielie, Admin.Asst.
35 W Water St., Ste.201
St. Paul, MN 55107
Ph: (651)665-9500
Fax: (651)665-9409
E-mail: azielie@greatrivergreening.org
URL: http://www.greatrivergreening.org
Local.

12422 ■ Hospitality Financial and Technology Professionals - Minneapolis/St. Paul Chapter
c/o Sue Sheridan
Midland Hills Country Club
2001 Fulham St.
St. Paul, MN 55113-5111
Ph: (651)631-0440
Fax: (651)633-3043
E-mail: ssheridan@midlandhillscc.org
URL: National Affiliate–www.hftp.org
Contact: Sue Sheridan, Pres.

Local. Provides opportunities to members through professional and educational development. **Affiliated With:** Hospitality Financial and Technology Professionals. **Conventions/Meetings:** quarterly meeting, with networking and educational activities - every fourth Wednesday.

12423 ■ Hostelling International, Minnesota AYH (HI-MN)
622 Selby Ave.
St. Paul, MN 55104
Ph: (651)251-1495
Fax: (651)251-1496
E-mail: info@himinnesota.org
URL: http://www.himinnesota.org
Contact: Jon Ridge, Exec.Dir.

Founded: 1953. **Members:** 5,000. **Membership Dues:** adult (age 18-54), $25 (annual) • senior (age 55 and over), $15 (annual). **Budget:** $325,000. **State.** Strives to help people of all ages gain a greater understanding of the world, locally and internationally, through educational programs, cultural connections, recreational activities and positive hostelling experiences. **Affiliated With:** Hostelling International-American Youth Hostels. **Publications:** *Minnesota Hosteller*, semiannual. Newsletter. **Conventions/Meetings:** monthly board meeting.

12424 ■ IABC Minnesota (IABC MN)
1821 Univ. Ave. W, No. S256
St. Paul, MN 55104
Ph: (612)333-4222
Fax: (651)917-1835
E-mail: iabcmn@nonprofitsolutions.com
URL: http://www.iabcmn.com
Contact: Martha Nevanen, Pres.

State. Public relations and communication professionals. Committed to improve the effectiveness of organizations through strategic, interactive and integrated business communication management. Provides products, services, and networking activities to help people and organizations excel in public relations, employee communication, marketing communication, public affairs and other forms of communication.

12425 ■ IFP Minnesota Center for Media Arts
2446 Univ. Ave. W, Ste.100
St. Paul, MN 55114
Ph: (651)644-1912
Fax: (651)644-5708
E-mail: word@ifpmn.org
URL: http://www.ifpmn.org
Contact: Jane Minton, Exec.Dir.

State. Supports and promotes the work of artists who create screenplays, film, video and photography in the Upper Midwest. **Affiliated With:** Independent Feature Project. **Formerly:** (2006) IFP Minneapolis/St. Paul.

12426 ■ INROADS, St. Paul, Minnesota
c/o Melvin Collins, Managing Dir.
2550 Univ. Ave. W, Ste.261-S
St. Paul, MN 55114
Ph: (651)644-4406
Fax: (651)649-3032
E-mail: mcollins@inroads.org
URL: National Affiliate–www.inroads.org
Contact: Melvin Collins, Managing Dir.
Local. Affiliated With: INROADS.

12427 ■ International Association of Business Communicators - Minnesota Chapter
1821 Univ. Ave. W, No. S-256
St. Paul, MN 55104
Ph: (612)333-4222
Fax: (612)917-1835
E-mail: iabcmn@nonprofitsolutions.com
URL: http://www.iabcmn.com
Contact: Brett Pyrtle, Pres.
State. Affiliated With: International Association of Business Communicators.

12428 ■ International Association of Heat and Frost Insulators and Asbestos Workers, AFL-CIO, CFL - Local Union 34
95 Empire Dr.
St. Paul, MN 55103
Ph: (651)312-1245
Fax: (651)312-1248
E-mail: insulators34@qwest.net
URL: National Affiliate–www.insulators.org
Contact: Richard Constable, Contact

Members: 370. **Local. Affiliated With:** International Association of Heat and Frost Insulators and Asbestos Workers.

12429 ■ International Association of Machinists and Aerospace Workers, LL-737
1399 Eustis St.
St. Paul, MN 55108
Ph: (651)646-7447
Fax: (651)645-7765
E-mail: toms@iam737.org
URL: http://www.iam737.org
Contact: Cindy Fisher, Admin.Asst.

Local. Affiliated With: International Association of Machinists and Aerospace Workers.

12430 ■ International Union, United Automobile, Aerospace and Agricultural Implement Workers of America, AFL-CIO - Local Union 879
2191 Ford Pkwy.
St. Paul, MN 55116
Ph: (651)699-4246
Fax: (651)699-3876
E-mail: uaw879@mtn.org
URL: http://www.uaw879.org
Contact: Rob McKenzie, Pres.

Members: 2,000. **Local.** AFL-CIO. **Affiliated With:** International Union, United Automobile, Aerospace and Agricultural Implement Workers of America.

12431 ■ Inventors' Network
23 Empire Dr.
St. Paul, MN 55103
Ph: (651)602-3175
URL: http://www.inventorsnetwork.org
Contact: Bill Baker, Contact

State. Affiliated With: United Inventors Association of the U.S.A.

12432 ■ Izaak Walton League of America Midwest Office
1619 Dayton Ave., Ste.202
St. Paul, MN 55104
Ph: (651)649-1446
Fax: (651)649-1494
E-mail: midwestoffice@iwla.org
URL: http://www.iwla.org
Contact: Paul Hansen, Exec.Dir.

Regional. Strive to improve America's air quality. Works to lead a Power Plant Campaign focused on cleaning up outdated coal-burning power plants. **Programs:** Conservation; Outdoor Ethics; Save Our Streams. **Projects:** Sustainability Education. **Affiliated With:** Izaak Walton League of America. **Publications:** *Outdoor America*, quarterly. Magazine. Features conservation issues. **Price:** $27.00 included in membership dues. ISSN: 0021-3314. **Advertising:** accepted • *Sustainability Communicator*, bimonthly. Newsletter. Features update on Sustainability Education Project. Alternate Formats: online • *Water Courses*, semiannual. Newsletter. Features update on the Save Our Streams Program. Alternate Formats: online. **Conventions/Meetings:** annual convention.

12433 ■ Izaak Walton League of America, Minnesota Division
c/o Office Administrator
555 Park St., No. 140
St. Paul, MN 55103-2110

Ph: (612)221-0215
E-mail: ikes@minnesotaikes.org
URL: http://www.minnesotaikes.org

Founded: 1932. **Members:** 1,300. **Membership Dues:** individual and family, $33-$65 (annual). **Staff:** 1. **State**. Conservation group devoted to protecting the environment. **Libraries: Type:** reference. **Holdings:** periodicals. **Subjects:** conservation, environment, energy, farming, hunting, fishing. **Awards:** Distinguished Conservationist. **Type:** recognition • Dr. Walter Breckenridge Conservation Education. **Type:** recognition • Ed Franey Conservation Media. **Type:** recognition • Membership Award. **Type:** recognition • Special Award. **Type:** recognition • Stewardship. **Type:** recognition • Sustainable Community. **Type:** recognition. **Affiliated With:** Izaak Walton League of America. **Publications:** *Waltonian*, quarterly. Newsletter. Includes member activities and conservation issues. **Price:** included in membership dues. **Circulation:** 1,300. Alternate Formats: online.

12434 ■ Jewish Community Action (JCA)
2375 Univ. Ave. W, Ste.150
St. Paul, MN 55114-1633
Ph: (651)632-2184
Fax: (651)632-2188
E-mail: carin@jewishcommunityaction.org
URL: http://www.jewishcommunityaction.org

Local.

12435 ■ Junior League of St. Paul
633 Snelling Ave. N
St. Paul, MN 55104
Ph: (651)291-7377
Fax: (651)291-8914
E-mail: webmaster@jlsp.org
URL: http://www.jlsp.org
Contact: Jennifer Birkeland Swenson, Pres.

Local.

12436 ■ Kitty Matchcover Club
c/o Nancy Bailey
1231 Edmund Ave.
St. Paul, MN 55104-2525
E-mail: sjbnab@aol.com
URL: National Affiliate–www.matchcover.org
Contact: Nancy Bailey, Contact

Local. **Affiliated With:** Rathkamp Matchcover Society.

12437 ■ Lake City Yacht Club (LCYC)
c/o Marie Dotseth
812 Farimount Ave.
St. Paul, MN 55105
E-mail: steveborchardt@charter.net
URL: http://www.lakecityyachtclub.com
Contact: Steve Borchardt, Commodore

Local.

12438 ■ Lakes Area Violet Growers
c/o Robert R. Aurandt
2144 Sloan St.
St. Paul, MN 55117
Ph: (651)771-9948
E-mail: robberaur@msn.com
URL: http://www.rosebudm.com/lavc
Contact: Robert R. Aurandt, Contact

Local. **Affiliated With:** African Violet Society of America.

12439 ■ Lauj Youth Society of Minnesota
c/o Cher Pao Lo
277 Univ. Ave. W, Ste.205
St. Paul, MN 55103
Ph: (651)644-2446
Fax: (651)644-2449
E-mail: svlys@yahoo.com
URL: http://www.laujyouth.org
Contact: See Vang, Exec.Dir.

State.

12440 ■ League of Minnesota Cities (LMC)
145 Univ. Ave. W
St. Paul, MN 55103
Ph: (651)281-1200 (651)281-1290
Fax: (651)281-1299
Free: (800)925-1122
E-mail: jmiller@lmnc.org
URL: http://www.lmnc.org
Contact: Jim Miller, Exec.Dir.

Founded: 1913. **Members:** 846. **Staff:** 70. **State**. Cities and townships working together to promote legislation favorable to local governments. Assists city officials in their efforts to improve services to citizens. **Libraries: Type:** by appointment only. **Holdings:** papers. **Subjects:** municipal governance. **Awards:** C.C. Ludwig Award. **Type:** recognition. **Recipient:** for outstanding service of elected/appointed city officials • City Achievement Award. **Type:** recognition. **Recipient:** for annual adjudicated projects. **Affiliated With:** National League of Cities. **Publications:** *Cities Bulletin*, weekly. Newsletter. Contains update on legislative action. **Price:** $60.00/year. **Advertising:** accepted • *Minnesota Cities*, 10/year. Magazine. Contains municipal issues. **Price:** $25.00/year. **Conventions/Meetings:** annual conference.

12441 ■ Libertarian Party of Minnesota
799 Raymond Ave.
St. Paul, MN 55114
Ph: (651)646-8980
Free: (800)788-2660
E-mail: info@lpmn.org
URL: http://www.lpmn.org
Contact: Ron Helwig, Chm.

Founded: 1972. **Members:** 650. **Membership Dues:** state only, $25 (annual) • combo, $40 (annual). **Local Groups:** 4. **State**. Official MN affiliate of the Libertarian party. Upholds the principle that the initiation of force or fraud is wrong as a means of achieving personal, social, or political goals. Conducts educational programs, runs candidates, and assists other liberty-oriented groups. **Affiliated With:** Libertarian National Committee. **Publications:** *Minnesota Libertarian*, quarterly. Newsletter. **Price:** $12.00. **Circulation:** 12,000. **Advertising:** accepted. Alternate Formats: online. **Conventions/Meetings:** annual convention, day long state convention, business and speakers (exhibits) • monthly meeting.

12442 ■ Macalester-Groveland Community Council (MGCC)
c/o Melissa Martinez-Sones, Exec.Dir.
320 Griggs St. S
St. Paul, MN 55105
Ph: (651)695-4000
E-mail: mgcc@macgrove.org
URL: http://www.macgrove.org
Contact: Melissa Martinez-Sones, Exec.Dir.

Local.

12443 ■ Meeting Professionals International - Minnesota Chapter
c/o Maria Huntley, Mgr.
1821 Univ. Ave. W, Ste.S256
St. Paul, MN 55104
Ph: (612)917-6243
Fax: (612)917-1835
E-mail: office@mnmpi.org
URL: http://www.mnmpi.org
Contact: Maria Huntley, Mgr.

State. **Affiliated With:** Meeting Professionals International.

12444 ■ Midwest Dairy Association
2015 Rice St.
St. Paul, MN 55113
Ph: (651)488-0261
Free: (800)642-3895
E-mail: dmoenning@midwestdairy.com
URL: http://www.midwestdairy.com
Contact: Donna Moenning, Dir., Industry Relations

Founded: 2000. **Members:** 18,000. **Staff:** 50. **Budget:** $23,000,000. **State Groups:** 9. **Regional**.

12445 ■ Midwest Society of Association Executives (MSAE)
c/o Kathy Johnson, Pres.
1885 Univ. Ave., Ste.222
St. Paul, MN 55104
Ph: (651)647-6388
Fax: (651)647-6416
E-mail: associations@msae.com
URL: http://www.msae.com
Contact: Kathy Johnson, Pres.

Regional. Professional society of paid executives of international, national, state, and local trade, professional, and philanthropic associations. Seeks to educate association executives on effective management, including: the proper objectives, functions, and activities of associations; the basic principles of association management; the legal aspects of association activity; policies relating to association management; efficient methods, procedures, and techniques of association management; the responsibilities and professional standards of association executives. **Affiliated With:** American Society of Association Executives.

12446 ■ Minneapolis Estate Planning Council
c/o Donna Harrington, Pres.
1371 Asbury St.
St. Paul, MN 55108
Ph: (651)221-0705
Fax: (651)298-0920
URL: http://councils.naepc.org/_cgi-bin/splashpage.web?CouncilID=222
Contact: Donna Harrington, Pres.

Local. Fosters understanding of the proper relationship between the functions of professionals in the estate planning field. Provides forum for estate planning professionals. Encourages cooperation among members. **Affiliated With:** National Association of Estate Planners and Councils.

12447 ■ Minneapolis/St. Paul Association for Computing Machinery SIGGRAPH
c/o Scott Moore, Chair
3032 Garfield Ave. S
St. Paul, MN 55108
Ph: (612)824-6949
Fax: (612)851-0094
E-mail: mpls-stpaul_chapter@siggraph.org

Local. Biological, medical, behavioral, and computer scientists; hospital administrators; programmers and others interested in application of computer methods to biological, behavioral, and medical problems. Stimulates understanding of the use and potential of computers in the Biosciences. **Affiliated With:** Association for Computing Machinery.

12448 ■ Minneapolis Twin City Airport Lions Club
c/o Jim Cohen, Sec.
4300 Glumack Dr., Ste.344
St. Paul, MN 55111
Ph: (952)949-1389
URL: http://www.5m5.org
Contact: Bob Weber, Pres.

Local. **Affiliated With:** Lions Clubs International.

12449 ■ Minnesota ACORN
c/o Becky Gomer
757 Raymond Ave.
St. Paul, MN 55114
Ph: (651)642-9639
Fax: (651)642-0060
E-mail: mnacornmsp@acorn.org
URL: http://www.acorn.org
Contact: Becky Gomer, Contact

State.

12450 ■ Minnesota AFL-CIO
c/o Ray Waldron, Pres.
175 Aurora Ave.
St. Paul, MN 55103

Ph: (651)227-7647
Fax: (651)227-3801
Free: (800)652-9004
E-mail: mnaflcio@mnaflcio.org
URL: http://www.mnaflcio.org
State. **Affiliated With:** AFL-CIO.

12451 ■ Minnesota Agri-Growth Council (MAGC)
408 St. Peter St., Ste.20
St. Paul, MN 55102
Ph: (651)905-8900
Fax: (651)905-8902
E-mail: daryn.mcbeth@agrigrowth.org
URL: http://www.agrigrowth.org
Contact: Daryn McBeth, Exec.Dir.
Founded: 1968. **State**. Functions as the umbrella organization that unites all of the various segments of the food and agriculture industries in Minnesota. Provides unity and consensus for the diverse voices in agriculture and rural Minnesota.

12452 ■ Minnesota Alliance for Progressive Action (MAPA)
c/o C. Scott Cooper, Exec.Dir.
1821 Univ. Ave., Ste.S-307
St. Paul, MN 55104
Ph: (651)641-4050
Fax: (651)641-4053
E-mail: cscooper@mapa-mn.org
URL: http://www.mapa-mn.org
State.

12453 ■ Minnesota Association of Cooperatives
400 Shelby Ave., Ste.Y
St. Paul, MN 55102
Ph: (651)228-0213
Fax: (651)228-1184
Contact: Maura Schwartz, Managing Dir.
State. Represents cooperatives doing business in Minnesota.

12454 ■ Minnesota Association of County Officers
c/o Luci Botzek, Administrator/Legislative Counsel
27 Exchange St. E, Ste.414
St. Paul, MN 55101-2264
Ph: (651)293-0953
Fax: (651)293-0373
State.

12455 ■ Minnesota Association for the Education of Young Children
1821 Univ. Ave., Ste.298S
St. Paul, MN 55104
Ph: (651)646-8689
Fax: (651)646-4514
E-mail: office@mnaeyc.org
URL: http://www.mnaeyc.org
Contact: Deborah Fitzwater-Dewey, Exec.Dir.
Founded: 1938. **Members:** 1,600. **Membership Dues:** comprehensive, $105 (annual) • regular, $70 (annual) • student, $55 (annual). **Staff:** 4. **Budget:** $350,000. **Regional Groups:** 1. **Local Groups:** 2. **State**. Early childhood educators, day care providers, and kindergarten and primary school teachers. Promotes high standards for the care and education of young children and advocates on their behalf. **Awards:** Distinguished Service Award. **Frequency:** annual. **Type:** recognition. **Recipient:** outstanding contribution to the field of improving the quality of life of children • Evelyn House Award. **Frequency:** annual. **Type:** recognition. **Recipient:** outstanding contribution to the field of improving the welfare of young children • Regional Services Award. **Frequency:** annual. **Type:** recognition. **Recipient:** outstanding contribution to the field of early childhood. **Computer Services:** Information services. **Additional Websites:** http://www.mnpdcouncil.org. **Councils:** Minnesota Professional Development. **Affiliated With:** National Association for the Education of Young Children. **Publications:** *News*, quarterly. Newsletter. Features early childhood practitioners in the state of Minnesota. **Circulation:** 1,600. **Advertising:** accepted • *Views*. Journal. **Conventions/Meetings:** annual conference, with workshops; tracks the target areas where early childhood education and care practitioners gather to study and learn new trends in this field (exhibits) - in Minneapolis, MN.

12456 ■ Minnesota Association of Library Friends (MALF)
1619 Dayton Ave., Ste.314
St. Paul, MN 55104
Ph: (651)227-0845
E-mail: malf@malf.info
URL: http://www.malf.info
Contact: Barbi Byers, Co-Pres.
State. Works to provide training, consultation and resources to further the development of support for libraries. **Affiliated With:** Friends of Libraries U.S.A.

12457 ■ Minnesota Association of School Administrators (MASA)
c/o Dr. Charles Kyte, Exec.Dir.
1884 Como Ave.
St. Paul, MN 55108
Ph: (651)645-6272
Fax: (651)645-7518
E-mail: ckyte@mnasa.org
URL: http://www.mnasa.org
Contact: Dr. Charles Kyte, Exec.Dir.
Founded: 1907. **Members:** 550. **Membership Dues:** $675 (annual). **Staff:** 5. **Regional Groups:** 9. **State**. School administrators, including superintendents, directors of curriculum, assistant superintendents, and other school business officials. **Awards:** Minnesota Superintendent of the Year. **Frequency:** annual. **Type:** monetary • Morris Bye Award. **Frequency:** annual. **Type:** monetary. **Publications:** *Leaders Forum*, quarterly. Newsletter. Includes association news, legal and legislative updates. **Price:** included in membership dues; $50.00/year. **Advertising:** accepted. **Conventions/Meetings:** semiannual conference.

12458 ■ Minnesota Association of Secondary School Principals (MASSP)
1667 N Snelling Ave., Ste.C-100
St. Paul, MN 55108-2131
Ph: (651)999-7333
Fax: (651)999-7331
E-mail: robert.schmidt@mail.massp.org
URL: http://www.massp.org
Contact: Robert J. Schmidt, Exec.Dir.
State.

12459 ■ Minnesota Association of Soil and Water Conservation Districts
c/o Lee Ann Buck, Exec.Dir.
790 Cleveland Ave. S, Ste.201
St. Paul, MN 55116-1958
Ph: (651)690-9028
Fax: (651)690-9065
Contact: Leann Buck, Exec.Dir.
State.

12460 ■ Minnesota Association of Women Police
c/o Mylan Masson, Pres.
Ctr. for Criminal Justice and Law Enforcement
1380 Energy Ln., No.104
St. Paul, MN 55108
Ph: (651)999-7600
E-mail: mylan.masson@minneapolis.edu
URL: National Affiliate–www.iawp.org
Contact: Mylan Masson, Pres.
State. Seeks to strengthen, unite and raise the profile of women in criminal justice. **Affiliated With:** International Association of Women Police.

12461 ■ Minnesota Bureau of Criminal Apprehension Agents' Association
1430 E Maryland Ave.
St. Paul, MN 55106
Ph: (651)793-7000
Fax: (651)793-1001
E-mail: bca.info@state.mn.us
URL: http://www.dps.state.mn.us/bca
Contact: Ms. Linda Finney, Superintendent
State.

12462 ■ Minnesota Cable Communications Association
c/o Michael Martin, Exec.Dir.
1886 Univ. Ave. W, Ste.320
St. Paul, MN 55104
Ph: (651)641-0268
Fax: (651)641-0319
E-mail: mncca@msn.com
State.

12463 ■ Minnesota Center for the Book
c/o Minnesota Humanities Commission
Humanities Educ. Ctr.
987 E Ivy Ave.
St. Paul, MN 55106-2046
Ph: (651)772-4245
Fax: (651)774-0205
Free: (866)268-7293
E-mail: martha@minnesotahumanities.org
URL: http://www.mnbooks.org
Contact: Ms. Martha Davis Beck, Program Officer
State. **Awards:** Minnesota Book Awards. **Frequency:** annual. **Type:** recognition. **Recipient:** for outstanding books by Minnesota authors. **Affiliated With:** Center for the Book.

12464 ■ Minnesota Chapter of the American College of Cardiology (ACC-MN)
1000 Westgate Dr.
St. Paul, MN 55114
Ph: (651)290-6261
Fax: (651)290-2266
E-mail: davide@ewald.com
URL: http://www.accmn.org
Contact: David Ewald CAE, Exec.Dir.
State. **Affiliated With:** American College of Cardiology.

12465 ■ Minnesota Chapter of American Society of Plumbing Engineers
c/o Ryan M. Hanson
NewMech Companies, Inc.
1633 Eustis St.
St. Paul, MN 55108
E-mail: ryhanson@newmech.com
URL: http://www.aspe.org/Minnesota
Contact: Ryan M. Hanson, Contact
State. Represents the interests of individuals dedicated to the advancement of the science of plumbing engineering. Seeks to resolve professional problems in plumbing engineering. Advocates greater cooperation among members and plumbing officials, contractors, laborers and the public. **Affiliated With:** American Society of Plumbing Engineers.

12466 ■ Minnesota Chapter of the Project Management Institute (PMI-MN)
1821 Univ. Ave. W, Ste.S256
St. Paul, MN 55104-2801
Ph: (651)917-6246
Fax: (651)917-1835
E-mail: administrator@pmi-mn.org
URL: http://www.pmi-mn.org
Contact: Mohamed Mandour, Pres.
State. Professional organization for project managers. **Affiliated With:** Project Management Institute.

12467 ■ Minnesota Coalition for Battered Women (MCBW)
590 Park St., Ste.410
St. Paul, MN 55103
Ph: (651)646-6177 (651)646-0994
Fax: (651)646-1527
Free: (800)289-6177
E-mail: mcbw@mcbw.org
URL: http://www.mcbw.org
Contact: Cyndi Cook, Exec.Dir.
Local.

12468 ■ Minnesota Coalition of Bicyclists (MCB)
PO Box 75452
St. Paul, MN 55175
Ph: (651)436-6666
E-mail: rtandems@winternet.com
URL: http://www.mtn.org/tcbc/mcb.html
Contact: Brian Rosenthal, Pres.
State.

12469 ■ Minnesota Coin Laundry Association (MNCLA)
c/o Jeff Gardner
428 Dayton Ave.
St. Paul, MN 55102-1784
Ph: (612)414-3310
E-mail: jgard97825@aol.com
URL: National Affiliate–www.coinlaundry.org
Contact: Jeff Gardner, Contact
State. Affiliated With: Coin Laundry Association.

12470 ■ Minnesota Concrete and Masonry Contractors Association (MC&MCA)
26 E Exchange St., Ste.414
St. Paul, MN 55101
Ph: (651)293-0892
Fax: (651)293-0373
E-mail: gary@capitolconnections.com
URL: http://www.mcmca.com
Contact: Gary Botzek, Exec.Dir.
Founded: 1964. **Members:** 125. **Membership Dues:** base company, $500 (annual). **Budget:** $150,000. **State.** Seeks to promote and encourage usage of concrete and masonry products and services in Minnesota. **Publications:** *Concrete & Masonry News*, monthly. Newsletter • Directory, annual. **Conventions/Meetings:** monthly board meeting • annual convention.

12471 ■ Minnesota Conservation Federation (MCF)
551 Snelling Ave. S, Ste.B
St. Paul, MN 55116-1525
Ph: (651)690-3077
Fax: (651)690-2208
Free: (800)531-3077
E-mail: mncf@mtn.org
URL: http://www.mncf.org
Contact: Barb Prindle, Pres.
Founded: 1936. **Members:** 12,000. **Membership Dues:** associate, $20 (annual) • junior, $10 (annual) • sponsor, $250 (annual) • supporting, $100 (annual) • contributing, $50 (annual) • family, $35 (annual) • life, $500. **Staff:** 1. **Budget:** $120,000. **State.** Works for the conservation, aesthetic appreciation, and restoration of wildlife and other natural resources. **Awards:** Conservationist of the Year. **Frequency:** annual. **Type:** recognition. **Recipient:** for accomplishments and efforts. **Publications:** *Minnesota-Out-of-Doors*, bimonthly. Magazine. **Price:** $15.00/year. **Circulation:** 12,000 • *Walk on the Wildside*, monthly. Magazine. **Circulation:** 1,000. **Conventions/Meetings:** annual general assembly.

12472 ■ Minnesota Council of Nonprofits (MCN)
c/o Jon Pratt
2314 Univ. Ave. W, No. 20
St. Paul, MN 55114
Ph: (651)642-1904
Fax: (651)642-1517
Free: (800)289-1904
E-mail: info@mncn.org
URL: http://www.mncn.org
Contact: Jon Pratt, Exec.Dir.
State. Affiliated With: National Council of Nonprofit Associations.

12473 ■ Minnesota Credit Union Network (MNCUN)
c/o Kevin Chandler, Pres.
555 Wabasha St. N, Ste.200
St. Paul, MN 55102
Ph: (651)288-5170
Fax: (651)288-5171
Free: (800)477-1034
E-mail: info@mncun.org
URL: http://www.mncun.org
Contact: Kevin Chandler, Pres.
State.

12474 ■ Minnesota Crop Improvement Association
c/o Gary M. Beil, Pres./CEO
1900 Hendon Ave.
St. Paul, MN 55108
Ph: (612)625-7766
Fax: (612)625-3748
Free: (800)510-6242
E-mail: mncia@tc.umn.edu
URL: http://www.mncia.org
Contact: Gary M. Beil, Pres./CEO
State. Offers NOP accredited organic producer and handler certification services (ISO65) compliant, seed certification and quality assurance, Non-GMO seed verification, Non-GMO IP grain certification, Foundation and Parent seed production, organic Foundation seed and seed and grain testing.

12475 ■ Minnesota Cultivated Wild Rice Council
4630 Churchill St., Ste.1
St. Paul, MN 55126
Ph: (651)638-1955
Fax: (651)638-0756
E-mail: mnwildrice@comcast.net
Contact: Beth Nelson, Pres.
State.

12476 ■ Minnesota Democratic Farmer Labor Party
255 E Plato Blvd.
St. Paul, MN 55107
Ph: (651)251-6300
Fax: (651)251-6325
Free: (800)999-7457
E-mail: bmelendez@dfl.org
URL: http://www.dfl.org
Contact: Brian Melendez, Chm.
Founded: 1944. **Staff:** 8. **State.** Works to strengthen state party structures. **Affiliated With:** Association of State Democratic Chairs. **Conventions/Meetings:** biennial convention.

12477 ■ Minnesota Dental Association (MDA)
2236 Marshall Ave., Ste.200
St. Paul, MN 55104
Ph: (651)646-7454
Fax: (651)646-8246
Free: (800)950-3368
E-mail: info@mndental.org
URL: http://www.mndental.org
Contact: Richard W. Diercks, Exec.Dir.
Founded: 1884. **State.**

12478 ■ Minnesota Division of the International Association for Identification
1246 Univ. Ave.
St. Paul, MN 55104-4101
Ph: (763)561-7526
E-mail: jlj6975@comcast.net
URL: http://www.wallylind.org
Contact: Jennifer Jaspersen, Sec.-Treas.
State. Organizes people in the profession of forensic identification, investigation and scientific examination of physical evidence, through education, training and research. Advances the scientific techniques of forensic identification and crime detection.

12479 ■ Minnesota Division - Izaak Walton League of America
555 Park St., Ste.140
St. Paul, MN 55103-2110
Ph: (651)221-0215
Fax: (651)221-0215
E-mail: ikes@minnesotaikes.org
URL: http://www.mtn.org/~mn-ikes
Contact: Dr. William Henke, Pres.
State. Individuals who seek the improvement, protection, and preservation of the great outdoors within the state of MN.

12480 ■ Minnesota Electronic Security and Technology Association (MNESTA)
161 St. Anthony Ave., Ste.820
St. Paul, MN 55103
Ph: (651)291-1900
E-mail: info@mbfaa.org
URL: http://www.mnbfaa.org
Contact: Russ Ernst, Pres.
State. Additional Websites: http://www.mnesta.org. **Affiliated With:** National Burglar and Fire Alarm Association. **Formerly:** (2006) Minnesota Burglar and Fire Alarm Association.

12481 ■ Minnesota Elementary School Principals' Association (MESPA)
1667 N Snelling Ave.
St. Paul, MN 55108
Ph: (651)999-7310
Fax: (651)999-7311
Free: (800)642-6807
E-mail: mespa@mespa.net
URL: http://www.mespa.net
Contact: P. Fred Storti, Exec.Dir.
State.

12482 ■ Minnesota Family Association
c/o Brannon Howse
PO Box 25062
St. Paul, MN 55125
Ph: (651)739-4112
Fax: (651)261-2152
E-mail: bhowse@afo.net
URL: http://www.familypolicy.com
State.

12483 ■ Minnesota Farm Bureau Federation (MFB)
PO Box 64370
St. Paul, MN 55164
Ph: (651)905-2100
Fax: (651)905-2159
E-mail: info@fbmn.org
URL: http://www.minnesotafarmbureau.org
Contact: Bob Shepard, Chief Administrator
State.

12484 ■ Minnesota Farmers Union (MFU)
600 County Rd. D W, Ste.14
St. Paul, MN 55112
Ph: (651)639-1223
Fax: (651)639-0421
Free: (800)969-3380
E-mail: mfu@mfu.org
URL: http://mfu.org
Contact: Doug Peterson, Pres.
Founded: 1929. **Members:** 25,000. **Membership Dues:** regular, $65 (annual). **State.** Rural advocacy and general farm organization that represents the concerns of rural communities and the people who live there. **Publications:** *Minnesota Agriculture*, monthly. Newspaper. **Conventions/Meetings:** quarterly board meeting • annual convention.

12485 ■ Minnesota Governor's Council on Developmental Disabilities
c/o Colleen Wieck, PhD, Exec.Dir.
370 Centennial Off. Bldg.
658 Cedar St.
St. Paul, MN 55155
Ph: (651)296-4018
Fax: (651)297-7200
Free: (877)348-0505
E-mail: admin.dd@state.mn.us
URL: http://www.mncdd.org
Contact: Colleen Wieck PhD, Exec.Dir.
Founded: 1971. **Members:** 25. **Staff:** 2. **Budget:** $1,000,000. **State.** Provides information, education, and training to build knowledge, develop skills, and change attitudes that will lead to increased independence, self determination, productivity, integration and inclusion of people with developmental disabilities and their families in the community. **Awards: Frequency:** annual. **Type:** grant. **Computer Services:** Online services, online products and services including publications, CD-ROM, e-learning courses.

Additional Websites: http://www.partnersinpolicymaking.com, http://www.mnddc.org. **Affiliated With:** National Association of Councils on Developmental Disabilities.

12486 ■ Minnesota Grocers Association (MGA)
c/o Nancy Christensen, Exec.Dir.
533 St. Clair Ave.
St. Paul, MN 55102
Ph: (651)228-0973
Fax: (651)228-1949
E-mail: mga@mngrocers.com
URL: http://www.mngrocers.com
State.

12487 ■ Minnesota Health and Housing Alliance (MHHA)
c/o Ms. Gayle M. Kvenvold, Pres./CEO
2550 Univ. Ave. W, Ste.350 S
St. Paul, MN 55114-1052
Ph: (651)645-4545
Fax: (651)645-0002
Free: (800)462-5368
URL: National Affiliate–www.aahsa.org
Contact: Ms. Gayle M. Kvenvold, Pres./CEO
Founded: 1967. **Members:** 700. **Staff:** 21. **Budget:** $2,300,000. **State**. Aims to provide representation and advocacy for nursing homes and senior housing facilities. **Affiliated With:** Assisted Living Federation of America. **Formerly:** (1979) Conference on Geriatric Care. **Publications:** *Issues Update*, periodic • *Monday Mailing*, weekly. **Conventions/Meetings:** annual meeting, in conjunction with MN Hospital and Healthcare Partnership - always September, Brainerd, MN • annual meeting - always February, Minneapolis, MN.

12488 ■ Minnesota Historical Society - Field Service Department (MNHS)
c/o Carol Felton, Office Administrator
345 W Kellogg Blvd.
St. Paul, MN 55102-1906
Ph: (651)296-6126
Fax: (651)297-1345
E-mail: carol.felton@mnhs.org
URL: http://www.mnhs.org
Contact: Carol Felton, Office Administrator
Local.

12489 ■ Minnesota HomeCare Association (MHCA)
c/o Neil Johnson, Exec.Dir.
1711 W County Rd. B, Ste.211S
St. Paul, MN 55113-4036
Ph: (651)635-0607
Fax: (651)635-0043
Free: (866)607-0607
E-mail: ldavidson@mnhomecare.org
URL: http://www.mnhomecare.org
Founded: 1970. **State. Affiliated With:** National Association for Home Care and Hospice.

12490 ■ Minnesota Housing Partnership (MHP)
1821 Univ. Ave. W, Ste.S137
St. Paul, MN 55104-2891
Ph: (651)649-1710
Fax: (651)649-1725
Free: (800)728-8916
E-mail: chalbach@mhponline.org
URL: http://www.mhponline.org
Contact: Chip Halbach, Exec.Dir.
Founded: 1987. **State.**

12491 ■ Minnesota International Educators (MIE)
c/o University of St. Thomas
Off. of Intl. Student Services
2115 Summit Ave.
St. Paul, MN 55105
Ph: (651)962-6650
Fax: (651)962-6655
E-mail: m-schn@umn.edu
URL: http://www.stthomas.edu/oiss/mie
Contact: Mark Schneider, Chm.
State. Advocates for increased awareness and support of international education and exchange on campuses, in government and in communities. Provides training, professional development and networking opportunities to individuals in the field of international education. **Affiliated With:** NAFSA/ Association of International Educators.

12492 ■ Minnesota Lath and Plaster Bureau
820 Transfer Rd.
St. Paul, MN 55114
Ph: (651)645-0208
Fax: (651)645-0209
E-mail: info@mnlath-plaster.com
URL: http://www.mnlath-plaster.com
Contact: Mr. Brian Mulcahy, Pres.
Founded: 1953. **State. Formerly:** (2005) Minnesota Lathing and Plastering Bureau.

12493 ■ Minnesota Library Association (MLA)
1619 Dayton Ave., Ste.314
St. Paul, MN 55104
Ph: (651)641-0982
Fax: (651)649-3169
Free: (877)867-0982
E-mail: barbara@mnlibraryassociation.org
URL: http://www.mnlibraryassociation.org
Contact: Barb Vaughan, Exec.Dir.
Founded: 1891. **Members:** 1,100. **Staff:** 2. **Budget:** $175,000. **State**. Represents all libraries and library workers in the state of Minnesota. Strives to improve library services and resources. Provides an opportunity to meet library peers and associates. **Affiliated With:** American Library Association. **Publications:** Directory, annual • Newsletter, bimonthly. **Conventions/Meetings:** annual conference - always near the 1st week in October.

12494 ■ Minnesota Licensed Beverage Association (MLBA)
1983 Sloan Pl., Ste.6
St. Paul, MN 55117
Ph: (651)772-0910
Fax: (651)772-0900
E-mail: info@mlba.com
URL: http://www.mlba.com
Contact: Tina Bellmore, Office Admin.
Founded: 1943. **Members:** 2,069. **Membership Dues:** individual, $279 (annual). **Staff:** 10. **Budget:** $500,000. **Regional Groups:** 12. **State**. Restaurants, taverns, hotels, nonprofit clubs, and package liquor stores. Promotes the alcohol beverage business at the retail level through lobbying and programs. **Affiliated With:** National Licensed Beverage Association. **Publications:** *MLBA Membership Directory*, annual. Magazine • *Proof Magazine*, bimonthly. **Price:** free to all liquior licences in MN. **Circulation:** 6,000. **Advertising:** accepted. **Conventions/Meetings:** annual Midwest Expo - convention, for retailers in the industry - always October.

12495 ■ Minnesota Literacy Council (MLC)
c/o Eric Nesheim, Exec.Dir.
756 Transfer Rd.
St. Paul, MN 55114-1404
Ph: (651)645-2277
Fax: (651)645-2272
Free: (800)225-READ
E-mail: enesheim@themlc.org
URL: http://www.theMLC.org
Contact: Eric Nesheim, Exec.Dir.
Founded: 1972. **State**. Provides direct and indirect literacy services to adults, children, volunteers and community programs around Minnesota.

12496 ■ Minnesota Manufactured Housing Association
c/o Mark J. Brunner, Exec.VP
1540 Humboldt Ave., Ste.205
St. Paul, MN 55118
Ph: (651)450-4700
Fax: (651)450-1110
E-mail: admin@mmmfghome.org
Contact: Mark Brunner, Exec.VP
State. Publications: Newsletter. **Conventions/ Meetings:** annual meeting.

12497 ■ Minnesota Mechanical Contractors Association (MMCA)
830 Transfer Rd.
St. Paul, MN 55114
Ph: (651)646-2121
Fax: (651)646-9678
Free: (800)816-8184
E-mail: info@mn-mca.org
URL: http://www.mn-mca.org
Contact: Steven Pettersen, Exec.VP
State.

12498 ■ Minnesota Medical Group Management Association
1821 Univ. Ave. W, Ste.S256
St. Paul, MN 55104
Ph: (651)917-6249
Fax: (651)917-1835
E-mail: info@mmgma.org
URL: http://www.mmgma.org
Contact: Tom P. Spiczka, Pres.
Founded: 1951. **State**. Helps in enabling medical practice executives and their organizations to recognize and improve the health status of the community of patients they serve. Focuses on enhancing a member's professional role, knowledge and skills. **Affiliated With:** Medical Group Management Association.

12499 ■ Minnesota Native Plant Society
250 Biological Sciences Center
1445 Gortner Ave.
Univ. of Minnesota
St. Paul, MN 55108
Ph: (651)870-8898
E-mail: contact@mnnps.org
URL: http://www.mnnps.org
Contact: Jason Husveth, Pres.
State.

12500 ■ Minnesota Neurosurgical Society
c/o Dr. Max E. Zarling
280 N Smith Ave., Ste.234
St. Paul, MN 55102-2475
Ph: (651)227-7088
Fax: (651)227-7066
URL: National Affiliate–www.aans.org
Contact: Dr. Max E. Zarling, Contact
State. Represents neurological surgeons united to promote excellence in neurological surgery and its related sciences. Provides funding to foster research in the neurosciences. **Affiliated With:** American Association of Neurological Surgeons.

12501 ■ Minnesota Nursery and Landscape Association (MNLA)
c/o Bob Fitch, Exec.Dir.
PO Box 130307
St. Paul, MN 55113-0003
Ph: (651)633-4987
Fax: (651)633-4986
Free: (888)886-6652
E-mail: mnla@mnla.biz
URL: http://www.mnlandscape.org
Founded: 1925. **Members:** 1,400. **Staff:** 4. **State**. Professional horticulture firms. Promotes the industry and continuing education. Sponsors nursery certification and seeks legislation beneficial to the industry. **Additional Websites:** http://www.mnla.biz. **Formerly:** (1988) Minnesota Nurserymen's Association. **Publications:** *MNLA News*, monthly. Newsletter. **Circulation:** 1,300. **Advertising:** accepted. **Conventions/Meetings:** semiannual convention (exhibits) - always January and August.

12502 ■ Minnesota Nurses Association (MNA)
1625 Energy Park Dr.
St. Paul, MN 55108
Ph: (651)646-4807
Fax: (651)647-5301
Free: (800)536-4662
E-mail: mnnurses@mnnurses.org
URL: http://www.mnnurses.org
Contact: Erin Murphy, Exec.Dir.

Founded: 1905. **Members:** 17,400. **Staff:** 38. **Budget:** $3,000,000. **State Groups:** 1. **Local Groups:** 13. **State**. Collective bargaining and professional advocacy organization for registered nurses. **Boards:** Minnesota Nurses Association Foundation; Minnesota Politically Involved Nurses. **Publications:** *Minnesota Nursing Accent*, 10/year. Newsletter. **Price:** $25.00. ISSN: 0026-5586. **Circulation:** 15,500. **Advertising:** accepted. Alternate Formats: CD-ROM. Also Cited As: *Accent*. **Conventions/Meetings:** annual convention (exhibits) - always October.

12503 ■ Minnesota Nurses Association - District 4
101 Westport Off. Bldg.
220 S Robert St.
St. Paul, MN 55107-1626
Ph: (651)222-7448
Fax: (651)222-7449
E-mail: district4nurses@prodigy.net
URL: http://www.mnnurses.org
Contact: Virginia Turba, Pres.

Local. Works to advance the nursing profession. Seeks to meet the needs of nurses and health care consumers. Fosters high standards of nursing practice. Promotes the economic and general welfare of nurses in the workplace. **Affiliated With:** American Nurses Association; Minnesota Nurses Association.

12504 ■ Minnesota Occupational Therapy Association (MOTA)
1000 Westgate Dr., Ste.252
St. Paul, MN 55114
Ph: (651)290-7498 (651)290-6277
Fax: (651)290-2266
E-mail: shannonp@ewald.com
URL: http://www.functionfirst.org
Contact: Shannon Pfarr Thompson, Exec.Dir.

State. Advances the quality, availability, use and support of occupational therapy through standard-setting, advocacy, education and research. **Affiliated With:** American Occupational Therapy Association.

12505 ■ Minnesota Organization of Leaders in Nursing (MOLN)
1821 Univ. Ave. W, Ste.S256
St. Paul, MN 55104
Ph: (651)999-5344
E-mail: office@moln.org
URL: http://www.moln.org
Contact: Peggy Siestema, Pres.

State. Represents nurse leaders who improve healthcare. Provides leadership, professional development, advocacy and research. Advances the nursing administration practice and patient care. **Affiliated With:** American Organization of Nurse Executives.

12506 ■ Minnesota Petroleum Marketers Association
3244 Rice St.
St. Paul, MN 55126
Ph: (651)484-7227
Fax: (651)484-9189
Free: (800)864-3813
E-mail: webmaster@mpmaonline.com
URL: http://www.mpmaonline.com
Contact: Alan Staples, Pres.

State.

12507 ■ Minnesota Pharmacists Association, East Metro District
c/o John V. Hoeschen, Chm.
St. Paul Corner Drug
240 S Snelling
St. Paul, MN 55105
Ph: (651)698-8859
E-mail: jhoeschen@stpaulcornerdrug.com
URL: http://www.mpha.org
Contact: John V. Hoeschen, Chm.

Local. Works to provide leadership for the pharmacy profession. Seeks to protect and enhance public health. Enhances the knowledge, ethics and skills of pharmacists through advocacy, education, research and the development of standards. **Affiliated With:** Minnesota Pharmacists Association.

12508 ■ Minnesota Planned Giving Council
1821 Univ. Ave. W, Ste.S256
St. Paul, MN 55104-2897
Ph: (651)917-6250
Fax: (651)917-1835
E-mail: office@mnpgc.org
URL: http://www.mnpgc.org
Contact: Jan Sickbert, Chair

State. Increases the quality and quantity of charitable planned gifts. Serves as the voice and professional resource for the gift planning community.

12509 ■ Minnesota Pollution Control Agency (MPCA)
520 Lafayette Rd.
St. Paul, MN 55155-4194
Ph: (651)296-6300 (651)649-5451
Fax: (800)657-3924
Free: (800)657-3864
E-mail: darlene.sigstad@pca.state.mn.us
URL: http://www.pca.state.mn.us
Contact: Darlene Sigstad, Sec.

Founded: 1972. **Staff:** 24. **State**. Works to provide technical presentations on pollution and the environment. Maintains speakers' bureau. **Telecommunication Services:** 24-hour hotline, crisis hotline, (800)422-0798 • teletype, emergency number, (651) 297-5353. **Formerly:** (1998) Pollution Control Agency of Rochester.

12510 ■ Minnesota Private College Council
c/o David B. Laird, Jr., Pres.
Bremer Tower
445 Minnesota St., Ste.500
St. Paul, MN 55101-2903
Ph: (651)228-9061
Fax: (651)228-0379
Free: (800)774-2655
E-mail: colleges@mnprivatecolleges.org
URL: http://www.mnprivatecolleges.com
Contact: David B. Laird Jr., Pres.

Founded: 1948. **Members:** 16. **Budget:** $1,200,000. **State**. Represents 17 of the MN's best four-year, liberal arts colleges and universities as well as more than 52,000 students. Seeks to create policy and funding conditions that allow any qualified Minnesota student the opportunity to attend a Minnesota private college or university. Serves member colleges through government relations and public policy development; research and analysis; communications; fundraising partnerships with corporations and foundations; grant acquisition and administration; and faculty development. **Affiliated With:** National Association of Independent Colleges and Universities. **Conventions/Meetings:** semiannual board meeting.

12511 ■ Minnesota Psychiatric Society (MPS)
c/o Linda Vukelich, Exec.Dir.
4707 Hwy. 61, No. 232
St. Paul, MN 55110-3227
Ph: (651)407-1873
Fax: (651)407-1754
E-mail: l.vukelich@comcast.net
URL: http://www.mnpsychsoc.org
Contact: Linda Vukelich, Exec.Dir.

State. **Affiliated With:** American Psychiatric Association.

12512 ■ Minnesota Psychological Association (MPA)
1000 Westgate Dr., Ste.252
St. Paul, MN 55114-1067
Ph: (651)203-7249
Fax: (651)290-2266
E-mail: davide@ewald.com
URL: http://mnpsych.org
Contact: David Ewald CAE, Exec.Dir.

Founded: 1936. **Members:** 1,100. **Membership Dues:** full, $230 (annual) • sustaining, $320 (annual) • academic, $98 (annual) • colleague, $133 (annual) • student, $50 (annual) • allied professional, $124 (annual) • couple (based on category as determined by the association), $146-$590 (annual). **Staff:** 3. **Budget:** $314,000. **Regional Groups:** 1. **State**. Promotes psychology together with its applications. Aims to develop public psychological interests. **Awards:** Donald G. Paterson Award. **Frequency:** annual. **Type:** monetary. **Recipient:** for outstanding undergraduate senior in psychology • Walter D. Mink Award. **Frequency:** annual. **Type:** recognition. **Recipient:** for outstanding undergraduate teacher. **Publications:** *Minnesota Psychologist*, bimonthly. Newsletter. **Price:** $33.00. **Circulation:** 1,300. **Advertising:** accepted. **Conventions/Meetings:** annual conference, with business meeting (exhibits).

12513 ■ Minnesota PTA
1667 Snelling Ave. N, Ste.111
St. Paul, MN 55108
Ph: (651)999-7320
Fax: (651)999-7321
Free: (800)672-0993
E-mail: mnpta@mnpta.org
URL: http://www.mnpta.org
Contact: Rosie Loeffler-Kemp, Pres.

Founded: 1923. **Members:** 27,500. **Membership Dues:** $4 (annual). **Local**. Seeks to support and speak on behalf of children and youth in the schools, in the community and before governmental bodies and other organizations that make decisions affecting children; to assist parents in developing the skills they need to raise and protect their children; and to encourage parent and public involvement in public schools. **Affiliated With:** National PTA - National Congress of Parents and Teachers. **Formerly:** (2005) Minnesota PTSA. **Publications:** *Voice of the Minnesota PTA*, quarterly. Newsletter. Alternate Formats: online. **Conventions/Meetings:** annual convention.

12514 ■ Minnesota Retailers Association (MnRA)
c/o Mr. Bruce W. Anderson, Pres.
400 Robert St. N, Ste.1540
St. Paul, MN 55101
Ph: (651)227-6631
Free: (800)227-6762
E-mail: mnra@mnretail.org
URL: http://www.mnretail.org
Contact: Mr. Bruce W. Anderson, Pres.

Founded: 1952. **State**. Works on behalf of the Minnesota retail industry. Represents the voice of retailers at the state capitol, publishes informative newsletters, a guidebook of laws and regulations that impact retailers in Minnesota and offers other legislative pieces that keep business owners informed of legislation in process. **Publications:** *Profit Line*. Newsletter. **Conventions/Meetings:** annual meeting.

12515 ■ Minnesota Safety Council
c/o Ms. Carol A. Bufton, CAE, Pres.
474 Concordia Ave.
St. Paul, MN 55103
Ph: (651)291-9150
Fax: (651)291-7584
Free: (800)444-9150
E-mail: msc@mnsafetycouncil.org
URL: http://www.mnsafetycouncil.org
Contact: Ms. Carol A. Bufton CAE, Pres.

Founded: 1928. **Members:** 2,400. **Membership Dues:** corporate (up to 100 employees), $325 (annual). **Staff:** 22. **Regional Groups:** 6. **State**. Prevents unintentional injuries at work, at home, at play and on the road. Offers workplace safety and health training courses, safety products, defensive driving training, consultation, print materials and other resources. **Libraries: Type:** reference. **Holdings:** books, periodicals. **Subjects:** workplace safety and health. **Additional Websites:** http://www.safe-a-rooni.org. **Publications:** *Memo to Members*, quarterly. Newsletter. **Price:** included in membership dues. **Circulation:** 4,000. Alternate Formats: online.

12516 ■ Minnesota St. Thomas More Chapter of the Catholics United for the Faith
c/o Andy Livingston
PO Box 131013
St. Paul, MN 55113
Ph: (612)280-8991
E-mail: acebilling@integrity.com
URL: http://www.mncuf.org
Contact: Andy Livingston, Contact
Local. Additional Websites: http://www.cuf.org/Member/chapters/chapterdetails.asp?chpID=41.

12517 ■ Minnesota School Age Care Alliance (MNSACA)
c/o Brian Siverson-Hall, Exec.Dir.
MNSACA
1000 Westgate Dr., Ste.252
St. Paul, MN 55114
Ph: (651)290-7478 (612)709-7157
Fax: (651)290-2266
E-mail: brians@mnsaca.org
URL: http://mnsaca.org
Contact: Brian J. Siverson-Hall, Exec.Dir.
Founded: 1985. **Members:** 600. **Membership Dues:** comprehensive, $70 (annual) • associate, $40 (annual) • student, $20 (annual). **Staff:** 1. **Budget:** $300,000. **State.** Child and youth focused professionals in the state of MN who provide school-age care in school, park, home, and agency settings during out-of-school hours. Promotes quality programs for children and youth through professional development and public advocacy. **Affiliated With:** National AfterSchool Association. **Publications:** *MNSACA Field Trip Fun*, annual. Book. Contains field trip listings in MN. **Price:** $15.00 • *Network News*, quarterly. Newsletter. **Conventions/Meetings:** annual conference - February • annual meeting - November.

12518 ■ Minnesota Science Teachers Association (MnSTA)
Hamline Univ.
1536 Hewitt Ave.
St. Paul, MN 55104
Ph: (651)523-2945
Fax: (651)523-3041
E-mail: ehessler01@hamline.edu
URL: http://www.mnsta.org
Contact: Ed Hessler, Exec.Dir.
State. Promotes excellence and innovation in science teaching and learning for all. Serves as the voice for excellence and innovation in science teaching and learning, curriculum and instruction, and assessment. Promotes interest and support for science education. **Affiliated With:** National Science Teachers Association.

12519 ■ Minnesota Senior Federation - Metropolitan Region
1885 Univ. Ave. W, Ste.190
St. Paul, MN 55104
Ph: (651)645-0261
Fax: (651)641-8969
Free: (877)645-0261
E-mail: info@mnseniors.org
URL: http://www.mnseniors.org
State. Conventions/Meetings: annual Metro Region Convention and State Convention (exhibits).

12520 ■ Minnesota Small Business Development Center
c/o Mary Kruger, State Dir.
First Natl. Bank Bldg.
332 Minnesota St., Ste.E200
St. Paul, MN 55101-1351
Ph: (651)297-5770
Fax: (651)296-5287
Free: (800)657-3858
E-mail: mary.kruger@state.mn.us
URL: http://www.mnsbdc.com
Contact: Mike Myhre, State Dir.
State. Offers free business management counseling and training seminars. **Affiliated With:** Association of Small Business Development Centers.

12521 ■ Minnesota Social Service Association
125 Charles Ave.
St. Paul, MN 55103
Ph: (651)644-0556
Fax: (651)224-6540
E-mail: mssa@mnsocialserviceassoc.org
URL: http://www.mnsocialserviceassoc.org
Contact: Rod Halvorson, Exec.Dir.
State.

12522 ■ Minnesota Society of Clinical Hypnosis
348 Prior Ave. N, Ste.101
St. Paul, MN 55104
Ph: (651)644-6616
Fax: (757)546-5754
E-mail: john@johnsowada.com
URL: National Affiliate–www.asch.net
Contact: John Sowada MA, Contact
State. Represents health and mental health care professionals using clinical hypnosis. Provides and encourages education programs to further the knowledge, understanding and application of hypnosis in health care. Works for the recognition and acceptance of hypnosis as an important tool in clinical health care. **Affiliated With:** American Society of Clinical Hypnosis.

12523 ■ Minnesota Society for Respiratory Care (MSRC)
c/o Laurie Tomaszewski, Pres.
Handi Medical
2505 Univ. Ave.
St. Paul, MN 55114
Ph: (651)644-9770
Fax: (651)523-8850
E-mail: ltomaszewski@handimedical.com
URL: http://msrcnet.com
Contact: Laurie Tomaszewski, Pres.
State. Fosters the improvement of educational programs in respiratory care. Advocates research in the field of respiratory care. **Affiliated With:** American Association for Respiratory Care.

12524 ■ Minnesota Soft Drink Association
c/o Joan Archer, Pres.
161 St. Anthony Ave., Ste.830
St. Paul, MN 55103
Ph: (651)291-2722
Fax: (651)291-2645
E-mail: msda@mn.state.net
State.

12525 ■ Minnesota State Chamber of Commerce
400 Robert St. N, Ste.1500
St. Paul, MN 55101
Ph: (651)292-4650
Fax: (651)292-4656
Free: (800)821-2230
E-mail: dolson@mnchamber.com
URL: http://www.mnchamber.com
Contact: David Olson, Pres.
Founded: 1909. **Members:** 3,000. **Staff:** 27. **State.** Promotes business and economic growth throughout the state. **Publications:** *Minnesota Business Views*, monthly. Newsletter. Contains timely, accurate information on legislative and regulatory issues that are important to business. Alternate Formats: online. **Conventions/Meetings:** monthly Energy Policy - meeting - every third Wednesday • monthly Environmental and Natural Resources Policy - meeting - every second Thursday.

12526 ■ Minnesota State Curling Association - St. Paul Curling Club
470 Selby Ave.
St. Paul, MN 55102
Ph: (651)224-7408
Fax: (651)224-6596
E-mail: managers@stpaulcurlingclub.org
URL: http://www.stpaulcurlingclub.org
Contact: Bob Nelson, Pres.
Local. Affiliated With: United States Curling Association.

12527 ■ Minnesota State University Student Association (MSUSA)
c/o Shannah Moore, Associate Dir. of Communications
106 Como Ave.
St. Paul, MN 55103
Ph: (651)224-1518
Fax: (651)224-9753
E-mail: msusa@msusa.net
URL: http://www.msusa.net
State.

12528 ■ Minnesota Taxpayers Association
85 E 7th Pl., Ste.250
St. Paul, MN 55101
Ph: (651)224-7477
Fax: (651)224-1209
Free: (800)322-8297
E-mail: info@mntax.org
URL: http://www.mntax.org
Contact: Mr. Lynn Edward Reed, Exec.Dir.
Founded: 1926. **Members:** 500. **Membership Dues:** individual (starting), $77 (annual) • businesses (based on employee size), $129 (annual) • trade association, $250 (annual). **Staff:** 4. **Budget:** $400,000. **State.** Seeks to further the awareness of the state and local policy makers about the impact of tax and spending policies by providing research and advocating sound public fiscal policy. **Affiliated With:** Governmental Research Association; National Tax Association - Tax Institute of America. **Publications:** *Fiscal Focus*, bimonthly. Newsletter. Contains fiscal information and news about Minnesota, legislators, and public. **Price:** $125.00/year. **Circulation:** 1,000. Alternate Formats: online.

12529 ■ Minnesota Telecom Alliance (MTA)
c/o Michael J. Nowick, Pres.
30 E 7th St., Ste.1650
St. Paul, MN 55101
Ph: (651)291-7311
Fax: (651)291-2795
E-mail: info@mnta.org
URL: http://www.mnta.org
Contact: Michael J. Nowick, Pres.
State. Formerly: (2005) Minnesota Telephone Alliance.

12530 ■ Minnesota Transport Services Association (MTSA)
840 Hampden Ave., Ste.207
St. Paul, MN 55114
Ph: (651)646-4075
Fax: (651)641-0764
URL: http://www.mtsa.org
Founded: 1936. **State.**

12531 ■ Minnesota Water Well Association (MWWA)
c/o Dave Schulenberg, Managing Dir.
1000 Westgate Dr., Ste.252
St. Paul, MN 55114
Ph: (651)290-6260 (651)290-6285
Fax: (651)290-2266
E-mail: mwwa@ewald.com
URL: http://www.mwwa.org
Contact: Joe Freeman, Pres.
Founded: 1923. **State.** Represents the well drilling industry throughout the state of Minnesota and maintains the quality of ground water. Serves contractors involved in well construction and repair. **Affiliated With:** National Ground Water Association. **Publications:** *When Citizens in Minnesota Need a Water*

Well, periodic. Pamphlet. Contains information about the process of well drilling, common problems and helpful information, and a guide to ensure safe water.

12532 ■ Minnesota Women's Consortium
550 Rice St.
St. Paul, MN 55103
Ph: (651)228-0338
Fax: (651)292-9417
E-mail: info@mnwomen.org
URL: http://www.mnwomen.org
Contact: Jan Jordet, Pres.
Founded: 1980. **Members:** 167. **State**. Works to improve the lives of women and their families in the state of Minnesota. **Publications:** *Capitol Bulletin*, periodic. Newsletter. **Conventions/Meetings:** weekly Brown Bag Issue Meetings.

12533 ■ Minnesotans for an Energy-Efficient Economy (ME3)
408 St. Peter St., Ste.220
St. Paul, MN 55102
Ph: (651)225-0878
Fax: (651)225-0870
E-mail: noble@me3.org
URL: http://www.me3.org
Contact: Michael Noble, Exec.Dir.
Membership Dues: basic, $35 (annual). **State**. **Publications:** *Sustainable Minnesota*, quarterly. Newsletter.

12534 ■ MMCA
830 Transfer Rd.
St. Paul, MN 55114
Ph: (651)646-2121
Fax: (651)646-9678
Free: (800)816-8154
E-mail: info@minnesotamca.org
URL: http://www.minnesotamca.org
Contact: Jen Distad, Admin.Asst.
State. Contractors who furnish, install, and service piping systems and related equipment for heating, cooling, refrigeration, ventilating, and air conditioning systems. **Affiliated With:** Mechanical Contractors Association of America. **Formerly:** (2005) Twin Cities Piping Industry Association.

12535 ■ Mothers Against Drunk Driving, Blue Earth/Nicollet
2429 Univ. Ave. W
St. Paul, MN 55114
Free: (800)487-6233
URL: National Affiliate–www.madd.org
Local. Victims of drunk driving crashes; concerned citizens. Encourages citizen participation in working towards reform of the drunk driving problem and the prevention of underage drinking. Acts as the voice of victims of drunk driving crashes by speaking on their behalf to communities, businesses, and educational groups. **Affiliated With:** Mothers Against Drunk Driving.

12536 ■ Mothers Against Drunk Driving, Carver County
2429 Univ. Ave. W
St. Paul, MN 55114
Free: (800)487-6233
URL: National Affiliate–www.madd.org
Local. Victims of drunk driving crashes; concerned citizens. Encourages citizen participation in working towards reform of the drunk driving problem and the prevention of underage drinking. Acts as the voice of victims of drunk driving crashes by speaking on their behalf to communities, businesses, and educational groups. **Affiliated With:** Mothers Against Drunk Driving.

12537 ■ Mothers Against Drunk Driving, Otter Tail County
2430 Univ. Ave. W
St. Paul, MN 55114
Ph: (218)739-9584
Free: (800)487-6233
URL: National Affiliate–www.madd.org
Contact: Judy Braddow, Contact
Local. Victims of drunk driving crashes; concerned citizens. Encourages citizen participation in working towards reform of the drunk driving problem and the prevention of underage drinking. Acts as the voice of victims of drunk driving crashes by speaking on their behalf to communities, businesses, and educational groups. **Affiliated With:** Mothers Against Drunk Driving.

12538 ■ Mothers Against Drunk Driving, State Office
2429 Univ. Ave. W
St. Paul, MN 55114
Ph: (651)523-0802
Fax: (651)523-0817
Free: (800)487-6233
E-mail: edcomm@maddmn.org
URL: http://www.maddmn.org
Contact: Bonnie Lobatt, Exec.Dir.
Local. Victims of drunk driving crashes; concerned citizens. Encourages citizen participation in working towards reform of the drunk driving problem and the prevention of underage drinking. Acts as the voice of victims of drunk driving crashes by speaking on their behalf to communities, businesses, and educational groups. **Affiliated With:** Mothers Against Drunk Driving.

12539 ■ NACE International, Twin Cities Section
c/o Steven M. Sweney, Chm.
Off. of Pipeline Safety
444 Cedar St.
St. Paul, MN 55101-5147
Ph: (651)296-9639
Fax: (651)296-9641
E-mail: steve.sweney@state.mn.us
URL: National Affiliate–www.nace.org
Contact: Steven M. Sweney, Chm.
Local. Promotes public safety by advancing the knowledge of corrosion engineering and science. Works to raise awareness of corrosion control and prevention technology among government agencies and legislators, businesses, professional societies and the general public. **Affiliated With:** NACE International: The Corrosion Society.

12540 ■ NARAL Pro-Choice Minnesota
c/o Timothy D. Stanley, Exec.Dir.
550 Rice St.
St. Paul, MN 55103
Ph: (651)602-7655
Fax: (651)602-7658
E-mail: info@prochoiceminnesota.org
URL: http://www.prochoiceminnesota.org
Contact: Timothy D. Stanley, Exec.Dir.
Founded: 1967. **Members:** 7,000. **Membership Dues:** member, $35 (annual) • student, $15 (annual) • choice defender, $50 (annual). **Budget:** $200,000. **State**. Works to develop and sustain a constituency that uses the political process to guarantee every woman the right to make personal decisions regarding the full range of reproductive choices, including preventing unintended pregnancy, bearing healthy children, and choosing legal abortion. **Affiliated With:** NARAL Pro-Choice America. **Formerly:** (2004) Minnesota National Abortion and Reproductive Rights Action League.

12541 ■ National Active and Retired Federal Employees Association - St. Paul 140
1752 Burns Ave.
St. Paul, MN 55106-6606
Ph: (651)776-8842
URL: National Affiliate–www.narfe.org
Contact: Janette Hoffman, Contact
Local. Protects the retirement future of employees through education. Informs members on issues affecting the retirement. **Affiliated With:** National Association of Retired Federal Employees.

12542 ■ National Active and Retired Federal Employees Association - White Bear Lake 1232
1623 E Sextant Ave.
St. Paul, MN 55109-2117
Ph: (651)777-4196
URL: National Affiliate–www.narfe.org
Contact: Joyce E. Spannbauer, Contact
Local. Protects the retirement future of employees through education. Informs members on issues affecting the retirement. **Affiliated With:** National Association of Retired Federal Employees.

12543 ■ National Association of Home Builders, Building Authority of Minnesota
570 Asbury St., Ste.301
St. Paul, MN 55104-1849
Ph: (651)646-7959
Fax: (651)646-2860
E-mail: pamw@bamn.org
URL: National Affiliate–www.nahb.org
Contact: Jeanie Palewizz, Admin.Asst.
Local. Single and multifamily home builders, commercial builders, and others associated with the building industry. **Affiliated With:** National Association of Home Builders.

12544 ■ National Association for Multicultural Education, Minnesota Chapter
c/o Paul C. Gorski, Pres.
Hamline Univ.
Graduate School of Educ.
300 4th St. E, No. 709
St. Paul, MN 55101
Ph: (651)523-2584
E-mail: gorski@earthlink.net
URL: National Affiliate–www.nameorg.org
Contact: Paul C. Gorski, Pres.
State. Represents individuals and groups with an interest in multicultural education from all levels of education, different academic disciplines and from diverse educational institutions and occupations. Provides leadership in national and state dialogues on equity, diversity and multicultural education. Works to fight injustices in schools and in communities. Seeks to ensure that all students receive an equitable education. **Affiliated With:** National Association for Multicultural Education.

12545 ■ National Association of Social Workers, Minnesota Chapter (NASW-MN)
Iris Park Pl., Ste.340
1885 Univ. Ave. W
St. Paul, MN 55104
Ph: (651)293-1935
Fax: (651)293-0952
E-mail: email@naswmn.org
URL: http://www.naswmn.org
Contact: Alan Ingram JD, Exec.Dir.
Members: 2,000. **State**. Works to enhance the professional growth and development of members. Promotes the profession of social work by establishing and maintaining professional standards, providing development opportunities to members, and advocating for clients through community education and political action. **Affiliated With:** National Association of Social Workers.

12546 ■ National Association of State Foresters, Minnesota
c/o Dave Epperly
Div. of Forestry
500 Lafayette Rd.
St. Paul, MN 55155
Ph: (651)259-5284
E-mail: dave.epperly@dnr.state.mn.us
URL: National Affiliate–www.stateforesters.org
Contact: Dave Epperly, Contact
State. **Affiliated With:** National Association of State Foresters.

12547 ■ National Association of Student Personnel Administrators, Minnesota
c/o Laurie Hamre, Coor.
Macalester Coll.
1600 Grand Ave. St.
St. Paul, MN 55105

Ph: (651)696-6220
Fax: (651)696-6630
E-mail: hamre@macalester.edu
URL: National Affiliate–www.naspa.org
Contact: Laurie Hamre, Coor.
State. Provides professional development and advocacy for student affairs educators and administrators. Seeks to promote, assess and support student learning through leadership. **Affiliated With:** National Association of Student Personnel Administrators.

12548 ■ National Association of Women Business Owners - Minnesota Chapter
c/o Sheila Ronning
1880 Livingston Ave., Ste.101
St. Paul, MN 55118
Ph: (952)929-7921
Fax: (952)926-0074
E-mail: info@nawbo-mn.org
URL: http://www.nawbo-mn.org
Contact: Sheila Ronning, Contact
State. **Affiliated With:** National Association of Women Business Owners.

12549 ■ National Council for Geocosmic Research, STARS Chapter
PO Box 11705
St. Paul, MN 55111-0705
Ph: (651)454-0073
E-mail: astrology@mnstars.com
URL: http://www.mnstars.com
Contact: Sally Blumenfeld, Pres.
Founded: 1982. **State**. **Affiliated With:** National Council for GeoCosmic Research.

12550 ■ National Federation of Independent Business - Minnesota
c/o Michael P. Hickey, State Dir.
332 Minnesota St., Ste.1316-E
First Natl. Bank Bldg.
St. Paul, MN 55101
Ph: (651)293-1283
Fax: (651)293-0084
E-mail: mike.hickey@nfib.org
State. **Affiliated With:** National Federation of Independent Business.

12551 ■ National Organization for Women - Minnesota
550 Rice St., No. 102
St. Paul, MN 55103
Ph: (651)222-1605
Fax: (651)292-9417
E-mail: mnnow@mnnow.org
URL: http://www.mnnow.org
State. **Affiliated With:** National Organization for Women.

12552 ■ National Results Council (NRC)
PO Box 9368
St. Paul, MN 55109-0368
Fax: (651)787-0576
Free: (888)604-2400
E-mail: nrc-mn@qwest.net
URL: http://www.nationalresultscouncil.org
Regional.

12553 ■ National Softball Association - Minnesota
2025 Sloan Pl., No. 32
St. Paul, MN 55117
Ph: (651)248-3314
Fax: (651)209-7399
E-mail: wedge@nsamn.com
URL: http://www.nsamn.com
Contact: Chad Wegscheider, Dir.
State. **Affiliated With:** National Softball Association.

12554 ■ National Youth Leadership Council (NYLC)
c/o Megan McKinnon, Exec.Asst.
1667 Snelling Ave. N, Ste.D300
St. Paul, MN 55108
Ph: (651)631-3672
Fax: (651)631-2955
URL: http://www.nylc.org
Regional.

12555 ■ North Star Gay Rodeo Association (NSGRA)
PO Box 11199
St. Paul, MN 55111-0199
Ph: (612)827-6336
E-mail: info@nsgra.org
URL: http://www.nsgra.org
Contact: Colin Smith, Pres.
Local. Represents individuals who promote the country western lifestyle and its facets such as western dance, arts and crafts, music, and skills such as horsemanship and roping; member of International Gay Rodeo Association. **Affiliated With:** International Association of Gay/Lesbian Country Western Dance Clubs.

12556 ■ Northern Lights American Eskimo Dog Association
c/o Mary Verness
1605 N Dunlap St.
St. Paul, MN 55108
Ph: (651)489-0074
E-mail: sundown41@hotmail.com
URL: National Affiliate–www.eskie.com/naeda
Contact: Mary Verness, Contact
Local.

12557 ■ Northwestern Society for Coatings Technology
c/o Ms. Kristin M. Halverson, Pres.
3M Co.
3M Center Bldg. 216-2N-07
St. Paul, MN 55144-1000
Ph: (651)733-4952
Fax: (651)736-2275
E-mail: khalverson@mmm.com
URL: National Affiliate–www.coatingstech.org
Contact: Ms. Kristin M. Halverson, Pres.
Regional. Represents chemists, chemical engineers, technologists and supervisory production personnel in the decorative and protective coatings industry and allied industries. Works to gather and disseminate practical and technical facts, data and standards fundamental to the manufacturing and use of paints, varnishes, lacquers, related protective coatings and printing inks. **Affiliated With:** Federation of Societies for Coatings Technology.

12558 ■ Osman Shriners
c/o Arthur G. Lemke
2750 Sibley Memorial Hwy.
St. Paul, MN 55121
Ph: (612)452-5660
Fax: (612)683-0231
URL: National Affiliate–www.shrinershq.org
Contact: Arthur G. Lemke, Contact
Local. **Affiliated With:** Imperial Council of the Ancient Arabic Order of the Nobles of the Mystic Shrine for North America.

12559 ■ Phi Theta Kappa, Beta Xi Alpha Chapter - Saint Paul College
c/o Nora Gibbons
235 Marshall Ave.
St. Paul, MN 55102
Ph: (651)846-1708
E-mail: nora.gibbons@saintpaul.edu
URL: http://www.ptk.org/directories/chapters/MN/21494-1.htm
Contact: Nora Gibbons, Advisor
Local.

12560 ■ Planned Parenthood of Minnesota, North Dakota and South Dakota
1965 Ford Pkwy.
St. Paul, MN 55116
Ph: (651)698-2401
Fax: (651)698-2405
E-mail: gifts@ppmns.org
URL: http://www.ppmns.org
Regional. **Formerly:** (2004) Planned Parenthood of Minnesota and South Dakota.

12561 ■ Prevent Child Abuse Minnesota
c/o Connie Skillingstad, Exec.Dir.
1821 Univ. Ave., Ste.202-S
St. Paul, MN 55104
Ph: (651)523-0099
Fax: (651)523-0380
Free: (800)621-6322
E-mail: pcamn@pcamn.org
URL: http://www.familysupport.org
Contact: Connie Skillingstad, Exec.Dir.
State. Strives to prevent child abuse and neglect by promoting positive parenting, healthy families and homes where children are valued and loved; provides statewide network of parent mutual support groups, child prevention events and materials. **Affiliated With:** Prevent Child Abuse.

12562 ■ Progressive Minnesota (PM)
2484 Univ. Ave. W
St. Paul, MN 55114
Ph: (651)641-6199
Fax: (651)645-1311
E-mail: pm@progressivemn.org
URL: http://www.progressivemn.org
Contact: Ben Goldfarb, Exec.Dir.
Founded: 1994. **State**. Brings social and economic justice and grassroots democracy through community organizing, education, coalition building and elections. **Affiliated With:** Working Families Party.

12563 ■ Psi Chi, National Honor Society in Psychology - Macalester College
c/o Dept. of Psychology
1600 Grand Ave.
St. Paul, MN 55105
Ph: (612)696-6223 (612)696-6114
Fax: (612)696-6348
E-mail: strauss@macalester.edu
URL: National Affiliate–www.psichi.org
Local. **Affiliated With:** Psi Chi, National Honor Society in Psychology.

12564 ■ Psi Chi, National Honor Society in Psychology - Metropolitan State University
c/o Dept. of Psychology
700 E 7th St.
St. Paul, MN 55106-5000
Ph: (651)793-1336
Fax: (651)793-1355
E-mail: gary.starr@metrostate.edu
URL: http://www.psichi.org/chapters/info.asp?chapter_id=948
Contact: Gary Starr PhD, Advisor
Local.

12565 ■ Public Relations Society of America, Minnesota
1821 Univ. Ave. W, Ste.S256
St. Paul, MN 55104
Ph: (651)917-6244
Fax: (651)917-1835
E-mail: prsamn@nonprofitsolutions.com
URL: http://www.mnprsa.com
Contact: Gail Liebl APR, Pres.
State. **Awards:** Donald G. Padilla Community Classic Award. **Frequency:** annual. **Type:** recognition. **Recipient:** for individuals who have demonstrated a long-term commitment to strengthening the community by sharing his or her expertise and knowledge • Minnesota PRSA Student Classic Awards. **Frequency:** annual. **Type:** recognition. **Recipient:** for best in student public relations program. **Affiliated With:** Public Relations Society of America.

12566 ■ Puppeteers of America - Great Plains Region
c/o Diane Rains, Dir.
2169 Upper Afton Rd.
St. Paul, MN 55119-4641
Ph: (651)739-2572
E-mail: freshwaterpearls@comcast.net
URL: National Affiliate–www.puppeteers.org
Contact: Diane Rains, Dir.
Regional.

12567 ■ Ramsey Co REACT
1600 Englewood Ave., No. 208
St. Paul, MN 55104-1228
Ph: (651)646-0259
E-mail: paul.oby@powermation.com
URL: http://www.reactintl.org/teaminfo/usa_teams/teams-usmn.htm
Local. Trained communication experts and professional volunteers. Provides volunteer public service and emergency communications through the use of radios (Citizen Band, General Mobile Radio Service, UHF and HAM). Coordinates with radio industries and government on safety communication matters and supports charitable activities and community organizations.

12568 ■ Ramsey County Historical Society (RCHS)
323 Landmark Center
75 W 5th St.
St. Paul, MN 55102
Ph: (651)222-0701
Fax: (651)223-8539
E-mail: info@rchs.com
URL: http://www.rchs.com
Contact: Priscilla Farnham, Contact
Founded: 1949. **Members:** 1,200. **Membership Dues:** individual, $30 (annual) • corporate, $100 (annual). **Staff:** 6. **Local**. The Ramsey County Historical Society's mission is to discover, collect, preserve, communicate, and interpret the history of the county for the general public, recreate the historical context, and make available the historical resources of the county. **Libraries: Type:** open to the public. **Holdings:** 4,000. **Subjects:** St. Paul and Ramsey county history. **Awards:** AASLH Award. **Type:** recognition. **Recipient:** for Ramsey County history. **Publications:** *Ramsey County History*, quarterly. Magazine. **Price:** $5.00. **Conventions/Meetings:** annual general assembly - November or December.

12569 ■ Ramsey Medical Society (RMS)
PO Box 131690
St. Paul, MN 55113
Ph: (612)362-3704
Fax: (612)623-2888
URL: http://www.metrodoctors.com
Contact: V. Stuart Cox MD, Pres.-Elect
Local. Represents the interests of physicians, residents and medical students. Promotes excellence in health care. Ensures a healthy practice environment. Preserves the professionalism of medicine. **Affiliated With:** Minnesota Medical Association.

12570 ■ Recycling Association of Minnesota (RAM)
PO Box 14497
St. Paul, MN 55114-0497
Ph: (651)641-4560
Fax: (651)641-4791
E-mail: ramrecycle@comcast.net
URL: http://www.recycleminnesota.org
Contact: Paul Gardner, Exec.Dir.
State. Advocates the use of recycled materials for environment conservation. Provides technical information on recycling methods, composting and reuse. Serves as a means of communication for recycling coordinators, environmental educators and other people advocating the importance of waste management. **Affiliated With:** National Recycling Coalition.

12571 ■ Refugee Mentoring Program (RMP)
c/o International Institute of Minnesota
1694 Como Ave.
St. Paul, MN 55108
Ph: (651)647-0191
Fax: (651)647-9268
E-mail: bstone@iimn.org
URL: http://www.iimn.org
Contact: Barbara Stone, Coor.
Founded: 2001. **Local**. Pairs volunteer mentors with refugee women and men in the Twin Cities. Mentors visit partners at home, offer friendship, help navigate the education, medical and social service systems, solve day-to-day problems, tutor English, provide life skills and introduces friends to the larger community. **Affiliated With:** World Pen Pals. **Formerly:** (2004) Refugee Women's Initiative. **Publications:** Newsletter. Contains cultural and events information related to refugees.

12572 ■ Reserve Officers Association - Department of Minnesota
PO Box 11769
St. Paul, MN 55111-0769
Ph: (763)421-2685 (651)746-3066
E-mail: jrosnow@hotmail.com
URL: http://www.mnroa.org
Contact: Maj. John F. Rosnow, Pres.
State. Promotes and supports the development and execution of a military policy for the United States. Provides professional development seminars, workshops and programs for its members. **Affiliated With:** Reserve Officers Association of the United States.

12573 ■ St. Croix Valley Kennel Club (SCVKC)
c/o Merle Schnepf, Corresponding Sec.
1795 Sargent Ave.
St. Paul, MN 55105
Ph: (651)407-7054 (651)436-2066
Fax: (651)407-7098
E-mail: clubinfo@scvkc.org
URL: http://www.scvkc.org
Contact: Merle Schnepf, Corresponding Sec.
Founded: 1969. **Members:** 76. **Membership Dues:** regular, $10 (annual). **Local**. **Affiliated With:** American Kennel Club. **Publications:** *The St. Croix Valley Scoup*, monthly. Newsletter. **Conventions/Meetings:** monthly meeting.

12574 ■ Saint Paul Area Association of Realtors
325 E Roselawn Ave.
St. Paul, MN 55117
Ph: (651)774-5206
Fax: (651)774-1177
E-mail: spaar@spaar.com
URL: http://www.spaar.com
Contact: Steve Hyland, Pres.
Local. Strives to develop real estate business practices. Advocates the right to own, use and transfer real property. Provides a facility for professional development, research and exchange of information among members. **Affiliated With:** National Association of Realtors.

12575 ■ St. Paul Area Chamber of Commerce
401 N Robert St., Ste.150
St. Paul, MN 55101
Ph: (651)223-5000
Fax: (651)223-5119
E-mail: larry@saintpaulchamber.com
URL: http://www.saintpaulchamber.com
Contact: Larry S. Dowell, Pres.
Founded: 1976. **Members:** 2,200. **Membership Dues:** base, $370. **Local**. Voice for business in St. Paul, MN and the east metro area. Strives to influence public policy; provide small business resources; create economic development; and shape the future workforce. **Affiliated With:** Community Leadership Association; Hispanic Chamber of Commerce of Minnesota; Minnesota State Chamber of Commerce.

12576 ■ St. Paul Association of Responsible Landlords (SPARL)
878 Payne Ave.
St. Paul, MN 55101
Ph: (651)647-6810
Fax: (651)647-6812
E-mail: sparl@sparl.org
URL: http://www.sparl.org
Contact: Paul Schmidt, Pres.
Founded: 1992. **Members:** 300. **Membership Dues:** regular, $45 (annual). **Staff:** 1. **Local**. Owners of rental properties in Twin Cities, MN. Educates rental property owners. Provides Landlord 101 classes quarterly. **Conventions/Meetings:** monthly meeting - always 3rd Tuesday.

12577 ■ Saint Paul Chapter IAAP
PO Box 65674
St. Paul, MN 55165
Ph: (651)765-5706
E-mail: blshaffer@landolakes.com
URL: http://www.iaap-saintpaul.org
Contact: Becki Shaffer, Pres.
Local. Professionals, corporations, academic institutions and students. Develops research and educational projects for administrative professionals. Provides training, seminars, conferences and educational programs.

12578 ■ St. Paul Chapter National Electrical Contractors Association
c/o Jerry Hein, Pres.
380 E Lafayette Frontage Rd., No. 216
St. Paul, MN 55107
Ph: (651)224-3377
Fax: (651)224-3638
E-mail: stpaulneca@cs.com
URL: National Affiliate–www.necanet.org
Contact: Mr. Jerry Hein, Pres.
Local. **Affiliated With:** National Electrical Contractors Association.

12579 ■ St. Paul Convention and Visitors Bureau
175 W Kellogg Blvd., Ste.502
St. Paul, MN 55102
Ph: (651)265-4900
Fax: (651)265-4999
Free: (800)627-6101
E-mail: kkirchgesler@stpaulcvb.org
URL: http://www.stpaulcvb.org
Contact: Karolyn Kirchgesler, Pres.
Members: 16. **Local**. Markets the greater St. Paul area to out-of-town visitors.

12580 ■ St. Paul District Dental Society
2233 Hamline Ave. N, Ste.512
St. Paul, MN 55113
Ph: (651)697-0831
Fax: (651)697-0839
E-mail: stpauldistrictde@qwest.net
URL: http://saintpaul.mndental.org
Contact: Kathy Krauter, Exec.Dir.
Local. Represents the interests of dentists committed to the public's oral health, ethics and professional development. Encourages the improvement of the public's oral health and promotes the art and science of dentistry. **Affiliated With:** American Dental Association; Minnesota Dental Association.

12581 ■ St. Paul Figure Skating Club
848 Pleasant Ave.
St. Paul, MN 55102
Ph: (651)297-9517
E-mail: lekastner@aol.com
URL: http://www.stpaulfsc.org
Contact: Lexie Kastner, Pres./Treas.
Local. Provides programs to encourage participation and achievement in the sport of figure skating on ice. Defines and maintains uniform standards of skating proficiency. Organizes and sponsors competitions and exhibitions for the purpose of stimulating interest in figure skating. **Affiliated With:** United States Figure Skating Association.

12582 ■ Saint Paul Jaycees
401 Robert St., Ste.150
St. Paul, MN 55101
Ph: (651)222-1708
Fax: (651)223-5119
E-mail: jcoffice@usinternet.com
URL: http://www.stpauljaycees.org
Contact: Laura Chesney, Contact
Founded: 1929. **Local**.

12583 ■ St. Paul Liberty Coin Club
c/o Don Lowry
586 Hazel St.
St. Paul, MN 55119
E-mail: libertycoinclub@usfamily.net
URL: National Affiliate–www.money.org
Contact: Don Lowry, Contact
Local. Affiliated With: American Numismatic Association.

12584 ■ St. Paul Ostomy Association (SPOA)
PO Box 75365
St. Paul, MN 55175
Ph: (651)455-6467
E-mail: gebohrer@usfamily.net
URL: http://www.ostomy.org
Contact: Richard K. Taylor, Pres.
Founded: 1978. **Members:** 100. **Membership Dues:** $25 (annual). **Budget:** $5,000. **Regional Groups:** 1. **State Groups:** 10. **Local.** Seeks to promote knowledge of ostomy and improve ostomy care. Provides support group. Disseminates information on ostomy rehabilitation through videos, seminars, and special scientific programs. **Affiliated With:** American Society for Clinical Laboratory Science. **Publications:** *The Pacesetter*, bimonthly. Newsletter. Contains educational information. **Price:** included in membership dues; free to members of the medical community. **Circulation:** 750. **Advertising:** accepted. Alternate Formats: online. **Conventions/Meetings:** monthly meeting, with ostomy appliances (exhibits) - every third Saturday, except June, July and August.

12585 ■ St. Paul Urban League
c/o Willie Mae Wilson, Pres.
401 Selby Ave.
St. Paul, MN 55102
Ph: (651)224-5771
E-mail: wmw@quest.net
URL: National Affiliate–www.nul.org
Contact: Willie Mae Wilson, Pres.
Local. Affiliated With: National Urban League.

12586 ■ SCORE St. Paul
c/o Martin Best, CHR
176 Snelling Ave. N, No. 300
St. Paul, MN 55104-4707
Ph: (651)632-8937
Fax: (651)632-8938
E-mail: stpaul@scoreminn.org
URL: http://www.score.org
Contact: Robert Baynton, Ch.
Affiliated With: SCORE.

12587 ■ Society of American Foresters, University of Minnesota Student Chapter
c/o Tara Bauer, Chair
135 NRAB
2003 Upper Buford Cir.
St. Paul, MN 55108
E-mail: dolp0002@umn.edu
URL: http://www.mnsaf.org
Contact: Tara Bauer, Chair
Local. Affiliated With: Society of American Foresters.

12588 ■ Society of Manufacturing Engineers - St. Paul Technical College S207
235 Marshall Ave.
St. Paul, MN 55102
Ph: (651)221-1354
Fax: (651)221-1416
E-mail: cadair@stp.tec.mn.us
URL: National Affiliate–www.sme.org
Contact: Clark V. Adair, Contact
Local. Advances manufacturing knowledge to gain competitive advantage. Improves skills and manufacturing solutions for the growth of economy. Provides resources and opportunities for manufacturing professionals. **Affiliated With:** Society of Naval Architects and Marine Engineers.

12589 ■ Society of Tribologists and Lubrication Engineers - Twin Cities Section
c/o Stephen O'Malley, Chm.
2719 Stillwater Rd.
St. Paul, MN 55119-3619
Ph: (651)739-6403
Fax: (651)739-6400
E-mail: somalley@yocumoil.com
URL: National Affiliate–www.stle.org
Contact: Stephen O'Malley, Chm.
Local. Promotes the advancement of tribology and the practice of lubrication engineering. Stimulates the study and development of lubrication tribology techniques. Promotes higher standards in the field. **Affiliated With:** Society of Tribologists and Lubrication Engineers.

12590 ■ Sons of Norway, Draxten Lodge 1-464
c/o Dean P. Stiller, Pres.
252 15th Ave. NW
St. Paul, MN 55112-7318
Ph: (612)821-4615
E-mail: dstiller@sofn.com
URL: National Affiliate–www.sofn.com
Contact: Dean P. Stiller, Pres.
Local. Affiliated With: Sons of Norway.

12591 ■ Sons of Norway, Fjell Syn Lodge 1-667
c/o Jill E. Burke, Pres.
5272 Red Oak Dr.
St. Paul, MN 55112-4847
Ph: (763)786-2544
E-mail: jeburke@landolakes.com
URL: National Affiliate–www.sofn.com
Contact: Jill E. Burke, Pres.
Local. Affiliated With: Sons of Norway.

12592 ■ Sons of Norway, Norsota Lodge 1-602
c/o Chris A. Larson, Pres.
4343 Andromeda Way
St. Paul, MN 55123-1823
Ph: (651)688-0698
E-mail: clarson@farmington.k12.mn.us
URL: National Affiliate–www.sofn.com
Contact: Chris A. Larson, Pres.
Local. Affiliated With: Sons of Norway.

12593 ■ Springboard for the Arts
308 Prince St., No. 270
St. Paul, MN 55101
Ph: (651)292-4381
Fax: (651)292-4315
E-mail: info@springboardforthearts.org
URL: http://www.springboardforthearts.org
Founded: 1978. **Staff:** 6. **Local.** Provides information, training, and affordable counseling for artists and arts groups in Minnesota and surrounding states. **Convention/Meeting:** none. **Formerly:** (2001) Resources and Counseling for the Arts. **Publications:** *R&C Workshop Brochure*, quarterly.

12594 ■ Suburban Corvettes of Minnesota
PO Box 17153
St. Paul, MN 55117-9998
E-mail: littleredcorvette@mn.rr.com
URL: http://www.suburbancorvettesofminnesota.com
Contact: Curt Callies, Pres.
Local. Affiliated With: National Council of Corvette Clubs.

12595 ■ Teleprofessional Managers Association - Minnesota
c/o Jennifer Carlson, Program Coor.
1821 Univ. Ave. W, Ste.S156
St. Paul, MN 55104-2892
Ph: (763)593-9419
Fax: (651)917-1835
Contact: Jennifer Carlson, Program Coor.
State.

12596 ■ Ten Thousand Villages-Minnesota
867 Grand Ave.
St. Paul, MN 55105-3024
Ph: (651)225-1043
Fax: (651)228-7266
URL: http://www.tenthousandvillages.org
Contact: Richard Martens, Pres.
State.

12597 ■ Twin Cities Compensation Network
PO Box 16122
St. Paul, MN 55116
Ph: (612)376-9282
Fax: (612)376-9876
E-mail: larry.morgan@lawson.com
URL: http://www.twincitiescomp.org
Contact: Larry Morgan, Pres.
Members: 260. **Membership Dues:** $50 (biweekly). **Regional.** Compensation and benefits professionals. Offers professional programs, information and educational opportunities for professionals in the field of human resources. **Affiliated With:** WorldatWork. **Conventions/Meetings:** monthly meeting.

12598 ■ Twin Cities Fencing Club
c/o Roberto Sobalvarro
741 Holly Ave.
St. Paul, MN 55128
Ph: (651)225-1990
E-mail: sobal001@tc.umn.edu
URL: http://www.ci.stpaul.mn.us/neighborhoods/supc/tcfc/
Local. Amateur fencers. **Affiliated With:** United States Fencing Association.

12599 ■ Twin City Figure Skating Association (TCFSA)
1570 Wheelock Ln., No. 306
St. Paul, MN 55117
E-mail: meharty@usfamily.net
URL: http://www.tcfsa.org
Contact: Elizabeth Harty, Contact
Local. Provides programs to encourage participation and achievement in the sport of figure skating on ice. Defines and maintains uniform standards of skating proficiency. Organizes and sponsors competitions and exhibitions for the purpose of stimulating interest in figure skating. **Affiliated With:** United States Figure Skating Association.

12600 ■ Two Wheel View/Trips for Kids - Twin Cities
PO Box 40084
St. Paul, MN 55104
Free: (866)858-2453
E-mail: info@twowheelview.org
URL: http://www.twowheelview.org
Contact: Rick McFerrin, Founder/Dir.
Founded: 2001. **Staff:** 1. **Budget:** $75,000. **Languages:** English, Norwegian, Spanish. **Local.** Connects young people to the social, cultural and physical environments through bicycle adventures. **Affiliated With:** International Mountain Bicycling Association. **Formerly:** (2004) Trips for Kids- Twin Cities.

12601 ■ United Brotherhood of Carpenters and Joiners of America, Lakes and Plains Regional Council 4020
700 Olive St.
St. Paul, MN 55101
Ph: (651)646-7207
Fax: (651)645-8318
E-mail: general.mail@mncarpenter.org
URL: http://www.mncarpenter.org
Regional. Affiliated With: United Brotherhood of Carpenters and Joiners of America.

12602 ■ United Cerebral Palsy Association of Minnesota
1821 Univ. Ave. W, Ste.219 S
St. Paul, MN 55104-2892

Ph: (651)646-7588
Fax: (651)646-3045
E-mail: ucpmn@cpinternet.com
URL: National Affiliate–www.ucp.org
Contact: Jo Ann Erbes, Exec.Dir.
Founded: 1953. **Budget:** $175,000. **State**. Advances the independence, productivity, and full citizenship of individuals with cerebral palsy and similar disabilities. Services include information and referral, advocacy, workshops and education seminars, and an augmentative and alternative communication equipment lending library for anyone with a communication disorder. **Affiliated With:** United Cerebral Palsy Associations. **Conventions/Meetings:** monthly board meeting • annual conference.

12603 ■ United Jewish Fund and Council (UJFC)
c/o Allen Levine, Pres.
790 Cleveland Ave. S, Ste.227
St. Paul, MN 55116
Ph: (651)690-1707
Fax: (651)690-0228
E-mail: webmaster@ujfc.org
URL: http://www.jewishminnesota.org
Local.

12604 ■ Women in the Trades
c/o Terry Clements, Exec.Dir.
550 Rice St.
St. Paul, MN 55103
Ph: (651)228-9955
Fax: (651)292-9417
Local. Promotes the employment and leadership of women in the construction trades and related fields. Provides career information, a speakers bureau, educational and advocacy programs.

12605 ■ Women on Wheels
PO Box 14180
St. Paul, MN 55114-0180
Ph: (651)647-4344
Free: (800)322-1969
URL: http://www.womenonwheels.org
Contact: Barb Grueschow, Board of Trustee
Founded: 1982. **Members:** 4,000. **Membership Dues:** $30 (annual). **Staff:** 2. **Local**. Unites all women motorcycle enthusiasts for recreation, education, mutual support, recognition and promotes a positive image of motorcycling.

12606 ■ Women's Art Registry of Minnesota (WARM)
Women's Consortium Bldg.
550 Rice St., No. 104
St. Paul, MN 55103
Ph: (651)292-1188
E-mail: info@thewarm.org
URL: http://www.thewarm.org
Contact: Barbara Harman, Pres.
Founded: 1972. **Members:** 200. **Membership Dues:** regular, $50 (annual). **State**. Organization of women artists that support and encourage women in the visual arts. Builds networks and programming that create educational, exhibition, and professional development opportunities. **Affiliated With:** Minnesota Women's Consortium; Women's Caucus for Art. **Publications:** *Warm-Ups*, bimonthly. Newsletter. **Price:** included in membership dues. **Advertising:** accepted. Alternate Formats: online. **Conventions/Meetings:** annual meeting, mentor/protegee exhibition; member juried show (exhibits).

12607 ■ WomenVenture
2324 Univ. Ave. W
St. Paul, MN 55114
Ph: (651)646-3808
E-mail: services@womenventure.org
URL: http://www.womenventure.org
Contact: Tene Wells, Pres.
Local. Helps women to start and grow their own business, plan rewarding careers, and train for non-traditional jobs.

12608 ■ Yellow Bike Coalition
210 E 10th St.
St. Paul, MN 55101
Ph: (651)222-2080
E-mail: ybc@yellowbikes.org
URL: http://www.yellowbikes.org
Contact: Andrew Koebrick, Pres.
Local.

12609 ■ Young Audiences of Minnesota
416 Landmark Ctr.
75 5th St. W
St. Paul, MN 55102-1414
Ph: (612)292-3399
Fax: (612)292-3397
E-mail: info@youngaudiencesofmn.org
URL: http://www.youngaudiencesofmn.org
Contact: Ms. Tia Simons, Exec.Dir.
Founded: 1963. **Staff:** 5. **Budget:** $500,000. **State**. Aims to inspire, empower and unite children and communities through education, arts and culture. **Affiliated With:** Young Audiences. **Also Known As:** (2005) Young Audiences of the Upper Midwest.

12610 ■ YWCA St. Paul
375 Selby Ave.
St. Paul, MN 55102
Ph: (651)222-3741
Fax: (651)222-6307
E-mail: info@ywcaofstpaul.org
URL: http://www.ywcaofstpaul.org
Contact: William Collins Jr., Exec.Dir.
Local.

St. Paul Park

12611 ■ American Legion, Richard Dingle Post 98
PO Box 6
St. Paul Park, MN 55071
Ph: (612)459-9079
Fax: (651)291-1057
URL: National Affiliate–www.legion.org
Local. Affiliated With: American Legion.

St. Peter

12612 ■ American Legion, Minnesota Post 37
c/o Lee C. Prentice
PO Box 444
St. Peter, MN 56082
Ph: (651)291-1800
Fax: (651)291-1057
URL: National Affiliate–www.legion.org
Contact: Lee C. Prentice, Contact
Local. Affiliated With: American Legion.

12613 ■ Association for Computing Machinery, Gustavus Adolphus College
c/o Barbara Kaiser, Sponsor
800 W Coll. Ave.
MCS Dept.
St. Peter, MN 56082
Ph: (507)933-7482
E-mail: kaiser@gac.edu
URL: National Affiliate–www.acm.org
Contact: Ryan Rud, Chm.
Local. Biological, medical, behavioral, and computer scientists; hospital administrators; programmers and others interested in application of computer methods to biological, behavioral, and medical problems. Stimulates understanding of the use and potential of computers in the Biosciences. **Affiliated With:** Association for Computing Machinery.

12614 ■ Glacial Ridge Appaloosa Horse Club
c/o Joanne Suchy
Rt. 1 Box 183
St. Peter, MN 56082
Ph: (507)931-2657
URL: National Affiliate–www.appaloosa.com
Contact: Joanne Suchy, Contact
Local. Affiliated With: Appaloosa Horse Club.

12615 ■ Minnesota Chapter of International Association of Campus Law Enforcement Administrators (MN-IACLEA)
c/o Ray Thrower, Pres.
Gustavus Adolphus Coll.
800 Coll. Ave.
St. Peter, MN 56082
Ph: (507)933-8809
URL: http://www.mn-iaclea.org
Contact: Ray Thrower, Pres.
State. Affiliated With: International Association of Campus Law Enforcement Administrators.

12616 ■ Minnesota Dollars for Scholars
c/o Deb Fichtner
PO Box 297
St. Peter, MN 56082
Ph: (952)835-7680
Fax: (952)831-2097
Free: (800)248-8080
E-mail: dollarsforscholars@scholarshipamerica.org
URL: http://mn.dollarsforscholars.org
Contact: Valerie McCullough, Exec.Dir.
State. Works to provide academic support and scholarships for local students pursuing higher education. **Affiliated With:** Dollars for Scholars.

12617 ■ Minnesota School Boards Association
c/o Robert Meeks, Exec.Dir.
1900 W Jefferson
St. Peter, MN 56082-3015
Ph: (507)934-2450
Fax: (507)931-1515
E-mail: rmeeks@mnmsba.org
URL: http://www.mnmsba.org
Contact: Robert Meeks, Exec.Dir.
State.

12618 ■ Nicollet County Historical Society
c/o Mark T. Morrison
1851 N Minnesota Ave.
St. Peter, MN 56082
Ph: (507)934-2160
Fax: (507)934-0172
E-mail: museum@nchsmn.org
URL: http://www.nchsmn.org
Contact: Ben Leonard, Dir.
Local.

12619 ■ Psi Chi, National Honor Society in Psychology - Gustavus Adolphus College
c/o Dept. of Psychology
800 W Coll. Ave.
St. Peter, MN 56082-1498
Ph: (507)933-7413 (507)933-7305
Fax: (507)933-6032
E-mail: jwotton2@gac.edu
URL: http://www.psichi.org/chapters/info.asp?chapter_id=656
Contact: Janine Wotton PhD, Advisor
Local.

12620 ■ St. Peter Area Chamber of Commerce
101 S Front St.
St. Peter, MN 56082
Ph: (507)934-3400
Fax: (507)934-8960
Free: (800)473-3404
E-mail: spchamb@hickorytech.net
URL: http://www.tourism.st-peter.mn.us
Contact: Larry Haugen, Contact
Local. Strives to provide leadership in order to enhance and promote economic development and quality of life in the St. Peter area. **Publications:** Newsletter.

12621 ■ United Way of St. Peter
PO Box 42
St. Peter, MN 56082-0042
Ph: (507)934-2423
URL: National Affiliate–national.unitedway.org
Local. **Affiliated With:** United Way of America.

Sanborn

12622 ■ American Legion, Colburn Post 286
PO Box 162
Sanborn, MN 56083
Ph: (651)291-1800
Fax: (651)291-1057
URL: National Affiliate–www.legion.org
Local. **Affiliated With:** American Legion.

12623 ■ American Legion, P.E. Post 650
12778 US Hwy. 71
Sanborn, MN 56083
Ph: (651)291-1800
Fax: (651)291-1057
URL: National Affiliate–www.legion.org
Local. **Affiliated With:** American Legion.

Sandstone

12624 ■ American Legion, Minnesota Post 151
c/o Hartley M. Robey
330 Minnesota St.
Sandstone, MN 55072
Ph: (651)291-1800
Fax: (651)291-1057
URL: National Affiliate–www.legion.org
Contact: Hartley M. Robey, Contact
Local. **Affiliated With:** American Legion.

12625 ■ National Active and Retired Federal Employees Association - Pine 1746
PO Box 311
Sandstone, MN 55072-0311
Ph: (320)245-2629
URL: National Affiliate–www.narfe.org
Contact: Marilyn E. Jokela, Contact
Local. Protects the retirement future of employees through education. Informs members on issues affecting the retirement. **Affiliated With:** National Association of Retired Federal Employees.

12626 ■ Sandstone Chamber of Commerce (SCC)
PO Box 23
Sandstone, MN 55072
Ph: (320)245-2271
Contact: Irene Sandell, Sec.
Members: 47. **Membership Dues:** private, $25 (annual) • business, $50 (annual). **Staff:** 4. **Budget:** $9,000. **Local**. Promotes business and community development in Sandstone, MN. **Awards:** Dollars for Scholars. **Frequency:** annual. **Type:** scholarship. **Conventions/Meetings:** annual Quarry Days Festival (exhibits) - always second weekend in August.

12627 ■ Sandstone Lions Club
PO Box 50
Sandstone, MN 55072
Ph: (320)245-5187
E-mail: bgaede@scicable.com
URL: http://www.lionwap.org/sandstonelionsmn
Contact: Bill Gaede, Pres.
Local. **Affiliated With:** Lions Clubs International.

Sartell

12628 ■ American Legion, Minnesota Post 277
c/o Lester Mc Neal
PO Box 6
Sartell, MN 56377
Ph: (651)291-1800
Fax: (651)291-1057
URL: National Affiliate–www.legion.org
Contact: Lester Mc Neal, Contact
Local. **Affiliated With:** American Legion.

12629 ■ Minnesota-Dakotas Society of PeriAnesthesia Nurses (MNDAKSPAN)
PO Box 344
Sartell, MN 56377
Ph: (320)529-8815
E-mail: deborahgp@clearwire.net
URL: http://www.mndakspan.com
Contact: Deb Greenwell-Plafcan RN, Pres.
Regional. Promotes quality and cost effective care for patients, their families and the community through public and professional education, research and standards of practice. **Affiliated With:** American Society of PeriAnesthesia Nurses.

12630 ■ National Active and Retired Federal Employees Association - St. Cloud 644
4332 Pine Point Rd.
Sartell, MN 56377-9749
Ph: (320)255-9292
URL: National Affiliate–www.narfe.org
Contact: Robert J. Kmitch, Contact
Local. Protects the retirement future of employees through education. Informs members on issues affecting the retirement. **Affiliated With:** National Association of Retired Federal Employees.

12631 ■ Trout Unlimited - Mid-Minnesota Chapter
c/o Wayne Killmer
906 Sunray Ct.
Sartell, MN 56377-4501
Ph: (320)654-9625
E-mail: wkillmer@charter.net
URL: http://www.tu.org
Contact: Wayne Killmer, Pres.
Regional.

Sauk Centre

12632 ■ American Legion, Sauk Centre Post 67
128 Main St. S
Sauk Centre, MN 56378
Ph: (651)291-1800
Fax: (651)291-1057
URL: National Affiliate–www.legion.org
Local. **Affiliated With:** American Legion.

12633 ■ Sauk Centre Area Chamber of Commerce (SCCC)
PO Box 222
Sauk Centre, MN 56378
Ph: (320)352-5201
Fax: (320)352-5202
E-mail: chamber@saukcentrechamber.com
URL: http://www.saukcentrechamber.com
Contact: Christine Brinkman, Exec.Dir.
Members: 125. **Local**. Promotes business and community development in Sauk Centre, MN. Holds festival. **Computer Services:** Online services, membership directory. **Publications:** Newsletter, bimonthly.

12634 ■ Sauk Centre Lions Club
c/o Bryan Olson, Pres.
11966 Bluegill Dr.
Sauk Centre, MN 56378
Ph: (320)352-2152 (320)352-2258
E-mail: bryan_olson@isd743.k12.mn.us
URL: http://www.5m4lions.org
Contact: Bryan Olson, Pres.
Local. **Affiliated With:** Lions Clubs International.

Sauk Rapids

12635 ■ American Legion, Frank Heinzel Post 254
109 N Benton Dr.
Sauk Rapids, MN 56379
Ph: (651)291-1800
Fax: (651)291-1057
URL: National Affiliate–www.legion.org
Local. **Affiliated With:** American Legion.

12636 ■ Rivers Council of Minnesota (RCM)
c/o Bruce Johnson, Exec.Dir.
1269 2nd St. N, Ste.200
Sauk Rapids, MN 56379
Ph: (320)259-6800
Fax: (320)259-6678
E-mail: bjohnson@riversmn.org
URL: http://www.riversmn.org
Contact: Bruce Johnson, Exec.Dir.
Founded: 1996. **Members:** 350. **Staff:** 3. **Budget:** $25,000. **State**. Seeks to help people protect, restore and enjoy Minnesota's 92,000 miles of rivers and streams. Works to anticipate issues that affect the health of the state's rivers and to provide tools for citizens and organizations to protect rivers effectively. **Publications:** *Advocate*, semiannual. Newsletter • *Thalweg*, monthly. Newsletter. Alternate Formats: online.

12637 ■ Sauk Rapids Riverside Lions Club
PO Box 662
Sauk Rapids, MN 56379
Ph: (320)656-0515
E-mail: vincethiel@yahoo.com
URL: http://www.lionwap.org/saukrapidsriversidelionsmn
Contact: Vince Thiel, Pres.
Local. **Affiliated With:** Lions Clubs International.

12638 ■ Works in Progress
c/o Michelle Massman, Exec.Dir.
PO Box 282
Sauk Rapids, MN 56379-0282
Ph: (320)259-1956
Fax: (320)656-1846
E-mail: winpinc@aol.com
URL: http://www.worksinprogress.org
Contact: Michelle Massman, Exec.Dir.
Local.

Savage

12639 ■ American Guild of Organists, Twin Cities (628)
c/o Judy Campen
9003 W. 136th St.
Savage, MN 55378
Ph: (952)496-0431 (612)916-1920
E-mail: jcampen@att.net
URL: http://TCAGO.org
Contact: Mrs. Judy A. Campen, Dean
Local. **Affiliated With:** American Guild of Organists. **Publications:** *Pipenotes*. Newsletter. **Price:** included in membership dues.

12640 ■ American Legion, Dan Patch Post 643
12375 Princeton Ave.
Savage, MN 55378
Ph: (651)291-1800
Fax: (651)291-1057
URL: National Affiliate–www.legion.org
Local. **Affiliated With:** American Legion.

12641 ■ Kaiteur Sports Club
14976 Oakcrest Cir.
Savage, MN 55378
URL: http://www.usaca.org/Clubs.htm
Contact: Talim Khan, Contact
Local.

12642 ■ North Western Insulator Club
c/o Ed Peters
5424 Dufferin Dr.
Savage, MN 55378
Ph: (952)447-2422
E-mail: nwic@clubs.insulators.com
URL: http://www.insulators.com/clubs/nwic.htm
Contact: Ed Peters, Contact
Regional. **Affiliated With:** National Insulator Association.

12643 ■ Savage Chamber of Commerce
First Community Bank Bldg.
14141 Glendale Rd., Ste.210
Savage, MN 55378
Ph: (952)894-8876
Fax: (952)894-9906
E-mail: mail@savagechamber.com
URL: http://www.savagechamber.com
Contact: Lori Anderson, Exec.Dir.
Founded: 1964. **Members:** 150. **Membership Dues:** business (based on number of employees), $215-$540 • non-profit organization, $215. **Local**. Strives to unite business and professional people who are dedicated to the ongoing development and support of business activities, industrial opportunities and civic enhancement of the Savage area. **Awards:** Business Person of the Year. **Frequency:** annual. **Type:** recognition. **Recipient:** for individuals who have given outstanding service to the chamber and community in general. **Committees:** Ambassador; Dan Patch Days; Golf; Map; Program.

12644 ■ STARFLEET Region 6
c/o Michael Urvand, Regional Coor.
12400 Inglewood Ave., No. 4
Savage, MN 55378
E-mail: mikeurvand@hotmail.com
URL: http://www.skypoint.com/~davidk50
Contact: Michael Urvand, Regional Coor.
Regional. **Affiliated With:** STARFLEET.

Scandia

12645 ■ East Central Dairy Goat Club
c/o Carol Amundson
15440 240th St. N
Scandia, MN 55073
Ph: (612)433-5119
URL: National Affiliate–adga.org
Contact: Carol Amundson, Contact
Local. **Affiliated With:** American Dairy Goat Association.

Seaforth

12646 ■ American Legion, Minnesota Post 275
c/o Ralph Lamb
PO Box 31
Seaforth, MN 56287
Ph: (651)291-1800
Fax: (651)291-1057
URL: National Affiliate–www.legion.org
Contact: Ralph Lamb, Contact
Local. **Affiliated With:** American Legion.

Sebeka

12647 ■ American Legion, Berg-Nylund Post 456
PO Box 127
Sebeka, MN 56477
Ph: (651)291-1800
Fax: (651)291-1057
URL: National Affiliate–www.legion.org
Local. **Affiliated With:** American Legion.

12648 ■ North Country Appaloosa Horse Club
c/o Malinda K. Dexter
19423 270th St.
Sebeka, MN 56477
Ph: (218)837-5412 (218)631-3195
Fax: (218)631-1625
E-mail: shadowap@uslink.net
URL: National Affiliate–www.appaloosa.com
Contact: Ms. Malinda K. Dexter, Pres.
Founded: 1982. **Members:** 85. **Membership Dues:** family, $15 (annual) • individual, $10 (annual). **Budget:** $8,000. **Regional Groups:** 5. **Regional**. Holds show and fundraiser. Presents year end award from the shows placing. **Awards:** Year End High Point Awards. **Frequency:** annual. **Type:** trophy. **Recipient:** for points earn at the shows. **Computer Services:** Mailing lists, shows result, entry, and placing. **Affiliated With:** Appaloosa Horse Club; Center of the Nation Appaloosa Horse Club; Glacial Ridge Appaloosa Horse Club; Indianhead Appaloosa Horse Club; Pride of the Prairie Appaloosa Club; Red River Valley Appaloosa Horse Club; Wissota Appaloosa Horse Club. **Publications:** Newsletter. Contains information about North Country. **Price:** free. **Circulation:** 85. **Advertising:** accepted. Alternate Formats: CD-ROM; online. **Conventions/Meetings:** monthly meeting, for Board of Directors and general membership - every 1st Saturday. Wadena, MN - Avg. Attendance: 10.

Shafer

12649 ■ American Legion, Minnesota Post 392
c/o Carl Linnell
19516 Furuby Rd.
Shafer, MN 55074
Ph: (651)291-1800
Fax: (651)291-1057
URL: National Affiliate–www.legion.org
Contact: Carl Linnell, Contact
Local. **Affiliated With:** American Legion.

Shakopee

12650 ■ American Legion, Shakopee Post 2
1266 1st Ave.
Shakopee, MN 55379
Ph: (651)291-1800
Fax: (651)291-1057
URL: National Affiliate–www.legion.org
Local. **Affiliated With:** American Legion.

12651 ■ Minnesota Corn Growers Association (MCGA)
738 First Ave. E
Shakopee, MN 55379
Ph: (952)233-0333
E-mail: info@mncorn.org
URL: http://www.mncorn.org/servlet/mcga/homepage
Contact: Duane Adams, Contact
State. **Affiliated With:** National Corn Growers Association.

12652 ■ Shakopee Chamber of Commerce
1801 County Rd. 101 E
PO Box 717
Shakopee, MN 55379-0717
Ph: (952)445-1660
Fax: (952)445-1669
Free: (800)574-2150
E-mail: chamber@shakopee.org
URL: http://www.shakopee.org
Contact: Carol Schultz, Exec.Dir.
Founded: 1955. **Members:** 250. **Staff:** 5. **Budget:** $376,250. **State Groups:** 1. **Local**. Promotes convention business and tourism in Shakopee, MN area. Operates tourist information center. **Computer Services:** Mailing lists, of members. **Formerly:** Shakopee Valley Convention and Visitors Bureau. **Publications:** *Chamber Reporter Insert*, monthly. Newsletter. **Circulation:** 400. **Advertising:** accepted.

12653 ■ Shakopee Jaycees
PO Box 133
Shakopee, MN 55379
Ph: (952)212-2957
E-mail: president@shakopeejaycees.org
URL: http://www.shakopeejaycees.org
Contact: Denise Olsen, Pres.
Local.

12654 ■ Shakopee Valley Lions Club
PO Box 621
Shakopee, MN 55379
E-mail: shakopeevalleylions@yahoo.com
URL: http://www.5m2lions.org
Local. **Affiliated With:** Lions Clubs International.

Sherburn

12655 ■ American Legion, Minnesota Post 356
c/o Thomas P. Saxton
PO Box 277
Sherburn, MN 56171
Ph: (651)291-1800
Fax: (651)291-1057
URL: National Affiliate–www.legion.org
Contact: Thomas P. Saxton, Contact
Local. **Affiliated With:** American Legion.

12656 ■ Minnesota Association of Agricultural Educators
c/o Kent Janssen, Pres.
457 160th St.
Sherburn, MN 56171
Ph: (507)764-4671 (507)639-7976
Fax: (507)764-4681
E-mail: kent_janssen@martin.k12.mn.us
URL: National Affiliate–www.naae.org
Contact: Kent Janssen, Pres.
State. Seeks to advance agricultural education and promotes the professional interests and growth of agriculture teachers. Provides agricultural education through visionary leadership, advocacy and service. **Affiliated With:** National Association of Agricultural Educators.

Shoreview

12657 ■ AMBUCS - Greater Twin Cities
c/o Sally R. Brown, Pres.
3210 Woodbridge St.
Shoreview, MN 55126
Ph: (651)270-6695 (651)765-1911
E-mail: sally.brown@comcast.net
URL: National Affiliate–www.ambucs.com
Contact: Sally R. Brown, Pres.
Local. Seeks to create mobility and independence for people with disabilities. Performs community service. Provides therapeutic tricycles to children with disabilities. Provides scholarships to therapists. **Affiliated With:** National AMBUCS.

12658 ■ American Legion, Jacobsen Memorial Post 487
3979 Virginia Cir.
Shoreview, MN 55126
Ph: (651)291-1800
Fax: (651)291-1057
URL: National Affiliate–www.legion.org
Local. **Affiliated With:** American Legion.

12659 ■ Friends of the St. Paul Farmers' Market
760 Larson Ct.
Shoreview, MN 55126-5806
Ph: (651)483-1367
Fax: (651)483-6508
E-mail: info@friendsofthemarket.org
URL: http://www.FriendsOfTheMarket.org
Contact: Patty Brand, Exec.Dir.
Founded: 1997. **Members:** 150. **Membership Dues:** fixed income, $15 (annual) • individual, $45 (annual)

• family, $65 (annual). **Budget:** $30,000. **Local.** Market supporters and growers. Seeks to educate, market, promote, and facilitate planning for construction of new market. **Publications:** *Friends of the St. Paul Farmers' Market Newsletter*, quarterly. **Circulation:** 3,000. **Conventions/Meetings:** board meeting - 6-8/year.

12660 ■ Minnesota Organization Development Network (MNODN)
c/o Jim Smith
3221 Woodbridge
Shoreview, MN 55126
Ph: (651)481-8103
E-mail: changeres@qwest.net
URL: http://www.mnodn.org
Contact: Jim Smith, Contact
State. Affiliated With: Organization Development Network. **Formerly:** (2005) Minnesota Organization Network.

12661 ■ Penn State Alumni Association, Minnesota Chapter
c/o Mick Kuban
1256 Bucher Ave.
Shoreview, MN 55126
E-mail: mickkuban@comcast.net
URL: http://www.psualum.com/chapter/minnesotachapter
Contact: Mick Kuban, Contact
State.

12662 ■ Ruffed Grouse Society, Twin Cities Chapter
c/o Chuck Blohm
591 Mercury Cir.
Shoreview, MN 55126
Ph: (651)486-3887
E-mail: chuck_blohm@hotmail.com
URL: http://www.twincitiesrgs.com
Contact: Chuck Blohm, Contact
Local. Affiliated With: Ruffed Grouse Society.

12663 ■ Sons of Norway, Synnove-Nordkap Lodge 1-8
c/o Mary Beth Mutchler, Pres.
3496 Nancy Pl.
Shoreview, MN 55126-8005
Ph: (651)484-8872
E-mail: mbe43@comcast.net
URL: http://home.comcast.net/~synnove1
Contact: Mary Beth Mutchler, Pres.
Local. Affiliated With: Sons of Norway.

Shorewood

12664 ■ American Legion, Clarence Clofer Post 259
24450 Smithtown Rd.
Shorewood, MN 55331
Ph: (651)291-1800
Fax: (651)291-1057
URL: National Affiliate–www.legion.org
Local. Affiliated With: American Legion.

12665 ■ National Academy of Television Arts and Sciences, Upper Midwest Chapter
4967 Kensington Gate
Shorewood, MN 55331
Ph: (952)474-7126
Fax: (952)474-7370
E-mail: info@ntauppermidwest.org
URL: http://www.natas-mn.org
Contact: Teresa Vickery, Contact
Membership Dues: active, $75 (annual) • associate, $200 (annual) • educator/student, $25 (annual). **Regional.** Promotes excellence in broadcasting. Inspires the next generation of broadcast journalists. Educates television viewers. **Affiliated With:** National Academy of Television Arts and Sciences.

12666 ■ Northwest Tonka Lions Club
c/o John Moonen, Pres.
25560 Smithtown Rd.
Shorewood, MN 55331
Ph: (952)470-8158
URL: http://www.5m5.org
Contact: John Moonen, Pres.
Local. Affiliated With: Lions Clubs International.

12667 ■ USA Track and Field Minnesota
c/o Janet Robertz, Managing Dir.
5355 Sylvan Ln.
Shorewood, MN 55331
Ph: (952)380-5823
Fax: (952)380-5823
E-mail: jlrobertz@msn.com
URL: http://www.usatfmn.org
Contact: Janet Robertz, Managing Dir.
State. Affiliated With: U.S.A. Track and Field.

Silver Lake

12668 ■ American Legion, Silver Lake Post 141
241 Main St. E
Silver Lake, MN 55381
Ph: (651)291-1800
Fax: (651)291-1057
URL: National Affiliate–www.legion.org
Local. Affiliated With: American Legion.

Slayton

12669 ■ ACF Southwestern Minnesota Chapter
c/o Martin Freeman, Pres.
2460 Ironwood Ave.
Slayton, MN 56172
Ph: (507)836-6008
E-mail: leftbank@iw.net
URL: National Affiliate–www.acfchefs.org
Contact: Martin L. Freeman, Pres.
Local. Promotes the culinary profession. Provides on-going educational training and networking for members. Provides opportunities for competition, professional recognition and access to educational forums with other culinarians at local, regional, national and international events. **Affiliated With:** American Culinary Federation.

12670 ■ American Legion, Erwin March Post 64
PO Box 92
Slayton, MN 56172
Ph: (651)291-1800
Fax: (651)291-1057
URL: National Affiliate–www.legion.org
Local. Affiliated With: American Legion.

12671 ■ Slayton Area Chamber of Commerce (SACC)
2635 Broadway Ave.
Slayton, MN 56172
Ph: (507)836-6902
Fax: (507)836-6650
E-mail: slaytoncham@iw.net
Contact: Ms. April Gangestad, Exec.Dir.
Local. Promotes business and community development in the Slayton, MN area. Conducts charitable activities. **Publications:** Directory, annual.

Sleepy Eye

12672 ■ American Legion, Minnesota Post 7
c/o Benjamin A. Remmele
113 1st Ave. S
Sleepy Eye, MN 56085
Ph: (651)291-1800
Fax: (651)291-1057
URL: National Affiliate–www.legion.org
Contact: Benjamin A. Remmele, Contact
Local. Affiliated With: American Legion.

12673 ■ Sleepy Eye Area Chamber of Commerce (SEACC)
232 E Main St.
Sleepy Eye, MN 56085
Ph: (507)794-4731
Fax: (507)794-4732
Free: (800)290-0588
E-mail: secofc@sleepyeyetel.net
URL: http://sleepyeye-mn.com
Contact: Mrs. Julie Schmitt, Exec.Dir.
Members: 110. **Staff:** 2. **Local.** Promotes business and community development in the Sleepy Eye, MN area. **Affiliated With:** U.S. Chamber of Commerce. **Publications:** Newsletter, monthly • Brochure, periodic. **Conventions/Meetings:** annual meeting.

South St. Paul

12674 ■ Alcoholics Anonymous
301 3rd Ave. S
South St. Paul, MN 55075
Ph: (651)451-2402
Local.

12675 ■ American Legion, Abner Rude Post 481
821 2nd St. N
South St. Paul, MN 55075
Ph: (651)291-1800
Fax: (651)291-1057
URL: National Affiliate–www.legion.org
Local. Affiliated With: American Legion.

12676 ■ Association of Residential Resources in Minnesota (ARRM)
c/o Bruce H. Nelson, Exec.Dir.
1185 N Concord St., Ste.424
South St. Paul, MN 55075
Ph: (651)291-1086
Fax: (651)293-9389
Free: (800)551-2211
E-mail: bnelson@arrm.org
URL: http://www.arrm.org
Founded: 1970. **State.**

12677 ■ Central Livestock Association (CLA)
c/o Donald Kampmeier, Pres./Gen.Mgr.
PO Box 419
South St. Paul, MN 55075
Ph: (651)451-1844
Fax: (651)451-1774
Free: (800)733-1844
URL: http://centrallivestock.aghost.net
State.

12678 ■ Connecting Business Men to Christ - Northland
820 Southview Blvd., Ste.9 S
South St. Paul, MN 55075
Ph: (651)455-0882
Fax: (651)455-0892
URL: http://www.northland.cbmc.com
Regional.

12679 ■ Dakota County Genealogical Society (DCGS)
130 3rd Ave. N
South St. Paul, MN 55075
Ph: (651)452-5926
E-mail: rthill04@yahoo.com
URL: http://www.geocities.com/Heartland/Flats/9284
Contact: Sue Kratsch, Corresponding Sec.
Founded: 1987. **Members:** 130. **Membership Dues:** senior, $20 (annual) • individual, $30 (annual) • family, $50 (annual). **Local.** Promotes interest in the people and history of Dakota County, MN. Operates library. **Formerly:** Dakota Genealogical Society. **Publications:** *Dakota County Genealogist*, quarterly.

Newsletter. **Price:** $10.00/year. ISSN: 1044-6524. **Circulation:** 250. **Advertising:** accepted. **Conventions/Meetings:** periodic workshop (exhibits).

12680 ■ Dakota County Historical Society (DCHS)
130 3rd Ave. N
South St. Paul, MN 55075
Ph: (651)552-7548
Fax: (651)552-7265
E-mail: dchs@mtn.org
URL: http://www.dakotahistory.org
Contact: Chad Roberts, Exec.Dir.

Founded: 1939. **Members:** 800. **Membership Dues:** individual, $30 (annual) • senior, $20 (annual) • family, $50 (annual) • sustaining, $100 (annual) • silver, $250 (annual) • gold, $500 (annual). **Staff:** 4. **Budget:** $130,000. **Local.** Strives to preserve, promote and interpret the history of the county. Sponsors programs and exhibitions each year, both off site and at the museum. Hosts a research library open to the public. **Libraries: Type:** open to the public. **Holdings:** 2,000; books, clippings, periodicals. **Subjects:** Dakota County history. **Computer Services:** database, Civil War and World War II • online services, searchable census, obituary. **Publications:** *Dakota County History*, 3/year. Newsletter. **Price:** included in membership dues. **Circulation:** 800 • *Over the Years*, 3/year. Magazine. **Price:** $5.00 for nonmembers; included in membership dues. **Conventions/Meetings:** annual meeting - always January.

12681 ■ Minnesota Veterinary Medical Association (MVMA)
101 Bridgepoint Way, Ste.100
South St. Paul, MN 55075
Ph: (651)645-7533
Fax: (651)645-7539
E-mail: info@mvma.org
URL: http://www.mvma.org
Contact: Sharon Vangsness, Exec.Dir.

Founded: 1891. **Members:** 1,200. **Membership Dues:** individual, $150 (annual). **State.** Missouri veterinarians. Seeks to advance, promote, educate, and safeguard the veterinary medical profession for the well being of people and animals. **Affiliated With:** American Veterinary Medical Association. **Formerly:** (2005) Missouri Veterinary Medical Association. **Publications:** *GLSVMA Newsletter*, monthly • *Messenger*, monthly. Newsletter • *Show Me Veterinarian*, monthly. Newsletter. **Conventions/Meetings:** annual convention.

12682 ■ National Speleological Society, Minnesota Speleological Survey
PO Box 763
South St. Paul, MN 55075
Ph: (763)784-3214
E-mail: mss@mss-caving.org
URL: http://www.mss-caving.org
Contact: Mark Sandmann, Pres.

State. Seeks to study, explore and conserve cave and karst resources. Protects access to caves and promotes responsible caving. Encourages responsible management of caves and their unique environments. **Affiliated With:** National Speleological Society.

12683 ■ Service Employees International Union, AFL-CIO, CLC - School Service Local Union 284
450 Southview Blvd.
South St. Paul, MN 55075
Ph: (651)256-9100
Fax: (651)256-9119
Free: (877)304-6042
E-mail: shanea@local284.com
URL: http://www.seiu284.org
Contact: Shane Allers, Exec.Dir.

Members: 7,169. **Local. Affiliated With:** Service Employees International Union.

12684 ■ South St. Paul Lions Club
1100 N Concord St.
South St. Paul, MN 55075
Ph: (651)451-8726
E-mail: gcos@visi.com
URL: http://www.ssplions.addr.com
Contact: Greg Cosgrove, Sec.

Local. Affiliated With: Lions Clubs International.

12685 ■ United Food and Commercial Workers International Union, AFL-CIO, CLC - Local Union 789
266 Hardman Ave.
South St. Paul, MN 55075
Ph: (651)451-6240
Fax: (651)451-8227
Free: (877)932-9789
E-mail: ufcw789@ufcw789.org
URL: http://www.ufcw789.org
Contact: Don Seaquist, Pres.

Members: 7,350. **Local. Affiliated With:** United Food and Commercial Workers International Union.

Spicer

12686 ■ American Legion, Henderson-Lewis Post 545
PO Box 296
Spicer, MN 56288
Ph: (651)291-1800
Fax: (651)291-1057
URL: National Affiliate–www.legion.org

Local. Affiliated With: American Legion.

12687 ■ Spicer Sunrise Lions Club
c/o John Woodhall, III, Pres.
9571 NE Hwy. 23
Spicer, MN 56288
Ph: (320)796-2951
E-mail: jawiii@charter.net
URL: http://www.5m4lions.org
Contact: John Woodhall III, Pres.

Local. Affiliated With: Lions Clubs International.

Spring Grove

12688 ■ American Legion, Dyrdal-Prolow Post 249
PO Box 451
Spring Grove, MN 55974
Ph: (651)291-1800
Fax: (651)291-1057
URL: National Affiliate–www.legion.org

Local. Affiliated With: American Legion.

12689 ■ Sons of Norway, Valheim Lodge 1-364
c/o Karen E. Fried, Pres.
RR 1, Box 472
Spring Grove, MN 55974-9801
Ph: (507)498-5611
E-mail: bfried@springgrove.coop
URL: http://www.valheimlodge.org
Contact: Karen E. Fried, Pres.

Local. Affiliated With: Sons of Norway.

12690 ■ Spring Grove Lions Club
c/o Roger Bender, Pres.
PO Box 246
Spring Grove, MN 55974
Ph: (507)498-3455
E-mail: drbender@springgrove.coop
URL: http://www.lions5m1.org/springgrove
Contact: Roger Bender, Pres.

Local. Affiliated With: Lions Clubs International.

Spring Lake Park

12691 ■ Minnesota Sports Federation Amateur Softball Association
7833 Hwy. 65 NE
Spring Lake Park, MN 55432
Ph: (763)241-1789
Fax: (763)241-1736
Free: (888)222-MSF1
E-mail: staff@msf1.org
URL: http://www.msf1.org

State. Affiliated With: Amateur Softball Association of America.

12692 ■ USA Diving - No. 21 Minnesota
c/o Lee Raihle
7990 Spring Lake Park Rd.
Spring Lake Park, MN 55432
Ph: (763)780-9748
E-mail: mnusd@iaxs.net
URL: National Affiliate–www.usdiving.org

State. Affiliated With: USA Diving.

Spring Valley

12693 ■ American Legion, Everett H. Hale Post 68
112 S Broadway
Spring Valley, MN 55975
Ph: (651)291-1800
Fax: (651)291-1057
URL: National Affiliate–www.legion.org

Local. Affiliated With: American Legion.

Springfield

12694 ■ American Ex-Prisoners of War, Prairieland Chapter
c/o Florian Wersal
45783 210th St.
Springfield, MN 56087
Ph: (507)723-5597
URL: National Affiliate–www.axpow.org

Local. Affiliated With: American Ex-Prisoners of War.

12695 ■ American Legion, Minnesota Post 257
c/o John Watson
PO Box 123
Springfield, MN 56087
Ph: (651)291-1800
Fax: (651)291-1057
URL: National Affiliate–www.legion.org
Contact: John Watson, Contact

Local. Affiliated With: American Legion.

12696 ■ Skills USA, Cottonwood River Cooperative Center
804 E Rock St.
Springfield, MN 56087
Ph: (507)723-6281
Fax: (507)723-4270
E-mail: sirksel@prairie.lakes.com
URL: http://www.mnskillsusa.org
Contact: Kristine Sellner, Contact

Local. Serves high school and college students enrolled in technical, skilled, and service and health occupations. Provides quality education experiences for students in leadership, teamwork, citizenship and character development. Builds and reinforces self-confidence, work attitudes and communication skills. Emphasizes total quality at work, high ethical standards, superior work skills, and life-long education. Promotes understanding of the free enterprise system and involvement in community service. **Affiliated With:** Skills USA - VICA.

12697 ■ Springfield Area Chamber of Commerce (SACC)
c/o Marlys Vanderwerf, Exec.Sec.
33 S Cass
Springfield, MN 56087
Ph: (507)723-3508
Fax: (507)723-4270
E-mail: spfdchamber@newulmtel.net
URL: http://www.springfieldmnchamber.org
Contact: Alan Fritch, VP
Founded: 1974. **Membership Dues:** major industry, $550 (annual) • large retailer, $220 (annual) • mid-sized retailer, $165 (annual) • small-scale retailer, $125 (annual) • service industry, $100 (annual) • small service industry, $70 (annual) • individual (for couple), $50 (annual) • friend of the chamber, $25 (annual) • associate, $5 (annual). **Local.** Promotes business and community development in the Springfield, MN area. **Publications:** *Chamber Chatter*, monthly. Newsletter.

Squaw Lake

12698 ■ Ruffed Grouse Society, Grand Rapids, Minnesota Chapter
c/o Gary Goltz
HC 2 Box 158
Squaw Lake, MN 56681
E-mail: goltz@paulbunyan.net
URL: National Affiliate–www.ruffedgrousesociety.org
Contact: Gary Goltz, Contact
Local. Affiliated With: Ruffed Grouse Society.

Stacy

12699 ■ American Legion, Peterson and Waller Post 312
7430 Lent Trail
Stacy, MN 55079
Ph: (651)291-1800
Fax: (651)291-1057
URL: National Affiliate–www.legion.org
Local. Affiliated With: American Legion.

12700 ■ Mothers Against Drunk Driving, Chisago/Isanti Counties (MADD)
PO Box 342
Stacy, MN 55079-0342
Ph: (651)209-3251
E-mail: maddprograms@yahoo.com
URL: National Affiliate–www.madd.org
Contact: John Barney, Chapter Pres.
Founded: 1997. **Members:** 40. **Local.** Victims of drunk driving crashes; concerned citizens. Encourages citizen participation in working towards reform of the drunk driving problem and the prevention of underage drinking. Acts as the voice of victims of drunk driving crashes by speaking on their behalf to communities, businesses, and educational groups. **Affiliated With:** Mothers Against Drunk Driving. **Conventions/Meetings:** monthly meeting - every last Friday.

12701 ■ Northern Flight Hunting Retriever Association (NFHRA)
c/o Deb Powell, Sec.
7275 261st Ave. NE
Stacy, MN 55079-9765
E-mail: d_c_powell@msn.com
URL: http://www.northernflighthuntingretrieversassociation.com
Contact: Deb Powell, Sec.
Local. Affiliated With: American Kennel Club.

Staples

12702 ■ American Legion, Ivan V. Sarff Post 70
PO Box 91
Staples, MN 56479
Ph: (651)291-1800
Fax: (651)291-1057
URL: National Affiliate–www.legion.org
Local. Affiliated With: American Legion.

12703 ■ Five Wings Arts Council
c/o Mark J. Turner
200 1st St. NE
Staples, MN 56479
Ph: (218)894-5485
Fax: (218)894-3045
E-mail: mturner@ncscmn.org
URL: http://www.fwac.org
Contact: Mark Turner, Exec.Dir.
Staff: 1. **Budget:** $180,000. **Nonmembership. Local. Awards:** Arts-related Grant Programs. **Frequency:** monthly. **Type:** grant.

12704 ■ National Active and Retired Federal Employees Association - Brainerd 738
10427 291st Ave.
Staples, MN 56479-3317
Ph: (218)894-2359
URL: National Affiliate–www.narfe.org
Contact: James A. Mohler, Contact
Local. Protects the retirement future of employees through education. Informs members on issues affecting the retirement. **Affiliated With:** National Association of Retired Federal Employees.

12705 ■ Region 5 Development Commission
611 Iowa Ave. NE
Staples, MN 56479
Ph: (218)894-3233
Fax: (218)894-1328
E-mail: info@regionfive.org
URL: http://www.regionfive.org
Contact: Cheryal Lee Hills, Exec.Dir.
Founded: 1973. **Local.**

Starbuck

12706 ■ American Legion, Magnus Grondahl Post 325
PO Box 751
Starbuck, MN 56381
Ph: (651)291-1800
Fax: (651)291-1057
URL: National Affiliate–www.legion.org
Local. Affiliated With: American Legion.

12707 ■ Starbuck Lions Club
c/o David Baukol, Sec.
PO Box 191
Starbuck, MN 56381
Ph: (320)239-2046
E-mail: djbaukol@hcinet.net
URL: http://www.5m4lions.org
Contact: David Baukol, Sec.
Local. Affiliated With: Lions Clubs International.

12708 ■ Sustainable Farming Association of Minnesota (SFA)
c/o Mary Jo Forbord, Exec.Dir.
29731 302 St.
Starbuck, MN 56381
Ph: (320)760-8732
Free: (866)760-8732
E-mail: mforbord@sfa-mn.org
URL: http://www.sfa-mn.org
Contact: Mary Jo Forbord, Exec.Dir.
Founded: 1988. **State.** Strives to create an information-sharing network about sustainable farming practices. Provides support to family farmers and seeks to acquire knowledge and understanding of economically and environmentally sound practices of production farming.

Stephen

12709 ■ American Legion, Stephen Post 390
PO Box 543
Stephen, MN 56757
Ph: (651)291-1800
Fax: (651)291-1057
URL: National Affiliate–www.legion.org
Local. Affiliated With: American Legion.

12710 ■ Stephen Lions Club
c/o Tim Paulson, Pres.
Box 354
Stephen, MN 56757
Ph: (218)478-3314 (218)478-3864
E-mail: timpaulson@sac.k12.mn.us
URL: http://lions5m11.org/sys-tmpl/door
Contact: Tim Paulson, Pres.
Local. Affiliated With: Lions Clubs International.

Stewart

12711 ■ American Legion, De-Gree-Fleisch Post 125
PO Box 214
Stewart, MN 55385
Ph: (651)291-1800
Fax: (651)291-1057
URL: National Affiliate–www.legion.org
Local. Affiliated With: American Legion.

Stewartville

12712 ■ American Legion, Ivan Stringer Post 164
1100 2nd Ave. NW
Stewartville, MN 55976
Ph: (651)291-1800
Fax: (651)291-1057
URL: National Affiliate–www.legion.org
Local. Affiliated With: American Legion.

12713 ■ South Eastern Minnesota Angus Association
c/o Robert Schunke, Pres.
7615 Co. Rd. 6 SW
Stewartville, MN 55976
Ph: (507)533-8013
URL: National Affiliate–www.angus.org
Contact: Robert Schunke, Pres.
Regional. Affiliated With: American Angus Association.

12714 ■ Stewartville Chamber of Commerce
417 1/2 S Main St.
PO Box 52
Stewartville, MN 55976
Ph: (507)533-6006
Fax: (507)533-6006
Free: (866)293-8107
E-mail: stewchamber@stewartville.com
Contact: Jodi Beck, Admin.
Local.

12715 ■ Stewartville Lions Club
c/o Darrel Jaeger, Sec.
406 SW 2nd St.
Stewartville, MN 55976
Ph: (507)533-4698
E-mail: djag239@aol.com
URL: http://www.lions5m1.org/stewartville
Contact: Darrel Jaeger, Sec.
Local. Affiliated With: Lions Clubs International.

Stillwater

12716 ■ American Legion, Stillwater Post 48
103 3rd St. S
Stillwater, MN 55082
Ph: (651)291-1800
Fax: (651)291-1057
URL: National Affiliate–www.legion.org
Local. Affiliated With: American Legion.

12717 ■ Buffet - Wyldlife
1151 Parkwood Ln.
Stillwater, MN 55082
Ph: (651)430-1873
URL: http://sites.younglife.org/_layouts/ylext/default.aspx?ID=C-3238
Local. Affiliated With: Young Life.

12718 ■ The Ethic of Citizenship Society
c/o William Dustin
7171 Mid Oaks Ave.
Stillwater, MN 55082
Ph: (651)430-3933
Fax: (651)430-0222
E-mail: william.dustin@ethicofcitizenship.com
URL: http://www.ethicofcitizenship.com/ECS.htm
Local.

12719 ■ Greater Stillwater Chamber of Commerce
106 S Main St.
PO Box 516
Stillwater, MN 55082
Ph: (651)439-4001
Fax: (651)439-4035
E-mail: info@ilovestillwater.com
URL: http://www.ilovestillwater.com
Contact: Curt Geissler, Pres.
Local. Promotes business and community development in Stillwater, MN.

12720 ■ In the Company of Ferrets
c/o Laura Palmer
PO Box 854
Stillwater, MN 55082
Ph: (651)439-5209
E-mail: luvfuzzies@aol.com
URL: http://www.itcoferrets.bravepages.com/index2.html
Contact: Liz Frolic, Pres.
Local.

12721 ■ Lily Lake Elementary Parent Teacher Organization
2003 W. Willard St.
Stillwater, MN 55082-5553
Local.

12722 ■ Minnesota Health Information Management Association (MHIMA)
c/o Karen Robey, RHIT, Central Office Coor.
PO Box 356
Stillwater, MN 55082
Ph: (651)342-0019
Fax: (763)494-5678
E-mail: mhima@comcast.net
URL: http://www.mnhima.org
Contact: Madonna LeBlanc MA, Pres.
State. Registered record administrators (RHIA); registered health information technicians (RHIT) with expertise in health information management, biostatistics, classification systems, and systems analysis. **Affiliated With:** American Health Information Management Association.

12723 ■ Neighborhood Service Exchange (NSE)
c/o Cathy Dyball, Program Mgr.
2300 Orleans St. W
Stillwater, MN 55082
Ph: (651)439-7434
Fax: (651)439-7616
E-mail: exchange@pressenter.com
URL: http://www.volunteercvs.org/index.php?id=neighborhood
Local.

12724 ■ St. Croix Area United Way
PO Box 305
Stillwater, MN 55082
Ph: (651)439-3838
E-mail: theunitedway@qwest.net
URL: http://www.unitedwaystillwater.org
Local. Affiliated With: United Way of America.

12725 ■ St. Croix Valley Lions Club
14846 18th St. N
Stillwater, MN 55082
Ph: (651)436-6102
E-mail: lionlund@hotmail.com
URL: http://stcroixvalleymn.lionwap.org
Contact: Pat Thron, Sec.
Local. Affiliated With: Lions Clubs International.

12726 ■ St. Paul Audubon Society
c/o Bob Sherman
14129-30th St.
Stillwater, MN 55082
Ph: (651)636-3462
E-mail: candresen@comcast.net
URL: http://www.saintpaulaudubon.net
Contact: Craig Andresen, Pres.
Founded: 1945. **Local. Formerly:** (2005) National Audubon Society - St. Paul.

12727 ■ Sweet Adelines International, Vallee de Croix Chorus
St. Paul's Lutheran Church
609 S 5th St.
Stillwater, MN 55082
Ph: (651)739-8635
E-mail: ebronson@pressenter.com
URL: http://www.valleedecroix.org
Contact: Marlys Bronson, Contact
Local. Advances the musical art form of barbershop harmony through education and performances. Provides education, training and coaching in the development of women's four-part barbershop harmony. **Affiliated With:** Sweet Adelines International.

12728 ■ Twin Cities Area Yorkshire Terrier Club
c/o Barbara Bedsted
16141-22nd St. N
Stillwater, MN 55082
Ph: (651)436-8776
Fax: (651)436-5657
URL: National Affiliate–www.ytca.org
Contact: Barbara Bedsted, Contact
Local. Affiliated With: Yorkshire Terrier Club of America.

12729 ■ Twin Cities Irish Water Spaniel Club (TCIWSC)
c/o Liz Weaver, Sec.
15430 58th St. N
Stillwater, MN 55082
URL: http://www.tciwsc.org
Contact: Jennifer Weaver, Pres.
Local.

12730 ■ Washington County Historical Society (WCHS)
PO Box 167
Stillwater, MN 55082
Ph: (651)439-5956
E-mail: information@wchsmn.org
URL: http://www.wchsmn.org
Contact: Brent T. Peterson, Exec.Dir.
Founded: 1934. **Members:** 500. **Membership Dues:** regular, $15 (annual) • family, $25 (annual) • student, senior, limited income, $10 (annual) • patron, $50 (annual) • sustaining, business, organization, $100 (annual) • life, $500. **Staff:** 3. **Budget:** $65,000. **Local.** Works to preserve, collect and disseminate the history of Minnesota and Washington County. **Libraries: Type:** open to the public. **Holdings:** 2,000. **Subjects:** Washington County, Minnesota military, school, lumbering, prison. **Publications:** *Historical Whisperings*, quarterly. Journal. Contains history related articles and staff reports. **Price:** included in membership dues. **Conventions/Meetings:** semiannual meeting, society doings over the year (exhibits) - always April and November.

12731 ■ Young Life St. Croix Valley
1151 Parkwood Ln.
Stillwater, MN 55082
Ph: (651)430-1873
Fax: (651)430-1651
URL: http://sites.younglife.org/sites/Stillwater/default.aspx
Local. Affiliated With: Young Life.

Storden

12732 ■ American Legion, Minnesota Post 391
c/o Herbert Reese
PO Box 162
Storden, MN 56174
Ph: (651)291-1800
Fax: (651)291-1057
URL: National Affiliate–www.legion.org
Contact: Herbert Reese, Contact
Local. Affiliated With: American Legion.

Strandquist

12733 ■ American Legion, Minnesota Post 466
c/o Sam R. Hougard
18946 380th St. NW
Strandquist, MN 56758
Ph: (651)291-1800
Fax: (651)291-1057
URL: National Affiliate–www.legion.org
Contact: Sam R. Hougard, Contact
Local. Affiliated With: American Legion.

Sturgeon Lake

12734 ■ Ruffed Grouse Society, Pine County Chapter
c/o Bryan Ketchmark
39424 W Shoreland Rd.
Sturgeon Lake, MN 55783
Ph: (218)372-4158
URL: National Affiliate–www.ruffedgrousesociety.org
Contact: Bryan Ketchmark, Contact
Local. Affiliated With: Ruffed Grouse Society.

Swanville

12735 ■ American Legion, Dolven-Wilcox Post 313
PO Box 243
Swanville, MN 56382
Ph: (651)291-1800
Fax: (651)291-1057
URL: National Affiliate–www.legion.org
Local. Affiliated With: American Legion.

Swatara

12736 ■ National Active and Retired Federal Employees Association - Pokegama 1800
39133 650th St.
Swatara, MN 55785
Ph: (218)697-8207
URL: National Affiliate–www.narfe.org
Contact: Margaret H. Niesen, Contact
Local. Protects the retirement future of employees through education. Informs members on issues affecting the retirement. **Affiliated With:** National Association of Retired Federal Employees.

Taconite

12737 ■ American Legion, Whittey Bennett Post 301
PO Box 406
Taconite, MN 55786
Ph: (651)291-1800
Fax: (651)291-1057
URL: National Affiliate–www.legion.org
Local. Affiliated With: American Legion.

Taunton

12738 ■ American Legion, Taunton Post 604
205 N Main Rte. 1
Taunton, MN 56291
Ph: (651)291-1800
Fax: (651)291-1057
URL: National Affiliate–www.legion.org
Local. Affiliated With: American Legion.

Taylors Falls

12739 ■ Communities Investing in Families (CIF)
c/o Martha E. Harding
Harding and Associates
38540 Reed Ave.
Taylors Falls, MN 55084
Free: (800)717-9363
E-mail: martyh@ecenet.com
URL: http://www.investinfamilies.org
Contact: Martha E. Harding, Contact
Local.

Thief River Falls

12740 ■ American Legion, Ecklund-Holmstrom Post 117
PO Box 7
Thief River Falls, MN 56701
Ph: (651)291-1800
Fax: (651)291-1057
URL: National Affiliate–www.legion.org
Local. Affiliated With: American Legion.

12741 ■ Goodridge Lions Club
c/o Marvin Hutchinson, Pres.
824 Horace Ave. N
Thief River Falls, MN 56701
Ph: (218)681-2940
URL: http://lions5m11.org/sys-tmpl/door
Contact: Marvin Hutchinson, Pres.
Local. Affiliated With: Lions Clubs International.

12742 ■ Lincoln High School Figure Skating Club
101 Knight Ave. S
Thief River Falls, MN 56701
Ph: (218)681-7432
E-mail: lsemanko@trf.k12.mn.us
URL: National Affiliate–www.usfigureskating.org
Contact: Lisa Semanko, Contact
Local. Provides programs to encourage participation and achievement in the sport of figure skating on ice. Defines and maintains uniform standards of skating proficiency. Organizes and sponsors competitions and exhibitions for the purpose of stimulating interest in figure skating. **Affiliated With:** United States Figure Skating Association.

12743 ■ Minnesota Nurses Association - District 1
110 Westview Ave. N, Apt. 202
Thief River Falls, MN 56701
Ph: (218)681-3396
E-mail: firstdistrict@hotmail.com
URL: http://www.mnnurses.org
Contact: Sheila LeTourneau, Pres.
Local. Works to advance the nursing profession. Seeks to meet the needs of nurses and health care consumers. Fosters high standards of nursing practice. Promotes the economic and general welfare of nurses in the workplace. **Affiliated With:** American Nurses Association; Minnesota Nurses Association.

12744 ■ Minnesota Senior Federation, Northwest Region
301 E 4th St.
Thief River Falls, MN 56701
Ph: (218)681-4507
URL: http://mnseniors.org
Local.

12745 ■ National Active and Retired Federal Employees Association - Thief River Falls 2328
17639 210th Ave. NW
Thief River Falls, MN 56701-9609
URL: National Affiliate–www.narfe.org
Contact: Raymond Berg, Contact
Local. Protects the retirement future of employees through education. Informs members on issues affecting the retirement. **Affiliated With:** National Association of Retired Federal Employees.

12746 ■ Phi Theta Kappa, Sigma Alpha Chapter - Northland Community and Technical College
c/o Jane Anderson
1101 Hwy. 1 E
Thief River Falls, MN 56701
Ph: (218)681-0836
E-mail: jane.anderson@northlandcollege.edu
URL: http://www.ptk.org/directories/chapters/MN/260-1.htm
Contact: Jane Anderson, Advisor
Local.

12747 ■ Ruffed Grouse Society, Agazzi Chapter
c/o Tony R. Dorn, Jr.
PO Box K
Thief River Falls, MN 56701
Ph: (218)681-6857
URL: National Affiliate–www.ruffedgrousesociety.org
Contact: Tony R. Dorn Jr., Contact
Local. Affiliated With: Ruffed Grouse Society.

12748 ■ St. Hilaire Lions Club
c/o John Kotaska, Pres.
15374 110th St. NE
Thief River Falls, MN 56701
Ph: (218)681-6327
E-mail: kotaska@wiktel.com
URL: http://lions5m11.org/sys-tmpl/door
Contact: John Kotaska, Pres.
Local. Affiliated With: Lions Clubs International.

12749 ■ Sons of Norway, Snorre Lodge 1-70
c/o Marlene J. Olson, Sec.
17325 120th Ave. NE
Thief River Falls, MN 56701-8556
Ph: (218)681-3587
URL: National Affiliate–www.sofn.com
Contact: Marlene J. Olson, Sec.
Local. Affiliated With: Sons of Norway.

12750 ■ Thief River Falls Area United Way
PO Box 276
Thief River Falls, MN 56701-0276
Ph: (218)681-3303
URL: National Affiliate–national.unitedway.org
Local. Affiliated With: United Way of America.

12751 ■ Thief River Falls Chamber of Commerce
2017 Hwy. 59 SE
Thief River Falls, MN 56701
Ph: (218)681-3720
Free: (800)827-1629
E-mail: trfchamb@wiktel.com
URL: http://www.visitthiefriverfalls.com
Contact: Stacy Myhrer, Pres.
Members: 250. **Local.** Works to establish Thief River Falls as the regional center of Northwest Minnesota. Promotes the welfare of all area citizens. **Telecommunication Services:** electronic mail, trfcvb@wiktel.com. **Committees:** Agribusiness; Ambassadors; Business and Community Issues; Business Boosters; School/Business Partnership.

12752 ■ Thief River Falls Lions Club
c/o Arlo Rude, Pres.
11878 US Hwy. 59 NE
Thief River Falls, MN 56701
Ph: (218)683-5816 (218)681-3653
E-mail: arude@wiktel.com
URL: http://lions5m11.org/sys-tmpl/door
Contact: Arlo Rude, Pres.
Local. Affiliated With: Lions Clubs International.

Tintah

12753 ■ American Legion, Jfb Post 610
PO Box 21
Tintah, MN 56583
Ph: (651)291-1800
Fax: (651)291-1057
URL: National Affiliate–www.legion.org
Local. Affiliated With: American Legion.

Tower

12754 ■ American Legion, Nelson-Jackson Post 245
PO Box 565
Tower, MN 55790
Ph: (651)291-1800
Fax: (651)291-1057
URL: National Affiliate–www.legion.org
Local. Affiliated With: American Legion.

12755 ■ Lake Vermilion Area Chamber of Commerce (LVACC)
Box 776-B
Tower, MN 55790
Ph: (218)753-2301
Free: (800)869-3766
E-mail: info@lakevermilionchamber.com
URL: http://www.lakevermilionchamber.com
Contact: Betsy Clark, Pres.
Local. Promotes business and community development in Tower, MN. Holds annual Fourth of July Celebration. **Formerly:** (1999) Towersoudan Chamber of Commerce. **Publications:** *Brochure*, annual. Directory • Directory, periodic.

Tracy

12756 ■ American Legion, Earle Ray Post 173
169 4th St.
Tracy, MN 56175
Ph: (651)291-1800
Fax: (651)291-1057
URL: National Affiliate–www.legion.org
Local. Affiliated With: American Legion.

12757 ■ Tracy Area Chamber of Commerce
372 Morgan St.
Tracy, MN 56175
Ph: (507)629-4021
Fax: (507)629-4345
E-mail: tracychamber@iw.net
URL: http://www.tracymnchamber.com
Contact: Kayla Hussong, Chair
Founded: 1910. **Members:** 110. **Local.** Promotes business and community development in the Tracy, MN area. Sponsors Box Car Days festival every Labor Day. **Computer Services:** Online services, membership directory. **Conventions/Meetings:** monthly board meeting - every 2nd Tuesday • semimonthly Business Partnership - meeting - every 1st and 3rd Tuesday • semimonthly meeting, for EDA - every 1st and 3rd Friday • monthly show, for sportsmen - every 3rd Thursday.

Trimont

12758 ■ American Legion, Foster-Bernhardt Post 373
PO Box 51
Trimont, MN 56176
Ph: (651)291-1800
Fax: (651)291-1057
URL: National Affiliate–www.legion.org
Local. Affiliated With: American Legion.

12759 ■ Korean War Veterans Association, Fairmont Chapter
c/o John J. Rabbe
PO Box 261
Trimont, MN 56176
Ph: (507)639-4081
E-mail: jr1929@frontiernet.net
URL: National Affiliate–www.kwva.org
Contact: John J. Rabbe, Contact
Local. Affiliated With: Korean War Veterans Association.

Truman

12760 ■ American Legion, Oles-Reader-Bosshart Post 115
PO Box 143
Truman, MN 56088
Ph: (651)291-1800
Fax: (651)291-1057
URL: National Affiliate–www.legion.org
Local. Affiliated With: American Legion.

Twig

12761 ■ Lake Superior Pointing Dog Club
c/o Liz Headley
PO Box 1066
Twig, MN 55791
Ph: (218)729-6328
URL: http://www.lspdc.com
Contact: Liz Headley, Sec.
Local.

Twin Valley

12762 ■ American Legion, Nesseth-Lien Post 431
204 2nd St. SW
Twin Valley, MN 56584
Ph: (651)291-1800
Fax: (651)291-1057
URL: National Affiliate–www.legion.org
Local. Affiliated With: American Legion.

12763 ■ Flom and Area Lions Club
c/o Marlyn Syverson, Pres.
RR No. 1, Box 132
Twin Valley, MN 56584
Ph: (218)567-8526
URL: http://lions5m11.org/sys-tmpl/door
Contact: Marlyn Syverson, Pres.
Local. Affiliated With: Lions Clubs International.

12764 ■ Sons of Norway, Nordland Lodge 1-492
c/o Alfield Erlien, Sec.
PO Box 9
Twin Valley, MN 56584-0009
Ph: (218)584-8166
URL: National Affiliate–www.sofn.com
Contact: Alfield Erlien, Sec.
Local. Affiliated With: Sons of Norway.

12765 ■ Twin Valley Lions Club
c/o Allan Matson, Sec.
500 E Main Ave.
Twin Valley, MN 56584
Ph: (218)584-5151 (218)584-8486
Fax: (218)584-5170
E-mail: allanm@nce.k12.mn.us
URL: http://lions5m11.org/sys-tmpl/door
Contact: Allan Matson, Sec.
Local. Affiliated With: Lions Clubs International.

Two Harbors

12766 ■ American Chemical Society, Lake Superior Section
c/o Roger Alden Anderson, Chm.
430 9th Ave.
Two Harbors, MN 55616-1320
E-mail: rogera62@lakenet.com
URL: National Affiliate–acswebcontent.acs.org
Contact: Roger Alden Anderson, Chm.
Local. Represents the interests of individuals dedicated to the advancement of chemistry in all its branches. Provides opportunities for peer interaction and career development. **Affiliated With:** American Chemical Society.

12767 ■ American Hiking Society - Superior Hiking Trail Association
731 7th Ave.
PO Box 4
Two Harbors, MN 55616
Ph: (218)834-2700
Fax: (218)834-3346
E-mail: suphike@mr.net
URL: http://www.americanhiking.org
Local.

12768 ■ American Legion, Anderson-Claffy Post 109
614 1st Ave.
Two Harbors, MN 55616
Ph: (651)291-1800
Fax: (651)291-1057
URL: National Affiliate–www.legion.org
Local. Affiliated With: American Legion.

12769 ■ Associated Contract Loggers and Truckers of Minnesota
PO Box 160
Two Harbors, MN 55616
Ph: (218)834-2796
E-mail: loggers@frontiernet.net
URL: http://www.forestresources.org/ALLIES/state-assoc.html
Contact: Ms. Sharon Hahn, Contact
State. Promotes the interests of forest products industry members. Advocates on issues relating to forestry, community and government relations, lumber quality control and forest education. Promotes sharing of information, facilitates networking and provides education for members.

12770 ■ East Lake County Chamber of Commerce
PO Box 26
1026 7th Ave.
Two Harbors, MN 55616
Ph: (218)226-4408 (218)834-2600
Fax: (800)777-7384
URL: National Affiliate–www.uschamber.com
Contact: Marvil LaCroix, Sec.
Members: 45. **Local.** Promotes business and community development in the Silver Bay, MN area. **Affiliated With:** U.S. Chamber of Commerce. **Formerly:** Silver Bay Area Chamber of Commerce. **Conventions/Meetings:** monthly meeting - always first Wednesday of the month.

12771 ■ Lake County Historical Society
c/o Rachelle Maloney, Dir.
PO Box 128
Two Harbors, MN 55616
Ph: (218)834-4898
Fax: (218)834-7198
E-mail: lakehist@lakenet.com
URL: http://www.lakecountyhistoricalsociety.org
Contact: Rachelle Maloney, Dir.
Founded: 1925. **Local.**

12772 ■ Minnesota State Curling Association - Two Harbors Curling Club
PO Box 183
Two Harbors, MN 55616
Ph: (218)834-2664
E-mail: n_oleary61@hotmail.com
URL: http://www.twoharborscurling.com
Contact: Norma O'Leary, Pres.
Local. Affiliated With: United States Curling Association.

12773 ■ Sons of Norway, Terje Viken Lodge 1-17
c/o F. Lucille Hansen, Pres.
1623 Hwy. 2
Two Harbors, MN 55616-4017
Ph: (218)834-4935
E-mail: hns682@aol.com
URL: National Affiliate–www.sofn.com
Contact: F. Lucille Hansen, Pres.
Local. Affiliated With: Sons of Norway.

12774 ■ Superior Hiking Trail Association (SHTA)
731 7th Ave.
PO Box 4
Two Harbors, MN 55616-0004
Ph: (218)834-2700
Fax: (218)834-3346
E-mail: suphike@mr.net
Contact: Gayle Coyer, Exec.Dir.
Founded: 1987. **Members:** 3,000. **Membership Dues:** individual, $25 (annual) • family, $35 (annual). **Staff:** 4. **Budget:** $200,000. **State.** Individuals and private and public firms and agencies in northeastern Minnesota. Works to promote, construct, and maintain a long distance hiking trail along Lake Superior from Duluth, MN to the Canadian border. Conducts hikes. **Boards:** Board of Directors. **Committees:** Fund Development; Membership; Promotion; Trail Development & Maintenance. **Affiliated With:** American Hiking Society. **Publications:** *Guide to the Superior Hiking Trail*, periodic, as needed. Book. **Price:** $15.95. ISSN: 0963-6598 • *The Ridgeline*, 5/year. Newsletter. **Price:** free. **Circulation:** 4,000. **Advertising:** accepted • *White Woods, Quiet Trails-Exploring Minnesota's North Shore in Winter*, periodic, as needed. Book. **Price:** $15.95. **Conventions/Meetings:** annual Membership Meeting - 1st Saturday in May each year. Two Harbors, MN - Avg. Attendance: 150.

12775 ■ Two Harbors Area Chamber of Commerce (THACC)
1026 7th Ave.
Two Harbors, MN 55616-1149
Ph: (218)834-2600
Fax: (218)834-4012
Free: (800)777-7384
E-mail: thchamber@twoharborschamber.com
URL: http://www.twoharbors.com/chamber
Contact: Gordy Anderson, Pres./CEO
Founded: 1947. **Members:** 160. **Staff:** 4. **Budget:** $76,000. **Local.** Promotes business and community development in the Two Harbors, MN area. **Computer Services:** Online services, member business directory. **Telecommunication Services:** electronic mail, info@premierspot.biz. **Publications:** *Chamber Chat*, quarterly. Newsletter.

12776 ■ Two Harbors Lions Club
c/o Robert Ostby, Pres.
1307 Press Camp Rd.
Two Harbors, MN 55616-4034
Ph: (218)834-5600
E-mail: ostbys@lakenet.com
URL: http://lions5m10.org
Contact: Robert Ostby, Pres.
Local. Affiliated With: Lions Clubs International.

Tyler

12777 ■ American Legion, A.C. Hansen Post 185
138 E Bradley Ave.
Tyler, MN 56178

Ph: (651)291-1800
Fax: (651)291-1057
URL: National Affiliate–www.legion.org
Local. Affiliated With: American Legion.

Ulen

12778 ■ American Legion, Minnesota Post 412
c/o Charles B. Rikhus
35909 County Hwy. 7
Ulen, MN 56585
Ph: (651)291-1800
Fax: (651)291-1057
URL: National Affiliate–www.legion.org
Contact: Charles B. Rikhus, Contact
Local. Affiliated With: American Legion.

12779 ■ Ulen Lions Club
c/o Gordon Nichols, Sec.
Box 125
Ulen, MN 56585
Ph: (218)596-8335
E-mail: gnichols@arvig.net
URL: http://lions5m11.org/sys-tmpl/door
Contact: Gordon Nichols, Sec.
Local. Affiliated With: Lions Clubs International.

Underwood

12780 ■ American Legion, George Bergem Post 489
112 Main St.
Underwood, MN 56586
Ph: (651)291-1800
Fax: (651)291-1057
URL: National Affiliate–www.legion.org
Local. Affiliated With: American Legion.

Upsala

12781 ■ American Legion, Upsala Post 350
PO Box 272
Upsala, MN 56384
Ph: (651)291-1800
Fax: (651)291-1057
URL: National Affiliate–www.legion.org
Local. Affiliated With: American Legion.

Vadnais Heights

12782 ■ Vadnais Heights Lions Club
800 E County Rd. E
Vadnais Heights, MN 55127
Ph: (651)736-2430 (651)653-1305
E-mail: didixon@att.net
URL: http://vadnaishts.lionwap.org
Contact: Deb Dixon, Membership Chair
Local. Affiliated With: Lions Clubs International.

Verndale

12783 ■ American Legion, Isaac Harrison Lyons Post 326
PO Box 33
Verndale, MN 56481
Ph: (651)291-1800
Fax: (651)291-1057
URL: National Affiliate–www.legion.org
Local. Affiliated With: American Legion.

12784 ■ Leader Area Lions Club
8498 56th St. SW
Verndale, MN 56481
Ph: (218)397-2378
E-mail: lazysranch@brainerd.net
URL: http://leadermn.lionwap.org
Contact: Lucille Sowers, Sec.
Local. Affiliated With: Lions Clubs International.

12785 ■ Minnesota Quarter Horse Association, District 6
c/o Ron Sundby
16498 US Hwy. 10
Verndale, MN 56481
Ph: (218)445-5849
URL: http://www.mnqha.com/index_main.htm
Contact: Ron Sundby, Contact
Local. Affiliated With: American Quarter Horse Association.

Vesta

12786 ■ American Legion, Minnesota Post 306
c/o Harvey E. Gladitsch
PO Box 83
Vesta, MN 56292
Ph: (651)291-1800
Fax: (651)291-1057
URL: National Affiliate–www.legion.org
Contact: Harvey E. Gladitsch, Contact
Local. Affiliated With: American Legion.

Victoria

12787 ■ American Legion, Victoria Post 1995
PO Box 36
Victoria, MN 55386
Ph: (651)291-1800
Fax: (651)291-1057
URL: National Affiliate–www.legion.org
Local. Affiliated With: American Legion.

Villard

12788 ■ American Legion, Minnesota Post 175
c/o Robert A. Lee
PO Box 83
Villard, MN 56385
Ph: (651)291-1800
Fax: (651)291-1057
URL: National Affiliate–www.legion.org
Contact: Robert A. Lee, Contact
Local. Affiliated With: American Legion.

12789 ■ American Legion, Westport Post 638
13632 120th St.
Villard, MN 56385
Ph: (651)291-1800
Fax: (651)291-1057
URL: National Affiliate–www.legion.org
Local. Affiliated With: American Legion.

Vining

12790 ■ Sons of Norway, Leif Erikson Lodge 1-32
c/o Carol A. Pagel, Sec.
45771 Chippewa Trail
Vining, MN 56588
Ph: (218)769-4329
E-mail: cpagel@prtel.com
URL: National Affiliate–www.sofn.com
Contact: Carol A. Pagel, Sec.
Local. Affiliated With: Sons of Norway.

Virginia

12791 ■ American Legion, Pratt-Volden-Mickelson Post 239
PO Box 17
Virginia, MN 55792
Ph: (651)291-1800
Fax: (651)291-1057
URL: National Affiliate–www.legion.org
Local. Affiliated With: American Legion.

12792 ■ American Welding Society, Arrowhead
c/o Loren Kantola, Chm.
Virginia High School
411 5th Ave. S
Virginia, MN 55792
Ph: (218)247-7880
E-mail: lorenkantola@usa.net
URL: National Affiliate–www.aws.org
Contact: Loren Kantola, Chm.
Local. Professional society of welders, welding supervisors, welding supply salespeople, welding business and welding related business owners, welding engineers, welding instructors, welding engineering professors, welding consultants, Certified Welding Inspectors, NDT technicians, pipefitters, plumbers, boilermakers, and anyone interested in promoting and advancing the education and science of joining. **Affiliated With:** American Welding Society.

12793 ■ Arrowhead RSVP
c/o Bonnie Ebnet, Dir.
702 3rd Ave. S
Virginia, MN 55792-2797
Ph: (218)749-2912
Fax: (218)749-2944
E-mail: bebnet@aeoa.org
URL: http://www.seniorcorps.gov/about/programs/rsvp_state.asp?usestateabbr=mn&Search4.x=18&Search4.y=13
Contact: Bonnie Ebnet, Dir.
Local. Affiliated With: Retired and Senior Volunteer Program.

12794 ■ Curl Mesabi
PO Box 500
Virginia, MN 55792
Ph: (218)744-1302 (218)749-5297
E-mail: curling@curlmesabi.com
URL: http://www.curlmesabi.com
Contact: Craig Wainio, Contact
Local. Affiliated With: United States Curling Association.

12795 ■ Laurentian Chamber of Commerce
403 1st St. N
PO Box 1072
Virginia, MN 55792-1072
Ph: (218)741-2717
Fax: (218)749-4913
E-mail: ppilney@laurentianchamber.org
URL: http://laurentianchamber.org
Contact: James Currie, Pres./CEO
Founded: 1922. **Members:** 325. **Local.** Promotes business and community development in Virginia, Eveleth, Mountain Iron, and Gilbert, MN. Educates on the value and importance of a thriving business community and on business issues impacting them; advocates for issues as appropriate; identifies the needs of the business community and becomes aware of its health; fosters participation and involvement in the chambers to build leaders; and serves as an information and referral resource for members. **Awards:** ATHENA Award. **Frequency:** periodic. **Type:** recognition • Award of Distinction. **Frequency:** periodic. **Type:** recognition • **Frequency:** periodic. **Type:** scholarship. **Computer Services:** Online services, community business directory. **Telecommunication Services:** electronic mail, ppilney@laurentianchamber.org. **Committees:** Charitable Gambling; Eveleth Heritage; Lakes Beautification; Legislative Affairs. **Councils:** Ambassadors. **Formerly:** (1999) Virginia Chamber of Commerce; (2005) Virginia Mountain Iron Gilbert Area Chamber of Commerce. **Publications:** *Youth Employment Directory*, periodic • Directory, annual. **Price:** $174.50/issue • Newsletter, monthly. **Conventions/Meetings:** monthly board meeting - 3rd Tuesday • annual meeting - always January • annual Midsummer Music Fest - festival.

12796 ■ Mesabi Range Youth for Christ
PO Box 474
Virginia, MN 55792
Ph: (218)749-3417
Fax: (218)749-3417
URL: National Affiliate–www.yfc.net
Local. Affiliated With: Youth for Christ/U.S.A.

12797 ■ Minnesota Iron Range Retriever Club
c/o Bob Haapala, Sec.
PO Box No. 661
Virginia, MN 55792
Ph: (218)741-8645
E-mail: rhaapala@cpinternet.com
URL: http://www.mirrc.org/
Contact: Bob Haapala, Sec.
State. Affiliated With: American Kennel Club.

12798 ■ Minnesota Senior Federation, North Star Region
c/o AEOA
702 Third Ave. S
Virginia, MN 55792
Ph: (218)749-2912
Fax: (218)749-2944
Free: (800)662-5711
E-mail: mnsfir@aeoa.org
URL: http://mnseniors.org
Local.

12799 ■ Minnesota State Curling Association - Curl Mesabi
PO Box 500
Virginia, MN 55792
Ph: (218)744-1302
E-mail: curling@curlmesabi.com
URL: http://www.curlmesabi.com
Local. Affiliated With: United States Curling Association.

12800 ■ Muskies Arrowhead Chapter
PO Box 82
Virginia, MN 55792
Ph: (218)290-4681
E-mail: dlswenson@hotmail.com
URL: National Affiliate–www.muskiesinc.org
Contact: David Swenson, Pres.
Local.

12801 ■ National Active and Retired Federal Employees Association - Queen City 1963
118 10th St. S
Virginia, MN 55792-2840
Ph: (218)741-5516
URL: National Affiliate–www.narfe.org
Contact: Robert H. Nyrhinen, Contact
Local. Protects the retirement future of employees through education. Informs members on issues affecting the retirement. **Affiliated With:** National Association of Retired Federal Employees.

12802 ■ North St. Louis County Habitat for Humanity (NSLCHFH)
PO Box 24
Virginia, MN 55792
Ph: (218)749-8910
Free: (866)749-8910
E-mail: habitat@nslchfh.org
URL: http://www.nslchfh.org
Contact: Nathan Thompson, Exec.Dir.
Local. Telecommunication Services: electronic mail, nathan@nslchfh.org. **Affiliated With:** Habitat for Humanity International.

12803 ■ Northern AIFA
c/o Mary Eddy Samuelson
PO Box 117
Virginia, MN 55792
Ph: (218)749-2001
Fax: (218)749-0841
E-mail: mary.samuelson.b43f@statefarm.com
URL: National Affiliate–naifa.org
Contact: Eddy Samuelson, Contact
Local. Represents the interests of insurance and financial advisors. Advocates for a positive legislative and regulatory environment. Enhances business and professional skills of members. **Affiliated With:** National Association of Insurance and Financial Advisors.

12804 ■ Phi Theta Kappa, Zeta Iota Chapter - Mesabi Range Community/Technical College
c/o Jennifer Willard
1001 Chestnut St. W
Virginia, MN 55792
Ph: (218)744-7524
E-mail: j.willard@mr.mnscu.edu
URL: http://www.ptk.org/directories/chapters/MN/261-1.htm
Contact: Jennifer Willard, Advisor
Local.

12805 ■ Plumbing-Heating-Cooling Contractors Association, Range
c/o Mr. Brian Heisel, Pres.
801 N 6th Ave., N Gate Plz.
Virginia, MN 55792-2308
Ph: (218)741-8381
Fax: (218)741-7642
URL: National Affiliate–www.phccweb.org
Contact: Mr. Brian Heisel, Pres.
Local. Represents the plumbing, heating and cooling contractors. Promotes the construction industry. Protects the environment, health, safety and comfort of society. **Affiliated With:** Plumbing-Heating-Cooling Contractors Association.

12806 ■ Ruffed Grouse Society, David Salsman Chapter
c/o R.C. Weidner
1021 S 2nd Ave.
Virginia, MN 55792
Ph: (218)741-5450
E-mail: rc@ridgeinn.com
URL: National Affiliate–www.ruffedgrousesociety.org
Contact: R.C. Weidner, Contact
Local. Affiliated With: Ruffed Grouse Society.

12807 ■ Sons of Norway, Haarfager Lodge 1-40
c/o Wayne G. Christiansen, Pres.
602 S 5th Ave.
Virginia, MN 55792-2738
Ph: (218)749-1366
E-mail: wchris@virginiamn.com
URL: National Affiliate–www.sofn.com
Contact: Wayne G. Christiansen, Pres.
Local. Affiliated With: Sons of Norway.

12808 ■ Virginia Area Historical Society
PO Box 736
Virginia, MN 55792
Ph: (218)741-1136
E-mail: virghist@virginiamn.com
URL: http://virginiamn.com/~historicalsociety
Contact: Betty Birnstihl, Museum Asst.
Members: 350. **Membership Dues:** individual, $10 (annual). **Staff:** 1. **Local.** Collects, preserves and disseminates the history of the Virginia, Minnesota area. Operates the Heritage Museum at Olcott Park with both permanent and changing exhibits. Conducts historical programs. **Libraries: Type:** open to the public. **Holdings:** archival material, audiovisuals, books, clippings, maps, photographs. **Publications:** Newsletter, quarterly.

12809 ■ Virginia Lions Club
c/o Timothy Riordan, Sec.
1214 N 7th Ave.
Virginia, MN 55792
Ph: (218)741-9106
E-mail: triordan@fortunebay.com
URL: http://lions5m10.org
Contact: Timothy Riordan, Sec.
Local. Affiliated With: Lions Clubs International.

Wabasha

12810 ■ American Legion, Minnesota Post 50
c/o Ben Krueger
155 Pembroke Ave.
Wabasha, MN 55981
Ph: (651)291-1800
Fax: (651)291-1057
URL: National Affiliate–www.legion.org
Contact: Ben Krueger, Contact
Local. Affiliated With: American Legion.

12811 ■ Izaak Walton League of America, Wapashaw Chapter
PO Box 172
Wabasha, MN 55981
Ph: (651)565-2283
E-mail: passe@wabasha.net
URL: National Affiliate–www.iwla.org
Contact: Tom Ellis, Pres.
Works to educate the public to conserve, maintain, protect, and restore the soil, forest, water, and other natural resources of the U.S; promotes the enjoyment and wholesome utilization of these resources. **Affiliated With:** Izaak Walton League of America.

12812 ■ Wabasha-Kellogg Area Chamber of Commerce
160 Main St.
PO Box 105
Wabasha, MN 55981-0105
Ph: (651)565-4158
Fax: (651)565-2808
Free: (800)565-4158
E-mail: info@wabashamn.org
URL: http://www.wabashamn.org
Contact: Randy Voth, Pres.
Founded: 1981. **Members:** 100. **Membership Dues:** business owner, $75-$600 (annual) • corporate, $1,000-$2,000 (annual) • social, $50 (annual). **Staff:** 1. **Regional Groups:** 1. **State Groups:** 1. **Local Groups:** 1. **Local.** Promotes business and community development in Wabasha, MN. Holds annual Riverboat Days Festival; sponsors annual Volksmarch event; established Eagle Watch Eagle Observatory; sponsors Annual Grumpy Old Men festival. **Libraries: Type:** open to the public. **Computer Services:** Online services, member listings. **Affiliated With:** Southeastern Minnesota Historic Bluff Country. **Publications:** *Business Directory*, annual. **Price:** free. **Advertising:** accepted • *Chamber*, monthly. Newsletter • *Visitor's Guide*. Directory. **Conventions/Meetings:** monthly conference • annual United Church of Christ Ham and Turkey Dinner.

12813 ■ Wabasha-Kellogg Area Chamber/CVB
PO Box 105
106 W Main St.
Wabasha, MN 55981
Ph: (651)565-4158
Fax: (651)565-2808
Free: (800)565-4158
E-mail: info@wabashamn.org
URL: http://www.wabashamn.org
Contact: Carolynn Klees, Mgr.
Founded: 1980. **Members:** 95. **Membership Dues:** one-star, $75 (annual) • two-star, $250 (annual) • three-star, $375 (annual). **Staff:** 2. **Budget:** $75,000. **Local.** Non-competitive sports enthusiasts. Supports local businesses and promotes tourism within Wabasha, MN. **Awards: Type:** monetary. **Recipient:** for corporate sponsors. **Telecommunication Services:** information service, tourism. **Affiliated With:** American Volkssport Association. **Formerly:** (2004) Wabasha River Walkers. **Publications:** *Wabasha-Kellogg Area Getaway Guide*, annual. Magazine. Features tourism related resources. **Price:** free. **Circulation:** 85,000. **Advertising:** accepted.

Wabasso

12814 ■ American Legion, Minnesota Post 263
c/o Victor Hirsch
PO Box 186
Wabasso, MN 56293

Ph: (651)291-1800
Fax: (651)291-1057
URL: National Affiliate–www.legion.org
Contact: Victor Hirsch, Contact
Local. Affiliated With: American Legion.

Waconia

12815 ■ American Legion, Waconia Post 150
233 S Olive St.
Waconia, MN 55387
Ph: (651)291-1800
Fax: (651)291-1057
URL: National Affiliate–www.legion.org
Local. Affiliated With: American Legion.

12816 ■ Carver County Historical Society (CCHS)
c/o Leann Brown
556 W First St.
Waconia, MN 55387-1203
Ph: (952)442-4234
Fax: (952)442-2530
Members: 400. **Local**. Individuals interested in preserving the history of Carver County, Minn. Sponsors exhibits, workshops, research, and tours. **Libraries: Type:** open to the public. **Holdings:** 300. **Publications:** Newsletter, quarterly. **Price:** for members.

12817 ■ Sons of Norway, Syttende Mai Lodge 1-517
c/o Eric A. Anderson, Pres.
1019 Fox Run Rd.
Waconia, MN 55387-9206
Ph: (952)448-5966
E-mail: sigrud@mchsi.com
URL: National Affiliate–www.sofn.com
Contact: Eric A. Anderson, Pres.
Local. Affiliated With: Sons of Norway.

12818 ■ South Metro ALU
c/o Martin Cole
PO Box 253
Waconia, MN 55387
Ph: (952)442-8461
Fax: (952)442-7549
URL: National Affiliate–www.naifa.org
Local. Represents the interest of insurance and financial advisors. Advocates for a positive legislative and regulatory environment. Enhances business and professional skills of members. **Affiliated With:** National Association of Insurance and Financial Advisors.

12819 ■ Waconia Area Chamber of Commerce
209 S Vine St.
Waconia, MN 55387
Ph: (952)442-5812
Fax: (952)856-4476
E-mail: dmcmillan@waconiachamber.org
URL: http://www.waconiachamber.org
Contact: Deb McMillan, Pres.
Membership Dues: educational institution, civic organization, county branch, city office, city branch, agricultural branch, individual, $165 • business (based on number of employees), $265-$1,250. **Local**. Seeks to enhance the economic and social health community by improving the business atmosphere of the area. **Committees:** Ambassadors; Events; Public Affairs; Retail; Tourism.

Wadena

12820 ■ American Legion, Wadena Post 171
PO Box 171
Wadena, MN 56482
Ph: (651)291-1800
Fax: (651)291-1057
URL: National Affiliate–www.legion.org
Local. Affiliated With: American Legion.

12821 ■ Leaf River Area, Habitat For Humanity
206 1st St. SE
Wadena, MN 56482
Ph: (218)632-6900
Fax: (218)632-6901
E-mail: h4h@arvig.net
URL: http://www.lrahfh.org
Contact: Mr. Michael Kramer, Exec.Dir.
Local. Works in partnership with God and people from all walks of life to develop communities with God's people in building and renovating houses so that there are decent houses in decent communities in which God's people can live and grow into all that God intended.

12822 ■ Minnesota Ambulance Association, Central
c/o Don Snorek, Dir.
Tri County Hosp.
415 N Jefferson St.
Wadena, MN 56482
Ph: (218)631-3510
Fax: (218)631-7511
E-mail: don.snorek@tricountyhospital.org
URL: http://www.mnems.org
Contact: Don Snorek, Dir.
Local. Seeks to maintain the financial viability of the EMS industry by advocating education, legislation and regulatory change. **Affiliated With:** Minnesota Ambulance Association.

12823 ■ Pets Abandoned Wanting Support (PAWS)
PO Box 62
Wadena, MN 56482
Ph: (218)639-7297
E-mail: gsrobben@arvig.net
URL: http://www.pawsmn.petfinder.com
Contact: Dr. Bridget King, Contact
Founded: 1998. **Members:** 86. **Membership Dues:** silver, $15 (annual) • gold, $25 (annual) • platinum, $50 (annual). **Staff:** 5. **Local**. Devoted to protecting animals from cruelty and neglect through education, vet care, sheltering of unwanted animals, and to find loving, adoptive homes to strengthen the human-animal bond.

12824 ■ United Way of Wadena Area
PO Box 22
Wadena, MN 56482-0022
Ph: (218)631-1414
URL: National Affiliate–national.unitedway.org
Local. Affiliated With: United Way of America.

Waite Park

12825 ■ American Legion, Silver Star Post 428
17 2nd Ave. N
Waite Park, MN 56387
Ph: (651)291-1800
Fax: (651)291-1057
URL: National Affiliate–www.legion.org
Local. Affiliated With: American Legion.

12826 ■ Girl Scouts - Land of Lakes Council
400 2nd Ave. S
Waite Park, MN 56387
Ph: (320)252-2952
Fax: (320)251-9403
Free: (800)955-6032
E-mail: ladavis@girlscoutslolc.org
URL: http://www.girlscoutslolc.org
Contact: Leigh Ann Davis, Exec.Dir.
Membership Dues: $10 (annual). **Staff:** 25. **Local**. Young girls and adult volunteers, corporate, government and individual supporters. Strives to develop potential and leadership skills among its members. Conducts trainings, educational programs and outdoor activities.

12827 ■ Minnesota Holstein Association (MHA)
411 28th Ave. S
Waite Park, MN 56387-1088
Ph: (320)259-0637
Fax: (320)259-0009
E-mail: jdingbaum@mnholstein.com
URL: http://www.mnholstein.com
Contact: Jennifer Dingbaum, Exec.Sec.
Founded: 1910. **Members:** 1,450. **Membership Dues:** regular, $50 (annual) • junior, $2 (annual) • life, adult (60 years and older), $250 • life, adult (70 years and older), $100. **Staff:** 3. **Budget:** $150,000. **Regional Groups:** 1. **State Groups:** 1. **Local Groups:** 31. **State**. Works to promote and improve the Holstein breed of dairy cattle. **Awards:** Distinguished Young Couple. **Frequency:** annual. **Type:** recognition. **Recipient:** for members who have made significant contributions to the industry • Longtime Meritorious Service. **Frequency:** annual. **Type:** recognition. **Recipient:** for a member who has made a significant contribution to the industry • Person of the Year. **Frequency:** annual. **Type:** recognition. **Recipient:** for a member who has made a significant contribution to the industry. **Publications:** *Midwest Holstein News*, quarterly. Newspaper. **Price:** $25.00/year. **Circulation:** 1,500. **Advertising:** accepted. Alternate Formats: microform • *Minnesota Holstein News*, quarterly. Magazine. **Price:** $25.00/year. **Circulation:** 1,500. **Advertising:** accepted. Alternate Formats: microform. **Conventions/Meetings:** annual convention, trade show (exhibits).

12828 ■ Veteran Motor Car Club of America - Brighton Chapter
c/o Leon Zimkiewicz, Pres.
1480 Winter Ln.
Waite Park, MN 56387
Ph: (810)226-6875
URL: National Affiliate–www.vmcca.org
Contact: Leon Zimkiewicz, Pres.
Local. Affiliated With: Veteran Motor Car Club of America.

Waldorf

12829 ■ American Legion, Minnesota Post 587
c/o Thomas L. Madden
PO Box 148
Waldorf, MN 56091
Ph: (651)291-1800
Fax: (651)291-1057
URL: National Affiliate–www.legion.org
Contact: Thomas L. Madden, Contact
Local. Affiliated With: American Legion.

Walker

12830 ■ American Legion, Spencer-Ross Post 134
PO Box 186
Walker, MN 56484
Ph: (651)291-1800
Fax: (651)291-1057
URL: National Affiliate–www.legion.org
Local. Affiliated With: American Legion.

12831 ■ Leech Lake Area Chamber of Commerce (LLACC)
PO Box 1089
Walker, MN 56484-1089
Ph: (218)547-1313
Fax: (218)547-1338
Free: (800)833-1118
E-mail: walker@eot.com
URL: http://www.leech-lake.com
Contact: Cindy Wannarka, Exec.Dir.
Founded: 1963. **Members:** 200. **Local**. Promotes business and community development in the Leech Lake, MN area. **Computer Services:** Online services, business directory. **Conventions/Meetings:** annual

Ethnic Festival • annual Leech Lake Regatta - competition • annual Muskie Northern Derby Days - festival.

12832 ■ Minnesota Chapter of American Fisheries Society
c/o Patrick Rivers, Sec.-Treas.
Walker Area Fisheries
07316 State Hwy. 371 NW
Walker, MN 56484
Ph: (218)547-1683 (218)847-7416
E-mail: pat.rivers@dnr.state.mn.us
URL: http://www.mnafs.org
Contact: Henry VanOffelen, Pres.

Founded: 1967. **Membership Dues:** general, $10 (annual). **State. Formerly:** (2005) American Fisheries Society - Minnesota Chapter. **Publications:** *RYBA*, quarterly. Newsletter. **Price:** included in membership dues. Alternate Formats: online.

12833 ■ Mississippi Headwaters Board (MHB)
c/o Jane E. Ekholm, Dir.
Cass County Courthouse
PO Box 3000
Walker, MN 56484
Ph: (218)547-7263
Fax: (218)547-7376
E-mail: cass.mhb@co.cass.mn.us
URL: http://www.mhbriverwatch.dst.mn.us
Contact: Jane E. Ekholm, Dir.

State.

Walnut Grove

12834 ■ American Legion, Minnesota Post 267
c/o Alfred Nelson
700 Main St.
Walnut Grove, MN 56180
Ph: (651)291-1800
Fax: (651)291-1057
URL: National Affiliate–www.legion.org
Contact: Alfred Nelson, Contact

Local. Affiliated With: American Legion.

Wanda

12835 ■ American Legion, Wanda Post 385
PO Box 244
Wanda, MN 56294
Ph: (651)291-1800
Fax: (651)291-1057
URL: National Affiliate–www.legion.org

Local. Affiliated With: American Legion.

12836 ■ Groundswell Inc. of Minnesota (MG)
PO Box 338
Wanda, MN 56294
Ph: (507)342-5797
Fax: (507)342-5797
Contact: Diane Irlbeck, Office Mgr.

Founded: 1974. **Members:** 2,500. **Budget:** $160,000. **State Groups:** 48. Farmers and other individuals who seek to preserve the existence of the family farm and to aid the rural economy in Minnesota and the U.S. as a whole. Educates farmers on their legal rights and the availability of assistance programs. Collects and distributes clothing, and other necessities to needy farmers. Supports legal, peaceful actions to improve the rural economy. Informs members of legislative activity and secures media attention for farmers and the rural economy in general. Maintains speakers' bureau. **Formerly:** (1992) Minnesota Groundswell. **Publications:** *Groundswell Newsletter*, monthly. **Conventions/Meetings:** annual board meeting.

Wannaska

12837 ■ Sons of Norway, Nordlys Lodge 1-498
c/o Marion E. Solom, Pres.
38198 County Rd. 1
Wannaska, MN 56761-9223
Ph: (218)425-7477
E-mail: marionsolom@hotmail.com
URL: National Affiliate–www.sofn.com
Contact: Marion E. Solom, Pres.

Local. Affiliated With: Sons of Norway.

Warba

12838 ■ American Legion, Truman Blakesley Post 432
PO Box 2701
Warba, MN 55793
Ph: (651)291-1800
Fax: (651)291-1057
URL: National Affiliate–www.legion.org

Local. Affiliated With: American Legion.

Warren

12839 ■ Agassiz Audubon Society
c/o Lori Becker, Dir.
RR2 Box 45A
Warren, MN 56762-9240
Ph: (218)745-5663
E-mail: wpp@wiktel.com
URL: http://www.wiktel.net/wpp
Contact: Lori Becker, Dir.

Local. Works to conserve and restore natural ecosystems, focusing on birds and other wildlife for the benefit of humanity and the earth's biological diversity. **Affiliated With:** National Audubon Society.

12840 ■ American Legion, Warren Post 27
424 N 1st St.
Warren, MN 56762
Ph: (651)291-1800
Fax: (651)291-1057
URL: National Affiliate–www.legion.org

Local. Affiliated With: American Legion.

12841 ■ Marshall County Mounted Posse
c/o Sheriff of Marshall County
208 E Colvin Ave.
Warren, MN 56762-1693
Ph: (218)745-5411 (218)745-5412
Fax: (218)745-9203
Contact: Herb Maurstad, Sheriff

Founded: 2000. **Members:** 80. **Staff:** 5. **Local.** Provides search and rescue for the County and surrounding area, secures crime scenes, assists the Marshall County Sheriff's Office.

12842 ■ Warren Lions Club - Minnesota
c/o Dennis M. Stalboerger, Pres.
417 S McKinley St.
Warren, MN 56762
Ph: (218)745-9200
URL: http://lions5m11.org/sys-tmpl/door
Contact: Dennis M. Stalboerger, Pres.

Local. Affiliated With: Lions Clubs International.

Warroad

12843 ■ American Legion, Minnesota Post 25
c/o Andrew O. Mattson
410 Lake St. NE
Warroad, MN 56763
Ph: (651)291-1800
Fax: (651)291-1057
URL: National Affiliate–www.legion.org
Contact: Andrew O. Mattson, Contact

Local. Affiliated With: American Legion.

12844 ■ Ruffed Grouse Society, Lake of the Woods Chapter
c/o Chuck Lindner
310 Main Ave.
Warroad, MN 56763
Ph: (218)386-9473
URL: National Affiliate–www.ruffedgrousesociety.org
Contact: Chuck Lindner, Contact

Local. Affiliated With: Ruffed Grouse Society.

12845 ■ Warroad Lions Club
c/o Dennis J. Thomson, Pres.
PO Box 510
Warroad, MN 56763
Ph: (218)386-2455 (218)386-9450
URL: http://lions5m11.org/sys-tmpl/door
Contact: Dennis J. Thomson, Pres.

Local. Affiliated With: Lions Clubs International.

Waseca

12846 ■ American Legion, Waseca Post 228
700 S State St.
Waseca, MN 56093
Ph: (651)291-1800
Fax: (651)291-1057
URL: National Affiliate–www.legion.org

Local. Affiliated With: American Legion.

12847 ■ Waseca Area Chamber of Commerce
108 E Elm Ave.
Waseca, MN 56093-2927
Ph: (507)835-3260
Fax: (507)835-3267
Free: (888)820-1243
E-mail: wchamber@hickorytech.net
URL: http://www.wasecamncc.com
Contact: Larry Dukes, Pres.

Local.

12848 ■ Waseca Area United Way
PO Box 268
Waseca, MN 56093
Ph: (507)234-5794
E-mail: wauwus@yahoo.com
URL: http://www.wasecaunitedway.org
Contact: Delores Dennis, Pres.

Local. Affiliated With: United Way of America.

12849 ■ Waseca County Chapter, American Red Cross
511 S State St.
Waseca, MN 56093
Ph: (507)835-8369
Fax: (507)835-8778
Free: (877)835-8369
E-mail: redcross@hickorytech.net
URL: http://wccarc.4mg.com
Contact: Robin Roberts, Mgr.

Founded: 1917. **Staff:** 18. **Local.** Strives to reduce the suffering of victims of disaster by helping communities to prepare, prevent and respond to disaster. Provides emergency communications to members of the armed forces, veterans and their families. Aids disaster victims and trains people in lifesaving skills and water safety. Provides other activities such as blood services, community services, and service opportunities for the youth. **Affiliated With:** American Red Cross National Headquarters.

12850 ■ Waseca Sleigh and Cutter Festival Association
c/o Ken Borgmann
5603 NW 102nd Ave.
Waseca, MN 56093-6305
Free: (877)833-8435
Contact: Ken Borgmann, Pres./COO

Founded: 1950. **Members:** 20. **Local Groups:** 1. **Local.** Volunteers interested in keeping part of history alive with horses, etc. Provides youth activities, including a festival, drawing, artwork, hockey, parade, scholarships (pending).

Watertown

12851 ■ American Legion, Minnesota Post 121
c/o Eugene Earley
PO Box 537
Watertown, MN 55388
Ph: (651)291-1800
Fax: (651)291-1057
URL: National Affiliate–www.legion.org
Contact: Eugene Earley, Contact
Local. Affiliated With: American Legion.

12852 ■ International Association of Administrative Professionals - Minnesota-North Dakota-South Dakota Division
715 Reo Rd.
Watertown, MN 55388
E-mail: debicain@rivord.org
URL: http://www.iaap-mnndsd-division.org
Contact: Debi Cain-Rivord, Pres.
State. Professionals, corporations, academic institutions and students. Develops research and educational projects for administrative professionals. Provides training, seminars, conferences and educational programs.

12853 ■ Watertown Lions Club - Minnesota
PO Box 791
Watertown, MN 55388
E-mail: info@watertownlions.org
URL: http://www.watertownlions.org
Local. Affiliated With: Lions Clubs International.

Watkins

12854 ■ American Legion, Watkins Post 453
PO Box 297
Watkins, MN 55389
Ph: (651)291-1800
Fax: (651)291-1057
URL: National Affiliate–www.legion.org
Local. Affiliated With: American Legion.

Watson

12855 ■ Watson Lions Club
c/o Jerry Lee, Pres.
9080 1st St. W
Watson, MN 56295
Ph: (320)269-7835
URL: http://www.5m4lions.org
Contact: Jerry Lee, Pres.
Local. Affiliated With: Lions Clubs International.

Waverly

12856 ■ American Legion, Charles Claessens Post 305
4359 70th St. SW
Waverly, MN 55390
Ph: (651)291-1800
Fax: (651)291-1057
URL: National Affiliate–www.legion.org
Local. Affiliated With: American Legion.

Wayzata

12857 ■ American Legion, Ernest Aselton Post 118
949 Wayzata Blvd. E
Wayzata, MN 55391
Ph: (651)291-1800
Fax: (651)291-1057
URL: National Affiliate–www.legion.org
Local. Affiliated With: American Legion.

12858 ■ Federalist Society for Law and Public Policy Studies - Minneapolis Chapter
c/o Mrs. Kimberly Reynolds Crockett
17900 Shavers Lake Dr.
Wayzata, MN 55391
Ph: (952)476-4478
Fax: (952)476-1067
E-mail: kimberlycrockett@mchsi.com
URL: National Affiliate–www.fed-soc.org
Contact: Mrs. Kimberly Reynolds Crockett, Contact
Local. Seeks to bring about a reordering of priorities within the U.S. legal system that will emphasize individual liberty, traditional values, and the rule of law. **Affiliated With:** Federalist Society for Law and Public Policy Studies.

12859 ■ Greater Twin Cities Golden Retriever Club
c/o Judy Thomas, Corresponding Sec.
150 Central Ave. S, No. 122
Wayzata, MN 55391
Ph: (952)473-6061
E-mail: goldenstc@aol.com
URL: http://www.gtcgrc.org
Contact: Judy Thomas, Corresponding Sec.
Local. Affiliated With: Golden Retriever Club of America.

12860 ■ Greater Wayzata Area Chamber of Commerce
402 E Lake St.
Wayzata, MN 55391-1651
Ph: (952)473-9595
Fax: (952)473-6266
E-mail: info@wayzatachamber.com
URL: http://www.wayzatachamber.com
Contact: Diane Wilson, Pres.
Founded: 1939. **Members:** 348. **Membership Dues:** business, $260-$676 (annual) • school, utility, government, $411 (annual) • associate, individual, $130 (annual) • nonprofit organization, $182 (annual). **Local**. Promotes business and community development in Wayzata, MN. Sponsors trolley rides and concerts in the summer, fall and winter golf outing, and annual festival in September. **Convention/Meeting:** none. **Computer Services:** Online services, member listings. **Publications:** *Discover Wayzata*. Catalog. **Advertising:** accepted • *Whistle Stop*, monthly. Newsletter. Alternate Formats: online • Membership Directory, annual. **Conventions/Meetings:** annual Holiday Open House and Tree Lighting - show • annual James J. Hill Days - festival.

12861 ■ North Central Chapter, Infectious Diseases Society of America (NCCIDSA)
c/o Susie Seashore, Exec.Sec.
PO Box 846
Wayzata, MN 55391
Ph: (612)274-7040
Fax: (952)476-0084
E-mail: seashore@citlink.net
URL: http://www.opitsourcebook.com/ncentral/ncentral.html
Contact: Paul J. Carson MD, Pres.
Local. Aims to improve the health of individuals, communities and society. Promotes education and research relating to infectious diseases. **Affiliated With:** Infectious Diseases Society of America.

12862 ■ United States Power Squadrons - District 10
c/o Robert Stierna, Commander
1930 Shoreline Dr.
Wayzata, MN 55391
Ph: (952)476-1951
E-mail: stobo76@chorus.net
URL: http://www.usps-d10.org
Contact: Robert Stierna, Commander
Regional. Affiliated With: United States Power Squadrons.

12863 ■ Wayzata Lions Club
c/o Barry Birkholz, Pres.
140 Benton Ave. N
Wayzata, MN 55391
Ph: (952)436-2768 (763)862-4528
URL: http://www.5m5.org
Contact: Barry Birkholz, Pres.
Local. Affiliated With: Lions Clubs International.

12864 ■ Z Owners of Minnesota
3935 Walden Ln.
Wayzata, MN 55391
Ph: (952)473-7919
Fax: (763)295-6379
E-mail: westlund@soncom.com
URL: National Affiliate–www.zcca.org
Contact: Bill Tapper, Pres.
State. Affiliated With: Z Car Club Association.

Welch

12865 ■ American Association for Medical Transcription, Twin Cities Chapter
c/o Jean Kehren, Pres.
1 Old Mystic Rd.
Welch, MN 55089
Ph: (651)388-1009
E-mail: kkehren@pressenter.com
URL: http://www.aamt.org/ca/twin
Contact: Jean Kehren, Pres.
Local. Works to represent and advance the profession of medical transcription and its practitioners. **Affiliated With:** American Association for Medical Transcription.

Welcome

12866 ■ American Legion, Welcome Post 553
PO Box 354
Welcome, MN 56181
Ph: (651)291-1800
Fax: (651)291-1057
URL: National Affiliate–www.legion.org
Local. Affiliated With: American Legion.

Wells

12867 ■ American Legion, Troska Post 210
PO Box 83
Wells, MN 56097
Ph: (651)291-1800
Fax: (651)291-1057
URL: National Affiliate–www.legion.org
Local. Affiliated With: American Legion.

12868 ■ Fairmont Area AIFA
c/o Dennis D. Pytleski, Pres.
224 S Broadway
Wells, MN 56097
Ph: (507)553-6318
Fax: (507)553-5156
E-mail: dezeray12115@hotmail.com
URL: National Affiliate–naifa.org
Contact: Dennis D. Pytleski, Pres.
Local. Represents the interests of insurance and financial advisors. Advocates for a positive legislative and regulatory environment. Enhances business and professional skills of members. **Affiliated With:** National Association of Insurance and Financial Advisors.

12869 ■ Wells Area Chamber of Commerce (WACC)
28 S Broadway
PO Box 134
Wells, MN 56097
Ph: (507)553-6450
Fax: (507)553-6451
Free: (866)553-6450
E-mail: wellscc@bevcomm.net
URL: http://wells.govoffice.com
Contact: Andrea Christensen, Exec.Dir.
Members: 73. **Local**. Promotes business and community development in the Wells, MN area. Sponsors Wells Kernel Days. **Computer Services:** Online

services, member listings. **Committees:** Agribusiness; Ambassador; Education; Fund Raising; Governmental; Retail/Service; Special Projects. **Publications:** Newsletter, monthly. Contains information on committee works and upcoming events. **Price:** for members. **Conventions/Meetings:** annual Kernel Days - festival.

Wendell

12870 ■ American Legion, Olson-Graminske Post 426
PO Box 73
Wendell, MN 56590
Ph: (651)291-1800
Fax: (651)291-1057
URL: National Affiliate–www.legion.org
Local. Affiliated With: American Legion.

12871 ■ Wendell Lions Club
c/o Brian Lacey, Pres.
33157 320th Ave.
Wendell, MN 56590
Ph: (218)458-2595
E-mail: bdlacey@runestone.net
URL: http://www.5m4lions.org
Contact: Brian Lacey, Pres.
Local. Affiliated With: Lions Clubs International.

West Concord

12872 ■ American Legion, Langemo Post 295
PO Box 195
West Concord, MN 55985
Ph: (651)291-1800
Fax: (651)291-1057
URL: National Affiliate–www.legion.org
Local. Affiliated With: American Legion.

12873 ■ Red River Valley Appaloosa Horse Club
c/o Valerie Townley
5902 NE 84th Ave.
West Concord, MN 55985
Ph: (507)527-2142
E-mail: horsesshows1@aol.com
URL: National Affiliate–www.appaloosa.com
Contact: Valerie Townley, Contact
Local. Affiliated With: Appaloosa Horse Club.

12874 ■ Wissota Appaloosa Horse Club
c/o Valerie Townley
5902 NE 84th Ave.
West Concord, MN 55985
Ph: (507)527-2141
E-mail: ez2spot@citilink.net
URL: National Affiliate–www.appaloosa.com
Contact: Valerie Townley, Contact
Local. Affiliated With: Appaloosa Horse Club.

West St. Paul

12875 ■ American Legion, Challenger Post 521
PO Box 18244
West St. Paul, MN 55118
Ph: (651)291-1800
Fax: (651)291-1057
URL: National Affiliate–www.legion.org
Local. Affiliated With: American Legion.

12876 ■ American Society of Mechanical Engineers, Minnesota Section
20 E Thompson Ave., Ste.206
West St. Paul, MN 55118
Ph: (651)699-4368
E-mail: krollm2@asme.org
URL: http://www.asme-mn.org
Contact: Mark Kroll, Chm.
State. Promotes the art, science and practice of Mechanical Engineering and allied arts and sciences. Encourages original research and fosters engineering education. Promotes the technical and societal contribution of engineers. **Affiliated With:** American Society of Mechanical Engineers.

12877 ■ DARTS of Minnesota
1645 Marthaler Ln.
West St. Paul, MN 55118
Ph: (651)455-1560 (651)455-1339
Fax: (651)234-2280
E-mail: info@darts1.org
URL: http://www.darts1.org
State.

12878 ■ Friends of Africa Education
c/o Matthew C. Dewey, Pres.
1670 S Robert St., Ste.326
West St. Paul, MN 55118
Ph: (651)457-8847
E-mail: foae@foae.org
URL: http://www.foae.org
Local.

12879 ■ Guild Incorporated
1025 Dodd Rd.
West St. Paul, MN 55118
Ph: (651)450-2220
Fax: (651)450-2221
E-mail: info@guildincorporated.org
URL: http://www.guildincorporated.org
Local. Helps individuals with mental illness lead quality lives.

12880 ■ Minnesota Society of Professional Engineers
c/o Mary Detloff, CAE, Exec.Dir.
20 E Thompson Ave., No. 206
West St. Paul, MN 55118
Ph: (651)457-2347
Fax: (651)457-6631
E-mail: mdetloff@mnspe.org
URL: http://www.mnspe.org
Contact: Mary Detloff CAE, Exec.Dir.
Founded: 1939. **Members:** 1,000. **Staff:** 2. **State.** Only society in MN whose voice speaks for all branches of engineering and is the only active, established organization devoting its entire effort to the professional, economic, social, and political aspects of engineering. State affiliate of the National Society of Professional Engineers. **Affiliated With:** National Society of Professional Engineers.

West Union

12881 ■ American Legion, Oscar Jacobson Post 417
321 Williams SE 3b
West Union, MN 56389
Ph: (651)291-1800
Fax: (651)291-1057
URL: National Affiliate–www.legion.org
Local. Affiliated With: American Legion.

Westbrook

12882 ■ American Legion, Westbrook Post 152
PO Box 236
Westbrook, MN 56183
Ph: (651)291-1800
Fax: (651)291-1057
URL: National Affiliate–www.legion.org
Local. Affiliated With: American Legion.

Whalan

12883 ■ American Legion, Erickson-Rose Post 637
624 Main St.
Whalan, MN 55949
Ph: (651)291-1800
Fax: (651)291-1057
URL: National Affiliate–www.legion.org
Local. Affiliated With: American Legion.

Wheaton

12884 ■ American Legion, Merton-Dale Post 80
PO Box 835
Wheaton, MN 56296
Ph: (651)291-1800
Fax: (651)291-1057
URL: National Affiliate–www.legion.org
Local. Affiliated With: American Legion.

12885 ■ Lake Traverse Association Corporation
1011 Broadway
Wheaton, MN 56296
Ph: (320)563-4610
Fax: (320)563-4987
E-mail: bdswd@traversenet.com
Contact: John Conroy, Pres.
Local.

12886 ■ Wheaton Area Chamber of Commerce (WACC)
PO Box 493
Wheaton, MN 56296-0493
Ph: (320)563-8271
Fax: (320)563-8274
URL: http://www.redrivermall.com
Contact: Mary Fox, Sec.
Members: 73. **Local.** Promotes business and community development in Wheaton, MN. **Formerly:** (1999) Wheaton Chamber of Commerce.

12887 ■ Wheaton Lions Club - Minnesota
c/o Robert Niss, Pres.
908 2nd Ave. N
Wheaton, MN 56296
Ph: (320)563-8583 (320)563-8112
E-mail: rln@traversenet.com
URL: http://www.5m4lions.org
Contact: Robert Niss, Pres.
Local. Affiliated With: Lions Clubs International.

White Bear Lake

12888 ■ American Chemical Society, Minnesota Section
c/o Dr. Joann Pfeiffer, Chair
Century Coll.
3300 Century Ave. N
White Bear Lake, MN 55110-1842
Ph: (651)779-3487
E-mail: j.pfeiffer@century.mnscu.edu
URL: National Affiliate–acswebcontent.acs.org
Contact: Dr. Joann Pfeiffer, Chair
State. Represents the interests of individuals dedicated to the advancement of chemistry in all its branches. Provides opportunities for peer interaction and career development. **Affiliated With:** American Chemical Society.

12889 ■ American Legion, West End Post 414
4780 Johnson Ave.
White Bear Lake, MN 55110
Ph: (612)429-4795
Fax: (651)291-1057
URL: National Affiliate–www.legion.org
Local. Affiliated With: American Legion.

12890 ■ American Legion, White Bear Lake Post 168
2210 3rd St.
White Bear Lake, MN 55110
Ph: (651)291-1800
Fax: (651)291-1057
URL: National Affiliate–www.legion.org
Local. Affiliated With: American Legion.

12891 ■ American Truck Historical Society, Minnesota Metro Chapter
c/o Bob Rowe
1266 Halper Pl.
White Bear Lake, MN 55110
Ph: (651)407-0017
E-mail: rarthurrowe@comcast.net
URL: National Affiliate–www.aths.org
Contact: Bob Rowe, Contact
Local.

12892 ■ Bald Eagle Sportsmen's Association
PO Box 10582
White Bear Lake, MN 55110
Ph: (651)429-9874
URL: National Affiliate–www.mynssa.com
Local. Affiliated With: National Skeet Shooting Association.

12893 ■ Black Bear Yacht Racing Association (BBYRA)
PO Box 10802
White Bear Lake, MN 55110
E-mail: carolrobertshaw@hotmail.com
URL: http://www.bbyra.com
Contact: Carol Robertshaw, Commodore
Local.

12894 ■ Central States Dressage and Eventing Association (CSDEA)
c/o St. Criox Saddlery
5960 Hwy. 61 N
White Bear Lake, MN 55110
Ph: (651)426-0831
E-mail: jmahrenholz@yahoo.com
URL: http://www.csdea.org
Contact: Jeanne Ahrenholz, Pres.
Membership Dues: individual, $45 (annual) • family, $55 (annual) • life, $500. **Local. Affiliated With:** United States Eventing Association.

12895 ■ Great Lakes Match Club
c/o Denise Alliegro
3702 Sun Terr.
White Bear Lake, MN 55110
E-mail: dalliegro@comcast.net
URL: National Affiliate–www.matchcover.org
Contact: Denise Alliegro, Contact
Regional. Affiliated With: Rathkamp Matchcover Society.

12896 ■ Heart of America Keeshond Club (HOAKC)
c/o James W. Parrish
5989 Hobe Ln.
White Bear Lake, MN 55110
E-mail: imagine@southslope.net
URL: http://www.geocities.com/hoakc
Local.

12897 ■ Mahtomedi - Young Life
PO Box 10725
White Bear Lake, MN 55110
Ph: (651)762-8483
URL: http://sites.younglife.org/_layouts/ylext/default.aspx?ID=C-3539
Local. Affiliated With: Young Life.

12898 ■ Phi Theta Kappa, Alpha Alpha Gamma Chapter - Century College
c/o Wade Warner
3300 Century Ave. N
White Bear Lake, MN 55110
Ph: (651)779-3329
E-mail: w.warner@century.mnscu.edu
URL: http://www.ptk.org/directories/chapters/MN/269-2.htm
Contact: Wade Warner, Advisor
Local.

12899 ■ Red Wing Soaring Association
PO Box 10828
White Bear Lake, MN 55110
Ph: (651)653-1631
E-mail: info@rwsa.org
URL: http://www.rwsa.org
Local. Affiliated With: Soaring Society of America.

12900 ■ St. Croix Valley Brittany Club
c/o Carol Heinel
2284 Birch St.
White Bear Lake, MN 55110
Ph: (651)426-7193
E-mail: mckummer@visi.com
URL: http://www.scvbc.org/
Contact: Marsha Kummer, Sec.
Local. Affiliated With: American Kennel Club.

12901 ■ Second Chance Animal Rescue
PO Box 10533
White Bear Lake, MN 55110-0533
Ph: (651)771-5662
E-mail: adopt@secondchancerescue.org
URL: http://www.secondchancerescue.org
Contact: Nancy Minion, Pres.
Local. Rescues, cares and places homeless companion animals. Checks animals for heartworm or feline leukemia and provides vaccination, spaying and neutering services. Places animals in volunteer foster homes until permanent adoptive homes are found. Works to educate the public on respect for all animal life, including the importance of spaying and neutering dogs and cats in order to reduce the number of healthy animals euthanized.

12902 ■ Sweet Adelines International, Lake Country Chorus
Redeemer Luthern Church
3770 Bellaire Ave.
White Bear Lake, MN 55110
Ph: (715)262-4203
E-mail: ppbc52@centurytel.net
URL: http://regionsix.org/chorus/lake_country.htm
Contact: Carolyn Plank, Contact
Local. Advances the musical art form of barbershop harmony through education and performances. Provides education, training and coaching in the development of women's four-part barbershop harmony. **Affiliated With:** Sweet Adelines International.

12903 ■ Twin Cities Chapter of the Society of Financial Service Professionals
2697 E County Rd. E, No. 282
White Bear Lake, MN 55110
Ph: (651)255-6556
Fax: (651)256-0285
E-mail: sfsptc@multiband.us
URL: http://www.sfsp.net/twincities
Contact: Sandy Beeson, Exec.Dir.
Local. Represents the interests of financial advisers. Fosters the development of professional responsibility. Helps clients achieve their personal and business-related financial goals. **Affiliated With:** Society of Financial Service Professionals.

12904 ■ Vadnais Lake Area Water Management Organization (VLAWMO)
c/o Stephanie McNamara, Administrator
4701 Hwy. 61
White Bear Lake, MN 55110
Ph: (651)429-8522
Fax: (651)429-8579
E-mail: office@vlawmo.org
URL: http://www.vlawmo.org
Contact: Stephanie McNamara, Administrator
Local.

12905 ■ White Bear Area Chamber of Commerce
4801 Hwy. 61, Ste.109
White Bear Lake, MN 55110
Ph: (651)429-8593
Fax: (651)429-8592
E-mail: info@whitebearchamber.com
URL: http://www.whitebearchamber.com
Contact: Patricia A. Brannan, Pres.
Founded: 1923. **Members:** 400. **Membership Dues:** business, $365-$1,025 (annual) • associate affiliation, $275 (annual) • retiree, government, educator, nonprofit organization, $230 (annual) • municipality, $540 (annual). **Local.** Promotes business and community development in the White Bear Lake, MN area. **Awards:** Business of the Year. **Frequency:** annual. **Type:** recognition • Volunteer of the Year. **Frequency:** annual. **Type:** recognition. **Computer Services:** Online services, member listings. **Committees:** Ambassadors; Chamber Annual Golf Outing; Community Relations; Fall Gala; Government Affairs/Local Issues; Networking; Scholarship; Technology. **Formerly:** (1994) White Bear Lake Area Chamber of Commerce. **Publications:** *Weekly Facts*. Newsletter. **Advertising:** accepted. Alternate Formats: online • Newsletter, monthly.

12906 ■ White Bear Lake/Mahtomedi - Wyldlife
PO Box 10725
White Bear Lake, MN 55110
Ph: (651)762-8483
URL: http://sites.younglife.org/_layouts/ylext/default.aspx?ID=C-3537
Local. Affiliated With: Young Life.

12907 ■ White Bear Lake - Young Life
PO Box 10725
White Bear Lake, MN 55110
Ph: (651)762-8483
URL: http://sites.younglife.org/_layouts/ylext/default.aspx?ID=C-1171
Local. Affiliated With: Young Life.

12908 ■ Young Life White Bear Lake - Mahtomedi Area
PO Box 10725
White Bear Lake, MN 55110
Ph: (651)762-8483
E-mail: jottaviani@mn25.younglife.org
URL: http://sites.younglife.org/sites/WhiteBear-MahtomediArea/default.aspx
Contact: John Ottaviani, Area Dir.
Local. Affiliated With: Young Life.

Willernie

12909 ■ American Legion, Kramer-Berg Post 507
PO Box 657
Willernie, MN 55090
Ph: (651)291-1800
Fax: (651)291-1057
URL: National Affiliate–www.legion.org
Local. Affiliated With: American Legion.

12910 ■ Minnesota West Coast Swing Dance Club
c/o Ray Stiff, Dir.
PO Box 193
Willernie, MN 55090
Ph: (651)247-7438
E-mail: dolores@usfamily.net
URL: http://www.visi.com/~randyg/wcs
Contact: Ray Stiff, Dir.
Local. Promotes and preserves the various Fast-Dance styles including Bop, Shag, East and West Coast Swing, Imperial Swing, Jitterbug, Hand Dance, Push, Whip, Lindy, and the music thereof. Encourages the resurgence of interest and participation in FastDance music and dance styles.

Willmar

12911 ■ American Cancer Society, Willmar
333 Litchfield Ave. SW
Willmar, MN 56201

Ph: (320)235-7237
Fax: (320)235-0796
Free: (800)481-3316
URL: http://www.cancer.org
Local. Affiliated With: American Cancer Society.

12912 ■ American Legion, Minnesota Post 167
c/o Austin F. Hanscom
PO Box 146
Willmar, MN 56201
Ph: (651)291-1800
Fax: (651)291-1057
URL: National Affiliate–www.legion.org
Contact: Austin F. Hanscom, Contact
Local. Affiliated With: American Legion.

12913 ■ Arc Kandiyohi County
201 SW 4th St., No. 12
Willmar, MN 56201-0801
Ph: (320)231-1777
E-mail: arckandi@uslink.net
URL: National Affiliate–www.TheArc.org
Founded: 1957. **Staff:** 1. **Local.** Parents, professional workers, and others interested in individuals with mental retardation. Works to promote services, research, public understanding, and legislation for people with mental retardation and their families. **Affiliated With:** Arc of the United States.

12914 ■ Easter Seals Minnesota - Willmar
2424 1st St. S
Willmar, MN 56201
Ph: (320)214-9238
Fax: (320)214-9140
URL: http://www.goodwilleasterseals.org
Contact: Ms. Melissa Peterson, Program Services Mgr.
Local. Works to help individuals with disabilities and special needs, and their families. Conducts programs to assist people of all ages with disabilities. Provides outpatient medical rehabilitation services. Advocates for the passage of legislation to help people with disabilities achieve independence, including the Americans with Disabilities Act (ADA). **Affiliated With:** Easter Seals.

12915 ■ Education Minnesota, Willmar
1708 First St. S, Ste.102
Box 1127
Willmar, MN 56201
Ph: (320)235-7220
Fax: (320)235-1733
Free: (800)642-3239
E-mail: mary.minnehan@educationminnesota.org
URL: http://www.educationminnesota.org
Contact: Mary Minnehan, Staff Person
Local. Affiliated With: American Federation of Teachers.

12916 ■ Habitat for Humanity of West Central Minnesota
PO Box 1171
Willmar, MN 56201
Ph: (320)231-2704
Fax: (320)231-0659
Free: (877)926-6434
E-mail: hfhwcm@habitatwcm.org
URL: http://www.habitatwcm.org
Founded: 1993. **Local.**

12917 ■ Kandiyohi County Pheasants Forever (KCPF)
PO Box 732
Willmar, MN 56201
Ph: (320)235-9788
E-mail: kandipf@charter.net
URL: http://www.kandipf.willmar.com
Contact: Greg Kamrowski, Pres.
Founded: 1982. **Local. Affiliated With:** Pheasants Forever.

12918 ■ Let's Go Fishing of Minnesota
c/o Michael O'Brien
1025 19th Ave. SW
Willmar, MN 56201
Ph: (320)235-8448
E-mail: info@letsgofishingofmn.com
URL: http://www.letsgofishingofmn.com
State.

12919 ■ Little Crow AIFA
c/o Elaine Peterson, Exec.
919 S 1st St.
Willmar, MN 56201
Ph: (320)235-0542
Fax: (320)235-0543
E-mail: rolmeister@willmar.com
URL: National Affiliate–naifa.org
Contact: Elaine Peterson, Exec.
Local. Represents the interests of insurance and financial advisors. Advocates for a positive legislative and regulatory environment. Enhances business and professional skills of members. **Affiliated With:** National Association of Insurance and Financial Advisors.

12920 ■ Minnesota Chapter of the Association for Healthcare Resource and Materials Management
c/o Charles Roelofs, Purchasing Agent
Rice Memorial Hosp.
301 Becker Ave. SW
Willmar, MN 56201-3302
Ph: (320)231-4116
Fax: (320)231-4852
E-mail: croe@rice.willmar.mn.us
URL: National Affiliate–www.ahrmm.org
Contact: Charles Roelofs, Purchasing Agent
State. Represents purchasing agents and materials managers active in the field of purchasing, inventory, distribution and materials management as performed in hospitals, related patient care institutions and government and voluntary health organizations. Provides networking and educational opportunities for members. Develops new business ventures that ensure the financial stability of members. **Affiliated With:** Association for Healthcare Resource and Materials Management.

12921 ■ Minnesota Senior Federation, Midwest Region
c/o Sue Johnson
PO Box 589
Willmar, MN 56201
Ph: (320)995-6633
Fax: (320)995-6634
Free: (877)995-6633
E-mail: sljohns@en-tel.net
URL: http://mnseniors.org
Contact: Sue Johnson, Contact
Local.

12922 ■ Minnesota Senior Federation, Minnesota Valley Region
c/o Sue Johnson
PO Box 589
Willmar, MN 56201
Ph: (320)995-6633
Fax: (320)995-6634
Free: (877)995-6633
E-mail: sljohns@en-tel.net
URL: http://mnseniors.org
Contact: Sue Johnson, Contact
Local.

12923 ■ Minnesota Senior Federation, Southwest Region
c/o Sue Johnson
PO Box 589
Willmar, MN 56201
Ph: (320)995-6633
Fax: (320)995-6634
Free: (877)995-6633
E-mail: sljohns@en-tel.net
URL: http://mnseniors.org
Contact: Sue Johnson, Contact
Local.

12924 ■ National Active and Retired Federal Employees Association - Willmar 2280
2201 SW 20th St.
Willmar, MN 56201-4987
Ph: (320)235-5153
URL: National Affiliate–www.narfe.org
Contact: Marvin D. Olson, Contact
Local. Protects the retirement future of employees through education. Informs members on issues affecting the retirement. **Affiliated With:** National Association of Retired Federal Employees.

12925 ■ Phi Theta Kappa, Alpha Eta Zeta Chapter - Ridgewater College
c/o Sarah Rhoda
PO Box 1097
Willmar, MN 56201
Ph: (320)231-2903
E-mail: sarah.rhoda@ridgewater.mnscu.edu
URL: http://www.ptk.org/directories/chapters/MN/268-1.htm
Contact: Sarah Rhoda, Advisor
Local.

12926 ■ Prairie Country Resource Conservation and Development Council
1005 High St., NE
Willmar, MN 56201-2667
Ph: (320)231-0008
Fax: (320)235-8751
E-mail: rwn2@mn.nrcs.usda.gov
URL: National Affiliate–www.rcdnet.org
Contact: Randy Nelson, Coor.
Local. Affiliated With: National Association of Resource Conservation and Development Councils.

12927 ■ Sons of Norway, Fedraheimen Lodge 1-59
c/o Earl O. Knutson, Pres.
722 2nd St. SW
Willmar, MN 56201-3514
Ph: (320)222-1613
E-mail: eoknutsn@en-tel.net
URL: National Affiliate–www.sofn.com
Contact: Earl O. Knutson, Pres.
Local. Affiliated With: Sons of Norway.

12928 ■ United Way of Kandiyohi County
PO Box 895
Willmar, MN 56201
Ph: (320)235-1050
Fax: (320)235-2774
E-mail: stacey@unitedwaykc.org
URL: http://www.unitedwaykc.org
Contact: Stacey Roberts, Exec.Dir.
Local. Affiliated With: United Way of America.

12929 ■ West Central Minnesota Youth for Christ
PO Box 625
Willmar, MN 56201
Ph: (320)235-0119
Fax: (320)235-0119
URL: http://www.yfcminnesota.com
Local. Affiliated With: Youth for Christ/U.S.A.

12930 ■ Willmar Evening Lions Club
c/o Don Lauver, Pres.
PO Box 1596
Willmar, MN 56201
Ph: (320)231-1492
E-mail: dl4110@msn.com
URL: http://www.5m4lions.org
Contact: Don Lauver, Pres.
Local. Affiliated With: Lions Clubs International.

12931 ■ Willmar Jaycees
PO Box 92
Willmar, MN 56201
Ph: (320)222-1982
E-mail: pddokken@en-tel.net
URL: http://jaycees.willmar.com
Contact: Patrick Dokken, Pres.
Founded: 1947. **Local.**

12932 ■ Willmar Lakes Area Chamber of Commerce (WLACC)
2104 E Hwy. 12
Willmar, MN 56201
Ph: (320)235-0300
Fax: (320)231-1948
E-mail: chamber@willmarareachamber.com
URL: http://www.willmarareachamber.com
Contact: Ken Warner, Pres.
Founded: 1929. **Members:** 585. **Membership Dues:** business, $280-$2,670 (annual) • retiree, $80 (annual) • individual, church, education, government, $140 (annual). **Staff:** 2. **Budget:** $286,000. **Local.** Promotes business and community development in the Willmar, MN area. **Awards: Frequency:** annual. **Type:** recognition. **Recipient:** to outstanding individuals and businesses for their contributions to the community. **Computer Services:** Online services, membership directory. **Committees:** Agri-Business; Ambassador; Membership Development; Public Policy; Special Events. **Publications:** *City and County Map.* Directory • Membership Directory • Newsletter, monthly. **Advertising:** accepted. Alternate Formats: online. **Conventions/Meetings:** annual banquet - always February • weekly Chamber Connections - meeting - every Friday.

12933 ■ Willmar Lakes Area Convention and Visitors Bureau
2104 E Hwy. 12
Willmar, MN 56201
Ph: (320)235-3552
Free: (800)845-8747
E-mail: info@seeyouinwillmar.com
URL: http://www.seeyouinwillmar.com
Contact: Stephanie Myogeto, Contact
Local. Formerly: (2006) Willmar Convention and Visitors Bureau.

12934 ■ Willmar Noon Lions Club
c/o Donn Winckler, Pres.
401 SE 19th St.
Willmar, MN 56201
Ph: (320)222-2073 (320)235-8504
E-mail: donn.wincker@mmrdc.org
URL: http://www.5m4lions.org
Contact: Donn Winckler, Pres.
Local. Affiliated With: Lions Clubs International.

Willow River

12935 ■ American Legion, Hanson-Anderson Post 361
PO Box 308
Willow River, MN 55795
Ph: (651)291-1800
Fax: (651)291-1057
URL: National Affiliate–www.legion.org
Local. Affiliated With: American Legion.

12936 ■ American Legion, Popek-Kostecky Post 163
PO Box 111
Willow River, MN 55795
Ph: (651)291-1800
Fax: (651)291-1057
URL: National Affiliate–www.legion.org
Local. Affiliated With: American Legion.

12937 ■ Society of American Foresters, Lake Superior Chapter
c/o Deb Moritz, Chair
PO Box 95
Willow River, MN 55795
Ph: (218)372-3182
E-mail: deb.moritz@dnr.state.mn.us
URL: http://www.mnsaf.org
Contact: Deb Moritz, Chair
Local. Affiliated With: Society of American Foresters.

Windom

12938 ■ American Legion, Windom Post 206
PO Box 184
Windom, MN 56101
Ph: (651)291-1800
Fax: (651)291-1057
URL: National Affiliate–www.legion.org
Local. Affiliated With: American Legion.

12939 ■ Education Minnesota, Windom
560 Second Ave.
Box 535
Windom, MN 56101
Ph: (507)831-5484
Fax: (507)831-0190
Free: (800)862-1176
URL: http://www.educationminnesota.org
Contact: Marion Wiering, Associate Staff
Local. Affiliated With: American Federation of Teachers.

12940 ■ Windom Area Chamber of Commerce and Visitors Bureau (WACCVB)
303 9th St.
PO Box 8
Windom, MN 56101-0008
Ph: (507)831-2752
Fax: (507)831-2755
Free: (800)7W1-NDOM
E-mail: windomchamber@qwest.net
URL: http://www.winwacc.com
Contact: Cheryl Hanson, Pres.
Members: 210. **Local.** Promotes business and community development in the Windom, MN area. Serves as a community information center. Sponsors community events including annual summer celebration, Riverfest. **Awards:** Community Honoree. **Frequency:** monthly. **Type:** recognition • Rural Stewardship. **Frequency:** annual. **Type:** recognition • WACC & VB Exceptional Achievement. **Frequency:** annual. **Type:** recognition • WACC & VB Volunteer of the Year. **Frequency:** annual. **Type:** recognition. **Formerly:** (1999) Windom Area +Chamber of Commerce. **Publications:** *Chamber Update*, monthly. Newsletter. **Conventions/Meetings:** annual meeting - always in October.

Winger

12941 ■ American Legion, Fengestad-Solie Post 200
PO Box 31
Winger, MN 56592
Ph: (651)291-1800
Fax: (651)291-1057
URL: National Affiliate–www.legion.org
Local. Affiliated With: American Legion.

12942 ■ Winger Lions Club
c/o Carsten Zahl, Sec.
Box 37
Winger, MN 56592
Ph: (218)938-4482
URL: http://lions5m11.org/sys-tmpl/door
Contact: Carsten Zahl, Sec.
Local. Affiliated With: Lions Clubs International.

Winnebago

12943 ■ American Legion, Winnebago Post 82
PO Box 642
Winnebago, MN 56098
Ph: (651)291-1800
Fax: (651)291-1057
URL: National Affiliate–www.legion.org
Local. Affiliated With: American Legion.

Winona

12944 ■ American Legion, Leon J. Wetzel Post 9
265 E 3rd St.
Winona, MN 55987
Ph: (651)291-1800
Fax: (651)291-1057
URL: National Affiliate–www.legion.org
Local. Affiliated With: American Legion.

12945 ■ American Red Cross, Winona County Chapter
1660 Kraemer Dr.
Winona, MN 55987
Ph: (507)452-4258
Fax: (507)452-0012
E-mail: winredc@luminet.net
URL: http://www.luminet.net/~winredc
Local.

12946 ■ Association for Computing Machinery, St. Mary's University of Minnesota
c/o John Bonomo, Sponsor
Dept. of Cmpt. Sci.
700 Terr. Heights
Winona, MN 55987-1399
Ph: (507)452-4430
Free: (800)635-5987
E-mail: ccombs@marys.smumn.edu
URL: National Affiliate–www.acm.org
Contact: Ann Smith, Chair
Local. Biological, medical, behavioral, and computer scientists; hospital administrators; programmers and others interested in application of computer methods to biological, behavioral, and medical problems. Stimulates understanding of the use and potential of computers in the Biosciences. **Affiliated With:** Association for Computing Machinery.

12947 ■ Association for Computing Machinery, Winona State University
c/o Gerald Cichanowski
PO Box 5838
Winona, MN 55987
Free: (800)342-5978
E-mail: wncesc@wind.winona.msus.edu
Contact: Gerald Cichanowski, Contact
Local. Biological, medical, behavioral, and computer scientists; hospital administrators; programmers and others interested in application of computer methods to biological, behavioral, and medical problems. Stimulates understanding of the use and potential of computers in the Biosciences. **Affiliated With:** Association for Computing Machinery.

12948 ■ Bluffview Montessori PTA
c/o Bluffview Montessorri School
1321 Gilmore Ave.
Winona, MN 55987
E-mail: tlieder@home.com
URL: http://familyeducation.com/MN/BluffviewMontessoriPTA
Contact: Terri Lieder, Contact
Local. Parents, teachers, students, and others interested in uniting the forces of home, school, and community. Promotes the welfare of children and youth.

12949 ■ Common Good RSVP
c/o Jennifer Halberg, Dir.
111 Market St.
Winona, MN 55987

Ph: (507)454-2270
Fax: (507)457-3027
E-mail: jhalberg@ccwinona.org
URL: http://www.seniorcorps.gov/about/programs/rsvp_state.asp?usestateabbr=mn&Search4.x=24&Search4.y=16
Contact: Jennifer Halberg, Dir.
Local. Affiliated With: Retired and Senior Volunteer Program.

12950 ■ Friends of the Upper Mississippi River Refuges
51 E 4th St.
Winona, MN 55987-3509
Ph: (507)454-6227
E-mail: info@friendsofuppermiss.org
URL: http://www.friendsofuppermiss.org
Contact: Jim Eddy, Pres.
Founded: 1997. **Members:** 260. **Membership Dues:** student, $15 (annual) • individual, $25 (annual) • family, $40 (annual) • contributor, $100 (annual) • benefactor, $500 (annual) • patron, $1,000 (annual). **Budget:** $23,000. **Local Groups:** 4. **Regional.** Works to conserve the natural and cultural resources of the Upper Mississippi River National Wildlife and Fish Refuge, the Trempealeau National Wildlife Refuge and the Driftless National Wildlife Refuge. **Formerly:** (1998) Friends of the Upper Mississippi. **Publications:** *Mississippi River Messenger*, quarterly. Newsletter. **Circulation:** 250. **Conventions/Meetings:** annual meeting - always May.

12951 ■ Habitat for Humanity Winona County, Minnesota
PO Box 1183
Winona, MN 55987
Ph: (507)457-0003
Fax: (507)457-0412
E-mail: info@habitatwinona.org
URL: http://www.habitatwinona.org
Contact: Nancy Iglesias, Exec.Dir.
Local. Affiliated With: Habitat for Humanity International.

12952 ■ Local 228C, Chemical Workers Council of the UFCW
628 Center St.
Winona, MN 55987
Ph: (507)454-4406
URL: National Affiliate–www.ufcw.org
Local. Affiliated With: United Food and Commercial Workers International Union.

12953 ■ Minnesota Buffalo Association (MNBA)
c/o Gail Griffin, Exec.Dir.
22627 Buffalo Ridge Rd.
Winona, MN 55987-6047
Ph: (507)454-2828
Fax: (208)361-5992
E-mail: info@mnbison.org
URL: http://www.mnbison.org
Contact: Gail Griffin, Exec.Dir.
Founded: 1993. **Members:** 172. **Membership Dues:** regular, $50 (annual). **Staff:** 1. **State Groups:** 1. **State.** Promotes and preserves the unique character have and the market potential of buffalo (bison) and buffalo products. **Publications:** *Bison New of the North*, 5/year. Newsletter. **Conventions/Meetings:** annual meeting.

12954 ■ Minnesota Business Educators Inc. (MBEI)
Winona State Univ.
175 W Mark St.
Winona, MN 55987-5838
Ph: (507)457-5601
Fax: (507)457-5697
E-mail: jkarjala@winona.edu
URL: http://www.mbei-online.org
Contact: Dr. Jeanette A. Karjala, Pres.
Founded: 1967. **Members:** 500. **Membership Dues:** $20 (annual). **Local Groups:** 7. **State.** Business education professionals. **Awards:** Distinguished Service. **Frequency:** annual. **Type:** recognition • Friend of Business Education. **Frequency:** annual. **Type:** recognition • Outstanding Post-Secondary Business Educator. **Frequency:** annual. **Type:** recognition • Outstanding Secondary Business Educator. **Frequency:** annual. **Type:** recognition. **Recipient:** for teaching experience, community service, publications, and services to business education. **Affiliated With:** National Business Education Association. **Publications:** *MBEL in Action*, 3/year. Newsletter. **Price:** included in membership dues. **Advertising:** accepted. **Conventions/Meetings:** annual conference, one day mini conference (exhibits) - always fall • annual convention (exhibits) - always spring.

12955 ■ Minnesota Native Wildflower Grass Producers Association
31837 Bur Oak Ln.
Winona, MN 55987
E-mail: ssns@springgrove.coop
URL: http://www.mnnwgpa.org
Contact: Garth Koste, Pres.
Founded: 1993. **Members:** 14. **Membership Dues:** voting, $200 (annual) • associate, $25 (annual). **State.** Promotes the diversity, quality and availability of regionally adapted native plant species; seeks to educate government agencies and the general public about the conservation, preservation, and restoration of habitats using native plant species. **Conventions/Meetings:** quarterly meeting.

12956 ■ Mothers Against Drunk Driving, Winona County
PO Box 28
Winona, MN 55987-0028
Ph: (507)452-0050
Fax: (507)454-7980
E-mail: vernh@hbci.com
URL: National Affiliate–www.madd.org/
Local. Victims of drunk driving crashes; concerned citizens. Encourages citizen participation in working towards reform of the drunk driving problem and the prevention of underage drinking. Acts as the voice of victims of drunk driving crashes by speaking on their behalf to communities, businesses, and educational groups. **Affiliated With:** Mothers Against Drunk Driving.

12957 ■ Psi Chi, National Honor Society in Psychology - Saint Mary's University of Minnesota
c/o Dept. of Psychology
700 Terr. Hts. No. 1464
Winona, MN 55987-1399
Ph: (507)457-6991
Fax: (507)457-1633
E-mail: mchurch@smumn.edu
URL: http://www.psichi.org/chapters/info.asp?chapter_id=265
Contact: Marcy Church PhD, Advisor
Local.

12958 ■ Sons of Norway, Nor-Win Lodge 1-505
c/o Robert H. Peterson, Pres.
2008 Clinton Dr.
Winona, MN 55987-9553
Ph: (507)452-4512
E-mail: upsbobber@charter.net
URL: National Affiliate–www.sofn.com
Contact: Robert H. Peterson, Pres.
Local. Affiliated With: Sons of Norway.

12959 ■ United Way of the Greater Winona Area
902 E 2nd St., Ste.330
Winona, MN 55987
Ph: (507)452-4624
Fax: (507)452-8786
E-mail: unitedway@hbci.com
URL: http://www.unitedwaywinona.org
Contact: Beth Forkner Moe, Exec.Dir.
Local. Affiliated With: United Way of America.

12960 ■ Winona Area Chamber of Commerce (WACC)
67 Main St.
PO Box 870
Winona, MN 55987-0870
Ph: (507)452-2272
Fax: (507)454-8814
E-mail: info@winonachamber.com
URL: http://www.winonachamber.com
Contact: Della Schmidt, Pres.
Founded: 1947. **Members:** 575. **Membership Dues:** business, $241-$1,803 (annual). **Staff:** 3. **For-Profit. Local.** Promotes business and community development in the Winona, MN area. **Committees:** Agriculture; Ambassador; Economic Development. **Subgroups:** Government Advocacy; Workforce Development. **Task Forces:** Annual Banquet; Business Appreciation Week; Transportation. **Publications:** *Business Advocate*. Newsletter. Alternate Formats: online.

12961 ■ Winona Area Mountain Bikers
178 Center St.
Winona, MN 55987
Ph: (507)452-4228
Fax: (507)452-4211
E-mail: adbcycle@hpci.com
URL: http://www.advcycle.com
Contact: Brad Walker, Contact
Local. Affiliated With: International Mountain Bicycling Association.

12962 ■ Winona County Historical Society (WCHS)
160 Johnson St.
Winona, MN 55987
Ph: (507)454-2723
Fax: (507)454-0006
E-mail: wchs@luminet.net
URL: http://www.winonahistory.org
Contact: Mark F. Peterson, Exec.Dir.
Founded: 1935. **Members:** 1,200. **Membership Dues:** senior, $20 (annual) • individual, $25 (annual) • family, $40 (annual) • senior household, $30 (annual) • contributing, $100 (annual) • sponsor, $250 (annual) • sustaining, $500 (annual) • Captain Orrin Smith Society, $1,000 (annual). **Staff:** 8. **Budget:** $200,000. **Local.** Promotes local history in Winona County, MN. **Libraries: Type:** open to the public. **Holdings:** 3,000. **Subjects:** Winona County. **Publications:** *Chronicles*, semiannual. Magazine. **Price:** included in membership dues • *Memo*, monthly. **Price:** included in membership dues • Newsletter, monthly. **Price:** included in membership dues. **Conventions/Meetings:** annual general assembly - during first quarter.

12963 ■ Winona Noon Lions Club
PO Box 424
Winona, MN 55987
E-mail: president@winonanoonlions.org
URL: http://www.winonanoonlions.org
Contact: Dr. Donald Budd, Pres.
Local. Affiliated With: Lions Clubs International.

12964 ■ Winona Rivertown Lions Club
PO Box 1002
Winona, MN 55987
Ph: (507)452-2687 (507)454-3021
URL: http://www.hbci.com/%7Emelr/lions.htm
Contact: Maureen Gorman, Contact
Local. Affiliated With: Lions Clubs International.

12965 ■ Winona Senior High School PTSA
901 Gilmore Ave.
Winona, MN 55987
Ph: (507)454-9500
E-mail: chuggenvik@ptamail.com
URL: http://familyeducation.com/MN/Winona_High_PTSA
Contact: Cindy Huggenvik, Pres.
Local. Parents, teachers, students, and others interested in uniting the forces of home, school, and community. Promotes the welfare of children and youth.

12966 ■ Winona Society for Human Resource Management
PO Box 71
Winona, MN 55987
Contact: Jeanne Hines, Pres.
Local. Represents the interests of human resource and industrial relations professionals and executives. Promotes the advancement of human resource management.

12967 ■ Winona - Young Life
250 Oak Leaf Dr.
Winona, MN 55987
Ph: (507)452-1388
URL: http://sites.younglife.org/_layouts/ylext/default.aspx?ID=C-3601
Local. Affiliated With: Young Life.

12968 ■ Young Life Winona
250 Oak Leaf Dr.
Winona, MN 55987
Ph: (507)452-1388
URL: http://sites.younglife.org/_layouts/ylext/default.aspx?ID=A-MN78
Local. Affiliated With: Young Life.

Winsted

12969 ■ American Legion, Martin Krueger Post 407
PO Box 360
Winsted, MN 55395
Ph: (320)485-4366
Fax: (651)291-1057
URL: National Affiliate–www.legion.org
Local. Affiliated With: American Legion.

Winthrop

12970 ■ American Legion, Gedig Post 314
106 Renville N
Winthrop, MN 55396
Ph: (651)291-1800
Fax: (651)291-1057
URL: National Affiliate–www.legion.org
Local. Affiliated With: American Legion.

12971 ■ Winthrop Area Chamber of Commerce
PO Box 594
Winthrop, MN 55396
Ph: (507)647-2627
Fax: (507)647-2627
Free: (800)647-9461
E-mail: winthropchamber@hotmail.com
Contact: Julie Trebelhom, Exec.Sec.
Members: 115. **Staff:** 1. **Local.** Promotes business in Winthrop. **Publications:** Newsletter, monthly. Brief news bulletin for members. **Price:** free. **Advertising:** accepted. **Conventions/Meetings:** monthly meeting.

Wolverton

12972 ■ American Legion, Nelson-Otteson Post 370
301 King of Trails Pkwy.
Wolverton, MN 56594
Ph: (651)291-1800
Fax: (651)291-1057
URL: National Affiliate–www.legion.org
Local. Affiliated With: American Legion.

Wood Lake

12973 ■ American Legion, Wood Lake Post 556
PO Box 103
Wood Lake, MN 56297
Ph: (651)291-1800
Fax: (651)291-1057
URL: National Affiliate–www.legion.org
Local. Affiliated With: American Legion.

Woodbury

12974 ■ American Legion, Woodbury Post 501
8301 Valley Creek Rd.
Woodbury, MN 55125
Ph: (651)291-1800
Fax: (651)291-1057
URL: National Affiliate–www.legion.org
Local. Affiliated With: American Legion.

12975 ■ American Society of Women Accountants, Minnesota/St. Paul Chapter No. 068
c/o Shelly Selby, CPA, Pres.
Transport Corp. of Am., Inc.
3780 Oxford Dr.
Woodbury, MN 55125
Ph: (651)905-2815 (651)578-0385
Fax: (651)994-5780
E-mail: shelly.selby@transportamerica.com
URL: National Affiliate–www.aswa.org
Contact: Shelly Selby CPA, Pres.
Local. Affiliated With: American Society of Women Accountants.

12976 ■ DeafArt Club (DAC)
c/o Michael Rosen
2254 Tower Ct.
Woodbury, MN 55125
Ph: (651)578-7649
E-mail: deafartclubmn@yahoo.com
URL: http://pages.sbcglobal.net/aslclay
Contact: Helene Oppenheimer, Exec.Dir.
Founded: 1999. **Languages:** English, German. **Local.** Seeks to educate about and facilitate the creation of deaf art; encourages participation at all levels, seeking to exhibit and sell deaf art both in person and on the Website. **Libraries: Type:** lending. **Holdings:** books.

12977 ■ Kiap Tu Wish Chapter of Trout Unlimited
c/o Greg Dietl, Pres.
10758 Falling Water Ln., Unit D
Woodbury, MN 55129-5304
Ph: (651)436-2604
E-mail: mccaiglee@hotmail.com
URL: http://www.lambcom.net/kiaptuwish
Contact: Greg Dietl, Pres.
Local. Affiliated With: Trout Unlimited. **Formerly:** (2005) Trout Unlimited, Kiap Tu Wish 168.

12978 ■ Minneapolis Central Lions Club
c/o Bridget S. Kohl, Pres.
8754 Summer Wind Cir.
Woodbury, MN 55125
Ph: (651)501-1573 (952)930-4216
URL: http://www.5m5.org
Contact: Bridget S. Kohl, Pres.
Local. Affiliated With: Lions Clubs International.

12979 ■ Minnesota Chiefs of Police Association
1951 Woodlane Dr.
Woodbury, MN 55125
Ph: (651)457-0677
Fax: (651)457-5665
Free: (800)377-4058
E-mail: harlan@mnchieff.org
Contact: Harlan Johnson, Exec.Dir.
State.

12980 ■ Minnesota Sheriffs' Association
c/o James Franklin, Exec.Dir.
1951 Woodlane Dr., Ste.200
Woodbury, MN 55125
Ph: (651)451-7216
Fax: (651)451-8087
E-mail: info@mnsheriffs.org
Contact: Mr. James D. Franklin, Exec.Dir.
Founded: 1885. **Membership Dues:** honorary and general, $25 (annual) • sustaining, $50 (annual). **Staff:** 3. **State Groups:** 1. **State. Publications:** *Minnesota Sheriff*, quarterly. Journal.

12981 ■ Minnesota Utility Contractors Association (MUCA)
c/o Jeff Hanson, Exec.Dir.
7616 Currell Blvd., Ste.155
Woodbury, MN 55125
Ph: (651)735-3908
Fax: (651)735-4018
Free: (800)567-6822
URL: http://www.muca.org
State.

12982 ■ Minnesota Working Rottweiler Association
c/o Warren Skura, Pres.
7033 Steeple View Rd.
Woodbury, MN 55125
Ph: (651)578-0141
E-mail: warsanrotts@yahoo.com
URL: http://www.mnworkingrottweiler.com
Contact: Warren Skura, Pres.
State.

12983 ■ National Association of Minority Contractors, Minnesota
7780 Somerset Rd.
Woodbury, MN 55125
Ph: (651)501-5813
E-mail: clifftonboyd@comcast.net
URL: National Affiliate–www.namcline.org
Contact: Clifton Boyd, Contact
State. Promotes the economic and legal interests of minority contracting firms. Provides education and training and identifies procurement opportunities for minority contractors. Advocates law and government actions which meet the concerns of minority contractors. **Affiliated With:** National Association of Minority Contractors.

12984 ■ Particle Society of Minnesota (PSM)
c/o Sara Gantner
2045 Wooddale Dr.
Woodbury, MN 55125-2904
Ph: (612)627-1480
Fax: (612)627-1444
E-mail: info@particlesociety.org
URL: http://particlesociety.org
Contact: Bruce Forsyth, Pres.
Founded: 1999. **Members:** 200. **Budget:** $10,000. **Regional Groups:** 1. **State Groups:** 1. **Local Groups:** 1. **State.** Promotes an interdisciplinary approach to particle science. Seeks to involve academic and industrial professionals in continuing education on particle science. **Conventions/Meetings:** annual conference (exhibits) - always fall.

12985 ■ Police and Firemen's Insurance Association - St. Paul Fire Department
c/o Al John
1733 Kerry Ln.
Woodbury, MN 55125
Ph: (651)730-1744
URL: National Affiliate–www.pfia.net
Contact: Al John, Contact
Local. Affiliated With: Police and Firemen's Insurance Association.

12986 ■ Woodbury Chamber of Commerce
7650 Currell Blvd., Ste.360
Woodbury, MN 55125
Ph: (651)578-0722
Fax: (651)578-7276
E-mail: chamber@woodburychamber.org
URL: http://www.woodburychamber.org
Contact: Tim Fallon, Chm.
Membership Dues: business (based on number of employees), $200-$1,500 (annual) • civic/volunteer organization, $150 (annual) • associate, $100 (annual). **Local.** Promotes business and community development in Woodbury, MN. **Awards:** Business of the Year. **Frequency:** annual. **Type:** recognition. **Recipient:** for outstanding contribution to the community • Citizen of the Year. **Frequency:** annual. **Type:** recognition. **Recipient:** for exemplary community service • Educational Team of the Year. **Frequency:** annual. **Type:** recognition. **Recipient:** for outstanding

contribution to education by a group • Elementary Educator of the Year. **Frequency:** annual. **Type:** recognition. **Recipient:** for outstanding contribution to elementary education • Secondary Educator of the Year. **Frequency:** annual. **Type:** recognition. **Recipient:** for outstanding contribution to secondary education. **Computer Services:** database, membership directory. **Committees:** Annual Chamber Gala; Community Events; Education; Government Relations/Business Development; Member Services; Web Site. **Publications:** *The Chamber Connection*. Newsletter. **Advertising:** accepted.

12987 ■ Woodbury Figure Skating Club
4125 Tower Dr.
Woodbury, MN 55125
E-mail: kwanfan@comcast.net
URL: http://www.skatewoodbury.org
Contact: Andrea Payne, Contact
Local. Provides programs to encourage participation and achievement in the sport of figure skating on ice. Defines and maintains uniform standards of skating proficiency. Organizes and sponsors competitions and exhibitions for the purpose of stimulating interest in figure skating. **Affiliated With:** United States Figure Skating Association.

12988 ■ Woodbury Jaycees
PO Box 25945
Woodbury, MN 55125
E-mail: woodburyjaycees@yahoo.com
URL: http://geocities.com/woodburyjaycees
Contact: Stacy Robertson, Pres.
Local.

12989 ■ Woodbury Young Life
7650 Currell Blvd., Ste.340
Woodbury, MN 55125
Ph: (651)739-4820
Fax: (651)739-8909
E-mail: troy@woodbury.younglife.org
URL: http://sites.younglife.org/sites/woodbury/default.aspx
Contact: Troy Daniels, Area Dir.
Local. **Affiliated With:** Young Life.

Worthington

12990 ■ American Legion, Calvin-Knuth Post 5
PO Box 292
Worthington, MN 56187
Ph: (651)291-1800
Fax: (651)291-1057
URL: National Affiliate–www.legion.org
Local. **Affiliated With:** American Legion.

12991 ■ Phi Theta Kappa, Alpha Nu Kappa Chapter - Minnesota West Community and Technical College
c/o Michael Fury
1450 Coll. Way
Worthington, MN 56187
Ph: (507)372-3407
E-mail: mfury@wr.mnwest.mnscu.edu
URL: http://www.ptk.org/directories/chapters/MN/2065-1.htm
Contact: Michael Fury, Advisor
Local.

12992 ■ RSVP of Southwest Minnesota
c/o Mary McLaughlin, Dir.
321 11th St.
Worthington, MN 56187-2450
Ph: (507)372-7374
Fax: (507)372-7918
E-mail: mmclaugh@rconnect.com
URL: http://www.seniorservice.org/southwest_mn_rsvp
Contact: Mary McLaughlin, Dir.
Local. **Affiliated With:** Retired and Senior Volunteer Program.

12993 ■ Worthington Area Chamber of Commerce
1121 Third Ave.
Worthington, MN 56187-2435
Ph: (507)372-2919
Fax: (507)372-2827
Free: (800)279-2919
E-mail: wcofc@frontiernet.net
URL: http://www.worthingtonmnchamber.com
Contact: Darlene S. Macklin, Contact
Local. Promotes business and community development in the Worthington, MN area. **Computer Services:** database, list of members • information services, facts about the community. **Publications:** Newsletter, monthly.

12994 ■ Worthington Area United Way
1121 3rd Ave.
Worthington, MN 56187-2435
Ph: (507)372-7541
URL: National Affiliate–national.unitedway.org
Local. **Affiliated With:** United Way of America.

Wykoff

12995 ■ American Legion, Stahl-Linnemeyer Post 369
222 Silver St. S
Wykoff, MN 55990
Ph: (651)291-1800
Fax: (651)291-1057
URL: National Affiliate–www.legion.org
Local. **Affiliated With:** American Legion.

12996 ■ Wykoff Lions Club
c/o Daniel J. Gleeson, Sec.
107 Gold St. N
Wykoff, MN 55990
Ph: (651)246-1841 (651)765-9903
E-mail: food@hmtel.com
URL: http://www.lions5m1.org/wykoff
Contact: Daniel J. Gleeson, Sec.
Local. **Affiliated With:** Lions Clubs International.

Wyoming

12997 ■ Sweet Adelines International, Lakes Area Chapter
Wyoming Community Church
5459 Viking Blvd.
Wyoming, MN 55092-9238
E-mail: gdf1933@msn.com
URL: http://www.regionsix.org/chorus/lakes_area.htm
Contact: Gail Frost, Contact
Local. Advances the musical art form of barbershop harmony through education and performances. Provides education, training and coaching in the development of women's four-part barbershop harmony. **Affiliated With:** Sweet Adelines International.

Zimmerman

12998 ■ American Legion, Kriesel-Jacobsen Post 560
12674 Fremont Ave.
Zimmerman, MN 55398
Ph: (651)291-1800
Fax: (651)291-1057
URL: National Affiliate–www.legion.org
Local. **Affiliated With:** American Legion.

12999 ■ Livonia Lions Club
c/o Joalyn Welte, Sec.
12410 243rd Ave.
Zimmerman, MN 55398
Ph: (763)441-2768
E-mail: livtownclrk@sherbtel.net
URL: http://www.livoniatownship.org/LivoniaLions.html
Contact: Joalyn Welte, Sec.
Local. **Affiliated With:** Lions Clubs International.

13000 ■ Minnesota Fox Trotter Association
c/o Mike Brinwall
28615 - 99 1/2 St.
Zimmerman, MN 55398
Ph: (763)633-3285
URL: National Affiliate–www.MFTHBA.com
Contact: Mike Brinwall, Contact
Local. **Affiliated With:** Missouri Fox Trotting Horse Breed Association.

13001 ■ Minnesota Quarter Horse Association, District 7
c/o Merv Hauge
12133 283rd Ave. N
Zimmerman, MN 55398
Ph: (763)389-2815
URL: http://www.mnqha.com/index_main.htm
Contact: Merv Hauge, Contact
Local. **Affiliated With:** American Quarter Horse Association.

Zumbro Falls

13002 ■ National Active and Retired Federal Employees Association - Rochester 391
RR 2, Box 2407
Zumbro Falls, MN 55991-9785
Ph: (507)753-3214
URL: National Affiliate–www.narfe.org
Contact: Allen J. Schacht, Contact
Local. Protects the retirement future of employees through education. Informs members on issues affecting the retirement. **Affiliated With:** National Association of Retired Federal Employees.

13003 ■ Zumbro Falls Lions Club
c/o Eugene Schmidt, Pres.
RR 1, Box 141
Zumbro Falls, MN 55991
Ph: (507)753-2459
URL: http://www.lions5m1.org/zumbrofalls
Contact: Eugene Schmidt, Pres.
Local. **Affiliated With:** Lions Clubs International.

Zumbrota

13004 ■ American Legion, Zumbrota Post 183
664 Pleasant Ave.
Zumbrota, MN 55992
Ph: (651)291-1800
Fax: (651)291-1057
URL: National Affiliate–www.legion.org
Local. **Affiliated With:** American Legion.

13005 ■ Zumbrota Chamber of Commerce (ZCC)
PO Box 2
Zumbrota, MN 55992-0002
Ph: (507)732-4282
URL: http://www.zumbrota.com
Contact: Andrea Kleinholz, Sec.
Members: 104. **Local**. Promotes business, community development, and tourism in Zumbrota, MN. Sponsors Covered Bridge Festival.

13006 ■ Zumbrota Lions Club
c/o Richard Whitaker, Sec.
797 2nd Ave.
Zumbrota, MN 55992
Ph: (507)732-7361
E-mail: rkwhit@charter.net
URL: http://www.lions5m1.org/zumbrota
Contact: Richard Whitaker, Sec.
Local. **Affiliated With:** Lions Clubs International.

Ada

13007 ■ American Chemical Society, Northwest Central Ohio Section
c/o Dr. Robert E. Lamb, Chm.
Ohio Northern Univ.
Dept. of Chemistry & Biochemistry
525 S Main St.
Ada, OH 45810-6000
Ph: (419)772-2343
Fax: (419)772-2330
E-mail: r-lamb@onu.edu
URL: National Affiliate–acswebcontent.acs.org
Contact: Dr. Robert E. Lamb, Chm.
Local. Represents the interests of individuals dedicated to the advancement of chemistry in all its branches. Provides opportunities for peer interaction and career development. **Affiliated With:** American Chemical Society.

13008 ■ American Legion, Foss-Agin-Meyer Post 185
109 N Main St.
Ada, OH 45810
Ph: (740)362-7478
Fax: (740)362-1429
URL: National Affiliate–www.legion.org
Local. Affiliated With: American Legion.

13009 ■ Association for Computing Machinery, Ohio Northern University
c/o Christina Gregg, Chair
525 S Main St.
Ada, OH 45810
Ph: (419)772-2000
URL: National Affiliate–www.acm.org
Contact: Lean Hall, Business Mgr.
Local. Biological, medical, behavioral, and computer scientists; hospital administrators; programmers and others interested in application of computer methods to biological, behavioral, and medical problems. Stimulates understanding of the use and potential of computers in the Biosciences. **Affiliated With:** Association for Computing Machinery.

13010 ■ Ohio Association of Student Financial Aid Administrators (OASFAA)
c/o Kacy L. Duling, Membership Chair
Ohio Northern Univ.
525 S Main St.
Ada, OH 45810
E-mail: k-duling@onu.edu
URL: http://www.oasfaa.org
Contact: Kacy L. Duling, Membership Chair
State. Represents the interests and needs of students, faculties and other persons involved in student financial aid. Promotes student aid legislation, regulatory analysis and professional development of financial aid legislators. Seeks to improve activities relating to the quality and improvement of student financial assistance in Higher Education institutions. **Affiliated With:** National Association of Student Financial Aid Administrators.

Adena

13011 ■ Adena Lions Club
c/o Dean Carter, Sec.
126 Park Ave.
Adena, OH 43901
Ph: (740)546-3684
E-mail: liondean@1st.net
URL: http://users.adelphia.net/~npssteve/district.htm
Contact: Dean Carter, Sec.
Local. Affiliated With: Lions Clubs International.

13012 ■ American Legion, Ohio Post 525
c/o Gilbert Koontz
PO Box 515
Adena, OH 43901
Ph: (740)362-7478
Fax: (740)362-1429
URL: National Affiliate–www.legion.org
Contact: Gilbert Koontz, Contact
Local. Affiliated With: American Legion.

13013 ■ Woman's Club of Adena
96 Park Ave.
Adena, OH 43901
Ph: (740)546-3464
E-mail: webmaster@adenanews.com
URL: http://www.adenanews.com/AWC.html
Contact: June McKim, Pres.
Local.

Akron

13014 ■ AAA Akron Auto Club
111 W Center St.
Akron, OH 44308
Ph: (330)896-7390
Fax: (330)762-9160
URL: http://www.aaa.com
Contact: Mr. Brian Thomas, Pres.
Local.

13015 ■ AAA Akron Automobile Club
506 Canton Rd.
Akron, OH 44312-2537
Ph: (330)798-0166
Local.

13016 ■ Akron Area Board of Realtors (AABOR)
PO Box 1663
Akron, OH 44309
Ph: (330)434-6677
Fax: (330)434-4641
E-mail: info@aabor.com
URL: http://www.aabor.com
Contact: Sandy Naragon, CEO
Local. Strives to develop real estate business practices. Advocates for the right to own, use and transfer real property. Provides a facility for professional development, research and exchange of information among members and the general public. **Affiliated With:** National Association of Realtors.

13017 ■ Akron Automobile Dealers Association
c/o Mr. Terry Metcalf, Exec.VP
688 Wolf Ledges Pkwy.
Akron, OH 44311
Ph: (330)434-3134
E-mail: aada1@msn.com
URL: National Affiliate–www.nada.org
Contact: Mr. Terry Metcalf, Exec.VP
Local. Affiliated With: National Automobile Dealers Association.

13018 ■ Akron BMW Motorcycle Club
c/o Michael Blum
PO Box 9059
Akron, OH 44305-0059
Ph: (330)665-1742
E-mail: mabdent@ix.netcom.com
URL: http://gozips.uakron.edu/%7Etmackey
Contact: Bill Vair, Pres.
Local.

13019 ■ Akron Character Counts
65 Steiner Ave.
Akron, OH 44301
Ph: (330)761-3067
Fax: (330)761-3240
E-mail: info@charactercountsakron.org
URL: http://charactercounts.bizland.com
Local.

13020 ■ Akron Council of Engineering and Scientific Societies
c/o Akron Public Library
808 W Market St.
Akron, OH 44303-1010
Ph: (330)535-8835
Local.

13021 ■ Akron Dental Society
565 Wolf Ledges Pkwy.
Akron, OH 44311
Ph: (330)376-3551
Fax: (330)376-2996
E-mail: info@akrondentalsociety.org
URL: http://www.akrondentalsociety.org
Contact: Rita Rocci, Exec.Dir.
Local. Represents the interests of dentists committed to the public's oral health, ethics and professional development. Encourages the improvement of the public's oral health and promotes the art and science of dentistry. **Affiliated With:** American Dental Association; Ohio Dental Association.

13022 ■ Akron Jewish Community Federation
c/o Robert Minster, Pres.
750 White Pond Dr.
Akron, OH 44320

Ph: (330)869-2424
Fax: (330)867-8498
E-mail: rminster@neo.rr.com
URL: http://www.jewishakron.org
Local.

13023 ■ Akron Society of Professional Photographers (ASPP)
Fineart Studios
2275 Manchester Rd.
Akron, OH 44314
Ph: (330)753-0312
E-mail: brent@fineartphotostudio.com
URL: http://www.akronphotographers.org
Contact: Dave Neldon, Pres.
Local. Affiliated With: Professional Photographers of America.

13024 ■ Akron Summit Convention and Visitors Bureau
77 E Mill St.
Akron, OH 44308
Ph: (330)374-7560
Fax: (330)374-7626
Free: (800)245-4254
E-mail: shamo@visitakronsummit.org
URL: http://www.visitakron-summit.org
Contact: Susan Hamo, Pres.
Local. Promotes conventions and tourism in Akron/Summit County, OH.

13025 ■ Akron Urban League
250 E Market St.
Akron, OH 44308
Ph: (330)434-3101
Fax: (330)434-2716
E-mail: aul250@aol.com
URL: http://www.akronul.org
Contact: Bernett L. Williams, Pres./CEO
Local. Affiliated With: National Urban League.

13026 ■ Alcoholics Anonymous World Services, Akron Intergroup Council
775 N Main St.
Akron, OH 44310
Ph: (330)253-8181
Fax: (330)253-8292
E-mail: info@akronaa.org
URL: http://www.akronaa.org
Local. Individuals recovering from alcoholism. AA maintains that members can solve their common problem and help others achieve sobriety through a twelve step program that includes sharing their experience, strength, and hope with each other. **Affiliated With:** Alcoholics Anonymous World Services.

13027 ■ Alzheimer's Association, Akron Tri-County Chapter
1815 W. Market St., Ste.301
Akron, OH 44313
Ph: (330)864-5646
Fax: (330)864-7336
URL: http://www.tricountyalz.org/
Family members of sufferers of Alzheimer's disease. Combats Alzheimer's disease and related disorders. (Alzheimer's disease is a progressive, degenerative brain disease in which changes occur in the central nervous system and outer region of the brain causing memory loss and other changes in thought, personality, and behavior.) Promotes research to find the cause, treatment, and cure for the disease. **Affiliated With:** Alzheimer's Association.

13028 ■ American Cancer Society, Summit Area
1900 W Market St.
Akron, OH 44313
Ph: (330)865-1200
Fax: (330)865-1205
Free: (888)227-6446
E-mail: monica.miller@cancer.org
URL: http://www.cancer.org
Contact: Monica Miller, Contact
Local. Works to eliminate cancer as a major health problem through research, education, advocacy and service. **Affiliated With:** American Cancer Society.

13029 ■ American Friends Service Committee, Northeast Ohio
c/o Kathleen Myrman, Program Support
513 W Exchange St.
Akron, OH 44302
Ph: (330)253-7151
Fax: (330)996-4664
E-mail: kmyrman@afsc.org
URL: http://www.afsc.org/greatlakes/akron.htm
Contact: Kathleen Myrman, Program Support
Local. Affiliated With: American Friends Service Committee.

13030 ■ American Legion, Akron Post 209
935 Brown St.
Akron, OH 44311
Ph: (330)785-1209
Fax: (740)362-1429
URL: National Affiliate–www.legion.org
Local. Affiliated With: American Legion.

13031 ■ American Legion, Ellet Post 794
270 High Grove Blvd.
Akron, OH 44312
Ph: (740)362-7478
Fax: (740)362-1429
URL: National Affiliate–www.legion.org
Local. Affiliated With: American Legion.

13032 ■ American Legion, Firestone Memorial Post 449
1090 Kenmore Blvd.
Akron, OH 44314
Ph: (740)362-7478
Fax: (740)362-1429
URL: National Affiliate–www.legion.org
Local. Affiliated With: American Legion.

13033 ■ American Legion, Garfield Memorial Post 566
2974 Cormany Rd.
Akron, OH 44319
Ph: (740)362-7478
Fax: (740)362-1429
URL: National Affiliate–www.legion.org
Local. Affiliated With: American Legion.

13034 ■ American Legion, Ohio Post 272
c/o John Fulton
65 N Summit St.
Akron, OH 44308
Ph: (740)362-7478
Fax: (740)362-1429
URL: National Affiliate–www.legion.org
Contact: John Fulton, Contact
Local. Affiliated With: American Legion.

13035 ■ American Legion, Viking Memorial Post 611
657 N Howard St.
Akron, OH 44310
Ph: (740)362-7478
Fax: (740)362-1429
URL: National Affiliate–www.legion.org
Local. Affiliated With: American Legion.

13036 ■ American Meteorological Society, Northeast Ohio
PO Box 8213
Akron, OH 44320-0213
Ph: (330)673-3783
E-mail: neocams@acorn.net
URL: http://www.ohioweather.net
Contact: Eric Wertz, Pres.
Founded: 1984. **Membership Dues:** $12 (annual). **Local**. People interested in meteorology/climatology. Strives to promote and educate the general public in meteorology and climatology through informative meetings and other educational activities. **Affiliated With:** American Meteorological Society. **Conventions/Meetings:** quarterly meeting, with speakers • annual picnic.

13037 ■ American Red Cross, Summit County Chapter
501 W Market St.
Akron, OH 44303
Ph: (330)535-6131
URL: http://summitcounty.redcross.org
Local.

13038 ■ American Society of Mechanical Engineers, Akron Section
c/o Brent C. Sisler, PE, Chair
2077 Stabler Rd.
Akron, OH 44313
Ph: (330)836-9238
E-mail: marybrentsisler@cs.com
URL: http://www.ecgf.uakron.edu/~asme/akron
Contact: Brent C. Sisler PE, Chair
Local. Promotes the art, science and practice of Mechanical Engineering and allied arts and sciences. Encourages original research and fosters engineering education. Promotes the technical and societal contribution of engineers. **Affiliated With:** American Society of Mechanical Engineers.

13039 ■ Association for Accounting Administration, Ohio Chapter
c/o James Fahey
106 S Main, Ste.1306
Akron, OH 44308-1418
Ph: (330)762-5022
Fax: (330)762-2727
E-mail: jim@brottmardis.com
URL: National Affiliate–www.cpaadmin.org
Contact: James Fahey, Pres.
State. Fosters the professional skills needed as firm administrators. Promotes accounting administration profession. Provides education to enhance the professional and personal competencies of accounting administration. **Affiliated With:** Association for Accounting Administration.

13040 ■ Association of Certified Fraud Examiners, Cleveland Area Chapter No. 13
207 Melody Ln.
Akron, OH 44321
Ph: (330)666-9616 (330)648-8400
E-mail: sgtfincl@aol.com
URL: National Affiliate–www.acfe.com
Contact: Mary Schultz CFE, Pres.
Local. Works to reduce the incidence of fraud and white-collar crime and to assist the members in its detection and deterrence. Sponsors training seminars on fraud and loss prevention. Administers credentialing programs for Certified Fraud Examiners. **Affiliated With:** Association of Certified Fraud Examiners.

13041 ■ Association of Community Organizations for Reform Now, Akron
19 N High St.
Akron, OH 44308
Ph: (330)376-2044
E-mail: ohacornak@acorn.org
URL: National Affiliate–www.acorn.org
Local. Affiliated With: Association of Community Organizations for Reform Now.

13042 ■ Association for Computing Machinery, University of Akron
c/o Roland Kopecky, Chair
235 Ayer Hall
Akron, OH 44325-4002
Ph: (330)972-7111
E-mail: acm@vonneumann.cs.uakron.edu
URL: http://www.cs.uakron.edu
Biological, medical, behavioral, and computer scientists; hospital administrators; programmers and others interested in application of computer methods to biological, behavioral, and medical problems. Stimulates understanding of the use and potential of computers in the Biosciences. **Affiliated With:** Association for Computing Machinery.

13043 ■ Association of Nurses in AIDS Care (ANAC)
c/o Adele Webb, PhD, RN, ACRN, FAAN
3538 Ridgewood Rd.
Akron, OH 44333
Ph: (330)670-0101
Fax: (330)670-0109
Free: (800)260-6780
E-mail: anac@anacnet.org
URL: http://www.anacnet.org/
Contact: Adele Webb PhD, Exec.Dir.
Local. **Affiliated With:** Association of Nurses in AIDS Care.

13044 ■ Association of the United States Army, Buckeye Landpower
c/o Wayne V. King
355 W Thornton St.
Akron, OH 44307
Ph: (330)762-7421
E-mail: nmonas5838@aol.com
URL: National Affiliate–www.ausa.org
Local. Represents the interests and concerns of American Soldiers. Fosters public support of the Army's role in national security. Provides professional education and information programs.

13045 ■ Autism Society of America, Ohio Chapter
701 S Main St.
Akron, OH 44311-1019
Ph: (330)376-0211
E-mail: askaso@autismohio.org
URL: http://www.autismohio.org
State. Works to improve the quality of life of all individuals with autism and their families through education, research and advocacy. Promotes public awareness and understanding of the symptoms and problems of individuals with autism.

13046 ■ Better Business Bureau of Akron
222 W Market St.
Akron, OH 44303-2111
Ph: (330)253-4590
Fax: (330)253-6249
Free: (800)825-8887
E-mail: vwlaszyn@akronbbb.org
URL: http://www.akronbbb.org
Contact: Victor J. Wlaszyn, Pres./CEO
Founded: 1920. **Members:** 2,400. **Staff:** 15. **Budget:** $1,107,000. **Local**. Provides business reliability reports and complaint handling, including informal mediation, arbitration and alternative dispute resolution, business/consumer education resources and materials, national and local charitable information and the promotion of ethical business standards and voluntary self-regulation. **Telecommunication Services:** electronic mail, info@akron.bbb.org. **Publications:** *Facts*, bimonthly. Newsletter. **Circulation:** 2,400.

13047 ■ Cable and Telecommunications Association for Marketing, Ohio Chapter
c/o Jeanie Lemond
Time Warner Cable
530 S Main St., Ste.1751
Akron, OH 44311
Ph: (330)630-7971
Fax: (330)633-2599
E-mail: jlemond@neo.rr.com
URL: http://www.ctamohio.com
Contact: Jeanie Lemond, Contact
State. Works for the development of consumer marketing excellence in cable television, new media and telecommunications services. Provides marketing education and networking opportunities to individuals who work for cable companies. **Affiliated With:** CTAM - Cable and Telecommunications Association for Marketing. **Publications:** *Ohio Connections*. Newsletter. Alternate Formats: online.

13048 ■ Christ Child Society of Akron
PO Box 5855
Akron, OH 44372
E-mail: christ_child_soc_akron@hotmail.com
URL: http://www.christchildsocietyakron.org
Local. **Affiliated With:** National Christ Child Society.

13049 ■ Cleveland/Akron 9to5
c/o Kathy Dean
215 Kenwood
Akron, OH 44313
Ph: (330)836-3217
URL: National Affiliate–www.9to5.org
Contact: Kathy Dean, Contact
Local. **Affiliated With:** 9 to 5, National Association of Working Women.

13050 ■ Easter Seals Northeast Ohio
3085 W Market St., Ste.124
Akron, OH 44333-3363
Ph: (330)836-9741
Fax: (330)836-4967
Free: (800)589-6834
E-mail: sdunn@eastersealsneo.org
URL: http://neohio.easterseals.com
Contact: Ms. Sheila Dunn, Pres./CEO
Local. Provides services for children and adults with disabilities or special needs, and supports their families. **Affiliated With:** Easter Seals.

13051 ■ Foster Grandparent Program of Summit County
250 Opportunity Pkwy.
Akron, OH 44307-2232
Ph: (330)253-8806
Fax: (330)253-8836
E-mail: ccooper@aksumcom.org
URL: National Affiliate–www.seniorcorps.org
Contact: Car Lee Cooper, Dir.
Local. Serves as mentors, tutors and caregivers for at-risk children and youth with special needs. Provides older Americans the opportunity to put their life experiences to work for local communities.

13052 ■ Funeral Consumers Alliance - Akron Region
3300 Morewood Rd.
Akron, OH 44333
Ph: (330)836-4418
Fax: (330)849-1030
E-mail: acams@neobright.net
URL: http://www.funerals.org/akron
Contact: Julia Glass, Membership Sec.
Local. Promotes a consumer's right to choose a dignified, meaningful, affordable funeral. Provides educational material to the public and affiliates. Monitors the funeral and cemetery industry for consumers nationwide. Responds to consumer complaints. Maintains speakers' bureau. **Affiliated With:** Funeral Consumers Alliance.

13053 ■ Girl Scouts of The Western Reserve
345 White Pond Dr.
Akron, OH 44320-1155
Ph: (330)864-9933
Fax: (330)864-5720
Free: (800)852-4474
E-mail: corporate@girlscoutswr.org
URL: http://www.girlscoutswr.org
Local. Young girls and adult volunteers, corporate, government and individual supporters. Strives to develop potential and leadership skills among its members. Conducts trainings, educational programs and outdoor activities.

13054 ■ Greater Akron Chamber of Commerce
1 Cascade Plaza, 17th Fl.
Akron, OH 44308-1192
Ph: (330)376-5550
Fax: (330)379-3164
Free: (800)621-8001
E-mail: info@greaterakronchamber.org
URL: http://www.greaterakronchamber.org
Contact: Daniel C. Colantone, CEO & Pres.
Members: 1,900. **Regional**. Serves business organizations to improve the economic and social status of Greater Akron. **Computer Services:** Mailing lists, of members and interested individuals. **Publications:** *Directions*, bimonthly. Newsletters. Contains information on the current and upcoming events of the Chapter, and other informative articles for the readers. **Advertising:** accepted. Alternate Formats: online.

13055 ■ Greater Akron Orchid Society
c/o Barbara Ford
2618 Mayfair Cir.
Akron, OH 44312
Ph: (216)644-3168
E-mail: baford@goodyear.com
URL: National Affiliate–www.orchidweb.org
Contact: Barbara Ford, Contact
Local. Professional growers, botanists, hobbyists, and others interested in extending the knowledge, production, use, and appreciation of orchids. **Affiliated With:** American Orchid Society.

13056 ■ Hands of Hope
c/o Tammy McIntosh-Palmer
62 N Summit St.
Akron, OH 44308
Ph: (330)434-7702
Fax: (330)434-7739
E-mail: handsofhope@quantum-mfg.com
URL: http://www.quantum-mfg.com
Contact: Tammy McIntosh, Dir.
Founded: 1999. **Budget:** $30,000. **Regional Groups:** 1. **Local**. Aims to meet natural, spiritual, and empowering needs of the community.

13057 ■ Home Builders Association of Portage and Summit Counties
c/o Carmine Torio, BIAE
799 White Pond Dr.
Akron, OH 44320-1136
Ph: (330)869-6800
Fax: (330)869-5506
E-mail: carminet@akronhba.com
URL: http://www.akronhba.com
Contact: Carmine Torio, Exec.Dir.
Local. Single and multifamily home builders, commercial builders, and others associated with the building industry. **Affiliated With:** National Association of Home Builders. **Formerly:** (2005) Home Builders Association of Greater Akron.

13058 ■ Institute of Management Accountants, Akron Chapter
c/o Diane L. Saulino, Pres.
Indus. Tube and Steel Corp.
1303 Home Ave.
Akron, OH 44310
Ph: (330)633-8541 (330)869-4933
Fax: (330)633-9756
E-mail: dsaulino@industrialtube.com
URL: http://www2.uakron.edu/ima
Contact: Diane L. Saulino, Pres.
Founded: 1939. **Members:** 345. **Local**. Promotes professional and ethical standards. Equips members and students with knowledge and training required for the accounting profession. **Affiliated With:** Institute of Management Accountants. **Publications:** *The Summit Report*. Newsletter. Alternate Formats: online. **Conventions/Meetings:** monthly dinner, with speakers and networking opportunities - every third Wednesday except December.

13059 ■ International Brotherhood of Electrical Workers, AFL-CIO, CFL - Local Union 306
2650 S Main St., Ste.200
Akron, OH 44319
Ph: (330)245-2240
Fax: (330)245-2209
E-mail: steve@ibew306.org
URL: http://www.ibew306.org
Contact: Michael D. Kammer, Pres.
Members: 768. **Local**. Works to elevate the moral, intellectual and social conditions of workers. **Affiliated With:** International Brotherhood of Electrical Workers.

13060 ■ International Brotherhood of Teamsters, Chauffeurs, Warehousemen and Helpers of America, AFL-CIO - Local Union 24
727 Grant St.
Akron, OH 44311-2197
E-mail: info@teamsters24.org
URL: http://teamsters24.org
Contact: Kenneth A. Ramser, Pres.
Members: 1,371. **Local. Affiliated With:** International Brotherhood of Teamsters.

13061 ■ Junior Achievement Akron
c/o David Best, Pres.
PO Box 26006
Akron, OH 44319
Ph: (330)434-1875
Fax: (330)434-2202
E-mail: staff@ja-akron.org
URL: http://akronarea.ja.org
Local.

13062 ■ Korean War Veterans Association, Akron Regional Chapter
c/o Edward P. Rose
1233 Lexington Ave.
Akron, OH 44310
Ph: (330)929-1633
URL: National Affiliate–www.kwva.org
Contact: Edward P. Rose, Contact
Local. Affiliated With: Korean War Veterans Association.

13063 ■ League of Women Voters in the Akron Area (LWVAA)
380 Mineola Ave.
Akron, OH 44320
Ph: (330)836-7079
E-mail: lwvaa@aol.com
URL: http://lwvaa.org
Contact: Mary Lou Gault, Pres.
Founded: 1920. **Members:** 100. **Membership Dues:** individual (in voting age), $45 (annual). **Local.** Aims to encourage the informed and active participation of all citizens in government and to influence public policy through education and advocacy. Sponsors voter's guide, candidate's meetings, and discussion of governmental issues. **Publications:** *Voter's Guide at Election Time*, monthly. Newsletter • Handbook, annual. **Price:** included in membership dues. **Conventions/Meetings:** monthly meeting.

13064 ■ Mason Contractors Associations of Akron and Vicinity
76 E North St.
Akron, OH 44304
Ph: (330)762-9951
Fax: (330)762-9960
E-mail: info@akronmca.org
URL: http://www.akronmca.com
Contact: Terry Moser, Pres.
Local. Promotes and encourages efficiency in the art of masonry construction. Encourages and aids in the education of apprentices in the industry, and to generally encourage the movement to build with brick and other masonry products. **Affiliated With:** Mason Contractors Association of America.

13065 ■ Medical Society of Greater Akron (MSGA)
653 W Market St., Ste.101
Akron, OH 44303-1438
Ph: (330)376-3222
Fax: (330)376-3331
E-mail: medicalsociety@choiceonemail.com
URL: http://www.msgaonline.com
Contact: Anita Rabaa, Exec.Dir.
Local. Advances the art and science of medicine. Promotes patient care and the betterment of public health. **Affiliated With:** Ohio State Medical Association.

13066 ■ Military Officers Association of America, Ohio Western Reserve Chapter
PO Box 1263
Akron, OH 44309-1263
E-mail: rakas1@aol.com
URL: National Affiliate–www.moaa.org
Local. Affiliated With: Military Officers Association of America.

13067 ■ Muslim Students' Association - University of Akron
c/o Musa Abdullah, Pres.
107 Wills Ave., Apt. 4
Akron, OH 44302
Ph: (330)762-3435
E-mail: msauakron@yahoo.com
URL: http://www.uakron.edu/msa
Contact: Musa Abdullah, Pres.
Local. Muslim students. Seeks to advance the interests of members; works to enable members to practice Islam as a complete way of life. **Affiliated With:** Muslim Students Association of the United States and Canada.

13068 ■ National Active and Retired Federal Employees Association - Portage Path 168
1693 Ewart Dr.
Akron, OH 44306-4111
Ph: (330)784-2558
URL: National Affiliate–www.narfe.org
Contact: Robert C. Graham, Contact
Local. Protects the retirement future of employees through education. Informs members on issues affecting the retirement. **Affiliated With:** National Association of Retired Federal Employees.

13069 ■ National Audubon Society - Greater Akron
PO Box 80056
Akron, OH 44308
Ph: (330)920-9138
E-mail: info@akronaudubon.org
URL: http://www.akronaudubon.org
Contact: Mark Purdy, Pres.
Local.

13070 ■ National Electrical Contractors Association, North Central Ohio Chapter (NECA)
495 Wolf Ledges Pkwy., Ste.No. 4
Akron, OH 44311-1049
Ph: (330)384-1242
Fax: (330)384-1244
E-mail: tshreves@necacontractors.org
URL: http://www.necacontractors.org
Contact: Thomas W. Shreves, Contact
Founded: 1948. **Members:** 50. **Staff:** 3. **Local.** Trade association. Provides contract negotiations, labor relations, pension administration and management, and supervisory education for electrical contractors in the greater Akron, Canton, and Steubenville, OH areas. **Affiliated With:** National Electrical Contractors Association.

13071 ■ National Federation of the Blind, Greater Summit County
2337 Newton St.
Akron, OH 44305
Ph: (330)733-8251
Fax: (330)733-8251
E-mail: everettg@stellarmerchandisers.com
URL: http://www.angelfire.com/oh2/nfbofakron
Contact: Beth Miller, Pres.
Local. Works to help blind persons achieve self-confidence and self-respect. Acts as a vehicle for collective self-expression by the blind. Provides education, information and referral services, scholarships, literature, and publications about blindness.

13072 ■ National Organization for Women - Akron Area
c/o Gail McWilliams, Pres.
513 W Exchange St.
Akron, OH 44302
Ph: (330)253-7151
E-mail: akronareanow@yahoo.com
URL: http://www.akrobiz.com/akronnow
Contact: Gail McWilliams, Pres.
Local. Affiliated With: National Organization for Women.

13073 ■ Navy League of the United States, Akron-Canton
c/o Anthony C. Marino, Pres.
255 N Portage Path, Apt. 410
Akron, OH 44303-1248
Ph: (330)869-9492
E-mail: marn862@aol.com
URL: National Affiliate–www.navyleague.org
Contact: Anthony C. Marino, Pres.
Local. Civilian organization that supports U.S. capability to keep the sea lanes open through a strong, viable Navy, Marine Corps, Coast Guard, and Merchant Marine. Seeks to awaken interest and cooperation of U.S. citizens in matters serving to aid, improve, and develop the efficiency of U.S. naval and maritime forces and equipment. **Affiliated With:** Navy League of the United States.

13074 ■ North Coast Woodturners (NCWT)
1789 Cynthia Cir.
Akron, OH 44333
Ph: (330)836-0147
E-mail: jmaier1@worldnet.att.net
URL: http://ncwt.org
Contact: Rick Maier, Pres.
Members: 100. **Membership Dues:** $15 (annual). **Local.** Promotes the art of woodturning. **Libraries: Type:** not open to the public. **Holdings:** 150. **Subjects:** woodturning, woodworking. **Affiliated With:** American Association of Woodturners. **Publications:** Newsletter, monthly. **Price:** free. **Conventions/Meetings:** monthly meeting (exhibits).

13075 ■ Northeast Ohio American Society for Training and Development (NEO-ASTD)
PO Box 2363
Akron, OH 44309
E-mail: president@neoastd.com
URL: http://www.neoastd.org
Contact: Hazel Tabor, Pres.
Local. Promotes workplace learning and the improvement of skills of workplace professionals. Provides resource and professional development to individuals in the field of learning and development. Recognizes and sets standards for learning and performance professionals. **Affiliated With:** American Society for Training and Development.

13076 ■ Ohio and Erie Canalway Coalition (OECC)
520 S Main St., Ste.2452
Akron, OH 44311
Ph: (330)434-5657
E-mail: info@ohioeriecanal.org
URL: http://www.ohioeriecanal.org
Contact: Daniel M. Rice, Pres./CEO
Founded: 1989. **Members:** 1,500. **Membership Dues:** individual, $15 (annual) • family, $25 (annual) • partner, $100 (annual) • corporate sponsor, $250 (annual) • corporate benefactor, $500 (annual) • heritage partner, $1,000 (annual) • student, senior, $10 (annual). **Budget:** $210,000. **Local.** Seeks to stimulate public interest and support for the protection, preservation, development and enhancement of the historical, natural and recreational resources along the route of the Ohio and Erie Canal, and the Ohio and Erie Canal Heritage Corridor. **Formerly:** (2006) Ohio and Erie Canal Corridor Coalition. **Publications:** *Heritage Partnership Handbook*. Examines the development of community partnerships. • *Towpath Companion: Travelers Guide to the Ohio and Erie Canal Towpath Trail*. Features an educational and interpretive guide to the Ohio and Erie Canal Towpath Trail. **Conventions/Meetings:** quarterly meeting, for the public • annual meeting.

13077 ■ Ohio Health Care Association, District 12
c/o Mary Harrison, Chair
Valley View Nursing & Rehabilitation
721 Hickory St.
Akron, OH 44303
Ph: (330)762-6486
Fax: (330)762-3517
E-mail: chcmary@hotmail.com
URL: http://www.ohca.org
Contact: Mary Harrison, Chair
Local. Promotes professionalism and ethical behavior of individuals providing long-term care delivery for patients and for the general public. Provides information, education and administrative tools to enhance the quality of long-term care. Improves the standards of service and administration of member nursing homes. **Affiliated With:** American Health Care Association.

13078 ■ Ohio Multi-County Development Corp. (OMCDC)
c/o Rose Juriga
680 E Market St., Ste.307
Akron, OH 44304-1614
Ph: (330)315-3718
Fax: (330)374-5117
E-mail: michael.gashash@commhealthcenter.org
URL: http://www.omcdc.org
Contact: John F. Herwick, Pres.
State.

13079 ■ Ohio Society of Radiologic Technologists (OSRT)
1985 Preston Ave.
Akron, OH 44305
Ph: (330)784-9042
Free: (866)405-OSRT
E-mail: osrt@neo.rr.com
URL: http://www.osrt.org
Contact: Dave Whipple RT, Exec.Sec.
State. Represents the professional society of radiologic technologists. Advances education and research in the radiologic sciences. Evaluates quality patient care. Improves the welfare and socioeconomics of radiologic technologists. **Affiliated With:** American Society of Radiologic Technologists.

13080 ■ Phi Theta Kappa - Alpha Alpha Psi Chapter
c/o Sheldon Wrice
Shrank Hall N 152
302 E Buchtel Ave.
Akron, OH 44325-6105
Ph: (330)972-6023
E-mail: swrice1@uakron.edu
URL: http://www.ptk.org/directories/chapters/OH/308-1.htm
Contact: Sheldon Wrice, Advisor
Local. Affiliated With: Phi Theta Kappa, International Honor Society.

13081 ■ Planned Parenthood of Summit, Portage, and Medina Counties (PPSPM)
444 W Exchange St.
Akron, OH 44302
Ph: (330)535-2671
Fax: (330)535-2987
Free: (800)230-PLAN
E-mail: questions@ppinfo.org
URL: http://ppinfo.org
Contact: Roberta E. Aber, Exec.Dir.
Founded: 1966. **Budget:** $2,300,000. **Nonmembership. Local.** Participants are individuals who support the organization through donations. Dedicated to meeting family planning, health care and educational needs through clinic services and school and community programs. **Libraries: Type:** reference. **Holdings:** books, periodicals, video recordings. **Subjects:** human sexuality, reproduction. **Affiliated With:** Planned Parenthood Federation of America. **Formerly:** (1983) Planned Parenthood Association of Summit County. **Publications:** *Agency Brochure* • *The Link* • *Nobody's Fool*. Booklet • *Planned Parenthood Voice*, semiannual. Newsletter • *SafeR Sex Card*. Brochure • *Spotlight*, 3/year. Newsletter • *Time Out*. **Conventions/Meetings:** annual meeting - always spring in Akron, OH.

13082 ■ Project: LEARN of Summit County
60 S High St.
Akron, OH 44326
Ph: (330)434-9461
Fax: (330)643-9195
E-mail: info@projectlearnsummit.org
URL: http://www.projectlearnsummit.org
Contact: Rick McIntosh, Exec.Dir.
Founded: 1982. **Membership Dues:** friends of literacy, $50 (annual). **Staff:** 19. **Budget:** $350,000. **Local.** Volunteer organization providing free, small group classes, and one-on-one tutoring in reading, math, computers, and writing to illiterate adults. GED and ESOL also offered. LEARN stands for Let Every Adult Read Now. Sponsors annual Corporate Spelling Bee and Scrabble Tournament for Literacy. **Special Interest Groups:** Friends of Literacy. **Affiliated With:** Laubach Literacy International. **Publications:** *Update*, quarterly. Newsletter • *Update Two*, monthly. Newsletter • Annual Report. **Conventions/Meetings:** monthly Tutor Training - seminar.

13083 ■ PRSA, Akron Area Chapter
PO Box 13038
Akron, OH 44334
Ph: (330)676-1101
Fax: (330)676-1101
E-mail: prsaaa@neo.rr.com
URL: http://www.PRSAAkron.org
Contact: Ms. Laura Guritza, Administrator
Members: 100. **Membership Dues:** regular, associate, retired, $40 (annual). **Local.** Seeks to advance the profession. Represents professionals from corporate, healthcare, nonprofit, agency, media, and academic realms. **Affiliated With:** Public Relations Society of America.

13084 ■ Psi Chi, National Honor Society in Psychology - University of Akron
c/o Dept. of Psychology
Box 206
302 E Buchtel Ave.
Akron, OH 44325-4301
Ph: (330)972-7280 (330)972-8372
Fax: (330)972-5174
E-mail: psi_ua@hotmail.com
URL: National Affiliate–www.psichi.org
Contact: Dennis Doverspike PhD, Advisor
Local.

13085 ■ RSVP Akron
c/o Inese Alvarez, Dir.
415 S Portage Path
Akron, OH 44320-2327
Ph: (330)762-8645
Fax: (330)762-5571
E-mail: rsvpsummit@matureservices.org
URL: http://www.seniorcorps.gov/about/programs/rsvp_state.asp?usestateabbr=oh&Search4.x=0&Search4.y=0
Contact: Inese Alvarez, Dir.
Local. Additional Websites: http://matureservices.org. **Affiliated With:** Retired and Senior Volunteer Program.

13086 ■ Ruffed Grouse Society, Northern Ohio Chapter
c/o Scott Galloway
Galloway Photography
2772 Copley Rd.
Akron, OH 44321
Ph: (330)666-9377
E-mail: galloway@raex.com
URL: National Affiliate–www.ruffedgrousesociety.org
Contact: Scott Galloway, Contact
Local. Affiliated With: Ruffed Grouse Society.

13087 ■ Scenic Ohio
c/o Christine Freitag, Chm.
PO Box 5835
Akron, OH 44372
Ph: (330)865-9715
E-mail: director@scenicohio.org
URL: http://www.scenicohio.org
Contact: Christine Freitag, Chm.
State. Affiliated With: Scenic America.

13088 ■ SCORE Akron
Natl. City Bank Bldg.
One Cascade Plz., 18th Fl.
Akron, OH 44308
Ph: (330)379-3163
Fax: (330)379-3164
Free: (877)257-2673
E-mail: akronsscore81@aol.com
URL: http://akronscore.org
Contact: Ron Stallings, Chm.
Founded: 1965. **Local.** Provides professional guidance and information to maximize the success of existing and emerging small businesses. Promotes entrepreneur education in Akron area, Ohio. **Affiliated With:** SCORE.

13089 ■ Society of Consumer Affairs Professionals in Business, Ohio Chapter
c/o Dana Allender, Dir. of New Business Development
InfoCision Mgt. Corp.
325 Springside Dr.
Akron, OH 44333
Ph: (330)670-5141
Fax: (330)668-3055
E-mail: ohio@socap.org
URL: National Affiliate–www.socap.org
State. Affiliated With: Society of Consumer Affairs Professionals in Business.

13090 ■ Special Libraries Association, Cleveland Chapter
c/o Susan Lloyd, Pres.-Elect
FirstEnergy Corp.
Bus. Info. Ctr.
76 S Main St.
Akron, OH 44308-1890
Ph: (330)384-4934
Fax: (330)255-1099
E-mail: lloyds@firstenergycorp.com
URL: http://www.sla.org/chapter/ccle
Contact: Susan Lloyd, Pres.-Elect
Local. Seeks to advance the leadership role of special librarians. Promotes and strengthens members through learning, advocacy and networking initiatives. **Affiliated With:** Special Libraries Association.

13091 ■ STARFLEET: USS Liberator
PO Box 13075
Akron, OH 44333
E-mail: liberator@regionone.net
URL: http://www.regionone.net/Liberator
Local. Affiliated With: STARFLEET.

13092 ■ Subcontractors Association of Northeast Ohio (SANEO)
76 E North St.
Akron, OH 44304
Ph: (330)762-9951
Fax: (330)762-9960
Free: (800)479-5557
E-mail: info@saneo.com
URL: http://www.asaneo.com
Contact: Lynne Black, Exec.Dir.
Founded: 1976. **Members:** 260. **Staff:** 4. **Local. Additional Websites:** http://www.saneo.com.

13093 ■ Summit County Chapter of Ohio Genealogical Society
PO Box 2232
Akron, OH 44309-2232
Ph: (330)699-1817
E-mail: summitogs@ald.net
URL: http://spot.acorn.net/gen
Contact: Gerald Huhn, Pres.
Membership Dues: individual, $10 (annual) • family, $11 (annual). **Local.** Works to create and build interests in preserving and collecting historical and

genealogical records of Summit County and the State of Ohio. **Affiliated With:** Ohio Genealogical Society.

13094 ■ Summit County Historical Society (SCHS)
550 Copley Rd.
Akron, OH 44320
Ph: (330)535-1120
Fax: (330)535-0250
E-mail: schs@summithistory.org
URL: http://www.summithistory.org
Contact: Paula G. Moran, Exec.Dir.
Founded: 1924. **Members:** 470. **Membership Dues:** general, $40 (annual). **Staff:** 6. **Budget:** $200,000. **Local**. Focuses on preservation, interpretation and education of Summit County, Ohio history. Maintains Perkins Stone Mansion, home of Akron's founding family, John Brown House, home of the famous abolitionist, and Old Stone School. **Affiliated With:** Western Reserve Historical Society. **Publications:** *Old Portage Trail Review*, bimonthly. Newsletter. **Price:** included in membership dues. **Circulation:** 1,000. **Conventions/Meetings:** annual meeting.

13095 ■ Summit County REACT
PO Box 281
Akron, OH 44309-0281
Ph: (330)560-5110
E-mail: react@personalizedsafetyservices.com
URL: http://www.reactintl.org/teaminfo/usa_teams/teams-usoh.htm
Local. Provides volunteer public service and emergency communications through the use of radios (Citizen Band, General Mobile Radio Service, UHF and HAM). Coordinates with radio industries and government on safety communication matters and supports charitable activities and community organizations.

13096 ■ Summit Education Initiative (SEI)
520 S Main St., Ste.2433-C
Akron, OH 44311-1010
Ph: (330)535-8833
Fax: (330)535-0242
E-mail: info@seisummit.org
URL: http://www.seisummit.org
Contact: Kym Lazar, Off.Mgr.
Local.

13097 ■ Tadmor Shriners
c/o D. L. Pepper, P.P.
3000 Krebs Dr.
Akron, OH 44319
Ph: (330)644-8494
Fax: (330)644-5008
E-mail: tadmor1@ezo.net
URL: National Affiliate–www.shrinershq.org
Contact: D. L. Pepper P.P., Contact
Local. Affiliated With: Imperial Council of the Ancient Arabic Order of the Nobles of the Mystic Shrine for North America.

13098 ■ Tire and Rim Association (TRA)
175 Montrose W Ave.
Akron, OH 44321
Ph: (330)666-8121
Fax: (330)666-8340
E-mail: tra@us-tra.org
URL: http://www.us-tra.org
State.

13099 ■ Tire Society
PO Box 1502
Akron, OH 44309-1502
Ph: (330)929-5238
Fax: (330)929-3576
E-mail: tiresociety@neo.rr.com
URL: http://www.tiresociety.org
Contact: Howard R. Snyder, Office Mgr.
Members: 300. **Membership Dues:** full, $200 (annual) • non-employed retiree, $100 (annual) • full-time student, $50 (annual). **Regional**. Seeks to increase and disseminate knowledge on the science and technology of tires. **Publications:** *Tire Science and Technology*, quarterly. Journal. ISSN: 0090-8657. **Conventions/Meetings:** annual conference, tire science and technology.

13100 ■ Tri-County National Association of The Remodeling Industry
c/o Pat Jones
1576 Akron Peninsula Rd.
Akron, OH 44313
Ph: (330)920-1379
Fax: (330)920-1618
E-mail: kera365@aol.com
URL: National Affiliate–www.nari.org
Contact: Pat Jones, Contact
Local. Remodeling contractors, manufacturers of building products, lending institutions, and wholesalers and distributors. Promotes the common business interests of those engaged in the home improvement and remodeling industries. Encourages ethical conduct, good business practices, and professionalism in the home improvement and remodeling industry. **Affiliated With:** National Association of the Remodeling Industry.

13101 ■ United Way of Summit County
c/o Bob Kulinski, Pres.
90 N Prospect St.
PO Box 1260
Akron, OH 44309-1260
Ph: (330)762-7601
Fax: (330)762-0317
E-mail: bkulinski@uwsummit.org
URL: http://www.uwsummit.org
Contact: Bob Kulinski, Pres.
Founded: 1919. **Staff:** 21. **Budget:** $10,200,000. **State Groups:** 1. **Local Groups:** 1. **Nonmembership. Local.** Conducts annual fund drive to support local health and human service agencies. **Affiliated With:** United Way of America. **Publications:** *Caring Connection*, bimonthly. Newsletter. Feature based newsletter on programs and services. **Price:** free. **Circulation:** 4,000.

13102 ■ USA Wrestling-Ohio (USAWO)
1679 Brookwood Dr.
Akron, OH 44313-5065
Ph: (330)867-6474
Fax: (330)252-5105
Free: (800)331-3044
E-mail: tknupp@claytongrp.com
URL: http://www.usawrestling-ohio.org
Contact: Tom Knupp, State Dir.
State. Affiliated With: U.S.A. Wrestling.

13103 ■ Women in the Wind - Akron Chapter
PO Box 4204
Akron, OH 44321
Ph: (330)848-0163
E-mail: witw@sbcglobal.net
URL: http://witw.netfirms.com
Contact: Sue B., VP
Founded: 1989. **Membership Dues:** regular, $35 (annual). **Local**. Women motorcyclists and enthusiasts. **Affiliated With:** Women in the Wind.

13104 ■ Women's Network
670 W. Exchange St.
Akron, OH 44303-1406
Ph: (330)379-2772
Fax: (330)379-9283
E-mail: jsparks@womennet.org
URL: http://www.womennet.org

13105 ■ World Future Society, Akron (Northeastern Ohio)
c/o William H. Fisher
Org. and Community Effectiveness
728 Kenmore Blvd.
Akron, OH 44314
Ph: (330)753-4995
Fax: (330)753-4915
E-mail: renovate@earthlink.net
URL: National Affiliate–www.wfs.org
Contact: William H. Fisher, Contact
Local. Individuals interested in forecasts and ideas about the future. **Affiliated With:** World Future Society.

Albany

13106 ■ Veterans of Foreign Wars 9893
Twp Rd. 3 & County Rd. 10
Albany, OH 45710
Ph: (740)698-8841
Local.

Alliance

13107 ■ Alliance Area Chamber of Commerce (AACC)
210 E Main St.
Alliance, OH 44601
Ph: (330)823-6260
Fax: (330)823-4434
E-mail: info@allianceohiochamber.org
URL: http://www.allianceohiochamber.org
Contact: R. Mark Locke, Pres.
Founded: 1915. **Members:** 380. **Local**. Promotes business and community development in the Alliance, OH area. Sponsors Carnation City Festival. **Affiliated With:** U.S. Chamber of Commerce. **Publications:** *Alliance for your Future*. Video • *Image Booklet*, triennial • *Update*, quarterly. Newsletter • *Who's Who*, biennial. Brochure. **Conventions/Meetings:** annual meeting.

13108 ■ The Alliance Genealogical Society (TAGS)
PO Box 3630
Alliance, OH 44601
E-mail: tag_ogs@hotmail.com
URL: http://www.rootsweb.com/~ohags
Contact: Janet Vogus, Pres.
Founded: 1982. **Membership Dues:** single/joint, $12 (annual). **Local**. Represents a group of Alliance residents who are interested in tracing ancestry. **Affiliated With:** Ohio Genealogical Society. **Publications:** *Atwater Township, Protage County Records 1808-1896*, periodic, published as necessary. Report. Includes cemetery and burial record. **Price:** $15.00 plus shipping and handling ($2.50) and $.90 sales tax for Ohio residents • *Early Marriage Records of Stark County, Ohio 1856-1870*, periodic, published as necessary. Report. **Price:** $22.00 plus shipping and handling ($2.50) • *Early Marriage Records of Stark County, Ohio 1841-1855*, periodic, published as necessary. Report. **Price:** $18.00 plus shipping and handling ($2.50) • *Early Marriages of Stark County, Ohio 1809-1840*, periodic, published as necessary. Report. Includes several nearby townships in Carroll and Summit Counties. **Price:** $12.00 plus shipping and handling ($2.50) and $.72 sales tax for Ohio residents • *Post Office Records of Alliance, Ohio Vol. 1*, periodic, published as necessary. Report. Includes money orders received, box rentals, dead letters, and key deposits. **Price:** $20.00 plus shipping and handling ($2.50).

13109 ■ Alliance-Salem ALU
430 N Union Ave.
Alliance, OH 44601
Ph: (330)821-9934
Fax: (330)823-1399
URL: National Affiliate–www.naifa.org
Local. Represents the interest of insurance and financial advisors. Advocates for a positive legislative and regulatory environment. Enhances business and professional skills of members. **Affiliated With:** National Association of Insurance and Financial Advisors.

13110 ■ American Legion, Alliance Post 166
c/o Charles C. Weybrecht, Adj.
141 W Main St.
Alliance, OH 44601
Ph: (740)362-7478
Fax: (740)362-1429
URL: National Affiliate–www.legion.org
Contact: Charles C. Weybrecht, Adj.
Local. Affiliated With: American Legion.

13111 ■ American Legion, Ohio Post 791
c/o William Taylor
78 S Webb Ave.
Alliance, OH 44601
Ph: (740)362-7478
Fax: (740)362-1429
URL: National Affiliate–www.legion.org
Contact: William Taylor, Contact
Local. **Affiliated With:** American Legion.

13112 ■ Association for Iron and Steel Technology Northeastern Ohio Chapter
c/o Mr. Rich Kurz, Sec.-Treas.
East Ohio Machinery Co.
22831 State Rte. 62
Alliance, OH 44601-9026
Ph: (330)821-7198
E-mail: rkurz@eohiomach.com
URL: http://www.aistech.org/chapters/mc_northeasternohio.htm
Contact: Mr. Rich Kurz, Sec.-Treas.
Local. Seeks to provide a medium of communication and cooperation among those interested in any phase of ferrous metallurgy and materials science and technology. Encourages interest in and the advancement of education in metallurgical and materials science and engineering related to the iron and steel industry. Conducts short continuing education courses. **Affiliated With:** Association for Iron and Steel Technology.

13113 ■ Hearts for Haiti
c/o Joel Nelson
2106 Watson Ave.
Alliance, OH 44601-4971
URL: http://www.hearts4haiti.com
Contact: Joel Nelson, Contact
Local.

13114 ■ International Union of Electronic, Electrical, Salaried, Machine and Furniture Workers, AFL-CIO-CLC - Local Union 750
22753 Lake Park
Alliance, OH 44601
Ph: (330)821-7274
E-mail: cwhaley@neo.rr.com
URL: http://www.genieunion.com
Contact: Clint Whaley, Pres.
Members: 175. **Local**. **Affiliated With:** International Union of Electronic, Electrical, Salaried, Machine, and Furniture Workers.

13115 ■ Limaville Lions Club
c/o V. Carmen Pritchard, Pres.
13910 Reeder Ave.
Alliance, OH 44601
Ph: (330)935-2948
E-mail: carmenp@aol.com
URL: http://www.lions13d.org
Contact: V. Carmen Pritchard, Pres.
Local. **Affiliated With:** Lions Clubs International.

13116 ■ Lions Club of Alliance
22625 State Rte. 62
Alliance, OH 44601
Ph: (330)823-2920 (330)821-1386
E-mail: elvin@barnett-insurance.com
URL: http://allianceoh.lionwap.org
Contact: Mark Mullet, Pres.
Local. **Affiliated With:** Lions Clubs International.

13117 ■ Mothers Against Drunk Driving, Stark County
PO Box 2125
Alliance, OH 44601
Ph: (330)821-0415
Free: (888)435-6233
E-mail: maddstarkcounty@aol.com
URL: National Affiliate–www.madd.org/
Contact: Milly Hurford, Coord.
Victims of drunk driving crashes; concerned citizens. Encourages citizen participation in working towards reform of the drunk driving problem and the prevention of underage drinking. Acts as the voice of victims of drunk driving crashes by speaking on their behalf to communities, businesses, and educational groups. **Affiliated With:** Mothers Against Drunk Driving.

13118 ■ Mount Union College Association for Computing Machinery Student Chapter
c/o James Klayder
1972 Clark Ave.
Alliance, OH 44601
E-mail: socs@muc.edu
URL: http://raider.muc.edu/Organizations/socs/index.htm
Contact: Gina Grisola, Treas.
Local. Biological, medical, behavioral, and computer scientists; hospital administrators; programmers and others interested in application of computer methods to biological, behavioral, and medical problems. Stimulates understanding of the use and potential of computers in the Biosciences. **Affiliated With:** Association for Computing Machinery.

13119 ■ National Association of Student Personnel Administrators, Ohio
c/o Douglas Oblander, Coor.
Mt. Union Coll.
1972 Clark Ave.
Alliance, OH 44601
Ph: (330)823-2243
Fax: (330)829-8737
E-mail: oblandda@muc.edu
URL: National Affiliate–www.naspa.org
Contact: Douglas Oblander, Coor.
State. Provides professional development and advocacy for student affairs educators and administrators. Seeks to promote, assess and support student learning through leadership. **Affiliated With:** National Association of Student Personnel Administrators.

13120 ■ Sons of Norway, Arctic Circle Lodge 5-662
c/o Joelle H. Mc Ilroy, Pres.
8754 Lynn Park St. NE
Alliance, OH 44601-9747
Ph: (330)935-2677
E-mail: rmcilroy@alliancelink.com
URL: http://www.sofn-arcticcircle.com
Contact: Joelle H. Mc Ilroy, Pres.
Local. **Affiliated With:** Sons of Norway.

13121 ■ STARFLEET: USS Arizona
c/o Kristin Keller-Williams
PO Box 3214
Alliance, OH 44601
E-mail: garfieldksk@aol.com
URL: http://www.regionone.net
Contact: Kristin Keller-Williams, Contact
State. **Affiliated With:** STARFLEET.

Amanda

13122 ■ American Legion, Ohio Post 57
c/o Clyde A. Smith
PO Box 102
Amanda, OH 43102
Ph: (740)362-7478
Fax: (740)362-1429
URL: National Affiliate–www.legion.org
Contact: Clyde A. Smith, Contact
Local. **Affiliated With:** American Legion.

13123 ■ Wrinkled Rescue/Chinese Shar-Pei Rescue
c/o Carol A.T. Lint
13689 Burns Rd.
Amanda, OH 43102
Ph: (740)969-2248
Fax: (740)969-2248
E-mail: wrinkledrsc@ohiohills.com
URL: http://www.geocities.com/WrinkledRescue
Contact: Carol A.T. Lint, Contact
Local. Works to rescue Chinese Shar-Pei. Finds homes for unwanted, abused and stray Shar-Pei. Provides spay/neuter, Heartworm test, Microchip identification, and other veterinary services. **Affiliated With:** Chinese Shar-Pei Club of America. **Formerly:** (2005) Wrinkled Rescue, Chinese Shar-Rescue Group.

Amelia

13124 ■ Amelia - Young Life
37 Wooded Ridge Dr.
Amelia, OH 45102
Ph: (513)218-6980
URL: http://sites.younglife.org/_layouts/ylext/default.aspx?ID=C-947
Local. **Affiliated With:** Young Life.

13125 ■ American Legion, Ohio Post 773
c/o Amelia Bicentennial
PO Box 773
Amelia, OH 45102
Ph: (740)362-7478
Fax: (740)362-1429
URL: National Affiliate–www.legion.org
Contact: Amelia Bicentennial, Contact
Local. **Affiliated With:** American Legion.

13126 ■ Anderson - Young Life
37 Wooded Ridge Dr.
Amelia, OH 45102
Ph: (513)218-6980
URL: http://sites.younglife.org/_layouts/ylext/default.aspx?ID=C-948
Local. **Affiliated With:** Young Life.

13127 ■ Greater Cincinnati Rottweiler Club
c/o Rocky Volpp
3120 St., Rt. 132
Amelia, OH 45102-2408
Ph: (513)797-7450
E-mail: rlvolpp@cs.com
URL: National Affiliate–www.amrottclub.org
Contact: Rocky Volpp, Contact
Local. **Affiliated With:** American Rottweiler Club.

13128 ■ New Richmond - Young Life
37 Wooded Ridge Dr.
Amelia, OH 45102
Ph: (513)218-6980
URL: http://sites.younglife.org/_layouts/ylext/default.aspx?ID=C-957
Local. **Affiliated With:** Young Life.

13129 ■ Young Life Southeast Cincinnati
37 Wooded Ridge Dr.
Amelia, OH 45102
Ph: (513)218-6980
URL: http://sites.younglife.org/_layouts/ylext/default.aspx?ID=A-OH159
Local. **Affiliated With:** Young Life.

Amherst

13130 ■ American Legion, Elmer Johnson Post 118
921 N Lake St.
Amherst, OH 44001
Ph: (740)362-7478
Fax: (740)362-1429
URL: National Affiliate–www.legion.org
Local. **Affiliated With:** American Legion.

13131 ■ Amherst Historical Society (AHS)
113 S Lake St.
Amherst, OH 44001
Ph: (440)988-7255
Fax: (440)988-2951
E-mail: amhersthistory@centurytel.net
Contact: John Dietrich, Bd.Pres.
Founded: 1973. **Members:** 218. **Staff:** 20. **Budget:** $40,000. **Local**. Individuals interested in the history of Amherst, OH. Operates museum; maintains one-room schoolhouse; conducts educational programs. Sponsors Old Time Jamboree. Offered to public genealogy information. **Libraries:** **Type:** by appoint-

ment only. **Holdings:** 800. **Subjects:** local history. **Awards:** Historic Homes Plaque Program. **Type:** recognition. **Affiliated With:** Ohio Association of Historical Societies and Museums. **Publications:** *Grindstone*, bimonthly. Newsletter. Offers information about current events within the society. **Price:** free. **Circulation:** 250. **Conventions/Meetings:** monthly Historical Interest - meeting (exhibits) - except June, July, August, fourth Wednesday.

13132 ■ Amherst Lions Club - Ohio
c/o Marty Plato, Pres.
717 Oakhurst Dr.
Amherst, OH 44001
Ph: (440)988-7131
E-mail: marty_plato@hotmail.com
URL: http://www.lions13b.org
Contact: Marty Plato, Pres.
Local. Affiliated With: Lions Clubs International.

13133 ■ J-Sak Snowboarding
c/o Jesse Csincsak, Pres.
924 Tarry Ln.
Amherst, OH 44001-2037
Ph: (440)988-5480
Fax: (440)988-5479
E-mail: wsinsak@apk.net
URL: http://www.jsaksnowboarding.com
Local.

13134 ■ Lorain County Association of Realtors (LoCAR)
8025 Leavitt Rd., Ste.B
Amherst, OH 44001
Ph: (440)986-9545
Fax: (440)986-9655
E-mail: contact@locar.org
URL: http://www.locar.org
Contact: Thomas Kowal, Exec. Officer
Local. Strives to develop real estate business practices. Advocates for the right to own, use and transfer real property. Provides a facility for professional development, research and exchange of information among members and the general public. **Affiliated With:** National Association of Realtors.

13135 ■ Lorain County Visitors Bureau (LCVB)
8025 Leavitt Rd.
Amherst, OH 44001
Ph: (440)984-5282
Fax: (440)984-7363
Free: (800)334-1673
E-mail: visitors@lorcnty.com
URL: http://www.lcvb.org
Contact: Patricia A. Cano, Contact
Local.

13136 ■ Lorain Harbor Lions Club
c/o Christine Burman, Pres.
137 Walnut Dr.
Amherst, OH 44001
Ph: (440)988-5504
E-mail: littlechri137@comcast.net
URL: http://www.lions13b.org
Contact: Christine Burman, Pres.
Local. Affiliated With: Lions Clubs International.

13137 ■ Lorain Lawn Bowling Club
c/o Bob Holfelder
818 Lincoln St.
Amherst, OH 44001
Ph: (440)984-2712
E-mail: bobbygeo@aol.com
URL: National Affiliate–www.bowlsamerica.org
Contact: Bob Holfelder, Contact
Local. Affiliated With: United States Lawn Bowls Association.

13138 ■ Main Street Amherst
255 Park Ave.
Amherst, OH 44001
Ph: (440)984-6709
Fax: (440)984-3293
E-mail: director@mainstreetamherst.org
URL: http://www.mainstreetamherst.org
Local.

13139 ■ National Association of Fleet Administrators, Western Reserve Chapter
c/o Mrs. Shari Szczepanski, Chair
Nordson Corp.
555 Jackson St.
Amherst, OH 44001-2408
Ph: (440)985-4138
Fax: (440)985-1417
E-mail: sszczepanski@nordson.com
URL: National Affiliate–www.nafa.org
Contact: Mrs. Shari Szczepanski, Chair
Local. Promotes the professional management of vehicles through education, government and industry relations and services to members. **Affiliated With:** National Association of Fleet Administrators.

13140 ■ National R90S Sport Owners Club No. 67
c/o Ken Claus
1206 Orchard Glen Dr.
Amherst, OH 44001
Ph: (440)988-3111
E-mail: fastr90s@aol.com
URL: http://bmwr90sownersclub.org
Contact: Kenneth Claus, VP
Local. Affiliated With: BMW Motorcycle Owners of America.

13141 ■ Penton Owners Group (POG)
PO Box 756
Amherst, OH 44001
Ph: (216)651-6559
E-mail: pentongroup@pentonusa.org
URL: http://www.pentonusa.org
Contact: Paul Danik, Pres.
Founded: 1998. **Members:** 300. **Membership Dues:** $20 (annual). **Local.** Penton motorcycle owners dedicated to preserving the era of the Penton motorcycle. Provides information about the history of the Penton motorcycle and the Penton company. **Affiliated With:** American Historic Racing Motorcycle Association; American Motorcyclist Association. **Publications:** *Still Keeping Track*, quarterly. Newsletter. **Price:** free for members. **Circulation:** 300. **Advertising:** accepted.

Andover

13142 ■ American Legion, Ohio Post 226
c/o Percy D. Hyatt
PO Box 164
Andover, OH 44003
Ph: (740)362-7478
Fax: (740)362-1429
URL: National Affiliate–www.legion.org
Contact: Percy D. Hyatt, Contact
Local. Affiliated With: American Legion.

Anna

13143 ■ American Legion, Heiland Post 446
PO Box 393
Anna, OH 45302
Ph: (740)362-7478
Fax: (740)362-1429
URL: National Affiliate–www.legion.org
Local. Affiliated With: American Legion.

13144 ■ Ohio National Farmers Organization
c/o Gary Schmiesing, Regional Dir.
8490 State Rte. 119
Anna, OH 45302
Ph: (419)628-3881
Fax: (419)628-2161
URL: National Affiliate–www.nfo.org
Contact: Gary Schmiesing, Dir.
State. Affiliated With: National Farmers Organization.

Ansonia

13145 ■ American Legion, Eck-Ary-Douglas-Dickey Post 353
PO Box 338
Ansonia, OH 45303
Ph: (740)362-7478
Fax: (740)362-1429
URL: National Affiliate–www.legion.org
Local. Affiliated With: American Legion.

Antwerp

13146 ■ American Legion, Cottrell-Boylan Post 253
PO Box 485
Antwerp, OH 45813
Ph: (740)362-7478
Fax: (740)362-1429
URL: National Affiliate–www.legion.org
Local. Affiliated With: American Legion.

13147 ■ Antwerp Chamber of Commerce
PO Box 1111
Antwerp, OH 45813
Ph: (419)258-1722
Contact: Cheryl Lichty, Sec.
Local.

13148 ■ Antwerp Preservation Society
c/o Randy Derck, Pres.
PO Box 981
Antwerp, OH 45813-0987
Ph: (419)258-5511
Fax: (419)258-2822

Apple Creek

13149 ■ American Legion, Ohio Post 147
c/o Wilbur Welty
8493 Hackett Rd.
Apple Creek, OH 44606
Ph: (740)362-7478
Fax: (740)362-1429
URL: National Affiliate–www.legion.org
Contact: Wilbur Welty, Contact
Local. Affiliated With: American Legion.

Archbold

13150 ■ American Legion, Buehrer-Lauber-Weckesser Post 311
PO Box 311
Archbold, OH 43502
Ph: (740)362-7478
Fax: (740)362-1429
URL: National Affiliate–www.legion.org
Local. Affiliated With: American Legion.

13151 ■ Archbold Area Chamber of Commerce
300 N Defiance St.
Archbold, OH 43502
Ph: (419)445-2222
E-mail: archchamber@bnnorth.net
URL: http://www.archbold.com
Contact: Dennis Howell, Village Administrator
Local. Promotes business and community development in Archbold, OH area.

13152 ■ Great Lakes Organization Development Network
c/o Steve Webster
Sauder Woodworking Co.
502 Middle St.
Archbold, OH 43502
Ph: (419)446-3491
Fax: (419)446-3483
E-mail: swebster@sauder.com
Regional. Affiliated With: Organization Development Network.

13153 ■ Maumee Valley Academy of Family Physicians
c/o Keith J. Lehman, MD
121 Westfield Dr.
Archbold, OH 43502
Ph: (419)445-2015
Fax: (419)445-8102
Members: 30. **Local.**

13154 ■ National Active and Retired Federal Employees Association - Fulton-Henry County 1856
501 Stryker St.
Archbold, OH 43502-1046
Ph: (419)445-6335
URL: National Affiliate–www.narfe.org
Contact: Verlene B. Lovejoy, Contact
Local. Protects the retirement future of employees through education. Informs members on issues affecting the retirement. **Affiliated With:** National Association of Retired Federal Employees.

13155 ■ Phi Theta Kappa - Alpha Omicron Mu Chapter
c/o Von Plessner
22-600 State Rte. 34
Archbold, OH 43502-9542
Ph: (419)267-5511
E-mail: vonpless@nscc.cc.oh.us
URL: http://www.ptk.org/directories/chapters/OH/4907-1.htm
Contact: Von Plessner, Advisor
Local. Affiliated With: Phi Theta Kappa, International Honor Society.

Arlington

13156 ■ Broken Bird Rod and Gun Club
11510 CR 24
Arlington, OH 45814
Ph: (419)273-2652
URL: National Affiliate–www.mynssa.com
Local. Affiliated With: National Skeet Shooting Association.

Ashland

13157 ■ AAA Ashland County
502 Claremont Ave.
Ashland, OH 44805-3091
Ph: (419)289-8133
Local.

13158 ■ American Chemical Society, Wooster Section
c/o Dr. Bruce Harry Bengtson, Chm.
1745 Cottage St.
Ashland, OH 44805-1237
Ph: (419)281-4033
E-mail: bhbengtson@ashland.com
URL: National Affiliate–acswebcontent.acs.org
Contact: Dr. Bruce Harry Bengtson, Chm.
Local. Represents the interests of individuals dedicated to the advancement of chemistry in all its branches. Provides opportunities for peer interaction and career development. **Affiliated With:** American Chemical Society.

13159 ■ American Legion, Ohio Post 88
c/o Harry Higgins
1338 Claremont Ave.
Ashland, OH 44805
Ph: (419)289-3633
Fax: (740)362-1429
URL: National Affiliate–www.legion.org
Contact: Harry Higgins, Contact
Local. Affiliated With: American Legion.

13160 ■ Ashland Area Chamber of Commerce (AACC)
10 W 2nd St., 2nd Fl.
Ashland, OH 44805
Ph: (419)281-4584
Fax: (419)281-4585
E-mail: chamber@ashlandoh.com
URL: http://www.ashlandohio.com
Contact: Marla Akridge, Pres.
Local. Promotes and enhances the economic well-being of the Ashland area.

13161 ■ Ashland Board of Realtors - Kentucky
19 W Main St., Ste.11-12
Ashland, OH 44805
Ph: (419)281-2700
Fax: (419)281-4349
E-mail: abor@zoominternet.net
URL: http://www.ashland-oh-homes.com
Contact: Sharon S. Sample, Exec. Officer
Local. Strives to develop real estate business practices. Advocates for the right to own, use and transfer real property. Provides a facility for professional development, research and exchange of information among members and the general public. **Affiliated With:** National Association of Realtors.

13162 ■ Ashland Evening Lions Club
c/o Forest Conrad, Jr., Pres.
937 Moss Hill Dr.
Ashland, OH 44805
Ph: (419)289-7207
E-mail: flconrad@quixnet.net
URL: http://www.ashlandeveninglions.com
Contact: Forest Conrad Jr., Pres.
Local. Affiliated With: Lions Clubs International.

13163 ■ Ashland Noon Lions Club
c/o James A. Click, Sec.
PO Box 452
Ashland, OH 44805
Ph: (419)281-0807
E-mail: jclick@ohio.aaa.com
URL: http://www.lions13b.org
Contact: James A. Click, Sec.
Local. Affiliated With: Lions Clubs International.

13164 ■ Association for Computing Machinery, Ashland University
c/o Dr. Boris Kerkez and Dr. Yanxia Jia, Faculty Advisors
Dept. of Mathematics and Cmpt. Sci.
401 Coll. Ave.
Ashland, OH 44805-3700
Ph: (419)289-5833 (419)289-5960
Fax: (419)289-5791
E-mail: bkerkez@ashland.edu
URL: http://www.ashland.edu/~msdnaa
Contact: Dr. Boris Kerkez, Faculty Advisor
Founded: 1997. **Members:** 15. **Local.** Students of Ashland University. Organized and operated exclusively for educational and scientific purpose. Promotes increased knowledge and interest in science, design and development, construction, language, management and applications of modern computing. Serves as a means of communication between persons having interest in computing. **Telecommunication Services:** electronic mail, yjia@ashland.edu. **Affiliated With:** Association for Computing Machinery.

13165 ■ Greater Mohican Audubon Society
c/o Louise Fleming
PO Box 907
Ashland, OH 44805
Ph: (419)289-5347
E-mail: lfleming@ashland.edu
URL: National Affiliate–www.audubon.org
Contact: Louise Fleming Ph.D., Pres.
Founded: 1999. **Members:** 450. **Membership Dues:** national, $20 (annual) • local, $10 (annual). **Regional.** Provides protection and promotes appreciation of birds and other wildlife through environmental education, conservation and restoration of habitats. **Affiliated With:** Audubon Ohio; National Audubon Society.

13166 ■ Habitat for Humanity of Ashland County (HFHAC)
Huntington Bank Bldg.
19 W Main St., Ste.4
Ashland, OH 44805
Ph: (419)281-9669
E-mail: hfhac@zoominternet.net
URL: http://users.zoominternet.net/~hfhac
Contact: Emmett Justice, Exec.Dir.
Local. Affiliated With: Habitat for Humanity International.

13167 ■ Mifflin Lions Club
c/o James L. Bittinger, Sec.
2078 Township Rd. 1095
Ashland, OH 44805
Ph: (419)368-3755
E-mail: jimbittinger@netzero.com
URL: http://www.lions13b.org
Contact: James L. Bittinger, Sec.
Local. Affiliated With: Lions Clubs International.

13168 ■ North Central Ohio Planned Giving Council (NCOPGC)
c/o Paul Ditlevson
Ashland Univ.
401 Coll. Ave.
Ashland, OH 44805
Ph: (419)289-5072 (419)289-5104
Fax: (419)289-5785
E-mail: pditlevs@ashland.edu
URL: http://www.ashland.edu/ncopgc
Contact: Mrs. Charleen Forrer, Liaison
Founded: 1994. **Members:** 35. **Membership Dues:** minimum individual and corporate person not seeking continuing education credit, $110 (annual) • corporate person seeking CLE and CE Credit for one person, $275 (annual) • corporate person seeking CLE and CE Credit for three persons, $550 (annual) • corporate person seeking CLE and CE Credit for seven persons, $1,000 (annual) • corporate person seeking CLE and CE Credit for fifteen persons, $2,000 (annual). **Staff:** 1. **Budget:** $14,000. **Local.** Seeks to disseminate continuing educational information in the latest and best estate planning options available for the public. Offers certified CLE and CEU credit for attorneys, accountants, CFPs and insurance agents. **Telecommunication Services:** electronic mail, cforrer@ashland.edu. **Affiliated With:** National Committee on Planned Giving. **Conventions/Meetings:** Continuing Education Seminars, for 4 hours of continuing education credit - 3-4 per year.

13169 ■ Ohio Amateur Softball Association
c/o Warren Jones, Commissioner
810 Township Rd. 1504
Ashland, OH 44805
Ph: (419)651-3335 (419)289-3978
Fax: (419)207-0785
E-mail: warrenjones@zoominternet.net
URL: http://www.ohioasasoftball.org
Contact: Warren Jones, Commissioner
State. Affiliated With: Amateur Softball Association of America.

13170 ■ Ohio Genealogical Society, Ashland County Chapter (AOGS)
PO Box 681
Ashland, OH 44805-0681
E-mail: shielascorner@ohio.net
URL: http://www.rootsweb.com/~ohacogs
Contact: Anne Budd, Pres.
Founded: 1970. **Members:** 280. **Membership Dues:** single, $10 • student under age 21, $5 • life - single, $150 • life - family, $225 • family, one address, $15. **Local. Libraries: Type:** open to the public. **Holdings:** 1,000; articles, books, periodicals. **Affiliated With:** Ohio Genealogical Society. **Publications:** *Pastfinder*, quarterly. Newsletter. Features Ashland County genealogy. **Conventions/Meetings:** monthly meeting - every third Tuesday, except December.

13171 ■ Pheasants Forever of Ashland Ohio
PO Box 837
Ashland, OH 44805
E-mail: magrum@mechcom.net
URL: http://www.ashlandpf.com
Contact: Katie Wright, Pres.
Local. Affiliated With: Pheasants Forever.

13172 ■ Psi Chi, National Honor Society in Psychology - Ashland University
c/o Dept. of Psychology
115 Andrews Hall
401 Coll. Ave.
Ashland, OH 44805-3702
Ph: (419)289-5391 (419)289-5381
Fax: (419)289-5665
E-mail: cickes@ashland.edu
URL: http://www.psichi.org/chapters/info.asp?chapter_id=787
Contact: Curt Ickes PhD, Advisor
Local.

13173 ■ Rowsburg Lions Club
c/o Dan Stone, Sec.
444 US 250 E
Ashland, OH 44805
Ph: (419)869-7614
E-mail: jdstone@bright.net
URL: http://www.lions13b.org
Contact: Dan Stone, Sec.
Local. Affiliated With: Lions Clubs International.

13174 ■ United Way of Ashland County
1011 E Main St., Ste.A
Ashland, OH 44805
Ph: (419)281-5551
Fax: (419)281-7622
E-mail: info@unitedwayashlandohio.com
URL: http://www.unitedwayashlandohio.com
Contact: Ms. Jan Broomall, Exec.Dir.
Founded: 1957. **Budget:** $800,000. **State Groups:** 1. **Local Groups:** 1. **Nonmembership. Local. Affiliated With:** United Way of America.

Ashley

13175 ■ American Legion, Ohio Post 518
c/o Clyde C. Keltner
PO Box 301
Ashley, OH 43003
Ph: (740)362-7478
Fax: (740)362-1429
URL: National Affiliate–www.legion.org
Contact: Clyde C. Keltner, Contact
Local. Affiliated With: American Legion.

Ashtabula

13176 ■ American Legion, Ohio Post 103
c/o Dewey Howlett
1804 W 19th St.
Ashtabula, OH 44004
Ph: (740)362-7478
Fax: (740)362-1429
URL: National Affiliate–www.legion.org
Contact: Dewey Howlett, Contact
Local. Affiliated With: American Legion.

13177 ■ Ashtabula Area Chamber of Commerce (AACC)
4536 Main Ave.
Ashtabula, OH 44004-6925
Ph: (440)998-6998
Fax: (440)992-8216
E-mail: mail@ashtabulachamber.net
URL: http://www.ashtabulachamber.net
Contact: Jim Timonere, Pres./CEO
Founded: 1887. **Membership Dues:** citizen, $75 • government, $200 • business (1-50 employees), $182-$200 • business (51; plus $1/employee), $250 • financial institution, $350 • utility, $600 • school, $200. **Local.** Promotes business and community development in the Ashtabula, OH area. **Computer Services:** Mailing lists, of members. **Publications:** *News and Views*, monthly. Newsletter. **Advertising:** accepted. Alternate Formats: online. **Conventions/Meetings:** semiannual meeting.

13178 ■ Ashtabula County AIFA
c/o Joseph Giangola, Sec.
1000 Lake Ave.
Ashtabula, OH 44004
Ph: (440)964-8211
Fax: (440)964-8912
E-mail: jgiangola@suite224.net
URL: National Affiliate–naifa.org
Contact: Joseph Giangola, Sec.
Local. Represents the interests of insurance and financial advisors. Advocates for a positive legislative and regulatory environment. Enhances business and professional skills of members. **Affiliated With:** National Association of Insurance and Financial Advisors.

13179 ■ Ashtabula County Board of Realtors
4310 Park Ave.
Ashtabula, OH 44004
Ph: (440)998-1152
Fax: (440)992-3709
E-mail: acbr@earthlink.net
URL: National Affiliate–www.realtor.org
Contact: Susan Mellin, Exec. Officer
Local. Strives to develop real estate business practices. Advocates for the right to own, use and transfer real property. Provides a facility for professional development, research and exchange of information among members and the general public. **Affiliated With:** National Association of Realtors.

13180 ■ Ashtabula County Society for Human Resource Management
c/o JoAnn Stewart
Hospice of the Western Reserve
1166 Lake Ave.
Ashtabula, OH 44004
Ph: (440)997-6619
Fax: (440)997-6478
E-mail: jstewart12@adelphia.net
Contact: JoAnn Stewart, Pres.
Local. Represents the interests of human resource and industrial relations professionals and executives. Promotes the advancement of human resource management.

13181 ■ Ashtabula River Partnership
PO BOX 1673
Ashtabula, OH 44005-1673
Ph: (440)964-0277
Fax: (440)964-5158
Contact: John Mahan PhD, Coor.
Local. Consortium of federal and state agencies, regional government officials, representatives of area industries, and other local citizens in Ashtabula, OH. Seeks to remove and safely dispose of contaminated sediments in the Ashtabula River.

13182 ■ Ashtabula Yacht Club
PO Box 225
Ashtabula, OH 44005-0225
Ph: (440)964-3129
E-mail: info@ashtabulayachtclub.com
URL: http://www.ashtabulayachtclub.com
Local.

13183 ■ National Active and Retired Federal Employees Association - Ashtabula 624
2638 W 8th St.
Ashtabula, OH 44004-2334
Ph: (440)964-2186
URL: National Affiliate–www.narfe.org
Contact: William H. Asuma, Contact
Local. Protects the retirement future of employees through education. Informs members on issues affecting the retirement. **Affiliated With:** National Association of Retired Federal Employees.

13184 ■ North End Club
517 Joseph Ave.
Ashtabula, OH 44004
Ph: (440)964-7291
Contact: Larry Frahm, Bar Mgr.
Local.

13185 ■ Northern Ohio Model "A" Club (NOMAC)
983 Stevenson Rd.
Ashtabula, OH 44004
Ph: (440)997-2442
E-mail: fargo@toolite.com
URL: http://clubs.hemmings.com/frameset.cfm?club=nomac
Contact: Ron Stebbins, Pres.
Local. Affiliated With: Model "A" Restorers Club.

13186 ■ Society of Manufacturing Engineers - Kent State University - Ashtabula U165
3325 W 13th St.
Ashtabula, OH 44004
Ph: (440)964-4266
Fax: (440)964-4269
E-mail: mczayka@kent.edu
URL: National Affiliate–www.sme.org
Contact: Michael Czayka, Contact
Local. Advances manufacturing knowledge to gain competitive advantage. Improves skills and manufacturing solutions for the growth of economy. Provides resources and opportunities for manufacturing professionals.

13187 ■ Sons of Italy
1412 Columbus Ave.
Ashtabula, OH 44004
Ph: (440)964-9260

13188 ■ United Way of Ashtabula County
2801 C Ct.
Ashtabula, OH 44004-4571
Ph: (440)998-4141
URL: National Affiliate–national.unitedway.org
Local. Affiliated With: United Way of America.

13189 ■ Vietnam Veterans of America, Chapter No. 231
c/o Bob Swanson, Pres.
PO Box 2847
Ashtabula, OH 44004
Ph: (440)275-9454
URL: http://www.vvabuckeyestatecouncil.com
Contact: Bob Swanson, Pres.
Local. Affiliated With: Vietnam Veterans of America.

Ashville

13190 ■ American Legion, Ashville Community Post 730
129 East St.
Ashville, OH 43103
Ph: (740)362-7478
Fax: (740)362-1429
URL: National Affiliate–www.legion.org
Local. Affiliated With: American Legion.

13191 ■ American Legion, Franklin Post 1
17358 Winchester Rd.
Ashville, OH 43103
Ph: (740)362-7478
Fax: (740)362-1429
URL: National Affiliate–www.legion.org
Local. Affiliated With: American Legion.

Athens

13192 ■ Alexander High School - Young Life
PO Box 1176
Athens, OH 45701-1176
Ph: (740)797-8387
URL: http://sites.younglife.org/sites/AlexanderHighSchool/default.aspx
Local. Affiliated With: Young Life.

13193 ■ American Legion, K.T. Crossen Post 21
520 W Union St.
Athens, OH 45701
Ph: (740)362-7478
Fax: (740)362-1429
URL: National Affiliate–www.legion.org
Local. Affiliated With: American Legion.

13194 ■ American Red Cross, Athens County Chapter
100 S May Ave.
Athens, OH 45701
Ph: (740)593-5273
E-mail: redcross@frognet.net
URL: http://www.athensohredcross.org
Local.

13195 ■ Appalachian Peace and Justice Network (APJN)
18 N Coll.
Athens, OH 45701
Ph: (740)592-2608
E-mail: apjn@frognet.net
URL: http://www.apjn.org
Contact: Mara Giglio, Training and Program Coor.
Founded: 1984. **Members:** 100. **Membership Dues:** regular, $25 (annual). **Staff:** 2. **Budget:** $40,000. **Local.** Serves all counties in Southeast OH. Empowers and challenges groups and individuals to work for peace and social justice. Educates, trains and builds coalitions among local regional groups and institutions. Trainings include: conflict resolution and peer mediation, and bias reduction. **Libraries: Type:** open to the public. **Holdings:** 1,000; books, video recordings. **Subjects:** peace organizing, conflict resolution, diversity. **Awards:** Appalachian Ohio Peace Prize. **Frequency:** annual. **Type:** monetary. **Recipient:** for students from grades 6 to 12 who submit an essay, poem, or artwork on a particular theme. **Publications:** *What's Happening*, annual. Newsletter. **Price:** free. **Circulation:** 1,000. **Conventions/Meetings:** workshop.

13196 ■ Art Libraries Society of North America - Ohio Valley
c/o Gary Ginther, Chm.
Alden Lib., Ohio Univ.
35 Park Pl.
Athens, OH 45701
Ph: (740)593-2663
Fax: (740)593-2708
E-mail: ginther@ohio.edu
URL: http://home.insightbb.com/~prunge2/arlisov
Contact: Gary Ginther, Chm.
Regional. Aims to address the needs of art libraries and other professionals. Serves as a means of communication between art librarians and other notable groups and individuals in the industry. Strives to assist in the publishing of articles on art. Advocates art appreciation. **Affiliated With:** Art Libraries Society/North America.

13197 ■ Athens Bicycle Club
6449 Luhrig Rd.
Athens, OH 45701
Ph: (740)592-1759
E-mail: info@athensbicycleclub.org
URL: http://athensbicycleclub.org
Local. Affiliated With: International Mountain Bicycling Association.

13198 ■ Athens County Board of Realtors
18 Old Coach Rd.
Athens, OH 45701
Ph: (740)592-1502
Fax: (740)593-5259
E-mail: sporter@soleandbloom.com
URL: National Affiliate–www.realtor.org
Contact: Sandra Porter, Exec. Officer
Local. Strives to develop real estate business practices. Advocates for the right to own, use and transfer real property. Provides a facility for professional development, research and exchange of information among members and the general public. **Affiliated With:** National Association of Realtors.

13199 ■ Athens High School - Young Life
PO Box 1176
Athens, OH 45701-1176
Ph: (740)797-8387
URL: http://sites.younglife.org/sites/AthensHighSchool/default.aspx
Local. Affiliated With: Young Life.

13200 ■ Athens Middle School - YoungLife
PO Box 1176
Athens, OH 45701-1176
Ph: (740)797-8387
URL: http://sites.younglife.org/sites/AthensMiddleSchool/default.aspx
Local. Affiliated With: Young Life.

13201 ■ Audio Engineering Society, Ohio University Section
c/o Erin M. Dawes
Ohio Univ., RTVC Bldg.
9 S Coll. St.
Athens, OH 45701
Ph: (740)597-6608
URL: National Affiliate–www.aes.org
Contact: Erin M. Dawes, Contact
Local. Represents the interests of engineers, administrators and technicians for radio, television and motion picture operation. Operates educational and research foundation. **Affiliated With:** Audio Engineering Society.

13202 ■ Big Brothers Big Sisters of Athens County
PO Box 1199
Athens, OH 45701-1199
Ph: (740)594-3395 (740)797-0037
Fax: (740)594-3395
E-mail: bbbs@frognet.net
URL: http://frognet.net/~bbbs
Contact: Amy Reinhardt, Exec.Dir.
Local. Seeks to make a positive difference in the lives of area youth through professionally supported relationships with mentors and volunteers; serves children between the ages of 6-16 within Athens County. Desires additional adult companionship, guidance and understanding. **Affiliated With:** Big Brothers Big Sisters of America.

13203 ■ Buckeye Forest Council (BFC)
PO Box 99
Athens, OH 45701
Ph: (740)594-6400
Fax: (740)594-6400
Free: (866)OHTREES
E-mail: info@buckeyeforestcouncil.org
URL: http://www.buckeyeforestcouncil.org
Contact: Susan Heitker, Exec.Dir.
Founded: 1993. **Members:** 500. **Membership Dues:** grassroots, $35 (annual) • understory, $50 (annual) • canopy, $100 (annual) • ecosystem, $500 (annual) • old growth, $1,000 • limited income, $20 (annual). **Staff:** 2. **Budget:** $100,000. **State Groups:** 1. **State.** Works to protect Ohio's native forests and its inhabitants through education, grassroots organizing, litigation and appeals, direct action, legislative education, lobbying and advocacy. **Affiliated With:** Heartwood. **Publications:** *Martha's Journal*, 3/year. Newsletter. Contains information on the work of the Buckeye Forest Council and general information about Ohio's forests. **Price:** included in membership dues. **Circulation:** 800. **Advertising:** accepted. Alternate Formats: online.

13204 ■ Federal Hocking High School - Young Life
PO Box 1176
Athens, OH 45701-1176
Ph: (740)797-8387
URL: http://sites.younglife.org/sites/FederalHocking/default.aspx
Local. Affiliated With: Young Life.

13205 ■ IT Alliance of Appalachian Ohio (ITAAO)
c/o Laura Hopstetter
340 W State St., Ste.142, Unit 20
Athens, OH 45701-3751
Ph: (740)597-1408
Fax: (740)597-1355
Free: (877)850-6367
E-mail: itaao@itaao.org
URL: http://www.itaao.org
Local.

13206 ■ Logan High School - Young Life
PO Box 1176
Athens, OH 45701-1176
Ph: (740)797-8387
E-mail: jb294502@ohiou.edu
URL: http://sites.younglife.org/sites/LoganHighSchool/default.aspx
Local. Affiliated With: Young Life.

13207 ■ Muslim Students Association - Ohio University at Athens (MSA)
c/o Islamic Center of Athens
13 Stewart St.
Athens, OH 45701
Ph: (740)594-3890
Fax: (740)594-3890
E-mail: muslimst@ohiou.edu
URL: http://cscwww.cats.ohiou.edu/~muslimst
Contact: Usame Tunagur, Pres.
Local. Muslim students. Seeks to advance the interests of members; works to enable members to practice Islam as a complete way of life. **Affiliated With:** Muslim Students Association of the United States and Canada.

13208 ■ NACE International, Ohio University Student Section
c/o Wei Sun, Chm.
Ohio Univ.
342 W State St.
Athens, OH 45701
Ph: (740)593-0164
Fax: (740)593-9949
E-mail: weisun@bobcat.ent.ohiou.edu
URL: National Affiliate–www.nace.org
Contact: Wei Sun, Chm.
Local. Promotes public safety by advancing the knowledge of corrosion engineering and science. Works to raise awareness of corrosion control and prevention technology among government agencies and legislators, businesses, professional societies and the general public. **Affiliated With:** NACE International: The Corrosion Society.

13209 ■ National Organization for Women - Athens
c/o Elaine Mather, Pres.
8627 Terrell Rd.
Athens, OH 45701

Ph: (740)593-6055
URL: http://www.ohionow.org
Contact: Elaine Mather, Pres.
Local. Affiliated With: National Organization for Women.

13210 ■ Neighbors Helping Neighbors of Athens County (NHN)
PO Box 2268
Athens, OH 45701-2268
Ph: (740)592-4477
E-mail: info@neighborhelp.org
URL: http://www.neighborhelp.org
Contact: Tracy Galway, Pres.
Founded: 1998. **Staff:** 3. **Local Groups:** 1. **Local.**

13211 ■ Nelsonville York - Young Life
PO Box 1176
Athens, OH 45701-1176
Ph: (740)797-8387
URL: http://sites.younglife.org/sites/NelsonvilleYorkHighSchool/default.aspx
Local. Affiliated With: Young Life.

13212 ■ Ohio Genealogical Society, Athens County Chapter
65 N Ct. St.
Athens, OH 45701-2506
E-mail: achsm@athenshistory.org
URL: http://www.athenshistory.org
Local. Affiliated With: Ohio Genealogical Society. **Also Known As:** (2005) Athens County Historical Society and Museum.

13213 ■ Ohio University Chapter of the Association for Computing Machinery
329 Stocker Ctr.
Ohio Univ.
Athens, OH 45701
Ph: (740)593-1568
Fax: (740)593-0007
E-mail: acm@oucsace.cs.ohiou.edu
Contact: Anthony J. Gress, Chair
Members: 150. **Local.** International scientific and educational organization. Dedicated to advancing the arts, sciences and applications of information technology. **Affiliated With:** Association for Computing Machinery. **Conventions/Meetings:** monthly meeting.

13214 ■ Ohio University Council of Teachers of Mathematics
c/o Lisa Smith, Representative
51A N Lancaster St.
Athens, OH 45701
E-mail: ls182902@ohio.edu
URL: http://www.ohio.edu/ouctm
Contact: Lisa Smith, Representative
Local. Aims to improve the teaching and learning of mathematics. Provides vision, leadership and professional development to support teachers in ensuring mathematics learning of the highest quality for all students. **Affiliated With:** National Council of Teachers of Mathematics.

13215 ■ Phi Beta Kappa, Ohio University
c/o Dr. Douglas Baxter, Chapter Sec.
Ohio Univ.
Dept. of History
Bentley Annex, 4th Fl.
Athens, OH 45701
Ph: (740)593-4354
E-mail: baxter@ohio.edu
URL: http://www.ohiou.edu/pbk
Contact: Dr. Douglas Baxter, Chapter Sec.
Local. Affiliated With: Phi Beta Kappa.

13216 ■ Planned Parenthood of Southeast Ohio
280 E State St.
Athens, OH 45701
Ph: (740)593-3375
URL: http://www.ppseo.org
Local. Affiliated With: Planned Parenthood Federation of America.

13217 ■ RSVP-Athens/Hockings County
c/o Alice Curtis, Dir.
20 Kern St.
Athens, OH 45701
Ph: (740)593-7382
Fax: (740)593-8006
E-mail: acsen@frognet.net
URL: http://www.joinseniorservice.org
Contact: Alice Curtis, Dir.
Local. Affiliated With: Retired and Senior Volunteer Program.

13218 ■ Society of Manufacturing Engineers - Ohio University S087
Ohio Univ., Dept. of Indus. Tech.
123 Stocker Ctr.
Athens, OH 45701-2979
Ph: (740)593-1450
Fax: (740)593-9382
E-mail: tscott@bobcat.ent.ohiou.edu
URL: http://www.ent.ohiou.edu/~sme
Contact: Thomas Scott, Contact
Local. Advances manufacturing knowledge to gain competitive advantage. Improves skills and manufacturing solutions for the growth of economy. Provides resources and opportunities for manufacturing professionals. **Affiliated With:** Oceanic Society.

13219 ■ Southern Ohio Council of Teachers of English (SOCTE)
c/o Jacqueline Glasgow, Pres.
Ohio Univ. English Dept.
Ellis Hall
Athens, OH 45701
Ph: (740)594-7297
E-mail: glasgowj@ohio.edu
URL: http://www.seorf.ohiou.edu/~xx144
Contact: Jacqueline Glasgow, Pres.
Regional. Affiliated With: National Council of Teachers of English.

13220 ■ Sweet Adelines International, Hocking Valley Chapter
Richland United Methodist Church
60 Pomeroy Rd.
Athens, OH 45701-9475
Ph: (614)575-3782
E-mail: lattelead1@aol.com
URL: National Affiliate–www.sweetadelineintl.org
Contact: Tawni Miller, Contact
Local. Advances the musical art form of barbershop harmony through education and performances. Provides education, training and coaching in the development of women's four-part barbershop harmony. **Affiliated With:** Sweet Adelines International.

13221 ■ Trimble High School - Young Life
PO Box 1176
Athens, OH 45701-1176
Ph: (740)797-8387
URL: http://sites.younglife.org/sites/TrimbleHighSchool/default.aspx
Local. Affiliated With: Young Life.

13222 ■ Young Life Athens County
PO Box 1176
Athens, OH 45701-1176
Ph: (740)797-8387
URL: http://sites.younglife.org/sites/AthensCounty/default.aspx
Local. Affiliated With: Young Life.

Attica

13223 ■ American Legion, Victory Post 260
17 W Tiffin St.
Attica, OH 44807
Ph: (740)362-7478
Fax: (740)362-1429
URL: National Affiliate–www.legion.org
Local. Affiliated With: American Legion.

13224 ■ Attica Lions Club
c/o Dwight Everhart, Pres.
PO Box 98
Attica, OH 44807
Ph: (419)426-2335
E-mail: wi080b@willard-oh.com
URL: http://www.lions13b.org
Contact: Dwight Everhart, Pres.
Local. Affiliated With: Lions Clubs International.

13225 ■ North Central Ohio Angus Association
c/o Nick Wagner, Pres.
13257 E Co. Rd. 56
Attica, OH 44807
Ph: (419)426-1406
URL: National Affiliate–www.angus.org
Contact: Nick Wagner, Pres.
Regional. Affiliated With: American Angus Association.

13226 ■ Northern Ohio Draft Pony Association (NODPA)
c/o Barb Featheringill, Sec.
15432 E Trail 8
Attica, OH 44807
Ph: (419)426-4835
Fax: (419)426-5336
E-mail: info@nodpa.org
URL: http://www.nodpa.org
Contact: Joe Gillett, Pres.
Local. Affiliated With: American Haflinger Registry.

Atwater

13227 ■ Atwater Lions Club - Ohio
c/o Danny Derreberry, Pres.
7179 Virginia Rd.
Atwater, OH 44201
Ph: (330)947-2837
URL: http://www.lions13d.org
Contact: Danny Derreberry, Pres.
Local. Affiliated With: Lions Clubs International.

13228 ■ Catholics United for the Faith - Our Lady of the Most Holy Eucharist Chapter
c/o Steve Marchand
764 Hartville Rd.
Atwater, OH 44201
Ph: (330)877-3787
E-mail: catholicbline@aol.com
URL: National Affiliate–www.cuf.org
Contact: Steve Marchand, Contact
Local.

13229 ■ Pinto Horse Association of Ohio (PTHAO)
c/o Dick Bredemeier, VP
4764 Fairgrounds Rd.
Atwater, OH 44201
Ph: (330)325-7506
E-mail: nbredem1@kent.edu
URL: http://www.members.tripod.com/ohiopinto
Contact: Barb Skrletts, Pres.
Members: 120. **Membership Dues:** youth individual, $15 (annual) • adult individual, $20 (annual) • family, $25 (annual). **State.** Persons interested in the promotion and improvement of the Pinto breed of horses. Sponsors competitions and educational activities. **Affiliated With:** Pinto Horse Association of America. **Publications:** *Spotcheck*, periodic. Newsletter. Contains association rules, news, and activities. **Price:** included in membership dues. **Circulation:** 100. **Advertising:** accepted. **Conventions/Meetings:** periodic meeting.

Aurora

13230 ■ Aurora Area Chamber of Commerce
549 S Chillicothe Rd.
Aurora, OH 44202

Ph: (330)562-3355
Fax: (330)995-2002
E-mail: jennifer@auroraohiochamber.com
URL: http://www.auroraohiochamber.com
Contact: Jennifer Natale, Exec.Dir.

Founded: 1976. **Members:** 140. **Membership Dues:** retiree, $45 • individual, clergy, $140 • nonprofit, $140 • professional, $275 • business (based on number of employees), $275-$660. **Staff:** 2. **Local**. Promotes business and community development in Aurora, OH. **Awards:** Adult. **Frequency:** annual. **Type:** recognition • Business. **Frequency:** annual. **Type:** recognition • Citizen of the Year. **Frequency:** annual. **Type:** recognition • Matching. **Frequency:** annual. **Type:** recognition • Youth. **Frequency:** annual. **Type:** recognition. **Committees:** Economic Development; Executive; Pro-Business/Merchants Association; Tourism. **Affiliated With:** Ohio Chamber of Commerce; U.S. Chamber of Commerce. **Publications:** *Community Profile & Map*. Newsletter • Membership Directory. **Conventions/Meetings:** semiannual banquet • monthly board meeting - every 2nd Thursday in Aurora, OH • monthly executive committee meeting - every 3rd Thursday in Aurora, OH • monthly meeting.

13231 ■ Hawthorne Valley Skeet Club
c/o G.M. McCullough
206 Chisholm Ct.
Aurora, OH 44202
Ph: (216)337-7682
URL: National Affiliate–www.mynssa.com
Contact: G.M. McCullough, Contact

Local. **Affiliated With:** National Skeet Shooting Association.

13232 ■ North East Ohio Vette Club (NEOVC)
c/o Tom Fetchik, Pres.
148 Royal Oak Dr.
Aurora, OH 44202
E-mail: tfetchik@aol.com
URL: http://www.neovc.org
Contact: Tom Fetchik, Pres.

Local. **Affiliated With:** National Council of Corvette Clubs.

13233 ■ Ohio Alpaca Breeders Association (OABA)
PO Box 624
Aurora, OH 44202
E-mail: info@alpaca-farms-breeders.com
URL: http://www.alpaca-farms-breeders.com
Contact: Eric Folkman, Pres.

State. **Affiliated With:** Alpaca Owners and Breeders Association.

Austinburg

13234 ■ Ohio Wine Producers Association (OWPA)
c/o Donniella Winchell, Exec.Dir.
PO Box 157
Austinburg, OH 44010
Ph: (440)466-4417
Fax: (440)466-4427
Free: (800)227-6972
E-mail: winchell@knownet.net
URL: http://www.ohiowines.org
Contact: Donniella Winchell, Exec.Dir.

Founded: 1975. **Members:** 485. **Membership Dues:** grower, $30 (annual) • associate, $75 (annual). **Budget:** $800,000. **State**. Seeks to provide an atmosphere in which wineries and growers can successfully do business. **Publications:** *Free Run*, bimonthly. Newsletter. **Price:** included in membership dues • *Ohio's Grapevine*, 3/year. Newspaper. **Price:** included in membership dues • *Vintage Views*. Newsletter. **Conventions/Meetings:** quarterly board meeting • annual meeting, industry.

Austintown

13235 ■ American Legion, Austintown Memorial Post 301
3652 Oakwood Ave.
Austintown, OH 44515
Ph: (740)362-7478
Fax: (740)362-1429
URL: National Affiliate–www.legion.org

Local. **Affiliated With:** American Legion.

13236 ■ Austintown Lions Club
c/o Brad Martin, Pres.
338 DeHoff Dr.
Austintown, OH 44515
Ph: (330)792-5851
URL: http://www.lions13d.org
Contact: Brad Martin, Pres.

Local. **Affiliated With:** Lions Clubs International.

13237 ■ Korean War Veterans Association, Mahoning Valley Chapter
c/o Zeno J. Foley
337 S Inglewood Ave.
Austintown, OH 44515-3935
Ph: (330)792-2735
E-mail: zenokwv@peoplepc.com
URL: National Affiliate–www.kwva.org
Contact: Zeno J. Foley, Contact

Local. **Affiliated With:** Korean War Veterans Association.

13238 ■ Youngstown South Side Lions Club
c/o William R. Cooper, Pres.
1003 Collins Ave.
Austintown, OH 44515
Ph: (330)799-0190
E-mail: thecoopers4@netzero.net
URL: http://www.lions13d.org
Contact: William R. Cooper, Pres.

Local. **Affiliated With:** Lions Clubs International.

Avon

13239 ■ American Association of Legal Nurse Consultants, Cleveland/NEO Chapter
c/o Linda Gartman, Pres.
PO Box 209
Avon, OH 44011-0209
Ph: (440)937-9474
E-mail: nickirn@aol.com
URL: http://www.aalnc-neocleveland.org
Contact: Linda Gartman, Pres.

Local. Promotes the professional advancement of registered nurses consulting within the legal arena. Provides a forum for continuing education, networking and mentoring. **Affiliated With:** American Association of Legal Nurse Consultants.

13240 ■ American Truck Historical Society, Northeast Ohio Chapter
c/o Donald Burge
37180 Chester Rd.
Avon, OH 44011
Ph: (440)934-6100
URL: National Affiliate–www.aths.org
Contact: Donald Burge, Contact

Local.

13241 ■ Avon Lions Club - Ohio
PO Box 22
Avon, OH 44011
Ph: (440)934-5739
E-mail: mjandpj@yahoo.com
URL: http://avonoh.lionwap.org
Contact: Paul Johnson, Pres.

Local. **Affiliated With:** Lions Clubs International.

13242 ■ Firelands Fly Fishers
PO Box 244
Avon, OH 44011
Ph: (440)937-5258
E-mail: r.mastnardo@firelandsflyfishers.org
URL: http://www.firelandsflyfishers.org
Contact: Bill Grake, Pres.

Local. **Affiliated With:** Federation of Fly Fishers.

Avon Lake

13243 ■ American Legion, Avon Lake Post 211
31972 Walker Rd.
Avon Lake, OH 44012
Ph: (740)362-7478
Fax: (740)362-1429
URL: National Affiliate–www.legion.org

Local. **Affiliated With:** American Legion.

13244 ■ North Coast Regional Chamber of Commerce
PO Box 275
Avon Lake, OH 44012-0275
Ph: (440)933-9311
E-mail: contact@northcoastchamber.com
URL: http://www.avonlakeavoncc.com
Contact: John Sobolewski, Exec.Dir.

Members: 600. **Membership Dues:** business (1 to 49 employees), $150 (annual) • business (50 or more employees), $200 (annual). **Local**. Strives to improve the quality of life in and around the local community. **Formerly:** Avon Lake - Avon Chamber of Commerce.

13245 ■ Ohio Association for Health, Physical Education, Recreation and Dance (OAHPERD)
631 Wellesley Cir.
Avon Lake, OH 44012
Fax: (440)930-7774
Free: (800)828-3468
E-mail: dianet@apk.net
URL: http://www.ohahperd.org
Contact: Diane Tomer, Exec.Dir.

Founded: 1930. **Members:** 2,300. **Membership Dues:** professional, $50 (annual) • student, retired, $25 (annual) • institution student, $20 (annual) • senior student, $40 (annual) • institution, $150 (annual). **Staff:** 1. **Budget:** $100,400. **Regional Groups:** 1. **State**. Athletic trainers, coaches, recreation personnel, safety/drivers education teachers, and health, physical, and dance instructors. Seeks to stimulate growth in the above disciplines as well as provide leadership and information for the continuous development of the field. **Awards:** Good Members of Season. **Frequency:** quarterly. **Type:** recognition • Memorial Scholarship. **Frequency:** annual. **Type:** scholarship • Research Grants. **Frequency:** annual. **Type:** grant. **Affiliated With:** American Alliance for Health, Physical Education, Recreation and Dance. **Publications:** *Future Focus*, semiannual. Journal. **Circulation:** 2,300. **Advertising:** accepted • *Newsline*, semiannual. Newsletter. **Conventions/Meetings:** annual conference (exhibits) - normally 1st week in December.

13246 ■ Young Life Lorain County
PO Box 193
Avon Lake, OH 44012
Ph: (440)315-2992
Fax: (440)892-2513
URL: http://sites.younglife.org/sites/LorainCounty/default.aspx
Contact: Mike Vonderau, Contact

Local. **Affiliated With:** Young Life.

Bainbridge

13247 ■ American Legion, Ohio Post 14
c/o Luther Giffin
105 W Third St.
Bainbridge, OH 45612

Ph: (740)362-7478
Fax: (740)362-1429
URL: National Affiliate–www.legion.org
Contact: Luther Giffin, Contact
Local. Affiliated With: American Legion.

Baltic

13248 ■ American Legion, Ohio Post 679
c/o Richard Regula
PO Box 384
Baltic, OH 43804
Ph: (740)362-7478
Fax: (740)362-1429
URL: National Affiliate–www.legion.org
Contact: Richard Regula, Contact
Local. Affiliated With: American Legion.

13249 ■ Baltic Lions Club
c/o E. Jack McQueen, Pres.
PO Box 59
Baltic, OH 43804
Ph: (330)897-6693
URL: http://users.adelphia.net/~npssteve/district.htm
Contact: E. Jack McQueen, Pres.
Local. Affiliated With: Lions Clubs International.

Baltimore

13250 ■ Baltimore Area Chamber of Commerce
PO Box 193
Baltimore, OH 43105
Ph: (740)438-0837
E-mail: dmaddux@rrohio.com
URL: http://www.baltimoreohiochamber.com
Contact: Dannette Maddux, Pres.
Founded: 1985. **Members:** 95. **Membership Dues:** $50 (annual). **Local.** Promotes business and community development in Baltimore, OH area. Sponsors Baltimore Festival. **Publications:** Newsletter, monthly.

Barberton

13251 ■ AAA Barberton Automobile Club
140 E Tuscarawas Ave.
Barberton, OH 44203
Ph: (330)753-7779
Local.

13252 ■ Akron-Canton Society of Radiologic Technologists
c/o Cheri Rollins
155 5th St. NE
Barberton, OH 44203
Ph: (330)848-7752
Fax: (330)745-0611
E-mail: cheri42@msn.com
URL: http://www.osrt.org
Contact: Cheri Rollins, Contact
Local. Represents the professional society of radiologic technologists. Advances education and research in the radiologic sciences. Evaluates quality patient care. Improves the welfare and socioeconomics of radiologic technologists. **Affiliated With:** American Society of Radiologic Technologists.

13253 ■ American Legion, Barberton Post 271
75 6th St. NW
Barberton, OH 44203
Ph: (740)362-7478
Fax: (740)362-1429
URL: National Affiliate–www.legion.org
Local. Affiliated With: American Legion.

13254 ■ American Red Cross, Barberton Chapter
600 W Park Ave.
Barberton, OH 44203
Ph: (330)753-7766
Fax: (330)848-2900
E-mail: arcbar@aol.com
URL: http://www.barbertonredcross.org
Local.

13255 ■ Barberton Community Foundation (BCF)
104 3rd St. NW, Ste.202
Barberton, OH 44203
Ph: (330)745-5995
Fax: (330)745-3990
E-mail: bcfcharity@aol.com
URL: http://www.miracomdesign.com/bcf/sites
Contact: Milan Pavkov, Chm.
Founded: 1996. **Staff:** 5. **Local.** Aims for improvement of the lives of citizens of Barberton Ohio. **Awards: Frequency:** quarterly. **Type:** grant • **Frequency:** quarterly. **Type:** scholarship. **Recipient:** must specifically benefit citizens/city of Barberton.

13256 ■ Ohio Bottle Club
c/o Alan DeMaison, Pres.
PO Box 585
Barberton, OH 44203-0585
E-mail: violinbottle@aol.com
URL: http://www.ohiobottles.freehomepage.com
Contact: Alan DeMaison, Pres.
State. Affiliated With: Federation of Historical Bottle Collectors.

13257 ■ STARFLEET: USS Ohio
c/o Barbara M. Buffington, Pres.
168 1/2 2nd St. NW, Apt. 1
Barberton, OH 44203
E-mail: ussohio@neo.rr.com
URL: http://www.regionone.net
Contact: Barbara M. Buffington, Contact
State. Affiliated With: STARFLEET.

Barnesville

13258 ■ American Legion, Barnesville Post 168
317 E South St.
Barnesville, OH 43713
Ph: (740)362-7478
Fax: (740)362-1429
URL: National Affiliate–www.legion.org
Local. Affiliated With: American Legion.

13259 ■ Barnesville Area Chamber of Commerce
130 W Main St.
Barnesville, OH 43713
Ph: (740)425-4300
Fax: (740)425-1048
E-mail: bacc@1st.net
URL: http://www.barnesvilleohio.com
Contact: Sherrie Wharton, Office Mgr.
Founded: 1939. **Members:** 100. **Staff:** 1. **Budget:** $5,000. **Local.** Promotes business and community development in Barnesville, OH. **Libraries: Type:** open to the public. **Holdings:** 25,000. **Awards:** Citizen of the Year. **Frequency:** annual. **Type:** recognition. **Committees:** Business and Industry; Doll Museum; Retail. **Formerly:** (1999) Barnesville Area Chamber of Commerce and Development Council. **Publications:** Newsletter, monthly. **Price:** free. **Circulation:** 125. **Conventions/Meetings:** monthly General Meeting - 2nd Thursday.

13260 ■ Barnesville Lions Club - Ohio
c/o Belmont Dodge
780 E Main St.
Barnesville, OH 43713
Ph: (740)425-1966 (412)596-6424
E-mail: steedle@1st.net
URL: http://users.adelphia.net/~npssteve/district.htm
Contact: Bill Steedle, Pres.
Local. Affiliated With: Lions Clubs International.

13261 ■ Belmont County Chapter of the Ohio Genealogical Society (BCCOGS)
PO Box 285
Barnesville, OH 43713
Ph: (614)484-4416
E-mail: president@bccogs.org
URL: http://www.rootsweb.com/~ohbelogs
Contact: Ann Clayton, Pres.
Founded: 1978. **Membership Dues:** single, $10 (annual) • joint, $12 (annual) • family, $14 (annual). **Staff:** 5. **Local.** Aims to promote genealogy. Encourages individuals of all ages to develop an interest, and to enlist their aid in preserving record. **Libraries: Type:** open to the public. **Holdings:** books, films. **Subjects:** genealogy. **Affiliated With:** Ohio Genealogical Society. **Publications:** *Belmont Co. Genealogy Newsletter*, quarterly. **Conventions/Meetings:** monthly meeting.

13262 ■ Estate Planning Council of Upper Ohio Valley
c/o Ronald A. Bischof
611 Park St.
PO Box 396
Barnesville, OH 43713
Ph: (740)425-1766
Fax: (740)425-3296
E-mail: rbischof@1st.net
URL: http://councils.naepc.org
Contact: Cynthia M. Perring, Pres.
Local. Fosters understanding of the proper relationship between the functions of various professions in the field of estate planning including CPAs, attorneys, trust officers, life underwriters and other parties having to do with estate planning. Encourages cooperation among members. **Affiliated With:** National Association of Estate Planners and Councils.

13263 ■ National Active and Retired Federal Employees Association - Belmont County 2175
62015 Tacoma Rd.
Barnesville, OH 43713-9615
Ph: (740)425-3265
URL: National Affiliate–www.narfe.org
Contact: Louis L. Dietrich, Contact
Local. Protects the retirement future of employees through education. Informs members on issues affecting the retirement. **Affiliated With:** National Association of Retired Federal Employees.

13264 ■ National Alliance for the Mentally Ill - Belmont, Harrison, Monroe
c/o Vicky Holland
34400 Holland Rd.
Barnesville, OH 43713
Ph: (740)425-2230
Free: (800)311-9454
URL: http://www.namiohio.org/affiliates_support.htm
Contact: Vicky Holland, Contact
Local. Strives to improve the quality of life of children and adults with severe mental illness through support, education, research and advocacy. **Affiliated With:** National Alliance for the Mentally Ill.

Batavia

13265 ■ American Legion, Ohio Post 237
c/o Frank W. Weaver
2215 Batavia Williamsburg Pike
Batavia, OH 45103
Ph: (740)362-7478
Fax: (740)362-1429
URL: National Affiliate–www.legion.org
Contact: Frank W. Weaver, Contact
Local. Affiliated With: American Legion.

13266 ■ Clermont County Genealogical Society (CCGS)
PO Box 394
Batavia, OH 45103-0394
Ph: (513)723-3423
E-mail: clermontgenealogy@hotmail.com
URL: http://www.rootsweb.com/~ohclecgs
Contact: Amy Schneider, Pres.

Founded: 1977. **Members:** 300. **Membership Dues:** single or family (same address), $12 (annual) • sustaining, $20 (annual) • life, $200. **Local.** Creates, fosters and maintains interest in local genealogies and history. Collects and preserves Clermont County genealogical records and information. Provides educational programs. **Libraries: Type:** open to the public. **Holdings:** articles, biographical archives, books, maps, periodicals, photographs. **Computer Services:** database. **Affiliated With:** Ohio Genealogical Society. **Publications:** *The Clermont County Genealogical Society Newsletter*, quarterly, February, May, August, November. Includes calendar of events, programs, record transcriptions, library reports and articles. **Price:** $12.00 included in membership dues. **Conventions/Meetings:** annual Heritage Day - luncheon, with a speaker on a genealogical topic and induction of the new members - in September • annual picnic, at different historic sites around the county - every summer.

13267 ■ Clermont County Historical Society (CCHS)
PO Box 14
Batavia, OH 45103
Ph: (513)753-8672
E-mail: clermonths@aol.com
URL: http://www.clermonthistoric.org
Contact: Cindy Johnson, Pres.

Founded: 1958. **Members:** 100. **Membership Dues:** individual, $15 (annual) • family, $20 (annual) • contributing, $30 (annual) • life, business/corporation (60 and older), $100 • life (under 60), $300. **Budget:** $55,000. **Local.** Individuals with interest in Clermont County, OH. Seeks to preserve and promote local history; conducts programs; oversees the Clermont County history archives. **Libraries: Type:** not open to the public. **Holdings:** 100; articles, books, periodicals. **Subjects:** county history. **Committees:** Monroe Township History. **Publications:** *Clermont Historian*, monthly. Newsletter. Contains amusing and historical items and current news. **Price:** included in membership dues. **Circulation:** 110. **Conventions/ Meetings:** monthly meeting (exhibits) - every 3rd Friday.

13268 ■ National Alliance for the Mentally Ill, Clermont County
1088 Wasserman Way
Batavia, OH 45103-1911
Ph: (513)732-5400
Fax: (513)732-5414
E-mail: kscherra@ccmhrb.org
URL: http://www.ccmhrb.org
Contact: Karen J. Scherra, Exec.Dir.

Local. Works to improve the life of people with mental illness and to promote mental wellness.

13269 ■ National Speleological Society, Greater Cincinnati Grotto (GCG)
c/o Rob Coomer, Ed.
4218 Muscovy Ln.
Batavia, OH 45103
Ph: (513)922-2687
E-mail: cavepig124@fuse.net
URL: http://www.gcgcavers.com
Contact: Rob Coomer, Ed.

Local. Seeks to study, explore and conserve cave and karst resources. Protects access to caves and promotes responsible caving. Encourages responsible management of caves and their unique environments. **Affiliated With:** National Speleological Society.

13270 ■ Phi Theta Kappa - Alpha Iota Theta Chapter
c/o Peggy Hager
Clermont Coll.
4200 Clermont Dr.
Batavia, OH 45103
Ph: (513)732-5207
E-mail: margaret.hager@uc.edu
URL: http://www.ptk.org/directories/chapters/OH/324-1.htm
Contact: Peggy Hager, Advisor

Local. Affiliated With: Phi Theta Kappa, International Honor Society.

13271 ■ Secrets of Speed Society (SOSS)
c/o Mr. Charles H. Yapp, Exec.Dir.
3860 Cain Run Rd.
Batavia, OH 45103
Ph: (513)724-0700
Fax: (513)724-0116
E-mail: cy4fn@aol.com
URL: http://www.secretsofspeed.com
Contact: Mr. Charles H. Yapp, Exec.Dir.

Founded: 1990. **Members:** 2,650. **Membership Dues:** full (with 1st class mail), $40 (annual) • full (with bulk mail), $33 (annual) • full overseas, $65 (annual) • full in Canada and Mexico, $43 (annual). **Staff:** 1. **Regional.** Works to celebrate the people, history, technology, and equipment of high performance Model A, T, and B Fords as used around the world for daily driving, cross country touring, and racing. **Libraries: Type:** by appointment only. **Holdings:** 1,100. **Subjects:** speedsters, racing, hot rods. **Awards:** Merit Award. **Frequency:** quarterly. **Type:** recognition. **Recipient:** for excellence in writing, research and photography of articles produced for the association's publication. **Computer Services:** Bibliographic search, contains complete outlines of articles written for research. **Publications:** *Secrets, The Ford Speed and Sport Magazine*, quarterly. **Price:** $10.00. **Circulation:** 2,650. **Advertising:** accepted. **Conventions/Meetings:** annual Speed Secrets Meet - general assembly, with workshops on historic and modern speed secrets (exhibits).

13272 ■ Vietnam Veterans of America, Chapter No. 649 - Clermont County
c/o David L. Murrell, Pres.
PO Box 426
Batavia, OH 45103
Ph: (513)575-0050
Fax: (513)248-8753
URL: http://www.vvabuckeyestatecouncil.com
Contact: David L. Murrell, Pres.

Local. Affiliated With: Vietnam Veterans of America.

Bay Village

13273 ■ Financial Planning Association of Northeast Ohio Chapter
28022 Osborn Rd.
Bay Village, OH 44140
Ph: (440)899-5055
Fax: (440)899-1010
E-mail: fpaneo@aol.com
URL: http://www.fpaneo.com
Contact: Michael A. Koler CFP, Pres.

Local. Promotes the value of the financial planning process and advances the financial planning profession. Provides forum for education and career development for its members. **Affiliated With:** Financial Planning Association.

13274 ■ Institute of Real Estate Management - Northern Ohio Chapter No. 41
c/o Heidi Langer
Langer Marketing
321 Florence Ct.
Bay Village, OH 44140
Ph: (440)892-7620
Fax: (440)617-0716
E-mail: heidi@langermarketing.com
URL: National Affiliate–www.irem.org
Contact: Heidi Langer, Contact

Local. Represents real property and asset management professionals. Works to promote professional ethics and standards in the field of property management. Strives to keep its members informed on the latest legislative actions and current industry trends. Provides classroom training, continuing education seminars, job referral service and candidate assistance services to enhance the effectiveness and professionalism of its members. **Affiliated With:** Institute of Real Estate Management.

13275 ■ International Facility Management Association, Northern Ohio (Cleveland)
c/o IFMA Northern Ohio
321 Florence Ct.
Bay Village, OH 44140
Ph: (440)892-7620
Fax: (440)617-0716
E-mail: ohioifma@comcast.net
URL: http://www.ifmanorthernohio.org
Contact: Mr. Gerald Zupancic CFM, Chapter Pres.

Local. Affiliated With: International Facility Management Association.

13276 ■ Public Relations Society of America, Cleveland
c/o Lynn Bracic, Chapter Facilitator
28022 Osborn Rd.
Bay Village, OH 44140
Ph: (440)899-1112
Fax: (440)899-1010
E-mail: lbprscleve@aol.com
URL: http://www.prsacleveland.org
Contact: Lynn Bracic, Chapter Facilitator

Members: 300. **Local. Affiliated With:** Public Relations Society of America. **Formerly:** (2005) Public Relations Society of America, Greater Cleveland.

13277 ■ Rocky River Power Squadron
c/o Susan Rothacker, Commander
PO Box 40185
Bay Village, OH 44140-0185
Ph: (440)315-1206
E-mail: sjrothacker@aol.com
URL: http://www.usps.org/localusps/rockyriver
Contact: Susan Rothacker, Commander

Local. Affiliated With: United States Power Squadrons.

13278 ■ Vietnam Veterans of America, Chapter No. 249
c/o John J. Hnylka, Pres.
PO Box 40271
Bay Village, OH 44140
Ph: (216)529-9366
URL: http://www.vvabuckeyestatecouncil.com
Contact: John J. Hnylka, Pres.

Local. Affiliated With: Vietnam Veterans of America.

Beach City

13279 ■ American Legion, Weimer-Widder Post 549
10141 Portland Ave.
Beach City, OH 44608
Ph: (740)362-7478
Fax: (740)362-1429
URL: National Affiliate–www.legion.org

Local. Affiliated With: American Legion.

13280 ■ Beach City Lions Club
c/o Clinton H. Garver, Pres.
432 2nd St. SW
Beach City, OH 44608
Ph: (330)756-2721
URL: http://www.lions13d.org
Contact: Clinton H. Garver, Pres.

Local. Affiliated With: Lions Clubs International.

13281 ■ Plumbing-Heating-Cooling Contractors Association, Stark
c/o Mr. Luke Grabill, Pres.
10235 Manchester Ave. SW
Beach City, OH 44608-9774
Ph: (330)756-2075
Fax: (330)756-2399
E-mail: luke@grabill.com
URL: National Affiliate–www.phccweb.org
Contact: Mr. Luke Grabill, Pres.
Local. Represents the plumbing, heating and cooling contractors. Promotes the construction industry. Protects the environment, health, safety and comfort of society. **Affiliated With:** Plumbing-Heating-Cooling Contractors Association.

Beachwood

13282 ■ American ORT, Cleveland Chapter
24100 Chagrin Blvd., No. 300
Beachwood, OH 44122
Ph: (216)464-3022
Fax: (216)464-8975
E-mail: cleveland@aort.org
URL: National Affiliate–www.aort.org
Contact: Roni R. Wallace, Dir.
Founded: 1960. **Members:** 500. **Local**. Provides quality technical education and training to students. Teaches the skills of more than 100 trades and professions ranging from auto mechanics and welding to biotechnology, robotics, computers, and fiber optics. **Affiliated With:** American ORT.

13283 ■ American Theatre Organ Society, Western Reserve Chapter
c/o Doug Powers, Pres.
3323 Belvoir Blvd.
Beachwood, OH 44122
Ph: (440)338-5233
E-mail: dmp50@ameritech.net
URL: National Affiliate–www.atos.org
Contact: Doug Powers, Pres.
Local. Aims to restore, preserve and promote the theatre pipe organ and its music. Encourages the youth to learn the instrument. Operates a committee that gathers history and old music from silent film days and information on theatre organists, theaters and organ installations of the silent film era. **Affiliated With:** American Theatre Organ Society.

13284 ■ Beachwood Chamber of Commerce (BCC)
Three Commerce Park Sq.
23230 Chagrin Blvd., Ste.835
Beachwood, OH 44122-5424
Ph: (216)831-0003
Fax: (216)360-7333
E-mail: mail@beachwood.org
URL: http://www.beachwood.org
Contact: Tom Sudow, Exec.Dir.
Founded: 1991. **Members:** 600. **Membership Dues:** business (based on number of employees), $125-$400 (annual) • nonprofit, bank, additional branch, $150 (annual) • retired, non-business resident, $75 (annual) • government agency officer/employee, $75 (annual) • restaurant, $200 (annual). **Staff:** 5. **Budget:** $150,000. **Regional Groups:** 1. **State Groups:** 2. **Local**. Promotes business and community development in Beachwood, OH. **Computer Services:** Information services, business directory. **Telecommunication Services:** electronic mail, tom@beachwood.org. **Committees:** Community Events; Economic Development; Educational Seminars; Golf/Tennis Outing; Hospitality; Marketing; Monthly Luncheons/Breakfasts; Networking. **Publications:** *The Business Link*, monthly. Newsletter • *Purchase Directory.*

13285 ■ Cleveland Society of Clinical Hypnosis
3690 Orange Pl., Ste.410
Beachwood, OH 44122
Ph: (216)464-3666
Fax: (216)464-3951
URL: National Affiliate–www.asch.net
Contact: Alvin Sutker PhD, Contact
Local. Represents health and mental health care professionals using clinical hypnosis. Provides and encourages education programs to further the knowledge, understanding and application of hypnosis in health care. Works for the recognition and acceptance of hypnosis as an important tool in clinical health care. **Affiliated With:** American Society of Clinical Hypnosis.

13286 ■ Commercial Finance Association, Ohio Chapter
c/o Timothy Griffin, Pres.
Comerica Bus. Credit
3201 Enterprise Pkwy., Ste.190
Beachwood, OH 44122
Ph: (216)514-6211
Fax: (216)514-6230
E-mail: tcgriffin@comerica.com
URL: National Affiliate–www.cfa.com
Contact: Timothy Griffin, Pres.
State. **Affiliated With:** Commercial Finance Association.

13287 ■ First Catholic Slovak Ladies Association - Beachwood Junior Branch HO
24950 Chagrin Blvd.
Beachwood, OH 44122
Ph: (216)464-8015
E-mail: irene@fcsla.com
URL: National Affiliate–www.fcsla.com
Local. **Affiliated With:** First Catholic Slovak Ladies Association.

13288 ■ First Catholic Slovak Ladies Association - Beachwood Senior Branch ZJ
24950 Chagrin Blvd.
Beachwood, OH 44122
Ph: (216)464-8015
E-mail: irene@fcsla.com
URL: National Affiliate–www.fcsla.com
Local. **Affiliated With:** First Catholic Slovak Ladies Association.

13289 ■ Mind-Body-Spirit Connected (MBSC)
c/o Donna R. Nowak, Exec.Dir.
23210 Chagrin Blvd., Ste.211
Beachwood, OH 44122-5425
Ph: (216)321-9181
E-mail: help@mbsconline.org
URL: http://mbsconline.org
Contact: Donna R. Nowak, Exec.Dir.
Founded: 2001. **Members:** 96. **Membership Dues:** student, $95 (annual) • associate, $175 (annual) • practitioner, $195 (annual). **Staff:** 1. **Local Groups:** 1. **Local**. Serves as a forum for convening holistic practitioners in complementary disciplines, firms, and individuals interested in complementary medicine. Promotes a mind-body-spirit approach to well being, and to exchange information, ideas and knowledge about the healing arts and holistic practice management. **Telecommunication Services:** electronic mail, help@mbsconline.org. **Publications:** *Connectives*, bimonthly. Newsletter. **Price:** $12.00 per year.

13290 ■ National Black MBA Association, Cleveland Chapter
PO Box 22839
Beachwood, OH 44122
Ph: (216)689-4294
E-mail: clevelandblackmbas@yahoo.com
URL: http://www.clevelandblackmbas.org
Contact: Alton A. Tinker, Pres.
Local. Aims to increase the number as well as the diversity of successful Blacks in the business community by providing innovative programs to stimulate members' intellectual and economic growth. **Affiliated With:** National Black MBA Association. **Also Known As:** (2005) National Black MBA Association, Euclid.

13291 ■ Orange Community Homeowners Association
3939 Pine Crest Dr.
Beachwood, OH 44122
Ph: (216)831-2920
Local.

Beallsville

13292 ■ American Legion, Beallsville Post 768
51921 Sr 145
Beallsville, OH 43716
Ph: (740)362-7478
Fax: (740)362-1429
URL: National Affiliate–www.legion.org
Local. **Affiliated With:** American Legion.

Beaver

13293 ■ Veterans of Foreign Wars 9942
2081 Adams Rd.
Beaver, OH 45613
Ph: (740)226-2900
Contact: Danny Schader, Quarter Master
Local.

Beavercreek

13294 ■ American Legion, Beavercreek Memorial Post 763
3200 Dayton Xenia Rd.
Beavercreek, OH 45434
Ph: (740)362-7478
Fax: (740)362-1429
URL: National Affiliate–www.legion.org
Local. **Affiliated With:** American Legion.

13295 ■ American Wine Society - Dayton
c/o Catherine A. Beard, Chair
3620 King Edward Way
Beavercreek, OH 45431-3791
Ph: (937)609-1534
E-mail: cathy@winegeeks.net
URL: National Affiliate–www.americanwinesociety.org
Contact: Catherine A. Beard, Chair
Local. **Affiliated With:** American Wine Society.

13296 ■ Beavercreek Chamber of Commerce (BCC)
3299 Kemp Rd.
Beavercreek, OH 45431-2550
Ph: (937)426-2202
Fax: (937)426-2204
E-mail: nancy@beavercreekchamber.org
Contact: Clete Buddelmeyer, Exec.Dir.
Founded: 1966. **Members:** 475. **Staff:** 2. **Budget:** $99,800. **Local**. Businesspersons, professionals, and individuals. Promotes the economic, civil, commercial, industrial, and educational interests of Beavercreek and Beavercreek Township, OH. **Awards:** Business Leadership Grant. **Frequency:** annual. **Type:** grant. **Telecommunication Services:** electronic mail, susan@beavercreekchamber.org. **Affiliated With:** U.S. Chamber of Commerce. **Publications:** *Chamber Link*, monthly. Newsletter. **Circulation:** 500. **Advertising:** accepted • *Membership Directory and Buyers' Guide*, periodic. **Conventions/Meetings:** annual meeting.

13297 ■ Greene County Convention and Visitors Bureau
1221 Meadowbridge Dr., Ste.A
Beavercreek, OH 45434
Ph: (937)429-9100
Fax: (937)429-7726
Free: (800)733-9109
E-mail: visitors@greenecountyohio.org
URL: http://www.greenecountyohio.org
Contact: John Abel, Exec.Dir.
Local.

13298 ■ National Active and Retired Federal Employees Association - Beavercreek 2217
2274 Apricot Dr.
Beavercreek, OH 45431-2662
Ph: (937)429-5967
URL: National Affiliate–www.narfe.org
Contact: Thomas Jones, Contact
Local. Protects the retirement future of employees through education. Informs members on issues affecting the retirement. **Affiliated With:** National Association of Retired Federal Employees.

13299 ■ National Active and Retired Federal Employees Association - Dayton 35
3463 Rome Beauty Dr.
Beavercreek, OH 45434-5929
Ph: (937)426-3977
URL: National Affiliate–www.narfe.org
Contact: Carol A. Blevins, Contact
Local. Protects the retirement future of employees through education. Informs members on issues affecting the retirement. **Affiliated With:** National Association of Retired Federal Employees.

13300 ■ National Association of Pastoral Musicians, Cincinnati-Miami Valley
c/o Ms. Loretta Feller
1378 Cowman Ct.
Beavercreek, OH 45434
Ph: (937)429-3396
E-mail: lkfeller@aol.com
URL: http://www.mvccm.org
Contact: Ms. Loretta Feller, Pres.
Local. Affiliated With: National Association of Pastoral Musicians.

13301 ■ Navy League of the United States, Dayton
c/o Robert F. Bauer, Pres.
1016 Grove Hill Dr.
Beavercreek, OH 45434-5906
Ph: (937)426-8725
URL: National Affiliate–www.navyleague.org
Contact: Robert F. Bauer, Pres.
Local. Civilian organization that supports U.S. capability to keep the sea lanes open through a strong, viable Navy, Marine Corps, Coast Guard, and Merchant Marine. Seeks to awaken interest and cooperation of U.S. citizens in matters serving to aid, improve, and develop the efficiency of U.S. naval and maritime forces and equipment. **Affiliated With:** Navy League of the United States.

13302 ■ Purple Penquins
c/o Helga Slade
2882 Hamden Dr.
Beavercreek, OH 45434-6456
Ph: (937)429-3946
E-mail: hslade2@sbcglobal.net
URL: National Affiliate–www.ava.org
Contact: Helga Slade, Contact
Local. Non-competitive sports enthusiasts. **Affiliated With:** American Volkssport Association.

Bedford

13303 ■ American Legion, Bedford Post 350
29 Ennis Ave.
Bedford, OH 44146
Ph: (740)362-7478
Fax: (740)362-1429
URL: National Affiliate–www.legion.org
Local. Affiliated With: American Legion.

13304 ■ Bedford Chamber of Commerce (BCC)
33 S Park
Bedford, OH 44146
Ph: (440)232-0115
Fax: (440)232-0521
URL: http://www.bedfordchamberoh.org
Contact: Melissa Tusai, Office Mgr.
Members: 75. **Local**. Promotes business and community development in Bedford, OH. Sponsors annual town picnic. **Publications:** *Business Directory of Bedford*, biennial. Newsletter • *Chamber Chatter*, monthly. Newsletter. **Price:** free • Newsletter, bimonthly. **Conventions/Meetings:** monthly meeting - always third Wednesday of the month.

13305 ■ Society of Broadcast Engineers, Chapter 70 - Northeast Ohio
c/o Mike Szabo, Chm.
169 W Glendale St.
Bedford, OH 44146
Ph: (216)344-3391
E-mail: sbe70@broadcast.net
URL: http://www.broadcast.net/~sbe70
Contact: Mike Szabo, Chm.
Local. Serves the interests of broadcast engineers. Promotes the profession and related fields for both theoretical and practical applications. Advocates for technical advancement of the industry. **Affiliated With:** Society of Broadcast Engineers. **Publications:** *70 Minutes*, monthly. Newsletter. **Advertising:** accepted. Alternate Formats: online.

Bedford Heights

13306 ■ American Legion, Ohio Post 94
c/o Lemuel T. Boydston
6042 White Pine Dr.
Bedford Heights, OH 44146
Ph: (740)362-7478
Fax: (740)362-1429
URL: National Affiliate–www.legion.org
Contact: Lemuel T. Boydston, Contact
Local. Affiliated With: American Legion.

13307 ■ Bedford Heights Chamber of Commerce
24816 Aurora Rd., Ste.C
Bedford Heights, OH 44146
Ph: (440)232-3369
Fax: (440)232-4862
E-mail: bedfordhtscofc@aol.com
URL: http://www.bedfordheightschamber.com
Contact: Dorothy Pirrung, Pres.
Membership Dues: business (based on the number of employees), $150-$750 (annual). **Local**. Represents the interests of businessmen and women associated together in a joint effort to preserve and protect the American free enterprise system.

Bellaire

13308 ■ American Legion, Bellaire Post 52
3600 Guernsey St.
Bellaire, OH 43906
Ph: (740)362-7478
Fax: (740)362-1429
URL: National Affiliate–www.legion.org
Local. Affiliated With: American Legion.

13309 ■ Bellaire Area Chamber of Commerce
PO Box 428
Bellaire, OH 43906
Ph: (740)676-9723
E-mail: information@bellairechamber.com
URL: http://www.bellairechamber.com
Contact: Barb Roman, Pres.
Local. Promotes the economic viability, cultural richness, environmental sensitivity, and the social needs of Bellaire.

13310 ■ Bellaire High School Alumni Association
c/o Scott Rataiczak
PO Box 307
Bellaire, OH 43906
E-mail: president@bellairealumni.org
URL: http://www.bellairealumni.org
Founded: 1905. **Staff:** 16. **Local**.

13311 ■ Bellaire Lions Club
c/o Rick Henry, Pres.
Box 262
Bellaire, OH 43906
Ph: (740)676-5156
URL: http://users.adelphia.net/~npssteve/district.htm
Contact: Rick Henry, Pres.
Local. Affiliated With: Lions Clubs International.

13312 ■ Korean War Veterans Association, Ohio Valley Chapter
c/o Stanley A. McCann
217 4th Ave.
Bellaire, OH 43906-1012
Ph: (740)676-4036
E-mail: vsmccann@stratuswave.net
URL: National Affiliate–www.kwva.org
Contact: Stanley A. McCann, Contact
Local. Affiliated With: Korean War Veterans Association.

Bellbrook

13313 ■ American Legion, Tuttle-Miller Post 761
26 N West St.
Bellbrook, OH 45305
Ph: (740)362-7478
Fax: (740)362-1429
URL: National Affiliate–www.legion.org
Local. Affiliated With: American Legion.

13314 ■ Bellbrook - Sugarcreek Area Chamber of Commerce (BSACC)
64 W Franklin St.
Bellbrook, OH 45305-1903
Ph: (937)848-4930
Fax: (937)848-4930
E-mail: bellbrooksugarcreek@juno.com
URL: http://bellbrooksugarcreekchamber.com
Contact: Chris Ewing, Exec.Dir.
Members: 135. **Membership Dues:** public entity, $50 (annual) • business, $90 (annual) • individual, $35 (annual) • service organization, $25 (annual) • auxiliary, $10 (annual). **Local**. Promotes business and community development in Bellbrook-Sugarcreek area of Ohio. **Awards:** Carl Valentine Scholarship. **Frequency:** annual. **Type:** scholarship. **Recipient:** for grades and need • The Chamber Pot. **Frequency:** annual. **Type:** recognition. **Recipient:** for service to community and chamber. **Affiliated With:** U.S. Chamber of Commerce. **Publications:** *Community Business Directory*, annual. **Price:** free. **Circulation:** 5,500. **Advertising:** accepted • *Newsgram*, semiannual. Newsletter. **Advertising:** accepted. **Conventions/Meetings:** monthly Business Meeting - always first Thursday, Bellbrook, OH.

13315 ■ Miami Valley Triumphs (MVT)
c/o Stan Seto, Pres.
PO Box 144
Bellbrook, OH 45305
Ph: (513)683-7974
E-mail: stans@fuse.net
URL: http://www.miamivalleytriumphs.org
Contact: Stan Seto, Pres.
Local. Affiliated With: Vintage Triumph Register.

Belle Center

13316 ■ American Legion, Ohio Post 266
c/o Willard Stout
PO Box 274
Belle Center, OH 43310
Ph: (740)362-7478
Fax: (740)362-1429
URL: National Affiliate–www.legion.org
Contact: Willard Stout, Contact
Local. Affiliated With: American Legion.

Belle Valley

13317 ■ American Legion, Belle Valley Post 641
131 Brown St.
Belle Valley, OH 43717
Ph: (740)362-7478
Fax: (740)362-1429
URL: National Affiliate–www.legion.org
Local. Affiliated With: American Legion.

Bellefontaine

13318 ■ AAA Ohio Automobile Club
1790 S Main St.
Bellefontaine, OH 43311
Ph: (937)599-5154
State.

13319 ■ American Legion, Ohio Post 173
c/o Harold Kerr
120 Colton Ave.
Bellefontaine, OH 43311
Ph: (740)362-7478
Fax: (740)362-1429
URL: National Affiliate–www.legion.org
Contact: Harold Kerr, Contact
Local. Affiliated With: American Legion.

13320 ■ Logan County Area Chamber of Commerce (LCCC)
100 S Main St.
Bellefontaine, OH 43311-2083
Ph: (937)599-5121
Fax: (937)599-2411
E-mail: info@logancountyohio.com
URL: http://www.logancountyohio.com
Contact: Ed Wallace, Pres./CEO
Founded: 1928. **Members:** 267. **Staff:** 3. **Budget:** $105,000. **Local.** Promotes business and community development in the Logan County, OH area. **Computer Services:** Online services, member listings. **Affiliated With:** U.S. Chamber of Commerce. **Formerly:** (1999) Greater Logan County Area Chamber of Commerce. **Publications:** *Tourist Directory*, annual • *Voice of Business*, bimonthly. Newsletter. **Price:** free for members. **Advertising:** accepted. Alternate Formats: online • Membership Directory, annual. **Price:** included in membership dues.

13321 ■ Logan County Historical Society and Logan County Museum
521 E Columbus Ave.
Bellefontaine, OH 43311
Ph: (937)593-7557
E-mail: lchsmuse@logan.net
URL: http://www.logancountymuseum.org
Contact: Todd McCormick, Curator/Dir.
Founded: 1946. **Members:** 600. **Membership Dues:** single, $15 (annual) • family, $20 (annual) • business, $30 (annual). **Staff:** 2. **Budget:** $150,000. **State Groups:** 1. **Local Groups:** 1. **Local.** Individuals interested in the history of Logan County, Ohio. Conducts educational programs and tours of the museum and mansion. Maintains archives library, photograph library, and Logan County Genealogical Society's Genealogy Library, all housed in the Logan County Museum. **Libraries: Type:** open to the public. **Holdings:** papers. **Subjects:** local history, Indian history (mainly local). **Committees:** Trustees. **Formerly:** Logan County Archaeological and Historical Society; (2001) Logan County Historical Society. **Publications:** *Logan County Historical Society Newsletter*, bimonthly. **Price:** included in membership dues. **Circulation:** 500. **Conventions/Meetings:** monthly meeting.

13322 ■ National Active and Retired Federal Employees Association - Logan County 2162
3265 Buckeye Dr. Southgate Acres
Bellefontaine, OH 43311-9626
Ph: (937)593-3176
URL: National Affiliate–www.narfe.org
Contact: Clayton W. Hill, Contact
Local. Protects the retirement future of employees through education. Informs members on issues affecting the retirement. **Affiliated With:** National Association of Retired Federal Employees.

13323 ■ Ohio Genealogical Society, Logan County
PO Box 36
Bellefontaine, OH 43311-0036
E-mail: logangs@loganrec.com
URL: http://www.co.logan.oh.us/museum/Geneology/geneology.html
Contact: Bonnie Hansen, Treas.
Founded: 1979. **Members:** 400. **Membership Dues:** single, $12 (annual) • joint, $17 (annual). **Regional.** Genealogists and others with an interest in the history of Logan County, OH. Catalogs and documents local cemetery records and other sources of genealogical information. **Libraries: Type:** reference. **Holdings:** 2,000; archival material, books. **Subjects:** genealogy, local history. **Affiliated With:** Ohio Genealogical Society. **Publications:** *Branches and Twigs*, quarterly. Newsletter. **Price:** $12.00. **Circulation:** 400. **Conventions/Meetings:** monthly meeting - November-April 3rd Wednesday; May-October 3rd Monday; no meeting in December.

13324 ■ Ohio Parents of Blind Children
c/o Crystal McClain, Pres.
1070 Township Rd. 181
Bellefontaine, OH 43311
Ph: (937)599-5782
E-mail: mcclain@loganrec.com
URL: http://www.nfbohio.org/parents.html
Contact: Crystal McClain, Pres.
State. Provides information and support to parents of blind children. Develops and expands resources available to parents and their children. Aims to eliminate discrimination and prejudice against the blind. **Affiliated With:** National Organization of Parents of Blind Children.

13325 ■ Puppeteers of America - Columbus Puppetry Guild
c/o David L. Greenbaum, Pres.
716 W Chillicothe Ave.
Bellefontaine, OH 43311
Ph: (937)593-2957
Fax: (937)593-2957
E-mail: starsonstringsxl@netzero.net
URL: http://cpg.brianwindsor.com
Contact: David L. Greenbaum, Pres.
Local.

13326 ■ United Way of Logan County, Ohio
122 N Main St.
Bellefontaine, OH 43311-2021
Ph: (937)592-2886
URL: National Affiliate–national.unitedway.org
Local. Affiliated With: United Way of America.

Bellevue

13327 ■ American Legion, Liberty Post 46
208 W Main St.
Bellevue, OH 44811
Ph: (740)362-7478
Fax: (740)362-1429
URL: National Affiliate–www.legion.org
Local. Affiliated With: American Legion.

13328 ■ Bellevue High School Alumni Association
c/o Sarah Phillips
PO Box 191
Bellevue, OH 44811
E-mail: sabes@hmcltd.net
URL: http://www.bellevuealumni.com
Contact: Dennis Sabo, Pres.
Members: 866. **Local.**

13329 ■ Bellevue Lions Club
c/o David Greene, Pres.
1060 Monroe St.
Bellevue, OH 44811
Ph: (419)483-8378
E-mail: dmgreene@cros.net
URL: http://www.lions13b.org
Contact: David Greene, Pres.
Local. Affiliated With: Lions Clubs International.

13330 ■ Historic Lyme Village Association (HLVA)
c/o Mrs. Alvina Schaeffer, Village Curator
8401 SR 113
Bellevue, OH 44811
Ph: (419)483-4949 (419)483-6052
E-mail: bdrown@woh.rr.com
URL: http://www.lymevillage.com
Contact: Mrs. Alvina Schaeffer, Village Curator
Founded: 1972. **Members:** 250. **Membership Dues:** student, $6 (annual) • single, $10 (annual) • couple, $15 (annual) • family, $25 (annual) • sustaining, $40 (annual) • patron, $100 (annual) • life, $200 • honorary, $10 (annual). **Local.** Individuals interested in historical preservation. Works for the preservation of Historic Lyme Village. Maintains museum; sponsors educational programs, tours, and special events. **Libraries: Type:** open to the public. **Holdings:** 100. **Projects:** Living History. **Formerly:** (1976) Historic Lyme Church Association. **Publications:** *The History of the School Houses in Lyme Township*. Book • *Life in Lyme*. Book • *Lyme Lines*, monthly. Newsletter. **Price:** included in membership dues • *1848 Butterfield's History of Seneca County and Burgner Family History*. Reprint • *1894 Erie County Atlas*. Reprint • *1874 Erie County Atlas*. Reprint • *Pioneers Progress*. Book • *World Grows Smaller*. Book. **Conventions/Meetings:** monthly meeting - during fall and winter.

13331 ■ Mad River and NKP Railroad Society
233 York St.
Bellevue, OH 44811-1377
Ph: (419)483-2222
E-mail: madriver@onebellevue.com
URL: http://www.onebellevue.com/madriver
Founded: 1972. **Members:** 650. **Membership Dues:** regular (age 0-60), $20 (annual) • regular (age over 60), $15 (annual) • family (parents & children under 18), $30 (annual) • sustaining, $75 (annual) • life, $350 • golden life, $500. **Budget:** $100,000. **Local.** Individuals interested in preserving railroad history. Promotes travel and shipping by rail. Operates railroad museum. **Libraries: Type:** reference. **Affiliated With:** Association of Railway Museums; Tourist Railway Association. **Publications:** *The Caboose Cable*, monthly. Newsletter. **Price:** included in membership dues. **Conventions/Meetings:** monthly general assembly - except March and December; always last Wednesday.

13332 ■ Ohio State Society of American Medical Technologists
c/o M. Beth Osher, MT, Pres.
146 Gunther St.
Bellevue, OH 44811
Ph: (419)483-5788
Fax: (419)483-1301
E-mail: bellevue146@yahoo.com
URL: http://www.ohioamt.org
Contact: M. Beth Osher MT, Pres.
State. Works to manage, promote and improve certification programs for allied health professionals who work in a variety of disciplines and settings. Administers certification examinations in accordance with the highest standards of accreditation. Provides continuing education, information and advocacy services to members. **Affiliated With:** American Medical Technologists.

13333 ■ Sweet Adelines International, Northern Buckeye Chapter
First United Methodist Church
901 Northwest St.
Bellevue, OH 44811-1029
Ph: (419)332-4566
E-mail: marhof@glis.cc
URL: National Affiliate–www.sweetadelineintl.org
Contact: Marjorie Hofelich, Contact
Local. Advances the musical art form of barbershop harmony through education and performances.

Provides education, training and coaching in the development of women's four-part barbershop harmony. **Affiliated With:** Sweet Adelines International.

Bellville

13334 ■ American Legion, Ohio Post 535
c/o Irvin Hiskey
77 Bell St.
Bellville, OH 44813
Ph: (740)362-7478
Fax: (740)362-1429
URL: National Affiliate–www.legion.org
Contact: Irvin Hiskey, Contact
Local. Affiliated With: American Legion.

13335 ■ Bellville Chamber of Commerce
142 Park Pl.
Bellville, OH 44813
Ph: (419)886-2245
Fax: (419)886-2297
URL: http://www.bellvilleohio.net
Contact: Larry Rose, Contact
Local.

13336 ■ Bellville-Jefferson Township Historical Society
c/o Donald C. Palm, Pres.
167 Main St.
Bellville, OH 44813
Ph: (419)886-3680
Fax: (419)886-4769
E-mail: edglea@aol.com
URL: http://www.angelfire.com/oh/bellville
Contact: Dean A. Thomas, Contact
Local.

13337 ■ Bellville Lions Club - Ohio
c/o Carolyn Brook, Sec.
598 Alexander Rd. W
Bellville, OH 44813
Ph: (419)886-4181
E-mail: csbrook@peoplepc.com
URL: http://www.lions13b.org
Contact: Carolyn Brook, Sec.
Local. Affiliated With: Lions Clubs International.

Beloit

13338 ■ American Legion, Ohio Post 574
c/o George D. Worth
3300 Westville Lake Rd.
Beloit, OH 44609
Ph: (740)362-7478
Fax: (740)362-1429
URL: National Affiliate–www.legion.org
Contact: George D. Worth, Contact
Local. Affiliated With: American Legion.

13339 ■ Homeworth Lions Club
c/o Merle Wasmire, Jr., Pres.
27424 Rainbow Lane Cir.
Beloit, OH 44609
Ph: (330)537-4107
URL: http://www.lions13d.org
Contact: Merle Wasmire Jr., Pres.
Local. Affiliated With: Lions Clubs International.

Belpre

13340 ■ American Legion, Blennerhassett Post 495
100 Washington Blvd.
Belpre, OH 45714
Ph: (740)362-7478
Fax: (740)362-1429
URL: National Affiliate–www.legion.org
Local. Affiliated With: American Legion.

13341 ■ Belpre Area Chamber of Commerce (BACC)
713 Park Dr.
PO Box 8
Belpre, OH 45714
Ph: (740)423-8934
Fax: (740)423-6616
E-mail: chamdir@charter.net
URL: http://www.belprechamber.com
Contact: Joan Knierim, Exec.Dir.
Founded: 1929. **Members:** 1,100. **Staff:** 17. **Budget:** $1,700,000. **Local.** Promotes business and community development in the Belpre, OH area. Conducts community social and promotional activities. **Publications:** *Chamberletter*, bimonthly. Newsletter. **Price:** free for members. Alternate Formats: online. **Conventions/Meetings:** monthly Business After Hours - meeting • annual dinner - always November • bimonthly meeting • monthly seminar.

13342 ■ Belpre Lions Club
PO Box 164
Belpre, OH 45714
Ph: (740)423-5171 (740)423-5677
E-mail: tlife@frognet.net
URL: http://belpreoh.lionwap.org
Contact: Teri L. Life, Sec.
Local. Affiliated With: Lions Clubs International.

Berea

13343 ■ American Legion, Ohio Post 91
c/o Albert E. Baesel
91 Amer. Legion Pkwy.
Berea, OH 44017
Ph: (740)362-7478
Fax: (740)362-1429
URL: National Affiliate–www.legion.org
Contact: Albert E. Baesel, Contact
Local. Affiliated With: American Legion.

13344 ■ American Sewing Guild, North Olmsted Chapter
c/o Nanka Pearce
80 Kraft St.
Berea, OH 44017
Ph: (440)826-0442
E-mail: nankapearce@hotmail.com
URL: http://www.geocities.com/asgnolm
Contact: Lynda Fazulak, Contact
Local. Affiliated With: American Sewing Guild.

13345 ■ Berea Chamber of Commerce
173 Front St.
PO Box 232
Berea, OH 44017
Ph: (440)243-8415
Fax: (440)243-8470
E-mail: chamber@bereaohio.com
URL: http://www.bereaohio.com
Contact: Kathy Kellums, Exec.Dir./Treas.
Founded: 1939. **Membership Dues:** individual, $35 (annual) • business (based on number of employees), $150-$550 (annual) • property owner, $250 (annual). **Local.** Advances and develops the commercial, industrial, civic and general interest for the residents and the City of Berea. **Awards:** Grindstone Award. **Frequency:** annual. **Type:** recognition. **Recipient:** to an outstanding citizen(s) who contributes their time and effort toward making Berea a better place to live. **Computer Services:** database, business members by category and name. **Publications:** Newsletter, bimonthly. Keeps the chamber in contact with the members.

13346 ■ Cleveland Shetland Sheepdog Club (CSSC)
c/o Louise Walter, Sec.
509 Chestnut Dr.
Berea, OH 44017
Ph: (440)243-3537
URL: http://www.clevelandshelties.com
Local.

13347 ■ Ohio Health Care Association, District 13
c/o Michael Coury, Chm.
Generations Hea. Care
2 Berea Commons, Ste.I
Berea, OH 44017
Ph: (440)243-8330
Fax: (440)243-3049
E-mail: mcoury@gerationshcm.com
URL: http://www.ohca.org
Contact: Michael Coury, Chm.
Local. Promotes professionalism and ethical behavior of individuals providing long-term care delivery for patients and for the general public. Provides information, education and administrative tools to enhance the quality of long-term care. Improves the standards of service and administration of member nursing homes. **Affiliated With:** American Health Care Association.

13348 ■ Psi Chi, National Honor Society in Psychology - Baldwin-Wallace College
c/o Dept. of Psychology
101 Carnegie Hall
275 Eastland Rd.
Berea, OH 44017
Ph: (440)826-2163 (440)826-2165
Fax: (440)826-8549
E-mail: bthomas@bw.edu
URL: National Affiliate–www.psichi.org
Local. Affiliated With: Psi Chi, National Honor Society in Psychology.

13349 ■ Siberian Husky Club of Greater Cleveland (SHCGC)
c/o Bobbie Palmer, Sec.
740 Prospect Rd., No. 2
Berea, OH 44017
Ph: (440)826-3653
Fax: (440)826-3653
E-mail: gramabobbie@ameritech.net
URL: http://www.siberiancleveland.org
Contact: Bobbie Palmer, Sec.
Founded: 1961. **Members:** 25. **Membership Dues:** single, $18 (annual) • couple, $27 (annual). **Local Groups:** 1. **Regional. Libraries: Type:** not open to the public. **Holdings:** articles, books, periodicals. **Subjects:** dogs, specifically Siberian Huskies, dog sledding. **Awards:** Conformation/Obedience/Special Awards. **Frequency:** annual. **Type:** recognition. **Affiliated With:** American Kennel Club. **Publications:** *Siberian X-Press*, monthly. Newsletter. Contains articles of interest to members and general information. **Price:** included in membership dues; $12.00/yr. for nonmembers. **Circulation:** 45. **Advertising:** accepted. **Conventions/Meetings:** monthly meeting - 2nd Monday of the month from September through June. Parma, OH • annual Punderson Sled Dog Race - competition • annual Spring Specialty Show and Obedience Trial - Berea, OH.

13350 ■ Young Life SW Cleveland
102 Baker St.
Berea, OH 44017
Ph: (440)243-7731
URL: http://sites.younglife.org/_layouts/ylext/default.aspx?ID=A-OH42
Local. Affiliated With: Young Life.

Berlin Center

13351 ■ Noah's Lost Ark
8424 Bedell Rd.
Berlin Center, OH 44401-9771
Ph: (330)584-7835
E-mail: noahslostark@aol.com
URL: http://www.noahslostark.org
Local.

Berlin Heights

13352 ■ American Legion, Berlin Heights Post 659
PO Box 143
Berlin Heights, OH 44814
Ph: (740)362-7478
Fax: (740)362-1429
URL: National Affiliate–www.legion.org
Local. Affiliated With: American Legion.

Bethel

13353 ■ American Legion, Ohio Post 406
c/o Archie Lee Boyce
3393 Legion Ln.
Bethel, OH 45106
Ph: (740)362-7478
Fax: (740)362-1429
URL: National Affiliate–www.legion.org
Contact: Archie Lee Boyce, Contact
Local. Affiliated With: American Legion.

Bethesda

13354 ■ American Legion, Epworth Post 90
PO Box 221
Bethesda, OH 43719
Ph: (740)362-7478
Fax: (740)362-1429
URL: National Affiliate–www.legion.org
Local. Affiliated With: American Legion.

Bettsville

13355 ■ American Legion, Ohio Post 733
c/o James W. Sullivan
PO Box 282
Bettsville, OH 44815
Ph: (740)362-7478
Fax: (740)362-1429
URL: National Affiliate–www.legion.org
Contact: James W. Sullivan, Contact
Local. Affiliated With: American Legion.

Beverly

13356 ■ American Legion, Ohio Post 389
c/o Russell Chadwick
PO Box 155
Beverly, OH 45715
Ph: (740)362-7478
Fax: (740)362-1429
URL: National Affiliate–www.legion.org
Contact: Russell Chadwick, Contact
Local. Affiliated With: American Legion.

13357 ■ Muskingum Valley Area Chamber of Commerce (MVACC)
PO Box 837
Beverly, OH 45715
Ph: (740)984-8259
E-mail: jawagner@aep.com
URL: http://www.mvacc.com
Contact: Glen Miller, Chm.
Membership Dues: individual, $30 (annual) • non-profit, $50 (annual) • government/government agency, educational institution, $100 (annual). **Local.** Advances the general welfare and prosperity of Muskingum Valley area. **Publications:** Articles. Alternate Formats: online.

Bexley

13358 ■ Bexley Area Chamber of Commerce (BACC)
2242 E Main St.
Bexley, OH 43209
Ph: (614)470-4500
E-mail: feedback@bexleyareachamber.org
URL: http://www.bexleyareachamber.org
Contact: Mark E. Cooper, Pres.
Membership Dues: individual, $35 (annual) • business, $70 (annual). **Local.** Promotes business and community development in the Bexley area. **Publications:** Newsletter, monthly. Contains information on upcoming events and featured businesses.

Bidwell

13359 ■ Southeastern Ohio Angus Association
c/o Mike Hemphill, Pres.
1075 SR 850
Bidwell, OH 45614
Ph: (740)245-5506
URL: National Affiliate–www.angus.org
Contact: Mike Hemphill, Pres.
Regional. Affiliated With: American Angus Association.

Big Prairie

13360 ■ Buckeye Appaloosa Horse Club
c/o Carlyn J. Wayland
12041 Township Rd. 521
Big Prairie, OH 44611
Ph: (303)378-2911
E-mail: appyacres@valkyrie.net
URL: National Affiliate–www.appaloosa.com
Contact: Carlyn J. Wayland, Contact
Local. Affiliated With: Appaloosa Horse Club.

Blanchester

13361 ■ American Legion, Marion Post 179
210 Lazenby St.
Blanchester, OH 45107
Ph: (740)362-7478
Fax: (740)362-1429
URL: National Affiliate–www.legion.org
Local. Affiliated With: American Legion.

13362 ■ Blanchester Area Chamber of Commerce (BACC)
PO Box 274
Blanchester, OH 45107
Ph: (937)783-3601
E-mail: blanchesterareacc@hotmail.com
Contact: Mark Paul, Pres.
Founded: 1980. **Members:** 56. **Local.** Promotes business and community development in the Blanchester, OH area. Sponsors annual Fun Fest. Holds monthly board meeting. **Publications:** Newsletter, bimonthly. **Conventions/Meetings:** annual meeting.

Bloomdale

13363 ■ Toledo Kennel Club
c/o Ms. Virginia Gray, Pres.
101 Lincoln St.
Bloomdale, OH 44817-9754
Ph: (419)454-3571
E-mail: info@toledokennelclub.org
URL: http://www.toledokennelclub.org
Contact: Ms. Virginia Gray, Pres.
Founded: 1878. **Membership Dues:** regular, $20 (annual). **Local.** Works to further the advancement of all breeds of purebred dogs; conducts dog shows, obedience trials and sanctioned matches under AKC rules; conducts educational programs on breeding, showing, training and the responsibilities of dog ownership; promotes charitable and other activities for the benefit of dogs and the community. **Affiliated With:** American Kennel Club. **Publications:** *Paw-Pouri*, monthly. Newsletter. **Price:** free to members. **Conventions/Meetings:** annual All-Breed Dog Show - specialty show • monthly meeting, membership meeting, public is invited - every 4th Thursday of the month • Obedience Trial - specialty show - 3/year.

Bloomville

13364 ■ American Legion, Caufield Post 434
PO Box 361
Bloomville, OH 44818
Ph: (740)362-7478
Fax: (740)362-1429
URL: National Affiliate–www.legion.org
Local. Affiliated With: American Legion.

Bluffton

13365 ■ American Legion, Bluffton Post 382
154 N Main St., 2nd Fl., Town Hall
Bluffton, OH 45817
Ph: (740)362-7478
Fax: (740)362-1429
URL: National Affiliate–www.legion.org
Local. Affiliated With: American Legion.

13366 ■ Bluffton Area Chamber of Commerce (BACC)
PO Box 142
Bluffton, OH 45817-0142
Ph: (419)358-5675
E-mail: bacc@sisna.com
Contact: Mrs. Betsy Lee, CEO
Members: 110. **Staff:** 1. **Budget:** $30,000. **Local.** Businesspeople, churches, and non-profit organizations organized to promote economic growth and community development in Bluffton, OH. Sponsors arts and crafts festival, antique car show, and Blaze of Lights Christmas Lighting ceremony. **Affiliated With:** U.S. Chamber of Commerce. **Formerly:** (1983) Bluffton +Businessmen Association. **Publications:** *Chamber Chat*, bimonthly. Newsletter. Includes updates on events and information. **Price:** free with membership. **Advertising:** accepted. **Conventions/Meetings:** quarterly Chamber Social Hour - meeting - always second Tuesday of the month • monthly meeting, membership - every 2nd Friday. Bluffton, OH.

13367 ■ Model T Ford Club of Northwest Ohio
c/o Jack Putnam
1215 Hancock Rd. 28
Bluffton, OH 45817
Ph: (419)358-6313
E-mail: jputnam@wcoil.com
URL: http://www.nwo-modelt.org
Contact: Jack Putnam, Contact
Local. Affiliated With: Model "T" Ford Club of America.

13368 ■ Psi Chi, National Honor Society in Psychology - Bluffton University
1 Univ. Dr.
Bluffton, OH 45817-2104
Ph: (419)358-3290
Fax: (419)358-3074
E-mail: nathp@bluffton.edu
URL: http://www.psichi.org/chapters/info.asp?chapter_id=969
Contact: Pamela S. Nath PhD, Advisor
Local.

13369 ■ United Way of Bluffton, Beaverdam, and Richland Township
215 S Lawn Ave.
Bluffton, OH 45817-1019
Ph: (419)358-8381 (419)358-3331
Fax: (419)358-3074
E-mail: flemingl@bluffton.edu
URL: National Affiliate–national.unitedway.org
Contact: Linda Fleming, Exec.Sec.
Budget: $19,500. **Local.** Works to assist in fundraising by conducting residential, door-to-door and

company wide employee campaigns and by encouraging corporate contributions. **Affiliated With:** United Way of America.

Boardman

13370 ■ American Legion, Boardman Memorial Post 565
749 Forest Ridge Dr.
Boardman, OH 44512
Ph: (740)362-7478
Fax: (740)362-1429
URL: National Affiliate–www.legion.org
Local. Affiliated With: American Legion.

13371 ■ American Red Cross, Mahoning Chapter
8392 Tod Ave.
Boardman, OH 44512
Ph: (330)726-6063
Fax: (330)726-6448
URL: http://mahoning.redcross.org
Local.

13372 ■ Boardman Lions Club
c/o Dennis Koch, Pres.
50 Buena Vista Ave.
Boardman, OH 44512
Ph: (330)758-4315
URL: http://www.lions13d.org
Contact: Dennis Koch, Pres.
Local. Affiliated With: Lions Clubs International.

13373 ■ Ice Zone Figure Skating Club
PO Box 3684
Boardman, OH 44513
E-mail: mkoman@zoominternet.net
URL: http://www.icezonefigureskatingclub.com
Contact: Denise Powell, Pres.
Local. Provides programs to encourage participation and achievement in the sport of figure skating on ice. Defines and maintains uniform standards of skating proficiency. Organizes and sponsors competitions and exhibitions for the purpose of stimulating interest in figure skating. **Affiliated With:** United States Figure Skating Association.

13374 ■ Independent Electrical Contractors, Western Reserve
c/o Anita Carano
PO Box 3279
Boardman, OH 44513
Ph: (330)629-9810
Fax: (330)629-9810
E-mail: acarano@zoominternet.net
URL: National Affiliate–www.ieci.org
Contact: Anita Carano, Contact
Local. Affiliated With: Independent Electrical Contractors.

13375 ■ Youngstown Diocesan Confederation of Teachers (YDCT)
c/o Barbara Demesko, Pres.
8090 Market St.
Boardman, OH 44512
Ph: (330)758-5312
Fax: (330)758-5312
E-mail: ydct3504@aol.com
URL: http://www.nacst.com/Youngstown/home.htm
Contact: Barbara Demesko, Pres.
Local. Affiliated With: National Association of Catholic School Teachers.

Bolivar

13376 ■ American Legion, Fort Laurens Post 190
PO Box 65
Bolivar, OH 44612
Ph: (740)362-7478
Fax: (740)362-1429
URL: National Affiliate–www.legion.org
Local. Affiliated With: American Legion.

13377 ■ Bolivar Lions Club
c/o William B. Clements, Pres.
9788 Lafort Cir. NE
Bolivar, OH 44612
Ph: (330)874-8007
E-mail: n3xut@aol.com
URL: http://users.adelphia.net/~npssteve/district.htm
Contact: William B. Clements, Pres.
Local. Affiliated With: Lions Clubs International.

Bowerston

13378 ■ American Legion, Ohio Post 581
c/o James O. Preston
91925 Derry Rd.
Bowerston, OH 44695
Ph: (740)362-7478
Fax: (740)362-1429
URL: National Affiliate–www.legion.org
Contact: James O. Preston, Contact
Local. Affiliated With: American Legion.

13379 ■ Ohio Valley Muskie Hunters
211 Mann St.
Bowerston, OH 44695
Ph: (740)269-1216
E-mail: michele_10869@msn.com
URL: National Affiliate–www.muskiesinc.org
Contact: Michele Uttermohlen, Pres.
Local.

Bowling Green

13380 ■ American Cancer Society, Wood Area
1045 N Main St., Ste.8
Bowling Green, OH 43402
Ph: (419)353-5645
Fax: (419)352-8041
Free: (888)227-6446
URL: http://www.cancer.org
Local. Affiliated With: American Cancer Society.

13381 ■ American Legion, Bowling Green Post 45
PO Box 392
Bowling Green, OH 43402
Ph: (740)362-7478
Fax: (740)362-1429
URL: National Affiliate–www.legion.org
Local. Affiliated With: American Legion.

13382 ■ American Statistical Association, Northwest Ohio Chapter
c/o James H. Albert, Sec.-Treas.
Bowling Green State Univ.
Dept. of Math & Statistics
Bowling Green, OH 43403-0001
Ph: (419)372-7456
E-mail: albert@bgnet.bgsu.edu
URL: National Affiliate–www.amstat.org
Contact: James H. Albert, Sec.-Treas.
Local. Promotes statistical practice, applications and research. Works for the improvement of statistical education at all levels. Seeks opportunities to advance the statistics profession. **Affiliated With:** American Statistical Association.

13383 ■ Bowling Green Skating Club (BGSC)
c/o BGSU Ice Arena
417 N Mercer Rd.
Bowling Green, OH 43403
Ph: (419)372-2264
Fax: (419)372-0303
E-mail: topper99@ix.netcom.com
URL: http://www.bgskateclub.org
Contact: Pat Rabb, Pres.
Local. Provides programs to encourage participation and achievement in the sport of figure skating on ice. Defines and maintains uniform standards of skating proficiency. Organizes and sponsors competitions and exhibitions for the purpose of stimulating interest in figure skating. **Affiliated With:** United States Figure Skating Association.

13384 ■ Bowling Green State University Council of Teachers of Mathematics
c/o Daniel Brahier, Membership Chm.
126 Life Sci Bldg., Rm. 126
Bowling Green, OH 43403
Ph: (419)372-0339
E-mail: brahier@bgnet.bgsu.edu
URL: http://bgmath.org/BGCTM/bgctm.htm
Contact: Daniel Brahier, Membership Chm.
Local. Aims to improve the teaching and learning of mathematics. Provides vision, leadership and professional development to support teachers in ensuring mathematics learning of the highest quality for all students. **Affiliated With:** National Council of Teachers of Mathematics.

13385 ■ Bowling Green Woman's Club
1446 Conneaut Ave.
Bowling Green, OH 43402
Ph: (419)352-8175
E-mail: jhgordon@dacor.net
URL: http://www.neighborhoodlink.com/org/bgwomansclub
Contact: Joan Gordon, Contact
Local.

13386 ■ Bowling Green - Young Life
PO Box 284
Bowling Green, OH 43402
Ph: (419)494-8556
URL: http://sites.younglife.org/_layouts/ylext/default.aspx?ID=C-1589
Local. Affiliated With: Young Life.

13387 ■ Bowling Green Youth Hockey Association (BGYHA)
Bowling Green State Univ.
Mercer Rd.
Bowling Green, OH 43403
Ph: (419)372-2365
E-mail: kramers@woh.rr.com
URL: http://www.bgyouthhockey.org
Contact: Jamie Ruffner, Coaching Coor.
Local.

13388 ■ Eastwood - Young Life
PO Box 284
Bowling Green, OH 43402
Ph: (419)494-8556
URL: http://sites.younglife.org/_layouts/ylext/default.aspx?ID=C-1590
Local. Affiliated With: Young Life.

13389 ■ Elmwood - Young Life
PO Box 284
Bowling Green, OH 43402
Ph: (419)494-8556
URL: http://sites.younglife.org/_layouts/ylext/default.aspx?ID=C-3114
Local. Affiliated With: Young Life.

13390 ■ Findlay Antique Bottle Club
PO Box 243
Bowling Green, OH 43402
E-mail: theglassapothecary@wcnet.org
URL: http://fabclub.freeyellow.com/home.html
Contact: Joe Terry, Pres.
Local. Affiliated With: Federation of Historical Bottle Collectors.

13391 ■ Great Lakes Curling Association - Bowling Green Curling Club
BGSU Ice Arena
Mercer Rd.
Bowling Green, OH 43403
Ph: (419)372-2264
E-mail: melanie@bgsu.edu
URL: http://www.goodcurling.net/basics/U.S.%20clubs/glakes.html
Contact: Melanie Rellinger, Pres.
Local. Affiliated With: United States Curling Association.

13392 ■ Humanists of Northwest Ohio
c/o Naomi Twining
20189 N Dixie Hwy.
Bowling Green, OH 43402-9255
Ph: (419)353-8353
E-mail: steel@buckeyeexpress.com
URL: National Affiliate–www.americanhumanist.org
Contact: Naomi Twining, Contact
Local. Affiliated With: American Humanist Association.

13393 ■ Main Street Bowling Green
121 E Wooster St.
Bowling Green, OH 43402
Ph: (419)354-4332
E-mail: downtown@wcnet.org
URL: http://www.wcnet.org/~downtown
Local.

13394 ■ National Active and Retired Federal Employees Association - Wood County 1942
11753 E Gypsy Ln. Rd.
Bowling Green, OH 43402-9518
Ph: (419)352-0276
URL: National Affiliate–www.narfe.org
Contact: Lloyd C. Borer, Contact
Local. Protects the retirement future of employees through education. Informs members on issues affecting the retirement. **Affiliated With:** National Association of Retired Federal Employees.

13395 ■ Northwest Ohio American Industrial Hygiene Association (NWO-AIHA)
c/o Heather Lorenz, Membership Chair
20488 Haskins Rd.
Bowling Green, OH 43402
E-mail: hlorenz@bgnet.bgsu.edu
URL: http://www.aiha.org/LocalSections/html/nwohio/nwohio.htm
Contact: Heather Lorenz, Membership Chair
Local. Represents the interests of occupational and environmental health professionals practicing in industry, government, labor and academic institutions and independent organizations. Promotes the certification of industrial hygienists. Administers educational programs for environmental health and safety professionals. **Affiliated With:** American Industrial Hygiene Association.

13396 ■ Ohio Genealogical Society, Wood County (OGS)
PO Box 722
Bowling Green, OH 43402-0722
E-mail: wcogs@wcnet.org
URL: National Affiliate–www.ogs.org
State. Affiliated With: Ohio Genealogical Society.

13397 ■ Portage Lions Club
c/o Jay Deutschman, Pres.
911 N Wintergarden Rd.
Bowling Green, OH 43402
Ph: (419)352-3568
E-mail: portagelions@dacor.net
URL: http://www.dacor.net/PortageLions
Contact: Jay Deutschman, Pres.
Local. Affiliated With: Lions Clubs International.

13398 ■ Psi Chi, National Honor Society in Psychology - Bowling Green State University
c/o Dept. of Psychology
Bowling Green State Univ.
Bowling Green, OH 43403-0228
Ph: (419)372-2301 (419)372-8161
Fax: (419)372-6013
E-mail: akg@bgnet.bgsu.edu
URL: http://www.psichi.org/chapters/info.asp?chapter_id=46
Contact: Anne K. Gordon PhD, Advisor
Local.

13399 ■ Society of Manufacturing Engineers - Bowling Green State University S102
252 Tech. Bldg.
Bowling Green, OH 43403
Ph: (419)372-2632
Fax: (419)372-6066
E-mail: wtodd@bgnet.bgsu.edu
URL: National Affiliate–www.sme.org
Contact: Dr. Todd Waggoner, Contact
Local. Advances manufacturing knowledge to gain competitive advantage. Improves skills and manufacturing solutions for the growth of economy. Provides resources and opportunities for manufacturing professionals. **Affiliated With:** American Oceanic Organization.

13400 ■ United Way of Greater Toledo Wood County Office
1616 E Wooster St., Unit 25
Bowling Green, OH 43402-2763
Ph: (419)352-2390
Fax: (419)353-0608
E-mail: woodcounty@uwgtol.org
URL: http://www.uwgtol.org
Contact: Bill Kitson, Pres./CEO
Local. Affiliated With: United Way of America.

13401 ■ Veterans of Foreign Wars 1148
720 S Main St.
Bowling Green, OH 43402
Ph: (419)353-6371
Contact: Norm Women, Quarter Master
Local.

13402 ■ Wood County Historical Society (WCHS)
13660 County Home Rd.
Bowling Green, OH 43402
Ph: (419)352-0967
Fax: (419)352-6220
E-mail: museum@woodcountyhistory.org
URL: http://www.woodcountyhistory.org
Contact: Christie Raber, Dir.
Founded: 1955. **Members:** 700. **Membership Dues:** senior (age 60 above), student, $10 (annual) • individual, $15 (annual) • family, $25 (annual) • business, $45 (annual) • sustaining, $60 (annual) • patron, $100 (annual) • life (individual), $300 • life (couple), $500. **Staff:** 4. **Local.** Works to educate the public about historical events with a focus on Wood County and the former infirmary. **Libraries: Type:** reference. **Subjects:** local history. **Awards:** Internship. **Frequency:** annual. **Type:** monetary. **Recipient:** for graduate and undergraduate students interested in museums. **Affiliated With:** Ohio Association of Historical Societies and Museums. **Publications:** *Black Swamp Chanticleer*, quarterly. Newsletter. Features information on events and local history. **Price:** included in membership dues. **Circulation:** 700. Alternate Formats: online. **Conventions/Meetings:** monthly board meeting • semiannual dinner, with lectures and living history presentations - always spring and fall.

13403 ■ Young Life Lake Erie West Region
PO Box 74
Bowling Green, OH 43402
Ph: (419)354-0838
Fax: (419)354-0717
URL: http://sites.younglife.org/_layouts/ylext/default.aspx?ID=A-AG157
Local. Affiliated With: Young Life.

13404 ■ Young Life Wood County
PO Box 284
Bowling Green, OH 43402
Ph: (419)494-8556
URL: http://sites.younglife.org/sites/WoodCounty/default.aspx
Local. Affiliated With: Young Life.

Bradner

13405 ■ American Legion, Ohio Post 36
c/o Carl Crowfoot
9531 Fostoria Rd.
Bradner, OH 43406
Ph: (740)362-7478
Fax: (740)362-1429
URL: National Affiliate–www.legion.org
Contact: Carl Crowfoot, Contact
Local. Affiliated With: American Legion.

13406 ■ American Legion, Ohio Post 338
c/o Albert Bowe
PO Box 351
Bradner, OH 43406
Ph: (740)362-7478
Fax: (740)362-1429
URL: National Affiliate–www.legion.org
Contact: Albert Bowe, Contact
Local. Affiliated With: American Legion.

Brecksville

13407 ■ American Legion, Brecksville-Excelsior Post 196
7400 Chippewa Rd.
Brecksville, OH 44141
Ph: (740)362-7478
Fax: (740)362-1429
URL: National Affiliate–www.legion.org
Local. Affiliated With: American Legion.

13408 ■ Brecksville Chamber of Commerce (BCC)
4450 Oakes Rd., Rm. 16
Brecksville, OH 44141
Ph: (440)526-7350
Fax: (440)526-7889
E-mail: bccthevoice@att.net
URL: http://www.brecksvillechamber.com
Contact: Michael J. Gorman, Pres.
Founded: 1968. **Members:** 160. **Membership Dues:** individual/small business, $125 (annual) • business (3-99 employees), $175 (annual) • corporate, $275 (annual). **Local.** Promotes business and community development in Brecksville, OH. **Publications:** *The Voice*, bimonthly. Newsletter. **Advertising:** accepted. Alternate Formats: online. **Conventions/Meetings:** monthly board meeting.

13409 ■ Brecksville Historical Association
c/o Ms. Sylvia Fowler, Pres.
PO Box 41403
Brecksville, OH 44141-0403
Ph: (440)526-7165
Fax: (440)546-0139
E-mail: b.association@att.net
URL: http://brecksville.oh.us
Contact: Ms. Sylvia Fowler, Pres.
Founded: 1925. **Members:** 343. **Membership Dues:** individual, $10 (annual) • family, $15 (annual) • patron, $25 (annual). **Budget:** $25,000. **Local.** Represents the interests of individual, family and residents of Brecksville. Promotes understanding and study of the history and heritage of Brecksville., Ohio. Conducts summer and fall festivals; preserves and collects artifacts and photographs. **Libraries: Type:** by appointment only. **Holdings:** archival material, clippings, papers, periodicals, photographs. **Subjects:** genealogy. **Awards:** Squire Charles Rich Award. **Frequency:** annual. **Type:** scholarship. **Recipient:** to Brecksville-Broadview Heights high school seniors. **Affiliated With:** Ohio Association of Historical Societies and Museums. **Formerly:** (1944) Early Settler's Association of Brecksville. **Publications:** Newsletter, quarterly.

13410 ■ Cleveland Model Boat Club No. 31
c/o Clyde Jones
7509 Winding Way
Brecksville, OH 44141

Ph: (440)526-8142
URL: http://www.clevelandmodelboat.com
Contact: Clyde Jones, Contact
Local.

13411 ■ Lupus Foundation of America, Greater Cleveland Chapter
12930 Chippewa Rd.
Brecksville, OH 44141
Ph: (440)717-0183
Fax: (440)717-0186
E-mail: info@lupuscleveland.org
URL: http://www.lupus.org
Contact: Suzanne Tierney, Exec.Dir.
Founded: 1977. **Members:** 1,000. **Membership Dues:** individual, $20 (annual) • family, $25 (annual) • sponsor, medical, $50 (annual) • patron, $100 (annual) • life, $200. **Local**. Works to increase knowledge and public awareness of lupus erythematosus, a non-contagious disease that may affect the skin alone or may manifest itself as a chronic, systemic, and inflammatory disease of the connective tissues. Assists lupus patients and their families, to cope with the daily problems associated with lupus. Collects and distributes funds for research. Works to bring lupus to the attention of the public. **Additional Websites:** http://www.lupuscleveland.org. **Affiliated With:** Lupus Foundation of America. **Publications:** *Clinician*, monthly. Newsletter • *Leaware*, monthly. Newsletter • *Lupus News*, monthly. Newsletter. **Conventions/Meetings:** monthly board meeting • periodic conference • annual convention.

13412 ■ National Active and Retired Federal Employees Association - Brecksville 2264
6712 Hidden Lake Trail
Brecksville, OH 44141-3179
Ph: (440)546-0809
URL: National Affiliate–www.narfe.org
Contact: Raymond Rapczynski, Contact
Local. Protects the retirement future of employees through education. Informs members on issues affecting the retirement. **Affiliated With:** National Association of Retired Federal Employees.

13413 ■ North Royalton Alumni Association
c/o Walter Zimlich
7005 Farview Rd.
Brecksville, OH 44141-1219
Ph: (440)526-8442
Fax: (440)526-0565
E-mail: wjzim1@sbcglobal.net
Founded: 1983. **Members:** 620. **Membership Dues:** life, $10. **Local Groups:** 1. **Local**. **Awards:** North Royalton Alumni Scholarship. **Frequency:** annual. **Type:** scholarship. **Recipient:** for internal revenue service. **Computer Services:** database • mailing lists. **Publications:** *NR Alumni Newsletter*, annual. **Price:** free. **Circulation:** 5,000. **Conventions/Meetings:** annual banquet • monthly meeting.

Bremen

13414 ■ American Legion, Ohio Post 20
c/o Oscar Mc Veigh
201 N Bd. St.
Bremen, OH 43107
Ph: (740)362-7478
Fax: (740)362-1429
URL: National Affiliate–www.legion.org
Contact: Oscar Mc Veigh, Contact
Local. **Affiliated With:** American Legion.

13415 ■ Bremen Chamber of Commerce
PO Box 105
Bremen, OH 43107
Ph: (740)569-4121
Fax: (740)681-3180
Contact: Brian Householder, Pres.
Local.

Brewster

13416 ■ American Legion, Harr-Reese Post 160
320 S Wabash Ave.
Brewster, OH 44613
Ph: (740)362-7478
Fax: (740)362-1429
URL: National Affiliate–www.legion.org
Local. **Affiliated With:** American Legion.

Brice

13417 ■ Automobile Dealers Alliance of Ohio
c/o Elizabeth A. Blair, Exec.VP
PO Box 216
Brice, OH 43109
Ph: (614)436-3393
State.

Bridgeport

13418 ■ American Legion, Bridgeport Post 227
118 S Lincoln Ave.
Bridgeport, OH 43912
Ph: (740)362-7478
Fax: (740)362-1429
URL: National Affiliate–www.legion.org
Local. **Affiliated With:** American Legion.

13419 ■ Bridgeport Area Chamber of Commerce
PO Box 86
Bridgeport, OH 43912
Ph: (740)635-3377
Contact: Ann Gallagher, Sec.
Local.

Brilliant

13420 ■ American Legion, Brilliant Post 573
212 Market St.
Brilliant, OH 43913
Ph: (740)362-7478
Fax: (740)362-1429
URL: National Affiliate–www.legion.org
Local. **Affiliated With:** American Legion.

13421 ■ Brilliant Lions Club
c/o James D. Emerson, Pres.
1111 Hyland Ave.
Brilliant, OH 43913
Ph: (740)598-4429
URL: http://users.adelphia.net/~npssteve/district.htm
Contact: James D. Emerson, Pres.
Local. **Affiliated With:** Lions Clubs International.

Broadview Heights

13422 ■ Al Koran Shriners
c/o Duncan McVean
1000 E Edgerton Rd.
Broadview Heights, OH 44147-3142
Ph: (440)546-9866
Fax: (440)546-1793
E-mail: moontartan@ameritech.net
URL: http://www.alkoran.org
Contact: Duncan McVean, Contact
Local. **Affiliated With:** Imperial Council of the Ancient Arabic Order of the Nobles of the Mystic Shrine for North America.

13423 ■ American Payroll Association, Greater Cleveland Chapter
PO Box 470147
Broadview Heights, OH 44147
Ph: (216)383-2207
E-mail: juliedrnek@aol.com
URL: http://www.apaclevelandchp.org
Contact: Julie Drnek CPP, Sec.
Local. Aims to increase the Payroll Professional's skill level through education and mutual support. Represents the Payroll Professional before legislative bodies. Administers the certified payroll professional program of recognition. Provides public service education on payroll and employment issues. **Affiliated With:** American Payroll Association.

13424 ■ Associated Builders and Contractors-Northern Ohio Chapter
9255 Market Pl. W
Broadview Heights, OH 44147
Ph: (440)717-0389
Fax: (440)746-0417
E-mail: ryan@nocabc.com
URL: http://www.nocabc.com
Contact: Ryan Martin, Pres.
Local. **Affiliated With:** Associated Builders and Contractors.

13425 ■ Broadview Heights Chamber of Commerce
1000 E Edgerton Rd.
Broadview Heights, OH 44147-3142
Ph: (440)838-4510
Fax: (440)717-0500
E-mail: bhcc@broadviewhts.org
URL: http://www.broadviewhts.org
Contact: Barb Consiglio, Office Mgr.
Members: 200. **Membership Dues:** business, $135 (annual). **Local**. Businesses, professionals, and government officials dedicated to advancing the prosperity of the Broadview Heights area, its residents, and business. Offers many free and low-cost promotional opportunities for members along with group benefits and discounts on products and services. **Conventions/Meetings:** monthly luncheon, provides an excellent atmosphere for meeting and establishing relationships with other area business owners and managers - every second Wednesday.

13426 ■ Broadview Heights Lions Club
c/o John Sims, Pres.
340 Countryside Dr.
Broadview Heights, OH 44147
Ph: (440)237-5711
E-mail: jbuick@andysimsbuick.com
URL: http://www.broadviewheightslions.org
Contact: John Sims, Pres.
Local. **Affiliated With:** Lions Clubs International.

13427 ■ Easter Seals Northeast Ohio
Corporate Off.
1929 A E Royalton Rd.
Broadview Heights, OH 44147
Ph: (440)838-0990
Fax: (440)838-8440
Free: (888)325-8532
E-mail: sdunn@eastersealsneo.org
URL: http://neohio.easterseals.com
Contact: Ms. Sheila Dunn, Pres./CEO
Local. Provides services for children and adults with disabilities or special needs, and supports their families. **Affiliated With:** Easter Seals.

13428 ■ Institute of Management Accountants, Cleveland Chapter
c/o Honey Wess, Pres.
763 Tollis Pkwy.
Broadview Heights, OH 44147
Ph: (216)834-0700
E-mail: honey_wess@yahoo.com
URL: http://www.cleveland.imanet.org
Contact: Honey Wess, Pres.
Members: 439. **Local**. Promotes professional and ethical standards. Equips members and students with knowledge and training required for the accounting

profession. **Affiliated With:** Institute of Management Accountants. **Conventions/Meetings:** monthly board meeting - every second Thursday.

13429 ■ Ohio Landscape Association (OLA)
9238 Broadview Rd.
Broadview Heights, OH 44147-2517
Ph: (440)717-0002
Fax: (440)717-0004
Free: (800)335-6521
E-mail: sandy@ohiolandscapers.org
URL: http://ohiolandscapers.org
Contact: Ms. Sandy Munley, Exec.Dir.

Founded: 1965. **Members:** 600. **Membership Dues:** business, $250 (annual). **Staff:** 3. **State**. Strives to encourage professionalism and ethical standards among landscape contractors through educational opportunities and to promote and improve the public image of the landscape industry. **Affiliated With:** Professional Landcare Network. **Formerly:** (2004) Ohio Landscapers Association. **Publications:** *The Growing Concern*, monthly. Newsletter. **Advertising:** accepted. **Conventions/Meetings:** monthly board meeting • annual dinner - January • meeting - 5/year, every 3rd Thursday evening of January, February, March, October, and November • annual meeting - November.

13430 ■ Reserve Officers Association - Department of Ohio, North Coast Cleveland Chapter 8
c/o Major Eldora Levert, Pres.
PO Box 470106
Broadview Heights, OH 44147
Ph: (216)464-1011
E-mail: eldoleve@aol.com
URL: http://www.roa.org/oh
Contact: Major Eldora Levert, Pres.

Local. Promotes and supports the development and execution of a military policy for the United States. Provides professional development seminars, workshops and programs for its members. **Affiliated With:** Reserve Officers Association of the United States.

13431 ■ SBC Pioneers Ohio Chapter
c/o Sally Willis, Pres.
2550 Boxberry Ln.
Broadview Heights, OH 44147
Ph: (440)237-6329
E-mail: salgal1995@sbcglobal.net
URL: http://sbcpioneers.org/chapters/ohio/ohio.html
Contact: Carol Novak, Sec.

State. **Affiliated With:** TelecomPioneers.

13432 ■ USO of Northern Ohio
MEPS
9199 Market Pl.
Broadview Heights, OH 44147
Ph: (440)717-0999
Fax: (440)526-7718
E-mail: usocleveland@aol.com
URL: http://www.usocleveland.org
Contact: Ms. Elizabeth A. Henderson, Dir.

Founded: 1941. **Members:** 500. **Staff:** 6. **Local**. Devoted to supporting the troops and their families in the northern 29 counties of Ohio. **Affiliated With:** USO World Headquarters.

Brook Park

13433 ■ American Legion, Brook Park Post 610
19944 Sheldon Rd.
Brook Park, OH 44142
Ph: (740)362-7478
Fax: (740)362-1429
URL: National Affiliate–www.legion.org

Local. **Affiliated With:** American Legion.

13434 ■ First Catholic Slovak Ladies Association - Cleveland Junior Branch 014
6312 Elmdale Rd.
Brook Park, OH 44142
Ph: (216)676-9332
URL: National Affiliate–www.fcsla.com

Local. **Affiliated With:** First Catholic Slovak Ladies Association.

13435 ■ International Union, United Automobile, Aerospace and Agricultural Implement Workers of America, AFL-CIO - Local Union 1250
17250 Hummel Rd.
Brook Park, OH 44142
Ph: (216)267-9900
E-mail: timlevandusky@uawlocal1250.org
URL: http://www.uawlocal1250.org
Contact: Tim Levandusky, Pres.

Local. Seeks for the dignity and equality of the workers. Strives to provide contractors with well-trained, productive employees. **Affiliated With:** International Union, United Automobile, Aerospace and Agricultural Implement Workers of America.

13436 ■ SW Suburban RSVP
c/o Yolanda A. Dambrosio, Dir.
5855 Smith Rd., Ste.9
Brook Park, OH 44142-2007
Ph: (216)676-6441
Fax: (216)676-6442
E-mail: swsubrsvp@aol.com
URL: http://www.seniorcorps.gov
Contact: Yolanda A. Dambrosio, Dir.

Local. **Affiliated With:** Retired and Senior Volunteer Program.

Brooklyn

13437 ■ Classical Attraction Dressage Society (CADS)
c/o Patti Gutwein
9300 Memphis Villas Blvd.
Brooklyn, OH 44144-2435
Ph: (216)749-5869
E-mail: gtelego@zoominternet.net
URL: http://www.cadsdressage.org
Contact: Ginny Telego, Pres.

Local. **Affiliated With:** United States Dressage Federation.

13438 ■ National Softball Association - Ohio
c/o John DeLuca, Dir.
9417 Morton
Brooklyn, OH 44144
Ph: (216)661-7408
E-mail: ohionsachief347@adelphia.net
URL: National Affiliate–www.playnsa.com
Contact: John DeLuca, Dir.

State. **Affiliated With:** National Softball Association.

Brookville

13439 ■ American Legion, Dale L. Binkley Memorial Post 289
321 N Wolf Creek St.
Brookville, OH 45309
Ph: (740)362-7478
Fax: (740)362-1429
URL: National Affiliate–www.legion.org

Local. **Affiliated With:** American Legion.

13440 ■ Brookville Fire Department Association
c/o Stacy Hanes
PO Box 10
Brookville, OH 45309-1717
Ph: (937)833-2345
Contact: James Nickel, Fire Chief

Local.

13441 ■ Miami Valley Beagle Club
c/o Earl A. Foreman
11937 Providence Rd.
Brookville, OH 45309-9306
URL: National Affiliate–clubs.akc.org
Contact: Earl A. Foreman, Contact

Local.

13442 ■ Precast/Prestressed Concrete Institute, Central Region (PCI)
c/o Phil Wiedemann, Exec.Dir.
9626 Upper Lewisburg Salem Rd.
Brookville, OH 45309
Ph: (937)833-3900
Fax: (937)833-3700
E-mail: phil@pci-central.org
URL: http://www.pcicentral.org
Contact: Phil Wiedemann, Exec.Dir.

Founded: 1954. **Members:** 1,400. **Regional**.

13443 ■ Veterans of Foreign Wars 3288
210 Carr Dr.
Brookville, OH 45309
Ph: (937)833-9921

Founded: 1981. **Members:** 537. **Staff:** 11. **Local**.

Brunswick

13444 ■ American Legion, Ohio Post 234
c/o Richard H. Davenport
5133 Center Rd.
Brunswick, OH 44212
Ph: (740)362-7478
Fax: (740)362-1429
URL: National Affiliate–www.legion.org
Contact: Richard H. Davenport, Contact

Local. **Affiliated With:** American Legion.

13445 ■ Brunswick Area Chamber of Commerce (BACC)
3511 Center Rd., Ste.AB
Brunswick, OH 44212
Ph: (330)225-8411
Fax: (330)273-8172
E-mail: exec@brunswickareachamber.org
URL: http://www.brunswickareachamber.org
Contact: Murray McDade, Pres.

Founded: 1931. **Members:** 275. **Membership Dues:** company, $240 (annual). **Staff:** 1. **Budget:** $45,000. **Local**. Businesses, organizations, and individuals interested in promoting the Brunswick, OH area. Holds seminars and social functions. **Computer Services:** Mailing lists, of members. **Affiliated With:** U.S. Chamber of Commerce. **Formerly:** (1999) Brunswick Chamber of Commerce. **Publications:** *Connections*, monthly. Newsletter. **Advertising:** accepted. Alternate Formats: online. **Conventions/Meetings:** monthly breakfast, with speaker; cost is $5/person - always third Wednesday, Brunswick, OH.

13446 ■ Buckeye Fox Trotter Association
c/o Terry Workman
PO Box 964
Brunswick, OH 44212
Ph: (330)220-7387
E-mail: terryworkman@adelphia.net
URL: National Affiliate–www.MFTHBA.com
Contact: Terry Workman, Contact

Local. **Affiliated With:** Missouri Fox Trotting Horse Breed Association.

13447 ■ Greater Cleveland Society of Association Executives (GCSAE)
3511 Center Rd.
Brunswick, OH 44212
Ph: (330)273-5756
Fax: (216)803-9900
E-mail: gcsae@core.com
URL: http://www.gcsae.com
Contact: Jackie Symons, Contact

Members: 90. **Membership Dues:** association professional, $150 (annual) • affiliate, $80 (annual) • retired, $35 (annual). **Local**. Works to enhance the professional development of northeast OH association executives through education, training, and networking. **Affiliated With:** American Society of Association Executives. **Publications:** *Association Advisor*, 9/year. Newsletter. **Advertising:** accepted. Alternate Formats: online.

13448 ■ Kidney Foundation of Medina County
c/o Jean Holland
4274 Manhattan Cir.
Brunswick, OH 44212-3523
Ph: (330)220-0945 (330)225-4446
Fax: (330)225-4039
E-mail: kidneyfo@apk.net
URL: http://medinakidneyfoundation.org
Contact: Jean Holland, Exec.Dir.
Staff: 1. **Budget:** $100,000. **Local. Awards:** Jack G. McCray Memorial Education Fund. **Type:** scholarship. **Publications:** Newsletter, monthly.

13449 ■ Media Communications Association International, Greater Cleveland Chapter
3511 Center Rd.
Brunswick, OH 44212
Ph: (330)273-5756
E-mail: adamhennessey247@yahoo.com
URL: http://www.clevelandmcai.org
Contact: Adam Hennessey, Pres.
Membership Dues: individual, $160 (annual) • student, $43 (annual) • organization (up to 3 employees, $155 add-on for each additional member), $455 (annual) • life, $1,000 • life 100 (limited to 100 members), $2,000. **Local.** Serves individuals engaged in multimedia communications. Seeks to advance the benefits and image of media communications professionals. **Affiliated With:** Media Communications Association International. **Publications:** *Inserts*, periodic. Newsletter. **Advertising:** accepted. Alternate Formats: online.

13450 ■ Medina County Youth for Christ
PO Box 626
Brunswick, OH 44212
Ph: (330)273-5794
Fax: (330)225-6921
URL: http://www.campuslifechat.org
Local. Affiliated With: Youth for Christ/U.S.A.

13451 ■ National Academy of Television Arts and Sciences, Cleveland Regional Chapter
3511 Center Rd.
Brunswick, OH 44212
Ph: (330)273-5756
Fax: (216)803-9900
E-mail: administrator@ntacleveland.com
URL: http://www.ntacleveland.com
Contact: Sheri Symons, Mgr.
Membership Dues: professional, $60 • student, $15. **Local.** Promotes excellence in broadcasting. Inspires the next generation of broadcast journalists. Educates television viewers. **Awards:** Emmy Awards. **Frequency:** annual. **Type:** recognition. **Recipient:** for outstanding achievement in broadcasting • Silver Circle Awards Program. **Frequency:** annual. **Type:** recognition. **Recipient:** for significant contributions to Chicago/Midwest broadcasting. **Affiliated With:** National Academy of Television Arts and Sciences.

13452 ■ Reserve Officers Association - Department of Ohio, Cleveland Coast Guard Chapter 10
c/o Lt. Michael P. Lavrenchik, USCGR, Pres.
4096 Sleepy Hollow Rd.
Brunswick, OH 44212
Ph: (330)225-1816 (216)987-5073
E-mail: miklav@ispwest.com
URL: http://www.roa.org/oh
Contact: Lt. Michael P. Lavrenchik USCGR, Pres.
Local. Promotes and supports the development and execution of a military policy for the United States. Provides professional development seminars, workshops and programs for its members. **Affiliated With:** Reserve Officers Association of the United States.

Bryan

13453 ■ American Legion, Ohio Post 284
c/o Charles E. Arnold
519 E Butler St.
Bryan, OH 43506
Ph: (740)362-7478
Fax: (740)362-1429
URL: National Affiliate–www.legion.org
Contact: Charles E. Arnold, Contact
Local. Affiliated With: American Legion.

13454 ■ Bryan Area Chamber of Commerce
c/o Daniel S. Yahraus, Exec.Dir.
138 S Lynn St.
Bryan, OH 43506
Ph: (419)636-2247
Fax: (419)636-5556
E-mail: bryancc@cityofbryan.net
URL: http://www.bryanchamber.org
Contact: Daniel S. Yahraus, Exec.Dir.
Founded: 1947. **Local.** Promotes Bryan and enhance the quality of life and economic stability of the community. **Divisions:** Bryan City Council; Leadership Williams County; Retail Merchants Association; William County Economic Development. **Publications:** *Top of Ohio Topics*, monthly. Newsletter. Contains information, fun and interesting facts as well as upcoming events. Alternate Formats: online.

13455 ■ National Active and Retired Federal Employees Association - Bryan 1136
414 Rosemont Ave.
Bryan, OH 43506-2541
Ph: (419)636-7935
URL: National Affiliate–www.narfe.org
Contact: Everett C. Flesher, Contact
Local. Protects the retirement future of employees through education. Informs members on issues affecting the retirement. **Affiliated With:** National Association of Retired Federal Employees.

13456 ■ National Reye's Syndrome Foundation - Support Group
c/o Terri J. Freudenberger
PO Box 829
Bryan, OH 43506-0829
Ph: (419)636-2679
Fax: (419)636-9897
Free: (800)233-7393
E-mail: nrsf@reyessyndrome.org
URL: http://www.reyessyndrome.org
Contact: Terri J. Freudenberger, Sec. and Co-founder
Founded: 1974. **Members:** 2,300. **Membership Dues:** individual/family, $25 (annual). **Staff:** 2. **Budget:** $90,000. **State Groups:** 47. **Languages:** English, Spanish. **Regional.** United to generate a concerted, organized lay movement to eradicate Reye's Syndrome. Has three main areas of concern: awareness - to aid in early detection and to educate the public and medical communities about the risk factor involved with the use of aspirin and other salicylates; service - to give families experiencing the trauma of Reye's Syndrome emotional support and guidance; and research - to support investigation of the disease, as well as study the impact the disease has on survivors. **Libraries: Type:** by appointment only. **Holdings:** articles, audiovisuals, video recordings. **Subjects:** Reye's Syndrome. **Awards: Type:** scholarship. **Recipient:** for research in Reye's Syndrome. **Computer Services:** Information services, case report pages set up for individuals wishing to report themselves or a family member who is a victim or survivor of Reye's Syndrome • online services, contains literature request page and information about Reye's Syndrome. **Telecommunication Services:** information service, answering machine that records incoming calls for individuals that have questions they would like to be answered. **Affiliated With:** National Reye's Syndrome Foundation. **Publications:** *In the News*, biennial. Newsletter. Provides information about Reye's Syndrome as becomes available, as well as different ways to help spread awareness. **Price:** free to members. **Circulation:** 5,000. Alternate Formats: online. **Conventions/Meetings:** quarterly board meeting, review of events and standings for the foundation • annual meeting - in June.

13457 ■ Ohio Genealogical Society, Williams County (OGS)
PO Box 293
Bryan, OH 43506-0293
E-mail: lashpamela@cityofbryan.net
URL: http://www.wcgs-ogs.com
Contact: Pamela Pattison Lash, Pres.
Founded: 1980. **Members:** 300. **Membership Dues:** single, $10 (annual). **Staff:** 2. **Local.** Individuals interested in preserving the history of Williams County, OH. Disseminates information. **Libraries: Type:** open to the public. **Holdings:** 400; books, films. **Subjects:** genealogy, history. **Awards:** Jennifer Lash Memorial Genealogical Award. **Frequency:** annual. **Type:** recognition. **Affiliated With:** Ohio Genealogical Society; Ohio Genealogical Society. **Publications:** *Atlas* • *Cemetery Records*. Directories • *Census Records*. Directories • *Marriage Records*. Directories • *Ohio's Last Frontier*, monthly. Newsletter. Includes genealogical information, society publications, records, and queries. **Price:** included in membership dues • *Research Guide*. **Conventions/Meetings:** monthly meeting - always 2nd Monday in Bryan, OH.

13458 ■ United Way of Williams County
PO Box 525
Bryan, OH 43506
Ph: (419)636-8603
Fax: (419)636-7306
E-mail: wecare@unitedwc.org
URL: http://www.unitedwaywc.org
Contact: Chris Malanga, Exec.Dir.
Founded: 1994. **Members:** 30. **Staff:** 2. **Budget:** $340,000. **Local Groups:** 29. **For-Profit. Local.** Strives to enhance the quality of life within the community. Facilitates financial giving, promotes voluntarism and coordinate with human service providers to unite the community's outreach efforts and to meet the true needs of citizens. Mobilizes the county's aggregate efforts to maximize the positive impact for children, families and senior citizens. **Awards: Frequency:** annual. **Type:** monetary. **Affiliated With:** United Way of America. **Formerly:** United Way of Bryan.

Buckeye Lake

13459 ■ Greater Buckeye Lake Chamber of Commerce
PO Box 5
Buckeye Lake, OH 43008
Ph: (740)242-5111
E-mail: info@buckeyelakecc.com
Contact: Darlene Murphy, Pres.
Local.

Bucyrus

13460 ■ American Legion, Colonel Crawford Post 181
123 E Rensselaer St.
Bucyrus, OH 44820
Ph: (740)362-7478
Fax: (740)362-1429
URL: National Affiliate–www.legion.org
Local. Affiliated With: American Legion.

13461 ■ American Red Cross, Crawford County Chapter
110 E Mary St.
Bucyrus, OH 44820
Ph: (419)562-4357
URL: http://crawfordcounty.redcross.org
Local.

13462 ■ American Rose Society, Buckeye District
c/o Terri Lady, Dir.
1440 Grandview Ave.
Bucyrus, OH 44820-3589
Ph: (419)562-1451
E-mail: rlady@earthlink.net
URL: http://www.buckeyerose.com
Contact: Terri Lady, Dir.
Regional. Affiliated With: American Rose Society.

13463 ■ Bucyrus Area Board of Realtors
PO Box 427
Bucyrus, OH 44820
Ph: (419)562-2278
Fax: (419)562-9311
E-mail: cherie@ohiorealtors.org
URL: National Affiliate–www.realtor.org
Contact: Dawn Hedges, Exec. Officer
Local. Strives to develop real estate business practices. Advocates for the right to own, use and transfer real property. Provides a facility for professional development, research and exchange of information among members and the general public. **Affiliated With:** National Association of Realtors.

13464 ■ Bucyrus Area Chamber of Commerce (BACC)
122 W Rensselaer St.
Bucyrus, OH 44820-2214
Ph: (419)562-4811
Fax: (419)562-9966
E-mail: bacc@bucyrusohio.com
URL: http://www.bucyrusohio.com
Contact: Deb Pinion, Exec.Dir.
Founded: 1925. **Members:** 223. **Budget:** $58,000. **Local.** Promotes business and community development in Crawford County, OH. **Convention/Meeting:** none. **Publications:** *Chamber of Commerce News*, bimonthly. Newsletter • *Quality of Life Book* • Directory, periodic. Alternate Formats: online.

13465 ■ Bucyrus Area United Way
PO Box 645
Bucyrus, OH 44820-0645
Ph: (419)562-9076
URL: National Affiliate–national.unitedway.org
Local. Affiliated With: United Way of America.

13466 ■ Bucyrus Lions Club
c/o Linda Spiegel, Sec.
1109 Hillcrest Dr.
Bucyrus, OH 44820
Ph: (419)562-0749
E-mail: lspiegel@columbus.rr.com
URL: http://www.lions13b.org
Contact: Linda Spiegel, Sec.
Local. Affiliated With: Lions Clubs International.

13467 ■ Richland Lithic and Lapidary Society
c/o Tom Kottyan, Pres.
PO Box 308
Bucyrus, OH 44820
E-mail: themineralhouse@netzero.com
URL: National Affiliate–www.amfed.org
Contact: Eva Clements, Sec.
Local. Aims to further the study of Earth Sciences and the practice of lapidary arts and mineralogy. **Affiliated With:** American Federation of Mineralogical Societies.

13468 ■ Veterans of Foreign Wars 8899
PO Box 1019
Bucyrus, OH 44820
Ph: (419)562-8301
Contact: Tom Hilbedbrand, Commander
Local.

Burton

13469 ■ American Legion, Atwood-Mauck Post 459
PO Box 261
Burton, OH 44021
Ph: (740)362-7478
Fax: (740)362-1429
URL: National Affiliate–www.legion.org
Local. Affiliated With: American Legion.

13470 ■ First Catholic Slovak Ladies Association - Bedford Junior Branch 380
12493 Jackson Blvd.
Burton, OH 44021
Ph: (440)834-4622
URL: National Affiliate–www.fcsla.com
Local. Affiliated With: First Catholic Slovak Ladies Association.

13471 ■ First Catholic Slovak Ladies Association - Bedford Senior Branch 475
12493 Jackson Blvd.
Burton, OH 44021
Ph: (440)834-4622
URL: National Affiliate–www.fcsla.com
Local. Affiliated With: First Catholic Slovak Ladies Association.

13472 ■ Garfield Heights Figure Skating Club
16022 Messenger Rd.
Burton, OH 44021
E-mail: jalange81@aol.com
URL: National Affiliate–www.usfigureskating.org
Contact: Joyce Lange, Contact
Local. Provides programs to encourage participation and achievement in the sport of figure skating on ice. Defines and maintains uniform standards of skating proficiency. Organizes and sponsors competitions and exhibitions for the purpose of stimulating interest in figure skating. **Affiliated With:** United States Figure Skating Association.

13473 ■ Geauga County Historical Society (GCHS)
PO Box 153
Burton, OH 44021
Ph: (440)834-1492
Fax: (440)834-4012
E-mail: info@geaugahistorical.org
URL: http://www.geaugahistorical.org/index.html
Contact: Dr. David P. Peltier PhD, Exec.Dir.
Founded: 1938. **Members:** 500. **Membership Dues:** individual, $35 (annual) • family/couple, $55 (annual) • senior individual, $25 (annual) • silver, $100 (annual) • gold, $250 (annual) • platinum/corporate, $500 (annual). **Staff:** 15. **Budget:** $400,000. **Regional.** Seeks to ensure that the history of the county is preserved for the education and appreciation of present and future generations. Conducts educational programs for schools and maintains a Western Reserve Village. **Libraries: Type:** by appointment only. **Holdings:** 2,000; books, papers, periodicals. **Subjects:** local history. **Affiliated With:** Western Reserve Historical Society. **Publications:** *The Quarterly*. Newsletter. **Price:** included in membership dues. **Circulation:** 1,000. **Advertising:** accepted. **Conventions/Meetings:** annual board meeting - in June.

13474 ■ Western Reserve Dairy Goat Association
c/o Kay Bright
PO Box 323
Burton, OH 44021
Ph: (440)834-4519
URL: National Affiliate–adga.org
Contact: Kay Bright, Contact
Local. Affiliated With: American Dairy Goat Association.

Butler

13475 ■ Butler Lions Club
c/o David Bellan, Pres.
1988 Snyder Rd.
Butler, OH 44822
Ph: (419)883-3387
E-mail: abssupply@bright.net
URL: http://www.lions13b.org
Contact: David Bellan, Pres.
Local. Affiliated With: Lions Clubs International.

13476 ■ Catholics United for the Faith - St. Therese of Lisieux Chapter, Ohio
c/o Michael and Cathy Worley
21696 Koppert Rd.
Butler, OH 44822
Ph: (740)599-7894
E-mail: mcjap@ecr.net
URL: National Affiliate–www.cuf.org
Contact: Michael Worley, Contact
Local.

Byesville

13477 ■ American Legion, Byesville Post 116
10335 Jackson St.
Byesville, OH 43723
Ph: (740)362-7478
Fax: (740)362-1429
URL: National Affiliate–www.legion.org
Local. Affiliated With: American Legion.

13478 ■ Byesville Board of Trade
PO Box 268
Byesville, OH 43723
Ph: (740)685-8625
Contact: Russ Valentine, Exec.Dir.
Local.

Cadiz

13479 ■ American Legion, Cadiz Post 34
336 E Spring St.
Cadiz, OH 43907
Ph: (740)362-7478
Fax: (740)362-1429
URL: National Affiliate–www.legion.org
Local. Affiliated With: American Legion.

13480 ■ Cadiz Lions Club
c/o C. Adrian Pincola, Pres.
618 Kerr Ave.
Cadiz, OH 43907
Ph: (740)942-2080 (740)942-1061
E-mail: bpincola@eohio.net
URL: http://users.adelphia.net/~npssteve/district.htm
Contact: C. Adrian Pincola, Pres.
Local. Affiliated With: Lions Clubs International.

13481 ■ Harrison Regional Chamber of Commerce (HRCC)
3780 Cadiz-Dennison Rd.
Cadiz, OH 43907
Ph: (740)942-3350
Fax: (740)942-0009
E-mail: hrcctour@eohio.net
URL: http://pages.eohio.net/harrisonchamber
Contact: Ed Coultrap, Exec.Dir.
Founded: 1975. **Members:** 176. **Membership Dues:** individual, $25 (annual) • service organization, $25 (annual) • business, $150 (annual). **Local.** Promotes business and community development in Harrison County, OH. Sponsors Ohio Business Week. Promotes tourism. Operates welcome station. **Awards: Type:** recognition. **Formerly:** (1999) Harrison Regional Chamber of Commerce and Tourism Information. **Publications:** *County Directory* • *HRCC Communicator*, bimonthly. Newsletter. Contains newsworthy articles and calendar of events. **Price:** free • *Plat Books*. Directory • *Tourism*. Directory. **Conventions/Meetings:** annual banquet, with awards presentation (exhibits) - always in February • periodic Business After Hours - meeting (exhibits) • annual Business Award "Harrison County's Best Award" - meeting - always in February • semiannual Business Expo - trade show (exhibits) • monthly Business Works - meeting • semiannual seminar - March

and October • annual Tourism/Beautification Awards - meeting - always in October.

13482 ■ Ohio Genealogical Society, Harrison County
45507 Unionvale Rd.
Cadiz, OH 43907-9723
E-mail: harrisonheritage@yahoo.com
URL: http://www.rootsweb.com/~ohharris/hcgs.htm
Contact: Susan Adams, Pres.
Membership Dues: single, $10 (annual) • joint, $15 (annual) • life - single, $150 • life - joint, $225. **Local. Libraries: Type:** by appointment only; open to the public. **Holdings:** archival material, articles, books. **Subjects:** family history. **Affiliated With:** Ohio Genealogical Society. **Publications:** *Our Harrison Heritage*, quarterly. Newsletter. **Price:** included in membership dues.

Calcutta

13483 ■ Calcutta Area Chamber of Commerce
15442 Pugh Rd.
Calcutta, OH 43920
Ph: (330)386-6060
Fax: (330)386-6060
URL: http://www.calcuttaohiochamber.com
Contact: Howard Claypool, Sec.-Treas.
Local. Promotes business and community development in Calcutta, OH.

13484 ■ Calcutta Lions Club
c/o Linda Metrovich, Pres.
48643 Lakeview Cir.
Calcutta, OH 43920
Ph: (330)385-4405
E-mail: lmetrovich@hotmail.com
URL: http://www.lions13d.org
Contact: Linda Metrovich, Pres.
Local. Affiliated With: Lions Clubs International.

Caldwell

13485 ■ American Legion, Noble Post 252
108 Lakeview Dr.
Caldwell, OH 43724
Ph: (740)362-7478
Fax: (740)362-1429
URL: National Affiliate–www.legion.org
Local. Affiliated With: American Legion.

13486 ■ Noble County Chamber of Commerce
PO Box 41
Caldwell, OH 43724-0041
Ph: (740)732-5288
Fax: (740)732-2377
Contact: Barry Parmiter, Pres.
Local.

Caledonia

13487 ■ American Legion, Caledonia Post 401
PO Box 415
Caledonia, OH 43314
Ph: (740)362-7478
Fax: (740)362-1429
URL: National Affiliate–www.legion.org
Local. Affiliated With: American Legion.

13488 ■ Michigan Association of Distributors
c/o Dan L. Schlosser, Exec.VP
PO Box 310
Caledonia, OH 43314-0310
Ph: (419)845-2023
Fax: (419)845-2026
E-mail: assnhq@gte.net
Trade association serving wholesale distributors of plumbing, heating, cooling and piping products.

13489 ■ National Active and Retired Federal Employees Association - Warren G Harding 329
4145 Roberts Rd.
Caledonia, OH 43314-9487
Ph: (740)389-2491
URL: National Affiliate–www.narfe.org
Contact: Loren A. Fulton, Contact
Local. Protects the retirement future of employees through education. Informs members on issues affecting the retirement. **Affiliated With:** National Association of Retired Federal Employees.

13490 ■ River Valley Lions Club
c/o John Kosto, Pres.
6075 Marion Edison Rd.
Caledonia, OH 43314-9413
Ph: (740)389-2306 (419)947-8676
E-mail: jekosto@verizon.net
URL: http://www.iwaynet.net/~lions13f
Contact: John Kosto, Pres.
Local. Affiliated With: Lions Clubs International.

Cambridge

13491 ■ American Legion, Antrim Post 461
PO Box 1801
Cambridge, OH 43725
Ph: (740)362-7478
Fax: (740)362-1429
URL: National Affiliate–www.legion.org
Local. Affiliated With: American Legion.

13492 ■ American Legion, Cambridge Post 84
PO Box 36
Cambridge, OH 43725
Ph: (740)362-7478
Fax: (740)362-1429
URL: National Affiliate–www.legion.org
Local. Affiliated With: American Legion.

13493 ■ Cambridge Area Chamber of Commerce (CCC)
918 Wheeling Ave.
Cambridge, OH 43725-0488
Ph: (740)439-6688
Fax: (740)439-6689
E-mail: info@cambridgeohiochamber.com
URL: http://www.cambridgeohiochamber.com
Contact: Michael A. Kachilla, Pres.
Members: 325. **Membership Dues:** $135 (annual). **Staff:** 3. **Budget:** $108,000. **Local.** Promotes business and community development in the Cambridge, OH area. **Affiliated With:** U.S. Chamber of Commerce. **Publications:** *Crossroads*, quarterly. Newsletter • Directory, annual. **Price:** free. **Circulation:** 2,500. **Conventions/Meetings:** annual Swing into Spring Homeshow - dinner (exhibits).

13494 ■ Cambridge Board of Realtors
PO Box 96
Cambridge, OH 43725
Ph: (740)826-7557
Fax: (740)826-4183
E-mail: cambridgeboardofrealtors@yahoo.com
URL: National Affiliate–www.realtor.org
Contact: Coleen Tiffner, Exec. Officer
Local. Strives to develop real estate business practices. Advocates for the right to own, use and transfer real property. Provides a facility for professional development, research and exchange of information among members and the general public. **Affiliated With:** National Association of Realtors.

13495 ■ Cambridge Lioness Club
c/o Teresa Bistor, Pres.
9450 E 77 Dr.
Cambridge, OH 43725
Ph: (740)439-4080
E-mail: trb4455@yahoo.com
URL: http://users.adelphia.net/~npssteve/district.htm
Contact: Teresa Bistor, Pres.
Local. Affiliated With: Lions Clubs International.

13496 ■ Cambridge Lions Club - Ohio
c/o David Conrath, Pres.
702 Clark St.
Cambridge, OH 43725
Ph: (937)445-2050 (740)432-1147
E-mail: dave.conrath@ncr.com
URL: http://users.adelphia.net/~npssteve/district.htm
Contact: David Conrath, Pres.
Local. Affiliated With: Lions Clubs International.

13497 ■ Cambridge - Young Life
PO Box 633
Cambridge, OH 43725
Ph: (740)432-8984
URL: http://sites.younglife.org/_layouts/ylext/default.aspx?ID=C-1570
Local. Affiliated With: Young Life.

13498 ■ Guernsey - Wyldlife
PO Box 633
Cambridge, OH 43725
Ph: (740)432-8984
URL: http://sites.younglife.org/_layouts/ylext/default.aspx?ID=C-4171
Local. Affiliated With: Young Life.

13499 ■ Ohio Mid-Eastern Governments Association (OMEGA)
326 Highland Ave.
PO Box 130
Cambridge, OH 43725
Ph: (740)439-4471
Fax: (740)439-7783
Free: (800)726-6342
E-mail: director@omega-ldd.org
Contact: Donald Myers, Exec.Dir.
Founded: 1967. **Members:** 66. **Staff:** 10. **Budget:** $500,000. **State.** Representatives of ten county and twelve municipal governments in mideastern Ohio. Assists members in obtaining federal grants from the Appalachian Regional Commission. Conducts educational and infrastructure development projects. Maintains in-house census office and Revolving Loan Fund. **Libraries: Type:** open to the public. **Subjects:** census data. **Publications:** *Omegazette*, quarterly. Newsletter. **Conventions/Meetings:** monthly board meeting • biennial meeting, of membership.

13500 ■ Southeastern Ohio Young Life
PO Box 633
Cambridge, OH 43725
Ph: (740)432-8984
URL: http://sites.younglife.org/sites/SoutheasternOhio/default.aspx
Contact: Kirk Wilson, Contact
Local. Affiliated With: Young Life.

13501 ■ Tri-County Estate Planning Council
c/o Frank A. McClure, Pres.
213 N 8th St.
Cambridge, OH 43725
Ph: (740)432-7844
Fax: (740)439-4950
E-mail: mcclure@frognet.net
URL: National Affiliate–councils.naepc.org
Contact: Frank A. McClure, Pres.
Local. Fosters understanding of the proper relationship between the functions of professionals in the estate planning field. Represents the interests of professionals involved in estate planning. Encourages cooperation among members. **Affiliated With:** National Association of Estate Planners and Councils.

13502 ■ United Way of Guernsey and Noble County
918 Wheeling Ave., Ste.1
Cambridge, OH 43725-2319
Ph: (740)439-2667
URL: National Affiliate–national.unitedway.org
Local. Affiliated With: United Way of America.

Camden

13503 ■ American Legion, Justice-Leibolt Post 377
PO Box 125
Camden, OH 45311
Ph: (740)362-7478
Fax: (740)362-1429
URL: National Affiliate–www.legion.org
Local. Affiliated With: American Legion.

13504 ■ Camden Area Chamber of Commerce
PO Box 90
Camden, OH 45311
Ph: (937)452-1684
Contact: Karen Feix, Pres.
Local.

13505 ■ Camden Lions Club - Ohio
155 N Main St.
Camden, OH 45311-1120
Ph: (937)452-3229
URL: http://www.lionwap.org/camdenoh
Contact: J. Mabry, Pres.
Local. Affiliated With: Lions Clubs International.

13506 ■ Miami Valley Pheasants Forever (MVPF)
6134 US, Rte. 127
Camden, OH 45311
E-mail: costanjp@muohio.edu
URL: http://www.orgs.muohio.edu/pheasantsforever/index.html
Contact: Jon Costanzo, Habitat Chm.
Founded: 2001. **Members:** 125. **Local.** Works to improve local wildlife habitat conditions and conserve natural resources. Assists the owners of local agricultural and recreational properties in their efforts to establish and manage nesting habitat, which is key to the survival of ring-necked pheasant and many other wildlife species. **Affiliated With:** Pheasants Forever.

Campbell

13507 ■ American Legion, Franklin D. Roosevelt Post 560
103 12th St.
Campbell, OH 44405
Ph: (740)362-7478
Fax: (740)362-1429
URL: National Affiliate–www.legion.org
Local. Affiliated With: American Legion.

13508 ■ First Catholic Slovak Ladies Association - Campbell Junior Branch 250
172 Gladstone St.
Campbell, OH 44405
Ph: (330)747-7302
URL: National Affiliate–www.fcsla.com
Local. Affiliated With: First Catholic Slovak Ladies Association.

13509 ■ GT Corp. Empowerment Organization
279 Whipple Ave.
Campbell, OH 44405-1544
Ph: (330)740-1982 (330)755-3130
Contact: Rev. Willie F. Peterson, CEO
Founded: 1999. **Staff:** 16. **Budget:** $240,000. **Local. Subgroups:** Faith Based Community Group; Pathway Partner Group. **Conventions/Meetings:** monthly Pathway Partner Workshops - 4th Thursday; Avg. Attendance: 20.

13510 ■ Western Reserve of Ohio Teachers of English (WROTE)
c/o Margaret Ford, Treas.
83 Creed Cir.
Campbell, OH 44405-1256
Ph: (330)799-6372
E-mail: camp_mf@access-k12.org
URL: http://www.octela.org/newoctela/newwrote.html
Contact: Margaret Ford, Treas.
Membership Dues: professional, $10 (annual). **Regional.** Supports English Language Arts instructors and instruction statewide. **Affiliated With:** National Council of Teachers of English.

Canal Fulton

13511 ■ American Association of Critical Care Nurses, Greater Akron Area Chapter
c/o John Schwendiman
725 Redwood Ave.
Canal Fulton, OH 44614
Ph: (330)854-5224
E-mail: gaac.info@aacn.org
URL: http://www.aacn.org/gaac
Contact: Jackie Gurnick, Pres.
Local. Represents the interests of professional critical care nurses. Provides education programs for nurses specializing in critical care and develops standards of nursing care of critically ill patients. **Affiliated With:** American Association of Critical-Care Nurses.

13512 ■ Canal Fulton Lions Club
c/o Floyd Gottsman, Pres.
11490 Lloyd St.
Canal Fulton, OH 44614
Ph: (330)882-5657
E-mail: patsy@sssnet.com
URL: http://www.lions13d.org
Contact: Floyd Gottsman, Pres.
Local. Affiliated With: Lions Clubs International.

13513 ■ Veteran Motor Car Club of America - Hall of Fame Chapter
c/o Tom Krake, Pres.
9619 Strausser St. NW
Canal Fulton, OH 44614
Ph: (330)854-3570
URL: National Affiliate–www.vmcca.org
Contact: Tom Krake, Pres.
Local. Affiliated With: Veteran Motor Car Club of America.

Canal Winchester

13514 ■ American Counseling Association, Ohio
c/o Tim Luckhaupt, Exec.
8312 Willowbridge Pl.
Canal Winchester, OH 43110
Ph: (614)833-1198
E-mail: tvluckhaupt@yahoo.com
URL: National Affiliate–www.counseling.org
State. Affiliated With: American Counseling Association.

13515 ■ American Legion, Leach-Benson Post 220
124 Beaty Ct.
Canal Winchester, OH 43110
Ph: (740)362-7478
Fax: (740)362-1429
URL: National Affiliate–www.legion.org
Local. Affiliated With: American Legion.

13516 ■ Canal Winchester Area Chamber of Commerce (CWACC)
58 E Waterloo St.
Canal Winchester, OH 43110
Ph: (614)837-1556
Fax: (614)837-9901
E-mail: chamber@canalwinchester.com
URL: http://www.canalwinchester.com
Contact: Kim Rankin, Exec.Dir.
Founded: 1985. **Members:** 225. **Membership Dues:** general (based on number of employees), $125-$575 (annual) • non-profit and community service organization, $75 (annual) • individual, $50 (annual). **Local.** Represents businesses, individuals and organizations dedicated to the promotion of business and the community. Promotes and fosters the free enterprise system through economic development. Advocates for local business interests, and provides investor benefits. **Publications:** *The Reporter*, monthly. Newsletter. **Advertising:** accepted. **Conventions/Meetings:** monthly Membership - luncheon - every second Wednesday.

13517 ■ Canal Winchester Lions Club
c/o Loretta Sweeney, Pres.
6171 Baybrook Dr.
Canal Winchester, OH 43110
Ph: (614)834-1516
E-mail: lorettasweeney@ameritech.net
URL: http://www.iwaynet.net/~lions13f
Contact: Loretta Sweeney, Pres.
Local. Affiliated With: Lions Clubs International.

13518 ■ Groveport Madison Lions Club
c/o Edwin Myers, Sec.
5157 Bixford Ave.
Canal Winchester, OH 43110
Ph: (614)836-5456
E-mail: edvamyers@aol.com
URL: http://www.iwaynet.net/~lions13f
Contact: Edwin Myers, Sec.
Local. Affiliated With: Lions Clubs International.

13519 ■ Mid-States Woolgrowers Cooperative Association
9449 Basil Western Rd. NW
Canal Winchester, OH 43110
Free: (800)841-9665
URL: http://www.midstateswoolgrowers.com
Regional. Affiliated With: American Sheep Industry Association.

13520 ■ Ohio Alliance for the Environment
c/oPeggy Smith, Executive Director
14 Beck St.
Canal Winchester, OH 43110
Ph: (614)833-4223
Fax: (614)833-4223
E-mail: smith@ohioalliance.org
URL: http://www.ohioalliance.org
Contact: Irene Probasco, Exec.Dir.
State. Provides environmental education programs for adults.

13521 ■ Ohio Association of Food and Environmental Sanitarians
Ohio Hea. Dept.
6855 Diley Rd. NW
Canal Winchester, OH 43110
Ph: (614)645-6195
E-mail: donb@columbus.gov
URL: National Affiliate–www.foodprotection.org
Contact: Donald Barrett, Contact
State. Provides food safety professionals with a forum to exchange information on protecting the food supply. Promotes sanitary methods and procedures for the development, production, processing, distribution, preparation and serving of food. **Affiliated With:** International Association for Food Protection.

13522 ■ Ohio Counseling Association
c/o Timothy V. Luckhaupt, Exec. Dir.
8312 Willowbridge Place
Canal Winchester, OH 43110
Ph: (614)833-6068
E-mail: ocaohio@yahoo.com

13523 ■ Ohio Heartland Chapter of the International Society for Performance Improvement (OHISPI)
6478 Winchester Blvd., Ste.120
Canal Winchester, OH 43110
Ph: (614)470-3551
E-mail: jyoung@rayandbarney.com
URL: http://www.ohispi.org
Contact: Jeff Young, Pres.
Local. Performance technologists, training directors, human resource managers, instructional designers,

human factors practitioners, and organizational development consultants who work in a variety of industries such as automotive, communications and telecommunications, computer, financial services, government agencies, health services, manufacturing, the military, travel/hospitality, and education. Dedicated to improving productivity and performance in the workplace through the application of performance and instructional technologies.

13524 ■ Rod Warriors Cruisin' Club
c/o Bill Enyart, Pres.
PO Box 42
Canal Winchester, OH 43110
Ph: (614)837-4235
E-mail: rodwarriors@ohiocarclubs.com
URL: http://www.ohiocarclubs.com
Contact: Bill Enyart, Pres.
Founded: 1996. **Members:** 5. **Membership Dues:** open, $35 (annual). **Local.** Individuals who love cars and love to cruise. Hosts cruiseins for charity.

Canfield

13525 ■ American Cancer Society, Mahoning County
525 N Broad St.
Canfield, OH 44406
Ph: (330)533-0546
Fax: (330)533-1678
Free: (888)227-6446
E-mail: alfred.stabilito@cancer.org
URL: http://www.cancer.org
Contact: Alfred Stabilito, Contact
Local. Works to eliminate cancer as a major health problem through research, education, advocacy and service. **Affiliated With:** American Cancer Society.

13526 ■ American Cancer Society, Trumbull Area
525 N Broad St.
Canfield, OH 44406
Ph: (330)533-0546
Fax: (330)533-1678
Free: (888)227-6446
URL: http://www.cancer.org
Local. Affiliated With: American Cancer Society.

13527 ■ American Legion, Canfield Post 177
23 E Main St.
Canfield, OH 44406
Ph: (740)362-7478
Fax: (740)362-1429
URL: National Affiliate–www.legion.org
Local. Affiliated With: American Legion.

13528 ■ American Society of Women Accountants, Youngstown Chapter No. 072
c/o Gertrude Martin, Pres.
4059 Canfield Rd.
5540 Tracy Dr.
Canfield, OH 44406
Ph: (330)792-1036
E-mail: catturney@aol.com
URL: National Affiliate–www.aswa.org
Contact: Gertrude Martin CPA, Pres.
Local. Affiliated With: American Society of Women Accountants.

13529 ■ Camp Fire USA Northeast Ohio Council
3712 Leffingwell Rd.
PO Box 516
Canfield, OH 44406
Ph: (330)533-4121
Fax: (330)533-9162
Free: (888)533-4426
E-mail: cfsmith99@yahoo.com
URL: http://www.cboss.com/campfire
Contact: Barbara A. Smith, CEO
Local. Affiliated With: Camp Fire USA.

13530 ■ Canfield Lions Club
PO Box 103
Canfield, OH 44406
Ph: (330)533-0422
E-mail: jrevans18@netzero.net
URL: http://canfieldoh.lionwap.org
Contact: John Evans, Pres.
Local. Affiliated With: Lions Clubs International.

13531 ■ Cystic Fibrosis Foundation, Mahoning County Chapter
7928 Herbert Rd.
Canfield, OH 44406
Ph: (330)533-3162 (330)759-0913
URL: National Affiliate–www.cff.org
Contact: Colleen Nouosel, Pres.
Founded: 1958. **Staff:** 1. **Local.** Cystic fibrosis patients, their families, and interested individuals. Provides patient care and educational programs; conducts research. **Affiliated With:** Cystic Fibrosis Foundation. **Publications:** Newsletter, periodic. **Conventions/Meetings:** periodic meeting.

13532 ■ Federation of Families for Children's Mental Health - First Ohio Chapter
4505 Quaker Ct.
Canfield, OH 44406
Ph: (330)726-9570
Fax: (330)726-9031
E-mail: xuparents@aol.com
URL: National Affiliate–www.ffcmh.org
Contact: Chrysanne Mitzel, Contact
Local. Affiliated With: Federation of Families for Children's Mental Health.

13533 ■ Irish American Archival Society
c/o Sally Murphy Pallante, Pres.
PO Box 454
5480 Mission Hills Dr.
Canfield, OH 44406-0454
Ph: (330)533-7542 (330)799-4544
Fax: (330)533-7542
E-mail: nana10eire@aol.com
URL: http://www.irishofyoungstown.com
Contact: Jim Dunn, Sec.
Founded: 1996. **Members:** 830. **Membership Dues:** individual, $15 (annual). **Budget:** $2,000. **Local Groups:** 1. **Regional.** Seeks to collect, research, and preserve documents, photos, memorabilia, and oral history of the Irish in the greater Mahoning Valley. Collects records of individuals, families, organizations, political groups, and businesses that influenced the growth and development of the Irish American community in the area. Develops a cultural exhibit and Irish cultural suitcase that is available for public and school educational activities. Conducts seminars open to the public that encourage Irish research of family genealogy, the preservation of old documents and to provide information on local Irish history. **Libraries: Type:** reference. **Holdings:** articles, audio recordings, books, photographs. **Subjects:** Irish history, Irish folk tales, Irish American events, oral histories. **Affiliated With:** Ancient Order of Hibernians. **Publications:** *The Harp*, quarterly. Newsletter. Features detailed calendar of local events, history information, photographs, seasonal recipes, and holiday articles about Irish culture. **Price:** included in membership dues. **Circulation:** 650 • *The Irish In Youngstown and the Greater Mahoning Valley.in Arcadia's Images of America Series*. Book. Local History. **Price:** $19.99 • *Irish Phone book*. Directory. Contains listing of local Irish organizations and contact numbers. **Price:** $3.00. **Conventions/Meetings:** quarterly meeting (exhibits) • quarterly meeting, membership • annual seminar.

13534 ■ Mahoning County Medical Association (MCMS)
565 E Main St., Ste.220
Canfield, OH 44406
Ph: (330)533-4880
E-mail: mcms1872@sbcglobal.net
URL: http://www.mahoningmed.org
Contact: Karen L. Frederick, Exec.Dir.
Local. Advances the art and science of medicine. Promotes patient care and the betterment of public health. **Affiliated With:** Ohio State Medical Association.

13535 ■ Marine Corps League Auxiliary - Sgt. Paul T. Varley Unit
c/o Patti C. Higgens
PO Box 241
Canfield, OH 44406-0241
Ph: (330)799-8190
Fax: (508)664-3079
E-mail: mclauxiliaryvarley@unitedstates.com
URL: http://www.mclauxiliaryVarley.unitedstates.com
Local.

13536 ■ National Active and Retired Federal Employees Association - Yarb 2122
4551 Canfield Rd.
Canfield, OH 44406-9349
Ph: (330)792-6026
URL: National Affiliate–www.narfe.org
Contact: Donald T. Hobbs, Contact
Local. Protects the retirement future of employees through education. Informs members on issues affecting the retirement. **Affiliated With:** National Association of Retired Federal Employees.

13537 ■ National Vocational-Technical Honor Society, Mahoning County Career and Technical Center
c/o Melissa Hackett
7300 N Palmyra Rd.
Canfield, OH 44406
Ph: (330)729-4000
Fax: (330)729-4050
E-mail: mjvs_mah@access-k12.org
URL: http://www.mahoningjvs.k12.oh.us
Contact: Melissa Hackett, Contact
Local. Honor students engaged in occupational and vocational-technical programs. Promotes vocational-technical education, career development, skilled workmanship, and individual qualities such as leadership and honesty. **Affiliated With:** National Technical Honor Society.

13538 ■ Plumbing-Heating-Cooling Contractors Association, Eastern Ohio
c/o Ms. Liana Driscoll, Pres.
55 Lisbon St.
Canfield, OH 44406-1415
Ph: (330)533-5559
Fax: (330)533-3668
E-mail: neffcoinc@aol.com
URL: National Affiliate–www.phccweb.org
Contact: Ms. Liana Driscoll, Pres.
Local. Represents the plumbing, heating and cooling contractors. Promotes the construction industry. Protects the environment, health, safety and comfort of society. **Affiliated With:** Plumbing-Heating-Cooling Contractors Association.

Canton

13539 ■ Alcoholics Anonymous World Services, Canton Area Intergroup Council
4125 Hills and Dales Rd. NW, Ste.400B
Canton, OH 44708-1676
Ph: (330)491-1989
E-mail: cantonintergroup@netscape.net
URL: http://www.cantonaa.org
Local. Individuals recovering from alcoholism. AA maintains that members can solve their common problem and help others achieve sobriety through a twelve step program that includes sharing their experience, strength, and hope with each other. **Affiliated With:** Alcoholics Anonymous World Services.

13540 ■ Alzheimer's Association, Greater East Ohio Area Chapter, Canton Office
4815 Munson St. NW
Canton, OH 44718
Ph: (330)966-7343
Fax: (330)966-7757
Free: (800)441-3322
E-mail: ruth.wright@alz.org
URL: National Affiliate–www.alz.org
Contact: Ruth Wright, RNC
Local. Provides comprehensive services to persons affected by Alzheimer's Disease and related disorders

through support, education, advocacy and research. **Affiliated With:** Alzheimer's Association.

13541 ■ American Institute of Chemical Engineers - Akron Section
c/o Tony Frank, Sec.
Marathon Ashland Petroleum LLC
2408 W Gambrinus Rd. SW
Canton, OH 44706
Ph: (330)479-7068
E-mail: afrank@mapllc.com
URL: http://members.core.com/~aiche
Contact: Tom Flynn, Chm.
Local. Represents the interests of chemical engineering professionals. Aims to contribute to the improvement of chemical engineering curricula offered in universities. Seeks to enhance the lifelong career development and financial security of chemical engineers through products, services, networking and advocacy. **Affiliated With:** American Institute of Chemical Engineers.

13542 ■ American Legion, Canton Post 44
1633 Cleveland Ave. NW
Canton, OH 44703
Ph: (740)362-7478
Fax: (740)362-1429
URL: National Affiliate–www.legion.org
Local. Affiliated With: American Legion.

13543 ■ American Legion, Ohio Post 204
c/o E.J. Jester, Adj.
2412 7th St. NE
Canton, OH 44704
Ph: (740)362-7478
Fax: (740)362-1429
URL: National Affiliate–www.legion.org
Contact: E.J. Jester, Adj.
Local. Affiliated With: American Legion.

13544 ■ American Legion, Ohio Post 440
c/o Stanley S. Bowman
PO Box 143
Canton, OH 44707
Ph: (740)362-7478
Fax: (740)362-1429
URL: National Affiliate–www.legion.org
Contact: Stanley S. Bowman, Contact
Local. Affiliated With: American Legion.

13545 ■ APICS, The Association for Operations Management - Canton Area Chapter
c/o John Cadden, Pres.
Combi Packaging Systems
5365 E Center Dr. NE
Canton, OH 44721
Ph: (330)458-0568
E-mail: cad@combi.com
URL: http://www.apicscanton.org
Contact: John Cadden, Pres.
Local. Provides information and services in production and inventory management and related areas to enable members, enterprises and individuals to add value to their business performance. **Affiliated With:** APICS - The Association for Operations Management.

13546 ■ Arc of Stark County
c/o Belden Village Tower
4450 Belden Village St. NW, Ste.307
Canton, OH 44718
Ph: (330)492-5225
Fax: (330)492-0593
E-mail: info@arcstark.org
URL: http://www.arcstark.org
Contact: Ronald Klonowski, Exec.Dir.
Local. Parents, professional workers, and others interested in individuals with mental retardation. Works to promote services, research, public understanding, and legislation for people with mental retardation and their families. **Affiliated With:** Arc of the United States.

13547 ■ Association of Christian Schools International, Ohio River Valley Region
c/o Dr. Randall Ross, EdD, Regional Dir.
3019 Cleveland Ave. SW, Ste.207
Canton, OH 44707
Ph: (330)484-7750
Fax: (330)484-7760
E-mail: randy_ross@acsi.org
URL: National Affiliate–www.acsi.org
Contact: Dr. Randall Ross EdD, Regional Dir.
Regional. Seeks to enable Christian educators and schools worldwide to effectively prepare students for life. **Telecommunication Services:** electronic mail, acsiorv@acsi.org. **Affiliated With:** Association of Christian Schools International.

13548 ■ Austin-Bailey Health and Wellness Foundation
2719 Fulton Rd. NW, Ste.D
Canton, OH 44718
Ph: (330)580-2380
Fax: (330)580-2381
E-mail: abfdn@cannet.com
URL: http://foundationcenter.org/grantmaker/austinbailey
Contact: Don A. Sultzbach, Exec.Dir.
Founded: 1996. **Staff:** 3. **Budget:** $600,000. **Nonmembership. Local.** Supports programs that promote health and wellness to the citizens of Holmes, Stark, Tuscarawas, and Wayne Counties in Ohio. **Awards: Frequency:** semiannual. **Type:** grant. **Recipient:** for health and wellness programs.

13549 ■ Better Business Bureau/Canton Regional and Greater West Virginia
PO Box 8017
Canton, OH 44711-8017
Ph: (330)454-9401
Fax: (330)456-8957
Free: (800)362-0494
E-mail: info@canton.bbb.org
URL: http://www.cantonbbb.org
Contact: Michael Paris, Pres./CEO
Regional. Seeks to promote and foster ethical relationship between businesses and the public through voluntary self-regulation, consumer and business education, and service excellence. Provides information to help consumers and businesses make informed purchasing decisions and avoid costly scams and frauds; settles consumer complaints through arbitration and other means. **Affiliated With:** BBB Wise Giving Alliance. **Formerly:** (2001) Better Business Bureau/Canton Regional.

13550 ■ Buckeye Corvettes
929 Cleveland Ave. NW
Canton, OH 44702-1895
Ph: (330)454-8011
Fax: (330)588-2042
URL: http://www.buckeyecorvettes.org
Contact: Greg Sohovich, Pres.
Local. Affiliated With: National Council of Corvette Clubs.

13551 ■ Buckeye SCORE
c/o Robert Forney, Chm.
Stark State Coll. of Tech., Advance Tech. Ctr.
6200 Frank Ave. NW, Rm. T101B
Canton, OH 44720-7299
Ph: (330)966-5465
Fax: (330)494-5280
E-mail: score@starkstate.edu
Local. Promotes business and community development in Canton, ID area. Conducts business education seminars and workshops to those wanting to start a business.

13552 ■ Builders Exchange of East Central Ohio
2521 - 34th St. NE
Canton, OH 44705
Ph: (330)452-8039
Fax: (330)452-4323
Free: (800)948-2244
E-mail: ggibson@bxofeco.com
URL: http://www.bxofeco.com
Contact: Gary Gibson, Exec.Dir.
Local. Represents the general contractors, subcontractors, suppliers, manufacturer's representatives and individual firms related to the construction industry. Provides information on construction and building procedures. **Affiliated With:** International Builders Exchange Executives.

13553 ■ Canton ALU
c/o William Burrow
220 Market S, Ste.1100
Canton, OH 44702
Ph: (330)452-2500
Fax: (330)452-2605
URL: National Affiliate–www.naifa.org
Local. Represents the interest of insurance and financial advisors. Advocates for a positive legislative and regulatory environment. Enhances business and professional skills of members. **Affiliated With:** National Association of Insurance and Financial Advisors.

13554 ■ Canton Area Chapter MOAA
c/o CWO4 George David
5835 Garth Cir. NW
Canton, OH 44718-1373
Ph: (330)493-8761
URL: National Affiliate–www.moaa.org
Contact: CWO4 George David, Contact
Local. Affiliated With: Military Officers Association of America.

13555 ■ Canton Audubon Society
PO Box 9586
Canton, OH 44711-9586
Ph: (330)832-2491
URL: http://www.audubon.org/chapter/oh/index.html
Contact: Alan R Dolan, Pres.
Local. Formerly: (2005) National Audubon Society - Canton.

13556 ■ Canton Lions Club - Ohio
c/o Salvatore Cammel, Sec.
1206 41st St. NW
Canton, OH 44709
Ph: (330)492-2547
E-mail: salcammel630@cs.com
URL: http://www.lions13d.org
Contact: Salvatore Cammel, Sec.
Local. Affiliated With: Lions Clubs International.

13557 ■ Canton Regional Chamber of Commerce
222 Market Ave. N
Canton, OH 44702-1418
Ph: (330)456-7253
Fax: (330)452-7786
Free: (800)533-4302
E-mail: info@cantonchamber.org
URL: http://www.cantonchamber.org
Contact: Dennis P. Saunier, Pres.
Founded: 1917. **Members:** 1,500. **Staff:** 50. **Budget:** $5,000,000. **Regional.** Provides services to members and helps advance the economic growth of Canton and the Stark County region. **Publications:** *ACTION*. Newsletter. **Price:** $25.00 for nonmembers. **Circulation:** 2,500.

13558 ■ Canton South Lions Club
c/o Jennifer Baylor, Sec.
6315 Melody Rd. NE
Canton, OH 44721
Ph: (330)494-4713
E-mail: jenbay2@juno.com
URL: http://www.lions13d.org
Contact: Jennifer Baylor, Sec.
Local. Affiliated With: Lions Clubs International.

13559 ■ Canton and Stark County Convention and Visitors Bureau
The Millennium Ctre.
222 Market Ave. N
Canton, OH 44702
Ph: (330)454-1439
Fax: (330)456-3600
Free: (800)533-4302
E-mail: cvbinfo@visitcantonohio.com
URL: http://www.visitcantonohio.com
Contact: John Kiste, Exec.Dir.
Local.

13560 ■ Canton Table Tennis Club
Canton YWCA
231 6th St. NE
Canton, OH 44702
Ph: (330)493-1457
E-mail: rdietz@neo.rr.com
URL: National Affiliate–www.usatt.org
Contact: Roy M. Dietz, Contact
Local. Affiliated With: U.S.A. Table Tennis.

13561 ■ Canton Urban League
1400 Sherrick Rd. SE
Canton, OH 44707
Ph: (330)456-3479
Fax: (330)456-3307
E-mail: jgordon@cantonul.org
URL: http://www.cantonul.org
Contact: Janet M. Gordon, Acting Pres./CEO
Local. Affiliated With: National Urban League.

13562 ■ Center Ice Skating Club
5421 Villa Padova Dr. NW
Canton, OH 44718
E-mail: carla@skatingsmylife.com
URL: http://www.skatingsmylife.com
Contact: Carl Yoder, Pres.
Local. Provides programs to encourage participation and achievement in the sport of figure skating on ice. Defines and maintains uniform standards of skating proficiency. Organizes and sponsors competitions and exhibitions for the purpose of stimulating interest in figure skating. **Affiliated With:** United States Figure Skating Association.

13563 ■ Easter Seals Northeast Ohio, Canton
3930 Fulton Dr. NW, Ste.107
Canton, OH 44718
Ph: (330)494-3642
Fax: (330)494-4538
Free: (800)341-0876
E-mail: sdunn@eastersealsneo.org
URL: http://neohio.easterseals.com
Contact: Ms. Sheila Dunn, Pres./CEO
Local. Provides services for children and adults with disabilities or special needs, and supports their families. **Affiliated With:** Easter Seals.

13564 ■ First Catholic Slovak Ladies Association - Canton Junior Branch 143
147 Raff Rd. NW
Canton, OH 44708
Ph: (330)454-3110
URL: National Affiliate–www.fcsla.com
Local. Affiliated With: First Catholic Slovak Ladies Association.

13565 ■ First Catholic Slovak Ladies Association - Canton Senior Branch 301
147 Raff Rd. NW
Canton, OH 44708
Ph: (330)454-3110
URL: National Affiliate–www.fcsla.com
Local. Affiliated With: First Catholic Slovak Ladies Association.

13566 ■ Friends of Stark Parks
c/o Greg Mencer
5300 Tyner St. NW
Canton, OH 44708-5041
Ph: (330)477-3552
Fax: (330)477-1211
E-mail: info@starkparks.com
Contact: Mr. Loren Souers Jr., Pres.
Founded: 1997. **Members:** 400. **Membership Dues:** $25 (annual). **Budget:** $25,000. **Local Groups:** 1. **Local.** Volunteer Organization that promotes development and use of parks and trails. Seeks to become a county-wide organization with a diverse volunteer and sponsorship base, to provide funds for development and expansion of existing parks and rails, and to support nature education for the enjoyment of park visitors. **Publications:** *Friends of Stark Parks*, quarterly. Newsletter. **Price:** included in membership dues. **Circulation:** 500. **Advertising:** accepted. **Conventions/Meetings:** annual meeting - in January.

13567 ■ Habitat for Humanity of Greater Canton (HFHGC)
2800 Leemont Ave. NW
Canton, OH 44709
Ph: (330)493-6500
Fax: (330)493-6501
E-mail: blechner@hfhcanton.org
URL: http://hfhcanton.org
Contact: Beth J. Lechner, Exec.Dir.
Founded: 1988. **Staff:** 11. **Budget:** $1,600,000. **Local.** Works to help meet the long-term housing needs of Canton's low income families who are inadequately housed. **Subgroups:** Thursday Crew. **Affiliated With:** Habitat for Humanity International. **Publications:** *Habitat Happenings*, quarterly. Newsletter. **Price:** free. **Circulation:** 8,500. Alternate Formats: online.

13568 ■ IEEE Akron/Canton Section
c/o Robert J. Voss, Pres.
3715 Eaton Rd. NW
Canton, OH 44708-1773
Ph: (330)454-1753
E-mail: rvoss@neo.rr.com
URL: http://ewh.ieee.org/r2/akroncanton
Contact: Robert J. Voss, Pres.
Local. Engineers and scientists in electrical engineering, electronics, and allied fields. Promotes creating, developing, integrating, sharing, and applying knowledge about electro and information technologies and sciences for the benefit of humanity and the profession. Conducts lectures on current engineering and scientific topics.

13569 ■ Indian Physicians Association of Greater Canton
c/o Balasubramanium Chitrabanu, MD
1470 Valentine Cir. NW
Canton, OH 44708
Ph: (330)452-6060
URL: National Affiliate–www.aapiusa.org
Contact: Balasubramanium Chitrabanu MD, Contact
Local. Represents Indian American physicians. Promotes excellence in patient care, teaching and research. Serves as a forum for scientific, educational and social interaction among members and other medical scientists of Indian heritage. Fosters the availability of medical assistance to indigent people in the United States. **Affiliated With:** American Association of Physicians of Indian Origin.

13570 ■ Junior Achievement of East Central Ohio
4353 Executive Cir. NW
Canton, OH 44718-2999
Ph: (330)433-0063
Fax: (330)433-0287
E-mail: staff@jaonline.org
URL: http://www.jaonline.org
Contact: Jody L. Levitt, Pres.
Local. Works to educate and inspire young people to value free enterprise, business and economics in improving the quality of their lives. Improves partnerships between the business and education communities through programs that develop future employees and encourage lifelong learning and citizenship. **Affiliated With:** Junior Achievement.

13571 ■ Massillon HS - Young Life
PO Box 9415
Canton, OH 44711
Ph: (330)453-2088
URL: http://sites.younglife.org/_layouts/ylext/default.aspx?ID=C-4309
Local. Affiliated With: Young Life.

13572 ■ National Active and Retired Federal Employees Association - Mckinley 341
4740 Fohl St. SW
Canton, OH 44706-3723
Ph: (330)484-4220
URL: National Affiliate–www.narfe.org
Contact: John Johnson, Contact
Local. Protects the retirement future of employees through education. Informs members on issues affecting the retirement. **Affiliated With:** National Association of Retired Federal Employees.

13573 ■ Ohio Association of Orthopaedic Technologists
8039 Blendwood NE Ave.
Canton, OH 44721
Ph: (330)832-2663
URL: National Affiliate–naot.org
Contact: Willie Suggs OTC, Contact
State. Promotes continued professional education for members and other orthopedic health care providers. Administers certification examinations. Seeks to enhance public understanding of orthopedics. **Affiliated With:** National Association of Orthopaedic Technologists.

13574 ■ Ohio Car Wash Association
1901 Mt. Vernon Blvd. NW
Canton, OH 44709
Ph: (330)492-8761
State.

13575 ■ Ohio Genealogical Society, Stark County Chapter
PO Box 9035
Canton, OH 44711-9035
E-mail: starkquery@yahoo.com
URL: National Affiliate–www.ogs.org
Contact: Dee Rondinella, Pres.
Local. Affiliated With: Ohio Genealogical Society.

13576 ■ Parents Anonymous of Stark County and Northern Ohio
800 Market Ave. N, Ste.1500B
Canton, OH 44702
Ph: (330)456-5470
Fax: (330)456-5841
E-mail: starkpa@familiesfirst-starkcounty.org
URL: http://www.familiesfirst-starkcounty.org
Contact: Shirley Walters, Dir.
Local.

13577 ■ Perry Township Lions Club
c/o Rebekah Ost, Sec.
4922 14th St. SW
Canton, OH 44710
Ph: (330)477-5854
E-mail: r_ost@hotmail.com
URL: http://www.geocities.com/perrylions
Contact: Rebekah Ost, Sec.
Local. Affiliated With: Lions Clubs International.

13578 ■ Phi Theta Kappa - Beta Gamma Epsilon Chapter
c/o Cherie Barth
6200 Frank Ave. NW
Canton, OH 44720
Ph: (330)966-5450
E-mail: cbarth@starkstate.edu
URL: http://www.ptk.org/directories/chapters/OH/20693-1.htm
Contact: Cherie Barth, Advisor
Local. Affiliated With: Phi Theta Kappa, International Honor Society.

13579 ■ Quilting Stars of Ohio
PO Box 80546
Canton, OH 44708
E-mail: quiltingstarsofohio@earthlink.net
URL: http://www.quiltingstars.org
Local.

13580 ■ RSVP of Stark County
c/o Jacqueline Dewey-Smith, Dir.
625 Cleveland Ave.
Canton, OH 44702
Ph: (330)455-0374
Fax: (330)455-2101
E-mail: rsvp1112@neo.rr.com
URL: http://www.joinseniorservice.org
Contact: Jacqueline Dewey-Smith, Dir.
Local. Affiliated With: Retired and Senior Volunteer Program.

13581 ■ Society of Manufacturing Engineers - Stark State College U172
6200 Frank Ave. NW
Canton, OH 44720-7299
Ph: (330)966-5461
E-mail: cjain@starkstate.edu
URL: National Affiliate–www.sme.org
Contact: Chandra Jain, Contact
Local. Advances manufacturing knowledge to gain competitive advantage. Improves skills and manufacturing solutions for the growth of economy. Provides resources and opportunities for manufacturing professionals. **Affiliated With:** Seafloor Geosciences Division.

13582 ■ Society of Tribologists and Lubrication Engineers - Canton Section
c/o Harvey Nixon, Chm.
PO Box 6930
Canton, OH 44706-0930
Ph: (330)471-2046
Fax: (330)458-6046
E-mail: harvey.nixon@timken.com
URL: National Affiliate–www.stle.org
Contact: Harvey Nixon, Chm.
Local. Promotes the advancement of tribology and the practice of lubrication engineering. Stimulates the study and development of lubrication tribology techniques. Promotes higher standards in the field. **Affiliated With:** Society of Tribologists and Lubrication Engineers.

13583 ■ Sons of the American Legion, Post 44
c/o Raymond Vensodale
1633 Cleveland Ave. NW
Canton, OH 44703
URL: http://www.legion.org/?content=post_locator
Local.

13584 ■ Stark County Association of Realtors Charitable Foundation
c/o Thomas Tuttle
4848 Munson St. NW
Canton, OH 44718-3631
Ph: (330)494-5630
Local.

13585 ■ Stark County Automobile Dealers Association
c/o Mr. James F. Kling, Exec.Dir.
2812 Whipple Ave. NW
Canton, OH 44708
Ph: (330)477-6655
Fax: (330)477-2595
E-mail: scada@neo.rr.com
URL: National Affiliate–www.nada.org
Contact: Mr. James F. Kling, Exec.Dir.
Local. Affiliated With: National Automobile Dealers Association.

13586 ■ Stark County Dental Society (SCDS)
4942 Higbee Ave. NW, Ste.K
Canton, OH 44718-2554
Ph: (330)493-1123
Fax: (330)493-1101
E-mail: scds@neo.rr.com
URL: http://www.starkcountydentalsociety.org
Contact: Ms. Barbara Weigand, Exec.Dir.
Local. Represents the interests of dentists committed to the public's oral health, ethics and professional development. Encourages the improvement of the public's oral health and promotes the art and science of dentistry. **Affiliated With:** American Dental Association; Ohio Dental Association.

13587 ■ Stark County Farm Bureau
1000 Market Ave. N
Canton, OH 44702
Ph: (330)456-4889
Fax: (330)456-7064
E-mail: cbaker@ofbf.org
URL: http://www.ofbf.org/ofbweb/ofbwebengine.nsf/counties
Contact: Nicholas Kennedy, Dir.
Local.

13588 ■ Stark County Human Resource Association
PO Box 20247
Canton, OH 44701
E-mail: teddybearhorn@hotmail.com
URL: http://www.starkhr.org
Contact: Debbie Horn, Pres.
Local. Represents the interests of human resource and industrial relations professionals and executives. Promotes the advancement of human resource management.

13589 ■ Stark County Medical Society (SCMS)
4942 Higbee Ave. NW, Ste.L
Canton, OH 44718
Ph: (330)492-3333
Fax: (330)492-3347
E-mail: starkmedical@ameritech.net
URL: http://www.starkmedical.org
Contact: JoAnn LaRocco, Exec.Dir.
Local. Advances the art and science of medicine. Promotes patient care and the betterment of public health. **Affiliated With:** Ohio State Medical Association.

13590 ■ Stark County Young Life
PO Box 9415
Canton, OH 44711
Ph: (330)453-2088
Fax: (330)453-2088
E-mail: hsizick@oh26.younglife.org
URL: http://sites.younglife.org/sites/YLStarkCounty/default.aspx
Contact: Heath D. Sizick, Area Dir.
Local. Affiliated With: Young Life.

13591 ■ Sweet Adelines International, City of Flags Chorus
Greenwood Christian Church
4425 Frazer Ave. NW
Canton, OH 44709-1319
Free: (800)SWEET-05
E-mail: t1hammer@neo.rr.com
URL: http://www.cityofflagschorus.com
Contact: Darryl Flinn, Dir.
Local. Advances the musical art form of barbershop harmony through education and performances. Provides education, training and coaching in the development of women's four-part barbershop harmony. **Affiliated With:** Sweet Adelines International.

13592 ■ Tuscarawas and Carroll REACT
PO Box 9603
Canton, OH 44711
Ph: (330)866-4386
URL: http://www.reactintl.org/teaminfo/usa_teams/teams-usoh.htm
Local. Trained communication experts and professional volunteers. Provides volunteer public service and emergency communications through the use of radios (Citizen Band, General Mobile Radio Service, UHF and HAM). Coordinates with radio industries and government on safety communication matters and supports charitable activities and community organizations.

13593 ■ United Way of Greater Stark County
4825 Higbee Ave. NW
Canton, OH 44718
Ph: (330)491-0445
Fax: (330)491-0477
E-mail: info@uwgsc.org
URL: http://www.uwgsc.org
Contact: Julie Blackledge, Exec.Dir.
Founded: 1924. **Members:** 27. **Staff:** 4. **Local.** Coordinates, plans and campaigns for 27 United Way agencies in Stark County, OH. **Affiliated With:** United Way of America.

13594 ■ Vietnam Veterans of America, Chapter No. 199
c/o Patricia A. Powell, Pres.
PO Box 21205
Canton, OH 44701
Ph: (330)453-7991
URL: http://www.vvabuckeyestatecouncil.com
Contact: Patricia A. Powell, Pres.
Local. Affiliated With: Vietnam Veterans of America.

13595 ■ Wood Truss Council of America Ohio Chapter Association (WTCAOCA)
c/o Stephen Yoder, Pres.
PO Box 80469
Canton, OH 44708
Ph: (330)478-2100
Fax: (330)478-6359
E-mail: steve.yoder@starktruss.com
URL: National Affiliate–www.sbcindustry.com
Contact: Stephen Yoder, Pres.
State. Represents manufacturers and suppliers of structural wood components. Protects and advances the interests of members, manufacturers and suppliers of related products. Encourages the use of structural wood components. Supports research, development and testing of wood trusses. **Affiliated With:** Wood Truss Council of America.

Cardington

13596 ■ American Legion, Jenkins-Vaughan Post 97
307 Park Ave., No. 26
Cardington, OH 43315
Ph: (740)362-7478
Fax: (740)362-1429
URL: National Affiliate–www.legion.org
Local. Affiliated With: American Legion.

13597 ■ Rotary Club of Cardington, Ohio
4380 US Rte. 42 N
Cardington, OH 43315
Ph: (419)864-8820
Fax: (740)725-1037
Contact: Jan Garverick, Contact
Founded: 1938. **Members:** 20. **State.** Service organization of business and professional executives. Promotes fellowship. Conducts community and international service. **Affiliated With:** Rotary International. **Conventions/Meetings:** weekly meeting.

Carey

13598 ■ American Legion, Earl Green Post 344
201 E Findlay St.
Carey, OH 43316
Ph: (740)362-7478
Fax: (740)362-1429
URL: National Affiliate–www.legion.org
Local. Affiliated With: American Legion.

13599 ■ Carey Area Chamber of Commerce
R119 W Findlay St.
PO Box 94
Carey, OH 43316-0094
Ph: (419)396-7856
Fax: (419)396-7856
E-mail: careychamber@udata.com
URL: http://www.wyandotonline.com/careychamber/default.htm
Contact: Nancy Maison, Exec.Dir.
Founded: 1993. **Members:** 105. **Membership Dues:** business (based on the number of employees), $60-$450 • individual, $25 • club group, $75 • utility, $250 • youth group, $50. **Budget:** $13,000. **Local.** Promotes business and community development in Carey, OH.

13600 ■ Carey United Way
PO Box 162
Carey, OH 43316-0162
Ph: (419)365-0600
URL: National Affiliate–national.unitedway.org
Local. Affiliated With: United Way of America.

Carlisle

13601 ■ Carlisle Lions Club - Ohio
465 Park Dr.
Carlisle, OH 45005-3352
Ph: (937)746-5619 (937)746-9098
E-mail: gminge@cinci.rr.com
URL: http://carlisleoh.lionwap.org
Contact: Greg Minge, Sec.
Local. Affiliated With: Lions Clubs International.

Carroll

13602 ■ Bloom Carroll Lions Club
95 Center St.
Carroll, OH 43112
Ph: (614)577-1758
E-mail: danielwaynefox@worldnet.att.net
URL: http://bcarrolloh.lionwap.org
Contact: Carolyn Fox, Pres.
Local. Affiliated With: Lions Clubs International.

Carrollton

13603 ■ American Legion, Carroll Post 428
PO Box 2
Carrollton, OH 44615
Ph: (740)362-7478
Fax: (740)362-1429
URL: National Affiliate–www.legion.org
Local. Affiliated With: American Legion.

13604 ■ Carroll County Chamber of Commerce and Economic Development (CCCED)
PO Box 277
Carrollton, OH 44615
Ph: (330)627-4811 (330)627-5500
Fax: (330)627-3647
E-mail: carrollchamber@eohio.net
Contact: Rhonda Cogan, Exec.Dir.
Founded: 1938. **Members:** 153. **Staff:** 2. **Local.** Retailers, manufacturers, professionals, and service organizations. Promotes business and community development in Carroll County, OH. Promotes tourism. Sponsors seminars and annual golf outing. **Awards:** Golden Shovel Ashton Scholarship. **Frequency:** annual. **Type:** scholarship. **Formerly:** (1979) Carrollton Chamber of Commerce; (1999) Carroll County Chamber of Commerce. **Publications:** Newsletter, monthly. **Conventions/Meetings:** annual meeting • monthly meeting.

13605 ■ Carrollton Lions Club
c/o Doris Streszoff, Sec.
6801 Luna Ln. SW
Carrollton, OH 44615
Ph: (330)627-5514
E-mail: dstrez@bright.net
URL: http://users.adelphia.net/~npssteve/district.htm
Contact: Doris Streszoff, Sec.
Local. Affiliated With: Lions Clubs International.

Castalia

13606 ■ Castalia Lions Club
c/o Joe Bias, Pres.
9010 Rogers Rd.
Castalia, OH 44824
Ph: (419)684-7575
E-mail: ajbias@aol.com
URL: http://www.lions13b.org
Contact: Joe Bias, Pres.
Local. Affiliated With: Lions Clubs International.

Cedarville

13607 ■ American Legion, Ohio Post 544
c/o Wallace C. Anderson
PO Box 544
Cedarville, OH 45314
Ph: (740)362-7478
Fax: (740)362-1429
URL: National Affiliate–www.legion.org
Contact: Wallace C. Anderson, Contact
Local. Affiliated With: American Legion.

13608 ■ Ohio Dairy Goat Association
c/o Sue Smart
3911 Fed. Rd.
Cedarville, OH 45314
Ph: (937)766-2619
URL: http://www.odga.org
Contact: Sue Smart, Contact
State. Affiliated With: American Dairy Goat Association.

Celina

13609 ■ American Legion, Celina Post 210
PO Box 52
Celina, OH 45822
Ph: (740)362-7478
Fax: (740)362-1429
URL: National Affiliate–www.legion.org
Local. Affiliated With: American Legion.

13610 ■ American Red Cross, Mercer County Chapter
117 S Main St., Ste.B
Celina, OH 45822
Ph: (419)586-2201
E-mail: cmbrunswick@hotmail.com
URL: http://mercercountyohio.redcross.org
Local.

13611 ■ AMVETS, Celina Post 91
8263 St., Rte. 703 E
Celina, OH 45822
E-mail: amvets91@hotmail.com
URL: http://www.amvets91.freeservers.com
Contact: John Brown, Commander
Local. Affiliated With: AMVETS - American Veterans.

13612 ■ Celina-Mercer County Chamber of Commerce
226 N Main St.
Celina, OH 45822-1663
Ph: (419)586-2219
Fax: (419)586-8645
E-mail: info@celinamercer.com
URL: http://www.celinamercer.com
Contact: Pam Buschur, Exec.Dir.
Founded: 1935. **Members:** 250. **Membership Dues:** nonprofit, $60 • associate 2, $30 • associate, $50 • business (retail/industrial/professional/hospital), $120. **Staff:** 2. **Local.** Promotes business and community development in the Mercer County, OH area. Sponsors area festival and operates Small Business Development Center. **Formerly:** (1995) Celina Area Chamber of Commerce. **Publications:** *Buyer's Guide and Membership Directory*, annual • Directory, periodic. **Price:** $5.00 for industrial directory; $6.00 for business directory • Newsletter, quarterly. **Advertising:** accepted. **Conventions/Meetings:** monthly Ambassador Committee Meeting - every 1st Thursday, 8 AM, Celina, OH • monthly executive committee meeting - every last Wednesday, 8 AM, Celina, OH.

13613 ■ Grand Lake Beagle Club
c/o Dan Nixon
4707 Cass Mont Rd.
Celina, OH 45822
URL: National Affiliate–clubs.akc.org
Contact: Dan Nixon, Contact
Local.

13614 ■ Mercer County Chapter of the Ohio Genealogical Society (MCCOGS)
PO Box 437
Celina, OH 45822-0437
Ph: (419)795-4494
E-mail: contact@mccogs.ohgenweb.net
URL: http://mccogs.ohgenweb.net
Contact: Carolyn Brandon, Pres.
Founded: 1980. **Members:** 400. **Membership Dues:** single, $10 (annual) • joint - family at same address, $12 (annual). **Budget:** $5,000. **Local. Libraries: Type:** open to the public; reference. **Holdings:** audio recordings, books, maps, periodicals. **Subjects:** genealogy. **Telecommunication Services:** electronic mail, cdmbrand@bright.net. **Affiliated With:** Ohio Genealogical Society. **Publications:** *The Mercer County Monitor*, quarterly. Newsletter. **Price:** included in membership dues. **Circulation:** 400.

13615 ■ National Technical Honor Society - Wright State University Lake Campus Ohio
7600 State Rte. 703
Celina, OH 45822-2952
Ph: (419)586-0300
Fax: (419)586-0358
Free: (800)237-1477
E-mail: anita.curry-jackson@wright.edu
Contact: Anita Curry-Jackson PhD, Contact
Local.

13616 ■ Veterans of Foreign Wars, Post 5713
PO Box 293
Celina, OH 45822-0293
Ph: (419)586-3140
E-mail: vfw@bright.net
URL: http://www.vfw5713.com
Contact: Mort Ward, Quarter Master
Local.

13617 ■ Vietnam Veterans of America, Chapter No. 783
c/o Steve Jones, Pres.
6686 Wabash Rd.
Celina, OH 45822
Ph: (419)942-1595
URL: http://www.vvabuckeyestatecouncil.com
Contact: Steve Jones, Pres.
Local. Affiliated With: Vietnam Veterans of America.

Centerburg

13618 ■ American Legion, Charles Andrews Post 460
5680 Sycamore Rd.
Centerburg, OH 43011
Ph: (740)362-7478
Fax: (740)362-1429
URL: National Affiliate–www.legion.org
Local. Affiliated With: American Legion.

Centerville

13619 ■ APICS, The Association for Operations Management - Dayton Chapter No. 64
c/o Jack Kerr, CPIM, Dir. of Education
6150 Gentry Woods Dr.
Centerville, OH 45459
Ph: (937)434-3201 (937)754-3245
E-mail: kerrcarguy@aol.com
URL: http://www.apicsdayton.org
Contact: Jack Kerr CPIM, Dir. of Education
Local. Provides information and services in production and inventory management and related areas to enable members, enterprises and individuals to add value to their business performance. **Affiliated With:** APICS - The Association for Operations Management.

13620 ■ Association of the United States Army, Major Samuel Woodfill - Cincinnati
c/o John M. Lusa
6872 Walnut Creek Ct.
Centerville, OH 45459
Ph: (937)433-4005
E-mail: jmlusa@earthlink.net
URL: National Affiliate–www.ausa.org
State. Represents the interests and concerns of American Soldiers. Fosters public support of the Army's role in national security. Provides professional education and information programs.

13621 ■ Association of Women's Health, Obstetric and Neonatal Nurses - Ohio Section
c/o Deborah Gresham, RNC, Chair
870 Vintage Lake Ct.
Centerville, OH 45458
Ph: (937)885-3401 (937)208-6205
E-mail: ddgresham@mvh.org
URL: National Affiliate–www.awhonn.org
Contact: Jennifer Doyle, Sec.-Treas.
State. Represents registered nurses and other health care providers who specialize in obstetric, women's health, and neonatal nursing. Advances the nursing profession by providing nurses with information and support to help them deliver quality care for women and newborns. **Affiliated With:** Association of Women's Health, Obstetric and Neonatal Nurses.

13622 ■ Explorers Club - George Rogers Clark Chapter
c/o Joseph E. Ricketts, Chm.
225 Hibberd Dr.
Centerville, OH 45458
Ph: (937)885-2477
Fax: (937)885-2477
E-mail: jer937@aol.com
URL: National Affiliate–www.explorers.org
Contact: Joseph E. Ricketts, Chm.
Local. Represents explorers and scientists. Promotes field research and scientific exploration. Encourages public interest in exploration and the sciences. **Affiliated With:** The Explorers Club.

13623 ■ Kettering Kilometer Climbers
c/o Jack Majni
6640 Green Br. Dr., No. 5
Centerville, OH 45459-6814
Ph: (937)438-9235
E-mail: jackemajni@earthlink.net
URL: National Affiliate–www.ava.org
Contact: Jack Majni, Contact
Founded: 1987. **Members:** 20. **Membership Dues:** family, $5 (annual). **Local.** Non-competitive sports enthusiasts. **Affiliated With:** American Volkssport Association. **Conventions/Meetings:** monthly meeting - always second Tuesday except for December.

13624 ■ National Organization for Women - Dayton
c/o Lisa Glaser
6640 Green Br. Dr., Apt. 8
Centerville, OH 45459-6814
Ph: (937)438-8530
E-mail: now_dayton@yahoo.com
URL: http://www.ohionow.org
Contact: Lisa Glaser, Contact
Local. Affiliated With: National Organization for Women.

13625 ■ Professional Photographers of Southwest Ohio (PPSO)
c/o Suzette McIntyre, VP
Photography by Suzette
411 Island Lake Ct.
Centerville, OH 45458
Ph: (937)885-9766
E-mail: suzetted@aol.com
URL: http://www.ppso.org
Contact: Dave Chambers, Pres.
Regional. Affiliated With: Professional Photographers of America.

13626 ■ Sweet Adelines International, Gem City Chorus
Gem City Music Hall
243 N Main St.
Centerville, OH 45459
Ph: (937)433-1014
E-mail: gemcityboard@yahoo.com
URL: http://www.harmonize.com/gemcity
Contact: Nancy Duffee, Asst.Dir.
Local. Advances the musical art form of barbershop harmony through education and performances. Provides education, training and coaching in the development of women's four-part barbershop harmony. **Affiliated With:** Sweet Adelines International.

Chagrin Falls

13627 ■ Air Conditioning Contractors of America - Ohio Chapter
18961 River's Edge Dr.
Chagrin Falls, OH 44023
Ph: (440)543-4011
Fax: (440)543-1699
Free: (800)353-2226
E-mail: accohio@aol.com
URL: http://www.accohio.org
Contact: Sandy Pogan CAE, Exec.Dir.
Founded: 1976. **Members:** 277. **Membership Dues:** contractor (heating, airconditioning and refrigeration), associate, $150 (annual). **Budget:** $100,000. **State Groups:** 1. **Local Groups:** 5. **State. Awards:** Contractor of the Year. **Frequency:** annual. **Type:** recognition. **Computer Services:** database. **Affiliated With:** Air Conditioning Contractors of America. **Publications:** *ACCO Newsletter*, quarterly. **Advertising:** accepted. Alternate Formats: online. **Conventions/Meetings:** annual meeting.

13628 ■ American Legion, Chagrin Falls Post 383
3803 Wiltshire Rd.
Chagrin Falls, OH 44022
Ph: (740)362-7478
Fax: (740)362-1429
URL: National Affiliate–www.legion.org
Local. Affiliated With: American Legion.

13629 ■ BMW Motorcycle Owners of Cleveland No. 196 (BMWMOC)
17115 Abbey Rd.
Chagrin Falls, OH 44023
E-mail: jgau@alltel.net
URL: http://www.bmwmoc.org
Contact: Roger Pivonka, Pres.
Membership Dues: individual, $10 (annual). **Local. Affiliated With:** BMW Motorcycle Owners of America.

13630 ■ Canine Resource Development (CRD)
c/o William J. Truax, Sr., Pres./Tres.
25 Easton Ln.
Chagrin Falls, OH 44022-2304
Ph: (440)336-3529
Fax: (440)498-0052
Free: (800)253-1244
E-mail: bill@k-9rd.org
URL: http://www.k-9rd.org
Contact: William J. Truax Sr., Pres./Treas.
Founded: 2000. **Members:** 2. **Staff:** 2. **Local.**

13631 ■ Chagrin Falls Parent Teacher Organization
c/o Liz O'Neil, Pres.
PO Box 131
Chagrin Falls, OH 44022-0131
URL: http://www.chagrin-falls.k12.oh.us/chagrinpto/index.htm
Local.

13632 ■ Chagrin Valley Chamber of Commerce (CVCC)
16 S Main St.
Chagrin Falls, OH 44022-3009
Ph: (440)247-6607
Fax: (440)247-6503
E-mail: info@cvcc.org
URL: http://www.cvcc.org
Contact: Mary Beth Wolfe, Exec.VP
Founded: 1943. **Members:** 500. **Membership Dues:** one time application (new members), $20 • general (based on number of persons), $100-$450 (annual) • resident/retiree, $75 (annual) • associate, $100 (annual) • dual COSE/CVCC (based on number of employees), $450-$600 (annual) • one time application (for dual COSE/CVCC), $50. **Local.** Serves as a powerful regional force, encouraging business to relocate to the Chagrin Valley. Presents the interests of business and industry before local and state governments. Supports the cultural and civic life of the communities and works to make the Valley a better place to live and do business. **Committees:** CVCC Annual Golf; Economic Development; Membership Development. **Subgroups:** Auburn/Bainbridge Business Group; Marketing Team; Visioneering. **Publications:** *Chagrin Valley*, annual. Directory. **Circulation:** 67,500. **Advertising:** accepted. Alternate Formats: online.

13633 ■ Chagrin Valley REACT
9921 Crystal Trail
Chagrin Falls, OH 44023-6207
Ph: (440)543-7325
E-mail: cvreact4995@aol.com
URL: http://www.reactintl.org/teaminfo/usa_teams/teams-usoh.htm
Local. Trained communication experts and professional volunteers. Provides volunteer public service and emergency communications through the use of radios (Citizen Band, General Mobile Radio Service, UHF and HAM). Coordinates with radio industries and government on safety communication matters and supports charitable activities and community organizations.

13634 ■ Chagrin Valley Women's League (CVWL)
PO Box 512
Chagrin Falls, OH 44022
URL: http://www.cvwl.org
Contact: Cheryl Abbarno, Pres.
Local.

13635 ■ Great Lakes Curling Association (GLCA)
c/o Bruce Listerman
250 Pheasant Run Dr.
Chagrin Falls, OH 44022
Ph: (440)893-9661
E-mail: ephman@aol.com
URL: http://personal.bgsu.edu/~rmmckay/GLCAIndex.html
Contact: Lynn Shaw, Sec.
Regional. Affiliated With: United States Curling Association.

13636 ■ Healthcare Executives Association of Northeast Ohio
18961 River's Edge Dr.
Chagrin Falls, OH 44023
Ph: (440)543-4011 (216)631-1852
Fax: (440)543-1699
E-mail: awoodw3369@aol.com
URL: http://www.heano.org
Contact: Anita B. Woodward CHE, Pres.
Local. Works to improve the health status of society by advancing healthcare leadership and management excellence. Conducts research, career development and public policy programs. **Affiliated With:** American College of Healthcare Executives.

13637 ■ Ohio State Association of Plumbing, Heating and Cooling Contractors
c/o Sandy Pogan, CAE, Exec.Mgr.
18961 Rivers Edge Dr.
Chagrin Falls, OH 44023-4965
Ph: (440)543-4011
Fax: (440)543-1699
Free: (800)686-7422
E-mail: ohiophcc@aol.com
URL: http://www.phccohio.org
Contact: Sandy Pogan CAE, Exec.Mgr.
Founded: 1890. **Members:** 275. **Membership Dues:** associate (supplier, wholesaler, manufacturer's representative), $150 (annual). **Local Groups:** 5. **State. Libraries: Type:** lending. **Holdings:** 150; audio recordings, video recordings. **Subjects:** technical information for the plumbing, heating and cooling contractor, safety and health, business management. **Awards:** Contractor of the Year. **Frequency:** annual. **Type:** recognition. **Recipient:** for serving the industry • Manufacturer's Representative of the Year. **Frequency:** annual. **Type:** recognition. **Recipient:** for serving the industry • Service Contractor of the Year. **Frequency:** annual. **Type:** recognition. **Recipient:** for serving the industry • Wholesaler/Supplier of the Year. **Frequency:** annual. **Type:** recognition. **Recipient:** for serving the industry. **Computer Services:** database. **Affiliated With:** National Fluid Power Association. **Publications:** *Ohio PHC Contractor*, quarterly. Magazine. Contains Ohio news for Ohio contractors. **Circulation:** 8,000. **Advertising:** accepted. Alternate Formats: online. **Conventions/Meetings:** annual convention, installation of officers (exhibits) • annual show (exhibits).

13638 ■ Pembroke Welsh Corgi Club of the Western Reserve (PWCCWR)
c/o Heather Lampman, Corresponding Sec.
18895 Thorpe Rd.
Chagrin Falls, OH 44023-2323
Ph: (440)708-0768
E-mail: hflampman@alltel.net
URL: http://www.pwccwr.org
Contact: Heather Lampman, Corresponding Sec.
Local. Affiliated With: Pembroke Welsh Corgi Club of America.

13639 ■ Warrensville Heights Reserve Police Color Guard
c/o William Zadeskey
8747 Apple Hill Rd.
Chagrin Falls, OH 44023-5819
Local.

Chardon

13640 ■ American Legion, Chardon Post 167
PO Box 123
Chardon, OH 44024
Ph: (740)362-7478
Fax: (740)362-1429
URL: National Affiliate–www.legion.org
Local. Affiliated With: American Legion.

13641 ■ American Legion, Mayfield Heights Post 163
14231 Chardon Windsor Rd.
Chardon, OH 44024
Ph: (740)362-7478
Fax: (740)362-1429
URL: National Affiliate–www.legion.org
Local. Affiliated With: American Legion.

13642 ■ Chardon Area Chamber of Commerce (CACC)
111 South St.
Chardon, OH 44024
Ph: (440)285-9050
Fax: (440)286-8964
E-mail: emabel@chardonchamber.com
URL: http://www.chardonchamber.com
Contact: Erna M. Leagan-Mabel, Exec.Sec.
Founded: 1927. **Members:** 162. **Membership Dues:** business (based on number of employees), $75-$400 (annual) • utility, $300 (annual). **Staff:** 1. **Budget:** $37,000. **Local.** Promotes business and community development in the Chardon, OH area. **Awards:** Business Person of the Year. **Frequency:** annual. **Type:** recognition. **Computer Services:** Mailing lists, of members. **Committees:** Community Programs; Fund Raising; General Operations; Marketing/Public Relations; Programming. **Publications:** *Chamber Chat*, 3/year. Newsletter. Alternate Formats: online. **Conventions/Meetings:** annual Community Business Seminar • monthly meeting, for members - every 1st Tuesday • annual Trade Fair - trade show (exhibits).

13643 ■ Compassionate Friends - Cuyahoga/Geauga Counties Chapter
c/o Marianne Lohrman
10 Wynewood Pl.
Chardon, OH 44024
Ph: (440)285-7658
E-mail: legacymom@excite.com
URL: http://www.tcfcleveland.org
Contact: Marianne Lohrman, Chapter Contact
Local.

13644 ■ Ohio Council of Teachers of Mathematics
c/o Mary Theresa Sharp, Membership Sec.
Notre Dame Educational Ctr.
13000 Auburn Rd.
Chardon, OH 44024-9330
Ph: (440)286-7101
E-mail: tsharp@ndec.org
URL: http://www.ohioctm.org
Contact: Mary Theresa Sharp, Membership Sec.
State. Aims to improve the teaching and learning of mathematics. Provides vision, leadership and professional development to support teachers in ensuring mathematics learning of the highest quality for all students. **Affiliated With:** National Council of Teachers of Mathematics.

13645 ■ United Way Services of Geauga County
209 Ctr. St.
Chardon, OH 44024-1189
Ph: (440)285-2261
Fax: (440)286-3442
Free: (888)386-3194
E-mail: info@uwsgc.org
URL: http://www.guws.org
Contact: Kimm Leininger LISW, Exec.Dir.
Local. Affiliated With: United Way of America.

Cherry Fork

13646 ■ American Legion, Morris-Baldridge Post 583
14467 State Rte. 136
Cherry Fork, OH 45618
Ph: (740)362-7478
Fax: (740)362-1429
URL: National Affiliate–www.legion.org
Local. Affiliated With: American Legion.

Chesapeake

13647 ■ American Legion, Chesapeake Memorial Post 640
10963 County Rd. 1
Chesapeake, OH 45619
Ph: (740)362-7478
Fax: (740)362-1429
URL: National Affiliate–www.legion.org
Local. Affiliated With: American Legion.

Chesterhill

13648 ■ Chesterhill Lions Club
8070 State Rte. 377 SW
Chesterhill, OH 43728
Ph: (740)554-6071
E-mail: bkskinner62@earthlink.net
URL: http://chesterhilloh.lionwap.org
Contact: Keith Skinner, Membership Chm.
Local. Affiliated With: Lions Clubs International.

Chesterland

13649 ■ American Society of Sanitary Engineering, Northern Ohio Chapter
c/o William Armstrong, Pres.
Reliance Mech. Corp.
763 Maple Grove Dr.
Chesterland, OH 44026
E-mail: barmstrong@hrp.every1.net
URL: National Affiliate–www.asse-plumbing.org
Contact: William Armstrong, Pres.
Local. Represents plumbing officials, sanitary engineers, plumbers, plumbing contractors, building officials, architects, engineers, designing engineers, physicians, and others interested in health. Conducts research on plumbing and sanitation and develops performance standards for components of the plumbing system. Sponsors disease research programs and other studies of water-borne epidemics. **Affiliated With:** American Society of Sanitary Engineering.

13650 ■ Chesterland Chamber of Commerce (CCC)
8228 Mayfield Rd., Ste.4B
Chesterland, OH 44026
Ph: (440)729-7297
Fax: (440)729-2690
E-mail: info@chesterlandchamber.com
URL: http://www.chesterlandchamber.com
Contact: Michelle Krysinski, Office Mgr.
Founded: 1962. **Members:** 207. **Membership Dues:** business (located in Geauga county, Kirtland and Gates Mills), $50 (annual) • individual (resident of Geauga county, Kirtland or Gates Mills), $25 (annual) • business (outside Geauga county, Kirtland and Gates Mills), $150 (annual). **Staff:** 2. **Local.** Promotes business and community development in Chester Township, Ohio and surrounding areas, including Geauga County and adjacent Cuyahoga and Lake counties. Publishes annual Chester telephone directory. **Awards:** Business Person of the Year Award. **Frequency:** annual. **Type:** recognition. **Recipient:** for outstanding contribution to the business and civic communities • **Frequency:** annual. **Type:** scholarship. **Recipient:** for qualified students who reside within the West Geauga Local School District. **Computer Services:** Online services, membership

directory. **Publications:** *The Communicator*, monthly. Newsletter. **Circulation:** 207. Alternate Formats: online • *Telephone Directory*, annual • Membership Directory, annual. **Conventions/Meetings:** annual Community Appreciation Dinner, open to the public and members • monthly meeting, for trustees - every 1st Thursday.

13651 ■ Huntington's Disease Society of America, Northeast Ohio Chapter
c/o Donald L. Barr, Chapter Pres.
7059 Old Mill Rd.
Chesterland, OH 44026
Ph: (440)423-4372
Fax: (440)423-0515
E-mail: dbarrhome@aol.com
URL: http://www.lkwdpl.org/hdsa
Contact: Donald L. Barr, Chapter Pres.
Founded: 1977. **Membership Dues:** individual, $15 (annual) • family, $25 (annual). **Local.** Volunteers concerned with Huntington's disease, an inherited and terminal neurological condition, which causes progressive brain and nerve deterioration. Seeks to identify HD families; to educate the public and professionals, with emphasis on increasing consumer awareness of HD; to promote and support basic and clinical research into the causes and cure of HD; to assist families in meeting the social, economic, and emotional problems resulting from HD. Works to change the attitude of the working community toward the HD patient, to enhance the HD patient's lifestyle, and to promote better health care and treatment, both in the community and in facilities. **Committees:** Medical Advisory. **Affiliated With:** Huntington's Disease Society of America. **Publications:** Newsletter, periodic, 4-5/year. **Conventions/Meetings:** semiannual meeting - May, September/October • monthly support group meeting.

13652 ■ The Littlest Heroes (TLH)
8228 Mayfield Rd., Ste.3B
Chesterland, OH 44026
Ph: (440)729-5200
Fax: (440)729-4014
E-mail: info@thelittlestheroes.org
URL: http://www.thelittlestheroes.org
Contact: Blazine Monaco, Exec.Dir.
Founded: 1999. **Staff:** 4. **Budget:** $450,000. **Local Groups:** 1. **Local.** Promotes spiritual, emotional and physical healing of children with cancer and their families by developing and providing a total system of support that complements traditional health care.

13653 ■ Ohio Motorists Association
12628 Chillicothe Rd.
Chesterland, OH 44026
Ph: (440)729-1938
Local.

Cheviot

13654 ■ American Legion, Schwab-Bailey Post 425
PO Box 11251
Cheviot, OH 45211
Ph: (740)362-7478
Fax: (740)362-1429
URL: National Affiliate–www.legion.org
Local. Affiliated With: American Legion.

Chillicothe

13655 ■ 1st Capital Federation of Families for Children's Mental Health
394 Chestnut St.
Chillicothe, OH 45601
Ph: (740)775-2674
Fax: (740)775-7834
E-mail: rmh1@adelphia.net
URL: National Affiliate–www.ffcmh.org
Contact: Rosemary Hill, Contact
Local. Affiliated With: Federation of Families for Children's Mental Health.

13656 ■ American Cancer Society, Ross Area
138 Marietta Rd., Ste.D
Chillicothe, OH 45601
Ph: (740)702-1160
Fax: (740)702-1163
Free: (888)227-6446
URL: http://www.cancer.org
Local. Affiliated With: American Cancer Society.

13657 ■ American Legion, Ohio Post 126
c/o Lorain Brown
976 Mutton Run Rd.
Chillicothe, OH 45601
Ph: (740)362-7478
Fax: (740)362-1429
URL: National Affiliate–www.legion.org
Contact: Lorain Brown, Contact
Local. Affiliated With: American Legion.

13658 ■ American Legion, Ohio Post 757
c/o Joseph W. Hoffman
289 Cooks Hill Rd.
Chillicothe, OH 45601
Ph: (740)362-7478
Fax: (740)362-1429
URL: National Affiliate–www.legion.org
Contact: Joseph W. Hoffman, Contact
Local. Affiliated With: American Legion.

13659 ■ American Legion, Ross County Post 62
53 W Main St.
Chillicothe, OH 45601
Ph: (740)362-7478
Fax: (740)362-1429
URL: National Affiliate–www.legion.org
Local. Affiliated With: American Legion.

13660 ■ American Red Cross, First Capital District Chapter
115 W Main St.
Chillicothe, OH 45601
Ph: (740)772-2014
Fax: (740)772-2000
URL: http://www.rossredcross.org
Local.

13661 ■ American Society for Quality, Scioto Valley Section 0815
PO Box 1947
Chillicothe, OH 45601-5947
E-mail: lc@asqsvs.org
URL: http://www.asqsvs.org
Contact: Oscar I. Phillips, Sec.
Local. Advances learning, quality improvement and knowledge exchange to improve business results and to create better workplaces and communities worldwide. Provides a forum for information exchange, professional development and continuous learning in the science of quality. **Affiliated With:** American Society for Quality.

13662 ■ Building Industry Association of South Central Ohio
c/o Judy Tomlinson
PO Box 346
Chillicothe, OH 45601-0346
Ph: (740)772-4113
Fax: (740)772-4113
E-mail: homebuilders@bright.net
URL: National Affiliate–www.nahb.org
Contact: Judy Tomlinson, Sec.
Local. Single and multifamily home builders, commercial builders, and others associated with the building industry. **Affiliated With:** National Association of Home Builders.

13663 ■ Chief Logan Reservation Staff Alumni Association (CLRAA)
c/o Dave McGhee, Pres.
PO Box 902
Chillicothe, OH 45601-0902
E-mail: davemcghee@clralumni.org
URL: http://www.clralumni.org
Local.

13664 ■ Chillicothe Ross Chamber of Commerce (CRCC)
45 E Main St.
Chillicothe, OH 45601
Ph: (740)702-2722
Fax: (740)702-2727
E-mail: ccinfo@chillicotheohio.com
URL: http://www.chillicotheohio.com
Contact: Marvin E. Jones, Exec.Dir.
Founded: 1912. **Members:** 600. **Membership Dues:** business (plus $4.2 for each employee above 8), $168-$273 (annual) • real estate business (plus $68 for each additional realtor), $168 (annual) • friend of the chamber (cannot own or operate a business), $68 (annual). **Local.** Promotes business and community development in Ross County, OH. **Awards:** Entrepreneur of the Year. **Frequency:** annual. **Type:** recognition. **Recipient:** for a business person who embodies the spirit and attributes of an entrepreneur • Volunteer of the Year. **Frequency:** annual. **Type:** recognition. **Computer Services:** Online services, membership directory. **Committees:** Golf; Governmental Affairs; Marketing and Membership; Networking. **Councils:** Ross County Safety. **Programs:** Pathfinders Leadership. **Affiliated With:** U.S. Chamber of Commerce. **Publications:** *Membership Directory and Buyer's Guide*, annual. **Circulation:** 600. **Advertising:** accepted • Newsletter, weekly. Contains the latest news on happenings within the chamber and the local business community. **Circulation:** 600. **Advertising:** accepted. Alternate Formats: online.

13665 ■ Easter Seals Central and Southeast Ohio
810 E Main St.
PO Box 354
Chillicothe, OH 45601
Ph: (740)773-1273
Fax: (740)773-0936
E-mail: pdupras@easterseals-cseohio.org
URL: http://centralohio.easterseals.com
Contact: Ms. Pandora Dupras, Program Mgr.
Local. Provides services for children and adults with disabilities or special needs, and supports their families. **Affiliated With:** Easter Seals.

13666 ■ Love Inc. of Ross County
c/o Valerie Searles
PO Box 6090
Chillicothe, OH 45601-6090
Ph: (740)773-0239 (740)773-0525
Fax: (740)773-0525
E-mail: val@horizonview.net
URL: http://www.loveinc.org
Contact: Jon James, Dir.
Founded: 2001. **Members:** 61. **Staff:** 1. **Regional Groups:** 62. **State Groups:** 8. **Local Groups:** 1. **Local.**

13667 ■ Masonic Lodge
57 E Main St.
Chillicothe, OH 45601
Ph: (740)774-3485
Fax: (740)774-1053
E-mail: sciotolodge6@horizonview.net
URL: http://www.chillicothemasons.org
Contact: Harley Thomas, Building Mgr.
Local.

13668 ■ National Active and Retired Federal Employees Association - Chillicothe 315
542 Mckellar St.
Chillicothe, OH 45601-3628
Ph: (740)772-4471
URL: National Affiliate–www.narfe.org
Contact: Joyce C. Peters, Contact
Local. Protects the retirement future of employees through education. Informs members on issues affecting the retirement. **Affiliated With:** National Association of Retired Federal Employees.

13669 ■ National Technical Honor Society - Pickaway-Ross Career and Technology Center - Ohio
895 Crouse Chapel Rd.
Chillicothe, OH 45601
Ph: (740)642-1200
Fax: (740)642-1399
E-mail: shara.cochenour@pickawayross.com
URL: http://www.pickawayross.com
Contact: Shara Cochenour, Contact
Local.

13670 ■ Ohio Health Care Association, District 9
c/o Christina Schramm, Chair
Chillicothe Nursing & Rehabilitation
60 Marietta Rd.
Chillicothe, OH 45601
Ph: (740)772-5900
E-mail: christina_schramm@kindredhealthcare.com
URL: http://www.ohca.org
Contact: Christina Schramm, Chair
Local. Promotes professionalism and ethical behavior of individuals providing long-term care delivery for patients and for the general public. Provides information, education and administrative tools to enhance the quality of long-term care. Improves the standards of service and administration of member nursing homes. **Affiliated With:** American Health Care Association.

13671 ■ Phi Theta Kappa - Alpha Psi Phi Chapter
c/o Dennis Bothel
Chillicothe Campus
571 W 5th St.
Chillicothe, OH 45601
Ph: (740)774-7229
E-mail: bothel@ohio.edu
URL: http://www.ptk.org/directories/chapters/OH/20598-1.htm
Contact: Dennis Bothel, Advisor
Local. Affiliated With: Phi Theta Kappa, International Honor Society.

13672 ■ Ross Co. Radio Pat. Svr REACT
746 England Hollow Rd.
Chillicothe, OH 45601
Ph: (740)775-5480
URL: http://www.reactintl.org/teaminfo/usa_teams/teams-usoh.htm
Local. Trained communication experts and professional volunteers. Provides volunteer public service and emergency communications through the use of radios (Citizen Band, General Mobile Radio Service, UHF and HAM). Coordinates with radio industries and government on safety communication matters and supports charitable activities and community organizations.

13673 ■ Ross County Genealogical Society
444 Douglas Ave.
PO Box 6352
Chillicothe, OH 45601-6352
Ph: (740)773-2715
E-mail: rcgs@bright.net
URL: http://www.rosscountyhistorical.org
Contact: Caroline Whitten, Pres.
Founded: 1973. **Members:** 500. **Membership Dues:** individual, $13 (annual). **Local**. Works to collect, preserve, and make available genealogical and historical records. Promotes historical education. **Libraries: Type:** reference. **Holdings:** books, periodicals. **Subjects:** Ross County, OH history. **Subgroups:** First Pioneers of Ross County. **Formerly:** (1999) Ohio Genealogical Society, Ross County Chapter. **Publications:** *Ross County Genealogical Society Newsletter*, quarterly. **Price:** included in membership dues. ISSN: 1057-185 • Books. **Conventions/Meetings:** monthly meeting • monthly meeting - always second Tuesday of each month. Chillicothe, OH • periodic workshop.

13674 ■ Scioto Society
PO Box 73
Chillicothe, OH 45601
Ph: (740)775-4100
Fax: (740)775-4349
Free: (866)775-0700
E-mail: tecumseh@bright.net
URL: http://www.tecumsehdrama.com
Contact: Marion N. Waggoner, Pres.
Founded: 1970. **Staff:** 5. **Budget:** $1,200,000. **Nonmembership. Local.** Works to promote the public image of Ross, Pike, and Pickaway Counties, OH, commonly referred to as the Scioto Valley. Sponsors outdoor drama "Tecumseh!". **Publications:** *Tecumseh Brochure*, annual.

13675 ■ South Central Ohio AIFA
c/o Robert L. Shoultz, Sec.
PO Box 6165
Chillicothe, OH 45601
Ph: (740)775-2886
Fax: (740)773-5302
E-mail: chuckhalm@horizonview.net
URL: National Affiliate–naifa.org
Contact: Robert L. Shoultz, Sec.
Local. Represents the interests of insurance and financial advisors. Advocates for a positive legislative and regulatory environment. Enhances business and professional skills of members. **Affiliated With:** National Association of Insurance and Financial Advisors.

13676 ■ Southcentral Ohio Academy of Family Physicians
c/o Kimber Alderson Jones D.O.
4439 St., Rt. 159, Ste.150
Chillicothe, OH 45601
Ph: (740)774-2263
Fax: (740)779-4524
Contact: Kimber A. Jones D.O., Contact
Members: 33. **Membership Dues:** $5 (annual). **Local**.

13677 ■ United Way of Ross County
53 E 2nd St.
Chillicothe, OH 45601-2543
Ph: (740)773-3280
Fax: (740)773-3281
E-mail: uwayross@bright.net
URL: National Affiliate–national.unitedway.org
Contact: Nancy O. Elliott, Exec.Dir.
Founded: 1935. **Staff:** 2. **Local. Affiliated With:** United Way of America.

13678 ■ Vietnam Veterans of America, Chapter No. 281
c/o Rudolph Walker
PO Box 5500
Chillicothe, OH 45601
Ph: (740)773-2616
URL: http://www.vvabuckeyestatecouncil.com
Contact: Rudolph Walker, Contact
Local. Affiliated With: Vietnam Veterans of America.

13679 ■ Vietnam Veterans of America, Chapter No. 645
c/o Richard Wozniak, Pres.
16149 SR 104 N
Chillicothe, OH 45601-7010
Ph: (740)774-7050
URL: http://www.vvabuckeyestatecouncil.com
Contact: Richard Wozniak, Pres.
Local. Affiliated With: Vietnam Veterans of America.

13680 ■ Vietnam Veterans of America, Ross County - Chapter No. 810
c/o John Daubert, Pres.
81 Amherst Dr.
Chillicothe, OH 45601
Ph: (740)779-0180
URL: http://www.vvabuckeyestatecouncil.com
Contact: John Daubert, Pres.
Local. Affiliated With: Vietnam Veterans of America.

Cincinnati

13681 ■ AAA Cincinnati
4750 Fields Ertel Rd.
Cincinnati, OH 45249
Ph: (513)683-5200
URL: http://www.aaa.com
Contact: Eleanor Boehle, Supervisor
Local.

13682 ■ AAA Cincinnati
2712 Erie Ave.
Cincinnati, OH 45208
Ph: (513)321-1222
E-mail: skeebaugh@aaaalliedgroup.com
URL: http://www.aaa.com
Contact: Shelly Keebaugh, Supervisor
Local.

13683 ■ AAA Cincinnati
8124 Beechmont Ave.
Cincinnati, OH 45255
Ph: (513)388-4222
Contact: Gevana Hicks, Supervisor
Local.

13684 ■ AAA Cincinnati
9718 Colerain Ave.
Cincinnati, OH 45251
Ph: (513)385-0909
URL: http://www.aaa.com
Contact: Debbie Doll, Supervisor
Local.

13685 ■ AAA Cincinnati
11711 Princeton Pike
Cincinnati, OH 45246
Ph: (513)671-1886
URL: http://www.aaa.com
Contact: Greg Couch, Supervisor
Local.

13686 ■ AAA Cincinnati
6558 Glenway Ave.
Cincinnati, OH 45211
Ph: (513)598-2500
Contact: Vicki Thorner, Supervisor
Local.

13687 ■ AAA Cincinnati
8176 Montgomery Rd.
Cincinnati, OH 45236
Ph: (513)984-3553
Local.

13688 ■ Accounting for Kids
c/o Crystal Faulkner
105 E 4th St., Ste.1600
Cincinnati, OH 45202
Ph: (513)768-6798
E-mail: cfaulkner@cfscpa.com
URL: http://www.accountingforkids.org
Contact: Crystal Faulkner, Contact
Local.

13689 ■ Acoustical Society of America - Cincinnati Chapter
c/o Jon W. Mooney, Pres.
586 Neeb Rd.
Cincinnati, OH 45233
E-mail: acoustics@jwmooney.com
URL: http://www.jwmooney.com/asa.htm
Contact: Jon W. Mooney, Pres.
Local. Represents the interests of individuals working in the field of acoustics. Aims to increase and diffuse the knowledge of acoustics and to promote its practical applications. **Affiliated With:** Acoustical Society of America.

13690 ■ Adams County Beagle Club
c/o Frank G. Stowell
4344 Cider Mill Dr.
Cincinnati, OH 45245-1402

Ph: (513)688-7887
E-mail: fgstow1@aol.com
URL: National Affiliate–www.akc.org
Contact: Frank G. Stowell, Contact

Founded: 1950. **Members:** 10. **Membership Dues:** general, $50 (annual). **Staff:** 5. **Budget:** $8,000. **Regional Groups:** 2. **Local**. Dedicated to the improvement and betterment of the breed; maintains land by farming and tilling, raises wild rabbits for club only; holds work parties, field trials and monthly meetings. **Awards:** Dog of the Year. **Frequency:** annual. **Type:** recognition. **Affiliated With:** American Kennel Club.

13691 ■ Advertising Club of Cincinnati
c/o Judy Thompson, Exec.Dir.
602 Main St., Ste.806
Cincinnati, OH 45202
Ph: (513)984-9990
Fax: (513)621-0213
E-mail: jthompson@adclubcincy.org
URL: http://www.adclubcincy.org
Contact: Judy Thompson, Exec.Dir.

Founded: 1904. **Members:** 240. **Membership Dues:** individual, $125 (annual). **Staff:** 1. **Local**. Strives to provide and promote a better understanding of the functions of advertising and of its values, to apply the skills, creativity and energy of the advertising industry, to advance the standards of advertising, to support voluntary self-regulation and to promote good fellowship and a free exchange of ideas. **Publications:** *Adrenaline*, monthly. Newsletter • *Advance*, 3/year. Magazine. **Conventions/Meetings:** monthly board meeting • monthly luncheon - September through May.

13692 ■ AHEPA 127
c/o George Karampas
7791 Twelve Oaks Ct.
Cincinnati, OH 45255-4318
Ph: (513)575-1820 (513)575-1823
Contact: Tammie Gilreath, Contact

Founded: 2002. **Staff:** 2. **Local**.

13693 ■ Aikido of Cincinnati (AoC)
4727 Red Bank Rd.
Cincinnati, OH 45227
Ph: (513)561-7202
E-mail: dojocho@aikidocincy.com
URL: http://www.aikidocincy.com
Contact: Charlie McGinnis, Instructor

Local. **Affiliated With:** United States Aikido Federation.

13694 ■ Air Conditioning Contractors of America, Greater Cincinnati Chapter
c/o Joyce Frank, Exec.Sec.
11020 Southland Rd.
Cincinnati, OH 45240
Ph: (513)651-1161
Fax: (513)742-8477
E-mail: jfrank@accagc.org
URL: National Affiliate–www.acca.org
Contact: Joyce Frank, Exec.Sec.

Local. Works to represent contractors involved in installation and service of heating, air conditioning, and refrigeration systems. **Affiliated With:** Air Conditioning Contractors of America.

13695 ■ Alcoholics Anonymous, Cincinnati Intergroup Office
3040 Madison Rd., Rm. 202
Cincinnati, OH 45209
Ph: (513)351-0422
E-mail: cso@aacincinnati.org
URL: http://www.aacincinnati.org

Local. Individuals recovering from alcoholism. Works to maintain that members can solve their common problem and to help others achieve sobriety through a twelve-step program that includes sharing their experience, strength, and hope with each other. **Affiliated With:** Alcoholics Anonymous World Services.

13696 ■ Alcoholism Council of the Cincinnati Area, National Council on Alcoholism and Drug Dependence
2828 Vernon Pl.
Cincinnati, OH 45219
Ph: (513)281-7880
E-mail: cincinnati.oh@ncadd.org
URL: National Affiliate–www.ncadd.org

Local. **Affiliated With:** National Council on Alcoholism and Drug Dependence.

13697 ■ Alliance of Guardian Angels, Cincinnati
4102 Glenway Ave.
Cincinnati, OH 45205
Ph: (513)921-2039
E-mail: cincinnati@guardianangels.org
URL: National Affiliate–www.guardianangels.org
Contact: Michael A. Schneider, Contact

Local. **Affiliated With:** Alliance of Guardian Angels.

13698 ■ Alzheimer's Association - Greater Cincinnati Chapter
644 Linn St., Ste.1026
Cincinnati, OH 45203-1742
Ph: (513)721-4284
Fax: (513)345-8446
Free: (800)272-3900
E-mail: sue.wilke@alz.org
URL: http://www.alz.org/grtrcinc
Contact: Sue Wilke, Exec.Dir.

Local. Family members of sufferers of Alzheimer's disease. Combats Alzheimer's disease and related disorders. (Alzheimer's disease is a progressive, degenerative brain disease in which changes occur in the central nervous system and outer region of the brain causing memory loss and other changes in thought, personality, and behavior.) Promotes research to find the cause, treatment, and cure for the disease. **Affiliated With:** Alzheimer's Association.

13699 ■ American Arbitration Association, Ohio
c/o James Noll, VP
250 E 5th St., Ste.420
Cincinnati, OH 45202
Ph: (513)241-8434
Fax: (513)241-8437
Free: (888)241-8434
E-mail: nollj@adr.org
URL: http://www.adr.org
Contact: James Noll, VP

State. Works to provide exceptional neutrals, proficient case management, dedicated personnel, advanced education and training, and innovative process knowledge to meet the conflict management and dispute resolution needs of the public now and in the future. **Affiliated With:** American Arbitration Association.

13700 ■ American Association of Blacks in Energy, Cincinnati
c/o Charles L. Sessions, Jr., Mgr.
Cinergy Corp.
426 Gest St., Rm. No. 304
Cincinnati, OH 45203
Ph: (513)287-5748
E-mail: csession@cinergy.com
URL: http://aabe.org
Contact: Charles L. Sessions Jr., Mgr.

Local. Represents the interests of African Americans and other minorities in the discussions and developments of energy policies and related fields. **Affiliated With:** American Association of Blacks in Energy.

13701 ■ American Association for Clinical Chemistry, Ohio Valley Section
c/o Michael W. Fowler, PhD, Chm.
Medpace Labs.
4620 Wesley Ave.
Cincinnati, OH 45212
Ph: (513)366-3270
Fax: (513)366-3273
URL: National Affiliate–www.aacc.org
Contact: Michael W. Fowler PhD, Chm.

Local. Represents the interests of clinical laboratory professionals, physicians, research scientists and other individuals involved with clinical chemistry and other clinical laboratory science-related disciplines. Seeks to improve the practice of clinical chemistry. Establishes standards for education and training in the field. **Affiliated With:** American Association for Clinical Chemistry.

13702 ■ American Association of Critical Care Nurses, Greater Cincinnati Chapter
c/o Pamela Bolton, Pres.
PO Box 19122
Cincinnati, OH 45219-0122
Ph: (513)723-5043
E-mail: gcc.info@aacn.org
URL: http://www.aacn.org
Contact: Pamela Bolton, Pres.

Members: 160. **Local**. Professional critical care nurses united to provide continuing education for nurses specializing in critical care and develop standards of nursing care of critically ill patients. Holds annual cardiac rehabilitation conference and trends in critical care symposium. **Affiliated With:** American Association of Critical-Care Nurses. **Conventions/Meetings:** annual symposium (exhibits) - April.

13703 ■ American Association for Laboratory Animal Science - Southern Ohio (SOB AALAS)
c/o Amy Gardner, Treas.
PO Box 19633
Cincinnati, OH 45219
E-mail: agardne9@eesus.jnj.com
URL: http://sob.d5aalas.org
Contact: Amy Gardner, Treas.

Local. Serves as a clearinghouse for the collection and exchange of information and expertise in the care and use of laboratory animals. Promotes and encourages the highest level of ethics within the profession of laboratory animal science. Provides educational and training programs for members and others who are professionally engaged in the production, care, use and study of laboratory animals. **Affiliated With:** American Association for Laboratory Animal Science.

13704 ■ American Association of Physics Teachers, Southern Ohio Section
c/o Bill Kuhlman, Pres.-Elect
St. Xavier High School
600 W North Bend Rd.
Cincinnati, OH 45224-1499
Ph: (513)761-7600
Fax: (513)761-3811
URL: http://www-physics.mps.ohio-state.edu/~aubrecht/sosaapt.html
Contact: Bill Kuhlman, Pres.-Elect

Local. Seeks to enhance the understanding and appreciation of physics through teaching. Aims to improve the pedagogical skills and physics knowledge of teachers at all levels. **Affiliated With:** American Association of Physics Teachers.

13705 ■ American Board of Trial Advocates - Cincinnati
2500 Cincinnati Commerce Ctr.
Cincinnati, OH 45202
Ph: (513)852-6000
Fax: (513)852-6087
E-mail: hgkorbee@woodlamping.com
Contact: Harold G. Korbee, Pres.

State. Improves the ethical and technical standards of practice in the field of advocacy. Elevates the standards of integrity, honor and courtesy in the legal profession. Promotes the efficient administration of justice and improvement of the law. **Affiliated With:** American Board of Trial Advocates.

13706 ■ American Cancer Society, Hamilton County
2808 Reading Rd.
Cincinnati, OH 45206
Ph: (513)891-1600
Fax: (513)891-5583
Free: (888)227-6446
E-mail: peter.osborne@cancer.org
URL: http://www.cancer.org
Contact: Peter Osborne, Contact
Local. Works to eliminate cancer as a major health problem through research, education, advocacy and service. **Affiliated With:** American Cancer Society.

13707 ■ American Chemical Society, Cincinnati Section
c/o Dr. Emel T. Yakali, Chm.
Raymond Walters Coll.
9555 Plainfield Rd.
Cincinnati, OH 45236-1007
Ph: (513)745-5686
E-mail: emel.yakali@uc.edu
URL: National Affiliate–acswebcontent.acs.org
Contact: Dr. Emel T. Yakali, Chm.
Local. Represents the interests of individuals dedicated to the advancement of chemistry in all its branches. Provides opportunities for peer interaction and career development. **Affiliated With:** American Chemical Society.

13708 ■ American Heart Association, Cincinnati
2936 Vernon Pl.
Cincinnati, OH 45219
Ph: (513)281-4048
Fax: (513)281-1433
E-mail: ray.meyer@heart.org
URL: http://americanheart.org
Contact: Ray Meyer, Contact
Budget: $1,400,000. **Local**. Attempts to reduce heart disease and stroke through education, public advocacy and by the funding of cardiovascular and stroke research. **Affiliated With:** American Heart Association. **Publications:** *Circulation*, monthly. Newsletter • Newsletters, periodic • Journals, periodic.

13709 ■ American Industrial Hygiene Association, Ohio Valley Section
c/o Joshua Harney, MS, Sec.
Cincinnati Children's Hosp. Medical Ctr.
3333 Burnet Ave., MCL 9007
Cincinnati, OH 45229
Ph: (513)636-7286
Fax: (513)636-2123
E-mail: josh.harney@cchmc.org
URL: http://www.aiha.org/localsections/html/ohiovalley/ohiovalley.htm
Contact: Joshua Harney MS, Sec.
Local. Promotes the study and control of environmental factors affecting the health and well being of workers. Sponsors continuing education courses in industrial hygiene, government affairs, and public relations. Conducts educational and research programs. **Affiliated With:** American Industrial Hygiene Association.

13710 ■ American Institute of Architects Cincinnati
c/o Longworth Hall Design Center
700 W Pete Rose Way
Cincinnati, OH 45203
Ph: (513)421-4661
Fax: (513)421-4665
E-mail: aiacinti@fuse.net
URL: http://www.aiacincinnati.org
Contact: Pat Daugherty, Exec.Dir.
Founded: 1870. **Members:** 350. **Membership Dues:** architect, $466 (annual) • associate, $225 (annual) • life, $500 • receive mail, $45 (annual). **Local Groups:** 9. **Local**. Strives to promote and forward the profession of architecture and the objectives of the American Institute of Architects in southwestern Ohio. **Awards:** Bettman Prize. **Frequency:** annual. **Type:** monetary. **Recipient:** for proposals of exemplary merit that seek to enrich the physical setting for urban life in greater Cincinnati through creativity and vision • Cincinnati Design Awards (CDA). **Frequency:** annual. **Type:** recognition. **Committees:** Architecture by Children; Beaux Arts Ball; Cincinnati Design Awards; Committee on the Environment; Golf; IDP/ARE; Urban Design; Young Architects and Interns Forum. **Affiliated With:** American Institute of Architects. **Publications:** *e-Architext*, monthly. Newsletter. Alternate Formats: online • Articles, periodic. Alternate Formats: online. **Conventions/Meetings:** monthly board meeting - every 2nd Tuesday.

13711 ■ American Institute of Chemical Engineers - Ohio Valley Section
PO Box 429139
Cincinnati, OH 45242
E-mail: imelnyk@keramida.com
URL: http://www.aicheovs.org
Contact: Ihor Melnyk, Chm.
Local. Represents the interests of chemical engineering professionals. Aims to contribute to the improvement of chemical engineering curricula offered in universities. Seeks to enhance the lifelong career development and financial security of chemical engineers through products, services, networking and advocacy. **Affiliated With:** American Institute of Chemical Engineers.

13712 ■ American Legion, Anderson Post 318
7551 Forest Rd.
Cincinnati, OH 45255
Ph: (740)362-7478
Fax: (740)362-1429
URL: National Affiliate–www.legion.org
Local. Affiliated With: American Legion.

13713 ■ American Legion, Bartley-Johnson-Bentley Post 437
5004 Willnet Dr.
Cincinnati, OH 45238
Ph: (740)362-7478
Fax: (740)362-1429
URL: National Affiliate–www.legion.org
Local. Affiliated With: American Legion.

13714 ■ American Legion, Bond-Hill-Roselawn Post 427
303 Glen Oaks Dr.
Cincinnati, OH 45238
Ph: (740)362-7478
Fax: (740)362-1429
URL: National Affiliate–www.legion.org
Local. Affiliated With: American Legion.

13715 ■ American Legion, Chambers-Hautman-Budde Post 534
4618 River Rd.
Cincinnati, OH 45204
Ph: (740)362-7478
Fax: (740)362-1429
URL: National Affiliate–www.legion.org
Local. Affiliated With: American Legion.

13716 ■ American Legion, Cincinnati Gas and Electric Post 410
481 Morrvue Dr.
Cincinnati, OH 45238
Ph: (740)362-7478
Fax: (740)362-1429
URL: National Affiliate–www.legion.org
Local. Affiliated With: American Legion.

13717 ■ American Legion, Fairfax Post 554
c/o Edward C. Gehlert
3809 Carlton St.
Cincinnati, OH 45227
Ph: (740)362-7478
Fax: (740)362-1429
URL: National Affiliate–www.legion.org
Contact: Edward C. Gehlert, Contact
Local. Affiliated With: American Legion.

13718 ■ American Legion, Guth Brothers Post 111
9854 Springfield Pike
Cincinnati, OH 45215
Ph: (740)362-7478
Fax: (740)362-1429
URL: National Affiliate–www.legion.org
Local. Affiliated With: American Legion.

13719 ■ American Legion, Hugh Watson Post 530
11100 Winton Rd.
Cincinnati, OH 45218
Ph: (740)362-7478
Fax: (740)362-1429
URL: National Affiliate–www.legion.org
Local. Affiliated With: American Legion.

13720 ■ American Legion, Hyde-Park-Mt-Lookout Post 744
224 Wilmer Ave.
Cincinnati, OH 45226
Ph: (740)362-7478
Fax: (740)362-1429
URL: National Affiliate–www.legion.org
Local. Affiliated With: American Legion.

13721 ■ American Legion, Mt. Washington Post 484
1837 Sutton Ave.
Cincinnati, OH 45230
Ph: (740)362-7478
Fax: (740)362-1429
URL: National Affiliate–www.legion.org
Local. Affiliated With: American Legion.

13722 ■ American Legion, Northeast Post 630
11330 Williamson Rd.
Cincinnati, OH 45241
Ph: (740)362-7478
Fax: (740)362-1429
URL: National Affiliate–www.legion.org
Local. Affiliated With: American Legion.

13723 ■ American Legion, Ohio Post 37
c/o Ralph L. Taylor
1646 W Galbraith Rd.
Cincinnati, OH 45239
Ph: (740)362-7478
Fax: (740)362-1429
URL: National Affiliate–www.legion.org
Contact: Ralph L. Taylor, Contact
Local. Affiliated With: American Legion.

13724 ■ American Legion, Ohio Post 72
c/o Stuart G. Luginbuhl
497 B Old State Rte. 74
Cincinnati, OH 45244
Ph: (740)362-7478
Fax: (740)362-1429
URL: National Affiliate–www.legion.org
Contact: Stuart G. Luginbuhl, Contact
Local. Affiliated With: American Legion.

13725 ■ American Legion, Ohio Post 631
c/o John R. Fox
PO Box 15719
Cincinnati, OH 45215
Ph: (740)362-7478
Fax: (740)362-1429
URL: National Affiliate–www.legion.org
Contact: John R. Fox, Contact
Local. Affiliated With: American Legion.

13726 ■ American Legion, Ohio Post 670
c/o Byron F. Hutchins, Jr., 1st Vice Commander
6280 Witherby Ave.
Cincinnati, OH 45224
Ph: (740)362-7478
Fax: (740)362-1429
URL: National Affiliate–www.legion.org
Contact: Byron F. Hutchins Jr., 1st Vice Commander
Local. Affiliated With: American Legion.

13727 ■ American Legion, Oola Khan Post 372
6919 Vine St.
Cincinnati, OH 45216
Ph: (740)362-7478
Fax: (740)362-1429
URL: National Affiliate–www.legion.org
Local. Affiliated With: American Legion.

13728 ■ American Legion, Wesley Werner Post 513
PO Box 31121
Cincinnati, OH 45231
Ph: (740)362-7478
Fax: (740)362-1429
URL: National Affiliate–www.legion.org
Local. Affiliated With: American Legion.

13729 ■ American Legion, Wittstein-Middleman Post 524
7521 Abbie Pl.
Cincinnati, OH 45237
Ph: (740)362-7478
Fax: (740)362-1429
URL: National Affiliate–www.legion.org
Local. Affiliated With: American Legion.

13730 ■ American Lung Association of Ohio, Southwest Branch
11113 Kenwood Rd.
Cincinnati, OH 45242
Ph: (513)985-3990
Fax: (513)985-3995
Free: (800)LUNG-USA
E-mail: jkaplan@ohiolung.org
URL: http://www.lungusa.org
Contact: Joel Kaplan, Exec.Dir.
Local. Works to fight lung disease in all its forms, with special emphasis on asthma, tobacco control, and environmental health. **Affiliated With:** American Lung Association.

13731 ■ American Parkinson Disease Association, Tri-State Parkinson's Wellness Chapter
c/o Richard Fagin, Pres.
151 W Galbrath Rd.
Cincinnati, OH 45216
Ph: (513)948-1100
Fax: (513)948-1120
Free: (800)840-2732
E-mail: info@parkinsonswellness.org
URL: http://www.parkinsonswellness.org
Contact: Richard Fagin, Pres.
Regional. Provides free Parkinson's Disease information and workshops to the community, holds fundraisers, and accepts donations. **Libraries: Type:** by appointment only; lending. **Holdings:** audio recordings, books, periodicals, video recordings. **Subjects:** Parkinson's Disease and related issues. **Affiliated With:** American Parkinson Disease Association.

13732 ■ American Red Cross, Cincinnati Area Chapter
720 Sycamore St.
Cincinnati, OH 45202-2115
Ph: (513)579-3000
URL: http://www.redcross.org/oh/cincy
Local.

13733 ■ American Society of Interior Designers, Ohio South/Kentucky
PO Box 498748
Cincinnati, OH 45249-8748
Free: (800)530-ASID
E-mail: asidohky@aol.com
URL: http://www.asidohky.org
Contact: Patricia Amburn ASID, Pres.
Regional. Represents practicing professional interior designers, students and industry partners. Strives to advance the interior design profession. Aims to demonstrate and celebrate the power of design to positively change people's lives. **Affiliated With:** American Society of Interior Designers.

13734 ■ American Society for Quality, Cincinnati Section 0900
c/o Steve Gemperline
5413 Bluesky Dr., Ste.11
Cincinnati, OH 45247
Ph: (513)741-2829
Free: (877)300-8364
E-mail: usasqcincinnati@onebox.com
URL: http://asqcincinnati.org
Contact: Steve Gemperline, Contact
Local. Advances learning, quality improvement and knowledge exchange to improve business results and to create better workplaces and communities worldwide. Provides a forum for information exchange, professional development and continuous learning in the science of quality. **Affiliated With:** American Society for Quality.

13735 ■ American Society for Training and Development, Greater Cincinnati Chapter (GCASTD)
11711 Princeton Pike, Ste.341, No. 132
Cincinnati, OH 45246
Ph: (513)575-0071
Fax: (317)841-8206
Free: (800)818-9564
E-mail: volunteers@gcastd.com
URL: http://www.gcastd.org
Contact: Tracy Sterling, Pres.
Membership Dues: professional, $50 (annual) • non-profit, $45 (annual) • student, retiree, $35 (annual). **Local.** Professional association for persons engaged in the training and development of business, industry, education, and government employees. **Telecommunication Services:** electronic mail, president@gcastd.com. **Affiliated With:** ASTD. **Publications:** *The HRD Edge*, quarterly. Newsletter. Alternate Formats: online.

13736 ■ American Statistical Association, Cincinnati Chapter
c/o Michael L. Schwiers, Pres.
Medpace Inc.
4620 Wesley Ave.
Cincinnati, OH 45212-2234
Ph: (513)579-9911
E-mail: m.schwiers@medpace.com
URL: National Affiliate–www.amstat.org
Contact: Michael L. Schwiers, Pres.
Local. Promotes statistical practice, applications and research. Works for the improvement of statistical education at all levels. Seeks opportunities to advance the statistics profession. **Affiliated With:** American Statistical Association.

13737 ■ American Subcontractors Association of Cincinnati (ASAC)
c/o Terry Phillips, Exec.Dir.
3 Kovach Dr.
Cincinnati, OH 45215
Ph: (513)475-5730
Fax: (513)678-2127
E-mail: tphillips@aci-construction.org
URL: http://www.asacincinnati.org
Contact: Ms. Terry Phillips, Exec.Dir.
Local. Affiliated With: American Subcontractors Association.

13738 ■ American Theatre Organ Society, Ohio Valley Chapter
c/o Joseph Hollmann, Pres.
1617 W Belmar Pl.
Cincinnati, OH 45224
Ph: (513)729-0786
E-mail: jhollmann@fuse.net
URL: National Affiliate–www.atos.org
Contact: Joseph Hollmann, Pres.
Regional. Aims to restore, preserve and promote the theatre pipe organ and its music. Encourages the youth to learn the instrument. Operates a committee that gathers history and old music from silent film days and information on theatre organists, theaters and organ installations of the silent film era. **Affiliated With:** American Theatre Organ Society.

13739 ■ American Truck Historical Society, Greater Cincinnati Chapter
c/o Jim Schrimpf
1231 Anderson Ferry Rd.
Cincinnati, OH 45238-4223
Ph: (513)451-1141
E-mail: jim_schrimpf@fuse.net
URL: National Affiliate–www.aths.org
Contact: Jim Schrimpf, Contact
Local.

13740 ■ American Volkssport Association, Mid-America Region
c/o Ginny Drumm
4432 Carnation Ave.
Cincinnati, OH 45238-4902
Ph: (513)471-7029
E-mail: ma_rd@ava.org
URL: National Affiliate–www.ava.org
Contact: Ginny Drumm, Contact
Regional.

13741 ■ American Wine Society - Cincinnati
c/o Richard Fruehwald, Co-Chm.
1034 Harbury Dr.
Cincinnati, OH 45224-2209
Ph: (513)541-7412
E-mail: winestr@aol.com
URL: http://www.awscincy.com
Contact: Richard Fruehwald, Co-Chm.
Local. Affiliated With: American Wine Society.

13742 ■ Anderson Area Chamber of Commerce (AACOC)
8072B Beechmont Ave.
Cincinnati, OH 45255-3177
Ph: (513)474-4802
Fax: (513)474-4857
E-mail: info@andersonareachamber.org
URL: http://andersonareachamber.org
Contact: Carolyn Moseley, Exec.Dir.
Founded: 1970. **Membership Dues:** individual/retired, $50 (annual) • associate/community organization, $65 (annual) • business (based on number of employees), $150-$430 (annual). **Staff:** 3. **Local.** Supports the area business community, develops programs to assure their success, and creates partnerships with government and residents for the overall benefit of the Anderson Area. Provides outstanding programs in the areas of business assistance, government affairs, community development, and membership services. **Awards:** Citizen of the Year. **Frequency:** annual. **Type:** recognition. **Committees:** After Hours; Citizen of the Year; Economic Development; Education/Professional Development; Finance; Greater Anderson Days Auction; Membership; Public Relations. **Publications:** *Chamber Notes*. Newsletter. Contains information about issues and Chamber opportunities. **Advertising:** accepted. **Conventions/Meetings:** periodic After Hours - meeting - usually January, March, May, August, and October • annual Citizen of the Year - meeting - every May • annual Golf Outing - competition - every June • annual Greater Anderson Days - festival - late July or early August • annual Prayer - breakfast - Wednesday before Thanksgiving.

13743 ■ APICS, The Association for Operations Management - Cincinnati Chapter
PO Box 14913
Cincinnati, OH 45250-0913
Ph: (513)607-3547
E-mail: president@apics-cincy.org
URL: http://www.apics-cincy.org
Contact: John J. Schuster CPIM, Pres.
Local. Provides information and services in production and inventory management and related areas to enable members, enterprises and individuals to add value to their business performance. **Affiliated With:** APICS - The Association for Operations Management.

13744 ■ Apple Siders of Cincinnati
5984 Cheviot Rd.
Cincinnati, OH 45247
Ph: (513)741-4325
E-mail: president@applesiders.com
URL: http://www.applesiders.com
Contact: Paul Galati, Pres.

Founded: 1978. **Members:** 350. **Membership Dues:** individual, family, $30 (annual). **Staff:** 12. **Budget:** $11,000. **Local**. Apple computer users from beginners to professionals. Seeks to share technical information, to educate, and to encourage newcomers to computing, and to further the art, science, and enjoyment of personal computing. **Libraries: Type:** open to the public. **Publications:** *Apple Press*, periodic. Newsletter. **Price:** included in membership dues. **Circulation:** 320. **Advertising:** accepted. **Conventions/Meetings:** annual AppleVention - convention, with Apple computer related hardware and software (exhibits) - usually November in Cincinnati, OH • monthly meeting - 3rd Wednesday.

13745 ■ ARMA, Greater Cincinnati Chapter
c/o Ray Beecraft
Procter and Gamble
TE-4 Box 1
Cincinnati, OH 45202
Ph: (513)698-6100
Fax: (513)983-5591
E-mail: beecraft.wr@pg.com
URL: National Affiliate–www.arma.org
Contact: Ray Beecraft, Board Member

Founded: 1975. **Members:** 70. **Membership Dues:** international, $115 (annual) • chapter, $35 (annual) • typical meeting attendance fee, $15. **Regional Groups:** 20. **State Groups:** 6. **Local Groups:** 1. **For-Profit**. **Local**. Information and knowledge management professionals. Includes records and information managers, MIS, ADP and operations professionals, imaging specialists, archivists, consultants, librarians and educators. Handles records retention; records center operations; integrated office technology; administrative services; vital records security; preservation of historical documents; information retrieval; files management; forms, reports and correspondence management; facilities management; teaching and research; human resources needs; and litigation support. **Libraries: Type:** reference. **Holdings:** 50; articles, books, video recordings. **Subjects:** records management. **Affiliated With:** ARMA International - The Association of Information Management Professionals. **Publications:** *The Information Management Journal*, bimonthly. Includes articles related to records management and the needs of the association. **Price:** included in membership dues. **Advertising:** accepted. **Conventions/Meetings:** annual conference.

13746 ■ Arthritis Foundation, Ohio River Valley Chapter (AFSOC)
7124 Miami Ave.
Cincinnati, OH 45243
Ph: (513)271-4545
Fax: (513)271-4703
Free: (800)383-6843
E-mail: info.orv@arthritis.org
URL: http://www.arthritis.org/communities/chapters/chapter.asp?chapid=65
Contact: Barbara Perez, Pres./CEO

Founded: 1957. **Members:** 12,000. **Membership Dues:** $25 (annual). **Staff:** 14. **Budget:** $1,200,000. **Local**. Individuals and businesses in southwestern Ohio, northern Kentucky and West Virginia united to discover the cause of, and cure for, arthritis. Conducts self-help, aquatic and land exercise, and educational programs. Maintains speaker's bureau. **Libraries: Type:** open to the public. **Holdings:** video recordings. **Subjects:** all arthritis related. **Boards:** Board of Trustees. **Committees:** Standing. **Affiliated With:** Arthritis Foundation. **Publications:** *Arthritis Today*, bimonthly. Magazine. **Price:** included in membership dues. **Advertising:** accepted • *In Touch*. Newsletter • Brochures, semiannual. **Conventions/Meetings:** annual dinner, volunteer recognition.

13747 ■ ASCnet Chapter of Southwest Ohio
c/o Hukill Hazlett Harrington Agy.
4601 Malsbary Rd.
Cincinnati, OH 45242
Ph: (513)793-1190
Fax: (513)793-5730
E-mail: bstern@hhhinsurance.com
URL: National Affiliate–www.ascnet.org
Contact: Brian Stern, Pres.

Local. Represents insurance agents and brokers using the Agency Manager software. Promotes successful automation and business practices through communication, education, and advocacy. **Affiliated With:** Applied Systems Client Network.

13748 ■ Assistance League of Greater Cincinnati
4527 Reading Rd., Ste.B
Cincinnati, OH 45229
Ph: (513)221-4447
Fax: (513)221-4447
E-mail: algc@fuse.net
URL: http://greatercincinnati.assistanceleague.org
Local. Affiliated With: Assistance League.

13749 ■ Associated Landscape Contractors of America, Cincinnati State Technical and Community College
c/o Claire Ehrlinger, Faculty Advisor
3520 Central Pkwy.
Cincinnati, OH 45223
Ph: (513)569-1644
Fax: (513)569-1467
E-mail: ehrlingc@cinstate.cc.oh.us
URL: National Affiliate–www.alca.org
Contact: Ben Wright, Faculty Advisor
Local. Affiliated With: Professional Landcare Network.

13750 ■ Association of Community Organizations for Reform Now, Cincinnati
1000 E McMillan St., Ste.1
Cincinnati, OH 45206
Ph: (513)221-1737
Fax: (513)221-1371
E-mail: ohacornciro@acorn.org
URL: National Affiliate–www.acorn.org
Local. Affiliated With: Association of Community Organizations for Reform Now.

13751 ■ Association for Computing Machinery, Xavier University
c/o Liz Johnson
Dept. of Mathematics and Cmpt. Sci.
3800 Victory Pkwy.
Cincinnati, OH 45207-4441
Ph: (513)745-3667
E-mail: heile@acm.org
URL: National Affiliate–www.acm.org
Contact: Tim Heile, Chm.

Local. Biological, medical, behavioral, and computer scientists; hospital administrators; programmers and others interested in application of computer methods to biological, behavioral, and medical problems. Stimulates understanding of the use and potential of computers in the Biosciences. **Affiliated With:** Association for Computing Machinery.

13752 ■ Association for Corporate Growth, Greater Cincinnati Chapter
c/o Richard Maier, Pres.
312 Walnut St., Ste.2450
Cincinnati, OH 45202
Ph: (513)929-0123
Fax: (513)929-0923
E-mail: rick.maier@abnamro.com
URL: http://www.acg.org/cincinnati
Contact: Richard Maier, Pres.

Local. Provides a forum for the exchange of ideas related to external and internal growth including acquisitions and divestitures, joint ventures, and new or expanded products and services. Assists members in improving their management skills and techniques in the field of corporate growth. **Affiliated With:** Association for Corporate Growth.

13753 ■ Association for Iron and Steel Technology Ohio Valley Chapter
c/o Ted Dageford, Sec.-Treas.
Xtek, Inc.
PO Box 415701
Cincinnati, OH 45241
Ph: (513)733-7842
Fax: (513)733-7820
E-mail: ted.dageford@xtek.com
URL: http://www.aistech.org/chapters/mc_ohiovalley.htm
Contact: Ted Dageford, Sec.-Treas.

Local. Seeks to provide a medium of communication and cooperation among those interested in any phase of ferrous metallurgy and materials science and technology. Encourages interest in and the advancement of education in metallurgical and materials science and engineering related to the iron and steel industry. Conducts short continuing education courses. **Affiliated With:** Association for Iron and Steel Technology.

13754 ■ Association for Preservation Technology International, Ohio Valley Chapter
c/o Robert Powell, Pres.
2 Garfield Pl., Ste.300
Cincinnati, OH 45202
Ph: (513)241-4422
Fax: (513)241-5560
E-mail: rap@ata-b.com
URL: http://www.apti.org/chapters/ohio
Contact: Robert Powell, Pres.

Local. Promotes the best technology for conserving historic structures and their settings. Promotes research and gathers technical information in all aspects of historic preservation. Encourages the training of craftsmen in the traditional techniques and skills required for historic preservation. **Affiliated With:** Association for Preservation Technology International.

13755 ■ Audio Engineering Society, University of Cincinnati Section
c/o Thomas A. Haines
Univ. of Cincinnati
Coll.-Conservatory of Music
M.L. 0003
Cincinnati, OH 45221
Ph: (513)556-9497
Fax: (513)556-0202
URL: National Affiliate–www.aes.org
Contact: Thomas A. Haines, Contact

Local. Represents the interests of engineers, administrators and technicians for radio, television and motion picture operation. Operates educational and research foundation. **Affiliated With:** Audio Engineering Society.

13756 ■ Audubon Society of Ohio - Cincinnati Chapter
3398 W Galbraith Rd.
Cincinnati, OH 45239
Ph: (513)741-7926
Fax: (513)741-7926
E-mail: audsocohio@earthlink.net
URL: http://home.earthlink.net/~audsocohio

Local. Formerly: (2005) National Audubon Society - Audubon Society of Ohio - Cincinnati Chapter.

13757 ■ Bankers Club
511 Walnut St., Ste.3000
Cincinnati, OH 45202
Ph: (513)651-3660
Fax: (513)651-0688
E-mail: contactus@bankers-cinn.com
URL: http://www.bankers-cinn.com
Contact: Charles W. Wilfong, Mgr.

Local. Facilitates exchange of ideas and encourages socialization between members.

13758 ■ Big Brothers Big Sisters of America Association of Cincinnati
8212 Blue Ash Rd.
Cincinnati, OH 45236
Ph: (513)761-3200
Fax: (513)761-3202
E-mail: info@bigbrobigsis.org
URL: http://www.bigbrobigsis.org
Local. Affiliated With: Big Brothers Big Sisters of America.

13759 ■ Bikers Against Child Abuse, Ohio Chapter
PO Box 53514
Cincinnati, OH 45253
Ph: (513)403-8501
URL: National Affiliate–www.bacausa.com
State.

13760 ■ Black Lawyers Association of Cincinnati
c/o Ken Parker, Pres.
PO Box 3181
Cincinnati, OH 45202
Ph: (513)684-3711
Fax: (513)684-6710
URL: National Affiliate–www.nationalbar.org
Contact: Ken Parker, Pres.
Local. Affiliated With: National Bar Association.

13761 ■ Black Nurses Association of Greater Cincinnati (18)
PO Box 37723
Cincinnati, OH 45222
Ph: (859)586-2559
URL: National Affiliate–www.nbna.org
Contact: Rhonda S. Robinson, Contact
Local. Represents registered nurses, licensed practical nurses, licensed vocational nurses, and student nurses. Builds consumer knowledge and understanding of health care issues. Facilitates the professional development and career advancement of nurses in emerging healthcare systems. Promotes economic development of nurses through entrepreneurial and other business initiatives. **Affiliated With:** National Black Nurses Association.

13762 ■ Bonsai Society of Greater Cincinnati
c/o Dave Radlinski
2715 Reading Rd.
Cincinnati, OH 45206
Ph: (513)831-6931
Fax: (513)831-3723
E-mail: dgradski@aol.com
URL: National Affiliate–www.bonsai-bci.com
Contact: Dave Radlinski, Contact
Local. Affiliated With: Bonsai Clubs International.

13763 ■ Boy Scouts of America - Dan Beard Council
2331 Victory Pkwy.
Cincinnati, OH 45206
Ph: (513)961-2336
Fax: (513)961-2688
Free: (800)872-6887
E-mail: operate@danbeard.org
URL: http://www.danbeard.org
Contact: Patrick M. Brown, Dir. of Operations
Local. Strives to prepare young people make ethical choices over lifetimes by instilling them with the values of the Scout Oath and Law. **Affiliated With:** Boy Scouts of America.

13764 ■ Buckeye United Fly Fishers (BUFF)
PO Box 42614
Cincinnati, OH 45242
Ph: (513)777-4854
E-mail: bdhaynes@one.net
URL: http://www.buckeyeflyfishers.com
Contact: Lou Haynes, Pres.
State. Affiliated With: Federation of Fly Fishers.

13765 ■ CDIC Society for Coatings Technology
c/o Mr. Neil J. Stubbers, Pres.
Deeks and Company
6615 Corporate Dr.
Cincinnati, OH 45242
Ph: (513)489-1300
Fax: (513)489-1303
E-mail: nstubbers@deeksandco.com
URL: http://www.cdicsociety.org
Contact: Mr. Neil J. Stubbers, Pres.
Regional. Represents chemists, chemical engineers, technologists and supervisory production personnel in the decorative and protective coatings industry and allied industries. Works to gather and disseminate practical and technical facts, data and standards fundamental to the manufacturing and use of paints, varnishes, lacquers, related protective coatings and printing inks. **Affiliated With:** Federation of Societies for Coatings Technology.

13766 ■ Charter Committee of Greater Cincinnati
811 Race St., Ste.300
Cincinnati, OH 45202
Ph: (513)241-0303
Fax: (513)241-0322
E-mail: charter@fuse.net
URL: http://chartercommittee.org
Contact: Jeffrey M. Cramerding, Exec.Dir.
Local. Works as an independent political party promoting a Cincinnati government that is free from partisan politics.

13767 ■ CHCA Young Life
PO Box 42171
Cincinnati, OH 45242-0171
Ph: (513)791-3730
URL: http://sites.younglife.org/sites/CHCA/default.aspx
Local. Affiliated With: Young Life.

13768 ■ Cheviot Westwood Lions Club
Westwood Town Ctr.
3017 Harrison Ave.
Cincinnati, OH 45211-5701
Ph: (513)471-9225
E-mail: icelog@worldnet.att.net
URL: http://cheviotwestwoodoh.lionwap.org
Contact: Irvin R. Huddleston, Pres.
Local. Affiliated With: Lions Clubs International.

13769 ■ Childbirth Education Association
c/o Elena Wolf, Pres.
PO Box 58573
Cincinnati, OH 45258-0573
Ph: (513)661-5655

13770 ■ Children's Defense Fund, Cincinnati
258 Erkenbrecher Ave.
Cincinnati, OH 45229
Ph: (513)751-2332
Fax: (513)751-2003
E-mail: kkahle@cdfcinti.org
URL: http://www.cdfcinti.org
Contact: Karen Kahle, Contact
Local. Affiliated With: Children's Defense Fund.

13771 ■ Children's Rights Council of South Ohio
PO Box 8805
Cincinnati, OH 45208
Ph: (513)624-7223
E-mail: kobrien@pacegroup.org
URL: http://www.pacegroup.org
Local. Affiliated With: Children's Rights Council.

13772 ■ Cincinnati 9to5
c/o Leonie Carter
4969 Oakland Dr.
Cincinnati, OH 45227
Ph: (513)271-4524
URL: National Affiliate–www.9to5.org
Contact: Leonie Carter, Contact
Local. Affiliated With: 9 to 5, National Association of Working Women.

13773 ■ Cincinnati African Violet Society
c/o Karen Malott
2131 Spinningwheel Ln.
Cincinnati, OH 45202
Ph: (513)232-8497
E-mail: kmalott@cinci.rr.com
URL: National Affiliate–www.avsa.org
Contact: Karen Malott, Contact
Local. Affiliated With: African Violet Society of America.

13774 ■ Cincinnati Area Board of Realtors (CABR)
c/o Gene Snavley, Exec.VP
14 Knollcrest Dr.
PO Box 37889
Cincinnati, OH 45222
Ph: (513)761-8800 (513)474-4800
Fax: (513)761-8813
E-mail: gene@cabr.org
URL: http://www.cabr.org
Contact: Dave Otto, Pres.
Local. Works to provide more business opportunities for its members and helps enhance the capabilities of real state professionals.

13775 ■ Cincinnati Area RSVP
c/o Michael Dutle, Dir.
3740 Glenway Ave.
Cincinnati, OH 45205-1742
Ph: (513)354-5704
Fax: (513)921-8222
E-mail: mdutle@fsmail.org
URL: http://www.servingfamilies.org/ProgramsServices/RSVP.htm
Contact: Michael Dutle, Dir.
Local. Affiliated With: Retired and Senior Volunteer Program.

13776 ■ Cincinnati Association for the Blind and Visually Impaired
c/o Kathy Gottschlich
2045 Gilbert Ave.
Cincinnati, OH 45202-1490
Ph: (513)221-8558
Fax: (513)221-2995
Free: (888)687-3935
E-mail: info@cincyblind.org
URL: http://www.cincyblind.org
Contact: Maureen Gregory, Dir. of Devel. & Comm. Rel.
Local. Offers counseling, rehabilitation, information and employment services to individuals who are blind visually impaired or print impaired in the Greater Cincinnati area.

13777 ■ Cincinnati Bar Association (CBA)
c/o Anne T. Gerhardt, Dir. of Development
225 E 6th St., 2nd Fl.
Cincinnati, OH 45202-3209
Ph: (513)381-8213
Fax: (513)381-0528
E-mail: info@cincybar.org
URL: http://www.cincybar.org
Contact: Anne T. Gerhardt, Dir. of Development
Local.

13778 ■ Cincinnati Better Business Bureau
7 W 7th St., Ste.1600
Cincinnati, OH 45202-2097
Ph: (513)421-3015
Fax: (513)621-0907
Free: (800)471-3015
E-mail: info@cinbbb.org
URL: http://www.cinbbb.org
Contact: Jocile Ehrlich, Pres./CEO
Local. Seeks to promote and foster the highest ethical relationship between businesses and the public through voluntary self-regulation, consumer and busi-

ness education, and service excellence. Provides information to help consumers and businesses make informed purchasing decisions and avoid costly scams and frauds; settles consumer complaints through arbitration and other means. **Affiliated With:** BBB Wise Giving Alliance.

13779 ■ Cincinnati Business and Professional Women's Club
c/o Amy M. McPike, Pres.
Herschede Bldg., 4 W 4th St.
Cincinnati, OH 45202
Ph: (513)241-9025
Local.

13780 ■ Cincinnati Computer Cooperative
49 Novner Dr.
Cincinnati, OH 45215
Ph: (513)771-3262
E-mail: c3@cinci.rr.com
URL: http://www.cincinnaticomputercooperative.org
Contact: Walt Fischer, Chm.
Local.

13781 ■ Cincinnati Contra Dancers
c/o John McCain
5638 Glenview Ave.
Cincinnati, OH 45224
Ph: (513)681-4768
E-mail: jwmccain1@hotmail.com
URL: http://cincinnaticontradance.org
Contact: John McCain, Treas.
Founded: 1985. **Members:** 43. **Membership Dues:** voting, $1 (annual). **Budget:** $30,000. **Local Groups:** 1. **Local.** Seeks to promote and teach old-time music and dance. **Affiliated With:** Country Dance and Song Society. **Publications:** *Monthly Flyer*, biennial. **Price:** free. Alternate Formats: online. **Conventions/Meetings:** annual New Year's Eve Dance and Potluck - dinner • annual Pigtown Fling - party, dance festival - April.

13782 ■ Cincinnati Corvette Club
PO Box 24184
Cincinnati, OH 45224
E-mail: cjenkins454@fuse.net
URL: http://www.cincinnati-corvettes.com
Contact: Jim Barbian, Pres.
Local. Affiliated With: National Council of Corvette Clubs.

13783 ■ Cincinnati Dental Society (CDS)
9200 Montgomery Rd., Ste.21A
Cincinnati, OH 45242
Ph: (513)984-3443
Fax: (513)984-3047
E-mail: cds@one.net
URL: http://www.cincinnatidental.org
Contact: Victoria J. Nixon, Exec.Dir.
Founded: 1886. **Members:** 650. **Staff:** 2. **State Groups:** 1. **Local.** Dentists in Brown, Clermont, Hamilton, and Warren counties, OH promoting public health and welfare through service and education. Seeks to advance the dental profession through continuing education and to cooperate with other health organizations. Holds seven postgraduate seminars a year. **Affiliated With:** American Dental Association; Ohio Dental Association. **Publications:** *Cincinnati Dental Society Bulletin*, monthly. Magazine. **Price:** free to members. **Conventions/Meetings:** annual Honors Night and Installation Dinner • monthly meeting, for members - first Monday; except in January, July and August • annual Scientific Meeting, with guest speaker.

13784 ■ Cincinnati Estate Planning Council
c/o Suzi Hoffman
4100 Executive Park Dr., No. 16
Cincinnati, OH 45241
Ph: (513)554-3074
Fax: (513)563-9743
E-mail: assocnnctn@aol.com
URL: National Affiliate–councils.naepc.org
Contact: Michael P. Daly, Pres.
Local. Represents the interests of professionals involved in estate planning. Promotes the understanding of the functions of estate planning professionals. **Affiliated With:** National Association of Estate Planners and Councils.

13785 ■ Cincinnati Folk Life (CFL)
PO Box 9008
Cincinnati, OH 45209-0008
Ph: (513)533-4822
E-mail: cfl@zoomtown.com
URL: http://www.cincinnatifolklife.com
Founded: 1981. **Members:** 300. **Local.** Aims to increase public awareness regarding folk music and its contribution to the culture of Cincinnati.

13786 ■ Cincinnati Habitat for Humanity (CHFH)
201 W Eighth St.
Cincinnati, OH 45202
Ph: (513)621-4147
Fax: (513)621-6869
E-mail: chfh@cincinnati-habitat.org
URL: http://www.cincinnati-habitat.org
Contact: Gabe Blumer, Acting Exec.Dir.
Founded: 1986. **Staff:** 3. **Budget:** $1,500,000. **Local.** Individuals interested in providing affordable housing for people in need. **Affiliated With:** Habitat for Humanity International. **Publications:** *Sharing the Good News*, bimonthly. Newsletter. **Price:** free. **Circulation:** 10,000. **Conventions/Meetings:** biennial conference.

13787 ■ Cincinnati-Hamilton County Community Action Agency Foundation
c/o Randal Bloch
2904 Woodburn Ave.
Cincinnati, OH 45206-1471
Ph: (513)569-1840
Local.

13788 ■ Cincinnati Horticultural Society (CHS)
3731 Eastern Hills Ln.
Cincinnati, OH 45209
Ph: (513)872-5194
Fax: (513)872-5193
Free: (800)670-6808
E-mail: chsevents@aol.com
URL: http://www.cincyflowershow.com
Contact: Jeane Elliott, Dir. of Administration
Membership Dues: single, $50 (annual) • family, $75 (annual) • sustaining, $300 (annual) • supporter, $650 (annual) • patron, $1,000 (annual) • platinum, $2,500 (annual). **Local.** Seeks to benefit organizations that promote the quality of life through horticulture.

13789 ■ Cincinnati Host Lions Club
15 W 6th St.
Cincinnati, OH 45202
Ph: (513)271-0516 (513)562-8683
E-mail: cincihostlionsclub@yahoo.com
URL: http://www.lionwap.org/cintioh
Contact: Larry Nurre, Pres.
Local. Affiliated With: Lions Clubs International.

13790 ■ Cincinnati-Kenwood Lions Club
9489 Raven Ln.
Cincinnati, OH 45242
Ph: (513)745-9931
E-mail: djm9489@fuse.net
URL: http://kenwoodoh.lionwap.org
Contact: Donna Ware, Pres.
Local. Affiliated With: Lions Clubs International.

13791 ■ Cincinnati Master Plumbers' Association (CMPA)
11020 Southland Rd.
Cincinnati, OH 45240
Ph: (513)742-CMPA
E-mail: info@cmpa-phcc.org
URL: http://www.cmpa-phcc.org
Contact: Joyce Frank, Exec.Mgr.
Founded: 1993. **Staff:** 6. **Local Groups:** 1. **Local.** Conducts plumbing apprenticeship program. Sponsors continuing education seminars for journeymen and contractors. **Awards:** Al Padur Scholarship Fund. **Frequency:** annual. **Type:** scholarship. **Recipient:** to a plumbing apprentice. **Conventions/Meetings:** annual Plumbing Industry Appreciation Night - dinner (exhibits).

13792 ■ Cincinnati Musicians' Association - Local 1, American Federation of Musicians
c/o Eugene V. Frey, Pres.
2145 Central Pkwy.
Cincinnati, OH 45214
Ph: (513)241-0900
Fax: (513)241-0902
URL: http://Musicians1.org
Contact: Eugene V. Frey, Pres.
Local. AFL-CIO. Musicians. Seeks to improve the wages and working conditions of professional musicians. **Additional Websites:** http://www.afm.org/1. **Affiliated With:** American Federation of Musicians of the United States and Canada.

13793 ■ Cincinnati Numismatic Association
c/o Emmett M. Ey
2816 Deerhaven Dr.
Cincinnati, OH 45244
E-mail: khcoins@fuse.net
URL: National Affiliate–www.money.org
Contact: Emmett M. Ey, Contact
Local. Affiliated With: American Numismatic Association.

13794 ■ Cincinnati Off Road Alliance
3307 Clifton Ave.
Cincinnati, OH 45220
E-mail: mitch@biowheels.com
URL: http://www.geocities.com/coratrails
Local. Affiliated With: International Mountain Bicycling Association.

13795 ■ Cincinnati Opera Association
1243 Elm St.
Cincinnati, OH 45202-7531
Ph: (513)241-2742 (513)768-5500
Fax: (513)768-5552
Free: (888)533-7149
E-mail: info@cincinnatiopera.com
URL: http://www.cincinnatiopera.com
Contact: Patricia K. Beggs, Gen.Dir./CEO
Founded: 1920. **Nonmembership. Local.**

13796 ■ Cincinnati Paralegal Association
PO Box 1515
Cincinnati, OH 45201
Ph: (513)244-1266
E-mail: cincinnati@cincinnatiparalegals.org
URL: http://www.cincinnatiparalegals.org
Contact: Jennifer M. McKinney-Taylor, Pres.
Founded: 1982. **Members:** 300. **Membership Dues:** active, associate, $60 (annual) • student, $35 (annual) • sustaining, $150 (annual). **Budget:** $25,000. **Local.** Paralegals in the Greater Cincinnati area who are committed to the development and growth of the paralegal profession. **Libraries: Type:** open to the public. **Subjects:** paralegal. **Awards:** New Member Award. **Frequency:** annual. **Type:** recognition. **Recipient:** for active member of less than 3 years • Professional Achievement Award. **Frequency:** annual. **Type:** recognition. **Recipient:** for active member • **Frequency:** annual. **Type:** scholarship. **Recipient:** for students enrolled in paralegal program. **Publications:** *The Paralegal Resource*, monthly. Newsletter. **Price:** $35.00/year. **Circulation:** 400. **Advertising:** accepted • *Paralegals in Greater Cincinnati*. Features guide to choosing a paralegal

program. • *2004 Salary Survey*, biennial. **Price:** included in membership dues. **Conventions/Meetings:** annual Career Path - seminar • annual CLE Seminar - always spring • monthly Membership Meeting.

13797 ■ Cincinnati Preservation Association (CPA)
342 W 4th St.
Cincinnati, OH 45202
Ph: (513)721-4506
Fax: (513)721-6832
E-mail: info@cincinnatipreservation.org
URL: http://www.cincinnatipreservation.org
Contact: Kendall Fisher, Exec.Dir.
Founded: 1964. **Members:** 900. **Membership Dues:** individual, $35 (annual) • household, $50 (annual) • student, $10 (annual) • capital, $100 (annual) • keystone, $250 (annual) • arch, $500 (annual) • cornerstone, $1,000 (annual). **Budget:** $250,000. **Local**. Promotes the preservation of historic buildings, sites, and monuments through education and advocacy. **Publications:** Newsletter, bimonthly. **Price:** included in membership dues.

13798 ■ Cincinnati Psychoanalytic Society
3001 Highland Ave.
Cincinnati, OH 45219
Ph: (513)961-8886
Fax: (513)961-0308
E-mail: cpiadministrator@3001.us
URL: National Affiliate–www.apsa.org
Contact: Bernard Foster MD, Co-Dir.
Local. Educates and promotes public awareness and interest in the science and art of psychoanalysis. Establishes and maintains standards for the training of psychoanalysts and for the practice of psychoanalysis. **Affiliated With:** American Psychoanalytic Association.

13799 ■ Cincinnati Society of Association Executives (CSAE)
c/o David R. LaFleche, Treas.
PO Box 42694
Cincinnati, OH 45242
Ph: (513)984-3443
Fax: (513)984-3047
E-mail: cdsnixon@one.net
URL: http://csaeonline.org
Contact: Ms. Victoria J. Nixon, Pres.
Membership Dues: regular, $50 (annual). **Local**. Represents paid executives of international, national, state, and local trade, professional, and philanthropic associations. Seeks to educate association executives on effective management, including: the proper objectives, functions, and activities of associations; the basic principles of association management; the legal aspects of association activity; policies relating to association management; efficient methods, procedures, and techniques of association management; the responsibilities and professional standards of association executives. **Affiliated With:** American Society of Association Executives.

13800 ■ Cincinnati Table Tennis Club
Xavier Field House
3900 Winding Way
Cincinnati, OH 45207
Ph: (513)961-2231 (513)558-5521
E-mail: john.monaco@uc.edu
URL: http://www.cincytt.org
Contact: John Monaco, Pres.
Local. **Affiliated With:** U.S.A. Table Tennis.

13801 ■ Cincinnati USA Regional Chamber (GCCC)
441 Vine St., Ste.300
Cincinnati, OH 45202-2812
Ph: (513)579-3100
Fax: (513)579-3101
E-mail: info@cincinnatichamber.com
URL: http://www.cincinnatichamber.com
Contact: Ellen van der Horst, Pres.
Founded: 1839. **Members:** 6,000. **Local**. Promotes business and community development in the Cincinnati, OH area. **Awards:** Great Living Cincinnatians Award. **Frequency:** annual. **Type:** recognition. **Recipient:** for community service • Outstanding Community Service Award. **Frequency:** annual. **Type:** recognition. **Recipient:** for contributions made by companies, groups or individuals to the area's charitable or service organizations. **Formerly:** (2006) Greater Cincinnati Chamber of Commerce. **Publications:** *Chamber Connect*, monthly. Newsletter. Alternate Formats: online • *Chambervision*, monthly. Newsletter • *Clubs and Organizations Directory*, periodic • *Greater Cincinnati Business Connections Directory*, annual. Catalog. Alternate Formats: online • *Greater Cincinnati Industrial Pinpointer*, periodic. Directory • *Greater Cincinnati Legislative Action Guide*, periodic. Directory • *International Trade Directory*, periodic • *Major Employers Directory*, annual. **Conventions/Meetings:** annual dinner • annual luncheon.

13802 ■ Cincinnati-Western Hills Lions Club
3338 Parkhill Dr.
Cincinnati, OH 45248
Ph: (513)574-5606
E-mail: dave_dornheggen@trihealth.com
URL: http://pricehilloh.lionwap.org
Contact: David Dornheggen, Sec.
Local. **Affiliated With:** Lions Clubs International.

13803 ■ Classical Association of Ohio
Xavier Univ.
Classics Dept.
3800 Victory Pkwy.
Cincinnati, OH 45207-4541
Ph: (513)745-3456
E-mail: delucej@muohio.edu
URL: http://www.camws.org
Contact: Edmund P. Cueva, VP
State. Represents university, college, secondary and elementary teachers of Latin, Greek and all other studies which focus on the world of classical antiquity. Supports and promotes the study of classical languages.

13804 ■ Clermont County Kennel Club (CCKC)
c/o Billie Thompston, Corresponding Sec.
4155 McLean Dr.
Cincinnati, OH 45255
Ph: (513)851-7117
E-mail: billie@sagenhaftweims.com
URL: http://www.clermontcountykc.org
Contact: Alan Margulies, Pres.
Local. **Affiliated With:** American Kennel Club.

13805 ■ Clifton Heights Community Urban Redevelopment Corp. (CHCURC)
2510 Ohio Ave., Ste.C
Cincinnati, OH 45219
Ph: (513)564-0078
Fax: (513)564-0093
URL: http://www.chcurc.org
Contact: Paul Pratt, Pres.
Local. **Publications:** *Reaching for New Heights*, annual. Newsletter.

13806 ■ Communities United for Action
3726 Llewellyn Ave.
Cincinnati, OH 45223
Ph: (513)541-4109
URL: National Affiliate–www.npa-us.org
Contact: Marlyn Evans, Exec.Dir.
Local. **Affiliated With:** National People's Action.

13807 ■ Community Development Corporations Association of Greater Cincinnati (CDCAGC)
c/o Patricia Garry, Exec.Dir.
2859 Colerain Ave., Ste.11
Cincinnati, OH 45225
Ph: (513)281-3774
Fax: (513)281-6600
E-mail: conact@cdcagc.org
URL: http://www.queencity.com/ndc
Contact: Patricia Garry, Exec.Dir.
Founded: 1979. **Membership Dues:** individual, $50 (annual) • nonprofit institution (based on the operating budget), $75-$100 (annual) • for profit financial institution, $415 (annual). **Local**. Provides technical support, training, and information to its members in order to improve their ability to serve the people of Cincinnati. Aims to increase economic development. **Formerly:** (2005) Neighborhood Development Corporations Association of Cincinnati.

13808 ■ Compassionate Friends - Greater Cincinnati-East Chapter
St. Timothy's Episcopal Church
8101 Beechmont Ave.
Cincinnati, OH 45230
Ph: (859)283-1926
E-mail: soccer17@fuse.net
URL: http://www.tcfcincy.org
Contact: Gary Christian, Contact
Local.

13809 ■ Cooperative for Education
2730 Hyde Park Ave.
Cincinnati, OH 45209
Ph: (513)731-2595
Fax: (513)731-2335
E-mail: coed@fuse.net
URL: http://www.coeduc.org
Contact: Joseph Berninger, Exec.Dir.
Founded: 1996. **Staff:** 4. **Budget:** $500,000. **Local**. Seeks to break the cycle of poverty in Guatemala through education. Projects include a self-sufficient textbook program, libraries, computer labs, and scholarships. **Formerly:** (2001) Cooperative for Educational Development.

13810 ■ Corbeau Ski Club
PO Box 17088
Cincinnati, OH 45217-0088
E-mail: bealewis@att.net
URL: http://www.corbeauski.org
Contact: Bea Lewis, Pres.
Local. **Affiliated With:** National Brotherhood of Skiers.

13811 ■ Cos Community Development Corp.
c/o Paula M. Jackson
65 E. Hollister St.
Cincinnati, OH 45219-1703
Local.

13812 ■ Crohn's and Colitis Foundation of American, Southwest Ohio Chapter
8 Triangle Park Dr., Ste.800
Cincinnati, OH 45246
Ph: (513)772-3550
Fax: (513)772-7599
Free: (877)283-7513
E-mail: swohio@ccfa.org
URL: National Affiliate–www.ccfa.org
Contact: Noel Balster, Development Dir.
Founded: 1995. **Membership Dues:** individual, $30 (annual) • family, $60 (annual) • physician, $300 (annual). **Staff:** 2. **Local**. Works to raise funds to support basic and clinical research to find the cause of, and cure for, Crohn's Disease and Ulcerative Colitis in addition to providing local education and support programs. **Affiliated With:** Crohn's and Colitis Foundation of America. **Publications:** *Focus on Crohn's and Colitis*, quarterly. Newsletter. **Conventions/Meetings:** bimonthly board meeting.

13813 ■ DanceCincinnati
PO Box 141345
Cincinnati, OH 45250-1345
Ph: (513)769-3088
URL: http://www.dancecincinnati.org
Contact: Patrick Hoffman, Pres.
Local. Encourages and promotes the physical, mental and social benefits of partner dancing.

Organizes and supports programs for the recreational enjoyment of ballroom dancing. Creates opportunities for the general public to participate in ballroom dancing and DanceSport.

13814 ■ Down Syndrome Association of Greater Cincinnati (DSAGC)
644 Linn St., Ste.408
Cincinnati, OH 45203-1734
Ph: (513)761-5400
Fax: (513)761-5401
E-mail: dsagc@fuse.net
URL: http://www.dsagc.com
Contact: Jane Page-Steiner, Exec.Dir.
Local. Functions as a support group for individuals with Down Syndrome and their families by providing information and resources.

13815 ■ Dress for Success Cincinnati
135 W 4th St.
Cincinnati, OH 45202
Ph: (513)651-3372
Fax: (513)651-3376
E-mail: cincinnati@dressforsuccess.org
URL: National Affiliate–www.dressforsuccess.org
Contact: Mary E. Ivers, Founder/CEO
Local.

13816 ■ EarthSave, Cincinnati
PO Box 3125
Cincinnati, OH 45201-3125
Ph: (513)929-2500
E-mail: cincinnati@earthsave.org
URL: http://cincinnati.earthsave.org
Local. Affiliated With: EarthSave International.

13817 ■ Easter Seals Southwestern Ohio
c/o Tammy Watson
231 Clark Rd.
Cincinnati, OH 45215
Ph: (513)821-9890
Fax: (513)821-9895
Free: (800)288-1123
E-mail: twatson@oh-sw.easter-seals.org
Contact: Tammy Watson, Pres./CEO
Local. Affiliated With: Easter Seals.

13818 ■ Ekklesia Development Corp.
c/o Kazava Smith
772 Whitter St.
Cincinnati, OH 45229-3336
Ph: (513)884-2608
E-mail: ekklesiadevcorp@prodigy.net
URL: http://www.projectgilead.org/contact.php
Local.

13819 ■ Elks Lodge
827 Lincoln Ave.
Cincinnati, OH 45206
Ph: (513)281-9670

13820 ■ Employers Resource Association (ERA)
1200 Edison Dr.
Cincinnati, OH 45216-2276
Ph: (513)679-4120 (614)538-9410
Fax: (513)679-4139
Free: (888)237-9554
E-mail: info@hrxperts.org
URL: http://www.hrxperts.org
Contact: Douglas J. Matthews, Pres.
Founded: 1946. **Members:** 1,165. **Membership Dues:** company with 50 employees or less, $425 (annual) • company with 51-99 employees (plus $2 per additional employee), $425 (annual) • company with over 100 employees (maximum; $5.25 per employee), $3,935 (annual). **Staff:** 19. **Budget:** $1,800,000. **Regional**. Employers in Ohio, Indiana, and northern Kentucky. Provides human resource services to businesses. **Convention/Meeting:** none. **Libraries: Type:** not open to the public. **Holdings:** 150; books. **Subjects:** human resources, general management. **Affiliated With:** American Society of Association Executives; Employer Association Group; Society for Human Resource Management. **Formerly:** (1946) Cincinnati Industrial Institute; (1985) Greater Cincinnati Employers Institute. **Publications:** *Briefs*, monthly. Newsletter. Contains information about human resources and general management. **Price:** included in membership dues.

13821 ■ Epilepsy Foundation of Greater Cincinnati
895 Central Ave., Ste.550
Cincinnati, OH 45202
Ph: (513)721-2905
Free: (877)804-2241
E-mail: ecgc@fuse.net
URL: http://www.epilepsyfoundation.org/cincinnati
Contact: Margie Frommeyer, Exec.Dir.
Local. Responds to the needs of the individual with epilepsy, their families and the community-at-large, by providing the following services: therapeutic camp for children, school support, job training, community education, group homes, support groups, counseling, and professional seminars.

13822 ■ Executive Suite Association, Cincinnati Local Member Network
c/o Cindy Petrey, General Mgr.
Off. Suites PLUS
11427 Reed Hartman Hwy.
Cincinnati, OH 45241
Ph: (513)469-1220 (513)618-6500
Fax: (513)618-6526
E-mail: blueash@officesuitesplus.com
URL: http://www.officesuitesplus.com
Contact: Cindy Petrey, General Mgr.
Local. Affiliated With: Office Business Center Association International.

13823 ■ Executive Women International, Cincinnati/Northern Kentucky Chapter
PO Box 9192
Cincinnati, OH 45209-0192
Ph: (513)585-6006 (513)784-7983
Fax: (513)585-6076
E-mail: millerve@healthall.com
URL: http://www.ewicincinky.com
Contact: Vetta Miller, Pres.
Founded: 1966. **Local**. Works to promote member firms and improve their communities. Provides opportunities for business and personal growth. **Committees:** Advisory; Long Range Planning; Major Fundraising Investigation; Nominating; Philanthropy; Program; Publication; Ways & Means. **Affiliated With:** Executive Women International. **Publications:** *Pulse*, monthly. Newsletter. Alternate Formats: online.

13824 ■ Fairfield Sportsmen's Association
10172 Bennington Dr.
Cincinnati, OH 45241
Ph: (513)779-7177
Fax: (513)779-2832
URL: National Affiliate–www.mynssa.com
Local. Affiliated With: National Skeet Shooting Association.

13825 ■ Family Firm Institute, Cincinnati Study Group
c/o Ellen Frankenberg, PhD
The Frankenberg Gp.
800 Compton Rd., No. 27
Cincinnati, OH 45231-3850
Ph: (513)729-1511
Fax: (513)729-1022
E-mail: ellen@frankenberggroup.com
URL: National Affiliate–www.ffi.org
Contact: Ellen Frankenberg PhD, Contact
Local. Affiliated With: Family Firm Institute.

13826 ■ Family Motor Coach Association - Just Friends
c/o Steve Czarsty
PMB F79148
3590 Round Bottom Rd.
Cincinnati, OH 45244
URL: National Affiliate–www.fmca.com
Contact: Steve Czarsty, Contact
Regional.

13827 ■ Federalist Society for Law and Public Policy Studies - Cincinnati Chapter
c/o Mr. John Nalbandian
Taft, Stettinius & Hollister, LLP
1800 FIRSTAR Ctr.
Cincinnati, OH 45202
Ph: (513)357-9634 (513)381-2838
Fax: (513)381-0205
E-mail: nalbandian@taftlaw.com
URL: National Affiliate–www.fed-soc.org
Contact: Mr. John Nalbandian, Contact
Local. Seeks to bring about a reordering of priorities within the U.S. legal system that will emphasize individual liberty, traditional values, and the rule of law. **Affiliated With:** Federalist Society for Law and Public Policy Studies.

13828 ■ Figure Skating Club of Cincinnati (FSCC)
c/o Jody Shelden, Pres.
6222 Ridge
Cincinnati, OH 45213
Ph: (513)531-7380
E-mail: gshelden@cinci.rr.com
URL: http://www.skatecincinnati.org
Contact: Jody Shelden, Pres.
Local. Provides programs to encourage participation and achievement in the sport of figure skating on ice. Defines and maintains uniform standards of skating proficiency. Organizes and sponsors competitions and exhibitions for the purpose of stimulating interest in figure skating. **Affiliated With:** United States Figure Skating Association.

13829 ■ Financial Managers Society, Ohio Chapter
c/o Robert J. Booth, Jr.
Winton Savings & Loan Co.
5511 Cheviot Rd.
Cincinnati, OH 45247
Ph: (513)385-3880
E-mail: rjbooth@wintonsavings.com
URL: National Affiliate–www.fmsinc.org
Contact: Robert J. Booth Jr., Pres.
State. Provides technical information exchange for financial personnel within financial institutions. **Affiliated With:** Financial Managers Society.

13830 ■ Franciscan Haircuts from the Heart
c/o Nancy Kinross
126 E 13th St.
Cincinnati, OH 45202-7639
Ph: (513)651-6468
E-mail: fhfhofc@queencity.com
URL: http://www.haircutsfromheart.org
Contact: Nancy Kinross, Exec.Dir.
Founded: 1999. **Staff:** 2. **Budget:** $95,000. **State Groups:** 1. **Nonmembership. For-Profit. Local**. Provides free professional hair cut services to the poor. **Boards:** Board of Trustees.

13831 ■ Free Inquiry Group of Greater Cincinnati and Northern Kentucky
c/o Margaret O'Kain, Pres.
PO Box 19034
Cincinnati, OH 45219
E-mail: figinfo@gofigger.org
URL: http://www.gofigger.org
Contact: Margaret O'Kain, Pres.
Founded: 1991. **Members:** 100. **Membership Dues:** regular, $25 (annual) • family, $35 (annual) • patron, $50 (annual) • sustaining, $100 (annual). **Local**. Persons who are devoted to humanism as a way of life. Humanism presupposes humanity's sole dependence on natural and social resources and acknowledges no supernatural power. Humanists believe that morality is based on the knowledge that humans are interdependent and, therefore, responsible to one another. **Affiliated With:** American Humanist Association.

13832 ■ Friends of WGUC
c/o Richard N. Eiswerth, Pres.
1223 Central Pkwy.
Cincinnati, OH 45214

Ph: (513)241-8282
Fax: (513)241-8456
E-mail: webmaster@wguc.org
URL: http://www.wguc.org
Local. Provides financial support for the station's ongoing operations.

13833 ■ Friends of Women's Studies
c/o Prof. Pat O'Reilly, PhD, Pres.
Univ. of Cincinnati
PO Box 210164
Cincinnati, OH 45221-0164
Ph: (513)556-6653
Fax: (513)556-6771
E-mail: friendsws@uc.edu
URL: http://www.artsci.uc.edu/womens_studies
Contact: Prof. Pat O'Reilly PhD, Pres.
Founded: 1980. **Members:** 200. **Membership Dues:** general, $25-$100 (annual). **Staff:** 1. **Budget:** $18,000. **Local Groups:** 1. **Local.** Works to support the activities, development, and growth of the Center for Women's Studies at the University of Cincinnati: Strives to disseminate knowledge about women's achievements, needs, and aspirations to the broader community. **Awards:** Student and Faculty Travel and Research Grants. **Frequency:** semiannual. **Type:** grant. **Recipient:** for University of Cincinnati Women's Studies graduate students and faculty applying for travel or research money to present papers at academic conferences.

13834 ■ Germania Volksmarch Gruppe
c/o Patty Galvin
3529 W Kemper Rd.
Cincinnati, OH 45251
Ph: (513)825-1355
E-mail: galvin4@aol.com
URL: http://www.germaniasociety.com
Contact: Patty Galvin, Contact
Local.

13835 ■ GFWC/Ohio Federation of Women's Clubs
8721 Tanager Woods Dr.
Cincinnati, OH 45249
E-mail: pwwilken@bright.net
URL: http://www.angelfire.com/oh2/ofwc
Contact: Lin Wilken, Pres.
State.

13836 ■ Girl Scouts-Great Rivers Council (GS-GRC)
c/o Barbara J. Bonifas, CEO
4930 Cornell Rd.
Cincinnati, OH 45242-1804
Ph: (513)489-1025
Fax: (513)489-1417
Free: (800)537-6241
E-mail: council@grgsc.org
URL: http://www.grgsc.org
Contact: Barbara J. Bonifas, CEO
Local. Promotes girl scouting; comes up with confidence enhancing programs and other activities that instill positive values to its members. **Formerly:** (2001) Great Rivers Girl Scout Council.

13837 ■ Greater Cincinnati Automobile Dealers Association
c/o Mr. Edward P. Ammann, Exec.VP
138 E Ct. St., Rm. 100
Cincinnati, OH 45202
Ph: (513)326-7100
Fax: (513)326-7106
E-mail: ace@gcada.net
URL: http://www.gcada.net
Contact: Mr. Edward P. Ammann, Exec.VP
Local. Affiliated With: National Automobile Dealers Association.

13838 ■ Greater Cincinnati Bird Club
c/o Raeann Richards
PO Box 40472
Cincinnati, OH 45240
Ph: (513)948-0089 (513)761-8934
E-mail: rrichards28@cinci.rr.com
URL: http://www.greatercincinnatibirdclub.org
Contact: Larry Wilson, Pres.
Founded: 1993. **Members:** 50. **Membership Dues:** single, $13 (annual) • family, $19 (annual). **Local.** People with exotic birds. Seeks to be a source of information to present and future bird owners; to address problems and issues which pertain to bird care, health and preservation; and to instill in future generations the importance of being responsible caretakers. Visits schools, libraries, nursing homes, etc. with outreach program. **Publications:** *As the Beak Speaks*, bimonthly. Newsletter. **Conventions/ Meetings:** meeting, with speakers - 5/year; February, April, June, October and December.

13839 ■ Greater Cincinnati Bowling Proprietors
c/o Frank Ruggerie, Pres.
9189 Colerain Ave.
Cincinnati, OH 45251
Ph: (513)385-8500
Fax: (513)385-8501
Local.

13840 ■ Greater Cincinnati Building and Construction Trades Council
c/o Joe Zimmer, Exec.Sec.
1550 Chase Ave.
Cincinnati, OH 45223
Ph: (513)541-0328
Fax: (513)541-2133
Local.

13841 ■ Greater Cincinnati Compensation and Benefits Association (GCCBA)
c/o Deb Ader, Dir., Compensation
Western and Southern Life Insurance Co.
400 Broadway
Cincinnati, OH 45202
Ph: (513)629-1140
E-mail: deb.ader@westernsouthernlife.com
URL: http://www.gccba.com
Contact: Deb Ader, Dir., Compensation
Local. Affiliated With: WorldatWork.

13842 ■ Greater Cincinnati Convention and Visitors Bureau (GCCVB)
300 W 6th St.
Cincinnati, OH 45202-2361
Ph: (513)621-2142
Fax: (513)621-5020
Free: (800)543-2613
E-mail: dlincoln@cincyusa.com
URL: http://www.cincyusa.com
Contact: Dan Lincoln, Pres.
Founded: 1945. **Members:** 750. **Membership Dues:** business (minimum), $425 (annual). **Budget:** $5,900,000. **Local.** Seeks to positively impact the greater Cincinnati area economy through convention, trade show, and visitor expenditures, and provide quality service to clients. **Publications:** *Destination Planning Guide*, annual. Directory • *Official Visitors Guide*, annual. Directory.

13843 ■ Greater Cincinnati Council of Teachers of Mathematics
c/o Anne Hambrick , Pres.
2821 Ridgewood Ave.
Cincinnati, OH 45231
Ph: (513)731-9642
E-mail: hambricka@olv-school.org
URL: http://www.gcctm.net
Contact: Anne Hambrick, Pres.
Local. Aims to improve the teaching and learning of mathematics. Provides vision, leadership and professional development to support teachers in ensuring mathematics learning of the highest quality for all students. **Affiliated With:** National Council of Teachers of Mathematics.

13844 ■ Greater Cincinnati Daylily and Hosta Society (GCDHS)
8497 Wetherfield Ln.
Cincinnati, OH 45236
Ph: (513)791-1311
E-mail: lilyman@fuse.net
URL: http://www.gcdhs.org/index.html
Contact: JR Blanton, Pres.
Local.

13845 ■ Greater Cincinnati Gas Dealers
3410 Glenway Ave.
Cincinnati, OH 45205
Ph: (513)921-3182
Contact: Mike Kunnen, Exec. Officer
Local.

13846 ■ Greater Cincinnati Golf Association (GCGA)
9200 Montgomery Rd., Ste.24B
Cincinnati, OH 45242
Ph: (513)522-4444
Fax: (513)521-4242
E-mail: gcga@gcga.org
URL: http://www.gcga.org
Contact: John T. Reis, Exec.Dir.
Local. Affiliated With: International Association of Golf Administrators.

13847 ■ Greater Cincinnati Golf Course Superintendents Association of America (GCSAA)
PO Box 45467
Cincinnati, OH 45242
Ph: (513)791-3163
E-mail: information@gcgcsa.org
URL: http://www.gcgcsa.org
Contact: John Lavelle, Exec. Administrator
Founded: 1931. **Local.** Represents the interests of golf course superintendents. Advances members' profession for career success. Enhances the enjoyment, growth and vitality in the game of golf. Educates members concerning efficient and economical management of golf courses. **Affiliated With:** Golf Course Superintendents Association of America.

13848 ■ Greater Cincinnati Health Council (GCHC)
2100 Sherman Ave., Ste.100
Cincinnati, OH 45212
Ph: (513)531-0200
Fax: (513)531-0278
E-mail: rdelewski@gchc.org
URL: http://www.gchc.org
Contact: Lynn Olman, Pres.
Membership Dues: business, $400 • non-profit organization, $200. **Regional.** Cooperates and coordinates with hospitals and other providers of health care in Southwestern Ohio, Northern Kentucky and Southern Indiana in order to ensure high quality patient care.

13849 ■ Greater Cincinnati Junior Chamber Foundation
PO Box 36444
Cincinnati, OH 45236-0444
Ph: (513)956-7704
E-mail: info@cincinnatijaycees.org
URL: http://www.cincinnatijaycees.org
Contact: Steve Miller, Pres.
Founded: 1999. **Members:** 100. **Budget:** $5,000. **Local.** Exists to support the mission and membership needs of the Greater Cincinnati Jaycees, including the communities in the Greater Cincinnati area.

13850 ■ Greater Cincinnati Mortgage Bankers Association
GMAC Mortgage Corp.
8044 Montgomery Rd., Ste.235
Cincinnati, OH 45236

Ph: (513)985-3000
Free: (888)453-4622
E-mail: trey.budke@gmacmc.com
URL: http://www.greatercincinnatimba.com
Contact: Trey Budke, Pres.
Local. Promotes fair and ethical lending practices and fosters professional excellence among real estate finance employees. Seeks to create an environment that enables members to invest in communities and achieve their business objectives. **Affiliated With:** Mortgage Bankers Association.

13851 ■ Greater Cincinnati and Northern Kentucky African-American Chamber of Commerce (GCNKAACC)
2945 Gilbert Ave.
Cincinnati, OH 45206
Ph: (513)751-9900
Fax: (513)751-9100
Free: (877)810-0245
E-mail: info@gcaacc.com
URL: http://www.gcaacc.com
Contact: Clarence R. McGill Sr., Chm.
Founded: 1996. **Members:** 700. **Membership Dues:** business (add $10/employee over 100), $200-$1,000 (annual) • non-profit, $250 (annual) • student, $20 (annual) • supporting - friend of the chamber, $25 (annual) • supporting - advocate of the chamber, $50 (annual) • supporting - ambassador of the chamber, $100 (annual). **Local**. Works to identify new market opportunities. Improves access to capital and economic growth for established and emerging African-American businesses. **Computer Services:** database, information on business members. **Programs:** Around the Nati; Chamber Moment; Chamber Speaks; ChamberNet.

13852 ■ Greater Cincinnati Orchid Society
c/o Janice Yates
4110 Rose Hill Ave.
Cincinnati, OH 45229-1527
Ph: (513)475-9771
E-mail: jyates11@earthlink.net
URL: National Affiliate–www.orchidweb.org
Contact: Janice Yates, Contact
Local. Professional growers, botanists, hobbyists, and others interested in extending the knowledge, production, use, and appreciation of orchids. **Affiliated With:** American Orchid Society.

13853 ■ Greater Cincinnati St. Bernard Club
c/o Melissa Koch, Sec.
2799 Pickmeier Ln.
Cincinnati, OH 45211
Ph: (513)661-3827
URL: National Affiliate–www.saintbernardclub.org
Contact: Melissa Koch, Sec.
Local. **Affiliated With:** Saint Bernard Club of America.

13854 ■ Greater Cincinnati Tall Stacks Commission
c/o Joe Warkany, Managing Dir.
PO Box 30435
Cincinnati, OH 45202
Ph: (513)721-0104
Fax: (513)639-2362
E-mail: info@tallstacks.com
URL: http://www.tallstacks.com
Local.

13855 ■ Greater Cincinnati Television Educational Foundation
1223 Central Pkwy.
Cincinnati, OH 45214-2890
Ph: (513)381-4033
E-mail: comments@cetconnect.org
URL: http://www.wcet.org
Contact: John H. Jacobs, Chm.
Local. Works to have a positive impact on teachers and the teaching process, improve student achievement, and foster a positive attitude toward and an appreciation of the arts by both students and teachers. **Telecommunication Services:** hotline, (800)808-0445. **Formerly:** (2003) Association for the Advancement of Arts Education.

13856 ■ Greater Cincinnati Venture Association
441 Vine St., Ste.300
Cincinnati, OH 45202
Ph: (513)579-3100 (513)686-2946
Fax: (513)762-3723
E-mail: info@gccc.com
URL: http://www.gccc.com
Contact: Ms. Alecia G. Jones, Program Mgr.
Membership Dues: individual, $125 (annual) • corporate, $300 (annual). **Regional**. **Telecommunication Services:** electronic mail, ajones@gcc.com.

13857 ■ Greater Cincinnati Weimaraner Club
c/o Jeni Rosen, Treas.
1725 Hudepohl Ln.
Cincinnati, OH 45231
Ph: (513)876-3231
E-mail: jeniroosen@cinci.rr.com
URL: http://cincyweimclub.org/
Contact: Bill Kuehnhold, Pres.
Local.

13858 ■ Hamilton County Board of Mental Retardation and Developmental Disabilities (HCBMR/DD)
4370 Malsbary Rd., Ste.200
Cincinnati, OH 45242
Ph: (513)794-3308 (513)794-3300
E-mail: hamcomrdd.communityrelations@hamilton-co.org
URL: http://hamilton-co.org/mrdd
Contact: Shelley F. Goering, Pres.
Local. Provides support services to people with disabilities and their families.

13859 ■ Hamilton County Chamber of Commerce (HCCC)
PO Box 42250
Cincinnati, OH 45242
Ph: (513)984-6555
Fax: (513)793-1063
E-mail: hccc@fuse.net
Contact: J. Gruber, Exec.Dir.
Founded: 1983. **Local**. Promotes business and community development in Hamilton County, OH. Sponsors seminars. **Publications:** Bulletin, periodic.

13860 ■ Hamilton County Compeer
c/o Nikki Irwin
2400 Reading Rd., Ste.412
Cincinnati, OH 45202
Ph: (513)287-8546
Fax: (513)287-8544
E-mail: nairwin@mhaswoh.org
URL: http://www.mentalhealthassn.org
Local.

13861 ■ Healthcare Financial Management Association, Southwestern Ohio Chapter
c/o Diana D. Feldman-Smith, Pres.-Elect
Adminastar Fed. Inc.
801a W 8th St.
Cincinnati, OH 45203-1606
Ph: (513)852-4236
E-mail: diana.fledman-smith@anthem.com
URL: http://www.swohfma.org
Contact: Diana D. Feldman-Smith, Pres.-Elect
Local. Provides education, analysis and guidance to healthcare finance professionals. Helps members and other individuals in advancing the financial management of health care and in improving the business performance of organizations serving the healthcare field. **Affiliated With:** Healthcare Financial Management Association.

13862 ■ High Cincinnatians Tall Club
PO Box 1811
Cincinnati, OH 45201-1811
Ph: (513)352-0281
E-mail: mail@highcincinnatians.com
URL: http://www.highcincinnatians.com
Contact: Denise McCoy, Pres.
Local. **Affiliated With:** Tall Clubs International.

13863 ■ Independent Electrical Contractors of Greater Cincinnati
c/o David Hittinger
586 Kings Run Dr.
Cincinnati, OH 45232
Ph: (513)542-0400
Fax: (513)542-0151
E-mail: dhittinger@iec-cincy.com
URL: http://www.iec-cincy.com
Contact: David Hittinger, Contact
Local. **Affiliated With:** Independent Electrical Contractors.

13864 ■ Indian Hill Historical Society (IHHS)
8100 Given Rd.
Cincinnati, OH 45243
Ph: (513)891-1873
Fax: (513)891-1873
E-mail: ihhist@one.net
URL: http://www.indianhill.org
Contact: Julie Brumleve, Administrator
Founded: 1974. **Members:** 550. **Membership Dues:** family, $45 (annual). **Staff:** 3. **Local**. Holds educational and historical programs; sponsors research. Maintains archives and local information on families, homes, and village history. **Libraries:** **Type:** open to the public. **Holdings:** 200; articles, books. **Subjects:** local history. **Formerly:** Indian Hill Historical Museum Association. **Publications:** *The Sampler*, monthly. Newsletter. **Price:** included in membership dues. **Circulation:** 600. **Conventions/Meetings:** monthly board meeting • annual meeting (exhibits) - always April • monthly meeting, with program presentation (exhibits).

13865 ■ Indian Hill Shooting Club
6053 Sebright Ct.
Cincinnati, OH 45230
Ph: (513)831-0994
URL: National Affiliate–www.mynssa.com
Local. **Affiliated With:** National Skeet Shooting Association.

13866 ■ Indian Hill Young Life
PO Box 42171
Cincinnati, OH 45242-0171
Ph: (513)791-3730
URL: http://sites.younglife.org/sites/IndianHill/default.aspx
Local. **Affiliated With:** Young Life.

13867 ■ Industrial Workers of the World - Ohio Valley
c/o Mark Damron
PO Box 42233
Cincinnati, OH 45242
E-mail: cincyiww@iww.org
URL: National Affiliate–www.iww.org
Contact: Mark Damron, Contact
Local. **Affiliated With:** Industrial Workers of the World.

13868 ■ Institute of Real Estate Management - Greater Cincinnati Chapter No. 9
1684 Nagel Rd.
Cincinnati, OH 45255
Ph: (513)388-9268
Fax: (513)388-0137
E-mail: aostigny@cinci.rr.com
URL: http://www.iremcincinnati.org
Contact: Amy Ostigny, Chapter Administrator
Local. Represents real property and asset management professionals. Works to promote professional ethics and standards in the field of property management. Strives to keep its members informed on the latest legislative activities and current industry

trends. Provides classroom training, continuing education seminars, job referral service and candidate assistance services to enhance the effectiveness and professionalism of its members. **Affiliated With:** Institute of Real Estate Management.

13869 ■ International Association of Business Communicators, Greater Cincinnati Chapter
c/o Patricia A. Frey
4801 Chapel Ridge Dr.
Cincinnati, OH 45223
Ph: (513)636-1286
E-mail: pfrey@fuse.net
URL: National Affiliate–www.iabc.com
Contact: Patricia A. Frey, Pres.
Local. Represents the interests of communication managers, public relations directors, writers, editors and audiovisual specialists. Encourages establishment of college-level programs in organizational communication. Conducts surveys on employee communication effectiveness and media trends. Conducts research in the field of communication. **Affiliated With:** International Association of Business Communicators.

13870 ■ International Brotherhood of Electrical Workers, AFL-CIO, CFL - Local Union 1347
4100 Colerain Ave.
Cincinnati, OH 45223
Ph: (513)541-6200
Fax: (513)541-2703
E-mail: ibew1347@fuse.net
URL: http://home.fuse.net/ibew1347
Contact: Kenneth Gross, Pres.
Members: 1,439. **Local**. Works to elevate the moral, intellectual and social conditions of workers. **Affiliated With:** International Brotherhood of Electrical Workers.

13871 ■ International Facility Management Association, Cincinnati
c/o Lou Miller, Pres.
4470 Hubble Rd.
Cincinnati, OH 45247
Ph: (513)404-1323
Fax: (513)741-8733
E-mail: lmiller497@aol.com
URL: http://www.ifmacincinnati.com
Contact: Lou Miller, Pres.
Founded: 1987. **Local**. **Affiliated With:** International Facility Management Association.

13872 ■ International Union, United Automobile, Aerospace and Agricultural Implement Workers of America, AFL-CIO - Local Union 863
10708 Reading Rd.
Cincinnati, OH 45241
Ph: (513)563-1252
Fax: (513)563-2903
Free: (877)305-6730
E-mail: webmaster@863uaw.org
URL: http://www.863uaw.org
Contact: Blust Phyllis, Pres.
Members: 2,660. **Local**. Seeks for the dignity and equality of the workers. Strives to provide contractors with well-trained, productive employees. **Affiliated With:** International Union, United Automobile, Aerospace and Agricultural Implement Workers of America.

13873 ■ Inventor's Council of Cincinnati
PO Box 42103
Cincinnati, OH 45242
Ph: (513)240-2870
E-mail: inventorscouncil@inventcinci.org
URL: http://www.inventcinci.org
Contact: Andrea Brady, Pres.
Local. Represents inventors' organizations and providers of services to inventors. Seeks to facilitate the development of innovation conceived by independent inventors. Provides leadership and support services to inventors and inventors' organizations. **Affiliated With:** United Inventors Association of the U.S.A.

13874 ■ Japan-America Society of Greater Cincinnati (JASGC)
300 Carew Tower
441 Vine St.
Cincinnati, OH 45202-2812
Ph: (513)579-3150
Fax: (513)579-3102
E-mail: jasgc@gccc.com
URL: http://www.cincinnatijas.com
Contact: Barry S. Myers, Exec.Dir.
Founded: 1988. **Members:** 950. **Membership Dues:** individual, $50 (annual) • corporate, $120 (annual). **Staff:** 2. **Budget:** $100,000. **Languages:** English, Japanese. **Local**. Promotes the U.S.-Japan relationship in Greater Cincinnati. **Committees:** Japanese Business Committee of Greater Cincinnati. **Affiliated With:** National Association of Japan-America Societies. **Also Known As:** Japan Society of Cincinnati. **Publications:** *Living in Greater Cincinnati* (in English and Japanese), biennial. Book. **Price:** $15.00 /year for members; $20.00 /year for nonmembers. **Advertising:** accepted. **Conventions/Meetings:** weekly meeting • monthly meeting.

13875 ■ Jewish Federation of Cincinnati
c/o Dean Richard E. Friedman, Pres.
4050 Executive Park Dr., Ste.300
Cincinnati, OH 45241
Ph: (513)985-1500
E-mail: sklebanow@jfedcin.org
URL: http://www.shalomcincy.org
Local.

13876 ■ Job Search Focus Group
c/o Randy Weaver, Pres.
1345 Grace Ave.
Cincinnati, OH 45208-2427
Ph: (513)871-0320
Fax: (513)871-3139

13877 ■ Junior League of Cincinnati (JLC)
3500 Columbia Pkwy.
Cincinnati, OH 45226
Ph: (513)871-9339
Fax: (513)871-8632
E-mail: jlcinti@aol.com
Contact: Sue Troller, Pres.
Founded: 1920. **Members:** 1,295. **Staff:** 3. **Budget:** $200,000. **Local**. Women over the age of 21. Promotes volunteerism in order to benefit the community. **Publications:** *Perspectives*, monthly. Newsletter. **Circulation:** 1,500. **Conventions/Meetings:** General Meeting - general assembly, business and training for members - 9/year; always 1st Tuesday of the month from September through May. Cincinnati, OH - Avg. Attendance: 150.

13878 ■ Juvenile Diabetes Research Foundation International, Greater Cincinnati Chapter
10901 Reed Hartman Hwy., No. 202
Cincinnati, OH 45242-3830
Ph: (513)793-3223
Fax: (513)936-5333
E-mail: cincinnati@jdrf.org
URL: http://www.jdf.org/cincinnati
Contact: Marie Uhlenbrock, Exec.Dir.
Founded: 1970. **Staff:** 5. **Local**. Strives to find a cure for diabetes and its complications through the support of research. **Affiliated With:** Juvenile Diabetes Research Foundation International.

13879 ■ Kidney Foundation of Greater Cincinnati
2200 Victory Pkwy., Ste.510
Cincinnati, OH 45206
Ph: (513)961-8105
Fax: (513)961-8120
E-mail: help@kidneycincinnati.org
URL: http://www.kidneycincinnati.org
Contact: Leslie Ostrander, Exec.Dir.
Founded: 1966. **Local**. Assists renal and transplant patients financially and provides grants for renal research.

13880 ■ Kings Young Life
PO Box 42171
Cincinnati, OH 45242-0171
Ph: (513)791-3730
URL: http://sites.younglife.org/sites/Kings/default.aspx
Local. **Affiliated With:** Young Life.

13881 ■ Korean War Veterans Association, Greater Cincinnati Chapter
c/o Robert L. McGeorge
3296 Blueacres Dr.
Cincinnati, OH 45239
Ph: (513)923-4920
E-mail: kwvmac1220@aol.com
URL: National Affiliate–www.kwva.org
Contact: Robert L. McGeorge, Contact
Local. **Affiliated With:** Korean War Veterans Association.

13882 ■ Lakota Thunderbird Youth Basketball
c/o Bob Leslie, Treas.
7442 Rodney Ct.
Cincinnati, OH 45241-1290
E-mail: rleslie@hamiltonsafe.com
URL: http://www.tbirdhoops.org
Local.

13883 ■ League of Women Voters of the Cincinnati Area (LWVCA)
103 William Howard Taft Rd.
Cincinnati, OH 45219
Ph: (513)281-8683
Fax: (513)281-8714
E-mail: lwvcincy@eos.net
URL: http://www.lwvcincinnati.org
Contact: Gail Wick, Sec.
Local. Advocates for public's participation in government matters and exerts efforts to widen people's understanding of valuable and major public policy issues. **Publications:** *The Voter*, monthly. Newsletter. Alternate Formats: online.

13884 ■ Legal Aid Society of Greater Cincinnati (LASGC)
215 E 9th St., Ste.200
Cincinnati, OH 45202
Ph: (513)241-9400
Fax: (513)241-0047
Free: (800)582-2682
E-mail: info@lascinti.org
URL: http://www.lascinti.org
Contact: Mary Asbury, Exec.Dir.
Local. Works to resolve serious legal problems of low-income people. Promotes economic stability, reduces poverty through effective legal assistance. Serves low-income residents of Hamilton, Butler, Clarmont, Warren and Brown Counties in southwest Ohio.

13885 ■ Les Chefs de Cuisine of Greater Cincinnati
4634 Laurelview Dr.
Cincinnati, OH 45244
Ph: (513)967-4067
Fax: (513)569-1467
E-mail: jkinsella@cinci.rr.com
URL: http://www.acfgc.org
Contact: John Kinsella CMC, Pres.
Local. Promotes the culinary profession and provides on-going educational training and networking for members. Provides opportunities for competition, professional recognition, and access to educational forums with other culinarians at local, regional, national, and international events.

13886 ■ Leukemia and Lymphoma Society, Southern Ohio Chapter
2300 Wall St., Ste.H
Cincinnati, OH 45212
Ph: (513)361-2100
Fax: (513)361-2109
E-mail: vanwinklej@oh-so.leukemia-lymphoma.org
URL: National Affiliate–www.leukemia-lymphoma.org
Contact: Jay E. Van Winkle, Exec.Dir.
Founded: 1979. **Staff:** 11. **Regional**. Raises funds to combat leukemia, lymphoma, Hodgkin's Disease

and myeloma through research, patient service, and public and professional education and advocacy. **Affiliated With:** Leukemia and Lymphoma Society.

13887 ■ License Beverage Association
1717 Sect. Rd., No. 201
Cincinnati, OH 45237
Ph: (513)731-0123
Local.

13888 ■ Loveland Beagle Club
c/o Frank G. Stowell, Sec.
2285 Jonathan Ct.
Cincinnati, OH 45255
Ph: (513)688-7887
E-mail: fgstow1@aol.com
URL: http://www.iwbeagles.co.uk/beagle/loveland.htm
Contact: Frank G. Stowell, Sec.
Founded: 1954. **Members:** 23. **Membership Dues:** general, $50 (annual). **Staff:** 6. **Budget:** $20,000. **Local.** Dedicated to improving the beagle breed, keeping the sport, and bettering it. Conducts work parties to farm and fill the land, provide food for and raise wild rabbits. Holds field trials and training for hounds. **Awards:** Dog of the Year. **Frequency:** annual. **Type:** recognition. **Recipient:** best trained dog. **Affiliated With:** American Kennel Club. **Conventions/Meetings:** monthly general assembly.

13889 ■ Madeira Woman's Club
7014 Miami Ave.
Cincinnati, OH 45243
E-mail: forgy@angelfire.com
URL: http://www.madeiracity.com/womansclub/index.html
Contact: Pat Foote, Contact
Local.

13890 ■ Madiera Young Life
PO Box 42171
Cincinnati, OH 45242-0171
Ph: (513)791-3730
URL: http://sites.younglife.org/sites/Madiera/default.aspx
Local. Affiliated With: Young Life.

13891 ■ Mail Systems Management Association, Ohio Valley Chapter
c/o Intrieve Inc.
PO Box 5412
Cincinnati, OH 45201-5412
Ph: (513)381-9420
Fax: (513)381-9616
URL: National Affiliate–www.msmanational.org
Contact: Donna L. Lanter, Pres.
Local. Provide a forum for people involved in the management, supervision and support of mail systems in business, industry, government and institutions. Raises the level of management prestige and esteem for managers employed in mail management.

13892 ■ Make-A-Wish Foundation of Southern Ohio
c/o Kevin Manley, Exec.Dir.
10260 Alliance Rd., Ste.200
Cincinnati, OH 45242
Ph: (513)745-9474
Fax: (513)745-9660
Free: (888)272-WISH
E-mail: southohio@makeawishohio.org
URL: http://www.makeawishohio.org
Contact: Kevin Manley, Exec.Dir.
Regional. Grants wishes to children with terminal or life-threatening illnesses, thereby providing these children and their families with special memories and a welcome respite from the daily stress of their situation. **Affiliated With:** Make-A-Wish Foundation of America.

13893 ■ Mariemont Young Life
PO Box 42171
Cincinnati, OH 45242-0171
Ph: (513)791-3730
URL: http://sites.younglife.org/sites/Mariemont/default.aspx
Local. Affiliated With: Young Life.

13894 ■ Mason Young Life
PO Box 42171
Cincinnati, OH 45242-0171
Ph: (513)791-3730
URL: http://sites.younglife.org/sites/MasonYL/default.aspx
Contact: Jason Shields, Contact
Local. Affiliated With: Young Life.

13895 ■ Mechanical Contractors Association of Cincinnati
1579 Summit Rd., Rm. 131
Cincinnati, OH 45237-1916
Ph: (513)761-5110
Fax: (513)761-5733
E-mail: rwtiemann@zoomtown.com
URL: National Affiliate–www.mcaa.org
Contact: Robert W. Tiemann, Exec.Dir.
Local. Contractors who furnish, install, and service piping systems and related equipment for heating, cooling, refrigeration, ventilating, and air conditioning systems. **Affiliated With:** Mechanical Contractors Association of America.

13896 ■ Media Heritage
c/o Michael Martini
1648 Herald Ave.
Cincinnati, OH 45207-1010
Ph: (513)458-3134
Fax: (513)745-3483
E-mail: mediaheritage@xstarnet.com
URL: http://www.mediaheritage.com
Founded: 2001. **Members:** 25. **Staff:** 3. **Budget:** $5,000. **Local.** Promotes preservation and research for researchers of broadcasting history by restoring and preserving original recordings, photographs and other memorabilia. Conducts oral histories. **Libraries: Type:** by appointment only. **Holdings:** audio recordings, books, photographs. **Subjects:** radio, television, film history.

13897 ■ Mental Health Association of Southwest Ohio
2400 Reading Rd., Ste.412
Cincinnati, OH 45202
Ph: (513)721-2910
Fax: (513)287-8544
E-mail: mha@mhaswoh.org
URL: http://www.mentalhealthassn.org
Contact: Nancy Minson, Exec.Dir.
Local. Seeks to promote mental health and prevent mental health disorders. Improves mental health of Americans through advocacy, public education, research and service. **Affiliated With:** National Mental Health Association.

13898 ■ Metro Cincinnati Amateur Softball Association
c/o Jerry Fick, Umpire-in-Chief
3016 Ambler Dr.
Cincinnati, OH 45241
Ph: (513)563-2755
E-mail: asauic@fuse.net
URL: http://www.metrocincinnati-asa.com
Contact: Jerry Fick, Umpire-in-Chief
Local. Affiliated With: Amateur Softball Association of America.

13899 ■ Metropolitan Sewer District of Greater Cincinnati (MSD-GC)
1600 Gest St.
Cincinnati, OH 45204
Ph: (513)244-5122 (513)352-4900
E-mail: michael.nalley@cincinnati-oh.gov
URL: http://www.msdgc.org
Contact: Bob Campbell, Dir.
Founded: 1968. **Local.** Takes care of wastewater removal in Hamilton County, Ohio. Serves the wastewater treatment needs of more than 800,000 customers.

13900 ■ Miami Valley Doberman Pinscher Club (MVDPC)
PO Box 62643
Cincinnati, OH 45262-0643
E-mail: mminnich@isoc.net
URL: http://www.miamivalleydpc.com
Contact: Micky Minnich, Convention Treas.
Founded: 1953. **Members:** 30. **Membership Dues:** full, $10 (annual). **Local. Affiliated With:** American Kennel Club. **Conventions/Meetings:** annual specialty show.

13901 ■ Miami Valley Orchid Society
10921 Thornview Dr.
Cincinnati, OH 45241
Ph: (513)733-9314
E-mail: rlyrrab@earthlink.net
URL: National Affiliate–www.orchidweb.org
Contact: Barry Rhinehart, Contact
Local. Professional growers, botanists, hobbyists, and others interested in extending the knowledge, production, use, and appreciation of orchids. **Affiliated With:** American Orchid Society.

13902 ■ Middletown AIFA
c/o Billy R. Fritts, Pres.
9990 Montomery Rd., No. 200
Cincinnati, OH 45242
Ph: (513)891-0777
Fax: (513)794-8741
E-mail: glen.castle@westernsouthernlife.com
URL: National Affiliate–naifa.org
Contact: Billy R. Fritts, Pres.
Local. Represents the interests of insurance and financial advisors. Advocates for a positive legislative and regulatory environment. Enhances business and professional skills of members. **Affiliated With:** National Association of Insurance and Financial Advisors.

13903 ■ Midwest Sign Association
c/o Dee Scott, CAE, CMP, Exec.Dir.
PO Box 36232
Cincinnati, OH 45236-3640
Ph: (513)984-8664
Fax: (513)984-1539

13904 ■ Milford Gun Club
PO Box 54457
Cincinnati, OH 45254
Ph: (513)248-0401
URL: http://www.milfordgunclub.com
Local. Affiliated With: National Skeet Shooting Association.

13905 ■ Milford - Young Life
PO Box 42171
Cincinnati, OH 45242-0171
Ph: (513)791-3730
URL: http://sites.younglife.org/sites/Milford/default.aspx
Local. Affiliated With: Young Life.

13906 ■ Military Officers Association of America, Greater Cincinnati Chapter
c/o Lt. Charles Kenny
8714 Weller Rd.
Cincinnati, OH 45249-2712
Ph: (513)489-2957
E-mail: ontos2@fuse.net
URL: http://www.cincymoaa.org
Contact: Lt. Charles Kenny, Pres.
Founded: 1973. **Local. Affiliated With:** Military Officers Association of America.

13907 ■ Mill Creek Watershed Council (MCWC)
One N Commerce Park Dr., Ste.222
Cincinnati, OH 45215
Ph: (513)563-8800
Fax: (513)563-8810
E-mail: nellwood@millcreekwatershed.org
URL: http://www.millcreekwatershed.org
Contact: Nancy Ellwood, Exec.Dir.
Founded: 1994. **Members:** 47. **Staff:** 1. **Budget:** $110,000. **Local. Libraries: Type:** by appointment

only. **Holdings:** 150; audiovisuals, books, photographs, reports, video recordings. **Subjects:** Mill Creek and its tributaries in the Cincinnati area. **Publications:** *Voice of the Mill Creek*, quarterly. Newsletter. **Price:** free. **Circulation:** 1,350. **Conventions/Meetings:** quarterly meeting, watershed Council - always last Friday in January, April, July, and October • annual New Realities for the Mill Creek - meeting - November • annual Outdoor Social - meeting.

13908 ■ Millcreek Valley Habitat for Humanity
420 W Wyoming Ave.
Cincinnati, OH 45215
Ph: (513)761-4687
Fax: (513)761-1334
E-mail: valleyhabitat@zoomtown.com
URL: http://www.millcreekvalleyhfh.org
Contact: Howard Runda, Pres.
Local. Affiliated With: Habitat for Humanity International.

13909 ■ Miniature Society of Cincinnati
c/o Marcine Wedig
661 Stanley Ave.
Cincinnati, OH 45226
Ph: (513)321-0278 (513)871-2823
URL: http://www.miniatures.org/states/OH.html
Contact: Marcine Wedig, Contact
Local. Affiliated With: National Association of Miniature Enthusiasts.

13910 ■ Montgomery Women's Club (MWC)
PO Box 42114
Cincinnati, OH 45242
E-mail: phylrobe@hotmail.com
URL: http://www.angelfire.com/oh3/montgomery
Contact: Suzanne Hurst, VP
Local.

13911 ■ Morgenroth Baseball
c/o Jack R. Morgenroth, Jr.
1252 Timberland Dr.
Cincinnati, OH 45215-1571
Ph: (513)771-5764
Fax: (513)771-5765
Contact: Jack Morgenroth, Contact
Founded: 1978. **Members:** 20. **Local.**

13912 ■ Mothers Against Drunk Driving, Southwestern Ohio
4015 Executive Park Dr., No. 215
Cincinnati, OH 45241
Ph: (513)769-6800
Fax: (513)769-6801
E-mail: maddswoh@fuse.net
URL: http://www.madd.org/oh/southwestern/
Contact: Andrea Rehkamp, Exec.Dir.
Founded: 1981. **Members:** 2,500. **Membership Dues:** individual, $20 (annual) • family, $40 (annual) • business, $150 (annual). **Local.** Victims of drunk driving crashes; concerned citizens. Encourages citizen participation in working towards reform of the drunk driving problem and the prevention of underage drinking. Acts as the voice of victims of drunk driving crashes by speaking on their behalf to communities, businesses, and educational groups. **Affiliated With:** Mothers Against Drunk Driving.

13913 ■ Nation Council for GeoCosmic Research, Ohio Valley Chapter
7485 Mountfort Ct.
Cincinnati, OH 45244
Ph: (513)231-4494
Fax: (513)231-4142
E-mail: kmunic8@aol.com
URL: National Affiliate–www.geocosmic.org
Contact: Ann Wood Schlesinger PhD, Contact
Local. Raises the standards of astrological education and research. Works to foster and publish research of a geocosmic nature and to pursue educational programs in various interdisciplinary fields related to geocosmic studies. **Affiliated With:** National Council for GeoCosmic Research.

13914 ■ National Academy of Television Arts and Sciences, Ohio Valley
9695 Sycamore Trace Ct.
Cincinnati, OH 45242
Ph: (513)793-9331
E-mail: ovnatas@fuse.net
URL: http://www.ohiovalleyemmy.org
Contact: Peg Ashbrock, Administrator
Founded: 1962. **Local.** Promotes excellence in broadcasting. Inspires the next generation of broadcast journalists. Educates television viewers. **Affiliated With:** National Academy of Television Arts and Sciences. **Publications:** Newsletter.

13915 ■ National Active and Retired Federal Employees Association - Campbell County 1760
8101 Sagamore Dr.
Cincinnati, OH 45236-2319
Ph: (513)793-5985
URL: National Affiliate–www.narfe.org
Contact: Barbara J. Shepherd, Contact
Local. Protects the retirement future of employees through education. Informs members on issues affecting the retirement. **Affiliated With:** National Association of Retired Federal Employees.

13916 ■ National Active and Retired Federal Employees Association - Cincinnati 265
6637 Iris Ave.
Cincinnati, OH 45213-1141
Ph: (513)351-2131
URL: National Affiliate–www.narfe.org
Contact: Nellie L. Hope, Contact
Local. Protects the retirement future of employees through education. Informs members on issues affecting the retirement. **Affiliated With:** National Association of Retired Federal Employees.

13917 ■ National Association of Black Journalists - Cincinnati Chapter
PO Box 14566
Cincinnati, OH 45250-0566
Ph: (513)421-0119
E-mail: tiana_rollinson@yahoo.com
URL: National Affiliate–www.nabj.org
Contact: Tiana Rollinson, Pres.
Local. Advocates the rights of black journalists. Provides informational and training services and professional development to black journalists and to the general public. **Affiliated With:** National Association of Black Journalists.

13918 ■ National Association of Church Business Administration, Greater Cincinnati Chapter
c/o Susan H. Siemer, Pres.
Armstrong Chapel UMC
5125 Drake Rd.
Cincinnati, OH 45243
Ph: (513)561-4220
Fax: (513)561-3062
E-mail: ssiemer@armstrongchapel.org
URL: http://cincinnati.nacba.net
Contact: Susan H. Siemer, Pres.
Membership Dues: active, $35 (annual) • associate, affiliate, $25 (annual) • business, $75 (annual). **Local. Affiliated With:** National Association of Church Business Administration.

13919 ■ National Association of Credit Managers Ohio, Cincinnati
38 Triangle Park Dr., Ste.3818
Cincinnati, OH 45246
Ph: (513)772-8200
Fax: (513)326-2040
URL: National Affiliate–www.nacm.org
Local. Affiliated With: National Association of Credit Management.

13920 ■ National Association of Home Builders of the U.S., Home Builders Association of Greater Cincinnati
415 Glensprings Dr.
Cincinnati, OH 45246-2357
Ph: (513)851-6300
Fax: (513)589-3211
E-mail: jmamone@cincybuilders.com
URL: http://www.cincybuilders.com
Contact: Mr. John Mamone CAE, Exec.Dir.
Founded: 1934. **Members:** 1,300. **Staff:** 12. **Budget:** $3,300,000. **Local.** Single and multifamily home builders, commercial builders, and others associated with the building industry. **Affiliated With:** National Association of Home Builders.

13921 ■ National Association of Industrial and Office Properties, Cincinnati-Northern Kentucky Chapter
c/o Amy Ostigny
1684 Nagel Rd.
Cincinnati, OH 45255-2546
Ph: (513)388-9268
Fax: (513)388-0137
E-mail: aostigny@cinci.rr.com
URL: National Affiliate–www.naiop.org
Contact: Ms. Amy Ostigny, Exec.Dir.
Local. Represents the interests of developers and owners of industrial, office and related commercial estate. Provides communication, networking, business opportunities and a forum to its members. Promotes effective public policy to create, protect and enhance property values. **Affiliated With:** National Association of Industrial and Office Properties. **Publications:** Newsletter, periodic. Alternate Formats: online.

13922 ■ National Association of Investors Corporation, OKI Tri-State Chapter
c/o Yolanda Moschella, Dir.
PO Box 19214
Cincinnati, OH 45219
Ph: (513)921-6188
E-mail: ymoschella@cinci.rr.com
URL: http://better-investing.org/chapter/okitri
Contact: Yolanda Moschella, Dir.
Regional. Teaches individuals how to become successful strategic long-term investors. Provides highly focused learning resources and investment tools that empower individuals to become better investors. **Affiliated With:** National Association of Investors Corporation.

13923 ■ National Association of Pastoral Musicians, Cincinnati Chapter
c/o Mr. Brian Bisig
11144 Spinner Ave.
Cincinnati, OH 45241-2632
Ph: (513)563-6377
E-mail: bisig_b@fuse.net
URL: National Affiliate–www.npm.org
Contact: Mr. Brian Bisig, Contact
Founded: 1996. **Members:** 100. **Local.** Fosters the art of musical liturgy. Serves the Catholic Church in the United States as musicians, clergy, liturgists, and other leaders of prayer. **Affiliated With:** National Association of Pastoral Musicians.

13924 ■ National Corvette Restorers Society, Queen City Chapter (NCRS QCC)
1122 Fuller St.
Cincinnati, OH 45202
Ph: (513)665-4607
E-mail: kjmeier@fuse.net
URL: http://www.ncrs.org/qc
Contact: Kurt Meier, Chm.
Founded: 1993. **Members:** 150. **Membership Dues:** $20 (annual). **Local.** Involved itself with the core principle that restoration undertaken as General Motors is paramount. Involved in monthly tech sessions, the Fall Meet and the annual swap meet. However, restoration should be fun and the Queen City Chapter has vast experience in that area as well. Monthly meetings, always with food, an annual Christmas

party, picnic runs and trips which concern Corvettes. **Affiliated With:** National Corvette Restorers Society.

13925 ■ National Electrical Contractors Association, Cincinnati (NECA)
7815 Cooper Rd., Ste.B
Cincinnati, OH 45242
Ph: (513)791-8777
Fax: (513)791-7738
E-mail: ctineca@cinci.rr.com
URL: http://ctineca.org
Contact: Don Bolling, Exec.Dir.
Founded: 1938. **Local**. Works to promote higher standards, quality workmanship and training for a skilled workforce. **Affiliated With:** National Electrical Contractors Association.

13926 ■ National Forum for Black Public Administrators, Cincinnati Chapter
c/o Bernice L. Walker, Dir., Small Business Dev.
138 E Court St., Rm. 607
Cincinnati, OH 45202-1226
Ph: (513)946-4323
Fax: (513)946-4330
E-mail: bernice.walker@hamilton-co.org
URL: National Affiliate–www.nfbpa.org
Contact: Bernice L. Walker, Dir., Small Business Dev.
Local. Works to promote, strengthen and expand the role of Blacks in public administration. Seeks to focus the influence of Black administrators toward building and maintaining viable communities. Develops specialized training programs for managers and executives. Works to further communication among Black public, private and academic institutions. Addresses issues that affect the administrative capacity of Black managers. **Affiliated With:** National Forum for Black Public Administrators.

13927 ■ National Human Resources Association, Cincinnati Chapter
c/o Patricia Hakes, Pres.
Westin Hotel
21 E 5th St.
Cincinnati, OH 45202
Ph: (513)852-2716
Fax: (513)852-2733
E-mail: patricia.hakes@westin.com
URL: National Affiliate–www.humanresources.org
Contact: Patricia Hakes, Pres.
Local. Seeks to advance the development of human resource professionals. Offers programs and services to interns and executives across the country. Provides networking forums and professional development for members.

13928 ■ National Multiple Sclerosis Society, Ohio Valley Chapter
c/o Linda Stetson, Chapter Pres.
4460 Lake Forest Dr., Ste.236
Cincinnati, OH 45242
Ph: (513)769-4400
Fax: (513)769-6019
E-mail: info@ohg.nmss.org
URL: http://nmss.org
Contact: Linda Stetson, Chapter Pres.
Staff: 13. **Local Groups:** 27. **Regional**. Stimulates, supports, and coordinates research into the cause, treatment, and cure of multiple sclerosis; provides services for persons with MS and related diseases and their families. **Affiliated With:** National Multiple Sclerosis Society.

13929 ■ National Organization of Black Law Enforcement Executives, Greater Cincinnati Chapter
c/o Gregory C. Hutchins
PO Box 1773
Cincinnati, OH 45202
Ph: (513)564-7562
Fax: (513)564-7587
E-mail: greg_c_hutchins@ohsp.uscourts.gov
URL: National Affiliate–www.noblenational.org
Contact: Gregory C. Hutchins, Contact
Local. **Affiliated With:** National Organization of Black Law Enforcement Executives.

13930 ■ National Organization for Women - Cincinnati
PO Box 9422
Cincinnati, OH 45209
Ph: (513)295-8969
E-mail: info@now-cincinnati.org
URL: http://www.now-cincinnati.org
Contact: Pamela Daniels, Pres.
Local. **Affiliated With:** National Organization for Women.

13931 ■ National Postal Mail Handlers Union, Local 304
6509 Montgomery Rd.
Cincinnati, OH 45213
Ph: (513)351-5501
Fax: (513)351-5501
URL: http://www.local304.com
Contact: Donald W Gephart, Treas.
Members: 3,080. **Regional**. **Affiliated With:** National Postal Mail Handlers Union.

13932 ■ National Society of Black Engineers - University of Cincinnati
PO Box 210018
Cincinnati, OH 45221-0018
E-mail: engn-eboard@listserv.uc.edu
URL: http://www.nsbe.uc.edu/nsbe
Contact: Michael J. Alexander, Pres.
Local. Strives to increase the number of culturally responsible Black engineers who excel academically, succeed professionally and positively impact the community. **Affiliated With:** National Society of Black Engineers.

13933 ■ National Technical Honor Society - Diamond Oaks - Ohio
6375 Harrison Ave.
Cincinnati, OH 45247
Ph: (513)574-1300
Fax: (513)574-3953
E-mail: brueninj@greatoaks.com
URL: http://www.greatoaks.com
Contact: Dave Buchwalter, Contact
Local.

13934 ■ Ohio Association for Infant Mental Health (OAIMH)
c/o Kathryn Merrilees, Pres.
512 Maxwell Ave.
Cincinnati, OH 45219
Ph: (812)926-3439
E-mail: cc44@ucmail.uc.edu
URL: http://www.oaimh.org
Contact: Kathryn Merrilees, Pres.
State. Provides public information on infant mental health. Advocates research on mental disorders that affect infants. Promotes the optimal development of infants and the treatment of mental disorders in the child's early years. **Affiliated With:** World Association for Infant Mental Health.

13935 ■ Ohio Bluebird Society
c/o Bernie Daniel
9211 Solon Dr.
Cincinnati, OH 45242
E-mail: ohbluebird@sssnet.com
URL: National Affiliate–www.nabluebirdsociety.org
Contact: Bernie Daniel, Contact
State. **Affiliated With:** North American Bluebird Society.

13936 ■ Ohio District Amateur Athletic Union
c/o Bill Kroth, Sec.
8047 New Brunswick Dr.
Cincinnati, OH 45241
Ph: (513)779-2709 (513)983-6708
Fax: (513)779-9640
E-mail: billkroth@aol.com
URL: http://www.ohioaau.org
Contact: Bill Kroth, Sec.
State. **Affiliated With:** Amateur Athletic Union.

13937 ■ Ohio Federation of Families for Children's Mental Health - Summit Behavioral Health
1101 Summit Rd.
Cincinnati, OH 45237
Ph: (513)948-3077
Fax: (513)761-6030
E-mail: terregarner@hotmail.com
URL: National Affiliate–www.ffcmh.org
Contact: Terre Garner, Dir.
Local. **Affiliated With:** Federation of Families for Children's Mental Health.

13938 ■ Ohio Genealogical Society, Hamilton County Chapter (OGSHC)
PO Box 15865
Cincinnati, OH 45215-0865
Ph: (513)956-7078
E-mail: hcgsohio@aol.com
URL: http://members.aol.com/ogshc
Contact: Kenny R. Burck, Pres.
Founded: 1973. **Members:** 1,250. **Membership Dues:** regular, $15 (annual) • sustaining, $20 (annual) • life-single, memorial-single, $150 • life-couple, memorial couple, $175. **Budget:** $35,000. **Local Groups:** 4. **Local**. Works to provide programs and resources for members to increase their knowledge of genealogy and family history. **Special Interest Groups:** African-American; Computer; German; Irish. **Affiliated With:** Ohio Genealogical Society. **Publications:** *The Gazette*, quarterly. Newsletter. Features 4 pages of news and information. **Price:** included in membership dues. **Circulation:** 1,600 • *The Tracer*, quarterly. Magazine. Features 32 pages of news and information of interest to the members. **Price:** included in membership dues; $2.00 for each back issue. **Circulation:** 1,600. **Conventions/Meetings:** monthly meeting, programs - Jan., Feb., March, April, May, Sept., Oct., and Nov. in various locations throughout the county.

13939 ■ Ohio Health Care Association, District 1
c/o Michael Scharfenberger, Chm.
Nursing Care Mgt.
7265 Kenwood Rd., Ste.300
Cincinnati, OH 45236
Ph: (513)793-8804
Fax: (513)793-8799
E-mail: mscharfenberger@fuse.net
URL: http://www.ohca.org
Contact: Michael Scharfenberger, Chm.
Local. Promotes professionalism and ethical behavior of individuals providing long-term care delivery for patients and for the general public. Provides information, education and administrative tools to enhance the quality of long-term care. Improves the standards of service and administration of member nursing homes. **Affiliated With:** American Health Care Association.

13940 ■ Ohio-Kentucky-Indiana Regional Council of Governments (OKI)
720 E Pete Rose Way, Ste.420
Cincinnati, OH 45202
Ph: (513)621-6300 (513)621-7063
Fax: (513)621-9325
E-mail: plan@oki.org
URL: http://www.oki.org
Contact: Mark R. Policinski, Exec.Dir.
Regional.

13941 ■ Ohio Northern Kentucky Indiana Vascular Technologists (ONKIVT)
2948 Cleinview Ave.
Cincinnati, OH 45206

Ph: (513)585-1439
Fax: (513)585-3068
E-mail: parlatdp@healthall.com
URL: National Affiliate–www.svunet.org
Contact: David P. Parlato BA, Contact
Regional. Represents vascular technologists and individuals in the field of noninvasive vascular technology. Seeks to establish an information clearinghouse providing reference and assistance in matters relating to noninvasive vascular technology. Facilitates cooperation among noninvasive vascular facilities and other health professions. Provides continuing education for individuals in the field. Represents members on various regulatory issues. **Affiliated With:** Society for Vascular Ultrasound.

13942 ■ Ohio Rifle and Pistol Association
c/o Alan Joseph
PO Box 43083
Cincinnati, OH 45243-0083
Ph: (513)891-1325
E-mail: capito@lek.net
URL: http://www.orpa.net
Contact: G. Martin Capito, Pres.
Founded: 1934. **Members:** 3,800. **State**. The association is composed of rifle and pistol owners in Ohio who promotes firearm safety, education and marksmanship. It also encourages and creates a public sentiment in favor of marksmanship, not only as a clean and wholesome sport, but also as an essential and vital means of national defense. Activities include an annual marksmanship clinic and Junior Olympic Rifle and Pistol Championship. **Publications:** *Gunsmoke*, bimonthly. Newsletter.

13943 ■ Ohio River Valley Water Sanitation Commission (ORSANCO)
5735 Kellogg Ave.
Cincinnati, OH 45228
Ph: (513)231-7719
Fax: (513)231-7761
E-mail: jison@orsanco.org
URL: http://www.orsanco.org
Contact: Ms. Jeanne Ison, Public Information Mgr.
Founded: 1948. **Staff:** 28. **State Groups:** 8. **Nonmembership**. **Regional**. Seeks to improve the water quality of Ohio River Basin by addressing programs and conducting special studies to ensure proper water sanitation.

13944 ■ Ohio Society of Certified Public Accountants - Cincinnati Chapter
c/o Eric Roth, CPA
Fifth Third Bank
38 Fountain Sq. Plz.
Cincinnati, OH 45263
Ph: (513)534-8912
Fax: (513)599-6249
E-mail: eric.roth@53.com
Contact: Eric Roth, Contact

13945 ■ Ohio Thoroughbred Breeders and Owners (OTBO)
6024 Harrison Ave., No. 13
Cincinnati, OH 45248
Ph: (513)574-5888 (513)574-0440
Fax: (513)574-2313
E-mail: gb.otbo@fuse.net
URL: http://www.otbo.com
Contact: G. Babst, Exec.Dir.
Founded: 1956. **Members:** 575. **Membership Dues:** regular, $40 (annual) • regular-family (2 people), $75 (annual) • gold single, $100 (annual) • gold family, $125 (annual). **Staff:** 1. **State**. **Awards:** Hall of Fame. **Frequency:** annual. **Type:** trophy. **Recipient:** for record and performance throughout the year • Horse of the Year & Divisional Champions. **Frequency:** annual. **Type:** trophy. **Recipient:** for record and performance throughout the year • Turfman of the Year. **Frequency:** annual. **Type:** trophy. **Recipient:** for record and performance throughout the year. **Committees:** Breeding; ByLaws/Finance; Legislative; Publicity; Race. **Publications:** *Stallion Register*, annual. Directory. Contains listings of stallion, farm, and supplier. **Circulation:** 1,100. **Advertising:** accepted.

13946 ■ Ohio Valley Business Travel Association (OVBTA)
PO Box 1113
Cincinnati, OH 45201-1113
Ph: (812)206-5200
E-mail: doug.payne@atswtstravel.com
URL: http://www.ovbta.org
Contact: Doug Payne CCTE, Pres.
Local. Represents travel managers and providers. Promotes the value of the travel manager in meeting corporate travel needs and financial goals. Cultivates a positive public image of the corporate travel industry. Protects the interests of members and their corporations in legislative and regulatory matters. Promotes safety, security, efficiency and quality travel. Provides a forum for the exchange of information and ideas among members. **Affiliated With:** National Business Travel Association.

13947 ■ Ohio Valley Section of the American Industrial Hygiene Association
c/o Joshua Harney, MS, Sec.
Cincinnati Children's Hosp. Medical Ctr.
3333 Burnet Ave., MCL 9007
Cincinnati, OH 45229
Ph: (513)636-7286
Fax: (513)636-2123
E-mail: josh.harney@cchmc.org
URL: http://www.aiha.org/localsections/html/ohiovalley/ohiovalley.htm
Contact: Joshua Harney MS, Sec.
Regional. Represents the interests of occupational and environmental health professionals practicing in industry, government, labor and academic institutions and independent organizations. Promotes the certification of industrial hygienists. Administers educational programs for environmental health and safety professionals. **Affiliated With:** American Industrial Hygiene Association.

13948 ■ Old Orchard Unit Owners Association
499 Mcintosh Dr.
Cincinnati, OH 45255
Ph: (513)528-2086
Local.

13949 ■ Over-The-Rhine Chamber of Commerce (OTRCC)
222 E 14th St.
Cincinnati, OH 45202-7309
Ph: (513)241-2690
Fax: (513)241-6770
E-mail: otrchamber@zoomtown.com
URL: http://www.otrchamber.com
Contact: Mario San Marco, Chm.
Founded: 1985. **Membership Dues:** business (based on number of employees), $100-$1,500 (annual) • nonprofit (1-9 employees), $75 (annual) • individual, $50 (annual). **Local**. Promotes business and community development in Over-the-Rhine, OH area. **Awards:** Architecture Award. **Frequency:** annual. **Type:** recognition • Arts Organization of the Year. **Frequency:** annual. **Type:** recognition • Business of the Year. **Frequency:** annual. **Type:** recognition • Chairman's Award. **Frequency:** annual. **Type:** recognition • Entrepreneur of the Year. **Frequency:** annual. **Type:** recognition • Individual Contribution Award. **Frequency:** annual. **Type:** recognition • New Business of the Year. **Frequency:** annual. **Type:** recognition • President's Award. **Frequency:** annual. **Type:** recognition. **Committees:** Events; Issues; Marketing and Public Relations; Safe and Clean.

13950 ■ Paper, Allied-Industrial, Chemical and Energy Workers International Union, AFL-CIO, CLC - Local Union 609
PO Box 36483
Cincinnati, OH 45254-1031
E-mail: pace50609@yahoo.com
URL: http://pace50609.homestead.com/pace50609.html
Contact: Andy Parker, Financial Sec.-Treas.
Members: 74. **Local**. **Affiliated With:** Pace International Union.

13951 ■ Parents And Children for Equality (PACE)
c/o Kevin O'Brien, Founder/Exec.Dir.
PO Box 8805
Cincinnati, OH 45208-0805
Ph: (513)624-7223
Fax: (513)624-7223
E-mail: cincinnati@pacegroup.org
URL: http://www.pacegroup.org
Contact: Kevin O'Brien, Founder/Exec.Dir.
Founded: 1995. **Members:** 1,000. **Membership Dues:** family/single, $20 (annual). **Staff:** 5. **Budget:** $50,000. **Regional Groups:** 2. **State Groups:** 5. **Local Groups:** 1. **State**. Provides educational and advocacy support to parents and children of divorced and never-married families. **Affiliated With:** Children's Rights Council. **Publications:** Newsletter, monthly. Distributed for educational purposes only. **Advertising:** accepted. **Conventions/Meetings:** monthly meeting.

13952 ■ Parents for Public Schools, Cincinnati Chapter
The Harriet Beacher Stowe House
2950 Gilbert Ave.
Cincinnati, OH 45206
Ph: (513)751-5437
Fax: (513)751-5435
URL: http://www.parents4publicschools.com/Cincinnati
Contact: Randie Marsh, Office Administrator
Local.

13953 ■ Parents Television Council - Cincinnati, Ohio Chapter
c/o Patricia Behne, Dir.
PO Box 58341
Cincinnati, OH 45258
Free: (800)297-2952
E-mail: cincinnatichapter@parentstv.org
URL: National Affiliate–www.parentstv.org
Contact: Patricia Behne, Dir.
Local.

13954 ■ Parents Without Partners, Cincinnati Chapter 203
PO Box 141076
Cincinnati, OH 45250-1076
Ph: (513)241-4744
E-mail: mbr203@mpowernet.com
URL: http://www.users.mpowernet.com/~pwp203
Founded: 1966. **Members:** 400. **Membership Dues:** single, $40 (annual). **Regional**. Custodial and non-custodial parents who are single by reason of widowhood, divorce, separation, or otherwise. Works to alleviate the problems of single parents in relation to the welfare and upbringing of their children and the acceptance into the general social order of single parents and their children. **Affiliated With:** Parents Without Partners. **Formerly:** (2005) Parents Without Partners, Cincinnati. **Publications:** Newsletter, monthly. **Price:** included in membership dues.

13955 ■ Partners in Community and Collaboration
c/o Dr. Lionel G. Walker
2815 Melrose Ave.
Cincinnati, OH 45206-1213
Contact: Dr. Robert Peoples, Contact
Local.

13956 ■ People Working Cooperatively - serving the Greater Cincinnati Community
c/o Kathy Campbell
4612 Paddock Rd.
Cincinnati, OH 45229
Ph: (513)351-7921 (859)331-1991
Fax: (513)351-2734
E-mail: campbellk@pwchomerepairs.org
URL: http://www.pwchomerepairs.org
Contact: Mr. Jock Pitts, Pres.
Staff: 65. **Nonmembership**. **Regional**. Performs essential repairs and services so that low-income ho-

meowners can remain in their homes, living independently in a safe, sound environment. **Publications:** Newsletter.

13957 ■ Phi Theta Kappa - Beta Gamma Sigma Chapter
c/o Tom Kober
3520 Central Pkwy.
Cincinnati, OH 45223
Ph: (513)569-1680
E-mail: member.services@ptk.org
URL: http://www.ptk.org/directories/chapters/OH/20700-1.htm
Contact: Tom Kober, Advisor
Local. Affiliated With: Phi Theta Kappa, International Honor Society.

13958 ■ Phi Theta Kappa - Upsilon Psi Chapter
c/o Eugene Kramer
Raymond Walter Coll.
9555 Plainfield Rd.
Cincinnati, OH 45236-1096
Ph: (513)936-7139
E-mail: eugene.f.kramer@uc.edu
URL: http://www.ptk.org/directories/chapters/OH/311-1.htm
Contact: Eugene Kramer, Advisor
Local. Affiliated With: Phi Theta Kappa, International Honor Society.

13959 ■ Pioneers Midwest Chapter 128
c/o Mark S. Williams
525 Vine St., Rm. 406
Cincinnati, OH 45202
Ph: (513)277-4545
Fax: (513)277-4489
E-mail: mswilliams@att.com
URL: http://www.attpioneersmidwest.org
Contact: Kattie M. Russey-Starnes, Treas.
Regional. Affiliated With: TelecomPioneers.

13960 ■ Planned Parenthood of Southwest Ohio Region
2314 Auburn Ave.
Cincinnati, OH 45219
Ph: (513)721-7635
Fax: (513)721-2313
URL: National Affiliate–www.plannedparenthood.org
Local. Affiliated With: Planned Parenthood Federation of America.

13961 ■ Product Development and Management Association, Tri-State
c/o Joe Kormos, Pres.
Innovative Development Associates
11977 Harbortown Dr.
Cincinnati, OH 45249
Ph: (513)683-1911
E-mail: joe@product-masters.com
URL: http://www.tristatepdma.org
Contact: Joe Kormos, Pres.
Local. Aims to build a community of practitioners, academics and service providers that share experiences and knowledge of the principles, practices and processes of effective product innovation. **Affiliated With:** Product Development and Management Association.

13962 ■ Professional Grounds Management Society, Greater Cincinnati
c/o Jennifer Gulick, Pres.
962 Summit Ave.
Cincinnati, OH 45246
Ph: (513)772-3159
Fax: (513)772-1297
E-mail: jgulick@davey.com
URL: National Affiliate–www.pgms.org
Contact: Jennifer Gulick, Pres.
Regional. Affiliated With: Professional Grounds Management Society.

13963 ■ Psi Chi, National Honor Society in Psychology - College of Mount St. Joseph
c/o Dept. of Psychology
5701 Delhi Rd.
Cincinnati, OH 45233-1670
Ph: (513)244-4271 (513)244-4862
Fax: (513)244-4222
E-mail: jim_bodle@mail.msj.edu
URL: http://www.psichi.org/chapters/info.asp?chapter_id=923
Contact: Jim Bodle PhD, Advisor
Local.

13964 ■ Psi Chi, National Honor Society in Psychology - Xavier University
c/o Dept. of Psychology
Elet Hall
3800 Victory Pkwy.
Cincinnati, OH 45207-6511
Ph: (513)745-3533 (513)745-3170
Fax: (513)745-3327
E-mail: mullins@xavier.edu
URL: http://www.psichi.org/chapters/info.asp?chapter_id=171
Contact: Morell Mullins PhD, Advisor
Local.

13965 ■ Public Allies Cincinnati
c/o David Wilke
2905 Burnet Ave.
Cincinnati, OH 45219
Ph: (513)559-1300
Fax: (513)559-1333
E-mail: davidwilke@publicallies.org
URL: http://www.publicallies.org
Contact: Dayle Deardurff, Exec.Dir.
Local.

13966 ■ Public Relations Society of America, Cincinnati
c/o Anna Campbell, Chapter Administrator
PO Box 43242
Cincinnati, OH 45243
Ph: (513)792-0402
Fax: (513)984-9191
E-mail: acampbell@fuse.net
URL: http://www.cincinnatiprsa.org
Contact: Carrie Krysanick APR, Board Member/Pres.
Local. Affiliated With: Public Relations Society of America.

13967 ■ Puli Club of America (PCA)
5032 Winton Ridge Ln.
Cincinnati, OH 45232
E-mail: cordonblue1@msn.com
URL: http://www.puliclub.org
Contact: Michael Rohe, Corresponding Sec.
State. Affiliated With: American Kennel Club.

13968 ■ Puppeteers of America - Cincinnati Area Puppetry Guild
c/o Linda Mason, Pres.
7014 Martha Rd.
Cincinnati, OH 45230
Ph: (513)231-0655
E-mail: bill.mason.how9@statefarm.com
URL: http://www.puppetrevolution.com/capg
Contact: Linda Mason, Pres.
Local.

13969 ■ Puppeteers of America - Great Lakes Region
c/o Aretta Baumgartner, Dir.
5097 Sumter Ave.
Cincinnati, OH 45238-3824
Ph: (513)471-2579
E-mail: hensonfan@fuse.net
URL: National Affiliate–www.puppeteers.org
Contact: Aretta Baumgartner, Dir.
Regional.

13970 ■ Queen City Figure Skating Club (QCFSC)
8294 Glenmill Ct.
Cincinnati, OH 45249
E-mail: dwett619@aol.com
URL: http://www.queencityfsc.com
Contact: Darlene Wetterich, Pres.
Local. Provides programs to encourage participation and achievement in the sport of figure skating on ice. Defines and maintains uniform standards of skating proficiency. Organizes and sponsors competitions and exhibitions for the purpose of stimulating interest in figure skating. **Affiliated With:** United States Figure Skating Association.

13971 ■ Queen City Skywalkers
c/o Ginny Drumm
4432 Carnation Ave.
Cincinnati, OH 45238-4902
Ph: (513)471-7029
E-mail: ginnydrumm@fuse.net
URL: National Affiliate–www.ava.org
Contact: Ginny Drumm, Contact
Local. Non-competitive sports enthusiasts. **Affiliated With:** American Volkssport Association.

13972 ■ R/C Sailing Club of Cincinnati No. 217
c/o Robert Bottenhorn
6405 Edwood Ave.
Cincinnati, OH 45224
Ph: (513)681-5705
URL: http://www.rcscc.org
Contact: Robert Bottenhorn, Contact
Local.

13973 ■ Rainbows, Cincinnati
c/o Sandy Keiser, LISW, Dir.
Catholic Social Services of Southwestern Ohio
100 E 8th St.
Cincinnati, OH 45202
Ph: (513)241-7745
Fax: (513)241-4333
E-mail: commed@cssdoorway.org
URL: http://www.rainbows.org
Contact: Sandy Keiser LISW, Dir.
Local Groups: 12. **Local.** Provides peer support for children and adults as they go through the grief process. **Affiliated With:** RAINBOWS.

13974 ■ Red River Valley Fighter Pilot Association - Cincinnati, Ohio
454 Fairview Pl.
Cincinnati, OH 45219
E-mail: joerr@eos.net
URL: National Affiliate–www.river-rats.org
Contact: Joe Richardson, Contact
Local. Affiliated With: Red River Valley Fighter Pilots Association.

13975 ■ Reserve Officers Association - Department of Ohio
c/o RADM Jan Timothy Riker, Pres.
6341 Parkman Pl.
Cincinnati, OH 45213
Ph: (513)631-6446 (513)621-2888
E-mail: jtriker@erlaw.org
URL: http://www.roa.org/oh
Contact: RADM Jan Timothy Riker, Pres.
State. Promotes and supports the development and execution of a military policy for the United States. Provides professional development seminars, workshops and programs for its members. **Affiliated With:** Reserve Officers Association of the United States.

13976 ■ Risk and Insurance Management Society, Ohio River Valley Chapter
c/o Jeffrey Meek
400 Broadway
Cincinnati, OH 45202

Ph: (513)357-4078
Fax: (513)629-1695
E-mail: jeff.meek@wslife.com
URL: http://cincinnati.rims.org
Contact: Melissa Bowman-Miller, Pres.
Local. Seeks to promote the discipline of risk management and enhance the image of professional risk managers. Fosters the educational and professional development of risk managers and others involved in the risk management and insurance industry. **Affiliated With:** Risk and Insurance Management Society.

13977 ■ River Dojo
2233 Eastern Ave.
Cincinnati, OH 45226
URL: http://www.usaikifed.com
Contact: Bruce Helwig, Instructor
Local. **Affiliated With:** United States Aikido Federation.

13978 ■ Rotary Club of Cincinnati
441 Vine St., Ste.2112
Cincinnati, OH 45202
Ph: (513)421-1080
Fax: (513)421-2070
E-mail: diane@cincinnatirotary.org
URL: http://www.cincinnatirotary.org
Contact: Diane Brasie, Exec.Dir.
Local. Provides humanitarian services by supporting needy children.

13979 ■ Save the Animals Foundation (STAF)
PO Box 9356
Cincinnati, OH 45209-0356
Ph: (513)561-7823
E-mail: pam@staf.org
URL: http://www.staf.org
Contact: Diana Malcontento, Pres.
Founded: 1988. **Members:** 20. **Local Groups:** 1. **Local**. Aims to provide the best quality care for animals. Provides a loving and safe home for abandoned, abused or neglected animals. **Awards:** Annual Veterinarian Award. **Frequency:** annual. **Type:** recognition. **Publications:** *Paws for Thought*, quarterly. Newsletter. Contains pet care articles and upcoming events. **Price:** free. **Circulation:** 3,000. **Advertising:** accepted.

13980 ■ SCDAA - Ohio Sickle Cell and Health Association
3770 Reading Rd.
Cincinnati, OH 45229-3128
Ph: (614)228-0157
Fax: (614)228-8089
E-mail: oscha@aol.com
URL: National Affiliate–www.sicklecelldisease.org
Contact: Wendy Berry-West, Exec.Dir.
State. Aims to create awareness of the negative impact of sickle cell disease on the health, economic, social and educational well being of the individual and his or her family. Encourages support for research activities leading to improved treatment and cure. **Affiliated With:** Sickle Cell Disease Association of America.

13981 ■ Sentinel Police Association
1890 Central Pkwy.
Cincinnati, OH 45214
Ph: (513)651-3507
Local.

13982 ■ Sharonville Federated Woman's Club
PO Box 621094
Cincinnati, OH 45262-1094
E-mail: sfwcinfo@aol.com
URL: http://sharonville-womans-club-gfwc.org/index.html
Contact: Ann Heath, Pres.
Local.

13983 ■ Sheet Metal Contractors Association of Greater Cincinnati
c/o Robert W. Tiemann
1579 Summit Rd., Ste.131
Cincinnati, OH 45237-1916
Ph: (513)761-5220
Fax: (513)761-5733
E-mail: rwtiemann@zoomtown.com
URL: National Affiliate–www.smacna.org
Contact: Robert W. Tiemann, Contact
Local. **Affiliated With:** Sheet Metal and Air Conditioning Contractors' National Association.

13984 ■ Sheet Metal Workers International Association LU 183/AFL-CIO
1579 Summit Rd., Rm. 129
Cincinnati, OH 45237
Ph: (513)821-9258 (513)821-9265
Fax: (513)821-9277
E-mail: smw183@fuse.net
URL: National Affiliate–www.aflcio.org
Members: 570. **Membership Dues:** production, $37 (monthly) • initiation fee, $125. **Staff:** 2. **Regional Groups:** 1. **Local**. **Affiliated With:** AFL-CIO. **Formerly:** (2004) Sheet Metal Workers AFL-CIO, LU 183.

13985 ■ Showbiz Players
c/o Bunny Arszman, Pres.
2727 Erlene Dr., No. 1059
Cincinnati, OH 45238
Ph: (513)981-7888 (513)385-9441
E-mail: bunny@showbizplayers.com
URL: http://www.showbizplayers.com
Contact: Bunny Arszman, Pres.
Founded: 1987. **Members:** 40. **Membership Dues:** producer, $15 (annual). **Budget:** $20,000. **Local**. Provides a creative outlet for all the people of community and produces quality theatre at an affordable price. **Affiliated With:** American Association of Community Theatre.

13986 ■ SHRM Ohio State Council
c/o Ann Byrnes
100 E 8th St.
Cincinnati, OH 45202-2129
Ph: (513)421-3134
Fax: (513)421-3085
E-mail: abyrnes@nacpa.org
URL: http://ohioshrm.org
Contact: Mr. Thomas Mobley SPHR, State Council Dir.
Members: 45. **State Groups:** 23. **State**. Promotes and develops the human resource profession through chapters, volunteer leaders, and human resource professionals. **Conventions/Meetings:** annual conference, with products and services associated with the HR industry (exhibits) • annual convention, state wide conference for the advancement of hr profession, attended by over 400 professional and 80 exhibitors (exhibits).

13987 ■ Sickle Cell Awareness Group
3458 Reading Rd.
Cincinnati, OH 45229
Ph: (513)281-9955 (513)281-0455
E-mail: sjohnson@gcul.org
URL: http://www.gcul.org
Contact: Anthony Thomas, Dir. of Health Initiative
Local.

13988 ■ Sickle Cell Awareness Group of Greater Cincinnati
3770 Reading Rd.
Cincinnati, OH 45229-3128
Ph: (513)872-8811
Fax: (513)872-8812
E-mail: sicklecell@fuse.net
URL: National Affiliate–www.sicklecelldisease.org
Contact: Antony Thomas, Exec.Dir.
Local. Aims to create awareness of the negative impact of sickle cell disease on the health, economic, social and educational well being of the individual and his or her family. Encourages support for research activities leading to improved treatment and cure. **Affiliated With:** Sickle Cell Disease Association of America.

13989 ■ Sister Cities Association of Greater Cincinnati (SCA)
441 Vine St., Ste.3601
Cincinnati, OH 45202
Ph: (513)241-8800
E-mail: sistercities@queencity.com
URL: http://www.queencity.com/sca
Contact: Sylvius Von Saucken, Interim Pres./Treas.
Founded: 1985. **Membership Dues:** corporate (based on number of employees), $100-$1,000 (annual). **Local**. Manages the international relationships of Cincinnati, OH by initiating relationships between cities that share common characteristics.

13990 ■ Society of American Military Engineers, Cincinnati Post
c/o Jim Bartley, Pres.
150 E 4th St., 6th Fl.
Cincinnati, OH 45202
Ph: (513)421-2265
URL: http://posts.same.org/cincinnati
Local. Works to advance the science of military engineering. Promotes and facilitates engineering support for national security. Develops and enhances relationships and competencies among uniformed services, public and private sector engineers and related professionals.

13991 ■ Society for Applied Spectroscopy, Cincinnati
c/o Mikhail Belkin, Chm.
Procter & Gamble
11511 Reed Hartman Hwy.
HB Box No. 326
Cincinnati, OH 45241
Ph: (513)626-0165
E-mail: belkin.m@pg.com
URL: http://www.s-a-s.org/local_sections.htm
Contact: Mikhail Belkin, Chm.
Local. **Affiliated With:** Society for Applied Spectroscopy.

13992 ■ Society of Broadcast Engineers, Chapter 33 - Southwest Ohio
c/o Wayne Chaney, Ed.
500 Central Ave.
Cincinnati, OH 45202
Ph: (513)852-4030 (937)220-1688
E-mail: wchaney@wcpo.com
URL: http://www.sbe33.org
Contact: George Hopstetter, Chm.
Local. Serves the interests of broadcast engineers. Promotes the profession and related fields for both theoretical and practical applications. Advocates for technical advancement of the industry. **Affiliated With:** Society of Broadcast Engineers. **Publications:** *The Modulator*. Newsletter.

13993 ■ Society of Manufacturing Engineers - University of Cincinnati S145
Univ. of Cincinnati, Center for Robotics
MINE Dept., ML 72
Cincinnati, OH 45221-0072
Ph: (513)556-2730
Fax: (513)556-3390
E-mail: ernie.hall@uc.edu
URL: National Affiliate–www.sme.org
Contact: Ernest L. Hall, Contact
Local. Advances manufacturing knowledge to gain competitive advantage. Improves skills and manufacturing solutions for the growth of economy. Provides resources and opportunities for manufacturing professionals. **Affiliated With:** Military Operations Research Society.

13994 ■ Society of Nuclear Medicine - Southeastern Chapters (SNM)
c/o Vincent J. Sodd, Chapter Administrator
5987 Turpin Hills Dr.
Cincinnati, OH 45244

Ph: (513)231-6955
E-mail: v.sodd@att.net
URL: http://www.snm.org
Contact: Vincent J. Sodd, Chapter Administrator
Regional. **Affiliated With:** Society of Nuclear Medicine.

13995 ■ Society of St. Vincent de Paul
1125 Bank St.
Cincinnati, OH 45214-2130
Ph: (513)562-8841
Fax: (513)562-8843
E-mail: info@svdpcincinnati.org
URL: http://www.svdpcincinnati.org
Contact: Ms. Liz Carter, Exec.Dir.
Local. Cares for the poor and needy of Cincinnati through person to person help with food, rent, utility assistance, clothing, furniture and companionship.

13996 ■ Society of Tribologists and Lubrication Engineers - Cincinnati Section
c/o Jerry Byers
3000 Disney St.
Cincinnati, OH 45208
Ph: (513)458-8156
Fax: (513)458-8170
E-mail: jerry_p_byers@milacron.com
URL: National Affiliate–www.stle.org
Contact: Jerry Byers, Contact
Local. Promotes the advancement of tribology and the practice of lubrication engineering. Stimulates the study and development of lubrication tribology techniques. Promotes higher standards in the field. **Affiliated With:** Society of Tribologists and Lubrication Engineers.

13997 ■ Solid Waste Association of North America, Ohio Buckeye Chapter
c/o Hamilton County Solid Waste District
250 William Howard Taft
Cincinnati, OH 45219
Ph: (513)946-7719
Fax: (513)946-7779
E-mail: jeffrey.aluotto@hamilton-co.org
URL: http://www.swanaohio.org
Contact: Mr. Jeffrey W. Aluotto, Pres.
State. **Affiliated With:** Solid Waste Association of North America.

13998 ■ South Central Ohio Minority Business Council (SCOMBC)
300 Carew Tower
441 Vine St.
Cincinnati, OH 45202-2812
Ph: (513)579-3104
Fax: (513)579-3101
E-mail: info@smbc.org
URL: http://www.scombc.com
Contact: Cathy Mock, Pres.
Membership Dues: basic, $1,500 (annual) • silver, $4,000 (annual) • gold, $7,000 (annual) • diamond, $10,000 (annual). **Local**. Aims to build a stronger society and to support business development.

13999 ■ Southern Ohio Association of Realtors (SOAR)
3848 McMann Rd.
Cincinnati, OH 45245
Ph: (513)528-2657
Fax: (513)528-2658
E-mail: soar@fuse.net
URL: http://www.soarealtors.com
Contact: Carol Culbertson, Pres.
Local. Strives to develop real estate business practices. Advocates for the right to own, use and transfer real property. Provides a facility for professional development, research and exchange of information among members and the general public. **Affiliated With:** National Association of Realtors.

14000 ■ Southern Ohio Board of Realtors
c/o Judith F. Buhr, Exec. Officer
523 Cincinnati-Batavia Pike
Cincinnati, OH 45244
Ph: (513)528-2657
Fax: (513)528-2658
Contact: Judith F. Buhr, Exec. Officer
Local. **Formerly:** (2001) Clermont County Board of Realtors.

14001 ■ Southwest Ohio Environmental Balancing Bureau
1579 Summit Rd., Rm. 131
Cincinnati, OH 45237-1915
Ph: (513)761-5220
Fax: (513)761-5733
E-mail: mechanic@iglou.com
URL: National Affiliate–www.nebb.org
Contact: Robert W. Tiemann, Chapter Coor.
Local. Works to help architects, engineers, building owners, and contractors produce buildings with HVAC systems. Establishes and maintains industry standards, procedures, and specifications for testing, adjusting, and balancing work. **Affiliated With:** National Environmental Balancing Bureau.

14002 ■ Southwest Ohio Senior Olympics
c/o Dina Hanks
805 Central Ave., Ste.800
Cincinnati, OH 45202
Ph: (513)421-5222
Fax: (513)871-1935
URL: http://www.ohioseniorolympics.org
Contact: Dina Hanks, Contact
Local. **Affiliated With:** National Senior Games Association.

14003 ■ Special Libraries Association, Cincinnati Chapter
c/o David Whelan, Pres.-Elect
Cincinnati Law Lib. Assn.
Hamilton County Courthouse
1000 Main St., Rm. 601
Cincinnati, OH 45202
Ph: (513)946-5263
Fax: (513)946-5252
E-mail: dwhelan@cms.hamilton-co.org
URL: http://www.sla.org/chapter/ccin/index.asp
Contact: David Whelan, Pres.-Elect
Local. Seeks to advance the leadership role of special librarians. Promotes and strengthens members through learning, advocacy and networking initiatives. **Affiliated With:** Special Libraries Association.

14004 ■ Starfire Council of Greater Cincinnati
c/o Tim Vogt
2330 Victory Pkwy., Ste.100A
Cincinnati, OH 45206
Ph: (513)281-2100
E-mail: tim@starfirecouncil.org
URL: http://www.starfirecouncil.org
Local.

14005 ■ Sweet Adelines International, Seven Hills Show Chorus
PO Box 42843
Cincinnati, OH 45242
Ph: (513)333-5426
E-mail: 7hills@cinci.rr.com
URL: http://www.evg.org/~7hills
Contact: Jason Remley, Dir.
Local. Advances the musical art form of barbershop harmony through education and performances. Provides education, training and coaching in the development of women's four-part barbershop harmony. **Affiliated With:** Sweet Adelines International.

14006 ■ Sycamore - Young Life
PO Box 42171
Cincinnati, OH 45242-0171
Ph: (513)791-3730
E-mail: ganaple@juno.com
URL: http://sites.younglife.org/sites/Sycamore/default.aspx
Contact: Gordon Anaple, Contact
Local. **Affiliated With:** Young Life.

14007 ■ Syrian Shriners
c/o Anthony M. Iacobucci, PhD, P.P.
217 William Howard Taft Rd.
Cincinnati, OH 45219
Ph: (513)751-3800
Fax: (513)751-4301
E-mail: tiacobucci@syrianshrine.org
URL: http://www.SyrianShrine.org
Contact: Anthony M. Iacobucci PhD, Recorder
Local. **Affiliated With:** Imperial Council of the Ancient Arabic Order of the Nobles of the Mystic Shrine for North America.

14008 ■ Ten Thousand Villages of Cincinnati
O'Bryonville
2011 Madison Rd.
Cincinnati, OH 45208
Ph: (513)871-5840
URL: National Affiliate–webbgui1088.cdgcommerce.com
State.

14009 ■ Transformation Cincinnati and Northern Kentucky (TCNKY)
PO Box 531266
Cincinnati, OH 45253-1266
Ph: (513)665-9100
E-mail: info@transformationcincinnati.com
URL: http://www.transformationcincinnati.com
Local.

14010 ■ Tri-State Athletics
c/o Mark Sutton, Pres.
1511 Lemontree Dr.
Cincinnati, OH 45240-2841
E-mail: mark@tristateathletics.com
URL: http://www.tristateathletics.com
Contact: Mark Sutton, Pres.
Regional.

14011 ■ Tri-State Catalysis Club
c/o Peter Smirniotis, Pres.
Univ. of Cincinnati
Coll. of Engg.
PO Box 210171
Cincinnati, OH 45221-0171
Ph: (513)556-1474
Fax: (513)556-3473
E-mail: panagiotis.smirniotis@uc.edu
URL: National Affiliate–www.nacatsoc.org
Contact: Peter Smirniotis, Pres.
Local. **Affiliated With:** North American Catalysis Society.

14012 ■ Tri-State Society for Healthcare Engineerings
c/o David Capal, Pres.
2100 Sherman Ave.
Cincinnati, OH 45212
Ph: (513)584-4585
Fax: (513)584-7984
E-mail: capaldf@healthall.com
URL: National Affiliate–www.ashe.org
Contact: David Capal, Pres.
Founded: 1978. **Members:** 180. **Budget:** $8,000. **Regional Groups:** 1. **Local Groups:** 1. **Regional**. **Affiliated With:** American Society for Healthcare Engineering of the American Hospital Association.

14013 ■ Tri-State Society for Healthcare Engineers (TSSHE)
c/o David Capal, Pres.
Univ. Hosp.
234 Goodman St.
Cincinnati, OH 45219-2316
Ph: (513)584-4585
Fax: (513)584-4583
E-mail: capaldf@healthall.com
URL: National Affiliate–www.ashe.org
Contact: David Capal, Pres.
Regional. Promotes better patient care by encouraging members to develop their knowledge and increase their competence in the field of facilities management. Cooperates with hospitals and allied associations in matters pertaining to facilities management. **Affili-**

ated With: American Society for Healthcare Engineering of the American Hospital Association.

14014 ■ United Association of Journeymen and Apprentices of the Plumbing and Pipe Fitting Industry of the United States and Canada - Local Union 392
c/o William Koester, Business Mgr.
1228 Central Pkwy.
Cincinnati, OH 45202-7500
Ph: (859)581-4060
Fax: (859)581-0096
E-mail: willie@local392.com
URL: http://www.local392.com
Contact: William Koester, Business Mgr.
Members: 2,377. **Local. Affiliated With:** United Association of Journeymen and Apprentices of the Plumbing, Pipe Fitting, Sprinkler Fitting Industry of the U.S. and Canada.

14015 ■ United Coalition for Animals (UCAN)
PO Box 42083
Cincinnati, OH 45242-0083
Ph: (513)981-7933
URL: http://www.cincinnatispayneuter.org
Local.

14016 ■ United Sales Associates
7537 State Rd.
Cincinnati, OH 45255-2438
Ph: (513)231-4266
Fax: (513)231-1456
E-mail: assocs@unitedsales.com
URL: http://www.unitedsales.com
Contact: George J. Hayward, Pres.
Local. Formerly: (2005) United Sales Association.

14017 ■ United States Naval Sea Cadet Corps - Cincinnati Division
3190 Gilbert Ave.
Cincinnati, OH 45207
E-mail: recruiter@cincyseacadets.org
URL: http://www.cincyseacadets.org
Contact: LTJG Belinda Witte, Commanding Officer
Local. Works to instill good citizenship and patriotism in youth. Encourages qualities such as personal neatness, loyalty, obedience, dependability, and responsibility to others. Offers courses in physical fitness and military drill, first aid, water safety, basic seamanship, and naval history and traditions. **Affiliated With:** Naval Sea Cadet Corps.

14018 ■ United Way of Greater Cincinnati
2400 Reading Rd.
Cincinnati, OH 45202-1458
Ph: (513)762-7100
Fax: (513)762-7146
URL: http://www.uwgc.org
Local. Affiliated With: United Way of America.

14019 ■ Urban League of Greater Cincinnati
3458 Reading Rd.
Cincinnati, OH 45229-3128
Ph: (513)281-9955
Fax: (513)281-0455
E-mail: djstanley@gcul.org
URL: http://www.gcul.org
Contact: Ms. Donna Jones Stanley, Pres./CEO
Membership Dues: equality circle, $1,000 (annual) • heritage, $500 (annual) • advocate, $250 (annual) • individual, $25 (annual) • senior citizen, $25 (annual). **Local.** Seeks to expand opportunity for African-Americans by promoting economic self-sufficiency through effective leadership in the areas of service delivery, research, planning, and advocacy. Conducts charitable activities. Offers teen pregnancy prevention program and skills training center. **Awards:** Oratorical Scholarship. **Type:** scholarship. **Affiliated With:** National Urban League. **Publications:** *Parity 2000*, quarterly. Newsletter • Annual Report, annual.

14020 ■ USA Weightlifting - Dearborn
c/o David Armstrong
Xavier Univ.
3800 Victory Pkwy.
Cincinnati, OH 45207-7510
Ph: (812)926-3579 (513)745-3226
Fax: (513)745-3226
URL: National Affiliate–www.usaweightlifting.org
Contact: David Armstrong, Contact
Local. Affiliated With: USA Weightlifting.

14021 ■ Valley of Cincinnati, Ancient Accepted Scottish Rite
317 E 5th St.
Cincinnati, OH 45202-3399
Ph: (513)421-3579
Fax: (513)562-2661
Free: (800)561-3579
E-mail: hccarpen@32masons.com
URL: http://www.rite32.org
Contact: Harry C. Carpenter, Exec.Sec.
Local. Upholds principles that revolve around brotherly love, relief and truth. **Formerly:** (2005) Valley of Cincinnati, Scottish Rite.

14022 ■ Vietnam Veterans of America Chapter No. 10
8418 Reading Rd.
Cincinnati, OH 45215
Ph: (513)761-8007
URL: National Affiliate–www.vva.org
Local. Affiliated With: Vietnam Veterans of America.

14023 ■ Volunteers of America Ohio River Valley
1063 Central Ave.
Cincinnati, OH 45202
Ph: (513)381-1954
Fax: (513)381-2171
URL: http://www.voa-orv.org
Local. Provides local human service programs and opportunities for individual and community involvement. **Affiliated With:** Volunteers of America.

14024 ■ Women of Reform Judaism: Isaac M. Wise Temple Sisterhood
8329 Ridge Rd.
Cincinnati, OH 45236
Ph: (513)793-2556
E-mail: welcome@wisetemple.org
URL: http://www.wisetemple.org
Local. Affiliated With: Women of Reform Judaism, The Federation of Temple Sisterhoods.

14025 ■ Women's Circuit (TWC)
c/o Suzanne Lachapelle, Pres.
PO Box 498968
Cincinnati, OH 45249-8968
E-mail: feedback@thewomenscircuit.com
URL: http://www.thewomenscircuit.net
Contact: Suzanne Lachapelle, Pres.
Local.

14026 ■ World Affairs Council of Greater Cincinnati
105 E 4th St., Ste.510
Fourth and Walnut Ctr.
Cincinnati, OH 45202
Ph: (513)621-2320
Fax: (513)562-4964
E-mail: wacgc@globalcincinnati.org
URL: http://www.worldaffairs-cin.org
Contact: Deborah A. Kittner, Dir. of Programs and Education
Membership Dues: diplomat individual, $75-$249 (annual) • ambassador, $250-$1,499 (annual) • President's Circle, $1,500 (annual) • student, $15 (annual) • associate, $250 (annual) • corporate diplomat, $500 (annual) • assistant secretary, $1,250 (annual) • under secretary, $2,500 (annual) • secretary of state, $5,000 (annual) • President's Circle corporate, $10,000 (annual). **Local.** Seeks to promote economic development by encouraging international awareness among business and community leaders, students and educators.

14027 ■ Young Life Cincinnati Metro
PO Box 42171
Cincinnati, OH 45242
Ph: (513)791-3730
URL: http://sites.younglife.org/_layouts/ylext/default.aspx?ID=A-AG225
Local. Affiliated With: Young Life.

14028 ■ Young Life Eastern Cincinnati
PO Box 42171
Cincinnati, OH 45242-0171
Ph: (513)791-3730
Fax: (513)791-3730
URL: http://sites.younglife.org/sites/EasternCincinnati/default.aspx
Local. Affiliated With: Young Life.

14029 ■ Zinzinnati Wanderers
c/o Joe Stigall, Pres.
618 Waycross Rd.
Cincinnati, OH 45240-3821
Ph: (513)385-1191 (513)681-4065
Fax: (513)851-8310
E-mail: jstigall@cinci.rr.com
URL: http://www.angelfire.com/oh3/zinzinnatiwanderers
Contact: Joe Stigall, Pres.
Local. Affiliated With: American Volkssport Association.

Circleville

14030 ■ American Legion, Hall-Adkins Post 134
PO Box 332
Circleville, OH 43113
Ph: (740)362-7478
Fax: (740)362-1429
URL: National Affiliate–www.legion.org
Local. Affiliated With: American Legion.

14031 ■ American Red Cross, Pickaway County Chapter
138A Watt St.
Circleville, OH 43113-1602
Ph: (740)474-5736
Fax: (740)420-3327
URL: http://www.pickaway-redcross.org
Local.

14032 ■ Circleville - Pickaway Chamber of Commerce
135 W Main St.
PO Box 462
Circleville, OH 43113
Ph: (740)474-4923
Fax: (740)477-6800
Free: (800)897-9424
E-mail: amy_elsea@thepickofohio.com
URL: http://www.pickaway.com
Contact: Amy Elsea, Dir.
Membership Dues: business (based on the number of employees), $170-$2,932 (annual) • special, $216 (annual). **Local.** Represents the interests of the business industry in Pickaway County. **Publications:** Newsletter, monthly. **Conventions/Meetings:** monthly board meeting • monthly Business After Business - meeting.

14033 ■ Ohio Genealogical Society, Pickaway County Historical Society
PO Box 85
Circleville, OH 43113
E-mail: pkwyhist@ohiohills.com
URL: http://www.rootsweb.com/~ohpickaw/gen.html
Membership Dues: regular (single or family), $25 (annual) • youth, $10 (annual) • business patron, $75 (annual) • industry patron, $125 (annual) • life, $500. **Local. Libraries: Type:** open to the public. **Holdings:** books, business records, archival material, articles, periodicals. **Subjects:** church histories and records, family genealogies, census records. **Affiliated With:** Ohio Genealogical Society. **Publications:** *Pickaway Quarterly*. Newsletter. Includes society

news, historical reports, genealogical articles and lists, and new acquisitions for both the Museum and the Genealogical Library. **Price:** included in membership dues.

14034 ■ Pickaway County Board of Realtors
208 N Scioto St.
Circleville, OH 43113
Ph: (740)420-9556
Fax: (740)474-9590
E-mail: pickawaycounty@aol.com
URL: National Affiliate–www.realtor.org
Contact: Carrie Meinert, Exec. Officer
Local. Strives to develop real estate business practices. Advocates for the right to own, use and transfer real property. Provides a facility for professional development, research and exchange of information among members and the general public. **Affiliated With:** National Association of Realtors.

14035 ■ Pickaway County Farm Bureau
24633 US Hwy. 23 S
Circleville, OH 43113
Ph: (740)474-6284
Contact: Cathy Hoile, Organization Dir.
Local.

14036 ■ Pickaway County Literacy Council
200 E High
Circleville, OH 43113
Ph: (740)477-6224
Fax: (740)474-9675
E-mail: pclc@rrohio.com
URL: http://www.pickaway.com
Contact: Catherine Robb, Coor.
Local. Affiliated With: ProLiteracy Worldwide.

14037 ■ Pickaway County Visitors Bureau
c/o Josephine Hall
PO Box 571
135 W Main St.
Circleville, OH 43113
Ph: (740)474-3636
Fax: (740)477-6800
Free: (888)770-7425
E-mail: pickofoh@ohiohills.com
URL: http://www.pickaway.com
Contact: Josephine Hall, Exec.Dir.
Staff: 1. **Local**. Located in central Ohio, promotes tourism countywide; offers historical museums, unique shopping, and outdoor adventure throughout the county.

14038 ■ United Way of Pickaway County
PO Box 292
Circleville, OH 43113-0292
Ph: (740)477-8171
URL: National Affiliate–national.unitedway.org
Local. Affiliated With: United Way of America.

Cleveland

14039 ■ 100 Black Men of Greater Cleveland
c/o Michael L. Nelson, Sr., Pres.
13110 Shaker Sq.
Cleveland, OH 44120
Ph: (216)491-3072
Fax: (216)491-1661
URL: National Affiliate–www.100blackmen.org
Contact: Michael L. Nelson Sr., Pres.
Local. Affiliated With: 100 Black Men of America.

14040 ■ Adoption Network Cleveland
1667 E 40th St.
Cleveland, OH 44103
Ph: (216)881-7511
Fax: (216)881-7510
E-mail: betsie@adoptionnetwork.org
URL: http://www.adoptionnetwork.org
Contact: Betsie Norris, Exec.Dir.
Founded: 1988. **Members:** 800. **Membership Dues:** individual, $30 (annual) • family, $40 (annual) • organization, $75 (annual). **Staff:** 4. **Budget:** $177,000. **Regional Groups:** 2. **Regional**. Educational, advocacy, support, and search group for adult adoptees, birth-parents, adoptive parents, and others interested in post-adoption issues and openness in adoption. **Libraries: Type:** lending. **Subjects:** adoption, child welfare. **Awards:** LND. **Type:** recognition • Triad Advocate of the Year Award. **Frequency:** annual. **Type:** recognition. **Affiliated With:** American Adoption Congress; North American Council on Adoptable Children. **Publications:** *Adoption Network News*, bimonthly. Newsletter. **Price:** included in membership dues. ISSN: 1097-5624. **Circulation:** 1,100. **Conventions/Meetings:** annual conference • weekly meeting.

14041 ■ Air and Waste Management Association - North Ohio Chapter (NOC-AWMA)
PO Box 31454
Cleveland, OH 44131-0454
E-mail: cinder@en.com
URL: http://www.nocawma.org
Local. Affiliated With: Air and Waste Management Association.

14042 ■ Alcoholics Anonymous World Services, Cleveland District Office
1701 E 12th St.
Reserve Sq. - Lower Commons
Cleveland, OH 44114
Ph: (216)241-7387
E-mail: info@aacleveland.com
URL: http://www.aacleveland.com
Contact: Ruth Dubin, Office Mgr.
Local. Individuals recovering from alcoholism. AA maintains that members can solve their common problem and help others achieve sobriety through a twelve step program that includes sharing their experience, strength, and hope with each other. **Affiliated With:** Alcoholics Anonymous World Services.

14043 ■ Alzheimer's Association, Cleveland Area Chapter
12200 Fairhill Rd.
Cleveland, OH 44120-1013
Ph: (216)721-8457
Fax: (216)721-1629
Free: (800)441-3322
E-mail: alzinfo@alzclv.org
URL: http://www.alzclv.org/index.htm
Contact: Mary K. Schwendeman, CEO
Local. Family members of sufferers of Alzheimer's disease. Combats Alzheimer's disease and related disorders. (Alzheimer's disease is a progressive, degenerative brain disease in which changes occur in the central nervous system and outer region of the brain causing memory loss and other changes in thought, personality, and behavior.) Promotes research to find the cause, treatment, and cure for the disease. **Affiliated With:** Alzheimer's Association.

14044 ■ American Association for Clinical Chemistry, Northeast Ohio Section
c/o Lisa Kubit, MBA, Chair
Prognostix Inc.
10265 Carnegie Ave.
Cleveland, OH 44106
Ph: (216)444-5301
Fax: (216)444-5335
URL: National Affiliate–www.aacc.org
Contact: Lisa Kubit MBA, Chair
Local. Represents the interests of clinical laboratory professionals, physicians, research scientists and other individuals involved with clinical chemistry and other clinical laboratory science-related disciplines. Seeks to improve the practice of clinical chemistry. Establishes standards for education and training in the field. **Affiliated With:** American Association for Clinical Chemistry.

14045 ■ American Cancer Society, Cuyahoga County
10501 Euclid Ave.
Cleveland, OH 44106
Ph: (216)241-1177
Fax: (216)241-0334
Free: (888)227-6446
E-mail: donna.korn@cancer.org
URL: http://www.cancer.org
Contact: Donna Korn, Contact
Local. Works to eliminate cancer as a major health problem through research, education, advocacy and service. **Affiliated With:** American Cancer Society.

14046 ■ American Chemical Society, Cleveland Section
c/o Dr. Robert Gerd Salomon, Chm.
Case Western Reserve Univ., Chemistry Dept.
10900 Euclid Ave.
Cleveland, OH 44106-1712
Ph: (216)368-2592
URL: National Affiliate–acswebcontent.acs.org
Contact: Dr. Robert Gerd Salomon, Chm.
Local. Represents the interests of individuals dedicated to the advancement of chemistry in all its branches. Provides opportunities for peer interaction and career development. **Affiliated With:** American Chemical Society.

14047 ■ American Civil Liberties Union, Ohio Affiliate (ACLUOH)
4506 Chester Ave.
Cleveland, OH 44103
Ph: (216)472-2200
Fax: (216)472-2210
E-mail: contact@acluohio.org
URL: http://www.acluohio.org
Contact: Christine Link, Exec.Dir.
Founded: 1920. **Members:** 17,900. **Membership Dues:** basic, $20-$30 (annual) • contributing, $35-$50 (annual) • supporting, $75 (annual) • sustaining, $125 (annual). **Staff:** 11. **Budget:** $700,000. **Regional Groups:** 3. **State**. Assists in maintaining constitutional and other fundamental rights in Ohio Chapter. **Libraries: Type:** lending. **Holdings:** books, video recordings. **Awards:** Civil Liberties Award. **Frequency:** annual. **Type:** recognition. **Recipient:** significant contribution in defending the bill of rights. **Affiliated With:** American Civil Liberties Union. **Publications:** *ACLU News*, periodic. Newsletter. Contains updates on civil liberties issues. **Price:** free. **Circulation:** 13,000 • *Civil Liberties: A Guide for the Perplexed*. Booklet • *Put Me in the Coach, The Rights of Girls and Women in Sports*. Newsletter • *Students: Know Your Rights*. Newsletter • *Teen Health Guide*. Booklet.

14048 ■ American College of Physicians - Ohio Chapter (ACP)
c/o Carla Biggert, Exec.Dir.
9500 Euclid Ave., S-13
Cleveland, OH 44195
Ph: (216)445-4020
E-mail: biggerc@ccf.org
URL: http://www.acponline.org/chapters/oh
Contact: Carla Biggert, Exec.Dir.
State. Affiliated With: American College of Physicians-American Society of Internal Medicine. **Conventions/Meetings:** annual meeting.

14049 ■ American Foundation for Suicide Prevention of Northeast Ohio
30195 Chagrin Blvd., Ste.210 N
Cleveland, OH 44124-5703
Ph: (216)464-3471
Fax: (216)831-0928
E-mail: afspneohio@aol.com
URL: http://www.afsp.org
Contact: Catherine Ferrer, Exec.Dir.
Founded: 1992. **Staff:** 1. **Budget:** $60,000. **Regional**. Individuals interested in the prevention of suicide through education and research programs. Sponsors programs for physicians, school counselors, teachers, social workers, nurses, clergy, home health aides, law enforcement officers, and parents. Emphasis is placed on the identification of individuals who may be at risk of major depression and/or suicide; effective response to them and their families; and effective referral to mental health professionals for assessment and, if appropriate, for treatment.

Presents "Recognizing Adolescent Depression and Suicide Prevention", A 2-period program for high school health classes. **Affiliated With:** American Foundation for Suicide Prevention. **Publications:** *Progress and Hope*, annual. Newsletter. **Price:** free.

14050 ■ American Hiking Society - Cleveland Hiking Club
PO Box 347097
Cleveland, OH 44134-7097
Ph: (216)238-6798
E-mail: rskuly@core.com
URL: National Affiliate–www.americanhiking.org
Local.

14051 ■ American Institute of Aeronautics and Astronautics, Case Western Reserve University
c/o Chih-Jen (Jackie) Sung, Associate Prof.
Glennan 415
Dept. of Mech. & Aero. Engg.
Case Western Reserve Univ.
Cleveland, OH 44106
Ph: (216)368-2942
Fax: (216)368-6445
E-mail: cjs15@po.cwru.edu
URL: http://www.aiaa.org
Contact: Prof. Chih-Jen (Jackie) Sung, Associate Prof.
Founded: 1980. **Members:** 30. **Membership Dues:** $20 (annual). **Budget:** $5,000. **Regional.** Committed to being the resource for the exchange of aeronautical and astronautical information. Seeks to help members get started on their career and professional development. Offers opportunities for educational assistance and financial aid. **Projects:** Design, Build, and Fly; Rocket Club. **Affiliated With:** American Institute of Aeronautics and Astronautics. **Conventions/Meetings:** monthly convention.

14052 ■ American Institute of Architects, Cleveland
1001 Huron Rd., No. 101
Cleveland, OH 44115
Ph: (216)575-1242
Fax: (216)575-1244
E-mail: aiacleve@en.com
URL: http://www.aiacleveland.com
Contact: Helen Miles, Admin.Asst.
Founded: 1890. **Members:** 500. **Staff:** 2. **Budget:** $200,000. **Regional Groups:** 3. **State Groups:** 7. **Local Groups:** 1. **Regional. Awards:** Design Award. **Frequency:** annual. **Type:** scholarship. **Telecommunication Services:** electronic mail, aiadocs@en.com. **Affiliated With:** American Institute of Architects. **Publications:** *Architecture*, monthly. **Circulation:** 700. **Advertising:** accepted • *Guide to Cleveland Architecture*. Book. **Price:** $19.95. ISSN: 0962-8742. **Circulation:** 700. **Advertising:** accepted. **Conventions/Meetings:** monthly meeting (exhibits); Avg. Attendance: 250.

14053 ■ American Legion, Army-Navy-Shaker Post 54
c/o Carl R. Withers
1000 Natl. City Bank Bldg.
Cleveland, OH 44114
Ph: (740)362-7478
Fax: (740)362-1429
URL: National Affiliate–www.legion.org
Contact: Carl R. Withers, Contact
Local. Affiliated With: American Legion.

14054 ■ American Legion, Cleveland Police Post 438
c/o The American Legion 13th District
5425 Fleet Ave.
Cleveland, OH 44105
Ph: (740)362-7478
Fax: (740)362-1429
URL: National Affiliate–www.legion.org
Local. Affiliated With: American Legion.

14055 ■ American Legion, Cleveland Post 2
c/o Dav Hall
1423 E 39th St.
Cleveland, OH 44114
Ph: (740)362-7478
Fax: (740)362-1429
URL: National Affiliate–www.legion.org
Contact: Dav Hall, Contact
Local. Affiliated With: American Legion.

14056 ■ American Legion, Fire Fighters Post 339
1645 Superior Ave.
Cleveland, OH 44114
Ph: (740)362-7478
Fax: (740)362-1429
URL: National Affiliate–www.legion.org
Local. Affiliated With: American Legion.

14057 ■ American Legion, Theodore Roosevelt Post 469
4910 Memphis Ave.
Cleveland, OH 44144
Ph: (740)362-7478
Fax: (740)362-1429
URL: National Affiliate–www.legion.org
Local. Affiliated With: American Legion.

14058 ■ American Legion, Western Reserve Post 315
769 E 105th St.
Cleveland, OH 44108
Ph: (740)362-7478
Fax: (740)362-1429
URL: National Affiliate–www.legion.org
Local. Affiliated With: American Legion.

14059 ■ American Planning Association - Ohio Chapter
c/o Terry Schwarz, Exec.Dir.
820 Prospect Ave.
Cleveland, OH 44115
Ph: (216)357-3436
Fax: (216)357-3430
E-mail: info@ohioplanning.org
URL: http://www.ohioplanning.org
Contact: Terry Schwarz, Exec.Dir.
State. Promotes the art and science of planning to meet the needs of people and society. Encourages the exchange of information and planning experiences. Advances the interests and welfare of the planning profession. **Affiliated With:** American Planning Association.

14060 ■ American Public Works Association, Ohio Chapter
c/o Ms. Phillis Fuller Clipps, Pres.
601 Lakeside Ave. E, Rm. 518
Cleveland, OH 44114-1015
Ph: (216)664-2371
Fax: (216)664-2289
E-mail: pfullerclipps@city.cleveland.oh.us
URL: http://ohio.apwa.net
Contact: Ms. Phillis Fuller Clipps, Pres.
State. Promotes professional excellence and public awareness through education, advocacy and the exchange of knowledge. **Affiliated With:** American Public Works Association.

14061 ■ American Red Cross, Greater Cleveland Chapter
3747 Euclid Ave.
Cleveland, OH 44115-2596
Ph: (216)431-3010
E-mail: info@redcross-cleveland.org
URL: http://www.redcross-cleveland.org
Founded: 1905. **Staff:** 55. **Budget:** $7,500,000. **Regional.**

14062 ■ American Red Cross Northern Ohio Blood Services Region
Ronald J. Warzel Donor Center
3636 Euclid Ave.
Cleveland, OH 44115
E-mail: brohclepr@usa.redcross.org
URL: http://www.redcross.org/br/northernohio
Regional.

14063 ■ American Society of Business Publication Editors, Cleveland Chapter (ASBPE-CC)
c/o Esther Durkalski, Pres.
7500 Old Oak Blvd.
Cleveland, OH 44130
Ph: (440)891-2698
Fax: (440)891-2733
E-mail: edurkalski@advanstar.com
URL: http://www.asbpe.org
Contact: Esther Durkalski, Pres.
Founded: 1964. **Members:** 650. **Membership Dues:** individual, $75 (annual). **Budget:** $3,500. **Regional.** Editors of business, trade, and technical publications. Serves as a forum for the exchange of ideas and conducts educational programming with journalism societies and schools of journalism. Sponsors editorial and graphics competition. **Awards: Frequency:** annual. **Type:** recognition. **Recipient:** trade press/business press. **Affiliated With:** American Society of Business Publication Editors. **Formerly:** (2001) American Society of Business Press Editors, Cleveland Chapter. **Publications:** *ASBPE Editor's Notes*, bimonthly. Newsletter. **Conventions/Meetings:** monthly luncheon.

14064 ■ American Society of Mechanical Engineers, Cleveland Section
3100 Chester Ave., Ste.216
Cleveland, OH 44114
Ph: (330)558-3919
URL: http://sections.asme.org/cleveland
Contact: Steve Weiler, Chm.
Local. Promotes the art, science and practice of Mechanical Engineering and allied arts and sciences. Encourages original research and fosters engineering education. Promotes the technical and societal contribution of engineers. **Affiliated With:** American Society of Mechanical Engineers.

14065 ■ American Society of Professional Estimators, Cleveland/North Ohio Chapter
c/o Timothy T. Calvey
Calvey Consulting, LLC
8473 Settlers Passage
Cleveland, OH 44141
Ph: (440)740-1132
Fax: (440)740-1134
E-mail: tcalvey@calveyconsulting.com
URL: National Affiliate–www.aspenational.com
Contact: Timothy T. Calvey, Contact
Local. Serves construction estimators through education, fellowship and opportunity for professional development.

14066 ■ American Society of Safety Engineers, Northern Ohio
1422 Euclid Ave., Ste.539
Cleveland, OH 44115
Ph: (216)621-0059
Fax: (216)621-0062
E-mail: aci@lubrizol.com
URL: http://nohio.asse.org
Contact: Angelo Cicconetti, Pres.
Local. Enhances the advancement of the safety profession and the safety professional. Promotes the technical, societal and economic well-being of safety practitioners. **Affiliated With:** American Society of Safety Engineers.

14067 ■ American Society for Training and Development - Greater Cleveland Chapter
c/o Camille Baron
1931 King James Pkwy., Ste.122
Cleveland, OH 44145

Ph: (440)835-3579
E-mail: astd@taskawayinc.com
URL: http://www.astdcleve.org
Contact: Lori Klepfer, Pres.
Local. Promotes workplace learning and the improvement of skills of workplace professionals. Provides resource and professional development to individuals in the field of learning and development. Recognizes and sets standards for learning and performance professionals. **Affiliated With:** American Society for Training and Development.

14068 ■ American Statistical Association, Cleveland Chapter
c/o John P. Holcomb, Pres.
Cleveland State Univ.
Dept. of Mathematics
2121 Euclid Ave., Rte. 1515
Cleveland, OH 44115-2214
Ph: (216)523-7157
E-mail: j.p.holcomb@csuohio.edu
URL: National Affiliate–www.amstat.org
Contact: John P. Holcomb, Pres.
Local. Promotes statistical practice, applications and research. Works for the improvement of statistical education at all levels. Seeks opportunities to advance the statistics profession. **Affiliated With:** American Statistical Association.

14069 ■ American Welding Society, Cleveland Section 006
c/o Paul Null, Sec.
The Lincoln Elec. Co.
22801 St. Claire Ave.
Cleveland, OH 44117
Ph: (216)383-4102
Fax: (216)383-8025
E-mail: paul_null@lincolnelectric.com
URL: National Affiliate–www.aws.org
Contact: Paul Null, Sec.
Local. Advances the science, technology and application of welding and related joining disciplines. **Affiliated With:** American Welding Society.

14070 ■ Amyotrophic Lateral Sclerosis Association, Northeast Ohio Chapter
2500 E 22nd St., Ste.102
Cleveland, OH 44115
Ph: (216)592-2572
Fax: (216)592-2575
E-mail: judy@alsaohio.org
URL: http://www.alsaohio.org
Contact: Sherrill Ann Moyer, Pres./CEO
Local. Works to find a cure and to enhance the quality of life for individuals suffering from ALS. **Affiliated With:** Amyotrophic Lateral Sclerosis Association.

14071 ■ APICS, The Association for Operations Management - Cleveland Chapter
PO Box 31357
Cleveland, OH 44131
E-mail: director1@apicscleveland.org
URL: http://www.apicscleveland.org
Contact: Monica Curley, Pres.
Local. Provides information and services in production and inventory management and related areas to enable members, enterprises and individuals to add value to their business performance. **Affiliated With:** APICS - The Association for Operations Management.

14072 ■ APMI Cleveland Chapter
c/o Larry Somrack, PMT
7650 Hub Pkwy.
Cleveland, OH 44125
Ph: (216)447-1550
Fax: (216)447-3835
E-mail: isomrack@nslanalytical.com
URL: National Affiliate–www.mpif.org
Contact: Larry Somrack, Chm.
Local. Maintains speakers' bureau and placement service. Serves the technical and informational needs of individuals interested or involved in the science and art of powder metallurgy. Provides the best source of information about the most up-to-date developments and advances in this dynamic, expanding technology through its publications, conferences and local section activities. **Affiliated With:** APMI International.

14073 ■ Arthritis Foundation Northeastern Ohio Chapter
4630 Richmond Rd., Ste.240
Cleveland, OH 44128
Ph: (216)831-7000
Fax: (216)831-1764
Free: (800)245-2275
E-mail: info.neoh@arthritis.org
URL: National Affiliate–www.arthritis.org
Contact: John T. Petures Jr., Pres.
Founded: 1950. **Members:** 8,000. **Membership Dues:** regular, $20 (annual). **Staff:** 25. **Budget:** $1,900,000. **Local**. Works to support research to find a cure for, and prevention of arthritis, and to improve the quality of life of those affected by arthritis. **Libraries: Type:** lending. **Holdings:** books, video recordings. **Awards: Frequency:** annual. **Type:** monetary. **Programs:** Joints in Motion. **Affiliated With:** Arthritis Foundation. **Publications:** *Arthritis Today*, bimonthly. Magazine. **Price:** included in membership dues; $12.95/issue for nonmembers. **Circulation:** 500,000. **Advertising:** accepted. Alternate Formats: online • *Joint Venture*. Newsletter. Keeps members up-to-date on local programs, exercise classes, seminars, and presentations. Alternate Formats: online. **Conventions/Meetings:** annual meeting (exhibits) - October.

14074 ■ Asian American Bar Association of Ohio
c/o James Wong Chin
526 Superior Ave. N
745 Leader Bldg.
Cleveland, OH 44114
Ph: (216)241-4246
Fax: (216)241-0646
E-mail: jimmychin@aol.com
URL: National Affiliate–www.napaba.org
Contact: James Wong Chin, Contact
State. Represents the interests of Asian Pacific American attorneys and their communities. Promotes justice, equity and opportunity for Asian Pacific Americans. Fosters professional development, legal scholarship, advocacy and community development. **Affiliated With:** National Asian Pacific American Bar Association.

14075 ■ Association of Community Organizations for Reform Now, Cleveland
3615 Superior Ave., 4th Fl.
Cleveland, OH 44114
Ph: (216)431-0573
Fax: (216)431-6077
E-mail: ohacorncv@acorn.org
URL: National Affiliate–www.acorn.org
Local. Affiliated With: Association of Community Organizations for Reform Now.

14076 ■ Association for Computing Machinery, Case Western Reserve University
c/o Paul Schneider, Staff Advisor
11111 Euclid Ave.
Thwing Ctr.
Cleveland, OH 44106-7103
Ph: (216)754-2034
E-mail: froggy@eecs.cwru.edu
URL: http://acm.cwru.edu
Local. Affiliated With: Association for Computing Machinery.

14077 ■ Association of Energy Engineers, Ohio/Northern - Cleveland/Akron
c/o Renee Benjamin
1642 Lakeside Ave.
Cleveland, OH 44114
Ph: (216)443-7636
Fax: (216)443-7663
E-mail: c0r1b@www.cuyahoga.oh.us
URL: National Affiliate–www.aeecenter.org
Contact: Renee Benjamin, Pres.
Local. Affiliated With: Association of Energy Engineers.

14078 ■ Association of Government Accountants - Cleveland Chapter
PO Box 99834
Cleveland, OH 44199
Ph: (216)204-7472
Fax: (216)204-1935
E-mail: agacleveland@agacleveland.org
URL: http://www.agacleveland.org
Contact: Bill Walsh CGFM, Pres.
Local. Provides quality education, professional development and certification to government accountants. Supports standards and research to advance government accountability. Seeks to encourage the interchange of ideas among financial managers in government service and among government and nongovernmental managers. **Affiliated With:** Association of Government Accountants.

14079 ■ Association of Legal Administrators, Cleveland Chapter
c/o Kristin A. Oliveri, Pres.
800 Superior Ave.
Cleveland, OH 44114
Ph: (216)622-8657
E-mail: koliveri@calfee.com
URL: http://www.alacleveland.org
Contact: Kristin A. Oliveri, Pres.
Local. Affiliated With: Association of Legal Administrators.

14080 ■ Athletics Directors Association, Division I-AAA
c/o NACDA
PO Box 16428
Cleveland, OH 44116
Ph: (440)892-4000
Fax: (440)892-4007
E-mail: carlon@uta.edu
URL: National Affiliate–www.nacda.collegesports.com
Contact: Mr. Pete Carlon, Pres.
Local.

14081 ■ Bakery, Confectionery, Tobacco Workers and Grain Millers International Union, AFL-CIO, CLC - Local Union 19
9665 Rockside Rd., Ste.B
Cleveland, OH 44125-6233
Ph: (216)771-5386
Fax: (216)520-1534
Free: (800)362-2120
E-mail: local19@bctgmlocal19.com
URL: http://www.bctgmlocal19.com
Contact: Paul LaBuda, Pres.
Members: 4,777. **Local. Affiliated With:** Bakery, Confectionery, Tobacco Workers and Grain Millers International Union.

14082 ■ Better Business Bureau, Cleveland
2217 E 9th St., Ste.200
Cleveland, OH 44115-1299
Ph: (216)241-7678
Fax: (216)861-6365
Free: (800)233-0361
E-mail: info@cleveland.bbb.org
URL: http://www.cleveland.bbb.org
Contact: David Weiss, Pres.
Local. Seeks to promote and foster ethical relationship between businesses and the public through voluntary self-regulation, consumer and business education, and service excellence. Provides information to help consumers and businesses make informed purchasing decisions and avoid costly scams and frauds; settles consumer complaints through arbitration and other means. **Affiliated With:** BBB Wise Giving Alliance.

14083 ■ Black Shield Police Association
c/o Lemgriffin
4097 E 131st St.
Cleveland, OH 44105-5564
Ph: (216)561-7777
Local.

14084 ■ Blacks In Government, Greater Cleveland Chapter
PO Box 811071
Cleveland, OH 44181-1071
E-mail: james.f.travis@grc.nasa.gov
URL: http://www.bignet.org/regional/greater.cleveland/index.htm
Contact: James F. Travis, Pres.
Local. Represents federal, state, and local government employees concerned with the present and future status of Blacks in government. Conducts seminars and workshops for professional and nonprofessional government employees. Advocates for equal opportunities for Blacks in government. **Affiliated With:** National Organization of Blacks in Government.

14085 ■ Business Volunteers Unlimited (BVU)
c/o Denise M. O'Brien, Dir., Administration
200 Public Sq., Ste.2650
Cleveland, OH 44114
Ph: (216)736-7711
Fax: (216)736-7710
E-mail: bvu@businessvolunteers.org
URL: http://www.businessvolunteers.org
Local.

14086 ■ Center for Mental Retardation (Cayuhoga)
3100 E 45th Pl., Ste.212
Cleveland, OH 44127
Ph: (216)341-5488
Fax: (216)341-5669
URL: http://www.cmr-cleveland.org
Contact: Charles P. Royer, Pres.
Founded: 1962. **Local**.

14087 ■ Chemical Coaters Association International, Northern Ohio
12703 Triskett Rd.
Cleveland, OH 44111
Ph: (216)476-8400
Fax: (216)476-1231
E-mail: mfr@chemicalmethods.com
URL: National Affiliate–www.ccaiweb.com
Contact: Michael Richards, Pres.
Local. Provides information and training on surface coating technologies. Raises the standards of finishing operations through educational meetings and seminars, training manuals, certification programs, and outreach programs with colleges and universities. **Affiliated With:** Chemical Coaters Association International.

14088 ■ Children's Rights Council of Cleveland
PO Box 771291
Cleveland, OH 44107
Ph: (216)249-3199
Fax: (216)731-4669
E-mail: crcofcleveland@juno.com
URL: National Affiliate–www.gocrc.com
Local. Affiliated With: Children's Rights Council.

14089 ■ City News Community Development Corporation
c/o James R. Crosby
1419 E 40th St.
Cleveland, OH 44103-1103
Ph: (216)881-0799
URL: http://www.citynewsohio.com
Contact: James Crosby, Contact
Local.

14090 ■ City Year Cleveland
c/o Christopher K. Larson
1007 Euclid Ave.
Cleveland, OH 44115
Ph: (216)574-2677
Fax: (216)574-2680
E-mail: clarson@cityyear.org
URL: http://www.cityyear.org
Local.

14091 ■ Cleveland AIFA
c/o Kimberly Hronek, Exec.
1120 Chester Ave., Ste.470
Cleveland, OH 44114
Ph: (216)241-3909
Fax: (216)696-2582
E-mail: khronek@mjmservices.org
URL: National Affiliate–naifa.org
Contact: Kimberly Hronek, Exec.
Local. Represents the interests of insurance and financial advisors. Advocates for a positive legislative and regulatory environment. Enhances business and professional skills of members. **Affiliated With:** National Association of Insurance and Financial Advisors.

14092 ■ Cleveland All-Breed Training Club (CABTC)
210 Hayes Dr., Ste.B
Cleveland, OH 44131
Ph: (216)398-1118
URL: http://www.cabtc.org
Contact: Elaine Moore, Corresponding Sec.
Local.

14093 ■ Cleveland Area Mountain Bike Association
PO Box 771471
Cleveland, OH 44107
E-mail: info@camba.us
URL: http://www.camba.us
Contact: Mr. Bill Braum, Pres.
Founded: 2001. **Members:** 225. **Membership Dues:** all, $20 (annual). **Budget:** $3,000. **Local Groups:** 1. **Local. Affiliated With:** International Mountain Bicycling Association.

14094 ■ Cleveland Association for Business Economics
c/o Dr. Michael Stoller, Pres.
PO Box 14003
Cleveland, OH 44114-0003
Ph: (440)543-7514
Fax: (440)543-7514
E-mail: mstoller1@adelphia.net
URL: http://www.bjkresearch.com/cabe
Local. Meets monthly during September through May to hear speakers on topics of current economic interest. **Affiliated With:** National Association for Business Economics.

14095 ■ Cleveland Chamber Collective
c/o Nicholas K. Underhill
17812 Landseer Rd.
Cleveland, OH 44119
Ph: (216)486-1884
E-mail: n.underhill@att.net
Contact: Nicholas Underhill, Dir.
Founded: 1992. **Members:** 7. **Staff:** 1. **Budget:** $1,500. **Local**.

14096 ■ Cleveland Chapter of the Society of Financial Service Professionals
1120 Chester Ave., Ste.470
Cleveland, OH 44114
Ph: (216)241-3910
Fax: (216)696-2582
E-mail: admin@clevelandsociety.org
URL: http://www.sfsp.net/cleveland
Contact: M. Joan McCarthy, Administrator
Local. Represents the interests of financial advisers. Fosters the development of professional responsibility. Helps clients achieve their personal and business-related financial goals. **Affiliated With:** Society of Financial Service Professionals.

14097 ■ Cleveland Council Black Nurses Association (17)
PO Box 221066
Cleveland, OH 44122
Ph: (216)426-1099
URL: National Affiliate–www.nbna.org
Contact: Dr. Rebecca Stitt-Fuller, Contact
Local. Represents registered nurses, licensed practical nurses, licensed vocational nurses, and student nurses. Builds consumer knowledge and understanding of health care issues. Facilitates the professional development and career advancement of nurses in emerging healthcare systems. Promotes economic development of nurses through entrepreneurial and other business initiatives. **Affiliated With:** National Black Nurses Association.

14098 ■ Cleveland Engineering Society (CES)
3100 Chester Ave., No. 216
Cleveland, OH 44114-4604
Ph: (216)361-3100
Fax: (216)361-1660
E-mail: info@cesnet.org
URL: http://www.cesnet.org
Contact: Carol A. Duane, Exec.Dir.
Founded: 1880. **Members:** 1,000. **Membership Dues:** active, $135 (annual) • executive, $260 (annual) • sustaining, $210 (annual) • senior, $55 (annual) • student, $25 (annual) • corporate, $750 (annual) • corporate partner (based on number of designates), $1,500-$5,000 (annual) • affiliate (based on number of members), $100-$200 (annual). **Staff:** 6. **Budget:** $375,000. **Local**. Engineers and other technical professional in northeast Ohio. Also offers educational programs, courses, tours, and networking. **Awards: Frequency:** annual. **Type:** scholarship. **Recipient:** for freshmen in college pursuing engineering or science related major. **Divisions:** Design & Construction; Energy; Environmental; Healthcare Facilities; Information Technology; Management of Technology; Senior; Young Profession. **Publications:** *CES Prospectus*, monthly. Newsletter. **Price:** included in membership dues; $20.00 /year for nonmembers. **Circulation:** 1,200. **Advertising:** accepted. **Conventions/Meetings:** annual Design and Construction Conference, Technology Conference, Energy Conference (exhibits) • biennial Infrastructure Conference • monthly Leadership Breakfast Series.

14099 ■ Cleveland Fellowship of Christian Athletes
PO Box 31780
Cleveland, OH 44131
Ph: (440)572-4242
E-mail: contact@fcacleveland.org
URL: http://www.fcacleveland.org
Contact: Jason Carthen, Dir.
Local.

14100 ■ Cleveland Memorial Society
21600 Shaker Blvd.
Cleveland, OH 44122
Ph: (216)751-5515
E-mail: info@clevememorialsociety.org
URL: http://www.clevememorialsociety.org
Founded: 1948. **Members:** 6,000. **Membership Dues:** life, $15. **Staff:** 1. **Budget:** $10,000. **Local**. Promotes dignified memorial services. Educates public regarding options in funeral and memorial arrangements. **Libraries: Type:** open to the public. **Holdings:** 100. **Subjects:** funeral industry, death, process of dying. **Affiliated With:** Funeral Consumers Alliance. **Publications:** Newsletter, annual. **Circulation:** 3,000. **Conventions/Meetings:** annual meeting.

14101 ■ Cleveland Peace Action
c/o Francis Chiappa
10916 Magnolia Dr.
Cleveland, OH 44106
Ph: (216)231-4245
E-mail: chiapski@aol.com
URL: http://www.peaceactioncleveland.org
Contact: Francis Chiappa, Pres.
Founded: 1981. **Members:** 975. **Budget:** $5,000. **State Groups:** 1. **Local Groups:** 1. **Regional**. Seeks to reduce violence, war and terrorism, through peaceful, just and democratic means-legislative action, media program, newsletter, informative and inspirational events. **Affiliated With:** Peace Action. **Formerly:** (1992) SANE/FREEZE of Greater Cleveland. **Publications:** *Cleveland Peace Action*, 5/year.

Newsletter. **Price:** free. **Circulation:** 2,500. **Conventions/Meetings:** quarterly Nuclearization of Space - meeting.

14102 ■ Cleveland Police Historical Society and Museum (CPHS)
1300 Ontario St.
Cleveland, OH 44113
Ph: (216)623-5055
E-mail: museum@stratos.net
URL: http://www.clevelandpolicemuseum.org
Contact: David C. Holcombe, Exec.Dir.
Founded: 1983. **Members:** 1,400. **Membership Dues:** family, $52 (annual) • retired, $10 (annual) • organ, business, $250 (annual) • life, $1,000 • corporate, $500 (annual) • individual, $26 (annual). **Staff:** 4. **Budget:** $10,000. **Regional Groups:** 1. **State Groups:** 2. **Local**. Individuals in Cleveland, OH interested in law enforcement history. Works to promote a better understanding of law enforcement, past and present. Works to preserve the history of the Cleveland, OH Police Department. Collects documents and artifacts. Maintains the Cleveland Police Museum, which conducts educational programs. **Libraries: Type:** open to the public. **Holdings:** archival material. **Awards:** Cleveland Police Historical Society Museum Hall of Fame. **Frequency:** annual. **Type:** recognition. **Recipient:** individuals who have made significant contributions to the safety and protection of Cleveland citizens. **Formerly:** Cleveland Police Historical Society, Inc. and Museum. **Publications:** *CPHS Newsletter*, quarterly • *The Hot Sheet*, quarterly. Newsletter.

14103 ■ Cleveland Society for Human Resource Management (CSHRM)
PO Box 32148
Cleveland, OH 44132
Ph: (216)556-3855
Fax: (216)261-3979
E-mail: michelle_m_flanik@keybank.com
URL: http://www.clevelandshrm.com
Contact: Michelle Flanik, Pres.
Local. Represents the interests of human resource and industrial relations professionals and executives. Promotes the advancement of human resource management.

14104 ■ Cleveland Society of Security Analysts
c/o Hilary A. Wiek, CFA
127 Public Sq., OH 01 27 2001
Cleveland, OH 44114
Ph: (216)696-8066
Fax: (216)689-3848
E-mail: hilary_a_wiek@keybank.com
Contact: Hillary Wiek, Pres.
Founded: 1950. **Members:** 320. **Membership Dues:** affiliate, $100 (annual) • regular, $100 (annual) • retired, $75 (annual). **Staff:** 1. **Local Groups:** 1. **Local**. Seeks to educate and inform members about companies and information concerning investment management. Members include financial analysts and portfolio managers in investment management businesses. **Formerly:** (1998) Association for Investment Management and Research, Cleveland Society. **Conventions/Meetings:** weekly luncheon, usually with topical speakers - Wednesdays. Cleveland, OH - Avg. Attendance: 50.

14105 ■ Cleveland Table Tennis Association
The Masonic Bldg.
3615 Euclid Ave., 4th Fl.
Cleveland, OH 44110
Ph: (216)268-1798 (216)391-2882
E-mail: dan1@eriecoast.com
URL: http://www.usatt.org/clubs
Contact: Dan Fondale, Contact
Local. Affiliated With: U.S.A. Table Tennis.

14106 ■ Communications Workers of America, AFL-CIO, CLC - Local Union 34001
1729 Superior Ave. E, Ste.450
Cleveland, OH 44114-2989
Ph: (216)621-6792
Fax: (216)621-6793
Free: (800)621-6202
E-mail: tnglocal1@sbcglobal.net
URL: http://tnglocal1.org
Contact: Richard Peery, Pres.
Members: 696. **Local. Affiliated With:** National Association Broadcast Employees and Technicians - Communications Workers of America.

14107 ■ Convention and Visitors Bureau of Greater Cleveland (CVBGC)
50 Public Sq., Ste.3100
Cleveland, OH 44113-2290
Ph: (216)621-4110
Fax: (216)621-5967
Free: (800)321-1004
E-mail: cvb@travelcleveland.com
URL: http://www.travelcleveland.com
Contact: Ms. DeAnn Hazey, Dir. of Communications
Local. Promotes business and community development in the Greater Cleveland area.

14108 ■ Cuyahoga County Planning Commission (CPC)
323 Lakeside Ave. W, Ste.400
Cleveland, OH 44113
Ph: (216)443-3700
Fax: (216)443-3737
E-mail: cpc@planning.co.cuyahoga.oh.us
URL: http://planning.co.cuyahoga.oh.us
Local.

14109 ■ Dress for Success Cleveland
2239 E 55th St.
Cleveland, OH 44103
Ph: (216)391-2301
Fax: (216)391-2380
URL: National Affiliate–www.dressforsuccess.org
Local.

14110 ■ Earth Day Coalition (EDC)
3606 Bridge Ave.
Cleveland, OH 44113
Ph: (216)281-6468
Fax: (216)281-5112
E-mail: edc@earthdaycoalition.org
URL: http://www.earthdaycoalition.org
Contact: Scott Sanders, Exec.Dir.
Founded: 1990. **Members:** 1,000. **Membership Dues:** basic, $35 (annual) • contributing, $50 (annual) • supporting, $100 (annual) • sponsoring, $250 (annual). **Staff:** 7. **Budget:** $400,000. **Languages:** English, Spanish. **Regional**. Promotes programs that include community pollution prevention and sustainable economic development with the Sustainable Cleveland Partnership; student leadership development and service learning with the student Environmental Congress; cleaner transportation with the Clean Cities Program; the Green Building project, creating environmentally friendly buildings; EMPACT, educating Northeast Ohio residents about and tracking progress of air quality; and many others. **Awards:** State Energy Program Grants. **Frequency:** annual. **Type:** grant. **Recipient:** for contribution in clean fuel programs. **Publications:** *Earth Day Coalition News*, quarterly. Newsletter • *Environmental Health Action Guide* • *Guide to the Green Scene*, annual. Directory. **Conventions/Meetings:** semiannual Advance the Choice Workshop, for alternative fuel vehicle fleet managers.

14111 ■ East Side Organizing Project
c/o Mark Seifert
1202 Miles Ave.
Cleveland, OH 44105
Ph: (216)429-0757
E-mail: esop_fighting_to_win@ameritech.net
URL: http://www.esop-cleveland.org
Local. Affiliated With: National People's Action.

14112 ■ Edgewater Yacht Club (EYC)
6700 Memorial Shoreway NW
Cleveland, OH 44102
Ph: (216)281-6470
Fax: (216)281-0265
E-mail: adam_zangerle@steris.com
URL: http://www.eycweb.com
Contact: Adam Zangerle, Commodore
Local.

14113 ■ Employee Assistance Professionals Association - Northern Ohio Chapter
PO Box 5167
Cleveland, OH 44101-0167
Ph: (216)491-4626
E-mail: lachell2@aol.com
URL: http://www.ohioeapa.com
Contact: Rochelle Keith, Pres.
Local. Affiliated With: Employee Assistance Professionals Association.

14114 ■ Epilepsy Association
2800 Euclid Ave., Ste.450
Cleveland, OH 44115-2418
Ph: (216)579-1330
Fax: (216)579-1336
Free: (800)653-4300
E-mail: info@epilepsyinfo.org
URL: http://www.epilepsyinfo.org
Founded: 1972. **Local**. Works to help people manage and cope with seizure disorders by improving their quality of life. **Boards:** Trustees. **Affiliated With:** Epilepsy Foundation. **Formerly:** (2005) Epilepsy Foundation of Northeast Ohio.

14115 ■ Esprit The Ultimate Ski and Sports Club
PO Box 94151
Cleveland, OH 44101-4151
E-mail: maryann608@yahoo.com
URL: http://www.espritsportsclub.com
Contact: Mary Ann Grayson, Pres.
Local. Affiliated With: National Brotherhood of Skiers.

14116 ■ Estate Planning Council of Cleveland
c/o Eleanor M. Spuhler
1120 Chester Ave., Ste.470
Cleveland, OH 44114-3514
Ph: (216)696-1228
Fax: (216)696-2582
E-mail: admin@epccleveland.org
URL: http://councils.naepc.org
Contact: J. Joseph Korpics, Pres.
Founded: 1930. **Members:** 430. **Local**. Advances estate planning knowledge and expertise. Represents the interests of professionals involved in estate planning field. Provides educational programs and forums to various professional disciplines. Encourages cooperation among members. **Affiliated With:** National Association of Estate Planners and Councils.

14117 ■ Euclid-St. Clair Development Corporation
17608 Euclid Ave.
Cleveland, OH 44112-1216
Ph: (216)486-9123
Fax: (216)486-9132
Contact: Ms. Sharonda Woodland, Admin.Asst.
Local.

14118 ■ Executive Women International/Cleveland
1331 Euclid Ave., United Way-Joanne Carter
Cleveland, OH 44115
Ph: (216)447-8960
Fax: (216)447-8967
E-mail: sherri.l.poore@aexp.com
URL: http://www.executivewomen.locality.com
Contact: Sherri L. Poore, Pres.
Local. Conducts networking educational and charitable programs. Enhances personal and professional development. Encourages community involvement. **Affiliated With:** Executive Women International.

14119 ■ Federalist Society for Law and Public Policy Studies - Cleveland Chapter
c/o Mr. David C. Tryon
Porter, Wright, Morris & Arthur
925 Euclid Ave., Ste.1700
Cleveland, OH 44115
Ph: (216)443-2560
Fax: (216)443-9011
E-mail: dtryon@porterwright.com
URL: National Affiliate–www.fed-soc.org
Contact: Mr. David C. Tryon, Contact

Local. Seeks to bring about a reordering of priorities within the U.S. legal system that will emphasize individual liberty, traditional values, and the rule of law. **Affiliated With:** Federalist Society for Law and Public Policy Studies.

14120 ■ Financial Executives International, Northeast Ohio Chapter
c/o Ms. Louise A. Walsh, Administrator
1120 Chester Ave., Ste.470
Cleveland, OH 44114
Ph: (216)696-5501
Fax: (216)696-2582
E-mail: admin@feineo.org
URL: http://fei.org/chapter/neohio
Contact: Mr. Ray Kalich, Pres.

Founded: 1935. **Local**. Promotes personal and professional development of financial executives. Provides peer networking opportunities and advocacy services. **Committees:** Career Services; Meeting Arrangements; Nominations; Professional Development; Programs; Retention; Sponsorship. **Affiliated With:** Financial Executives International. **Publications:** Newsletter, monthly. Alternate Formats: online. **Conventions/Meetings:** monthly meeting - every 2nd Tuesday; September through May (excluding January).

14121 ■ First Catholic Slovak Ladies Association - Cleveland Junior Branch 240
c/o Betty J. Kuchta
3304 W 30th St.
Cleveland, OH 44109
Ph: (216)671-2044
URL: National Affiliate–www.fcsla.com
Contact: Betty J. Kuchta, Contact

Local. Affiliated With: First Catholic Slovak Ladies Association.

14122 ■ First Catholic Slovak Ladies Association - Cleveland Senior Branch 010
17807 Nottingham Rd.
Cleveland, OH 44119
Ph: (216)464-8015
E-mail: irene@fcsla.com
URL: National Affiliate–www.fcsla.com

Local. Affiliated With: First Catholic Slovak Ladies Association.

14123 ■ First Catholic Slovak Ladies Association - Cleveland Senior Branch 360
3304 W 30th St.
Cleveland, OH 44109
Ph: (216)351-0338
URL: National Affiliate–www.fcsla.com

Local. Affiliated With: First Catholic Slovak Ladies Association.

14124 ■ First Catholic Slovak Ladies Association - Cleveland Senior Branch 530
c/o Rev. Albert Marflak
10510 Buckeye Rd.
Cleveland, OH 44104
Ph: (216)721-5300
URL: National Affiliate–www.fcsla.com
Contact: Rev. Albert Marflak, Contact

Local. Affiliated With: First Catholic Slovak Ladies Association.

14125 ■ Germany Philatelic Society, No. 19 Cleveland
c/o Wilton S. Sogg
1800 Midland Bldg.
101 W Prospect Ave.
Cleveland, OH 44115-1088
Ph: (216)621-0150
URL: National Affiliate–www.gps.nu
Contact: Wilton S. Sogg, Contact

Local. Affiliated With: Germany Philatelic Society.

14126 ■ Girl Scouts of Lake Erie Council (GSLEC)
19201 Villaview Rd.
Cleveland, OH 44119-4073
Ph: (216)481-1313
Fax: (216)692-4060
Free: (800)362-0215
E-mail: girlscouts@gslec.org
URL: http://www.gslec.org

Local.

14127 ■ Gr. Cleveland YoungLives - YoungLives
3178 W 94th St.
Cleveland, OH 44102
Ph: (216)281-5812
URL; http://sites.younglife.org/_layouts/ylext/default.aspx?ID=C-1481

Local. Affiliated With: Young Life.

14128 ■ Great Lakes REACT
PO Box 44405
Cleveland, OH 44144
Ph: (216)324-2061
E-mail: greatlakesreact@usa.com
URL: http://www.reactintl.org/teaminfo/usa_teams/teams-usoh.htm

Local. Trained communication experts and professional volunteers. Provides volunteer public service and emergency communications through the use of radios (Citizen Band, General Mobile Radio Service, UHF and HAM). Coordinates with radio industries and government on safety communication matters and supports charitable activities and community organizations.

14129 ■ Greater Cleveland Chapter National Electrical Contractors Association
PO Box 348001
950 Keynote Cir., Ste.20
Cleveland, OH 44131
Ph: (216)398-8440
Fax: (216)398-7928
Free: (800)229-NECA
E-mail: gccneca@gccneca.org
URL: http://www.gccneca.org
Contact: Richard L. Newcomer, Exec.Dir.

Local. Represents contractors erecting, installing, repairing, servicing, and maintaining electric wiring, equipment, and appliances. **Affiliated With:** National Electrical Contractors Association.

14130 ■ Greater Cleveland Dental Society (GCDS)
200 Treeworth Blvd.
Cleveland, OH 44147
Ph: (440)717-1891
Fax: (440)717-1894
E-mail: calderdice@gcds.org
URL: http://www.gcds.org
Contact: Ms. Carla J. Alderdice, Exec.Dir.

Local. Represents the interests of dentists committed to the public's oral health, ethics and professional development. Encourages the improvement of the public's oral health and promotes the art and science of dentistry. **Affiliated With:** American Dental Association; Ohio Dental Association.

14131 ■ Greater Cleveland Ecology Association
323 Lakeside Ave. W., Ste.400
Cleveland, OH 44113
Ph: (216)687-1266 (216)443-3706
Fax: (216)443-3737
E-mail: clh1@nacs.net
Contact: Sheila Carlson, Acting Dir.

Local.

14132 ■ Greater Cleveland Habitat for Humanity (GCHFH)
6920 Union Ave.
Cleveland, OH 44105
Ph: (216)429-1299
Fax: (216)429-3629
E-mail: ed@gchfh.org
URL: http://www.gchfh.org
Contact: Jeffrey Bowen, Exec.Dir.

Local. Affiliated With: Habitat for Humanity International.

14133 ■ Greater Cleveland Media Development Corp.
50 Public Sq., Ste.825
Cleveland, OH 44113-2239
Ph: (216)623-3910
Fax: (216)623-0876
Free: (888)746-FILM
E-mail: ccarmody@clevelandfilm.com
URL: http://www.clevelandfilm.com
Contact: Chris Carmody, Pres.

Founded: 1998. **Staff:** 3. **Local. Affiliated With:** Association of Film Commissioners International. **Also Known As:** (2004) Greater Cleveland Film Commission.

14134 ■ Greater Cleveland Partnership (GCP)
Tower City Center
50 Public Sq., Ste.200
Cleveland, OH 44113-2291
Ph: (216)621-3300
Fax: (216)621-4617
Free: (888)304-GROW
E-mail: customerservice@clevegrowth.com
URL: http://www.clevelandgrowth.com
Contact: David Goss, Senior Dir.

Founded: 1983. **Members:** 7. **Staff:** 3. **Budget:** $250,000. **Local**. Public works infrastructure advocacy. Develops community capital investment strategy (biannually). Offers technical support to members. **Publications:** *Community Capital Investment Strategy*, biennial.

14135 ■ Greater Cleveland Youth for Christ
2230 W 110th
Cleveland, OH 44102
Ph: (216)252-9881
Fax: (216)252-9882
URL: http://www.yfccleveland.org

Local. Affiliated With: Youth for Christ/U.S.A.

14136 ■ Grounds Managers Association
c/o Paul J. Pfeifer, Pres.
PO Box 606246
Cleveland, OH 44106
Ph: (216)721-1600
Fax: (216)368-3080
Free: (800)421-8722
E-mail: gmaohio@aol.com
URL: National Affiliate–www.pgms.org
Contact: Diane Gerlach, Exec.Sec.

Local. Affiliated With: Professional Grounds Management Society.

14137 ■ Healthcare Financial Management Association, Northeast Ohio Chapter
c/o Christopher Milligan, Pres.
1457 E 40th St.
Cleveland, OH 44103-1103

Ph: (216)426-3535
E-mail: cmilligan@humanarc.com
URL: http://www.neohfma.org
Contact: Christopher Milligan, Pres.

Local. Provides education, analysis and guidance to healthcare finance professionals. Helps members and other individuals in advancing the financial management of health care and in improving the business performance of organizations serving the healthcare field. **Affiliated With:** Healthcare Financial Management Association.

14138 ■ Heather McNally Milko (HMP)
c/o Heather McNally Milko
5882 Pearl Rd.
Cleveland, OH 44130
Ph: (440)888-3575
Fax: (440)888-6330
Free: (866)888-3575
E-mail: hmp@hmpevents.com
URL: http://www.hmpevents.com
Contact: Heather McNally Milko, Exec.Dir.

Local.

14139 ■ High Technology Crime Investigation Association - Ohio
PO Box 99242
Cleveland, OH 44199
E-mail: info@ohiohtcia.org
URL: http://www.ohiohtcia.org
Contact: Leonard Drinkard, Pres.

State. Promotes the voluntary interchange of data, information, experience, ideas and knowledge about methods, processes, and techniques relating to investigations and security in advanced technologies. **Affiliated With:** High Technology Crime Investigation Association International.

14140 ■ IEEE Lasers and Electro-Optics Society, Cleveland
c/o M. Tabib-Azar
Case Western Reserve Univ.
Elecl. Engg. Dept.
10900 Euclid Ave.
Cleveland, OH 44106-7221
Ph: (216)368-6431
Fax: (216)368-6039
E-mail: mxt7@case.edu
URL: National Affiliate–www.i-LEOS.org
Contact: Massod Tabib-Avar, Contact

Local. **Affiliated With:** IEEE Lasers and Electro-Optics Society.

14141 ■ Information Systems Audit and Control Association, Northeast Ohio Chapter
c/o Karen Doubrava, CISA
2060 E 9th St.
Cleveland, OH 44115-1355
Ph: (216)687-7932
E-mail: karen.doubrava@mmoh.com
URL: http://www.isaca-neohio.org
Contact: Karen Doubrava CISA, Contact

Local. **Affiliated With:** Information Systems Audit and Control Association and Foundation.

14142 ■ International Alliance of Theatrical Stage Employees, Moving Picture Technicians, Artists, MPP, OandVT 160
2900 Euclid Ave.
Cleveland, OH 44115-2416
Ph: (216)621-7854
Fax: (216)621-9123
E-mail: iatse160@usa.com
URL: National Affiliate–www.iatse.lm.com
Contact: John A. Galinac, Contact

Members: 66. **Local**. **Affiliated With:** International Alliance of Theatrical Stage Employees, Moving Picture Technicians, Artists and Allied Crafts of the United States, Its Territories and Canada.

14143 ■ International Association of Gay/Lesbian Country Western Dance Clubs, Rainbow Wranglers
PO Box 99327
Cleveland, OH 44199-0327
Ph: (216)228-7145
E-mail: president@rainbowwranglers.org
URL: http://rainbowwranglers.org
Contact: Leslie Nelson, Pres.

Local. **Affiliated With:** International Association of Gay/Lesbian Country Western Dance Clubs.

14144 ■ International Association of Gay Square Dance Clubs - Cleveland City Country Dancers (CCCD)
PO Box 5592
Cleveland, OH 44101-0592
E-mail: hawk22@ameritech.net
URL: http://www.cccdohio.org
Contact: Jerry W., Pres.

Local. Fosters educational, recreational, and social opportunities within the framework of Modern Western square dancing for the gay and lesbian community. Works to increase the enjoyment of square dancing for everyone. Promotes better understanding between the straight world and the gay and lesbian community. **Affiliated With:** International Association of Gay Square Dance Clubs.

14145 ■ International Brotherhood of Magicians, Ring 23
c/o David C. Boyce, Treas.
4403 Denison Ave.
Cleveland, OH 44109
Ph: (216)739-1522
E-mail: info@ring23.org
URL: http://www.magician.org
Contact: Dr. Bruce Averbook, Pres.

Local. Professional and semiprofessional magicians; suppliers, assistants, agents, and others interested in magic. Seeks to advance the art of magic in the field of amusement, entertainment, and culture. Promotes proper means of discouraging false or misleading advertising of effects, tricks, literature, merchandise, or actions appertaining to the magical arts; opposes exposures of principles of the art of magic, except in books on magic and magazines devoted to such art for the exclusive use of magicians and devotees of the art; encourages humane treatment and care of live animals whenever employed in magical performances. **Affiliated With:** International Brotherhood of Magicians.

14146 ■ International Customer Service Association, Cleveland/Northcoast
c/o Rita Tormento
McGean-Rohco, Inc.
2910 Harvard Ave.
Cleveland, OH 44105
Ph: (216)441-4900
Fax: (216)441-1377
E-mail: rita.tormento@mcgean-rohco.com
URL: National Affiliate–www.icsa.com
Contact: Rita Tormento, Mgr.

Local. **Affiliated With:** International Customer Service Association.

14147 ■ International Union of Bricklayers and Allied Craftworkers, AFL-CIO-CLC Local Union 36
c/o Daniel Zavagno, Business Mgr./Field Representative
4205 Chester Ave.
Cleveland, OH 44103
Ph: (216)426-8552
Fax: (216)426-8549
E-mail: zavagno_local36@noadc97.org
URL: National Affiliate–www.bacweb.org
Contact: Daniel Zavagno, Business Mgr./Field Representative

Members: 110. **Local**. **Affiliated With:** International Union of Bricklayers and Allied Craftworkers.

14148 ■ International Union of Operating Engineers, Local 018
3515 Prospect Ave.
Cleveland, OH 44115
Ph: (216)432-3138
Fax: (216)432-0370
URL: http://www.iuoelocal18.org
Contact: Patrick L. Sink, Business Mgr.

Local. AFL-CIO. **Affiliated With:** International Union of Operating Engineers.

14149 ■ Japanese American Citizens League - Cleveland Chapter
2783 Lancashire, No. 15
Cleveland, OH 44106
Ph: (216)556-2277
E-mail: cleveland@jacl.org
URL: http://www.lkwdpl.org/jacl

Local. **Affiliated With:** Japanese American Citizens League.

14150 ■ Jewish Community Federation of Cleveland
c/o Stephen H. Hoffman, Pres.
1750 Euclid Ave.
Cleveland, OH 44115
Ph: (216)566-9200
Fax: (216)861-1230
E-mail: info@jcfcleve.org
URL: http://www.jewishcleveland.org
Contact: Stephen H. Hoffman, Pres.

Founded: 1839. **Local**.

14151 ■ Juvenile Diabetes Research Foundation International, Northeast Ohio Chapter
5000 Rockside Rd., Ste.310
Cleveland, OH 44131
Ph: (216)524-6000
Fax: (216)328-8340
Free: (888)718-3061
E-mail: northeastohio@jdrf.org
URL: http://www.jdrf.org
Contact: Laura Maciag, Exec.Dir.

Nonprofit, nongovernmental funder of diabetes research. Mission is to find a cure for diabetes and its complications through the support of research. **Affiliated With:** Juvenile Diabetes Research Foundation International.

14152 ■ Knights of Columbus, Cleveland Council No. 733
2132 E 9th St., Ste.319
Cleveland, OH 44115
Ph: (216)771-4811
Fax: (216)619-4812
E-mail: council733@kofc733.org
URL: http://www.kofc733.org
Contact: Henry L. Tucker, Grand Knight

Local. **Affiliated With:** Knights of Columbus.

14153 ■ Lake Carriers' Association (LCA)
614 W Superior Ave., Ste.915
Cleveland, OH 44113-1383
Ph: (216)621-1107 (216)861-0590
Fax: (216)241-8262
E-mail: ggn@lcaships.com
URL: http://www.lcaships.com
Contact: James H.I. Weakly, Pres.

Founded: 1880. **Members:** 12. **Staff:** 4. **Budget:** $700,000. Represents operators of U.S.-Flag Great Lakes bulk carriers before federal and state agencies. **Computer Services:** database, marketing contacts. **Committees:** Advisory; Captains; Fleet Engineers; International Joint Conference; Navigation; Vessel Personnel and Safety. **Absorbed:** (1892) Cleveland Vessel Owners Association. **Publications:** *Great Lakes Shipping and Michigan: Partners in Commerce.* Brochure • *Great Lakes Shipping: The Vital Link for Ohio Industry*. Brochure • *Lake Carriers' Association*, annual. Annual Report. **Price:** $10.00/individual, not directly involved with industry • *Tonnage Statistics*, monthly • *US-Flag Shipping on the Great Lakes.* Brochures • Videos. Feature the benefits of Great Lakes shipping. **Conventions/Meetings:** annual

International Joint Conference - alternates between U.S. and Canada.

14154 ■ Lake View Cemetery Association
12316 Euclid Ave.
Cleveland, OH 44106-4313
Ph: (216)421-2665
Fax: (216)421-2415
E-mail: info@lakeviewcemetery.com
URL: http://www.lakeviewcemetery.com
Contact: Mary C. Krohmer, Sec.
Local. Presents discoveries in architecture, geology, sculpture, animal life and horticulture. Offers a diverse year-round schedule of educational and cultural events. Strives to maintain the natural beauty and dignity of this historic non-sectarian cemetery.

14155 ■ League of Women Voters of the Cleveland Area (LWV)
1148 Euclid Ave., Ste.500
Cleveland, OH 44115
Ph: (216)781-8375
Fax: (216)781-8381
E-mail: info@lwvcef.org
URL: http://www.lwvcef.org
Contact: Barbara Stones, Pres.
Local.

14156 ■ League of Women Voters of Cuyahoga County
50 Public Sq., Rm. 938
Cleveland, OH 44113
Ph: (216)781-0555
E-mail: lwvcra@sbcglobal.net
URL: http://www.lwvcra.org
Contact: Carol E. Gibson, Contact
Founded: 1963. **Membership Dues:** local league (assessment), $2 (annual). **Budget:** $7,000. **Local Groups:** 11. **Local**. Studies county issues. Provides advocacy and educational services. **Publications:** *County Voter's Guide*, biennial, even-numbered years. Brochure.

14157 ■ Lesbian/Gay Community Center of Greater Cleveland
6600 Detroit Ave.
Cleveland, OH 44102
Ph: (216)651-5428
Fax: (216)651-6439
Free: (888)429-8761
E-mail: info@lgcsc.org
URL: http://www.lgcsc.org
Contact: Sue Doerfer, Exec.Dir.
Founded: 1975. **Members:** 1,000. **Membership Dues:** individual, $25 (annual) • family, $40 (annual) • senior, student, $15 (annual) • organizer, $150 (annual) • activist, $250 (annual) • pioneer, $600 (annual) • advocate, $1,200 (annual) • benefactor, $2,500 (annual) • patron, $5,000 (annual) • visionary, $10,000 (annual). **Staff:** 5. **Local**. Works as a community based service organization that serves the gay, lesbian, bisexual, and transgender communities in Northeast OH. Provides service to HIV/AIDS community and members of the larger community affected by sexual orientation and gender identity issues. Offers a drop-in for people living with HIV and AIDS. Maintains a resource center, peer support groups, speaker's bureau, youth group, safe school programs, anti-violence project and community outreach. **Formerly:** (1999) Pride and Respect for Youth in a Sexual Minority. **Publications:** *The Center Attraction*, quarterly. Newsletter. **Conventions/Meetings:** annual meeting.

14158 ■ Leukemia and Lymphoma Society of America, Northern Ohio
902 Westpoint Pkwy., Ste.300
Cleveland, OH 44145
Ph: (440)617-2873
Fax: (440)617-2880
E-mail: crossn@lls.org
URL: http://www.leukemia.org
Contact: Nathaniel A. Cross, Exec.Dir.
Founded: 1971. **Local**. Works to cure leukemia, lymphoma, Hodgkin's disease, and myeloma, and to improve the quality of life of patients and their families. **Affiliated With:** Leukemia and Lymphoma Society. **Formerly:** (2000) Leukemia Society of America, Northern Ohio.

14159 ■ Make-A-Wish Foundation of Greater Ohio and Kentucky
The Hanna Bldg.
1422 Euclid Ave., Ste.239
Cleveland, OH 44115
Ph: (216)241-3670
Fax: (216)241-3618
Free: (888)272-WISH
E-mail: neohio@makeawishohio.org
URL: http://www.makeawishohio.org
Contact: Susan McConnell, Pres./CEO
Founded: 1983. **Budget:** $4,000,000. **Local**. Grants wishes to children with life-threatening illnesses to enrich the human experience with hope, strength and joy. **Affiliated With:** Make-A-Wish Foundation of America. **Formerly:** (2001) Make-A-Wish Foundation of Northeast, Central, and Southern Ohio. **Publications:** *Wish-o-gram*, quarterly. Newsletter. **Conventions/Meetings:** bimonthly board meeting.

14160 ■ Make-A-Wish Foundation of Northeast Ohio
1422 Euclid Ave., Ste.239
Cleveland, OH 44115
Ph: (216)241-3670
Fax: (216)241-3618
Free: (888)272-WISH
E-mail: neohio@makeawishohio.org
URL: http://www.makeawishohio.org
Contact: Mary Coll, Admin.Coor.
Regional. Grants wishes to children with terminal or life-threatening illnesses, thereby providing these children and their families with special memories and a welcome respite from the daily stress of their situation. **Affiliated With:** Make-A-Wish Foundation of America.

14161 ■ Mechanical Contractors Association
981 Keynote Cir.
Cleveland, OH 44131
Ph: (216)459-0770
Fax: (216)459-1342
E-mail: mapic@mapic.org
URL: http://www.mapic.org
Contact: Thomas Wanner, Exec.Dir.
Local.

14162 ■ Mechanical and Plumbing Industry Council (MAPIC)
c/o Thomas J. Wanner, Exec.Dir.
981 Keynote Cir., Ste.30
Cleveland, OH 44131-1842
Ph: (216)459-0770
Fax: (216)459-1342
E-mail: mapic@mapic.org
URL: http://www.mapic.org
Contact: Thomas J. Wanner, Exec.Dir.
Local. Contractors who furnish, install, and service piping systems and related equipment for heating, cooling, refrigeration, ventilating, and air conditioning systems. **Affiliated With:** Mechanical Contractors Association of America. **Formerly:** (2005) Mechanical Contractors Association of Cleveland.

14163 ■ Medina County ALU
614 Superior Ave. NW, Ste.604
Cleveland, OH 44113
Ph: (216)696-1057
Fax: (330)722-5599
URL: National Affiliate–www.naifa.org
Local. Represents the interest of insurance and financial advisors. Advocates for a positive legislative and regulatory environment. Enhances business and professional skills of members. **Affiliated With:** National Association of Insurance and Financial Advisors.

14164 ■ Metro Cleveland Amateur Softball Association
601 Lakeside Ave., Rm. 8
Cleveland, OH 44144
Ph: (216)664-2326
Fax: (216)861-1709
E-mail: donnaddante_clevelandasa@msn.com
URL: http://www.asametrocleveland.com
Contact: Donn Addante, Commissioner
Local. **Affiliated With:** Amateur Softball Association of America.

14165 ■ MidTown Cleveland (MTC)
4019 Prospect Ave., No. 200
Cleveland, OH 44103
Ph: (216)391-5080
Fax: (216)391-6285
E-mail: info@midtowncleveland.org
URL: http://www.midtowncleveland.org
Contact: James A. Haviland, Exec.Dir.
Founded: 1982. **Members:** 255. **Membership Dues:** area business, $250 (annual). **Staff:** 8. **Budget:** $490,000. **Local**. Businesses interested in the revitalization of MidTown, a two square mile area of industrial, commercial, and residential properties in Cleveland, OH. **Awards: Frequency:** annual. **Type:** recognition. **Telecommunication Services:** electronic mail, jhaviland@midtowncleveland.org. **Formerly:** Midtown Corridor. **Publications:** *MidTown Momentum*, quarterly. Newsletter • *Restaurant Guide* • *Security Guides* • *Service*. Brochure • Annual Report, annual. Contains highlights, committees, and awards. **Circulation:** 2,200 • Directory, semiannual. **Conventions/Meetings:** annual Business After Hours - trade show (exhibits) - always March • biennial Forums - meeting • annual meeting - always May in Cleveland, OH.

14166 ■ Mothers Against Drunk Driving, North Coast Chapter
1323 Old River Rd., 1st Fl.
Cleveland, OH 44113
Ph: (216)685-0880
Fax: (216)685-0884
Free: (800)691-6233
E-mail: maddnorthcoast@spcglobal.net
URL: http://www.maddnorthcoast.org
Regional. Victims of drunk driving crashes; concerned citizens. Encourages citizen participation in working towards reform of the drunk driving problem and the prevention of underage drinking. Acts as the voice of victims of drunk driving crashes by speaking on their behalf to communities, businesses, and educational groups. **Affiliated With:** Mothers Against Drunk Driving.

14167 ■ Muscular Dystrophy Association, Northeast Ohio (MDA)
16600 W Sprague Rd., No. 190
Cleveland, OH 44130
Ph: (440)816-0916
E-mail: northeastohioservices@mdausa.org
Contact: Irwin B. Jacobs MD, Dir.
Founded: 1950. **Languages:** English, Spanish. **Local**. Provides services tailored to the individual needs of members. Provides opportunities for members to interact and exchange ideas. Visits tertiary institutions and gives presentations about neuromuscular conditions. Offers consultation services and check-ups for members. Assists in accessing equipment and facilities. **Affiliated With:** Muscular Dystrophy Association. **Formerly:** (2002) Muscular Dystrophy Association, Midpark. **Publications:** Brochures (in English and Spanish), periodic. Contains information on various diseases. **Price:** free.

14168 ■ Muslim Student's Association of Cleveland State University (MSA/CSU)
Univ. Ctr., 9th Fl.
UC 102 Box 29
Cleveland, OH 44115

Ph: (216)768-8803
E-mail: csu_msa@yahoo.com
URL: http://www.csuohio.edu/msa
Contact: Eman Dughly, Pres.
Local. Muslim students in North America. Seeks to advance the interests of members; works to enable members to practice Islam as a complete way of life. **Affiliated With:** Muslim Students Association of the United States and Canada.

14169 ■ Na'amat U.S.A., Cleveland Council
14055 Cedar Rd., Rm. 300
Cleveland, OH 44118
Ph: (216)321-2002
Contact: Florence Dobrin, Pres.
Founded: 1925. Professional women and homemakers who work for the rehabilitation, integration, and education of women, children, and youth in Israel. Promotes education and culture in the U.S. **Affiliated With:** Na'amat U.S.A. **Publications:** Newsletter, periodic.

14170 ■ NARAL Pro-Choice Ohio
12000 Shaker Blvd.
Cleveland, OH 44120
Ph: (216)283-2180
Fax: (216)283-2184
Free: (800)GO-NARAL
E-mail: choice@prochoiceohio.org
URL: http://www.naralohio.org
Contact: Kellie Copeland, Exec.Dir.
Founded: 1978. **Members:** 15,000. **Membership Dues:** student, $15 (annual) • standard, $35 (annual) • family, $60 (annual) • bronze, $100 (annual) • silver, $250 (annual) • gold, $500 (annual). **Staff:** 5. **Budget:** $200,000. **State**. Works to use the political process to guarantee every woman the right to make personal reproductive decisions, including preventing unintended pregnancy, bearing healthy children, and choosing safe and legal abortion. **Libraries: Type:** open to the public. **Holdings:** articles, books, periodicals, video recordings. **Subjects:** reproductive health issues. **Computer Services:** Information services, fact sheets and talking points on current issues and events • information services, online newsroom that provides comprehensive information about reproductive rights in Ohio. **Programs:** Friends; Student Organizing. **Projects:** Choice Action Teams; Contraceptive Equity; Emergency Contraception; Unmasking Fake Clinics. **Affiliated With:** NARAL Pro-Choice America. **Formerly:** (2004) National Abortion and Reproductive Rights Action League Ohio. **Publications:** *The Voice of Choice*, quarterly. Newsletter. Alternate Formats: online.

14171 ■ National Active and Retired Federal Employees Association - Cleveland East 2232
1348 E 115th St.
Cleveland, OH 44106-1347
Ph: (216)791-1347
URL: National Affiliate–www.narfe.org
Contact: Fannie C. Cockfield, Contact
Local. Protects the retirement future of employees through education. Informs members on issues affecting the retirement. **Affiliated With:** National Association of Retired Federal Employees.

14172 ■ National Association of Industrial and Office Properties, Northern Ohio Chapter
c/o Donna Haders
Chap. Administrators Ent.
30200 Detroit Rd.
Cleveland, OH 44145-1967
Ph: (440)899-0010
Fax: (440)892-1404
E-mail: naiop@wherryassoc.com
URL: National Affiliate–www.naiop.org
Contact: Ms. Sheila Westfall, Exec.Dir.
Local. Represents the interests of developers and owners of industrial, office and related commercial estate. Provides communication, networking, business opportunities and a forum to its members. Promotes effective public policy to create, protect and enhance property values. **Awards:** Member of the Year. **Frequency:** annual. **Type:** recognition. **Recipient:** to chapter member who has given an extraordinary amount of time and dedication to the chapter. **Committees:** Charity Golf. **Affiliated With:** National Association of Industrial and Office Properties. **Publications:** *Chapter Connection*, quarterly. Newsletter. Alternate Formats: online. **Conventions/Meetings:** annual meeting.

14173 ■ National Association of Rocketry - Tri-City Sky Busters
c/o Les Kramer
16603 Lucille Ave.
Cleveland, OH 44111
Ph: (216)941-4554
E-mail: phoenix@skybusters.org
URL: http://www.skybusters.org
Contact: Les Kramer, Contact
Local.

14174 ■ National Electrical Contractors Association, Greater Cleveland Chapter
950 Keynote Cir., No. 20
Cleveland, OH 44131
Ph: (216)398-8440
Fax: (216)398-7928
Free: (800)229-NECA
Contact: Richard L. Newcomer, Exec.Dir.
Founded: 1945. **Members:** 58. **Membership Dues:** application fee, $150. **Staff:** 3. **Budget:** $600,000. **Local**. Electrical contractors in northeastern Ohio. Conducts collective bargaining activities. Sponsors seminars and workshops. **Affiliated With:** National Electrical Contractors Association. **Publications:** *Electrical Contractor*, monthly. Magazine. **Price:** free • *NECA Review*, monthly. Newsletter. **Conventions/Meetings:** annual convention, electrical equipment, tools and ancillary equipment (exhibits) - usually October.

14175 ■ National Forum for Black Public Administrators, Cleveland Chapter
c/o Dwight D. Wilson, Asst. Commissioner
4600 Harvard Ave.
Cleveland, OH 44105
Ph: (216)348-7277
Fax: (216)420-7116
E-mail: dwight_wilson@clevelandwater.com
URL: National Affiliate–www.nfbpa.org
Contact: Dwight D. Wilson, Asst. Commissioner
Local. Works to promote, strengthen and expand the role of Blacks in public administration. Seeks to focus the influence of Black administrators toward building and maintaining viable communities. Develops specialized training programs for managers and executives. Works to further communication among Black public, private and academic institutions. Addresses issues that affect the administrative capacity of Black managers. **Affiliated With:** National Forum for Black Public Administrators.

14176 ■ National Multiple Sclerosis Society, Ohio Buckeye
c/o Janet Kramer, Pres.
1422 Euclid Ave., Ste.333
Cleveland, OH 44115
Ph: (216)696-8220
Fax: (216)696-2817
Free: (800)667-7131
E-mail: oha@nmss.org
URL: National Affiliate–www.nmss.org
Contact: Ms. Janet Kramer, Pres.
Founded: 1953. **Members:** 8,000. **Membership Dues:** general, $25 (annual). **Staff:** 38. **Budget:** $3,500,000. **Local**. Stimulates, supports, and coordinates research into the cause, treatment, and cure of multiple sclerosis; provides services for persons with MS and related diseases and their families. **Libraries: Type:** lending. **Holdings:** 711; articles, books, video recordings. **Subjects:** multiple sclerosis. **Awards:** Arnold and Gerrie King Lifetime Achievement Award. **Frequency:** annual. **Type:** recognition. **Recipient:** for volunteers who help others with MS • Carolyn P. Konnert Achievement. **Frequency:** annual. **Type:** recognition. **Recipient:** for volunteers who help others with MS • Development Volunteer. **Frequency:** annual. **Type:** recognition. **Recipient:** for volunteers who help others with MS • Isroff Program Volunteer. **Frequency:** annual. **Type:** recognition. **Recipient:** for volunteers who help others with MS • Norman Cohn Hope Award. **Frequency:** annual. **Type:** recognition. **Recipient:** for volunteers who help others with MS • Taubman Community. **Frequency:** annual. **Type:** recognition. **Recipient:** for volunteers who help others with MS • Walk/Bike Top Team. **Frequency:** annual. **Type:** recognition. **Recipient:** for volunteers who help others with MS • Woman of Courage. **Frequency:** annual. **Type:** recognition. **Recipient:** for volunteers who help others with MS. **Affiliated With:** National Multiple Sclerosis Society. **Publications:** *MS Connections*, quarterly. Newsletter. Covers broad audience and people with Multiple Sclerosis. **Circulation:** 13,500. **Advertising:** accepted. Alternate Formats: online • *MS Program Connections*, quarterly. Newsletter. Covers broad audience and people with Multiple Sclerosis. **Circulation:** 8,500. **Advertising:** accepted. Alternate Formats: online.

14177 ■ National Technical Honor Society - Remington College - Cleveland Campus - Ohio
14445 Broadway Ave.
Cleveland, OH 44125-1957
Ph: (216)475-7520
Fax: (216)475-6055
URL: http://www.remingtoncollege.com
Local.

14178 ■ Norman S. Minor Bar Association
c/o Anthony Jordan, Pres.
PO Box 99823
Cleveland, OH 44199
Ph: (216)622-7853
E-mail: nsmba-owner@yahoogroups.com
URL: http://www.nsmba.org
Contact: Anthony Jordan, Pres.
Founded: 1980. **Local**. **Affiliated With:** National Bar Association.

14179 ■ North Coast Chief Petty Officers Association (NCCPOA)
PO Box 99205
Cleveland, OH 44199
Ph: (216)676-6766
E-mail: cporetuscg@yahoo.com
URL: http://www.nccpoa.org
Contact: Gary Seifert, Pres.
Local. **Affiliated With:** United States Coast Guard Chief Petty Officers Association.

14180 ■ North Eastern Ohio American Association of Diabetes Educators (NEOAADE)
c/o Diabetes Association of Greater Cleveland
3601 S Green Rd., Ste.100
Cleveland, OH 44122
Ph: (216)591-0800
E-mail: webmaster@neoaade.org
URL: http://www.neoaade.org
Contact: MaryEllen Eichman-Fiala RD, Pres.
Local. Promotes the development of quality diabetes education for the diabetic consumer. Fosters communication and cooperation among individuals and organizations involved in diabetes patient education. Provides educational opportunities for the professional growth and development of members. **Affiliated With:** American Association of Diabetes Educators.

14181 ■ North Eastern Ohio Orienteering Club (NEOOC)
PO Box 5703
Cleveland, OH 44101-0703
Ph: (440)729-3255
E-mail: katkat@neo.rr.com
URL: http://neooc.home.att.net
Local. **Affiliated With:** United States Orienteering Federation.

14182 ■ Northeast Ohio Alumni Extension - National Society of Black Engineers (NEO-NSBEAE)
PO Box 6351
Cleveland, OH 44101-1351
Free: (877)891-5544
E-mail: information@neo-nsbe.org
URL: http://www.neo-nsbe.org
Contact: Keshia Johnson, Pres.
Local. Strives to increase the number of culturally responsible Black engineers who excel academically, succeed professionally and positively impact the community. **Affiliated With:** National Society of Black Engineers.

14183 ■ Northeast Ohio Apartment Association (NOAA)
408 W St. Clair Ave., No. 200
Cleveland, OH 44113
Ph: (216)241-1635
E-mail: info@noaaonline.com
URL: http://www.noaaonline.com
Contact: Ralph W. Mcgreevy, Exec.VP
Regional.

14184 ■ Northeast Ohio Association for Computing Machinery SIGGRAPH
c/o Michael Hilliard, Chm.
The Cleveland Museum of Art
Attention New Media Initiatives
11150 E Blvd.
Cleveland, OH 44106
Ph: (216)707-2647
E-mail: mhilliard@clevelandart.org
URL: National Affiliate–www.acm.org
Contact: Michael Hilliard, Chm.
Local. Biological, medical, behavioral, and computer scientists; hospital administrators; programmers and others interested in application of computer methods to biological, behavioral, and medical problems. Stimulates understanding of the use and potential of computers in the Biosciences. **Affiliated With:** Association for Computing Machinery.

14185 ■ Northeast Ohio Coalition for the Homeless (NEOCH)
c/o Brian Davis, Exec.Dir.
3631 Perkins Ave. 3A-3, 3rd Fl.
Cleveland, OH 44114
Ph: (216)432-0540
Fax: (216)432-0620
E-mail: neoch@neoch.org
URL: http://www.neoch.org
Local.

14186 ■ Northeast Ohio Health Information Management Association (NOHIMA)
c/o David Lasky, RHIT, Pres.
MetroHealth Medical Center
2500 MetroHealth Dr.
Cleveland, OH 44109-1998
Ph: (440)312-4729
E-mail: dlasky@cchseast.org
URL: http://www.ohima.org/reg.associations/regassocnohima.html
Contact: David Lasky RHIT, Pres.
Local. Represents the interests of individuals dedicated to the effective management of personal health information needed to deliver quality healthcare to the public. Provides career, professional development and practice resources. Sets standards for education and certification. Advocates public policy that advances Health Information Management (HIM) practice. **Affiliated With:** American Health Information Management Association; Ohio Health Information Management Association.

14187 ■ Northeast Ohio's Northcoast Naturists (NN)
PO Box 33673
Cleveland, OH 44133-0673
Ph: (216)556-2533
E-mail: club@northcoast-naturists.org
URL: http://www.northcoast-naturists.org
State. Clothes-optional recreation organization. **Affiliated With:** The Naturist Society. **Also Known As:** (2005) Northcoast Naturists.

14188 ■ Northern Ohio Vascular Association (NOVA)
4788 Lindsey Ln.
Cleveland, OH 44143-2926
Ph: (216)382-8999
Fax: (216)839-4513
E-mail: ambenet@aol.com
URL: National Affiliate–www.svunet.org
Contact: Angela M. Jagan RN, Contact
Local. Represents vascular technologists and individuals in the field of noninvasive vascular technology. Seeks to establish an information clearinghouse providing reference and assistance in matters relating to noninvasive vascular technology. Facilitates cooperation among noninvasive vascular facilities and other health professions. Provides continuing education for individuals in the field. Represents members on various regulatory issues. **Affiliated With:** Society for Vascular Ultrasound.

14189 ■ Not In Your Name, Ohio - Cleveland
PO Box 609034
Cleveland, OH 44109
Ph: (216)633-6200
E-mail: no_more_war_us@yahoo.com
URL: http://www.nioncleveland.org
Local.

14190 ■ Ohio Association for Healthcare Quality (OAHQ)
PO Box 461045
Cleveland, OH 44146-7071
Ph: (937)641-3363
E-mail: oahq@juno.com
URL: http://www.geocities.com/oahq
Contact: Carol Wise, Pres.
Membership Dues: individual, $30 (annual) • retired, $15 (annual). **State**. Works to improve the delivery of healthcare by advancing the theory and practice of quality management by supporting the professional growth ad development of healthcare professionals. **Affiliated With:** National Association for Healthcare Quality.

14191 ■ Ohio Center for the Book
Main Lib.
325 Superior Ave. NE
Cleveland, OH 44114
Ph: (216)623-2800
E-mail: ohiocenterforthebook@cpl.org
URL: http://www.ohiocenterforthebook.org
Contact: Andrew A. Venable Jr., Dir.
State. **Affiliated With:** Center for the Book.

14192 ■ Ohio Citizen Action
c/o Sandy Buchanan, Exec.Dir.
614 W Superior Ave., Ste.1200
Cleveland, OH 44113
Ph: (216)861-5200
Fax: (216)694-6904
Free: (888)777-7135
E-mail: staff@ohiocitizen.org
URL: http://www.ohiocitizen.org
Contact: Sandy Buchanan, Exec.Dir.
State.

14193 ■ Ohio City Design Review Committee
c/o Laura M. Noble
2525 Market Ave.
Cleveland, OH 44113
Ph: (216)781-3222
Fax: (216)781-3252
Local.

14194 ■ Ohio Disabled American Veterans
1240 E 9th St., Rm. 1015
Cleveland, OH 44199
Ph: (216)522-3508
URL: National Affiliate–www.dav.org
State. **Affiliated With:** Disabled American Veterans.

14195 ■ Ohio Genealogical Society, Greater Cleveland
PO Box 40254
Cleveland, OH 44140-0254
Ph: (440)759-4666
E-mail: mjfc99@core.com
URL: http://www.rootsweb.com/~ohgcgg
Contact: Mrs. Marilyn Carlson, Past Pres.
Founded: 1971. **Members:** 95. **Membership Dues:** individual, $15 (annual) • family, $20 (annual) • contributing, $30 (annual) • sustaining, $45 (annual). **Regional**. **Libraries: Type:** reference; open to the public. **Holdings:** biographical archives, books, maps, periodicals. **Computer Services:** database, names in the 1900 federal census for Cleveland. **Special Interest Groups:** Cuyahoga County Pioneers Lineage Society. **Affiliated With:** Ohio Genealogical Society. **Publications:** *The Certified Copy*, quarterly. Newsletter. **Price:** included in membership dues. ISSN: 0749-5684. **Conventions/Meetings:** monthly meeting, with speakers - every 3rd Monday of the month except July & December.

14196 ■ Ohio Glass Association (OGA)
25550 Chagrin Blvd., Ste.403
Cleveland, OH 44122
Fax: (216)595-8230
Free: (800)858-2572
E-mail: oga1@ohioglass.org
URL: http://www.ohioglass.org
Contact: Avery H. Fromet, Administrator
State. **Affiliated With:** National Glass Association.

14197 ■ Ohio-Israel Chamber of Commerce (OICC)
PO Box 39007
Cleveland, OH 44139-0007
Ph: (216)965-4474
Fax: (440)248-4888
E-mail: ohioisraelchamber@ameritech.net
URL: http://ohioisraelchamber.com
Contact: Howard Gudell, Pres.
Founded: 1996. **Members:** 140. **Staff:** 2. **Languages:** English, Hebrew. **State**. Promotes business between Ohio and Israeli companies by programming, matchmaking, and government contacts. **Committees:** Biotechnology/Healthcare; Marketing and PR; Professional and Business Advisory; Program; Technology and Communications. **Affiliated With:** America-Israel Chamber of Commerce, Central Atlantic Region; Federation of Israeli Chambers of Commerce; Israel Export and International Cooperation Institute. **Publications:** *Business Barometer*, quarterly. Newsletter. **Price:** free. **Circulation:** 1,000. **Advertising:** accepted.

14198 ■ Ohio League for Nursing
c/o Jane F. Mahowald, MA, RN, Exec.Dir.
20545 Center Ridge Rd., Ste.205
Cleveland, OH 44116
Ph: (440)331-2721
Fax: (440)331-2744
E-mail: jfmahowald@aol.com
URL: http://www.ohioleaguefornursing.org
Contact: Jane F. Mahowald MA, RN, Exec.Dir.
State.

14199 ■ Ohio Planning Conference (OPC)
c/o Terry Schwarz, Exec.Dir.
820 Prospect Ave.
Cleveland, OH 44115
Ph: (216)357-3436
Fax: (216)357-3430
E-mail: info@ohioplanning.org
URL: http://www.ohioplanning.org
Contact: Terry Schwarz, Exec.Dir.
State.

14200 ■ Ohio State Neurosurgical Society
c/o Dr. Alan R. Cohen
11100 Euclid Ave., Rm. B501
Cleveland, OH 44106-1736

Ph: (216)844-5741
Fax: (216)844-5710
URL: National Affiliate–www.aans.org
Contact: Dr. Alan R. Cohen, Contact
State. Represents neurological surgeons united to promote excellence in neurological surgery and its related sciences. Provides funding to foster research in the neurosciences. **Affiliated With:** American Association of Neurological Surgeons.

14201 ■ Ohio Supreme Court Historical Society
c/o Thomas S. Kilbane, Chm.
127 Public Sq., Ste.4900
Cleveland, OH 44114-1304
Ph: (216)479-8500
Fax: (216)479-8780
E-mail: tkilbane@ssd.com
URL: National Affiliate–www.supremecourthistory.org
Contact: Thomas S. Kilbane, Chm.
State. Collects and preserves the history of the Supreme Court of the United States. Conducts educational programs and supports historical research. Collects antiques and artifacts related to the Court's history. Increases public awareness of the Court's contributions to the nation's constitutional heritage. **Affiliated With:** Supreme Court Historical Society.

14202 ■ Ohio Venture Association (OVA)
1120 Chester Ave., Ste.470
Cleveland, OH 44114-3514
Ph: (216)566-8884
Fax: (216)696-2582
E-mail: admin@ohioventure.org
URL: http://www.ohioventure.org
Contact: Ms. Joan McCarthy, Administrator
Membership Dues: individual, $160 (annual) • corporate/institutional, $400 (annual). **State. Formerly:** (2005) Ohio Association of College and University Business Officers. **Publications:** Newsletter, quarterly. Alternate Formats: online.

14203 ■ Organization Development Connection of Northeast Ohio
c/o Brad Shrock
2111 Center St.
Cleveland, OH 44113-2303
Ph: (216)861-5178
E-mail: odconnection@odconnection.org
URL: http://www.odconnection.org
Contact: Brad Shrock, Contact
Regional. Affiliated With: Organization Development Network.

14204 ■ Phi Theta Kappa - Alpha Zeta Delta Chapter
c/o Marcia Romoser
2900 Community Coll. Ave.
Cleveland, OH 44115
Ph: (216)987-4162
E-mail: marcia.romoser@ptk.org
URL: http://www.ptk.org/directories/chapters/OH/316-1.htm
Contact: Marcia Romoser, Advisor
Local. Affiliated With: Phi Theta Kappa, International Honor Society.

14205 ■ Planned Parenthood of Greater Cleveland
3500 Lorain Ave., Ste.400
Cleveland, OH 44113
Ph: (216)961-8804
Fax: (216)334-2211
E-mail: info@ppgc.org
URL: National Affiliate–www.plannedparenthood.org
Local. Affiliated With: Planned Parenthood Federation of America.

14206 ■ Policy Matters Ohio
c/o Amy B. Hanauer, Exec.Dir.
2912 Euclid Ave.
Cleveland, OH 44115-2637
Ph: (216)931-9922 (216)931-9921
Fax: (216)931-9924
E-mail: ahanauer@policymattersohio.org
URL: http://www.policymattersohio.org
Contact: Amy B. Hanauer, Exec.Dir.
Founded: 2000. **Staff:** 7. **Budget:** $350,000. **State Groups:** 1. **State**. Policy research institute focused on issued related to worker well-being.

14207 ■ Project: LEARN
2728 Euclid Ave., Ste.200
Cleveland, OH 44115
Ph: (216)621-9483
Fax: (216)696-5637
E-mail: prolearn@projectlearn.org
URL: http://www.projectlearn.com
Local. Affiliated With: ProLiteracy Worldwide.

14208 ■ Psi Chi, National Honor Society in Psychology - Case Western Reserve University
c/o Dept. of Psychology
109 Mather Memorial Bldg.
10900 Euclid Ave.
Cleveland, OH 44106-7123
Ph: (216)368-2686 (216)368-6467
Fax: (216)368-4891
E-mail: rlg2@case.edu
URL: National Affiliate–www.psichi.org
Contact: Robert L. Greene PhD, Advisor
Local.

14209 ■ Puppeteers of America - Puppetry Guild of Northeastern Ohio
c/o Jean Jackson, Pres.
2980 Washington Blvd.
Cleveland, OH 44118
Ph: (216)932-3730
E-mail: jeanjackson@ameritech.net
URL: National Affiliate–www.puppeteers.org
Contact: Jean Jackson, Pres.
Local.

14210 ■ Real Estate Investors Association
5011 Lorain Ave.
Cleveland, OH 44102
Ph: (216)651-6655
Local.

14211 ■ Risk and Insurance Management Society, Northeast Ohio Chapter
c/o John Hach
22801 St. Clair Ave.
Cleveland, OH 44117-1199
Ph: (216)383-2377
Fax: (801)697-4277
E-mail: jhach@lincolnelectric.com
URL: http://northeastohio.rims.org
Contact: Mark Tucker, Pres.
Local. Seeks to promote the discipline of risk management and enhance the image of professional risk managers. Fosters the educational and professional development of risk managers and others involved in the risk management and insurance industry. **Affiliated With:** Risk and Insurance Management Society.

14212 ■ RSVP Cleveland
c/o Joy Banish, Dir.
4614 Prospect Ave., Ste.205
Cleveland, OH 44103
Ph: (216)391-9500
Fax: (216)391-9010
E-mail: mailbox@rsvpclev.org
URL: http://www.seniorcorps.gov/about/programs/rsvp_state.asp?usestateabbr=oh&Search4.x=0&Search4.y=0
Contact: Joy Banish, Dir.
Local. Affiliated With: Retired and Senior Volunteer Program.

14213 ■ Scottish Rite Valley of Cleveland
3615 Euclid Ave.
Cleveland, OH 44115
Ph: (216)432-2370
Fax: (216)391-3159
E-mail: secretary@aasrcleveland.org
URL: http://www.aasrcleveland.org
Contact: Mr. Alan Jones, Sec.
Local.

14214 ■ Self Insurers' Group of Ohio (SIGO)
101 W Prospect Ave.
Cleveland, OH 44115
Ph: (216)566-3095
E-mail: info@sigo-ohio.org
URL: http://www.sigo-ohio.org
Contact: Anthony J. Colangelo, Contact
State.

14215 ■ Shaker Square Area Development
c/o Reid Robbins, Exec.Dir.
11811 Shaker Blvd. No. 206
Cleveland, OH 44120-1927
Ph: (216)421-2100
Fax: (216)421-2200
Local.

14216 ■ Sheet Metal and Air Conditioning Contractors' National Association of North Central Ohio (SMACNA/NCO)
950 Keynote Cir., Ste.10
Cleveland, OH 44131-1802
Ph: (216)398-9860
Fax: (216)398-9801
E-mail: mlaskey@ceacisp.org
URL: http://www.ceacisp.org
Contact: Mark Laskey, Exec.Dir.
Founded: 1969. **Members:** 10. **Staff:** 2. **Budget:** $49,000. **Local**. Air conditioning and sheet metal contractors. Establishes standards and codes in the field. Sponsors sheet metal apprentice contest; offers apprenticeship; conducts charitable activities, collective bargaining agreement with local sheetmetal union 33. **Affiliated With:** Construction Industry Employers Association; Sheet Metal and Air Conditioning Contractors' National Association. **Publications:** Newsletter, bimonthly • Directory, annual. **Conventions/Meetings:** convention - 5/year.

14217 ■ Sheet Metal Workers' Local Union 33 Cleveland District
c/o Reggie Hohenberger, Pres./Business Mgr.
3666 Carnegie Ave.
Cleveland, OH 44115-2714
Ph: (216)391-1645
Fax: (216)391-4335
Free: (800)527-3834
E-mail: presbusmgr@smwlu33.org
URL: http://www.smwlu33.org
Contact: Andy Farmer, Contact
Members: 5,066. **Local. Affiliated With:** Sheet Metal Workers' International Association.

14218 ■ Society of American Registered Architects - Northern Ohio Chapter
c/o Celso Gilberti, Pres.
GSI Architects, Inc.
1240 Huron Rd.
Cleveland, OH 44115
Ph: (216)363-0000
Fax: (216)363-1990
E-mail: cgilberti@gsiarchitects.com
URL: National Affiliate–www.sara-national.org
Contact: Celso Gilberti, Pres.
Local. Seeks to provide a link between the architect and the user of architectural services. Supports the concept of profitable professionalism for all members. **Affiliated With:** Society of American Registered Architects.

14219 ■ Society for Marketing Professional Services/Northeast Ohio
c/o Jeffery A. Dentzer, Pres.
5430 Warner Rd.
Cleveland, OH 44125

Ph: (216)524-6800
Fax: (216)642-3216
E-mail: info@smpsneo.org
URL: http://www.smpsneo.org
Contact: Jeffery A. Dentzer, Pres.
Founded: 2001. **Local.** Strives to be the primary resource for education, team building and strategic and marketing information for SMPS members and others involved in the built environment. **Affiliated With:** Society for Marketing Professional Services.

14220 ■ Society of Northern Ohio Professional Photographers
c/o Mike Andonov, Pres.
PO Box 91787
Cleveland, OH 44101
E-mail: milesphoto@aol.com
URL: http://www.sonopp.com
Local. Professional society of portrait, wedding, commercial, and industrial, and specialized photographers. **Affiliated With:** Professional Photographers of America.

14221 ■ Society of Physics Students - Cleveland State University Chapter No. 1247
2121 Euclid Ave., SI 124
Cleveland, OH 44115
Ph: (216)687-2433
Fax: (216)523-7268
E-mail: k.streletzky@csuohio.edu
URL: National Affiliate–www.spsnational.org
Contact: Kiril Streletzky, Faculty Advisor
Local. Offers opportunities for the students to enrich their experiences and skills about physics. Helps students to become professional in the field of physics. **Affiliated With:** Society of Physics Students.

14222 ■ Three Trackers of Ohio
PO Box 44121
Cleveland, OH 44144
Ph: (216)556-0787
E-mail: md1053@aol.com
URL: http://www.3trackers.org
Contact: Mark Deitz, Pres.
State. Affiliated With: Disabled Sports USA.

14223 ■ United Brotherhood of Carpenters and Joiners of America, Cleveland Local Union No. 21
3615 Chester Ave.
Cleveland, OH 44114
Ph: (216)391-2828
Fax: (216)391-1029
URL: http://www.ovrcc.com
Local. Affiliated With: United Brotherhood of Carpenters and Joiners of America.

14224 ■ United Brotherhood of Carpenters and Joiners of America, Cleveland Local Union No. 509
3615 Chester Ave.
Cleveland, OH 44114
Ph: (440)473-0017
Fax: (216)391-1029
E-mail: mcahill@ovrcc.com
URL: http://www.ovrcc.com
Local. Affiliated With: United Brotherhood of Carpenters and Joiners of America.

14225 ■ United Brotherhood of Carpenters and Joiners of America, Ohio and Vicinity Regional Council of Carpenters
3615 Chester Ave.
Cleveland, OH 44114
Ph: (216)391-2828
E-mail: info@ovrcc.org
URL: http://www.ovrcc.com
Contact: Roberto Peto, Exec.Sec.-Treas.
Regional. Affiliated With: United Brotherhood of Carpenters and Joiners of America. **Formerly:** (2005) United Brotherhood of Carpenters and Joiners of America, Ohio and Vicinity Regional Council of Carpenters 4046.

14226 ■ United Cerebral Palsy Association of Greater Cleveland
10011 Euclid Ave.
Cleveland, OH 44106
Ph: (216)791-8363
Fax: (216)721-3372
E-mail: sdean@ucpcleveland.org
URL: National Affiliate–www.ucp.org
Contact: Susan A. Dean, Exec.Dir.
Local. Aids persons with cerebral palsy and other disabilities, and their families. Goals are to, minimize its effects, and improve the quality of life for persons with cerebral palsy and other disabilities, and their families. **Affiliated With:** United Cerebral Palsy Associations.

14227 ■ United Food and Commercial Workers International Union, AFL-CIO, CLC - Local Union 880
2828 Euclid Ave.
Cleveland, OH 44115
Ph: (216)241-5930
Fax: (216)241-2826
Free: (800)241-5930
E-mail: ufcwlocal880@adelphia.net
URL: http://www.ufcwlocal880.com
Contact: Thomas H. Robertson, Pres.
Members: 26,039. **Local. Affiliated With:** United Food and Commercial Workers International Union.

14228 ■ United States Naval Sea Cadet Corps - Cleveland Division
Cleveland Naval Reserve Center
1089 E 9th St.
Cleveland, OH 44114-1091
E-mail: phoenix@uhrad.com
URL: http://www.nscccleveland.org
Contact: LCDR Joseph Molter, Commanding Officer
Local. Works to instill good citizenship and patriotism in youth. Encourages qualities such as personal neatness, loyalty, obedience, dependability, and responsibility to others. Offers courses in physical fitness and military drill, first aid, water safety, basic seamanship, and naval history and traditions. **Affiliated With:** Naval Sea Cadet Corps.

14229 ■ United Way Services of Greater Cleveland
1331 Euclid Ave.
Cleveland, OH 44115-1819
Ph: (216)436-2100
E-mail: marketing@uws.org
URL: http://www.uws.org
Local. Affiliated With: United Way of America.

14230 ■ Urban League of Greater Cleveland
2930 Prospect Ave.
Cleveland, OH 44115
Ph: (216)622-0999
Fax: (216)622-0997
E-mail: info@ulcleveland.org
URL: http://www.ulcleveland.org
Contact: Myron F. Robinson, Pres./CEO
Local. Affiliated With: National Urban League.

14231 ■ USA Weightlifting - Olympic Health Club
c/o John Schubert
3159 W 98th St.
Cleveland, OH 44102
Ph: (216)281-7410 (216)631-9200
Fax: (216)631-9200
URL: National Affiliate–www.usaweightlifting.org
Contact: John Schubert, Contact
Local. Affiliated With: USA Weightlifting.

14232 ■ USA Weightlifting - West Park YMCA
c/o Terry Shusta
15501 Lorain Ave.
Cleveland, OH 44111
Ph: (216)941-5410 (440)886-2757
Fax: (440)886-2757
URL: National Affiliate–www.usaweightlifting.org
Contact: Terry Shusta, Contact
Local. Affiliated With: USA Weightlifting.

14233 ■ Vietnam Veterans of America, Greater Cleveland - Chapter No. 15
c/o James Quisenberry, Pres.
1041 Starkweather Ave.
Cleveland, OH 44113
Ph: (216)830-8515
URL: http://www.vvabuckeyestatecouncil.com
Contact: James Quisenberry, Pres.
Local. Affiliated With: Vietnam Veterans of America.

14234 ■ Visiting Nurse Association HealthCare and Partners of Ohio
2500 E 22nd St.
Cleveland, OH 44115-3204
Ph: (216)931-1400
E-mail: info@vnacleveland.org
URL: http://www.vnacleveland.org
Contact: Diane Gallagher, Dir. of Advancements
State. Formerly: (2005) Visiting Nurse Association of Ohio.

14235 ■ Volunteers of America of Northeast and North Central Ohio
8225 Brecksville Rd., Ste.206
Cleveland, OH 44141-1362
Ph: (440)717-1500
Fax: (440)717-1508
URL: http://www.voa-nenc-ohio.org
Regional. Provides local human service programs and opportunities for individual and community involvement. **Affiliated With:** Volunteers of America.

14236 ■ VSA Arts of Ohio/Cleveland Area Service Division
c/o Veta Groth
1275 Lakeside Ave. E
Cleveland, OH 44114-1132
Ph: (216)344-1761
Fax: (216)861-0253
E-mail: vgroth@adelphia.net
Contact: Mr. Jerry Devis, Board Pres.
Founded: 1982. **Members:** 7. **Budget:** $8,000. **State Groups:** 1. **Local Groups:** 8. **Local.** Promotes the creative power in people with disabilities; sponsors arts festivals in the Cleveland area throughout the year; conducts art classes jointly with The Beck Center for the Arts. **Committees:** Planning. **Publications:** *Very Special Notes*, semiannual. Newsletter. Contains four pages and distribute to teachers and staff. **Circulation:** 600. **Conventions/Meetings:** annual festival, arts festival for children with disabilities.

14237 ■ Western Cuyahoga Audubon Society (WCAS)
c/o Mary Anne Romito, Pres.
4310 Bush Ave.
Cleveland, OH 44109
Ph: (216)267-7111
E-mail: romito@wcasohio.org
URL: http://www.audubon.org/chapter/oh/index.html
Contact: Mary Anne Romito, Pres.
Regional. Formerly: (2005) National Audubon Society - Western Cuyahoga.

14238 ■ Western Reserve Historical Society (WRHS)
c/o Patrick Reymann, Exec.Dir.
10825 E Blvd.
Cleveland, OH 44106
Ph: (216)721-5722
E-mail: preymann@wrhs.org
URL: http://www.wrhs.org
Contact: Tamera Brown, Dir. of External Affairs
Local. Cultural institution in Cleveland's University Circle.

14239 ■ YL Cleveland Young Lives
3178 W 94th St.
Cleveland, OH 44102
Ph: (216)281-5812
URL: http://sites.younglife.org/_layouts/ylext/default.aspx?ID=A-OH138
Local. Affiliated With: Young Life.

14240 ■ YMCA of Greater Cleveland
2200 Prospect Ave., Ste.900
Cleveland, OH 44115-2602
Ph: (216)344-0095
Fax: (216)344-3901
E-mail: ghaley@clevelandymca.org
URL: http://www.ymcacleveland.org/content/home.aspx
Contact: Glenn Haley, Pres./CEO
Founded: 1854. **Local**. Seeks to develop and improve the spiritual, social, mental, and physical well-being of young people and adults. Programs include health and fitness, swimming, youth sports, childcare, and camping. **Also Known As:** YMCA of Cleveland; Cleveland Young Men's Christian Association. **Publications:** *Y-Link*, quarterly. Newsletter. Alternate Formats: online • Annual Report, annual. Alternate Formats: online.

14241 ■ Young Audiences of Greater Cleveland (YAGC)
c/o Marsha Dobrzynski, Exec.Dir.
13110 Shaker Sq., Ste.C203
Cleveland, OH 44120-2313
Ph: (216)561-5005
Fax: (216)561-3444
E-mail: info@yagc.org
URL: http://www.yagc.org
Contact: Marsha Dobrzynski, Exec.Dir.
Founded: 1953. **Members:** 5. **Budget:** $600,000. **Local**. Enriches the lives of children and promotes creative learning by uniting arts with education. **Awards:** Sunshine Award. **Frequency:** annual. **Type:** recognition. **Recipient:** for community service in arts education. **Affiliated With:** Young Audiences. **Conventions/Meetings:** annual conference - always June.

14242 ■ Young Life Cleveland Metro
1362 E 124th St.
Cleveland, OH 44106
Ph: (216)408-8558
URL: http://sites.younglife.org/_layouts/ylext/default.aspx?ID=A-OH33
Local. **Affiliated With:** Young Life.

14243 ■ YWCA of Greater Cleveland
4019 Prospect Ave.
Cleveland, OH 44103
Ph: (216)881-6878
Fax: (216)881-9922
E-mail: smiller@ywcaofcleveland.org
URL: http://www.ywcaofcleveland.org
Contact: Sondra Miller, Dir. of Resource Development
Membership Dues: regular, $100 (annual). **Local**. Works to empower women and eliminate racism through three program areas: domestic violence education and prevention, teen services, and child care. **Awards:** YWCA Women of Achievement Awards. **Frequency:** annual. **Type:** recognition. **Recipient:** for women who demonstrate outstanding leadership qualities. **Affiliated With:** Girls Inc. **Publications:** *Our Voice*, seasonal. Newsletter. **Price:** free. Alternate Formats: online.

Cleveland Heights

14244 ■ Association of Jewish Libraries - Cleveland (Greater Cleveland)
c/o Linda Silver, Pres.
Ratner Media & Tech. Ctr.
Jewish Educ. Ctr. of Cleveland
2030 Taylor Rd.
Cleveland Heights, OH 44118
Ph: (216)371-8288
E-mail: lsilver@jecc.org
URL: National Affiliate–www.jewishlibraries.org
Contact: Linda Silver, Pres.
Local. Aims to maintain high professional standards for Jewish librarians. Promotes the enhancement of facilities found in Jewish libraries. Encourages the publication of materials, especially involving children's literature. **Affiliated With:** Association of Jewish Libraries.

14245 ■ Cleveland Psychoanalytic Center (CPC)
2460 Fairmount Blvd., Ste.312
Cleveland Heights, OH 44106-3648
Ph: (216)229-5959
Fax: (216)229-7321
E-mail: cpcwebmaster@gmail.com
URL: http://www.psychoanalysiscleveland.org
Contact: Ms. Deborah Morse, Admin.Coor.
Local. Educates and promotes public awareness and interest in the science and art of psychoanalysis. Establishes and maintains standards for the training of psychoanalysts and for the practice of psychoanalysis. **Affiliated With:** American Psychoanalytic Association.

14246 ■ Future Heights
c/o Julie Langan, Exec.Dir.
2163 Lee Rd., Ste.103
Cleveland Heights, OH 44118-2975
Ph: (216)320-1423
E-mail: info@futureheights.org
URL: http://www.futureheights.org
Contact: Julie Langan, Exec.Dir.
Founded: 2000. **Members:** 300. **Staff:** 1. **Budget:** $100,000. **Local Groups:** 1. **Local**. Strives to preserve and strengthen neighborhoods and commercial districts in Cleveland Heights. Advocates citizen participation in planning and development. **Computer Services:** Online services, community calendar. **Publications:** *FutureHeights News*, quarterly. Newsletter. **Price:** free. **Circulation:** 2,000.

14247 ■ Heights Regional Chamber of Commerce (HRCC)
3109 Mayfield Rd., Ste.202
Cleveland Heights, OH 44118
Ph: (216)397-7322
Fax: (216)397-7353
E-mail: info@hrcc.org
URL: http://www.hrcc.org
Contact: Angie Pohlman, Dir.
Founded: 1948. **Membership Dues:** business (depending on the number of employees), $125-$400 • government, school, $300 • citizen, $75 • utility company, $600 • platinum, $2,500. **Local**. Represents the interests of businesses and professionals in the cities of Cleveland Heights, Lyndhurst, Richmond Heights, Shaker Heights, South Euclid and University Heights.

14248 ■ Physicians for Social Responsibility, Northeast Ohio
c/o Jason Chao, Pres.
PO Box 181418
Cleveland Heights, OH 44118
Ph: (216)368-3886
E-mail: jason.chao@case.edu
URL: National Affiliate–www.psr.org
Contact: Jason Chao, Pres.
Local. **Affiliated With:** Physicians for Social Responsibility.

14249 ■ Project Repair
2520 Noble Rd.
Cleveland Heights, OH 44121
Ph: (216)381-9560
Contact: Rebecca Stager, Program Coor.
Local.

14250 ■ Tasters Guild International - Cleveland, Chapter No. 070
2727 Lanchashire Rd., Apt. A501
Cleveland Heights, OH 44106
Ph: (216)371-1291
URL: National Affiliate–www.tastersguild.com
Contact: Larry Weingarten, Contact
Local. Aims to educate consumers and spread the word of responsible wine and food consumption. Provides opportunity to encounter the best in wine and culinary delights. **Affiliated With:** Tasters Guild International.

Cleves

14251 ■ American Legion, Miller-Stockum Post 485
29 E State Rd.
Cleves, OH 45002
Ph: (740)362-7478
Fax: (740)362-1429
URL: National Affiliate–www.legion.org
Local. **Affiliated With:** American Legion.

14252 ■ East Coast 4 Wheel Drive Association (EC4WDA)
101 S Miami Ave.
Cleves, OH 45002
Fax: (513)941-1479
Free: (800)ECST4WD
E-mail: ec4wda@ec4wda.org
URL: http://www.ec4wda.org
Contact: Barry Kellerman, Pres.
Founded: 1969. **Members:** 1,500. **Membership Dues:** individual, $26 (annual) • associate, $35 (annual). **Regional Groups:** 5. **Regional**. Sponsors 4x4 racing events and recreational trail riding events. **Publications:** *East Coaster*, quarterly. Newsletter. **Price:** included in membership dues. **Advertising:** accepted. **Conventions/Meetings:** annual convention - always November.

14253 ■ International Thomas Merton Society - Cincinnati, OH
c/o Tony Russo
8087 Bridgetown Rd.
Cleves, OH 45002
E-mail: trusso@fuse.net
URL: National Affiliate–www.merton.org
Contact: Tony Russo, Contact
Local. Promotes the knowledge of the life and writings of Thomas Merton. Organizes retreats and conferences devoted to Merton and his works. Supports the general writing of general-interest and scholarly books and articles about Merton.

Clinton

14254 ■ Akron-Canton Muskie Maniacs
1354 Johns Rd.
Clinton, OH 44216
Ph: (330)882-9512
E-mail: m_mihalko@msn.com
URL: National Affiliate–www.muskiesinc.org
Contact: Michael Mihalko, Pres.
Local.

Clyde

14255 ■ American Legion, Ohio Post 122
c/o Orrin G. Franks
PO Box 366
Clyde, OH 43410
Ph: (740)362-7478
Fax: (740)362-1429
URL: National Affiliate–www.legion.org
Contact: Orrin G. Franks, Contact
Local. **Affiliated With:** American Legion.

14256 ■ Clyde Business and Professional Association
c/o Rebecca R. Brooks
PO Box 351
Clyde, OH 43410-0351
Ph: (419)547-9194
Local.

Coldwater

14257 ■ American Legion, Patriotism Post 470
601 N 2nd St.
Coldwater, OH 45828
Ph: (740)362-7478
Fax: (740)362-1429
URL: National Affiliate–www.legion.org
Local. Affiliated With: American Legion.

14258 ■ Coldwater Area Chamber of Commerce
PO Box 57
Coldwater, OH 45828
Ph: (419)678-4881
E-mail: coldwater@bright.net
URL: National Affiliate–www.joinsoca.com
Contact: Janet Gels, Contact
Local. Promotes social and economic development in Coldwater, OH.

Columbiana

14259 ■ American Legion, Ohio Post 290
c/o Benjamin Firestone
44403 State Rte. 14
Columbiana, OH 44408
Ph: (740)362-7478
Fax: (740)362-1429
URL: National Affiliate–www.legion.org
Contact: Benjamin Firestone, Contact
Local. Affiliated With: American Legion.

14260 ■ Columbiana Area Chamber of Commerce
104-1/2 S Main St.
Columbiana, OH 44408
Ph: (330)482-3822
URL: http://www.columbianachamber.com
Contact: Chris Davis, Pres.
Members: 108. **Membership Dues:** business, $50-$250 (annual) • institution, $50 (annual) • associate, $35 (annual). **Staff:** 1. **Local.** Promotes business and community development in the Columbiana, OH area. Sponsors Christmas decorating contest, Street Fair photo contest, and 4th of July fireworks. **Libraries: Type:** open to the public. **Awards:** Community Awards. **Frequency:** annual. **Type:** recognition. **Computer Services:** Online services, membership directory. **Publications:** *Chamber Chatter*, monthly. Newsletter. **Price:** free. Alternate Formats: online. **Conventions/Meetings:** monthly board meeting - always second Tuesday • annual Community Awards Banquet.

14261 ■ Columbiana Area Lions Club
44240 Crestview Rd.
Columbiana, OH 44408
Ph: (330)482-2039
E-mail: ruperaa@peoplepc.com
URL: http://columbianaareaoh.lionwap.org
Contact: Becky Rupert, Sec.-Treas.
Local. Affiliated With: Lions Clubs International.

Columbus

14262 ■ 100 Black Men of Central Ohio
1409 E Livingston Ave.
Columbus, OH 43205
Fax: (614)253-4448
E-mail: info@100bmco.org
URL: http://www.100bmco.org
Local. Affiliated With: 100 Black Men of America.

14263 ■ AAA Ohio Automobile Club
2625 Northland Plz. Dr.
Columbus, OH 43231
Ph: (614)899-1222
State.

14264 ■ AAA Ohio Automobile Club
4701 Reed Rd.
Columbus, OH 43220
Ph: (614)457-2614
State.

14265 ■ AAA Ohio Automobile Club
6023 E Main St.
Columbus, OH 43213
Ph: (614)866-4420
State.

14266 ■ AARP, Ohio
17 S High St., Ste.800
Columbus, OH 43215-3467
Ph: (614)224-9800
Fax: (614)224-9801
E-mail: ohaarp@aarp.org
URL: http://www.aarp.org/oh
Persons 50 years of age or older, working or retired. Seeks to improve every aspect of living for older people. **Affiliated With:** American Association of Retired Persons.

14267 ■ Academic Library Association of Ohio (ALAO)
c/o Ohio College Association
PO Box 3082
Columbus, OH 43210-0082
Ph: (740)587-6389
Fax: (740)587-6285
E-mail: watsona@denison.edu
URL: http://www.alaoweb.org
Contact: Ann Watson, VP/Pres.-Elect
State. Enhances the ability of academic library and information professionals to serve the information needs of the higher education community and to improve learning, teaching and research. **Affiliated With:** Association of College and Research Libraries.

14268 ■ Action Ohio Coalition For Battered Women
36 W Gay St., Ste.311
Columbus, OH 43215
Ph: (614)221-1255
Fax: (614)221-6357
Free: (888)622-9315
E-mail: actionoh@ee.net
URL: http://www.actionohio.org
Contact: Hilda M. Stotts, Pres.
State. Affiliated With: National Coalition Against Domestic Violence.

14269 ■ Adaptive Adventure Sports Coalition
c/o Steve Ricker
1139 Dodd Hall
480 W 9th Ave.
Columbus, OH 43210
Ph: (614)293-4963
E-mail: info@taasc.org
URL: http://www.taasc.org
Founded: 1997. **State. Affiliated With:** Disabled Sports USA.

14270 ■ Aikido of Columbus
221 Piedmont Rd.
Columbus, OH 43214
Ph: (614)262-3355
E-mail: paullinden@aol.com
URL: http://www.usaikifed.com
Contact: Paul Linden, Instructor
Local. Affiliated With: United States Aikido Federation.

14271 ■ Aladdin Shriners
c/o P. Daniel Martin
3850 Stelzer Rd.
Columbus, OH 43219-3044
Ph: (614)475-2609
Fax: (614)475-8225
Free: (800)475-3850
E-mail: aladdinshrine@aladdinshrine.org
URL: http://www.aladdinshrine.org
Contact: P. Daniel Martin, Recorder
Local. Affiliated With: Imperial Council of the Ancient Arabic Order of the Nobles of the Mystic Shrine for North America.

14272 ■ Alcoholics Anonymous World Services, Central Ohio Fellowship Intergroup
1561 Old Leonard Ave.
Columbus, OH 43219-2580
Ph: (614)253-8501
Fax: (614)253-5554
Free: (800)870-3795
E-mail: cogf@aacentralohio.org
URL: http://www.aacentralohio.org
Local. Individuals recovering from alcoholism. AA maintains that members can solve their common problem and help others achieve sobriety through a twelve step program that includes sharing their experience, strength, and hope with each other. **Affiliated With:** Alcoholics Anonymous World Services.

14273 ■ ALS Association, Western Ohio
1810 MacKenzie Dr., Ste.120
Columbus, OH 43220
Ph: (614)273-2572
Fax: (614)273-2573
Free: (866)273-2572
E-mail: alsohio@alsohio.org
URL: http://www.alsohio.org
Contact: Marlin Seymour, Exec.Dir.
Membership Dues: $25 (annual). **Staff:** 2. **Regional Groups:** 55. **State.** ALS patients, families, and friends providing support and communication to fellow members. **Conventions/Meetings:** annual convention (exhibits) - held in May, Washington, DC.

14274 ■ American Association of Airport Executives, Ohio
c/o Ronald E. Newland
Port Columbus Intl. Airport
4600 Intl. Gateway
Columbus, OH 43219-1779
Ph: (616)239-4084
Fax: (614)238-7867
E-mail: rnewland@columbusairports.com
URL: http://www.glcaaae.org
Contact: Ronald E. Newland, Contact
State. Represents airport management personnel at public airports. Promotes professionalism and financial stability in the administration of airports. Furthers airport safety and operational efficiency. Seeks to develop a systematic exchange of information and experience in the development, maintenance and operation of airports. **Affiliated With:** American Association of Airport Executives.

14275 ■ American Board of Trial Advocates - Ohio
37 W Broad St., No. 480
Columbus, OH 43215
Ph: (614)228-6599
Fax: (614)241-2215
E-mail: tking@craiggroup.com
Contact: Tom King, Pres.
State. Improves the ethical and technical standards of practice in the field of advocacy. Elevates the standards of integrity, honor and courtesy in the legal profession. Promotes the efficient administration of justice and improvement of the law. **Affiliated With:** American Board of Trial Advocates.

14276 ■ American Cancer Society, Franklin County
870 Michigan Ave.
Columbus, OH 43215

Ph: (614)228-8466
Fax: (614)228-4456
Free: (888)227-6446
E-mail: sheri.richardson@cancer.org
URL: http://www.cancer.org
Contact: Sheri Richardson, Contact
Local. Works to eliminate cancer as a major health problem through research, education, advocacy and service. **Affiliated With:** American Cancer Society.

14277 ■ American Chemical Society, Columbus Section
c/o Dr. Thomas J. Weeks, Chm.
2655 Camden Rd.
Columbus, OH 43221-3221
E-mail: tomweeks@aol.com
URL: National Affiliate–acswebcontent.acs.org
Contact: Dr. Thomas J. Weeks, Chm.
Local. Represents the interests of individuals dedicated to the advancement of chemistry in all its branches. Provides opportunities for peer interaction and career development. **Affiliated With:** American Chemical Society.

14278 ■ American Concrete Institute, Central Ohio Chapter
c/o David A. Holtzapple
Korda/Nemeth Engrg.
1650 Watermark Dr., Ste.200
Columbus, OH 43215
Ph: (614)487-1650
Fax: (614)487-8981
URL: National Affiliate–www.aci-int.org
Contact: Dave Holtzapple, Structural Engr.
Local. Technical society of engineers, architects, contractors, educators, and others interested in improving techniques of design construction and maintenance of concrete products and structures. **Affiliated With:** American Concrete Institute.

14279 ■ American Council of the Blind of Ohio (ACB-O)
PO Box 21488
Columbus, OH 43221
Fax: (614)451-0539
Free: (800)835-2226
E-mail: kmorlock@gcfn.org
URL: http://www.acbohio.org
Contact: Ken Morlock, Exec.Dir.
State. Strives to improve the well-being of all blind and visually impaired individuals. Seeks to elevate the social, economic and cultural levels of blind people. Improves educational and rehabilitation facilities and opportunities for the visually impaired. **Affiliated With:** American Council of the Blind.

14280 ■ American Council of the Blind of Ohio
c/o Ken Morlock, Exec.Dir.
PO Box 21488
Columbus, OH 43221
Fax: (614)451-0539
Free: (800)835-2226
E-mail: kmorlock@gcfn.org
URL: http://www.acbohio.org
Contact: Ken Morlock, Exec.Dir.
State. Strives to improve the well being of all blind and visually impaired people. Aims to elevate the social, economic and cultural levels of blind people. Cooperates with the public and private institutions and organizations concerned with blind services. Conducts a public education program to promote greater understanding of blindness and the capabilities of blind people. **Affiliated With:** American Council of the Blind.

14281 ■ American Council of Engineering Companies of Ohio (ACEC Ohio)
1650 Lake Shore Dr., Ste.200
Columbus, OH 43204
Ph: (614)487-8844
Fax: (614)487-8841
E-mail: info@acecohio.org
URL: http://www.acecohio.org
Contact: Donald L. Mader, Exec.Dir.
Founded: 1977. **Members:** 160. **Staff:** 2. **Budget:** $310,000. **Regional Groups:** 6. **State**. Serves the needs of privately owned engineering companies. **Awards:** Engineering Excellence Award. **Frequency:** annual. **Type:** recognition. **Formerly:** (2002) Consulting Engineers Council of Ohio. **Publications:** *Ohio Consulting Engineer*, monthly. Newsletter. **Conventions/Meetings:** annual conference.

14282 ■ American Culinary Federation Columbus Chapter
PO Box 16130
Columbus, OH 43216-6130
Ph: (614)470-2002
E-mail: acf@acfcolumbus.org
URL: http://www.acfcolumbus.org
Contact: Sharon Pallas CEPC, Pres.
Local. Promotes the culinary profession and provides on-going educational training and networking for members. Provides opportunities for competition, professional recognition, and access to educational forums with other culinarians at local, regional, national, and international events.

14283 ■ American Federation of Teachers, AFL-CIO - Professional Guild of Ohio Local Union 1960
PO Box 7139
Columbus, OH 43205-0139
Ph: (614)258-4401
Fax: (614)258-4465
Free: (800)331-5428
E-mail: cdoerfler@professionalsguild.org
URL: http://professionalsguild.org
Contact: Christine Doerfler, Organizing Dir.
Members: 1,391. **Local**. **Affiliated With:** American Federation of Teachers.

14284 ■ American Industrial Hygiene Association, Central Ohio Section (CO-AIHA)
c/o William J. Frost, CIH, Pres.
PO Box 2219
Columbus, OH 43216
Ph: (614)790-3078
E-mail: jfrost@ashland.com
URL: http://www.aiha.org/localsections/html/coaiha/homepage.htm
Contact: William J. Frost CIH, Pres.
Local. Promotes the study and control of environmental factors affecting the health and well being of workers. Sponsors continuing education courses in industrial hygiene, government affairs, and public relations. Conducts educational and research programs. **Affiliated With:** American Industrial Hygiene Association.

14285 ■ American Institute of Aeronautics and Astronautics, Columbus Section
c/o Pro. Gerald Gregorek
8292 Breckenridge Way
Columbus, OH 43235
E-mail: gregorek.1@osu.edu
URL: National Affiliate–www.aiaa.org/
Contact: Dr. Corso Padova, Sect.Chm.
Local. **Affiliated With:** American Institute of Aeronautics and Astronautics.

14286 ■ American Institute of Architects Columbus
21 W. Broad St., Ste.200
Columbus, OH 43215-4100
Ph: (614)469-1973
Fax: (614)469-1976
E-mail: info@aiacolumbus.org
URL: http://www.aiacolumbus.org
Local. Professional society of architects. Fosters professionalism and accountability among members through continuing education and training; promotes design excellence by influencing change in the industry. **Affiliated With:** American Institute of Architects.

14287 ■ American Institute of Architects Ohio
17 S High St., Ste.200
Columbus, OH 43215
Ph: (614)221-1900
Fax: (614)221-1989
E-mail: aiaohio@assnoffices.com
URL: http://www.aiaohio.org
Contact: Kate Brunswick CAE, Dir. of Service
Founded: 1857. **Members:** 2,000. **Local Groups:** 7. **State**. Seeks to further architectural profession and practice by influencing legislative and public policy of state through its government affairs program. **Awards:** Design Award. **Type:** recognition • Gold Medal Award. **Frequency:** annual. **Type:** recognition. **Recipient:** for exemplary efforts and significant accomplishments in the field of architecture • Gold Medal Firm Award. **Frequency:** annual. **Type:** recognition. **Recipient:** for consistently producing distinguished architecture • Mentor Award. **Type:** recognition. **Recipient:** for individual who has demonstrated the ability to assist and mentor in the community • Public Service Award. **Type:** recognition. **Recipient:** for individual who has significant impact in community through public service • Twenty Five Year Award. **Type:** recognition. **Recipient:** for designing unique and effective architectural projects. **Affiliated With:** American Institute of Architects. **Publications:** *ArchiTypes*. Newsletter. Contains information, updates, and profile regarding the organization. Alternate Formats: online. **Conventions/Meetings:** annual convention (exhibits).

14288 ■ American Legion, Bexley Post 430
3227 E Livingston Ave.
Columbus, OH 43227
Ph: (740)362-7478
Fax: (740)362-1429
URL: National Affiliate–www.legion.org
Local. **Affiliated With:** American Legion.

14289 ■ American Legion, Camp Chase Post 98
PO Box 44141
Columbus, OH 43204
Ph: (740)362-7478
Fax: (740)362-1429
URL: National Affiliate–www.legion.org
Local. **Affiliated With:** American Legion.

14290 ■ American Legion, Columbus Post 82
5475 Sandalwood Blvd.
Columbus, OH 43229
Ph: (740)362-7478
Fax: (740)362-1429
URL: National Affiliate–www.legion.org
Local. **Affiliated With:** American Legion.

14291 ■ American Legion, Comrade Whitehall Post 490
1117 S Hamilton Rd.
Columbus, OH 43227
Ph: (740)362-7478
Fax: (740)362-1429
URL: National Affiliate–www.legion.org
Local. **Affiliated With:** American Legion.

14292 ■ American Legion, Don Gentile Post 532
1571 Demorest Rd.
Columbus, OH 43228
Ph: (740)362-7478
Fax: (740)362-1429
URL: National Affiliate–www.legion.org
Local. **Affiliated With:** American Legion.

14293 ■ American Legion, Galloway Post 799
47 Maple Dr.
Columbus, OH 43228
Ph: (740)362-7478
Fax: (740)362-1429
URL: National Affiliate–www.legion.org
Local. **Affiliated With:** American Legion.

14294 ■ American Legion, Navy-Marine Post 276
334 S Gould Rd.
Columbus, OH 43209
Ph: (740)362-7478
Fax: (740)362-1429
URL: National Affiliate–www.legion.org
Local. Affiliated With: American Legion.

14295 ■ American Legion, Northwest Post 443
PO Box 21014
Columbus, OH 43221
Ph: (740)362-7478
Fax: (740)362-1429
URL: National Affiliate–www.legion.org
Local. Affiliated With: American Legion.

14296 ■ American Legion, Ohio Post 157
c/o A.L. Brooks
2954 E 5th Ave.
Columbus, OH 43219
Ph: (740)362-7478
Fax: (740)362-1429
URL: National Affiliate–www.legion.org
Contact: A.L. Brooks, Contact
Local. Affiliated With: American Legion.

14297 ■ American Legion, Ohio Post 182
c/o Raymond Scott
1569 Republic Ave.
Columbus, OH 43211
Ph: (740)362-7478
Fax: (740)362-1429
URL: National Affiliate–www.legion.org
Contact: Raymond Scott, Contact
Local. Affiliated With: American Legion.

14298 ■ American Legion, Ohio Post 465
c/o Malcolm D. Jeffrey
1441 N Grant Ave.
Columbus, OH 43201
Ph: (740)362-7478
Fax: (740)362-1429
URL: National Affiliate–www.legion.org
Contact: Malcolm D. Jeffrey, Contact
Local. Affiliated With: American Legion.

14299 ■ American Legion, Ohio Post 486
c/o Robert Dutro
250 W Broad St., No. m21
Columbus, OH 43215
Ph: (740)362-7478
Fax: (740)362-1429
URL: National Affiliate–www.legion.org
Contact: Robert Dutro, Contact
Local. Affiliated With: American Legion.

14300 ■ American Legion, Ohio Post 770
c/o Sergeant Donald R. Long
1500 E 17th Ave.
Columbus, OH 43219
Ph: (740)362-7478
Fax: (740)362-1429
URL: National Affiliate–www.legion.org
Contact: Sergeant Donald R. Long, Contact
Local. Affiliated With: American Legion.

14301 ■ American Legion, Sam Mason Post 690
PO Box 09750
Columbus, OH 43209
Ph: (740)362-7478
Fax: (740)362-1429
URL: National Affiliate–www.legion.org
Local. Affiliated With: American Legion.

14302 ■ American Legion, Southway Post 144
3253 S High St.
Columbus, OH 43207
Ph: (740)362-7478
Fax: (740)362-1429
URL: National Affiliate–www.legion.org
Local. Affiliated With: American Legion.

14303 ■ American Lung Association of Ohio (ALAO)
1950 Arlingate Ln.
Columbus, OH 43228-4102
Ph: (614)279-1700
Fax: (614)279-4940
Free: (800)LUNG-USA
E-mail: molly1@ohiolung.org
URL: http://www.ohiolung.org
Contact: Tracy Ross, Interim Pres./CEO
Founded: 1901. **Members:** 35. **Staff:** 48. **Budget:** $5,000,000. **Regional Groups:** 8. **State.** Works to prevent and control lung disease. **Awards:** Stocklen Lung Research Fund. **Frequency:** annual. **Type:** monetary. **Affiliated With:** American Lung Association.

14304 ■ American Mothers - Ohio Chapter
c/o Judy Hardin, Pres.
1015 Norris Dr.
Columbus, OH 43224
Ph: (614)262-9604
E-mail: jhardin247@aol.com
URL: National Affiliate–www.americanmothers.org
Contact: Judy Hardin, Pres.
State. Affiliated With: American Mothers, Inc.

14305 ■ American Payroll Association, Columbus Area Chapter
PO Box 26894
Columbus, OH 43226-0894
E-mail: patterb6@nationwide.com
URL: http://www.apacolumbus.org
Contact: Brad Patterson CPP, Pres.
Local. Aims to increase the Payroll Professional's skill level through education and mutual support. Represents the Payroll Professional before legislative bodies. Administers the certified payroll professional program of recognition. Provides public service education on payroll and employment issues. **Affiliated With:** American Payroll Association.

14306 ■ American Red Cross, Central Ohio Blood Services Region
c/o Catherine West, Dir. of Communications
995 E Broad St.
Columbus, OH 43205
Ph: (614)253-2740
Fax: (614)253-1544
Free: (800)GIVELIFE
E-mail: westc@usa.redcross.org
URL: http://www.bloodsaveslives.org
Contact: Catherine West, Dir. of Communications
Local. Strives to provide life-saving units of blood to 58 hospitals within a 27 county area in central Ohio. Conducts "Youth Blood Program.".

14307 ■ American Red Cross of Greater Columbus
995 E Broad St.
Columbus, OH 43205
Ph: (614)253-2740
Fax: (614)253-1544
Free: (800)750-0750
URL: http://columbus.redcross.org
Regional.

14308 ■ American Society for Quality, Columbus Section 0801
c/o Mustafa Shraim
PO Box 218132
Columbus, OH 43221
Fax: (614)573-7238
E-mail: mus@shraimqps.com
URL: http://www.asq-columbus.org
Contact: Mustafa Shraim, Contact
Local. Advances learning, quality improvement and knowledge exchange to improve business results and to create better workplaces and communities worldwide. Provides a forum for information exchange, professional development and continuous learning in the science of quality. **Affiliated With:** American Society for Quality.

14309 ■ American Society of Safety Engineers, Central Ohio Chapter
c/o Nick Minto, Pres.
Turner Constr. Co.
250 E Wilson Bridge Rd.
Columbus, OH 43085
Ph: (614)781-8550
Fax: (614)781-8553
E-mail: nminto@centralohioasse.org
URL: http://www.centralohioasse.org
Contact: Nick Minto, Pres.
Local. Enhances the advancement of the safety profession and the safety professional. Promotes the technical, societal and economic well-being of safety practitioners. **Affiliated With:** American Society of Safety Engineers.

14310 ■ American Society of Sanitary Engineering, Central Ohio Chapter
c/o Ronald Graves, Pres.
Plumbers & Pipefitters Local Union 189
1226 Kinnear Rd.
Columbus, OH 43212
E-mail: rgraves@columbusmail.com
URL: National Affiliate–www.asse-plumbing.org
Contact: Ronald Graves, Pres.
Local. Represents plumbing officials, sanitary engineers, plumbers, plumbing contractors, building officials, architects, engineers, designing engineers, physicians, and others interested in health. Conducts research on plumbing and sanitation and develops performance standards for components of the plumbing system. Sponsors disease research programs and other studies of water-borne epidemics. **Affiliated With:** American Society of Sanitary Engineering.

14311 ■ American Society for Training and Development - Central Ohio Chapter
PO Box 1322
Columbus, OH 43216-1322
Ph: (614)249-5196
Free: (877)517-4131
E-mail: info@centralohioastd.org
URL: http://www.centralohioastd.org
Contact: Gary Rybak, Pres.
Local. Promotes workplace learning and the improvement of skills of workplace professionals. Provides resource and professional development to individuals in the field of learning and development. Recognizes and sets standards for learning and performance professionals. **Affiliated With:** American Society for Training and Development.

14312 ■ American Statistical Association, Columbus Chapter
c/o Mark E. Irwin
Dept. of Statistics
Ohio State Univ.
1958 Neil Ave.
Columbus, OH 43210
Ph: (614)292-0779
Fax: (614)292-2096
E-mail: irwin@stat.ohio-state.edu
URL: National Affiliate–www.amstat.org
Contact: Mark E. Irwin, Pres.
Founded: 1929. **Local.** Professional society of persons interested in the theory, methodology, and application of the use and compilation of statistics. Offers science fair judging. **Publications:** none. **Affiliated With:** American Statistical Association. **Conventions/Meetings:** semiannual symposium.

14313 ■ American Welding Society, Columbus Section 036
c/o John Lawmon, Treas.
Edison Welding Inst.
1250 Arthur E Adams Dr.
Columbus, OH 43221
Ph: (614)688-5054
Fax: (614)688-5001
E-mail: johnlawmon@msn.com
URL: National Affiliate–www.aws.org
Contact: Jerry Van Meter, Chm.
Local. Professional engineering society in the field of welding. **Affiliated With:** American Welding Society.

14314 ■ American Women in Radio and Television, Buckeye of Central Ohio
Radio One
1500 W Third Ave., No. 300
Columbus, OH 43212
Ph: (614)487-1444
Fax: (614)487-5873
E-mail: bspencer@bluechipbroadcasting.com
URL: National Affiliate–www.awrt.org
Contact: Brenda Spencer, Contact
Local. Affiliated With: American Women in Radio and Television.

14315 ■ Americans United for Separation of Church and State, Central Ohio
PO Box 1142
Columbus, OH 43216
E-mail: info@auohio.org
URL: http://www.auohio.org
Local. Affiliated With: Americans United for Separation of Church and State.

14316 ■ ARC of Ohio
1335 Dublin Rd., Ste.205-C
Columbus, OH 43215
Ph: (614)487-4720
Fax: (614)487-4725
Free: (800)875-2723
E-mail: info@thearcofohio.org
URL: http://www.thearcofohio.org
Contact: Gary Tonks, Exec.Dir.
Founded: 1953. **Membership Dues:** $20 (annual). **State.** Parents, self-advocates, and other interested individuals organized to promote the human rights, personal dignity, and community participation of citizens with mental retardation, other developmental disabilities and their families. **Formerly:** Association of Retarded Citizens of Ohio. **Publications:** *The Arc News*, quarterly. Newsletter. **Price:** included in membership dues. **Conventions/Meetings:** annual conference.

14317 ■ Assistance League of Metro Columbus
PO Box 340406
Columbus, OH 43234
Ph: (614)781-1002
Fax: (614)888-8603
E-mail: cabauer42@aol.com
URL: http://www.almetrocolumbus.org
Local. Affiliated With: Assistance League.

14318 ■ Associated General Contractors of Ohio (AGC)
c/o Richard J. Hobbs, Exec.VP
1755 Northwest Blvd.
Columbus, OH 43212
Ph: (614)486-6446
Fax: (614)486-6498
E-mail: rjh@agcohio.com
URL: http://www.agcohio.com
Contact: Richard J. Hobbs, Exec.VP
State.

14319 ■ Associated Landscape Contractors of America, Columbus State Community College
c/o Steven O'Neal, Faculty Advisor
Academic Center B
PO Box 1609
Columbus, OH 43216-1609
Ph: (614)287-5417
Fax: (614)287-3644
E-mail: soneal@cscc.edu
URL: http://www.cscc.edu
Contact: Steven O'Neal, Faculty Advisor
Local. Affiliated With: Professional Landcare Network.

14320 ■ Associated Landscape Contractors of America, Ohio State University
c/o Martin Quigley, Faculty Advisor
Dept. of Hort. and Crop. Sci.
2001 Fyffe, Howlett Hall
Columbus, OH 43210-1096
Ph: (614)292-3136
Fax: (614)292-3505
E-mail: quigley.30@osu.edu
URL: National Affiliate–www.alca.org
Contact: Martin Quigley, Faculty Advisor
Local. Affiliated With: Professional Landcare Network.

14321 ■ Association for Community Organization and Social Administration, Midwest Region
c/o Richard Boettcher
Ohio State Univ.
1670 Cambridge Blvd.
Columbus, OH 43212
Ph: (313)577-4441
Fax: (614)292-6940
E-mail: boettcher.1@osu.edu
URL: National Affiliate–www.acosa.org
Contact: Richard Boettcher, Contact
Regional. Affiliated With: Association for Community Organization and Social Administration.

14322 ■ Association of Community Organizations for Reform Now, Columbus
379 N 20th Lower Level
Columbus, OH 43203
Ph: (614)258-8854
Fax: (614)258-9487
E-mail: ohacorncoro@acorn.org
URL: National Affiliate–www.acorn.org
Local. Affiliated With: Association of Community Organizations for Reform Now.

14323 ■ Association for Computing Machinery, Ohio State University
395 Dreese Labs, 2015 Neil Ave.
Columbus, OH 43210
Ph: (614)231-0929
E-mail: gurari@cis.ohio-state.edu
Contact: Eitan Gurari, Contact
Founded: 1947. **Members:** 50. **Membership Dues:** individual, $5 (annual). **Budget:** $500. **Local.** Biological, medical, behavioral, and computer scientists; hospital administrators; programmers and others interested in application of computer methods to biological, behavioral, and medical problems. Stimulates understanding of the use and potential of computers in the Biosciences. **Affiliated With:** Association for Computing Machinery.

14324 ■ Association of Government Accountants - Central Ohio Chapter
c/o Lisa Plaga, Sec.
155 E Broad St.
Columbus, OH 43215
Ph: (614)341-1921 (614)885-5380
E-mail: dmiller@ci.powell.oh.us
URL: http://www.coaga.org
Contact: Debra Miller, Pres.
Local. Provides quality education, professional development and certification to government accountants. Supports standards and research to advance government accountability. Seeks to encourage the interchange of ideas among financial managers in government service and among government and nongovernmental managers. **Affiliated With:** Association of Government Accountants.

14325 ■ Association of Independent Colleges and Universities of Ohio (AICUO)
c/o Larry H. Christman, Pres.
17 S High St., Ste.1020
Columbus, OH 43215-3473
Ph: (614)228-2196
Fax: (614)228-8406
E-mail: lchristm@aicuo.edu
URL: http://www.aicuo.edu
State. Affiliated With: National Association of Independent Colleges and Universities.

14326 ■ Association of Late-Deafened Adults - Midwest
c/o Martha Mattox-Baker
1535 Glenn Ave.
Columbus, OH 43212
Ph: (466)085-6142
E-mail: buckeyemarty@core.com
URL: National Affiliate–www.alda.org
Contact: Martha Mattox-Baker, Contact
Regional. Advocates for the needs of late-deafened people. Provides information, support and social opportunities through self-help groups, meetings and social events. **Affiliated With:** Association of Late-Deafened Adults.

14327 ■ Association of Legal Administrators, Columbus Chapter
c/o Jane Lagusch, Office Administrator
Bailey Cavalieri LLC
10 W Broad St., Ste.2100
Columbus, OH 43215-3422
Ph: (614)227-8888
E-mail: meisenbarth@bricker.com
URL: http://www.alacolumbus.org
Contact: Jane Lagusch, Contact
Local. Affiliated With: Association of Legal Administrators.

14328 ■ Association of Ohio Health Commissioners (AOHC)
50 W Broad St., No. 1614
Columbus, OH 43215
Ph: (614)221-5994
Fax: (614)221-5998
E-mail: aohc_1@aohc.net
URL: http://www.aohc.net
Contact: Beth Bickford, Exec.Dir.
State.

14329 ■ Association of Ohio Life Insurance Companies (AOLIC)
c/o Kurtis A. Tunnell, Legislative Counsel
100 S 3rd St.
Columbus, OH 43215-4291
Ph: (614)227-4860
Fax: (614)227-2390
E-mail: info@aolic.com
URL: http://www.aolic.com
State.

14330 ■ Association of Ohio Philanthropic Homes and Housing and Services for the Aging (AOPHA)
c/o Mr. John Alfano, Pres./CEO
855 S Wall St.
Columbus, OH 43206-1921
Ph: (614)444-2882
Fax: (614)444-2974
E-mail: info@aopha.org
URL: http://www.aopha.org
Contact: Mr. John Alfano, Pres./CEO
State.

14331 ■ Association for Psychological Type - Columbus
c/o Janet Wilks
43 E North Broadway St.
Columbus, OH 43214
Ph: (614)447-9855 (614)752-6442
E-mail: j.wilks@earthlink.net
URL: National Affiliate–www.aptinternational.org
Contact: Janet Wilks, Contact
Local. Promotes the practical application and ethical use of psychological type. Provides members with opportunities for continuous learning, sharing experiences and creating understanding and knowledge through research. **Affiliated With:** Association for Psychological Type.

14332 ■ Association of the United States Army, Central Ohio
c/o Michael W. McHenry
2205 Tuliphee Ave.
Columbus, OH 43229-5357

Ph: (614)336-7202
URL: National Affiliate–www.ausa.org
Local. Represents the interests and concerns of American Soldiers. Fosters public support of the Army's role in national security. Provides professional education and information programs.

14333 ■ Association for Women in Science, Central Ohio (AWISCO)
c/o Raquel Diaz-Sprague
484 W 12th Ave.
Columbus, OH 43210
Ph: (614)268-1488
Fax: (614)267-9019
E-mail: diaz-sprague.1@osu.edu
URL: http://awisco.osu.edu
Contact: Raquel Diaz-Sprague, Contact
Founded: 1977. **Membership Dues:** regular, $15 (annual) • retired, $10 (annual) • student, $5 (annual). **Local**. Promotes equal opportunities for women to enter the scientific workforce and to achieve their career goals; provides educational information to women planning careers in science; networks with other women's groups; monitors scientific legislation and the status of women in science. **Affiliated With:** Association for Women in Science. **Publications:** Newsletter, quarterly. **Conventions/Meetings:** quarterly meeting.

14334 ■ Audubon Ohio
692 N. High St., Ste.208
Columbus, OH 43215-1585
Ph: (614)224-3303
Fax: (614)224-3305
E-mail: ohio@audubon.org
URL: National Affiliate–www.audubon.org
Affiliated With: National Audubon Society.

14335 ■ Better Business Bureau of Central Ohio
1335 Dublin Rd., Ste.30A
Columbus, OH 43215
Ph: (614)486-6336
Fax: (614)486-6631
Free: (800)759-2400
E-mail: info@columbus-ohbbb.org
URL: http://www.centralohiobbb.org
Contact: Kip Morse, Pres.
Local. Seeks to promote and foster ethical relationship between businesses and the public through voluntary self-regulation, consumer and business education, and service excellence. Provides information to help consumers and businesses make informed purchasing decisions and avoid costly scams and frauds; settles consumer complaints through arbitration and other means. **Affiliated With:** BBB Wise Giving Alliance. **Also Known As:** (2005) Better Business Bureau serving Columbus and Central Ohio.

14336 ■ Big Brothers Big Sisters of Central Ohio
1855 E Dublin-Granville Rd., 1st Fl.
Columbus, OH 43229-3516
Ph: (614)839-2447
Fax: (614)839-5437
Free: (866)892-2447
E-mail: bbbs@bbbscentralohio.org
URL: http://www.bbbscentralohio.org
Contact: Mr. Dave Schirner, Exec.VP
Founded: 1933. **Staff:** 43. **Nonmembership. For-Profit. Local.** Works for child mentoring. **Affiliated With:** Big Brothers Big Sisters of America. **Formerly:** (2004) Big Brothers Big Sisters Association of Central Ohio.

14337 ■ Bloom-Carroll - Young Life
1515 W Lane Ave.
Columbus, OH 43221
Ph: (614)485-5433
URL: http://sites.younglife.org/_layouts/ylext/default.aspx?ID=C-3696
Local. Affiliated With: Young Life.

14338 ■ BMW Car Club of America, Buckeye Chapter
c/o Ken Price, Pres.
PO Box 21880
Columbus, OH 43221
Ph: (513)735-2032
Fax: (513)735-4087
E-mail: kenprice@fuse.net
URL: http://www.buckeyebmwcca.org
Contact: Ken Price, Pres.
Local. Affiliated With: BMW Car Club of America.

14339 ■ Box 15 Club
c/o Paul Freedman
PO Box 82510
Columbus, OH 43202
E-mail: box15cmh@hotmail.com
Contact: Paul Freedman, Contact
Local.

14340 ■ Brain Injury Association of Ohio (BIAOH)
1335 Dublin Rd., Ste.217D
Columbus, OH 43215-1000
Ph: (614)481-7100
Fax: (614)481-7103
Free: (866)644-6242
E-mail: help@biaoh.org
URL: http://www.biaoh.org
Contact: Suzanne Minnich, Exec.Dir.
Founded: 1983. **Members:** 500. **Membership Dues:** regular, $35 (annual). **Staff:** 11. **Local Groups:** 50. **State**. Works to expand the capacity of services for individuals and families coping with brain injury; increase the knowledge and expertise of professional service providers; raise public awareness of the impact of brain injury; promote ways to reduce the threat, or the disabling after-effects of brain injury. **Libraries: Type:** open to the public. **Subjects:** brain injury education, recovery. **Affiliated With:** Brain Injury Association of America. **Conventions/Meetings:** annual convention, provides educational workshops and social events for individuals with brain injury, their family and friends, professionals and other interested people (exhibits).

14341 ■ Buckeye Association of School Administrators (BASA)
c/o Jerry Klenke, Exec.Dir.
8050 N High St., Ste.150
Columbus, OH 43235-6486
Ph: (614)846-4080
Fax: (614)846-4081
E-mail: klenke@basa-ohio.org
URL: http://www.basa-ohio.org
Contact: Jerry Klenke, Exec.Dir.
Founded: 1969. **Staff:** 10. **State**.

14342 ■ Buckeye Beemers No. 99
c/o Eric Nyrop
PO Box 154
Columbus, OH 43216-0154
Ph: (614)444-9409
E-mail: ericnyrop@ameritech.net
URL: http://www.buckeyebeemers.org
Contact: Molly Cruze-Nyrop, Pres.
Local. BMW motorcycle owners organized for pleasure, recreation, safety, and dissemination of information concerning BMW motorcycles. **Affiliated With:** BMW Motorcycle Owners of America.

14343 ■ Buckeye Model Yachtsmen No. 188
c/o Ken Szakelyhidi
1359 Island Bay Dr.
Columbus, OH 43235-7561
Ph: (614)459-5448
URL: National Affiliate–www.amya.org
Contact: Ken Szakelyhidi, Contact
Local.

14344 ■ Buckeye Sertoma Club
c/o April Rhea
1306 Nautical Dr.
Columbus, OH 43207
Ph: (614)292-3988 (614)861-5261
E-mail: boster@units.ohio-state.edu
URL: http://members.aol.com/bsc10331
Contact: Liz Boster, Pres.
Local.

14345 ■ Buckeye State Sheriff's Association
c/o Robert A. Cornwell, Exec.Dir.
6230 Busch Blvd., Ste.260
Columbus, OH 43229
Ph: (614)431-5500
Fax: (614)431-5665
Local.

14346 ■ Buckeye Wander Freunde
c/o Mike Mosser
6565 Estel Rd.
Columbus, OH 43235
Ph: (614)761-9629
E-mail: michael.r.mosser@jpmchase.com
URL: National Affiliate–www.ava.org
Contact: Mike Mosser, Contact
Local. Non-competitive sports enthusiasts. **Affiliated With:** American Volkssport Association.

14347 ■ Builders Exchange of Central Ohio (BX)
c/o Ms. Catherine Blackford, Exec.Dir.
PO Box 369
Columbus, OH 43216
Ph: (614)486-9521
Fax: (614)486-7620
E-mail: info@bx.org
URL: http://www.bx.org
Contact: Ms. Catherine Blackford, Exec.Dir.
Founded: 1892. **Members:** 1,100. **Local**. Represents the general contractors, subcontractors, suppliers, manufacturer's representatives and individual firms related to the construction industry. Provides information on construction and building procedures. **Affiliated With:** International Builders Exchange Executives. **Publications:** *The BX Products & Services Guide*, annual. Membership Directory. Contains resources for BX members and products/services they provide. **Advertising:** accepted. Alternate Formats: online • *The Exchange*, weekly. Newsletter. Features highlights of upcoming events, programs, classes, awards and other member information. **Advertising:** accepted. Alternate Formats: online.

14348 ■ Builders Exchange Foundation
1175 Dublin Rd.
Columbus, OH 43215-1026
Ph: (614)486-9521

14349 ■ Canal Winchester - Young Life
1515 W Lane Ave.
Columbus, OH 43221
Ph: (614)485-5433
URL: http://sites.younglife.org/_layouts/ylext/default.aspx?ID=C-3700
Local. Affiliated With: Young Life.

14350 ■ Capital City Organizational Development Network
c/o Jeffrey R. Young
5710 Sovereign St.
Columbus, OH 43235
Ph: (614)764-2650
Fax: (614)764-2650
E-mail: jyoung@rayandbarney.com
URL: National Affiliate–www.odnetwork.org
Contact: Mr. Jeff Young, VP of Communications
Founded: 2004. **Members:** 15. **Membership Dues:** normal, $25 (annual) • student, $10 (annual). **Local**. Provides opportunities for members, clients, prospective clients and other related professionals to meet and discuss OD topics, share OD and training opportunities, resources and to network. Provides a networking and educational forum for members to learn and promote OD, form alliances, pursue publishing opportunities, and become actively involved in community outreach projects. **Affiliated With:** Organization Development Network. **Formerly:**

(2004) Central Ohio Regional Organization Development Network. **Publications:** *Organizational Development.* Newsletter.

14351 ■ Center for Effective Discipline (CED)
155 W Main St., Ste.1603
Columbus, OH 43215
Ph: (614)221-8829
Fax: (614)221-2110
E-mail: nblock@infinet.com
URL: http://www.stophitting.org
Contact: Nadine Block, Exec.Dir.
Founded: 1983. **Members:** 35. **State**. Provides information about the effects of corporal punishment of children and alternatives to it. **Formerly:** (1993) Ohio Coalition for More Effective School Discipline. **Publications:** Newsletter, periodic • Books.

14352 ■ Central Ohio Alpine Ski Troop
3202 Palomar Ave.
Columbus, OH 43231
E-mail: acox@moodynolan.com
URL: National Affiliate–www.nbs.org
Contact: Arthur N. Cox, Pres.
Local. Affiliated With: National Brotherhood of Skiers.

14353 ■ Central Ohio Association for Computing Machinery SIGCHI (BuckCHI)
c/o Eric Myers, Chm.
PO Box 20187
Columbus, OH 43220
E-mail: bukchi-officers@acm.org
URL: http://www.acm.org/chapters/buckchi
Contact: Eric Myers, Chm.
Local. Represents the biological, medical, behavioral, and computer scientists; hospital administrators; programmers and others interested in application of computer methods to biological, behavioral, and medical problems. Stimulates understanding of the use and potential of computers in biosciences. **Affiliated With:** Association for Computing Machinery.

14354 ■ Central Ohio Chapter of American Society of Plumbing Engineers
PO Box 2571
Columbus, OH 43216-2571
Ph: (614)487-1650
E-mail: mark.simpson@korda.com
URL: http://www.aspe.org/Central_Ohio
Contact: Mark G. Simpson, Pres.
Local. Represents the interests of individuals dedicated to the advancement of the science of plumbing engineering. Seeks to resolve professional problems in plumbing engineering. Advocates greater cooperation among members and plumbing officials, contractors, laborers and the public. **Affiliated With:** American Society of Plumbing Engineers.

14355 ■ Central Ohio Chapter of the Human Factors and Ergonomics Society
210 Baker Systems Bldg.
1971 Neil Ave.
Columbus, OH 43210
E-mail: sommerich.1@osu.edu
URL: http://www-iwse.eng.ohio-state.edu/ISEFaculty/sommerich/centralohhfes
Contact: Dr. Carolyn M. Sommerich, Contact
Founded: 1987. **Local**. Represents practitioners, students, and academicians with interests in human factors, ergonomics, safety or related areas. Promotes and advances the understanding of the human factors involved in the design, manufacture, and use of machines, systems, and devices of all kinds. **Affiliated With:** Human Factors and Ergonomics Society.

14356 ■ Central Ohio Chapter of International Facility Management Association
PO Box 340647
Columbus, OH 43234-0647
Ph: (614)688-3993
Fax: (614)688-3248
E-mail: leachman.8@osu.edu
URL: http://www.ifmacentralohio.org
Contact: Dorothy Leachman, Pres.
Founded: 1988. **Members:** 175. **Local**. Comprised of facility managers representing all types of organizations including banks, insurance companies, hospitals, colleges and universities, utility companies, electronic equipment manufacturers, petroleum companies, museums, auditoriums, and federal, state, provincial, and local governments. Works to enhance the professional goals of persons involved or interested in the field of facility management (the planning, designing, and managing of workplaces). **Affiliated With:** International Facility Management Association. **Formerly:** (2001) International Facility Management Association, Columbus.

14357 ■ Central Ohio Chapter of Muskies
3975 Ritamarie Dr.
Columbus, OH 43220
Ph: (614)451-0485
E-mail: ohiomuskieshow@yahoo.com
URL: http://www.centralohiochaptermuskiesinc.org
Contact: Ross L. Wagner, Pres.
Local.

14358 ■ Central Ohio Chapter, National Electrical Contractors Association
c/o Gregory E. Stewart, Pres.
3070 Riverside Dr., Ste.165
Columbus, OH 43221-2547
Ph: (614)481-8558
Fax: (614)481-8565
E-mail: cohneca@attglobal.net
URL: National Affiliate–www.necanet.org
Founded: 1953. **Members:** 36. Contractors erecting, installing, repairing, servicing, and maintaining electric wiring, equipment, and appliances. Seeks to represent, promote, and enhance the management interests of members through labor relations, education, management skill improvement, apprentice and journeyman training, marketing, services, public relations, information, communication, and creation of a better business environment; and to coordinate the collective activities of the electrical contracting industry in the areas of government relations, technical, standards, public relations, communication, information, and business ethics. **Affiliated With:** National Electrical Contractors Association. **Conventions/Meetings:** bimonthly board meeting • quarterly Chapter Membership Meeting.

14359 ■ Central Ohio Diabetes Association
1100 Dennison Ave.
Columbus, OH 43201
Ph: (614)884-4400
Fax: (614)884-4484
E-mail: coda@diabetesohio.org
URL: http://www.diabetesohio.org
Contact: Jeanne Grothaus, Exec.Dir.
Founded: 1964. **Members:** 600. **Membership Dues:** individual, $25 (annual) • student, senior (over 65 years old), $20 (annual) • friend, $50 (annual) • pacesetter (with bracelet/necklace), $100 (annual) • benefactor (with bracelet/necklace), $500 (annual) • life (with necklace/bracelet), $1,000. **Staff:** 13. **Budget:** $1,122,000. **Regional Groups:** 10. **Local**. Promotes research, information and advocacy to find a prevention and cure for diabetes and to improve the lives of all people with diabetes. Promotes public awareness of diabetes as a serious disease. Conducts educational programs and provides information to people with diabetes. **Libraries: Type:** open to the public. **Holdings:** articles, books, periodicals, video recordings. **Subjects:** diabetes. **Awards: Frequency:** semiannual. **Type:** grant. **Recipient:** for Ohio based diabetes related research projects. **Publications:** *Diabetes Directions*, 3/year. Newsletter. Contains articles on diabetes. **Price:** $25.00/year. **Circulation:** 1,500. **Advertising:** accepted. **Conventions/Meetings:** annual Diabetes Health Fair - meeting, with speakers; offers free screenings for blood sugar and blood pressure, foot exams, cholesterol screenings, eye exams (exhibits) - first week in November • annual meeting - always May in Columbus, OH • annual symposium, open to healthcare professionals; with speakers (exhibits) - first week in November.

14360 ■ Central Ohio Minority Business Association (COMBA)
1393 E Broad St.
Columbus, OH 43205
Ph: (614)252-8005
Fax: (614)258-9667
E-mail: mcbap@comba.com
URL: http://www.comba.com
Contact: Frank W. Watson, Pres.
Local. Provides business counseling and technical assistance to small business owners. Offers assistance to members in start-up, bookkeeping, business plan writing, loan and bond packaging and private and government contract opportunities.

14361 ■ Central Ohio Orchid Society (COOS)
c/o Jonathan Young, Membership Chm.
1752 Marsdale Ave.
Columbus, OH 43223
Ph: (614)272-5256
E-mail: jnthnyoun@aol.com
URL: http://www.coosinfo.info
Contact: Jonathan Young, Membership Chm.
Regional. Affiliated With: American Orchid Society.

14362 ■ Central Ohio Planned Giving Council (COPGC)
c/o CIVIC
PO Box 20129
Columbus, OH 43220-0129
Ph: (614)884-7780
Fax: (614)884-7783
E-mail: copgc@cs.com
URL: http://www.copgc.com
Contact: Wayne Jenkins, Pres.
Local. Consists of individuals from the fundraising, accounting, estate planning, insurance, and related fields. Provides education and networking opportunities. **Affiliated With:** National Committee on Planned Giving.

14363 ■ Central Ohio Senior Olympics
c/o Maryann Tilley
2100 Morse Rd., Ste.4625
Columbus, OH 43229
Ph: (614)645-3320
Fax: (614)645-0647
E-mail: mntilley@columbus.gov
URL: http://www.ohioseniorolympics.org
Contact: Maryann Tilley, Contact
Local. Affiliated With: National Senior Games Association.

14364 ■ Central Ohio Youth for Christ
PO Box 14804
Columbus, OH 43214
Ph: (614)848-4870
Fax: (614)431-8111
URL: National Affiliate–www.yfc.net
Local. Affiliated With: Youth for Christ/U.S.A.

14365 ■ Children's Defense Fund, Ohio
52 E Lynn St., Ste.400
Columbus, OH 43215-3507
Ph: (614)221-2244
Fax: (614)221-2247
E-mail: cdfohio@cdfohio.org
URL: http://www.cdfohio.org
Contact: Ronald Browder, Dir.
Founded: 1981. **State. Affiliated With:** Children's Defense Fund.

14366 ■ Children's Hunger Alliance
c/o William J. Dolan, CEO
370 S Fifth St.
Columbus, OH 43215
Ph: (614)341-7700
Fax: (614)341-7701
Free: (800)227-6446
E-mail: 4kids@childrenshungeralliance.org
URL: http://www.childrenshungeralliance.org
State.

14367 ■ City Year Columbus
c/o David Ciccone
35 N 4th St.
Columbus, OH 43215
Ph: (614)224-9569 (614)586-1434
E-mail: dciccone01@cityyear.org
URL: http://www.cityyear.org/columbus
Contact: David Ciccone, Recruitment Mgr.

Local. Brings together young people, age 17-24, from diverse backgrounds for a ten-month program focusing on civic leadership, team building, and mobilizing citizens to civic action.

14368 ■ Coalition on Homelessness and Housing in Ohio
c/o Susan Francis
35 E. Gay St., Ste.210
Columbus, OH 43215-3138
Ph: (614)280-1984
Fax: (614)463-1060
E-mail: cohhio@cohhio.org
URL: http://www.cohhio.org

State.

14369 ■ Columbus AIDS Task Force (CATF)
1751 E Long St.
Columbus, OH 43203
Ph: (614)299-2437 (614)291-7162
Fax: (614)291-7163
E-mail: rickharrison@catf.net
URL: http://www.catf.net
Contact: Aaron M. Riley, Exec.Dir.

Founded: 1984. **Staff:** 40. **Budget:** $2,600,000. **Nonmembership. Local**. Provides services and referrals to persons with HIV/AIDS. Promotes community education. Sponsors Art for Life auction. Conducts charitable activities. Maintains Ohio AIDS/HIV/STD hotline. **Libraries: Type:** open to the public. **Subjects:** HIV/AIDS. **Publications:** *The CATF News*, bimonthly. Newsletter • Brochures. Alternate Formats: online. **Conventions/Meetings:** meeting.

14370 ■ Columbus Association of Black Journalists (CABJ)
PO Box 1924
Columbus, OH 43216
E-mail: krichards@dispatch.com
URL: http://cabjcolumbus.org
Contact: Kirk Richards, Pres.

Local. Advocates the rights of black journalists. Provides informational and training services and professional development to black journalists and to the general public. **Affiliated With:** National Association of Black Journalists.

14371 ■ Columbus Beagle Club
c/o John E. Blair
1008 Bricker Blvd.
Columbus, OH 43221-1644
URL: National Affiliate–clubs.akc.org
Contact: John E. Blair, Contact

Local.

14372 ■ Columbus Black Nurses Association (82)
PO Box 13518
Columbus, OH 43213
Ph: (614)836-8225
URL: National Affiliate–www.nbna.org
Contact: Pauline Bryant, Contact

Local. Represents registered nurses, licensed practical nurses, licensed vocational nurses, and student nurses. Builds consumer knowledge and understanding of health care issues. Facilitates the professional development and career advancement of nurses in emerging healthcare systems. Promotes economic development of nurses through entrepreneurial and other business initiatives. **Affiliated With:** National Black Nurses Association.

14373 ■ Columbus Blues Alliance (CBA)
1350 W 5th Ave., Ste.10-D
Columbus, OH 43212
Ph: (614)486-4575
E-mail: info@columbusblues.com
URL: http://www.colsbluesalliance.org

Founded: 1989. **Members:** 300. **Membership Dues:** basic (includes bi-monthly publication and T-shirt), $25 (annual) • publication only, $15 (annual). **Staff:** 10. **Local**. Musicians and others with an interest in the Blues. Works to preserve Blues heritage and tradition. Conducts performances, Blues jams, and seminars. **Awards:** Lifetime Achievement Awards. **Frequency:** periodic. **Type:** recognition. **Recipient:** for blues musicians. **Publications:** *Columbus Blues Alliance Magazine*, bimonthly. Reviews of current blues products, regional and national blues news. **Price:** $15.00/year. **Circulation:** 5,000. **Advertising:** accepted. **Conventions/Meetings:** monthly Business Meeting - always first Sunday, Columbus, OH • Presentation - meeting • annual Traditional Blues Festival, features acoustic Delta, Country, and Piedmont Blues by national and local musicians; concert performances and a jam plus southern foods.

14374 ■ Columbus Board of Realtors (CBR)
2700 Airport Dr.
Columbus, OH 43219
Ph: (614)475-4000
Fax: (614)475-4091
E-mail: lmetzger@columbusrealtors.org
URL: http://www.columbusrealtors.com
Contact: Larry L. Metzger, CEO

Local. Strives to develop real estate business practices. Advocates for the right to own, use and transfer real property. Provides a facility for professional development, research and exchange of information among members and the general public. **Affiliated With:** National Association of Realtors.

14375 ■ Columbus Bonsai Society
c/o Mark Passerrello
PO Box 1981
Columbus, OH 43216-1981
Ph: (614)890-1995
E-mail: mpasserr@columbus.rr.com
URL: National Affiliate–www.bonsai-bci.com
Contact: Mark Passerrello, Contact

Local. Affiliated With: Bonsai Clubs International.

14376 ■ Columbus Campaign for Arms Control
c/o Mark Stansbery
1101 Bryden Rd.
Columbus, OH 43205
Ph: (614)252-9255
E-mail: walk@igc.org
URL: http://sif.org.ohio-state.edu/
Contact: Mark D. Stansbery, Contact

Local. Work for global nuclear disarmament through education and action campaigns designed to organize community of solidarity and peace. **Affiliated With:** Peace Action.

14377 ■ Columbus Chamber
37 N High St.
Columbus, OH 43215
Ph: (614)221-1321
Fax: (614)221-1408
E-mail: ty_marsh@columbus.org
URL: http://www.columbus-chamber.org
Contact: Ty D. Marsh, Pres./CEO

Local. Fosters economic growth and business development in Greater Columbus community. **Formerly:** (2004) Greater Columbus Chamber of Commerce.

14378 ■ Columbus Chapter of the National Stuttering Association
4598 Sandy Ln.
Columbus, OH 43224
Ph: (614)447-8568
Free: (800)364-1677
E-mail: scarbrough.1@osu.edu
URL: http://www.geocities.com/nsacolumbus/
Contact: Dave Scarbrough, Chap.Ldr.

Founded: 1989. **Members:** 10. **Membership Dues:** $35 (annual). **Staff:** 2. **Local**. Support group and information clearinghouse geared towards individuals who stutter. **Affiliated With:** National Stuttering Association.

14379 ■ Columbus Chorus of Sweet Adelines International
PO Box 13081
Columbus, OH 43213
Ph: (614)470-3104
URL: http://home.columbus.rr.com/columbuschorus
Contact: Mary Ellen Guntzelman, Dir.

Local. Advances the musical art form of barbershop harmony through education and performances. Provides education, training and coaching in the development of women's four-part barbershop harmony. **Affiliated With:** Sweet Adelines International.

14380 ■ Columbus Compensation Association (CCA)
PO Box 164022
Columbus, OH 43216-4022
Ph: (614)529-8803
E-mail: info@columbuscomp.org
URL: http://www.columbuscomp.org
Contact: Mary Ellis, Pres.

Membership Dues: individual, $50-$170 (annual). **Local. Affiliated With:** WorldatWork.

14381 ■ Columbus Council on World Affairs (CCWA)
280 N High St., Ste.705
Columbus, OH 43215
Ph: (614)249-8450
Fax: (614)249-6011
E-mail: info@columbusworldaffairs.org
URL: http://www.columbuscwa.org
Contact: Tina Humphrey, Contact

Local. Seeks to increase international education in central Ohio.

14382 ■ Columbus District Golf Association (CDGA)
1570 W First Ave.
Columbus, OH 43212
Ph: (614)487-1207
Fax: (614)487-1209
E-mail: golfmaster@ohiogolf.org
URL: http://www.ohiogolf.org
Contact: Miles Cumberland, Pres.

Local. Affiliated With: International Association of Golf Administrators.

14383 ■ Columbus Downtown Development Corporation
c/o Bob McLaughlin, Admininistrator
20 E Broad St., Ste.100
Columbus, OH 43215
Ph: (614)645-5001
Fax: (614)724-0276
E-mail: aehickman@columbus.gov
URL: http://www.downtowncolumbus.com/cddc.php
Contact: Bob McLaughlin, Administrator

Local.

14384 ■ Columbus Downtown Lions Club
c/o Steve Tucker, Pres.
330 E Markison Ave.
Columbus, OH 43207
Ph: (614)221-4286 (614)445-1034
E-mail: stucker@rweiler.com
URL: http://www.iwaynet.net/~lions13f
Contact: Steve Tucker, Pres.

Local. Affiliated With: Lions Clubs International.

14385 ■ Columbus Figure Skating Club (CFSC)
Ohio State Univ. Ice Rink
390 Woody Hayes Dr.
Columbus, OH 43210-1167
E-mail: jwells@lah4law.com
URL: http://www.columbusfsc.com
Contact: Jamie Wells, Pres.

Local. Provides programs to encourage participation and achievement in the sport of figure skating on ice.

Defines and maintains uniform standards of skating proficiency. Organizes and sponsors competitions and exhibitions for the purpose of stimulating interest in figure skating. **Affiliated With:** United States Figure Skating Association.

14386 ■ Columbus High Society Tall Club
PO Box 393
Columbus, OH 43216-0393
Ph: (614)470-0785
E-mail: columbustallclub@sbcglobal.net
URL: http://clubs.tall.org/ohio/columbus
Local. Affiliated With: Tall Clubs International.

14387 ■ Columbus Hilltop Lions Club
c/o Roderick Fuller, Pres.
1929 Beverly Rd.
Columbus, OH 43220
Ph: (614)486-7821
URL: http://www.iwaynet.net/~lions13f
Contact: Roderick Fuller, Pres.
Local. Affiliated With: Lions Clubs International.

14388 ■ Columbus House Rabbit Society
c/o Karalee Curry, Chapter Mgr.
PO Box 29444
Columbus, OH 43229
Ph: (614)895-0004
E-mail: karalee@columbusrabbit.org
URL: http://columbusrabbit.org
Contact: Karalee Curry, Chapter Mgr.
Local.

14389 ■ Columbus Inner City Lions Club
c/o Annie M. Hooks, Pres.
2219 Dartmouth Ave.
Columbus, OH 43219
Ph: (614)258-1786
URL: http://www.iwaynet.net/~lions13f
Contact: Annie M. Hooks, Pres.
Local. Affiliated With: Lions Clubs International.

14390 ■ Columbus Jewish Federation (CJF)
1175 Coll. Ave.
Columbus, OH 43209
Ph: (614)237-7686
Fax: (614)237-2221
E-mail: mhurwitz@tcjf.org
URL: http://www.tcjf.org
Contact: Marsha F. Hurwitz, Pres./CEO
Founded: 1926. **Local.**

14391 ■ Columbus Jewish Historical Society (CJHS)
1175 Coll. Ave.
Columbus, OH 43209-2890
Ph: (614)238-6977
Fax: (614)237-2221
E-mail: cjhs1@tcjf.org
URL: http://www.columbusjewishhistoricalsociety.org
Contact: Skip Yassenoff, Pres.
Membership Dues: individual, $45 (annual) • family, $60 (annual) • organization, $50 (annual). **Local.** Documents, preserves, and disseminates historical and educational information on the Jewish communities of Columbus and Central Ohio. **Affiliated With:** American Jewish Historical Society.

14392 ■ Columbus Literacy Council (CLC)
195 N Grant Ave.
Columbus, OH 43215
Ph: (614)221-5013
E-mail: columbusliteracy@columbusliteracy.org
URL: http://columbusliteracy.org
Local. Provides one-to-one tutoring, small group instruction, and computer-assisted learning to adults who are either new readers or have limited English as a Second Language (ESL) proficiency. **Affiliated With:** Laubach Literacy International.

14393 ■ Columbus Medical Association (CMA)
431 E Broad St.
Columbus, OH 43215
Ph: (614)240-7410
E-mail: yourthoughts@goodhealthcolumbus.org
URL: http://www.cma-ohio.org
Contact: Philip Cass PhD, CEO
Local. Advances the art and science of medicine. Promotes patient care and the betterment of public health. **Affiliated With:** Ohio State Medical Association.

14394 ■ Columbus Mortgage Bankers Association
PO Box 30826
Columbus, OH 43230
Ph: (614)475-0032
Fax: (614)475-0032
E-mail: cmba@columbus.rr.com
URL: http://www.columbusmba.org
Contact: Bob Niemi, Pres.
Local. Promotes fair and ethical lending practices and fosters professional excellence among real estate finance employees. Seeks to create an environment that enables members to invest in communities and achieve their business objectives. **Affiliated With:** Mortgage Bankers Association.

14395 ■ Columbus Northeast Lions Club
c/o George Empson, Pres.
3938 Eisenhower Rd.
Columbus, OH 43224
Ph: (614)268-8999
E-mail: gempson@juno.com
URL: http://www.iwaynet.net/~lions13f
Contact: George Empson, Pres.
Local. Affiliated With: Lions Clubs International.

14396 ■ Columbus Northern Lions Club
c/o Lawrence Smith, Pres.
359 Chase Rd.
Columbus, OH 43214
Ph: (614)888-3707
E-mail: smuff2@hotmail.com
URL: http://www.iwaynet.net/~lions13f
Contact: Lawrence Smith, Pres.
Local. Affiliated With: Lions Clubs International.

14397 ■ Columbus Northland Lions Club
c/o Jacqueline Giles, Pres.
3975 Wynding Dr.
Columbus, OH 43214
Ph: (614)267-1818
URL: http://www.iwaynet.net/~lions13f
Contact: Jacqueline Giles, Pres.
Local. Affiliated With: Lions Clubs International.

14398 ■ Columbus Ohio Catholic Alumni Club
PO Box 695
Columbus, OH 43215
Ph: (614)575-0518
E-mail: dwdoell@yahoo.com
URL: http://www.angelfire.com/oh/CatholicAlumniClub/index.html
Local. Affiliated With: Catholic Alumni Clubs, International.

14399 ■ Columbus Outdoor Pursuits (COP)
PO Box 14384
Columbus, OH 43214-0384
Ph: (614)442-7901
E-mail: office@outdoor-pursuits.org
URL: http://www.outdoor-pursuits.org
Contact: Ann Gerckens, Office Mgr.
Founded: 1937. **Members:** 3,000. **Membership Dues:** adult, $25 (annual) • family, $35 (annual) • youth, $10 (annual) • senior, $15 (annual). **Staff:** 3. **Budget:** $500,000. **State.** Sponsor outdoor activities including bicycling, backpacking, whitewater boating, caving, climbing, cross country skiing, and hiking. Sponsors educational programs. **Additional Websites:** http://www.goba.com. **Formerly:** Columbus Outdoor Club. **Publications:** *Columbus Outdoors*, monthly. Newsletter. Contains a schedule of activities, educational programs, program registration forms, and articles. **Price:** included in membership dues. **Circulation:** 3,000. **Advertising:** accepted. **Conventions/Meetings:** monthly Program Meeting, with general information about COP plus information about activity of the month - always 3rd Tuesday of each month, Sept. through June; Avg. Attendance: 50.

14400 ■ Columbus Philatelic Club (CPC)
c/o Walton U. Beauvais, Dir.
PO Box 20582
Columbus, OH 43220-0582
E-mail: information@colopex.com
URL: http://ourworld.compuserve.com/homepages/wbeau/
Contact: Walton U. Beauvais, Dir.
Local. Affiliated With: American Philatelic Society.

14401 ■ Columbus SCORE
280 N High St., Ste.1400
Columbus, OH 43215-2542
Ph: (614)469-2357
Fax: (614)469-5848
E-mail: info@scorecolumbus.org
URL: http://www.scorecolumbus.org
Contact: Mr. Bob Stern, Chm.
Local. Assists individuals with their decisions to begin or to operate small businesses. Provides educational seminars and business counseling.

14402 ■ Columbus Softball Association (CSA)
c/o Randy Lykins, Pres.
1160 N High St.
Columbus, OH 43201-2411
Ph: (812)498-7825
E-mail: leanneeberts@yahoo.com
URL: http://www.columbussoftball.org
Contact: Randy Lykins, Pres.
Local.

14403 ■ Columbus Southern Pines Lions Club
c/o Lisa Barnes, Pres.
2705 Millview Dr.
Columbus, OH 43207
Ph: (614)491-3863
E-mail: gcorwin@columbus.rr.com
URL: http://www.iwaynet.net/~lions13f
Contact: Lisa Barnes, Pres.
Local. Affiliated With: Lions Clubs International.

14404 ■ Columbus Table Tennis Club (CTTC)
7663 New Market Center Way
Columbus, OH 43235-1979
Ph: (614)263-5207
E-mail: anne_f_43202@yahoo.com
URL: http://www.geocities.com/alrayfish
Contact: Anne F. Fish, Pres.
Founded: 1937. **Members:** 80. **Membership Dues:** adult, $205 (annual) • family, $240 (annual) • seniors, $185 (annual) • 15 and under, $150 (annual). **Staff:** 5. **Regional Groups:** 1. **State Groups:** 1. **Local Groups:** 1. **Languages:** Chinese, English, Greek, Indian Dialects, Italian, Russian, Spanish, Vietnamese. **Local.** Supports and promotes the game of table tennis. **Libraries: Type:** open to the public. **Affiliated With:** U.S.A. Table Tennis. **Conventions/Meetings:** annual Columbus Macy Block Fall Open Table Tennis Tournament - competition • annual Columbus Round Robin Tournament - competition, must have U.S.A. Table Tennis Association rating to participate • weekly Table Tennis League - competition - always Thursday.

14405 ■ Columbus Urban League
788 Mt. Vernon Ave.
Columbus, OH 43203-1408
Ph: (614)257-6300
Fax: (614)257-6327
E-mail: scephas@cul.org
URL: http://www.cul.org
Contact: Sandra Cephas, Senior VP
Founded: 1918. **Membership Dues:** individual, $40 (annual). **Staff:** 60. **Budget:** $4,000,000. **Local.**

Promotes the full participation of African-Americans and disadvantaged individuals in the social and economic fabric of the society. Sponsors programs in education, training, employment, housing, and family services. **Departments:** Career Development Services; Education and Youth Services; Family Development; Housing Services; Mature Adult Services. **Subgroups:** Columbus Urban League Circle of Friends; Columbus Urban League Guild; Columbus Urban League Young Professionals. **Affiliated With:** National Urban League. **Publications:** *Columbus Urban League Solutions*, quarterly. Newsletter. Keeps customers, supporters, employees, and friends informed of agency activities and issues that affect the community at large. Alternate Formats: online. **Conventions/Meetings:** annual meeting - late September.

14406 ■ Columbus Weightlifting Club
c/o Daniel F. Bell
4358 Indianola Ave.
Columbus, OH 43202
Ph: (614)262-4904
E-mail: info@columbusweightlifting.com
URL: http://www.columbusweightlifting.com
Contact: Daniel F. Bell, Contact
Local.

14407 ■ Columbus West Indian Association (CWIA)
c/o Henry Bacchas, Pres.
PO Box 29704
Columbus, OH 43229
Ph: (614)895-9645
E-mail: webmaster@cwiaonline.org
URL: http://www.cwiaonline.org
Contact: Henry Bacchas, Pres.
Local.

14408 ■ Common Cause - Ohio
50 W Broad St., No. 1750
Columbus, OH 43215
Ph: (614)224-2497
E-mail: commoncauseohio@aol.com
URL: http://www.commoncause.org/
Contact: Sibley Amebeck, Mgr.
Founded: 1970. **State.**

14409 ■ Community Bankers Association of Ohio (CBAO)
8800 Lyra Dr., Ste.570
Columbus, OH 43240
Ph: (614)846-8124
Fax: (614)846-4999
Free: (800)THE-CBAO
E-mail: rlpalmer@cbao.com
URL: http://www.cbao.com
Contact: Robert L. Palmer, Pres./CEO
Founded: 1974. **State.**

14410 ■ Community Financial Education
c/o Tom Kelly, Exec.Dir.
30 E Broad St., 10th Fl.
Columbus, OH 43215-3461
Ph: (614)752-2748
Free: (800)228-1102
E-mail: tom.kelly@tos.state.oh.us
URL: http://ohiowomenandmoney.org
Founded: 1999. **Local.** Funding source for free financial seminars titled "Women & Money" and presented by State Treasurer, Joseph T. Deters.

14411 ■ Community Organizing Center - For Mother Earth
Old First Presbyterian Bldg.
1101 Bryden Rd.
Columbus, OH 43205
Ph: (614)252-9255
Fax: (614)443-2651
URL: http://www.motherearth.org
Contact: Patricia Brown, Pres.
Founded: 1993. **Nonmembership.** Provides logistical support for citizen participation and safe environments for communication. Trains community organizers. Maintains speakers' bureau. **Libraries:** **Type:** reference; open to the public. **Holdings:** audiovisuals, books, business records, clippings, monographs, periodicals. **Subjects:** human and native rights, community organizing, disarmament, environmental justice. **Committees:** Middle East Peace. **Projects:** Alternatives to Militarism; Columbus-Copapayo Sister City; Economic & Environmental Justice Networking; Indigenious Peoples Obeservance; Ohio Cuba Action Group; Ohio Empowerment Coalition. **Subgroups:** Columbus Campaign for Arms Control; Ohio Cuba Action Group. **Affiliated With:** For Mother Earth. **Formerly:** (1988) Walkacross America for Mother Earth/Ohio Peace March. **Publications:** *For Mother Earth News*, semiannual. Newsletter. Links local and international actions for disarmament, human rights, and ecojustice. **Price:** donation plus shipping and handling. **Circulation:** 5,000. **Advertising:** accepted. Alternate Formats: online. **Conventions/Meetings:** biennial conference (exhibits).

14412 ■ Compassionate Friends - Central Ohio Chapter
PO Box 29132
Columbus, OH 43229-0132
Ph: (614)882-8986
E-mail: edean234@aol.com
URL: http://www.tcfcolumbusoh.org
Local.

14413 ■ Consortium for Entrepreneurship Education
c/o Dr. Cathy Ashmore, Exec.Dir.
1601 W Fifth Ave., Ste.199
Columbus, OH 43212
Ph: (614)486-6538
Fax: (419)791-8922
E-mail: cashmore@entre-ed.org
URL: http://www.entre-ed.org
Contact: Dr. Cathy Ashmore, Exec.Dir.
Founded: 1982. **Members:** 60. **Membership Dues:** corporate, $3,000 (annual) • partner, $500 (annual). **State Groups:** 20. **Regional.** Provides advocacy, leadership, networking, technical assistance, and resources nationally across all levels and disciplines of education, promoting quality practices and programs. **Awards:** Entrepreneurship Education FORUM Scholarships. **Frequency:** annual. **Type:** scholarship. **Recipient:** for outstanding educational program in entrepreneurship education. **Computer Services:** database, of programs and resources supporting entrepreneurship education. **Publications:** *EntrepreNews & Views*, quarterly. Newsletter. **Price:** free for members. **Conventions/Meetings:** annual Entrepreneurship Education FORUM - conference, sharing programs and resources (exhibits).

14414 ■ Corporation for National and Community Service - Oklahoma
c/o Paul Schrader
51 N High St., Ste.800
Columbus, OH 43215
Ph: (614)469-7441
Fax: (614)469-2125
E-mail: oh@cns.gov
URL: http://www.nationalservice.gov/about/role_impact/state_profiles_detail.asp?tbl_profiles_state=OK
Contact: Paul Schrader, Contact
State.

14415 ■ Council for Exceptional Children, Ohio
c/o Janice Kelley-Stafford
1722 Bedford Rd.
Columbus, OH 43212-2002
Ph: (614)365-6513
E-mail: janicek@columbus.rr.com
URL: http://www.cec.sped.org/ab/federati.html
Contact: Janice Kelley-Stafford, Contact
State. Additional Websites: http://www.cec-ohio.org.

14416 ■ Council of Residential Specialists, Ohio Chapter
c/o Greg Stitz, Operations Mgr.
200 E Town St.
Columbus, OH 43215-4682
Ph: (614)228-6675
Fax: (614)228-2601
E-mail: stitz@ohiorealtors.org
URL: http://www.ohiocrs.org
Contact: Ralph Renninger CRS, Pres.
State.

14417 ■ Counselors of Real Estate, Ohio/Kentucky Chapter
c/o Eric E. Belfrage, CRE, Chm.
Integra Realty Rsrcs., Hosp.ity Specialty Practice
1900 Crown Park Ct.
Columbus, OH 43235
Ph: (614)451-3211
Fax: (614)451-9599
E-mail: ebelfrage@irr.com
URL: National Affiliate–www.cre.org
Contact: Eric E. Belfrage CRE, Chm.
Regional. Affiliated With: Counselors of Real Estate.

14418 ■ County Commissioners' Association of Ohio (CCAO)
c/o Larry L. Long, Exec.Dir.
37 W Broad St., Ste.650
Columbus, OH 43215-4195
Ph: (614)221-5627
Fax: (614)221-6986
Free: (888)757-1904
E-mail: info@ccao.org
URL: http://www.ccao.org
Contact: Larry L. Long, Exec.Dir.
Founded: 1880. **State.** County commissioners in Ohio. Unites county commissioners of Ohio to promote practices and policies in the county government for the benefit of Ohio citizens.

14419 ■ County Engineers Association of Ohio (CEAO)
c/o Glenn W. Sprowls, Exec.Dir.
6500 Busch Blvd., Ste.100
Columbus, OH 43229
Ph: (614)221-0707
Fax: (614)221-5761
E-mail: gsprowls@ceao.org
URL: http://www.ceao.org
Contact: Glenn W. Sprowls, Exec.Dir.
State. Affiliated With: National Association of County Engineers.

14420 ■ County Treasurers Association of Ohio
51 N High St., Ste.888
Columbus, OH 43215
Ph: (614)233-6818
Fax: (614)221-1946
E-mail: ctao@iwaynet.net
State. Elected county treasurers from the 88 counties. Collects all county revenues, including taxes from real estate, manufactured homes and personal property. Invests all county money in order to bring the best returns. Monitors and responds to all introduced legislation affecting treasurers.

14421 ■ Crohn's and Colitis Foundation of America, Central Ohio Chapter
2021 E Dublin Granville Rd., Ste.125
Columbus, OH 43229
Ph: (614)781-9970
Fax: (614)781-9972
Free: (800)625-5977
E-mail: centralohio@ccfa.org
URL: National Affiliate–www.ccfa.org
Contact: Kim Houf, Development Mgr.
Founded: 1996. **Members:** 580. **Staff:** 3. **Local.** Promotes chapter awareness and corporate sponsorship; activities include bowlathon, tribute dinner, golf tournament, walkathon, education programs, and support groups. **Affiliated With:** Community Health Charities. **Publications:** *Chapter Newsletter*, periodic

• Brochures, periodic. Covers diseases and the commonly asked questions. • Books. Contains various topics covering the diseases.

14422 ■ Democratic Socialists of America, Columbus
c/o Simone Morgen
PO Box 82588
Columbus, OH 43202-9998
E-mail: smorgen@juno.com
URL: http://dsco1.tripod.com
Contact: Ms. Simone Morgan, Co-Chm.
Founded: 1990. **Members:** 35. **Membership Dues:** low-income, $20 (annual) • regular, $45 (annual). **Budget:** $5,000. **Local Groups:** 1. **Local.** Seeks to educate the public about Socialist ideals and viewpoints concerning economic, social and political equality. **Awards:** Debs-Thomas-Harrington. **Frequency:** annual. **Type:** recognition. **Recipient:** for service and activism in labor, faith and community work. **Computer Services:** Information services, web site with news and upcoming events and books, links, issues of interest to members and the community. **Additional Websites:** http://dsco.org. **Affiliated With:** Democratic Socialists of America. **Also Known As:** (2004) Democratic Socialists of Central Ohio (DSCO).

14423 ■ Dignity - USA, Columbus Chapter
PO Box 82001
Columbus, OH 43202
Ph: (614)447-6546
E-mail: dignity@columbus.rr.com
URL: http://www.dignitygc.org
Local.

14424 ■ Dublin Coffman/Jerome - Young Life
1515 Lane Ave., Ste.LL
Columbus, OH 43221
Ph: (614)485-5433
URL: http://sites.younglife.org/_layouts/ylext/default.aspx?ID=C-1513
Local. Affiliated With: Young Life.

14425 ■ Dublin Scioto - Young Life
1515 Lane Ave., Ste.LL
Columbus, OH 43221
Ph: (614)485-5433
URL: http://sites.younglife.org/_layouts/ylext/default.aspx?ID=C-1514
Local. Affiliated With: Young Life.

14426 ■ Earth Share of Ohio
3528 N High St., Ste.E
Columbus, OH 43214-4090
Ph: (614)263-6367
Fax: (614)263-6327
Free: (877)434-2357
E-mail: info@earthshareofohio.org
URL: http://www.earthshareofohio.org
Contact: Paul Bingle, Exec.Dir.
State. Affiliated With: Earth Share.

14427 ■ Easter Seals Central and Southeast Ohio
PO Box 7166
Columbus, OH 43205-0166
Ph: (614)228-5523
Fax: (614)443-1848
Free: (800)860-5523
E-mail: kzuckerm@eaterseals-cseohio.org
URL: http://www.centralohio.easterseals.com
Contact: Ms. Karin Zuckerman, CEO
Local. Provides services for children and adults with disabilities or special needs, and supports their families. **Affiliated With:** Easter Seals.

14428 ■ Electrical Industry of Central Ohio Labor Management Cooperation
c/o Brian Damant
PO Box 163128
Columbus, OH 43216
Ph: (614)224-4408
Fax: (614)224-1847
E-mail: coh.neca@electricaltrades.org
Contact: Brian Damant, Chapter Mgr.
Local.

14429 ■ English Country Dancers of Columbus
c/o Sue Wartell
410 Clinton Heights
Columbus, OH 43202-1277
Ph: (614)263-9501
E-mail: swartell@cas.org
URL: http://www.bigscioty.com/english.html
Contact: Sue Wartell, Contact
Founded: 1975. **Membership Dues:** individual (per dance session), $5 (biweekly) • individual, $80 (annual). **Local Groups:** 1. **Local.** Works to enjoy and promote English Country Dancing as a social activity. Hosts dances 2-3 times per month with live music, for anyone wishing to join. **Libraries: Type:** reference; not open to the public. **Holdings:** 20; audio recordings, books. **Subjects:** english country dancing, english country dancers of Columbus. **Affiliated With:** Country Dance and Song Society.

14430 ■ Epilepsy Foundation of Central Ohio (EFCO)
510 E N Broadway, Ste.400
Columbus, OH 43214
Ph: (614)261-1100
Fax: (614)261-1248
Free: (800)878-3226
E-mail: epilepsyohio@epilepsy-ohio.org
URL: http://www.epilepsy-ohio.org
Contact: Nancy Brantner, Exec.Dir.
Founded: 1957. **Local.** Provides information, support, and education on epilepsy to children and adults in Ohio. **Affiliated With:** Epilepsy Foundation. **Publications:** Newsletter. Alternate Formats: online.

14431 ■ Experience Columbus
90 N High St.
Columbus, OH 43215-9457
Ph: (614)221-6623
Fax: (614)221-5618
Free: (800)354-2657
E-mail: visitorinfo@experiencecolumbus.com
URL: http://www.experiencecolumbus.com
Contact: Paul D. Astleford, Pres./CEO
Local.

14432 ■ Federal Bar Association, Columbus Chapter
c/o Mr. Mark Landes, Esq., Pres.
250 E Broad St., Ste.900
Columbus, OH 43215
Ph: (614)221-2121
Fax: (614)365-9516
E-mail: marklandes@isaacbrant.com
URL: National Affiliate–www.fedbar.org
Contact: Mr. Mark Landes Esq., Pres.
Founded: 1920. **Regional. Affiliated With:** Federal Bar Association.

14433 ■ Federalist Society for Law and Public Policy Studies - Columbus Chapter
c/o Mr. Chad A. Readler, Pres.
Jones, Day, Reavis & Pogue
1900 Huntington Ctr.
Columbus, OH 43215
Ph: (614)469-3891 (614)469-3939
Fax: (614)461-4198
E-mail: careadler@jonesday.com
URL: National Affiliate–www.fed-soc.org
Contact: Mr. Chad A. Readler, Pres.
Local. Seeks to bring about a reordering of priorities within the U.S. legal system that will emphasize individual liberty, traditional values, and the rule of law. **Affiliated With:** Federalist Society for Law and Public Policy Studies.

14434 ■ Fostoria Coin Club
c/o Gary Moran
PO Box 28707
Columbus, OH 43228
Ph: (614)272-6440
E-mail: big4ce1@aol.com
URL: http://www.fostoriacoinclub.org
Contact: Gary Moran, Contact
Local. Affiliated With: American Numismatic Association.

14435 ■ Franklin County Genealogical and Historical Society (FCGHS)
PO Box 44309
Columbus, OH 43204-0309
Ph: (614)469-1300
E-mail: fcghs@yahoo.com
URL: http://www.rootsweb.com/~ohfcghs
Founded: 1970. **Members:** 550. **Membership Dues:** primary, $15 (annual) • patron, $50 (annual) • corporate, $1,000 (annual) • life, $300 • life, joint, $500. **Staff:** 1. **Local.** Genealogical researchers and historians. Collects, preserves, and promotes genealogical and historical materials. Conducts seminars and lectures. Sponsors essay contests. **Libraries: Type:** reference. **Awards:** Pioneer Families of Franklin Co. **Frequency:** annual. **Type:** recognition. **Recipient:** for ancestors in Franklin County, Ohio by 1830. **Special Interest Groups:** African-American Genealogy; Computer. **Affiliated With:** Ohio Genealogical Society; Ohio Genealogical Society. **Publications:** *Franklintonian*, bimonthly. Newsletter. Contains information on surname file and material research ideas. **Price:** included in membership dues. ISSN: 1059-4051. **Conventions/Meetings:** annual meeting - always November.

14436 ■ Franklinton Board of Trade
456 W Broad St.
Columbus, OH 43215-2756
Ph: (614)224-7550
Local.

14437 ■ Fraternal Order of Police of Ohio, State Lodge
c/o Denise Young, Office Administrator
222 E Town St.
Columbus, OH 43215-4611
Ph: (614)224-5700
Fax: (614)224-5775
E-mail: dyoung@fopohio.org
URL: http://www.fopohio.org
Contact: Denise Young, Office Administrator
State. Affiliated With: Fraternal Order of Police, Grand Lodge.

14438 ■ Friends of the Conservatory
c/o Paul Redman
1778 E Broad St.
Columbus, OH 43203-2040
Ph: (614)645-1800
Local.

14439 ■ Friends of the Lower Olentangy Watershed (FLOW)
3528 N High St., Ste.F
Columbus, OH 43214
Ph: (614)267-3386
Fax: (614)262-8922
E-mail: emily-dick@franklinswcd.org
URL: http://www.olentangywatershed.org
Contact: Emily Dick, Chair
Founded: 1997. **Members:** 160. **Membership Dues:** individual, $25 (annual) • family, $40 (annual) • supporting, $50 (annual) • business, $175 (annual) • bronze, $200 (annual) • silver, $300 (annual) • gold, $500 (annual) • sustaining, $1,000 (annual). **Staff:** 1. **Budget:** $10,000. **Local.** Increases public awareness of the extensive environmental, recreational, cultural and historical resources of the Lower Olentangy River Watershed. Promotes responsible uses and policies of the river. **Formerly:** (2005) Friends of the Lower Olentangy Watershed Flow.

14440 ■ Funeral Consumers Alliance of Central Ohio (FCACO)
PO Box 14835
Columbus, OH 43214-0835
Ph: (614)263-4632
E-mail: info@funeralsohio.org
URL: http://www.funeralsohio.org
Founded: 1953. **Members:** 2,000. **Membership Dues:** life, $40. **Local.** Promotes low cost cremations and funerals with dignity and simplicity. **Affiliated With:** Funeral Consumers Alliance. **Conventions/Meetings:** annual meeting - always May.

14441 ■ Gahanna - Young Life
1515 W Lane Ave.
Columbus, OH 43221
Ph: (614)485-5433
URL: http://sites.younglife.org/_layouts/ylext/default.aspx?ID=C-1592
Local. Affiliated With: Young Life.

14442 ■ Girl Scouts - Seal of Ohio Council
1700 WaterMark Dr.
Columbus, OH 43215-1097
Ph: (614)487-8101
Fax: (614)487-8189
Free: (800)621-7042
E-mail: mlane@sealofohio.org
URL: http://www.gsheart.org
Local. Young girls and adult volunteers, corporate, government and individual supporters. Strives to develop potential and leadership skills among its members. Conducts trainings, educational programs and outdoor activities.

14443 ■ Goodwill Columbus
1331 Edgehill Rd.
Columbus, OH 43212
Ph: (614)294-5181
Fax: (614)294-6895
E-mail: anne.ransone@gwcols.com
URL: http://www.goodwillcolumbus.org
Local.

14444 ■ Grandview High School - Young Life
1515 Lane Ave., Ste.LL
Columbus, OH 43221
Ph: (614)485-5433
URL: http://sites.younglife.org/_layouts/ylext/default.aspx?ID=C-2789
Local. Affiliated With: Young Life.

14445 ■ Great Lakes Association of Orthodontists (GLAO)
17 S High St., Ste.200
Columbus, OH 43215
Fax: (614)221-1989
Free: (877)274-6420
E-mail: glao@assnoffices.com
URL: http://www.glao.org
Contact: Debbie Nunner, Exec.Dir.
Founded: 1926. **Members:** 1,250. **Staff:** 1. **Budget:** $100,000. **State Groups:** 5. **Regional.** Orthodontists and others seeking to advance the field of orthodontics and promote high standards of ethical and professional conduct. **Affiliated With:** American Association of Orthodontists. **Formerly:** (1989) Great Lakes Society of Orthodontists. **Publications:** *GLAO News*, semiannual. Newsletter. **Conventions/Meetings:** annual convention.

14446 ■ Greater Columbus Area Chamber of Commerce
37 N High St.
Columbus, OH 43215
Ph: (614)221-1321
Fax: (614)221-1408
E-mail: ty_marsh@columbus.org
URL: http://www.columbus.org
Contact: Mr. Ty D. Marsh, Pres./CEO
Founded: 1884. **Members:** 3,000. **Local.** Promotes business and community development in Columbus, OH area. **Formerly:** (2004) Columbus Chamber.

14447 ■ Greater Columbus Habitat for Humanity (GCHFH)
3140 Westerville Rd.
Columbus, OH 43224
Ph: (614)414-0427
Fax: (614)414-0432
E-mail: ejthomas@habitat-columbus.org
URL: http://www.habitat-columbus.org
Contact: E.J. Thomas, Exec.Dir.
Local. Affiliated With: Habitat for Humanity International.

14448 ■ Green Energy Ohio (GEO)
7870 Olentangy River Rd., Ste.209
Columbus, OH 43235
Ph: (614)985-6131
Fax: (614)888-9716
Free: (866)473-3664
E-mail: geo@greenenergyohio.org
URL: http://www.greenenergyohio.org
Contact: William A. Spratley, Exec.Dir.
Founded: 2000. **Members:** 220. **Membership Dues:** benefactor/corporate benefactor, $300 (annual) • patron/corporate patron, $150 (annual) • contributing, $60 (annual) • regular, $35 (annual) • limited income, $20 (annual) • basic, $34 (annual). **Budget:** $125,000. **State.** Dedicated to promote environmentally and economically sustainable energy policies and practices in OH. Conducts wind monitoring and development. Present educational workshops on solar power. Acts as a state clearinghouse with educational materials on renewable energy. Works toward statewide aggregation of green power for OH electric customers. **Formerly:** (2001) Ohio Solar Energy Society. **Publications:** Newsletter, quarterly. **Conventions/Meetings:** bimonthly board meeting • monthly GEO Wind and Solar Committee Meeting.

14449 ■ Grove City, OH - Young Life
1515 W Lane Ave.
Columbus, OH 43221
Ph: (614)485-5433
URL: http://sites.younglife.org/_layouts/ylext/default.aspx?ID=C-1498
Local. Affiliated With: Young Life.

14450 ■ Healthcare Financial Management Association, Central Ohio Chapter
c/o Jackie Nussbaum
Ernst & Young, LLP
41 S High St.
1100 Huntington Ctr.
Columbus, OH 43251
Ph: (614)463-7346
E-mail: centralohio@centralohiohfma.org
URL: http://www.centralohiohfma.org
Contact: George M. Gevas, Pres.-Elect
Local. Provides education, analysis and guidance to healthcare finance professionals. Helps members and other individuals in advancing the financial management of health care and in improving the business performance of organizations serving the healthcare field. **Affiliated With:** Healthcare Financial Management Association.

14451 ■ Hearing Loss Association of America, Ohio
c/o Hermine Willey, Coor.
689 Olde Orchard Ct.
Columbus, OH 43213-3409
Ph: (614)861-7956
E-mail: cohear@aol.com
URL: National Affiliate–www.hearingloss.org
Contact: Hermine Willey, Coor.
State. Promotes understanding of the nature, causes, complications and remedies of hearing loss. Raises public awareness of the special needs of people who are hard of hearing through information, education, advocacy and support. **Affiliated With:** Hearing Loss Association of America.

14452 ■ Heart of Ohio Hikers 522
c/o Max Rhoades
599 Lummisford Ln. N
Columbus, OH 43214
Ph: (614)451-2905 (614)447-3600
Fax: (614)447-5471
E-mail: mrhoade1@columbus.rr.com
URL: National Affiliate–www.ava.org
Contact: Max Rhoades, Pres.
Founded: 1988. **Members:** 20. **Membership Dues:** $7 (annual). **State Groups:** 1. **Local Groups:** 3. **Local.** Seeks to organize fun activities such as trails and walking routes. **Awards: Type:** medal. **Recipient:** for walk completion. **Affiliated With:** American Volkssport Association. **Publications:** *The American Wanderer*, bimonthly. Newspaper. **Price:** $15.00/year. **Advertising:** accepted. Alternate Formats: online • *International Events*. Newspaper • *OVA for Ohio Events*. Journal. **Conventions/Meetings:** biennial workshop (exhibits).

14453 ■ Heritage Ohio
846 1/2 E Main St.
Columbus, OH 43205
Ph: (614)258-6200
Fax: (614)258-6400
E-mail: info@heritageohio.org
URL: http://www.heritageohio.org
Contact: Curtis Burris, Office Mgr.
Founded: 1989. **Members:** 312. **Membership Dues:** student, $20 (annual) • household, $35 (annual) • Transom Society, $125 (annual) • Palladium Society, $250 (annual) • Prism Society, $500 (annual) • Keystone Society, $1,000 (annual) • Finial Society, $5,000 (annual) • organization, $75-$300 (annual) • business, $150-$300 (annual) • local government, $150-$750 (annual). **Staff:** 2. **State.** Statewide organization that encourages development, redevelopment, and improvement of downtowns throughout OH. **Formerly:** (2000) Downtown Ohio Development Foundation; (2003) Downtown Ohio. **Publications:** *Resource Guide*, annual. Serves as a guide for businesses in the industry. • *StreetScapes*, quarterly. Newsletter. **Conventions/Meetings:** annual conference • semiannual workshop - always spring and fall.

14454 ■ HI-USA, Central and Southern Ohio Council
c/o HI-Columbus
PO Box 41
Columbus, OH 43216-0041
Ph: (614)470-4276
E-mail: ayh@netwalk.com
URL: http://www.netwalk.com/~ayh/index.htm
Contact: Allan South, Pres.
Local. Affiliated With: Hostelling International-American Youth Hostels.

14455 ■ Hilliard Darby - Young Life
1515 Lane Ave., Ste.LL
Columbus, OH 43221
Ph: (614)485-5433
URL: http://sites.younglife.org/_layouts/ylext/default.aspx?ID=C-1515
Local. Affiliated With: Young Life.

14456 ■ Hilliard Davidson - Young Life
1515 Lane Ave., Ste.LL
Columbus, OH 43221
Ph: (614)485-5433
URL: http://sites.younglife.org/_layouts/ylext/default.aspx?ID=C-1516
Local. Affiliated With: Young Life.

14457 ■ Hilliard Lions Club
c/o Thomas Barton, Sec.
3539 Rochfort Bridge Dr.
Columbus, OH 43221
Ph: (614)777-0668
E-mail: tabarton@earthlink.net
URL: http://www.iwaynet.net/~lions13f
Contact: Thomas Barton, Sec.
Local. Affiliated With: Lions Clubs International.

14458 ■ Holocaust Education Council
c/o Brad Hoffman
1175 Coll. Ave.
Columbus, OH 43209
E-mail: mking@tcjf.org
URL: http://www.holocausteducationcouncil.com
Local.

14459 ■ The Home Network Center (THNC)
c/o John K. Farnlacher
1708 Huy Rd.
Columbus, OH 43224
Ph: (614)262-6574 (614)288-1524
Fax: (614)262-6647
E-mail: jack@thnc.org
URL: http://www.thnc.org/
Contact: Mr. Jack Farnlacher, Exec.Dir.
Founded: 2000. **Members:** 1. **Membership Dues:** student, $25 (annual) • individual, $35 (annual) • family, $60 (annual) • life, $1,500 • professional, $250 (annual) • organizational, $1,250 (annual) • supporting, $2,500 (annual). **Staff:** 1. **Regional. Libraries: Type:** not open to the public. **Holdings:** 350; articles, books, periodicals. **Subjects:** home construction, networking, general topics.

14460 ■ Humanist Community of Central Ohio (HCCO)
PO Box 141373
Columbus, OH 43214-6373
Ph: (614)470-0811
E-mail: prez@hcco.org
URL: http://www.hcco.org
Contact: Amy Birtcher, Pres.
Regional. Affiliated With: American Humanist Association.

14461 ■ Humanist Society of Columbus
c/o Lawrence Earl Wurdlow
2233 Summit St.
Columbus, OH 43201-1392
Ph: (614)263-1193
E-mail: earlword@msn.com
URL: National Affiliate–www.americanhumanist.org
Contact: Lawrence Earl Wurdlow, Contact
Local. Affiliated With: American Humanist Association.

14462 ■ Huntington's Disease Society of America, Central Ohio Chapter
c/o Sarah Morrison, Pres.
490 City Park Ave., Ste.C
Columbus, OH 43215
Ph: (614)460-8800
Fax: (614)460-8801
Free: (866)877-4372
E-mail: centralohiohdsa@yahoo.com
URL: http://www.hdsacentralohio.org
Contact: Sarah Morrison, Pres.
Membership Dues: special, $50 (annual) • family, $25 (annual) • individual, $15 (annual). **Local.** Individuals and groups of volunteers concerned with Huntington's disease, an inherited and terminal neurological condition causing progressive brain and nerve deterioration. Goals are to: identify HD families; educate the public and professionals, with emphasis on increasing consumer awareness of HD; promote and support basic and clinical research into the causes and cure of HD; to assist families in meeting the social, economic, and emotional problems resulting from HD. Aims to change the attitude of the working community toward the HD patient, enhance the HD patient's lifestyle, and promote better health care and treatment, both in the community and in facilities. **Awards:** Hope Leadership Award. **Frequency:** annual. **Type:** recognition. **Recipient:** for significant contributions to Columbus and surrounding areas. **Computer Services:** Information services, fact sheet. **Programs:** In-service Training. **Affiliated With:** Huntington's Disease Society of America. **Publications:** *Our Voice*, semiannual. Newsletter. Alternate Formats: online. **Conventions/Meetings:** monthly support group meeting, bringing up of concerns, sharing of experiences, asking questions, with speaker at times - every 2nd Thursday.

14463 ■ IABC/Columbus
PO Box 12528
Columbus, OH 43212
Ph: (614)445-2877
E-mail: iabc_columbus@hotmail.com
URL: http://columbus.iabc.com
Contact: Beth Varcho, Pres.
Local. Public relations and communication professionals. Committed to improve the effectiveness of organizations through strategic, interactive and integrated business communication management. Provides products, services, and networking activities to help people and organizations excel in public relations, employee communication, marketing communication, public affairs and other forms of communication.

14464 ■ IEEE Computer Society, Columbus Chapter
c/o Joanne E Degroat
205 Dreese Laboratory
2015 Neil Ave.
Columbus, OH 43210-1272
Ph: (614)292-2439
Fax: (614)292-7596
E-mail: degroat@ee.eng.ohio-state.edu
URL: National Affiliate–www.computer.org
Local. Affiliated With: IEEE Computer Society.

14465 ■ IEEE Computer Society, Ohio State University
c/o Ming T. Liu
Dept. of Comp. and Info Sci.
2036 Neil Ave.
Columbus, OH 43210
Ph: (614)292-6552
E-mail: mayhew@cis.ohio-state.edu
URL: http://www.cse.ohio-state.edu/ieee
Contact: Michael Mayhew, Pres.
Local. Affiliated With: IEEE Computer Society.

14466 ■ Independent Electrical Contractors, Central Ohio
c/o Barbara Tipton
3128-H E 17th Ave.
Columbus, OH 43219
Ph: (614)473-1050
Fax: (614)473-1359
E-mail: batipton@aol.com
URL: National Affiliate–www.ieci.org
Contact: Barbara Tipton, Contact
Local. Affiliated With: Independent Electrical Contractors.

14467 ■ Independent Insurance Agents Association of Ohio
c/o Thomas H. Hardy, Exec.VP
1330 Dublin Rd.
Columbus, OH 43215
Ph: (614)464-3100
Fax: (614)486-9797
Free: (800)282-4424

14468 ■ Industrial Energy Users-Ohio (IEU-OHIO)
21 E State St., 17th Fl.
Columbus, OH 43215
Ph: (614)469-8000
Fax: (614)469-4653
E-mail: srandazzo@mwncmh.com
URL: http://www.ieu-ohio.org
Contact: Michael W. Brakey, Chm.
Founded: 1990. **Members:** 38. **State.** Promotes customer-driven outcomes on matters affecting the price and availability of energy on OH and the Midwest region. Members consume about $3,000,000 per year in electricity and natural gas to operate their OH plants.

14469 ■ Information Systems Audit and Control Association, Central Ohio Chapter
PO Box 151152
Columbus, OH 43215
Ph: (614)249-8075
E-mail: mckitrj@nationwide.com
URL: http://www.isaca-centralohio.org
Contact: Jason McKitrick CISA, Pres.
Local. Affiliated With: Information Systems Audit and Control Association and Foundation.

14470 ■ International Alliance of Theatrical Stage Employees, Moving Picture Technicians, Artists, S 12
555 E Rich St., Ste.217
Columbus, OH 43215
Ph: (614)221-3753
Fax: (614)221-0078
E-mail: office@iatse12.org
URL: National Affiliate–www.iatse.lm.com
Members: 155. **Local. Affiliated With:** International Alliance of Theatrical Stage Employees, Moving Picture Technicians, Artists and Allied Crafts of the United States, Its Territories and Canada.

14471 ■ International Association of Business Communicators, Columbus Chapter
PO Box 12528
Columbus, OH 43212
E-mail: iabc_columbus@hotmail.com
URL: http://columbus.iabc.com
Local. Represents the interests of communication managers, public relations directors, writers, editors and audiovisual specialists. Encourages establishment of college-level programs in organizational communication. Conducts surveys on employee communication effectiveness and media trends. Conducts research in the field of communication. **Affiliated With:** International Association of Business Communicators.

14472 ■ International Association of Gay/Lesbian Country Western Dance Clubs, Columbus Stompers
PO Box 163131
Columbus, OH 43216-3131
Ph: (614)445-0885
E-mail: jchak@aol.com
URL: http://stompers.org
Contact: Dan Poeppelman, Pres.
Founded: 1990. **Members:** 75. **Membership Dues:** all, $30 (annual). **Local. Computer Services:** Mailing lists, of members. **Committees:** Dance; Executive. **Affiliated With:** International Association of Gay/Lesbian Country Western Dance Clubs.

14473 ■ International Association of Heat and Frost Insulators and Asbestos Workers, Local 44
947 Goodale Blvd., Ste.244
Columbus, OH 43212
Ph: (614)221-7177
Fax: (614)221-8669
URL: http://www.insulators.org
Local.

14474 ■ International Facility Management Association, Central Ohio Chapter (IFMA)
c/o Dorothy Leachman, Pres.
PO Box 340647
Columbus, OH 43234-0647
Ph: (614)688-3993
Fax: (614)688-3248
E-mail: leachman.8@osu.edu
URL: http://www.ifmacentralohio.org
Contact: Dorothy Leachman, Pres.
Membership Dues: professional, associate, retired, $92 (annual) • student, $10 (annual). **State.** Facility managers representing all types of organizations including banks, insurance companies, hospitals, colleges and universities, utility companies, electronic equipment manufacturers, petroleum companies, museums, auditoriums, and federal, state, provincial, and local governments. Works to enhance the professional goals of persons involved or interested in the

field of facility management (the planning, designing, and managing of workplaces). **Affiliated With:** International Facility Management Association.

14475 ■ International Federation of Professional and Technical Engineers Local 7
PO Box 13125
Columbus, OH 43213-0125
Ph: (614)692-3399
Fax: (614)692-3562
E-mail: danny_tipton@dla.mil
URL: National Affiliate–www.ifpte.org
Contact: Danny Tipton, Pres.

Founded: 1968. **Membership Dues:** union, $10 (biweekly). **Local**. Represents engineers, scientists, architects, and technicians. **Affiliated With:** International Federation of Professional and Technical Engineers. **Publications:** *Outlook Newsletter*, quarterly. **Conventions/Meetings:** triennial convention.

14476 ■ International Visitors Council - Columbus
57 Jefferson Ave.
Columbus, OH 43215
Ph: (614)225-9057
Fax: (614)225-0656
E-mail: info@columbusivc.org
URL: http://www.columbusivc.org
Contact: Kevin R. Webb, Exec.Dir.

Founded: 1965. **Members:** 300. **Membership Dues:** individual, $25 (annual) • family, $50 (annual). **Staff:** 4. **Budget:** $500,000. **Local Groups:** 1. **Languages:** English, French, German, Russian, Spanish. **For-Profit**. **Local**. Arranges cultural exchanges between distinguished international visitors and their counterparts in Central Ohio. **Awards:** Citizen Diplomat Award. **Frequency:** annual. **Type:** recognition. **Recipient:** for outstanding community volunteerism in international activities. **Affiliated With:** Greater Columbus Chamber of Commerce; National Council for International Visitors. **Publications:** *IVC Interpreter*, quarterly. Newsletter. **Price:** included in membership dues. **Circulation:** 300. **Conventions/Meetings:** periodic Global Connection Forum - meeting - always in Columbus, OH.

14477 ■ Inventors Network
c/o Bob Stonecypher
1383 Fahlander Dr. S
Columbus, OH 43229
Ph: (614)888-0805
Fax: (614)840-9126
E-mail: 13832667@msn.com

Affiliated With: United Inventors Association of the U.S.A.

14478 ■ Iranian Cultural Association of Greater Columbus
c/o Mina Mokhtari
PO Box 3434
Columbus, OH 43210
Ph: (614)457-2049
E-mail: amahdi@columbus.rr.com
URL: http://www.pazhvak.org
Contact: Ms. Naraghi, Contact

Local. Provides educational and cultural services to the Iranian community in Central Ohio. **Formerly:** (2005) Iranian +Cultural Association.

14479 ■ Jobs for Ohio's Graduates
c/o Lee Blanton, COO
21 E State St., Ste.900
Columbus, OH 43215
Ph: (614)224-7955
Fax: (614)224-7966
E-mail: lee.blanton.jog@sbcglobal.net
URL: http://ohio.jag.org
Contact: Lee Blanton, COO

State. **Affiliated With:** Jobs for America's Graduates.

14480 ■ John Mercer Langston Bar Association (JMLBA)
c/o James Barnes, Pres.
PO Box 1551
Columbus, OH 43216
Ph: (614)728-8537
E-mail: info@jmlba.org
URL: http://www.jmlba.org
Contact: James Barnes, Pres.

Membership Dues: first admitted to the practice of law more than 3 years, $100 (annual) • first admitted to the practice of law from 1 to 3 years, $50 (annual). **Local**. **Affiliated With:** National Bar Association.

14481 ■ Jonathan Alder - Young Life
1515 Lane Ave., Ste.LL
Columbus, OH 43221
Ph: (614)485-5433
URL: http://sites.younglife.org/_layouts/ylext/default.aspx?ID=C-1517

Local. **Affiliated With:** Young Life.

14482 ■ Juvenile Diabetes Research Foundation International, Mid-Ohio Chapter
c/o Amy J. Morgan, Exec.Dir.
134 A-2 Northwoods Blvd.
Columbus, OH 43235
Ph: (614)464-CURE
Fax: (614)464-2877
E-mail: midohio@jdrf.org
URL: http://www.jdrf.org/midohio
Contact: Mary Prusak, Spec. Events Coord.

Local. Nonprofit, nongovernmental funder of diabetes research. Mission is to find a cure for diabetes and its complications through the support of research. **Affiliated With:** Juvenile Diabetes Research Foundation International.

14483 ■ Kaleidoscope Youth Coalition (KYC)
c/o Kaleidoscope Youth Center
PO Box 8104
Columbus, OH 43201
Ph: (614)294-7886
E-mail: info@kaleidoscope.org
URL: http://www.kaleidoscope.org
Contact: Angie Wellman, Exec.Dir.

Founded: 1994. **Members:** 200. **Staff:** 1. **Budget:** $20,000. **Local**. Represents gay, lesbian, bisexual, transgendered, and questioning youth. **Libraries: Type:** not open to the public. **Holdings:** 500; books, periodicals. **Subjects:** gay, lesbian, bisexual, transgender, health, social competency.

14484 ■ Karrer MS - Wyldlife
1515 Lane Ave., Ste.LL
Columbus, OH 43221
Ph: (614)485-5433
URL: http://sites.younglife.org/_layouts/ylext/default.aspx?ID=C-1519

Local. **Affiliated With:** Young Life.

14485 ■ Khmers Kampuchea-Krom Federation (KKF)
PO Box 28674
Columbus, OH 43228
Ph: (614)272-8452
Fax: (614)272-8452
E-mail: info@khmerkrom.org
URL: http://www.khmerkrom.org

Local.

14486 ■ Kilbourne - Young Life
1515 W Lane Ave.
Columbus, OH 43221
Ph: (614)485-5433
URL: http://sites.younglife.org/_layouts/ylext/default.aspx?ID=C-1483

Local. **Affiliated With:** Young Life.

14487 ■ Knights of Columbus, Columbus
212 E Broad St.
Columbus, OH 43215
Ph: (614)873-4533
URL: http://www.kofccolumbus.org
Contact: Deacon Bonacci, Chaplain

Local. **Affiliated With:** Knights of Columbus.

14488 ■ Korean War Veterans Association, Central Ohio Chapter
c/o James L. Kay
PO Box 236134
Columbus, OH 43222
Ph: (614)279-2428
E-mail: kwvadoh@msn.com
URL: National Affiliate–www.kwva.org
Contact: James L. Kay, Contact

Local. **Affiliated With:** Korean War Veterans Association.

14489 ■ Korean War Veterans Association, Department of Ohio
c/o Michael Mahoney
35 E Chestnut St., 4th Fl.
Columbus, OH 43215
Ph: (614)225-0540
E-mail: kwvadoh@msn.com
URL: National Affiliate–www.kwva.org
Contact: Michael Mahoney, Contact

State. **Affiliated With:** Korean War Veterans Association.

14490 ■ Labor and Employment Relations Association, Central Ohio
c/o Darrell Hughes, Sec.-Treas.
400 S 5th St., Ste.200
Columbus, OH 43215
Ph: (614)221-1216
Fax: (614)221-8769
E-mail: dhughes@dhflaw.com
URL: http://www.lera.uiuc.edu/chapters/Profiles/OH-Central.html
Contact: Greg Scott, Pres.

Local.

14491 ■ League of Women Voters of Ohio (LWVO)
17 S High St., Ste.650
Columbus, OH 43215-3413
Ph: (614)469-1505
Fax: (614)469-7918
Free: (877)598-6446
E-mail: jbarbee@lwvohio.org
URL: http://www.lwvohio.org
Contact: Jerolyn Barbee, Exec.Dir.

Founded: 1920. **Staff:** 3. **Budget:** $100,000. **Local Groups:** 37. **State**. Promotes informed and active participation of citizens in government and to act on selected governmental issues. Maintains League of Women Voters Education Fund. **Affiliated With:** League of Women Voters of the United States. **Publications:** *Know Your Ohio Government (Ninth Edition) 2004*. Book. Serves as a guide for citizens who wants to learn how to influence government policies. **Price:** $23.00 • *OhioVOTER*, quarterly. Newsletter. Alternate Formats: online. **Conventions/Meetings:** biennial meeting.

14492 ■ Libertarian Party of Ohio (LPO)
700 Morse Rd., Ste.208
Columbus, OH 43214-1879
Ph: (614)547-0290
Fax: (877)496-9010
Free: (800)669-6542
E-mail: hq@lpo.org
URL: http://www.lpo.org
Contact: Robert Butler, Exec.Dir.

State. Promotes smaller, more effective government and civil liberty. **Affiliated With:** Libertarian National Committee.

14493 ■ LifeCare Alliance
c/o Teri Ryan
1699 W Mound St.
Columbus, OH 43223

Ph: (614)278-3130
Fax: (614)278-3143
E-mail: csc@lifecarealliance.org
URL: http://www.lifecarealliance.org
Local.

14494 ■ Lines West Buckeye Region Chapter, Pennsylvania Railroad Technical and Historical Society
c/o Gary Cost, Pres.
455 Lombard Rd.
Columbus, OH 43228-1933
E-mail: gcost@columbus.rr.com
URL: National Affiliate–www.prrths.com
Contact: Gary Cost, Pres.
Local. Brings together people who are interested in the history of the Pennsylvania Railroad. Promotes the preservation and recording of all information regarding the organization, operation, facilities and equipment of the Pennsylvania Railroad. **Affiliated With:** Pennsylvania Railroad Technical and Historical Society.

14495 ■ Lupus Foundation of America, Columbus, Marcy Zitron Chapter
6119 E Main St., Ste.207
Columbus, OH 43213
Ph: (614)755-5077
Fax: (614)755-5066
E-mail: office@lupusohio.org
URL: http://www.lupusohio.org
Contact: Dollean Harmon, Pres.
Members: 300. **Membership Dues:** individual, $15 (annual) • family, $25 (annual) • patron, $50 (annual) • sponsor, $100 (annual) • life, $500. **Local**. Works to increase knowledge and public awareness of lupus erythematosus, a noncontagious disease that may affect the skin alone or may manifest itself as a chronic, systemic, and inflammatory disease of the connective tissues. Assists lupus patients and their families, to cope with the daily problems associated with lupus. Collects and distributes funds for research. Works to bring lupus to the attention of the public. **Affiliated With:** Lupus Foundation of America. **Publications:** *The Lupus Sundial*, quarterly. Newsletter.

14496 ■ Make-A-Wish Foundation of Central Ohio
2545 Farmers Dr., Ste.300
Columbus, OH 43235
Ph: (614)923-0555
Fax: (614)923-0573
Free: (877)206-9474
E-mail: centralohio@makeawishohio.org
URL: http://www.makeawishohio.org
Contact: Susan McConnell, Pres./CEO
State. Grants wishes to children with terminal or life-threatening illnesses, thereby providing these children and their families with special memories and a welcome respite from the daily stress of their situation. **Affiliated With:** Make-A-Wish Foundation of America.

14497 ■ Mechanical Contractors Association of Central Ohio (MCACO)
c/o William H. McNally, Exec.Dir.
1550 Old Henderson Rd., Ste.N-232
Columbus, OH 43220
Ph: (614)459-0770
Fax: (614)457-0770
E-mail: mcaco@mcaco.ldmi.net
URL: http://www.mcaofcentralohio.com
Contact: William H. McNally, Exec.Dir.
Founded: 1937. **Members:** 85. **Membership Dues:** active, $400 (annual). **Staff:** 2. **Budget:** $200,600. **Local**. Owners and managers of plumbing and mechanical contracting firms. Promotes the industry; provides educational programs. **Affiliated With:** Mechanical Contractors Association of America. **Publications:** *Pipeline*, periodic. Newsletter • Directory, annual. Contains listing of all area firms, principals, addresses, and phone and fax numbers. **Price:** free. **Conventions/Meetings:** monthly general assembly - always second Tuesday.

14498 ■ Medical Group Management Association Ohio
PO Box 14882
Columbus, OH 43214
Ph: (614)470-3923
Fax: (614)442-3150
E-mail: mderamo@maternohio.com
URL: http://www.ohiomgma.com
Contact: Michael D'Eramo FACMPE, Pres.
State. Promotes program of mutual education in the field of medical group practice administration. Disseminates information of mutual interest. Improves administration in medical groups in order to serve its members, the medical groups they represent and medical group practice. Cooperates with other organizations having similar aims and objectives. **Affiliated With:** Medical Group Management Association.

14499 ■ Mental Health Association of Franklin County (MHAFC)
538 E Town St., Ste.D
Columbus, OH 43215
Ph: (614)221-1441
Fax: (614)221-1491
E-mail: info@mhafc.org
URL: http://www.mhafc.org
Contact: Laura Moskow Sigal MA, Exec.Dir.
Founded: 1956. **Members:** 550. **Membership Dues:** bellringer, $500 • pacesetter, $250-$499 • patron, $110-$249 • professional, $50-$99 • family, $40 • individual, $25. **Staff:** 7. **Budget:** $400,000. **Local**. Works to improve the mental health of Franklin County residents by providing information and referrals, education, advocacy, support groups, depression screening, and ombudsman services. **Libraries: Type:** lending. **Holdings:** video recordings. **Subjects:** mental health and recovery, depression, self-esteem, stress management. **Computer Services:** Online services, free online anxiety and depression screenings. **Subgroups:** Depression Support Group; Families in Touch; Schizophrenics Anonymous. **Affiliated With:** National Mental Health Association. **Publications:** *The Advocate*, quarterly. Newsletter. Provides timely information about mental health issues affecting the Franklin County area. **Price:** included in membership dues. **Circulation:** 3,000 • *Mental Health & Recovery Services Directory*, biennial. Provides a listing of not-for-profit organizations in Franklin County that provide mental health, drug, and alcohol services. **Price:** included in membership dues • *Parentalk Newsletter* (in English and Spanish). Provides educational information for new parents. **Price:** $25.00 QNQ • Annual Report, annual. Alternate Formats: online. **Conventions/Meetings:** conference, for professional development (exhibits) - 3/year.

14500 ■ Metro Columbus - Young Life
1515 W Lane Ave.
Columbus, OH 43221
Ph: (614)485-5433
Fax: (614)485-2278
E-mail: steve@ylcolumbus.com
URL: http://sites.younglife.org/sites/columbus/default.aspx
Contact: Steve Gardner, Metro Dir.
Local. Affiliated With: Young Life.

14501 ■ Miami Valley DX Club (MVDXC)
Box 292132
Columbus, OH 43229-8132
Ph: (614)848-9410
E-mail: mvdxc@att.net
URL: http://www.anarc.org/mvdxc
Contact: David Hammer, Publisher
Founded: 1973. **Members:** 60. **Membership Dues:** open to all, $10 (annual). **Staff:** 3. **Local**. Promotes the hobby of communications monitoring. **Affiliated With:** Association of North American Radio Clubs. **Publications:** *DX World*, monthly. Newsletter. Features coverage of all bands. **Price:** $1.00 sample. **Advertising:** accepted.

14502 ■ Miami Valley Vizsla Club (MVVC)
c/o Pam Williams
1379 Goldmill Way
Columbus, OH 43204
Ph: (614)351-0242
Fax: (614)308-0437
E-mail: goosielu@infinet.com
URL: http://www.mvvc.org
Contact: Pam Williams, Rescue Coor.
Founded: 1969. **Local**.

14503 ■ Mid-Ohio Central Service Professionals
c/o Marie Long, Pres.
Mt. Carmel East Hosp.
6001 E Broad St.
Columbus, OH 43213
Ph: (614)234-6736
E-mail: mlong2@mchs.com
URL: National Affiliate–www.ashcsp.org
Contact: Marie Long, Pres.
Local. Promotes healthcare central service, sterile processing and inventory management practices. Provides education, professional and organization development, advocacy and communication to healthcare service professionals. **Affiliated With:** American Society for Healthcare Central Service Professionals.

14504 ■ Mid Ohio District Nurses Association (MODNA)
1520 Henderson Rd., Ste.100
Columbus, OH 43220
Ph: (614)326-1630
Fax: (614)326-1633
E-mail: modna@sbcglobal.net
URL: http://www.modna.org
Contact: Barbara Nash, Pres.
Founded: 1926. **Members:** 1,800. **Membership Dues:** voluntary, $295. **Staff:** 3. **Local**. Serves as a professional support organization for registered nurses. Conducts continuing education programs and community volunteer projects. **Awards:** Dorothy A. Cornelius Scholarship. **Frequency:** annual. **Type:** scholarship. **Affiliated With:** American Nurses Association; Ohio Nurses Association. **Publications:** *Professionally Speaking*, bimonthly. Newsletter. **Circulation:** 2,000. **Advertising:** accepted. **Conventions/Meetings:** annual meeting (exhibits).

14505 ■ Mid-Ohio Regional Planning Commission (MORPC)
285 E Main St.
Columbus, OH 43215
Ph: (614)228-2663
Fax: (614)228-1904
E-mail: morpmail@morpc.org
URL: http://www.morpc.org
Contact: Ms. Marilyn Brown, Public Affairs Dir.
Regional. Serves as a community resource for the region by providing comprehensive planning, programming and intergovernmental coordinating services in the areas of transportation, land use, energy conservation, the environment and housing. Designated as the region's metropolitan planning organization for transportation planning.

14506 ■ Midwest Affordable Housing Management Association (MAHMA)
c/o Steven D. Gladman, CAE, Exec.Dir.
PO Box 12204
Columbus, OH 43212-0204
Ph: (614)481-6949
Fax: (614)481-6951
Free: (888)242-9472
E-mail: mahma@columbusapts.org
URL: http://www.mahma.com
Contact: Steven D. Gladman CAE, Exec.Dir.
Regional.

14507 ■ Midwest Dairy Foods Association
3280 Riverside Dr., Ste.10
Columbus, OH 43221
Ph: (614)326-6433
Fax: (614)442-5516
Regional. Represents dairy processing companies located in Illinois, Indiana and Ohio.

14508 ■ Mothers Against Drunk Driving, Franklin County
2700 E Main St., Ste.103
Columbus, OH 43209
Ph: (614)231-6233
Fax: (614)231-1750
E-mail: maddfranklinco@aol.com
URL: http://www.madd.org/oh/franklin
Contact: Louanne Jones, Exec.Dir.
Local. Victims of drunk driving crashes; concerned citizens. Encourages citizen participation in working towards reform of the drunk driving problem and the prevention of underage drinking. Acts as the voice of victims of drunk driving crashes by speaking on their behalf to communities, businesses, and educational groups. **Affiliated With:** Mothers Against Drunk Driving.

14509 ■ Mothers Against Drunk Driving, Ohio
5900 Roche Dr., Ste.250
Columbus, OH 43229
Ph: (614)885-6233
Fax: (614)885-0105
E-mail: info@maddohio.org
URL: http://www.madd.org
Contact: Doug Scoles, Exec.Dir.
State. Victims of drunk driving crashes; concerned citizens. Encourages citizen participation in working towards reform of the drunk driving problem and the prevention of underage drinking. Acts as the voice of victims of drunk driving crashes by speaking on their behalf to communities, businesses, and educational groups. **Affiliated With:** Mothers Against Drunk Driving.

14510 ■ Muscular Dystrophy Association, Columbus
960 Kingsmill Pkwy.
Columbus, OH 43229
Ph: (614)436-7744
Fax: (614)436-7743
URL: National Affiliate–www.mdausa.org
Local. Affiliated With: Muscular Dystrophy Association.

14511 ■ Muslim Students' Association - Ohio State University (MSA-OSU)
Enarson Hall
154 W 12th Ave.
Columbus, OH 43210
Ph: (614)292-OHIO
E-mail: msa@osu.edu
URL: http://www.osu.edu/students/msa
Contact: Mahin Islam, Pres.
Local. Muslim students in North America. Seeks to advance the interests of members; works to enable members to practice Islam as a complete way of life. **Affiliated With:** Muslim Students Association of the United States and Canada.

14512 ■ NAMI Ohio
747 E Broad St.
Columbus, OH 43205
Ph: (614)224-2700
Fax: (614)224-5400
Free: (800)686-AMIO
E-mail: amiohio@amiohio.org
URL: http://www.namiohio.org
Contact: Terry L. Russell, Exec.Dir.
Founded: 1982. **Membership Dues:** professional, $30 (annual). **State**. Provides mutual support, education, and advocacy for individuals and families affected by serious brain disorders. **Committees:** Jails and Prisons. **Programs:** Family to Family Education; Provider Education. **Publications:** *News Briefs*, quarterly. Newsletter. Includes information about brain disorders, new treatment options, research, political and legislative news.

14513 ■ National Association of Fleet Administrators, Tri-State
c/o Diana Wolfe, Chair
PO Box 1498
Columbus, OH 43216-1498
Ph: (614)559-2521
Fax: (614)559-2598
E-mail: wolfed@whitecastle.com
URL: http://www.tristatenafa.org
Contact: Diana Wolfe, Chair
Regional. Promotes the professional management of vehicles through education, government and industry relations and services to members. **Affiliated With:** National Association of Fleet Administrators.

14514 ■ National Association of Industrial and Office Properties, Central Ohio Chapter
c/o Bill Baumgardner
Pizzuti Companies
2 Miranova Pl., Ste.800
Columbus, OH 43215-5098
Ph: (614)280-4000
Fax: (614)280-5000
E-mail: debbielee@centralohionaiop.org
URL: National Affiliate–www.naiop.org
Contact: DebbieLee Dougherty, Chapter Exec.
Local. Represents the interests of developers and owners of industrial, office and related commercial estate. Provides communication, networking, business opportunities and a forum to its members. Promotes effective public policy to create, protect and enhance property values. **Affiliated With:** National Association of Industrial and Office Properties.

14515 ■ National Association of Industrial and Office Properties, Ohio Chapter
c/o DebbieLee Dougherty
2500 E Main St., Ste.100
Columbus, OH 43209-2483
Ph: (614)235-0311
Fax: (614)235-0880
E-mail: debbielee@centralohio.org
URL: National Affiliate–www.naiop.org
Contact: DebbieLee Dougherty, Exec.Dir.
State. Represents the interests of developers and owners of industrial, office and related commercial estate. Provides communication, networking, business opportunities and a forum to its members. Promotes effective public policy to create, protect and enhance property values. **Affiliated With:** National Association of Industrial and Office Properties.

14516 ■ National Association of Minority Contractors, Central Ohio
c/o Dan Moncrief
2188 Oriole Pl.
Columbus, OH 43219-2038
Ph: (614)258-5673
Fax: (614)372-0333
E-mail: dmoncrief@mcdanielsconstruction.com
URL: National Affiliate–www.namcline.org
Contact: Dan Moncrief, Contact
Local. Promotes the economic and legal interests of minority contracting firms. Provides education and training and identifies procurement opportunities for minority contractors. Advocates law and government actions which meet the concerns of minority contractors. **Affiliated With:** National Association of Minority Contractors.

14517 ■ National Association of Rocketry - Columbus Society for the Advancement of Rocketry (CSAR)
c/o Larry Rice, Pres.
1416 Aven Dr.
Columbus, OH 43227
Ph: (614)235-1339
E-mail: larryr33323@yahoo.com
URL: http://csarnar113.tripod.com
Contact: Larry Rice, Pres.
Local.

14518 ■ National Association of Social Workers - Ohio Chapter (NASW-OC)
33 N 3rd St., Ste.530
Columbus, OH 43215
Ph: (614)461-4484
Fax: (614)461-9793
E-mail: ohnasw@ameritech.net
URL: http://www.naswoh.org
Contact: C. Elaine Stepp MSW, Exec.Dir.
Founded: 1976. **Members:** 5,250. **Membership Dues:** associate, $142 (annual) • doctoral student, $134 (annual) • regular, $117 (annual). **Staff:** 5. **Budget:** $390,000. **Regional Groups:** 8. **State**. Professional social workers. Provides professional development opportunities, legislative advocacy, social action, and membership services; establishes professional standards. **Awards:** Public Official of the Year. **Type:** recognition • Student of the Year. **Frequency:** annual. **Type:** recognition. **Recipient:** for outstanding scholarship, community involvement and adherence to code of ethics • SW of the Year. **Type:** recognition • Volunteer of the Year. **Type:** recognition. **Affiliated With:** National Association of Social Workers. **Publications:** *Ohio Chapter NASW Newsletter*, 8/year. **Price:** included in membership dues; $15.00 /year for nonmembers. **Circulation:** 5,300. **Advertising:** accepted. **Conventions/Meetings:** annual conference (exhibits) - always March • monthly Continuing Education Programs - meeting - except March in all major cities in Ohio • monthly workshop (exhibits).

14519 ■ National Association of State Foresters, Ohio
c/o John Dorka
Div. of Forestry
1855 Fountain Square Ct., H-1
Columbus, OH 43224
Ph: (614)265-6690
E-mail: john.dorka@dnr.state.oh.us
URL: National Affiliate–www.stateforesters.org
Contact: John Dorka, Contact
State. Affiliated With: National Association of State Foresters.

14520 ■ National Audubon Society - Columbus
PO Box 141350
Columbus, OH 43214
Ph: (740)549-0333
E-mail: information@columbusaudubon.org
URL: http://www.columbusaudubon.org
Contact: Kristan Leedy, Pres.
Founded: 1913. **Local**. Promotes the appreciation, understanding, and conservation of birds and their habitats.

14521 ■ National Federation of Independent Business - Ohio
c/o Roger R. Geiger, State Dir.
50 W Broad St., Ste.3100
Columbus, OH 43215
Ph: (614)221-4107
Fax: (614)221-8677
E-mail: roger.geiger@nfib.org
URL: National Affiliate–www.nfib.com
Contact: Roger R. Geiger, State Dir.
State. Affiliated With: National Federation of Independent Business.

14522 ■ National Horseshoe Pitchers Association - Ohio
c/o Dan Sanders
6687 Merwin Rd.
Columbus, OH 43235-2841
Ph: (614)761-3357
E-mail: dsanderling@yahoo.com
URL: National Affiliate–www.horseshoepitching.com
Contact: Dan Sanders, Regional Dir.
State.

14523 ■ National Kidney Foundation of Ohio
1373 Grandview Ave., Ste.200
Columbus, OH 43212-2804
Ph: (614)481-4030
Fax: (614)481-4038
E-mail: mcampbell@nkfohio.org
URL: http://www.nkfofohio.org
Contact: Orelle Jackson, Exec.Dir.
Founded: 1987. **Members:** 200. **Staff:** 7. **Budget:** $500,000. **Local Groups:** 2. **State**. Unites to prevent and treat kidney and related diseases. Maintains speakers' bureau. Conducts professional education programs for health care providers. **Libraries: Type:** open to the public. **Holdings:** 100. **Subjects:** kidney and related diseases, organ donation. **Awards:** Mary Jo Cosio, RN Award. **Frequency:** annual. **Type:** grant. **Recipient:** for renal disease research. **Boards:** Medical Advisory. **Committees:** Fundraising; Minority Initiative; Patient Services; Professional Education; Public Education; Public Policy. **Affiliated With:** National Kidney Foundation. **Publications:** *Kidney Comments*, periodic. Newsletter. Contains information for renal patients and families. **Price:** free. **Circulation:** 8,500.

14524 ■ National Management Association, Columbus Public Service Chapter
c/o Linda Rightor
Trans. Div.
1800 E 17th Ave.
Columbus, OH 43219
E-mail: lvrightor@columbus.gov
URL: National Affiliate–www.nma1.org
Contact: Linda Rightor, Contact
Local. Business and industrial management personnel; membership comes from supervisory level, with the remainder from middle management and above. Seeks to develop and recognize management as a profession and to promote the free enterprise system. **Affiliated With:** National Management Association.

14525 ■ National Organization for Women - Columbus
c/o Randi Organ, Pres.
PO Box 82455
Columbus, OH 43202
Ph: (614)675-1200
E-mail: contactus@columbusnow.net
URL: http://www.columbusnow.net
Contact: Randi Organ, Pres.
Local. **Affiliated With:** National Organization for Women.

14526 ■ National Organization for Women - Ohio
PO Box 8134
Columbus, OH 43201-0134
Ph: (614)485-0996
E-mail: ohionow@ohionow.org
URL: http://www.ohionow.org
State. **Affiliated With:** National Organization for Women.

14527 ■ National Sojourners, Columbus No. 10
c/o Lt.Col. Davy L. Winkle
5760 Firwood Pl.
Columbus, OH 43229-3406
Ph: (614)846-4661
E-mail: dlwinkle@aol.com
URL: National Affiliate–www.nationalsojourners.org
Contact: Lt.Col. Davy L. Winkle, Contact
Local.

14528 ■ National Speleological Society, Shady Grove Grotto
c/o Aaron Snyder
2874 Melva Ave.
Columbus, OH 43224
E-mail: jill.buss@osumc.edu
URL: National Affiliate–www.caves.org
Contact: Aaron Snyder, Contact
Local. Seeks to study, explore and conserve cave and karst resources. Protects access to caves and promotes responsible caving. Encourages responsible management of caves and their unique environments. **Affiliated With:** National Speleological Society.

14529 ■ Near Earth Object Search Society (NEOSS)
c/o Gregory D. Peisert, Exec.Dir.
4615 Hiton Corporate Dr.
Columbus, OH 43232-0000
Ph: (937)427-4199
E-mail: greg.peisert@neoss.org
Local.

14530 ■ New Albany - Young Life
1515 W Lane Ave.
Columbus, OH 43221
Ph: (614)485-5433
URL: http://sites.younglife.org/sites/NewAlbany/default.aspx
Local. **Affiliated With:** Young Life.

14531 ■ Nigerian Friendship Association of Greater Columbus, Ohio
c/o Emeka Okafor
6048 Leafridge Ln.
Columbus, OH 43232-7718
Local.

14532 ■ Ohio Academy of Family Physicians (OAFP)
c/o Ann M. Spicer, Exec.VP
4075 N High St.
Columbus, OH 43214
Ph: (614)267-7867
Fax: (614)267-9191
Free: (800)742-7327
E-mail: mail@ohioafp.org
URL: http://www.ohioafp.org
Contact: Ann M. Spicer, Exec.VP
State. Professional society of family physicians who provide continuing comprehensive care to patients. **Affiliated With:** American Academy of Family Physicians.

14533 ■ Ohio Academy of Nursing Homes
2 Miranova Pl.
Columbus, OH 43215
Ph: (614)461-1922
Fax: (614)461-0434
Free: (800)999-6264
State.

14534 ■ Ohio Academy of Science (OAS)
1500 W 3rd Ave., Ste.228
Columbus, OH 43212-2817
Ph: (614)488-2228
Fax: (614)488-7629
Free: (800)OHI-OSCI
E-mail: oas@iwaynet.net
URL: http://www.ohiosci.org
Contact: Mr. Lynn E. Elfner, CEO
Founded: 1891. **Members:** 2,000. **Membership Dues:** $65 (quarterly). **Staff:** 4. **Budget:** $400,000. **Regional Groups:** 16. **State**. Scientists, engineers, industrial researchers, science and math teachers, and students dedicated to promoting the study of science. Seeks to foster curiosity, discovery, and innovation for the benefit of society. **Publications:** *OAS News*, periodic. Newsletter. **Price:** included in membership dues • *Ohio Journal of Science*, quarterly. **Price:** $50.00 in U.S.; $55.00 outside U.S. **Conventions/Meetings:** annual assembly, scientific research presentation (exhibits).

14535 ■ Ohio Academy of Trial Lawyers (OATL)
395 E Broad St., Ste.200
Columbus, OH 43215-3844
Ph: (614)341-6800
Fax: (614)341-6810
E-mail: oatl@oatlaw.org
URL: http://www.oatlaw.org
Contact: Jill Snitcher McQuain, Exec.Dir.
State.

14536 ■ Ohio AFL-CIO
395 E Broad St., Ste.300
Columbus, OH 43215
Ph: (614)224-8271
Fax: (614)224-2671
URL: http://www.ohaflcio.org
Contact: William A. Burga, Pres.
State. **Affiliated With:** AFL-CIO.

14537 ■ Ohio AgriBusiness Association (OABA)
5151 Reed Rd., Ste.200-A
Columbus, OH 43220
Ph: (614)326-7520
Fax: (614)326-7519
E-mail: info@oaba.net
URL: http://www.oaba.net
Contact: Gary King, Pres./CEO
State. **Publications:** *Industry Directory*, annual • Newsletter, monthly. **Conventions/Meetings:** annual meeting - always February.

14538 ■ Ohio Apartment Association (OAA)
1224 Dublin Rd.
Columbus, OH 43215
Ph: (614)488-4355
Fax: (614)488-8526
URL: National Affiliate–www.naahq.org
Contact: Steven D. Gladman, Governmental Affairs Coor.
Founded: 1987. **Staff:** 1. **Local Groups:** 11. **Local**. Trade association representing apartment owners and management companies. Seeks to advance the general welfare of the industry; advocates for the enactment of beneficial legislation; provides network for exchange of information. Promotes continuing education. **Affiliated With:** National Apartment Association. **Formerly:** Ohio Apartment and Condominiums Association. **Publications:** *Capital Watch*, weekly. Newsletter. Legislative update. **Conventions/Meetings:** quarterly meeting.

14539 ■ Ohio Art League
954 N High St.
Columbus, OH 43201
Ph: (614)299-8225
Fax: (614)299-8225
E-mail: oal@rrcol.com
URL: http://www.oal.org
Contact: Ellen Grevey, Exec.Dir.
Founded: 1909. **Members:** 600. **Membership Dues:** artist, $50 (annual) • student, $35 (annual) • family of two, $90 (annual) • associate, $100 (annual) • award patron, $500 (annual) • sponsor, $1,000 (annual) • corporate, $5,000 (annual). **Staff:** 2. **State**. Open to all Ohio artists, curators, and individuals interested in the arts. **Awards: Frequency:** semiannual. **Type:** monetary. **Recipient:** for outstanding artwork. **Formerly:** (1998) Columbus Art League. **Publications:** *Details*, quarterly. Newsletter. **Price:** included in membership dues • *Ohio Art*, semiannual. Journal. **Price:** free. **Circulation:** 3,000. **Advertising:** accepted. **Conventions/Meetings:** monthly Exhibitions - meeting (exhibits) • semiannual Juried Exhibition - meeting (exhibits) - always spring and fall • Lecture Series - meeting - 3-4/year • monthly Member Curated Exhibits - meeting (exhibits) • periodic workshop.

14540 ■ Ohio Assisted Living Association (OALA)
c/o Jean Thompson, Exec.Dir.
1335 Dublin Rd., Ste.211-B
Columbus, OH 43215-7037
Ph: (614)481-1950
Fax: (614)481-1954
E-mail: oala@ohioassistedliving.org
URL: http://www.ohioassistedliving.org
Contact: Jean Thompson, Exec.Dir.
State. **Affiliated With:** Assisted Living Federation of America.

14541 ■ Ohio Association of Alcoholism and Drug Abuse Counselors (OAADAC)
c/o Patricia Liggett, Admin.Asst.
5900 Roche Dr., Ste.440
Columbus, OH 43229
Ph: (614)888-2695
Fax: (614)841-9680
Free: (800)721-2841
E-mail: info@oaadac.org
URL: http://www.oaadac.org
Contact: Patricia Liggett, Admin.Asst.
Local. **Affiliated With:** NAADAC The Association for Addiction Professionals.

14542 ■ Ohio Association of Area Agencies on Aging (OAAAA)
c/o Jane Taylor, Exec.Dir.
1335 Dublin Rd., Ste.200A
Columbus, OH 43215
Ph: (614)481-3511
Fax: (614)481-3566
E-mail: oaaaa@ohioaging.org
URL: http://www.ohioaging.org
Contact: Jane Taylor, Exec.Dir.
State.

14543 ■ Ohio Association of Broadcasters (OAB)
88 E Broad St., Ste.1180
Columbus, OH 43215-3525
Ph: (614)228-4052
Fax: (614)228-8133
E-mail: oab@oab.org
URL: http://www.oab.org
Contact: Christine H. Merritt, Exec.VP
Founded: 1937. **Members:** 400. **Staff:** 3. **State**. Provides legislative advocacy, educational programs, and station inspections.

14544 ■ Ohio Association of Career Colleges and Schools (OACCS)
1857 NW Blvd. Annex
Columbus, OH 43212
Ph: (614)487-8180
Fax: (614)487-8190
E-mail: oaccs@aol.com
URL: http://www.members.aol.com/oaccs
Contact: Max J. Lerner, Exec.Dir.
Founded: 1973. **Members:** 58. **Staff:** 3. **State**.

14545 ■ Ohio Association for Career and Technical Education
5080 Sinclair Rd., Ste.100
Columbus, OH 43229
Ph: (614)885-1881
Fax: (614)885-1975
Free: (800)522-5519
E-mail: ohioacte@ohiohills.com
URL: http://www.ohioacte.org
Contact: Dr. Darrell Parks, Exec.Dir.
Founded: 1922. **Members:** 3,800. **Membership Dues:** affiliate, $40 (annual) • full-time student, $15 (annual) • retired educator, $31 (annual) • business community, $135 (annual) • life, $400. **Staff:** 2. **Budget:** $275,000. **Local Groups:** 14. **State**. Career and technical educational teachers and administrators. Represents the field before governmental bodies; provides public relations services; promotes professional growth. **Awards:** Career/Technical Educator of the Year. **Frequency:** annual. **Type:** recognition • Distinguished Service Award. **Frequency:** annual. **Type:** recognition • Man or Woman of the Year in Career and Technical Education. **Type:** recognition • New Professional Award. **Type:** recognition • Outstanding Career/Technical Education Teacher in Community Service. **Frequency:** annual. **Type:** recognition • Outstanding New Career/Technical Education Teacher. **Frequency:** annual. **Type:** recognition • Pacesetter Awards. **Frequency:** annual. **Type:** recognition • Person of the Year. **Frequency:** annual. **Type:** recognition. **Recipient:** for continuing efforts to support and promote career technical and adult education throughout Ohio • Policy Maker of the Year. **Frequency:** annual. **Type:** recognition • Teacher of the Year. **Frequency:** annual. **Type:** recognition. **Divisions:** Adult Workforce Development; Affiliation of Tech Prep Academics; Career Based Intervention; Family & Consumer Sciences; Health Careers and Technology; Special Needs; Trade & Industrial. **Affiliated With:** Association for Career and Technical Education. **Also Known As:** Ohio ACTE. **Formerly:** (1998) Ohio Vocational Association. **Publications:** Newsletter, quarterly. **Conventions/Meetings:** annual conference (exhibits).

14546 ■ Ohio Association of Child Caring Agencies (OACCA)
50 W Broad St., Ste.1900
Columbus, OH 43215
Ph: (614)461-0014
Fax: (614)228-7004
E-mail: pwyman@oacca.org
URL: http://www.oacca.org
Contact: Penny Wyman, Exec.Dir.
Founded: 1973. **Members:** 75. **Staff:** 4. **For-Profit. State**. Social service providers. Conduct educational/training; advocate on behalf of children, families and member agencies with focus on foster care, adoption, chilren's behavioral health, juvenile justice and special education. **Publications:** *Advocate*, monthly. Newsletter • Membership Directory, annual. **Conventions/Meetings:** semiannual conference (exhibits).

14547 ■ Ohio Association of Civil Trial Attorneys (OACTA)
17 S High St., Ste.200
Columbus, OH 43215
Ph: (614)221-1900
Fax: (614)221-1989
E-mail: oacta@assnoffices.com
URL: http://www.oacta.org
Contact: Nancy S. Waterhouse, Exec.Dir.
Members: 760. **Membership Dues:** active, $125 (annual) • inactive, $30 (annual) • new attorney (less than 5 years in practice), associate (paralegal or equivalent), $60 (annual) • sustaining, $50 (annual). **Staff:** 2. **State**. Defense lawyers. Professional organization seeking to improve the administration of justice with respect to civil law suits. **Formerly:** Ohio Association of Civil Trial Lawyers. **Publications:** *OACTA Update*, periodic. Newsletter • Magazine, quarterly. **Conventions/Meetings:** semiannual meeting (exhibits) - always spring and fall.

14548 ■ Ohio Association of Collegiate Registrars and Admissions Officers (OACRAO)
c/o Connie Goodman, Asst. to Registrar/Web Coor.
The Ohio State Univ.
1800 Cannon Dr., No. 730
730 Lincoln Tower
Columbus, OH 43210
Ph: (614)292-1556
Fax: (614)292-7199
E-mail: goodman.7@osu.edu
URL: http://www.oacrao.ohiou.edu
Contact: Connie Goodman, Asst. to Registrar/Web Coor.
Founded: 1926. **Members:** 710. **State**. Provides professional development regarding best practices, and standards and guidelines in records management, admissions, enrollment management, administrative information technology and student services to higher education officials in Ohio. **Affiliated With:** American Association of Collegiate Registrars and Admissions Officers. **Formerly:** (2001) American Association of Collegiate Registrars and Admission Officers, Ohio. **Conventions/Meetings:** annual conference.

14549 ■ Ohio Association of Community Action Agencies (OACAA)
c/o Philip E. Cole, Exec.Dir.
50 W Broad St., Ste.1616
Columbus, OH 43215
Ph: (614)224-8500
Fax: (614)224-2587
E-mail: info@oaccaa.org
URL: http://www.oacaa.org
Contact: Philip E. Cole, Exec.Dir.
State.

14550 ■ Ohio Association of Community Colleges (OACC)
41 S High St., Ste.3625
Columbus, OH 43215
Ph: (614)221-6222
Fax: (614)221-6239
Free: (888)533-6222
E-mail: info@ohiocc.org
URL: http://www.ohiocc.org
Contact: Mr. Terry M. Thomas CAE, Exec.Dir.
Founded: 1993. **Members:** 24. **Membership Dues:** institution, $20,000 (annual). **Staff:** 4. **Budget:** $438,750. **State**. Strives to promote and represent the interest of community colleges. Advocates for the interests of students and their education. **Awards:** All-Ohio Academic Team. **Frequency:** annual. **Type:** scholarship. **Recipient:** for outstanding two-year college students. **Subgroups:** All-Ohio Academic Team; Legislation; Trustee Education. **Publications:** *Community College Connection*, semiannual. Newsletter. **Circulation:** 550. **Conventions/Meetings:** semiannual meeting, trustee education.

14551 ■ Ohio Association of Convention and Visitor Bureaus (OACVB)
c/o Molly McKee
37 W Broad St., Ste.480
Columbus, OH 43215
Ph: (614)241-2226
Fax: (614)241-2215
Free: (888)505-9552
E-mail: oacvb@aol.com
URL: http://www.oacvb.org
Contact: Molly McKee, Contact
State.

14552 ■ Ohio Association of Elementary School Administrators (OAESA)
8050 N High St., Ste.170
Columbus, OH 43235-6487
Ph: (614)430-8590
Fax: (614)430-8596
E-mail: info@oaesa.org
URL: http://www.oaesa.org
Contact: Ronald A. Stebelton, Exec.Dir.
Founded: 1923. **Members:** 2,200. **Membership Dues:** active, $225 (annual) • associate, $55 (annual) • institutional, $150 (annual). **Staff:** 6. **Budget:** $850,000. **Regional Groups:** 10. **Local Groups:** 30. **State**. Professional organization of elementary and middle school principals and central office administrators. **Awards:** Hall of Fame - Distinguished Principal. **Frequency:** annual. **Type:** recognition. **Affiliated With:** National Association of Elementary School Principals. **Formerly:** Ohio Association of Elementary School Principals. **Publications:** *Capitol Update*, biweekly • *Keeping You Informed*, monthly • *Letter of the Law* • *Quarterly*. **Conventions/Meetings:** annual conference (exhibits) - always in Columbus, OH.

14553 ■ Ohio Association for Gifted Children (OAGC)
501 Morrison Rd., Ste.103
Columbus, OH 43230
Ph: (614)337-0386
Fax: (614)337-9298
E-mail: president@oagc.com
URL: http://www.oagc.com
Contact: Judy Back, Pres.
Founded: 1952. **State**. Advances interest in programs for the gifted. Seeks to further education of the gifted and enhances their potential creativity. Unites to address the unique needs of children and youth with demonstrated gifts and talents as well as those children who may be able to develop their talent potentials with appropriate educational experiences. Encourages and responds to the diverse expressions of gifts and talents in children

and youth from all cultures, racial and ethnic backgrounds, and socioeconomic groups. **Affiliated With:** National Association for Gifted Children.

14554 ■ Ohio Association of Health Plans (OAHP)
230 E Town St.
Columbus, OH 43215-3842
Ph: (614)228-4662
Fax: (614)228-5816
E-mail: info@oahp.org
URL: http://www.oahp.org
Contact: William Epling, Chm.
Founded: 1980. **State**. **Formerly:** (2001) Ohio HMO Association.

14555 ■ Ohio Association of Historical Societies and Museums (OAHSM)
c/o Bonnie Such, Sec.
1982 Velma Ave.
Columbus, OH 43211-2497
Ph: (614)297-2340
Fax: (614)297-2233
E-mail: bsuch@ohiohistory.org
URL: http://www.ohiohistory.org/resource/oahsm
Contact: Bonnie Such, Sec.
Founded: 1959. **Members:** 550. **Membership Dues:** student, $15 (annual) • individual, $20 (annual) • low budget organization, $25 (annual) • high budget organization and benefactor, $45 (annual). **Staff:** 3. **Regional Groups:** 8. **State**. A network of historical organizations in Ohio which exists to encourage an appreciation for and an understanding of Ohio's heritage by assisting efforts to collect preserve, and interpret local history. **Awards:** Achievement. **Frequency:** annual. **Type:** recognition. **Publications:** *Directory of Historical Organizations in Ohio*, triennial. **Price:** $18.00. **Circulation:** 750. **Advertising:** accepted • *Local Historian*, bimonthly. Newsletter • *Timeline*, quarterly. Magazine. **Conventions/Meetings:** annual meeting (exhibits) - first Friday and Saturday in November • annual regional meeting - always spring.

14556 ■ Ohio Association of Institutional Research and Planning (OAIRP)
c/o Dr. Kevin W. Sayers
One Coll. and Main Sts.
Columbus, OH 43209
Ph: (614)236-6943
Fax: (614)236-6926
E-mail: ksayers@capital.edu
URL: National Affiliate–www.airweb.org
Contact: Dr. Kevin W. Sayers, Contact
State. Represents individuals interested in institutional research. Fosters research leading to improved understanding, planning, and operation of institutions of postsecondary education. **Affiliated With:** Association for Institutional Research.

14557 ■ Ohio Association of Insurance and Financial Advisors (OAIFA)
c/o Robert P. Freed, Pres.
17 S High St., No. 200
Columbus, OH 43215-3458
Ph: (614)228-4539
Fax: (614)221-1989
E-mail: naifa-ohio@assnoffices.com
URL: http://www.naifaohio.org
Contact: Robert P. Freed, Pres.
State. Provides services to individuals engaged in the financial services industries including continuing education, legislative/regulatory representation, public relations, public service programs and political involvement and action programs.

14558 ■ Ohio Association of Medical Equipment Services (OAMES)
17 S High St., Ste.1000
Columbus, OH 43215
Ph: (614)876-2424
Fax: (614)876-2490
E-mail: kam@oames.org
URL: http://www.oames.org
Contact: Kamela Yuricich, Exec.Dir.
Founded: 1981. **Members:** 200. **Membership Dues:** regular, associate, $600 (annual). **Staff:** 1. **Budget:** $130,000. **State**. Owners, managers, and staff members of home medical equipment companies. Provides a forum for the exchange of information on the home-based health services industry. **Formerly:** Ohio Association of Durable Medical Equipment Companies. **Publications:** *OAMES Update*, monthly. Bulletin • Newsletter, quarterly. **Conventions/Meetings:** annual conference, executive level education program (exhibits) - October • periodic meeting • periodic seminar.

14559 ■ Ohio Association of Movers (OAM)
c/o Ed Bramer, Exec.Dir.
5300 E Main St., Ste.104
Columbus, OH 43213
Ph: (614)866-4349
Fax: (614)866-2644
E-mail: kbrown@ohiomovers.org
URL: http://www.ohiomovers.org
Contact: Karen Brown, Associate Dir.
State.

14560 ■ Ohio Association of Nonprofit Organizations (OANO)
100 E Broad St., Ste.2440
Columbus, OH 43215-3119
Ph: (614)280-0233
Fax: (614)280-0657
E-mail: info@oano.org
URL: http://www.ohiononprofits.org
Contact: Jennifer Campbell, Exec.Dir.
Membership Dues: non-profit (based on budget), $65-$500 (annual) • for-profit company, $500 (annual) • individual, $100 (annual). **State**. **Affiliated With:** National Council of Nonprofit Associations.

14561 ■ Ohio Association of Polygraph Examiners
161 Busch Blvd., Ste.336
Columbus, OH 43229
Ph: (614)781-0255
Fax: (614)781-0257
E-mail: redategf@aol.com
URL: http://www.ohiopolygraph.org
Contact: Jack P. Lonier, Contact
State. Represents individuals dedicated to providing a valid and reliable means to verify the truth and establish the highest standards of moral, ethical, and professional conduct in the polygraph field. Establishes standards of ethical practices, techniques, instrumentation, research, advanced training and continuing educational programs. Provides a forum for the presentation and exchange of information derived from such research, training and education. **Affiliated With:** American Polygraph Association.

14562 ■ Ohio Association of Professional Fire Fighters
1380 Dublin Rd., No. 104
Columbus, OH 43215-1025
Ph: (614)488-9920
Fax: (614)488-9925
E-mail: msandl48@aol.com
URL: http://www.oapff.com
Contact: Mark Sanders, Pres.
State.

14563 ■ Ohio Association of Public School Employees (OAPSE)
c/o Joseph P. Rugola, Exec.Dir.
6805 Oak Creek Dr.
Columbus, OH 43229
Ph: (614)890-4770
Fax: (614)890-3540
Free: (800)786-2773
URL: http://www.oapse.org
State.

14564 ■ Ohio Association of Realtors (OAR)
c/o Donald W. Freels, CEO
200 E Town St.
Columbus, OH 43215-4648
Ph: (614)228-6675
Fax: (614)228-2601
E-mail: info@ohiorealtors.org
URL: http://www.ohiorealtors.org
Contact: Donald W. Freels, CEO
State.

14565 ■ Ohio Association of School Business Officials (OASBO)
8050 N High St., Ste.130
Columbus, OH 43235
Ph: (614)431-9116
Fax: (614)431-9137
Free: (800)OH-OASBO
E-mail: info@oasbo-ohio.org
URL: http://oasbo-ohio.org
Contact: Barbara Shaner, Interim Exec.Dir.
State. Serves the professional needs of Ohio school district treasures and business managers. **Affiliated With:** Association of School Business Officials International. **Publications:** *Business Chronicle*, 5/year, during school year. Magazine • *Legislative Bulletin*, biweekly. Newsletter • *News Line*, biweekly. Newsletter. **Conventions/Meetings:** annual conference • periodic seminar.

14566 ■ Ohio Association of Secondary School Administrators (OASSA)
8050 N High St., Ste.180
Columbus, OH 43235-6484
Ph: (614)430-8311
Fax: (614)430-8315
E-mail: sraines@oassa.org
URL: http://www.oassa.org
Contact: Steven E. Raines, Exec.Dir.
Founded: 1922. **Members:** 2,500. **Membership Dues:** professional, $230 (annual) • associate, retiree, $40 (annual) • patron, $100 (annual). **Staff:** 7. **Budget:** $930,000. **State**. Athletic directors and vocational and secondary school administrators. Provides support to the profession. Sponsors cheerleading competition. **Affiliated With:** National Association of Secondary School Principals. **Publications:** *Legal Notes*, monthly. Newsletter • *Legislative Report*, bimonthly. Newsletter • *Middle Level News and Supervisors Digest*, monthly. Newsletter • *Update*, biweekly. Newsletter. **Conventions/Meetings:** annual conference (exhibits) - always fall in Columbus, OH.

14567 ■ Ohio Association of Security and Investigation Services (OASIS)
c/o Jim Silvania, Exec.Dir.
41 S High St.
Columbus, OH 43215
Ph: (614)227-4595 (614)227-2109
Fax: (614)227-2100
E-mail: jsilvania@porterwright.com
URL: http://www.ohoasis.org
Contact: Jim Silvania, Exec.Dir.
State. Represents Ohio's licensed private investigation and security professionals.

14568 ■ Ohio Association of Textile Services
c/o David W. Field, CAE, Exec.Dir.
17 S High St., Ste.200
Columbus, OH 43215
Ph: (614)221-1900
Fax: (614)221-1989
E-mail: oats@assnoffices.com
State.

14569 ■ Ohio Association of Wholesale Distributors
c/o John C. Mahaney, Jr., Exec.Dir.
50 W Broad St., Ste.2020
Columbus, OH 43215-5912
Ph: (614)221-7833
Fax: (614)221-7020
Free: (800)256-4670
State.

14570 ■ Ohio Auctioneers Association
c/o Peggy Metzger, Exec.Dir.
17 S High St., Ste.200
Columbus, OH 43215-3458
Ph: (614)221-3245
Fax: (614)221-1989
E-mail: oaa@assnoffices.com
State.

14571 ■ Ohio Automatic Merchandising Association
c/o John C. Mahaney, Jr., Exec.Dir.
50 W. Broad St., Ste.2020
Columbus, OH 43215
Ph: (614)221-7833
Fax: (614)221-7020
Free: (800)256-4670
State.

14572 ■ Ohio Bankers League (OBL)
4249 Easton Way, Ste.150
Columbus, OH 43219
Ph: (614)340-7595
Fax: (614)340-7596
Free: (800)686-6755
E-mail: webmaster@ohiobankersleague.com
URL: http://www.ohiobankersleague.com
Contact: Michael M. Van Buskirk, Pres./CEO
State. Formerly: (2005) Ohio Bankers Association. **Publications:** *Ohio Banker*, annual. Magazine • *Ohio Banker*, monthly. Newsletter • *Ohio Directory*, annual. **Conventions/Meetings:** annual meeting - always May.

14573 ■ Ohio Bed and Breakfast Association (OBBA)
5310 E Main St., Ste.104
Columbus, OH 43213
Ph: (614)868-5567
Fax: (614)868-1177
E-mail: obba@travelohio.com
URL: http://www.ohiobba.com
State.

14574 ■ Ohio Burglar and Fire Alarm Association (OBFAA)
c/o Darrel T. Shaw, Jr., Pres.
1145 Slade Ave.
Columbus, OH 43235-4052
Ph: (614)457-1748
Fax: (614)447-8927
Free: (800)746-2322
E-mail: beverlygbailey@aol.com
URL: http://www.secureohio.org
Contact: Darrel T. Shaw Jr., Pres.
Founded: 1986. **State. Telecommunication Services:** electronic mail, beverlygbailey@secureohio.com. **Affiliated With:** National Burglar and Fire Alarm Association.

14575 ■ Ohio Cable Telecommunications Association (OCTA)
c/o Edward Kozelek, Exec.VP
50 W Broad St., Ste.1118
Columbus, OH 43215
Ph: (614)461-4014
Fax: (614)461-9326
E-mail: octaed@octa.org
URL: http://www.octa.org
Contact: Edward Kozelek, Exec.VP
State. Represents the cable television and telecommunications industry in the Ohio General Assembly, the Public Utilities Commission of Ohio and the United States Congress on issues of importance to current and future businesses. Conducts and coordinates a number of public affairs programs for members and works with the media to communicate issues and events of importance.

14576 ■ Ohio Cast Metals Association
2970 Scioto Pl.
Columbus, OH 43221
Ph: (614)876-5100
Local.

14577 ■ Ohio Chamber of Commerce (OCC)
c/o Andrew E. Doehrel, Pres./CEO
230 E Town St.
PO Box 15159
Columbus, OH 43215-0159
Ph: (614)228-4201
Fax: (614)228-6403
Free: (800)622-1893
E-mail: occ@ohiochamber.com
URL: http://www.ohiochamber.com
Contact: Andrew Doehrel, Pres./CEO
Founded: 1893. **Members:** 4,000. **Membership Dues:** business, $250 (annual). **Staff:** 24. **Budget:** $2,000,000. **State.** Businesses organized to foster economic and industrial growth in Ohio. Serves as liaison between government and business. Keeps members informed of employment conditions, economic developments, and pertinent regulations. Conducts lobbying activities. **Councils:** Ohio Small Business. **Publications:** *The Complete Wage and Hour Manual*. Contains information about minimum wage, overtime pay, wage payment, garnishment, and other related issues. • *Environmental and Safety Directory*, annual. Contains information on the Ohio EPA, permitting and fees, and state regulatory contacts. • *Membership Notes*, bimonthly. Newsletter. Contains special happenings and new member services. • *Ohio and Federal Employment Law Manual*. Contains federal and state information concerning workplace. • *Ohio Matters*, bimonthly. Magazine. Includes information about business and legislative activities. **Advertising:** accepted. **Conventions/Meetings:** annual meeting.

14578 ■ Ohio Chapter American College of Emergency Physicians (OHACEP)
3510 Snouffer Rd., Ste.100
Columbus, OH 43235
Ph: (614)792-6506
Fax: (614)792-6508
Free: (888)642-2374
E-mail: info@ohacep.org
URL: http://www.ohacep.org
Contact: Catherine A. Marco MD, Pres.
State. Affiliated With: American College of Emergency Physicians.

14579 ■ Ohio Chapter of the American College of Surgeons
c/o Brad L. Feldman, MPA, Exec.Dir.
PO Box 1715
Columbus, OH 43216-1715
Ph: (614)221-9814
Fax: (614)221-2335
Free: (877)677-3227
E-mail: ocacs@ohiofacs.org
URL: http://www.ohiofacs.org
Contact: Brad L. Feldman MPA, Exec.Dir.
Members: 1,500. **State.** Strives to educate members and public about surgical care and to improve the standards of surgical care in Ohio. **Affiliated With:** American College of Surgeons.

14580 ■ Ohio Chemistry Technology Council (OCTC)
c/o Jack R. Pounds, Pres.
88 E Broad St., Ste.1490
Columbus, OH 43215
Ph: (614)224-1730
Fax: (614)224-5168
E-mail: info@ohiochemistry.org
URL: http://www.ohiochem.org
Contact: Jack R. Pounds, Pres.
State.

14581 ■ Ohio Christmas Tree Association (OCTA)
Two Nationwide Plz.
PO Box 182383
Columbus, OH 43215-2383
Fax: (614)249-2200
Free: (800)288-1225
E-mail: darnold@ofbf.org
URL: http://www.ohiochristmastree.com
Contact: Dale Arnold, Exec.Dir.
State. Christmas tree growers in the state of Ohio.

14582 ■ Ohio Cleaners Association
c/o David W. Field, CAE, Exec.Dir.
17 S High St., Ste.200
Columbus, OH 43215-3458
Ph: (614)221-1900
Fax: (614)221-1989
State.

14583 ■ Ohio Coal Association
17 S High St., Ste.215
Columbus, OH 43215
Ph: (614)228-6336
Fax: (614)228-6349
E-mail: info@ohiocoal.com
URL: http://www.ohiocoal.com
Contact: Michael T. Carey, Pres.
State. Coal owners and operators working with elected and appointed government officials to relay the importance of a vibrant coal industry to Ohio's economic well-being.

14584 ■ Ohio Coin Machine Association (OCMA)
c/o Judith A. Martin, Exec.Dir.
3757 Indianola Ave.
Columbus, OH 43214
Ph: (614)784-9772
Fax: (614)784-9771
E-mail: ocma@the-ocma.org
URL: http://www.the-ocma.org
Contact: Judith A. Martin, Exec.Dir.
State.

14585 ■ Ohio College Personnel Association (OCPA)
c/o Dwayne Todd, Pres.
Columbus Coll. of Art and Design
107 N 9th St.
Columbus, OH 43215
Ph: (614)222-4015
Fax: (614)222-4034
E-mail: dtodd@ccad.edu
URL: http://www.ocpaonline.org
Contact: Dwayne Todd, Pres.
State. Provides outreach, advocacy, research and professional development to foster college student learning. **Affiliated With:** American College Personnel Association.

14586 ■ Ohio Community Development Corp. Association (OCDCA)
33 N Third St., 2nd Fl.
Columbus, OH 43215
Ph: (614)461-6392
Fax: (614)461-1011
E-mail: pkbarnes@ohiocdc.org
URL: http://www.ohiocdc.org
Contact: Patricia Barnes, Exec.Dir.
Founded: 1984. **Members:** 200. **Budget:** $788,934. **State.** Represents 200 Community Development Corporations (CDCs) and their partners. **Affiliated With:** National Congress for Community Economic Development. **Publications:** *Microenterprise*. Directory • *Microlending Guide* • Newsletter, monthly. **Conventions/Meetings:** annual conference • periodic Training Workshop for CDCs.

14587 ■ Ohio Contractors Association
PO Box 909
Columbus, OH 43216
Ph: (614)488-0724
Fax: (614)488-0728
Free: (800)229-1388
E-mail: info@ohiocontractors.org
URL: http://www.ohiocontractors.org
Contact: C. Clark Street, Pres.
State. Affiliated With: American Road and Transportation Builders Association.

14588 ■ Ohio Council of Behavioral Healthcare Providers
36 E Gay St., Ste.401
Columbus, OH 43215
Ph: (614)228-0747
Fax: (614)228-0740
Contact: Mr. Hubert Wirtz, CEO
Founded: 1979. **Members:** 170. **Staff:** 6. **Budget:** $1,000,000. **State.** Professional trade association for private, nonprofit, and corporate community mental health, and drug/alcohol treatment agencies. Seeks to improve community mental health and substance abuse services. Provides training, education, technical assistance, lobbying, products, and services. **Divisions:** Financial Management Group (FMG). **Formerly:** Ohio Council of Community Mental Health and Recovery Organizations. **Publications:** *Ohio Council News*, monthly. Newsletter. **Price:** for members. Alternate Formats: online • *Policy and Marketplace Update*, monthly. Newsletter. **Price:** for members. Alternate Formats: online • *Salary Survey*, biennial • Membership Directory, annual. **Conventions/Meetings:** biennial Best Practices Conference • annual meeting, includes educational training for membership (exhibits).

14589 ■ Ohio Council of Churches (OCC)
6230 Busch Blvd., Ste.430
Columbus, OH 43229
Ph: (614)885-9590
Fax: (614)885-6097
Free: (800)760-9590
E-mail: info@ohcouncilchs.org
URL: http://www.ohcouncilchs.org
Contact: Rev. Rebecca J. Tollefson, Exec.Dir.
Founded: 1919. **Members:** 18. **Staff:** 7. **Budget:** $385,000. **State.** Religious denominations. Comprised of 28 judicatories working together for the common good through social advocacy and public policy efforts. **Committees:** Finance; Interfaith Global Warming; Personnel; Review and Planning. **Special Interest Groups:** Faith; Issues. **Task Forces:** Child Care/Children; Christian/Jewish; Education/Funding; Health Care; Ohio Ministries Convocation; Poverty and Welfare; Racism/Race Relations; Rural Life, Farm Crisis, and Environment. **Publications:** *Legislative Brief*, biweekly. Newsletter. Deals with current national and state issues before legislation. **Price:** $10.00/year. **Circulation:** 750. Also Cited As: *Ohio Impace Newsletter* • *The Ohio Christian News*, quarterly. Newspaper. **Price:** $5.00. ISSN: 0030-0845. **Circulation:** 13,000. Alternate Formats: diskette. **Conventions/Meetings:** annual The Ohio Ministries Convocation - assembly, for clergy and laity (exhibits) - January.

14590 ■ Ohio Council for Home Care (OCHC)
1395 E Dublin-Granville Rd., Ste.350
Columbus, OH 43229
Ph: (614)885-0434
Fax: (614)885-0413
E-mail: ochc@homecareohio.org
URL: http://www.homecareohio.org
Contact: Kathleen Anderson CAE, Exec.Dir.
Founded: 1965. **Members:** 309. **Staff:** 8. **Budget:** $700,000. **For-Profit. State.** Home health agencies, companies, and individuals. Provides information on the home health care industry; monitors and supports legislation; offers workshops and seminars. **Awards:** Dorothy Royce Award. **Frequency:** annual. **Type:** recognition. **Committees:** Education Oversight. **Affiliated With:** National Association for Home Care and Hospice. **Publications:** *The Advocate*, weekly. Newsletter. Contains up-to-date information about the home care industry. **Price:** included in membership dues • *The Bulletin*, weekly. Newsletter. Faxed to OCHC members. **Price:** included in membership dues. **Circulation:** 309 • *Home Care and the Law*, 2-4/year. Newsletter • *Hospice Insider*, monthly. Newsletter • *Ohio Home Health Observer*, quarterly. Newsletter. **Advertising:** accepted • *Resource Guide*, annual. Directory. Provides listing of home care and hospice agencies. **Advertising:** accepted. **Conventions/Meetings:** annual Policy Conference - always spring, in Columbus, OH • annual Remembering Our Past-Celebrating Our Future - conference, plus trade show - always fall, in Columbus, OH.

14591 ■ Ohio Council of Retail Merchants (OCRM)
c/o John C. Mahaney, Jr., Pres./CEO
50 W Broad St., Ste.2020
Columbus, OH 43215
Ph: (614)221-7833
Fax: (614)221-7020
Free: (800)256-4670
URL: http://www.ocrm.net
Contact: John C. Mahaney Jr., Pres./CEO
State. Affiliated With: National Retail Federation.

14592 ■ Ohio Council of Teachers of English Language Arts
c/o Ruth McClain
644 Overlook Dr.
Columbus, OH 43214
Ph: (614)457-0626
E-mail: rmcclain@bright.net
URL: http://www.octela.org
Contact: Ruth McClain, Exec.Dir.
Founded: 1957. **Members:** 2,200. **Membership Dues:** regular, $35 (annual) • student and retiree, $12 (annual). **Staff:** 3. **Regional Groups:** 3. **For-Profit. State. Affiliated With:** National Council of Teachers of English. **Publications:** *OCTELA Newsletter* • *Ohio Journal of English Language Arts*. **Price:** included in membership dues • *Ohio Teachers Write*. Magazine.

14593 ■ Ohio Democratic Party
271 E State St.
Columbus, OH 43215
Ph: (614)221-6563
Fax: (614)221-0721
E-mail: todd@ohiodems.org
URL: http://www.ohiodems.org
Contact: Todd Rensi, Development Dir.
State. Affiliated With: Democratic National Committee.

14594 ■ Ohio Dental Association (ODA)
c/o David Owsiany, JD, Exec.Dir.
1370 Dublin Rd.
Columbus, OH 43215-1098
Ph: (614)486-2700
Fax: (614)486-0381
E-mail: david@oda.org
URL: http://www.oda.org
Contact: David Owsiany JD, Exec.Dir.
Founded: 1866. **Members:** 5,400. **State.** Aims to improve oral health and strengthen dentistry in Ohio by providing resources to advance the dental profession.

14595 ■ Ohio Designer Craftsmen (ODC)
1665 W 5th Ave.
Columbus, OH 43212
Ph: (614)486-4402 (614)486-7119
Fax: (614)486-4402
E-mail: info@ohiocraft.org
URL: http://www.ohiocraft.org
Founded: 1963. **Members:** 2,100. **State.**

14596 ■ Ohio Developmental Disabilities Planning Council
c/o David Zwyer, Exec.Dir.
Ohio Developmental Disabilities Coun.
8 E Long St., Atlas Bldg., 12th Fl.
Columbus, OH 43215
Ph: (614)466-5205
Fax: (614)466-0298
E-mail: david.zwyer@dmr.state.oh.us
Contact: David Zwyer, Exec.Dir.
State. People with developmental disabilities, families and guardians of people with developmental disabilities, representatives from state agencies, nonprofit organizations and agencies that serve people with developmental disabilities. National network of state councils serving people with developmental disabilities. **Affiliated With:** National Association of Councils on Developmental Disabilities.

14597 ■ Ohio Division of Travel and Tourism
PO Box 1001
Columbus, OH 43216-1001
Ph: (614)466-8844
Fax: (614)466-6744
URL: http://www.ohiotourism.com
Contact: Amir Eylon, Interim State Tourism Dir.
State.

14598 ■ Ohio Domestic Violence Network
4807 Evanswood Dr., No. 201
Columbus, OH 43229
Ph: (614)781-9651
Fax: (614)781-9652
Free: (800)934-9840
E-mail: info@odvn.org
URL: http://www.odvn.org
State. Affiliated With: National Coalition Against Domestic Violence.

14599 ■ Ohio Ecological Food and Farm Association (OEFFA)
c/o Laura Weis, Membership Coor./Office Administrator
PO Box 82234
Columbus, OH 43202
Ph: (614)421-2022
Fax: (614)421-2011
E-mail: oeffa@oeffa.com
URL: http://www.oeffa.com
Contact: Laura Weis, Membership Coor./Office Administrator
Founded: 1979. **Members:** 1,000. **Membership Dues:** individual, $35 (annual) • family/non-profit organization, $50 (annual) • small business, $60 (annual) • large business, $100 (annual) • student, $10 (annual) • life, $500. **Staff:** 3. **Budget:** $50,000. **Regional Groups:** 5. **State Groups:** 1. **State.** Farmers, gardeners, and consumers. Works to promote sustainable and healthful agriculture in Ohio and elsewhere. Supports wider study and adoption of resource conserving farm and garden practices, preservation of family farms, use of appropriate technology, greater regional food self-reliance, and the wise development of rural and urban landscape. **Publications:** *OEFFA News*, bimonthly. Newsletter. Includes sustainable agricultural news. **Price:** free for members. **Circulation:** 2,000. **Advertising:** accepted.

14600 ■ Ohio Education Association (OEA)
c/o Dennis M. Reardon, Exec.Dir.
225 E Broad St.
Columbus, OH 43215
Ph: (614)228-4526
Fax: (614)228-8771
Free: (800)282-1500
E-mail: exdirweb@ohea.org
URL: http://www.ohea.org
Contact: Dennis M. Reardon, Exec.Dir.
State.

14601 ■ Ohio Educational Library Media Association (OELMA)
17 S High St., Ste.200
Columbus, OH 43215
Ph: (614)221-1900
Fax: (614)221-1989
E-mail: kate@assnoffices.com
URL: http://www.oelma.org
Contact: Sue Rahn, Pres.
Founded: 1976. **Members:** 1,200. **Membership Dues:** active, $75 (annual) • retired/student, $35 (annual). **Staff:** 1. **Regional Groups:** 6. **State.** Serves as the premier organization for teacher-librarians within the state of Ohio. Promotes professional development, student literacy and achievement, and technological excellence in Ohio's schools. Supports members' efforts to implement guidelines and standards through educational programs, publications, and networking of state affiliate organizations. **Publications:** *OELMA News*. Newsletter • *Ohio Media Spectrum*, quarterly. Journal. **Conventions/Meetings:** annual conference, with trade show - always fall • periodic regional meeting.

14602 ■ Ohio Educational Service Center Association (OESCA)
8050 N High St., Ste.150
Columbus, OH 43235
Ph: (614)846-4080 (614)561-6818
Fax: (614)846-4081
E-mail: info@oesca.org
URL: http://www.oesca.org
Contact: Craig Burford, Exec.Dir.
Members: 60. **Staff:** 2. **Regional Groups:** 11. **State. Awards:** Franklin B. Walter All Scholastic Award. **Frequency:** annual. **Type:** recognition. **Recipient:** for student academic achievement. **Committees:** Accountability and Best Practices; Critical Issues; Special Projects. **Publications:** *The Torch*, quarterly. Newsletter. Contains association news and state policy updates. **Circulation:** 500.

14603 ■ Ohio Electric Utility Institute (OEUI)
PO Box 164203
Columbus, OH 43216-4203
Ph: (614)221-3422
Fax: (614)221-8976
E-mail: bam156@aol.com
URL: http://www.oeui.org
Contact: Beverly Martin, Managing Dir.
Founded: 1951. **State.**

14604 ■ Ohio Environmental Council (OEC)
1207 Grandview Ave., Ste.201
Columbus, OH 43212-3449
Ph: (614)487-7506
Fax: (614)487-7510
E-mail: oec@theoec.org
URL: http://www.theoec.org
Contact: Vicki L. Deisner, Exec.Dir.
State.

14605 ■ Ohio Family Care Association (OFCA)
PO Box 82185
Columbus, OH 43202
Ph: (614)268-7776
Fax: (614)262-7004
E-mail: handers1@columbus.rr.com
URL: http://www.ofcaonline.org
Contact: Bill Anderson, Pres.
State. Seeks to identify and advocate the needs of children in foster care and those who care for them. Works to improve the foster parenting image nationwide and educate the courts, legislators, and the public to the needs of children in the foster care system. Informs foster parents of their legal rights; encourages mandatory parenting skills training and a minimum requirement of pre-service training for all foster parents. Maintains speakers' bureau. **Affiliated With:** National Foster Parent Association.

14606 ■ Ohio Farm Bureau Federation
PO Box 182383
Columbus, OH 43218-2383
Ph: (614)249-2400
Fax: (614)249-2200
URL: http://www.ofbf.org
Contact: John C. Fisher, Exec.VP
Founded: 1919. **Members:** 207,386. **Staff:** 60. **State.** Farmers and others involved in agriculture and related businesses. Represents members' interests. **Publications:** *Buckeye Farm News*, monthly. Magazine. **Circulation:** 207,386. **Advertising:** accepted. **Conventions/Meetings:** annual meeting - always December.

14607 ■ Ohio Farmers Union
175 S 3rd St., Ste.1020
Columbus, OH 43215
Ph: (614)221-9520
Fax: (614)221-7083
Free: (888)610-4400
E-mail: columbus@ohfarmersunion.org
URL: http://www.ohfarmersunion.org
Contact: Gregg Hargett, Government Relations Dir.
State.

14608 ■ Ohio Federation of Soil and Water Conservation Districts (OFSWCD)
PO Box 24518
Columbus, OH 43224
Ph: (614)784-1900
Fax: (614)784-9181
E-mail: jeaneen.hooks@ofswcd.org
Contact: Jeaneen Hooks, Admin.Coor.
State. Formerly: (2005) Ohio Federation of Soil and Water Conservation Districts Soil and Water.

14609 ■ Ohio Federation of Teachers (OFT)
1251 E Broad St.
Columbus, OH 43205-1487
Ph: (614)258-3240
Free: (800)821-1722
E-mail: info@oft-aft.org
URL: http://www.oft-aft.org
Contact: Tom Mooney, Pres.
Members: 20,000. **State.**

14610 ■ Ohio Florists' Association (OFA)
2130 Stella Ct.
Columbus, OH 43215
Ph: (614)487-1117
Fax: (614)487-1216
E-mail: ofa@ofa.org
URL: http://www.ofa.org
Contact: John R. Holmes, Exec.Dir.
Founded: 1929. **Members:** 3,500. **Membership Dues:** business (based on production greenhouse space), $85-$185 (annual) • associate (active member employee, educator, student), $50 (annual). **Staff:** 9. **Regional.** Bedding plant growers, garden centers, interior plantscapers, wholesale and retail florists, educators and professionals in floriculture and horticulture. Offers educational programs and tours. **Publications:** *OFA First News*, 3/year. Newsletter. Contains news and information of interest to the membership. **Price:** included in membership dues. **Circulation:** 3,200 • *Ohio Florists' Association Bulletin*, monthly. Features technical information. **Circulation:** 3,200 • *Tips on Growing.*. Booklet. Series on floriculture. **Conventions/Meetings:** annual trade show, educational; short course (exhibits) - always mid-July, Columbus, OH.

14611 ■ Ohio Flyers Hang Gliding Association
1049 S Washington Ave.
Columbus, OH 43206
Ph: (614)444-6701
E-mail: jalden55@hotmail.com
URL: National Affiliate–www.ushga.org
State. Affiliated With: U.S. Hang Gliding Association.

14612 ■ Ohio Forestry Association
c/o Robert Romig, Exec.Dir.
4080 S High St.
Columbus, OH 43207
Ph: (614)497-9580
Fax: (614)497-9581
E-mail: info@ohioforest.org
URL: http://www.ohioforest.org
Contact: Robert Romig, Exec.Dir.
Founded: 1903. **State.**

14613 ■ Ohio Fruit Growers Society (OFGS)
c/o Tom Sachs, Exec.Dir.
PO Box 182383
Columbus, OH 43218-2383
Ph: (614)246-8292
Fax: (614)249-2200
E-mail: growohio@ofbf.org
URL: http://www.ohiofruit.org
Contact: Jennifer Hungerford, Program Asst.
State.

14614 ■ Ohio Funeral Directors Association (OFDA)
PO Box 21760
Columbus, OH 43221-0760
Ph: (614)486-5339
Fax: (614)486-5358
Free: (800)589-6332
E-mail: steve@ofdaonline.org
URL: http://www.ohiofda.org
Contact: Stephen J. Gehlert, Exec.Dir.
State.

14615 ■ Ohio Gas Association
200 Civic Ctr. Dr., Ste.100
Columbus, OH 43215
Ph: (614)224-1036
Fax: (614)224-1097
E-mail: ohiogas@aol.com
URL: http://www.ohiogasassoc.org
Contact: Roy Rushing, Pres.
Founded: 1971. **Members:** 111. **Membership Dues:** affiliate, $245 (annual). **Staff:** 2. **Regional.** Natural gas trade organization. **Awards:** Safety Award. **Frequency:** annual. **Type:** recognition. **Publications:** Newsletter, periodic. **Advertising:** accepted. **Conventions/Meetings:** annual convention - always September • annual Marketing Seminar (exhibits) - always June • annual Technical Seminar (exhibits) - always March, Columbus, OH.

14616 ■ Ohio Geological Society
c/o Nicole Venteris, Pres.
PO Box 14304
Columbus, OH 43214
Ph: (740)927-6731
E-mail: president@ohgeosoc.org
URL: http://www.ohgeosoc.org
Contact: Nicole Venteris, Pres.
State. Fosters scientific research and advances the science of geology. Promotes technology and inspires high professional conduct. **Affiliated With:** American Association of Petroleum Geologists.

14617 ■ Ohio Golf Association (OGA)
1570 W First Ave.
Columbus, OH 43212
Ph: (614)487-1207
Fax: (614)487-1209
E-mail: golfmaster@ohiogolf.org
URL: http://www.ohiogolf.org
Contact: Hugh Wall III, Pres.
State. Affiliated With: International Association of Golf Administrators.

14618 ■ Ohio Government Finance Officers Association
c/o Nancy Waterhouse, Exec.Dir.
17 S High St., Ste.200
Columbus, OH 43215
Ph: (614)221-1900
Fax: (614)221-1989
E-mail: gfoa@assnoffices.com
URL: http://www.ohgfoa.com
Contact: Nancy Waterhouse, Exec.Dir.
Membership Dues: non-governmental institution, $140 (annual) • associate (student, intern, and retiree), $20 (annual) • government institution (based on annual revenue), $40-$70 (annual). **State.** Works to meet the challenges of the ever-evolving profession of government finance and fosters increased cooperation among governments and private financial institutes by promoting the exchange of information among finance officers of all local governments. Gives wealthy information concerning government and private finance through programs and publications.

14619 ■ Ohio Grantmakers Forum (OGF)
c/o George E. Espy, Pres.
37 W Broad St., Ste.800
Columbus, OH 43215-4198
Ph: (614)224-1344
Fax: (614)224-1388
E-mail: info@ohiograntmakers.org
URL: http://www.ohiograntmakers.org
Contact: George E. Espy, Pres.
State. Functions as a resource for organized philanthropy in Ohio.

14620 ■ Ohio Grocers Association (OGA)
3280 Riverside Dr., Ste.10
Columbus, OH 43221
Ph: (614)442-5511
Fax: (614)442-5516
E-mail: tom@ohiogrocers.org
URL: http://www.ohiogrocers.org
Contact: Mr. Thomas S. Jackson CAE, Pres./CEO
Founded: 1899. **Members:** 600. **Membership Dues:** retailer (based on annual sales), $145-$2,295 (an-

nual) • associate (based on annual sales), $395-$1,995 (annual) • food broker (based on annual sales), $125-$225 (annual) • wholesaler (minimum), $2,500 (annual). **Staff:** 9. **Budget:** $1,000,000. **State Groups:** 1. **Local Groups:** 3. **State**. Trade association for the grocery industry in OH. **Awards:** Hall of Fame. **Frequency:** annual. **Type:** recognition. **Recipient:** for excellence in industry • Pinnacle. **Frequency:** annual. **Type:** recognition. **Recipient:** for excellence in industry. **Computer Services:** Online services, membership services and benefits. **Committees:** Loss Prevention. **Publications:** *Action Report*, as needed. Newsletter. **Price:** included in membership dues. **Circulation:** 800 • *OhioGrocer*, quarterly. Magazine. **Price:** included in membership dues. **Circulation:** 1,100. **Advertising:** accepted.

14621 ■ Ohio Harness Horsemen's Association (OHHA)
c/o Jerry Knappenberger, Gen.Mgr.
800 Michigan Ave.
Columbus, OH 43215-1166
Ph: (614)221-3650
Fax: (614)221-8726
Free: (800)353-6442
E-mail: jlknappenberger@ohha.com
URL: http://www.ohha.com
State.

14622 ■ Ohio Health Care Association, District 7
c/o David Parker, Chm.
HCR Manorcare
1876 Wyandotte Rd.
Columbus, OH 43212
Ph: (614)486-9112
Fax: (614)573-7668
E-mail: dparker@hcr-manorcare.com
URL: http://www.ohca.org
Contact: David Parker, Chm.
Local. Promotes professionalism and ethical behavior of individuals providing long-term care delivery for patients and for the general public. Provides information, education and administrative tools to enhance the quality of long-term care. Improves the standards of service and administration of member nursing homes. **Affiliated With:** American Health Care Association.

14623 ■ Ohio High School Athletic Association (OHSAA)
c/o Daniel B. Ross, PhD, Commissioner
4080 Roselea Pl.
Columbus, OH 43214
Ph: (614)267-2502
Fax: (614)267-1677
E-mail: dross@ohsaa.org
URL: http://www.ohsaa.org
Contact: Daniel B. Ross PhD, Commissioner
State. Works to regulate, supervise and administer interscholastic athletic competition among its member schools. Strives to make interscholastic programs become integral factor in the total educational program of the schools. **Affiliated With:** National Federation of State High School Associations.

14624 ■ Ohio Historical Society (OHS)
1982 Velma Ave.
Columbus, OH 43211-2453
Ph: (614)297-2300
Fax: (614)297-2352
E-mail: bneale@ohiohistory.org
URL: http://www.ohiohistory.org
Contact: Dr. William K. Laidlaw Jr., Exec.Dir.
Founded: 1885. **Members:** 9,600. **Membership Dues:** lover, $75 (annual) • seer, $50 (annual) • student, $30 (annual) • patriot, $175 (annual) • preserver, $150 (annual) • entrepreneur, $300 (annual). **State**. Interprets, preserves, collects and makes available evidence of the past. Provides leadership on furthering knowledge, understanding and appreciation of the prehistory and history of Ohio. **Libraries: Type:** open to the public. **Holdings:** 317,000; archival material, articles, audiovisuals, books, maps, periodicals. **Subjects:** Ohio history from settlement to the present, Ohio archaeology and natural history. **Computer Services:** Online services, collections catalog via email. **Publications:** *Echoes*, monthly. Newsletter. **Price:** included in membership dues • *Ohio History*. Journal. Alternate Formats: online • *TIMELINE*, bimonthly. Magazine.

14625 ■ Ohio Home Builders Association
c/o Vincent Squillace, CAE BIAE
17 S High St., Ste.700
Columbus, OH 43215-3413
Ph: (614)228-6647
Fax: (614)228-5149
E-mail: vsquillace@ohiohba.com
URL: http://www.ohiohba.com
Contact: Vince Squillace, Exec.Dir.
State. Single and multifamily home builders, commercial builders, and others associated with the building industry. **Affiliated With:** National Association of Home Builders.

14626 ■ Ohio Hospital Association (OHA)
155 E Broad St., 15th Fl.
Columbus, OH 43215-3620
Ph: (614)221-7614
Fax: (614)221-4771
E-mail: oha@ohanet.org
URL: http://www.ohanet.org
Contact: James R. Castle, Pres./CEO
Founded: 1915. **Members:** 4,250. **Staff:** 45. **Budget:** $5,000,000. **Regional Groups:** 4. **State**. Hospitals (250); individuals and organizations that support hospitals (4000). Assists hospitals and related organizations in serving community health care needs. **Publications:** *Health e-NEWS Plus*, weekly. Newsletter. Alternate Formats: online • *Return on Investment*, annual. Annual Report. Alternate Formats: online. **Conventions/Meetings:** annual convention - always April.

14627 ■ Ohio Hotel and Lodging Association (OH&LA)
692 N High St., Ste.212
Columbus, OH 43215
Ph: (614)461-6462
Fax: (614)224-4714
Free: (800)589-6462
E-mail: info@ohla.org
URL: http://www.ohla.org
Contact: Amir Eylon, Exec.VP
Founded: 1893. **Members:** 550. **Membership Dues:** active (with 5 rooms or less), property under construction, $165 • bed and breakfast, $100 • allied, $400. **Staff:** 5. **Budget:** $500,000. **State**. Hotels and motels. Provides representation, information and resources for the Ohio lodging industry, promotes the Ohio travel and tourism industry, and increases membership value. **Affiliated With:** American Hotel and Lodging Association. **Formerly:** (1998) Ohio Hotel & Motel Association. **Publications:** *Inn-House*, quarterly. Newsletter. **Price:** $75.00 per issue (50 words of copy). **Circulation:** 1,200. **Advertising:** accepted. Alternate Formats: online • *Purchasing Directory*, annual. Contains listings of allied vendor. **Price:** free. **Advertising:** accepted • *Travel Directory*, annual. Membership Directory. **Conventions/Meetings:** annual meeting (exhibits) - always November.

14628 ■ Ohio Humanities Council (OHC)
471 E Broad St., Ste.1620
Columbus, OH 43215-3857
Ph: (614)461-7802
Fax: (614)461-4651
Free: (800)293-9774
E-mail: ohc@ohiohumanities.org
URL: http://www.ohiohumanities.org
Contact: Gale E. Peterson, Exec.Dir.
State. Encourages public understanding and utilization of the humanities. Promotes the application of the humanities in American life. **Affiliated With:** Federation of State Humanities Councils.

14629 ■ Ohio Insurance Institute (OII)
PO Box 816
Columbus, OH 43215-4321
Ph: (614)228-1593
Fax: (614)228-1678
E-mail: info@ohioinsurance.org
URL: http://www.ohioinsurance.org
Contact: Daniel J. Kelso, Pres.
Founded: 1968. **State**.

14630 ■ Ohio Jewelers Association
c/o Adriana A. Sfalcin, Exec.Dir.
51 W Broad St., Ste.2020
Columbus, OH 43215
Ph: (614)221-2237
Fax: (614)221-7020
Free: (800)652-6257
State.

14631 ■ Ohio Land Improvement Contractors Association (OLICA)
c/o Dale Arnold, Exec.Dir.
PO Box 182383
Columbus, OH 43218-2383
Ph: (614)246-8294
Fax: (614)249-2200
E-mail: darnold@ofbf.org
URL: http://www.olica.org
Contact: Dale Arnold, Exec.Dir.
State. Organization of conservation, environmental and land improvement construction companies, support businesses, soil scientists and interested parties. Conduct seminars, meeting, field days and training schools on conservation/environmental construction, safety and small business management.

14632 ■ Ohio Land Title Association (OLTA)
c/o Daniel H. Dozer, CAE, Exec.Dir.
2500 E Main St., Ste.100
Columbus, OH 43209-2483
Ph: (614)235-5001
Fax: (614)235-0880
Free: (888)292-6582
E-mail: dan@olta.org
URL: http://www.olta.org
Contact: Daniel H. Dozer CAE, Exec.Dir.
State.

14633 ■ Ohio League of Conservation Voters (OLCV)
c/o Bill Demora
1200 W Fifth Ave.
Columbus, OH 43212-3449
Ph: (614)481-0517
E-mail: olcv_info@ohiolcv.org
URL: http://www.ohiolcv.org
Contact: Bill Demora, Exec.Dir.
Founded: 1999. **Membership Dues:** $35 (annual). **State**. **Formerly:** (2005) Ohio League of +Conservation +Voters +Education Fund.

14634 ■ Ohio Licensed Beverage Association (OLBA)
c/o Phil Craig, Exec.Dir.
37 W Broad St., Ste.480
Columbus, OH 43215
Ph: (614)224-3840
Fax: (614)241-2215
Free: (800)678-5995
E-mail: pcraig@craiggroup.com
URL: http://www.olba.org
Contact: Phil Craig, Exec.Dir.
Founded: 1935. **State**. Protects and advances the interests and welfare of retail and liquor permit holders in Ohio. **Affiliated With:** National Licensed Beverage Association. **Publications:** *Ohio Beverage Journal*, periodic • *Ohio Tavern News*, periodic. Newsletter. **Conventions/Meetings:** quarterly meeting - always March, June, September, and December.

14635 ■ Ohio Literacy Network (OLN)
c/o Maureen O'Rourke, Exec.Dir.
6161 Busch Blvd., Ste.340
Columbus, OH 43229

Ph: (614)505-0716
Fax: (614)505-0718
Free: (800)228-READ
E-mail: info@ohioliteracynetwork.org
URL: http://www.ohioliteracynetwork.org
Contact: Maureen O'Rourke, Exec.Dir.

Founded: 1987. **Members:** 300. **Membership Dues:** individual, $25 (annual) • nonprofit organization, $65 (annual) • literacy student/volunteer, $5 (annual). **State.** Seeks to increase adult literacy and to create awareness of adult literacy issues, needs and services. **Affiliated With:** Laubach Literacy International. **Publications:** *Literacy Communicator*, bimonthly. Newsletter. Alternate Formats: online. **Conventions/Meetings:** quarterly board meeting • annual meeting.

14636 ■ Ohio Lumbermen's Association (OLA)
41 Croswell Rd.
Columbus, OH 43214
Ph: (614)267-7817 (614)267-7816
Fax: (614)267-6448
Free: (800)282-4632
E-mail: olaoffices@ohiolumber.org
URL: http://www.ohiolumber.org
Contact: John C. Benson, Exec.VP

Founded: 1881. **Members:** 450. **Membership Dues:** affiliate, $60 (annual) • associate, $460 (annual). **Staff:** 6. **State.** Lumber dealers and manufacturers. Informs members of industry activity. Organizes lobbying activities. Sponsors seminars and educational programs. Conducts analyses of operating costs and salaries. **Libraries: Type:** open to the public. **Awards:** The Charles E. and Marian Benson Scholarship Fund. **Frequency:** annual. **Type:** scholarship. **Recipient:** to OSU forestry student. **Affiliated With:** National Lumber and Building Material Dealers Association. **Publications:** *Building Material Dealer*, monthly. Magazine. **Price:** $24.00/year. **Circulation:** 9,000. **Advertising:** accepted • *Buyer's Guide & Dealer Directory*, annual • *Timber Talk*, monthly. Newsletter. **Conventions/Meetings:** annual trade show (exhibits).

14637 ■ Ohio Manufacturers' Association (OMA)
33 N High St.
Columbus, OH 43215
Ph: (614)224-5111
Fax: (614)224-1012
Free: (800)662-4463
E-mail: oma@ohiomfg.com
URL: http://www.ohiomfg.com
Contact: Eric L. Burkland, Pres.

State.

14638 ■ Ohio Middle School Association (OMSA)
c/o Philip Binkley
PO Box 20363
Columbus, OH 43220
Ph: (614)457-3750
Fax: (614)457-5099
E-mail: pbinkley@hotmail.com
URL: http://www.ohiomsa.org
Contact: Philip Binkley, Exec.Dir.

Founded: 1972. **Members:** 7,200. **Membership Dues:** individual, $25 (annual) • building, $150 (annual). **Staff:** 1. **Regional Groups:** 8. **State.** Individuals interested in education in middle and junior high schools. Promotes new, innovative, and exemplary programs. Holds regional workshops, in-service programs, and visitations to model schools. **Awards:** OMSA Recognition and Component Awards. **Frequency:** annual. **Type:** recognition. **Recipient:** for student/staff recognition, exemplary middle level programs. **Affiliated With:** National Middle School Association. **Publications:** *In the Middle*, 3/year. Newsletter. **Price:** included in membership dues • *OMSA Journal*, 3/year. **Price:** included in membership dues. **Conventions/Meetings:** annual conference (exhibits).

14639 ■ Ohio Mortgage Bankers Association (OMBA)
PO Box 2405
Columbus, OH 43216-2405
Ph: (614)221-9493
Fax: (614)221-2335
E-mail: omba@ohiomba.org
URL: http://www.ohiomba.org
Contact: Brad L. Feldman MPA, Exec.VP/Exec.Dir.

Founded: 1961. **Members:** 150. **Staff:** 2. **State Groups:** 1. **Local Groups:** 5. **State. Publications:** *Capital Comments*, quarterly. Newsletter. **Advertising:** accepted. **Conventions/Meetings:** annual meeting (exhibits) - always May.

14640 ■ Ohio Municipal League (OML)
c/o Susan J. Cave, Exec.Dir.
175 S 3rd St., Ste.510
Columbus, OH 43215
Ph: (614)221-4349
Fax: (614)221-4390
E-mail: omunileague@copper.net
URL: http://www.omunileague.org
Contact: Susan J. Cave, Exec.Dir.

State. Affiliated With: National League of Cities.

14641 ■ Ohio Museums Association
c/o Mrs. Therese M. Potenzini, Exec.Dir.
1982 Velma Rd.
Columbus, OH 43211
Ph: (614)297-2375
Fax: (614)297-2376
E-mail: oma@ohiohistory.org
URL: http://ohiomuseums.org
Contact: Mrs. Therese M. Potenzini, Exec.Dir.

Founded: 1976. **Members:** 380. **Membership Dues:** all (depending on budget), $35-$500 (annual). **Staff:** 2. **Budget:** $68,000. **State Groups:** 1. **State.** Museums and museum employees in Ohio. Strive to enhance the ability of Ohio Museums in serving the public interests by providing a forum for support and communication. **Libraries: Type:** not open to the public; lending; reference. **Holdings:** 100; articles, books. **Subjects:** museums. **Awards:** Outstanding Achievement, Distinguished Museum Professional. **Frequency:** annual. **Type:** trophy. **Recipient:** for museums or individuals who demonstrate going above or beyond the call of duty • Visual Communication Award. **Frequency:** annual. **Type:** recognition. **Recipient:** for success of a visual piece such as a catalogue, brochure, ad campaign, annual report and poster. **Computer Services:** Mailing lists. **Boards:** Board of Trustees. **Publications:** *Ohio Museums*, biennial. Magazine. **Price:** free. **Circulation:** 800. **Advertising:** accepted • *Ohio Museums*, monthly. Newsletter. **Price:** free. **Circulation:** 420. **Advertising:** accepted. **Conventions/Meetings:** annual conference, with 16 sessions, awards banquet, tours of museums (exhibits) - 2 1/2 day.

14642 ■ Ohio National Congress of Parents and Teachers
40 Northwoods Blvd.
Columbus, OH 43235
Ph: (614)781-6344
Fax: (614)781-6349
E-mail: oh_office@pta.org
URL: http://www.ohiopta.org

State. Libraries: Type: reference; not open to the public. **Subjects:** children, education. **Awards: Frequency:** annual. **Type:** recognition. **Recipient:** for achieving the mission of the PTA. **Computer Services:** Online services. **Affiliated With:** National PTA - National Congress of Parents and Teachers. **Also Known As:** (2004) Ohio PTA. **Publications:** *Ohio PTA - The News*, 8/year. Newsletter. Contains information about the Ohio PTA. **Price:** $12.00/year. ISSN: 01990918. **Circulation:** 1,500. **Advertising:** accepted. **Conventions/Meetings:** annual meeting.

14643 ■ Ohio Native Plant Society, Central Ohio Chapter
1411 Cambridge Rd.
Columbus, OH 43212
Ph: (614)488-3671
URL: http://groups.msn.com/NativePlantSocietyofNortheastOhio/chapters.msnw
Contact: Susan Ramser, Pres.

Local.

14644 ■ Ohio Network of Children's Advocacy Centers (ONCAC)
c/o Ben Murray, Exec.Dir.
131 N High St., Ste.620
Columbus, OH 43215
Ph: (614)221-7994
Fax: (614)221-8442
E-mail: mail@oncac.org
URL: http://www.oncac.org
Contact: Ben Murray, Exec.Dir.

State.

14645 ■ Ohio Newspaper Association (ONA)
1335 Dublin Rd., Ste.216 B
Columbus, OH 43215
Ph: (614)486-6677
Fax: (614)486-4940
E-mail: fdeaner@ohionews.org
URL: http://www.ohionews.org
Contact: Frank E. Deaner, Exec.Dir.

Founded: 1933. **State.**

14646 ■ Ohio Nurses Association
4000 E Main St.
Columbus, OH 43213-2950
Ph: (614)237-5414
Fax: (614)237-6074
Contact: Michele Prater, Marketing Specialist

Founded: 1904. **Members:** 9,000. **Staff:** 30. **State Groups:** 1. **Local Groups:** 1. **State.** Advocate for professional nursing, nurses, and quality health care in Ohio. **Libraries: Type:** not open to the public. **Subjects:** nursing, law, public health. **Affiliated With:** American Nurses Association. **Publications:** *Ohio Nurses Review*, monthly. Magazine. Professional journal of OMA for registered nurses. **Price:** $30.00/year. ISSN: 0030-0993. **Circulation:** 9,000. **Advertising:** accepted. **Conventions/Meetings:** biennial convention (exhibits).

14647 ■ Ohio Nursing Students' Association (ONSA)
c/o Ohio Nurses Association
4000 E Main St.
Columbus, OH 43213
E-mail: info@choosenursingoh.com
URL: http://www.choosenursingoh.com
Contact: Jessica Galaska, Pres.

State. Promotes the nursing profession. Encourages programs and learning opportunities connected with nursing and health. Advocates the participation of nursing students in developing health care methods offered to the public. **Affiliated With:** National Student Nurses' Association.

14648 ■ Ohio Occupational Therapy Association (OOTA)
PO Box 32252
Columbus, OH 43232
Fax: (614)231-0830
Free: (888)231-7319
E-mail: webmaster@oota.org
URL: http://www.oota.org
Contact: Jan Seabaugh, Exec.Sec.

State. Advances the quality, availability, use and support of occupational therapy through standard-setting, advocacy, education and research. **Affiliated With:** American Occupational Therapy Association.

14649 ■ Ohio Osteopathic Association (OOA)
c/o Jon F. Wills, Exec.Dir.
PO Box 8130
Columbus, OH 43201

Ph: (614)299-2107
Fax: (614)294-0457
Free: (800)234-4848
E-mail: jwills@ooanet.org
URL: http://www.ooanet.org
Contact: Jon F. Wills, Exec.Dir.
Founded: 1898. **Members:** 1,350. **Staff:** 6. **State.**

14650 ■ Ohio Petroleum Council
c/o Terry P. Fleming, Exec.Dir.
88 E. Broad St., Ste.1460
Columbus, OH 43215
Ph: (614)221-5439
Fax: (614)221-1914

14651 ■ Ohio Petroleum Gas Association
18 S High St., Ste.200
Columbus, OH 43215
Ph: (614)221-1900
Fax: (614)221-1989
Contact: Anita Field, Exec.Sec
State.

14652 ■ Ohio Pharmacists Association (OPA)
2155 Riverside Dr.
Columbus, OH 43221-4052
Ph: (614)586-1497
Fax: (614)586-1545
E-mail: info@ohiopharmacists.org
URL: http://www.ohiopharmacists.org
Contact: Ernest E. Boyd CAE, Exec.Dir.
Founded: 1879. **State.**

14653 ■ Ohio Podiatric Medical Association (OPMA)
5310 McKitrick Blvd.
Columbus, OH 43235
Ph: (614)457-6269
Fax: (614)457-3375
E-mail: info@opma.org
URL: http://www.opma.org
Contact: Ms. Debbie Bratka CAE, Operations Mgr.
Founded: 1915. **Members:** 500. **Staff:** 3. **Local Groups:** 8. **State. Affiliated With:** American Podiatric Medical Association. **Publications:** *Ohio Podiatric Medical Association News Journal*, quarterly. **Advertising:** accepted. Alternate Formats: online.

14654 ■ Ohio Pork Producers Council (OPPC)
c/o Richard Isler, Exec.VP
5930 Sharon Woods Blvd., Ste.101
Columbus, OH 43229
Ph: (614)882-5887
Fax: (614)882-6077
Free: (800)320-7991
E-mail: oppc@ohiopork.org
URL: http://www.ohiopork.org
Contact: Tony Bornhorst, Pres.
Founded: 1968. **State.**

14655 ■ Ohio Poultry Association (OPA)
5930 Sharon Wood Blvd., Ste.102
Columbus, OH 43229
Ph: (614)882-6111
URL: http://www.ohiopoultry.org
Contact: David White, Contact
Founded: 1948. **Members:** 600. **Staff:** 3. **Budget:** $750,000. **State Groups:** 4. **State.** Serves and promotes Ohio's poultry farms. **Affiliated With:** National Turkey Federation. **Publications:** *Ohio Poultry Association Newsletter*, quarterly. **Price:** included in membership dues. **Advertising:** accepted. **Conventions/Meetings:** annual conference.

14656 ■ Ohio Primary Care Association (OPCA)
4150 Indianola Ave.
Columbus, OH 43214
Ph: (614)884-3101
Fax: (614)884-3108
Free: (888)884-3101
E-mail: sfrick@ohiopca.org
URL: http://www.ohiopca.org
Contact: Shawn Frick, Exec.Dir.
Founded: 1983. **State.**

14657 ■ Ohio Professionals for School-Age Children
c/o Becky Ketron, Pres.
2425 Bethel Rd.
Columbus, OH 43220
Ph: (937)416-5174
E-mail: ketronrr@aol.com
URL: National Affiliate–www.nsaca.org
Contact: Becky Ketron, Pres.
Founded: 1986. **Members:** 300. **Membership Dues:** individual, student, $35 (annual) • agency with 5-25 staff, $125-$625 (annual). **State Groups:** 1. **Local Groups:** 12. **State.** Dedicated to advocating, supporting and educating for quality school-age programming for all children in Ohio. Provides technical assistance and professional development opportunities for individuals who work with school-age children. **Awards:** Pursuit of Excellence. **Frequency:** annual. **Type:** recognition. **Recipient:** for individuals who work directly with school age children at least 50% of their time; must be a member in good standing of OPSAC; must be nominated, reviewed, and observed. **Committees:** Coalition Building; Communications; Governance; Professional Development; Public Policy; Pursuit of Excellence; Resource Development. **Affiliated With:** National AfterSchool Association. **Formerly:** (2004) Ohio Professionals for School-Age Care. **Publications:** Newsletter. **Price:** for members. **Advertising:** accepted. Alternate Formats: online. **Conventions/Meetings:** annual Spring Extravaganza - conference, for school age and youth development program professionals (exhibits).

14658 ■ Ohio Program Evaluators' Group (OPEG)
c/o Sandy Lock, Treas.
PO Box 992
Columbus, OH 43216
Ph: (216)368-2711 (216)658-1879
E-mail: fischer@case.edu
URL: http://www.opeg.org
Contact: Rob Fischer, Pres.
State. Seeks to improve evaluation practices and methods. Provides a forum for professional development, networking and exchange of practical, methodological and theoretical knowledge in the field of evaluation. Promotes evaluation as a profession. **Affiliated With:** American Evaluation Association.

14659 ■ Ohio Propane Gas Association (OPGA)
17 S High St., Ste.200
Columbus, OH 43215
Ph: (614)221-1900
Fax: (614)221-1989
E-mail: opga@assnoffices.com
URL: http://www.ohiopropanegas.org
Contact: David Archer, Pres.
Founded: 1948. **Members:** 200. **Membership Dues:** associate, $235 (annual) • individual, cylinder retailer, $125 (annual) • independent marketer (first plant; plus 315 for each additional branch), $800 (annual). **State.** Promotes and develops the propane gas industry in the state of OH. **Publications:** *Ohio Propane News*, bimonthly. Newsletter. **Conventions/Meetings:** annual convention - always August in Huron, OH • quarterly meeting, membership meeting.

14660 ■ Ohio Prosecuting Attorneys Association (OPAA)
196 E State St., Ste.200
Columbus, OH 43215
Ph: (614)221-1266
Fax: (614)221-0753
E-mail: delores@ohiopa.org
URL: http://www.ohiopa.org
Contact: Delores Wilson, Admin.Asst.
State.

14661 ■ Ohio Provider Resource Association (OPRA)
30 Spruce St.
Columbus, OH 43215
Ph: (614)224-6772
Fax: (614)224-3340
E-mail: opra@opra.org
URL: http://www.opra.org
Contact: Dorothy Saunders, Office Mgr.
Founded: 1974. **Members:** 230. **Staff:** 4. **Budget:** $500,000. **Regional Groups:** 8. **State.** Advocates for community based service provider to persons with developmental disabilities. **Formerly:** Ohio Private Residential Association. **Publications:** *Agenda*, monthly. Newsletter. **Conventions/Meetings:** biennial meet (exhibits).

14662 ■ Ohio Psychiatric Association (OPA)
c/o Janet Shaw, MD, Exec.Dir.
1350 W 5th Ave., Ste.218
Columbus, OH 43212
Ph: (614)481-7555
Fax: (614)481-7559
E-mail: jshaw@ohiopsych.org
URL: http://www.ohiopsych.org
Contact: Janet Shaw MD, Exec.Dir.
State. Promotes the study of mental disorders. **Affiliated With:** American Psychiatric Association. **Publications:** *Insight Matters*, quarterly. Newsletter.

14663 ■ Ohio Psychological Association (OPA)
400 E Town St., Ste.200
Columbus, OH 43215
Ph: (614)224-0034
Fax: (614)224-2059
Free: (800)783-1983
E-mail: postmaster@ohpsych.org
URL: http://www.ohpsych.org
Contact: Michael O. Ranney MPA, Exec.Dir.
Founded: 1947. **Members:** 1,600. **Staff:** 5. **State.** Advances psychology as a science, profession, and as a means of promoting human welfare. **Publications:** *Ohio Psychologist*, bimonthly. Magazine. **Price:** $25.00 /year for nonmembers; included in membership dues. **Conventions/Meetings:** annual convention.

14664 ■ Ohio Public Interest Research Group
36 W Gay St., Ste.315
Columbus, OH 43215
Ph: (614)460-8732
E-mail: info@ohiopirg.org
URL: http://www.ohiopirg.org
State.

14665 ■ Ohio Ready Mixed Concrete Association (ORMCA)
PO Box 29190
Columbus, OH 43229-0190
Ph: (614)891-0210
Fax: (614)891-2675
E-mail: ormca@infinet.com
URL: http://www.ohioconcrete.org
Contact: Kenneth L. Caubble, Pres./Exec.Dir.
Founded: 1938. **State.**

14666 ■ Ohio Region of Narcotics Anonymous
PO Box 546
Columbus, OH 43216
Ph: (614)252-1700
Free: (800)587-4232
URL: http://www.naohio.org
State. Affiliated With: Narcotics Anonymous.

14667 ■ Ohio Restaurant Association (ORA)
1525 Bethel Rd., Ste.301
Columbus, OH 43220-2054
Ph: (614)442-3535
Fax: (614)442-3550
Free: (800)282-9049
E-mail: info@ohiorestaurant.org
URL: http://www.ohiorestaurant.org
Contact: Geoff Hetrick, Pres./CEO
Founded: 1920. **Members:** 2,500. **Membership Dues:** restaurant, $195-$4,600 (annual) • purveyor, $200-$500 (annual) • associate, $80 (annual). **Staff:** 10. **Local Groups:** 10. **State.** Works for the represen-

tation, education, assistance and promotion of the Ohio restaurant industry. **Libraries: Type:** open to the public. **Subjects:** restaurant information. **Awards:** Lifetime Achievement. **Frequency:** annual. **Type:** recognition. **Publications:** *AlaCarte*, monthly. Newsletter • *Membership Directory and Hotline*, annual. **Circulation:** 2,500. **Advertising:** accepted • Magazine, monthly. **Conventions/Meetings:** annual Mid-America Softserve and Pizza Show - convention (exhibits) - always in February.

14668 ■ Ohio Right to Life Society
2238 S Hamilton Rd., Ste.200
Columbus, OH 43232-2000
Ph: (614)864-5200
Fax: (614)864-5222
E-mail: life@ohiolife.org
URL: http://www.ohiolife.org
Contact: Denise Mackura, Exec.Dir.

State. Affiliated With: National Right to Life Committee.

14669 ■ Ohio Rural Electric Cooperatives (OREC)
c/o Anthony Ahern, Pres./CEO
PO Box 26036
Columbus, OH 43226-0036
Ph: (614)846-5757
URL: http://www.buckeyepower.com

State.

14670 ■ Ohio School Boards Association (OSBA)
c/o John M. Brandt, Exec.Dir.
8050 N High St., Ste.100
Columbus, OH 43235-6482
Ph: (614)540-4000
Fax: (614)540-4100
Free: (800)589-6722
E-mail: j_brandt@osba-ohio.org
URL: http://www.osba-ohio.org
Contact: John M. Brandt, Exec.Dir.

Founded: 1955. **Members:** 738. **Staff:** 49. **Budget:** $4,600,000. **Regional Groups:** 5. **State.** Boards of education. Acts as an educational service organization to all the public school boards in the state of Ohio. **Affiliated With:** National School Boards Association. **Publications:** *OSBA Briefcase*, bimonthly. Newsletter • *OSBA Journal*, 10/year. Magazine • *OSBA Legislative Report*, weekly, during legislative session. **Conventions/Meetings:** annual conference (exhibits) - always in Columbus, OH.

14671 ■ Ohio Self Insurers Association
PO Box 1008
Columbus, OH 43216-1008
Ph: (614)464-5660
Fax: (614)464-6350
E-mail: rrobetz@vssp.com
Contact: Mr. Robin Obetz, Exec.Sec.

Founded: 1974. **Members:** 600. **Staff:** 1. **Budget:** $700,000. **Local Groups:** 4. **State.** Self insured employers. Supports workers compensation. **Publications:** *C-Me*, quarterly. Newsletter • Directory, annual. **Price:** included in membership dues. **Conventions/Meetings:** annual conference - always June; Avg. Attendance: 300.

14672 ■ Ohio Sheep Improvement Association (OSIA)
c/o Roger High, Exec.Dir.
PO Box 182383
Columbus, OH 43218-2383
Ph: (614)246-8299
Fax: (614)246-8699
E-mail: rmayhugh@ofbf.org
URL: http://www.ohiosheep.org
Contact: Roger High, Exec.Dir.

State. Affiliated With: American Sheep Industry Association.

14673 ■ Ohio Society of Anesthesiologists (OSA)
3757 Indianola Ave.
Columbus, OH 43214-3753
Ph: (614)784-9721
Fax: (614)784-9771
E-mail: osa@osainc.org
URL: http://www.osainc.org
Contact: Jerome F. O'Hara Jr., Pres.-Elect

State. Strives to raise and maintain the standards of the medical practice of anesthesiology. Seeks to improve the care of the patient. Encourages education, research and scientific progress in anesthesiology. **Affiliated With:** American Society of Anesthesiologists.

14674 ■ Ohio Society of Professional Engineers (OSPE)
c/o Tim Schaffer, Exec.Dir.
4795 Evanswood Dr., Ste.201
Columbus, OH 43229-7216
Ph: (614)846-1144
Fax: (614)846-1131
Free: (800)654-9481
E-mail: ospe@iwaynet.net
URL: http://www.ohioengineer.com
Contact: Tim Schaffer, Exec.Dir.

State.

14675 ■ Ohio Soft Drink Association
1525 Bethel Rd., Ste.302
Columbus, OH 43220-2054
Ph: (614)442-1803
Fax: (614)442-1830
E-mail: osda@rrcol.com

Local.

14676 ■ Ohio Soybean Council
c/o John Lumpe, Exec.Dir.
4625 Morse Rd., Ste.101
Columbus, OH 43230
Ph: (614)476-3100
Fax: (614)476-9576
Free: (888)SOY-OHIO
E-mail: jlumpe@soyohio.org
URL: http://www.soyohio.org
Contact: John Lumpe, Exec.Dir.

State. Invests "soybean check-off funds" in order to maximize the profits of soybean farmers in Ohio.

14677 ■ Ohio Spill Planning Prevention and Emergency Response Association
c/o Joel Hogue
PO Box 261045
Columbus, OH 43226-1045
URL: National Affiliate–www.naroil.com

State.

14678 ■ Ohio State Assembly of the Association of Surgical Technologists
PO Box 20588
Columbus, OH 43220-0588
E-mail: rturner125@adelphia.net
URL: http://www.ohioast.org
Contact: Jean Carty-Turner, Pres.

State. Represents surgical technologists. Aims to study, discuss, and exchange knowledge, experience, and ideas in the field of surgical technology. Promotes a high standard of surgical technology performance in the community for quality patient care. **Affiliated With:** Association of Surgical Technologists.

14679 ■ Ohio State Association of Nurse Anesthetists (OSANA)
17 S High St., Ste.200
Columbus, OH 43215
Ph: (614)221-1900
Fax: (614)221-1989
E-mail: peggy@assnoffices.com
URL: http://www.osana.org
Contact: Peggy Blankenship, Dir. of Services

State.

14680 ■ Ohio State Bar Association (OSBA)
c/o Denny L. Ramey, CAE, Exec.Dir.
PO Box 16562
Columbus, OH 43216-6562
Ph: (614)487-2050
Fax: (614)487-1008
Free: (800)282-6556
E-mail: osba@ohiobar.org
URL: http://www.ohiobar.org
Contact: Mr. Ken Brown, Dir. of PR

Founded: 1880. **Members:** 30,000. **State.** Represents more than 25000 Ohio lawyers and judges, nearly 75 percent of Ohio law practitioners which includes legal assistant and law student associate members. Works for the advancement of science of jurisprudence; promotes improvement of the law and administration of justice; upholds integrity, honor and courtesy in the legal profession and encourage and enforce adherence to high standards of professional conduct; takes positions on matters of public interest as deemed advisable; encourages thorough legal education; cultivates cordial relations among members of the Bar and perpetuate the history of the profession and the Association. **Computer Services:** Electronic publishing, legal research; weekly caselaw updates. **Telecommunication Services:** electronic bulletin board, discussion lists.

14681 ■ Ohio State Buckeye University Lions Club
c/o Erica Braatz, Pres.
5028 Dierker Rd., Apt. A6
Columbus, OH 43220
Ph: (614)405-9250 (419)450-0290
E-mail: froggygrleb@hotmail.com
URL: http://www.iwaynet.net/~lions13f
Contact: Erica Braatz, Pres.

Local. Affiliated With: Lions Clubs International.

14682 ■ Ohio State Chiropractic Association (OSCA)
PO Box 1836
Columbus, OH 43216-1836
Ph: (614)221-9933
Fax: (614)221-9933
Free: (800)837-6721
E-mail: osca@oscachiro.org
URL: http://www.oscachiro.org
Contact: Anthony R. Battaglia DC, Pres.

State.

14683 ■ Ohio State University Fencing Club
c/o Vladimir Nazlymov, Head Coach
Steelwood Training Fac.
1160 Steelwood Dr.
Columbus, OH 43210
Ph: (614)292-9323
Fax: (614)292-8480
URL: http://www.fansonly.com/schools/osu/sports/c-fenc/osu-c-fenc-body.html
Contact: Vladimir Nazlymov, Head Coach

State. Amateur fencers. **Affiliated With:** United States Fencing Association.

14684 ■ Ohio State University - Great Lakes Aquatic Ecosystem Research Consortium
Ohio Sea Grant
Ohio State University
1314 Kinnear Rd.
Columbus, OH 43212
Ph: (614)292-8949
Fax: (614)292-4364
E-mail: rheath@kent.edu
Contact: Robert T Heath, Colloquium Coord.

Works to facilitate inter-university collaborative research and the formation of large research teams to investigate topics of concern in the North American Great Lakes, their tributaries and coastal wetlands. Holds occasional meetings at member universities or at the F.T. Stone Laboratory on South Bass Island in Lake Erie.

14685 ■ Ohio State University Lions Club
c/o Danielle Poole, Pres.
1210 Minuteman Ct.
Columbus, OH 43220
Ph: (330)446-4581
E-mail: dpoole@optometry.osu.edu
URL: http://www.iwaynet.net/~lions13f
Contact: Danielle Poole, Pres.
Local. Affiliated With: Lions Clubs International.

14686 ■ Ohio Storage Owner's Society
c/o Mike Lane
6956 E Broad St., No. 212
Columbus, OH 43213
Fax: (217)241-4683
Free: (866)528-5230
E-mail: mike@p-a-m-s.com
URL: National Affiliate–www.selfstorage.org
Contact: Mike Lane, Contact
State. Represents owners and operators of self storage facilities. Works to improve the quality of management, customer service and facilities. Promotes public awareness of the self storage industry. Conducts educational meetings on management, marketing, security, and related topics. Lobbies for state legislation protecting and recognizing self storage owners and operators. **Affiliated With:** Self Storage Association.

14687 ■ Ohio Subcontractors Council
808 Frank Rd.
Columbus, OH 43223-3855
Ph: (614)341-9780
Fax: (614)278-2184
Free: (877)482-7263
E-mail: bryang@capitalcitycrane.com
URL: http://www.capitalcitycrane.com
Contact: Brian Gibson, VP
State. Affiliated With: American Subcontractors Association.

14688 ■ Ohio Telecom Association (OTA)
17 S High St., Ste.600
Columbus, OH 43215
Ph: (614)221-3231
Fax: (614)221-0048
E-mail: ota@ohiotelecom.com
URL: http://www.ohiotelecom.com
Contact: Charles R. Moses, Pres.
Founded: 1895. **Members:** 46. **Staff:** 4. **Budget:** $500,000. **State.** Telephone companies providing local exchange service. Seeks to protect the interests of local exchange carriers. **Affiliated With:** United States Telecom Association. **Formerly:** Ohio Independent Telephone Association; Ohio Telephone Association; Ohio Telecommunications Industry Association. **Publications:** *Regulatory Review*, weekly • *State House Report*, monthly. Newsletter • *Telecom Today*. Newsletter. Alternate Formats: online • Directory, annual. **Advertising:** accepted • Membership Directory, annual. **Advertising:** accepted. **Conventions/Meetings:** annual conference.

14689 ■ Ohio Tire Dealers and Retreaders Association (OTDRA)
50 W Broad St., Ste.2020
Columbus, OH 43215
Ph: (614)221-7950
Fax: (614)221-7020
URL: http://www.otdra.com
Contact: Gordon Gough, Exec.Dir.
Founded: 1967. **Members:** 240. **State. Affiliated With:** Ohio Council of Retail Merchants. **Formerly:** (2005) Ohio Tire Dealers and Retreaders. **Publications:** *Buckeye Footprints*. Newsletter. **Conventions/Meetings:** annual Convention and Suppliers Showcase.

14690 ■ Ohio Township Association (OTA)
c/o Michael H. Cochran, Exec.Dir.
5969 E Livingston Ave., Ste.110
Columbus, OH 43232-2970
Ph: (614)863-0045
Fax: (614)863-9751
E-mail: ota@ohiotownships.org
URL: http://www.ohiotownships.org
Contact: Michael H. Cochran, Exec.Dir.
Founded: 1928. **State.**

14691 ■ Ohio Travel Association (OTA)
c/o Marc McQuaid, Exec.Dir.
130 E Chestnut St., Ste.301
Columbus, OH 43215
Ph: (614)572-1931
Fax: (614)572-1937
Free: (800)896-4682
E-mail: info@ohiotravel.org
URL: http://www.ohiotravel.org
Contact: Marc McQuaid, Exec.Dir.
Founded: 1976. **Members:** 880. **State.** Represents travel and tourism professionals from hotels, restaurants, attractions, and destination marketing organizations as well as individuals from tour companies who package and sell group tour vacations.

14692 ■ Ohio Trucking Association (OTA)
50 W Broad St., Ste.1111
Columbus, OH 43215
Ph: (614)221-5375
Fax: (614)221-3717
Free: (888)382-1574
E-mail: info@ohiotruckingassn.org
URL: http://www.ohiotruckingassn.org
Contact: Larry A. Davis, Pres.
Founded: 1918. **Members:** 1,200. **Membership Dues:** Ohio domiciled motor carrier (based on number of vehicles), $350-$4,000 (annual) • out-of-state carrier (minimum), $350 (annual) • allied industry (local/regional customer base), $350 (annual) • allied industry (statewide customer base), $450 (annual) • allied industry (national customer base), $550 (annual). **Staff:** 8. **Regional Groups:** 5. **State.** Promotes and protects the interests of the trucking industry in Ohio. **Councils:** Ohio Truck Maintenance; Ohio Truck Safety. **Publications:** *Government Directory*, biennial. Includes pictures and biographies of new legislators and government officials. **Price:** $15.00 plus tax. **Circulation:** 1,500. **Advertising:** accepted • *News Briefs*, bimonthly. Newsletter. **Circulation:** 1,300. **Advertising:** accepted. **Conventions/Meetings:** annual convention (exhibits).

14693 ■ Ohio United Way
88 E Broad St., Ste.620
Columbus, OH 43215-3506
Ph: (614)224-8146
Fax: (614)224-6597
E-mail: juliet_rowland@ouw.org
URL: http://www.ouw.org
Contact: Juliet Coles Rowland, Pres./CEO
State. Affiliated With: United Way of America.

14694 ■ Ohio Valley Pembroke Welsh Corgi Club (OVPWCC)
c/o Pam Hudson, Sec.
5192 Hitesman Way
Columbus, OH 43214
Ph: (614)433-0253
E-mail: pamhudson@columbus.rr.com
URL: http://www.ohiovalleycorgi.org
Contact: Lanalee Jorgensen, Pres.
Local. Affiliated With: Pembroke Welsh Corgi Club of America.

14695 ■ Ohio Valley Regional Chapter of the Society of Environmental Toxicology and Chemistry (OVC SETAC)
c/o Tyler K. Linton, Pres.
Great Lakes Environmental Ctr.
1295 King Ave.
Columbus, OH 43230
E-mail: tlinton@glec.com
URL: http://chapters.setac.org/ohiovalley
Contact: Tyler K. Linton, Pres.
Regional. Supports the development of principles and practices for protection, enhancement and management of sustainable environmental quality and ecosystem integrity. Promotes research, education, communication and training in the environmental sciences. Provides a forum for individuals and institutions engaged in the study of environmental issues, management and conservation of natural resources, and environmental research and development. **Affiliated With:** Society of Environmental Toxicology and Chemistry.

14696 ■ Ohio Vegetable and Potato Growers Association (OVPGA)
c/o Tom Sachs, Exec.Dir.
PO Box 182383
Columbus, OH 43218-2383
Ph: (614)246-8292
Fax: (614)249-2200
E-mail: growohio@ofbf.org
URL: http://www.ohiovegetables.org
Contact: Tom Sachs, Exec.Dir.
State.

14697 ■ Ohio Veterinary Medical Association (OVMA)
3168 Riverside Dr.
Columbus, OH 43221
Ph: (614)486-7253
Fax: (614)486-1325
Free: (800)662-OVMA
E-mail: ohiovma@ohiovma.org
URL: http://www.ohiovma.org
Contact: Dr. Tod Schadler, Pres.
Founded: 1893. **Members:** 2,400. **Membership Dues:** associate, $55 (annual) • sustaining, $50 (annual). **Staff:** 6. **Budget:** $1,000,000. **State.** Represents veterinarians practicing in various fields and specialties. Fosters life-long learning, stewardship, compassion and community in veterinary medicine. Provides services to its members in the areas of continuing education, advocacy on public policy matters, and access to variety of professional resources. **Publications:** *Newsline*, monthly. Newsletter. **Price:** included in membership dues. **Circulation:** 2,300. **Advertising:** accepted. **Conventions/Meetings:** annual Midwest Veterinary Conference (exhibits).

14698 ■ Ohio Wholesale Marketers Association
c/o Beth Wymer, Exec.Dir.
88 E Broad St., Ste.1240
Columbus, OH 43215
Ph: (614)224-3435
Founded: 1942. **Members:** 90. **Staff:** 2. **Budget:** $200,000. **State.** Wholesale tobacco and candy distributors, product manufacturers, brokers and other industry associates. Represents members' interests in governmental relations and industry matters. Holds educational seminars and trade show. Various membership service programs. **Awards: Frequency:** annual. **Type:** scholarship. **Recipient:** essay requirement; college enrollment. **Formerly:** (2005) Ohio Association of Tobacco and Candy Distributors. **Publications:** *OATCD Membership Directory*, annual. Contains comprehensive membership listings; product information; industry information. **Circulation:** 300. **Advertising:** accepted • *Ohio Distributor*, monthly. Newsletter. **Conventions/Meetings:** annual TriState Tobacco and Candy Distributors Convention, held jointly with the Indiana and Kentucky associations (exhibits) - September; Avg. Attendance: 300.

14699 ■ Ohio Women's Business Resource Network (OWBRN)
c/o Mary Ann McClure, Dir.
PO Box 1001
Columbus, OH 43215-1001
Ph: (614)466-2682
Fax: (614)466-0829
Free: (800)848-1300
E-mail: msacct@eurekanet.com
URL: http://www.ohiobiz.org
Contact: Linda Steward, Contact
Founded: 1992. **Members:** 12. **Membership Dues:** organization (women's business centers), $300 (annual). **State.** Promotes successful women's

entrepreneurship throughout the state of OH. Provides private sector 3rd party certification of women business enterprises in Ohio and surrounding states.

14700 ■ Ohio Women's Law Enforcement Network
c/o Teri Ruslander, Pres.
PO Box 23073
Columbus, OH 43223
Ph: (614)645-4624
E-mail: dteri37@aol.com
URL: National Affiliate–www.iawp.org
Contact: Teri Ruslander, Pres.

State. Seeks to strengthen, unite and raise the profile of women in criminal justice. **Affiliated With:** International Association of Women Police.

14701 ■ Ohio Young Democrats
c/o Jonathan Varner, Pres.
271 E State St.
Columbus, OH 43215
Ph: (614)221-6563
E-mail: info@ohioyd.org
URL: http://www.ohioyd.org

State.

14702 ■ Ohioans to Stop Executions (OTSE)
9 E Long St., Ste.201
Columbus, OH 43215
Ph: (614)560-0654
Fax: (614)224-7150
E-mail: eunice@ijpc-cincinnati.org
URL: http://www.otse.org
Contact: Alice Gerdeman, Chair

State. **Affiliated With:** National Coalition to Abolish the Death Penalty.

14703 ■ Olentangy Liberty - Young Life
1515 W Lane Ave.
Columbus, OH 43221
Ph: (614)485-5433
URL: http://sites.younglife.org/_layouts/ylext/default.aspx?ID=C-3795

Local. **Affiliated With:** Young Life.

14704 ■ Olentangy - Young Life
1515 W Lane Ave.
Columbus, OH 43221
Ph: (614)485-5433
URL: http://sites.younglife.org/_layouts/ylext/default.aspx?ID=C-1487

Local. **Affiliated With:** Young Life.

14705 ■ Operation Lifesaver, Ohio
c/o Sheldon Senek, Coor.
5075 Fisher Rd.
Columbus, OH 43228-9145
Ph: (614)771-3071
Fax: (614)771-3273
E-mail: oplifeohio@aol.com
URL: http://www.ohol.org
Contact: Sheldon Senek, Coor.

State. Seeks to reduce the incidence of grade-crossing collisions in the U.S. Works to increase public awareness on the frequencies of grade-crossing collisions and to correct driver behavior to avoid collisions. Also works to prevent trespasser pedestrian fatalities and injuries along railroad rights-of-way. **Affiliated With:** Operation Lifesaver.

14706 ■ Organization of Chinese Americans - Columbus Chapter
PO Box 20623
Columbus, OH 43220
E-mail: oca@columbus.rr.com
URL: http://www.ocacolumbus.org/main/index.htm
Contact: Grace Chen, Pres.

Local.

14707 ■ Parents Anonymous of Central and Southern Ohio
197 E Gay St.
Columbus, OH 43215
Ph: (614)221-5891
Fax: (614)228-1125
E-mail: lcormier@colscss.org
URL: http://www.colscss.org
Contact: Lucy Cormier, Program Coor.

Local.

14708 ■ Payments Central
1550 Old Henderson Rd., Ste.N-160
Columbus, OH 43220
Fax: (614)457-4824
Free: (800)288-2204
E-mail: jerry@paymentcentral.org
URL: http://www.paymentscentral.org
Contact: Mr. Gerald P. Woessner AAP, Pres./CEO

Regional. Promotes the development of electronic solutions to improve payments systems. **Affiliated With:** NACHA: The Electronic Payments Association.

14709 ■ People's Rights Organization (PRO)
4444 Indianola Ave.
Columbus, OH 43214-2226
Ph: (614)268-0122
Fax: (614)268-0122
E-mail: brentgreer@peoplesrights.org
URL: http://www.peoplesrights.org
Contact: Brent Greer, Sec.

Founded: 1989. **Members:** 2,700. **Membership Dues:** individual, $35 (annual) • life, $360. **Staff:** 5. **Regional Groups:** 1. **State Groups:** 1. **Local Groups:** 1. **Local**. Seeks to educate the public about the safe use of firearms, offers classes for the recently passed Concealed Carry law in Ohio. Sponsors many Eddie Eagle Gun Safety Seminars and Refuse to be a Victim seminars throughout Central Ohio. Works with other groups in Ohio to pass laws protecting rights as guaranteed by the Second Amendment. **Libraries: Type:** by appointment only; open to the public. **Holdings:** 100; articles. **Subjects:** Second Amendment issues. **Awards:** People's Rights Organization Founding Fathers Second Amendment Award. **Frequency:** annual. **Type:** recognition. **Recipient:** for outstanding efforts in defense and support of the Second Amendment. **Additional Websites:** http://www.pro-training.info. **Affiliated With:** Citizens Committee for the Right to Keep and Bear Arms; Second Amendment Foundation. **Publications:** *Proponent*, monthly. Newsletter. **Conventions/Meetings:** monthly board meeting (exhibits) - 3rd Tuesday • monthly meeting - 3rd Tuesday.

14710 ■ Phi Theta Kappa - Alpha Rho Epsilon Chapter
c/o Charles Gallucci
Student Activities
550 E Spring St.
Union Hall 053
Columbus, OH 43215-1722
Ph: (614)287-5499
E-mail: cgallucc@cscc.edu
URL: http://www.ptk.org/directories/chapters/OH/8983-1.htm
Contact: Charles Gallucci, Advisor

Local. **Affiliated With:** Phi Theta Kappa, International Honor Society.

14711 ■ Prevent Blindness Ohio
1500 W 3rd Ave., Ste.200
Columbus, OH 43212-2874
Ph: (614)464-2020
Fax: (614)481-9670
Free: (800)301-2020
E-mail: info@pbohio.org
URL: http://www.pbohio.org
Contact: Sherry Williams, Pres./CEO

Founded: 1957. **Staff:** 25. **Budget:** $1,500,000. **Nonmembership**. **State**. Consumer advocate for sight conservation, promotes eye health and safety while working to find the cure for blinding eye diseases. **Awards:** Predoctoral Student Fellowship Research Awards For Females Pursuing Careers in Vision Research. **Frequency:** annual. **Type:** grant. **Recipient:** for partial support to younger investigators • Prevent Blindness America Investigator Award. **Frequency:** annual. **Type:** grant. **Recipient:** for research that relates to clinically important eye diseases and promotes sight preservation and preventing blindness. **Computer Services:** Online services, e-mail newsletter. **Affiliated With:** Prevent Blindness America. **Formerly:** (2004) National Society to Prevent Blindness-Ohio Affiliate. **Publications:** *Vision Problems in Ohio*. Survey. Features demographics of vision problems in Ohio county-by-county. **Price:** $10.00. Alternate Formats: online.

14712 ■ Prevent Child Abuse Ohio
700 Children's Dr., H-130
Columbus, OH 43205
Ph: (614)722-6800
Fax: (614)722-5510
Free: (800)CHILDREN
E-mail: pcao@chi.osu.edu
URL: http://www.pcao.org

State. Provides a variety of programs and services aimed at preventing child abuse in the state of OH. **Telecommunication Services:** information service, resource line for families for safe quality child care as well as other needed resources. **Formerly:** (2000) Center for Child Abuse Prevention. **Publications:** *Prevent Child Abuse Ohio*, quarterly. Newsletters. Newsletter highlighting PCAO programs and events, state news, community news and save the date. Alternate Formats: online. **Conventions/Meetings:** annual Protecting Ohio's Children: Together We Can Prevent Child Abuse and Neglect - conference (exhibits).

14713 ■ Professional Land Surveyors of Ohio (PLSO)
2865 W Dublin-Granville Rd., Ste.700
Columbus, OH 43235-2203
Ph: (614)761-2313
Fax: (614)761-2317
E-mail: plso@ohiosurveyor.org
URL: http://www.ohiosurveyor.org

State. **Affiliated With:** National Society of Professional Surveyors.

14714 ■ Professional Photographers of Central Ohio (PPCO)
c/o Robert Hughes, 1st VP
1041 Broadview Ave.
Columbus, OH 43212
Ph: (614)488-2769
E-mail: roberthughes@ameritech.net
URL: http://www.ppco.org
Contact: Ron Burgess, Board Chm.

Local. **Affiliated With:** Professional Photographers of America.

14715 ■ Professional Photographers of Ohio (PPO)
c/o Philip Craig
37 W Broad St., Ste.480
Columbus, OH 43215
Ph: (614)228-6703
Fax: (614)241-2215
E-mail: carol@ppofohio.org
URL: http://www.ppofohio.org
Contact: Mary Ann Porinchak, Pres.

State. **Affiliated With:** Professional Photographers of America.

14716 ■ Project Management Institute, Central Ohio Chapter
1500 W 3rd Ave., Ste.120
Columbus, OH 43212-2816
Ph: (614)485-0333
Fax: (614)485-0366
E-mail: admin@pmicentralohio.com
URL: http://www.pmicentralohio.com
Contact: Twyla Southall PMP, Pres.

Local. Corporations and individuals engaged in the practice of project management; project management students and educators. Seeks to advance the study, teaching, and practice of project management. **Affiliated With:** Project Management Institute.

14717 ■ Psi Chi, National Honor Society in Psychology - Ohio Dominican University
c/o Dept. of Psychology
1216 Sunbury Rd.
Columbus, OH 43219-2099
Ph: (614)251-4686
Fax: (614)252-0776
E-mail: crimmina@ohiodominican.edu
URL: http://www.psichi.org/chapters/info.asp?chapter_id=469
Contact: Anne M. Crimmings PhD, Advisor
Local.

14718 ■ Public Children Service Association of Ohio (PCSAO)
510 E Mound St., Ste.200
Columbus, OH 43215
Ph: (614)224-5802
Fax: (614)228-5150
E-mail: pcsao@sbcglobal.net
URL: http://www.pcsao.org
Contact: Crystal Ward Allen, Exec.Dir.
Founded: 1980. **Members:** 70. **Staff:** 3. **State**.

14719 ■ Public Interest Research Group - Ohio (Ohio PIRG)
36 W Gay St., Ste.315
Columbus, OH 43215
Ph: (614)460-8732
E-mail: info@ohiopirg.org
URL: http://ohiopirg.org
Contact: Erin Bowser, State Dir.
State.

14720 ■ Religious Coalition for Reproductive Choice - Ohio Chapter
PO Box 82204
Columbus, OH 43202
Ph: (614)221-3636
Free: (800)587-2330
E-mail: ohiorcrc@sbcglobal.net
URL: http://www.ohiorcrc.org
State. Affiliated With: Religious Coalition for Reproductive Choice.

14721 ■ Resolve of Ohio
PO Box 141277
Columbus, OH 43214
Free: (800)414-OHIO
E-mail: info@resolveofohio.org
URL: http://www.resolveofohio.org
Contact: Carole White, Pres.
Founded: 1987. **Members:** 200. **Membership Dues:** basic, $55 (annual) • contributing, $65 (annual) • supporting, $75 (annual) • circle of friend, $100 (annual) • professional, $125 (annual) • limited income, $35 (annual). **Regional Groups:** 5. **State**. Provides support and information to those experiencing infertility and increases awareness of infertility issues through advocacy and public education. **Libraries: Type:** lending; not open to the public. **Holdings:** 50; articles, books, periodicals, video recordings. **Subjects:** medical treatment, adoption, emotional issues. **Computer Services:** Information services. **Affiliated With:** Resolve, The National Infertility Association. **Publications:** *Family Building Magazine*, quarterly. **Price:** included in membership dues • Newsletter, bimonthly. **Price:** included in membership dues.

14722 ■ Risk and Insurance Management Society, Central Ohio Chapter
c/o Marc Hrusch
Risk Mgt. Dept.
Bravo Development, Inc.
4644 Kenny Rd.
Columbus, OH 43220
Ph: (614)249-7690
E-mail: chizevd@nationwide.com
URL: http://centralohio.rims.org
Contact: Dan Chizever, Pres.
Local. Seeks to promote the discipline of risk management and enhance the image of professional risk managers. Fosters the educational and professional development of risk managers and others involved in the risk management and insurance industry. **Affiliated With:** Risk and Insurance Management Society.

14723 ■ RSVP Franklin County
c/o Martha Weger, Dir.
195 N Grant Ave.
Columbus, OH 43215
Ph: (614)221-6766
Fax: (614)224-6866
E-mail: rsvp@firstlink.org
URL: http://www.seniorcorps.gov/about/programs/rsvp_state.asp?usestateabbr=oh&Search4.x=0&Search4.y=0
Contact: Martha Weger, Dir.
Local. Affiliated With: Retired and Senior Volunteer Program.

14724 ■ Ruffed Grouse Society, Ohio Chapter
c/o Todd Scarborough
4271 Boulder Creek Dr.
Columbus, OH 43230
Ph: (419)875-5036
E-mail: rgs@ruffedgrousesociety.org
URL: National Affiliate–www.ruffedgrousesociety.org
Contact: Todd Scarborough, Contact
State. Affiliated With: Ruffed Grouse Society.

14725 ■ St. Leo Preservation Society
c/o Loris M. Mitchell
1451 Linwood Ave.
Columbus, OH 43206-3152
Contact: Loris M. Mitchell, Pres./Treas.
Founded: 2002. **Members:** 7. **Staff:** 7. **Local**. Aims to preserve St. Leo Church and Parish from destruction; to continue charitable works in the name of St. Leo the Great, and to inform others as to the plight and importance of all faith communities to local neighborhoods. **Publications:** *St. Leo Newsletter*, quarterly. **Circulation:** 1,000. **Advertising:** not accepted.

14726 ■ Share the Vision of Ohio
c/o Sally Harris, Exec.Dir.
2053 Ridgecliff Rd.
Columbus, OH 43221
Ph: (614)273-9999 (614)451-8995
Fax: (614)451-8995
E-mail: sharethevision@columbus.rr.com
URL: http://www.sharethevisionohio.org
Contact: Sally Harris, Exec.Dir.
Local. Formerly: (2005) Share the Vision.

14727 ■ Short North Business Association
120 W Goodale St.
Columbus, OH 43215-2357
Ph: (614)228-8050
Fax: (614)228-8035
E-mail: snbacols@aol.com
URL: http://www.shortnorth.org
Contact: John Angelo, Exec.Dir.
Founded: 1983. **Members:** 200. **Membership Dues:** small business, $90 (annual) • patron, $250 (annual) • corporate, $500 (annual). **Staff:** 1. **Local**. Seeks to support and promote its members and businesses in the Columbus, OH area; to advocate the development and revitalization of this historic neighborhood; and to celebrate and encourage the diversity of the urban arts district. **Publications:** *Short North Visitors Guide*, annual. Pamphlet. **Price:** free. **Circulation:** 50,000.

14728 ■ Sierra Club, Ohio Chapter
36 W Gay St., Ste.314
Columbus, OH 43215-2811
Ph: (614)461-0734
Fax: (614)461-0730
E-mail: enid.nagel@thomson.com
URL: http://ohio.sierraclub.org
Contact: Enid Nagel, Chm.
Founded: 1969. **Members:** 17,000. **Membership Dues:** $35 (annual). **Staff:** 2. **Local Groups:** 7. **Local**. Individuals dedicated to improving the quality of the environment through activism, education, and lobbying. Sponsors workshops and activist training programs. Issues publications. **Affiliated With:** Sierra Club. **Publications:** *Sierran Magazine*, monthly. Journal. **Advertising:** accepted. **Conventions/Meetings:** periodic meeting.

14729 ■ Skeptics and Agnostics for Christian Culture
c/o Kurt Weiland
2700 E Main St., Ste.208
Columbus, OH 43209-2536
Ph: (614)235-2929
Fax: (614)235-3008
E-mail: ngoo@prodigy.net
Contact: Kurt Weiland, Treas.
Founded: 2000. **Members:** 3. **Local**.

14730 ■ Society of the 173D Airborne Brigade, Midwest Chapter XVII
c/o 1st Sgt. James L. Haynes, Jr.
408 Bernhard Rd.
Columbus, OH 43213-1936
Ph: (614)239-8436
E-mail: jhaynes173d@yahoo.com
URL: http://www.skysoldier.org
Contact: James L. Haynes, Contact
Founded: 2000. **Members:** 600. **Membership Dues:** $20 (annual) • life, $173. **Staff:** 20. **Regional Groups:** 6. **State Groups:** 1. **Local Groups:** 1. **Local**. Locates members of the 173D Airborne and Associates. Upholds the legency of the unit. Provides scholarships, circulates newsletters and search graves of fallen comrades. **Computer Services:** database • mailing lists.

14731 ■ Society of American Foresters, Ohio (OSAF)
c/o Mark Ervin, Chm.
ODNR-Div. of Forestry
1855 Fountain Sq., H-1
Columbus, OH 43224
Ph: (614)265-6667
E-mail: mark.ervin@dnr.state.oh.us
URL: http://www.ohiosaf.org
Contact: Mark Ervin, Chm.
State. Affiliated With: Society of American Foresters.

14732 ■ Society of Antique Modelers - Ohio 6
334 N Remington
Columbus, OH 43209
Ph: (614)237-8722
E-mail: dhale2@aol.com
URL: National Affiliate–www.antiquemodeler.org
Local. Affiliated With: Society of Antique Modelers.

14733 ■ Society of Financial Service Professionals - Columbus, Ohio Chapter
17 S High St., Ste.200
Columbus, OH 43215
Ph: (614)221-1900
Fax: (614)221-1989
E-mail: sfsp@assnoffices.com
URL: http://www.sfsp.net/columbusoh
Contact: Victoria A. Green RHU, Pres.
Local. Represents the interests of financial advisers. Fosters the development of professional responsibility. Helps clients achieve their personal and business-related financial goals. **Affiliated With:** Society of Financial Service Professionals.

14734 ■ Society of Manufacturing Engineers - Columbus State Community College S092
Columbus State Community Coll., Mech. Engg. Tech.
550 E Spring St.
Columbus, OH 43215
Ph: (614)227-2677
Fax: (614)287-5146
E-mail: dbickers@cscc.edu
URL: National Affiliate–www.sme.org
Contact: Dick Bickerstaff, Contact
Local. Advances manufacturing knowledge to gain competitive advantage. Improves skills and manufacturing solutions for the growth of economy. Provides resources and opportunities for manufacturing professionals. **Affiliated With:** Estuarine Research Federation.

14735 ■ Society of Manufacturing Engineers - Ohio State University S205
Ohio State Univ., 210 Baker Syss. Bldg.
1971 Neil Ave.
Columbus, OH 43210-1271
Ph: (614)292-0177
Fax: (614)292-7852
E-mail: brevick.1@osu.edu
URL: National Affiliate–www.sme.org
Contact: Dr. Jerald R. Brevick, Contact
Local. Advances manufacturing knowledge to gain competitive advantage. Improves skills and manufacturing solutions for the growth of economy. Provides resources and opportunities for manufacturing professionals. **Affiliated With:** National Ocean Industries Association.

14736 ■ Society for Marketing Professional Services/Columbus Chapter
c/o Mitchel R. Levitt, FSMPS
99 E Main St.
Columbus, OH 43215
Ph: (614)255-3710
Fax: (614)255-3810
E-mail: mlevitt@karlsberger.com
URL: http://www.smpscolumbus.org
Contact: Mitchel R. Levitt FSMPS, Pres.
Founded: 1982. **Local**. Strives to be the primary resource for education, team building and strategic and marketing information for SMPS members and others involved in the built environment. Offers each member a variety of ways to gain new contacts and relationships and further their professional development. **Affiliated With:** Society for Marketing Professional Services.

14737 ■ Society of Physics Students - Ohio State University Chapter No. 5175
174 W 18th Ave.
Columbus, OH 43210-1106
Ph: (614)292-5713
Fax: (614)292-7557
E-mail: furnstahl.1@osu.edu
URL: National Affiliate–www.spsnational.org
Local. Offers opportunities for the students to enrich their experiences and skills about physics. Helps students to become professional in the field of physics. **Affiliated With:** Society of Physics Students.

14738 ■ Songwriters and Poets Critique (SPC)
PO Box 21065
Columbus, OH 43221
Ph: (614)877-1727
E-mail: dmeyers@songwriterscritique.com
URL: http://www.songwriterscritique.com
Contact: Dallas Meyers, Pres.
Founded: 1985. **Members:** 100. **Membership Dues:** regular, $30 (annual). **Local**. Specializes in the craft of writing songs and poems through critiques, workshops, concerts, demos, and more. Gives opportunity to members to collaborate with other writers and musicians.

14739 ■ Special Libraries Association, Central Ohio Chapter
c/o John Holtzclaw, Pres.-Elect
Nationwide Lib.
One Nationwide Plz., 1-01-05
Columbus, OH 43215-2220
Ph: (614)249-6414
Fax: (614)249-2218
E-mail: holtzcj@nationwide.com
URL: http://www.sla.org/chapter/ccno
Contact: John Holtzclaw, Pres.-Elect
Local. Seeks to advance the leadership role of special librarians. Promotes and strengthens members through learning, advocacy and networking initiatives. **Affiliated With:** Special Libraries Association.

14740 ■ Special Olympics, Ohio
c/o Bob Rickard, Exec.Dir.
3303 Winchester Pike
Columbus, OH 43232
Ph: (614)239-7050
Fax: (614)239-1873
E-mail: rwrsooh@aol.com
URL: http://www.ohiospoly.org
State. **Affiliated With:** Special Olympics.

14741 ■ STARFLEET: USS Columbus
c/o Steve Harper
4456 Collingdale Rd.
Columbus, OH 43231
E-mail: starfleetmarine2002@yahoo.com
URL: http://www.regionone.net
Contact: Steve Harper, Contact
Local. **Affiliated With:** STARFLEET.

14742 ■ Step 1 All-Stars
c/o Kelly Maynard
3895 Bus. Park Dr.
Columbus, OH 43204
Ph: (614)272-STEP
E-mail: info@step1allstars.com
URL: http://www.step1allstars.com
Contact: Kelly Maynard, Contact
Local.

14743 ■ Sweet Adelines International, Capitol Showcase Chapter
Dominion Middle School
330 E Dominion Blvd.
Columbus, OH 43214-2212
Ph: (614)864-8924
E-mail: grahamk@fcmcclerk.com
URL: National Affiliate–www.sweetadelineintl.org
Contact: Kate Graham, Contact
Local. Advances the musical art form of barbershop harmony through education and performances. Provides education, training and coaching in the development of women's four-part barbershop harmony. **Affiliated With:** Sweet Adelines International.

14744 ■ Thomas - Young Life
1515 W Lane Ave.
Columbus, OH 43221
Ph: (614)485-5433
URL: http://sites.younglife.org/_layouts/ylext/default.aspx?ID=C-1482
Local. **Affiliated With:** Young Life.

14745 ■ Tourette Syndrome Association of Ohio
PO Box 28345
Columbus, OH 43228
Ph: (614)272-1824
Fax: (614)272-1824
Free: (800)543-2675
E-mail: admin@tsaohio.org
URL: http://www.tsaohio.org
Contact: Debbie Meyer, Admin.Coord.
State. Provides current information, advocacy resources, public education, and social opportunities to improve the lives of families affected by this neurological disorder.

14746 ■ Tri-Village Lions Club
PO Box 12721
Columbus, OH 43212
Ph: (614)481-9800 (614)459-0592
E-mail: a.sulser@ws-architects.com
URL: http://columbusoh.lionwap.org
Contact: Bill Shelley, Pres.
Local. **Affiliated With:** Lions Clubs International.

14747 ■ Tri-Village Noon Lions Club
c/o Scott Stevenson, Pres.
7107 Ashville Park Dr.
Columbus, OH 43235
Ph: (614)451-6313 (614)793-0073
E-mail: scott@nwtitle.com
URL: http://www.iwaynet.net/~lions13f
Contact: Scott Stevenson, Pres.
Local. **Affiliated With:** Lions Clubs International.

14748 ■ UNICEF, Columbus Chapter
c/o Global Gallery
683 N High St.
Columbus, OH 43215
Ph: (614)228-5437
URL: http://www.unicef.org
Contact: Sue Wolford, Contact
Local. **Affiliated With:** U.S. Fund for Unicef.

14749 ■ United Food and Commercial Workers, Local 1059, Central Region
4150 E Main St., 2nd Fl.
Columbus, OH 43213-2966
Ph: (614)237-7671
Free: (800)282-6488
URL: http://www.ufcw1059.com
Local. **Affiliated With:** United Food and Commercial Workers International Union.

14750 ■ United States Harness Writers Association, Ohio Chapter (USHWA-OH)
c/o Paul G. Ramlow
750 Michigan Ave.
Columbus, OH 43215
Ph: (614)224-2291
Fax: (614)228-1385
E-mail: pramlow@ustrotting.com
URL: http://www.ustrotting.com
Contact: Paul G. Ramlow, Sec.
Founded: 1943. **Members:** 45. **Membership Dues:** $50 (annual). **State**. Writers, reporters, editors, broadcasters, columnists, and cartoonists who cover harness racing for the press. **Affiliated With:** United States Harness Writers' Association. **Publications:** Newsletter, semiannual. **Conventions/Meetings:** annual meeting.

14751 ■ United States Power Squadrons - District 29
c/o Lt. Samuel A. Woodruff, Jr., Exec. Officer
1616 Scottsdale Ave.
Columbus, OH 43235
Ph: (614)457-9423
E-mail: skipwood@aol.com
URL: http://www.usps.org/localusps/d29
Contact: Lt. Samuel A. Woodruff Jr., Exec. Officer
Regional. **Affiliated With:** United States Power Squadrons.

14752 ■ United Transportation Union, AFL-CIO - Local Union 1397
3594 High Creek Dr.
Columbus, OH 43223-3416
E-mail: ptcampbell@utulocal1397.org
URL: http://www.utulocal1397.org/
Contact: Paul Campbell, Pres.
Members: 112. **Local**. **Affiliated With:** United Transportation Union.

14753 ■ United Way of Central Ohio
360 S 3rd St.
Columbus, OH 43215
Ph: (614)227-2700
Fax: (614)224-5835
E-mail: scoffman@uwcentralohio.org
URL: http://www.uwcentralohio.org
Contact: Janet E. Jackson, Pres./CEO
Founded: 1923. **Staff:** 74. **Budget:** $5,200,000. **Local**.

14754 ■ Upper Arlington Community Orchestra
c/o Barbara Keith
PO Box 20069
Columbus, OH 43220
E-mail: info@uaorchestra.com
URL: http://www.uaorchestra.com
Contact: Barbara Keith, Treas.
Local. Community orchestra.

14755 ■ Upper Arlington - Young Life
1515 Ln. Ave., Ste.LL
Columbus, OH 43221
Ph: (614)485-5433
URL: http://sites.younglife.org/_layouts/ylext/default.aspx?ID=C-1518
Local. Affiliated With: Young Life.

14756 ■ Veterans of Foreign Wars 3424
3177 S High St.
Columbus, OH 43207
Ph: (614)497-9100
Contact: Dan Meeks, Contact
Local.

14757 ■ Victorian Village Society
PO Box 10792
Columbus, OH 43201-7792
Ph: (614)228-2912
E-mail: info@victorianvillage.org
URL: http://www.victorianvillage.org
Contact: Rob Pettit, Pres.
Local. Focuses on building a strong community through representation, advocacy and sponsorship of social events for the Victorian village area.

14758 ■ Vietnam Veterans of America, Buckeye State Council
35 E Chestnut St.
Columbus, OH 43215
Ph: (614)228-0188
Fax: (614)228-2711
URL: http://www.vvabuckeyestatecouncil.com
State. Affiliated With: Vietnam Veterans of America.

14759 ■ Vietnam Veterans of America, Chapter No. 670
c/o Steve Fulton, Pres.
PO Box 2555
Columbus, OH 43216-2555
Ph: (614)751-8820
Fax: (614)751-8903
URL: http://www.vvabuckeyestatecouncil.com
Contact: Steve Fulton, Pres.
Local. Affiliated With: Vietnam Veterans of America.

14760 ■ Volunteers of America of Central Ohio
1776 E Broad St.
Columbus, OH 43203
Ph: (614)253-6100
Fax: (614)253-6000
URL: http://www.voa.org/centralohio
Local. Affiliated With: Volunteers of America.

14761 ■ W. North - Young Life
1515 W Lane Ave.
Columbus, OH 43221
Ph: (614)485-5433
URL: http://sites.younglife.org/_layouts/ylext/default.aspx?ID=C-1595
Local. Affiliated With: Young Life.

14762 ■ W. South - Young Life
1515 W Lane Ave.
Columbus, OH 43221
Ph: (614)485-5433
URL: http://sites.younglife.org/_layouts/ylext/default.aspx?ID=C-1593
Local. Affiliated With: Young Life.

14763 ■ West Central - Young Life
1515 W Lane Ave.
Columbus, OH 43221
Ph: (614)485-5433
URL: http://sites.younglife.org/_layouts/ylext/default.aspx?ID=C-3699
Local. Affiliated With: Young Life.

14764 ■ Westland - Young Life
1515 W Lane Ave.
Columbus, OH 43221
Ph: (614)485-5433
URL: http://sites.younglife.org/sites/Westland/default.aspx
Contact: Mandee Lower, Contact
Local. Affiliated With: Young Life.

14765 ■ Wholesale Beer and Wine Association of Ohio (WBWAO)
37 W Broad St., Ste.710
Columbus, OH 43215-4132
Ph: (614)224-3500
Fax: (614)224-1348
Free: (800)282-7639
E-mail: info@wbwao.org
URL: http://www.wbwao.org
Contact: Andrew W. Herf, VP - Legislative Affairs
State. Telecommunication Services: electronic mail, wbwao@aol.com.

14766 ■ Women of Reform Judaism: Temple Israel Sisterhood, Columbus
c/o Liz Plotnick-Snay, Co-Pres.
5419 E Broad St.
Columbus, OH 43213
Ph: (614)866-0010
Fax: (614)866-9046
E-mail: sisterhood@templeisrael.org
URL: http://www.templeisrael.org/sisterhood
Contact: Elaine Tenenbaum, Exec.Dir.
Local. Affiliated With: Women of Reform Judaism, The Federation of Temple Sisterhoods.

14767 ■ World of Children
222 E Campus View Blvd.
Columbus, OH 43235
Ph: (614)491-5784
E-mail: suzan@worldofchildren.org
URL: http://www.worldofchildren.org
Contact: Suzan Nocella, Dir. Operations
Local.

14768 ■ Worthington Lions Club
c/o Robert E. Medley, Sec.
7402 Golden Springs Dr.
Columbus, OH 43235
Ph: (614)781-8847 (614)264-0057
Fax: (614)781-8845
E-mail: robert.medley@morganstanley.com
URL: http://www.iwaynet.net/~lions13f
Contact: Robert E. Medley, Sec.
Local. Affiliated With: Lions Clubs International.

14769 ■ Young Life Columbus North
1515 W Lane Ave.
Columbus, OH 43221
Ph: (614)485-5433
Fax: (614)485-2278
URL: http://sites.younglife.org/_layouts/ylext/default.aspx?ID=A-OH149
Local. Affiliated With: Young Life.

14770 ■ Young Life Columbus Northeast
1515 W Lane Ave.
Columbus, OH 43221
Ph: (614)485-5433
Fax: (614)485-2278
URL: http://sites.younglife.org/sites/ColumbusNortheast/default.aspx
Local. Affiliated With: Young Life.

14771 ■ Young Life Columbus Northwest
1515 Ln. Ave., Ste.LL
Columbus, OH 43221
Ph: (614)485-5433
Fax: (614)485-2278
URL: http://sites.younglife.org/_layouts/ylext/default.aspx?ID=A-OH28
Local. Affiliated With: Young Life.

14772 ■ Young Life Columbus Southeast
1515 W Lane Ave.
Columbus, OH 43221
Ph: (614)485-5433
Fax: (614)485-2278
URL: http://sites.younglife.org/sites/ColumbusSoutheast/default.aspx
Local. Affiliated With: Young Life.

14773 ■ Young Life Columbus Southwest
1515 W Lane Ave.
Columbus, OH 43221
Ph: (614)485-5433
Fax: (614)485-2278
URL: http://sites.younglife.org/sites/ColumbusSouthwest/default.aspx
Local. Affiliated With: Young Life.

14774 ■ Z Car and Roadster Owner Club (ZROC)
3743 Montclair Dr.
Columbus, OH 43219
E-mail: eelawson5@yahoo.com
URL: http://www.zroc.org
Contact: Ernie Lawson, Pres.
Local. Affiliated With: Z Car Club Association.

Columbus Grove

14775 ■ American Legion, Bowers-Slusser Post 516
412 Plum St.
Columbus Grove, OH 45830
Ph: (740)362-7478
Fax: (740)362-1429
URL: National Affiliate–www.legion.org
Local. Affiliated With: American Legion.

14776 ■ Gardeners of America/Men's Garden Clubs of America - Gardeners Club of Bluffton-Pandora Area
c/o Joyce A. Fuerst, Pres.
18044 Rd. 11R
Columbus Grove, OH 45830-9756
Ph: (419)659-5638
URL: National Affiliate–www.tgoa-mgca.org
Contact: Joyce A. Fuerst, Pres.
Local.

Concord Township

14777 ■ American Cancer Society, Geauga Area
7861 Crile Rd.
Concord Township, OH 44077
Ph: (440)358-0864
Fax: (440)358-9073
Free: (888)227-6446
URL: http://www.cancer.org
Local. Affiliated With: American Cancer Society.

14778 ■ Northcoast (Lake County-Cleveland) Senior Olympics
c/o Fran Ward
11189 Spear Rd.
Concord Township, OH 44077
Ph: (440)585-3045
Fax: (440)358-7280
E-mail: fward@lakemetroparks.com
URL: http://www.ohioseniorolympics.org
Contact: Fran Ward, Contact
Local. Affiliated With: National Senior Games Association.

Concord Twp

14779 ■ American Wine Society - Cleveland
c/o Judith Kesler, Chair
10391 Misty Ridge
Concord Twp, OH 44077

Ph: (440)352-9331
E-mail: jecekesler@aol.com
URL: National Affiliate–www.americanwinesociety.org
Contact: Judith Kesler, Chair
Local. Affiliated With: American Wine Society.

Conneaut

14780 ■ American Legion, Cowle Post 151
272 Bd. St.
Conneaut, OH 44030
Ph: (740)362-7478
Fax: (740)362-1429
URL: National Affiliate–www.legion.org
Local. Affiliated With: American Legion.

14781 ■ Conneaut Area Chamber of Commerce (CACC)
235 Main St.
PO Box 722
Conneaut, OH 44030-0722
Ph: (440)593-2402
Fax: (440)593-2401
URL: National Affiliate–www.uschamber.com
Contact: Geoffrey Klein, Exec.Dir.
Founded: 1906. **Members:** 165. **Staff:** 1. **Local.** Promotes business and community development in the Conneaut, OH area. Sponsors annual Community Appreciation Week in August, flag program in downtown area and harbor area, lights of love tree in November and December. **Affiliated With:** U.S. Chamber of Commerce. **Publications:** *Chamber Communicator*, periodic. Newsletter. **Conventions/Meetings:** quarterly meeting.

14782 ■ Conneaut Historical Society
402 S Amboy Rd.
Conneaut, OH 44030-3004
Ph: (440)593-4896
E-mail: suarn@suite224.net
Contact: Sue Howard, Sec.
Founded: 1986. **Members:** 125. **Membership Dues:** individual, $10 (annual) • couple, $15 (annual) • family, $20 (annual) • patron, $50 (annual). **Local.** To preserve, display, and teach about area artifacts and history. Sponsors monthly meetings, speakers, 50/50 raffle, auction, refreshments and social time.

Continental

14783 ■ American Legion, Winnow-Arn Post 541
PO Box 306
Continental, OH 45831
Ph: (740)362-7478
Fax: (740)362-1429
URL: National Affiliate–www.legion.org
Local. Affiliated With: American Legion.

Convoy

14784 ■ American Legion, Lewis Post 208
PO Box 216
Convoy, OH 45832
Ph: (740)362-7478
Fax: (740)362-1429
URL: National Affiliate–www.legion.org
Local. Affiliated With: American Legion.

14785 ■ West Central Health Information Management Association (WCHIMA)
c/o LaDonna Etzler, Pres.
4091 Monmouth Rd.
Convoy, OH 45832
Ph: (419)749-2270
E-mail: frisbie@bright.net
URL: http://www.ohima.org
Contact: LaDonna Etzler, Pres.
Local. Represents the interests of individuals dedicated to the effective management of personal health information needed to deliver quality healthcare to the public. Provides career, professional development and practice resources. Sets standards for education and certification. Advocates public policy that advances Health Information Management (HIM) practice. **Affiliated With:** American Health Information Management Association; Ohio Health Information Management Association.

Coolville

14786 ■ Coolville Lions Club
PO Box 204
Coolville, OH 45723
E-mail: amy111@1st.net
URL: http://coolvilleoh.lionwap.org
Contact: Amy Wilfong, Sec.
Local. Affiliated With: Lions Clubs International.

Copley

14787 ■ American Legion, Ohio Post 473
c/o Frank Bender
PO Box 4091
Copley, OH 44321
Ph: (740)362-7478
Fax: (740)362-1429
URL: National Affiliate–www.legion.org
Contact: Frank Bender, Contact
Local. Affiliated With: American Legion.

Corning

14788 ■ American Legion, Corning Post 327
PO Box 356
Corning, OH 43730
Ph: (740)362-7478
Fax: (740)362-1429
URL: National Affiliate–www.legion.org
Local. Affiliated With: American Legion.

Cortland

14789 ■ Cortland Lions Club
197 W Main St.
Cortland, OH 44410
Ph: (330)637-1991 (330)637-2731
E-mail: hjhallett@aol.com
URL: http://cortlandoh.lionwap.org
Contact: Bill Hallett, Pres.
Local. Affiliated With: Lions Clubs International.

14790 ■ Mosquito Beemers
c/o Bob Woofter
PO Box 673
Cortland, OH 44410
Ph: (330)638-1009
E-mail: kuul2@aol.com
URL: http://www.mosquitobeemers.com
Contact: Ernie Conover, Pres.
Local.

14791 ■ Newton Falls Lions Club
c/o Betty Robbins, Pres.
199 Stahl Ave.
Cortland, OH 44410
Ph: (330)638-7649
E-mail: betdrobbins@aol.com
URL: http://www.lions13d.org
Contact: Betty Robbins, Pres.
Local. Affiliated With: Lions Clubs International.

14792 ■ USA Weightlifting - Team Pendragon
c/o Lou DeMarco
3900 Greenville Rd.
Cortland, OH 44410
Ph: (330)924-3663
E-mail: lpdem@aol.com
URL: National Affiliate–www.usaweightlifting.org
Contact: Lou DeMarco, Contact
Local. Affiliated With: USA Weightlifting.

Coshocton

14793 ■ American Legion, Ohio Post 65
c/o Ralph Courtright
652 Main St.
Coshocton, OH 43812
Ph: (740)362-7478
Fax: (740)362-1429
URL: National Affiliate–www.legion.org
Contact: Ralph Courtright, Contact
Local. Affiliated With: American Legion.

14794 ■ American Red Cross, Coshocton County Chapter
245 N 4th St.
Coshocton, OH 43812
Ph: (740)622-0228
Fax: (740)622-6763
E-mail: cosharc@sbcglobal.net
URL: http://coshocton.redcross.org
Contact: Jackie Mishler, Exec.Dir.
Local.

14795 ■ Big Brothers Big Sisters of Coshocton County
733 Cambridge Rd.
Coshocton, OH 43812
Ph: (740)623-8110
E-mail: agency@bbbscoshco.org
URL: http://www.bbbscoshco.org
Contact: Geneva Martin, Program Dir.
Local. Affiliated With: Big Brothers Big Sisters of America.

14796 ■ Coshocton Co REACT
PO Box 937
Coshocton, OH 43812
Ph: (740)622-6282
E-mail: jarmstrong-re40@sbcglobal.net
URL: http://www.reactintl.org/teaminfo/usa_teams/teams-usoh.htm
Local. Trained communication experts and professional volunteers. Provides volunteer public service and emergency communications through the use of radios (Citizen Band, General Mobile Radio Service, UHF and HAM). Coordinates with radio industries and government on safety communication matters and supports charitable activities and community organizations.

14797 ■ Coshocton County ALU
c/o M. Leach
PO Box 757
Coshocton, OH 43812
Ph: (740)622-3421
Fax: (740)622-0788
URL: National Affiliate–www.naifa.org
Local. Represents the interest of insurance and financial advisors. Advocates for a positive legislative and regulatory environment. Enhances business and professional skills of members. **Affiliated With:** National Association of Insurance and Financial Advisors.

14798 ■ Coshocton County Board of Realtors
115 N 3rd St.
Coshocton, OH 43812
Ph: (740)622-7678
Fax: (740)622-5123
E-mail: cmgriffith@aol.com
URL: National Affiliate–www.realtor.org
Contact: Marlene Griffith, Exec. Officer
Local. Strives to develop real estate business practices. Advocates for the right to own, use and transfer real property. Provides a facility for professional development, research and exchange of information among members and the general public. **Affiliated With:** National Association of Realtors.

14799 ■ Coshocton County Chamber of Commerce
101 N Whitewoman St.
Coshocton, OH 43812
Ph: (740)622-5411 (740)622-5412
Fax: (740)622-9902
Free: (800)589-2430
E-mail: info@coshoctonchamber.com
URL: http://www.coshoctonchamber.com
Contact: Mr. Scott Thompson, Exec.Dir.

Members: 450. **Local.** Promotes business and community development in Coshocton County, OH. Sponsors annual Coshocton Canal Festival, Coshocton Hot Air Balloon Race, and T.V. Auction. **Awards:** Community Improvement Award of the Year. **Frequency:** annual. **Type:** recognition • Richard Rea Small Business of the Year Award. **Frequency:** annual. **Type:** recognition • Rotary Club Employee of the Year Award. **Frequency:** annual. **Type:** recognition. **Computer Services:** Mailing lists, current membership, retail district, safety council • online services, membership directory. **Committees:** Business After Hours; Canal Festival Parade; Education; Hot Air Balloon Festival; TV Auction. **Councils:** Safety. **Also Known As:** (2005) Coshocton Area Chamber of Commerce; (2005) Coshocton Chamber of Commerce. **Publications:** *Chamber Chatter*, 10/year. Newsletter. Features updates, calendar of events, special announcements, advertisements, legislative updates, and new member information. **Circulation:** 450. **Advertising:** accepted • Membership Directory, annual, updates are made every year and a half to two years. Contains listing of current members names, address, phone, email and web site information. **Advertising:** accepted. **Conventions/Meetings:** annual meeting - always April.

14800 ■ Coshocton Friends of the Library
c/o Coshocton County Public Library
655 Main St.
Coshocton, OH 43812-1614
Ph: (740)622-0956
Fax: (740)622-4331
URL: http://www.coshoctonpl.org
Contact: Ann Miller, Dir.
Local.

14801 ■ Coshocton Lions Club
c/o Charles Hathaway, III, Sec.
2078 Fulton Dr.
Coshocton, OH 43812
Ph: (740)622-8443 (740)498-8025
URL: http://users.adelphia.net/~npssteve/district.htm
Contact: Lisa Kowalski, Pres.
Local. Affiliated With: Lions Clubs International.

14802 ■ Johnson-Humrickhouse Museum (JHM)
c/o Jeff Gill, Pres.
300 N Whitewoman St.
Coshocton, OH 43812
Ph: (740)622-8710
Fax: (740)622-8710
E-mail: jhmuseum@sbcglobal.net
URL: http://www.jhmuseum.org
Contact: Jeff Gill, Pres.
Founded: 1931. **Members:** 275. **Local.** Seeks to support the Johnson-Humrickhouse Museum. **Publications:** Newsletter, quarterly.

14803 ■ Korean War Veterans Association, Coshocton Chapter
c/o Ivan J. Loos
1870 Walnut St.
Coshocton, OH 43812
Ph: (740)622-7168
URL: National Affiliate–www.kwva.org
Contact: Ivan J. Loos, Contact
Local. Affiliated With: Korean War Veterans Association.

14804 ■ Roscoe Village Foundation
381 Hill St.
Coshocton, OH 43812
Ph: (740)622-9310
Fax: (740)623-6555
Free: (800)877-1830
URL: http://www.roscoevillage.com
Local. Preserves the history of Roscoe Village.

14805 ■ United Way of Coshocton County
PO Box 84
Coshocton, OH 43812-0084
Ph: (740)622-4567
URL: National Affiliate–national.unitedway.org
Local. Affiliated With: United Way of America.

Covington

14806 ■ American Legion, Ohio Post 80
c/o A.B. Cole
PO Box 33
Covington, OH 45318
Ph: (740)362-7478
Fax: (740)362-1429
URL: National Affiliate–www.legion.org
Contact: A.B. Cole, Contact
Local. Affiliated With: American Legion.

Crestline

14807 ■ American Legion, Mc Whirter Post 488
PO Box 151
Crestline, OH 44827
Ph: (740)362-7478
Fax: (740)362-1429
URL: National Affiliate–www.legion.org
Local. Affiliated With: American Legion.

14808 ■ Crestline Area United Way
PO Box 163
Crestline, OH 44827-0163
Ph: (419)683-4418
URL: National Affiliate–national.unitedway.org
Contact: Dorothy Strickler, Contact
Founded: 1960. **Members:** 7. **Staff:** 2. **Local.**

14809 ■ Crestline Lions Club - Ohio
c/o H. L. Barker, PDG, Sec.
789 State Rte. 181
Crestline, OH 44827
Ph: (419)683-1478
E-mail: sonnyb@bright.net
URL: http://www.lions13b.org
Contact: H. L. Barker PDG, Sec.
Local. Affiliated With: Lions Clubs International.

14810 ■ Ontario Lions Club
c/o Randall Hanlon, Pres.
1115 Brookdale Dr.
Crestline, OH 44827
Ph: (419)683-4266
E-mail: rhanlon@columbus.rr.com
URL: http://www.lions13b.org
Contact: Randall Hanlon, Pres.
Local. Affiliated With: Lions Clubs International.

14811 ■ Organic Crop Improvement Association, Ohio- Chapter 2
c/o Kathleen Paynter
7950 Oldfield Rd.
Crestline, OH 44827-9782
Ph: (419)683-3961
Fax: (419)683-3961
E-mail: ohioocia2contact@hotmail.com
URL: National Affiliate–www.ocia.org
Contact: Kathleen Paynter, Contact
Local. Affiliated With: Organic Crop Improvement Association.

Creston

14812 ■ American Legion, Creston Post 497
PO Box 1112
Creston, OH 44217
Ph: (740)362-7478
Fax: (740)362-1429
URL: National Affiliate–www.legion.org
Local. Affiliated With: American Legion.

14813 ■ Creston Lions Club
c/o James C. Murray, Sec.
PO Box 25
Creston, OH 44217
Ph: (330)435-6670 (330)435-4404
Fax: (330)435-4770
E-mail: pjmurray@valkyrie.net
URL: http://users.adelphia.net/~npssteve/district.htm
Contact: James C. Murray, Sec.
Local. Affiliated With: Lions Clubs International.

Crooksville

14814 ■ American Legion, Basil Grimes Post 222
200 N Buckeye St.
Crooksville, OH 43731
Ph: (740)362-7478
Fax: (740)362-1429
URL: National Affiliate–www.legion.org
Local. Affiliated With: American Legion.

Croton

14815 ■ Central Ohio Theatre Organ Society (COTOS)
c/o Duane King, Pres.
PO Box 211
Croton, OH 43013
Ph: (614)374-8808
E-mail: dking70@hotmail.com
URL: http://theatreorgans.com/cotos/index.htm
Contact: Duane King, Pres.
Local. Affiliated With: American Theatre Organ Society.

Cuyahoga Falls

14816 ■ AAA Akron Automobile Club
1945 23rd St.
Cuyahoga Falls, OH 44223-1483
Ph: (330)923-4826
Local.

14817 ■ Akron Mineral Society
244 Chestnut Blvd.
Cuyahoga Falls, OH 44221
E-mail: rlee@neo.rr.com
URL: National Affiliate–www.amfed.org
Contact: Terry Warner, Pres.
Local. Aims to further the study of Earth Sciences and the practice of lapidary arts and mineralogy. **Affiliated With:** American Federation of Mineralogical Societies.

14818 ■ American Legion, Ohio Post 281
c/o Charles Faust
1601 Front St.
Cuyahoga Falls, OH 44221
Ph: (740)362-7478
Fax: (740)362-1429
URL: National Affiliate–www.legion.org
Contact: Charles Faust, Contact
Local. Affiliated With: American Legion.

14819 ■ BMW Car Club of America, Northern Ohio Chapter
c/o John Black, Membership Chm.
PO Box 3228
Cuyahoga Falls, OH 44223-0528

Ph: (440)808-9826
E-mail: membership@nohiobmwcca.org
URL: http://www.nohiobmwcca.org
Contact: John Black, Membership Chm.
Local. Affiliated With: BMW Car Club of America.

14820 ■ Catalina 22 National Sailing Association, Fleet 131 Atwood Lake, Ohio
c/o Fred Denning
1757 Eleventh St.
Cuyahoga Falls, OH 44221-4515
Ph: (330)928-7313
E-mail: fdenning@yahoo.com
URL: http://www.acorn.net/catalina22fleet131
Contact: Fred Denning, Contact
Membership Dues: $10 (annual). **Local. Affiliated With:** Catalina 22 National Sailing Association.

14821 ■ Cuyahoga Falls Chamber of Commerce (CFCC)
2020 Front St., Ste.103
Cuyahoga Falls, OH 44221-3200
Ph: (330)929-6756
Fax: (330)929-4278
E-mail: info@cfchamber.com
URL: http://www.cuyahogafallschamberofcommerce.com
Contact: Laura Petrella, Exec.Dir.
Founded: 1926. **Members:** 300. **Membership Dues:** business, $225-$530 (annual) • associate, $75 (annual) • non-profit, $125 (annual) • individual, $225 (annual) • retired, $95 (annual). **Local.** Promotes economic growth and development by encouraging programs designed to support, strengthen and expand the local businesses in Cuyahoga Falls. Supports activities of a civic, social and cultural nature which are designed to increase the functional and aesthetic values of the community. **Publications:** Membership Directory, annual. Features chamber members for recognition and exposure purposes. **Price:** included in membership dues. Alternate Formats: online. **Conventions/Meetings:** semiannual Coffee and Contacts - meeting, free and limited to first 20 members • monthly Falls After Five - meeting, offers opportunity to meet new people and network • monthly luncheon, with business speakers.

14822 ■ Cuyahoga Valley Spaziergangers
c/o Bob Evans
3425 E Prescott Cir.
Cuyahoga Falls, OH 44223-3386
Ph: (330)923-2359
E-mail: bobnancyevans@msn.com
URL: National Affiliate–www.ava.org
Contact: Bob Evans, Contact
Local.

14823 ■ Lupus Foundation of America, Akron Area Chapter
2769 Front St.
Cuyahoga Falls, OH 44221
Ph: (330)945-6767
Free: (877)635-8787
E-mail: lupusakron@msn.com
URL: http://www.lupusakron.org
Contact: Patricia Michael, Pres.
Founded: 1977. **Members:** 300. **Membership Dues:** individual, $15 (annual) • family, $18 (annual) • professional, $25 (annual). **Staff:** 1. **Budget:** $15,000. **Local Groups:** 4. **Local.** Lupus erythematosus patients and their families and friends. Supports research and education. Provides public awareness services. **Libraries: Type:** lending; not open to the public. **Affiliated With:** Lupus Foundation of America. **Publications:** *Lupus Gram*, quarterly. Newsletter. Contains medical articles on lupus and local chapter events and news. **Price:** included in membership dues. **Circulation:** 500. **Conventions/Meetings:** annual Living with Lupus - conference - always September or October. Akron, OH - Avg. Attendance: 35.

14824 ■ Mental Health Association of Summit County (MHASC)
PO Box 639
Cuyahoga Falls, OH 44222
Ph: (330)923-0688
Fax: (330)923-7573
Free: (800)991-1311
E-mail: questions@mhasc.net
URL: http://www.mhasc.net
Contact: Rudolph J. Libertini, Exec.Dir.
Founded: 1956. **Members:** 500. **Staff:** 26. **Budget:** $600,000. **State Groups:** 1. **Local.** Family and friends of individuals who suffer from mental illness; interested individuals. Advocates for the elimination of the social stigma attached to mental illnesses. Supports services, research, and funding for the mentally ill. **Libraries: Type:** open to the public. **Holdings:** 100. **Subjects:** mental illness. **Affiliated With:** National Mental Health Association. **Publications:** *The Advocate*, quarterly. Newsletter. **Price:** free. **Circulation:** 6,000. **Conventions/Meetings:** annual conference (exhibits).

14825 ■ STARFLEET: USS Lagrange
c/o Robert Swiger, Pres.
PO Box 1193
Cuyahoga Falls, OH 44223
Ph: (330)923-7854
E-mail: usslagrange3916b@aol.com
URL: http://www.angelfire.com/oh2/usslagrange
Contact: Robert Swiger, Pres.
Local. Affiliated With: STARFLEET.

14826 ■ Vietnam Veterans of America, Chapter No. 34
c/o Mike Arnold, Pres.
PO Box 30
Cuyahoga Falls, OH 44222
Ph: (330)773-6434
URL: http://www.vvabuckeyestatecouncil.com
Contact: Mike Arnold, Pres.
Local. Affiliated With: Vietnam Veterans of America.

14827 ■ Vietnam Veterans of America, Chapter No. 717
c/o John Darmstadt, Pres.
PO Box 4091
Cuyahoga Falls, OH 44223
Ph: (330)923-2709
URL: http://www.vvabuckeyestatecouncil.com
Contact: John Darmstadt, Pres.
Local. Affiliated With: Vietnam Veterans of America.

14828 ■ Western Reserve Carriage Association
3919 Wyoga Lake Rd.
Cuyahoga Falls, OH 44224
E-mail: drales@ix.netcom.com
URL: http://www.wrcarriageassociation.org
State.

Dalton

14829 ■ Dalton Area Chamber of Commerce
PO Box 168
Dalton, OH 44618
Ph: (330)832-9582
E-mail: chamber@leedaservices.com
Contact: Joseph B. Knetzer, Pres.
Local. Conventions/Meetings: annual Dalton Holidays - festival, features various entertainment, lots of food, and plenty of crafts to see and purchase - first weekend in December • monthly meeting - every first Wednesday.

14830 ■ Dalton Lions Club - Ohio
c/o William Baringer, Pres.
13950 Arnold Rd.
Dalton, OH 44618
Ph: (330)857-8479
URL: http://users.adelphia.net/~npssteve/district.htm
Contact: William Baringer, Pres.
Local. Affiliated With: Lions Clubs International.

14831 ■ National Active and Retired Federal Employees Association - Wayne County 2218
1315 Deerfield SW
Dalton, OH 44618
Ph: (330)828-2359
URL: National Affiliate–www.narfe.org
Contact: Helena P. Schloneger, Contact
Local. Protects the retirement future of employees through education. Informs members on issues affecting the retirement. **Affiliated With:** National Association of Retired Federal Employees.

14832 ■ Ohio State Trappers Association (OSTA)
18336 Goudy Rd.
Dalton, OH 44618
URL: http://www.ohiostatetrapper.org
Founded: 1940. **State.**

14833 ■ Scottish Terrier Club of Northern Ohio
c/o Tonna Hines, Sec.
1862 Deerfield NW
Dalton, OH 44618
Ph: (330)828-8899
E-mail: tandem@raex.com
URL: http://www.members.tripod.com/stcno
Local.

Damascus

14834 ■ Teachers Saving Children (TSC)
PO Box 125
Damascus, OH 44619-0125
Ph: (330)821-2747
E-mail: tsc-life@juno.com
URL: http://www.teacherssavingchildren.org
Contact: Ms. Connie Bancroft, Exec.Dir.
Founded: 1991. **Membership Dues:** regular, $25 (annual) • retired educator, college student, $10 (annual). **State Groups:** 1. **Local.** Pro-life teachers and other concerned citizens. Aims to establish respect for all human life from conception to natural death. **Publications:** *Teaching Saving Children*, bimonthly. Newsletter • Brochure.

Dayton

14835 ■ ACF Greater Dayton Chapter
c/o Keith E. Davis, CEC, Pres.
PO Box 736
Dayton, OH 45409
Ph: (937)253-1010
E-mail: ceckeithra@aol.com
URL: National Affiliate–www.acfchefs.org
Contact: Keith E. Davis CEC, Pres.
Local. Promotes the culinary profession and provides on-going educational training and networking for members. Provides opportunities for competition, professional recognition, and access to educational forums with other culinarians at local, regional, national, and international events.

14836 ■ Alpha Iota Delta, Pi Chapter
c/o Joseph W. Coleman
Wright State Univ.
Info. Syss., 212Q Rike Hall
3640 Colonel Glenn Hwy.
Dayton, OH 45435-0001
Ph: (937)775-2648
Fax: (937)775-2421
E-mail: joseph.coleman@wright.edu
URL: National Affiliate–www.alphaiotadelta.com
Contact: Dr. Joseph W. Coleman, Sponsor
Founded: 1972. **Members:** 130. **Local.** Management science undergraduates at Wright State University. Promotes professional fellowship among students and faculty members. Confers distinctions for academic excellence. Participates in National Scholastic Honorary Society. **Publications:** none.

Libraries: Type: open to the public. **Holdings:** 583,979; periodicals. **Affiliated With:** Alpha Iota Delta.

14837 ■ Alzheimer's Association, Miami Valley Chapter
3797 Summit Glen Dr., Ste.G100
Dayton, OH 45449
Ph: (937)291-3332
Fax: (937)291-0463
Free: (800)441-3322
E-mail: judy.turner@alz.org
Contact: Judy Turner, Exec.Dir.
Local. Assists people with Alzheimer's disease and related dementia. **Affiliated With:** Alzheimer's Association.

14838 ■ American Cancer Society, Montgomery Area
40 S Perry St., Ste.120
Dayton, OH 45402
Ph: (937)223-8521
Fax: (937)223-5435
Free: (888)227-6446
E-mail: paula.reed@cancer.org
URL: http://www.cancer.org
Contact: Paula Reed, Contact
Local. Works to eliminate cancer as a major health problem through research, education, advocacy and service. **Affiliated With:** American Cancer Society.

14839 ■ American Federation of Government Employees, AFL-CIO - DOD Local Union 1138
5337 Huberville Rd.
Dayton, OH 45431
Ph: (937)254-2343
Fax: (937)254-2330
E-mail: prez@afgecouncil214.org
URL: http://www.afgecouncil214.org/1138/
Contact: Pamela McGinnis, Pres.
Members: 310. **Local.** Federal employees including food inspectors, nurses, printers, cartographers, lawyers, police officers, census workers, OSHA inspectors, janitors, truck drivers, secretaries, artists, plumbers, immigration inspectors, scientists, doctors, cowboys, botanists, park rangers, computer programmers, foreign service workers, airplane mechanics, environmentalists, and writers. Seeks to help provide good government services, while ensuring that government workers are treated fairly and with dignity. **Affiliated With:** American Federation of Government Employees.

14840 ■ American Federation of Musicians, Local 101-473
PO Box 60026
Dayton, OH 45406
Ph: (937)567-9300
Fax: (937)567-9301
E-mail: daytonmusicians@yahoo.com
URL: http://daytonmusicians.org
Contact: Donald Sutton, Sec.-Treas.
Founded: 1899. **Members:** 278. **Local.** AFL-CIO. Musicians. Seeks to improve the wages and working conditions of professional musicians. **Affiliated With:** American Federation of Musicians of the United States and Canada.

14841 ■ American Friends Service Committee - Dayton, Ohio
c/o Patricia Trammell, Eastern Area Coor.
915 Salem Ave.
Dayton, OH 45406
Ph: (937)278-4225
Fax: (937)278-2778
E-mail: afscpat@aol.com
URL: http://www.afsc.org/greatlakes/dayton/default.htm
Contact: Patricia Trammell, Eastern Area Coor.
Local.

14842 ■ American Institute of Architects Dayton
5816 Daffodil Circle
Dayton, OH 45449
Ph: (937)291-1913
Fax: (937)436-4994
E-mail: aiadayton@donet.com
URL: National Affiliate–www.aia.org
Local. Professional society of architects. Fosters professionalism and accountability among members through continuing education and training; promotes design excellence by influencing change in the industry. **Affiliated With:** American Institute of Architects.

14843 ■ American Legion, Dayton Post 5
PO Box 31321
Dayton, OH 45437
Ph: (740)362-7478
Fax: (740)362-1429
URL: National Affiliate–www.legion.org
Local. Affiliated With: American Legion.

14844 ■ American Legion, J.C. Trigg Memorial Post 328
143 W Hudson Ave.
Dayton, OH 45405
Ph: (740)362-7478
Fax: (740)362-1429
URL: National Affiliate–www.legion.org
Local. Affiliated With: American Legion.

14845 ■ American Legion, Northridge Memorial Post 746
7015 N Dixie Dr.
Dayton, OH 45414
Ph: (740)362-7478
Fax: (740)362-1429
URL: National Affiliate–www.legion.org
Local. Affiliated With: American Legion.

14846 ■ American Legion, Ohio Post 619
c/o Tony Stein
1510 Webster St.
Dayton, OH 45404
Ph: (740)362-7478
Fax: (740)362-1429
URL: National Affiliate–www.legion.org
Contact: Tony Stein, Contact
Local. Affiliated With: American Legion.

14847 ■ American Legion, Ohio Post 776
c/o Gen. Daniel Chappie James
5350 Burkhardt Rd.
Dayton, OH 45431-2110
Ph: (740)362-7478
Fax: (740)362-1429
E-mail: adj776@aol.com
URL: National Affiliate–www.legion.org
Contact: Gen. Daniel Chappie James, Contact
Local. Affiliated With: American Legion.

14848 ■ American Legion, South Park Memorial Post 675
228 Obell Ct.
Dayton, OH 45409
Ph: (740)362-7478
Fax: (740)362-1429
URL: National Affiliate–www.legion.org
Local. Affiliated With: American Legion.

14849 ■ American Payroll Association, Miami Valley Chapter
PO Box 1301
Dayton, OH 45401-1301
Ph: (937)425-8482
Fax: (937)425-8414
E-mail: info@apamiamivalleyoh.org
URL: http://www.apamiamivalleyoh.org
Contact: Gloria Adams CPP, Pres.
Local. Aims to increase the Payroll Professional's skill level through education and mutual support. Represents the Payroll Professional before legislative bodies. Administers the certified payroll professional program of recognition. Provides public service education on payroll and employment issues. **Affiliated With:** American Payroll Association.

14850 ■ American Red Cross, Dayton Area Chapter
370 W First St.
Dayton, OH 45401
Ph: (937)222-6711
E-mail: volunteer@dac.redcross.org
URL: http://www.dayton.oh.redcross.org
Local.

14851 ■ American Society of Heating, Refrigerating and Air-Conditioning Engineers - Dayton
PO Box 3202
Dayton, OH 45401-3202
Ph: (937)264-4343
Fax: (937)264-4360
E-mail: daytonashrae@operamail.com
URL: http://www.sinclair.edu/community/daytonashrae
Contact: Mike Kirchens, Pres.
Local. Advances the arts and sciences of heating, ventilation, air-conditioning and refrigeration. Provides a source of technical and educational information, standards and guidelines. Conducts seminars for professional growth. **Affiliated With:** American Society of Heating, Refrigerating and Air-Conditioning Engineers.

14852 ■ American Society for Training and Development - Western Ohio Chapter
140 E Monument Ave.
Dayton, OH 45402
Ph: (937)775-4473
E-mail: scott.graham@wright.edu
URL: http://wocastd.org
Contact: Scott Graham, Pres.
Local. Promotes workplace learning and the improvement of skills of workplace professionals. Provides resource and professional development to individuals in the field of learning and development. Recognizes and sets standards for learning and performance professionals. **Affiliated With:** American Society for Training and Development.

14853 ■ Antioch Shriners
c/o H. Dale Biddle
107 E First St.
Dayton, OH 45402-1214
Ph: (937)461-4740
Fax: (937)461-3904
Free: (800)790-4740
E-mail: larrymcornett@aol.com
URL: http://www.antiochshrine.com
Contact: H. Dale Biddle, Recorder
Local. Affiliated With: Imperial Council of the Ancient Arabic Order of the Nobles of the Mystic Shrine for North America.

14854 ■ Association of Community Organizations for Reform Now, Dayton
3665 Otterbein St.
Dayton, OH 45406
Ph: (937)776-0761
E-mail: ohacornda@acorn.org
URL: National Affiliate–www.acorn.org
Local. Affiliated With: Association of Community Organizations for Reform Now.

14855 ■ Association for Computing Machinery, Wright State University (ACM)
c/o Parag Sharma, Pres.
Dept. of CS & Engg.
303 Russ
3640 Colonel Glenn Hwy.
Dayton, OH 45435
Ph: (937)775-5117
E-mail: acm@cs.wright.edu
URL: http://www.cs.wright.edu/cecs/clubs/acm
Contact: Parag Sharma, Pres.
Local. Biological, medical, behavioral, and computer scientists; hospital administrators; programmers and others interested in application of computer methods

to biological, behavioral, and medical problems. Stimulates understanding of the use and potential of computers in the Biosciences. **Affiliated With:** Association for Computing Machinery.

14856 ■ Association of Energy Engineers, Ohio/West Central Ohio
c/o John O'Brien Sr., Mechanical Engr.
Heapy Engg. LLC
1400 W Dorothy Ln.
Dayton, OH 45409-1310
Ph: (937)224-0861
Fax: (937)224-5777
E-mail: jpobrien@heapy.com
URL: National Affiliate–www.aeecenter.org
Contact: John O'Brien, Sr. Mechanical Engr.
State. Affiliated With: Association of Energy Engineers.

14857 ■ Association for Women in Science, Miami Valley
c/o Dept. of Biochemistry and Molecular Biology
Wright State Univ.
3640 Colonel Glen Hwy.
Dayton, OH 45435
E-mail: ina.bicknell@wright.edu
URL: National Affiliate–www.awis.org
Contact: Ina Rea Bicknell, Contact
Local. Professional women and students in life, physical, and social sciences and engineering; men are also members. Promotes equal opportunities for women to enter the scientific workforce and to achieve their career goals; provides educational information to women planning careers in science; networks with other women's groups; monitors scientific legislation and the status of women in science. **Affiliated With:** Association for Women in Science.

14858 ■ Aullwood Audubon Center and Farm
1000 Aullwood Rd.
Dayton, OH 45414
Ph: (937)890-7360
Fax: (937)890-2382
E-mail: aullwood@gemair.com
URL: http://aullwood.center.audubon.org
Contact: Charity Krueger, Exec.Dir.
Founded: 1957. **Members:** 1,800. **Membership Dues:** family, $35 (annual). **Staff:** 12. **Budget:** $600,000. **Local.** Provides activities that increase understanding and preservation of the planet by children and adults through education, research and recreation. **Libraries: Type:** reference. **Holdings:** 2,000; books, periodicals. **Subjects:** natural history. **Formerly:** (1991) National Audubon Society, Dayton Chapter; (1995) National Audubon Aullwood Center. **Publications:** *Aullwood Center and Farm*, bimonthly. Newsletter. **Price:** free to members. ISSN: 1097-1548. **Circulation:** 2,000 • *EE Bulletin*, periodic.

14859 ■ Beavercreek - Young Life
555 Clareridge Ln.
Dayton, OH 45458
Ph: (937)434-3484
URL: http://sites.younglife.org/sites/Beavercreek/default.aspx
Local. Affiliated With: Young Life.

14860 ■ Bellbrook - Young Life
555 Clareridge Ln.
Dayton, OH 45458
Ph: (937)434-3484
URL: http://sites.younglife.org/sites/Bellbrook/default.aspx
Local. Affiliated With: Young Life.

14861 ■ Better Business Bureau of Dayton/Miami Valley
15 W 4th St., Ste.300
Dayton, OH 45402
Ph: (937)222-5825
Fax: (937)222-3338
Free: (800)776-5301
E-mail: info@dayton.bbb.org
URL: http://www.dayton.bbb.org
Contact: Donna Childs, Pres.
Local. Seeks to promote and foster ethical relationship between businesses and the public through voluntary self-regulation, consumer and business education, and service excellence. Provides information to help consumers and businesses make informed purchasing decisions and avoid costly scams and frauds; settles consumer complaints through arbitration and other means. **Affiliated With:** BBB Wise Giving Alliance.

14862 ■ Blacks In Government, Greater Dayton Chapter
PO Box AMC 33684
Dayton, OH 45433-0684
E-mail: greater.dayton@bignet.org
URL: http://www.bignet.org/regional/greater.dayton/index.htm
Contact: Mr. Leonard T. Stone, Pres.
Local. Represents federal, state, and local government employees concerned with the present and future status of Blacks in government. Conducts seminars and workshops for professional and nonprofessional government employees. Advocates for equal opportunities for Blacks in government. **Affiliated With:** National Organization of Blacks in Government.

14863 ■ Bowling Centers Association of Ohio (BCAO)
PO Box 750996
Dayton, OH 45475
Ph: (937)433-8363
Fax: (937)433-2597
E-mail: bpao@siscom.net
URL: http://www.bowlohio.com
Contact: Pat Marazzi, Exec.Dir.
State.

14864 ■ Butler/Warren County Society for Human Resource Management
c/o Rich Lencyk
Crane Am. Sers.
3440 Off. Park Dr.
Dayton, OH 45439
Ph: (937)293-6526
Fax: (937)395-0396
E-mail: rich.lencyk@craneamerica.com
URL: http://www.ohioshrm.org/butler
Contact: Rich Lencyk, Pres.
Local. Represents the interests of human resource and industrial relations professionals and executives. Promotes the advancement of human resource management.

14865 ■ Camp Fire USA Greater Dayton Area Council
4301 Powell Rd.
Dayton, OH 45424
Ph: (937)236-6115
Fax: (937)236-9115
E-mail: daytoncampfire@sbcglobal.net
URL: http://home.woh.rr.com/mainweb/campfireusa/home.htm
Local. Affiliated With: Camp Fire USA.

14866 ■ Cityfolk
126 N Main St., Ste.220
Dayton, OH 45402
Ph: (937)223-3655 (937)496-3863
Fax: (937)223-2842
E-mail: cityfolk@cityfolk.org
URL: http://www.cityfolk.org
Contact: John Harris, Exec.Dir.
Founded: 1980. **Members:** 500. **Membership Dues:** individual, $40 (annual). **Staff:** 10. **Budget:** $1,000,000. **Local.** Promotes traditional, folk, and ethnic arts in Dayton, OH through concerts, educational activities, and major summer festival. **Publications:** Newsletter, 3/year. Contains updates on current Cityfolk events. **Price:** free. **Circulation:** 500. **Conventions/Meetings:** annual festival, traditional and ethnic music and dance performances, craftspeople, food and vending (exhibits) - always 3rd weekend of June in Dayton, OH.

14867 ■ Dayton Area Auto Dealers Association (DAADA)
c/o Mr. Michael A. McCall, Exec.VP
220 S Edwin C. Moses Blvd., Ste.No. 20-210
Dayton, OH 45402-8400
Ph: (937)222-4911
Fax: (937)512-4913
E-mail: mike.mccall@daada.org
URL: http://www.daada.org
Contact: Mr. Michael A. McCall, Exec.VP
Local. Affiliated With: National Automobile Dealers Association.

14868 ■ Dayton Area Board of Realtors (DABR)
1515 S Main St.
Dayton, OH 45409
Ph: (937)223-0900
Fax: (937)223-1084
E-mail: jlivesay@dabr.com
URL: http://www.dabr.com
Contact: Dale M. Berry, Pres.
Local. Strives to develop real estate business practices. Advocates for the right to own, use and transfer real property. Provides a facility for professional development, research and exchange of information among members and the general public. **Affiliated With:** National Association of Realtors.

14869 ■ Dayton Area Chamber of Commerce
c/o Phillip L. Parker, CAE, Pres./CEO
1 Chamber Plz.
Dayton, OH 45402-2400
Ph: (937)226-1444
Fax: (937)226-8254
E-mail: info@dacc.org
URL: http://www.daytonchamber.org
Contact: Phillip L. Parker CAE, Pres./CEO
Founded: 1907. **Members:** 3,657. **Membership Dues:** business (1-99 employees), $335-$110 (annual) • business (100-299 employees), $1,225-$2,220 (annual) • charitable organization, $335 (annual). **Budget:** $3,500,000. **Local.** Promotes business and community development in Dayton, OH area. **Computer Services:** Information services, membership directory. **Boards:** Workforce policy. **Committees:** CEO Development; Executive Dialogue; HR Policy Review; Quality Dayton. **Councils:** Research Advisory. **Task Forces:** Internet. **Formerly:** (1999) Dayton Area Chamber of Commerce Economic Development Division. **Publications:** *ChamberWatch*, bimonthly. Newsletter. Contains information about issues being considered at the statehouse and the Congress. • *Focus*, quarterly. Newsletter. **Advertising:** accepted. Alternate Formats: online • *Membership Directory and Community Guide*, annual. **Circulation:** 22,000. **Advertising:** accepted. **Conventions/Meetings:** quarterly board meeting • annual Membership Meeting.

14870 ■ Dayton Association of Insurance and Financial Advisors
1524 E Stroop Rd., Ste.102
Dayton, OH 45429-5083
Ph: (937)298-5558
Fax: (937)298-5727
E-mail: adminoffice@erinet.com
Contact: Patricia A. Croft, Exec. Officer
Founded: 1915. **Members:** 361. **Membership Dues:** individual, $306 (annual). **Staff:** 1. **Budget:** $100,000. **Local.** Life and health insurance agents and affiliates in southwestern Ohio. Supports the principles of, and seeks to educate both the members and public about, legal reserve life and health insurance. **Formerly:** (2000) Dayton Association of Life Underwriters. **Publications:** *Lifelines*, monthly. Newsletter. **Advertising:** accepted • *Who's Who*, annual. Directory. **Conventions/Meetings:** annual Exhibitors Day (exhibits) - April • monthly meeting - always third Thursday.

14871 ■ Dayton Audubon Society (DAS)
1375 E Siebenthaler Ave.
Dayton, OH 45414-5398
Ph: (937)886-0092
E-mail: audubon@dayton.net
URL: http://www.dayton.net/Audubon
Contact: Dick Balk, Pres.
Founded: 1923. **Local.**

14872 ■ Dayton Builders Exchange
2077 Embury Park Rd.
Dayton, OH 45414
Ph: (937)278-5723
Fax: (937)278-3843
E-mail: daytonbx@aol.com
URL: http://www.daytonbx.org
Founded: 1910. **Members:** 275. **Membership Dues:** regular, $520 (annual) • associate, $195 (annual). **Staff:** 3. **Budget:** $200,000. **Local.** Construction contractors, suppliers, architects, and engineers in southwestern Ohio. Provides members with professional services and works to improve the construction industry. **Libraries: Type:** not open to the public. **Holdings:** 50; periodicals. **Subjects:** job bid work/public court records. **Awards:** Craftsmanship Award. **Frequency:** annual. **Type:** recognition. **Recipient:** for skills on jobsite • Trade/Architectural Awards. **Type:** recognition. **Publications:** *Construction Journal*, weekly. Includes construction project info/financial (courts). **Price:** $50.00. **Circulation:** 240. **Advertising:** accepted. **Conventions/Meetings:** annual Meeting and Inaugural Ball - always April • quarterly seminar.

14873 ■ Dayton Chapter of the Society of Financial Service Professionals
c/o Patricia A. Croft, Chapter Exec.
DAIFA/SFSP
1524 E Stroop Rd., Ste.102
Dayton, OH 45429
Ph: (937)298-5558
Fax: (937)298-5727
E-mail: adminoffice@erinet.com
URL: http://www.sfsp.net/dayton
Contact: Patricia A. Croft, Chapter Exec.
Local. Represents the interests of financial advisers. Fosters the development of professional responsibility. Helps clients achieve their personal and business-related financial goals. **Affiliated With:** Society of Financial Service Professionals.

14874 ■ Dayton Cycling Club
c/o Kay Wert Minardi, Ed.
PO Box 94
Dayton, OH 45409
Ph: (937)235-1196 (937)299-2454
E-mail: spokenlink@earthlink.net
URL: http://www.daytoncyclingclub.org
Contact: Anita Patten, Pres.
Founded: 1963. **Members:** 700. **Membership Dues:** individual, $20 (annual) • family, $30 (annual). **Local.** Strives to promote and popularize active participation in bicycling in all of its forms. Encourages the safe use of bicycles for recreation and transportation purposes. Provides educational and social functions for the benefit of its members and others. **Affiliated With:** Adventure Cycling Association; International Mountain Bicycling Association; League of American Bicyclists; Ultra Marathon Cycling Association. **Publications:** *Spoke 'N Link*, monthly. Newsletter. **Price:** included in membership dues. **Circulation:** 700. **Advertising:** accepted.

14875 ■ Dayton Dental Society
436 Patterson Rd.
Dayton, OH 45419-4306
Ph: (937)294-2808
Fax: (937)294-7099
E-mail: daytondentalsoc@aol.com
URL: http://www.daytondentalsociety.com
Contact: Gregory Shelhouse, Pres.
Local. Represents the interests of dentists committed to the public's oral health, ethics and professional development. Encourages the improvement of the public's oral health and promotes the art and science of dentistry. **Affiliated With:** American Dental Association; Ohio Dental Association.

14876 ■ Dayton Downtown Lions Club
E 1st St.
Dayton, OH 45402
Ph: (937)832-0881
URL: http://daytonoh.lionwap.org
Contact: Todd Trautwein, Pres.
Local. Affiliated With: Lions Clubs International.

14877 ■ Dayton Gem and Mineral Society (DGMS)
Riverbend Art Ctr.
1301E Siebenthaler Rd.
Dayton, OH 45414
E-mail: andrea.koziol@notes.udayton.edu
URL: http://homepages.udayton.edu/~koziolam/dgms/dgmsmain.html
Contact: Dr. Andrea Koziol, Pres.
Local. Aims to further the study of Earth Sciences and the practice of lapidary arts and mineralogy. **Affiliated With:** American Federation of Mineralogical Societies.

14878 ■ Dayton/Miami Valley Safety Council
1 Chamber Plz.
Dayton, OH 45402-2400
Ph: (937)226-8227
Fax: (937)226-8254
URL: National Affiliate–www.nsc.org
Contact: Ms. Amy Schrimpf, Exec.Dir.
Founded: 1952. **Members:** 200. **Staff:** 2. **State Groups:** 1. **Local.** Works to promote a safe and healthy environment at home, in the workplace, and in the community by increasing safety and health awareness. **Libraries: Type:** reference. **Holdings:** video recordings. **Subjects:** safety and health. **Affiliated With:** National Safety Council. **Publications:** *Safety Net*, bimonthly. Newsletter. **Price:** for members. **Circulation:** 1,000. **Advertising:** accepted. **Conventions/Meetings:** annual conference (exhibits) - September.

14879 ■ Dayton and Montgomery County Convention and Visitors Bureau
1 Chamber Plz., No. A
Dayton, OH 45402-2400
Ph: (937)226-8211
Fax: (937)226-8294
Free: (800)221-8235
E-mail: cvbureau@dnaco.net
URL: http://www.daytoncvb.com
Local.

14880 ■ Dayton Ohio Habitat for Humanity (DOHH)
1041 S Patterson Rd.
Dayton, OH 45402
Ph: (937)586-0860
Fax: (937)586-0861
E-mail: dpesce@daytonhabitat.org
URL: http://www.daytonhabitat.org
Contact: Frank Gorman, Exec.Dir.
Local. Telecommunication Services: electronic mail, fgorman@daytonhabitat.org. **Affiliated With:** Habitat for Humanity International.

14881 ■ Dayton Table Tennis Club
Lohrey Center
2366 Glenarm Ave.
Dayton, OH 45420
Ph: (937)433-6956 (937)253-1417
URL: http://www.usatt.org/clubs
Contact: John Dichiaro, Contact
Local. Affiliated With: U.S.A. Table Tennis.

14882 ■ Dayton Urban League
c/o Willie F. Walker, Pres.
907 W Fifth St.
Dayton, OH 45402
Ph: (937)220-6650
E-mail: williewalker@earthlink.net
URL: National Affiliate–www.nul.org
Contact: Willie F. Walker, Pres.
Local. Affiliated With: National Urban League.

14883 ■ Dignity - Dayton
PO Box 3304
Dayton, OH 45401
Ph: (937)640-2468
URL: http://dignitydayton.org
Local.

14884 ■ Foster Grandparent Program of Greater Dayton
105 S Wilkerson St.
Dayton, OH 45402
Ph: (937)223-2390
Fax: (937)223-6078
E-mail: srcvolser@aol.com
URL: http://www.seniorresourceconnection.com
Contact: Nanci McGuire, Dir.
Local. Serves as mentors, tutors and caregivers for at-risk children and youth with special needs. Provides older Americans the opportunity to put their life experiences to work for local communities.

14885 ■ Gem City Gliders Ski and Bike Club
535 Alameda Pl.
Dayton, OH 45406
Ph: (937)275-5439
E-mail: sheriski@att.net
URL: http://www.nbs.org/clubs/clubsbystate.php
Contact: Ms. Sheri Wise, Pres.
Local. Affiliated With: National Brotherhood of Skiers.

14886 ■ Girl Scouts of Buckeye Trails Council
450 Shoup Mill Rd.
Dayton, OH 45415
Ph: (937)275-7601
Free: (800)233-4845
E-mail: webmaster@btgirlscouts.org
URL: http://www.btgirlscouts.org
Contact: Caroline Su, Contact
Local. Young girls and adult volunteers, corporate, government and individual supporters. Strives to develop potential and leadership skills among its members. Conducts trainings, educational programs and outdoor activities.

14887 ■ Goodwill Industries of the Miami Valley (GID)
1511 Kuntz Rd.
Dayton, OH 45404-1297
Ph: (937)461-4800
Fax: (937)461-2750
E-mail: communications@goodwilldayton.org
URL: http://www.dayton.net/goodwill
Contact: Amy Lutrell, Pres.
Founded: 1934. **Members:** 475. **Local.** Provides employment, training, evaluation, counseling, job placement, vision services, and opportunities for personal growth to people with vocational disadvantages and disabilities. **Affiliated With:** Goodwill Industries International. **Publications:** *Focus*, quarterly. Newsletter. **Price:** free to donors.

14888 ■ Greater Dayton ACM Chapter
c/o William Davis, Chm.
140 E Monument Ave.
Dayton, OH 45402-1211
Ph: (937)224-8513
E-mail: dayton@acm.org
URL: National Affiliate–www.acm.org
Contact: William Davis, Chm.
Local. Works to advance the art, science, engineering, and application of information technology. Strives to promote technical awareness and professionalism in the computing community of Greater Dayton area. **Affiliated With:** Association for Computing Machinery. **Formerly:** (2005) Greater Dayton Association for Computing Machinery Chapter. **Conventions/Meetings:** monthly meeting - every second Thursday.

14889 ■ Greater Dayton Apartment Association (GDAA)
2555 S Dixie Dr., Ste.100
Dayton, OH 45409
Ph: (937)293-1170
Fax: (937)293-1180
E-mail: info@gdaa.org
URL: http://www.gdaa.org
Contact: Joanna Coyle, Exec.Dir.
Local. Promotes professionalism in the multi-housing industry through education and legislation.

14890 ■ Greater Dayton Association of Black Journalists
PO Box 1091
Dayton, OH 45401
Ph: (937)239-1282
E-mail: arobinson@daytonadailynews.com
URL: National Affiliate–www.nabj.org
Contact: Amelia Robinson, Pres.
Local. Advocates the rights of black journalists. Provides informational and training services and professional development to black journalists and to the general public. **Affiliated With:** National Association of Black Journalists.

14891 ■ Greater Dayton Corvette Club (GDCC)
PO Box 2307
Dayton, OH 45401-2307
E-mail: mjones@donet.com
URL: http://www.dayton-corvette-club.com
Contact: Mike Jones, Pres.
Local. Affiliated With: National Council of Corvette Clubs.

14892 ■ Greater Dayton Planned Giving Council
c/o Kevin McDonald
Key Bank
34 N Main St.
PO Box 1809
Dayton, OH 45401-1809
Ph: (937)586-7553
Fax: (937)586-7553
E-mail: kmcdonald@keybank.com
URL: National Affiliate–www.ncpg.org
Contact: Kevin McDonald, Pres.
Founded: 1995. **Members:** 82. **Membership Dues:** local individual, $100 (annual) • national, $90 (annual). **Local.** Professional association of individuals from the fundraising, accounting, estate planning, insurance, and related fields. Provides education and networking opportunities. **Affiliated With:** National Committee on Planned Giving.

14893 ■ IEEE - Dayton Section
140 E Monument Ave.
Dayton, OH 45402
Ph: (937)775-5052
E-mail: krattan@cs.wright.edu
URL: http://ewh.ieee.org/r2/dayton
Contact: Dr. Kuldip Rattan, Chm.
Local. Engineers and scientists in electrical engineering, electronics, and allied fields. Promotes creating, developing, integrating, sharing, and applying knowledge about electro and information technologies and sciences for the benefit of humanity and the profession. Conducts lectures on current engineering and scientific topics.

14894 ■ Infusion Nurses Society, Buckeye
6674 Munger Rd.
Dayton, OH 45459
Ph: (937)436-2472
E-mail: dbing@toast.net
URL: National Affiliate–www.ins1.org
Contact: Debbie Bingley, Pres.
Local. Represents the interests of healthcare professionals who are involved with the practice of infusion therapy. Seeks to advance the delivery of quality therapy to patients. Promotes research and education in the practice of infusion nursing. **Affiliated With:** Infusion Nurses Society.

14895 ■ International Association of Business Communicators, Dayton Chapter
c/o Mary Z. Bogan
6700 Statesboro Rd.
Dayton, OH 45459
Ph: (937)438-9708
E-mail: mbogan1@woh.rr.com
URL: http://www.iabcdayton.com
Contact: Mary Z. Bogan, Pres.
Local. Represents the interests of communication managers, public relations directors, writers, editors and audiovisual specialists. Encourages establishment of college-level programs in organizational communication. Conducts surveys on employee communication effectiveness and media trends. Conducts research in the field of communication. **Affiliated With:** International Association of Business Communicators.

14896 ■ International Association of Machinists and Aerospace Workers, AFL-CIO, CLC - Lodge 225
60 Commerce Park Dr.
Dayton, OH 45404-1212
Ph: (937)275-3978 (937)233-9007
Fax: (937)233-0437
E-mail: br20ak@aol.com
URL: http://ll225.goiam.org
Contact: Dennis Pennington, Pres.
Members: 499. **Local. Affiliated With:** International Association of Machinists and Aerospace Workers.

14897 ■ International Union of Electronic, Electrical, Salaried, Machine and Furniture Workers, AFL-CIO-CLC - Local Union 755
1675 Woodman Dr.
Dayton, OH 45432
Ph: (937)253-3565
Fax: (937)253-4269
E-mail: lwest@iuelocal755.com
URL: http://www.iuelocal755.com
Contact: Larry West, Pres.
Members: 2,000. **Local. Affiliated With:** International Union of Electronic, Electrical, Salaried, Machine, and Furniture Workers.

14898 ■ International Union, United Automobile, Aerospace and Agricultural Implement Workers of America, AFL-CIO - Local Union 696
1543 Alwildy Ave.
Dayton, OH 45408
Ph: (937)228-2142
E-mail: info@uaw696.com
URL: http://www.uaw696.com
Contact: Joe Buckley, Pres.
Members: 1,780. **Local.** Seeks for the dignity and equality of the workers. Strives to provide contractors with well-trained, productive employees. **Affiliated With:** International Union, United Automobile, Aerospace and Agricultural Implement Workers of America.

14899 ■ Inventors Council of Dayton
Wright Bros. Sta.
PO Box 611
Dayton, OH 45409
Ph: (937)224-8513 (937)256-9698
E-mail: swfday@aol.com
URL: http://groups.yahoo.com/group/inventors_council
Contact: Stephen W. Frey, Pres.
Founded: 1982. **Membership Dues:** all, $40 (annual). **Local.** Seeks to promote commercialization efforts for inventors and provide education resources for members. Activities are monthly meetings, conferences, lab and factory tours, and patent searching seminars. **Affiliated With:** United Inventors Association of the U.S.A. **Conventions/Meetings:** monthly meeting, presentations about "from mind to market place" range of subjects; Show and Tell and Question and Answer sessions; tours on various facilities; participates in TechFest during the month of February (exhibits) - first Wednesday of each month. Kettering, OH - Avg. Attendance: 50.

14900 ■ Jane Austen Society of North America, Ohio, Dayton
c/o Gary Mitchner
108 Patterson Rd.
Dayton, OH 45419
Ph: (937)299-1663
E-mail: gary.mitchner@sinclair.edu
URL: National Affiliate–www.jasna.org
Contact: Gary Mitchner, Contact
Local. Affiliated With: Jane Austen Society of North America.

14901 ■ Jewish Federation of Greater Dayton
c/o Barbara Sanderow, Pres.
4501 Denlinger Rd.
Dayton, OH 45426-2395
Ph: (937)854-4150
Fax: (937)854-2850
E-mail: jphares@jfgd.net
URL: http://www.jewishdayton.org
Contact: Ms. Jodi Phares, Sec.
Local.

14902 ■ Juvenile Diabetes Research Foundation International, Greater Dayton Chapter
1293-H Lyons Rd.
Dayton, OH 45458
Ph: (937)439-2873
Fax: (937)439-4086
E-mail: dayton@jdrf.org
URL: http://www.jdrf.org/dayton
Contact: Karen Myers, Exec.Dir.
Local. Nongovernmental funder of diabetes research. Mission is to find a cure for diabetes and its complications through the support of research. **Affiliated With:** Juvenile Diabetes Research Foundation International.

14903 ■ Kettering - Young Life
555 Clareridge Ln.
Dayton, OH 45458
Ph: (937)434-3484
URL: http://sites.younglife.org/sites/Kettering/default.aspx
Local. Affiliated With: Young Life.

14904 ■ League of Women Voters of the Greater Dayton Area (LWVGDA)
131 N Ludlow St., Talbott Tower, Ste.1208
Dayton, OH 45402-1703
Ph: (937)228-4041 (937)372-4148
Fax: (937)228-4104
E-mail: league@lwvdayton.org
URL: http://www.lwvdayton.org
Contact: Penny Wolff, Pres.
Founded: 1920. **Members:** 300. **Membership Dues:** individual, $50 (annual). **Staff:** 3. **Budget:** $38,000. **Local Groups:** 1. **Regional.** Voting age citizens in the Dayton, Ohio area. Promotes political responsibility through active, informed participation in government. Conducts voter registration activities, candidate meetings, cable TV interviews, informational meetings, referrals to proper source, etc. **Libraries: Type:** open to the public. **Holdings:** 70; books, video recordings. **Subjects:** politics, history, women's issues. **Affiliated With:** League of Women Voters of the United States. **Publications:** *Directory of Public Officials in for Montgomery County and Greene County*, annual. Lists all local elected officials in Montgomery and Greene counties. **Price:** $2.00 plus shipping and handling. **Circulation:** 3,500 • *The Voter*, monthly. Newsletter. **Conventions/Meetings:** quarterly meeting, specific topics which change every year • monthly Unit Meetings - September-May.

14905 ■ Macedonia Community Development Corp.
c/o Dr. Robert E. Baines, Jr.
27 N Gettysburg Ave.
Dayton, OH 45417-1701
Ph: (937)268-2011 (937)268-7175
Fax: (937)268-4988
Contact: Daphene Baines, Manager
Founded: 1974. **Staff:** 7. **Local.** Provides housing and youth activities.

14906 ■ Master Electrical Contractors Independent Electrical Contractors of Dayton
c/o Howard Honious
2523 Roanoke Ave.
Dayton, OH 45419-1529

Ph: (937)299-4809
Fax: (937)299-4809
E-mail: hhonious@aol.com
URL: National Affiliate–www.ieci.org
Local. **Affiliated With:** Independent Electrical Contractors.

14907 ■ Mathematical Association of America, University of Dayton Student Chapter
300 Coll. Park
Dayton, OH 45469
Ph: (937)229-1000
E-mail: mary.hickey@notes.udayton.edu
URL: http://www.udayton.edu/%7Emathclub
Contact: Mary Hickey, Pres.
Local. Promotes the general understanding and appreciation of mathematics. Advances and improves the education in the mathematical sciences at the collegiate level. Provides resources and activities that foster scholarship, professional growth and cooperation among teachers, other professionals and students. **Affiliated With:** Mathematical Association of America.

14908 ■ Mechanical Contractors Association of Greater Dayton (MCA)
c/o Robert H. Pope
2077 Embury Park Rd.
Dayton, OH 45414
Ph: (937)278-0102
Fax: (937)278-0317
E-mail: mca@assnsoffice.com
URL: http://www.mcadayton.com
Contact: Robert H. Pope, Contact
Local. Contractors who furnish, install, and service piping systems and related equipment for heating, cooling, refrigeration, ventilating, and air conditioning systems. **Affiliated With:** Mechanical Contractors Association of America.

14909 ■ Media Communications Association International, Ohio Valley Chapter
PO Box 2046
Dayton, OH 45401-2046
Ph: (937)254-9763
E-mail: president@mcai-ohiovalley.org
URL: http://www.mcai-ohiovalley.org
Contact: John Pugnale, Pres.
Local. Provides networking and education opportunities to media communications professionals. Facilitates effective communication using new technology and with sound communication principles. **Publications:** *In-Sync*. Newsletter.

14910 ■ Miami Valley Fire-EMS Alliance
c/o Charles A. Wiltrout, Exec.Dir.
444 W Third St., Ste.20-231
Dayton, OH 45402-1460
Ph: (937)512-5103 (937)512-5108
Fax: (937)512-5124
E-mail: cwiltrout@voyager.net
URL: http://www.mvfea.com
Contact: Charles A. Wiltrout, Exec.Dir.
Founded: 1995. **Members:** 30. **Membership Dues:** associate, $500 (annual). **Staff:** 2. **Budget:** $160,000. **Local**. Represents the Council of Governments in a two county area of 20 communities seeking ways to improve services and/or save money in Fire and EMS services. **Publications:** *The Advisor*, monthly. Newsletter. **Price:** free. **Circulation:** 350. Alternate Formats: online.

14911 ■ Miami Valley Golf Association (MVGA)
555 Kramer Rd.
Dayton, OH 45419
Ph: (937)294-6842 (937)608-6169
Fax: (937)294-7003
E-mail: steve@miamivalleygolf.org
URL: http://www.miamivalleygolf.org
Contact: Steve Jurick, Exec.Dir.
Local. **Affiliated With:** International Association of Golf Administrators.

14912 ■ Miami Valley Golf Course Superintendents Association (MVGA)
555 Kramer Rd.
Dayton, OH 45419
Ph: (937)294-6842 (937)608-6169
Fax: (937)294-7003
E-mail: steve@miamivalleygolf.org
URL: http://www.miamivalleygolf.org
Contact: Steve Jurick, Exec.Dir.
Founded: 1997. **Local**. Represents the interests of golf course superintendents. Advances members' profession for career success. Enhances the enjoyment, growth and vitality in the game of golf. Educates members concerning efficient and economical management of golf courses. **Affiliated With:** Golf Course Superintendents Association of America.

14913 ■ Miami Valley Health Information Management Association (MVHIMA)
c/o Julie Hamiel, RHIT, Pres.
Children's Medical Ctr.
1 Children's Plz.
Dayton, OH 45404
Ph: (937)641-3000
E-mail: hamielj@childrensdayton.org
URL: http://www.ohima.org/reg.associations/regassocmvhima.html
Contact: Julie Hamiel RHIT, Pres.
Local. Represents the interests of individuals dedicated to the effective management of personal health information needed to deliver quality healthcare to the public. Provides career, professional development and practice resources. Sets standards for education and certification. Advocates public policy that advances Health Information Management (HIM) practice. **Affiliated With:** American Health Information Management Association; Ohio Health Information Management Association.

14914 ■ Miami Valley Model Yacht Association No. 73
c/o Donald Peacock
468 Walden Trail
Dayton, OH 45440
Ph: (513)427-1088
URL: National Affiliate–www.amya.org
Contact: Donald Peacock, Contact
Local.

14915 ■ Miami Valley NARI
c/o Jeff Miller, CR, CLC, Pres.
136 S Keowee St.
Dayton, OH 45402
Ph: (937)222-6274
Fax: (937)222-5794
Free: (800)498-6274
E-mail: dayton@naripro.org
URL: http://www.naridayton.org
Contact: Kimberly Fantaci, Exec.Dir.
Members: 130. **Membership Dues:** all, $315 (annual). **Staff:** 5. **For-Profit**. **Local**. **Awards:** Local Contractor of the Year Awards. **Frequency:** annual. **Type:** recognition. **Affiliated With:** National Association of the Remodeling Industry. **Also Known As:** (2004) Miami Valley National Association of the Remodeling Industry. **Publications:** *The Remodeler*, monthly. Newsletter. **Circulation:** 200. **Conventions/Meetings:** monthly Membership Meeting, educational sessions.

14916 ■ Miami Valley Orienteering Club (MVOC)
c/o Frederick Dudding
2533 Far Hills Ave.
Dayton, OH 45419-1547
Ph: (937)294-2228
URL: http://www.geocities.com/mvoclub
Contact: Frederick Dudding, Contact
Local. **Affiliated With:** United States Orienteering Federation.

14917 ■ Miami Valley Regional Planning Commission (MVRPC)
1 S Main St., Ste.260
Dayton, OH 45402
Ph: (937)223-6323
Fax: (937)223-9750
E-mail: mrobinette@mvrpc.org
URL: http://www.mvrpc.org
Contact: Mr. P. Michael Robinette, Exec.Dir.
Members: 63. **Local**. Serves as the Metropolitan Planning Organization for Montgomery, Miami, Greene Counties, plus a portion of Warren County. Provides regional and environmental planning support for members in seven counties. **Publications:** *Regional Perspective*, quarterly. Newsletter. **Advertising:** accepted. Alternate Formats: online • Annual Report. **Advertising:** accepted. Alternate Formats: online.

14918 ■ Miami Valley Restaurant Association
2207 Cybelle Ct.
Dayton, OH 45390
Ph: (937)461-6872
URL: http://www.themvra.org
Contact: Amy Zahora, Exec.Dir.
Local. **Formerly:** (2005) Miami Valley Venture Association.

14919 ■ Miami Valley Water Garden Society
PO Box 13293
Dayton, OH 45413-0293
E-mail: mvwgs@aol.com
URL: http://www.mvwgs.org
Contact: Mr. Jerry Woodbury, Pres.
Founded: 1992. **Membership Dues:** family, $20 (annual). **Local Groups:** 1. **Local**. Aims to promote the hobby of water gardening and outdoor fish keeping, and to educate others in greater Dayton, Ohio area. **Libraries: Type:** lending; not open to the public. **Holdings:** 100; books, video recordings. **Subjects:** water gardening, outdoor fish keeping. **Affiliated With:** Associated Koi Clubs of America; Goldfish Society of America; International Waterlily and Water Gardening Society. **Publications:** *Water Garden Ways*, monthly, except December. Newsletter. **Price:** free to members. **Advertising:** accepted. **Conventions/Meetings:** monthly meeting, with speakers, discusses water garden topics (exhibits) - every 4th Wednesday.

14920 ■ Microscopy Society of the Ohio River Valley (MSORV)
c/o William R. Ragland, Pres.
Univ. of Dayton Res. Inst.
300 Coll. Park Dr.
Dayton, OH 45469
Ph: (937)255-1142
Fax: (937)258-8075
E-mail: william.ragland@wpafb.af.mil
URL: http://www.ascdayton.org/msorv.html
Contact: William R. Ragland, Pres.
Local. **Affiliated With:** Microscopy Society of America.

14921 ■ Montgomery County Chapter, Ohio Genealogical Society (MCC-OGS)
PO Box 1584
Dayton, OH 45401-1584
Ph: (937)859-7824
E-mail: carolynjburns@woh.rr.com
URL: http://www.rootsweb.com/~ohmontgs
Contact: Carolyn Johnson-Burns, Publicity Officer
Founded: 1974. **Members:** 330. **Membership Dues:** individual, $12 (annual) • family, $15 (annual) • sustaining, $25 (annual). **Local**. Individuals interested in genealogy. Conducts public educational programs and lectures; holds trade days, ethnic days, and workshops. **Awards:** First Families of Montgomery County, Ohio. **Frequency:** annual. **Type:** recognition. **Recipient:** any member of OGS who is a direct descendant of an individual who settled in the area once defined as Montgomery County before December 31, 1830. **Affiliated With:** Ohio Genealogical Society; Ohio Genealogical Society. **Publications:** *Cemetery Inscriptions, Montgomery County, Ohio*. Book • *Dayton City Directory* • *Family Tree*, monthly.

Newsletter. Features subjects about genealogy. **Price:** $10.00. ISSN: 10470956. **Circulation:** 400. **Conventions/Meetings:** monthly meeting - usually 2nd Saturday.

14922 ■ Montgomery County Historical Society (MCHS)
224 N St. Clair St.
Dayton, OH 45402
Ph: (937)228-6271
E-mail: mchs@daytonhistory.org
URL: http://www.daytonhistory.org
Contact: Claudia Watson, Dir.

Founded: 1896. **Members:** 500. **Membership Dues:** family, $40 (annual) • individual, $25 (annual) • senior citizen, $15 (annual) • sustaining, $100 (annual) • patron, $500 (annual) • benefactor, $1,000 (annual) • corporate, $100-$1,000 (annual). **Staff:** 9. **Budget:** $450,000. **Local.** Individuals interested in the history of Montgomery County, OH. Maintains an educational research center and manages the NCR Corporate Archive and DP and L Collection. Administers the Patterson Homestead Museum and Rental Facility. **Libraries: Type:** by appointment only. **Holdings:** 750. **Subjects:** Montgomery County. **Awards:** Preservation Awards. **Frequency:** annual. **Type:** recognition. **Publications:** *Columns*, quarterly. Newsletter. **Price:** included in membership dues. **Conventions/Meetings:** annual meeting.

14923 ■ Montgomery County Medical Society - Ohio
40 S Perry St.
Dayton, OH 45402
Ph: (937)223-0990
E-mail: info@mcmsoh.org
URL: http://www.mcmsoh.org
Contact: Constance M. Mahle, Exec.Dir.

Local. Advances the art and science of medicine. Promotes patient care and the betterment of public health. **Affiliated With:** Ohio State Medical Association.

14924 ■ Montgomery County, Ohio - Young Democrats
c/o Scott Murphy, Pres.
131 S Wilkinson St.
Dayton, OH 45402
E-mail: info@montgomeryyd.org
URL: http://www.montgomeryyd.org

Local.

14925 ■ Montgomery/Greene Counties RSVP
c/o Nanci McGuire, Dir.
105 S Wilkinson St.
Dayton, OH 45402
Ph: (937)223-2390
Fax: (937)223-2510
E-mail: srcvolser@aol.com
URL: http://www.seniorcorps.gov/about/programs/rsvp_state.asp?usestateabbr=oh&Search4.x=0&Search4.y=0
Contact: Nanci McGuire, Dir.

Local. Affiliated With: Retired and Senior Volunteer Program.

14926 ■ Muscular Dystrophy Association, Dayton
2621 Dryden Rd., Ste.306
Dayton, OH 45439
Ph: (937)296-1160
Fax: (937)296-1243
E-mail: daytondistrict@mdausa.org
URL: http://www.mdausa.org
Contact: Vincent Hopkins, Contact

Staff: 5. **Local.** Local chapter for voluntary national health agency, which provides direct patient care plus a worldwide research effort into 40 neuromuscular disease entities. **Affiliated With:** Muscular Dystrophy Association.

14927 ■ National Association of Catholic Family Life Ministers (NACFLM)
300 Coll. Park
Dayton, OH 45469-2512
Ph: (937)229-3324
Fax: (937)229-4902
E-mail: nacflm@udayton.edu
URL: http://www.nacflm.org
Contact: Steve Beirne, Pres.

Regional. Affiliated With: National Association of Catholic Family Life Ministers.

14928 ■ National Association of Credit Management Ohio (NACM)
41 White Allen Ave.
Dayton, OH 45405
Ph: (937)228-6124
Fax: (937)228-6114
Free: (800)875-6124
E-mail: info@nacmohio.com
URL: http://www.nacmohio.com
Contact: E. Pat O'Brien CAE, Pres./CEO/Sec.

State. Affiliated With: National Association of Credit Management. **Formerly:** (2005) National Association of Credit Managers Ohio.

14929 ■ National Association of Industrial and Office Properties, Dayton Chapter
c/o Kim Bramlage
PO Box 552
Dayton, OH 45401-0522
Ph: (937)837-5281
Fax: (937)854-4194
E-mail: kbramlage@aol.com
URL: National Affiliate–www.naiop.org
Contact: Ms. Kim Bramlage, Exec.Dir.

Local. Represents the interests of developers and owners of industrial, office and related commercial estate. Provides communication, networking, business opportunities and a forum to its members. Promotes effective public policy to create, protect and enhance property values. **Affiliated With:** National Association of Industrial and Office Properties.

14930 ■ National Forum for Black Public Administrators, Dayton Chapter
c/o Carolyn E. Wright, Pres.
1946 Haverhill Dr.
Dayton, OH 45406
E-mail: carolynwri@msn.com
URL: National Affiliate–www.nfbpa.org
Contact: Carolyn E. Wright, Pres.

Local. Works to promote, strengthen and expand the role of Blacks in public administration. Seeks to focus the influence of Black administrators toward building and maintaining viable communities. Develops specialized training programs for managers and executives. Works to further communication among Black public, private and academic institutions. Addresses issues that affect the administrative capacity of Black managers. **Affiliated With:** National Forum for Black Public Administrators.

14931 ■ National Management Association, Greater Dayton Leadership Association
c/o Sue Kappeler
Natl. Mgt. Assn.
2210 Arbor Blvd.
Dayton, OH 45439
E-mail: sue@nma1.org
URL: National Affiliate–www.nma1.org
Contact: Sue Kappeler CM, Contact

Local. Business and industrial management personnel; membership comes from supervisory level, with the remainder from middle management and above. Seeks to develop and recognize management as a profession and to promote the free enterprise system. **Affiliated With:** National Management Association.

14932 ■ National Speleological Society, Dayton Underground Grotto (DUG)
c/o Andy Niekamp
1515 Cordell Dr.
Dayton, OH 45439
Ph: (937)252-2978
E-mail: officers@dugcaves.com
URL: http://www.dugcaves.com
Contact: Mike Hood, Chm.

Local. Seeks to study, explore and conserve cave and karst resources. Protects access to caves and promotes responsible caving. Encourages responsible management of caves and their unique environments. **Affiliated With:** National Speleological Society.

14933 ■ National Technical Honor Society - ITT Technical Institute - Dayton Ohio
3325 Stop Eight Rd.
Dayton, OH 45414
Ph: (937)454-2267
Free: (800)568-3241
URL: http://www.itt-tech.edu

Local.

14934 ■ North American Die Casting Association Southern Ohio Chapter 14
c/o Tim Tilk
2520 Needmore Rd.
Dayton, OH 45414
E-mail: ttilk@yoderindustries.com
URL: National Affiliate–www.diecasting.org
Contact: Tim Tilk, Vice Chm.

Local. Develops product standards; compiles trade statistics on metal consumption trends; conducts promotional activities; provides information on chemistry, mechanics, engineering, and other arts and sciences related to die casting. Provides training materials and short, intensive courses in die casting. Maintains speakers' bureau. **Affiliated With:** North American Die Casting Association.

14935 ■ Oak Tree Corner
2312 Far Hills Ave., PMB 108
Dayton, OH 45419
Ph: (937)285-0199
E-mail: oaktreecorner@mail.com
URL: http://www.oaktreecorner.com

Founded: 1996. **Budget:** $20,000. **Local Groups:** 2. **Local.** Provides support groups for grieving children and teens in southwest OH. **Conventions/Meetings:** semiannual workshop, training for volunteer facilitators - always January and August in Kettering, OH.

14936 ■ Ohio Agri-Women
c/o Peggy Clark, Pres.
2274 E Lytle Five Points Rd.
Dayton, OH 45458
Ph: (937)885-5965
Fax: (937)885-5942
E-mail: paclark@starband.net
URL: http://www.ohioaginfo.com/resources_women.htm
Contact: Peggy Clark, Pres.

State. Organization of women in agriculture-related businesses who "stand up and speak out for agriculture" by education consumers and legislators.

14937 ■ Ohio Health Care Association, District 2
c/o Kenn Daily, Chm.
Miami Shores of Moraine
3421 Pinnacle Rd.
Dayton, OH 45418
Ph: (937)268-3488
Fax: (937)267-5021
E-mail: kdaily@miamishoresmoraine.com
URL: http://www.ohca.org
Contact: Kenn Daily, Chm.

Local. Promotes professionalism and ethical behavior of individuals providing long-term care delivery for patients and for the general public. Provides information, education and administrative tools to enhance the quality of long-term care. Improves the standards of service and administration of member nursing homes. **Affiliated With:** American Health Care Association.

14938 ■ Ohio Native Plant Society, Miami Valley Chapter
c/o Nancy Bain
444 Acorn Dr.
Dayton, OH 45419
Ph: (937)698-6426
URL: http://groups.msn.com/NativePlantSocietyofNortheastOhio/chapters.msnw
Contact: Nancy Bain, Contact
Local.

14939 ■ Ohio Physiological Society (OPS)
c/o Dan R. Halm, Pres.
Wright State Univ.
Dept. of Neuroscience Cell Biology and Physiology
3640 Colonel Glenn Hwy.
Dayton, OH 45435
Ph: (937)775-2742 (937)775-3067
Fax: (937)775-3391
URL: http://www.med.wright.edu/ncbp/ops/index.html
Contact: Dan R. Halm, Pres.
State. Fosters education, scientific research and dissemination of information in the Physiological sciences. **Affiliated With:** American Physiological Society.

14940 ■ Ohio Prospect Research Network (OPRN)
c/o Rob Boley, Associate Dir. of Advancement
Off. of Advancement
Wright State Univ. School of Medicine
3640 Colonel Glenn Hwy.
Dayton, OH 45435
Ph: (937)775-3903
Fax: (937)775-3254
E-mail: robert.boley@wright.edu
URL: http://www.oprn.org
Contact: Rob Boley, Associate Dir. of Advancement
Regional. Resource for individuals working in non-profit fundraising, development and advancement.

14941 ■ Ohio Regional Association of Law Libraries (ORALL)
Univ. of Dayton Zimmerman Law Lib.
300 Coll. Park
Dayton, OH 45469-2780
Ph: (513)229-2444
E-mail: hanley@udayton.edu
URL: http://www.orall.org
Contact: Thomas Hanley, Contact
Founded: 1949. **Members:** 350. **Membership Dues:** $15 (annual). **Regional.** Law libraries located in Indiana, Kentucky, Michigan, and Ohio. Promotes the growth, advancement, and improvement of law librarians and the development of law libraries. **Affiliated With:** American Association of Law Libraries. **Publications:** *ORALL Newsletter*, quarterly. **Advertising:** accepted • Directory, annual. ISSN: 1048-2199. **Conventions/Meetings:** annual meeting.

14942 ■ Ohio State Society of Enrolled Agents - Greater Dayton Chapter
c/o John Tishaus, Pres.
7069-B Taylorsville Rd.
Dayton, OH 45424
Ph: (937)236-7362
Fax: (937)236-7362
E-mail: tishnassoc@aol.com
URL: http://www.ossea.org/pdf/0804newsletter.pdf
Contact: John Tishaus EA, Pres.
Local. Affiliated With: National Association of Enrolled Agents.

14943 ■ Ohio Valley NARI
136 S Keowee St.
Dayton, OH 45402
Fax: (937)222-5794
Free: (800)498-6274
E-mail: cincinnati@naripro.org
URL: http://www.naricincinnati.org
Contact: Dan Lea, Assoc.Exec.
Founded: 1996. **Local. Affiliated With:** National Association of the Remodeling Industry. **Also Known As:** (2004) Ohio Valley National Association of the Remodeling Industry.

14944 ■ Outreach for Animals
c/o Timothy A. Harrison
PO Box 24114
Dayton, OH 45424
Ph: (937)436-0727
E-mail: harrison@outreachforanimals.com
URL: http://www.outreachforanimals.org
Contact: Mr. Russell H. Muntz, Administrator
Founded: 2001. **Staff:** 1. **Budget:** $20,000. **Nonmembership. Regional.**

14945 ■ Parents Without Partners, Dayton
PO Box 884
Dayton, OH 45401-0884
Ph: (937)640-1877
URL: National Affiliate–www.parentswithoutpartners.org
Local. Works to provide single parents and their children with an opportunity for enhancing personal growth, self-confidence and sensitivity towards others by offering an environment for support, friendship and the exchange of parenting techniques. **Affiliated With:** Parents Without Partners.

14946 ■ Phi Theta Kappa - Nu Pi Chapter
c/o Bill Kamil
444 W 3rd St.
Dayton, OH 45402-1460
Ph: (937)512-4598
E-mail: tarik.kamil@sinclair.edu
URL: http://www.ptk.org/directories/chapters/OH/307-1.htm
Contact: Bill Kamil, Advisor
Local. Affiliated With: Phi Theta Kappa, International Honor Society.

14947 ■ Plumbing-Heating-Cooling Contractors Association, Dayton Area
c/o Michael L. Byrd, Pres.
3691 Southbrook Dr.
Dayton, OH 45430-1449
Ph: (937)429-2159
Fax: (937)427-1326
E-mail: adependable@hotmail.com
URL: National Affiliate–www.phccweb.org
Contact: Michael L. Byrd, Pres.
Local. Represents the plumbing, heating and cooling contractors. Promotes the construction industry. Protects the environment, health, safety and comfort of society. **Affiliated With:** Plumbing-Heating-Cooling Contractors Association.

14948 ■ Project Management Institute - Dayton/Miami Valley Chapter
c/o Bill Bierlein, Pres.
140 E Monument St.
Dayton, OH 45402
Ph: (937)656-2953
E-mail: william_bierlein@reyrey.com
URL: http://www.daytonpmi.org
Contact: Bill Bierlein, Pres.
Local. Corporations and individuals engaged in the practice of project management; project management students and educators. Seeks to advance the study, teaching, and practice of project management. **Affiliated With:** Project Management Institute.

14949 ■ Public Relations Society of America, Dayton/Miami Valley
c/o Beth Ling, Dir. of Public Relations
Design Forum
7575 Paragon Rd.
Dayton, OH 45459
Ph: (937)312-8803
E-mail: bling@designforum.com
URL: http://www.prsadayton.org
Contact: Beth Ling, Dir. of Public Relations
Founded: 1966. **Local. Affiliated With:** Public Relations Society of America.

14950 ■ Sassafras Star Sailing Society No. 160
c/o Bob Luther
4433 Tangent Dr.
Dayton, OH 45440
Ph: (937)293-7809
URL: National Affiliate–www.amya.org
Contact: Bob Luther, Contact
Local.

14951 ■ SCORE Chapter 107
Fed. Bldg., Rm. 104
200 W 2nd St.
Dayton, OH 45402
Ph: (937)225-2887
Fax: (937)225-7667
E-mail: score@daytonscore.org
URL: http://www.daytonscore.org
Contact: John Houston, Sec.
Founded: 1970. **Members:** 40. **Staff:** 2. **Budget:** $15,000. **Regional Groups:** 2. **State Groups:** 5. **Local Groups:** 1. **Local.** Volunteer businessmen and women. Provides free small business management assistance to individuals in Dayton, OH, and surrounding counties. **Libraries: Type:** open to the public. **Holdings:** 500. **Subjects:** starting a business. **Publications:** Newsletter, monthly. **Price:** free. **Circulation:** 80. **Conventions/Meetings:** monthly workshop, educational workshop (exhibits) - every 3rd Thursday except December.

14952 ■ Sheet Metal and Roofing Contractors Association of Miami Valley
c/o Robert H. Pope
2077 Embury Park Rd.
Dayton, OH 45414
Ph: (937)278-0308
Fax: (937)278-0317
E-mail: bpope@assnsoffice.com
URL: National Affiliate–www.smacna.org
Contact: Robert H. Pope, Contact
Local. Affiliated With: Sheet Metal and Air Conditioning Contractors' National Association.

14953 ■ Society for the Advancement of Material and Process Engineering, Midwest Chapter
c/o Donald A. Klosterman, Dir.
Univ. of Dayton
937 New England Ave.
Dayton, OH 45459-5922
Ph: (937)229-2528
Fax: (937)229-2503
E-mail: klosterman@udri.udayton.edu
URL: http://www.midwestsampe.org
Contact: Donald A. Klosterman, Dir.
Regional. Represents individuals engaged in the development of advanced materials and processing technology in airframe, missile, aerospace, propulsion, electronics, life sciences, management, and related industries. Provides scholarships for science students seeking financial assistance. Provides placement services for members. **Affiliated With:** Society for the Advancement of Material and Process Engineering.

14954 ■ Society of Antique Modelers - Western Ohio Oldtimers
7712 Eagle Creek Dr.
Dayton, OH 45459-3414
Ph: (937)433-2592
E-mail: wd8ncr@earthlink.net
URL: National Affiliate–www.antiquemodeler.org
Local. Affiliated With: Society of Antique Modelers.

14955 ■ Society of Manufacturing Engineers - Sinclair Community College U156
Indus. Engg. Tech., Sinclair Community Coll.
444 W Third St.
Dayton, OH 45402-1460
Ph: (937)512-2311
Fax: (937)512-4530
E-mail: dmeyer@sinclair.edu
URL: National Affiliate–www.sme.org
Contact: David Meyer, Contact
Local. Advances manufacturing knowledge to gain competitive advantage. Improves skills and manufacturing solutions for the growth of economy. Provides resources and opportunities for manufacturing professionals. **Affiliated With:** Sea Grant Association.

14956 ■ Society of Manufacturing Engineers - University of Dayton S070
Univ. of Dayton, Dept. Engg. Tech.
300 Coll. Park Ave.
Dayton, OH 45469-0249
Ph: (937)229-2972
Fax: (937)229-4975
E-mail: robert.wolff@notes.udayton.edu
URL: National Affiliate–www.sme.org
Contact: Robert L. Wolff, Contact
Local. Advances manufacturing knowledge to gain competitive advantage. Improves skills and manufacturing solutions for the growth of economy. Provides resources and opportunities for manufacturing professionals. **Affiliated With:** Institute for Operations Research and the Management Sciences.

14957 ■ South Metro Regional Chamber of Commerce
7887 Washington Village Dr., Ste.265
Dayton, OH 45459
Ph: (937)433-2032
Fax: (937)433-6881
E-mail: linda.gibney@smrcoc.org
URL: http://www.smrcoc.org
Contact: Linda Gibney, Contact
Founded: 1969. **Members:** 900. **Local**. Promotes business and community development in the Southern Dayton, OH metropolitan area. Holds Business After Hours parties and monthly board of directors meeting. **Formerly:** (2005) South Metro Dayton Area Chamber of Commerce. **Publications:** *The Business Advisor*, monthly. Newsletter • *Comprehensive Guide to Members*, annual. Directory. **Advertising:** accepted • *South Metro Monthly Magazine*. Newsletter. Contains information on chamber networking events, regional economic, workforce development, and school-to-work program. • Report, annual. Alternate Formats: online. **Conventions/Meetings:** quarterly luncheon.

14958 ■ Southern Ohio Chapter of the Human Factors and Ergonomics Society (SOCHFES)
PO Box 31052
Dayton, OH 45437-0052
Ph: (937)255-8848
E-mail: timothy.barry@wpafb.af.mil
URL: http://www.cs.wright.edu/sochfes
Contact: Tim Barry, Pres.
Local. Offers opportunities for professional and social interaction. Provides forum for the stimulating exchange of human factors information, methods, and ideas. **Affiliated With:** Human Factors and Ergonomics Society.

14959 ■ Special Wish Foundation, Dayton
436 Valley St.
Dayton, OH 45404
Ph: (937)223-9474
Fax: (937)223-0374
Free: (800)611-3232
E-mail: aspecialwish@childrensdayton.org
URL: http://aspecialwish.org
Contact: Jim Heikes, Chm.
Local. Grants wishes to children birth through age 20 who have been diagnosed with a life-threatening disorder. **Affiliated With:** A Special Wish Foundation.

14960 ■ State Guard Association of the United States, Ohio
c/o Ronnie R. Pitsinger, Col.
10132 Stroud Ln.
Dayton, OH 45458
Ph: (937)885-7385
Fax: (937)885-7385
URL: National Affiliate–www.sgaus.org
Contact: Ronnie R. Pitsinger, Col.
State. **Affiliated With:** State Guard Association of the United States.

14961 ■ Technical Association of the Pulp and Paper Industry - Ohio Section
c/o Steve Axtell, Sec.
2000 Courthouse Plz. NE
10 W Second St.
Dayton, OH 45402
Ph: (937)443-6877
Fax: (937)443-6805
E-mail: steve.axtell@thompsonhine.com
URL: http://www.ohiotappi.org
Contact: Steve Axtell, Sec.
State. Furthers the application of science, engineering and technology in paper and other related industries. Serves as a forum for the collection, dissemination and interchange of technical concepts and information about the pulp and paper industry. Provides education, training and professional growth opportunities to members. **Affiliated With:** TAPPI - Technical Association of the Pulp and Paper Industry.

14962 ■ Thurgood Marshall Law Society (TMLS)
c/o Mia Wortham Spells, Pres.
PO Box 60792
Dayton, OH 45406
Ph: (937)224-4600
Fax: (937)224-4707
E-mail: spellslaw@aol.com
URL: National Affiliate–www.nationalbar.org
Contact: Mia Wortham Spells, Pres.
Local. **Affiliated With:** National Bar Association.

14963 ■ Trout Unlimited - Madmen
c/o Mark Blauvelt
2124 Southlea Dr.
Dayton, OH 45459
Ph: (513)865-6800 (937)291-1016
E-mail: markblauvelt@hormail.com
URL: http://www.tu.org
Contact: Mark Blauvelt, Pres.
Local.

14964 ■ Trout Unlimited - Ohio Council
c/o Mark Blauvelt, Pres.
2124 Southlea Dr.
Dayton, OH 45459-3639
Ph: (937)974-2908
E-mail: markblauvelt@hotmail.com
URL: National Affiliate–www.tu.org
Contact: Mark Blauvelt, Pres.
State.

14965 ■ United Way of the Greater Dayton Area
184 Salem Ave.
Dayton, OH 45406-5804
Ph: (937)225-3001
E-mail: president@dayton-unitedway.org
URL: http://www.dayton-unitedway.org
Contact: Marc Levy, Pres./CEO
Local. **Affiliated With:** United Way of America.

14966 ■ USATF Ohio Association
c/o Karen Krsak, Pres.
PO Box 5848
Dayton, OH 45405-0848
Ph: (937)235-9436
E-mail: usatf-ohio@msn.com
URL: http://www.usatf.org/assoc/oh
Contact: Karen Krsak, Pres.
Membership Dues: youth, adult, $15 (annual). **State**. **Affiliated With:** U.S.A. Track and Field.

14967 ■ Vegetarian Society of the Greater Dayton Area (VSGDA)
c/o Mary Sue Gmeiner
PO Box 750742
Dayton, OH 45475-0742
Ph: (937)849-6109 (937)837-3576
E-mail: vsgda@yahoo.com
URL: http://www.dayton.vegetariansociety.org
Contact: Mary Sue Gmeiner, Coor.
Nonmembership. **Local**. Promotes the nutritional, economical, ecological, and ethical benefits of a vegetarian diet. **Affiliated With:** North American Vegetarian Society. **Publications:** *VSGDA E-News*, monthly. Newsletters. Provides schedule of events, recipes, and articles of interest. **Conventions/Meetings:** monthly meeting, potluck; occasional speaker (exhibits) - 2nd Friday.

14968 ■ Vietnam Veterans of America, Chapter No. 97 Miami Valley
c/o Tom Istvan, Pres.
PO Box 2707
Dayton, OH 45401-2707
Ph: (937)233-9750
URL: http://www.vvabuckeyestatecouncil.com
Contact: Tom Istvan, Pres.
Local. **Affiliated With:** Vietnam Veterans of America.

14969 ■ Waynesville - Young Life
555 Clareridge Ln.
Dayton, OH 45458
Ph: (937)434-3484
URL: http://sites.younglife.org/sites/Waynesville/default.aspx
Local. **Affiliated With:** Young Life.

14970 ■ Western Ohio Chapter, National Electrical Contractors Association
2210 Arbor Blvd.
Dayton, OH 45439-1506
Ph: (937)299-0384
Fax: (937)299-7322
E-mail: dan@wocneca.org
URL: http://www.wocneca.org
Contact: Dana W. Neal, Exec.Mgr.
Local. **Affiliated With:** National Electrical Contractors Association.

14971 ■ Wright Dunbar
1105 W Third St.
Dayton, OH 45402
Ph: (937)443-0249
Fax: (937)443-0270
E-mail: ineal@wright-dunbar.org
URL: http://www.wright-dunbar.org
Contact: Idotha Bootsie Neal, Exec.Dir.
Local.

14972 ■ Wright State University Area Council of Teachers of Mathematics
c/o Barbara Carruth, Membership Chair
5601 Winterberry Ct.
Dayton, OH 45431-2814
E-mail: jccbsc@attglobal.net
URL: National Affiliate–www.nctm.org
Contact: Barbara Carruth, Membership Chair
Local. Aims to improve the teaching and learning of mathematics. Provides vision, leadership and professional development to support teachers in ensuring mathematics learning of the highest quality for all students. **Affiliated With:** National Council of Teachers of Mathematics.

14973 ■ Young Life Dayton North
473 King Oak Ln.
Dayton, OH 45415
Ph: (937)890-0486
URL: http://sites.younglife.org/_layouts/ylext/default.aspx?ID=A-OH157
Local. **Affiliated With:** Young Life.

14974 ■ Young Life Dayton, OH
555 Clareridge Ln.
Dayton, OH 45458
Ph: (937)434-3484
Fax: (937)434-3484
URL: http://sites.younglife.org/sites/Dayton/default.aspx
Local. **Affiliated With:** Young Life.

14975 ■ YWCA of Dayton
141 W Third St.
Dayton, OH 45402
Ph: (937)461-5550
Fax: (937)222-0610
E-mail: ksnow@ywcadayton.org
URL: http://www.ywcadayton.org
Contact: Donna Audette, Pres.
Local. Conducts daily programs in careers and life planning, health and sexuality, leadership and com-

munication, sports and adventure, and life skills and self-reliance. Works to create an environment in which girls can learn and grow to their fullest potential. **Affiliated With:** Girls Inc.

De Graff

14976 ■ American Legion, Miami Valley Post 652
221 W Miami St.
De Graff, OH 43318
Ph: (740)362-7478
Fax: (740)362-1429
URL: National Affiliate–www.legion.org
Local. Affiliated With: American Legion.

Deerfield

14977 ■ American Legion, Deerfield Post 713
PO Box 195
Deerfield, OH 44411
Ph: (740)362-7478
Fax: (740)362-1429
URL: National Affiliate–www.legion.org
Local. Affiliated With: American Legion.

14978 ■ Deerfield Chamber of Commerce
PO Box 193
Deerfield, OH 44411-0193
Ph: (330)584-8440
Fax: (330)686-8880
E-mail: sandie@neorr.com
Contact: Sandie Welch, Pres.
Local.

14979 ■ Society of Petrophysicists and Well Log Analysts - Ohio Chapter
c/o Steve George
PO Box 160
Deerfield, OH 44411
Ph: (544)343-3306
Fax: (330)654-4916
E-mail: segeorge@atlasamerica.com
URL: National Affiliate–www.spwla.org
Contact: Steve George, Contact
State. Advances the science of petrophysics and formation evaluation through well logging and other formation evaluation techniques. Provides information services to scientists in the petroleum and mineral industries. Strives to strengthen petrophysical education and to increase awareness of the role of petrophysics in the Oil and Gas Industry and the scientific community. **Affiliated With:** Society of Petrophysicists and Well Log Analysts.

Defiance

14980 ■ American Cancer Society, Defiance Area
419 Fifth St., Ste.2030
Defiance, OH 43512
Ph: (419)782-6866
Fax: (419)782-4372
Free: (888)227-6446
URL: http://www.cancer.org
Local. Affiliated With: American Cancer Society.

14981 ■ American Cancer Society, Henry County Unit (ACSHCU)
419 5th St., No. 1090
Defiance, OH 43512-2626
Ph: (419)782-6866
Free: (800)ACS-2345
URL: http://www.cancer.org
Contact: Jessica Stewart, Exec.Dir.
Local. Volunteers supporting education and research in cancer prevention, diagnosis, detection, and treatment. Conducts patient service programs. **Affiliated With:** American Cancer Society.

14982 ■ American Legion, Ohio Post 117
c/o Herbert E. Anderson
648 S Clinton St.
Defiance, OH 43512
Ph: (740)362-7478
Fax: (740)362-1429
URL: National Affiliate–www.legion.org
Contact: Herbert E. Anderson, Contact
Local. Affiliated With: American Legion.

14983 ■ American Red Cross, Defiance County Chapter
Box No. 351
1220 S Clinton St.
Defiance, OH 43512-0351
Ph: (419)782-0136
Fax: (419)782-8337
E-mail: dredcros@bright.net
URL: http://www.bright.net/~dredcros
Local.

14984 ■ Defiance Area Chamber of Commerce
615 W 3rd St.
Defiance, OH 43512
Ph: (419)782-7946
Fax: (419)782-0111
E-mail: fculver@defiancechamber.com
URL: http://www.defiancechamber.com
Contact: Floyd A. Culver, Pres.
Members: 450. **Membership Dues:** real estate/medical professional/insurance/accounting/law/architecture/surveying/engineering, $120 (annual) • service/newspaper/radio/construction/industrial/utility (base), $120 (annual) • professional/associate, $50 (annual) • bank/savings & loan (per million in asset), $37 (annual) • non-business/non-profit/educational institution/fast food eatery/caterer, $120 (annual) • restaurant/tavern, $220 (annual). **Local.** Office holders, business leaders, educators, youth professionals and small business owners. Acts as a respected voice of advocacy for business and education in Defiance County. **Affiliated With:** Ohio Chamber of Commerce; U.S. Chamber of Commerce. **Publications:** *The Chamber Network*, monthly. Newsletter. **Advertising:** accepted. Alternate Formats: online.

14985 ■ Defiance Area Young Men's Christian Association
1599 Palmer Dr.
Defiance, OH 43512
Ph: (419)784-4747
Fax: (419)782-4497
E-mail: ymca_gk@defnet.com
URL: http://defianceymca.org
Contact: Glenn Kuhn, Exec.Dir.
Founded: 1965. **Members:** 6,000. **Staff:** 100. **Budget:** $1,000,000. **Local.** Seeks to develop and improve the spiritual, social, mental, and physical well-being of young people and adults. Sponsors annual River Run on July 4, Corporate Olympics each July, Healthy Kids Day in Spring, and Polar Bear Run in December. **Publications:** *Program Schedule*, 7/year. Newsletter.

14986 ■ Defiance Area Youth for Christ
PO Box 111
Defiance, OH 43512
Fax: (419)782-0599
Free: (888)782-0656
URL: http://www.yfcohio.com
Local. Affiliated With: Youth for Christ/U.S.A.

14987 ■ Defiance County Chapter of the Ohio Genealogical Society
PO Box 7006
Defiance, OH 43512-7006
E-mail: defiancegenealogy2002@yahoo.com
URL: http://www.rootsweb.com/~ohdcgs
Contact: Cecelia Brown, Pres.
Founded: 1977. **Members:** 142. **Membership Dues:** single, $12 (annual) • family, $15 (annual). **Local.** Gathering together to share and learn how to trace family lineage and to help people who are working on their family genealogy. Meetings monthly with programs and speakers. **Libraries: Type:** open to the public. **Affiliated With:** Ohio Genealogical Society. **Formerly:** Ohio Genealogical Society, Defiance County Chapter. **Publications:** *Yesteryears Trails*, quarterly. Newsletter. Contains articles of interest for those tracing family history and lineage in Defiance County, OH. **Price:** included in membership dues; $7.00 single; $10.00 joint. ISSN: 1047-0077. **Conventions/Meetings:** First Families Banquet • monthly meeting - always fourth Monday, except August and December; Defiance, OH.

14988 ■ Home Builders Association of Northwestern Ohio
c/o Richard Kahle
26761 Behrens Rd.
Defiance, OH 43512-8114
Ph: (419)782-7756
Fax: (419)782-7756
URL: National Affiliate–www.nahb.org
Local. Single and multifamily home builders, commercial builders, and others associated with the building industry. **Affiliated With:** National Association of Home Builders.

14989 ■ International Union, United Automobile, Aerospace and Agricultural Implement Workers of America, AFL-CIO - Local Union 211
2120 Baltimore St.
Defiance, OH 43512
Ph: (419)784-5399
Fax: (419)784-5838
URL: http://www.uawlocal211.org
Contact: Paul Murcko, Pres.
Members: 2,775. **Local.** AFL-CIO. **Affiliated With:** International Union, United Automobile, Aerospace and Agricultural Implement Workers of America.

14990 ■ National Active and Retired Federal Employees Association - Ft Defiance 1862
1709 Wldwood Dr.
Defiance, OH 43512-2532
Ph: (419)784-2634
URL: National Affiliate–www.narfe.org
Contact: Leo J. Swary, Contact
Local. Protects the retirement future of employees through education. Informs members on issues affecting the retirement. **Affiliated With:** National Association of Retired Federal Employees.

14991 ■ Northwestern Ohio Board of Realtors
322 Clinton St.
Sam Switzer Realty
Defiance, OH 43512-2162
Ph: (419)782-4116
Fax: (419)782-6658
E-mail: nwob@adelphia.net
URL: National Affiliate–www.realtor.org
Contact: Sharnaine Kondas, Exec. Officer
Local. Strives to develop real estate business practices. Advocates for the right to own, use and transfer real property. Provides a facility for professional development, research and exchange of information among members and the general public. **Affiliated With:** National Association of Realtors.

14992 ■ Psi Chi, National Honor Society in Psychology - Defiance College
c/o Dept. of Psychology
701 N Clinton St.
Defiance, OH 43512-1695
Ph: (419)783-2337 (419)783-2449
E-mail: ddalke@defiance.edu
URL: http://www.psichi.org/chapters/info.asp?chapter_id=739
Contact: Deborah E. Dalke PhD, Advisor
Local.

14993 ■ United Way of Defiance County
PO Box 351
Defiance, OH 43512-0351
Ph: (419)782-3510
URL: National Affiliate–national.unitedway.org
Local. Affiliated With: United Way of America.

14994 ■ Veteran Motor Car Club of America - Defiance Chapter
c/o James W. Foster, Pres.
14668 Dohoney Rd.
Defiance, OH 43512
Ph: (419)395-1456
E-mail: jrfoster@defnet.com
URL: National Affiliate–www.vmcca.org
Contact: James W. Foster, Pres.
Local. Affiliated With: Veteran Motor Car Club of America.

Delaware

14995 ■ American Legion, Deutschle-Annick-Memorial Post 888
PO Box 8007
Delaware, OH 43015
Ph: (740)362-7478
Fax: (740)362-1429
URL: National Affiliate–www.legion.org
Local. Affiliated With: American Legion.

14996 ■ American Legion of Ohio
c/o William K. Balser, Commander
PO Box 8007
Delaware, OH 43015
Ph: (740)362-7478
Fax: (740)362-1429
Free: (800)930-8961
E-mail: ohlegion@iwaynet.net
URL: http://www.ohioamericanlegion.org
Contact: Mr. Thomas M. Wiswell, Dir. of Internal Affairs
Founded: 1919. **Members:** 145,000. **Membership Dues:** all, $18 (annual). **Staff:** 22. **Budget:** $1,300,000. **Regional Groups:** 14. **Local Groups:** 605. **State.** Provides service to veterans and their families through programs and the local Posts. **Libraries: Type:** by appointment only. **Holdings:** 600; books, periodicals, video recordings. **Subjects:** organizational records. **Awards:** College Scholarships. **Frequency:** annual. **Type:** scholarship. **Recipient:** for descendant of member. **Affiliated With:** American Legion. **Publications:** *Ohio Legion News*, quarterly. Newspaper. **Price:** $2.00 /year for members. **Circulation:** 145,000. **Advertising:** accepted. Alternate Formats: online. **Conventions/Meetings:** annual convention.

14997 ■ American Legion, Ohio Post 115
c/o Raymond B. Austin
PO Box 432
Delaware, OH 43015
Ph: (740)362-7478
Fax: (740)362-1429
URL: National Affiliate–www.legion.org
Contact: Raymond B. Austin, Contact
Local. Affiliated With: American Legion.

14998 ■ American Red Cross, Delaware County Chapter
5 W Winter St.
Delaware, OH 43015
Ph: (740)362-2021 (740)548-7300
URL: http://delawarecounty.redcross.org
Local.

14999 ■ American Society for Microbiology - Ohio Branch
c/o Laura Tuhela-Reuning, Sec.-Treas.
Wesleyan Univ.
90 S Henry St.
Delaware, OH 43015
Ph: (740)368-3511
Fax: (740)368-3999
E-mail: lmtuhela@owu.edu
URL: National Affiliate–www.asm.org
Contact: Donald E. Langworthy, Pres.
State. Advances the knowledge in the field of microbiology. Improves educational programs and encourages fundamental and applied research in microbiological sciences. Supports training and public information. **Affiliated With:** American Society for Microbiology.

15000 ■ Association for Computing Machinery, Ohio Wesleyan University
c/o Mohammad S. Mehkari, Chair
ACM-Dept. of Mathematical Sci.
Stewart Hall
61 S Sandusky St.
Delaware, OH 43015
Ph: (740)368-3188
Fax: (740)368-3199
E-mail: msmehkar@owu.edu
URL: http://www.owu.edu/~aaacm
Contact: Mohammad S. Mehkari, Chair
State. Biological, medical, behavioral, and computer scientists; hospital administrators; programmers and others interested in application of computer methods to biological, behavioral, and medical problems. Stimulates understanding of the use and potential of computers in the Biosciences. **Affiliated With:** Association for Computing Machinery.

15001 ■ Central Ohio ASCnet User Group
c/o Trimble Insurance Agency Inc.
PO Box 280
Delaware, OH 43015
Ph: (740)369-6711
Fax: (740)369-1981
E-mail: gtrimble@trimbleins.com
URL: National Affiliate–www.ascnet.org
Contact: Greg Trimble, Pres.
Local. Represents insurance agents and brokers using the Agency Manager software. Promotes successful automation and business practices through communication, education, and advocacy. **Affiliated With:** Applied Systems Client Network.

15002 ■ Delaware Area Chamber of Commerce (DACC)
23 N Union St.
Delaware, OH 43015
Ph: (740)369-6221
Fax: (740)369-4817
E-mail: dachamber@delawareohiochamber.com
URL: http://www.delawareohiochamber.com
Contact: Charlotte Joseph, Pres.
Founded: 1907. **Members:** 500. **Membership Dues:** full business (plus $4 per full-time employee and $2 per part-time employee), $200 (annual) • individual, $50 (annual). **Staff:** 2. **Budget:** $115,000. **Local.** Promotes business and community development in Delaware County, OH. **Libraries: Type:** not open to the public. **Computer Services:** Online services, membership directory. **Formerly:** Delaware County Chamber of Commerce. **Publications:** *ChamberNotes*. Newsletter. Alternate Formats: online • *Manufacturer Directory*, annual • *Welcome Book*, quadrennial. Contains general overview of Delaware area. **Price:** $1.00 additional copies. **Advertising:** accepted • Membership Directory, annual • Book, bimonthly. **Conventions/Meetings:** annual meeting - always January • monthly meeting.

15003 ■ Delaware Community Lions Club
c/o Sheila Milligan, Pres.
321 Rutherford Ave.
Delaware, OH 43015
Ph: (740)369-5898
URL: http://www.iwaynet.net/~lions13f
Contact: Sheila Milligan, Pres.
Local. Affiliated With: Lions Clubs International.

15004 ■ Delaware County Board of Realtors
21 N Sandusky St.
Delaware, OH 43015
Ph: (740)363-3227
Fax: (740)363-3227
E-mail: dcbr@midohio.net
URL: National Affiliate–www.realtor.org
Contact: Cheryl Inscho, Exec. Officer
Local. Strives to develop real estate business practices. Advocates for the right to own, use and transfer real property. Provides a facility for professional development, research and exchange of information among members and the general public. **Affiliated With:** National Association of Realtors.

15005 ■ Delaware County Genealogical Society
PO Box 1126
157 E William St.
Delaware, OH 43015-8126
Ph: (740)369-3831
E-mail: dchsdcgs@midohio.net
URL: http://www.rootsweb.com/~ohdchs
Contact: Mr James Freed, Pres.
Founded: 1984. **Members:** 250. **Membership Dues:** individual, $10 (annual) • joint, $12 (annual) • life - individual, $150 • life - joint, $200. **Budget:** $7,000. **Local.** Strives to encourage individual research, support the objectives of the Ohio Genealogical Society, collect and preserve genealogical and historical records and publish such records if advisable. **Libraries: Type:** open to the public; reference. **Holdings:** 500; books, periodicals, photographs, reports. **Subjects:** genealogical and local history. **Awards:** Delaware County Pioneers. **Frequency:** annual. **Type:** recognition. **Recipient:** for documented ancestor in Delaware County prior to 1850. **Subgroups:** Delaware County Pioneers. **Affiliated With:** Ohio Genealogical Society; Ohio Genealogical Society. **Publications:** *The Delaware Genealogist*, quarterly. Newsletter. Contains topics about genealogy. **Price:** included in membership dues. **Circulation:** 400.

15006 ■ Delaware County Habitat for Humanity (DCHFH)
305 Curtis St.
Delaware, OH 43015
Ph: (740)363-9950
Fax: (740)363-0462
E-mail: mjkuhns@owu.edu
URL: http://www.habitatdelawareco.org
Contact: Jackie Kuhns, Exec.Dir.
Local. Affiliated With: Habitat for Humanity International.

15007 ■ Delaware County Historical Society (DCHS)
PO Box 317
Delaware, OH 43015-0317
Ph: (740)369-3831
E-mail: dchsdcgs@midohio.net
URL: http://www.midohio.net/dchsdcgs
Contact: Marilyn Cryder, Contact
Founded: 1938. **Members:** 300. **Membership Dues:** individual, $10 (annual) • husband and wife, $15 (annual) • patron/business member, $35 (annual) • sponsor, $100 (annual) • benefactor, $500 (annual) • life, $250. **Budget:** $36,000. **Local.** Individuals and families. Collects, preserves, and disseminates local genealogical material and historical memorabilia. Maintains museum. Supports local activities. **Libraries: Type:** reference. **Holdings:** 3,000. **Publications:** Newsletter, quarterly. **Conventions/Meetings:** quarterly meeting.

15008 ■ Great Lakes Appaloosa Horse Club (GLApHC)
c/o Charles Schroeder, Pres.
387 Lawrence
Delaware, OH 43015
E-mail: corjschroeder@aol.com
URL: http://www.glaphc.com
Contact: Charles Schroeder, Pres.
Local. Affiliated With: Appaloosa Horse Club.

15009 ■ Mothers Against Drunk Driving, Delaware County
141 N Sandusky St.
Delaware, OH 43015
Ph: (740)833-2710
Fax: (740)368-1979
Free: (877)677-6233
URL: National Affiliate–www.madd.org
Contact: Chrystal Alexander, Dir.
Local. Victims of drunk driving crashes; concerned citizens. Encourages citizen participation in working towards reform of the drunk driving problem and the

prevention of underage drinking. Acts as the voice of victims of drunk driving crashes by speaking on their behalf to communities, businesses, and educational groups. **Affiliated With:** Mothers Against Drunk Driving.

15010 ■ Psi Chi, National Honor Society in Psychology - Ohio Wesleyan University
c/o Dept. of Psychology
52 Phillips Hall
61 S Sandusky St.
Delaware, OH 43015-2398
Ph: (740)368-3800 (740)368-3807
Fax: (740)368-3812
E-mail: nksmith@owu.edu
URL: http://www.psichi.org/chapters/info.asp?chapter_id=87
Contact: Kyle Smith PhD, Advisor
Local.

15011 ■ Tauheed (Islamic Society) - Ohio Wesleyan University
c/o Mohammad Munibullah Khan
HWCC Box No. 233
Delaware, OH 43015
Ph: (740)368-2244
Fax: (740)368-3073
E-mail: tauheed@owu.edu
URL: http://www.owu.edu/~tauheed
Contact: Mohammad Munibullah Khan, Contact
Local. Muslim students in North America. Seeks to advance the interests of members; works to enable members to practice Islam as a complete way of life. **Affiliated With:** Muslim Students Association of the United States and Canada.

15012 ■ United Way of Delaware County, Ohio
PO Box 319
Delaware, OH 43015
Ph: (740)369-9618 (740)548-6801
Fax: (740)369-9080
E-mail: feedback@uwaydelaware.org
URL: http://www.uwaydelaware.org
Contact: Katherine Tatterson, Pres.
Local. Affiliated With: United Way of America.

Delphos

15013 ■ American Legion, Commemorative Post 268
413 N State St.
Delphos, OH 45833
Ph: (740)362-7478
Fax: (740)362-1429
URL: National Affiliate–www.legion.org
Local. Affiliated With: American Legion.

15014 ■ Delphos Area Chamber of Commerce (DACC)
310 N Main St.
Delphos, OH 45833
Ph: (419)695-1771
Fax: (419)695-1771
E-mail: dchamber1@wcoil.com
URL: http://www.delphos-ohio.com
Contact: Diane Sterling, Exec.Dir.
Founded: 1929. **Local.** Promotes business and community development in the Delphos, OH area. Sponsors annual Canal Days Festival. **Affiliated With:** U.S. Chamber of Commerce.

Delta

15015 ■ American Legion, A. E. E. E. W. Post 373
5939 Sr 109
Delta, OH 43515
Ph: (740)362-7478
Fax: (740)362-1429
URL: National Affiliate–www.legion.org
Local. Affiliated With: American Legion.

15016 ■ Delta Chamber of Commerce
PO Box 96
Delta, OH 43515-0096
Ph: (419)822-3089 (419)822-4055
URL: http://www.deltaohio.com
Contact: Marcy LeFevre, Pres.
Local. Promotes business and community development in Delta, OH.

15017 ■ Izaak Walton League of America, Delta Chapter
402 Adrian St.
Delta, OH 43515-1124
Ph: (419)822-4468
URL: National Affiliate–www.iwla.org
Local. Works to educate the public to conserve, maintain, protect, and restore the soil, forest, water, and other natural resources of the U.S; promotes the enjoyment and wholesome utilization of these resources. **Affiliated With:** Izaak Walton League of America.

Dennison

15018 ■ American Legion, Ohio Post 491
c/o William J. Linehan
402 Logan St.
Dennison, OH 44621
Ph: (740)362-7478
Fax: (740)362-1429
URL: National Affiliate–www.legion.org
Contact: William J. Linehan, Contact
Local. Affiliated With: American Legion.

15019 ■ Clayland Lions Club
c/o Beth Johnson, Pres.
6219 Wolf Run Rd. SE
Dennison, OH 44621
Ph: (740)922-4641 (740)922-1929
E-mail: ejohnson@claymont.k12.oh.us
URL: http://users.adelphia.net/~npssteve/district.htm
Contact: Beth Johnson, Pres.
Local. Affiliated With: Lions Clubs International.

Deshler

15020 ■ American Legion, Deshler Post 316
505 S Stearns Ave.
Deshler, OH 43516
Ph: (740)362-7478
Fax: (740)362-1429
URL: National Affiliate–www.legion.org
Local. Affiliated With: American Legion.

15021 ■ Deshler Chamber of Commerce
PO Box 123
Deshler, OH 43516
Ph: (419)278-1826
Contact: Jackie Arps, Sec.-Treas.
Local.

15022 ■ Ohio Genealogical Society, Henry County
c/o Lucille Van Scoyoc, Treas.
PO Box 231
Deshler, OH 43516
E-mail: information@henrycountyohiogenealogy.org
URL: http://www.henrycountyohiogenealogy.org
Contact: Lucille Van Scoyoc, Treas.
Founded: 1986. **Membership Dues:** family, $10 (annual). **Local.** Preserves records of Henry County and related areas of Ohio. **Affiliated With:** Ohio Genealogical Society. **Publications:** *Henry County Birth Record, Vol. 1 (1867-1877)*, periodic. Directory. **Price:** $12.00 plus $2 postage • *Henry County Death Records, Vol. 1 (1867-1877)*, periodic. Directory. **Price:** $10.00 plus $2 postage • *1857 Tax Duplicates*, periodic. Directory. **Price:** $12.00 plus $2 postage.

Diamond

15023 ■ Portage County Beagle Club
c/o George Gealy
3373 Mcclintocksburg Rd.
Diamond, OH 44412-9732
URL: National Affiliate–clubs.akc.org
Contact: George Gealy, Contact
Local.

Dillonvale

15024 ■ Muskies Hopedale Chapter
15 Township Rd. 125
Dillonvale, OH 43917
Ph: (740)769-7269
E-mail: jlctrngng@1st.net
URL: National Affiliate–www.muskiesinc.org
Contact: Michael A. Uscio, Pres.
Local.

Dover

15025 ■ American Cancer Society, Tuscarawas Area
201A W Ohio Ave.
Dover, OH 44622
Ph: (330)602-5062
Fax: (330)602-5062
Free: (888)227-6446
URL: http://www.cancer.org
Local. Affiliated With: American Cancer Society.

15026 ■ American Legion, Dover Post 205
128 E 3rd St.
Dover, OH 44622
Ph: (740)362-7478
Fax: (740)362-1429
URL: National Affiliate–www.legion.org
Local. Affiliated With: American Legion.

15027 ■ Dover Historical Society
c/o James D. Nixon, Pres.
325 E Iron Ave.
Dover, OH 44622
Ph: (330)343-7040
Fax: (330)343-6290
Free: (800)815-2794
E-mail: reeves@tusco.net
URL: http://www.doverhistory.org
Contact: James D. Nixon, Pres.
Members: 1,000. **Local.** Promotes historical studies and investigations, more especially pertaining to the state of Ohio, County of Tuscarawas and City of Dover, through the discovery, collection, preservation, organization, and, if practical, the publication of historical fact pertaining to state, county and city. Cooperates with state, county and local schools in the teaching of state and local history and assists libraries, other museums, and historical focused groups and organizations in doing all things necessary to identify, promote, maintain and preserve the history of state, county and city.

15028 ■ National Active and Retired Federal Employees Association - Tuscarawas Valley 635
2717 Delaware Cir.
Dover, OH 44622-9427
Ph: (330)343-5983
URL: National Affiliate–www.narfe.org
Contact: Violet A. Schimitzer, Contact
Local. Protects the retirement future of employees through education. Informs members on issues affecting the retirement. **Affiliated With:** National Association of Retired Federal Employees.

15029 ■ National Alliance for the Mentally Ill - Tuscarawas County
c/o Polly Patin-Mellor
1228 Walnut St.
Dover, OH 44622

Ph: (330)364-6068
URL: http://www.namiohio.org/affiliates_support.htm
Contact: Polly Patin-Mellor, Contact
Local. Strives to improve the quality of life of children and adults with severe mental illness through support, education, research and advocacy. **Affiliated With:** National Alliance for the Mentally Ill.

15030 ■ Ohio Chapter National Association of Tax Professionals
c/o Randal R. Longacher, CPA LUTCF, Pres.
PO Box 473
Dover, OH 44622-0473
Ph: (330)364-8647
Fax: (330)343-9434
E-mail: tuscotax@tusco.net
URL: National Affiliate–www.natptax.com
Contact: Randal R. Longacher CPA, Pres.
State. Affiliated With: National Association of Tax Professionals.

15031 ■ Ohio Health Care Association, District 10
c/o David Hennis, Chm.
Hennis Care Ctre.
1720 Cross St.
Dover, OH 44622
Ph: (330)364-8849
Fax: (330)364-2128
E-mail: hdhennis@tusco.net
URL: http://www.ohca.org
Contact: David Hennis, Chm.
Local. Promotes professionalism and ethical behavior of individuals providing long-term care delivery for patients and for the general public. Provides information, education and administrative tools to enhance the quality of long-term care. Improves the standards of service and administration of member nursing homes. **Affiliated With:** American Health Care Association.

15032 ■ Society for Human Resource Management - Tuscora Chapter
c/o Dawn Brogan
Walt Disney World
301 E 12th St.
Dover, OH 44622
Ph: (330)364-5124
E-mail: dawn.brogan@disney.com
URL: http://www.ohioshrm.org/tuscora
Contact: Dawn Brogan, Pres.
Local. Represents the interests of human resource and industrial relations professionals and executives. Promotes the advancement of human resource management.

15033 ■ Tuscarawas County ALU
2620-B N Wooster Ave.
Dover, OH 44622
Fax: (330)364-2206
URL: National Affiliate–www.naifa.org
Local. Represents the interest of insurance and financial advisors. Advocates for a positive legislative and regulatory environment. Enhances business and professional skills of members. **Affiliated With:** National Association of Insurance and Financial Advisors.

15034 ■ Tuscarawas County Coin Club
c/o Ted Fisher
811 N Tuscarawas Ave.
Dover, OH 44622
E-mail: suephil@tusco.net
URL: National Affiliate–www.money.org
Contact: Ted Fisher, Contact
Local. Affiliated With: American Numismatic Association.

Doylestown

15035 ■ American Legion, D. W. M. D. Post 407
49 Black Dr.
Doylestown, OH 44230
Ph: (740)362-7478
Fax: (740)362-1429
URL: National Affiliate–www.legion.org
Local. Affiliated With: American Legion.

15036 ■ American Legion, Ohio Post 777
c/o Earnest F. Kerr, Jr.
11804 Clinton Rd.
Doylestown, OH 44230
Ph: (740)362-7478
Fax: (740)362-1429
URL: National Affiliate–www.legion.org
Contact: Earnest F. Kerr Jr., Contact
Local. Affiliated With: American Legion.

15037 ■ Friends of the Paullin Library
c/o Daniel O. Waller
24 1/2 S Portage St.
Doylestown, OH 44230-1571
Ph: (330)658-4677
E-mail: doylestown@wayne.lib.oh.us
URL: http://www.wayne.lib.oh.us
Contact: Lora Goman, Branch Mgr.
Local.

Dresden

15038 ■ American Legion, Ohio Post 399
c/o Charles M. Mitchell
1385 S Main St.
Dresden, OH 43821
Ph: (740)362-7478
Fax: (740)362-1429
URL: National Affiliate–www.legion.org
Contact: Charles M. Mitchell, Contact
Local. Affiliated With: American Legion.

15039 ■ Dresden REACT
38 W 9th St.
Dresden, OH 43821
Ph: (740)754-3881
URL: http://www.reactintl.org/teaminfo/usa_teams/teams-usoh.htm
Local. Trained communication experts and professional volunteers. Provides volunteer public service and emergency communications through the use of radios (Citizen Band, General Mobile Radio Service, UHF and HAM). Coordinates with radio industries and government on safety communication matters and supports charitable activities and community organizations.

Dublin

15040 ■ Air Conditioning Contractors of America, Greater Dayton Chapter
c/o Betty Clark, Exec.Dir.
6047 Frantz Rd., Ste.105
Dublin, OH 43017
Fax: (614)717-4915
Free: (866)630-1247
URL: http://www.accadayton.org
Contact: Betty Clark, Exec.Dir.
Local. Strives to promote the reputation of the HVAC industry in the Miami Valley by adhering to the highest ethical business standards of members. Fosters professionalism through ongoing educational programs. **Affiliated With:** Air Conditioning Contractors of America.

15041 ■ American Camp Association Ohio
5244 Bandon Ct.
Dublin, OH 43016-4312
Ph: (614)766-4519
Fax: (614)766-4519
Free: (800)837-2269
E-mail: info@acaohio.org
URL: http://www.acaohio.org
Contact: Jerry Duffie, Pres.
State. Represents the organized camping industry and all segments of the camp profession, including agencies serving youth and adults, independent camps, religious and fraternal organizations and public/municipal agencies. Serves as a knowledge center for the camping industry, educating camp owners and directors in the administration of camp operations, particularly program quality, health and safety, and assisting parents, families and caregivers nationwide in selecting camps that meet industry-accepted and government recognized standards. **Formerly:** (2004) American Camping Association - Ohio Section.

15042 ■ American Wine Society - Columbus
c/o Linda Stahl, Treas.
5957 Kirkwall Ct. E
Dublin, OH 43017
Ph: (614)855-3804
E-mail: bernthurn@aol.com
URL: http://www.columbusaws.com
Contact: Jerome J. Substanley, Co-Chm.
Local. Affiliated With: American Wine Society.

15043 ■ Central Ohio Air Conditioning Contractors of America (COACCA)
c/o Betty J. Clark, Exec.Dir.
6047 Frantz Rd., Ste.105
Dublin, OH 43017
Ph: (614)923-1057
Fax: (614)717-4915
URL: http://coacca.org
Contact: Betty J. Clark, Exec.Dir.
Founded: 1906. **Members:** 100. **Local.** Contractors involved in installation and service of heating, air conditioning, and refrigeration systems. **Awards:** Hall of Honor. **Frequency:** annual. **Type:** recognition. **Affiliated With:** Air Conditioning Contractors of America. **Publications:** Directory, annual • Newsletter, monthly.

15044 ■ Central Ohio Kennel Club (COKC)
c/o Barbara Alexander
4200 Bright Rd.
Dublin, OH 43016-9513
Ph: (614)792-3232
E-mail: cokc_info@ohiodogs.com
URL: http://ohiodogs.com
Contact: Barbara Alexander, Contact
Regional. Affiliated With: American Kennel Club.

15045 ■ Chiller Figure Skating Club (ChFSC)
PO Box 3621
Dublin, OH 43016-0310
E-mail: info@achillerfsc.com
URL: http://www.chillerfsc.com
Contact: Stormy Holderman, Pres.
Local. Provides programs to encourage participation and achievement in the sport of figure skating on ice. Defines and maintains uniform standards of skating proficiency. Organizes and sponsors competitions and exhibitions for the purpose of stimulating interest in figure skating. **Affiliated With:** United States Figure Skating Association.

15046 ■ Financial Planning Association of Central Ohio
5481 Haverhill Dr.
Dublin, OH 43017
Ph: (614)336-9333
Fax: (614)793-1946
E-mail: darmstrong@kdaadvisors.com
URL: http://www.fpacentralohio.org
Contact: Diane Armstrong CFP, Pres.
Local. Orchestrates the promotion and education of the financial planning profession to its members and the Central Ohio community. **Affiliated With:** Financial Planning Association.

15047 ■ Golden Retriever Club of Columbus, Ohio (GRCCO)
c/o Nancy Burns
9035 Picardy Ct.
Dublin, OH 43017

Ph: (614)889-0786
E-mail: ayrshires@aol.com
URL: http://www.grcco.org
Contact: Nancy Burns, Contact
Local. **Affiliated With:** Golden Retriever Club of America.

15048 ■ Human Resources Association of Central Ohio
PO Box 3021
Dublin, OH 43016
Ph: (614)760-0400
E-mail: support@hraco.com
URL: http://www.hraco.com
Contact: Carole Lassak, Coor.
Local. Represents the interests of human resource and industrial relations professionals and executives. Promotes the advancement of human resource management.

15049 ■ Irish Baseball Backers
c/o Dublin Scioto High School
4000 Hard Rd.
Dublin, OH 43016-8349
Local.

15050 ■ NAIFA-Columbus (OH)
c/o Karen Shepherd, Exec.
8457 Invergordon Ct.
Dublin, OH 43017
Ph: (614)766-8472
Fax: (614)766-8474
E-mail: exec@naifa-columbus.org
URL: http://www.naifa-columbus.org
Contact: Karen Shepherd, Exec.
Local. Represents the interests of insurance and financial advisors. Advocates for a positive legislative and regulatory environment. Enhances business and professional skills of members. **Affiliated With:** National Association of Insurance and Financial Advisors.

15051 ■ National Technical Honor Society - Northwest Career Center - Ohio
2960 Cranston Dr.
Dublin, OH 43017
Ph: (614)365-5325
Fax: (614)365-5621
E-mail: northwest_career_center@hotmail.com
URL: http://www.columbus.k12.oh.us
Contact: Charles Richardson, Dir.
Local.

15052 ■ Nature Conservancy, Ohio Chapter
6375 Riverside Dr., Ste.50
Dublin, OH 43017
Ph: (614)717-2770
Fax: (614)717-2777
E-mail: ohio@tnc.org
URL: National Affiliate–www.nature.org
Contact: Dr. Richard L. Shank, State Dir.
State. Works to preserve plants, animals, and natural communities that represent the diversity of life on Earth by protecting the lands and waters they need to survive. **Affiliated With:** Nature Conservancy.

15053 ■ Ohio Association of Chiefs of Police (OACP)
c/o Todd N. Wurschmidt, PhD, Exec.Dir.
6277 Riverside Dr., Ste.2N
Dublin, OH 43017-5067
Ph: (614)761-0330
Fax: (614)761-9509
E-mail: oacp@oacp.org
URL: http://www.oacp.org
Contact: Todd N. Wurschmidt PhD, Exec.Dir.
Founded: 1928. **State**.

15054 ■ Ohio Court Reporters Association (OCRA)
5021 Winchell Ct.
Dublin, OH 43017
Ph: (614)336-2045
Fax: (614)336-2604
E-mail: info@ocraonline.com
URL: http://www.ocraonline.com
Contact: Tracy Schiefferle, Exec.Dir.
Members: 400. **Membership Dues:** active reporter, $115 (annual) • associate, $45 (annual) • student, retired, $25 (annual). **Staff:** 1. **State Groups:** 1. **State**. **Awards:** Diplomat Award. **Frequency:** annual. **Type:** trophy • Fincun Award. **Frequency:** annual. **Type:** trophy • Hagestrom Speed Cup. **Frequency:** annual. **Type:** trophy • Realtime Award. **Frequency:** annual. **Type:** trophy • Rosalie Stevens Student Scholarship. **Frequency:** annual. **Type:** monetary • Stiles Award. **Frequency:** annual. **Type:** trophy. **Publications:** *Buckeye Record*, quarterly. Newsletter. **Price:** included in membership dues. **Advertising:** accepted. Alternate Formats: online. **Conventions/Meetings:** annual conference (exhibits) - always fall • annual meeting (exhibits).

15055 ■ Ohio Credit Union League (OCUL)
c/o Paul Mercer, Pres.
5815 Wall St.
Dublin, OH 43017
Ph: (614)336-2894
Fax: (614)336-2895
Free: (800)486-2917
E-mail: oculmail@ohiocul.org
URL: http://www.ohiocul.org
Contact: Paul Mercer, Pres.
State.

15056 ■ Ohio Equipment Distributors Association (OEDA)
c/o David L. Kahler, Exec.Sec.-Treas.
PO Box 68
Dublin, OH 43017
Ph: (614)889-1309
Fax: (614)889-0463
E-mail: ostaff@omeda.org
URL: http://www.omeda.org
State. Represents approximately 100 construction equipment distributors in Ohio.

15057 ■ Ohio Hospice and Palliative Care Organization (OHPCO)
555 Metro Pl. N, Ste.650
Dublin, OH 43017-1375
Ph: (614)763-0036
Fax: (614)763-0050
Free: (800)776-9513
E-mail: info@ohpco.org
URL: http://www.ohpco.org
Contact: Jeff Lycan RN, BS, Pres./CEO
Founded: 1978. **Members:** 74. **Membership Dues:** individual, $30 (annual) • associate, $300 (annual) • provider, $740-$6,400 (annual). **Staff:** 5. **Budget:** $450,000. **State**. Hospice organizations and individuals interested in the promotion of the hospice concept and program of care. Promotes standards of care in program planning and implementation; monitors health care legislation and regulation relevant to hospice care. Sponsors professional liaison and peer group networking. Collects data for the purpose of demonstrating definitive national trends in the hospice movement; encourages recognized medical and other health teaching institutions to provide instruction in hospice care of terminally ill patients and their families. Compiles statistics. Conducts educational and training programs in numerous aspects of hospice care for administrators and care-givers. **Libraries: Type:** open to the public. **Holdings:** 1,000; articles, books. **Subjects:** end of life care. **Awards:** Friend of Hospice. **Frequency:** annual. **Type:** recognition • Person of the Year. **Frequency:** annual. **Type:** recognition. **Recipient:** for significant contribution to end of life care • Stein Award. **Frequency:** annual. **Type:** recognition. **Recipient:** for hospice excellence • Volunteer of the Year. **Frequency:** annual. **Type:** recognition. **Recipient:** for service to end of life care. **Affiliated With:** National Association for Home Care and Hospice. **Formerly:** (2000) Ohio Hospice Organization. **Publications:** *Advance Directives* (in English and Spanish), annual. Brochure. Contains directives about Ohio Living will and Durable Power of Attorney. Alternate Formats: online • *In Touch* (in English and Spanish), annual. Journal. **Price:** $3.00. **Conventions/Meetings:** annual conference, educational (exhibits) - three days.

15058 ■ Ohio Manufactured Homes Association (OMHA)
201 Bradenton Ave., Ste.100
Dublin, OH 43017-3540
Ph: (614)799-2340
Fax: (614)799-0616
Telex: 0
E-mail: info@welcomehomeohio.com
URL: http://www.welcomehomeohio.com
Contact: Tim Williams, Exec.VP
Founded: 1947. **Members:** 670. **Membership Dues:** retailer (manufactured/modular homes, with annual sales of 1-12 units), $147 • retailer (manufactured/modular homes, with annual sales of 13-25 units), $263 • retailer (manufactured/modular homes, with annual sales of 26-50 units), $378 • retailer (manufactured/modular homes, with annual sales of 51 or more units), $609 • associate (exclusive manufactured home broker), $315 • associate (community developer), $609 • associate (supplier and service firms), $494 • associate (lending institutions), $174 • associate (insurance company), $520 • associate (insurance agency), $263 • associate (utility company), $609 • associate (transporters-intrastate), $263 • associate (transporters-interstate), $494 • associate (independent parts, accessories, or service), $174. **Staff:** 5. **Budget:** $850,000. **Regional Groups:** 20. **Local Groups:** 89. **State**. Retailers, community owners, manufacturers, service and supply firms, utility companies, transporters, financial institutions, and insurance companies. Promotes the manufactured housing. Funds political action committee; monitors pertinent legislation; lobbies on behalf of the industry. **Awards:** Ohio Industry Awards. **Frequency:** annual. **Type:** recognition. **Affiliated With:** Manufactured Housing Institute. **Formerly:** (1982) Ohio Mobile Home and Recreational Vehicle Association. **Publications:** *Access*, bimonthly. Newsletter. **Price:** free for members. **Circulation:** 800. **Advertising:** accepted • *Data-Grams*, periodic • Membership Directory, biennial. **Conventions/Meetings:** annual conference • periodic seminar.

15059 ■ Ohio-Michigan Equipment Dealers Association (OMEDA)
PO Box 68
Dublin, OH 43017
Ph: (614)889-1309
Fax: (614)889-0463
E-mail: ostaff@omeda.org
URL: http://www.omeda.org
Contact: David L. Kahler, Exec.VP/CEO
State.

15060 ■ Ohio Petroleum Marketers and Convenience Store Association (OPMCA)
4242 Tuller Rd., Unit B
Dublin, OH 43017
Ph: (614)792-5212
Fax: (614)792-1706
E-mail: info@opmca.org
URL: http://www.opmca.org
Contact: Roger F. Dreyer, Pres.
State. **Formerly:** (2005) Ohio Petroleum Marketers Association.

15061 ■ Ohio Scientific Education and Research Association (OSERA)
7652 Sawmill Rd., No. 337
Dublin, OH 43016
Ph: (614)784-1961
E-mail: director@osera.org
URL: http://www.osera.org
Contact: M. Sue Benford PhD, Exec.Dir.
Founded: 1991. **Members:** 30. **Staff:** 1. **Budget:** $140,000. **State**. Fosters understanding of the responsible use of animals in education, biomedical, product safety, and environmental protection research. Supports humane use of animals in these efforts until scientifically valid non-animal methods are developed.

15062 ■ Ohio Seed Improvement Association (OSIA)
c/o John Armstrong, Sec./Mgr.
PO Box 477
Dublin, OH 43017-0477
Ph: (614)889-1136
Fax: (614)889-8979
E-mail: osia@ohseed.org
URL: http://www.ohseed.org
State.

15063 ■ Ohio Valley Retriever Club (OVRC)
c/o David Berk, Corresponding Sec.
5585 Wilcox Rd.
Dublin, OH 43016
Ph: (614)889-5871
E-mail: martybell@zande.com
URL: http://home.insight.rr.com/ovrc/
Contact: Marty Bell, Pres.
State. **Affiliated With:** American Kennel Club.

15064 ■ Ohio Vehicle Leasing Association (OVLA)
6083 O'Sweeney Ln.
Dublin, OH 43016
Free: (800)369-5633
URL: http://www.uautolease.com
State. Promotes sound public policy with respect to the leasing of motor vehicles, to collect and disseminate information concerning present and proposed national, state, and local legislation and regulations pertaining to all phases of motor vehicle leasing, to present the views of motor vehicle lessors to national, state, and local legislative and regulatory bodies, to cooperate with other organizations and groups having similar objectives, and to encourage the formation of local groups of motor vehicle lessors for the accomplishment of the foregoing purposes. **Affiliated With:** Truck Renting and Leasing Association.

15065 ■ Olive Branch Farm Skeet Club
178 Marion St.
Dublin, OH 43017
Ph: (740)380-2731
URL: National Affiliate–www.mynssa.com
Local. **Affiliated With:** National Skeet Shooting Association.

15066 ■ Sweet Adelines International, Scioto Valley Chorus
Northwest Presbyterian Church
6400 Post Rd.
Dublin, OH 43016-1226
Ph: (614)876-8106
E-mail: sciotovalleychorus@harmonize.com
URL: http://www.harmonize.com/svc
Contact: Kathie Holloway, Contact
Local. Advances the musical art form of barbershop harmony through education and performances. Provides education, training and coaching in the development of women's four-part barbershop harmony. **Affiliated With:** Sweet Adelines International.

15067 ■ Turkish American Association of Central Ohio (TAACO)
PO Box 3566
Dublin, OH 43016
Ph: (614)270-2574
E-mail: taacomail@yahoo.com
URL: http://www.taaco.org
Contact: Bulent Bekcioglu, Pres.
Founded: 1969. **Membership Dues:** individual, $25 (annual) • family, $40 (annual) • student, senior, $10 (annual). **Local**. **Affiliated With:** Assembly of Turkish American Associations.

15068 ■ Young Life Buckeye Region
75 S High St., No. 7
Dublin, OH 43017
Ph: (614)889-7545
Fax: (614)889-8250
URL: http://sites.younglife.org/sites/BuckeyeRegion/default.aspx
Local. **Affiliated With:** Young Life.

Duncan Falls

15069 ■ American Legion, Ohio Post 246
c/o Ernest G. Walsh
PO Box 7
Duncan Falls, OH 43734
Ph: (740)362-7478
Fax: (740)362-1429
URL: National Affiliate–www.legion.org
Contact: Ernest G. Walsh, Contact
Local. **Affiliated With:** American Legion.

East Canton

15070 ■ American Legion, Ohio Post 667
c/o Lowell D. Oberly
204 Wood St. NE
East Canton, OH 44730
Ph: (740)362-7478
Fax: (740)362-1429
URL: National Affiliate–www.legion.org
Contact: Lowell D. Oberly, Contact
Local. **Affiliated With:** American Legion.

15071 ■ East Canton Lions Club
c/o Earl Haslam, Pres.
221 Noble St.
East Canton, OH 44730
Ph: (330)488-2838
E-mail: eastcantonlionsclub@yahoo.com
URL: http://www.lions13d.org
Contact: Earl Haslam, Pres.
Local. **Affiliated With:** Lions Clubs International.

East Fultonham

15072 ■ American Legion, Newton Post 726
PO Box 132
East Fultonham, OH 43735
Ph: (740)362-7478
Fax: (740)362-1429
URL: National Affiliate–www.legion.org
Local. **Affiliated With:** American Legion.

East Liberty

15073 ■ American Legion, Wood-Rosebrook Post 745
PO Box 132
East Liberty, OH 43319
Ph: (740)362-7478
Fax: (740)362-1429
URL: National Affiliate–www.legion.org
Local. **Affiliated With:** American Legion.

East Liverpool

15074 ■ AAA Columbiana County
516 Broadway
East Liverpool, OH 43920
Ph: (330)385-2020
Local.

15075 ■ American Legion, Glenmoor Post 736
45940 Y & O Rd.
East Liverpool, OH 43920
Ph: (740)362-7478
Fax: (740)362-1429
URL: National Affiliate–www.legion.org
Local. **Affiliated With:** American Legion.

15076 ■ American Legion, Ohio Post 374
c/o Alfred H. Wedgewood
1824 Parkway
East Liverpool, OH 43920
Ph: (740)362-7478
Fax: (740)362-1429
URL: National Affiliate–www.legion.org
Contact: Alfred H. Wedgewood, Contact
Local. **Affiliated With:** American Legion.

15077 ■ Beaver Creek Area Association of Realtors
1332 St. Clair
East Liverpool, OH 43920
Ph: (330)385-4900
Fax: (330)385-7500
E-mail: hilbertagency@mtn-state.com
URL: National Affiliate–www.realtor.org
Contact: Beth A. Hilbert, Exec. Officer
Local. Strives to develop real estate business practices. Advocates for the right to own, use and transfer real property. Provides a facility for professional development, research and exchange of information among members and the general public. **Affiliated With:** National Association of Realtors.

15078 ■ East Liverpool Area Chamber of Commerce
529 Market St.
East Liverpool, OH 43920-5094
Ph: (330)385-0845
Fax: (330)385-0581
E-mail: office@elchamber.com
URL: http://www.elchamber.com
Contact: Pamela Hoppel, Exec.Dir.
Founded: 1916. **Local**. Promotes business and community development in the East Liverpool area.

15079 ■ East Liverpool Lions Club
c/o Fred Crawford, Pres.
2988 Kingsridge Dr.
East Liverpool, OH 43920
Ph: (330)385-6950
E-mail: spyder64@core.com
URL: http://www.lions13d.org
Contact: Fred Crawford, Pres.
Local. **Affiliated With:** Lions Clubs International.

15080 ■ Korean War Veterans Association, Tri-State Chapter
c/o Donald R. Wolf
829 Louise Ave.
East Liverpool, OH 43920
Ph: (330)385-7403
URL: National Affiliate–www.kwva.org
Contact: Donald R. Wolf, Contact
Regional. **Affiliated With:** Korean War Veterans Association.

15081 ■ Masonic Temple
422 Broadway St.
East Liverpool, OH 43920
Ph: (330)385-0172
Contact: Gerald C. Goodballet, Sec.-Treas.

15082 ■ United Way of Southern Columbiana County
PO Box 646
East Liverpool, OH 43920-5646
Ph: (330)385-2082
URL: National Affiliate–national.unitedway.org
Local. **Affiliated With:** United Way of America.

East Palestine

15083 ■ American Legion, Ohio Post 31
c/o George F. Mc Bane
140 N Walnut St.
East Palestine, OH 44413
Ph: (740)362-7478
Fax: (740)362-1429
URL: National Affiliate–www.legion.org
Contact: George F. Mc Bane, Contact
Local. **Affiliated With:** American Legion.

East Sparta

15084 ■ American Legion, Ohio Post 244
c/o Isaac L. Kinney
9516 Chestnut Ave. SE
East Sparta, OH 44626
Ph: (740)362-7478
Fax: (740)362-1429
URL: National Affiliate–www.legion.org
Contact: Isaac L. Kinney, Contact
Local. Affiliated With: American Legion.

Eastlake

15085 ■ Eastlake Women's Club
PO Box 7152
Eastlake, OH 44097
Ph: (440)951-1416
E-mail: ewceohio@yahoo.com
URL: http://www.geocities.com/ewceohio/index.html
Contact: Arlene Balchak, Pres.
Local.

Eaton

15086 ■ American Hiking Society - Preble County Historical Society
7693 Swartsel Rd.
Eaton, OH 45320-9437
Ph: (937)787-4256
Fax: (937)787-9662
E-mail: prcohs-admin@core.com
URL: http://pchs.preblecounty.com
Local.

15087 ■ American Legion, St. Clair Post 215
1000 Rte. 35 W
Eaton, OH 45320
Ph: (740)362-7478
Fax: (740)362-1429
URL: National Affiliate–www.legion.org
Local. Affiliated With: American Legion.

15088 ■ Eaton - Preble County Chamber of Commerce
Eaton Natl. Bank Bldg.
PO Box 303
Eaton, OH 45320-0303
Ph: (937)456-4949
Fax: (937)456-4949
E-mail: chamberoffices@preblecountyohio.com
URL: http://preblecountyohio.com
Contact: Bonnie Norris, Chair
Founded: 1952. **Members:** 180. **Staff:** 2. **Local. Awards: Frequency:** annual. **Type:** scholarship. **Recipient:** for high school seniors of current year usually nominated by their teacher or school administrator. **Publications:** Newsletter, monthly.

15089 ■ Preble County Chapter - Ohio Genealogical Society
c/o Tom Crumbaker, Pres.
450 Barron St.
Eaton, OH 45320-2402
Ph: (937)456-4970
Fax: (937)456-6092
E-mail: pcroom@oplin.org
URL: http://www.pcdl.lib.oh.us
Contact: Nancy Crowell, Lib.
Founded: 1987. **Members:** 75. **Membership Dues:** individual, $15 (annual). **Local.** Formed through the interest created from classes offered at the library and through the growing of genealogical and local history collections in the county. Projects include compiling various family and governmental records, and providing research for those who cannot visit the area. **Libraries: Type:** open to the public; reference. **Holdings:** 11,000; archival material, biographical archives, books, films, papers, photographs. **Subjects:** genealogical and local history of Preble county. **Awards:** First Families of Preble County Ohio. **Frequency:** periodic. **Type:** recognition. **Recipient:** to a member who has proved that their ancestors resided in Preble County, Ohio on or prior to December 31, 1820. **Affiliated With:** Ohio Genealogical Society. **Publications:** *Preble's Pride*, quarterly. Newsletter. **Price:** included in membership dues. **Conventions/ Meetings:** quarterly meeting.

15090 ■ Preble County Habitat for Humanity
160 Woodland Dr.
Eaton, OH 45320
Ph: (937)456-4950
Fax: (513)456-6037
E-mail: waynepresb@voyager.net
URL: National Affiliate–www.habitat.org
Local. Affiliated With: Habitat for Humanity International.

15091 ■ Preble County Historical Society (PCHS)
7693 Swartsel Rd.
Eaton, OH 45320
Ph: (937)787-4256
Fax: (937)787-9662
E-mail: prcohs@core.com
URL: http://pchs.preblecounty.com
Contact: Jane Lightner, Exec.Dir.
Founded: 1971. **Members:** 550. **Membership Dues:** family, $20 (annual) • individual, $10 (annual) • business, $25 (annual) • covered bridge, $50 (annual) • Lewisburg log house, $75 (annual) • Swartsel house, $100 (annual) • Swartsel gold, $250 (annual). **Staff:** 2. **Budget:** $75,000. **Local.** Individuals interested in the history of Preble County, OH. Promotes knowledge of the area's history. Maintains historical center. Sponsors annual Farm Tour Day and monthly open houses in May through October and December. Offers school tours and outreach programs. **Publications:** *1881 Preble County History Book* • *1992 Preble County, OH History Book* • *Telltales*, quarterly. Newsletters. **Advertising:** accepted. **Conventions/ Meetings:** annual Farm Tour Day - first Sunday in October • annual Historic House Tour - summer • annual meeting, membership.

Edgerton

15092 ■ American Legion, J.D. Smith Memorial Post 10
PO Box 775
Edgerton, OH 43517
Ph: (740)362-7478
Fax: (740)362-1429
URL: National Affiliate–www.legion.org
Local. Affiliated With: American Legion.

15093 ■ Edgerton Chamber of Commerce
PO Box 399
Edgerton, OH 43517
Ph: (419)298-2335
Contact: Roger Strup, Sec.
Local.

15094 ■ National Sojourners, Maumee Valley No. 518
c/o CAP'F Dale A. Mathys
PO Box 381
Edgerton, OH 43517-0381
Ph: (419)298-3558
E-mail: usmcdam@adelphia.net
URL: National Affiliate–www.nationalsojourners.org
Contact: CAP'F Dale A. Mathys, Contact
Local.

Edon

15095 ■ American Legion, Edon Post 662
308 Walz St.
Edon, OH 43518
Ph: (740)362-7478
Fax: (740)362-1429
URL: National Affiliate–www.legion.org
Local. Affiliated With: American Legion.

Eldorado

15096 ■ Eldorado Lions Club
150 N Monroe St.
Eldorado, OH 45321
Ph: (937)273-2511
URL: http://eldoradooh.lionwap.org
Contact: Ray Kimmel, Pres.
Local. Affiliated With: Lions Clubs International.

Elida

15097 ■ National Active and Retired Federal Employees Association - John Folk 317
4055 Gomer Rd.
Elida, OH 45807-9504
Ph: (419)331-9963
URL: National Affiliate–www.narfe.org
Contact: Clyde E. Neinas, Contact
Local. Protects the retirement future of employees through education. Informs members on issues affecting the retirement. **Affiliated With:** National Association of Retired Federal Employees.

15098 ■ West Central Ohio Angus Association
c/o Brent English, Pres.
9859 Zion Church Rd.
Elida, OH 45807
Ph: (419)339-3417
URL: National Affiliate–www.angus.org
Contact: Brent English, Pres.
State. Affiliated With: American Angus Association.

Elkton

15099 ■ American Federation of Government Employees, AFL-CIO - Local Union 607
PO Box 146
Elkton, OH 44415
Ph: (303)402-0129
URL: http://www.afgelocal607.com
Contact: Carl Halt, Pres.
Founded: 1997. **Members:** 230. **Local.** Federal employees including food inspectors, nurses, printers, cartographers, lawyers, police officers, census workers, OSHA inspectors, janitors, truck drivers, secretaries, artists, plumbers, immigration inspectors, scientists, doctors, cowboys, botanists, park rangers, computer programmers, foreign service workers, airplane mechanics, environmentalists, and writers. Seeks to help provide good government services, while ensuring that government workers are treated fairly and with dignity. **Affiliated With:** American Federation of Government Employees.

Elmore

15100 ■ American Legion, Community Post 279
PO Box 612
Elmore, OH 43416
Ph: (740)362-7478
Fax: (740)362-1429
URL: National Affiliate–www.legion.org
Local. Affiliated With: American Legion.

15101 ■ Elmore Lions Club
c/o Leslie Willey, Pres.
16751 W Smith Rd.
Elmore, OH 43416
Ph: (419)862-3094
E-mail: 6409@accesstoledo.com
URL: http://www.lions13b.org
Contact: Leslie Willey, Pres.
Local. Affiliated With: Lions Clubs International.

15102 ■ Sugar Creek Protection Society
PO Box 151
Elmore, OH 43416
Ph: (419)862-3386
Fax: (419)372-7243
E-mail: jmagsi@bgnet.bgsu.edu
Contact: Justine Magsig, Publicity Chm.
Founded: 1974. **Members:** 400. **Membership Dues:** all, $5. **Local**. Assists landowners and farmers in the Sugar Creek watershed with service and information. Keeps the creek clear of obstructions at no cost to watershed landowners. Provides scholarships for students of local schools to attend summer Forestry Camp.

Elyria

15103 ■ American Cancer Society, Lorain Area
43099 N Ridge Rd.
Elyria, OH 44035
Ph: (440)324-2211
Fax: (440)324-4217
Free: (888)227-6446
E-mail: monica.miller@cancer.org
URL: http://www.cancer.org
Contact: Monica Miller, Contact
Local. Works to eliminate cancer as a major health problem through research, education, advocacy and service. **Affiliated With:** American Cancer Society.

15104 ■ American Legion, Elyria Post 12
393 Ohio St.
Elyria, OH 44035
Ph: (740)362-7478
Fax: (740)362-1429
URL: National Affiliate–www.legion.org
Local. Affiliated With: American Legion.

15105 ■ American Legion, North Ridgeville Post 802
307 Columbus St.
Elyria, OH 44035
Ph: (740)362-7478
Fax: (740)362-1429
URL: National Affiliate–www.legion.org
Local. Affiliated With: American Legion.

15106 ■ American Red Cross, Lorain County Chapter
2929 W River Rd. N
Elyria, OH 44035
Ph: (440)324-2929
URL: http://loraincounty.redcross.org
Local.

15107 ■ AMVETS, Elyria Post 32
11087 S Middle Ave.
Elyria, OH 44035
Ph: (440)458-8544
E-mail: post32@ohamvets.org
URL: http://www.ohamvets.org/post32.htm
Contact: Edward E. Gardiner Sr., Commander
Local. Affiliated With: AMVETS - American Veterans.

15108 ■ Antique Automobile Club of America, Ohio Region - Commodore Perry Chapter
c/o Maureen Davie
43260 Dellefield Rd.
Elyria; OH 44035
Ph: (440)233-8245
URL: http://www.aaca.org/ohio/CommPerrry.htm
Contact: Peter R. Davie, Pres.
Local. Collectors, hobbyists, and others interested in the preservation, maintenance, and restoration of automobiles and in automotive history. **Affiliated With:** Antique Automobile Club of America.

15109 ■ Black River Audubon Society
c/o Jack Smith, Co-Editor
304 West Ave.
Elyria, OH 44035
Ph: (440)322-0820
E-mail: mvhoff@en.com
URL: National Affiliate–www.audubon.org
Contact: Jack Smith, Co-Editor
Local. Works to conserve and restore natural ecosystems, focusing on birds and other wildlife for the benefit of humanity and the earth's biological diversity. **Affiliated With:** National Audubon Society.

15110 ■ Elyria Evening Lions Club
c/o Robert Bohn, Pres.
283 Washington Ave., No. 302
Elyria, OH 44035
Ph: (440)323-9313 (440)365-5222
E-mail: armygreen2@yahoo.com
URL: http://www.lions13b.org
Contact: Robert Bohn, Pres.
Local. Affiliated With: Lions Clubs International.

15111 ■ Firelands Lions Club
c/o Richard Temple, Pres.
7444 Lake Ave.
Elyria, OH 44035
Ph: (440)324-2662
URL: http://www.lions13b.org
Contact: Richard Temple, Pres.
Local. Affiliated With: Lions Clubs International.

15112 ■ Friends of Wetlands (FOWL)
PO Box 2016
Elyria, OH 44036
Ph: (440)324-7522
E-mail: john@fowl.org
URL: http://www.fowl.org
Contact: John Katko, Contact
Founded: 1991. **Local**.

15113 ■ Greater Cleveland Nurses Association
1289 East Ave.
Elyria, OH 44035
Ph: (216)771-6922
Fax: (440)322-3466
E-mail: gcna@clevelandnurse.org
URL: http://www.clevelandnurse.org
Contact: Diane Winfrey RN, Pres.
Local. Works to advance the nursing profession. Seeks to meet the needs of nurses and health care consumers. Fosters high standards of nursing practice. Promotes the economic and general welfare of nurses in the workplace. **Affiliated With:** American Nurses Association; Ohio Nurses Association.

15114 ■ Greater Lorain County Chapter of the Society for Human Resource Management (GLCC SHRM)
c/o Kelley Turner
Riddell Sports Gp., Inc.
669 Sugar Ln.
Elyria, OH 44035
Ph: (440)366-8225
Fax: (440)365-9629
E-mail: kturner@riddellsales.com
URL: http://www.ohioshrm.org/lorain
Contact: Kelley Turner, Pres.
Members: 75. **Local**. Provides members of the Human Resources profession an environment where professional development can flourish through networking and educational opportunities. Serves as a link to the national Society for Human Resource Management and a resource to the greater Lorain County area business community. **Affiliated With:** SHRM Ohio State Council.

15115 ■ LaGrange Lions Club - Ohio
c/o Noel Fox, Pres.
10788 LaGrange Rd.
Elyria, OH 44035
Ph: (440)458-6781
E-mail: lagrangelions@glwb.net
URL: http://www.lions13b.org
Contact: Noel Fox, Pres.
Local. Affiliated With: Lions Clubs International.

15116 ■ Lorain County AIFA
c/o Bill Long
PO Box 1635
Elyria, OH 44036
Ph: (440)322-3774
Fax: (440)322-3689
E-mail: longgroup@comcast.net
URL: National Affiliate–naifa.org
Contact: Bill Long, Contact
Local. Represents the interests of insurance and financial advisors. Advocates for a positive legislative and regulatory environment. Enhances business and professional skills of members. **Affiliated With:** National Association of Insurance and Financial Advisors.

15117 ■ Lorain County Bar Association
202 Robinson Bldg.
401 Broad St.
Elyria, OH 44035
Ph: (440)323-8416
Fax: (440)323-1922
URL: National Affiliate–www.abanet.org
Members: 359. **Membership Dues:** individual, $125 (annual). **Staff:** 1. **Local**. **Awards:** John Mercer Livingston Essay Contest Award. **Frequency:** periodic. **Type:** scholarship. **Recipient:** for high school students in the contest.

15118 ■ Lorain County Chapter of the Ohio Genealogical Society
PO Box 865
Elyria, OH 44036-0865
Ph: (440)323-5080
E-mail: margcheney@aol.com
URL: http://home.centurytel.net/lorgen
Contact: Margaret Cheney, Pres.
Founded: 1983. **Members:** 200. **Membership Dues:** family, $12 (annual). **Local**. Works to promote genealogical research and to preserve and publish local historical records of a genealogical nature. **Affiliated With:** Ohio Genealogical Society. **Publications:** *The Researcher*, quarterly. Newsletter.

15119 ■ Lorain County Medical Society
5320 Hoag Dr., Ste.D
Elyria, OH 44035
Ph: (440)934-6825
Fax: (440)934-1059
E-mail: lcmed@centurytel.net
URL: http://www.lcmedicalsociety.org
Contact: Eileen Novello, Exec.Dir.
Local. Advances the art and science of medicine. Promotes patient care and the betterment of public health. **Affiliated With:** Ohio State Medical Association.

15120 ■ Lorain County RSVP
c/o Dawn Millerm, Dir.
320 N Gateway Blvd.
Elyria, OH 44035-4928
Ph: (440)326-4805
Fax: (440)326-4828
E-mail: lcrsvp@alltel.net
URL: http://www.seniorcorps.gov/about/programs/rsvp_state.asp?usestateabbr=oh&Search4.x=17&Search4.y=6
Contact: Dawn Millerm, Dir.
Local. Affiliated With: Retired and Senior Volunteer Program.

15121 ■ Lorain County Urban League
401 Broad St., Ste.205
Elyria, OH 44035
Ph: (440)323-3364
Fax: (440)323-5299
E-mail: fwright@lcul.org
URL: http://www.lcul.org
Contact: Fred Wright, Pres./CEO
Local. Affiliated With: National Urban League.

15122 ■ Main Street Elyria
104 Middle Ave.
Elyria, OH 44035
Ph: (440)322-5000
Fax: (440)322-5999
URL: http://www.mainstreetelyria.com
Local.

15123 ■ National Active and Retired Federal Employees Association - Lorain Cnty 1592
108 California Dr.
Elyria, OH 44035-8206
Ph: (440)366-8826
URL: National Affiliate–www.narfe.org
Contact: Phyllis R. Merrell, Contact
Local. Protects the retirement future of employees through education. Informs members on issues affecting the retirement. **Affiliated With:** National Association of Retired Federal Employees.

15124 ■ Phi Theta Kappa - Phi Pi Chapter
c/o George Vourlojianis
1005 N Abbe Rd.
Elyria, OH 44035-1691
Ph: (440)366-7165
E-mail: gvourloj@lorainccc.edu
URL: http://www.ptk.org/directories/chapters/OH/323-1.htm
Contact: George Vourlojianis, Advisor
Local. Affiliated With: Phi Theta Kappa, International Honor Society.

15125 ■ Society of Manufacturing Engineers - Lorain County Community College S254
1005 Abbe Rd. N
Elyria, OH 44035-1691
Ph: (440)365-7024
Fax: (440)366-4105
E-mail: rzitek@lorainccc.edu
URL: National Affiliate–www.sme.org
Contact: Scott itek, Contact
Local. Advances manufacturing knowledge to gain competitive advantage. Improves skills and manufacturing solutions for the growth of economy. Provides resources and opportunities for manufacturing professionals. **Affiliated With:** International Oceanographic Foundation.

15126 ■ STARFLEET: USS Gallifrey
c/o Capt. Thomas B. Heffner
150 Ridge Cir. Ln., Apt. A
Elyria, OH 44035
E-mail: ussgallifrey@alltel.net
URL: http://www.regionone.net
Contact: Capt. Thomas B. Heffner, Contact
Local. Affiliated With: STARFLEET.

15127 ■ Sweet Adelines International, Lake Ridge Chorus
First United Methodist Church
312 3rd St.
Elyria, OH 44035-5618
Ph: (440)245-1231
E-mail: barbershopdiva2004@yahoo.com
URL: http://www.mysweetadelines.com
Contact: Betty Pekare, Contact
Local. Advances the musical art form of barbershop harmony through education and performances. Provides education, training and coaching in the development of women's four-part barbershop harmony. **Affiliated With:** Sweet Adelines International.

15128 ■ Volunteer Guardianship Program of Lorain County
5201 Abbe Rd.
Elyria, OH 44035
Ph: (440)934-3613
E-mail: nbring@lutheranmetro.org
URL: http://www.charityadvantage.com/lutheranmetro/vgplorain.asp
Contact: Nita Bring-Mazurek, Program Dir.
Founded: 1993. **Staff:** 4. **Budget:** $85,000. **Local.**

Englewood

15129 ■ American Legion, Randolph Post 707
PO Box 194
Englewood, OH 45322
Ph: (740)362-7478
Fax: (740)362-1429
E-mail: post707adjutant@hotmail.com
URL: National Affiliate–www.legion.org
Local. Affiliated With: American Legion.

15130 ■ Dayton-Buckeye Model 'A' Club
c/o Roger Kauffman
PO Box 322
Englewood, OH 45322
Ph: (937)884-7438 (937)332-1733
URL: http://www.modelaford.org/states/oh.html
Contact: Roger Kauffman, Contact
Local. Affiliated With: Model "A" Restorers Club.

15131 ■ Englewood-Northmont Chamber of Commerce (ENCC)
PO Box 62
Englewood, OH 45322-0062
Ph: (937)836-2550
Fax: (937)836-2485
E-mail: info@englewood-northmontcoc.com
URL: http://www.englewood-northmontcoc.com
Contact: Cathy Hutton, Exec.Dir.
Founded: 1977. **Members:** 180. **Membership Dues:** business (based on number of employees), $125-$475 (annual). **Staff:** 1. **Local.** Promotes business and economic growth in northern Montgomery County, OH. **Publications:** *Chamber Directory*. **Price:** included in membership dues • *The Informer*, monthly. Newsletter. **Price:** included in membership dues • *The Outlook*, monthly. Newsletter. Includes a schedule of community activities for the coming month. **Circulation:** 180. **Advertising:** accepted.

15132 ■ Northmont Lions Club
555 W Natl. Rd.
Englewood, OH 45322-1153
Ph: (937)890-0443
URL: http://northmontoh.lionwap.org
Contact: William G. Schindell, Pres.
Local. Affiliated With: Lions Clubs International.

15133 ■ Ohio Volkssport Association
c/o Randy Adams
4128 Kinsey Rd.
Englewood, OH 45322
Ph: (937)269-4635
E-mail: ovapres@yahoo.com
URL: http://us.geocities.com/ovawalker
Contact: Randy Adams, Contact
State.

15134 ■ Trail Trolls
c/o Randy Adams
4128 Kinsey Rd.
Englewood, OH 45322
Ph: (937)269-4635
E-mail: ovapres@yahoo.com
URL: http://www.geocities.com/shiningstarofmydistrict/TrailTrolls.html
Contact: Randy Adams, Contact
Local.

15135 ■ Veterans of Foreign Wars 5434
116 N Main St.
Englewood, OH 45322
Ph: (937)836-4405
Contact: Thillis Gannon, Commander
Local.

Enon

15136 ■ Enon Community Historical Society (ECHS)
PO Box 442
Enon, OH 45323
Ph: (937)864-7080
E-mail: echs@core.com
URL: http://www.enonhistory.org
Contact: Mike Barry, Pres.
Founded: 1977. **Members:** 230. **Membership Dues:** individual, $7 (annual) • family, $10 (annual) • life, individual, $100 • life, business, $150. **Budget:** $25,000. **State Groups:** 1. **Local.** Individuals interested in the history of Enon, OH. Operates Heritage Room (library and museum). Sponsors community social activities. **Libraries: Type:** open to the public. **Holdings:** 1,000. **Subjects:** local, genealogy. **Awards:** Fowble Award. **Frequency:** annual. **Type:** recognition. **Recipient:** for service to the Society. **Publications:** *Images*, quarterly. Newsletter. **Price:** included in membership dues. **Circulation:** 150 • *Our Heritage, Enon, Ohio, Mad River Township History*. Book. **Conventions/Meetings:** annual Apple Butter Festival - 2nd weekend in October in Enon, OH • monthly board meeting • annual Ice Cream Social - meeting • quarterly meeting (exhibits) • annual meeting • annual Tree Lighting - meeting - 1st Saturday of December in Enon, OH.

15137 ■ Society of Antique Modelers - Springfield Antique Modelers
3034 Willow Run Cir.
Enon, OH 45323
Ph: (937)882-6775
E-mail: bobsam832@aol.com
URL: National Affiliate–www.antiquemodeler.org
Local. Affiliated With: Society of Antique Modelers.

Euclid

15138 ■ American Legion, Euclid Post 343
20750 Arbor Ave.
Euclid, OH 44123
Ph: (740)362-7478
Fax: (740)362-1429
URL: National Affiliate–www.legion.org
Local. Affiliated With: American Legion.

15139 ■ Buckeye Chapter Paralyzed Veterans of America
c/o Robert Burtin Jr., Pres.
25100 Euclid Ave., Ste.117
Euclid, OH 44117
Ph: (216)731-1017
Fax: (216)731-6404
Free: (800)248-2548
E-mail: donorinfo@buckeyepva.org
URL: http://www.buckeyepva.org
Contact: Robert Burtin Jr., Pres.
Local. Veterans who have incurred an injury or disease affecting the spinal cord and causing paralysis. **Affiliated With:** Paralyzed Veterans of America. **Formerly:** (2005) Paralyzed Veterans of America, Ohio; Buckeye Chapter.

15140 ■ Euclid Blade and Edge Figure Skating Club
252 E 242
Euclid, OH 44132
E-mail: euclidskating@yahoo.com
URL: National Affiliate–www.usfigureskating.org
Local. Provides programs to encourage participation and achievement in the sport of figure skating on ice. Defines and maintains uniform standards of skating proficiency. Organizes and sponsors competitions and exhibitions for the purpose of stimulating interest in figure skating. **Affiliated With:** United States Figure Skating Association.

15141 ■ Euclid Chamber of Commerce (ECC)
21935 Lakeshore Blvd.
Euclid, OH 44123
Ph: (216)731-9322
Fax: (216)731-8354
E-mail: info@euclidchamberofcommerce.com
URL: http://www.euclidchamberofcommerce.com
Contact: Richard Kretschman, Pres.
Founded: 1930. **Members:** 200. **Membership Dues:** bank (plus $10 per million in deposits), $165 •

commercial/retail/industrial/institutional (plus $1.65 per employee), $165 • professional, $220 • part-time business/student, $115 • utility (plus $.01 per Euclid based customer), $165. **Staff:** 1. **Budget:** $92,000. **Local**. Individuals from business, industry, the professions, and the public sector interested in promoting business and community development in Euclid, OH. **Affiliated With:** U.S. Chamber of Commerce. **Publications:** *Chamber News*, monthly. Newsletter. **Circulation:** 350. **Advertising:** accepted. Alternate Formats: online • *Club List*, monthly. Directory • *Membership Directory and Buyer's Guide*, annual. **Conventions/Meetings:** annual Awards Dinner • periodic Business After Hours - meet • monthly luncheon • periodic Small Business Breakfasts.

15142 ■ Euclid Public Schools Alumni Association
711 E 222 St.
Euclid, OH 44123-2090
Ph: (216)797-7895
Fax: (216)797-7900
E-mail: jmayer@euclid.k12.oh.us
URL: http://www.euclid.k12.oh.us
Contact: Joseph Mayer, Alumni Dir.
Founded: 1991. **Members:** 36,400. **Membership Dues:** individual, $5 (annual) • life, $50. **Local**. Seeks to establish and maintain communications between the Euclid Public Schools and its former students, staff, and friends. Gathers and shares information about alumni to demonstrate the success and effectiveness of the Euclid Public Schools. Collects and preserves memorabilia and information, sets up and administers a charitable foundation which will fund scholarships, provide additional educational and training opportunities for students and/or staff, and support recognition activities and other related matters. **Publications:** *Euclid Alumni News*, quarterly. Newsletter. **Price:** $5.00/year. **Conventions/Meetings:** annual meeting.

15143 ■ Euclid Stamp Club (ESC)
PO Box 32211
Euclid, OH 44132
E-mail: zoretich6@cs.com
URL: http://www.members.aol.com/eupex
Contact: Mr. Frank Zoretich Jr., Sec.
Founded: 1966. **Members:** 60. **Membership Dues:** individual, $7 (annual) • couple, $10 (annual). **Local**. Collectors of stamps and related items. Organized to help members buy and sell stamps, promote philatelic research, and stimulate interest in postal history. **Libraries: Type:** by appointment only; lending; not open to the public. **Holdings:** 100; archival material, books. **Subjects:** literature, stamp catalogs. **Awards:** Eupex Medals. **Frequency:** annual. **Type:** medal. **Recipient:** for popular show exhibit. **Computer Services:** Online services, web site with meeting and show announcement, exhibitor prospectuses, show covers for sale, and links of philatelic interest. **Affiliated With:** American Philatelic Society. **Conventions/Meetings:** annual EUPEX Stamp Show, stamp exhibit and dealer bourse (exhibits).

15144 ■ National Management Association, Argo-Tech Leadership Chapter
c/o Jeff Curtis
Argo-Tech Corp.
23555 Euclid Ave., No. 703-C
Euclid, OH 44117
Ph: (216)692-5813
Fax: (216)692-6862
E-mail: curtis@argo-tech.com
URL: National Affiliate–www.nma1.org
Contact: Jeff Curtis, Pres.
Local. Business and industrial management personnel; membership comes from supervisory level, with the remainder from middle management and above. Seeks to develop and recognize management as a profession and to promote the free enterprise system. **Affiliated With:** National Management Association.

15145 ■ Ohio Society for the Elevation of Kites
248 E 274th St.
Euclid, OH 44132
Ph: (330)274-2818
E-mail: osek-cleve@adelphia.net
URL: http://users.adelphia.net/~osekcleve/
Contact: Harry Gregory, Pres.
Local. **Affiliated With:** American Kitefliers Association.

Fairborn

15146 ■ American Legion, Dignam-Whitmore Post 526
526 Legion Ln.
Fairborn, OH 45324
Ph: (740)362-7478
Fax: (740)362-1429
URL: National Affiliate–www.legion.org
Local. **Affiliated With:** American Legion.

15147 ■ Dayton Area Chapter - MOAA
c/o Capt. Terence Cooney
PO Box 12
Fairborn, OH 45324-0012
Ph: (937)427-0590
E-mail: tcooney@woh.rr.com
Contact: Capt. Terence Cooney, Contact
Local. **Affiliated With:** Military Officers Association of America.

15148 ■ Fairborn Area Chamber of Commerce (FACC)
12 N Central Ave.
Fairborn, OH 45324-5097
Ph: (937)878-3191
Fax: (937)878-3197
E-mail: chamber@fairborn.com
URL: http://www.fairborn.com
Contact: John G. Dalton, Exec.Dir.
Founded: 1944. **Members:** 510. **Membership Dues:** financial institution, $600 (annual) • utility (plus $4 per employee up to 100 and $3 each over 100), $250 (annual) • developer (plat builder), $600 (annual) • professional (plus $50 each partner; plus $15 per employee up to 4 and $4 each over 4), $100 (annual) • real estate (plus $50 each partner; plus $15 per employee up to 4 and $4 each over 4), $100 (annual) • apartment (plus $1 per unit), $100 (annual) • motel, hotel (plus $1 per room and $50 for each bar or restaurant), $100 (annual) • automobile dealership (plus $4 per employee), $150 (annual) • industrial (plus $4 per employee up to 100, $3 each up to 200, $2 each over 200), $250 (annual) • retail, amusement, restaurant, lounge, sub-contractor, finance and loan office, grocery, diversified contractor and service, $100 (annual) • civic organization and church, $100 (annual). **Budget:** $100,000. **Local**. Promotes business and community development in the Fairborn, OH area. Bestows Citizen of the Year Award. Participates in the annual Sweet Corn Festival and 4th of July parade. **Awards:** Outstanding AFJROTC. **Type:** grant. **Recipient:** for cadets • President's Award. **Frequency:** annual. **Type:** recognition • W. Ed Duncan Distinguished Citizen Award. **Frequency:** annual. **Type:** recognition. **Computer Services:** Online services, membership directory. **Affiliated With:** U.S. Chamber of Commerce. **Publications:** *Chamber Update*, monthly. Newsletter. **Price:** free for members. Alternate Formats: online • *Membership Directory and Buyers' Guide*, annual. **Circulation:** 3,000. **Conventions/Meetings:** annual Chamber Chat - meeting • monthly Christmas Open House - festival • annual Easter Egg Hunt - festival • annual Golf Outing - competition • annual Greene County Business Expo - banquet - always third Friday in April • annual meeting.

15149 ■ Fairborn Performing Arts and Cultural Association (FPACA)
c/o Raleigh A. Sandy, Jr., Pres.
PO Box 564
Fairborn, OH 45324
Ph: (937)885-1868
Fax: (937)885-1864
E-mail: restoretheater@aol.com
URL: http://fairbornperformingartsandculturalcenter.org
Local.

15150 ■ Independent Order of Odd Fellows, Mad River Lodge 243
PO Box 243
Fairborn, OH 45324
Ph: (937)879-5020
URL: http://www.madriverlodge243.org
Contact: Joe C. Jarrell, Noble Grand
Local.

15151 ■ Midwest Archives Conference (MAC)
33 N Grand Ave.
Fairborn, OH 45324
Ph: (937)879-7241
E-mail: jc65000@worldnet.att.net
URL: http://www.midwestarchives.org
Contact: Shari Christy, Sec.
Founded: 1972. **Members:** 1,000. **Membership Dues:** individual, $30 (annual) • U.S. institution, $60 (annual) • institution, in Canada, $70 (annual) • other, outside U.S., $80 (annual). **Budget:** $50,000. **Regional Groups:** 1. Represents archivists, genealogists, historians, librarians, local historical society and museum personnel, manuscript curators, oral historians, records managers, and related professionals (membership is international). Promotes cooperation and exchange of information among individuals and institutions interested in the preservation and use of archives and manuscript materials. Disseminates information on research materials and the methodology and theory in current archival practice. Provides a forum for discussion among members. Awards emeritus status to retired members who have made significant contributions to the profession or the organization. **Libraries: Type:** reference. **Holdings:** archival material. **Awards:** Archie Motley Minority Scholarship Award. **Frequency:** annual. **Type:** scholarship. **Recipient:** to a minority student studying archival methods • Louisa Bowen Memorial Scholarship Award. **Frequency:** annual. **Type:** scholarship. **Recipient:** to archival studies students. **Committees:** Education; Local Arrangements; Nominating; Program. **Publications:** *Archival Issues*, semiannual. Journal. Contains issues and problems confronting the contemporary archivist. **Price:** included in membership dues; $16.00/issue for nonmembers. ISSN: 0363-888X. **Circulation:** 1,100. **Advertising:** accepted. Also Cited As: *Midwestern Archivist* • *MAC Newsletter*, quarterly. Includes employment opportunities, conference reports, financial statements, meeting minutes, news of members, and listing of publications available. **Price:** included in membership dues; $6.00 for nonmembers. ISSN: 0741-0379. **Circulation:** 1,100. Also Cited As: *Midwest Archives Conference Newsletter*. **Conventions/Meetings:** semiannual conference and workshop, for archival vendors (exhibits) - always May and fall, in various locations • seminar.

15152 ■ National Active and Retired Federal Employees Association - Fairborn 610
1907 Glenrose Dr.
Fairborn, OH 45324-2508
Ph: (937)684-6945
URL: National Affiliate–www.narfe.org
Contact: John C. Peters, Contact
Local. Protects the retirement future of employees through education. Informs members on issues affecting the retirement. **Affiliated With:** National Association of Retired Federal Employees.

Fairfield

15153 ■ Association of Certified Fraud Examiners, Southwest Ohio Chapter No. 46
c/o George Grossenbaugh, CFE, Pres.
Cincinnati Financial Corp.
6200 S Gilmore Rd.
Fairfield, OH 45014-5141

Ph: (513)870-2124
E-mail: george_grossenbaugh@cinfin.com
URL: National Affiliate–www.cfenet.com
Contact: George Grossenbaugh CFE, Pres.
Local. Affiliated With: Association of Certified Fraud Examiners.

15154 ■ Colerain - Young Life
5850 Boymel Dr., Ste.6
Fairfield, OH 45014
Ph: (513)874-5750
URL: http://sites.younglife.org/_layouts/ylext/default.aspx?ID=C-1536
Local. Affiliated With: Young Life.

15155 ■ Fairfield Chamber of Commerce
670 Wessel Dr.
Fairfield, OH 45014
Ph: (513)881-5500
Fax: (513)881-5503
URL: http://www.fairfieldchamber.com
Contact: Ginger Shawver, Pres./CEO
Founded: 1956. **Members:** 500. **Membership Dues:** business (plus $3.25 per employee), $230 (annual) • bank (plus $3.25 per employee), $330 (annual) • associate or retiree, $130 (annual). **Local.** Promotes business and community development in the Fairfield, OH area. Sponsors Indian Summer Days Festival. **Committees:** Ambassadors; Business Education; Business Networking; Business Showcase; Community Appearance Award; Golf Outing; Legislative/Economic Development; Special Projects. **Publications:** *The Fairfield Advantage*, monthly. Newsletter. **Advertising:** accepted. Alternate Formats: online • Membership Directory, annual. Includes buyers' guide. **Price:** $25.00 for nonmembers; free for members.

15156 ■ Finneytown - Young Life
5850 Boymel Dr., Ste.6
Fairfield, OH 45014
Ph: (513)874-5750
URL: http://sites.younglife.org/_layouts/ylext/default.aspx?ID=C-1538
Local. Affiliated With: Young Life.

15157 ■ Greater Cincinnati Philatelic Society
c/o Mr. Rick Wilkins
6351 Robert E. Lee Dr.
Fairfield, OH 45014
E-mail: rmaifeld@fuse.net
URL: National Affiliate–www.stamps.org
Contact: Mr. Rick Wilkins, Contact
Local. Affiliated With: American Philatelic Society.

15158 ■ Hamilton Dog Training Club
c/o Katie Maess, Treas.
2716 Symmes Rd.
Fairfield, OH 45014
E-mail: ktmaess@earthlink.net
URL: http://www.hamiltondogtraining.com
Local.

15159 ■ Hamilton Fairfield Oxford Board of Realtors (HFOBR)
1251 Nilles Rd., Ste.11
Fairfield, OH 45014
Ph: (513)939-2881
Fax: (513)939-2991
E-mail: hfobr@fuse.net
URL: http://www.theboardofrealtors.com
Contact: Leslie A. Besl, Exec. Officer
Local. Strives to develop real estate business practices. Advocates for the right to own, use and transfer real property. Provides a facility for professional development, research and exchange of information among members and the general public. **Affiliated With:** National Association of Realtors.

15160 ■ Hamilton - Young Life
5850 Boymel Dr., Ste.6
Fairfield, OH 45014
Ph: (513)874-5750
URL: http://sites.younglife.org/_layouts/ylext/default.aspx?ID=C-1539
Local. Affiliated With: Young Life.

15161 ■ Jaguar Club of Greater Cincinnati
5649 Venus Ln.
Fairfield, OH 45014
Ph: (513)874-0644
E-mail: info@cincijagclub.org
URL: http://www.cincijagclub.org
Contact: Janice Flanagan, Pres.
Local. Affiliated With: Jaguar Clubs of North America.

15162 ■ Lakota East - Young Life
5850 Boymel Dr., Ste.6
Fairfield, OH 45014
Ph: (513)874-5750
URL: http://sites.younglife.org/_layouts/ylext/default.aspx?ID=C-1540
Local. Affiliated With: Young Life.

15163 ■ Lakota West - Young Life
5850 Boymel Dr., Ste.6
Fairfield, OH 45014
Ph: (513)874-5750
URL: http://sites.younglife.org/_layouts/ylext/default.aspx?ID=C-1541
Local. Affiliated With: Young Life.

15164 ■ Mt. Healthy - Young Life
5850 Boymel Dr., Ste.6
Fairfield, OH 45014
Ph: (513)874-5750
URL: http://sites.younglife.org/_layouts/ylext/default.aspx?ID=C-1543
Local. Affiliated With: Young Life.

15165 ■ Oak Hills - Young Life
5850 Boymel Dr., Ste.6
Fairfield, OH 45014
Ph: (513)874-5750
URL: http://sites.younglife.org/_layouts/ylext/default.aspx?ID=C-1545
Local. Affiliated With: Young Life.

15166 ■ Our Lady of the Rosary - Young Life
5850 Boymel Dr., Ste.6
Fairfield, OH 45014
Ph: (513)874-5750
URL: http://sites.younglife.org/_layouts/ylext/default.aspx?ID=C-1542
Local. Affiliated With: Young Life.

15167 ■ Princeton - Young Life
5850 Boymel Dr., Ste.6
Fairfield, OH 45014
Ph: (513)874-5750
URL: http://sites.younglife.org/_layouts/ylext/default.aspx?ID=C-1546
Local. Affiliated With: Young Life.

15168 ■ Ross - Young Life
5850 Boymel Dr., Ste.6
Fairfield, OH 45014
Ph: (513)874-5750
URL: http://sites.younglife.org/_layouts/ylext/default.aspx?ID=C-1547
Local. Affiliated With: Young Life.

15169 ■ St. Xavier - Young Life
5850 Boymel Dr., Ste.6
Fairfield, OH 45014
Ph: (513)874-5750
URL: http://sites.younglife.org/_layouts/ylext/default.aspx?ID=C-1548
Local. Affiliated With: Young Life.

15170 ■ Talawanda - Young Life
5850 Boymel Dr., Ste.6
Fairfield, OH 45014
Ph: (513)874-5750
URL: http://sites.younglife.org/_layouts/ylext/default.aspx?ID=C-1549
Local. Affiliated With: Young Life.

15171 ■ Taylor - Young Life
5850 Boymel Dr., Ste.6
Fairfield, OH 45014
Ph: (513)874-5750
URL: http://sites.younglife.org/_layouts/ylext/default.aspx?ID=C-1550
Local. Affiliated With: Young Life.

15172 ■ Venice Cemetery Association
2307 Beechwood Dr.
Fairfield, OH 45014
Ph: (513)738-1193
Local.

15173 ■ Wyoming - Young Life
5850 Boymel Dr., Ste.6
Fairfield, OH 45014
Ph: (513)874-5750
URL: http://sites.younglife.org/_layouts/ylext/default.aspx?ID=C-1554
Local. Affiliated With: Young Life.

15174 ■ Young Life Greater Cincinnati
5850 Boymel Dr., Ste.6
Fairfield, OH 45014
Ph: (513)874-5750
Fax: (513)874-5751
URL: http://sites.younglife.org/sites/GreaterCincinnati/default.aspx
Contact: Kolia Lutow, Contact
Local. Affiliated With: Young Life.

15175 ■ Young Life Western Cincinnati Urban
5850 Boymel Dr., Ste.6
Fairfield, OH 45014-5500
Ph: (513)874-5750
Fax: (513)825-1128
URL: http://sites.younglife.org/_layouts/ylext/default.aspx?ID=A-OH162
Local. Affiliated With: Young Life.

15176 ■ Z Car Club of Ohio
174 Palm Springs Dr.
Fairfield, OH 45014-8633
E-mail: fdjonesjr@aol.com
URL: National Affiliate–www.zcca.org
Contact: Fred Jones, Pres.
State. Affiliated With: Z Car Club Association.

Fairlawn

15177 ■ AAA Akron Automobile Club
2710 W Market St.
Fairlawn, OH 44333
Ph: (330)867-0694
Local.

Fairport Harbor

15178 ■ Fairport Harbor Historical Society (FHHS)
129 2nd St.
Fairport Harbor, OH 44077
Ph: (440)354-4825
E-mail: fhhs@ncweb.com
URL: http://fairportlighthouse.com
Contact: Valerie A. Laczko, Pres.
Founded: 1945. **Members:** 257. **Membership Dues:** $10 (annual). **Local.** Individuals interested in local and marine history. Gathers and preserves items related to local history and Great Lakes shipping. Maintains tower and keeper's dwelling and conducts tours. **Libraries: Type:** not open to the public. **Holdings:** 1,500; articles, books, periodicals. **Subjects:** local and marine history, Great Lakes, lighthouses. **Also Known As:** Fairport Marine Museum and Lighthouse. **Publications:** *A View Through the Porthole*, quarterly. Newsletter. **Conventions/Meetings:** monthly meeting - except November and December; every fourth Wednesday in Fairport Harbor, OH.

15179 ■ Fairport Harbor Rod and Reel Association (FHRRA)
PO Box 1038
Fairport Harbor, OH 44077
Ph: (440)354-9931
E-mail: secretary@fhrra.org
URL: http://www.fhrra.org
Local.

Fairview Park

15180 ■ American Chemical Society, Louisiana Section
c/o Dr. Jane Sheldon Murray, Chair
18860 Timber Ln.
Fairview Park, OH 44126-1758
E-mail: jsmurray@uno.edu
URL: National Affiliate–acswebcontent.acs.org
Contact: Dr. Jane Sheldon Murray, Chair
State. Represents the interests of individuals dedicated to the advancement of chemistry in all its branches. Provides opportunities for peer interaction and career development. **Affiliated With:** American Chemical Society.

15181 ■ American Legion, Clifton Post 421
22001 Brookpark Rd.
Fairview Park, OH 44126
Ph: (740)362-7478
Fax: (740)362-1429
URL: National Affiliate–www.legion.org
Local. Affiliated With: American Legion.

15182 ■ American Legion, Fairview Post 738
19311 Lorain Rd.
Fairview Park, OH 44126
Ph: (740)362-7478
Fax: (740)362-1429
URL: National Affiliate–www.legion.org
Local. Affiliated With: American Legion.

15183 ■ American Legion, Hellenic Post 453
4558 Orchard Rd.
Fairview Park, OH 44126
Ph: (740)362-7478
Fax: (740)362-1429
URL: National Affiliate–www.legion.org
Local. Affiliated With: American Legion.

15184 ■ Ohio Genealogical Society, Cuyahoga West Chapter
PO Box 26196
Fairview Park, OH 44126-0196
E-mail: cuyahogawest@att.net
URL: National Affiliate–www.ogs.org
Local. Affiliated With: Ohio Genealogical Society; Ohio Genealogical Society, Cuyahoga West Chapter. **Also Known As:** (2005) Cuyahoga West Chapter of the Ohio Genealogical Society.

Farmdale

15185 ■ Mahoning Valley AIFA
c/o Pamela Kuhn, Exec.
8724 Rte. 193
Farmdale, OH 44417
Ph: (330)876-0888
Fax: (330)876-0888
E-mail: mvaifa@yahoo.com
URL: National Affiliate–naifa.org
Contact: Pamela Kuhn, Exec.
Local. Represents the interests of insurance and financial advisors. Advocates for a positive legislative and regulatory environment. Enhances business and professional skills of members. **Affiliated With:** National Association of Insurance and Financial Advisors.

Farmer

15186 ■ American Legion, Farmer Post 137
PO Box 60
Farmer, OH 43520
Ph: (740)362-7478
Fax: (740)362-1429
URL: National Affiliate–www.legion.org
Local. Affiliated With: American Legion.

Fayette

15187 ■ American Legion, Ohio Post 143
c/o John Dale
424 S Fayette St.
Fayette, OH 43521
Ph: (740)362-7478
Fax: (740)362-1429
URL: National Affiliate–www.legion.org
Contact: John Dale, Contact
Local. Affiliated With: American Legion.

15188 ■ Friends of Harrison Lake State Park
c/o Susan K. Long
26246 Harrison Lake Rd.
Fayette, OH 43521-9779
Ph: (419)237-2593
Local.

Felicity

15189 ■ American Legion, Ohio Post 224
c/o Wiley Croswell
PO Box 99
Felicity, OH 45120
Ph: (740)362-7478
Fax: (740)362-1429
URL: National Affiliate–www.legion.org
Contact: Wiley Croswell, Contact
Local. Affiliated With: American Legion.

15190 ■ Veterans of Foreign Wars 7496
3251 Tyfe Rd.
Felicity, OH 45120
Ph: (513)876-2031
Affiliated With: Veterans of Foreign Wars of the United States.

Findlay

15191 ■ American Cancer Society, Hancock
110 S Main St.
Findlay, OH 45840
Ph: (419)423-0456
Fax: (419)423-1120
Free: (888)227-6446
URL: http://www.cancer.org
Local. Affiliated With: American Cancer Society.

15192 ■ American Legion, Ohio Post 3
c/o Ralph D. Cole
120 W Front St.
Findlay, OH 45840
Ph: (740)362-7478
Fax: (740)362-1429
URL: National Affiliate–www.legion.org
Contact: Ralph D. Cole, Contact
Local. Affiliated With: American Legion.

15193 ■ American Red Cross, Hancock County Chapter
125 Fair St.
Findlay, OH 45840
Ph: (419)422-9322
E-mail: arc@hancock-redcross.org
URL: http://www.hancock-redcross.org
Local.

15194 ■ American Vaulting Association - University of Findlay Vaulters
c/o Lori Cramer, Coach
11178 County Rd. 201
Findlay, OH 45840
Ph: (419)424-4859
E-mail: cramer@findlay.edu
URL: National Affiliate–www.americanvaulting.org
Contact: Lori Cramer, Coach
Local. Affiliated With: American Vaulting Association.

15195 ■ Blanchard Valley AIFA
c/o Thomas J. Wagner, Pres.
510 S Main St.
Findlay, OH 45840
Ph: (419)423-8311
Fax: (419)424-8986
E-mail: william92@aol.com
URL: National Affiliate–naifa.org
Contact: Thomas J. Wagner, Pres.
Local. Represents the interests of insurance and financial advisors. Advocates for a positive legislative and regulatory environment. Enhances business and professional skills of members. **Affiliated With:** National Association of Insurance and Financial Advisors.

15196 ■ Blanchard Valley Volkssporters
c/o Elizabeth Behrendt
425 W Melrose Ave.
Findlay, OH 45840
Ph: (419)425-5636
E-mail: elizabeth@aputnammallets.com
URL: National Affiliate–www.ava.org
Contact: Elizabeth Behrendt, Contact
Founded: 1987. **Members:** 16. **Membership Dues:** individual, $8 (annual). **State Groups:** 35. **Local Groups:** 1. **Local.** Non-competitive sports enthusiasts. **Awards: Frequency:** periodic. **Type:** recognition. **Recipient:** for participation in events. **Affiliated With:** American Volkssport Association. **Conventions/Meetings:** monthly meeting - always 2nd Thursday, Sky Bank Community Room, in Findlay, OH.

15197 ■ Camp Fire USA Northwest Ohio Council
305 W Hardin St.
Findlay, OH 45840
Ph: (419)422-5415 (419)435-2639
Fax: (419)422-5499
E-mail: fun@campfireusa-nwohi.com
URL: http://www.campfireusa-nwohio.com
Contact: Linda Hamilton, CEO
Founded: 1923. **Members:** 6,000. **Staff:** 32. **Budget:** $350,000. **Local Groups:** 1. **Local.** Provides opportunities for youth to realize their potential and to function effectively as caring and self-directed individuals, through informal education programs. Seeks to improve those conditions in society which affect youth. **Affiliated With:** Camp Fire USA. **Formerly:** (1996) NO-WE-OH- Council of Campfire, Inc.

15198 ■ Elks Lodge
601 S. Main St.
Findlay, OH 45840
Ph: (419)422-2442

15199 ■ Findlay Area Human Resource Association (FAHRA)
c/o Sally L. Siferd, Pres.
PO Box 366
Findlay, OH 45839
Ph: (419)306-8619
Fax: (419)422-0063
E-mail: sally@hrhousecall.com
URL: http://www.ohioshrm.org/findlay
Contact: Sally L. Siferd, Pres.
Local. Represents the interests of human resource and industrial relations professionals and executives. Promotes the advancement of human resource management.

15200 ■ Findlay Area Youth for Christ
PO Box 514
Findlay, OH 45839
Ph: (419)422-7452
Fax: (419)422-7452
URL: http://www.campuslifeweb.org
Local. Affiliated With: Youth for Christ/U.S.A.

15201 ■ Findlay-Hancock County Chamber of Commerce
123 E Main Cross St.
Findlay, OH 45840
Ph: (419)422-3313
Fax: (419)422-9508
E-mail: info@findlayhancockchamber.com
URL: http://www.findlayhancockchamber.com
Contact: Douglas S. Peters, Pres./CEO
Local. Promotes the growth of the community by concentrating on the needs of businesses. Provides medical and business opportunities for the members and interested individuals. **Publications:** *Investor Report*, bimonthly. Newsletters. Contains information on the current and upcoming events of the organization. **Advertising:** accepted. Alternate Formats: online.

15202 ■ Gardeners of America/Men's Garden Clubs of America - Findlay Men and Women's Garden Club
c/o William Lanning, Pres.
9374 SR 12
Findlay, OH 45840
Ph: (419)423-1010
E-mail: bilan2@bright.net
URL: National Affiliate–www.tgoa-mgca.org
Contact: William Lanning, Pres.
Local.

15203 ■ German Shepherd Dog Club of Toledo
c/o Linda Hall
421 W. Lincoln St.
Findlay, OH 45840-3145
URL: National Affiliate–www.akc.org
Affiliated With: American Kennel Club.

15204 ■ Heartland Board of Realtors
655 Fox Run Rd., Ste.M
Findlay, OH 45840
Ph: (419)422-3833
Fax: (419)422-1453
E-mail: heartboard@woh.rr.com
URL: http://www.heartlandboardofrealtors.org
Contact: Jim Slough, Pres.
Local. Strives to develop real estate business practices. Advocates for the right to own, use and transfer real property. Provides a facility for professional development, research and exchange of information among members and the general public. **Affiliated With:** National Association of Realtors.

15205 ■ Liberty Benton Parent Teacher Organization
9190 County Rd. 9
Findlay, OH 45840
Ph: (419)422-8526
Fax: (419)422-5108
URL: http://www.noacsc.org/hancock/lb/PTO/PTO.htm
Contact: Cindy Frankart, Pres.
Local.

15206 ■ Lupus Foundation of America Northwest Ohio Chapter
1710 Manor Hill Rd.
Findlay, OH 45840
Ph: (419)423-9313
Fax: (419)423-5959
Free: (888)33-LUPUS
E-mail: info@lupusnwoh.org
URL: http://www.lupusnwoh.org
Contact: Ms. Jody Noble, Pres./CEO
Founded: 1986. **Members:** 250. **Membership Dues:** single, $15 (annual) • family, $25 (annual). **Staff:** 3. **Regional Groups:** 3. **State Groups:** 2. **Local Groups:** 2. **Regional**. Provides education and support to lupus patients and their families, also promotes public awareness of the disease and its symptoms, and supports research relating to the diagnosis, treatment and cure of lupus. **Libraries: Type:** open to the public. **Holdings:** 35; periodicals. **Subjects:** lupus and chronic illness. **Awards:** Rosemary Cook Award. **Frequency:** annual. **Type:** recognition. **Affiliated With:** Lupus Foundation of America. **Publications:** *Lupus Friend*, bimonthly. Newsletter. Contains articles on lupus and related topics. **Price:** free to members. **Circulation:** 350. **Conventions/Meetings:** bimonthly meeting, with doctors and other professionals speaking on topics related to lupus - always 4th Sunday; February, April, June, August, October.

15207 ■ Midwest Association of Student Employment Administrators (MASEA)
c/o Patti Beck, Pres.
The Univ. of Findlay
1000 N Main St.
Findlay, OH 45840
Ph: (419)434-5338
Fax: (419)434-5505
E-mail: pbeck@findlay.edu
URL: http://www.masea.org
Contact: Patti Beck, Pres.
Regional. Promotes and supports student employment through research, publications, exchange of information and professional development opportunities. **Affiliated With:** National Student Employment Association.

15208 ■ Midwest Association of Student Financial Aid Administrators (MASFAA)
c/o Arman J. Habegger, Chm.
Univ. of Findlay
1000 N Main St.
Findlay, OH 45840
Ph: (419)434-6923
Fax: (419)434-4898
E-mail: habegger@findlay.edu
URL: http://www.masfaaweb.org
Contact: Arman J. Habegger, Chm.
Regional. Represents the interests and needs of students, faculties and other persons involved in student financial aid. Promotes student aid legislation, regulatory analysis and professional development of financial aid legislators. Seeks to improve activities relating to the quality and improvement of student financial assistance in Higher Education institutions. **Affiliated With:** National Association of Student Financial Aid Administrators.

15209 ■ National Active and Retired Federal Employees Association - Hancock County 2278
1538 Burson Dr.
Findlay, OH 45840-6520
Ph: (419)422-6534
URL: National Affiliate–www.narfe.org
Contact: Arlyn P. Grooms, Contact
Local. Protects the retirement future of employees through education. Informs members on issues affecting the retirement. **Affiliated With:** National Association of Retired Federal Employees.

15210 ■ National Association of Home Builders of the U.S., Hancock County Home Builders Association
c/o Irene Putnam
Local No. 3639
1655 Tiffin Ave., Ste.B
Findlay, OH 45840
Ph: (419)420-1846
Fax: (419)420-1856
E-mail: info@hancockhomebuilders.com
URL: http://www.hancockhomebuilders.com
Contact: Irene F. Putnam, Contact
Local. Single and multifamily home builders, commercial builders, and others associated with the building industry. **Affiliated With:** National Association of Home Builders.

15211 ■ National Association of Miniature Enthusiasts - Mini-Magic Miniatures
c/o Cheryl McNish
2767 Whitespire Ct.
Findlay, OH 45840
Ph: (419)423-9494
E-mail: hmcnish@aol.com
URL: http://www.miniatures.org/states/OH.html
Contact: Cheryl McNish, Contact
Local. Affiliated With: National Association of Miniature Enthusiasts.

15212 ■ Northwestern Ohio Golf Course Superintendents Association
18580 Treetop Ct.
Findlay, OH 45840
Ph: (419)894-4653
E-mail: redhawkrun@tds.net
URL: http://www.nwogcsa.com
Contact: Tim Glorioso, Pres.
Membership Dues: regular, facility, $65 • retired, $15 • affiliate, $100. **Local**. Represents the interests of golf course superintendents. Advances members' profession for career success. Enhances the enjoyment, growth and vitality in the game of golf. Educates members concerning efficient and economical management of golf courses. **Affiliated With:** Golf Course Superintendents Association of America. **Publications:** *On the Ball*. Newsletter. Alternate Formats: online.

15213 ■ Ohio Partners for Affordable Energy
PO Box 1793
Findlay, OH 45839-1793
Ph: (419)425-8860
Fax: (419)425-8862
E-mail: drinebolt@aol.com
Contact: David C. Rinebolt, Exec.Dir.
Founded: 1995. **Members:** 70. **State**. Works to ensure affordable, environmentally-sound energy options for low and moderate income consumers. **Publications:** *OPAE Update*, monthly. Newsletter. **Conventions/Meetings:** quarterly board meeting • annual conference.

15214 ■ Society of Manufacturing Engineers - Owens Community College S217
Owens Community Coll., Engg. Technologies
300 Davis St.
Findlay, OH 45840
Ph: (419)429-3563
E-mail: grettig@owens.cc.oh.us
URL: National Affiliate–www.sme.org
Contact: Glenn A. Rettig, Contact
Local. Advances manufacturing knowledge to gain competitive advantage. Improves skills and manufacturing solutions for the growth of economy. Provides resources and opportunities for manufacturing professionals. **Affiliated With:** Oceanic Society Expeditions.

15215 ■ United Way of Hancock County
245 Standford Pkwy.
Findlay, OH 45840
Ph: (419)423-1432
E-mail: kduv@uwhancock.org
URL: http://www.uwhancock.org
Contact: Keith G. DuVernay, Pres./CEO
Local. Affiliated With: United Way of America.

15216 ■ Veterans of Foreign Wars 5645
315 Walnut St.
Findlay, OH 45840
Ph: (419)423-0023
Local.

15217 ■ Wheelmen, Ohio
1210 South St.
Findlay, OH 45840-6449
E-mail: dnichols@bright.net
URL: National Affiliate–www.thewheelmen.org
State.

15218 ■ Young Men's Christian Association of Findlay, Ohio
300 E Lincoln St.
Findlay, OH 45840
Ph: (419)422-4424
Fax: (419)422-8249
E-mail: rgartner@findlayymca.com
URL: http://findlayymca.com
Contact: Mr. Russ Gartner, CEO
Founded: 1889. **Members:** 8,500. **Membership Dues:** youth, $116 (annual) • adult, $384 (annual) • senior youth, $144 (annual). **Staff:** 150. **Budget:** $3,200,000. **Local Groups:** 1. **Local**. Seeks to put Christian principles into practice through programs that build Spirit, Mind, and Body for all regardless of race, religion, or ability to pay for services. **Publications:** *Program Schedule*, 3/year • Newsletter, quarterly.

Flushing

15219 ■ American Legion, Flushing Post 366
PO Box 427
Flushing, OH 43977
Ph: (740)362-7478
Fax: (740)362-1429
URL: National Affiliate–www.legion.org
Local. Affiliated With: American Legion.

Forest

15220 ■ American Legion, Lehman-Zimmerman Post 259
204 W Lima St.
Forest, OH 45843
Ph: (740)362-7478
Fax: (740)362-1429
URL: National Affiliate–www.legion.org
Local. Affiliated With: American Legion.

Fort Jennings

15221 ■ American Legion, Colonel Jennings Post 715
240 W 4th St.
Fort Jennings, OH 45844
Ph: (740)362-7478
Fax: (740)362-1429
URL: National Affiliate–www.legion.org
Local. Affiliated With: American Legion.

15222 ■ Midwest National Show Horse Association (MNSHA)
c/o Jan Pohlman, Sec.
19759 SR 189
Fort Jennings, OH 45844
Ph: (937)962-4336
E-mail: cindyc@infinet.com
Contact: Cindy Clinton, Pres.
Local. Affiliated With: National Show Horse Registry.

Fort Loramie

15223 ■ American Legion, Fort Loramie Post 355
PO Box 351
Fort Loramie, OH 45845
Ph: (740)362-7478
Fax: (740)362-1429
URL: National Affiliate–www.legion.org
Local. Affiliated With: American Legion.

Fort Recovery

15224 ■ American Legion, Emmet Mannix Post 345
PO Box 577
Fort Recovery, OH 45846
Ph: (740)362-7478
Fax: (740)362-1429
URL: National Affiliate–www.legion.org
Local. Affiliated With: American Legion.

15225 ■ Fort Recovery Chamber of Commerce
PO Box 671
Fort Recovery, OH 45846-0671
Ph: (419)375-2530
Fax: (419)375-4709
E-mail: fortrecovery@bright.net
URL: http://www.fortrecovery.org
Local. Publications: Newsletter, periodic. Alternate Formats: online.

15226 ■ National Association of Home Builders, Mercer County Building Authority
c/o Stacy Laux
PO Box 708
Fort Recovery, OH 45846
Ph: (419)375-4247
Fax: (419)375-4247
E-mail: tlaux@bright.net
URL: National Affiliate–www.nahb.org
Local. Single and multifamily home builders, commercial builders, and others associated with the building industry. **Affiliated With:** National Association of Home Builders.

Fostoria

15227 ■ Alliance of Guardian Angels, Fostoria
213 S Main St.
Fostoria, OH 44830-1007
Ph: (419)435-8282
E-mail: fostoria@guardianangels.org
URL: National Affiliate–www.guardianangels.org
Contact: Mayor John Davoli, Contact
Local. Affiliated With: Alliance of Guardian Angels.

15228 ■ American Legion, Earl Foust Post 73
550 E Zeller Rd.
Fostoria, OH 44830
Ph: (740)362-7478
Fax: (740)362-1429
URL: National Affiliate–www.legion.org
Local. Affiliated With: American Legion.

15229 ■ Bascom Lions Club
c/o David L. Cramer, Pres.
2765 N County Rd. 39
Fostoria, OH 44830
Ph: (419)435-8524
E-mail: cramerfarms@aol.com
URL: http://www.lions13b.org
Contact: David L. Cramer, Pres.
Local. Affiliated With: Lions Clubs International.

15230 ■ Fostoria Area Chamber of Commerce (FACC)
121 N Main St.
Fostoria, OH 44830-2215
Ph: (419)435-0486
Fax: (419)435-0936
E-mail: chamberfost@aol.com
URL: http://www.fostoriachamber.org
Contact: Beverly K. Barber, Admin.Asst.
Founded: 1951. **Members:** 240. **Staff:** 2. **State Groups:** 1. **Local**. Promotes business and community development in the Fostoria, OH area. **Computer Services:** Online services, membership directory. **Councils:** Legislative Affairs. **Affiliated With:** U.S. Chamber of Commerce. **Publications:** Newsletter. Alternate Formats: online.

15231 ■ Fostoria Lions Club
c/o Mona DiCesare, Pres.
1033 Kennedy Ln.
Fostoria, OH 44830
Ph: (419)435-3249
E-mail: afirechf@bright.net
URL: http://www.lions13b.org
Contact: Mona DiCesare, Pres.
Local. Affiliated With: Lions Clubs International.

15232 ■ United Way of Fostoria
PO Box 186
Fostoria, OH 44830-0186
Ph: (419)435-4484
URL: National Affiliate–national.unitedway.org
Contact: Dennis Studrawa, Exec.Dir.
Founded: 1957. **Staff:** 2. **State Groups:** 1. **Local**. Works to assist in fundraising by conducting company-wide employee campaigns and encourages corporate contributions. Helps administer additional funds for the purpose of building a stronger community. **Affiliated With:** United Way of America. **Publications:** *United Way at Work*, bimonthly. Newsletter • *United Way at Work Bulletin*, bimonthly. Newsletter. Contains agency summaries.

15233 ■ Vietnam Veterans of America, Chapter No. 400
PO Box 101
Fostoria, OH 44830
Ph: (419)436-0552
URL: http://www.vvabuckeyestatecouncil.com
Local. Affiliated With: Vietnam Veterans of America.

15234 ■ Vietnam Veterans of America, Chapter No. 440
c/o David Short, Pres.
PO Box 101
Fostoria, OH 44830
Ph: (419)436-0552
Fax: (775)521-0161
URL: http://www.vvabuckeyestatecouncil.com
Contact: David Short, Pres.
Local. Affiliated With: Vietnam Veterans of America.

Frankfort

15235 ■ American Legion, Ohio Post 483
c/o Joseph Ellsworth White
PO Box 4
Frankfort, OH 45628
Ph: (740)362-7478
Fax: (740)362-1429
URL: National Affiliate–www.legion.org
Contact: Joseph Ellsworth White, Contact
Local. Affiliated With: American Legion.

Franklin

15236 ■ American Legion, Ohio Post 149
c/o Russell Mc Elfresh
126 E 4th St.
Franklin, OH 45005
Ph: (740)362-7478
Fax: (740)362-1429
URL: National Affiliate–www.legion.org
Contact: Russell Mc Elfresh, Contact
Local. Affiliated With: American Legion.

15237 ■ American Society of Safety Engineers, Kitty Hawk Chapter
c/o Bill Search, Pres.
3300 State Rte. 122
Franklin, OH 45005
Ph: (937)865-3827 (937)746-5135
E-mail: wsearch@ehstech.com
URL: http://kittyhawk.asse.org
Contact: Bill Search, Pres.
Local. Enhances the advancement of the safety profession and the safety professional. Promotes the technical, societal and economic well-being of safety practitioners. **Affiliated With:** American Society of Safety Engineers.

15238 ■ Franklin Area Chamber of Commerce (FACC)
201 E 2nd St., Ste.9
PO Box 721
Franklin, OH 45005-0721
Ph: (937)746-8457
Fax: (937)746-2461
E-mail: franklincc@dayton99.com
URL: http://www.franklinohio.org/chamber/chamber.asp
Contact: Cheryl Cooper-Darragh, Exec.Dir.
Founded: 1947. **Members:** 105. **Local**. Promotes business and community development in the Franklin, OH area. **Conventions/Meetings:** monthly meeting, with speaker - every 3rd Monday.

Frazeysburg

15239 ■ Frazeysburg Revitalization Association
PO Box 448
Frazeysburg, OH 43822-0448
Local.

15240 ■ Ohio Association of Meat Processors (OAMP)
c/o Valerie Parks Graham, Exec.Sec.
6870 Licking Valley Rd.
Frazeysburg, OH 43822
Ph: (740)828-9900
Fax: (740)828-2635
E-mail: val@oamp.org
URL: http://www.oamp.org
Contact: Valerie Parks Graham, Exec.Sec.
Founded: 1940. **State**.

Fredericksburg

15241 ■ American Legion, Fredericksburg Memorial Post 651
County Rd. 2 Harrison
Fredericksburg, OH 44627
Ph: (740)362-7478
Fax: (740)362-1429
URL: National Affiliate–www.legion.org
Local. **Affiliated With:** American Legion.

Fredericktown

15242 ■ American Legion, Ohio Post 500
c/o Joe Cocanour
81 Mt. Vernon Ave.
Fredericktown, OH 43019
Ph: (740)362-7478
Fax: (740)362-1429
URL: National Affiliate–www.legion.org
Contact: Joe Cocanour, Contact
Local. **Affiliated With:** American Legion.

15243 ■ German Shepherd Dog Club of Central Ohio
c/o Rosemary Booth, Sec.
RR 1, 16199 N Liberty Rd.
Fredericktown, OH 43019
Ph: (740)397-0865
URL: http://jmadesign.com/gsdcco
Local.

15244 ■ Heart of Ohio Angus Association
c/o Greg VanHouten, Pres.
9480 Bryant Rd.
Fredericktown, OH 43019
Ph: (740)694-9519
URL: National Affiliate–www.angus.org
Contact: Greg VanHouten, Pres.
Local. **Affiliated With:** American Angus Association.

Fremont

15245 ■ American Legion, Thurston-Zwir Post 121
2000 Buckland Ave.
Fremont, OH 43420
Ph: (740)362-7478
Fax: (740)362-1429
URL: National Affiliate–www.legion.org
Local. **Affiliated With:** American Legion.

15246 ■ American Red Cross, Sandusky County Chapter
1245 Napoleon St.
Fremont, OH 43420
Ph: (419)332-5574
Fax: (419)332-5598
E-mail: arcsandco@sbcglobal.net
URL: http://www.srcredcross.org
Local.

15247 ■ Fremont Noon Lions Club
c/o Colleen Carmack, Pres.
200 S Granville Blvd.
Fremont, OH 43420
Ph: (419)332-3583
URL: http://www.lions13b.org
Contact: Colleen Carmack, Pres.
Local. **Affiliated With:** Lions Clubs International.

15248 ■ Izaak Walton League of America, Fremont Chapter
43 Westwood Dr.
Fremont, OH 43420-9637
Ph: (419)334-3095
URL: National Affiliate–www.iwla.org
Contact: Melvin Balduf, Pres.
Local. Works to educate the public to conserve, maintain, protect, and restore the soil, forest, water, and other natural resources of the U.S; promotes the enjoyment and wholesome utilization of these resources. **Affiliated With:** Izaak Walton League of America.

15249 ■ North Coast Estate Planning Council
c/o Nora E. Gallagher, 2nd VP
323 Croghan St.
Fremont, OH 43420
Ph: (419)355-2170
Fax: (419)355-2175
E-mail: ngallagher@croghan.com
URL: National Affiliate–councils.naepc.org
Contact: Steve Furey, Pres.
Local. Fosters understanding of the proper relationships between the functions of professionals in the estate planning field. Represents the interests of professionals involved in estate planning. Encourages cooperation among members. **Affiliated With:** National Association of Estate Planners and Councils.

15250 ■ Phi Theta Kappa - Alpha Mu Epsilon Chapter
c/o Gina Staccone-Smeal
2830 Napoleon Rd.
Fremont, OH 43420
Ph: (419)334-8400
E-mail: gstacconesmeal@terra.edu
URL: http://www.ptk.org/directories/chapters/OH/322-1.htm
Contact: Gina Staccone-Smeal, Advisor
Local. **Affiliated With:** Phi Theta Kappa, International Honor Society.

15251 ■ President R.B. Hayes Audubon Society
PO Box 92
Fremont, OH 43420
URL: http://www.audubon.org/chapter/oh/index.html
Local. **Formerly:** (2005) National Audubon Society - President R.B. Hayes.

15252 ■ Sandusky County Builders Association
PO Box 721
Fremont, OH 43420
Ph: (419)332-3844
Local.

15253 ■ Sandusky County Convention and Visitors Bureau
712 North St., Ste.102
Fremont, OH 43420
Ph: (419)332-4470
Fax: (419)332-4359
E-mail: info@sanduskycounty.org
URL: http://www.sanduskycounty.org
Contact: Connie Dundel, Contact
Local.

15254 ■ Sandusky River Basin LUA
c/o Rick Frank
814 W State St.
Fremont, OH 43420
Ph: (419)332-8481
Fax: (419)332-4754
URL: National Affiliate–www.naifa.org
Local. Represents the interest of insurance and financial advisors. Advocates for a positive legislative and regulatory environment. Enhances business and professional skills of members. **Affiliated With:** National Association of Insurance and Financial Advisors.

15255 ■ United Way of Sandusky County
103 S Front St.
Fremont, OH 43420-3021
Ph: (419)334-8938
Fax: (419)334-8938
E-mail: lhavens@uwsandco.org
URL: http://www.uwsandco.org
Local. **Affiliated With:** United Way of America.

Fresno

15256 ■ Ohio National Barrel Horse Association
49308 CR 186
Fresno, OH 43824
Ph: (740)622-4047
URL: National Affiliate–www.nbha.com
Contact: Ellen McKee, Dir.
State. Promotes the sport of barrel horse racing. Conducts barrel racing competitions. Establishes standard rules for the sport. **Affiliated With:** National Barrel Horse Association.

Gahanna

15257 ■ American Legion, Gahanna Post 797
PO Box 30843
Gahanna, OH 43230
Ph: (740)362-7478
Fax: (740)362-1429
URL: National Affiliate–www.legion.org
Local. **Affiliated With:** American Legion.

15258 ■ American Society of Women Accountants, Columbus Chapter No. 016 (ASWA)
c/o Angela Wheeler, CPA, Pres.
Schiffman, Grow and Co., PC
4064 Blendon Way Dr.
Gahanna, OH 43230
Ph: (614)261-0600 (614)476-4024
Fax: (614)268-6363
E-mail: president@aswa-cols-oh.org
URL: http://www.aswa-cols-oh.org
Contact: Angela Wheeler CPA, Pres.
Local. Women from CPAs to students. United to enable women in accounting and related fields to further themselves and their profession. Sponsors CPE days and gives scholarships to women students in accounting. Offers networking and availability of job

opportunities. **Affiliated With:** American Society of Women Accountants. **Conventions/Meetings:** monthly dinner, with speakers.

15259 ■ ARMA International - The Information Management Professionals, Greater Columbus Ohio Chapter
c/o R. Michael Johnson
Amer. Elec. Power Co.
700 Morrison Rd., 4th Fl.
Gahanna, OH 43230-6642
Ph: (614)883-7446
Fax: (614)883-7452
E-mail: rmjohnson@aep.com
URL: National Affiliate–www.arma.org
Contact: Mike Johnson, Pres.
Local. Affiliated With: ARMA International - The Association of Information Management Professionals.

15260 ■ Association of Certified Fraud Examiners, Central Ohio Chapter No. 39
c/o Heinz E. Ickert, CFE, Pres.
PO Box 30607
Gahanna, OH 43230
Ph: (614)464-3343
E-mail: heinz.ickert@reacpa.com
URL: http://www.cocfe.homestead.com
Contact: Heinz E. Ickert CFE, Pres.
Membership Dues: associate student, $20 (annual). **Local. Affiliated With:** Association of Certified Fraud Examiners.

15261 ■ Bexley Lions Club
c/o Jason Gunsorek, Pres.
848 Hensel Woods Rd.
Gahanna, OH 43230
Ph: (614)229-4610 (614)775-9176
E-mail: gunsorek@hbgcpas.com
URL: http://www.iwaynet.net/~lions13f
Contact: Jason Gunsorek, Pres.
Local. Affiliated With: Lions Clubs International.

15262 ■ Central Ohio American Industrial Hygiene Association (CO-AIHA)
c/o Tom Finnegan, CSP, Treas.
5113 Wolf Run Dr.
Gahanna, OH 43230
Ph: (614)645-5638
E-mail: tgfinnegan@columbus.org
URL: http://www.aiha.org/localsections/html/coaiha
Contact: Tom Finnegan CSP, Treas.
Local. Represents the interests of occupational and environmental health professionals practicing in industry, government, labor and academic institutions and independent organizations. Promotes the certification of industrial hygienists. Administers educational programs for environmental health and safety professionals. **Affiliated With:** American Industrial Hygiene Association.

15263 ■ Gahanna Area Chamber of Commerce
94 N High St.
Gahanna, OH 43230
Ph: (614)471-0451
Fax: (614)471-5122
E-mail: info@gahannaareachamber.com
URL: http://www.gahannaareachamber.com
Contact: Mrs. Leslee Blake, Pres.
Founded: 1981. **Members:** 403. **Staff:** 2. **Local.** Promotes business and community development in Gahanna, OH. **Publications:** Directory, annual • Newsletter, monthly.

15264 ■ Gahanna Lions Club
c/o Herbert Docken, Pres.
415 Emory St.
Gahanna, OH 43230
Ph: (614)476-4859
URL: http://www.iwaynet.net/~lions13f
Contact: Herbert Docken, Pres.
Local. Affiliated With: Lions Clubs International.

15265 ■ International Brotherhood of Magicians, Ring 7
c/o Steven Parlette, Sec.
4306 Secludedwood Ct.
Gahanna, OH 43230
Ph: (614)428-5966
E-mail: pipernospam@beol.net
URL: http://www.ring7.org
Contact: Glenn Mackie, Pres.
Local. Professional and semi-professional magicians; suppliers, assistants, agents, and others interested in magic. Seeks to advance the art of magic in the field of amusement, entertainment, and culture. Promotes proper means of discouraging false or misleading advertising of effects, tricks, literature, merchandise, or actions appertaining to the magical arts; opposes exposures of principles of the art of magic, except in books on magic and magazines devoted to such art for the exclusive use of magicians and devotees of the art; encourages humane treatment and care of live animals whenever employed in magical performances. **Affiliated With:** International Brotherhood of Magicians.

15266 ■ National Association of Pastoral Musicians, Columbus
c/o Mr. Mark Shaffer, Dir.
699 Whirlaway Ct.
Gahanna, OH 43230
Ph: (614)855-3909
E-mail: coreteam@npm-columbus.org
URL: http://www.npm-columbus.org
Contact: Mr. Mark Shaffer, Dir.
Local. Affiliated With: National Association of Pastoral Musicians.

15267 ■ National Association of Professional Insurance Agents, Indiana
c/o George W. Haenszel, Exec.VP
600 Cross Pointe Rd.
Gahanna, OH 43230
Ph: (614)552-8000
Fax: (614)552-0115
Free: (800)555-9742
E-mail: inpia@indianapia.com
URL: http://www.indianapia.com
Contact: George Haenszel, Exec.VP
State. Affiliated With: National Association of Professional Insurance Agents.

15268 ■ Ohio Aggregates and Industrial Minerals Association (OAIMA)
162 N Hamilton Rd.
Gahanna, OH 43230
Fax: (614)428-7919
Free: (800)647-6257
E-mail: rocks@oaima.org
URL: http://www.oaima.org
Contact: Pat Jacomet, Exec.Dir.
State. Represents operators who mine sand, gravel, stone, dolomite, slag, salt, clay and aglime.

15269 ■ Ohio Physical Therapy Association (OPTA)
c/o Nancy J. Garland, CEO/Exec.Dir.
1085 Beecher Crossing N, Ste.B
Gahanna, OH 43230
Ph: (614)855-4109 (614)855-5029
Fax: (614)855-5914
E-mail: opt@ohiopt.org
URL: http://www.ohiopt.org
Contact: Nancy J. Garland, CEO/Exec.Dir.
State. Affiliated With: American Physical Therapy Association. **Formerly:** (2005) American Physical Therapy Association - Ohio Chapter.

15270 ■ Ohio School Psychologists Association (OSPA)
104 Mill St., Ste.F
Gahanna, OH 43230
Ph: (614)414-5980
Fax: (614)414-5982
E-mail: mail@ospaonline.org
URL: http://www.ospaonline.org
Contact: Erich R. Merkle, Contact
Founded: 1945. **Members:** 832. **Membership Dues:** full, $100 • student, intern, $20 • first year post intern, $75 • retired, unemployed, affiliate, $50. **Staff:** 2. **Budget:** $83,000. **State Groups:** 10. **State.** School psychologists and others interested in the psychology of school children. Promotes appropriate school psychological services in order to meet the needs of children. **Awards:** Bartlett Ohio School Psychologist of the Year. **Frequency:** annual. **Type:** recognition. **Affiliated With:** National Association of School Psychologists. **Publications:** *Ohio School Psychologist*, quarterly. Newsletter. **Price:** included in membership dues. **Conventions/Meetings:** semiannual conference (exhibits) - always spring and fall, usually the beginning of May and October.

15271 ■ Professional Insurance Agents Association of Ohio (PIA)
600 Cross Pointe Rd.
Gahanna, OH 43230
Ph: (614)552-8000
Fax: (614)552-0115
Free: (800)555-1742
E-mail: ohpia@ohiopia.com
URL: http://www.ohiopia.com
Contact: Lynne McGuire, Dir. of Administration
Founded: 1934. **Membership Dues:** active agency, $454-$853 (annual) • company, $491 (annual) • individual, $231 (annual) • consumer, $25 (annual). **Staff:** 20. **Budget:** $2,000,000. **State.** Independent insurance agents. Provides legislative representation. Offers educational programs and insurance benefits. **Affiliated With:** National Association of Professional Insurance Agents. **Formed by Merger of:** Ohio Association of Mutual Insurance Agents. **Publications:** *Client*, quarterly. Newsletter. Alternate Formats: online • *ProAction*, bimonthly. Newsletter. Alternate Formats: online • Magazine. **Advertising:** accepted. Alternate Formats: online. **Conventions/Meetings:** annual convention (exhibits) - spring in Ohio.

15272 ■ Reserve Officers Association - Department of Ohio, General Orton Chapter 26
c/o LTC Charles Tom Liszkay, Pres.
457 Tresham Rd.
Gahanna, OH 43230
Ph: (614)827-1626 (614)476-2044
Fax: (614)827-1627
E-mail: tom.liszkay@juno.com
URL: http://www.roa.org/oh
Contact: LTC Charles Tom Liszkay, Pres.
Local. Promotes and supports the development and execution of a military policy for the United States. Provides professional development seminars, workshops and programs for its members. **Affiliated With:** Reserve Officers Association of the United States.

Galena

15273 ■ American Legion, Young-Budd Post 171
6921 Big Walnut Rd.
Galena, OH 43021
Ph: (740)362-7478
Fax: (740)362-1429
URL: National Affiliate–www.legion.org
Local. Affiliated With: American Legion.

15274 ■ Mid-Ohio Dressage Association (MODA)
c/o Nancy Wentz
11850 Overbrook Ln.
Galena, OH 43021
Ph: (740)965-4700
E-mail: marys@midohiodressage.org
URL: http://www.midohiodressage.org
Contact: Mary Saint, Pres.
Local. Affiliated With: United States Dressage Federation.

15275 ■ National Speleological Society, Central Ohio Grotto (COG)
c/o Bill Walden, Ed.
1672 S Galena Rd.
Galena, OH 43021-9540

Ph: (740)965-2942
E-mail: wwalden@columbus.rr.com
URL: http://www.tuningoracle.com/COG
Contact: Bill Walden, Ed.
Local. Seeks to study, explore and conserve cave and karst resources. Protects access to caves and promotes responsible caving. Encourages responsible management of caves and their unique environments. **Affiliated With:** National Speleological Society.

Galion

15276 ■ Air Vair Group
5474 State Rte. 19
Galion, OH 44833
E-mail: airvair@richnet.net
URL: http://www.corvair.org/chapters/airvairs
Contact: Mark Corbin, Pres.
Local. Enthusiasts of the Corvair automobile united for technical assistance and parts availability. **Affiliated With:** Corvair Society of America.

15277 ■ American Legion, Ohio Post 758
c/o Eugene L. Morton
9668 Ketterman Dr.
Galion, OH 44833
Ph: (740)362-7478
Fax: (740)362-1429
URL: National Affiliate–www.legion.org
Contact: Eugene L. Morton, Contact
Local. Affiliated With: American Legion.

15278 ■ American Legion, Scarbrough Post 243
118 S Market St.
Galion, OH 44833
Ph: (740)362-7478
Fax: (740)362-1429
URL: National Affiliate–www.legion.org
Local. Affiliated With: American Legion.

15279 ■ American Red Cross, Galion Area Chapter
124 N Union St.
Galion, OH 44833-1735
Ph: (419)468-5611
Fax: (419)468-4673
URL: http://galionchapter.redcross.org
Local.

15280 ■ Galion Area Chamber of Commerce (GACC)
106 Harding Way E
Galion, OH 44833-1901
Ph: (419)468-7737
Fax: (419)462-5487
E-mail: galionchamber@galionchamber.org
URL: http://www.galionchamber.org
Contact: Joe Kleinknecht, Pres./CEO
Members: 270. **Membership Dues:** bank and savings institution (plus $25 per million in Galion deposits), $175 (annual) • professional, real estate and insurance (plus $30 each partner and $4 per employee), $175 (annual) • retail, service, social club (plus $4 per employee), $175 (annual) • industry (with below 100 employees; plus $4 per employee), $175 (annual) • industry (with over 100 employees; plus $3 per employee), $550 (annual) • associate, $75 (annual). **Local.** Promotes business and community development in the Galion, OH area. **Computer Services:** Online services, membership directory. **Divisions:** Advocacy; Economic Development; Investor Benefits. **Publications:** *Galion Today*, bimonthly. Newsletter. **Advertising:** accepted. Alternate Formats: online.

15281 ■ Galion Area United Way
PO Box 242
Galion, OH 44833-0242
Ph: (419)468-4291
URL: National Affiliate–national.unitedway.org
Local. Affiliated With: United Way of America.

15282 ■ Galion Board of Realtors
244 Erie St.
Galion, OH 44833-1409
Ph: (419)777-2128
Fax: (419)777-2128
E-mail: tlswank@columbus.rr.com
URL: National Affiliate–www.realtor.org
Contact: Arthur B. Miller, Pres.
Local. Strives to develop real estate business practices. Advocates for the right to own, use and transfer real property. Provides a facility for professional development, research and exchange of information among members and the general public. **Affiliated With:** National Association of Realtors.

15283 ■ Galion Lions Club
c/o Tom Jeffers, Sec.
1105 Cherington Dr.
Galion, OH 44833
Ph: (419)468-2952
E-mail: genlib@juno.com
URL: http://www.lions13b.org
Contact: Tom Jeffers, Sec.
Local. Affiliated With: Lions Clubs International.

15284 ■ German Village Wander Volk
c/o Russell Brown
7700 RD 58
Galion, OH 44833
Ph: (419)946-6773
E-mail: baron6773@aol.com
URL: National Affiliate–www.ava.org
Contact: Russell Brown, Contact
Local. Non-competitive sports enthusiasts. **Affiliated With:** American Volkssport Association.

15285 ■ Habitat for Humanity in Crawford County, Ohio
PO Box 131
Galion, OH 44833-0131
Fax: (419)468-2735
Free: (800)893-2030
E-mail: lantz_cjs@hotmail.com
URL: National Affiliate–www.habitat.org
Local. Affiliated With: Habitat for Humanity International.

15286 ■ Main Street Galion
106 Harding Way E
Galion, OH 44833
Ph: (419)468-4812
Fax: (419)468-9622
E-mail: mainst@galionoh.com
URL: http://www.galionohio.com/mainst/mainsthome.html
Local.

15287 ■ Ohio Genealogical Society, Crawford County
PO Box 92
Galion, OH 44833-0092
E-mail: ccgs_oh@yahoo.com
URL: http://www.rootsweb.com/~ohccgs
Contact: Mary Fox, Pres.
Founded: 1974. **Members:** 500. **Membership Dues:** single, $8 (annual) • joint, $10 (annual) • sustaining, $15 (annual). **For-Profit. Local.** Preserves and publishes genealogy records in the Crawford County, OH area. **Affiliated With:** Ohio Genealogical Society. **Publications:** *Tracking*, 9/year. Newsletter. **Price:** included in membership dues. **Conventions/Meetings:** meeting - 8/year.

15288 ■ Ohio/West Virginia State Association of Emblem Club
c/o Debbie Blubaugh
668 Brookside Dr.
Galion, OH 44833
Ph: (419)468-9945
E-mail: mblubau@columbus.it.com
URL: http://www.emblemclub.com/html/ohio.html
Contact: Debbie Blubaugh, Contact
Regional. Affiliated With: Supreme Emblem Club of the United States of America.

Gallipolis

15289 ■ American Legion, Lafayette Post 27
1839 Mccormick Rd.
Gallipolis, OH 45631
Ph: (740)362-7478
Fax: (740)362-1429
URL: National Affiliate–www.legion.org
Local. Affiliated With: American Legion.

15290 ■ Gallia County Chamber of Commerce
16 State St.
PO Box 465
Gallipolis, OH 45631-0465
Ph: (740)446-0596 (740)446-3662
E-mail: lneal@galliacounty.org
URL: http://www.galliacounty.org
Contact: Ryan Smith, Contact
Membership Dues: individual, associate, elected official, senior (60 years old or older), $50 • bank, $500 • privately owned farm (with a maximum of 5 employees), civic, charitable organization (Jaycees, REDA, etc.), $100 • school, $250 • business, $150-$1,000. **Local.** Promotes business and community development in Gallipolis, OH. **Committees:** Annual Dinner; Business Appreciation; Community Service; Golf; Legislative; Promotions; River Recreation Festival; Transportation. **Publications:** Newsletter, monthly. **Price:** included in membership dues • Membership Directory. **Price:** $10.00. Alternate Formats: online • Annual Report, annual. Alternate Formats: online.

15291 ■ Gallia County Genealogical Society, Ohio Genealogical Chapter
PO Box 1007
Gallipolis, OH 45631-1007
Ph: (740)446-0320 (740)446-1775
E-mail: hcevans@eurekanet.com
URL: http://www.zoomnet.net/~histsoc
Contact: Henny Evans, Pres.
Founded: 1983. **Members:** 500. **Membership Dues:** individual, $15 (annual). **Staff:** 1. **State Groups:** 1. **Local.** Individuals with an interest in genealogy. Locates, restores, and preserves historic genealogical and demographic records. **Libraries: Type:** open to the public. **Holdings:** 100. **Subjects:** Gallia County, general history, revolutionary soldiers who lived in Gallia County, first family files. **Awards:** Jane Roush McCafferty Award. **Frequency:** annual. **Type:** recognition. **Recipient:** for contribution to society. **Additional Websites:** http://galliagenealogy.org. **Affiliated With:** Ohio Genealogical Society. **Formerly:** (1999) Ohio Genealogical Society, Gallia County Chapter. **Publications:** *Gallia County Glade*, quarterly. Newsletter. **Price:** included in membership dues • Book. Contains indexes of books for sale, births, marriages, wills and deaths. **Conventions/Meetings:** monthly workshop - always second Thursday except July, August, and December.

15292 ■ Gallipolis Junior Woman's Club
PO Box 911
Gallipolis, OH 45631
E-mail: gallipolisjrwomen@yahoo.com
URL: http://gallipolisjrwomen.tripod.com
Contact: Beth Covey, Pres.
Local.

15293 ■ Ohio BASS Chapter Federation (OBCF)
43 Portsmouth Rd.
Gallipolis, OH 45631
Ph: (740)446-9810
Fax: (740)446-9819
E-mail: jdoss@ohiobass.org
URL: http://www.ohiobass.org
Contact: Jim Doss, Pres.
State. Bass tournament organization dedicated to youth and the environment.

15294 ■ Ohio Valley Bicycle Club
PO Box 63 226 First Ave.
Gallipolis, OH 45631
Ph: (740)446-4639
E-mail: ohiovalleybikeclub@yahoo.com
URL: http://www.ohiovalleybicycleclub.org
State. Affiliated With: International Mountain Bicycling Association.

15295 ■ Sweet Adelines International, French Colony Chapter
Grace United Methodist Church
600 2nd Ave.
Gallipolis, OH 45631-1221
Ph: (304)525-8319
E-mail: mpmadsen@adelphia.net
URL: National Affiliate–www.sweetadelineintl.org
Contact: Mary Madsen, Contact
Local. Advances the musical art form of barbershop harmony through education and performances. Provides education, training and coaching in the development of women's four-part barbershop harmony. **Affiliated With:** Sweet Adelines International.

15296 ■ United Way of Gallia County
PO Box 771
Gallipolis, OH 45631
Ph: (740)446-2442
Fax: (740)446-0322
E-mail: unitedwaygallia@voyager.net
URL: http://www.unitedwaygallia.org
Contact: Liz Rumley, Pres.
Local.

15297 ■ Vietnam Veterans of America, Chapter No. 709
c/o Larry Marr, Pres.
39 Hilda Ext.
Gallipolis, OH 45631
Ph: (740)446-9629
URL: http://www.vvabuckeyestatecouncil.com
Contact: Larry Marr, Pres.
Local. Affiliated With: Vietnam Veterans of America.

Galloway

15298 ■ National Association of Church Business Administrators, Columbus Chapter
c/o Barry Hines, FCBA, Pres.
Cypress Wesleyan Church
PO Box 360
Galloway, OH 43119-0360
Ph: (614)878-8192
Fax: (614)878-2174
E-mail: barryh@cypressonline.net
URL: http://columbus.nacba.net
Contact: Barry Hines FCBA, Pres.
Local. Business administrators and managers employed by local churches or institutions of the Christian church. Provides a program of study, service, fellowship, training, information exchange, and problem discussion. **Affiliated With:** National Association of Church Business Administration.

15299 ■ Ohio Athletic Trainers' Association (OATA)
c/o Michael Medich, Pres.-Elect
Westland High School
146 Galloway Dr.
Galloway, OH 43119
Ph: (614)851-7082
Fax: (614)870-5531
E-mail: medichm@oata.org
URL: http://www.oata.org
Contact: Michael Medich, Pres.-Elect
State. Affiliated With: National Athletic Trainers' Association.

15300 ■ Ohio State Society of Enrolled Agents - Greater Columbus Chapter
c/o Kenneth Maykowski, Pres.
848 Claytonbend Dr.
Galloway, OH 43119
Ph: (614)878-6186
E-mail: kpmski@columbus.rr.com
URL: http://www.ossea.org/pdf/0804newsletter.pdf
Contact: Kenneth Maykowski EA, Pres.
Local. Affiliated With: National Association of Enrolled Agents.

Garfield Heights

15301 ■ American Legion, Garfield Heights
13112 Thraves Ave.
Garfield Heights, OH 44125
Ph: (216)662-9515
URL: National Affiliate–www.legion.org
Local. Affiliated With: American Legion.

15302 ■ Garfield Heights Chamber of Commerce
c/o Mary Stamler, Exec.Dir.
5284 Trans. Blvd.
Garfield Heights, OH 44125
Ph: (216)475-7775
Fax: (216)475-2237
E-mail: mstamler@garfieldchamber.com
URL: http://www.garfieldchamber.com
Contact: Mary Stamler, Exec.Dir.
Local. Works to promote and serve the local business, civic and social interests in the Garfield Heights, OH area. **Computer Services:** database, membership directory. **Publications:** *Communique*, periodic. Newsletter. **Advertising:** accepted. Alternate Formats: online.

15303 ■ Reserve Officers Association - Department of Ohio, General Patton Chapter 25
c/o Capt. Kevin Trewhella, USAR, Pres.
11016 McCraken Rd.
Garfield Heights, OH 44125
Ph: (216)475-9904 (330)467-0051
E-mail: ktrewhella@hotmail.com
URL: http://www.roa.org/oh
Contact: Capt. Kevin Trewhella USAR, Pres.
Local. Promotes and supports the development and execution of a military policy for the United States. Provides professional development seminars, workshops and programs for its members. **Affiliated With:** Reserve Officers Association of the United States.

Garrettsville

15304 ■ Garrettsville - Hiram Area Chamber of Commerce (GHACC)
PO Box 1
Garrettsville, OH 44231
Ph: (330)527-5850 (330)527-2411
E-mail: patrick@apk.net
URL: http://www.garrettsvillehiramarea.com
Contact: Rick Patrick, Pres.
Members: 55. **Local.** Promotes business and community development in Portage County, OH. Helps operate People Tree for the needy. Sponsors Silver Crik Turkey Daze Festival. **Formerly:** (1999) Garrettsville Area Chamber of Commerce. **Publications:** *Garrettsville: New England Charm Today - We Have it All.* **Conventions/Meetings:** monthly meeting.

15305 ■ Garrettsville Lions Club
c/o Brian Gorby, Pres.
8210 Clover Ln.
Garrettsville, OH 44231
Ph: (330)527-2891
E-mail: bgorgy@neo.rr.com
URL: http://www.lions13d.org
Contact: Brian Gorby, Pres.
Local. Affiliated With: Lions Clubs International.

15306 ■ Masonic Lodge No. 246
8120 Main St.
Garrettsville, OH 44231
Ph: (330)527-2675
E-mail: php144@yahoo.com
URL: http://www.masonic-lodges.org/Garrettsville-246
Contact: William B. Owen, Sec.
Founded: 1854. **Local. Awards:** President Garfield Humanitarian Award. **Frequency:** annual. **Type:** scholarship. **Recipient:** for members with outstanding grades, leadership, and need.

Geneva

15307 ■ American Legion, George Call Post 124
PO Box 150
Geneva, OH 44041
Ph: (740)362-7478
Fax: (740)362-1429
URL: National Affiliate–www.legion.org
Local. Affiliated With: American Legion.

15308 ■ Ashtabula County Genealogical Society (ACGS)
Geneva Public Lib.
860 Sherman St.
Geneva, OH 44041-9101
Ph: (440)466-4521
E-mail: acgs@ashtabulagen.org
URL: http://www.ashtabulagen.org
Contact: Troy Bailey, Pres.
Local.

15309 ■ Geneva Area Chamber of Commerce (GACC)
866 E Main St.
PO Box 84
Geneva, OH 44041-0084
Ph: (440)466-8694
Fax: (440)466-0823
E-mail: info@genevachamber.org
URL: http://www.genevachamber.org
Contact: Sue Ellen Foote, Exec.Dir.
Members: 250. **Staff:** 1. **Local.** Promotes business and community development in the Geneva, OH area. **Publications:** Newsletter, monthly. **Advertising:** accepted.

15310 ■ Geneva-on-the-Lake Chamber of Commerce
5536 Lake Rd.
Geneva, OH 44041
Ph: (440)466-8600
Fax: (440)466-8911
Free: (800)862-9948
E-mail: gol@ncweb.com
URL: http://www.visitgenevaonthelake.com
Contact: Marge Milliken, Tourism Spec.
Local.

Genoa

15311 ■ American Legion, Genoa Post 324
302 West St.
Genoa, OH 43430
Ph: (740)362-7478
Fax: (740)362-1429
URL: National Affiliate–www.legion.org
Local. Affiliated With: American Legion.

Georgetown

15312 ■ American Legion, Ohio Post 180
c/o Carey Bavis
1001 S Main St.
Georgetown, OH 45121

Ph: (740)362-7478
Fax: (740)362-1429
URL: National Affiliate–www.legion.org
Contact: Carey Bavis, Contact
Local. Affiliated With: American Legion.

15313 ■ Brown County Chamber of Commerce
110 E State St.
Georgetown, OH 45121
Ph: (937)378-4784
Fax: (937)378-1634
Free: (888)BRO-WNOH
E-mail: brchcom@bright.net
Contact: Ray Becraft, Exec.Dir.
Local.

15314 ■ Ohio Genealogical Society, Brown County (OGS)
PO Box 83
Georgetown, OH 45121-0083
E-mail: ogs@ogs.org
URL: National Affiliate–www.ogs.org
Founded: 1977. **Members:** 300. **Membership Dues:** individual, $7 (annual) • family, $9 (annual). **Local.** Individuals engaged in genealogical research. Works to preserve Brown County, OH history and family records in order to help those searching for their ancestors. Holds annual seminar; operates library. Sponsors annual Heritage Harvest programs. **Libraries: Type:** reference. **Subjects:** surrounding coutries; eastern states. **Affiliated With:** Ohio Genealogical Society; Ohio Genealogical Society. **Publications:** *On the Trail*, quarterly. **Price:** free to members. **Conventions/Meetings:** monthly meeting - always third Thursday of the month.

Germantown

15315 ■ Dayton Amateur Softball Association
c/o Clyde Brewer, Commissioner
10476 Germantown-Middletown Rd.
Germantown, OH 45327
Ph: (937)855-7745
E-mail: cbrewerasa@copper.net
URL: National Affiliate–www.asasoftball.com
Contact: Clyde Brewer, Commissioner
Local. Affiliated With: Amateur Softball Association of America.

15316 ■ Germantown Lions Club
201 W Market St.
Germantown, OH 45327-1220
Ph: (937)855-2005 (513)243-2136
E-mail: liontim@woh.rr.com
URL: http://germantownoh.lionwap.org
Contact: Tim Emley, Pres.
Local. Affiliated With: Lions Clubs International.

15317 ■ Hamilton Middletown Beagle Club
c/o Mr. Clyde S. Focht
8947 Preble Co Line Rd.
Germantown, OH 45327-9416
URL: National Affiliate–clubs.akc.org
Contact: Mr. Clyde S. Focht, Contact
Local.

Gibsonburg

15318 ■ American Legion, Welker-Smith Post 17
300 S Main St.
Gibsonburg, OH 43431
Ph: (740)362-7478
Fax: (740)362-1429
URL: National Affiliate–www.legion.org
Local. Affiliated With: American Legion.

Gilboa

15319 ■ American Legion, Harter-Williams Post 536
126 Franklin St.
Gilboa, OH 45875
Ph: (740)362-7478
Fax: (740)362-1429
URL: National Affiliate–www.legion.org
Local. Affiliated With: American Legion.

Girard

15320 ■ American Legion, Dewitt McConnell Post 235
11 High St.
Girard, OH 44420
Ph: (740)362-7478
Fax: (740)362-1429
URL: National Affiliate–www.legion.org
Local. Affiliated With: American Legion.

15321 ■ Big Brothers Big Sisters of Mahoning Valley
325 N State St.
Girard, OH 44420
Ph: (330)545-0002
Fax: (330)545-0104
E-mail: bbbs@bbbsmv.com
URL: http://www.bbbsmv.com
Contact: Brian Higgins LSW, Exec.Dir.
Regional. Affiliated With: Big Brothers Big Sisters of America. **Formerly:** (2005) Big Brothers Big Sisters of America of Mahoning Valley.

15322 ■ Girard Lions Club
c/o Joseph M. Barnot, Sec.
1021 Park Circle Dr.
Girard, OH 44420
Ph: (330)545-5286
E-mail: btxjoe@hotmail.com
URL: http://www.lions13d.org
Contact: Joseph M. Barnot, Sec.
Local. Affiliated With: Lions Clubs International.

15323 ■ Greater Girard Area Chamber of Commerce (GGACC)
PO Box 457
Girard, OH 44420
Ph: (330)545-8616
E-mail: knightlinemb@aol.com
URL: http://www.girardchamber.org
Contact: Patrick Rubinic, Pres.
Local. Publications: Newsletter, monthly.

15324 ■ Junior Achievement of Mahoning Valley
1920 Churchill Rd.
Girard, OH 44420
Ph: (330)539-5268
Fax: (330)539-9550
E-mail: juniorachievement@onecom.com
URL: http://warren-youngstown.ja.org
Contact: John Church, Chm.
Founded: 1952. **Staff:** 3. **Budget:** $215,000. **Nonmembership. Regional.** Educates and inspires young people to value free enterprise, business, and economics to improve the quality of their lives. **Affiliated With:** Junior Achievement.

Glencoe

15325 ■ American Legion, Glencoe Post 632
6363 Main St.
Glencoe, OH 43928
Ph: (740)362-7478
Fax: (740)362-1429
URL: National Affiliate–www.legion.org
Local. Affiliated With: American Legion.

Glouster

15326 ■ American Legion, Mc-Cann-Frederick Post 414
PO Box 161
Glouster, OH 45732
Ph: (740)362-7478
Fax: (740)362-1429
URL: National Affiliate–www.legion.org
Local. Affiliated With: American Legion.

15327 ■ Ohio Valley Dairy Goat Association
c/o Deb Schneider
7110 Cox-Kolbe Rd.
Glouster, OH 45732
Ph: (740)767-4557
URL: http://kelpies.us/ovdga
Contact: Deb Schneider, Contact
Local. Affiliated With: American Dairy Goat Association.

Gnadenhutten

15328 ■ American Legion, Gnadenhutten Post 154
PO Box 164
Gnadenhutten, OH 44629
Ph: (740)362-7478
Fax: (740)362-1429
URL: National Affiliate–www.legion.org
Local. Affiliated With: American Legion.

15329 ■ Gnadenhutten Historical Society (GHS)
PO Box 396
Gnadenhutten, OH 44629
Ph: (614)254-4143 (740)254-4756
Fax: (740)254-4992
E-mail: gnadmuse@tusco.net
URL: http://www.gnaden.tusco.net
Contact: Barbara S. McKeown, Sec.-Treas.
Founded: 1843. **Members:** 100. **Membership Dues:** individual, $3 (annual) • family, $5 (annual) • business, $20 (annual). **State Groups:** 1. **Local Groups:** 1. **Local.** Individuals interested in the history of Gnadenhutten, OH. Operates Gnadenhutten Historical Society Museum; conducts special events, including Pioneer Days and craft shows. **Awards:** OAHSM Award of Achievement. **Frequency:** annual. **Type:** recognition • Rosenberry Foundation. **Frequency:** annual. **Type:** monetary. **Publications:** *Monumental News*, semiannual. Newsletter. **Conventions/Meetings:** monthly meeting.

Goshen

15330 ■ Cincinnati Mineral Society
c/o Judy Budnik, Pres.
2948 Rontina Dr.
Goshen, OH 45122
Ph: (513)575-1990
E-mail: wisoh@email.msn.com
URL: http://www.mineralsociety.org
Contact: Marie Huizing, Sec.
Local. Aims to further the study of Earth Sciences and the practice of lapidary arts and mineralogy. **Affiliated With:** American Federation of Mineralogical Societies.

15331 ■ Geological Alliance
2948 Rotina Dr.
Goshen, OH 45122-9300
Ph: (513)575-1990
E-mail: wisoh@msn.com
URL: National Affiliate–www.amfed.org
Contact: Judy Budnik, Treas.
Local. Aims to further the study of Earth Sciences and the practice of lapidary arts and mineralogy. **Affiliated With:** American Federation of Mineralogical Societies.

15332 ■ Goshen Lions Club
6710 Goshen Rd.
Goshen, OH 45122-9200
Ph: (513)831-0632
URL: http://goshenoh.lionwap.org
Contact: Andrew W. Evans, Pres.
Local. Affiliated With: Lions Clubs International.

Grafton

15333 ■ Midview High School Key Club
38199 W Capel Rd.
Grafton, OH 44044
Ph: (440)748-2124
E-mail: ashovery@msn.com
URL: http://www.keyclub.org/club/midview
Contact: Katie Wittenbrook, Pres.
Local.

15334 ■ Ohio Morgan Horse Association
c/o Dayan Adell Birchler, Pres.
9865 Avon-Belden Rd.
Grafton, OH 44044
Ph: (440)748-2619
E-mail: mudicreck@aol.com
URL: http://www.ohiomorgan.com
Contact: Dayan Adell Birchler, Pres.
State. Affiliated With: American Morgan Horse Association.

15335 ■ Veterans of Foreign Wars 3341
783 Huron St.
Grafton, OH 44044
Ph: (440)926-3341
Local. Conventions/Meetings: monthly meeting.

15336 ■ Vietnam Veterans of America, Chapter No. 559
c/o Modesto Garcia, Pres.
2500 S Avon-Belden Rd.
Grafton, OH 44044-9802
Ph: (440)748-1161
URL: http://www.vvabuckeyestatecouncil.com
Contact: Modesto Garcia, Pres.
Local. Affiliated With: Vietnam Veterans of America.

Grand Rapids

15337 ■ American Legion, Ohio Post 232
c/o Alva N. Sidle
PO Box 218
Grand Rapids, OH 43522
Ph: (740)362-7478
Fax: (740)362-1429
URL: National Affiliate–www.legion.org
Contact: Alva N. Sidle, Contact
Local. Affiliated With: American Legion.

15338 ■ Grand Rapids Area Chamber of Commerce
PO Box 391
Grand Rapids, OH 43522-0391
Ph: (419)832-1106
Fax: (419)832-1106
URL: http://www.grandrapidsohio.com
Local.

Grandview Heights

15339 ■ National Association of Professional Organizers, Ohio Chapter
c/o Melanie Haack, Treas.
903 Palmer Rd.
Grandview Heights, OH 43212-3714
E-mail: dheimann@wowway.com
URL: http://www.j2consult.com/napoohio
Contact: Debra Heimann, Pres.
State. Promotes the profession of professional organizing. Educates the public about the field of professional organizing. Supports, educates, and provides a networking forum for members.

Granville

15340 ■ American Baptist Churches of Ohio (ABC/OHIO)
c/o Dr. Lawrence O. Swain, Exec. Minister
PO Box 376
Granville, OH 43023-0376
Ph: (740)587-0804
Fax: (740)587-0807
E-mail: dwest@abc-ohio.org
URL: http://www.abc-ohio.org
Contact: Dr. Lawrence O. Swain, Exec. Minister
Founded: 1826. **Members:** 292. **Budget:** $1,300,000. **Local Groups:** 20. **State.** American Baptist churches in Ohio, excluding Cuyahoga County, representing 65,000 individuals. **Conventions/Meetings:** annual conference (exhibits) - always October.

15341 ■ American Legion, Granville Post 398
PO Box 2
Granville, OH 43023
Ph: (740)362-7478
Fax: (740)362-1429
URL: National Affiliate–www.legion.org
Local. Affiliated With: American Legion.

15342 ■ Granville - Young Life
PO Box 90
Granville, OH 43023
Ph: (740)360-9982
URL: http://sites.younglife.org/_layouts/ylext/default.aspx?ID=C-1579
Local. Affiliated With: Young Life.

15343 ■ Heath High School - Young Life
PO Box 90
Granville, OH 43023
Ph: (740)360-9982
URL: http://sites.younglife.org/_layouts/ylext/default.aspx?ID=C-4430
Local. Affiliated With: Young Life.

15344 ■ Licking County Rock and Mineral Society
c/o Robert Pflaumer, Pres.
2429 Deeds Rd.
Granville, OH 43023
E-mail: jlahr@ecr.net
URL: National Affiliate–www.amfed.org
Contact: Paul Green, Sec.
Local. Aims to further the study of Earth Sciences and the practice of lapidary arts and mineralogy. **Affiliated With:** American Federation of Mineralogical Societies.

15345 ■ Ohio Mushroom Society (OMS)
c/o Dick Doyle, Treas.
14 Sunset Hill
Granville, OH 43023-1162
Ph: (740)587-0019
E-mail: doyle@denison.edu
URL: http://www.ohiomushroom.org/oldoms
Contact: Dick Doyle, Treas.
Founded: 1973. **State.** Amateur and professional mycologists, mycophagists, devotees of mushroom lore, students, and botanists. Promotes amateur mycology (the study of fungi, such as mushrooms, puffballs, molds, rusts, and smuts). **Affiliated With:** North American Mycological Association.

15346 ■ Ohio Oil and Gas Association (OOGA)
PO Box 535
Granville, OH 43023-0535
Ph: (740)587-0444
Fax: (740)587-0446
E-mail: rreda@ooga.org
URL: http://www.ooga.org
Contact: Thomas E. Stewart, Exec.VP
Founded: 1947. **Members:** 1,350. **Staff:** 5. **Budget:** $500,000. **State.** Individuals involved in the exploration, development and production of crude oil and natural gas within the State of Ohio. Works to protect, promote, foster and advance the common interests of those engaged in all aspects of the Ohio crude oil and natural gas producing industry. **Publications:** *Scout Report*, monthly • Membership Directory, annual • Bulletin, monthly. **Conventions/Meetings:** annual meeting (exhibits) - always March.

15347 ■ Young Life Licking County
PO Box 90
Granville, OH 43023
Ph: (740)360-9982
URL: http://sites.younglife.org/_layouts/ylext/default.aspx?ID=A-OH54
Local. Affiliated With: Young Life.

Gratiot

15348 ■ American Legion, National Trail Post 756
10 County Line Rd.
Gratiot, OH 43740
Ph: (740)362-7478
Fax: (740)362-1429
URL: National Affiliate–www.legion.org
Local. Affiliated With: American Legion.

Graytown

15349 ■ American Welding Society, Northwest Ohio Section 046
c/o Richard West, Chm.
1956 N Stange Rd.
Graytown, OH 43432
Ph: (419)862-2933
URL: National Affiliate–www.aws.org
Contact: Richard West, Chm.
Local. Promotes the interests of professional engineering society in the field of welding. **Affiliated With:** American Welding Society.

Green

15350 ■ Green Chamber of Commerce
c/o Paul Miller
PO Box 547
Green, OH 44232-0547
Ph: (330)896-3023
Fax: (330)896-3178
E-mail: info@greencoc.org
Contact: Connie Romig, CEO
Founded: 2000. **Members:** 210. **Staff:** 3. **Budget:** $60,000. **Local.** Works to advance the interest of business and professional firms in the City of Green, Ohio and the surrounding communities.

Green Springs

15351 ■ American Legion, Ohio Post 295
c/o Marion H. Peck
211 Smith St.
Green Springs, OH 44836
Ph: (740)362-7478
Fax: (740)362-1429
URL: National Affiliate–www.legion.org
Contact: Marion H. Peck, Contact
Local. Affiliated With: American Legion.

15352 ■ Green Springs Lions Club
c/o Ted Rutherford, PDG, Sec.
PO Box 185
Green Springs, OH 44836
Ph: (419)639-2931
E-mail: tedj34@hotmail.com
URL: http://www.lions13b.org
Contact: Ted Rutherford PDG, Sec.
Local. Affiliated With: Lions Clubs International.

Greenhills

15353 ■ American Sewing Guild, Cincinnati Chapter
c/o Galina Radford
9 Bradnor Pl.
Greenhills, OH 45218
Ph: (513)825-8238
E-mail: galina@cinci.rr.com
URL: http://www.asgcincinnati.org
Contact: Galina Radford, Contact
Local. Affiliated With: American Sewing Guild.

Greentown

15354 ■ American Legion, Ohio Post 436
c/o Howard D. Miller
PO Box 113
Greentown, OH 44630
Ph: (740)362-7478
Fax: (740)362-1429
URL: National Affiliate–www.legion.org
Contact: Howard D. Miller, Contact
Local. Affiliated With: American Legion.

Greenville

15355 ■ American Legion, Erk Cottrell Post 140
325 N Ohio St.
Greenville, OH 45331
Ph: (513)548-7077
Fax: (740)362-1429
URL: National Affiliate–www.legion.org
Local. Affiliated With: American Legion.

15356 ■ APICS, The Association for Operations Management - Lima Area Chapter No. 290
c/o Charles King, CIRM, Pres.
1164 Evergreen Dr.
Greenville, OH 45331
Ph: (937)547-9229
E-mail: spitzen2002@hotmail.com
URL: http://www.lima-apics.org
Contact: Charles King CIRM, Pres.
Local. Provides information and services in production and inventory management and related areas to enable members, enterprises and individuals to add value to their business performance. **Affiliated With:** APICS - The Association for Operations Management.

15357 ■ Darke County Association of Realtors
306 Sycamore St.
Greenville, OH 45331
Ph: (937)548-5462
Fax: (937)548-6164
E-mail: dcar@erinet.com
URL: National Affiliate–www.realtor.org
Contact: Kelly K. Barney, Exec. Officer
Local. Strives to develop real estate business practices. Advocates for the right to own, use and transfer real property. Provides a facility for professional development, research and exchange of information among members and the general public. **Affiliated With:** National Association of Realtors.

15358 ■ Darke County Chamber of Commerce
622 S Broadway
PO Box 237
Greenville, OH 45331-0237
Ph: (937)548-2102
Fax: (937)548-5608
E-mail: info@darkecountyohio.com
URL: http://www.darkecountyohio.com
Contact: Louanna Gwinn, Pres.
Founded: 1927. **Members:** 500. **Membership Dues:** contractor, distributor, farmer, motel, retail, service, transportation, wholesaler, $165-$500 (annual) • barber, beautician, independent garage, service station, $165 (annual) • attorney, accountant, physician, hospital, medical center, funeral home, insurance agency, real estate firm, $165 (annual) • educator, elected/government employee, professional, $85 (annual) • charitable not-for-profit association, professional association, church, $85 (annual) • non-active businessperson, $60 (annual) • automobile dealer (plus $.25 per unit on lot), $165 (annual) • bank, building and loan association, financial institution (plus $15 for each additional $1 million in assets), $310 (annual) • personal loan association (plus $15 for each additional $500000 in assets), $165 (annual) • industry, processor (plus $2 per employee), $165 (annual) • utility (plus $.05 per meter), $165 (annual). **Local.** Promotes business and community development in the Greenville, OH area. **Computer Services:** database, membership directory. **Committees:** Agriculture; Business; Economic Development; Education; Government Relations; Industrial; Leadership. **Councils:** Small Business. **Affiliated With:** U.S. Chamber of Commerce. **Publications:** *Business Start-up Guide*. Book • *Darke County Image Book* • *Industrial Directory* • *Organizations and Clubs List*. Directory • Newsletter, periodic. Alternate Formats: online • Annual Report, annual. Alternate Formats: online.

15359 ■ Darke County, Ohio Habitat for Humanity
PO Box 1015
Greenville, OH 45331
Ph: (937)548-3635
Fax: (937)548-3635
E-mail: darkecountyhabitat@countystart.com
URL: http://www.darkecountyhabitat.org
Local. Affiliated With: Habitat for Humanity International.

15360 ■ Darke County United Way
PO Box 716
Greenville, OH 45331-0716
Ph: (937)547-1272
URL: National Affiliate–national.unitedway.org
Local. Affiliated With: United Way of America.

15361 ■ Darke County Youth for Christ
PO Box 266
Greenville, OH 45331
Ph: (937)548-2477
Fax: (937)548-9165
URL: http://www.dcyfc.org
Local. Affiliated With: Youth for Christ/U.S.A.

15362 ■ Friends of Bears Mill
c/o Terry L. Clark, Pres.
6450 Arcanum Bear's Mill Rd.
Greenville, OH 45331-9617
Ph: (937)548-5112
Fax: (937)547-6044
E-mail: bearsmill@woh.rr.com
URL: http://www.bearsmill.com
Contact: Terry Clark, Pres.
Local. Works to preserve and keep the mill open to the public for touring and educational purposes.

15363 ■ Miami Valley RSVP
c/o Mary Ann Nieberding, Dir.
116 E 3rd St.
Greenville, OH 45331-0459
Ph: (937)548-8002
Fax: (937)548-2664
E-mail: mnieberding@corsp.org
URL: http://www.seniorcorps.gov/about/programs/rsvp_state.asp?usestateabbr=oh&Search4.x=0&Search4.y=0
Contact: Mary Ann Nieberding, Dir.
Local. Affiliated With: Retired and Senior Volunteer Program.

15364 ■ Ohio Genealogical Society, Darke County
PO Box 908
Greenville, OH 45331-0908
Ph: (937)526-3953
E-mail: ahuffman@wesnet.com
URL: http://dcgs.dcoweb.org
Contact: Alice Huffman, Pres.
Membership Dues: single or joint, $14 (annual). **Local. Affiliated With:** Ohio Genealogical Society.

Greenwich

15365 ■ American Legion, Mil-Bow-Mar Post 280
RR 224 E
Greenwich, OH 44837
Ph: (740)362-7478
Fax: (740)362-1429
URL: National Affiliate–www.legion.org
Local. Affiliated With: American Legion.

Grove City

15366 ■ American Legion, Paschall Post 164
3363 Mcdowell Rd.
Grove City, OH 43123
Ph: (740)362-7478
Fax: (740)362-1429
E-mail: americanlegion164@sbcglobal.net
URL: National Affiliate–www.legion.org
Local. Affiliated With: American Legion.

15367 ■ Columbus Rotor Wing
6690 Ridpath Rd.
Grove City, OH 43123
Ph: (614)539-9268
E-mail: dillrc1@aol.com
URL: http://torchs.org/clubs/clubs.htm
Contact: Mike Dillon, Contact
Local.

15368 ■ Grove City Area Chamber of Commerce (GCACC)
4069 Broadway
Grove City, OH 43123
Ph: (614)875-9762
Fax: (614)875-1510
Free: (877)870-5393
E-mail: info@gcchamber.org
URL: http://www.gcchamber.org
Contact: Lynn A. Smith, Exec.Dir.
Founded: 1978. **Members:** 400. **Membership Dues:** business, $135-$495 (annual) • individual, $95 (annual) • nonprofit organization, church, association, $110 (annual). **Staff:** 3. **Budget:** $100,000. **Local.** Business, industry, and professional persons interested in promoting business and community development in the southwestern Franklin County, OH area. Sponsors flea and farmer's markets. **Awards:** Community Service Award. **Type:** recognition • Ohio Business Week Scholarships. **Type:** scholarship • School and Business Awards. **Type:** recognition. **Computer Services:** Online services, membership directory. **Affiliated With:** U.S. Chamber of Commerce. **Publications:** *Quality of Life Magazine*, biennial • Membership Directory, annual • Newsletter, monthly. **Conventions/Meetings:** quarterly luncheon • annual meeting - always January or February.

15369 ■ Grove City Lions Club - Ohio
c/o David Walters, Pres.
3174 Kingswood Dr.
Grove City, OH 43123
Ph: (614)871-9160
URL: http://www.iwaynet.net/~lions13f
Contact: David Walters, Pres.
Local. Affiliated With: Lions Clubs International.

15370 ■ National Model Railroad Association, Mid-Central Region
c/o Howard Smith, MMR, Pres.
3255 Big Run S Rd.
Grove City, OH 43123
Ph: (614)871-0500
E-mail: president@midcentral-region-nmra.org
URL: http://www.midcentral-region-nmra.org
Contact: Howard Smith MMR, Pres.
Regional. Affiliated With: National Model Railroad Association.

15371 ■ Ohio State Trapshooting Foundation
5854 Willow Lake Dr.
Grove City, OH 43123-8845
Ph: (614)539-5623
Fax: (614)539-5624
E-mail: ohiotrap@juno.com
URL: http://www.ohiotrap.com
Contact: Vivian Webb, Sec.
Founded: 1995. **State.**

15372 ■ Weimaraner Club of Columbus (WCC)
c/o Jennifer Marple, Sec.
3688 Larchmere Dr.
Grove City, OH 43123
Ph: (614)539-5617
E-mail: heychickie@gmail.com
URL: http://www.weimclubcolumbus.org
Contact: Jennifer Marple, Sec.
Members: 52. **Membership Dues:** regular, $13 (annual). **Local. Affiliated With:** American Kennel Club.

Groveport

15373 ■ Navy League of the United States, Greater Columbus
c/o Joe M. Hart
5565 Ebright Rd.
Groveport, OH 43125-9742
Fax: (614)836-2831
E-mail: jhart@kingthompson.com
URL: National Affiliate–www.navyleague.org
Contact: William F. Hanf, Contact
Local. Civilian organization that supports U.S. capability to keep the sea lanes open through a strong, viable Navy, Marine Corps, Coast Guard, and Merchant Marine. Seeks to awaken interest and cooperation of U.S. citizens in matters serving to aid, improve, and develop the efficiency of U.S. naval and maritime forces and equipment. **Affiliated With:** Navy League of the United States.

15374 ■ Southeastern Franklin County Chamber of Commerce
5151 Berger Rd.
Groveport, OH 43125-9722
Ph: (614)836-1138
Fax: (614)836-1138
E-mail: chambersefc@aol.com
URL: http://www.chambersefc.com
Contact: Susan Brobst, Exec.Dir.
Membership Dues: individual, $100 (annual) • business (based on number of employees), $100-$300 (annual). **Local.** Promotes business and community development in Southeastern Franklin County, OH. **Formerly:** (2000) Groveport-Madison Area Chamber of Commerce. **Publications:** Newsletter, monthly • Membership Directory, annual. **Conventions/Meetings:** monthly meeting - every 3rd Wednesday.

Hamden

15375 ■ Ohio Genealogical Society, Vinton County
c/o Lawrence McWhorter, Pres.
PO Box 306
Hamden, OH 45634-0306
Ph: (740)384-2467 (740)384-6305
URL: http://www.rootsweb.com/~ohvinton/vinton.htm
Contact: Mr. Lawrence McWhorter, Pres.
Founded: 1950. **Members:** 84. **Membership Dues:** single, family, $10 (annual). **Local.** Individuals interested in the people and history of Vinton County, OH. **Libraries: Type:** open to the public. **Affiliated With:** Ohio Genealogical Society. **Publications:** *Vinton County Heritage*, quarterly. Newsletter. **Price:** included in membership dues. **Conventions/Meetings:** monthly meeting - always 2nd Sunday.

Hamilton

15376 ■ AAA Ohio Automobile Club
744 NW Washington Blvd.
Hamilton, OH 45013
Ph: (513)863-3200
Contact: Lorraine Espel, Mgr.
State.

15377 ■ American Legion, Durwin-Schantz Post 138
427 S 3rd St.
Hamilton, OH 45011
Ph: (740)362-7478
Fax: (740)362-1429
URL: National Affiliate–www.legion.org
Local. Affiliated With: American Legion.

15378 ■ American Legion, Lewis-Whitaker Post 520
727 Central Ave.
Hamilton, OH 45011
Ph: (740)362-7478
Fax: (740)362-1429
URL: National Affiliate–www.legion.org
Local. Affiliated With: American Legion.

15379 ■ American Legion, Ohio Post 681
c/o Havelock D. Nelson
3377 Indian Ct.
Hamilton, OH 45011
Ph: (740)362-7478
Fax: (740)362-1429
URL: National Affiliate–www.legion.org
Contact: Havelock D. Nelson, Contact
Local. Affiliated With: American Legion.

15380 ■ Badin ROKS (ROKS)
c/o Pat Meehan
1306 Southern Hills Blvd.
Hamilton, OH 45013
Ph: (513)368-7535
E-mail: jenn8504@hotmail.com
URL: http://orunner.net/BadinROKS
Contact: Jenny Meehan, Pres.
Local. Affiliated With: United States Orienteering Federation.

15381 ■ Butler County Historical Society
327 N Second St.
Hamilton, OH 45011
Ph: (513)896-9930
E-mail: bcomuseum@fuse.net
URL: http://home.fuse.net/butlercountymuseum
Contact: Marjorie Brown, Dir.
Local. Seeks to make the heritage of the county more accessible to the public through its museum and outreach programs. **Publications:** Newsletter, 10/year.

15382 ■ Butler County United Way
323 N 3rd St.
Hamilton, OH 45011
Ph: (513)863-0800
Fax: (513)863-3467
E-mail: bcuw@bc-unitedway.org
URL: http://www.bc-unitedway.org
Contact: Maureen Noe, Pres./CEO
Founded: 1920. **Staff:** 6. **Budget:** $500,000. **Local.** Works to raise and distribute funds to agencies and programs which help people in need, improving the quality of life in the communities. **Affiliated With:** United Way of America. **Formerly:** United Way of the Hamilton Fairfield, Ohio Area and Vicinity.

15383 ■ Cincinnati Celiac Support Group (CCSG)
c/o Jill Perkins, Pres.
1107 Goodman Ave.
Hamilton, OH 45013
Ph: (513)533-0382
E-mail: jillian.perkins@fuse.net
URL: http://www.geocities.com/cinci_celiac/index.html
Contact: Jill Perkins, Pres.
Local.

15384 ■ Greater Hamilton Chamber of Commerce (GHCC)
201 Dayton St.
Hamilton, OH 45011-1633
Ph: (513)844-1500
Fax: (513)844-1999
URL: http://www.hamilton-ohio.com
Contact: Kenny Craig, Pres./CEO
Founded: 1911. **Members:** 570. **Membership Dues:** financial institution, manufacturing and processor, professional, real estate, general business, insurance, nonprofit (base), $280 (annual) • public utility/publisher (per meter, trunk line, subscriber), $0 (annual) • retiree (individual/non-business), $85 (annual). **Staff:** 7. **Local.** Promotes business and community development in the Hamilton, OH area. **Awards:** Citizen of Year. **Frequency:** annual. **Type:** recognition. **Computer Services:** Online services, membership directory. **Programs:** Leadership Hamilton. **Publications:** *ChamberLetter*, monthly. Newsletter. Features upcoming event, news on members, and latest topic. **Circulation:** 1,200. **Advertising:** accepted. Alternate Formats: online • Membership Directory, annual. **Price:** $20.00.

15385 ■ Greater Hamilton Convention and Visitors Bureau
One Riverfront Plz.
Hamilton, OH 45011
Ph: (513)844-8080
Fax: (513)844-8090
Free: (800)311-5353
URL: http://www.hamilton-cvb.com
Contact: Debra Fescina Bridge, Exec.Dir.
Founded: 1993. **Staff:** 2. **Budget:** $100,000. **Nonmembership. Local.** Promotes Hamilton, Ohio as a tourist destination.

15386 ■ Hamilton, Ohio City of Sculpture
PO Box 545
Hamilton, OH 45012
Ph: (513)895-3934
E-mail: hamiltonohiocityofsculpture@fuse.net
URL: http://www.cityofsculpture.org
Founded: 2000. **Local.** Works to promote the recognition of Hamilton as a cultural community through obtaining sculptures to be placed in public spaces for the enjoyment of citizens and visitors.

15387 ■ Izaak Walton League of America, Anthony Wayne Chapter
c/o Raymond C. Zehler
900 Morman Rd.
Hamilton, OH 45013-4358
Ph: (513)868-3179
E-mail: zehleriwla@email.msn.com
URL: National Affiliate–www.iwla.org
Local. Works to educate the public to conserve, maintain, protect, and restore the soil, forest, water, and other natural resources of the U.S.; promotes the enjoyment and wholesome utilization of these resources. **Affiliated With:** Izaak Walton League of America.

15388 ■ Izaak Walton League of America, Buckeye All-State Chapter
5990 Fairham Rd.
Hamilton, OH 45011
Ph: (513)868-2848
E-mail: ferrislawoffice@aol.com
URL: National Affiliate–www.iwla.org
Contact: Mr. Donald L. Ferris, Contact
Local. Works to educate the public to conserve, maintain, protect, and restore the soil, forest, water, and other natural resources of the U.S; promotes the enjoyment and wholesome utilization of these resources. **Affiliated With:** Izaak Walton League of America.

15389 ■ Izaak Walton League of America, Dry Fork Chapter
c/o Donald L. Ferris
5990 Fairham Rd.
Hamilton, OH 45011
Ph: (513)868-2848
E-mail: ferrislawoffice@aol.com
URL: National Affiliate–www.iwla.org
Contact: Mr. Donald L. Ferris, Contact
Local. Works to educate the public to conserve, maintain, protect, and restore the soil, forest, water, and other natural resources of the U.S; promotes the enjoyment and wholesome utilization of these resources. **Affiliated With:** Izaak Walton League of America.

15390 ■ Izaak Walton League of America, Fairfield Chapter
c/o Robert Kraft, Sec.-Treas.
3725 Rose Ave.
Hamilton, OH 45015-3016
Ph: (513)868-3430
E-mail: bobkraft@fuse.net
URL: http://home.fuse.net/fairfieldiwla
Contact: Robert Kraft, Sec.-Treas.
Founded: 1976. **Membership Dues:** regular, $45 (annual). **Local**. Works to educate the public to conserve, maintain, protect and restore the soil forest, water and other natural resources of the U.S. **Affiliated With:** Izaak Walton League of America.

15391 ■ Izaak Walton League of America, Hamilton Chapter
5990 Fairham Rd.
Hamilton, OH 45011
Ph: (513)868-2848
E-mail: ferrislawoffice@aol.com
URL: National Affiliate–www.iwla.org
Contact: Mr. Donald L. Ferris, Contact
Local. Works to educate the public to conserve, maintain, protect, and restore the soil, forest, water, and other natural resources of the U.S; promotes the enjoyment and wholesome utilization of these resources. **Affiliated With:** Izaak Walton League of America.

15392 ■ Izaak Walton League of America, National Youth Convention Chapter
c/o Yvonne Hayes
953 Greenwood Ave.
Hamilton, OH 45011-1817
Ph: (513)863-8018
E-mail: ych48@aol.com
URL: National Affiliate–www.iwla.org
Contact: Yvonne Hayes, Contact
Local. Works to educate the public to conserve, maintain, protect and restore the soil forest, water and other natural resources of the U.S.

15393 ■ Izaak Walton League of America - Ohio Division
900 Morman Rd.
Hamilton, OH 45013-4358
E-mail: tanfam5@powersupply.net
URL: http://www.iwlaohiodivision.org
Contact: Mr. Scott Tanner, VP
Members: 2,134. **Local Groups:** 23. **State**. Works to effect changes in laws and regulations by way of resolutions. Acts as a liaison between Ohio chapters and the National Headquarters. Represents members of all races, creeds, colors, and sex. **Awards:** Izaak Walton League of America - Ohio Division Scholarship. **Frequency:** annual. **Type:** scholarship. **Recipient:** to a graduating high school senior that is following a course of study in the environmental science field. **Affiliated With:** Izaak Walton League of America, Anthony Wayne Chapter; Izaak Walton League of America, Buckeye All-State Chapter; Izaak Walton League of America, Cincinnati Chapter; Izaak Walton League of America, Delta Chapter; Izaak Walton League of America, Dry Fork Chapter; Izaak Walton League of America Midwest Office; Izaak Walton League of America - Western Reserve. **Conventions/Meetings:** annual convention.

15394 ■ Miami Indian Trekkers
c/o Patricia McCormick
21 Fairborn Ct.
Hamilton, OH 45013
Ph: (513)868-7471
E-mail: jandpmcc@aol.com
URL: National Affiliate–www.ava.org
Contact: Patricia McCormick, Contact
Founded: 1982. **Members:** 101. **Membership Dues:** $2 (annual). **Local**. Non-competitive sports enthusiasts. **Awards:** Butler County Metroparks; Hamilton City Park Dept. **Frequency:** annual. **Type:** grant. **Affiliated With:** American Volkssport Association. **Publications:** Newsletter, annual. **Conventions/Meetings:** semiannual Volksmarch - meeting - always May and September.

15395 ■ Miami Valley Angus Association
c/o Dave Long, Dir.
3107 Layhigh Rd.
Hamilton, OH 45013-9406
Ph: (513)738-3933 (937)456-7868
E-mail: stewart@infinet.com
URL: http://www.angus1.com/mvaa
Contact: Dave Long, Dir.
Founded: 1954. **Local**. **Affiliated With:** American Angus Association.

15396 ■ National Active and Retired Federal Employees Association Butler/Warren Counties 569
3131 Pleasant Ave.
Hamilton, OH 45015-1740
Ph: (513)893-6777
URL: National Affiliate–www.narfe.org
Contact: Russell P. Sick, Contact
Local. Protects the retirement future of employees through education. Informs members on issues affecting the retirement. **Affiliated With:** National Association of Retired Federal Employees.

15397 ■ Ohio Public Employer Labor Relations Association (OHPELRA)
c/o Ms. Laura Joy Campbell, Pres.
315 High St., 6th Fl.
Hamilton, OH 45011
Ph: (513)887-3595
Fax: (513)785-5199
E-mail: campbellj@butlercountyohio.org
URL: http://www.ohpelra.org
Contact: Ms. Laura Joy Campbell, Pres.
Founded: 1983. **Members:** 280. **Membership Dues:** individual, $185 (annual). **Budget:** $79,800. **State**. Professional association of labor-relations and human resources professionals serving Ohio public employers, including the state, cities, counties, townships, colleges and universities, and public schools. Offers professional education and advocacy, and three training programs annually. **Affiliated With:** National Public Employer Labor Relations Association. **Conventions/Meetings:** annual conference.

15398 ■ Ohio Water Well Association (OWWA)
c/o Dan Schlosser, Exec.Dir.
3271 Springcrest Dr.
Hamilton, OH 45011
Ph: (513)895-0695
Fax: (513)895-1739
Free: (800)537-6585
E-mail: dan310@earthlink.net
URL: http://www.ohiowaterwell.org
Contact: Dave Yeager, Pres.
State. Ground water drilling contractors; manufacturers and suppliers of drilling equipment; ground water scientists such as geologists, engineers, public health officials, and others interested in the problems of locating, developing, preserving, and using ground water supplies. **Affiliated With:** National Ground Water Association.

15399 ■ Orienteering Club of Cincinnati (OCIN)
c/o Pat Meehan
1306 Southern Hills Blvd.
Hamilton, OH 45013
Ph: (513)523-9279
E-mail: mikeminium@aol.com
URL: http://www.ocin.org
Contact: Pat Meehan, Contact
Local. **Affiliated With:** United States Orienteering Federation.

15400 ■ Ross Lions Club
2575 Cincinnati-Brookville Rd.
Hamilton, OH 45014-6001
Ph: (513)738-4453
URL: http://rossoh.lionwap.org
Contact: David Nevin, Pres.
Local. **Affiliated With:** Lions Clubs International.

15401 ■ Southern Ohio Beagle Club
c/o Annette Adkins
2741 Hamilton Mason Rd.
Hamilton, OH 45011-5370
URL: National Affiliate–www.akc.org
Contact: Annette Adkins, Contact
Local.

15402 ■ TriState Habitat for Humanity
8200 Beckett Park Dr., Ste.111
Hamilton, OH 45011
Ph: (513)942-9211
Fax: (513)942-9311
E-mail: tristate@habitat-tristate.org
URL: http://www.habitat-tristate.org
Contact: Tonya Dutze, Office Admin.
Regional. **Affiliated With:** Habitat for Humanity International.

Hamler

15403 ■ American Legion, Ohio Post 262
c/o Warren L. Mc Intire
PO Box 391
Hamler, OH 43524
Ph: (740)362-7478
Fax: (740)362-1429
URL: National Affiliate–www.legion.org
Contact: Warren L. Mc Intire, Contact
Local. **Affiliated With:** American Legion.

Hammondsville

15404 ■ American Legion, Hammondsville Post 742
PO Box 162
Hammondsville, OH 43930
Ph: (740)362-7478
Fax: (740)362-1429
URL: National Affiliate–www.legion.org
Local. **Affiliated With:** American Legion.

Hannibal

15405 ■ American Legion, Ohio Valley Post 760
PO Box 273
Hannibal, OH 43931
Ph: (740)362-7478
Fax: (740)362-1429
URL: National Affiliate–www.legion.org
Local. **Affiliated With:** American Legion.

Harrison

15406 ■ American Legion, Ohio Post 199
c/o Jennings Bryan Yeager
PO Box 603
Harrison, OH 45030

Ph: (740)362-7478
Fax: (740)362-1429
URL: National Affiliate–www.legion.org
Contact: Jennings Bryan Yeager, Contact
Local. Affiliated With: American Legion.

15407 ■ Crosby Township Historical Society
8910 Willey Rd.
Box 12
Harrison, OH 45030-9774
Ph: (513)738-1440
E-mail: crosbytwp@aol.com
Contact: Sara Waugh, Historian
Founded: 1996. **Members:** 100. **Membership Dues:** life, $100 • family, $12 (annual) • single, $5 (annual). **Local.** Strives to preserve the history of Crosby Township. Collects local and family histories, photos and other artifacts for the education and appreciation of everyone. **Publications:** *Crosby Township Historical*, quarterly. Newsletter. **Conventions/Meetings:** monthly meeting, features topics of local or general history - third Thursday.

Hartford

15408 ■ Hartford Youth Baseball and Softball
c/o Constance J. Humenik
PO Box 70
Hartford, OH 44424-0070
Local.

Hartville

15409 ■ American Welding Society, Stark Central Section 085
c/o Mike Medal, Chm.
12071 Market Ave. N
Hartville, OH 44632
Ph: (330)575-7123
E-mail: sirmm58@aol.com
URL: National Affiliate–www.aws.org
Contact: Mike Medal, Contact
Local. Promotes the interests of professional engineering society in the field of welding. **Affiliated With:** American Welding Society.

15410 ■ Hartville Lions Club
c/o Chuck Moyer, Sec.
PO Box 273
Hartville, OH 44632
Ph: (330)877-1118
E-mail: moyerc@neo.rr.com
URL: http://www.lions13d.org
Contact: Chuck Moyer, Sec.
Local. Affiliated With: Lions Clubs International.

15411 ■ Lake Township Chamber of Commerce (LTCC)
PO Box 1207
Hartville, OH 44632
Ph: (330)877-5500
E-mail: president@lakechamber.com
URL: http://www.lakechamber.com
Contact: Paul Tarr, Pres.
Membership Dues: business (based on number of employees), $145-$215 (annual) • business (new), $75 (annual) • individual, non-profit organization, $50 (annual). **Local.** Promotes business and community development in the Hartville, OH area. **Computer Services:** database, membership directory. **Committees:** Economic Development; Marketing and Tourism;- Pro-Business Advocacy; Resource Support. **Conventions/Meetings:** monthly board meeting - every 2nd Wednesday • monthly Pro-Business Advocacy Committee Meeting - every 1st Monday • monthly Resource Committee Meeting - every 1st Tuesday.

15412 ■ North American Butterfly Association - Northeastern Ohio
Chrysalis In Time
PO Box 1183
Hartville, OH 44632
Ph: (330)699-6213
E-mail: c_liebson@hotmail.com
URL: http://www.naba.org/chapters/nabano/publish/index.html
Contact: Judy Semroc, Pres.
Membership Dues: local chapter, $5 (annual) • life, $50. **Local. Affiliated With:** North American Butterfly Association.

Heath

15413 ■ Heath Lions Club
1141 Conn Way Dr.
Heath, OH 43056
Ph: (740)522-4408 (740)364-0845
E-mail: wesisco@alltel.net
URL: http://heathoh.lionwap.org
Contact: Ken Scott, Pres.
Local. Affiliated With: Lions Clubs International.

Hebron

15414 ■ American Fisheries Society, Ohio Chapter (OCAFS)
c/o Stacy Xenakis, Sec.-Treas.
10517 Canal Rd.
Hebron, OH 43025
URL: http://www.biosci.ohio-state.edu/~ocafs
Contact: Stacy Xenakis, Sec.-Treas.
Founded: 1974. **Members:** 100. **Membership Dues:** all, $100 (annual). **State.** Promotes conservation of fisheries and aquatic resources. Provides information, professional services, and opportunities for aquatic stewardship to Ohio's fisheries professionals, educators, students, and conservationists. **Awards:** AFS Professional Certification Grant. **Frequency:** annual. **Type:** grant. **Recipient:** to a qualified fisheries professional • Ohio Academy of Science, Milt Austin Award. **Frequency:** annual. **Type:** monetary. **Recipient:** for best aquatic science project • OSU Stone Laboratory Scholarship. **Frequency:** annual. **Type:** scholarship. **Recipient:** to a qualified student • Travel Grant, Midwest Fish and Wildlife Conference. **Frequency:** annual. **Type:** grant. **Recipient:** to a qualified student. **Subgroups:** Aquatic Stewardship; Information Transfer and Outreach. **Affiliated With:** American Fisheries Society.

15415 ■ American Legion, Hebron Post 285
108 Water St.
Hebron, OH 43025
Ph: (740)362-7478
Fax: (740)362-1429
URL: National Affiliate–www.legion.org
Local. Affiliated With: American Legion.

15416 ■ Reynoldsburg Lions Club
c/o Richard Manifold, Sec.
77 Lakeshore Dr.
Hebron, OH 43025
Ph: (740)928-1718
E-mail: rmani@earthlink.net
URL: http://www.iwaynet.net/~lions13f
Contact: Richard Manifold, Sec.
Local. Affiliated With: Lions Clubs International.

Hicksville

15417 ■ American Legion, Ohio Post 223
c/o Edward C. Smart
PO Box 15
Hicksville, OH 43526
Ph: (740)362-7478
Fax: (740)362-1429
URL: National Affiliate–www.legion.org
Contact: Edward C. Smart, Contact
Local. Affiliated With: American Legion.

15418 ■ International Association of Machinists and Aerospace Workers, AFL-CIO, CLC - Local Lodge 2484
207 Dixon Ave.
Hicksville, OH 43526
E-mail: dinky@highstream.net
URL: http://ll2484.goiam.org/index.htm
Contact: Gene Starbuck, Pres.
Members: 148. **Local. Affiliated With:** International Association of Machinists and Aerospace Workers.

Highland Heights

15419 ■ American Institute of Chemical Engineers - Cleveland Section
837 Eastlawn Dr.
Highland Heights, OH 44143
Ph: (216)509-2806
E-mail: clroe12@aol.com
URL: http://www.ctsc.org/aichecle
Contact: Chuck Roe, Vice Chm.
Local. Represents the interests of chemical engineering professionals. Aims to contribute to the improvement of chemical engineering curricula offered in universities. Seeks to enhance the lifelong career development and financial security of chemical engineers through products, services, networking and advocacy. **Affiliated With:** American Institute of Chemical Engineers.

Highland Hills

15420 ■ Associated Landscape Contractors of America, Cuyahoga Community College
c/o David Emmitt, Faculty Advisor
Plant Sci. and Landscape Tech.
4250 Richmond Rd.
Highland Hills, OH 44122
Ph: (216)987-2235
Fax: (216)987-2237
E-mail: dave.emmitt@tri.c.edu
URL: National Affiliate–www.alca.org
Contact: David Emmitt, Faculty Advisor
Local. Affiliated With: Professional Landcare Network.

15421 ■ College Reading and Learning Association, Ohio River Valley
c/o Sandie Crawford
Cuyahoga Community Coll.
4250 Richmond Rd.
Highland Hills, OH 44122-6104
Ph: (216)987-2111
Fax: (216)987-2520
E-mail: sandie.crawford@tri-c.edu
URL: National Affiliate–www.crla.net
Contact: Sandie Crawford, Contact
State. Represents student-oriented professionals active in the fields of reading, learning assistance, developmental education and tutorial services at the college/adult level. Provides a forum for the interchange of ideas, methods and information to improve student learning and to facilitate the professional growth of members. **Affiliated With:** College Reading and Learning Association.

15422 ■ Phi Theta Kappa - Alpha Epsilon Eta Chapter
c/o Michael Rowan
E Campus
4250 Richmond Rd.
Highland Hills, OH 44122-6104

Ph: (216)987-2368
E-mail: michael.rowan@tri-c.edu
URL: http://www.ptk.org/directories/chapters/OH/314-1.htm
Contact: Michael Rowan, Advisor
Local. Affiliated With: Phi Theta Kappa, International Honor Society.

Hilliard

15423 ■ AAA Ohio Automobile Club
4601 Leap Ct.
Hilliard, OH 43026
Ph: (614)771-5777
State.

15424 ■ Acoustical Society of America - Central Ohio Chapter
c/o Angelo Campanella, Chm.
3201 Ridgewood Dr.
Hilliard, OH 43026-2453
Ph: (614)876-5108
E-mail: acampane@postbox.acs.ohio-state.edu
URL: National Affiliate–asa.aip.org
Contact: Angelo Campanella, Chm.
Local. Represents the interests of individuals working in the field of acoustics. Aims to increase and diffuse the knowledge of acoustics and to promote its practical applications. **Affiliated With:** Acoustical Society of America.

15425 ■ American Legion, Memorial Post 614
3898 Lattimer St.
Hilliard, OH 43026
Ph: (740)362-7478
Fax: (740)362-1429
URL: National Affiliate–www.legion.org
Local. Affiliated With: American Legion.

15426 ■ Arthritis Foundation, Central Ohio Chapter
3740 Ridge Mill Dr.
Hilliard, OH 43026
Ph: (614)876-8200
Fax: (614)876-8363
Free: (888)382-4673
E-mail: info.coh@arthritis.org
URL: National Affiliate–www.arthritis.org
Contact: Irene Baird, Pres./Exec.Dir.
Founded: 1954. **Members:** 13,500. **Staff:** 11. **Budget:** $750,000. **Local.** Seeks to discover the causes of and cure for arthritis. **Computer Services:** Information services, local physician referral list. **Programs:** Joints in Motion; Local Political Advocacy. **Subgroups:** Volunteer. **Affiliated With:** Arthritis Foundation.

15427 ■ ASIS International, Columbus Ohio Chapter 27
c/o Tom E. Ingstrum, CPP, Pres.
YUM Brands, Inc.
5383 Carina Ct.
Hilliard, OH 43026
Ph: (614)876-6040
Fax: (614)876-6040
E-mail: tom.ingstrum@yum.com
URL: http://www.asis27.org
Contact: Tom E. Ingstrum CPP, Pres.
Local. Seeks to increase the effectiveness and productivity of security practices by developing educational programs and materials that address security concerns. **Affiliated With:** ASIS International.

15428 ■ Brookfield Village Homeowners Association (BVHA)
c/o Rob Healy, Treas.
PO Box 244
Hilliard, OH 43026
E-mail: rlmhealy@columbus.rr.com
URL: http://www.bvha.info
Contact: Rob Healy, Treas.
Founded: 2001. **Members:** 500. **Staff:** 4. **Local. Publications:** *Brookfield Village View*, quarterly. Newsletter. **Advertising:** accepted.

15429 ■ Central Ohio Council of Teachers of Mathematics
6111 Parkmeadow Ln.
Hilliard, OH 43026
Ph: (614)777-2926 (614)921-7104
Fax: (614)777-2424
E-mail: jerome_mescher@fclass.hilliard.k12.oh.us
URL: http://www.ohioctm.org
Contact: Vicky Kirschner, District Dir.
Local. Aims to improve the teaching and learning of mathematics. Provides vision, leadership and professional development to support teachers in ensuring mathematics learning of the highest quality for all students. **Affiliated With:** National Council of Teachers of Mathematics.

15430 ■ Columbus African Violet Society (CAVS)
c/o Mary Martin
6033 Heritage View Ct.
Hilliard, OH 43026
Ph: (614)529-0589
E-mail: martin6033@sbcglobal.net
URL: National Affiliate–www.avsa.org
Contact: Mary Martin, Contact
Local. Affiliated With: African Violet Society of America.

15431 ■ Columbus Miniature Society
c/o Linda Patterson
3579 Braidwood Dr.
Hilliard, OH 43026
Ph: (614)876-3579
E-mail: lindapatterson@columbus.rr.com
URL: http://www.miniatures.org/states/OH.html
Contact: Linda Patterson, Contact
Local. Affiliated With: National Association of Miniature Enthusiasts.

15432 ■ DADS America, Ohio
c/o Chris Tock, Representative
5599 Sandbrook Ln.
Hilliard, OH 43026
Ph: (614)527-1411
E-mail: ctock@columbus.rr.com
URL: http://www.dadsamerica.org/OH/oh.htm
Contact: Chris Tock, Representative
State. Affiliated With: Dads Against Discrimination.

15433 ■ Hilliard Area Chamber of Commerce (HACC)
4081 Main St.
Hilliard, OH 43026-1501
Ph: (614)876-7666
Fax: (614)876-3113
E-mail: info@hilliardchamber.org
URL: http://www.hilliardchamber.org
Contact: Libby Gierach, Pres./CEO
Founded: 1973. **Members:** 370. **Membership Dues:** business, $140-$460 (annual) • individual, $80 (annual) • nonprofit organization and church, $115 (annual). **Staff:** 1. **Local.** Businesses, organizations, and government officials organized to promote business and community development in northwestern Franklin County, OH. Sponsors seminars; holds luncheons and Business After Hours parties. Awards scholarships. Sponsors Hollyfest auction and art fair. **Awards:** Business/Business Person of the Year. **Frequency:** annual. **Type:** recognition. **Recipient:** for outstanding contributions to the business and community • Galbreath Award. **Type:** recognition. **Recipient:** for excellence in volunteer service • Hollyfest Scholarship Foundation. **Frequency:** annual. **Type:** scholarship. **Recipient:** to a graduating student of Hilliard High School. **Computer Services:** Online services, membership directory. **Publications:** *Hilliard Area Chamber of Commerce Professional Directory*, annual • *News and Views*, monthly. Newsletter. **Advertising:** accepted. Alternate Formats: online • Membership Directory, annual. **Advertising:** accepted.

15434 ■ Hilliard Davidson Athletic Boosters
PO Box 1302
Hilliard, OH 43026
E-mail: david_banyots@fclass.hilliard.k12.oh.us
URL: http://eteamz.active.com/hdaboosters
Contact: Aristotle Hutrus, Pres.
Local.

15435 ■ Mid-Ohio Vair Force
4673 NW Pkwy.
Hilliard, OH 43026
E-mail: VairForceOne@webtv.net
URL: National Affiliate–www.corvair.org
Founded: 1983. **Members:** 30. **Membership Dues:** $12 (annual). **Local.** Corvair owners in central Ohio. Provides technical assistance and assists in locating parts. Sponsors technical sessions and social events. **Affiliated With:** Corvair Society of America. **Publications:** *Meeting Notice*, monthly. Newsletter • *Vair Voice*, monthly. **Conventions/Meetings:** monthly meeting.

15436 ■ National Association of Disability Examiners, Great Lakes
c/o Susan Smith, Dir.
5781 Coldcreek Dr.
Hilliard, OH 43026
Ph: (614)438-1879
Free: (888)672-5261
E-mail: susan.x.smith@ssa.gov
URL: National Affiliate–www.nade.org
Contact: Susan Smith, Dir.
Regional. Develops the art and science of disability evaluation. Enhances public awareness of disability evaluation. Furthers the professional recognition for disability evaluation practitioners. **Affiliated With:** National Association of Disability Examiners.

15437 ■ National Association for Multicultural Education, Ohio Chapter
c/o Robin Brenneman, Pres.
Hilliard-Davison Public Schools
4105 Saturn Rd.
Hilliard, OH 43026
Ph: (614)527-4407
E-mail: kenrob@columbus.rr.com
URL: http://www.nameorg.org/Chapters/Ohio/OH.html
Contact: Robin Brenneman, Pres.
State. Represents individuals and groups with an interest in multicultural education from all levels of education, different academic disciplines and from diverse educational institutions and occupations. Provides leadership in national and state dialogues on equity, diversity and multicultural education. Works to fight injustices in schools and in communities. Seeks to ensure that all students receive an equitable education. **Affiliated With:** National Association for Multicultural Education.

15438 ■ National Spa and Pool Institute Central Ohio Chapter
c/o Steven Ramey, Pres.
Suburban Pool and Spa
3920 Scioto Darby Rd.
Hilliard, OH 43026-9701
Ph: (614)777-0100
URL: National Affiliate–www.nspi.org
State. Affiliated With: Association of Pool and Spa Professionals.

15439 ■ Ohio Council for the Social Studies (OCSS)
c/o Linda Logan, Membership Dir.
3258 Scioto Farms Dr.
Hilliard, OH 43026
E-mail: llogan@columbus.rr.com
URL: http://www.ocss.org
Contact: Linda Logan, Membership Dir.
State. Represents teachers of elementary and secondary social studies, including instructors of civics, geography, history, law, economics, political science, psychology, sociology, and anthropology. Promotes the teaching of social studies. Provides members with opportunities to share strategies, have

access to new material, and keep abreast of the national education scene. **Affiliated With:** National Council for the Social Studies.

15440 ■ Ohio Ophthalmological Society (OOS)
3401 Mill Run Dr.
Hilliard, OH 43026
Ph: (614)527-6799
Fax: (614)527-6763
E-mail: oos@ohioeye.org
URL: http://www.ohioeye.org
Contact: Todd Baker, Exec.Dir.
Founded: 1961. **State**.

15441 ■ Ohio State Medical Association (OSMA)
c/o Brent Mulgrew, Exec.Dir.
3401 Mill Run Dr.
Hilliard, OH 43026
Ph: (614)527-6762
Fax: (614)527-6763
Free: (800)766-6762
E-mail: info@osma.org
URL: http://www.osma.org
Contact: Brent Mulgrew, Exec.Dir.
State.

Hillsboro

15442 ■ American Legion, Ohio Post 129
c/o Raymond R. Stout
185 Montz St.
Hillsboro, OH 45133
Ph: (740)362-7478
Fax: (740)362-1429
URL: National Affiliate–www.legion.org
Contact: Raymond R. Stout, Contact
Local. Affiliated With: American Legion.

15443 ■ Appalachian Appaloosa Association
c/o Tim Sheeley
11325 State, Rte. 506
Hillsboro, OH 45133
Ph: (937)466-2124
E-mail: ksheeley@intouch.net
URL: National Affiliate–www.appaloosa.com
Contact: Tim Sheeley, Contact
Local. Affiliated With: Appaloosa Horse Club.

15444 ■ Highland Beagle Club
c/o Mike Wilson
2185 Grooms Ln.
Hillsboro, OH 45133
URL: National Affiliate–clubs.akc.org
Contact: Mike Wilson, Contact
Local.

15445 ■ Highland County Board of Realtors
216 N High St.
Hillsboro, OH 45133
Ph: (937)393-1948
Fax: (937)393-1940
E-mail: bonamey@yahoo.com
URL: National Affiliate–www.realtor.org
Contact: Bonnie Amey, Exec. Officer
Local. Strives to develop real estate business practices. Advocates for the right to own, use and transfer real property. Provides a facility for professional development, research and exchange of information among members and the general public. **Affiliated With:** National Association of Realtors.

15446 ■ Highland County Chamber of Commerce (HACC)
1575 N High St., Ste.400
Hillsboro, OH 45133-0296
Ph: (937)393-1111
Fax: (937)393-2697
E-mail: hccoc@cinci.rr.com
Contact: Melody Johnson, Pres./CEO
Local. Promotes business and community development in the Highland County, OH area. **Affiliated With:** U.S. Chamber of Commerce. **Formerly:** Hillsboro Area Chamber of Commerce. **Publications:** Membership Directory, periodic • Newsletter, monthly. **Conventions/Meetings:** annual meeting - always in March.

15447 ■ Ohio Association of Agricultural Educators (OAAE)
c/o Tom Oglesby, Pres.
3925 W New Market Rd.
Hillsboro, OH 45133
Ph: (937)288-9802 (740)828-3832
E-mail: mvgraham@agristar.net
URL: http://www.oaae.info
Contact: Tom Oglesby, Pres.
State. Seeks to advance agricultural education and promotes the professional interests and growth of agriculture teachers. Provides agricultural education through visionary leadership, advocacy and service. **Affiliated With:** National Association of Agricultural Educators.

15448 ■ Ohio Health Care Association, District 8
c/o Tim McGowan, Chm.
Laurels Of Hillsboro
175 Chillicothe Ave.
Hillsboro, OH 45133
Ph: (937)393-1925
Fax: (937)393-3666
E-mail: tmcgowan@laurelhealth.com
URL: http://www.ohca.org
Contact: Tim McGowan, Chm.
Local. Promotes professionalism and ethical behavior of individuals providing long-term care delivery for patients and for the general public. Provides information, education and administrative tools to enhance the quality of long-term care. Improves the standards of service and administration of member nursing homes. **Affiliated With:** American Health Care Association.

15449 ■ Phi Theta Kappa - Alpha Omicron Eta Chapter
c/o Jessica Wise, Advisor
100 Hobart Dr.
Hillsboro, OH 45133
Ph: (937)393-3431
E-mail: jwise@sscc.edu
URL: http://www.ptk.org/directories/chapters/OH/5919-1.htm
Contact: Ms. Jessica Wise, Advisor
Local. Affiliated With: Phi Theta Kappa, International Honor Society.

15450 ■ Reserve Officers Association - Department of Ohio, General Grant Chapter 28
c/o Capt. Phyllis Clousner, Pres.
6910 Beechwood Rd.
Hillsboro, OH 45133-8449
Ph: (937)393-4917
URL: http://www.roa.org/oh
Contact: Capt. Phyllis Clousner, Pres.
Local. Promotes and supports the development and execution of a military policy for the United States. Provides professional development seminars, workshops and programs for its members. **Affiliated With:** Reserve Officers Association of the United States.

15451 ■ Southern Ohio Draft Horse Association
6831 US Hwy. 50 W
Hillsboro, OH 45133
Ph: (937)393-3525
URL: National Affiliate–www.nasdha.net/RegionalAssoc.htm
Contact: Ruth Bloom, Pres.
State.

Hinckley

15452 ■ North Coast Fossil Club (NCFC)
c/o Tony Verdi, Pres.
1225 Ledge Rd.
Hinckley, OH 44233
E-mail: vicepresident@ncfclub.org
URL: http://www.ncfclub.org
Contact: Sharon McKanze, Sec.
Regional. Aims to further the study of Earth Sciences and the practice of lapidary arts and mineralogy. **Affiliated With:** American Federation of Mineralogical Societies.

Hiram

15453 ■ Muslim Students' Association - Hiram College
c/o Muntazir Dhala
PO Box 67
Hiram, OH 44234
Ph: (330)569-3211
URL: http://www.geocities.com/TheTropics/Resort/2012
Contact: Muntazir Dhala, Contact
Local. Muslim students in North America. Seeks to advance the interests of members; works to enable members to practice Islam as a complete way of life. **Affiliated With:** Muslim Students Association of the United States and Canada.

Holgate

15454 ■ American Legion, Wm. F. Helmke Post 340
215 Elm St.
Holgate, OH 43527
Ph: (740)362-7478
Fax: (740)362-1429
URL: National Affiliate–www.legion.org
Local. Affiliated With: American Legion.

Holland

15455 ■ American Chemical Society, Toledo Section
c/o Joseph A. Grappin, Chm.
2141 Longacre Ln.
Holland, OH 43528-9694
Ph: (419)897-9000
E-mail: ja.grappin@sbcglobal.net
URL: National Affiliate–acswebcontent.acs.org
Contact: Joseph A. Grappin, Chm.
Local. Represents the interests of individuals dedicated to the advancement of chemistry in all its branches. Provides opportunities for peer interaction and career development. **Affiliated With:** American Chemical Society.

15456 ■ American Legion, Holland Post 646
1074 Clarion Ave.
Holland, OH 43528
Ph: (740)362-7478
Fax: (740)362-1429
URL: National Affiliate–www.legion.org
Local. Affiliated With: American Legion.

15457 ■ Glass Center Coin Club
c/o Royce S. Hutchinson
7331 Sioux Trail
Holland, OH 43528
Ph: (419)861-3954
E-mail: hpborden_62@msn.com
URL: http://www.geocities.com/glasscentercoin
Contact: Royce S. Hutchinson, Contact
Local. Affiliated With: American Numismatic Association.

15458 ■ Holland - Springfield Chamber of Commerce
1032 S McCord Rd.
Holland, OH 43528
Ph: (419)865-2110
Fax: (419)865-4888
E-mail: info@hollandspringfieldcoc.org
URL: http://www.hollandspringfieldcoc.org
Contact: Mary Green, Pres.
Founded: 1990. **Membership Dues:** business (based on number of employees), $130-$470 (annual). **Local**. Represents businesses. Provides business endorsements and referrals to members. **Publications:** Newsletter, monthly.

15459 ■ Toledo Youth for Christ
PO Box 12
Holland, OH 43528
Ph: (419)865-1442
URL: National Affiliate–www.yfc.net
Local. Affiliated With: Youth for Christ/U.S.A.

15460 ■ United Food and Commercial Workers, Local 911
PO Box 966
Holland, OH 43528
Ph: (419)865-1341
Fax: (419)865-8674
Free: (800)232-8279
E-mail: ufcw911@buckeye-express.com
URL: http://www.ufcw911.com
Local. Affiliated With: United Food and Commercial Workers International Union.

Hollansburg

15461 ■ American Legion, Ohio Post 708
c/o Niles Richards
PO Box 20
Hollansburg, OH 45332
Ph: (740)362-7478
Fax: (740)362-1429
URL: National Affiliate–www.legion.org
Contact: Niles Richards, Contact
Local. Affiliated With: American Legion.

Holmesville

15462 ■ American Legion, Ohio Post 551
c/o Melvin Mc Clure
9150 Sr 83
Holmesville, OH 44633
Ph: (740)362-7478
Fax: (740)362-1429
URL: National Affiliate–www.legion.org
Contact: Melvin Mc Clure, Contact
Local. Affiliated With: American Legion.

15463 ■ Prairie Township Volunteer Fire Dept
118 E Jackson St.
Holmesville, OH 44633-0000
Ph: (330)279-2552
Contact: Mose Yoder, Fire Chief
Local.

Homerville

15464 ■ American Saddlebred Horse Association of Ohio
c/o Marcia Belcher
7972 Firestone Rd.
Homerville, OH 44235
Ph: (330)625-1009
E-mail: mbelcher@directway.com
URL: http://www.ohiosaddlebred.com
Contact: Marcia Belcher, Contact
State. Affiliated With: American Saddlebred Horse Association.

15465 ■ Rustbelt 4x4 Trailriders Association
PO Box 0023
Homerville, OH 44235
Ph: (330)648-2470
E-mail: rustpilot@aol.com
URL: http://www.ufwda.org/showmembers.php?cat=A75
Local. Affiliated With: United Four-Wheel Drive Associations.

Hopedale

15466 ■ American Legion, Hopedale Post 682
PO Box 486
Hopedale, OH 43976
Ph: (740)362-7478
Fax: (740)362-1429
URL: National Affiliate–www.legion.org
Local. Affiliated With: American Legion.

Howard

15467 ■ East Knox Lions Club
PO Box 3
Howard, OH 43028
Ph: (740)392-4994
E-mail: avjemb@ecr.net
URL: http://eastknoxlionscluboh.lionwap.org
Contact: Howard Cherry, Pres.
Local. Affiliated With: Lions Clubs International.

15468 ■ NACM Hartland
PO Box 339
Howard, OH 43028
Fax: (740)397-6915
Free: (888)222-1447
E-mail: wcroyle@nacmhartland.com
Contact: William Croyle, Chief Operating Officer
Local. Affiliated With: National Association of Credit Management. **Formerly:** (2005) National Association of Credit Management Heartland Unit.

Hubbard

15469 ■ American Legion, Hubbard Post 51
27 Hager St.
Hubbard, OH 44425
Ph: (740)362-7478
Fax: (740)362-1429
URL: National Affiliate–www.legion.org
Local. Affiliated With: American Legion.

15470 ■ First Catholic Slovak Ladies Association - Struthers Junior Branch 066
47 Westview
Hubbard, OH 44425
Ph: (330)534-3280
URL: National Affiliate–www.fcsla.com
Local. Affiliated With: First Catholic Slovak Ladies Association.

15471 ■ Hubbard Lions Club
c/o Elmer Berstling, Sec.
448 Sunset Dr.
Hubbard, OH 44425
Ph: (330)534-1788
E-mail: guinsfans@aol.com
URL: http://www.lions13d.org
Contact: Elmer Berstling, Sec.
Local. Affiliated With: Lions Clubs International.

Huber Heights

15472 ■ American Legion, Huber Heights Post 200
5046 Nebraska Ave.
Huber Heights, OH 45424
Ph: (937)236-9283
Fax: (740)362-1429
URL: National Affiliate–www.legion.org
Local. Affiliated With: American Legion.

15473 ■ Antique Automobile Club of America, Ohio Region - Southern Chapter
c/o Ronald L. Taylor, Trustee
6793 Bellefontaine Rd.
Huber Heights, OH 45424
Ph: (937)233-8748
E-mail: s1913d@aol.com
URL: http://local.aaca.org/ohio/southern.htm
Contact: Jay Kolb, Pres.
Founded: 1954. **Local.** Collectors, hobbyists, and others interested in the preservation, maintenance, and restoration of automobiles and in automotive history. **Affiliated With:** Antique Automobile Club of America.

15474 ■ Clark County Beagle Club
c/o Don Bringman
6911 Citrus Cir.
Huber Heights, OH 45424-7011
URL: National Affiliate–clubs.akc.org
Contact: Don Bringman, Contact
Local.

15475 ■ Epilepsy Foundation of Western Ohio
7523 Brandt Park
Huber Heights, OH 45424-2337
Ph: (937)233-2500
Fax: (937)233-5439
Free: (800)360-3296
E-mail: jpoppa@ohioepilepsy.org
URL: http://www.epilepsyfoundation.org/westernohio
Contact: Janine Poppa, Pres./CEO
Founded: 1974. **Local.** Ensures that people with seizures are able to participate in all life experiences. Aims to prevent, control and cure epilepsy through research, education, advocacy and services. **Affiliated With:** Epilepsy Foundation.

15476 ■ Huber Heights Chamber of Commerce
4756 Fishburg Rd.
Huber Heights, OH 45424-4046
Ph: (937)233-5700
Fax: (937)233-5769
E-mail: hhchamber@sbcglobal.net
URL: http://www.huberheightschamber.com
Contact: Pat Stephens, Exec.Dir.
Founded: 1980. **Members:** 300. **Membership Dues:** business (based on number of employees), $140-$585 • realtor, $210 • bank, $315 • utility, $500. **For-Profit. Local.** Promotes business and community development in Huber Heights, OH. **Computer Services:** Information services, membership directory. **Publications:** Newsletter, monthly.

15477 ■ National Active and Retired Federal Employees Association - Huber Heights 2238
7100 Encanto Pl.
Huber Heights, OH 45424-3141
Ph: (937)236-2489
URL: National Affiliate–www.narfe.org
Contact: Lawrence E. Reed, Contact
Local. Protects the retirement future of employees through education. Informs members on issues affecting the retirement. **Affiliated With:** National Association of Retired Federal Employees.

15478 ■ United States Naval Sea Cadet Corps - Dayton Division
St. Peters Church
6161 Chamersburg Rd.
Huber Heights, OH 45424-3808
E-mail: lashton@sbp-in.com
URL: http://dolphin.seacadets.org/US_units/UnitDetails.asp?UnitID=041DAY
Contact: LCDR Lee D. Ashton NSCC, Commanding Officer
Local. Works to instill good citizenship and patriotism in youth. Encourages qualities such as personal neatness, loyalty, obedience, dependability, and responsibility to others. Offers courses in physical fitness and military drill, first aid, water safety, basic seamanship, and naval history and traditions. **Affiliated With:** Naval Sea Cadet Corps.

Hudson

15479 ■ AAA Akron Automobile Club
179 W Sts.boro Rd.
Hudson, OH 44236-2708
Ph: (330)650-6727
Local.

15480 ■ American Legion, Lee-Bishop Post 464
5790 Hudson Dr.
Hudson, OH 44236
Ph: (740)362-7478
Fax: (740)362-1429
URL: National Affiliate–www.legion.org
Local. Affiliated With: American Legion.

15481 ■ Hudson Area Chamber of Commerce (HACC)
156 N Main St.
Hudson, OH 44236-0700
Ph: (330)650-0621
Fax: (330)656-1646
E-mail: info@hudsoncoc.org
URL: http://www.hudsoncoc.org
Contact: Carolyn Konefal, Exec.Dir.
Founded: 1983. **Members:** 280. **Membership Dues:** business, $195-$900 (annual) • self employed (no employee), $130 (annual) • associate (representative of current member business), $130 (annual) • retiree, $50 (annual) • executive, $2,500 (annual). **Local.** Promotes business and community development in the Hudson, OH area. Holds annual dinner. **Computer Services:** Online services, member listings. **Committees:** Ambassadors; Downtown Development; Fund Raising; Golf Outing; Legislative Affairs; Nominating; Policy/By-Laws; Scholarship/Education. **Affiliated With:** U.S. Chamber of Commerce. **Publications:** *Bulletin*, monthly. Newsletter. **Advertising:** accepted • *Business Link*, monthly. Newsletter. **Advertising:** accepted. Alternate Formats: online • *Community Profile*, annual • *Industrial Guide*. **Conventions/Meetings:** monthly meeting.

15482 ■ Hudson Genealogical Study Group (HGSG)
Hudson Lib. and Historical Soc., Dept. G
96 Lib. St.
Hudson, OH 44236
Ph: (330)653-6658
E-mail: hgsg@bigfoot.com
URL: http://www.rootsweb.com/~ohhudogs/hudson.htm
Contact: Jack Bowers, Pres.
Founded: 1990. **Members:** 120. **Membership Dues:** individual, $10 (annual) • family, $12 (annual). **Budget:** $6,500. **State Groups:** 1. **Local.** Individuals interested in genealogy. Works to promote interest in genealogical research. Provides support to the archives of the Hudson Library and Historical Society. Conducts educational activities, including professional training in research techniques. **Libraries: Type:** open to the public. **Holdings:** articles, books, periodicals. **Subjects:** local history, genealogy. **Affiliated With:** Ohio Genealogical Society. **Also Known As:** Ohio Genealogical Society, Hudson Chapter. **Publications:** *The Hudson Green*, quarterly. Newsletter. Alternate Formats: online • Books • Directory, periodic. **Conventions/Meetings:** quarterly meeting, with lecture • weekly meeting.

15483 ■ Hudson Library and Historical Society (HLHS)
96 Lib. St.
Hudson, OH 44236
Ph: (330)653-6658
Fax: (330)650-4693
E-mail: mailref@hudson.lib.oh.us
URL: http://hudsonlibrary.org
Contact: E. Leslie Polott, Dir./Curator
Founded: 1910. **Staff:** 46. **Budget:** $1,200,000. **Local.** Individuals interested in the history of Hudson and Summit County, OH. Operates genealogical research facilities. Supports and provides assistance to the local public library. **Libraries: Type:** reference. **Holdings:** 128,904. **Publications:** *Books to Bytes*, quarterly. Newsletter. **Price:** free to every household in Hudson. **Conventions/Meetings:** quarterly Baldwin-Babcock Lecture Series.

15484 ■ Hudson Premier Table Tennis Club
Hudson High School
2400 Hudson Rd.
Hudson, OH 44236
Ph: (330)655-2502
E-mail: hudsonpremierttc@yahoo.com
URL: National Affiliate–www.usatt.org
Contact: Robert Salone, Contact
Local. Affiliated With: U.S.A. Table Tennis.

15485 ■ Hudson - Young Life
7169 Huntington
Hudson, OH 44236
Ph: (330)655-7688
URL: http://sites.younglife.org/_layouts/ylext/default.aspx?ID=C-1532
Local. Affiliated With: Young Life.

15486 ■ Kent Figure Skating Club
5750 Nicholson Dr.
Hudson, OH 44236
E-mail: johnandmeg@adelphia.net
URL: http://www.kentskatingclub.com
Contact: John Faust, Contact
Local. Provides programs to encourage participation and achievement in the sport of figure skating on ice. Defines and maintains uniform standards of skating proficiency. Organizes and sponsors competitions and exhibitions for the purpose of stimulating interest in figure skating. **Affiliated With:** United States Figure Skating Association.

15487 ■ Ohio Genealogical Society, Hudson Genealogical Study Group
c/o Hudson Library and Historical Society
96 Lib. St.
Hudson, OH 44236
E-mail: jackbowers2002@yahoo.com
URL: http://www.rootsweb.com/~ohhudogs/hudson.htm
Contact: Jack Bowers, Pres.
Local. Affiliated With: Ohio Genealogical Society.

15488 ■ Young Life Western Reserve
7169 Huntington
Hudson, OH 44236
Ph: (330)655-7688
Fax: (330)655-7688
URL: http://sites.younglife.org/_layouts/ylext/default.aspx?ID=A-OH34
Local. Affiliated With: Young Life.

Huntsville

15489 ■ American Legion, Ohio Post 381
c/o Charles Collins
PO Box 272
Huntsville, OH 43324
Ph: (740)362-7478
Fax: (740)362-1429
URL: National Affiliate–www.legion.org
Contact: Charles Collins, Contact
Local. Affiliated With: American Legion.

Huron

15490 ■ Fraternal Order of Eagles, Huron No. 2875
PO Box 454
Huron, OH 44839
Ph: (419)433-4611
Fax: (419)433-8854
E-mail: eagle310@buckeye-express.com
URL: http://www.foe2875.com
Contact: Harold Edwards, Pres.
Local. Affiliated With: Grand Aerie, Fraternal Order of Eagles.

15491 ■ Huron Chamber of Commerce (HCC)
PO Box 43
Huron, OH 44839
Ph: (419)433-5700
Fax: (419)433-5700
E-mail: chamber@huron.net
URL: http://www.huron.net
Contact: Sheila Ehrhardt, Dir.
Members: 175. **Membership Dues:** associate, civic group, community service, education, religious, individual, $55 (annual) • food service, marina, lodging, broker, insurance, professional, retail, wholesale, service, automotive, $125-$300 (annual) • industrial/manufacturing, financial, utility, $175-$400 (annual). **Local.** Promotes business and community development in Huron, OH. **Affiliated With:** U.S. Chamber of Commerce. **Publications:** *The Wave*, monthly. Newsletter. Alternate Formats: online. **Conventions/Meetings:** monthly luncheon.

15492 ■ Huron Lions Club
c/o Tony Lisa, Pres.
317 Chevy Dr.
Huron, OH 44839
Ph: (419)433-6861
E-mail: clemsboy@aol.com
URL: http://www.lions13b.org
Contact: Tony Lisa, Pres.
Local. Affiliated With: Lions Clubs International.

Independence

15493 ■ American Association of Healthcare Administrative Management, Western Reserve Chapter No. 18
c/o Gloria Dlugo, CPAM, Chair
Cleveland Clinic Hea. Sys.
6801 Brecksville Rd.
Independence, OH 44131
Ph: (216)636-8051
Fax: (216)636-8088
E-mail: dlugog@ccf.org
URL: National Affiliate–www.aaham.org
Contact: Gloria Dlugo CPAM, Chair
Local. Represents the interests of healthcare administrative management professionals. Seeks proper recognition for the financial aspect of hospital and clinic management. Provides member services and leadership in the areas of education, communication, representation, professional standards and certification. **Affiliated With:** American Association of Healthcare Administrative Management.

15494 ■ American Society of Sanitary Engineering, Region No. 6 - East
c/o Robert Tesar, Dir.
6973 Carol Dr.
Independence, OH 44131-5309
Ph: (216)524-6541
URL: National Affiliate–www.asse-plumbing.org
Contact: Robert Tesar, Dir.
Regional. Represents plumbing officials, sanitary engineers, plumbers, plumbing contractors, building officials, architects, engineers, designing engineers, physicians, and others interested in health. Conducts research on plumbing and sanitation and develops performance standards for components of the plumbing system. Sponsors disease research programs and other studies of water-borne epidemics. **Affiliated With:** American Society of Sanitary Engineering.

15495 ■ Cleveland Area Board of Realtors, Ohio (CABOR)
5633 Brecksville Rd.
Independence, OH 44131
Ph: (216)901-0130
Fax: (216)901-0149
E-mail: croehl@cabor.com
URL: http://www.cabor.com
Contact: Carla Roehl, CEO
Local. Strives to develop real estate business practices. Advocates for the right to own, use and transfer real property. Provides a facility for professional development, research and exchange of

information among members and the general public. **Affiliated With:** National Association of Realtors.

15496 ■ Energy Industries of Ohio
c/o Casting Development Center
6100 Oak Tree Blvd., Ste.200
Independence, OH 44131-2597
Ph: (216)643-2952
State.

15497 ■ Home Builders Association of Greater Cleveland (HBA)
c/o Nate Coffman, Exec. Officer
6140 W Creek Rd. Blvd.
Independence, OH 44131
Ph: (216)447-8700
Fax: (216)524-0758
E-mail: info@hbacleveland.com
URL: http://www.hbacleveland.com
Contact: Shavon Williams, Admin.Asst.
Founded: 1943. **Local.** Single and multifamily home builders, commercial builders, and others associated with the building industry. **Affiliated With:** National Association of Home Builders.

15498 ■ Independence Music Boosters
c/o Peggy Fritz
6111 Archwood Rd.
Independence, OH 44131
Ph: (216)328-1928
E-mail: imb44131@netscape.net
URL: http://www.independence.k12.oh.us/hs/clubs/imb/index.htm
Contact: Peggy Fritz, Contact
Local.

15499 ■ International Association of Business Communicators, Cleveland Chapter
c/o Joel H. Head
Park One Ctr., 6100 Oak Tree Blvd.
Independence, OH 44131
Ph: (216)662-5090
E-mail: joel.head@headwindsltd.com
URL: National Affiliate–www.iabc.com
Contact: Joel H. Head, Pres.
Local. Represents the interests of communication managers, public relations directors, writers, editors and audiovisual specialists. Encourages establishment of college-level programs in organizational communication. Conducts surveys on employee communication effectiveness and media trends. Conducts research in the field of communication. **Affiliated With:** International Association of Business Communicators.

15500 ■ Juvenile Diabetes Research Foundation International, East Central Ohio Branch
5000 Rockside Rd., Ste.No. 310
Independence, OH 44131
Ph: (216)524-6000
Fax: (216)328-8340
Free: (888)718-3061
E-mail: momalley@jdrf.org
URL: http://www.jdrf.org
Contact: George F. Voinovich, Pres.
Founded: 1970. **Local.** Strives to find a cure for diabetes and its complications through the support of research. **Affiliated With:** Juvenile Diabetes Research Foundation International. **Publications:** *Countdown*, quarterly. Magazine. Provides articles on the effects of research on the way people with diabetes must live their lives. **Price:** included in membership dues • *Discoveries*, quarterly. Newsletter. **Conventions/Meetings:** monthly board meeting.

15501 ■ Labor and Employment Relations Association - Northeast Ohio Chapter
c/o Federal Mediation and Conciliation Service
6161 Oak Tree Blvd.
Independence, OH 44131-2516
Ph: (216)520-4800
Fax: (216)520-4815
E-mail: admin@irra-neohio.org
URL: http://www.irra-neohio.org
Contact: John F. Buettner, Pres.
Founded: 1972. **Members:** 230. **Membership Dues:** regular, $30 (annual) • organization (add $25/individual more than four), $100 (annual). **Local.** Labor professionals. Provides a forum for management, labor and neutrals to explore all aspects of labor and employment relations in an atmosphere of cooperation and academic inquiry. Promotes exchanges among labor and employment relations' practitioners seeking a favorable climate for labor-management relations. **Affiliated With:** Labor and Employment Relations Association. **Formerly:** (2006) Industrial Relations Research Association - Northeast Ohio Chapter. **Conventions/Meetings:** quarterly meeting.

15502 ■ Ohio SADD
c/o Ohio Motorists Safety Foundation
5700 Brecksville Rd.
Independence, OH 44131
Ph: (216)606-6023
Fax: (216)606-6315
E-mail: kgroll@aaaoma.com
URL: http://www.aaa.com/aaa/128/home/Safety/sadd/sadd_nl.htm
Contact: Ken Groll, Coor.
State. Affiliated With: Students Against Destructive Decisions, Students Against Drunk Driving.

15503 ■ Precision Metalforming Association (PMA)
c/o William E. Gaskin, CAE, Pres./Sec.
6363 Oak Tree Blvd.
Independence, OH 44131-2500
Ph: (216)901-8800
Fax: (216)901-9190
E-mail: pma@pma.org
URL: http://www.metalforming.com
Local.

15504 ■ Professional Remodelers of Ohio
c/o Brenda Callaghan, Exec.Dir.
5755 Granger Rd., Ste.750
Independence, OH 44131
Ph: (216)619-6274
Fax: (216)619-6278
Free: (888)448-6274
E-mail: info@proohio.org
URL: http://www.proohio.org
Contact: Brenda Callaghan, Exec.Dir.
Founded: 1962. **Members:** 325. **Membership Dues:** all, initially ($425 thereafter), $450 (annual). **Staff:** 7. **State Groups:** 1. **State.** Works to enhance its members' ability to grow their businesses through consumer awareness, educational programs and legislative action. Serves as the remodeling industry resource in NE Ohio for information and advocacy for consumers, community, and members. Represents professional remodeling contractors, product manufacturers, distributors, wholesalers, trade and consumer publications, utilities and lending institutions. **Libraries: Type:** not open to the public. **Holdings:** 150; articles, books, periodicals, video recordings. **Subjects:** home remodeling, associations, builders, small businesses, sales, business, architecture, certification, remodeling/building codes, laws information, permit information, OSHA information, EPA information. **Awards:** Professional Remodeler of the Year. **Frequency:** annual. **Type:** recognition. **Recipient:** based on project scope. **Computer Services:** Mailing lists. **Affiliated With:** National Association of the Remodeling Industry. **Formerly:** (2004) Greater Cleveland NARI. **Publications:** Membership Directory, biennial. Contains lists of members, winners of Professional Remodeler of the Year Awards, and articles on home remodeling. **Price:** free. **Circulation:** 125,000. **Advertising:** accepted • Newsletter, monthly. Contains updated information on members, the remodeling industry, upcoming events, etc. **Price:** free. **Circulation:** 400. **Advertising:** accepted. **Conventions/Meetings:** annual Professional Home Improvement - trade show, with variety of exhibitors mainly focusing on home improvement, with a celebrity guest and promotional contests every year (exhibits).

15505 ■ Skyscraper Club of Cleveland
PO Box 31252
Independence, OH 44131-0252
Ph: (216)556-1494
E-mail: cleveland@tall.org
URL: http://tall.org/clubs/ohio/cleveland
Contact: Barbe Kilroy, Pres.
Founded: 1946. **Members:** 100. **Membership Dues:** personal, $25 (annual). **Local.** Social club for women 5'10" and taller and men 6'2" and taller, 21 years or older. Open to singles and married couples, who meet the requirements. Works to promote awareness and provide support and activities for tall people. Makes charitable contributions to Marfan's Syndrome Association. **Additional Websites:** http://tall.org. **Affiliated With:** Tall Clubs International. **Publications:** *Scraper*, monthly. Newsletter. Contains monthly calendar and articles of interest to members. **Price:** free to members. **Advertising:** accepted. **Conventions/Meetings:** monthly meeting - always second Wednesday of the month • triennial Weekend Convention - usually in November near Cleveland, OH.

15506 ■ Sweet Adelines International, Greater Cleveland Chorus
Independence United Methodist Church
6615 Brecksville Rd.
Independence, OH 44131
E-mail: president2005@greaterclevelandchorus.com
URL: http://www.GreaterClevelandChorus.com
Contact: Mary Schwartz, Pres.
Local. Advances the musical art form of barbershop harmony through education and performances. Provides education, training and coaching in the development of women's four-part barbershop harmony. **Affiliated With:** Sweet Adelines International.

Ironton

15507 ■ American Legion, Downey-Pogue-Scott Post 590
720 Quincy St.
Ironton, OH 45638
Ph: (740)362-7478
Fax: (740)362-1429
URL: National Affiliate–www.legion.org
Local. Affiliated With: American Legion.

15508 ■ American Legion, Ironton Post 433
PO Box 443
Ironton, OH 45638
Ph: (740)362-7478
Fax: (740)362-1429
URL: National Affiliate–www.legion.org
Local. Affiliated With: American Legion.

15509 ■ Wurtland Beagle Club
c/o Lloyd Pancake
3941 State Rte. 141
Ironton, OH 45638-8765
Ph: (740)533-0319
URL: National Affiliate–clubs.akc.org
Contact: Lloyd Pancake, Contact
Local.

Jackson

15510 ■ AAA South Central Ohio
126 E Gay St.
Jackson, OH 45640
Ph: (740)286-5077
Contact: Judy Kearns, Mgr.
Local.

15511 ■ American Legion, Ohio Post 81
c/o Jefferson Howe
185 Morton St.
Jackson, OH 45640
Ph: (740)362-7478
Fax: (740)362-1429
URL: National Affiliate–www.legion.org
Contact: Jefferson Howe, Contact
Local. Affiliated With: American Legion.

15512 ■ Gallia/Jackson/Vinton Counties RSVP
c/o Susan M. Rogers, Dir.
102 Broadway St.
Jackson, OH 45640
Ph: (740)286-4918
Fax: (740)288-7032
E-mail: srogers@rio.edu
URL: http://www.seniorcorps.gov/about/programs/rsvp_state.asp?usestateabbr=oh&Search4.x=14&Search4.y=5
Contact: Susan M. Rogers, Dir.
Local. Affiliated With: Retired and Senior Volunteer Program.

15513 ■ Jackson Area Chamber of Commerce (JACC)
234 Broadway St.
Jackson, OH 45640-1702
Ph: (740)286-2722
Fax: (740)286-8443
E-mail: info@jacksonohio.org
URL: http://www.jacksonohio.org
Contact: Randy R. Heath, Exec.Dir.
Founded: 1911. **Members:** 360. **Staff:** 1. **Budget:** $35,000. **Local.** Promotes business and community development in Jackson, OH. **Awards:** Entrepreneur of the Year. **Frequency:** annual. **Type:** recognition • Person of the Year. **Frequency:** annual. **Type:** recognition. **Computer Services:** Online services, membership listing. **Publications:** *The Chamber Bulletin*, monthly. Newsletter. Contains monthly update of Chamber Business. **Price:** free. **Circulation:** 100. **Advertising:** accepted. Alternate Formats: diskette; online. **Conventions/Meetings:** annual banquet (exhibits) - always in October.

15514 ■ Jackson County Beagle Club
c/o Rodney L. Smith
24 Payne St.
Jackson, OH 45640-1868
URL: National Affiliate–clubs.akc.org
Contact: Rodney L. Smith, Contact
Local.

15515 ■ Ohio Genealogical Society, Jackson County Chapter
PO Box 807
Jackson, OH 45640-0807
URL: National Affiliate–www.ogs.org
Contact: Ruth Hayth, Pres.
Local. Affiliated With: Ohio Genealogical Society.

15516 ■ Veterans of Foreign Wars 8402
283 E Main St.
Jackson, OH 45640
Ph: (740)286-1550
Contact: Harry Erabtree, Commander
Local.

15517 ■ Vietnam Veterans of America, Chapter No. 634
c/o Ralph Miller, Pres.
2572 Smith Bridge Rd.
Jackson, OH 45640
Ph: (740)286-3417
URL: http://www.vvabuckeyestatecouncil.com
Contact: Ralph Miller, Pres.
Local. Affiliated With: Vietnam Veterans of America.

Jackson Center

15518 ■ All American City Chorus of Sweet Adelines
201 Hamer Ave., Box 6
Jackson Center, OH 45334
Ph: (937)596-6431
E-mail: info@allamericancitychorus.com
URL: http://www.allamericancitychorus.com
Contact: Alma Mae Helmlinger, Dir.
Local. Advances the musical art form of barbershop harmony through education and performances. Provides education, training and coaching in the development of women's four-part barbershop harmony. **Affiliated With:** Sweet Adelines International.

15519 ■ American Legion, Scherer Post 493
PO Box 575
Jackson Center, OH 45334
Ph: (740)362-7478
Fax: (740)362-1429
URL: National Affiliate–www.legion.org
Local. Affiliated With: American Legion.

Jacobsburg

15520 ■ Belmont County - Young Life
PO Box 23
Jacobsburg, OH 43933-0023
Ph: (740)686-2580
URL: http://sites.younglife.org/_layouts/ylext/default.aspx?ID=C-1531
Local. Affiliated With: Young Life.

15521 ■ Martin's Ferry/Bridgeport - Young Life
PO Box 23
Jacobsburg, OH 43933-0023
Ph: (740)686-2580
URL: http://sites.younglife.org/_layouts/ylext/default.aspx?ID=C-3473
Local. Affiliated With: Young Life.

15522 ■ Young Life Ohio Valley West
PO Box 23
Jacobsburg, OH 43933-0023
Ph: (740)686-2580
Fax: (740)526-9302
URL: http://sites.younglife.org/_layouts/ylext/default.aspx?ID=A-OH32
Regional. Affiliated With: Young Life.

Jamestown

15523 ■ American Legion, Ohio Post 155
c/o Wilbur Thomas
PO Box 38
Jamestown, OH 45335
Ph: (740)362-7478
Fax: (740)362-1429
URL: National Affiliate–www.legion.org
Contact: Wilbur Thomas, Contact
Local. Affiliated With: American Legion.

Jefferson

15524 ■ American Legion, Baylor Post 152
395 E Erie St.
Jefferson, OH 44047
Ph: (740)362-7478
Fax: (740)362-1429
URL: National Affiliate–www.legion.org
Local. Affiliated With: American Legion.

15525 ■ Jefferson Area Chamber of Commerce
PO Box 100
Jefferson, OH 44047-0100
Ph: (440)576-3070
Fax: (440)576-4352
E-mail: membership@jeffersonchamber.com
URL: http://www.jeffersonchamber.com
Contact: Peggy Stadler, Corresponding Sec.
Membership Dues: business, $75 (annual) • individual, $35 (annual). **Local.** Aims to advance the commercial, industrial, professional, civic and general interests of the Jefferson trades areas. **Awards:** Citizen of the Year. **Frequency:** annual. **Type:** recognition. **Computer Services:** database, membership directory. **Committees:** Annual Appreciation Golf Outing; Citizen of the Year Banquet; Community Center Benefit; County Chamber Rep/Home Show; Easter Egg Hunt; Manna Food Drive; Scholarship. **Subcommittees:** Merchants. **Conventions/Meetings:** monthly meeting - every 1st Tuesday.

15526 ■ National Organization for Women - Astabula
c/o Phyllis Duffy-Zala, Pres.
987 Webster Rd.
Jefferson, OH 44047
Ph: (440)576-7958
E-mail: lighthouse51@adelphia.net
URL: http://www.ohionow.org
Contact: Phyllis Duffy-Zala, Pres.
Local. Affiliated With: National Organization for Women.

Jeromesville

15527 ■ American Legion, Jerome Post 749
PO Box 6
Jeromesville, OH 44840
Ph: (740)362-7478
Fax: (740)362-1429
URL: National Affiliate–www.legion.org
Local. Affiliated With: American Legion.

15528 ■ Jeromesville Lions Club
c/o Lawrence Bair, Sec.
310 County Rd. 30A
Jeromesville, OH 44840
Ph: (419)368-1047
E-mail: lbair1@neo.rr.com
URL: http://www.lions13b.org
Contact: Lawrence Bair, Sec.
Local. Affiliated With: Lions Clubs International.

Jerusalem

15529 ■ National Active and Retired Federal Employees Association - Monroe County 2193
52303 Wells Rd.
Jerusalem, OH 43747
Ph: (740)472-1906
URL: National Affiliate–www.narfe.org
Contact: Eugene S. Wells, Contact
Local. Protects the retirement future of employees through education. Informs members on issues affecting the retirement. **Affiliated With:** National Association of Retired Federal Employees.

Jewell

15530 ■ American Legion, Community Memorial Post 635
PO Box 30012
Jewell, OH 43530
Ph: (740)362-7478
Fax: (740)362-1429
URL: National Affiliate–www.legion.org
Local. Affiliated With: American Legion.

Johnstown

15531 ■ American Legion, Johnstown Post 254
PO Box 413
Johnstown, OH 43031
Ph: (740)362-7478
Fax: (740)362-1429
URL: National Affiliate–www.legion.org
Local. Affiliated With: American Legion.

15532 ■ Buckeye Triumphs
c/o Buck Henry, Pres.
9023 Concord Rd.
Johnstown, OH 43031
Ph: (614)733-0563
E-mail: info@buckeyetriumphs.org
URL: http://www.buckeyetriumphs.org
Contact: Buck Henry, Pres.
Local. Affiliated With: Vintage Triumph Register.

15533 ■ Mideastern Farrier's Association No. 17
c/o Steven J. Muir, Pres.
10811 Jug St., Rd. NW
Johnstown, OH 43031-9366
Ph: (740)967-7463
URL: National Affiliate–www.americanfarriers.org
Contact: Steven J. Muir, Pres.
Regional. Affiliated With: American Farrier's Association.

Junction City

15534 ■ American Legion, Ohio Post 376
c/o James E. Fisher
PO Box 135
Junction City, OH 43748
Ph: (740)362-7478
Fax: (740)362-1429
URL: National Affiliate–www.legion.org
Contact: James E. Fisher, Contact
Local. Affiliated With: American Legion.

Kelleys Island

15535 ■ Kelleys Island Chamber of Commerce (KICC)
PO Box 783-F
Kelleys Island, OH 43438-0783
Ph: (419)746-2360
Fax: (419)746-2360
URL: http://www.kelleysislandchamber.com
Contact: Lisa Klonaris, Dir.
Local. Promotes tourism on Kelleys Island. Develops increased cooperation between the Kelleys Island Village Council and the business community.

Kensington

15536 ■ Ohio Chapter of the MFTHBA
c/o David Baldwin, Pres.
11900 Lynchburg Rd.
Kensington, OH 44427
Ph: (330)894-2789
E-mail: baldwin_david@hotmail.com
Affiliated With: Missouri Fox Trotting Horse Breed Association.

Kent

15537 ■ American Legion, Portage Post 496
1945 Mogadore Rd.
Kent, OH 44240
Ph: (740)362-7478
Fax: (740)362-1429
URL: National Affiliate–www.legion.org
Local. Affiliated With: American Legion.

15538 ■ American Library Association/Associated Library Science Students of Ohio, Kent State University (KSU ALA/ALSSO)
c/o Jason Holmes, Faculty Advisor
Student Chap., School of Lib. Sci.
Kent State Univ.
PO Box 5190
Kent, OH 44242
Ph: (330)672-2782
Fax: (330)672-7965
E-mail: alsso@slis.kent.edu
URL: http://www.slis.kent.edu/~alsso
Contact: Ms. Heather Bryan, Co-Pres.
Founded: 1989. **Local.** Aims to maintain a strong working relationship with the ALA, to fulfill a leadership role within the SLIS community, and to serve as a clearinghouse for ideas and issues between its members and the larger world of Library and Information Science. Seeks to encourage and facilitate participation in the ALA and works to promote scholarly achievement and professional awareness among its members. Provides an avenue for communication between members and the ALA, and SLIS students and faculty. Provides data on timely issues and concerns while acting as a local forum for the exchange of ideas. Promotes networking, information sharing, or act as a sounding board in identifying real world trends and competencies important for current students. **Affiliated With:** American Library Association.

15539 ■ Association for Computing Machinery, Kent State University (ACM/KSU)
Math and Cmpt. Sci. Bldg.
Kent, OH 44242
Ph: (330)672-9980
E-mail: acm@cs.kent.edu
URL: http://acm.cs.kent.edu
Contact: Michael Collard, Advisor
Local. Biological, medical, behavioral, and computer scientists; hospital administrators; programmers and others interested in application of computer methods to biological, behavioral, and medical problems. Stimulates understanding of the use and potential of computers in the biosciences. **Affiliated With:** Association for Computing Machinery.

15540 ■ Brimfield Area Chamber of Commerce
PO Box 3414
Kent, OH 44240-3414
Ph: (330)348-3573
E-mail: sbennett@landam.com
URL: http://www.brimfieldchamber.com
Contact: Sabrina Christian-Bennett, Pres.
Founded: 1960. **Members:** 60. **Local.** Promotes business and community development in the Brimfield, OH area. Organizes community donations for schools and police. **Awards: Frequency:** periodic. **Type:** scholarship. **Recipient:** for local high school seniors. **Publications:** *Monthly Minutes*. Newsletter • Directory. **Conventions/Meetings:** annual Brimfield Sausage Fest - festival • monthly Fashion Show - meeting - always first Tuesday • annual meeting.

15541 ■ Kent Area Chamber of Commerce (KACC)
c/o Daniel D. Smith, Exec.Dir.
Portage Travel Bldg.
138 E Main St.
Kent, OH 44240
Ph: (330)673-9855
Fax: (330)673-9860
E-mail: dsmith@kentbiz.com
URL: http://www.kentbiz.com
Contact: Daniel D. Smith, Exec.Dir.
Membership Dues: general business/organization (plus $6 per employee above 3), not-for-profit, government agency (plus $2 per employee above 3), $200 (annual) • associate, $70 (annual) • associate department, $190 (annual) • individual (not affiliated with any organization), retiree, religious/service organization, $100 (annual) • utility, $550 (annual). **Local.** Promotes business and community development in the Kent, OH area. **Awards:** Kent Medal for Public Service. **Frequency:** annual. **Type:** medal. **Recipient:** to an individual, institution or organization whose community service has resulted in the advancement of the common good, promotion of public welfare, or stimulation of public service • Small Business Award. **Frequency:** annual. **Type:** recognition. **Computer Services:** database, membership directory. **Committees:** Economic Development/Pro Business Advocacy. **Affiliated With:** Greater Akron Chamber of Commerce; Ohio Chamber of Commerce; U.S. Chamber of Commerce. **Formerly:** (2005) Kent Area Chamber of Commerce and Information Center. **Publications:** *KACC Member Newsletter*, monthly. **Price:** included in membership dues; $15.00 for additional subscription. Alternate Formats: online. **Conventions/Meetings:** monthly board meeting - 3rd Thursday • monthly board meeting - last Thursday • monthly Finance Committee - meeting - every 1st Tuesday.

15542 ■ Kent Fencing Club
c/o Derek Wilkinson
20 Loop Rd.
Kent, OH 44243-1020
Ph: (330)798-0153
E-mail: derek.wilkinson@pbs.proquest.com
URL: http://dept.kent.edu/recserv/fencing/
Local. Amateur fencers. **Affiliated With:** United States Fencing Association.

15543 ■ Kent Lions Club
c/o Rob Dinehart, Pres.
911 Crain Ave.
Kent, OH 44240
Ph: (330)678-7547
E-mail: robdhart@aol.com
URL: http://www.kentohiolions.org
Contact: Rob Dinehart, Pres.
Local. Affiliated With: Lions Clubs International.

15544 ■ Ohio Lake Management Society (OLMS)
PO Box 463
Kent, OH 44240
Ph: (440)708-2439
Fax: (330)672-3713
E-mail: oleskie@olms.org
URL: http://www.olms.org
Contact: Dana Oleskiewicz, Pres.
State. United to promote the sharing of information on water management issues; foster the development of local lake restoration projects; support programs, policies and legislation in water protection; and encourage cooperation between organizations, agencies, government and individuals. Provides workshop training and technical assistance and sponsors the Citizen Lake Awareness and Monitoring (CLAM) program, a statewide education and volunteer monitoring project in Ohio. **Affiliated With:** North American Lake Management Society. **Publications:** Newsletter, quarterly. **Conventions/Meetings:** annual conference.

15545 ■ Psi Chi, National Honor Society in Psychology - Kent State University
c/o Dept. of Psychology
PO Box 5190
Kent, OH 44242-0999
Ph: (330)672-2166 (330)672-3787
Fax: (330)672-3786
E-mail: rjoynes@kent.edu
URL: http://www.psichi.org/chapters/info.asp?chapter_id=38
Contact: Robin Joynes PhD, Advisor
Local.

15546 ■ Ravenna Lions Club
c/o Jamison Stone, Pres.
3501 Verner Rd.
Kent, OH 44240
Ph: (330)297-1491
E-mail: jamison_stone@yahoo.com
URL: http://www.lions13d.org
Contact: Jamison Stone, Pres.
Local. Affiliated With: Lions Clubs International.

15547 ■ RSVP of Ashtabula County
c/o Laurie Scharf, Dir.
218 Gougler Ave.
Kent, OH 44240
Ph: (440)992-6789
E-mail: srvolpro@erie.net
URL: http://www.seniorcorps.gov/about/programs/rsvp_state.asp?usestateabbr=oh&Search4.x=0&Search4.y=0
Contact: Laurie Scharf, Dir.
Local. Affiliated With: Retired and Senior Volunteer Program.

15548 ■ RSVP of Portage County
c/o Kathleen Long, Dir.
218 Gougler Ave.
Kent, OH 44240
Ph: (330)678-0076
Fax: (330)673-6765
E-mail: rsvpofpc@raex.com
URL: http://www.portagefamilies.org/rsvp/index.html
Contact: Kathleen Long, Dir.
Local. Additional Websites: http://www.homestead.com/rsvpofpc/home.html. **Affiliated With:** Retired and Senior Volunteer Program.

15549 ■ Society for the Advancement of Material and Process Engineering, Northern Ohio Chapter
c/o Brent K. Larson, PhD, Dir.
Sr. R&D Engineer
Schneller, Inc.
6019 Powdermill Rd.
Kent, OH 44240
Ph: (330)676-7138
Fax: (330)673-7327
E-mail: blarson@schneller.com
URL: National Affiliate–www.sampe.org
Contact: Brent K. Larson PhD, Dir.
Local. Represents individuals engaged in the development of advanced materials and processing technology in airframe, missile, aerospace, propulsion, electronics, life sciences, management, and related industries. Provides scholarships for science students seeking financial assistance. Provides placement services for members. **Affiliated With:** Society for the Advancement of Material and Process Engineering.

15550 ■ Society of Manufacturing Engineers - Kent State University S050
Kent State Univ., School of Tech.
209A Van Duesen Hall
Kent, OH 44242-0001
Ph: (330)672-1445
Fax: (330)672-2894
E-mail: efilppi@kent.edu
URL: National Affiliate–www.sme.org
Contact: Ed Filppi, Contact
Local. Advances manufacturing knowledge to gain competitive advantage. Improves skills and manufacturing solutions for the growth of economy. Provides resources and opportunities for manufacturing professionals. **Affiliated With:** Coastal Engineering Research Council.

15551 ■ U.S.A. Volleyball Ohio Valley Region
c/o Ron Wyzynski, Exec.Dir./CEO/Registrar
315 Johnson Rd.
Kent, OH 44240
Fax: (330)673-2514
Free: (888)873-9478
E-mail: wyzynski@ovr.org
URL: http://www.ovr.org
Contact: Ron Wyzynski, Exec.Dir./CEO/Registrar
Regional. Promotes and establishes quality volleyball through participation by both adults and juniors, according to the standards set forth by USA Volleyball and the Amateur Sports Act of 1978. **Affiliated With:** United States Volleyball Association/United States Volleyball Association.

Kenton

15552 ■ American Legion, Kenton Post 198
PO Box 393
Kenton, OH 43326
Ph: (740)362-7478
Fax: (740)362-1429
URL: National Affiliate–www.legion.org
Local. Affiliated With: American Legion.

15553 ■ Hardin County Chamber of Commerce
United Community Bldg.
225 S Detroit St.
Kenton, OH 43326
Ph: (419)673-4131
Fax: (419)674-4876
E-mail: chamber@hardinohio.org
URL: http://www.hardinohio.org
Contact: Sue Harrison, Pres.
Founded: 1921. **Members:** 250. **Membership Dues:** individual, $80 (annual) • general (plus $2.25 per employee), $160 (annual) • heavy industrial and utility (plus $1.75 per employee), $310 (annual) • professional, $160 (annual) • financial institution, $430 (annual). **Staff:** 1. **Local.** Business, industry, and professional persons dedicated to business and community development in the Hardin County, OH area. **Awards:** Citizen of the Year. **Frequency:** annual. **Type:** recognition • Community Service Awards. **Type:** recognition. **Subgroups:** Hardin County Ambassadors. **Affiliated With:** U.S. Chamber of Commerce. **Publications:** *Commerce Connection*, quarterly. Newsletters • Membership Directory, annual. **Advertising:** accepted.

15554 ■ United Way of Hardin County
225 S Detroit St.
Kenton, OH 43326-1903
Ph: (419)675-1860
URL: National Affiliate–national.unitedway.org
Local. Affiliated With: United Way of America.

Kettering

15555 ■ AAA Miami Valley
1218 E Stroop Rd.
Kettering, OH 45429
Ph: (937)294-1695 (937)294-3941
Free: (800)457-6674
Contact: Brenda Lawson, Office Mgr.
Local.

15556 ■ American Ex-Prisoners of War, Dayton Area Chapter
c/o Kenneth Castor
4841 Shadyhill Ln.
Kettering, OH 45429
Ph: (937)434-5605
URL: National Affiliate–www.axpow.org
Local. Affiliated With: American Ex-Prisoners of War.

15557 ■ American Legion, Kettering Post 598
5700 Kentshire Dr.
Kettering, OH 45440
Ph: (740)362-7478
Fax: (740)362-1429
URL: National Affiliate–www.legion.org
Local. Affiliated With: American Legion.

15558 ■ Arthritis Foundation, Dayton Branch
c/o Jill Lewis
Kettering Sports Medicine
3490 Far Hills Ave.
Kettering, OH 45429
Ph: (937)293-5211
Fax: (937)293-5493
Free: (800)383-6843
E-mail: jelewis@arthritis.org
URL: National Affiliate–www.arthritis.org
Local. Seeks to: discover the cause and improve the methods for the treatment and prevention of arthritis and other rheumatic diseases; increase the number of scientists investigating rheumatic diseases; provide training in rheumatic diseases for more doctors; extend knowledge of arthritis and other rheumatic diseases to the lay public, emphasizing the socioeconomic as well as medical aspects of these diseases. **Affiliated With:** Arthritis Foundation.

15559 ■ The Compassionate Friends - Miami Valley, Ohio Chapter (TCF)
PO Box 292112
Kettering, OH 45429
Ph: (937)640-2621
E-mail: miamivalleytcf@yahoo.com
URL: http://www.miamivalleytcf.com
Nonmembership. Local.

15560 ■ Kettering Lions Club
5700 Kentshire Dr.
Kettering, OH 45440-4248
Ph: (937)298-2576
URL: http://ketteringoh.lionwap.org
Contact: Basil Morrison, Pres.
Local. Affiliated With: Lions Clubs International.

15561 ■ Kettering - Moraine - Oakwood Chamber of Commerce (KMOCC)
2977 Far Hills Ave.
Kettering, OH 45419
Ph: (937)299-3852
Fax: (937)299-3851
URL: http://www.kmo-coc.org
Contact: Rod J. Sommer, Pres.
Founded: 1957. **Members:** 750. **Local.** Promotes business and community development in Kettering, Moraine, and Oakwood, OH. **Awards:** Enterprise Spirit Award. **Frequency:** annual. **Type:** recognition. **Recipient:** for businesses that contribute to community development. **Computer Services:** Online services, membership directory. **Affiliated With:** U.S. Chamber of Commerce. **Formerly:** (1995) Kettering Chamber of Commerce. **Publications:** Membership Directory, annual. **Price:** $25.00/issue • Newsletter, bimonthly. **Advertising:** accepted. Alternate Formats: online. **Conventions/Meetings:** annual Golf Outing - competition • annual Holiday Program Enterprise Spirit Award - show • monthly meeting.

15562 ■ National Active and Retired Federal Employees Association - Ket-Cent-Oak 1927
4427 Jonathan Dr.
Kettering, OH 45440-1628
Ph: (937)298-5388
URL: National Affiliate–www.narfe.org
Contact: Victor H. Bilek, Contact
Local. Protects the retirement future of employees through education. Informs members on issues affecting the retirement. **Affiliated With:** National Association of Retired Federal Employees.

15563 ■ Ohio Valley Chapter of Associated Locksmiths of America
c/o Mehdi Zahedi
Accu-Key Lock & Safe Inc.
3116 Allendale Dr.
Kettering, OH 45409
Ph: (937)294-4241
URL: National Affiliate–www.aloa.org
Contact: Mehdi Zahedi, Contact
Local. Affiliated With: Associated Locksmiths of America.

15564 ■ Red River Valley Fighter Pilot Association - Wright Patterson AFB/Dayton, Ohio
716 Oakview Dr.
Kettering, OH 45429
E-mail: jollyfe@att.net
URL: National Affiliate–www.river-rats.org
Contact: Charles Rouhier, Contact
Local. Affiliated With: Red River Valley Fighter Pilots Association.

15565 ■ South Dayton Figure Skating Club (SDFSC)
c/o Trish Burke-Williams, Pres.
PO Box 293003
Kettering, OH 45429
E-mail: trishbwilliams@hotmail.com
URL: http://www.sdfsc.org
Contact: Trish Burke-Williams, Pres.
Members: 150. **Membership Dues:** regular, $50 (annual). **Local. Affiliated With:** United States Figure Skating Association.

Killbuck

15566 ■ Veterans of Foreign Wars 7079
PO Box 413
Killbuck, OH 44637
Ph: (330)276-1987
Contact: Robert Arnold, Contact
Local.

Kimbolton

15567 ■ National Active and Retired Federal Employees Association Guernsey-Noble 2189
18378 Anderson Rd.
Kimbolton, OH 43749-9767
Ph: (740)489-5347
URL: National Affiliate–www.narfe.org
Contact: Cecil R. Carlson, Contact
Local. Protects the retirement future of employees through education. Informs members on issues affecting the retirement. **Affiliated With:** National Association of Retired Federal Employees.

Kingston

15568 ■ American Legion, Kingston Post 291
PO Box 111
Kingston, OH 45644
Ph: (740)362-7478
Fax: (740)362-1429
URL: National Affiliate–www.legion.org
Local. Affiliated With: American Legion.

Kingsville

15569 ■ American Legion, Neal Post 743
6120 State Rte. 193
Kingsville, OH 44048
Ph: (740)362-7478
Fax: (740)362-1429
URL: National Affiliate–www.legion.org
Local. Affiliated With: American Legion.

Kinsman

15570 ■ American Legion, Ohio Post 506
c/o Harry Lees
6336 State Rte. 87
Kinsman, OH 44428
Ph: (740)362-7478
Fax: (740)362-1429
URL: National Affiliate–www.legion.org
Contact: Harry Lees, Contact
Local. Affiliated With: American Legion.

Kirkersville

15571 ■ American Legion, Ohio Post 107
c/o Milon Edward Rardon
PO Box 21
Kirkersville, OH 43033
Ph: (740)362-7478
Fax: (740)362-1429
URL: National Affiliate–www.legion.org
Contact: Milon Edward Rardon, Contact
Local. Affiliated With: American Legion.

Kirtland

15572 ■ American Legion, Ohio Post 609
c/o Barber Williams
7232 Chardon Rd.
Kirtland, OH 44094
Ph: (740)362-7478
Fax: (740)362-1429
URL: National Affiliate–www.legion.org
Contact: Barber Williams, Contact
Local. Affiliated With: American Legion.

15573 ■ Phi Theta Kappa - Alpha Psi Rho Chapter
c/o Irene Yuen
7700 Clocktower Dr.
Kirtland, OH 44094-5198
Ph: (440)975-4765
E-mail: irene.yuen@ptk.org
URL: http://www.ptk.org/directories/chapters/OH/20596-1.htm
Contact: Irene Yuen, Advisor
Local. Affiliated With: Phi Theta Kappa, International Honor Society.

Kirtland Hills

15574 ■ Lake County Historical Society
8610 Mentor Rd.
Kirtland Hills, OH 44060
Ph: (440)255-8979
Fax: (440)255-8980
E-mail: information@lakehistory.org
URL: http://www.lakehistory.org
Contact: Harry W. Hopes, Pres.
Local. Works as a historical organization that operates a fifteen-acre historic site housing a museum, research library and staff officers. Sponsors the "Little Mountain Folk Festival".

La Rue

15575 ■ American Legion, Phillippi-Clement Post 101
c/o Larry Knapp, Finance Officer
8874 Larue Prospect Rd.
La Rue, OH 43332
Ph: (740)362-7478
Fax: (740)362-1429
URL: National Affiliate–www.legion.org
Contact: Larry Knapp, Finance Officer
Local. Affiliated With: American Legion.

15576 ■ La Rue Lions Club
c/o Dan Hicks, Sec.
181 S Chestnut St.
La Rue, OH 43332
Ph: (740)528-2115 (740)499-3938
E-mail: chicks80@columbus.rr.com
URL: http://www.iwaynet.net/~lions13f
Contact: Dan Hicks, Sec.
Local. Affiliated With: Lions Clubs International.

Lagrange

15577 ■ Friends of Lagrange Community Park
c/o Larry Shaw
PO Box 137
Lagrange, OH 44050
E-mail: dave@tuttlemedia.com
URL: http://www.friendsofthepark.org
Contact: Guy Page, Chm.
Local.

Lake Milton

15578 ■ American Legion, Lake Post 737
PO Box 100
Lake Milton, OH 44429
Ph: (740)362-7478
Fax: (740)362-1429
URL: National Affiliate–www.legion.org
Local. Affiliated With: American Legion.

Lakeside

15579 ■ Marblehead Peninsula Lions Club
c/o Maryanne Laubner, Sec.
457 N Erie Beach Rd.
Lakeside, OH 43440
Ph: (419)798-5791
E-mail: mary@cros.net
URL: http://www.lions13b.org
Contact: Maryanne Laubner, Sec.
Local. Affiliated With: Lions Clubs International.

Lakewood

15580 ■ Easter Seals Northeast Ohio
14701 Detroit Ave., Ste.252
Lakewood, OH 44107
Ph: (216)228-5170
Fax: (216)228-1018
E-mail: info@eastersealsneo.org
URL: http://www.neohio.easterseals.com
Contact: Ms. Sheila Dunn, Pres./CEO
Local. Provides services for children and adults with disabilities or special needs, and supports their families. **Affiliated With:** Easter Seals.

15581 ■ First Catholic Slovak Ladies Association - Lakewood Junior Branch 429
1578 Ridgewood Ave.
Lakewood, OH 44107-5039
Ph: (330)226-0068
URL: National Affiliate–www.fcsla.com
Local. Affiliated With: First Catholic Slovak Ladies Association.

15582 ■ First Catholic Slovak Ladies Association - Lakewood Senior Branch 432
1578 Ridgewood Ave.
Lakewood, OH 44107
Ph: (330)226-0068
URL: National Affiliate–www.fcsla.com
Local. Affiliated With: First Catholic Slovak Ladies Association.

15583 ■ Gardeners of America/Men's Garden Clubs of America - Greater Cleveland Men's Garden Club
c/o Jeff Pierpont
12911 Lake Ave.
Lakewood, OH 44107
Ph: (216)221-4429
E-mail: jeff.pierpont@nationalcity.com
URL: National Affiliate–www.tgoa-mgca.org
Contact: Jeff Pierpont, Contact
Local.

15584 ■ International Personnel Management Association, Cleveland
c/o Kevin Reynolds, Pres.
12650 Detroit Ave.
Lakewood, OH 44107
Ph: (216)529-6613
Fax: (216)529-5669
E-mail: kevin.reynolds@lakewoodoh.net
URL: National Affiliate–www.ipma-hr.org
Contact: Kevin Reynolds, Pres.
Local. Affiliated With: International Public Management Association for Human Resources.

15585 ■ IPMA-HR Cleveland Chapter
c/o Kevin Reynolds, Pres.
12650 Detroit Ave.
Lakewood, OH 44107
Ph: (216)529-6613
Fax: (216)529-5669
E-mail: kevin.reynolds@lakewoodoh.net
URL: National Affiliate–www.ipma-hr.org
Contact: Kevin Reynolds, Pres.
Local. Seeks to improve human resource practices in government through provision of testing services, advisory service, conferences, professional development programs, research and publications. Sponsors seminars, conferences and workshops on various phases of public personnel administration.

15586 ■ Lakewood Chamber of Commerce (LCC)
14701 Detroit Ave., Ste.130
Lakewood, OH 44107-4109
Ph: (216)226-2900
Fax: (216)226-1340
E-mail: info@lakewoodchamber.org
URL: http://www.lakewoodchamber.org
Contact: Kathy Berkshire, Exec.Dir.
Founded: 1911. **Members:** 375. **Membership Dues:** business (depends on the number of employees), $130-$450 (annual) • freight forward, $375 (annual) • associate, $75 (annual). **Staff:** 2. **Local**. Promotes business and community development in Lakewood, OH. **Committees:** Business Person of the Year; Economic Development; Education; Legislative and Governmental Affairs. **Affiliated With:** U.S. Chamber of Commerce. **Publications:** Directory, annual • Newsletter, monthly.

15587 ■ Lakewood Historical Society
14710 Lake Ave.
Lakewood, OH 44107
Ph: (216)221-7343
E-mail: lakewoodhistory@bge.net
URL: http://www.lakewoodhistory.org
Contact: Mazie M. Adams, Exec.Dir.
Local.

15588 ■ Navy League of the United States, Cleveland
c/o William R. Keller, Pres.
18173 Clipton Rd.
Lakewood, OH 44107
Ph: (216)226-4456
Fax: (216)226-8144
E-mail: bkeller5@cs.com
URL: National Affiliate–www.navyleague.org
Contact: William R. Keller, Pres.
Local. Civilian organization that supports U.S. capability to keep the sea lanes open through a strong, viable Navy, Marine Corps, Coast Guard, and Merchant Marine. Seeks to awaken interest and cooperation of U.S. citizens in matters serving to aid, improve, and develop the efficiency of U.S. naval and maritime forces and equipment. **Affiliated With:** Navy League of the United States.

15589 ■ North Coast Women's Sailing Association (NCWSA)
PO Box 732
Lakewood, OH 44107
E-mail: bethski_98@yahoo.com
URL: http://www.ncwsa.net
Contact: Beth Tyson-Fitzhugh, Commodore
Founded: 1995. **Members:** 185. **Membership Dues:** full, $40 (annual) • junior, $25 (annual). **Local**. Promotes women's sailboat experiences through educational and racing programs. **Libraries: Type:** not open to the public. **Holdings:** 20. **Subjects:** beginning to advanced racing, cruising. **Awards:** Competition Fund Award. **Frequency:** quarterly. **Type:** monetary. **Recipient:** to member. **Publications:** *Racer*, monthly. Newsletter. Describes monthly events and member activities. **Price:** included in membership dues. **Advertising:** accepted. Alternate Formats: online. **Conventions/Meetings:** annual Regatta - September • monthly workshop.

15590 ■ Northern Ohio Electrical Contractors Association (NOECA)
c/o Harry Lieben
1567 Mars Ave.
Lakewood, OH 44107-3822
Ph: (216)521-2908
Fax: (216)226-2811
E-mail: harrylieben@earthlink.net
URL: National Affiliate–www.ieci.org
Local. **Affiliated With:** Independent Electrical Contractors. **Formerly:** (2004) Independent Electrical Contractors, Northern Ohio. **Publications:** Newsletter, monthly.

15591 ■ West Shore Orchid Society
c/o Allan Lund
1460 Waterbury Rd.
Lakewood, OH 44107
Ph: (216)226-4866
URL: National Affiliate–www.orchidweb.org
Contact: Allan Lund, Contact
Local. Professional growers, botanists, hobbyists, and others interested in extending the knowledge, production, use, and appreciation of orchids. **Affiliated With:** American Orchid Society.

15592 ■ Winterhurst Figure Skating Club (WFSC)
14740 Lakewood Heights Blvd.
Lakewood, OH 44107
Ph: (216)228-4030
URL: http://www.winterhurstfsc.com
Contact: Pam Eifel, Contact
Local. Provides programs to encourage participation and achievement in the sport of figure skating on ice. Defines and maintains uniform standards of skating proficiency. Organizes and sponsors competitions and exhibitions for the purpose of stimulating interest in figure skating. **Affiliated With:** United States Figure Skating Association.

Lancaster

15593 ■ American Boer Goat Association - Region 10
2610 Crawfis Rd.
Lancaster, OH 43130
E-mail: dcboers@buckeyeinternet.com
URL: National Affiliate–www.abga.org
Contact: David Carter, Contact
Regional.

15594 ■ American Cancer Society, Fairfield Area
649 E Main St.
Lancaster, OH 43130
Ph: (740)653-5632
Fax: (740)653-5677
Free: (888)227-6446
E-mail: sheri.richardson@cancer.org
URL: http://www.cancer.org
Contact: Sheri Richardson, Contact
Local. Works to eliminate cancer as a major health problem through research, education, advocacy and service. **Affiliated With:** American Cancer Society.

15595 ■ American Cancer Society, Pickaway Area
649 E Main St.
Lancaster, OH 43130
Ph: (740)653-5632
Fax: (740)474-6078
Free: (888)227-6446
E-mail: sheri.richardson@cancer.org
URL: http://www.cancer.org
Contact: Sheri Richardson, Contact
Local. Works to eliminate cancer as a major health problem through research, education, advocacy and service. **Affiliated With:** American Cancer Society.

15596 ■ American Legion, Fairfield Post 11
154 E Main St.
Lancaster, OH 43130
Ph: (740)362-7478
Fax: (740)362-1429
URL: National Affiliate–www.legion.org
Local. **Affiliated With:** American Legion.

15597 ■ Chief Tarhe Beagle Club
c/o Bill Bay
314 Lake Rd. NE
Lancaster, OH 43130-9376
URL: National Affiliate–clubs.akc.org
Contact: Bill Bay, Contact
Local.

15598 ■ Environmental Education Council of Ohio (EECO)
PO Box 1004
Lancaster, OH 43130
Ph: (740)653-2649 (330)332-3953
Fax: (740)653-6100
E-mail: director@eeco-online.org
URL: http://www.eeco-online.org
Contact: Ms. Brenda Metcalf, Exec.Dir.
Founded: 1968. **Members:** 500. **Membership Dues:** student, senior citizen, $20 (annual) • individual, professional, $35 (annual) • organization, $70 (annual). **Staff:** 2. **Budget:** $1,000,000. **Regional Groups:** 12. **State Groups:** 1. **State**. Promotes understanding of the natural, physical, and social systems that make up the environment. Motivates people to work to conserve and protect the environment. **Awards:** Outstanding Environmental Educator in the Field of Formal Education. **Frequency:** annual. **Type:** trophy. **Recipient:** for preschool, elementary, middle school, high school or college teacher, administrator or curriculum specialist • Outstanding Environmental in the Field of Nonformal Education. **Frequency:** annual. **Type:** trophy. **Recipient:** for nonformal educator. **Computer Services:** database, link to website • online services. **Publications:** Newsletter. **Conventions/Meetings:** annual meeting.

15599 ■ Fairfield County Youth Football League (FCYFL)
c/o Robert Burkhart
1544 Wheeling Rd.
Lancaster, OH 43130
Ph: (614)249-3974 (614)732-0188
E-mail: fcyfl@columbus.rr.com
URL: http://www.fcyflohio.org
Contact: Robert Burkhart, Contact
Local.

15600 ■ Fairfield Heritage Association (FHA)
105 E Wheeling St.
Lancaster, OH 43130
Ph: (740)654-9923
E-mail: fairheritage@greenapple.com
URL: http://www.fairfieldheritage.org
Contact: Joyce Harvey, Pres.
Local. Preserves and promotes the understanding of Fairfield County history.

15601 ■ Habitat for Humanity of Fairfield County
3476 Cincinnati-Zanesville Rd. NE
PO Box 2392
Lancaster, OH 43130-5392
Ph: (740)654-3434
Fax: (740)654-3434
E-mail: fairhfh@fairfield-habitat.org
URL: http://www.fairfield-habitat.org
Contact: Robert J. Sulick, Exec.Dir.
Founded: 1992. **Local**. **Affiliated With:** Habitat for Humanity International.

15602 ■ Lancaster Area Society for Human Resource Management (LASHRM)
c/o Janet Rankin
Fairfield Medical Center
401 N Ewing St.
Lancaster, OH 43130

Ph: (740)687-8122
Fax: (740)687-8633
E-mail: janetr@smchealth.org
URL: http://www.ohioshrm.org/lancaster
Contact: Janet Rankin, Pres.

Local. Represents the interests of human resource and industrial relations professionals and executives. Promotes the advancement of human resource management.

15603 ■ Lancaster Board of Realtors
127 W Wheeling St.
Lancaster, OH 43130
Ph: (740)653-1861
Fax: (740)653-7409
E-mail: lancasterboard@lancasterboardofrealtors.com
URL: http://www.lancasterboardofrealtors.com
Contact: Debbie Hoelscher, Exec. Officer

Local. Strives to develop real estate business practices. Advocates for the right to own, use and transfer real property. Provides a facility for professional development, research and exchange of information among members and the general public. **Affiliated With:** National Association of Realtors.

15604 ■ Lancaster Fairfield County Chamber of Commerce
109 N Broad St.
PO Box 2450
Lancaster, OH 43130-5450
Ph: (740)653-8251
Fax: (740)653-7074
E-mail: info@lancoc.org
URL: http://www.lancoc.org
Contact: Christopher L. Agnitsch, Pres.

Members: 700. **Membership Dues:** accountant, funeral director, insurance, real estate and all health related professional (plus $15 per employee or associate), $225 (annual) • public official, nonprofit organization, individual not actively engaged in business, $165 (annual) • manufacturing, processor, construction, transportation, retail, wholesale, hotel, motel, automotive, publisher, radio, TV, $225 (annual) • second small business with the same owner, $70 (annual) • retired, $55 (annual). **Staff:** 3. **Local**. Promotes business and community development in the Lancaster, OH area. **Computer Services:** database, membership directory. **Telecommunication Services:** electronic mail, chris@lancoc.org. **Councils:** Legislative Action; Safety. **Divisions:** Information Technology; Resource Center; Small Business; Women's Resource Network. **Publications:** *Chamber Report*, monthly. Newsletter. **Price:** included in membership dues. **Advertising:** accepted. Alternate Formats: online • *Images of Fairfield County*. Magazine. **Advertising:** accepted. Alternate Formats: online. **Conventions/Meetings:** monthly Info Tech Meeting - 3rd Thursday • monthly Legislative Action Council Meeting - 3rd Friday • monthly Safety Council Meeting - every 1st Tuesday except July and August.

15605 ■ Lancaster Sertoma Club
PO Box 471
Lancaster, OH 43130
Ph: (740)654-7972
E-mail: rsmith@greenapple.com
URL: http://www.greenapple.com/%7Esertoma
Contact: Ron Smith, Sec.

Local.

15606 ■ Ohio Art Education Association (OAEA)
c/o Dennis Eckert, Treas.
621 Oak Hollow Way
Lancaster, OH 43130
E-mail: golubiem@zoomtown.com
URL: http://oaea.org
Contact: Dr. Mary Golubieski, Pres.

State. Promotes art education through professional development, service, advancement of Knowledge, and leadership.

15607 ■ Ohio Genealogical Society, Fairfield County Chapter
PO Box 1470
Lancaster, OH 43130-0570
Ph: (740)653-2745
E-mail: chapter@fairfieldgenealogy.org
URL: http://www.fairfieldgenealogy.org
Contact: Karen S. Smith, Pres.

Founded: 1978. **Members:** 375. **Membership Dues:** individual, $10 (annual) • family, $11 (annual). **State Groups:** 1. **Local**. Individuals with an interest in local history and genealogy. Maintains genealogical collection at Fairfield County District Library; conducts educational programs. **Libraries: Type:** open to the public. **Awards:** 4H Genealogy Award. **Frequency:** annual. **Type:** recognition. **Recipient:** chosen by 4H. **Affiliated With:** Ohio Genealogical Society. **Also Known As:** Fairfield County Genealogical Society. **Publications:** *Fairfield Trace*, quarterly. Newsletter. Contains church, cemetery, newspaper, military and biographical info pertaining to Fairfield Co., OH. **Price:** included in membership dues. **Circulation:** 450. **Advertising:** accepted. **Conventions/Meetings:** monthly meeting, with speakers (exhibits) - always third Thursday of each month. Lancaster, OH - Avg. Attendance: 25.

15608 ■ Phi Theta Kappa - Beta Beta Theta Chapter
c/o John Furlow, Jr.
1570 Granville Pike
Lancaster, OH 43130
Ph: (740)654-6711
E-mail: furlow@ohio.edu
URL: http://www.ptk.org/directories/chapters/OH/20679-1.htm
Contact: John Furlow Jr., Advisor

Local. Affiliated With: Phi Theta Kappa, International Honor Society.

15609 ■ Plumbing-Heating-Cooling Contractors Association, Central Ohio
c/o Mr. Jeffrey D. Noll, Pres.
PO Box 2573
Lancaster, OH 43130-5573
Ph: (740)687-9073
Fax: (740)687-1960
E-mail: jeffnoll@greenapple.com
URL: National Affiliate–www.phccweb.org
Contact: Mr. Jeffrey D. Noll, Pres.

Local. Represents the plumbing, heating and cooling contractors. Promotes the construction industry. Protects the environment, health, safety and comfort of society. **Affiliated With:** Plumbing-Heating-Cooling Contractors Association.

15610 ■ Quail Unlimited, Ohio Valley Chapter
2942 Elder Rd. NE
Lancaster, OH 43130
Ph: (740)536-7853 (614)325-2553
E-mail: jalbert@ruffwing.com
URL: National Affiliate–www.qu.org

Local. Affiliated With: Quail Unlimited.

15611 ■ STARFLEET: USS Asgard
c/o Cynthia Walter
435 Busby Ave.
Lancaster, OH 43130
E-mail: cyndwa@prodigy.net
URL: http://www.regionone.net
Contact: Cynthia Walter, Contact

Local. Affiliated With: STARFLEET.

15612 ■ United States Psychiatric Rehabilitation Association - Ohio Chapter
c/o Fairfield County Mental Health & Recovery Services Board
1560 Sheridan Dr.
Lancaster, OH 43130
Ph: (740)654-0829
Fax: (740)654-7621
E-mail: holley@mh.state.oh.us
URL: National Affiliate–www.uspra.org
Contact: Don Halley, Pres.

State. Promotes the advancement of the role, scope, and quality of service designed to facilitate the readjustment into the community of adults with psychiatric disabilities. Provides a forum for the exchange of ideas, experiences, and contributions to the field. Encourages the development of improved concepts and methodologies in the field of psychiatry. **Affiliated With:** United States Psychiatric Rehabilitation Association.

15613 ■ United Way of Fairfield County, Ohio
115 S Broad St.
Lancaster, OH 43130
Ph: (740)653-0643
Fax: (740)653-1139
E-mail: sorlando@uwayfairfieldco.org
URL: http://www.uwayfairfieldco.org
Contact: Sherry Orlando, Exec.Dir.

Local. Affiliated With: United Way of America.

15614 ■ Women's Division of the Lancaster Chamber of Commerce
Lancaster Fairfield County Chamber of Commerce
109 N Broad St.
PO Box 2450
Lancaster, OH 43130
Ph: (740)653-8251
Fax: (740)653-7074
E-mail: info@lancoc.org
URL: http://www.lancoc.org
Contact: Nanciann Rosier, Chair

Local.

Leavittsburg

15615 ■ American Legion, Elmer Dade Memorial Post 699
201 S Leavitt Rd.
Leavittsburg, OH 44430
Ph: (614)392-4961
Fax: (740)362-1429
URL: National Affiliate–www.legion.org

Local. Affiliated With: American Legion.

Lebanon

15616 ■ AAA Cincinnati
102 E Mulberry St.
Lebanon, OH 45036
Ph: (513)932-3300

State.

15617 ■ American Legion, Ohio Post 186
c/o Ralph P. Snook
PO Box 186
Lebanon, OH 45036
Ph: (740)362-7478
Fax: (740)362-1429
URL: National Affiliate–www.legion.org
Contact: Ralph P. Snook, Contact

Local. Affiliated With: American Legion.

15618 ■ American Meteorological Society, Central Ohio
c/o Robin L. Belton
1111 Deerfield Rd., Unit 111
Lebanon, OH 45036
E-mail: belton.6@pop.service.ohio-state.edu
URL: National Affiliate–www.ametsoc.org/AMS
Contact: Robin L. Belton, Contact

Regional. Affiliated With: American Meteorological Society.

15619 ■ American Society of Appraisers, Dayton - Cincinnati Chapter
c/o James A. Garrett, Pres.
Garrett Appraisal Ser.
PO Box 359
Lebanon, OH 45036-0359
Ph: (513)932-0005
Fax: (513)932-0005
E-mail: garrett@go-concepts.com
URL: http://www.appraisers.org/dayton_cincinnati
Contact: James A. Garrett, Pres.
Local. Serves as a professional appraisal educator, testing and accrediting society. Sponsors mandatory recertification program for all members. Offers consumer information service to the public. **Affiliated With:** American Society of Appraisers.

15620 ■ American Society of Media Photographers, Ohio Valley Chapter
c/o Todd Joyce, Co-Pres.
2174 S Waynesville Rd.
Lebanon, OH 45036
Ph: (513)899-2727
Fax: (513)421-1209
E-mail: todd@joycephotography.com
URL: http://www.asmpohiovalley.org
Contact: Todd Joyce, Co-Pres.
Regional. **Affiliated With:** American Society of Media Photographers.

15621 ■ Lebanon Area Chamber of Commerce (LACC)
20 N Broadway
Lebanon, OH 45036
Ph: (513)932-1100
Fax: (513)932-9050
E-mail: info@lebanonchamber.org
URL: http://www.lebanonchamber.org
Contact: Sara Arseneau, Exec.Dir.
Founded: 1924. **Membership Dues:** sole proprietor with no employees, $195 (annual) • business with employees (plus $5 per employee), $195 (annual) • business with independent contractors working in Warren County (plus $5 per contractor), $195 (annual) • nonprofit (plus $2.50 per employee), $97 (annual) • associate (no voting and no benefits), $125 (annual). **Local**. Promotes business and community development in the Lebanon, OH area. Sponsors Christmas Festival and Artstreet. **Computer Services:** Online services, member listings. **Affiliated With:** U.S. Chamber of Commerce. **Publications:** *Business and Industry Directory*, periodic • Newsletter, bimonthly. Lists new members, upcoming events and programs, community activities, government issues, and member activities.

15622 ■ Lebanon Lions Club - Ohio
122 E Silver St.
Lebanon, OH 45036-1812
Ph: (513)932-7070
URL: http://lebanon1oh.lionwap.org
Contact: Jeffery Bour, Pres.
Local. **Affiliated With:** Lions Clubs International.

15623 ■ Ohio Genealogical Society, Warren County Chapter
Admin. Bldg., Lower Level
406 Justice Dr.
Lebanon, OH 45036
Ph: (513)695-1144
E-mail: wcgs@co.warren.oh.us
URL: http://www.co.warren.oh.us/genealogy/index.htm
Contact: Diana Linkous, Pres.
Founded: 1981. **Members:** 165. **Staff:** 10. **Local**. Genealogists and others with an interest in family history in Warren County, OH. Gathers and publishes local birth, marriage, court, death, and cemetery records. **Libraries: Type:** open to the public. **Holdings:** archival material, books, periodicals. **Subjects:** genealogy, history. **Affiliated With:** Ohio Genealogical Society. **Publications:** *Heir-Lines*, quarterly. **Price:** included in membership dues • Books. **Conventions/Meetings:** monthly meeting - always third Wednesday, except January-March.

15624 ■ Warren County Convention and Visitors Bureau
313 E Warren St.
Lebanon, OH 45036
Ph: (513)933-1138
Free: (800)791-4FUN
E-mail: lmcintosh@wccvb.org
URL: http://www.ohio4fun.org
Contact: Shirley Bonekemper, Exec.Dir.
Local.

15625 ■ Warren County Historical Society (WCHS)
105 S Broadway
Lebanon, OH 45036-1707
Ph: (513)932-1817
Fax: (513)932-8560
E-mail: wchs@go-concepts.com
URL: http://wchsmuseum.com
Contact: Ms. Shirley Ray, Museum Dir.
Founded: 1940. **Members:** 632. **Membership Dues:** individual, $20 (annual) • family, $30 (annual) • sustaining, $60 (annual) • patron, $125 (annual) • gold card, $500 (annual) • non-profit business, $45 (annual) • small business, $150 (annual) • sustaining business, $275 (annual) • patron business, $550 (annual) • gold business, $1,000 (annual). **Staff:** 3. **Local**. Individuals interested in preserving the history of Warren County, OH. Operates the Warren County Historical Society Museum, gift shop and genealogy/research library all year-round, as well as the nearby Glendower Mansion, which is opened seasonally. Provides advance notice of special events and lectures to the members. Offers an annual quilt show, two antiques shows, a Civil War Encampment, History Camp for Kids, Christmas at Glendower, and flea market fund-raisers for the museum. **Libraries: Type:** reference. **Holdings:** 3,000; archival material, books, clippings, maps, papers, photographs. **Subjects:** Warren County history, genealogy, Shaker. **Awards:** Lena Iorns History Award. **Frequency:** annual. **Type:** recognition. **Recipient:** to two eighth-grade students from each Warren County junior high school for their achievement in and love of history. **Publications:** *HistoricaLog*, quarterly. Newsletter. Features a story on some historical event, person or place in Warren County, and advance notice of upcoming society events. **Price:** included in membership dues. **Conventions/Meetings:** annual meeting.

15626 ■ Warren County Kennel Club of Ohio (WCKC)
PO Box 1144
Lebanon, OH 45036
E-mail: warrencountykc@aol.com
URL: http://warrencountykc.com
Founded: 1975. **Local**.

15627 ■ Warren County Retired and Senior Volunteer Program
c/o Dolcee Hoffman, Dir.
570 N State, Rte. 741
Lebanon, OH 45036
Ph: (513)695-2252
Fax: (513)695-2277
E-mail: dolceeh@wccsinc.org
URL: http://www.wccsi.org
Contact: Dolcee Hoffman, Dir.
Local. **Affiliated With:** Retired and Senior Volunteer Program.

15628 ■ Warren County United Way, Ohio
645 Oak St.
Lebanon, OH 45036
Ph: (513)932-3987
Fax: (513)932-4496
URL: http://www.warrencountyunitedway.org
Contact: Michael Schepers, Exec.Dir.
Local. **Affiliated With:** United Way of America.

Leesburg

15629 ■ American Legion, Leesburg Post 568
6 W Main St.
Leesburg, OH 45135
Ph: (740)362-7478
Fax: (740)362-1429
URL: National Affiliate–www.legion.org
Local. **Affiliated With:** American Legion.

Leetonia

15630 ■ American Legion, Ohio Post 131
c/o Joe Williams
420 Columbia St.
Leetonia, OH 44431
Ph: (740)362-7478
Fax: (740)362-1429
URL: National Affiliate–www.legion.org
Contact: Joe Williams, Contact
Local. **Affiliated With:** American Legion.

15631 ■ Leetonia-Washingtonville Area Chamber of Commerce
300 E Main St.
Leetonia, OH 44431-1137
Ph: (330)427-6721
Fax: (330)427-8080
Local.

Leipsic

15632 ■ American Legion, Ohio Post 287
c/o Charles J. Wagner
815 Mathias St.
Leipsic, OH 45856
Ph: (740)362-7478
Fax: (740)362-1429
URL: National Affiliate–www.legion.org
Contact: Charles J. Wagner, Contact
Local. **Affiliated With:** American Legion.

15633 ■ Leipsic Area Chamber of Commerce
142 E Main St.
Leipsic, OH 45856
Ph: (419)943-2009
E-mail: info@leipsic.com
URL: http://www.leipsic.com
Contact: Greg Warnimont, Pres.
Local. Represents businesses in Leipsic, OH.

Lewis Center

15634 ■ Automotive Service Association of Ohio
6081 Columbus Pike, State Rte. 23
Lewis Center, OH 43035
Ph: (740)548-4889
Fax: (740)548-5746
Free: (800)441-6518
E-mail: asaohio@infinet.com
URL: http://www.asashop.org/asaohio
Contact: Lisa Clark, Exec.Dir.
State. **Affiliated With:** Automotive Service Association.

15635 ■ Columbus Southeast Lions Club
c/o Steven Aumiller, Pres.
7740 Pinehill Rd.
Lewis Center, OH 43035
Ph: (740)657-8077
E-mail: swaumiller@insight.com
URL: http://www.iwaynet.net/~lions13f
Contact: Steven Aumiller, Pres.
Local. **Affiliated With:** Lions Clubs International.

Lewisburg

15636 ■ American Legion, Paul Sodder Post 213
PO Box 507
Lewisburg, OH 45338
Ph: (740)362-7478
Fax: (740)362-1429
URL: National Affiliate–www.legion.org
Local. **Affiliated With:** American Legion.

15637 ■ Lewisburg Lions Club
US 40 W
Lewisburg, OH 45338
Ph: (937)962-2457
URL: http://lewisburgoh.lionwap.org
Contact: Ken Wright, Pres.
Local. Affiliated With: Lions Clubs International.

Lexington

15638 ■ Vintage Chevrolet Club of America, Lake Erie (Ohio) Region No. 7
c/o Gaye Kanz, Dir.
3835 State Rte. 546
Lexington, OH 44904
Ph: (419)884-9320
URL: National Affiliate–www.vcca.org
Contact: Gaye Kanz, Dir.
Local. Affiliated With: Vintage Chevrolet Club of America.

Liberty Center

15639 ■ American Legion, Ohio Post 492
c/o Gilbert Baughman
103 N Pleasantview Dr.
Liberty Center, OH 43532
Ph: (740)362-7478
Fax: (740)362-1429
URL: National Affiliate–www.legion.org
Contact: Gilbert Baughman, Contact
Local. Affiliated With: American Legion.

15640 ■ Friends of the Liberty Center Public Library
c/o Mary Beth Slee
PO Box 66
Liberty Center, OH 43532
Ph: (419)533-5721
Fax: (419)533-4849
E-mail: libctr@oplin.org
URL: http://library.norweld.lib.oh.us/libertycenter/friends.htm
Contact: Mary Beth Slee, Contact
Founded: 1997. **Members:** 314. **Membership Dues:** individual, $5 (annual) • family, $10 (annual) • lifetime, $100. **Budget:** $7,000. **Local.** Individuals interested in providing support to the Liberty Center Public Library in Liberty Center, OH. Sponsors fundraising events for the library. **Libraries: Type:** open to the public. **Holdings:** 12,500. **Conventions/Meetings:** monthly meeting.

Lima

15641 ■ AAA Ohio Automobile Club
2115 Allentown Rd.
Lima, OH 45805
Ph: (419)228-1022
State.

15642 ■ Allen County REACT
PO Box 981
Lima, OH 45802
Ph: (419)296-0958
E-mail: allencoreact@aol.com
URL: http://www.reactintl.org/teaminfo/usa_teams/teams-usoh.htm
Local. Trained communication experts and professional volunteers. Provides volunteer public service and emergency communications through the use of radios (Citizen Band, General Mobile Radio Service, UHF and HAM). Coordinates with radio industries and government on safety communication matters and supports charitable activities and community organizations.

15643 ■ Alzheimer's Association, Northwest Ohio Chapter, Lima Office
892-A S Cable Rd.
Lima, OH 45805
Ph: (419)227-9700
Fax: (419)222-6212
Free: (800)441-3322
E-mail: wcodot@bright.net
URL: National Affiliate–www.alz.org
Contact: Dorothy Wildermuth, Contact
Local. Family members of sufferers of Alzheimer's disease. Combats Alzheimer's disease and related disorders. (Alzheimer's disease is a progressive, degenerative brain disease in which changes occur in the central nervous system and outer region of the brain causing memory loss and other changes in thought, personality, and behavior.) Promotes research to find the cause, treatment, and cure for the disease. **Affiliated With:** Alzheimer's Association.

15644 ■ American Cancer Society, Mercer Area
616 Collett St.
Lima, OH 45805
Ph: (419)225-8860
Fax: (419)486-3490
Free: (888)227-6446
URL: http://www.cancer.org
Local. Affiliated With: American Cancer Society.

15645 ■ American Legion, Ohio Post 96
c/o William Paul Gallagher
711 S Shore Dr.
Lima, OH 45804
Ph: (740)362-7478
Fax: (740)362-1429
URL: National Affiliate–www.legion.org
Contact: William Paul Gallagher, Contact
Local. Affiliated With: American Legion.

15646 ■ American Legion, Stover-Harrod Post 133
1375 E State Rd.
Lima, OH 45801
Ph: (740)362-7478
Fax: (740)362-1429
URL: National Affiliate–www.legion.org
Local. Affiliated With: American Legion.

15647 ■ American Red Cross, Allen County Chapter
610 S Collett St.
Lima, OH 45805
Ph: (419)227-5121
Fax: (419)222-0416
E-mail: director@allenohrc.org
URL: http://www.allenohrc.org
Contact: David Collins, Exec.Dir.
Local.

15648 ■ Apollo Education Association
3325 Shawnee Rd.
Lima, OH 45806-1454
Ph: (419)998-2999
URL: http://www.apollocareercenter.com
Contact: J. Chris Pfister, Superintendent
Local.

15649 ■ Arc of Allen County
547 S Collett
Lima, OH 45805
Ph: (419)225-6285
Fax: (419)228-7770
E-mail: arc@wcoil.com
URL: http://www.arcallencounty.org
Contact: Joshua Ebling, Exec.Dir.
Local. Parents, professional workers, and others interested in individuals with mental retardation. Works to promote services, research, public understanding, and legislation for people with mental retardation and their families. **Affiliated With:** Arc of the United States.

15650 ■ Better Business Bureau of West Central Ohio
219 N McDonel St.
Lima, OH 45801
Ph: (419)223-7010
Fax: (419)229-2029
E-mail: info@limabbb.org
URL: http://www.wcohio.bbb.org
Contact: Neil Winget, Pres./CEO
Local. Seeks to promote and foster ethical relationship between businesses and the public through voluntary self-regulation, consumer and business education, and service excellence. Provides information to help consumers and businesses make informed purchasing decisions and avoid costly scams and frauds; settles consumer complaints through arbitration and other means. **Affiliated With:** BBB Wise Giving Alliance.

15651 ■ Downtown Lima
147 N Main St.
Lima, OH 45801
Ph: (419)222-6045
Fax: (419)229-0266
E-mail: info@downtownlimaohio.com
URL: http://www.downtownlimaohio.com
Local.

15652 ■ Gardeners of America/Men's Garden Clubs of America - Gardeners of Lima
c/o Wayne Thelan, Pres.
4612 Kitamat Trail
Lima, OH 45805
Ph: (419)999-2842
E-mail: thelan@wcoil.com
URL: National Affiliate–www.tgoa-mgca.org
Contact: Wayne Thelan, Pres.
Local.

15653 ■ Girl Scouts of Appleseed Ridge
1870 W Robb Ave.
Lima, OH 45805
Ph: (419)225-4085
Fax: (419)229-7570
Free: (800)962-7753
E-mail: council@gsar.org
URL: http://www.gsar.org
Contact: Jane P. Krites, CEO
Local. Young girls and adult volunteers, corporate, government and individual supporters. Strives to develop potential and leadership skills among its members. Conducts trainings, educational programs and outdoor activities.

15654 ■ Habitat for Humanity - Lima Area
119 N Cole St.
Lima, OH 45805
Ph: (419)222-4937
E-mail: habitat@wcoil.com
URL: http://www.habitatlima.org
Contact: Lavon J. Welty, Exec.Dir.
Local. Affiliated With: Habitat for Humanity International.

15655 ■ International Brotherhood of Magicians, Ring 205
c/o Gene Craft, Sec.
Lima Tech. Coll.
4240 Campus Dr.
Lima, OH 45804-3597
Ph: (419)995-8303
Fax: (419)995-8095
E-mail: ring205@hotmail.com
URL: http://www.angelfire.com/oh/ring205
Contact: Paul Ricksecker, Pres.
Local. Professional and semi-professional magicians; suppliers, assistants, agents, and others interested in magic. Seeks to advance the art of magic in the field of amusement, entertainment, and culture. Promotes proper means of discouraging false or misleading advertising of effects, tricks, literature, merchandise, or actions appertaining to the magical arts; opposes exposures of principles of the art of magic, except in books on magic and magazines devoted to such art for the exclusive use of magicians and devotees of

the art; encourages humane treatment and care of live animals whenever employed in magical performances. **Affiliated With:** International Brotherhood of Magicians.

15656 ■ International Union, United Automobile, Aerospace and Agricultural Implement Workers of America, AFL-CIO - Local Union 2075
1440 Bellefontaine Ave.
Lima, OH 45804
Ph: (419)229-7593
E-mail: monroej@gdls.com
URL: http://www.uawlocal2075-2147.org
Contact: Jeff Monroe, Pres.
Members: 438. **Local**. AFL-CIO. **Affiliated With:** International Union, United Automobile, Aerospace and Agricultural Implement Workers of America.

15657 ■ Korean War Veterans Association, Johnny Johnson Chapter
c/o Dillon Staas
2636 Debbie Dr.
Lima, OH 45807
Ph: (419)225-7177
E-mail: dstaas@woh.rr.com
URL: National Affiliate–www.kwva.org
Contact: Dillon Staas, Contact
Local. Affiliated With: Korean War Veterans Association.

15658 ■ Lima/Allen County Chamber of Commerce
147 N Main St.
Lima, OH 45801-4927
Ph: (419)222-6045
Fax: (419)229-0266
E-mail: chamber@limachamber.com
URL: http://www.limachamber.com
Contact: Jed E. Metzger, Pres./CEO
Founded: 1887. **Membership Dues:** business (based on number of employees), $185-$4,580 (annual) • board of advisor, $25,000 (annual) • gold key, $4,000 (annual) • second location, $100 (annual) • individual, $125 (annual) • church, social/charitable organization, $150 (annual). **Staff:** 8. **Local**. Promotes business and community development in the Lima, OH area. **Computer Services:** Online services, business directory. **Telecommunication Services:** electronic mail, jmetzger@limachamber.com. **Committees:** Agri-Business; Education; Minority Business Advisory; Retail; Small Business; Wake, Rattle and Roll. **Councils:** Lima/Allen County Trades; Manufacturer. **Publications:** *Allen County Business Directory*. Contains lists of businesses from the public, private and not-for-profit sectors. **Price:** $75. 00. Alternate Formats: CD-ROM • *Allen County Interactive CD-ROM*. Video. Contains over 2.5 hours of text and audio, in addition to over 500 images, for relocating families, prospective businesses, etc. **Price:** $3.00 for members; $6.00 for nonmembers. Alternate Formats: CD-ROM • *Business Network*, monthly. Newsletter. **Circulation:** 80,000 • *Membership Directory and Buyers' Guide*, annual. **Price:** included in membership dues; $7.00 for nonmembers. **Circulation:** 3,500. **Advertising:** accepted. Alternate Formats: online • *Minority Business/Professional Directory*. Contains listings for minority-owned Chamber member businesses and organizations. **Price:** included in membership dues; $5.00 for nonmembers. **Conventions/Meetings:** monthly Safety Council Meeting - every 2nd Tuesday • monthly Wake, Rattle and Roll - meeting - every last Friday.

15659 ■ Lima Area Senior Olympics
c/o Mary Lou Paisley
3400 W Elm
Lima, OH 45807
Ph: (419)991-8811
Fax: (419)991-3312
E-mail: wellness@seniorcitizens.ws
URL: http://www.ohioseniorolympics.org
Contact: Mary Lou Paisley, Contact
Local. Affiliated With: National Senior Games Association.

15660 ■ Lima Beagle Club
c/o Doug Rowe
1502 Garland Ave.
Lima, OH 45804-2734
URL: National Affiliate–clubs.akc.org
Contact: Doug Rowe, Contact
Local.

15661 ■ Lima Exchange Club
PO Box 774
Lima, OH 45802
E-mail: mbowker@limachamber.com
URL: http://www.limaexchangeclub.com
Contact: Marc Bowker, Pres.
Local.

15662 ■ Lima Society for Human Resource Management (LSHRM)
c/o Tillie A. Schiffler
Clemans Nelson & Associates
417 Northwest St.
Lima, OH 45801
Ph: (419)227-4945
Fax: (419)229-8617
URL: http://www.limashrm.org
Contact: Tillie A. Schiffler, Pres.
Local. Represents the interests of human resource and industrial relations professionals and executives. Promotes the advancement of human resource management.

15663 ■ Mothers Against Drunk Driving, Allen/Putnam Counties
PO Box 1491
Lima, OH 45802
Ph: (419)224-6233
Fax: (419)523-6126
URL: National Affiliate–www.madd.org
Local. Victims of drunk driving crashes; concerned citizens. Encourages citizen participation in working towards reform of the drunk driving problem and the prevention of underage drinking. Acts as the voice of victims of drunk driving crashes by speaking on their behalf to communities, businesses, and educational groups. **Affiliated With:** Mothers Against Drunk Driving.

15664 ■ Navy Club of Adam G. Stelzer - Ship No. 9
605 Seriff Rd.
Lima, OH 45805
Ph: (419)991-2142
URL: National Affiliate–www.navyclubusa.org
Contact: Doyle Keith, Commander
Local. Represents individuals who are, or have been, in the active service of the U.S. Navy, Naval Reserve, Marine Corps, Marine Corps Reserve, and Coast Guard. Promotes and encourages further public interest in the U.S. Navy and its history. Upholds the spirit and ideals of the U.S. Navy. Acts as a public forum for members' views on national defense. Assists the Navy Recruiting Command whenever and wherever possible. Conducts charitable activities. **Affiliated With:** Navy Club of the United States of America.

15665 ■ Ohio Genealogical Society, Allen County
PO Box 1104
Lima, OH 45802
E-mail: dcarder2@woh.rr.com
URL: http://allencogenealogysociety.homestead.com/main.html
Contact: Debbie Carder, VP
Local. Affiliated With: Ohio Genealogical Society.

15666 ■ Ohio Health Care Association, District 3
c/o James W. Unverferth, Chm.
HCF Mgt., Inc.
1100 Shawnee Rd.
Lima, OH 45805
Ph: (419)999-2010
Fax: (419)999-4162
E-mail: jim.unverferth@hcfmanagement.com
URL: http://www.ohca.org
Contact: James W. Unverferth, Chm.
Local. Promotes professionalism and ethical behavior of individuals providing long-term care delivery for patients and for the general public. Provides information, education and administrative tools to enhance the quality of long-term care. Improves the standards of service and administration of member nursing homes, **Affiliated With:** American Health Care Association.

15667 ■ Ohio Thoracic Society
c/o Nancy J. Nedilsky, Administrator
PO Box 870
Lima, OH 45802-0870
Ph: (419)991-5464
E-mail: njnedilsky@wcoil.com
URL: National Affiliate–www.thoracic.org
Contact: James Willey MD, Pres.
State. Aims to improve the study and practice of thoracic surgery and related disciplines. Seeks to prevent and fight respiratory diseases through research, education and patient advocacy. **Affiliated With:** American Thoracic Society.

15668 ■ Phi Theta Kappa - Alpha Tau Mu Chapter
c/o Sean Lause
Galvin Hall
4240 Campus Dr.
Lima, OH 45804
Ph: (419)995-8374
E-mail: lause.s@rhodesstate.edu
URL: http://www.ptk.org/directories/chapters/OH/14269-1.htm
Contact: Sean Lause, Advisor
Local. Affiliated With: Phi Theta Kappa, International Honor Society.

15669 ■ Society of Manufacturing Engineers - James A. Rhodes State College S226
James A. Rhodes State Coll., Engg. Tech.
4240 Campus Dr.
Lima, OH 45804-3776
Ph: (419)995-8073
Fax: (419)995-8095
E-mail: hill.j@rhodesstate.edu
URL: National Affiliate–www.sme.org
Contact: Jack E. Hill, Contact
Local. Advances manufacturing knowledge to gain competitive advantage. Improves skills and manufacturing solutions for the growth of economy. Provides resources and opportunities for manufacturing professionals. **Affiliated With:** Center for Oceans Law and Policy.

15670 ■ Sweet Adelines International, Sisters in Song Chapter
Market St. Presbyterian Church
1100 W Market
Lima, OH 45805
Ph: (419)225-7359
E-mail: janicek@wcoil.com
URL: National Affiliate–www.sweetadelineintl.org
Contact: Janice Comeskey, Contact
Local. Advances the musical art form of barbershop harmony through education and performances. Provides education, training and coaching in the development of women's four-part barbershop harmony. **Affiliated With:** Sweet Adelines International.

15671 ■ Tri-Moraine Audubon Society
PO Box 5648
Lima, OH 45802
Ph: (937)596-5330
E-mail: webmaster@tri-moraineaudubon.org
URL: http://www.tri-moraineaudubon.org
Contact: Mary Rosenbeck, Pres.
Local. Formerly: (2005) National Audubon Society - Tri-Moraine.

15672 ■ United Way of Greater Lima
616 S Collett St.
Lima, OH 45805
Ph: (419)227-6341
Fax: (419)222-2479
E-mail: uw@unitedwaylima.com
URL: http://www.unitedwaylima.org
Contact: Beverly J. Prueter, Pres.
Founded: 1955. **Nonmembership**. **Local**. Raises funds through community and corporate campaigns to support various nonprofit organizations. **Affiliated With:** United Way of America. **Publications:** *In Touch*, quarterly. Newsletter. **Price:** free. **Circulation:** 2,000.

15673 ■ Vietnam Veterans of America, Chapter No. 89 LZ-Lima
c/o Bill Riepenhoff, Pres.
130 W Elm St.
Lima, OH 45801
Ph: (419)222-2136
URL: http://www.vvabuckeyestatecouncil.com
Contact: Bill Riepenhoff, Pres.
Local. **Affiliated With:** Vietnam Veterans of America.

15674 ■ West Central Association of Realtors, Ohio
400 S Cable Rd.
Lima, OH 45805-3112
Ph: (419)227-5432
Fax: (419)229-1842
E-mail: tim_s@yocumrealty.com
URL: http://www.wcare.net
Contact: Tim Stanford, Pres.
Local. Strives to develop real estate business practices. Advocates for the right to own, use and transfer real property. Provides a facility for professional development, research and exchange of information among members and the general public. **Affiliated With:** National Association of Realtors.

Lindsey

15675 ■ Lindsey Lions Club
c/o Rod Opelt, Pres.
313 Walnut St.
Lindsey, OH 43442
Ph: (419)665-2532 (419)547-2619
E-mail: rod_opelt@whirlpool.com
URL: http://www.lions13b.org
Contact: Rod Opelt, Pres.
Local. **Affiliated With:** Lions Clubs International.

Lisbon

15676 ■ American Legion, Ohio Post 275
c/o John J. Welsh
419 E Lincoln Way
Lisbon, OH 44432
Ph: (740)362-7478
Fax: (740)362-1429
URL: National Affiliate–www.legion.org
Contact: John J. Welsh, Contact
Local. **Affiliated With:** American Legion.

15677 ■ East Liverpool Beagle Club
c/o Gary Johnson
118 W Washington St.
Lisbon, OH 44432-1242
URL: National Affiliate–clubs.akc.org
Contact: Gary Johnson, Contact
Local.

15678 ■ Lisbon Area Chamber of Commerce (LACC)
PO Box 282
Lisbon, OH 44432
Ph: (330)424-1803
Fax: (330)424-0717
E-mail: info@lisbonohiochamber.com
URL: http://www.lisbonohiochamber.com/index.html
Contact: Fred Capel, Exec.Dir.
Founded: 1964. **Members:** 121. **Local**. Promotes business and community development in the Lisbon, OH area. Sponsors annual Johnny Appleseed Festival. **Publications:** *Chamber of Commerce Newsletter*, quarterly. **Conventions/Meetings:** bimonthly board meeting • annual meeting - always January.

15679 ■ Lisbon Lions Club - Ohio
c/o Ed Cusick, Pres.
64 North St.
Lisbon, OH 44432
Ph: (330)424-5234
E-mail: lisbonlionsclub@yahoo.com
URL: http://www.lions13d.org
Contact: Ed Cusick, Pres.
Local. **Affiliated With:** Lions Clubs International.

15680 ■ Ohio Health Care Association, District 11
c/o Tim Chesney, Chm.
Pleasant View Nursing Home
7451 Pleasant View Dr.
Lisbon, OH 44432
Ph: (330)424-3721
Fax: (330)424-0316
E-mail: chesneytim@hotmail.com
URL: http://www.ohca.org
Contact: Tim Chesney, Chm.
Local. Promotes professionalism and ethical behavior of individuals providing long-term care delivery for patients and for the general public. Provides information, education and administrative tools to enhance the quality of long-term care. Improves the standards of service and administration of member nursing homes. **Affiliated With:** American Health Care Association.

15681 ■ RSVP of Columbiana County
c/o Kathy Birch, Dir.
PO Box 355
Lisbon, OH 44432
Ph: (330)424-7877
Fax: (330)424-0910
E-mail: rsvpofcc@sky-access.com
URL: http://www.seniorcorps.gov/about/programs/rsvp.asp
Contact: Kathy Birch, Dir.
Local. **Affiliated With:** Retired and Senior Volunteer Program.

15682 ■ West Point Lions Club - Ohio
c/o Joan J. Plunkett, Sec.
42290 State Rte. 518
Lisbon, OH 44432
Ph: (330)424-7773
E-mail: joan@firstlocal.net
URL: http://www.lions13d.org
Contact: Joan J. Plunkett, Sec.
Local. **Affiliated With:** Lions Clubs International.

Lithopolis

15683 ■ American Legion, Walker-Hecox-Hickle Post 677
PO Box 181
Lithopolis, OH 43136
Ph: (740)362-7478
Fax: (740)362-1429
URL: National Affiliate–www.legion.org
Local. **Affiliated With:** American Legion.

Little Hocking

15684 ■ Muskies West Virginia Chapter 9
1270 Fed. Rd.
Little Hocking, OH 45742
Ph: (740)667-3471
E-mail: jimoor@frognet.net
URL: http://www.muskies.org/chapters/09
Contact: Jim Moore, Pres.
Local.

Lodi

15685 ■ American Legion, Lodi Post 523
120 Bank St.
Lodi, OH 44254
Ph: (740)362-7478
Fax: (740)362-1429
URL: National Affiliate–www.legion.org
Local. **Affiliated With:** American Legion.

15686 ■ Lodi Area Chamber of Commerce
PO Box 6
Lodi, OH 44254
Ph: (330)948-8047
E-mail: info@lodiohiochamber.com
URL: http://www.lodiohiochamber.com
Contact: Paul Bayus, Pres.
Founded: 1949. **Membership Dues:** regular, $50 (annual). **Local**. Promotes businesses in Lodi, OH. Provides networking and information services to members. **Awards:** Business/Community Person of the Year. **Frequency:** annual. **Type:** recognition. **Computer Services:** database, membership directory • mailing lists, of members. **Committees:** Civic; Government Affairs; Industrial; Public Relations; Retail. **Affiliated With:** Ohio Chamber of Commerce.

15687 ■ North Ohio National Organization for the Reform of Marijuana Laws
c/o Cher Neufer
107 Wooster St.
Lodi, OH 44254
Ph: (330)948-WEED
E-mail: nonorml@420.com
Affiliated With: National Organization for the Reform of Marijuana Laws.

Logan

15688 ■ American Legion, Ohio Post 78
c/o Lawrence Neal Helber
12845 State Rte. 664 S
Logan, OH 43138
Ph: (740)362-7478
Fax: (740)362-1429
URL: National Affiliate–www.legion.org
Contact: Lawrence Neal Helber, Contact
Local. **Affiliated With:** American Legion.

15689 ■ Korean War Veterans Association, Hocking Valley Chapter
c/o Larry G. McKinniss
31478 Harsh Rd.
Logan, OH 43138-9059
Ph: (740)380-0181
URL: National Affiliate–www.kwva.org
Contact: Larry G. McKinniss, Contact
Local. **Affiliated With:** Korean War Veterans Association.

15690 ■ Logan - Hocking Chamber of Commerce
4 E Hunter St.
PO Box 838
Logan, OH 43138
Ph: (740)385-6836
Fax: (740)385-7259
E-mail: contact@logan-hockingchamber.com
URL: http://www.logan-hockingchamber.com
Contact: Bill Rienhart, Exec.Dir.
Membership Dues: individual associate, $35 (annual) • retired, $50 (annual) • associate business, $95 (annual) • professional, $125-$1,350 (annual) • financial institution, $350-$1,350 (annual) • utility, $575 (annual) • other business (based on number of employees), $100-$1,350 (annual). **Local**. Aims to keep Logan area's economic condition at a level where businesses will risk their resources in the hope of making a profit. **Committees:** Chamber Benefits. **Councils:** Chamber and Community Development; Economic Development; Logan Business. **Programs:** First Impressions. **Publications:** Membership Directory. Alternate Formats: online. **Conventions/**

Meetings: monthly Chamber and Community Development Council Meeting - 4th Thursday • monthly Economic Development Council Meeting - 1st Thursday • monthly Logan Business Council Meeting - 1st Wednesday.

15691 ■ United Way of Hocking County
PO Box 567
Logan, OH 43138-9087
Ph: (740)385-1389
URL: National Affiliate–national.unitedway.org
Local. Affiliated With: United Way of America.

London

15692 ■ American Legion, Madison Memorial Post 105
PO Box 11
London, OH 43140
Ph: (740)362-7478
Fax: (740)362-1429
URL: National Affiliate–www.legion.org
Local. Affiliated With: American Legion.

15693 ■ Correctional Education Association - Region III
c/o Wesley Jones, Treas.
PO Box 740
London, OH 43140-0740
Ph: (740)852-9777
URL: http://cea.com
Contact: Joanna Leftwich, Dir.
Founded: 1951. **Members:** 1,000. **Membership Dues:** individual, $50 (annual). **Budget:** $8,000. **State Groups:** 6. **Regional. Awards:** Teacher of the Year. **Frequency:** annual. **Type:** grant. **Recipient:** for outstanding teacher. **Affiliated With:** American Correctional Association. **Publications:** *CEA Region III*. Newsletter. **Conventions/Meetings:** annual conference.

15694 ■ London Lions Club
c/o Dana Fisher, Sec.
10540 State Rte. 38 SW
London, OH 43140
Ph: (740)852-2345 (740)874-9201
E-mail: rr1363@dragonbbs.com
URL: http://www.iwaynet.net/~lions13f
Contact: Dana Fisher, Sec.
Local. Affiliated With: Lions Clubs International.

15695 ■ Madison County Chamber of Commerce
730 Keny Blvd.
London, OH 43140-1074
Ph: (740)852-2250
Fax: (740)852-5133
E-mail: nancymorcher@madisoncountychamber.org
URL: http://www.madisoncountychamber.org
Contact: Nancy Morcher, Pres.
Members: 300. **Membership Dues:** business (based on number of employees), $350-$850 (annual) • associate, $50 (annual) • utilities, financial institution, $550 (annual) • basic, $200 (annual). **Local.** Promotes business and community development in the London, OH area. **Computer Services:** Online services, member directory. **Formerly:** (2000) London Area Chamber of Commerce. **Publications:** Newsletter, monthly. Contains upcoming events and current developments. Alternate Formats: online.

15696 ■ Ohio Festivals and Events Association (OFEA)
c/o Donna Warner, Sec.-Treas.
2055 Cherokee Dr.
London, OH 43140
Ph: (740)852-9499
E-mail: info@ofea.org
URL: http://www.ofea.org
Contact: Donna Warner, Sec.-Treas.
Founded: 1961. **Members:** 55. **Membership Dues:** festival and event, $200 (annual). **State.** Promotes festivals, events, and tourism. **Awards:** Legion of Honor. **Frequency:** annual. **Type:** recognition. **Recipient:** for individuals who have contributed to the organization • President's Award. **Frequency:** annual. **Type:** recognition. **Recipient:** for individuals who best represent the ideals and principles of the organization. **Affiliated With:** International Festivals and Events Association. **Publications:** Directory, annual • Newsletter, bimonthly • Brochures, annual. **Conventions/Meetings:** annual convention (exhibits) - always November • semiannual meeting.

15697 ■ Vietnam Veterans of America, Chapter No. 746
c/o Jerry V. Collier, Jr., Pres.
PO Box 531
London, OH 43140-0531
Ph: (740)852-9303
URL: http://www.vvabuckeyestatecouncil.com
Contact: Jerry V. Collier Jr., Pres.
Local. Affiliated With: Vietnam Veterans of America.

Lorain

15698 ■ Alcoholics Anonymous World Services, Lorain County Central Office
PO Box 563
577 Broadway
Lorain, OH 44052
Ph: (440)246-1800
URL: National Affiliate–www.aa.org
Local. Individuals recovering from alcoholism. AA maintains that members can solve their common problem and help others achieve sobriety through a twelve step program that includes sharing their experience, strength, and hope with each other. **Affiliated With:** Alcoholics Anonymous World Services.

15699 ■ American Legion, Lorain Post 30
1112 W Erie Ave.
Lorain, OH 44052
Ph: (740)362-7478
Fax: (740)362-1429
URL: National Affiliate–www.legion.org
Local. Affiliated With: American Legion.

15700 ■ Association of Clinical Research Professionals - Northeastern Ohio Chapter
c/o Denise Theisen, Pres.
5416 Rosecliff Dr.
Lorain, OH 44053
E-mail: dtheisen@nohc.com
URL: http://www.acrpnet.org/chapters/neoh/index.html
Contact: Denise Theisen, Pres.
Local. Promotes professional growth in the field of clinical research. Provides networking opportunities for members. Advocates for the enhancement of education and knowledge in the field of clinical research. **Affiliated With:** Association of Clinical Research Professionals.

15701 ■ Big Brothers Big Sisters of America of Lorain County
1917 N Ridge Rd. E, A
Lorain, OH 44055
Ph: (440)277-6541
Fax: (440)277-6583
Free: (888)222-7371
E-mail: big@bigloraincounty.org
URL: http://www.bigloraincounty.org
Contact: Lise Day, Pres./CEO
Founded: 1994. **Members:** 400. **Staff:** 7. **Budget:** $250,000. **Languages:** English, Spanish. **Local.** Works to help children in the community to reach their full potential and become responsible adults by facilitating long-term, personal relationships between children and adults/mentors who serve as friends and role models. **Affiliated With:** Big Brothers Big Sisters of America.

15702 ■ Community Health Partners of Ohio Consolidated
3700 Kolbe Rd.
Lorain, OH 44053-1611
Ph: (440)960-4000
Fax: (440)960-4630
URL: http://www.community-health-partners.com
Contact: Rita Klima, Ofc.Mgr.
Local.

15703 ■ Easter Seals Northwestern Ohio
1909 N Ridge Rd., No. 6
Lorain, OH 44055
Ph: (440)277-7337
Fax: (440)277-7339
Free: (888)723-5602
URL: http://www.nwohio.easterseals.com
Local. Provides services for children and adults with disabilities or special needs, and supports their families. **Affiliated With:** Easter Seals.

15704 ■ First Catholic Slovak Ladies Association - Lorain Senior Branch 114
2235 E Erie Ave.
Lorain, OH 44052
Ph: (440)288-1492
URL: National Affiliate–www.fcsla.com
Local. Affiliated With: First Catholic Slovak Ladies Association.

15705 ■ Lorain County Chamber of Commerce
6100 S Broadway Ave., Ste.201
Lorain, OH 44053-3875
Ph: (440)233-6500 (440)323-9424
Fax: (440)246-4050
E-mail: fdetillio@loraincountychamber.com
URL: http://loraincountychamber.com
Contact: Frank P. DeTillio, Pres.
Founded: 1883. **Members:** 400. **Membership Dues:** business (plus $5 per each additional employee over 5), $275 (annual) • church, individual, government and nonprofit organization, $275-$550 (annual). **Staff:** 5. **Budget:** $250,000. **Local.** Businesses and individuals promoting economic and community development and social programs in Lorain County, OH. **Formerly:** (1999) Greater Lorain Chamber of Commerce. **Publications:** *Take Action*, periodic. Newsletter • *Vista*, quarterly • Report, annual. Alternate Formats: online.

15706 ■ Lorain County Tropical Greenhouse and Museum Association
c/o Dr. Ibrahim Eren
1366 W 2nd St.
Lorain, OH 44052-1332
Ph: (440)244-3296 (440)965-4027
Fax: (440)989-4876
Contact: Dr. Ibrahim Eren, Exec. Officer
Local.

15707 ■ Lorain Lions Club
PO Box 298
Lorain, OH 44052
Ph: (440)244-4390
E-mail: liondansmith@yahoo.com
URL: http://lorainoh.lionwap.org
Contact: Bruce Diso, Pres.
Local. Affiliated With: Lions Clubs International.

15708 ■ National Association of Rocketry - NARScouts
c/o Dan Bihary
2923 N Jefferson Blvd.
Lorain, OH 44052
Ph: (440)288-3409
E-mail: narscouts@yahoo.com
URL: http://nar.org/NARseclist.asp
Contact: Dan Bihary, Contact
Local.

15709 ■ National Organization for Women - Greater Cleveland
c/o Barbara Padgett, Pres.
107 1/2 Arizona Ave.
Lorain, OH 44052
Ph: (440)288-2251
E-mail: greaterclevelandnow@yahoo.com
URL: http://www.akrobiz.com/clevelandnow
Contact: Barbara Padgett, Pres.
Local. Affiliated With: National Organization for Women.

15710 ■ Sheffield Lions Club
c/o Waite Staller, Sec.
290 N Ridge Rd. E
Lorain, OH 44055
Ph: (440)233-6297
E-mail: bigbitebud@adelphia.net
URL: http://www.lions13b.org
Contact: Waite Staller, Sec.
Local. Affiliated With: Lions Clubs International.

15711 ■ Sophisticated Gents
2062 E 28th St.
Lorain, OH 44055-1909
Ph: (440)277-4879
Local.

15712 ■ United Way of Greater Lorain County
1875 N Ridge Rd. E, Ste.H
Lorain, OH 44055
Ph: (440)277-6530
Fax: (440)277-7409
Free: (800)275-6106
E-mail: admin@uwglc.net
URL: http://www.loraincountyunitedway.org
Contact: Gerald E. Skully, Exec.Dir.
Local. Affiliated With: United Way of America.

Loudonville

15713 ■ American Legion, Loudon Post 257
131 S Water St.
Loudonville, OH 44842
Ph: (740)362-7478
Fax: (740)362-1429
URL: National Affiliate–www.legion.org
Local. Affiliated With: American Legion.

15714 ■ Loudonville Lions Club
c/o Beckie Conway, Pres.
104 W Campbell St.
Loudonville, OH 44842
Ph: (419)994-5236
E-mail: beckietigger01@netzero.com
URL: http://www.lions13b.org
Contact: Beckie Conway, Pres.
Local. Affiliated With: Lions Clubs International.

15715 ■ Loudonville - Mohican Area Convention and Visitor's Bureau
249 W Main St.
Loudonville, OH 44842
Ph: (419)994-2519
Fax: (419)994-5950
E-mail: info@loudoville-mohican.com
URL: http://www.loudonville-mohican.com
Founded: 1957. **Members:** 200. **Staff:** 2. **Local Groups:** 3. **Local.** Promotes business and community development in the Loudonville, OH area. **Affiliated With:** U.S. Chamber of Commerce. **Formerly:** (1999) Loudonville-Greater Mohican Area Chamber of Commerce; (2006) Loudonville - Mohican Area Chamber of Commerce. **Publications:** Newsletter, monthly • Newsletter, periodic. Features events of interest in the area and special savings on services by merchants. Alternate Formats: online. **Conventions/Meetings:** annual meeting - always January.

Louisville

15716 ■ American Legion, Monnier-Duplain Post 548
925 W St. Louis Ct.
Louisville, OH 44641
Ph: (740)362-7478
Fax: (740)362-1429
URL: National Affiliate–www.legion.org
Local. Affiliated With: American Legion.

15717 ■ Korean War Veterans Association, Buckeye Chapter
c/o Hubert L. Bair
716 E Main
Louisville, OH 44641
Ph: (330)875-1526
E-mail: hlb427@webtv.net
URL: National Affiliate–www.kwva.org
Contact: Hubert L. Bair, Contact
Local. Affiliated With: Korean War Veterans Association.

15718 ■ Louisville Area Chamber of Commerce
c/o Cheryle Casar, Pres.
229 E Main St.
PO Box 67
Louisville, OH 44641
Ph: (330)875-7371
Fax: (330)875-3839
E-mail: cheryle@louisvilleohchamber.com
URL: http://www.louisvilleohchamber.com
Contact: Cheryle Casar, Pres.
Founded: 1991. **Members:** 113. **Staff:** 1. **Local.** Strives to develop and enhance the economic and business environment in the Louisville area through leadership, advocacy, and investor benefits. **Telecommunication Services:** electronic mail, lcoc@neo.rr.com • electronic mail, christine@louisvilleohchamber.com.

15719 ■ Louisville Lions Club - Ohio
PO Box 45
Louisville, OH 44641
E-mail: navydadlion@yahoo.com
URL: http://www.lionwap.org/LOUISVILLEOH
Contact: Leroy Truby, Sec.
Local. Affiliated With: Lions Clubs International.

15720 ■ Marlboro Lions Club - Ohio
8234 Columbus Rd. NE
Louisville, OH 44641
Ph: (330)875-9200
E-mail: gtate@neo.rr.com
URL: http://www.lionwap.org/marlborooh
Contact: Gary Tate, Sec.
Local. Affiliated With: Lions Clubs International.

Loveland

15721 ■ American Legion, Loveland Post 256
897 Oakland Rd.
Loveland, OH 45140
Ph: (740)362-7478
Fax: (740)362-1429
URL: National Affiliate–www.legion.org
Local. Affiliated With: American Legion.

15722 ■ Eagle Creek Beagle Club
c/o Richard E. Baumann
665 Wards Corner Rd.
Loveland, OH 45140-9047
URL: National Affiliate–clubs.akc.org
Contact: Richard E. Baumann, Contact
Local.

15723 ■ Greater Cincinnati BMW Club No. 18
c/o Mike LaBar
6293 Br. Hill Guinea Pike
Loveland, OH 45140
Ph: (513)774-9609
E-mail: mlabar@amig.com
URL: http://www.gcbmwc.org
Contact: Jerry Cummins, Pres.
Local. BMW motorcycle owners organized for pleasure, recreation, safety, and dissemination of information concerning BMW motorcycles. **Affiliated With:** BMW Motorcycle Owners of America.

15724 ■ Greater Cincinnati/Dayton Organization Development Network
c/o Jackie Gibson, Admin.
6401 Northward Dr.
Loveland, OH 45140
Ph: (513)881-5864
Fax: (513)697-9110
E-mail: info@odncincy.org
URL: http://www.odncincy.org
Local. Affiliated With: Organization Development Network.

15725 ■ Greater Loveland Historical Society
c/o Mrs. Janet Beller, Dir.
201 Riverside Dr.
Loveland, OH 45140-8627
Ph: (513)683-5692
Fax: (513)683-7409
E-mail: glhsm@fuse.net
URL: http://www.lovelandmuseum.org
Contact: Mrs. Janet Beller, Dir.
Founded: 1975. **Members:** 400. **Membership Dues:** all, $10-$1,000 (annual). **Staff:** 1. **Local.** Works to collect, preserve, and make available historical material and information pertaining to the Greater Loveland, Ohio area. Seeks to institute and encourage inquiry into the said area. **Libraries: Type:** reference. **Holdings:** archival material, maps. **Subjects:** local history, genealogy. **Boards:** Trustees. **Publications:** *Passages Through Time*. Book. **Price:** $15.00 • Newsletter, quarterly. **Price:** included in membership dues. **Circulation:** 400.

15726 ■ Izaak Walton League of America, Cincinnati Chapter
544 Br. Hill-Loveland Rd.
Loveland, OH 45140
Ph: (513)683-7233 (513)697-6100
E-mail: kflowers@fuse.net
URL: http://tinpan.fortunecity.com/wellerville/702/index.html
Contact: Kevin S. Flowers, Contact
Founded: 1943. **Local.** Aims to protect America's rich resources to ensure a high quality of life for all people, now and in the future. **Affiliated With:** Izaak Walton League of America.

15727 ■ KYOVA Morgan Horse Association
c/o Elise Becht
9564 Stonemasters Dr.
Loveland, OH 45140-6207
Ph: (513)697-8290
URL: National Affiliate–www.morganhorse.com
Contact: Elise Becht, Contact
Local. Affiliated With: American Morgan Horse Association.

15728 ■ Loveland Area Chamber of Commerce
510 W Loveland Ave.
PO Box 111
Loveland, OH 45140-0111
Ph: (513)683-1544
Fax: (513)683-5449
E-mail: info@lovelandchamber.org
URL: http://www.lovelandchamber.org
Contact: Paulette Leeper, Exec.Dir.
Founded: 1965. **Members:** 200. **Membership Dues:** business, $110-$250 (annual) • family entrepreneur, corporate associate, $100 (annual) • individual, nonprofit organization, $50 (annual). **State Groups:** 1. **Local.** Promotes business and community development in the Loveland, OH area. Sponsors Music in the Park concerts, valentine stamping program, and golf outing. **Awards: Frequency:** annual. **Type:** scholarship. **Computer Services:** Online services,

members' directory. **Committees:** Executive; Golf; Nominating; Scholarship; Valentine; Web Site. **Publications:** Directory, annual. **Advertising:** accepted • Newsletter, bimonthly. **Conventions/Meetings:** annual Christmas in Loveland - festival.

15729 ■ National Speleological Society, Red-Eye Karst Team
c/o Brian Heckman
6438 Snider Rd.
Loveland, OH 45140-9589
Ph: (513)722-0459
E-mail: cavescoob@aol.com
URL: National Affiliate–www.caves.org
Contact: Brian Heckman, Contact
Local. Seeks to study, explore and conserve cave and karst resources. Protects access to caves and promotes responsible caving. Encourages responsible management of caves and their unique environments. **Affiliated With:** National Speleological Society.

15730 ■ Reserve Officers Association - Department of Ohio, Cincinnati Navy Chapter 71
c/o Ralph W. Popp, Pres.
2483 Lilac St.
Loveland, OH 45140
Ph: (513)697-9596
E-mail: rwpopp@fuse.net
URL: http://www.roa.org/oh
Contact: Ralph W. Popp, Pres.
Local. Promotes and supports the development and execution of a military policy for the United States. Provides professional development seminars, workshops and programs for its members. **Affiliated With:** Reserve Officers Association of the United States.

15731 ■ Women in Insurance and Financial Services, Cincinnati Chapter
c/o Marilyn Hospodar
Hospodar Insurance Agency
200 W Loveland Ave.
Loveland, OH 45140
Ph: (513)677-2158
Fax: (513)677-8158
E-mail: hospodar@fuse.net
URL: National Affiliate–www.w-wifs.org
Contact: Marilyn Hospodar, Contact
Local. Affiliated With: Women in Insurance and Financial Services.

Lowell

15732 ■ American Legion, Lowell Post 750
226 Main St.
Lowell, OH 45744
Ph: (740)362-7478
Fax: (740)362-1429
URL: National Affiliate–www.legion.org
Local. Affiliated With: American Legion.

Lowellville

15733 ■ American Legion, Lowellville Post 247
140 E Liberty St.
Lowellville, OH 44436
Ph: (740)362-7478
Fax: (740)362-1429
URL: National Affiliate–www.legion.org
Local. Affiliated With: American Legion.

Lucas

15734 ■ Lucas Lions Club
c/o William Spohn, Pres.
4203 Tucker Rd.
Lucas, OH 44843
Ph: (419)892-2640
URL: http://www.lions13b.org
Contact: William Spohn, Pres.
Local. Affiliated With: Lions Clubs International.

15735 ■ Madison Township Lions Club
c/o Richard Groff, Sec.
361 W Shore Dr.
Lucas, OH 44843
Ph: (419)892-3068
E-mail: rgroff3973@aol.com
URL: http://www.lions13b.org
Contact: Richard Groff, Sec.
Local. Affiliated With: Lions Clubs International.

Lucasville

15736 ■ American Legion, Wm. A. Baker Post 363
PO Box 1292
Lucasville, OH 45648
Ph: (740)362-7478
Fax: (740)362-1429
URL: National Affiliate–www.legion.org
Local. Affiliated With: American Legion.

15737 ■ National Technical Honor Society - Scioto County JVS - Ohio (SCJVS)
951 Vern Riffe Dr.
Lucasville, OH 45648
Ph: (740)259-2632
URL: http://www.sciotojvs.k12.oh.us
Local.

Luckey

15738 ■ American Legion, Troy-Webster Post 240
PO Box 141
Luckey, OH 43443
Ph: (740)362-7478
Fax: (740)362-1429
URL: National Affiliate–www.legion.org
Local. Affiliated With: American Legion.

Ludlow Falls

15739 ■ Echo Hills Kennel Club of Ohio (EHKC)
c/o Charley McMaster
9771 W Fenner Rd.
Ludlow Falls, OH 45339-9742
Ph: (937)947-2059
E-mail: contact@echohillskennelclub.com
URL: http://www.echohillskennelclub.com
Contact: Charley McMaster, Pres.
Local.

Lyndhurst

15740 ■ First Catholic Slovak Ladies Association - Cleveland Junior Branch 461
1636 Brainard Rd.
Lyndhurst, OH 44124
Ph: (216)641-0949
URL: National Affiliate–www.fcsla.com
Local. Affiliated With: First Catholic Slovak Ladies Association.

15741 ■ First Catholic Slovak Ladies Association - Cleveland Senior Branch 378
1635 Brainard Rd.
Lyndhurst, OH 44124
Ph: (216)641-0949
URL: National Affiliate–www.fcsla.com
Local. Affiliated With: First Catholic Slovak Ladies Association.

Macedonia

15742 ■ Air Conditioning Contractors of America, Greater Cleveland Chapter
PO Box 207
Macedonia, OH 44056
Ph: (330)467-1390
Fax: (330)467-1390
E-mail: info@acca-cleve.net
URL: http://www.acca-cleve.net
Contact: Jerry Collins, Pres.
Local. Assists members to acquire, serve, and satisfy their customers. Provides quality technical and management information and services. Promotes good business ethics and sound business practices. **Affiliated With:** Air Conditioning Contractors of America. **Publications:** Newsletter, monthly. Alternate Formats: online.

15743 ■ American Legion, Nordonia Hills Post 801
PO Box 560157
Macedonia, OH 44056
Ph: (740)362-7478
Fax: (740)362-1429
URL: National Affiliate–www.legion.org
Local. Affiliated With: American Legion.

15744 ■ ESOP Association, Executive Committee of the State and Regional Chapter Council
c/o Floyd J. Griffin, Chm.
Patio Enclosures, Inc.
700 E Highland Rd.
Macedonia, OH 44056-2112
Ph: (330)468-0700
Fax: (330)468-0785
E-mail: fjgriffin@patioenclosuresinc.com
URL: http://www.patioenclosuresinc.com
Contact: Floyd J. Griffin, Chm.
Regional. Affiliated With: ESOP Association.

Madison

15745 ■ American Legion, North Madison Memorial Post 601
1725 Hubbard Rd.
Madison, OH 44057
Ph: (740)362-7478
Fax: (740)362-1429
URL: National Affiliate–www.legion.org
Local. Affiliated With: American Legion.

15746 ■ American Legion, Ohio Post 112
c/o Jay Wilson
6671 Middle Ridge Rd.
Madison, OH 44057
Ph: (740)362-7478
Fax: (740)362-1429
URL: National Affiliate–www.legion.org
Contact: Jay Wilson, Contact
Local. Affiliated With: American Legion.

15747 ■ American Wine Society - Covered Bridge
c/o Steve Henderson, Co-Chm.
PO Box 41
Madison, OH 44057
Ph: (440)428-5900
E-mail: hendersontrav@alltel.net
URL: National Affiliate–www.americanwinesociety.org
Contact: Steve Henderson, Co-Chm.
Local. Affiliated With: American Wine Society.

15748 ■ Madison - Perry Area Chamber of Commerce
5965 N Ridge Rd.
PO Box 4
Madison, OH 44057

Ph: (440)428-3760
Fax: (440)428-6668
E-mail: exec@mpacc.org
URL: http://www.mpacc.org
Contact: Nancy Currie, Pres.

Local. Represents businesses in Madison and Perry, OH. Stimulates community leadership and economic development. **Publications:** Newsletter, monthly • Membership Directory, annual. Alternate Formats: online.

15749 ■ Ohio Health Care Association, District 14
c/o Joyce Humphrey, Chair
Cardinal Woods
6831 Chapel Rd.
Madison, OH 44057
Ph: (440)428-5103
Fax: (440)428-9003
E-mail: joycefool158@aol.com
URL: http://www.ohca.org
Contact: Joyce Humphrey, Chair

Local. Promotes professionalism and ethical behavior of individuals providing long-term care delivery for patients and for the general public. Provides information, education and administrative tools to enhance the quality of long-term care. Improves the standards of service and administration of member nursing homes. **Affiliated With:** American Health Care Association.

15750 ■ Rabbit Run Community Arts Association (RRCAA)
49 Park St.
Madison, OH 44057-0235
Ph: (440)428-5913
Fax: (440)428-2130
E-mail: office@rabbitrunonline.com
URL: http://www.rabbitrunonline.com
Contact: Mr. Brint Learned, Exec.Dir.
Local.

Magnolia

15751 ■ Magnolia Lions Club - Ohio
PO Box 331
Magnolia, OH 44643
Ph: (330)866-2084
E-mail: rleach@sssnet.com
URL: http://magnoliaoh.lionwap.org
Contact: Bob Leach, Sec.
Local. Affiliated With: Lions Clubs International.

Maineville

15752 ■ Ballet Tech Ohio Performing Arts Association (BTOPAA)
c/o Marvel Gentry Davis
7623 Old 3C Hwy.
Maineville, OH 45039
Ph: (513)683-6860
E-mail: btpoaa@ballettechohiopaa.org
URL: http://www.ballettechohiopaa.org
State.

Malinta

15753 ■ American Legion, Bevelhymer-Gilliland Post 400
Box 48
Malinta, OH 43535
Ph: (740)362-7478
Fax: (740)362-1429
URL: National Affiliate–www.legion.org
Local. Affiliated With: American Legion.

Malvern

15754 ■ American Legion, Valley Post 375
PO Box 406
Malvern, OH 44644
Ph: (740)362-7478
Fax: (740)362-1429
URL: National Affiliate–www.legion.org
Local. Affiliated With: American Legion.

15755 ■ Pleasant Valley Beagle Club
c/o Paul Holmes
PO Box 63
Malvern, OH 44644-0063
URL: National Affiliate–clubs.akc.org
Contact: Paul Holmes, Contact
Local.

Manchester

15756 ■ American Legion, Matthews-Carter Post 325
211 Pearl St.
Manchester, OH 45144
Ph: (740)362-7478
Fax: (740)362-1429
URL: National Affiliate–www.legion.org
Local. Affiliated With: American Legion.

15757 ■ Ohio Onsite Wastewater Association (OOWA)
672 State Rte. 247
Manchester, OH 45144
Fax: (937)549-8175
Free: (866)843-4429
E-mail: oowa@ohioonsite.org
URL: http://www.ohioonsite.org
Contact: Susan Ruehl, Administrative Asst.

Founded: 1998. **Members:** 190. **Membership Dues:** individual, $85 (annual). **State**. Aims to improve the conditions of the onsite wastewater recycling industry. Seeks to establish throughout Ohio a relationship, among all those concerned with the onsite wastewater recycling industry, that will increase the flow of information, not only among members but also among all organizations, agencies and individuals. Works to compile and to disseminate statistics, experiences and other information affecting the onsite wastewater recycling industry. Works to inform and educate the general public concerning the value of recycling wastewater. Aims to protect the environment by assisting the development of sound ecological practices in the manufacture, design, installation, maintenance and management of onsite wastewater treatment and disposal systems. **Awards:** Distinguished Service Award. **Frequency:** annual. **Type:** recognition. **Recipient:** for outstanding service in helping advance the onsite industry in Ohio.

Mansfield

15758 ■ AAA Ohio Automobile Club
2114 Park Ave. W
Mansfield, OH 44906
Ph: (419)529-8500
State.

15759 ■ American Legion, Ohio Post 16
c/o Earl D. Mc Vey
1106 Park Ave. E
Mansfield, OH 44905
Ph: (740)362-7478
Fax: (740)362-1429
URL: National Affiliate–www.legion.org
Contact: Earl D. Mc Vey, Contact
Local. Affiliated With: American Legion.

15760 ■ American Legion, Ohio Post 676
c/o Eugene Hicks
460 Harmon Ave.
Mansfield, OH 44903
Ph: (740)362-7478
Fax: (740)362-1429
URL: National Affiliate–www.legion.org
Contact: Eugene Hicks, Contact
Local. Affiliated With: American Legion.

15761 ■ American Red Cross, Richland County Chapter
39 N Park St.
Mansfield, OH 44902-1732
Ph: (419)524-0311
Fax: (419)522-7848
URL: http://richlandcounty.redcross.org
Local.

15762 ■ American Society for Quality, Mansfield Section 0811
c/o Randy Stromer
835 Tanglewood Dr.
Mansfield, OH 44906
Ph: (330)263-3308
E-mail: randy.stroemer@boschrexroth-us.com
URL: http://groups.asq.org/811
Contact: Randy Stromer, Contact

Local. Advances learning, quality improvement and knowledge exchange to improve business results and to create better workplaces and communities worldwide. Provides a forum for information exchange, professional development and continuous learning in the science of quality. **Affiliated With:** American Society for Quality.

15763 ■ Astronomy for Youth
470 Rudy Rd.
Mansfield, OH 44903
E-mail: tgoff@neo.rr.com
URL: http://astronomyforyouth.tripod.com

Local. Promotes the science of astronomy. Works to encourage and coordinate activities of amateur astronomical societies. Fosters observational and computational work and craftsmanship in various fields of astronomy. **Affiliated With:** Astronomical League.

15764 ■ Building Industry Association of North Central Ohio
1183 Lexington Ave.
Mansfield, OH 44907-2252
Ph: (419)774-7996
Fax: (419)774-7966
E-mail: bianco@sisna.com
URL: National Affiliate–www.nahb.org
Contact: Bob Ashbrook, Exec.Dir.

Local. Single and multifamily home builders, commercial builders, and others associated with the building industry. **Affiliated With:** National Association of Home Builders.

15765 ■ Catholics United for the Faith - Our Lady, Help of Christians Chapter
c/o Don Marcum
1898 Beal Rd.
Mansfield, OH 44903
Ph: (419)589-2981
E-mail: dumbox@kosinet.com
URL: National Affiliate–www.cuf.org
Contact: Don Marcum, Contact
Local.

15766 ■ Concerned Black Men of Mansfield
Ocie Hill Neighborhood Ctr.
445 Bowman St.
Mansfield, OH 44903
Ph: (419)522-4565
Fax: (419)612-6625
E-mail: ebenson@neo.rr.com
URL: National Affiliate–www.cbmnational.org
Local.

15767 ■ Girl Scouts of Heritage Trails Council
35 N Park
Mansfield, OH 44902
Ph: (419)522-0391
Free: (800)433-1290
E-mail: execsec@girlscoutsht.org
URL: http://www.girlscoutsht.org
Contact: Sandy Shelley, Exec.Sec.
Local. Young girls and adult volunteers, corporate, government and individual supporters. Strives to develop potential and leadership skills among its members. Conducts trainings, educational programs and outdoor activities.

15768 ■ Helping Other People Prepare and Endure
c/o Helen J. Black
478 Allison Ave.
Mansfield, OH 44903-1002

15769 ■ Korean War Veterans Association, Richland County Chapter
c/o Frank J. Russo
618 Orchard Dr. E
Mansfield, OH 44904
Ph: (419)756-1468
E-mail: fpb@earthlink.net
URL: National Affiliate–www.kwva.org
Contact: Frank J. Russo, Contact
Local. **Affiliated With:** Korean War Veterans Association.

15770 ■ Lexington Lions Club - Ohio
c/o Joe Saunier, Pres.
1295 W Cook Rd.
Mansfield, OH 44906
Ph: (419)756-0797
E-mail: lionblackstone@earthlink.net
URL: http://www.lions13b.org
Contact; Joe Saunier, Pres.
Local. **Affiliated With:** Lions Clubs International.

15771 ■ Mansfield Area AIFA
PO Box 1087
Mansfield, OH 44901-1087
Fax: (419)589-9482
URL: National Affiliate–www.naifa.org
Local. Represents the interest of insurance and financial advisors. Advocates for a positive legislative and regulatory environment. Enhances business and professional skills of members. **Affiliated With:** National Association of Insurance and Financial Advisors.

15772 ■ Mansfield Board of Realtors (MBR)
1101 Lexington Ave.
Mansfield, OH 44907
Ph: (419)756-1130
Fax: (419)756-4080
E-mail: mfdboard@mansfieldboard.com
URL: http://www.mansfieldboard.com
Contact: Barbara Murray, Exec. Officer
Local. Strives to develop real estate business practices. Advocates for the right to own, use and transfer real property. Provides a facility for professional development, research and exchange of information among members and the general public. **Affiliated With:** National Association of Realtors.

15773 ■ Mansfield Evening Lions Club
c/o Edwin H. Pfahler, Pres.
62 Chestnut Ct.
Mansfield, OH 44906
Ph: (419)747-1111
E-mail: atp1111@aol.com
URL: http://www.lions13b.org
Contact: Edwin H. Pfahler, Pres.
Local. **Affiliated With:** Lions Clubs International.

15774 ■ Mansfield Noon Lions
c/o Waterford of Mansfield
1296 S Trimble Rd.
Mansfield, OH 44906
Ph: (419)775-1013
E-mail: sglasgo@neo.rr.com
URL: http://www.lions13b.org
Contact: Stephen Glasgo, Pres.
Local. **Affiliated With:** Lions Clubs International.

15775 ■ Mansfield Reformatory Preservation Society (MRPS)
100 Reformatory Rd.
Mansfield, OH 44905
Ph: (419)522-2644
Fax: (419)522-8492
E-mail: info@mrps.org
URL: http://www.mrps.org
Contact: Christina Grozik, Operations Dir.
Founded: 1992. **Staff:** 5. **Nonmembership**. **Local**. **Formerly:** (2004) Ohio State Reformatory Historic Site.

15776 ■ Mansfield-Richland Area Chamber of Commerce (MRACC)
55 N Mulberry St.
Mansfield, OH 44902
Ph: (419)522-3211
Fax: (419)526-6853
E-mail: info@mrachamber.com
URL: http://www.mrachamber.com
Contact: Kevin Nestor, Pres.
Founded: 1899. **Members:** 700. **Staff:** 4. **Local**. Promotes business and community development in the Richland County, OH area. **Committees:** Business Advocacy; Business and Economic Development; Membership Services; Resources. **Programs:** Leadership Unlimited; Leadership Unlimited Members. **Subgroups:** Chamber Education Foundation; Young Leaders Institute. **Publications:** Newsletter, monthly. Alternate Formats: online. **Conventions/Meetings:** weekly Business After Hours - meeting, networking - every Thursday • annual Chamber Golf Classic - competition - 1st Friday of August • annual meeting - last Thursday of January.

15777 ■ Mansfield and Richland County Convention and Visitors Bureau
124 N Main St.
Mansfield, OH 44902-1603
Ph: (419)525-1300
Fax: (419)524-7722
Free: (800)642-8282
E-mail: visitors@mansfieldtourism.com
URL: http://www.mansfieldtourism.com
Local.

15778 ■ NAMI, Richland County, Ohio
34 Park Ave. W
Mansfield, OH 44902-1602
Ph: (419)522-6264
Fax: (419)525-2524
E-mail: mpierce5@neo.rr.com
Contact: Mary K Pierce, Exec.Dir.
Local.

15779 ■ National Active and Retired Federal Employees Association - Johnny Appleseed 612
2510 Fairway Xing
Mansfield, OH 44903-6507
Ph: (419)589-2913
URL: National Affiliate–www.narfe.org
Contact: Joseph W. Cinadr, Contact
Local. Protects the retirement future of employees through education. Informs members on issues affecting the retirement. **Affiliated With:** National Association of Retired Federal Employees.

15780 ■ North Central Ohio SCORE
c/o Clare Clemes, Chair
Chamber of Commerce
55 N Mulberry St.
Mansfield, OH 44902
Ph: (419)522-3211
Contact: Merris Welge, Office Mgr.
Local.

15781 ■ North Central Ohio Youth for Christ
147 S Main St.
Mansfield, OH 44902
Ph: (419)522-1122
Fax: (419)524-7431
URL: http://www.seethechange.org
Local. **Affiliated With:** Youth for Christ/U.S.A.

15782 ■ Ohio Genealogical Society (OGS)
713 S Main St.
Mansfield, OH 44907-1644
Ph: (419)756-7294
Fax: (419)756-8681
E-mail: ogs@ogs.org
URL: http://www.ogs.org
Contact: Thomas Stephen Neel, Library Dir.
Founded: 1959. **Members:** 6,550. **Membership Dues:** controlled, $27 (annual). **Staff:** 3. **Budget:** $357,925. **Regional Groups:** 3. **State Groups:** 2. **Local Groups:** 96. **For-Profit**. Genealogists, historians, libraries, and other interested individuals from throughout the U.S. Promotes genealogical research and the preservation of historical records in Ohio. Facilitates the exchange of ideas and information. Sponsors educational programs on family lineage in Ohio. Maintains speakers' bureau. **Libraries: Type:** reference. **Holdings:** 25,000; periodicals. **Subjects:** genealogy, Ohio history. **Awards:** Ohio Book Award. **Frequency:** annual. **Type:** recognition. **Computer Services:** database, on web site. **Divisions:** Cemetery; Education; Library; Publicity. **Publications:** *Chapter Directory*, periodic. Includes Ohio genealogical books being sold by local chapters. **Price:** $10.00. **Circulation:** 500. **Advertising:** accepted • *First Families of Ohio Roster* • *Ohio Cemeteries* • *Ohio Civil War Genealogy Journal*, quarterly. Magazine. Contains information on family history and documentation on Ohio's Civil War soldiers. **Price:** $20.00. **Circulation:** 1,000. **Advertising:** accepted • *Ohio Genealogical Society Quarterly*. Magazine. **Price:** included in membership dues. **Circulation:** 6,550. **Advertising:** accepted • *Ohio Genealogy News*, bimonthly. Magazine. Includes calendar of events, chapter announcements, library acquisitions, queries, and membership information. **Price:** included in membership dues. **Circulation:** 6,550. **Advertising:** accepted • *Ohio Records and Pioneer Families*, quarterly. Contains cemetery and family records, court abstracts, and genealogical articles. **Price:** $20.00. **Circulation:** 1,400. **Conventions/Meetings:** annual Chapter Management Seminar - competition, training for chapter officers • annual conference (exhibits).

15783 ■ Ohio Housing Authorities Conference (OHAC)
PO Box 1029
Mansfield, OH 44901
Ph: (419)524-9116
Fax: (419)524-1535
E-mail: ohacoffice@earthlink.net
URL: http://www.ohac.com
Founded: 1939. **Members:** 70. **Staff:** 2. **State**. Fosters and promotes affordable housing in Ohio through education and training of members, exchange of information, mutual support and collaborative efforts. **Publications:** *The Journal*, quarterly. Newsletter. Discusses current issues. **Conventions/Meetings:** semiannual conference - always spring and fall.

15784 ■ Ohio Native Plant Society, Mohican Chapter
1778 Dougwood Dr.
Mansfield, OH 44904
Ph: (419)774-0077
E-mail: mklein@neo.rr.com
URL: http://groups.msn.com/NativePlantSocietyofNortheastOhio/chapters.msnw
Contact: Mike Klein, Pres.
Local.

15785 ■ Ohio Prairie Association (OPA)
3360 SR 546
Mansfield, OH 44904-9238

Ph: (419)433-5639
E-mail: ohioprairie@aol.com
URL: http://www.ohioprairie.org
Contact: Mr. John A. Blakeman, Pres.
Founded: 2000. **Members:** 200. **Membership Dues:** regular, $20 (annual) • student, $10 (annual) • family, $25 (annual) • friend, library, $35 (annual) • institution, $50 (annual) • supporting, $75 (annual) • contributing, $150 (annual) • life, $500. **Budget:** $4,000. **State Groups:** 1. **For-Profit. State.** Prairie scientists, managers, enthusiasts, and others who support and promote prairies in OH. **Publications:** *Ohio Prairie Gazette*, quarterly. Journal. Features articles on Ohio prairies. **Price:** free. **Circulation:** 200. **Conventions/Meetings:** annual conference, with prairie field trips (exhibits).

15786 ■ Olentangy Beagle Club
c/o Lewis Steele
3470 State Rte. 545
Mansfield, OH 44903-9003
URL: National Affiliate–www.akc.org
Contact: Lewis Steele, Contact
Local. Affiliated With: American Kennel Club.

15787 ■ Phi Theta Kappa - Beta Theta Eta Chapter
c/o Diane Hipsher
2441 Kenwood Cir.
Mansfield, OH 44906
Ph: (419)755-4803
E-mail: dhipsher@ncstatecollege.edu
URL: http://www.ptk.org/directories/chapters/OH/21408-1.htm
Contact: Diane Hipsher, Advisor
Local. Affiliated With: Phi Theta Kappa, International Honor Society.

15788 ■ Project Management Institute, Northwest Ohio
c/o Kevin F. Cukrowicz, PMP, Pres.
Sprint
665 Lexington Ave.
OHMANB0205
Mansfield, OH 44907-1504
Ph: (419)755-8461
Fax: (419)756-0754
E-mail: kevin.f.cukrowicz@mail.sprint.com
Affiliated With: Project Management Institute.

15789 ■ Reserve Officers Association - Department of Ohio, Col. Coleman Todd Chapter 53
c/o CDR Edward W. Olson, Pres.
572 Edgewood Rd.
Mansfield, OH 44907-1526
Ph: (419)774-5695 (419)526-0206
Fax: (419)774-5862
E-mail: eolson@richlandcountyoh.us
URL: http://www.roa.org/oh
Contact: Edward W. Olson, Pres.
Local. Promotes and supports the development and execution of a military policy for the United States. Provides professional development seminars, workshops and programs for its members. **Affiliated With:** Reserve Officers Association of the United States.

15790 ■ Richland County Genealogical Society
PO Box 3823
Mansfield, OH 44907-3823
E-mail: sunda@prodigy.net
URL: http://www.rootsweb.com/~ohrichgs
Contact: Sunda Peters, Pres.
Founded: 1959. **Local. Affiliated With:** Ohio Genealogical Society. **Formerly:** (1964) Richland County Chapter - Ohio Genealogical Society.

15791 ■ Richland County Habitat for Humanity
201 E Fifth St., Ste.2105
Mansfield, OH 44902
Ph: (419)524-8361
Fax: (419)524-2860
E-mail: rchfh@richnet.net
Contact: Veronna K. Drane, Exec.Dir.
Local. Affiliated With: Habitat for Humanity International.

15792 ■ Richland County Regional Planning Commission
35 N Park St., Ste.230
Mansfield, OH 44902
Ph: (419)774-5684
Fax: (419)774-5685
E-mail: rplanning@rcrpc.org
URL: http://rcrpc.org
Contact: Richard D. Adair, Exec.Dir.
Founded: 1959. **Local.**

15793 ■ RSVP Richland County
c/o Barbara Balsley, Dir.
35 N Park St.
Mansfield, OH 44902-1775
Ph: (419)525-2816
Fax: (419)524-3467
E-mail: rsvp@unitedwayofrichlandcounty.org
URL: http://www.unitedwayofrichlandcounty.org
Contact: Ms. Kathi Cutlip, Dir.
Local. Recruits individuals 55 and above to volunteer in Richland County. Volunteers sites include area schools, not for profit organizations, government entities and health care related facilities. **Affiliated With:** Retired and Senior Volunteer Program.

15794 ■ STARFLEET: USS Intrepid
c/o Suzanne Maurer
145 Elmridge Rd.
Mansfield, OH 44907
E-mail: missouri145@aol.com
URL: http://www.regionone.net
Contact: Suzanne Maurer, Contact
Local. Affiliated With: STARFLEET.

15795 ■ United Way of Richland County
35 N Park St.
Mansfield, OH 44902-1722
Ph: (419)525-2816
Fax: (419)524-3467
E-mail: skippo@unitedwayofrichlandcounty.org
URL: http://www.unitedwayofrichlandcounty.org
Contact: Skip Allman, Exec.Dir.
Local. Affiliated With: United Way of America.

15796 ■ Veteran's of Foreign Wars 3494
853 Ashland Rd.
Mansfield, OH 44905
Ph: (419)589-6728
Contact: Marylou Finley, Bartender
Local.

15797 ■ Vietnam Veterans of America, Chapter No. 616
c/o John A. Johnston, Pres.
1150 N Main St.
Mansfield, OH 44901
Ph: (419)525-4455
Fax: (419)524-8023
URL: http://www.vvabuckeyestatecouncil.com
Contact: John A. Johnston, Pres.
Local. Affiliated With: Vietnam Veterans of America.

Mantua

15798 ■ American Legion, Mantua Post 193
PO Box 252
Mantua, OH 44255
Ph: (740)362-7478
Fax: (740)362-1429
URL: National Affiliate–www.legion.org
Local. Affiliated With: American Legion.

15799 ■ Crestwood Lions Club
PO Box 40
Mantua, OH 44255
Ph: (330)274-0837
E-mail: crestwoodlionsoh@yahoo.com
URL: http://crestwoodlionsoh.lionwap.org
Contact: Timothy McDermott, Sec.
Local. Affiliated With: Lions Clubs International.

15800 ■ Plumbing-Heating-Cooling Contractors Association, Akron
c/o Mr. Raymond Harner, Pres.
2480 Bartlett Rd.
Mantua, OH 44255-8764
Ph: (330)626-5551
Fax: (330)274-8764
E-mail: hp2480@hotmail.com
URL: National Affiliate–www.phccweb.org
Contact: Mr. Raymond Harner, Pres.
Local. Represents the plumbing, heating and cooling contractors. Promotes the construction industry. Protects the environment, health, safety and comfort of society. **Affiliated With:** Plumbing-Heating-Cooling Contractors Association.

Maple Heights

15801 ■ American Legion, Garfield Heights Post 304
15609 Ramage Ave.
Maple Heights, OH 44137
Ph: (740)362-7478
Fax: (740)362-1429
URL: National Affiliate–www.legion.org
Local. Affiliated With: American Legion.

15802 ■ American Legion, Maple Heights Post 309
15521 Broadway Ave.
Maple Heights, OH 44137
Ph: (740)362-7478
Fax: (740)362-1429
URL: National Affiliate–www.legion.org
Local. Affiliated With: American Legion.

15803 ■ American Legion, Ohio Post 22
c/o Harold B. Harris
PO Box 37040
Maple Heights, OH 44137
Ph: (740)362-7478
Fax: (740)362-1429
URL: National Affiliate–www.legion.org
Contact: Harold B. Harris, Contact
Local. Affiliated With: American Legion.

15804 ■ American Legion, Ohio Post 569
c/o Frank J. Petrarca
15805 Libby Rd.
Maple Heights, OH 44137
Ph: (740)362-7478
Fax: (740)362-1429
URL: National Affiliate–www.legion.org
Contact: Frank J. Petrarca, Contact
Local. Affiliated With: American Legion.

Marblehead

15805 ■ American Legion, Ohio Post 555
c/o Louis Feuma
PO Box 282
Marblehead, OH 43440
Ph: (740)362-7478
Fax: (740)362-1429
URL: National Affiliate–www.legion.org
Contact: Louis Feuma, Contact
Local. Affiliated With: American Legion.

15806 ■ Bay Point Yacht Club
10948 E Bay Shore Rd.
Marblehead, OH 43440
E-mail: buster@bathtownship.info
URL: http://www.bpyc.org
Contact: Tom Frascella, Commodore
Local.

15807 ■ Catholics United for the Faith - Servants of Christ Through Mary Chapter
c/o Raymond Bush
1681 N Trader Crossing
Marblehead, OH 43440

Ph: (419)734-0001
URL: National Affiliate–www.cuf.org
Contact: Raymond Bush, Contact
Local.

15808 ■ Marblehead Peninsula Chamber of Commerce
210B W Main St.
Marblehead, OH 43440
Ph: (419)798-9777
Fax: (419)798-9777
E-mail: info@marbleheadpeninsula.com
URL: http://www.marbleheadpeninsula.com
Contact: Katrina Webb, Sec.
Local. Promotes business and community development in the Marblehead, OH area. **Formerly:** (2002) Peninsula Chamber of Commerce.

Marengo

15809 ■ American Legion, Marengo Memorial Post 710
1549 County Rd. 26
Marengo, OH 43334
Ph: (740)362-7478
Fax: (740)362-1429
URL: National Affiliate–www.legion.org
Local. Affiliated With: American Legion.

15810 ■ Ohio State Pony of the Americas Club (OSPOAC)
c/o Rodney Miller, Pres.
7044 State Rt. 229
Marengo, OH 43334
Ph: (419)768-2730
E-mail: celspoas@neo.rr.com
URL: http://www.ohiopoa.org
Contact: Rodney Miller, Pres.
Membership Dues: family, $20 (annual). **State. Affiliated With:** Pony of the Americas Club.

Maria Stein

15811 ■ American Legion, Ohio Post 571
c/o Maria Stein
8140 State Rte. 119
Maria Stein, OH 45860
Ph: (740)362-7478
Fax: (740)362-1429
URL: National Affiliate–www.legion.org
Contact: Maria Stein, Contact
Local. Affiliated With: American Legion.

Marietta

15812 ■ American Cancer Society, Washington Area
607 Putnam St.
Marietta, OH 45750
Ph: (740)374-5464
Free: (888)227-6446
URL: http://www.cancer.org
Local. Affiliated With: American Cancer Society.

15813 ■ American Legion, Marietta Post 64
PO Box 16
Marietta, OH 45750
Ph: (740)362-7478
Fax: (740)362-1429
URL: National Affiliate–www.legion.org
Local. Affiliated With: American Legion.

15814 ■ American Red Cross, Washington County Chapter
401 Fourth St.
Marietta, OH 45750
Ph: (740)373-0281
Fax: (740)373-3065
E-mail: wcarc@frognet.net
URL: http://www.frognet.net/~wcarc
Local.

15815 ■ Buckeye Hills-Hocking Valley Regional Development District (BH-HVRDD)
Rte. 1, Box 299D
Marietta, OH 45750
Ph: (740)374-9436
Fax: (740)374-8038
E-mail: bretallphin@buckeyehills.org
URL: http://www.buckeyehills.org
Contact: C. Boyer Simcox, Exec.Dir.
Founded: 1968. **Members:** 65. **Staff:** 47. **Budget:** $2,000,000. **Regional Groups:** 2. **State Groups:** 2. **Local.** Seeks to foster a cooperative effort in regional planning, programming, and the implementing of regional plans and programs. **Libraries: Type:** open to the public. **Holdings:** 150. **Publications:** *Regional Developments*, 3/year. Newsletter.

15816 ■ Easter Seals Central and Southeast Ohio
PO Box 31
Marietta, OH 45750
Ph: (740)374-8876
Free: (800)860-5523
E-mail: kzuckerm@easterseals-cseohio.org
URL: http://www.centralohio.easterseals.com
Contact: Mr. Karin Zuckerman, CEO
Local. Provides services for children and adults with disabilities or special needs, and supports their families. **Affiliated With:** Easter Seals.

15817 ■ Economic Roundtable of the Ohio Valley
c/o Dr. Jacqueline Khorassani
Dept. of Economics
Marietta Coll.
215 5th St.
Marietta, OH 45750
Ph: (740)376-4621
Fax: (740)376-7501
E-mail: jackie.khorassani@marietta.edu
Contact: Dr. Jacqueline Khorassani, VP of Programs
Founded: 1983. **Members:** 210. **Membership Dues:** regular, $25 (annual) • student, $5 (annual) • distinguished, life, $1,000 • life, $250 • sustaining, $50 (annual). **Staff:** 1. **Budget:** $20,000. **Local.** Businesspeople and professionals, students and faculty, and other interested individuals. Arranges lectures by distinguished speakers to raise public awareness of current economic issues and events. **Publications:** *Economic Roundtable of the Ohio Valley*, annual. Brochure. **Price:** free • *MACRO and micro*, 5/year. Newsletter. **Conventions/Meetings:** periodic Luncheon Speakers - lecture.

15818 ■ Greater Marietta United Way
307 LL Putnam St.
Marietta, OH 45750
Ph: (740)373-3333
E-mail: uway@frognet.net
URL: http://www.mariettauw.org
Contact: Mary Anne Bush, Exec.Dir.
Local. Affiliated With: United Way of America.

15819 ■ Home Builders Association of Washington County
c/o Tim Strahler
PO Box 1048
Marietta, OH 45750-6048
Ph: (740)749-3536
Fax: (740)749-3552
URL: National Affiliate–www.nahb.org
Local. Single and multifamily home builders, commercial builders, and others associated with the building industry. **Affiliated With:** National Association of Home Builders.

15820 ■ Marietta AIFA
c/o Don Neehouse
PO Box 1140
Marietta, OH 45750
Ph: (740)373-2604
Fax: (740)373-8827
E-mail: neehoud@nationwide.com
URL: National Affiliate–naifa.org
Contact: Don Neehouse, Contact
Local. Represents the interests of insurance and financial advisors. Advocates for a positive legislative and regulatory environment. Enhances business and professional skills of members. **Affiliated With:** National Association of Insurance and Financial Advisors.

15821 ■ Marietta Area Chamber of Commerce
316 3rd St.
Marietta, OH 45750
Ph: (740)373-5176
Fax: (740)373-7808
E-mail: info@mariettachamber.com
URL: http://www.mariettachamber.com
Contact: Charlotte Keim, Pres.
Members: 580. **Membership Dues:** auto dealer (based on number of units), $170-$290 (annual) • hospital, nursing home (plus $1.25 per bed), $170 (annual) • hotel, motel, bed and breakfast (plus $1.25 per unit), $170 (annual) • utility (per meter installation), $0 (annual) • construction, transportation, oil/gas (plus $5 per employee), $170 (annual) • general retailer, loan company, funeral home, restaurant, theater (plus $6.50 per employee above 41), $170-$360 (annual) • industrial (plus $3.25 for 1-50 employees; $2.25 for 51-200 employees; $1.25 for more than 200 employees), $170 (annual) • professional (plus $50 each additional professional & $4.50 each additional employee), $170 (annual) • service, wholesale (based on number of employees, plus $6.50 per employee above 40), $170-$310 (annual) • nonprofit association, $170 (annual) • affiliate, associate, $50 (annual) • commercial bank (per million of assets), $30 (annual) • savings, loan association (per million of assets), $22 (annual). **Staff:** 5. **Local.** Promotes business and community development in the Marietta, OH area. **Computer Services:** Mailing lists, of members. **Committees:** Economic Development; Governmental Affairs; Special Events. **Programs:** Leads Exchange. **Publications:** *The Entrepreneur*, monthly. Newsletter. Features current activities, legislation, and news items about the members. **Circulation:** 1,000. **Advertising:** accepted • *Industrial Guide*. Directory. **Price:** included in membership dues • Membership Directory, annual. Features all individuals who are business members, listed alphabetically with their telephone numbers. **Price:** included in membership dues; $5.00 additional copy for members; $20.00 for nonmembers. Alternate Formats: online.

15822 ■ Marietta Beagle Club
c/o Gracie Moore
Rte. 7, Box 357
Marietta, OH 45750
URL: National Affiliate–www.akc.org
Contact: Gracie Moore, Contact
Local. Affiliated With: American Kennel Club.

15823 ■ Marietta Board of Realtors
324 Fourth St., Ste.200
Marietta, OH 45750
Ph: (740)373-8194
Fax: (740)373-7727
E-mail: mariettarealtors@sbcglobal.net
URL: http://www.mariettarealtors.com
Contact: Elizabeth Keener, Exec. Officer
Local. Strives to develop real estate business practices. Advocates for the right to own, use and transfer real property. Provides a facility for professional development, research and exchange of information among members and the general public. **Affiliated With:** National Association of Realtors.

15824 ■ National Active and Retired Federal Employees Association - Belpre 865
103 Sierra Rd.
Marietta, OH 45750-9353
Ph: (740)374-2099
URL: National Affiliate–www.narfe.org
Contact: James A. Jones, Contact
Local. Protects the retirement future of employees through education. Informs members on issues af-

fecting the retirement. **Affiliated With:** National Association of Retired Federal Employees.

15825 ■ National Technical Honor Society - The Career Center - Ohio
21740 State Rt 676
Marietta, OH 45750
Ph: (740)373-2766
URL: http://www.thecareercenter.net
Contact: Roger Bartunek, Contact
Local.

15826 ■ Ohio Society of Health-System Pharmacists (OSHP)
50 Greenwood Cir.
Marietta, OH 45750
Ph: (740)373-8595
Fax: (740)373-8595
E-mail: ohioshp@ohioshp.org
URL: http://www.ohioshp.org
Contact: Bob Parsons, Exec.VP
State. Advances and supports the professional practice of pharmacists in hospitals and health systems. Serves as the collective voice on issues related to medication use and public health. **Affiliated With:** American Society of Health System Pharmacists.

15827 ■ Phi Theta Kappa - Alpha Rho Gamma Chapter
c/o Cindy Carbone
710 Colegate Dr.
Marietta, OH 45750
Ph: (740)374-8716
E-mail: cindy.carbone@ptk.org
URL: http://www.ptk.org/directories/chapters/OH/8857-1.htm
Contact: Cindy Carbone, Advisor
Local. **Affiliated With:** Phi Theta Kappa, International Honor Society.

15828 ■ Psi Chi, National Honor Society in Psychology - Marietta College
c/o Dept. of Psychology
304 Erwin Hall
215 5th St.
Marietta, OH 45750-4033
Ph: (740)376-4794 (740)374-4766
Fax: (740)376-4459
E-mail: maye@marietta.edu
URL: http://www.psichi.org/chapters/info.asp?chapter_id=532
Contact: Dr. Ryan May, Advisor
Local.

15829 ■ Reno Lions Club
101 Summit Rd.
Marietta, OH 45750
Ph: (740)374-9355 (740)373-2206
E-mail: keith.young@bdoil.com
URL: http://renooh.lionwap.org
Contact: Keith Young, VP
Local. **Affiliated With:** Lions Clubs International.

15830 ■ Sandhill Water and Sewer Association
107 Brant Dr.
Marietta, OH 45750
Ph: (740)373-1941
Local.

15831 ■ Washington County (Ohio) Habitat for Humanity (WCHFH)
PO Box 4092
Marietta, OH 45750
Ph: (740)373-9764
E-mail: director@wchfh.com
URL: http://www.wchfh.com
Contact: Mr. Dennis Thomas, Exec.Dir.
Local. **Affiliated With:** Habitat for Humanity International.

15832 ■ Washington County RSVP
c/o Judith A. Grize, Dir.
333 4th St.
Marietta, OH 45750-2002
Ph: (740)373-3107
Fax: (740)373-7251
E-mail: rsvpwashingtoncounty@yahoo.com
URL: http://www.seniorcorps.gov
Contact: Judith A. Grize, Dir.
Founded: 1973. **Members:** 430. **Staff:** 2. **Local**. **Affiliated With:** Retired and Senior Volunteer Program.

Marion

15833 ■ American Cancer Society, Marion Area
1105 Mt. Vernon Ave.
Marion, OH 43302
Ph: (740)389-3074
Fax: (740)389-5906
Free: (888)227-6446
E-mail: sheri.richardson@cancer.org
URL: http://www.cancer.org
Contact: Sheri Richardson, Contact
Local. Works to eliminate cancer as a major health problem through research, education, advocacy and service. **Affiliated With:** American Cancer Society.

15834 ■ American Legion, Bird Mc Ginnis Post 162
531 Bellefontaine Ave.
Marion, OH 43302
Ph: (740)362-7478
Fax: (740)362-1429
URL: National Affiliate–www.legion.org
Local. **Affiliated With:** American Legion.

15835 ■ American Legion, Marion G.I. Post 584
142 Olney Ave.
Marion, OH 43302
Ph: (740)362-7478
Fax: (740)362-1429
URL: National Affiliate–www.legion.org
Local. **Affiliated With:** American Legion.

15836 ■ American Red Cross, Marion County Chapter
1849 Summerset Dr.
Marion, OH 43302-5843
Ph: (740)725-9141
Fax: (740)725-9182
URL: http://www.marionoh-redcross.org
Local.

15837 ■ Bereaved Parents of the USA, Marion Chapter - Ohio
c/o Kathy Fremont
1212 Prospect Upper Sandusky Rd. N
Marion, OH 43302
Ph: (740)382-2068
E-mail: kmfcook@yahoo.com
URL: National Affiliate–www.bereavedparentsusa.org
Contact: Kathy Fremont, Contact
Local.

15838 ■ Kingwood Orchid Society
c/o Kennet E. Lehner
392 S Vine St.
Marion, OH 43302
Ph: (740)382-8603
E-mail: pepper19@gte.net
URL: National Affiliate–www.orchidweb.org
Contact: Kenneth E. Lehner, Contact
Local. Professional growers, botanists, hobbyists, and others interested in extending the knowledge, production, use, and appreciation of orchids. **Affiliated With:** American Orchid Society.

15839 ■ Marion Area AIFA
c/o Ralph F. Behner
235 S Seffner Ave.
Marion, OH 43302
Ph: (740)223-3088
Fax: (740)223-2867
E-mail: rfbehner@yahoo.com
URL: National Affiliate–naifa.org
Contact: Ralph F. Behner, Contact
Local. Represents the interests of insurance and financial advisors. Advocates for a positive legislative and regulatory environment. Enhances business and professional skills of members. **Affiliated With:** National Association of Insurance and Financial Advisors.

15840 ■ Marion Area Chamber of Commerce
205 W Center St.
Marion, OH 43302
Ph: (740)382-2181
Fax: (740)387-7722
E-mail: chamber@marion.net
URL: http://www.marion.net/chamber
Contact: Pamela S. Hall, Pres.
Membership Dues: employer (with less than 500 employees, plus $4 per employee), educational institution, church, service club, $200 (annual) • elected official, government office, $200 (annual) • individual, $75 (annual). **Staff:** 3. **Local**. Represents businesses in Marion, OH. Provides leadership for improvement of the economic prosperity and quality of life in the local community. **Committees:** Ambassadors; Business Retention and Expansion; Legislative Affairs. **Councils:** Human Resource; Manufacturers; Marion Area Safety; Women's Business. **Subgroups:** Marion Industrial Club. **Publications:** *Progressing Together*, monthly. Newsletter. **Price:** included in membership dues.

15841 ■ Marion Area Independent Insurance Agents Association
c/o Steven R. Simpson
602 E Center St.
Marion, OH 43302-4236
Ph: (740)387-3296
Fax: (740)387-7922
Free: (800)262-5932
Contact: Mr. Steven R. Simpson, Exec. Officer
Local.

15842 ■ Marion Board of Realtors
516 E Center St.
Marion, OH 43302-4244
Ph: (740)387-2928
Fax: (740)382-9420
Contact: Ms. Lori Dye, Exec. Officer
Local.

15843 ■ Marion County Historical Society (MCHS)
Heritage Hall
169 E Church St.
Marion, OH 43302-3819
Ph: (740)387-4255
Fax: (740)387-0117
E-mail: mchs@historymarion.org
URL: http://www.historymarion.org
Contact: Ms. Gale E. Martin, Dir.
Founded: 1969. **Members:** 450. **Membership Dues:** individual, $15 (annual) • family, $25 (annual) • sustaining, $50 (annual) • student, $5 (annual) • major benefactor, $3,000 (annual) • benefactor, $1,000-$2,999 (annual) • sponsor, $500-$999 (annual) • patron, $250-$499 (annual) • advocate, $100-$249 (annual). **Staff:** 3. **Budget:** $85,000. **Local**. Individuals interested in the history of Marion County, OH. Operates Heritage Hall, County Historical Museum, Rinker-Howser Resource Center, Harding Presidential Collections, Marion County Hall of Fame, 1897 brick schoolhouse, 1851 log cabin and a railroad prairie remnant. Conducts educational programs; sponsors Civil War reenactment unit and Civil War round table. **Libraries:** **Type:** reference. **Holdings:** archival material, books, periodicals. **Subjects:** genealogy, local history. **Awards:** **Frequency:** annual. **Type:** scholarship. **Affiliated With:** Ohio Association of Historical Societies and Museums. **Also Known As:** Heritage Hall. **Publications:** *Day Before Yesterday: A Collection of Marion, Ohio, Vignettes* • *Hallmarks*, quarterly. Newsletter. **Price:**

included in membership dues • *Jim Thorpe and the Oorang Indians: NFL's Most Colorful Franchise* • *Marion County History, 1979* • *1907 History of Marion County* • *The Scioto Ordinance Plant and Marion Engineer Depot* • *Tales from the Sage of Salt Rock.* **Conventions/Meetings:** Public Program Meeting - at least 4/year.

15844 ■ Marion and Crawford Counties RSVP
c/o Brenda L. Tharp, Dir.
PO Box 779
Marion, OH 43302
Ph: (740)387-0175
Fax: (740)224-1210
E-mail: rsvpwap@gte.net
URL: http://www.seniorcorps.gov/about/programs/rsvp_state.asp?usestateabbr=oh&Search4.x=0&Search4.y=0
Contact: Brenda L. Tharp, Dir.
Local. Affiliated With: Retired and Senior Volunteer Program.

15845 ■ Marion Evening Lions Club
c/o Randall K. Drazba, Sec.
659 Lark St.
Marion, OH 43302
Ph: (614)888-3100 (740)387-2616
Fax: (614)888-0043
E-mail: randuke1@yahoo.com
URL: http://www.iwaynet.net/~lions13f
Contact: Randall K. Drazba, Sec.
Local. Affiliated With: Lions Clubs International.

15846 ■ Marion Noon Lions Club
c/o Victoria Sheskey, Sec.
218 Washington Ave. E
Marion, OH 43302
Ph: (740)387-9523
E-mail: vsheskey@adelphia.net
URL: http://www.iwaynet.net/~lions13f
Contact: Victoria Sheskey, Sec.
Local. Affiliated With: Lions Clubs International.

15847 ■ Masonic Lodge
119 W. Church St.
Marion, OH 43302
Ph: (740)382-4017

15848 ■ Ohio Corn Growers Association (OCGA)
1100 E Center St.
Marion, OH 43302
Ph: (740)382-0483 (740)383-2676
Fax: (740)387-0144
E-mail: dsiekman@ohiocorn.org
URL: http://www.ohiocorn.org
Contact: Dwayne Siekman, Exec.Dir.
State. Publications: *Corn Talk*, monthly.

15849 ■ Ohio Genealogical Society, Marion Area
PO Box 844
Marion, OH 43301-0844
E-mail: meeker@gte.net
URL: http://www.rootsweb.com/~ohmags
Contact: Steve Eckard, Pres.
Membership Dues: single, $10 (annual) • joint, $12 (annual). **Local.** Supports the objectives of the Ohio Genealogical Society. Collects records and makes them available for use in genealogical research. Preserves genealogical and historical records of related areas in Ohio. **Telecommunication Services:** electronic mail, marshall1067@aol.com. **Affiliated With:** Ohio Genealogical Society. **Publications:** *Marion Memories*, quarterly. Newsletter. **Price:** included in membership dues • *1880 Marion Co., OH Census Index*, periodic. Directory. **Price:** $11.56 plus shipping and handling • *1850 Marion Co., OH Census*, periodic. Directory. **Price:** $25.40 plus shipping and handling • *1900 Marion Co., OH Census Index*, periodic. Directory. **Price:** $13.70 plus shipping and handling • *St. Mary's (Catholic) Cemetery - Marion, OH*, periodic. Directory. Includes tombstone listings. **Price:** $27.54 plus shipping and handling.

15850 ■ Palace Cultural Arts Association
c/o Elaine Merchant, Exec.Dir.
276 W Center St.
Marion, OH 43302
Ph: (740)383-2101
Fax: (740)387-3425
E-mail: marionpalace@marion.net
URL: http://www.marionpalace.org
Contact: Elaine Merchant, Exec.Dir.
Local. Works to foster and promote the public's appreciation and understanding of the cultural arts by coordination, information and common services to organizations engaged in cultural activities by attracting, sponsoring and presenting cultural performances, by operating a public place or places for such cultural performances and educational activities. Operates and maintains the Palace Theatre.

15851 ■ Phi Theta Kappa - Beta Nu Pi Chapter
c/o Teresa Plummer
1467 Mt. Vernon Ave.
Marion, OH 43302
Ph: (740)389-4636
E-mail: plummert@mtc.edu
URL: http://www.ptk.org/directories/chapters/OH/21347-1.htm
Contact: Teresa Plummer, Advisor
Local. Affiliated With: Phi Theta Kappa, International Honor Society.

15852 ■ Pleasant Lions Club
c/o Joseph A. Kume, Sec.
830 Chambord Cir.
Marion, OH 43302
Ph: (740)389-4476 (740)389-2559
E-mail: joe_k@treca.org
URL: http://www.iwaynet.net/~lions13f
Contact: Joseph A. Kume, Sec.
Local. Affiliated With: Lions Clubs International.

15853 ■ Reserve Officers Association - Department of Ohio, Col. Copeland Chapter 43
c/o Capt. Norman W. Fogt, Sec.
644 Girard Ave.
Marion, OH 43302-4920
Ph: (740)382-4446
URL: http://www.roa.org/oh
Contact: Capt. Norman W. Fogt, Sec.
Local. Promotes and supports the development and execution of a military policy for the United States. Provides professional development seminars, workshops and programs for its members. **Affiliated With:** Reserve Officers Association of the United States.

15854 ■ Ridgedale Lions Club
c/o Jim Rohler, PDG, Sec.
3624 Marion-Buckeye Rd.
Marion, OH 43302
Ph: (740)383-2548
E-mail: therohlers@hotmail.com
URL: http://www.iwaynet.net/~lions13f
Contact: Jim Rohler PDG, Sec.
Local. Affiliated With: Lions Clubs International.

15855 ■ Tri-Rivers Education Association
2222 Marion Mt. Gilead Rd.
Marion, OH 43302-8914
Ph: (740)389-4681
URL: http://www.tririvers.com
Contact: Dr. Charles Barr, Superintendent
Local.

15856 ■ United Way Marion County
PO Box 473
Marion, OH 43301-0473
Ph: (740)383-3108
Fax: (740)382-4357
E-mail: unitedwaypam@marion.net
URL: http://unitedwaymarion.org
Local. Affiliated With: United Way of America.

15857 ■ Vietnam Veterans of America, Chapter No. 822 - Col. Harold F. Lyon Memorial
c/o Joseph Smith, Pres.
PO Box 1812
Marion, OH 43301-1812
Ph: (740)387-7040
URL: http://www.vvabuckeyestatecouncil.com
Contact: Joseph Smith, Pres.
Local. Affiliated With: Vietnam Veterans of America.

Mark Center

15858 ■ Ohio Boer Goat Association
c/o Yvonne Blosser
9263 Wonderly Rd.
Mark Center, OH 43536
E-mail: fawn@bright.net
URL: National Affiliate–usbga.org
Contact: Yvonne Blosser, Contact
State.

Marshallville

15859 ■ American Legion, Marshallville Post 718
PO Box 252
Marshallville, OH 44645
Ph: (740)362-7478
Fax: (740)362-1429
URL: National Affiliate–www.legion.org
Local. Affiliated With: American Legion.

Martins Ferry

15860 ■ Martins Ferry Area Chamber of Commerce (MFACC)
418 Walnut St.
Martins Ferry, OH 43935
Ph: (740)633-2565
Fax: (740)633-2641
E-mail: mfchamber@aol.com
Contact: Dorothy Powell, Exec.Dir.
Founded: 1901. **Members:** 115. **Staff:** 2. **Local.** Promotes business and community development in the Martins Ferry, OH area.

Martinsville

15861 ■ South Western Ohio Dairy Goat Association
c/o Lisa Begley
481 Oak Grove Rd.
Martinsville, OH 45146
Ph: (937)685-2026
URL: http://www.geocities.com/swodga2001
Contact: Lisa Begley, Contact
Local. Affiliated With: American Dairy Goat Association.

Marysville

15862 ■ American Legion, Union Post 79
PO Box 408
Marysville, OH 43040
Ph: (740)362-7478
Fax: (740)362-1429
URL: National Affiliate–www.legion.org
Local. Affiliated With: American Legion.

15863 ■ Marysville Association of Realtors
PO Box 187
Marysville, OH 43040
Ph: (937)644-0661
Fax: (937)644-0661
E-mail: mar@imetweb.net
URL: National Affiliate–www.realtor.org
Contact: Suzanne M. Juzwiak, Exec. Officer
Local. Strives to develop real estate business practices. Advocates for the right to own, use and

transfer real property. Provides a facility for professional development, research and exchange of information among members and the general public. **Affiliated With:** National Association of Realtors.

15864 ■ National Association of Home Builders, Union County Building Authority
c/o Betty Koltenbah
881 Catalpa Pl.
Marysville, OH 43040-2102
Ph: (937)642-7578
Fax: (937)642-7547
URL: National Affiliate–www.nahb.org

Local. Single and multifamily home builders, commercial builders, and others associated with the building industry. **Affiliated With:** National Association of Home Builders.

15865 ■ Ohio Beef Council
c/o Elizabeth Harsch, Exec.Dir.
10600 U.S. Hwy. 42
Marysville, OH 43040
Ph: (614)873-6736
Fax: (614)873-6835

State.

15866 ■ Ohio Genealogical Society, Union County Chapter
PO Box 438
Marysville, OH 43040-0438
E-mail: vsmit8@columbus.rr.com
URL: http://www.rootsweb.com/~ohuniogs
Contact: Virginia Smith, Pres.

Founded: 1979. **Membership Dues:** single, $10 (annual) • family at the same address, $12 (annual). **Local. Affiliated With:** Ohio Genealogical Society. **Publications:** *Union County Echoes*, bimonthly. Newsletter. **Price:** included in membership dues.

15867 ■ Union County Chamber of Commerce
227 E 5th St.
Marysville, OH 43040-1297
Ph: (937)642-6279
Fax: (937)644-0422
Free: (800)642-0087
E-mail: chamber@unioncounty.org
URL: http://www.unioncounty.org
Contact: Eric S. Phillips, CEO/Dir.

Members: 512. **Membership Dues:** agriculture, individual, $55 (annual) • retail or service company, $110-$182 (annual) • professional, $182 (annual) • non-profit organization, educational institution, school, $152 (annual) • medical care facility, $212 (annual) • industrial, manufacturing, $152-$484 (annual) • financial institution, $363-$726 (annual) • utility company, $726 (annual). **Local**. Promotes business and community development in the Union County, Marysville, OH area. **Committees:** Ambassadors; Legislative; Team Union County; URT Group. **Councils:** Safety; Union County Business, Education and Workforce Team. **Study Groups:** Union County Safety Council. **Subgroups:** Industrial Parkway Association; Marysville Business Association; Plain City Business Association; Richwood Area Business Association. **Working Groups:** Leadership Institute. **Publications:** *Bridge Tour*, annual. Brochures • *Convention & Visitors Bureau*, monthly. Newsletters • *Quality of Life Book & Membership Directory*, annual. Alternate Formats: online • Newsletter, periodic.

15868 ■ United Way of Union County, Ohio
PO Box 145
Marysville, OH 43040-0145
Ph: (937)644-8381
Fax: (937)644-2512
Free: (877)644-8381
E-mail: unitedwayuc@imetweb.net
URL: http://www.unitedwayofunioncounty.org
Contact: Shari Marsh, Exec.Dir.

Local. Affiliated With: United Way of America.

15869 ■ Veterans of Foreign Wars 3320
15237 Indus. Pkwy.
Marysville, OH 43040
Ph: (937)644-1080
Fax: (937)644-1090
Contact: Gary Miller, Canteen Mgr.

Local.

Mason

15870 ■ American Cancer Society, Southwest Ohio Area
5378-A Cox Smith Rd.
Mason, OH 45040
Ph: (513)229-0616
Fax: (513)229-4994
Free: (888)227-6446
URL: http://www.cancer.org

Local. Affiliated With: American Cancer Society.

15871 ■ American Legion, Ohio Post 194
c/o Joe Barr
401 Reading Rd.
Mason, OH 45040
Ph: (740)362-7478
Fax: (740)362-1429
URL: National Affiliate–www.legion.org
Contact: Joe Barr, Contact

Local. Affiliated With: American Legion.

15872 ■ Audio Engineering Society, Cincinnati Section
c/o Dan Scherbarth
Digital Groove Prdt.ions
5392 Conifer Dr.
Mason, OH 45040
Ph: (513)325-5329
Fax: (513)336-9625
URL: National Affiliate–www.aes.org
Contact: Dan Scherbarth, Contact

Local. Represents the interests of engineers, administrators and technicians for radio, television and motion picture operation. Operates educational and research foundation. **Affiliated With:** Audio Engineering Society.

15873 ■ Chamber of Northeast Cincinnati
316 W Main St.
Mason, OH 45040
Ph: (513)336-0125
Fax: (513)398-6371
E-mail: jharris@necchamber.org
URL: http://www.necchamber.org
Contact: John Harris, Pres.

Local. Provides valuable services to its members, advocates for a positive business environment, and stimulates economic development. Works closely with township, city, and county officials to help attract new business and assist with planned growth and development. **Formerly:** (2005) Mason Chamber of Commerce. **Publications:** *The Navigator*, monthly. Newsletter. Contains timely reports and current issues on what is going on in business community. **Circulation:** 1,000.

15874 ■ Cincinnati Astronomical Society
9583 Sparrow Pl.
Mason, OH 45040
Ph: (513)941-1981
E-mail: wknesel@cinci.rr.com
URL: http://www.cinastro.org
Contact: Wally Knesel, Contact

Local. Promotes the science of astronomy. Works to encourage and coordinate activities of amateur astronomical societies. Fosters observational and computational work and craftsmanship in various fields of astronomy. **Affiliated With:** Astronomical League.

15875 ■ International Customer Service Association, Greater Cincinnati
c/o Scott Farmer, Dir.
Luxottica Retail
4000 Luxottica Pl.
Mason, OH 45040
Ph: (513)765-6282
E-mail: sfarmer@luxotticaretail.com
URL: National Affiliate–www.icsa.com
Contact: Scott Farmer, Dir.

Local. Affiliated With: International Customer Service Association.

15876 ■ Mason Lions Club
401 Reading Rd.
Mason, OH 45040-1513
Ph: (513)336-7879 (513)494-1967
URL: http://masonoh.lionwap.org
Contact: Ken Strosnider, Pres.

Local. Affiliated With: Lions Clubs International.

15877 ■ Northeast Cincinnati Chamber of Commerce
316 W Main St.
Mason, OH 45040
Ph: (513)336-0125
Fax: (513)398-6371
E-mail: lfergus@necchamber.org
URL: http://www.mlkchamber.org
Contact: John Harris, Pres.

Staff: 4. **Local**. Promotes business and community development in the Mason, OH area. **Formerly:** (2005) Mason Landen Kings Chamber of Commerce. **Publications:** *The Navigator*, monthly. Newsletter. Contains reports and current issues on what is going on in the business community. • Membership Directory.

15878 ■ Veterans of Foreign Wars Post 9622
120 W Main St.
Mason, OH 45040
Ph: (513)398-9622
Contact: Roger Yost, Commander

Local.

Massillon

15879 ■ AAA Massillon Automobile Club
1972 Whales Rd. NE
Massillon, OH 44646
Ph: (330)833-1084

Local.

15880 ■ American Legion, Massillon Post 221
PO Box 757
Massillon, OH 44648
Ph: (216)833-4930
Fax: (740)362-1429
URL: National Affiliate–www.legion.org

Local. Affiliated With: American Legion.

15881 ■ American Red Cross, Western Stark County Chapter
c/o Victoria L. Wood, Exec.Dir.
3140 Lincoln Way E, Ste.201
Massillon, OH 44646
Ph: (330)833-9943
Fax: (330)830-2538
E-mail: wstkcty@sssnet.com
URL: http://massillongateway.com/redcross
Contact: Victoria L. Wood, Exec.Dir.

Founded: 1917. **Local**. Humanitarian organization, led by volunteers and guided by its Congressional Charter and Fundamental Principles of the International Red Cross Movement. Provides relief to victims of disasters and helps people prevent, prepare for, and respond to emergencies. **Awards:** Volunteer of the Year. **Frequency:** annual. **Type:** recognition. **Computer Services:** Information services, web pages that contain information about disaster services and help. **Affiliated With:** American

Red Cross National Headquarters. **Publications:** *Pulse*, quarterly. Newsletter. Alternate Formats: online.

15882 ■ Antique Automobile Club of America, Ohio Region
c/o Bill Briner, Treas.
2524 Schuler NW
Massillon, OH 44647
Ph: (330)833-2555
E-mail: merlehoover@dragonbbs.com
URL: http://local.aaca.org/ohio/index.htm
Contact: Merle Hoover, Pres.
Founded: 1946. **Membership Dues:** individual, $15 (annual). **State.** Collectors, hobbyists, and others interested in the preservation, maintenance, and restoration of automobiles and in automotive history. **Affiliated With:** Antique Automobile Club of America.

15883 ■ Big Brothers Big Sisters of America of Massillon
730 Duncan St. SW
Massillon, OH 44647-7960
Ph: (330)833-1997
Fax: (330)833-5366
E-mail: bgcmtigers@aol.com
URL: National Affiliate–www.bbbsa.org
Founded: 1973. **Members:** 100. **Staff:** 2. **Budget:** $40,000. **Local.** Seeks to create a one-on-one relationship between adults and children who are from single parent homes. **Affiliated With:** Big Brothers Big Sisters of America. **Publications:** *What's Happening!*, quarterly. Newsletter.

15884 ■ Jackson - Beldon Chamber of Commerce
5735 Wales Ave. NW
Massillon, OH 44646-9097
Ph: (330)833-4400
Fax: (330)833-4456
E-mail: info@jbcc.org
URL: http://www.jbcc.org
Contact: Ruthanne Wilkof, Exec.Dir.
Membership Dues: business (1-9 employees), $175 • business (10-49 employees), $275 • business (50-99 employees), $450 • business (100 or more employees), $550 • non-profit, $75. **Local.** Works to promote integrity, good faith, just, and equitable principles in business and to foster, protect, and advance the commercial, mercantile, industrial, professional, social and civic interests of Jackson Township and its citizens. Strives to be an advocate of business in Jackson and Stark County. Helps in servicing the needs of businesses and develops program that benefit the members. **Computer Services:** Online services, membership listings. **Affiliated With:** Ohio Chamber of Commerce; U.S. Chamber of Commerce. **Publications:** Newsletter. Contains information on the current events in the Jackson-Belden Chamber and the surrounding Canton area. Alternate Formats: online.

15885 ■ Jackson Township Lions Club
c/o John Whitmer, Pres.
6373 Kilkenny Cir. NW
Massillon, OH 44646
Ph: (330)837-9412
E-mail: jwhitmer@sssnet.com
URL: http://www.jacksontownshiplions.org
Contact: John Whitmer, Pres.
Local. Affiliated With: Lions Clubs International.

15886 ■ Masonic Lodge
333 2nd St. SW
Massillon, OH 44646
Ph: (330)833-7615

15887 ■ Massillon Area Chamber of Commerce (MACC)
137 Lincoln Way E
Massillon, OH 44646
Ph: (330)833-3146
Fax: (330)833-8944
E-mail: info@massillonohchamber.com
URL: http://massillongateway.com
Founded: 1915. **Membership Dues:** small and professional business (plus $3 per full-time employee and $1.50 per part-time employee), $160 (annual) • retiree, $75 (annual) • social service organization, $130 (annual). **Local.** Promotes business and community development in the Massillon, OH area. **Publications:** *Buyers Guide*, annual. Directory. **Circulation:** 20,000.

15888 ■ Massillon Lions Club
PO Box 215
Massillon, OH 44648
Ph: (330)832-2173
E-mail: bheadcarl1@aol.com
URL: http://www.massillonlionsclub.org
Contact: Carl Leonhardt, Pres.
Local. Affiliated With: Lions Clubs International.

15889 ■ Massillon-Stark County REACT
PO Box 483
Massillon, OH 44648
Ph: (330)837-4018
E-mail: mscrc260@juno.com
URL: http://www.reactintl.org/teaminfo/usa_teams/teams-usoh.htm
Local. Trained communication experts and professional volunteers. Provides volunteer public service and emergency communications through the use of radios (Citizen Band, General Mobile Radio Service, UHF and HAM). Coordinates with radio industries and government on safety communication matters and supports charitable activities and community organizations.

15890 ■ Massillon Urban League
c/o Beverly Lewis, Interim Pres.
35 Erie St. N, Ste.205
Massillon, OH 44646
Ph: (330)833-2804
E-mail: bevlewis7@hotmail.com
URL: National Affiliate–www.nul.org
Contact: Beverly Lewis, Interim Pres.
Local. Affiliated With: National Urban League.

15891 ■ Meals on Wheels of Stark and Wayne Counties
2363 Nave St. SE
Massillon, OH 44646
Free: (800)466-8010
E-mail: info@mow-starkwayne.org
URL: http://www.mow-starkwayne.org
Local. Affiliated With: Meals on Wheels Association of America.

15892 ■ Northwest Lions Club
1737 Clearbrook Rd. NW
Massillon, OH 44646
Ph: (330)833-2271
E-mail: ngmlpt@aol.com
URL: http://northwestoh.lionwap.org
Contact: Nancy McEwen, Sec.-Treas.
Local. Affiliated With: Lions Clubs International.

15893 ■ Ohio Chapter of the Myasthenia Gravis Foundation
2907 B Lincoln Way E
Massillon, OH 44646
Ph: (330)834-9066
Fax: (330)834-9067
E-mail: emailohiochaptermgf@nci2000.net
URL: http://www.ohiochaptermgf.org
State. Provides ongoing public education and patient services through local support group meetings, newsletters, medical programs, and personal contact. **Affiliated With:** Myasthenia Gravis Foundation of America.

15894 ■ Ohio Music Education Association (OMEA)
c/o Roger Hall, Exec.Dir.
8227 Audubon St. NW
Massillon, OH 44646-7834
Ph: (330)833-5677
Fax: (330)833-4774
E-mail: execdirector@omea-ohio.org
URL: http://www.omea-ohio.org
Contact: Roger Hall, Exec.Dir.
State. Works to promote and advance music education. Advances the personal and professional growth of music educators. **Affiliated With:** MENC: The National Association for Music Education.

15895 ■ Tuslaw Lions Club
PO Box 273
Massillon, OH 44648
Ph: (330)833-0615
E-mail: jhfowler@sssnet.com
URL: http://www.tuslawlions.com
Contact: Linda Fowler, Pres.
Local. Affiliated With: Lions Clubs International.

15896 ■ Utility Workers Union of America, AFL-CIO - Local Union 116 (UWUA)
966 Norwich Ave. NW
Massillon, OH 44646-3049
Ph: (330)834-3445
Fax: (330)834-3446
E-mail: uwua116@juno.com
URL: http://www.uwualocal116.org
Contact: Joseph L Helbling, Contact
Members: 130. **Local. Affiliated With:** Utility Workers Union of America, AFL-CIO.

15897 ■ Vietnam Veterans of America, Chapter No. 646 - Western Stark County
c/o Bob Jones, Pres.
PO Box 251
Massillon, OH 44648
Ph: (330)833-3100
URL: http://www.vvabuckeyestatecouncil.com
Contact: Bob Jones, Pres.
Local. Affiliated With: Vietnam Veterans of America.

Maumee

15898 ■ AAA Northwest Ohio
316 W Dussel Dr.
Maumee, OH 43537
Ph: (419)897-4455 (419)897-5075
Fax: (419)897-0789
URL: http://www.aaa.com
Contact: Ms. Cathy Mossing, Travel Agent
State.

15899 ■ American Cancer Society, Lucas County
135 Chesterfield Dr., Ste.100
Maumee, OH 43537
Ph: (419)891-9200
Fax: (419)891-9223
Free: (888)227-6446
URL: http://www.cancer.org
Local. Affiliated With: American Cancer Society.

15900 ■ American Legion, Maumee Post 320
204 Illinois Ave.
Maumee, OH 43537
Ph: (740)362-7478
Fax: (740)362-1429
URL: National Affiliate–www.legion.org
Local. Affiliated With: American Legion.

15901 ■ Anthony Wayne HS - Young Life
PO Box 412
Maumee, OH 43537
Ph: (419)514-5433
URL: http://sites.younglife.org/_layouts/ylext/default.aspx?ID=C-1582
Local. Affiliated With: Young Life.

15902 ■ Anthony Wayne Wyldlife
PO Box 412
Maumee, OH 43537
Ph: (419)514-5433
URL: http://sites.younglife.org/_layouts/ylext/default.aspx?ID=C-3606
Local. Affiliated With: Young Life.

15903 ■ Association of Certified Fraud Examiners, Toledo Chapter No. 122
145 Chesterfield Ln.
Maumee, OH 43537
Ph: (419)891-1040
E-mail: arndt@wvco.com
URL: National Affiliate–www.acfe.com
Contact: Greg Arndt CFE, Pres.
Local. Works to reduce the incidence of fraud and white-collar crime and to assist the members in its detection and deterrence. Sponsors training seminars on fraud and loss prevention. Administers credentialing programs for Certified Fraud Examiners. **Affiliated With:** Association of Certified Fraud Examiners.

15904 ■ Bowsher HS - Young Life
PO Box 412
Maumee, OH 43537
Ph: (419)514-5433
URL: http://sites.younglife.org/_layouts/ylext/default.aspx?ID=C-1583
Local. Affiliated With: Young Life.

15905 ■ Gateway - Wyldlife
PO Box 412
Maumee, OH 43537
Ph: (419)514-5433
URL: http://sites.younglife.org/_layouts/ylext/default.aspx?ID=C-1587
Local. Affiliated With: Young Life.

15906 ■ Golden Retriever Club of Greater Toledo (GRCGT)
c/o Barbara Bumcrots, Pres.
2509 Seventh Ave.
Maumee, OH 43537
Ph: (419)891-0232
E-mail: babsbuggy@yahoo.com
URL: http://www.wcnet.org/~grcgt
Contact: Barbara Bumcrots, Pres.
Local. Affiliated With: Golden Retriever Club of America.

15907 ■ Home Builders Association of Greater Toledo
c/o Daniel Saevig
1911 Indian Wood Cir.
Maumee, OH 43537-4002
Ph: (419)473-2507
Fax: (419)473-3015
E-mail: dsaevig@toledohba.com
URL: http://www.toledohba.com
Contact: Tony Plath, Exec.VP
Local. Single and multifamily home builders, commercial builders, and others associated with the building industry. **Affiliated With:** National Association of Home Builders.

15908 ■ IEEE Computer Society, Toledo Chapter
c/o Donald Ewing, Jr.
608 Pierce St.
Maumee, OH 43537-3624
Ph: (419)893-3562
E-mail: djewing@computer.org
URL: http://ewh.ieee.org/r4/toledo/comp-cont/comp-cont.html
Contact: Gerald Heuring, Chair
Local. Affiliated With: IEEE Computer Society.

15909 ■ Maumee Chamber of Commerce
605 Conant St.
Maumee, OH 43537-3356
Ph: (419)893-5805
Fax: (419)893-8699
E-mail: info@maumeechamber.com
URL: http://www.maumeechamber.com
Contact: Brenda Clixby, Exec.Dir.
Founded: 1955. **Members:** 325. **Membership Dues:** business, individual, $125-$275 (annual). **Staff:** 2. **Local.** Promotes business and community development in Maumee, OH. **Awards:** College Scholarships. **Frequency:** annual. **Type:** recognition. **Publications:** *Members Bulletin*, 8/year. **Conventions/Meetings:** meeting - 8/year.

15910 ■ Maumee Council for the Arts (MCA)
c/o Tom Wagner, Pres.
400 Conant St.
Maumee, OH 43537-3380
E-mail: wagsprc@msn.com
URL: http://www.maumeearts.org
Contact: Tom Wagner, Pres.
Local.

15911 ■ Maumee HS - Young Life
PO Box 412
Maumee, OH 43537
Ph: (419)514-5433
URL: http://sites.younglife.org/_layouts/ylext/default.aspx?ID=C-1584
Local. Affiliated With: Young Life.

15912 ■ Maumee Valley Historical Society
1031 River Rd.
Maumee, OH 43537
Ph: (419)893-9602
Fax: (419)893-3108
E-mail: mvhs@accesstoledo.com
URL: http://www.maumee.org/recreation/wolcott.htm
Contact: Mr. Jack Hiles, Exec.Dir.
Founded: 1864. **Members:** 300. **Staff:** 5. **Budget:** $200,000. **Local.** Works to disseminate information, maintain museum, offer educational tours; hosts an Annual Antiques Show and Sale. **Publications:** *Northwest Ohio Quarterly*. Journal • *Ohio Cues*, monthly, except during summer. Newsletter. **Conventions/Meetings:** annual meeting.

15913 ■ Maumee Valley Volkssporters
c/o Craig Gauger
606 W Dudley St.
Maumee, OH 43537
Ph: (419)893-0540
E-mail: gcgauger@hotmail.com
URL: http://www.geocities.com/Yosemite/Gorge/4120
Contact: Craig Gauger, Contact
Local. Affiliated With: American Volkssport Association.

15914 ■ Ohio Council of Chapters, MOAA
c/o Capt. John MacDonald
6629 Fawn Ln.
Maumee, OH 43537-1176
Ph: (419)868-3039
E-mail: jmac.donald@adelphia.net
URL: National Affiliate–www.moaa.org
Contact: Capt. John MacDonald, Contact
State. Affiliated With: Military Officers Association of America.

15915 ■ Perrysburg HS - Young Life
PO Box 412
Maumee, OH 43537
Ph: (419)514-5433
URL: http://sites.younglife.org/_layouts/ylext/default.aspx?ID=C-1585
Local. Affiliated With: Young Life.

15916 ■ Perrysburg - Wyldlife
PO Box 412
Maumee, OH 43537
Ph: (419)514-5433
URL: http://sites.younglife.org/_layouts/ylext/default.aspx?ID=C-1588
Local. Affiliated With: Young Life.

15917 ■ Rossford HS - Young Life
PO Box 412
Maumee, OH 43537
Ph: (419)514-5433
URL: http://sites.younglife.org/_layouts/ylext/default.aspx?ID=C-1586
Local. Affiliated With: Young Life.

15918 ■ Society for Applied Spectroscopy, Toledo
c/o Joseph A. Grappin, Chm.
Monarch Analytical Labs
349 Tomahawk Dr.
Maumee, OH 43537
Ph: (419)897-9000
E-mail: ja.grappin@worldnet.att.net
URL: National Affiliate–www.s-a-s.org
Contact: Joseph A. Grappin, Chm.
Local. Affiliated With: Society for Applied Spectroscopy.

15919 ■ Toledo South Side - Young Life
PO Box 412
Maumee, OH 43537
Ph: (419)514-5433
Fax: (419)865-3579
E-mail: southsideyounglife@yahoo.com
URL: http://sites.younglife.org/sites/ToledoSouthSide/default.aspx
Local. Affiliated With: Young Life.

15920 ■ Women's Entrepreneurial Network (WEN)
PO Box 514
Maumee, OH 43537
Ph: (419)536-6732
Fax: (419)534-3007
URL: http://www.wentoledo.org
Contact: Bobbi Quackenbush, Pres.
Founded: 1994. **Members:** 300. **Membership Dues:** individual, $75 (annual) • corporate, $150 (annual). **Local.** Strives to encourage and support women in business and women-friendly businesses with successful entrepreneurial development. **Computer Services:** Online services, members' blog. **Publications:** *WEN Newsletter - Connecting with Success*, monthly. **Conventions/Meetings:** annual conference • weekly meeting, networking.

Mayfield Heights

15921 ■ Cleveland-Akron Swing and Hustle Club
1226 Elmwood Rd.
Mayfield Heights, OH 44124
E-mail: cash-club@neo.rr.com
URL: http://www.cashdanceclub.org
Contact: Tina Price, Treas.
Local.

15922 ■ Friends of Freedom Society Ohio Underground Railroad Association (FOFS)
c/o Douglas Thomas, Pres.
PO Box 24823
Mayfield Heights, OH 44124-0823
Ph: (614)596-5335
E-mail: info@ohioundergroundrailroad.org
URL: http://www.ohioundergroundrailroad.org
Contact: Douglas Thomas, Pres.
Founded: 1996. **Membership Dues:** regular, $35 (annual). **Local.** Seeks to raise and maintain public awareness about the lives of enslaved African Americans as it relates to the Underground Railroad movement. Preserves and commemorates the cultural landscapes and its connections to the lives of the people associated with the Underground Railroad. Documents past history of the Underground Railroad as being one of the first civil rights movements in the U.S. **Awards:** Conductor of the Year. **Frequency:** annual. **Type:** recognition. **Recipient:** for outstanding contributions toward the preservation and education of the Underground Railroad history.

15923 ■ National Association of Investors Corporation, Northeast Ohio Chapter (NAIC)
PO Box 248126
Mayfield Heights, OH 44124
Ph: (440)449-1427 (216)556-3014
E-mail: suzettecohen@yahoo.com
URL: http://www.betterinvesting.org/chapter/neohio
Contact: Suzette Cohen, Dir.
Local. Provides support services to investment clubs and individual members throughout the chapter area.

Schedules several investment-related programs and classes throughout the year, all of which are open to members and non-members. **Affiliated With:** National Association of Investors Corporation.

Maynard

15924 ■ American Legion, Community Post 666
PO Box 343
Maynard, OH 43937
Ph: (740)362-7478
Fax: (740)362-1429
URL: National Affiliate–www.legion.org
Local. Affiliated With: American Legion.

McArthur

15925 ■ American Legion, Ohio Post 303
c/o Robert Wyckoff
PO Box 1
McArthur, OH 45651
Ph: (740)362-7478
Fax: (740)362-1429
URL: National Affiliate–www.legion.org
Contact: Robert Wyckoff, Contact
Local. Affiliated With: American Legion.

15926 ■ Veterans of Foreign Wars 5299
401 Veterans Memorial Dr.
McArthur, OH 45651
Ph: (740)596-2497
Contact: John Barber, Commander
Local.

15927 ■ Vinton County Chamber of Commerce
104 W Main St.
PO Box 307
McArthur, OH 45651
Ph: (740)596-5033
Fax: (740)596-9262
E-mail: dboothe@vintoncounty.com
URL: http://www.vintoncounty.com
Contact: David M. Boothe, Exec.Dir.
Local. Promotes business and community development in the McArthur, OH area. **Awards:** Student of the Year. **Frequency:** annual. **Type:** recognition.

15928 ■ Vinton County Convention and Visitors Bureau
c/o Bobbie Davis
104 W Main St.
McArthur, OH 45651-0307
Ph: (740)596-5033
E-mail: info@vintoncounty.com
URL: http://www.vintoncountytravel.com
Contact: Bobbie Davis, Contact
Local.

McClure

15929 ■ American Legion, Roberts-Mc-Millen Post 332
East St., RR 65
McClure, OH 43534
Ph: (740)362-7478
Fax: (740)362-1429
URL: National Affiliate–www.legion.org
Local. Affiliated With: American Legion.

McComb

15930 ■ American Legion, Mulford-Butler Post 511
PO Box 489
McComb, OH 45858
Ph: (740)362-7478
Fax: (740)362-1429
URL: National Affiliate–www.legion.org
Local. Affiliated With: American Legion.

15931 ■ Korean War Veterans Association, Hancock County Chapter
c/o Robert L. Wilson
219 Andrew Dr.
McComb, OH 45858
Ph: (419)293-3071
E-mail: chaldafarm@yahoo.com
URL: National Affiliate–www.kwva.org
Contact: Robert L. Wilson, Contact
Local. Affiliated With: Korean War Veterans Association.

McConnelsville

15932 ■ American Legion, Malconta Post 24
61 S Kennebec Ave.
McConnelsville, OH 43756
Ph: (740)362-7478
Fax: (740)362-1429
URL: National Affiliate–www.legion.org
Local. Affiliated With: American Legion.

15933 ■ National Active and Retired Federal Employees Association - Zanesville 648
85 Leeper Rd.
McConnelsville, OH 43756-9001
Ph: (740)962-6514
URL: National Affiliate–www.narfe.org
Contact: James Mckibben, Contact
Local. Protects the retirement future of employees through education. Informs members on issues affecting the retirement. **Affiliated With:** National Association of Retired Federal Employees.

15934 ■ Ohio Genealogical Society, Morgan County Chapter
PO Box 418
McConnelsville, OH 43756-0418
E-mail: morgancochapterogs@hotmail.com
URL: http://www.ogs.org
Contact: C. Reed, Contact
Founded: 1981. **Members:** 150. **Membership Dues:** individual, $10 (annual) • family, $12 (annual). **Local.** Dedicated to the collection and distribution of genealogical material relating to past or present residents of Morgan County, Ohio; provides educational and informative programs pertaining to genealogy. **Libraries: Type:** open to the public. **Holdings:** books. **Subjects:** local history, genealogy. **Affiliated With:** Ohio Genealogical Society. **Publications:** *Morgan Link*, quarterly. Newsletter. **Price:** included in membership dues. **Circulation:** 200. **Conventions/Meetings:** quarterly meeting, regular chapter meeting and program - 3rd Tuesday of February, May, August, and November at Kate Love Simpson Library, McConnelsville, OH.

McDonald

15935 ■ McDonald Lions Club
c/o Mathew Hull, Sec.
522 Illinois Ave.
McDonald, OH 44437
E-mail: getz@ada.k12.on.su
URL: http://www.lions13d.org
Contact: Mathew Hull, Sec.
Local. Affiliated With: Lions Clubs International.

15936 ■ Ohio Browns Boosters
c/o Jeff Joseph, Pres.
480 Dakota Ave.
McDonald, OH 44437
Ph: (330)506-7194
Free: (866)276-9671
E-mail: moreinfo@brownsboosters.com
URL: http://www.brownsboosters.com
Contact: Jeff Joseph, Pres.
Local.

Mechanicsburg

15937 ■ American Legion, Ohio Post 238
c/o Donald Cannon
24 S Locust St.
Mechanicsburg, OH 43044
Ph: (740)362-7478
Fax: (740)362-1429
URL: National Affiliate–www.legion.org
Contact: Donald Cannon, Contact
Local. Affiliated With: American Legion.

Medina

15938 ■ American Legion, Courtney Lawrence Post 202
620 N Broadway St.
Medina, OH 44256
Ph: (740)362-7478
Fax: (740)362-1429
URL: National Affiliate–www.legion.org
Local. Affiliated With: American Legion.

15939 ■ American Red Cross, Medina County Chapter
704 N Court St.
Medina, OH 44256
Ph: (330)723-4565
Fax: (330)725-3000
URL: http://www.medinaredcross.org
Local.

15940 ■ Friends of Medina County Parks
6364 Deerview Ln.
Medina, OH 44256-8008
Ph: (330)722-9364
Fax: (330)722-9366
E-mail: parks@medinacountyparks.com
URL: http://www.medinacountyparks.com
Contact: Thomas James, Dir.
Local.

15941 ■ Great Dane Club of Cleveland
c/o Karen VanBoxel
7915 Br. Rd.
Medina, OH 44256
Ph: (330)725-1184
Fax: (330)723-6212
E-mail: vanboxelt@nobleknights.com
URL: http://www.grafton1.com/GDCC
Founded: 1944. **Local. Conventions/Meetings:** monthly meeting - every 4th Tuesday of the month.

15942 ■ Izaak Walton League of America, Medina Chapter
581 S Broadway St.
Medina, OH 44256-2607
Ph: (330)722-6853
E-mail: cafajaz@aol.com
URL: National Affiliate–www.iwla.org
Contact: Faye Jessie, Sec.
Local. Works to educate the public to conserve, maintain, protect, and restore the soil, forest, water, and other natural resources of the U.S; promotes the enjoyment and wholesome utilization of these resources. **Affiliated With:** Izaak Walton League of America.

15943 ■ Leadership Medina County (LMC)
1101 W Liberty St.
Medina, OH 44256
Ph: (330)725-8461
Fax: (330)725-5870
E-mail: info@leadershipmedinaccounty.org
URL: http://www.leadershipmedinacounty.org
Contact: Lucy P. Sondles, Exec.Dir.
Founded: 1991. **Regional Groups:** 1. **State Groups:** 1. **Local.** Administers education and leadership development program. Facilitates communication and cooperation among members. **Publications:** *Directory of Alumni*, annual. Membership Directory. Lists program membership and current community involvement activities. **Price:** free for members;

$10.00 for nonmembers • *Leading Edge*. Newsletter. Alternate Formats: online.

15944 ■ Medina Area Chamber of Commerce
145 N Court St.
Medina, OH 44256-1927
Ph: (330)723-8773
Fax: (330)722-6844
E-mail: info@medinaohchamber.com
URL: http://www.medinaohchamber.com
Contact: Debra Lynn-Schmitz, Pres./CEO
Members: 500. **Membership Dues:** amusement/entertainment, apartment/mobile home, automotive, diversified, hotel/motel (based on number of employees), $212-$407 (annual) • construction, insurance, investment/finance, professional service, real estate (based on number of employees), $212-$780 (annual) • business outside Medina County ($67 each additional representative), $363 (annual) • non-profit organization ($28 for each additional representative), $212 (annual) • associate, $140 (annual). **Staff:** 5. **Local.** Unites hundreds of businesses and professional firms and serves as the central agency that works to improve business and build a better community. **Computer Services:** Electronic publishing, e-link informs members of issues or events occurring in between regular issues of The Chamber Link • mailing lists, of members. **Committees:** Business Advocacy; Business Development; Economic Development; Event Planning; Miniature Golf Outing. **Councils:** Business Corridor; Human Resource; Safety. **Publications:** *The Chamber Link*, monthly, except August. Newsletter. Provides current member news and updates on local issues affecting business, plus a calendar of events and informative articles. **Price:** included in membership dues. **Advertising:** accepted. Alternate Formats: online • Membership Directory, annual. **Advertising:** accepted. Alternate Formats: online • Annual Report, annual. Alternate Formats: online.

15945 ■ Medina County Board of Realtors
421 N Court St.
Medina, OH 44256
Ph: (330)722-1000
Local.

15946 ■ Medina County Convention and Visitors Bureau
PO Box 486
Medina, OH 44258
Ph: (330)722-5502
Fax: (330)723-4713
Free: (800)860-2943
E-mail: info@visitmedinacounty.com
URL: http://www.visitmedinacounty.com
Contact: Daniel D. Hostetler III, Exec.Dir.
Founded: 1991. **Members:** 225. **Membership Dues:** local business base, $25 (annual). **Staff:** 2. **Budget:** $220,000. **Local.** Promotes tourism and conventions in Medina County, OH. **Libraries: Type:** not open to the public. **Holdings:** 54; books. **Subjects:** local information. **Publications:** *Medina Traveler*, biennial. Newsletter. **Price:** free. **Circulation:** 1,700. **Conventions/Meetings:** annual meeting - always October, Medina County, OH.

15947 ■ Medina County Department of Planning Services (MCDPS)
124 W Washington St., Ste.B-4
Medina, OH 44256
Ph: (330)722-9219
Fax: (330)764-8456
E-mail: ptheken@medinaco.org
URL: http://www.planning.co.medina.oh.us
Contact: Ms. Patrice Theken, Dir.
Local. Publications: Newsletter, monthly. Alternate Formats: online.

15948 ■ Medina County Home Builders Association
c/o James Owen
4081 N Jefferson St.
Medina, OH 44256
Ph: (330)725-2371
Fax: (330)725-0461
E-mail: jowen@medinacountyhba.com
URL: http://www.medinacountyhba.com
Contact: Tim VanderLaan, Exec.Dir.
Local. Single and multifamily home builders, commercial builders, and others associated with the building industry. **Affiliated With:** National Association of Home Builders.

15949 ■ Medina County REACT
PO Box 0562
Medina, OH 44258
Ph: (330)225-3702
E-mail: medinacoreact@aol.com
URL: http://www.reactintl.org/teaminfo/usa_teams/teams-usoh.htm
Local. Trained communication experts and professional volunteers. Provides volunteer public service and emergency communications through the use of radios (Citizen Band, General Mobile Radio Service, UHF and HAM). Coordinates with radio industries and government on safety communication matters and supports charitable activities and community organizations.

15950 ■ Medina Summit Land Conservancy
PO Box 141
Medina, OH 44258-0141
Ph: (330)723-7313
Fax: (330)722-6592
E-mail: info@mslconservancy.org
URL: http://www.mslconservancy.org
Contact: Chris Bunch, Exec.Dir.
Founded: 1999. **Members:** 750. **Membership Dues:** senior, $20 (annual) • family, $50 (annual) • supporting, $100 (annual). **Staff:** 3. **Budget:** $300. **Local.** Works for conservation of natural, agricultural and rural land in and around Medina and Summit Counties, Ohio. **Affiliated With:** Land Trust Alliance. **Publications:** *The Conservator*, quarterly. Newsletter. **Price:** free membership. **Circulation:** 1,000. Alternate Formats: online.

15951 ■ NACE International, Cleveland Section
c/o Otto J. Esterle, Chm.
Corrpro Companies Inc.
1055 W Smith Rd.
Medina, OH 44256
Ph: (330)723-5082
Fax: (330)722-7654
E-mail: oesterle@corrpro.com
URL: National Affiliate–www.nace.org
Contact: Otto J. Esterle, Chm.
Local. Promotes public safety by advancing the knowledge of corrosion engineering and science. Works to raise awareness of corrosion control and prevention technology among government agencies and legislators, businesses, professional societies and the general public. **Affiliated With:** NACE International: The Corrosion Society.

15952 ■ National Earth Science Teachers Association, East Central Chapter
6800 Wolff Rd.
Medina, OH 44256
Ph: (330)225-7731
E-mail: rfabick@zoominternet.net
URL: National Affiliate–www.nestanet.org
Contact: Ron Fabick, Contact
Regional. Represents the community of Earth Science educators. Seeks to advance Earth Science education at all educational levels. **Affiliated With:** National Earth Science Teachers Association.

15953 ■ Ohio Genealogical Society, Medina County
c/o Maggie Stewart-Zimmerman, Coor.
PO Box 804
Medina, OH 44258-0804
Ph: (330)725-4257
E-mail: ohmedina@ev1.net
URL: http://www.rootsweb.com/~ohmedina/index.htm
Contact: Maggie Stewart-Zimmerman, Coor.
Founded: 1976. **Members:** 75. **Membership Dues:** individual, $10 (annual) • family, $12 (annual). **Local.** Individuals interested in genealogy and local history. Conducts research; assists beginning genealogists. **Libraries: Type:** reference. **Holdings:** archival material, books, periodicals. **Subjects:** genealogy, local history. **Affiliated With:** Ohio Genealogical Society. **Publications:** Books • Newsletter, periodic.

15954 ■ Ohio Parents of Children with Visual Impairments (OPVI)
c/o Rachel Miller, Pres.
5786 Arlyne Ln.
Medina, OH 44256
Ph: (330)722-6609
E-mail: rachel@jmiller.us
URL: National Affiliate–www.spedex.com/napvi
Contact: Rachel Miller, Pres.
State. Represents individuals committed to providing support to the parents of children who have visual impairments. Promotes public understanding of the needs and rights of children who are visually impaired. **Affiliated With:** National Association for Parents of Children With Visual Impairments.

15955 ■ Prader-Willi Syndrome Association of Ohio
c/o Steve Fetsko, Pres.
1087 Dover Dr.
Medina, OH 44256
Ph: (330)723-0004
E-mail: pwsaohio@aol.com
URL: http://www.pwsaohio.org
Contact: Steve Fetsko, Pres.
State. Affiliated With: Prader-Willi Syndrome Association (U.S.A.).

15956 ■ Project: LEARN of Medina County
222 S Broadway
Medina, OH 44256
Ph: (330)723-1314
Fax: (330)764-9305
E-mail: dmorawski@zoominternet.net
URL: http://www.projectlearnmedina.org
Contact: Diane Morawski, Exec.Dir.
Founded: 1983. **Members:** 300. **Budget:** $112,000. **Local.** Seeks to reduce adult illiteracy. Motivates and supports teaching of illiterate adults and older youths to a level of listening, speaking, reading, writing, and basic computational skills enabling them to solve their daily problems. **Affiliated With:** Laubach Literacy International. **Formerly:** (2006) Literacy Council of Medina County, Project Learn Program. **Publications:** *Changing Lives*, quarterly. Newsletter. **Conventions/Meetings:** annual meeting - always in March.

15957 ■ United Way of Medina County
704 N Court St.
Medina, OH 44256-1731
Ph: (330)725-3926
Fax: (330)725-3000
Free: (877)725-3926
E-mail: uwmc@unitedwaymedina.org
URL: http://www.unitedwaymedina.org
Contact: Julie A. King, Exec.Dir.
Local. Affiliated With: United Way of America.

15958 ■ Vietnam Veterans of America, Medina County - Chapter No. 385
c/o Edward S. Jones, Pres.
PO Box 1267
Medina, OH 44258
Ph: (440)779-1198
Fax: (815)377-1383
URL: http://www.vvabuckeyestatecouncil.com
Contact: Edward S. Jones, Pres.
Local. Affiliated With: Vietnam Veterans of America.

Medway

15959 ■ American Legion, New Carlisle Post 286
1587 1/2 Lake Rd.
Medway, OH 45341
Ph: (937)845-9353
Fax: (740)362-1429
URL: National Affiliate–www.legion.org
Local. Affiliated With: American Legion.

Mentor

15960 ■ Aikido of Cleveland
6160 Meadowbrook Dr.
Mentor, OH 44060
Ph: (440)946-5112
Fax: (440)946-8508
E-mail: aikido@aikidoofcleveland.com
URL: http://pages.prodigy.net/clevelandaikikai
Contact: Linda Lee-Vecchio, Instructor
Local. Affiliated With: United States Aikido Federation.

15961 ■ Alcohol and Drug Abuse Self-Help Network, d.b.a. SMART Recovery
c/o Mrs. Shari Allwood, Exec.Dir.
7537 Mentor Ave., Ste.No. 306
Mentor, OH 44060
Ph: (440)951-5357
Fax: (440)951-5358
Free: (866)951-5357
E-mail: srmail1@aol.com
URL: http://www.smartrecovery.org
Contact: Mrs. Shari Allwood, Exec.Dir.
Founded: 1994. **Members:** 2. **Languages:** English, Spanish. **For-Profit. Regional.** Strives to support people recover from any type of addictive behaviors (substances or activities), by teaching how to change self-defeating thinking, emotions, and actions; and to work towards long-term satisfactions and quality of life. Offers free face-to-face mutual help groups. **Computer Services:** Online services, mutual help groups. **Formerly:** (2004) SMART Recovery. **Publications:** Newsletter, quarterly • Handbook • Manual • Videos.

15962 ■ American Legion, Mentor Post 352
5359 Lorrey Pl.
Mentor, OH 44060
Ph: (740)362-7478
Fax: (740)362-1429
URL: National Affiliate–www.legion.org
Local. Affiliated With: American Legion.

15963 ■ American Legion, Richmond Heights Post 775
6745 Olde Field Ct.
Mentor, OH 44060
Ph: (740)362-7478
Fax: (740)362-1429
URL: National Affiliate–www.legion.org
Local. Affiliated With: American Legion.

15964 ■ Blackbrook Audubon Society
c/o Harriet Pedone, VP
7573 Dahlia Dr.
Mentor, OH 44060
Ph: (440)255-0961
E-mail: maryannelizabeth@aol.com
URL: National Affiliate–www.audubon.org
Contact: Mary Ann Wagner, Contact
Local. Works to conserve and restore natural ecosystems, focusing on birds and other wildlife for the benefit of humanity and the earth's biological diversity. **Affiliated With:** National Audubon Society.

15965 ■ Competition Corvette Association (CCA)
PO Box 1291
Mentor, OH 44061
E-mail: vettehelper@comcast.net
URL: http://home.comcast.net/~vettehelper/ccainfo.html
Local. Affiliated With: National Council of Corvette Clubs.

15966 ■ Eastlake Coin Club
c/o Lenny Kramer
8634 Sta. St.
Mentor, OH 44060
E-mail: kramerprinting@sbcglobal.net
URL: National Affiliate–www.money.org
Contact: Lenny Kramer, Contact
Local. Affiliated With: American Numismatic Association.

15967 ■ Greater Cleveland Chapter of Parents of Murdered Children
8226 Windham Dr.
Mentor, OH 44060-5915
Ph: (440)974-0948
Fax: (440)255-9974
E-mail: clv9@aol.com
URL: http://www.pomc.com/chapters.cfm
Contact: Debbi Melaragno, Chapter Leader
Local. Affiliated With: Parents of Murdered Children.

15968 ■ Lake County Democratic Party
7547 Mentor Ave., Ste.107
Mentor, OH 44060
Ph: (440)951-9662
E-mail: doug@lakedems.com
URL: http://www.lakedems.com
Contact: Mr. Thomas Tagliamonte, Chm.
Languages: English, Spanish. **Local.** Represents Lake County's registered Democrats. Promotes the ideals, issues, and candidates of the Democratic Party at all levels of government and specifically those that impact the residents of Lake County at the county, state, and local levels. **Affiliated With:** Democratic National Committee.

15969 ■ Lake and Geauga Area Association of Realtors
8334 Mentor Ave., Ste.100
Mentor, OH 44060
Ph: (440)974-8506
Fax: (440)974-1399
E-mail: lgaar@sbsglobal.net
URL: http://www.lgaar.org
Contact: Patricia Rathz, Exec. Officer
Local. Strives to develop real estate business practices. Advocates for the right to own, use and transfer real property. Provides a facility for professional development, research and exchange of information among members and the general public. **Affiliated With:** National Association of Realtors.

15970 ■ Mentor Area Chamber of Commerce (MACC)
6972 Spinach Dr.
Mentor, OH 44060
Ph: (440)255-1616 (440)255-0777
Fax: (440)255-1717
E-mail: info@mentorchamber.org
URL: http://www.mentorchamber.org
Contact: Marie S. Pucak, Exec.Dir.
Founded: 1960. **Members:** 550. **Local.** Promotes business and community development in the Mentor, OH area. **Computer Services:** Online services, member listing. **Divisions:** Activities/Revenue Generation; Administration; Business Development; Membership Development/Retention. **Affiliated With:** U.S. Chamber of Commerce. **Publications:** *Chamber News*, monthly. Newsletter. **Circulation:** 700. **Advertising:** accepted. **Conventions/Meetings:** annual Golf Outing - competition • monthly luncheon - always 4th Tuesday.

15971 ■ Mentor Figure Skating Club
Mentor Civic Arena
8600 Munson Rd.
Mentor, OH 44060
Ph: (440)205-8498
URL: http://www.mentorfsc.org
Contact: Suzanne Clemente, Pres.
Local. Provides programs to encourage participation and achievement in the sport of figure skating on ice. Defines and maintains uniform standards of skating proficiency. Organizes and sponsors competitions and exhibitions for the purpose of stimulating interest in figure skating. **Affiliated With:** United States Figure Skating Association.

15972 ■ National Association of Telecommunications Officers and Advisors, Ohio
c/o Kathie Pohl, Public Information Officer
The Mentor Channel
8500 Civic Center Blvd.
Mentor, OH 44060
Ph: (440)974-5794
Fax: (440)974-5710
E-mail: kpohl@apk.net
URL: National Affiliate–www.natoa.org
Contact: Kathie Pohl, Public Information Officer
State. Represents cable television and telecommunications administrators, staff personnel from local governments and public interest groups. Seeks to establish an information-sharing network among local telecommunications regulators and users in the public sector. Provides education and training for local government officials to enhance their capacity to deal with cable and telecommunications issues. Provides technical and policy development assistance to members. Maintains speakers' bureau. **Affiliated With:** National Association of Telecommunications Officers and Advisors.

15973 ■ National Audubon Society - Blackbrook
7573 Dahlia Dr.
Mentor, OH 44060
Ph: (440)255-0961
E-mail: maryannelizebeth@aol.com
URL: http://www.blackbrookaudubon.org
Contact: Mary Anne Wagner, Pres.
Local.

15974 ■ Northeast Ohio Chapter of Project Management Institute (NEOPMI)
6068 Seminole Trail
Mentor, OH 44060
Ph: (440)951-1396
Fax: (866)316-5831
E-mail: info@pmineo.org
URL: http://www.pmineo.org
Contact: Maxine Hare, Office Mgr.
Founded: 1990. **Members:** 500. **Membership Dues:** individual, $125 (annual). **Local.** Corporations and individuals engaged in the practice of project management; project management students and educators. Seeks to advance the study, teaching, practice, and promotion of the project management profession. **Affiliated With:** Project Management Institute. **Formerly:** (2001) Project Management Institute, Northeast Ohio. **Publications:** *PM Network*, monthly. Magazine • Newsletter, quarterly. **Conventions/Meetings:** annual conference • monthly meeting - always in the evening.

15975 ■ Northeast Ohio Coin Club
c/o Arthur L. Jaklic
8250 Deepwood Blvd., No. 8
Mentor, OH 44060
Ph: (440)974-2871
URL: National Affiliate–www.money.org
Contact: Arthur L. Jaklic, Contact
Local. Affiliated With: American Numismatic Association.

15976 ■ Parents Without Partners, Lake Geauga
PO Box 121
Mentor, OH 44061-0121
Ph: (216)556-3399
E-mail: bpageski77@aol.com
URL: http://www.geocities.com/pwp412
Founded: 1975. **Members:** 190. **Membership Dues:** $35 (annual). **Local. Affiliated With:** Parents Without Partners.

15977 ■ Project Management Institute, Northeast Ohio (NEOPMI)
6068 Seminole Trail
Mentor, OH 44060
Ph: (440)951-1396
Fax: (866)316-5831
E-mail: info@pmineo.org
URL: http://www.pmineo.org
Contact: Kevin Cukrowicz PMP, Pres.
Local. Promotes project management as a recognized discipline. Creates an environment that fosters professional development and networking and guides the next generation of project managers. **Affiliated With:** Project Management Institute.

15978 ■ Single Volunteers of Lake County (SVLC)
PO Box 1853
Mentor, OH 44061-1853
Ph: (440)954-4247
E-mail: singlevolunteer@yahoo.com
URL: http://www.svlc.us
Founded: 1999. **Local.** Aims to meet different people and promotes friendship while volunteering for non-profit groups around Lake County and Northeast Ohio areas. **Affiliated With:** Single Volunteers of Lake County; Single Volunteers of Twin Cities.

15979 ■ Society for Human Resource Management - Lake/Geauga Chapter
PO Box 5125
Mentor, OH 44061
E-mail: christine_holroyd@progressive.com
URL: http://www.lgashrm.org
Contact: Christine Holroyd, Pres.
Local. Represents the interests of human resource and industrial relations professionals and executives. Promotes the advancement of human resource management.

15980 ■ Sweet Adelines International, Maple Mountain Chapter
Mentor Christian Church
8751 Mentor Ave.
Mentor, OH 44060-6256
Ph: (440)255-5259
URL: National Affiliate–www.sweetadelineintl.org
Contact: Janice Yanoscsik, Contact
Local. Advances the musical art form of barbershop harmony through education and performances. Provides education, training and coaching in the development of women's four-part barbershop harmony. **Affiliated With:** Sweet Adelines International.

15981 ■ United Way of Lake County, Ohio
9285 Progress Pkwy.
Mentor, OH 44060
Ph: (440)352-3166 (440)946-7375
Fax: (440)975-1220
E-mail: link@uwlc.org
URL: http://www.uwlc.org
Contact: Glen Gilbert, Chm.
Local. Affiliated With: United Way of America.

15982 ■ USA Dance - North Coast Ohio
c/o Jeri Parks, Treas.
9086 Lake Overlook Dr.
Mentor, OH 44060-1170
Ph: (440)257-3649
E-mail: jeri@parksweb.com
URL: http://parksweb.com/whp/usabda/index.htm
Contact: Jeri Parks, Treas.
Local. Encourages and promotes the physical, mental and social benefits of partner dancing. Organizes and supports programs for the recreational enjoyment of ballroom dancing. Creates opportunities for the general public to participate in ballroom dancing and DanceSport.

Miamisburg

15983 ■ American Legion, Miamisburg Post 165
35 N Main St.
Miamisburg, OH 45342
Ph: (740)362-7478
Fax: (740)362-1429
URL: National Affiliate–www.legion.org
Local. Affiliated With: American Legion.

15984 ■ ARMA International - Information Management Professionals, Greater Dayton Chapter
c/o Lorraine Northern
3232 Newmark Dr.
Miamisburg, OH 45342
Ph: (937)910-3140
Fax: (937)910-3678
E-mail: lori.northern@ncmc.com
URL: National Affiliate–www.arma.org
Contact: Lorraine Northern, Contact
Members: 40. **Local.** Holds monthly dinner meetings with educational presentations. **Affiliated With:** ARMA International - The Association of Information Management Professionals.

15985 ■ Clinical Laboratory Management Association, Six Rivers Chapter
c/o Cynthia Griffith, Pres.
Middletown Regional Hosp. Lab
8892 S Union Rd.
Miamisburg, OH 45342
Ph: (513)420-5029
E-mail: cynthia.griffith@middletownhospital.org
URL: http://www.sixriversclma.org
Contact: Cynthia Griffith, Pres.
Regional. Provides clinical laboratory leaders with resources to balance science and technology with the art of management. Promotes efficient, productive, and high quality operations. Enhances the professional, managerial and leadership skills of members. **Affiliated With:** Clinical Laboratory Management Association.

15986 ■ Dayton Chapter of the International Facility Management Association
PO Box 603
Miamisburg, OH 45343
Ph: (937)865-4052
Fax: (937)865-4431
E-mail: fbullock@mound.com
URL: http://www.dayton-ifma.com
Contact: Frank Bullock PE, Pres.
Founded: 1989. **Members:** 100. **Membership Dues:** business, $275 (annual). **Local.** Comprised of facility managers representing all types of organizations including banks, insurance companies, hospitals, colleges and universities, utility companies, electronic equipment manufacturers, petroleum companies, museums, auditoriums, and federal, state, provincial, and local governments. Works to enhance the professional goals of persons involved or interested in the field of facility management (the planning, designing, and managing of workplaces). **Affiliated With:** International Facility Management Association. **Publications:** *Facility Management Journal*, bimonthly. Magazine. **Conventions/Meetings:** annual conference • annual convention.

15987 ■ Miami Valley Human Resource Association
c/o Mark Ording
Primerica
1 Prestige Plz.
Miamisburg, OH 45342
Ph: (937)748-9636
Fax: (937)748-9636
E-mail: markording@msn.com
URL: http://www.mvhra.org
Contact: Mark Ording, Pres.
Local. Represents the interests of human resource and industrial relations professionals and executives. Promotes the advancement of human resource management.

15988 ■ Miamisburg Lion Club
15 W Linden Ave.
Miamisburg, OH 45342-2829
Ph: (937)859-7872
E-mail: rogfullmnbbq@aol.com
URL: http://miamisburgoh.lionwap.org
Contact: Roger Dixon, Sec.
Local. Affiliated With: Lions Clubs International.

15989 ■ Quail Unlimited, Butler County Chapter
c/o Mark Metzger, Chm.
521 Byers Rd.
Miamisburg, OH 45342
Ph: (937)839-5735
E-mail: cmomark@siscom.net
URL: National Affiliate–www.qu.org
Contact: Mark Metzger, Chm.
Local. Affiliated With: Quail Unlimited.

Miamitown

15990 ■ Community Associations Institute, Ohio Valley Chapter
PO Box 697
Miamitown, OH 45041-0697
Ph: (513)353-3810
Fax: (513)353-1064
E-mail: ohvccai@aol.com
URL: http://www.caiohiovalley.org
Contact: Jackie Rogenstengel, Exec.Dir.
Local. Enhances the environment in which the members operate. Improves the image of community association professionals and volunteers. Helps members develop personal and professional skills needed for success. **Affiliated With:** Community Associations Institute. **Publications:** *Quorum*, monthly. Magazine. Provides quality, expert articles and information about daily operations and issues.

Middle Bass

15991 ■ Middle Bass Island Yacht Club (MBIYC)
PO Box 81
Middle Bass, OH 43446
Ph: (419)285-9971
E-mail: mbiyc@mbiyc.com
URL: http://www.mbiyc.com
Local.

Middle Point

15992 ■ NAIFA-Lima
c/o Doris Dickman
PO Box 256
Middle Point, OH 45863
Ph: (419)233-3078
URL: National Affiliate–www.naifa.org
Local. Represents the interest of insurance and financial advisors. Advocates for a positive legislative and regulatory environment. Enhances business and professional skills of members. **Affiliated With:** National Association of Insurance and Financial Advisors.

Middleburg Heights

15993 ■ American Institute of Aeronautics and Astronautics, Northern ohio
c/o Ian Halliwell
Modern Technologies Corp.
Islander 2, Ste.206
7530 Lucerne Dr.
Middleburg Heights, OH 44130-6557
E-mail: ihalliwell_mtc@crusolutions.com
URL: National Affiliate–www.aiaa.org/
Scientists and engineers in the field of aeronautics and astronautics. Facilitates interchange of techno-

logical information through publications and technical meetings in order to foster overall technical progress in the field and increase the professional competence of members. **Affiliated With:** American Institute of Aeronautics and Astronautics.

15994 ■ First Catholic Slovak Ladies Association - Cleveland Junior Branch 503
c/o Dolores Sirocky
15547 Hickox Blvd.
Middleburg Heights, OH 44130
Ph: (216)676-9226
URL: National Affiliate–www.fcsla.com
Contact: Dolores Sirocky, Contact
Local. Affiliated With: First Catholic Slovak Ladies Association.

15995 ■ First Catholic Slovak Ladies Association - Cleveland Senior Branch 578
c/o Dolores Sirocky
15547 Hickox Blvd.
Middleburg Heights, OH 44130
Ph: (216)676-9226
URL: National Affiliate–www.fcsla.com
Contact: Dolores Sirocky, Contact
Local. Affiliated With: First Catholic Slovak Ladies Association.

15996 ■ National Association to Advance Fat Acceptance, Northern Ohio Chapter
PO Box 30106
Middleburg Heights, OH 44130
Ph: (440)327-7364
E-mail: ohionaafa@yahoo.com
URL: http://www.ltech.net/naafa
Contact: Pat Dobrovic, Pres.
Members: 40. **Membership Dues:** low income, student, senior, $13 (annual) • regular, $17 (annual) • joint, $23 (annual). **Local.** Believes that all people, regardless of size or shape, have the right to live peacefully, free of harassment, ridicule and size-related guilt; be hired or not hired based on their gifts and abilities; fair and adequate compensation for their labor; access to public facilities, insurance and quality health care; freedom of exploitation by commercial interests who profit by perpetrating social stigma of being fat; and the respect of the community based on their achievements, contributions and citizenship in the human family. Seeks to secure these rights through education, activism, support and by cultivating size-positive social situations for fat people, their friends and admirers in the Northern Ohio area. **Affiliated With:** National Association to Advance Fat Acceptance. **Publications:** *Northern Ohio Buckeye Bulletin*, monthly. Newsletter.

15997 ■ National Association of Women in Construction, Region 4
c/o Debbie Gregoire, Dir.
6800 Eastland Rd.
Middleburg Heights, OH 44130
Ph: (440)243-3535
Fax: (440)243-9993
E-mail: dgregoire@brewer-garrett.com
URL: http://www.geocities.com/nawic4
Contact: Debbie Gregoire, Dir.
Regional. Serves as the voice of women in the construction industry. Contributes to the development of the industry. Encourages women to pursue and establish career in construction. Promotes cooperation, fellowship and understanding among members of the association. **Affiliated With:** National Association of Women in Construction. **Publications:** *NAWIC Region 4*. Newsletter. Alternate Formats: online.

15998 ■ Northern Ohio Painting and Taping Contractors Association
c/o Guy C. Gallo
7550 Lucerne Dr., Ste.301
Middleburg Heights, OH 44130-2683
Ph: (440)826-9300
Contact: Guy Gallo, Exec.Dir.
Local.

Middlefield

15999 ■ Experimental Aircraft Association, Chapter 5
c/o Ed Malovic, Pres.
Geauga County Airport 7G8
Middlefield, OH 44062
Ph: (440)636-5287
E-mail: biplane@alltel.net
URL: http://www.eaa5.org
Contact: Ed Malovic, Pres.
Founded: 1954. **Members:** 50. **Membership Dues:** individual, family, $25 (annual). **Local.** Promotes general aviation in Geauga County, OH. Assists members with maintenance and construction of aircraft. **Affiliated With:** Experimental Aircraft Association. **Publications:** *Plane and Simple*, monthly. Newsletter. Alternate Formats: online. **Conventions/Meetings:** EAA Annual Convention and Fly-In, aviation related (exhibits) - held the 1st week in August.

16000 ■ Middlefield Chamber of Commerce
PO Box 801
Middlefield, OH 44062
Ph: (440)632-5705
Fax: (440)632-5705
E-mail: mccinfo@middlefieldcc.com
URL: http://www.geaugalink.com/extlinks/mfdccfrm.html
Contact: Jean Young, Pres.
Membership Dues: business, $75-$200 (annual). **Local.** Promotes business and community development in Middlefield Township, OH. **Computer Services:** Mailing lists, of members. **Publications:** Newsletter, monthly. **Conventions/Meetings:** monthly meeting.

Middleport

16001 ■ American Legion, Feeney-Bennett Post 128
PO Box 128
Middleport, OH 45760
Ph: (740)362-7478
Fax: (740)362-1429
URL: National Affiliate–www.legion.org
Local. Affiliated With: American Legion.

Middletown

16002 ■ American Legion, Blythe-Williams Post 789
112 S Clinton, No. 413
Middletown, OH 45044
Ph: (740)362-7478
Fax: (740)362-1429
URL: National Affiliate–www.legion.org
Local. Affiliated With: American Legion.

16003 ■ American Legion, Middletown Post 218
116 S Main St.
Middletown, OH 45044
Ph: (740)362-7478
Fax: (740)362-1429
URL: National Affiliate–www.legion.org
Local. Affiliated With: American Legion.

16004 ■ American Red Cross, Butler County Chapter
1227 Central Ave.
Middletown, OH 45044
Ph: (513)423-9233
Fax: (513)423-1265
URL: http://www.butlercountyredcross.org
Local.

16005 ■ Bulls Run Ramblers
c/o Michael Perkins
8459 Ora Ln.
Middletown, OH 45042
Ph: (513)423-1733
E-mail: perkma@hotmail.com
URL: National Affiliate–www.ava.org
Contact: Michael Perkins, Contact
Local. Non-competitive sports enthusiasts. **Affiliated With:** American Volkssport Association.

16006 ■ Butler County Chapter of Ohio Genealogical Society
PO Box 2011
Middletown, OH 45042-2011
E-mail: da120757@cinci.rr.com
URL: http://da120757.tripod.com/bcogs
Contact: Deb Morrison, Pres.
Founded: 1977. **Members:** 150. **Membership Dues:** single, $10 (annual) • joint, $12 (annual). **Staff:** 6. **State Groups:** 1. **State. Awards:** First Families of Butler County. **Frequency:** annual. **Type:** recognition. **Recipient:** for individual in Butler County before 1820. **Affiliated With:** Ohio Genealogical Society. **Publications:** *Pathways*, quarterly. Newsletter. **Price:** included in membership dues. **Circulation:** 200. **Conventions/Meetings:** monthly meeting - second Saturday, except July and August.

16007 ■ Citizens Against Domestic Violence (CADV)
c/o Elsa Croucher
2105 Central Ave.
Middletown, OH 45042
Ph: (513)423-0044 (513)539-8272
Fax: (513)539-8289
E-mail: cadv@core.com
URL: http://WWW.CADV-Ohio.com
Contact: Mr. James Croucher, Treas.
Founded: 1996. **Members:** 12. **Staff:** 1. **Local.**

16008 ■ International Brotherhood of Magicians, Ring 324
c/o Anthony Day, VP
1936 Erie Ave.
Middletown, OH 45042
Ph: (513)422-3047
E-mail: antondrakon@aol.com
URL: http://www.magician.org/member/ring324/home
Contact: Ron Evans, Pres.
Local. Professional and semi-professional magicians; suppliers, assistants, agents, and others interested in magic. Seeks to advance the art of magic in the field of amusement, entertainment, and culture. Promotes proper means of discouraging false or misleading advertising of effects, tricks, literature, merchandise, or actions appertaining to the magical arts; opposes exposures of principles of the art of magic, except in books on magic and magazines devoted to such art for the exclusive use of magicians and devotees of the art; encourages humane treatment and care of live animals whenever employed in magical performances. **Affiliated With:** International Brotherhood of Magicians.

16009 ■ InWord Resources
PO Box 531
Middletown, OH 45042
Ph: (513)422-2143
Fax: (513)422-3178
Free: (888)422-3060
E-mail: info@inword.org
URL: http://www.inword.org
Contact: Barry Shafer, Dir.
Local. Promotes biblical literacy among teens. Works to strengthen youth ministry with inductive methods, tools, and materials for personal Bible understanding and for small group settings.

16010 ■ Lebanon - Young Life
PO Box 1124
Middletown, OH 45042
Ph: (513)253-3858
URL: http://sites.younglife.org/sites/Lebanon/default.aspx
Local. Affiliated With: Young Life.

16011 ■ Miami Valley Astronomical Society (MVAS)
c/o Ron Sherman, Pres.
307 Stanley St.
Middletown, OH 45044
Ph: (513)423-4717 (513)919-2100
URL: http://www.mvas.org
Contact: Ron Sherman, Pres.
Local. Promotes the science of astronomy. Works to encourage and coordinate activities of amateur astronomical societies. Fosters observational and computational work and craftsmanship in various fields of astronomy. **Affiliated With:** Astronomical League.

16012 ■ Mid-Miami Valley Chamber of Commerce
1500 Central Ave.
Middletown, OH 45044
Ph: (513)422-4551
Fax: (513)422-6831
E-mail: bill@thechamberofcommerce.org
URL: http://www.mmvchamber.org
Contact: Bill Triick, Pres./CEO
Founded: 1944. **Members:** 500. **Membership Dues:** business (plus $6.50 per full-time employee), $305 (annual) • financial institution (minimum of $500; based on millions of deposit), $500 (annual) • public utility/publisher (per meter, trunk line, subscriber in The Chamber of Commerce area), $0 (annual) • non-profit and not-for-profit, $305 (annual) • retiree (individual/non-business), $100 (annual). **Staff:** 3. **Budget:** $180,000. **Local**. Businesses, industries, and individuals. Promotes economic growth, job development, and improved quality of life in Butler County, OH. **Computer Services:** Online services, members' directory. **Programs:** Leadership. **Subgroups:** Small Business Development Center. **Affiliated With:** American Chamber of Commerce Executives; U.S. Chamber of Commerce. **Also Known As:** (2005) Chamber of Commerce Serving Middletown, Monroe and Trenton. **Formerly:** Middletown Area Chamber of Commerce. **Conventions/Meetings:** monthly luncheon - every 1st Thursday • annual meeting - always January.

16013 ■ Middletown Board of Realtors
20 N Main St.
Middletown, OH 45042
Ph: (513)423-3445
Local.

16014 ■ Middletown Convention and Visitors Bureau
PO Box 1245
Middletown, OH 45042
Ph: (513)422-3030
Fax: (513)422-3030
Free: (888)664-3353
E-mail: info@visitmiddletown.org
Contact: Ms. Ann Mort, Exec.Dir.
Founded: 1992. **Staff:** 1. **Budget:** $113,000. **Nonmembership**. **Local**. Promotes Middletown, OH as a tourist destination.

16015 ■ Middletown Pee Wee Football and Cheerleading (MPWFC)
PO Box 44921
Middletown, OH 45044-0921
Ph: (513)422-3973
E-mail: jettieb1@hotmail.com
URL: http://www.leaguelineup.com/welcome.asp?url=middletownpeewee
Contact: Jettie Bailey, Pres.
Founded: 1953. **Members:** 60. **Membership Dues:** regular, $2 (annual). **Budget:** $75,000. **Local**. Promotes youth football and cheerleading. **Awards:** Middletown Pee Wee Football Scholarship Award. **Frequency:** annual. **Type:** scholarship. **Recipient:** for active participation in football or cheerleading as high school senior and carrying good GPA. **Conventions/Meetings:** annual Thanksgiving Football Autumn Classic - competition - 3rd weekend in November.

16016 ■ Middletown - Young Life
PO Box 1124
Middletown, OH 45042
Ph: (513)253-3858
URL: http://sites.younglife.org/_layouts/ylext/default.aspx?ID=C-1496
Local. **Affiliated With:** Young Life.

16017 ■ Ohio Society for Healthcare Engineering (OSHE)
c/o John McKinney, III, Pres.
Middletown Regional Hosp.
105 McKnight Dr.
Middletown, OH 45044-4838
Ph: (513)420-5204
Fax: (513)420-5178
E-mail: john.mckinney@middletownhospital.org
URL: National Affiliate–www.ashe.org
Contact: John McKinney III, Pres.
State. Promotes better patient care by encouraging members to develop their knowledge and increase their competence in the field of facilities management. Cooperates with hospitals and allied associations in matters pertaining to facilities management. **Affiliated With:** American Society for Healthcare Engineering of the American Hospital Association.

16018 ■ Phi Theta Kappa - Beta Epsilon Delta Chapter
c/o James Janik
4200 E Univ. Blvd.
Middletown, OH 45042
Ph: (513)727-3230
E-mail: janikjm@muohio.edu
URL: http://www.ptk.org/directories/chapters/OH/20742-1.htm
Contact: James Janik, Advisor
Local. **Affiliated With:** Phi Theta Kappa, International Honor Society.

16019 ■ Springboro - Young Life
PO Box 1124
Middletown, OH 45042
Ph: (513)253-3858
URL: http://sites.younglife.org/sites/Springboro/default.aspx
Local. **Affiliated With:** Young Life.

Milan

16020 ■ American Legion, Colvin-Dale Post 527
PO Box 527
Milan, OH 44846
Ph: (740)362-7478
Fax: (740)362-1429
URL: National Affiliate–www.legion.org
Local. **Affiliated With:** American Legion.

16021 ■ Edison Birthplace Association (EBA)
c/o Edison Birthplace Museum
PO Box 451
Milan, OH 44846
Ph: (419)499-2135
Fax: (419)499-2135
E-mail: edisonbp@accnorwalk.com
URL: http://www.tomedison.org
Contact: Robert K.L. Wheeler, Pres.
Founded: 1950. **Members:** 97. **Membership Dues:** student, $5 (annual) • individual, $25 (annual) • family, $50 (annual) • special friend, $100 (annual) • life, $1,000 (annual) • corporate sponsor, $5,000 (annual). **Staff:** 2. **Budget:** $70,000. Persons who contribute to an endowment fund for the purpose of perpetuating the Thomas Alva Edison Birthplace Museum, which opened in 1947 in Milan, OH. Edison (1847-1931), the inventor, was born in Milan, and the museum has been designated as a National Historic Landmark. Provides specialized education program. **Conventions/Meetings:** annual meeting, for trustees • tour.

16022 ■ Milan Edison Lions Club
c/o Christopher S. Tatem, Pres.
20 Chippewa Dr.
Milan, OH 44846
Ph: (419)499-8210
E-mail: ctatem@neo.rr.com
URL: http://www.lions13b.org
Contact: Christopher S. Tatem, Pres.
Local. **Affiliated With:** Lions Clubs International.

Milford

16023 ■ American Legion, Ohio Post 450
c/o Victor Stier
450 Victor Stier Dr.
Milford, OH 45150
Ph: (740)362-7478
Fax: (740)362-1429
URL: National Affiliate–www.legion.org
Contact: Victor Stier, Contact
Local. **Affiliated With:** American Legion.

16024 ■ Association for Psychological Type - Greater Cincinnati
100 Miami Lakes Dr.
Milford, OH 45150
Ph: (513)563-2583
E-mail: gossman@blueharborcpi.com
URL: National Affiliate–www.aptinternational.org
Contact: Linda Gossman, Contact
Local. Promotes the practical application and ethical use of psychological type. Provides members with opportunities for continuous learning, sharing experiences and creating understanding and knowledge through research. **Affiliated With:** Association for Psychological Type.

16025 ■ Clermont County Chamber of Commerce (CCC)
553 Chamber Dr.
Milford, OH 45150
Ph: (513)576-5000
E-mail: clermontchamber@clermontchamber.com
URL: http://www.clermontchamber.com
Contact: Matthew Van Sant, Pres./CEO
Members: 1,300. **Membership Dues:** business (based on the number of employees), $274-$2,091 (annual). **Local**. Encourages businesses to relocate to Clermont, existing businesses to stay in Clermont, and new and growing businesses to establish their operations in the county. Provides economic development assistance to companies interested in Clermont County, including assistance with financing, expansion, relocation, site identification, and labor force development. **Awards:** Business Advocate Award. **Frequency:** annual. **Type:** recognition. **Recipient:** for an organization or individual actively advancing and/or protecting the interests of small businesses • Customer Focus. **Frequency:** annual. **Type:** recognition. **Recipient:** for an organization that implemented policies that demonstrate a commitment to customers • Emerging Small Business Award. **Frequency:** annual. **Type:** recognition. **Recipient:** for an organization with entrepreneurial spirit that is positioning itself to grow substantially into the future • Innovative Business Practice. **Frequency:** annual. **Type:** recognition. **Recipient:** for an organization demonstrating unique and inventive practices, products, or procedures • New Member of the Year. **Frequency:** annual. **Type:** recognition. **Recipient:** for an organization that become a chamber member within the past 24 months and is an active participant in chamber activities. **Publications:** *Images of Clermont County*, annual. Magazine • *Intercom*, monthly. Newsletter. Contains chamber information. **Circulation:** 1,600. **Advertising:** accepted. Alternate Formats: online.

16026 ■ Greater Cincinnati Chapter of American Orff-Schulwerk Association
c/o John Crandall
36 Concord Woods Dr.
Milford, OH 45150
E-mail: opus62@cinci.rr.com
URL: http://www.geocities.com/cincyorff
Contact: Leslie Hicks, Pres.
Local. Provides a forum for the continued growth and development of Orff Schulwerk. Promotes the value and use of Orff Schulwerk.

16027 ■ Milford - Miami Township Chamber of Commerce
100 Cemetery Rd.
Milford, OH 45150
Ph: (513)831-2411
Fax: (513)831-3547
E-mail: director@milfordmiamitownship.com
URL: http://www.milfordmiamitownship.com
Contact: Jo Ann Weigel, Acting Exec.Dir.
Membership Dues: business, $95-$350 (annual). **Local. Computer Services:** Mailing lists, mailing list of members. **Committees:** Business Dinner; Candidate Night; Education; Frontier Days; Office Remodeling; Parliamentarian; Special Events. **Task Forces:** The Mildford. **Publications:** *Chamber Update*, monthly. Newsletter. Contains listings of new members, upcoming events, programs, community activities, government issues, and member activities. **Price:** included in membership dues.

16028 ■ Milford Theatre Guilde (MTG)
c/o Linda Roll, Sec.
5775 Tall Oaks Dr.
Milford, OH 45150-2557
Ph: (513)575-9351
E-mail: info@milfordtheatreguilde.org
URL: http://www.milfordtheatreguilde.org
Contact: Marta Tillson, Pres.
Local.

16029 ■ National Association of Rocketry - Queen City Area Rocket Club (QUARK)
c/o Mark Fisher
5953 Pinto Pl.
Milford, OH 45150
Ph: (513)575-9332
E-mail: microzen@hotmail.com
URL: http://quarkers.org
Contact: Mark Fisher, Contact
Local.

16030 ■ USA Diving - Dive Cincinnati
PO Box 268
Milford, OH 45150
Ph: (513)697-9509
Fax: (513)697-9609
E-mail: divecincinnati@cinci.rr.com
URL: http://www.divecincinnati.com
Local. Affiliated With: USA Diving.

16031 ■ World Future Society, Cincinnati
c/o Thomas Mantel
PO Box 157
Milford, OH 45150
Ph: (513)527-7129 (513)576-0525
URL: National Affiliate–www.wfs.org
Contact: Thomas Mantel, Contact
Local. Affiliated With: World Future Society.

Milford Center

16032 ■ Dublin Lions Club - Ohio
c/o Jeff Parren, Pres.
6 Reed St.
Milford Center, OH 43045
Ph: (614)791-0990 (614)738-0041
E-mail: jparren@agentsbrokerage.com
URL: http://www.iwaynet.net/~lions13f
Contact: Jeff Parren, Pres.
Local. Affiliated With: Lions Clubs International.

Miller City

16033 ■ American Legion, Diemer-Dobmeyer Post 172
PO Box 8
Miller City, OH 45864
Ph: (740)362-7478
Fax: (740)362-1429
URL: National Affiliate–www.legion.org
Local. Affiliated With: American Legion.

Millersburg

16034 ■ American Legion, Holmes Post 192
264 W Jackson St.
Millersburg, OH 44654
Ph: (740)362-7478
Fax: (740)362-1429
URL: National Affiliate–www.legion.org
Local. Affiliated With: American Legion.

16035 ■ Holmes County Chamber of Commerce
35 N Monroe St.
Millersburg, OH 44654
Ph: (330)674-3975
Fax: (330)674-3976
E-mail: info@holmescountychamber.com
URL: http://www.holmescountychamber.com
Contact: Shasta Mast, Exec.Dir.
Local. Promotes business and community development in the Millersburg, OH area. **Computer Services:** database, membership directory. **Councils:** Economic Development; Industry. **Subgroups:** Tourism Bureau. **Publications:** Directory, annual.

16036 ■ Holmes County Habitat for Humanity
PO Box 418
Millersburg, OH 44654
Ph: (330)674-4663
E-mail: kmohler@valkyrie.net
URL: http://www.habitatofholmescounty.org
Local. Affiliated With: Habitat for Humanity International.

16037 ■ Holmes County Humane Society (HCHS)
PO Box 442
Millersburg, OH 44654
Ph: (330)231-5439
URL: http://www.holmeshumane.org
Contact: Robyn Miller, Contact
Local.

16038 ■ Ohio Genealogical Society, Holmes County Chapter
PO Box 136
Millersburg, OH 44654-0136
Ph: (330)378-2314 (330)378-2657
E-mail: hcgen@valkyrie.net
URL: http://www.rootsweb.com/~ohholmes
Contact: Ed Thomas, Contact
Founded: 1983. **Members:** 400. **Membership Dues:** single, $10 (annual) • couple/family, $12 (annual) • life (single), $100 • life (couple/family), $125. **Local.** Individuals interested in preserving the history of Holmes County, OH. Donates books and genealogical records to local libraries. **Libraries: Type:** reference. **Holdings:** audiovisuals, papers, reports. **Subjects:** original records of County Courthouse from 1825. **Affiliated With:** Ohio Genealogical Society. **Publications:** *Holmes County Heirs*, bimonthly. Newsletter. **Price:** included in membership dues. **Conventions/Meetings:** monthly meeting - always fourth Thursday; third Thursday in November; except December.

Millersport

16039 ■ American Legion, Millersport Post 637
PO Box 611
Millersport, OH 43046
Ph: (740)362-7478
Fax: (740)362-1429
URL: National Affiliate–www.legion.org
Local. Affiliated With: American Legion.

16040 ■ Ruffed Grouse Society, Ohio Hills Chapter
c/o Chuck Wolfgang
12371 Cherry Ln.
Millersport, OH 43046
Ph: (614)478-8059
E-mail: todd.scarborough@epa.state.oh.us
URL: National Affiliate–www.ruffedgrousesociety.org
Contact: Chuck Wolfgang, Contact
Local. Affiliated With: Ruffed Grouse Society.

Mineral City

16041 ■ American Legion, Carr-Bailey Post 519
PO Box 416
Mineral City, OH 44656
Ph: (740)362-7478
Fax: (740)362-1429
URL: National Affiliate–www.legion.org
Local. Affiliated With: American Legion.

16042 ■ East Central Ohio Home Building Industry Association
c/o Sharon Fulton
7984 Dawn Rd. NE
Mineral City, OH 44656-9321
Ph: (330)364-3598
Fax: (330)364-3598
E-mail: ecobia1957@aol.com
URL: http://ECOBIA1957.com
Contact: Sharon A. Fulton, Exec.Dir.
Trade association involved in Parade of Homes, Spring Home & Garden Show, Circuit of New Homes; single family residential, multifamily, light commercial. **Affiliated With:** National Association of Home Builders.

16043 ■ Huff Run Watershed Restoration Partnership
c/o Marlene Harsha
PO Box 55
Mineral City, OH 44656-0055
Ph: (330)859-2192
Contact: Ms. Maureen Wise, Coor.
Local.

Minerva

16044 ■ American Legion, Ohio Post 357
c/o Don V. Cross
103 E Line St.
Minerva, OH 44657
Ph: (740)362-7478
Fax: (740)362-1429
URL: National Affiliate–www.legion.org
Contact: Don V. Cross, Contact
Local. Affiliated With: American Legion.

16045 ■ Minerva Area Chamber of Commerce (MACOC)
301 Valley St.
Minerva, OH 44657-1853
Ph: (330)868-7979
Fax: (330)868-3347
E-mail: minervachamber@adelphia.net
URL: http://www.minervachamber.com
Contact: W. John Soliday, Exec.Dir.
Local. Promotes the advancement of the industrial, retail, commercial, and professional environment in Minerva Area, OH.

16046 ■ Shaw Land Conservancy
c/o Hilda E. Beach
8059 Magnet Rd. NE
Minerva, OH 44657-8752
Ph: (330)895-4642
Fax: (330)895-4642
E-mail: hbeach@tusco.net
URL: National Affiliate–www.lta.org
Contact: Hilda E. Beach, Contact
Local.

Minford

16047 ■ American Legion, Minford Post 622
c/o James Irwin, Commander
PO Box 2
Minford, OH 45653
Ph: (740)362-7478
Fax: (740)362-1429
URL: National Affiliate–www.legion.org
Contact: James Irwin, Commander
Local. Affiliated With: American Legion.

Mingo Junction

16048 ■ American Legion, Mingo Junction Post 351
666 Commercial St.
Mingo Junction, OH 43938
Ph: (740)362-7478
Fax: (740)362-1429
URL: National Affiliate–www.legion.org
Local. Affiliated With: American Legion.

Minster

16049 ■ American Legion, Minster Post 387
PO Box 79
Minster, OH 45865
Ph: (740)362-7478
Fax: (740)362-1429
URL: National Affiliate–www.legion.org
Local. Affiliated With: American Legion.

Mogadore

16050 ■ American Institute of Architects Akron
13152 Sugarbush Ave. NW
Mogadore, OH 44260
Ph: (330)699-9788
Fax: (330)699-9788
E-mail: aiakron@worldnet.att.net
URL: National Affiliate–www.aia.org
Contact: Rebecca Boyes, Exec.Dir.
Local. Professional society of architects. Fosters professionalism and accountability among members through continuing education and training; promotes design excellence by influencing change in the industry. **Affiliated With:** American Institute of Architects.

16051 ■ American Legion, Park Etter Post 452
PO Box 246
Mogadore, OH 44260
Ph: (740)362-7478
Fax: (740)362-1429
URL: National Affiliate–www.legion.org
Local. Affiliated With: American Legion.

16052 ■ American Payroll Association, Hall of Fame Chapter
PO Box 399
Mogadore, OH 44260
Ph: (330)264-7400
Fax: (330)264-7974
E-mail: kathyalmasy@dsdistribution.com
URL: http://www.apahofohio.org
Contact: Kathy Almasy, Sec.
Local. Aims to increase the Payroll Professional's skill level through education and mutual support. Represents the Payroll Professional before legislative bodies. Administers the certified payroll professional program of recognition. Provides public service education on payroll and employment issues. **Affiliated With:** American Payroll Association.

16053 ■ Brimfield Lions Club
3074 State Rte. 43
Mogadore, OH 44260-9773
Ph: (330)673-4391
E-mail: realshar@ameritech.net
URL: http://brimfieldlionscluboh.lionwap.org
Contact: Sharon M. Ebie, VP/Treas.
Local. Affiliated With: Lions Clubs International.

16054 ■ Randolph Lions Club - Ohio
c/o Leonard McKay, Sec.
3797 Randolph Rd.
Mogadore, OH 44260
Ph: (330)325-2855
URL: http://www.lions13d.org
Contact: Terry Baker, Pres.
Local. Affiliated With: Lions Clubs International.

Monroe

16055 ■ Monroe Lions Club - Ohio
PO Box 220
Monroe, OH 45050-0220
Ph: (513)539-7500 (513)423-1287
E-mail: rkremer@cshco.com
URL: http://monroeoh.lionwap.org
Contact: Joe Beatty, Pres.
Local. Affiliated With: Lions Clubs International.

16056 ■ United Food and Commercial Workers, Local 1099, Central Region
913 Lebanon St.
Monroe, OH 45050-1495
Ph: (513)539-9961
E-mail: ufcw1099@aol.com
URL: http://www.ufcw1099.org
Local. Affiliated With: United Food and Commercial Workers International Union.

Monroeville

16057 ■ American Legion, Sch-Loe-Man Post 547
8 S Main St.
Monroeville, OH 44847
Ph: (740)362-7478
Fax: (740)362-1429
URL: National Affiliate–www.legion.org
Local. Affiliated With: American Legion.

16058 ■ Ohio North Coast Chapter of Associated Locksmiths of America
c/o Ronald Betschman, CML, Chm.
Betschman Security Inc.
2 Horseshoe Dr.
Monroeville, OH 44847
Ph: (419)465-4153
Fax: (419)465-4448
E-mail: betschlk@accnorwalk.com
URL: National Affiliate–www.aloa.org
Contact: Ronald Betschman CML, Chm.
Local. Affiliated With: Associated Locksmiths of America.

Montpelier

16059 ■ American Legion, Montpelier Post 109
216 Empire St.
Montpelier, OH 43543
Ph: (740)362-7478
Fax: (740)362-1429
URL: National Affiliate–www.legion.org
Local. Affiliated With: American Legion.

16060 ■ GK Riverbottom Hunt Club
08962 County Rd. I-50
Montpelier, OH 43543
Ph: (419)485-8717
URL: National Affiliate–www.mynssa.com
Local. Affiliated With: National Skeet Shooting Association.

16061 ■ Montpelier Area Chamber of Commerce (MACC)
410 W Main
Montpelier, OH 43543
Ph: (419)485-4416
Fax: (419)495-4416
E-mail: macc@bright.net
URL: http://www.montpelieroh.com
Contact: Ms. Terry Buntain, Exec.Dir.
Members: 104. **Local.** Promotes business and community development in the Montpelier, OH area. Sponsors annual Bean Days Festival and Blue Water train excursion. Maintains retail division. Holds bimonthly board meeting. Sponsors Bean Days Festival. **Publications:** *Directory of Members*, annual. Newsletter • Newsletter, bimonthly. **Conventions/Meetings:** annual meeting.

16062 ■ Montpelier Industrial Development Committee
c/o John Bitler, Pres.
PO Box 148
Montpelier, OH 43543
Ph: (419)485-5543 (419)485-4416
Fax: (419)485-4947
E-mail: jbitler@montpelieroh.org
URL: http://www.montpelieroh.com
Contact: John Bitler, Pres.
Local. Formerly: (1998) Montpelier Independent Development Comm.

16063 ■ Society of Study of Male Psychology
321 Iuka Dr.
Montpelier, OH 43543
Ph: (419)485-3602
E-mail: jbergman@northweststate.edu
Contact: Dr. Jerry Bergman, Dir.
Local.

16064 ■ Williams County Area Crime Stoppers
c/o Laura Gray
221 Empire St.
Montpelier, OH 43543-1315
Ph: (419)485-3121 (419)485-9302
Contact: Laura Gray, Pres.
Founded: 2002. **Members:** 32. **Budget:** $10,000. **Local.** Community organization geared toward public involvement in fighting crime by offering cash rewards to anonymous persons giving tips to solve a crime.

Montville

16065 ■ Buckeye Military Vehicle Collectors
c/o Dennis Burger, Pres.
10450 Plank Rd.
Montville, OH 44064-8707
Ph: (440)968-3779
URL: National Affiliate–www.mvpa.org
Contact: Dennis Burger, Pres.
Local. Affiliated With: Military Vehicle Preservation Association.

Moraine

16066 ■ Dayton Dog Training Club (DDTC)
3040 E River Rd.
Moraine, OH 45439-1414
Ph: (937)293-5219
URL: http://www.daytondogtraining.com
Contact: Lynn Luikart, Corresponding Sec.
Local.

Morrow

16067 ■ Veterans of Foreign Wars 351
351 2nd St.
Morrow, OH 45152
Ph: (513)899-2986
Local.

Mount Gilead

16068 ■ American Red Cross, Morrow County Chapter
37 W Centre St.
Mount Gilead, OH 43338
Ph: (419)946-2811
E-mail: arcmorow@bright.net
URL: http://morrowcounty.redcross.org
Local.

16069 ■ Habitat for Humanity of Morrow County
PO Box 341
Mount Gilead, OH 43338-0341
Ph: (419)947-6142
E-mail: cfidler@redbird.net
Founded: 1998. **Members:** 15. **Local**. **Affiliated With:** Habitat for Humanity International.

16070 ■ Morrow County Chamber of Commerce and Visitors' Bureau (MCCCVB)
17-1/2 W High St.
PO Box 174
Mount Gilead, OH 43338
Ph: (419)946-2821
Fax: (419)946-3861
E-mail: chamuway@bright.net
URL: http://www.morrowcochamber.com
Contact: Rosemary Kay Levings, Exec.Dir.
Founded: 1968. **Members:** 200. **Staff:** 2. **Budget:** $81,000. **Local**. Promotes economic growth and community development in Morrow County, OH. **Awards:** Career Passport Award. **Frequency:** annual. **Type:** scholarship. **Recipient:** to one senior in each 5 schools for outstanding career passport • Citizen of the Year. **Frequency:** annual. **Type:** recognition. **Recipient:** for outstanding person of the year that has accomplished many avenues for the county as a whole • Student of the Month. **Frequency:** bimonthly. **Type:** recognition. **Recipient:** for outstanding senior in 5 county schools recognized at chamber noon luncheon. **Committees:** Business-Education; Economic Development; Small Business. **Councils:** HR. **Affiliated With:** Ohio Chamber of Commerce; United Way of America. **Formerly:** (1960) Mount Gilead Area Chamber of Commerce; (1999) Morrow County Chamber of Commerce. **Publications:** Newsletter, quarterly. **Circulation:** 200. **Advertising:** accepted.

16071 ■ Mount Gilead Lions Club - Ohio
c/o Alvin Miller, Pres.
3935 Township Rd. 110
Mount Gilead, OH 43338
Ph: (419)946-3666
URL: http://www.iwaynet.net/~lions13f
Contact: Alvin Miller, Pres.
Local. **Affiliated With:** Lions Clubs International.

16072 ■ Ohio Association for the Education of Young Children
c/o Kimberly Tice, Exec.Dir.
PO Box 71
Mount Gilead, OH 43338
Ph: (419)946-6693
Fax: (419)946-6515
Free: (800)626-2392
E-mail: exedirector@oaeyc.org
URL: http://www.oaeyc.org
Contact: Kimberly Tice, Exec.Dir.
State. Improves well-being of young children, with particular focus on the quality of educational and developmental services for the children. **Affiliated With:** National Association for the Education of Young Children.

16073 ■ Ohio Genealogical Society, Morrow County Chapter
PO Box 401
Mount Gilead, OH 43338-0401
Ph: (419)947-5866 (614)397-4855
E-mail: morrowco.gen.society@myaxiom.net
URL: http://www.rootsweb.com/~ohmorrow
Contact: Betty Meier, Pres.
Founded: 1976. **Members:** 120. **Membership Dues:** single, $5 (annual) • joint, $7 (annual). **Local**. Persons interested in genealogy. Compiles cemetery books, conducts speaker meetings, donates materials to library. **Libraries:** **Type:** open to the public. **Awards:** 4-H Genealogy at Fair. **Frequency:** annual. **Type:** trophy. **Affiliated With:** Ohio Genealogical Society. **Publications:** *The Monument*, quarterly. Newsletter. **Conventions/Meetings:** monthly meeting - every fourth Saturday.

16074 ■ United Way of Morrow County
c/o Mrs. Rosemary Levings, Exec.Dir./Sec.
17 1/2 W High St.
PO Box 84
Mount Gilead, OH 43338
Ph: (419)946-2821
Fax: (419)946-3861
E-mail: chamuway@bright.net
URL: http://www.morrowcounty.net/unitedway
Contact: Mrs. Rosemary Levings, Exec.Dir./Sec.
Founded: 1960. **Members:** 11. **Staff:** 2. **Budget:** $155,000. **State Groups:** 1. **Local**. Supports and finances United Way Agencies so they may service the county. **Affiliated With:** United Way of America. **Publications:** Newsletter, quarterly.

Mount Orab

16075 ■ National Speleological Society, Miami Valley Grotto
c/o Daryl Robinson
15602 Hillcrest Rd.
Mount Orab, OH 45154
Ph: (513)623-3008
E-mail: jeschenck@hotmail.com
URL: National Affiliate–www.caves.org
Contact: Daryl Robinson, Contact
Local. Seeks to study, explore and conserve cave and karst resources. Protects access to caves and promotes responsible caving. Encourages responsible management of caves and their unique environments. **Affiliated With:** National Speleological Society.

Mount Pleasant

16076 ■ Dillonvale-Mt. Pleasant Lions Club
c/o Donald Thompson, Pres.
Box 4
Mount Pleasant, OH 43939
Ph: (740)769-2804 (740)769-7411
URL: http://users.adelphia.net/~npssteve/district.htm
Contact: Donald Thompson, Pres.
Local. **Affiliated With:** Lions Clubs International.

Mount Sterling

16077 ■ American Legion, Mt. Sterling Post 417
27 N Clark St., No. 17
Mount Sterling, OH 43143
Ph: (740)362-7478
Fax: (740)362-1429
URL: National Affiliate–www.legion.org
Local. **Affiliated With:** American Legion.

Mount Vernon

16078 ■ American Legion, Ohio Post 136
c/o Dan C. Stone, Jr.
606 W Chestnut St.
Mount Vernon, OH 43050
Ph: (614)392-4961
Fax: (740)362-1429
URL: National Affiliate–www.legion.org
Contact: Dan C. Stone Jr., Contact
Local. **Affiliated With:** American Legion.

16079 ■ American Red Cross, Knox County Chapter
300 N Mulberry St.
Mount Vernon, OH 43050-3402
Ph: (740)397-6300
Fax: (740)397-6093
E-mail: arcofknox@earthlink.net
URL: http://knoxcounty.redcross.org
Local.

16080 ■ Association for Computing Machinery, Mount Vernon Nazarene University (MVNU)
c/o Tom Beutel
800 Martinsburg Rd.
Mount Vernon, OH 43050
Ph: (740)392-6868
E-mail: tbeutel@mvnu.edu
URL: http://www.mvnc.edu
Local. **Affiliated With:** Association for Computing Machinery.

16081 ■ Kno Ho County RSVP
c/o Margaret Summers, Dir.
PO Box 251
Mount Vernon, OH 43050
Ph: (740)393-3633
Fax: (740)397-3306
E-mail: msrsvp@ecr.net
URL: http://www.seniorcorps.gov/about/programs/rsvp_state.asp?usestateabbr=oh&Search4.x=22&Search4.y=6
Contact: Margaret Summers, Dir.
Local. **Affiliated With:** Retired and Senior Volunteer Program.

16082 ■ Knox County Board of Realtors
PO Box 488
Mount Vernon, OH 43050
Ph: (740)392-8490
Fax: (740)392-8429
E-mail: knoxrealtors@earthlink.net
URL: National Affiliate–www.realtor.org
Contact: Jeri L. Scott, Exec. Officer
Local. Strives to develop real estate business practices. Advocates for the right to own, use and transfer real property. Provides a facility for professional development, research and exchange of information among members and the general public. **Affiliated With:** National Association of Realtors.

16083 ■ Knox County Convention and Visitors Bureau
c/o Patrick L. Crow
107 S Main St.
Mount Vernon, OH 43050-3325
Ph: (740)392-6102
Fax: (740)392-7840
Free: (800)837-5282
E-mail: info@visitknoxohio.org
URL: http://www.visitknoxohio.org
Local.

16084 ■ Knox County Habitat for Humanity
200 Main St.
Mount Vernon, OH 43050
Ph: (740)393-1434
Fax: (740)393-1157
E-mail: hfhkc@ecr.net
URL: http://www.hfhknoxoh.org
Contact: Joyce Klein, Pres.
Local. **Telecommunication Services:** electronic mail, kleinj@kenyon.edu. **Affiliated With:** Habitat for Humanity International.

16085 ■ Licking-Knox AIFA
c/o Kevin Spearman
744 Southridge Dr.
Mount Vernon, OH 43050
Ph: (740)397-0731
Fax: (740)393-0733
E-mail: kevin@spearmanfinancial.com
URL: National Affiliate–naifa.org
Contact: Kevin Spearman, Contact
Local. Represents the interests of insurance and financial advisors. Advocates for a positive legislative and regulatory environment. Enhances business and professional skills of members. **Affiliated With:** National Association of Insurance and Financial Advisors.

16086 ■ Mount Vernon - Knox County Chamber of Commerce
7 E Ohio Ave.
Mount Vernon, OH 43050
Ph: (740)393-1111
Fax: (740)393-1590
E-mail: chamber@knoxchamber.com
URL: http://www.knoxchamber.com
Local. Represents businesses in Mount Vernon, OH.

16087 ■ Ohio Health Care Association, District 6
c/o William Levering, Chm.
Levering Mgt.
201 N Main St.
Mount Vernon, OH 43050
Ph: (740)397-8940
Fax: (740)392-6075
E-mail: bill@leveringmanagement.com
URL: http://www.ohca.org
Contact: William Levering, Chm.
Local. Promotes professionalism and ethical behavior of individuals providing long-term care delivery for patients and for the general public. Provides information, education and administrative tools to enhance the quality of long-term care. Improves the standards of service and administration of member nursing homes. **Affiliated With:** American Health Care Association.

16088 ■ People First of Ohio
PO Box 988
Mount Vernon, OH 43050
Ph: (740)397-6100
Fax: (740)397-6118
Free: (888)959-8838
E-mail: peoplefirst@ecr.net
URL: http://www.peoplefirstofohio.org
State. **Affiliated With:** People First International.

16089 ■ Sweet Adelines International, Dogwood Blossoms Chapter
Big Brothers/Big Sisters
8868 Columbus Rd.
Mount Vernon, OH 43050-4404
Ph: (740)668-7222
E-mail: mahunter@ecr.net
URL: National Affiliate–www.sweetadelineintl.org
Contact: Maureen Hunter, Contact
Local. Advances the musical art form of barbershop harmony through education and performances. Provides education, training and coaching in the development of women's four-part barbershop harmony. **Affiliated With:** Sweet Adelines International.

16090 ■ United Way of Knox County, Ohio
110 E High St.
Mount Vernon, OH 43050-3402
Ph: (740)397-5721
URL: National Affiliate–national.unitedway.org
Local. **Affiliated With:** United Way of America.

16091 ■ Veterans of Foreign Wars 4027
307 W Chestnut St.
Mount Vernon, OH 43050
Ph: (740)393-4027
Contact: Don Wilson, Quarter Master
Local.

Mowrystown

16092 ■ American Legion, Ohio Post 694
c/o Carl Harris, Adj.
PO Box 301
Mowrystown, OH 45155
Ph: (740)362-7478
Fax: (740)362-1429
URL: National Affiliate–www.legion.org
Contact: Carl Harris, Adj.
Local. **Affiliated With:** American Legion.

Munroe Falls

16093 ■ Sales and Marketing Executives
471 Belmont Park Dr.
Munroe Falls, OH 44262
Ph: (330)945-7740
Local.

16094 ■ Sweet Adelines International, Heart of Ohio Show Chorus
Twin Falls United Methodist Church
60 N River Rd.
Munroe Falls, OH 44262-1308
Ph: (330)633-8705
URL: http://www.heartofohiosings.org
Contact: David Wallace, Dir.
Local. Advances the musical art form of barbershop harmony through education and performances. Provides education, training and coaching in the development of women's four-part barbershop harmony. **Affiliated With:** Sweet Adelines International.

Murray City

16095 ■ American Legion, Murray Post 420
150 Locust and Main
Murray City, OH 43144
Ph: (740)362-7478
Fax: (740)362-1429
URL: National Affiliate–www.legion.org
Local. **Affiliated With:** American Legion.

N Canton

16096 ■ American Society of Media Photographers, Ohio/North Coast Chapter (ASMP/ONC)
c/o Shawn Wood, Pres.
2440 State St. NE
N Canton, OH 44721
Ph: (330)877-6774
E-mail: studio7@sssnet.com
URL: http://www.asmponc.org
Contact: Shawn Wood, Pres.
Regional. **Affiliated With:** American Society of Media Photographers.

Napoleon

16097 ■ American Legion, Ohio Post 300
c/o Bert G. Taylor
500 Glenwood Ave.
Napoleon, OH 43545
Ph: (740)362-7478
Fax: (740)362-1429
URL: National Affiliate–www.legion.org
Contact: Bert G. Taylor, Contact
Local. **Affiliated With:** American Legion.

16098 ■ LISTEN for Life
c/o Ray Witte
377 Maumee Ln.
Napoleon, OH 43545
Ph: (419)592-3265
E-mail: listen4life@yahoo.com
URL: http://www.geocities.com/listen4life
Contact: Ray Witte, Pres.
Founded: 2001. **Languages:** Chichewa, English, Telugu. **Local**. Bible teaching ministry through speaking, writing and recordings. **Libraries: Type:** open to the public. **Holdings:** audio recordings. **Subjects:** God, Christian life. **Publications:** *Life Line Report*, quarterly. Newsletter. Report of responses and correspondence. **Price:** free.

16099 ■ Napoleon - Henry County Chamber of Commerce
611 N Perry St.
Napoleon, OH 43545
Ph: (419)592-1786
Fax: (419)592-4945
E-mail: hcncoc@ohiohenrycounty.com
URL: http://www.naphcchamber.com
Contact: Joel Miller, Dir.
Founded: 1952. **Members:** 250. **Staff:** 2. **Budget:** $95,000. **Local**. Promotes business and community development in Napoleon, OH. Sponsors new teacher breakfast, tourism activities, and business after hours. **Formerly:** Napoleon Area Chamber of Commerce. **Publications:** Newsletter, monthly. **Price:** $75.00. **Advertising:** accepted • Directory, biennial. **Conventions/Meetings:** monthly Business After Hours - meeting - always first Thursday.

16100 ■ United Way of Henry County
611 N Perry St.
Napoleon, OH 43545-1701
Ph: (419)599-8176
URL: National Affiliate–national.unitedway.org
Local. **Affiliated With:** United Way of America.

16101 ■ Veterans of Foreign Wars 8218
1008 N Perry St.
Napoleon, OH 43545
Ph: (419)599-1456
Contact: Ken Baker, Commander
Local.

Nashport

16102 ■ Central Ohio Golf Course Superintendents Association (COGCSA)
6835 Dillon Hills Dr.
Nashport, OH 43830
Ph: (614)834-4020
Fax: (614)834-4020
E-mail: spmagg@earthlink.net
URL: http://www.cogcsa.org
Contact: Sean Magginis, Pres.
Founded: 1926. **Membership Dues:** student, $25 (annual) • regular, $75 (annual). **Local**. Represents the interests of golf course superintendents. Advances members' profession for career success. Enhances the enjoyment, growth and vitality in the game of golf. Educates members concerning efficient and economical management of golf courses. **Awards:** Glenn B. Hudson Memorial Fund and Scholarship. **Frequency:** annual. **Type:** scholarship. **Recipient:** for turfgrass management student. **Affiliated With:** Golf Course Superintendents Association of America. **Publications:** Newsletter, monthly.

16103 ■ Ohio Angus Association
c/o Jerry Ballard, Sec./Field Mgr.
6425 Ballard Rd.
Nashport, OH 43830
Ph: (740)452-8821
Fax: (740)452-8821
E-mail: ohioangus@msmisp.com
Contact: Jerry Ballard, Sec./Fieldman
Members: 475. **Membership Dues:** $25 (annual). **Staff:** 1. **Regional Groups:** 9. **State Groups:** 1. **State**. Production and sale of purebred angus cattle. **Publications:** *Ohio Angus Association*, monthly. Newsletter. **Price:** free. **Circulation:** 625. **Advertising:** accepted. **Conventions/Meetings:** annual meeting; Avg. Attendance: 200.

Navarre

16104 ■ Antique Automobile Club of America, Ohio Region - Canton Chapter
c/o Darrin Troyer, VP
5912 Drenta Cir. SW
Navarre, OH 44662
Ph: (330)484-5099
E-mail: troyersolds@aol.com
URL: http://local.aaca.org/ohio/canton.htm
Contact: John Simmons, Pres.
Founded: 1965. **Local**. Collectors, hobbyists, and others interested in the preservation, maintenance, and restoration of automobiles and in automotive history. **Affiliated With:** Antique Automobile Club of America.

Neapolis

16105 ■ Ruffed Grouse Society, Northwest Ohio Chapter
c/o Dan Lane
PO Box 587
Neapolis, OH 43547-0587
Ph: (330)666-9377
E-mail: galloway@raex.com
URL: National Affiliate–www.ruffedgrousesociety.org
Contact: Dan Lane, Contact
Local. **Affiliated With:** Ruffed Grouse Society.

Neffs

16106 ■ American Legion, Neffs Post 77
PO Box 292
Neffs, OH 43940
Ph: (740)362-7478
Fax: (740)362-1429
URL: National Affiliate–www.legion.org
Local. **Affiliated With:** American Legion.

Nelsonville

16107 ■ American Legion, Ohio Post 229
c/o Glenford Dugan
135 W Columbus St.
Nelsonville, OH 45764
Ph: (740)362-7478
Fax: (740)362-1429
URL: National Affiliate–www.legion.org
Contact: Glenford Dugan, Contact
Local. **Affiliated With:** American Legion.

16108 ■ Phi Theta Kappa - Alpha Mu Delta Chapter
c/o Abigail Cox
3301 Hocking Pkwy.
Nelsonville, OH 45764-9588
Ph: (740)753-3591
E-mail: abigailfo@yahoo.com
URL: http://www.ptk.org/directories/chapters/OH/320-1.htm
Contact: Abigail Cox, Advisor
Local. **Affiliated With:** Phi Theta Kappa, International Honor Society.

16109 ■ Vietnam Veterans of America, Chapter No. 676
c/o Steve Phillips, Pres.
PO Box 59
Nelsonville, OH 45764
Ph: (740)753-1917
URL: http://www.vvabuckeyestatecouncil.com
Contact: Steve Phillips, Pres.
Local. **Affiliated With:** Vietnam Veterans of America.

Nevada

16110 ■ American Legion, Ohio Post 462
c/o Robert D. Case
115 1/2 N Main St.
Nevada, OH 44849
Ph: (740)362-7478
Fax: (740)362-1429
URL: National Affiliate–www.legion.org
Contact: Robert D. Case, Contact
Local. **Affiliated With:** American Legion.

16111 ■ Nevada Lions Club - Ohio
c/o Harold Kinsey, Sec.
13288 E Township Hwy. 10
Nevada, OH 44849
Ph: (740)482-2200
E-mail: ahkinsey@wcnet.org
URL: http://www.lions13b.org
Contact: Harold Kinsey, Sec.
Local. **Affiliated With:** Lions Clubs International.

New Albany

16112 ■ American Legion, National Defense Employees Post 792
8359 Morse Rd.
New Albany, OH 43054
Ph: (740)362-7478
Fax: (740)362-1429
URL: National Affiliate–www.legion.org
Local. **Affiliated With:** American Legion.

16113 ■ New Albany Lions Club
c/o Eldoris J. McFarland, Sec.
4308 Bridgelane Pl.
New Albany, OH 43054
Ph: (614)855-7959
E-mail: emcfarl@insight.com
URL: http://www.iwaynet.net/~lions13f
Contact: Eldoris J. McFarland, Sec.
Local. **Affiliated With:** Lions Clubs International.

16114 ■ Ohio Dietetic Association
c/o Denise Hill, Exec.Dir.
34 N High St.
New Albany, OH 43054
Ph: (614)895-1253
Fax: (614)895-3466
E-mail: oda@eatrightohio.org
URL: http://www.eatrightohio.org
Contact: Denise Hill, Exec.Dir.
Members: 2,800. **Staff:** 1. **Local Groups:** 10. **State**. **Affiliated With:** American Dietetic Association.

New Boston

16115 ■ City Limits Table Tennis Club
Limits Family Fun Ctr.
3432 Rhodes Ave.
New Boston, OH 45662
Ph: (740)820-4427 (740)456-2489
E-mail: rdnoel14@cs.com
URL: http://www.cjhardin.siteblast.com
Contact: Rick Noel, Contact
Local. **Affiliated With:** U.S.A. Table Tennis.

New Bremen

16116 ■ American Legion, New Bremen Post 241
PO Box 94
New Bremen, OH 45869
Ph: (740)362-7478
Fax: (740)362-1429
URL: National Affiliate–www.legion.org
Local. **Affiliated With:** American Legion.

16117 ■ Auglaize County Arc
428 W Haven Dr.
New Bremen, OH 45869
Ph: (419)629-2419
URL: National Affiliate–www.TheArc.org
Local. Parents, professional workers, and others interested in individuals with mental retardation. Works to promote services, research, public understanding, and legislation for people with mental retardation and their families. **Affiliated With:** Arc of the United States.

16118 ■ Lock One Community Arts
c/o Scott Kuenning
15 N Walnut St.
New Bremen, OH 45869
Ph: (419)733-0139
Fax: (419)629-3336
E-mail: lockone@nktelco.net
URL: http://www.nktelco.net/lockone
Contact: Scott Kuenning, Contact
Local.

16119 ■ Southwestern Auglaize County Chamber of Commerce
PO Box 3
107 W Monroe St., Ste.2
New Bremen, OH 45869
Ph: (419)629-0313
Fax: (419)629-0411
E-mail: swauglaizechamber@nktelco.net
URL: http://www.swauglaizechamber.com
Contact: Greg Myers, Dir.
Founded: 1998. **Membership Dues:** commercial (plus $3 per employee for more than 25 employees), $145-$200 (annual) • industrial (plus $2.50 per employee for more than 25 employees), $300 (annual) • professional (plus $5 per employee for more than 25 employees), $250 (annual) • financial (plus $5 per employee for more than 25 employees), $400 (annual) • hospital and nursing home (plus $1.50 per employee for more than 25 employees), $300 (annual) • utility, $400 (annual) • education, $250 (annual) • government, $1,000 (annual) • nonprofit organization, associate, individual, $60 (annual). **Local**. Works to improve the economy and quality of life in Southwest Auglaize and the surrounding areas. **Computer Services:** database, membership listings.

New Carlisle

16120 ■ All Ohio Scanner Club (AOSC)
20 Phillip Dr.
New Carlisle, OH 45344-9108
E-mail: n8oay@qsl.net
URL: http://www.aosc.org
Contact: Dave Marshall, Managing Ed.
Founded: 1979. **Members:** 591. **Membership Dues:** in U.S., $24 (annual) • in Canada and Mexico, $30 (annual) • outside U.S. and Canada and Mexico, $42 (annual). **Regional**. Shares information and improves the hobby of monitoring two-way radio communications. **Publications:** *American Scanner-gram*, bimonthly. Newsletter. Contains information exchange for scanner and short wave radio listeners. **Price:** included in membership dues. **Circulation:** 600.

16121 ■ National Active and Retired Federal Employees Association - Wright 1840
170 Weinland Dr.
New Carlisle, OH 45344-2926
Ph: (937)849-6626
URL: National Affiliate–www.narfe.org
Contact: William E. Gardner, Contact
Local. Protects the retirement future of employees through education. Informs members on issues affecting the retirement. **Affiliated With:** National Association of Retired Federal Employees.

16122 ■ Photographic Art Specialist of Ohio
c/o Catherine Harvey
410 Kennison
New Carlisle, OH 45344

Ph: (937)845-0674
URL: National Affiliate–ppa.com
Contact: Myle Antro, Pres.
Local. Promotes the interests of individuals involved in portrait, wedding, commercial and industrial photography. **Affiliated With:** Professional Photographers of America.

16123 ■ Reserve Officers Association - Department of Ohio, Col. John E. Coleman Chapter 16
c/o Maj.Gen. Earl A. Aler, Jr., Pres.
6423 Winding Tree Dr.
New Carlisle, OH 45344
Ph: (937)882-6498 (937)882-6489
Fax: (937)882-9213
E-mail: earlaler@aol.com
URL: http://www.roa.org/oh
Contact: Maj.Gen. Earl A. Aler Jr., Pres.
Local. Promotes and supports the development and execution of a military policy for the United States. Provides professional development seminars, workshops and programs for its members. **Affiliated With:** Reserve Officers Association of the United States.

New Concord

16124 ■ Association for Computing Machinery, Muskingum College
c/o Ty James, Pres.
163 Stormont St.
New Concord, OH 43762
Ph: (740)826-8332
Fax: (740)826-8404
E-mail: acm@muskingum.edu
URL: http://www.muskingum.edu/~acm
Contact: Ty James, Pres.
Local. Promotes an increased knowledge of the science, design, development, construction, languages, and applications of modern computing machinery; a greater interest in computing machinery and its applications; and a means of communication between persons having interest in computing machinery. **Affiliated With:** Association for Computing Machinery.

16125 ■ Ohio Meat Goat Association
13140 Stoney Point Rd.
New Concord, OH 43762
E-mail: morrowfarm@aol.com
URL: National Affiliate–www.abga.org
Contact: Mary Morrow, Contact
State.

16126 ■ Psi Chi, National Honor Society in Psychology - Muskingum College
c/o Dept. of Psychology
153 Stormont St.
New Concord, OH 43762-1199
Ph: (740)826-8350 (740)826-8355
Fax: (740)826-8357
E-mail: larryn@muskingum.edu
URL: http://www.psichi.org/chapters/info.asp?chapter_id=247
Contact: Dr. Larry Normansell, Advisor
Local.

16127 ■ Sweet Adelines International, Friendship VII Chapter
United Presbyterian Church
2 W High St.
New Concord, OH 43762-1209
Ph: (740)489-5811
E-mail: ritatuck@aol.com
URL: National Affiliate–www.sweetadelineintl.org
Contact: Rita Tucker, Contact
Local. Advances the musical art form of barbershop harmony through education and performances. Provides education, training and coaching in the development of women's four-part barbershop harmony. **Affiliated With:** Sweet Adelines International.

New Holland

16128 ■ American Legion, Arch Post 477
10 E Front St.
New Holland, OH 43145
Ph: (740)362-7478
Fax: (740)362-1429
URL: National Affiliate–www.legion.org
Local. Affiliated With: American Legion.

New Knoxville

16129 ■ American Legion, Washington Post 444
PO Box 555
New Knoxville, OH 45871
Ph: (740)362-7478
Fax: (740)362-1429
URL: National Affiliate–www.legion.org
Local. Affiliated With: American Legion.

New Lebanon

16130 ■ American Legion, New Lebanon Post 762
35 W Main St.
New Lebanon, OH 45345
Ph: (740)362-7478
Fax: (740)362-1429
URL: National Affiliate–www.legion.org
Local. Affiliated With: American Legion.

16131 ■ New Lebanon Lions Club
32 S Church St.
New Lebanon, OH 45345-1214
Ph: (937)687-2077
URL: http://newlebanonoh.lionwap.org
Contact: John Lantis, Pres.
Local. Affiliated With: Lions Clubs International.

New Lexington

16132 ■ American Legion, Ohio Post 188
c/o John Tague
PO Box 602
New Lexington, OH 43764
Ph: (740)362-7478
Fax: (740)362-1429
URL: National Affiliate–www.legion.org
Contact: John Tague, Contact
Local. Affiliated With: American Legion.

16133 ■ Perry County Agriculture Society
5446 State Rte. 37 E
New Lexington, OH 43764
Ph: (740)342-3047
Local.

16134 ■ Perry County Chamber of Commerce
103 W Brown St.
New Lexington, OH 43764
Ph: (740)342-3547
Fax: (740)342-3547
E-mail: pccoc@netpluscom.com
Contact: Larry Rentschler, Pres.
Founded: 1983. **Members:** 130. **Local**. Promotes business and community development in the New Lexington, OH area.

16135 ■ Perry County RSVP
c/o Rita Bartimusm, Dir.
PO Box 605
New Lexington, OH 43764-0605
Ph: (740)342-2149
Fax: (740)342-7206
E-mail: pcrsvp@netpluscom.com
URL: http://www.seniorcorps.gov/about/programs/rsvp_state.asp?usestateabbr=oh&Search4.x=0&Search4.y=0
Contact: Rita Bartimusm, Dir.
Local. Affiliated With: Retired and Senior Volunteer Program.

16136 ■ Phi Theta Kappa - Beta Lambda Nu Chapter
c/o Patrick Chute
Perry Campus
5454 Rte. 37E
New Lexington, OH 43764-9723
Ph: (740)342-3337
E-mail: chute_p@hocking.edu
URL: http://www.ptk.org/directories/chapters/OH/21719-1.htm
Contact: Patrick Chute, Advisor
Local. Affiliated With: Phi Theta Kappa, International Honor Society.

New London

16137 ■ American Legion, Broome-Wood Post 292
185 N Main St.
New London, OH 44851
Ph: (740)362-7478
Fax: (740)362-1429
URL: National Affiliate–www.legion.org
Local. Affiliated With: American Legion.

16138 ■ Ohio Rifle and Pistol Association (ORPA)
c/o Mr. Keith V. Bailey, Sec.
PO Box 205
New London, OH 44851
Ph: (419)929-0307
Fax: (775)898-2744
E-mail: kvbguns@msn.com
URL: http://www.orpa.net
Contact: Mr. Keith V. Bailey, Sec.
Founded: 1934. **Members:** 4,000. **Membership Dues:** individual, $21 (annual) • junior, $5 (annual) • associate, $9 (annual) • club/league, $20 (annual) • life (individual), $350 • life (senior), $210. **Local Groups:** 54. **State**. Works to defend the second amendment and to promote firearm safety and shooting sports. **Awards:** Donna J. Deal Memorial Award. **Frequency:** annual. **Type:** scholarship. **Affiliated With:** National Rifle Association of America. **Publications:** *Gunsmoke*, bimonthly. Newsletter.

New Madison

16139 ■ American Legion, Laroy Farst Post 245
PO Box 127
New Madison, OH 45346
Ph: (740)362-7478
Fax: (740)362-1429
URL: National Affiliate–www.legion.org
Local. Affiliated With: American Legion.

New Matamoras

16140 ■ American Legion, New Matamoras Post 378
PO Box 324
New Matamoras, OH 45767
Ph: (740)362-7478
Fax: (740)362-1429
URL: National Affiliate–www.legion.org
Local. Affiliated With: American Legion.

New Middletown

16141 ■ Antique Automobile Club of America, Ohio Region - Meander Chapter
c/o Darryl Parisi
9852 Deltona Dr.
New Middletown, OH 44442
E-mail: tcopeland@neo.rr.com
URL: http://www.aaca.org/ohio/meander/
Contact: Darryl Parisi, Contact
Local. Collectors, hobbyists, and others interested in the preservation, maintenance, and restoration of automobiles and in automotive history. **Affiliated With:** Antique Automobile Club of America.

16142 ■ New Middletown Lions Club
c/o Ed Salata, Pres.
5335 Sycamorehill Dr.
New Middletown, OH 44442
Ph: (330)542-8987
E-mail: salata@sbcglobal.net
URL: http://www.lions13d.org
Contact: Ed Salata, Pres.
Local. Affiliated With: Lions Clubs International.

New Paris

16143 ■ American Legion, Ohio Post 360
c/o Clarence Teaford
215 N Washington St.
New Paris, OH 45347
Ph: (740)362-7478
Fax: (740)362-1429
URL: National Affiliate–www.legion.org
Contact: Clarence Teaford, Contact
Local. Affiliated With: American Legion.

New Philadelphia

16144 ■ AAA Tuscarawas County
1112 Fourth St. NW
New Philadelphia, OH 44663
Ph: (330)343-4481
URL: http://www.aaa.com
Contact: Richard Brinkman, Mgr.
Local.

16145 ■ American Legion, Tuscarawas Post 139
111 3rd St. SW
New Philadelphia, OH 44663
Ph: (330)343-8436
Fax: (740)362-1429
URL: National Affiliate–www.legion.org
Local. Affiliated With: American Legion.

16146 ■ American Red Cross, Muskingum Lakes Chapter
113 W High St.
New Philadelphia, OH 44663
Ph: (330)343-8633
E-mail: info@mlcredcross.org
URL: http://www.mlcredcross.org
Local.

16147 ■ Big Brothers Big Sisters of East Central Ohio
151 N Broadway
New Philadelphia, OH 44663
Ph: (330)364-3800
Fax: (330)343-3194
Free: (888)364-5965
E-mail: bbbs@tusco.net
URL: http://www.bbbseco.com
Contact: Jamie L. Orr, Exec.Dir.
Local. Serves children ages 6-14 by matching them with an adult volunteer to spend a minimum of 4 hours per month together. **Affiliated With:** Big Brothers Big Sisters of America. **Formerly:** (2005) Big Brothers Big Sisters of Tuscarawas, Carroll and Harrison Counties, and also serving Holmes County.

16148 ■ Buckeye Beagle Club
c/o Betty Buss
101 Sea Gull Ln. SE
New Philadelphia, OH 44663-3129
E-mail: jgbeagles@aol.com
URL: National Affiliate–www.akc.org
Contact: Betty Buss, Contact
Local. Affiliated With: American Kennel Club.

16149 ■ Dover Lions Club - Ohio
c/o Mary Ellen Sherer, Pres.
1090 Thomas Dr. SW
New Philadelphia, OH 44663
Ph: (330)364-7105 (330)339-6060
E-mail: shererm@dover.k12.oh.us
URL: http://users.adelphia.net/~npssteve/district.htm
Contact: Mary Ellen Sherer, Pres.
Local. Affiliated With: Lions Clubs International.

16150 ■ Harcatus RSVP
c/o Gail Baldwin, Dir.
1324 3rd St. NW
New Philadelphia, OH 44663
Ph: (330)364-9251
Fax: (330)343-6526
E-mail: rsvp@bright.net
URL: http://www.seniorcorps.gov/about/programs/rsvp_state.asp?usestateabbr=oh&Search4.x=0&Search4.y=0
Contact: Gail Baldwin, Dir.
Local. Affiliated With: Retired and Senior Volunteer Program.

16151 ■ Local 20C, Chemical Workers Council of the UFCW
PO Box 945
New Philadelphia, OH 44663
Ph: (330)343-7701
URL: National Affiliate–www.ufcw.org
Local. Affiliated With: United Food and Commercial Workers International Union.

16152 ■ Ohio Genealogical Society, Tuscarawas County
PO Box 141
New Philadelphia, OH 44663-0141
Ph: (740)922-0531
E-mail: tcgs1@aol.com
URL: http://web.tusco.net/tcgs/index.htm
Contact: Emma McMannamy, Pres.
Founded: 1968. **Membership Dues:** single, $12 (annual) • couple, $15 (annual) • life - single, $150 • life - couple, $200. **Local. Libraries: Type:** open to the public. **Holdings:** films, archival material, periodicals, software, maps, biographical archives. **Subjects:** family history/registry, birth, deaths, wills, marriage, guardianship, American Genealogy. **Affiliated With:** Ohio Genealogical Society.

16153 ■ Society of Manufacturing Engineers - Kent State University - Tuscarawas S180
Kent State Univ. - Tuscarawas, Engg. Tech.
330 Univ. Dr. NE
New Philadelphia, OH 44663
Ph: (330)308-7414
Fax: (330)339-3321
E-mail: dkandray@tusc.kent.edu
URL: National Affiliate–www.sme.org
Contact: Dan Kandray, Contact
Local. Advances manufacturing knowledge to gain competitive advantage. Improves skills and manufacturing solutions for the growth of economy. Provides resources and opportunities for manufacturing professionals. **Affiliated With:** International Association for the Physical Sciences of the Oceans.

16154 ■ Tuscarawas County Chamber of Commerce (TCCC)
1323 4th St. NW
New Philadelphia, OH 44663
Ph: (330)343-4474
Fax: (330)343-6526
E-mail: info@tuschamber.com
URL: http://www.tuschamber.com
Contact: Lois F. Rembert, Pres.
Founded: 1959. **Members:** 500. **Membership Dues:** business, $230-$740 (annual) • basic, financial (based on asset), $275 (annual) • basic, hotel/lodging (based on bed count), $250 (annual) • professional, firm ($105 per additional professional), $250 (annual) • non-profit, individual, $150 (annual) • school/education, $250 (annual) • utility (based on number of employees), $485-$1,185 (annual). **Staff:** 4. **Budget:** $200,000. **Regional Groups:** 2. **State Groups:** 1. **Local.** Promotes business and community development in Tuscarawas County, OH. Operates safety council and export resource center. **Committees:** Ambassadors; Business/Education; Communications; Legislative; Membership; Retention and Expansion. **Councils:** Agriculture; Tuscarawas Valley Safety. **Affiliated With:** U.S. Chamber of Commerce. **Publications:** *Economic and Demographics of Tuscarawas County* • *Images of Tuscarawas County*, annual. Magazine. Features a unique and in-depth showcase of the community and the businesses that make an impression on it. **Advertising:** accepted. Alternate Formats: online • *Strictly Business*, quarterly. Newsletter. **Price:** $5.00. **Circulation:** 1,000. **Advertising:** accepted. Alternate Formats: online • Newsletter, annual. **Conventions/Meetings:** monthly board meeting.

16155 ■ Tuscarawas County Rabbit Breeders Association
3386 Henderson School Rd.
New Philadelphia, OH 44663
Ph: (330)343-8407
E-mail: okhaven@tusco.net
URL: National Affiliate–www.arba.net
Contact: Deborah A. Brown, Exec. Officer
Local. Breeders of cavies and rabbits. **Affiliated With:** American Rabbit Breeders Association. **Conventions/Meetings:** monthly meeting.

16156 ■ Tuscarawas County Young Democrats
c/o Zachary Cummings, Treas.
1260 Monroe St. NW
New Philadelphia, OH 44663
E-mail: info@tcyd.org
URL: http://www.tcyd.org/who.html
Local.

16157 ■ United Way of Tuscarawas County
PO Box 525
New Philadelphia, OH 44663-0525
Ph: (330)343-7772
URL: http://www.tuscunitedway.org
Contact: Scott Robinson, Exec.Dir.
Founded: 1942. **Local. Affiliated With:** United Way of America.

16158 ■ Vietnam Veterans of America, Chapter No. 857 - New Philadelphia
c/o Tom Burke, Pres.
PO Box 170
New Philadelphia, OH 44663
Ph: (330)339-6814
URL: http://www.vvabuckeyestatecouncil.com
Contact: Tom Burke, Pres.
Local. Affiliated With: Vietnam Veterans of America.

New Richmond

16159 ■ American Legion, Ohio Post 550
c/o John Farina
311 Caroline St.
New Richmond, OH 45157
Ph: (740)362-7478
Fax: (740)362-1429
URL: National Affiliate–www.legion.org
Contact: John Farina, Contact
Local. Affiliated With: American Legion.

New Riegel

16160 ■ American Legion, Ohio Post 354
c/o Edward Grine
20 E South St.
New Riegel, OH 44853

Ph: (740)362-7478
Fax: (740)362-1429
URL: National Affiliate–www.legion.org
Contact: Edward Grine, Contact
Local. Affiliated With: American Legion.

New Washington

16161 ■ American Legion, Ohio Post 405
c/o Carl A. Geiger
PO Box 386
New Washington, OH 44854
Ph: (740)362-7478
Fax: (740)362-1429
URL: National Affiliate–www.legion.org
Contact: Carl A. Geiger, Contact
Local. Affiliated With: American Legion.

New Waterford

16162 ■ New Waterford Fireman's Association
3767 E Main St.
New Waterford, OH 44445
Ph: (330)457-2363
Local.

16163 ■ New Waterford Lions Club
PO Box 313
New Waterford, OH 44445
Ph: (330)482-4271
E-mail: wisoh@comcast.net
URL: http://newwaterfordoh.lionwap.org
Contact: Darryl Jones, Pres.
Local. Affiliated With: Lions Clubs International.

Newark

16164 ■ Alcoholics Anonymous World Services, Intergroup Office
PO Box 11
Newark, OH 43058-0011
Ph: (740)345-7060
URL: National Affiliate–www.aa.org
Contact: Brenda Brown, Contact
Local. Individuals recovering from alcoholism. AA maintains that members can solve their common problem and help others achieve sobriety through a twelve step program that includes sharing their experience, strength, and hope with each other. **Affiliated With:** Alcoholics Anonymous World Services.

16165 ■ American Legion, Hanover Post 764
1989 W High St. NE
Newark, OH 43055
Ph: (740)362-7478
Fax: (740)362-1429
URL: National Affiliate–www.legion.org
Local. Affiliated With: American Legion.

16166 ■ American Legion, Heath Post 771
c/o William P. Callis
201 S Westmoor Ave., Apt. B
Newark, OH 43055
Ph: (740)362-7478
Fax: (740)362-1429
URL: National Affiliate–www.legion.org
Contact: William P. Callis, Contact
Local. Affiliated With: American Legion.

16167 ■ American Legion, Ohio Post 85
c/o Levi Phillips
85 S 6th St.
Newark, OH 43055
Ph: (740)362-7478
Fax: (740)362-1429
URL: National Affiliate–www.legion.org
Contact: Levi Phillips, Contact
Local. Affiliated With: American Legion.

16168 ■ American Red Cross, Licking County Chapter
PO Box 4337
Newark, OH 43058-4337
Ph: (740)349-9442
Fax: (740)349-9446
URL: http://lickingcounty.redcross.org
Local.

16169 ■ Great Lakes Curling Association - Newark Curling Club
c/o Graham Campbell, Sec.
40 W Main St.
Newark, OH 43055
Ph: (740)349-6727
Fax: (740)349-6788
E-mail: parkssec@prodigy.net
URL: http://www.usacurl.org/basics/U.S.%20clubs/glakes.html
Contact: Graham Campbell, Sec.
Local. Affiliated With: United States Curling Association.

16170 ■ Licking County Board of Realtors (LCBR)
57 N Third St.
Newark, OH 43055
Ph: (740)345-2151
Fax: (740)345-5040
E-mail: lcbrphil@alltel.net
URL: http://www.lickingcountyrealtors.com
Contact: Phil Frye, Exec. Officer
Local. Strives to develop real estate business practices. Advocates for the right to own, use and transfer real property. Provides a facility for professional development, research and exchange of information among members and the general public. **Affiliated With:** National Association of Realtors.

16171 ■ Licking County United Way
PO Box 4490
Newark, OH 43058-4490
Ph: (740)345-6685
Fax: (740)345-7712
Free: (877)264-1082
E-mail: dcarpenter@lcuw.net
URL: http://www.unitedwayoflickingcounty.org
Contact: Donna L. Carpenter, Exec.Dir.
Local. Affiliated With: United Way of America.

16172 ■ Mental Health Association of Licking County
65 Messimer Dr.
Newark, OH 43055
Ph: (740)522-1341
Fax: (740)522-4464
Free: (888)260-2613
E-mail: mhalc@alink.com
URL: http://www.mhalc.org
Contact: Paddy Kutz, Exec.Dir.
Local. Seeks to promote mental health and prevent mental health disorders. Improves mental health of Americans through advocacy, public education, research and service. **Affiliated With:** National Mental Health Association.

16173 ■ Muskingum Valley Beagle Club
c/o Dennis Shirk
16313 Brushy Fork Rd.
Newark, OH 43056-9412
URL: National Affiliate–clubs.akc.org
Contact: Dennis Shirk, Contact
Local.

16174 ■ National Active and Retired Federal Employees Association - Licking County 310
12208 Fairview Rd. SE
Newark, OH 43056-9040
Ph: (740)323-2356
URL: National Affiliate–www.narfe.org
Contact: Sondra K. Gartner, Contact
Local. Protects the retirement future of employees through education. Informs members on issues affecting the retirement. **Affiliated With:** National Association of Retired Federal Employees.

16175 ■ National Audubon Society - East Central Ohio
209 Fairfield Ave.
Newark, OH 43055
E-mail: rbniccum@ecr.net
URL: National Affiliate–www.audubon.org
Contact: Richard Niccum, Pres.
Local.

16176 ■ National Technical Honor Society - Career and Technology Education Centers - Ohio (C-TEC)
C-TEC Secondary Center
150 Price Rd.
Newark, OH 43055
Ph: (740)366-3351
Free: (800)875-1587
E-mail: rcassidy@c-tec.edu
URL: http://www.c-tec.edu
Contact: Ronald Cassidy, Superintendent
Local.

16177 ■ National Technical Honor Society - CTEC Satellite Programs - Ohio
C-TEC Satellite Center
1179 Univ.Dr.
LeFevre Hall
Rm. 154
Newark, OH 43055
Ph: (740)366-9190
E-mail: rcassidy@c-tec.edu
URL: http://www.c-tec.edu
Contact: Ronald Cassidy, Contact
Local.

16178 ■ Newark Alliance
PO Box 733
Newark, OH 43058-0733
Ph: (740)349-7304
E-mail: info@newarkalliance.com
Contact: Amy Rule, Admin.Asst.
Founded: 1999. **Members:** 45. **Staff:** 1. **Budget:** $120,000. **Local.** Professionals, groups, corporations, and individuals dedicated to revitalizing downtown Newark, OH economically, culturally, and historically. **Committees:** Design; Economic Development; Organizations and Fundraising; Promotions. **Absorbed:** (2000) Newark Downtown Association. **Publications:** *Revitalization Update*, quarterly. Newsletter. **Circulation:** 200. Alternate Formats: online. **Conventions/Meetings:** periodic board meeting • annual meeting • monthly meeting, committees.

16179 ■ Newark Table Tennis Club
Advantage Club
1845 W Main St.
Newark, OH 43055
Ph: (740)467-2132 (740)928-7555
URL: http://www.usatt.org/clubs
Contact: Paul Miller, Contact
Local. Affiliated With: U.S.A. Table Tennis.

16180 ■ Newark Teacher's Association (NTA)
52 N 3rd St., No. 306
Newark, OH 43055
Ph: (740)345-0274
Fax: (740)345-8091
E-mail: ntateach@alltel.net
URL: http://www.ntateach.ohea.us
Contact: Barry Moore, Pres.
Local.

16181 ■ Ohio Genealogical Society, Licking County (LCGS)
101 W Main St., Rm. 228
Newark, OH 43055-5054
Ph: (740)349-5510
E-mail: lcgs@npls.org
URL: http://www.rootsweb.com/~ohlcgs2/index.html
Contact: Nola Miles Rogers, Pres.
Founded: 1972. **Members:** 600. **Membership Dues:** individual, $12 (annual) • double, $14 (annual). **For-Profit. Local.** Individuals interested in the genealogy of the Licking County, OH area. Aids people who wish to trace their genealogical ancestry. **Libraries: Type:**

reference; open to the public. **Holdings:** 5,000; books, films. **Subjects:** genealogy and history, family histories, obituary files. **Awards:** Volunteerism. **Frequency:** annual. **Type:** recognition. **Recipient:** dedication to work. **Computer Services:** database, genealogical databases and research. **Boards:** Executive. **Affiliated With:** Ohio Genealogical Society. **Publications:** *The Licking Lantern*, quarterly. Newsletter. **Price:** $3.00/issue; free to members. ISSN: 0748-1012. **Circulation:** 600. **Conventions/Meetings:** monthly meeting, business and educational programs - always first Monday (except January, February, March) in Newark, OH.

16182 ■ Ohio Gourd Society
11341 Eddyburg Rd.
Newark, OH 43055
Ph: (740)345-4864
E-mail: clark@foothillsfarm.com
URL: http://ohiogourdsociety.org
Contact: Gary Clark, Pres.
State. Affiliated With: American Gourd Society.

16183 ■ Phi Theta Kappa - Alpha Theta Zeta Chapter
c/o Cris Clark
Hopewell Hall 161
1179 Univ. Dr.
Newark, OH 43055-1767
Ph: (740)364-9594
E-mail: cclark@cotc.edu
URL: http://www.ptk.org/directories/chapters/OH/319-1.htm
Contact: Cris Clark, Advisor
Local. Affiliated With: Phi Theta Kappa, International Honor Society.

16184 ■ Southeastern Ohio Dairy Goat Association
c/o Christina Ritchey
PO Box 722
Newark, OH 43058-0722
Ph: (614)345-6066
URL: National Affiliate–adga.org
Contact: Christina Ritchey, Contact
Local. Affiliated With: American Dairy Goat Association.

16185 ■ Special Wish Foundation, Newark
c/o Pat Hinger
PO Box 4292
Newark, OH 43058-4292
Ph: (740)349-9474
Fax: (740)345-7732
E-mail: kphinger@alink.com
URL: National Affiliate–www.spwish.org
Local. Affiliated With: A Special Wish Foundation.

16186 ■ Sweet Adelines International, Newark Chapter
St. Paul's Lutheran Church
67 N 5th
Newark, OH 43055
Ph: (740)668-7007
E-mail: millerlynn_d@yahoo.com
URL: National Affiliate–www.sweetadelineintl.org
Contact: Lynn Miller, Contact
Local. Advances the musical art form of barbershop harmony through education and performances. Provides education, training and coaching in the development of women's four-part barbershop harmony. **Affiliated With:** Sweet Adelines International.

16187 ■ United Way of Licking County
PO Box 4490
Newark, OH 43058-4490
Ph: (740)345-6685
Fax: (740)345-7712
Free: (877)264-1082
E-mail: dcarpenter@lcuw.net
URL: http://www.unitedwayoflickingcounty.org
Contact: Donna L. Carpenter, Exec.Dir.
Local. Affiliated With: United Way of America.

16188 ■ Vietnam Veterans of America, Chapter No. 55
c/o Mark A. Rehl, Pres.
PO Box 624
Newark, OH 43055
Ph: (740)927-6272
URL: http://www.vvabuckeyestatecouncil.com
Contact: Mark A. Rehl, Pres.
Local. Affiliated With: Vietnam Veterans of America.

Newburgh Heights

16189 ■ American Legion, Newburgh Heights Post 627
c/o Teddy M. Zieja
3935 E 42nd St.
Newburgh Heights, OH 44105
Ph: (740)362-7478
Fax: (740)362-1429
URL: National Affiliate–www.legion.org
Contact: Teddy M. Zieja, Contact
Local. Affiliated With: American Legion.

Newbury

16190 ■ American Legion, Newbury Post 663
PO Box 26
Newbury, OH 44065
Ph: (740)362-7478
Fax: (740)362-1429
URL: National Affiliate–www.legion.org
Local. Affiliated With: American Legion.

16191 ■ Catholic Men's Fellowship of Northeastern Ohio
c/o Dave Douglas, Pres.
PO Box 464
Newbury, OH 44065
Ph: (216)382-9366
E-mail: dbradner@cmfneo.org
URL: http://www.cmfneo.org
Contact: Dave Douglas, Pres.
Founded: 1999. **Local.** Catholic men promoting spiritual growth, participation in parish-based faith sharing and fellowship groups. **Conventions/Meetings:** annual Answer The Call - conference.

16192 ■ Habitat for Humanity of Geauga County
PO Box 21
Newbury, OH 44065
Ph: (440)564-5848
Fax: (440)564-5808
E-mail: geaugahabitat@alltel.net
URL: http://www.habitatgeauga.org
Local. Affiliated With: Habitat for Humanity International.

16193 ■ Ohio Native Plant Society, Northeastern Ohio Chapter
10761 Pekin Rd.
Newbury, OH 44065-9762
Ph: (440)286-9504
E-mail: npsohio@hotmail.com
URL: http://groups.msn.com/NativePlantSocietyofNortheastOhio/_homepage
Contact: Judy Barnhart, Pres.
Local.

16194 ■ Western Reserve Kennel Club (WRKC)
c/o Ann Yuhasz, Corresponding Sec.
10606 Pekin Rd.
Newbury, OH 44065
E-mail: wrkcleve@core.com
URL: http://www.westernreservekc.com
Contact: Peg Gross, Pres.
Local. Affiliated With: American Kennel Club.

Newcomerstown

16195 ■ American Legion, Ohio Post 431
c/o Thomas C. Montgomery
1 Canal Ct.
Newcomerstown, OH 43832
Ph: (740)362-7478
Fax: (740)362-1429
URL: National Affiliate–www.legion.org
Contact: Thomas C. Montgomery, Contact
Local. Affiliated With: American Legion.

16196 ■ Briar Patch Beagle Club
c/o June Roe
604 S River St.
Newcomerstown, OH 43832-1448
URL: National Affiliate–www.akc.org
Contact: June Roe, Contact
Local. Affiliated With: American Kennel Club.

16197 ■ Newcomerstown Chamber of Commerce
PO Box 456
Newcomerstown, OH 43832-0456
Ph: (740)498-7244
Fax: (740)498-6310
E-mail: gjc@sota-oh.com
URL: National Affiliate–www.ohiochamber.com
Contact: Gary Chaney, Treas.
Local. Promotes business and community development in Newcomerstown, OH area.

16198 ■ Vietnam Veterans of America, Chapter No. 532 - Roger D. Lewis Memorial
c/o James Ross, Pres.
PO Box 129
Newcomerstown, OH 43832-0129
Ph: (740)498-8561
URL: http://www.vvabuckeyestatecouncil.com
Contact: James Ross, Pres.
Local. Affiliated With: Vietnam Veterans of America.

Newton Falls

16199 ■ American Legion, Newton Post 236
2025 E River Rd.
Newton Falls, OH 44444
Ph: (740)362-7478
Fax: (740)362-1429
URL: National Affiliate–www.legion.org
Local. Affiliated With: American Legion.

16200 ■ Reserve Officers Association - Department of Ohio, M.G. Geisman Chapter 46
c/o Capt. Frances M. Frantz, USAR, Pres.
5214 W Main St.
Newton Falls, OH 44444-1832
Ph: (330)872-0651 (330)872-7912
E-mail: saturns1@prodigy.net
URL: http://www.roa.org/oh
Contact: Capt. Frances M. Frantz USAR, Pres.
Local. Promotes and supports the development and execution of a military policy for the United States. Provides professional development seminars, workshops and programs for its members. **Affiliated With:** Reserve Officers Association of the United States.

16201 ■ Western Reserve Amateur Radio Association
c/o Randall L. Stokes
PO Box 481
Newton Falls, OH 44444-0481
Ph: (440)548-3352 (330)872-3727
Fax: (330)872-3727
E-mail: kc8ibr@msn.com
Contact: Ronald D. Miller, Contact
Founded: 1997. **Members:** 25. **Membership Dues:** $10 (annual). **Staff:** 5. **Budget:** $1,000. **Local. Subgroups:** Emergency Services.

Newtown

16202 ■ Ohio State African Violet Society
c/o Sharon Holtzman
6971 Olentangy Ln.
Newtown, OH 45244
Ph: (513)271-5678
E-mail: msviolet@att.net
URL: National Affiliate–www.avsa.org
Contact: Sharon Holtzman, Contact
State. Affiliated With: African Violet Society of America.

Ney

16203 ■ American Legion, Ney Community Post 680
PO Box 242
Ney, OH 43549
Ph: (740)362-7478
Fax: (740)362-1429
URL: National Affiliate–www.legion.org
Local. Affiliated With: American Legion.

Niles

16204 ■ American Legion, Ohio Post 106
823 Nancy Ave.
Niles, OH 44446
Ph: (740)362-7478
Fax: (740)362-1429
URL: National Affiliate–www.legion.org
Local. Affiliated With: American Legion.

16205 ■ Girl Scouts of Lake to River Council
980 Warren Ave.
Niles, OH 44446
Ph: (330)652-5876
Fax: (330)544-7959
Free: (800)362-9430
E-mail: contact@girlscoutslaketoriver.org
URL: http://www.girlscoutslaketoriver.org
Contact: Karen Conklin, CEO
Local. Young girls and adult volunteers, corporate, government and individual supporters. Strives to develop potential and leadership skills among its members. Conducts trainings, educational programs and outdoor activities.

16206 ■ International Brotherhood of Magicians, Ring 2
c/o Mr. Nick Verina, Sec.
1453 Kearney St.
Niles, OH 44446
Ph: (330)652-6506
E-mail: merlin44446@yahoo.com
Contact: Mr. Nick Verina, Sec.
Members: 50. **Membership Dues:** regular, $15 (annual). **Local.** Professional and semiprofessional magicians; suppliers, assistants, agents, and others interested in magic. Seeks to advance the art of magic in the field of amusement, entertainment, and culture. Promotes proper means of discouraging false or misleading advertising of effects, tricks, literature, merchandise, or actions appertaining to the magical arts; opposes exposures of principles of the art of magic, except in books on magic and magazines devoted to such art for the exclusive use of magicians and devotees of the art; encourages humane treatment and care of live animals whenever employed in magical performances. **Affiliated With:** International Brotherhood of Magicians.

16207 ■ Niles Lions Club
c/o Marian Nori, Sec.
2670 Deer Trail
Niles, OH 44446
Ph: (330)544-6820
E-mail: menamarian@aol.com
URL: http://www.lions13d.org
Contact: Marian Nori, Sec.
Local. Affiliated With: Lions Clubs International.

16208 ■ Trumbull County Convention and Visitors Bureau
650 Youngstown-Warren Rd.
Niles, OH 44446
Ph: (330)544-3468
Fax: (330)544-5615
Free: (800)672-9555
URL: http://www.trumbullcountycvb.org
Local.

16209 ■ Youngstown Air Reserve Base Community Council
c/o Richard F. Alberini
1201 Youngstown Warren Rd.
Niles, OH 44446-4615
Local.

North Baltimore

16210 ■ American Legion, North Baltimore Post 539
PO Box 243
North Baltimore, OH 45872
Ph: (740)362-7478
Fax: (740)362-1429
URL: National Affiliate–www.legion.org
Local. Affiliated With: American Legion.

16211 ■ North Baltimore Area Chamber of Commerce (NBACC)
PO Box 284
North Baltimore, OH 45872
Ph: (419)257-3523 (419)257-3514
E-mail: nboh@wcnet.org
Contact: Bonnie Knaggs, Pres.
Members: 75. **Membership Dues:** $40 (annual). **Local.** Businesses, professionals, organizations, and individuals. Promotes business and community development in the North Baltimore, OH area. Sponsors Good Old Summer Time Festival. **Publications:** none. **Awards:** Citizen of the Year. **Frequency:** annual. **Type:** monetary. **Conventions/Meetings:** biennial convention (exhibits) - always in April • monthly meeting.

North Canton

16212 ■ Akron-Canton Boxer Rescue of Ohio (ACBR)
c/o Debra M. Steidl
325 W Maple St.
North Canton, OH 44720-2717
Ph: (330)499-4418
E-mail: akroncantonboxerrescue@yahoo.com
URL: http://www.geocities.com/akroncantonboxerrescue/home.html
Contact: Debra M. Steidl, Contact
State.

16213 ■ American Cancer Society, Stark Area
925 S Main St.
North Canton, OH 44720
Ph: (330)497-7100
Fax: (330)966-0436
Free: (888)227-6446
E-mail: monica.miller@cancer.org
URL: http://www.cancer.org
Contact: Monica Miller, Contact
Local. Works to eliminate cancer as a major health problem through research, education, advocacy and service. **Affiliated With:** American Cancer Society.

16214 ■ American Chemical Society, Akron Section
c/o Daryl Lee Stein, Chair
6125 Sandy Ridge Cir. NW
North Canton, OH 44720-6689
Ph: (330)343-7711
E-mail: dstein1@neo.rr.com
URL: National Affiliate–acswebcontent.acs.org
Contact: Daryl Lee Stein, Chair
Local. Represents the interests of individuals dedicated to the advancement of chemistry in all its branches. Provides opportunities for peer interaction and career development. **Affiliated With:** American Chemical Society.

16215 ■ Building Industry Association of Stark County
c/o Joe Race
4345 Metro Cir. NW
North Canton, OH 44720-7715
Ph: (330)494-5700
Fax: (330)494-6665
E-mail: jrace@biastark.org
URL: http://www.biastark.com
Contact: Joe Race, Exec.Dir.
Local. Single and multifamily home builders, commercial builders, and others associated with the building industry. **Affiliated With:** National Association of Home Builders.

16216 ■ Girl Scouts - Great Trail Council
1010 Applegrove St. NW
North Canton, OH 44720
Ph: (330)433-9485
Fax: (330)499-4475
E-mail: greattrail@ezo.net
URL: http://www.greattrail.org
Local. Young girls and adult volunteers, corporate, government and individual supporters. Strives to develop potential and leadership skills among its members. Conducts trainings, educational programs and outdoor activities.

16217 ■ Inventors Council of Canton
c/o Frank Fleischer
303 55th St. NW
North Canton, OH 44720
Ph: (330)499-1262
E-mail: president@inventorscouncilofcanton.org
Local. Affiliated With: United Inventors Association of the U.S.A.

16218 ■ National Association of Miniature Enthusiasts - Society of Miniature Memories
c/o Ruthie Pay
2335 Greenburg Rd.
North Canton, OH 44720-1415
Ph: (330)899-0231
URL: http://www.miniatures.org/states/OH.html
Contact: Ruthie Pay, Contact
Local. Affiliated With: National Association of Miniature Enthusiasts.

16219 ■ North Canton Area Chamber of Commerce (NCACC)
121 S Main St.
North Canton, OH 44720-3021
Ph: (330)499-5100
Fax: (330)499-7181
E-mail: cathy@northcantonchamber.org
URL: http://www.northcantonchamber.org
Contact: Cathy Dunlap, Pres.
Founded: 1959. **Members:** 500. **Membership Dues:** business with less than 100 employees, $150-$250 (annual) • associate, $90 (annual) • business with more than 100 employees, $375 (annual). **Local.** Businesses, schools, churches, and individuals united to promote business in the North Canton, OH area. **Computer Services:** Online services, member directory. **Affiliated With:** Ohio Chamber of Commerce; U.S. Chamber of Commerce. **Publications:** Newsletter, bimonthly.

16220 ■ North Canton Lions Club
c/o Jim Puperi, Pres.
8344 Willowhurst Cir. NW
North Canton, OH 44720

Ph: (330)494-0672
E-mail: eripup@aol.com
URL: http://www.lions13d.org
Contact: Jim Puperi, Pres.
Local. Affiliated With: Lions Clubs International.

16221 ■ Ohio Association of Mortgage Brokers (OAMB)
c/o Mary Ellen Addessi, Administration VP/Board Consultant
170 Bancorp Bldg.
5686 Dressler Rd. NW
North Canton, OH 44720
Ph: (330)497-7233
Fax: (330)497-6533
Free: (800)218-OAMB
E-mail: mea@oamb.org
URL: http://www.oamb.org
Contact: Mary Ellen Addessi, Administration VP/Board Consultant
State.

16222 ■ Ohio State Skeet Association
PO Box 2393
North Canton, OH 44720
Ph: (330)492-5490
E-mail: ossatresurer@neo.rr.com
URL: National Affiliate–www.mynssa.com
State. Affiliated With: National Skeet Shooting Association.

16223 ■ Oldsmobile Club of America, Northern Ohio Chapter
c/o Mike Cibulas, Pres.
3560 Alpine St. NE
North Canton, OH 44721
Ph: (330)492-8154
E-mail: mcibulas@neo.rr.com
URL: http://www.northernohiooldsclub.com
Contact: Mike Cibulas, Pres.
Founded: 1972. **Membership Dues:** individual, $10 (annual). **Local. Affiliated With:** Oldsmobile Club of America. **Publications:** Newsletter, quarterly.

16224 ■ West Highland White Terrier Club of Northern Ohio
c/o Gary Hahn, Pres.
2795 Byron Dr.
North Canton, OH 44720
E-mail: mombales@aol.com
URL: http://www.geocities.com/petsburgh/yard/6266
Contact: Gary Hahn, Pres.
Regional.

North Fairfield

16225 ■ American Legion, Firelands Memorial Post 706
PO Box 204
North Fairfield, OH 44855
Ph: (740)362-7478
Fax: (740)362-1429
URL: National Affiliate–www.legion.org
Local. Affiliated With: American Legion.

16226 ■ American Legion, Fitchville Memorial Post 729
1488 State Rte. 162 E
North Fairfield, OH 44855
Ph: (740)362-7478
Fax: (740)362-1429
URL: National Affiliate–www.legion.org
Local. Affiliated With: American Legion.

16227 ■ North Fairfield Lions Club
c/o Dave Hicks, Pres.
136 Ridge Rd. N
North Fairfield, OH 44855
Ph: (419)744-2831
E-mail: hicks@accnorwalk.com
URL: http://www.lions13b.org
Contact: Dave Hicks, Pres.
Local. Affiliated With: Lions Clubs International.

North Hampton

16228 ■ Ohio Association of Independent Accountants (OAIA)
c/o Richard E. Ayers, EA, ATA, Exec.Dir.
PO Box 250
North Hampton, OH 45349-0250
Free: (800)926-3156
E-mail: ayresats@donet.com
URL: National Affiliate–www.nsacct.org
Contact: Richard E. Ayers EA, Exec.Dir.
State. Affiliated With: National Society of Accountants.

North Jackson

16229 ■ National Active and Retired Federal Employees Association - Charles Hogg 14
PO Box 638
North Jackson, OH 44451-0638
Ph: (330)547-3327
URL: National Affiliate–www.narfe.org
Contact: Frances Artin, Contact
Local. Protects the retirement future of employees through education. Informs members on issues affecting the retirement. **Affiliated With:** National Association of Retired Federal Employees.

16230 ■ Youngstown All Breed Training Club (YABTC)
PO Box 397
11801 Mahoning Ave.
North Jackson, OH 44451-0397
Ph: (330)538-2907
E-mail: perri@cboss.com
URL: http://yabtccom.temp.powweb.com
Contact: Perri Graf, Pres.
Founded: 1952. **Members:** 125. **Membership Dues:** applied, $60 (annual). **Local. Affiliated With:** American Kennel Club. **Publications:** *Wag-N-Tales*, monthly. Newsletter. **Advertising:** accepted. Alternate Formats: online.

North Kingsville

16231 ■ Ashtabula Lighthouse Restoration and Preservation Society
c/o Joe Santiana, Pres.
PO Box 221
North Kingsville, OH 44068
E-mail: straitliner@suite224.net
URL: http://www.ashtabulalighthouse.com
Contact: Joe Santiana, Pres.
Local.

16232 ■ Children's Rights Council of Northeast Ohio
2804 E Center St.
North Kingsville, OH 44068
Ph: (440)224-0694
URL: National Affiliate–www.gocrc.com
Local. Affiliated With: Children's Rights Council.

North Lewisburg

16233 ■ American Legion, Ohio Post 258
c/o Chester Mc Crery
PO Box 301
North Lewisburg, OH 43060
Ph: (740)362-7478
Fax: (740)362-1429
URL: National Affiliate–www.legion.org
Contact: Chester Mc Crery, Contact
Local. Affiliated With: American Legion.

North Olmsted

16234 ■ American Society of Appraisers, Akron - Cleveland Chapter
PO Box 363
North Olmsted, OH 44070
Ph: (216)222-3006
Fax: (216)222-3926
E-mail: roseoh@sbcglobal.net
URL: http://www.appraisers.org/akron_cleveland
Contact: Rose Rooney, Sec.
Local. Serves as a professional appraisal educator, testing and accrediting society. Sponsors mandatory recertification program for all members. Offers consumer information service to the public. **Affiliated With:** American Society of Appraisers.

16235 ■ Greater Cleveland Norwegian Elkhound Club (GCNEC)
c/o Katherine Ausse, Sec.
30924 Old Shore Dr.
North Olmsted, OH 44070
Ph: (440)779-0703
E-mail: causse@wideopenwest.com
URL: http://www.elkhounds.net/gcnec
Local.

16236 ■ North Olmsted Chamber of Commerce (NOCC)
25045 Lorain Rd.
North Olmsted, OH 44070-2054
Ph: (440)777-3368
Fax: (440)777-9361
E-mail: dsebri@leeca.org
URL: http://www.nolmstedchamber.org
Contact: John Sobolewski, Exec.Dir.
Founded: 1954. **Members:** 220. **Membership Dues:** business, $180-$500 (annual) • bank, utility, $500 (annual) • nonprofit organization, associate (non-voting), $100 (annual). **Staff:** 2. **Budget:** $35,000. **Local.** Businesses, industries, and individuals. Promotes business and community development in North Olmsted, OH. **Awards:** Scholarship Award. **Frequency:** annual. **Type:** scholarship. **Computer Services:** Online services, business directory. **Committees:** Awards; Legislation; Long Range Planning; Media Relations; Newsletter; Nominating; Programs; Website. **Affiliated With:** U.S. Chamber of Commerce. **Formerly:** North Olmsted Businessmen's Association. **Publications:** *Chamber Insider*, monthly. Newsletter. Features the latest information about chamber events, programs, committees, and initiatives. Alternate Formats: online • Directory, annual.

16237 ■ Northern Ohio Golf Association (NOGA)
One Golfview Ln.
North Olmsted, OH 44070
Ph: (440)686-1070
Fax: (440)686-1075
E-mail: noga@usga.org
URL: http://www.noga.org
Contact: Scotte Rorabaugh, Exec.Dir.
Founded: 1917. **Regional.** Conducts tournaments, holds seminars, and awards scholarships. **Affiliated With:** International Association of Golf Administrators.

16238 ■ Ohio Public Facilities Maintenance Association (OPFMA)
PO Box 835
North Olmsted, OH 44070
Ph: (440)716-8518
Fax: (440)716-8519
Free: (866)570-7880
E-mail: alexandra@opfma.org
URL: http://www.opfma.org
Contact: Alexandra Schneider, Administrator
Founded: 1987. **State. Telecommunication Services:** electronic mail, info@opfma.org.

16239 ■ Parmatown African Violet Club
c/o Pat Schreiber
25978 Tallwood Dr.
North Olmsted, OH 44070

Ph: (440)777-4558
E-mail: patschreiber@excite.com
URL: National Affiliate–www.avsa.org
Contact: Pat Schreiber, Contact
Local. Affiliated With: African Violet Society of America.

16240 ■ Union and League of RSA
c/o Georgeta Washington
23203 Lorain Rd.
North Olmsted, OH 44070-1625
E-mail: uleague@aol.com
URL: http://www.romaniansocieties.com
Local. Publications: *America*, monthly. Newsletter.

North Ridgeville

16241 ■ Greater Cleveland Council Figure Skating Club
5795 Tree Moss Ln.
North Ridgeville, OH 44039
Ph: (440)808-1995
Fax: (440)327-1094
E-mail: cleveskate@aol.com
URL: http://www.clevelandskating.com
Contact: Diane Murphy, Office Dir.
Local. Provides programs to encourage participation and achievement in the sport of figure skating on ice. Defines and maintains uniform standards of skating proficiency. Organizes and sponsors competitions and exhibitions for the purpose of stimulating interest in figure skating. **Affiliated With:** United States Figure Skating Association.

16242 ■ North Ridgeville Chamber of Commerce/Visitors Bureau
c/o Ms. Dayle Noll, Exec.Dir.
34845 Lorain Rd.
North Ridgeville, OH 44039-4448
Ph: (440)327-3737
Fax: (440)327-1474
E-mail: nrcoc@nrchamber.com
URL: http://www.nrchamber.com
Contact: Ms. Dayle Noll, Exec.Dir.
Founded: 1976. **Members:** 200. **Membership Dues:** individual, $100 (annual) • business, $200 (annual). **Staff:** 1. **Local.** Advances the commercial, industrial, civic, professional and general business interests of the city; to strive for a stable and dynamic economy; and to encourage a unified public spirit of all citizens and groups in the interest of the general welfare. **Publications:** Newsletter, monthly. **Conventions/Meetings:** monthly board meeting - first Thursday • monthly meeting - third Thursday.

16243 ■ North Ridgeville Lions Club
c/o Dick Brent, Pres.
8659 Harris Dr.
North Ridgeville, OH 44039
Ph: (440)740-2437
E-mail: dbrent8659@hotmail.com
URL: http://www.lions13b.org
Contact: Dick Brent, Pres.
Local. Affiliated With: Lions Clubs International.

North Royalton

16244 ■ Buckeye Vintage Thunderbird Club of Ohio
15044 Highland Dr.
North Royalton, OH 44133
Ph: (440)582-3589
E-mail: birds2nv@aol.com
URL: National Affiliate–www.vintagethunderbirdclub.org
Local. Affiliated With: Vintage Thunderbird Club International.

16245 ■ Forestwood Figure Skating Club of Parma Ohio
14160 Heather Ln.
North Royalton, OH 44133
E-mail: lorimargevicius@wideopenwest.com
URL: National Affiliate–www.usfigureskating.org
Contact: Lori Margevicius, Contact
Local. Provides programs to encourage participation and achievement in the sport of figure skating on ice. Defines and maintains uniform standards of skating proficiency. Organizes and sponsors competitions and exhibitions for the purpose of stimulating interest in figure skating. **Affiliated With:** United States Figure Skating Association.

16246 ■ North Royalton Chamber of Commerce (NRCC)
13737 State Rd.
PO Box 33122
North Royalton, OH 44133
Ph: (440)237-6180
Fax: (440)237-6181
E-mail: rrnews@aol.com
Contact: Ronald Matye, Pres.
Founded: 1918. **Members:** 210. **Local.** Promotes business and community development in North Royalton, OH. Sponsors monthly luncheons, after-hours networking, Community Festival, Golf Outing, Community School Breakfast, Mayor's State of the City Address. **Awards: Type:** scholarship. **Publications:** *Royalton Recorder*, semimonthly. Newspaper. **Conventions/Meetings:** periodic meeting.

16247 ■ North Royalton Lions Club
PO Box 33123
North Royalton, OH 44133
E-mail: nrlions@aol.com
URL: http://www.northroyaltonlions.org
Contact: Doug Demian, Pres.
Local. Affiliated With: Lions Clubs International.

16248 ■ North Royalton - Young Life
11680 Royalton Rd.
North Royalton, OH 44133
Ph: (440)237-7958
URL: http://sites.younglife.org/sites/NorthRoyalton/default.aspx
Contact: Hollie Fish, Contact
Local. Affiliated With: Young Life.

16249 ■ Royalton Hills Lions Club
PO Box 33476
North Royalton, OH 44133
Ph: (440)717-0031
E-mail: royaltonhills@aol.com
URL: http://royaltonhillsoh.lionwap.org
Contact: Pat Worton, Pres.
Local. Affiliated With: Lions Clubs International.

16250 ■ Sheet Metal and Air Conditioning Contractors' National Association - Cleveland
c/o James L. Shoaff
6058 Royalton Rd.
Royalton Plz.
North Royalton, OH 44133-5104
Ph: (440)877-3500
Fax: (440)877-3502
E-mail: smacnacle@aol.com
URL: National Affiliate–www.smacna.org
Contact: James L. Shoaff, Contact
Local. Affiliated With: Sheet Metal and Air Conditioning Contractors' National Association.

16251 ■ Western Reserve Insulator Club
c/o John Hovanec
PO Box 33661
North Royalton, OH 44133
Ph: (440)237-2242
E-mail: wric@clubs.insulators.com
URL: http://www.insulators.com/clubs/wric.htm
Contact: John Hovanec, Contact
Founded: 1999. **Membership Dues:** individual age of 16, $2 (annual) • adult, family, $7 (annual). **Regional. Affiliated With:** National Insulator Association. **Publications:** *Twiggs Times*, quarterly. Newsletter.

16252 ■ Young Life Cleveland South
11680 Royalton Rd.
North Royalton, OH 44133
Ph: (440)237-7958
Fax: (440)237-6992
E-mail: kevin@clevelandsouth.younglife.org
URL: http://sites.younglife.org/sites/ClevelandSouth/default.aspx
Contact: Kevin Sorg, Contact
Local. Affiliated With: Young Life.

North Star

16253 ■ American Legion, Buckeye Post 174
PO Box 67
North Star, OH 45350
Ph: (740)362-7478
Fax: (740)362-1429
URL: National Affiliate–www.legion.org
Local. Affiliated With: American Legion.

Northfield

16254 ■ Nordonia Hills Chamber of Commerce
PO Box 34
Northfield, OH 44067-0034
Ph: (330)467-8956
Fax: (330)468-4901
E-mail: laura@nordoniahillschamber.org
URL: http://www.nordoniahillschamber.org
Contact: Laura Sparano, Exec.Dir.
Membership Dues: business (based on number of employees), $160-$1,000 (annual) • associate, $100 (annual) • individual, retiree, religious/service organization, second business, $75 (annual) • government agency, $150 (annual) • resident, $50 (annual). **Local.** Promotes business and community development in the Northfield, OH area. **Telecommunication Services:** electronic mail, chamber@nordoniahillschamber.org. **Publications:** Newsletter, bimonthly.

16255 ■ Rough Rangers Off Road club (RRORC)
c/o Sean Campbell, Sec.
PO Box 670160
Northfield, OH 44067
Ph: (330)908-0254
E-mail: chubby@rrorc.com
URL: http://www.rrorc.com
Contact: Sean Campbell, Sec.
Local. Affiliated With: United Four-Wheel Drive Associations.

Northwood

16256 ■ Safety Council of Northwest Ohio (SCNWO)
8015 Rinker Pointe Ct.
Northwood, OH 43619
Ph: (419)662-7777
Fax: (419)662-8888
Free: (877)457-1818
E-mail: mail@scnwo.com
URL: http://www.scnwo.com
Contact: Dennis W. McMickens, Pres.
Founded: 1960. **Members:** 350. **Membership Dues:** business (1-75 employees), $125 (annual) • business (76-200 employees), $250 (annual) • business (201 or more employees), $375 (annual). **Staff:** 4. **State Groups:** 1. **Regional.** Improves the quality of life through enhancement of the safety and health of people, the economy, and the environment and by providing education and resources to Northwest Ohio. **Libraries: Type:** not open to the public. **Holdings:** 500; video recordings. **Subjects:** safety issues on

and off the job. **Awards:** Certificate of Appreciation. **Frequency:** annual. **Type:** recognition. **Recipient:** life saving attempt • Good Samaritan. **Frequency:** annual. **Type:** recognition • Hero. **Frequency:** annual. **Type:** recognition. **Recipient:** those who go above and beyond the norm to help those in harms way. **Formerly:** Toledo Lucas County Safety Council. **Publications:** *The Safety Source*, bimonthly. Newsletter. **Price:** free. **Conventions/Meetings:** annual Safety Day in Toledo - conference, presented and coordinated by professional volunteers; more than 20 specialty sessions throughout the day and over 30 vendors all in one place plus a keynote speaker to open the program.

Norton

16257 ■ Tasters Guild International - Akron, Chapter No. 079
3044 Wadsworth Rd.
Norton, OH 44203
Ph: (330)825-8280
E-mail: milkovichmike@yahoo.com
URL: National Affiliate–www.tastersguild.com
Contact: Michael Milkovich, Contact
Local. Aims to educate consumers and spread the word of responsible wine and food consumption. Provides opportunity to encounter the best in wine and culinary delights. **Affiliated With:** Tasters Guild International.

Norwalk

16258 ■ American Legion, Ken-Bur-Bel Post 41
1544 US Rte. 20 W
Norwalk, OH 44857
Ph: (740)362-7478
Fax: (740)362-1429
URL: National Affiliate–www.legion.org
Local. Affiliated With: American Legion.

16259 ■ American Lung Association of Ohio, Northwest Branch (ALAOSSB)
c/o Patricia J. Volz, Exec.Dir.
226 State Rte. 61
Norwalk, OH 44857-9705
Ph: (419)663-5864
Fax: (419)668-2575
Free: (800)231-5864
E-mail: pjvolz@ohiolung.org
URL: http://www.ohiolung.org
Contact: Patricia J. Volz, Exec.Dir.
Founded: 1903. **Members:** 8. **Staff:** 4. **Budget:** $375,000. **Local.** Physicians, nurses, and laymen in north central Ohio. Promotes the prevention and control of lung disease; conducts research and educational activities. **Libraries: Type:** open to the public. **Holdings:** articles. **Subjects:** lung health. **Affiliated With:** American Lung Association. **Formerly:** South Shore Lung Association; (2004) American Lung Association of Ohio, South Shore Branch. **Publications:** Newsletter, semiannual. **Price:** free • Newsletter, bimonthly. For patients.

16260 ■ Easter Seals Northwestern Ohio
226 State Rte. 61 E
Norwalk, OH 44857
Ph: (419)668-6791
Fax: (419)663-4529
Free: (800)696-5601
E-mail: ksolomon@eastersealsnwohio.org
URL: http://www.nwohio.easterseals.com
Contact: Mrs. Karen Solomon, Home Care Coor.
Local. Provides services for children and adults with disabilities or special needs, and supports their families. **Affiliated With:** Easter Seals.

16261 ■ National Active and Retired Federal Employees Association - Firelands 382
1500 Ridge Rd. N
Norwalk, OH 44857-9740
Ph: (419)668-8726
URL: National Affiliate–www.narfe.org
Contact: Mary A. Newland, Contact
Local. Protects the retirement future of employees through education. Informs members on issues affecting the retirement. **Affiliated With:** National Association of Retired Federal Employees.

16262 ■ Norwalk Area Chamber of Commerce (NACC)
10 W Main St.
Norwalk, OH 44857
Ph: (419)668-4155
Fax: (419)663-6173
E-mail: chamber@accnorwalk.com
URL: http://www.norwalkareachamber.com
Contact: Melissa James, Exec.Dir.
Founded: 1938. **Members:** 306. **Staff:** 2. **Local.** Promotes the general welfare and prosperity of the citizens, businesses, and industries of the Norwalk, OH area. **Publications:** Book, annual. **Price:** free for members • Newsletter, monthly.

16263 ■ Norwalk Lions Club
c/o Jon Christman, Pres.
34 Marshall St.
Norwalk, OH 44857
Ph: (419)663-7834
URL: http://www.lions13b.org
Contact: Jon Christman, Pres.
Local. Affiliated With: Lions Clubs International.

16264 ■ Ohio Genealogical Society, Huron County Chapter
PO Box 923
Norwalk, OH 44857-0923
E-mail: tito@accnorwalk.com
URL: http://www.rootsweb.com/~ohhuron
Contact: Tom Neel, Pres.
Founded: 1986. **Membership Dues:** single, $10 (annual) • joint, $12 (annual) • student, $2 (annual) • life, $200. **Local. Awards: Frequency:** annual. **Type:** recognition. **Recipient:** for ancestors proven to be in Huron County by 1850; for Civil War families of Huron County. **Affiliated With:** Ohio Genealogical Society. **Publications:** *Kinologist*, quarterly. Newsletter. **Price:** included in membership dues. **Conventions/Meetings:** monthly meeting - always fourth Monday except December.

Norwood

16265 ■ American Legion, Ohio Post 123
c/o Leland M. Barnett
5129 Montgomery Rd.
Norwood, OH 45212
Ph: (740)362-7478
Fax: (740)362-1429
URL: National Affiliate–www.legion.org
Contact: Leland M. Barnett, Contact
Local. Affiliated With: American Legion.

16266 ■ International Brotherhood of Magicians, Ring 71
c/o David Jones, Pres.
2514 Leslie Ave.
Norwood, OH 45212-4206
Ph: (513)531-6548 (513)561-1060
Fax: (513)531-0707
E-mail: ibmring71@gmail.com
URL: http://www.ring71.com
Contact: David Jones, Pres.
Local. Professional and semi-professional magicians; suppliers, assistants, agents, and others interested in magic. Seeks to advance the art of magic in the field of amusement, entertainment, and culture. Promotes proper means of discouraging false or misleading advertising of effects, tricks, literature, merchandise, or actions appertaining to the magical arts; opposes exposures of principles of the art of magic, except in books on magic and magazines devoted to such art for the exclusive use of magicians and devotees of the art; encourages humane treatment and care of live animals whenever employed in magical performances. **Affiliated With:** International Brotherhood of Magicians.

Nova

16267 ■ American Legion, Lucas Vaughn Post 219
336 Tr. 791
Nova, OH 44859
Ph: (740)362-7478
Fax: (740)362-1429
URL: National Affiliate–www.legion.org
Local. Affiliated With: American Legion.

16268 ■ Nova Lions Club
c/o Kenneth Myers, Pres.
950 Township Rd. 150
Nova, OH 44859
Ph: (419)652-3861
E-mail: aharsar@bright.net
URL: http://www.lions13b.org
Contact: Kenneth Myers, Pres.
Local. Affiliated With: Lions Clubs International.

Oak Harbor

16269 ■ American Legion, Ohio Post 114
c/o John A. Fader
221 W Park St.
Oak Harbor, OH 43449
Ph: (740)362-7478
Fax: (740)362-1429
URL: National Affiliate–www.legion.org
Contact: John A. Fader, Contact
Local. Affiliated With: American Legion.

16270 ■ American Society of Farm Managers and Rural Appraisers Ohio Chapter
c/o Gary Pfeiffer, Pres.
1867 N Benton Carroll
Oak Harbor, OH 43449
Ph: (419)898-0914
Fax: (419)898-7410
E-mail: gpfeiffer@coastalwave.net
URL: National Affiliate–www.asfmra.org
Contact: Gary Pfeiffer, Pres.
State. Affiliated With: American Society of Farm Managers and Rural Appraisers.

16271 ■ Black Swamp Angus Association
c/o John Moore, Pres.
2865 North St., Rte. 19
Oak Harbor, OH 43449
Ph: (419)898-1526
URL: National Affiliate–www.angus.org
Contact: John Moore, Pres.
Local. Affiliated With: American Angus Association.

16272 ■ National Active and Retired Federal Employees Association - Vacationland 1030
207 Portage St.
Oak Harbor, OH 43449-1439
Ph: (419)898-6065
URL: National Affiliate–www.narfe.org
Contact: Carolyn S. Baldwin, Contact
Local. Protects the retirement future of employees through education. Informs members on issues affecting the retirement. **Affiliated With:** National Association of Retired Federal Employees.

16273 ■ Oak Harbor Area Chamber of Commerce (OHACC)
178 W Water St.
Oak Harbor, OH 43449
Ph: (419)898-0479
Fax: (419)898-2429
E-mail: chamber@oakharborohio.net
URL: http://www.oakharborohio.net
Contact: Lisa Hoover, Exec.Dir.
Founded: 1970. **Members:** 120. **Local.** Promotes business and community development in the Oak Harbor, OH area. **Publications:** *Chamber Chatter*,

periodic. Newsletter. **Advertising:** accepted. **Conventions/Meetings:** monthly board meeting - always 3rd Thursday.

16274 ■ Oak Harbor Lions Club
c/o Chris DeTray, Pres.
2520 S State Rte. 19
Oak Harbor, OH 43449
Ph: (419)898-9074
E-mail: cdetray@crosserfuneralhome.com
URL: http://www.lions13b.org
Contact: Chris DeTray, Pres.
Local. Affiliated With: Lions Clubs International.

Oak Hill

16275 ■ American Legion, Kent-Metzler Post 261
PO Box 47
Oak Hill, OH 45656
Ph: (740)362-7478
Fax: (740)362-1429
URL: National Affiliate–www.legion.org
Local. Affiliated With: American Legion.

Oakwood

16276 ■ American Legion, Giltz-Brown Post 341
621 Walnut St.
Oakwood, OH 45873
Ph: (740)362-7478
Fax: (740)362-1429
URL: National Affiliate–www.legion.org
Local. Affiliated With: American Legion.

Oakwood Village

16277 ■ Northern Ohio Beagle Club
c/o Tom Kormanec
23307 Alexander Rd.
Oakwood Village, OH 44146-6251
URL: National Affiliate–clubs.akc.org
Contact: Tom Kormanec, Contact
Local.

Oberlin

16278 ■ American Legion, Ohio Post 102
c/o Karl Wilson Locke
25 W Coll. St.
Oberlin, OH 44074
Ph: (740)362-7478
Fax: (740)362-1429
URL: National Affiliate–www.legion.org
Contact: Karl Wilson Locke, Contact
Local. Affiliated With: American Legion.

16279 ■ American Legion, Ohio Post 656
c/o Willard B. Holmes
200 N Park St.
Oberlin, OH 44074
Ph: (740)362-7478
Fax: (740)362-1429
URL: National Affiliate–www.legion.org
Contact: Willard B. Holmes, Contact
Local. Affiliated With: American Legion.

16280 ■ Association for Computing Machinery, Oberlin College
c/o Rhys Price Jones, Sponsor
King 223C
10 N. Professor St.
Oberlin, OH 44074-1019
Ph: (216)775-8697
Fax: (216)775-8124
E-mail: rhyspj@cs.oberlin.edu
URL: http://www.cs.oberlin.edu/
Affiliated With: Association for Computing Machinery.

16281 ■ First Catholic Slovak Ladies Association - Elyria Junior Branch 478
189 W Coll. St., Apt. E
Oberlin, OH 44074-1573
Ph: (440)775-0371
URL: National Affiliate–www.fcsla.com
Local. Affiliated With: First Catholic Slovak Ladies Association.

16282 ■ First Catholic Slovak Ladies Association - Elyria Senior Branch 476
189 W Coll. St., Apt. E
Oberlin, OH 44074
Ph: (440)775-0371
URL: National Affiliate–www.fcsla.com
Local. Affiliated With: First Catholic Slovak Ladies Association.

16283 ■ Lorain County Farm Bureau
PO Box 0157
Oberlin, OH 44074-0157
Ph: (440)774-2211
Fax: (440)775-2921
E-mail: cward@ofbf.org
Contact: Connie Ward, Organization Dir.
Local.

16284 ■ Main Street Oberlin
20 E Coll. St.
Oberlin, OH 44074
Ph: (440)774-6262
Fax: (440)775-2423
E-mail: oberlinchamber@oberlin.net
URL: http://www.oberlin.org
Local.

16285 ■ National Federation of the Blind of Ohio
c/o Barbara Pierce, Pres.
237 Oak St.
Oberlin, OH 44074-1517
Ph: (440)775-2216
E-mail: bbpierce@pobox.com
URL: http://www.nfbohio.org
Contact: Barbara Pierce, Pres.
State. Works to help blind persons achieve self-confidence and self-respect. Acts as a vehicle for collective self-expression by the blind. Provides education, information and referral services, scholarships, literature, and publications about blindness.

16286 ■ National Organization for Women - Oberlin
c/o Marion Campbell, Pres.
44 Walnut St.
Oberlin, OH 44074
Ph: (419)668-9187
E-mail: negrophile@aol.com
URL: http://www.ohionow.org
Contact: Marion Campbell, Pres.
Local. Affiliated With: National Organization for Women.

16287 ■ Oberlin African-American Genealogy and History Group
c/o Phyllis Yarber Hogan, VP
M.P.O. 09374
Oberlin, OH 44074-0374
E-mail: oberlinaagenealogy@afrigeneas.net
URL: http://www.geocities.com/oberlinaagenealogy
Contact: Phyllis Yarber Hogan, VP
Local.

16288 ■ Oberlin Area Chamber of Commerce
20 E Coll. St.
Oberlin, OH 44074
Ph: (440)774-6262
Fax: (440)775-2423
E-mail: oberlinchamber@oberlin.net
URL: http://www.oberlin.org
Contact: Ron Pierre, Pres.
Members: 170. **Membership Dues:** business (based on number of employees), $150-$800 (annual) • individual, household, $50 (annual). **Local.** Aims to advance the general welfare and prosperity of Oberlin area.

16289 ■ Oberlin College Flaming Blades (OCFC)
Wilder Box 77
135 W Lorain St.
Oberlin, OH 44074
Ph: (440)774-3261
E-mail: flamingblades@fencingmail.com
URL: http://www.oberlin.edu/~fencing
Local. Amateur fencers. **Affiliated With:** United States Fencing Association. **Formerly:** (2005) Oberlin College Fencing Club.

16290 ■ Oberlin College National Organization for the Reform of Marijuana Laws
c/o Blake Wilder
Wilder Box 60
135 W Lorain
Oberlin, OH 44074
E-mail: ocnorml@oberlin.edu
URL: National Affiliate–www.norml.org
Contact: Jami Creason, Sec.
Local. Affiliated With: National Organization for the Reform of Marijuana Laws.

16291 ■ Ohio Health Care Association, District 5
c/o Jill Herron, Chair
Welcome Nursing Home
417 S Main St.
Oberlin, OH 44074
Ph: (440)775-1491
Fax: (440)774-3378
E-mail: jherron@verizon.net
URL: http://www.ohca.org
Contact: Jill Herron, Chair
Local. Promotes professionalism and ethical behavior of individuals providing long-term care delivery for patients and for the general public. Provides information, education and administrative tools to enhance the quality of long-term care. Improves the standards of service and administration of member nursing homes. **Affiliated With:** American Health Care Association.

16292 ■ Parents for Public Schools, Oberlin Chapter
372 Elm St.
Oberlin, OH 44074
Ph: (440)774-1566
URL: National Affiliate–www.parents4publicschools.com
Contact: Debbi Walsh, Co-Chair
Local.

Ohio City

16293 ■ American Legion, Ohio Post 346
c/o Harvey Lewis
306 Lambert St.
Ohio City, OH 45874
Ph: (740)362-7478
Fax: (740)362-1429
URL: National Affiliate–www.legion.org
Contact: Harvey Lewis, Contact
Local. Affiliated With: American Legion.

Old Fort

16294 ■ Old Fort Lions Club
c/o Robert Colson, Sec.
PO Box 242
Old Fort, OH 44861
Ph: (419)992-4773
E-mail: ninefe66@hotmail.com
URL: http://www.lions13b.org
Contact: Robert Colson, Sec.
Local. Affiliated With: Lions Clubs International.

Olmsted Falls

16295 ■ American Legion, Community Post 403
PO Box 38403
Olmsted Falls, OH 44138
Ph: (740)362-7478
Fax: (740)362-1429
URL: National Affiliate–www.legion.org
Local. Affiliated With: American Legion.

16296 ■ American Legion, Strongsville Post 795
26948 Adele Ln.
Olmsted Falls, OH 44138
Ph: (740)362-7478
Fax: (740)362-1429
URL: National Affiliate–www.legion.org
Local. Affiliated With: American Legion.

16297 ■ First Catholic Slovak Ladies Association - North Olmsted Junior Branch 499
27328 Bagley Rd.
Olmsted Falls, OH 44138-1009
Ph: (440)235-5414
URL: National Affiliate–www.fcsla.com
Local. Affiliated With: First Catholic Slovak Ladies Association.

16298 ■ First Catholic Slovak Ladies Association - North Olmsted Senior Branch 573
27328 Bagley Rd.
Olmsted Falls, OH 44138
Ph: (440)235-5414
URL: National Affiliate–www.fcsla.com
Local. Affiliated With: First Catholic Slovak Ladies Association.

16299 ■ Ohio District, The Lutheran Church-Missouri Synod
PO Box 38277
Olmsted Falls, OH 44138-0277
Ph: (440)235-2297
Fax: (440)235-1970
E-mail: albrechtk@oh.lcms.org
URL: http://www.oh.lcms.org
Contact: Rev. Ronald Bergen, Pres.
Regional.

Oregon

16300 ■ AAA Northwest Ohio
3237 Navarre Ave.
Oregon, OH 43616
Ph: (419)691-2439
Local.

16301 ■ American Legion, Ohio Post 537
c/o Christ Dunberger
4925 Pickle Rd.
Oregon, OH 43616
Ph: (740)362-7478
Fax: (740)362-1429
URL: National Affiliate–www.legion.org
Contact: Christ Dunberger, Contact
Local. Affiliated With: American Legion.

16302 ■ Eastern Maumee Bay Chamber of Commerce
4209 Corduroy Rd.
Oregon, OH 43616
Ph: (419)693-5580
Fax: (419)693-9990
E-mail: director@embchamber.org
URL: http://www.embchamber.org
Contact: Deb Warnke, Exec.Dir.
Membership Dues: senior citizen, $50 (annual) • non-business individual, $65 (annual) • franchise manager (base), $70 (annual) • business (based on number of employees), $135-$375 (annual). **Local.** Strives to improve the quality of life, general welfare and prosperity of Eastern Maumee Bay community. **Publications:** *Chamber Hi-Lites*, monthly. Newsletter.

16303 ■ Northwest Ohio Dietary Managers Association
c/o Rebecca J. Massey, CDM
2326 Taft Ave.
Oregon, OH 43616
Ph: (419)693-2071 (419)698-4331
URL: http://www.nwdma.com
Contact: Rebecca J. Massey CDM, Contact
Local. Represents dietary managers. Maintains a high level of competency and quality in dietary departments through continuing education. Provides optimum nutritional care through foodservice management. **Affiliated With:** Dietary Managers Association.

16304 ■ Toledo Industrial Recreation and Employee Services Council (TIRES)
2460 Navarre Ave., Ste.8
Oregon, OH 43616
Ph: (419)691-5060
Fax: (419)691-5061
E-mail: tires@solarstop.net
URL: http://www.tires-toledo.com
Contact: Carol McGowan, Pres.
Founded: 1970. **Members:** 420. **Membership Dues:** regular, $275 (annual). **Staff:** 3. **Budget:** $108,000. **Local Groups:** 1. **Local.** Companies, government agencies, schools and universities, hospitals, and community service organizations. Promotes positive relations between employers and employees. **Libraries: Type:** not open to the public. **Holdings:** 30; articles, books, periodicals. **Awards:** Melvin Byers Scholarship. **Frequency:** annual. **Type:** scholarship. **Recipient:** to a graduating senior, son or daughter of a member. **Publications:** *'Round TIRES*, monthly. Newsletter. **Price:** included in membership dues. Alternate Formats: online • *TIRES Services Directory*, semiannual. **Conventions/Meetings:** monthly meeting - always third Tuesday.

16305 ■ Veterans of Foreign Wars 9816
1802 Ashcroft Dr.
Oregon, OH 43618
Ph: (419)698-8178
Local.

16306 ■ Vintage Chevrolet Club of America, Glass Capitol Region No. 7
c/o Harold Cuthbertson, Dir.
PO Box 167211
Oregon, OH 43616
Ph: (419)351-1427
URL: National Affiliate–www.vcca.org
Contact: Harold Cuthbertson, Dir.
Local. Affiliated With: Vintage Chevrolet Club of America.

Orrville

16307 ■ American Legion, Ohio Post 282
c/o Frank E. Cook
237 E Market St.
Orrville, OH 44667
Ph: (740)362-7478
Fax: (740)362-1429
URL: National Affiliate–www.legion.org
Contact: Frank E. Cook, Contact
Local. Affiliated With: American Legion.

16308 ■ NAIFA-Wayne Holmes
c/o Tom Gregory
PO Box 3
Orrville, OH 44667
Ph: (330)683-1050
Fax: (330)683-1169
E-mail: andyb@hummelgrp.com
URL: National Affiliate–naifa.org
Contact: Tom Gregory, Contact
Local. Represents the interests of insurance and financial advisors. Advocates for a positive legislative and regulatory environment. Enhances business and professional skills of members. **Affiliated With:** National Association of Insurance and Financial Advisors.

16309 ■ Orrville Area United Way
PO Box 214
Orrville, OH 44667-0214
Ph: (330)683-8181
Fax: (330)683-4021
E-mail: meyers330@earthlink.net
URL: http://www.orrvilleareaunitedway.org
Contact: Helen V. Meyers, Exec.Dir.
Founded: 1958. **Members:** 24. **Staff:** 2. **Budget:** $389,637. **Local.** Strives to make Dalton, Marshallville, Orrville, and surrounding areas better places to live by partnering with Wayne County social service agencies to raise, allocate, and expend funds for needed services in a fiscally responsible manner; continuously evaluate and improve these services; communicate their availability; and encourage social service volunteerism. **Awards:** Manges Memorial Scholarship. **Frequency:** annual. **Type:** scholarship. **Recipient:** for volunteerism. **Affiliated With:** United Way of America. **Publications:** *Directory of Partner Agencies*, annual. **Conventions/Meetings:** monthly board meeting.

16310 ■ Paper, Allied-Industrial, Chemical and Energy Workers International Union, AFL-CIO, CLC - Local Union 801
2056 Portage Rd.
Orrville, OH 44667-1833
E-mail: mburgess@pacelocal4-801.com
URL: http://www.pacelocal4-801.com
Contact: Ben Johnson, Pres.
Members: 379. **Local. Affiliated With:** Pace International Union.

16311 ■ Phi Theta Kappa - Alpha Zeta Chi Chapter
c/o Michele Turner
Wayne Coll.
1901 Smucker Rd.
Orrville, OH 44667
Ph: (330)972-8925
E-mail: cmt@uakron.edu
URL: http://www.ptk.org/directories/chapters/OH/317-1.htm
Contact: Michele Turner, Advisor
Local. Affiliated With: Phi Theta Kappa, International Honor Society.

16312 ■ Professional Grounds Management Society, Midwest Region
c/o Gene Pouly, Dir.
E.F. Pouly Co.
9088 Back Orrville Rd.
Orrville, OH 44667
Ph: (330)683-2037
Fax: (330)683-3530
E-mail: poulygene@aol.com
URL: http://www.efpouly.com
Contact: Lorna Duskey, Sec.
Local. Affiliated With: Professional Grounds Management Society.

Orwell

16313 ■ American Legion, Orwell Memorial Post 719
215 N Maple St.
Orwell, OH 44076
Ph: (740)362-7478
Fax: (740)362-1429
URL: National Affiliate–www.legion.org
Local. Affiliated With: American Legion.

Osgood

16314 ■ American Legion, Osgood Post 588
PO Box 121
Osgood, OH 45351
Ph: (740)362-7478
Fax: (740)362-1429
URL: National Affiliate–www.legion.org
Local. Affiliated With: American Legion.

Ottawa

16315 ■ American Legion, Kerner-Slusser Post 63
218 W Main St.
Ottawa, OH 45875
Ph: (740)362-7478
Fax: (740)362-1429
URL: National Affiliate–www.legion.org
Local. Affiliated With: American Legion.

16316 ■ Ohio Farmers Union
c/o Joseph Logan, Pres.
PO Box 363
Ottawa, OH 45875
Ph: (419)523-5300
Fax: (419)523-5913
Free: (800)321-3671
E-mail: ottawa@ohfarmersunion.org
URL: http://www.ohfarmersunion.org
Contact: Steve Maurer, Exec.Dir.
Founded: 1974. **Members:** 8,000. **Membership Dues:** $35 (annual). **Staff:** 13. **Budget:** $780,000. **Local Groups:** 1. **State**. Works for legislation that puts profit back in family agriculture. Promotes improved economic prospects for family farms. Conducts legislative, cooperative, and educational programs. **Libraries: Type:** open to the public. **Subjects:** agriculture, health, safety. **Awards:** Essay Contest. **Frequency:** annual. **Type:** scholarship. **Affiliated With:** National Farmers Union. **Publications:** *Ohio Union Farmer*, monthly. Newsletter. **Price:** $35. 00/year. **Circulation:** 8,000. **Conventions/Meetings:** annual convention - January or February; Avg. Attendance: 350.

16317 ■ Ohio Genealogical Society, Putnam County
PO Box 403
Ottawa, OH 45875-0403
E-mail: putnamgenalogy@yahoo.com
URL: http://www.putnamgenealogy.com
Contact: Linda Hermiller, Pres.
Founded: 1984. **Members:** 190. **Membership Dues:** individual, $10 (annual) • double, $12 (annual) • life, $110 • junior, $5 (annual). **Local**. Individuals interested in the history and genealogy of Putnam County, OH. Gathers, preserves, and disseminates genealogical and historical information. **Additional Websites:** http://www.ogs.org. **Affiliated With:** Ohio Genealogical Society. **Formerly:** (2004) Ohio Genealogical Society, Putnam County Chapter. **Publications:** *Cemetery*. Books • *Putnam Pastfinder*, quarterly. Newsletter. **Price:** included in membership dues. **Conventions/Meetings:** monthly general assembly.

16318 ■ Ottawa Area Chamber of Commerce
129 Court St.
PO Box 68
Ottawa, OH 45875
Ph: (419)523-3141
Fax: (419)523-5860
E-mail: ottawachamber@earthlink.net
URL: http://www.ottawaohiochamber.com
Contact: Mary Bockrath, Exec.Dir.
Founded: 1950. **Members:** 278. **Local**. Promotes businesses in Ottawa, OH. Provides resources, referrals and promotional opportunities to members.

16319 ■ Ottawa Lions Club
PO Box 281
Ottawa, OH 45875
Ph: (419)523-5526
E-mail: ottawalions@yahoo.com
URL: http://ottawaoh.lionwap.org
Contact: Carol Schnipke, Pres.
Local. Affiliated With: Lions Clubs International.

16320 ■ United Way of Putnam County, Ohio
PO Box 472
Ottawa, OH 45875
Ph: (419)523-4505
E-mail: unitedway@bright.net
URL: http://www.unitedwaypc.com
Contact: Jeanne Beutler, Contact
Local. Affiliated With: United Way of America.

Owensville

16321 ■ Northeastern Lions Club
457 Broadway
Owensville, OH 45160
Ph: (513)625-9268 (513)831-2274
E-mail: kermitjr@cinci.rr.com
URL: http://northeasternoh.lionwap.org
Contact: Kermit Beckworth Jr., Pres.
Local. Affiliated With: Lions Clubs International.

16322 ■ Ruffed Grouse Society, Gilbert R. Symons Chapter
c/o Mark Sabo
309 E Main St.
Owensville, OH 45160
Ph: (513)732-0950
E-mail: sabomj@aol.com
URL: National Affiliate–www.ruffedgrousesociety.org
Contact: Mark Sabo, Contact
Local. Affiliated With: Ruffed Grouse Society.

Oxford

16323 ■ Association for Computing Machinery, Miami University at Ohio
c/o Tom Gould, Pres.
Cmpt. Sci. and Systems Anal.
123 Kreger Hall
Oxford, OH 45056
Ph: (513)529-5928
Fax: (513)529-1524
E-mail: gouldtj@muohio.edu
URL: http://www.eas.muohio.edu/organizations/acm
Contact: Tom Gould, Pres.
Local. Biological, medical, behavioral, and computer scientists; hospital administrators; programmers and others interested in application of computer methods to biological, behavioral, and medical problems. Stimulates understanding of the use and potential of computers in the biosciences. **Additional Websites:** http://www.eas.muohio.edu/csa. **Affiliated With:** Association for Computing Machinery.

16324 ■ Miami University Council of Teachers of Mathematics
c/o Nicole Walton, Representative
219 W Walnut St., Apt. 3
Oxford, OH 45056
E-mail: takagit@muohio.edu
URL: http://www.orgs.muohio.edu/muctm
Contact: Nicole Walton, Representative
Local. Aims to improve the teaching and learning of mathematics. Provides vision, leadership and professional development to support teachers in ensuring mathematics learning of the highest quality for all students. **Affiliated With:** National Council of Teachers of Mathematics.

16325 ■ Oxford Audubon Society
c/o Liz Woedl
PO Box 556
Oxford, OH 45056
URL: National Affiliate–www.audubon.org
Local.

16326 ■ Oxford Chamber of Commerce (OCC)
30 W Park Pl., 2nd Fl.
Oxford, OH 45056
Ph: (513)523-5200
Fax: (513)523-2308
E-mail: exec@oxfordchamber.org
URL: http://www.oxfordchamber.org
Contact: JoNell Rowan, Exec.Dir.
Founded: 1979. **Members:** 300. **Membership Dues:** commercial (minimum; based on number of employees), $150 (annual) • financial (plus $25 per million dollars in deposits in Oxford), $160 (annual) • professional (plus $12 additional professional), $150 (annual) • utility company (minimum; 10 cents per meter of service), $125 (annual) • local social service organization, $75 (annual) • student in Miami, $25 (annual) • company affiliate, $20 (annual) • associate, $50 (annual). **Staff:** 4. **Budget:** $60,000. **Local**. Businesspersons and professionals interested in promoting business and community development in Oxford, OH. **Computer Services:** Mailing lists, of members. **Publications:** Newsletter. Alternate Formats: online. **Conventions/Meetings:** annual Casino Night - meeting • annual Christmas Festival - always summer • annual meeting • annual Music Festival - conference • annual Red Brick Rally Car Show.

16327 ■ Oxford Lions Club - Ohio
Miami Univ.
1809 E Spring St.
Oxford, OH 45056
Ph: (513)523-5264
E-mail: sales@oxford-real-estate.com
URL: http://oxfordoh.lionwap.org
Contact: Jeff Schrorer, Pres.
Local. Affiliated With: Lions Clubs International.

16328 ■ Society of Manufacturing Engineers - Miami University S076
142 Kreger Hall
Oxford, OH 45056
Ph: (513)529-2647
Fax: (513)529-1454
E-mail: baileym@muohio.edu
URL: National Affiliate–www.sme.org
Contact: Michael Bailey-VanKuren, Contact
Local. Advances manufacturing knowledge to gain competitive advantage. Improves skills and manufacturing solutions for the growth of economy. Provides resources and opportunities for manufacturing professionals. **Affiliated With:** Marine Technology Society.

16329 ■ United Way of Oxford, Ohio and Vicinity
PO Box 262
Oxford, OH 45056-0262
Ph: (513)523-0991
URL: National Affiliate–national.unitedway.org
Local. Affiliated With: United Way of America.

Painesville

16330 ■ American Cancer Society, Geauga, Lake Ashtabula Area Office
7861 Crile Rd.
Painesville, OH 44077-9180
Fax: (440)358-9073
Free: (888)227-6446
URL: National Affiliate–www.cancer.org
Contact: Vida Prekler, Area Dir.
Founded: 1946. **Staff:** 7. **Local**. Volunteers supporting education and research into cancer prevention,

diagnosis, detection, and treatment. Offers information and referral, provides service and rehabilitation programs and Fresh Start stop smoking clinic. Sponsors speakers, films, and I Can Cope educational programs; offers Reach to Recovery volunteer visitation program for mastectomy patients; operates Good Buys Resale Shops. **Libraries: Type:** open to the public. **Subjects:** cancer prevention, nutrition, legacies, diagnostic. **Affiliated With:** American Cancer Society. **Publications:** Newsletter, annual. Updates American Cancer Society events and programs. **Price:** free. **Circulation:** 12,000.

16331 ■ American Legion, Brakeman-King Post 336
60 Chester St.
Painesville, OH 44077
Ph: (740)362-7478
Fax: (740)362-1429
URL: National Affiliate–www.legion.org
Local. Affiliated With: American Legion.

16332 ■ American Legion, Chesterland Post 780
54 Middleton Dr.
Painesville, OH 44077
Ph: (740)362-7478
Fax: (740)362-1429
URL: National Affiliate–www.legion.org
Local. Affiliated With: American Legion.

16333 ■ American Red Cross, Lake County Chapter
1016 Bank St.
Painesville, OH 44077
Ph: (440)352-3171
E-mail: info@lakecountyredcross.org
URL: http://www.lakecountyredcross.org
Local.

16334 ■ Grand River Partners, Inc. (GRPI)
c/o Lake Erie College
391 W Washington St.
Painesville, OH 44077
Ph: (440)375-7311
Fax: (440)375-7314
E-mail: grpi@grandriverpartners.org
URL: http://www.grandriverpartners.org
Contact: Eddie Dengg, Exec.Dir.
Local. Works to protect the Grand River, its tributaries and watershed.

16335 ■ Lake County Planning Commission (LCPC)
125 E Erie St.
Painesville, OH 44077
Ph: (440)350-2740
E-mail: dwebster@lakecountyohio.org
URL: http://www.lakecountyohio.org/planning
Contact: Darrell C. Webster, Dir.
Founded: 1957. **Members:** 11. **Staff:** 7. **Budget:** $301,860. **Local. Committees:** Lake County Coastal Plan; Land Use and Zoning.

16336 ■ Mothers Against Drunk Driving, Western Reserve
1585 Birdie Ln.
Painesville, OH 44077
Ph: (440)350-6233
Fax: (440)350-2933
URL: National Affiliate–www.madd.org
Local. Victims of drunk driving crashes; concerned citizens. Encourages citizen participation in working towards reform of the drunk driving problem and the prevention of underage drinking. Acts as the voice of victims of drunk driving crashes by speaking on their behalf to communities, businesses, and educational groups. **Affiliated With:** Mothers Against Drunk Driving.

16337 ■ National Technical Honor Society - Auburn Career Center - Ohio
8140 Auburn Rd.
Painesville, OH 44077
Ph: (440)357-7542
Free: (800)544-9750
E-mail: mbittner@auburncc.org
URL: http://www.auburncc.org
Contact: Mary Ann Bittner, Contact
Local.

16338 ■ North Coast Corvair Enthusiasts
PO Box 902
Painesville, OH 44077
E-mail: corsaone@usa.com
URL: http://www.65corsa.freehosting.net
Contact: Karen Fisher, Sec.
Local. Enthusiasts of the Corvair automobile united for technical assistance and parts availability. **Affiliated With:** Corvair Society of America.

16339 ■ North Coast Fly Fishers (NCFF)
PO Box 312
Painesville, OH 44077
E-mail: president@ncff.net
URL: http://www.ncff.net
Contact: Dick Erickson, Pres.
Local. Affiliated With: Federation of Fly Fishers.

16340 ■ Northeast Ohio AIFA
c/o Mary Jahn, Exec.
2303 Northway Dr.
Painesville, OH 44077-4720
Ph: (440)354-8402
Fax: (440)720-3005
E-mail: maryfjahn@aol.com
URL: National Affiliate–naifa.org
Contact: Mary Jahn, Exec.
Local. Represents the interests of insurance and financial advisors. Advocates for a positive legislative and regulatory environment. Enhances business and professional skills of members. **Affiliated With:** National Association of Insurance and Financial Advisors.

16341 ■ Ohio Society, Sons of the American Revolution, Samuel Huntington Chapter (OHSSAR)
c/o Robert Parvin, Pres.
6366 Indian Point Rd.
Painesville, OH 44077-8844
E-mail: parvlinc@ncweb.com
URL: http://www.sar.org/ohssar/samuel_huntington_chapter.htm
Contact: Robert Parvin, Pres.
Local. Affiliated With: National Society, Sons of the American Revolution.

16342 ■ Painesville Area Chamber of Commerce
391 W Washington St.
Lake Erie Coll.
Coll. Hall
Painesville, OH 44077
Ph: (440)357-7572
Fax: (440)357-8752
E-mail: exec@painesvilleohchamber.org
URL: http://www.painesvilleohchamber.org
Contact: Linda Reed, Exec.Dir.
Staff: 3. **Local.** Promotes business and community development to enrich the economic, civic, social, cultural and environmental well being of Painesville area. **Awards:** Citizen of the Year. **Frequency:** annual. **Type:** recognition. **Telecommunication Services:** electronic mail, office@painesvilleohchamber.org. **Publications:** Newsletter, monthly.

16343 ■ Painesville Area Habitat for Humanity
89 Chester St.
Painesville, OH 44077
Ph: (440)354-4404
E-mail: djoss@pahfh.org
URL: http://www.pahfh.org
Contact: Donald Joss, Exec.Dir.
Founded: 1990. **Staff:** 1. **Budget:** $150,000. **Local.** Builds simple, decent, affordable homes for low income families. **Affiliated With:** Habitat for Humanity International.

16344 ■ Psi Chi, National Honor Society in Psychology - Lake Erie College
c/o Dept. of Psychology
391 W Washington St.
Painesville, OH 44077-3389
Ph: (440)375-7181
Fax: (440)352-3533
E-mail: yachanin@lec.edu
URL: http://www.psichi.org/chapters/info.asp?chapter_id=229
Contact: Stephen A. Yachanin PhD, Advisor
Local.

16345 ■ Sons of the American Revolution - Ohio Society (OHSSAR)
c/o Robert Parvin, Pres.
6366 Indian Point Rd.
Painesville, OH 44077-8844
Ph: (440)254-4557
E-mail: parvlinc@ncweb.com
URL: http://www.sar.org/ohssar/ohssar.html
Contact: Robert Parvin, Pres.
State.

16346 ■ Town and Country African Violet Society
c/o Gertrude Morabito
7057 Brightwood Dr.
Painesville, OH 44077
Ph: (440)352-9119
URL: National Affiliate–www.avsa.org
Contact: Gertrude Morabito, Contact
Local. Affiliated With: African Violet Society of America.

16347 ■ Vacationland Corvairs
11903 Concord Hambden Rd.
Painesville, OH 44077
E-mail: rampside@ncweb.com
URL: National Affiliate–www.corvair.org
Local. Enthusiasts of the Corvair automobile united for technical assistance and parts availability. **Affiliated With:** Corvair Society of America.

16348 ■ Veterans of Foreign Wars 2595
570 Liberty St.
Painesville, OH 44077
Ph: (440)354-9090
Contact: Marjorie Heraga, Contact
Local.

Pandora

16349 ■ American Legion, Pandora Post 616
108 W Main
Pandora, OH 45877
Ph: (740)362-7478
Fax: (740)362-1429
URL: National Affiliate–www.legion.org
Local. Affiliated With: American Legion.

Paris

16350 ■ Paris Lions Club - Ohio
c/o Linnie Seaburn, Pres.
2321 Freedmont Rd. SE
Paris, OH 44669
Ph: (330)862-2210
E-mail: sassy@raex.com
URL: http://www.lions13d.org
Contact: Linnie Seaburn, Pres.
Local. Affiliated With: Lions Clubs International.

Parma

16351 ■ American Legion, Al Sirat Grotto Post 392
7667 York Rd.
Parma, OH 44130
Ph: (740)362-7478
Fax: (740)362-1429
URL: National Affiliate–www.legion.org
Local. Affiliated With: American Legion.

16352 ■ American Legion, Brooklyn Post 233
3119 Russell Ave.
Parma, OH 44134
Ph: (740)362-7478
Fax: (740)362-1429
URL: National Affiliate–www.legion.org
Local. Affiliated With: American Legion.

16353 ■ American Legion, Ohio Post 212
c/o Raymond W. Enea
7103 Hampstead Ave.
Parma, OH 44129
Ph: (740)362-7478
Fax: (740)362-1429
URL: National Affiliate–www.legion.org
Contact: Raymond W. Enea, Contact
Local. Affiliated With: American Legion.

16354 ■ American Legion, Ohio Post 572
c/o Joseph J. Jacubic
6483 State Rd.
Parma, OH 44134
Ph: (740)362-7478
Fax: (740)362-1429
URL: National Affiliate–www.legion.org
Contact: Joseph J. Jacubic, Contact
Local. Affiliated With: American Legion.

16355 ■ American Legion, Parma Heights Post 703
7667 York Rd.
Parma, OH 44130
Ph: (740)362-7478
Fax: (740)362-1429
URL: National Affiliate–www.legion.org
Local. Affiliated With: American Legion.

16356 ■ American Society of Women Accountants, Cleveland Chapter No. 013
c/o Sonia Shellito, CPA, Pres.
Ft. Dearborn Life Insurance Co.
9621 Elsmere Dr.
Parma, OH 44130
Ph: (216)696-7700 (440)843-8403
Fax: (216)696-5860
E-mail: jennyearley@yahoo.com
URL: http://www.aswacleveland.org
Contact: Jennifer Earley CPA, Membership Chair
Local. Strives to enable women in all fields of accounting to achieve their personal, professional and economic potential and to contribute to the future development of the profession. **Affiliated With:** American Society of Women Accountants.

16357 ■ Association for Computing Machinery, Bryant and Stratton Parma Campus
c/o Jean M. Simbach
12955 Snow Rd.
Parma, OH 44130
Ph: (216)265-3151
E-mail: jmsimbach@bryantstratton.edu
URL: National Affiliate–www.acm.org
Contact: Jean M. Simbach, Contact
Local. Biological, medical, behavioral, and computer scientists; hospital administrators; programmers and others interested in application of computer methods to biological, behavioral, and medical problems. Stimulates understanding of the use and potential of computers in the Biosciences. **Affiliated With:** Association for Computing Machinery.

16358 ■ Consortium of Healthy and Immunized Communities (CHIC)
5550 Venture Dr.
Parma, OH 44130
Ph: (216)201-2001
URL: http://www.chicohio.com
Contact: Cindy Modie, Chair
Founded: 1995. **Members:** 125. **Membership Dues:** $25 (annual). **Staff:** 5. **Local.** Seeks to improve the health and immunization status of northern ohio communities.

16359 ■ Cuyahoga Valley Space Society
3433 N Ave.
Parma, OH 44134-1252
Ph: (216)749-0017
E-mail: geocooper3@aol.com
URL: National Affiliate–www.nss.org
Contact: George F. Cooper III, Contact
Local. Works for the creation of a spacefaring civilization. Encourages the establishment of self-sustaining human settlements in space. Promotes large-scale industrialization and private enterprise in space.

16360 ■ East View Rod and Gun Club
7778 Hoertz Rd.
Parma, OH 44134
Ph: (440)885-4746
URL: National Affiliate–www.mynssa.com
Local. Affiliated With: National Skeet Shooting Association.

16361 ■ First Catholic Slovak Ladies Association - Cleveland Junior Branch 057
7277 Barton Cir.
Parma, OH 44129
Ph: (440)884-5463
URL: National Affiliate–www.fcsla.com
Local. Affiliated With: First Catholic Slovak Ladies Association.

16362 ■ First Catholic Slovak Ladies Association - Cleveland Junior Branch 441
2123 Tuxedo Ave.
Parma, OH 44134
Ph: (216)749-6494
E-mail: bertaj@aol.com
URL: National Affiliate–www.fcsla.com
Local. Affiliated With: First Catholic Slovak Ladies Association.

16363 ■ First Catholic Slovak Ladies Association - Cleveland Junior Branch 481
7140 Thorncliffe Blvd.
Parma, OH 44134
Ph: (440)845-0282
URL: National Affiliate–www.fcsla.com
Local. Affiliated With: First Catholic Slovak Ladies Association.

16364 ■ First Catholic Slovak Ladies Association - Cleveland Junior Branch 485
7140 Thorncliffe Blvd.
Parma, OH 44134
Ph: (440)845-0282
URL: National Affiliate–www.fcsla.com
Local. Affiliated With: First Catholic Slovak Ladies Association.

16365 ■ First Catholic Slovak Ladies Association - Cleveland Senior Branch 141
6177 Norfolk Dr.
Parma, OH 44134
Ph: (440)888-0480
URL: National Affiliate–www.fcsla.com
Local. Affiliated With: First Catholic Slovak Ladies Association.

16366 ■ First Catholic Slovak Ladies Association - Cleveland Senior Branch 221
7277 Barton Cir.
Parma, OH 44129
Ph: (440)884-5463
URL: National Affiliate–www.fcsla.com
Local. Affiliated With: First Catholic Slovak Ladies Association.

16367 ■ First Catholic Slovak Ladies Association - Cleveland Senior Branch 238
2123 Tuxedo Ave.
Parma, OH 44134
Ph: (216)749-6494
E-mail: bertaj@aol.com
URL: National Affiliate–www.fcsla.com
Local. Affiliated With: First Catholic Slovak Ladies Association.

16368 ■ First Catholic Slovak Ladies Association - Cleveland Senior Branch 557
7140 Thorncliffe Blvd.
Parma, OH 44134
Ph: (440)845-0282
URL: National Affiliate–www.fcsla.com
Local. Affiliated With: First Catholic Slovak Ladies Association.

16369 ■ First Catholic Slovak Ladies Association - Lakewood Junior Branch 457
12921 List Ln.
Parma, OH 44131
Ph: (440)884-7333
URL: National Affiliate–www.fcsla.com
Local. Affiliated With: First Catholic Slovak Ladies Association.

16370 ■ First Catholic Slovak Ladies Association - Lakewood Senior Branch 524
12920 List Ln.
Parma, OH 44130
Ph: (440)884-7333
URL: National Affiliate–www.fcsla.com
Local. Affiliated With: First Catholic Slovak Ladies Association.

16371 ■ Korean War Veterans Association, Greater Cleveland Chapter
c/o Paul Romanovich
5400 Sandy Hook Dr.
Parma, OH 44134-6124
Ph: (440)885-5101
E-mail: sandyvalley@msn.com
URL: National Affiliate–www.kwva.org
Contact: Paul Romanovich, Contact
Local. Affiliated With: Korean War Veterans Association.

16372 ■ Lake Erie Association, USA Track and Field
c/o Larry Seifert, Pres.
8280 Craigleigh Dr.
Parma, OH 44129
Ph: (440)842-2142
Fax: (440)842-2142
E-mail: lns1955@juno.com
URL: http://www.lakeerie.org
Contact: Larry Seifert, Pres.
Local. Affiliated With: U.S.A. Track and Field.

16373 ■ National Active and Retired Federal Employees Association - Cleveland 470
5704 Edgehill Dr.
Parma, OH 44130-1603
Ph: (440)884-5720
URL: National Affiliate–www.narfe.org
Contact: Mary An Ann Stevans, Contact
Local. Protects the retirement future of employees through education. Informs members on issues affecting the retirement. **Affiliated With:** National Association of Retired Federal Employees.

16374 ■ Northeast Ohio Applied Systems Users Group
c/o Four Star Insurance Agency Inc.
5835 Pearl Rd.
Parma, OH 44130-2110
Ph: (440)882-2000
Fax: (440)888-0320
E-mail: joe@fourstarinsurance.com
URL: National Affiliate–www.ascnet.org
Contact: Joseph Germana, Pres.
Local. Represents insurance agents and brokers using the Agency Manager software. Promotes successful automation and business practices through communication, education, and advocacy. **Affiliated With:** Applied Systems Client Network.

16375 ■ Ohio Division of the International Association for Identification
10830 Johnson Dr.
Parma, OH 44130
E-mail: masilonisjb@aol.com
URL: http://www.oioa.org
Contact: Joseph Masilonis, Pres.
Founded: 1967. **State.** Organizes people in the profession of forensic identification, investigation and scientific examination of physical evidence, through education, training and research. Encourages research in scientific crime detection by employing the collective of the profession to advance the scientific techniques of forensic identification and crime detection.

16376 ■ Parma Area Chamber of Commerce
7908 Day Dr.
Parma, OH 44129
Ph: (440)886-1700
Fax: (440)886-1770
E-mail: chamber@parmaareachamber.org
URL: http://parmaareachamber.org
Contact: Patricia A. Pell, Exec.Dir.
Founded: 1955. **Members:** 500. **Membership Dues:** business (varies with the number of employees), $175-$400 (annual) • non-business, $75 (annual). **Staff:** 2. **Local.** Provides benefits and opportunities to over 500 business and organization members including networking referrals, sponsorships, advertising, direct marketing, discounts on insurance, payroll, timekeeping and credit card processing, workers' compensation group programs, member to member discounts and more. Supports community and member events, regional and local partnerships, legislative impact, leadership, and volunteer roles. **Libraries: Type:** reference. **Publications:** *Insight*, monthly. Newsletter. Alternate Formats: online.

16377 ■ Phi Theta Kappa - Chi Omega Chapter
c/o Mary Hovanec
Western Campus
11000 Pleasant Valley Rd.
Rm. B149
Parma, OH 44130-5199
Ph: (216)987-5482
E-mail: mary.hovanec@tri-c.edu
URL: http://www.ptk.org/directories/chapters/OH/313-1.htm
Contact: Mary Hovanec, Advisor
Local. Affiliated With: Phi Theta Kappa, International Honor Society.

16378 ■ U.S.A. Track and Field Lake Erie
c/o Larry Seifert, Pres.
8280 Craigleigh Dr.
Parma, OH 44129
Ph: (440)842-2142
Fax: (440)842-2142
E-mail: lns1955@juno.com
URL: http://www.lakeerie.org
Contact: Larry Seifert, Pres.
Local. Affiliated With: U.S.A. Track and Field.

16379 ■ West Creek Preservation Committee (WCPC)
c/o David M. Lincheck, Dir.
PO Box 347113
Parma, OH 44134
Ph: (216)749-3720
Fax: (216)749-3730
E-mail: dlincheck@westcreek.org
URL: http://www.westcreek.org
Contact: Derek Schafer, Watershed Associate
Local. Works as a watershed stewardship organization focused on riparian corridor protection and education and outreach on the West Creek tributary of the Cuyahoga River.

Parma Heights

16380 ■ First Catholic Slovak Ladies Association - Cleveland Senior Branch 517
7042 Greenleaf Ave.
Parma Heights, OH 44130
Ph: (440)845-1575
URL: National Affiliate–www.fcsla.com
Local. Affiliated With: First Catholic Slovak Ladies Association.

16381 ■ North Eastern Ohio Education Association (NEOEA)
6929 W 130th St., Ste.301
Parma Heights, OH 44130
Ph: (440)845-2030
Fax: (440)845-2695
Free: (800)354-6794
E-mail: info@neoea.org
URL: http://www.neoea.org
Contact: William S. Lavezzi, Exec.Dir.
Founded: 1869. **Members:** 34,000. **Membership Dues:** active, $20 (annual). **Staff:** 3. **Budget:** $800,000. **Regional Groups:** 1. **State Groups:** 1. **Local Groups:** 193. **Local.** Membership consists of teachers and support personnel in public K-12 schools, colleges, and MR/DD boards in the northeastern OH. Affiliate of the Ohio Education Association and the National Education Association. Seeks to improve professional standards and promote compensation and working conditions for members. Sponsors annual "NEOEA Day", on the second Friday of each school year, offering an extensive array of leadership, professional, and personal development workshops. **Libraries: Type:** not open to the public. **Holdings:** 12; periodicals. **Subjects:** education, consumer affairs. **Awards:** Five Star Local Award. **Frequency:** annual. **Type:** recognition. **Recipient:** for local affiliates that are leaders in involvement with the association • Legislative Action Award. **Frequency:** annual. **Type:** recognition. **Recipient:** for local affiliates with strong programs of legislative activity • Newsletter Award. **Frequency:** annual. **Type:** recognition. **Recipient:** for local affiliates with strong local newsletters • Positive Image Award. **Frequency:** annual. **Type:** recognition • Public Relations Minigrant. **Frequency:** annual. **Type:** grant. **Recipient:** for local affiliates with approved public relations activities. **Committees:** Credentials; Economic Security and Retirement; Elections; Environmental Concerns; History; Internal Political Action; Leadership Development; Resolutions. **Affiliated With:** National Education Association; Ohio Education Association. **Publications:** *News and Views*, 7/year. Newsletter. **Price:** free. **Circulation:** 34,200. **Advertising:** accepted. Alternate Formats: online. **Conventions/Meetings:** semiannual Representative Assembly - X.

16382 ■ Society of Fire Protection Engineers - Northeast Ohio Chapter
c/o Thomas Eakin, Sec.-Treas.
6617 Bennington Dr.
Parma Heights, OH 44130-4004
Ph: (216)433-3948
E-mail: thomas.g.eakin@grc.nasa.gov
URL: http://ctsc.org/sfpe/about_neo.htm
Contact: Jeff Spiesz, Pres.
Local. Advances the science and practice of fire protection engineering. Aims to maintain high professional and ethical standards among members. Fosters fire protection engineering education. **Affiliated With:** Society of Fire Protection Engineers.

Pataskala

16383 ■ American Subcontractors Association-Central Ohio Chapter
c/o Jady Johnson
PO Box 779
Pataskala, OH 43062
Ph: (740)964-3550
Fax: (740)927-9457
E-mail: info@asa-centralohio.org
URL: http://www.asa-centralohio.org
Contact: Marla Graham, Exec.Dir.
Represents commercial construction subcontractors, material suppliers and service companies, both union and non-union ranging in size from the smallest private firms to the nation's largest specialty contractors. Seeks to improve the business environment for subcontractors, specialty contractors and suppliers through advocacy, communication, education and networking. **Affiliated With:** American Subcontractors Association.

16384 ■ American Truck Historical Society, Buckeye Vintage Haulers
c/o Donald Stewart
DBA Denni Brook Farm
10120 Jersey Mill Rd.
Pataskala, OH 43062
Ph: (740)924-6355
URL: National Affiliate–www.aths.org
Contact: Donald Stewart, Contact
Local.

16385 ■ Indian Springs Beagle Club
c/o Ken Stump
81 Ohio Ave. SW
Pataskala, OH 43062-8433
URL: National Affiliate–clubs.akc.org
Contact: Ken Stump, Contact
Local.

16386 ■ Ohio Dressage Society (OSDS)
c/o Chris Gemmel-Gnidovec, Treas.
4380 Blacklid Rd. NW
Pataskala, OH 43062
Ph: (740)862-8640
E-mail: kathypainter@hotmail.com
URL: http://www.ohiodressagesociety.com
Contact: Amy Rothe-Hietter, Pres.
State. Affiliated With: United States Dressage Federation.

Paulding

16387 ■ Habitat for Humanity of Paulding County
PO Box 328
Paulding, OH 45879
Ph: (419)399-3848
E-mail: president@habitatpc.com
URL: http://www.habitatpc.com
Local. Affiliated With: Habitat for Humanity International.

16388 ■ Paulding County United Way
PO Box 357
Paulding, OH 45879-0357
Ph: (419)399-5300
Fax: (419)399-2047
E-mail: pcuw@paulding-net.com
URL: National Affiliate–national.unitedway.org
Contact: Nancy Hessler, Exec.Dir.
Local. Conducts an annual systematic, countywide fund drive for the benefit of member agencies and organizations and Paulding County, Ohio.

Payne

16389 ■ American Legion, Ohio Post 297
c/o Reuben J. Smith
230 N Main St.
Payne, OH 45880
Ph: (740)362-7478
Fax: (740)362-1429
URL: National Affiliate–www.legion.org
Contact: Reuben J. Smith, Contact
Local. Affiliated With: American Legion.

16390 ■ National Active and Retired Federal Employees Association - Van Wert-Paulding 630
RR 2, 4801 Rd. 72
Payne, OH 45880-9401
Ph: (419)263-3086
URL: National Affiliate–www.narfe.org
Contact: Leo F. Davis, Contact
Local. Protects the retirement future of employees through education. Informs members on issues affecting the retirement. **Affiliated With:** National Association of Retired Federal Employees.

Pedro

16391 ■ Izaak Walton League of America, Lawrence County Chapter
554 Township Rd. 140 E
Pedro, OH 45659
Ph: (740)532-2342 (740)532-3824
URL: National Affiliate–www.iwla.org
Contact: Phillip Hardy, Pres.
Local. Works to educate the public to conserve, maintain, protect, and restore the soil, forest, water, and other natural resources of the U.S; promotes the enjoyment and wholesome utilization of these resources. **Affiliated With:** Izaak Walton League of America.

Peebles

16392 ■ American Legion, Thompson-Wallingford Post 594
122 N Main St.
Peebles, OH 45660
Ph: (740)362-7478
Fax: (740)362-1429
URL: National Affiliate–www.legion.org
Local. Affiliated With: American Legion.

Pemberville

16393 ■ American Legion, Freedom Post 183
PO Box 765
Pemberville, OH 43450
Ph: (740)362-7478
Fax: (740)362-1429
URL: National Affiliate–www.legion.org
Local. Affiliated With: American Legion.

Peninsula

16394 ■ Hostelling International-Northeast Ohio Council
6093 Stanford Rd.
Peninsula, OH 44264
Ph: (330)467-8711
Fax: (330)467-8711
E-mail: hi-stanfordhostel@juno.com
URL: http://www.hiayh.org
Contact: Sarah Jaquay, Pres.
Founded: 1985. **Members:** 1,200. **Membership Dues:** adult (18-54 years old), $28 (annual) • adult (55 years old and over), $18 (annual) • youth (17 years old and under), $17 (annual) • life, $250. **Local.** Works to help the young gain a greater understanding of the world and its people through hostelling. **Additional Websites:** http://www.stanfordhostel.com. **Affiliated With:** Hostelling International-American Youth Hostels; Hostelling International - American Youth Hostels, Metropolitan Chicago Council. **Formerly:** American Youth Hostels-Northeast Ohio Council. **Publications:** *Backroads*, bimonthly. Newsletter.

Pepper Pike

16395 ■ Cleveland Hiking Club
c/o John Nelson
PO Box 24508
Pepper Pike, OH 44124
Ph: (440)449-2588
E-mail: jdn33333@cs.com
URL: http://www.clevelandhikingclub.com
Contact: Joe Shaffer, Pres.
Local. Promotes hiking for health and recreation. **Affiliated With:** American Hiking Society.

16396 ■ Hunting Valley Gun Club
31000 E Landerwood Dr.
Pepper Pike, OH 44124
Ph: (216)464-0248
E-mail: jkoch39@sbcgldbal.net
URL: National Affiliate–www.mynssa.com
Local. Affiliated With: National Skeet Shooting Association.

16397 ■ Orange Alumni Association
32000 Chagrin Blvd.
Pepper Pike, OH 44124
Ph: (216)831-8601
Fax: (216)831-4209
E-mail: info@orangerec.com
URL: http://www.orangeschools.org
Contact: Laura Guentner, Dir.
Founded: 1988. **Membership Dues:** $10 (annual) • life, $100. **Regional.** Maintains hall of fame. Assists in organizing reunions. Provides scholarships. **Awards:** Alumni Scholarship. **Frequency:** annual. **Type:** scholarship. **Recipient:** graduating high school seniors (child of an Alumnus). **Committees:** Chairpersons. **Publications:** *Talk and Tales*, 3/year. Newsletter. **Circulation:** 6,000. **Advertising:** accepted. **Conventions/Meetings:** meeting - 5/year.

16398 ■ Society of Otorhinolaryngology and Head/Neck Nurses - Greater Cleveland Area Chapter
3 Louis Dr.
Pepper Pike, OH 44124
Ph: (216)721-1040
Fax: (216)721-1072
E-mail: ctuckerrnfa@msn.com
URL: National Affiliate–www.sohnnurse.com
Contact: Cynthia Tucker RNFA, Contact
Local. Advances the professional growth and development of nurses dedicated to the specialty of Otorhinolaryngology nursing through education and research. Promotes innovations in practice, research and healthcare policy initiatives. **Affiliated With:** Society of Otorhinolaryngology and Head/Neck Nurses.

Perry

16399 ■ American Legion, Perry Memorial Post 697
PO Box 31
Perry, OH 44081
Ph: (740)362-7478
Fax: (740)362-1429
URL: National Affiliate–www.legion.org
Local. Affiliated With: American Legion.

16400 ■ Perry Historical Society of Lake County Ohio
PO Box 216
Perry, OH 44081
Ph: (440)259-4541
E-mail: mlplatko@ncweb.com
URL: http://www.webzar.com/perryhistorical
Contact: Joyce Phillips, Pres.
Founded: 1992. **Members:** 140. **Budget:** $5,000. **Local.** Works to collect and preserve for future generations, historic items that originated in Perry for preservation and display. Disseminates information to the public regarding the history and culture of Perry of Lake County. **Libraries: Type:** open to the public. **Holdings:** 150; articles, books, photographs. **Subjects:** history, genealogy. **Publications:** *The Perry Heritage*, quarterly. Newsletter. Includes membership information, historical information, and cartoons. **Price:** free for members. **Circulation:** 175. **Conventions/Meetings:** monthly workshop, history related and general programs - 2nd Saturday in Lakeco, OH.

Perrysburg

16401 ■ American Legion, Perrysburg Post 28
PO Box 100
Perrysburg, OH 43552
Ph: (740)362-7478
Fax: (740)362-1429
URL: National Affiliate–www.legion.org
Local. Affiliated With: American Legion.

16402 ■ American Nuclear Society, Ohio Section
c/o Larry Grime, Chm.
L.A. Grrime & Assoc., Inc. AcroServices
860 Sandalwood Rd. W
Perrysburg, OH 43551
Ph: (419)872-9999
URL: National Affiliate–www.ans.org
Contact: Larry Grime, Chm.
State. Works to advance science and engineering in the nuclear industry. Works with government agencies, educational institutions, and other organizations dealing with nuclear issues. **Affiliated With:** American Nuclear Society.

16403 ■ Black Swamp Air Force
PO Box 43552-0671
Perrysburg, OH 43551
Ph: (419)833-2462
E-mail: kkilgoar56@hotmail.com
URL: http://www.bsaf.org
Contact: Kevin Kilgoar, Commandant
Local. Affiliated With: American Kitefliers Association.

16404 ■ Black Swamp Conservancy (BSC)
PO Box 332
Perrysburg, OH 43552-0332
Ph: (419)872-5263
Fax: (419)872-8197
E-mail: bsc@blackswamp.org
URL: http://www.blackswamp.org
Contact: Kevin Joyce, Exec.Dir.
Local.

16405 ■ Greater Toledo Council of Teachers of Mathematics
c/o Debra Shelt, Pres.
510 Arrowhead Dr.
Perrysburg, OH 43551
Ph: (419)873-8223 (419)372-9188
E-mail: dshelt@bgnet.bgsu.edu
URL: National Affiliate–www.nctm.org
Contact: Debra Shelt, Pres.
Local. Aims to improve the teaching and learning of mathematics. Provides vision, leadership and professional development to support teachers in ensuring mathematics learning of the highest quality for all students. **Affiliated With:** National Council of Teachers of Mathematics.

16406 ■ Humane Ohio
PO Box 820
Perrysburg, OH 43552
Ph: (419)266-5607
E-mail: info@humaneohio.org
URL: http://www.humaneohio.org
State.

16407 ■ International Brotherhood of Magicians, Ring 68
c/o David Sieja, Pres.
336 Queensland Blvd.
Perrysburg, OH 43551
Ph: (419)874-4552
E-mail: evadsmagic@earthlink.net
URL: http://www.ring68.cjb.net
Contact: David Sieja, Pres.
Local. Professional and semi-professional magicians; suppliers, assistants, agents, and others interested in magic. Seeks to advance the art of magic in the field of amusement, entertainment, and culture. Promotes proper means of discouraging false or misleading advertising of effects, tricks, literature, merchandise, or actions appertaining to the magical arts; opposes exposures of principles of the art of magic, except in books on magic and magazines devoted to such art for the exclusive use of magicians and devotees of the art; encourages humane treatment and care of live animals whenever employed in magical performances. **Affiliated With:** International Brotherhood of Magicians.

16408 ■ Juvenile Diabetes Research Foundation International, Northwest Ohio Chapter
27475 Holiday Ln., Ste.No. 1
Perrysburg, OH 43551
Ph: (419)873-1377
Fax: (419)873-1365
Free: (888)533-9255
E-mail: northwestohio@jdrf.org
URL: http://www.jdrf.org
Contact: Sarah Berndt, Pres.
Founded: 1970. **Membership Dues:** $25 (annual). **Budget:** $500,000. **Local.** Strives to find a cure for diabetes and its complications through the support of research. **Affiliated With:** Juvenile Diabetes Research Foundation International. **Publications:** *Countdown*, quarterly. Magazine. Provides articles on the effects of research on the way people with diabetes must live their lives. **Price:** included in membership dues • *Discoveries Newsletter*, quarterly. **Conventions/Meetings:** annual meeting - always June.

16409 ■ National Spinal Cord Injury Association - Northwest Ohio Chapter
10117 Woodmont Way
Perrysburg, OH 43551
Ph: (419)872-5347
E-mail: jbeckley@woh.rr.com
URL: National Affiliate–www.spinalcord.org
Contact: Jim Beckley, Pres.
Local. Empowers individuals who are suffering from spinal cord injury. Provides information on the causes and prevention of spinal cord injuries. **Affiliated With:** National Spinal Cord Injury Association.

16410 ■ Ohio Fair Managers Association (OFMA)
PO Box 422
Perrysburg, OH 43551
Ph: (419)874-0170
E-mail: ofma@buckeye-express.com
URL: http://www.ohiofairs.org
Contact: Howard L. Call, Exec.Dir.
State.

16411 ■ Perrysburg Area Chamber of Commerce
105 W Indiana Ave.
Perrysburg, OH 43551
Ph: (419)874-9147
Fax: (419)872-9347
E-mail: director@perrysburgchamber.com
URL: http://www.perrysburgchamber.com
Contact: Sandy Latchem, Exec.Dir.
Membership Dues: business, $115 (annual) • charitable organization, $60 (annual). **Local.** Promotes business, community development and free enterprise system in the Perrysburg, OH area. **Computer Services:** Information services, membership directory • mailing lists, of members. **Publications:** *Chamber Connection*, monthly. Newsletter. Contains business' issues, and chamber and community developments. Alternate Formats: online.

16412 ■ Three Meadows Home Owners Association
905 Oak Knoll Dr.
Perrysburg, OH 43551
Ph: (419)874-7644
Local.

16413 ■ Veteran Motor Car Club of America - Great Lakes Region
c/o Bob Ward, Dir.
907 Shearwood Dr.
Perrysburg, OH 43551
Ph: (419)874-3627
URL: National Affiliate–www.vmcca.org
Contact: Bob Ward, Dir.
Regional. Affiliated With: Veteran Motor Car Club of America.

16414 ■ Veteran Motor Car Club of America - Toledo Chapter
c/o David Knepper, Pres.
2431 Fremont Pike
Perrysburg, OH 43551
Ph: (419)837-6559
URL: National Affiliate–www.vmcca.org
Contact: David Knepper, Pres.
Local. Affiliated With: Veteran Motor Car Club of America.

Perrysville

16415 ■ Perrysville Lions Club
c/o Julianne Zody, Sec.
PO Box 236
Perrysville, OH 44864
Ph: (419)938-6156
E-mail: cozcurl@earthlink.net
URL: http://www.lions13b.org
Contact: Julianne Zody, Sec.
Local. Affiliated With: Lions Clubs International.

Pettisville

16416 ■ American Legion, Pettisville Post 445
PO Box 53224
Pettisville, OH 43553
Ph: (740)362-7478
Fax: (740)362-1429
URL: National Affiliate–www.legion.org
Local. Affiliated With: American Legion.

Pickerington

16417 ■ American Legion, David Johnston Memorial Post 283
PO Box 114
Pickerington, OH 43147
Ph: (740)362-7478
Fax: (740)362-1429
URL: National Affiliate–www.legion.org
Local. Affiliated With: American Legion.

16418 ■ Arc of Fairfield County
9095 Cotswold Dr.
Pickerington, OH 43147
Ph: (614)863-9372
Fax: (614)863-0883
URL: http://www.thearcofohio.org
Contact: Debbie Willitte, Exec.Dir.
Local.

16419 ■ Central Ohio Kennel Club (COKC)
c/o Joan Barrett, Sec.
11374 Rockwood Ct. NW
Pickerington, OH 43147-9113
E-mail: cokc_info@ohiodogs.com
URL: http://ohiodogs.com
Contact: Joan Barrett, Sec.
Regional.

16420 ■ Central Ohio Orienteering (COO)
c/o RW Heubner
8545 Appleridge Cir.
Pickerington, OH 43147
Ph: (614)751-9961
E-mail: krogers@netset.com
URL: http://centralohioorienteers.org
Contact: RW Heubner, Contact
Local. Affiliated With: United States Orienteering Federation.

16421 ■ Naval Reserve Association, 4-218 Columbus Chapter
c/o Capt. George F. Williams
10076 Oxford Dr.
Pickerington, OH 43147-9668
E-mail: roanavy1@aol.com
URL: National Affiliate–www.navy-reserve.org
Contact: Capt. George F. Williams, Contact
Local. Promotes the interests of the Department of the Navy and the Naval Reserve. Supports the military and naval policies of the United States. Advocates for an adequate naval establishment including a well-trained and readily available Naval Reserve. **Affiliated With:** Naval Reserve Association.

16422 ■ Ohio Public Health Association (OPHA)
PO Box 294
Pickerington, OH 43147
Ph: (614)833-2600
Fax: (614)833-2600
E-mail: ohiopha@iwaynet.net
URL: http://www.ohiopha.org
Contact: David Heisel DDS, Pres.
Founded: 1925. **Membership Dues:** active, $48 (annual) • round up, $50 (annual) • full-time student, $15 (annual) • retired, $20 (annual). **State.** Works to promote and protect personal, community, and environmental health in Ohio by stimulating public action, educating and mobilizing health professionals and promoting research and teaching in areas of public health. **Awards:** John D. Porterfield Distinguished Service Award. **Frequency:** annual. **Type:** recognition. **Recipient:** for an OPHA member who has demonstrated an outstanding performance in public health • Ohio Public Health Association Young Public Health Professionals Award. **Frequency:** annual. **Type:** recognition. **Recipient:** for a public health professional aged 30 or less who made a contribution within their agency or state • Outstanding Public Health Nurse Award. **Frequency:** annual. **Type:** recognition. **Recipient:** to the most outstanding public health nurse. **Committees:** Coalition for Affordable Prescription; Services Block Grant Advisory. **Sections:** Vital Statistics. **Special Interest Groups:** Maternal and Child Health. **Affiliated With:** American Public Health Association. **Publications:** *Interaction*, bimonthly. Newsletter. Contains information on the organization and its members. **Conventions/Meetings:** monthly meeting, general membership - every 2nd Tuesday.

16423 ■ Ohio Thimble Seekers
c/o Sandra Woodyard
10892 Grant Ln.
Pickerington, OH 43147
E-mail: sandwood@aol.com
URL: National Affiliate–www.thimblecollectors.com
Contact: Sandra Woodyard, Contact
State. Affiliated With: Thimble Collectors International.

16424 ■ Pickerington Area Chamber of Commerce (PACC)
13 W Columbus St.
Pickerington, OH 43147
Ph: (614)837-1958
Fax: (614)837-6420
E-mail: president@pickeringtonchamber.com
URL: http://www.pickeringtonchamber.com
Contact: Helen Mayle, Pres.
Founded: 1978. **Members:** 349. **Membership Dues:** business (based on number of employees), $144-$456 (annual) • nonprofit, $100 (annual). **Staff:** 2. **Local.** Promotes business and community development in Pickerington, OH. **Awards:** PACC Scholarship. **Frequency:** annual. **Type:** scholarship. **Recipient:** for Pickerington School District students. **Committees:** Ambassadors; Benefits; Economic Development; Event; Leadership; LEADS; Legislative Affairs; Technology. **Publications:** *Businews*, monthly. Newsletter. **Advertising:** accepted • *Community Guide and Profile* • *Pickerington Area Map*. Membership Directory.

Piney Fork

16425 ■ American Legion, Ohio Post 735
c/o Gwyn Allen
350 Township Rd. 39
Piney Fork, OH 43941
Ph: (740)362-7478
Fax: (740)362-1429
URL: National Affiliate–www.legion.org
Contact: Gwyn Allen, Contact
Local. Affiliated With: American Legion.

Pioneer

16426 ■ American Legion, Agnew-Shinabarger Post 307
PO Box 446
Pioneer, OH 43554
Ph: (740)362-7478
Fax: (740)362-1429
URL: National Affiliate–www.legion.org
Local. Affiliated With: American Legion.

16427 ■ Midstates Mule and Donkey Show Society
18817 Rd. 1050
Pioneer, OH 43554
Ph: (419)459-4694
E-mail: mgilcher@webtv.net
Contact: Maribel Gilcher, Sec.
Founded: 1973. **Members:** 318. **Membership Dues:** $15 (annual). **Local.** Owners of donkeys and mules in Illinois, Indiana, Kentucky, Michigan, and Ohio. Promotes appreciation of donkeys and mules. **Awards: Type:** scholarship. **Recipient:** student with good grade point average and active showing of donkeys and mules. **Publications:** Newsletter, bimonthly. **Price:** $15.00. **Conventions/Meetings:** annual meeting - always November.

Piqua

16428 ■ AAA Cincinnati
116 E High St.
Piqua, OH 45356
Ph: (937)773-3753
Local.

16429 ■ American Association for Medical Transcription, Buckeye Area Chapter (AAMT-BAC)
c/o Sandra L. Reagan, CMT, FAAMT, Pres.
1844 Carol Dr.
Piqua, OH 45356
E-mail: sreagan@woh.rr.com
URL: http://buckeyechapteraamt.com
Contact: Ms. Peggy Allwardt CMT, E-newsletter Ed.
Local. Works to represent and advance the profession of medical transcription and its practitioners. **Affiliated With:** American Association for Medical Transcription.

16430 ■ American Legion, Schnell-Westfall Post 184
301 W Water St.
Piqua, OH 45356
Ph: (740)362-7478
Fax: (740)362-1429
URL: National Affiliate–www.legion.org
Local. Affiliated With: American Legion.

16431 ■ Breakfast Discipleship - Young Life
325 W Ash St.
Piqua, OH 45356
Ph: (937)778-1118
URL: http://sites.younglife.org/_layouts/ylext/default.aspx?ID=C-3770
Local. Affiliated With: Young Life.

16432 ■ Korean War Veterans Association, Western Ohio Chapter
c/o Ken Williamson
PO Box 19
Piqua, OH 45356
Ph: (937)698-7150
URL: National Affiliate–www.kwva.org
Contact: Ken Williamson, Contact
Local. Affiliated With: Korean War Veterans Association.

16433 ■ Main Street Piqua
326 N Main St.
Piqua, OH 45356
Ph: (937)773-9355
Fax: (937)773-8553
E-mail: info@mainstreetpiqua.com
URL: http://www.mainstreetpiqua.com
Contact: Lorna Swisher, Exec.Dir.
Local.

16434 ■ New Knoxville - Young Life
325 W Ash St.
Piqua, OH 45356
Ph: (937)778-1118
URL: http://sites.younglife.org/_layouts/ylext/default.aspx?ID=C-3204
Local. Affiliated With: Young Life.

16435 ■ Ohio Mathematics Association of Two-Year Colleges
c/o Janet Cook, Pres.
1973 Edison Dr.
Piqua, OH 45356
Ph: (937)778-8600
E-mail: cook@edisonohio.edu
URL: http://www.terra.edu/ohiomatyc
Contact: Janet Cook, Pres.
State. Promotes and increases awareness of the role of two-year colleges in mathematics education. Provides a forum for the improvement of mathematics instruction in the first two years of college. Provides professional development opportunities for educators interested in the first two years of collegiate mathematics instruction. **Affiliated With:** American Mathematical Association of Two-Year Colleges.

16436 ■ Phi Theta Kappa - Alpha Lambda Eta Chapter
c/o Jane Kretschmann
1973 Edison Dr.
Piqua, OH 45356
Ph: (937)778-8600
E-mail: kretschmann@edison.cc.oh.us
URL: http://www.ptk.org/directories/chapters/OH/318-1.htm
Contact: Jane Kretschmann, Advisor
Local. Affiliated With: Phi Theta Kappa, International Honor Society.

16437 ■ Piqua Area Chamber of Commerce (PACC)
326 N Main St.
PO Box 1142
Piqua, OH 45356
Ph: (937)773-2765
Fax: (937)773-8553
E-mail: ksdyas@piquaareachamber.com
URL: http://www.piquaareachamber.com
Contact: Mr. David E. Vollette, Pres.
Membership Dues: small business, regular, professional, out of town, $300 (annual) • financial institution, school, $425 (annual) • utility, publisher, $400 (annual) • nonprofit organization, $160 (annual) • retired individual, $135 (annual). **Staff:** 4. **Local.** Promotes business and community development in the Piqua, OH area. **Councils:** Miami County Safety; Miami County Small Business; Piqua Area Human Resource.

16438 ■ Piqua Area United Way
PO Box 631
Piqua, OH 45356-0631
Ph: (937)773-6786
URL: National Affiliate–national.unitedway.org
Local. Affiliated With: United Way of America.

16439 ■ Piqua Jr. High - Wyldlife
325 W Ash St.
Piqua, OH 45356
Ph: (937)778-1118
URL: http://sites.younglife.org/_layouts/ylext/default.aspx?ID=C-1568
Local. Affiliated With: Young Life.

16440 ■ Piqua - Young Life
325 W Ash St.
Piqua, OH 45356
Ph: (937)778-1118
URL: http://sites.younglife.org/_layouts/ylext/default.aspx?ID=C-1567
Local. Affiliated With: Young Life.

16441 ■ Young Life Miami-Shelby County
325 W Ash St.
Piqua, OH 45356
Ph: (937)778-1118
URL: http://sites.younglife.org/_layouts/ylext/default.aspx?ID=A-OH38
Local. Affiliated With: Young Life.

Plain City

16442 ■ American Legion, Plain City Post 248
241 Maple St.
Plain City, OH 43064
Ph: (740)362-7478
Fax: (740)362-1429
URL: National Affiliate–www.legion.org
Local. Affiliated With: American Legion.

16443 ■ Plain City Lions Club
c/o Dale Rausch, Pres.
17401 State Rte. 161
Plain City, OH 43064
Ph: (614)873-4384
E-mail: ecrso@msn.com
URL: http://www.iwaynet.net/~lions13f
Contact: Dale Rausch, Pres.
Local. Affiliated With: Lions Clubs International.

The Plains

16444 ■ Veterans of Foreign Wars 7174
12 Pine St.
The Plains, OH 45780
Ph: (740)797-4946
Contact: Billy Warren, Commander
Local.

Pleasant Plain

16445 ■ Clermont County Stamp Club
c/o Janet R. Klug
6854 Newtonsville Rd.
Pleasant Plain, OH 45162-9616
E-mail: tongajan@aol.com
URL: http://hometown.aol.com/TongaJan/ccsc.html
Contact: Janet R. Klug, Contact
Local. Affiliated With: American Philatelic Society.

16446 ■ Sons of Norway, Edvard Grieg Lodge 5-657
c/o G. Karl Flem, Pres.
9436 Morrow Woodville Rd.
Pleasant Plain, OH 45162-9309
Ph: (513)877-3005
E-mail: flem1973@yahoo.com
URL: http://www.evensens.net/sons
Contact: G. Karl Flem, Pres.
Local. Affiliated With: Sons of Norway.

Pleasantville

16447 ■ American Legion, Ohio Post 9
c/o Ross George
PO Box 5871
Pleasantville, OH 43148
Ph: (740)362-7478
Fax: (740)362-1429
URL: National Affiliate–www.legion.org
Contact: Ross George, Contact
Local. Affiliated With: American Legion.

Plymouth

16448 ■ American Legion, Ehret-Parsel Post 447
112 Trux St.
Plymouth, OH 44865
Ph: (740)362-7478
Fax: (740)362-1429
URL: National Affiliate–www.legion.org
Local. Affiliated With: American Legion.

Poland

16449 ■ American Legion, Mahoning Valley Post 15
35 Cortland St.
Poland, OH 44514
Ph: (740)362-7478
Fax: (740)362-1429
URL: National Affiliate–www.legion.org
Local. Affiliated With: American Legion.

16450 ■ Poland Lions Club
c/o Paul Young, Pres.
PO Box 5424
Poland, OH 44514
Ph: (330)757-9805
E-mail: jmyump@earthlink.net
URL: http://www.lions13d.org
Contact: Paul Young, Pres.
Local. Affiliated With: Lions Clubs International.

16451 ■ Shenango Valley Beagle Club
c/o Don Ginnetti
2457 Country Ln.
Poland, OH 44514-1515
URL: National Affiliate–clubs.akc.org
Contact: Don Ginnetti, Contact
Local.

Polk

16452 ■ Hayesville Lions Club
c/o Robin Bowman, Pres.
176 US 250 E
Polk, OH 44866
Ph: (419)869-7286
E-mail: flamebowman@aol.com
URL: http://www.lions13b.org
Contact: Robin Bowman, Pres.
Local. Affiliated With: Lions Clubs International.

16453 ■ Polk Lions Club
c/o Ronald Wiley, Pres.
328 S Main St.
Polk, OH 44866
Ph: (419)945-2338
E-mail: rdslwiley@aol.com
URL: http://www.lions13b.org
Contact: Ronald Wiley, Pres.
Local. Affiliated With: Lions Clubs International.

Pomeroy

16454 ■ American Legion, Drew Webster Post 39
PO Box 401
Pomeroy, OH 45769
Ph: (740)362-7478
Fax: (740)362-1429
URL: National Affiliate–www.legion.org
Local. Affiliated With: American Legion.

16455 ■ Meigs County Chamber of Commerce (MCCC)
238 W Main St.
Pomeroy, OH 45769
Ph: (740)992-5005
Fax: (740)992-7942
E-mail: director@meigscountyohio.com
URL: http://www.meigscountychamber.com
Contact: Steve Story, Pres.
Founded: 1980. **Members:** 200. **Membership Dues:** business, $90-$300 (annual) • individual, $50 (annual) • civic, charitable organization, church, $75 (annual) • academic institution, $250 (annual) • utility company, $500 (annual) • financial institution, $1,000 (annual) • retiree/senior, $35 (annual) • elected official, $75 (annual) • professional, $150 (annual). **Staff:** 3. **Local.** Promotes business and community development in Meigs County, OH. **Computer Services:** Online services, membership directory. **Committees:** Assessment; Auditing; Bridge and Beautification; Expansion and Retention; Fundraising; Nominating; Public Relations/Imaging; Transportation. **Formed by Merger of:** Pomeroy Chamber of Commerce; Middleport Chamber of Commerce. **Formerly:** (1990) Pomeroy Area Chamber of Commerce. **Publications:** Newsletter, monthly. **Conventions/Meetings:** monthly meeting.

16456 ■ Meigs RSVP
c/o Diana Coates, Dir.
PO Box 722
Pomeroy, OH 45769-0722
Ph: (740)992-2161
Fax: (740)992-7886
E-mail: rsvp@meigsseniors.com
URL: http://www.seniorcorps.gov/about/programs/rsvp_state.asp?usestateabbr=oh&Search4.x=24&Search4.y=6
Contact: Diana Coates, Dir.
Local. Affiliated With: Retired and Senior Volunteer Program.

Port Clinton

16457 ■ American Legion, Ohio Post 113
c/o Alfred G. Dodway
PO Box 535
Port Clinton, OH 43452
Ph: (740)362-7478
Fax: (740)362-1429
URL: National Affiliate–www.legion.org
Contact: Alfred G. Dodway, Contact
Local. Affiliated With: American Legion.

16458 ■ Camp Perry Shooting Club
PO Box 427
Port Clinton, OH 43452
Ph: (419)635-2682
URL: National Affiliate–www.mynssa.com
Local. Affiliated With: National Skeet Shooting Association.

16459 ■ National Organization for Women - Port Clinton
c/o Jane Held, Co-Pres.
PO Box 805
Port Clinton, OH 43452
Ph: (419)797-2684 (419)734-4870
E-mail: smothers@cros.net
URL: http://www.ohionow.org
Contact: Jane Held, Co-Pres.
Local. Affiliated With: National Organization for Women.

16460 ■ Ohio Genealogical Society, Ottawa County Chapter
PO Box 193
Port Clinton, OH 43452-0193
Ph: (419)898-6662
E-mail: ocgs@cros.net
URL: http://www.rootsweb.com/~ohoccgs
Contact: Donna Schell, Sec.
Founded: 1969. **Members:** 200. **Membership Dues:** single, $16 (annual) • family, $20 (annual) • contributing, $30 (annual). **Local.** Individuals in the Ottawa County, OH area interested in the preservation of the local genealogy. Collects and preserves historical records and makes these records available to all members and the general public. Provides aid to individuals who are doing genealogical research. **Affiliated With:** Ohio Genealogical Society. **Publications:** *Marshland to Heartland*, quarterly. Newsletter. Contains genealogical data of Ottawa County, Ohio. **Price:** included in membership dues. **Advertising:** accepted. **Conventions/Meetings:** monthly meeting - always third Tuesday except July.

16461 ■ Port Clinton Lions Club
c/o Denice Day, Sec.
4476 E Konker Rd.
Port Clinton, OH 43452
Ph: (419)797-4586
E-mail: dday@admirals-pointe.net
URL: http://www.lions13b.org
Contact: Denice Day, Sec.
Local. Affiliated With: Lions Clubs International.

16462 ■ United Way of Greater Toledo Ottawa County Office
127 W Perry St., Ste.105
Port Clinton, OH 43452-1039
Ph: (419)734-6645
Fax: (419)734-4841
Free: (800)650-4357
E-mail: ottawacounty@uwgtol.org
URL: http://www.uwgtol.org
Contact: Bill Kitson, Pres./CEO
Local. Affiliated With: United Way of America.

16463 ■ Veterans of Foreign Wars
214 Madison St.
Port Clinton, OH 43452
Ph: (419)734-9981 (419)734-1360
Fax: (419)734-0486
E-mail: vfw2480@cros.net
Contact: Teresia Sloan, Center Mgr.
Local.

Portage

16464 ■ American Legion, Portage Memorial Post 725
PO Box 212
Portage, OH 43451
Ph: (740)362-7478
Fax: (740)362-1429
URL: National Affiliate–www.legion.org
Local. Affiliated With: American Legion.

Portsmouth

16465 ■ AAA South Central Ohio
1414 12th St.
Portsmouth, OH 45662
Ph: (740)354-5614
URL: http://www.aaa.com
Contact: Brenda Thacker, Mgr.
Local.

16466 ■ American Legion, Ohio Post 23
c/o James Dickey
705 Court St., No. 186
Portsmouth, OH 45662
Ph: (740)362-7478
Fax: (740)362-1429
URL: National Affiliate–www.legion.org
Contact: James Dickey, Contact
Local. Affiliated With: American Legion.

16467 ■ American Legion, Ohio Post 471
c/o Russell D. Williams
950 Gallia St.
Portsmouth, OH 45662
Ph: (740)362-7478
Fax: (740)362-1429
URL: National Affiliate–www.legion.org
Contact: Russell D. Williams, Contact
Local. Affiliated With: American Legion.

16468 ■ American Red Cross, Ohio River Valley Chapter
614 Glover St.
Portsmouth, OH 45662
Ph: (740)354-3293
Fax: (740)353-8735
URL: http://ohiorivervalley.redcross.org
Local.

16469 ■ Arthritis Foundation, Scioto Valley Branch
c/o Diane Boster
602 Chillicothe St., No. 338
Portsmouth, OH 45662
Ph: (740)353-4774
Free: (800)358-0380
E-mail: info.orv@arthritis.org
URL: National Affiliate–www.arthritis.org
Local. Seeks to: discover the cause and improve the methods for the treatment and prevention of arthritis and other rheumatic diseases; increase the number of scientists investigating rheumatic diseases; provide training in rheumatic diseases for more doctors; extend knowledge of arthritis and other rheumatic diseases to the lay public, emphasizing the socioeconomic as well as medical aspects of these diseases. **Affiliated With:** Arthritis Foundation.

16470 ■ National Active and Retired Federal Employees Association - Portsmouth 2121
2921 Sunrise Ave.
Portsmouth, OH 45662-2250
Ph: (740)353-7266
URL: National Affiliate–www.narfe.org
Contact: Donald W. Snively, Contact
Local. Protects the retirement future of employees through education. Informs members on issues affecting the retirement. **Affiliated With:** National Association of Retired Federal Employees.

16471 ■ Ohio River REACT Team
419 Bloom St.
Portsmouth, OH 45662-5412
Ph: (740)776-9937
URL: http://www.reactintl.org/teaminfo/usa_teams/teams-usoh.htm
Local. Trained communication experts and professional volunteers. Provides volunteer public service and emergency communications through the use of radios (Citizen Band, General Mobile Radio Service, UHF and HAM). Coordinates with radio industries and government on safety communication matters and supports charitable activities and community organizations.

16472 ■ Portsmouth ALU
c/o Ray McGinnis
1110 Gay St.
Portsmouth, OH 45662
Ph: (740)353-1702
URL: National Affiliate–www.naifa.org
Local. Represents the interest of insurance and financial advisors. Advocates for a positive legislative and regulatory environment. Enhances business and professional skills of members. **Affiliated With:** National Association of Insurance and Financial Advisors.

16473 ■ Portsmouth Area Chamber of Commerce
324 Chillicothe St.
PO Box 509
Portsmouth, OH 45662
Ph: (740)353-7647
Fax: (740)353-5824
Free: (800)648-2574
E-mail: sogp@portsmouth.org
Contact: Robert Huff, Pres./CEO
Local.

16474 ■ RSVP of Scioto County
c/o Vicki Daily, Dir.
PO Box 407
Portsmouth, OH 45662-0407
Ph: (740)354-3137
Fax: (740)353-4965
E-mail: rsvpscio@sciotowireless.net
URL: http://www.joinseniorservice.org
Contact: Vicki Daily, Dir.
Local. Affiliated With: Retired and Senior Volunteer Program.

16475 ■ Scioto County Chapter of the Ohio Genealogical Society (SCCOGS)
PO Box 812
Portsmouth, OH 45662
E-mail: sccogsnews@earthlink.net
URL: http://www.sccogs.com
Contact: Gladys Reynolds, Pres.
Membership Dues: $15 (annual). **Local.** Supports the objective of Ohio Genealogical Society. Preserves and collects historical records of related areas of Ohio, and makes them available for use in genealogical research. **Telecommunication Services:** electronic mail, gnreynolds@verizon.net. **Affiliated With:** Ohio Genealogical Society. **Publications:** *SCCOGS News*, bimonthly. Newsletter. **Price:** included in membership dues; $2.00 for nonmembers.

16476 ■ Southern Ohio Growth Partnership
c/o Robert D. Huff
PO Box 509
Portsmouth, OH 45662
Ph: (740)353-7647
Fax: (740)353-5824
Contact: Mr. Robert D. Huff, Pres./CEO
Founded: 1992. **Membership Dues:** active, $2,000 (annual). **Staff:** 5. **Budget:** $250,000. **Local.**

16477 ■ United Way of Scioto County
2919 Walnut St.
Portsmouth, OH 45662-4827
Ph: (740)353-5121
Fax: (740)353-9014
E-mail: unitedway@sciotowireless.net
URL: http://www.uwsciotocounty.org
Contact: Tess Midkiff, Pres.
Local. Affiliated With: United Way of America.

Powell

16478 ■ Associated Risk Managers of Ohio (ARM)
c/o Cynthia R. Mills, Exec.Dir.
3956 N Hampton Dr.
Powell, OH 43065
Ph: (614)764-7730
Fax: (614)764-7737
Free: (800)336-2228
E-mail: cmills@rrohio.com
Contact: Cynthia R. Mills, Exec.Dir.
State. Ohio insurance marketing organization with members located in 22 key economic trade centers throughout the state.

16479 ■ Ohio Golf Course Owners Association (OGCOA)
74 S Liberty St.
Powell, OH 43065
Ph: (614)436-9299
Fax: (614)436-2625
Free: (800)826-4394
E-mail: ohiogolf@netset1.com
URL: http://www.buckeyegolf.com
Contact: Gary Wilkins, Pres.
Members: 300. **State.**

16480 ■ Powell Area Chamber of Commerce
30 W Olentangy St.
PO Box 2008
Powell, OH 43065-2008
Ph: (614)888-1090
Fax: (614)888-4803
URL: http://www.powellchamber.com
Contact: Julie Zdanowicz, Pres./CEO
Founded: 1990. **Members:** 120. **Membership Dues:** gold, $500 (annual) • business, $150 (annual) • business member with web link, $170 (annual). **Staff:** 1. **Local.** Promotes business and community development in the greater Powell, OH area. **Awards:** Business Person of the Year. **Frequency:** annual. **Type:** recognition • Citizen of the Year. **Frequency:** annual. **Type:** recognition • Restoration of the Year. **Frequency:** annual. **Type:** recognition. **Recipient:** to a restorer of an old building. **Computer Services:** Information services, member directory. **Additional Websites:** http://www.olentangycommerce.com. **Formerly:** (1999) Greater Powell Area Chamber of Commerce. **Publications:** *Greater Powell Area Chamber of Commerce Directory and Community Guide*, annual. **Price:** free. **Circulation:** 10,000. **Advertising:** accepted • Newsletter, monthly. **Advertising:** accepted.

16481 ■ Powell Sertoma Club
PO Box 169
Powell, OH 43065
Ph: (614)888-1090
E-mail: info@powellsertoma.com
URL: http://www.powellsertoma.com
Contact: Greg Jaudzems, Pres.
Local.

Powhatan Point

16482 ■ American Legion, Saner Post 228
279 Hwy. 7 N
Powhatan Point, OH 43942
Ph: (740)362-7478
Fax: (740)362-1429
URL: National Affiliate–www.legion.org
Local. Affiliated With: American Legion.

Proctorville

16483 ■ Lawrence County Genealogical Society, OGS Chapter 74
PO Box 1035
Proctorville, OH 45669-1035

Ph: (740)886-7230
E-mail: lawcoloreman@aol.com
URL: http://www.lawrencecountyohio.com/gensoc/gensoc.htm
Contact: Judy Carpenter, Pres.

Founded: 1984. **Members:** 250. **Membership Dues:** household, $10 (annual). **Local**. Strives to preserve and publish local records and genealogical research in Lawrence County, OH. **Libraries: Type:** reference. **Subjects:** local history, genealogy. **Awards:** Lawrence County 4-H Genealogy Project Winner. **Type:** recognition. **Subgroups:** Civil War Society; First Families of Lawrence County. **Affiliated With:** Ohio Genealogical Society. **Publications:** *Lawco Lore*, quarterly. Newsletter. **Price:** included in membership. **Circulation:** 315.

Prospect

16484 ■ American Legion, Ohio Post 368
c/o Verne I. Mounts
PO Box 187
Prospect, OH 43342
Ph: (740)362-7478
Fax: (740)362-1429
URL: National Affiliate–www.legion.org
Contact: Verne I. Mounts, Contact

Local. Affiliated With: American Legion.

16485 ■ American Theatre Organ Society, Heart Of Ohio Chapter
c/o Angela Carbetta, Pres.
785 Prospect-Mt. Vernon Rd.
Prospect, OH 43342
Ph: (740)726-2520
E-mail: accarbetta@aol.com
URL: National Affiliate–www.atos.org
Contact: Angela Carbetta, Pres.

Local. Aims to restore, preserve and promote the theatre pipe organ and its music. Encourages the youth to learn the instrument. Operates a committee that gathers history and old music from silent film days and information on theatre organists, theaters and organ installations of the silent film era. **Affiliated With:** American Theatre Organ Society.

16486 ■ Green Camp Lions Club
c/o Charles Long, Sec.
4263 LaRue-Prospect Rd. S
Prospect, OH 43342
Ph: (740)382-1818 (740)528-2797
Fax: (740)528-2797
E-mail: kestrel@marion.net
URL: http://www.iwaynet.net/~lions13f
Contact: Charles Long, Sec.

Local. Affiliated With: Lions Clubs International.

16487 ■ Korean War Veterans Association, Marion Chapter
c/o Robert Kerr
2122 Prospect Norton Rd.
Prospect, OH 43342-9313
Ph: (740)494-2568
E-mail: dcrkerr@wmconnect.com
URL: National Affiliate–www.kwva.org
Contact: Robert Kerr, Contact

Local. Affiliated With: Korean War Veterans Association.

16488 ■ Prospect Lions Club - Ohio
c/o Thomas R. Stiffler, Pres.
6362 Hughes Rd.
Prospect, OH 43342
Ph: (740)494-2019
URL: http://www.iwaynet.net/~lions13f
Contact: Thomas R. Stiffler, Pres.

Local. Affiliated With: Lions Clubs International.

Put In Bay

16489 ■ American Legion, Scheible-Downing Post 542
PO Box 56
Put In Bay, OH 43456
Ph: (740)362-7478
Fax: (740)362-1429
URL: National Affiliate–www.legion.org

Local. Affiliated With: American Legion.

16490 ■ Put-in-Bay Chamber of Commerce (PBCC)
148 Delaware Ave.
PO Box 250
Put In Bay, OH 43456
Ph: (419)285-2832
Fax: (419)285-4702
E-mail: islandinfo@put-in-bay.com
URL: http://www.put-in-bay.com
Contact: Maggie Beckford, Exec.Dir.

Members: 140. **Membership Dues:** full, $65 (annual) • associate, $100 (annual). **Staff:** 2. **Budget:** $96,000. **Local**. Seeks to attract business and tourism to the Put-in-Bay, OH area. **Committees:** Finance; Island Guide. **Publications:** *Island Guide*, annual. Magazine. Contains tourist information. **Price:** included in membership dues. **Circulation:** 225,000. **Advertising:** accepted. **Conventions/Meetings:** bimonthly general assembly.

Quaker City

16491 ■ American Legion, Beaver Post 578
224 Beaver St.
Quaker City, OH 43773
Ph: (740)362-7478
Fax: (740)362-1429
URL: National Affiliate–www.legion.org

Local. Affiliated With: American Legion.

16492 ■ American Legion, Ohio Post 337
c/o Earl Conner
PO Box 265
Quaker City, OH 43773
Ph: (740)362-7478
Fax: (740)362-1429
URL: National Affiliate–www.legion.org
Contact: Earl Conner, Contact

Local. Affiliated With: American Legion.

Racine

16493 ■ American Legion, Racine Post 602
PO Box 36
Racine, OH 45771
Ph: (740)362-7478
Fax: (740)362-1429
URL: National Affiliate–www.legion.org

Local. Affiliated With: American Legion.

16494 ■ Meigs County Beagle Club
c/o Roger Birch
48784 State Rte. 124
Racine, OH 45771-9020
URL: National Affiliate–www.akc.org
Contact: Roger Birch, Contact

Members: 16. **Membership Dues:** $25 (annual). **Staff:** 5. **Local. Affiliated With:** American Kennel Club.

Ravenna

16495 ■ American Legion, Garrettsville Post 32
865 Overlook Ave.
Ravenna, OH 44266
Ph: (740)362-7478
Fax: (740)362-1429
URL: National Affiliate–www.legion.org

Local. Affiliated With: American Legion.

16496 ■ American Legion, Ravenna Post 331
109 Elm St., No. 747
Ravenna, OH 44266
Ph: (740)362-7478
Fax: (740)362-1429
URL: National Affiliate–www.legion.org

Local. Affiliated With: American Legion.

16497 ■ Gardeners of America/Men's Garden Clubs of America - Garden Club of Kent
c/o Rick Strebler, Pres.
3456 State Rte. 59
Ravenna, OH 44266
Ph: (330)296-9300
E-mail: hybridperpetual@aol.com
URL: National Affiliate–www.tgoa-mgca.org
Contact: Rick Strebler, Pres.

Local.

16498 ■ Habitat for Humanity of Portage County (HFHPC)
PO Box 306
Ravenna, OH 44266-0306
Ph: (330)296-2880
Fax: (330)296-5263
E-mail: hfhofpc@aol.com
URL: http://www.habitatofportage.com

Local. Affiliated With: Habitat for Humanity International.

16499 ■ Mothers Against Drunk Driving, Portage County
250 S. Chestnut St. No. 16
Ravenna, OH 44266
Ph: (330)297-6701
Fax: (330)297-1012
E-mail: maddpc@juno.com

Victims of drunk driving crashes; concerned citizens. Encourages citizen participation in working towards reform of the drunk driving problem and the prevention of underage drinking. Acts as the voice of victims of drunk driving crashes by speaking on their behalf to communities, businesses, and educational groups. **Affiliated With:** Mothers Against Drunk Driving.

16500 ■ Muskies Cleveland Chapter 23
5608 Brave Chief Ln.
Ravenna, OH 44266
Ph: (330)296-2398
E-mail: fffffish@aol.com
URL: http://www.muskiesinc23.com
Contact: Richard E. Burke, Pres.

Local.

16501 ■ North Coast Triumph Association (NCTA)
c/o Bob Brown, Pres.
230 S Diamond St.
Ravenna, OH 44266-2846
E-mail: spanksbox@aol.com
URL: http://www.nctaweb.com
Contact: Bob Brown, Pres.

Local. Affiliated With: Vintage Triumph Register.

16502 ■ Portage County Association of Realtors
PO Box 509
Ravenna, OH 44266
Ph: (330)296-5451
Fax: (330)296-2060
E-mail: pcar@neo.rr.com
URL: National Affiliate–www.realtor.org
Contact: Laurie Summers, Exec. Officer

Local. Strives to develop real estate business practices. Advocates for the right to own, use and transfer real property. Provides a facility for professional development, research and exchange of information among members and the general public. **Affiliated With:** National Association of Realtors.

16503 ■ Portage County Chapter of the Ohio Genealogical Society (PCCOGS)
PO Box 821
Ravenna, OH 44266-0821
Ph: (330)296-3523
URL: http://www.history.portage.oh.us/genealogy_society.html
Contact: Claudia Bissler, Pres.

Membership Dues: single, $10 (annual) • two or more at one address, $12 (annual). **Local. Affiliated With:** Ohio Genealogical Society. **Publications:** *Portage Path of Genealogy*, bimonthly. Newsletter. Contains information relating to meeting dates and subjects, member activities, and queries. **Price:** included in membership dues; $1.00 for nonmembers.

16504 ■ Ravenna Area Chamber of Commerce (RACC)
135 E Main St.
Ravenna, OH 44266
Ph: (330)296-3886
Fax: (330)296-6986
E-mail: director@ravennachamber.com
URL: http://www.ravennachamber.com
Contact: Pat Artz, Exec.Dir.

Founded: 1912. **Members:** 250. **Local**. Promotes business and community development in the Ravenna, OH area. **Awards:** Raven Awards. **Frequency:** annual. **Type:** recognition. **Recipient:** to organizations whose new construction, renovations or facade treatments help advance the Ravenna area. **Committees:** Economic Development; Education; Fundraising; Marketing; Membership Services; Networking; Ravenna Pride. **Affiliated With:** U.S. Chamber of Commerce. **Publications:** Newsletter, bimonthly.

16505 ■ Reed Memorial Library
167 E Main St.
Ravenna, OH 44266
Ph: (330)296-2827
Fax: (330)296-3780
E-mail: refreed@oplin.org
URL: http://www.reed.lib.oh.us
Contact: James Wichman, Pres.

Founded: 1999. **Members:** 150. **Membership Dues:** single, $10 (biennial) • family, $20 (biennial) • senior citizen, $6 (biennial) • institution, $50 (biennial) • life, $100. **Local**. Supports the public library in the community. **Computer Services:** database, CD-ROM • information services, business and investment, consumer product • online services, web catalog, reference service. **Formerly:** (2005) Friends of Reed Memorial Library. **Publications:** *Read the News*, quarterly. Newsletter. Alternate Formats: online • Annual Report, annual. Alternate Formats: online.

Reading

16506 ■ American Legion, Halker-Flege Post 69
9000 Reading Rd.
Reading, OH 45215
Ph: (740)362-7478
Fax: (740)362-1429
URL: National Affiliate–www.legion.org
Local. Affiliated With: American Legion.

16507 ■ Reading Chamber of Commerce
PO Box 15164
Reading, OH 45215
Ph: (513)733-5500
Fax: (513)733-5604
E-mail: jims@gentool.com
URL: http://www.readingohiochamber.org
Contact: Jim Stewart, Pres.

Membership Dues: 1 to 5 employees, $75 (annual) • 6 to 50 employees, $150 (annual) • 51 plus employees, $300 (annual). **Local.**

16508 ■ Reading Police Officers Association
c/o Scott Snow
1000 Market St.
Reading, OH 45215-3209
Ph: (513)733-5126
Local.

Republic

16509 ■ American Legion, Wade Benfer Post 404
112 Washington St.
Republic, OH 44867
Ph: (740)362-7478
Fax: (740)362-1429
URL: National Affiliate–www.legion.org
Local. Affiliated With: American Legion.

16510 ■ American Truck Historical Society, Black Swamp Chapter
c/o Jim Peters
5271 ESR No.18
Republic, OH 44867
Ph: (418)585-4251
URL: National Affiliate–www.aths.org
Contact: Jim Peters, Contact
Local.

16511 ■ Republic Lions Club
c/o Phillip Benner, Pres.
308 N Kilbourne St.
Republic, OH 44867
Ph: (419)585-7331
E-mail: phillipbenner@hotmail.com
URL: http://www.lions13b.org
Contact: Phillip Benner, Pres.
Local. Affiliated With: Lions Clubs International.

Reynoldsburg

16512 ■ American Legion, Reynoldsburg Post 798
1114 Roundelay Rd. E
Reynoldsburg, OH 43068
Ph: (740)362-7478
Fax: (740)362-1429
URL: National Affiliate–www.legion.org
Local. Affiliated With: American Legion.

16513 ■ IEEE Communications Society, Columbus Chapter
c/o Sol Black
6910 Prior Pl.
Reynoldsburg, OH 43068-1730
Ph: (614)864-5893
E-mail: sblack@celestica.com
URL: National Affiliate–www.comsoc.org
Contact: Sol Black, Contact

Local. Industry professionals with a common interest in advancing all communications technologies. Seeks to foster original work in all aspects of communications science, engineering, and technology and encourages the development of applications that use signals to transfer voice, data, image, and/or video information between locations. Promotes the theory and use of systems involving all types of terminals, computers, and information processors; all pertinent systems and operations that facilitate transfer; all transmission media; switched and unswitched networks; and network layout, protocols, architectures, and implementations. **Affiliated With:** IEEE Communications Society.

16514 ■ National Association of Drug Diversion Investigators of Ohio
c/o Rob Amiet, Pres.
Ohio State Bd. of Pharmacy
1818 Chimney Hill Ct.
Reynoldsburg, OH 43068
Ph: (614)861-5531
Fax: (212)417-2099
E-mail: ramiet@bop.state.oh.us
URL: National Affiliate–www.naddi.org
Contact: Rob Amiet, Pres.

State. Represents the interests of individuals who are responsible for investigating and prosecuting pharmaceutical drug diversion. Seeks to improve the members' ability to investigate and prosecute pharmaceutical drug diversion. **Affiliated With:** National Association of Drug Diversion Investigators.

16515 ■ National School Public Relations Association, Ohio
c/o Karen Kaiser, Exec.Dir.
PO Box 664
Reynoldsburg, OH 43068
Ph: (614)871-2222
E-mail: director@nspraohio.org
URL: http://www.nspraohio.org
Contact: Susan Cross, Pres.

Founded: 1983. **Members:** 200. **Membership Dues:** individual, $45 (annual) • institutional, $110 (annual). **Budget:** $35,000. **State**. Educators with responsibilities in the area of communications, public relations, and community relations. Seeks to strengthen education by assisting members in listening to and communicating with their publics, and by enhancing the image and role of public relations in educational management. **Affiliated With:** National School Public Relations Association. **Conventions/Meetings:** annual conference - always spring.

16516 ■ Ohio Rural Development Partnership (ORDP)
A.B. Graham Bldg.
8995 E Main St.
Reynoldsburg, OH 43068-3399
Ph: (614)728-4937
Fax: (614)728-2652
Free: (800)282-1955
E-mail: ruraldev@mail.agri.state.oh.us
URL: http://www.ohioagriculture.gov/ordp.stm
Contact: Fred L. Dailey, Dir.

Founded: 1992. **Members:** 650. **Staff:** 2. **Regional Groups:** 3. **State Groups:** 1. **State. Formerly:** (2005) Ohio Rural Partners.

16517 ■ Public Relations Society of America, Central Ohio
c/o Dr. Steve Iseman, Pres.
PO Box 374
Reynoldsburg, OH 43068
Ph: (614)470-2762 (419)772-5053
Fax: (419)772-1856
E-mail: administrator@centralohioprsa.org
URL: http://www.centralohioprsa.org
Contact: Dr. Steve Iseman, Pres.
Local. Affiliated With: Public Relations Society of America.

16518 ■ Reserve Officers Association - Department of Ohio, Columbus Navy Chapter 12
c/o LCDR Timothy L. Thickstun, Pres.
325 Deer Tail Rd.
Reynoldsburg, OH 43068-9725
Ph: (614)252-8422 (614)863-9565
E-mail: tim@advfuel.com
URL: http://www.roa.org/oh
Contact: LCDR Timothy L. Thickstun, Pres.

Local. Promotes and supports the development and execution of a military policy for the United States. Provides professional development seminars, workshops and programs for its members. **Affiliated With:** Reserve Officers Association of the United States.

16519 ■ Reynoldsburg Area Chamber of Commerce
1580 Brice Rd.
Reynoldsburg, OH 43068
Ph: (614)866-4753
Fax: (614)866-7313
E-mail: jan@reynoldsburgchamber.com
URL: http://www.reynoldsburgchamber.com
Contact: Jan Hills, Exec.Dir.

Membership Dues: business (based on number of employees), $140-$350 (annual) • associate, $35 (annual). **Local**. Promotes and supports business environment within the community by representing its interests. Enhances the general welfare of the community through economic prosperity. **Publications:** Newsletter. Alternate Formats: online.

16520 ■ Whitehall Area Lions Club
c/o Karen Risen, Pres.
1219 Hilton Dr.
Reynoldsburg, OH 43068
Ph: (614)752-8463 (614)864-9819
E-mail: drisen@insight.rr.com
URL: http://www.iwaynet.net/~lions13f
Contact: Karen Risen, Pres.
Local. Affiliated With: Lions Clubs International.

Richfield

16521 ■ AMVETS, Richfield Post 176
3944 Wheatley Rd.
Richfield, OH 44286
Ph: (330)659-3924
URL: http://www.ohamvets.org/post176.htm
Local. Affiliated With: AMVETS - American Veterans.

16522 ■ Antique Automobile Club of America, Ohio Region - Northern Chapter
c/o Regina Jandrey, Sec.
4373 Broadview Rd.
Richfield, OH 44286
Ph: (330)659-4637
E-mail: jandrey3@aol.com
URL: http://local.aaca.org/ohio/norther.htm
Contact: Moses Dannenhirsh, Pres.
Local. Collectors, hobbyists, and others interested in the preservation, maintenance, and restoration of automobiles and in automotive history. **Affiliated With:** Antique Automobile Club of America.

16523 ■ IEEE Computer Society, Cleveland
c/o Steve Belovich, Exec. Officer
4816 Brecksville Rd., Ste.No. 1
Richfield, OH 44286
Ph: (330)659-2660
E-mail: belovich@smart-data.com
Contact: Dr. Steve Belovich, CEO
Founded: 1988. **Members:** 12. **Staff:** 12. **Languages:** English, Spanish. **For-Profit. Regional.** Specializes in industrial process automation, time data acquisition, quality management, spc/sec and software development for factory floor and enterprise integration. **Affiliated With:** IEEE Computer Society.

Richmond

16524 ■ American Legion, Honored Seven Post 740
PO Box 322
Richmond, OH 43944
Ph: (740)362-7478
Fax: (740)362-1429
URL: National Affiliate–www.legion.org
Local. Affiliated With: American Legion.

Richmond Heights

16525 ■ Forest Hill Lawn Bowling Club
c/o Jean Sinzinger
759 Edgewood Rd.
Richmond Heights, OH 44143
Ph: (216)449-5058
E-mail: ionams@aol.com
URL: http://www.members.aol.com/uslbacentral/index.htm
Contact: Jean Sinzinger, Contact
Local. Affiliated With: United States Lawn Bowls Association.

16526 ■ Lake-Geauga Helicopter Association
4845 Monticello Blvd.
Richmond Heights, OH 44143
Ph: (216)381-1412
URL: http://torchs.org/clubs/clubs.htm
Contact: Robert A. Voss, Contact
Local.

Richwood

16527 ■ American Legion, Baccarat Post 40
105 N Franklin St.
Richwood, OH 43344
Ph: (740)362-7478
Fax: (740)362-1429
URL: National Affiliate–www.legion.org
Local. Affiliated With: American Legion.

16528 ■ International Union, United Automobile, Aerospace and Agricultural Implement Workers of America, AFL-CIO - Local Union 2269
297 Grove St.
Richwood, OH 43344
URL: http://www.uawlocal2269.org
Contact: Rick Nye, Pres.
Members: 203. **Local**. AFL-CIO. **Affiliated With:** International Union, United Automobile, Aerospace and Agricultural Implement Workers of America.

16529 ■ Ohio Quarter Horse Association (OQHA)
101 Tawa Rd.
PO Box 209
Richwood, OH 43344-0209
Ph: (740)943-2346 (740)943-2389
Fax: (740)943-3752
E-mail: qtrhorse@oqha.com
URL: http://www.oqha.com
Contact: Dennis Hales, Exec.VP
State. State affiliate of the American Quarter Horse Association. Promotes the breeding and competition of registered American Quarter Horses around the state through awards and educational programs as well as donations to state FFA and 4-H programs and equine research. Sponsors the All American Quarter Horse Congress single breed horse show annually in October at the Ohio Expo Center in Columbus, Ohio.

16530 ■ Veterans of Foreign Wars 870
9 W. Blagrove St.
Richwood, OH 43344
Ph: (740)943-3808
Affiliated With: Veterans of Foreign Wars of the United States.

Ridgeville Corners

16531 ■ American Legion, Ohio Post 454
c/o Ward L. Adams
PO Box 172
Ridgeville Corners, OH 43555
Ph: (740)362-7478
Fax: (740)362-1429
URL: National Affiliate–www.legion.org
Contact: Ward L. Adams, Contact
Local. Affiliated With: American Legion.

Rio Grande

16532 ■ Ohio Association of College Stores (OACS)
c/o David Ding, VP/Pres.-Elect
Rio Grande Univ. Bookstore
218 N Coll. Ave.
Rio Grande, OH 45674
Ph: (740)245-7274
E-mail: dding@rio.edu
URL: http://www.oacsohio.org
Contact: David Ding, VP/Pres.-Elect
State. Promotes the collegiate retailing industry. Enhances the college store industry through service, education and research. Promotes high standards of business practices and ethics within the industry. **Affiliated With:** National Association of College Stores.

16533 ■ Phi Theta Kappa - Beta Nu Phi Chapter
c/o Beverly Crabtree
218 N Coll. Ave.
Rio Grande, OH 45674
Ph: (740)245-5353
E-mail: beverlyc@rio.edu
URL: http://www.ptk.org/directories/chapters/OH/21603-1.htm
Contact: Beverly Crabtree, Advisor
Local. Affiliated With: Phi Theta Kappa, International Honor Society.

16534 ■ RiverBend Society for Human Resource Management
c/o Phyllis J. Mason
PO Box 500
Rio Grande, OH 45674
Ph: (740)245-7228
Fax: (740)245-4909
E-mail: pmason@rio.edu
URL: http://ohioshrm.org/riverbend
Contact: Phyllis L. Mason, Pres.
Local. Represents the interests of human resource and industrial relations professionals and executives. Promotes the advancement of human resource management.

Ripley

16535 ■ American Legion, Courts-Fussnecker Post 367
2944 Elk River Rd.
Ripley, OH 45167
Ph: (740)362-7478
Fax: (740)362-1429
URL: National Affiliate–www.legion.org
Local. Affiliated With: American Legion.

Rittman

16536 ■ American Legion, Ohio Post 423
c/o Howard A. Bair
77 Warren St.
Rittman, OH 44270
Ph: (740)362-7478
Fax: (740)362-1429
URL: National Affiliate–www.legion.org
Contact: Howard A. Bair, Contact
Local. Affiliated With: American Legion.

16537 ■ Doylestown Lions Club
15077 Mt. Eaton Rd.
Rittman, OH 44270
Ph: (330)347-6831
E-mail: markystang@yahoo.com
URL: http://doylestownoh.lionwap.org
Contact: Jerry Foyse, Pres.
Local. Affiliated With: Lions Clubs International.

16538 ■ Gemutlich Wanderers
c/o Leon Brandes
127 N 2nd St.
Rittman, OH 44270-0000
Ph: (330)927-5635
E-mail: lbrandes@neo.rr.com
URL: National Affiliate–www.ava.org
Contact: Leon Brandes, Contact
Local. Non-competitive sports enthusiasts. **Affiliated With:** American Volkssport Association.

16539 ■ Rittman Area Chamber of Commerce
12 N Main St., Ste.2
Rittman, OH 44270
Ph: (330)925-4828
Fax: (330)925-4828
E-mail: rittmanchamber@aol.com
URL: http://www.rittman.com
Contact: John Landers, Exec.Dir.
Local. Promotes businesses in Rittman, OH.

Rock Creek

16540 ■ Antique Automobile Club of America, Ohio Region - Western Reserve Chapter
c/o Kenneth C. Pobuda, Pres.
2851 Trask Rd.
Rock Creek, OH 44084
Ph: (440)474-4398
URL: http://www.aaca.org/ohio/WestReserve.htm
Contact: Kenneth C. Pobuda, Pres.
Local. Collectors, hobbyists, and others interested in the preservation, maintenance, and restoration of automobiles and in automotive history. **Affiliated With:** Antique Automobile Club of America.

Rockford

16541 ■ American Legion, Ohio Post 508
c/o Glen D. Eckhart
PO Box 251
Rockford, OH 45882
Ph: (740)362-7478
Fax: (740)362-1429
URL: National Affiliate–www.legion.org
Contact: Glen D. Eckhart, Contact
Local. **Affiliated With:** American Legion.

Rocky River

16542 ■ American Association of Physics Teachers, Ohio Section
c/o Lawrence J. Badar, Representative
Case Western Univ.
20802 Beachwood Dr.
Rocky River, OH 44116-1408
Ph: (440)331-2586
E-mail: larrybadar@oal.com
URL: National Affiliate–www.aapt.org
Contact: Lawrence J. Badar, Representative
State. Seeks to enhance the understanding and appreciation of physics through teaching. Aims to improve the pedagogical skills and physics knowledge of teachers at all levels. **Affiliated With:** American Association of Physics Teachers.

16543 ■ American Legion, Rocky River Post 451
c/o Henry J. Morgan
19911 Lake Rd.
Rocky River, OH 44116
Ph: (740)362-7478
Fax: (740)362-1429
URL: National Affiliate–www.legion.org
Contact: Henry J. Morgan, Contact
Local. **Affiliated With:** American Legion.

16544 ■ Cleveland Southeast Lions Club
2878 Wagar Rd.
Rocky River, OH 44116
E-mail: cleselions@yahoo.com
URL: http://www.geocities.com/cleselions
Contact: David Gutfranski, Pres.
Local. **Affiliated With:** Lions Clubs International.

16545 ■ Greater Cleveland FEIS Society
20245 Orchard Grove Ave.
Rocky River, OH 44116-3526
E-mail: clevelandfeis@yahoo.com
URL: http://www.clevelandfeis.com
Contact: Teresa Reilly Kowalski, Pres.
Local.

16546 ■ Health Physics Society, Northern Ohio Chapter
3901 Linden Rd.
Rocky River, OH 44116
E-mail: radiationguy@earthlink.net
URL: National Affiliate–www.hps.org
Contact: John M. Wills, Pres.
Local. Promotes the practice of radiation safety. Encourages research in radiation science and disseminates radiation safety information. **Affiliated With:** Health Physics Society.

16547 ■ Latin Liturgy Association
c/o Mr. James F. Pauer, Pres.
PO Box 16517
Rocky River, OH 44116
E-mail: jfpauer@juno.com
URL: http://www.latinliturgy.com
Contact: Mr. James F. Pauer, Pres.
Local.

16548 ■ Rocky River Chamber of Commerce (RRCC)
20160 Detroit Rd.
Rocky River, OH 44116-2444
Ph: (440)331-1140
Fax: (440)331-3485
E-mail: info@rockyriverchamber.com
URL: http://www.rockyriverchamber.com
Contact: Pat Krizansky, Exec.Dir.
Founded: 1938. **Members:** 250. **Membership Dues:** associate, $55 (annual) • public official, $80 (annual) • business, $130-$360 (annual). **Staff:** 1. **Local**. Promotes business and community development in Rocky River, OH. Holds annual Christmas party to benefit Rocky River Assistance Program. **Awards: Type:** scholarship. **Committees:** Communications; Education; Government Affairs/Economic Development; Legal; Strategic Planning/Financial/Budget. **Affiliated With:** U.S. Chamber of Commerce. **Publications:** *River Biz*, monthly. Newsletter. **Advertising:** accepted. Alternate Formats: online • *Rocky River Residence Reference Guide*, annual. Directory. **Conventions/Meetings:** Business Mixers - meeting - 3/year • monthly luncheon, with informative program - every 4th Thursday • annual New Teachers' Luncheon.

Rootstown

16549 ■ Buckeye Woodworkers and Turners (BWWT)
c/o Larry McCardel, Pres.
4577 Hattrick Rd.
Rootstown, OH 44272
Ph: (330)325-2158
E-mail: lbmccardel@aol.com
URL: http://www.bwwt.org
Contact: Larry McCardel, Pres.
Local. Represents amateur and professional woodturners, gallery owners, wood and equipment suppliers, and collectors. **Affiliated With:** American Association of Woodturners.

16550 ■ Microscopy Society of Northeastern Ohio (MSNO)
c/o Jeanette Killius, Pres. Elect
Dept. of Res. and Sponsored Programs
NEOU Coll. of Medicine
PO Box 95
Rootstown, OH 44272-0095
Ph: (330)325-6311
Fax: (330)325-5910
E-mail: jkillius@neoucom.edu
URL: http://www.msneo.org
Contact: Jeanette Killius, Pres. Elect
Membership Dues: professional, $20 (annual) • corporate, $50 (annual) • student, retiree, $5 (annual). **Regional**. **Affiliated With:** Microscopy Society of America.

16551 ■ Rootstown Area Chamber of Commerce
PO Box 254
Rootstown, OH 44272
Ph: (330)325-2379
E-mail: website@rootstownchamber.org
URL: http://www.rootstownchamber.org
Contact: Ken Cain, Pres.
Membership Dues: general, $50 (annual). **Local**. Promotes interest of its members and of business in general. **Computer Services:** Information services, membership directory. **Conventions/Meetings:** monthly meeting - every 2nd Tuesday.

16552 ■ Rootstown Lions Club
c/o Paul Jay, Pres.
4928 Judy Dr.
Rootstown, OH 44272
Ph: (330)325-8310
E-mail: yajeulbone@yahoo.com
URL: http://www.rootstownlions.homestead.com
Contact: Paul Jay, Pres.
Local. **Affiliated With:** Lions Clubs International.

16553 ■ Rootstown Soccer Club (RSC)
PO Box 72
Rootstown, OH 44272-0072
E-mail: k.w.moss@att.net
URL: http://www.rootstownsoccerclub.org
Contact: Ken Moss, Pres.
Local.

Roseville

16554 ■ American Legion, Ohio Post 71
c/o Forest L. Mumford
74 S Main St.
Roseville, OH 43777
Ph: (740)362-7478
Fax: (740)362-1429
URL: National Affiliate–www.legion.org
Contact: Forest L. Mumford, Contact
Local. **Affiliated With:** American Legion.

Rossburg

16555 ■ Darke County Pheasants Forever
147 E Star Rd.
Rossburg, OH 45362
Ph: (419)336-5104
E-mail: darkepheasants4ever@lycos.com
URL: http://darkepheasants4ever.tripod.com
Contact: Doug Hesson, Pres.
Local. **Affiliated With:** Pheasants Forever.

Rossford

16556 ■ American Legion, Rossford Post 533
145 Bergin St., No. 23
Rossford, OH 43460
Ph: (740)362-7478
Fax: (740)362-1429
URL: National Affiliate–www.legion.org
Local. **Affiliated With:** American Legion.

16557 ■ BMW Riders of Toledo No. 16 (BMWRoT)
c/o Gary Haydel
134 Vineyard Dr.
Rossford, OH 43460

Ph: (419)666-3126
E-mail: bmwtoledocampout@bex.net
URL: http://www.BMWRidersOfToledo.org
Contact: Gary Haydel, Contact
Local. Affiliated With: BMW Motorcycle Owners of America.

16558 ■ Toledo Chapter National Electrical Contractors Association
c/o Dan Saad, Governor
727 Lime City Rd., No. 100
Rossford, OH 43460
Ph: (419)666-6040
Fax: (419)666-6080
E-mail: todd@necaohmi.org
URL: National Affiliate–www.necanet.org
Contact: Mr. Daniel L. Bollin, Pres.
Regional. Contractors erecting, installing, repairing, servicing, and maintaining electric wiring, equipment, and appliances. **Affiliated With:** National Electrical Contractors Association.

16559 ■ United Brotherhood of Carpenters and Joiners of America, Toledo Local Union No. 248
9278 E Arena Dr.
Rossford, OH 43460
Ph: (419)893-3782
Fax: (419)893-4021
URL: http://www.carpenters.org
Contact: Timothy Moran, Pres.
Local. Affiliated With: United Brotherhood of Carpenters and Joiners of America.

Roundhead

16560 ■ Scioto River Hunting Club (SRHC)
PO Box 275
Roundhead, OH 43346
Ph: (937)464-6560
Fax: (937)464-7464
E-mail: lindatussing@srhuntclub.com
URL: http://www.srhuntclub.com
Contact: Linda Tussing, Mgr.
Local. Affiliated With: National Skeet Shooting Association.

Russell Township

16561 ■ Geauga Humane Society / Rescue Village
15463 Chillicothe Rd.
Russell Township, OH 44072
Ph: (440)338-4819
E-mail: info@geaugahumane.org
URL: http://www.geaugahumane.org
Local.

Russells Point

16562 ■ Indian Lake Area Chamber of Commerce (ILACoC)
126 N Orchard Island Rd.
PO Box 717
Russells Point, OH 43348-0717
Ph: (937)843-5392
Fax: (937)843-9051
E-mail: office@indianlakechamber.org
URL: http://www.indianlakechamber.org
Contact: Frank Dietz, Pres.
Founded: 1957. **Members:** 317. **Membership Dues:** business (varies with number of employees), $60-$180 (annual) • organization, $30 (annual) • individual associate, $20 (annual). **Staff:** 2. **Local.** Individuals, businesses, churches, and organizations united to promote business and community development in the Russells Point, OH area. **Awards:** Citizen of the Year. **Frequency:** annual. **Type:** recognition. **Recipient:** for outstanding contributions to the improvement of the Indian Lake area. **Computer Services:** Online services, membership directory. **Affiliated With:** U.S. Chamber of Commerce. **Publications:** *Soundings*, monthly. Newsletter. Alternate Formats: online. **Conventions/Meetings:** monthly board meeting - every 1st Thursday • annual meeting.

Russellville

16563 ■ American Legion, Walter Miller Post 394
PO Box 44
Russellville, OH 45168
Ph: (740)362-7478
Fax: (740)362-1429
URL: National Affiliate–www.legion.org
Local. Affiliated With: American Legion.

Rutland

16564 ■ American Legion, Eli Denison Post 467
PO Box 419
Rutland, OH 45775
Ph: (740)362-7478
Fax: (740)362-1429
URL: National Affiliate–www.legion.org
Local. Affiliated With: American Legion.

Sagamore Hills

16565 ■ American Hiking Society - Cuyahoga Valley Trails Council
714 Fieldcrest Ct.
Sagamore Hills, OH 44067
Ph: (330)467-9593
URL: National Affiliate–www.americanhiking.org
Local.

16566 ■ Ohio Association of Parliamentarians (OAP)
927 Trimble Pl.
Sagamore Hills, OH 44067-2239
Ph: (216)225-6447
E-mail: parliscrib@aol.com
URL: National Affiliate–www.parliamentarians.org
Contact: James Williams, Pres.
Founded: 1968. **Members:** 200. **Membership Dues:** regular, retired, student, $15 (annual). **Budget:** $60,000. **Local Groups:** 16. **State.** Persons interested in study of, research on, and practice of parliamentary procedures. **Libraries: Type:** open to the public. **Holdings:** 406; books. **Subjects:** parliamentary law and procedure. **Affiliated With:** National Association of Parliamentarians. **Publications:** *The Parliagram*, periodic. Newsletter • *The Parliagraph*, quarterly. Directory. **Conventions/Meetings:** annual convention - usually September.

St. Bernard

16567 ■ Reserve Officers Association - Department of Ohio, Alfred Gus Karger Chapter 7
c/o Major Michael A. Clark, Pres.
4312 Sullivan Ave.
St. Bernard, OH 45217-1747
Ph: (513)771-4740
E-mail: michael.a.clark@us.army.mil
URL: http://www.roa.org/oh
Contact: Major Michael A. Clark, Pres.
Local. Promotes and supports the development and execution of a military policy for the United States. Provides professional development seminars, workshops and programs for its members. **Affiliated With:** Reserve Officers Association of the United States.

St. Clairsville

16568 ■ AAA Ohio Auto Club
107 S Marietta St.
St. Clairsville, OH 43950
Ph: (740)695-4030
Fax: (740)695-9432
Free: (800)288-4467
Contact: Ms. Maryjo Bumbico, Mgr.
Local.

16569 ■ American Legion, St. Clairsville Post 159
PO Box 495
St. Clairsville, OH 43950
Ph: (740)362-7478
Fax: (740)362-1429
URL: National Affiliate–www.legion.org
Local. Affiliated With: American Legion.

16570 ■ Easter Seals St. Clairsville, Ohio
330 Fox-Shannon Pl., Ste.2
St. Clairsville, OH 43950
Ph: (740)695-5979
Fax: (740)695-6764
E-mail: ateaster@comcast.net
URL: http://wv.easterseals.com
Contact: Mrs. Lorie Untch, Pres./CEO
Local. Provides assistance and services to people with disabilities and their families. **Affiliated With:** Easter Seals.

16571 ■ Northern Ohio Valley Astronomy Educators (NOVAE)
c/o Ralph J. Hadley, Jr., VP
9080 Randall Dr.
St. Clairsville, OH 43950
Ph: (740)699-0685
E-mail: henrywin05@comcast.net
URL: http://novaeastronomy.tripod.com
Contact: Henry Winchester, Pres.
Local. Promotes the science of astronomy. Works to encourage and coordinate activities of amateur astronomical societies. Fosters observational and computational work and craftsmanship in various fields of astronomy. **Affiliated With:** Astronomical League.

16572 ■ Phi Theta Kappa - Beta Theta Mu Chapter
c/o Virginia Moore
120 Fox-Shannon Pl.
St. Clairsville, OH 43950
Ph: (740)695-9500
E-mail: gmoore@btc.edu
URL: http://www.ptk.org/directories/chapters/OH/21025-1.htm
Contact: Virginia Moore, Advisor
Local. Affiliated With: Phi Theta Kappa, International Honor Society.

16573 ■ RSVP of Belmont County
c/o Judith Hartman, Dir.
CAC
153 1/2 W Main St.
St. Clairsville, OH 43950
Ph: (740)695-0293
Fax: (740)695-3602
E-mail: jhartman@cacbelmont.org
URL: http://www.seniorcorps.gov/about/programs/rsvp_state.asp?usestateabbr=oh&Search4.x=0&Search4.y=0
Contact: Judith Hartman, Dir.
Local. Affiliated With: Retired and Senior Volunteer Program.

16574 ■ Society of Antique Modelers - Flyers 79
108 Spring St.
St. Clairsville, OH 43950
Ph: (740)695-1920
URL: National Affiliate–www.antiquemodeler.org
Local. Affiliated With: Society of Antique Modelers.

St. Henry

16575 ■ American Legion, St. Henry Post 648
341 W Main St.
St. Henry, OH 45883
Ph: (740)362-7478
Fax: (740)362-1429
URL: National Affiliate–www.legion.org
Local. Affiliated With: American Legion.

16576 ■ St. Henry Academic Promoters
c/o Lyn M. Brophy
371 Columbus St.
St. Henry, OH 45883-0000
Local.

St. Marys

16577 ■ American Legion, St. Marys Post 323
PO Box 104
St. Marys, OH 45885
Ph: (740)362-7478
Fax: (740)362-1429
URL: National Affiliate–www.legion.org
Local. Affiliated With: American Legion.

16578 ■ Gardeners of America/Men's Garden Clubs of America - St. Marys Gardeners of America
c/o Deb Morrisey, Pres.
1119 Nagel St.
St. Marys, OH 45885
Ph: (419)394-2967
E-mail: deb@bright.net
URL: National Affiliate–www.tgoa-mgca.org
Contact: Deb Morrisey, Pres.
Local.

16579 ■ Lima Society of Professional Photographers
c/o Cheryl Walter
407 N Main St.
St. Marys, OH 45885
Ph: (419)394-4678
E-mail: sgstudio@hotmail.com
URL: National Affiliate–ppa.com
Contact: Michael K. Lamm, Pres.
Founded: 1992. **Members:** 30. **Local. Affiliated With:** Professional Photographers of America.

16580 ■ Northwest Ohio Applied Systems Users Group
c/o RJ Burke Insurance Agency
121 N Wayne St.
St. Marys, OH 45885
Ph: (419)394-3381
Fax: (419)394-8593
E-mail: joe@rjburke.com
URL: National Affiliate–www.ascnet.org
Contact: Joe Burke, Pres.
Local. Represents insurance agents and brokers using the Agency Manager software. Promotes successful automation and business practices through communication, education, and advocacy. **Affiliated With:** Applied Systems Client Network.

16581 ■ United Way of Auglaize County
PO Box 236
St. Marys, OH 45885
Ph: (419)394-3944
Fax: (419)394-1999
E-mail: uwa@bright.net
URL: http://www.auglaizeunitedway.org
Contact: Cathy Yohey, Dir.
Local. Affiliated With: United Way of America.

16582 ■ West Central Ohio ALU
c/o Steve Schmitmeyer
PO Box 67
St. Marys, OH 45885
Ph: (419)394-2414
Fax: (419)394-8695
URL: National Affiliate–www.naifa.org
Local. Represents the interest of insurance and financial advisors. Advocates for a positive legislative and regulatory environment. Enhances business and professional skills of members. **Affiliated With:** National Association of Insurance and Financial Advisors.

St. Paris

16583 ■ American Legion, Ohio Post 148
c/o Keith Cretors
144 S Springfield St.
St. Paris, OH 43072
Ph: (740)362-7478
Fax: (740)362-1429
URL: National Affiliate–www.legion.org
Contact: Keith Cretors, Contact
Local. Affiliated With: American Legion.

Salem

16584 ■ American Legion, Ohio Post 56
c/o Charles H. Carey
713 E State St., Ste.A
Salem, OH 44460
Ph: (740)362-7478
Fax: (740)362-1429
URL: National Affiliate–www.legion.org
Contact: Charles H. Carey, Contact
Local. Affiliated With: American Legion.

16585 ■ Camp Fire Boys and Girls Tayanoka Council
PO Box 177
Salem, OH 44460
Ph: (330)337-6413
E-mail: campfire@salemohio.com
URL: http://www.salemohio.com/campfire
Local. Affiliated With: Camp Fire USA. **Formerly:** (2005) Camp Fire U.S.A. Tayanoka Council.

16586 ■ Columbiana County Chapter of the Ohio Genealogical Society (CCCOGS)
PO Box 861
Salem, OH 44460
Ph: (330)782-8380
E-mail: askier1@earthlink.net
URL: http://www.rootsweb.com/~ohcolumb/index.htm
Contact: Arlene Obertance, Contact
Founded: 1976. **Members:** 300. **Membership Dues:** individual, $12 (annual). **Local Groups:** 1. **Local.** Individuals interested in researching ancestors who were/are from the Columbiana County, OH area. Preserves and safeguards manuscripts, books, records, and memorandum of people living in the county, and then print, publish, and circulate this information to those who can benefit from it. **Libraries: Type:** open to the public. **Holdings:** articles, books, reports. **Subjects:** genealogy, census records, church records. **Affiliated With:** Ohio Genealogical Society. **Publications:** *Columbiana County Connection*, monthly. Newsletter. Contains genealogy information associated with Columbiana County. **Price:** included in membership dues. **Circulation:** 300.

16587 ■ Habitat for Humanity of Northern Columbiana County (HFHNCC)
468 Prospect St.
Salem, OH 44460
Ph: (330)337-1003
Fax: (330)337-7281
E-mail: habitatncc@sbcglobal.net
URL: National Affiliate–www.habitat.org
Local. Affiliated With: Habitat for Humanity International.

16588 ■ Ruffed Grouse Society, Beaver Creek Chapter
c/o Chuck Firestone
390 Hickory Ln.
Salem, OH 44460
Ph: (330)332-5644
E-mail: sran_paf@access-k12.org
URL: National Affiliate–www.ruffedgrousesociety.org
Contact: Chuck Firestone, Contact
Local. Affiliated With: Ruffed Grouse Society.

16589 ■ Salem Area Chamber of Commerce (SACC)
713 E State St.
Salem, OH 44460-2911
Ph: (330)337-3473
Fax: (330)337-3474
E-mail: chamber@salemohio.com
URL: http://www.salemohio.com/chamber
Founded: 1956. **Members:** 300. **Staff:** 2. **Budget:** $85,000. **Local.** Promotes business and community development in the Salem, OH area. Sponsors Salem Jubilee festival. **Computer Services:** Mailing lists, of members. **Divisions:** Greater Salem Retail Merchants Association. **Subgroups:** Salem Area Industrial Development Corp. **Affiliated With:** U.S. Chamber of Commerce. **Publications:** *Buyer's Guide and Membership Directory*, periodic • *Salem Industrial Directory*, biennial • *Salem Update*, monthly. Newsletter. Contains the latest information on the activities of the chamber.

16590 ■ Salem Community Center (SCC)
1098 N Ellsworth Ave.
Salem, OH 44460
Ph: (330)332-5885
E-mail: mail@salemcommunitycenter.com
URL: http://www.salemcommunitycenter.com
Contact: Mark Equizi, Dir.
Founded: 2000. **Local. Formerly:** (2005) Salem Community Center Association.

16591 ■ Salem Lions Club - Ohio
PO Box 421
Salem, OH 44460
E-mail: wxsalemoh@neo.rr.com
URL: http://www.salemohio.com/lionsclub
Local. Affiliated With: Lions Clubs International.

16592 ■ Tayanoka Council of Camp Fire
671 E State St.
PO Box 177
Salem, OH 44460
Ph: (330)337-6413
E-mail: campfire@salemohio.com
URL: http://www.salemohio.com/campfire
Local. Provides programs that include mentoring opportunities, environmental education, camping, and direct child care services. **Affiliated With:** Camp Fire USA.

16593 ■ United Way Services of Northern Columbiana County
713 E State St.
Salem, OH 44460-2911
Ph: (330)337-0310
URL: National Affiliate–national.unitedway.org
Local. Affiliated With: United Way of America.

16594 ■ Veteran Motor Car Club of America - Nickel Age Touring Chapter
c/o John Tarleton, Pres.
449 W 5th St.
Salem, OH 44460-2107
Ph: (330)332-0116
URL: National Affiliate–www.vmcca.org
Contact: John Tarleton, Pres.
Local. Affiliated With: Veteran Motor Car Club of America.

Salineville

16595 ■ American Legion, Ohio Post 442
c/o John Adams
51 W Main St.
Salineville, OH 43945
Ph: (740)362-7478
Fax: (740)362-1429
URL: National Affiliate–www.legion.org
Contact: John Adams, Contact
Local. **Affiliated With:** American Legion.

16596 ■ Southern Local - Young Life
16669 Steubenville Pike Rd.
Salineville, OH 43945
Ph: (330)708-1090
URL: http://sites.younglife.org/_layouts/ylext/default.aspx?ID=C-1580
Local. **Affiliated With:** Young Life.

16597 ■ Young Life Columbiana County
16669 Steubenville Pike Rd.
Salineville, OH 43945
Ph: (330)708-1090
URL: http://sites.younglife.org/_layouts/ylext/default.aspx?ID=A-OH58
Local. **Affiliated With:** Young Life.

Sandusky

16598 ■ AAA Ohio Automobile Club
1437 Sycamore Line
Sandusky, OH 44870
Ph: (419)625-5831
State.

16599 ■ ACF Sandusky Bay Area Chefs Chapter
c/o Michael Edwards, Pres.
505 Lawrence St.
Sandusky, OH 44870
Ph: (419)627-9665
E-mail: chefmichael0693@sbcglobal.net
URL: National Affiliate–www.acfchefs.org
Contact: Michael Edwards, Pres.
Local. Promotes the culinary profession and provides on-going educational training and networking for members. Provides opportunities for competition, professional recognition, and access to educational forums with other culinarians at local, regional, national, and international events.

16600 ■ Alcoholics Anonymous World Services, North Central Ohio Area Intergroup
PO Box 338
Sandusky, OH 44871-0338
Ph: (419)625-5995
Free: (888)683-9768
Local. Individuals recovering from alcoholism. AA maintains that members can solve their common problem and help others achieve sobriety through a twelve step program that includes sharing their experience, strength, and hope with each other. **Affiliated With:** Alcoholics Anonymous World Services.

16601 ■ American Legion, Commodore Denig Post 83
3615 S Hayes Ave.
Sandusky, OH 44870
Ph: (740)362-7478
Fax: (740)362-1429
URL: National Affiliate–www.legion.org
Local. **Affiliated With:** American Legion.

16602 ■ American Red Cross, Firelands Chapter
300 Central Ave.
Sandusky, OH 44870
Ph: (419)626-1641
Free: (800)589-2286
E-mail: info@firelandsredcross.org
URL: http://www.firelandsredcross.org
Local.

16603 ■ Arc of Erie County
c/o The Kaleidoscope Ctr.
4405 Galloway Rd., No. 112
Sandusky, OH 44870
Ph: (419)625-9677
URL: National Affiliate–www.TheArc.org
Local. Parents, professional workers, and others interested in individuals with mental retardation. Works to promote services, research, public understanding, and legislation for people with mental retardation and their families. **Affiliated With:** Arc of the United States.

16604 ■ Big Brothers Big Sisters of America of Erie County
904 W Washington St.
Sandusky, OH 44870
Ph: (419)626-8694
Fax: (419)626-8695
E-mail: eriebbbs@aol.com
URL: http://www.bigbrothersbigsisterseriecounty.org
Membership Dues: $30. **For-Profit**. **Local**. **Affiliated With:** Big Brothers Big Sisters of America.

16605 ■ Bird Strike Committee, U.S.A. (BSC-USA)
c/o Richard A. Dolbeer, Chm.
6100 Columbus Ave.
Sandusky, OH 44870
Ph: (419)625-0242
Fax: (419)625-8465
E-mail: richard.a.dolbeer@aphis.usda.gov
URL: http://www.birdstrike.org
Contact: Richard A. Dolbeer, Chm.
Local.

16606 ■ Boys and Girls Club of Sandusky
PO Box 626
Sandusky, OH 44871-0626
Ph: (419)624-9250 (419)624-9460
Fax: (419)627-1760
URL: http://www.bgcsandusky.org
Contact: Gil Vaulghn, Contact
Founded: 1998. **Members:** 470. **Membership Dues:** youth, $5 (annual). **Staff:** 7. **Budget:** $110,000. **Regional Groups:** 1. **State Groups:** 1. **Local Groups:** 1. **Local**. Provides youth development programs. Sponsors various youth activities and educational programs.

16607 ■ Easter Seals Northwestern Ohio
279 E Market St.
Sandusky, OH 44870
Ph: (419)626-8447
Fax: (419)627-9063
Free: (866)626-8447
E-mail: lross@easterseals nwohio.org
URL: http://www.nwohio.easterseals.com
Contact: Mrs. Lavinda Ross, Contact
Local. Provides services for children and adults with disabilities or special needs, and supports their families. **Affiliated With:** Easter Seals.

16608 ■ Erie County Chapter of the Ohio Genealogical Society (ECOGS)
PO Box 1301
Sandusky, OH 44871-1301
URL: http://www.rootsweb.com/~oheccogs
Contact: Janis Burke, Pres.
Membership Dues: individual, $10 (annual). **Local**. **Affiliated With:** Ohio Genealogical Society.

16609 ■ Erie County MR-DD Employees Association
c/o Edward C. Ostheimer
4405 Galloway Rd.
Sandusky, OH 44870-6026
Ph: (419)627-7790
URL: http://www.eriemrdd.org
Local.

16610 ■ Firelands Association of Realtors
2710 Campbell St.
Sandusky, OH 44870
Ph: (419)625-5787 (419)625-3802
Fax: (419)625-3442
E-mail: eoeio@aol.com
URL: http://www.faor.com
Contact: Ruth E. DeHenning, CEO
Local. Strives to develop real estate business practices. Advocates for the right to own, use and transfer real property. Provides a facility for professional development, research and exchange of information among members and the general public. **Affiliated With:** National Association of Realtors.

16611 ■ Firelands Audubon Society
PO Box 967
Sandusky, OH 44870
Ph: (419)639-3097
E-mail: chickadee1956@yahoo.com
URL: National Affiliate–www.audubon.org
Contact: Carol Andres, Pres.
Local. **Formerly:** (2005) National Audubon Society - Firelands.

16612 ■ Gardeners of America/Men's Garden Clubs of America - Erie County Men's Garden Club
c/o Scott Fulton, Pres.
314 Fulton St.
Sandusky, OH 44870
Ph: (419)625-5281
URL: National Affiliate–www.tgoa-mgca.org
Contact: Scott Fulton, Pres.
Local.

16613 ■ Greater Erie County Marketing Group (GEM)
247 Columbus Ave., Ste.126
Sandusky, OH 44870
Ph: (419)627-7791
Fax: (419)627-7595
E-mail: mdlitten@gem.org
URL: http://www.gem.org
Contact: Mark D. Litten, Exec.Dir.
Founded: 1988. **Nonmembership**. **Local**. Aims to create and retain jobs within Erie County. Works with the private sector and government agencies to increase economic opportunities for individuals and businesses through a comprehensive economic development program.

16614 ■ Korean War Veterans Association, William J. Sanpozzi Chapter
c/o Karl W. Lynn
318 Michigan Ave.
Sandusky, OH 44870
Ph: (419)626-3421
E-mail: johnwasylik@sbcglobal.net
URL: National Affiliate–www.kwva.org
Contact: Karl W. Lynn, Contact
Local. **Affiliated With:** Korean War Veterans Association.

16615 ■ Lake Shore Corvette Club (LSCC)
PO Box 647
Sandusky, OH 44870
E-mail: vettsmith@accnorwalk.com
URL: http://www.lakeshorecorvettes.com
Contact: Earl Smith, Pres.
Local. **Affiliated With:** National Council of Corvette Clubs.

16616 ■ North Central Ohio AIFA
c/o Nora E. Gallagher, Pres.
PO Box 395
Sandusky, OH 44871-0395
Ph: (419)625-8934
Fax: (419)625-3579
E-mail: ngallagher@croghan.com
URL: National Affiliate–naifa.org
Contact: Nora E. Gallagher, Pres.
Local. Represents the interests of insurance and financial advisors. Advocates for a positive legislative and regulatory environment. Enhances business and

professional skills of members. **Affiliated With:** National Association of Insurance and Financial Advisors.

16617 ■ Sandusky/Erie County Convention and Visitors Bureau
4424 Milan Rd., Ste.A
Sandusky, OH 44870
Ph: (419)625-2984
Fax: (419)625-5009
Free: (800)255-3743
E-mail: vcbstaff@buckeyenorth.com
URL: http://www.sanduskyohiocedarpoint.com
Contact: Joan Van Offeren, Exec.Dir.
Local. Offers free information and services for visitors, motor coach tours, and meeting/convention planners.

16618 ■ Sandusky Lions Club
c/o Craig Hecht, Pres.
222 46th St.
Sandusky, OH 44870
Ph: (419)625-9608 (419)627-6635
E-mail: hechtcraig@aol.com
URL: http://www.lions13b.org
Contact: Craig Hecht, Pres.
Local. Affiliated With: Lions Clubs International.

16619 ■ Sandusky Main Street Association
160 Columbus Ave.
Sandusky, OH 44870
Ph: (419)627-5942
Fax: (419)609-1156
E-mail: info@sanduskymainstreet.com
URL: http://www.sanduskymainstreet.com
Local.

16620 ■ Society of Antique Modelers - Ohio 39
5807 Cambridge Cir.
Sandusky, OH 44870
Ph: (419)625-9078
E-mail: buckysam1@cs.com
URL: National Affiliate–www.antiquemodeler.org
Local. Affiliated With: Society of Antique Modelers.

16621 ■ United Way of Erie County, Ohio
416 Columbus Ave.
Sandusky, OH 44870
Ph: (419)625-4672
Fax: (419)625-4673
URL: http://www.unitedwayeriecounty.org
Contact: Phyllis Bransky, Pres.
Local. Affiliated With: United Way of America.

Sardinia

16622 ■ American Legion, Ohio Post 755
c/o George A. Lambert
PO Box 336
Sardinia, OH 45171
Ph: (740)362-7478
Fax: (740)362-1429
URL: National Affiliate–www.legion.org
Contact: George A. Lambert, Contact
Local. Affiliated With: American Legion.

Scio

16623 ■ American Legion, Scio Post 482
PO Box 482
Scio, OH 43988
Ph: (740)362-7478
Fax: (740)362-1429
URL: National Affiliate–www.legion.org
Local. Affiliated With: American Legion.

Sebring

16624 ■ American Legion, Mc Kinley Post 76
395 W California Ave.
Sebring, OH 44672
Ph: (740)362-7478
Fax: (740)362-1429
URL: National Affiliate–www.legion.org
Local. Affiliated With: American Legion.

16625 ■ Sebring Lions Club
306 W Texas Ave.
Sebring, OH 44672
Ph: (330)938-2347
E-mail: esummers@alliancelink.com
URL: http://sebringoh.lionwap.org
Contact: Elva Summers, Pres.
Local. Affiliated With: Lions Clubs International.

Senecaville

16626 ■ Eastern Ohio Angus Association
c/o Tammy Hill, Sec.-Treas.
56450 Sarahsville Rd.
Senecaville, OH 43780
Ph: (740)685-5312
E-mail: thill@clover.net
URL: National Affiliate–www.angus.org
Contact: Tammy Hill, Sec.-Treas.
Local. Affiliated With: American Angus Association.

Seven Hills

16627 ■ Northeast Ohio Concrete Promotion Council
c/o David Bentkowski
6213 Cabrini
Seven Hills, OH 44131-2848
Ph: (216)447-9854
Contact: David Bentkowski Esq., Exec.Dir.
Founded: 2000. **Local.** Provides information about concrete pavements.

16628 ■ Society of Tribologists and Lubrication Engineers - Cleveland Section
c/o Michael Cesa, Chm.
5920 Mural Dr.
Seven Hills, OH 44131-1951
Ph: (216)642-3929
Fax: (216)642-0708
E-mail: mcesa@etna.com
URL: National Affiliate–www.stle.org
Contact: Michael Cesa, Chm.
Local. Promotes the advancement of tribology and the practice of lubrication engineering. Stimulates the study and development of lubrication tribology techniques. Promotes higher standards in the field. **Affiliated With:** Society of Tribologists and Lubrication Engineers.

16629 ■ Western Reserve Numismatic Club
c/o Terry M. Stahurski
549 Mapleview Dr.
Seven Hills, OH 44131
Ph: (216)573-0761
URL: National Affiliate–www.money.org
Contact: Terry M. Stahurski, Contact
Local. Affiliated With: American Numismatic Association.

Seville

16630 ■ Akron - Canton Area Cooks and Chefs Association
c/o David St. John-Grubb, Chapter Pres.
7345 Meadow View Dr.
Seville, OH 44273-9202
E-mail: foodworks@neo.rr.com
URL: http://www.acfakron-canton.org
Contact: David St. John-Grubb, Chapter Pres.
Founded: 1976. **Local.** Promotes the culinary profession and provides on-going educational training and networking for members. Provides opportunities for competition, professional recognition, and access to educational forums with other culinarians at local, regional, national, and international events.

16631 ■ North East Ohio Dairy Goat Association
c/o Pat Cornell
3717 Good Rd.
Seville, OH 44273
Ph: (330)334-6109
URL: National Affiliate–adga.org
Contact: Pat Cornell, Contact
Local. Affiliated With: American Dairy Goat Association.

16632 ■ Society For The Handicapped Of Medina County
4283 Paradise Rd.
Seville, OH 44273
Ph: (330)725-7041
URL: National Affiliate–www.thearc.org
Local. Parents, professional workers, and others interested in individuals with mental retardation. Works to promote services, research, public understanding, and legislation for people with mental retardation and their families. **Affiliated With:** Arc of the United States.

Shadyside

16633 ■ American Legion, Shadyside Post 521
3809 Central Ave.
Shadyside, OH 43947
Ph: (740)362-7478
Fax: (740)362-1429
URL: National Affiliate–www.legion.org
Local. Affiliated With: American Legion.

Shaker Heights

16634 ■ Cleveland Skating Club
2500 Kemper Rd.
Shaker Heights, OH 44120
Ph: (216)791-2800
Fax: (216)791-9501
E-mail: mzcsc@isgwebnet.com
URL: http://www.clevelandskatingclub.org
Local. Affiliated With: United States Curling Association.

16635 ■ Club Managers Association of America - Greater Cleveland Chapter
c/o Nancy Kaska, Exec.Sec.
2500 Kemper Rd.
Shaker Heights, OH 44120
Ph: (216)791-2800
E-mail: cmaakaska@disnow.com
URL: http://www.gccmaa.org
Contact: Nancy Kaska, Exec.Sec.
Local. Promotes and advances friendly relations between and among persons connected with the management of clubs. Encourages the education and advancement of members in the field of club management. **Affiliated With:** Club Managers Association of America.

16636 ■ Greater Cleveland Chapter, MOAA
3150 Woodbury Rd.
Shaker Heights, OH 44120-2443
Ph: (216)751-7274
E-mail: foxreinhardt@usa.net
URL: National Affiliate–www.moaa.org
Contact: Maj. Heath Reinhardt, Contact
Local. Affiliated With: Military Officers Association of America.

16637 ■ International Association of Torch Clubs, Region 5
3008 Fontenay Rd.
Shaker Heights, OH 44120-1729
Ph: (216)752-8448
Fax: (216)295-8820
E-mail: johnmagnolia@aol.com
URL: National Affiliate–www.torch.org
Contact: John A. Horner Jr., Dir.
Regional. Represents the interests of men and women of diverse professions. Fosters high standards of professional ethics and civic well-being. **Affiliated With:** International Association of Torch Clubs.

16638 ■ Ohio Nursing Administration in Long Term Care (ODONA/LTC)
2898 Kingsley Rd.
Shaker Heights, OH 44122
Ph: (216)991-2400
Fax: (216)991-2400
Free: (866)226-3662
E-mail: odonaltc@aol.com
URL: http://www.odonaltc.org
Contact: Nancy George RNC, Pres.
Founded: 1990. **Membership Dues:** active, $20 (annual) • associate, $85 (annual) • patron, $500 (annual). **State**. Establishes professional relationships with the various disciplines in long term care. Represents nursing administrators, nurse managers and nurses dedicated in long term care. Promotes quality of care and quality of life for long term care residents of Ohio. **Affiliated With:** National Association of Directors of Nursing Administration in Long Term Care.

16639 ■ Ohio Vegetarian Advocates
c/o Stephen R. Kaufman, MD, Pres.
3200 Morley Rd.
Shaker Heights, OH 44122-2863
Ph: (216)283-6702
Fax: (216)283-6702
Free: (866)202-9170
E-mail: stkaufman@mindspring.com
URL: http://www.vegsource.com/vegadvocates
Contact: Stephen R. Kaufman MD, Pres.
Founded: 1996. **Members:** 2,500. **Membership Dues:** regular, $20 (annual). **Staff:** 1. **Budget:** $50,000. **Regional Groups:** 1. **Languages:** English, French, Spanish. **Regional**. Promotes vegetarianism through education, public outreach, and social events. **Libraries: Type:** by appointment only; open to the public. **Holdings:** 500; books, periodicals, video recordings. **Subjects:** vegetarianism, animal protectionism. **Also Known As:** (2001) Vegetarian Advocates. **Publications:** Newsletter, weekly. **Price:** free. **Conventions/Meetings:** bimonthly meeting, with potluck dinner.

16640 ■ Shaker Figure Skating Club
2931 Carlton Rd.
Shaker Heights, OH 44122
E-mail: gibbons@bqmlaw.com
URL: National Affiliate–www.usfigureskating.org
Contact: Sandy Gibbons, Contact
Local. Provides programs to encourage participation and achievement in the sport of figure skating on ice. Defines and maintains uniform standards of skating proficiency. Organizes and sponsors competitions and exhibitions for the purpose of stimulating interest in figure skating. **Affiliated With:** United States Figure Skating Association.

16641 ■ Shaker Historical Society (SHS)
16740 S Park Blvd.
Shaker Heights, OH 44120
Ph: (216)921-1201
Fax: (216)921-2615
E-mail: shakhist@bright.net
URL: http://www.cwru.edu/affil/shakhist/shaker.htm
Contact: Catherine R. Winans, Exec.Dir.
Founded: 1947. **Members:** 450. **Membership Dues:** individual, $25 (annual) • family, $35 (annual). **Staff:** 5. **Budget:** $85,000. **Regional**. Individuals and organizations interested in preserving and promoting appreciation of the Shakers, especially North Union; the history of the settlers of Warrensville Township; and the history of Shaker Heights, Ohio. Maintains museum and library. **Libraries: Type:** open to the public. **Holdings:** 3,500. **Subjects:** the Shakers, local history. **Committees:** Women's Committee. **Publications:** *The Journal*, quarterly. Newsletter. **Price:** for members.

16642 ■ Shaker Youth Soccer Association (SYSA)
c/o Tom Roberts, Treas.
2873 Huntington Rd.
Shaker Heights, OH 44120-2403
E-mail: tfowler@thewritingroom.com
URL: http://www.shakeryouthsoccer.org
Contact: Tom Roberts, Treas.
Local.

16643 ■ Stiga Shaker Heights Table Tennis Club
Shaker Heights Community Bldg.
3450 Lee Rd.
Shaker Heights, OH 44120
Ph: (216)691-1767
E-mail: valeriye@yahoo.com
URL: National Affiliate–www.usatt.org
Contact: Valeriy Elnatanov, Contact
Local. **Affiliated With:** U.S.A. Table Tennis.

16644 ■ United Synagogue of Conservative Judaism, Great Lakes and Rivers Region
3645 Warrensville Center Rd., No. 220
Shaker Heights, OH 44122
Ph: (216)751-0606
Fax: (216)751-0607
E-mail: glr@uscj.org
URL: http://www.uscj.org/glr
Contact: Dr. Richard Lederman, Exec.Dir.
Founded: 1913. **Regional**. Umbrella organization for the affiliated conservative congregations and Solomon Schechter schools in North America. **Affiliated With:** United Synagogue Youth.

Sharon Center

16645 ■ Air Conditioning Contractors of America, Akron Canton Chapter
PO Box 425
Sharon Center, OH 44274
Ph: (330)762-9951
Free: (800)479-5557
E-mail: acca239@aol.com
Contact: Lynne Black, Exec.Dir.
Local. Works to represent contractors involved in installation and service of heating, air conditioning, and refrigeration systems. **Affiliated With:** Air Conditioning Contractors of America. **Publications:** *Keynotes*, monthly. Newsletter. Alternate Formats: online.

16646 ■ Science Education Council of Ohio (SECO)
PO Box 349
Sharon Center, OH 44274
Ph: (330)239-1371
Fax: (330)239-1371
E-mail: tshiverdecker@ohiorc.org
URL: http://www.secoonline.org
Contact: Terry Shiverdecker, Exec.Dir.
State. Promotes excellence and innovation in science teaching and learning for all. Serves as the voice for excellence and innovation in science teaching and learning, curriculum and instruction, and assessment. Promotes interest and support for science education. **Affiliated With:** National Science Teachers Association.

Sharonville

16647 ■ American Legion, Ohio Post 790
c/o William E. Grace
3318 E Sharon Rd.
Sharonville, OH 45241
Ph: (740)362-7478
Fax: (740)362-1429
URL: National Affiliate–www.legion.org
Contact: William E. Grace, Contact
Local. **Affiliated With:** American Legion.

16648 ■ Sharonville Chamber of Commerce
11006 Reading Rd., Ste.301
Sharonville, OH 45241
Ph: (513)554-1722
Fax: (513)956-5522
E-mail: info@sharonvillechamber.com
URL: http://www.sharonvillechamber.com
Contact: Pat Madyda, Exec.Dir.
Local.

Shauck

16649 ■ American Legion, E.B. Rinehart Post 754
PO Box 201
Shauck, OH 43349
Ph: (740)362-7478
Fax: (740)362-1429
URL: National Affiliate–www.legion.org
Local. **Affiliated With:** American Legion.

Sheffield Village

16650 ■ International Union, United Automobile, Aerospace and Agricultural Implement Workers of America, AFL-CIO - Local Union 2000
3151 Abbe Rd.
Sheffield Village, OH 44054
Ph: (440)934-3151
Fax: (440)934-3150
E-mail: unionhall@uawlocal2000.org
URL: http://www.uawlocal2000.org
Contact: Tim Donovan, Pres.
Members: 1,997. **Local**. AFL-CIO. **Affiliated With:** International Union, United Automobile, Aerospace and Agricultural Implement Workers of America.

16651 ■ International Union, United Automobile, Aerospace and Agricultural Implement Workers of America, AFL-CIO - Lorain County CAP Council Local 2000
3151 Abbe Rd.
Sheffield Village, OH 44054
Ph: (440)934-3151
Fax: (440)934-3150
E-mail: unionhall@uawlocal2000.org
URL: http://www.uawlocal2000.org
Contact: Tim Donovan, Pres.
Members: 5,850. **Local**. AFL-CIO. **Affiliated With:** International Union, United Automobile, Aerospace and Agricultural Implement Workers of America.

16652 ■ North Coast Building Industry Association (NCBIA)
c/o Rocco Fana, Jr., Exec. Officer
5201 Waterford Dr.
Sheffield Village, OH 44035
Ph: (440)934-1090
Fax: (440)934-1089
Free: (800)947-5381
E-mail: rfanajr@northcoastbia.com
URL: http://www.northcoastbia.com
Contact: Rocco Fana Jr., Exec. Officer
Founded: 1944. **Members:** 600. **Membership Dues:** builder, developer, remodeler, $515-$2,515 (annual) • associate, $475 (annual) • affiliate, $170 (annual) • remodeler council, $150 (annual) • sales/marketing council, $50 (annual). **Local**. Represents single and multifamily home builders, commercial builders and others associated with the building industry. **Committees:** Ambassadors Club; Codes; Government Affairs; Home Show. **Councils:** Sales and Marketing. **Subgroups:** Anthem Blue Cross/Blue Shield; Installation Banquet/Hall of Fame; Workers Compensation Group Plan. **Affiliated With:** National Association of

Home Builders. **Publications:** *Builder*, monthly. Newsletter. **Advertising:** accepted. Alternate Formats: online • Membership Directory. **Conventions/ Meetings:** monthly board meeting • monthly meeting.

Shelby

16653 ■ American Legion, O'Brien Post 326
89 E Main St.
Shelby, OH 44875
Ph: (740)362-7478
Fax: (740)362-1429
URL: National Affiliate–www.legion.org
Local. Affiliated With: American Legion.

16654 ■ Ohio Genealogical Society, Richland County-Shelby Chapter
PO Box 766
Shelby, OH 44875-0766
E-mail: clabaugh@richnet.net
URL: http://www.rootsweb.com/~ohscogs
Founded: 1985. **Membership Dues:** single, $10 (annual) • joint, $12 (annual). **Local. Affiliated With:** Ohio Genealogical Society. **Publications:** *Shelby Spirits*, monthly. Newsletter. **Price:** included in membership dues.

16655 ■ Shelby Chamber of Commerce
142 N Gamble, Ste.A
Shelby, OH 44875
Ph: (419)342-2426
Fax: (419)342-2189
Free: (888)245-2426
E-mail: chamber@shelbyoh.com
URL: http://www.shelbyoh.com
Contact: Carol Knapp, Pres.
Local. Promotes the interests of local businesses and enhance the quality of life of Shelby community.

Sherrodsville

16656 ■ American Legion, Dellroy Post 475
2276 Lodge Rd.
Sherrodsville, OH 44675
Ph: (740)362-7478
Fax: (740)362-1429
URL: National Affiliate–www.legion.org
Local. Affiliated With: American Legion.

16657 ■ American Legion, Ohio Post 660
c/o Charles Caldwell
80 Hill Dr.
Sherrodsville, OH 44675
Ph: (740)362-7478
Fax: (740)362-1429
URL: National Affiliate–www.legion.org
Contact: Charles Caldwell, Contact
Local. Affiliated With: American Legion.

Shiloh

16658 ■ American Legion, Garrett-Riest Post 503
PO Box 253
Shiloh, OH 44878
Ph: (740)362-7478
Fax: (740)362-1429
URL: National Affiliate–www.legion.org
Local. Affiliated With: American Legion.

16659 ■ Savannah Lions Club - Ohio
c/o Steve Willeke, Pres.
1520 McMillan Rd.
Shiloh, OH 44878
Ph: (419)895-1005
URL: http://www.lions13b.org
Contact: Steve Willeke, Pres.
Local. Affiliated With: Lions Clubs International.

Shreve

16660 ■ American Legion, Forest Post 67
10094 Shreve Rd.
Shreve, OH 44676
Ph: (740)362-7478
Fax: (740)362-1429
URL: National Affiliate–www.legion.org
Local. Affiliated With: American Legion.

16661 ■ International Association of Electrical Inspectors, Ohio Chapter (IAEI-OC)
c/o Tim McClintock
11813 Township Rd. 516
Shreve, OH 44676
Ph: (330)567-3330
Fax: (330)567-3330
E-mail: curryelec@aol.com
URL: National Affiliate–www.iaei.org
Contact: Timothy D. Curry, Sec.-Treas.
Founded: 1926. **Members:** 1,200. **Local Groups:** 6. **State.** Certified electrical safety inspectors; representatives from manufacturers and utilities; and consultants. Provides educational programs and information in order to establish consistent and knowledgeable code interpretations. **Awards:** Fred O. Evertz. **Frequency:** annual. **Type:** recognition. **Recipient:** for dedication and service to organization. **Affiliated With:** International Association of Electrical Inspectors. **Publications:** *Meeting Program*, annual. **Advertising:** accepted. **Conventions/Meetings:** annual meeting • annual Professional Development Seminar (exhibits) - always May.

Sidney

16662 ■ AAA Shelby County
920 Wapakoneta Ave.
Sidney, OH 45365-1471
Ph: (937)492-3167
Local.

16663 ■ American Legion, Sidney Post 217
1265 N 4th Ave.
Sidney, OH 45365
Ph: (740)362-7478
Fax: (740)362-1429
URL: National Affiliate–www.legion.org
Local. Affiliated With: American Legion.

16664 ■ Big Brothers Big Sisters of Shelby and Darke County
PO Box 885
Sidney, OH 45365-0885
Ph: (937)492-7611 (937)547-9622
E-mail: info@bigbrobigsis-shelbydarke.org
URL: http://www.bigbrobigsis-shelbydarke.org
Contact: Lisa Brown, Exec.Dir.
Local. Affiliated With: Big Brothers Big Sisters of America.

16665 ■ National Active and Retired Federal Employees Association - Upper Miami Valley 325
2370 Brierwood Trail
Sidney, OH 45365-3722
Ph: (937)497-0846
URL: National Affiliate–www.narfe.org
Contact: Karl H. Reinhardt, Contact
Local. Protects the retirement future of employees through education. Informs members on issues affecting the retirement. **Affiliated With:** National Association of Retired Federal Employees.

16666 ■ Ohio Association of Emergency Medical Services (OAEMS)
c/o Karen Beavers, Pres.
PO Box 4158
Sidney, OH 45365
Ph: (937)497-0542
Fax: (937)492-6335
Free: (800)382-9960
E-mail: karen.beavers@oaems.org
URL: http://www.oaems.org
State.

16667 ■ Shelby County Coin Club
c/o Bernard Nagengast
PO Box 4128
Sidney, OH 45365
Ph: (937)394-4812
E-mail: nagetke@bright.net
URL: National Affiliate–www.money.org
Contact: Bernard Nagengast, Contact
Local. Affiliated With: American Numismatic Association.

16668 ■ Shelby County Historical Society
c/o Tilda Phlipot, Exec.Dir.
PO Box 376
Sidney, OH 45365-0376
Ph: (937)498-1653
Fax: (937)492-0876
E-mail: info@shelbycountyhistory.org
URL: http://www.shelbycountyhistory.org
Contact: Tilda Phlipot, Exec.Dir.
Local.

16669 ■ Shelby County United Way
PO Box 751
Sidney, OH 45365-0751
Ph: (937)492-2101
E-mail: iandrews@shelbycounitedway.org
URL: http://www.shelbycounitedway.org
Contact: Iddy Andrews, Exec.Dir.
Local. Affiliated With: United Way of America.

16670 ■ Sidney-Shelby County Young Men's Christian Association
300 E Parkwood St.
Sidney, OH 45365
Ph: (937)492-9134
Fax: (937)492-4705
E-mail: info@sidney-ymca.org
URL: http://www.sidney-ymca.org
Contact: Ed Thomas, Exec.Dir.
Founded: 1968. **Members:** 5,500. **Staff:** 100. **Budget:** $2,100,000. **Local Groups:** 2. **Local.** Seeks to develop and improve the spiritual, social, mental, and physical well-being of young people and adults. Operates childcare centers. **Awards:** Lee E. Schauer Memorial Scholarship. **Frequency:** annual. **Type:** scholarship. **Recipient:** for graduating high school senior with minimum GPA of 2.5, heavy consideration given to volunteer activities and leadership abilities. **Publications:** *Program Brochure*, 3/year. Contains listing of classes and programs. Alternate Formats: online • Annual Report, annual. Alternate Formats: online. **Conventions/Meetings:** monthly board meeting.

16671 ■ West Ohio Development Council
c/o Lew Blackford, Dir.
101 S Ohio Ave., 2nd Fl.
Sidney, OH 45365
Ph: (937)498-9554
Fax: (937)498-2472
E-mail: lblackford@westohiodevelopment.com
URL: http://www.westohiodevelopment.com
Contact: Lewis A. Blackford, Exec.Dir.
Founded: 1983. **Budget:** $106,425. **Local.** Creates employment opportunities for individuals in this sector of the state of Ohio. Council consists of eight chamber of commerce and eight Community Improvement Corporation Members.

Smithfield

16672 ■ American Legion, Burriss-Smith Post 396
1075 Main St.
Smithfield, OH 43948
Ph: (740)362-7478
Fax: (740)362-1429
URL: National Affiliate–www.legion.org
Local. Affiliated With: American Legion.

Smithville

16673 ■ American Hiking Society - Camp Tuscazoar Foundation
667 Dennis Cir.
Smithville, OH 44677
Ph: (330)345-8100
Fax: (330)345-8775
E-mail: camptuscazoar@aol.com
URL: http://www.tuscazoar.org
Local.

16674 ■ American Legion, Smithville Post 711
162 Holley Dr.
Smithville, OH 44677
Ph: (740)362-7478
Fax: (740)362-1429
URL: National Affiliate–www.legion.org
Local. **Affiliated With:** American Legion.

Solon

16675 ■ American Legion, Collinwood Post 759
c/o Basil J. Lopilo
7632 Lindsay Ln.
Solon, OH 44139
Ph: (740)362-7478
Fax: (740)362-1429
URL: National Affiliate–www.legion.org
Contact: Basil J. Lopilo, Contact
Local. **Affiliated With:** American Legion.

16676 ■ First Catholic Slovak Ladies Association - Cleveland Junior Branch 483
6594 Arbordale Ave.
Solon, OH 44139
Ph: (440)248-8537
URL: National Affiliate–www.fcsla.com
Local. **Affiliated With:** First Catholic Slovak Ladies Association.

16677 ■ First Catholic Slovak Ladies Association - Cleveland Senior Branch 555
6594 Arbordale Ave.
Solon, OH 44139
Ph: (216)464-8015
URL: National Affiliate–www.fcsla.com
Local. **Affiliated With:** First Catholic Slovak Ladies Association.

16678 ■ Gilmour Academy Figure Skating Club
34375 Ada Dr.
Solon, OH 44139
Ph: (216)851-7000
URL: National Affiliate–www.usfigureskating.org
Contact: Carren Kay, Contact
Local. Provides programs to encourage participation and achievement in the sport of figure skating on ice. Defines and maintains uniform standards of skating proficiency. Organizes and sponsors competitions and exhibitions for the purpose of stimulating interest in figure skating. **Affiliated With:** United States Figure Skating Association.

16679 ■ Hospitality Financial and Technology Professionals - Cleveland/Akron Chapter
c/o Mark Batey, CPA, Pres.
32125 Solon Rd., Ste.200
Solon, OH 44139-3557
Ph: (440)248-8787
Fax: (440)248-0841
E-mail: mbatey@ssandg.com
URL: National Affiliate–www.hftp.org
Contact: Mark Batey, Pres.
Local. Provides opportunities to members through professional and educational development. **Affiliated With:** Hospitality Financial and Technology Professionals. **Conventions/Meetings:** monthly meeting - every third Wednesday of the month.

16680 ■ Lake Erie District Amateur Athletic Union
c/o Michele Dula, Registrar
37960 Fox Run Dr.
Solon, OH 44139
Ph: (216)691-2246
Fax: (216)691-3491
E-mail: dula5@sbcglobal.net
URL: National Affiliate–aausports.org
Contact: Michele Dula, Registrar
Local. **Affiliated With:** Amateur Athletic Union.

16681 ■ Northeast Ohio Translators Association (NOTA)
c/o Jill Sommer, Pres.
33425 Bainbridge Rd.
Solon, OH 44139
Ph: (440)519-0161
E-mail: pres@ohiotranslators.org
URL: http://www.ohiotranslators.org
Contact: Jill Sommer, Pres.
Regional. **Affiliated With:** American Translators Association. **Publications:** *NOTA BENE*, 5/year. Newsletter.

16682 ■ Northern Ohio Branch of the International Dyslexia Association (NOB/IDA)
31705 Burlwood Dr.
Solon, OH 44139
Ph: (216)556-0883
Fax: (440)248-4104
URL: http://www.dyslexia-nohio.org
Contact: Julie Mawaka, Exec.Dir.
Founded: 1989. **Members:** 235. **Membership Dues:** individual, $70 (annual) • family, $110 (annual) • institutional (non-profit), $395 (annual) • college student, $40 (annual) • retired (more than 65 years of age and not employed full time), $45 (annual) • life, $2,000. **Staff:** 1. **Local**. Individuals interested in the study, treatment, and prevention of the problems of dyslexia or specific language disability. **Affiliated With:** International Dyslexia Association. **Formerly:** (1999) Northern Ohio Branch of the Orton Dyslexia Society. **Publications:** Newsletter, semiannual. Contains articles/research on reading and language issues. **Price:** included in membership dues. **Advertising:** accepted. **Conventions/Meetings:** annual symposium (exhibits) - always spring.

16683 ■ Northern Ohio Dressage Association (NODA)
c/o Alice Brightup
27925 Louise Dr.
Solon, OH 44139
Ph: (440)564-9463
E-mail: janice@paddocksaddlery.com
URL: http://www.nodarider.org
Contact: Janice Lawrenz, Pres.
Local. **Affiliated With:** United States Dressage Federation.

16684 ■ Solon Chamber of Commerce (SCC)
33595 Bainbridge Rd., Ste.101
Solon, OH 44139-2942
Ph: (440)248-5080
Fax: (440)248-9121
E-mail: staff@solonchamber.com
URL: http://www.solonchamber.com
Contact: Nancy Traum, Pres./CEO
Founded: 1927. **Members:** 540. **Membership Dues:** business, $150-$1,500 (annual) • community organization, $150 (annual). **Local**. Promotes business and community development in Solon, OH. **Publications:** *News and Views*, monthly. Newsletter. Contains information on chamber events, civic affairs, legislative issues, and other information helpful to business profession. Alternate Formats: online • *The Solon Community Directory*. Features listing of all retail, commercial, and professional businesses in Solon. **Price:** $5.00 additional copy • *The Solon Industrial Directory*. Features listing of all industrial companies in Solon. **Price:** free for members; $25.00 for nonmembers. **Conventions/Meetings:** monthly Coffee Connection - meeting - every 2nd Friday.

16685 ■ Warrensville Heights Coin Club
c/o William J. Krizsan
PO Box 391441
Solon, OH 44139
Ph: (330)963-0482
URL: National Affiliate–www.money.org
Contact: William J. Krizsan, Contact
Local. **Affiliated With:** American Numismatic Association.

16686 ■ Z Association of Cleveland, Ohio
27480 Solon Rd.
Solon, OH 44139
Ph: (440)232-8228
E-mail: zacohio@aol.com
URL: National Affiliate–www.zcca.org
Contact: Bonnie Swirsky, Pres.
Local. **Affiliated With:** Z Car Club Association.

Somerset

16687 ■ American Legion, Ohio Post 58
c/o Leo Ryan
PO Box 552
Somerset, OH 43783
Ph: (740)362-7478
Fax: (740)362-1429
URL: National Affiliate–www.legion.org
Contact: Leo Ryan, Contact
Local. **Affiliated With:** American Legion.

South Amherst

16688 ■ American Legion, South Amherst Post 197
204 Erie St.
South Amherst, OH 44001
Ph: (740)362-7478
Fax: (740)362-1429
URL: National Affiliate–www.legion.org
Local. **Affiliated With:** American Legion.

South Charleston

16689 ■ American Legion, Allen-Myers-Hohn Post 176
PO Box 108
South Charleston, OH 45368
Ph: (740)362-7478
Fax: (740)362-1429
URL: National Affiliate–www.legion.org
Local. **Affiliated With:** American Legion.

South Euclid

16690 ■ American Legion, Heightshillcrest Post 104
1939 Green Rd., No. 305
South Euclid, OH 44121
Ph: (740)362-7478
Fax: (740)362-1429
URL: National Affiliate–www.legion.org
Local. **Affiliated With:** American Legion.

16691 ■ Great Lakes Curling Association - Mayfield Curling Club
1545 Sheridan Dr.
South Euclid, OH 44121
Ph: (216)381-0826
E-mail: robertrosenfeld@ameritech.net
URL: http://www.usacurl.org/basics/U.S.%20clubs/glakes.html
Contact: Robert Rosenfeld, Pres.
Local. **Affiliated With:** United States Curling Association.

16692 ■ Korean War Veterans Association, Lake Erie Chapter
c/o Steve Szekely
1516 Laclede Rd.
South Euclid, OH 44121-3012
Ph: (216)381-9080
E-mail: sxdszek@earthlink.net
URL: National Affiliate–www.kwva.org
Contact: Steve Szekely, Contact
Local. Affiliated With: Korean War Veterans Association.

16693 ■ NAMD Cleveland
c/o Camille Bridges-Erkins
PO Box No. 210016
South Euclid, OH 44121-7016
Ph: (216)214-4143
Fax: (216)381-0459
E-mail: namdoh2002@yahoo.com
URL: National Affiliate–www.namdntl.org
Contact: Camille Bridges-Erkins, Pres.
Local. Engages in marketing, sales, sales promotion, advertising, or public relations that are concerned with the delivery of goods and services to the minority consumer market. **Affiliated With:** National Alliance of Market Developers.

16694 ■ National Sojourners, Cleveland No. 23
c/o Lt. Wilfrid A. Grose, Jr.
3905 Princeton Blvd.
South Euclid, OH 44121-2336
Ph: (216)381-7050
URL: National Affiliate–www.nationalsojourners.org
Contact: Lt. Wilfrid A. Grose Jr., Contact
Local.

16695 ■ Ohio St. Bernard Club
1347 Frances Ct.
South Euclid, OH 44121
Ph: (216)381-2726
E-mail: fmalat1347@acninc.net
URL: National Affiliate–www.saintbernardclub.org
Contact: Joanne Riccio, Chair
State. Affiliated With: Saint Bernard Club of America.

South Point

16696 ■ Greater Lawrence County Area Chamber of Commerce (GLCACC)
216 Collins Ave.
PO Box 488
South Point, OH 45680-0488
Ph: (740)377-4550
Fax: (740)377-2091
Free: (800)408-1334
E-mail: dingus@ohio.edu
URL: http://www.lawrencecountyohio.org
Contact: Patricia L. Clonch, Exec.Dir.
Founded: 1983. **Members:** 350. **Membership Dues:** business (varies with number of employees), $125-$750 • financial institution ($20 per $1000 of Lawrence County deposits), $750-$1,500 • utility/media, $750 • academic institution, $150-$400 • professional, $150 • elected official/retiree, $75. **Staff:** 9. **Local.** Promotes business and community development in Lawrence County, OH. Conducts seminars and workshops. **Awards: Type:** recognition. **Publications:** Newsletter, quarterly • Annual Report, annual. Alternate Formats: online. **Conventions/Meetings:** annual banquet, with awards presentation.

16697 ■ Tri-State Pilots Association
9654 County Rd. 1
South Point, OH 45680-8978
Ph: (740)894-5867
Local.

South Zanesville

16698 ■ Muskingum Co REACT
47 Hazel Ave.
South Zanesville, OH 43701-6307
Ph: (740)453-2833
URL: http://www.reactintl.org/teaminfo/usa_teams/teams-usoh.htm
Local. Trained communication experts and professional volunteers. Provides volunteer public service and emergency communications through the use of radios (Citizen Band, General Mobile Radio Service, UHF and HAM). Coordinates with radio industries and government on safety communication matters and supports charitable activities and community organizations.

Southington

16699 ■ American Legion, Southington Post 751
2822 Warren Burton Rd.
Southington, OH 44470
Ph: (740)362-7478
Fax: (740)362-1429
URL: National Affiliate–www.legion.org
Local. Affiliated With: American Legion.

16700 ■ American Orff-Schulwerk Association, Greater Cleveland Chapter No. 1
c/o BethAnn Hepburn, Pres.
4377 Helsey-Susselmen
Southington, OH 44470
Ph: (330)898-4158
E-mail: hepburn4music@aol.com
URL: http://www.clevelandorff.org
Contact: BethAnn Hepburn, Pres.
Local. Provides a forum for the continued growth and development of Orff Schulwerk. Promotes the value and use of Orff Schulwerk.

Spencer

16701 ■ American Legion, Spencer Post 608
PO Box 265
Spencer, OH 44275
Ph: (740)362-7478
Fax: (740)362-1429
URL: National Affiliate–www.legion.org
Local. Affiliated With: American Legion.

Spencerville

16702 ■ American Legion, Ohio Post 191
c/o Harry J. Reynolds
PO Box 38
Spencerville, OH 45887
Ph: (740)362-7478
Fax: (740)362-1429
URL: National Affiliate–www.legion.org
Contact: Harry J. Reynolds, Contact
Local. Affiliated With: American Legion.

Spring Valley

16703 ■ Spring Valley Area Chamber of Commerce (SVACC)
PO Box 396
Spring Valley, OH 45370
Ph: (937)862-4110
URL: http://springvalleyoh.com/springvalley/svcc/svcc.htm
Contact: Judy Madden, Pres.
Local. Promotes business and community development in Spring Valley, OH.

Springboro

16704 ■ Associated Builders and Contractors-Ohio Valley Chapter
33 Greenwood Ln.
Springboro, OH 45066-3034
Ph: (937)704-0111
Fax: (937)704-9394
Free: (800)686-6440
E-mail: ovabc@ovabc.org
URL: http://www.ovabc.org
Contact: Kathleen Somers, Pres.
Founded: 1974. **Members:** 400. **Staff:** 8. **Budget:** $1,200,000. **State Groups:** 1. **Local Groups:** 1. **Local.** Promotes free enterprise and open competition in the construction industry, as well as merit-based rewards for workers. **Awards:** Accredited Quality Contractor. **Type:** recognition • Award of Excellence/Merit. **Type:** recognition. **Affiliated With:** Associated Builders and Contractors. **Publications:** *Construction Connection*, quarterly. Newsletter. Contains construction industry news. **Price:** $50.00 /year for nonmembers. **Circulation:** 1,000. **Advertising:** accepted. Alternate Formats: online. **Conventions/Meetings:** annual conference.

16705 ■ Ohio Valley Construction Education Foundation (OVCEF)
33 Greenwood Ln.
Springboro, OH 45066-3034
Ph: (937)704-0111
Fax: (937)704-9394
Free: (800)686-6440
E-mail: ovabc@ovabc.org
URL: http://www.ovabc.org
Contact: Gary Bambauer, VP of Education
Founded: 1993. **Members:** 300. **Staff:** 3. **State Groups:** 1. **Local Groups:** 1. **Local.** Provides education and training for the construction industry. **Publications:** *Construction Trainer*, semiannual. Newsletter.

16706 ■ Oldsmobile Club of America, Gem City Rockets
c/o Jim Hosey, Pres.
155 Sesame St.
Springboro, OH 45066
Ph: (513)748-3540
E-mail: 71w30@w-30.com
URL: http://www.w-30.com/gcr.htm
Contact: Jim Hosey, Pres.
Founded: 1989. **Membership Dues:** individual, $15 (annual). **Local. Affiliated With:** Oldsmobile Club of America.

16707 ■ Reserve Officers Association - Department of Ohio, Kittyhawk Chapter 70
c/o Capt. Sharon M. Donlinger, USAFR, Pres.
710 W Market St.
Springboro, OH 45066
Ph: (937)255-4745 (937)748-0491
E-mail: sharonandgraham@earthlink.net
URL: http://www.roa.org/oh
Contact: Capt. Sharon M. Donlinger USAFR, Pres.
Local. Promotes and supports the development and execution of a military policy for the United States. Provides professional development seminars, workshops and programs for its members. **Affiliated With:** Reserve Officers Association of the United States.

16708 ■ Rural Land Alliance
c/o Charles S. Gulas
PO Box 366
Springboro, OH 45066-7434
E-mail: landalliance@yahoo.com
URL: http://www.landalliance.org
Local.

16709 ■ Springboro Chamber of Commerce
325 S Main St.
Springboro, OH 45066
Ph: (937)748-0074
Fax: (937)748-0525
E-mail: chamber@springboroohio.org
URL: http://www.springboroohio.com
Contact: Anne Stremanos, Exec.Dir.
Founded: 1975. **Members:** 375. **Staff:** 2. **Local.** Promotes and supports local business and

community. **Libraries: Type:** reference. **Holdings:** 4. **Computer Services:** Mailing lists, of members • online services, members listed by business category. **Committees:** Ambassadors; Annual Dinner; Expo; Golf. **Affiliated With:** Ohio Chamber of Commerce; U.S. Chamber of Commerce. **Publications:** *Business Update*, monthly. Newsletter. **Price:** free for members. **Circulation:** 400. **Advertising:** accepted.

16710 ■ Springboro Lions Club
60 E North St.
Springboro, OH 45066-1367
Ph: (937)748-1411
E-mail: schrimpf9@aol.com
URL: http://springborooh.lionwap.org
Contact: Marguerite Weser, Pres.
Local. Affiliated With: Lions Clubs International.

Springdale

16711 ■ Springdale-Forest Park Lions Club
11999 Lawnview Ave.
Springdale, OH 45246
Ph: (513)793-1782 (513)742-8945
E-mail: ljones1@cinci.rr.com
URL: http://springdaleoh.lionwap.org
Contact: Robert C. Bowman, Sec.
Local. Affiliated With: Lions Clubs International.

Springfield

16712 ■ American Cancer Society, Clark/Miami Area
1130 Vester Ave.
Springfield, OH 45503
Ph: (937)399-0809
Fax: (937)399-2060
Free: (888)227-6446
URL: http://www.cancer.org
Local. Affiliated With: American Cancer Society.

16713 ■ American Legion, Bailey-Frey Post 125
c/o Harvey E. Howard, Adj.
1055 Heard Ave.
Springfield, OH 45506
Ph: (740)362-7478
Fax: (740)362-1429
URL: National Affiliate–www.legion.org
Contact: Harvey E. Howard, Adj.
Local. Affiliated With: American Legion.

16714 ■ American Legion, Clark Post 362
839 E Cecil St.
Springfield, OH 45503
Ph: (740)362-7478
Fax: (740)362-1429
URL: National Affiliate–www.legion.org
Local. Affiliated With: American Legion.

16715 ■ American Legion, Cultice-Ward Post 6
1913 E Pleasant St.
Springfield, OH 45505
Ph: (740)362-7478
Fax: (740)362-1429
URL: National Affiliate–www.legion.org
Local. Affiliated With: American Legion.

16716 ■ American Legion, Ohio Post 787
c/o Roger L. Vickers
3039 Sturbridge St.
Springfield, OH 45503
Ph: (740)362-7478
Fax: (740)362-1429
URL: National Affiliate–www.legion.org
Contact: Roger L. Vickers, Contact
Local. Affiliated With: American Legion.

16717 ■ American Red Cross, Clark County Chapter
1830 N Limestone
Springfield, OH 45503
Ph: (937)399-3872
Fax: (937)399-6111
URL: http://clarkcountyohio.redcross.org
Local.

16718 ■ American Society of Dowsers, Southwestern Ohio Dowsers
c/o William Sheline, Pres.
1048 W Sparrow
Springfield, OH 45502
Ph: (937)325-5433
URL: National Affiliate–dowsers.new-hampshire.net
Local. Affiliated With: American Society of Dowsers.

16719 ■ American Statistical Association, Dayton Chapter
c/o Douglas M. Andrews, Representative
PO Box 720
Springfield, OH 45501
Ph: (937)327-7863
E-mail: dandrews@wittenberg.edu
URL: National Affiliate–www.amstat.org
Contact: Douglas M. Andrews, Representative
Local. Promotes statistical practice, applications and research. Works for the improvement of statistical education at all levels. Seeks opportunities to advance the statistics profession. **Affiliated With:** American Statistical Association.

16720 ■ American Wine Society - Springfield
c/o Michael A. Farren, Co-Chm.
420 Bowman Rd.
Springfield, OH 45505
Ph: (937)325-5864
E-mail: mafarren@prodigy.net
URL: National Affiliate–www.americanwinesociety.org
Contact: Michael A. Farren, Co-Chm.
Local. Affiliated With: American Wine Society.

16721 ■ Association for Computing Machinery, Wittenberg University
c/o Nancy Saks
Department of Mathematics and Computer Science
PO Box 720
Springfield, OH 45501
Ph: (937)327-7855
Fax: (937)327-7851
E-mail: nsaks@wittenberg.edu
URL: National Affiliate–www.acm.org
Contact: Nancy K. Saks, Faculty Adviser
Founded: 2002. **Membership Dues:** all, $5 (annual). **Local.** Biological, medical, behavioral, and computer scientists; hospital administrators; programmers and others interested in application of computer methods to biological, behavioral, and medical problems. Stimulates understanding of the use and potential of computers in the Biosciences. **Affiliated With:** Association for Computing Machinery.

16722 ■ Center City Neighborhood Association
c/o Michael G. Morris
PO Box 1291
Springfield, OH 45501-1291
Ph: (937)325-0047
Fax: (937)325-0735
URL: http://www.center-city.org
Contact: Horton Hobbs, Exec.Dir.
Local.

16723 ■ Clark County Audubon Society
c/o John F. Gallagher, Pres.
121 Larchmont Ave.
Springfield, OH 45503
Ph: (513)323-0782
URL: http://www.audubon.org/chapter/oh/index.html
Contact: John F. Gallagher, Pres.
Local. Formerly: (2005) National Audubon Society - Clark County.

16724 ■ Clark County Coin Club
c/o Rodney A. Riggle
4324 Midfield St.
Springfield, OH 45503
Ph: (937)399-5976
E-mail: lugger1@netzero.com
URL: National Affiliate–www.money.org
Contact: Mr. Rodney A. Riggle, Past Pres.
Founded: 1957. **Members:** 50. **Membership Dues:** all, $5 (annual). **State Groups:** 1. **Local Groups:** 1. **Local.** Approximately 50 members from starting to advanced Numismatists, promoting the hobby through monthly meetings, Spring and Fall Coin Shows and an annual Youth Scholarship. **Libraries: Type:** not open to the public; by appointment only; lending. **Holdings:** books, video recordings. **Subjects:** numismatics, history. **Awards:** Larry Brooks Memorial Scholarship. **Frequency:** annual. **Type:** scholarship. **Recipient:** for study and essay on a selected numismatic subject. **Affiliated With:** American Numismatic Association. **Publications:** *C.C.C.C. Newsletter*, monthly. Contains numismatic news, history and minutes of the most recent meeting. **Price:** included in membership dues. **Circulation:** 50.

16725 ■ Clark County Literacy Coalition (CCLC)
137 E High St.
Springfield, OH 45502-1215
Ph: (937)323-8617
Fax: (937)328-6911
E-mail: priscilla.marshall@clarkcountyliteracy.org
URL: http://www.clarkcountyliteracy.org
Contact: Mrs. Priscilla Marshall, Exec.Dir.
Founded: 1989. **Members:** 13. **Staff:** 5. **Budget:** $241,548. **Languages:** English, Spanish. **Local.** Agencies and organizations that are interested in promoting literacy. Provides monthly tutor training, one-on-one literacy instruction for adults and children, English for Speakers of other languages instruction, and an Educational Resources Center for tutors, students and staff. Promotes literacy and the importance of basic reading skills, and reading/speaking English skills in the Clark County community. **Libraries: Type:** not open to the public. **Holdings:** 1,000; books, periodicals, video recordings. **Awards:** Edith Stager Memorial Award. **Frequency:** annual. **Type:** recognition. **Recipient:** for student and tutor who demonstrated hard work and dedication to literacy. **Computer Services:** Information services, student computer lab for work with ESL and basic reading software, and Internet access. **Telecommunication Services:** hotline, referral hotline for literacy services in the community, (937)323-8617. **Committees:** Income Development; Nominating/Recruiting. **Affiliated With:** Ohio Literacy Network; United Way of America. **Also Known As:** (1988) Warder Literacy Center. **Publications:** *Partners In Literacy*, quarterly. Newsletter. Includes upcoming events of the Warder Literacy Center and current happenings of its programs, students' progress, services and general information. **Price:** free. **Circulation:** 350. Alternate Formats: online. **Conventions/Meetings:** monthly Tutor Training Workshops, trains volunteer tutors in student curriculum, reporting student progress, and working with learning disabilities.

16726 ■ Clark County Planning Commission
25 W Pleasant St.
Springfield, OH 45506
Ph: (937)328-2498
Fax: (937)328-2621
Local. Formerly: (2005) Canton County Planning Commission.

16727 ■ Clark - YoungLife
PO Box 1465
Springfield, OH 45501-1465
Ph: (937)342-4494
URL: http://sites.younglife.org/sites/Clark/default.aspx
Local. Affiliated With: Young Life.

16728 ■ Doberman Pinscher Club of Greater Dayton
c/o E.A. Thielen, Pres.
2934 Ironwood Dr.
Springfield, OH 45504-4116
Ph: (937)324-2014
E-mail: skipthielen@hotmail.com
URL: http://hometown.aol.com/Doberdawn/DPCDayton.html
Local.

16729 ■ Great Dane Club of America (GDCA)
c/o Mrs. Linda Ridder, Pres.
2933 Archer Ln.
Springfield, OH 45503
E-mail: lindaridder@sbcglobal.net
URL: http://www.gdca.org
Contact: Mrs. Linda Ridder, Pres.
State. Affiliated With: American Kennel Club.

16730 ■ Hayward - YoungLife
PO Box 1465
Springfield, OH 45501-1465
Ph: (937)342-4494
URL: http://sites.younglife.org/sites/Hayward/default.aspx
Local. Affiliated With: Young Life.

16731 ■ International Union, United Automobile, Aerospace and Agricultural Implement Workers of America, AFL-CIO - Local Union 402
3671 Urbana Rd.
Springfield, OH 45502
Ph: (937)390-3327
Fax: (937)390-0043
Free: (800)832-0402
E-mail: local402@iapdatacom.net
URL: http://www.uawlocal402.org
Contact: Charlie Hayden, Pres.
Members: 3,680. **Local.** Seeks for the dignity and equality of the workers. Strives to provide contractors with well-trained, productive employees. **Affiliated With:** International Union, United Automobile, Aerospace and Agricultural Implement Workers of America.

16732 ■ Kenton Ridge - Young Life
PO Box 1465
Springfield, OH 45501-1465
Ph: (937)342-4494
URL: http://sites.younglife.org/sites/KR/default.aspx
Local. Affiliated With: Young Life.

16733 ■ Miami Valley Mineral and Gem Club (MVMGC)
c/o Edward Hugh Fulton, Pres.
231 W State St.
Springfield, OH 45506-2634
Ph: (937)322-1021
E-mail: info@mvmgc.org
URL: http://www.mvmgc.org
Contact: Dick Faux, Sec.
Local. Aims to further the study of Earth Sciences and the practice of lapidary arts and mineralogy. **Affiliated With:** American Federation of Mineralogical Societies.

16734 ■ National Active and Retired Federal Employees Association Springfield-Clark 187
2362 Kingswood Dr. W
Springfield, OH 45503-2309
Ph: (937)399-7512
URL: National Affiliate–www.narfe.org
Contact: Evard Linn, Contact
Local. Protects the retirement future of employees through education. Informs members on issues affecting the retirement. **Affiliated With:** National Association of Retired Federal Employees.

16735 ■ National Association of Miniature Enthusiasts - Springfield Mini Ma'ams
c/o Toni Miller
6405 Morris Rd.
Springfield, OH 45502
Ph: (937)399-9508
E-mail: millertfwc@aol.com
URL: http://www.miniatures.org/states/OH.html
Contact: Toni Miller, Contact
Local. Affiliated With: National Association of Miniature Enthusiasts.

16736 ■ Northwestern - Young Life
PO Box 1465
Springfield, OH 45501-1465
Ph: (937)342-4494
URL: http://sites.younglife.org/sites/NW/default.aspx
Local. Affiliated With: Young Life.

16737 ■ Ohio Association of Cardiovascular and Pulmonary Rehabilitation (OACVPR)
c/o Suzy Jones, Sec.-Treas.
1955 N Fountain Blvd.
Springfield, OH 45504
URL: http://www.oacvpr.org
State.

16738 ■ Ohio Valley District of Precision Metalforming Association
c/o Steve Heitbrink
Pentaflex, Inc.
4981 Gateway Blvd.
Springfield, OH 45502
Ph: (937)325-5551
Fax: (937)325-2620
E-mail: sheitbrink@pentaflex.com
URL: http://ohiovalley.pma.org
Contact: Steve Heitbrink, Contact
Local. Promotes and safeguards the interests of the metalforming industry. Conducts technical and educational programs. Provides legislative and regulatory assistance to members. **Affiliated With:** Precision Metalforming Association.

16739 ■ Phi Theta Kappa - Alpha Nu Lambda Chapter
c/o Tom Marshall
570 E Leffels Ln.
Springfield, OH 45501-0570
Ph: (937)328-6095
E-mail: marshallt@clarkstate.edu
URL: http://www.ptk.org/directories/chapters/OH/2067-1.htm
Contact: Tom Marshall, Advisor
Local. Affiliated With: Phi Theta Kappa, International Honor Society.

16740 ■ Reserve Officers Association - Department of Ohio, Buckeye Chapter 5
c/o Col. William D. Widdows, Pres.
725 Donnelly Ave.
Springfield, OH 45503
Ph: (937)629-0740
E-mail: wdwassoc@earthlink.net
URL: http://www.roa.org/oh
Contact: Col. William D. Widdows, Pres.
Local. Promotes and supports the development and execution of a military policy for the United States. Provides professional development seminars, workshops and programs for its members. **Affiliated With:** Reserve Officers Association of the United States.

16741 ■ Roosevelt - Wyldlife
PO Box 1465
Springfield, OH 45501-1465
Ph: (937)342-4494
URL: http://sites.younglife.org/_layouts/ylext/default.aspx?ID=C-4183
Local. Affiliated With: Young Life.

16742 ■ RSVP of Clark County, Ohio
c/o Norma Knowlton, Dir.
101 S Fountain Ave.
Springfield, OH 45502-1902
Ph: (937)324-5705
Fax: (937)324-9005
E-mail: eursvp@aol.com
URL: http://www.seniorcorps.gov/about/programs/rsvp_state.asp?usestateabbr=oh&Search4.x=0&Search4.y=0
Contact: Norma Knowlton, Dir.
Local. Affiliated With: Retired and Senior Volunteer Program.

16743 ■ Shawnee - Young Life
PO Box 1465
Springfield, OH 45501-1465
Ph: (937)342-4494
URL: http://sites.younglife.org/sites/Shawnee/default.aspx
Local. Affiliated With: Young Life.

16744 ■ Society of Physics Students - Wittenberg University Chapter No. 8379
PO Box 720
Springfield, OH 45501
Ph: (937)327-7823
Fax: (937)327-6340
E-mail: pvoytas@wittenberg.edu
URL: National Affiliate–www.spsnational.org
Local. Offers opportunities for the students to enrich their experiences and skills about physics. Helps students to become professional in the field of physics. **Affiliated With:** Society of Physics Students.

16745 ■ Southeastern - Young Life
PO Box 1465
Springfield, OH 45501-1465
Ph: (937)342-4494 (937)462-8479
URL: http://sites.younglife.org/sites/Southeastern/default.aspx
Contact: Mike Parker, Contact
Local. Affiliated With: Young Life.

16746 ■ Springfield Board of Realtors
322 W Columbia St.
Springfield, OH 45504
Ph: (937)323-6489
Local.

16747 ■ Springfield-Clark County Chamber of Commerce (SACC)
333 N Limestone St., Ste.201
Springfield, OH 45503
Ph: (937)325-7621
Fax: (937)325-8765
Free: (800)803-1553
E-mail: chamber@springfieldnet.com
URL: http://www.springfieldnet.com
Contact: Kathy McPommell, VP
Founded: 1894. **Membership Dues:** enrollment fee (new members), $50 • base, $275 (annual). **Local.** Promotes business and community development in the Springfield, OH area. **Affiliated With:** American Chamber of Commerce Executives; U.S. Chamber of Commerce. **Formerly:** Springfield Area Chamber of Commerce. **Publications:** *Business and Professional Directory*, annual. **Price:** $30.00 for nonmembers; $15.00 for members (one copy free) • Newspaper, monthly.

16748 ■ Springfield Council of the National Committee on Planned Giving
c/o Kenneth E. Hershberger, Dir. of Planned Giving
The Ohio Masonic Home Benevolent Endowment Found., Inc.
5 Masonic Dr.
Springfield, OH 45504-3658
Ph: (937)525-4973
Fax: (937)525-8342
E-mail: khershberger@ohiomasonichome.org
URL: National Affiliate–www.ncpg.org
Contact: Kenneth E. Hershberger, Dir. of Planned Giving
Local. Represents people whose work involves charitable gift planning. Works to increase both the quality and quantity of planned gifts for donors, clients, community and nation. Sponsors the program, Leave A Legacy (TM). Holds meetings the fourth

Friday of each month at the Springfield Inn, an annual symposium on planned giving is also held. **Affiliated With:** National Committee on Planned Giving. **Formerly:** (2005) Springfield Chapter of the National Committee on Planned Giving.

16749 ■ Springfield Exchange Club
PO Box 1482
Springfield, OH 45501
E-mail: join@springfieldexchangeclub.org
URL: http://www.springfieldexchangeclub.org
Contact: Lee Thompson, Pres.
Local.

16750 ■ Springfield Human Resources Management Association
PO Box 2144
Springfield, OH 45501
E-mail: jennifer.borden@health-partners.org
URL: http://www.ohioshrm.org/springfield
Contact: Jennifer Borden, Pres.
Local. Represents the interests of human resource and industrial relations professionals and executives. Promotes the advancement of human resource management.

16751 ■ Springfield North - Young Life
PO Box 1465
Springfield, OH 45501-1465
Ph: (937)342-4494
URL: http://sites.younglife.org/_layouts/ylext/default.aspx?ID=C-1505
Local. Affiliated With: Young Life.

16752 ■ Tecumseh - Young Life
PO Box 1465
Springfield, OH 45501-1465
Ph: (937)342-4494
URL: http://sites.younglife.org/sites/Tecumseh/default.aspx
Local. Affiliated With: Young Life.

16753 ■ United Way of Clark and Champaign Counties
PO Box 59
Springfield, OH 45501
Ph: (937)324-5551
Fax: (937)324-2605
E-mail: unitedway@uwccc.org
URL: http://uwccc.org
Contact: Douglas Lineberger, Exec.Dir.
Local. Aims to nurture a safe, healthy and caring community that builds on the strengths of its citizens, neighborhoods, businesses and human services delivery systems. **Affiliated With:** United Way of America.

16754 ■ Western Buckeye Rottweiler Club
c/o Kathy Yontz
1051 Shrine Rd.
Springfield, OH 45504-3937
Ph: (937)323-8329
E-mail: kathy@glasscity.com
URL: National Affiliate–www.amrottclub.org
Contact: Kathy Yontz, Contact
Local. Affiliated With: American Rottweiler Club.

16755 ■ Wittenberg University Speleological Society (WUSS)
c/o Dept. of Biology
PO Box 720
Springfield, OH 45501-0720
E-mail: kmkviper@yahoo.com
URL: http://www4.wittenberg.edu/student_organizations/wuss
Contact: Kevin Kissell, Pres.
Local. Seeks to study, explore and conserve cave and karst resources. Protects access to caves and promotes responsible caving. Encourages responsible management of caves and their unique environments. **Affiliated With:** National Speleological Society.

16756 ■ Young Life Springfield
PO Box 1465
Springfield, OH 45501-1465
Ph: (937)342-4494
Fax: (937)629-9278
URL: http://sites.younglife.org/sites/springfield/default.aspx
Local. Affiliated With: Young Life.

Steubenville

16757 ■ AAA South Central Ohio
2716 Sunset Blvd.
Steubenville, OH 43952
Ph: (740)264-7717
Local.

16758 ■ American Legion, Argonne Post 33
PO Box 4166
Steubenville, OH 43952
Ph: (740)362-7478
Fax: (740)362-1429
URL: National Affiliate–www.legion.org
Local. Affiliated With: American Legion.

16759 ■ American Legion, Ohio Post 274
c/o David Walker
PO Box 4106
Steubenville, OH 43952
Ph: (740)362-7478
Fax: (740)362-1429
URL: National Affiliate–www.legion.org
Contact: David Walker, Contact
Local. Affiliated With: American Legion.

16760 ■ Association for Computing Machinery, Franciscan University of Steubenville
c/o Edward G. Kovach
1235 Univ. Blvd.
Steubenville, OH 43952
Ph: (614)284-7211
Fax: (614)283-6401
E-mail: ekovach@franuniv.edu
URL: National Affiliate–www.acm.org
Contact: Edward G. Kovach, Contact
Local. Biological, medical, behavioral, and computer scientists; hospital administrators; programmers and others interested in application of computer methods to biological, behavioral, and medical problems. Stimulates understanding of the use and potential of computers in the Biosciences. **Affiliated With:** Association for Computing Machinery.

16761 ■ Brooke-Hancock-Jefferson Metropolitan Planning Commission (BHJMPC)
124 N 4th St.
Steubenville, OH 43952
Ph: (740)282-3685 (304)797-9666
Fax: (740)282-1821
Free: (888)819-6110
E-mail: bhjmpc@bhjmpc.org
URL: http://www.bhjmpc.org
Contact: Dr. John Brown, Exec.Dir.
Founded: 1965. **Members:** 33. **Staff:** 9. **Budget:** $500,000. **Regional.** Designated Metropolitan Planning Organization (MPO) for ISTEA. Creates transportation planning for designated local development districts for Appalachian Regional Commission LDD for ARC and Economic Planning and Development Council. **Libraries: Type:** reference. **Holdings:** 1,000. **Subjects:** transportation, sewer and water, regional government. **Boards:** Brooke-Hancock; Council Policy; Planning and Development. **Committees:** Transportation Advisory. **Formerly:** (1992) Brooke-Hancock Planning & Development Council; WV Region XI. **Publications:** *Regional Review*, quarterly. Newsletter. Contains BHJ activities. **Price:** free. **Circulation:** 500. Alternate Formats: online. **Conventions/Meetings:** bimonthly BHJ Full Commission - meeting, commission member governments (exhibits).

16762 ■ Jefferson County Chamber of Commerce
630 Market St.
PO Box 278
Steubenville, OH 43952
Ph: (740)282-6226
Fax: (740)282-6285
E-mail: info@jeffersoncountychamber.com
URL: http://www.jeffersoncountychamber.com
Contact: William Chesson, Pres.
Local.

16763 ■ Mothers Against Drunk Driving, Ohio Valley Chapter
PO Box 1574
Steubenville, OH 43952
Ph: (304)748-6233
Fax: (304)748-6233
URL: National Affiliate–www.madd.org
Local. Victims of drunk driving crashes; concerned citizens. Encourages citizen participation in working towards reform of the drunk driving problem and the prevention of underage drinking. Acts as the voice of victims of drunk driving crashes by speaking on their behalf to communities, businesses, and educational groups. **Affiliated With:** Mothers Against Drunk Driving.

16764 ■ National Active and Retired Federal Employees Association - Fort Steuben 2191
2818 Cleveland Aue
Steubenville, OH 43952-1139
Ph: (740)264-3971
URL: National Affiliate–www.narfe.org
Contact: Salvatore Pate, Contact
Local. Protects the retirement future of employees through education. Informs members on issues affecting the retirement. **Affiliated With:** National Association of Retired Federal Employees.

16765 ■ Ohio Genealogy Society, Jefferson County Chapter
PO Box 4712
Steubenville, OH 43952-8712
URL: http://www.rootsweb.com/~ohjefogs
Contact: Julia A. Krutilla, Pres.
Founded: 1986. **Members:** 200. **Membership Dues:** single, $10 (annual) • joint, $12 (annual). **Staff:** 4. **Budget:** $6,000. **State Groups:** 1. **Local Groups:** 1. **Local.** Works to promote and educate about family history through monthly meetings. Provides various Jefferson County genealogy books to promote advancement of the organization goals. **Libraries: Type:** open to the public. **Holdings:** 3,000. **Subjects:** genealogy, local history. **Publications:** *Jefferson County Lines Newsletter*, annual. **Conventions/Meetings:** monthly general assembly - always first Tuesday of each month. Steubenville, OH - Avg. Attendance: 30.

16766 ■ Ohio Valley Coin Association
c/o Robert C. Leist
2610 Devonshire St.
Steubenville, OH 43952-1110
Ph: (614)264-7081
E-mail: terbec_43964@yahoo.com
URL: National Affiliate–www.money.org
Contact: Robert C. Leist, Contact
Local. Affiliated With: American Numismatic Association.

16767 ■ Phi Theta Kappa - Alpha Omicron Nu Chapter
c/o Mary Beth Ruthem
4000 Sunset Blvd.
Steubenville, OH 43953
Ph: (740)264-5591
E-mail: mbruthem@jcc.edu
URL: http://www.ptk.org/directories/chapters/OH/6530-1.htm
Contact: Mary Beth Ruthem, Advisor
Local. Affiliated With: Phi Theta Kappa, International Honor Society.

16768 ■ Psi Chi, National Honor Society in Psychology - Franciscan University of Steubenville
c/o Dept. of Psychology
100 Franciscan Way
Steubenville, OH 43952-1707
Ph: (740)283-6486 (740)283-3771
Fax: (740)537-9533
E-mail: gseverance@franciscan.edu
URL: http://www.psichi.org/chapters/info.asp?chapter_id=667
Contact: Gary Severance PhD, Advisor
Local.

16769 ■ United Way of Jefferson County, Ohio
PO Box 1463
501 Washington St.
Steubenville, OH 43952
Ph: (740)284-9000
Fax: (740)283-2103
E-mail: smk@unitedway-jc.org
URL: http://www.unitedway-jc.org
Contact: Suzanne Kresser, Exec.Dir.
Local. Affiliated With: United Way of America.

16770 ■ Veteran Motor Car Club of America - Tri-State Region
c/o Albert Pavlik, Jr., Dir.
1803 Norton Pl.
Steubenville, OH 43952
Ph: (740)282-7197
URL: National Affiliate–www.vmcca.org
Contact: Albert Pavlik Jr., Dir.
Regional. Affiliated With: Veteran Motor Car Club of America.

Stony Ridge

16771 ■ Greater Toledo Orchid Society
c/o Caroline Carpenter
5940 Freemont Pike
Box 322
Stony Ridge, OH 43463
Ph: (419)837-5259
E-mail: carorchid@aol.com
URL: National Affiliate–www.orchidweb.org
Contact: Caroline Carpenter, Contact
Local. Professional growers, botanists, hobbyists, and others interested in extending the knowledge, production, use, and appreciation of orchids. **Affiliated With:** American Orchid Society.

Stoutsville

16772 ■ Institute of Real Estate Management - Columbus Chapter No. 42
9640 Thomas Hill Rd.
Stoutsville, OH 43154
Ph: (614)871-1023
Fax: (614)871-1023
E-mail: tctaylor@mac.com
URL: http://www.iremcolumbus.org
Contact: Cheryl J. Taylor, Chapter Administrator
Local. Represents real property and asset management professionals. Works to promote professional ethics and standards in the field of property management. Strives to keep its members informed on the latest legislative activities and current industry trends. Provides classroom training, continuing education seminars, job referral service and candidate assistance services to enhance the effectiveness and professionalism of its members. **Affiliated With:** Institute of Real Estate Management.

Stow

16773 ■ Akron AIFA
c/o Lori Lamancusa
4198 Hampton Cir.
Stow, OH 44224
Ph: (330)294-1049
Fax: (330)294-1049
E-mail: helbob@mac.com
URL: http://www.aaifa.org
Contact: Lori Lamancusa, Contact
Local. Represents the interests of insurance and financial advisors. Advocates for a positive legislative and regulatory environment. Enhances business and professional skills of members. **Affiliated With:** National Association of Insurance and Financial Advisors.

16774 ■ American Legion, Ohio Post 175
c/o Roger Moore
3733 Fishcreek Rd.
Stow, OH 44224
Ph: (740)362-7478
Fax: (740)362-1429
URL: National Affiliate–www.legion.org
Contact: Roger Moore, Contact
Local. Affiliated With: American Legion.

16775 ■ Gardeners of America/Men's Garden Clubs of America - Stow Community Garden Club
c/o Geraldine Herman, Pres.
2139 Maple Rd.
Stow, OH 44224
Ph: (330)688-5782
E-mail: ga71herman@sbcglobal.net
URL: National Affiliate–www.tgoa-mgca.org
Contact: Geraldine Herman, Pres.
Local.

16776 ■ Greater Akron Mathematics Educators' Society
c/o Kim Yoak, Pres.
Lakeview Intermediate School
1819 Graham Rd.
Stow, OH 44224
Ph: (330)689-5200
E-mail: st_kyoak@mail.neonet.k12.oh.us
URL: http://www3.uakron.edu/games
Contact: Kim Yoak, Pres.
Local. Aims to improve the teaching and learning of mathematics. Provides vision, leadership and professional development to support teachers in ensuring mathematics learning of the highest quality for all students. **Affiliated With:** National Council of Teachers of Mathematics.

16777 ■ National Association of Rocketry - Mantua Township Missile Agency (MTMA)
c/o Mark Recktenwald
2800 Williamsburg Cir.
Stow, OH 44224
Ph: (440)968-3220
E-mail: markrecktenwald@yahoo.com
URL: http://mtma.x3fusion.com
Contact: Mark Recktenwald, Pres.
Local.

16778 ■ Stow-Munroe Falls Chamber of Commerce (SMFCC)
4381 Hudson Dr., Ste.K2
Stow, OH 44224
Ph: (330)688-1579
Fax: (330)688-6234
E-mail: smfcc@smfcc.com
URL: http://www.smfcc.com
Contact: Cindy Smith Lewis, Exec.Dir.
Founded: 1964. **Members:** 300. **Staff:** 3. **Budget:** $50,000. **Regional Groups:** 1. **State Groups:** 2. **Local.** Promotes business and community development in the Stow-Munroe Falls area. Sponsors annual Pride Week, golf outing and Community Showcase, Candidates and Issues Night, Public Officials Reception and more. Conducts charitable activities. **Awards:** Business Person of Year. **Frequency:** annual. **Type:** recognition • Friend of the Community Award. **Frequency:** annual. **Type:** recognition • Lifetime Membership. **Frequency:** annual. **Type:** recognition • 25 Year Members. **Frequency:** annual. **Type:** recognition. **Committees:** Business/Education Advisory; Community Showcase; Economic Development; Government Affairs; Member Benefits; Membership; Program; Technology. **Affiliated With:** U.S. Chamber of Commerce. **Publications:** *Moving a Business to Stow*. **Price:** free • *Opening a Business in Stow*. Directory • *Stow-Munroe Falls Chamber of Commerce Member Business Directory* • *Stow-Munroe Falls Chamber of Commerce Membership Directory and Resource Guide*, annual • Newsletter, monthly. **Conventions/Meetings:** monthly luncheon - always third Tuesday.

Strasburg

16779 ■ American Legion, Charles Hofer Post 522
PO Box 11
Strasburg, OH 44680
Ph: (740)362-7478
Fax: (740)362-1429
URL: National Affiliate–www.legion.org
Local. Affiliated With: American Legion.

16780 ■ Veteran Motor Car Club of America - Buckeye-Keystone Region
c/o Walter Stockert, Dir.
985 Weber Ave. SW
Strasburg, OH 44680
Ph: (330)878-5008
URL: National Affiliate–www.vmcca.org
Contact: Walter Stockert, Dir.
Local. Affiliated With: Veteran Motor Car Club of America.

Streetsboro

16781 ■ American Legion, Streetsboro Post 685
PO Box 2411
Streetsboro, OH 44241
Ph: (740)362-7478
Fax: (740)362-1429
URL: National Affiliate–www.legion.org
Local. Affiliated With: American Legion.

16782 ■ Streetsboro Chamber of Commerce
9205 State Rte. 43, Ste.106
Streetsboro, OH 44241-5323
Ph: (330)626-4769
Fax: (330)422-1118
E-mail: sacc@streetsborochamber.org
URL: http://www.streetsborochamber.org/
Contact: Cathy Bieterman, Pres.
Local. Conventions/Meetings: monthly luncheon - every 2nd Wednesday of the month.

Strongsville

16783 ■ American Legion, Buckeye Road Post 559
c/o Jim Nagy
20322 Berkshire Cir.
Strongsville, OH 44149
Ph: (740)362-7478
Fax: (740)362-1429
URL: National Affiliate–www.legion.org
Contact: Jim Nagy, Contact
Local. Affiliated With: American Legion.

16784 ■ Association of the United States Army, Newton D. Baker
c/o Richard A. Harris
17588 Brandywine Dr.
Strongsville, OH 44136
Ph: (216)441-8614 (440)238-7397
E-mail: usma76@ameritech.net
URL: National Affiliate–www.ausa.org
Local. Represents the interests and concerns of American Soldiers. Fosters public support of the Army's role in national security. Provides professional education and information programs.

16785 ■ Berea Power Squadron
8076 Priem Rd.
Strongsville, OH 44149
E-mail: dmbar@att.net
URL: http://www.bereapowersquadron.org
Local. Affiliated With: United States Power Squadrons.

16786 ■ Cleveland Coatings Society (CCS)
c/o Mr. Steven J. Alessandro, Pres.
PPG Indus., Inc.
19699 Progress Dr.
Strongsville, OH 44149
Ph: (440)572-6972
Fax: (440)572-0848
E-mail: salessandro@ppg.com
URL: http://www.clevelandcoatingssociety.org
Contact: Mr. Steven J. Alessandro, Pres.
Local. Represents chemists, chemical engineers, technologists and supervisory production personnel in the decorative and protective coatings industry and allied industries. Works to gather and disseminate practical and technical facts, data and standards fundamental to the manufacturing and use of paints, varnishes, lacquers, related protective coatings and printing inks. **Affiliated With:** Federation of Societies for Coatings Technology.

16787 ■ Dalmatians Off the Streets Rescue Group (DOTS)
c/o Susan L. Weeden
8536 W 130th St.
Strongsville, OH 44136-1907
Ph: (440)582-4600
E-mail: dal1rescue@aol.com
Contact: Susan L. Weeden, Contact
Founded: 1998. **Local.** Protects the welfare of Dalmatians through provision of shelter, veterinary check up and needed vaccines and medical treatment, and spay/neuter to prevent reproduction. House incoming Dalmatians until we are able to find foster or permanent homes for them.

16788 ■ First Catholic Slovak Ladies Association - Lakewood Junior Branch 088
8311 Litto Dr.
Strongsville, OH 44136
Ph: (440)238-4177
URL: National Affiliate–www.fcsla.com
Local. Affiliated With: First Catholic Slovak Ladies Association.

16789 ■ Greater Cleveland Council of Teachers of Mathematics
c/o Frederick Dillon, Membership Chm.
15690 Balmoral Ct.
Strongsville, OH 44136-2594
E-mail: fdillon@strongnet.org
URL: http://www.jcu.edu/math/faculty/mtedwards/gcctm/index.html
Contact: Frederick Dillon, Membership Chm.
Local. Aims to improve the teaching and learning of mathematics. Provides vision, leadership and professional development to support teachers in ensuring mathematics learning of the highest quality for all students. **Affiliated With:** National Council of Teachers of Mathematics.

16790 ■ Institute of Management Accountants, Cleveland East Chapter
c/o Bob Miller, Dir. of Special Activities
10393 Forestview Dr.
Strongsville, OH 44136
Ph: (440)846-1021 (216)429-4148
E-mail: emhm@aol.com
URL: http://www.cleveast.imanet.org
Contact: Carol Kuczer, Pres.
Founded: 1969. **Members:** 175. **Local.** Promotes professional and ethical standards. Equips members and students with knowledge and training required for the accounting profession. **Awards:** H.T. Farr Member of the Year. **Frequency:** annual. **Type:** recognition. **Recipient:** for chapter member. **Affiliated With:** Institute of Management Accountants. **Publications:** Newsletter. Alternate Formats: online.

16791 ■ International Brotherhood of Painters and Allied Trades of the United States and Canada AFL-CIO-CFL - District Council 6
8257 Dow Cir.
Strongsville, OH 44136
Ph: (440)239-4575
Fax: (440)234-6527
Free: (866)239-4575
E-mail: membersinput@iupat-dc6.org
URL: http://www.iupat-dc6.org
Contact: Terrance Conroy, Contact
Members: 2,641. **Local.**

16792 ■ Inventors Connection of Greater Cleveland (ICGC)
PO Box 360804
Strongsville, OH 44136
Ph: (216)226-9681
E-mail: icgc@aol.com
URL: http://members.aol.com/icgc
Contact: Mr. Donald Bergquist, Sec.
Founded: 1984. **Members:** 60. **Membership Dues:** $35 (annual). **Budget:** $1,500. **Local Groups:** 1. **Regional.** Composed of inventors and others interested in the innovative process and its entrepreneurial followup. Seeks to encourage innovation, assist innovators through education, and offer networking opportunities. Not intended to offer or replace legal or financial advice. Does not provide endorsements or invention evaluation. **Computer Services:** Electronic publishing, monthly newsletter as email attachment or viewed in Adobe Acrobat and MS Word • mailing lists. **Affiliated With:** United Inventors Association of the U.S.A. **Publications:** *Invention in Greater Cleveland*, monthly. Newsletter. Features news and summary of past meetings and announcement of upcoming meetings. **Price:** included in membership dues. **Circulation:** 200. Alternate Formats: online. **Conventions/Meetings:** monthly meeting, with speaker - every first Monday in Brooklyn, OH.

16793 ■ National Active and Retired Federal Employees Association - Region IV
10429 Oak Br. Trail
Strongsville, OH 44149-1278
Ph: (440)878-1833
URL: National Affiliate–www.narfe.org
Contact: Tom Johnson, VP
Regional. Protects the retirement future of employees through education. Informs members on issues affecting the retirement. **Affiliated With:** National Treasury Employees Union.

16794 ■ Ohio Genealogical Society, Southwest Cuyahoga
13305 Pearl Rd.
Strongsville, OH 44136-3403
E-mail: gmtjaden@aol.com
URL: http://members.aol.com/gmtjaden
Contact: Eva Williamson, Pres.
Membership Dues: individual, $10 (annual) • family, $12 (annual). **Local. Affiliated With:** Ohio Genealogical Society.

16795 ■ Ohio State Society of Enrolled Agents - Greater Cleveland Chapter
c/o Jerome Wisniewski, Pres.
14400 Pearl Rd., No. 4
Strongsville, OH 44136
Ph: (440)572-8773
Fax: (440)572-8762
E-mail: wiese@nacs.net
Contact: Jerome Wisniewski EA, Pres.
Local. Affiliated With: National Association of Enrolled Agents.

16796 ■ Olympia Homeowners Association
12657 Olympus Way
Strongsville, OH 44136
Ph: (440)238-8186

16797 ■ Plumbing-Heating-Cooling Contractors Association, North East Ohio
c/o Mr. Chris Gates, Pres.
12652 Prospect Rd.
Strongsville, OH 44149-2970
Ph: (440)238-7885
Fax: (440)238-7886
E-mail: gatesplumbing@sbcglobal.net
URL: National Affiliate–www.phccweb.org
Contact: Mr. Chris Gates, Pres.
Local. Represents the plumbing, heating and cooling contractors. Promotes the construction industry. Protects the environment, health, safety and comfort of society. **Affiliated With:** Plumbing-Heating-Cooling Contractors Association.

16798 ■ Strongsville Chamber of Commerce (SCC)
18829 Royalton Rd.
Strongsville, OH 44136-5130
Ph: (440)238-3366
Fax: (440)238-7010
E-mail: strongsvillecofc@earthlink.net
URL: http://www.strongsvillecofc.com
Contact: Douglas M. Kawiecki, Pres.
Local. Promotes business and community development in Strongsville, OH. Monitors legislation. Sponsors annual homecoming festival. **Affiliated With:** U.S. Chamber of Commerce. **Formerly:** (1999) Strongsville Area Chamber of Commerce. **Publications:** *Christmas Catalogue*, annual. Directory • *Stongsville Chamber of Commerce News*, periodic • Newsletter, periodic.

16799 ■ Strongsville Skating Club
PO Box 361764
Strongsville, OH 44136-0030
Ph: (440)268-2800
Fax: (440)268-2801
E-mail: mtrizio@aol.com
URL: http://www.strongsvilleskating.com
Contact: Barb Trizio, Pres.
Local. Provides programs to encourage participation and achievement in the sport of figure skating on ice. Defines and maintains uniform standards of skating proficiency. Organizes and sponsors competitions and exhibitions for the purpose of stimulating interest in figure skating. **Affiliated With:** United States Figure Skating Association.

16800 ■ Valley Vagabonds
c/o Deva Simon
13317 Tradewinds Dr.
Strongsville, OH 44136
Ph: (440)572-1675
E-mail: deval17@aol.com
URL: http://www.geocities.com/valleyvclv
Contact: Deva Simon, Pres.
Founded: 1980. **Members:** 124. **Local.** Promotes walking, cross-country skiing, swimming, and biking in northeastern Ohio. **Affiliated With:** American Volkssport Association. **Publications:** Newsletter, semiannual. **Price:** free to members. **Conventions/Meetings:** monthly symposium.

Struthers

16801 ■ American Legion, Struthers Post 158
PO Box 44
Struthers, OH 44471
Ph: (740)362-7478
Fax: (740)362-1429
URL: National Affiliate–www.legion.org
Local. Affiliated With: American Legion.

Stryker

16802 ■ American Legion, Yackee-Strong-Memorial Post 60
PO Box 204
Stryker, OH 43557
Ph: (740)362-7478
Fax: (740)362-1429
URL: National Affiliate–www.legion.org
Local. Affiliated With: American Legion.

Sugar Grove

16803 ■ National Speleological Society, Standing Stone Grotto
c/o Mike Oatney
PO Box 231
Sugar Grove, OH 43155-0231
Ph: (740)746-8337
E-mail: moatney@columbus.rr.com
URL: National Affiliate–www.caves.org
Contact: Mike Oatney, Contact
Local. Seeks to study, explore and conserve cave and karst resources. Protects access to caves and promotes responsible caving. Encourages responsible management of caves and their unique environments. **Affiliated With:** National Speleological Society.

Sugarcreek

16804 ■ American Legion, Homer Weiss Post 494
PO Box 341
Sugarcreek, OH 44681
Ph: (740)362-7478
Fax: (740)362-1429
URL: National Affiliate–www.legion.org
Local. Affiliated With: American Legion.

16805 ■ Garaway Young Life
PO Box 490
Sugarcreek, OH 44681
Ph: (330)852-2002
URL: http://sites.younglife.org/sites/sugarcreek/default.aspx
Local. Affiliated With: Young Life.

16806 ■ Young Life Tuscarawas County
PO Box 490
Sugarcreek, OH 44681
Ph: (330)852-2002
URL: http://sites.younglife.org/sites/TuscCounty/default.aspx
Local. Affiliated With: Young Life.

Sullivan

16807 ■ Sullivan Lions Club
c/o Jack Taylor, Pres.
648 Township Rd. 150
Sullivan, OH 44880
Ph: (419)736-2458
URL: http://www.lions13b.org
Contact: Jack Taylor, Pres.
Local. Affiliated With: Lions Clubs International.

Summerfield

16808 ■ American Legion, Summerfield Post 415
601 E Cross St.
Summerfield, OH 43788
Ph: (740)362-7478
Fax: (740)362-1429
URL: National Affiliate–www.legion.org
Local. Affiliated With: American Legion.

Summitville

16809 ■ Northeastern Ohio Angus Association
c/o Stuart Moore, Pres.
PO Box 147
Summitville, OH 43962
Ph: (330)223-2214
URL: National Affiliate–www.angus.org
Contact: Stuart Moore, Pres.
Regional. Affiliated With: American Angus Association.

Sunbury

16810 ■ American Legion, Ohio Post 457
c/o Col. Benson Hough
230 Otis St.
Sunbury, OH 43074
Ph: (740)362-7478
Fax: (740)362-1429
URL: National Affiliate–www.legion.org
Contact: Col. Benson Hough, Contact
Local. Affiliated With: American Legion.

16811 ■ Big Walnut Breakfast Lions Club
c/o Joan Shaw, Pres.
PO Box 388
Sunbury, OH 43074
Ph: (740)965-3752
E-mail: mshaw106@columbus.rr.com
URL: http://www.iwaynet.net/~lions13f
Contact: Joan Shaw, Pres.
Local. Affiliated With: Lions Clubs International.

16812 ■ Mid America Miniature Horse Club (MAMHC)
13040 N Old 3C Rd.
Sunbury, OH 43074
Ph: (740)965-1994
E-mail: mistyrosen@hotmail.com
URL: http://www.mamhc1.com
Contact: Phoebe Kerby, Pres.
Founded: 1984. **Members:** 190. **Membership Dues:** family, farm, $25 (annual). **Regional Groups:** 1. **State Groups:** 1. **Local Groups:** 1. **Regional.** Works to promote the miniature horse. **Awards:** High Point. **Frequency:** annual. **Type:** recognition. **Affiliated With:** American Miniature Horse Association. **Publications:** *Gazette*, bimonthly. Newsletter. **Price:** included in membership dues.

16813 ■ National Active and Retired Federal Employees Association - Columbus 235
2352 St. Rt 61
Sunbury, OH 43074-8410
Ph: (740)965-4844
URL: National Affiliate–www.narfe.org
Contact: Audrey Jo Eastham, Contact
Local. Protects the retirement future of employees through education. Informs members on issues affecting the retirement. **Affiliated With:** National Association of Retired Federal Employees.

16814 ■ Sunbury - Big Walnut Area Chamber of Commerce
130 Stelzer Ct.
PO Box 451
Sunbury, OH 43074
Ph: (740)965-2860
Fax: (740)965-9969
E-mail: info@sunburybigwalnutchamber.com
URL: http://www.sunburybigwalnutchamber.com
Contact: Chris Quinlan, Pres.
Local.

16815 ■ Sunbury Lions Club
c/o Jim Christian, Pres.
PO Box 361
Sunbury, OH 43074
Ph: (740)965-4686
E-mail: quaybaby69@hotmail.com
URL: http://www.iwaynet.net/~lions13f
Contact: Jim Christian, Pres.
Local. Affiliated With: Lions Clubs International.

Swanton

16816 ■ American Legion, Murbach-Siefert Post 479
200 S Hallett Ave.
Swanton, OH 43558
Ph: (740)362-7478
Fax: (740)362-1429
URL: National Affiliate–www.legion.org
Local. Affiliated With: American Legion.

16817 ■ Fulton County Chapter, Ohio Genealogical Society
PO Box 337
Swanton, OH 43558
Ph: (419)826-5207
E-mail: kariscot@accesstoledo.com
URL: http://www.rootsweb.com/~ohfulton
Contact: Karen Szabo, Sec.
Founded: 1980. **Members:** 121. **Membership Dues:** single, $12 (annual). **Local.** Seeks to support the objectives of the Ohio Genealogical Society; to create and build interest in preservation and collection of historical records of Fulton County and related areas in OH; to encourage active membership in this chapter and in the Ohio Genealogical Society; to take an active part in collecting records and in making them available for use in genealogical research; to publish genealogical materials compiled by the chapter members; and to secure and hold appropriate copyrights and master copies. **Libraries: Type:** open to the public. **Holdings:** 300. **Subjects:** Fulton County, Lucas County, Williams County, Henry County, Ohio. **Awards:** First Families. **Frequency:** annual. **Type:** recognition. **Recipient:** to individuals with heritage dating back to 1860 in the Fulton County area. **Affiliated With:** Ohio Genealogical Society; Ohio Genealogical Society. **Formerly:** (2001) Ohio Genealogical Society, Fulton County Chapter. **Publications:** *Fulton Footprints*, quarterly. Newsletter. **Price:** included in membership dues. **Conventions/Meetings:** monthly meeting - every first Wednesday excluding July and August.

16818 ■ Ohio Health Care Association, District 15
c/o Lisa Mitchell, Chair
Swanton Hea. Care & Retirement
214 S Munson Rd.
Swanton, OH 43558
Ph: (419)825-1145
Fax: (419)825-5044
E-mail: lmitchell@earthlink.net
URL: http://www.ohca.org
Contact: Lisa Mitchell, Chair
Local. Promotes professionalism and ethical behavior of individuals providing long-term care delivery for patients and for the general public. Provides information, education and administrative tools to enhance the quality of long-term care. Improves the standards of service and administration of member nursing homes. **Affiliated With:** American Health Care Association.

16819 ■ Swanton Area Chamber of Commerce (SACC)
100 Broadway
Swanton, OH 43558
Ph: (419)826-1941
Fax: (419)826-3242
E-mail: swantoncc@aol.com
URL: http://www.swantonareacoc.com
Contact: Neil Toeppe, Exec.Dir.
Founded: 1975. **Members:** 85. **Membership Dues:** business, $80-$275 (annual) • utility, financial institution, $275 (annual) • individual, civic, $50 (annual). **Local.** Businesses, factories, retail stores, wholesalers, professional and fraternal organizations, and individuals interested in promoting business and community development in eastern Fulton and western Lucas counties, OH. Conducts workshops. **Committees:** Community Affairs; Economic Development; Finance and Budget; Government Affairs; Infrastructure; Membership; Public Relations. **Affiliated With:** U.S. Chamber of Commerce. **Publications:** Newsletter, bimonthly. **Conventions/Meetings:** annual dinner • quarterly meeting.

16820 ■ Veterans of Foreign Wars 8598
105 S Main St.
Swanton, OH 43558
Ph: (419)826-3935
Contact: Gilbert Urban, Commander
Local.

Sycamore

16821 ■ American Legion, Sycamore Post 250
PO Box 83
Sycamore, OH 44882
Ph: (740)362-7478
Fax: (740)362-1429
URL: National Affiliate–www.legion.org
Local. Affiliated With: American Legion.

16822 ■ Sycamore Lions Club
c/o Ronald Roberts, Sec.
PO Box 323
Sycamore, OH 44882
Ph: (419)927-2219
E-mail: ronrob@bright.net
URL: http://www.lions13b.org
Contact: Ronald Roberts, Sec.
Local. Affiliated With: Lions Clubs International.

Sylvania

16823 ■ AAA Northwest Ohio
5700 Monroe St.
Sylvania, OH 43560
Ph: (419)885-3555
Local.

16824 ■ American Legion, Ohio Post 468
c/o Joseph W. Diehn
5580 Centennial Rd.
Sylvania, OH 43560
Ph: (740)362-7478
Fax: (740)362-1429
URL: National Affiliate–www.legion.org
Contact: Joseph W. Diehn, Contact
Local. Affiliated With: American Legion.

16825 ■ Maumee Valley Chefs Chapter ACF
c/o Edward W. Gozdowski, CEC, Pres.
6060 Centennial Rd.
Sylvania, OH 43560
Ph: (419)885-8608
E-mail: edgchef@aol.com
URL: National Affiliate–www.acfchefs.org
Contact: Edward W. Gozdowski CEC, Pres.
Local. Promotes the culinary profession and provides on-going educational training and networking for members. Provides opportunities for competition, professional recognition, and access to educational forums with other culinarians at local, regional, national, and international events.

16826 ■ Mothers Against Drunk Driving, Greater Toledo Area
6465 Monroe St., Ste.211
Sylvania, OH 43560
Ph: (419)885-6233
Fax: (419)882-8667
E-mail: toledomadd@pngusa.net
URL: http://www.madd.org/oh/toledo
Contact: Dale A. Jones Jr., Pres.
Local. Victims of drunk driving crashes; concerned citizens. Encourages citizen participation in working towards reform of the drunk driving problem and the prevention of underage drinking. Acts as the voice of victims of drunk driving crashes by speaking on their behalf to communities, businesses, and educational groups. **Affiliated With:** Mothers Against Drunk Driving.

16827 ■ Northview - Young Life
PO Box 226
Sylvania, OH 43560
Ph: (419)351-9787
URL: http://sites.younglife.org/_layouts/ylext/default.aspx?ID=C-1491
Local. Affiliated With: Young Life.

16828 ■ Northwest Ohio District of Precision Metalforming Association
c/o Candy Villarreal, Administrator/Sec.-Treas.
PO Box 642
Sylvania, OH 43560-0642
Ph: (419)450-1480
E-mail: nwohiopma@yahoo.com
URL: http://nwohio.pma.org
Contact: Candy Villarreal, Administrator/Sec.-Treas.
Local. Promotes and safeguards the interests of the metalforming industry. Conducts technical and educational programs. Provides legislative and regulatory assistance to members. **Affiliated With:** Precision Metalforming Association.

16829 ■ Northwest Ohio Traditional Music and Dance (NOTMAD)
c/o Cathy Whitaker
5505 Wadsworth Dr.
Sylvania, OH 43560
Ph: (419)283-3430
E-mail: info@notmad.org
URL: http://notmad.org
Contact: Cathy Whitaker, Pres.
Local. Affiliated With: Country Dance and Song Society.

16830 ■ Ohio Health Care Association, District 4
c/o Debra Kriner, Chair
D. Kriner & Assoc.
7608 Shadywood Ln.
Sylvania, OH 43560
Ph: (419)882-2171
Fax: (419)882-2101
E-mail: debbie@dkriner.com
URL: http://www.ohca.org
Contact: Debra Kriner, Chair
Local. Promotes professionalism and ethical behavior of individuals providing long-term care delivery for patients and for the general public. Provides information, education and administrative tools to enhance the quality of long-term care. Improves the standards of service and administration of member nursing homes. **Affiliated With:** American Health Care Association.

16831 ■ Racing for Recovery (R4R)
c/o Todd Crandell
6936 Clare Ct.
Sylvania, OH 43560
Ph: (419)824-8462
Fax: (419)824-8463
Free: (866)SOB-ER01
E-mail: racing4recovery@aol.com
URL: http://www.racingforrecovery.com
Contact: Todd Crandell, Exec.Dir.
Founded: 2001. **Members:** 8. **Regional Groups:** 1. **State Groups:** 2. **Local Groups:** 1. **Local.** Committed to preventing all forms of substance abuse and to provide positive alternatives to those currently battling addictions by encouraging a lifestyle of fitness and health through 5K run/walk events across the nation. **Subgroups:** R4R Support Groups. **Conventions/Meetings:** annual 5K Run/Walk - tour.

16832 ■ Southview - Young Life
PO Box 226
Sylvania, OH 43560
Ph: (419)351-9787
URL: http://sites.younglife.org/_layouts/ylext/default.aspx?ID=C-1492
Local. Affiliated With: Young Life.

16833 ■ Springfield - Young Life
PO Box 226
Sylvania, OH 43560
Ph: (419)351-9787
URL: http://sites.younglife.org/_layouts/ylext/default.aspx?ID=C-1493
Local. Affiliated With: Young Life.

16834 ■ Sylvania Area Chamber of Commerce (SACC)
6616 Monroe St., Ste.8
Sylvania, OH 43560
Ph: (419)882-2135
Fax: (419)885-7740
E-mail: sylvania.chamber@sev.org
URL: http://www.sylvaniachamber.org
Contact: Ms. Candy Baker, Exec.Dir.
Founded: 1954. **Members:** 500. **Membership Dues:** firm (with 1-4 employees), $175 (annual) • firm (with 5-9 employees), $250 (annual) • firm (with 10-25 employees), $300 (annual) • firm (with 26-49 employees), $350 (annual) • firm (with 50 or more employees), $400 (annual). **Staff:** 2. **For-Profit. Local.** Promotes business and community development in the Sylvania, OH area. Sponsors annual Arts and Crafts Festival. **Publications:** Newsletter, monthly. **Conventions/Meetings:** monthly luncheon.

16835 ■ Young Life West Toledo
PO Box 226
Sylvania, OH 43560
Ph: (419)351-9787
Fax: (419)865-3579
E-mail: moshea_yl@yahoo.com
URL: http://sites.younglife.org/sites/westtoledo/default.aspx
Local. Affiliated With: Young Life.

Tallmadge

16836 ■ Akron Black Nurses Association (16)
c/o Bertha Solomon, LPN
29 Oliver Rd.
Tallmadge, OH 44278
Ph: (330)633-1157
URL: National Affiliate–www.nbna.org
Contact: Bertha Solomon LPN, Contact
Local. Represents registered nurses, licensed practical nurses, licensed vocational nurses, and student nurses. Builds consumer knowledge and understanding of health care issues. Facilitates the professional development and career advancement of nurses in emerging healthcare systems. Promotes economic development of nurses through entrepreneurial and other business initiatives. **Affiliated With:** National Black Nurses Association.

16837 ■ Akron-Canton Bonsai Society
c/o Art Krummel
320 Hanna Dr.
Tallmadge, OH 44278
Ph: (330)633-1519
E-mail: akrummel@neo.rr.com
URL: National Affiliate–www.bonsai-bci.com
Contact: Art Krummel, Contact
Local. Affiliated With: Bonsai Clubs International.

16838 ■ Akron Turner Club (ATC)
547 S Munroe Falls Rd.
Tallmadge, OH 44278
Ph: (330)733-4540
Contact: Kenny Hines, Pres.
Founded: 1885. **Members:** 550. **Membership Dues:** regular and auxillary, $35 (annual). **Staff:** 2. **Budget:** $150,000. **Regional Groups:** 1. **State Groups:** 10. **Languages:** English, German. **Local.** Promotes health and physical education for the family through gymnastics, swimming, games, bowling, golf, social events and cultural education. Offers classes in music, painting, and handicrafts. **Affiliated With:** American Turners. **Publications:** *ATC Newsletter*, quarterly. **Price:** included in membership dues. **Circulation:** 500. **Advertising:** accepted. **Conventions/Meetings:** annual District Convention (exhibits) - always March or April; Avg. Attendance: 35.

16839 ■ All Breed Training Club of Akron (ABTCA)
E Howe Rd.
Tallmadge, OH 44278
Ph: (330)630-0418
E-mail: info@abtca.org
URL: http://www.abtca.mysaga.net
Contact: Lois Orlando, Corresponding Sec.
Local.

16840 ■ American Legion, Kneil-Lawrentz Post 255
PO Box 255
Tallmadge, OH 44278
Ph: (740)362-7478
Fax: (740)362-1429
URL: National Affiliate–www.legion.org
Local. Affiliated With: American Legion.

16841 ■ American Society for Quality, Akron-Canton Section 0810
c/o Jeffrey Pfouts, Chm.
PO Box 392
Tallmadge, OH 44278-0392
E-mail: jpfouts@alliedmachine.com
URL: http://www.asq810.org
Contact: Jeffrey Pfouts, Chm.
Local. Advances learning, quality improvement and knowledge exchange to improve business results and to create better workplaces and communities worldwide. Provides a forum for information exchange, professional development and continuous learning in the science of quality. **Affiliated With:** American Society for Quality.

16842 ■ Gardeners of America/Men's Garden Clubs of America - Akron Men's Garden Club
c/o David Hawkins
461 Perry Rd.
Tallmadge, OH 44278
Ph: (330)784-1956
URL: http://www.acorn.net/mgcakron
Contact: David Hawkins, Contact
Local.

16843 ■ Suffield Lions Club
c/o Steve Wartko, Sec.
1039 Southeast Ave.
Tallmadge, OH 44278
Ph: (330)630-9099
E-mail: gravepick@sbcglobal.net
URL: http://www.lions13d.org
Contact: Dale Williams, Pres.
Local. Affiliated With: Lions Clubs International.

16844 ■ Tallmadge Chamber of Commerce
80 Community Dr.
Tallmadge, OH 44278
Ph: (330)633-5417
Fax: (330)633-5415
E-mail: tallmadgechamber@sbcglobal.net
URL: http://www.tallmadge-chamber.com
Contact: Nikole L. Dack, Exec.Dir.
Founded: 1955. **Members:** 167. **Membership Dues:** business, $175-$280 (annual) • non-profit, $75 (annual) • home-based business, $145 (annual) • individual, $90 (annual). **Staff:** 2. **Local.** Promotes business and community development in Tallmadge, OH. Sponsors arts and crafts festival. Conducts charitable activities. **Awards:** Business Person of the Year. **Frequency:** annual. **Type:** recognition • Citizen of the Year. **Frequency:** annual. **Type:** recognition • **Frequency:** periodic. **Type:** scholarship. **Telecommunication Services:** electronic mail, tallmadgechamber@rrbiznet.com. **Publications:** *Business Notes*, monthly. Newsletter. Alternate Formats: online • Bulletin, monthly. **Conventions/ Meetings:** annual banquet, recognizes long-standing Tallmadge businesses, and honoring the Citizen and Business Persons of the Year - every November • annual Golf Scramble - competition, a fundraiser, a great networking opportunity with a little friendly competition - always August • monthly meeting - every third Wednesday.

16845 ■ USA Weightlifting - American College of Modern Weightlifting
c/o Carl E. Hughes, II -
1174 East Ave.
Tallmadge, OH 44278-2510
Ph: (330)630-2471
E-mail: cascade1@voyager.net
URL: National Affiliate–www.usaweightlifting.org
Contact: Carl E. Hughes II, Contact
Local. Affiliated With: USA Weightlifting.

Terrace Park

16846 ■ Cincinnati AIFA
PO Box 208
Terrace Park, OH 45174
Ph: (513)248-1125
Fax: (513)248-1147
URL: National Affiliate–www.naifa.org
Local. Represents the interest of insurance and financial advisors. Advocates for a positive legislative and regulatory environment. Enhances business and professional skills of members. **Affiliated With:** National Association of Insurance and Financial Advisors.

16847 ■ Cincinnati Chapter of the Society of Financial Service Professionals
PO Box 208
Terrace Park, OH 45174
Ph: (513)248-1125
Fax: (513)248-1147
E-mail: adminoffice@naifa-cincinnati.com
URL: http://www.sfsp.net/cincinnati
Contact: Cynthia J. Palmer, Exec.Dir.
Local. Represents the interests of financial advisers. Fosters the development of professional responsibility. Helps clients achieve their personal and business-related financial goals. **Affiliated With:** Society of Financial Service Professionals.

16848 ■ Terrace Park Historical Society
c/o Carol B. Cole, Treas.
725 Wooster Pike
Terrace Park, OH 45174
E-mail: carolcole@fuse.net
URL: http://www.tphistoricalsociety.org
Local.

Thornville

16849 ■ American Legion, Ohio Post 342
c/o Edgar A. Orr
155 S Church St.
Thornville, OH 43076
Ph: (740)362-7478
Fax: (740)362-1429
URL: National Affiliate–www.legion.org
Contact: Edgar A. Orr, Contact
Local. Affiliated With: American Legion.

Tiffin

16850 ■ American Legion, Tiffin Post 169
280 S Washington St.
Tiffin, OH 44883
Ph: (740)362-7478
Fax: (740)362-1429
URL: National Affiliate–www.legion.org
Local. Affiliated With: American Legion.

16851 ■ Bloomville Lions Club
c/o Richard Lease, Pres.
4951 E County Rd., No. 16
Tiffin, OH 44883
Ph: (419)447-5677
E-mail: ezlease@wcnet.org
URL: http://www.lions13b.org
Contact: Richard Lease, Pres.
Local. Affiliated With: Lions Clubs International.

16852 ■ Catholics United for the Faith - Cardinal Newman Chapter
c/o Jo Patuto
276 Clay St., Box 575
Tiffin, OH 44883
Ph: (419)447-6593
URL: National Affiliate–www.cuf.org
Contact: Jo Patuto, Contact
Local.

16853 ■ Izaak Walton League of America, Tiffin-Seneca County Chapter
c/o Kenneth Sarka
PO Box 724
Tiffin, OH 44883
Ph: (419)447-5060
E-mail: kmsarka@bright.net
URL: National Affiliate–www.iwla.org
Local. Works to educate the public to conserve, maintain, protect, and restore the soil, forest, water, and other natural resources of the U.S; promotes the enjoyment and wholesome utilization of these resources. **Affiliated With:** Izaak Walton League of America.

16854 ■ Miami Valley Boxer Club (MVBC)
c/o Charles W. Coull, Corresponding Sec.
3215 W County Rd. 26
Tiffin, OH 44883
Ph: (419)447-8308
E-mail: winland@thewavz.com
URL: http://ohioboxers.com
Local.

16855 ■ National Active and Retired Federal Employees Association - Tiffin 504
310 Riverside Dr.
Tiffin, OH 44883-1607
Ph: (419)447-8266
URL: National Affiliate–www.narfe.org
Contact: Robert L. Booth, Contact
Local. Protects the retirement future of employees through education. Informs members on issues affecting the retirement. **Affiliated With:** National Association of Retired Federal Employees.

16856 ■ National Technical Honor Society - Vanguard-Sentinel Career Centers Ohio
793 E Twp.201
Tiffin, OH 44883
Ph: (419)448-1212
E-mail: sentinel@vscc.k12.oh.us
URL: http://www.vscc.k12.oh.us
Contact: Hank Elchert, Dir.
Local.

16857 ■ Ohio Association for Employment in Education
c/o Andrea Domachowski, Dir.
Career Development
Heidelberg Coll.
310 E Market St.
Tiffin, OH 44883
Ph: (419)448-2058
E-mail: agrata@heidelberg.edu
URL: National Affiliate–www.aaee.org
Contact: Andrea Domachowski, Dir.
State. Serves the staffing needs of education professionals at colleges, universities and school districts whose members are school personnel/HR administrators and college and university career center administrators. Promotes ethical standards and practices in the employment processes. **Affiliated With:** American Association for Employment in Education.

16858 ■ Ohio Choral Directors Association (OCDA)
c/o Jacqueline A. Nielsen, Treas.
PO Box 567
Tiffin, OH 44883
E-mail: ocdatreasurer@woh.rr.com
URL: http://www.ohiocda.org
Contact: Mark Munson, Pres.
Members: 700. **Membership Dues:** associate/ active, $75 (annual) • student, $30 (annual) • life, $2,000 • retired, $35 (annual) • institutional, $100 (annual) • industry, $125 (annual). **State.** Serves the choral musicians of Ohio through the promotion of choral excellence. **Subgroups:** Repertoire and Standards; Technology. **Affiliated With:** American Choral Directors Association. **Publications:** *OCDA News*, 3/year. Newsletter. **Advertising:** accepted. Alternate Formats: online. **Conventions/Meetings:** annual conference - 2007 Feb. 8-10, Columbus, OH.

16859 ■ Psi Chi, National Honor Society in Psychology - Heidelberg College
c/o Dept. of Psychology
310 E Market St.
Tiffin, OH 44883-2462
Ph: (419)448-2000 (419)448-2238
Fax: (419)448-2236
E-mail: estrahan@heidelberg.edu
URL: http://www.psichi.org/chapters/info.asp?chapter_id=587
Contact: Esther Strahan PhD, Advisor
Local.

16860 ■ Sandusky Valley Amateur Astronomy Club
650 S Washington St.
Tiffin, OH 44883
Ph: (419)448-9377
E-mail: tfretz@friendlynet.com
URL: National Affiliate–www.astroleague.org
Contact: Thomas Fretz, Contact
Local. Promotes the science of astronomy. Works to encourage and coordinate activities of amateur astronomical societies. Fosters observational and computational work and craftsmanship in various fields of astronomy. **Affiliated With:** Astronomical League.

16861 ■ Seneca County Genealogical Society (SCGS)
PO Box 157
Tiffin, OH 44883-0157
E-mail: history@popmailbox.com
URL: http://www.senecasearchers.org
Contact: Steve Hartzell, Recording Sec.
Founded: 1981. **Members:** 397. **Membership Dues:** regular, $10 (annual). **Local.** Genealogists united to gather, preserve, and disseminate genealogical and historical information pertaining to Seneca County, OH. **Awards:** First Families of Seneca County Gold Award. **Frequency:** annual. **Type:** recognition. **Recipient:** for people with ancestors who resided in Seneca County prior to 1841 • First Families of Seneca County Silver Award. **Frequency:** annual. **Type:** recognition. **Recipient:** for people with ancestors who resided in Seneca County during the period 1841-1860. **Affiliated With:** Ohio Genealogical Society. **Also Known As:** (2005) Ohio Genealogical Society, Seneca County. **Publications:** *Seneca Searchers*, bimonthly. Newsletter. Features society news and genealogical and historical information about Seneca County Ohio. **Price:** included in membership dues. **Circulation:** 480. **Conventions/Meetings:** monthly meeting - every first Tuesday in Tiffin, OH; except in July, August, and December.

16862 ■ Seneca County Home Builders Association
c/o Kim Ernst
PO Box 712
Tiffin, OH 44883-0712
Ph: (419)447-7241
Fax: (419)448-7349
E-mail: schba@acctiffin.com
URL: National Affiliate–www.nahb.org
Local. Single and multifamily home builders, commercial builders, and others associated with the building industry. **Affiliated With:** National Association of Home Builders.

16863 ■ Seneca Habitat for Humanity
PO Box 917
Tiffin, OH 44883
Ph: (419)447-4270
E-mail: senecahfh@yahoo.com
URL: National Affiliate–www.habitat.org
Local. Affiliated With: Habitat for Humanity International.

16864 ■ Tiffin Area Chamber of Commerce
62 S Washington St.
Tiffin, OH 44883
Ph: (419)447-4141
Fax: (419)447-5141
E-mail: tiffinchamber@bpsom.com
URL: http://www.tiffinchamber.com
Contact: Richard Focht Jr., CEO & Pres.
Local. Seeks to promote and support community enhancement activities that are beneficial to Tiffin area. **Committees:** Ambassador's Club; Annual Dinner; Around the Town; Community Plan; Fundraising Event; Legislative Series. **Councils:** Safety; Tiffin Area Industrial Management. **Publications:** *Chamber Vision*, periodic. Newsletter. Alternate Formats: online.

16865 ■ Tiffin Lions Club
c/o Richard Steinmetz, Pres.
185 Minerva St.
Tiffin, OH 44883
Ph: (419)447-8810
E-mail: tiffinlions@woh.rr.com
URL: http://www.lions13b.org
Contact: Richard Steinmetz, Pres.
Local. Affiliated With: Lions Clubs International.

16866 ■ Tiffin-Seneca United Way
174 Jefferson St.
Tiffin, OH 44883
Ph: (419)448-0355
Fax: (419)448-0709
E-mail: tsunitedway@bpsom.com
URL: http://www.tiffinohio.com/UnitedWay
Local. Affiliated With: United Way of America.

Tiltonsville

16867 ■ American Legion, Y. T. R. Post 153
PO Box 73
Tiltonsville, OH 43963
Ph: (740)362-7478
Fax: (740)362-1429
URL: National Affiliate–www.legion.org
Local. Affiliated With: American Legion.

Tipp City

16868 ■ American Legion, Ohio Post 586
c/o Frank E. Robinson
377 N 3rd St., No. 118
Tipp City, OH 45371
Ph: (740)362-7478
Fax: (740)362-1429
URL: National Affiliate–www.legion.org
Contact: Frank E. Robinson, Contact
Local. Affiliated With: American Legion.

16869 ■ Ohio Association of School Nurses (OASN)
c/o Renee Besecker, Exec.Dir.
PO Box 150
Tipp City, OH 45371
Ph: (937)667-0850
Fax: (937)667-3366
E-mail: exdirector@oasn.org
URL: http://www.oasn.org
Contact: Renee Besecker, Exec.Dir.
State. Advances the delivery of professional school health services. Increases the awareness of students on the necessity of health and learning. Improves the health of children by developing school nursing practices. **Affiliated With:** National Association of School Nurses.

16870 ■ Tipp City Area Chamber of Commerce
12 S 3rd St.
Tipp City, OH 45371-0134
Ph: (937)667-8300
Fax: (937)667-8867
E-mail: tippcham@core.com
Contact: Ms. Vicki Marie Lowery, Pres./C.E.O.
Founded: 1954. **Members:** 150. **Membership Dues:** individual or employee, $117 (annual). **Staff:** 1. **Budget:** $70,000. **For-Profit. Local. Libraries: Type:** not open to the public. **Awards:** Business of the Year. **Frequency:** annual. **Type:** trophy • Citizen of the Year. **Frequency:** annual. **Type:** trophy. **Recipient:** for contributions to community • Small Business of the Year. **Frequency:** annual. **Type:** trophy. **Publications:** *The Chamber Connection*, bimonthly. Newsletter. **Circulation:** 250. **Advertising:** accepted.

16871 ■ Tipp City Area United Way
PO Box 95
Tipp City, OH 45371
Ph: (937)669-3863
Fax: (937)667-8862
E-mail: director@tippcityauw.org
URL: http://www.tippcityauw.org
Contact: Deborah Carr, Exec.Dir.
Local. Affiliated With: United Way of America.

Tiro

16872 ■ Col. Crawford Lions Club
c/o Linda Efaw, Pres.
6598 Loss Creek Rd.
Tiro, OH 44887
Ph: (419)683-2473
E-mail: efaw1@bright.net
URL: http://www.lions13b.org
Contact: Linda Efaw, Pres.
Local. Affiliated With: Lions Clubs International.

Toledo

16873 ■ Alcoholics Anonymous World Services, Northwest Ohio and Southeastern Michigan Central Office
2747 Glendale Ave.
Toledo, OH 43614
Ph: (419)380-9862
Fax: (419)380-9978
E-mail: toledoaa@accesstoledo.com
URL: http://www.toledoaa.com
Local. Individuals recovering from alcoholism. AA maintains that members can solve their common problem and help others achieve sobriety through a twelve step program that includes sharing their experience, strength, and hope with each other. **Affiliated With:** Alcoholics Anonymous World Services.

16874 ■ Alzheimer's Association, Northwest Ohio Chapter
2500 N Reynolds Rd.
Toledo, OH 43615
Ph: (419)537-1999
Fax: (419)536-5591
Free: (800)441-3322
E-mail: alzheimers@nwoalz.org
URL: http://www.nwoalz.org
Local. Assists people with Alzheimer's disease and related dementia. **Affiliated With:** Alzheimer's Association.

16875 ■ American Association of Critical-Care Nurses, Greater Toledo Area Chapter (GTAC-AACN)
PO Box 351203
Toledo, OH 43635-1203
E-mail: kzsarnay@meduohio.edu
URL: http://www.gtac.org
Contact: Kathleen McCarthy BSN, Pres.-Elect
Local. Professional critical care nurses. Works to provide continuing education programs for nurses specializing in critical care and to develop standards of nursing care of critically ill patients. **Affiliated With:** American Association of Critical-Care Nurses.

16876 ■ American Legion, Adams Township Post 553
206 S Byrne Rd.
Toledo, OH 43615
Ph: (740)362-7478
Fax: (740)362-1429
URL: National Affiliate–www.legion.org
Local. Affiliated With: American Legion.

16877 ■ American Legion, Argonne Post 545
2715 Tamarack Dr.
Toledo, OH 43614
Ph: (740)362-7478
Fax: (740)362-1429
URL: National Affiliate–www.legion.org
Local. Affiliated With: American Legion.

16878 ■ American Legion, Conn-Weissenberger Post 587
2020 W Alexis Rd.
Toledo, OH 43613
Ph: (740)362-7478
Fax: (740)362-1429
URL: National Affiliate–www.legion.org
Local. Affiliated With: American Legion.

16879 ■ American Legion, Dean Horton Navy Post 108
2913 Stoneleigh Dr.
Toledo, OH 43617
Ph: (740)362-7478
Fax: (740)362-1429
URL: National Affiliate–www.legion.org
Local. Affiliated With: American Legion.

16880 ■ American Legion, Hyatt-Allen Post 538
4818 Thobe Rd.
Toledo, OH 43615
Ph: (740)362-7478
Fax: (740)362-1429
URL: National Affiliate–www.legion.org
Local. Affiliated With: American Legion.

16881 ■ American Legion, North End Post 576
5267 N Detroit Ave.
Toledo, OH 43612
Ph: (740)362-7478
Fax: (740)362-1429
URL: National Affiliate–www.legion.org
Local. Affiliated With: American Legion.

16882 ■ American Legion, Ohio Post 18
c/o Tony Wroblewski
2237 Farm View Ct.
Toledo, OH 43615
Ph: (740)362-7478
Fax: (740)362-1429
URL: National Affiliate–www.legion.org
Contact: Tony Wroblewski, Contact
Local. Affiliated With: American Legion.

16883 ■ American Legion, Ohio Post 99
c/o Harry E. Pond
3247 E Manhattan Blvd.
Toledo, OH 43611
Ph: (740)362-7478
Fax: (740)362-1429
URL: National Affiliate–www.legion.org
Contact: Harry E. Pond, Contact
Local. Affiliated With: American Legion.

16884 ■ American Legion, Ohio Post 132
c/o Vernon Mc Cune
PO Box 140273
Toledo, OH 43614
Ph: (740)362-7478
Fax: (740)362-1429
URL: National Affiliate–www.legion.org
Contact: Vernon Mc Cune, Contact
Local. Affiliated With: American Legion.

16885 ■ American Legion, Ohio Post 135
c/o Walter Weller
2404 W Sylvania Ave.
Toledo, OH 43613
Ph: (740)362-7478
Fax: (740)362-1429
URL: National Affiliate–www.legion.org
Contact: Walter Weller, Contact
Local. Affiliated With: American Legion.

16886 ■ American Legion, Ohio Post 334
c/o Arthur Daly
502-504 Main St.
Toledo, OH 43605
Ph: (740)362-7478
Fax: (740)362-1429
URL: National Affiliate–www.legion.org
Contact: Arthur Daly, Contact
Local. Affiliated With: American Legion.

16887 ■ American Legion, Ohio Post 786
c/o Donald Dunbar
863 W Central Ave.
Toledo, OH 43610
Ph: (740)362-7478
Fax: (740)362-1429
URL: National Affiliate–www.legion.org
Contact: Donald Dunbar, Contact
Local. Affiliated With: American Legion.

16888 ■ American Legion, Point Place Post 110
5119 N Summit St.
Toledo, OH 43611
Ph: (740)362-7478
Fax: (740)362-1429
URL: National Affiliate–www.legion.org
Local. Affiliated With: American Legion.

16889 ■ American Legion, Przybylski Post 642
2810 Airport Hwy.
Toledo, OH 43609
Ph: (740)362-7478
Fax: (740)362-1429
URL: National Affiliate–www.legion.org
Local. Affiliated With: American Legion.

16890 ■ American Legion, South Side Post 531
881 Geneva Ave.
Toledo, OH 43609
Ph: (740)362-7478
Fax: (740)362-1429
URL: National Affiliate–www.legion.org
Local. Affiliated With: American Legion.

16891 ■ American Legion, Toledo Police Post 512
540 Independence Rd.
Toledo, OH 43607
Ph: (740)362-7478
Fax: (740)362-1429
URL: National Affiliate–www.legion.org
Local. Affiliated With: American Legion.

16892 ■ American Legion, Toledo Post 335
601 Monroe St.
Toledo, OH 43604
Ph: (740)362-7478
Fax: (740)362-1429
URL: National Affiliate–www.legion.org
Local. Affiliated With: American Legion.

16893 ■ American Payroll Association, Toledo Area Chapter
541 N Superior St.
Toledo, OH 43660
Ph: (419)724-6028
Fax: (419)724-6080
E-mail: pemery@toledoblade.com
URL: http://www.apatoledo.org
Contact: Paula M. Emery, Pres.
Members: 75. **Membership Dues:** $40 (annual). **Local.** Aims to increase the Payroll Professional's skill level through education and mutual support. Represents the Payroll Professional before legislative bodies. Administers the certified payroll professional program of recognition. Provides public service education on payroll and employment issues. **Affiliated With:** American Payroll Association.

16894 ■ American Red Cross, Greater Toledo Area Chapter
3100 W Central Ave.
Toledo, OH 43606
Ph: (419)329-2900
E-mail: toloharc@usa.redcross.org
URL: http://www.redcrosstoledo.org
Regional.

16895 ■ American Society of Appraisers, Toledo Chapter
c/o Michael J. Binkowski, Pres.
Toledo Bldg., Ste.620
316 N Michigan St.
Toledo, OH 43624
Ph: (419)243-6108
Fax: (419)824-0487
E-mail: mbink@buckeye-express.com
URL: http://www.appraisers.org/toledo
Contact: Michael J. Binkowski, Pres.
Local. Serves as a professional appraisal educator, testing and accrediting society. Sponsors mandatory recertification program for all members. Offers consumer information service to the public. **Affiliated With:** American Society of Appraisers.

16896 ■ American Society of Mechanical Engineers, Northwest Ohio Section
c/o Len Anderson, PE
PO Box 920
Toledo, OH 43697-0920
Ph: (419)698-6765
Fax: (419)697-6549
E-mail: nwo@asme.org
URL: http://sections.asme.org/nwohio
Contact: Len Anderson PE, Contact
Local. Promotes the art, science and practice of Mechanical Engineering and allied arts and sciences. Encourages original research and fosters engineering education. Promotes the technical and societal contribution of engineers. **Affiliated With:** American Society of Mechanical Engineers.

16897 ■ American Society for Quality, Toledo Section 1006
c/o Aimee L. Smith, Chair
3161 N Republic Blvd.
Toledo, OH 43615
Ph: (419)848-6691
E-mail: aimee.smith@benchmark-usa.com
URL: http://www.toledo-asq.org
Contact: Aimee L. Smith, Chair
Local. Advances learning, quality improvement and knowledge exchange to improve business results and to create better workplaces and communities worldwide. Provides a forum for information exchange, professional development and continuous learning in the science of quality. **Affiliated With:** American Society for Quality.

16898 ■ American Welding Society, Whitmer Career and Technical Center
c/o Craig Donnell
Welding and Metal Constr. Dept.
5719 Clegg Dr.
Toledo, OH 43613
Ph: (419)473-8455
Fax: (419)473-8309
E-mail: cdonnell@washloc.k12.oh.us
URL: National Affiliate–www.aws.org
Contact: Craig Donnell, Contact
Founded: 1997. **Members:** 27. **Staff:** 1. **Budget:** $200. **Local.** Offers secondary education/SENSE Program. **Affiliated With:** American Welding Society.

16899 ■ AMVETS, Toledo Post 222
4133 N Summit St.
Toledo, OH 43611
Ph: (419)726-0724
URL: http://groups.msn.com/amvetspost222toledooh
Local. Affiliated With: AMVETS - American Veterans.

16900 ■ Ancient Order of Hibernians - John P. Kelly, Division 1, Toledo, OH
c/o Matt Cassidy, Pres.
5940 Murnen Rd.
Toledo, OH 43623
E-mail: tolaoh@aol.com
URL: http://www.tolaoh.com
Contact: Matt Cassidy, Pres.
Local. Affiliated With: Ancient Order of Hibernians in America.

16901 ■ APICS, The Association for Operations Management - Toledo Chapter
PO Box 2823
Toledo, OH 43606
Ph: (419)662-7531
Fax: (419)662-9234
E-mail: president@apicstoledo.org
URL: http://www.apicstoledo.org
Contact: Bruce Brechin CPIM, Pres.
Local. Provides information and services in production and inventory management and related areas to enable members, enterprises and individuals to add value to their business performance. **Affiliated With:** APICS - The Association for Operations Management.

16902 ■ Arthritis Foundation, Northwestern Ohio
310 N Reynolds Rd., Ste.F
Toledo, OH 43615
Ph: (419)537-0888
URL: National Affiliate–www.arthritis.org
Local. Seeks to: discover the cause and improve the methods for the treatment and prevention of arthritis and other rheumatic diseases; increase the number of scientists investigating rheumatic diseases; provide training in rheumatic diseases for more doctors; extend knowledge of arthritis and other rheumatic diseases to the lay public, emphasizing the socioeconomic as well as medical aspects of these diseases. **Affiliated With:** Arthritis Foundation.

16903 ■ ASIS International, Toledo Chapter No. 56
c/o Robert J. Bilek, Chm.
5555 Airport Hwy., Ste.130
Toledo, OH 43615
Ph: (419)861-7645
Fax: (419)861-7704
E-mail: robert.bilek@fedex.com
URL: http://www.asistoledo.org
Contact: Robert J. Bilek, Chm.
Local. Seeks to increase the effectiveness and productivity of security practices by developing educational programs and materials that address security concerns. **Affiliated With:** ASIS International.

16904 ■ Association of Community Organizations for Reform Now, Toledo
316 N Michigan
Toledo, OH 43624
Ph: (419)244-7250
E-mail: ohacornto@acorn.org
URL: National Affiliate–www.acorn.org
Local. Affiliated With: Association of Community Organizations for Reform Now.

16905 ■ Association for Computing Machinery, University of Toledo
Nitschke Hall, Rm. 2020
2801 W Bancroft
Toledo, OH 43606
Ph: (419)530-8169
E-mail: acm@eng.utoledo.edu
URL: http://www.eecs.utoledo.edu/~acm
Contact: Artur Maryamov, Chm.
Local. Represents computer scientists, programmers, and information systems specialists. Encourages individuals in the computing industry to meet together, share ideas, plan events, and engage in life-long learning. **Affiliated With:** Association for Computing Machinery.

16906 ■ Association for Professionals in Infection Control and Epidemiology, Northwest Ohio
c/o Macy Anne, RN, Treas.
St. Vincent Medical Ctr.
2213 Cherry St.
Toledo, OH 43608
Ph: (419)251-0480
E-mail: anne_macy@mhsnr.org
URL: http://www.apic93.org
Contact: Brenda Dubilzig, Pres.
Local. Works to influence, support and improve the quality of healthcare through the development of educational programs and standards. Promotes quality research and standardization of practices and procedures. **Affiliated With:** Association for Professionals in Infection Control and Epidemiology.

16907 ■ Better Business Bureau, Northwest Ohio and Southeastern Michigan
3103 Executive Pkwy., Ste.200
Toledo, OH 43606-1312
Ph: (419)531-3116
Fax: (419)578-6001
E-mail: info@toledobbb.org
URL: http://www.toledobbb.org
Contact: Richard T. Eppstein, Pres./CEO
Founded: 1919. **Members:** 4,300. **Budget:** $1,000,000. **Regional**. Businesses in the Toledo, OH area. Seeks to promote and foster ethical relationship between businesses and the public through voluntary self-regulation, consumer and business education, and service excellence. Provides information to help consumers and businesses make informed purchasing decisions and avoid costly scams and frauds; settles consumer complaints through arbitration and other means. **Affiliated With:** BBB Wise Giving Alliance.

16908 ■ Big Brothers Big Sisters Northwestern Ohio
1 Stranahan Sq., Ste.252
Toledo, OH 43604
Ph: (419)243-4600
Fax: (419)243-2402
Free: (888)393-2767
E-mail: bbbsnwo@juno.com
URL: National Affiliate–www.bbbsa.org
Contact: Tami Hrebic, Program Specialist
Regional. Works to provide quality mentoring relationships between children and qualified adults in Northwestern Ohio, and promote their development into competent, confident and caring individuals. **Affiliated With:** Big Brothers Big Sisters of America.

16909 ■ Children's Rights Council of Ohio
c/o Margaret Wuwert, Coor.
4069 W Sylvania Ave.
Toledo, OH 43623
Ph: (419)473-8955
Fax: (419)473-8984
Free: (866)473-8957
E-mail: hummelfan7@aol.com
URL: National Affiliate–www.gocrc.com
Contact: Margaret Wuwert, Coor.
State. Works to assure a child the frequent, meaningful and continuing contact with two parents and extended family the child would normally have during a marriage. Strives to strengthen families through education, favoring family formation and family preservation. **Affiliated With:** Children's Rights Council.

16910 ■ Dignity - Toledo
PO Box 1388
Toledo, OH 43603
Ph: (419)242-9057
URL: http://www.fripro.com/DIGNITYTOLEDO.htm
Local.

16911 ■ Easter Seals Northwestern Ohio
435 S Hawley St., Ste.A
Toledo, OH 43609
Ph: (419)241-2600
Fax: (419)241-5046
Free: (877)855-2601
E-mail: kharris@eastersealsnwohio.org
URL: http://nwohio.easterseals.com
Contact: Ms. Kelli Harris, Community Relations Dir.
Local. Provides assistance and services to people with disabilities and their families. **Affiliated With:** Easter Seals.

16912 ■ Elks Lodge
3520 N. Holland Sylvania Rd.
Toledo, OH 43615
Ph: (419)841-6654

16913 ■ Employee Assistance Professionals Association - Greater Toledo Chapter
PO Box 1981
Toledo, OH 43603
Ph: (419)251-1444
Fax: (419)251-0616
E-mail: linda_lindsey@mhsnr.org
URL: http://www.ohioeapa.com/toledo/gt-eapa_brochure.html
Contact: Linda K. Lindsey, Pres.
Local. Affiliated With: Employee Assistance Professionals Association.

16914 ■ Epilepsy Foundation of Northwest Ohio
PMB129 6725 W Central Ave., Ste.M
Toledo, OH 43617
Ph: (248)351-7979
Fax: (248)351-2101
Free: (800)377-6226
URL: National Affiliate–www.epilepsyfoundation.org
Contact: Arlene Gorelick, Pres.
Local. Affiliated With: Epilepsy Foundation.

16915 ■ Financial Executives International, Toledo Chapter
c/o Mrs. Jane Kervin, Membership Chair
2859 135th St.
Toledo, OH 43611
Ph: (419)662-4330
Fax: (419)662-4340
E-mail: jkervin@namsa.com
URL: http://www.fei.org/eWeb/startpage.aspx?site=ch_tol
Contact: Mr. Richard Sterling, Pres.
Regional. Promotes personal and professional development of financial executives. Provides peer networking opportunities and advocacy services. **Committees:** Academic Relations; Career Services; Communications; Meeting Arrangements; National Liaison; Nominations; Professional Development; Programs. **Affiliated With:** Financial Executives International.

16916 ■ First Catholic Slovak Ladies Association - Toledo Junior Branch 149
740 Woodford St.
Toledo, OH 43605
Ph: (419)691-2809
URL: National Affiliate–www.fcsla.com
Local. Affiliated With: First Catholic Slovak Ladies Association.

16917 ■ Funeral Consumers' Alliance of Northwest Ohio (FCANWO)
2210 Collingwood Blvd.
Toledo, OH 43620
Ph: (419)874-6666
E-mail: fcanwo@yahoo.com
URL: http://www.funerals.org/nwo
Contact: Rebecca Locke-Gagnon, Pres.
Founded: 1968. **Members:** 1,003. **Membership Dues:** life, $30. **Local**. Provides education-advocacy-protection of a consumers right to choose a meaningful, dignified, and affordable funeral. **Affiliated With:** Funeral Consumers Alliance. **Publications:** Newsletter, annual. Contains a notice of annual membership

meeting. **Price:** free. **Circulation:** 1,003. **Conventions/Meetings:** annual meeting - usually April or May in Toledo, OH.

16918 ■ Gardeners of America/Men's Garden Clubs of America - Forget-Me-Not Garden Club
c/o James Sigrist, Pres.
5263 Brandon Rd.
Toledo, OH 43615
Ph: (419)536-1837
URL: National Affiliate–www.tgoa-mgca.org
Contact: James Sigrist, Pres.
Local.

16919 ■ Greater Toledo Convention and Visitors Bureau (GTCVB)
401 Jefferson Ave.
Toledo, OH 43604-1067
Ph: (419)321-6404 (419)241-1111
Fax: (419)255-7731
Free: (800)243-4667
E-mail: jdonnely@dotoledo.org
URL: http://www.dotoledo.org
Contact: Jim Donnely, Pres./CEO
Local.

16920 ■ Greater Toledo Urban League
608 Madison Ave., Ste.1525
Toledo, OH 43604
Ph: (419)243-3343
E-mail: gtul557@aol.com
URL: http://www.gtul.org
Contact: Johnny M. Mickler Sr., Pres./CEO
Local. **Affiliated With:** National Urban League.

16921 ■ Healthcare Financial Management Association, Northwest Ohio Chapter
c/o Samantha M. Platzke, CPA, Pres.-Elect
2200 Jefferson Ave.
Toledo, OH 43624-1120
Ph: (419)251-2046
E-mail: samantha.platzke@mhsnr.org
URL: http://www.nwohiohfma.org
Contact: Samantha M. Platzke CPA, Pres.-Elect
Local. Provides education, analysis and guidance to healthcare finance professionals. Helps members and other individuals in advancing the financial management of health care and in improving the business performance of organizations serving the healthcare field. **Affiliated With:** Healthcare Financial Management Association.

16922 ■ Hostelling International - Toledo Area Council
PO Box 352736
Toledo, OH 43635-2736
Ph: (419)419-0087
E-mail: toledoareacouncil@ekit.com
URL: http://www.freewheel.com/hiayh
Contact: Judy Wright, Pres.
Membership Dues: adult (18-54 years old), $28 (annual) • senior (55 years old and above), $18 (annual) • life, $250. **Local**. Helps individuals, especially the young, gain a greater understanding of the world and its people through hostelling. **Affiliated With:** Hostelling International-American Youth Hostels.

16923 ■ International Facility Management Association, Northwest Ohio Chapter
Lucas County Facilities
Facilities Dept.
761 Berdan Ave.
Toledo, OH 43610
Ph: (419)213-6437
Fax: (419)241-7039
E-mail: kgochen641@aol.com
URL: National Affiliate–www.ifma.org
Contact: Kathleen Gochenour, Pres.
Local. Works to enhance the professional goals of persons involved in the field of facility management. Conducts educational and research programs. Cultivates cooperation, understanding and interest among individuals, firms and associations.

16924 ■ International Union, United Automobile, Aerospace and Agricultural Implement Workers of America, AFL-CIO - Local Union 12
2300 Ashland Ave.
Toledo, OH 43620
Ph: (419)241-9126
URL: http://www.uawlocal12.org
Contact: Bruce Baumhower, Pres.
Members: 8,626. **Local**. AFL-CIO. **Affiliated With:** International Union, United Automobile, Aerospace and Agricultural Implement Workers of America.

16925 ■ International Union, United Automobile, Aerospace and Agricultural Implement Workers of America, AFL-CIO - Local Union 14
5411 Jackman Rd.
Toledo, OH 43613
Ph: (419)473-2854
URL: http://www.uawlocal14.org
Contact: Oscar Bunch, Pres.
Members: 3,560. **Local**. Seeks for the dignity and equality of the workers. Strives to provide contractors with well-trained, productive employees. **Affiliated With:** International Union, United Automobile, Aerospace and Agricultural Implement Workers of America.

16926 ■ Korean War Veterans Association, Northwest Ohio Chapter
c/o Thomas J. Van Buren
PO Box 5455
Toledo, OH 43613
Ph: (419)475-0885
E-mail: jovanburen@aol.com
URL: National Affiliate–www.kwva.org
Contact: Thomas J. Van Buren, Contact
Local. **Affiliated With:** Korean War Veterans Association.

16927 ■ Log Cabin Republicans of Northwest Ohio
c/o David Schulz, Chm.
PO Box 118050
Toledo, OH 43611
E-mail: nwohio@logcabin.org
URL: National Affiliate–online.logcabin.org
Contact: David Schulz, Chm.
Regional. **Affiliated With:** Log Cabin Republicans.

16928 ■ Make-A-Wish Foundation of Northwest Ohio
405 Madison Ave., Ste.210
Toledo, OH 43604
Ph: (419)244-9474
Fax: (419)244-9221
Free: (800)666-8539
E-mail: nwohio@northwestohio.wish.org
URL: http://www.northwestohio.wish.org
Contact: Jay Salvage, Exec.Dir.
Founded: 1984. **Staff:** 3. **Local**. Grants wishes to children under the age of 18 who have a life-threatening or terminal illness, thereby providing the family with special memories and respite from the stress of their situation. **Affiliated With:** Make-A-Wish Foundation of America.

16929 ■ Maumee Valley Habitat for Humanity
223-229 S Fearing Blvd.
Toledo, OH 43609
Ph: (419)382-1946
Fax: (419)382-4397
E-mail: cthayer@mvhabitat.org
URL: http://www.mvhabitat.org
Contact: Charles F. Thayer, Exec.Dir.
Founded: 1988. **Staff:** 3. **Budget:** $700,000. **For-Profit**. **Regional**. Volunteers build simple, decent, single family houses and sell them below market value to partner families. Provides 100% financing for each house on a 0% interest twenty year mortgage. **Affiliated With:** Habitat for Humanity International. **Publications:** Newsletter, quarterly. **Price:** free. **Circulation:** 2,000. **Conventions/Meetings:** monthly Board of Trustees - board meeting - 3rd Monday.

16930 ■ Mortgage Bankers Association Of Northwest Ohio (Toledo) (MBANWO)
PO Box 9208
Toledo, OH 43697
Ph: (419)885-8520
E-mail: patton4806@covad.net
URL: http://www.mbanwo.com
Contact: Karen Patton, Administrator
Local. Promotes fair and ethical lending practices and fosters professional excellence among real estate finance employees. Seeks to create an environment that enables members to invest in communities and achieve their business objectives. **Affiliated With:** Mortgage Bankers Association.

16931 ■ Mothers' Center of Greater Toledo
PO Box 351713
Toledo, OH 43635
Ph: (419)389-8275
E-mail: ctyo@buckeye-express.com
URL: http://www.motherscenter.net
Contact: Christine Tyo, Contact
Local. Provides an open forum for learning about child development and parenting. Creates an environment of inquiry and research regarding the needs and experiences of women and families. Validates and builds on participants' skills and talents. Offers on-site programming at corporations. A new initiative focuses on the economic impact of motherhood. **Affiliated With:** National Association of Mothers' Centers.

16932 ■ Muslim Students' Association - University of Toledo
Student Union
2801 Bancroft St.
Toledo, OH 43606-3390
Ph: (419)530-4636
Fax: (419)878-6215
URL: http://homepages.utoledo.edu/msa/
Local. Muslim students in North America. Seeks to advance the interests of members; works to enable members to practice Islam as a complete way of life. **Affiliated With:** Muslim Students Association of the United States and Canada.

16933 ■ National Active and Retired Federal Employees Association - Toledo 226
6104 Douglas Rd.
Toledo, OH 43613-1250
Ph: (419)474-0868
URL: National Affiliate–www.narfe.org
Contact: John R. Huff, Contact
Local. Protects the retirement future of employees through education. Informs members on issues affecting the retirement. **Affiliated With:** National Association of Retired Federal Employees.

16934 ■ National Association of Investors Corporation, Northwest Buckeye Chapter
3020 Barrington Dr.
Toledo, OH 43606
Ph: (419)874-8088
E-mail: dtcomo@buckeye-express.com
URL: http://better-investing.org/chapter/nwohio
Contact: Doris Como, Contact
Local. Teaches individuals how to become successful strategic long-term investors. Provides highly focused learning resources and investment tools that empower individuals to become better investors. **Affiliated With:** National Association of Investors Corporation.

16935 ■ National Association of Rocketry - Toledo Area Rocket Society (TARS)
PO Box 351301
Toledo, OH 43635
Ph: (419)841-1051
E-mail: info@toledorocketry.com
URL: http://www.toledorocketry.com
Contact: John J. Schmidt Jr., Contact
Local.

16936 ■ National Association of Women in Construction, Toledo Chapter
c/o Kathie Weaver
The Collaborative Inc.
500 Madison Ave.
Toledo, OH 43604
Ph: (419)242-7405
Fax: (419)242-7400
E-mail: kweaver@thecollaborativeinc.com
URL: http://www.nawictoledo.org
Contact: Kathie Weaver, Contact
Founded: 1980. **Local**. Serves as the voice of women in the construction industry. Contributes to the development of the industry. Encourages women to pursue and establish career in construction. Promotes cooperation, fellowship and understanding among members of the association. **Affiliated With:** National Association of Women in Construction.

16937 ■ National Organization for Women - Toledo Area
c/o Amy McLoughlin, Coor.
2251 Portsmouth Ave.
Toledo, OH 43613
Ph: (419)260-5477
E-mail: femails@toledonow.org
URL: http://www.ohionow.org
Contact: Amy McLoughlin, Coor.
Local. **Affiliated With:** National Organization for Women.

16938 ■ Navy League of the United States, Toledo-Erie Islands
c/o James L. Black, Pres.
2403 Parliament Sq.
Toledo, OH 43617
Ph: (419)535-1363
E-mail: jimblack@toast.net
URL: National Affiliate–www.navyleague.org
Contact: James L. Black, Pres.
Local. Civilian organization that supports U.S. capability to keep the sea lanes open through a strong, viable Navy, Marine Corps, Coast Guard, and Merchant Marine. Seeks to awaken interest and cooperation of U.S. citizens in matters serving to aid, improve, and develop the efficiency of U.S. naval and maritime forces and equipment. **Affiliated With:** Navy League of the United States.

16939 ■ Northwest Ohio Black Media Association (NOBMA)
PO Box 322
Toledo, OH 43697-0322
Ph: (419)244-2579
E-mail: clyde1@buckeye-access.com
URL: http://www.nobma.org
Contact: Clyde Hughes, Pres.
Local. Advocates the rights of black journalists. Provides informational and training services and professional development to black journalists and to the general public. **Affiliated With:** National Association of Black Journalists.

16940 ■ Northwest Ohio Chapter of the Association of Legal Administrators
c/o Mark C. Elliott, Pres.
PO Box 2088
Toledo, OH 43603-2088
Ph: (419)247-2506
E-mail: mce@fullerhenry.com
URL: http://www.alanwohio.org
Contact: Mark C. Elliott, Pres.
Local. **Affiliated With:** Association of Legal Administrators.

16941 ■ Northwest Ohio Health Information Management Association (NWOHIMA)
c/o Jill Buathier, Pres.
Medical Univ. of Ohio
Hea. Info. Mgt.
3065 Arlington Ave., Dowling Hall 70
Toledo, OH 43614
Ph: (419)383-3908
E-mail: jbuathier@meduohio.edu
URL: http://www.ohima.org
Contact: Jill Buathier, Pres.
Local. Represents the interests of individuals dedicated to the effective management of personal health information needed to deliver quality healthcare to the public. Provides career, professional development and practice resources. Sets standards for education and certification. Advocates public policy that advances Health Information Management (HIM) practice. **Affiliated With:** American Health Information Management Association; Ohio Health Information Management Association.

16942 ■ Northwest Ohio Hemophilia Foundation
241 N Superior St., 2nd Fl.
Toledo, OH 43604
Ph: (419)242-9587
Fax: (419)242-4951
E-mail: info@nwohiohemophilia.org
URL: http://www.nwohiohemophilia.org
Contact: Stephanie Branco, Dir.
Local. Promotes the health and well-being of those affected by bleeding disorders in Northwest Ohio. Provides outreach services, including education, information and referral, advocacy, and family networking meetings. Maintains a Family Crisis Fund, provides medical alert bracelets, and funds camperships for youth affected by bleeding disorders. **Affiliated With:** National Hemophilia Foundation.

16943 ■ Northwest Ohio Mayors and Managers Association
300 Madison Ave., Ste.270
Toledo, OH 43604
Ph: (419)252-2700
Fax: (419)252-2724
E-mail: nomma@rgp.org
URL: http://www.nomma.us
Contact: Eileen Granata, Contact
Founded: 1990. **Local**. Unified regional network and voice promoting municipal interests and strategic growth in Northwest Ohio.

16944 ■ Ohio Association for Developmental Education (OADE)
c/o Marge Bartelt, Pres.-Elect
PO Box 10000
Toledo, OH 43699-1947
Ph: (614)227-5372
E-mail: dhall@cscc.edu
URL: http://www.oade.org
Contact: Marge Bartelt, Pres.-Elect
State. Seeks to improve the theory and practice of developmental education. Enhances the professional capabilities of development educators. Supports student learning and provides public leadership. **Affiliated With:** National Association for Developmental Education.

16945 ■ Ottawa River Beagle Club
c/o Andrew Owczarzak, Jr.
921 Southover Rd.
Toledo, OH 43612-3134
URL: National Affiliate–clubs.akc.org
Contact: Andrew Owczarzak Jr., Contact
Local.

16946 ■ Paralegal Association of Northwest Ohio (PANO)
PO Box 1322
Toledo, OH 43603-1322
URL: http://www.panonet.org
Contact: Jean A. McIntyre, Contact
Local. Provides continuing education and professional development programs for paralegal professionals. Works to improve the quality and effectiveness of the delivery of legal services.

16947 ■ Parents for Public Schools of Toledo
PO Box 6972
Toledo, OH 43612
Ph: (419)473-0875
E-mail: ppstoledo@buckeye-express.com
URL: http://www.ppstoledo.org
Contact: Darlene K. Fisher, Pres.
Local.

16948 ■ Phi Theta Kappa - Alpha Omega Pi Chapter
c/o Chuck Bohleke
PO Box 10000
Toledo, OH 43699
Ph: (567)661-7209
E-mail: chuck.bohleke@ptk.org
URL: http://www.ptk.org/directories/chapters/OH/20606-2.htm
Contact: Chuck Bohleke, Advisor
Local. **Affiliated With:** Phi Theta Kappa, International Honor Society.

16949 ■ Planned Parenthood of Northwest Ohio
1301 Jefferson Ave.
Toledo, OH 43624-1838
Ph: (419)255-1123
Fax: (419)255-5216
URL: http://www.ppnwo.org
Local. **Affiliated With:** Planned Parenthood Federation of America.

16950 ■ Pontiac-Oakland Club International, Northwest Ohio Chapter
c/o Virgene Toth
833 Kingston Ave.
Toledo, OH 43605
URL: National Affiliate–www.poci.org
Contact: Virgene Toth, Contact
Local. **Affiliated With:** Pontiac-Oakland Club International.

16951 ■ Portage River Basin Council
PO Box 9508
Toledo, OH 43697
Ph: (419)241-9155
Fax: (419)241-9116
E-mail: kurt@tmacog.org
URL: http://www.tmacog.org
Contact: Kurt Erichsen, Dir. of Environmental Planning
Local.

16952 ■ Pride of Toledo Chorus of Sweet Adelines International
Common Space Too
10 S Holland-Sylvania Rd.
Toledo, OH 43615-5620
Ph: (419)539-2220
E-mail: prideoftoledo@yahoo.com
URL: http://www.prideoftoledo.org
Contact: Sue Metz, Pres.
Local. Advances the musical art form of barbershop harmony through education and performances. Provides education, training and coaching in the development of women's four-part barbershop harmony. **Affiliated With:** Sweet Adelines International.

16953 ■ Professional Musicians of NW Ohio - Local No. 15-286, American Federation of Musicians
1700 N Reynolds Rd.
Toledo, OH 43615
Ph: (419)531-9933
E-mail: nwmusic@mindspring.com
URL: http://www.geocities.com/local15286
Contact: Bernard Sanchez, Pres.
Local. AFL-CIO. Musicians. Seeks to improve the wages and working conditions of professional musicians. **Affiliated With:** American Federation of Musicians of the United States and Canada. **Formerly:** (2005) Toledo Federation of Musicians - Local 15-286, American Federation of Musicians.

16954 ■ Project Management Institute, Western Lake Erie Chapter
PO Box 6867
Toledo, OH 43612
E-mail: info@pmiwlec.org
URL: http://www.pmiwlec.org
Contact: Jeff Panning PMP, Pres.
Local. Strives to promote the profession of project management by and for its members. Provides opportunities for project management education and professional development of its members. Provides a framework for professional networking and social interaction among its members. **Affiliated With:** Project Management Institute.

16955 ■ Public Relations Society of America, Northwest Ohio
c/o Kari Bucher, Chapter Administrator
5743 Larkhall Dr.
Toledo, OH 43614
Ph: (419)867-8792
E-mail: klbmomof4@spcglobal.net
URL: http://www.nwohioprsa.org
Contact: Kari Bucher, Chapter Administrator
Founded: 1951. **Members:** 70. **Local. Affiliated With:** Public Relations Society of America.

16956 ■ Refrigeration Services Engineers
220 Matzinger Rd.
Toledo, OH 43612
Ph: (419)476-2370
Local.

16957 ■ RSVP of Northwestern Ohio
c/o Sally Davies, Dir.
930 Detroit Ave.
Toledo, OH 43614
Ph: (419)382-7060
Fax: (419)382-7099
E-mail: sdavies@areaofficeonaging.com
URL: http://www.areaofficeonaging.com/aoavol.html
Contact: Sally Davies, Dir.
Local. Affiliated With: Retired and Senior Volunteer Program.

16958 ■ Secret Victoria's No. 190
c/o Peter Siek
3831 Drummond Rd.
Toledo, OH 43613
Ph: (419)474-2090
URL: National Affiliate–www.amya.org
Contact: Peter Siek, Contact
Regional.

16959 ■ Sheet Metal Contractors Association of Nortwest Ohio
c/o William Brennan
1845 Collingwood Blvd.
Toledo, OH 43624-1049
Ph: (419)241-3601
Fax: (419)241-8636
E-mail: wbrennan@cccouncil.com
URL: http://www.cccouncil.com
Local. Affiliated With: Sheet Metal and Air Conditioning Contractors' National Association.

16960 ■ Society of Manufacturing Engineers - University of Toledo S319
Univ. of Toledo, MIME Dept.
4046 Nitschke Hall
Toledo, OH 43606
Ph: (419)530-3631
Fax: (419)530-8206
E-mail: imarines@eng.utoledo.edu
URL: National Affiliate–www.sme.org
Contact: Dr. Loan D. Marinescu, Contact
Local. Advances manufacturing knowledge to gain competitive advantage. Improves skills and manufacturing solutions for the growth of economy. Provides resources and opportunities for manufacturing professionals. **Affiliated With:** Optical Society of America.

16961 ■ Toledo AIFA
c/o Lynn Schmenk, Exec.
PO Box 23266
Toledo, OH 43623
Ph: (419)725-7201
Fax: (419)725-7723
E-mail: michelle.burkhart@savageandassociates.com
URL: National Affiliate–naifa.org
Contact: Lynn Schmenk, Exec.
Local. Represents the interests of insurance and financial advisors. Advocates for a positive legislative and regulatory environment. Enhances business and professional skills of members. **Affiliated With:** National Association of Insurance and Financial Advisors.

16962 ■ Toledo Area Chamber of Commerce (TACC)
Enterprise Ste.200
300 Madison Ave.
Toledo, OH 43604-1575
Ph: (419)243-8191
Fax: (419)241-8302
E-mail: joinus@toledochamber.com
URL: http://www.toledochamber.com
Contact: Mark A. V'Soske CAE, Pres.
Members: 4,000. **Local.** Businesses. Promotes business and community development in the Toledo, OH area. Offers cost-saving benefits and networking opportunities to members. **Awards:** ATHENA Award. **Frequency:** annual. **Type:** recognition. **Committees:** Ambassadors; Government Affairs; Small Business Development Center (SBDC) Advisory; Solicitations Review; Toledo Area Small Business Association (TASBA) Program; Workforce Development. **Affiliated With:** U.S. Chamber of Commerce. **Publications:** *Insider*, monthly. Newspaper. **Price:** free for members. **Advertising:** accepted • *Membership Reference Guide*, annual. Directory. **Price:** $35.00/issue • *Toledo Profile Series*. **Conventions/Meetings:** periodic Business After Hours - meeting, networking opportunity to gain new customers and suppliers - September through May • annual meeting.

16963 ■ Toledo Area Human Resources Association
PO Box 776
Toledo, OH 43697
E-mail: sheri.caldwell@toledozoo.org
URL: http://www.toledohr.org
Contact: Sheri Caldwell, Pres.
Local. Represents the interests of human resource and industrial relations professionals and executives. Promotes the advancement of human resource management.

16964 ■ Toledo Area Military Officers Association of America
c/o Lt.Col. Harry Weiss
PO Box 8754
Toledo, OH 43623-0754
E-mail: toledojones@earthlink.net
URL: http://www.roa.org/oh/ch060/MOAA%20Site/index.html
Contact: Col. Denman Jones, Pres.
Founded: 1953. **Local. Affiliated With:** Military Officers Association of America.

16965 ■ Toledo Area Planned Giving Council
c/o United Way
One Stranahan Sq.
Toledo, OH 43604
Ph: (419)254-4616
Fax: (419)246-4614
E-mail: grichter@uwgtol.org
URL: http://www.ncpg.org/councils/homepages/index.asp?id=11
Contact: Glenn Richter, Contact
Local. Increases the quality and quantity of charitable planned gifts. Serves as the voice and professional resource for the gift planning community.

16966 ■ Toledo Area Theatre Organ Society (TATOS)
c/o Nelda Reno, Pres.
4220 Garden Park Dr.
Toledo, OH 43613-4011
Ph: (419)478-5959
E-mail: momreno@buckeye-express.com
URL: http://www.theatreorgans.com/tatos
Contact: Nelda Reno, Pres.
Local. Aims to restore, preserve and promote the theatre pipe organ and its music. Encourages the youth to learn the instrument. Operates a committee that gathers history and old music from silent film days and information on theatre organists, theaters and organ installations of the silent film era. **Affiliated With:** American Theatre Organ Society.

16967 ■ Toledo Automobile Dealers Association
c/o Clay P. Hepler, Exec.VP
6150 Fantasy Dr.
Toledo, OH 43615
Ph: (419)843-2611
URL: National Affiliate–www.nada.org
Contact: Mr. Clay P. Hepler, Exec.VP
Local. Affiliated With: National Automobile Dealers Association.

16968 ■ Toledo Bar Association (TBA)
c/o Trish Branam, Exec.Dir.
311 N Superior St.
Toledo, OH 43604
Ph: (419)242-9363
Fax: (419)242-3614
E-mail: tba@toledobar.org
URL: http://www.toledobar.org
Contact: Trish Branam, Exec.Dir.
Founded: 1878. **Members:** 1,750. **Membership Dues:** affiliate, retired, $155 (annual). **Staff:** 14. **Budget:** $1,051,000. **Local.** Attorneys licensed to practice in Ohio. Seeks to improve the administration of civil and criminal justice, and the availability of legal services to the public. Sponsors legal education programs. **Publications:** *Toledo Bar Association Legal Directory*, annual. **Price:** $25.00 including tax. **Advertising:** accepted • *Toledo Bar Association Newsletter*, monthly, except July and August.

16969 ■ Toledo Board of Realtors
2961 S Republic Blvd.
Toledo, OH 43615
Ph: (419)535-3222
Local.

16970 ■ Toledo Dental Society (TDS)
4895 Monroe St., Ste.103
Toledo, OH 43623-4383
Ph: (419)474-8611
Fax: (419)473-0860
E-mail: toledodental@sbcglobal.net
URL: National Affiliate–www.ada.org
Contact: Ms. Beverly Graham, Exec.Dir.
Local. Represents the interests of dentists committed to the public's oral health, ethics and professional development. Encourages the improvement of the public's oral health and promotes the art and science of dentistry. **Affiliated With:** American Dental Association; Ohio Dental Association.

16971 ■ Toledo District Golf Association (TDGA)
5533 Southwyck Blvd., Ste.204
Toledo, OH 43614
Ph: (419)866-4771
Fax: (419)866-0388
E-mail: tdgagolf@ameritech.net
URL: http://www.tdgagolf.org
Contact: Marianne Reece, Exec.Dir.
Local. Affiliated With: International Association of Golf Administrators.

16972 ■ Toledo Estate Planning Council (TEPC)
c/o Mary Ann Pontius, Exec.Dir.
PO Box 140666
Toledo, OH 43614
Ph: (419)381-1717
Fax: (419)381-1797
E-mail: mapattao@buckeye-express.com
URL: National Affiliate–councils.naepc.org
Contact: Alyce Juby, Pres.
Founded: 1960. **Local**. Fosters understanding of the proper relationship among estate planning specialists from different disciplines. Provides informed guidance and education in the creation, conservation and distribution of estates. Increases public understanding of the need for competent estate planning. Encourages cooperation among members. **Affiliated With:** National Association of Estate Planners and Councils.

16973 ■ Toledo Jazz Society
425 N St. Clair St.
Toledo, OH 43604
Ph: (419)241-5299
Fax: (419)241-4777
E-mail: toledojazz@toledojazzsociety.org
URL: http://www.toledojazzsociety.org
Contact: Jon Richardson, Pres.
Founded: 1980. **Members:** 480. **Membership Dues:** individual, $25 (annual) • family, $40 (annual) • sponsor, $75 (annual) • patron/musician sponsor, $100 (annual) • benefactor, $300 (annual) • corporate, $500 (annual). **Staff:** 4. **Local**. **Publications:** *Jazz Notes*, bimonthly. Newsletter. **Advertising:** accepted.

16974 ■ Toledo Police Patrolman's Association
1947 Franklin Ave.
Toledo, OH 43624
Ph: (419)241-8914
Fax: (419)241-8333
E-mail: ttpa@aol.com
Contact: Rose Owens, Office Mgr.
Local.

16975 ■ Toledo Power Squadron
PO Box 498
Toledo, OH 43697-0498
Ph: (419)874-2169
E-mail: marykay@amobility.com
URL: http://www.usps.org/localusps/toledo
Contact: Audie L. Jaqua, Commander
Local. **Affiliated With:** United States Power Squadrons.

16976 ■ Toledo Rotary Club Foundation
c/o Thomas Klein
1 Stranahan Sq., Ste.246
Toledo, OH 43604-1429
Ph: (419)241-7060
E-mail: info@toledorotary.org
URL: http://www.toledorotary.org
Contact: Christina Dunn, Exec.Dir.
Local.

16977 ■ Toledo Senior Olympics
c/o Justin Moor
Area Off. on Aging
2155 Arlington Ave.
Toledo, OH 43609
Fax: (419)382-4560
Free: (800)472-7277
E-mail: jmoor@areaofficeonaging.com
URL: http://www.ohioseniorolympics.org
Contact: Justin Moor, Contact
Local. **Affiliated With:** National Senior Games Association.

16978 ■ Toledo Surgical Society
3065 Arlington Ave.
Toledo, OH 43614
Ph: (419)383-6462
E-mail: webmaster@mco.edu
URL: http://www.mco.edu/depts/surgery/tss/index.html
Contact: Valerie Fine, Admin.Asst.
Founded: 1963. **Members:** 159. **Membership Dues:** fellowship, $75 (annual). **Staff:** 1. **Budget:** $12,000. **Regional Groups:** 1. **Local**.

16979 ■ United Way of Greater Toledo
One Stranahan Sq.
Toledo, OH 43604
Ph: (419)248-2424
E-mail: unitedway@uwgtol.org
URL: http://www.uwgtol.org
Contact: Bill Kitson, Pres./CEO
Local. **Affiliated With:** United Way of America.

16980 ■ University of Toledo Police Patrolman's Association (UTPPA)
c/o University of Toledo
2801 W Bancroft St.
Toledo, OH 43606
Ph: (419)530-4162
Fax: (419)530-4505
E-mail: adier@utnet.utoledo.edu
URL: http://www.utppa.utoledo.edu
Contact: Mick Dier, Contact
Founded: 1986. **Local**.

16981 ■ USA Weightlifting - Toledo
c/o Todd Baden
Synergy Sports and Fitness
5400 Central Ave.
Toledo, OH 43615
Ph: (419)537-0001
E-mail: toddbaden@yahoo.com
URL: National Affiliate–www.usaweightlifting.org
Contact: Todd Baden, Contact
Local. **Affiliated With:** USA Weightlifting.

16982 ■ Veterans of Foreign Wars 4906
2161 Consaul St.
Toledo, OH 43605
Ph: (419)698-4411

16983 ■ Vietnam Veterans of America, Chapter No. 35
c/o Charles M. Kries, Pres.
2300 Ashland Ave., Rm. 229
Toledo, OH 43620
Ph: (419)242-4293
Fax: (419)242-6773
URL: http://www.vvabuckeyestatecouncil.com
Contact: Charles M. Kries, Pres.
Local. **Affiliated With:** Vietnam Veterans of America.

16984 ■ Vietnam Veterans of America, Region 5
c/o Leverett Hobbs, Dir.
830 W Alexis Rd., No. 5
Toledo, OH 43612
E-mail: lhobbs@vva.org
URL: National Affiliate–www.vva.org
Contact: Leverett Hobbs, Dir.
Regional. **Affiliated With:** Vietnam Veterans of America.

16985 ■ Women in the Wind (WITW)
PO Box 8392
Toledo, OH 43605
E-mail: witw@womeninthewind.org
URL: http://www.womeninthewind.org
Contact: Becky Brown, Founder/Treas.
Founded: 1979. **Members:** 1,300. **Membership Dues:** individual, $15 (annual). **Staff:** 5. **Local Groups:** 68. **Local**. Women motorcyclists and enthusiasts. **Awards:** Safe Mileage Award. **Frequency:** annual. **Type:** recognition. **Affiliated With:** Women in the Wind. **Formerly:** (2001) Women in the Wind, Toledo Chapter. **Publications:** *Shootin' the Breeze*, bimonthly. Newsletter. **Price:** included in membership dues. **Circulation:** 1,300. **Conventions/Meetings:** semiannual conference.

16986 ■ Zenobia Shriners
c/o E. LeRoy Williams
1511 Madison Ave.
Toledo, OH 43624-1477
Ph: (419)241-3189
Fax: (419)241-9751
E-mail: zenobia@amplex.net
URL: http://www.amplex.net/zenobiashrine
Contact: E. LeRoy Williams, Recorder
Local. **Affiliated With:** Imperial Council of the Ancient Arabic Order of the Nobles of the Mystic Shrine for North America.

Tontogany

16987 ■ American Legion, Lybarger-Grimm Post 441
PO Box 131
Tontogany, OH 43565
Ph: (740)362-7478
Fax: (740)362-1429
URL: National Affiliate–www.legion.org
Local. **Affiliated With:** American Legion.

Toronto

16988 ■ American Legion, St. Mihiel Post 86
PO Box 56
Toronto, OH 43964
Ph: (740)362-7478
Fax: (740)362-1429
URL: National Affiliate–www.legion.org
Local. **Affiliated With:** American Legion.

16989 ■ Toronto - Young Life
PO Box 30
Toronto, OH 43964
Ph: (740)537-2917
URL: http://sites.younglife.org/_layouts/ylext/default.aspx?ID=C-1597
Local. **Affiliated With:** Young Life.

16990 ■ Young Life Upper Jefferson Cnty
PO Box 30
Toronto, OH 43964
Ph: (740)537-2917
URL: http://sites.younglife.org/_layouts/ylext/default.aspx?ID=A-OH91
Local. **Affiliated With:** Young Life.

Trenton

16991 ■ Trenton Lions Club - Ohio
604 W State St.
Trenton, OH 45067-1432
Ph: (513)988-6272 (513)988-9651
E-mail: acadia412@yahoo.com
URL: http://trentonoh.lionwap.org
Contact: Alan Burley, Sec.
Local. **Affiliated With:** Lions Clubs International.

Trotwood

16992 ■ American Legion, Fort Mc Kinley Memorial Post 613
27 S Meadow Dr.
Trotwood, OH 45416
Ph: (937)276-9566
Fax: (740)362-1429
URL: National Affiliate–www.legion.org
Local. **Affiliated With:** American Legion.

16993 ■ Trotwood Chamber of Commerce (TCC)
400 Lake Ctr. Dr.
Trotwood, OH 45426
Ph: (937)837-1484
Fax: (937)837-1508
E-mail: trotwoodchamber@aol.com
Contact: Marie Battle, Exec.Dir.
Founded: 1977. **Members:** 101. **Membership Dues:** 1-10, $85 (annual) • 11 up, $125 (annual). **Staff:** 1. **Budget:** $12,000. **Local**. Business and professional

people united to promote business and community development in Trotwood and Madison Township, OH. Sponsors Heritage Days festival. **Task Forces:** R & E. **Affiliated With:** U.S. Chamber of Commerce. **Publications:** *Trotwood Newsletter*, monthly. **Advertising:** accepted. Alternate Formats: online. **Conventions/Meetings:** monthly board meeting - every third Wednesday. Trotwood, OH • monthly meeting (exhibits) - always fourth Wednesday of the month.

16994 ■ Trotwood-Madison Historical Society
PO Box 26434
Trotwood, OH 45426
Ph: (937)837-5387 (937)837-0355
E-mail: trotwoodhistory@juno.com
URL: http://www.trotwood.org
Contact: Claude Keeling, Treas.

Founded: 1979. **Members:** 208. **Membership Dues:** adult, $10 (annual) • family, $15 (annual). **State Groups:** 1. **Local.** Purchased 150-year-old home to be restored for a museum, now open second Sunday each month and other times by appointment. **Awards:** Certification by Ohio Association of Historical Societies and Museums (OAHSM). **Type:** recognition. **Committees:** Junior Historical Society; Youth Group - Team Hope. **Publications:** Newsletter, monthly. **Circulation:** 200. **Conventions/Meetings:** monthly meeting.

Troy

16995 ■ AAA Cincinnati
1042 S Dorset Rd.
Troy, OH 45373
Ph: (937)339-0112
Local.

16996 ■ American Legion, Ohio Post 43
c/o Clifford Thompson
622 S Market St.
Troy, OH 45373
Ph: (740)362-7478
Fax: (740)362-1429
URL: National Affiliate–www.legion.org
Contact: Clifford Thompson, Contact
Local. Affiliated With: American Legion.

16997 ■ American Red Cross of the Northern Miami Valley
1314 Barnhart Rd.
Troy, OH 45373
Ph: (937)332-1414
URL: http://northernmiamivalley.redcross.org
Regional.

16998 ■ Brukner Gem and Mineral Club
5995 Horseshoe Bend Rd.
Troy, OH 45373-9485
E-mail: kstrucksis@aol.com
URL: National Affiliate–www.amfed.org
Contact: Yvonne Owen, Pres.

Local. Aims to further the study of Earth Sciences and the practice of lapidary arts and mineralogy. **Affiliated With:** American Federation of Mineralogical Societies.

16999 ■ Corvette Troy (CT)
PO Box 125
Troy, OH 45373
E-mail: twitt2@choiceonemail.com
URL: http://www.corvette-troy.com
Contact: Tom Witt, Pres.
Local. Affiliated With: National Council of Corvette Clubs.

17000 ■ Home Builders Association of Miami County
c/o Mark Bourelle, Pres.
1200 Archer Dr.
Troy, OH 45373
Ph: (937)339-7963
Fax: (937)440-1574
E-mail: info@hbamiamicounty.com
URL: http://www.hbamiamicounty.com
Contact: Mark Bourelle, Pres.

Founded: 1956. **Members:** 270. **Membership Dues:** builder, $390 • associate, $360 • industry supporter, $290. **Local.** Works to promote the policies that make housing a national priority. **Affiliated With:** National Association of Home Builders. **Formerly:** (2005) National Association of Home Builders of the U.S., Home Builders Association of Miami County.

17001 ■ Institute of Management Accountants, Dayton Chapter
c/o Paul Myers, Dir. of Communications/Webmaster
ITW Food Equip. Gp.
701 S Ridge Ave.
Troy, OH 45374-0001
Ph: (937)332-2304
Fax: (937)332-2042
E-mail: paul.myers@itwfeg.com
URL: http://www.dayton.imanet.org
Contact: Paul Myers, Dir. of Communications/ Webmaster

Founded: 1926. **Members:** 500. **Local.** Promotes professional and ethical standards. Equips members and students with knowledge and training required for the accounting profession. **Affiliated With:** Institute of Management Accountants. **Publications:** *Balance Sheet*. Newsletter. Alternate Formats: online. **Conventions/Meetings:** monthly board meeting - every first Tuesday.

17002 ■ Mental Health Association of Miami County (MHAMC)
1100 Wayne St.
Box 4002
Troy, OH 45373
Ph: (937)332-9293
Fax: (937)332-9293
Free: (800)351-7347
E-mail: mhamc@verizon.net
URL: http://www.mhamc.com
Contact: Karen L. Schultz MEd, Exec.Dir.

Local. Seeks to promote mental health and prevent mental health disorders. Improves mental health of Americans through advocacy, public education, research and service. **Affiliated With:** National Mental Health Association.

17003 ■ Miami County Historical and Genealogical Society, Chapter of OGS
PO Box 305
Troy, OH 45373-0305
Ph: (937)778-9869 (937)277-4450
E-mail: vljbrown@bright.net
URL: http://www.rootsweb.com/~ohmchgs
Contact: Rodney Young, Pres.

Founded: 1952. **Members:** 250. **Membership Dues:** individual, family, $14 (annual) • life (individual/family), $140. **Local.** Persons interested in genealogical research, objective, and finding their ancestors. Works to document and preserve the history of Miami County, Ohio. **Awards:** Miami Co. Heritage Award. **Frequency:** annual. **Type:** recognition. **Affiliated With:** Ohio Genealogical Society. **Formerly:** (1998) Ohio Historical and Genealogical Society, Miami County Chapter. **Publications:** *Miami Meanderings*, quarterly. Newsletter. Miami County information. **Circulation:** 250. **Conventions/Meetings:** annual Routes to Roots - workshop, genealogy related topics (exhibits).

17004 ■ Miami Valley ALU
405 Public Sq., Ste.252
Troy, OH 45373
Ph: (937)339-6523
Fax: (937)335-8692
URL: National Affiliate–www.naifa.org

Local. Represents the interest of insurance and financial advisors. Advocates for a positive legislative and regulatory environment. Enhances business and professional skills of members. **Affiliated With:** National Association of Insurance and Financial Advisors.

17005 ■ Midwestern Ohio Association of Realtors
1087 N Market St.
Troy, OH 45373
Ph: (937)335-8501
Fax: (937)335-8201
Free: (888)886-8267
E-mail: moar@moarrealtors.com
URL: http://www.moarrealtors.com
Contact: Roger Rude, Pres.

Local. Strives to develop real estate business practices. Advocates for the right to own, use and transfer real property. Provides a facility for professional development, research and exchange of information among members and the general public. **Affiliated With:** National Association of Realtors.

17006 ■ Stillwater Leisure Sport Association
c/o Ray Holmes
2225 Fenner Rd.
Troy, OH 45373-8416
Ph: (937)339-6433
E-mail: rholmes5@woh.rr.com
URL: National Affiliate–www.ava.org
Contact: Ray Holmes, Contact
Local.

17007 ■ Stillwater Stargazers
Bruckner Nature Center
5995 Horseshoe Bend Rd.
Troy, OH 45373
Ph: (937)252-3005
E-mail: kmhitzeman@hitzeman.com
URL: http://www.dma.org/~wagner
Contact: Keba Hitzeman, Contact

Local. Promotes the science of astronomy. Works to encourage and coordinate activities of amateur astronomical societies. Fosters observational and computational work and craftsmanship in various fields of astronomy. **Affiliated With:** Astronomical League.

17008 ■ Troy Area Chamber of Commerce
405 SW Public Sq., Ste.330
Troy, OH 45373
Ph: (937)339-8769 (937)339-1716
Fax: (937)339-4944
E-mail: tacc@troyohiochamber.com
URL: http://www.troyohiochamber.com
Contact: Charles E. Cochran, Pres.

Members: 400. **Membership Dues:** business base, $300 (annual) • non-profit/executive/elected official, $150 (annual). **Local.** Seeks to enhance the quality of life of Troy community through promotion of economic vitality and growth, stimulation of business environment and advancement of free enterprise system. **Awards:** Community Service Award. **Frequency:** annual. **Type:** recognition • Distinguished Citizen. **Frequency:** annual. **Type:** recognition • Educator of the Year. **Frequency:** annual. **Type:** recognition • Young Man/Woman of the Year. **Frequency:** annual. **Type:** recognition. **Committees:** Ambassadors; Awards; Business Advisory to Education; Legislative; Women's in Networking. **Councils:** Human Resource; Industrial; Small Business. **Publications:** *Chamber News*, monthly. Newsletter. Alternate Formats: online.

17009 ■ Troy Lions Club - Ohio
PO Box 355
Troy, OH 45373
E-mail: troy42lions@earthlink.net
URL: http://www.lionsdist13e.org/troy
Contact: Jeff Feierstein, Pres.
Local. Affiliated With: Lions Clubs International.

17010 ■ Troy Main Street
405 SW Public Sq., Ste.231
Troy, OH 45373
Ph: (937)339-5455
Fax: (937)339-6765
E-mail: troymainstreet@bizwoh.rr.com
URL: http://www.troymainstreet.org
Local.

17011 ■ Troy Skating Club (TSC)
255 Adams St.
Troy, OH 45373
Ph: (937)339-8521
Fax: (937)339-7074
E-mail: kslack9907@aol.com
URL: http://www.troyskatingclub.org
Contact: Kathy Slack, Pres.

Local. Provides programs to encourage participation and achievement in the sport of figure skating on ice. Defines and maintains uniform standards of skating proficiency. Organizes and sponsors competitions and exhibitions for the purpose of stimulating interest in figure skating. **Affiliated With:** United States Figure Skating Association.

17012 ■ United Way of Troy, Ohio
PO Box 36
Troy, OH 45373-0036
Ph: (937)335-8410
URL: National Affiliate–national.unitedway.org

Local. Affiliated With: United Way of America.

Twinsburg

17013 ■ American Mold Builders Association, Northern Ohio Chapter
c/o Dave Kuhary, Pres.
Indus. Mold & Machine
2057 E Aurora Rd.
Twinsburg, OH 44087
Ph: (330)425-7374
Fax: (330)425-9433
E-mail: indmold@industrialmold.com
URL: National Affiliate–www.amba.org
Contact: Dave Kuhary, Pres.

Local.

17014 ■ First Catholic Slovak Ladies Association - Cleveland Senior Branch 176
10336 Merriam Ln.
Twinsburg, OH 44087
Ph: (330)425-3102
URL: National Affiliate–www.fcsla.com

Local. Affiliated With: First Catholic Slovak Ladies Association.

17015 ■ Northeast Ohio CoDA Community (NEOCC)
PO Box 158
Twinsburg, OH 44087-0158
Ph: (440)954-4281
E-mail: info@neocoda.info
URL: http://www.neocoda.info
Contact: Cynthy D., Contact

Local. Affiliated With: Co-Dependents Anonymous.

17016 ■ Ohio State Numismatic Association (OSNA)
c/o Bill Krizsan, Membership Chm.
PO Box 784
Twinsburg, OH 44087
E-mail: big4ce1@aol.com
URL: http://www.eosna.org
Contact: Bill Krizsan, Membership Chm.

State. Affiliated With: American Numismatic Association.

17017 ■ Tinkers Creek Land Conservancy
PO Box 805
Twinsburg, OH 44087
Ph: (330)425-4159
E-mail: treewlkr@aol.com
URL: http://www.tinkerscreek.org
Contact: Ms. Marion Olson, Pres.

Local.

17018 ■ Twinsburg Chamber of Commerce (TCC)
9044 Church St.
Twinsburg, OH 44087
Ph: (330)963-6249
Fax: (330)963-6995
E-mail: djohnson@twinsburgchamber.com
URL: http://www.twinsburgchamber.com
Contact: Mr. Douglas H. Johnson, Exec.Dir.

Founded: 1921. **Members:** 300. **Membership Dues:** business, $175-$575 (annual) • nonprofit/retiree, $75 (annual) • platinum club, $2,000 (annual) • gold club, $1,500 (annual) • silver club, $1,000 (annual). **Staff:** 15. **Budget:** $100,000. **Regional Groups:** 1. **State Groups:** 1. **Local**. Promotes business in the Twinsburg, OH area. **Computer Services:** database, list of people who are desiring for employment in Twinsburg. **Divisions:** Twinsburg Visitors Center. **Affiliated With:** U.S. Chamber of Commerce. **Publications:** *Chamber News*, monthly. Newsletter. Includes member news, upcoming events, listing of member to member discounts, and other articles of interest to the business community. **Price:** free to members. Alternate Formats: online • *Twinsburg Industrial and Commercial Directory*, annual. Contains a list of all businesses known in Twinsburg at the time of publication. **Price:** free to members • *Twinsburg Quick Facts*. Brochure. Contains demographic information, statistics on population, income, age, diversity, geographic information, and community information. **Price:** free. **Conventions/Meetings:** annual Golf Outing - competition, networking with other businesses - every June • monthly luncheon - always third Thursday.

Uhrichsville

17019 ■ American Legion, Waterford Post 230
PO Box 109
Uhrichsville, OH 44683
Ph: (740)362-7478
Fax: (740)362-1429
URL: National Affiliate–www.legion.org

Local. Affiliated With: American Legion.

17020 ■ Twin City Chamber of Commerce (TCCC)
210 E 3rd St.
PO Box 49
Uhrichsville, OH 44683
Ph: (740)922-5623
Fax: (740)922-1371
E-mail: twincityinfo@sbcglobal.net
URL: http://www.twincitychamber.org
Contact: Teri Edwards, Exec.Dir.

Founded: 1913. **Members:** 220. **Staff:** 2. **Local**. Manufacturers, retail store owners, and interested individuals organized to promote business and community development in the Dennison and Uhrichsville, OH area. Sponsors various community activities. **Awards: Frequency:** annual. **Type:** recognition. **Recipient:** for member nomination • **Frequency:** annual. **Type:** scholarship. **Recipient:** for member nomination. **Affiliated With:** U.S. Chamber of Commerce. **Publications:** Newsletter, monthly. **Circulation:** 220. **Advertising:** accepted • Directory, periodic.

Uniontown

17021 ■ Eastern Ohio Health Information Management Association (EOHIMA)
c/o Jan Gerzina, RHIT
10785 Market Ave. N
Uniontown, OH 44685
Ph: (330)297-2868
E-mail: gneff@rmh2.org
URL: http://www.ohima.org/reg.associations/regassoceohima.html
Contact: Gabriella Neff, Pres.-Elect

Local. Represents the interests of individuals dedicated to the effective management of personal health information needed to deliver quality healthcare to the public. Provides career, professional development and practice resources. Sets standards for education and certification. Advocates public policy that advances Health Information Management (HIM) practice. **Affiliated With:** American Health Information Management Association; Ohio Health Information Management Association.

17022 ■ Uniontown Lions Club
PO Box 427
Uniontown, OH 44685-0427
Ph: (330)877-1088
E-mail: s.sinsabaugh@att.net
URL: http://www.uniontownLions.org
Contact: Ron Mikula, Pres.

Local. Affiliated With: Lions Clubs International.

University Heights

17023 ■ American Accounting Association, Ohio Region
c/o Gerald P. Weinstein, Pres.
John Carroll Univ.
Boler School of Bus.
Dept. of Accountancy
20700 N Park Blvd.
University Heights, OH 44118
Ph: (216)397-4609
Fax: (216)397-3063
E-mail: weinstein@jcu.edu
URL: http://aaahq.org/ohio/index.html
Contact: Gerald P. Weinstein, Pres.

State. Promotes excellence in accounting education, research and practice. Advances accounting instruction and encourages qualified individuals to enter careers in the teaching of accounting. Promotes the development and uses of accounting for internal management purposes. **Affiliated With:** American Accounting Association.

17024 ■ Association for Computing Machinery, John Carroll University
c/o Marc Kirschenbaum, Dr.
Dept. of Math & Cmpt. Sci.
20700 N Park Blvd.
University Heights, OH 44118
Ph: (216)397-4351
Fax: (216)397-3033
E-mail: acm@jcu.edu
URL: National Affiliate–www.acm.org
Contact: Will Lanphear, Chm.

Local. Biological, medical, behavioral, and computer scientists; hospital administrators; programmers and others interested in application of computer methods to biological, behavioral, and medical problems. Stimulates understanding of the use and potential of computers in the Biosciences. **Affiliated With:** Association for Computing Machinery.

17025 ■ Easter Seals Northeast Ohio
2175 Taylor Rd.
University Heights, OH 44118
Fax: (440)838-8440
Free: (888)325-8532
E-mail: spowers@eastersealsneo.org
URL: http://neohio.easterseals.com
Contact: Susan Powers, Contact

Local. Provides assistance and services to people with disabilities and their families. **Affiliated With:** Easter Seals.

17026 ■ John Carroll University Students In Free Enterprise
John Carroll Univ.
20700 N Park Blvd.
University Heights, OH 44118
E-mail: alextenenbaum@hotmail.com
URL: http://www.jcu.edu/sife
Contact: Alex Tenanbaum, Pres.

Local.

17027 ■ Society of Physics Students - John Carroll University Chapter No. 3329
20700 N Park Blvd.
University Heights, OH 44118
Ph: (216)397-4301
Fax: (216)397-4499
E-mail: lacueva@jcu.edu
URL: National Affiliate–www.spsnational.org
Local. Offers opportunities for the students to enrich their experiences and skills about physics. Helps students to become professional in the field of physics. **Affiliated With:** Society of Physics Students.

Upper Arlington

17028 ■ Ohio Grocers Association
3280 Riverside Dr., Ste.10
Upper Arlington, OH 43221
Ph: (614)442-5511
Fax: (614)442-5516
URL: http://www.ohiogrocers.org
Contact: Tom Jackson, Pres.
State.

17029 ■ Society of Antique Modelers - Heart of Ohio Chapter
3111 Tremont Rd.
Upper Arlington, OH 43221
Ph: (614)442-8800
E-mail: bworley@iopener.net
URL: National Affiliate–www.antiquemodeler.org
Local. Affiliated With: Society of Antique Modelers.

17030 ■ Upper Arlington Area Chamber of Commerce
2120 Tremont Ctr.
Upper Arlington, OH 43221
Ph: (614)481-5710
Fax: (614)481-5711
E-mail: admin@uachamber.org
URL: http://www.uachamber.org
Contact: Ms. Brenda Schwandt, Pres.
Founded: 1977. **Members:** 660. **Membership Dues:** business, $164-$452 (annual) • professional/self employed/individual/independent contractor, $133 (annual) • civic/service organization, $102 (annual). **Staff:** 2. **For-Profit**. **Local**. Promotes business and community development in Upper Arlington, OH. **Publications:** *Directions*, monthly. Newsletter. **Circulation:** 600. **Advertising:** accepted. Alternate Formats: online.

Upper Sandusky

17031 ■ American Legion, Wyandot Post 225
122 N Sandusky Ave.
Upper Sandusky, OH 43351
Ph: (740)362-7478
Fax: (740)362-1429
URL: National Affiliate–www.legion.org
Local. Affiliated With: American Legion.

17032 ■ United Way of Upper Sandusky and Pitt Township
PO Box 152
Upper Sandusky, OH 43351-0152
Ph: (419)294-2131
URL: National Affiliate–national.unitedway.org
Local. Affiliated With: United Way of America.

17033 ■ Upper Sandusky Area Chamber of Commerce (USACC)
108 E Wyandot Ave.
PO Box 223
Upper Sandusky, OH 43351
Ph: (419)294-3349
Fax: (419)294-3531
E-mail: upsancc@bright.net
URL: http://www.uppersanduskychamber.com
Contact: Monica Bess, Exec.Dir.
Founded: 1947. **Members:** 190. **Staff:** 1. **Local**. Promotes business and community development in Wyandot County, OH. **Publications:** *Compass*, bimonthly. Newsletter. **Advertising:** accepted. Alternate Formats: online • *Industry Business*, periodic. Directory • Brochures, periodic. **Conventions/Meetings:** monthly board meeting - every second Tuesday.

17034 ■ Upper Sandusky Lions Club
c/o Rebecca Krock, Sec.
9527 County Hwy. 111
Upper Sandusky, OH 43351
Ph: (419)294-5365
E-mail: rkrock@woh.rr.com
URL: http://www.lions13b.org
Contact: Rebecca Krock, Sec.
Local. Affiliated With: Lions Clubs International.

17035 ■ Wyandot County Humane Society (WCHS)
9640 County Hwy. 330
Upper Sandusky, OH 43351-9668
Ph: (419)294-4477
Free: (888)294-4477
E-mail: wyhumaneone@cs.com
URL: http://www.wyhumane.org
Contact: David A Balz, Contact
Local. Sponsors animal shelter, animal rescue, equine rescue, low-cost spay/neuter clinic, and wildlife rehabilitation in the Wyandot County, OH area.

Urbana

17036 ■ American Legion, Pearce-Kerns Post 120
414 N Main St.
Urbana, OH 43078
Ph: (740)362-7478
Fax: (740)362-1429
URL: National Affiliate–www.legion.org
Local. Affiliated With: American Legion.

17037 ■ American Legion, Urbana Post 741
c/o Clarence Tallman
589 Jackson Hill Rd.
Urbana, OH 43078
Ph: (740)362-7478
Fax: (740)362-1429
URL: National Affiliate–www.legion.org
Contact: Clarence Tallman, Contact
Local. Affiliated With: American Legion.

17038 ■ American Red Cross, Champaign County Chapter
658 Bodey Cir.
Urbana, OH 43078
Ph: (937)653-7276
Fax: (937)653-6570
URL: http://champaigncounty.redcross.org
Local.

17039 ■ Central Ohio Theatre Organ Society (COTOS)
236 New Haven Dr.
Urbana, OH 43078
Ph: (614)374-8808
E-mail: dking700@hotmail.com
URL: http://theatreorgans.com/cotos/index.htm
Contact: Duane King, Pres.
Local. Aims to restore, preserve and promote the theatre pipe organ and its music. Encourages the youth to learn the instrument. Operates a committee that gathers history and old music from silent film days and information on theatre organists, theaters and organ installations of the silent film era. **Affiliated With:** American Theatre Organ Society.

17040 ■ Champaign County Chamber of Commerce
113 Miami St.
Urbana, OH 43078
Ph: (937)653-5764
Free: (877)873-5764
E-mail: info@champaignohio.com
URL: http://www.champaignohio.com/chamber.htm
Contact: Ms. Kelly Evans-Wilson PhD, Exec.Dir.
Founded: 1950. **Members:** 250. **Membership Dues:** financial institution, $800 (annual) • public utility, $750 (annual) • manufacturing/publishing, $325-$1,500 (annual) • retail/service/business/retail/dealer/lodging/restaurant/contractor, $135-$700 (annual) • professional/professional service, $150-$350 (annual) • school, $225 (annual) • university, $500 (annual) • government office/agency, $135 (annual) • non-profit organization, $85-$1,000 (annual) • individual, $135 (annual). **Staff:** 2. **Local**. Promotes business and community development in Champaign County, OH. Holds monthly board meeting. **Programs:** Leadership Champaign County. **Formerly:** (2006) Urbana - Champaign County Chamber of Commerce. **Publications:** *Chamber News*, bimonthly. Newsletter. **Advertising:** accepted.

17041 ■ Champaign County REACT Team
225 Logan St., Apt. 203
Urbana, OH 43078
Ph: (937)484-4633
E-mail: greeneyemini@yahoo.com
URL: http://www.reactintl.org/teaminfo/usa_teams/teams-usoh.htm
Local. Trained communication experts and professional volunteers. Provides volunteer public service and emergency communications through the use of radios (Citizen Band, General Mobile Radio Service, UHF and HAM). Coordinates with radio industries and government on safety communication matters and supports charitable activities and community organizations.

17042 ■ Ohio Historical Society - Cedar Bog Nature Preserve
980 Woodburn Rd.
Urbana, OH 43078-9417
Ph: (937)484-3744
Free: (800)860-0147
URL: http://www.ohiohistory.org/places/cedarbog
Local.

17043 ■ Tecumseh Trailblazers
c/o Gil Stempfly
4830 Stony Creek Rd.
Urbana, OH 43078-8456
Ph: (937)788-2290
E-mail: swisswalker@aol.com
URL: National Affiliate–www.ava.org
Contact: Gil Stempfly, Contact
Membership Dues: $10 (annual). **State Groups:** 1. **Local Groups:** 1. **Local**. Non-competitive sports enthusiasts. **Affiliated With:** American Volkssport Association. **Conventions/Meetings:** bimonthly meeting.

Utica

17044 ■ American Legion, Ohio Post 92
c/o Lawrence Lightner
PO Box 2
Utica, OH 43080
Ph: (740)362-7478
Fax: (740)362-1429
URL: National Affiliate–www.legion.org
Contact: Lawrence Lightner, Contact
Local. Affiliated With: American Legion.

Valley City

17045 ■ Medina Corvette Club
PO Box 214
Valley City, OH 44280
E-mail: medinacorvette@aol.com
URL: http://www.eornccc.org/medina.htm
Local. Affiliated With: National Council of Corvette Clubs.

17046 ■ Valley City Chamber of Commerce
PO Box 304
Valley City, OH 44280-0304
Ph: (330)483-1111
E-mail: webmaster@valleycity.org
URL: http://www.valleycity.org
Contact: Mary Ann Bauer, Pres.
Local.

Van Wert

17047 ■ American Legion, Ohio Post 178
c/o Isaac Van Wert
PO Box 326
Van Wert, OH 45891
Ph: (740)362-7478
Fax: (740)362-1429
URL: National Affiliate–www.legion.org
Contact: Isaac Van Wert, Contact
Local. Affiliated With: American Legion.

17048 ■ American Welding Society, Johnny Appleseed Section 191
c/o Denny Keoster, Chm.
Vantage Career Ctr.
818 N Franklin St.
Van Wert, OH 45891
Ph: (419)238-5411
Fax: (419)238-4058
Free: (800)686-3944
Contact: Jim Grant, Dir.
Local. Professional engineering society in the field of welding. **Affiliated With:** American Welding Society.

17049 ■ Gardeners of America/Men's Garden Clubs of America - Gardeners of Van Wert County
c/o Dale Davies, Pres.
PO Box 524
Van Wert, OH 45891
Ph: (419)238-9351
E-mail: ihenny@bright.net
URL: National Affiliate–www.tgoa-mgca.org
Contact: Dale Davies, Pres.
Local.

17050 ■ National Technical Honor Society - Vantage Career Center - Ohio
818 N Franklin St.
Van Wert, OH 45891
Ph: (419)238-5411
Fax: (419)238-4058
Free: (800)686-3944
E-mail: vt_supt@noacsc.org
URL: http://www.vantagecareercenter.com
Contact: Dr. Stephen Mercer, Contact
Local.

17051 ■ Navy Club of the USS Ohio - Ship No. 726
430 Boyd Ave.
Van Wert, OH 45891
Ph: (419)232-6134
URL: National Affiliate–www.navyclubusa.org
Contact: Kenneth Myers, Commander
Local. Represents individuals who are, or have been, in the active service of the U.S. Navy, Naval Reserve, Marine Corps, Marine Corps Reserve, and Coast Guard. Promotes and encourages further public interest in the U.S. Navy and its history. Upholds the spirit and ideals of the U.S. Navy. Acts as a public forum for members' views on national defense. Assists the Navy Recruiting Command whenever and wherever possible. Conducts charitable activities. **Affiliated With:** Navy Club of the United States of America.

17052 ■ Ohio Genealogical Society, Van Wert County Ohio Chapter
PO Box 485
Van Wert, OH 45891-0485
E-mail: daberkmh@bright.net
URL: http://www.rootsweb.com/~ohvwogs
Local. Affiliated With: Ohio Genealogical Society.

17053 ■ United Way of Van Wert County
109 W Main St.
Van Wert, OH 45891-1703
Ph: (419)238-6689
URL: National Affiliate–national.unitedway.org
Local. Affiliated With: United Way of America.

17054 ■ Van Wert Area County Chamber of Commerce (VWCCC)
118 W Main St.
Van Wert, OH 45891
Ph: (419)238-4390
Fax: (419)238-4589
E-mail: info@vanwertchamber.com
URL: http://www.vanwertchamber.com
Contact: Jodie A. Perry, Pres./CEO
Founded: 1926. **Members:** 300. **Membership Dues:** individual (no business affiliation), $103 (annual) • basic, utility (add $.04/meter), $328 (annual) • city, village, township government, $109 (annual) • non-profit/organization, $158 (annual) • hotel/motel/bed and breakfast (add $2/room), $165 (annual) • home-based business (with no employees), $109 (annual) • banks/savings and loan (add $20/employee over 10), $710 (annual) • finance company/credit union (add $20/employee over 10),, $274 (annual) • education, $274 (annual) • professional (add $2.50/employee), $191 (annual). **Staff:** 2. **Local.** Promotes business and community development in the Van Wert, OH area. Sponsors annual Home Show. **Telecommunication Services:** electronic mail, amcconn@vanwertchamber.com. **Committees:** Agribusiness; Ambassadors; Annual Dinner; Finance; Home Show; Leadership; Legislative; Membership Services. **Affiliated With:** U.S. Chamber of Commerce. **Publications:** *Chamber Viewpoint*, monthly. Newsletter. Includes membership information. **Price:** included in membership dues. **Advertising:** accepted. Alternate Formats: online • *Membership Directory and Buyer's Guide*, biennial. **Circulation:** 1,500. **Advertising:** accepted • *Van Wert Community Guide*, semiannual. Magazine. Showcases the community and markets the quality of life to entice and welcome new businesses and residents to the Van Wert area. **Circulation:** 2,500. **Advertising:** accepted. Alternate Formats: online. **Conventions/Meetings:** monthly board meeting • periodic Business After Hours - meeting, networking - usually third or fourth Thursday • annual Membership Dinner and Awards Ceremony • annual Van Wert Home and Garden Show - trade show, features home related products and weekend family event (exhibits) - always March.

17055 ■ Van Wert County Historical Society
PO Box 621
Van Wert, OH 45891-0621
Ph: (419)238-5297
E-mail: vwmuseum@bright.net
URL: http://www.geocities.com/Heartland/Woods/9479
Local. Preserves Van Wert County history and culture. Maintains a Victorian mansion, gazebo, schoolhouse, log house, Conrail caboose, and barn.

17056 ■ Youth for Christ/West Central Ohio (YC-WCO)
PO Box 422
Van Wert, OH 45891
Ph: (419)238-1370
Fax: (419)238-2416
E-mail: wcoyfc@bright.net
URL: National Affiliate–www.gospelcom.net/yfc
Contact: Eric Hancock, Exec.Dir.
Founded: 1950. **Staff:** 3. **Budget:** $80,000. **Nonmembership. Local.** Interdenominational organization promoting the evangelization of teenagers. Conducts social events and trips. **Affiliated With:** Youth for Christ/U.S.A.

Vandalia

17057 ■ American Legion, Vandalia Memorial Post 668
PO Box 104
Vandalia, OH 45377
Ph: (740)362-7478
Fax: (740)362-1429
URL: National Affiliate–www.legion.org
Local. Affiliated With: American Legion.

17058 ■ American Line Builders Chapter National Electrical Contractors Association
63-C N Dixie Dr.
Vandalia, OH 45377-2059
Ph: (937)898-5824
Fax: (937)898-6361
E-mail: alb@albneca.org
URL: http://www.albneca.org
Contact: Mr. Robert G. La Lumiere, Contact
Regional. Affiliated With: National Electrical Contractors Association.

17059 ■ Rathkamp Matchcover Society, Vandalia
1359 Surrey Rd., No. Y
Vandalia, OH 45377-1646
Ph: (937)890-8684
URL: http://www.matchcover.org
Contact: Mary Anne Pertuis, Sec.
Founded: 1941. **Members:** 1,050. **Membership Dues:** $15 (annual). **Staff:** 6. **Regional Groups:** 30. **Local Groups:** 3. **Local.** Promotes interest in matchcover collecting. **Affiliated With:** Rathkamp Matchcover Society. **Publications:** *RMS Bulletin*, bimonthly. Newsletter. **Price:** for members. **Circulation:** 1,050. **Advertising:** accepted. **Conventions/Meetings:** annual convention (exhibits) - usually August.

17060 ■ Sister Cities of Vandalia
c/o Roger Pratt
245 Timberwind Ln.
Vandalia, OH 45377-0000
Ph: (937)898-1287
URL: National Affiliate–www.ava.org
Contact: Roger Pratt, Contact
Local. Affiliated With: American Volkssport Association.

17061 ■ Vandalia Butler Pee Wee Youth Sports Association
c/o Gary Kronenberger, Pres.
PO Box 512
Vandalia, OH 45377
E-mail: gary.kronenberger@sbcglobal.net
URL: http://www.eteamz.com/VandaliaButlerWeeAviators
Contact: Gary Kronenberger, Pres.
Local.

Vanlue

17062 ■ Flag City REACT
PO Box 237
Vanlue, OH 45890
Ph: (419)387-7829
URL: http://www.reactintl.org/teaminfo/usa_teams/teams-usoh.htm
Local. Trained communication experts and professional volunteers. Provides volunteer public service and emergency communications through the use of radios (Citizen Band, General Mobile Radio Service, UHF and HAM). Coordinates with radio industries and government on safety communication matters and supports charitable activities and community organizations.

Vermilion

17063 ■ American Legion, Fiebirch Post 397
2713 State Rd.
Vermilion, OH 44089
Ph: (740)362-7478
Fax: (740)362-1429
URL: National Affiliate–www.legion.org
Local. Affiliated With: American Legion.

17064 ■ American Legion, Memorial-Square Post 61
219 Barnes Rd.
Vermilion, OH 44089
Ph: (740)362-7478
Fax: (740)362-1429
URL: National Affiliate–www.legion.org
Local. Affiliated With: American Legion.

17065 ■ Great Lakes Historical Society (GLHS)
c/o Inland Seas Maritime Museum
480 Main St.
PO Box 435
Vermilion, OH 44089-0435
Ph: (440)967-3467
Fax: (440)967-1419
Free: (800)893-1485
E-mail: glhs1@inlandseas.org
URL: http://www.inlandseas.org
Contact: Christopher H. Gillcrist, Exec.Dir.
Founded: 1944. **Members:** 3,000. **Membership Dues:** individual, $49 (annual) • senior (over 65), $32 (annual) • contributing, $100 (annual) • sustaining, $64 (annual) • benefactor, $200 (annual) • patron, $500 (annual) • life, $1,000. **Staff:** 8. Libraries, historical societies, museums, schools, and individuals interested in the Great Lakes region. Promotes interest in discovering and preserving material on the Great Lakes and the Great Lakes area of the U.S. and Canada, such as books, documents, records, and objects relating to the history, geology, commerce, and folklore of the Great Lakes. Conducts research programs; maintains museum. **Libraries: Type:** reference. **Holdings:** 6,000; business records, papers, photographs. **Subjects:** Great Lakes and shipping. **Publications:** *The Chadburn*, quarterly. Newsletter. **Price:** included in membership dues. **Circulation:** 3,000. **Advertising:** accepted • *Inland Seas*, quarterly. Journal. Includes articles relating to the past and present history of the Great Lakes. Includes Great Lakes calendar, book reviews, and roundtable. **Price:** included in membership dues. ISSN: 0020-1537. **Circulation:** 3,000. **Advertising:** accepted. **Conventions/Meetings:** semiannual meeting (exhibits) - always May and October, Vermilion, OH • annual Model Shipwrights Competition.

17066 ■ Vermilion Chamber of Commerce (VCC)
5495 Liberty Ave.
Vermilion, OH 44089
Ph: (440)967-4477
Fax: (440)967-2877
E-mail: vermilionchamber@centurytel.net
URL: http://vermilionohio.com
Contact: Maureen Coe, Pres.
Founded: 1962. **Members:** 300. **Membership Dues:** business, $100-$300 (annual) • associate, individual, $50 (annual). **Local**. Promotes business and community development in Vermilion, OH. Sponsors annual dinner, Festival of Fish, Woollybear Festival, and an awards luncheon. **Publications:** *Directory of Members*, annual • *Vermilion Chamber Bulletin*, monthly. **Conventions/Meetings:** meeting - 2-3/year.

17067 ■ Vermilion Lions Club
c/o John Showalter, Pres.
941 Exchange St.
Vermilion, OH 44089
Ph: (440)967-3332
E-mail: beatdjjohn@yahoo.com
URL: http://www.lions13b.org
Contact: John Showalter, Pres.
Local. Affiliated With: Lions Clubs International.

Versailles

17068 ■ American Legion, Versailles Post 435
106 S Center St.
Versailles, OH 45380
Ph: (740)362-7478
Fax: (740)362-1429
URL: National Affiliate–www.legion.org
Local. Affiliated With: American Legion.

Vienna

17069 ■ Builders Association of Eastern Ohio and Western Pennsylvania
c/o Kevin M. Reilly, Exec.VP
PO Box 488
1372 Youngstown-Kingsville Rd.
Vienna, OH 44473
Ph: (330)539-6050
E-mail: buildersassociation@neo.rr.com
URL: http://www.buildersassoc.org
Contact: Kevin M. Reilly, Exec.VP
Regional. Affiliated With: Sheet Metal and Air Conditioning Contractors' National Association.

17070 ■ National Organization for Women - Youngstown S
c/o Justin Hite
1279 Youngstown-Kingsville Rd.
Vienna, OH 44473
E-mail: cuddlemonster84@yahoo.com
URL: http://www.ohionow.org
Contact: Justin Hite, Contact
Local. Affiliated With: National Organization for Women.

17071 ■ Teen Straight Talk
1393 Youngstown-Kingsville Rd. SE
Vienna, OH 44473-9534
Ph: (330)539-6040
Fax: (330)539-6041
E-mail: tstoffice@aol.com
URL: http://members.aol.com/sexualabstinence
Contact: Mary L. Duke, Exec.Dir.
Founded: 1989. **Staff:** 5. **Budget:** $140,000. **Regional Groups:** 1. **Nonmembership. Regional.** Equips young people with truth, unaltered by cultural standards, providing them with a foundation to evaluate behaviors, choosing those which will result in physical, emotional, social and moral health. **Libraries: Type:** by appointment only. **Holdings:** 25; articles, books, video recordings. **Subjects:** abstinence, purity, relationships. **Additional Websites:** http://www.teenstraighttalk.cjb.net. **Telecommunication Services:** electronic mail, sexualabstinence@aol.com. **Publications:** *Veracity*. Newsletter. **Circulation:** 500. **Advertising:** accepted. **Conventions/Meetings:** monthly board meeting - every 2nd Monday in Vienna, OH.

Vinton

17072 ■ American Legion, Vinton Post 161
1263 Jones Rd.
Vinton, OH 45686
Ph: (740)362-7478
Fax: (740)362-1429
URL: National Affiliate–www.legion.org
Local. Affiliated With: American Legion.

Wadsworth

17073 ■ American Legion, Wadsworth Post 170
PO Box 142
Wadsworth, OH 44281
Ph: (740)362-7478
Fax: (740)362-1429
URL: National Affiliate–www.legion.org
Local. Affiliated With: American Legion.

17074 ■ Copley - Young Life
111 Broad St., Ste.200
Wadsworth, OH 44281
Ph: (330)620-5448
URL: http://sites.younglife.org/_layouts/ylext/default.aspx?ID=C-1488
Local. Affiliated With: Young Life.

17075 ■ County Line - Wyldlife
111 Broad St., Ste.200
Wadsworth, OH 44281
Ph: (330)620-5448
URL: http://sites.younglife.org/_layouts/ylext/default.aspx?ID=C-1489
Local. Affiliated With: Young Life.

17076 ■ Izaak Walton League of America, Wadsworth Chapter
PO Box 743
Wadsworth, OH 44282-0743
Ph: (330)334-4815
E-mail: blumaan@aol.com
URL: National Affiliate–www.iwla.org
Local. Works to educate the public to conserve, maintain, protect, and restore the soil, forest, water, and other natural resources of the U.S; promotes the enjoyment and wholesome utilization of these resources. **Affiliated With:** Izaak Walton League of America.

17077 ■ Masonic Lodge
660 High St.
Wadsworth, OH 44281
Ph: (330)336-8350

17078 ■ National Association of the Remodeling Industry East Central Ohio
PO Box 140
Wadsworth, OH 44282
Ph: (330)334-5117
Fax: (330)336-7575
E-mail: nari@wadsnet.com
URL: National Affiliate–www.nari.org
Contact: Gerry Streator, Pres.
Local. Brings together people who work in the remodeling industry. Provides resources for knowledge and training in the industry. Encourages ethical conduct, sound business practices and professionalism. Promotes the remodeling industry's products. **Affiliated With:** National Association of the Remodeling Industry.

17079 ■ Wadsworth Area Chamber of Commerce (WACC)
125 W Boyer St., Ste.B
Wadsworth, OH 44281
Ph: (330)336-6150
Fax: (330)336-2672
E-mail: business@wadsworthchamber.com
URL: http://www.wadsworthchamber.com
Contact: Beth Workman, CEO
Founded: 1954. **Members:** 350. **Membership Dues:** new business (base rate including up to 3 full time employees), $155 (annual) • financial institution (add $25 each full-time employee), $180 (annual) • associate, non-profit, $75 (annual). **Local**. Promotes business and community development in the Wadsworth, OH area. Evaluates and responds to the needs of local businesses; provides programs and services to members. **Publications:** Newsletter, monthly. **Advertising:** accepted • Directory, biennial. Alternate Formats: online. **Conventions/Meetings:** monthly board meeting • monthly luncheon - always last Wednesday • annual Sidewalk Sale and Flea Market Cruise - meeting.

17080 ■ Wadsworth - Young Life
111 Broad St., Ste.200
Wadsworth, OH 44281
Ph: (330)620-5448
URL: http://sites.younglife.org/_layouts/ylext/default.aspx?ID=C-2824
Local. Affiliated With: Young Life.

17081 ■ Young Life County Line
111 Broad St., Ste.200
Wadsworth, OH 44281
Ph: (330)620-5448
URL: http://sites.younglife.org/_layouts/ylext/default.aspx?ID=A-OH156
Local. Affiliated With: Young Life.

Wakeman

17082 ■ American Legion, Wakeman Post 689
PO Box 252
Wakeman, OH 44889
Ph: (740)362-7478
Fax: (740)362-1429
URL: National Affiliate–www.legion.org
Local. Affiliated With: American Legion.

17083 ■ Wakeman Lions Club
PO Box 405
Wakeman, OH 44889
Ph: (440)839-2926
E-mail: cmsbook@adelphia.net
URL: http://wakemanoh.lionwap.org
Contact: Christine Staller, Sec.
Local. Affiliated With: Lions Clubs International.

Walbridge

17084 ■ American Federation of Government Employees, AFL-CIO - Council 164
302 Raymond St.
Walbridge, OH 43465
Ph: (515)256-8367
Fax: (515)256-8421
E-mail: michael.dennis@iadesm.ang.af.mil
URL: http://www.civ-tech164.org
Contact: Michael Dennis, Pres.
Members: 14. **Local.** Federal employees including food inspectors, nurses, printers, cartographers, lawyers, police officers, census workers, OSHA inspectors, janitors, truck drivers, secretaries, artists, plumbers, immigration inspectors, scientists, doctors, cowboys, botanists, park rangers, computer programmers, foreign service workers, airplane mechanics, environmentalists, and writers. Seeks to help provide good government services, while ensuring that government workers are treated fairly and with dignity. **Affiliated With:** American Federation of Government Employees.

Waldo

17085 ■ American Legion, Porter-Snyder Post 605
367 W Main St.
Waldo, OH 43356
Ph: (740)726-2506
Fax: (740)362-1429
URL: National Affiliate–www.legion.org
Local. Affiliated With: American Legion.

Walhonding

17086 ■ American Legion, Ohio Post 650
c/o Joseph Colopy, Jr.
30065 Stricker Rd.
Walhonding, OH 43843
Ph: (740)362-7478
Fax: (740)362-1429
URL: National Affiliate–www.legion.org
Contact: Joseph Colopy Jr., Contact
Local. Affiliated With: American Legion.

Walton Hills

17087 ■ Northern Ohio Wellness Connection (NOWC)
c/o Jim Toth, Dir.
19357 Rashell Dr.
Walton Hills, OH 44146
Ph: (440)232-0442
E-mail: to_nowc@yahoo.com
URL: http://www.nowc.homestead.com
Contact: Jim Toth, Dir.
Regional.

Wapakoneta

17088 ■ American Legion, Auglaize Post 330
PO Box 241
Wapakoneta, OH 45895
Ph: (740)362-7478
Fax: (740)362-1429
URL: National Affiliate–www.legion.org
Local. Affiliated With: American Legion.

17089 ■ Auglaize County Genealogical Society
PO Box 2021
Wapakoneta, OH 45895-0521
E-mail: acgsogs@rootsweb.com
URL: http://www.rootsweb.com/~ohaugogs/index.html
Contact: Dan Bennett, Treas.
Membership Dues: single, $10 (annual) • family, $13 (annual) • life, $200. **Local. Affiliated With:** Ohio Genealogical Society. **Formerly:** (2005) Ohio Genealogical Society, Auglaize County Chapter. **Publications:** *Fallen Timbers Ances-Tree*, quarterly. Newsletter. **Price:** included in membership dues • Newsletter, periodic. **Conventions/Meetings:** monthly meeting - always first Saturday.

17090 ■ National Active and Retired Federal Employees Association Auglaize-Mercer 2170
12289 State Rte. 219
Wapakoneta, OH 45895-8349
Ph: (937)693-2293
URL: National Affiliate–www.narfe.org
Contact: Gilbert L. Atkinson, Contact
Local. Protects the retirement future of employees through education. Informs members on issues affecting the retirement. **Affiliated With:** National Association of Retired Federal Employees.

17091 ■ Ohio Suffolk Sheep Association
c/o Pat Wiford, Sec.-Treas.
19785 Santa Fe-New Knoxville Rd.
Wapakoneta, OH 45895
Ph: (937)596-5229
URL: National Affiliate–www.u-s-s-a.org
Contact: Pat Wiford, Sec.-Treas.
State. Affiliated With: United Suffolk Sheep Association.

17092 ■ Ohio Toy Fox Terrier Association
c/o Bernice McDermitt, Pres.
17020 Buckland Holden Rd.
Wapakoneta, OH 45895
E-mail: foxchasetfts@charter.net
URL: National Affiliate–www.ntfta.netfirms.com
Contact: Bernice McDermitt, Pres.
State. Affiliated With: National Toy Fox Terrier Association.

17093 ■ Reserve Officers Association - Department of Ohio, Anthony Wayne Chapter 4
c/o Major Donald K. Hauenstein, Pres.
816 Aster Dr.
Wapakoneta, OH 45895-1007
Ph: (419)738-2366 (419)394-8252
Fax: (419)394-4187
E-mail: dknrmh@bright.net
URL: http://www.roa.org/oh
Contact: Major Donald K. Hauenstein, Pres.
Local. Promotes and supports the development and execution of a military policy for the United States. Provides professional development seminars, workshops and programs for its members. **Affiliated With:** Reserve Officers Association of the United States.

17094 ■ Wapakoneta Area Chamber of Commerce (WACC)
16 E Auglaize St.
PO Box 208
Wapakoneta, OH 45895
Ph: (419)738-2911
Fax: (419)739-2298
E-mail: wapcofc@bright.net
URL: http://www.wapakoneta.com
Contact: Dan Graf, Dir.
Membership Dues: small business (add $5/employee over 5), $150 (annual) • extended care (add $5/bed over 5), $150 (annual) • financial institution (add $5/employee over 5), $635 (annual) • lodging (add $5/employee over 5), $150 (annual) • utility (add $5/employee over 5), $340 (annual) • professional (add $30/additional professional and $5/employee over 5), $150 (annual) • education institution, $150 (annual) • associate, non-profit organization, $75 (annual) • friend, $40 (annual). **Staff:** 2. **Local.** Promotes business and community development in the Wapakoneta, OH area. Sponsors the Indian Summer Festival. **Publications:** *Chamber Chat*, monthly. Newsletter.

Warren

17095 ■ American Legion, Howland Post 700
PO Box 8735
Warren, OH 44484
Ph: (740)362-7478
Fax: (740)362-1429
URL: National Affiliate–www.legion.org
Local. Affiliated With: American Legion.

17096 ■ American Legion, Ohio Post 278
c/o Clarence Hyde
2237 N Park Ave.
Warren, OH 44483
Ph: (740)362-7478
Fax: (740)362-1429
URL: National Affiliate–www.legion.org
Contact: Clarence Hyde, Contact
Local. Affiliated With: American Legion.

17097 ■ American Legion, Ohio Post 540
c/o Roger Gardner
5789 Louise Ave. NW
Warren, OH 44483
Ph: (740)362-7478
Fax: (740)362-1429
URL: National Affiliate–www.legion.org
Contact: Roger Gardner, Contact
Local. Affiliated With: American Legion.

17098 ■ American Legion, Ohio Post 564
c/o John Gilliam
234 Bane St. SW
Warren, OH 44485
Ph: (740)362-7478
Fax: (740)362-1429
URL: National Affiliate–www.legion.org
Contact: John Gilliam, Contact
Local. Affiliated With: American Legion.

17099 ■ Champion Lions Club
3771 Mahoning Ave.
Warren, OH 44483-1919
Ph: (330)847-9215
E-mail: tristar2380@aol.com
URL: http://championlions.lionwap.org
Contact: Worthy Cottrill Jr., Pres.
Local. Affiliated With: Lions Clubs International.

17100 ■ Dress for Success Warren-Youngstown
418 Main St.
Warren, OH 44485
Ph: (330)399-3800
E-mail: classfour1@aol.com
URL: National Affiliate–www.dressforsuccess.org
Contact: Felicia Pruitt-Davis, Founder/CEO
Local.

17101 ■ Easter Seals Trumbull County, Ohio
155 S Park Ave.
Warren, OH 44481
Ph: (330)399-1001
Fax: (330)743-1168
E-mail: easterseals@mtc.easterseals.com
URL: http://mtc.easterseals.com
Contact: Mr. Kenan Sklener, CEO
Local. Provides services to children and adults with disabilities and other special needs, and to support their families. **Affiliated With:** Easter Seals.

17102 ■ International Union of Bricklayers and Allied Craftworkers, AFL-CIO-CLC Local Union 43
c/o Jerre Riggle
684 N Park Ave.
Warren, OH 44484-4803

Ph: (330)394-9325
Fax: (330)394-9325
E-mail: riggle_local43@noadc97.org
URL: National Affiliate–www.bacweb.org
Contact: Jerre Riggle, Field Representative
Members: 234. **Local**. **Affiliated With:** International Union of Bricklayers and Allied Craftworkers.

17103 ■ International Union, United Automobile, Aerospace and Agricultural Implement Workers of America, AFL-CIO - Local Union 1112
11471 Reuther Dr. SW
Warren, OH 44481-9532
E-mail: tfeens@onecom.com
URL: http://www.uaw1112.com
Contact: Jim Graham, Pres.
Members: 4,262. **Local**. AFL-CIO. **Affiliated With:** International Union, United Automobile, Aerospace and Agricultural Implement Workers of America.

17104 ■ International Union, United Automobile, Aerospace and Agricultural Implement Workers of America, AFL-CIO - Local Union 1714
2121 Salt Springs Rd. SW
Warren, OH 44481
Ph: (330)824-2527
E-mail: uaw1714@hotmail.com
URL: http://www.uaw1714.com
Contact: Jim Kaster, Pres.
Members: 2,176. **Local**. Seeks for the dignity and equality of the workers. Strives to provide contractors with well-trained, productive employees. **Affiliated With:** International Union, United Automobile, Aerospace and Agricultural Implement Workers of America.

17105 ■ Lordstown Lions Club
7887 Tod St. SW
Warren, OH 44481
Ph: (330)824-3722
E-mail: lordstown_lions@cebridge.net
URL: http://lordstownlions.lionwap.org
Contact: Rick Albrecht Sr., Pres.
Local. **Affiliated With:** Lions Clubs International.

17106 ■ Musicians AFL-CIO, LU 118
116 Pine Ave. NE
Warren, OH 44481-1232
Ph: (330)399-1541
Fax: (330)399-6047
E-mail: local118@afm.org
URL: http://www.afm.org/118
Contact: Karen L.B. Ferren, Sec.-Treas.
Founded: 1900. **Members:** 300. **Membership Dues:** regular, $105 (annual). **Local**. Provides work for members, referral system. **Affiliated With:** AFL-CIO. **Publications:** *The Musician*, quarterly. Journal. **Circulation:** 300. **Advertising:** accepted. **Conventions/Meetings:** biennial convention (exhibits) - always June • annual Tri-State Musicians Conference (exhibits) - always May.

17107 ■ Navy League of the United States, Western Reserve
c/o George S. Lardis, Pres.
414 Darlington Rd. NE
Warren, OH 44484-2007
Ph: (330)656-5433
URL: National Affiliate–www.navyleague.org
Contact: George S. Lardis, Pres.
Local. Civilian organization that supports U.S. capability to keep the sea lanes open through a strong, viable Navy, Marine Corps, Coast Guard, and Merchant Marine. Seeks to awaken interest and cooperation of U.S. citizens in matters serving to aid, improve, and develop the efficiency of U.S. naval and maritime forces and equipment. **Affiliated With:** Navy League of the United States.

17108 ■ Ohio Coin Laundry Association
c/o Mike Keriotis
2781 Hoffman Cir. NE
Warren, OH 44483-3007
Ph: (330)506-3688
URL: National Affiliate–www.coinlaundry.org
Contact: Mike Keriotis, Contact
State. Provides education and service to the entrepreneurs of the coin laundry industry. **Affiliated With:** Coin Laundry Association.

17109 ■ Society of Manufacturing Engineers - Trumbull Career and Technical Center S301
4314 Mahoning Ave. NW
Warren, OH 44483
Ph: (330)675-8834
Fax: (330)675-7676
E-mail: wdulaney@excite.com
URL: National Affiliate–www.sme.org
Contact: Walter Dulaney, Contact
Local. Advances manufacturing knowledge to gain competitive advantage. Improves skills and manufacturing solutions for the growth of economy. Provides resources and opportunities for manufacturing professionals. **Affiliated With:** U.S. National Committee for the Scientific Committee on Oceanic Research.

17110 ■ Struthers Lions Club
c/o Renee McCaman, Pres.
317 Raymond Ave. NW
Warren, OH 44483
Ph: (330)847-8478
E-mail: lions2005newsletter@yahoo.com
URL: http://www.lions13d.org
Contact: Renee McCaman, Pres.
Local. **Affiliated With:** Lions Clubs International.

17111 ■ Trumbull County Bar Association (TCBA)
c/o Dee Bloom, Sec.
PO Box 422
Warren, OH 44482
Ph: (330)675-2415
Fax: (330)675-2412
E-mail: secretary@tcba.net
URL: http://www.tcba.net
Contact: Dee Bloom, Sec.
Founded: 1879. **Members:** 427. **Staff:** 2. **Local Groups:** 27. **Local**. Attorneys in good standing. Seeks to improve the administration of civil and criminal justice, and the availability of legal services to the public. Sponsors social activities. **Awards:** Outstanding Achievements Award. **Type:** recognition • 25 and 50 Yr. Members Annual. **Type:** trophy. **Conventions/Meetings:** monthly seminar.

17112 ■ Trumbull County Genealogical Society
PO Box 309
Warren, OH 44482-0309
E-mail: cwoodward@neo.rr.com
URL: http://www.rootsweb.com/~ohtcgs
Contact: Cindy Woodward, Contact
Founded: 1969. **Members:** 225. **Membership Dues:** single, $10 (annual) • joint, $12 (annual). **Local**. Strives to educate its members and the public as a whole by acquiring, preserving and disseminating genealogical and historical information. **Affiliated With:** Ohio Genealogical Society. **Publications:** *Ancestry Trails*, monthly. Newsletter. **Price:** free for members.

17113 ■ Trumbull County Medical Society (TCMS)
PO Box 23
Warren, OH 44482
Ph: (330)847-6352
Free: (866)377-6474
URL: http://www.trumbullmed.org
Contact: Marla Fraelich, Exec.Sec.
Local. Advances the art and science of medicine. Promotes patient care and the betterment of public health. **Affiliated With:** Ohio State Medical Association.

17114 ■ United Way of Trumbull County
3601 Youngstown Rd. SE
Warren, OH 44484-2832
Ph: (330)369-1000
Fax: (330)369-5555
E-mail: info@unitedwaytrumbull.org
URL: http://www.unitedwaytrumbull.org
Contact: Thomas J. Krysiek, Pres./CPO
Local. **Affiliated With:** United Way of America.

17115 ■ USA Dance - Chapter 2015
c/o Brenda Eckenrode, VP
3265 Reeves Rd. NE
Warren, OH 44483
Ph: (330)718-0166
E-mail: peanut9999@aol.com
URL: http://usabda215.tripod.com
Contact: Brenda Eckenrode, VP
Local. Encourages and promotes the physical, mental and social benefits of partner dancing. Organizes and supports programs for the recreational enjoyment of ballroom dancing. Creates opportunities for the general public to participate in ballroom dancing and DanceSport.

17116 ■ Warren Area Miniature Club
c/o Susan Gillespie
149 Warrenton Dr.
Warren, OH 44481
Ph: (330)847-6330
E-mail: wamcminis@hotmail.com
URL: http://www.miniatures.org/states/OH.html
Contact: Susan Gillespie, Contact
Local. **Affiliated With:** National Association of Miniature Enthusiasts.

17117 ■ Warren Area Stamp Club
c/o Alexander J. Savakis
PO Box 609
Warren, OH 44482-0609
E-mail: warrenstampclub@aol.com
URL: http://hometown.aol.com/warrenstampclub
Contact: Alexander J. Savakis, Sec.
Founded: 1926. **Members:** 20. **Membership Dues:** regular membership, $2 (annual). **Local**. **Libraries: Type:** not open to the public. **Holdings:** 18; articles, books. **Subjects:** philately. **Affiliated With:** American Philatelic Society. **Publications:** *The Western Reserve Philatelist*, monthly. Newsletter. **Price:** free at monthly meetings.

17118 ■ Warren Lions Club - Ohio
PO Box 251
Warren, OH 44482-0251
Ph: (330)847-7549
E-mail: johardman@netdotcom.com
URL: http://warrenoh.lionwap.org
Contact: John Hardman, Sec.
Local. **Affiliated With:** Lions Clubs International.

17119 ■ Warren, OH 9to5
c/o Gale Johnson
1145 Miller St. SW
Warren, OH 44485
Ph: (330)395-6913
URL: National Affiliate–www.9to5.org
Contact: Gale Johnson, Contact
Local. **Affiliated With:** 9 to 5, National Association of Working Women.

17120 ■ Warren Striders Track Club
c/o Jack C. Thornton, Jr.
PO Box 3440
Warren, OH 44485-0440
E-mail: jthorntonjr1@msn.com
URL: http://www.warrenstriderstrackclubinc.com
Contact: Jack C. Thornton Jr., Contact
Local.

17121 ■ Warren - Trumbull Urban League
c/o Thomas S. Conley, Pres.
290 W Market St.
Warren, OH 44481

Ph: (330)394-4316
E-mail: 1warrentrumbull@neo.rr.com
URL: National Affiliate–www.nul.org
Contact: Thomas S. Conley, Pres.
Local. Affiliated With: National Urban League.

Warrensville Heights

17122 ■ International Association of Ministers Wives and Ministers Widows, Ohio
23673 Banbury Cir., No. 4
Warrensville Heights, OH 44128
Ph: (216)662-7721
URL: National Affiliate–www.iamwmw.org
Contact: Ruth Mosely, Pres.
State. Affiliated With: International Association of Ministers Wives and Ministers Widows.

17123 ■ United Steelworkers of America, Sub District Office
c/o Rose Jones
25111 Miles Rd., Ste.H
Warrensville Heights, OH 44128
Ph: (216)292-5683
URL: http://www.uswa.org
Contact: Garry Steinbeck, District Dir.
Members: 110. **Local. Affiliated With:** United Steelworkers of America. **Formerly:** (2005) United Steelworkers of America, AFL-CIO-CLC - Local Union 77.

Warsaw

17124 ■ American Legion, Walhonding Valley Post 634
PO Box 353
Warsaw, OH 43844
Ph: (740)362-7478
Fax: (740)362-1429
URL: National Affiliate–www.legion.org
Local. Affiliated With: American Legion.

Washington Court House

17125 ■ American Legion, Homer Lawson Post 653
c/o Charles T. Harris
825 Sycamore St.
Washington Court House, OH 43160
Ph: (740)362-7478
Fax: (740)362-1429
URL: National Affiliate–www.legion.org
Contact: Charles T. Harris, Contact
Local. Affiliated With: American Legion.

17126 ■ American Legion, Ohio Post 25
c/o Paul H. Hughey
1240 US Hwy. 22 NW
Washington Court House, OH 43160
Ph: (740)362-7478
Fax: (740)362-1429
URL: National Affiliate–www.legion.org
Contact: Paul H. Hughey, Contact
Local. Affiliated With: American Legion.

17127 ■ Fayette County Chamber of Commerce
101 E E. St.
Washington Court House, OH 43160
Ph: (740)335-0761
Fax: (740)335-0762
Free: (800)479-7797
E-mail: fayettechamber@yahoo.com
URL: http://www.fayettecountyohio.com
Contact: Roger Blackburn, Pres.
Local. Seeks to promote and enhance the business environment within the area. **Awards: Frequency:** annual. **Type:** scholarship. **Computer Services:** Mailing lists, mailing lists of members. **Publications:** Newsletter, annual. **Circulation:** 500. Alternate Formats: online.

17128 ■ Fayette County Historical Society (FCHS)
517 Columbus Ave.
Washington Court House, OH 43160
Ph: (740)335-2953
Contact: Carol A. Carey, Curator
Founded: 1948. **Members:** 500. **Membership Dues:** adult, $10 (annual) • life, $100 • student, $5 (annual). **Staff:** 1. **Budget:** $25,000. **State Groups:** 2. **Local.** Individuals interested in the history of Fayette County, OH. Operates Fayette County Museum. **Libraries: Type:** open to the public. **Holdings:** 300; books. **Subjects:** ohio and local history, civil war. **Affiliated With:** Ohio Association of Historical Societies and Museums. **Publications:** *Fayette County, Ohio: A Pictorial History*. Book. **Price:** $37.00 plus shipping and handling $5.00. **Conventions/Meetings:** annual meeting - always 1st Thursday of November. Washington Court House, OH - Avg. Attendance: 75.

17129 ■ Local 776C, Chemical Workers Council of the UFCW
57 Country Manor Dr. NE
Washington Court House, OH 43160
Ph: (614)474-3161
URL: National Affiliate–www.ufcw.org
Local. Affiliated With: United Food and Commercial Workers International Union.

17130 ■ Mothers Against Drunk Driving, Fayette/Pickaway Counties
141 Eastview Dr.
Washington Court House, OH 43160
Ph: (740)636-9960
URL: National Affiliate–www.madd.org
Local. Victims of drunk driving crashes; concerned citizens. Encourages citizen participation in working towards reform of the drunk driving problem and the prevention of underage drinking. Acts as the voice of victims of drunk driving crashes by speaking on their behalf to communities, businesses, and educational groups. **Affiliated With:** Mothers Against Drunk Driving.

17131 ■ Ohio Genealogical Society, Fayette County (FCGS)
PO Box 342
Washington Court House, OH 43160-0342
E-mail: db9620@dragonbbs.com
URL: http://www.fayettecogs.org
Contact: Pamela Rhoads, Pres.
Founded: 1981. **Membership Dues:** individual, family (living at the same address), $10 (annual) • person, family (living at the same address), $100 (10/year). **Local Groups:** 1. **Local.** Assists people to find their ancestors for their own satisfaction or admittance to an organizations that requires certain decendancy from a specific ancestor. Volunteers at the Archives to index the old records. Publish old records. **Libraries: Type:** lending; open to the public; reference. **Holdings:** archival material, articles, biographical archives, books, maps, periodicals. **Subjects:** family genealogies, researchable records. **Awards:** Annual Membership. **Frequency:** biennial. **Type:** recognition. **Recipient:** for non-members • Certificate of Appreciation. **Frequency:** annual. **Type:** recognition. **Recipient:** to members who volunteer their services for the betterment of the organization. **Computer Services:** Information services, look-ups of certain information, names of researchers. **Affiliated With:** Ohio Genealogical Society.

17132 ■ South Central Ohio Angus Association
c/o Wayne Baird, Pres.
5838 Wash-Goodhope Rd. SE
Washington Court House, OH 43160-9230
Ph: (740)335-6483
URL: National Affiliate–www.angus.org
Contact: Wayne Baird, Pres.
Local. Affiliated With: American Angus Association.

17133 ■ United Way of Fayette County, Ohio
132 1/2 E Ct. St., Ste.204
Washington Court House, OH 43160
Ph: (740)335-8932
URL: National Affiliate–national.unitedway.org
Local. Affiliated With: United Way of America.

Washingtonville

17134 ■ Vietnam Veterans of America, Chapter No. 40
c/o Thomas S. Schahill, Pres.
PO Box 305
Washingtonville, OH 44490-0305
Ph: (330)337-3090
URL: http://www.vvabuckeyestatecouncil.com
Contact: Thomas S. Schahill, Pres.
Local. Affiliated With: Vietnam Veterans of America.

Waterville

17135 ■ American Legion, Waterville Post 463
c/o John Rosebrock
6661 Waterville Monclova Rd.
Waterville, OH 43566
Ph: (740)362-7478
Fax: (740)362-1429
URL: National Affiliate–www.legion.org
Contact: John Rosebrock, Contact
Local. Affiliated With: American Legion.

17136 ■ Waterville Area Chamber of Commerce (WACC)
122 Farnsworth Rd.
Waterville, OH 43566
Ph: (419)878-5188
Fax: (419)878-5199
E-mail: watervillechamber@toast.net
URL: http://www.watervillechamber.com/index.html
Contact: Dawn Bly, Exec.Dir.
Founded: 1970. **Members:** 138. **Membership Dues:** retail, $100 (annual). **Staff:** 2. **Local.** Businesspersons, professionals, retail and service merchants, manufacturers representatives, and industry interested in promoting business and community development in the Waterville, OH area. Assists new business; provides input for economic development. Sponsors Riverfest and annual Roche de Boeuf Festival. **Awards:** Scholarship. **Frequency:** annual. **Type:** scholarship. **Publications:** *Business and Community Directory*, quarterly. Newsletter. **Price:** included in membership dues • Newsletter, quarterly. **Conventions/Meetings:** monthly meeting - always first Thursday.

Wauseon

17137 ■ American Legion, Robinson-Gibbs Post 265
1105 N Shoop Ave.
Wauseon, OH 43567
Ph: (740)362-7478
Fax: (740)362-1429
URL: National Affiliate–www.legion.org
Local. Affiliated With: American Legion.

17138 ■ American Red Cross, Fulton County Ohio
PO Box 156
Wauseon, OH 43567-0156
Ph: (419)335-4636
Fax: (419)335-4633
E-mail: executive@fultoncountyredcross.org
URL: http://www.fultoncoredcross.org
Local.

17139 ■ Fulton County Historical Society (FCHS)
229 Monroe St.
Wauseon, OH 43567
Ph: (419)337-7922
E-mail: museum@fultoncountyhs.org
URL: http://rootsweb.com/~ohfulton/HistoricalSociety.html
Contact: Barbara Berry, Dir.
Founded: 1883. **Members:** 200. **Membership Dues:** single, $20 (annual) • family, $30 (annual) • life, $200 • student, $5 (annual). **Staff:** 1. **Budget:** $32,000. **Local.** Works to collect artifacts and written records pertaining to Fulton County, Ohio. Maintains the Fulton County Historical Museum, the 1896 Lake Shore and Michigan Southern Railroad Depot, the 1861 Raphael Reighard Blacksmith Shop, and the 1838 Canfield Log Cabin. **Libraries: Type:** open to the public. **Holdings:** 200; archival material, books, papers, periodicals, photographs. **Subjects:** Fulton County history, Ohio history. **Awards:** Centennial Farm Awards. **Frequency:** periodic. **Type:** recognition. **Additional Websites:** http://www.fultoncountyhs.org. **Affiliated With:** Fulton County Chapter, Ohio Genealogical Society. **Publications:** *Fulton County Pioneer*, quarterly. Newsletter. **Price:** included in membership dues. **Circulation:** 250. **Conventions/Meetings:** bimonthly board meeting - January through October • annual meeting, with dinner and entertainment - always last Monday of October.

17140 ■ Gardeners of America/Men's Garden Clubs of America - Fulton County Garden Club
c/o George Dobransky, Pres.
650 Pine St.
Wauseon, OH 43567
Ph: (419)337-1436
URL: National Affiliate–www.tgoa-mgca.org
Contact: George Dobransky, Pres.
Local.

17141 ■ United Way of Fulton County, Ohio
604 S Shoop Ave., Ste.122
Wauseon, OH 43567-1725
Ph: (419)337-9606
URL: National Affiliate–national.unitedway.org
Local. Affiliated With: United Way of America.

17142 ■ Veterans of Foreign Wars 7424
1133 N. Ottokee St.
Wauseon, OH 43567
Ph: (419)335-1301
Affiliated With: Veterans of Foreign Wars of the United States.

17143 ■ Wauseon Chamber of Commerce (WCC)
115 N Fulton St.
PO Box 217
Wauseon, OH 43567
Ph: (419)335-9966
Fax: (419)335-7693
E-mail: debbie@wauseonchamber.com
URL: http://www.wauseonchamber.com
Contact: Debbie Nelson, Exec.Dir.
Founded: 1937. **Members:** 234. **Membership Dues:** one-time admin fee (new members), $15 • business and industry, $150-$440 (annual) • bank, credit union, utility, hospital, $440 (annual) • associate, school, church, service club, charity, public official, government, $90 (annual) • home based business (with no employees), $70 (annual) • individual/retiree, $25 (annual). **Staff:** 1. **State Groups:** 1. **Local.** Promotes business and community development in the Wauseon, OH area. **Supersedes:** Wauseon Commerce Club.

Waverly

17144 ■ American Legion, Merritt Post 142
PO Box 124
Waverly, OH 45690
Ph: (740)362-7478
Fax: (740)362-1429
URL: National Affiliate–www.legion.org
Local. Affiliated With: American Legion.

17145 ■ AMVETS, Waverly Post 58
210 N Market St.
Waverly, OH 45690
Ph: (740)947-8627
E-mail: commander@amvetspost58.freeservers.com
URL: http://amvetspost58.freeservers.com
Contact: Bill Walsh, Adj.
Local. Affiliated With: AMVETS - American Veterans.

17146 ■ Ohio Genealogical Society, Pike County
PO Box 224
Waverly, OH 45690
E-mail: pikeweb2003@yahoo.com
URL: http://www.rootsweb.com/~ohpcgs
Contact: Fred Shoemaker, Pres.
Founded: 1973. **Membership Dues:** single, $10 (annual) • family, $12 (annual). **Local. Affiliated With:** Ohio Genealogical Society. **Publications:** *Beaver and Marion Townships*, periodic. Book. **Price:** $15.00 plus shipping and handling • *Evergreen-Union of Waverly*, periodic. Book. **Price:** $25.00 plus shipping and handling • *Newton and Camp Creek Townships*, periodic. Book. **Price:** $15.00 plus shipping and handling • *Seal Township*, periodic. Book. **Price:** $15.00 plus shipping and handling • Newsletter, quarterly. Contains information about Pike County. **Price:** included in membership dues.

17147 ■ Pike County Chamber of Commerce (PCCC)
12455 State Rte. 104
PO Box 107
Waverly, OH 45690
Ph: (740)947-7715
Fax: (740)947-7716
E-mail: mail@pikechamber.org
URL: http://www.pikechamber.org
Contact: Blaine Beekman, Exec.Dir.
Founded: 1960. **Local.** Promotes business and community development in Pike County, OH. **Affiliated With:** U.S. Chamber of Commerce. **Publications:** *Accent*, monthly. Newsletter. **Advertising:** accepted. Alternate Formats: online • Bulletin, monthly. **Conventions/Meetings:** annual banquet - always in January • monthly Business After Hours - meeting - always 3rd Thursday.

17148 ■ Waverly Lawn Bowling Club
c/o Ada Mendez
320 Oak Ave.
Waverly, OH 45690
E-mail: adax@bright.net
URL: National Affiliate–www.bowlsamerica.org
Contact: Ada Mendez, Contact
Local. Affiliated With: United States Lawn Bowls Association.

Waynesburg

17149 ■ American Legion, Sandy Valley Post 432
166 E Lisbon St.
Waynesburg, OH 44688
Ph: (740)362-7478
Fax: (740)362-1429
URL: National Affiliate–www.legion.org
Local. Affiliated With: American Legion.

Waynesfield

17150 ■ American Legion, Wayne Post 395
521 N Westminster St.
Waynesfield, OH 45896
Ph: (740)362-7478
Fax: (740)362-1429
URL: National Affiliate–www.legion.org
Local. Affiliated With: American Legion.

Waynesville

17151 ■ American Legion, Wayne Township Veterans Post 615
PO Box 154
Waynesville, OH 45068
Ph: (740)362-7478
Fax: (740)362-1429
URL: National Affiliate–www.legion.org
Local. Affiliated With: American Legion.

17152 ■ Waynesville Area Chamber of Commerce
PO Box 281
10-B N Main St.
Waynesville, OH 45068-0281
Ph: (513)897-8855
Fax: (513)897-9833
E-mail: waynsville@aol.com
URL: http://www.waynesvilleohio.com
Contact: Joseph Coons, Exec.Dir.
Founded: 1969. **Members:** 300. **Membership Dues:** business (1-10 employees), $75 (annual) • business (11-50 employees), $100 (annual) • business (51-100 employees), $150 (annual) • business (101-300 employees), $250 (annual) • business (301-500 employees), $500 (annual) • business (501 or more employees), $1,000 (annual) • associate, $30 (annual). **Local.** Works to advance, protect, and preserve the civic, economic, business, and individual interest of the Waynesville area. **Publications:** *Getting It Right The First Time: A Pocket Guide For New Business*. Brochure • Newsletter, bimonthly. **Conventions/Meetings:** annual festival.

17153 ■ Waynesville Historical Preservation Board
c/o Rod Smith, Village Mgr.
1400 Lytle Rd.
Waynesville, OH 45068
Ph: (513)897-8015
Fax: (513)897-2015
E-mail: info@waynesville-ohio.org
URL: http://www.waynesville-ohio.org
Contact: Rod Smith, Village Mgr.
Local. Enforces the Waynesville Historic Preservation Board Rules and Regulations and provides the formal process to approve or disprove the external design of proposed new buildings within the Historic Preservation District.

17154 ■ Waynesville Lions Club
387 Victoria Pl.
Waynesville, OH 45068
Ph: (513)897-2736
URL: http://waynesvilleoh.lionwap.org
Contact: Ed Andres, Pres.
Local. Affiliated With: Lions Clubs International.

Wellington

17155 ■ American Legion, Spirit of 76 Post 8
518 S Main St.
Wellington, OH 44090
Ph: (740)362-7478
Fax: (740)362-1429
URL: National Affiliate–www.legion.org
Local. Affiliated With: American Legion.

17156 ■ Main Street Wellington
PO Box 1
Wellington, OH 44090
Ph: (440)647-3987
E-mail: info@mainstreetwellington.com
URL: http://www.mainstreetwellington.com
Local.

17157 ■ Wellington Area Chamber of Commerce
226 Wenner St.
PO Box 42
Wellington, OH 44090

Ph: (440)647-2222
Contact: Virginia Haynes, Pres.
Local.

17158 ■ Wellington Education Association
c/o Virginia P. Mateer
218 Wenner St.
Wellington, OH 44090-1019
Local.

Wellston

17159 ■ American Legion, Wellston Post 371
1001 S Pennsylvania Ave.
Wellston, OH 45692
Ph: (740)362-7478
Fax: (740)362-1429
URL: National Affiliate–www.legion.org
Local. Affiliated With: American Legion.

17160 ■ Ruffed Grouse Society, Hocking River Valley Chapter
c/o Steve Benson
23473 State Rte. 93
Wellston, OH 45692
Ph: (304)645-7039
E-mail: tms1987@charter.net
URL: National Affiliate–www.ruffedgrousesociety.org
Contact: Steve Benson, Contact
Local. Affiliated With: Ruffed Grouse Society.

Wellsville

17161 ■ American Legion, Wellsville Post 70
229 Wells Ave.
Wellsville, OH 43968
Ph: (740)362-7478
Fax: (740)362-1429
URL: National Affiliate–www.legion.org
Local. Affiliated With: American Legion.

17162 ■ Wellsville Lions Club
c/o Randy Dillard, Pres.
1487 Mick Rd.
Wellsville, OH 43968
Ph: (330)532-4542
URL: http://www.lions13d.org
Contact: Randy Dillard, Pres.
Local. Affiliated With: Lions Clubs International.

West Alexandria

17163 ■ American Legion, Ohio Post 322
c/o James E. Ryan
PO Box 2
West Alexandria, OH 45381
Ph: (740)362-7478
Fax: (740)362-1429
URL: National Affiliate–www.legion.org
Contact: James E. Ryan, Contact
Local. Affiliated With: American Legion.

17164 ■ Ohio Simmental Association (OSA)
c/o Melissa Ulrich, Sec.
5353 Enterprise Rd.
West Alexandria, OH 45381
Ph: (937)839-4169 (937)787-3203
E-mail: tvah@bright.net
URL: http://ohiosimmental.com
Contact: Melissa Ulrich, Sec.
Founded: 1971. **Members:** 177. **Membership Dues:** regular, $20 (annual). **Staff:** 2. **State Groups:** 1. **State.** Represents Simmental breeders. Promotes Simmental breed of cattle. **Conventions/Meetings:** annual meeting.

17165 ■ West Alexandria Lions Club
16 N Main St.
West Alexandria, OH 45381
Ph: (937)839-4972
URL: http://alexandriaoh.lionwap.org
Contact: Tom Welsh, Pres.
Local. Affiliated With: Lions Clubs International.

West Carrollton

17166 ■ American Welding Society, Dayton
c/o Chris Anderson, Chm.
Motoman, Inc.
805 Liberty Ln.
West Carrollton, OH 45449
Ph: (937)847-6200
Fax: (937)847-3355
E-mail: chris.anderson@motoman.com
URL: National Affiliate–www.aws.org
Contact: Chris Anderson, Chm.
Local. Professional engineering society in the field of welding. **Affiliated With:** American Welding Society.

West Chester

17167 ■ African Violet Society of Dayton
c/o Pat Hancock
PO Box 8085
West Chester, OH 45069
Ph: (513)777-2524
E-mail: avsd@gesneriad.org
URL: National Affiliate–www.avsa.org
Contact: Pat Hancock, Contact
Local. Affiliated With: African Violet Society of America.

17168 ■ American Diabetes Association, Southwest Ohio/Northern Kentucky Area
8899 Brookside Ave., Ste.102
West Chester, OH 45069
Ph: (513)759-9330
Fax: (513)759-9335
Free: (800)DIABETES
E-mail: srichard@diabetes.org
URL: National Affiliate–www.diabetes.org
Contact: Sylvia A. Richard, Exec.Dir.
Local. Affiliated With: American Diabetes Association.

17169 ■ American Hellenic Educational Progressive Association - District 11
c/o George Sampanis
6437 Tylers Crossing
West Chester, OH 45069
Ph: (513)779-0842
E-mail: georgegds@hotmail.com
URL: http://www.ahepa.org/district11
Contact: George Sampanis, Contact
Regional. Affiliated With: American Hellenic Educational Progressive Association.

17170 ■ Chessie System Historical Society (CSHS)
c/o Randy Broadwater, Pres.
7158 Dimmick Rd.
West Chester, OH 45069
E-mail: chessieengineer@aol.com
URL: http://www.moosevalley.org/cshs/
Contact: Randy Broadwater, Pres.
Founded: 1998. **Members:** 275. **Membership Dues:** in U.S., $30 (annual) • foreign, $45 (annual). **Staff:** 9. **Local. Conventions/Meetings:** annual convention.

17171 ■ Cincinnati Model Yacht Club No. 191
c/o Pablo Godel
8515 Breezewood Ct., No. 208
West Chester, OH 45069
Free: (877)876-2941
URL: http://www.regatta1.com/cmyc/index.html
Contact: Pablo Godel, Contact
Local.

17172 ■ Dachshund Club of Southwestern Ohio
c/o Terri Dickmann, Sec.
7350 Hamilton-Mason Rd., Unit A
West Chester, OH 45069
E-mail: kittentcd@hotmail.com
URL: National Affiliate–www.dachshund-dca.org
Local. Affiliated With: Dachshund Club of America.

17173 ■ Financial Executives International, Cincinnati Chapter (FEI)
c/o Ms. Rosemary Deitzer, Administrator
PO Box 1862
West Chester, OH 45071-1862
Ph: (513)779-4495
Fax: (513)777-4461
E-mail: deitzer@one.net
URL: http://www.fei.org/eWeb/startpage.aspx?site=ch_cin
Contact: Mr. Jeffery Bastian, Pres.
Members: 185. **Local.** Promotes personal and professional development of financial executives. Provides peer networking opportunities and advocacy services. **Committees:** Academic Relations; Attendance; Career Services; Communications; Government Issues Coordination; Professional Development; Programs; Strategic Partners. **Affiliated With:** Financial Executives International.

17174 ■ Institute of Management Accountants, Cincinnati North Chapter
c/o Mary Donisi
Contech Constr. Products, Inc.
9025 Centre Pointe Dr., Ste.400
West Chester, OH 45069
Ph: (513)645-7987
E-mail: bpkoniak@fuse.net
URL: http://www.cincynorth.imanet.org
Contact: Brian Koniak, Pres.
Local. Promotes professional and ethical standards. Equips members and students with knowledge and training required for the accounting profession. **Affiliated With:** Institute of Management Accountants. **Publications:** *By All Accounts*, monthly. Newsletter. Alternate Formats: online. **Conventions/Meetings:** monthly meeting - every third Wednesday except December.

17175 ■ Junior Achievement OKI Partners
9361 Allen Rd.
West Chester, OH 45069
Ph: (513)346-7100
Fax: (513)346-7105
E-mail: information@japartners.org
URL: http://partners.ja.org
Contact: Jennifer P. Smith, Contact
Local. Affiliated With: Junior Achievement.

17176 ■ National Association of Miniature Enthusiasts - A-3 Regional Miniaturists
c/o Lynne Joehnk
7240 Walnut Creek Dr.
West Chester, OH 45069-5555
Ph: (513)860-3044
URL: http://www.miniatures.org/states/OH.html
Contact: Lynne Joehnk, Contact
Local. Affiliated With: National Association of Miniature Enthusiasts.

17177 ■ National Association of Miniature Enthusiasts - Married with Minis
c/o Lynne Joehnk
7240 Walnut Creek Dr.
West Chester, OH 45069-5555
Ph: (513)860-3044
URL: http://www.miniatures.org/states/OH.html
Contact: Lynne Joehnk, Contact
Local. Affiliated With: National Association of Miniature Enthusiasts.

17178 ■ Pediatric Heart Research Association
c/o Dodie Weisbrod, Pres.
PO Box 1547
West Chester, OH 45071

Ph: (513)759-0250
URL: http://www.pediatricheart.org
Contact: Dodie Weisbrod, Pres.
Local.

17179 ■ Southeastern Butler County Chamber of Commerce
8945 Brookside Ave., Ste.101
West Chester, OH 45069
Ph: (513)777-3600
Fax: (513)777-0188
URL: http://www.sebcchamber.com
Contact: Joseph A. Hinson, Pres./CEO
Local.

West Farmington

17180 ■ Summit Beagle Club
c/o Betty Ratini
3542 G P Easterly Rd.
West Farmington, OH 44491-8700
URL: National Affiliate–clubs.akc.org
Contact: Betty Ratini, Contact
Local.

West Jefferson

17181 ■ American Legion, Jefferson Post 201
9701 W Broad St.
West Jefferson, OH 43162
Ph: (740)362-7478
Fax: (740)362-1429
URL: National Affiliate–www.legion.org
Local. **Affiliated With:** American Legion.

West Lafayette

17182 ■ American Legion, West Lafayette Post 466
PO Box 134
West Lafayette, OH 43845
Ph: (740)362-7478
Fax: (740)362-1429
URL: National Affiliate–www.legion.org
Local. **Affiliated With:** American Legion.

West Liberty

17183 ■ American Legion, Woodard-Mc-Govern Post 426
PO Box 483
West Liberty, OH 43357
Ph: (740)362-7478
Fax: (740)362-1429
URL: National Affiliate–www.legion.org
Local. **Affiliated With:** American Legion.

17184 ■ Bellefontaine ALU
PO Box 633
West Liberty, OH 43357
Ph: (937)465-2551
Fax: (937)465-8976
URL: National Affiliate–www.naifa.org
Local. Represents the interest of insurance and financial advisors. Advocates for a positive legislative and regulatory environment. Enhances business and professional skills of members. **Affiliated With:** National Association of Insurance and Financial Advisors.

17185 ■ Mac-A-Cheek Foundation for the Humanities (MFH)
c/o Margaret Piatt
PO Box 166
West Liberty, OH 43357
Ph: (937)465-2821
Fax: (937)465-7774
E-mail: macochee@logan.net
URL: http://www.piattcastles.org
Contact: Margaret Piatt, Contact
Founded: 1994. **Members:** 40. **Membership Dues:** patron, $35 (annual) • contributor, $60 (annual) • supporter, $100 (annual). **Staff:** 2. **Local**. Provides research for publications and public programs in the humanities areas. **Awards:** Ohio Humanities Council. **Frequency:** annual. **Type:** grant. **Recipient:** for humanities programs • **Frequency:** periodic. **Type:** recognition. **Recipient:** for high school writing contest. **Publications:** *That New World*. Book. Contains scholarly analysis and poems. **Price:** $11.95 • Newsletter, quarterly. Provides program updates. **Price:** included in membership dues. **Circulation:** 50.

West Manchester

17186 ■ American Legion, Priddy-Walters Post 665
450 N Main St.
West Manchester, OH 45382
Ph: (740)362-7478
Fax: (740)362-1429
URL: National Affiliate–www.legion.org
Local. **Affiliated With:** American Legion.

West Mansfield

17187 ■ American Legion, West Mansfield Post 603
PO Box 113
West Mansfield, OH 43358
Ph: (740)362-7478
Fax: (740)362-1429
URL: National Affiliate–www.legion.org
Local. **Affiliated With:** American Legion.

West Milton

17188 ■ American Legion, Gingrich-Poince Post 487
2334 S Miami St.
West Milton, OH 45383
Ph: (740)362-7478
Fax: (740)362-1429
URL: National Affiliate–www.legion.org
Local. **Affiliated With:** American Legion.

17189 ■ NACE International, Southwest Ohio Section
c/o Alfred J. Daum, Chm.
Miami Valley Corrosion Tech.
903 S Main St.
West Milton, OH 45383-1364
Ph: (937)698-4265
Fax: (937)656-7031
E-mail: alfred.daum@wpafb.af.mil
URL: National Affiliate–www.nace.org
Contact: Alfred J. Daum, Chm.
Local. Promotes public safety by advancing the knowledge of corrosion engineering and science. Works to raise awareness of corrosion control and prevention technology among government agencies and legislators, businesses, professional societies and the general public. **Affiliated With:** NACE International: The Corrosion Society.

West Salem

17190 ■ American Legion, Ohio Post 499
c/o James Stevenson
13893 Cong. St.
West Salem, OH 44287
Ph: (740)362-7478
Fax: (740)362-1429
URL: National Affiliate–www.legion.org
Contact: James Stevenson, Contact
Local. **Affiliated With:** American Legion.

17191 ■ National Speleological Society, Ohio Cavers and Climbers
c/o Laura Stine
3277 Arrick Dr.
West Salem, OH 44287
Ph: (419)945-2092
E-mail: cavefrk@copper.net
URL: National Affiliate–www.caves.org
Contact: Laura Stine, Contact
State. Seeks to study, explore and conserve cave and karst resources. Protects access to caves and promotes responsible caving. Encourages responsible management of caves and their unique environments. **Affiliated With:** National Speleological Society.

17192 ■ Organic Crop Improvement Association, Ohio- Chapter 1
c/o Steve Sears
9665 Kline Rd.
West Salem, OH 44287
Ph: (419)853-4060
E-mail: ssears@direcway.com
URL: National Affiliate–www.ocia.org
Contact: Steve Sears, Contact
State. **Affiliated With:** Organic Crop Improvement Association.

West Union

17193 ■ Adams County Chamber of Commerce
111 W Main St.
PO Box 398
West Union, OH 45693
Ph: (937)544-5454
Fax: (937)544-6957
Free: (888)223-5454
E-mail: acchamber@bright.net
URL: http://www.adamscountyohchamber.org
Contact: John Holden, Exec.Dir.
Founded: 1989. **Staff:** 5. **Local**. Seeks to improve and preserve the physical and economic development of the county. **Publications:** Newsletter, monthly.

17194 ■ American Legion, Ohio Post 633
c/o Charles H. Eyre
166 Rigdon Rd.
West Union, OH 45693
Ph: (740)362-7478
Fax: (740)362-1429
URL: National Affiliate–www.legion.org
Contact: Charles H. Eyre, Contact
Local. **Affiliated With:** American Legion.

17195 ■ American Legion, Young-Moore Post 100
PO Box 335
West Union, OH 45693
Ph: (740)362-7478
Fax: (740)362-1429
URL: National Affiliate–www.legion.org
Local. **Affiliated With:** American Legion.

17196 ■ American Society of Dowsers, Great Serpent Mound Chapter
c/o Douglas E. McIlwain, Pres.
217 W Main St.
West Union, OH 45693

Ph: (937)544-7900
Fax: (937)544-2919
E-mail: douglasmcilwainlaw@dragonbbs.com
URL: National Affiliate–dowsers.new-hampshire.net
Contact: Doug Mcilwain, Chapter Pres.
Local. Promotes fellowship and the teaching of dowsing skills. Informs the public on the significance and uses of dowsing. **Affiliated With:** American Society of Dowsers.

17197 ■ Dream Factory of Southern Ohio
c/o Deana Grooms, Area Coor.
PO Box 492
West Union, OH 45693
Ph: (937)544-7137
E-mail: southernohio@dreamfactoryinc.com
URL: National Affiliate–www.dreamfactoryinc.org
Contact: Deana Grooms, Area Coor.
Local. **Affiliated With:** Dream Factory.

17198 ■ National Technical Honor Society - Ohio Valley and Technical Center Ohio
175 Lloyd Rd.
West Union, OH 45693
Ph: (937)544-2336
Fax: (937)544-5176
E-mail: tmitchell_ov@scoca-k12.org
URL: http://www.ohiovalley.k12.oh.us
Contact: Tad Mitchell, Dir.
Local.

17199 ■ West Union Firemens' Building Association
c/o Terry Lacy
57 Logans Ln.
West Union, OH 45693-1083
Ph: (937)544-3121
Local.

West Unity

17200 ■ American Legion, West Unity Post 669
PO Box 785
West Unity, OH 43570
Ph: (740)362-7478
Fax: (740)362-1429
URL: National Affiliate–www.legion.org
Local. **Affiliated With:** American Legion.

17201 ■ West Unity Area Chamber of Commerce (WUACC)
PO Box 263
West Unity, OH 43570-0263
Ph: (419)924-2952
Fax: (419)924-2952
Contact: Jean Gerig, Pres.
Founded: 1972. **Members:** 75. **Membership Dues:** single, $20 (annual) • retail, $35 (annual) • industry, $70 (annual). **Staff:** 1. **Local**. Promotes business and community development in the West Unity, OH area. **Publications:** none. **Formerly:** (1999) West Unity Chamber of Commerce. **Conventions/Meetings:** monthly meeting.

Westerville

17202 ■ American Federation of State, County and Municipal Employees, AFL-CIO - Civil Service Employees Association Local Union 11
c/o Ronald Alexander, Pres.
390 Worthington Rd., Ste.A
Westerville, OH 43082-8331
Ph: (614)865-4700
Fax: (614)865-4777
Free: (888)OCS-EA11
E-mail: ocseacs@ocsea.org
URL: http://www.ocsea.org
Contact: Ronald Alexander, Pres.
Members: 35,691. **Local**. AFL-CIO. **Affiliated With:** American Federation of State, County and Municipal Employees.

17203 ■ American Legion, Dublin Post 800
5517 Ben Patrick Ct.
Westerville, OH 43081
Ph: (740)362-7478
Fax: (740)362-1429
URL: National Affiliate–www.legion.org
Local. **Affiliated With:** American Legion.

17204 ■ American Society of Appraisers, Columbus Chapter
c/o John W. Peck, Pres.
Porter and Peck Inc.
1001 Eastwind Dr., Ste.103
Westerville, OH 43081
Ph: (614)890-8384
Fax: (614)890-7351
E-mail: johnpeck@porterandpeck.com
URL: http://www.appraisers.org/columbus
Contact: John W. Peck, Pres.
Local. Serves as a professional appraisal educator, testing and accrediting society. Sponsors mandatory recertification program for all members. Offers consumer information service to the public. **Affiliated With:** American Society of Appraisers.

17205 ■ APICS, The Association for Operations Management - Columbus Chapter No. 99
PO Box 2068
Westerville, OH 43086
Ph: (614)286-4651
E-mail: sean.ryman@scotts.com
URL: http://www.apics-col.org
Contact: Sean Ryman CPIM, Pres.
Local. Provides information and services in production and inventory management and related areas to enable members, enterprises and individuals to add value to their business performance. **Affiliated With:** APICS - The Association for Operations Management.

17206 ■ Buckeye Bop Club (BBC)
4994 Wintersong Ln.
Westerville, OH 43081
Ph: (614)865-0764
E-mail: info@buckeyebop.org
URL: http://www.buckeyebop.org
Contact: Donna Conley, Pres.
Local. Promotes and preserves bop, swing, shag and jitterbug dance styles and the heritage of those styles of music that center on the beat and rhythm. Strives to enhance communication and promotional coordination of activities throughout the membership.

17207 ■ Central Ohio Association of Catholic Educators (COACE)
PO Box 1871
Westerville, OH 43086-1871
Fax: (614)775-0875
E-mail: coace@coace.com
URL: http://www.coace.com
Contact: Kathleen Mahoney, Pres.
Founded: 1968. **Staff:** 7. **Regional**. **Affiliated With:** National Association of Catholic School Teachers.

17208 ■ Central Ohio Shetland Sheepdog Association (COSSA)
c/o Lisa Harler, Sec.
7177 Northgate Way
Westerville, OH 43082
Ph: (614)797-4364
E-mail: meadowind@juno.com
URL: http://www.cossashelties.com
Contact: Lisa Harler, Sec.
Regional.

17209 ■ Columbus Beechcroft Lions Club
c/o TR Theis, Pres.
527 Tansy Ln.
Westerville, OH 43081
Ph: (614)296-6933
E-mail: trtheman@aol.com
URL: http://www.iwaynet.net/~lions13f
Contact: TR Theis, Pres.
Local. **Affiliated With:** Lions Clubs International.

17210 ■ Columbus Dental Society
663 Park Meadow Rd., Ste.F
Westerville, OH 43081-2880
Ph: (614)895-2371
Fax: (614)895-0060
E-mail: polly.cds@rrohio.com
URL: http://www.columbusdentalsociety.com
Contact: Ms. Polly Mowery, Exec.Dir.
Local. Represents the interests of dentists committed to the public's oral health, ethics and professional development. Encourages the improvement of the public's oral health and promotes the art and science of dentistry. **Affiliated With:** American Dental Association; Ohio Dental Association.

17211 ■ Delaware Lions Club
c/o Brian Vincent, Pres.
6615 Burbank Pl.
Westerville, OH 43082
Ph: (614)523-0517
URL: http://www.iwaynet.net/~lions13f
Contact: Brian Vincent, Pres.
Local. **Affiliated With:** Lions Clubs International.

17212 ■ Financial Executives International, Central Ohio Chapter
c/o Ms. Christina Leezer, Administrator
PO Box 0156
Westerville, OH 43086-0156
Ph: (614)565-5039
Fax: (614)901-0743
E-mail: cleezer@wowway.com
URL: http://www.fei.org/eWeb/startpage.aspx?site=ch_ohc
Contact: Mr. James May, Pres.
Local. Promotes personal and professional development of financial executives. Provides peer networking opportunities and advocacy services. **Affiliated With:** Financial Executives International. **Publications:** Newsletter. Alternate Formats: online.

17213 ■ Grove City Noon Lions Club
c/o James Anderson, Pres.
1239 Chatham Ridge Rd.
Westerville, OH 43081
Ph: (614)875-6333 (614)818-4588
E-mail: janderson@schoedinger.com
URL: http://www.iwaynet.net/~lions13f
Contact: James Anderson, Pres.
Local. **Affiliated With:** Lions Clubs International.

17214 ■ Home Builders Association of Central Ohio
c/o Thomas Hart
495 Executive Campus Dr.
Westerville, OH 43082
Ph: (614)891-0575
Fax: (614)891-0535
E-mail: tom@biahomebuilders.com
URL: http://www.biahomebuilders.com
Contact: James Hilz, Exec.Dir.
Local. Single and multifamily home builders, commercial builders, and others associated with the building industry. **Affiliated With:** National Association of Home Builders.

17215 ■ Military Officers Club of Central Ohio
c/o Lt.Col. Martin Stires
718 Linncrest Dr.
Westerville, OH 43081-2437
Ph: (614)882-4285
E-mail: stires718@aol.com
URL: National Affiliate–www.moaa.org
Contact: Lt.Col. Martin Stires, Contact
Local. **Affiliated With:** Military Officers Association of America.

17216 ■ National Association of the Remodeling Industry of Central Ohio
c/o Jim Turner, Pres.
285 N State St., Ste.102
Westerville, OH 43081

Ph: (614)895-3080
Fax: (614)895-3085
E-mail: info@nariofcentralohio.org
URL: http://www.nariofcentralohio.org
Contact: Shari Bates, Exec.Dir.
Founded: 1985. **Local**. **Affiliated With:** National Association of the Remodeling Industry.

17217 ■ Ohio Nursery and Landscape Association
72 Dorchester Sq.
Westerville, OH 43081-3350
Ph: (614)899-1195
Fax: (614)899-9489
Free: (800)825-5062
E-mail: billstalter@onla.org
URL: http://www.onla.org
Contact: Bill Stalter, Exec.Dir.
Founded: 1908. **Members:** 1,700. **Membership Dues:** corporate, $150-$400 (annual) • individual, $10-$75. **Staff:** 5. **Budget:** $1,820,275. **State**. Works to provide proactive leadership and guidance to the Green Industry. Offers services to increase the profitability of member firms, through personal and professional growth, addressing legislative and regulatory issues, research, marketing, education and technology. **Awards:** Award of Merit. **Frequency:** annual. **Type:** recognition • Distinguished Contribution Award. **Frequency:** annual. **Type:** recognition • Scholarship Awards. **Frequency:** annual. **Type:** scholarship. **Additional Websites:** http://BuckeyeGardening.com. **Publications:** *The Buckeye*, monthly. Magazine. Includes association news, Green Industry news, legislative update and article of contributing authors. **Price:** $25.00. **Circulation:** 2,200. **Advertising:** accepted. Alternate Formats: online • *Membership Yearbook*, annual • *Nursery Stock Survey*, annual. **Conventions/Meetings:** annual Central Environmental Nursery Trade Show (CENTS), with educational sessions provided by Ohio State University (exhibits) - always January. 2007 Jan. 22-24, Columbus, OH; 2008 Jan. 21-23, Columbus, OH.

17218 ■ Ohio Parks and Recreation Association (OPRA)
c/o Michelle Park, CPRP, Exec.Dir.
1069A W Main St.
Westerville, OH 43081
Ph: (614)895-2222
Fax: (614)895-3050
Free: (800)238-1108
E-mail: opra@opraonline.org
URL: http://www.opraonline.org
Contact: Michelle Park CPRP, Exec.Dir.
State.

17219 ■ Ohio Racquetball Association
6449 Lake Trail Dr.
Westerville, OH 43082
Ph: (614)890-6073
Fax: (614)890-9986
E-mail: ganim@earthlink.net
URL: http://www.ohioracquetball.com
Contact: Doug Ganim, Contact
State. **Affiliated With:** United States Racquetball Association.

17220 ■ Printing Industries Association
88 Dorchester Sq.
PO Box 819
Westerville, OH 43086-0819
Ph: (614)794-2300
Fax: (614)794-2049
Free: (888)576-1971
E-mail: pianko@pianko.org
URL: http://www.pianko.org
Contact: James A. Cunningham, Pres.
Members: 600. **Staff:** 15. **Regional**. Printing companies and suppliers to the graphic arts industry in Northern KY and OH. Provides programs, offers services, and promotes an environment that assists members to be community responsive and seeks to improve the industry. **Awards:** Print Excellence Award. **Frequency:** annual. **Type:** recognition. **Affiliated With:** Graphic Arts Technical Foundation; Printing Industries of America. **Publications:** *The Communicator*, quarterly. Magazine. Includes articles of interest to members. **Circulation:** 1,000. **Advertising:** accepted. **Conventions/Meetings:** annual conference, targets executives at member companies to assist them in growing their business.

17221 ■ Society of Physics Students - Otterbein College Chapter No. 5413
One Otterbein Coll.
Westerville, OH 43081
Ph: (614)823-1316
Fax: (614)823-1968
E-mail: drobertson@otterbein.edu
URL: National Affiliate–www.spsnational.org
Local. Offers opportunities for the students to enrich their experiences and skills about physics. Helps students to become professional in the field of physics. **Affiliated With:** Society of Physics Students.

17222 ■ Sweet Adelines International, Ohio Heartland Chapter
135 S Hempstead Rd.
Westerville, OH 43081
Ph: (614)891-0998
E-mail: wesing@ohioheartlandsings.com
URL: http://www.ohioheartlandsings.com
Contact: Donna Davis, Dir.
Local. Advances the musical art form of barbershop harmony through education and performances. Provides education, training and coaching in the development of women's four-part barbershop harmony. **Affiliated With:** Sweet Adelines International.

17223 ■ Westerville Area Chamber of Commerce
99 Commerce Park Dr.
Westerville, OH 43082
Ph: (614)882-8917
Fax: (614)882-2085
E-mail: info@westervillechamber.com
URL: http://www.westervillechamber.com
Contact: Janet Tressler-Davis, Pres./CEO
Founded: 1968. **Members:** 760. **Staff:** 3. **For-Profit**. **Local**. **Awards:** Outstanding Business Person of the Year. **Frequency:** annual. **Type:** recognition. **Recipient:** for involvement in business and the community. **Affiliated With:** Ohio Chamber of Commerce. **Publications:** *The Communicator*, monthly. Newsletter. **Price:** for members. **Circulation:** 850. **Advertising:** accepted. **Conventions/Meetings:** annual Westerville Music and Arts Festival (exhibits) - Westerville, OH - Avg. Attendance: 40000.

17224 ■ Westerville Lions Club
PO Box 597
Westerville, OH 43081
E-mail: info@westervillelions.org
URL: http://www.westervillelions.org
Contact: Kerry Robinson, Pres.
Local. **Affiliated With:** Lions Clubs International.

17225 ■ World Future Society, Columbus
c/o David J. Staley
The DStaley Gp.
8162 Baltimore Ave.
Westerville, OH 43081
Ph: (419)448-2173
Fax: (419)448-2124
E-mail: david@staleygroup.com
URL: National Affiliate–www.wfs.org
Contact: David J. Staley, Contact
Local. **Affiliated With:** World Future Society.

Westlake

17226 ■ American Association of Physicians of Indian Origin, Northern Ohio
c/o Vasu Pandrangi, MD
2314 Beaver Creek
Westlake, OH 44145
Ph: (440)816-2725
URL: National Affiliate–www.aapiusa.org
Contact: Vasu Pandrangi MD, Contact
Local. Represents Indian American physicians. Promotes excellence in patient care, teaching and research. Serves as a forum for scientific, educational and social interaction among members and other medical scientists of Indian heritage. Fosters the availability of medical assistance to indigent people in the United States. **Affiliated With:** American Association of Physicians of Indian Origin.

17227 ■ American Legion, Bay Village Post 385
PO Box 45075
Westlake, OH 44145
Ph: (740)362-7478
Fax: (740)362-1429
URL: National Affiliate–www.legion.org
Local. **Affiliated With:** American Legion.

17228 ■ Cuy-Lor Stamp Club
c/o Dennis Sadowski, Pres.
PO Box 45042
Westlake, OH 44145
E-mail: napoleon@voyager.net
URL: http://www.virtualstampclub.com/apschap_cuylor.html
Contact: Dennis Sadowski, Pres.
Local. Offers stamp collectors in western suburbs or Cleveland a chance to share their love of stamp collection, meets on second and fourth Friday monthly, sponsors annual show and bourse in October. **Affiliated With:** American Philatelic Society.

17229 ■ Greater Cleveland Mortgage Bankers Association (GCMBA)
Wherry & Associates
30200 Detroit Rd.
Westlake, OH 44145
Ph: (440)899-0010
Fax: (440)892-1404
URL: http://www.gcmba.net
Contact: Arthur Rotatori, Pres.
Local. Promotes fair and ethical lending practices and fosters professional excellence among real estate finance employees. Seeks to create an environment that enables members to invest in communities and achieve their business objectives. **Affiliated With:** Mortgage Bankers Association.

17230 ■ Lakewood Wyldlife
27070 Detroit Rd., Ste.202
Westlake, OH 44145
Ph: (440)808-9888
URL: http://sites.younglife.org/_layouts/ylext/default.aspx?ID=C-4479
Local. **Affiliated With:** Young Life.

17231 ■ National Association of Credit Management Greater Cleveland (NACMGC)
23850 Ctr. Ridge Rd., Ste.4
Westlake, OH 44145-4218
Ph: (440)871-7878
Fax: (440)871-8068
E-mail: nacmcleveland@aol.com
URL: http://www.nacmcleveland.com/document_1.html
Contact: Mr. Gary A. Paul CBA, Chm./CEO
Founded: 1986. **Members:** 250. **Local**. Works to promote credit management. Offers services and information to assist its members in all facets of their work activity. Provides a forum through which members come together for education, networking, and other business purposes. **Affiliated With:** National Association of Credit Management.

17232 ■ National Speleological Society, Cleveland Grotto
29242 Detroit Rd.
Westlake, OH 44145
E-mail: treasurer@clevelandgrotto.org
URL: http://www.clevelandgrotto.org
Contact: Bill Nordgren, Treas.
Local. Seeks to study, explore and conserve cave and karst resources. Protects access to caves and

promotes responsible caving. Encourages responsible management of caves and their unique environments. **Affiliated With:** National Speleological Society.

17233 ■ Northeast Ohio Romance Writers of America (NEORWA)
c/o Erin McCarthy
PO Box 45397
Westlake, OH 44145
E-mail: dkayc@aol.com
URL: http://www.neorwa.com
Contact: Debby Conrad, Pres.
Local. Works to provide networking and support to individuals seriously pursuing a career in romance fiction. Helps writers become published and established in their writing field. **Affiliated With:** Romance Writers of America.

17234 ■ Ohio Association of Ambulatory Surgery Centers (OAASC)
c/o Alexander Rintoul, Chm.
960 Clague Rd.
Westlake, OH 44145
Ph: (440)250-2447
Fax: (440)250-2498
E-mail: alexander.rintoul@uhhs.com
URL: http://www.oaasc.net
Contact: Lisa Spoden PhD, Exec.Dir.
Founded: 1997. **Members:** 6. **Local.** Works to enhance the quality of care in Ohio ambulatory surgery centers; provide legislative and regulatory representation for ambulatory surgery centers to advocate their interests and those of their patients; promote public awareness of ambulatory surgery centers; encourage high standards of professional conduct by organizations providing ambulatory surgical care. **Formerly:** (2001) Health Partners Select.

17235 ■ Ohio Speedskating Association
2418 Bassett Rd.
Westlake, OH 44145-2909
Ph: (440)892-9029
Fax: (440)899-0109
E-mail: info@ohiospeedskating.com
URL: http://www.ohiospeedskating.com
Contact: Tom Frank, Pres.
Members: 125. **State.** Seeks to encourage, advance, improve, and govern amateur ice speed skating in the state of Ohio. Sponsors competitions. **Publications:** *Racing Blade*, bimonthly. **Advertising:** accepted. Alternate Formats: diskette. **Conventions/Meetings:** annual meeting - always May.

17236 ■ Rocky River High School - Young Life
27070 Detroit Rd., Ste.202
Westlake, OH 44145
Ph: (440)808-9888
URL: http://sites.younglife.org/sites/ylriver/default.aspx
Local. Affiliated With: Young Life.

17237 ■ Trout Unlimited - Emerald Necklace Chapter
30182 Washington Way
Westlake, OH 44145
Ph: (440)835-0670
Contact: Christopher Steffen, Pres.

17238 ■ West Shore Chamber of Commerce
24600 Center Ridge Rd., Ste.480
Westlake, OH 44145-5617
Ph: (440)835-8787
Fax: (440)835-8798
URL: http://www.westshorechamber.org
Contact: John Sobolewski, Exec.Dir.
Founded: 1979. **Local.**

17239 ■ Young Life Cleveland West Shore
27070 Detroit Rd., Ste.202
Westlake, OH 44145
Ph: (440)808-9888
URL: http://sites.younglife.org/sites/clevelandwestshore/default.aspx
Contact: Andy Reid, Contact
Local. Affiliated With: Young Life.

17240 ■ Young Life North Coast Development
27070 Detroit Rd., No. 202
Westlake, OH 44145
Ph: (440)835-6555
Fax: (440)892-2513
URL: http://sites.younglife.org/_layouts/ylext/default.aspx?ID=A-AG224
Regional. Affiliated With: Young Life.

17241 ■ Young Life North Coast Region
27070 Detroit Rd., Ste.206
Westlake, OH 44145
Ph: (440)835-6555
Fax: (440)892-2513
URL: http://sites.younglife.org/_layouts/ylext/default.aspx?ID=A-AG83
Regional. Affiliated With: Young Life.

Weston

17242 ■ American Legion, Norcross-Meyers Post 305
12152 Roundhead Rd.
Weston, OH 43569
Ph: (740)362-7478
Fax: (740)362-1429
URL: National Affiliate–www.legion.org
Local. Affiliated With: American Legion.

17243 ■ American Legion, Weston Post 409
13160 Mill St.
Weston, OH 43569
Ph: (740)362-7478
Fax: (740)362-1429
URL: National Affiliate–www.legion.org
Local. Affiliated With: American Legion.

Wharton

17244 ■ Wharton Lions Club
c/o Thomas Kotterman, Pres.
8673 County Hwy. 78
Wharton, OH 43359
Ph: (419)458-2683
URL: http://www.lions13b.org
Contact: Thomas Kotterman, Pres.
Local. Affiliated With: Lions Clubs International.

Wheelersburg

17245 ■ Greater Portsmouth Area Board of Realtors
PO Box 388
Wheelersburg, OH 45694
Ph: (740)574-2974
Fax: (740)574-5713
E-mail: realtors1@adelphia.net
URL: National Affiliate–www.realtor.org
Contact: Pamela Jane Blume, Exec. Officer
Local. Strives to develop real estate business practices. Advocates for the right to own, use and transfer real property. Provides a facility for professional development, research and exchange of information among members and the general public. **Affiliated With:** National Association of Realtors.

17246 ■ Huntington Beagle Club
c/o Brian S. Partlow
24 Inlet Ct.
Wheelersburg, OH 45694-8643
URL: National Affiliate–clubs.akc.org
Contact: Brian S. Partlow, Contact
Local.

17247 ■ West Virginia Quarter Horse Association (WVQHA)
c/o Jerry Collingsworth
241 Burkes Ln.
Wheelersburg, OH 45694
Ph: (740)992-7519 (740)574-6707
URL: http://www.westvirginiaquarterhorseassociation.com
Contact: Tom Karr, Pres.
State. Affiliated With: American Quarter Horse Association.

Whitehall

17248 ■ USO of Central Ohio
c/o Jake Brewer, Exec.Dir.
161-185 N Yearling Rd.
In the Army Reserve Ctr.
Whitehall, OH 43213-1365
Ph: (614)692-3929
Fax: (614)692-3967
E-mail: usojake@cs.com
URL: http://www.allmilitary.com/coluso.htm
Contact: Jake Brewer, Exec.Dir.
Founded: 1942. **Members:** 200. **Local.** Serves the social, welfare, spiritual, recreational, and community involvement needs of U.S. service persons and their dependents. Seeks to provide programs and services that enhance the quality of life and improve morale. **Affiliated With:** USO World Headquarters.

17249 ■ Whitehall Area Chamber of Commerce
PO Box 13607
Whitehall, OH 43213
Ph: (614)237-7792
Fax: (614)238-3863
E-mail: whitehallchamber@hotmail.com
URL: http://www.whitehallchamber.org
Contact: Diane Hopper, Exec.Dir.
Membership Dues: business (varies with the number of employees), $120-$370 (annual). **Local.** Seeks to preserve and enhance the positive image of Whitehall community. **Awards:** Beautification Award. **Frequency:** annual. **Type:** recognition. **Recipient:** for showing pride in landscaping and creating building. **Computer Services:** Online services, message board. **Publications:** *Chamber Chronicle*. Newsletter. Alternate Formats: online.

Whitehouse

17250 ■ American Legion, Whitehouse Post 384
PO Box 2818
Whitehouse, OH 43571
Ph: (740)362-7478
Fax: (740)362-1429
URL: National Affiliate–www.legion.org
Local. Affiliated With: American Legion.

17251 ■ Glass City Corvette Club (GCCC)
11649 Reed Rd.
Whitehouse, OH 43571
E-mail: webmaster@glasscitycorvettes.com
URL: http://www.glasscitycorvettes.com
Local. Affiliated With: National Council of Corvette Clubs.

17252 ■ Veteran Motor Car Club of America - Black Swamp Chapter
c/o John Zimmerman, Pres.
6127 Texas St.
Whitehouse, OH 43571
Ph: (419)877-0885
URL: National Affiliate–www.vmcca.org
Contact: John Zimmerman, Pres.
Local. Affiliated With: Veteran Motor Car Club of America.

Wickliffe

17253 ■ American Legion, Brewer-Tarasco Post 7
29919 Euclid Ave.
Wickliffe, OH 44092

Ph: (740)362-7478
Fax: (740)362-1429
URL: National Affiliate–www.legion.org
Local. Affiliated With: American Legion.

17254 ■ Boys Hope Girls Hope of Cleveland
c/o Anne O'Donnell, Exec.Dir.
28700 Euclid Ave.
Wickliffe, OH 44092
Ph: (440)943-7615
Fax: (440)943-7614
E-mail: hopeneoh@bhgh.org
URL: National Affiliate–www.boyshopegirlshope.org
Contact: Anne O'Donnell, Exec.Dir.
Local. Affiliated With: Boys Hope Girls Hope.

17255 ■ First Catholic Slovak Ladies Association - Cleveland Junior Branch 453
1527 E 296th St.
Wickliffe, OH 44092
Ph: (440)944-4657
E-mail: fcsla_s522j453@hotmail.com
URL: National Affiliate–www.fcsla.com
Local. Affiliated With: First Catholic Slovak Ladies Association.

17256 ■ First Catholic Slovak Ladies Association - Cleveland Senior Branch 522
1527 E 296th St.
Wickliffe, OH 44092
Ph: (440)944-4657
E-mail: fcsla_s522j453@hotmail.com
URL: National Affiliate–www.fcsla.com
Local. Affiliated With: First Catholic Slovak Ladies Association.

17257 ■ Lake County Medical Society - Ohio (LCMS)
PO Box 103
Wickliffe, OH 44092
Ph: (440)833-0444
Fax: (440)833-0475
E-mail: info@lcms.net
URL: http://www.lcms.net
Contact: Mary Elyn Bove, Exec.Dir.
Local. Advances the art and science of medicine. Promotes patient care and the betterment of public health. **Affiliated With:** Ohio State Medical Association.

17258 ■ Wickliffe Area Chamber of Commerce
28855 Euclid Ave.
The Provo House
Wickliffe, OH 44092-2538
Ph: (440)943-1134
Fax: (440)943-1114
E-mail: chamber@wickliffechamber.org
URL: http://www.wickliffechamber.org
Contact: Susan E. Peters, Exec.Dir.
Founded: 1929. **Members:** 500. **Local.** Promotes business and community development in Wickliffe, OH. Makes available member benefits including workers' compensation and group health insurance and discount telecommunications programs. **Awards: Frequency:** annual. **Type:** scholarship. **Recipient:** for local high school seniors. **Affiliated With:** U.S. Chamber of Commerce. **Publications:** *Business Network*, monthly. Newsletter. **Advertising:** accepted • *Directory of Businesses*, periodic. **Price:** $10.00/copy. Alternate Formats: online. **Conventions/Meetings:** monthly board meeting - always second Tuesday, Wickliffe, OH • monthly breakfast • monthly luncheon.

Wilberforce

17259 ■ Central State University Association for Computing Machinery Student Chapter
c/o Robert L. Marcus
PO Box 1400
1004 Brush Row Rd.
Wilberforce, OH 45384
Ph: (937)376-6362
E-mail: rmarcus@csu.ces.edu
URL: National Affiliate–www.acm.org
Contact: Robert L. Marcus, Contact
Local. Biological, medical, behavioral, and computer scientists; hospital administrators; programmers and others interested in application of computer methods to biological, behavioral, and medical problems. Stimulates understanding of the use and potential of computers in the Biosciences. **Affiliated With:** Association for Computing Machinery.

17260 ■ Psi Chi, National Honor Society in Psychology - Central State University
c/o Dept. of Social and Behavioral Sciences
328 Wesley Hall - Box 1004
1400 Brush Row Rd.
Wilberforce, OH 45384-1004
Ph: (937)376-6144 (937)376-6052
Fax: (937)376-6468
E-mail: eperdomo@centralstate.edu
URL: http://www.psichi.org/chapters/info.asp?chapter_id=547
Contact: Edison Perdomo PhD, Advisor
Local.

17261 ■ Society of Manufacturing Engineers - Central State University S307
Central State Univ., Mfg. Engg. Dept.
PO Box 457
Wilberforce, OH 45384
Ph: (937)376-6525
Fax: (937)376-6679
E-mail: ajayi-majebi@csu.ces.edu
URL: National Affiliate–www.sme.org
Contact: Dr. Abayomi Ajayi-Majebi, Contact
Local. Advances manufacturing knowledge to gain competitive advantage. Improves skills and manufacturing solutions for the growth of economy. Provides resources and opportunities for manufacturing professionals. **Affiliated With:** American Society of Limnology and Oceanography.

Wilkesville

17262 ■ American Legion, Ohio Post 476
c/o Joseph Freeman
PO Box 2
Wilkesville, OH 45695
Ph: (740)362-7478
Fax: (740)362-1429
URL: National Affiliate–www.legion.org
Contact: Joseph Freeman, Contact
Local. Affiliated With: American Legion.

Willard

17263 ■ American Legion, Buckingham-Dermer Post 514
PO Box 148
Willard, OH 44890
Ph: (740)362-7478
Fax: (740)362-1429
URL: National Affiliate–www.legion.org
Local. Affiliated With: American Legion.

17264 ■ Ohio Motorists Association
106 Blossom Centre Blvd.
Willard, OH 44890-9312
Ph: (419)935-0950
State.

17265 ■ Plymouth Lions Club - Ohio
c/o Dan Melick, Pres.
271 Portage Path
Willard, OH 44890
Ph: (419)935-3802
E-mail: bigbasslak@aol.com
URL: http://www.lions13b.org
Contact: Dan Melick, Pres.
Local. Affiliated With: Lions Clubs International.

17266 ■ Veterans of Foreign Wars 3430
19 Woodland Ave.
Willard, OH 44890
Ph: (419)935-8532
Contact: Bob DeHoya, Commander
Local.

17267 ■ Willard Area Chamber of Commerce
PO Box 73
Willard, OH 44890
Ph: (419)935-1888
Contact: Todd Shininger, Dir.
Local.

Williamsburg

17268 ■ American Legion, Williamsburg Post 288
208 E Main St.
Williamsburg, OH 45176
Ph: (740)362-7478
Fax: (740)362-1429
URL: National Affiliate–www.legion.org
Local. Affiliated With: American Legion.

Williamsport

17269 ■ American Legion, Johnson-Miner Post 618
PO Box 246
Williamsport, OH 43164
Ph: (740)362-7478
Fax: (740)362-1429
URL: National Affiliate–www.legion.org
Local. Affiliated With: American Legion.

Willoughby

17270 ■ American Chemical Society, Northeastern Ohio Section
c/o Matt Gieselman, Chm.
2255 Par Ln., Apt. 1105
Willoughby, OH 44094-2900
E-mail: mtgi@lubrizol.com
URL: National Affiliate–acswebcontent.acs.org
Contact: Matt Gieselman, Chm.
Local. Represents the interests of individuals dedicated to the advancement of chemistry in all its branches. Provides opportunities for peer interaction and career development. **Affiliated With:** American Chemical Society.

17271 ■ American Legion, Palmer-Roberts Post 214
4304 Center St.
Willoughby, OH 44094
Ph: (740)362-7478
Fax: (740)362-1429
E-mail: alpost214@sbcyahoo.com
URL: National Affiliate–www.legion.org
Local. Affiliated With: American Legion.

17272 ■ Chagrin River Watershed Partners (CRWP)
PO Box 229
Willoughby, OH 44096-0229
Ph: (440)975-3870
E-mail: kdw@crwp.org
URL: http://www.crwp.org
Contact: Ms. Kyle Dreyfuss-Wells, Dir.
Local. Strives to preserve and enhance the scenic and environmental quality of the ecosystem of the Chagrin River.

17273 ■ Izaak Walton League of America - Western Reserve
c/o Jim Storer
1264 Tioga Trail
Willoughby, OH 44094

Ph: (513)868-3179
URL: http://www.iwla.org
Contact: Jim Storer, Contact
Local. Educates the public to conserve, maintain, protect, and restore the soil, forest, water, and other natural resources of the U.S. Promotes the utilization of these resources. Sponsors environmental programs.

17274 ■ League of Women Voters - Lake Erie Basin Committee
37081 Beech Hills Dr.
Willoughby, OH 44094
Ph: (440)942-8145
E-mail: claralm1@juno.com
Contact: Clara L. Maurus, Corresponding Sec.
Local.

17275 ■ National Active and Retired Federal Employees Association - Lake County2182
5357 Oakridge Dr.
Willoughby, OH 44094-3150
Ph: (216)585-2097
URL: National Affiliate–www.narfe.org
Contact: Richard F. Debaltzo, Contact
Local. Protects the retirement future of employees through education. Informs members on issues affecting the retirement. **Affiliated With:** National Association of Retired Federal Employees.

17276 ■ North Coast Lions Club
31701 Chardon Rd.
Willoughby, OH 44094
Ph: (440)944-3947
E-mail: wdburnet@aol.com
URL: http://northcoastlions.bravehost.com
Contact: Wallie Burnett, Sec.
Local. Affiliated With: Lions Clubs International.

17277 ■ USA Diving - Jeff Arnold Diving Enterprises
38432 Sheerwater Ln.
Willoughby, OH 44094
Ph: (440)975-0048
E-mail: warnold@ameritech.net
URL: National Affiliate–www.usdiving.org
Contact: Jeff Arnold, Contact
Local. Programs: Cleveland Area Diving. **Affiliated With:** USA Diving.

17278 ■ Willoughby Area Chamber of Commerce (WACC)
28 Public Sq.
Willoughby, OH 44094
Ph: (440)942-1632
Fax: (440)942-0586
E-mail: info@willoughbyareachamber.com
URL: http://www.wacoc.com
Contact: Nikki Matala, Exec.Dir.
Founded: 1903. **Members:** 452. **Membership Dues:** business (based on number of employees), $135-$325 (annual) • utility, bank, government, $350 (annual) • civic, $70 (annual). **Staff:** 2. **Budget:** $120,000. **Local**. Promotes business and community development in the Willoughby, Willoughby Hills, and Kirtland, OH area. Offers Workers' Compensation and Health Insurance at greatly reduced premiums. **Awards:** Distinguished Business. **Frequency:** annual. **Type:** recognition • Distinguished Citizen. **Frequency:** annual. **Type:** recognition • Distinguished Civic Organization. **Frequency:** annual. **Type:** recognition • **Type:** scholarship. **Recipient:** for a graduating senior. **Affiliated With:** U.S. Chamber of Commerce. **Publications:** *Membership Directory and Buyer's Guide*, annual • Newsletter, monthly. **Conventions/Meetings:** monthly board meeting • monthly meeting, networking opportunities.

17279 ■ Willoughby South High Instrumental Music Boosters
PO Box 1381
Willoughby, OH 44096-1381
E-mail: info@southbands.org
URL: http://www.southbands.org
Contact: Dennis Brothers, Contact
Local. Formerly: (2005) Willoughby South Instrumental Music Boosters.

Willoughby Hills

17280 ■ Veterans of Foreign Wars 4358
29412 White Rd.
Willoughby Hills, OH 44092
Ph: (440)944-1642
Local.

Willowick

17281 ■ American Culinary Federation Cleveland Chapter
PO Box 5124
Willowick, OH 44095
Ph: (216)621-2231
E-mail: timr_1@juno.com
URL: http://www.acfcleveland.com
Contact: Tim Rios CEC, Pres.
Local. Promotes the culinary profession and provides on-going educational training and networking for members. Provides opportunities for competition, professional recognition, and access to educational forums with other culinarians at local, regional, national, and international events.

17282 ■ American Legion, Willowick-Eastlake Post 678
570 E 328th St.
Willowick, OH 44095
Ph: (740)362-7478
Fax: (740)362-1429
URL: National Affiliate–www.legion.org
Local. Affiliated With: American Legion.

17283 ■ Lake and Geauga County Federation of Musicians - Local 657, American Federation of Musicians
c/o Mr. Frank Hess, Jr., Pres.
31755 Vine St.
Willowick, OH 44095
Ph: (440)943-9816
Fax: (440)943-9872
E-mail: local657@afm.org
URL: http://www.ncweb.com/org/mulocal657/index.html
Contact: Mr. Frank Hess Jr., Pres.
Founded: 1939. **Members:** 75. **Membership Dues:** individual, $150 (annual) • regular, $160 (annual) • life, $106. **Local**. Professional musicians. Seeks to improve the wages and working conditions of professional musicians. Provides opportunities for individuals and groups to participate in community summer concert programs and referrals for private performances. **Libraries: Type:** by appointment only. **Holdings:** audio recordings, video recordings. **Subjects:** local musicians. **Telecommunication Services:** electronic mail, local657@adelphia.net. **Affiliated With:** American Federation of Musicians of the United States and Canada. **Publications:** *Notes To You*, quarterly. Newsletter. **Advertising:** accepted. Alternate Formats: online. **Conventions/Meetings:** monthly board meeting • quarterly meeting.

17284 ■ Willowick Chamber of Commerce
30435 Lakeshore Blvd.
Willowick, OH 44095
Ph: (440)585-5765
E-mail: info@willowickchamber.org
URL: http://www.willowickchamber.org
Contact: Mary Elyn Bove, Exec.Dir.
Local. Promotes business and community development in Willowick, OH. **Publications:** Newsletter, annual, published 6 times.

Willshire

17285 ■ American Legion, Ohio Post 207
c/o Homer Pierson
PO Box 55
Willshire, OH 45898
Ph: (740)362-7478
Fax: (740)362-1429
URL: National Affiliate–www.legion.org
Contact: Homer Pierson, Contact
Local. Affiliated With: American Legion.

Wilmington

17286 ■ American Legion, Wilmington Veterans Post 49
PO Box 531
Wilmington, OH 45177
Ph: (740)362-7478
Fax: (740)362-1429
URL: National Affiliate–www.legion.org
Local. Affiliated With: American Legion.

17287 ■ Association for Computing Machinery, Wilmington College
c/o Jim FitzSimmons
ACM Cmpt. Club
251 Ludovic St.
Wilmington, OH 45177
Ph: (937)383-8590
Free: (800)341-9318
E-mail: acm@wilmington.edu
URL: http://www.wilmington.edu
Contact: Kathryn Springsteen, Dean of Faculty
Local. Biological, medical, behavioral, and computer scientists; hospital administrators; programmers and others interested in application of computer methods to biological, behavioral, and medical problems. Stimulates understanding of the use and potential of computers in the Biosciences. **Affiliated With:** Association for Computing Machinery.

17288 ■ Clinton County Board of Realtors, Ohio
PO Box 772
Wilmington, OH 45177
Ph: (937)382-4427
Fax: (937)382-6199
E-mail: borton-mcdermont@cinci.rr.com
URL: National Affiliate–www.realtor.org
Contact: Robert Germann, Exec. Officer
Local. Strives to develop real estate business practices. Advocates for the right to own, use and transfer real property. Provides a facility for professional development, research and exchange of information among members and the general public. **Affiliated With:** National Association of Realtors.

17289 ■ Clinton County Farmers and Sportsman's Association
PO Box 223
Wilmington, OH 45177
Ph: (513)382-1178
URL: National Affiliate–www.mynssa.com
Local. Affiliated With: National Skeet Shooting Association.

17290 ■ Clinton County Historical Society (CCHS)
149 E Locust St.
PO Box 529
Wilmington, OH 45177
Ph: (937)382-4684
Fax: (937)382-5634
E-mail: info@clintoncountyhistory.org
URL: http://www.clintoncountyhistory.org
Contact: Kay Fisher, Dir.
Founded: 1948. **Members:** 335. **Membership Dues:** individual, $20 (annual) • family, $30 (annual) • patron, corporate, $100 (annual). **Staff:** 2. **Local**. Individuals interested in the history of Clinton County, OH. Maintains Rombach Place, museum, and genealogy library. **Libraries: Type:** reference. **Holdings:** 2,000. **Subjects:** genealogy and history. **Publications:** *Clinton Chronicle*, quarterly. Newsletter. **Price:** included in membership dues • *Rombach Recorder*, quarterly. Newsletter. **Price:** included in membership dues.

17291 ■ Human Resources Association of Western Ohio
c/o Julie Butcher, Pres.
PO Box 930
Wilmington, OH 45177
Ph: (937)283-6034
Fax: (937)283-3877
E-mail: julie@sfminsurance.com
Contact: Julie Butcher, Pres.
Local. Represents the interests of human resource and industrial relations professionals and executives. Promotes the advancement of human resource management.

17292 ■ National Active and Retired Federal Employees Association - Clinton City 2204
317 Kenyon Dr.
Wilmington, OH 45177-1108
Ph: (937)382-5157
URL: National Affiliate–www.narfe.org
Contact: Russell H. Smart, Contact
Local. Protects the retirement future of employees through education. Informs members on issues affecting the retirement. **Affiliated With:** National Association of Retired Federal Employees.

17293 ■ Orienteering Wilmington College (OWC)
c/o Gregory Garland
251 Ludovic St., No. 413
Wilmington, OH 45177
Ph: (513)252-6453
E-mail: ggarland@wilmington.edu
URL: National Affiliate–www.us.orienteering.org
Contact: Gregory Garland, Contact
Local. **Affiliated With:** United States Orienteering Federation.

17294 ■ United Way of Clinton County
31 W Main St.
Wilmington, OH 45177-2236
Ph: (937)383-4846
URL: National Affiliate–national.unitedway.org
Local. **Affiliated With:** United Way of America.

17295 ■ Wilmington - Clinton County Chamber of Commerce (WCCCC)
40 N South St.
Wilmington, OH 45177
Ph: (937)382-2737
Fax: (937)383-2316
Free: (888)922-2250
E-mail: karenhaley@wccchamber.com
URL: http://www.wccchamber.com
Contact: Karen M. Haley, Pres.
Founded: 1957. **Local**. Promotes business and community development in the Clinton County, OH area. **Convention/Meeting:** none. **Publications:** *Buyer's Guide*, annual. Directory • Newsletter, bimonthly. **Advertising:** accepted. Alternate Formats: online.

Winchester

17296 ■ American Legion, Cameron-Ellis Post 242
PO Box 458
Winchester, OH 45697
Ph: (740)362-7478
Fax: (740)362-1429
URL: National Affiliate–www.legion.org
Local. **Affiliated With:** American Legion.

17297 ■ National Active and Retired Federal Employees Association - Highland County 2230
4660 Eckmansville Rd.
Winchester, OH 45697-9719
Ph: (937)695-1443
URL: National Affiliate–www.narfe.org
Contact: Charles W. Mercer, Contact
Local. Protects the retirement future of employees through education. Informs members on issues affecting the retirement. **Affiliated With:** National Association of Retired Federal Employees.

Windham

17298 ■ American Legion, Windham Post 674
PO Box 446
Windham, OH 44288
Ph: (740)362-7478
Fax: (740)362-1429
URL: National Affiliate–www.legion.org
Local. **Affiliated With:** American Legion.

17299 ■ Windham Lions Club - Ohio
c/o Walter Lininger, Sec.
8988 Wil-Verne Dr.
Windham, OH 44288
Ph: (330)326-2852
E-mail: judylin@config.com
URL: http://www.lions13d.org
Contact: Walter Lininger, Sec.
Local. **Affiliated With:** Lions Clubs International.

Wintersville

17300 ■ American Legion, Stevens-Christian-Memorial Post 557
1212 Two Ridge Rd.
Wintersville, OH 43953
Ph: (740)362-7478
Fax: (740)362-1429
E-mail: legionpost557@yahoo.com
URL: http://www.geocities.com/legionpost557
Local. **Affiliated With:** American Legion.

17301 ■ Belmont County Board of Realtors
406 Overlook Dr.
Wintersville, OH 43952
Ph: (740)264-0001
Fax: (740)266-6137
E-mail: tristmls@1st.net
URL: National Affiliate–www.realtor.org
Contact: JoAnn McClain, Exec. Officer
Local. Strives to develop real estate business practices. Advocates for the right to own, use and transfer real property. Provides a facility for professional development, research and exchange of information among members and the general public. **Affiliated With:** National Association of Realtors.

17302 ■ Steubenville AIFA
c/o Ronald E. Rutter
125 Main St.
Wintersville, OH 43953
Ph: (740)264-7458
Fax: (740)264-7852
E-mail: taxmen@prodigy.net
URL: National Affiliate–naifa.org
Contact: Ronald E. Rutter, Contact
Local. Represents the interests of insurance and financial advisors. Advocates for a positive legislative and regulatory environment. Enhances business and professional skills of members. **Affiliated With:** National Association of Insurance and Financial Advisors.

17303 ■ Steubenville Area Board of Realtors
406 Overlook Dr.
Wintersville, OH 43952
Ph: (740)264-0001
Fax: (740)266-6137
E-mail: tristmls@comcast.net
URL: National Affiliate–www.realtor.org
Contact: Russell Kuntz, Pres.
Local. Strives to develop real estate business practices. Advocates for the right to own, use and transfer real property. Provides a facility for professional development, research and exchange of information among members and the general public. **Affiliated With:** National Association of Realtors.

17304 ■ Veteran Motor Car Club of America - Steel Valley Chapter
c/o Robert H. Kaine, Pres.
159 Gumps Ln.
Wintersville, OH 43953
Ph: (740)264-7219
URL: National Affiliate–www.vmcca.org
Contact: Robert H. Kaine, Pres.
Local. **Affiliated With:** Veteran Motor Car Club of America.

Woodsfield

17305 ■ American Legion, Monroe Post 87
111 Home Ave.
Woodsfield, OH 43793
Ph: (740)362-7478
Fax: (740)362-1429
URL: National Affiliate–www.legion.org
Local. **Affiliated With:** American Legion.

17306 ■ Monroe County Chamber of Commerce (SOCC)
PO Box 643
Woodsfield, OH 43793
Ph: (740)472-5499
Fax: (740)472-5499
E-mail: monroechamber@gmn4u.com
URL: http://www.monroechamber.com
Founded: 1974. **Nonmembership**. **Local**. Promotes business and community development in Monroe County, OH. Sponsors festival. **Formerly:** (1991) Switzerland of Ohio Chamber of Commerce. **Publications:** Directory, periodic • Newsletter, periodic. **Conventions/Meetings:** annual Black Walnut - festival, features a variety of timber-related activities, stream engines, antiques, crafts, entertainment, classic and antique car show, and antique auction, along with fine foods - every second full weekend in October • annual dinner, officers update the members on activities of the past year and goals for the coming year, with guest speakers and entertainment - always March.

17307 ■ Monroe County Chapter of the Ohio Genealogical Society
PO Box 641
Woodsfield, OH 43793-0641
Ph: (740)483-1481
E-mail: karo@1st.net
URL: http://www.rootsweb.com/~ohmccogs
Contact: Karen Romick, Contact
Membership Dues: individual, $10 (annual). **Local**. **Affiliated With:** Ohio Genealogical Society.

Wooster

17308 ■ American Association of Bovine Practitioners, District 4
c/o Richard Wiley, DVM, Dir.
W Old Lincoln Way
Wooster, OH 44691
Ph: (330)264-7787
Fax: (330)262-5251
E-mail: npvc@bright.net
URL: National Affiliate–www.aabp.org
Contact: Richard Wiley DVM, Dir.
Regional. Works to promote the interests, improve the public stature, and increase the knowledge of veterinarians in the field of dairy and beef cattle practice. Elevates standards of bovine practice. Promotes understanding and goodwill among members. **Affiliated With:** American Association of Bovine Practitioners.

17309 ■ American Dairy Science Association - Ohio State University - Ag Tech Institute
c/o Wesley Greene
1328 Dover Rd.
Wooster, OH 44691
E-mail: greene.2@osu.edu
URL: National Affiliate–www.adsa.org
Contact: Wesley Greene, Contact
Local. **Affiliated With:** American Dairy Science Association.

17310 ■ American Legion, Wooster Post 68
PO Box 162
Wooster, OH 44691
Ph: (740)362-7478
Fax: (740)362-1429
URL: National Affiliate–www.legion.org
Local. Affiliated With: American Legion.

17311 ■ American Red Cross, Wayne County Chapter
124 N Walnut St.
Wooster, OH 44691
E-mail: jgareis@arcwayne.org
URL: http://www.arc-wayne.org
Local.

17312 ■ Apple Creek Lions Club
c/o Wilbur M. Miller, Sec.
478 Barnard Rd.
Wooster, OH 44691
Ph: (330)264-3591
E-mail: wilann@bright.net
URL: http://users.adelphia.net/~npssteve/district.htm
Contact: Wilbur M. Miller, Sec.
Local. Affiliated With: Lions Clubs International.

17313 ■ Ash YL club - Young Life
PO Box 1561
Wooster, OH 44691
Ph: (330)264-9077
URL: http://sites.younglife.org/_layouts/ylext/default.aspx?ID=C-1523
Local. Affiliated With: Young Life.

17314 ■ Asia's Hope
c/o David C. Atkins
PO Box 185
343 N Milltown Rd.
Wooster, OH 44691-0185
E-mail: dcatkins@yahoo.com
URL: http://www.asiashope.org
Contact: David C. Atkins, Contact
Local.

17315 ■ Associated Landscape Contractors of America, Ohio State University/Agricultural Technical Institute
c/o Kent Hammond, Faculty Advisor
1328 Dover Rd.
Wooster, OH 44691
Ph: (330)264-3911 (330)287-1331
Fax: (330)287-1333
E-mail: hammond.4@osu.edu
Contact: Gloria Wirt, Sec.
Local. Affiliated With: Professional Landcare Network.

17316 ■ Boys' Village - Young Life
PO Box 1561
Wooster, OH 44691
Ph: (330)264-9077
URL: http://sites.younglife.org/_layouts/ylext/default.aspx?ID=C-3033
Local. Affiliated With: Young Life.

17317 ■ Goodwill Industries of Wayne County (GIWC)
c/o Judy Delaney, Pres.
1034 Nold Ave.
PO Box 1188
Wooster, OH 44691
Ph: (330)264-1300
Fax: (330)264-3400
E-mail: goodwill@woostergoodwill.org
URL: http://www.woostergoodwill.org
Contact: Judy Delaney, Pres.
Founded: 1979. **Staff:** 25. **Budget:** $3,000,000. **State Groups:** 2. **Local.** Provides employment, training, evaluation, counseling, placement, and other workforce development services and opportunities for personal growth for persons with employment barriers. **Affiliated With:** Goodwill Industries International. **Publications:** *Bulletin Board*, quarterly. Newsletter. **Price:** free. **Circulation:** 1,000 • *Growing Goodwill Development*, quarterly. Newsletter. **Price:** free. **Circulation:** 500.

17318 ■ Habitat for Humanity in Wayne County, Ohio
1022 Heyl Rd.
Wooster, OH 44691
Ph: (330)263-1713
Fax: (330)263-1714
E-mail: habitat@sssnet.com
URL: http://wooster.net/habitat
Local. Affiliated With: Habitat for Humanity International.

17319 ■ Home Builders Association of Wayne and Holmes Counties
c/o Debbie Arnette
4973 Cleveland Rd., Ste.A
Wooster, OH 44691
Ph: (330)345-1293
Fax: (330)345-4820
E-mail: whhbainfo@aol.com
URL: http://whhba.com
Contact: Mindy Roberts, Pres.
Local. Single and multifamily home builders, commercial builders, and others associated with the building industry. **Affiliated With:** National Association of Home Builders.

17320 ■ Izaak Walton League of America, Wayne County Chapter
4859 Angling Rd. Ext.
Wooster, OH 44691-3206
Ph: (330)264-5497
E-mail: jk915@bright.net
URL: National Affiliate–www.iwla.org
Local. Works to educate the public to conserve, maintain, protect, and restore the soil, forest, water, and other natural resources of the U.S; promotes the enjoyment and wholesome utilization of these resources. **Affiliated With:** Izaak Walton League of America.

17321 ■ Lamplighter's Civic and Social Organization
PO Box 295
Wooster, OH 44691
Ph: (330)262-8426
E-mail: service@i3themes.com
URL: http://www.lamplighters.info
Contact: Anthony Yacapraro, Pres.
Local.

17322 ■ Main Street Wooster
377 W Liberty St.
Wooster, OH 44691
Ph: (330)262-6222
Fax: (330)262-5745
E-mail: downtown@mainstreetwooster.org
URL: http://www.mainstreetwooster.org
Contact: Sandra Hull, Exec.Dir.
Local.

17323 ■ Norwayne - Young Life
PO Box 1561
Wooster, OH 44691
Ph: (330)264-9077
URL: http://sites.younglife.org/_layouts/ylext/default.aspx?ID=C-4066
Local. Affiliated With: Young Life.

17324 ■ Ohio Haflinger Association (OHA)
c/o Sharon D. Leisure, Sec.-Treas.
1066 Bell Rd.
Wooster, OH 44691
E-mail: info@ohiohaflinger.com
URL: http://ohiohaflinger.com
Contact: Sharon D. Leisure, Sec.-Treas.
State. Affiliated With: American Haflinger Registry.

17325 ■ Phi Theta Kappa - Alpha Mu Xi Chapter
c/o Roger Baur
Agricultural Tech. Inst.
1328 Dover Rd.
Wooster, OH 44691-8905
Ph: (330)264-3911
E-mail: baur.1@osu.edu
URL: http://www.ptk.org/directories/chapters/OH/1014-1.htm
Contact: Roger Baur, Advisor
Local. Affiliated With: Phi Theta Kappa, International Honor Society.

17326 ■ Trout Unlimited, Clear Fork River 667 (CFRTU)
c/o Skip Nault, Pres.
2722 Taylor Dr.
Wooster, OH 44691
E-mail: nault.1@osu.edu
URL: http://www.cfrtu.org
Contact: Skip Nault, Pres.
Local. Affiliated With: Trout Unlimited.

17327 ■ United Way of Wayne and Holmes Counties
215 S Walnut St.
Wooster, OH 44691
Ph: (330)263-6363
Fax: (330)264-5607
Free: (800)247-9473
URL: http://www.uwwayneholmes.org
Contact: Peggy Schmitz, Pres.
Local. Affiliated With: United Way of America.

17328 ■ Vietnam Veterans of America, Chapter No. 255
c/o Gary Engelhardt, Pres.
PO Box 324
Wooster, OH 44691
Ph: (330)345-7914
URL: http://www.vvabuckeyestatecouncil.com
Contact: Gary Engelhardt, Pres.
Local. Affiliated With: Vietnam Veterans of America.

17329 ■ Wayne Area Human Resources Association (WAHRA)
c/o Lila Woods, Pres.
FJ Designs
2163 Great Trails Dr.
Wooster, OH 44691
Ph: (330)567-2906
Fax: (330)567-3925
E-mail: rlilley@rbbsystems.com
URL: http://www.ohioshrm.org/wayne
Contact: Ross Lilley, Pres. Elect
Local. Represents the interests of human resource and industrial relations professionals and executives. Promotes the advancement of human resource management.

17330 ■ Wayne County Genealogical Society
PO Box 856
Wooster, OH 44691-0856
Ph: (330)262-0916
URL: http://www.rootsweb.com/~ohwayne/wcgs.htm
Founded: 1964. **Members:** 200. **Local. Affiliated With:** Ohio Genealogical Society.

17331 ■ Wayne County Genealogical Society
c/o Corresponding Sec.
Box 856
Wooster, OH 44691-0856
Ph: (330)695-2122
E-mail: cag@bright.net
URL: http://www.rootsweb.com/~ohwayne/wcgs.htm
Contact: Cheryl Abernathy, Contact
Founded: 1965. **Members:** 135. **Membership Dues:** individual, $12 (annual) • family, $16 (annual). **Local Groups:** 1. **Local.** Preserves the history of Wayne County, OH and the history of its families. **Publications:** *Wayne Ancestors*, quarterly. Newsletter. **Price:** included in membership dues. **Conventions/Meetings:** monthly meeting - every 1st Saturday, except December in Wooster, OH.

17332 ■ Wayne County Historical Society (WCHS)
546 E Bowman St.
Wooster, OH 44691
Ph: (330)264-8856
Fax: (330)264-8823
E-mail: host@waynehistorical.org
URL: http://www.waynehistorical.org
Contact: Jeff Musselman, Pres.
Founded: 1904. **Members:** 650. **Membership Dues:** individual, age 60 and up, $15 (annual) • individual, $20 (annual) • family, $25 (annual) • patron, $50 (annual) • benefactor, $100 (annual) • corporate (silver, gold, platinum), $100-$500 (annual) • life (individual), $350. **Staff:** 2. **Budget:** $45,000. **Local**. Individuals interested in Wayne County, OH history. Seeks to preserve and display the history and artifacts of the area. Conducts educational program. **Libraries: Type:** open to the public. **Subjects:** county history and genealogy. **Affiliated With:** Ohio Association of Historical Societies and Museums. **Publications:** Newsletter, quarterly. **Price:** free for members. **Circulation:** 650 • Brochure, periodic. **Conventions/Meetings:** periodic workshop.

17333 ■ Wayne-Holmes Association of Realtors
145 E Liberty St.
Wooster, OH 44691
Ph: (330)264-8062
Fax: (330)263-4625
E-mail: wayneholmesrealtors@earthlink.net
URL: http://www.wayneholmesrealtors.com
Contact: Amy L. Scott, Exec. Officer
Local. Strives to develop real estate business practices. Advocates for the right to own, use and transfer real property. Provides a facility for professional development, research and exchange of information among members and the general public. **Affiliated With:** National Association of Realtors.

17334 ■ Wilson's Disease Association
c/o Kimberly Symonds, Exec.Dir.
1802 Brookside Dr.
Wooster, OH 44691
Ph: (330)264-1450
Fax: (509)757-6418
Free: (800)399-0266
E-mail: info@wilsonsdisease.org
URL: http://www.wilsonsdisease.org
Contact: Kimberly Symonds, Exec.Dir.
Local.

17335 ■ Woo YL Club - Young Life
PO Box 1561
Wooster, OH 44691
Ph: (330)264-9077
URL: http://sites.younglife.org/_layouts/ylext/default.aspx?ID=C-1528
Local. **Affiliated With:** Young Life.

17336 ■ Wooster Area Chamber of Commerce (WACC)
377 W Liberty St.
Wooster, OH 44691
Ph: (330)262-5735
Fax: (330)262-5745
E-mail: peeples@neobright.net
URL: http://www.woosterchamber.com
Contact: Sue Peeples, Associate Exec.Dir.
Founded: 1900. **Members:** 600. **Membership Dues:** base rate, commercial/professional/special service, $180 (annual) • financial institution (per million dollars of deposit), $21 (annual) • base rate, industrial (add $4.40/employee over 5), $180 (annual) • retiree, church, $40 (annual) • associate (employees of chamber members), $75 (annual) • non-profit (under 25 employees), $180 (annual) • non-profit (over 25 employees), $320 (annual). **Local**. Promotes business and community development in Wayne County, OH. **Awards:** Business of the Year. **Frequency:** annual. **Type:** recognition • New Business of the Year. **Frequency:** annual. **Type:** recognition • Small Business Person of the Year. **Frequency:** annual. **Type:** recognition. **Recipient:** for small business owners • Wall of Fame. **Frequency:** annual. **Type:** recognition. **Councils:** Wooster Area Safety. **Divisions:** Administration/Finance; Community Affairs; Industrial/Commercial Economic Development; Membership Retention; Retail Service Economic Development. **Programs:** Leadership Wooster; Legislative Affairs. **Publications:** *Chamber Connection*, monthly. Newsletter. **Circulation:** 1,300. **Advertising:** accepted • *Wayne County Industrial*, annual. Directory. Contains list of all manufacturers in the area. **Price:** free for members; $10.00 for nonmembers • *Wayne County Plat Book*. Contains the names of landowners in Wayne County. **Price:** $15.00 • Membership Directory, annual. Contains list of members alphabetically, by category and by contact name. **Conventions/Meetings:** annual dinner, introduction of the chamber's new board of directors - every January • annual Wayne County Home and Garden - show, features products for home and garden (exhibits) - every spring.

17337 ■ Young Life Wayne and Ashland Counties
PO Box 1561
Wooster, OH 44691
Ph: (330)264-9077
Fax: (330)828-0810
URL: http://sites.younglife.org/sites/wayneash/default.aspx
Local. **Affiliated With:** Young Life.

Worthington

17338 ■ American Academy of Pediatrics, Ohio Chapter
c/o Sandra Aured, Exec.Dir.
6641 N High St., Ste.200
Worthington, OH 43085
Ph: (614)846-6258
Fax: (614)846-4025
E-mail: ohaap@sbcglobal.net
URL: http://www.ohioaap.org
Contact: Sandra Aured, Exec.Dir.
Members: 1,300. **State**. Pediatricians. **Affiliated With:** American Academy of Pediatrics. **Publications:** *Ohio Pediatrics*, quarterly. Newsletter. **Conventions/Meetings:** annual symposium (exhibits).

17339 ■ American Federation of State, County and Municipal Employees Council 8 Ohio
c/o Patricia Moss, Pres.
6800 N High St.
Worthington, OH 43085-2512
Ph: (614)841-1918
Fax: (614)841-1299
Free: (800)282-3014
E-mail: organize@ohcouncil8.org
URL: http://www.ohcouncil8.org
State. **Affiliated With:** American Federation of State, County and Municipal Employees.

17340 ■ American Hiking Society - Buckeye Trail Association
PO Box 254
Worthington, OH 43085
Ph: (740)585-2603
E-mail: hhullss@frognet.net
URL: National Affiliate–www.americanhiking.org
Local.

17341 ■ American Legion, Leasure-Blackston Post 239
700 Morning St.
Worthington, OH 43085
Ph: (740)362-7478
Fax: (740)362-1429
URL: National Affiliate–www.legion.org
Local. **Affiliated With:** American Legion.

17342 ■ Buckeye Trail Association (BTA)
PO Box 254
Worthington, OH 43085
Free: (800)881-3062
E-mail: info@buckeyetrail.org
URL: http://www.buckeyetrail.org
Contact: Herb Hulls, Pres.
Local. **Affiliated With:** American Hiking Society.

17343 ■ Central Ohio Woodturners
c/o Craig Wright, Treas.
7634 Whitneyway Dr.
Worthington, OH 43085-5311
Ph: (614)481-3184 (614)885-9419
E-mail: centralohiowoodturners@yahoo.com
URL: http://www.centralohiowoodturners.org
Contact: Andi Wolfe, Pres.
Local. Represents amateur and professional woodturners, gallery owners, wood and equipment suppliers, and collectors. **Affiliated With:** American Association of Woodturners.

17344 ■ Institute of Internal Auditors, Central Ohio Chapter
c/o Amy Schwartz
1469 Clovenstone Dr.
Worthington, OH 43085
Ph: (614)466-9431 (614)331-9352
E-mail: mukesh.singh@bwc.state.oh.us
URL: National Affiliate–www.theiia.org
Contact: Mukesh K. Singh, Pres.
Membership Dues: regular, $115 (annual) • educator, $65 (annual) • student, retired, $30 (annual) • life, $2,100 • sustainer (government auditors only), $50 (annual) • organization ($65 per staff member over 5; $50 per staff member over 100), $425-$6,600 (annual). **Local**. Serves as advocate for the internal audit profession. Provides certification, education, research, and technological guidance for the profession. **Committees:** Attendance; Audit; Budget; Communications/Website; Government Relations; Marketing; Nominating; Research. **Affiliated With:** Institute of Internal Auditors. **Publications:** *The Spreadsheet*, monthly. Newsletter. **Advertising:** accepted. Alternate Formats: online.

17345 ■ Masonic Lodge
634 High St.
Worthington, OH 43085
Ph: (614)885-5318
Fax: (614)885-5319
URL: http://www.freemason.com
Contact: Mr. George O. Braatz PGM, Grand Sec.
Local.

17346 ■ National Association of Investors Corporation (NAIC)
PO Box 420
Worthington, OH 43085
Ph: (614)885-1480
E-mail: stocksmith@hotmail.com
URL: http://www.betterinvesting.org/chapter/centohio
Contact: Doug Smith, Pres.
Local. Teaches individuals how to become successful strategic long-term investors. Provides highly focused learning resources and investment tools that empower individuals to become better investors. **Affiliated With:** National Association of Investors Corporation.

17347 ■ Ohio Association of County Boards of MRDD (OACBMRDD)
73 E Wilson Bridge Rd., Ste.B-1
Worthington, OH 43085
Ph: (614)431-0616
Fax: (614)431-6457
E-mail: dohler@oacbmrdd.org
URL: http://www.oacbmrdd.org
Contact: Dan Ohler, Exec.Dir.
State.

17348 ■ Ohio Association of Physician Assistants (OAPA)
c/o Beth Adamson, CAE, Exec.Dir.
579 High St.
Worthington, OH 43085-4132
Ph: (614)436-4457
Free: (800)292-4997
E-mail: oapa@ohiopa.com
URL: http://www.ohiopa.com
Contact: Ray Wawrowski, Pres.
State. Physician assistants who have graduated from an accredited program and/or are certified by the National Commission on Certification of Physician Assistants; individuals who are enrolled in an accredited PA educational program. Purposes are to: enhance public access to quality, cost-effective health care, educate the public about the physician assistant profession; represent physician assistants' interests before Congress, government agencies, and health-related organizations; assure the competence of physician assistants through development of educational curricula and accreditation programs; provide services for members. **Affiliated With:** American Academy of Physician Assistants.

17349 ■ Ohio Health Information Management Association
c/o Amy Dotts, RHIA, Exec.Dir.
PO Box 824
Worthington, OH 43085-0824
Ph: (614)847-0160
Fax: (614)847-0153
E-mail: ohima-info@ohima.org
URL: http://www.ohima.org
Contact: Amy Dotts RHIA, Exec.Dir.
Founded: 1986. **Members:** 1,700. **Budget:** $200,000. **State**. United to ensure that timely and accurate health information is complete and available for the benefit of patients and providers, while playing a vital role in healthcare planning and research. **Affiliated With:** American Health Information Management Association. **Conventions/Meetings:** annual convention, health information management education, meeting and trade show (exhibits).

17350 ■ Ohio Optometric Association
PO Box 6036
Worthington, OH 43085
Ph: (614)781-0708
Fax: (614)781-6521
Free: (800)999-4939
E-mail: info@ooa.org
URL: http://www.ooa.org
Contact: Richard Cornett, Exec.Dir.
Founded: 1902. **Members:** 1,200. **Staff:** 8. **State**. **Affiliated With:** American Optometric Association. **Formerly:** American Optometric Association - Ohio Chapter. **Publications:** *Perspectives*, bimonthly. Newsletter. **Circulation:** 1,600. **Advertising:** accepted. **Conventions/Meetings:** annual East West Eye - conference (exhibits).

17351 ■ Ohio Society of Association Executives
c/o Mary Anne Knapke, Exec.Dir.
500 W Wilson Bridge Rd., Ste.80
Worthington, OH 43085
Ph: (614)846-0998
Fax: (614)846-1924
E-mail: osae@osae.org
URL: National Affiliate–www.asaenet.org
Founded: 1938. **Members:** 850. **Membership Dues:** individual, $135 (annual) • business, $60 (annual). **Staff:** 2. **Budget:** $250,000. **State**. Trade and professional association of chief executive officers and staff specialists. Promotes trade and professional groups. Provides educational seminars; monitors legislation. **Awards:** OSAE Achievement Awards Competition. **Frequency:** annual. **Type:** recognition. **Affiliated With:** American Society of Association Executives. **Formerly:** (1982) Ohio Trade Association Executives. **Publications:** *Executive News*, monthly. Newsletter • *OSAE Membership Roster*, annual • Newsletter. **Conventions/Meetings:** annual conference - August • monthly luncheon • annual Trade Show - workshop - Columbus.

17352 ■ Worthington Area Chamber of Commerce (WACC)
25 W New England Ave., Ste.100
PO Box 209
Worthington, OH 43085
Ph: (614)888-3040
Fax: (614)841-4842
E-mail: connect@worthingtonchamber.org
Contact: John Butterfield, Exec.Dir.
Founded: 1913. **Members:** 600. **Staff:** 3. **Local**. Promotes business and community development in the Worthington, OH area. Sponsors community social and promotional events. Maintains resource center. **Awards:** Small Businessperson of the Year. **Frequency:** annual. **Type:** recognition. **Affiliated With:** U.S. Chamber of Commerce. **Publications:** *Directory/Buyer's Guide*, annual • Newsletter, monthly. **Conventions/Meetings:** monthly Business After Hours - luncheon • monthly Coffee - meeting • monthly general assembly.

17353 ■ Worthington Convention and Visitors Bureau
579 High St.
PO Box 225
Worthington, OH 43085
Ph: (614)841-2545
Fax: (614)841-2551
Free: (800)997-9935
E-mail: cvbwmace@aol.com
URL: http://www.worthington.org
Local.

Wright-Patterson AFB

17354 ■ American Chemical Society, Dayton Section
c/o Dr. Hilmar Koerner, Chm.
Afrl/Mlbp Bldg. 654, Rm. 305
2941 Hobson Way
Wright-Patterson AFB, OH 45433-7749
Ph: (937)904-5091
Fax: (937)255-9157
E-mail: hkoerner@woh.rr.com
URL: National Affiliate–acswebcontent.acs.org
Contact: Dr. Hilmar Koerner, Chm.
Local. Represents the interests of individuals dedicated to the advancement of chemistry in all its branches. Provides opportunities for peer interaction and career development. **Affiliated With:** American Chemical Society.

17355 ■ American Meteorological Society, Wright Memorial
c/o Peter B. Roohr, Pres.
88 WS/WEA
2049 Monohan Way, Bldg. 91, Area B
Wright-Patterson AFB, OH 45433-7204
Ph: (937)255-2316
E-mail: peter.roohr@wpafb.af.mil
URL: http://www.geocities.com/ametsoc/
Contact: Peter B. Roohr, Pres.
Local. **Affiliated With:** American Meteorological Society.

17356 ■ Association for Unmanned Vehicle Systems International, Wright Kettering Chapter
c/o David Lanman, AFRL/VAOT
2130 8th St., Rm. 146
Wright-Patterson AFB, OH 45433
Ph: (937)904-8602
Fax: (937)656-9022
E-mail: david.lanman@wpafb.af.mil
Contact: David Lanman, Pres.
Founded: 1972. **Membership Dues:** individual, corporate, $50 (annual). **Local**. Government, industry and academic people interested in the promotion of unmanned systems. **Affiliated With:** Association for Unmanned Vehicle Systems International. **Publications:** *Unmanned Systems*, bimonthly. Magazine. **Conventions/Meetings:** annual conference (exhibits).

17357 ■ International Personnel Management Association, Dayton, Ohio
c/o Lisa M. Clinch, Pres.
4040 Ogdon Ave.
Wright-Patterson AFB, OH 45433
Ph: (937)255-0781
Fax: (937)255-7712
URL: National Affiliate–www.ipma-hr.org
Contact: Lisa M. Clinch, Pres.
Local. **Affiliated With:** International Public Management Association for Human Resources.

17358 ■ National Management Association, Van Kuren
NASIC/SCXD
4180 Watson Way
Wright-Patterson AFB, OH 45433-5648
Ph: (937)257-4694
E-mail: kbierley@dayton.net
URL: http://www.dayton.net/nma
Contact: Raelynn Bryan, Pres.
Local. Business and industrial management personnel; membership comes from supervisory level, with the remainder from middle management and above. Seeks to develop and recognize management as a profession and to promote the free enterprise system. **Affiliated With:** National Management Association.

17359 ■ National Management Association, Wright Chapter
c/o Betsy Combs
AFRL/HEOR
PO Box 33894
Wright-Patterson AFB, OH 45433
E-mail: betsy.combs@wpafb.af.mil
URL: National Affiliate–www.nma1.org
Contact: Betsy Combs, Contact
Local. Business and industrial management personnel; membership comes from supervisory level, with the remainder from middle management and above. Seeks to develop and recognize management as a profession and to promote the free enterprise system. **Affiliated With:** National Management Association.

17360 ■ Ohio Section of the American Physical Society (OSAPS)
c/o Robert L. Hengehold
Air Force Inst. of Tech.
Dept. of Engg. Physics
2950 Hobson Way
Wright-Patterson AFB, OH 45433
Ph: (937)255-3636
E-mail: robert.hengehold@afit.edu
URL: http://www.aps.org/units/osaps
Contact: Robert L. Hengehold, Contact
State. Represents individuals dedicated to the advancement and the diffusion of knowledge of physics. Develops and implements programs in physics education and outreach. Fosters the health of the profession through career and development initiatives and committees on women and minorities. **Affiliated With:** American Physical Society.

17361 ■ Society for Applied Spectroscopy, Ohio Valley
c/o James R. Gord, Chm.
AFRL/PRTS Bldg. 490
1790 Loop Rd. N
Wright-Patterson AFB, OH 45433-7103
Ph: (937)255-7431
E-mail: james.gord@wpafb.af.mil
URL: National Affiliate–www.s-a-s.org
Contact: James R. Gord, Chm.
Local. **Affiliated With:** Society for Applied Spectroscopy.

17362 ■ Society of Tribologists and Lubrication Engineers - Dayton Section
c/o Dr. Carl Hager
AFRL/MLBT, Bldg. 654
2941 Hobson Way, Rm. 136
Wright-Patterson AFB, OH 45433

Ph: (937)255-9016
Fax: (937)255-2176
E-mail: carl.hager@wpafb.af.mil
URL: National Affiliate–www.stle.org
Contact: Dr. Carl Hager, Contact

Local. Promotes the advancement of tribology and the practice of lubrication engineering. Stimulates the study and development of lubrication tribology techniques. Promotes higher standards in the field. **Affiliated With:** Society of Tribologists and Lubrication Engineers.

Wyoming

17363 ■ Sweet Adelines International, Queen City Chorus
Valley Temple
145 Springfield Pike
Wyoming, OH 45215-4261
Ph: (513)554-2648
E-mail: queencitychorus@yahoo.com
URL: http://www.queencitychorus.org
Contact: Lynn Hartmurt, Dir.

Local. Advances the musical art form of barbershop harmony through education and performances. Provides education, training and coaching in the development of women's four-part barbershop harmony. **Affiliated With:** Sweet Adelines International.

Xenia

17364 ■ Air Force Association, Wright Memorial Chapter No. 212
c/o Dennis Drayer, Pres.
Teradata - NCR
1639 Ashmont Ct., Ste.1000
Xenia, OH 45385
E-mail: dennis.drayer@ncr.com
URL: http://www.afadaytonwright.com
Contact: Dennis Drayer, Pres.

Local. Promotes public understanding of aerospace power and the role it plays in the security of the nation. Sponsors symposia and disseminates information through outreach programs. **Affiliated With:** Air Force Association.

17365 ■ American Legion, Foody-Cornwell Post 95
203 Bellbrook Ave.
Xenia, OH 45385
Ph: (740)362-7478
Fax: (740)362-1429
URL: National Affiliate–www.legion.org

Local. Affiliated With: American Legion.

17366 ■ American Legion, Ohio Post 517
c/o John Roan
610 E Main St.
Xenia, OH 45385
Ph: (740)362-7478
Fax: (740)362-1429
URL: National Affiliate–www.legion.org
Contact: John Roan, Contact

Local. Affiliated With: American Legion.

17367 ■ Dayton Miniature Society
c/o Roberta Sponenbergh
2120 Stewart Rd.
Xenia, OH 45385
Ph: (937)376-4218
E-mail: difrntdrumr@netzero.net
URL: http://www.miniatures.org/states/OH.html
Contact: Roberta Sponenbergh, Contact

Local. Affiliated With: National Association of Miniature Enthusiasts.

17368 ■ Fariborn High School - Young Life
PO Box 333
Xenia, OH 45385
Ph: (937)768-0049
URL: http://sites.younglife.org/_layouts/ylext/default.aspx?ID=C-4093

Local. Affiliated With: Young Life.

17369 ■ Greene County Chapter of the Ohio Genealogical Society (GCCOGS)
PO Box 706
Xenia, OH 45385-0706
Ph: (513)897-4862
E-mail: blindsey58@woh.rr.com
URL: http://www.rootsweb.com/~ohgccogs
Contact: Barb Lindsey, Pres.

Membership Dues: individual, $10 (annual) • family (2 people, same address), $13 (annual) • outside U.S., $15 (annual) • life - single, $100 • life - married couple, $150. **Local**. Collects and preserves historical records in the Greene County area of Ohio. Publishes genealogical materials compiled by the members of the chapter. **Telecommunication Services:** electronic mail, grapewin1@aol.com. **Affiliated With:** Ohio Genealogical Society. **Publications:** *Index to Dora C. Brentlinger's Beside the Stillwater*, periodic. Directory. **Price:** $6.00 plus shipping and handling • *Marriage Records, Volume A (1803-1840)*, periodic. Directory. **Price:** $15.00 plus shipping and handling • *Revolutionary War Ancestors of Greene County, Ohio*, periodic. Directory. **Price:** $25.00 • *Riddell's 1896 Atlas of Green County*, periodic. Directory. **Price:** $10.00 plus shipping and handling.

17370 ■ Greene County Historical Society (GCHS)
74 W Church St.
Xenia, OH 45385
Ph: (937)372-4606
Fax: (937)376-5660
E-mail: gchsxo@aol.com
Contact: Joan Baxter, Exec.Dir.

Founded: 1929. **Members:** 430. **Membership Dues:** family, $25 (annual) • single, $13 (annual) • senior citizen family, $15 (annual) • senior citizen single, student, $8 (annual) • sustaining, $100 (annual). **Staff:** 2. **Budget:** $65,000. **State Groups:** 2. **Local**. Current and former residents of Greene County, OH; business firms interested in the county's history. Promotes knowledge of Greene County history. Sponsors presentations; conducts annual Christmas Holiday of Homes Tour, Railroad Dinners, special exhibits, escorted tours, etc. **Libraries: Type:** open to the public. **Holdings:** 200. **Publications:** *Our Heritage*, monthly. Newsletter. **Conventions/Meetings:** monthly meeting - always second Monday.

17371 ■ Greene County Right To Life
PO Box 883
Xenia, OH 45385-0883
Ph: (937)376-5483
URL: http://www.pregnantpause.org
Contact: Ms. Lois Moore, Treas.

Founded: 1990. **Members:** 900. **State Groups:** 1. **Local**. Promotes the rights of the unborn., handicapped, minorities and any other innocent person whose right to life is threatened.

17372 ■ Habitat for Humanity of Greene County
PO Box 866
Xenia, OH 45385
Ph: (937)374-8726
E-mail: webmaster@greenecountyhabitat.org
URL: http://www.greenecountyhabitat.org
Contact: Jolene Westafer, Pres.

Local. Telecommunication Services: electronic mail, dwestafer@att.net. **Affiliated With:** Habitat for Humanity International.

17373 ■ Korean War Veterans Association, Greene County Chapter
c/o Howard W. Camp
430 S Stadium Dr.
Xenia, OH 45385
Ph: (937)372-6403
E-mail: campl19@aol.com
URL: National Affiliate–www.kwva.org
Contact: Howard W. Camp, Contact

Local. Affiliated With: Korean War Veterans Association.

17374 ■ Mothers Against Drunk Driving, Greene County
PO Box 83
Xenia, OH 45385
Ph: (937)372-1220
Free: (800)552-8641
URL: National Affiliate–www.madd.org

Local. Victims of drunk driving crashes; concerned citizens. Encourages citizen participation in working towards reform of the drunk driving problem and the prevention of underage drinking. Acts as the voice of victims of drunk driving crashes by speaking on their behalf to communities, businesses, and educational groups. **Affiliated With:** Mothers Against Drunk Driving.

17375 ■ National Active and Retired Federal Employees Association - Xenia 2163
757 Country Club Dr.
Xenia, OH 45385-1641
Ph: (937)372-5232
URL: National Affiliate–www.narfe.org
Contact: Bruce G. Conner, Contact

Local. Protects the retirement future of employees through education. Informs members on issues affecting the retirement. **Affiliated With:** National Association of Retired Federal Employees.

17376 ■ Ohio Bicycle Federation (OBF)
c/o Chuck Smith, Chm.
PO Box 253
Xenia, OH 45385-0253
Ph: (937)656-0814 (937)890-6689
Fax: (937)890-6689
E-mail: chuck@ohiobike.org
URL: http://www.ohiobike.org
Contact: Chuck Smith, Chm.

State.

17377 ■ Ohio Volkssports Association
c/o Thelma Goris
92 Kinsey Rd.
Xenia, OH 45385
Ph: (765)966-0391
E-mail: thelmajg@infocom.com
URL: http://us.geocities.com/ovawalker/
Contact: Thelma Goris, Contact

Local. Affiliated With: American Volkssport Association.

17378 ■ Xenia Area Chamber of Commerce (XACC)
334 W Market St.
Xenia, OH 45385-2843
Ph: (937)372-3591
Fax: (937)372-2192
E-mail: xacc@xacc.com
URL: http://www.xacc.com
Contact: Barbara Zajbel, Pres.

Founded: 1949. **Members:** 500. **Membership Dues:** business (base rate), $220 (annual) • club/organization, $85 (annual) • individual, $55 (annual). **Staff:** 2. **Local**. Promotes business and community development in the Xenia, OH area. **Affiliated With:** U.S. Chamber of Commerce. **Publications:** *Chamber News*, monthly. Newsletter. Contains information about business issues and community activities. **Advertising:** accepted. Alternate Formats: online • *Community Profile Book*, biennial. Booklets.

17379 ■ Xenia - Young Life
PO Box 333
Xenia, OH 45385
Ph: (937)768-0049
URL: http://sites.younglife.org/_layouts/ylext/default.aspx?ID=C-1480

Local. Affiliated With: Young Life.

17380 ■ Young Life Xenia/Fairborn
PO Box 333
Xenia, OH 45385
Ph: (937)768-0049
URL: http://sites.younglife.org/sites/Xenia/default.aspx
Local. Affiliated With: Young Life.

Yellow Springs

17381 ■ Dayton Dog Training Club
c/o Barbara Mann, Pres.
120 W South Coll. St.
Yellow Springs, OH 45387-1542
Ph: (937)293-5219
URL: http://www.daytondogtraining.com
Contact: Lynn Luikart, Corresponding Sec.
Local. Affiliated With: American Kennel Club.

17382 ■ ESOP Association, Ohio
c/o Ms. Deborah Stottlemyer, Pres.
YSI, Inc.
PO Box 279
Yellow Springs, OH 45387-0279
Ph: (937)767-7241
Fax: (937)767-9320
E-mail: dstottlemyer@ysi.com
URL: National Affiliate–www.esopassociation.org
Contact: Ms. Deborah Stottlemyer, Pres.
State. Affiliated With: ESOP Association.

17383 ■ Yellow Springs Chamber of Commerce
101 Dayton St.
Yellow Springs, OH 45387-1817
Ph: (937)767-2686
Fax: (937)767-7876
E-mail: info@yellowspringsohio.org
URL: http://www.yellowspringsohio.org
Contact: Elizabeth Newman, Exec.Dir.
Local. Promotes business and community development in Yellow Springs, OH area.

Youngstown

17384 ■ Alcoholics Anonymous World Services, Youngstown Area Intergroup
4445 Mahoning Ave.
Youngstown, OH 44515
Ph: (330)270-3000
URL: National Affiliate–www.aa.org
Contact: Beth Reese, Chm.
Local. Individuals recovering from alcoholism. AA maintains that members can solve their common problem and help others achieve sobriety through a twelve step program that includes sharing their experience, strength, and hope with each other. **Affiliated With:** Alcoholics Anonymous World Services.

17385 ■ American Institute of Architects Eastern Ohio
Ohio One Bldg., Ste.324
Youngstown, OH 44503
Ph: (330)743-1800
Fax: (330)743-1800
E-mail: mchristoff@olsjam.com
URL: http://aiaeoc.com
Contact: Mollie Christoff, Exec.Sec.
Professional society of architects. Fosters professionalism and accountability among members through continuing education and training; promotes design excellence by influencing change in the industry. **Affiliated With:** American Institute of Architects.

17386 ■ American Legion, Kelly-Ward-Varley-Memorial Post 732
2225 Glenwood Ave.
Youngstown, OH 44511
Ph: (740)362-7478
Fax: (740)362-1429
URL: National Affiliate–www.legion.org
Local. Affiliated With: American Legion.

17387 ■ American Legion, Mary P. Klaser Memorial Post 727
113 Green Bay Dr.
Youngstown, OH 44512
Ph: (740)362-7478
Fax: (740)362-1429
URL: National Affiliate–www.legion.org
Local. Affiliated With: American Legion.

17388 ■ American Legion, Ohio Post 504
c/o George W. Carver
408 Kenmore Ave.
Youngstown, OH 44511
Ph: (740)362-7478
Fax: (740)362-1429
URL: National Affiliate–www.legion.org
Contact: George W. Carver, Contact
Local. Affiliated With: American Legion.

17389 ■ American Legion, Road of Remembrance Post 472
323 E Indianola Ave.
Youngstown, OH 44507
Ph: (740)362-7478
Fax: (740)362-1429
URL: National Affiliate–www.legion.org
Local. Affiliated With: American Legion.

17390 ■ American Payroll Association, Youngstown, Ohio Chapter
c/o Carol Franket
Simon Property Gp.
100 DeBartolo Pl.
Youngstown, OH 44513
Ph: (330)965-5281
E-mail: cfranket@simon.com
URL: http://www.apayoungstownchp.org
Contact: Carol Franket, Pres.
Local. Aims to increase the Payroll Professional's skill level through education and mutual support. Represents the Payroll Professional before legislative bodies. Administers the certified payroll professional program of recognition. Provides public service education on payroll and employment issues. **Affiliated With:** American Payroll Association.

17391 ■ American Postal Workers Union, AFL-CIO - Youngstown Local Union 443
PO Box 443
Youngstown, OH 44501
Ph: (330)759-9626
URL: http://www.ypwu.com
Contact: Ray Stanar, Pres.
Members: 354. **Local.** AFL-CIO. **Affiliated With:** American Postal Workers Union.

17392 ■ Automobile Dealers Association of Eastern Ohio
c/o Mr. Steve Chos, Exec.VP
5353 Belmont Ave.
Youngstown, OH 44505
Ph: (330)759-1111
E-mail: adaeo@sbcglobal.net
Contact: Mr. Steve Chos, Exec.VP
Local. Affiliated With: National Automobile Dealers Association.

17393 ■ Better Business Bureau of Mahoning Valley
PO Box 1495
Youngstown, OH 44501-1495
Ph: (330)744-3111
Fax: (330)744-7336
E-mail: info@youngstownbbb.org
URL: http://www.youngstownbbb.org
Contact: Patricia B. Rose, Pres.
Local. Seeks to promote and foster ethical relationship between businesses and the public through voluntary self-regulation, consumer and business education, and service excellence. Provides information to help consumers and businesses make informed purchasing decisions and avoid costly scams and frauds; settles consumer complaints through arbitration and other means. **Affiliated With:** BBB Wise Giving Alliance.

17394 ■ Children's Rights Council of Tri-county, Ohio
2308 Bears Den Rd.
Youngstown, OH 44511
Ph: (330)789-3057
URL: National Affiliate–www.gocrc.com
Local. Affiliated With: Children's Rights Council.

17395 ■ Corydon Palmer Dental Society
985 Churchill Hubbard Rd.
Youngstown, OH 44505-1338
Ph: (330)759-5085
Fax: (330)759-7374
E-mail: cr@vrubenstein.com
URL: http://www.oda.org
Contact: Ms. Carolyn Rubenstein, Exec.Dir.
Local. Represents the interests of dentists committed to the public's oral health, ethics and professional development. Encourages the improvement of the public's oral health and promotes the art and science of dentistry. **Affiliated With:** American Dental Association; Ohio Dental Association.

17396 ■ Easter Seals Youngstown
299 Edwards St.
Youngstown, OH 44502
Ph: (330)743-1168
Fax: (330)743-1616
E-mail: easterseals@mtc.easterseals.com
URL: http://mtc.easterseals.com
Contact: Mr. Kenan Sklener, CEO
Local. Provides assistance and services to people with disabilities and their families. **Affiliated With:** Easter Seals.

17397 ■ Eastern Ohio Council of Teachers of Mathematics
6835 Colleen Dr.
Youngstown, OH 44512-3834
Ph: (330)758-4669
E-mail: dh@zoominternet.net
URL: http://www.ohioctm.org
Contact: Debbie Haverstock, District Dir.
Local. Aims to improve the teaching and learning of mathematics. Provides vision, leadership and professional development to support teachers in ensuring mathematics learning of the highest quality for all students. **Affiliated With:** National Council of Teachers of Mathematics.

17398 ■ First Catholic Slovak Ladies Association - Youngstown Junior Branch 029
2239 Oran Dr.
Youngstown, OH 44512
Ph: (330)792-5345
URL: National Affiliate–www.fcsla.com
Local. Affiliated With: First Catholic Slovak Ladies Association.

17399 ■ First Catholic Slovak Ladies Association - Youngstown Junior Branch 192
1403 E Florida Ave.
Youngstown, OH 44509
Ph: (330)782-2864
URL: National Affiliate–www.fcsla.com
Local. Affiliated With: First Catholic Slovak Ladies Association.

17400 ■ First Catholic Slovak Ladies Association - Youngstown Senior Branch 030
2239 Oran Dr.
Youngstown, OH 44511
Ph: (330)792-5345
URL: National Affiliate–www.fcsla.com
Local. Affiliated With: First Catholic Slovak Ladies Association.

17401 ■ Gardeners of America/Men's Garden Clubs of America - Men's Garden Club of Youngstown
c/o Joseph Alessi, Jr., Pres.
3857 Baymor Dr.
Youngstown, OH 44511

Ph: (330)792-4355
E-mail: alessijoepat@juno.com
URL: National Affiliate–www.tgoa-mgca.org
Contact: Joseph Alessi Jr., Pres.
Local.

17402 ■ Habitat for Humanity of Mahoning County (HFHMC)
1151 Manning Ave.
Youngstown, OH 44502
Ph: (330)743-7244
Fax: (330)743-0660
E-mail: hfhmc@sbcglobal.net
URL: http://www.hfhofmc.org
Local. **Affiliated With:** Habitat for Humanity International.

17403 ■ Mahoning County Chapter of Ohio Genealogical Society
PO Box 9333
Youngstown, OH 44513-9333
E-mail: mccogs@zoominternet.net
URL: http://mahoningcountychapterogs.org
Contact: Mr. Louis J. Joseph, Treas.
Founded: 1972. **Members:** 260. **Membership Dues:** single, $15 (annual) • family - living in same residence, $17 (annual). **Local**. Gathers and disseminates genealogical data. Assists local and out-of-town members in their research. **Awards:** Pioneer Families of Mahoning County Award. **Frequency:** periodic. **Type:** recognition. **Recipient:** for families with ancestors living in the county prior to 1851. **Affiliated With:** Ohio Genealogical Society. **Publications:** *Mahoning Meanderings*, 9/year. Newsletter. Contains local general news and queries. **Price:** included in membership dues. **Conventions/Meetings:** monthly meeting, educational and business - 3rd Monday; Austintown, OH • annual seminar (exhibits) - always in September.

17404 ■ Mahoning Valley Audubon Society
c/o Jeff Harvey, Pres.
PO Box 3214
Youngstown, OH 44512
URL: National Affiliate–www.audubon.org
Local. Works to conserve and restore natural ecosystems, focusing on birds and other wildlife for the benefit of humanity and the earth's biological diversity. **Affiliated With:** National Audubon Society.

17405 ■ National Electrical Contractors Association - Penn-Ohio Chapter
c/o Robert J. Lidle, Mgr.
755 Bd.man-Canfield Rd., No. J7
Youngstown, OH 44512-4300
Ph: (330)726-5525
Fax: (330)726-4906
E-mail: info@pennohioneca.org
URL: http://www.pennohioneca.org
Contact: Mr. Brian W. Keeling, Pres.
Regional. **Affiliated With:** National Electrical Contractors Association.

17406 ■ National Organization for Women - Greater Youngstown
c/o Mary Ann Baker, Pres.
4025 Market St.
Youngstown, OH 44512
Ph: (330)782-1511
URL: http://www.ohionow.org
Contact: Mary Ann Baker, Pres.
Local. **Affiliated With:** National Organization for Women.

17407 ■ National Safety Council, Northern Ohio Chapter
25 E Boardman St., Ste.338
Youngstown, OH 44503
Ph: (330)747-8657
Fax: (330)747-6141
Free: (800)715-0358
E-mail: info@nscnohio.org
URL: http://www.nscnohio.org
Contact: Larry Kingston, Exec.Dir.
Founded: 1952. **Members:** 414. **Membership Dues:** level 1 (1-10 employees), $215 (annual) • level 2 (11-49 employees), $250 (annual) • level 3 (50-100 employees), $275 (annual) • level 4 (101 employees, plus $.65 for each over 101), $300 (annual). **Staff:** 2. **Budget:** $200,000. **Regional**. Serving corporations and organizations in 30 counties of Northern Ohio. Promotes safety and health in the workplace, home and community. Provides training, including Advanced Safety Certification, OSHA compliance, Defensive Driving, First Aid, Bloodborne Pathogens, CPR and AED. Courses on-site and online. **Libraries: Type:** reference; lending; by appointment only. **Holdings:** periodicals, video recordings. **Subjects:** occupational safety, traffic safety, community safety, general safety and health. **Awards: Type:** recognition. **Computer Services:** Information services, links to many safety resources • online services, safety courses. **Boards:** Control; Executive. **Committees:** Budget; Program. **Affiliated With:** National Safety Council. **Publications:** *Safety Spot*, quarterly. Newsletter. Provides safety and health information. **Price:** free. **Circulation:** 1,000. **Advertising:** accepted • Bulletins, monthly. Provides safety and health information. **Advertising:** accepted.

17408 ■ Ohio Nurses Association - District Three
Williamsburg W
5669 Mahoning Ave., Ste.C
Youngstown, OH 44515
Ph: (330)799-4199
Fax: (330)799-5930
E-mail: d3ona5669@yahoo.com
URL: http://www.d3ona.org
Contact: Linda Warino, Exec.Dir.
Local. Works to advance the nursing profession. Seeks to meet the needs of nurses and health care consumers. Fosters high standards of nursing practice. Promotes the economic and general welfare of nurses in the workplace. **Affiliated With:** American Nurses Association; Ohio Nurses Association.

17409 ■ Ohio Senior Olympics
c/o Ms. Deanna Clifford, Sec.
25 E Boardman St.
Youngstown, OH 44503
Ph: (330)746-2938
Fax: (330)746-6700
E-mail: info@ohioseniorolympics.org
URL: http://www.ohioseniorolympics.org
Contact: Ms. Deanna Clifford, Sec.
Founded: 1979. **Regional Groups:** 8. **State Groups:** 1. **Nonmembership**. **State**. Promotes healthy lifestyles for people ages 50 and over through education, fitness and sports. Comprised of 8 regional games around the state of Ohio; hosts an annual sporting competition.

17410 ■ Penn-Ohio Chapter National Electrical Contractors Association
c/o Robert J. Lidle, Mgr.
755 Bd.man-Canfield Rd., No. J7
Youngstown, OH 44512-4300
Ph: (330)726-5525
Fax: (330)726-4906
E-mail: lidle@pennohioneca.org
URL: National Affiliate–www.necanet.org
Contact: Mr. Robert J. Lidle, Mgr.
Regional. Contractors erecting, installing, repairing, servicing, and maintaining electric wiring, equipment, and appliances. **Affiliated With:** National Electrical Contractors Association.

17411 ■ Planned Parenthood of Mahoning Valley
77 E Midlothian Blvd.
Youngstown, OH 44507
Ph: (330)788-6506
URL: National Affiliate–www.plannedparenthood.org
Regional. **Affiliated With:** Planned Parenthood Federation of America.

17412 ■ Reserve Officers Association - Department of Ohio, Mahoning County Chapter 42
c/o Col. Walter M. Duzzny, USAR, Pres.
66 Parkgate Ave.
Youngstown, OH 44515-3236
Ph: (330)740-2200 (330)792-7068
Fax: (330)740-2188
E-mail: wduzzny@mahoningcountyoh.gov
URL: http://www.roa.org/oh
Contact: Col. Walter M. Duzzny USAR, Pres.
Local. Promotes and supports the development and execution of a military policy for the United States. Provides professional development seminars, workshops and programs for its members. **Affiliated With:** Reserve Officers Association of the United States.

17413 ■ RSVP of Mahoning and Southern Trumbull Counties
c/o Donna M. Bruno, Dir.
5500 Market St., Ste.106
Youngstown, OH 44512-2616
Ph: (330)782-5877
Fax: (330)782-5001
E-mail: dbruno@volunteerservicesagency.org
URL: http://www.joinseniorservice.org
Contact: Donna M. Bruno, Dir.
Local. **Affiliated With:** Retired and Senior Volunteer Program.

17414 ■ Society of Industrial Archeology, Northern Ohio Chapter
c/o Tom Leary
4317 Chester Dr.
Youngstown, OH 44512
Ph: (330)788-8793
E-mail: teleary@ysu.edu
URL: National Affiliate–www.siahq.org
Contact: Tom Leary, Contact
Regional. Encourages the study, interpretation, and preservation of historically significant industrial sites, structures, artifacts, and technology. Promotes public awareness and appreciation of the value of preserving the country's industrial heritage. **Affiliated With:** Society for Industrial Archeology.

17415 ■ STARFLEET: USS Renegade
c/o John Hoppa
3980 Nassau Ct.
Youngstown, OH 44511
E-mail: ussrenegade2547@yahoo.com
URL: http://www.regionone.net
Contact: John Hoppa, Contact
Local. **Affiliated With:** STARFLEET.

17416 ■ Sweet Adelines International, Spirit of the Valley Chapter
Faith Community Church
1919 E Midlothian Blvd.
Youngstown, OH 44502-2909
Ph: (330)536-6547
E-mail: cookiemom51@msn.com
URL: National Affiliate–www.sweetadelineintl.org
Contact: Beverly Miller, Contact
Local. Advances the musical art form of barbershop harmony through education and performances. Provides education, training and coaching in the development of women's four-part barbershop harmony. **Affiliated With:** Sweet Adelines International.

17417 ■ Systems of Help Unlimited
c/o Sandra L. Robinson
PO Box 6483
Youngstown, OH 44501-6483

17418 ■ United Brotherhood of Carpenters and Joiners of America, Youngstown Local Union No. 171
348 W Rayen Ave.
Youngstown, OH 44502-1151
Ph: (330)747-6715
Fax: (330)746-6837
E-mail: carpenters171@att.net
URL: http://www.ovrcc.com
Local. **Affiliated With:** United Brotherhood of Carpenters and Joiners of America.

17419 ■ Vietnam Veterans of America, Chapter No. 135
c/o Thomas Moschella, Pres.
24 N Brockway Ave.
Youngstown, OH 44509
Ph: (330)799-3319
URL: http://www.vvabuckeyestatecouncil.com
Contact: Thomas Moschella, Pres.
Local. Affiliated With: Vietnam Veterans of America.

17420 ■ Visiting Nurse Association of Greater Youngstown
519 E Indianola Ave.
Youngstown, OH 44502
Ph: (330)782-5606
Fax: (330)782-5600
E-mail: vna@visitingnurseassn.com
URL: http://www.visitingnurseassn.com
Contact: Ms. Suzanne Tucci, Exec.Dir.
Founded: 1904. **Staff:** 85. **Budget:** $3,000,000. **Local.** Nursing professionals and allied health personnel working to bring medical skills, therapy, counseling, and personal care to homebound patients. **Libraries: Type:** not open to the public. **Holdings:** 50. **Subjects:** health. **Publications:** Newsletter. Alternate Formats: online.

17421 ■ Youngstown AFL-CIO Council
25 N Canfield
Niles Rd., Ste.80
Youngstown, OH 44515
Ph: (330)792-0861
Fax: (330)793-0611
Contact: Larry Fauver, Pres.
Local. Labor unions. Represents the interests of labor; lobbies for favorable legislation. **Affiliated With:** AFL-CIO.

17422 ■ Youngstown Aikikai
3624 Valerie Dr.
Youngstown, OH 44502
URL: http://www.usaikifed.com
Contact: Charles Cycyk, Instructor
Local. Affiliated With: United States Aikido Federation.

17423 ■ Youngstown Area Grocers Association
7301 W Blvd., Ste.C4
Youngstown, OH 44512-5270
Ph: (330)629-8383
URL: National Affiliate–www.fmi.org
Contact: Eileen Stanton, Admin.Asst.
Founded: 1899. **Members:** 250. **Staff:** 3. **Local.** Grocers, Store owners, and other food industry representatives in Mahoning, Trumbull, and Columbiana counties, OH. Provides information and education services to the food industry. **Awards: Frequency:** annual. **Type:** scholarship. **Affiliated With:** Food Marketing Institute; National Grocers Association. **Publications:** Bulletin, biweekly.

17424 ■ Youngstown BMW No. 120
c/o Don Jessop
4474 Lanterman Rd.
Youngstown, OH 44515
Ph: (330)799-3108
E-mail: ybmwrick@zoominternet.net
URL: National Affiliate–www.bmwmoa.org
Contact: Don Jessop, Contact
Local. BMW motorcycle owners organized for pleasure, recreation, safety, and dissemination of information concerning BMW motorcycles. **Affiliated With:** BMW Motorcycle Owners of America.

17425 ■ Youngstown Columbiana Association of Realtors (YCAR)
5405 Market St.
Youngstown, OH 44512
Ph: (330)788-7026
Fax: (330)788-4329
E-mail: sharyn@ycar.org
URL: http://www.ycar.org
Contact: Sharyn Braunstein, CEO
Local. Strives to develop real estate business practices. Advocates for the right to own, use and transfer real property. Provides a facility for professional development, research and exchange of information among members and the general public. **Affiliated With:** National Association of Realtors.

17426 ■ Youngstown Lions Club
c/o Josephine Polis, Pres.
6009 Frontier Dr.
Youngstown, OH 44514
Ph: (330)757-7294
E-mail: jpolis@parkvista.oprs.org
URL: http://www.lions13d.org
Contact: Josephine Polis, Pres.
Local. Affiliated With: Lions Clubs International.

17427 ■ Youngstown/Mahoning Valley United Way
255 Watt St.
Youngstown, OH 44505
Ph: (330)746-8494
Fax: (330)746-4525
E-mail: mzubick@ymvunitedway.org
URL: http://www.ymvunitedway.org
Contact: Donald Cagigas, Pres./CPO
Local. Affiliated With: United Way of America.

17428 ■ Youngstown Numismatic Club
c/o Thomas Linebaugh
3781 Baymar Dr.
Youngstown, OH 44511
Ph: (216)792-8030
URL: National Affiliate–www.money.org
Contact: Thomas Linebaugh, Contact
Local. Affiliated With: American Numismatic Association.

17429 ■ Youngstown SCORE
c/o Flora Pamer, Chm.
Williamson Hall, Rm. 306
Youngstown State Univ.
1 Univ. Plz.
Youngstown, OH 44555
Ph: (330)746-2687
Fax: (330)746-0872
E-mail: ysuscore@aol.com
URL: http://youngstown-score.org
Contact: Warren Jensen, Pres.
Founded: 1970. **Local.** Promotes business and community development in Youngstown, OH area. Conducts business education seminars and workshops to those wanting to start a business.

17430 ■ Youngstown State University Students In Free Enterprise
Dept. of Commun. and Theater
Youngstown State Univ.
1 Univ. Plz.
Youngstown, OH 44555-3631
Ph: (330)941-3633
URL: http://www.ysu.edu/stu_org/sife
Contact: Dr. Lawrence Hugenberg, Contact
Local.

17431 ■ Youngstown-Warren Inventors Association
McLaughlin & McNally
500 City Centre 1
Youngstown, OH 44503
Ph: (330)744-4481
E-mail: rjh@mm-lawyers.com
URL: National Affiliate–www.uiausa.org
Contact: Robert J. Herberger, Contact
Local. Represents inventors' organizations and providers of services to inventors. Seeks to facilitate the development of innovation conceived by independent inventors. Provides leadership and support services to inventors and inventors' organizations. **Affiliated With:** United Inventors Association of the U.S.A.

17432 ■ Youngstown/Warren Regional Chamber of Commerce
11 Fed. Plz. Central, Ste.1600
Youngstown, OH 44503
Ph: (330)744-2131
Fax: (330)746-0330
E-mail: kim@regionalchamber.com
URL: http://www.regionalchamber.com
Contact: Thomas M. Humphries, Pres./CEO
Local.

Zanesfield

17433 ■ Christian Camp and Conference Association, Ohio Section
c/o Matt Wiley, Pres.
Marmon Valley Farm Camp
7754 State Rte. 292 S
Zanesfield, OH 43360
Ph: (937)593-8000
URL: http://ohio.ccca-us.org
Contact: Matt Wiley, Pres.
State. Affiliated With: Christian Camping International/U.S.A.

Zanesville

17434 ■ American Cancer Society, Muskingum Area
3612 Maple Ave.
Zanesville, OH 43702
Ph: (740)454-2589
Fax: (740)374-5168
Free: (888)227-6446
URL: http://www.cancer.org
Local. Affiliated With: American Cancer Society.

17435 ■ American Legion Auxiliary of Ohio
c/o Pamela Jackson, Sec.-Treas.
PO Box 2760
Zanesville, OH 43702
Ph: (740)452-8245
Fax: (740)452-2620
E-mail: ala_pam@rrohio.com
Contact: Pamela Jackson, Sec.-Treas.
Founded: 1920. **Members:** 56,000. **Staff:** 4. **Local Groups:** 480. **State. Affiliated With:** American Legion Auxiliary.

17436 ■ American Legion, Zanesville Post 29
27 S 3rd St.
Zanesville, OH 43701
Ph: (740)362-7478
Fax: (740)362-1429
URL: National Affiliate–www.legion.org
Local. Affiliated With: American Legion.

17437 ■ Duncan Falls-Philo Lions Club
1770 Candlestick Dr.
Zanesville, OH 43701
Ph: (740)452-6667
E-mail: dstyo@msmisp.com
URL: http://duncanfallsphilooh.lionwap.org
Contact: Gerald Tyo, Sec.
Local. Affiliated With: Lions Clubs International.

17438 ■ Girl Scouts - Heart of Ohio
PO Box 370
Zanesville, OH 43702-0370
Ph: (740)454-8563
Fax: (740)454-8111
Free: (800)292-6759
E-mail: info@gsheart.org
URL: http://www.gsheart.org
Contact: Yvette Livers, Exec.Dir.
Local. Young girls and adult volunteers, corporate, government and individual supporters. Strives to develop potential and leadership skills among its members. Conducts trainings, educational programs and outdoor activities.

17439 ■ International Brotherhood of Teamsters, Chauffeurs, Warehousemen and Helpers of America, AFL-CIO - Local Union 637
PO Box 2746
100 Timber Run Rd.
Zanesville, OH 43702-2746
Ph: (740)453-2102
Fax: (740)453-2410
E-mail: teamsters@y-city.net
URL: http://my.sota-oh.com/~teamsters
Contact: Doug Greiner, Pres./Business Representative
Members: 1,200. **Local. Affiliated With:** International Brotherhood of Teamsters.

17440 ■ National Organization for Women - Zanesville
c/o Lace Lynch
PO Box 3524
Zanesville, OH 43702
Ph: (740)452-4411
E-mail: lacel@core.com
URL: http://www.ohionow.org
Contact: Lace Lynch, Contact
Local. Affiliated With: National Organization for Women.

17441 ■ Ohio Turfgrass Foundation (OTF)
c/o Kevin Thompson, Exec.Dir.
1100-H Brandywine Blvd.
Zanesville, OH 43702-3388
Fax: (740)452-2552
Free: (888)683-3445
E-mail: info@ohioturfgrass.org
URL: http://www.ohioturfgrass.org
Contact: Kevin Thompson, Exec.Dir.
State. Works for the improvement of turfgrass for golf courses, athletic fields, parks, roadsides, cemeteries, commercial and residential lawns.

17442 ■ Phi Theta Kappa - Alpha Alpha Alpha Chapter
c/o Ronald Huth
1555 Newark Rd.
Zanesville, OH 43701-2626
Ph: (740)588-1348
E-mail: rhuth@zanestate.edu
URL: http://www.ptk.org/directories/chapters/OH/315-1.htm
Contact: Ronald Huth, Advisor
Local. Affiliated With: Phi Theta Kappa, International Honor Society.

17443 ■ Ruffed Grouse Society, Three Rivers Chapter
c/o Joe Miller
445 Airport Rd.
Zanesville, OH 43701
Ph: (740)452-9664
URL: National Affiliate–www.ruffedgrousesociety.org
Contact: Joe Miller, Contact
Local. Affiliated With: Ruffed Grouse Society.

17444 ■ Salt Creek Beagle Club
c/o Marilyn J. Hartman
4250 Arch Hill Rd.
Zanesville, OH 43701-7131
URL: National Affiliate–clubs.akc.org
Contact: Marilyn J. Hartman, Contact
Local.

17445 ■ United Way of Muskingum, Perry, and Morgan Counties
526 Putnam Ave.
Zanesville, OH 43701-4933
Ph: (740)454-6872
URL: National Affiliate–national.unitedway.org
Local. Affiliated With: United Way of America.

17446 ■ Vietnam Veterans of America, Chapter No. 42
c/o Jerry B. Combs, Pres.
334 Shinnick St.
Zanesville, OH 43701
Ph: (740)455-3895
URL: http://www.vvabuckeyestatecouncil.com
Contact: Jerry B. Combs, Pres.
Local. Affiliated With: Vietnam Veterans of America.

17447 ■ Voice of the Retarded, Ohio
3805 Old Wheeling Rd.
Zanesville, OH 43701
Ph: (740)453-4737
E-mail: redbud@1st.net
URL: National Affiliate–www.vor.net
Contact: Tawny S. Gregg, Dir.
State. Affiliated With: Voice of the Retarded.

17448 ■ Zanesville Area AIFA
c/o Kenneth A. Johnson, Pres.
309 Main St.
Zanesville, OH 43701
Ph: (740)450-1550
Fax: (740)450-1987
E-mail: brown11@nationw.de.com
URL: National Affiliate–naifa.org
Contact: Kenneth A. Johnson, Pres.
Local. Represents the interests of insurance and financial advisors. Advocates for a positive legislative and regulatory environment. Enhances business and professional skills of members. **Affiliated With:** National Association of Insurance and Financial Advisors.

17449 ■ Zanesville - Muskingum County Chamber of Commerce
205 N 5th St.
Zanesville, OH 43701
Ph: (740)455-8282
Fax: (740)454-2963
Free: (800)743-2303
E-mail: kashby@zmchamber.com
URL: http://www.zmchamber.com
Contact: Thomas C. Poorman, Pres.
Founded: 1905. **Members:** 825. **Membership Dues:** business (based on number of employees), $195-$3,895 (annual) • individual, professional firm (per associate), $95 (annual) • farm, $140 (annual) • bank (per million in deposits), $15 (annual) • nonprofit, $85 (annual) • education/government (base), mobile home park (base), $195 (annual). **Staff:** 3. **Local.** Promotes business and community development in the Muskingum County, OH area. **Computer Services:** Information services, directory search • online services, free listing for members in 2 websites. **Publications:** *Commerce*, annual. Handbook. Includes membership directory. Alternate Formats: online • *Legislative Directory*, annual. Contains information about Ohio's state and federal legislators. • *Voice*, monthly. Newsletter. **Advertising:** accepted. Alternate Formats: online.

Abrams

17450 ■ American Legion, Machickanee Post 523
5970 Cedar St.
Abrams, WI 54101
Ph: (608)745-1090
Fax: (608)745-0179
URL: National Affiliate–www.legion.org
Local. Affiliated With: American Legion.

17451 ■ Wisconsin Choral Directors Association (WCDA)
6802 Miller Rd.
Abrams, WI 54101-9799
Ph: (920)826-2832
Fax: (920)826-2832
E-mail: wcda@wischoral.org
URL: http://www.ensemble.org/assoc/wcda/
Contact: Lynn Seidl, Pres.
Membership Dues: associate/active, $75 (annual) • student, $30 (annual) • life, $2,000. **State.** Maintains the choral music of Wisconsin. Generates activities and interests in the choral arts. Encourages choral directors in all areas of choral life. **Awards:** Morris D. Hayes Award. **Frequency:** annual. **Type:** recognition. **Recipient:** for outstanding contribution to choral music in Wisconsin • Outstanding Church Musician Award. **Frequency:** annual. **Type:** recognition. **Recipient:** for exemplary contribution to music in the church • Outstanding Young Choral Director Award. **Frequency:** annual. **Type:** recognition. **Recipient:** for creating an impact on the quality and visibility of choral music • The Stanley Custer Distinguished Service Award. **Frequency:** annual. **Type:** recognition. **Recipient:** for exemplary contribution to the organization. **Boards:** Advisory. **Subgroups:** Repertoire and Standards. **Affiliated With:** American Choral Directors Association. **Publications:** *Soundings*, 3/year. Newsletter. **Conventions/Meetings:** annual Men's and Women's Choir - festival.

Adams

17452 ■ Adams County Chamber of Commerce and Tourism (ACCC&T)
252 S Main St.
PO Box 576
Adams, WI 53910
Ph: (608)339-6997
Fax: (608)339-8079
Free: (888)339-6997
E-mail: chamber@adamscountywi.com
URL: http://www.adamscountywi.com
Contact: Alice Parr, Exec.Dir.
Founded: 1945. **Members:** 126. **Membership Dues:** basic small business, $154 (annual). **Staff:** 1. **Budget:** $48,000. **Local.** Promotes business and community development in Adams County, WI. Sponsors annual Crazy Days business and retail festival, Castle Rock Triathlon, Waterfest Boat Parade and Holiday Parade & seasonal events. **Awards:** High School Outstanding Student/s. **Frequency:** annual. **Type:** recognition • JEM Grant from the Wisconsin State Department of Tourism. **Frequency:** annual. **Type:** recognition. **Computer Services:** Mailing lists. **Subcommittees:** Marketing. **Formerly:** Adams-Friendship Chamber of Commerce. **Publications:** *Adams County Chamber of Commerce Newsletter*, quarterly • *Adams County Visitors Guide*, annual. Membership Directory. **Conventions/Meetings:** monthly meeting - always 4th Tuesday.

17453 ■ American Legion, Red Cloud Post 250
PO Box 755
Adams, WI 53910
Ph: (608)745-1090
Fax: (608)745-0179
URL: National Affiliate–www.legion.org
Local. Affiliated With: American Legion.

17454 ■ Paws
c/o V. I. Nelson
417 Linden, Box 585
Adams, WI 53910-9514
Ph: (608)339-9572 (608)339-9383
Fax: (608)339-9383
Contact: Vi Nelson, Dir.
Founded: 2001. **Members:** 400. **Staff:** 6. **Regional Groups:** 5. **State Groups:** 2. **Local Groups:** 3. **Local.**

Adell

17455 ■ American Legion, Triangle B Post 193
RR 1
Adell, WI 53001
Ph: (608)745-1090
Fax: (608)745-0179
URL: National Affiliate–www.legion.org
Local. Affiliated With: American Legion.

17456 ■ American Legion, Wisconsin Post 462
c/o Russell W. Mulder
214 Osius St.
Adell, WI 53001
Ph: (608)745-1090
Fax: (608)745-0179
URL: National Affiliate–www.legion.org
Contact: Russell W. Mulder, Contact
Local. Affiliated With: American Legion.

17457 ■ Plumbing-Heating-Cooling Contractors Association, Sheboygan County
c/o Mr. Jim Eberhardt
400 Wisconsin St., Box 98
Adell, WI 53001
Ph: (920)994-9203
Fax: (920)994-2346
E-mail: jnhardt@excel.net
URL: National Affiliate–www.phccweb.org
Contact: Mr. Jim Eberhardt, Contact
Local. Represents the plumbing, heating and cooling contractors. Promotes the construction industry. Protects the environment, health, safety and comfort of society. **Affiliated With:** Plumbing-Heating-Cooling Contractors Association.

Albany

17458 ■ American Legion, Mc-Dermott-Steindorf Post 144
300 N Water
Albany, WI 53502
Ph: (608)745-1090
Fax: (608)745-0179
URL: National Affiliate–www.legion.org
Local. Affiliated With: American Legion.

Algoma

17459 ■ Algoma Area Chamber of Commerce (AACC)
1226 Lake St.
Algoma, WI 54201
Ph: (920)487-2041
Fax: (920)487-5519
Free: (800)498-4888
E-mail: chamber@algoma.org
URL: http://www.algoma.org
Founded: 1946. **Members:** 210. **Membership Dues:** business, $175 (annual). **Staff:** 4. **Budget:** $100,000. **Local Groups:** 4. **Local.** Individuals seeking to improve the business climate and promote community development in the Algoma, WI area. Sponsors festivals, promotes tourism and operates visitor center. **Libraries: Type:** open to the public; reference. **Subjects:** local history, Algoma record Herald 1873-present, birth/death/marriage records. **Awards:** Business of the Year. **Frequency:** annual. **Type:** recognition • Educator of the Year. **Frequency:** annual. **Type:** recognition • Industry of the Year. **Frequency:** annual. **Type:** recognition. **Publications:** *Chamber Beacon*, quarterly. Newsletter. **Conventions/Meetings:** annual Doll and Teddy Bear Show and Sale • annual Harvestfest - festival • annual Heritage Day - meeting • annual Holiday Park of Lights and Parade - show (exhibits) • annual meeting • annual Shanty Days - meeting • annual Wet Whistle Wine Fest - festival.

17460 ■ American Legion, Wisconsin Post 236
c/o Ernest Haucke
94 Clark St.
Algoma, WI 54201

Ph: (608)745-1090
Fax: (608)745-0179
URL: National Affiliate–www.legion.org
Contact: Ernest Haucke, Contact
Local. Affiliated With: American Legion.

Allenton

17461 ■ American Legion, Fohl-Martin Post 483
PO Box 143
Allenton, WI 53002
Ph: (608)745-1090
Fax: (608)745-0179
URL: National Affiliate–www.legion.org
Local. Affiliated With: American Legion.

Alma Center

17462 ■ American Legion, Adams-Helwig-Randles Post 162
PO Box 83
Alma Center, WI 54611
Ph: (608)745-1090
Fax: (608)745-0179
URL: National Affiliate–www.legion.org
Local. Affiliated With: American Legion.

Almena

17463 ■ Almena Commercial Club
PO Box 175
Almena, WI 54805
Ph: (715)357-6103
Contact: Kay Rundhaug, Pres.
Local.

17464 ■ Northwest Wisconsin Gem and Mineral Society
c/o Roy Wickman, Pres.
1127 7th St.
Almena, WI 54805
E-mail: rktswick@chibarbun.net
URL: National Affiliate–www.amfed.org
Contact: Neil Sitenga, Sec.
Local. Aims to further the study of Earth Sciences and the practice of lapidary arts and mineralogy. **Affiliated With:** American Federation of Mineralogical Societies.

Almond

17465 ■ American Legion, Mead-Rath-Gutke Post 339
1401 Div. St.
Almond, WI 54909
Ph: (608)745-1090
Fax: (608)745-0179
URL: National Affiliate–www.legion.org
Local. Affiliated With: American Legion.

Altoona

17466 ■ American Cancer Society, Altoona
2427 N Hillcrest Pkwy.
Altoona, WI 54720
Ph: (715)832-0181
URL: National Affiliate–www.cancer.org
Local. Affiliated With: American Cancer Society.

17467 ■ American Cancer Society, Eau Claire
2427 N Hillcrest Pkwy., Ste.7
Altoona, WI 54720
Ph: (715)832-0181
Fax: (715)832-8570
URL: National Affiliate–www.cancer.org
Local. Affiliated With: American Cancer Society.

17468 ■ American Legion, Post 545 Altoona
611 S Willson Dr.
Altoona, WI 54720
Ph: (608)745-1090
Fax: (608)745-0179
URL: National Affiliate–www.legion.org
Local. Affiliated With: American Legion.

17469 ■ River Country Resource Conservation and Development Council
PO Box 207
Altoona, WI 54720
Ph: (715)834-9672
Fax: (715)834-8663
URL: http://www.rivercountryrcd.org
Local. Affiliated With: National Association of Resource Conservation and Development Councils.

Amberg

17470 ■ American Legion, Mullaney-Mc-Trusty Post 428
PO Box 104
Amberg, WI 54102
Ph: (608)745-1090
Fax: (608)745-0179
URL: National Affiliate–www.legion.org
Local. Affiliated With: American Legion.

Amery

17471 ■ American Legion, Larson-Torgerson Post 169
320 Memorial Dr.
Amery, WI 54001
Ph: (608)745-1090
Fax: (608)745-0179
URL: National Affiliate–www.legion.org
Local. Affiliated With: American Legion.

Amherst

17472 ■ American Legion, Wisconsin Post 22
c/o Selma E. Voigt
PO Box 252
Amherst, WI 54406
Ph: (608)745-1090
Fax: (608)745-0179
URL: National Affiliate–www.legion.org
Contact: Selma E. Voigt, Contact
Local. Affiliated With: American Legion.

Antigo

17473 ■ American Legion, Sparks-Doernenburg Post 3
PO Box 294
Antigo, WI 54409
Ph: (608)745-1090
Fax: (608)745-0179
URL: National Affiliate–www.legion.org
Local. Affiliated With: American Legion.

17474 ■ Antigo Area Chamber of Commerce
329 Superior St.
PO Box 339
Antigo, WI 54409
Ph: (715)623-4134
Fax: (715)623-4135
Free: (888)526-4523
E-mail: antigocc@newnorth.net
Contact: Denise Wendt, Exec.Dir.
Local.

17475 ■ Triple R Club
c/o Diane Resch
W16061 Evergreen Rd.
Antigo, WI 54409-9801
Founded: 1950. **Members:** 30. **Local.** Promotes education, activities and trial development of horses. **Awards:** Triple R Scholarship. **Frequency:** annual. **Type:** scholarship.

17476 ■ Trout Unlimited - Antigo Chapter
c/o Scott Henricks, Pres.
213 Mary St.
Antigo, WI 54409-2536
Ph: (715)623-3867
E-mail: henricks51@g2a.net
URL: National Affiliate–www.tu.org
Contact: Scott Henricks, Pres.
Local.

17477 ■ United Way of Langlade County
PO Box 594
Antigo, WI 54409-0594
Ph: (715)623-7696
URL: National Affiliate–national.unitedway.org
Local. Affiliated With: United Way of America.

17478 ■ Wisconsin Health Care Association, District 7
c/o Wanda Hose, Pres.
Eastview Med & Rehabilitation
729 Park St.
Antigo, WI 54409
Ph: (715)623-2356
URL: http://www.whca.com
Contact: Wanda Hose, Pres.
Local. Promotes professionalism and ethical behavior of individuals providing long-term care delivery for patients and for the general public. Provides information, education and administrative tools to enhance the quality of long-term care. Improves the standards of service and administration of member nursing homes. **Affiliated With:** American Health Care Association; Wisconsin Health Care Association.

17479 ■ Wisconsin Mint Board
PO Box 327
Antigo, WI 54409-0327
Ph: (715)623-7683
Fax: (715)623-3176
Contact: Julie Braun, Exec.Ast.
State. Provides funding for research, hold Board of Directors meetings and annual meeting with growers.

17480 ■ Wisconsin Potato and Vegetable Growers Association
700 5th Ave.
PO Box 327
Antigo, WI 54409-0327
Ph: (715)623-7683
Fax: (715)623-3176
E-mail: wpvga@wisconsinpotatoes.com
URL: http://www.wisconsinpotatoes.com
Contact: Mike Carter, Exec.Dir.
Founded: 1948. **Members:** 442. **Membership Dues:** grower, $40 (annual) • associate, $125 (annual). **Staff:** 6. **Budget:** $1,000,000. **State.** Organized to protect and advance the interests of potato and vegetable farmers. Sponsors seminars, research station field days, training workshops, conferences, and special receptions. **Libraries: Type:** open to the public. **Holdings:** 48. **Subjects:** potato and vegetable industry. **Awards:** WPVGA Associate Division Scholarship. **Frequency:** annual. **Type:** scholarship. **Affiliated With:** National Potato Council. **Publications:** *The Badger Common'Tater*, monthly. Magazine. Contains news about the potato and vegetable industry in Wisconsin and the United States. **Price:** $18.00 1 yr. subscription; $30.00 2 yr. subscription; $30.00 1 yr. foreign subscription; $50.00 2 yr. foreign subscription. **Circulation:** 3,800. **Advertising:** accepted. **Conventions/Meetings:** annual Wisconsin Potato and Vegetable Industry Show - trade show (exhibits) - always October.

Appleton

17481 ■ ACF Fox Valley Chapter
c/o Kari Schoening
PO Box 2842
Appleton, WI 54912
Ph: (920)738-5555
E-mail: chefjeff@fvtc.edu
URL: National Affiliate–www.acfchefs.org
Contact: Jeffrey S. Igel, Pres.

Local. Promotes the culinary profession and provides on-going educational training and networking for members. Provides opportunities for competition, professional recognition, and access to educational forums with other culinarians at local, regional, national, and international events.

17482 ■ American Association for Medical Transcription, Four Lakes Chapter
c/o Debra Behnke, CMT, Pres.
928 S Weimar St.
Appleton, WI 54915-3405
E-mail: dbehnke3@new.rr.com
URL: http://www.aamt.org/ca/flc
Contact: Debra Behnke CMT, Pres.

Local. Works to represent and advance the profession of medical transcription and its practitioners. **Affiliated With:** American Association for Medical Transcription.

17483 ■ American Legion, Oney-Johnston-Edward-Blessman Post 38
3220 W Coll. Ave.
Appleton, WI 54914
Ph: (608)745-1090
Fax: (608)745-0179
URL: National Affiliate–www.legion.org

Local. **Affiliated With:** American Legion.

17484 ■ American Legion, Wisconsin Post 265
c/o Leo Van Roy
N178 County Rd. N
Appleton, WI 54915
Ph: (608)745-1090
Fax: (608)745-0179
URL: National Affiliate–www.legion.org
Contact: Leo Van Roy, Contact

Local. **Affiliated With:** American Legion.

17485 ■ American Welding Society, Fox Valley Section
c/o Al Sherrill, Chm.
1635 W Spencer St.
Appleton, WI 54914
Ph: (920)735-4069
Fax: (920)735-4168
E-mail: asherr@millerwelds.com
URL: http://www.awsfoxvalley.org
Contact: Al Sherrill, Chm.

Founded: 1919. **Members:** 450. **Membership Dues:** non-profit organization, $78 (annual). **Local**. Welders and students interested in the welding industry. Seeks to expand the knowledge of welding and advance the science, technology and application of welding and related joining disciplines. Activities include technical sessions, plant tours and leisure activities. **Affiliated With:** American Welding Society. **Publications:** Journal, monthly.

17486 ■ Appleton Curling Club
307 N Westhill Blvd.
Appleton, WI 54914
Ph: (920)733-9662
E-mail: mdavis280@earthlink.net
URL: http://www.appletoncurlingclub.com
Contact: Mark Davis, Pres.

Local. **Affiliated With:** United States Curling Association.

17487 ■ Appleton Noon Lions Club
PO Box 762
Appleton, WI 54912
E-mail: appletonnoonlions@tponet.com
URL: http://appletonnoonlions.com
Contact: Otto Cox, Pres.

Local. **Affiliated With:** Lions Clubs International.

17488 ■ Association of Wisconsin Snowmobile Clubs (AWSC)
5497 Waterford Ln., Ste.B
Appleton, WI 54913
Ph: (920)734-5530
Fax: (920)734-5528
E-mail: awsc@awsc.org
URL: http://awsc.org

Founded: 1969. **Members:** 32,000. **Membership Dues:** club, $10 (annual) • associate, $20 (annual) • commercial, $35 (annual). **Staff:** 2. **State**. Snowmobile owners and individuals interested in the snowmobile and related industries. Works with government agencies to create and maintain snowmobile trails. Promotes safe snowmobiling. **Publications:** *Wisconsin Snowmobile News*, 8/year. Magazine. **Price:** included in membership dues; $20.00 for nonmembers. **Advertising:** accepted. **Conventions/Meetings:** annual convention - always March • annual workshop - always October.

17489 ■ Big Brothers Big Sisters of the Fox Valley Region
117 S Locust St., No. 1
Appleton, WI 54914-5228
Ph: (920)739-3542
Fax: (920)739-6887
E-mail: khawkinson@mail.bbbsfvr.com
URL: http://www.bemybig.com
Contact: Kari Hawkinson, Exec.Dir.

Founded: 1968. **Members:** 400. **Staff:** 7. **Budget:** $460,000. **Languages:** English, Spanish. **Local**. Members/volunteers are between the ages of 16 and 80. These individuals desire to make a difference in the lives of the youth in the community through an ongoing friendship. Primary focus is to assist youth in becoming confident, competent and caring individuals through a positive relationship with a caring mentor. **Committees:** Executive; Fund Development; Marketing; Planning/Board Dev.; Program. **Affiliated With:** Big Brothers Big Sisters of America.

17490 ■ Fox Cities Chamber of Commerce and Industry (FCCCI)
PO Box 1855
Appleton, WI 54912-1855
Ph: (920)734-7101
Fax: (920)734-7161
E-mail: information@foxcitieschamber.com
URL: http://www.foxcitieschamber.com
Contact: William J. Welch, Pres./CEO

Founded: 1976. **Members:** 1,500. **Membership Dues:** $213 (annual). **Staff:** 18. **Budget:** $1,700,000. **Local**. Business, industry, and individuals in east central Wisconsin. Works to enhance the community's economic well-being, promote balanced development, and assure continued improvement of the quality of life. **Awards:** Athena Award. **Frequency:** annual. **Type:** trophy. **Recipient:** for outstanding contributions to company, industry, community, to other women and to the chamber • Manufacturer of the Year. **Frequency:** annual. **Type:** recognition. **Recipient:** for a manufacturing firm that has excellence, innovation, ability to adapt, quality improvement efforts, and overall success in the marketplace • Small Business of the Year. **Frequency:** annual. **Type:** recognition. **Recipient:** for companies at least 5 years old, a member in good standing and provide documentation of accomplishments and quality initiatives. **Formed by Merger of:** Appleton Chamber of Commerce; Neenah-Menasha Chamber of Commerce. **Publications:** *Fox Cities Business*, monthly. Newsletter • *Manufacturer Directory*, periodic • *Organizations Guide*. Directory • Membership Directory, periodic. **Conventions/Meetings:** periodic License to Cruise - show, classic car show; with food and live music (exhibits) • annual meeting • periodic Morning Business Advice - breakfast, with guests.

17491 ■ Fox Cities Convention and Visitors Bureau
3433 W Coll. Ave.
Appleton, WI 54914
Ph: (920)734-3358
Fax: (920)734-1080
Free: (800)236-6673
E-mail: tourism@foxcities.org
URL: http://www.foxcities.org
Contact: Lyn Peters, Exec.Dir.

Local.

17492 ■ Fox Valley Literacy Coalition
c/o David Vaclavik, Exec.Dir.
103 E Washington St.
Appleton, WI 54911-5466
Ph: (920)991-9840
Fax: (920)991-1012
E-mail: foxvalleylit@milwpc.com
URL: http://www.focol.org/literacy
Contact: Ms. Rosemarie Burns, Exec.Dir.

Local. **Affiliated With:** ProLiteracy Worldwide.

17493 ■ Fox Valley National Association of The Remodeling Industry
c/o Rick Willer, Regional Board Representative
PO Box 1152
Appleton, WI 54912
Ph: (920)832-9003
Fax: (920)731-5028
E-mail: info@remodelfoxvalley.com
URL: http://www.remodelfoxvalley.com
Contact: Rick Willer, Regional Board Representative

Founded: 1994. **Members:** 37. **Membership Dues:** local business, individual, $350 (annual). **Local**. Represents the remodeling contractors, building products manufacturers, lending institutions, wholesalers and distributors. Promotes the common business interests of those engaged in the home improvement and remodeling industries. Encourages ethical conduct, good business practices, and professionalism in the home improvement and remodeling industry. Supports community service efforts, partners with other nonprofit organizations and governmental agencies to assist the elderly, medically needy and low-income residents to maintain home ownership. **Affiliated With:** National Association of the Remodeling Industry. **Publications:** *NARI News*, monthly. Newsletter. **Conventions/Meetings:** monthly board meeting, networking/educational - every 3rd Wednesday • monthly General Membership - meeting - every 3rd Wednesday.

17494 ■ Fox-Wolf Watershed Alliance
c/o Linda Stoll
PO Box 1861
Appleton, WI 54912-1861
Ph: (920)722-2151
E-mail: foxwolf@fwwa.org
URL: http://www.fwwa.org

Local.

17495 ■ Franklin Elementary School PTA
2212 N Jarchow St.
Appleton, WI 54911
Ph: (920)832-6246
E-mail: jon@imccentral.com
URL: http://myschoolonline.com/wi/franklin_elementary
Contact: Liz Heck, Pres.

Local. Parents, teachers, students, and others interested in uniting the forces of home, school, and community. Promotes the welfare of children and youth.

17496 ■ Friends of the Fox
PO Box 741
Appleton, WI 54912-0741
Ph: (920)707-2065
URL: http://www.friendsofthefox.org
Contact: Doug Dobbe, Pres.

Founded: 1982. **Membership Dues:** basic, $25 (annual) • gold, $50 (annual) • executive, $250 (annual)

• corporate, $500 (annual). **Local. Publications:** Newsletter, quarterly. Alternate Formats: online.

17497 ■ Funeral Consumers Alliance of the Fox Valley
PO Box 1422
Appleton, WI 54912-1422
Ph: (920)738-0228
E-mail: bspencer@new.rr.com
URL: http://www.funerals.org/FoxValley/
Contact: Ms. Beth Spencer, Pres.

Members: 120. **For-Profit. Local. Affiliated With:** Funeral Consumers Alliance.

17498 ■ Girl Scouts of the Fox River Area
4693 Lynndale Dr.
Appleton, WI 54913-9614
Ph: (920)734-4559
Fax: (920)734-1304
Free: (800)924-1211
E-mail: cmutschler@girlscoutsfoxriverarea.org
URL: http://www.girlscoutsfoxriverarea.org
Contact: Cathryn Mutschler, CEO

Local. Young girls and adult volunteers, corporate, government and individual supporters. Strives to develop potential and leadership skills among its members. Conducts trainings, educational programs and outdoor activities.

17499 ■ Great Lakes Maintenance Association (GLMA)
PO Box 1916
Appleton, WI 54912-1916
Ph: (920)380-9565
Fax: (920)380-9565
E-mail: gr8lakesma@aol.com
Contact: John F. Bulter, Pres.

Founded: 2000. **Members:** 150. **Membership Dues:** $30 (annual). **Regional.** Works for the advancement of people in the maintenance field, and related professions. **Awards: Frequency:** annual. **Type:** scholarship. **Publications:** *Great Lakes Maintenance Messenger*, monthly. Newsletter. **Conventions/Meetings:** annual show (exhibits).

17500 ■ Indus of Fox Valley
c/o Dr. Ramakant T. Shet, Board Member
3600 N Shawnee Ave.
Appleton, WI 54914
E-mail: indusfoxvalley@focol.org
URL: http://www.focol.org/indusfoxvalley
Contact: Dr. Ramakant T. Shet, Board Member

Local.

17501 ■ International Association of Machinists and Aerospace Workers, AFL-CIO, CLC - Local Lodge 2575
1632 N Eugene
Appleton, WI 54914
E-mail: president@iamll2575.org
URL: http://www.iamll2575.org
Contact: Jerry Lemke, Pres.

Members: 689. **Local. Affiliated With:** International Association of Machinists and Aerospace Workers.

17502 ■ Mothers Against Drunk Driving, Upper Fox Valley
PO Box 2131
Appleton, WI 54913
Ph: (920)734-6233
Fax: (920)734-6943
URL: National Affiliate–www.madd.org

Local. Victims of drunk driving crashes; concerned citizens. Encourages citizen participation in working towards reform of the drunk driving problem and the prevention of underage drinking. Acts as the voice of victims of drunk driving crashes by speaking on their behalf to communities, businesses, and educational groups. **Affiliated With:** Mothers Against Drunk Driving.

17503 ■ Mothers Against Drunk Driving, Wisconsin State
PO Box 536
Appleton, WI 54912-0536
Ph: (920)831-6540
Fax: (920)831-6542
Free: (800)799-6233
E-mail: maddwi@powercom.net
URL: http://shells.powercom.net/~maddwi/
Victims of drunk driving crashes; concerned citizens. Encourages citizen participation in working towards reform of the drunk driving problem and the prevention of underage drinking. Acts as the voice of victims of drunk driving crashes by speaking on their behalf to communities, businesses, and educational groups. **Affiliated With:** Mothers Against Drunk Driving.

17504 ■ NAIFA-Wisconsin-Fox River Valley
PO Box 1994
Appleton, WI 54912-1994
Ph: (920)734-1310
Fax: (920)830-2458
URL: National Affiliate–www.naifa.org
Local. Represents the interest of insurance and financial advisors. Advocates for a positive legislative and regulatory environment. Enhances business and professional skills of members. **Affiliated With:** National Association of Insurance and Financial Advisors.

17505 ■ National Alliance on Mental Illness - Fox Valley
516 W 6th St.
Appleton, WI 54911
Ph: (920)954-1550
Fax: (920)954-0490
E-mail: info@namifoxvalley.org
URL: http://www.namifoxvalley.org
Contact: Karen J. Aspenson, Exec.Dir.
Local. Strives to improve the quality of life of children and adults with severe mental illness through support, education, research and advocacy. **Affiliated With:** National Alliance for the Mentally Ill.

17506 ■ National Association of Home Builders of the U.S., Valley Home Builders Association (VHBA)
c/o Pauline Meyer
920 W Assn. Dr.
Appleton, WI 54914-1493
Ph: (920)731-7931
Fax: (920)731-7968
E-mail: info@vhba.com
URL: http://www.vhba.com
Contact: Pauline Meyer, Exec.VP
Local. Single and multifamily home builders, commercial builders, and others associated with the building industry. **Affiliated With:** National Association of Home Builders.

17507 ■ National Association of Miniature Enthusiasts - Retreat Into Miniatures
c/o Bette Smith
1 Wittmann Ct.
Appleton, WI 54915
Ph: (920)733-8414
E-mail: desmith@famvid.com
URL: http://www.miniatures.org/states/WI.html
Contact: Bette Smith, Contact
Local. Affiliated With: National Association of Miniature Enthusiasts.

17508 ■ National Association of Women Business Owners, Wisconsin
c/o Ms. Tammy Schultz, Internet Marketing Coor.
2700 W Coll. Ave., Box 188
Appleton, WI 54914
E-mail: tammy@virtualtech.com
URL: http://www.weofwisconsin.org
Contact: Ms. Tammy Schultz, Internet Marketing Coor.

Membership Dues: individual, $75 (annual). **State.** Aims to bring together businesswomen of many occupations in a non-competitive setting and to assist women business owners and those with an entrepreneurial spirit on their journey to building and maintaining successful businesses. Provides opportunities, support, resources and information in a fun and relaxed environment. Seeks to be recognized as the professional organization of choice for businesswomen in Northeastern Wisconsin.

17509 ■ North Central Region of the Astronomical League (N.C.R.A.L.)
c/o Mr. Ty Westbrook, Chair
330 W Brewster St.
Appleton, WI 54911
Ph: (920)733-7264
E-mail: tyimail@sbcglobal.net
URL: http://www.ncral.org
Contact: Mr. Ty Westbrook, Chair
Founded: 1947. **Members:** 2,300. **Local Groups:** 39. **Regional.** Promotes the hobby of astronomy. Works to encourage and coordinate activities of amateur astronomical societies. Fosters observational and computational work and craftsmanship in various fields of astronomy. **Awards:** N.C.R.A.L. Regional Award. **Frequency:** annual. **Type:** recognition. **Recipient:** to amateur astronomy through a member's local astronomy club, public outreach, the NCRAL or the astronomical league. **Affiliated With:** Astronomical League. **Conventions/Meetings:** annual convention, with speakers (exhibits).

17510 ■ Northeast Wisconsin Building and Construction Trades Council
c/o Gary Ruhl
2828 N Ballard Rd., Rm. No. 202
Appleton, WI 54911-8703
Ph: (920)733-3136
Fax: (920)733-2391
URL: National Affiliate–www.milwbuildingtrades.org
Contact: Gary Ruhl, Contact
Local. Formerly: (2005) Northeast Wisconsin Building and Trades Council.

17511 ■ Oshkosh Earth Science Club
c/o Gary Richards, Pres.
900 N State St.
Appleton, WI 54911
E-mail: woofnpur@famvid.com
URL: National Affiliate–www.amfed.org
Contact: Dolly Hollander, Sec.
Local. Aims to further the study of Earth Sciences and the practice of lapidary arts and mineralogy. **Affiliated With:** American Federation of Mineralogical Societies.

17512 ■ Outagamie County Historical Society (OCHS)
330 E Coll. Ave.
Appleton, WI 54911
Ph: (920)733-8445
Fax: (920)733-8636
E-mail: ochs@foxvalleyhistory.org
URL: http://www.foxvalleyhistory.org
Contact: Terry Bergen, Exec.Dir.
Founded: 1872. **Members:** 750. **Membership Dues:** adult, $15 (annual) • family, $30 (annual). **Staff:** 11. **Local.** Individuals, families, and educators in Outagamie County and the lower Fox River Valley, in Wisconsin, interested in collecting, preserving, and exhibiting local history. Owns and operates the Outagamie Museum, Houdini Historical Center in Appleton, and Charles A. Grignon Mansion in Kaukauna. Conducts public events, exhibits, genealogy classes. Holds library, archival and three-dimensional collections. **Libraries: Type:** by appointment only. **Holdings:** 2,000; books, maps, photographs. **Subjects:** local history, Harry Houdini. **Awards:** Carolyn Kellogg Historic Preservation Award. **Frequency:** annual. **Type:** recognition • Lillian Mackesy Historian of the Year. **Frequency:** annual. **Type:** recognition. **Additional Websites:** http://www.houdinihistory.org. **Affiliated With:** American Association of Museums; American Association for State and Local History; National Trust for Historic Preservation; Wisconsin Historical Society. **Formerly:** (1968) Outagamie County Pioneer and Historical Society. **Publications:**

History Today, quarterly. Newsletter • *Mystifier*, quarterly • *Report to the Community*, annual. Annual Report.

17513 ■ Outagamie Philatelic Society (OPS)
PO Box 11
Appleton, WI 54912-0011
Ph: (920)734-2417
E-mail: corosec@sbcglobal.net
URL: National Affiliate–www.stamps.org
Contact: Verna Shackleton, Treas.
Founded: 1942. **Members:** 26. **Membership Dues:** adult, $5 (annual) • youth, $3 (annual). **Staff:** 5. **Local**. Individuals in northeastern Wisconsin organized to promote the hobby of stamp collecting. **Affiliated With:** American Philatelic Society. **Publications:** *Valley Philatelist*, bimonthly. Newsletter. **Circulation:** 26. **Conventions/Meetings:** monthly meeting - except June, July, and August; always third Thursday • annual Outapex Stamp Show - always spring.

17514 ■ PFLAG Appleton/Fox Cities
128 N Oneida St.
Appleton, WI 54911
Ph: (920)882-4056
E-mail: pflagfc@focol.org
URL: http://www.pflagfoxcities.org
Local. Affiliated With: Parents, Families, and Friends of Lesbians and Gays.

17515 ■ Phi Theta Kappa, Beta Epsilon Omicron Chapter - Fox Valley Technical College
c/o Vicky Barke
1825 N Bluemound Dr.
Appleton, WI 54914
Ph: (920)735-2468
E-mail: barke@fvtc.edu
URL: http://www.ptk.org/directories/chapters/WI/20753-1.htm
Contact: Vicky Barke, Advisor
Local.

17516 ■ Points of Light Foundation - Volunteer Center of East Central Wisconsin
2616 S Oneida St., Ste.2
Appleton, WI 54915-2101
Ph: (920)832-9360
Fax: (920)832-9317
E-mail: jdrobeck@volunteercenter.net
URL: National Affiliate–www.pointsoflight.org
Contact: Julia Drobeck, Contact
Local. Affiliated With: Points of Light Foundation.

17517 ■ Psi Chi, National Honor Society in Psychology - Lawrence University
c/o Dept. of Psychology
PO Box 599
Appleton, WI 54912-0599
Ph: (920)832-6706
Fax: (920)832-6962
E-mail: terry.l.rew-gottfried@lawrence.edu
URL: National Affiliate–www.psichi.org
Local. Affiliated With: Psi Chi, National Honor Society in Psychology.

17518 ■ Public Relations Society of America, Northeast Wisconsin Chapter
PO Box 1673
Appleton, WI 54913-1673
E-mail: info@prsanewis.org
URL: http://www.prsanewis.org
Contact: Don Klein, Pres.
Founded: 2000. **Members:** 60. **Membership Dues:** full, $60 (annual) • associate, $40 (annual). **Regional**. Dedicated to advancing the professional practice of public relations in northeast Wisconsin. Seeks to unify, strengthen, and advance the profession of public relations within the region. **Affiliated With:** Public Relations Society of America. **Also Known As:** (2004) PRSA. **Conventions/Meetings:** monthly meeting - every 4th Tuesday.

17519 ■ Pulp and Paper Manufacturers Association
2000 S Memorial Dr.
Appleton, WI 54915
Ph: (920)734-5778
Fax: (920)734-0176
E-mail: info@ppmausa.com
URL: http://www.ppmausa.com
Contact: Dick Kendall, Exec.Dir.
Local.

17520 ■ Realtors Association of Northeast Wisconsin (RANW)
PO Box 2637
Appleton, WI 54912-2637
Ph: (920)739-9108
Fax: (920)739-9149
E-mail: mchapman@ranw.org
URL: http://www.ranw.org
Contact: Marg Chapman, Exec.VP
Local. Strives to develop real estate business practices. Advocates the right to own, use and transfer real property. Provides a facility for professional development, research and exchange of information among members and to the general public. **Affiliated With:** National Association of Realtors.

17521 ■ The Retired Enlisted Association Chapter 66 (TREA)
c/o Holly Hoppe, Pres.
1820 S Wilson St.
Appleton, WI 54915-4261
Ph: (920)993-8560
Fax: (920)834-6805
E-mail: r.langan@earthlink.net
URL: National Affiliate–www.trea.org
Local. Affiliated With: The Retired Enlisted Association.

17522 ■ RSVP Outagamie County
c/o Carol Bloemer, Dir.
2616 S Oneida St., Ste.2
Appleton, WI 54915
Ph: (920)832-9360
Fax: (920)832-9317
E-mail: rsvp@volunteercenter.net
URL: http://www.volunteercenter.net
Contact: Carol Bloemer, Dir.
Local. Affiliated With: Retired and Senior Volunteer Program.

17523 ■ SCORE Fox Cities
125 N Superior St.
PO Box 1855
Appleton, WI 54913
Ph: (920)734-7101
Fax: (920)734-7161
E-mail: score@foxcitiesbusiness.com
URL: http://www.foxcitiesbusiness.com/score/index.htm
Contact: William Devine, Chm.
Regional. Provides free counseling and low-cost workshops within the Fox Valley. **Affiliated With:** SCORE.

17524 ■ Society for Human Resource Management - Fox Valley Chapter
c/o Teri Pedersen
Lutheran Social Sers.
3003A N Richmond St.
Appleton, WI 54911
E-mail: tpedersen@lsswis.org
URL: http://www.wishrm.org/chapter/foxval/index.html
Contact: Teri Pedersen, Pres.
Local. Represents the interests of human resource and industrial relations professionals and executives. Promotes the advancement of human resource management.

17525 ■ Sons of Norway, Norse Valley Lodge 5-491
c/o Mary Colleen Myers, Pres.
508 W Foster St.
Appleton, WI 54915-1510
Ph: (920)733-6820
E-mail: cmyersm@aol.com
URL: National Affiliate–www.sofn.com
Contact: Mary Colleen Myers, Pres.
Local. Affiliated With: Sons of Norway.

17526 ■ Sweet Adelines International, Fox Valley Chorus
Grace Lutheran Church, Lower Level
900 N Mason St.
Appleton, WI 54915
Ph: (920)734-5131
E-mail: anniezentner@hotmail.com
URL: http://www.foxvalleychorus.org
Contact: Ann Zentner, Contact
Regional. Advances the musical art form of barbershop harmony through education and performances. Provides education, training and coaching in the development of women's four-part barbershop harmony. **Affiliated With:** Sweet Adelines International.

17527 ■ Teamsters Local Union 563
PO Box 174
Appleton, WI 54912
Ph: (920)725-7086 (920)725-7087
Fax: (920)725-6990
E-mail: local563@tds.net
URL: National Affiliate–www.aflcio.org
Contact: Robert Schlieve Jr., Sec.-Treas.
Members: 1,636. **Staff:** 4. **State Groups:** 1. **Local**. Represent truck drivers, dairy, warehouse, construction and public sector. **Awards:** Robert Schlieve Sr. Scholarship. **Frequency:** annual. **Type:** scholarship. **Recipient:** awarded to local union 563 members.

17528 ■ Trout Unlimited, Fox Valley
c/o Tom Deer
N9628 Chadbury Ln.
Appleton, WI 54915
Ph: (920)830-2322
E-mail: trouttricks@netzero.net
URL: http://www.foxvalleytu.org
Contact: Mr. Tony Treml, Pres.
Local. Affiliated With: Trout Unlimited.

17529 ■ United Food and Commercial Workers, Local 78T, Northcentral Region
4408 Windingbrook Dr.
Appleton, WI 54913-7762
Ph: (920)882-8944
URL: National Affiliate–www.ufcw.org
Local. Affiliated With: United Food and Commercial Workers International Union.

17530 ■ Vietnam Veterans of America, Chapter 351
PO Box 1862
Appleton, WI 54912-1862
E-mail: contact@vva351.com
URL: http://www.vva351.com
Local. Affiliated With: Vietnam Veterans of America.

17531 ■ Wisconsin Association for Talented and Gifted (WATG)
1608 W Cloverdale Dr.
Appleton, WI 54914
Ph: (920)991-9177
Fax: (920)991-1225
E-mail: watg@focol.org
URL: http://www.focol.org/watg
Contact: Nancy Woodward, Exec.Asst.
Founded: 1993. **Membership Dues:** individual, $35 • family, $45 • institutional, $80. **State**. Advances interest in programs for the gifted. Seeks to further education of the gifted and enhances their potential creativity. Unites to address the unique needs of children and youth with demonstrated gifts and talents as well as those children who may be able to develop their talent potentials with appropriate educational experiences. Encourages and responds to the diverse expressions of gifts and talents in children and youth from all cultures, racial and ethnic backgrounds, and socioeconomic groups. **Affiliated With:** National Association for Gifted Children.

17532 ■ Wisconsin Fox Valley Sheet Metal Contractors Association
c/o David C. Seitz, Pres.
3315 N Ballard Rd., Ste.D
Appleton, WI 54911-8988
Ph: (920)734-3148
Fax: (920)734-6754
Free: (877)625-8304
E-mail: david@omswi.com
URL: http://www.omswi.com
Contact: Ms. Joyce Kabat, VP/Office Mgr./Admin. Asst.
Local. Affiliated With: Sheet Metal and Air Conditioning Contractors' National Association.

17533 ■ Wisconsin Regional Writers' Association (WRWA)
510 W Sunset Ave.
Appleton, WI 54911
Ph: (920)734-3724
E-mail: president@wrwa.net
URL: http://www.WRWA.net
Contact: Patricia Dunson Boverhuis, Pres.
Founded: 1948. **Members:** 800. **Membership Dues:** regular, $25 (annual) • senior citizen, $10 (annual) • full time student, $10 (annual). **Regional Groups:** 55. **State Groups:** 1. **State**. Statewide organization of amateur and professional writers dedicated to self-improvement, service to others, and to the writer's craft. Conducts two conferences each year: spring and fall. Annual writing competitions are open to all members. **Awards: Frequency:** annual. **Type:** scholarship. **Recipient:** based on financial need and professionalism. **Publications:** *Wisconsin Regional Writer*, quarterly. Newsletter. **Price:** included in membership dues. **Circulation:** 800. **Advertising:** accepted. **Conventions/Meetings:** semiannual conference, with speakers, workshops, and awards presentation - always spring and fall.

Arcadia

17534 ■ American Legion, Tickfer-Erickson Post 17
PO Box 184
Arcadia, WI 54612
Ph: (608)745-1090
Fax: (608)745-0179
URL: National Affiliate–www.legion.org
Local. Affiliated With: American Legion.

17535 ■ Arcadia Chamber of Commerce
PO Box 81
Arcadia, WI 54612-0081
Ph: (608)323-2319
E-mail: arcadia@triwest.net
URL: http://arcadiawi.org
Contact: Noreen Haines, Exec.Sec.
Local. Works to enhance the business community of Arcadia. **Committees:** Retail. **Projects:** Arcadia Avenue of Lights. **Subcommittees:** Ag Day; Arcadia Memorial Ride; Development/Tourism; Easter Egg Hunt; Holiday Fair; Programs/Special Events.

Argyle

17536 ■ American Legion, Argyle Post 251
PO Box 125
Argyle, WI 53504
Ph: (608)745-1090
Fax: (608)745-0179
URL: National Affiliate–www.legion.org
Local. Affiliated With: American Legion.

Arkdale

17537 ■ Wisconsin Woodland Owners Association, Central Sands Chapter
c/o Ruthanne Horning, Chair
PO Box 71
Arkdale, WI 54613
Ph: (608)564-7640
E-mail: cookie@maqs.net
URL: http://www.wisconsinwoodlands.org
Contact: Ruthanne Horning, Chair
Local. Affiliated With: Wisconsin Woodland Owners Association.

Arlington

17538 ■ Wisconsin Curling Association - Arlington Curling Club
PO Box 224
Arlington, WI 53911
Ph: (608)635-4013
E-mail: bonsplr@sbcglobal.net
URL: http://www.goodcurling.net/basics/U.S.%20clubs/wisconsin.html
Contact: Gary Hellenbrand, Pres.
Local. Affiliated With: United States Curling Association.

Armstrong Creek

17539 ■ Ruffed Grouse Society, Nicolet Wild River Chapter
c/o David Ziolkowski
2420 Ziolkowski Rd.
Armstrong Creek, WI 54103
Ph: (715)336-2523
URL: National Affiliate–www.ruffedgrousesociety.org
Contact: David Ziolkowski, Contact
Local. Affiliated With: Ruffed Grouse Society.

Arpin

17540 ■ American Legion, Ebert-Wunrow Post 475
8346 State Rd. 186
Arpin, WI 54410
Ph: (715)421-1461
Fax: (608)745-0179
URL: National Affiliate–www.legion.org
Local. Affiliated With: American Legion.

Ashland

17541 ■ American Legion, Kelly-Johnson Post 90
220 Main St. E
Ashland, WI 54806
Ph: (608)745-1090
Fax: (608)745-0179
URL: National Affiliate–www.legion.org
Local. Affiliated With: American Legion.

17542 ■ American Meteorological Society, Northland College
c/o Kevin L. Huyck, Pres.
1411 Ellis Ave.
Ashland, WI 54806-3999
Ph: (715)682-1425
E-mail: kb9wob@yahoo.com
URL: National Affiliate–www.ametsoc.org/AMS
Local. Professional meteorologists, oceanographers, and hydrologists; interested students and nonprofessionals. **Affiliated With:** American Meteorological Society.

17543 ■ Ashland Area Chamber of Commerce (AACC)
PO Box 746
Ashland, WI 54806
Ph: (715)682-2500
Fax: (715)682-9404
Free: (800)284-9484
E-mail: ashchamb@centurytel.net
URL: http://www.visitashland.com
Contact: Mary McPhetridge, Exec.Dir.
Founded: 1888. **Members:** 250. **Local.** Retailers and businesses. Promotes business and community development in the Ashland, WI area. **Conventions/Meetings:** annual Apostle Islands Lighthouse Celebration - tour, lighthouse cruises and tours • annual CenturyTel WhistleStop - festival.

17544 ■ Ashland Lions Club - Wisconsin
PO Box 832
Ashland, WI 54806
Ph: (715)682-4504
E-mail: twaby@charter.net
URL: http://ashlandlionsclub.com
Contact: Greg Tobisch, Pres.
Local. Affiliated With: Lions Clubs International.

17545 ■ Northwest RSVP
c/o Janet Washnieski, Dir.
400 Chapple Ave.
Ashland, WI 54806
Ph: (715)682-6502
Fax: (715)682-2062
E-mail: washrsvp@ncis.net
URL: http://www.seniorcorps.gov/about/programs/rsvp_state.asp?usestateabbr=wi&Search4.x=0&Search4.y=0
Contact: Janet Washnieski, Dir.
Local. Affiliated With: Retired and Senior Volunteer Program.

17546 ■ Psi Chi, National Honor Society in Psychology - Northland College
c/o Dept. of Psychology
1411 Ellis Ave.
Ashland, WI 54806-3999
Ph: (715)682-1397
Fax: (715)682-1849
E-mail: pnorris@northland.edu
URL: National Affiliate–www.psichi.org
Local. Affiliated With: Psi Chi, National Honor Society in Psychology.

17547 ■ Ruffed Grouse Society, Chequamegon Chapter
c/o Mike Hanson
1205 Main St. W
Ashland, WI 54806
Ph: (715)682-2194
URL: National Affiliate–www.ruffedgrousesociety.org
Contact: Mike Hanson, Contact
Local. Affiliated With: Ruffed Grouse Society.

17548 ■ Trout Unlimited - Wild Rivers Chapter
66625 Highland Rd.
Ashland, WI 54806-2662
Ph: (715)682-4703 (715)682-5307
E-mail: wwheart@cheqnet.net
URL: National Affiliate–www.tu.org
Contact: Bill Heart, Pres.
Local.

Athelstane

17549 ■ American Legion, Parker-Jose-Stockwell Post 66
N 11452 Pkwy. Rd.
Athelstane, WI 54104
Ph: (608)745-1090
Fax: (608)745-0179
URL: National Affiliate–www.legion.org
Local. Affiliated With: American Legion.

Athens

17550 ■ American Legion, Chapman-Belter Post 4
PO Box 13
Athens, WI 54411
Ph: (608)745-1090
Fax: (608)745-0179
URL: National Affiliate–www.legion.org
Local. Affiliated With: American Legion.

Auburndale

17551 ■ United Brotherhood of Carpenters and Joiners of America, Marshfield Local Union No. 2958
908 Rangeline Rd.
Auburndale, WI 54412
Ph: (715)389-1990
E-mail: dfinsec@northsidecomp.com
URL: National Affiliate–www.carpenters.org/home.html
Local. Affiliated With: United Brotherhood of Carpenters and Joiners of America.

Augusta

17552 ■ American Legion, Spondley Post 291
PO Box 300
Augusta, WI 54722
Ph: (608)745-1090
Fax: (608)745-0179
URL: National Affiliate–www.legion.org
Local. Affiliated With: American Legion.

Avoca

17553 ■ American Legion, Wisconsin Post 335
c/o Frank O. Brien
PO Box 233
Avoca, WI 53506
Ph: (608)745-1090
Fax: (608)745-0179
URL: National Affiliate–www.legion.org
Contact: Frank O. Brien, Contact
Local. Affiliated With: American Legion.

17554 ■ American Rabbit Breeders Association, Misty Hills Rabbit Club
c/o Danielle Kohlmeyer, Sec.
604 Clyde St.
Avoca, WI 53506
E-mail: abby@mhtc.net
URL: http://www.geocities.com/wisconsin_state_rba/Local_Clubs.html
Contact: Danielle Kohlmeyer, Sec.
Local. Affiliated With: American Rabbit Breeders Association.

Bagley

17555 ■ American Legion, Abraham-Hickok-Wetmore Post 148
c/o David J. Meoska
11988 County Rd. A
Bagley, WI 53801
Ph: (608)745-1090
Fax: (608)745-0179
URL: National Affiliate–www.legion.org
Contact: David J. Meoska, Contact
Local. Affiliated With: American Legion.

17556 ■ American Legion, Liscum Brothers Post 482
225 S Bagley Ave.
Bagley, WI 53801
Ph: (608)745-1090
Fax: (608)745-0179
URL: National Affiliate–www.legion.org
Local. Affiliated With: American Legion.

Baileys Harbor

17557 ■ Baileys Harbor Community Association (BHCA)
PO Box 31
Baileys Harbor, WI 54202
Ph: (920)839-2366
Fax: (920)839-2366
E-mail: bhinfo@dcwis.com
URL: http://www.baileysharbor.com
Contact: Stephanie Heald-Fisher, Pres.
Founded: 1979. **Membership Dues:** business, $50 (annual) • individual, $50 (annual) • associate, $75 (annual). **Local.** Works to advance the commercial, financial, industrial and civic interests of the area. **Publications:** *Fall is a Favorite Time of Year.* Newsletter. Alternate Formats: online. **Conventions/Meetings:** annual Collector Car and Truck Show (exhibits) • annual festival, features craft show, food, bake sale, antique car show, raffle, and souvenir booth.

Baldwin

17558 ■ American Legion, Cave-Dahl Post 240
PO Box 738
Baldwin, WI 54002
Ph: (608)745-1090
Fax: (608)745-0179
URL: National Affiliate–www.legion.org
Local. Affiliated With: American Legion.

17559 ■ Baldwin Area Chamber of Commerce
PO Box 813
Baldwin, WI 54002
Ph: (715)684-2221 (715)684-3153
URL: http://www.baldwinchamber.com
Contact: Sheryl Marshall, Pres.
Founded: 1982. **Local. Additional Websites:** http://www.baldwin.org. **Conventions/Meetings:** monthly meeting - every 3rd Thursday of the month.

17560 ■ Miniature Pinscher Club of Greater Twin Cities
c/o Paula Bondarenko, Sec.
2392 US Hwy. 12
Baldwin, WI 54002
Ph: (715)684-4797
E-mail: bondspins@hotmail.com
Contact: Gretchen Hofheins, Pres.
Local.

17561 ■ St. Croix Valley District Nurses Association - No. 13
355 County Rd. Y
Baldwin, WI 54002
Ph: (715)684-3088
E-mail: bammfin@baldwin-telecom.net
URL: http://www.wisconsinnurses.org
Contact: Ann Findlay, Pres.
Local. Works to advance the nursing profession. Seeks to meet the needs of nurses and health care consumers. Fosters high standards of nursing practice. Promotes the economic and general welfare of nurses in the workplace. **Affiliated With:** American Nurses Association; Wisconsin Nurses' Association.

Balsam Lake

17562 ■ American Legion, Wisconsin Post 278
c/o Ellis Hagler
625 N State Rd. 46
Balsam Lake, WI 54810
Ph: (608)745-1090
Fax: (608)745-0179
URL: National Affiliate–www.legion.org
Contact: Ellis Hagler, Contact
Local. Affiliated With: American Legion.

17563 ■ National Active and Retired Federal Employees Association - Indianhead 1581
1651 70th St.
Balsam Lake, WI 54810-2419
Ph: (715)268-8618
URL: National Affiliate–www.narfe.org
Contact: Ken Chapdelaine, Contact
Local. Protects the retirement future of employees through education. Informs members on issues affecting the retirement. **Affiliated With:** National Association of Retired Federal Employees.

Bancroft

17564 ■ American Legion, Yonke-Christenson Post 533
8340 Tennessee Walker Rd.
Bancroft, WI 54921
Ph: (608)745-1090
Fax: (608)745-0179
URL: National Affiliate–www.legion.org
Local. Affiliated With: American Legion.

Bangor

17565 ■ American Legion, Anderson-Good Post 40
401 S 15th Ave.
Bangor, WI 54614
Ph: (608)745-1090
Fax: (608)745-0179
URL: National Affiliate–www.legion.org
Local. Affiliated With: American Legion.

17566 ■ Bangor Business Club
PO Box 2
Bangor, WI 54614
Ph: (608)486-4060
Local.

17567 ■ Bangor Lions Club - Wisconsin
c/o Bonnie Horstman, Pres.
1601 Labus Dr.
Bangor, WI 54614
Ph: (608)486-2711
E-mail: cmsisobonnie@wmconnect.com
URL: http://www.md27d2.org
Contact: Bonnie Horstman, Pres.
Local. Affiliated With: Lions Clubs International.

17568 ■ International Association of Machinists and Aerospace Workers, AFL-CIO, CLC - Lodge 1771
1815 Wheldon St.
Bangor, WI 54614-8807
E-mail: strawberryerickson@yahoo.com
URL: http://home.centurytel.net/IAMDL66/1771/index.htm
Contact: Adam Adams, Pres.
Members: 377. **Local. Affiliated With:** International Association of Machinists and Aerospace Workers.

Baraboo

17569 ■ American Legion, Baraboo Post 26
113 2nd St.
Baraboo, WI 53913
Ph: (608)745-1090
Fax: (608)745-0179
URL: National Affiliate–www.legion.org
Local. Affiliated With: American Legion.

17570 ■ American Legion, Post 556 Sanford White Eagle
E10619 N Reedsburg Rd.
Baraboo, WI 53913
Ph: (608)745-1090
Fax: (608)745-0179
URL: National Affiliate–www.legion.org
Local. Affiliated With: American Legion.

17571 ■ Baraboo Area Chamber of Commerce (BCC)
PO Box 442
Baraboo, WI 53913
Ph: (608)356-8333
Fax: (608)356-8422
Free: (800)BAR-ABOO
E-mail: chamber@baraboo.com
URL: http://www.baraboo.com/chamber
Contact: Gene Dalhoff, Exec.Dir.
Founded: 1950. **Members:** 280. **Membership Dues:** retail, manufacturing, agri-business, professional

(base up to 5 employees) and financial institution (minimum), $195 (annual) • institution governed by Public Service Commission, $510 (annual) • nonprofit organization/associate, $115 (annual) • individual, $58 (annual) • 18 hole Golf Course/Ski Hill, $555 (annual). **Local**. Agribusiness, manufacturing, professional, retail, and tourism businesses. Promotes business and community development in Baraboo, WI. **Publications:** *Chamber Review*, monthly. Newsletter. Highlights activities of the Chamber and member businesses. Provides other information of use to members. **Price:** included in membership dues • Membership Directory, annual. Contains data regarding all member businesses. **Price:** included in membership dues. **Conventions/Meetings:** annual Golf Outing - meeting • annual Holiday Open House - meeting • annual Radio/TV Auction - meeting • annual Summer Begins in Baraboo - festival.

17572 ■ Baraboo Area United Way
PO Box 290
Baraboo, WI 53913-0290
Free: (866)307-4160
URL: National Affiliate–national.unitedway.org
Local. Affiliated With: United Way of America.

17573 ■ Baraboo Lions Club
c/o Kandie Beckwith, Pres.
601 15th St.
Baraboo, WI 53913
Ph: (608)356-5088
URL: http://www.md27d2.org
Contact: Kandie Beckwith, Pres.
Local. Affiliated With: Lions Clubs International.

17574 ■ Kiwanis Club of Baraboo
PO Box 462
Baraboo, WI 53913
Ph: (608)253-7594
E-mail: catherine.sperl@verizon.net
URL: http://www.baraboo.com/kiwanis
Contact: Cathy Sperl, Pres.
Local.

17575 ■ National Alliance for the Mentally Ill - South Central
c/o Donna Meier, Pres.
PO Box 371
Baraboo, WI 53913-0371
Ph: (608)768-5375
URL: http://www.namiwisconsin.org/library/directory
Contact: Donna Meier, Pres.
Local. Strives to improve the quality of life of children and adults with severe mental illness through support, education, research and advocacy. **Affiliated With:** National Alliance for the Mentally Ill.

17576 ■ Phi Theta Kappa, Beta Kappa Eta Chapter - University of Wisconsin-Baraboo/Sauk
c/o Diann Kiesel
1006 Connie Rd.
Baraboo, WI 53913
Ph: (608)356-8351
E-mail: dkiesel@uwc.edu
URL: http://www.ptk.org/directories/chapters/WI/21673-1.htm
Contact: Diann Kiesel, Advisor
Local.

17577 ■ Sauk County Historical Society (SCHS)
PO Box 651
Baraboo, WI 53913
Ph: (608)356-1001
E-mail: history@saukcounty.com
URL: http://www.saukcounty.com/schs
Contact: Peter Shrake, Exec.Dir.
Founded: 1906. **Members:** 360. **Membership Dues:** single, $15 (annual) • family, $25 (annual) • friend, $35 (annual) • supporter, $50 (annual) • sponsor, $100 (annual) • patron, $250 (annual) • benefactor, $500 (annual). **Local.** Individuals interested in the history of Sauk County, WI. Seeks to collect and preserve artifacts and information of historical significance to the area. Encourages historical education and research including genealogical research. Expanded the local library with many family histories. Holds lectures throughout the year and sponsors a biannual parade of homes. Maintains Van Orden Mansion Museum. **Affiliated With:** Wisconsin Historical Society. **Publications:** *Old Sauk Trails*, quarterly. Newsletter. **Conventions/Meetings:** monthly board meeting.

17578 ■ South Central Wisconsin AIFA
c/o Patricia Boehlke
313 Oak St.
Baraboo, WI 53913
Ph: (608)356-6606
Fax: (608)356-9305
E-mail: patti@don-rick.com
URL: National Affiliate–naifa.org
Contact: Patricia Boehlke, Contact
Local. Represents the interests of insurance and financial advisors. Advocates for a positive legislative and regulatory environment. Enhances business and professional skills of members. **Affiliated With:** National Association of Insurance and Financial Advisors.

17579 ■ Wisconsin Holstein Association (WHA)
902 8th Ave.
Baraboo, WI 53913
Fax: (608)356-6312
Free: (800)223-4269
E-mail: chrisw@wisholsteins.com
URL: http://www.wisholsteins.com
Contact: Bruce Towns, Mgr.
Founded: 1890. **Members:** 5,200. **Membership Dues:** adult, $35 (annual) • junior, $12 (annual). **Staff:** 4. **Budget:** $435,000. **State.** Holstein dairy farmers. Promotes Holstein dairy farming. Holds cattle shows, seminars, and workshops. **Publications:** *Wisconsin Holstein News*, monthly. Newsletter. **Price:** $35.00/year. **Conventions/Meetings:** annual convention.

Barnes

17580 ■ Barnes Area Development Corporation
c/o Town of Barnes
3360 Co. Hwy. N
Barnes, WI 54873-9515
Ph: (715)795-2782
Fax: (715)795-2784
E-mail: clerk@barnes-wi.com
Contact: Arthur Smith, Pres.
Founded: 1999. **Members:** 8. **Local.** Local industrial park.

Barneveld

17581 ■ American Legion, Eveland-Trainor Post 433
101 Wood St.
Barneveld, WI 53507
Ph: (608)745-1090
Fax: (608)745-0179
URL: National Affiliate–www.legion.org
Local. Affiliated With: American Legion.

Barron

17582 ■ American Legion, Brown-Selvig Post 212
PO Box 12
Barron, WI 54812
Ph: (608)745-1090
Fax: (608)745-0179
URL: National Affiliate–www.legion.org
Local. Affiliated With: American Legion.

Bay City

17583 ■ American Legion, Harding-Hall-Darrington Post 357
PO Box 156
Bay City, WI 54723
Ph: (608)745-1090
Fax: (608)745-0179
URL: National Affiliate–www.legion.org
Local. Affiliated With: American Legion.

Bayfield

17584 ■ American Legion, Toutloff-Saunders-Duffy Post 49
PO Box 807
Bayfield, WI 54814
Ph: (608)745-1090
Fax: (608)745-0179
URL: National Affiliate–www.legion.org
Local. Affiliated With: American Legion.

17585 ■ Bayfield Chamber of Commerce
42 S Broad St.
PO Box 138
Bayfield, WI 54814
Ph: (715)779-3335
Fax: (715)779-5080
Free: (800)447-4094
E-mail: chamber@bayfield.org
URL: http://www.bayfield.org
Contact: Cari Obst, Exec.Dir.
Members: 250. **Membership Dues:** attraction, financial, utility, restaurant/bar (over 10 seats), marina (over 50 slips), $400 (annual) • lodging (add $10/room over two rooms), orchard, campground, recreational service, professional service, $250 (annual) • non-profit, $195 (annual). **Staff:** 3. **Local.** Promotes business and community development in Bayfield, WI area. **Awards:** Good Neighbor Award. **Frequency:** annual. **Type:** recognition. **Recipient:** for beautification efforts of individuals, businesses and nonprofit organizations. **Publications:** Newsletter, monthly.

17586 ■ Chequamegon Audubon Society
105 S Seventh St.
Bayfield, WI 54814
E-mail: larshowk@cheqnet.net
URL: http://www.audubon.org/chapter/wi/index.html
Contact: Neil Howk, Pres.
Local. Formerly: (2005) National Audubon Society - Chequamegon Chapter.

17587 ■ Pike's Creek Keel Club
34480 Port Superior Rd.
Bayfield, WI 54814
E-mail: treasurer@pckc.org
URL: http://www.pckc.org
Contact: Pat Noordsij, Treas.
Local.

17588 ■ Sons of Norway, Birkebeiner Lodge 5-611
c/o Steven R. Kurtz, Pres.
85360 County Hwy. J
Bayfield, WI 54814-4454
Ph: (715)779-3165
E-mail: kurtz@cheqnet.net
URL: National Affiliate–www.sofn.com
Contact: Steven R. Kurtz, Pres.
Local. Affiliated With: Sons of Norway.

Beaver Dam

17589 ■ American Legion, Wisconsin Post 146
c/o John E. Miller
PO Box 146
Beaver Dam, WI 53916

Ph: (608)745-1090
Fax: (608)745-0179
URL: National Affiliate–www.legion.org
Contact: John E. Miller, Contact
Local. Affiliated With: American Legion.

17590 ■ Beaver Dam Area Chamber of Commerce (BDACC)
127 S Spring St.
Beaver Dam, WI 53916
Ph: (920)887-8879
Fax: (920)887-9750
E-mail: info@beaverdamchamber.com
URL: http://www.beaverdamchamber.com
Contact: Philip Fritsche, Exec.Dir.
Founded: 1922. **Local.** Promotes business and community development in the Beaver Dam, WI area. Offers a Beaver Dam Health Program to members. **Affiliated With:** American Chamber of Commerce Executives; Community Leadership Association; U.S. Chamber of Commerce. **Publications:** *News From Your Chamber*, monthly. Newsletter. **Conventions/Meetings:** annual Legislative Dialogue - meeting • annual Recognition Dinner.

17591 ■ Classical Association of Wisconsin
Wayland Acad.
101 N Univ. Ave.
Beaver Dam, WI 53916
Ph: (920)885-3373
E-mail: klake@wayland.org
URL: http://www.camws.org
Contact: Keely Lake, VP
State. Represents university, college, secondary and elementary teachers of Latin, Greek and all other studies which focus on the world of classical antiquity. Supports and promotes the study of classical languages.

17592 ■ Dodge County Area District Nurses Association - No. 15
N8411 Fairway Dr.
Beaver Dam, WI 53916
Ph: (920)887-2633
E-mail: mossv@uwosh.edu
URL: http://www.wisconsinnurses.org
Contact: Vicki Moss, Pres.
Local. Works to advance the nursing profession. Seeks to meet the needs of nurses and health care consumers. Fosters high standards of nursing practice. Promotes the economic and general welfare of nurses in the workplace. **Affiliated With:** American Nurses Association; Wisconsin Nurses' Association.

17593 ■ Dodge County Fair Association
PO Box 654
Beaver Dam, WI 53916
Ph: (920)885-3586 (920)887-1522
Fax: (920)386-4437
E-mail: fair@dodgecountyfairgrounds.com
URL: http://www.dodgecountyfairgrounds.com
Contact: James Schoenike, Pres.
Founded: 1887. **Members:** 9. **Local.** Organizes Dodge County Fair.

17594 ■ Habitat for Humanity of Dodge County, Wisconsin (HFHDC)
PO Box 471
Beaver Dam, WI 53916-0471
Ph: (920)356-9812
E-mail: hfhdc@powerweb.net
URL: National Affiliate–www.habitat.org
Local. Provides housing projects for families in Dodge County. **Affiliated With:** Habitat for Humanity International.

17595 ■ Society for Human Resource Management - Dodge County Chapter
c/o Mary Rothschadl
707 S Univ. Ave.
Beaver Dam, WI 53916
Ph: (920)887-4100
Fax: (920)887-4101
URL: http://www.wishrm.org/chapter/dodgeCo/index.html
Contact: Steve Foerster, Pres.
Local. Represents the interests of human resource and industrial relations professionals and executives. Promotes the advancement of human resource management.

17596 ■ Swan City Ice Skaters
216 Haskell St.
Beaver Dam, WI 53916
E-mail: betswan@ameritech.net
URL: National Affiliate–www.usfigureskating.org
Contact: Bette Swanke, Contact
Local. Provides programs to encourage participation and achievement in the sport of figure skating on ice. Defines and maintains uniform standards of skating proficiency. Organizes and sponsors competitions and exhibitions for the purpose of stimulating interest in figure skating. **Affiliated With:** United States Figure Skating Association.

17597 ■ Trout Unlimited - Aldo Leopold Chapter
805 S Center St.
Beaver Dam, WI 53916-2807
Ph: (920)356-0081
E-mail: barniskis@yahoo.com
URL: http://www.tu.org
Contact: Clinton Byrnes, Pres.
Local.

17598 ■ United Way of Dodge County, Wisconsin
PO Box 158
Beaver Dam, WI 53916-0158
Ph: (920)885-2488
URL: National Affiliate–national.unitedway.org
Local. Affiliated With: United Way of America.

Beetown

17599 ■ American Legion, Thorpe-Taylor Post 551
PO Box 751
Beetown, WI 53802
Ph: (608)745-1090
Fax: (608)745-0179
URL: National Affiliate–www.legion.org
Local. Affiliated With: American Legion.

Belgium

17600 ■ American Legion, Belgium Memorial Post 412
PO Box 186
Belgium, WI 53004
Ph: (608)745-1090
Fax: (608)745-0179
URL: National Affiliate–www.legion.org
Local. Affiliated With: American Legion.

Belleville

17601 ■ American Legion, Duppler-Smith Post 460
PO Box 455
Belleville, WI 53508
Ph: (608)745-1090
Fax: (608)745-0179
URL: National Affiliate–www.legion.org
Local. Affiliated With: American Legion.

17602 ■ Belleville Community Club
Box 16
Belleville, WI 53508
Ph: (608)424-3747 (608)424-3147
Contact: Mr. Dan Edge, Pres.
Founded: 1942. **Members:** 220. **Membership Dues:** individual, couple, $5 (annual) • business, $10 (annual). **Budget:** $90,000. **Local.**

Belmont

17603 ■ American Legion, Hinkins-Moody Post 453
c/o Ken Leahy
134 Engelke Dr.
Belmont, WI 53510
Ph: (608)745-1090
Fax: (608)745-0179
URL: National Affiliate–www.legion.org
Contact: Ken Leahy, Contact
Local. Affiliated With: American Legion.

Beloit

17604 ■ American Ex-Prisoners of War, Southern Wisconsin Chapter
2489 Austin Pl.
Beloit, WI 53511-2324
Ph: (608)365-3591
URL: National Affiliate–www.axpow.org
Contact: Jean Meade, Sec.
Local. Affiliated With: American Ex-Prisoners of War.

17605 ■ American Legion, West-Field Post 48
236 St. Lawrence Ave.
Beloit, WI 53511
Ph: (608)745-1090
Fax: (608)745-0179
URL: National Affiliate–www.legion.org
Local. Affiliated With: American Legion.

17606 ■ Beloit Fencing Club
c/o Jeffrey Ozanne, Pres.
600 Emerson St.
Beloit, WI 53511
Ph: (608)363-4275
E-mail: fencing@beloit.edu
URL: http://www.beloit.edu/~fencing
Local. Amateur fencers. **Affiliated With:** United States Fencing Association.

17607 ■ Girl Scouts of Badger Council
1201 Big Hill Ct.
Beloit, WI 53511
Ph: (608)362-8922
Fax: (608)362-4084
Free: (800)362-3226
E-mail: info@gsbadger.com
URL: http://www.gsbadger.org
Local. Young girls and adult volunteers, corporate, government and individual supporters. Strives to develop potential and leadership skills among its members. Conducts trainings, educational programs and outdoor activities.

17608 ■ GRASLand Conservancy
c/o Bill Hallstrom, Chair.
2042 Meridith Dr.
Beloit, WI 53511
Ph: (608)365-5884
E-mail: audubonman@aol.com
Contact: Bill Hallstrom, Chair.
Founded: 1991. **Members:** 360. **Budget:** $250,000. **For-Profit. Local.** Works to acquire land, conservation easements, and farm preservation easements in Green, Eastern Lafayette, and Rock counties as well as portions of Dane, Iowa, and Jefferson counties. **Committees:** East Branch Raccoon Creek Advisory Committee; Executive Committee; Land Management Committee.

17609 ■ Greater Beloit Chamber of Commerce (GBCC)
520 E Grand Ave.
Beloit, WI 53511
Ph: (608)365-8835
Fax: (608)365-9345
E-mail: info@greaterbeloitchamber.com
URL: http://www.greaterbeloitchamber.com
Contact: Nancy Forbeck, Pres.

Founded: 1927. **Members:** 350. **Local**. Promotes business and community development in the Beloit, WI area. Holds annual festival, seminars, and high school career expo. Maintains speaker's bureau. **Commissions:** Stateline Community Marketing. **Councils:** Stateline Leadership Academy. **Affiliated With:** U.S. Chamber of Commerce. **Formerly:** Greater Beloit Association. **Publications:** *CCGB News*, monthly. Newsletter. **Price:** $15.00 /year for individuals • *The Network*. Newsletter. **Advertising:** accepted. Alternate Formats: online • Directory, annual. **Conventions/Meetings:** annual dinner - always in February.

17610 ■ Green-Rock Audubon Society (GRAS)
2042 Meridith
Beloit, WI 53511
Ph: (608)365-5884
E-mail: audubonman@aol.com
URL: http://www.audubon.org/chapter/wi/index.html
Contact: Bill Hallstrom, Pres.

Founded: 1991. **Members:** 360. **Membership Dues:** chapter, $15 (annual) • senior and student, $10 (annual) • joint (with national audubon society), $20 (annual). **Budget:** $15,000. **For-Profit**. **Local**. **Awards:** Environmental Business of the Year. **Frequency:** annual. **Type:** recognition. **Recipient:** for outstanding effort by a business to reduce pollution, protect wildlife, recycle, and/or promote environmental education • Environmental Teacher of the Year. **Frequency:** annual. **Type:** monetary. **Recipient:** for making children aware of protecting and appreciating environment • Environmentalist of the Year. **Frequency:** annual. **Type:** recognition. **Recipient:** for outstanding environmental work operation • Meritorious Service Award. **Frequency:** annual. **Type:** recognition. **Recipient:** for long and caring service in the field of the environment. **Computer Services:** Online services, environmental alerts through e-mail. **Committees:** Semi-Autonomous. **Subgroups:** Grassland Conservancy. **Affiliated With:** National Audubon Society. **Also Known As:** (2004) National Audubon Society - Green Rock. **Publications:** *The NAturalist*, quarterly. Newsletter. Describes what the organization is doing. **Price:** free with membership. **Circulation:** 525.

17611 ■ Izaak Walton League of America - Beloit
c/o James Dencker
751 E Morning Glory
Beloit, WI 53511
Ph: (608)362-5574
URL: http://www.iwla.org
Contact: James Dencker, Contact

Local. Educates the public to conserve, maintain, protect, and restore the soil, forest, water, and other natural resources of the U.S. Promotes the utilization of these resources. Sponsors environmental programs.

17612 ■ Kiwanis Club of Beloit Stateline Golden K
c/o Larry Durben, Pres.
2521 Lori Ann Dr.
Beloit, WI 53511
Ph: (608)365-8526
URL: http://kc_beloit_sl_gk.tripod.com/beloitstatelinegoldenk
Contact: Larry Durben, Pres.

Local.

17613 ■ Mothers Against Drunk Driving, Rock/Walworth Counties
2240 Prairie Ave. PMB1954
Beloit, WI 53511
Ph: (608)365-8100
Fax: (608)365-8100
URL: National Affiliate–www.madd.org
Contact: Virginia Boran, Pres.

Local. Victims of drunk driving crashes; concerned citizens. Encourages citizen participation in working towards reform of the drunk driving problem and the prevention of underage drinking. Acts as the voice of victims of drunk driving crashes by speaking on their behalf to communities, businesses, and educational groups. **Affiliated With:** Mothers Against Drunk Driving.

17614 ■ Northern Illinois Beagle Club
c/o Dwain Hoefer
3520 W Spring Creek Rd.
Beloit, WI 53511-8444
URL: National Affiliate–clubs.akc.org
Contact: Dwain Hoefer, Contact

Local.

17615 ■ Overflowing Cup Total Life Center (OFCTLC)
306 State St.
PO Box 1075
Beloit, WI 53512-1075
Ph: (608)365-0365
Fax: (608)364-8971
E-mail: ofctlc@aol.com
URL: http://www.overflowingcup.org
Contact: Pastor Dave Fogderud, Pres.

Founded: 1974. **Staff:** 10. **Budget:** $50,000. **Nonmembership**. **Regional**. Charitable and religious organization which provides food, clothing, emergency shelter, and guidance counseling to individuals in southern Wisconsin and northern Illinois. Operates an extended care facility and a youth center, The Fun House. Holds concerts and worship services. **Libraries: Type:** open to the public. **Holdings:** 4,000; books. **Subjects:** Christian oriented. **Telecommunication Services:** electronic mail, ofctlcbooking@tds.net. **Formerly:** (1986) Overflowing Cup Christian Coffee House Ministry. **Publications:** *Calendar of Coffee House Activities*, periodic • *The Overflow*, periodic. Newsletter. **Conventions/Meetings:** weekly Alpha Recovery Group and Bible Study - workshop (exhibits) - Friday, Saturday, Monday, and Tuesday nights • festival, outdoor music.

17616 ■ Retired and Senior Volunteer Program of Rock County
c/o Robert W. Harlow, Exec.Dir.
81 Beloit Mall
Beloit, WI 53511
Ph: (608)362-9593
E-mail: rsvp@rsvp-rock.org
URL: http://www.seniorcorps.gov/about/programs/rsvp_state.asp?usestateabbr=wi&Search4.x=26&Search4.y=7
Contact: Robert W. Harlow, Exec.Dir.

Local. Affiliated With: Retired and Senior Volunteer Program.

17617 ■ Rock Valley Youth for Christ
PO Box 1113
Beloit, WI 53512-1113
Ph: (608)758-3610
Fax: (608)758-3615
URL: http://www.rvyfc.org

Local. Affiliated With: Youth for Christ/U.S.A.

17618 ■ South Central Professional Photographers Association (SCPA)
c/o Dawn Schreier, Pres.
1629 E Inman Pkwy., No. 4
Beloit, WI 53511
Ph: (608)712-3686
E-mail: dawnklitzke@hotmail.com
URL: http://www.southcentralppa.com
Contact: Dawn Schreier, Pres.

Local. Affiliated With: Professional Photographers of America.

17619 ■ Stateline United Way
400 E Grand Ave., Ste.101
Beloit, WI 53511-6200
Ph: (608)365-4451
URL: National Affiliate–national.unitedway.org

Local. Affiliated With: United Way of America.

Benton

17620 ■ American Legion, Wisconsin Post 290
c/o Milton B. Wiseman
489 Galena St.
Benton, WI 53803
Ph: (608)745-1090
Fax: (608)745-0179
URL: National Affiliate–www.legion.org
Contact: Milton B. Wiseman, Contact

Local. Affiliated With: American Legion.

17621 ■ Izaak Walton League of America, Southwestern Chapter
c/o Sandy Crabtree
5186 County I
Benton, WI 53803
Ph: (608)759-4083
E-mail: leadmine@mhtc.net
URL: National Affiliate–www.iwla.org

Regional. Works to educate the public to conserve, maintain, protect, and restore the soil, forest, water, and other natural resources of the U.S; promotes the enjoyment and wholesome utilization of these resources. **Affiliated With:** Izaak Walton League of America.

17622 ■ Puppeteers of America - Wisconsin Puppetry Guild
c/o Sandye Voight, Pres.
362 E Main
Benton, WI 53803
Ph: (608)759-4425
E-mail: info@wipuppetry.org
URL: http://www.wipuppetry.org
Contact: Sandye Voight, Pres.

State.

Berlin

17623 ■ American Legion, O.-Connor-Chiers Post 340
140 S Adams Ave.
Berlin, WI 54923
Ph: (608)745-1090
Fax: (608)745-0179
URL: National Affiliate–www.legion.org

Local. Affiliated With: American Legion.

17624 ■ Berlin Chamber of Commerce (BCC)
161 W Hurin St.
Berlin, WI 54923
Ph: (920)361-3636
Fax: (920)361-5439
Free: (800)979-9334
E-mail: berlinchamber@dotnet.com
Contact: Lisa Schilling, Exec.Dir.

Founded: 1948. **Members:** 110. **Membership Dues:** diamond (40 and above employees), $950 • emerald (31-39 employees), $850 • ruby (21-30 employees), $750 • sapphire (11-20 employees), $600 • pearl (4-10 employees), $400 • licensed professional, $250 • opal (1-3 employees), $195 • club and organization, $50. **Local**. Promotes business and community development in Berlin, WI. **Publications:** *CommUNITY*, quarterly. Newsletter. Features upcoming chamber events and local articles of interest. • *Visi-*

tor's Guide. Directory. **Conventions/Meetings:** quarterly meeting - every 1st and 3rd Thursday in Berlin, WI • annual meeting.

17625 ■ Berlin Community Development Corporation (BCDC)
c/o Scott Larson, Dir.
PO Box 64
108 N Capron St.
Berlin, WI 54923-0064
Ph: (920)361-5402
Fax: (920)361-5431
E-mail: berlinchamber@dotnet.com
URL: http://www.1berlin.com
Contact: Scott Larson, Contact
Founded: 1991. **Members:** 9. **Staff:** 1. **Local**. Strives to facilitate community growth and revitalization through enhanced economic and social development.

Big Bend

17626 ■ Big Bend-Vernon Lions Club
W231 S9205 Riverside St.
Big Bend, WI 53103
Ph: (262)662-2260
E-mail: president@bigbendvernonlions.org
URL: http://www.bigbendvernonlions.org
Contact: Joan Weber, Pres.
Local. Affiliated With: Lions Clubs International.

Birnamwood

17627 ■ American Legion, Darling-Gunderson Post 341
PO Box 121
Birnamwood, WI 54414
Ph: (608)745-1090
Fax: (608)745-0179
URL: National Affiliate–www.legion.org
Local. Affiliated With: American Legion.

17628 ■ National Active and Retired Federal Employees Association - Wausau 689
PO Box 236
Birnamwood, WI 54414-0236
Ph: (715)449-3988
URL: National Affiliate–www.narfe.org
Contact: Michael F. Smith, Contact
Local. Protects the retirement future of employees through education. Informs members on issues affecting the retirement. **Affiliated With:** National Association of Retired Federal Employees.

Black Creek

17629 ■ American Legion, Duhm-Masch Post 332
PO Box 202
Black Creek, WI 54106
Ph: (608)745-1090
Fax: (608)745-0179
URL: National Affiliate–www.legion.org
Local. Affiliated With: American Legion.

Black Earth

17630 ■ American Legion, Mickelsons-Martin Post 313
PO Box 283
Black Earth, WI 53515
Ph: (608)745-1090
Fax: (608)745-0179
URL: National Affiliate–www.legion.org
Local. Affiliated With: American Legion.

Black River Falls

17631 ■ American Legion, Miles-Hagen Post 200
421 Hwy. 54
Black River Falls, WI 54615
Ph: (608)745-1090
Fax: (608)745-0179
URL: National Affiliate–www.legion.org
Local. Affiliated With: American Legion.

17632 ■ Black River Falls Figure Skating Club
PO Box 853
Black River Falls, WI 54615
E-mail: dunnfour@cuttingedge.net
URL: National Affiliate–www.usfigureskating.org
Contact: Judy Dunneisen, Contact
Local. Provides programs to encourage participation and achievement in the sport of figure skating on ice. Defines and maintains uniform standards of skating proficiency. Organizes and sponsors competitions and exhibitions for the purpose of stimulating interest in figure skating. **Affiliated With:** United States Figure Skating Association.

17633 ■ National Active and Retired Federal Employees Association - Tri-County 1386
1013 Fillmore St.
Black River Falls, WI 54615-1528
Ph: (715)284-1693
URL: National Affiliate–www.narfe.org
Contact: Robert C. Uhrig, Contact
Local. Protects the retirement future of employees through education. Informs members on issues affecting the retirement. **Affiliated With:** National Association of Retired Federal Employees.

17634 ■ Sons of Norway, Fossen Lodge 5-534
c/o Lucy J. Anderson, Pres.
N7375 S Odeen Rd.
Black River Falls, WI 54615-5817
Ph: (715)284-7590
E-mail: lucymerl@jackelec.com
URL: National Affiliate–www.sofn.com
Contact: Lucy J. Anderson, Pres.
Local. Affiliated With: Sons of Norway.

17635 ■ Sweet Adelines International, Rhythm of the River Chapter
United Methodist Church
100 N 4th St.
Black River Falls, WI 54615-1230
Ph: (715)488-4304
URL: http://www.rhythmoftheriver.com
Contact: Judy Andersen, Team Leader
Local. Advances the musical art form of barbershop harmony through education and performances. Provides education, training and coaching in the development of women's four-part barbershop harmony. **Affiliated With:** Sweet Adelines International.

Blair

17636 ■ American Legion, Knudtson-Mattison Post 231
231 W Broadway St.
Blair, WI 54616
Ph: (608)745-1090
Fax: (608)745-0179
URL: National Affiliate–www.legion.org
Local. Affiliated With: American Legion.

17637 ■ Blair Chamber of Commerce
PO Box 413
Blair, WI 54616
Ph: (608)989-2517
Contact: Dale Olson, Pres.
Local.

17638 ■ Sons of Norway, Fagernes Lodge 5-616
c/o Eddie M. Thompson, Pres.
N25966 Joe Coulee Rd.
Blair, WI 54616-9032
Ph: (608)525-6067
E-mail: latemt@msn.com
URL: National Affiliate–www.sofn.com
Contact: Eddie M. Thompson, Pres.
Local. Affiliated With: Sons of Norway.

17639 ■ Wisconsin Health Care Association, District 9
c/o Stacy Suchla, Pres.
Grand View Care Ctr.
620 Grand View Ave.
Blair, WI 54616
Ph: (608)989-2511
URL: http://www.whca.com
Contact: Stacy Suchla, Pres.
Local. Promotes professionalism and ethical behavior of individuals providing long-term care delivery for patients and for the general public. Provides information, education and administrative tools to enhance the quality of long-term care. Improves the standards of service and administration of member nursing homes. **Affiliated With:** American Health Care Association; Wisconsin Health Care Association.

Blanchardville

17640 ■ American Legion, Dobson-Johnson Post 142
100 Mason St.
Blanchardville, WI 53516
Ph: (608)523-4016
Fax: (608)745-0179
URL: National Affiliate–www.legion.org
Local. Affiliated With: American Legion.

Bloomer

17641 ■ American Legion, Wisconsin Post 295
c/o Martin A. Treptow
PO Box 71
Bloomer, WI 54724
Ph: (608)745-1090
Fax: (608)745-0179
URL: National Affiliate–www.legion.org
Contact: Martin A. Treptow, Contact
Local. Affiliated With: American Legion.

17642 ■ Bloomer Chamber of Commerce
PO Box 273
Bloomer, WI 54724
Ph: (715)568-3339
Fax: (715)568-3345
E-mail: bchamber@bloomer.net
URL: http://www.bloomer.net/~bchamber
Contact: Rod Turner, Exec.Dir.
Local. Promotes business and community development in Bloomer, WI area. **Publications:** Newsletter. Alternate Formats: online.

Bloomington

17643 ■ Wisconsin Association of Meat Processors
PO Box 505
Bloomington, WI 53804
Ph: (608)994-3173
Fax: (608)994-3173
E-mail: kbisarek@hotmail.com
URL: http://www.wi-amp.com
Contact: Kenneth J. Bisarek, Exec.Sec.
State. Works for the advancement and improvement of the Meat Processing industry by encouraging and fostering high ethical standards of good business practices in the industry and the cooperation of all engaged in the industry by the interchange of ideas

and business methods as a means of increasing efficiency and usefulness of the industry to the general public. **Affiliated With:** American Association of Meat Processors.

Blue River

17644 ■ American Legion, Wisconsin Post 443
c/o Robert R. Shattuck
PO Box 85
Blue River, WI 53518
Ph: (608)745-1090
Fax: (608)745-0179
URL: National Affiliate–www.legion.org
Contact: Robert R. Shattuck, Contact
Local. Affiliated With: American Legion.

Bonduel

17645 ■ American Legion, Wisconsin Post 392
c/o William H. Meyer
W 4969 Resort Rd.
Bonduel, WI 54107
Ph: (608)745-1090
Fax: (608)745-0179
URL: National Affiliate–www.legion.org
Contact: William H. Meyer, Contact
Local. Affiliated With: American Legion.

17646 ■ American Legion, Zernicke-Wegner Post 217
PO Box 156
Bonduel, WI 54107
Ph: (608)745-1090
Fax: (608)745-0179
URL: National Affiliate–www.legion.org
Local. Affiliated With: American Legion.

Boscobel

17647 ■ American Legion, Blake-Semrad Post 134
PO Box 134
Boscobel, WI 53805
Ph: (608)745-1090
Fax: (608)745-0179
URL: National Affiliate–www.legion.org
Local. Affiliated With: American Legion.

17648 ■ Boscobel Chamber of Commerce
800 Wisconsin Ave.
Boscobel, WI 53805
Ph: (608)375-2672 (608)375-6050
E-mail: bchamber@centurytel.net
URL: http://www.boscobelwisconsin.com
Contact: Corey Grassel, Pres.
Local. Promotes business and community development in Boscobel, WI area.

17649 ■ Wisconsin Educational Media Association (WEMA)
c/o Courtney Rounds, Association Mgr.
PO Box 206
Boscobel, WI 53805
Ph: (608)375-6020
E-mail: wema@centurytel.net
URL: http://wemaonline.org
Contact: Courtney Rounds, Association Mgr.
Founded: 1948. **Members:** 1,100. **Membership Dues:** professional, $40 (annual). **Budget:** $60,000. **Regional Groups:** 12. **State.** School library media professionals. Sponsors school media fair. **Awards:** Media Grants. **Frequency:** annual. **Type:** grant • WEMA Awards. **Type:** recognition. **Affiliated With:** American Association of School Librarians; Association for Educational Communications and Technology. **Formerly:** Wisconsin Audiovisual Association. **Publications:** *WEMA Dispatch*, bimonthly. Newsletter • *Wisconsin Ideas in Media*, annual. Journal • Membership Directory, annual. **Conventions/Meetings:** annual conference (exhibits) - always spring.

Boulder Junction

17650 ■ Boulder Junction Chamber of Commerce
PO Box 286
Boulder Junction, WI 54512-0286
Ph: (715)385-2400
Fax: (715)385-2379
Free: (800)466-8759
E-mail: boulderjct@boulderjct.org
URL: http://www.boulderjct.org
Local. Promotes business and community development in Boulder Junction, WI area.

Bowler

17651 ■ American Legion, Davenport-Lang Post 414
PO Box 65
Bowler, WI 54416
Ph: (608)745-1090
Fax: (608)745-0179
URL: National Affiliate–www.legion.org
Local. Affiliated With: American Legion.

Boyceville

17652 ■ American Legion, Harmon-Harris Post 314
PO Box 157
Boyceville, WI 54725
Ph: (608)745-1090
Fax: (608)745-0179
URL: National Affiliate–www.legion.org
Local. Affiliated With: American Legion.

17653 ■ Sons of Norway, Solheim Lodge 5-278
c/o Victoria L. Maves, Sec.
E4990 920th Ave.
Boyceville, WI 54725-5039
Ph: (715)632-2486
E-mail: cvmaves@wwt.net
URL: National Affiliate–www.sofn.com
Contact: Victoria L. Maves, Sec.
Local. Affiliated With: Sons of Norway.

Boyd

17654 ■ American Legion, Wisconsin Post 326
c/o Walter Nelson
PO Box 95
Boyd, WI 54726
Ph: (608)745-1090
Fax: (608)745-0179
URL: National Affiliate–www.legion.org
Contact: Walter Nelson, Contact
Local. Affiliated With: American Legion.

Brandon

17655 ■ American Legion, Mattox-Henslin Post 378
100 Maria St.
Brandon, WI 53919
Ph: (608)745-1090
Fax: (608)745-0179
URL: National Affiliate–www.legion.org
Local. Affiliated With: American Legion.

Briggsville

17656 ■ American Legion, Wisconsin Post 329
c/o Carl E. Grabman
PO Box 211
Briggsville, WI 53920
Ph: (608)745-1090
Fax: (608)745-0179
URL: National Affiliate–www.legion.org
Contact: Carl E. Grabman, Contact
Local. Affiliated With: American Legion.

Brillion

17657 ■ American Legion, Bloedorn-Becker-Jensen Post 126
216 Washington St.
Brillion, WI 54110
Ph: (608)745-1090
Fax: (608)745-0179
URL: National Affiliate–www.legion.org
Local. Affiliated With: American Legion.

17658 ■ Brillion Area Chamber of Commerce
PO Box 123
Brillion, WI 54110
Ph: (920)756-3575
E-mail: kgolaw@charter.net
URL: http://www.brillionchamber.com
Contact: Keith G. Ondrasek, Pres.
Local. Promotes business and community development in Brillion, WI area.

Bristol

17659 ■ Wisconsin Rifle and Pistol Association (WRPA)
c/o Eric Obermeyer, Pres.
PO Box 263
Bristol, WI 53104
Ph: (262)843-3537
E-mail: ejobermeyer@yahoo.com
URL: http://www.wrpa.com
Contact: Eric Obermeyer, Pres.
State. Affiliated With: National Rifle Association of America.

Brodhead

17660 ■ American Legion, Swann-Gehr Post 197
809 E Exchange St.
Brodhead, WI 53520
Ph: (608)745-1090
Fax: (608)745-0179
URL: National Affiliate–www.legion.org
Local. Affiliated With: American Legion.

17661 ■ Brodhead Chamber of Commerce
PO Box 16
Brodhead, WI 53520-0016
Ph: (608)897-8411
E-mail: nancy@brodheadchamber.org
URL: http://www.brodheadchamber.org
Contact: Nancy Sutherland, Sec.
Membership Dues: business (based on number of employees), $115-$275 (annual) • associate, $30 (annual). **Local.** Promotes business and community development in Brodhead, WI area. **Conventions/Meetings:** monthly meeting - every 3rd Monday.

Brookfield

17662 ■ American Hellenic Educational Progressive Association - Milwaukee, Chapter 43
c/o Demetrios Mavraganis, Pres.
3445 Avalon Dr.
Brookfield, WI 53045

Ph: (262)790-0232
E-mail: dmavraganis@aol.com
URL: http://www.ahepafamily.org/d13
Contact: Demetrios Mavraganis, Pres.
Local. Affiliated With: American Hellenic Educational Progressive Association.

17663 ■ American Legion, Behling-Kutchera Post 296
PO Box 315
Brookfield, WI 53008
Ph: (608)745-1090
Fax: (608)745-0179
URL: National Affiliate–www.legion.org
Local. Affiliated With: American Legion.

17664 ■ American Legion, Stenz-Griesell-Smith Post 449
3245 N 124th St.
Brookfield, WI 53005
Ph: (608)745-1090
Fax: (608)745-0179
URL: National Affiliate–www.legion.org
Local. Affiliated With: American Legion.

17665 ■ American Lung Association of Wisconsin (ALAW)
13100 W Lisbon Rd., Ste.700
Brookfield, WI 53005-2508
Ph: (262)703-4200
Fax: (262)781-5180
Free: (800)LUNG-USA
E-mail: amlung@lungwisconsin.org
URL: http://lungusa2.org/wisconsin
Contact: Margaret MacLeod Brahm, Pres./CEO
Founded: 1908. **Staff:** 19. **Budget:** $2,000,000. **Regional Groups:** 1. **State.** Promotes lung health and works to prevent lung disease through research, public policy, education and community service by focusing on asthma, tobacco and environmental health. **Awards: Frequency:** annual. **Type:** grant. **Recipient:** for research related to lung disease and lung health. **Affiliated With:** American Lung Association. **Formerly:** (1980) Wisconsin Lung Association. **Publications:** *Fight for Life*, semiannual. Newsletter. **Circulation:** 100,000. **Conventions/Meetings:** annual conference, conferences for health professionals/various topics.

17666 ■ American Society of Appraisers, Wisconsin Chapter
c/o James W. Volkman, Pres.
Corporate Valuation Advisors
250 N Sunny Slope Rd., Ste.110
Brookfield, WI 53005-4811
Ph: (262)821-5996
Fax: (262)821-1666
E-mail: jvolkman@corporatevaluationadvisors.com
URL: http://www.appraisers.org/wisconsin
Contact: James W. Volkman, Pres.
State. Serves as a professional appraisal educator, testing and accrediting society. Sponsors mandatory recertification program for all members. Offers consumer information service to the public. **Affiliated With:** American Society of Appraisers.

17667 ■ American Society of Golf Course Architects (ASGCA)
125 N Executive Dr., Ste.106
Brookfield, WI 53005
Ph: (262)786-5690
Fax: (262)786-5919
E-mail: info@asgca.org
URL: http://www.asgca.org
Regional. Affiliated With: International Association of Golf Administrators.

17668 ■ Greater Brookfield Chamber of Commerce (GBCC)
1305 N Barker Rd., Ste.5
Brookfield, WI 53045
Ph: (262)786-1886
Fax: (262)786-1959
E-mail: carol@brookfieldchamber.com
URL: http://www.brookfieldchamber.com
Contact: Carol White, Exec.Dir.
Membership Dues: business (with 1-75 employees), $275-$600 (annual) • business (with 76-300 employees), $710-$1,195 (annual). **Local.** Promotes business and community development in Brookfield, WI. **Formerly:** (1999) Brookfield Chamber of Commerce. **Publications:** *Net Works*, monthly. Newsletter. Alternate Formats: online • Membership Directory, biennial. **Conventions/Meetings:** monthly Active Business Leader Exchange - meeting - every 2nd and 4th Wednesday in Wauwatosa, WI.

17669 ■ Information Systems Security Association, Milwaukee Chapter
c/o Mr. Andrew Pretzl, CISSP, Pres.
Norlight Telecommunications
13935 Bishops Dr.
Brookfield, WI 53005
Ph: (262)792-7799
E-mail: president@issa-milwaukee.org
URL: http://www.issa-milwaukee.org
Contact: Mr. Andrew Pretzl CISSP, Pres.
Local. Represents information security professionals and practitioners. Enhances the knowledge, skill and professional growth of members. Provides educational forums and peer interaction opportunities. **Affiliated With:** Information Systems Security Association.

17670 ■ Infusion Nurses Society, Southern Wisconsin
c/o Jean Bennett
3360 Fiebrantz Dr.
Brookfield, WI 53005
Ph: (414)805-6449
E-mail: mhunter@fmlh.edu
URL: National Affiliate–www.ins1.org
Contact: Mark Hunter RN, Pres.
Local. Represents the interests of healthcare professionals who are involved with the practice of infusion therapy. Seeks to advance the delivery of quality therapy to patients. Promotes research and education in the practice of infusion nursing. **Affiliated With:** Infusion Nurses Society.

17671 ■ Kiwanis Club of Brookfield, Wisconsin
PO Box 294
Brookfield, WI 53005
Ph: (262)751-6040
E-mail: brookfieldkiwanis@hotmail.com
URL: http://my.execpc.com/~kruschep/kiwanis.htm
Local.

17672 ■ Learning Disabilities Association of Wisconsin
13035 W Bluemound Rd., Ste.100
Brookfield, WI 53005
Ph: (414)299-9002
Fax: (414)425-5113
Free: (866)LDA-WISC
E-mail: ldawisconsin@hotmail.com
URL: http://www.ldawisconsin.com
Contact: Linda Lehmann, Pres.
Founded: 1970. **Members:** 1,000. **Membership Dues:** regular, $35 (annual). **State Groups:** 1. **Local Groups:** 10. **State.** Individuals united to promote the interests of learning disabled youths and adults. **Libraries: Type:** not open to the public. **Holdings:** 150; articles, books. **Subjects:** learning disabilities, attention deficit disorders. **Telecommunication Services:** electronic mail, info@ldawisconsin.com. **Publications:** *Connections*. Newsletter. Alternate Formats: online • *Newsbrief*, quarterly. Newsletter. **Price:** included in membership dues. **Advertising:** accepted. **Conventions/Meetings:** annual conference (exhibits) - October.

17673 ■ Milwaukee Optometric Society
c/o Valerie Frazer, OD, Pres.
13255 W Bluemound Rd., Ste.200
Brookfield, WI 53005
Ph: (262)784-9201
Fax: (262)784-9206
E-mail: drvalod@yahoo.com
URL: http://www.woa-eyes.org
Contact: Valerie Frazer OD, Pres.
Local. Aims to improve the quality, availability and accessibility of eye and vision care. Promotes high standards of patient care. Monitors and promotes legislation concerning the scope of optometric practice and other issues relevant to eye/vision care. **Affiliated With:** American Optometric Association; Wisconsin Optometric Association.

17674 ■ National Association of Investors Corporation, Milwaukee Chapter
12655 Falcon Dr.
Brookfield, WI 53005
Ph: (262)786-8683
E-mail: eahurst@mail2world.com
URL: http://better-investing.org/chapter/milwaukee
Contact: Evonne Hurst, Pres.
Local. Teaches individuals how to become successful strategic long-term investors. Provides highly focused learning resources and investment tools that empower individuals to become better investors. **Affiliated With:** National Association of Investors Corporation.

17675 ■ National Kidney Foundation of Wisconsin
16655 W Bluemound Rd., Ste.240
Brookfield, WI 53005
Ph: (262)821-0705
Fax: (262)821-5641
Free: (800)543-6393
E-mail: nkfw@kidneywi.org
Affiliated With: National Kidney Foundation.

17676 ■ Nevada Funeral Directors Association (NFDA)
13625 Bishop's Dr.
Brookfield, WI 53005
Ph: (262)789-1880
Fax: (262)789-6977
Free: (800)228-6332
E-mail: nfda@nfda.org
URL: http://www.nfda.org
Contact: R.Dogget Whitacker Jr., Pres.
Founded: 1882. **Members:** 20,300. **Membership Dues:** retired licensee, $65 (annual) • apprentice, $55 (annual) • individual licensee, $290 (annual) • mortuary science student, $35 (annual) • life, $888. **Staff:** 49. **State.** Provides services and disseminates information to help members in providing better service to families especially during bereavement. **Computer Services:** database, member directory, trends and statistics, state associations • information services, fact sheets, funeral service and consumer resources • online services, resource store • online services, supplier dispatch, classified advertising, bulletin. **Telecommunication Services:** teleconference, speakerphone for staff training. **Programs:** For A Life Worth Saving; Funeral Service Consumer Assistance Program. **Affiliated With:** National Funeral Directors Association. **Publications:** *The Director*, monthly. Magazine. Offers in-depth features regarding funeral service. Alternate Formats: online. **Conventions/Meetings:** annual conference, about leadership • annual convention, with expo, workshops, seminars and networking opportunities (exhibits).

17677 ■ Public Relations Society of America, Southeastern Wisconsin Chapter
c/o Carol Weber
250 N Sunnyslope Rd.
Brookfield, WI 53005
Ph: (262)796-2220
Fax: (262)796-2000
E-mail: info@prsawis.org
URL: http://www.prsawis.org
Contact: Ms. Leslie Bonk, Website Mgr.
State. Affiliated With: Public Relations Society of America.

17678 ■ Tasters Guild International - Milwaukee, Chapter No. 017
17000 W Capital Dr.
Brookfield, WI 53005

Ph: (262)781-5575
Fax: (262)781-5472
E-mail: vineyardconsultants@yahoo.com
URL: National Affiliate–www.tastersguild.com
Contact: Bill Tobin, Mgr.
Local. Aims to educate consumers and spread the word of responsible wine and food consumption. Provides opportunity to encounter the best in wine and culinary delights. **Affiliated With:** Tasters Guild International.

17679 ■ Volunteers of America of Wisconsin
275 Regency Ct., Ste.104
Brookfield, WI 53045
Ph: (262)432-0118
Free: (800)481-3611
E-mail: info@voawi.org
URL: http://www.voawi.org
Contact: Jim Stewart, Pres./CEO
State. Affiliated With: Volunteers of America.

17680 ■ Waukesha Kennel Club
c/o Mrs. Lindley Henson, Pres.
1750 Jean Marie Ct.
Brookfield, WI 53005
Ph: (262)782-1758
E-mail: larrydhenson@yahoo.com
URL: http://www.waukeshakennelclub.com
Contact: Mrs. Lindley Henson, Pres.
Local.

17681 ■ Wisconsin Chapter, Leukemia and Lymphoma Society
c/o Bede Barth, Exec.Dir.
4125 N 124th St., Unit A
Brookfield, WI 53005
Ph: (262)790-4701
Fax: (262)790-4706
Free: (800)261-7399
E-mail: barthb@lls.org
URL: http://www.lls.com
Contact: Bede Barth, Exec.Dir.
State. Raises funds to combat leukemia, lymphoma, Hodgkin's Disease and myeloma through research, patient service, and public and professional education and advocacy. **Affiliated With:** Leukemia and Lymphoma Society.

17682 ■ Wisconsin Golf Course Superintendents Association (WGCSA)
Bishops Way, Ste.104
Brookfield, WI 53005
Ph: (262)786-4303 (920)887-0030
Fax: (262)786-4202
E-mail: mike@oldhickorycc.com
URL: http://www.wgcsa.com
Contact: Mike Lyons, Pres.
Membership Dues: class A, B, C, D, $150 (annual). **State**. Represents the interests of golf course superintendents. Advances members' profession for career success. Enhances the enjoyment, growth and vitality in the game of golf. Educates members concerning efficient and economical management of golf courses. **Affiliated With:** Golf Course Superintendents Association of America.

17683 ■ Wisconsin Innkeepers Association (WIA)
1025 S Moorland Rd., Ste.200
Brookfield, WI 53005
Ph: (262)782-2851
Fax: (262)782-0550
E-mail: wia@lodging-wi.com
URL: http://www.lodging-wi.com
Contact: Lola Roeh, Chm.
Membership Dues: lodging, $145-$198 (annual) • associate, $340 (annual) • educational institution, $280 (annual) • chamber, $200-$325 (annual) • student, $20 (annual). **State**. Aims to provide services and benefits for members to improve the profitability and success of the lodging industry in Wisconsin. **Affiliated With:** American Hotel and Lodging Association.

17684 ■ Wisconsin Institute of Certified Public Accountants (WICPA)
PO Box 1010
Brookfield, WI 53005
Ph: (262)785-0445
Fax: (262)785-0838
Free: (800)772-6939
E-mail: comments@wicpa.org
URL: http://www.wicpa.org
Founded: 1905. **State**.

17685 ■ Wisconsin Self-Service Laundry Association (WSLA)
17125C No. 204, W Bluemound Rd.
Brookfield, WI 53005
Ph: (262)662-4387
Fax: (262)662-4387
E-mail: dshine1@aol.com
URL: http://www.wsla.org
Contact: Don Shine, Pres.
State. Represents owners/managers of laundromats in Wisconsin. Sponsors twice-yearly trade shows and conventions for self-service laundry owners and managers. **Affiliated With:** Coin Laundry Association.

17686 ■ Wisconsin Senior Olympics
c/o Helen Ramon, Coor.
125 N Executive Dr., Ste.102
Brookfield, WI 53005
Ph: (262)821-4444
E-mail: info@wiseniorolympics.com
URL: http://www.wiseniorolympics.com
Contact: Helen Ramon, Coor.
Founded: 1984. **State**. Provide Wisconsin's older adults, men and women age 50 and over, the opportunity to improve their overall fitness and wellness through recreational, social and competitive events. **Affiliated With:** National Senior Games Association.

17687 ■ Wisconsin State Golf Association (WSGA)
333 Bishops Way, Ste.104
Brookfield, WI 53005
Fax: (262)786-4202
Free: (888)786-4301
E-mail: tom@wsga.org
URL: http://www.wsga.org
Contact: Thomas J. Schmidt, Exec.Dir.
Founded: 1901. **Members:** 378. **Membership Dues:** club, $125 (annual). **State**. Exists for the general purpose of promoting and conserving the best interests and the true spirit of the game of golf throughout the state of Wisconsin. **Affiliated With:** International Association of Golf Administrators.

17688 ■ Wisconsin Thoracic Society
c/o Michelle Mercure, Administrator
13100 W Lisbon Ave., Ste.700
Brookfield, WI 53005-2508
Ph: (262)703-4200
E-mail: tsandy@lungwisconsin.org
URL: National Affiliate–www.thoracic.org
Contact: Alan Pratt MD, Pres.
State. Aims to improve the study and practice of thoracic surgery and related disciplines. Seeks to prevent and fight respiratory diseases through research, education and patient advocacy. **Affiliated With:** American Thoracic Society.

Brooklyn

17689 ■ American Legion, Wisconsin Post 160
c/o Benjamin Johnson
PO Box 262
Brooklyn, WI 53521
Ph: (608)745-1090
Fax: (608)745-0179
URL: National Affiliate–www.legion.org
Contact: Benjamin Johnson, Contact
Local. Affiliated With: American Legion.

17690 ■ Brooklyn Area Chamber of Commerce
PO Box 33
108 Hotel St.
Brooklyn, WI 53521
Ph: (608)455-1627
Fax: (608)455-1627
E-mail: brooklyn@quicksitemaker.com
URL: http://www.brooklynwisconsin.com
Contact: LaVorn Dvorak, Pres.
Membership Dues: associate, $35 (annual) • self-employed, home-based business, $65 (annual) • professional/small business (1-5 employees), $125 (annual) • medium business (6-20 employees), $200 (annual) • industry/utility/large business (21 and up employees), $300 (annual) • very large business, $500 (annual). **Local**. Promotes and develop Brooklyn area business and at the same time provides education and supports its members businesses.

Brown Deer

17691 ■ Brown Deer Chamber of Commerce
3900 W Brown Deer Rd.
Brown Deer, WI 53209
Ph: (414)371-3055
Fax: (414)355-7879
E-mail: dausavich@ckrueger.net
URL: http://www.browndeerchamber.org
Contact: Diane Ausavich, Pres.
Local. Promotes business and community development in Brown Deer, WI.

17692 ■ Milwaukee Cricket Club
8041 N Sherman Blvd.
Brown Deer, WI 53209
URL: http://www.usaca.org/Clubs.htm
Contact: Dowen Virgo, Contact
Local.

17693 ■ USA Diving - No. 19 Wisconsin
c/o Gary Cox
9250 N Green Bay Rd.
Brown Deer, WI 53209
Ph: (414)357-2803
E-mail: gcox.sa@ymcamke.org
URL: National Affiliate–www.usdiving.org
State. Affiliated With: USA Diving.

Bruce

17694 ■ American Legion, Wisconsin Post 268
c/o Earl J. Conley
834 N Main
Bruce, WI 54819
Ph: (608)745-1090
Fax: (608)745-0179
URL: National Affiliate–www.legion.org
Contact: Earl J. Conley, Contact
Local. Affiliated With: American Legion.

Burlington

17695 ■ American Legion, Wisconsin Post 79
c/o Ross Wilcox
PO Box 2
Burlington, WI 53105
Ph: (608)745-1090
Fax: (608)745-0179
URL: National Affiliate–www.legion.org
Contact: Ross Wilcox, Contact
Local. Affiliated With: American Legion.

17696 ■ Burlington Area Chamber of Commerce (BACC)
113 E Chestnut St.
Burlington, WI 53105
Ph: (262)763-6044
E-mail: eherter@burlingtonchamber.org
URL: http://www.burlingtonchamber.org
Contact: Janice Ludtke, Exec.Dir.
Founded: 1944. **Staff:** 2. **Local**. Promotes business and community development in the Burlington, WI

area. Holds festival. **Committees:** Community Marketing. **Affiliated With:** U.S. Chamber of Commerce. **Publications:** *Burlington, Discover the Treasures*, monthly. Newspaper • *FOCUS*, monthly. Newsletter. Contains member news, committee reports, and other valuable information. **Price:** free for members only. **Conventions/Meetings:** monthly board meeting - every 1st Wednesday in Burlington, WI.

17697 ■ Burlington Lions Club (BLC)
PO Box 154
Burlington, WI 53105
Ph: (262)763-4484 (262)763-9322
Fax: (262)767-0190
Contact: Dennis Yanny, Pres.
Founded: 1950. **Members:** 71. **Membership Dues:** $63 (quarterly). **Budget:** $57,000. **Local.** Seeks to aid the blind and hearing impaired. Also serves community projects and charitable organizations. **Awards:** Hefty Scholarships (2). **Frequency:** annual. **Type:** scholarship. **Recipient:** high school graduate attending a vocational school. **Affiliated With:** Lions Clubs International. **Conventions/Meetings:** semimonthly meeting - always 2nd and 4th Monday of the month. Burlington, WI.

Butler

17698 ■ Butler Area Chamber of Commerce (BACC)
12810 W Hampton Ave.
Butler, WI 53007-1606
Ph: (262)781-5195
Fax: (262)781-7870
E-mail: info@butlerchamber.org
URL: http://www.butlerchamber.org
Contact: Linda C. Ryfinski, Exec.Dir.
Founded: 1970. **Members:** 200. **Membership Dues:** business (based on number of employees), $185-$480. **Local.** Promotes business and community development in the Butler, WI area. Offers special health insurance program for small businesses and real estate and employment referrals. **Awards:** Distinguished Business of the Year. **Frequency:** annual. **Type:** recognition • Distinguished Citizen of the Year. **Frequency:** annual. **Type:** recognition. **Committees:** Ambassador; Business/Economic Development/Government; Business Education/Speakers; Chamber Liaison; Golf; Retail. **Affiliated With:** U.S. Chamber of Commerce. **Publications:** *Butler Area Chamber of Commerce Newsletter*, monthly. **Price:** included in membership dues. **Conventions/Meetings:** annual Christmas Business After Hours - meeting - 2006 Dec. 7, Menomonee Falls, WI • annual dinner.

17699 ■ Butler Lions Club - Wisconsin
5154 N 127th St.
Butler, WI 53007
Ph: (262)781-8670
E-mail: sandicatwoman@aol.com
URL: http://butlerwi.lionwap.org
Contact: Sandi Thomas, 1st VP
Local. Affiliated With: Lions Clubs International.

17700 ■ Make-A-Wish Foundation of Wisconsin
13195 W Hampton Ave.
Butler, WI 53007
Ph: (262)781-4445
Fax: (262)781-3736
Free: (800)236-9474
E-mail: info@wisconsin.wish.org
URL: http://wisconsin.wish.org
Contact: Patti Gorsky, Pres.
Founded: 1984. **State.** Grants the wishes of children with life-threatening medical conditions to enrich the human experience with hope, strength, and joy. **Telecommunication Services:** electronic mail, pgorsky@wisconsin.wish.org. **Affiliated With:** Make-A-Wish Foundation of America.

Butternut

17701 ■ American Legion, Wisconsin Post 272
c/o Thaddeus K. Zyk
PO Box 22
Butternut, WI 54514
Ph: (608)745-1090
Fax: (608)745-0179
URL: National Affiliate–www.legion.org
Contact: Thaddeus K. Zyk, Contact
Local. Affiliated With: American Legion.

Cable

17702 ■ American Legion, Stokes-Liebman Post 487
43495 Trail Inn Rd. S
Cable, WI 54821
Ph: (608)745-1090
Fax: (608)745-0179
URL: National Affiliate–www.legion.org
Local. Affiliated With: American Legion.

17703 ■ American Rabbit Breeders Association, Lumberjack Rabbit Club
c/o Candis Hankins, Sec.
44995 S Lake Owen Dr.
Cable, WI 54821
URL: http://www.geocities.com/wisconsin_state_rba/Local_Clubs.html
Contact: Candis Hankins, Sec.
Local. Affiliated With: American Rabbit Breeders Association.

17704 ■ Cable Area Chamber of Commerce
PO Box 217
Cable, WI 54821
Ph: (715)798-3833
Fax: (715)798-4456
Free: (800)533-7454
E-mail: info@cable4fun.com
URL: http://www.cable4fun.com
Contact: Holly Henry, Exec.Dir.
Membership Dues: regular, $175 (annual). **Local.**

17705 ■ Chequamegon Area Mountain Bike Association (CAMBA)
PO Box 141
Cable, WI 54821
Ph: (715)798-3130
Fax: (715)798-3599
Free: (800)533-7454
E-mail: camba@cheqnet.net
URL: http://www.cambatrails.org
Local. Affiliated With: International Mountain Bicycling Association.

Cadott

17706 ■ American Legion, Wisconsin Post 159
c/o Henry P. Svetlik
PO Box 22
Cadott, WI 54727
Ph: (608)745-1090
Fax: (608)745-0179
URL: National Affiliate–www.legion.org
Contact: Henry P. Svetlik, Contact
Local. Affiliated With: American Legion.

17707 ■ Cadott Area Chamber of Commerce
PO Box 84
Cadott, WI 54727
Ph: (715)289-3338
Contact: Jim Buetow, Sec.-Treas.
Local.

Cambria

17708 ■ American Legion, Cambria Post 401
W 4033 Crown Rd.
Cambria, WI 53923
Ph: (608)745-1090
Fax: (608)745-0179
URL: National Affiliate–www.legion.org
Local. Affiliated With: American Legion.

Cambridge

17709 ■ American Legion, Wisconsin Post 195
c/o James Munro
PO Box 141
Cambridge, WI 53523
Ph: (608)745-1090
Fax: (608)745-0179
URL: National Affiliate–www.legion.org
Contact: James Munro, Contact
Local. Affiliated With: American Legion.

17710 ■ Cambridge Chamber of Commerce
PO Box 572
Cambridge, WI 53523-0572
Ph: (608)423-3780
Fax: (608)423-7558
E-mail: chamber@smallbytes.net
URL: http://www.cambridgewi.com
Contact: Craig Carpenter, Pres.
Local. Promotes business and community development in Cambridge, WI area.

17711 ■ Wisconsin Woodland Owners Association, Blackhawk Chapter
c/o Joe Arington, Chm.
2935 Evergreen Dr.
Cambridge, WI 53523
Ph: (608)423-3713
E-mail: joearington@hotmail.com
URL: http://www.wisconsinwoodlands.org
Contact: Joe Arington, Chm.
Local. Affiliated With: Wisconsin Woodland Owners Association.

Cameron

17712 ■ American Legion, Pieper-Marsh Post 194
604 Main St.
Cameron, WI 54822
Ph: (608)745-1090
Fax: (608)745-0179
URL: National Affiliate–www.legion.org
Local. Affiliated With: American Legion.

Camp Douglas

17713 ■ American Legion, Wisconsin Post 133
c/o Earl Guilligan
PO Box 133
Camp Douglas, WI 54618
Ph: (608)745-1090
Fax: (608)745-0179
URL: National Affiliate–www.legion.org
Contact: Earl Guilligan, Contact
Local. Affiliated With: American Legion.

17714 ■ Camp Douglas Lions Club
c/o Gary Frei, Pres.
W10384 26th St.
Camp Douglas, WI 54618
Ph: (608)427-6581
URL: http://www.md27d2.org
Contact: Gary Frei, Pres.
Local. Affiliated With: Lions Clubs International.

17715 ■ Great Lakes Belted Galloway Association
c/o Lyndall Mack
33745 Co. Hwy.
Camp Douglas, WI 54618
Ph: (608)427-6745
E-mail: rbmacklm@mwt.net
URL: National Affiliate–www.beltie.org
Regional. Affiliated With: Belted Galloway Society.

17716 ■ Inventors and Entrepreneurs Club of Juneau County
PO Box 322
Camp Douglas, WI 54618
Ph: (608)427-2070
E-mail: jcedcsm@mwt.net
URL: National Affiliate–www.uiausa.org
Contact: Terry Whipple, Contact
Local. Represents inventors' organizations and providers of services to inventors. Seeks to facilitate the development of innovation conceived by independent inventors. Provides leadership and support services to inventors and inventors' organizations. **Affiliated With:** United Inventors Association of the U.S.A.

Caroline

17717 ■ American Legion, Blashe-Peters-Tober Post 456
W12850 County Rd. M
Caroline, WI 54928
Ph: (608)745-1090
Fax: (608)745-0179
URL: National Affiliate–www.legion.org
Local. Affiliated With: American Legion.

Cascade

17718 ■ American Legion, Ambelang-Ebelt-Lau Post 386
305 W Water St.
Cascade, WI 53011
Ph: (608)745-1090
Fax: (608)745-0179
URL: National Affiliate–www.legion.org
Local. Affiliated With: American Legion.

Casco

17719 ■ American Legion, Thibadeau-Drossart Post 319
N 6145 Village Ln.
Casco, WI 54205
Ph: (608)745-1090
Fax: (608)745-0179
URL: National Affiliate–www.legion.org
Local. Affiliated With: American Legion.

Cashton

17720 ■ American Legion, Wisconsin Post 445
c/o Gunwald Overgard
720 Broadway St.
Cashton, WI 54619
Ph: (608)745-1090
Fax: (608)745-0179
URL: National Affiliate–www.legion.org
Contact: Gunwald Overgard, Contact
Local. Affiliated With: American Legion.

17721 ■ Cashton Development Corporation
c/o Scott Wall, Pres.
PO Box 1
Cashton, WI 54619
Ph: (608)654-5121 (608)654-7713
Fax: (608)654-5297
Contact: Mr. Scott Wall, Pres.
Founded: 1968. **Members:** 9. **Budget:** $11,000. **Local.** Works for the development of overall Cashton area by way of practical assistance to desirable industries and businesses. **Libraries: Type:** reference. **Holdings:** 7,500.

17722 ■ Cashton Lions Club
c/o Mary Jo Moore, Sec.
E8626 Rognstad Ridge Rd.
Cashton, WI 54619
Ph: (608)634-4598
E-mail: tmmoore@mwt.net
URL: http://www.md27d2.org
Contact: Mary Jo Moore, Sec.
Local. Affiliated With: Lions Clubs International.

Cassville

17723 ■ American Legion, Mumm-Welsh Post 352
PO Box 362
Cassville, WI 53806
Ph: (608)745-1090
Fax: (608)745-0179
URL: National Affiliate–www.legion.org
Local. Affiliated With: American Legion.

17724 ■ Cassville Lions Club
PO Box 704
Cassville, WI 53806-0704
Ph: (608)725-5693
E-mail: thelimey53@hotmail.com
URL: http://cassvillewi.lionwap.org
Contact: Tom Matchett, Sec.-Treas.
Local. Affiliated With: Lions Clubs International.

Cecil

17725 ■ Northeastern Wisconsin Orchid Society
c/o Marie Bergsbaken
W2030 Cty. Hwy. E
Cecil, WI 54111
Ph: (715)745-6398
E-mail: marielb@frontiernet.net
Contact: Ms. Marie Bergsbaken, Contact
Local. Professional growers, botanists, hobbyists, and others interested in extending the knowledge, production, use, and appreciation of orchids. **Affiliated With:** American Orchid Society.

Cedar Grove

17726 ■ American Legion, Van-Der-Jagt-De-Bruine Post 338
PO Box 171
Cedar Grove, WI 53013
Ph: (608)745-1090
Fax: (608)745-0179
URL: National Affiliate–www.legion.org
Local. Affiliated With: American Legion.

Cedarburg

17727 ■ Cedarburg Chamber of Commerce (CCC)
PO Box 104
Cedarburg, WI 53012
Ph: (262)377-5856 (262)377-9620
Fax: (262)377-6470
Free: (800)237-2874
E-mail: info@cedarburg.org
URL: http://www.cedarburg.org
Contact: Kristine Hage, Exec.Dir.
Founded: 1902. **Members:** 275. **Local.** Businesses and individuals. Promotes business and community development in Cedarburg, WI. **Conventions/Meetings:** annual Radio Auction - meeting.

17728 ■ Cedarburg Lions Club
PO Box 754
Cedarburg, WI 53012
Ph: (414)228-4402
E-mail: mail@cedarburglionsclub.org
URL: http://www.cedarburglionsclub.org
Contact: Lee Owen, Pres.
Local. Affiliated With: Lions Clubs International.

17729 ■ IEEE Electromagnetic Compatibility Society, Milwaukee
c/o James Blaha
L.S.Compliance, Inc.
W66 N220 Commerce Ct.
Cedarburg, WI 53012
Ph: (262)421-4969
Fax: (262)375-4248
E-mail: jblaha@lsr.com
URL: http://www.ewh.ieee.org/r4/milwaukee
Contact: James Blaha, Contact
Local. Affiliated With: IEEE Electromagnetic Compatibility Society.

17730 ■ Society of Consumer Affairs Professionals in Business, Wisconsin Chapter
c/o Dennis E. Garrett
Marquette Univ.
W72 N815 Harrison Ave.
Cedarburg, WI 53012
Ph: (414)288-3371
Fax: (414)288-7638
E-mail: wisconsin@socap.org
URL: National Affiliate–www.socap.org
Affiliated With: Society of Consumer Affairs Professionals in Business.

17731 ■ Wisconsin Health Care Association, District 6
c/o Angela Willms, Pres.
Cedar Springs Hea. & Rehabilitation
N27 W5707 Lincoln Blvd.
Cedarburg, WI 53012
Ph: (262)376-7676
URL: http://www.whca.com
Contact: Angela Willms, Pres.
Local. Promotes professionalism and ethical behavior of individuals providing long-term care delivery for patients and for the general public. Provides information, education and administrative tools to enhance the quality of long-term care. Improves the standards of service and administration of member nursing homes. **Affiliated With:** American Health Care Association; Wisconsin Health Care Association.

17732 ■ Wisconsin Parents of Blind Children
c/o Elizabeth Buhrke, Pres.
N41 W 5403 Spring St.
Cedarburg, WI 53012
Ph: (262)377-7110
E-mail: ej_buhrke@hotmail.com
URL: National Affiliate–www.nfb.org
Contact: Elizabeth Buhrke, Pres.
State. Provides information and support to parents of blind children. Develops and expands resources available to parents and their children. Aims to eliminate discrimination and prejudice against the blind. **Affiliated With:** National Organization of Parents of Blind Children.

17733 ■ Wisconsin Sporting Clays Association (WSCA)
c/o Jeff Knorr
PO Box 265
Cedarburg, WI 53012
Ph: (920)864-7070
E-mail: hunterspark@earthlink.net
URL: http://www.wi-sportingclays.org
Contact: Greg VanDenPlas, Pres.
State.

Centuria

17734 ■ American Legion, Wisconsin Post 346
c/o Adolph Timm
PO Box 452
Centuria, WI 54824
Ph: (608)745-1090
Fax: (608)745-0179
URL: National Affiliate–www.legion.org
Contact: Adolph Timm, Contact
Local. Affiliated With: American Legion.

Chaseburg

17735 ■ American Legion, Chaseburg Post 202
304 Gilbertson St.
Chaseburg, WI 54621
Ph: (608)745-1090
Fax: (608)745-0179
URL: National Affiliate–www.legion.org
Local. Affiliated With: American Legion.

17736 ■ Chaseburg Lions Club
c/o Ron Bell, Sec.
205 Carriage Dr.
Chaseburg, WI 54621
Ph: (608)483-2250
E-mail: ronb@mwt.net
URL: http://www.md27d2.org
Contact: Ron Bell, Sec.
Local. Affiliated With: Lions Clubs International.

17737 ■ La Crosse District Nurses Association
c/o Rose S. Presser, Pres.
1601 Overson Ln.
Chaseburg, WI 54621
Ph: (608)483-2775
E-mail: rspresse@gundluth.org
URL: http://www.ldna.org
Contact: Rose S. Presser, Pres.
Local. Works to advance the nursing profession. Seeks to meet the needs of nurses and health care consumers. Fosters high standards of nursing practice. Promotes the economic and general welfare of nurses in the workplace. **Affiliated With:** American Nurses Association; Wisconsin Nurses' Association.

Chetek

17738 ■ Chetek Area Chamber of Commerce
PO Box 747
Chetek, WI 54728
Fax: (715)924-4496
Free: (800)317-1720
E-mail: info@chetekwi.net
URL: http://www.chetekwi.net
Members: 120. **Local.** Promotes business and community development in Chetek, WI area. **Formerly:** (1999) Chetek Chamber of Commerce.

Chili

17739 ■ United Food and Commercial Workers, Local 717, Northcentral Region
N5721 Catlin Ave.
Chili, WI 54420
Ph: (715)384-2626
URL: National Affiliate–www.ufcw.org
Local. Affiliated With: United Food and Commercial Workers International Union.

Chilton

17740 ■ American Legion, Grassold-Schmidlkofer Post 125
PO Box 65
Chilton, WI 53014
Ph: (608)745-1090
Fax: (608)745-0179
URL: National Affiliate–www.legion.org
Local. Affiliated With: American Legion.

17741 ■ Chilton Chamber of Commerce
PO Box 351
Chilton, WI 53014
Ph: (920)849-1585 (920)418-1650
E-mail: info@chiltonchamber.com
URL: http://www.chiltonchamber.com
Contact: Tammy Pethan, Sec.
Founded: 1948. **Members:** 165. **Membership Dues:** $85 (annual). **Local.** Strives to unite and promote the commercial mercantile and manufacturing interests of the City of Chilton. Improves civic, industrial, and business principles among its members. **Awards:** Citizens of the Year. **Frequency:** annual. **Type:** recognition.

Chippewa Falls

17742 ■ American Legion, Meuli-Kelean-Kramer-Dannenberg Post 77
PO Box 241
Chippewa Falls, WI 54729
Ph: (608)745-1090
Fax: (608)745-0179
URL: National Affiliate–www.legion.org
Local. Affiliated With: American Legion.

17743 ■ American Rabbit Breeders Association, Indianhead
c/o Pam Celesnik, Sec.
5706 Co Rd. T
Chippewa Falls, WI 54729
URL: http://www.geocities.com/wisconsin_state_rba/Local_Clubs.html
Contact: Pam Celesnik, Sec.
Local. Affiliated With: American Rabbit Breeders Association.

17744 ■ American Rabbit Breeders Association, Red Cedar
c/o Mary Steinmetz, Sec.
7341 100th Ave.
Chippewa Falls, WI 54729
URL: http://www.geocities.com/wisconsin_state_rba/Local_Clubs.html
Contact: Mary Steinmetz, Sec.
Local. Affiliated With: American Rabbit Breeders Association.

17745 ■ American Red Cross
404 1/2 N. Bridge St.
Chippewa Falls, WI 54729
Ph: (715)723-4655
Fax: (715)723-5056
Free: (800)261-4182
E-mail: ericksons@atscvcredcross.org
Local.

17746 ■ Badgerland Gordon Setter Club
c/o Clyde Sippel, Pres.
1880 Paint Creek Rd.
Chippewa Falls, WI 54729
Ph: (715)726-1923
E-mail: paintcrk@ecol.net
URL: http://www.badgerlandgordonsetterclub.com
Contact: Clyde Sippel, Pres.
Membership Dues: individual, $12 (annual) • family, $15 (annual) • junior, $6 (annual). **Regional. Affiliated With:** Gordon Setter Club of America.

17747 ■ Chippewa County Humane Association (CCHA)
PO Box 562
Chippewa Falls, WI 54729-0562
Ph: (715)382-4832
Fax: (715)382-4832
E-mail: ccha@ecol.net
URL: http://www.chippewahumane.com
Contact: Linda Burlingame, Pres.
Members: 250. **Membership Dues:** standard, $15 (annual) • senior and student, $10 (annual) • family, $25 (annual) • humanitarian, $50 (annual) • corporate, $100 (annual) • pet, $2 (annual). **Staff:** 10. **State Groups:** 1. **Local.** Works for the humane treatment of animals. Fosters a humane ethic and philosophy through educational, legislative, investigative, and legal activities. Operates animal shelter. **Formerly:** Chippewa Falls Humane Society; (2005) Chippewa County Humane Society. **Publications:** *Shelter Friends*, periodic. Newsletter. **Conventions/Meetings:** monthly board meeting - always second Monday • annual general assembly.

17748 ■ Chippewa County Tourism Council
10 S Bridge St.
Chippewa Falls, WI 54729-2812
Ph: (715)723-7150
Free: (866)723-0331
E-mail: info@chippewachamber.org
URL: http://www.chippewacounty.com
Contact: Judy Gilles, Pres.
Founded: 1997. **Members:** 11. **Local.** Promotes Chippewa County in its entirety. Aims to enhance communication dealing with tourism issues at the local, county and regional levels.

17749 ■ Chippewa Falls Area Chamber of Commerce
10 S Bridge St.
Chippewa Falls, WI 54729
Ph: (715)723-0331
Fax: (715)723-0332
Free: (866)723-0340
E-mail: info@chippewachamber.org
URL: http://www.chippewachamber.org
Contact: Mike D. Jordan, Pres.
Founded: 1910. **Members:** 500. **Membership Dues:** minimum, $185. **Local.** Works to improve quality of life in the community by providing leadership to promote business interest of members. **Awards:** Excellence in Education. **Frequency:** annual. **Type:** recognition. **Committees:** Ambassadors; Excellence in Education; Industrial; June Dairy Days; Public Affairs; Small Business; Tourism Planning; Workforce. **Publications:** *Chamber News*, monthly. Newsletter. Includes information about business news and events. • Annual Report. Alternate Formats: online. **Conventions/Meetings:** monthly meeting, meets to socialize and makes new contacts - every 4th Monday.

17750 ■ Chippewa Falls Industrial Development Corporation (IDC)
c/o Jayson C. Smith, Sec.-Treas.
30 W Central St.
Chippewa Falls, WI 54729
Ph: (715)726-2729
Fax: (715)726-2750
E-mail: jsmith@ci.chippewa-falls.wi.us
URL: http://chippewaidc.org
Contact: Jayson C. Smith, Sec.-Treas.
Founded: 1953. **Local.** Promotes industrial and economic growth in Chippewa falls.

17751 ■ Chippewa Falls Main Street
c/o Jim Schuh, Dir.
10 S Bridge St., Ste.1
Chippewa Falls, WI 54729-2812
Ph: (715)723-6661 (715)723-7858
Fax: (715)720-4882
E-mail: info@chippewafallsmainst.org
URL: http://www.chippewafallsmainst.org
Contact: Jim Schuh, Dir.
Founded: 1989. **Members:** 190. **Staff:** 3. **Budget:** $140,000. **State Groups:** 3. **Local.** Promotes business and community development in Chippewa Falls,

WI. Sponsors downtown revitalization program. **Libraries: Type:** open to the public. **Holdings:** 25; articles, audio recordings, books, periodicals, video recordings. **Subjects:** downtown revitalization. **Telecommunication Services:** electronic mail, jim. cfms@charter.net. **Publications:** *Chippewa Falls Main Street Promotion Calendar*, annual • *Downtown Chippewa Falls Business Directory*, annual • *Historic Walking Tour of Downtown Chippewa Falls* • *Main Stream*, bimonthly. Newsletter. Contains news about Downtown activities and programs. **Circulation:** 800 • *150 Great Things to do for a Perfect Day in Chippewa Falls, WI.* **Conventions/Meetings:** annual meeting, membership.

17752 ■ Chippewa Valley Gem and Mineral Society
c/o Roger Goss, Pres.
922 Dover
Chippewa Falls, WI 54729
E-mail: rgoss@cvol.net
URL: National Affiliate–www.amfed.org
Contact: Judy Goss, Sec.
Local. Aims to further the study of Earth Sciences and the practice of lapidary arts and mineralogy. **Affiliated With:** American Federation of Mineralogical Societies.

17753 ■ Eau Claire Horseshoe Club
c/o Robert J. Rehm, Treas.
614 Grant Ct.
Chippewa Falls, WI 54729-3423
Ph: (715)720-9298
E-mail: echc@cvol.net
URL: http://members.cvol.net/echc
Contact: Robert J. Rehm, Treas.
Membership Dues: $20 (annual). **Local**. Promotes the sport of horseshoes. **Publications:** *Four Dead*, annual. Contains lists of averages, winners of leagues, and other horseshoe information. **Price:** included in membership dues.

17754 ■ Food and Commercial Workers AFL-CIO, LU 268
PO Box 126
Chippewa Falls, WI 54729
URL: http://www.ufcw.org/
Contact: John Ray, Contact
Founded: 1920. **Members:** 308. **Membership Dues:** $17 (monthly). **State Groups:** 1. **Local**. Union local representing workers at the Mason companies in the footwear industry. Members represents work in shipping, receiving, and manufacturing. **Affiliated With:** United Food and Commercial Workers International Union. **Formerly:** (1979) Boot and Shoe Workers Union. **Conventions/Meetings:** monthly Local Union Meeting - general assembly - third Thursday of the month. Chippewa Falls, WI - Avg. Attendance: 50.

17755 ■ Indianhead Optometric Society
c/o Denise Arneson, OD, Pres.
113 N Bridge St.
Chippewa Falls, WI 54729
Ph: (715)723-9187
Fax: (715)723-1755
E-mail: nweyecare@sbcglobal.net
URL: http://www.woa-eyes.org
Contact: Denise Arneson OD, Pres.
Local. Aims to improve the quality, availability and accessibility of eye and vision care. Promotes high standards of patient care. Monitors and promotes legislation concerning the scope of optometric practice and other issues relevant to eye/vision care. **Affiliated With:** American Optometric Association; Wisconsin Optometric Association.

17756 ■ Muskies First Wisconsin Chapter
PO Box 122
Chippewa Falls, WI 54729
Ph: (715)863-7463
E-mail: firstwi@muskiesinc.org
URL: http://www.muskiesinc.org/chapters/06
Contact: Mark Hintz, Pres.
Local.

17757 ■ PFLAG Eau Claire/Greater Chippewa Valley
18718 65th Ave.
Chippewa Falls, WI 54729
Ph: (715)723-3476
E-mail: apopko2003@yahoo.com
URL: http://www.pflag.org/Wisconsin.246.0.html
Local. **Affiliated With:** Parents, Families, and Friends of Lesbians and Gays.

17758 ■ Wisconsin Farmers Union (WFU)
117 W Spring St.
Chippewa Falls, WI 54729
Ph: (715)723-5561
Fax: (715)723-7011
Free: (800)272-5531
E-mail: info@wisconsinfarmersunion.com
URL: http://www.wisconsinfarmersunion.com
Contact: Sue Beitlich, Pres.
State.

17759 ■ Wisconsin Indianhead Chapter of Associated Locksmiths of America
c/o Kenneth W. Briggs, Chair
Chippewa Valley Lock & Key
20 Bay St.
Chippewa Falls, WI 54729
Ph: (715)726-0687
E-mail: info@chippewavalleylockandkey.com
URL: National Affiliate–www.aloa.org
Contact: Kenneth W. Briggs, Chair
Local. **Affiliated With:** Associated Locksmiths of America.

17760 ■ Wisconsin Regional Lily Society (WRLS)
c/o Helen Corbett, Treas.
7634 185th St.
Chippewa Falls, WI 54729
E-mail: asns@indianheadtel.net
URL: http://www.wrls.org
Contact: Darrel Roeder, Pres.
State. **Affiliated With:** North American Lily Society.

Clear Lake

17761 ■ American Legion, Wisconsin Post 108
c/o Wiley Davis
284 Golf Dr.
Clear Lake, WI 54005
Ph: (608)745-1090
Fax: (608)745-0179
URL: National Affiliate–www.legion.org
Contact: Wiley Davis, Contact
Local. **Affiliated With:** American Legion.

17762 ■ Clear Community Club
PO Box 266
Clear Lake, WI 54005
Ph: (715)263-2755
Fax: (715)263-2267
Contact: Matt Anderson, Pres.
Local. **Formerly:** (2005) Clear Lake Civic and Community Association.

17763 ■ International Association of Machinists and Aerospace Workers, AFL-CIO, CLC - Local Lodge 1217
105 South Ave. W
Clear Lake, WI 54005
E-mail: heiny@pressenter.com
URL: http://ll1217.goiam.org
Contact: Robert Plecko, VP
Members: 142. **Local**. Seeks for the dignity and equality of the workers. Strives to provide contractors with well-trained, productive employees. **Affiliated With:** International Association of Machinists and Aerospace Workers.

17764 ■ Sons of Norway, Sjoland Lodge 5-635
c/o Gregory D. Warner, Pres.
383 55th St.
Clear Lake, WI 54005-3403
Ph: (715)263-2776
E-mail: joleewarner@hotmail.com
URL: National Affiliate–www.sofn.com
Contact: Gregory D. Warner, Pres.
Local. **Affiliated With:** Sons of Norway.

Cleveland

17765 ■ Cleveland Chamber of Commerce
PO Box 56
Cleveland, WI 53015-0056
Ph: (920)693-8256
E-mail: information@chamberofcleveland.com
URL: http://www.chamberofcleveland.com
Contact: Tim Schueler, Sec.-Treas.
Local. Strives to bring new business and industry to Cleveland while helping the existing ones to become more viable.

17766 ■ Lakeshore Beagle Club
c/o Randy Pfrang
PO Box 75
Cleveland, WI 53015-0075
Ph: (920)693-8495
E-mail: rpfrang@intella.net
URL: National Affiliate–www.akc.org
Contact: Randy Pfrang, Contact
Founded: 1950. **Members:** 48. **Membership Dues:** $65 (annual). **Local**. Promotes education and competition of the field trial beagle. **Affiliated With:** American Kennel Club. **Conventions/Meetings:** monthly meeting.

17767 ■ Phi Theta Kappa, Beta Lambda Sigma Chapter - Lakeshore Technical College
c/o Scott Lieburn
1290 North Ave.
Cleveland, WI 53015
Ph: (920)693-1378
E-mail: scott.lieburn@gotoltc.edu
URL: http://www.ptk.org/directories/chapters/WI/21316-1.htm
Contact: Scott Lieburn, Advisor
Local.

Clinton

17768 ■ American Legion, Dary-Paulsen Post 440
PO Box 451
Clinton, WI 53525
Ph: (608)745-1090
Fax: (608)745-0179
URL: National Affiliate–www.legion.org
Local. **Affiliated With:** American Legion.

Clintonville

17769 ■ American Association of Bovine Practitioners, District 5
c/o Andy Johnson, DVM, Dir.
W8275 Clover Leaf Lake Rd.
Clintonville, WI 54929
Ph: (715)823-7933
Fax: (715)823-7880
E-mail: drandy@theudderdoctor.com
URL: National Affiliate–www.aabp.org
Contact: Andy Johnson DVM, Dir.
Regional. Works to promote the interests, improve the public stature, and increase the knowledge of veterinarians in the field of dairy and beef cattle practice. Elevates standards of bovine practice. Promotes understanding and goodwill among members. **Affiliated With:** American Association of Bovine Practitioners.

17770 ■ American Legion, Veterans Memorial Post 63
20 Memorial Cir.
Clintonville, WI 54929
Ph: (608)745-1090
Fax: (608)745-0179
URL: National Affiliate–www.legion.org
Local. Affiliated With: American Legion.

17771 ■ Clintonville Area Chamber of Commerce
18 S Main St.
PO Box 56
Clintonville, WI 54929
Ph: (715)823-4606
Fax: (715)823-7318
E-mail: cvlchmbr@frontiernet.net
URL: http://www.clintonvillewi.org/chamber
Contact: Joanne Doornink, Exec.Dir.
Founded: 1910. **Local.** Works to encourage communication and cooperation among business, industry, education, and community by providing leadership to promote the community.

17772 ■ Wisconsin Curling Association - Clintonville Curling Club
65 Sixth St.
Clintonville, WI 54929
Ph: (715)823-4160
E-mail: mschultz@vadtek.com
URL: http://www.goodcurling.net/basics/U.S.%20clubs/wisconsin.html
Contact: Mark Schultz, Pres.
Local. Affiliated With: United States Curling Association.

Cobb

17773 ■ American Legion, Fingerson-Rule Post 463
PO Box 143
Cobb, WI 53526
Ph: (808)623-2375
Fax: (608)745-0179
URL: National Affiliate–www.legion.org
Local. Affiliated With: American Legion.

Colby

17774 ■ American Legion, Wisconsin Post 266
c/o Arnold Krueger
408 N 2nd St.
Colby, WI 54421
Ph: (608)745-1090
Fax: (608)745-0179
URL: National Affiliate–www.legion.org
Contact: Arnold Krueger, Contact
Local. Affiliated With: American Legion.

17775 ■ Colby Chamber of Commerce
Box 444
Colby, WI 54421-0444
Ph: (715)223-2342
E-mail: colbych@charter.net
Contact: Tod Smith, Pres.
Local.

17776 ■ Midstate District Nurses Association - No. 8
W157 Clover Dale Rd.
Colby, WI 54421
Ph: (715)223-4872
E-mail: sharong@waushosp.org
URL: http://www.wisconsinnurses.org
Contact: Sharon Groschwitz, Pres.
Local. Works to advance the nursing profession. Seeks to meet the needs of nurses and health care consumers. Fosters high standards of nursing practice. Promotes the economic and general welfare of nurses in the workplace. **Affiliated With:** American Nurses Association; Wisconsin Nurses' Association.

Coleman

17777 ■ American Legion, Kalbes-Seewald Post 280
PO Box 229
Coleman, WI 54112
Ph: (608)745-1090
Fax: (608)745-0179
URL: National Affiliate–www.legion.org
Local. Affiliated With: American Legion.

Colfax

17778 ■ American Legion, Russell-Toycen Post 131
PO Box 414
Colfax, WI 54730
Ph: (608)745-1090
Fax: (608)745-0179
URL: National Affiliate–www.legion.org
Local. Affiliated With: American Legion.

17779 ■ Sweet Adelines International, Red Cedar Sounds Chapter
Colfax United Methodist Church
501 Cedar St.
Colfax, WI 54730-9081
Ph: (715)962-3903
E-mail: eggert.patricia@mayo.edu
URL: National Affiliate–www.sweetadelineintl.org
Contact: Pat Eggert, Contact
Local. Advances the musical art form of barbershop harmony through education and performances. Provides education, training and coaching in the development of women's four-part barbershop harmony. **Affiliated With:** Sweet Adelines International.

Colgate

17780 ■ Jayco Jafari International Travel Club, Flight 106 Jaybirds of Milwaukee
c/o Kevin Breutzmann, Pres.
3169 Upper Woodland Dr.
Colgate, WI 53017
E-mail: milwaukeejaybirds@hotmail.com
URL: National Affiliate–www.jaycorvclub.com
Contact: Kevin Breutzmann, Pres.
Local. Affiliated With: Jayco Travel Club.

17781 ■ Milwaukee Audubon Society
3873 Wooded Ridge Trail
Colgate, WI 53017
Ph: (262)251-9080
E-mail: wildbird@charter.net
URL: http://www.audubon.org/chapter/wi/index.html
Contact: Steven Mahler, Pres.
Local. Formerly: (2005) National Audubon Society - Milwaukee Chapter.

Columbus

17782 ■ American Legion, Lange-Ostrander-Hurd Post 62
229 E Poet St.
Columbus, WI 53925
Ph: (608)745-1090
Fax: (608)745-0179
URL: National Affiliate–www.legion.org
Local. Affiliated With: American Legion.

17783 ■ Columbus Area Chamber of Commerce
PO Box 362
Columbus, WI 53925
Ph: (920)623-3699
Fax: (920)623-0171
Contact: Beverly Hartl, Pres.
Local.

Coon Valley

17784 ■ American Legion, Coon Valley Post 116
105 Park St.
Coon Valley, WI 54623
Ph: (608)745-1090
Fax: (608)745-0179
URL: National Affiliate–www.legion.org
Local. Affiliated With: American Legion.

17785 ■ Coon Valley Lions Club
c/o Paul Lewison, Pres.
501 Central Ave.
Coon Valley, WI 54623
Ph: (608)542-3946
URL: http://www.md27d2.org
Contact: Paul Lewison, Pres.
Local. Affiliated With: Lions Clubs International.

Cornell

17786 ■ American Legion, Weinsch-Gilbert-Patten-Gillett Post 353
309 S 2nd St.
Cornell, WI 54732
Ph: (608)745-1090
Fax: (608)745-0179
URL: National Affiliate–www.legion.org
Local. Affiliated With: American Legion.

17787 ■ Indianhead Chapter MOAA
c/o Lt.Cdr. Paul Johnson
PO Box 267
Cornell, WI 54732-0267
Ph: (715)239-6346
E-mail: paulrose@centurytel.net
URL: National Affiliate–www.moaa.org
Contact: Lt.Cdr. Paul Johnson, Contact
Local. Affiliated With: Military Officers Association of America.

Cottage Grove

17788 ■ American Legion, Galvin-Struckmeyer Post 248
PO Box 215
Cottage Grove, WI 53527
Ph: (608)745-1090
Fax: (608)745-0179
URL: National Affiliate–www.legion.org
Local. Affiliated With: American Legion.

Crandon

17789 ■ Crandon Area Chamber of Commerce
PO Box 88
Crandon, WI 54520
Ph: (715)478-3450
Fax: (715)478-4650
Free: (800)334-3387
E-mail: info@crandonwi.com
URL: http://www.crandonwi.com
Founded: 1978. **Members:** 100. **Membership Dues:** sole proprietor, $125 (annual) • large business, $525 (annual) • municipal, corporate, $2,000 (annual). **Local.** Seeks to promote the tourism and economic development of Crandon and Forest County. **Publications:** Newsletter. **Conventions/Meetings:** monthly meeting - every 1st Thursday.

17790 ■ Sokaogon-Chippewa Committee
3086 State Hwy. 55
Crandon, WI 54520-8878
Ph: (715)478-5180
Fax: (715)478-5904
Contact: Timmy Retzlaff, Contact
Local.

Crivitz

17791 ■ American Legion, Netzel-Zenz Post 413
PO Box 324
Crivitz, WI 54114
Ph: (608)745-1090
Fax: (608)745-0179
URL: National Affiliate–www.legion.org
Local. Affiliated With: American Legion.

Cross Plains

17792 ■ American Legion, Kerl-Endres-Brannan Post 245
2217 Amer. Legion Dr.
Cross Plains, WI 53528
Ph: (608)745-1090
Fax: (608)745-0179
URL: National Affiliate–www.legion.org
Local. Affiliated With: American Legion.

17793 ■ Cross Plains Lions Club
2501 Center St.
Cross Plains, WI 53528
Ph: (608)798-2147
E-mail: lcesser@chorus.net
URL: http://www.geocities.com/crossplainslions
Local. Affiliated With: Lions Clubs International.

Cuba City

17794 ■ American Legion, Wisconsin Post 104
c/o Henry Pinch
413 E Calhoun St.
Cuba City, WI 53807
Ph: (608)745-1090
Fax: (608)745-0179
URL: National Affiliate–www.legion.org
Contact: Henry Pinch, Contact
Local. Affiliated With: American Legion.

17795 ■ Cuba City Chamber of Commerce
PO Box 706
Cuba City, WI 53807
Ph: (608)744-3456
Contact: Tim Gile, Pres.
Local.

17796 ■ Cuba City Community Development Corporation
c/o Kathy Schultz, Sec.
108 N Main St.
Cuba City, WI 53807
Ph: (608)744-2152
Fax: (608)744-2151
E-mail: cubacity@pcii.net
Local.

Cudahy

17797 ■ American Legion, Kerlin Farina Post 16
PO Box 100304
Cudahy, WI 53110
Ph: (608)745-1090
Fax: (608)745-0179
URL: National Affiliate–www.legion.org
Local. Affiliated With: American Legion.

17798 ■ Cudahy Historical Society
PO Box 332
Cudahy, WI 53110-0332
Ph: (414)747-1892
E-mail: koszuth@execpc.com
URL: http://www.ci.cudahy.wi.us/Historical_Society/index.htm
Contact: John Hundseder, Pres.
Founded: 1977. **Members:** 138. **Membership Dues:** student, $3 (annual) • individual, $7 (annual) • family, $10 (annual) • business, $25 (annual) • life, $100. **Budget:** $8,000. **Local.** Individuals interested in preserving the history of Cudahy, WI. Sponsors museum. **Affiliated With:** Wisconsin Historical Society. **Publications:** Newsletter, 3/year, always spring, fall, and winter. **Conventions/Meetings:** meeting - 3rd Tuesday of September, November, February, April, and June.

Cumberland

17799 ■ Cumberland Chamber of Commerce (CCC)
PO Box 665
Cumberland, WI 54829
Ph: (715)822-3378
E-mail: bagafest@chibardun.net
URL: http://www.cumberland-wisconsin.com
Contact: Starr Avery, Exec.Sec.
Founded: 1966. **Members:** 140. **Staff:** 1. **Budget:** $100,000. **Local.** Businesses and professionals promoting economic and community development in Cumberland, WI. Sponsors annual Rutabaga Festival. **Publications:** Newsletter, quarterly. **Conventions/Meetings:** annual meeting.

17800 ■ Cumberland PTA
c/o Barb Bangsberg, Pres.
789 22 3/4 Ave.
Cumberland, WI 54829
E-mail: barb@bangsberg.com
URL: http://www.cumberlandpta.com
Contact: Barb Bangsberg, Pres.
Local. Parents, teachers, students, and others interested in uniting the forces of home, school, and community. Promotes the welfare of children and youth.

Cushing

17801 ■ American Legion, Wisconsin Post 269
c/o Arndt T. Johnson
PO Box 454
Cushing, WI 54006
Ph: (608)745-1090
Fax: (608)745-0179
URL: National Affiliate–www.legion.org
Contact: Arndt T. Johnson, Contact
Local. Affiliated With: American Legion.

Custer

17802 ■ Midwest Renewable Energy Association (MREA)
c/o Tehri Parker, Exec.Dir.
7558 Deer Rd.
Custer, WI 54423
Ph: (715)592-6595
Fax: (715)592-6596
E-mail: info@the-mrea.org
URL: http://www.the-mrea.org
Contact: Tehri Parker, Exec.Dir.
Founded: 1990. **Members:** 2,100. **Membership Dues:** basic, individual, $35 (annual) • basic, family, $50 (annual) • basic, senior/student, $20 (annual) • empowered, individual, $65 (annual) • empowered, family, $85 (annual) • life, individual, $500 • life, family, $750 • individual, ASES/MREA, $100 (annual) • senior/student, ASES/MREA, $55 (annual) • basic business, private, $100 (annual) • basic business, non-profit, $50 (annual) • premier business, private, $150 (annual) • premier business, non-profit, $100 (annual) • sustaining corporate business, private, $1,000 (annual) • sustaining corporate business, non-profit, $750 (annual). **Staff:** 3. **Budget:** $115,000. **State Groups:** 38. **Regional.** Serves as network for sharing ideas, resources, and information with individuals, businesses, and communities to promote a sustainable future through renewable energy and energy efficiency. Works to protect the environment by educating the public about appropriate use of natural resources to meet the energy needs. **Affiliated With:** American Solar Energy Society. **Publications:** *Re News*, quarterly. Newsletter. Contains articles and calendar of events pertaining to renewable energy issues. **Price:** $6.00. **Advertising:** accepted. **Conventions/Meetings:** annual Renewable Energy and Sustainable Living Fair - festival (exhibits) - always June; Central WI • annual Solar Homes and Businesses - tour - every October • periodic workshop.

Dane

17803 ■ American Legion, Havlik-Koltes-Thaden Post 503
PO Box 62
Dane, WI 53529
Ph: (608)745-1090
Fax: (608)745-0179
URL: National Affiliate–www.legion.org
Local. Affiliated With: American Legion.

Darien

17804 ■ American Legion, Wilkins-Kelly Post 450
21 Market St.
Darien, WI 53114
Ph: (608)745-1090
Fax: (608)745-0179
URL: National Affiliate–www.legion.org
Local. Affiliated With: American Legion.

Darlington

17805 ■ American Legion, Bates-O'Brien-Howe-Wiegel Post 214
299 Spring St.
Darlington, WI 53530
Ph: (608)745-1090
Fax: (608)745-0179
URL: National Affiliate–www.legion.org
Local. Affiliated With: American Legion.

17806 ■ Darlington Chamber of Commerce
439 Main St., Ste.B
Darlington, WI 53530
Ph: (608)776-3067
Fax: (608)776-3067
Free: (888)506-6553
E-mail: dtonmain@mhtc.net
URL: http://www.darlingtonwi.org
Local. Promotes business and community development in Darlington, WI area.

17807 ■ South West Wisconsin Optometric Society
c/o Paul Lueck, OD, Pres.
PO Box 154
Darlington, WI 53530
Ph: (262)776-4413
Fax: (262)776-4414
E-mail: eccdarl@mhtc.net
URL: http://www.woa-eyes.org
Contact: Paul Lueck OD, Pres.
Local. Aims to improve the quality, availability and accessibility of eye and vision care. Promotes high standards of patient care. Monitors and promotes legislation concerning the scope of optometric practice and other issues relevant to eye/vision care. **Affiliated With:** American Optometric Association; Wisconsin Optometric Association.

De Forest

17808 ■ American Legion, Olson-Grinde Post 348
PO Box 180
De Forest, WI 53532

Ph: (608)745-1090
Fax: (608)745-0179
URL: National Affiliate–www.legion.org
Local. Affiliated With: American Legion.

17809 ■ Badger Kennel Club (BKC)
5925 Haase Rd.
De Forest, WI 53532-2976
Ph: (608)588-2606
E-mail: info@badgerkennelclub.com
URL: http://www.badgerkennelclub.com
Contact: Robbin Polivka, Sec.
Local. Affiliated With: American Kennel Club.

17810 ■ De Forest Area Chamber of Commerce
201 De Forest St.
De Forest, WI 53532
Ph: (608)846-2922
E-mail: info@deforestchamber.com
URL: http://www.deforestchamber.com
Contact: Rhonda Gilbertson, Exec.Dir.
Members: 150. **Membership Dues:** non-profit, associate, $58 (annual) • business (based on number of employees), $145-$578 (annual). **Local.** Strives to provide leadership to improve business environment and promote economic growth through membership participation and involvement. **Telecommunication Services:** electronic mail, dacc@chorus.net. **Committees:** Ambassador; Annual Meeting; 4th of July - Parade; 4th of July - Setup/Cleanup; 4th of July - Volunteer Recruitment; Golf Outing; Publicity; Tourism. **Publications:** Newsletters.

De Pere

17811 ■ American Cancer Society, Green Bay
3311 S Packerland Dr.
De Pere, WI 54115
Free: (800)ACS-2345
URL: http://www.cancer.org
Local. Affiliated With: American Cancer Society.

17812 ■ American Legion, Heesaker-Brown Post 230
c/o Kenneth Van De Hei
3186 Williams Grant Dr.
De Pere, WI 54115
Ph: (608)745-1090
Fax: (608)745-0179
URL: National Affiliate–www.legion.org
Contact: Kenneth Van De Hei, Contact
Local. Affiliated With: American Legion.

17813 ■ ARMA International - Fox Valley/Green Bay Chapter - The Information Management Professionals
c/o Rick Griesser
A.R.M.S.
1850 Enterprise Dr.
De Pere, WI 54115
Ph: (920)339-0135
E-mail: rickg@arms4rim.com
URL: National Affiliate–www.arma.org
Contact: Rick Griesser, Pres.
Founded: 1985. **Members:** 35. **Membership Dues:** regular, includes national dues, $150 (annual). **Local.** Strives to be a valuable resource for education, guidance and networking on records and information management topics. **Libraries: Type:** not open to the public; lending. **Holdings:** 100; articles, books, reports, video recordings. **Subjects:** records, information management. **Affiliated With:** ARMA International - The Association of Information Management Professionals.

17814 ■ Packerland Theatre Organ Society
802 Bolles St.
De Pere, WI 54115
Ph: (920)339-8501
E-mail: pcc28@netnet.net
URL: http://packerlandtos.tripod.com
Contact: Thomas McNeely, Pres.
Local. Aims to restore, preserve and promote the theatre pipe organ and its music. Encourages the youth to learn the instrument. Operates a committee that gathers history and old music from silent film days and information on theatre organists, theaters and organ installations of the silent film era. **Affiliated With:** American Theatre Organ Society.

17815 ■ Wisconsin Athletic Trainers' Association, Northeast
c/o Jill Murphy
1656 Remington Ridge Way
De Pere, WI 54115-9378
Ph: (920)430-4750
E-mail: jillmurph30@yahoo.com
URL: http://www.watainc.org
Contact: Jill Murphy, Contact
Local. Affiliated With: National Athletic Trainers' Association.

De Soto

17816 ■ De Soto Area Lions Club
c/o Margaret M. Spalla, Sec.
PO Box 32
De Soto, WI 54624
Ph: (608)648-3661
E-mail: sparlt@frontiernet.net
URL: http://www.md27d2.org
Contact: Margaret M. Spalla, Sec.
Local. Affiliated With: Lions Clubs International.

Deer Park

17817 ■ American Legion, Wisconsin Post 213
c/o Erick Vick
131 N Main St.
Deer Park, WI 54007
Ph: (608)745-1090
Fax: (608)745-0179
URL: National Affiliate–www.legion.org
Contact: Erick Vick, Contact
Local. Affiliated With: American Legion.

17818 ■ Northern Lights Peruvian House Club
c/o Patricia Wienke, Pres.
2102 Hwy. 63
Deer Park, WI 54007
Ph: (715)263-2814 (715)263-3619
E-mail: up-rite@cltcomm.net
URL: http://www.northernlightsperuvianclub.org
Contact: Patricia Wienke, Pres.
Regional. Affiliated With: North American Peruvian Horse Association.

Deerbrook

17819 ■ Ruffed Grouse Society, Langlade Chapter
c/o Gary Strasser
PO Box 20
Deerbrook, WI 54424
Ph: (715)542-4541
URL: National Affiliate–www.ruffedgrousesociety.org
Contact: Gary Strasser, Contact
Local. Affiliated With: Ruffed Grouse Society.

Deerfield

17820 ■ American Legion, Draeger-Fencil Post 260
48 N Main St.
Deerfield, WI 53531
Ph: (608)745-1090
Fax: (608)745-0179
URL: National Affiliate–www.legion.org
Local. Affiliated With: American Legion.

Delafield

17821 ■ American Legion, Delafield Post 196
333 N Laphim Peak Rd.
Delafield, WI 53018
Ph: (608)745-1090
Fax: (608)745-0179
URL: National Affiliate–www.legion.org
Local. Affiliated With: American Legion.

17822 ■ Delafield Chamber of Commerce (DCC)
PO Box 180171
Delafield, WI 53018
Ph: (262)646-8100
Fax: (262)646-8237
Free: (888)294-1082
E-mail: info@delafieldchamber.org
URL: http://www.delafieldchamber.org
Contact: Cate Rahmlow, Exec.Dir.
Founded: 1930. **Local.** Promotes business and community development in Delafield, WI.

17823 ■ Hawks Inn Historical Society (HIHS)
PO Box 180104
Delafield, WI 53018
Ph: (262)646-4794
URL: http://www.hawksinn.org
Contact: Norman Seltzer, Pres.
Founded: 1960. **Members:** 375. **Membership Dues:** individual, $15 (annual) • family, $20 (annual). **Staff:** 20. **Local.** Individuals interested in mid-19th century social customs. Features costumed tour guides. Maintains mid-19th century stagecoach stop in Delafield, WI. **Libraries: Type:** not open to the public. **Holdings:** 50. **Subjects:** Wisconsin history, local history. **Affiliated With:** Wisconsin Historical Society. **Publications:** *Young America*. Book • Newsletter, quarterly. **Price:** included in membership dues. **Conventions/Meetings:** monthly meeting - every 3rd Monday.

17824 ■ Izaak Walton League of America - Waukesha County
c/o Lillian McNulty
817 Mill St.
Delafield, WI 53018-1515
Ph: (262)646-3482
URL: http://www.iwla.org
Contact: Lillian McNulty, Contact
Local. Educates the public to conserve, maintain, protect, and restore the soil, forest, water, and other natural resources of the U.S. Promotes the utilization of these resources. Sponsors environmental programs.

17825 ■ Ruffed Grouse Society, Kettle Moraine Chapter
c/o Dale Arenz
W324N1198 Lapham Peak Rd.
Delafield, WI 53018
Ph: (262)646-3252
URL: National Affiliate–www.ruffedgrousesociety.org
Contact: Dale Arenz, Contact
Local. Affiliated With: Ruffed Grouse Society.

Delavan

17826 ■ American Legion, Rutledge-Boviall Post 95
111 S 2nd St.
Delavan, WI 53115
Ph: (608)745-1090
Fax: (608)745-0179
URL: National Affiliate–www.legion.org
Local. Affiliated With: American Legion.

17827 ■ Delavan - Delavan Lake Area Chamber of Commerce
53 E Walworth Ave.
Delavan, WI 53115

Ph: (262)728-5095
Fax: (262)728-9199
Free: (800)624-0052
E-mail: info@delavanwi.org
URL: http://www.delavanwi.org
Contact: Jackie Baar, Exec.Dir.
Local. Promotes business and community development in Delavan, WI area. **Publications:** Newsletter, monthly. Alternate Formats: online.

17828 ■ Southern Wisconsin AIFA
c/o William Duesterbeck, Treas.
1407 Racine St., Unit 5
Delavan, WI 53115-1467
Ph: (262)742-4004
Fax: (262)742-3333
E-mail: bill.duesterbeck@thrivent.com
URL: National Affiliate–naifa.org
Contact: William Duesterbeck, Treas.
Local. Represents the interests of insurance and financial advisors. Advocates for a positive legislative and regulatory environment. Enhances business and professional skills of members. **Affiliated With:** National Association of Insurance and Financial Advisors.

17829 ■ United Way of Delavan-Darien
PO Box 30
Delavan, WI 53115-0030
Ph: (262)882-3736
URL: National Affiliate–national.unitedway.org
Local. Affiliated With: United Way of America.

17830 ■ Walworth County Genealogical Society (WCGS)
PO Box 159
Delavan, WI 53115
Ph: (608)363-0554 (608)752-8816
E-mail: kjendlie@charter.net
URL: http://www.rootsweb.com/~wiwalwor
Contact: Donna Long Kjendlie, Pres.
Founded: 1988. **Members:** 180. **Membership Dues:** individual, $10 (annual) • family, $12 (annual) • contributing, $25 (annual). **Local**. Provides educational and resourceful workshops, preserves documents, publishes and reprints such items as atlases and cemetery records, educational information to the public, speakers for groups, and classes when needed. Opened genealogical research library. Publications are for sale. **Libraries: Type:** open to the public. **Holdings:** 400; articles, books, maps, periodicals. **Subjects:** genealogy. **Publications:** *Cemetery Publications*, periodic • *Declaration of Intent and Naturalization Records* • *Indexes to the 1882 and 1912 Walworth County Histories* • *Lagrange Pioneers* • *1873 Walworth County Atlas* • *1919 Prairie Farmer's Directory and Newspaper Obits* • *UW-Whitewater ARC Guide to Researching* • *WCGS Newsletter*, bimonthly. Features genealogical newsletter. **Price:** free for members. ISSN: 1088-5765. **Circulation:** 220. **Conventions/Meetings:** monthly board meeting • periodic Hands-On Meeting • monthly meeting • annual workshop, books, photos, genealogy, family history and cemetery materials (exhibits).

Denmark

17831 ■ American Legion, Johnson-Hershman Post 363
PO Box 481
Denmark, WI 54208
Ph: (608)745-1090
Fax: (608)745-0179
URL: National Affiliate–www.legion.org
Local. Affiliated With: American Legion.

17832 ■ Denmark Community Business Association
PO Box 97
Denmark, WI 54208-0097
Ph: (920)863-6400 (920)863-2161
Fax: (920)863-3237
E-mail: markl@denmarkstate.com
Contact: Mark Looker, VP
Local.

17833 ■ USA Weightlifting - Power Sports Athletic Center
c/o David Gremore
450 S Wall, Lot 21A
Denmark, WI 54208
Ph: (920)863-6888
URL: National Affiliate–www.usaweightlifting.org
Contact: David Gremore, Contact
Local. Affiliated With: USA Weightlifting.

Dodgeville

17834 ■ American Legion, Wisconsin Post 97
c/o Gomer E. Lewis
322 N Douglas St.
Dodgeville, WI 53533
Ph: (608)745-1090
Fax: (608)745-0179
URL: National Affiliate–www.legion.org
Contact: Gomer E. Lewis, Contact
Local. Affiliated With: American Legion.

17835 ■ Bike Wisconsin
PO Box 10
Dodgeville, WI 53533-0010
Free: (888)575-3640
E-mail: wisbike@mhtc.net
URL: http://www.bikewisconsin.org
State.

17836 ■ Dodgeville Area Chamber of Commerce
338 N Iowa
Dodgeville, WI 53533
Ph: (608)935-9200
Fax: (608)930-5324
Free: (877)863-6343
E-mail: info@dodgeville.com
URL: http://www.dodgeville.com
Contact: Ron Dentinger, Exec.Dir.
Local. Promotes business and community development in Dodgeville, WI area. **Formerly:** (2004) Dodgeville Chamber of Commerce.

17837 ■ Friends of Folklore Village
c/o Douglas R. Miller, Exec.Dir.
3210 County Hwy. BB
Dodgeville, WI 53533-0000
Ph: (608)924-4000
Fax: (608)924-3725
E-mail: staff@folklorevillage.org
URL: http://www.folklorevillage.org
Contact: Douglas Miller, Exec.Dir.
Local.

17838 ■ Friends of Governor Dodge State Park
c/o Scott Wippermann
4175 State Rd. 23
Dodgeville, WI 53533-8915
Ph: (608)935-2315
Fax: (608)935-3959
Local.

17839 ■ Southwest Chain Gang Bicycle Club
PO Box 66
Dodgeville, WI 53533
Ph: (608)935-RIDE
E-mail: dmataya@cyfi.com
URL: http://www.madpeople.com/dmataya/chaingang
Contact: Bill Hauda, Newsletter Ed.
Regional.

Dorchester

17840 ■ American Legion, Leach-Paulson Post 517
PO Box 444
Dorchester, WI 54425
Ph: (608)745-1090
Fax: (608)745-0179
URL: National Affiliate–www.legion.org
Local. Affiliated With: American Legion.

Dousman

17841 ■ American Legion, Jones-Mehltretter Post 405
111 Grove St.
Dousman, WI 53118
Ph: (608)745-1090
Fax: (608)745-0179
URL: National Affiliate–www.legion.org
Local. Affiliated With: American Legion.

17842 ■ Horses Have Hope and Other Animals Too
c/o Judith E. Ashley
S30 W36160 Hwy. D, PO Box 161
Dousman, WI 53118-0161
Ph: (262)965-4845 (414)828-6832
Fax: (262)965-4845
E-mail: horseshavehope@earthlink.net
Contact: Judy Ashley, Pres.
Founded: 1999. **Members:** 20. **Budget:** $40,000. **Local.**

Downing

17843 ■ American Legion, Downing Winterling Post 232
404 Forest St.
Downing, WI 54734
Ph: (608)745-1090
Fax: (608)745-0179
URL: National Affiliate–www.legion.org
Local. Affiliated With: American Legion.

Durand

17844 ■ American Legion, Wisconsin Post 181
c/o Robert E. Morsbach
PO Box 71
Durand, WI 54736
Ph: (608)745-1090
Fax: (608)745-0179
URL: National Affiliate–www.legion.org
Contact: Robert E. Morsbach, Contact
Local. Affiliated With: American Legion.

Eagle

17845 ■ Eagle Historical Society (EHS)
PO Box 454
217 W Main St.
Eagle, WI 53119
E-mail: mm@eaglewi.org
URL: http://www.eaglewi.org/eaglehs.org
Contact: Bea Marquardt, Sec.
Founded: 1998. **Members:** 300. **Membership Dues:** individual, $10 (annual) • family, $15 (annual) • senior (65 and over), $8 (annual) • sustaining, $25-$49 (annual) • sponsor, $50-$99 (annual) • patron, $100 (annual). **Budget:** $7,000. **Local**. Seeks to preserve the history of the Eagle, WI area. Operates museum where local historical artifacts are stored and displayed. **Publications:** Newsletter, quarterly. **Price:** included in membership dues. Alternate Formats: online. **Conventions/Meetings:** monthly meeting.

Eagle River

17846 ■ American Legion, Wisconsin Post 114
c/o Frederick J. Walsh
520 Hwy. 45 S
Eagle River, WI 54521
Ph: (608)745-1090
Fax: (608)745-0179
URL: National Affiliate–www.legion.org
Contact: Frederick J. Walsh, Contact
Local. Affiliated With: American Legion.

17847 ■ Headwaters Search and Rescue Dog Association (HSAR)
PO Box 332
Eagle River, WI 54521
Ph: (715)479-4441
Free: (800)472-7290
URL: http://www.hsark9.org
Contact: Tony Campion, Contact
Local. Affiliated With: American Rescue Dog Association.

17848 ■ Muskies Headwaters Chapter
PO Box 652
Eagle River, WI 54521
Ph: (715)477-2913
E-mail: promusky@newnorth.net
URL: http://www.headwatersmuskies.com
Contact: Bill Jacobs, Pres.
Local.

17849 ■ Plumbing-Heating-Cooling Contractors Association, Northern Wisconsin
c/o Lionel Kliss, Pres.
1030 Hwy. 45 S
Eagle River, WI 54521
Ph: (715)479-9712
Fax: (715)479-9675
E-mail: mkkliss@yahoo.com
URL: National Affiliate–www.phccweb.org
Contact: Lionel Kliss, Pres.
Local. Represents the plumbing, heating and cooling contractors. Promotes the construction industry. Protects the environment, health, safety and comfort of society. **Affiliated With:** Plumbing-Heating-Cooling Contractors Association.

17850 ■ Vilas County Chamber of Commerce
330 Court St.
Eagle River, WI 54521
Ph: (715)479-3649
Fax: (715)479-1978
Contact: Cindy Burzinski, Sec.
Local. Formerly: (1999) Eagle River Area Chamber of Commerce.

17851 ■ Wisconsin Amateur Hockey Association (WAHA)
PO Box 1509
Eagle River, WI 54521-1509
Ph: (715)479-3955
Contact: Don Kohlman, Sec.
Founded: 1947. **Members:** 1,000. **Staff:** 1. Amateur hockey teams. Promotes ice hockey and acts as a governing body for the sport. Sponsors competitions; conducts charitable programs. **Awards:** Hockey Hall of Fame/WAHA. **Frequency:** annual. **Type:** scholarship. **Publications:** *WAHA Directory*, annual • *WAHA Newsletter*, quarterly. **Conventions/Meetings:** annual convention - always May; Avg. Attendance: 300.

East Troy

17852 ■ American Legion, Loomis-Martin Post 188
PO Box 775
East Troy, WI 53120
Ph: (608)745-1090
Fax: (608)745-0179
URL: National Affiliate–www.legion.org
Local. Affiliated With: American Legion.

17853 ■ Badger State Matchcover Club
c/o Evelyn Ramlow
2743 Main St., No. 224
East Troy, WI 53120-1380
E-mail: evelyntiger@aol.com
URL: National Affiliate–www.matchcover.org
Contact: Evelyn Ramlow, Contact
State. Affiliated With: Rathkamp Matchcover Society.

17854 ■ Badger State Morgan Horse Club
c/o Mary Beth Weber, Pres.
PO Box 735
East Troy, WI 53120
Ph: (262)642-7789
E-mail: crmorgans@aol.com
URL: http://www.badgerstatemorganhorseclub.com
Contact: Mary Beth Weber, Pres.
State. Affiliated With: American Morgan Horse Association.

17855 ■ East Troy Area Chamber of Commerce
PO Box 312
East Troy, WI 53120
Ph: (262)642-3770
Fax: (262)642-8769
E-mail: info@easttroywi.org
URL: http://www.easttroywi.org
Contact: Linda Kaplan, Pres.
Local. Promotes business and community development in East Troy, WI area.

17856 ■ Field Spaniel Society of America
c/o Terry Middleton, Sec.
W845 Hwy. 20
East Troy, WI 53120-0901
E-mail: terryfssa@yahoo.com
URL: http://clubs.akc.org/fssa
Contact: Terry Middleton, Sec.
Local.

17857 ■ International Facility Management Association, Southeast Wisconsin (Milwaukee) (SEW IFMA)
PO Box 21
East Troy, WI 53120-0021
Ph: (414)297-1125
E-mail: tony.lillibridge@gsa.com
URL: http://www.sewifma.org
Contact: Tony Lillibridge, Pres.
Local. Affiliated With: International Facility Management Association.

17858 ■ Wisconsin English Springer Spaniel Association (WESSA)
c/o Sue Myers
W754 Harmony Ln.
East Troy, WI 53120
E-mail: wessa@execpc.com
URL: http://my.execpc.com/~wessa
Contact: Mary Molter, Pres.
State.

17859 ■ Wisconsin/Illinois Show Horse Society
c/o Diane Bergeman, Pres.
W4690 Little Prairie Rd.
East Troy, WI 53120
Ph: (262)495-4379
URL: National Affiliate–www.nshregistry.org
Contact: Diane Bergeman, Pres.
State. Affiliated With: National Show Horse Registry.

Eastman

17860 ■ American Legion, Fisher-Lechnir-Wall Post 252
PO Box 156
Eastman, WI 54626
Ph: (608)745-1090
Fax: (608)745-0179
URL: National Affiliate–www.legion.org
Local. Affiliated With: American Legion.

Eau Claire

17861 ■ American Association of Physics Teachers, Wisconsin Section (WAPT)
c/o Dr. Erik Hendrickson, Sec.-Treas.
Univ. of Wisconsin, Eau Claire
Dept. of Physics and Astronomy
Eau Claire, WI 54702-4004
Ph: (715)836-5834
Fax: (715)836-3955
E-mail: hendrije@uwec.edu
URL: http://www.uwec.edu/physics/wapt
Contact: Dr. Erik Hendrickson, Sec.-Treas.
Founded: 1945. **Members:** 150. **Membership Dues:** all, $10 (annual). **State.** High school and college physics teachers. Promotes a professional approach to the teaching of physics. **Awards:** Excellence in Teaching Physics. **Frequency:** annual. **Type:** recognition. **Recipient:** for an excellent high school or college/university physics teacher • Lifetime Achievement. **Frequency:** annual. **Type:** recognition. **Recipient:** for persons who have devoted serious energy and effort toward WAPT during their professional career. **Affiliated With:** American Association of Physics Teachers. **Publications:** *Spectrum*, 3/year. Newsletter. **Conventions/Meetings:** annual conference, a 2-day conference (Friday/Saturday) on last weekend of October; with workshops for teachers, poster presentations, oral paper presentations, banquet, business meeting.

17862 ■ American Legion, Johnson-Nicoles-Kuhlman-Olson Post 53
634 Water St.
Eau Claire, WI 54702
Ph: (608)745-1090
Fax: (608)745-0179
URL: National Affiliate–www.legion.org
Local. Affiliated With: American Legion.

17863 ■ American Red Cross, Chippewa Valley Chapter
218 N Barstow St.
Eau Claire, WI 54703
Ph: (715)834-4182
E-mail: chapter@cvcredcross.org
URL: http://www.wwt.net/~eauarc
Local.

17864 ■ Arc Eau Claire
513 S. Barstow St.
Eau Claire, WI 54701
Ph: (715)834-7204
E-mail: thearcec@execpc.com
URL: National Affiliate–www.TheArc.org
Local. Parents, professional workers, and others interested in individuals with mental retardation. Works to promote services, research, public understanding, and legislation for people with mental retardation and their families. **Affiliated With:** Arc of the United States.

17865 ■ Association for Computing Machinery, University of Wisconsin/Eau Claire
c/o Chris Andringa, Chm.
132 Davis Center
Eau Claire, WI 54702
Ph: (715)836-2637
Fax: (715)836-2923
E-mail: wagnerpj@uwec.edu
URL: National Affiliate–www.acm.org
Contact: Chris Andringa, Chm.
Local. Biological, medical, behavioral, and computer scientists; hospital administrators; programmers and others interested in application of computer methods to biological, behavioral, and medical problems. Stimulates understanding of the use and potential of computers in the biosciences. **Affiliated With:** Association for Computing Machinery.

17866 ■ Big Brothers Big Sisters of Northwestern Wisconsin
312 S Barstow, Ste.S1
Eau Claire, WI 54701
Ph: (715)835-0161
Fax: (715)835-2636
Free: (800)648-1696
E-mail: info@bbbsnw.org
URL: http://www.bbbsnw.org
Contact: Jason Plante, Pres.
State. Affiliated With: Big Brothers Big Sisters of America.

17867 ■ Big Rivers AIFA
c/o Amanda Thompson, Exec.
4233 Southtowne Dr., Ste.1
Eau Claire, WI 54701
Ph: (715)835-3176
URL: National Affiliate–naifa.org
Contact: Amanda Thompson, Exec.

Local. Represents the interests of insurance and financial advisors. Advocates for a positive legislative and regulatory environment. Enhances business and professional skills of members. **Affiliated With:** National Association of Insurance and Financial Advisors.

17868 ■ Boy Scouts of America, Chippewa Valley Council
710 S Hastings Way
Eau Claire, WI 54701-3425
Ph: (715)832-6671
Fax: (715)832-6711
E-mail: gclay@bsa-cvc.org
URL: http://www.bsa-cvc.org
Contact: George Clay, Scout Exec.

Local. Affiliated With: Boy Scouts of America. **Also Known As:** (2005) Boy Scouts of America, Eau Claire.

17869 ■ Chippewa Valley Apartment Association
c/o Mr. Dale Goshaw, Exec. Officer
907 Piedmont Rd.
Eau Claire, WI 54703
Ph: (715)836-7507
E-mail: goshawdr@uwec.edu
Contact: Mr. Dale Goshaw, Exec. Officer

Founded: 1981. **Members:** 50. **Membership Dues:** business or apartment owner, $140 (annual) • associate, $130 (annual). **Budget:** $7,000. **State Groups:** 1. **Local.** A group of apartment owners in the Chippewa Valley which includes Eau Claire, Chippewa, Menomonee, and surrounding areas that educate, promote and protect CVAA members interests in the state and local housing market. **Libraries: Type:** open to the public. **Subjects:** information on all phases of landlording in Wisconsin. **Publications:** *The Valley Dweller*, monthly. Newsletter. **Price:** $140.00 for members. **Advertising:** accepted. Alternate Formats: online. **Conventions/Meetings:** monthly meeting - every 2nd Monday.

17870 ■ Chippewa Valley Convention and Visitors Bureau
3625 Gateway Dr., Ste.F
Eau Claire, WI 54701
Ph: (715)831-2345
Fax: (715)831-2340
Free: (888)523-FUNN
E-mail: info@chippewavalley.net
URL: http://www.eauclaire-info.com

Local.

17871 ■ Chippewa Valley Young Life Club
PO Box 1305
Eau Claire, WI 54702-1305
Ph: (715)831-1444
URL: http://sites.younglife.org/sites/chippewavalleyclub/default.aspx

Local. Affiliated With: Young Life.

17872 ■ Council for Exceptional Children, Wisconsin
c/o Amy Schlieve
2109 Sherman Creek
Eau Claire, WI 54703
Ph: (715)232-1332
E-mail: schlievea@uwstout.edu
URL: http://www.cec.sped.org/ab/federati.html
Contact: Amy Schlieve, Contact

State.

17873 ■ Eau Claire Area Chamber of Commerce (GECACC)
101 N Farwell St., Ste.101
Eau Claire, WI 54702
Ph: (715)834-1204
Fax: (715)834-1956
E-mail: information@eauclairechamber.org
URL: http://www.eauclairechamber.org
Contact: Robert S. McCoy, Pres.

Founded: 1915. **Members:** 1,100. **Membership Dues:** general business, $225-$7,886 • professional, $225 • individual, $117. **Local.** Promotes business and community development in the Eau Claire, WI area. **Awards:** Ambassador of the Year. **Frequency:** annual. **Type:** recognition. **Recipient:** to active ambassador • Athena Award. **Frequency:** annual. **Type:** recognition. **Recipient:** for an individual who strives toward the highest level of professional accomplishment for women, who excels in her chosen field, and has devoted time and energy to her community in a meaningful way • Outstanding Volunteer. **Frequency:** annual. **Type:** recognition. **Recipient:** for an active volunteer in the chamber for many years and is heavily involved with many chamber projects including acting as chairman • Small Business Person. **Frequency:** annual. **Type:** recognition. **Recipient:** for increase in sales and/or unit volume, financial success, entrepreneurship, innovativeness of product or service, offered response to adversity, community involvement, and innovative effort shown in area of local and national interest. **Committees:** Agri-Business; Ambassadors; Annual Meeting; Business Expo; Downtown Revitalization; Excellence in Education. **Councils:** Business. **Task Forces:** Business Salutes Eau Claire. **Publications:** *Valley Business*, monthly. Newsletter. **Advertising:** accepted • Directory, annual.

17874 ■ Eau Claire Area Economic Development Corporation
c/o Mr. Brian Doudna, Exec.Dir.
PO Box 1108
Eau Claire, WI 54702
Ph: (715)834-0070
Fax: (715)834-1956
Free: (800)944-2449
E-mail: info@eauclaire-wi.com
URL: http://www.eauclaire-wi.com
Contact: Mr. Brian Doudna, Exec.Dir.

Local. Formerly: (2005) Eau Claire Area Industrial Development Corporation.

17875 ■ Eau Claire Area Foundation
PO Box 511
Eau Claire, WI 54702-0511
Ph: (715)552-3801
Fax: (715)552-3802
E-mail: info@ecareafoundation.org
URL: http://www.ecareafoundation.org
Contact: Janice Ninneman, Exec.Dir.

Founded: 1997. **Members:** 11. **Staff:** 1. **Regional.** Provides opportunities by which individuals, families and businesses may make gifts to enhance the quality of life in the Eau Claire Area. **Libraries: Type:** open to the public.

17876 ■ Eau Claire Curling Club
5530 Fairview Dr.
Eau Claire, WI 54701
Ph: (715)834-4898
E-mail: questions@curlingclub.com
URL: http://www.curlingclub.com
Contact: Pat Layde, Pres.

Founded: 1995. **Local. Affiliated With:** United States Curling Association.

17877 ■ Eau Claire Figure Skating Club
PO Box 8224
Eau Claire, WI 54702-8224
Ph: (715)334-1575
E-mail: retherk@uwec.edu
URL: National Affiliate–www.usfigureskating.org
Contact: Kris Retherford, Contact

Local. Provides programs to encourage participation and achievement in the sport of figure skating on ice. Defines and maintains uniform standards of skating proficiency. Organizes and sponsors competitions and exhibitions for the purpose of stimulating interest in figure skating. **Affiliated With:** United States Figure Skating Association.

17878 ■ Epilepsy Foundation of Western Wisconsin
1812 Brackett Ave., Ste.5
Eau Claire, WI 54701
Ph: (715)834-4455
Fax: (715)834-4465
Free: (800)924-2105
E-mail: kbergefww@sbcglobal.net
URL: http://www.epilepsyfoundation.org/westernwisc
Contact: Eric R. Hargis, Pres./CEO

Founded: 1972. **Members:** 100. **Membership Dues:** general, $25 (annual). **Staff:** 4. **Budget:** $187,000. **Regional Groups:** 1. **Local.** Seeks to improve life opportunities for individuals with epilepsy and their families through advocacy, support, and individual and community education. **Libraries: Type:** open to the public. **Holdings:** 200; archival material, books, periodicals, video recordings. **Subjects:** epilepsy, medications, social. **Awards:** Stars in Epilepsy. **Frequency:** annual. **Type:** recognition. **Affiliated With:** Epilepsy Foundation. **Formerly:** Epilepsy Center of Western Wisconsin. **Publications:** *Wave Length*, quarterly. Newsletter. **Circulation:** 1,500 • Annual Report, annual. Alternate Formats: online. **Conventions/Meetings:** annual Managing Epilepsy Conference (exhibits) - April in Eau Claire, WI.

17879 ■ Indianhead Professional Photographers Association (IPPA)
c/o Thomas W. Giles, Membership Chm.
1412A S Hastings Way
Eau Claire, WI 54701
Ph: (715)834-2993
E-mail: indianhead@gilesphoto.com
URL: http://www.indianheadphotographers.org
Contact: Thomas W. Giles, Membership Chm.

Members: 100. **Membership Dues:** active, aspiring, $60 (annual) • active associate, sustaining, $57 (annual) • husband and wife, $67 (annual). **Budget:** $1,000. **Local.** Professional photographers and suppliers to the photographic industry in northwestern Wisconsin. Sponsors programs to increase professional skills. **Awards:** Photographer of the Year. **Frequency:** annual. **Type:** trophy • Print of the Year. **Frequency:** annual. **Type:** trophy. **Affiliated With:** Professional Photographers of America. **Publications:** *Indianhead Photographer*, 7/year. Newsletter. **Price:** free for members. **Circulation:** 110. **Advertising:** accepted. Alternate Formats: online. **Conventions/Meetings:** monthly meeting.

17880 ■ Institute of Management Accountants, Chippewa Valley
c/o Michael T. Pynch, Pres.
Wipfli, LLP
3703 Oakwood Hills Pkwy.
Eau Claire, WI 54702-0690
Ph: (715)723-9766 (715)858-6630
E-mail: mpynch@wipfli.com
URL: http://www.ima-northernlights.imanet.org
Contact: Michael T. Pynch, Pres.

Local. Promotes professional and ethical standards. Equips members and students with knowledge and training required for the accounting profession. **Affiliated With:** Institute of Management Accountants.

17881 ■ International Brotherhood of Teamsters, Chauffeurs, Warehousemen and Helpers of America, AFL-CIO - Local Union 662
1280 W Clairmont, Ste.5
Eau Claire, WI 54702
Ph: (715)835-6106
E-mail: 662ec@charter.net
URL: http://teamsters662.com
Contact: David Reardon, Sec.-Treas.

Members: 4,513. **Local. Affiliated With:** International Brotherhood of Teamsters.

17882 ■ Junior Achievement of Wisconsin Northwest District
c/o Sherrie Mohr, Dir.
505 Dewey St. S, Ste.204
Eau Claire, WI 54701
Ph: (715)835-5566
Fax: (715)831-0274
E-mail: jaw-nw@charter.net
URL: http://www.jawis.org
Contact: Sherrie Mohr, Dir.
Regional.

17883 ■ Lower Long Lake Foundation
c/o Jake Farrell
1263 Graham Ave.
Eau Claire, WI 54701-3953
Ph: (715)835-2787 (715)552-7210
Fax: (715)552-7215
Contact: Jake Farrell, Sec.-Treas.
Founded: 1997. **Members:** 20. **Staff:** 6. **Local.** Strives to preserve Lower Long Lake.

17884 ■ Mid-American Association for Behavior Analysis
Univ. of Wisconsin-Eau Claire
Dept. of Psychology
Eau Claire, WI 54702-4004
Ph: (715)836-3995
Fax: (715)836-5733
E-mail: klattkp@uwec.edu
URL: http://psyc.uwec.edu/maba/maba.html
Contact: Kevin Klatt, Contact
Regional. Represents individuals interested in the applied, experimental, and theoretical analysis of behavior. Promotes the development of behavior analysis as a profession and as a science. Provides a forum for the discussion of issues related to behavior analysis. **Affiliated With:** Association for Behavior Analysis.

17885 ■ Moose International, Family Center 1408 - Eau Claire
3606 Curvue Rd.
Eau Claire, WI 54703
Ph: (715)835-6522
URL: National Affiliate–www.mooseintl.org
Founded: 1914. **Members:** 800. **Membership Dues:** moose member, $40 (annual). **Staff:** 2. **Budget:** $100,000. **Regional Groups:** 1. **State Groups:** 1. **Local.** Fraternal society. Supports civic and charitable projects. Holds fundraising events. **Affiliated With:** Moose, International. **Publications:** *Moose Antler*, monthly. Newsletter. **Price:** free to members. **Advertising:** accepted. **Conventions/Meetings:** annual Charity Ball - meeting • bimonthly meeting • semiannual meeting, held in conjunction with the State Moose Association.

17886 ■ Mothers Against Drunk Driving, Eau Claire County
1536 Howard Ave.
Eau Claire, WI 54703
Ph: (715)552-8176
E-mail: stopdrunkdriving@hotmail.com
URL: National Affiliate–www.madd.org
Local. Victims of drunk driving crashes; concerned citizens. Encourages citizen participation in working towards reform of the drunk driving problem and the prevention of underage drinking. Acts as the voice of victims of drunk driving crashes by speaking on their behalf to communities, businesses, and educational groups. **Affiliated With:** Mothers Against Drunk Driving.

17887 ■ National Active and Retired Federal Employees Association - Eau Claire 371
1705 Oaklawn Dr.
Eau Claire, WI 54703-1681
Ph: (715)838-0464
URL: National Affiliate–www.narfe.org
Contact: Vernon R. Thalacker, Contact
Local. Protects the retirement future of employees through education. Informs members on issues affecting the retirement. **Affiliated With:** National Association of Retired Federal Employees.

17888 ■ National Alliance for the Mentally Ill - Eau Claire
c/o DeeAnne Peterson-Hagen, Exec.Dir.
505 S Dewey St., Ste.206
Eau Claire, WI 54701
Ph: (715)836-9977
Fax: (715)836-7450
E-mail: petersond200@yahoo.com
URL: http://www.namiwisconsin.org/library/directory
Contact: DeeAnne Peterson-Hagen, Exec.Dir.
Local. Strives to improve the quality of life of children and adults with severe mental illness through support, education, research and advocacy. **Affiliated With:** National Alliance for the Mentally Ill.

17889 ■ National Association of Home Builders of the U.S., Chippewa Valley Home Builders Association (CVHBA)
c/o Lance C. Clark
3410 Oakwood Mall Dr., Ste.400
Eau Claire, WI 54701
Ph: (715)835-2526
Fax: (715)835-2905
E-mail: info@cvhomebuilders.com
URL: http://www.cvhomebuilders.com
Contact: Gregory Haselwander, Pres.
Local. Provides quality products and services to homeowners and residents in Chippewa Valley area. Assists their members in growing their business and enhancing their professional development through continuing education. **Telecommunication Services:** electronic mail, lancec@cvhomebuilders.com. **Committees:** Building and Grounds; Ethics and Grievance; Government Affairs; Home and Garden Show; Nominations; Parade of Homes; Philanthropic Outreach; Strategic Planning. **Affiliated With:** National Association of Home Builders.

17890 ■ Northwest Regional Builders Exchange
PO Box 3003
Eau Claire, WI 54702
Ph: (715)834-2934
Fax: (715)834-3590
E-mail: info@nwrbx.com
URL: http://www.nwrbx.com
Contact: Matt Faulkner, Pres.
Founded: 1954. **Regional.** Represents the general contractors, subcontractors, suppliers, manufacturer's representatives and individual firms related to the construction industry. Provides information on construction and building procedures. **Affiliated With:** International Builders Exchange Executives.

17891 ■ Realtors Association of Northwestern Wisconsin
1903 Keith St.
Eau Claire, WI 54701
Ph: (715)835-0923
Fax: (715)835-4621
Free: (888)221-0112
E-mail: staff@ranww.org
URL: http://www.ranww.org
Contact: Margo Katterhagen, Pres.
Local. Strives to develop real estate business practices. Advocates the right to own, use and transfer real property. Provides a facility for professional development, research and exchange of information among members and to the general public. **Affiliated With:** National Association of Realtors.

17892 ■ Retired Enlisted Association, 77
c/o Melvin Rude
3315 Curvue Rd.
Eau Claire, WI 54703-9205
Ph: (715)834-5137
URL: National Affiliate–www.trea.org
Contact: Melvin Rude, Contact
Local. Affiliated With: The Retired Enlisted Association.

17893 ■ Ruffed Grouse Society, Chippewa Valley Chapter
c/o Don Betthauser
961 Dorbe St.
Eau Claire, WI 54701
Ph: (715)834-9864
URL: National Affiliate–www.ruffedgrousesociety.org
Contact: Don Betthauser, Contact
Local. Affiliated With: Ruffed Grouse Society.

17894 ■ SBC Pioneers Wisconsin Chapter
c/o Gloria Grabowski, Pres.
304 S Dewey
Eau Claire, WI 54701
Ph: (715)839-5946
Fax: (715)839-5929
E-mail: gg1898@sbc.com
URL: http://sbcpioneers.org/chapters/wisconsin/wisconsin.html
Contact: Barb Keehn, Treas.
State. Affiliated With: TelecomPioneers.

17895 ■ SCORE Eau Claire
Fed. Bldg., Rm. B11
500 S Barstow St.
Eau Claire, WI 54701
Ph: (715)834-1573
Fax: (715)834-6047
Free: (877)888-2985
E-mail: score@ecol.net
URL: http://www.score-eauclaire.org
Contact: Robert Kamphaus, Chm.
Local. Provides professional guidance, mentoring services and financial assistance to maximize the success of existing and emerging small businesses. **Telecommunication Services:** electronic mail, score@score-eauclaire.org. **Affiliated With:** SCORE.

17896 ■ Sierra Club - John Muir Chapter - Chippewa Valley Group
3352 Fear St.
Eau Claire, WI 54701
Ph: (715)834-2864
URL: http://www.sierraclub.org/chapters/wi/
Contact: Kris Mason, Co-Chm.
Local.

17897 ■ Society of Broadcast Engineers, Chapter 112 - Western Wisconsin
c/o Todd Zschernitz, Sec.
5545 Hwy. 93
Eau Claire, WI 54701
Ph: (715)835-1818
Fax: (715)835-8009
E-mail: tritchie@pressenter.com
URL: http://www.broadcast.net/~sbe112
Contact: Todd Ritchie, Chm.
Local. Serves the interests of broadcast engineers. Promotes the profession and related fields for both theoretical and practical applications. Advocates for technical advancement of the industry. **Affiliated With:** Society of Broadcast Engineers. **Publications:** Newsletter. Alternate Formats: online.

17898 ■ Society for Human Resource Management - Chippewa Valley Chapter
c/o Jill Thornton
Kelly Sers.
2004 Highland Ave., Ste.D
Eau Claire, WI 54701
E-mail: jill_thornton@kellyservices.com
URL: http://www.wishrm.org/chapter/chpval/index.html
Contact: Jill Thornton, Pres.
Local. Represents the interests of human resource and industrial relations professionals and executives. Promotes the advancement of human resource management.

17899 ■ Society of Manufacturing Engineers - Chippewa Valley Technological College S170
Chippewa Valley Tech. Coll., Trade & Indus. Div.
620 W Clairemont Ave.
Eau Claire, WI 54701

Ph: (715)874-4612
Fax: (715)874-4603
E-mail: tvanderloop@chippewa.tec.wi.us
URL: National Affiliate–www.sme.org
Contact: Thomas J. Vanderloop, Contact
Local. Advances manufacturing knowledge to gain competitive advantage. Improves skills and manufacturing solutions for the growth of economy. Provides resources and opportunities for manufacturing professionals. **Affiliated With:** U.S. Psychotronics Association.

17900 ■ Society of Physics Students - University of Wisconsin-Eau Claire Chapter No. 8289
230 Phillips Sci. Hall
Eau Claire, WI 54702
Ph: (715)836-3148
Fax: (715)836-3955
E-mail: hendrije@uwec.edu
URL: National Affiliate–www.spsnational.org
Contact: Dr. J. Erik Hendrickson, Faculty Advisor
Local. Offers opportunities for the students to enrich their experiences and skills about physics. Helps students to become professional in the field of physics. **Affiliated With:** Society of Physics Students.

17901 ■ Sons of Norway, Loven Lodge 5-29
c/o Evelyn A. Krigsvold, Pres.
2830 13th St.
Eau Claire, WI 54703-2730
Ph: (715)835-8718
E-mail: larsenfolk@hotmail.com
URL: National Affiliate–www.sofn.com
Contact: Evelyn A. Krigsvold, Pres.
Local. Affiliated With: Sons of Norway.

17902 ■ Sweet Adelines International, Chippewa Valley Chapter
Grace Lutheran Church
202 W Grand Ave.
Eau Claire, WI 54703-5327
E-mail: ssb65@localnet.com
URL: http://www.cvsweetadelines.org
Contact: Sue Gunn, Pres.
Local. Advances the musical art form of barbershop harmony through education and performances. Provides education, training and coaching in the development of women's four-part barbershop harmony. **Affiliated With:** Sweet Adelines International.

17903 ■ Trout Unlimited - Ojibleau Chapter
PO Box 822
Eau Claire, WI 54702-0822
Ph: (715)232-2311
E-mail: vandenbloomd@uwstout.edu
URL: National Affiliate–www.tu.org
Contact: Dennis Vanden Bloomen, Pres.
Local.

17904 ■ United Way of Greater Eau Claire
131 S Barstow St.
Eau Claire, WI 54701
Ph: (715)834-5043
Fax: (715)834-0425
Free: (800)411-8929
E-mail: info@unitedwayeauclaire.org
URL: http://www.unitedwayeauclaire.org
Contact: Kris Becker, Exec.Dir.
Founded: 1966. **Staff:** 5. **Local. Affiliated With:** United Way of America. **Publications:** Newsletter, quarterly.

17905 ■ University of Wisconsin Ice Skating Club - Eau Claire
Univ. Recreation
105 Hilltop Ctr.
Eau Claire, WI 54701
E-mail: horsagsc@uwec.edu
URL: National Affiliate–www.usfigureskating.org
Local. Provides programs to encourage participation and achievement in the sport of figure skating on ice. Defines and maintains uniform standards of skating proficiency. Organizes and sponsors competitions and exhibitions for the purpose of stimulating interest in figure skating. **Affiliated With:** United States Figure Skating Association.

17906 ■ USA Weightlifting - Team Janz
c/o Jonathon Janz
624 E Tyler Ave.
Eau Claire, WI 54701
Ph: (608)385-8688
E-mail: jonathonjanz@yahoo.com
URL: National Affiliate–www.usaweightlifting.org
Contact: Jonathon Janz, Contact
Local. Affiliated With: USA Weightlifting.

17907 ■ Western Dairyland RSVP
c/o Kathy Diel, Dir.
1300 First Ave.
Eau Claire, WI 54703
Ph: (715)985-2391
Fax: (715)985-3239
E-mail: kdiel@westerndairyland.org
URL: http://www.seniorcorps.gov
Contact: Kathy Diel, Dir.
Local. Affiliated With: Retired and Senior Volunteer Program.

17908 ■ Wisconsin Council of Teachers of English Language Arts (WCTELA)
c/o Dr. Scott Oates, Treas.
Dept. of English
UW-Eau Claire
PO Box 4004
Eau Claire, WI 54702-4004
Ph: (715)836-4953
E-mail: oatessf@uwec.edu
URL: http://www.wctela.org
Contact: Lynn Aprill, Pres.
Membership Dues: standard, $30 (annual) • contributing, $40 (annual) • sustaining, $50 (annual) • new teacher, $20 (annual) • retiree, $15 (annual) • student, $5 (annual). **State. Affiliated With:** National Council of Teachers of English.

17909 ■ Wisconsin Curling Association - Loch Wissota Curling Club
c/o Jonathan Stolp, Pres.
2805 Fourth St.
Eau Claire, WI 54703
Ph: (715)832-3180
E-mail: stolpn@aol.com
URL: http://www.goodcurling.net/basics/U.S.%20clubs/wisconsin.html
Contact: Jonathan Stolp, Pres.
Local. Affiliated With: United States Curling Association.

17910 ■ Wisconsin Electronic Service Association, Indianhead Chapter
c/o Roger Wood
Woods Electronics
3335 London Rd.
Eau Claire, WI 54701
Ph: (715)834-3822 (715)832-7143
Fax: (715)839-9149
Free: (800)924-3474
E-mail: woodelec@charter.net
URL: National Affiliate–www.nesda.com
Contact: Roger Wood, Pres.
Founded: 1966. **Members:** 15. **State Groups:** 1. **Local Groups:** 1. **Local**. Electronic service companies. **Libraries: Type:** not open to the public. **Subjects:** electronic library state only. **Affiliated With:** National Electronics Service Dealers Association. **Formerly:** Wisconsin Electronic Sales and Service Association, Indianhead Chapter. **Publications:** *The WESA Newsletter*, quarterly. **Advertising:** accepted. **Conventions/Meetings:** annual convention, electronic displays (exhibits) - always June; Avg. Attendance: 150.

17911 ■ Wisconsin Health Care Association, District 10
c/o Jim Deignan, Pres.
Dove Hea. Care Nursing & Rehabilitation
1405 Truax Blvd.
Eau Claire, WI 54703
Ph: (715)552-1030
URL: http://www.whca.com
Contact: Jim Deignan, Pres.
Local. Promotes professionalism and ethical behavior of individuals providing long-term care delivery for patients and for the general public. Provides information, education and administrative tools to enhance the quality of long-term care. Improves the standards of service and administration of member nursing homes. **Affiliated With:** American Health Care Association; Wisconsin Health Care Association.

17912 ■ Young Life Chippewa Valley
PO Box 1305
Eau Claire, WI 54702-1305
Ph: (715)831-1444
Fax: (715)831-3343
URL: http://sites.younglife.org/sites/chippewavalley/default.aspx
Local. Affiliated With: Young Life.

Eau Galle

17913 ■ American Legion, Wood-Gasteyer Post 542
N 486 County Rd. D
Eau Galle, WI 54737
Ph: (608)745-1090
Fax: (608)745-0179
URL: National Affiliate–www.legion.org
Local. Affiliated With: American Legion.

Edgar

17914 ■ American Legion, Sawyer-Drumm Post 393
PO Box 74
Edgar, WI 54426
Ph: (608)745-1090
Fax: (608)745-0179
URL: National Affiliate–www.legion.org
Local. Affiliated With: American Legion.

Edgerton

17915 ■ American Legion, Wisconsin Post 30
c/o Ralph Amundson
5643 W Stone Farm Rd.
Edgerton, WI 53534
Ph: (608)745-1090
Fax: (608)745-0179
URL: National Affiliate–www.legion.org
Contact: Ralph Amundson, Contact
Local. Affiliated With: American Legion.

17916 ■ Classic Peruvian's Horse Club
c/o Karen Lee-Molkenthen
W9160 Bussey Rd.
Edgerton, WI 53534
Ph: (608)884-2011
E-mail: parkviewfarm@aol.com
URL: National Affiliate–www.aaobpph.org
Contact: Karen Lee-Molkenthen, Contact
Local. Affiliated With: American Association of Owners and Breeders of Peruvian Paso Horses.

17917 ■ Edgerton Area Chamber of Commerce (EACC)
20 S Main St.
Edgerton, WI 53534
Ph: (608)884-4408
Fax: (608)884-4408
Free: (888)298-4408
E-mail: info@edgertonwisconsin.com
URL: http://www.edgertonwisconsin.com
Contact: Diane Everson, Pres.
Members: 108. **Local**. Promotes business and community development in the Edgerton, WI area.

17918 ■ Trout Unlimited, Blackhawk
c/o Dave Patrick
107 Lord St.
Edgerton, WI 53534-2015
Ph: (608)884-6948
URL: National Affiliate–www.tu.org
Contact: Mr. Terry Vaughn, Pres.
Local. Affiliated With: Trout Unlimited.

Egg Harbor

17919 ■ Memorial Societies of Wisconsin
6900 Lost Lake Rd.
Egg Harbor, WI 54209-9231
Ph: (920)868-3136
Free: (800)374-1109
E-mail: memorialsociety@itol.com
URL: http://memorialsocietywi.org
Contact: Mr. John Blake, Exec.Dir.
Founded: 1986. **Members:** 2,000. **Membership Dues:** individual, $15. **Staff:** 2. **Budget:** $10,000. **State.** Provides dignity, simplicity and low-cost funerals, cremations and memorial services through a statewide network of cooperating funeral homes. **Publications:** *MEMO*, quarterly. Newsletter. Contains funeral plans. **Price:** free to members. **Circulation:** 300.

Eleva

17920 ■ American Legion, Hopland-Moen Post 459
PO Box 187
Eleva, WI 54738
Ph: (608)745-1090
Fax: (608)745-0179
URL: National Affiliate–www.legion.org
Local. Affiliated With: American Legion.

Elk Mound

17921 ■ American Legion, Howe-Paff Post 37
PO Box 22
Elk Mound, WI 54739
Ph: (608)745-1090
Fax: (608)745-0179
URL: National Affiliate–www.legion.org
Local. Affiliated With: American Legion.

17922 ■ Pony of the Americas Club, Wisconsin - North
c/o Dennis Coombs, Pres.
535 S Buena Vista Rd.
Elk Mound, WI 54739
Ph: (715)874-5322
E-mail: email@rockinsockinponies.com
URL: National Affiliate–www.poac.org
Contact: Dennis Coombs, Pres.
State. Affiliated With: Pony of the Americas Club.

17923 ■ West Wisconsin Dressage Association
c/o Michelle Marquart, Pres.
N2844 960th St.
Elk Mound, WI 54739
Ph: (715)874-4436
URL: National Affiliate–www.usdf.org
Contact: Michelle Marquart, Pres.
Local. Affiliated With: United States Dressage Federation.

Elkhart Lake

17924 ■ American Legion, Friedrichs-Mueller-Norgaard Post 149
N 9015 Highview Rd.
Elkhart Lake, WI 53020
Ph: (608)745-1090
Fax: (608)745-0179
URL: National Affiliate–www.legion.org
Local. Affiliated With: American Legion.

17925 ■ Elkhart Lake Area Chamber of Commerce
41 E Rhine St.
Elkhart Lake, WI 53020
Ph: (920)876-2922
Free: (877)ELK-HART
E-mail: elcoc@bizwi.rr.com
URL: http://www.elkhartlake.com
Local. Promotes business and community development in Elkhart Lake, WI area.

Elkhorn

17926 ■ American Legion, Kelley-Gardner-Katzman-Stoflet Post 45
PO Box 501
Elkhorn, WI 53121
Ph: (608)745-1090
Fax: (608)745-0179
URL: National Affiliate–www.legion.org
Local. Affiliated With: American Legion.

17927 ■ Elkhorn Area Chamber of Commerce (EACC)
114 W Court St.
PO Box 41
Elkhorn, WI 53121
Ph: (262)723-5788
Fax: (262)723-5784
E-mail: elkchamber@elkhorn-wi.org
URL: http://www.elkhorn-wi.org
Contact: Diane Riese, Exec.Dir.
Members: 257. **Membership Dues:** retail/profession and service (1-5 employees), $175 (annual) • retail/profession and service (6-15 employees), $215 (annual) • retail/profession and service (16-35 employees), $265 (annual) • financial institution (based on local deposits), $250-$800 (annual) • hotel/motel/bed and breakfast (based on number of rooms), $175-$440 (annual). **Staff:** 1. **Local.** Promotes business and community development in the Elkhorn, WI area. Holds annual Christmas Carol town parade. **Libraries: Type:** open to the public. **Holdings:** audio recordings, books, periodicals, video recordings. **Awards:** $500 Scholarship. **Frequency:** annual. **Type:** scholarship. **Recipient:** for a graduating senior attending a two-year technical college. **Formerly:** (1999) Bighorn Area Chamber of Commerce. **Publications:** *Commerce Comments*, monthly. Newsletter. **Circulation:** 325. **Advertising:** accepted. **Conventions/Meetings:** annual meeting, to approve board of directors.

17928 ■ Kiwanis Club of Elkhorn, Wisconsin
PO Box 553
Elkhorn, WI 53121
E-mail: info@elkhornkiwanis.org
URL: http://www.elknet.net/kiwanis
Contact: Sheila Reiff, Pres.
Local.

17929 ■ Lakes Area Realtors Association
5 S Ridgway Ct., Ste.1-C
Elkhorn, WI 53121
Ph: (262)723-6851
Fax: (262)723-3256
E-mail: mvanderbunt@charterinternet.com
URL: http://www.lakesrealtors.com
Contact: Mike Vanderbunt, Exec.Dir.
Local.

17930 ■ Southern Wisconsin Appaloosa Horse Club
c/o Ronald A. Person
N 5827 Oakcreek Dr.
Elkhorn, WI 53121
Ph: (262)723-2747
E-mail: ingenuity@elknet.net
URL: National Affiliate–www.appaloosa.com
Contact: Ronald A. Person, Contact
Regional. Affiliated With: Appaloosa Horse Club.

17931 ■ Walworth County Land Conservancy
c/o Robert Mann
PO Box 533
Elkhorn, WI 53121-0048
Ph: (262)741-6557
Fax: (262)723-3463
E-mail: rmann@mannbrosinc.com
URL: http://www.walcntylc.org
Contact: Paul Ormson, Admn.Dir.
Founded: 2001. **Members:** 60. **Local.**

Ellsworth

17932 ■ American Legion, Kinne-Engelhart Post 204
PO Box 205
Ellsworth, WI 54011
Ph: (608)745-1090
Fax: (608)745-0179
URL: National Affiliate–www.legion.org
Local. Affiliated With: American Legion.

17933 ■ Ellsworth Chamber of Commerce
PO Box 927
Ellsworth, WI 54011
Ph: (715)273-6442
E-mail: ellsworthchamber@sbcglobal.net
URL: http://www.ellsworthchamber.com
Contact: Joanne Hines, Pres.
Members: 100. **Local.** Works to promote the development of Ellsworth community. **Publications:** Newsletter, monthly. Includes information about meetings and events in the community. **Advertising:** accepted. Alternate Formats: online.

Elm Grove

17934 ■ Wisconsin Off-Road Bicycling Association (WORBA)
PO Box 5184
Elm Grove, WI 53122-5184
E-mail: mac@worba.org
URL: http://www.worba.org
Contact: John Watson, Pres.
State. Promotes and preserve environmentally responsible mountain biking opportunities. **Affiliated With:** International Mountain Bicycling Association.

Elmwood

17935 ■ American Legion, Crain and Ottman Post 207
PO Box 283
Elmwood, WI 54740
Ph: (608)745-1090
Fax: (608)745-0179
URL: National Affiliate–www.legion.org
Local. Affiliated With: American Legion.

17936 ■ Ruffed Grouse Society, Durand Area Chapter
c/o Don Konsela
E2297 150th Ave.
Elmwood, WI 54740
Ph: (715)672-8862
URL: National Affiliate–www.ruffedgrousesociety.org
Contact: Don Konsela, Contact
Local. Affiliated With: Ruffed Grouse Society.

Elroy

17937 ■ American Legion, Cleary-Miller Post 115
PO Box 72
Elroy, WI 53929
Ph: (608)745-1090
Fax: (608)745-0179
URL: National Affiliate–www.legion.org
Local. Affiliated With: American Legion.

17938 ■ American Legion, Wisconsin Post 504
c/o Conrad Shaker
W10704 Mack Valley Rd.
Elroy, WI 53929
Ph: (608)745-1090
Fax: (608)745-0179
URL: National Affiliate–www.legion.org
Contact: Conrad Shaker, Contact
Local. Affiliated With: American Legion.

17939 ■ Crosstown African Violet Club
c/o Arlene Garvens
30630 Outboard Rd.
Elroy, WI 53929
Ph: (608)463-7775
E-mail: rag@elroynet.com
URL: National Affiliate–www.avsa.org
Contact: Arlene Garvens, Contact
Local. Affiliated With: African Violet Society of America.

17940 ■ Elroy Area Advancement Corporation
PO Box 52
Elroy, WI 53929
Ph: (608)462-5872
E-mail: elroywi@mwt.net
URL: http://www.elroywi.com
Contact: Joan Sartori, Pres.
Local. Promotes community advancement in the Elroy, WI area.

17941 ■ Elroy Lions Club
c/o Gary Board, Pres.
N2426 Weger Rd.
Elroy, WI 53929
Ph: (608)462-8121
E-mail: ggboard@hotmail.com
URL: http://www.elroylions.org
Contact: Gary Board, Pres.
Local. Affiliated With: Lions Clubs International.

Emerald

17942 ■ American Legion, Wisconsin Post 404
c/o Guy R. Mc Cluskey
PO Box 302
Emerald, WI 54013
Ph: (608)745-1090
Fax: (608)745-0179
URL: National Affiliate–www.legion.org
Contact: Guy R. Mc Cluskey, Contact
Local. Affiliated With: American Legion.

Ettrick

17943 ■ American Legion, Runnestrand-Pederson Post 354
PO Box 356
Ettrick, WI 54627
Ph: (608)745-1090
Fax: (608)745-0179
URL: National Affiliate–www.legion.org
Local. Affiliated With: American Legion.

17944 ■ North Bend Lions Club
c/o Bill Suttie, Pres.
W12409 State Hwy. 54
Ettrick, WI 54627
Ph: (608)582-4076
URL: http://www.md27d2.org
Contact: Bill Suttie, Pres.
Local. Affiliated With: Lions Clubs International.

Evansville

17945 ■ American Legion, Mc-Kinney-Hatlevig Post 35
6542 N South 5th St.
Evansville, WI 53536
Ph: (608)745-1090
Fax: (608)745-0179
URL: National Affiliate–www.legion.org
Local. Affiliated With: American Legion.

17946 ■ American Rabbit Breeders Association, Badger Rabbit Breeders
c/o Sue Dietzman, Sec.
15416 W Butts Corner Rd.
Evansville, WI 53536
Ph: (608)882-5853
E-mail: brabbitman@jvlnet.com
URL: http://www.geocities.com/badgerrba
Contact: Sue Dietzman, Sec.
Local. Affiliated With: American Rabbit Breeders Association.

17947 ■ Evansville Chamber of Commerce
PO Box 51
Evansville, WI 53536
Ph: (608)882-5131
E-mail: chamber-info@evansville-wi.com
URL: http://www.evansville-wi.com
Contact: Trish Graves, Admin.Asst.
Members: 85. **Membership Dues:** for 1-2 full time employees (increases with full time employee equivalency), $95 (annual). **Staff:** 1. **Local Groups:** 1. **Local.** Promotes business and community development in Evansville, WI. **Publications:** *Chamber News*, quarterly. Newsletter. **Price:** included in membership dues. **Circulation:** 85. **Conventions/ Meetings:** semimonthly meeting.

17948 ■ Rock River Speleological Society (RRSS)
c/o Bruce Foyer, Pres.
1947 N State Hwy. 213
Evansville, WI 53536
Ph: (608)876-6080
E-mail: alcaver@hotmail.com
URL: http://www.caves.org/grotto/rrss
Contact: Bruce Foyer, Pres.
Regional. Seeks to study, explore and conserve cave and karst resources. Protects access to caves and promotes responsible caving. Encourages responsible management of caves and their unique environments. **Affiliated With:** National Speleological Society.

Fairchild

17949 ■ American Legion, Neuman-Mc-Gaver Post 466
309 N Front St.
Fairchild, WI 54741
Ph: (608)745-1090
Fax: (608)745-0179
URL: National Affiliate–www.legion.org
Local. Affiliated With: American Legion.

Fall Creek

17950 ■ American Legion, Bever Post 550
W 9150 Beaver Creek Rd.
Fall Creek, WI 54742
Ph: (608)745-1090
Fax: (608)745-0179
URL: National Affiliate–www.legion.org
Local. Affiliated With: American Legion.

17951 ■ American Legion, Voight Post 376
PO Box 423
Fall Creek, WI 54742
Ph: (608)745-1090
Fax: (608)745-0179
URL: National Affiliate–www.legion.org
Local. Affiliated With: American Legion.

17952 ■ Chippewa Valley Astronomical Society
S1 County Rd. K
Fall Creek, WI 54742
Ph: (715)839-0995
E-mail: elliott@uwec.edu
URL: http://www.cvastro.org
Contact: Ray Forsgren, Contact
Local. Promotes the science of astronomy. Works to encourage and coordinate activities of amateur astronomical societies. Fosters observational and computational work and craftsmanship in various fields of astronomy. **Affiliated With:** Astronomical League.

17953 ■ White Pine Wildlife Rehabilitation Center
S. 3091 Oak Knoll Rd.
Fall Creek, WI 54742-9312
Ph: (715)877-2372
Fax: (715)877-3119
E-mail: critter@ecol.net
Contact: John J. Owens, Pres.
Founded: 1990. **Local.** Tax deductible registered charity volunteer organization. Works to care for injured and orphaned wild animals and to educate the public about wildlife.

Fall River

17954 ■ Central Wisconsin Vizsla Club (CWVC)
c/o Rebecca Smith
N4355 County Rd., DG
Fall River, WI 53932
Ph: (920)484-6443
E-mail: jzsilver@sbcglobal.net
URL: http://www.cwvc.org
Contact: Janet Silverman, Contact
Founded: 1994. **Members:** 100. **Membership Dues:** single, $15 (annual) • family, $20 (annual). **Regional Groups:** 25. **State Groups:** 1. **Local.** Promotes the welfare of the Vizsla breed and encourages high standards in breeding, training, and competition. **Awards: Frequency:** annual. **Type:** recognition. **Affiliated With:** American Kennel Club. **Publications:** *The Paw's Print*, quarterly. Newsletter. **Price:** free for members; $10.00 /year for nonmembers. **Advertising:** accepted. **Conventions/Meetings:** quarterly meeting.

Fence

17955 ■ National Alliance for the Mentally Ill - Wishigan
c/o Fumico McLain, Pres.
708 Homestead Joint Rd.
Fence, WI 54120
Ph: (715)336-2744
Fax: (715)336-2744
E-mail: fhm@czo.net
URL: http://www.namiwisconsin.org/library/directory
Contact: Fumico McLain, Pres.
Local. Strives to improve the quality of life of children and adults with severe mental illness through support, education, research and advocacy. **Affiliated With:** National Alliance for the Mentally Ill.

Fennimore

17956 ■ American Legion, Whitish-Funk Post 184
PO Box 75
Fennimore, WI 53809

Ph: (608)745-1090
Fax: (608)745-0179
URL: National Affiliate–www.legion.org
Local. Affiliated With: American Legion.

17957 ■ Fennimore Area Chamber of Commerce
850 Lincoln Ave.
Fennimore, WI 53809
Ph: (608)822-3599
Fax: (608)822-6007
E-mail: promo@fennimore.com
URL: http://fennimore.com
Contact: Linda Parrish, Promotions Coor.
Founded: 1970. **Members:** 80. **Budget:** $12,000. **Local.** Promotes business, tourism, and community development in Fennimore, WI. **Publications:** Newsletter, quarterly.

17958 ■ Sons of Norway, Sor Vest Viskonsin Lodge 5-629
c/o Harriet C. Copus, Sec.
1525 Jackson St.
Fennimore, WI 53809-2052
Ph: (608)822-3195
E-mail: hcopus@tds.net
URL: National Affiliate–www.sofn.com
Contact: Harriet C. Copus, Sec.
Local. Affiliated With: Sons of Norway.

17959 ■ Southwestern Wisconsin Angus Association
c/o Roger Kreul, Pres.
12035 Rogers Rd.
Fennimore, WI 53809
Ph: (608)822-6092
E-mail: twokcattlekr@netscape.net
URL: National Affiliate–www.angus.org
Contact: Roger Kreul, Pres.
State. Affiliated With: American Angus Association.

17960 ■ Wisconsin Educational Media Association
1300 Industrial Dr.
Fennimore, WI 53809
Ph: (608)822-6884
Fax: (608)822-3828
E-mail: wema@centurytel.net
URL: http://www.wemaonline.org
Contact: Mary Lou Zuege, Pres.
Strives to promote learning and information access through the development and effective utilization of all forms of media and technology; to provide leadership for the educational media field in Wisconsin; to offer services and professional growth opportunities to all members; and to work cooperatively with other educational organizations and agencies. **Publications:** *WEMA Dispatch*. Contains local and state news of the profession. **Conventions/Meetings:** annual conference - spring • annual workshop - fall.

Fifield

17961 ■ American Legion, Fifield Post 532
PO Box 85
Fifield, WI 54524
Ph: (608)745-1090
Fax: (608)745-0179
URL: National Affiliate–www.legion.org
Local. Affiliated With: American Legion.

Fish Creek

17962 ■ Door County Environmental Council
PO Box 114
Fish Creek, WI 54212
Ph: (920)743-6003
Fax: (920)743-6727
E-mail: jerrymv@itol.com
URL: http://tourpages.com
Contact: Jerome M. Viste, Exec.Dir.
Founded: 1970. **Members:** 550. **Membership Dues:** $15 (annual). **Staff:** 1. **Local.** Citizens of northeast Wisconsin interested in the preservation of natural resources for future generations. Testifies on critical issues and takes legal action. Offers educational programs. Conducts essay contest and scholarship for high school county students. **Awards:** Annual Essay Contest Award. **Frequency:** annual. **Type:** monetary. **Recipient:** for grades 5 to 12; top six essays • Rosner/Johnson Memorial Scholarships. **Frequency:** annual. **Type:** scholarship. **Recipient:** Door County high school students with environmental interests. **Publications:** Newsletter, quarterly. Contains in-depth reports on activities and challenges. **Price:** free to members. **Conventions/Meetings:** Sustainable Agriculture Institute - general assembly - 8/year.

Fitchburg

17963 ■ Madison District Nurses Association - No. 3
2724 Jacquelyn Dr.
Fitchburg, WI 53711
Ph: (608)221-0383
E-mail: megan@wisconsinnurses.org
URL: http://www.wisconsinnurses.org
Contact: Linda Szalkucki, Pres.
Local. Works to advance the nursing profession. Seeks to meet the needs of nurses and health care consumers. Fosters high standards of nursing practice. Promotes the economic and general welfare of nurses in the workplace. **Affiliated With:** American Nurses Association; Wisconsin Nurses' Association.

17964 ■ National Association of Watch and Clock Collectors, Chapter 171
5510 Lacy Rd.
Fitchburg, WI 53711-5318
E-mail: dale.beske@doit.wisc.edu
URL: http://www.geocities.com/nawcc171
Contact: Dale Beske, Sec.
Local.

Florence

17965 ■ American Legion, Meyers-Youngell Post 211
PO Box 568
Florence, WI 54121
Ph: (608)745-1090
Fax: (608)745-0179
URL: National Affiliate–www.legion.org
Local. Affiliated With: American Legion.

17966 ■ Commonwealth Sportsmen's Club
c/o Sean Franklin
HC 3, Box 19A
Florence, WI 54121-9703
E-mail: comsport@charter.net
URL: http://commonwealthclub.tripod.com
Founded: 1947. **Members:** 70. **Membership Dues:** $5 (annual). **Local Groups:** 1. **Local.**

Fond du Lac

17967 ■ Alcoholics Anonymous World Services, Winnebago Land Central Office
280 N Main St.
Fond du Lac, WI 54935
Ph: (920)922-7512
URL: National Affiliate–www.aa.org
Local. Individuals recovering from alcoholism. AA maintains that members can solve their common problem and help others achieve sobriety through a twelve step program that includes sharing their experience, strength, and hope with each other. **Affiliated With:** Alcoholics Anonymous World Services.

17968 ■ American Legion, Trier-Puddy Post 75
500 Fond Du Lac Ave.
Fond du Lac, WI 54935
Ph: (608)745-1090
Fax: (608)745-0179
URL: National Affiliate–www.legion.org
Local. Affiliated With: American Legion.

17969 ■ American Red Cross, Fond du Lac County Chapter
272 N Main St.
Fond du Lac, WI 54935
Ph: (920)922-3450
Fax: (920)922-3225
E-mail: redcrfdl@charter.net
URL: http://fonddulaccounty.redcross.org
Local.

17970 ■ Association for Psychological Type - Interest Group, Fox River Valley
c/o Lori McEathron
PO Box 1303
Fond du Lac, WI 54936-1303
Ph: (920)929-7581
Fax: (920)929-7126
E-mail: lmceathron@fcedc.com
URL: National Affiliate–www.aptinternational.org
Contact: Lori McEathron, Contact
Local. Promotes the practical application and ethical use of psychological type. Provides members with opportunities for continuous learning, sharing experiences and creating understanding and knowledge through research. **Affiliated With:** Association for Psychological Type.

17971 ■ Downtown Fond du Lac Partnership
207 N Main St.
Fond du Lac, WI 54935
Ph: (920)921-9500
Fax: (920)921-9559
E-mail: terrif@fdlac.com
URL: http://www.fdlac.com
Contact: Terri Fleming, Dir.
Local.

17972 ■ Fond du Lac Area Association of Commerce (FDLAAC)
207 N Main St.
Fond du Lac, WI 54935
Ph: (920)921-9500
Fax: (920)921-9559
E-mail: info@fdlac.com
URL: http://www.fdlac.com
Contact: Joe Reitemeier, Pres./CEO
Founded: 1912. **Members:** 800. **Staff:** 11. **Budget:** $750,000. **Local.** Promotes business and community development in the Fond du Lac, WI area. **Awards:** Community Awards. **Frequency:** annual. **Type:** recognition • **Frequency:** annual. **Type:** scholarship. **Committees:** Education. **Councils:** Agri-Business; Communications Council; Safety Council. **Formerly:** Fond du Lac Area Chamber of Commerce. **Publications:** *FDLAC*, monthly. Newsletter. Alternate Formats: online • Directory, annual.

17973 ■ Fond du Lac Area Convention and Visitors Bureau
171 S Pioneer Rd.
Fond du Lac, WI 54935
Ph: (920)923-3010
Fax: (920)929-6846
Free: (800)937-9123
E-mail: visitor@fdl.com
URL: http://www.fdl.com
Contact: Michael Schmal, CEO
Founded: 1975. **Staff:** 9. **Budget:** $350,000. **Nonmembership. Local.**

17974 ■ Fond du Lac Area United Way
74 S Main St.
Fond du Lac, WI 54935
Ph: (920)921-7010
Fax: (920)921-2808
E-mail: info@fdlunitedway.org
URL: http://www.fdlunitedway.org
Contact: Tina Potter, Exec.Dir.
Local. Affiliated With: United Way of America.

17975 ■ Fond du Lac Area Youth for Christ
303 E 9th St.
Fond du Lac, WI 54935
Ph: (920)923-1416
Fax: (920)923-4090
URL: http://www.fdlyfc.org
Local. Affiliated With: Youth for Christ/U.S.A.

17976 ■ Fond du Lac Blue Line Figure Skating
N5583 Glacier Ct.
Fond du Lac, WI 54935
E-mail: sk8rmom_1c@charter.net
URL: National Affiliate–www.usfigureskating.org
Contact: Suzanne Schlecht, Contact
Local. Provides programs to encourage participation and achievement in the sport of figure skating on ice. Defines and maintains uniform standards of skating proficiency. Organizes and sponsors competitions and exhibitions for the purpose of stimulating interest in figure skating. **Affiliated With:** United States Figure Skating Association.

17977 ■ Fond du Lac County Audubon Society
PO Box 84
Fond du Lac, WI 54935
URL: National Affiliate–www.audubon.org
Local. Works to conserve and restore natural ecosystems, focusing on birds and other wildlife for the benefit of humanity and the earth's biological diversity. **Affiliated With:** National Audubon Society.

17978 ■ Fond du Lac County-Farm Bureau
343 N Peters Ave.
Fond du Lac, WI 54935
Ph: (920)921-4520
Contact: Linda Jahn, Office Mgr.
Local.

17979 ■ Fond du Lac County Kennel Club
c/o Joanne Brault, Corresponding Sec.
W2588 Poplar Rd.
Fond du Lac, WI 54935-8941
E-mail: rbrault@thesurf.com
URL: http://www.geocities.com/fdlckc
Contact: Joanne Brault, Corresponding Sec.
Local.

17980 ■ Fond du Lac County REACT
PO Box 1081
Fond du Lac, WI 54935-1081
Ph: (920)923-4291
E-mail: 4364@wireact.org
URL: http://www.reactintl.org/teaminfo/usa_teams/teams-uswi.htm
Contact: Ed Beltz, Pres.
Local. Trained communication experts and professional volunteers. Provides volunteer public service and emergency communications through the use of radios (Citizen Band, General Mobile Radio Service, UHF and HAM). Coordinates with radio industries and government on safety communication matters and supports charitable activities and community organizations.

17981 ■ Fond du Lac Home Builders
490 W Rolling Meadows Dr.
Fond du Lac, WI 54937
Ph: (920)922-9067
E-mail: info@homebuildersfdldodge.com
URL: http://www.homebuildersfdldodge.com
Contact: Joan Van de Castle, Exec. Officer
Local.

17982 ■ Habitat for Humanity of Fond du Lac County
PO Box 2311
Fond du Lac, WI 54936-2311
Ph: (920)921-6623
Fax: (920)921-2893
E-mail: habitatfdl@dotnet.com
URL: http://habitatfdl.org
Local. Affiliated With: Habitat for Humanity International.

17983 ■ Hearty Sole Walkers
c/o Renee Soles
200E Pioneer Rd.
Fond du Lac, WI 54935
Ph: (920)922-3239
E-mail: solesrr@thesurf.com
URL: National Affiliate–www.ava.org
Contact: Renee Soles, Contact
Local.

17984 ■ Izaak Walton League of America - A.D. Sutherland Chapter
451 E 2nd St.
Fond du Lac, WI 54935
Ph: (920)923-5891
E-mail: lroy@fdldotnet.com
URL: http://www.iwla.org
Contact: Mr. Tom Wilhelms, Membership Sec.
Founded: 1927. **Members:** 150. **Membership Dues:** single, $57 (annual). **Local Groups:** 1. **Local.**

17985 ■ Mail Systems Management Association, Wisconsin Chapter
c/o Society Insurance
150 Camelot Dr.
Fond du Lac, WI 54935-8030
Ph: (920)922-1220
Fax: (920)922-9810
URL: National Affiliate–www.msmanational.org
Contact: Christy Warner, Pres.
State. Provide a forum for people involved in the management, supervision and support of mail systems in business, industry, government and institutions. Raises the level of management prestige and esteem for managers employed in mail management.

17986 ■ NAIFA-Fond du Lac
c/o Mike Immel
343 N Peters Ave.
Fond du Lac, WI 54935
Ph: (920)924-6751
Fax: (920)921-5834
URL: National Affiliate–naifa.org
Contact: Mike Immel, Contact
Local. Represents the interests of insurance and financial advisors. Advocates for a positive legislative and regulatory environment. Enhances business and professional skills of members. **Affiliated With:** National Association of Insurance and Financial Advisors.

17987 ■ National Active and Retired Federal Employees Association - Fond du Lac 708
137 E Div. St.
Fond du Lac, WI 54935-4307
Ph: (920)921-2806
URL: National Affiliate–www.narfe.org
Contact: George E. Layher, Contact
Local. Protects the retirement future of employees through education. Informs members on issues affecting the retirement. **Affiliated With:** National Association of Retired Federal Employees.

17988 ■ National Alliance for the Mentally Ill - Fond du Lac
c/o Donn Stout, Pres.
459 E First St.
Fond du Lac, WI 54935
Ph: (920)929-3309
E-mail: nami@namifonddulac.org
URL: http://www.namifonddulac.org
Contact: Donn Stout, Pres.
Local. Strives to improve the quality of life of children and adults with severe mental illness through support, education, research and advocacy. **Affiliated With:** National Alliance for the Mentally Ill.

17989 ■ Oshkosh Philatelic Society
c/o Don Halverson
N9196 Willow Ln. Beach
Fond du Lac, WI 54935-9537
E-mail: artcoy@vbe.com
URL: http://www.virtualstampclub.com/apsoshkosh.html
Contact: Mr. Don Halverson, Pres.
Founded: 1930. **Members:** 35. **Membership Dues:** full membership, $3 (annual). **State Groups:** 1. **For-Profit. Local. Libraries: Type:** not open to the public. **Holdings:** 10; books. **Subjects:** philatelics only. **Computer Services:** Online services, e-mail only. **Committees:** Ad Hoc Committee. **Affiliated With:** American Philatelic Society; Wisconsin Federation of Stamp Clubs.

17990 ■ Phi Theta Kappa, Beta Mu Kappa Chapter - Moraine Park Technical College
c/o Lawrence Pasquini
235 N Natl. Ave.
Fond du Lac, WI 54936-1940
Ph: (920)924-3193
E-mail: lpasquini@morainepark.edu
URL: http://www.ptk.org/directories/chapters/WI/21380-1.htm
Contact: Lawrence Pasquini, Advisor
Local.

17991 ■ Points of Light Foundation - Volunteer Center of Fond du Lac County
650 N Main St.
Fond du Lac, WI 54935-1928
Ph: (920)926-1414
E-mail: volunteercenter@fdlvolunteer.com
URL: http://www.fdlvolunteer.com
Contact: Kay Vandervort, Contact
Local. Affiliated With: Points of Light Foundation.

17992 ■ Society for Human Resource Management - Fond du Lac Chapter
207 N Main St.
Fond du Lac, WI 54935
Ph: (920)921-9500
Fax: (920)921-9559
E-mail: info@fdlac.com
URL: http://wishrm.org/chapter/fdlac/index.html
Contact: Jeffrey Reed, Pres.
Local. Represents the interests of human resource and industrial relations professionals and executives. Promotes the advancement of human resource management.

17993 ■ Society of Manufacturing Engineers - Moraine Park Tech. College S234
PO Box 1940
Fond du Lac, WI 54936-1940
Ph: (920)924-3144
Fax: (920)924-3443
E-mail: troehlr@morainepark.edu
URL: National Affiliate–www.sme.org
Contact: Tom Roehl, Contact
Local. Advances manufacturing knowledge to gain competitive advantage. Improves skills and manufacturing solutions for the growth of economy. Provides resources and opportunities for manufacturing professionals. **Affiliated With:** Fine Particle Society.

17994 ■ Wisconsin Chapter of the Tourette Syndrome Association (WTSA)
173 E 11th St.
Fond du Lac, WI 54935
Ph: (920)960-5459 (920)923-0175
E-mail: wtsa@voyager.net
URL: http://my.voyager.net/~wtsa
Contact: Charles Sosinski, Pres.
State. Works to identify the cause of, find the cure for and control the effects of Tourette Syndrome (TS).

Offers resources and referrals to help people and their families cope with the problems that occur with TS. Raises public awareness and counter media stereotypes about TS. **Affiliated With:** Tourette Syndrome Association.

Footville

17995 ■ American Legion, Devins-Teehan Post 237
Old Hwy. 11
Footville, WI 53537
Ph: (608)745-1090
Fax: (608)745-0179
URL: National Affiliate–www.legion.org
Local. Affiliated With: American Legion.

17996 ■ Late Bloomers African Violet Society
c/o Linda Wendler
123 Depot St.
Footville, WI 53537
Ph: (608)876-6294
URL: National Affiliate–www.avsa.org
Contact: Linda Wendler, Contact
Local. Affiliated With: African Violet Society of America.

Forestville

17997 ■ American Legion, Wisconsin Post 372
c/o George W. Goetz
PO Box 305
Forestville, WI 54213
Ph: (608)745-1090
Fax: (608)745-0179
URL: National Affiliate–www.legion.org
Contact: George W. Goetz, Contact
Local. Affiliated With: American Legion.

Fort Atkinson

17998 ■ American Rabbit Breeders Association, Tri-County Rabbit Breeders
c/o Melissa Carlson, Sec.
W8779 Advent Rd.
Fort Atkinson, WI 53538
URL: http://www.geocities.com/wisconsin_state_rba/Local_Clubs.html
Contact: Melissa Carlson, Sec.
Local. Affiliated With: American Rabbit Breeders Association.

17999 ■ Fort Atkinson Area Chamber of Commerce (FAACC)
244 N Main St.
Fort Atkinson, WI 53538
Ph: (920)563-3210
Fax: (920)563-8946
Free: (888)SEE-FORT
E-mail: evp@fortchamber.com
URL: http://www.fortchamber.com
Contact: Dianne A. Hrobsky, Exec.VP
Founded: 1889. **Members:** 242. **Local.** Commercial, industrial, professional, retail, and service businesses. Promotes business and community development in the Fort Atkinson, WI area. **Affiliated With:** American Chamber of Commerce Executives; U.S. Chamber of Commerce. **Publications:** *Focus on Fort Atkinson*, monthly. Newsletter. Features articles of interest to keep the member informed and abreast of important issues. **Circulation:** 600. **Advertising:** accepted.

18000 ■ Navy League of the United States, Madison
c/o George E. Burlingame, Pres.
9020 E County Line Rd.
Fort Atkinson, WI 53538-9208
Ph: (920)563-6005
E-mail: phylburl@idonet.com
URL: National Affiliate–www.navyleague.org
Contact: George E. Burlingame, Pres.
Local. Civilian organization that supports U.S. capability to keep the sea lanes open through a strong, viable Navy, Marine Corps, Coast Guard, and Merchant Marine. Seeks to awaken interest and cooperation of U.S. citizens in matters serving to aid, improve, and develop the efficiency of U.S. naval and maritime forces and equipment. **Affiliated With:** Navy League of the United States.

18001 ■ United Way of Jefferson and North Walworth Counties
611 Grove St.
Fort Atkinson, WI 53538
Ph: (920)563-8880
Fax: (920)563-0051
URL: http://www.ourunitedway.com
Contact: Dan McCrea, Exec.Dir.
Founded: 1943. **Staff:** 2. **State Groups:** 1. **Nonmembership. Local.** Fundraising organization for communities of Jefferson, Fort Atkinson, Lake Mills, Rome, Whitewater, Sullivan, Helenville and Palmyra and Elkhorn. All proceeds go to 38 non-profit community health and social programs. **Affiliated With:** United Way of America. **Formerly:** (1998) Land of Blackhawk Chapter of the United Way. **Conventions/Meetings:** monthly Board of Directors - board meeting - always second Monday • annual meeting, campaign.

Fountain City

18002 ■ American Legion, Fountain City Post 56
PO Box 445
Fountain City, WI 54629
Ph: (608)745-1090
Fax: (608)745-0179
URL: National Affiliate–www.legion.org
Local. Affiliated With: American Legion.

Fox Lake

18003 ■ Fox Lake Area Chamber of Commerce
PO Box 94
Fox Lake, WI 53933-0094
Ph: (920)928-3777
Fax: (920)928-2033
Free: (800)858-4904
E-mail: foxlake@powercom.net
URL: http://www.foxlake.com
Contact: Lorraine Mund, Administrator
Members: 70. **Local.** Promotes economic, industrial, and community development and tourism in Fox Lake, WI. **Formerly:** (1999) Fox Lake Chamber of Commerce. **Publications:** *Fox Lake Visitors Guide*, annual. Newspaper. **Price:** free.

18004 ■ Wisconsin Association of Agricultural Educators
c/o Richard Aide, Exec.Dir.
N10496 Buckhorn Rd.
Fox Lake, WI 53933
Ph: (920)324-8787
E-mail: dick@waae.com
URL: http://www.waae.com
Contact: Keith Gundlach, Pres.
State. Seeks to advance agricultural education and promotes the professional interests and growth of agriculture teachers. Provides agricultural education through visionary leadership, advocacy and service. **Affiliated With:** National Association of Agricultural Educators.

Fox Point

18005 ■ Labor and Employment Relations Association, Wisconsin
c/o Cary Silverstein, Sec.
1615 E Dean Rd.
Fox Point, WI 53217
Ph: (414)352-5140
Fax: (414)351-2969
E-mail: cslive1013@aol.com
URL: http://www.uwm.edu/Org/IRRA
Contact: Marcia Pulich, Pres.
State.

18006 ■ National Association of Miniature Enthusiasts - Wisconsin Wee World Society
c/o Louise Potter
7220 N Barnett Ln.
Fox Point, WI 53217
Ph: (414)352-9209
URL: http://www.miniatures.org/states/WI.html
Contact: Louise Potter, Contact
State. Affiliated With: National Association of Miniature Enthusiasts.

Franklin

18007 ■ American Cancer Society, Franklin
9809 S Franklin Dr., Ste.102
Franklin, WI 53132
Ph: (414)423-8570
Fax: (414)423-8538
URL: http://www.cancer.org
Local. Affiliated With: American Cancer Society.

18008 ■ American Legion, Willey-Herda Post 192
PO Box 320152
Franklin, WI 53132
Ph: (608)745-1090
Fax: (608)745-0179
URL: National Affiliate–www.legion.org
Local. Affiliated With: American Legion.

18009 ■ American Welding Society, Milwaukee Section
c/o John Kozeniecki, Chm.
Image Indus. Inc.
4105 W Southwood Dr.
Franklin, WI 53132
Ph: (414)423-9129
Fax: (414)423-9168
Free: (888)475-7883
E-mail: john.kozeniecki@stork.com
URL: National Affiliate–www.aws.org
Contact: John Kozeniecki, Chm.
Local. Professional engineering society in the field of welding. **Affiliated With:** American Welding Society.

18010 ■ Friends of the Franklin Public Library
9229 W Loomis Rd.
Franklin, WI 53132
Ph: (414)425-8214
Fax: (414)425-9498
E-mail: broark@franklinwi.gov
URL: http://www.terrenceberres.com/fplf.html
Contact: Carole Donovan, Pres.
Founded: 1980. **Members:** 52. **Membership Dues:** regular, $5 (annual). **Budget:** $1,500. **State Groups:** 1. **Local.** Works to increase public awareness of library services. Sponsors activities, raises funds, purchases library materials. **Libraries: Type:** open to the public. **Holdings:** 50,000; audio recordings, books, periodicals, video recordings. **Publications:** *Friends Newsletter*, bimonthly. Contains library happenings, book lovers' reviews. **Price:** free. **Circulation:** 200. **Conventions/Meetings:** annual meeting, with election of officers - May. Franklin, WI • monthly meeting - 4th Thursday of every month except December.

18011 ■ Hugs for Homeless Animals (H4HA)
c/o Rae French, Pres.
PO Box 320245
Franklin, WI 53132-0245
Ph: (262)514-2085
Free: (888)483-8180
E-mail: info@h4ha.org
URL: http://www.h4ha.org
Local.

18012 ■ United Transportation Union, AFL-CIO - Local Union 322
6610 S 122nd St.
Franklin, WI 53132
E-mail: railjag@aol.com
URL: http://www.geocities.com/gcira
Contact: Robert Alba, Chair
Members: 80. **Local. Affiliated With:** United Transportation Union.

18013 ■ Wehr Astronomical Society
Wehr Nature Center
9701 W Coll. Ave.
Franklin, WI 53132
Ph: (262)675-0941
E-mail: grdupree@netwurx.net
URL: http://www.wehrastro.org
Contact: Charlotte Du Pree, Contact
Local. Promotes the science of astronomy. Works to encourage and coordinate activities of amateur astronomical societies. Fosters observational and computational work and craftsmanship in various fields of astronomy. **Affiliated With:** Astronomical League.

18014 ■ Wisconsin Metro Audubon Society (WMAS)
c/o Diane Lembck, Pres.
6492 S 121
Franklin, WI 53132
Ph: (414)425-9616
E-mail: dluvs2hike@core.com
URL: http://www.audubon.org/chapter/wi/index.html
Contact: Lavone Reis, Pres.
State. Formerly: (2005) National Audubon Society - Wisconsin Metro.

Franksville

18015 ■ American Legion, Wisconsin Post 494
c/o Harvey K. Funk
4277 Hwy. 41
Franksville, WI 53126
Ph: (608)745-1090
Fax: (608)745-0179
URL: National Affiliate–www.legion.org
Contact: Harvey K. Funk, Contact
Local. Affiliated With: American Legion.

18016 ■ American Rabbit Breeders Association, Southern Lakes Rabbit Club
c/o Lisa Woelbing, Sec.
2689 Waukesha Rd.
Franksville, WI 53126
URL: http://www.geocities.com/wisconsin_state_rba/Local_Clubs.html
Contact: Lisa Woelbing, Sec.
Local. Affiliated With: American Rabbit Breeders Association.

18017 ■ Wisconsin Dietary Managers Association
c/o Dianna Bartlet, CDM, Pres.
10218 Dunkelow Rd.
Franksville, WI 53126
Ph: (414)607-4100
E-mail: dianna.bartlet@vmp.org
URL: http://www.dmaonline.org/WI
Contact: Dianna Bartlet CDM, Pres.
State. Represents dietary managers. Maintains a high level of competency and quality in dietary departments through continuing education. Provides optimum nutritional care through foodservice management. **Affiliated With:** Dietary Managers Association.

Frederic

18018 ■ American Legion, Wisconsin Post 249
c/o Paul G. Johnson
PO Box 184
Frederic, WI 54837
Ph: (608)745-1090
Fax: (608)745-0179
URL: National Affiliate–www.legion.org
Contact: Paul G. Johnson, Contact
Local. Affiliated With: American Legion.

18019 ■ Frederic Area Community Association
PO Box 250
Frederic, WI 54837-0250
Ph: (715)327-4836
Contact: Rebecca Harlander, Sec.-Treas.
Local.

Fredonia

18020 ■ American Legion, Hamm-Miller Post 145
c/o Gary R. Dotzauer
11988 County Rd. A
Fredonia, WI 53021
Ph: (608)745-1090
Fax: (608)745-0179
URL: National Affiliate–www.legion.org
Contact: Gary R. Dotzauer, Contact
Local. Affiliated With: American Legion.

18021 ■ American Legion, Wisconsin Post 410
c/o Robert Weyker
123 Wisconsin St.
Fredonia, WI 53021
Ph: (608)745-1090
Fax: (608)745-0179
URL: National Affiliate–www.legion.org
Contact: Robert Weyker, Contact
Local. Affiliated With: American Legion.

18022 ■ Fox Valley Retriever Club
c/o James Coggins, Sec.
4838 Blueberry Rd.
Fredonia, WI 53021
E-mail: coggins@uwn.edu
URL: http://www.foxvalleyrc.com
Contact: James Coggins, Sec.
Local. Affiliated With: American Kennel Club.

Fremont

18023 ■ American Legion, Wolf River Post 391
322 Waupaca St.
Fremont, WI 54940
Ph: (608)745-1090
Fax: (608)745-0179
URL: National Affiliate–www.legion.org
Local. Affiliated With: American Legion.

18024 ■ Fremont Area Chamber of Commerce
PO Box 114
Fremont, WI 54940
Ph: (920)446-3838
E-mail: uberfrau9@centurytel.net
URL: http://www.fremontwis.com
Contact: Debby Gramer, Pres.
Local. Promotes business and community development in Fremont, WI area.

Friesland

18025 ■ Friesland Chamber of Commerce
PO Box 127
Friesland, WI 53935-0127
Ph: (920)348-5267
Contact: Don DeYoung, Pres.
Local.

Galesville

18026 ■ Galesville Area Chamber of Commerce
PO Box 196
Galesville, WI 54630
Ph: (608)582-2868
Contact: Einar Daffinson, Pres.
Local.

18027 ■ PFLAG Galesville/Western Wisconsin
17150 N 4th St.
Galesville, WI 54630
Ph: (608)582-2114
E-mail: marinuka@aol.com
URL: http://www.pflag.org/Wisconsin.246.0.html
Local. Affiliated With: Parents, Families, and Friends of Lesbians and Gays.

18028 ■ Veteran Motor Car Club of America - Coulee Chapter
c/o Ken Gunderson, Pres.
W 17999 Silver Creek Rd.
Galesville, WI 54630
Ph: (608)582-4332
E-mail: klgunderson@aol.com
URL: National Affiliate–www.vmcca.org
Contact: Ken Gunderson, Pres.
Local. Affiliated With: Veteran Motor Car Club of America.

18029 ■ Veteran Motor Car Club of America - Upper Mississippi Region
c/o Ken Gunderson, Dir.
W 17999 Silver Creek Rd.
Galesville, WI 54630
Ph: (608)582-4332
E-mail: klgunderson@aol.com
URL: National Affiliate–www.vmcca.org
Contact: Ken Gunderson, Dir.
State. Affiliated With: Veteran Motor Car Club of America.

Gays Mills

18030 ■ American Legion, Mc-Cormick-Rose Post 308
217 Orin St.
Gays Mills, WI 54631
Ph: (608)745-1090
Fax: (608)745-0179
URL: National Affiliate–www.legion.org
Local. Affiliated With: American Legion.

18031 ■ Gays Mills Lions Club
c/o Gary Bell, Pres.
628 Mulberry St.
Gays Mills, WI 54631
Ph: (608)735-4958
URL: http://www.md27d2.org
Contact: Gary Bell, Pres.
Local. Affiliated With: Lions Clubs International.

18032 ■ Soldiers Grove Lions Club
c/o Bill McCormick, Pres.
43323 State Hwy. 171
Gays Mills, WI 54631
Ph: (608)624-5716
URL: http://www.md27d2.org
Contact: Bill McCormick, Pres.
Local. Affiliated With: Lions Clubs International.

Genoa

18033 ■ American Legion, Genoa-De-Soto Post 246
PO Box 147
Genoa, WI 54632
Ph: (608)745-1090
Fax: (608)745-0179
URL: National Affiliate–www.legion.org
Local. Affiliated With: American Legion.

Genoa City

18034 ■ American Legion, Sponholtz-Deignan Post 183
PO Box 553
Genoa City, WI 53128
Ph: (608)745-1090
Fax: (608)745-0179
URL: National Affiliate–www.legion.org
Local. Affiliated With: American Legion.

18035 ■ Genoa City Lions Club
N1798 N Daisy Dr.
Genoa City, WI 53128
Ph: (262)279-3000 (815)678-7820
E-mail: rookie177@charter.net
URL: http://genoacitywi.lionwap.org
Contact: Eric Torstenson, Pres.
Local. Affiliated With: Lions Clubs International.

Germantown

18036 ■ ACF Chefs of Milwaukee
PO Box 0894
Germantown, WI 53022
E-mail: micmp2@hotmail.com
URL: http://www.acfchefsofmilwaukee.com
Contact: Mic Pietrykowski, Pres.
Local. Promotes the culinary profession and provides on-going educational training and networking for members. Provides opportunities for competition, professional recognition, and access to educational forums with other culinarians at local, regional, national, and international events.

18037 ■ American Legion, Germantown, Post 1
PO Box 321
Germantown, WI 53022
Ph: (262)251-5470
URL: National Affiliate–www.legion.org
Contact: Gilbert A. Lucka, Cmdr.
Founded: 1919. **Members:** 400. **Membership Dues:** $25 (annual). **State Groups:** 50. **Local.** Individuals who have served in U.S. Armed Forces during wartime. **Affiliated With:** American Legion. **Publications:** *No. 1 News and Views*, bimonthly. Newsletter. **Conventions/Meetings:** annual convention • monthly meeting.

18038 ■ Association for Corporate Growth, Wisconsin Chapter
c/o Jim Kettinger, Pres.
W175 N11117 Stonewood Dr., Ste.204
Germantown, WI 53022
Ph: (262)532-2440
Fax: (262)532-2430
E-mail: acgwisconsin@acg.org
URL: http://www.acg.org/wisconsin
Contact: Jim Kettinger, Pres.
State. Affiliated With: Association for Corporate Growth.

18039 ■ Germantown Area Chamber of Commerce (GACC)
PO Box 12
Germantown, WI 53022
Ph: (262)255-1812
Fax: (262)255-9033
E-mail: lgrgich@germantownchamber.org
URL: http://germantownchamber.org
Contact: Lynn Grgich, Admin.Asst.
Founded: 1982. **Members:** 230. **Staff:** 2. **Budget:** $100,000. **Local.** Promotes business and community development in the Germantown, WI area. Sponsors seminars, parades, social events, and annual dinner. **Publications:** Booklets • Newsletter, bimonthly.

18040 ■ Germantown Junior Women's Club
PO Box 62
Germantown, WI 53022
Ph: (262)255-9425
E-mail: germantownjwc@sbcglobal.net
URL: http://www.gjwc.com
Contact: Jean Morin, Contact
Local.

18041 ■ Milwaukee Area Compensation Association (MACA)
W175 N11117 Stonewood Dr., Ste.204
Germantown, WI 53022
Ph: (262)532-2440
Fax: (262)532-2430
E-mail: maca@teamwi.com
URL: http://www.macaonline.org
Contact: Jill Franke CCP, Pres.
Local. Affiliated With: WorldatWork.

18042 ■ National Active and Retired Federal Employees Association Oconomowoc-Watertown 1112
W180 9817 Rivers Bend Cir. W
Germantown, WI 53022
Ph: (262)251-1463
URL: National Affiliate–www.narfe.org
Contact: George L. Oncken, Contact
Local. Protects the retirement future of employees through education. Informs members on issues affecting the retirement. **Affiliated With:** National Association of Retired Federal Employees.

18043 ■ Project Management Institute - Milwaukee/SE WI Chapter (PMI)
W175 N11117 Stonewood Dr., Ste.204
Germantown, WI 53022
E-mail: president@pmi-milwaukee.org
URL: http://www.pmi-milwaukee.org
Contact: David Becher PMP, Pres.
Local. Administers the Project Management Professional certification program. Provides local membership services through a network of chapters and puts on international and regional seminars. **Affiliated With:** Project Management Institute.

18044 ■ WACHA - The Premier Payments Resource
W177 N9886 River Crest Dr., Ste.112
Germantown, WI 53022
Ph: (262)345-1245
Fax: (262)345-1246
Free: (800)453-1843
E-mail: info@wacha.org
URL: http://www.wacha.org
Contact: Ms. Mary M. Gilmeister AAP, Pres.
State. Promotes the development of electronic solutions to improve payments systems. **Affiliated With:** NACHA: The Electronic Payments Association.

18045 ■ Wisconsin Mathematics Council
W175 N11117 Stonewood Dr., Ste.204
Germantown, WI 53022
Ph: (262)437-0174
Fax: (262)532-2430
E-mail: wmc@wismath.org
URL: http://www.wismath.org
Contact: Sue Hanson-Otis, Pres.
State. Aims to improve the teaching and learning of mathematics. Provides vision, leadership and professional development to support teachers in ensuring mathematics learning of the highest quality for all students. **Affiliated With:** National Council of Teachers of Mathematics.

18046 ■ Wisconsin Retail Lumber Association (WRLA)
c/o David L. Rosenmeier, Exec.VP
W175 N11086 Stonewood Dr.
Germantown, WI 53022
Ph: (262)250-1835
Fax: (262)250-1842
Free: (800)236-3534
E-mail: wrla@wrlamsi.com
URL: http://www.wrlamsi.com
Contact: David L. Rosenmeier, Exec.VP
State. Affiliated With: National Lumber and Building Material Dealers Association.

Gillett

18047 ■ American Legion, Krause-Simpson Post 300
105 W Main St.
Gillett, WI 54124
Ph: (608)745-1090
Fax: (608)745-0179
URL: National Affiliate–www.legion.org
Local. Affiliated With: American Legion.

18048 ■ Revitalize Gillett
PO Box 304
Gillett, WI 54124-0304
Ph: (920)855-1414
Fax: (920)855-1451
URL: http://www.revitalizegillett.org
Contact: Diane Nichols, Program Mgr.
Founded: 2002. **Staff:** 1. **Budget:** $68,000. **Local.** A nonprofit organization that revitalizes the downtown area of Gillett through economic development and historic preservation.

18049 ■ Trout Unlimited - Oconto River Watershed 385
c/o Jerry and Tess Paluch
13019 Little Creek Ln.
Gillett, WI 54124-9152
Ph: (920)855-1706
E-mail: jerrytess@ez-net.com
URL: National Affiliate–www.tu.org
Contact: Jerry Paluch, Pres.
Local. Formerly: (2005) Trout Unlimited - Oconto River Chapter.

Gilman

18050 ■ American Legion, Western Taylor County Post 359
W14635 Trucker Ln.
Gilman, WI 54433
Ph: (608)745-1090
Fax: (608)745-0179
URL: National Affiliate–www.legion.org
Local. Affiliated With: American Legion.

Gilmanton

18051 ■ American Legion, Forrest-Gunderson-Klevgard Post 264
PO Box 6
Gilmanton, WI 54743
Ph: (608)745-1090
Fax: (608)745-0179
URL: National Affiliate–www.legion.org
Local. Affiliated With: American Legion.

Glendale

18052 ■ Glendale Association of Commerce
5909 N Milwaukee River Pkwy.
Glendale, WI 53209-3815
Ph: (414)228-1716
Fax: (414)332-6182
Contact: Bob Porsche, Pres.
Local. Aims to foster tourism, as well as to protect and advance the commercial, industrial, cultural, educational, and civic interests of the City of Glendale.

18053 ■ IABC Southeastern Wisconsin
c/o Rebecca Dahlman, Pres.
5757 N Green Bay Ave.
Glendale, WI 53209
Ph: (414)524-2945
Fax: (414)524-3200
E-mail: rebecca.a.dahlman@jci.com
URL: http://www.iabc-sewis.com
Contact: Rebecca Dahlman, Pres.
Local. Public relations and communication professionals. Committed to improve the effectiveness of organizations through strategic, interactive and integrated business communication management. Provides products, services, and networking activities to help people and organizations excel in public relations, employee communication, marketing communication, public affairs and other forms of communication.

18054 ■ International Association of Business Communicators, Southeastern Wisconsin Chapter
c/o Rebecca Dahlman
Johnson Controls, Inc.
5757 N Green Bay Ave.
Glendale, WI 53209
Ph: (414)524-2945
Fax: (414)524-3200
E-mail: rebecca.a.dahlman@jci.com
Contact: Rebecca Dahlman, Pres.
Local. Represents the interests of communication managers, public relations directors, writers, editors and audiovisual specialists. Encourages establishment of college-level programs in organizational communication. Conducts surveys on employee communication effectiveness and media trends. Conducts research in the field of communication. **Affiliated With:** International Association of Business Communicators.

18055 ■ Old English Sheepdog Club of America (OESCA)
c/o Barbara Mooers, Corresponding Sec.
5554 N Navajo Ave.
Glendale, WI 53217
Ph: (414)963-1828
E-mail: bmooers@wi.rr.com
URL: http://www.oldenglishsheepdogclubofamerica.org
Contact: Marilyn O'Cuilinn, Pres.
Regional.

Glenwood City

18056 ■ American Legion, Curry-Ainsworth Post 168
PO Box 134
Glenwood City, WI 54013
Ph: (608)745-1090
Fax: (608)745-0179
URL: National Affiliate–www.legion.org
Local. Affiliated With: American Legion.

Glidden

18057 ■ American Legion, Prosser-Curtis-Kubley Post 247
RR 1, Box 376
Glidden, WI 54527
Ph: (715)264-3363
Fax: (608)745-0179
URL: National Affiliate–www.legion.org
Local. Affiliated With: American Legion.

Goodman

18058 ■ American Legion, Martell-Musiaw Post 325
W 14350 Hwy. 8
Goodman, WI 54125
Ph: (715)336-2268
Fax: (608)745-0179
URL: National Affiliate–www.legion.org
Local. Affiliated With: American Legion.

Gordon

18059 ■ American Legion, Lockman-Jensen Post 499
PO Box 206
Gordon, WI 54838
Ph: (608)745-1090
Fax: (608)745-0179
URL: National Affiliate–www.legion.org
Local. Affiliated With: American Legion.

18060 ■ Eau Claire Lakes Business Association of Barnes and Gordon
13702 S Crystal Beach Rd.
Gordon, WI 54838
Ph: (715)376-2322
Free: (800)299-7506
E-mail: vacation@eauclairelakes.com
URL: http://www.eauclairelakes.com
Contact: Andrea Babcock, Sec.
Local. Works to provide recreation and vacation place for families.

Grafton

18061 ■ American Legion, Rose-Harms Post 355
1540 13th Ave.
Grafton, WI 53024
Ph: (608)745-1090
Fax: (608)745-0179
URL: National Affiliate–www.legion.org
Local. Affiliated With: American Legion.

18062 ■ Big Brothers and Sisters of Ozaukee County (BBBS Ozaukee)
885 Badger Cir.
Grafton, WI 53024
Ph: (262)377-0784
Fax: (262)377-7370
E-mail: bbbsoz@sbcglobal.net
URL: http://bigs-ozaukee.org
Contact: Denise M. Shaffer, Exec.Dir.
Founded: 1974. **Members:** 90. **Staff:** 5. **Budget:** $170,000. **Local**. Provides a child from single parent home with an adult friend who can offer regular guidance, understanding, and acceptance. Makes available training and resources for volunteers and parents; sponsors educational and recreational programs and special events; conducts fundraising activities. **Affiliated With:** Big Brothers Big Sisters of America. **Publications:** *Big Connection*, bimonthly. Newsletter. **Advertising:** accepted. **Conventions/Meetings:** annual meeting - usually in March.

18063 ■ Grafton Area Chamber of Commerce (GACC)
1634 Wisconsin Ave.
PO Box 132
Grafton, WI 53024
Ph: (262)377-1650
Fax: (262)375-7087
E-mail: info@grafton-wi.org
URL: http://grafton-wi.org
Contact: Nancy Hundt, Exec.Dir.
Founded: 1975. **Members:** 170. **Staff:** 1. **Local**. Promotes commercial, financial, industrial, and civic development in the Grafton, WI area. Sponsors annual Christmas Party, Holiday Tree Lighting, Farmer's Market, and Grafton Grand Prix. **Publications:** *Business Directory*, annual • Newsletter, bimonthly • Brochures, bimonthly. **Conventions/Meetings:** monthly meeting.

18064 ■ Grafton Lions Club - Wisconsin
PO Box 0211
Grafton, WI 53024
Ph: (262)377-0943
E-mail: davenan75@wi.rr.com
URL: http://www.graftonlions.org
Contact: Dave Antoine, Membership Chm.
Local. Affiliated With: Lions Clubs International.

18065 ■ Ozaukee Humane Society (OHS)
2073 Hwy. W
Grafton, WI 53024
Ph: (262)377-7580
Fax: (262)377-4811
E-mail: info@ozaukeehumane.org
URL: http://www.ozaukeehumane.org
Contact: Victoria Wellens, Exec.Dir.
Founded: 1977. **Local.**

18066 ■ Ozaukee Realtors Association
1525 Wisconsin Ave.
Grafton, WI 53024
Ph: (262)375-4730
Fax: (262)375-1019
E-mail: maryz@ozaukeerealtorsassociation.com
URL: http://ora53024.tripod.com
Contact: Mary J. Zielski, Exec. Officer
Local. Strives to develop real estate business practices. Advocates the right to own, use and transfer real property. Provides a facility for professional development, research and exchange of information among members and to the general public. **Affiliated With:** National Association of Realtors.

18067 ■ Pheasants Forever Ozaukee County
PO Box 201
Grafton, WI 53024
Ph: (262)284-7268
URL: http://www.ozpf.com
Contact: Jeff Stolen, Pres.
Local. Affiliated With: Pheasants Forever.

Grand Marsh

18068 ■ American Legion, Snider-Richardson Post 273
PO Box 22
Grand Marsh, WI 53936
Ph: (608)745-1090
Fax: (608)745-0179
URL: National Affiliate–www.legion.org
Local. Affiliated With: American Legion.

18069 ■ Wisconsin Trappers Association (WTA)
3048 10th Ct.
Grand Marsh, WI 53936-9636
Ph: (608)584-4681
E-mail: wtatreas@maqs.net
URL: http://www.wistrap.org
Contact: Gwen Campbell, Treas.
Founded: 1963. **Members:** 3,000. **Membership Dues:** regular or family (with T&P Caller subscription), $25 (annual) • regular or family (without T&P Caller subscription), $11 (annual) • individual life (under the age of 62 with T&P Caller subscription for life), $300 • life (over the age of 62 with the T&P Caller subscription for life), $100 • junior (ages 17 & under with T&P Caller subscription), $12 (annual) • new life (add spouse to existing), $100. **Staff:** 2. **Regional Groups:** 11. **State Groups:** 1. **State. Telecommunication Services:** electronic mail, virjo4t@msn.com. **Affiliated With:** National Trappers Association.

Grantsburg

18070 ■ American Legion, Brask-Fossum-Janke Post 185
PO Box 215
Grantsburg, WI 54840
Ph: (608)745-1090
Fax: (608)745-0179
URL: National Affiliate–www.legion.org
Local. Affiliated With: American Legion.

18071 ■ Grantsburg Chamber of Commerce
PO Box 451
Grantsburg, WI 54840
Ph: (715)463-2405
URL: http://www.grantsburgwi.com
Contact: Ted Gerber, Pres.
Local.

Gratiot

18072 ■ American Legion, Wisconsin Post 177
c/o Gille Mc Glynn
PO Box 321
Gratiot, WI 53541
Ph: (608)745-1090
Fax: (608)745-0179
URL: National Affiliate–www.legion.org
Contact: Gille Mc Glynn, Contact
Local. Affiliated With: American Legion.

Green Bay

18073 ■ Alliance of Guardian Angels, Green Bay
1607 Mason St.
Green Bay, WI 54302
Ph: (920)265-1284
E-mail: greenbay@guardianangels.org
URL: National Affiliate–www.guardianangels.org
Contact: Jason Costa, Contact
Local. Affiliated With: Alliance of Guardian Angels.

18074 ■ Alzheimer's Association of Greater Wisconsin
2900 Curry Ln., Ste.A
Green Bay, WI 54311
Ph: (920)469-2110
Fax: (920)469-2131
Free: (800)272-3900
E-mail: mary.bouche@alz.org
URL: http://www.alzgw.org
Contact: Mary B. Bouche, Exec.Dir.
Founded: 1985. **Membership Dues:** family, $25 (annual) • professional, $50 (annual) • organization, $100 (annual). **Staff:** 16. **Budget:** $1,200,000. **Regional Groups:** 7. **State Groups:** 3. **For-Profit. State.** Family members of sufferers of Alzheimer's disease. Combats Alzheimer's disease and related disorders. (Alzheimer's disease is a progressive, degenerative brain disease in which changes occur in the central nervous system and outer region of the brain causing memory loss and other changes in thought, personality, and behavior.) Promotes research to find the cause, treatment, and cure for the disease. **Libraries: Type:** open to the public. **Holdings:** 350; audio recordings, books, video recordings. **Computer Services:** Information services. **Affiliated With:** Alzheimer's Association.

18075 ■ American Legion, Suburban Green Bay Post 518
3611 Glen Kent Ct.
Green Bay, WI 54313
Ph: (608)745-1090
Fax: (608)745-0179
URL: National Affiliate–www.legion.org
Local. Affiliated With: American Legion.

18076 ■ American Legion, Sullivan-Wallen Post 11
PO Box 1262
Green Bay, WI 54305
Ph: (608)745-1090
Fax: (608)745-0179
URL: National Affiliate–www.legion.org
Local. Affiliated With: American Legion.

18077 ■ American Legion, Wisconsin Post 539
c/o Delores E. Mueller, Adj.
725 Marshall Ave.
Green Bay, WI 54303
Ph: (608)745-1090
Fax: (608)745-0179
URL: National Affiliate–www.legion.org
Contact: Delores E. Mueller, Adj.
Local. Affiliated With: American Legion.

18078 ■ American Meteorological Society, Packerland Chapter
c/o Peg Zenko, Treas.
240 Lau St.
Green Bay, WI 54302
E-mail: amschapter@yahoo.com
URL: http://www.ametsoc.org/chapters/packerland
Contact: Dr. Steve Meyer, Pres.
Local. Affiliated With: American Meteorological Society.

18079 ■ American Public Works Association, Wisconsin Chapter
c/o Jennifer Barlas, Membership Chair
2737 S Ridge Rd.
Green Bay, WI 54304
Ph: (920)497-2500
Fax: (920)497-8516
E-mail: jbarlas@foth.com
URL: http://wisconsin.apwa.net
Contact: Jennifer Barlas, Membership Chair
State. Promotes professional excellence and public awareness through education, advocacy and the exchange of knowledge. **Affiliated With:** American Public Works Association.

18080 ■ American Red Cross, Lakeland Chapter
PO Box 8295
Green Bay, WI 54308-8295
Ph: (920)468-8535
Fax: (920)468-1290
E-mail: arcgbw@arclakeland.org
URL: http://www.arclakeland.org
Local.

18081 ■ American Society of Safety Engineers, Nicolet Chapter
PO Box 13422
Green Bay, WI 54307-3422
Ph: (920)405-9162
E-mail: johnc@mmmins.com
URL: http://nicolet.asse.org
Contact: John A. Corpus, Pres.
Local. Enhances the advancement of the safety profession and the safety professional. Promotes the technical, societal and economic well-being of safety practitioners. **Affiliated With:** American Society of Safety Engineers.

18082 ■ Arthritis Foundation, Northeastern District Office
2921 S Webster Ave., Ste.A
Green Bay, WI 54301-1500
Ph: (920)330-0592
Fax: (920)330-0596
E-mail: info.wi.nedo@arthritis.org
URL: http://www.arthritis.org
Contact: Ms. Laura Libert, Dir.
Regional. Seeks to: discover the cause and improve the methods for the treatment and prevention of arthritis and other rheumatic diseases; increase the number of scientists investigating rheumatic diseases; provide training in rheumatic diseases for more doctors; extend knowledge of arthritis and other rheumatic diseases to the lay public, emphasizing the socioeconomic as well as medical aspects of these diseases. **Affiliated With:** Arthritis Foundation.

18083 ■ Bay-Lake Regional Planning Commission
Old Ft. Sq.
211 N Broadway, Ste.211
Green Bay, WI 54303-2757
Ph: (920)448-2820
Fax: (920)448-2823
E-mail: mwalter@baylakerpc.org
URL: http://www.baylakerpc.org
Contact: Mr. Mark A. Walter, Exec.Dir.
Founded: 1972. **Staff:** 11. **Budget:** $900,000. **Local.** Seeks to provide planning service on area-wide issues, grant writing assistance, economic development, and sewer service area planning, represent local interests on state and federal planning program activities, and provide local planning assistance to communities and counties within the region of Brown, Door, Florence, Kewaunee, Manitowoc, Marinette, Oconto, and Sheboygan in Northeast Wisconsin. **Libraries: Type:** open to the public. **Subjects:** community plans, government reports. **Publications:** *Comprehensive Economic Development Strategy*, annual. Annual Report • Newsletter, quarterly. **Conventions/Meetings:** monthly meeting - always second Friday.

18084 ■ Bay Port High School - Young Life
PO Box 11014
Green Bay, WI 54307-1014
Ph: (920)434-5854 (920)217-5708
E-mail: nathanashmead@hotmail.com
URL: http://sites.younglife.org/sites/bayport/default.aspx
Contact: Nate Ashmead, Contact
Local. Affiliated With: Young Life.

18085 ■ Beja Shriners
c/o Charles Zanzig
PO Box 13537
Green Bay, WI 54307-3537
Ph: (920)498-1985
Fax: (920)498-0290
E-mail: beja@gbonline.com
URL: National Affiliate–www.shrinershq.org
Contact: Charles Zanzig, Contact
Local. Affiliated With: Imperial Council of the Ancient Arabic Order of the Nobles of the Mystic Shrine for North America.

18086 ■ Big Brothers Big Sisters of America of Northeastern Wisconsin
1345 W Mason St.
Green Bay, WI 54303-2049
Ph: (920)498-2227
Fax: (920)498-2249
E-mail: info@bbbsnew.org
URL: http://www.bbbsnew.org
Contact: Mr. Jan V. Malchow, Exec.Dir.
Local. Matches children, primarily from single-parent families, with qualified caring adult volunteers on a one adult or one couple to one child basis. **Affiliated With:** Big Brothers Big Sisters of America.

18087 ■ Brown County 4-H and Youth Program
1150 Bellevue St.
Green Bay, WI 54302
Ph: (920)391-4610
Fax: (920)391-4617
E-mail: karla.voss@ces.uwex.edu
URL: http://www.browncountyextension.org
Contact: Karla Voss, Advisor
Founded: 1918. **Members:** 700. **Staff:** 3. **Local Groups:** 25. **Local.** Positive youth development program for youth ages 5 to 19 years old. Educational programming focuses on building life skills, leadership and civic involvement. **Affiliated With:** National 4-H Council. **Publications:** *4-H Newsletter*, monthly. **Conventions/Meetings:** monthly Leaders Association Meeting - always first Tuesday • quarterly Youth Advisory Council Meeting.

18088 ■ Brown County Association for Retarded Citizens (BCARC)
c/o Nancy Fennema
PO Box 12770
1673 Dousman St.
Green Bay, WI 54307

Ph: (920)498-2599
Fax: (920)498-2652
Contact: Nancy Fennema, Exec.Dir.
Founded: 1957. **Members:** 475. **Staff:** 100. **Budget:** $5,000,000. **Local**. Parents, professionals, and other interested individuals organized to promote services, research, public understanding, and legislation for individuals with mental retardation and their families. Conducts charitable activities. **Publications:** *Echoes*, monthly. Newsletter. **Price:** for members.

18089 ■ Brown County Civic Music Association (BCCMA)
c/o Rita Kilmer, Exec.Sec.
511 St. Mary's Blvd.
Green Bay, WI 54301
Ph: (920)469-7999 (920)338-1808
Fax: (920)338-1802
E-mail: civicmusic@athenet.net
URL: http://www.foxcitiesbusiness.com/bccivicmusic
Contact: Rita Kilmer, Exec.Sec.
Founded: 1926. **Members:** 1,500. **Membership Dues:** adult, $75 (annual) • student, $25 (annual). **Staff:** 1. **Budget:** $86,000. **State Groups:** 1. **Local Groups:** 1. **Local**. Educational and cultural organization for classical music and dance enthusiasts. Sponsors performing arts events. **Telecommunication Services:** electronic mail, civicmusic@aol.com. **Publications:** *Civic Music Association News*, annual. Newsletter.

18090 ■ Brown County Historical Society (BCHS)
PO Box 1411
Green Bay, WI 54305-1411
Ph: (920)437-1840
Fax: (920)455-4518
E-mail: bchs@netnet.net
URL: http://www.browncohistoricalsoc.org
Contact: Wendy Barszcz, Exec.Dir.
Founded: 1899. **Members:** 700. **Membership Dues:** individual, $25 (annual) • family, $35 (annual) • supporter, $50 (annual) • centennial, $100 (annual) • provider, $250 (annual) • founder, $500 (annual). **Staff:** 5. **Budget:** $180,000. **Local**. Individuals, businesses and foundations with an interest in local history. Seeks to advance, preserve and disseminate knowledge about the history of Brown County, WI. Operates a historic house museum and publishes a regional history magazine and newsletter. **Libraries: Type:** open to the public. **Holdings:** books, periodicals. **Subjects:** building preservation. **Affiliated With:** Wisconsin Historical Society.

18091 ■ Brown County Sportsmen's Club
1711 W Deerfield Ave.
Green Bay, WI 54313
Ph: (920)434-9930
URL: National Affiliate–www.mynssa.com
Local. Affiliated With: National Skeet Shooting Association.

18092 ■ Catholics United for the Faith - Our Lady of Good Help Chapter
c/o Ed and Carole Hummel
563 Hilltop Dr.
Green Bay, WI 54301
Ph: (920)336-0370
E-mail: eahumm@msn.com
URL: National Affiliate–www.cuf.org
Contact: Ed Hummel, Contact
Local.

18093 ■ Clean Water Action Council of Northeast Wisconsin
1270 Main St., Ste.120
Green Bay, WI 54302
Ph: (920)437-7304
Fax: (920)437-7326
E-mail: cleanwater@cwac.net
URL: http://cwac.net
Contact: Ms. Rebecca Katers, Exec.Dir.
Membership Dues: benefactor, $120 (annual) • sponsor, $60 (annual) • supporting, $36 (annual) • subscriber, $24 (annual) • low income, $15 (annual). **Local**. Works in order to protect public health and the environment. **Affiliated With:** Clean Water Action.

18094 ■ Clinical Laboratory Management Association of Wisconsin
c/o Gary Rogaczewski, Pres.
St. Vincent Hosp.
835 S Van Buren St.
Green Bay, WI 54307
Ph: (920)433-8179
Fax: (920)431-3245
URL: http://www.wiclma.org
Contact: Gary Rogaczewski, Pres.
State. Provides clinical laboratory leaders with resources to balance science and technology with the art of management. Promotes efficient, productive, and high quality operations. Enhances the professional, managerial and leadership skills of members. **Affiliated With:** Clinical Laboratory Management Association.

18095 ■ Diva Adventures
834 Christiana St.
Green Bay, WI 54303-1642
Ph: (920)432-0004
E-mail: coriemtbiker@new.rr.com
URL: http://www.divadventures.com
Local. Affiliated With: International Mountain Bicycling Association.

18096 ■ Employers Workforce Development Network (EWDN)
c/o Wendy Seronko, Exec.Dir.
201 W Walnut
Green Bay, WI 54303-5711
Ph: (920)435-4540
E-mail: wendyse@sbsglobal.net
URL: http://www.ewdn.org
Contact: Wendy Seronko, Exec.Dir.
Local.

18097 ■ Financial Executives International, Northeast Wisconsin Chapter
c/o Ms. Patti L. Ayala, Administrator
WG&R Furniture Co.
900 Challenger Dr.
Green Bay, WI 54311
Ph: (920)406-5019
Fax: (920)406-5003
E-mail: patti.ayala@wgrfurniture.com
URL: http://fei.org/chapter/newisc
Contact: Mr. Donald Noskowiak, Pres.
Founded: 1978. **Members:** 85. **Local**. Promotes personal and professional development of financial executives. Provides peer networking opportunities and advocacy services. **Committees:** Academic Relations; Auditing; Career Services; National Liaison; Professional Development; Programs; Retention; Sponsorship. **Affiliated With:** Financial Executives International. **Publications:** Membership Directory. Alternate Formats: online • Newsletter. Alternate Formats: online.

18098 ■ Fraternal Order of Police, Wisconsin State Lodge
c/o Kathy Martin, Pres.
PO Box 1561
Green Bay, WI 54305-1561
Ph: (608)572-0088
E-mail: statelodge@wifop.org
URL: http://www.wifop.org
Contact: Kathy Martin, Pres.
State. Affiliated With: Fraternal Order of Police, Grand Lodge.

18099 ■ Gardeners of America/Men's Garden Clubs of America - Gardeners Club of Green Bay
c/o Julie Vlasnik, Pres.
2825 Heartland Terr.
Green Bay, WI 54313
Ph: (920)434-9351
E-mail: vlasnik9050@sbcglobal.net
URL: http://gardeners_club.home.att.net
Contact: Julie Vlasnik, Pres.
Membership Dues: individual, $35 (annual). **Local**.

18100 ■ Glacierland Resource Conservation and Development Council
3086 Voyager Dr., Ste.1
Green Bay, WI 54311
Ph: (920)465-3006
Fax: (920)465-3010
E-mail: greg.hines@wi.usda.gov
URL: http://www.glacierlandrcd.org
Contact: Greg Hines, Coor.
Local. Affiliated With: National Association of Resource Conservation and Development Councils.

18101 ■ Greater Green Bay Figure Skating Club (GGBFSC)
PO Box 11204
Green Bay, WI 54307-1204
Ph: (920)336-1874
E-mail: dejardinb@aol.com
URL: http://home.new.rr.com/ggbfsc
Contact: Barbara DeJardin, Contact
Local. Provides programs to encourage participation and achievement in the sport of figure skating on ice. Defines and maintains uniform standards of skating proficiency. Organizes and sponsors competitions and exhibitions for the purpose of stimulating interest in figure skating. **Affiliated With:** United States Figure Skating Association.

18102 ■ Green Bay Area Chamber of Commerce (GBACC)
400 S Washington St.
PO Box 1660
Green Bay, WI 54305-1660
Ph: (920)437-8704
Fax: (920)437-1024
E-mail: info@titletown.org
URL: http://www.titletown.org
Contact: Paul Jadin, Pres.
Founded: 1917. **Members:** 2,000. **Staff:** 33. **Budget:** $2,300,000. **Local**. Promotes business and community development in the Green Bay, WI area. **Committees:** Bay Area Community Health Partnership; Government Affairs; Leadership Green Bay; Marketing Communications; Partners in Education; SBC Group Services. **Councils:** Small Business. **Publications:** *Bay Business Journal*, bimonthly. Features editorials about chamber members, a tech watch, art spotlight and viewpoint article. • Membership Directory, annual. Features a complete listing of chamber members. **Circulation:** 5,000. **Conventions/Meetings:** monthly Power Networking Breakfast - every 1st Tuesday in Green Bay, WI.

18103 ■ Green Bay Chapter Chief Petty Officers Association
PO Box 307
Green Bay, WI 54305-0307
Ph: (414)432-7568
E-mail: d9rcmcuscg@gbonline.com
URL: http://www.uscgcpoa.org/1-cpoa/1-cpoa_index.htm
Contact: Raymond Borchert, Pres.
Local. Affiliated With: United States Coast Guard Chief Petty Officers Association.

18104 ■ Green Bay Chess Association
2191 Allouez Ave.
Green Bay, WI 54311
Ph: (920)465-9859
E-mail: dyounkle@yahoo.com
URL: http://www.greenbaychess.org
Contact: Doug Younkle, Pres.
Founded: 2000. **Members:** 15. **Membership Dues:** regular, $5 (annual). **Local Groups:** 1. **Local**. Chess players interested in teaching others, young and old, about the game of chess as a means of improving intellectual abilities, social skills, and quality of life. Conducts classes about chess and club or tournament organization; also starts chess clubs and runs

tournaments. **Libraries: Type:** reference. **Holdings:** 280; books, periodicals. **Subjects:** chess. **Affiliated With:** United States Chess Federation. **Conventions/ Meetings:** annual meeting.

18105 ■ Green Bay Curling Club
781 Potts Ave.
Green Bay, WI 54304
Ph: (920)494-9931
E-mail: president@curlgb.com
URL: http://www.curlgb.com
Contact: Mike Hannon, Pres.
Local. Affiliated With: United States Curling Association.

18106 ■ Green Bay Education Association (GBEA)
2256 Main St.
Green Bay, WI 54311
Ph: (920)468-4232
Fax: (920)468-6766
E-mail: gbea@gbea.org
URL: http://www.gbea.org
Contact: Keith Patt, Exec.Dir.
Founded: 1912. **Members:** 1,600. **Staff:** 4. **Budget:** $594,000. **State Groups:** 1. **Local.** Full-time and part-time certified teachers employed by the Green Bay, WI area public school district. Seeks to protect and advance the interests of teachers. Acts as collective bargaining agent. **Awards:** GBEA Scholarship Trust. **Frequency:** annual. **Type:** scholarship. **Recipient:** one for high school student for college and one for high school student for tech school. **Affiliated With:** National Education Association; Wisconsin Education Association Council. **Publications:** *Calendar Handbook*, annual. **Price:** $3.00. **Advertising:** accepted • *Common Ground, Common Voices* • *Counterpoint* • *Green Bay Education Association Perspective*, weekly. Newsletter. **Conventions/Meetings:** monthly Representative Assembly - meeting - always 4th Monday.

18107 ■ Green Bay Film Society
c/o David Coury, Dir.
1917 Lakeside Pl.
Green Bay, WI 54302-1220
Ph: (920)465-2097
E-mail: gbfilm@uwgb.edu
URL: http://www.uwgb.edu/gbfilm
Contact: David Coury, Dir.
Founded: 2000. **Members:** 150. **Membership Dues:** voluntary, $20 (annual). **Staff:** 4. **Budget:** $5,000. **Local.** Works to bring international and independent film to northeast Wisconsin and provide a forum for discussion.

18108 ■ Institute of Internal Auditors, Fox Valley/Central Wisconsin Chapter
c/o Michael Machesney, Pres.
Wisconsin Public Ser. Corp.
PO Box 19002
Green Bay, WI 54307-9002
Ph: (920)433-1666
E-mail: mmaches@wpsr.com
URL: http://www.theiia.org/chapters/index.cfm/home.page/cid/167
Contact: Michael Machesney, Pres.
Membership Dues: regular, $115 (annual) • educator, $65 (annual) • student, retired, $30 (annual) • life, $2,100 • sustainer (government auditors only), $50 (annual) • organization ($65 per staff member over 5; $50 per staff member over 100), $425-$6,600 (annual). **Regional.** Serves as advocate for the internal audit profession. Provides certification, education, research, and technological guidance for the profession. **Computer Services:** database, membership directory. **Committees:** Academic Relations; Audit; Employment; Newsletter/Directory; Nominating; Program/Meeting; Research; Website. **Affiliated With:** Institute of Internal Auditors.

18109 ■ International Facility Management Association, Northeast Wisconsin Chapter
c/o Randy Steele, Pres.
PO Box 792
Green Bay, WI 54305-0792
Ph: (920)468-2153
Fax: (920)468-2154
E-mail: randy.steele@ki.com
URL: http://www.ifmanewisconsin.org
Contact: Randy Steele, Pres.
Regional. Affiliated With: International Facility Management Association.

18110 ■ International Union of Operating Engineers, Local 310
PO Box 8323
Green Bay, WI 54308
Ph: (920)437-2750
Fax: (920)437-3122
E-mail: office@local310.org
URL: http://local310.org
Contact: Tom Rosenberg, Business Mgr.
Local. Works to bring economic justice to the workplace and to improve the lives of working families. **Telecommunication Services:** electronic mail, tom@local310.org. **Affiliated With:** International Union of Operating Engineers.

18111 ■ Inventors Network of Wisconsin
1749 Chateau Dr.
Green Bay, WI 54304
Ph: (920)429-0331 (920)810-2267
E-mail: inventorgb@sbcglobal.net
URL: National Affiliate–www.uiausa.org
Contact: Tobias Andropolis, Pres.
State. Represents inventors' organizations and providers of services to inventors. Seeks to facilitate the development of innovation conceived by independent inventors. Provides leadership and support services to inventors and inventors' organizations. **Affiliated With:** United Inventors Association of the U.S.A.

18112 ■ Jayco Jafari International Travel Club, Flight 41 Jay Pack
c/o Bruce Borley, Pres.
807 E Allovez Ave.
Green Bay, WI 54301
E-mail: jaypack41@yahoo.com
URL: http://geocities.com/jaypack41
Contact: Bruce Borley, Pres.
Local. Affiliated With: Jayco Travel Club.

18113 ■ Junior Achievement of Brown County
c/o Laura Bilotti, Dir.
2301 Riverside Dr. Ste.B16
Green Bay, WI 54301
Ph: (920)437-2444
Fax: (920)437-2452
E-mail: bcja@itol.com
URL: http://www.jawis.org
Contact: Laura Bilotti, Dir.
Local. Works to educate and inspire young people to value free enterprise, understand business and economics, and be better prepared for the workforce.

18114 ■ MOC of Northeastern Wisconsin
c/o Col. Charles Wood
322 Orchard Ln.
Green Bay, WI 54301-2869
Ph: (920)592-1094
E-mail: dl@cdwoodfin.com
URL: National Affiliate–www.moaa.org
Contact: Col. Charles Wood, Contact
Local. Affiliated With: Military Officers Association of America.

18115 ■ Mothers Against Drunk Driving, Brown/Marinette Counties
PO Box 433
Green Bay, WI 54305
Ph: (920)496-8950
Fax: (920)496-9858
Free: (800)799-6233
URL: National Affiliate–www.madd.org/
Local. Victims of drunk driving crashes; concerned citizens. Encourages citizen participation in working towards reform of the drunk driving problem and the prevention of underage drinking. Acts as the voice of victims of drunk driving crashes by speaking on their behalf to communities, businesses, and educational groups. **Affiliated With:** Mothers Against Drunk Driving.

18116 ■ NAIFA-Northeastern Wisconsin
c/o Aleta Kauffman, Exec.Sec.
713 N Locust St.
Green Bay, WI 54303
Ph: (920)884-0282
Fax: (920)884-0282
E-mail: naifa-new@new.rr.com
URL: http://naifanet.com/northeasternwisconsin
Contact: Aleta Kauffman, Exec.Sec.
Local. Represents the interests of insurance and financial advisors. Advocates for a positive legislative and regulatory environment. Enhances business and professional skills of members. **Affiliated With:** National Association of Insurance and Financial Advisors.

18117 ■ National Alliance for the Mentally Ill - Brown County
c/o Lucy Seidel, Pres.
PO Box 398
Green Bay, WI 54305-0398
Ph: (920)430-7460
URL: http://www.namiwisconsin.org/library/directory
Contact: Lucy Seidel, Pres.
Local. Strives to improve the quality of life of children and adults with severe mental illness through support, education, research and advocacy. **Affiliated With:** National Alliance for the Mentally Ill.

18118 ■ Navy Club of Green Bay - Ship No. 18
816 Div. St.
Green Bay, WI 54303
Ph: (920)437-8639
URL: National Affiliate–www.navyclubusa.org
Contact: Orville Thayer, Commander
Local. Represents individuals who are, or have been, in the active service of the U.S. Navy, Naval Reserve, Marine Corps, Marine Corps Reserve, and Coast Guard. Promotes and encourages further public interest in the U.S. Navy and its history. Upholds the spirit and ideals of the U.S. Navy. Acts as a public forum for members' views on national defense. Assists the Navy Recruiting Command whenever and wherever possible. Conducts charitable activities. **Affiliated With:** Navy Club of the United States of America.

18119 ■ Neville Public Museum Astronomical Society
1081 Raleigh St.
Green Bay, WI 54304
Ph: (920)405-8534
E-mail: ddewitt@tds.net
URL: http://www.npmas.com
Contact: Don DeWitt, Contact
Local. Promotes the science of astronomy. Works to encourage and coordinate activities of amateur astronomical societies. Fosters observational and computational work and craftsmanship in various fields of astronomy. **Affiliated With:** Astronomical League.

18120 ■ Neville Public Museum Geology Club
c/o Randy E. Phillips, Pres.
1139 Crooks St.
Green Bay, WI 54301
E-mail: lillianpkgrl@aol.com
URL: National Affiliate–www.amfed.org
Contact: Sandra A. Phillips, Sec.
Local. Aims to further the study of Earth Sciences and the practice of lapidary arts and mineralogy. **Affiliated With:** American Federation of Mineralogical Societies.

18121 ■ Nicolet Coin Club
c/o D. Long
1018 Bellevue St.
Green Bay, WI 54302

Ph: (920)468-7760
E-mail: dlong1@new.rr.com
URL: National Affiliate–www.money.org
Contact: D. Long, Contact
Local. Affiliated With: American Numismatic Association.

18122 ■ Northeast Wisconsin Chapter of the APA
PO Box 19070
Green Bay, WI 54307
Ph: (920)272-1588
Fax: (920)496-4720
E-mail: sherih@prevea.com
URL: http://www.apanewi.org
Contact: Sherri Hoffman, Pres.
Local. Aims to increase the Payroll Professional's skill level through education and mutual support. Represents the Payroll Professional before legislative bodies. Administers the certified payroll professional program of recognition. Provides public service education on payroll and employment issues. **Affiliated With:** American Payroll Association.

18123 ■ Northeast Wisconsin Technical College (NWTC)
c/o H. Jeffrey Rafn, PhD, Pres.
PO Box 19042
Green Bay, WI 54307-9042
Ph: (920)498-5400
Fax: (920)498-6883
Free: (800)422-NWTC
E-mail: jrafn@nwtc.edu
URL: http://www.nwtc.edu
Contact: H. Jeffrey Rafn PhD, Pres.
Local. Supports technical educators and technical education at all levels throughout northeast WI. Raises funds for scholarships. Sponsors professional development activities for members and works to make the voice of technical education loud and clear in WI government. **Formerly:** (2001) Northeast Wisconsin Vocational Association; (2005) Northeast Wisconsin Association for Career and Technical Education.

18124 ■ Northeastern Wisconsin Area Local American Postal Workers Union
PO Box 10324
Green Bay, WI 54307-0324
URL: http://newal.org
Local. AFL-CIO. **Affiliated With:** American Postal Workers Union.

18125 ■ Northeastern Wisconsin Beagle Club
c/o Brian Gau
2612 Libal St.
Green Bay, WI 54301-2866
URL: National Affiliate–clubs.akc.org
Contact: Brian Gau, Contact
Local.

18126 ■ Packer Country Sports and Ports
c/o Kari Sliva, Pres./CEO
PO Box 10596
1901 S Oneida St.
Green Bay, WI 54307-0596
Ph: (920)494-9507
Fax: (920)494-9229
Free: (888)867-3342
E-mail: visitorinfo@packercountry.com
URL: http://www.packercountry.com
Contact: Kari Sliva, Pres./CEO
Local.

18127 ■ Packerland Kennel Club (PKC)
PO Box 2282
Green Bay, WI 54306
Ph: (920)468-5580
E-mail: packerlandkc@sbcglobal.net
URL: http://packerlandkennelclub.com
Contact: Sue Werner, Pres.
Founded: 1957. **Local. Publications:** *The Paw Print.* Newsletter. Alternate Formats: online.

18128 ■ Psi Chi, National Honor Society in Psychology - University of Wisconsin-Green Bay
c/o Dept. of Psychology
MACH C318, 2420 Nicolet Dr.
Green Bay, WI 54311
Ph: (920)465-5038 (920)465-5679
Fax: (920)465-5044
E-mail: gurungr@uwgb.edu
URL: National Affiliate–www.psichi.org
Local. Affiliated With: Psi Chi, National Honor Society in Psychology.

18129 ■ RSVP of Brown County
c/o Jim Radey, Dir.
984 9th St.
Green Bay, WI 54304-3441
Ph: (920)429-9445
Fax: (920)429-9449
E-mail: jradey@new.rr.com
URL: http://www.seniorcorps.gov/about/programs/rsvp_state.asp?usestateabbr=wi&Search4.x=0&Search4.y=0
Contact: Jim Radey, Dir.
Local. Affiliated With: Retired and Senior Volunteer Program.

18130 ■ Ruffed Grouse Society, Northeastern Wisconsin Chapter
c/o Joel A. Ehrfurth
2114 Kingfisher Ln.
Green Bay, WI 54313
Ph: (920)434-6444
E-mail: jehrfurth@spancrete.com
URL: National Affiliate–www.ruffedgrousesociety.org
Contact: Joel A. Ehrfurth, Contact
Local. Affiliated With: Ruffed Grouse Society.

18131 ■ SCORE Green Bay
Bus. Assistance Center, Rm. 130
2701 Larsen Rd.
Green Bay, WI 54303
Ph: (920)496-8930
Fax: (920)496-6009
E-mail: deboth@titletown.org
URL: http://www.greenbayscore.org
Contact: Jim McCormick, Chm.
Local. Provides free and confidential business counseling tailored to meet the needs of small business owners and personal objectives. **Telecommunication Services:** electronic mail, cgokey@titletown.org. **Committees:** Marketing; Program; Work Shops. **Affiliated With:** SCORE.

18132 ■ Society for Human Resource Management - Green Bay Area
PO Box 12761
Green Bay, WI 54307
E-mail: info@gbshrm.org
URL: http://www.gbshrm.org
Contact: Cheryl Scholtz-Fischer, Pres.
Local. Represents the interests of human resource and industrial relations professionals and executives. Promotes the advancement of human resource management.

18133 ■ Society of Manufacturing Engineers - ITT Technical Institute S347
470 Security Blvd.
Green Bay, WI 54313
Ph: (920)662-9000
E-mail: ejpederson@aol.com
URL: National Affiliate–www.sme.org
Contact: Erik Pederson, Contact
Local. Advances manufacturing knowledge to gain competitive advantage. Improves skills and manufacturing solutions for the growth of economy. Provides resources and opportunities for manufacturing professionals. **Affiliated With:** American Society of Parasitologists.

18134 ■ Solid Waste Association of North America, Wisconsin Badger Chapter
c/o Stevan Keith
PO Box 19012
Green Bay, WI 54307
Ph: (608)266-4029
Fax: (608)267-1533
E-mail: skeith@milwcnty.com
URL: National Affiliate–www.swana.org
Contact: Steve Keith, Pres.
State. Affiliated With: Solid Waste Association of North America.

18135 ■ Sons of Norway, Gronnvik Lodge 5-632
c/o Myron A. Vedvik, Financial Sec.
1945 Wood Ln.
Green Bay, WI 54304-1915
Ph: (920)497-0878
E-mail: uffda@tds.net
URL: http://gronnvik.tripod.com
Contact: Myron A. Vedvik, Financial Sec.
Local. Affiliated With: Sons of Norway.

18136 ■ Taxpayers Network
721 Cardinal Ln., Ste.105
Green Bay, WI 54313
Ph: (920)434-3100
Fax: (920)662-1517
E-mail: mail@taxpayersnetwork.org
URL: http://www.taxpayersnetwork.org
Contact: Amy McGee Polasky, Exec.Dir.
Founded: 1992. **Members:** 75,000. **Membership Dues:** standard, $84 (annual) • association, $60 (annual) • senior citizen, $25 (annual) • legislative, $50 (annual). **Budget:** $3,000,000. **Local.** Seeks to educate members and the general public about government and public policy; conducts and publishes research with the goal of generating policy discussions in areas which impact American citizens. **Publications:** *Network News*, quarterly. Newsletter. **Conventions/Meetings:** annual Critical Issues Policy Summit - conference.

18137 ■ Trout Unlimited - Green Bay Chapter
1326 14th Ave.
Green Bay, WI 54304
Ph: (920)336-8008
E-mail: lmeyers@new.rr.com
URL: http://www.greenbaytu.com
Contact: Lee Meyers, Contact
Founded: 1969. **Local.**

18138 ■ United States Naval Sea Cadet Corps - VADM James H. Flatley, Jr. Division
NMCRC Green Bay
2949 Ramada Way
Green Bay, WI 54303
E-mail: nsccdad@yahoo.com
URL: http://dolphin.seacadets.org/US_units/UnitDetails.asp?UnitID=091AJF
Contact: LTJG Gary L. Frost NSCC, Commanding Officer
Local. Works to instill good citizenship and patriotism in youth. Encourages qualities such as personal neatness, loyalty, obedience, dependability, and responsibility to others. Offers courses in physical fitness and military drill, first aid, water safety, basic seamanship, and naval history and traditions. **Affiliated With:** Naval Sea Cadet Corps.

18139 ■ Wisconsin Council on Problem Gambling (WCPG)
1825 Riverside Dr.
Green Bay, WI 54301
Ph: (920)437-8888
Free: (800)426-2535
E-mail: wcpgamble5-rose@new.rr.com
URL: http://www.wi-problemgamblers.org
Contact: Rose Gruber, Exec.Dir.
State. Affiliated With: National Council on Problem Gambling.

18140 ■ Wisconsin Health Care Association, District 8
c/o Joe Scherwinski, Pres.
Western Village
1640 Shawano Ave.
Green Bay, WI 54303
Ph: (920)499-5177
URL: http://www.whca.com
Contact: Joe Scherwinski, Pres.
Local. Promotes professionalism and ethical behavior of individuals providing long-term care delivery for patients and for the general public. Provides information, education and administrative tools to enhance the quality of long-term care. Improves the standards of service and administration of member nursing homes. **Affiliated With:** American Health Care Association; Wisconsin Health Care Association.

18141 ■ Wisconsin National Organization for the Reform of Marijuana Laws
c/o Chris Kelly
PO Box 1923
Green Bay, WI 54305-1923
Ph: (608)294-9178
E-mail: emailus@winorml.org
URL: http://www.winorml.org
State. Affiliated With: National Organization for the Reform of Marijuana Laws.

18142 ■ Wisconsin Organization of Nurse Executives (W-ONE)
c/o Carol Winegarden, Pres.
St. Mary's Hosp. Medical Ctr.
1726 Shawano Ave.
Green Bay, WI 54303
Ph: (608)268-1806 (920)498-4604
Fax: (920)498-1861
E-mail: cwinegar@stmgb.org
URL: http://www.w-one.org
Contact: Carol Winegarden, Pres.
State. Represents nurse leaders who improve healthcare. Provides leadership, professional development, advocacy and research. Advances the nursing administration practice and patient care. **Affiliated With:** American Organization of Nurse Executives.

18143 ■ YoungLife Green Bay
PO Box 11014
Green Bay, WI 54307-1014
Ph: (920)434-5854
URL: http://sites.younglife.org/sites/GreenBay/default.aspx
Local. Affiliated With: Young Life.

Green Lake

18144 ■ American Legion, Willis-Chapel Post 306
PO Box 448
Green Lake, WI 54941
Ph: (608)745-1090
Fax: (608)745-0179
URL: National Affiliate–www.legion.org
Local. Affiliated With: American Legion.

18145 ■ Dartford Historical Society (DHS)
501 Mill St.
PO Box 638
Green Lake, WI 54941
Ph: (920)294-6194
URL: National Affiliate–www.aaslh.org
Contact: Lawrence Behlen, Pres.
Founded: 1956. **Members:** 120. **Membership Dues:** individual, $10 (annual) • business, family, $15 (annual). **Budget:** $25,000. **Local.** Individuals interested in the collection, preservation, and education related to the history of Green Lake, WI area. Operates museum, research center, and exhibit gallery. **Libraries: Type:** open to the public. **Holdings:** 1,000. **Subjects:** Green Lake area history. **Affiliated With:** American Association for State and Local History; Wisconsin Historical Society. **Publications:** *Dartford News*, 6/yr. Newsletter. **Circulation:** 150. **Advertising:** not accepted. **Conventions/Meetings:** quarterly workshop; Avg. Attendance: 50.

18146 ■ Green Lake Area Chamber of Commerce (GLACC)
550 Mill St.
PO Box 337
Green Lake, WI 54941-0337
Ph: (920)294-3231
Fax: (920)294-3415
Free: (800)253-7354
E-mail: info@visitgreenlake.com
URL: http://www.visitgreenlake.com
Contact: Dusty Walker, Exec.Dir.
Founded: 1965. **Staff:** 2. **Local.** Promotes business and community development in the Green Lake, WI area. Sponsors community social and promotional activities. **Publications:** *Visitors Guide*, annual. Directory. **Price:** available to members only. **Conventions/Meetings:** annual Harvest Days Festival.

18147 ■ Wisconsin Association of Local Health Department and Boards (WALHDAB)
c/o Ms. Kathy Munsey, RN, Co-Pres.
Green Lake County Dept. of Hea. and Human Services
PO Box 588
Green Lake, WI 54941
Ph: (920)294-4070
E-mail: kmunsey@co.green-lake.wi.us
URL: http://www.walhdab.org
Contact: Ms. Kathy Munsey RN, Co-Pres.
Members: 92. **Regional Groups:** 5. **State Groups:** 1. **State. Affiliated With:** National Association of Local Boards of Health.

Greenbush

18148 ■ American Legion, Haslee-Doebert-Schmidt Post 261
PO Box 51
Greenbush, WI 53026
Ph: (608)745-1090
Fax: (608)745-0179
URL: National Affiliate–www.legion.org
Local. Affiliated With: American Legion.

Greendale

18149 ■ American Legion, Greendale Post 416
6351 W Grange Ave.
Greendale, WI 53129
Ph: (608)745-1090
Fax: (608)745-0179
URL: National Affiliate–www.legion.org
Local. Affiliated With: American Legion.

18150 ■ Greendale Chamber of Commerce (GCC)
PO Box 467
Greendale, WI 53129
Ph: (414)423-3900
E-mail: info@greendalechamber.com
URL: http://www.greendalechamber.com
Contact: Lynn M. Magner, Pres.
Founded: 1980. **Members:** 44. **Budget:** $10,000. **Local.** Promotes business and community development in Greendale, WI area.

18151 ■ Greendale Lions Club
PO Box 241
Greendale, WI 53129
Ph: (414)421-5643
E-mail: kenc@milwpc.com
URL: http://www.greendalelions.com
Local. Affiliated With: Lions Clubs International.

18152 ■ Timber Wolf Preservation Society (TWPS)
6669 S 76th St.
Greendale, WI 53129
Ph: (414)425-6107
URL: http://www.timberwolfinformation.org/info/world/twps.htm
Founded: 1979. **State.**

18153 ■ Wisconsin Park and Recreation Association (WPRA)
c/o Steven J. Thompson, CPRP, Exec.Dir.
6601-C Northway
Greendale, WI 53129
Ph: (414)423-1210
Fax: (414)423-1296
E-mail: wpra@wpraweb.org
URL: http://www.wpraweb.org
Contact: Steven J. Thompson CPRP, Exec.Dir.
Founded: 1965. **Members:** 1,100. **Staff:** 2. **Budget:** $1,250,000. **State Groups:** 4. **State.** Park, recreation, and therapeutic recreation professionals. Provides voluntary certification and legislative advocacy. Sponsors workshops. **Libraries: Type:** open to the public. **Subjects:** park, recreation and therapeutic recreation. **Awards:** WPRA Foundation. **Frequency:** annual. **Type:** scholarship. **Recipient:** Professional Development. **Affiliated With:** American Society of Association Executives. **Absorbed:** Wisconsin Recreation Association. **Publications:** *Impact*, quarterly. Journal • *Leisure Line*, monthly. Newsletter • Directory, annual. **Conventions/Meetings:** annual conference (exhibits) - always November.

Greenfield

18154 ■ German Shepherd Dog Club of Wisconsin
c/o Cheri Graupp
4606 W Morgan Ave.
Greenfield, WI 53220
Ph: (414)327-9912
E-mail: karenlacosse@aol.com
URL: http://www.gsdcw.com/
Contact: Ron Labinski, Pres.
State. Affiliated With: American Kennel Club.

18155 ■ Greenfield Chamber of Commerce
4818 S 76th St., Ste.129
PO Box 20786
Greenfield, WI 53220
Ph: (414)327-8500
E-mail: support@greenfieldchamber.org
URL: http://www.greenfieldchamber.org
Contact: Cindy M. Leranth, Pres.
Founded: 1957. **Local.** Promotes business and community development in Greenfield, WI area. **Awards:** Business (Person) of the Year. **Frequency:** annual. **Type:** recognition • Educator of the Year. **Frequency:** annual. **Type:** recognition • Student of the Year. **Frequency:** annual. **Type:** recognition • Volunteer of the Year. **Frequency:** annual. **Type:** recognition. **Conventions/Meetings:** monthly Business After Five - meeting, networking - every 3rd Wednesday • monthly Good Morning Greenfield - breakfast - every 1st Friday.

18156 ■ Illinois Sign Association (ISA)
12342 W Layton Ave.
Greenfield, WI 53228
Ph: (414)529-4235
Fax: (414)529-4722
E-mail: membership@toriiphillips.com
URL: http://www.isa-sign.com
Contact: Brian Swingle, Exec.Dir.
Local. Works in cooperation with planners and businesses to provide guidelines necessary to formulate legislation essential to insure improved community appearance. **Publications:** *Images*, bimonthly. Newsletter. **Price:** included in membership dues. **Advertising:** accepted. **Conventions/Meetings:** annual ISA Fall Conference and Golf Outing • annual ISA Spring Conference and Golf Outing.

18157 ■ Libertarian Party of Wisconsin (LPWI)
c/o Arif Khan, Chm.
PO Box 20815
Greenfield, WI 53220-0815
Fax: (414)727-9182
Free: (800)236-9236
E-mail: director@lpwi.org
URL: http://www.lpwi.org
Contact: Arif Khan, Chm.
Founded: 1973. **State. Affiliated With:** Libertarian National Committee.

18158 ■ Muskies Milwaukee Chapter
PO Box 28842
Greenfield, WI 53228
Ph: (414)541-5840
E-mail: rjw@randell.com
Contact: Rick Wyrwas, Pres.
Local.

18159 ■ Wisconsin Association of Textile Services
c/o Brian Swingle, Exec.Dir.
12342 W Layton Ave.
Greenfield, WI 53228
Ph: (414)529-4703
Fax: (414)529-4722
E-mail: membership@toriiphillips.com

18160 ■ Wisconsin Fabricare Institute (WFI)
12342 W Layton Ave.
Greenfield, WI 53228
Ph: (414)529-4707
Fax: (414)529-4722
E-mail: info@wisecleaners.com
URL: http://www.wiscleaners.com
Contact: Susan Doolin, Pres.
State.

18161 ■ Wisconsin Landscape Federation
12342 W. Layton Ave.
Greenfield, WI 53228
Ph: (414)529-4705
Fax: (414)529-4722
E-mail: membership@toriiphillips.com
URL: http://www.wislf.org
Contact: Brian Swingle, Exec.Dir.
State. Publications: *Green Side Up*, monthly. Newsletter. **Price:** included in membership dues. **Circulation:** 750. **Advertising:** accepted. **Conventions/Meetings:** annual convention.

18162 ■ Wisconsin Nursery Association
c/o Brian Swingle
12342 W Layton Ave.
Greenfield, WI 53228
Ph: (414)529-4705
Fax: (414)529-4722
E-mail: membership@toriiphillips.com
State.

Greenleaf

18163 ■ Izaak Walton League of America - Southern Brown Conservation
c/o John Leick
6503 Blake Rd.
Greenleaf, WI 54126
Ph: (920)864-2581
URL: http://www.iwla.org
Contact: John Leick, Contact
Local. Educates the public to conserve, maintain, protect, and restore the soil, forest, water, and other natural resources of the U.S. Promotes the utilization of these resources. Sponsors environmental programs.

Greenville

18164 ■ Greenville Lions Club - Wisconsin
PO Box 23
Greenville, WI 54942
Ph: (920)757-6197
E-mail: info@greenvillelions.org
URL: http://www.greenvillelions.org
Local. Affiliated With: Lions Clubs International.

Greenwood

18165 ■ Greenwood Chamber of Commerce
PO Box 86
Greenwood, WI 54437
Ph: (715)267-7221
Contact: Patricia Lindner, Pres.
Local.

Gresham

18166 ■ American Legion, Gresham Post 390
951 Main St.
Gresham, WI 54128
Ph: (608)745-1090
Fax: (608)745-0179
URL: National Affiliate–www.legion.org
Local. Affiliated With: American Legion.

Gurney

18167 ■ American Legion, Mercier-Kero Post 371
HC 1, Box 787
Gurney, WI 54559
Ph: (715)893-2255
Fax: (608)745-0179
URL: National Affiliate–www.legion.org
Local. Affiliated With: American Legion.

Hales Corners

18168 ■ American Legion, Hales Corners Memorial Post 299
PO Box 141
Hales Corners, WI 53130
Ph: (608)745-1090
Fax: (608)745-0179
URL: National Affiliate–www.legion.org
Local. Affiliated With: American Legion.

18169 ■ English Cocker Spaniel Club of America (ECSCA)
c/o Mrs. Kate Romanski, Corresponding Sec.
PO Box 252
Hales Corners, WI 53130
E-mail: kathy@kabree.com
URL: http://www.ecsca.org
Contact: Kathleen Moore, Pres.
State. Affiliated With: American Kennel Club.

18170 ■ French Canadian-Acadian Genealogists of Wisconsin
PO Box 414
Hales Corners, WI 53130-0414
Ph: (414)443-9429
E-mail: kdupuis@wi.rr.com
URL: http://www.fcgw.org/
Contact: Kateri Dupuis, Pres.
Founded: 1982. **Members:** 150. **Membership Dues:** individual, $20 (annual). **State.** Members are genealogists researching French Canadian and Acadian Lines with ties to Wisconsin. Objectives are to foster and encourage interest and research in French Canadian and Acadian genealogy, heritage, and culture. **Libraries: Type:** not open to the public. **Holdings:** books, periodicals. **Subjects:** genealogy. **Publications:** *FCWG Quarterly*. Journal. Contains informative articles, genealogies, and queries free to members. **Price:** included in membership dues. ISSN: 1057-3488 • *We Remember*. Papers • Papers. **Conventions/Meetings:** monthly meeting - except January and December, second Thursday of the month.

18171 ■ Milwaukee Area Land Conservancy
c/o Delene Hanson, Pres.
10203 W Ridge Rd.
Hales Corners, WI 53130-1437
Ph: (414)425-4608
E-mail: malc@execpc.com
URL: National Affiliate–www.gatheringwaters.org
Contact: Delene Hanson, Pres.
Local.

18172 ■ Wisconsin Health Care Association, District 5
c/o John Sauer, Pres.
Hales Corners Care Ctr.
9449 W Forest Home Ave.
Hales Corners, WI 53130
Ph: (414)529-6888
URL: http://www.whca.com
Contact: John Sauer, Pres.
Local. Promotes professionalism and ethical behavior of individuals providing long-term care delivery for patients and for the general public. Provides information, education and administrative tools to enhance the quality of long-term care. Improves the standards of service and administration of member nursing homes. **Affiliated With:** American Health Care Association; Wisconsin Health Care Association.

Hammond

18173 ■ American Legion, Deneen-Mc-Cabe Post 432
PO Box 432
Hammond, WI 54015
Ph: (608)745-1090
Fax: (608)745-0179
URL: National Affiliate–www.legion.org
Local. Affiliated With: American Legion.

18174 ■ American Legion, Johnson-Whistler Post 323
1305 2nd St.
Hammond, WI 54015
Ph: (608)745-1090
Fax: (608)745-0179
URL: National Affiliate–www.legion.org
Local. Affiliated With: American Legion.

Hancock

18175 ■ American Legion, Roger-Oestrich-Hancock-Coloma Post 343
128 E South Lake St.
Hancock, WI 54943
Ph: (608)745-1090
Fax: (608)745-0179
URL: National Affiliate–www.legion.org
Local. Affiliated With: American Legion.

Hartford

18176 ■ American Legion, Courtney-Carr-Milner Post 19
PO Box 27022
Hartford, WI 53027
Ph: (608)745-1090
Fax: (608)745-0179
URL: National Affiliate–www.legion.org
Local. Affiliated With: American Legion.

18177 ■ Hartford Area Chamber of Commerce
225 N Main St.
Hartford, WI 53027
Ph: (262)673-7002
Fax: (262)673-7057
Free: (866)222-5401
E-mail: info@hartfordchamber.org
URL: http://www.hartfordwi.net
Contact: Doreen Buntrock, Exec.Dir.
Local. Works to support and foster development in Hartford area. **Committees:** Chamber Operations; Community Issues; Economic Development; Education; Government Affairs; Tourism. **Subgroups:** Ambassadors.

18178 ■ Voice of the Retarded, Wisconsin
669 McCarthy Dr. N
Hartford, WI 53027
Ph: (920)474-4201
Fax: (920)474-4129
E-mail: res08i8g@verizon.net
URL: National Affiliate–www.vor.net
Contact: Kevin Underwood, Dir.
State. **Affiliated With:** Voice of the Retarded.

18179 ■ Wisconsin Onsite Waste Disposal Association
c/o Gretchen McQuestion
783 Tipperary Ln.
Hartford, WI 53027-9049
Ph: (262)966-2942
Fax: (262)966-0471
Free: (800)377-6672
Contact: Gretchen McQuestion, Contact
Founded: 1976. **Members:** 250. **State**. **Publications:** *WOWDA News*, monthly. Newsletter. **Price:** available to members only. **Circulation:** 270. **Advertising:** accepted. **Conventions/Meetings:** annual meeting.

Hartland

18180 ■ American Legion, Flanagan-Dorn Post 294
231 Goodwin Ave.
Hartland, WI 53029
Ph: (608)745-1090
Fax: (608)745-0179
URL: National Affiliate–www.legion.org
Local. **Affiliated With:** American Legion.

18181 ■ Arrowhead Young Life
151 E Capitol Dr.
Hartland, WI 53029
Ph: (262)367-5453
URL: http://sites.younglife.org/sites/Arrowhead/default.aspx
Local. **Affiliated With:** Young Life.

18182 ■ Five-Os Young Life - Oconomowoc
151 E Capitol Dr.
Hartland, WI 53029
Ph: (262)367-5453
URL: http://sites.younglife.org/sites/Five-Os/default.aspx
Local. **Affiliated With:** Young Life.

18183 ■ Hartland Area Chamber of Commerce
140 E Capitol Dr.
Hartland, WI 53029-2104
Ph: (262)367-7059
Fax: (262)367-2980
E-mail: admin@hartland-wi.org
URL: http://www.hartland-wi.org
Contact: Ms. Lynn Minturn, Exec.Dir.
Local. Serves the members by providing programs and services, which enhance the business climate and community. **Publications:** *Chamber Member Directory & Community Guide*, annual • *Hartland Matters*, semiweekly. Newsletter. Contains information on the association news and updates. Alternate Formats: online.

18184 ■ Kettle Moraine Young Life
151 E Capitol Dr.
Hartland, WI 53029
Ph: (262)367-5453
URL: http://sites.younglife.org/sites/KettleMoraine/default.aspx
Local. **Affiliated With:** Young Life.

18185 ■ National Multiple Sclerosis Society, Wisconsin
c/o Colleen Kalt, Pres./CEO
1120 James Dr., Ste.A
Hartland, WI 53029
Ph: (262)369-4400
Fax: (262)369-4410
Free: (800)242-3358
E-mail: info@wisms.org
URL: http://www.wisms.org
Contact: Colleen Kalt, Pres./CEO
State. Provides programs, services and advocacy efforts for people with MS and related diseases and their families, as well as supports research into the cause, treatment and cure of MS. **Libraries: Type:** lending; open to the public; reference. **Holdings:** articles, audio recordings, books, films, periodicals, reports. **Affiliated With:** National Multiple Sclerosis Society.

18186 ■ ULS - Wyldlife
151 E Capitol Dr.
Hartland, WI 53029
Ph: (262)367-5453
URL: http://sites.younglife.org/_layouts/ylext/default.aspx?ID=C-4217
Local. **Affiliated With:** Young Life.

18187 ■ Vintage Triumphs of Wisconsin (VTOW)
c/o Mary Stockinger, Pres.
W305 N6546 Beaver View Rd.
Hartland, WI 53029
Ph: (262)521-1072
E-mail: john.stokinger@gte.net
URL: http://vtow.northwoodsoft.com
Contact: Mary Stockinger, Pres.
Founded: 1976. **Members:** 105. **Membership Dues:** individual, $25 (annual) • commercial, $40 (annual). **Local**. Individuals from southeastern Wisconsin who are interested in Triumph automobiles. Provides restoration resources; sponsors technical sessions and social activities. **Affiliated With:** Vintage Triumph Register. **Publications:** *Coventry Commentator*, monthly. Newsletter. **Advertising:** accepted. **Conventions/Meetings:** monthly meeting.

18188 ■ Wisconsin Curling Association - Kettle Moraine Curling Club (KMCC)
2360 Oakwood Rd.
Hartland, WI 53029
Ph: (262)367-8862
E-mail: marypat_shandor@yahoo.com
URL: http://www.kmcurlingclub.com/home/home.cfm
Contact: MaryPat Shandor, Pres.
Local. **Affiliated With:** United States Curling Association.

18189 ■ Wisconsin Waterfowl Association (WWA)
614 W Capitol Dr.
Hartland, WI 53029
Ph: (262)369-6309
Fax: (262)369-7813
Free: (800)524-8460
E-mail: h2ofowl@powercom.net
URL: http://www.wisducks.org
Contact: Jeff Nania, Exec.Dir.
Founded: 1983. **Members:** 7,400. **Membership Dues:** regular, $25 (annual) • contributing, $50 (annual) • habitat sponsor, $200 (annual) • youth, $10 (annual). **Staff:** 3. **Budget:** $400,000. **State Groups:** 30. **State**. Conservationists seeking to preserve Wisconsin's wetlands, waterfowl habitat, and related wildlife. Provides legislative advocacy. Sponsors educational programs on conservation and Waterfowl Hunter's Skills Clinic. **Awards:** Canvasback Award. **Frequency:** annual. **Type:** recognition • Chevron-Times Magazine's Conservation Award. **Frequency:** annual. **Type:** recognition • Partners for Wildlife Award. **Frequency:** annual. **Type:** recognition. **Affiliated With:** Wisconsin Waterfowl Association. **Formerly:** (1989) Wisconsin Waterfowlers Association. **Publications:** *Wisconsin Waterfowl*, quarterly. Brochures. **Circulation:** 10,000. **Advertising:** accepted. Alternate Formats: CD-ROM • *Wisconsin Waterfowl Magazine*, quarterly • *Wood Duck Nest Boxes*. Booklet.

18190 ■ Young Life Lake Country
151 E Capitol Dr.
Hartland, WI 53029
Ph: (262)367-5453
Fax: (262)367-5453
URL: http://sites.younglife.org/sites/LakeCountry/default.aspx
Local. **Affiliated With:** Young Life.

Hatley

18191 ■ American Legion, Hatley Post 471
1238 Koskey Rd.
Hatley, WI 54440
Ph: (608)745-1090
Fax: (608)745-0179
URL: National Affiliate–www.legion.org
Local. **Affiliated With:** American Legion.

Haugen

18192 ■ American Legion, Brunclik-Konop Post 540
c/o Jim Hill
PO Box 140
Haugen, WI 54841
Ph: (608)745-1090
Fax: (608)745-0179
URL: National Affiliate–www.legion.org
Contact: Jim Hill, Contact
Local. **Affiliated With:** American Legion.

Hawkins

18193 ■ American Legion, Cuff-Patricki Post 174
412 South Ave.
Hawkins, WI 54530
Ph: (608)745-1090
Fax: (608)745-0179
URL: National Affiliate–www.legion.org
Local. **Affiliated With:** American Legion.

Hayward

18194 ■ American Legion, Butler-Lindner Post 218
PO Box 524
Hayward, WI 54843
Ph: (608)745-1090
Fax: (608)745-0179
URL: National Affiliate–www.legion.org
Local. **Affiliated With:** American Legion.

18195 ■ Hayward Area Chamber of Commerce (HCC)
PO Box 726
Hayward, WI 54843
Ph: (715)634-8662
Fax: (715)634-8498
Free: (800)724-2992
E-mail: info@haywardareachamber.com
URL: http://www.haywardareachamber.com
Contact: Kevin Ruetten, Exec.Dir.
Membership Dues: investment, $190 (annual) • financial institution, $300 (annual) • associate business, non-profit, $80 (annual) • non-business indi-

vidual, $50 (annual). **Local**. Promotes business and community development in Hayward, WI. **Affiliated With:** U.S. Chamber of Commerce. **Publications:** *The Endeavor*, monthly. Newsletter • *Hayward's Calendar of Events*, annual. Newsletter • Directory, annual. **Conventions/Meetings:** annual Hayward Fall Festival.

18196 ■ Hayward Figure Skating Club
PO Box 172
Hayward, WI 54843
E-mail: 2yk@cheqnet.net
URL: National Affiliate–www.usfigureskating.org
Contact: Bonnie Danczyk, Contact
Local. Provides programs to encourage participation and achievement in the sport of figure skating on ice. Defines and maintains uniform standards of skating proficiency. Organizes and sponsors competitions and exhibitions for the purpose of stimulating interest in figure skating. **Affiliated With:** United States Figure Skating Association.

18197 ■ Muskies Hayward Lakes Chapter
PO Box 609
Hayward, WI 54843
Ph: (715)634-4543
E-mail: muskiemike@cheqnet.net
URL: National Affiliate–www.muskiesinc.org
Contact: Michael Persson, Pres.
Local.

18198 ■ Northland Area Builders Association
PO Box 1189
Hayward, WI 54843-1189
Ph: (715)634-5127
Fax: (715)634-5127
E-mail: naba@cheqnet.net
URL: http://www.nabaonline.net
Contact: Pam Ruetten, Exec. Officer
Local. Single and multifamily home builders, commercial builders, and others associated with the building industry. **Affiliated With:** National Association of Home Builders. **Formerly:** (2005) Northland Area Building Authority.

18199 ■ Ruffed Grouse Society, Wilderness Wings Chapter
c/o Don Aderman
15167 W Spring Creek Rd.
Hayward, WI 54843
Ph: (715)634-3055
E-mail: djaderman@johnsontimber.com
URL: National Affiliate–www.ruffedgrousesociety.org
Contact: Don Aderman, Contact
Local. Affiliated With: Ruffed Grouse Society.

Hazel Green

18200 ■ American Legion, Temperly-Duncan Post 526
PO Box 276
Hazel Green, WI 53811
Ph: (608)745-1090
Fax: (608)745-0179
URL: National Affiliate–www.legion.org
Local. Affiliated With: American Legion.

Hazelhurst

18201 ■ Sons of Norway, Nordlandet Lodge 5-620
c/o Jeanne L. Julseth-Heinrich, Pres.
6002 Interlocken Rd.
Hazelhurst, WI 54531-9650
Ph: (715)356-6786
E-mail: jeannesings@nnex.net
URL: National Affiliate–www.sofn.com
Contact: Jeanne L. Julseth-Heinrich, Pres.
Local. Affiliated With: Sons of Norway.

High Bridge

18202 ■ National Alliance for the Mentally Ill - Chequamegon Bay Area
c/o Sue Sederholm, Pres.
RR1 Box 255
High Bridge, WI 54846
Ph: (715)682-4563
URL: http://www.namiwisconsin.org/library/directory
Contact: Sue Sederholm, Pres.
Local. Strives to improve the quality of life of children and adults with severe mental illness through support, education, research and advocacy. **Affiliated With:** National Alliance for the Mentally Ill.

Highland

18203 ■ American Legion, Wisconsin Post 422
c/o Robert Kail
PO Box 185
Highland, WI 53543
Ph: (608)745-1090
Fax: (608)745-0179
URL: National Affiliate–www.legion.org
Contact: Robert Kail, Contact
Local. Affiliated With: American Legion.

Hilbert

18204 ■ American Legion, Kupsh-Brockmann Post 127
W 909 River View Rd.
Hilbert, WI 54129
Ph: (608)745-1090
Fax: (608)745-0179
URL: National Affiliate–www.legion.org
Local. Affiliated With: American Legion.

18205 ■ Wisconsin Draft Horse Breeders
W5072 Faro Springs RD.
Hilbert, WI 54129
Ph: (920)989-1131
URL: National Affiliate–www.nasdha.net/RegionalAssoc.htm
Contact: Mary Alice Lee, Sec.-Treas.
State.

Hillsboro

18206 ■ American Legion, Harrison-Jones Post 223
PO Box 67
Hillsboro, WI 54634
Ph: (608)745-1090
Fax: (608)745-0179
URL: National Affiliate–www.legion.org
Local. Affiliated With: American Legion.

18207 ■ Hillsboro Lions Club - Wisconsin
c/o Dean Muller, Pres.
E18034 Heights Rd.
Hillsboro, WI 54634
Ph: (608)489-4590
E-mail: dean.muller@wi.ngb.army.mil
URL: http://www.md27d2.org
Contact: Dean Muller, Pres.
Local. Affiliated With: Lions Clubs International.

Hingham

18208 ■ American Legion, Higby-Oglan-Soerens Post 345
W 4426 Water St.
Hingham, WI 53031
Ph: (608)745-1090
Fax: (608)745-0179
URL: National Affiliate–www.legion.org
Local. Affiliated With: American Legion.

Hixton

18209 ■ American Legion, Hanson-Lien Post 368
PO Box 132
Hixton, WI 54635
Ph: (608)745-1090
Fax: (608)745-0179
URL: National Affiliate–www.legion.org
Local. Affiliated With: American Legion.

18210 ■ American Legion, Thomas and Leonard Johnson Post 541
Town of Northfield
W 15682 Hwy. 121
Hixton, WI 54635
Ph: (608)745-1090
Fax: (608)745-0179
URL: National Affiliate–www.legion.org
Local. Affiliated With: American Legion.

Holcombe

18211 ■ American Legion, Verhulst-Willmarth-Paulsen Post 311
26495 278th St.
Holcombe, WI 54745
Ph: (608)745-1090
Fax: (608)745-0179
URL: National Affiliate–www.legion.org
Local. Affiliated With: American Legion.

Hollandale

18212 ■ American Legion, Hollandale Post 510
1820 Long Valley Rd.
Hollandale, WI 53544
Ph: (608)745-1090
Fax: (608)745-0179
URL: National Affiliate–www.legion.org
Local. Affiliated With: American Legion.

Horicon

18213 ■ American Legion, Horicon Post 157
735 S Hubbard St.
Horicon, WI 53032
Ph: (608)745-1090
Fax: (608)745-0179
URL: National Affiliate–www.legion.org
Local. Affiliated With: American Legion.

18214 ■ American Society of Agricultural and Biological Engineers, District 3 - Wisconsin
c/o Bob Loehr
300 N Vine St.
Horicon, WI 53032
Ph: (920)485-5365
Fax: (920)485-5169
E-mail: loehrrobertj@johndeere.com
URL: http://www.asabe.org/membership/sections/dist3wi.html
Contact: Bob Loehr, Contact
Regional. Promotes the science and art of engineering in agricultural, food and biological systems. Encourages the professional improvement of members. Fosters education and develops engineering standards used in agriculture, food and biological systems. **Affiliated With:** American Society of Agricultural and Biological Engineers.

18215 ■ Horicon Chamber of Commerce (HCC)
PO Box 23
Horicon, WI 53032-0023
Ph: (920)485-3200
E-mail: writeus@horiconchamber.com
URL: http://www.horiconchamber.com
Members: 100. **Local**. Promotes business and community development in Horicon, WI.

18216 ■ International Association of Machinists and Aerospace Workers, LL-873
258 Barstow St.
Horicon, WI 53032
Ph: (920)485-2631
Fax: (920)485-4941
URL: http://www.powerweb.net/local873
Contact: Jim Geidd, Pres.
Members: 1,617. **Local. Affiliated With:** International Association of Machinists and Aerospace Workers.

Hortonville

18217 ■ American Legion, Hammond-Schmit Post 55
PO Box 355
Hortonville, WI 54944
Ph: (608)745-1090
Fax: (608)745-0179
URL: National Affiliate–www.legion.org
Local. Affiliated With: American Legion.

18218 ■ Fox Valley District Nurses Association - No. 6
W 8553 Hickory Ct.
Hortonville, WI 54944
E-mail: marnocha@uwosh.edu
URL: http://www.wisconsinnurses.org
Contact: Suzanne Marnocha, Pres.
Local. Works to advance the nursing profession. Seeks to meet the needs of nurses and health care consumers. Fosters high standards of nursing practice. Promotes the economic and general welfare of nurses in the workplace. **Affiliated With:** American Nurses Association; Wisconsin Nurses' Association.

18219 ■ Wisconsin Woodland Owners Association, Wolf River Chapter
c/o Chris Wyman, Chm.
45 Parkview Ln.
Hortonville, WI 54944
Ph: (920)779-4195
E-mail: wyhome@sbcglobal.net
URL: http://www.wisconsinwoodlands.org
Contact: Chris Wyman, Chm.
Local. Affiliated With: Wisconsin Woodland Owners Association.

Hubertus

18220 ■ American Legion, Goetz St. Louis Post 522
1096 County Rd. J
Hubertus, WI 53033
Ph: (608)745-1090
Fax: (608)745-0179
URL: National Affiliate–www.legion.org
Local. Affiliated With: American Legion.

18221 ■ Sweet Adelines International, Harmony of the Hill Chapter
Shepherd of the Hills Church
1350 Hwy. 175
Hubertus, WI 53033
Ph: (414)354-7294
E-mail: jcprice2@execpc.com
URL: National Affiliate–www.sweetadelineintl.org
Contact: Irene Price, Contact
Local. Advances the musical art form of barbershop harmony through education and performances. Provides education, training and coaching in the development of women's four-part barbershop harmony. **Affiliated With:** Sweet Adelines International.

Hudson

18222 ■ American Legion, Wisconsin Post 50
c/o Otis H. King
PO Box 347
Hudson, WI 54016
Ph: (608)745-1090
Fax: (608)745-0179
URL: National Affiliate–www.legion.org
Contact: Otis H. King, Contact
Local. Affiliated With: American Legion.

18223 ■ Hudson Area Chamber of Commerce and Tourism Bureau
502 Second St.
Hudson, WI 54016
Ph: (715)386-8411
Fax: (715)386-8432
Free: (800)657-6775
E-mail: info@hudsonwi.org
URL: http://www.hudsonwi.org
Contact: Kim Heinemann, Pres.
Founded: 1953. **Members:** 470. **Local.** Strives to serve its members by promoting the local economy and advocating the interests of the business community while advancing the recreational and cultural opportunities in the Hudson area. **Committees:** Ambassadors; Autumn Taste Talk; Golf Outing; Public Affairs; Retail; Service; Tourism. **Councils:** Industry. **Publications:** Membership Directory, annual. Contains listing of all chamber members and active volunteers/representatives of company and organization. **Circulation:** 470. **Advertising:** accepted • Newsletter. **Circulation:** 600. Alternate Formats: online.

18224 ■ Hudson Lions Club - Wisconsin
PO Box 691
Hudson, WI 54016
Ph: (715)386-3965
E-mail: jschmitt@pressenter.com
URL: http://hudsonlionsclub.org
Contact: Dan Gaeu, Pres.
Local. Affiliated With: Lions Clubs International.

18225 ■ Ruffed Grouse Society, St. Croix Valley Chapter
c/o Michael Juhnke
404 4th St. N
Hudson, WI 54016
Ph: (715)386-9424
URL: National Affiliate–www.ruffedgrousesociety.org
Contact: Michael Juhnke, Contact
Local. Affiliated With: Ruffed Grouse Society.

18226 ■ St. Croix County Historical Society (SCCHS)
1004 3rd St.
Hudson, WI 54016
Ph: (715)386-2654
E-mail: octagonhouse@juno.com
URL: http://www.pressenter.com/~octagon
Contact: Dolores Taavola, Pres.
Founded: 1948. **Members:** 200. **Membership Dues:** individual, $10 (annual) • family, $15 (annual) • contributing/silver, $25 (annual) • supporting/gold, $50 (annual) • benefactor/platinum, $100 (annual). **Staff:** 3. **Local.** Individuals interested in the history of St. Croix County, WI. Maintains Carriage House, Garden House, and Octagon House. Sponsors tours. **Awards:** Volunteer of the Year. **Frequency:** annual. **Type:** medal. **Recipient:** to a volunteer for significant contribution to the society. **Committees:** Acquisition Cataloguing and Research; Building; Finance; Garden; House (Museum); Publication; Publicity, Promotion, and Newsletter; Tour. **Affiliated With:** Wisconsin Historical Society. **Publications:** *The Bulletin*, periodic. Newsletter • Brochure. **Conventions/Meetings:** semiannual meeting - always spring and fall.

18227 ■ United Way of St. Croix County
c/o John M. Coughlin, Exec.Dir.
911 4th St., Ste.5
Hudson, WI 54016
Ph: (715)377-0203
Fax: (715)377-0774
E-mail: givehope@unitedwaystcroix.org
URL: http://www.unitedwaystcroix.org/uwscc
Contact: John M. Coughlin, Exec.Dir.
Local.

Humbird

18228 ■ American Legion, Melcher-Matti Post 320
3049 King St.
Humbird, WI 54746
Ph: (608)745-1090
Fax: (608)745-0179
URL: National Affiliate–www.legion.org
Local. Affiliated With: American Legion.

Hurley

18229 ■ American Legion, Cossette-Woitkielewicz Post 58
201 Iron St.
Hurley, WI 54534
Ph: (608)745-1090
Fax: (608)745-0179
URL: National Affiliate–www.legion.org
Local. Affiliated With: American Legion.

18230 ■ Hurley Area Chamber of Commerce (HACC)
316 Silver St.
Hurley, WI 54534
Ph: (715)561-4334
Fax: (715)561-3742
Free: (866)340-4334
E-mail: hurley@hurleywi.com
URL: http://www.hurleywi.com
Contact: Tina Paruolo, Exec.Dir.
Local. Promotes business and community development in the Hurley, WI area. Holds Poker Run, Red Light Snowmobile Rally, and Paavo Nurmi Marathon. **Computer Services:** Mailing lists, of members. **Publications:** Newsletter, quarterly.

18231 ■ Iron County Historical Society (ICHS)
303 Iron St.
Hurley, WI 54534
Ph: (715)561-2244
URL: http://www.hurleywi.com/ironcountyhistory
Contact: Gene Cisewski, Pres.
Founded: 1964. **Members:** 116. **Membership Dues:** individual, $5 (annual) • family, $10 (annual) • business, $25 (annual) • life, $100. **Languages:** English, Finnish, German. **Regional.** Individuals interested in the history of Iron County, WI. Operates Old Iron County Courthouse Museum. **Libraries: Type:** open to the public. **Subjects:** Gogebic County, MI; Iron County, WI. **Computer Services:** Record retrieval services, digital microfilm reproduction. **Affiliated With:** Wisconsin Historical Society. **Conventions/Meetings:** annual meeting, first Tuesday of month - membership meetings monthly except for January and February. Old Courthouse Museum.

Independence

18232 ■ American Legion, Sura-Wiersgalla Post 186
PO Box 57
Independence, WI 54747
Ph: (608)745-1090
Fax: (608)745-0179
URL: National Affiliate–www.legion.org
Local. Affiliated With: American Legion.

Iola

18233 ■ American Legion, Sheveland-Taylor Post 14
PO Box 67
Iola, WI 54945
Ph: (608)745-1090
Fax: (608)745-0179
URL: National Affiliate–www.legion.org
Local. Affiliated With: American Legion.

18234 ■ Employee Stock Ownership Plan Association, Wisconsin
c/o Ross Hubbard
Krause Publications
700 E State
Iola, WI 54990
Ph: (715)445-2214 (920)437-1617
E-mail: carol.wheeler@sficorp.com
URL: National Affiliate–www.esopassociation.org
Contact: Ms. Carol Wheeler, Pres.
State. Affiliated With: ESOP Association.

18235 ■ Iola - Scandinavia Area Chamber of Commerce
PO Box 167
Iola, WI 54945
Ph: (715)445-4000
E-mail: mike@iolaoldcarshow.com
URL: http://www.ischamber.org
Contact: Terry Murphy, Pres.
Local. Promotes business and community development in Iola and Scandinavia, WI.

18236 ■ Sons of Norway, Norskeland Lodge 5-580
c/o Mitch L. Taylor, Pres.
N8269 Anderson Rd.
Iola, WI 54945-9415
Ph: (715)445-2727
E-mail: rudy@athenet.net
URL: National Affiliate–www.sofn.com
Contact: Mitch L. Taylor, Pres.
Local. Affiliated With: Sons of Norway.

Irma

18237 ■ Foster Grandparent Program of Lincoln Hills School
W4380 Cooper Lake Rd.
Irma, WI 54442
Ph: (715)536-8386
Fax: (715)536-8236
E-mail: donna.nash@doc.state.wi.us
URL: National Affiliate–www.seniorcorps.org
Contact: Donna Nash, Dir.
Local. Serves as mentors, tutors and caregivers for at-risk children and youth with special needs. Provides older Americans the opportunity to put their life experiences to work for local communities.

Iron River

18238 ■ American Legion, Hanson-Maki Post 506
68470 Maine St.
Iron River, WI 54847
Ph: (608)745-1090
Fax: (608)745-0179
URL: National Affiliate–www.legion.org
Local. Affiliated With: American Legion.

18239 ■ Friends of the Library
PO Box 806
Iron River, WI 54847-0806
Ph: (715)372-5451
Contact: Linda Watlers, Pres.
Local. Libraries: Type: open to the public. **Holdings:** 8,000.

Ixonia

18240 ■ Western Waukesha County Dog Training Club (WWCDTC)
PO Box 223
Ixonia, WI 53036-0223
Ph: (920)206-9334
Free: (877)706-9334
E-mail: info@seespotsit.com
URL: http://www.seespotsit.com
Contact: Julie Lentz-Andrus, VP
Founded: 1975. **Members:** 200. **Membership Dues:** single/junior, $100 (annual). **Local Groups:** 1. **Local. Libraries: Type:** not open to the public. **Holdings:** 100. **Subjects:** dog training, breeds. **Awards:** Achievement Award. **Frequency:** annual. **Type:** recognition. **Affiliated With:** American Kennel Club. **Publications:** *The ReCall*, monthly. Newsletter. Contains clubs news, events information, and schedule of events. **Price:** free for members. **Circulation:** 200. **Conventions/Meetings:** annual AKC Trial - specialty show • annual UKC Trial - specialty show.

Jackson

18241 ■ American Legion, Wisconsin Post 486
c/o Sgt. Henry F. Gumm
PO Box 485
Jackson, WI 53037
Ph: (608)745-1090
Fax: (608)745-0179
URL: National Affiliate–www.legion.org
Contact: Sgt. Henry F. Gumm, Contact
Local. Affiliated With: American Legion.

Janesville

18242 ■ American Legion, Wisconsin Post 205
c/o Richard Ellis
PO Box 382
Janesville, WI 53547
Ph: (608)745-1090
Fax: (608)745-0179
URL: National Affiliate–www.legion.org
Contact: Richard Ellis, Contact
Local. Affiliated With: American Legion.

18243 ■ American Red Cross, South Central Wisconsin Chapter
211 N Parker Dr.
Janesville, WI 53545
Ph: (608)754-4497
Fax: (608)754-8119
URL: http://southcentralwisconsin.redcross.org
Regional.

18244 ■ Blackhawk Curling Club (BCC)
1400 Craig Ave.
Janesville, WI 53547
Ph: (608)754-9714
E-mail: info@blackhawkcurlingclub.com
URL: http://www.blackhawkcurlingclub.com
Local. Affiliated With: United States Curling Association.

18245 ■ Blackhawk Human Resource Association
c/o Jennifer Anderson
PO Box 1488
Janesville, WI 53546
Ph: (608)754-2710
Fax: (608)754-1322
E-mail: anderjl@freedomplastics.com
URL: http://www.bhraonline.org
Contact: Jacqueline Swanson, Pres.
Local. Represents the interests of human resource and industrial relations professionals and executives. Promotes the advancement of human resource management.

18246 ■ Epilepsy Foundation of Southern Wisconsin
205 N. Main St., Ste.106
Janesville, WI 53545-3062
Ph: (608)755-1821
Fax: (608)741-0718
Free: (800)693-2287
E-mail: efsw@ticon.net
URL: http://efa.org/southwisc
Contact: Ms. Patricia C. Robinson, Exec.Dir.
Founded: 1981. **Membership Dues:** general, $25 (annual). **Staff:** 6. **Budget:** $200,000. **State Groups:** 5. **Local Groups:** 3. **Languages:** English, Spanish. **Nonmembership. Local. Libraries: Type:** not open to the public. **Holdings:** films, video recordings. **Subjects:** various aspects of epilepsy. **Awards:** Employer of the Year. **Frequency:** annual. **Type:** recognition. **Recipient:** for outstanding participation in the organization • School of the Year. **Frequency:** annual. **Type:** recognition. **Recipient:** for outstanding participation in the organization. **Affiliated With:** Epilepsy Foundation. **Publications:** *Epilepsy Foundation of Southern Wisconsin*, 2-3 times per year. Newsletter. Contains information about the agency and developments in epilepsy research and medications. **Price:** no charge. **Circulation:** 1,500. Alternate Formats: online.

18247 ■ Forward Janesville (FJI)
51 S Jackson St.
Janesville, WI 53548
Ph: (608)757-3160
Fax: (608)757-3170
E-mail: forward@forwardjanesville.com
URL: http://www.forwardjanesville.com
Contact: Mr. John Beckord, Pres.
Founded: 1991. **Members:** 600. **Staff:** 7. **Budget:** $643,500. **Regional.** Leads private sector economic and community development efforts to ensure the continued health and prosperity of business and industry in Janesville. **Publications:** *The Report*, quarterly. Newsletter. **Advertising:** accepted.

18248 ■ Good Shepherd K-9 Rescue
c/o Karen A. Frank
PO Box 1291
Janesville, WI 53547
Ph: (608)868-2050
Fax: (608)868-2050
Contact: Karen Frank, Pres.
Founded: 2001. **Members:** 4. **Membership Dues:** $10 (annual). **Staff:** 4. **Regional Groups:** 1. **State Groups:** 1. **Local Groups:** 1. **Local.** Dedicated to saving and finding good homes for unwanted, abused or homeless purebred German Shepherd dogs; seeks to educate the public on the breed and responsibility of owning a German Shepherd; conducts fundraisers, training and educational activities.

18249 ■ Green-Rock Audubon Society
c/o Neil Deupree, Pres.
419 S Franklin St.
Janesville, WI 53545
Ph: (608)752-8342
E-mail: deupreen@inwave.com
Contact: Neil Deupree, Pres.
Local. Environmental conservation. Works to protect the environment, especially wildlife and its habitat through education, activism, advocacy, and conservancy.

18250 ■ Janesville Area Rental Property Association
PO Box 1061
Janesville, WI 53547-1061
Ph: (608)757-1610
E-mail: dandtrentals@sbcglobal.net
URL: http://www.jarpa.org
Contact: Dale Hicks, Pres.
Founded: 1979. **Members:** 44. **Membership Dues:** $200 (annual). **State Groups:** 1. **Local.** Landlords of rental properties, mainly residential. Provides services and training for members. **Affiliated With:** Wisconsin Apartment Association. **Formerly:** (2004) Janesville Area Apartment Association. **Publications:** *For the Record/WAA News*, monthly. Newsletter. Contains local information/state news. **Price:** free to members. **Circulation:** 100. **Advertising:** accepted. **Conventions/Meetings:** monthly general assembly, with speakers, seminars, and social events - 3rd Thursday, Janesville, WI.

18251 ■ Janesville Figure Skating Club
1610 N Lexington Dr.
Janesville, WI 53545
E-mail: debtatroe@yahoo.com
URL: National Affiliate–www.usfigureskating.org
Contact: Deb Tatroe, Contact
Local. Provides programs to encourage participation and achievement in the sport of figure skating on ice.

Defines and maintains uniform standards of skating proficiency. Organizes and sponsors competitions and exhibitions for the purpose of stimulating interest in figure skating. **Affiliated With:** United States Figure Skating Association.

18252 ■ Janesville Masonic Center
2322 E. Milwaukee St.
Janesville, WI 53545
Ph: (608)752-3098
Local.

18253 ■ Janesville Noon Kiwanis Club
PO Box 51
Janesville, WI 53547-0051
Free: (877)479-4493
E-mail: info@janesvillekiwanis.org
URL: http://janesvillekiwanis.org
Contact: Tom Waller, Pres.
Local.

18254 ■ Junior Achievement, Rock County
c/o Shelly Stefanczyk, District Dir.
PO Box 85
Janesville, WI 53547-0085
Ph: (608)754-8760
Fax: (608)754-8762
E-mail: jarockdir@sbcglobal.net
URL: http://rockcounty.ja.org
Contact: Shelly Stefanczyk, District Dir.
Local. Affiliated With: Junior Achievement.

18255 ■ League of Women Voters of Janesville
PO Box 8064
Janesville, WI 53547-8064
Ph: (608)868-9180
E-mail: lwv@lwvjvl.org
URL: http://www.3dccc.com/LWV
Contact: Ethel Himmel, Pres.
Local. Encourages the active participation of citizens in government. Influences public policy through education and advocacy.

18256 ■ Mentoring Moms
c/o Phyllis B. Baxter
2020 E Milwaukee St.
Janesville, WI 53545
Ph: (608)754-0197
Fax: (608)314-9009
Contact: Phyllis Baxter, Dir.
Founded: 2000. **Staff:** 3.

18257 ■ National Federation of the Blind, Rock County Chapter
c/o Jennifer Wenzel, Pres.
2502 Elizabeth St.
Janesville, WI 53545
Ph: (608)754-4785
E-mail: rockcounty@nfbwis.org
URL: http://www.nfbwis.org
Contact: Jennifer Wenzel, Pres.
Local. Works to help blind persons achieve self-confidence and self-respect. Acts as a vehicle for collective self-expression by the blind. Provides education, information and referral services, scholarships, literature, and publications about blindness.

18258 ■ National Federation of the Blind of Wisconsin
2502 Elizabeth St.
Janesville, WI 53548
Ph: (608)758-4800
E-mail: president@nfbwis.org
URL: http://www.nfbwis.org
Contact: Dan Wenzel, Pres.
State. Works to help blind persons achieve self-confidence and self-respect. Acts as a vehicle for collective self-expression by the blind. Provides education, information and referral services, scholarships, literature, and publications about blindness.

18259 ■ Phi Theta Kappa, Beta Mu Chi Chapter - University of Wisconsin-Rock County
c/o Linda Reinhardt
2909 Kellogg Ave.
Janesville, WI 53546
Ph: (608)758-6535
E-mail: lreinhar@uwc.edu
URL: http://www.ptk.org/directories/chapters/WI/22253-1.htm
Contact: Linda Reinhardt, Advisor
Local.

18260 ■ Rock County Historical Society
PO Box 8096
Janesville, WI 53547-8096
Ph: (608)756-4509
E-mail: rchs@rchs.us
URL: http://www.rchs.us
Contact: Melissa de Bie, Contact
Founded: 1948. **Members:** 650. **Membership Dues:** student, $5 (annual) • senior individual, $15 (annual) • individual, $25 (annual) • household, $45 (annual) • patron, $100 (annual) • benefactor, $250 (annual) • corporate, $500 (annual) • life, $1,000. **Staff:** 9. **Budget:** $300,000. **Local.** Individuals in southern Wisconsin interested in history and genealogy. Preserves artifacts and disseminates knowledge of area history. Sponsors the Tallman Arts Festival; offers annual Historic House Tour, regular guided tours at the 1857 Lincoln-Tallman Restorations, and exhibits and programs at the Helen Jeffris Wood Museum Center. **Libraries: Type:** reference. **Holdings:** 3,000; archival material, books, papers, photographs. **Subjects:** local history, genealogy, business, industry, school and public records. **Publications:** *Rock County Recorder*, quarterly. Newsletter. **Price:** included in membership dues. **Circulation:** 650. **Conventions/Meetings:** periodic meeting (exhibits).

18261 ■ Rock Green Realtors Association
4451 Woodgate Dr., Unit E
Janesville, WI 53546
Ph: (608)755-4854
Fax: (608)755-4843
E-mail: mls@rockgreenhomes.com
URL: http://rockgreenrealtors.com
Contact: Lee Kessler, Exec. Officer
Local. Strives to develop real estate business practices. Advocates the right to own, use and transfer real property. Provides a facility for professional development, research and exchange of information among members and to the general public. **Affiliated With:** National Association of Realtors.

18262 ■ Rock River Valley Pheasants Forever
c/o Jeff Jacoby
5637 W Miles Rd.
Janesville, WI 53545
E-mail: dstelter@ticon.net
URL: http://www.rockrivervalleypf.com
Contact: Jeff Jacoby, Contact
Local. Affiliated With: Pheasants Forever.

18263 ■ Ruffed Grouse Society, Blackhawk Area Chapter
c/o Ronald Stegeman
414 Winnebago Dr.
Janesville, WI 53545
Ph: (608)755-5702
E-mail: stegeman5@aol.com
URL: National Affiliate–www.ruffedgrousesociety.org
Contact: Ronald Stegeman, Contact
Local. Affiliated With: Ruffed Grouse Society.

18264 ■ South Central Wisconsin Builders Association
c/o Carol Engebretson
PO Box 563
Janesville, WI 53547-0563
Ph: (608)752-8075
Fax: (608)752-7721
E-mail: scwba@inwave.com
URL: http://www.scwbaonline.com
Contact: Carol Engebretson, Exec. Officer
Local. Single and multifamily home builders, commercial builders, and others associated with the building industry. **Affiliated With:** National Association of Home Builders. **Formerly:** (2005) South Central Wisconsin Building Authority.

18265 ■ Tri City REACT
833 Cornelia St.
Janesville, WI 53545
Ph: (608)752-4547
E-mail: 4365@wireact.org
URL: http://www.reactintl.org/teaminfo/usa_teams/teams-uswi.htm
Contact: Mark Fry, Pres.
Local. Trained communication experts and professional volunteers. Provides volunteer public service and emergency communications through the use of radios (Citizen Band, General Mobile Radio Service, UHF and HAM). Coordinates with radio industries and government on safety communication matters and supports charitable activities and community organizations.

18266 ■ United Way of North Rock County
205 N Main St., Ste.101
Janesville, WI 53545-3062
Ph: (608)757-3040
Fax: (608)757-3055
E-mail: gsmith@unitedwayjanesville.org
URL: http://www.unitedwayjanesville.org
Contact: Gary L. Smith, Pres.
Founded: 1943. **Members:** 41. **Staff:** 7. **Budget:** $2,020,000. **Local.** Conducts charitable activities.

18267 ■ Wisconsin Collectors Association
PO Box 816
Janesville, WI 53547
Ph: (608)754-4425
Fax: (608)754-0637
Free: (800)354-6951
Contact: Denis Donahue, Gen.Mgr.
State. An association of Wisconsin Licensed Collection Agency.

18268 ■ Wisconsin School-Age Care Alliance
c/o Stacy Randall
WCCIP
813 Princeton Rd.
Janesville, WI 53546
Ph: (608)758-8721
Fax: (608)758-8721
E-mail: stacyrandall@prodigy.net
URL: National Affiliate–www.nsaca.org
Local. Affiliated With: National AfterSchool Association.

18269 ■ Wisconsin State Grange
25 S Martin Dr.
Janesville, WI 53545
Ph: (608)756-0545
E-mail: al_arner@ticon.net
URL: National Affiliate–www.nationalgrange.org
Contact: Alan Arner, Master
State. Rural family service organization with a special interest in agriculture. Promotes mission and goals through legislative, social, educational, community service, youth, and member services programs. **Affiliated With:** National Grange.

Jefferson

18270 ■ American Legion, Reinhardt-Windl Post 164
214 Hillebrandt Dr.
Jefferson, WI 53549
Ph: (608)745-1090
Fax: (608)745-0179
URL: National Affiliate–www.legion.org
Local. Affiliated With: American Legion.

18271 ■ Jefferson Chamber of Commerce
108 S Main St.
Jefferson, WI 53549-1717
Ph: (920)674-4511
Fax: (920)674-1499
E-mail: coc@jefnet.com
URL: http://www.jeffersonchamberwi.com
Contact: Janet Werner, Exec.Dir.
Local. Promotes business and community development in Jefferson, WI area.

18272 ■ Jefferson County Literacy Council (JCLC)
c/o Jill Ottow, Exec.Dir.
621 W Racine St.
Jefferson, WI 53549
Ph: (920)675-0500
Fax: (920)675-0510
E-mail: info@jclc.us
URL: http://www.jclc.us
Contact: Jill Ottow, Exec.Dir.
Founded: 1996. **Members:** 50. **Budget:** $2,500. **Local**. Works to provide one-on-one training in general literacy or ESL. **Affiliated With:** ProLiteracy Worldwide. **Publications:** *Jefferson County Literacy Council News*. Newsletter. Alternate Formats: online.

18273 ■ National Alliance for the Mentally Ill - Jefferson County, Wisconsin
c/o Kathi Cauley
PO Box 133
Jefferson, WI 53549
Ph: (920)674-8198
URL: http://www.namiwisconsin.org/library/directory
Contact: Kathi Cauley, Contact
Local. Strives to improve the quality of life of children and adults with severe mental illness through support, education, research and advocacy. **Affiliated With:** National Alliance for the Mentally Ill.

18274 ■ Tomorrow's Hope
c/o Barbara Endl
147 W Rockwell St.
Jefferson, WI 53549
Ph: (920)674-8967
Fax: (920)674-9849
URL: http://www.tomorrowshope.org
Contact: Barbara Endl, Contact
Local.

18275 ■ Wisconsin Outdoor Access (WOA)
c/o Steve Frye, VP
PO Box 172
Jefferson, WI 53549
Ph: (920)605-5015
E-mail: ryevok@idcnet.com
URL: http://climbingcentral.com
Members: 140. **Staff:** 3. **State**. Provides environmentally sensible access to climbing areas. **Libraries: Type:** open to the public. **Subjects:** climbing policies. **Awards:** Start Up Grant. **Type:** monetary. **Publications:** Newsletter, periodic. **Price:** free. **Circulation:** 200. **Advertising:** accepted. Alternate Formats: CD-ROM; online. **Conventions/Meetings:** party.

Johnson Creek

18276 ■ Continental Trucking Association
321 N Watertown St.
Johnson Creek, WI 53038
Ph: (920)699-5010
Local.

18277 ■ Johnson Creek Area Chamber of Commerce
PO Box 238
Johnson Creek, WI 53038-0527
Ph: (920)699-2296
Contact: Steve Meloy, Pres.
Local.

Junction City

18278 ■ American Legion, Furo-Heinen Post 281
c/o Leroy Wanta
PO Box 114
Junction City, WI 54443
Ph: (608)745-1090
Fax: (608)745-0179
URL: National Affiliate–www.legion.org
Contact: Leroy Wanta, Contact
Local. Affiliated With: American Legion.

Juneau

18279 ■ American Legion, Hustisford Memorial Post 420
c/o Randy L. Nehls
N 2903 County Rd. Dj
Juneau, WI 53039
Ph: (608)745-1090
Fax: (608)745-0179
URL: National Affiliate–www.legion.org
Contact: Randy L. Nehls, Contact
Local. Affiliated With: American Legion.

18280 ■ American Legion, Juneau Post 15
162 E Oak St.
Juneau, WI 53039
Ph: (608)745-1090
Fax: (608)745-0179
URL: National Affiliate–www.legion.org
Local. Affiliated With: American Legion.

18281 ■ Dodge County Dairy Testing
PO Box 122
Juneau, WI 53039
Ph: (920)386-2637
Contact: Jim Schoenike, Mgr.
Founded: 1975. **Members:** 30. **Budget:** $12,000. **Local**. Farmers and agribusiness people united to promote dairy products. Sponsors annual Farm Dairy Brunch. **Formerly:** (2005) Dodge County Dairy Promotion.

18282 ■ Juneau Chamber of Commerce
PO Box 4
Juneau, WI 53039
Ph: (920)386-3359
E-mail: juneau@juneauwi.org
URL: http://www.juneauwi.org
Contact: Gretchen Last, Pres.
Local. Promotes business and community development in Juneau, WI area.

18283 ■ Wooden Canoe Heritage Association, Wisconsin
c/o Brian Downey, Pres.
Galleria Cabinet & Wooden Boat Works
N 3183 Hwy. 26
Juneau, WI 53039
Ph: (920)696-3526
E-mail: brian@benchmarkdrives.com
URL: National Affiliate–www.wcha.org
Contact: Brian Downey, Pres.
State. Affiliated With: Wooden Canoe Heritage Association.

Kaukauna

18284 ■ American Ex-Prisoners of War, Northeastern Wisconsin Chapter
c/o Milford Roehrborn
N2401 Co. U
Kaukauna, WI 54130
Ph: (920)766-3227
URL: National Affiliate–www.axpow.org
Local. Affiliated With: American Ex-Prisoners of War.

18285 ■ American Legion, Kaukauna Post 41
PO Box 227
Kaukauna, WI 54130
Ph: (608)745-1090
Fax: (608)745-0179
URL: National Affiliate–www.legion.org
Local. Affiliated With: American Legion.

18286 ■ Freedom Business Association
N3989 Washington Ave.
Kaukauna, WI 54130-7557
Local.

18287 ■ Heart of the Valley Chamber of Commerce
101 E Wisconsin Ave.
Kaukauna, WI 54130-2153
Ph: (920)766-1616
Fax: (920)766-5504
E-mail: bbeckman@heartofthevalleychamber.com
URL: http://www.heartofthevalleychamber.com
Contact: Bobbie Beckman, Exec.Dir.
Founded: 1927. **Local**.

18288 ■ Kiwanis Club of Kaukauna
c/o Jon Olson, Pres.
116 1/2 E 5th St.
Kaukauna, WI 54130
Ph: (920)419-3220
URL: http://kc_kau.tripod.com
Contact: Jon Olson, Pres.
Local.

18289 ■ United Brotherhood of Carpenters and Joiners of America, Northern Wisconsin Regional Council of Carpenters 4183 (NWRCC)
N2216 Bodde Rd.
Kaukauna, WI 54130
Ph: (920)996-2300
Fax: (920)996-2308
E-mail: team1@nwrcc.org
URL: http://www.nwrcc.org
Contact: James E. Moore, Exec.Sec.-Treas.
Regional. Affiliated With: United Brotherhood of Carpenters and Joiners of America.

Kendall

18290 ■ American Legion, Wisconsin Post 309
c/o William J. Schriver
414 Medbury St.
Kendall, WI 54638
Ph: (608)745-1090
Fax: (608)745-0179
URL: National Affiliate–www.legion.org
Contact: William J. Schriver, Contact
Local. Affiliated With: American Legion.

18291 ■ Kendall Lions Club
c/o Allen Vlasak, Pres.
30438 Ostrich Rd.
Kendall, WI 54638
Ph: (608)463-7242
E-mail: ahvlasak@mwt.net
URL: http://www.md27d2.org
Contact: Allen Vlasak, Pres.
Local. Affiliated With: Lions Clubs International.

Kennan

18292 ■ American Legion, Ray-S.-Neilson-John-H.-Winter Post 362
W 10268 Lawrence St.
Kennan, WI 54537
Ph: (608)745-1090
Fax: (608)745-0179
URL: National Affiliate–www.legion.org
Local. Affiliated With: American Legion.

Kenosha

18293 ■ Alcohol and Other Drugs Council of Kenosha County
611 56th St., Ste.200
Kenosha, WI 53140-3667
Ph: (262)658-8166
E-mail: kenosha.wi@ncadd.org
URL: National Affiliate–www.ncadd.org
Affiliated With: National Council on Alcoholism and Drug Dependence.

18294 ■ American Legion, Kenosha-Paul-Herrick Post 21
504 58th St.
Kenosha, WI 53140
Ph: (414)657-7464
Fax: (608)745-0179
URL: National Affiliate–www.legion.org
Local. Affiliated With: American Legion.

18295 ■ American Society for Quality, Racine-Kenosha-Walworth Section 1204
c/o Dave Prins, Chm.
5307 95th Ave.
Kenosha, WI 53144
E-mail: dprins@execpc.com
URL: http://members.busynet.net/asq1204
Contact: Dave Prins, Chm.
Local. Advances learning, quality improvement and knowledge exchange to improve business results and to create better workplaces and communities worldwide. Provides a forum for information exchange, professional development and continuous learning in the science of quality. **Affiliated With:** American Society for Quality.

18296 ■ American Welding Society, Racine Kenosha Section 132
c/o David Henry, Chm.
Rockford Ind. Welding Sup
4719 70th Ave.
Kenosha, WI 53144
Ph: (262)635-9000
Fax: (262)653-9100
E-mail: dhenry@riws.com
URL: National Affiliate–www.aws.org
Local. Professional engineering society in the field of welding. **Affiliated With:** American Welding Society.

18297 ■ Belle City Beemers 20/20 Riders No. 201
c/o Nicole Moss, Ed.
1368 Sheridan Rd.
Kenosha, WI 53140
Ph: (262)551-9305
E-mail: nsmoss@wi.rr.com
URL: National Affiliate–www.bmwmoa.org
Contact: Nicole Moss, Ed.
Membership Dues: individual, $10. **Local.** BMW motorcycle owners organized for pleasure, recreation, safety, and dissemination of information concerning BMW motorcycles. **Awards:** High Mileage. **Frequency:** annual. **Type:** monetary. **Recipient:** motorcycle tire. **Affiliated With:** BMW Motorcycle Owners of America.

18298 ■ Girl Scout Council of Kenosha County
2303 37th St.
Kenosha, WI 53140
Ph: (262)657-7102
Fax: (262)657-7104
Free: (800)834-5440
E-mail: gscout@kenoshagirlscouts.org
URL: http://www.kenoshagirlscouts.org
Contact: Dan Hartstern, Pres.
Local. Young girls and adult volunteers, corporate, government and individual supporters. Strives to develop potential and leadership skills among its members. Conducts trainings, educational programs and outdoor activities.

18299 ■ Kenosha Aikikai
4211 Green Bay Rd.
Kenosha, WI 53144
Ph: (262)637-1476
E-mail: kenosha-aikikai@earthlink.net
URL: http://home.earthlink.net/~kenosha-aikikai
Contact: M. Rock-Lazo, Instructor
Local. Affiliated With: United States Aikido Federation.

18300 ■ Kenosha Area Chamber of Commerce
PO Box 518
Kenosha, WI 53140
Ph: (262)654-1234
Fax: (262)654-4655
E-mail: info@kenoshaareachamber.com
URL: http://www.kenoshaareachamber.com
Contact: Cory Ann St. Marie-Carls, Exec.Dir.
Founded: 1916. **Local.**

18301 ■ Kenosha County RSVP
c/o Darleen R. Coleman, Dir.
7730 Sheridan Rd.
Kenosha, WI 53143
Ph: (262)658-3508
Fax: (262)658-2263
E-mail: kenosharsvp@mcleodusa.net
URL: http://www.kafasi.org
Contact: Darleen R. Coleman, Dir.
Local. Affiliated With: Retired and Senior Volunteer Program.

18302 ■ Kenosha History Center (KCHS)
220 51st Pl.
Kenosha, WI 53140
Ph: (262)654-5770
Fax: (262)654-1730
E-mail: kchs@acronet.net
URL: http://www.kenoshahistorycenter.org
Contact: Tom Schleif, Exec.Dir.
Founded: 1878. **Members:** 600. **Membership Dues:** senior, $15 (annual) • individual, $20 (annual) • family, $30 (annual) • homesteader, $100 (annual) • settler, $250 (annual) • lighthouse keeper, $500 (annual) • rambler, $1,000 (annual) • ambassador, $5,000 (annual). **Staff:** 5. **Budget:** $200,000. **Local.** Individuals interested in the history of Kenosha County, WI. Provides educational programs for area schools. Operates museum and archives of local history. **Libraries: Type:** reference. **Holdings:** 500; books, maps, photographs. **Subjects:** local history. **Awards:** Award of Merit. **Frequency:** annual. **Type:** recognition. **Recipient:** for significant contribution to preserving Kenosha County's history. **Committees:** Southport Lighthouse Preservation. **Affiliated With:** Wisconsin Historical Society. **Publications:** *Kenosha: From Pioneer Village to Modern City*. Book. Includes history of Kenosha 1835-1935. • *Kenosha: Historical Sketches* • *Kenosha Kaleidoscope* • *Lighthouse: A History of the Lighthouse at Southport, WI* • *The Photographs of Louis Thiers*. Book • *Southport Newsletter*, quarterly • *Time Traveler*, periodic. Pamphlet. **Conventions/Meetings:** annual Membership Meeting, election of directors, presentation of award of merit - always October in Kenosha, WI.

18303 ■ Kenosha Realtors Association (KRA)
7347 57th Ave.
Kenosha, WI 53142
Ph: (262)942-0592
Fax: (262)942-0940
URL: http://www.krainc.com
Contact: Janet Stroud, Associate Exec.
Local.

18304 ■ National Active and Retired Federal Employees Association - Kenosha 1436
2130 22nd Ave.
Kenosha, WI 53143-1707
Ph: (262)551-7589
URL: National Affiliate–www.narfe.org
Contact: James H. Moldenauer, Contact
Local. Protects the retirement future of employees through education. Informs members on issues affecting the retirement. **Affiliated With:** National Association of Retired Federal Employees.

18305 ■ National Alliance for the Mentally Ill - Kenosha
c/o Richard Guenther, Co-Pres.
PO Box 631
Kenosha, WI 53141
Ph: (262)652-3606
URL: http://www.namiwisconsin.org/library/directory
Contact: Richard Guenther, Co-Pres.
Local. Strives to improve the quality of life of children and adults with severe mental illness through support, education, research and advocacy. **Affiliated With:** National Alliance for the Mentally Ill.

18306 ■ Navy Club of Kenosha - Ship No. 40
5125 41st St.
Kenosha, WI 53144
Ph: (262)654-0083
URL: National Affiliate–www.navyclubusa.org
Contact: Thomas A. Fredericksen, Commander
Local. Represents individuals who are, or have been, in the active service of the U.S. Navy, Naval Reserve, Marine Corps, Marine Corps Reserve, and Coast Guard. Promotes and encourages further public interest in the U.S. Navy and its history. Upholds the spirit and ideals of the U.S. Navy. Acts as a public forum for members' views on national defense. Assists the Navy Recruiting Command whenever and wherever possible. Conducts charitable activities. **Affiliated With:** Navy Club of the United States of America.

18307 ■ Phi Theta Kappa, Alpha Xi Iota Chapter - Gateway Technical College
c/o Bernard O'Connell
3520 30th Ave.
Kenosha, WI 53142-1690
Ph: (262)564-3066
E-mail: oconnellb@gtc.edu
URL: http://www.ptk.org/directories/chapters/WI/4180-1.htm
Contact: Bernard O'Connell, Advisor
Local.

18308 ■ Psi Chi, National Honor Society in Psychology - Carthage College
c/o Dept. of Psychology
2001 Alford Park Dr.
Kenosha, WI 53140
Ph: (262)551-5838 (262)551-5801
Fax: (262)551-6208
E-mail: lcameron@carthage.edu
URL: National Affiliate–www.psichi.org
Local. Affiliated With: Psi Chi, National Honor Society in Psychology.

18309 ■ Psi Chi, National Honor Society in Psychology - University of Wisconsin-Parkside
c/o Dept. of Psychology
PO Box 2000
Kenosha, WI 53141-2000
Ph: (262)595-2658 (262)595-2313
Fax: (262)595-2602
E-mail: edward.conrad@uwp.edu
URL: National Affiliate–www.psichi.org
Local. Affiliated With: Psi Chi, National Honor Society in Psychology.

18310 ■ Racine-Kenosha AIFA
c/o Michael Leonardelli
2215 63rd St.
Kenosha, WI 53143-4351
Ph: (262)654-0427
Fax: (262)654-3311
E-mail: mleonardelli@ruralins.com
URL: http://www.rkaifa.org
Contact: Michael Leonardelli, Contact
Local. Represents the interests of insurance and financial advisors. Advocates for a positive legislative and regulatory environment. Enhances business and professional skills of members. **Affiliated With:** National Association of Insurance and Financial Advisors.

18311 ■ Society of Physics Students - Carthage College Chapter No. 1015
2001 Alford Park Dr.
Kenosha, WI 53140-1900
Ph: (262)551-5856
Fax: (262)551-6208
E-mail: jmq@carthage.edu
URL: National Affiliate–www.spsnational.org
Local. Offers opportunities for the students to enrich their experiences and skills about physics. Helps students to become professional in the field of physics. **Affiliated With:** Society of Physics Students.

18312 ■ Sons of Norway, Hafrsfjord Lodge 5-206
c/o Greg D. Rismoen, Pres.
3206 13th Pl.
Kenosha, WI 53144-3061
Ph: (262)552-8272
E-mail: gregris@aol.com
URL: National Affiliate–www.sofn.com
Contact: Greg D. Rismoen, Pres.
Local. **Affiliated With:** Sons of Norway.

18313 ■ United Way of Kenosha County
3601 30th Ave., Ste.202
Kenosha, WI 53144
Ph: (262)658-4104
Fax: (262)658-2005
E-mail: unitedway@kenoshaunitedway.org
URL: http://www.kenoshaunitedway.org
Contact: Peter Walcott, Exec.Dir.
Local. Seeks to raise funds for local human services conducting company-wide employee campaigns and by encouraging corporate and individual contributions, and to distribute funds to not-for-profit agencies, based upon local priorities and agencies' needs. **Affiliated With:** United Way of America. **Conventions/Meetings:** annual Day of Caring - meeting.

18314 ■ Wisconsin Health Care Association, District 1
c/o Dave Egan, Pres.
The Clairidge House
1519 60th St.
Kenosha, WI 53140
Ph: (262)656-7500
URL: http://www.whca.com
Contact: Dave Egan, Pres.
Local. Promotes professionalism and ethical behavior of individuals providing long-term care delivery for patients and for the general public. Provides information, education and administrative tools to enhance the quality of long-term care. Improves the standards of service and administration of member nursing homes. **Affiliated With:** American Health Care Association; Wisconsin Health Care Association.

Keshena

18315 ■ American Legion, Menominee Post 497
PO Box 508
Keshena, WI 54135
Ph: (608)745-1090
Fax: (608)745-0179
URL: National Affiliate–www.legion.org
Local. **Affiliated With:** American Legion.

Kewaskum

18316 ■ American Legion, Wisconsin Post 384
c/o Robert G. Romaine
1538 Fond Du Lac Ave., No. 650
Kewaskum, WI 53040
Ph: (414)626-2420
Fax: (608)745-0179
URL: National Affiliate–www.legion.org
Contact: Robert G. Romaine, Contact
Local. **Affiliated With:** American Legion.

18317 ■ Kewaskum Lions Club
PO Box 642
Kewaskum, WI 53040
E-mail: president@kewaskumlionsclub.org
URL: http://www.kewaskumlionsclub.org
Contact: Brian Kleinke, Pres.
Local. **Affiliated With:** Lions Clubs International.

Kewaunee

18318 ■ American Legion, Kewaunee Post 29
1113 Juneau St.
Kewaunee, WI 54216
Ph: (608)745-1090
Fax: (608)745-0179
URL: National Affiliate–www.legion.org
Local. **Affiliated With:** American Legion.

18319 ■ Green Bay Rackers Homebrewing Club
c/o Michael Conard
1021 Juneau St.
Kewaunee, WI 54216-1127
Ph: (920)388-3747
URL: http://www.rackers.org
Founded: 1982. **Members:** 55. **Local**.

18320 ■ Kewaunee Area Chamber of Commerce (KCC)
PO Box 243
Kewaunee, WI 54216
Ph: (920)388-4822 (920)388-0444
Fax: (920)388-4901
Free: (800)666-8214
E-mail: kewchamber@itol.com
URL: http://www.kewaunee.org
Contact: April Dahl, Pres.
Membership Dues: business (based on number of employees), $250-$500 (annual) • seasonal, $100 (annual) • self-employed in home business, $75 (annual) • non-profit, $50 (annual) • friend, $30 (annual) • professional, $150 (annual). **Local**. Seeks to provide the leadership necessary to promote Kewaunee's tourism, business and industrial development, while preserving its maritime heritage. Sponsors Trout Festival and Parade.

18321 ■ Organic Crop Improvement Association, Northeast Wisconsin
c/o Karen Kinstetter
N5364 Hemlock Ln.
Kewaunee, WI 54216
Ph: (920)388-4369
Fax: (920)388-3408
E-mail: kkinstetter@itol.com
URL: National Affiliate–www.ocia.org
Contact: Karen Kinstetter, Contact
Local. **Affiliated With:** Organic Crop Improvement Association.

Kiel

18322 ■ Kiel Area Association of Commerce
PO Box 44
Kiel, WI 53042-0044
Ph: (920)894-4638
E-mail: secretary@kielwi.org
URL: http://www.kielwi.org
Contact: Linda Bauman, Sec.
Local. Promotes business and community development in Kiel, WI.

18323 ■ Sheboygan Space Society
728 Center St.
Kiel, WI 53042
Ph: (920)894-2376
E-mail: willf@tcei.com
URL: http://www.tcei.com/sss
Contact: Wilbert G. Foerster, Contact
Local. Works for the creation of a spacefaring civilization. Encourages the establishment of self-sustaining human settlements in space. Promotes large-scale industrialization and private enterprise in space.

Kimberly

18324 ■ American Legion, Wisconsin Post 60
c/o William Verhagen
515 W Kimberly Ave.
Kimberly, WI 54136
Ph: (608)745-1090
Fax: (608)745-0179
URL: National Affiliate–www.legion.org
Contact: William Verhagen, Contact
Local. **Affiliated With:** American Legion.

18325 ■ Wisconsin Association of School Nurses (WASN)
c/o Cindy Vandenberg, Pres.
Kimberly Area School District
217 E Kimberly Ave.
Kimberly, WI 54136
Ph: (920)788-7900
E-mail: cvandenberg@kimberly.k12.wi.us
URL: http://www.wisconsinschoolnurses.org
Contact: Cindy Vandenberg, Pres.
State. Advances the delivery of professional school health services. Increases the awareness of students on the necessity of health and learning. Improves the health of children by developing school nursing practices. **Affiliated With:** National Association of School Nurses.

King

18326 ■ American Legion, Shipley-Robinson-Moen-Will Post 161
PO Box 237
King, WI 54946
Ph: (608)745-1090
Fax: (608)745-0179
URL: National Affiliate–www.legion.org
Local. **Affiliated With:** American Legion.

Kingston

18327 ■ American Legion, Wisconsin Post 395
c/o George Thompson
PO Box 2
Kingston, WI 53939
Ph: (608)745-1090
Fax: (608)745-0179
URL: National Affiliate–www.legion.org
Contact: George Thompson, Contact
Local. **Affiliated With:** American Legion.

Kohler

18328 ■ American Society for Quality, Winnebago Section 1206
PO Box 272
Kohler, WI 53044-0272
Ph: (920)225-6127
URL: http://www.asqsection1206.org
Contact: Ron Jochimsen, Chm.
Local. Advances learning, quality improvement and knowledge exchange to improve business results and to create better workplaces and communities worldwide. Provides a forum for information exchange, professional development and continuous learning in the science of quality. **Affiliated With:** American Society for Quality.

18329 ■ Ruffed Grouse Society, Lake Shore Chapter
c/o Dave Lukaszewski
127 Greenview Ct.
Kohler, WI 53044

Ph: (920)467-0682
URL: National Affiliate–www.ruffedgrousesociety.org
Contact: Dave Lukaszewski, Contact
Local. **Affiliated With:** Ruffed Grouse Society.

Krakow

18330 ■ Northeast Wisconsin District Nurses Association - No. 9
N4821 Center St.
Krakow, WI 54137
Ph: (920)899-3461
E-mail: pjzeeman@netnet.net
URL: http://www.wisconsinnurses.org
Contact: Julie Zeeman, Pres.
Local. Works to advance the nursing profession. Seeks to meet the needs of nurses and health care consumers. Fosters high standards of nursing practice. Promotes the economic and general welfare of nurses in the workplace. **Affiliated With:** American Nurses Association; Wisconsin Nurses' Association.

La Crosse

18331 ■ Alzheimer's Association of Greater WI, LaCrosse Regional Office
116 Fifth Ave. S, Ste.421
La Crosse, WI 54601
Ph: (608)784-5011
Fax: (608)784-4428
Free: (800)272-3900
E-mail: laura.moriarty@alz.org
URL: National Affiliate–www.alz.org
Contact: Mary Ihle, Contact
Local. Family members of sufferers of Alzheimer's disease. Combats Alzheimer's disease and related disorders. (Alzheimer's disease is a progressive, degenerative brain disease in which changes occur in the central nervous system and outer region of the brain causing memory loss and other changes in thought, personality, and behavior.) Promotes research to find the cause, treatment, and cure for the disease. **Affiliated With:** Alzheimer's Association.

18332 ■ American Chemical Society, Lacrosse-Winona Section
c/o Curtis J. Czerwinski, Chm.
Univ. of Wisconsin, Dept. of Chemistry
1725 State St.
La Crosse, WI 54601-3742
Ph: (608)785-8701
Fax: (608)785-8281
E-mail: czerwins.curt@uwlax.edu
URL: National Affiliate–acswebcontent.acs.org
Contact: Curtis J. Czerwinski, Chm.
Local. Represents the interests of individuals dedicated to the advancement of chemistry in all its branches. Provides opportunities for peer interaction and career development. **Affiliated With:** American Chemical Society.

18333 ■ American Legion, Wisconsin Post 52
c/o Roy L. Vingers
711 6th St. S
La Crosse, WI 54601
Ph: (608)745-1090
Fax: (608)745-0179
URL: National Affiliate–www.legion.org
Contact: Roy L. Vingers, Contact
Local. **Affiliated With:** American Legion.

18334 ■ American Rabbit Breeders Association, Friendly Rabbit of Trempealeau
c/o Linda Wenger, Sec.
1522 Weston Ln.
La Crosse, WI 54601
URL: http://www.geocities.com/wisconsin_state_rba/Local_Clubs.html
Contact: Linda Wenger, Sec.
Local. **Affiliated With:** American Rabbit Breeders Association.

18335 ■ American Red Cross-Scenic Bluffs Chapter
2928 Losey Blvd. S
La Crosse, WI 54601
Ph: (608)788-1000
Fax: (608)787-8507
Free: (800)837-6313
Contact: Jamie Harmon, Comm. Services Specialist
Local.

18336 ■ American Society of Heating, Refrigerating and Air-Conditioning Engineers La Crosse Area Chapter
c/o William Fox, Pres.
3600 Pammel Creek Rd.
La Crosse, WI 54601
Ph: (608)787-2460
E-mail: bfox@trane.com
URL: http://www.ashraelacrosse.org
Contact: William Fox, Pres.
Local. Advances the arts and sciences of heating, ventilation, air-conditioning and refrigeration. Provides a source of technical and educational information, standards and guidelines. Conducts seminars for professional growth. **Affiliated With:** American Society of Heating, Refrigerating and Air-Conditioning Engineers.

18337 ■ Association for Psychological Type - LaCrosse
c/o Gary Gilmore
Univ. of Wisconsin
201 Mitchell Hall
La Crosse, WI 54601
Ph: (608)785-8163
Fax: (608)785-6792
E-mail: gilmore@mail.uwlax.edu
URL: National Affiliate–www.aptinternational.org
Contact: Gary Gilmore, Contact
Local. Promotes the practical application and ethical use of psychological type. Provides members with opportunities for continuous learning, sharing experiences and creating understanding and knowledge through research. **Affiliated With:** Association for Psychological Type.

18338 ■ Automatic Transmission Rebuilders Association, Midwest Chapter
c/o Brad Benrud, Pres.
N 2995 Smith Valley
La Crosse, WI 54601
Ph: (608)781-9900
E-mail: allentrans@charter.net
URL: National Affiliate–www.atra.com
Contact: Brad Benrud, Pres.
Regional. Provides training, support and technical information based on the needs, trends and opportunities of the Transmission/Powertrain industry. Promotes the highest level in ethical business and rebuilding practices for professionals within the industry. **Affiliated With:** Automatic Transmission Rebuilders Association.

18339 ■ Blackhawk Retriever Club (BRC)
c/o Christine Rynearson, Sec.
PO Box 1942
La Crosse, WI 54602-1942
Ph: (608)582-4406
E-mail: eagleseye2222@charter.net
URL: http://www.homestead.com/brc
Contact: Christine Rynearson, Sec.
Founded: 1956. **Members:** 50. **Membership Dues:** voting, $25 (annual). **Regional**. **Affiliated With:** American Kennel Club. **Conventions/Meetings:** monthly meeting.

18340 ■ Cloudbase Flyers
3507 Lakeshore Dr.
La Crosse, WI 54603
Ph: (507)895-4240
E-mail: nroland@centurytel.net
URL: National Affiliate–www.ushga.org
Local. **Affiliated With:** U.S. Hang Gliding Association.

18341 ■ Coulee Region Audubon Society
c/o Bobbie Wilson, Pres.
PO Box 2573
La Crosse, WI 54602
Ph: (608)788-8831
E-mail: pbwilson@centurytel.net
URL: http://www.couleeaudubon.org
Contact: Bobbie Wilson, Pres.
Local. **Formerly:** (2005) National Audubon Society - Coulee Region.

18342 ■ Coulee Region Orchid Guild
c/o Charles Drake, Pres.
2829 Hamilton St.
La Crosse, WI 54603
Ph: (608)781-7648
E-mail: miaelipebutterbrodt@yahoo.com
URL: http://www.couleeorchids.com
Contact: Mi Ae Butterbrodt, Contact
Local. Professional growers, botanists, hobbyists, and others interested in extending the knowledge, production, use, and appreciation of orchids. **Affiliated With:** American Orchid Society.

18343 ■ Coulee Region RSVP
c/o Lynnetta P. Kopp, Exec.Dir.
2025 S Ave., Ste.200
La Crosse, WI 54601
Ph: (608)785-0500
Fax: (608)785-2573
Free: (888)822-1295
E-mail: rsvplax@fflax.net
URL: http://www.rsvplacrosse.org
Contact: Lynnetta P. Kopp, Exec.Dir.
Local. **Affiliated With:** Retired and Senior Volunteer Program.

18344 ■ French Island Lions Club
c/o David Peterson, Pres.
2540 1st Ave. E
La Crosse, WI 54603
Ph: (608)783-0799
URL: http://www.md27d2.org
Contact: David Peterson, Pres.
Local. **Affiliated With:** Lions Clubs International.

18345 ■ Gateway Optometric Society
c/o Ann Wonderling, OD, Pres.
W5224 Knoblock Rd.
La Crosse, WI 54601
Ph: (608)788-4300
Fax: (608)788-4325
E-mail: wonderbama@hotmail.com
URL: http://www.woa-eyes.org
Contact: Ann Wonderling OD, Pres.
Local. Aims to improve the quality, availability and accessibility of eye and vision care. Promotes high standards of patient care. Monitors and promotes legislation concerning the scope of optometric practice and other issues relevant to eye/vision care. **Affiliated With:** American Optometric Association; Wisconsin Optometric Association.

18346 ■ Girl Scouts of Riverland Council
2710 Quarry Rd.
La Crosse, WI 54601-3993
Ph: (608)784-3693
Free: (800)787-2688
E-mail: gscouts@centurytel.net
URL: http://www.gsriverland.com
Contact: Mary Rohrer, Exec.Dir.
Local. Young girls and adult volunteers, corporate, government and individual supporters. Strives to develop potential and leadership skills among its members. Conducts trainings, educational programs and outdoor activities.

18347 ■ International Association of Machinists and Aerospace Workers, District Lodge 66
1307 Market St.
La Crosse, WI 54601

Ph: (608)784-2025
Fax: (608)784-8817
E-mail: districtlodge66@centurytel.net
URL: http://home.centurytel.net/IAMDL66
Contact: Rick Mickschl, Directing Business Representative
Members: 2,000. **Local**. Represents workers. Strives to provide contractors with well-trained and productive employees. **Affiliated With:** International Association of Machinists and Aerospace Workers.

18348 ■ International Association of Machinists and Aerospace Workers, Local Lodge 21
2219 E Ave. S
La Crosse, WI 54601
Ph: (608)788-6575
Fax: (608)788-8182
E-mail: lodge21@centurytel.net
URL: http://home.centurytel.net/IAMDL66/21
Contact: James Urbanek, Sec.-Treas.
Members: 1,798. **Local**. **Affiliated With:** International Association of Machinists and Aerospace Workers.

18349 ■ International Association of Machinists and Aerospace Workers, Local Lodge 1115
1307 Market St.
La Crosse, WI 54601
Ph: (608)784-2025
URL: http://home.centurytel.net/IAMDL66/1115
Contact: Larry Klukas, Pres.
Members: 247. **Local**. **Affiliated With:** International Association of Machinists and Aerospace Workers.

18350 ■ Korean War Veterans Association, West Central Wisconsin Chapter
c/o Edward Jack Adams
PO Box 3423
La Crosse, WI 54602
Ph: (608)788-4850
E-mail: dsnbrn@earthlink.net
URL: National Affiliate–www.kwva.org
Contact: Edward Jack Adams, Contact
Local. **Affiliated With:** Korean War Veterans Association.

18351 ■ La Crosse Area Astronomical Society (LAAS)
c/o Prof. Robert H. Allen, Pres.
Univ. of Wisconsin
Cowley Hall
Physics Dept.
La Crosse, WI 54601
Ph: (608)785-8669
Fax: (608)785-8403
E-mail: allen.robe@uwlax.edu
URL: http://www.uwlax.edu/planetarium
Contact: Prof. Robert H. Allen, Pres.
Founded: 1978. **Members:** 50. **Membership Dues:** full, $15 (annual) • associate, $6 (annual) • student, $10 (annual). **Budget:** $1,000. **Regional Groups:** 1. **Local**. Amateur astronomers and other individuals in West Central Wisconsin. Seeks to promote amateur astronomy. **Affiliated With:** Astronomical League. **Publications:** Newsletter, monthly. **Price:** $15.00 /year for nonmembers; included in membership dues. **Circulation:** 50. **Conventions/Meetings:** monthly meeting, with speakers; videos and telescopic observing sessions.

18352 ■ La Crosse Area Chamber of Commerce
712 Main St.
La Crosse, WI 54601
Ph: (608)784-4880
Fax: (608)784-4919
E-mail: lse_chamber@centurytel.net
URL: http://www.lacrossechamber.com
Contact: Dick Granchalek, Pres.
Members: 800. **Membership Dues:** business (based on number of full time employees), $210-$2,919 • individual (non-business), $114. **Local**. Works to improve the business community and regional economy of La Crosse area. **Committees:** Ambassadors; Business and Student Education; Business Exposition; Cracker Barrel; Government Action; Intercultural Network; Oktoberfest in the Capitol. **Programs:** Member to Member Discount. **Affiliated With:** U.S. Chamber of Commerce. **Publications:** *Chamber Connection*, monthly. Newsletter. Contains member information and chamber events. **Price:** included in membership dues; $15.00 /year for nonmembers. **Circulation:** 1,500. **Advertising:** accepted • Membership Directory, annual. Lists member businesses and organizations including contact information and brief description of services provided. **Price:** $40.00 for nonmembers; $10.00 for members.

18353 ■ La Crosse Area Convention and Visitors Bureau (LACVB)
410 Veterans Memorial Dr.
La Crosse, WI 54601
Ph: (608)782-2366
Fax: (608)782-4082
Free: (800)658-9424
E-mail: info@explorelacrosse.com
URL: http://www.explorelacrosse.com
Contact: David Clements, Exec.Dir.
Local.

18354 ■ La Crosse Area Development Corporation (LADCO)
c/o James P. Hill, Exec.Dir.
712 Main St.
La Crosse, WI 54601
Ph: (608)784-5488
Fax: (608)784-5408
Free: (888)208-0698
E-mail: ladco@centurytel.net
URL: http://www.ladcoweb.org
Contact: James P. Hill, Exec.Dir.
Founded: 1971. **Members:** 135. **Staff:** 3. **Budget:** $160,000. **Local**. Offers assistance with site search/ analysis, financial program coordination, data for market comparisons, new small business development, assembly of private/public sector project team. **Awards:** Coulee Region Entrepreneurial Award. **Frequency:** annual. **Type:** monetary. **Recipient:** for a business plan; evaluated on feasibility, potential for growth, job creation, and marketability • Director's Award. **Frequency:** annual. **Type:** recognition. **Recipient:** for individual who has performed great service to the organization or who is retiring from the Board of Directors • Distinguished Service Award. **Frequency:** annual. **Type:** recognition. **Recipient:** for contributions to the development of the area economy • President's Award. **Frequency:** annual. **Type:** recognition. **Recipient:** for a current, major contribution or accomplishment. **Publications:** *Economic Profile*, biennial. Booklet. Contains demographic and quality of life information for the La Crosse MSA. **Price:** free • *La Crosse County Econowatch*, semiannual. Booklet. Contains detailed information relating to local economic trends. • *The LADCO Link*, monthly. Newsletter. Contains update on corporation activities and projects. **Circulation:** 300. **Conventions/Meetings:** semiannual The Economic Forum - meeting - usually one every spring and one every fall in La Crosse, WI • annual meeting (exhibits) - every November or December in La Crosse, WI.

18355 ■ La Crosse Area Realtors Association (LARA)
111 6th St. S
La Crosse, WI 54601
Ph: (608)785-7744
Fax: (608)785-7742
E-mail: cglocke@larawebsite.com
URL: http://www.larawebsite.com
Contact: Char Glocke, Exec. Officer
Local. Strives to develop real estate business practices. Advocates the right to own, use and transfer real property. Provides a facility for professional development, research and exchange of information among members and to the general public. **Affiliated With:** National Association of Realtors.

18356 ■ La Crosse Builders Exchange
427 Gillette St.
La Crosse, WI 54603
Ph: (608)781-1819
Fax: (608)781-1718
E-mail: sandyb@laxbx.com
URL: http://www.laxbx.com
Contact: Sandy Bakalars, Mgr.
Local. Represents the general contractors, subcontractors, suppliers, manufacturer's representatives and individual firms related to the construction industry. Provides information on construction and building procedures. **Affiliated With:** International Builders Exchange Executives.

18357 ■ La Crosse County Historical Society (LCHS)
PO Box 1272
La Crosse, WI 54602
Ph: (608)782-1980
Fax: (608)793-1359
E-mail: lchs@centurytel.net
URL: http://www.lchsweb.org
Contact: Dr. Carl R. Miller, Exec.Dir.
Founded: 1898. **Members:** 400. **Membership Dues:** basic, $35 (annual) • century, $125 (annual) • heritage, $1,000 (annual) • family, $50 (annual) • patron, $250 (annual) • life, $5,000. **Staff:** 3. **Budget:** $182,000. **Local**. Individuals, families, and businesses. Seeks to preserve, protect, collect, and exhibit writings and artifacts concerning the history of La Crosse County, WI. Sponsors educational programs, ice cream social, and holiday showcase. Operates two museums and a historic house. **Libraries:** **Type:** reference; open to the public. **Holdings:** archival material. **Subjects:** local history. **Awards:** Volunteer of the Year. **Frequency:** annual. **Type:** recognition. **Recipient:** for most number of volunteer hours during the year. **Publications:** *Past, Present, and Future*, quarterly. Newsletter. Writes on historical topics. **Price:** $25.00/year. **Advertising:** accepted. Alternate Formats: online. **Conventions/Meetings:** annual dinner, reopening of Hixon House after complete renovation - always May.

18358 ■ La Crosse Education Association
2020 Caroline St.
La Crosse, WI 54603
Ph: (608)781-5116

18359 ■ La Crosse Kiwanis Club
PO Box 61
La Crosse, WI 54602-0061
Ph: (608)784-2684
Fax: (608)784-8077
E-mail: bethndav@centurytel.net
URL: http://lackiwanis.tripod.com
Local.

18360 ■ La Crosse Lions Club
c/o Art Marson, Pres.
717 S 19th St.
La Crosse, WI 54601
Ph: (608)784-5578
E-mail: marsona@wwtc.edu
URL: http://www.md27d2.org
Contact: Art Marson, Pres.
Local. **Affiliated With:** Lions Clubs International.

18361 ■ La Crosse North Lions Club
c/o Tom Price, Pres.
1025 S 25th St.
La Crosse, WI 54601
Ph: (608)787-6515
E-mail: gurvisl1@yahoo.com
URL: http://www.md27d2.org
Contact: Tom Price, Pres.
Local. **Affiliated With:** Lions Clubs International.

18362 ■ La Crosse Scenic Bluffs Chapter of the American Theatre Organ Society (LCSBCATOS)
c/o Michael Hengelsberg, Pres.
1616 Jackson St.
La Crosse, WI 54601

Ph: (608)784-4976
E-mail: hengelsber@aol.com
URL: http://www.angelfire.com/music3/scenicbluffsatos
Contact: Michael Hengelsberg, Pres.

Local. Aims to restore, preserve and promote the theatre pipe organ and its music. Encourages the youth to learn the instrument. Operates a committee that gathers history and old music from silent film days and information on theatre organists, theaters and organ installations of the silent film era. **Affiliated With:** American Theatre Organ Society.

18363 ■ La Crosse Scenic Bluffs Chapter of the American Theatre Organ Society (LCSBCATOS)
c/o Michael Hengelsberg, Pres.
1616 Jackson St.
La Crosse, WI 54601
Ph: (608)784-4976
E-mail: lacrosseorgans@aol.com
URL: http://www.angelfire.com/music3/scenicbluffsatos
Contact: Michael Hengelsberg, Pres.

Founded: 2001. **Membership Dues:** individual, family, $20 (annual) • donor, $50 (annual) • sponsor, $100 (annual) • mentor, $250 (annual) • student, $10 (annual) • benefactor, $1,000 (annual). **Local. Affiliated With:** American Theatre Organ Society.

18364 ■ La Crosse Velo Club
Smith's Cycling and Fitness
7th cor. State St.
La Crosse, WI 54601
Ph: (608)784-1175
E-mail: cripp71@yahoo.com
URL: http://www.lacrossevelo.com
Contact: Chris Ripp, Pres.

Membership Dues: individual, $15 (annual) • family, $25 (annual). **Local. Affiliated With:** International Mountain Bicycling Association.

18365 ■ Lacrosse Area Communications Consortium (LACC)
c/o John Sarnowski, Pres.
300 4th St. N
La Crosse, WI 54601
Ph: (608)785-9593 (608)783-5321
Fax: (608)789-4808
E-mail: lacc@normicro.com
URL: http://www.la-crosse.wi.us
Contact: John Sarnowski, Pres.

Founded: 1995. **Local.** Exists for the purpose of facilitating the organization and sharing of community-wide information resources through voice, video and/or data technology. Seeks to serve the interests of the citizens, business, public/private institutions and government agencies of the La Crosse area. **Conventions/Meetings:** monthly meeting - always 2nd Tuesday at 7:30 AM.

18366 ■ Military Officers Association of America, La Crosse Chapter
c/o Col. Kenneth Kempf
5337 W Norseman Dr.
La Crosse, WI 54601-2455
Ph: (608)788-6522
E-mail: kenlindakempf@earthlink.net
URL: National Affiliate–www.moaa.org
Contact: Col. Kenneth Kempf, Contact

Local. Affiliated With: Military Officers Association of America.

18367 ■ Mississippi River Regional Planning Commission (MRRPC)
1707 Main St., Ste.240
La Crosse, WI 54601
Ph: (608)785-9396
Fax: (608)785-9394
E-mail: plan@mrrpc.com
URL: http://www.mrrpc.com
Contact: Gregory D. Flogstad, Dir.

Founded: 1964. **Local.**

18368 ■ MOAA Wisconsin Council of Chapters
c/o Lt.Col. Barry Miller
426 22nd St. N
La Crosse, WI 54601-3803
Ph: (608)782-3676
E-mail: miller.barr@uwlax.edu
URL: National Affiliate–www.moaa.org
Contact: Lt.Col. Barry Miller, Contact

State. Affiliated With: Military Officers Association of America.

18369 ■ Mormon Coulee Lions Club
c/o Margaret Lueck, Sec.
2922 S 23rd St.
La Crosse, WI 54601
Ph: (608)788-3739
URL: http://www.md27d2.org
Contact: Frank Moldenhauer, Pres.

Local. Affiliated With: Lions Clubs International.

18370 ■ Mothers Against Drunk Driving, La Crosse County
3307 Meadow Ln. Pl.
La Crosse, WI 54601
Ph: (608)788-2006
E-mail: maddmomlar@aol.com
URL: National Affiliate–www.madd.org

Local. Victims of drunk driving crashes; concerned citizens. Encourages citizen participation in working towards reform of the drunk driving problem and the prevention of underage drinking. Acts as the voice of victims of drunk driving crashes by speaking on their behalf to communities, businesses, and educational groups. **Affiliated With:** Mothers Against Drunk Driving.

18371 ■ Muskies God's Country Chapter
PO Box 1461
La Crosse, WI 54602
Ph: (608)582-4700
E-mail: malibumuskie@peoplepc.com
URL: National Affiliate–www.muskiesinc.org
Contact: Bill Green, Pres.

Local.

18372 ■ NAIFA-Western Wisconsin
505 King St., Ste.124
La Crosse, WI 54601
Ph: (608)793-1400
URL: National Affiliate–www.naifa.org

Local. Represents the interest of insurance and financial advisors. Advocates for a positive legislative and regulatory environment. Enhances business and professional skills of members. **Affiliated With:** National Association of Insurance and Financial Advisors.

18373 ■ National Alliance for the Mentally Ill - La Crosse
c/o Helen Buehler, Co-Pres.
4062 Terrace Dr.
La Crosse, WI 54601-7510
Ph: (608)784-7532
URL: http://www.namiwisconsin.org/library/directory
Contact: Helen Buehler, Co-Pres.

Local. Strives to improve the quality of life of children and adults with severe mental illness through support, education, research and advocacy. **Affiliated With:** National Alliance for the Mentally Ill.

18374 ■ PFLAG La Crosse
PO Box 3655
La Crosse, WI 54602
Ph: (608)787-0466
E-mail: info@pflaflacrosse.org
URL: http://go.to/pflaglacrosse

Local. Affiliated With: Parents, Families, and Friends of Lesbians and Gays.

18375 ■ Phi Theta Kappa, Beta Nu Chi Chapter - Western Wisconsin Technical College
c/o Daniel Rooney
304 Sixth St. N
La Crosse, WI 54601
Ph: (608)785-9200
E-mail: rooneyd@wwtc.edu
URL: http://www.ptk.org/directories/chapters/WI/21583-1.htm
Contact: Daniel Rooney, Advisor

Local.

18376 ■ Ruffed Grouse Society, Coulee Region Chapter
c/o Robert D. Clark
N3762 Scenic Dr.
La Crosse, WI 54601
Ph: (608)781-3497
E-mail: jclark3762@aol.com
URL: National Affiliate–www.ruffedgrousesociety.org
Contact: Robert D. Clark, Contact

Local. Affiliated With: Ruffed Grouse Society.

18377 ■ SCORE La Crosse
712 Main St.
La Crosse, WI 54601
Ph: (608)784-4880
E-mail: scorelax@centurytel.net
URL: National Affiliate–www.score.org

Local. Provides professional guidance, mentoring services and financial assistance to maximize the success of existing and emerging small businesses. **Affiliated With:** SCORE.

18378 ■ Society for Human Resource Management - La Crosse Chapter
c/o Jodi Roesler
PO Box 817
La Crosse, WI 54602
E-mail: kkastan@gundluth.org
Contact: Linda Kastantin, Pres.

Local. Represents the interests of human resource and industrial relations professionals and executives. Promotes the advancement of human resource management.

18379 ■ Trout Unlimited, Coulee Region
c/o Rich Bain, Pres.
2302 Onalaska Ave.
La Crosse, WI 54603-4207
Ph: (608)792-8044
Free: (800)546-4392
E-mail: info@couleeregiontu.org
URL: http://www.couleeregiontu.org
Contact: Rich Bain, Pres.

Local. Affiliated With: Trout Unlimited.

18380 ■ University of Wisconsin - La Crosse Branch Lions Club
c/o Erica Nedland, Pres.
222 S 8th St.
La Crosse, WI 54601
Ph: (608)784-3530
E-mail: nedland01@yahoo.com
URL: http://www.uwlax.edu/uwl%2Dlions
Contact: Erica Nedland, Pres.

Local. Affiliated With: Lions Clubs International.

18381 ■ Western Wisconsin AFL-CIO
1920 Ward Ave., Ste.2
La Crosse, WI 54601-6761
Ph: (608)782-5851
Fax: (608)782-8015
E-mail: hickswi@centurytel.net
URL: http://westernwisconsinaflcio.org
Contact: Mr. Terry L. Hicks, Pres.

Founded: 1897. **Members:** 5,280. **Staff:** 1. **Budget:** $18,000. **State Groups:** 2. **Local Groups:** 3. **For-Profit. Regional.** Organization of labor unions in La Crosse, Monroe, and Vernon Counties, WI representing 8,000 workers. Public and private. **Committees:** Community Services; Dan Hanson; Labor Liaison. **Affiliated With:** AFL-CIO; Minnesota AFL-CIO. **Also Known As:** La Crosse AFL-CIO Council; La Crosse

AFL-CIO Central Labor Council. **Publications:** *Union Herald, Inc.*, monthly. Newspaper. **Price:** $6.00/year. **Circulation:** 5,500. **Advertising:** accepted. Alternate Formats: online. **Conventions/Meetings:** annual Labor Day Rally and Parade, commemoration of Labor Day holiday - always first Monday in September • bimonthly meeting - always 1st and 3rd Thursday • Workers Memorial Day Event - meeting, workers Memorial Day commemoration - always 28th of April.

18382 ■ Wisconsin Chapter of the National Emergency Number Association (WINENA)
c/o Al Blencoe, Pres.
La Crosse County Emergency Services
333 Vine St.
La Crosse, WI 54601
Ph: (608)785-5955
Fax: (608)785-9858
E-mail: blencoe.al@co-la-crosse.wi.us
URL: http://www.winena.org
Contact: Al Blencoe, Pres.
State. Promotes the technical advancement, availability, and implementation of a universal emergency telephone number system. **Affiliated With:** National Emergency Number Association.

18383 ■ Wisconsin Health Information Management Association (WHIMA)
2350 South Ave., Ste.107
La Crosse, WI 54601
Ph: (608)787-0168
Fax: (608)787-0169
E-mail: sbissen@execpc.com
URL: http://www.whima.org
Contact: Cassandra Bissen RHIA, Exec.Dir.
Founded: 1935. **Members:** 1,250. **Staff:** 2. **Regional Groups:** 6. **State**. Health information professionals. **Awards:** Health Information Management Scholarship. **Frequency:** annual. **Type:** scholarship. **Recipient:** to a student in accredited health information management or a health information technology program enrollee. **Computer Services:** Mailing lists • online services. **Affiliated With:** American Health Information Management Association. **Publications:** *Health Information Link*, bimonthly. Newsletter. **Price:** $20.00/year. **Circulation:** 1,200. **Advertising:** accepted. Alternate Formats: online • *Legal Resource Material for Patient Health Care Information* • *Management Services in Long Term Care Facilities* • *Professional Practice Standards for Health Information*. Alternate Formats: diskette. **Conventions/Meetings:** annual conference, with educational program (exhibits) - usually late April or early May • annual conference - always September.

La Farge

18384 ■ La Farge Lions Club
c/o Becky Hooker, Pres.
306 N Bird St.
La Farge, WI 54639
Ph: (608)625-2585
E-mail: hookerb@lafarge.k12.wi.us
URL: http://www.md27d2.org
Contact: Becky Hooker, Pres.
Local. **Affiliated With:** Lions Clubs International.

La Pointe

18385 ■ Madeline Island Chamber of Commerce
PO Box 274
La Pointe, WI 54850
Ph: (715)747-2801
Free: (888)475-3386
E-mail: info@madelineisland.com
URL: http://www.madelineisland.com
Local. Promotes business and community development in Madeline Island, WI.

La Valle

18386 ■ American Legion, Kropp-Braund Post 242
PO Box 46
La Valle, WI 53941
Ph: (608)745-1090
Fax: (608)745-0179
URL: National Affiliate–www.legion.org
Local. **Affiliated With:** American Legion.

18387 ■ Reedsburg Lions Club
c/o Bob Roloff, Pres.
S1561 Fox Ct.
La Valle, WI 53941
Ph: (608)985-8167
URL: http://www.md27d2.org
Contact: Bob Roloff, Pres.
Local. **Affiliated With:** Lions Clubs International.

Lac Du Flambeau

18388 ■ Dillman's Creative Arts Foundation (DCAF)
PO Box 98
Lac Du Flambeau, WI 54538-0098
Ph: (715)588-3143 (715)588-7322
Fax: (715)588-3110
E-mail: frontdesk@dillmans.com
URL: http://www.dillmans.com
Contact: Dennis Robertson, Pres.
Founded: 1989. **Staff:** 3. **Regional**. Promotes public awareness and appreciation of the arts in Lac Du Flambeau, WI. **Libraries:** **Type:** open to the public. **Holdings:** 500; books, video recordings. **Subjects:** art. **Awards:** Dillman's Creative Arts Scholarship Award. **Frequency:** annual. **Type:** scholarship. **Recipient:** for specific needs and interests. **Publications:** Brochure, annual. Contains descriptions of workshops, dates, costs, and instructor bios. **Price:** free. Alternate Formats: online.

18389 ■ Lac Du Flambeau Chamber of Commerce
602 Peace Pipe Rd.
Lac Du Flambeau, WI 54538
Ph: (715)588-3346
Fax: (715)588-9408
Free: (877)588-3346
E-mail: info@lacduflambeauchamber.com
Contact: Randy Soulier, Pres.
Members: 50. **Local**.

Ladysmith

18390 ■ American Legion, Moore-Long Post 64
PO Box 181
Ladysmith, WI 54848
Ph: (608)745-1090
Fax: (608)745-0179
URL: National Affiliate–www.legion.org
Local. **Affiliated With:** American Legion.

18391 ■ Indianhead Community Action
PO Box 40
Ladysmith, WI 54848
Ph: (715)532-5594 (715)532-7542
E-mail: info@indianheadcaa.org
URL: http://www.indianheadcaa.org
Contact: Jerome Drahos, Exec.Dir.
Local.

18392 ■ Wisconsin Timberline Hare Beagle Club
c/o Robert Kelley
W10348 Polack Ave.
Ladysmith, WI 54848-9424
URL: National Affiliate–clubs.akc.org
Contact: Robert Kelley, Contact
Local.

18393 ■ Wisconsin Woodland Owners Association, Northwest Chapter
c/o William Fucik, Chm.
N9197 Fedyn Rd.
Ladysmith, WI 54848-9739
Ph: (715)532-6606
E-mail: wolfhill@chipvalley.com
URL: http://www.wisconsinwoodlands.org
Contact: William Fucik, Chm.
Local. **Affiliated With:** Wisconsin Woodland Owners Association.

Lake Geneva

18394 ■ ACF Greater Geneva Lakes Professional Chefs Association
PO Box 904
Lake Geneva, WI 53147
Ph: (262)275-1516
E-mail: forpetewad@charter.net
URL: National Affiliate–www.acfchefs.org
Contact: Peter Wadlund, Pres.
Local. Promotes the culinary profession and provides on-going educational training and networking for members. Provides opportunities for competition, professional recognition, and access to educational forums with other culinarians at local, regional, national and international events.

18395 ■ American Legion, Wisconsin Post 24
c/o Frank Kresen
PO Box 24
Lake Geneva, WI 53147
Ph: (414)248-5555
Fax: (608)745-0179
URL: National Affiliate–www.legion.org
Contact: Frank Kresen, Contact
Local. **Affiliated With:** American Legion.

18396 ■ American Rabbit Breeders Association, Lakeland
c/o Kathy Benhart, Sec.
W3975 Willow Bend Rd.
Lake Geneva, WI 53147
URL: http://www.geocities.com/wisconsin_state_rba/Local_Clubs.html
Contact: Kathy Benhart, Sec.
Local. **Affiliated With:** American Rabbit Breeders Association.

18397 ■ Geneva Lake Area Chamber of Commerce (GLACC)
201 Wrigley Dr.
Lake Geneva, WI 53147-2004
Ph: (262)248-4416
Fax: (262)248-1000
Free: (800)345-1020
E-mail: lgcc@lakegenevawi.com
URL: http://www.lakegenevawi.com
Contact: George F. Hennerley, Exec.VP
Founded: 1947. **Membership Dues:** professional (with 1-over 21 employees; plus $23 per associate), $285-$600 (annual) • industrial (with 1-over 331 employees), $300-$975 (annual) • individual, $200 (annual) • nonprofit/charitable, $250 (annual) • associate, $450 (annual) • retail business (with 1-over 51 employees; plus $20 per additional employee), $335-$1,000 (annual). **Local**. Promotes business and community development in the Geneva Lakes, WI area. **Publications:** Newsletter, monthly.

18398 ■ Geneva Lakes Area United Way
PO Box 455
Lake Geneva, WI 53147
Ph: (262)249-1100
URL: National Affiliate–national.unitedway.org
Local. **Affiliated With:** United Way of America.

18399 ■ Sweet Adelines International, Spirit of the Lakes Chorus
Horticultural Hall
300 Broad St.
Lake Geneva, WI 53147-1812

Ph: (414)248-6350
E-mail: smithhaus@genevaonline.com
URL: National Affiliate–www.sweetadelineintl.org
Contact: Joyce Schmidt, Contact

Local. Advances the musical art form of barbershop harmony through education and performances. Provides education, training and coaching in the development of women's four-part barbershop harmony. **Affiliated With:** Sweet Adelines International.

18400 ■ Wisconsin Boer Goat Association
c/o Sue Slack
W 3695 Willow Bend Rd.
Lake Geneva, WI 53147
E-mail: kslacksuffolks@yahoo.com
URL: National Affiliate–usbga.org
Contact: Sue Slack, Contact

State.

18401 ■ Young Life Geneva Lakes
Covenant Harbour Bible Camp
1724 Main St.
Lake Geneva, WI 53147
Ph: (262)248-3600
Fax: (262)248-6814
URL: http://sites.younglife.org/sites/GenevaLakes/default.aspx

Local. Affiliated With: Young Life.

Lake Mills

18402 ■ American Legion, Clarence-Bean-Warren-George Post 67
PO Box 113
Lake Mills, WI 53551
Ph: (608)745-1090
Fax: (608)745-0179
URL: National Affiliate–www.legion.org

Local. Affiliated With: American Legion.

18403 ■ Lake Mills Area Chamber of Commerce (LMCC)
200C Water St.
Lake Mills, WI 53551
Ph: (920)648-3585
Fax: (920)648-6751
E-mail: chamber@lakemills.org
URL: http://www.lakemills.org
Contact: Teri Nelson, Pres.

Members: 70. **Local.** Works to enhance, preserve, and protect the quality of life and business in the Lake Mills, WI area.

18404 ■ Lake Mills Lions Club
PO Box 294
Lake Mills, WI 53551
Ph: (920)648-8636 (920)648-2287
E-mail: bobplumber@charter.net
URL: http://lakemillswi.lionwap.org
Contact: Bob Metzker, Pres.

Local. Affiliated With: Lions Clubs International.

18405 ■ NAIFA-Southeast Wisconsin
c/o Scott A. Coenen, Pres.
PO Box 219
Lake Mills, WI 53551
Ph: (920)648-7715
Fax: (920)648-7815
E-mail: naifa-se-wi@charter.net
URL: National Affiliate–naifa.org
Contact: Scott A. Coenen, Pres.

Local. Represents the interests of insurance and financial advisors. Advocates for a positive legislative and regulatory environment. Enhances business and professional skills of members. **Affiliated With:** National Association of Insurance and Financial Advisors.

Lake Nebagamon

18406 ■ Nebagamon Community Association
11507 E Waterfront Dr.
Lake Nebagamon, WI 54849
Ph: (715)374-2283 (715)374-3101
Fax: (715)374-3766
E-mail: nca@pressenter.com
URL: http://www.lakenebagamonwi.com
Contact: Catherine Coletta, Prog. Chair

Local. Departments: Lake Nebagamon Volunteer Fire. **Programs:** Senior Nutrition. **Subgroups:** Lake Nebagamon Lakeshore Property Owners Association; Nebagamon Community Association.

Lake Tomahawk

18407 ■ American Legion, Wisconsin Post 318
c/o Colin F. Shultz
PO Box 318
Lake Tomahawk, WI 54539
Ph: (608)745-1090
Fax: (608)745-0179
URL: National Affiliate–www.legion.org
Contact: Colin F. Shultz, Contact

Local. Affiliated With: American Legion.

Lakewood

18408 ■ Lakewood Area Chamber of Commerce
PO Box 87
Lakewood, WI 54138
Ph: (715)276-6500
Fax: (715)276-6458
E-mail: lkwd@ez-net.com
URL: http://www.lakewoodareachamber.com
Contact: Ruth Benoit, Exec.Sec.

Members: 75. **Local.** Promotes business and community development and tourism in the Lakewood, WI area. Sponsors Lakewood Mardi Gras Spring Fling festival. **Formerly:** (1987) Lakes Country Chamber of Commerce. **Publications:** *Chamber Newsletter*, monthly.

Lancaster

18409 ■ American Legion, Wisconsin Post 109
c/o Richard Burns
PO Box 22
Lancaster, WI 53813
Ph: (608)723-2173
Fax: (608)745-0179
URL: National Affiliate–www.legion.org
Contact: Richard Burns, Contact

Local. Affiliated With: American Legion.

18410 ■ Grant Regional Health Center Auxiliary
c/o Mary Lou Bausch
507 S Monroe St.
Lancaster, WI 53813-2054
Ph: (608)723-2143
URL: http://www.grantregional.com
Contact: Mary Lou Bausch, Contact

Local.

18411 ■ Lancaster Area Chamber of Commerce
206 S Madison St.
PO Box 292
Lancaster, WI 53813
Ph: (608)723-2820
Fax: (608)723-7409
E-mail: lanchamber@pcii.net
URL: http://www.lancasterwisconsin.com
Contact: Marge Sherwin, Exec.Dir.

Members: 95. **Local.** Promotes agricultural, business, community, and industrial development in the Lancaster, WI area. **Committees:** Ambassadors; Retail; Tourism. **Formerly:** (1999) Lancaster Chamber of Commerce. **Publications:** Newsletter, monthly. **Conventions/Meetings:** monthly board meeting - 3rd Tuesday.

18412 ■ United Way of Grant County, Wisconsin
PO Box 308
Lancaster, WI 53813-0308
Ph: (608)723-2239
URL: National Affiliate–national.unitedway.org

Local. Affiliated With: United Way of America.

18413 ■ Wisconsin Pork Association (WPA)
c/o Keri M. Retallick, Exec.VP
PO Box 327
Lancaster, WI 53813
Ph: (608)723-7551
Fax: (608)723-7553
Free: (800)822-7675
E-mail: wppa@wppa.org
URL: http://www.wppa.org

State.

Land O' Lakes

18414 ■ American Legion, Soquist-Binder-Kirk Post 464
PO Box 844
Land O' Lakes, WI 54540
Ph: (608)745-1090
Fax: (608)745-0179
URL: National Affiliate–www.legion.org

Local. Affiliated With: American Legion.

18415 ■ Land O'Lakes Chamber of Commerce (LOLCC)
PO Box 599
Land O' Lakes, WI 54540
Ph: (715)547-3432
Fax: (715)547-8010
Free: (800)236-3432
E-mail: lolinfo@nnex.net
Contact: Sandy Wait, Exec.Sec.

Founded: 1925. **Members:** 115. **Staff:** 2. **Budget:** $30,000,000. **Local.** Promotes business and community development in Land O'Lakes, WI. Holds annual Headwaters Classic Dogsled Races, Family Fun Day, Colorama, Winter Festival, and Art Impressions art show. **Libraries: Type:** open to the public. **Holdings:** 20,000. **Publications:** *Directory of Business Firms and Professional Services*, annual • Brochures. **Price:** free. **Circulation:** 10,000. **Advertising:** accepted. **Conventions/Meetings:** monthly meeting, business oriented, sometimes exhibits are featured - always 2nd Thursday of the month.

Lena

18416 ■ American Legion, Doney-Degrave Post 342
PO Box 232
Lena, WI 54139
Ph: (608)745-1090
Fax: (608)745-0179
URL: National Affiliate–www.legion.org

Local. Affiliated With: American Legion.

18417 ■ Caballo Norte
c/o Michele Ripley, Pres.
6489 Cty. Rd. 1
Lena, WI 54139

Ph: (920)546-0566
E-mail: mripley@ez-net.com
URL: National Affiliate–www.pphrna.org
Contact: Michele Ripley, Pres.

Founded: 2000. **Members:** 31. **Membership Dues:** all, $25 (annual). **State**. Works to the advancement of the Peruvian horse and education of the Peruvian horse owner in Wisconsin. Holds monthly meetings at various locations in the Green Bay area, local parades, and horse festivals. **Libraries: Type:** not open to the public. **Holdings:** 1,000; articles, books, periodicals, video recordings. **Subjects:** Peruvian Paso horse. **Affiliated With:** North American Peruvian Horse Association. **Publications:** *What's News*, quarterly. Newsletter. **Price:** included in membership dues. **Circulation:** 31. **Advertising:** accepted.

18418 ■ Lena Community Development Corp.
PO Box 59
Lena, WI 54139
Ph: (920)829-5525
Contact: A. H. Schuettpelz, Treas.
Local.

Linden

18419 ■ American Legion, Linden Post 493
PO Box 466
Linden, WI 53553
Ph: (608)745-1090
Fax: (608)745-0179
URL: National Affiliate–www.legion.org
Local. **Affiliated With:** American Legion.

Little Chute

18420 ■ American Legion, Wisconsin Post 258
c/o Jacob Coppus
PO Box 22
Little Chute, WI 54140
Ph: (608)745-1090
Fax: (608)745-0179
URL: National Affiliate–www.legion.org
Contact: Jacob Coppus, Contact
Local. **Affiliated With:** American Legion.

Lodi

18421 ■ American Legion, Maynard-Schulgen Post 216
PO Box 216
Lodi, WI 53555
Ph: (608)745-1090
Fax: (608)745-0179
URL: National Affiliate–www.legion.org
Local. **Affiliated With:** American Legion.

18422 ■ Canned Vegetable Council (CVC)
PO Box 303
Lodi, WI 53555
Ph: (608)592-4236
Fax: (608)592-4742
Local.

18423 ■ Lodi Chamber of Commerce
PO Box 43
Lodi, WI 53555
Ph: (608)592-4412
Fax: (608)712-4414
E-mail: lodichamber@lodicommerce.com
Contact: Sally Pierick, Exec.Sec.

Membership Dues: $115 (annual). **Local**. Works to promote economic growth, fostering community development and interaction, and initiating and supporting the civic, educational, recreational, and economic welfare of the Lodi area.

18424 ■ Wisconsin Angus Association
c/o Ardel Quam, Sec.-Treas.
N 706 St., Rd. 113
Lodi, WI 53555
Ph: (608)592-3649
E-mail: quam@chorus.net
URL: http://www.wisconsinangus.org
Contact: Jim Ward, Pres.
State. **Telecommunication Services:** electronic mail, thewards@ticon.net. **Affiliated With:** American Angus Association.

18425 ■ Wisconsin Curling Association - Lodi Curling Club
704 Fair St.
Lodi, WI 53555
Ph: (608)592-7372
E-mail: pjohnson@lathropclark.com
URL: http://www.goodcurling.net/basics/U.S.%20clubs/wisconsin.html
Contact: Paul Johnson, Pres.
Local. **Affiliated With:** United States Curling Association.

Lomira

18426 ■ American Legion, Bintzler-Waehler Post 347
412 Pleasant Hill Ave.
Lomira, WI 53048
Ph: (608)745-1090
Fax: (608)745-0179
URL: National Affiliate–www.legion.org
Local. **Affiliated With:** American Legion.

18427 ■ Lomira Area Chamber of Commerce
PO Box 386
Lomira, WI 53048
Ph: (920)269-7229 (920)269-4112
E-mail: warehousewebs@charter.net
URL: http://www.lomira.com/Servgrop/COC/Index-COC.htm
Contact: Jim Bisek, Pres.
Local. Promotes business and community development in Lomira, WI.

Lone Rock

18428 ■ American Legion, Wisconsin Post 383
PO Box 7
Lone Rock, WI 53556
Ph: (608)745-1090
Fax: (608)745-0179
URL: National Affiliate–www.legion.org
Local. **Affiliated With:** American Legion.

18429 ■ Ithaca Lions Club - Wisconsin
c/o Dean Rinehart, Sec.
30035 Old Sextonville Dr.
Lone Rock, WI 53556
Ph: (608)647-6120
E-mail: rinehart_2000_2001@yahoo.com
URL: http://www.md27d2.org
Contact: Dean Rinehart, Sec.
Local. **Affiliated With:** Lions Clubs International.

Long Lake

18430 ■ Wisconsin League for Nursing (WLN)
c/o Mary Ann Tanner, Exec.Sec.
PO Box 107
Long Lake, WI 54542
Ph: (414)332-6271
E-mail: modtech@att.net
URL: http://www.cuw.edu/AdultEd_Graduate/programs/nursing/wln
Contact: Mary Ann Tanner, Exec.Sec.
State.

Loretta

18431 ■ American Legion, Jensen-Hansen Post 394
4039 W North Clover Rd.
Loretta, WI 54896
Ph: (608)745-1090
Fax: (608)745-0179
URL: National Affiliate–www.legion.org
Local. **Affiliated With:** American Legion.

Loyal

18432 ■ Wisconsin Woodland Owners Association, Black River Chapter
c/o Larry Eggman, Chm.
N8466 Cardinal Ln.
Loyal, WI 54446
Ph: (715)255-9830
E-mail: epongratz@charter.net
URL: http://www.wisconsinwoodlands.org
Contact: Larry Eggman, Chm.
Local. **Affiliated With:** Wisconsin Woodland Owners Association.

Lublin

18433 ■ American Legion, Abramowicz-Kaczmarczyk-Cwikla Post 547
W 13315 South St.
Lublin, WI 54447
Ph: (608)745-1090
Fax: (608)745-0179
URL: National Affiliate–www.legion.org
Local. **Affiliated With:** American Legion.

Luck

18434 ■ American Legion, Victor Post 255
PO Box 498
Luck, WI 54853
Ph: (608)745-1090
Fax: (608)745-0179
URL: National Affiliate–www.legion.org
Local. **Affiliated With:** American Legion.

Luxemburg

18435 ■ American Legion, Private Ralph Kline Post 262
PO Box 91
Luxemburg, WI 54217
Ph: (608)745-1090
Fax: (608)745-0179
URL: National Affiliate–www.legion.org
Local. **Affiliated With:** American Legion.

18436 ■ Luxemburg Chamber of Commerce (LCC)
PO Box 141
Luxemburg, WI 54217-0307
Ph: (920)845-2722
Fax: (920)845-2902
E-mail: info@luxemburgusa.com
URL: http://www.luxemburgusa.com
Contact: Bernadine Mathu, Sec.

Founded: 1945. **Members:** 150. **Local**. Promotes business and community development in the Luxemburg, WI area. **Computer Services:** Information services, business directory. **Publications:** *Business Directory*, biennial. **Conventions/Meetings:** monthly meeting.

18437 ■ Wisconsin Woodland Owners Association, NEWFO Chapter
c/o Charles Wagner, Chm.
E1934 City Rd. S
Luxemburg, WI 54217

Ph: (920)837-7712
E-mail: crwagner@itol.com
URL: http://www.wisconsinwoodlands.org
Contact: Charles Wagner, Chm.
Local. Affiliated With: Wisconsin Woodland Owners Association.

Lyndon Station

18438 ■ International Association of Machinists and Aerospace Workers, AFL-CIO, CLC - Lodge 2269
W1972 60th St.
Lyndon Station, WI 53944
E-mail: lshonk@merr.com
URL: http://ll2269.goiam.org
Contact: Lois Andres, Pres.
Members: 327. **Local. Affiliated With:** International Association of Machinists and Aerospace Workers.

18439 ■ Mauston Lions Club
c/o Kieran Powers, Pres.
W3857 Hwy. 12/16
Lyndon Station, WI 53944
Ph: (608)666-4782
URL: http://www.md27d2.org
Contact: Kieran Powers, Pres.
Local. Affiliated With: Lions Clubs International.

Lyons

18440 ■ American Legion, Rice-Lemmerhart-Smith Post 327
PO Box 281
Lyons, WI 53148
Ph: (608)745-1090
Fax: (608)745-0179
URL: National Affiliate–www.legion.org
Local. Affiliated With: American Legion.

Madison

18441 ■ 1000 Friends of Wisconsin
16 N Carroll St., Ste.810
Madison, WI 53703
Ph: (608)259-1000
Fax: (608)259-1621
E-mail: friends@1kfriends.org
URL: http://www.1kfriends.org
Contact: Steve Hiniker, Exec.Dir.
Founded: 1996. **Members:** 2,000. **Membership Dues:** friend, $100 (annual) • society, $500 (annual) • circle, $1,000 (annual). **Staff:** 6. **State.** Works to protect and enhance Wisconsin's urban and rural landscapes by providing citizens with the inspiration, information and tools needed to effectively participate in the decisions having the greatest impact on community health. **Publications:** *Wisconsin Landscapes*, quarterly. Newsletter. **Price:** free to members.

18442 ■ Acacia, Wisconsin Chapter
c/o Kevin May
222 Langdon St.
Madison, WI 53703
Ph: (414)467-2076
E-mail: kmay@wisc.edu
URL: http://www.acaciawisconsin.com
Contact: Kevin May, Pres.
State. Affiliated With: Acacia.

18443 ■ AFT-Wisconsin
6602 Normandy Ln., 1st Fl.
Madison, WI 53719
Ph: (608)662-1444
Fax: (608)662-1443
Free: (800)362-7390
E-mail: gussert@aft-wisconsin.org
URL: http://www.aft-wisconsin.org
Contact: Andy Gussert, Pres.
Founded: 1932. **Members:** 16,000. **Staff:** 20. **Local Groups:** 52. **State. Awards:** Scholarships. **Frequency:** annual. **Type:** monetary. **Recipient:** to children or grandchildren of AFT-Wisconsin members. **Boards:** Executive. **Councils:** Graduate Employees; Higher Education; K-12 Teachers; Paraprofessional and School-Related Personnel; State Employees; Wisconsin Technical College System. **Subgroups:** Retiree Chapter. **Formerly:** (2004) Wisconsin Federation of Teachers. **Publications:** *The Professional*, bimonthly. Newsletter. **Price:** free. **Advertising:** accepted. Alternate Formats: online. **Conventions/Meetings:** annual convention - always the 4th Thursday and Friday of October in Wisconsin, USA.

18444 ■ Aggregate Producers of Wisconsin
c/o Patrick J. Osborne, Exec.Dir.
PO Box 2157
Madison, WI 53701-2157
Ph: (608)283-2595
Fax: (608)283-2589
State.

18445 ■ AIDS Network
600 Williamson St.
Madison, WI 53703
Ph: (608)252-6540
Fax: (608)252-6559
E-mail: info@madisonaidsnetwork.org
URL: http://www.aidsnetwork.org
Contact: Bob Power, Exec.Dir.
Founded: 1985. **Staff:** 22. **Budget:** $1,600,000. **Local.** Provides support, education and assistance to people with HIV/AIDS. **Libraries: Type:** reference. **Holdings:** books, periodicals. **Subjects:** AIDS, public service providers. **Formerly:** Madison Aids Support. **Publications:** *Positive Times*, quarterly. Newsletter. **Price:** free. **Circulation:** 3,000. **Advertising:** accepted. **Conventions/Meetings:** annual workshop.

18446 ■ Alcoholics Anonymous World Services, Madison Area Intergroup/Central Office
6400 Monona Dr.
Madison, WI 53716
Ph: (608)222-8989
URL: National Affiliate–www.aa.org
Local. Individuals recovering from alcoholism. AA maintains that members can solve their common problem and help others achieve sobriety through a twelve step program that includes sharing their experience, strength, and hope with each other. **Affiliated With:** Alcoholics Anonymous World Services.

18447 ■ Alliance for Animals, Madison
122 State St., Ste.406
Madison, WI 53703-2500
Ph: (608)257-6333
E-mail: alliance@allanimals.org
URL: http://www.allanimals.org
Contact: Tina Kaske, Dir.
Founded: 1984. **Members:** 700. **Membership Dues:** $25 (annual). **Staff:** 1. **Local.** Helps in the protection of animals. **Libraries: Type:** reference. **Holdings:** books, video recordings. **Subjects:** animal protection. **Committees:** Companion Animals/Animals Used in Entertainment; Farm; Laboratory Animals; Wildlife. **Publications:** *Animal News*, quarterly. Newsletter. **Price:** $25.00/year. **Conventions/Meetings:** monthly general assembly - always second Monday of the month.

18448 ■ Alzheimer's Association, South Central Wisconsin Chapter
517 N Segoe Rd., Ste.301
Madison, WI 53705
Ph: (608)232-3400
Fax: (608)232-3407
Free: (800)272-3900
E-mail: familysupport@alzwisc.org
URL: http://www.alzwisc.org
Contact: Paul Rusk, Exec.Dir.
Staff: 12. **Local Groups:** 8. **State.** Provides programs and services for people with Alzheimer's disease or related dementias. **Libraries: Type:** reference. **Holdings:** books, video recordings. **Subjects:** issues related to Alzheimer's disease, dementia, and caregiving. **Affiliated With:** Alzheimer's Association. **Publications:** Newsletter, quarterly. Contains articles specifically for caregivers, latest research updates, and news about upcoming events.

18449 ■ American Academy of Pediatrics, Wisconsin Chapter
c/o Carolyn Evenstad, Exec.Dir.
PO Box 1109
Madison, WI 53701
Ph: (608)222-7751
E-mail: cmewcaap@aol.com
URL: http://www.wisaap.org
Contact: Lu Ann Moraski MD, Sec.-Treas.
State. Affiliated With: American Academy of Pediatrics.

18450 ■ American Association of Airport Executives, Wisconsin
c/o David C. Jensen
Dane County Regional Airport
4000 Intl. Ln.
Madison, WI 53704
Ph: (608)246-3387
Fax: (608)246-3385
E-mail: jensen.david@co.dane.wi.us
URL: http://www.glcaaae.org
Contact: David C. Jensen, Contact
State. Represents airport management personnel at public airports. Promotes professionalism and financial stability in the administration of airports. Furthers airport safety and operational efficiency. Seeks to develop a systematic exchange of information and experience in the development, maintenance and operation of airports. **Affiliated With:** American Association of Airport Executives.

18451 ■ American Association for Clinical Chemistry, Chicago Section
c/o Craig C. Foreback, PhD, Chm.
Univ. of Wisconsin Medical School
Pathology and Lab. Medicine, CLS Prog.
1300 Univ. Ave.
Madison, WI 53706-1510
Ph: (608)262-6651
Fax: (608)262-9520
URL: National Affiliate–www.aacc.org
Contact: Craig C. Foreback PhD, Chm.
Local. Represents the interests of clinical laboratory professionals, physicians, research scientists and other individuals involved with clinical chemistry and other clinical laboratory science-related disciplines. Seeks to improve the practice of clinical chemistry. Establishes standards for education and training in the field. **Affiliated With:** American Association for Clinical Chemistry.

18452 ■ American Association of Retired Persons, Wisconsin
222 W Washington Ave., Ste.600
Madison, WI 53703
Ph: (608)251-2277
Fax: (608)251-7612
Free: (866)448-3611
E-mail: wistate@aarp.org
URL: National Affiliate–www.aarp.org
Contact: D'anna Bowman, State Dir.
State. Persons 50 years of age or older, working or retired. Seeks to improve every aspect of living for older people. **Affiliated With:** American Association of Retired Persons.

18453 ■ American Brittany Club, Badger
c/o Jim Brigham, Sec.
4130 Cherokee Dr.
Madison, WI 53711
Ph: (608)233-3909
E-mail: jwbrigham03@sbcglobal.net
URL: http://www.badgerbrittanyclub.com
Contact: Jim Brigham, Sec.
Local. Affiliated With: American Brittany Club.

18454 ■ American Camp Association, Wisconsin (ACA-WI)
3217 Sandwood Way
Madison, WI 53713
Ph: (608)663-0051
E-mail: acawisconsin@charter.net
URL: http://www.acawisconsin.org
Contact: Peg Smith, Exec.Dir.

Founded: 1938. **Members:** 225. **Membership Dues:** professional (owners/directors of camps), $400 (annual) • professional (other type of staff), $300 (annual) • professional (standards visitors, retirees, or professional educator, additional individual), $150 (annual) • associate, $100 (annual) • associate (standards visitor, retirees and volunteer), $50 (annual). **Staff:** 2. **State Groups:** 1. **For-Profit. State.** Camp owners, directors, and counselors; businesses and students interested in organized camping. **Libraries: Type:** lending. **Holdings:** 100; audiovisuals, books. **Subjects:** camp management and programming. **Awards:** Acorn Award. **Frequency:** annual. **Type:** recognition. **Recipient:** to member contributing to camping movement. **Affiliated With:** American Camping Association. **Formerly:** (2004) American Camping Association, Wisconsin Section. **Publications:** *Badger Tracks*, 5/year. Newsletter. Contains news about Wisconsin camping and national camping issues. **Price:** free. **Circulation:** 225. **Conventions/Meetings:** annual workshop (exhibits).

18455 ■ American Cancer Society, Madison
8317 Elderberry Rd.
Madison, WI 53717
Ph: (608)833-4555
Fax: (608)833-1195
Free: (877)423-9123
URL: http://www.cancer.org
Contact: Kelly McClyman, Receptionist

Local. Affiliated With: American Cancer Society.

18456 ■ American Chemical Society, Wisconsin Section
c/o Dr. Frank Albert Weinhold, Chm.
Univ. of Wisconsin, Chemistry Dept.
1101 Univ. Ave.
Madison, WI 53706-1322
Ph: (608)262-0263
URL: National Affiliate–acswebcontent.acs.org
Contact: Dr. Frank Albert Weinhold, Chm.

State. Represents the interests of individuals dedicated to the advancement of chemistry in all its branches. Provides opportunities for peer interaction and career development. **Affiliated With:** American Chemical Society.

18457 ■ American Council of Engineering Companies of Wisconsin (ACEC WI)
3 S Pinckney St., Ste.800
Madison, WI 53703
Ph: (608)257-9223
Fax: (608)257-0009
E-mail: acecwi@acecwi.org
URL: http://www.acecwi.org
Contact: John Boldt PE, Pres.

Founded: 1959. **Members:** 64. **Membership Dues:** principal, $415 (annual). **Staff:** 2. **Budget:** $250,000. **State Groups:** 1. **State.** Represents private practice consulting engineering firms. **Awards:** Engineering Excellence Awards. **Frequency:** annual. **Type:** recognition. **Affiliated With:** American Council of Engineering Companies. **Formerly:** (2005) Wisconsin Association of Consulting Engineers. **Publications:** *Update*, monthly. Newsletter. **Circulation:** 600. Alternate Formats: online. **Conventions/Meetings:** annual meeting - every spring in Sheboygan, WI.

18458 ■ American Ex-Prisoners of War, Badger Chapter
c/o Clifford Syverud
201 N Albridge Ave., Apt. 212
Madison, WI 53714
Ph: (608)244-8827
URL: National Affiliate–www.axpow.org
Contact: Clifford Syverud, Contact

Local. Affiliated With: American Ex-Prisoners of War.

18459 ■ American Guild of Organists, Madison (644)
PO Box 5321
Madison, WI 53705
Ph: (608)249-7288
Fax: (608)244-3773
E-mail: acm@madisonacm.org
URL: http://www.madisonacm.org

Founded: 1953. **Members:** 104. **Membership Dues:** regular, $84 (annual) • special, $60 (annual) • full-time student, $32 (annual) • partner (second member at same address), $58 (annual). **Local.** Promotes organ and choral music. **Affiliated With:** American Guild of Organists. **Also Known As:** (1984) Association of Church Musicians. **Publications:** *Church Music Notes*, monthly. Newsletter. **Price:** included in membership dues. **Circulation:** 400. **Advertising:** accepted.

18460 ■ American Heart Association, Madison
2850 Dairy Dr., Ste.300
Madison, WI 53718
Ph: (608)221-8866
Fax: (608)221-9233
URL: http://www.americanheart.org

Local. Affiliated With: American Heart Association.

18461 ■ American Hellenic Educational Progressive Association - Madison, Chapter 369
c/o John A. Scocos, Pres.
4154 Nakoma Rd.
Madison, WI 53711
Ph: (608)266-4348
E-mail: john.scocos@dva.state.wi.us
URL: http://www.ahepafamily.org/d13
Contact: John A. Scocos, Pres.

Local. Affiliated With: American Hellenic Educational Progressive Association.

18462 ■ American Institute of Architects, Wisconsin (AIAW)
c/o William M. Babcock, Exec.Dir.
321 S Hamilton St.
Madison, WI 53703-4000
Ph: (608)257-8477
Fax: (608)257-0242
Free: (800)272-4483
E-mail: aiaw@aiaw.org
URL: http://www.aiaw.org
Contact: William M. Babcock Hon., Exec.Dir.

Members: 1,450. **Membership Dues:** architect, firm principal (new member), $307 (annual) • architect, employee (new member), $279 (annual) • associate (new member), $129 (annual) • professional affiliate, $200 (annual) • student affiliate, $10 (annual). **State.** Seeks to advance the science and art of planning and building by advancing the standards of architectural education, training and practice. Aims to coordinate the building industry and profession of architecture; promotes the aesthetic, scientific and practical efficiency of the profession. **Committees:** Component Affairs; Education and Practice; Executive and Administrative; Government Affairs; State Programs. **Affiliated With:** American Institute of Architects. **Publications:** *Wisconsin Architect*, quarterly. Magazine. **Circulation:** 2,800. **Advertising:** accepted • *Wisconsin Architect Consultant Directory*, annual. **Price:** free. **Circulation:** 2,900. **Advertising:** accepted • Membership Directory, annual. Contains list of names, firm, daytime phone and address for AIA Wisconsin members. **Price:** free for members. **Circulation:** 1,450.

18463 ■ American Legion, Blackhawk Post 553
5599 Barbara Dr.
Madison, WI 53711
Ph: (608)745-1090
Fax: (608)745-0179
URL: National Affiliate–www.legion.org
Local. Affiliated With: American Legion.

18464 ■ American Legion, West Side Memorial Post 151
PO Box 44702
Madison, WI 53744
Ph: (608)745-1090
Fax: (608)745-0179
URL: National Affiliate–www.legion.org
Local. Affiliated With: American Legion.

18465 ■ American Legion, William-B.-Cairns-Victory Post 57
PO Box 45259
Madison, WI 53744
Ph: (608)745-1090
Fax: (608)745-0179
URL: National Affiliate–www.legion.org
Local. Affiliated With: American Legion.

18466 ■ American Legion, Wisconsin Post 501
c/o Donald C. Severson
PO Box 14255
Madison, WI 53708
Ph: (608)745-1090
Fax: (608)745-0179
URL: National Affiliate–www.legion.org
Contact: Donald C. Severson, Contact
Local. Affiliated With: American Legion.

18467 ■ American Nuclear Society, Wisconsin
c/o Michelle Blanchard
1513 Univ. Ave.
Madison, WI 53706
Ph: (608)262-3392
URL: National Affiliate–www.ans.org
Contact: Michelle Blanchard, Contact

State. Works to advance science and engineering in the nuclear industry. Works with government agencies, educational institutions, and other organizations dealing with nuclear issues. **Affiliated With:** American Nuclear Society.

18468 ■ American Red Cross, Badger Chapter
PO Box 5905
Madison, WI 53705-0905
Ph: (608)227-1297
Fax: (608)227-1439
URL: http://www.arcbadger.org
Local.

18469 ■ American Red Cross Badger-Hawkeye Blood Services Region
4860 Sheboygan Ave.
Madison, WI 53705
Ph: (608)233-9300
Fax: (608)233-8318
URL: http://www.redcrossblood.com
Regional.

18470 ■ American Society of Farm Managers and Rural Appraisers Wisconsin Chapter (WCASFMRA)
c/o Arlin Brannstrom, MS, MBA, AAC, Sec.-Treas.
7310 Farmington Way
Madison, WI 53717
Ph: (608)265-3030
Fax: (608)833-1965
E-mail: ajbranns@wisc.edu
URL: National Affiliate–www.asfmra.org
Contact: Larry Foltz, Pres.

State. Affiliated With: American Society of Farm Managers and Rural Appraisers.

18471 ■ American Society for Healthcare Food Service Administrators, Wisconsin Chapter
c/o Jane Dunn, MS, R.D., Asst.Dir. Food and Nutrition Services
Univ. of Wisconsin Hosp. & Clinic
600 Highland Ave., F4/120-1510
Madison, WI 53792
Ph: (608)263-8227 (608)263-8231
Fax: (608)262-1636
E-mail: jm.dunn@hosp.wisc.edu
URL: http://www.uwhealth.org
Contact: Mr. Ricardo Crespo, Sec.

State. **Affiliated With:** American Society for Healthcare Food Service Administrators.

18472 ■ American Society of Heating, Refrigerating and Air-Conditioning Engineers Madison Chapter
PO Box 8030
Madison, WI 53708-8030
Ph: (608)276-9200
Fax: (608)276-9204
E-mail: kimball@strang-inc.com
URL: http://www.ashraemadison.org
Contact: Bruce Kimball, Pres.

Local. Advances the arts and sciences of heating, ventilation, air-conditioning and refrigeration. Provides a source of technical and educational information, standards and guidelines. Conducts seminars for professional growth. **Affiliated With:** American Society of Heating, Refrigerating and Air-Conditioning Engineers.

18473 ■ American Society for Training and Development - South Central Wisconsin (ASTD-SCWC)
1 E Main St., No. 305
Madison, WI 53703
Ph: (608)212-2783
Fax: (262)569-1540
E-mail: astdscwc@astdscwc.org
URL: http://www.astdscwc.org
Contact: Patti Coan, Pres.

Local. Promotes workplace learning and the improvement of skills of workplace professionals. Provides resource and professional development to individuals in the field of learning and development. Recognizes and sets standards for learning and performance professionals. **Affiliated With:** American Society for Training and Development.

18474 ■ American Trauma Society, Wisconsin
c/o Martha Florey, JD
PO Box 7936
Madison, WI 53707-7936
Ph: (608)266-3557
E-mail: martha.florey@dot.state.wi.us
URL: National Affiliate–www.amtrauma.org
Contact: Martha Florey JD, Contact

State. Seeks to prevent trauma and improve trauma care. Advocates for injury care and prevention in the community. **Affiliated With:** American Trauma Society.

18475 ■ American Woman's Society of Certified Public Accountants, Madison
c/o Dawn Fischer
PO Box 1764
Madison, WI 53701-1764
Ph: (608)836-7500
Fax: (608)836-7505
E-mail: dawn.fisher@sgcpa.com
URL: http://www.awscpa.org/madison
Contact: Kathy Chandler, Pres.

Membership Dues: professional, $25 (annual) • student, $5 (annual). **Local**. Provides support to women in accounting profession through continuing education. **Awards:** Scholarship. **Frequency:** annual. **Type:** monetary. **Recipient:** for accounting major with a GPA greater than 3.0. **Committees:** Hospitality; Newsletter; Program; Scholarship. **Affiliated With:** American Woman's Society of Certified Public Accountants. **Publications:** Newsletter. Alternate Formats: online.

18476 ■ Arc-Wisconsin Disability Association
600 Williamson St., Ste.J
Madison, WI 53703
Ph: (608)251-9272
Fax: (608)251-1403
Free: (877)272-8400
E-mail: arcw@chorus.net
URL: http://www.arc-wisconsin.org
Contact: Mr. Jim Hoegemeier, Exec.Dir.

Founded: 1949. **Members:** 10,000. **Membership Dues:** individual, $30 (annual). **Staff:** 14. **Budget:** $908,435. **Local Groups:** 32. **State**. Parents, self-advocates, professionals, and other interested individuals organized to promote quality of life opportunities for people with developmental and related disabilities and their families through public policy, advocacy, training, and information and assistance services. **Formerly:** Association for Retarded Citizens. **Publications:** *Arc-Wisconsin News*, 3/year. Newsletter. **Advertising:** accepted • *State Membership Directory*, annual • Bulletin, monthly. **Conventions/Meetings:** annual State Conference (exhibits).

18477 ■ ARMA, Madison Chapter
c/o Ana Aquino-Perez, Pres.
Wisconsin Dept. of Trans.
4802 Sheboygan Ave., Rm. 751
Madison, WI 53707
Ph: (608)266-5290
E-mail: ana.aquino-perez@dot.state.wi.us
URL: http://archives.library.wisc.edu/armad/armad.htm
Contact: Ana Aquino-Perez, Pres.

Founded: 1979. **Members:** 55. **Membership Dues:** individual, $20 (annual). **Local**. Strives to provide education, research and networking opportunities to information professionals to enable them to use their skills to leverage the value of records, information and knowledge as corporate assets and as contributions to organizational success. **Affiliated With:** ARMA International - The Association of Information Management Professionals. **Publications:** *Armadison*, monthly. Newsletter. **Conventions/Meetings:** annual conference • monthly meeting.

18478 ■ Associated Builders and Contractors of Wisconsin (ABC)
5330 Wall St.
Madison, WI 53718
Ph: (608)244-5883
Fax: (608)244-2401
Free: (800)244-2224
E-mail: sstone@abcwi.org
URL: http://www.abcwi.org
Contact: Stephen L. Stone, Pres.

State. **Affiliated With:** Associated Builders and Contractors.

18479 ■ Associated General Contractors of Wisconsin
c/o Robert L. Barker, Exec.VP
4814 E Broadway
Madison, WI 53716
Ph: (608)221-3821
Fax: (608)221-4446
E-mail: bbarker@agcwi.org
URL: http://www.agcwi.org
Contact: Robert L. Barker, Exec.VP

Founded: 1927. **Membership Dues:** full regular, $750 (annual) • specialty contractor, $725 (annual) • visiting regular, $375 (annual). **State**.

18480 ■ Associated Students of Madison (ASM)
c/o Alison Rice
800 Langdon St.
512 Mem Union
Madison, WI 53706
Ph: (608)265-4276 (608)265-9020
Fax: (608)265-5637
E-mail: asm@studentorg.wisc.edu
URL: http://www.asm.wisc.edu

Founded: 1994. **Members:** 40,000. **Staff:** 7. **Budget:** $650,000. **State Groups:** 1. **Local**. Promotes students participation in governance and policy development, events and activities, grievances, and actions to take for the welfare of the students and the university. **Awards: Type:** grant • **Type:** monetary. **Boards:** Nominations. **Committees:** Academic Affairs; Campus Relations; Diversity; Legislative Affairs; Shared Governance; Students Services Finance. **Affiliated With:** United Council of University of Wisconsin Students; United States Student Association. **Also Known As:** (2004) Associated Students of Madison, the Student Government at the University of Wisconsin - Madison.

18481 ■ Association of Community Organizations for Reform Now, Madison
2349 Allied Dr., No. 126
Madison, WI 53711
Ph: (608)277-0655
E-mail: wiacornmaro@acorn.org
URL: National Affiliate–www.acorn.org

Local. **Affiliated With:** Association of Community Organizations for Reform Now.

18482 ■ Association for Computing Machinery, University of Wisconsin/Madison
c/o Prof. Gurindar Sohi, Chm.
1210 W Dayton St.
Cmpt. Sci. Dept.
Madison, WI 53706-1613
Ph: (608)262-1204
Fax: (608)262-9777
E-mail: sohi@cs.wisc.edu
URL: http://www.cs.wisc.edu
Contact: Prof. Gurindar Sohi, Chm.

Local. Biological, medical, behavioral, and computer scientists; hospital administrators; programmers and others interested in application of computer methods to biological, behavioral, and medical problems. Stimulates understanding of the use and potential of computers in the biosciences. **Affiliated With:** Association for Computing Machinery.

18483 ■ Association of Government Accountants - Southern Wisconsin Chapter
PO Box 1454
Madison, WI 53701-1454
Ph: (608)267-9818
E-mail: admin@aga-wi.org
URL: http://www.aga-wis.org
Contact: Sherri Voigt CPA, Pres.

Local. Provides quality education, professional development and certification to government accountants. Supports standards and research to advance government accountability. Seeks to encourage the interchange of ideas among financial managers in government service and among government and nongovernmental managers. **Affiliated With:** Association of Government Accountants.

18484 ■ Association for Institutional Research in the Upper Midwest (AIRUM)
c/o Clare Huhn
Univ. of Wisconsin-Madison
170-A Bascom Hall
500 Lincoln Dr.
Madison, WI 53706
Ph: (608)265-9276
E-mail: chuhn@vc.wisc.edu
URL: National Affiliate–www.airweb.org
Contact: Clare Huhn, Contact

Regional. Represents individuals interested in institutional research. Fosters research leading to improved understanding, planning, and operation of institutions of postsecondary education. **Affiliated With:** Association for Institutional Research.

18485 ■ Association for Psychological Type - Madison
c/o Dee Relyea
6806 Winstone Dr.
Madison, WI 53711
Ph: (608)513-9675 (608)274-9179
Fax: (608)274-5131
E-mail: dee@careerlifecoaching.com
URL: National Affiliate–www.aptinternational.org
Contact: Dee Relyea, Contact
Local. Promotes the practical application and ethical use of psychological type. Provides members with opportunities for continuous learning, sharing experiences and creating understanding and knowledge through research. **Affiliated With:** Association for Psychological Type.

18486 ■ Association of Wisconsin School Administrators (AWSA)
4797 Hayes Rd., Ste.103
Madison, WI 53704-3288
Ph: (608)241-0300
Fax: (608)249-4973
E-mail: tbeattie@awsa.org
URL: http://www.awsa.org
Contact: Tom Beattie, Exec.Dir.
Founded: 1978. **State**.

18487 ■ Autism Society of America, Madison Area Chapter (ASGM)
2935 S Fish Hatchery Rd., No. 101
Madison, WI 53711
Ph: (608)213-8519
E-mail: autismmadison@gmail.com
URL: http://www.autismmadison.org
Local. Works to improve the quality of life of all individuals with autism and their families through education, research and advocacy. Promotes public awareness and understanding of the symptoms and problems of individuals with autism.

18488 ■ Badger Bonsai Society
c/o Bob Eskeitz
126 S Marquette St.
Madison, WI 53704
Ph: (608)249-5227
Fax: (608)249-0213
E-mail: bonsaibobs@charter.net
URL: National Affiliate–www.bonsai-bci.com
Contact: Bob Eskeitz, Contact
Local. **Affiliated With:** Bonsai Clubs International.

18489 ■ Badger Stamp Club
c/o Curt Shawkey, Pres.
4817 Martha Ln.
Madison, WI 53714
E-mail: cshawkey@netscape.net
URL: http://www.virtualstampclub.com/apschapbadger.html
Contact: Curt Shawkey, Pres.
Local. **Affiliated With:** American Philatelic Society.

18490 ■ Bicycle Federation of Wisconsin (BFW)
c/o Marjorie Ward, Exec.Dir.
106 E Doty St., Ste.400
Madison, WI 53703
Ph: (608)251-4456
Fax: (608)251-4594
E-mail: info@bfw.org
URL: http://www.bfw.org
Contact: Marjorie Ward, Exec.Dir.
State.

18491 ■ Big Brothers Big Sisters of Dane County
2059 Atwood Ave.
Madison, WI 53704
Ph: (608)661-5437
Fax: (608)663-5444
Free: (800)890-KIDS
E-mail: friends@bbbsmadison.org
URL: http://www.bbbsmadison.org
Contact: Dora Zuniga, Exec.Dir.
Local. Develops and supports long-lasting friendships between children and caring, responsible adult volunteers to provide a positive experience for both child and adult. **Affiliated With:** Big Brothers Big Sisters of America.

18492 ■ Bio-Diversity Project
214 N Henry St., No. 201
Madison, WI 53703
Ph: (608)250-9876
Fax: (608)257-3513
E-mail: project@biodiverse.org
URL: http://www.biodiversityproject.org
Contact: Jane Elder, Exec.Dir.
Founded: 2000. **Staff:** 6. **Local**.

18493 ■ Boy Scouts of America, Glacier's Edge Council
c/o Madison Scout Service Center
34 Schroeder Ct.
Madison, WI 53711-6222
Ph: (608)273-1005
Fax: (608)273-8686
Free: (800)213-1418
E-mail: stheck@bsamail.org
URL: http://www.glaciersedge.org
Contact: Stephen Heck, Scout Exec.
Local. **Affiliated With:** Boy Scouts of America. **Also Known As:** (2005) Boy Scouts of America, Madison. **Formerly:** (2005) Boy Scouts of America, Four Lakes Council.

18494 ■ Camp Randall Rowing Club
c/o Steven Schaefer, Pres.
15 N Butler St., Ste.404
Madison, WI 53703-4216
Ph: (608)256-3636
Fax: (608)661-9200
E-mail: info@camprandallrc.org
URL: http://www.camprandallrc.org
Contact: Mr. Steven T. Schaefer, Pres.
Founded: 1995. **Members:** 100. **Membership Dues:** individual, $35 (annual). **Local**. Provides competitive rowing programs for adults and high school students. **Publications:** *Brittingham Bruit*, quarterly. Newsletter. **Price:** free. **Circulation:** 220.

18495 ■ Capital City Corvair Club (CCCC)
2795 Allegheny Dr.
Madison, WI 53719
Ph: (608)845-7580
E-mail: lmfry@aol.com
URL: http://www.capitalcitycorvairs.com
Contact: Larry Fry, Pres.
Founded: 1963. **Membership Dues:** regular, $12 (annual). **Local**. Enthusiasts of the Corvair automobile united for technical assistance and parts availability. **Affiliated With:** Corvair Society of America. **Publications:** *Exhaust*, monthly. Newsletter. **Price:** included in membership dues.

18496 ■ Church World Service/CROP, Wisconsin Region
1955 W Broadway, Ste.102
Madison, WI 53713
Ph: (608)222-7008 (608)222-4875
Free: (888)297-2767
Contact: Gaston Razafy, Regional Dir.
Founded: 1945. **Members:** 36. **Regional Groups:** 26. **State Groups:** 1. **Regional**. Volunteers dedicated to organizing communities for understanding, action, and fundraising for world hunger. **Affiliated With:** Church World Service. **Formerly:** Church World Service/Crop, Wisconsin-Northern Illinois Region. **Publications:** *The Cropwalker*, biennial. Newsletter. **Price:** free • *Service Illustrated*, 3/year. Newsletter.

18497 ■ Citizens Utility Board (CUB)
16 N Carroll St., Ste.720
Madison, WI 53703
Ph: (608)251-3322
Fax: (608)251-7609
E-mail: staff@wiscub.org
URL: http://www.wiscub.org
Contact: Charles Higley, Exec.Dir.
Founded: 1980. **Members:** 8,000. **Staff:** 3. **Budget:** $250,000. **State Groups:** 1. **State**. **Publications:** *Citizen's Utility Board Reporter*, 3/year. Newsletter. **Circulation:** 5,000.

18498 ■ Coalition of Wisconsin Aging Groups (CWAG)
c/o Thomas L. Frazier, Exec.Dir.
2850 Dairy Dr., Ste.100
Madison, WI 53718-6751
Ph: (608)224-0606
Fax: (608)224-0607
Free: (800)366-2990
E-mail: cwag@cwag.org
URL: http://www.cwag.org
Contact: Mary Jorgensen, Contact
Founded: 1978. **Members:** 125,000. **Membership Dues:** group, $25 (annual) • individual, $15 (annual) • business (25 or fewer employees), $50 (annual) • business (26 or more employees), $100 (annual) • life, $150. **Staff:** 26. **Budget:** $1,000,000. **State Groups:** 600. **State**. Groups interested in issues relating to older citizens. Conducts educational, legal, and advocacy activities; lobbies and encourages members to lobby. **Libraries: Type:** not open to the public. **Subjects:** elder law. **Publications:** *Action Alert*, 5/year • *CWAG Advocate*, quarterly. Newspaper • *Guardianship*. Newsletter • *Legislative Update*, 5/year. Newsletter. **Conventions/Meetings:** quarterly board meeting • annual convention • regional meeting - 2-4/year.

18499 ■ Common Cause Wisconsin (CC/WI)
PO Box 2597
Madison, WI 53701-2597
Ph: (608)256-2686
Fax: (608)256-2686
E-mail: ccwisjwh@itis.com
URL: http://commoncause.sitemanager.ims.net
Contact: Jay Heck, Exec.Dir.
Founded: 1975. **Members:** 4,300. **Membership Dues:** individual, $25 (annual) • family, $40 (annual) • contributing, $75-$200. **Staff:** 2. **Budget:** $90,000. **State**. Promotes government and political openness and accountability through research, advocacy, and lobbying. Campaigns finance, ethics and lobby reform, open meetings law and other issues concerning the promotion and maintenance of "clean," open, responsive and accountable government. Works on issues at the state and federal levels. **Affiliated With:** Common Cause. **Publications:** *Common Sense*, quarterly. Newsletter. Features updates on issues and activities for statewide membership. **Price:** free. **Circulation:** 4,500. Alternate Formats: online. **Conventions/Meetings:** quarterly board meeting, with legislative agenda, budget, other issues - always January, April, July and October in Madison, WI.

18500 ■ Community Analysis and Planning Division (CAPD)
30 W Mifflin St., Rm. 402
Madison, WI 53703
Ph: (608)266-4137
Fax: (608)266-9117
E-mail: info@danecorpc.org
Contact: William N. Lane, Exec.Dir.
Local. Regional planning agency.

18501 ■ Community Bankers of Wisconsin (CBW)
c/o Daryll J. Lund, Pres./CEO
455 County Rd. M, Ste.101
Madison, WI 53719
Ph: (608)833-4229
Fax: (608)833-8114
E-mail: info@communitybankers.org
URL: http://www.communitybankers.org
Contact: Daryll J. Lund, Pres./CEO
State.

18502 ■ Construction Labor-Management Association
718 Post Rd., Ste.D
Madison, WI 53713
Ph: (608)271-5501
Fax: (608)271-5981
E-mail: cmlcgw@ett.net
URL: http://www.clmcwisc.com
Local.

18503 ■ Dane County Humane Society (DCHS)
5132 Voges Rd.
Madison, WI 53718
Ph: (608)838-0413
Fax: (608)838-0368
URL: http://giveshelter.org
Contact: Pam McCloud-Smith, Exec.Dir.
Local.

18504 ■ Democratic Party of Wisconsin (DPW)
222 W Washington St., Ste.150
Madison, WI 53703
Ph: (608)255-5172
Fax: (608)255-8919
E-mail: party@wisdems.org
URL: http://www.wisdems.org
Contact: Linda Harold, Chair
Founded: 1948. **Membership Dues:** general, $20 (annual). **Local Groups:** 72. **State**. Individuals united to promote the Democratic Party platform and elect Democrats to government office. **Libraries: Type:** open to the public. **Holdings:** articles. **Subjects:** public policy, campaigns. **Affiliated With:** Democratic National Committee. **Publications:** *The Wisconsin Democrat*, periodic. Newsletter. **Conventions/Meetings:** annual convention (exhibits) - always June.

18505 ■ Durendal Fencing Club
c/o Jessie Glaeser, Sec. and Instructor
Neighborhood House Community Ctr.
29 S Mills St.
Madison, WI 53715
Ph: (608)231-9215 (608)233-1612
E-mail: jessieglaeser@yahoo.com
URL: http://www.geocities.com/~dvrendal
Contact: Jessie Glaeser, Sec. and Instructor
Local. Amateur fencers. **Affiliated With:** United States Fencing Association.

18506 ■ East Side Business Men's Association (ESBMA)
3735 Monona Dr.
Madison, WI 53714
Ph: (608)222-9131
Fax: (608)222-9132
E-mail: office@esbma.com
URL: http://www.esbma.com
Contact: James Veloff, Contact
Local.

18507 ■ Easter Seals Wisconsin
101 Nob Hill Rd., Ste.301
Madison, WI 53713
Ph: (608)277-8288
Fax: (608)277-8333
Free: (800)422-2324
E-mail: wawbeek@wi.easterseals.com
URL: http://wi.easterseals.com
Contact: William J. Holley, Chm.
State. Supporters, public and private partners, and volunteers. Strives to help people with disabilities by creating solutions and enhancing quality of life. **Affiliated With:** Easter Seals.

18508 ■ Employee Assistance Professionals Association - South Central Wisconsin Chapter
PO Box 252
Madison, WI 53701-0252
Ph: (608)240-5458
E-mail: david.rutter@doc.state.wi.us
URL: http://www.eapa.info/ChaptBranch/WI03/SCentralWisconsin.htm
Contact: David Rutter, Pres.
Local. Affiliated With: Employee Assistance Professionals Association.

18509 ■ Epilepsy Foundation South Central Wisconsin
1302 Mendota St., No. 100
Madison, WI 53714-1024
Ph: (608)442-5555
Fax: (608)442-7474
Free: (800)657-4929
E-mail: ataggart@wisc.edu
URL: http://www.epilepsyfoundation.org/socentralwisc
Contact: Arthur Taggart, Exec.Dir.
Founded: 1980. **Budget:** $250,000. **Local Groups:** 15. **Local**. Enhances the quality of life for individuals affected by epilepsy. Aims to educate and support individuals with epilepsy and their families, to increase awareness in the general community, and to facilitate prevention and management of epilepsy. **Affiliated With:** Epilepsy Foundation.

18510 ■ Four Lakes Ice Yacht Club (4LIYC)
c/o Jerry Simon, Interim Treas.
3788 Highridge Rd.
Madison, WI 53718
Ph: (608)233-9744
E-mail: debwhitehorse@iceboat.org
URL: http://www.iceboat.org
Contact: Jerry Simon, Interim Treas.
Local.

18511 ■ Friends of Madison School and Community Recreation
c/o Friends of MSCR
3802 Regent St.
Madison, WI 53705-5221
Ph: (608)204-3000 (608)204-3015
E-mail: lchaffin@madison.k12.wi.us
URL: http://www.mscr.org
Contact: Ms. Lucy Chaffin, Dir.
Founded: 2000. **Members:** 200. **Membership Dues:** regular, $10-$100 (annual). **Budget:** $10,000. **Local Groups:** 1. **Local**. **Awards:** Friends of MSCR Mini-Grants. **Frequency:** annual. **Type:** monetary. **Recipient:** for program development within MSCR.

18512 ■ Friends of Troy Gardens (FTG)
c/o Sundee Wislow, Exec.Dir.
Rm. 171 Bldg. 14
3601 Memorial Dr.
Madison, WI 53704
Ph: (608)240-0409
E-mail: info@troygardens.org
URL: http://www.troygardens.org
Contact: Sundee Wislow, Exec.Dir.
Local.

18513 ■ Friends of WHA-TV
c/o Wisconsin Public Television
821 Univ. Ave.
Madison, WI 53706
Ph: (608)263-2121
Free: (800)253-1158
URL: http://www.wpt.org
Contact: Jon Miskowski, Exec.Dir.
Local.

18514 ■ German Shepherd Rescue Alliance of Wisconsin (GSRAW)
c/o Sue Hasey, Pres.
PO Box 7354
Madison, WI 53707-7354
Ph: (608)839-8833 (608)334-1832
E-mail: gsdrescue@gmx.net
URL: http://www.gsraw.com
Contact: Sue Hasey, Pres.
Founded: 2000. **Members:** 18. **State**. Works to increase public awareness against animal cruelty and overpopulation, while rescuing and finding homes for displaced and unwanted German shepherds throughout Wisconsin and further, if necessary. **Conventions/Meetings:** monthly meeting - 2nd Wednesday.

18515 ■ Girl Scouts of Black Hawk Council
2710 Ski Ln.
Madison, WI 53713
Ph: (608)276-8500
E-mail: info@girlscoutsofblackhawk.org
Founded: 1927. **Members:** 11,000. **Local**. Provides informal education for girls ages 5-17.

18516 ■ Greater Madison Area Society for Human Resource Management
2830 Agriculture Dr.
Madison, WI 53718
Ph: (608)204-9814
Fax: (608)204-9818
E-mail: chapteradmin@gmashrm.org
URL: http://www.gmashrm.org
Contact: Belinda Weber, Pres.
Local. Represents the interests of human resource and industrial relations professionals and executives. Promotes the advancement of human resource management.

18517 ■ Greater Madison Chamber of Commerce (GMCC)
PO Box 71
615 E Washington Ave., 2nd Fl.
Madison, WI 53701-0071
Ph: (608)256-8348
Fax: (608)256-0333
E-mail: info@greatermadisonchamber.com
URL: http://www.greatermadisonchamber.com
Contact: Mrs. Jennifer Alexander, Pres.
Founded: 1913. **Members:** 1,500. **Membership Dues:** basic, $200 (annual). **Staff:** 10. **Budget:** $380,000. **Local**. Promotes business and community development in Dane County, WI. **Councils:** Greater Madison Collaboration. **Affiliated With:** U.S. Chamber of Commerce. **Formerly:** Madison Chamber of Commerce. **Publications:** *Business Beat*, monthly. Newsletter. **Advertising:** accepted. **Conventions/Meetings:** annual meeting - always in February.

18518 ■ Greater Madison Convention and Visitors Bureau (GMCVB)
615 E Washington Ave.
Madison, WI 53703
Ph: (608)255-2537
Fax: (608)258-4950
Free: (800)373-6376
E-mail: gmcvb@visitmadison.com
URL: http://www.visitmadison.com
Contact: Deb Archer CDME, Pres./CEO
Founded: 1972. **Members:** 600. **Local**. Area businesses representing all facets of the tourism industry. Strives to promote Madison and Dane County as a convention and tourism destination. **Publications:** *Group Tour Planner*, annual • *Kid's Guide to Greater Madison*, annual • *Visitors Guide*, semiannual • Membership Directory, annual. **Conventions/Meetings:** annual Business Card Exchange - meeting • annual Meeting Planners' Marketplace • semiannual New Member Orientation - meeting.

18519 ■ Habitat for Humanity of Dane County
PO Box 258128
Madison, WI 53725-8128
Ph: (608)255-1549
Fax: (608)255-1823
E-mail: hfh@chorus.net
URL: http://www.habitatdane.org/home.cfm
Contact: Brian Miller, Exec.Dir.
Local. Affiliated With: Habitat for Humanity International.

18520 ■ IABC/Madison
PO Box 5101
Madison, WI 53705
Ph: (608)261-2415
E-mail: hearivl@swib.state.wi.us
URL: http://madison.iabc.com
Contact: Vicki Hearing, Pres.
Local. Public relations and communication professionals. Committed to improve the effectiveness of organizations through strategic, interactive and integrated business communication

management. Provides products, services, and networking activities to help people and organizations excel in public relations, employee communication, marketing communication, public affairs and other forms of communication.

18521 ■ IEEE Madison Section
1126 Hathaway Dr.
Madison, WI 53711-3137
Ph: (608)278-0377
E-mail: rotter@ieee.org
URL: http://www.bugsoft.com/ieee
Contact: Sandy Rotter, Chair

Local. Engineers and scientists in electrical engineering, electronics, and allied fields. Promotes creating, developing, integrating, sharing, and applying knowledge about electro and information technologies and sciences for the benefit of humanity and the profession. Conducts lectures on current engineering and scientific topics.

18522 ■ Independent Business Association of Wisconsin (IBAW)
c/o Steve Sobiek, Exec.Dir.
1400 E Washington Ave., Ste.282
Madison, WI 53703
Ph: (608)251-5546
Fax: (608)251-5952
Free: (800)362-8027
E-mail: iba@ibaw.com
URL: http://www.ibaw.com
Contact: Steve Sobiek, Exec.Dir.

Founded: 1971. **Members:** 500. **State**. Established for networking and educational programming on a monthly basis, as well as political advocacy. **Publications:** *Small Business Today*, quarterly. Newsletter. Alternate Formats: online.

18523 ■ Industrial Workers of the World - Lakeside Press
1334 Williamson St.
Madison, WI 53703
Ph: (608)255-1800
URL: National Affiliate–www.iww.org

Local. Affiliated With: Industrial Workers of the World.

18524 ■ Industrial Workers of the World - Railroad Workers
PO Box 3010
Madison, WI 53704
Ph: (773)255-5412
E-mail: baltimored1@yahoo.com
URL: National Affiliate–www.iww.org

Local. Affiliated With: Industrial Workers of the World.

18525 ■ Institute of Internal Auditors, Madison Chapter
c/o Dawn Vogel
Great Lakes Educal. Loan Sers., Inc.
2401 Intl. Ln.
Madison, WI 53704-3192
Ph: (608)246-1691
E-mail: admin@iiamad.org
URL: http://iiamad.org
Contact: Dawn Vogel, Pres.

Membership Dues: regular, $115 (annual) • educator, $65 (annual) • student, retired, $30 (annual) • life, $2,100 • sustainer (government auditors only), $50 (annual) • organization ($65 per staff member over 5; $50 per staff member over 100), $425-$6,600 (annual). **Local**. Serves as advocate for the internal audit profession. Provides certification, education, research, and technological guidance for the profession. **Committees:** Academic Relations; Government Relations; Historian; Long Range Planning; Meeting Arrangements; Programs & Seminars; Research. **Affiliated With:** Institute of Internal Auditors. **Publications:** Newsletter, periodic. Alternate Formats: online.

18526 ■ Institute of Real Estate Management - Madison Chapter No. 82
c/o Kevin King
4801 Forest Run Rd., Ste.101
Madison, WI 53704-7337
Ph: (608)240-2800
Fax: (608)240-2801
E-mail: kking@wisre.com
URL: National Affiliate–www.irem.org
Contact: Kevin King, Contact

Local. Represents real property and asset management professionals. Works to promote professional ethics and standards in the field of property management. Strives to keep its members informed on the latest legislative activities and current industry trends. Provides classroom training, continuing education seminars, job referral service and candidate assistance services to enhance the effectiveness and professionalism of its members. **Affiliated With:** Institute of Real Estate Management.

18527 ■ International Alliance of Theatrical Stage Employees, Moving Picture Technicians, Artists, M 251
418 Farley Ave.
Madison, WI 53705
Ph: (608)244-0909 (608)238-3492
Fax: (608)238-3492
E-mail: justinavic@charter.net
URL: National Affiliate–www.iatse.lm.com
Contact: Ms. Justina Vickerman, Sec.

Members: 99. **Local. Affiliated With:** International Alliance of Theatrical Stage Employees, Moving Picture Technicians, Artists and Allied Crafts of the United States, Its Territories and Canada.

18528 ■ International Association of Business Communicators, Madison Chapter
PO Box 5101
Madison, WI 53705
Ph: (608)261-2415
E-mail: hearivl@swib.state.wi.us
Contact: Vicki Hearing, Pres.

Local. Represents the interests of communication managers, public relations directors, writers, editors and audiovisual specialists. Encourages establishment of college-level programs in organizational communication. Conducts surveys on employee communication effectiveness and media trends. Conducts research in the field of communication. **Affiliated With:** International Association of Business Communicators.

18529 ■ International Association of Gay/Lesbian Country Western Dance Clubs, Dairyland Cowboys and Cowgirls
621 Emerson St.
Madison, WI 53715
Ph: (608)255-9131
Fax: (815)301-9573
E-mail: info@dcandc.org
URL: http://www.dcandc.org
Contact: Richard Kilmer, Contact

Local. Affiliated With: International Association of Gay/Lesbian Country Western Dance Clubs.

18530 ■ International Facility Management Association, Madison
c/o Laura J.S. Huttner, Pres.
1202 Northport Dr.
Madison, WI 53704
Ph: (608)242-6260
Fax: (608)242-6293
E-mail: huttner@co.dane.wi.us
URL: http://www.ifmadison.org
Contact: Laura J.S. Huttner, Pres.

Founded: 1984. **Local**. Comprised of facility managers representing all types of organizations including banks, insurance companies, hospitals, colleges and universities, utility companies, electronic equipment manufacturers, petroleum companies, museums, auditoriums, and federal, state, provincial, and local governments. Works to enhance the professional goals of persons involved or interested in the field of facility management (the planning, designing, and managing of workplaces). **Affiliated With:** International Facility Management Association.

18531 ■ International Interior Design Association, Wisconsin Chapter
c/o Linda B. Page, VP Membership
Kee Architecture
621 Williamson St.
Madison, WI 53703-3691
Ph: (608)255-9202
Fax: (608)255-9011
E-mail: keearch@keearch.com
Contact: Ms. Erica Neal, Contact

Founded: 1994. **Members:** 250. **Membership Dues:** professional, $405 (annual) • student, $40 (annual). **State**. Interior designers and others associated with the industry. Focuses on the needs of members and the profession of interior design by providing networking opportunities and continuing education programs aimed at keeping members up to date on changes in the profession. **Affiliated With:** International Interior Design Association. **Publications:** *Reflections*, 3/year. Newsletter. **Conventions/Meetings:** monthly board meeting • quarterly meeting, membership • semiannual State-Wide Educational Event - meeting.

18532 ■ International Personnel Management Association, Wisconsin
c/o Pamela Dollard, Pres.
Univ. of Wisconsin-Madison
1552 Univ. Ave., Rm. 418
Madison, WI 53706
Ph: (608)265-5534
E-mail: dollard@wisc.edu
URL: National Affiliate–www.ipma-hr.org
Contact: Pamela Dollard, Pres.

State. Affiliated With: International Public Management Association for Human Resources.

18533 ■ InterVarsity Christian Fellowship/USA
6400 Schroeder Rd.
PO Box 7895
Madison, WI 53707-7895
Ph: (608)274-9001
Fax: (608)274-7882
E-mail: information@intervarsity.org
URL: http://www.ivcf.org
Contact: Alec Hill, CEO/Pres.

Founded: 1941. **State**.

18534 ■ Invasive Plants Association of Wisconsin
c/o David Hamel, Sec.
PO Box 5274
Madison, WI 53705-0274
E-mail: info@ipaw.org
URL: http://www.ipaw.org
Contact: Mr. David O. Hamel, Sec.

Founded: 2001. **Members:** 200. **Membership Dues:** individual, $20 (annual) • organization/agency, $100 (annual). **Staff:** 1. **Budget:** $10,000. **Regional Groups:** 12. **State**. Advances understanding of invasive plants and encourage their control to promote stewardship of the natural resources of Wisconsin. **Publications:** *Plants Out of Place*, quarterly. Newsletter. Contains 9 to 16 pages b/w 8 1/2" x 11". **Advertising:** accepted. Alternate Formats: online. **Conventions/Meetings:** biennial Plants Out of Place - conference.

18535 ■ IPMA-HR Wisconsin Chapter
c/o Pamela Dollard, Pres.
Univ. of Wisconsin-Madison
1552 Univ. Ave., Rm. 418
Madison, WI 53706
Ph: (608)265-5534
E-mail: dollard@wisc.edu
URL: National Affiliate–www.ipma-hr.org
Contact: Pamela Dollard, Pres.

Local. Seeks to improve human resource practices in government through provision of testing services, advisory service, conferences, professional development programs, research and publications. Sponsors seminars, conferences and workshops on various phases of public personnel administration.

18536 ■ Jane Austen Society of North America, Wisconsin
3611 Sunset Dr.
Madison, WI 53705
Ph: (608)238-9272
E-mail: coop6@charter.net
URL: National Affiliate–www.jasna.org
Contact: Liz Philosophos Cooper, Contact
State. Affiliated With: Jane Austen Society of North America.

18537 ■ Juvenile Diabetes Research Foundation International, Western Wisconsin Chapter
c/o Western Wisconsin Chapter
7818 Big Sky Dr., Ste.No. 118
Madison, WI 53719
Ph: (608)833-2873
Fax: (608)833-9214
E-mail: westernwi@jdrf.org
URL: National Affiliate–www.jdrf.org
Contact: Nicole Schult, Exec.Dir.
Languages: English, Spanish. **Local.** Works to find a cure for diabetes and its complications through the support of research. Provides support for families and individuals battling insulin-dependent diabetes. Membership outreach and support group meetings and activities are scheduled throughout the year. Major fundraising events include WALK To Cure Diabetes, Spring Gala, RIDE To Cure Diabetes. **Affiliated With:** Juvenile Diabetes Research Foundation International.

18538 ■ Knights of Columbus, Madison
4297 W Beltline Hwy.
Madison, WI 53711
Ph: (608)274-5750
Fax: (608)274-8522
E-mail: eripp@wikofc.com
URL: http://www.wikofc.com
Contact: Eileen Ripp, Admin.Mgr.
Local. Affiliated With: Knights of Columbus.

18539 ■ Korean War Veterans Association, South Central Wisconsin Chapter
c/o Wayne Pickarts
6303 Kilpatrick Ln.
Madison, WI 53718
Ph: (608)222-2566
E-mail: wppickarts@aol.com
URL: National Affiliate–www.kwva.org
Contact: Wayne Pickarts, Contact
Local. Affiliated With: Korean War Veterans Association.

18540 ■ League of Wisconsin Municipalities
c/o Dan Thompson, Exec.Dir.
202 State St., Ste.300
Madison, WI 53703-2215
Ph: (608)267-2380
Fax: (608)267-0645
Free: (800)991-5502
E-mail: league@lwm-info.org
URL: http://www.lwm-info.org
Contact: Dan Thompson, Exec.Dir.
State. Affiliated With: National League of Cities.

18541 ■ Legislative Reference Bureau - Wisconsin (LRB)
PO Box 2037
Madison, WI 53701-2037
Ph: (608)266-3561
Fax: (608)264-6948
E-mail: lrb.library@legis.state.wi.us
URL: http://www.legis.state.wi.us/lrb
Contact: Stephen R. Miller, Chief
State. Provides information on legislative activity to the general public.

18542 ■ Mad Town Talls
c/o Dave Janiszewski
PO Box 5263
Madison, WI 53705
Ph: (608)829-2969
E-mail: madison@tall.org
URL: National Affiliate–www.tall.org
Contact: Dave Janiszewski, Contact
Local. Affiliated With: Tall Clubs International.

18543 ■ Madcap Squares
61 Waunona Woods Ct.
Madison, WI 53713-1769
E-mail: sqdnznut@charter.net
URL: National Affiliate–www.iagsdc.org
Local. Affiliated With: International Association of Gay Square Dance Clubs.

18544 ■ Madison Area Builders Association
c/o Nancy Caldwell CAE BIAE
5936 Seminole Centre Ct.
Madison, WI 53711-5164
Ph: (608)288-1133
Fax: (608)288-1136
E-mail: builders@maba.org
URL: http://www.maba.org
Local. Single and multifamily home builders, commercial builders, and others associated with the building industry. **Affiliated With:** National Association of Home Builders. **Formerly:** (2004) Madison Area Building Authority.

18545 ■ Madison Area Compensation Network
c/o Joan Provencher, CCP, Human Resource Dir.
Gp. Hea. Cooperative
PO Box 44971
Madison, WI 53744-4971
Ph: (608)251-4156
Fax: (608)828-9333
Free: (800)605-4327
E-mail: joan_provencher@ghc-hmo.com
Contact: Mr. Mike R., Admin. Reception Board
Local. Affiliated With: WorldatWork.

18546 ■ Madison Area Literacy Council (MLC)
c/o Melissa Cooley, Volunteer Coor.
1118 S Park St.
Madison, WI 53715
Ph: (608)244-3911
Fax: (608)244-3899
E-mail: melissa@madisonarealiteracy.org
URL: http://www.madisonarealiteracy.org
Contact: Melissa Cooley, Volunteer Coor.
Founded: 1974. **Members:** 800. **Staff:** 5. **Budget:** $300,000. **Languages:** English, Spanish. **Local.** Tutors, adult learners, and interested individuals in Dane County, WI. Seeks to improve literacy. Trains volunteers for tutoring adults in basic literacy and English as a second language. Provides tutoring and learners placement, follow-up, and support. **Publications:** *The Learning Connection*, quarterly. Newsletter. **Conventions/Meetings:** annual meeting.

18547 ■ Madison Area Quality Improvement Network (MAQIN)
2909 Landmark Pl.
Madison, WI 53713
Ph: (608)277-7800
Fax: (608)277-7810
E-mail: info@maqin.org
URL: http://www.maqin.org
Contact: Pat Lund, Member Services Dir.
Local. Promotes learning for business and community success.

18548 ■ Madison Area Technical College's Electron Microscopy (MATC-EM)
Madison Area Tech. Coll.
3550 Anderson St.
Madison, WI 53704
Ph: (608)243-4309 (608)246-6100
Fax: (608)246-6880
E-mail: wcarmichael@matcmadison.edu
URL: http://matcmadison.edu/electronmicros
Contact: William Carmichael, Contact
Local. Affiliated With: Microscopy Society of America. **Formerly:** (2005) Madison Area Technical College Society for Electron Microscopy.

18549 ■ Madison Association of Plumbing Contractors (MAPC)
c/o Marcie M. Marquardt, Exec.Mgr.
5940 Seminole Ctre. Ct., Ste.102
Madison, WI 53711
Ph: (608)288-1414
Fax: (608)288-1515
E-mail: mapcwi@aol.com
URL: http://www.mapcwi.com
Contact: Marcie M. Marquardt, Exec.Mgr.
Local. Contractors who furnish, install, and service plumbing systems. Promotes standardization of materials and methods in the industry.

18550 ■ Madison Atheists, University of Wisconsin
c/o Patrick Meade, Pres.
716 Langdon St.
Madison, WI 53706
Ph: (608)264-0845
E-mail: madison_atheists@lists.services.wisc.edu
URL: National Affiliate–www.atheists.org
Contact: Patrick Meade, Pres.
Local. Affiliated With: American Atheists.

18551 ■ Madison Audubon Society (MAS)
222 S Hamilton St., Ste.1
Madison, WI 53703-3201
Ph: (608)255-2473
Fax: (608)255-2489
E-mail: masoffice@mailbag.com
URL: http://madisonaudubon.org
Contact: Joanne Herfel, Pres.
Founded: 1936. **Members:** 2,500. **Membership Dues:** regular, $35 (annual) • senior, student, $15 (annual). **Staff:** 5. **For-Profit. Local.** Aims to educate members and public about the natural world and the threats that natural ecosystems are facing. Advocates preservation and protection of ecosystems. Develops and maintains sanctuaries to save and restore natural habitats. Chairs the WI Bird Conservation Initiative, which gave them the authority to manage over 2500 acres of protected area for wildlife. Activities include free field trips and public education programs and sponsors major events such as the Art Fair and Prairies Jubilee. **Committees:** Population and Habitat. **Affiliated With:** National Audubon Society. **Publications:** *The Audubon Caws*, monthly. Newsletter. Alternate Formats: online. **Conventions/Meetings:** monthly Madison Audubon Society Free Public Programs - meeting, natural history theme talks by invited speakers - every third Tuesday except July, August and December.

18552 ■ Madison Gem and Mineral Club
PO Box 55024
Madison, WI 53705
Ph: (608)831-6562 (608)712-2697
E-mail: klrmsk2@yahoo.com
URL: http://www.madison.com/communities/madisonrockclub
Contact: Steve Harsy, Pres.
Local. Aims to further the study of Earth Sciences and the practice of lapidary arts and mineralogy. **Affiliated With:** American Federation of Mineralogical Societies.

18553 ■ Madison Hours
c/o Jon Hain, Pres./Treas.
1202 Williamson St.
Madison, WI 53703
Ph: (608)259-9050
E-mail: postmaster@madisonhours.org
URL: http://www.madisonhours.org
Contact: Jon Hain, Pres./Treas.
Membership Dues: $5-$10 (annual). **Local.** Promotes economic equity and well-being, as well as

cooperation among community members. **Affiliated With:** HOUR Money Network.

18554 ■ Madison Jewish Community Council (MJCC)
6434 Enterprise Ln.
Madison, WI 53719-1117
Ph: (608)278-1808
Fax: (608)278-7814
E-mail: mjcc@mjcc.net
URL: http://www.jewishmadison.org
Contact: Mr. Steven H. Morrison, Exec.Dir.
Founded: 1940. **Staff:** 20. **Budget:** $900,000. **Local.** Works to provide coordination, consolidation and centralization of charitable, educational and cultural fund-raising activities in Madison toward building a strong and unified Jewish community. **Affiliated With:** Jewish Council for Public Affairs; United Jewish Communities. **Also Known As:** (2004) Jewish Federation. **Formerly:** (2004) Madison Jewish Welfare Fund. **Publications:** *Monthly Reporter*, 11/year, September to July. Newspaper. Contains local, national and international news of interest to the Madison Jewish community. **Price:** free. **Advertising:** accepted. Alternate Formats: online.

18555 ■ Madison Lakes Yacht Club (MLYC)
PO Box 7032
Madison, WI 53707-7032
Ph: (608)221-4696
E-mail: jasalvo@facstaff.wisc.edu
URL: http://www.mlyc.org
Contact: Jay Salvo, Commodore
Local.

18556 ■ Madison West Coast Swing Club
c/o Mark Jacobson, Pres.
PO Box 258067
Madison, WI 53713
Ph: (608)222-7750
E-mail: m.jacobson15@verizon.net
URL: http://www.madisonwestcoastswing.org
Founded: 1996. **Members:** 200. **Membership Dues:** regular, $20 (annual). **Budget:** $25,000. **Local.** Social club dedicated to enjoying and promoting West Coast Swing dancing, provides lessons, places to dance on a weekly and monthly basis and workshops with professionals. **Publications:** Newsletter, 3-4/year. Features club news. **Price:** included in membership dues. **Advertising:** accepted.

18557 ■ Madison West Kiwanis Club
c/o Rich Grooms, Pres.
329 Cheyenne Tr.
Madison, WI 53705
Ph: (608)661-0272 (608)712-2827
E-mail: rgrooms@mhtc.net
URL: http://madisonwestkiwanis.tripod.com
Contact: Rich Grooms, Pres.
Local.

18558 ■ Magic Soccer Club
c/o Julie Friesler
5329 Lacy Rd.
Madison, WI 53711
Ph: (608)288-9390
E-mail: administrator@magicsoccer.org
URL: http://www.magicsoccer.org
Contact: Julie Friesler, Coaching Dir.
Local.

18559 ■ Mathematical Association of America, Wisconsin Section
c/o Jeganathan Sriskandarajah, Chm.-Elect
3550 Anderson St.
Madison, WI 53704
Ph: (608)243-4313
E-mail: jsriskandara@matcmadison.edu
URL: http://www.maa.org/Wisconsin
Contact: Jeganathan Sriskandarajah, Chm.-Elect
State. Promotes the general understanding and appreciation of mathematics. Advances and improves the education in the mathematical sciences at the collegiate level. Provides resources and activities that foster scholarship, professional growth and cooperation among teachers, other professionals and students. **Affiliated With:** Mathematical Association of America.

18560 ■ Media Communications Association-International, Madison Chapter
PO Box 5315
Madison, WI 53705-0135
Ph: (608)831-9242
E-mail: mcaimadison@aol.com
URL: http://www.mcai-madison.org
Contact: Steve Schumacher, Pres.
Members: 60. **Membership Dues:** individual, $160 (annual) • organizational, $455 (annual) • commercial, $1,250-$7,500 (annual) • life, $1,000-$2,000 • retired, $45 (annual) • student, $43 (annual). **Local.** Serves individuals engaged in multimedia communications. Seeks to advance the benefits and image of media communications professionals. **Libraries: Type:** lending. **Holdings:** video recordings. **Computer Services:** Mailing lists, of members. **Affiliated With:** Media Communications Association International. **Publications:** *Storyboard*, bimonthly. Newsletter. **Advertising:** accepted. Alternate Formats: online • Membership Directory, annual. Alternate Formats: online.

18561 ■ Meeting Professionals International, Wisconsin Chapter
2830 Agriculture Dr.
Madison, WI 53718
Ph: (608)204-9816
Fax: (608)204-9818
E-mail: admin@mpiwi.org
URL: http://www.mpiwi.org
Contact: Kim Marie Ball CMP, Pres.
Members: 325. **Membership Dues:** planner/supplier, $325 (annual). **Staff:** 1. **Budget:** $100,000. **State. Awards:** Supplier and Planner of the Year. **Frequency:** annual. **Type:** recognition. **Affiliated With:** Meeting Professionals International. **Publications:** *Agenda*, periodic. Newsletter. **Conventions/Meetings:** monthly meeting.

18562 ■ Midwest Environmental Advocates (MEA)
c/o Melissa K. Scanlan, Founder and Exec.Dir.
702 E Johnson St.
Madison, WI 53703
Ph: (608)251-5047
Fax: (608)268-0205
E-mail: advocate@midwestadvocates.org
URL: http://www.midwest-e-advocates.org
Founded: 1999. **Staff:** 3. **Regional.**

18563 ■ Midwest Equipment Dealers Association (MEDA)
c/o Gary W. Manke, CAE, Exec.VP
5330 Wall St., Ste.100
Madison, WI 53718
Ph: (608)240-4700
Fax: (608)240-2069
E-mail: meda@medaassn.com
URL: http://www.meda-online.com
Contact: Gary W. Manke CAE, Exec.VP
Founded: 1991. **Regional.** Committed to building the best business environment for equipment dealers in Illinois and Wisconsin.

18564 ■ Midwest Food Processors Association (MWFPA)
PO Box 1297
Madison, WI 53701-1297
Ph: (608)255-9946
Fax: (608)255-9838
E-mail: info@mwfpa.org
URL: http://www.mwfpa.org
Contact: John Exner, Pres.
Founded: 1903. **Members:** 245. **Membership Dues:** processor, $2,015-$6,660 (annual) • associate, $360 (annual). **Staff:** 4. **Budget:** $300,000. **State.** Serves food processors in Illinois, Minnesota and Wisconsin. **Publications:** *MWFPA News*. Newsletter • Directory, annual. **Conventions/Meetings:** annual meeting (exhibits).

18565 ■ Mining Impact Coalition of Wisconsin
PO Box 55372
Madison, WI 53705
Ph: (608)233-8455
Fax: (608)233-8455
E-mail: burroak15@aol.com
URL: http://www.miningimpacts.net
Contact: Dave Blouin, Treas./Coor.
Founded: 1994. **Members:** 800. **Budget:** $25,000. **State.** Conducts research and educate people on the impacts of metallic and nonmetallic mining.

18566 ■ Muscular Dystrophy Association of Southwestern Wisconsin
2744 Agriculture Dr.
Madison, WI 53718
Ph: (608)222-3269
Fax: (608)222-6171
E-mail: madisondistrict@mdausa.org
URL: http://www.mdausa.org
Contact: Cheryl Balazs, District Dir.
Founded: 1950. **Members:** 500. **Staff:** 4. **Budget:** $791,000. **For-Profit. Local.** Individuals with Muscular Dystrophy and their families and friends. Offers assistance with wheelchairs and braces plus a MDA clinic based at University of Wisconsin Hospital in Madison, WI. Sponsors free summer camp for kids 6-21 with a neuromuscular disease, support groups for ALS or Lou Gehrig's Disease, and pays for research in order to find a cure. Also sponsors local fundraising. **Affiliated With:** Muscular Dystrophy Association. **Publications:** *MDA Matters*, quarterly. Newsletter. **Price:** free. **Circulation:** 700. **Conventions/Meetings:** quarterly executive committee meeting • annual regional meeting.

18567 ■ Musicians AFM, LU 166 - AFL-CIO (MAMA)
6414 Copps Ave., Ste.121
Madison, WI 53716
Ph: (608)222-3030
Free: (877)222-3942
E-mail: afm166madison@chorus.net
Contact: Leatrice Sorem, Sec.-Treas.
Founded: 1901. **Members:** 171. **Membership Dues:** regular, $103 (annual). **Local. Affiliated With:** American Federation of Musicians of the United States and Canada. **Also Known As:** Madison Area Musicians Association Local 166. **Publications:** *Newscast*, 4-6/year. Newsletter. **Advertising:** accepted.

18568 ■ Muskies Capital City Chapter
PO Box 8862
Madison, WI 53708
Ph: (608)241-0210
E-mail: info@capitalcitymuskiesinc.org
URL: http://www.capitalcitymuskiesinc.org
Contact: Steve Reinstra, Pres.
State.

18569 ■ NACE International, Wisconsin Section
c/o Larry Capps, Chm.
PO Box 1231
Madison, WI 53701-1231
Ph: (608)252-7224
Fax: (608)252-5658
E-mail: lcapps@mge.com
URL: National Affiliate–www.nace.org
Contact: Larry Capps, Chm.
State. Promotes public safety by advancing the knowledge of corrosion engineering and science. Works to raise awareness of corrosion control and prevention technology among government agencies and legislators, businesses, professional societies and the general public. **Affiliated With:** NACE International: The Corrosion Society.

18570 ■ NAMI Wisconsin
4233 W Beltline Hwy.
Madison, WI 53711

Ph: (608)268-6000
Fax: (608)268-6004
Free: (800)236-2988
E-mail: nami@namiwisconsin.org
URL: http://www.namiwisconsin.org
Contact: Donna Wrenn, Exec.Dir.
Founded: 1980. **Membership Dues:** professional, $40 (annual) • individual/family, $30 (annual) • low income, $7 (annual) • open door, $3 (annual). **State**. Strives to improve the quality of life of persons who are affected by mental illnesses throughout Wisconsin. **Libraries: Type:** lending. **Holdings:** audio recordings, books, video recordings. **Subjects:** mental illness. **Publications:** *Advocate*, bimonthly. Newsletter • *The Iris*, bimonthly. Newsletter. Contains information about national, state and local affiliate activities.

18571 ■ Nation Council for GeoCosmic Research, Madison Chapter
6701 Seyfield Rd., Ste.119
Madison, WI 53719
Ph: (608)442-5156
URL: National Affiliate–www.geocosmic.org
Contact: Jacquelyn Archer, Contact
Local. Raises the standards of astrological education and research. Works to foster and publish research of a geocosmic nature and to pursue educational programs in various interdisciplinary fields related to geocosmic studies. **Affiliated With:** National Council for GeoCosmic Research.

18572 ■ National Abortion and Reproductive Action League of Wisconsin
122 State St., Ste.201
Madison, WI 53703-2500
Ph: (608)287-0016
Fax: (608)287-0176
Free: (800)752-8024
E-mail: info@prochoicewisconsin.org
URL: http://www.naralwi.org
State. **Affiliated With:** NARAL Pro-Choice America.

18573 ■ National Alliance for the Mentally Ill - Dane County
2059 Atwood Ave.
Madison, WI 53704
Ph: (608)249-7188
E-mail: namidane@chorus.net
URL: http://www.namidanecounty.org
Contact: Jim Hinsberger, Office Asst.
Local. Strives to improve the quality of life of children and adults with severe mental illness through support, education, research and advocacy. **Affiliated With:** National Alliance for the Mentally Ill.

18574 ■ National Association of Investors Corporation, South Central Wisconsin Chapter
PO Box 44682
Madison, WI 53744
Ph: (608)755-1283
E-mail: investor@cindystover.com
URL: http://better-investing.org/chapter/swiscon
Contact: Cindy Stover, Pres.
Local. Teaches individuals how to become successful strategic long-term investors. Provides highly focused learning resources and investment tools that empower individuals to become better investors. **Affiliated With:** National Association of Investors Corporation.

18575 ■ National Association of Social Workers - Wisconsin Chapter (NASW-WI)
16 N Carroll St., Ste.220
Madison, WI 53703
Ph: (608)257-6334
Fax: (608)257-8233
E-mail: naswwi@tds.net
URL: National Affiliate–www.naswdc.org
Contact: Marc D. Herstand, Exec.Dir.
Founded: 1974. **Members:** 2,550. **Staff:** 2. **Budget:** $165,000. **Local Groups:** 7. **State**. Professional social workers, students, and interested persons organized to: create professional standards for social work practice; advocate sound public social policies through political and legislative action; provide continuing education opportunities. Presents Social Worker of the Year, Public Citizen of the Year. Presents awards at annual conference. **Affiliated With:** National Association of Social Workers. **Publications:** *Wisconsin Social Worker*, bimonthly. Newsletter. Contains current and relevant information on SW issues in Wisconsin. **Price:** included in membership dues. **Circulation:** 2,700. **Advertising:** accepted. **Conventions/Meetings:** annual conference (exhibits) - always spring; Avg. Attendance: 200.

18576 ■ National Association of State Foresters, Wisconsin
c/o Paul DeLong
PO Box 7921
Madison, WI 53707
Ph: (608)264-9224
E-mail: paul.delong@dnr.state.wi.us
URL: National Affiliate–www.stateforesters.org
Contact: Paul DeLong, Contact
State. **Affiliated With:** National Association of State Foresters.

18577 ■ National Association of The Remodeling Industry of Madison
4269 W Beltline Hwy., Ste.B
Madison, WI 53711-3859
Ph: (608)222-0670
Fax: (608)222-0061
E-mail: info@remodelingmadison.org
URL: http://www.remodelingmadison.org
Contact: Kathy Raab, Exec.Dir.
Founded: 1979. **Members:** 206. **Membership Dues:** local, $395 (annual) • local national, $270 (annual). **Staff:** 2. **Budget:** $325,600. **Local Groups:** 1. **Local**. Remodeling contractors, manufacturers of building products, lending institutions, and wholesalers and distributors. Promotes the common business interests of those engaged in the home improvement and remodeling industries. Encourages ethical conduct, good business practices, and professionalism in the home improvement and remodeling industry. **Libraries: Type:** not open to the public. **Holdings:** 50; books, films, periodicals, video recordings. **Subjects:** remodeling techniques, business practices. **Awards:** Contractor of the Year Awards. **Frequency:** annual. **Type:** recognition • Individual Achievement Awards. **Frequency:** annual. **Type:** trophy. **Affiliated With:** National Association of the Remodeling Industry. **Publications:** *NARI Home Remodeling Directory*, annual. **Price:** free. **Circulation:** 10,000. **Advertising:** accepted. Alternate Formats: CD-ROM • *NARI Remodeled Homes Tour Guide*, annual. Brochure. **Price:** free. **Circulation:** 10,000. **Advertising:** accepted. Alternate Formats: CD-ROM • *Remodeling News*, monthly. Newsletter. **Price:** free. **Circulation:** 10,000. **Advertising:** accepted. Alternate Formats: CD-ROM. **Conventions/Meetings:** annual convention, showcases home improvement products and services (exhibits).

18578 ■ National Federation of Independent Business - Wisconsin
c/o Bill G. Smith, State Dir.
10 East Doty St., Ste.201
Madison, WI 53703
Ph: (608)255-6083
Fax: (608)255-4909
E-mail: bill.smith@nfib.org
Founded: 1943. **Members:** 600,000. **State**. Acts as an advocacy group for small businesses. **Affiliated With:** National Federation of Independent Business.

18579 ■ National Organization of Circumcision Information Resource Centers of Wisconsin - Madison
c/o Stan Emerson
PO Box 81
Madison, WI 53701
Ph: (608)246-3963
Fax: (608)246-3963
E-mail: nocirc@danenet.wicip.org
URL: http://danenet.danenet.org/nocirc
Contact: Stan Emerson, Contact
Local. Seeks to educate professionals and the public about routine infant male circumcision and the practice of female genital mutilation. **Affiliated With:** National Organization of Circumcision Information Resource Centers.

18580 ■ National Organization for Women - Wisconsin
122 State St., Ste.403
Madison, WI 53703
Ph: (608)255-3911
Fax: (608)255-1139
E-mail: admin@winow.org
URL: http://www.winow.org
State. **Affiliated With:** National Organization for Women.

18581 ■ National Society of Black Engineers - Wisconsin Black Engineering Student Society (NSBE-WBESS)
1083 Engineer Centers Bldg.
1550 Engg. Dr.
Madison, WI 53706
Ph: (608)263-5550
E-mail: wbess@cae.wisc.edu
URL: http://homepages.cae.wisc.edu/~wbess
Contact: Ninrat Datiri, Pres.
Local. Strives to increase the number of culturally responsible Black engineers who excel academically, succeed professionally and positively impact the community. **Affiliated With:** National Society of Black Engineers.

18582 ■ Natural Heritage Land Trust
303 S Paterson St., Ste.6
Madison, WI 53703
Ph: (608)258-9797
Fax: (608)258-8184
E-mail: meg@nhlt.org
URL: http://www.nhlt.org
Contact: Jim Welsh, Exec.Dir.
Founded: 1983. **Local**. Works to conserve the natural areas and open space in Dane and surrounding counties. **Formerly:** (2004) Dane County Natural Heritage Foundation.

18583 ■ Nature Conservancy, Wisconsin Field Office
633 W Main St.
Madison, WI 53703
Ph: (608)251-8140
Fax: (608)251-8535
E-mail: wisconsin@tnc.org
URL: http://www.tnc.org/wisconsin
Contact: Mary Jean Huston, State Dir.
Founded: 1959. **Members:** 25,000. **Membership Dues:** basic, $25 (annual). **State**. Works to preserve the plants, animals, and natural communities that represent the diversity of life on earth by protecting the lands and waters they need to survive. **Affiliated With:** Nature Conservancy. **Publications:** *The Places We Save*, periodic. **Price:** $16.95/copy • Newsletter, quarterly. **Conventions/Meetings:** annual meeting - always in September or October.

18584 ■ NIRS Forage and Feed Testing Consortium
c/o Dan Undersander
1975 Linden Dr.
Madison, WI 53706-1108
Ph: (608)263-5070
Fax: (608)262-5217
E-mail: djunders@facstaff.wisc.edu
URL: http://www.uwex.edu/ces/forage/nirs/home-page.htm
Contact: Don Sapienza, Pres.
Local.

18585 ■ Nonprofit Tech
266 Waubesa St., Ste.2
Madison, WI 53704
Ph: (608)241-3616
Fax: (608)241-3709
E-mail: help@nonprofit-tech.org
URL: http://www.nonprofit-tech.org/
Contact: Alnisa Allgood, Exec.Dir.
Founded: 1998. **Members:** 100. **Membership Dues:** affiliate member, $100-$1,000 (annual). **Regional**.

Libraries: Type: open to the public. **Holdings:** 600; articles. **Subjects:** nonprofit technology. **Computer Services:** database • electronic publishing • information services. **Also Known As:** (2004) Nonprofit Tech Association.

18586 ■ North American Lake Management Society (NALMS)
PO Box 5443
Madison, WI 53705-0443
Ph: (608)233-2836
Fax: (608)233-3186
E-mail: nalms@nalms.org
URL: http://www.nalms.org
Contact: Carol Winge, Office Mgr.
Local.

18587 ■ North Central College Health Association (NCCHA)
c/o Kathleen Poi, RN, Sec.
Univ. of Wisconsin-Madison
1552 Univ. Ave.
Madison, WI 53726
Ph: (608)262-1885
Fax: (608)262-4701
E-mail: kmpoi@wisc.edu
URL: http://www.acha.org/about_acha/affiliates/NCCHA
Contact: Kathleen Poi RN, Sec.
Regional. Serves as an advocate and leadership organization for college and university health. Promotes research and practices that advance the health of students and the campus community. Provides education, communication, programs and services that address the health issues of post-secondary students. **Affiliated With:** American College Health Association.

18588 ■ North Central Hearth, Patio and Barbecue Association (NCHPBA)
PO Box 259282
Madison, WI 53725-9282
Ph: (608)829-2580
Fax: (608)831-3590
E-mail: nchbpa@chorus.net
URL: http://www.nchpba.org
Contact: Karen Teske-Osborne, Exec.Dir.
Founded: 1992. **Regional**. Provides professional member services and industry support, including education, statistics, government relations, marketing, advertising, and consumer education. **Affiliated With:** Hearth Patio and Barbeque Association.

18589 ■ Office and Professional Employees International Union, AFL-CIO, CLC -Local Union 39
c/o John Peterson, Business Mgr.
1602 S Park St., Ste.226
Madison, WI 53715
Ph: (608)257-4734
Fax: (608)257-1155
E-mail: union@opeiu39.com
URL: http://www.opeiu39.com
Contact: John Peterson, Business Mgr.
Members: 1,813. **State**. **Affiliated With:** Office and Professional Employees International Union.

18590 ■ Olbrich Botanical Society
3330 Atwood Ave.
Madison, WI 53704
Ph: (608)246-4550
Fax: (608)246-4719
E-mail: scybart@cityofmadison.com
URL: http://www.olbrich.org
Contact: Sharon Cybart, Mgr. of Mktg. & PR
Founded: 1952. **Members:** 4,850. **Membership Dues:** single, $35 (annual) • family, $45 (annual). **Staff:** 32. **Local**. Strives to improve the quality of life and promote the art, science and knowledge of the plant world in partnership with Olbrich Botanical Gardens, which is owned and operated by the City of Madison Parks Department. The gardens feature 16 acres of outdoor display gardens, including the only Thia Pavilion and Garden in the continental U.S., and a year-round tropical conservatory. Supports all fund-raising, events, and educational programming at the gardens. **Libraries: Type:** open to the public. **Holdings:** articles, books, periodicals. **Subjects:** gardening. **Publications:** *Olbrich Garden News*, quarterly. Newsletter. **Price:** included in membership dues.

18591 ■ Operation Lifesaver, Wisconsin
c/o Jim Tracey
PO Box 7914
Madison, WI 53707-7914
Ph: (608)267-7946
Free: (800)WIS-RAIL
E-mail: james.tracey@dot.state.wi.us
URL: National Affiliate–www.oli.org
State. Seeks to reduce the incidence of grade-crossing collisions in the U.S. Works to increase public awareness on the frequencies of grade-crossing collisions and to correct driver behavior to avoid collisions and reduce pedestrian, trespasser incidents at grade-crossings and on railroad property through free educational presentations. **Affiliated With:** Operation Lifesaver. **Conventions/Meetings:** bimonthly meeting - 2nd Thursday of Jan., March, May, July, Sept., and Nov.

18592 ■ Orchid Growers Guild (OGG)
PO Box 5432
Madison, WI 53705
Ph: (608)238-5871
E-mail: egadzicki@charter.net
URL: http://www.orchidguild.org
Contact: Elaine Malter, Pres.
Local. Professional growers, botanists, hobbyists, and others interested in extending the knowledge, production, use, and appreciation of orchids. **Affiliated With:** American Orchid Society.

18593 ■ Outdoor Advertising Association of Wisconsin
c/o Janet Swandby, Exec.Dir.
44 E Mifflin St., Ste.101
Madison, WI 53703
Ph: (608)286-0764
Fax: (608)286-0766
E-mail: swandby@aol.com
State.

18594 ■ OutReach
600 Williamson St.
Madison, WI 53703-3588
Ph: (608)255-8582
E-mail: outreach@outreachinc.com
URL: http://www.outreachinc.com
Contact: Scott Mickelson, Sec.
Founded: 1973. **Staff:** 3. **Budget:** $180,000. **Local**. Gay and lesbian social service agency in Madison, WI. Seeks to be a vibrant and inclusive agent, dedicated to positive change for the lesbian, gay, bisexual, and transgender communities by providing services which nurture, strengthen, and celebrate the community. Educates and informs the public and members and advocates for social justice. **Libraries: Type:** open to the public. **Holdings:** 2,800; books, periodicals. **Subjects:** gay, lesbian, bisexual, transgender issues. **Awards: Frequency:** annual. **Type:** recognition. **Recipient:** for contributions to the community. **Formerly:** The United; Madison Gay/Lesbian Resource Center; (1998) Madison Community United. **Publications:** *Equal Time*, quarterly. Newsletter. **Price:** free. **Circulation:** 5,000.

18595 ■ Petroleum Marketers Association of Wisconsin/Wisconsin Association of Convenience Stores (PMAW/WACS)
121 S Pinkney St., Ste.300
Madison, WI 53703-5116
Ph: (608)256-7555
Fax: (608)256-7666
E-mail: pmawinfo@pmawwacs.org
URL: http://www.pmawwacs.org
Contact: Robert J. Bartlett, Pres.
Founded: 1926. **Members:** 573. **Staff:** 5. **State**. Petroleum marketers and convenience store owners. Represents members' interests; conducts educational programs; keeps members informed on industry activities. **Committees:** Budget and Audit; Convenience Store and PAC; Fuel Oil; Government Affairs; Nominating; Planning; Truck Stop Operators. **Affiliated With:** National Association of Convenience Stores; Petroleum Marketers Association of America. **Formerly:** Oil Jobbers of Wisconsin. **Publications:** *The Informer*, monthly. **Conventions/Meetings:** annual trade show.

18596 ■ Pharmacy Society of Wisconsin (PSW)
c/o Christopher J. Decker, RPh, Exec.VP
701 Heartland Trail
Madison, WI 53717
Ph: (608)827-9200
Fax: (608)827-9292
E-mail: dfargen@pswi.org
URL: http://www.pswi.org
Contact: Christopher J. Decker RPh, Exec.VP
State. **Publications:** *Fast Facts*, semimonthly. Newsletter • Journal, bimonthly.

18597 ■ Phi Theta Kappa, Beta Beta Psi Chapter - Madison Area Technical College
c/o Timothy Twohill
3550 Anderson St.
Madison, WI 53704-2599
Ph: (608)246-6293
E-mail: ttwohill@matcmadison.edu
URL: http://www.ptk.org/directories/chapters/WI/20685-1.htm
Contact: Timothy Twohill, Advisor
Local.

18598 ■ Physicians for Social Responsibility, Madison
c/o Alfred Meyer, Exec.Dir.
2712 Marshall Ct., Ste.2
Madison, WI 53705
Ph: (608)232-9945
Fax: (608)232-9464
E-mail: mail@psrmadison.org
URL: http://www.psrmadison.org
Contact: Alfred Meyer, Exec.Dir.
Local. **Affiliated With:** Physicians for Social Responsibility.

18599 ■ Prevent Child Abuse Wisconsin (PCAW)
211 S Paterson St., Ste.250
Madison, WI 53703
Ph: (608)256-3374
Fax: (608)256-3378
Free: (800)CHILDREN
E-mail: pcawi@preventchildabusewi.org
URL: http://www.preventchildabusewi.org
Contact: Patti Herman PhD, Exec.Dir.
State. Seeks to prevent child maltreatment through education, advocacy, resources and support for families. **Affiliated With:** Prevent Child Abuse.

18600 ■ Professional Insurance Agents of Wisconsin (PIAW)
6401 Odana Rd.
Madison, WI 53719
Ph: (608)274-8188
Fax: (608)274-8195
Free: (800)261-7429
E-mail: piaw@piaw.org
URL: http://www.piaw.org
Contact: Ronald Von Haden CIC, Exec.VP
Founded: 1950. **Members:** 3,400. **Membership Dues:** agency, $335-$1,400 (annual) • associate, company, $450 (annual). **Staff:** 5. **Budget:** $1,400,000. **State**. Independent insurance agents. **Awards:** Professional Agent of the Year. **Frequency:** annual. **Type:** recognition. **Publications:** *Wisconsin Professional Agent*, monthly. Magazine. **Circulation:** 2,900. **Advertising:** accepted. **Conventions/Meetings:** annual convention (exhibits) - July or August.

18601 ■ Progressive Dane (PD)
PO Box 1222
Madison, WI 53701
Ph: (608)257-4985
Fax: (608)257-6400
E-mail: office@prodane.org
URL: http://www.prodane.org
Local. Serves as a progressive political party based in Dane County, Wisconsin. **Affiliated With:** Working Families Party.

18602 ■ Project Management Institute, Madison/S. Central Wisconsin
PO Box 5392
Madison, WI 53705-5392
Ph: (608)661-7840
E-mail: mark.treiber@inacom.com
URL: http://www.pmi-madison.org
Contact: Mark Treiber PMP, Pres.
Local. Provides opportunities for professional growth through educational programs, professional development, networking opportunities, and support. Holds monthly meetings from September through May. **Affiliated With:** Project Management Institute.

18603 ■ Public Relations Society of America, Madison
c/o Paula M. Symons, APR, Membership Chair
RTI Donor Services-Allograft Resources Div.
6502 Odana Rd.
Madison, WI 53719
Ph: (608)231-9050
Fax: (608)231-9776
E-mail: psymons@rtix.com
URL: http://www.prsamadison.org
Contact: Paula M. Symons APR, Membership Chair
Local. **Affiliated With:** Public Relations Society of America.

18604 ■ Rainbow Families Wisconsin
c/o Outreach
722 Wedgewood Way
Madison, WI 53711-1137
E-mail: pjm8356@aol.com
URL: http://www.geocities.com/rainbowfamilieswisconsin
Contact: Allan Beatty, Chm.
State.

18605 ■ Realtors Association of South Central Wisconsin
4801 Forest Run Rd., Ste.101
Madison, WI 53704-7337
Ph: (608)240-2800
Fax: (608)240-2801
E-mail: jsmith@wisre.com
URL: http://www.rascw.org
Contact: Janine Smith, Contact
Local. Strives to develop real estate business practices. Advocates the right to own, use and transfer real property. Provides a facility for professional development, research and exchange of information among members and to the general public. **Affiliated With:** National Association of Realtors.

18606 ■ Rehabilitation for Wisconsin (RFW)
1302 Mendota St., Ste.200
Madison, WI 53714-1024
Ph: (608)244-5310
Fax: (608)244-9097
E-mail: rfw@rfw.org
URL: http://www.rfw.org
Contact: Michael Kirby, Exec.Dir.
Founded: 1977. **Members:** 55. **Staff:** 8. **Budget:** $474,789. **State**. Community rehabilitation programs for persons with disabilities. Seeks to assist members in helping people with disabilities achieve independence and employment. **Libraries: Type:** not open to the public. **Holdings:** 200; articles, books, periodicals. **Subjects:** rehabilitation, management ADA. **Awards: Frequency:** annual. **Type:** recognition. **Publications:** *Proform*, quarterly. Newsletter • Directory, annual. **Conventions/Meetings:** annual Catch the Wave - conference, with rehab products, computer products, insurance, packaging equipment - always spring.

18607 ■ Religious Coalition for Reproductive Choice - Wisconsin Chapter
900 Univ. Bay Dr.
Madison, WI 53705
Ph: (608)233-9774
E-mail: info@rcrcwi.org
URL: National Affiliate–www.rcrc.org
State. **Affiliated With:** Religious Coalition for Reproductive Choice.

18608 ■ Rotary Club of Madison (RCM)
22 N Carroll St., Ste.202
Madison, WI 53703
Ph: (608)255-9164
Fax: (608)255-9007
E-mail: office@rotarymadison.org
URL: http://rotarymadison.org
Contact: Patricia L. Jenkins, Exec.Dir.
Founded: 1913. **Members:** 500. **Membership Dues:** individual, $885 (annual). **Staff:** 2. **Budget:** $400,000. **Local**. Service organization of business and professional leaders. **Awards:** Joseph G. Werner Meritorious Service. **Frequency:** annual. **Type:** recognition. **Recipient:** for outstanding club service • Manfred E. Swarsensky Humanitarian Service. **Frequency:** annual. **Type:** recognition. **Recipient:** for individuals • Senior Service. **Frequency:** annual. **Type:** recognition. **Recipient:** for individuals aged 65 or older. **Affiliated With:** Rotary International. **Publications:** *Rotary News*, weekly. Newsletter. **Price:** $30.00/year. **Conventions/Meetings:** annual Rotary District Conference - convention (exhibits).

18609 ■ RSVP of Dane County
c/o D. Teztlaff, Dir.
517 N Segoe Rd., Ste.300
Madison, WI 53705-3108
Ph: (608)238-7901
Fax: (608)238-7931
E-mail: dtetzlaff@rsvpdane.org
URL: http://www.rsvpdane.org
Contact: D. Teztlaff, Dir.
Local. **Affiliated With:** Retired and Senior Volunteer Program.

18610 ■ Ruffed Grouse Society, John M. Keener Chapter
c/o James F. Shurts
2811 Chamberlain Ave.
Madison, WI 53705
E-mail: robertmclemore@carmax.com
URL: National Affiliate–www.ruffedgrousesociety.org
Contact: James F. Shurts, Contact
Local. **Affiliated With:** Ruffed Grouse Society.

18611 ■ Safe Community Coalition of Madison and Dane County
PO Box 6652
Madison, WI 53716-0652
Ph: (608)256-6713
Fax: (608)256-6795
E-mail: scc@safecommunitycoalition.org
URL: http://www.safecommunitycoalition.org
Contact: Ms. Cheryl Wittke, Exec.Dir.
Local. Seeks to reduce injuries through countywide, collaborative, educational safety campaigns.

18612 ■ Sand County Foundation
PO Box 3186
Madison, WI 53704-3186
Ph: (608)663-4605
E-mail: info@sandcounty.net
URL: http://www.sandcounty.net
Contact: David Allen, VP of Operations
Founded: 1965. **Staff:** 4. **Budget:** $1,000,000. **Nonmembership. Local**.

18613 ■ SCORE Madison
MG&E Innovation Center
505 S Rosa Rd.
Madison, WI 53719
Ph: (608)441-2820
Fax: (608)441-2821
E-mail: rlw-score145@charter.net
URL: http://www.madison.com/communities/score
Contact: Kent Anderson, Chm.
Local. Provides entrepreneur education for the formation, growth and success of small businesses in the area. **Affiliated With:** SCORE.

18614 ■ Sierra Club - John Muir Chapter (SC-JMC)
c/o Wisconsin Sierra Club
222 S Hamilton St., No. 1
Madison, WI 53703-3201
Ph: (608)256-0565
E-mail: john.muir.chapter@sierraclub.org
URL: http://www.sierraclub.org
Contact: Caryl Terrell, Dir.
Founded: 1965. **Members:** 14,000. **Membership Dues:** regular, $39 (annual) • introductory, $25 (annual) • senior, student, limited income, $24 (annual) • supporting, $75 (annual) • contributing, $150 (annual). **Staff:** 2. **Regional Groups:** 1. **State Groups:** 1. **Local Groups:** 8. **State**. Provides the public with opportunities to preserve, restore, protect and enjoy a clean and healthy environment, for the future of all living things. Empowers people to influence public policy that protects or improves Wisconsin's environment through grassroots activism, public education, outings, electoral process, lobbying, and when necessary, litigation. Promotes smart growth that protects wetlands, farms and forests and provides families with livable communities; reduces reliance on polluting, non-renewable sources of power through energy efficiency and conservation and promoting renewable sources of energy; and restores integrity of state government.

18615 ■ Sierra Club - Midwest Office
214 N Henry St., Ste.203
Madison, WI 53703-2200
Ph: (608)257-4994
Fax: (608)257-3513
E-mail: mw.field@sierraclub.org
URL: http://www.sierraclub.org
Contact: Alison Horton, Staff Dir.
Founded: 1892. **Members:** 600,000. **Membership Dues:** individual (after $25 introductory payment), $39 (annual). **Regional**. **Affiliated With:** Sierra Club.

18616 ■ Sisters of the Moon
c/o Lauranne Bailey
PO Box 7683
Madison, WI 53707-7683
E-mail: mcjourney@charter.net
URL: http://www.freewebs.com/witw_sotm
Contact: Lauranne Bailey, Contact
Local. **Affiliated With:** Women in the Wind.

18617 ■ Society of Broadcast Engineers, Chapter 24 Madison Wisconsin
c/o James Magee, Chm.
6400 Enterprise Ln., Ste.200
Madison, WI 53719
Ph: (608)288-5152
E-mail: jim.magee@inewsroom.com
URL: http://www.sbe24.org
Contact: James Magee, Chm.
Local. Serves the interests of broadcast engineers. Promotes the profession and related fields for both theoretical and practical applications. Advocates for technical advancement of the industry. **Affiliated With:** Society of Broadcast Engineers. **Publications:** Newsletter. Alternate Formats: online.

18618 ■ Society of Manufacturing Engineers - University of Wisconsin - Madison S133
Univ. of Wisconsin - Madison, Dept. of Indus. Engg.
1513 Univ. Ave.
Madison, WI 53706-1572

Ph: (608)262-9534
Fax: (608)262-8454
E-mail: szhou@engr.wisc.edu
URL: National Affiliate–www.sme.org
Contact: Shiyu Zhou, Contact
Local. Advances manufacturing knowledge to gain competitive advantage. Improves skills and manufacturing solutions for the growth of economy. Provides resources and opportunities for manufacturing professionals. **Affiliated With:** Classification Society of North America.

18619 ■ South Central Federation of Labor, AFL-CIO (SCFL)
1602 S Park St., No. 228
Madison, WI 53715
Ph: (608)256-5111
Fax: (608)256-6661
E-mail: thefed@scfl.org
URL: http://www.scfl.org
Contact: James A. Cavanaugh, Pres.
Founded: 1893. **Members:** 31,000. **Staff:** 3. **Local Groups:** 85. **Local**. Local unions. Seeks to secure united action of AFL-CIO unions; to advance the interests of organized labor and its members; to increase public understanding of the labor movement. Makes available scholarships; participates in United Way programs; sponsors annual Labor Day festival. **Affiliated With:** AFL-CIO. **Formed by Merger of:** (1988) Dane County Labor Council; Sauk County Federation of Labor. **Formerly:** (1984) Madison Federation of Labor; (1988) Dane County Labor Council. **Publications:** *Union Labor News*, monthly. Newspaper. **Price:** $6.00/year. ISSN: 0041-6924. **Circulation:** 19,000. **Advertising:** accepted. **Conventions/Meetings:** monthly meeting - always third Monday.

18620 ■ South Metropolitan Planning Council (SMPC)
2300 S Park St.
Madison, WI 53713
Ph: (608)260-8078 (608)260-8098
Fax: (608)260-8133
E-mail: smpc@terracom.net
Contact: Ms. Jean Nielsen, Facilitator/Admin.
Founded: 1997. **Members:** 13. **Staff:** 2. **Budget:** $164,000. **Local Groups:** 1. **Local**. Represents the coalition of Southside Madison neighborhood and business organizations whose purpose is to increase the civic capacity of community members, neighborhood groups, and partnerships and collaborations. Identifies issues for action, creates spaces where everyone's voice is heard, creates opportunities to get involved and to learn by doing, providing information and education, and leading and nurturing collective action. Works in Park Street revitalization, housing research, neighborhood organizing, and a community newspaper. **Awards:** Hands Across South Madison. **Frequency:** annual. **Type:** monetary. **Recipient:** to southside neighborhood associations and community organizations for projects that increase access to community-based programs, services, and activities for southside neighborhoods and residents. **Special Interest Groups:** Business Association; Neighborhood Associations. **Publications:** *Southern Exposure* (in English and Spanish), quarterly. Newspaper. **Price:** free. **Circulation:** 13,000. **Advertising:** accepted. **Conventions/Meetings:** monthly board meeting.

18621 ■ Special Libraries Association, Wisconsin Chapter
c/o Diane Gurtner, Pres.-Elect
Global Tech. Knowledge Kraft Foods
910 Mayer Ave.
Madison, WI 53704
Ph: (608)285-4025
E-mail: diane.gurtner@kraft.com
URL: http://www.sla.org/chapter/cwi
Contact: Diane Gurtner, Pres.-Elect
State. Seeks to advance the leadership role of special librarians. Promotes and strengthens members through learning, advocacy and networking initiatives. **Affiliated With:** Special Libraries Association.

18622 ■ Special Olympics Wisconsin (SOWI)
5900 Monona Dr., Ste.301
Madison, WI 53716
Ph: (608)222-1324
Fax: (608)222-3578
Free: (800)552-1324
E-mail: info@specialolympicswisconsin.org
URL: http://www.specialolympicswisconsin.org
Contact: Dennis H. Alldridge, Pres.
Members: 25,500. **Budget:** $4,500,000. **State**. Promotes physical fitness, sports training, and athletic competition for children and adults with mental retardation. Seeks to contribute to the physical, social, and psychological development of persons with mental retardation. Participants range in age from 8 years to adult and compete in 17 different sports. **Telecommunication Services:** electronic mail, dalldridge@specialolympicswisconsin.org. **Affiliated With:** Special Olympics. **Publications:** *Teammates*, quarterly. Newsletter. Alternate Formats: online. **Conventions/Meetings:** annual conference.

18623 ■ State Bar of Wisconsin
PO Box 7158
Madison, WI 53718-2101
Ph: (608)257-3838
Fax: (608)257-5502
Free: (800)728-7788
E-mail: service@wisbar.org
URL: http://www.wisbar.org
Contact: D. Michael Guerin, Pres.
Founded: 1957. **Members:** 14,800. **Staff:** 70. **State**. Regulates attorneys in Wisconsin and promotes professional development. Supports legal education of attorneys and lobbies on behalf of members. **Publications:** *Directory of Committees and Boards*, annual. Bulletin • Newsletter, monthly. **Conventions/Meetings:** semiannual meeting - always winter and spring.

18624 ■ Sweet Adelines International, Sound of Madison Chapter
Lake Edge Lutheran
4032 Monona Dr.
Madison, WI 53716-1138
Ph: (608)244-6777
E-mail: gloriab@uwdc.org
URL: National Affiliate–www.sweetadelineintl.org
Contact: Gloria Borchert, Contact
Local. Advances the musical art form of barbershop harmony through education and performances. Provides education, training and coaching in the development of women's four-part barbershop harmony. **Affiliated With:** Sweet Adelines International.

18625 ■ Sweet Adelines International, Yahara River Chapter
St. Paul Lutheran Church
2126 N Sherman Ave.
Madison, WI 53704-3933
Ph: (920)887-0732
E-mail: admackey@charter.net
URL: National Affiliate–www.sweetadelineintl.org
Contact: Annette Mackey, Contact
Local. Advances the musical art form of barbershop harmony through education and performances. Provides education, training and coaching in the development of women's four-part barbershop harmony. **Affiliated With:** Sweet Adelines International.

18626 ■ Tavern League of Wisconsin
2817 Fish Hatchery
Madison, WI 53713
Ph: (608)270-8591
Fax: (608)270-8595
Free: (800)445-9221
E-mail: info@tlw.org
Contact: Pete Madland, CEO
State.

18627 ■ Tobacco-Free Dane County Coalition (TFDCC)
c/o Teresa Ryan, Coor.
1202 Northport Dr.
Madison, WI 53704
Ph: (608)242-6442
E-mail: tobacofreedanecounty@yahoo.com
Contact: Teresa Ryan, Coor.
Local.

18628 ■ Trout Unlimited - Southern Wisconsin Chapter
c/o Mark Maffitt, Newscasts Ed.
6306 Bradley Pl.
Madison, WI 53711
Ph: (608)273-2140
E-mail: mark.maffitt@invitrogen.com
URL: http://www.swtu.org
Contact: Susan Fey, Pres.
Regional.

18629 ■ United Council of University of Wisconsin Students
c/o Exec.Dir.
14 W Mifflin St., Ste.212
Madison, WI 53703
Ph: (608)263-3422
Fax: (608)265-4070
E-mail: executive@unitedcouncil.net
URL: http://www.unitedcouncil.net
Founded: 1960. **Staff:** 9. **Local**. Wisconsin's statewide student association.

18630 ■ United States Naval Sea Cadet Corps - Badger Division
NMCRC Madison
1430 Wright St.
Madison, WI 53704-4192
E-mail: badgerdivision@yahoo.com
URL: http://dolphin.seacadets.org/US_units/UnitDetails.asp?UnitID=091BDR
Contact: LTJG Werner L. Gade NSCC, Commanding Officer
Local. Works to instill good citizenship and patriotism in youth. Encourages qualities such as personal neatness, loyalty, obedience, dependability, and responsibility to others. Offers courses in physical fitness and military drill, first aid, water safety, basic seamanship, and naval history and traditions. **Affiliated With:** Naval Sea Cadet Corps.

18631 ■ United Transportation Union, AFL-CIO - Wisconsin State Legislative Board 56
7 N Pinckney St.
Ste.50 C
Madison, WI 53703-2840
Free: (800)362-9472
E-mail: wisconsinutu@msn.com
URL: http://www.mailbag.com/users/utulo56/index.html
Contact: Thomas P. Dwyer II, Dir.-Chair
Members: 903. **Local**. **Affiliated With:** United Transportation Union.

18632 ■ United Way of Dane County
2059 Atwood Ave.
Madison, WI 53704
Ph: (608)246-4350
Fax: (608)246-4349
E-mail: lhoward@uwdc.org
URL: http://www.uwdc.org
Contact: Leslie Ann Howard, Pres.
Local. **Affiliated With:** United Way of America.

18633 ■ United Way of Wisconsin
PO Box 7548
Madison, WI 53707
Ph: (608)246-8272
Fax: (608)246-2126
E-mail: uww@unitedwaywi.org
URL: http://www.unitedwaywi.org
Contact: Stephen A. Webster PhD, Exec.Dir.
Staff: 3. **Budget:** $120,000. **State Groups:** 1. **State**. **Affiliated With:** United Way of America.

18634 ■ University of Wisconsin Aikido
2314 Coolidge St.
Madison, WI 53703
Ph: (608)249-1037
URL: http://www.usaikifed.com
Contact: Robert Felt, Instructor
Local. Affiliated With: United States Aikido Federation.

18635 ■ Urban League of Greater Madison
151 E Gorham St.
Madison, WI 53703
Ph: (608)251-8550
Fax: (608)251-0944
E-mail: ulgm@ulgm.org
URL: http://www.ulgm.org
Contact: Stephen L. Braunginn, Pres./CEO
Local. Affiliated With: National Urban League.

18636 ■ U.S.A. Track and Field, Wisconsin (WIUSATF)
c/o Mary Stroud
5203 Whitcomb Dr.
Madison, WI 53711
Ph: (608)274-4270
E-mail: mary.stroud@wiusatf.org
URL: http://www.wiusatf.org
Contact: Mary Stroud, Contact
Membership Dues: youth, $12 (annual) • adult, $15 (annual). **State. Affiliated With:** U.S.A. Track and Field. **Formerly:** (2005) U.S.A. Track and Field, Wisconsin Top.

18637 ■ VSA arts of Wisconsin
c/o Kathie Wagner, Pres.
4785 Hayes Rd., Ste.201
Madison, WI 53704-7364
Ph: (608)241-2131
Fax: (608)241-1982
E-mail: vsawis@vsawis.org
URL: http://www.vsawis.org
Contact: Ms. Kathie Wagner, Pres.
State. Works to expand the capabilities, confidence and quality of life for children and adults with disabilities by providing programs in dance, drama, creative writing, music and visual art. **Affiliated With:** VSA arts.

18638 ■ Wisconsin 4-H Foundation
610 Langdon St.
428 Lowell Hall
Madison, WI 53703
Ph: (608)262-1597
Fax: (608)265-6407
E-mail: donna.faulkner@uwex.edu
URL: http://www.uwex.edu/ces/4h/foundation
Contact: Donna Faulkner, Asst.
Founded: 1954. **State.**

18639 ■ Wisconsin Academy of Physician Assistants
PO Box 1109
330 E Lakeside St.
Madison, WI 53701
Ph: (608)283-5410
Fax: (608)283-5424
Free: (800)762-8965
E-mail: kathym@wismed.org
URL: http://www.wapa.org
Contact: Kathy Mohelnitzky, Contact
State. Supports and promotes the professional interests of physician assistants. **Affiliated With:** American Academy of Physician Assistants. **Publications:** *The Spectator*, 8/year. Newsletter. **Conventions/Meetings:** semiannual meeting (exhibits).

18640 ■ Wisconsin Academy of Trial Lawyers (WATL)
c/o Ms. Jane E. Garrott, Exec.Dir.
44 E Mifflin St., Ste.103
Madison, WI 53703
Ph: (608)257-5741
Fax: (608)255-9285
E-mail: contact@watl.org
URL: http://www.watl.org
Contact: Ms. Jane E. Garrott, Exec.Dir.
Founded: 1957. **Members:** 1,000. **Membership Dues:** active (based on number of years in legal practice), $55-$225 (annual) • sustaining, $750 (annual) • paralegal, legal assistant affiliate, $50 (annual) • inactive, $80 (annual). **Staff:** 7. **State.**

18641 ■ Wisconsin Agri-Service Association (WASA)
6000 Gisholt Dr., Ste.208
Madison, WI 53713
Ph: (608)223-1111
Fax: (608)223-1147
E-mail: info@wasa.org
URL: http://www.wasa.org
Contact: Tom Stehr, Pres.
Founded: 1994. **Members:** 500. **Membership Dues:** regular, $220 (annual) • associate, $1,100 (annual). **Staff:** 3. **State.** Represents the feed, seed, grain, and farm supply industries of WI. **Awards:** Eldon Roesler Scholarship. **Frequency:** annual. **Type:** scholarship. **Recipient:** for an individual with a GPA of 3.0 or greater who has completed 1 year of college and is studying an agricultural related field. **Affiliated With:** American Feed Industry Association; American Seed Trade Association; National Grain and Feed Association. **Publications:** *WASA Directory*, annual. **Price:** $30.00. **Advertising:** accepted. **Conventions/Meetings:** annual convention (exhibits).

18642 ■ Wisconsin Agribusiness Council (WAC)
PO Box 46100
Madison, WI 53744-6100
Fax: (877)947-2475
Free: (877)947-2474
E-mail: fhavenswac@mhtc.net
URL: http://www.wisagri.com
Contact: Ferron K. Havens, Pres./CEO
Founded: 1971. **State.** Dedicated to improving the business environment for agriculture in Wisconsin.

18643 ■ Wisconsin Alliance of Cities
c/o Edward J. Huck, Exec.Dir.
14 W Mifflin St., Ste.206
Madison, WI 53703-2568
Ph: (608)257-5881
Fax: (608)257-5882
E-mail: ed@wiscities.org
URL: http://www.wiscities.org
Contact: Edward J. Huck, Exec.Dir.
Members: 38. **State.**

18644 ■ Wisconsin Alliance of Hearing Professionals
c/o Douglas Q. Johnson
1 E Mark St., Ste.305
Madison, WI 53703
Ph: (608)257-3541
Fax: (608)257-8755
URL: National Affiliate–www.ihsinfo.org/
Contact: Douglas Q. Johnson, Exec.Dir. and Gen. Counsel
Founded: 1963. **Members:** 125. **State.** Hearing instrument specialists and audiologists. Disseminates information on hearing health care to the public and on the use and care of hearing instruments to the hearing impaired. **Affiliated With:** International Hearing Society. **Publications:** Newsletter, monthly. **Conventions/Meetings:** annual conference.

18645 ■ Wisconsin Apartment Association (WAA)
PO Box 2051
Madison, WI 53701-2051
Ph: (608)227-1024
Fax: (608)227-1002
E-mail: admin@waaonline.org
URL: http://www.waaonline.org
Contact: Karen Miskimen, Admin.
Founded: 1986. **Members:** 2,000. **Membership Dues:** regular, $80 (annual) • member-at-large, $165 (annual) • associate, $230 (annual). **Staff:** 6. **Budget:** $300,000. **Regional Groups:** 22. **Local Groups:** 22. **State.** Owners and managers of multi-family rental properties in Wisconsin. Promotes and provides education and information exchange on matters relating to the industry. Provides legislative advocacy. **Publications:** *Wisconsin Apartment News*, monthly. Magazine. **Price:** included in membership dues. **Circulation:** 2,200. **Advertising:** accepted. **Conventions/Meetings:** annual convention, seminars, booths and trade show (exhibits) • annual meeting.

18646 ■ Wisconsin Arts Board (WAB)
101 E Wilson St., 1st Fl.
Madison, WI 53702
Ph: (608)266-0190
Fax: (608)267-0380
E-mail: artsboard@arts.state.wi.us
URL: http://www.arts.state.wi.us
Contact: George Tzougros, Exec.Dir.
Founded: 1973. **Staff:** 12. **State.** Promotes the development of the arts throughout the state of WI. Supports artists and arts organizations with funds from the state legislature and the National Endowment for the Arts. **Awards: Frequency:** annual. **Type:** fellowship. **Recipient:** to Wisconsin residents • **Frequency:** annual. **Type:** grant. **Recipient:** to Wisconsin residents. **Publications:** *WI Art and Craft Fair Directory*, annual. Contains museum and gallery guide. **Price:** free. **Circulation:** 60,000.

18647 ■ Wisconsin Asphalt Pavement Association (WAPA)
c/o Gerald J. Waelti, PE, LS, Exec.VP
122 State St., Ste.507
Madison, WI 53703
Ph: (608)255-3114
Fax: (608)255-3371
E-mail: wiasppav@execpc.com
URL: http://www.wispave.org
Contact: Gerald J. Waelti P.E., Exec.VP
Founded: 1957. **Members:** 100. **Staff:** 2. **State.** Contracting companies (17); associate members are interested individuals (75). Works to promote the use of asphalt in road construction. Sponsors six educational seminars per year. **Publications:** *Wisconsin Asphalt Pavement Association Newsletter*, quarterly. **Price:** free. **Circulation:** 400. Alternate Formats: CD-ROM; online. **Conventions/Meetings:** annual convention (exhibits) - always December.

18648 ■ Wisconsin Assisted Living Association (WALA)
c/o Jim Murphy, Exec.Dir.
2875 Fish Hatchery Rd.
Madison, WI 53713-3120
Ph: (608)288-0246
Fax: (608)288-0734
E-mail: info@ewala.org
URL: http://www.ewala.org
Contact: Jim Murphy, Exec.Dir.
Founded: 1995. **Members:** 600. **Staff:** 3. **State. Affiliated With:** Assisted Living Federation of America.

18649 ■ Wisconsin Association on Alcohol and Other Drug Abuse (WAAODA)
6601 Grand Teton Plz., Ste.A
Madison, WI 53719
Ph: (608)276-3400
Fax: (608)276-3402
Free: (800)787-9979
E-mail: waaoda@artists.net
URL: http://www.waaoda.org
Contact: Yvonne Nair-Gill, Exec.Dir.
Founded: 1966. **Members:** 500. **Membership Dues:** small business (under 30 employees), $150 (annual) • individual, $25 (annual) • student/retired, $15 (annual) • corporate sponsor, $500 (annual) • corporate benefactor, $1,000 (annual). **Staff:** 2. **State.** Works to develop more effective response to alcohol and drug abuse/addiction problems, through education, prevention, and advocacy. **Committees:** Conference; Nominations; Personnel; Public Policy. **Publications:** *The Voice*, quarterly. Newsletter. Devoted to AODA education, prevention and advocacy. **Price:** free. **Circulation:** 530. **Conventions/Meetings:** quarterly

board meeting • annual conference, with training program (exhibits) - always spring.

18650 ■ Wisconsin Association for Career and Technical Education
c/o Bette Lou Esser, Exec.Dir.
518 Potomac Ln.
Madison, WI 53719-1115
Ph: (608)833-5858
Fax: (608)833-3011
E-mail: wacteorg@chorus.net
URL: http://www.wacteonline.org
Contact: Bette Lou Esser, Exec.Dir.
State. Supports vocational technical education that will assure students' successful roles in families, communities, and society. **Affiliated With:** Association for Career and Technical Education.

18651 ■ Wisconsin Association of Central Service Professionals
c/o Jean Hodge, Pres.
Meriter Hosp.
202 S Park St.
Madison, WI 53715
Fax: (608)267-5787
E-mail: jhodge@meriter.com
URL: National Affiliate–www.ashcsp.org
Contact: Jean Hodge, Pres.
State. Promotes healthcare central service, sterile processing and inventory management practices. Provides education, professional and organization development, advocacy and communication to healthcare service professionals. **Affiliated With:** American Society for Healthcare Central Service Professionals.

18652 ■ Wisconsin Association of Family and Children's Agencies
c/o John R. Grace, Exec.Dir.
131 W Wilson St., Ste.901
Madison, WI 53703
Ph: (608)257-5939
Fax: (608)257-6067
State.

18653 ■ Wisconsin Association of Health Plans
c/o Nancy J. Wenzel, Exec.Dir.
10 E Doty St., Ste.503
Madison, WI 53703
Ph: (608)255-8599
Fax: (608)255-8627
E-mail: pdougherty@tds.net
URL: http://www.wihealthplans.org
Contact: Nancy J. Wenzel, Exec.Dir.
State. **Formerly:** (2001) Association of Wisconsin Health Maintenance Organizations.

18654 ■ Wisconsin Association of Health Underwriters (WAHU)
4600 Amer. Pkwy., Ste.208
Madison, WI 53718
Ph: (608)268-0200
Fax: (608)241-7790
E-mail: dan@ewahu.org
URL: http://www.ewahu.org
Contact: Dan Schwartzer, Exec.Dir.
State.

18655 ■ Wisconsin Association for Healthcare Quality (WAHQ)
c/o Linda Buel, Pres.
UW Hosp. and Clinics
600 Highland Ave.
Madison, WI 53792
Ph: (608)203-4616
Fax: (608)203-4627
E-mail: la.buel@hosp.wisc.edu
URL: http://www.wahq.org
Contact: Linda Buel, Pres.
Founded: 1979. **Membership Dues:** general, $45 (annual). **State**. Focuses in healthcare quality across the continuum. Works as a state organization used for networking among members. **Affiliated With:** National Association for Healthcare Quality.

18656 ■ Wisconsin Association of Homes and Services for the Aging (WAHSA)
c/o Mr. John R. Sauer, Exec.Dir.
204 S Hamilton St.
Madison, WI 53703-3212
Ph: (608)255-7060
Fax: (608)255-7064
E-mail: info@wahsa.org
URL: http://www.wahsa.org
Contact: Mr. John R. Sauer, Exec.Dir.
Founded: 1960. **Members:** 200. **Staff:** 6. **Budget:** $1,100,000. **Regional Groups:** 6. **State Groups:** 1. **State**. Works to serve the elderly and disabled, comprised of 190 religious, fraternal, private and governmental organizations which own, operate and/or sponsor 94 nursing homes, 22 facilities for the developmentally disabled, 56 community-based residential facilities, 91 independent living facilities, and over 310 community service agencies, which provide programs such as Alzheimer's support, adult day care, child day care, home health, hospice, homecare, and Meals on Wheels. Provides programs and services to assist members in meeting the needs of elderly and disabled individuals. **Affiliated With:** American Association of Homes and Services for the Aging. **Publications:** Annual Report. Contains the profile, service and works of the organization. **Conventions/Meetings:** conference - spring • conference - fall.

18657 ■ Wisconsin Association of Independent Colleges and Universities (WAICU)
122 W Washington Ave., Ste.700
Madison, WI 53703-2718
Ph: (608)256-7761
Fax: (608)256-7065
Free: (800)4DEGREE
E-mail: mail@waicuweb.org
URL: http://www.wisconsinmentor.org
Contact: Rolf Wegenke PhD, Pres.
Founded: 1961. **Members:** 20. **Staff:** 13. **State**. Presidents of nonprofit, 4-year degree granting colleges and universities in WI. Promotes the interests of member institutions and private higher education. **Affiliated With:** National Association of Independent Colleges and Universities. **Publications:** *Guide to Admissions and Financial Aid*, annual. Manual • *The Independent*, quarterly • *The WTG Achievers*, monthly. Newsletters. Contains stories of students benefiting from the Wisconsin Tuition Grant.

18658 ■ Wisconsin Association of Insurance and Financial Advisors
c/o Cynthia L. Bong, Pres.
2702 Intl. Ln., Ste.207
Madison, WI 53704
Ph: (608)244-3131
Fax: (608)244-0476
E-mail: info@naifawisconsin.org
URL: http://wisconsin.naifa.org
Contact: Cynthia L. Bong, Pres.
State. **Formerly:** (2001) Wisconsin Association of Life Underwriters.

18659 ■ Wisconsin Association of Lakes (WAL)
c/o Peter Murray, Exec.Dir.
One Point Pl., Ste.101
Madison, WI 53719-2809
Ph: (608)662-0923
Fax: (608)833-7179
Free: (800)542-5253
E-mail: ptmurray@wisconsinlakes.org
URL: http://wisconsinlakes.org
Contact: Peter Murray, Exec.Dir.
Members: 350. **State**. Works to protect, restore, and conserve clean, safe, healthy lakes for everyone. Provides unified voice for public policy that will protect and preserve lakes, advance public knowledge of lakes, their watersheds and ecosystems, help local leaders manage and restore lakes and their watersheds, and assist lake groups and lake users in efforts to carry out this mission. Works in partnership with the Wisconsin Department of Natural Resources and the University of Wisconsin Extension Lakes Partnership Program to provide a strong technical, financial, and social support system for local lake organizations and lake users. **Affiliated With:** North American Lake Management Society.

18660 ■ Wisconsin Association of Mortgage Brokers (WAMB)
16 N Carroll St., No. 900
Madison, WI 53703
Ph: (608)259-9262
Fax: (608)251-8192
E-mail: info@wambrokers.com
URL: http://www.wambrokers.com
Contact: Lloyd Levin, Pres.
State. Promotes the mortgage broker industry through education, programs, professional certification and government affairs representation. Seeks to increase professionalism and to foster business relationships among members. **Affiliated With:** National Association of Mortgage Brokers.

18661 ■ Wisconsin Association of Parliamentarians (WAP)
c/o Robert Schuck, Pres.
22 N Franklin St., Apt. C3
Madison, WI 53703
Ph: (608)215-4668
E-mail: robertschuckprp@aol.com
URL: http://www.parliamentarians.org/WI
Contact: Robert Schuck, Pres.
State. Aims to study, teach, promote and disseminate the democratic principles of parliamentary law and procedure. **Affiliated With:** National Association of Parliamentarians.

18662 ■ Wisconsin Association for Perinatal Care (WAPC)
McConell Hall
1010 Mound St.
Madison, WI 53715
Ph: (608)267-6060
Fax: (608)267-6089
E-mail: wapc@perinatalweb.org
URL: http://www.perinatalweb.org
Contact: Ann E. Conway MPA, Exec.Dir.
State.

18663 ■ Wisconsin Association of School Boards (WASB)
c/o Ken Cole, Exec.Dir.
122 W Washington Ave., Ste.400
Madison, WI 53703-2718
Ph: (608)257-2622
Fax: (608)257-8386
E-mail: kcole@wasb.org
URL: http://www.wasb.org
Contact: Ken Cole, Exec.Dir.
State.

18664 ■ Wisconsin Association of School Business Officials (WASBO)
c/o Dr. Donald Mrdjenovich, Exec.Dir.
4797 Hayes Rd., Ste.101
Madison, WI 53704
Ph: (608)249-8588
Fax: (608)249-3163
E-mail: wasbo@wasbo.com
URL: http://www.wasbo.com
Contact: Dr. Donald Mrdjenovich, Exec.Dir.
Founded: 1947. **Members:** 550. **Membership Dues:** active, service affiliate, $125 (annual). **Staff:** 2. **Regional Groups:** 7. **State**. Seeks advanced school business management. **Awards:** Business Official of the Year. **Frequency:** annual. **Type:** monetary • Business Services Award. **Frequency:** annual. **Type:** grant • Wallace E. Zastrow Award. **Frequency:** annual. **Type:** monetary. **Affiliated With:** Association of School Business Officials International. **Publications:** *Taking Care of Business*, bimonthly. Newsletter. **Circulation:** 550. **Advertising:** accepted. **Conventions/Meetings:** annual conference (exhibits) - every spring.

18665 ■ Wisconsin Association of School Councils (WASC)
4797 Hayes Rd., No. 202
Madison, WI 53704
Ph: (608)241-7107
Fax: (608)241-7139
Free: (866)572-WASC
E-mail: roger@wasc.org
URL: National Affiliate–www.principals.org
Contact: Mary Price, Associate Dir.
Founded: 1934. **Members:** 500. **Membership Dues:** school group, $70 (annual). **Staff:** 3. **Budget:** $190,000. **State**. Public, private, and parochial school student decision-making organization. Provides student leadership training; offers counseling to members; facilitates interaction among school leadership organizations. Sponsors in-service programs, seminars, workshops, and regional meetings. **Awards: Frequency:** annual. **Type:** scholarship. **Affiliated With:** Association of Wisconsin School Administrators; National Association of Secondary School Principals. **Publications:** *Directory of Members*, annual • *News Notes*, 10/year. Newsletter • Booklet. **Conventions/Meetings:** annual JAM State Conference (exhibits) - last weekend in April • annual SHA State Conference (exhibits) - first weekend in May.

18666 ■ Wisconsin Association of School District Administrators (WASDA)
c/o Dr. Miles E. Turner, Exec.Dir.
4797 Hayes Rd., Ste.201
Madison, WI 53704-3292
Ph: (608)242-1090
Fax: (608)242-1290
E-mail: mturner@wasda.org
URL: http://www.wasda.org
Contact: Dr. Miles E. Turner, Exec.Dir.
State.

18667 ■ Wisconsin Association of Student Financial Aid Administrators (WASFAA)
c/o Karyn Graham, Data Base Mgr.
Univ. of Wisconsin, Madison
Off. of Student Financial Services
432 N Murray St.
Madison, WI 53706
Ph: (920)748-8101
E-mail: schuetzs@ripon.edu
URL: http://www.wasfaa.net
Contact: Steve Schuetz, Pres.
State. Represents the interests and needs of students, faculties and other persons involved in student financial aid. Promotes student aid legislation, regulatory analysis and professional development of financial aid legislators. Seeks to improve activities relating to the quality and improvement of student financial assistance in Higher Education institutions. **Affiliated With:** National Association of Student Financial Aid Administrators.

18668 ■ Wisconsin Association of Women Police (WAWP)
PO Box 2338
Madison, WI 53701-2338
E-mail: president@atswawp.org
URL: http://www.wawp.org
Contact: Kathy Schult, Pres.
State. Seeks to strengthen, unite and raise the profile of women in criminal justice. **Affiliated With:** International Association of Women Police.

18669 ■ Wisconsin Athletic Trainers' Association
c/o Joseph J. Greene, Pres.
621 Sci. Dr.
Madison, WI 53711
Ph: (608)265-8382
Fax: (608)265-8340
E-mail: jjogreene@charter.net
URL: http://www.watainc.org
Contact: Joseph J. Greene, Pres.
State. **Affiliated With:** National Athletic Trainers' Association.

18670 ■ Wisconsin Athletic Trainers' Association, Southwest
c/o John McKinley
3245 Stonecreek Dr.
Madison, WI 53719-5296
Ph: (608)263-5321
E-mail: jmckinleyatc@hotmail.com
URL: http://www.watainc.org
Contact: John McKinley, Contact
Local. **Affiliated With:** National Athletic Trainers' Association.

18671 ■ Wisconsin Automobile and Truck Dealers Association (WATDA)
PO Box 5345
Madison, WI 53705
Ph: (608)251-5577
Fax: (608)251-4379
E-mail: watda-info@watda.org
URL: http://www.watda.org
Contact: Mr. Gary D. Williams CAE, Pres.
Founded: 1929. **Members:** 900. **Budget:** $3,200,000. **State**. **Affiliated With:** National Automobile Dealers Association.

18672 ■ Wisconsin Bankers Association
c/o Harry J. Argue, Exec.VP
PO Box 8880
Madison, WI 53708-8880
Ph: (608)441-1200
Fax: (608)661-9381
Contact: Barbara Croucher, Contact
State.

18673 ■ Wisconsin Beef Council
c/o John W. Freitag, Exec.Dir.
680 Grand Canyon Dr.
Madison, WI 53719
Ph: (608)833-7177
Fax: (608)833-4725
E-mail: jwf@beeftips.com
URL: http://www.beeftips.com
Contact: John W. Freitag, Exec.Dir.
State. Represents the interests of educators, dietitians, home economists, restaurateurs, meat managers, nurses, physician assistants, and various other thought leaders to strengthen beef's position in the marketplace and to maintain and expand domestic and foreign markets. **Affiliated With:** Cattlemen's Beef Promotion and Research Board.

18674 ■ Wisconsin Broadcasters Association (WBA)
44 E Mifflin St., Ste.900
Madison, WI 53704
Ph: (608)255-2600
Fax: (608)256-3986
Free: (800)236-1922
E-mail: kristenb@wi-broadcasters.org
URL: http://www.wi-broadcasters.org
Contact: John Laabs, Pres./CEO
Founded: 1951. **State**.

18675 ■ Wisconsin Business Women's Coalition
c/o Gene Boyer, Pres.
46 Waterford Cir., No. 202
Madison, WI 53719
Ph: (608)273-9760 (954)389-1879
Fax: (608)273-9761
E-mail: geneboyer@aol.com
Contact: Gene Boyer, Pres.
Founded: 1986. **Membership Dues:** women business owners in business less than 3 years, $35 (annual) • in business more than 3 years, $60 (annual) • individuals whose interests and concerns parallel those of women business owners, $35 (annual) • friends of the coalition, $60 (annual) • corporate sponsors, coalition partners, organizations, government agencies, $100 (annual) • student, $15 (annual). **Budget:** $3,000. **Nonmembership**. **State**. Affiliation of grassroots organizations and individuals committed to identifying and representing the collective interests of Wisconsin women in business. Promotes equal opportunity and economic security for women in business and the self-employed. **Publications:** *Going Into Business Right*, periodic. Manual. Instructional manual that accompanies seminar presentation. **Conventions/Meetings:** periodic workshop - as scheduled.

18676 ■ Wisconsin Cable Communications Association
c/o Thomas S. Hanson, Exec.Dir.
22 E Mifflin St., Ste.1010
Madison, WI 53703
Ph: (608)256-1683
Fax: (608)256-6222
State.

18677 ■ Wisconsin Center for the Book (WCFB)
Wisconsin Acad. of Sci., Arts and Letters
1922 Old Univ. Ave.
Madison, WI 53726
Ph: (608)263-1692
Fax: (608)265-3039
E-mail: contact@wisconsinacademy.org
URL: http://www.wisconsinacademy.org/book/index.html
State. **Affiliated With:** Center for the Book.

18678 ■ Wisconsin Chapter of the American Planning Association (WAPA)
c/o Gary L. Peterson, Pres.
621 N Sherman Ave.
Madison, WI 53704
Ph: (608)249-2514
Fax: (608)249-6615
E-mail: maps@maps-inc.com
URL: http://www.wisconsinplanners.org
Contact: Gary L. Peterson, Pres.
State. Promotes the art and science of planning to meet the needs of people and society. Encourages the exchange of information and planning experiences. Advances the interests and welfare of the planning profession. **Affiliated With:** American Planning Association.

18679 ■ Wisconsin Chapter National Electrical Contractors Association
2200 Kilgust Rd.
Madison, WI 53713-4820
Ph: (608)221-4650
Fax: (608)221-4652
E-mail: loyal@wisneca.com
URL: http://www.wisneca.com
Contact: Loyal O'Leary, Exec.VP
Founded: 1962. **State**. Provides management services and labor relations programs for electrical contractors; conducts seminars for contractor sales and training. Conducts research and educational programs; compiles statistics. **Affiliated With:** National Electrical Contractors Association.

18680 ■ Wisconsin Chapter Triangle Fraternity
148 Breese Terr.
Madison, WI 53705
Ph: (608)233-2583
E-mail: atwitt@wisc.edu
URL: http://www.cae.wisc.edu/~triangle
Contact: Adam Witt, Pres.
Founded: 1913. **State**.

18681 ■ Wisconsin Cheese Makers' Association (WCMA)
8030 Excelsior Dr., Ste.305
Madison, WI 53717-1950
Ph: (608)828-4550
Fax: (608)828-4551
E-mail: office@wischeesemakersassn.org
URL: http://www.wischeesemakersassn.org
Contact: John Umhoefer, Exec.Dir.
Founded: 1891. **Members:** 300. **Staff:** 3. Active licensed cheese plants; active licensed cheese making employees; suppliers of goods and services to the industry. Seeks to educate members for better work in the art of making cheese, the care and management of factories, and the sale of the product.

Works to curb in competency in the business and to provide and enforce laws that will protect the manufacturer against deceitful imitations. **Awards: Frequency:** annual. **Type:** recognition. **Publications:** *Convention Book*, annual • Newsletter, monthly. **Conventions/Meetings:** annual International Cheese Technology - convention (exhibits) - always April even years in Madison, WI • biennial Wisconsin Cheese Industry Conference - convention - 2007 Apr. 18-19, La Crosse, WI.

18682 ■ Wisconsin Chiropractic Association (WCA)
c/o Russel A. Leonard, Exec.Dir.
521 E Washington Ave.
Madison, WI 53703-2914
Ph: (608)256-7023
Fax: (608)256-7123
E-mail: rleonard@aol.com
URL: http://www.wisconsinchiropractic.com
Contact: Russel A. Leonard, Exec.Dir.
State. Publications: *FYI*. **Conventions/Meetings:** annual meeting.

18683 ■ Wisconsin Citizen Action (WCA)
1202 Williamson St., Ste.B
Madison, WI 53703
Ph: (608)256-1250
Fax: (608)256-1177
E-mail: madison@citizenactionwi.org
URL: http://www.wi-citizenaction.org
Contact: Bob Hudek, Exec.Dir.
Founded: 1979. **Members:** 53,000. **Membership Dues:** coalition (based on the number of organizations), $150-$225 (annual) • organization (based on the number of members), $30-$575 (annual). **Staff:** 50. **Budget:** $1,000,000. **State Groups:** 1. **State**. Works for social, economic, and environmental justice. Current issues include campaign finance reform, public education reform, health care reform, lead poisoning prevention, family issues, and the environment. **Publications:** *Wisconsin Citizen Action Forum*, quarterly. Newsletter. **Price:** included in membership dues. **Circulation:** 54,000. **Advertising:** accepted. **Conventions/Meetings:** annual conference - always March, Milwaukee or Madison, WI.

18684 ■ Wisconsin Coalition Against Domestic Violence
307 S Paterson St., No. 1
Madison, WI 53703
Ph: (608)255-0539
Fax: (608)255-3560
E-mail: wcadv@wcadv.org
URL: http://www.wcadv.org
Contact: Linda Mayfield, Chair-Elect
State. Affiliated With: National Coalition Against Domestic Violence.

18685 ■ Wisconsin College Personnel Association (WCPA)
c/o Louise Paskey, Pres.
Edgewood Coll.
1000 Edgewood Coll. Dr.
Madison, WI 53711
Ph: (608)663-3228
E-mail: lpaskey@edgewood.edu
URL: http://www.myacpa.org/sid/wi
Contact: Louise Paskey, Pres.
State. Provides outreach, advocacy, research and professional development to foster college student learning. **Affiliated With:** American College Personnel Association.

18686 ■ Wisconsin Conservation Congress
c/o Wisconsin Department of Natural Resources
PO Box 7921
Madison, WI 53707-7921
Ph: (608)266-2621
Fax: (608)261-4380
E-mail: amy.lemberger@dnr.state.wi.us
URL: http://www.dnr.state.wi.us/org/nrboard/congress
Contact: Al Phelan, Liaison
Founded: 1934. **Members:** 360. **State Groups:** 1. **State**. Elected volunteers. Serves in an advisory capacity to the Natural Resources Board (the ruling board of the Department of Natural Resources). **Conventions/Meetings:** periodic meeting.

18687 ■ Wisconsin Coordinating Council on Nicaragua (WCCN)
PO Box 1534
Madison, WI 53701
Ph: (608)257-7230 (608)742-8408
Fax: (608)257-7904
E-mail: wccn@wccnica.org
URL: http://www.wccnica.org
Contact: Carlos Arenas, Exec.Dir.
Founded: 1984. **Members:** 1,100. **Membership Dues:** regular, $35 (annual). **Staff:** 6. **Budget:** $350,000. **Languages:** English, Spanish. WCCN is a nation-wide, non-profit, membership-supported organization working in partnership with Nicaraguans to promote social and economic justice through alternative models of development and activism. **Telecommunication Services:** electronic mail, exdir@wccnica.org. **Committees:** Loan Fund Oversight; Outreach; Women's Empowerment Project. **Projects:** NICA Fund; US-Nicaragua Women's Empowerment. **Publications:** *Bibliography on Alternative Credit in Nicaragua*. Alternate Formats: online • *Friends in Deed: The Story of U.S. Nicaragua Sister Cities*, quarterly. Book. **Price:** $10.00 • *Nicaraguan Developments*, quarterly. Newsletter. **Price:** included in membership dues. Alternate Formats: online • Annual Report, annual. Alternate Formats: online • Reports. Alternate Formats: online. **Conventions/Meetings:** annual meeting.

18688 ■ Wisconsin Council on Children and Families
c/o Charity Eleson, Exec.Dir.
16 N Carroll St., Ste.600
Madison, WI 53703
Ph: (608)284-0580
Fax: (608)284-0583
E-mail: celeson@wccf.org
URL: http://www.wccf.org
Contact: Charity Eleson, Exec.Dir.
Membership Dues: individual, $40 (annual). **State**. Promotes the well-being of children and families in Wisconsin. Advocates for effective and efficient health, education and human service delivery systems. **Affiliated With:** Voices for America's Children. **Publications:** *Capitol Comments*. Newsletter. **Price:** included in membership dues; $1.00 for nonmembers.

18689 ■ Wisconsin Council of County and Municipal Employees AFSCME, Council 40 AFL-CIO
c/o Bob Chybowski, Exec.Dir.
8033 Excelsior Dr., Ste.B
Madison, WI 53717-1903
Ph: (608)836-4040
Fax: (608)836-4444
Free: (800)362-8261
E-mail: webmaster@afscmecouncil40.org
URL: http://www.afscmecouncil40.org
Contact: Bob Chybowski, Exec.Dir.
State. Affiliated With: AFL-CIO.

18690 ■ Wisconsin Council on Developmental Disabilities (WCDD)
c/o Jennifer Ondrejka, Exec.Dir.
201 W Washington Ave., Ste.110
Madison, WI 53703
Ph: (608)266-7826 (608)266-6660
Fax: (608)267-3906
E-mail: help@wcdd.org
URL: http://www.wcdd.org
Contact: Helen Hartman, Office Mgr.
State. Plans ways to improve support for people with developmental disabilities, advocates for their civil rights, and plans ways that communities can increase their capacity to be welcoming, supportive, affirming places for people with developmental disabilities. Sponsors DAWN (Disability Advocates: Wisconsin Network), which works to establish a system of community supports and services that will enable all people with disabilities to enjoy the full rights and responsibilities that come w/citizenship. **Affiliated With:** National Association of Councils on Developmental Disabilities.

18691 ■ Wisconsin Council of Hostelling International - American Youth Hostels
141 S Butler St.
Madison, WI 53703
Ph: (608)441-0144
E-mail: madisonhostel@yahoo.com
URL: http://hostellingwisconsin.org
State. Provides access to overnight accommodations both nationally and internationally for travelers of all ages. Sponsors fund raising activities including a Midnight Bicycle Ride and a bicycle and canoe program in addition to volunteer opportunities at hostels in Wisconsin. **Affiliated With:** Hostelling International-American Youth Hostels.

18692 ■ Wisconsin Council of Safety (WCS)
PO Box 352
Madison, WI 53701-0352
Ph: (608)258-3400
Fax: (608)258-3413
Free: (800)236-3400
E-mail: broessler@wischamberfoundation.org
URL: http://www.wischamberfoundation.org/wcs
Contact: Bryan Roessler, Dir.
Founded: 1923. **Members:** 6,500. **Membership Dues:** level 1 (1-10 employees), $215 (annual) • level 2 (11-49 employees), $250 (annual) • level 3 (50-100 employees), $275 (annual) • level 4 (additional $.65 per employee over 100), $300 (annual). **Staff:** 4. **State**. Dedicated to educating and motivating people to live safer and healthier lives - whether at home, work, school, play or on the highway. **Awards:** Wisconsin Corporate Safety Award. **Frequency:** annual. **Type:** recognition. **Telecommunication Services:** electronic mail, wcs@wischamberfoundation.org. **Affiliated With:** National Safety Council. **Publications:** *WI Safety and Health News*, bimonthly. Newsletter. Contains safety and health compliance. **Price:** included in membership dues; $25.00 /year for nonmembers. **Circulation:** 8,000. **Advertising:** accepted. **Conventions/Meetings:** annual Wisconsin Safety and Health Congress Expo - conference (exhibits) - usually in April.

18693 ■ Wisconsin Counties Association (WCA)
c/o Mark D. O'Connell, Exec.Dir.
22 E Mifflin St., Ste.900
Madison, WI 53703
Ph: (608)663-7188
Fax: (608)663-7189
Free: (866)404-2700
E-mail: mail@wicounties.org
URL: http://www.wicounties.org
Contact: Mark D. O'Connell, Exec.Dir.
State.

18694 ■ Wisconsin Court Reporters Association (WCRA)
Circuit Ct., Br. 16, Rm. 306
210 Martin Luther King Jr. Blvd.
Madison, WI 53703
Ph: (608)267-1568
Fax: (608)267-4151
E-mail: kelly120958@aol.com
URL: http://www.tripod.com
Contact: Roberta Bitler, Pres.
State. Affiliated With: National Court Reporters Association.

18695 ■ Wisconsin Crop Improvement Association (WCIA)
c/o Eugene R. Amberson, Gen.Mgr.
554 Moore Hall
Univ. of Wisconsin-Madison
1575 Linden Dr.
Madison, WI 53706-1597

Ph: (608)262-1341
Fax: (608)262-0210
E-mail: wcia@mailplus.wisc.edu
URL: http://www.wisc.edu/wcia
Contact: Eugene R. Amberson, Gen.Mgr.
Founded: 1901. **State**. Conducts third party field, seed, and facility inspections. Acts as the official seed certifying agency in Wisconsin.

18696 ■ Wisconsin Early Childhood Association (WECA)
c/o Mary Babula, Dir. of Membership Services
744 Williamson St., Ste.200
Madison, WI 53703
Ph: (608)240-9880
Fax: (608)240-9890
Free: (800)783-9322
E-mail: weca@wecanaeyc.org
URL: http://www.wecanaeyc.org
Contact: Mary Babula, Dir. of Membership Services
State. Works to improve child care and early education. **Affiliated With:** National Association for the Education of Young Children.

18697 ■ Wisconsin Economic Development Association (WEDA)
4600 Amer. Pkwy., Ste.208
Madison, WI 53718
Ph: (608)255-5666
Fax: (608)241-7790
Free: (800)581-4941
E-mail: weda@weda.org
URL: http://www.weda.org
Contact: James Otterstein, Pres.
State.

18698 ■ Wisconsin Education Association Council (WEAC)
PO Box 8003
Madison, WI 53708-8003
Ph: (608)276-7711
Fax: (608)276-8203
Free: (800)362-8034
E-mail: askonweac@weac.org
URL: http://www.weac.org
State.

18699 ■ Wisconsin Electric Cooperative Association (WECA)
131 W Wilson St., Ste.400
Madison, WI 53703
Ph: (608)258-4400
Fax: (608)258-4407
E-mail: david.jenkins@wfcmac.coop
URL: http://www.weca.coop
Contact: David Jenkins, Division Mgr.
State.

18700 ■ Wisconsin Energy Conservation Corporation (WECC)
211 S Paterson St., 3rd Fl.
Madison, WI 53703
Ph: (608)249-9322
Fax: (608)249-0339
Free: (800)969-9322
E-mail: jbrandt@weccusa.org
URL: http://www.weccusa.org
Contact: Janet Brandt, Exec.Dir.
State. Works to ensure that customers are provided with high-quality, valuable, and affordable opportunities to increase their energy efficiency. Assists with the development and effective delivery of coordinated, comprehensive programs that strive to transform markets to a higher-level of energy efficiency.

18701 ■ Wisconsin Family Ties (WFT)
16 N Carroll St., Ste.640
Madison, WI 53703
Ph: (608)267-6888
Fax: (608)267-6801
Free: (800)422-7145
E-mail: info@wifamilyties.org
URL: http://www.wifamilyties.org
Contact: Hugh Davis, Exec.Dir.
Founded: 1987. **Staff:** 21. **Budget:** $343,000. **Local Groups:** 12. **Nonmembership**. **State**. Parents, children, and mental health and related professionals. Seeks to ensure the rights to full citizenship, support, and access to services for children and youth with mental disorders and their families. Works to address the needs of children and youth with emotional, behavioral, and mental disorders. **Libraries: Type:** open to the public. **Holdings:** 1,100. **Subjects:** children's mental health. **Awards:** Educational Scholarship. **Frequency:** annual. **Type:** scholarship. **Recipient:** for individual planning to attend educational/training events. **Affiliated With:** Federation of Families for Children's Mental Health. **Publications:** *Family Ties*, quarterly. Newsletter. **Price:** free. **Circulation:** 6,000. **Conventions/Meetings:** semiannual meeting • periodic workshop.

18702 ■ Wisconsin Farm Bureau Federation (WFBF)
PO Box 5550
Madison, WI 53705-0550
Ph: (608)828-5701 (608)836-5575
Free: (800)261-FARM
E-mail: info.demingway@wfbf.com
URL: http://www.wfbf.com
Contact: Bill Bruins, Pres.
Founded: 1919. **Members:** 46,700. **Staff:** 20. **State**. Individuals involved in the agriculture industry. Conducts lobbying activities. Sponsors workshops and youth education programs. **Awards:** WFBF Scholarship Program. **Frequency:** annual. **Type:** scholarship. **Recipient:** for students in agriculture related fields. **Affiliated With:** American Farm Bureau Federation. **Publications:** *Farm Bureau's Rural Route*, 8/year. Newspaper. **Circulation:** 3,500. **Advertising:** accepted. **Conventions/Meetings:** annual convention (exhibits) - usually December.

18703 ■ Wisconsin Fathers for Children and Families (WFCF)
PO Box 1742
Madison, WI 53701
Ph: (608)255-3237
E-mail: info@wisconsinfathers.org
URL: http://wisconsinfathers.org
Contact: Jan Raz, Pres.
Founded: 1987. **Members:** 175. **Membership Dues:** regular, $30 (annual). **State**. Promotes joint custody and placement of children of divorce. Holds monthly meetings. Sponsors Father's Day picnic. Offers lawyer referrals for members. **Formerly:** (1995) Coalition for Fathers Rights; (1998) Wisconsin Fathers for Equal Justice. **Publications:** *Today's Dads*, monthly. Newsletter. **Price:** included in membership dues. **Conventions/Meetings:** bimonthly meeting.

18704 ■ Wisconsin Federation of Cooperatives (WFC)
131 W Wilson, Ste.400
Madison, WI 53703
Ph: (608)258-4400 (608)258-4414
Fax: (608)258-4407
E-mail: lori.weaver@wfcmac.coop
URL: http://www.wfcmac.coop
Contact: Lori Weaver, VP Communication and Dairy
State. Represents all types of cooperatives (farm supply, dairy, healthcare, credit union, marketing, mutual insurance, electric, telephone, etc.).

18705 ■ Wisconsin Fertilizer and Chemical Association (WFCA)
2317 Intl. Ln., Ste.115
Madison, WI 53704
Ph: (608)249-4070
Fax: (608)249-5311
E-mail: wfca@aol.com
URL: http://www.wfca.biz
Contact: Elizabeth Anther, Contact
Founded: 1961. **Members:** 450. **Staff:** 2. **State**. Fertilizer and agricultural chemical dealers, vendors, and manufacturers. Works to: establish higher standards of business ethics; improve business efficiency; promote equitable trade practices. **Awards:** Member Scholarship. **Frequency:** annual. **Type:** scholarship. **Recipient:** for incoming college freshman in agriculture related field; members, children only. **Publications:** *WFCA News*, monthly. Newsletter. **Conventions/Meetings:** annual Wisconsin Fertilizer, Agleam and Pest Management Conference (exhibits) - always third week in January.

18706 ■ Wisconsin Financial Services Association
c/o Thomas S. Hanson, Exec.Dir.
22 E Mifflin St., Ste.1010
Madison, WI 53703
Ph: (608)256-6413
Fax: (608)256-6222
State.

18707 ■ Wisconsin Forum for Healthcare Strategy
c/o Lauren Cnare, Treas.
5218 Kevins Way
Madison, WI 53714
Ph: (608)224-1292
E-mail: speckson@charter.net
URL: http://www.wfhs.org
Contact: Steven Quade, Pres.
State. Persons in hospitals, health systems and networks, managed care plans, and physician groups who are engaged in strategic planning, business development, marketing, or public relations activities. **Affiliated With:** Society for Healthcare Strategy and Market Development of the American Hospital Association.

18708 ■ Wisconsin Geological and Natural History Survey
3817 Mineral Point Rd.
Madison, WI 53705-5100
Ph: (608)262-1705
Fax: (608)262-8086
E-mail: jmrober1@wisc.edu
URL: http://www.uwex.edu/wgnhs
Contact: James M Robertson, Dir./State Geologist
State.

18709 ■ Wisconsin Grocers Association (WGA)
One S Pinckney St., Ste.504
Madison, WI 53703
Ph: (608)244-7150
Fax: (608)244-9030
E-mail: brandon@wisconsingrocers.com
URL: http://www.wisconsingrocers.com
Contact: Brandon Scholz, Pres./CEO
State.

18710 ■ Wisconsin Health Care Association
c/o Thomas P. Moore
121 S Pinckney St., Ste.500
Madison, WI 53703
Ph: (608)257-0125
Fax: (608)257-0025
E-mail: info@whca.com
URL: http://www.whca.com
Contact: Thomas P. Moore, Exec.Dir.
State. Provides professional services necessary and intimately linked to achievement of the quality of care. **Affiliated With:** American Health Care Association.

18711 ■ Wisconsin Historical Society (WHS)
816 State St.
Madison, WI 53706-1482
Ph: (608)264-6400 (608)264-6448
Fax: (608)264-6545
E-mail: whsmember@whs.wisc.edu
URL: http://www.wisconsinhistory.org
Contact: Ellsworth H. Brown, Dir.
Founded: 1846. **Members:** 7,700. **Membership Dues:** individual, senior citizen's family, $40 (annual) • family, $50 (annual) • senior, $30 (annual) • institution, $65 (annual). **Staff:** 150. **Budget:** $17,700,000. **Local Groups:** 300. **Regional**. Offers residents a glimpse of life as it was and makes the past relevant to life as it is. Provides the state's residents with direct access to resources that can help in tracing family roots, understanding social and political trends and movements and acquiring a sense of the daily lives of people in the Midwest over the centuries by col-

lecting, caring for and sharing the historical record and artifacts of Wisconsin and its people. **Libraries: Type:** open to the public. **Holdings:** 3,600,000; archival material, books, periodicals. **Subjects:** Wisconsin history, labor history, social action, western settlement. **Awards:** Alice E. Smith Fellowship. **Frequency:** annual. **Type:** grant. **Recipient:** for a woman conducting a graduate research on the history of Wisconsin or the Midwest • Amy Louise Hunter Fellowship. **Frequency:** biennial. **Type:** grant. **Recipient:** for graduate research on the history of women and public policy • John C. Geilfuss Fellowship. **Frequency:** annual. **Type:** grant. **Recipient:** for graduate research on Wisconsin business or economic history. **Boards:** Curators. **Publications:** *Columns*, bimonthly. Newsletter. **Price:** included in membership dues • *Exchange*, bimonthly. Newsletter • *Wisconsin Magazine of History*, quarterly. Journal. **Conventions/Meetings:** annual meeting - always June.

18712 ■ Wisconsin Homecare Organization (WHO)
c/o Russell King, Exec.Dir.
5610 Medical Cir., Ste.33
Madison, WI 53719
Ph: (608)278-1115
Fax: (608)278-4009
E-mail: wishomecare@earthlink.net
URL: http://www.wishomecare.org
Contact: Russell King, Exec.Dir.
State. Providers of home health care, hospice, and homemaker-home health aide services; interested individuals and organizations. Develops and promotes high standards of patient care in home care services. **Affiliated With:** National Association for Home Care and Hospice.

18713 ■ Wisconsin Hospital Association (WHA)
PO Box 259038
Madison, WI 53725-9038
Ph: (608)274-1820
Fax: (608)274-8554
E-mail: sbrenton@wha.org
URL: http://www.wha.org
Contact: Steve Brenton, Pres.
State.

18714 ■ Wisconsin House Rabbit Society (WHRS)
PO Box 46473
Madison, WI 53744-6473
Ph: (608)232-7044
E-mail: karla@wisconsinhrs.org
URL: http://www.wisconsinhrs.org
Contact: George R. Flentke, Mgr.
Founded: 1992. **Members:** 450. **Membership Dues:** regular, $12 (annual). **State.** Assists humane societies in fostering and rehabilitation of domestic rabbits. Offers education program that helps decrease impulse buying of domestic rabbits and increases the awareness of rabbits as house pets. **Affiliated With:** House Rabbit Society. **Publications:** *Wisconsin House Rabbit News*, quarterly. Newsletter. **Price:** included in membership dues. **Circulation:** 600. **Advertising:** accepted.

18715 ■ Wisconsin Housing Alliance
202 State St., Ste.200
Madison, WI 53703
Ph: (608)255-3131
Fax: (608)255-5595
E-mail: info@wmha.org
URL: http://www.wmha.org
Contact: Ross Kinzler, Exec.Dir.
State. Members represent all segments of the manufactured housing industry. **Formerly:** (2003) Wisconsin Manufactured Housing Association.

18716 ■ Wisconsin Intergenerational Network (WIN)
c/o Bonnie Schmidt, Dir.
PO Box 6664
Madison, WI 53716
Ph: (608)221-6118
Fax: (608)224-0607
E-mail: info@wi-win.org
Contact: Bonnie Schmidt, Dir.
Founded: 1992. **Members:** 100. **State.** Represents individuals, agencies, and organizations, including representatives from education, volunteerism, prevention, recreation, faith communities, and government, that believe that interaction and cooperation among generations contribute to the health and well being of individuals and society. Encourages and supports intergenerational programming and advocacy. **Libraries: Type:** by appointment only; lending. **Holdings:** 30; books, business records, periodicals, video recordings. **Subjects:** intergenerational programming. **Affiliated With:** Colorado Intergenerational Network; Generations United; Generations United of Central Pennsylvania; Hawaii Intergenerational Network; Intergenerational Strategies; Massachusetts Intergenerational Network; Nebraska Generations United; New York State Intergenerational Network; Oregon Generations Together; Sanilac County Intergenerational Coalition. **Publications:** *WIN Quarterly Newsletter*. **Price:** available to members only. Alternate Formats: online. **Conventions/Meetings:** annual conference.

18717 ■ Wisconsin Interlibrary Services (WILS)
728 State St., Rm. 464
Madison, WI 53706-1494
Ph: (608)263-4981
Fax: (608)263-3684
E-mail: schneid@wils.wisc.edu
URL: http://www.wils.wisc.edu
Contact: Kathy Schneider, Dir.
Founded: 1972. **Members:** 500. **Membership Dues:** basic, $160-$800 (annual) • resource sharing, $425 (annual) • CatExpress, CatExpress-group, $325 (annual) • full, $875-$1,000 (annual) • group, $1,000 (annual). **Staff:** 22. **Budget:** $7,000,000. **State.** Provides information service, discounted purchasing, and training. Maintains statewide interlibrary loan network. **Affiliated With:** Wisconsin Library Services. **Publications:** *Access*. Newsletter. Alternate Formats: online • Annual Report, annual. **Conventions/Meetings:** annual conference, new technologies for libraries - usually in May.

18718 ■ Wisconsin Jewelers Association
c/o Mary Kaja, Exec.Dir.
1 E Main St.
Madison, WI 53703
Ph: (608)257-3541
Fax: (608)257-8755
E-mail: mkaja@supranet.net
Contact: Mary Kaja, Exec.Dir.
State.

18719 ■ Wisconsin Land and Water Conservation Association (WLWCA)
c/o Rebecca Baumann, Exec.Dir.
One Point Pl., Ste.101
Madison, WI 53719
Ph: (608)833-1833
Fax: (608)833-7179
E-mail: ginakaminski@wlwca.org
URL: http://www.wlwca.org
State.

18720 ■ Wisconsin Library Association (WLA)
5250 E Terrace Dr., Ste.A1
Madison, WI 53718-8345
Ph: (608)245-3640
Fax: (608)245-3646
E-mail: wla@scls.lib.wi.us
URL: http://www.wla.lib.wi.us
Contact: Lisa K. Strand, Exec.Dir.
Founded: 1891. **Members:** 2,100. **Staff:** 3. **Budget:** $300,000. **State.** Public, academic, school, and special librarians; library support staff; library trustees. Seeks to improve library services and provide educational services. **Awards:** Library Service Awards. **Frequency:** annual. **Type:** recognition • Literary Awards. **Frequency:** annual. **Type:** recognition. **Affiliated With:** American Library Association. **Publications:** *Middle Readers Handbook*, annual. **Price:** $14.00 • *WLA Membership Directory and Handbook*. **Price:** $12.00 for members; $18.00 for nonmembers. **Circulation:** 2,100. **Advertising:** accepted • *WLA Newsletter*, bimonthly. **Conventions/Meetings:** annual conference (exhibits).

18721 ■ Wisconsin Library Services (WILS)
728 State St., Rms. 464 and B106B
Madison, WI 53706-1494
Ph: (608)263-4962
Fax: (608)262-6067
E-mail: slmarcus@wils.wisc.edu
URL: http://www.wils.wisc.edu
Contact: Sarah Marcus, Contact
Founded: 1972. **Members:** 535. **Local.** Represents all types of libraries in the state of WI. **Conventions/Meetings:** quarterly board meeting.

18722 ■ Wisconsin Liquid Waste Carriers Association
c/o Patrick J. Essie
16 N Carroll St.
Madison, WI 53703
Ph: (608)256-7701
Fax: (608)251-8192
E-mail: pessie@essieconsulting.com
URL: http://www.wlwca.com
Contact: Patrick J. Essie, Contact
Founded: 1970. **Members:** 180. **State.**

18723 ■ Wisconsin Manufacturers and Commerce (WMC)
PO Box 352
501 E Washington Ave.
Madison, WI 53701-0352
Ph: (608)258-3400
Fax: (608)258-3413
E-mail: jhaney@wmc.org
URL: http://www.wmc.org
Contact: James S. Haney, Pres.
Founded: 1911. **Members:** 4,300. **Budget:** $6,000,000. **State.** Wisconsin manufacturers and service companies. Fosters and advances policies which are in the public interest of the state and nation. **Awards:** The Besadny Scholarship. **Frequency:** annual. **Type:** scholarship. **Recipient:** to a University of Wisconsin student pursuing a career in the environmental area • Business Friend of the Environment Awards. **Frequency:** annual. **Type:** recognition • Excellence in Education Award. **Frequency:** annual. **Type:** recognition. **Recipient:** for successful school districts, educators, businesses and service organizations • Wisconsin Business Friend of the Environment Award. **Frequency:** annual. **Type:** recognition. **Recipient:** for companies whose projects go beyond regulatory compliance • Wisconsin Corporate Safety Award. **Frequency:** annual. **Type:** recognition. **Recipient:** for employers exemplifying occupational safety and health excellence • Wisconsin Manufacturer of the Year Award. **Frequency:** annual. **Type:** recognition. **Recipient:** for outstanding achievements • Working for Wisconsin Award. **Frequency:** biennial. **Type:** recognition. **Recipient:** for outstanding legislators. **Affiliated With:** American Chamber of Commerce Executives; U.S. Chamber of Commerce; Wisconsin Manufacturers and Commerce. **Publications:** *Capitol Watch*, weekly. Newsletter. Alternate Formats: online • *Chamber to Chamber*. Newsletter. Alternate Formats: online • *Human Resources Report*, periodic. Newsletter. Alternate Formats: online • *Insight*, monthly. Newsletter. Contains the latest information about the legislative action that affect the organization. Alternate Formats: online • *Manufacturing Report*, periodic. Newsletter. Alternate Formats: online • *Member Service Update*. Newsletter. Includes the latest service and advantage of WMC membership. Alternate Formats: online • *Sales and Exchange*, monthly. Newsletter. Alternate Formats: online. **Conventions/Meetings:** annual Wisconsin Safety Congress.

18724 ■ Wisconsin Mathematical Association of Two-Year Colleges (WisMATYC)
c/o George Alexander, Pres.
3550 Anderson St.
Madison, WI 53704
Ph: (608)246-6187
E-mail: galexander@matcmadison.edu
URL: http://www.wis.matyc.org
Contact: George Alexander, Pres.
State. Promotes and increases awareness of the role of two-year colleges in mathematics education. Provides a forum for the improvement of mathematics instruction in the first two years of college. Provides professional development opportunities for educators interested in the first two years of collegiate mathematics instruction. **Affiliated With:** American Mathematical Association of Two-Year Colleges.

18725 ■ Wisconsin Medical Group Management Association
c/o SueAnn Darre
PO Box 1109
Madison, WI 53701-1109
Fax: (608)283-5424
Free: (800)762-8968
E-mail: sdarre@wismed.org
URL: http://www.wmgma.org
Contact: SueAnn Darre, Exec.Dir.
Founded: 1989. **State**. Promotes the art and science of medical practice management to improve the health of the community. Advances group practice management in order to improve the delivery of health care in Wisconsin. **Affiliated With:** Medical Group Management Association.

18726 ■ Wisconsin Medical Society
330 E Lakeside St.
PO Box 1109
Madison, WI 53701-1109
Ph: (608)442-3800
Fax: (608)442-3802
Free: (866)442-3800
E-mail: membership@wismed.org
URL: http://www.wisconsinmedicalsociety.org
Contact: Dr. Susan L. Turney MD, Exec.VP/CEO
Founded: 1841. **Members:** 10,000. **Membership Dues:** young physician (based on years of practice), $99-$499 • initial, $510. **Staff:** 80. **Local Groups:** 55. **State**. Represents the interests of physicians. Seeks to advance the art and science of medicine and improve the health of Wisconsin residents. Promotes the passage and enforcement of just medical laws. **Affiliated With:** American Medical Association. **Publications:** *Medigram*, monthly. Alternate Formats: online • *Wisconsin Medical Journal*, bimonthly. **Advertising:** accepted. Alternate Formats: online. **Conventions/Meetings:** annual meeting.

18727 ■ Wisconsin Merchants Federation
c/o Chris C. Tackett, Pres. & CEO
One E Main St., Ste.305
Madison, WI 53703
Ph: (608)257-3541
Fax: (608)257-8755
URL: National Affiliate–www.nrf.com
Contact: Mary Kaja, VP
Founded: 1960. **Members:** 1,500. **Staff:** 5. **State**. Retailers and merchants. Represents members' interests in legislative activities. **Affiliated With:** National Retail Federation. **Publications:** *Wisconsin Merchant Federation Bulletin*, monthly. **Conventions/ Meetings:** annual meeting.

18728 ■ Wisconsin Milk Haulers Association
562 Grand Canyon Dr.
Madison, WI 53719
Ph: (608)833-8200
Fax: (608)833-2875
E-mail: ctuhus@witruck.org
URL: http://www.wimilkhauler.org
State. Promotes increased efficiency, productivity, and competitiveness in the trucking industries. **Affiliated With:** American Trucking Associations.

18729 ■ Wisconsin Mortgage Bankers Association (WMBA)
PO Box 1606
Madison, WI 53701
Ph: (608)255-4180
Fax: (608)283-2589
Free: (800)532-1091
E-mail: johni@wimort.com
URL: http://www.wimba.org
Contact: John Inzeo, Pres.
Members: 200. **Staff:** 3. **Budget:** $80,000. **Local Groups:** 3. **State**. Companies involved or interested in the mortgage banking industry. Maintains political action committee; conducts state advocacy, educational conferences, seminars, and workshops. **Publications:** *Brief*, monthly. Newsletter. **Price:** free. **Circulation:** 650 • Membership Directory, annual. **Conventions/Meetings:** annual Real Estate Finance Conference (exhibits).

18730 ■ Wisconsin Motor Carriers Association
PO Box 44849
Madison, WI 53744-4849
Ph: (608)833-8200
Fax: (608)833-2875
URL: http://www.witruck.org
Contact: David Batterman, Board of Dir.
State. Promotes increased efficiency, productivity, and competitiveness in the trucking industries. **Affiliated With:** American Trucking Associations.

18731 ■ Wisconsin Movers Association
c/o Michael Dehaan, Exec.Dir.
PO Box 44849
Madison, WI 53744-4849
Ph: (608)833-8200
Fax: (608)833-2875
E-mail: ctuhus@witruck.org
URL: http://www.wismovers.org
Contact: Ms. Cherie Tuhus, Division Administrator
Founded: 1944. **Members:** 46. **Staff:** 2. **Budget:** $15,000. **State Groups:** 1. **State**.

18732 ■ Wisconsin National Congress of Parents and Teachers
4797 Hayes Rd., Ste.102
Madison, WI 53704-3256
Ph: (608)244-1455
Fax: (608)244-4785
E-mail: wi_office@pta.org
URL: http://www.wisconsinpta.org
Contact: Cyndi Barbian, Pres.
Founded: 1910. **Members:** 50,000. **Staff:** 2. **State**. Works to improve the health and welfare of Wisconsin school children; focuses on issues such as parenting skills and drug abuse awareness. Offers leadership training and workshops; holds quarterly board meeting. **Committees:** Building Successful Partnership; Bulletin Editor; ByLaws; Convention; Executive; Reflections. **Affiliated With:** National PTA - National Congress of Parents and Teachers. **Publications:** *Wisconsin Parent Teacher*, 9/year. Bulletin. **Price:** $9.00/year. **Conventions/Meetings:** annual convention.

18733 ■ Wisconsin National Guard Association (WINGA)
2400 Wright St., Rm. 208
Madison, WI 53704-2572
Ph: (608)242-3114
Fax: (608)242-3513
E-mail: wingainc@terracom.net
URL: http://winga.org
Contact: Lt.Col.(Ret.) Ronald R. Wagner, Exec.Dir.
Founded: 1951. **Members:** 1,800. **Membership Dues:** depends on military grade, $5-$15 (annual) • life, active, $80 • life, retired, $15. **Staff:** 6. **Budget:** $340,000. **State**. Officers, warrant officers, and active and retired Wisconsin National Guard personnel. Promotes the national security of the United States of America. **Affiliated With:** Adjutants General Association of the United States; National Guard Association of the United States. **Publications:** *Your Communicator*, quarterly. Newsletter. **Price:** included in membership dues. **Circulation:** 1,900. Alternate Formats: online. **Conventions/Meetings:** annual conference (exhibits) - in April or May.

18734 ■ Wisconsin Network for Peace and Justice (WNPJ)
122 State St., Ste.402
Madison, WI 53703
Ph: (608)250-9240
E-mail: info@wnpj.org
URL: http://www.wnpj.org
Contact: Alfred Meyer, Chm.
Founded: 1991. **Members:** 400. **Membership Dues:** individual, $25 (annual) • family, $35 (annual) • sustaining, $52 (annual) • organization without paid staff, $40 (annual) • organization with paid staff, $60 (annual) • A-Dollar-A-Day-For-Peace, $365 (annual) • life, $1,000 • fixed income, $10 (annual). **Staff:** 1. **Budget:** $37,000. **State**. Facilitates activities, cooperation, and communication among Wisconsin organizations and individuals working toward the creation of a world free from violence and injustice. **Task Forces:** Corporate Accountability. **Publications:** *Networks News*, bimonthly. Newsletter. **Circulation:** 600. **Conventions/Meetings:** annual conference (exhibits) - always fall • quarterly executive committee meeting • annual Steering Committee Meeting, organizational representatives - 1st Saturday in April.

18735 ■ Wisconsin Neurosurgical Society
c/o Dr. Gregory R. Trost
600 Highland Ave., K4/8 CSC
Madison, WI 53792-0001
Ph: (608)263-1411
Fax: (608)263-1728
URL: National Affiliate–www.aans.org
Contact: Dr. Gregory R. Trost, Contact
State. Represents neurological surgeons united to promote excellence in neurological surgery and its related sciences. Provides funding to foster research in the neurosciences. **Affiliated With:** American Association of Neurological Surgeons.

18736 ■ Wisconsin Newspaper Association (WNA)
c/o Peter D. Fox, Exec.Dir.
PO Box 5580
3822 Mineral Point Rd.
Madison, WI 53705
Ph: (608)238-7171
Fax: (608)238-4771
Free: (800)261-4242
E-mail: peter.fox@wnanews.com
URL: http://www.wnanews.com
Contact: Peter D. Fox, Exec.Dir.
Founded: 1853. **Members:** 270. **Staff:** 15. **For-Profit**. **State**. Wisconsin daily and weekly newspapers united to promote the interests of the newspaper-publishing industry. **Affiliated With:** National Newspaper Association. **Publications:** *Annual Directory and Rate Book*, annual. **Price:** $25.00 • *WNA Bulletin*, weekly. **Conventions/Meetings:** semiannual meeting - always June and mid-winter.

18737 ■ Wisconsin Nurses' Association (WNA)
c/o Gina Dennik-Champion, MSN, Exec.Dir.
6117 Monona Dr.
Madison, WI 53716
Ph: (608)221-0383
Fax: (608)221-2788
E-mail: info@wisconsinnurses.org
URL: http://www.wisconsinnurses.org
Contact: Gina Dennik-Champion MSN, Exec.Dir.
Founded: 1910. **Members:** 2,200. **Staff:** 5. **Regional Groups:** 5. **Local Groups:** 16. **State**. Professional organization for registered nurses. **Publications:** *STAT Bulletin*, monthly. Newsletter. **Price:** $45.00. **Circulation:** 2,500. **Advertising:** accepted. Alternate Formats: online. **Conventions/Meetings:** annual convention (exhibits) - usually third week in October.

18738 ■ Wisconsin Occupational Therapy Association (WOTA)
122 E Olin Ave., Ste.165
Madison, WI 53713
Ph: (608)287-1606
Fax: (608)287-1608
Free: (800)728-1992
E-mail: wota@execpc.com
URL: http://www.homestead.com/wota
Contact: Linda Anderson, Pres.
State. Advances the quality, availability, use and support of occupational therapy through standard-setting, advocacy, education and research. **Affiliated With:** American Occupational Therapy Association.

18739 ■ Wisconsin Optometric Association (WOA)
5721 Odana Rd., Ste.110
Madison, WI 53719
Ph: (608)274-4322
Fax: (608)274-8646
Free: (800)678-5357
E-mail: petertheo@tds.net
URL: http://www.woa-eyes.org
Contact: Peter Theo, Exec.Dir.
State. Affiliated With: American Optometric Association.

18740 ■ Wisconsin Physical Therapy Association
c/o Karen Oshman, Exec.Dir.
802 W Broadway, Ste.208
Madison, WI 53713
Ph: (608)221-9191
Fax: (608)221-9697
E-mail: wpta@wpta.org
URL: http://www.wpta.org
Contact: Karen Oshman, Exec.Dir.
Founded: 1928. **Members:** 2,000. **State. Publications:** *PT Connections*, quarterly. Newsletter. **Advertising:** accepted. **Conventions/Meetings:** semiannual conference - always spring and fall.

18741 ■ Wisconsin Planned Giving Council
c/o Eugene R. Schramka
Grant Thornton
PO Box 8100
Madison, WI 53708
Ph: (608)286-6962
Fax: (608)257-6760
E-mail: eugene.schramka@gt.com
URL: National Affiliate–www.ncpg.org
Contact: Eugene R. Schramka, Contact
State. Affiliated With: National Committee on Planned Giving.

18742 ■ Wisconsin Pottery Association (WPA)
c/o Timothy J. Holthaus, Sec.
PO Box 46105
Madison, WI 53744-6105
E-mail: webmaster@wisconsinpottery.org
URL: http://www.wisconsinpottery.org
Contact: Timothy J. Holthaus, Sec.
Founded: 1993. **Members:** 100. **Membership Dues:** individual, $20 (annual) • dual, $30 (annual). **Budget:** $10,000. **State.** Collectors of antique art pottery and crockery. Works to educate the public on the history of various potteries and their contribution to art and culture. **Publications:** *WPA Press*, quarterly. Newsletter. **Price:** included in membership dues. **Circulation:** 100. **Conventions/Meetings:** annual Comprehensive Pottery Exhibit - convention, pottery exhibit (exhibits) - always August.

18743 ■ Wisconsin Primary Health Care Association
c/o Sarah V. Lewis, Exec.Dir.
49 Kessel Ct., Ste.210
Madison, WI 53711
Ph: (608)277-7477
Fax: (608)277-7474
E-mail: wphca@wphca.org
URL: http://www.wphca.org
Founded: 1982. **State.**

18744 ■ Wisconsin Professional Police Association (WPPA)
340 Coyier Ln.
Madison, WI 53713
Ph: (608)273-3840
Fax: (608)273-3904
Free: (800)362-8838
E-mail: bahr@wppa.com
URL: http://www.wppa.com
Contact: Thomas Bahr, Exec.Dir.
Founded: 1932. **Members:** 9,000. **Membership Dues:** full-time, $28 (monthly) • part-time, $24 (monthly) • fraternal, $6 (monthly). **Staff:** 23. **Budget:** $1,900,000. **Local Groups:** 350. **State.** Union of certified professional and retired law enforcement officers. Provides bargaining, contract negotiations, educational programs, legislative advocacy, and fraternal opportunities. **Awards: Frequency:** annual. **Type:** scholarship. **Recipient:** Wisconsin students pursuing degree in police science or criminal justice. **Affiliated With:** National Association of Police Organizations. **Formerly:** Wisconsin Professional Policemen's Association. **Publications:** *Wisconsin Police Journal*, bimonthly. Contains information on professional issues, collective bargaining, and governmental relations. **Price:** included in membership dues. ISSN: 1086-5187. **Circulation:** 7,000. **Advertising:** accepted. **Conventions/Meetings:** annual convention - always May.

18745 ■ Wisconsin Psychiatric Association (WPA)
PO Box 1109
Madison, WI 53701
Fax: (608)283-5424
Free: (800)762-8967
E-mail: wpa@smswi.org
URL: http://www.thewpa.org
Contact: Mr. Edward Levin, Exec.Dir.
State. Seeks to further the study of the nature, treatment, and prevention of mental disorders. **Affiliated With:** American Psychiatric Association.

18746 ■ Wisconsin Psychological Association (WPA)
126 S Franklin St.
Madison, WI 53703
Ph: (608)251-1450
Fax: (608)251-5480
E-mail: wispsych@execpc.com
URL: http://www.wipsychology.org
Contact: Kaye Price Laud PhD, Pres.
State. Affiliated With: American Psychological Association. **Publications:** *Wisconsin Psychologist*. **Conventions/Meetings:** semiannual meeting.

18747 ■ Wisconsin Public Health Association (WPHA)
PO Box 1109
Madison, WI 53701
Ph: (414)464-8340
Fax: (608)283-5424
Free: (800)567-4494
E-mail: wpha@wamllc.net
URL: http://www.wpha.org
Contact: Sue Kunferman, Pres.
Founded: 1948. **State.** Protects and promotes personal and public health improvement through educational and scientific programs. Exercises leadership with health professionals and general public in health policy development and action. **Affiliated With:** American Public Health Association.

18748 ■ Wisconsin Public Interest Research Group (WISPIRG)
210 N Bassett St., Ste.200
Madison, WI 53703
Ph: (608)251-1918
Fax: (608)287-0865
E-mail: info@wispirg.org
URL: http://www.wispirg.org
Contact: Jennifer Giegerich, State Dir.
State. Works to protect the environment, protect consumers and promote democracy.

18749 ■ Wisconsin Ready Mixed Concrete Association
16 N Carroll St., Ste.925
Madison, WI 53703
Ph: (608)250-6304
Fax: (608)250-6306
E-mail: info@wrmca.com
URL: http://www.wrmca.com
Contact: Patrick Essie, Exec.Dir.
Founded: 1939. **Members:** 130. **Budget:** $500,000. **State.** Serves the ready mixed concrete producers and its suppliers through education, promotion and legislative activities. **Publications:** *The Report*, quarterly. Newsletter. **Conventions/Meetings:** bimonthly board meeting • annual convention.

18750 ■ Wisconsin Restaurant Association (WRA)
c/o Edward J. Lump, Pres./CEO
2801 Fish Hatchery Rd.
Madison, WI 53713
Ph: (608)270-9950
Fax: (608)270-9960
Free: (800)589-3211
URL: http://www.wirestaurant.org
Contact: Edward J. Lump, Pres./CEO
State.

18751 ■ Wisconsin School Public Relations Association (WSPRA)
122 W Washington Ave., Ste.400
Madison, WI 53703
Ph: (608)257-3220
Fax: (608)257-8386
E-mail: pwelch@wasb.org
URL: http://www.wspra.org
Contact: Anne Egan-Waukau, Pres.-Elect
State. Affiliated With: National School Public Relations Association. **Formerly:** (2005) National School Public Relations Association, Wisconsin.

18752 ■ Wisconsin Small Business Development Center (WSBDC)
Univ. of Wisconsin-Madison
975 Univ. Ave., Rm. 3260
Madison, WI 53706
Ph: (608)263-7680
Fax: (608)263-0818
Free: (800)940-7232
E-mail: sbdc@bus.wisc.edu
URL: http://www.wisconsinsbdc.org
Contact: Mary Avery, Contact
Nonmembership. State. Provides educational services for entrepreneurs and small business owners. **Affiliated With:** Association of Small Business Development Centers.

18753 ■ Wisconsin Society of Clinical Hypnosis
2545 Marshall Pkwy.
Madison, WI 53713
Ph: (608)276-9191
Fax: (608)276-9144
E-mail: mmbailey@facstaff.wisc.edu
URL: National Affiliate–www.asch.net
Contact: Melinda Bailey PhD, Contact
State. Represents health and mental health care professionals using clinical hypnosis. Provides and encourages education programs to further the knowledge, understanding and application of hypnosis in health care. Works for the recognition and acceptance of hypnosis as an important tool in clinical health care. **Affiliated With:** American Society of Clinical Hypnosis.

18754 ■ Wisconsin Space Institute
c/o Eric E. Rice
Space Ctr.
1212 Fourier Dr.
Madison, WI 53717

Ph: (608)827-5000
Fax: (608)827-5050
E-mail: ricee@orbitec.com
Contact: Eric E. Rice PhD, Contact
Founded: 1990. **Local**. Educational and research institute related to space.

18755 ■ Wisconsin State Genealogical Society (WSGS)
PO Box 5106
Madison, WI 53705-0106
E-mail: wsgs@chorus.net
URL: http://www.wsgs.org
Contact: Jane Radloff, Pres.
Founded: 1939. **Members:** 1,390. **Membership Dues:** individual, $18 (annual) • family, $20 (annual) • affiliate, $25 (annual) • institutional, $25 (annual). **Regional Groups:** 13. **Local Groups:** 12. **State**. Persons interested in Wisconsin genealogy; libraries and organizations with genealogical collections. **Awards:** Pioneer Family Certificates and Century Family Certificates. **Frequency:** annual. **Type:** recognition. **Recipient:** for descendants of pioneer families • WSGS Book Award. **Frequency:** annual. **Type:** recognition. **Recipient:** Wisconsin family history. **Affiliated With:** Wisconsin Historical Society. **Publications:** *Chapter Chatter*, periodic. Newsletter. **Price:** $5.00. **Circulation:** 90 • *WSGS Newsletter*, quarterly. **Conventions/Meetings:** semiannual convention, booksellers (exhibits) - always May and October.

18756 ■ Wisconsin State Telecommunications Association (WSTA)
121 E Wilson St., Ste.102
Madison, WI 53703
Ph: (608)256-8866
Fax: (608)256-2676
URL: http://www.wsta.info
Contact: Bill Esbeck, Exec.Dir.
Founded: 1910. **State**. **Publications:** *PSC Open Meetings Report* • *WSTA Bulletin* • *WSTA Legislative Update*. **Conventions/Meetings:** annual meeting.

18757 ■ Wisconsin Stewardship Network (WSN)
122 State St., Ste.510
Madison, WI 53703
Ph: (608)268-1218
Fax: (608)268-1218
E-mail: stewardship@wsn.org
URL: http://www.wsn.org
Contact: Alice McCombs, Contact
State.

18758 ■ Wisconsin Taxpayers Alliance (WISTAX)
401 N Lawn Ave.
Madison, WI 53704-5033
Ph: (608)241-9789
Fax: (608)241-5807
E-mail: wistax@wistax.org
URL: http://www.wistax.org
Contact: Beulah M. Poulter, Operations Dir.
Founded: 1932. **Staff:** 9. **Nonmembership**. **State**. Dedicated to improving the Wisconsin system of representative government. Conducts educational programs in schools; provides research and serves as a consultant on government administration, tax policy, and legislation for municipal officials, legislators, the media, and other organizations. **Libraries: Type:** reference. **Holdings:** 628; books, papers, periodicals. **Subjects:** state and local government and taxation. **Publications:** *Directory of the Wisconsin Legislative and Congressional Districts*, biennial • *Focus*, 2 or 3 times per month. Newsletter • *Framework of Your Wisconsin Government*, periodic, usually every 2 or 3 years. Book • *MunicipalFacts*, annual. Annual Report • *SchoolFacts*, annual. Book • *The Wisconsin Taxpayer*, monthly. Magazine • Brochures • Videos.

18759 ■ Wisconsin Transportation Builders Association (WTBA)
1 S Pinckney St., Ste.818
Madison, WI 53703
Ph: (608)256-6891
Fax: (608)256-1670
E-mail: info@wtba.org
URL: http://www.wtba.org
Contact: Patrick Stevens, Exec.Dir.
Membership Dues: contractor, associate, $500 (annual). **State**. **Affiliated With:** American Road and Transportation Builders Association.

18760 ■ Wisconsin Utilities Association (WUA)
PO Box 2117
Madison, WI 53701
Ph: (608)257-3151
Fax: (608)257-9124
E-mail: bskewes@wiutilities.org
URL: http://www.wiutilities.org/contact.htm
Contact: William R. Skewers, Exec.Dir.
Founded: 1922. **Members:** 11. **Staff:** 4. **Budget:** $600,000. **State**. Investor owned gas and electric companies organized to represent the interests of the utility industry in Wisconsin. **Publications:** *F.Y.I.*, bimonthly. Newsletter • *WUA Annual Directory*, annual. **Conventions/Meetings:** annual conference • annual workshop.

18761 ■ Wisconsin Veterinary Medical Association (WVMA)
301 N Broom St.
Madison, WI 53703
Ph: (608)257-3665
Fax: (608)257-8989
Free: (888)254-5202
E-mail: wvma@wvma.org
URL: http://www.wvma.org
Contact: Mr. Rob Poehnelt, Communications Dir.
Founded: 1915. **Members:** 2,050. **Staff:** 3. **State**. Aims to provide quality professional and humane animal care by conducting annual conference and continuing education programs; promotes veterinary research, animal disease prevention and control, humane care and treatment of all animals; advances science, art and business of veterinary medicine through coordinated group effort; informs the public of the purpose and role of the veterinary medical professional; and takes positions on legislative and social issues affecting the profession. **Affiliated With:** American Veterinary Medical Association.

18762 ■ Wisconsin Waste Facility Siting Board
5005 Univ. Ave., Ste.201
Madison, WI 53705
Ph: (608)267-7854
Fax: (608)264-9885
Contact: David Schwarz, Administrator
State.

18763 ■ Wisconsin Wetlands Association (WWA)
222 S Hamilton St., Ste.1
Madison, WI 53703
Ph: (608)250-9971
Fax: (608)287-1179
E-mail: info@wiscwetlands.org
URL: http://www.wiscwetlands.org
Contact: Becky Abel, Exec.Dir.
Founded: 1969. **Members:** 850. **Membership Dues:** basic, $30 (annual) • sustainer, $50 (annual) • contributor, $100 (annual) • patron, $250 (annual) • heritage circle, $500 (annual) • student/low income, $15 (annual). **Staff:** 4. **State**. Dedicated to the protection, restoration and enjoyment of wetlands and associated ecosystems through science-based programs, education and advocacy. **Conventions/Meetings:** annual Wetland Science Forum - conference, convince members of the wetland community in Wisconsin and the Great Lakes region to discuss a variety of wetland issues (exhibits) - usually January or February.

18764 ■ Wisconsin Wine and Spirit Institute
c/o Eric Peterson, Exec.VP
22 N Carroll St., Ste.200
Madison, WI 53703
Ph: (608)256-5223
Fax: (608)256-3493
E-mail: ejp@tds.net
State.

18765 ■ Wisconsin Women's Network (WWN)
122 State St., No. 404
Madison, WI 53703
Ph: (608)255-9809
E-mail: wiwomen@execpc.com
URL: http://www.wiwomensnetwork.org
Contact: Nora Cusack, Chair
Founded: 1979. **State**. Coalition of organizations and individuals working to improve the status of women in Wisconsin. **Awards:** Stateswoman of the Year. **Frequency:** annual. **Type:** recognition. **Publications:** *The Stateswoman*, quarterly. Newsletter. **Conventions/Meetings:** annual Milwaukee Legislative Breakfast • annual Stateswoman of the Year Brunch - dinner.

18766 ■ Women in Focus
PO Box 44013
Madison, WI 53744-4013
Founded: 1983. **Members:** 25. Professional women committed to supporting the education of minority children and youth through developing and maintaining programs and providing funding through scholarships, grants and educational materials. **Awards: Frequency:** annual. **Type:** scholarship.

18767 ■ Wood Truss Council of America (WTCA)
c/o Anna L. Stamm, Membership Dir.
6300 Enterprise Ln.
Madison, WI 53719
Ph: (608)274-4849
Fax: (608)274-3329
E-mail: wtca@woodtruss.com
URL: http://www.sbcindustry.com
Contact: Anna L. Stamm, Membership Dir.
Founded: 1983. **Local**. **Affiliated With:** Wood Truss Council of America. **Formerly:** (2005) South Carolina Component Manufacturers Association.

18768 ■ Zor Shriners
c/o James L. Stelsel
575 Zor Shrine Pl.
Madison, WI 53719-2094
Ph: (608)833-6343
Fax: (608)833-6348
E-mail: zortemp@chorus.net
URL: http://www.zorshriners.com
Contact: James L. Stelsel, Contact
Local. **Affiliated With:** Imperial Council of the Ancient Arabic Order of the Nobles of the Mystic Shrine for North America.

Maiden Rock

18769 ■ American Legion, Wisconsin Post 158
c/o William E. Geer
PO Box 141
Maiden Rock, WI 54750
Ph: (608)745-1090
Fax: (608)745-0179
URL: National Affiliate–www.legion.org
Contact: William E. Geer, Contact
Local. **Affiliated With:** American Legion.

Manawa

18770 ■ American Legion, Jim Falls Post 276
c/o Bill Squires
PO Box 913
Manawa, WI 54949

Ph: (608)745-1090
Fax: (608)745-0179
URL: National Affiliate–www.legion.org
Contact: Bill Squires, Contact
Local. Affiliated With: American Legion.

18771 ■ Manawa Area Chamber of Commerce
PO Box 221
Manawa, WI 54949
Ph: (920)596-2495
E-mail: manawa@wolfnet.net
URL: http://www.manawachamber.com/
Contact: Lola Bonikowske, Sec.
Local. Strives to promote cooperation among all branches of industry, agriculture, and commerce for the economic and civic development of Manawa City and the surrounding area. **Conventions/Meetings:** monthly General Membership Meeting - every 1st Thursday of the month.

18772 ■ Trout Unlimited - Shaw-Paca Chapter
324 E 4th St.
Manawa, WI 54949-9225
Ph: (920)596-3089
E-mail: skyonna@netnet.net
URL: National Affiliate–www.tu.org
Contact: Dave Ehrenberg, Pres.
Local.

Manitowish Waters

18773 ■ Manitowish Waters Chamber of Commerce (MWCC)
PO Box 251
Manitowish Waters, WI 54545
Ph: (715)543-8488
Fax: (715)543-2519
Free: (888)626-9877
E-mail: funinfo@manitowishwaters.org
Contact: Jodi McMahon, Dir.
Founded: 1939. **Members:** 126. **Staff:** 2. **Local**. Promotes business and community development in Manitowish Waters, WI. Sponsors festival; holds gun show. **Publications:** Directory, periodic.

Manitowoc

18774 ■ American Legion, Drews-Bleser Post 88
811 Jay St.
Manitowoc, WI 54220
Ph: (608)745-1090
Fax: (608)745-0179
URL: National Affiliate–www.legion.org
Local. Affiliated With: American Legion.

18775 ■ American Red Cross, Manitowoc/Calumet Chapter
205 N 8 th St.
Manitowoc, WI 54220
Ph: (920)684-6601
Fax: (920)864-5252
Free: (877)822-4207
E-mail: arc@redcross-mtwc-cal.org
URL: http://chapters.redcross.org/wi/manitowoc-calumet
Local.

18776 ■ AMVETS, Manitowoc Post 99
4310 Conroe St.
Manitowoc, WI 54220
Ph: (920)684-6577
URL: http://amvets99.g3z.com
Local. Affiliated With: AMVETS - American Veterans.

18777 ■ Bikers Against Child Abuse, Maritime Chapter
PO Box 2123
Manitowoc, WI 54221-2123
Ph: (920)905-5437
E-mail: maritime@bacausa.com
URL: National Affiliate–www.bacausa.com
Local.

18778 ■ Lakeshore AIFA
4533 CTH B
Manitowoc, WI 54220
Ph: (920)684-1804
Fax: (920)684-1850
URL: National Affiliate–www.naifa.org
Local. Represents the interest of insurance and financial advisors. Advocates for a positive legislative and regulatory environment. Enhances business and professional skills of members. **Affiliated With:** National Association of Insurance and Financial Advisors.

18779 ■ Lakeshore Area Human Resources Association (LAHRA)
c/o Kristen Kracaw
ABR Employment Sers.
1011 Washington St.
Manitowoc, WI 54220
Ph: (920)684-8324
E-mail: kkracaw@abrjobs.com
URL: http://www.wishrm.org/chapter/lkshr/index.html
Contact: Kristen Kracaw, Pres.
Local. Represents the interests of human resource and industrial relations professionals and executives. Promotes the advancement of human resource management.

18780 ■ Lakeshore Estate Planning Council
c/o Robert W. Brown
PO Box 787
Manitowoc, WI 54221-0787
Ph: (920)683-2424
Fax: (920)683-1569
E-mail: bob.brown@associatedbank.com
URL: http://councils.naepc.org
Contact: Robert W. Brown CTFA, Pres.
Local. Fosters understanding of the proper relationship between the functions of various professions in the field of estate planning including CPAs, attorneys, trust officers, life underwriters and other parties having to do with estate planning. Encourages cooperation among members. **Affiliated With:** National Association of Estate Planners and Councils.

18781 ■ Lakeshore Humane Society
1551 N 8th St.
Manitowoc, WI 54220
Ph: (920)684-5401
Fax: (920)684-5885
E-mail: lakeshorehumane@sbcglobal.net
URL: http://lhs.petfinder.com
Contact: Linda Willman, Dir.
Founded: 1970. **Members:** 400. **Membership Dues:** individual, $15 (annual) • household, $25 (annual) • senior (62 and over), $5 (annual) • junior (under 18), $18 (annual). **Staff:** 3. **Budget:** $180,000. **State Groups:** 1. **Local**. Works for the humane treatment of animals. Fosters a humane ethic and philosophy through educational, legislative, investigative, and legal activities. Conducts charitable activities; holds semiannual bazaar, annual walk for kindness, open house, and dinner/dance. Operates retail store selling pet supplies. **Libraries: Type:** open to the public. **Holdings:** 30; books, video recordings. **Subjects:** pet species. **Awards:** Certificate of Appreciation. **Frequency:** annual. **Type:** recognition. **Recipient:** for volunteers or promoters of the humane treatment of animals. **Formerly:** (1980) Manitowoc Humane Society. **Publications:** *Wags and Whiskers*, quarterly. Newsletter. **Price:** free for members. **Circulation:** 700. **Advertising:** accepted. **Conventions/Meetings:** monthly board meeting • quarterly meeting, membership.

18782 ■ Manitowoc City Centre Association
c/o Gary Stolp
PO Box 845
Manitowoc, WI 54221
Ph: (920)652-2390
E-mail: lgstolp@lsol.net
URL: National Affiliate–www.ava.org
Contact: Gary Stolp, Contact
Local.

18783 ■ Manitowoc County Figure Skating Club (MCFSC)
PO Box 357
Manitowoc, WI 54221-0357
Ph: (920)684-8496
E-mail: admin@manitowoccountyfsc.org
URL: http://www.manitowoccountyfsc.org
Local. Provides programs to encourage participation and achievement in the sport of figure skating on ice. Defines and maintains uniform standards of skating proficiency. Organizes and sponsors competitions and exhibitions for the purpose of stimulating interest in figure skating. **Affiliated With:** United States Figure Skating Association.

18784 ■ Manitowoc County Historical Society (MCHS)
1701 Michigan Ave.
Manitowoc, WI 54220
Ph: (920)684-4445
Fax: (920)684-0573
E-mail: mchistsoc@lakefield.net
URL: http://www.mchistsoc.org
Contact: Sarah Johnson, Exec.Dir.
Founded: 1906. **Members:** 1,725. **Membership Dues:** individual, $20 (annual) • family, $30 (annual) • student, $5 (annual) • friend, $35 (annual) • contributor, $50 (annual) • patron, $100 (annual) • corporate, $125-$1,000 (annual) • life, $1,000. **Staff:** 3. **Budget:** $208,000. **Local**. Corporations, institutions, businesses, families, and individuals. Promotes interest in the history of Manitowoc County, WI. Collects and preserves historical records and artifacts. Holds educational programs, ethnic festivals, and special events. Operates Pinecrest Historical Village, a 60-acre outdoor museum and the Manitowoc County Heritage Center. **Libraries: Type:** reference. **Holdings:** 5,000; articles, audio recordings, books, periodicals. **Subjects:** local and state history, education. **Awards:** Historic Preservation Achievement Awards. **Frequency:** annual. **Type:** recognition. **Affiliated With:** Wisconsin Historical Society. **Publications:** *Edward Ehlert Series on Manitowoc County History*, periodic. Newsletter • *Heritage News*, quarterly. Newsletter • Monograph, annual. **Conventions/Meetings:** annual meeting - January.

18785 ■ Manitowoc County Kennel Club
c/o Karleen Cole, Corresponding Sec.
40 Albert Dr.
Manitowoc, WI 54220
Ph: (920)684-1911
E-mail: lwckfc@lakefield.net
URL: http://www.mc-kc.com
Contact: Karleen Cole, Corresponding Sec.
Founded: 1921. **Members:** 200. **Membership Dues:** single, $25 (annual). **Local**. Promotes the sport and breeding of purebred dogs. Offers all facets of the sport: agility, conformation, field and obedience. **Affiliated With:** American Kennel Club.

18786 ■ Manitowoc/Two Rivers Area Chamber of Commerce
1515 Memorial Dr.
PO Box 903
Manitowoc, WI 54221-0903
Ph: (920)684-5575
Fax: (920)684-1915
Free: (800)262-7892
E-mail: chamber@lakefield.net
URL: http://www.manitowocchamber.com
Contact: Betsy Alles, Exec.Dir.
Founded: 1970. **Members:** 610. **Membership Dues:** business, $308 (annual). **Local**. Businesses. Promotes business and community development in Manitowoc County, WI. **Awards:** Athena Award. **Fre-**

quency: annual. **Type:** recognition. **Recipient:** to a businesswoman • Industry of the Year. **Frequency:** annual. **Type:** recognition • Non-Profit of the Year. **Frequency:** annual. **Type:** recognition • Small Business of the Year. **Frequency:** annual. **Type:** recognition. **Committees:** Small Business. **Affiliated With:** U.S. Chamber of Commerce. **Publications:** *Chamber Talk*, monthly. Newsletter. Features an update on all chamber activities. • *Visitor Guide*, annual. Directory. Includes attractions, restaurants, hotels/motels, and other pertinent visitor information. **Circulation:** 60,000 • Membership Directory, annual. Includes profiles of the chamber and the community.

18787 ■ National Active and Retired Federal Employees Association - Manitowoc 710
3423 Edgewood Rd.
Manitowoc, WI 54220-2309
Ph: (920)682-2221
URL: National Affiliate–www.narfe.org
Contact: Robert R. Stangel, Contact
Local. Protects the retirement future of employees through education. Informs members on issues affecting the retirement. **Affiliated With:** National Association of Retired Federal Employees.

18788 ■ National Alliance for the Mentally Ill - Manitowoc
c/o Anne Bermann, Pres.
706 N 8th St., No. 106
Manitowoc, WI 54220
Ph: (920)686-1011
URL: http://www.namiwisconsin.org/library/directory
Contact: Anne Bermann, Pres.
Local. Strives to improve the quality of life of children and adults with severe mental illness through support, education, research and advocacy. **Affiliated With:** National Alliance for the Mentally Ill.

18789 ■ National Association of Home Builders of the U.S., Manitowoc County Home Builders Association
820 S 8th St.
Manitowoc, WI 54220
Ph: (920)684-6222
Fax: (920)684-6277
E-mail: mchba@lakefield.net
URL: National Affiliate–www.nahb.org
Contact: Brando Bartow, Pres.
Local. Single and multifamily home builders, commercial builders, and others associated with the building industry. **Affiliated With:** National Association of Home Builders.

18790 ■ Phi Theta Kappa, Alpha Sigma Lambda Chapter - University of Wisconsin-Manitowoc
c/o Brian Murphy
705 Viebahn St.
Manitowoc, WI 54220-6601
Ph: (920)683-4732
E-mail: bmurphy@uwc.edu
URL: http://www.ptk.org/directories/chapters/WI/11184-1.htm
Contact: Brian Murphy, Advisor
Local.

18791 ■ Trout Unlimited - Lakeshore Chapter
c/o Wayne Trupke
10723 English Lake Rd.
Manitowoc, WI 54220
Ph: (920)758-2357
E-mail: ctrupke@yahoo.com
URL: National Affiliate–www.tu.org
Contact: Wayne Trupke, Contact
Local.

18792 ■ United Way of Manitowoc County
1704 Memorial Dr.
Manitowoc, WI 54220
Ph: (920)682-8888
Fax: (920)682-8889
E-mail: unitedway@lakefield.net
URL: http://www.unitedwaymanitowoc.org
Contact: Dale K. Moschea, Exec.Dir.
Local. Affiliated With: United Way of America.

18793 ■ Vintage Chevrolet Club of America, Packerland Region No. 4
c/o Fred Schnell, Dir.
4327 Madison Rd.
Manitowoc, WI 54220-9745
Ph: (920)999-4781
URL: National Affiliate–www.vcca.org
Contact: Fred Schnell, Dir.
Local. Affiliated With: Vintage Chevrolet Club of America.

18794 ■ Wisconsin Society of Enrolled Agents
c/o Donald L. Wollersheim, Exec.Dir.
116 E Waldo Blvd.
Manitowoc, WI 54220
Ph: (920)686-1040
Fax: (920)684-8208
Contact: Donald Wollersheim, Exec.Dir.
State.

Maple

18795 ■ Laurentian Shield Resources for Nonviolence
12833E Hwy. 13
Maple, WI 54854
Ph: (715)364-8533
E-mail: thastings@northland.edu
URL: http://www.serve.com/gvaughn/laurentian
Contact: Tom Howard-Hastings, Non-violence Trainer
Local. Affiliated With: War Resisters League.

Marathon

18796 ■ American Legion, Wisconsin Post 469
c/o Alois Dreikosen
PO Box 516
Marathon, WI 54448
Ph: (608)745-1090
Fax: (608)745-0179
URL: National Affiliate–www.legion.org
Contact: Alois Dreikosen, Contact
Local. Affiliated With: American Legion.

Marinette

18797 ■ American Legion, Teddy-Budlong-Robert-Smith Post 39
PO Box 477
Marinette, WI 54143
Ph: (608)745-1090
Fax: (608)745-0179
URL: National Affiliate–www.legion.org
Local. Affiliated With: American Legion.

18798 ■ American Nurses Association - Bay Area Medical Center, Prof LSC
N2184 Krause Rd.
Marinette, WI 54143
URL: National Affiliate–www.nursingworld.org
Members: 180. **Local.** Represents registered nurses. Facilitates high standards of nursing practice. Advocates issues relevant to nursing and health care. **Affiliated With:** American Nurses Association.

18799 ■ Marinette Area Chamber of Commerce
601 Marinette Ave.
Marinette, WI 54143
Ph: (715)735-6681
Fax: (715)735-6682
Free: (800)236-6681
E-mail: chamber@centurytel.net
URL: http://www.marinettechamber.com
Contact: Gary A. Nadolny, Exec.Dir./CEO
Founded: 1939. **Members:** 310. **Local.** Promotes business and community development in Marinette, WI area. **Committees:** Education; Event Planning; Governmental Affairs; Tourism; Voyageurs. **Programs:** Gift Certificate. **Publications:** *Marinette Chamber Memo*, monthly. Newsletter. Contains information about chamber events. **Circulation:** 700. **Advertising:** accepted • Directory, annual. **Conventions/Meetings:** monthly board meeting.

18800 ■ Marinette and Menominee Counties Youth Suicide Prevention
1113 Elizabeth Ave.
Marinette, WI 54143
Fax: (906)864-3058
E-mail: jmharper@cybrzn.com
URL: http://www.lakeshore-counseling.com
Contact: Jeanne M. Harper, Coord.
Founded: 1985. **Staff:** 1. **Budget:** $1,000. **State Groups:** 1. **State.** Concerned individuals, counselors, teachers, hospitals, parents, and churches united to reduce the number of completed and attempted youth suicides. Acts as a clearinghouse for public information and education resources regarding youth suicide; supports research and the development of suicide prevention programs; advocates for pertinent legislation. Has developed community standards for suicide prevention. Sponsors annual Be A Life Saver Week and speaker's bureau. **Libraries: Type:** open to the public. **Holdings:** 1,000. **Subjects:** suicide, grief. **Publications:** *Legal and Ethical Aspects in WI*. Report. **Price:** $5.00. **Advertising:** not accepted. **Conventions/Meetings:** annual Be A Life Saver Month, educational - always March • annual National Depression Awareness Month, educational - always October • annual National Suicide Prevention Awareness Month, educational - always May.

18801 ■ National Association For Uniformed Services - Northern Wisconsin, Chapter 1
c/o Robert D. Saxton
1501 Grant St.
Marinette, WI 54143-2321
Ph: (715)732-4363
URL: National Affiliate–www.naus.org
Contact: Robert D. Saxton, Contact
Local. Provides assistance and support to active or retired military uniformed service officers. Protects and improves the compensation, entitlements and benefits earned by members of the uniformed services for themselves, their families and survivors and all American citizens with common interests. **Affiliated With:** National Association for Uniformed Services.

18802 ■ Phi Theta Kappa, Alpha Epsilon Theta Chapter - University of Wisconsin-Marinette
c/o Daniel Kallgren
750 W Bay Shore St.
Marinette, WI 54143
Ph: (715)735-4317
E-mail: dkallgre@uwc.edu
URL: http://www.ptk.org/directories/chapters/WI/1006-1.htm
Contact: Daniel Kallgren, Advisor
Local.

18803 ■ River Cities Habitat for Humanity, Wisconsin
PO Box 304
Marinette, WI 54143-0304
Ph: (715)732-6280
Fax: (715)735-7589
E-mail: rivercitieshfh@unitedwaymarinette.org
URL: National Affiliate–www.habitat.org
Local. Serves the counties of Menominee Michigan and Marinette Wisconsin. **Affiliated With:** Habitat for Humanity International.

18804 ■ Ruffed Grouse Society, Marinette County Chapter
c/o Robert Zutter
504 W Bay Shore St.
Marinette, WI 54143

Ph: (715)453-4702
E-mail: 5hilgys@klinktech.net
URL: National Affiliate–www.ruffedgrousesociety.org
Contact: Robert Zutter, Contact
Local. Affiliated With: Ruffed Grouse Society.

18805 ■ Tri-City Area United Way
PO Box 1143
Marinette, WI 54143
Ph: (715)735-7785
Fax: (715)735-7589
E-mail: amykretz@unitedwaymarinette.org
URL: http://www.unitedwaymarinette.org
Local. Affiliated With: United Way of America.

18806 ■ Trout Unlimited - Marinette County Chapter
c/o Steve Wilke
2526 Shore Dr.
Marinette, WI 54143-4041
Ph: (715)732-4911 (715)732-0717
Fax: (715)732-0596
E-mail: swilke@new.rr.com
URL: http://www.tu.org
Contact: Steve Wilke, Pres.
Local.

Marion

18807 ■ American Legion, Wisconsin Post 198
c/o William Bertram
712 W Ramsdell St.
Marion, WI 54950
Ph: (608)745-1090
Fax: (608)745-0179
URL: National Affiliate–www.legion.org
Contact: William Bertram, Contact
Local. Affiliated With: American Legion.

18808 ■ Wisconsin Jersey Breeders Association
E6261 Schoneck Rd.
Marion, WI 54950
Ph: (715)754-4886
E-mail: laswls@frontiernet.net
Contact: Lori Schoneck, Sec.
Members: 160. **Membership Dues:** $15 (annual). **State.** Promotes the Jersey Breed. **Awards:** Youth awards - various. **Frequency:** annual. **Type:** monetary. **Recipient:** complete award application. **Publications:** *Wisconsin Jersey Booster*, 3/year. Magazine. **Price:** $10.00 or membership. **Advertising:** accepted. **Conventions/Meetings:** Wisconsin Jersey Breeders Annual Meeting - late Feb. or early March; Avg. Attendance: 90.

Markesan

18809 ■ American Legion, Abendroth-Connolly Post 282
11 E Charles St.
Markesan, WI 53946
Ph: (608)745-1090
Fax: (608)745-0179
URL: National Affiliate–www.legion.org
Local. Affiliated With: American Legion.

18810 ■ Ripon Jr. High - Wyldlife
PO Box 24
Markesan, WI 53946-0024
Ph: (920)748-9088
URL: http://sites.younglife.org/_layouts/ylext/default.aspx?ID=C-4215
Local. Affiliated With: Young Life.

18811 ■ Ripon Sr. High - Young Life
PO Box 24
Markesan, WI 53946-0024
Ph: (920)748-9088
URL: http://sites.younglife.org/_layouts/ylext/default.aspx?ID=C-2534
Local. Affiliated With: Young Life.

18812 ■ Young Life Ripon
PO Box 24
Markesan, WI 53946-0024
Ph: (920)748-9088
URL: http://sites.younglife.org/_layouts/ylext/default.aspx?ID=A-WI26
Local. Affiliated With: Young Life.

Marshall

18813 ■ American Legion, Luther-Hamshire-Pearsall Post 279
PO Box 51
Marshall, WI 53559
Ph: (608)745-1090
Fax: (608)745-0179
URL: National Affiliate–www.legion.org
Local. Affiliated With: American Legion.

18814 ■ Madison Area Volkssport Association
c/o Tom Doyle
5824 Lachinvars Trail
Marshall, WI 53559-9720
Ph: (608)655-3141
E-mail: tjdoyle98@msn.com
URL: http://www.dairylandwalkers.com
Contact: Tom Doyle, Contact
Local. Affiliated With: American Volkssport Association.

18815 ■ Marshall Lions Club - Wisconsin
PO Box 655
Marshall, WI 53559
E-mail: webmaster@sightfirst.com
URL: http://sightfirst.com
Local. Affiliated With: Lions Clubs International.

Marshfield

18816 ■ Knights of Columbus, Marshfield
PO Box 446
Marshfield, WI 54449
Ph: (715)384-2488
Fax: (715)387-3338
E-mail: clubhouse@kofcmarshfield.org
URL: http://www.kofcmarshfield.org
Contact: Richard Podsiadlik, Treas.
Local. Affiliated With: Knights of Columbus.

18817 ■ Marshfield Area Chamber of Commerce and Industry (MACCI)
700 S Central Ave.
PO Box 868
Marshfield, WI 54449
Ph: (715)384-3454
Fax: (715)387-8925
E-mail: info@marshfieldchamber.com
URL: http://www.marshfieldchamber.com
Contact: Barbara Fleisner, Exec.Dir.
Founded: 1946. **Members:** 500. **Local.** Promotes business and community development in the Marshfield, WI area. Sponsors annual Dairy Fest and Arts Weekend. Holds monthly board of directors meeting. **Councils:** Industry; Leadership Marshfield Advisory; Retail Coordinating; Small Business. **Affiliated With:** U.S. Chamber of Commerce. **Publications:** *Perspectives*, monthly. Newsletter. Alternate Formats: online • Annual Report, annual.

18818 ■ Marshfield Area Kennel Club
c/o Renee Danhof, Pres.
9815 Stadt Rd.
Marshfield, WI 54449
E-mail: info@makc.org
URL: http://www.makc.org
Contact: Renee Danhof, Pres.
Local.

18819 ■ Marshfield Area United Way
PO Box 771
Marshfield, WI 54449-0771
Ph: (715)384-9992
Fax: (715)384-0043
E-mail: unitedway@tznet.com
URL: http://www.marshfieldareaunitedway.org
Contact: Michelle Boernke, Exec.Dir.
Local. Affiliated With: United Way of America.

18820 ■ Marshfield Lions Club - Wisconsin
PO Box 732
Marshfield, WI 54449
E-mail: marshfieldlions@charter.net
URL: http://www.tznet.com/lions
Local. Affiliated With: Lions Clubs International.

18821 ■ Northern Flyway Golden Retriever Club of America (NFGRC)
c/o Lori Waltonen, Sec.
11778 Sunset Dr.
Marshfield, WI 54449
E-mail: ariell@wi-net.com
URL: http://www.nfgrc.com
Contact: Ellen Hardin, Pres.
Local. Affiliated With: Golden Retriever Club of America.

18822 ■ Phi Theta Kappa, Alpha Xi Kappa Chapter - University of Wisconsin-Marshfield/Wood County
c/o Ruth Elderbrook
PO Box 150
Marshfield, WI 54449-0150
Ph: (715)389-6531
E-mail: relderbr@uwc.edu
URL: http://www.ptk.org/directories/chapters/WI/4200-1.htm
Contact: Ruth Elderbrook, Advisor
Local.

18823 ■ SCORE Central Wisconsin
700 S Central Ave.
Marshfield, WI 54449
Ph: (715)384-3454
E-mail: cwscore@centralwisconsinscore.org
URL: http://www.centralwisconsinscore.org
Local. Provides free counseling and low-cost workshops for the Stevens Point, Marshfield and Wisconsin Rapids area. **Affiliated With:** SCORE.

18824 ■ Sons of Norway, Myrmarken Lodge 5-609
c/o Roberta A. Johansson, Sec.
10656 MacArthur Dr.
Marshfield, WI 54449-9795
Ph: (715)676-2182
E-mail: johanyr@webtv.net
URL: National Affiliate–www.sofn.com
Contact: Roberta A. Johansson, Sec.
Local. Affiliated With: Sons of Norway.

18825 ■ Sweet Adelines International, Heart O' Wisconsin Chapter
Wesley United Methodist Church
205 E 3rd St.
Marshfield, WI 54449-3708
Ph: (715)652-2153
E-mail: kurtdeb@tznet.com
URL: National Affiliate–www.sweetadelineintl.org
Contact: Debbie Fleming, Contact
Local. Advances the musical art form of barbershop harmony through education and performances. Provides education, training and coaching in the

development of women's four-part barbershop harmony. **Affiliated With:** Sweet Adelines International.

Mason

18826 ■ American Legion, Hogaj-Francisco Post 516
PO Box 146
Mason, WI 54856
Ph: (608)745-1090
Fax: (608)745-0179
URL: National Affiliate–www.legion.org
Local. Affiliated With: American Legion.

Mattoon

18827 ■ American Legion, Wisconsin Post 287
c/o John Owen
PO Box 153
Mattoon, WI 54450
Ph: (608)745-1090
Fax: (608)745-0179
URL: National Affiliate–www.legion.org
Contact: John Owen, Contact
Local. Affiliated With: American Legion.

Mauston

18828 ■ American Legion, Burton-Koppang Post 81
1055 E State St.
Mauston, WI 53948
Ph: (608)745-1090
Fax: (608)745-0179
URL: National Affiliate–www.legion.org
Local. Affiliated With: American Legion.

18829 ■ Greater Mauston Area Chamber of Commerce
PO Box 171
Mauston, WI 53948
Ph: (608)847-4142
Fax: (608)847-4142
E-mail: chamber@mauston.com
URL: http://www.mauston.com
Contact: Stacy Havill, Office Administrator
Founded: 1945. **Members:** 200. **Staff:** 1. **Local.** Promotes business and community development in the Mauston, WI area. Sponsors 4th of July Freedomfest. **Affiliated With:** U.S. Chamber of Commerce. **Formerly:** (1999) Greater Mauston Area Chamber of Commerce; (2006) Mauston Chamber of Commerce. **Publications:** Newsletter, monthly. **Price:** free. **Circulation:** 200. **Advertising:** accepted.

18830 ■ Greater Mauston Area Development Corporation (GMADC)
c/o JoAnne Ehasz, CEcD, Exec.Dir.
103 Div. St.
Mauston, WI 53948-1314
Ph: (608)847-7483
Fax: (608)847-5814
Free: (888)AT-GMADC
E-mail: gmadc@mwt.net
URL: http://www.gmadcmauston.org
Contact: JoAnne Ehasz CEcD, Exec.Dir.
Founded: 1960. **Members:** 45. **Staff:** 1. **Local.** Promotes economic development for the city of Mauston.

18831 ■ South Central Wisconsin Optometric Society
c/o John Schaefer, OD, Pres.
205 Div. St.
Mauston, WI 53948
Ph: (608)847-6264
Fax: (608)847-7279
E-mail: schaef@mwt.net
URL: http://www.woa-eyes.org
Contact: John Schaefer OD, Pres.
Local. Aims to improve the quality, availability and accessibility of eye and vision care. Promotes high standards of patient care. Monitors and promotes legislation concerning the scope of optometric practice and other issues relevant to eye/vision care. **Affiliated With:** American Optometric Association; Wisconsin Optometric Association.

Mayville

18832 ■ Mayville Area Chamber of Commerce (MCC)
12 S Main St.
PO Box 185
Mayville, WI 53050-0185
Ph: (920)387-5776
E-mail: info@mayvillechamber.com
URL: http://www.mayvillechamber.com
Contact: Linda Turk, Chamber Staff
Founded: 1945. **Members:** 110. **Staff:** 2. **Local.** Area business personnel striving to promote business and community development in Mayville, WI. Supports community projects, children's holiday programs, and the Audubon Days festival. Provides opportunities to network, "to belong, and to make a difference.". **Awards:** Citizen of the Year. **Frequency:** annual. **Type:** recognition. **Recipient:** individuals who are nominated by letter to the MCC board of directors. **Computer Services:** Information services. **Additional Websites:** http://www.audubondays.com. **Boards:** Board of Directors.

18833 ■ Mayville Historical Society (MHS)
PO Box 82
Mayville, WI 53050
Ph: (920)387-7900
E-mail: lliebenow@mayvillecity.com
URL: http://www.mayvillecity.com/organizations/historical_society.html
Contact: Larry Liebenow, Pres.
Founded: 1968. **Members:** 200. **Membership Dues:** individual, $5 (annual) • family, $10 (annual) • business/organization, $15 (annual). **State Groups:** 1. **Local Groups:** 1. **State.** Individuals interested in the history of Mayville, WI. Maintains Mayville Historical Society Museum. **Affiliated With:** Wisconsin Historical Society. **Publications:** *Wagon Wheels*, quarterly. Newsletter. **Price:** free. **Circulation:** 225. **Conventions/Meetings:** monthly board meeting - always first Monday • annual Strawberry Ice Cream Social - party - always 4th Sunday in June.

18834 ■ Wisconsin District of Precision Metalforming Association
c/o Jerry Moede, Membership Chm.
351 Pinecrest Ct.
Mayville, WI 53050
Ph: (920)387-3403
Fax: (920)387-3403
E-mail: sales@wellerusa.com
URL: http://wisconsin.pma.org
Contact: Jerry Moede, Membership Chm.
State. Promotes and safeguards the interests of the metalforming industry. Conducts technical and educational programs. Provides legislative and regulatory assistance to members. **Affiliated With:** Precision Metalforming Association.

Mazomanie

18835 ■ American Legion, Greening-Buelow Post 437
PO Box 42
Mazomanie, WI 53560
Ph: (608)745-1090
Fax: (608)745-0179
URL: National Affiliate–www.legion.org
Local. Affiliated With: American Legion.

18836 ■ Mazomanie Chamber of Commerce
11 Brodhead St.
PO Box 142
Mazomanie, WI 53560-0142
Ph: (608)795-2117
Fax: (608)795-2102
URL: http://www.villageofmazomanie.com
Contact: Dan Viste, Pres.
Local.

18837 ■ Wisconsin Beagle Club
c/o Fred Kalsow
6314 Old Settlers Rd.
Mazomanie, WI 53560-9745
URL: National Affiliate–clubs.akc.org
Contact: Fred Kalsow, Contact
Local.

McFarland

18838 ■ American Legion, Edwards-Foye Post 534
4911 Burma Rd.
McFarland, WI 53558
Ph: (608)745-1090
Fax: (608)745-0179
URL: National Affiliate–www.legion.org
Local. Affiliated With: American Legion.

18839 ■ Madison BMW Club No. 7
PO Box 152
McFarland, WI 53558-0152
Ph: (608)831-4439
E-mail: president@madisonbmwclub.org
URL: http://www.madisonbmwclub.org
Contact: Todd Herbst, Pres.
Membership Dues: individual, $20 (annual) • couple, $25 (annual). **Local. Affiliated With:** BMW Motorcycle Owners of America.

18840 ■ Madison Curling Club
4802 Marsh Rd.
McFarland, WI 53558
Ph: (608)838-5875
E-mail: info@madisoncurlingclub.com
URL: http://www.madisoncurlingclub.com
Contact: Sharon Kelley, Pres.
Founded: 1931. **Local. Affiliated With:** United States Curling Association.

18841 ■ McFarland Chamber of Commerce
5124 Farwell St.
PO Box 372
McFarland, WI 53558
Ph: (608)838-4011
Fax: (608)838-4011
E-mail: m.mcfarlandchamber@verizon.net
URL: http://www.mcfarlandchamber.com
Founded: 1980. **Members:** 100. **Local.** Seeks to unite and direct the various businesses in the McFarland area in development and stimulation of the civic, industrial and commercial life. Activities include Family Festival, Citizen of the Year Banquet and Christmas in the Village festivities. **Awards:** Citizen of the Year. **Frequency:** annual. **Type:** recognition. **Recipient:** for outstanding members of the community. **Publications:** Newsletter, monthly. **Conventions/Meetings:** monthly board meeting • annual meeting.

18842 ■ Southern Wisconsin Figure Skating Club (SWFSC)
PO Box 367
McFarland, WI 53558
E-mail: southernwisconsinfsc@yahoo.com
URL: http://www.madison.com/communities/swfsc
Local. Provides programs to encourage participation and achievement in the sport of figure skating on ice. Defines and maintains uniform standards of skating proficiency. Organizes and sponsors competitions and exhibitions for the purpose of stimulating interest in figure skating. **Affiliated With:** United States Figure Skating Association.

Medford

18843 ■ American Legion, Landua-Jensen Post 147
224 S 2nd St.
Medford, WI 54451
Ph: (608)745-1090
Fax: (608)745-0179
URL: National Affiliate–www.legion.org
Local. Affiliated With: American Legion.

18844 ■ Medford Area Chamber of Commerce
104 E Perkins St.
PO Box 172
Medford, WI 54451
Ph: (715)748-4729
Fax: (715)748-6899
Free: (888)682-9567
E-mail: chamber@dwave.net
URL: http://www.medfordwis.com
Contact: Susan Emmerich, Exec.Dir.
Local. Promotes business and community development in Medford, WI area.

18845 ■ Medford Curling Club
525 S Whelen Ave.
Medford, WI 54451
Ph: (715)748-4050
E-mail: steve_delonay@hotmail.com
URL: http://www.medfordcurling.com
Contact: Steve DeLonay, Pres.
Founded: 1913. **Local. Affiliated With:** United States Curling Association.

18846 ■ Muskies Central Wisconsin Chapter
PO Box 263
Medford, WI 54451
Ph: (715)748-4072
E-mail: teamrooster@tds.net
URL: National Affiliate–www.muskiesinc.org
Contact: Tim Reinke, Pres.
Local.

18847 ■ National Association of Rocketry - Medford Association of Rocket Science (MARS)
c/o Tater Schuld
342 N 2nd St.
Medford, WI 54451
Ph: (715)748-9669
E-mail: marsclub@charter.net
URL: http://www.mars-rocketry.com
Contact: Tater Schuld, Contact
Local.

18848 ■ Pri-Ru-Ta Resource Conservation and Development Council
925 Donald St., Rm. 102
Medford, WI 54451
Ph: (715)748-2008
Fax: (715)748-4836
E-mail: chris.borden@wi.usda.gov
URL: http://www.pcpros.net/~debessel/Pri-Ru-Ta/pri-ru-ta.html
Contact: Chris Borden, Coor.
Local. Affiliated With: National Association of Resource Conservation and Development Councils.

18849 ■ United Way of Taylor County
PO Box 85
Medford, WI 54451-0085
Ph: (715)748-3000
URL: National Affiliate–national.unitedway.org
Local. Affiliated With: United Way of America.

18850 ■ Veterans of Foreign Wars
240 S. 8th St.
Medford, WI 54451
Ph: (715)748-3322

Mellen

18851 ■ Mellen Area Chamber of Commerce
PO Box 193
Mellen, WI 54546
Ph: (715)274-2330 (715)274-2898
E-mail: mellen001@centurytel.net
URL: http://www.mellenwi.org
Contact: Jerry Parker, Contact
Local. Promotes business and community development in Mellen, WI.

18852 ■ Wisconsin Health Care Association, District 12
c/o Gwen Lawver, Pres.
Mellen Manor
450 Lake Dr.
Mellen, WI 54546
Ph: (715)274-5706
URL: http://www.whca.com
Contact: Gwen Lawver, Pres.
Local. Promotes professionalism and ethical behavior of individuals providing long-term care delivery for patients and for the general public. Provides information, education and administrative tools to enhance the quality of long-term care. Improves the standards of service and administration of member nursing homes. **Affiliated With:** American Health Care Association; Wisconsin Health Care Association.

Melrose

18853 ■ American Legion, Wisconsin Post 439
c/o Neil S. Lewison
PO Box 171
Melrose, WI 54642
Ph: (608)745-1090
Fax: (608)745-0179
URL: National Affiliate–www.legion.org
Contact: Neil S. Lewison, Contact
Local. Affiliated With: American Legion.

Menasha

18854 ■ Alcoholics Anonymous World Services, Fox Valley Central Office
324 Nicolet Blvd.
Menasha, WI 54952
Ph: (920)720-0522
URL: National Affiliate–www.aa.org
Local. Individuals recovering from alcoholism. AA maintains that members can solve their common problem and help others achieve sobriety through a twelve step program that includes sharing their experience, strength, and hope with each other. **Affiliated With:** Alcoholics Anonymous World Services.

18855 ■ American Chemical Society, Northeast Wisconsin Section
c/o Dr. Martin David Rudd, Chm.
Univ. of Wisconsin Fox Valley
1478 Midway Rd.
Menasha, WI 54952-1224
Ph: (920)832-2694
E-mail: martindrudd@yahoo.com
URL: National Affiliate–acswebcontent.acs.org
Contact: Dr. Martin David Rudd, Chm.
Local. Represents the interests of individuals dedicated to the advancement of chemistry in all its branches. Provides opportunities for peer interaction and career development. **Affiliated With:** American Chemical Society.

18856 ■ American Legion, Lenz-Gazecki Post 152
PO Box 441
Menasha, WI 54952
Ph: (608)745-1090
Fax: (608)745-0179
URL: National Affiliate–www.legion.org
Local. Affiliated With: American Legion.

18857 ■ Arc of Neenah-Menasha
375 Winnebago Ave.
Menasha, WI 54952
Ph: (920)725-0943
Fax: (920)725-1531
E-mail: info@arcofnm.com
URL: http://www.arcofnm.com
Contact: Susan Vander Heiden, Exec.Dir.
Local. Parents, professional workers, and others interested in individuals with mental retardation. Works to promote services, research, public understanding, and legislation for people with mental retardation and their families. **Affiliated With:** Arc of the United States.

18858 ■ East Central Wisconsin Regional Planning Commission (ECWRPC)
132 Main St.
Menasha, WI 54952
Ph: (920)751-4770
Fax: (920)751-4771
E-mail: staff@eastcentralrpc.org
URL: http://www.eastcentralrpc.org
Contact: Eric Fowle, Exec.Dir.
Founded: 1972. **Members:** 28. **Staff:** 20. **Budget:** $1,020,000. **Regional Groups:** 8. **State Groups:** 2. **Local Groups:** 12. **Local.** County and local government representatives (28) who promote economic development and intergovernmental coordination in 8 participating and 2 non-participating Wisconsin counties. **Publications:** *Rapport*, quarterly. Newsletter • Annual Report, annual. **Conventions/Meetings:** quarterly board meeting.

18859 ■ Greater Fox Cities Area Habitat for Humanity
1800 Appleton Rd.
Menasha, WI 54952
Ph: (920)954-8702
Fax: (920)954-8390
E-mail: jweyenberg_hfh@gwicc.org
URL: http://www.foxcitieshabitat.org
Contact: John Weyenberg, Exec.Dir.
Founded: 1993. **Staff:** 55. **Budget:** $1,800,000. **Local. Affiliated With:** Habitat for Humanity International.

18860 ■ Juvenile Diabetes Research Foundation, Northeast Wisconsin Chapter
1800 Appleton Rd., Ste.2
Menasha, WI 54952
Ph: (920)997-0038
Fax: (920)997-0039
Free: (866)233-3354
E-mail: northeastwi@jdrf.org
URL: http://www.jdrf.org/chapters/WI/Northeast-Wisconsin
Contact: Julie Kersten, Exec.Dir.
Founded: 1977. **Members:** 400. **Staff:** 1. **State.** Works to find a cure for diabetes and its complications through the support of research. **Committees:** Bike; Gala/Day of Volunteers; Outreach/PR; Walk Day Volunteers. **Affiliated With:** Juvenile Diabetes Research Foundation International. **Also Known As:** JDF. **Publications:** *Discoveries*, quarterly. Newsletter. Alternate Formats: online • *Needle Point*, bimonthly. Newsletter • Directory, annual.

18861 ■ Menasha Bluejay Football Club (MBFC)
Menasha High School
420 7th St.
Menasha, WI 54952
E-mail: jkschmid@new.rr.com
URL: http://menashabluejayfootball.homestead.com
Contact: Kathy Schmid, Pres.
Local.

18862 ■ National Active and Retired Federal Employees Association - Fox Valley 437
PO Box 512
Menasha, WI 54952-0512
Ph: (920)722-4504
URL: National Affiliate–www.narfe.org
Contact: Giles F. Clark, Contact
Local. Protects the retirement future of employees through education. Informs members on issues af-

fecting the retirement. **Affiliated With:** National Association of Retired Federal Employees.

18863 ■ Northeast Wisconsin Families with Children from China (NEW FCC)
c/o Sharyl LaFaive, Sec.
338 Park St.
Menasha, WI 54952
Ph: (920)751-0535
E-mail: samlafaive@new.rr.com
URL: http://www.newfcc.org
Contact: Sharyl LaFaive, Sec.
Local.

18864 ■ Phi Theta Kappa, Alpha Theta Tau Chapter - University of Wisconsin-Fox Valley
c/o Rex Hieser
Fox Valley Ctr.
1478 Midway Rd.
Menasha, WI 54952-1297
Ph: (920)832-2873
E-mail: rhieser@uwc.edu
URL: http://www.ptk.org/directories/chapters/WI/345-1.htm
Contact: Rex Hieser, Advisor
Local.

18865 ■ Trout Unlimited - Fox Valley Chapter
316 Naymut St.
Menasha, WI 54952-3423
Ph: (920)722-8015
E-mail: rahagen@execpc.com
URL: http://www.foxvalleytu.org
Contact: Tom Deer, Pres.
Local. Protect and preserve cold water resources.

18866 ■ United Way Fox Cities
1820 Appleton Rd.
Menasha, WI 54952-1110
Ph: (920)954-7210
E-mail: peter.kelly@unitedway.org
URL: http://www.unitedwayfoxcities.org
Contact: Peter C. Kelly, Pres./CEO
Local. Affiliated With: United Way of America.

18867 ■ University of Wisconsin at Fox Valley National Organization for the Reform of Marijuana Laws
c/o Anthony Capener
1561 Brighton Beach Rd.
Menasha, WI 54952
Ph: (920)540-9938
E-mail: capea9484@uwc.edu
URL: http://www.norml.org
Local. Affiliated With: National Organization for the Reform of Marijuana Laws.

Menomonee Falls

18868 ■ American Legion, Henrizi-Schneider Post 382
PO Box 323
Menomonee Falls, WI 53052
Ph: (608)745-1090
Fax: (608)745-0179
URL: National Affiliate–www.legion.org
Local. Affiliated With: American Legion.

18869 ■ Antique Automobile Club of America, Wisconsin Region
c/o Vern Kamholtz
W1 48N7739 Menomonee Manor Dr.
Menomonee Falls, WI 53051
E-mail: wraaca@hotmail.com
URL: http://www.aaca.org/wisconsin
Contact: Stanley Larson, Pres.
State. Collectors, hobbyists, and others interested in the preservation, maintenance, and restoration of automobiles and in automotive history. **Affiliated With:** Antique Automobile Club of America.

18870 ■ Chicagoland Bearded Collie Club (CBCC)
c/o Ms. Nancy Steckel, Sec.
W152 N6977 Westwood Dr.
Menomonee Falls, WI 53051-5045
E-mail: wagmoor@ispwest.com
URL: http://my.execpc.com/~gmoulton/cbcc/index.html
Contact: Ms. Nancy Steckel, Sec.
Founded: 1972. **Membership Dues:** $25 (annual). **Local.** Seeks to encourage and promote health and quality in the breeding of purebred Bearded Collies. Protects and advances the interests of the breed by encouraging sportsmanlike competition at dog shows, obedience trails and herding tests. Conducts sanctioned matches, sanctioned and licensed specialty shows and obedience trials, and herding tests under the rules and regulations of The American Kennel Club. Encourages training and competition in herding, obedience and tracking. Educates the public about the history, standard, care and training of the Bearded Collie. Provides a vehicle for rescue and placement of lost, abandoned or unwanted Bearded Collies. Provides a means of bringing together those genuinely interested in Bearded Collies.

18871 ■ Habitat for Humanity of Waukesha
PO Box 1143
Menomonee Falls, WI 53052
Ph: (262)502-4289
E-mail: habitatwaukesha@wauknet.com
URL: http://www.hfhwaukesha.com
Local. Affiliated With: Habitat for Humanity International.

18872 ■ IEEE Communications Society, Milwaukee Chapter
c/o Howard Haugstad
Automated Control Technologies
W172N8866 Shady Ln.
Menomonee Falls, WI 53051-2002
Ph: (262)255-9599
E-mail: hhaugstad@voyager.net
URL: National Affiliate–www.comsoc.org
Contact: Howard Haugstad, Contact
Local. Affiliated With: IEEE Communications Society.

18873 ■ IEEE Computer Society, Milwaukee Chapter
c/o John G. Safar, Chm.
PO Box 172
Menomonee Falls, WI 53051
Ph: (262)251-4435
E-mail: safar@juno.com
URL: National Affiliate–www.computer.org
Contact: John G. Safar, Chm.
Local. Affiliated With: IEEE Computer Society.

18874 ■ Illinois Society of Professional Farm Managers and Rural Appraisers
c/o Carroll Merry, Exec.Dir.
N78W14573 Appleton Ave., No. 287
Menomonee Falls, WI 53051
Ph: (262)253-6902
Fax: (262)253-6903
E-mail: ispfmra@countryside-marketing.com
URL: http://www.ispfmra.org
Contact: Carroll Merry, Exec.Dir.
Founded: 1938. **Members:** 300. **Budget:** $100,000. **State. Affiliated With:** American Society of Farm Managers and Rural Appraisers. **Formerly:** (2004) American Society of Farm Managers and Rural Appraisers Illinois Chapter.

18875 ■ K-9 Obedience Training Club of Menomonee Falls
N56 W20326 Silver Spring Rd.
Menomonee Falls, WI 53051
Ph: (262)252-3569
E-mail: training@k9otc.com
URL: http://www.k9otc.com
Contact: Barbara Borchert, Corresponding Sec.
Founded: 1956. **Membership Dues:** associate, $150 (annual) • regular, $132 (annual) • family, $156 (annual). **Local.**

18876 ■ Kiwanis Club of Menomonee Falls
PO Box 585
Menomonee Falls, WI 53052-0585
E-mail: email@fallskiwanis.com
URL: http://www.mfkiwanis.homestead.com
Contact: John H. Rousseau, Pres.
Local.

18877 ■ Menomonee Falls Chamber of Commerce (MFCC)
N88 W16621 Appleton Ave.
PO Box 73
Menomonee Falls, WI 53052-0073
Ph: (262)251-2430
Fax: (262)251-0969
Free: (800)801-6565
E-mail: jan@fallschamber.com
URL: http://www.menomoneefallschamber.com
Contact: Jenny Polachowski, Exec.Dir.
Founded: 1932. **Members:** 425. **Membership Dues:** regular, $285 (annual). **Staff:** 3. **Budget:** $300,000. **Local.** Provides support and services for the ongoing economic development in the area. Brings together business and community leaders to promote, develop and support the economic, educational, and civic interests of the community. **Awards:** Business of the Year Award. **Frequency:** annual. **Type:** recognition. **Recipient:** for the business member who has given outstanding support to the organization and its programs, projects, and events • Chairperson of the Year Award. **Frequency:** annual. **Type:** recognition. **Recipient:** for the organization's chairperson(s) who have done an outstanding job of committee leadership in producing a successful program, project, or event • Citizen of the Year. **Frequency:** annual. **Type:** recognition. **Recipient:** for outstanding leadership qualities, community service, performance and contribution to the benefit and betterment of the area and its citizens • Community Betterment Award. **Frequency:** annual. **Type:** recognition. **Recipient:** to an organization, business or person for their work and accomplishments • Community Improvement Award. **Frequency:** annual. **Type:** recognition. **Recipient:** to a business or organization for their efforts toward the enhancement of the community or their facilities in the village • Leadership Menomonee Falls Award. **Frequency:** annual. **Type:** recognition. **Recipient:** to the nominee(s) displaying emerging leadership, qualities of service and accomplishments • Leading the Way/Women of Achievement Award. **Frequency:** periodic. **Type:** recognition. **Recipient:** to honorees for their qualities of outstanding leadership, exceptional business acumen, and selfless service to the community • President's Award. **Frequency:** annual. **Type:** recognition. **Recipient:** for individual who has promoted and given service to the organization in numerous capacities by giving of their time and talent to some projects and programs. **Telecommunication Services:** information service, for general community about business and cultural information regarding the area. **Committees:** Active Legislative Economic Resource Team; Ambassadors; CEO Round Table; Education; Leadership Menomonee Falls; Marketing & Communication; Tourism. **Affiliated With:** U.S. Chamber of Commerce; Wisconsin Manufacturers and Commerce. **Formerly:** (1999) Menomonee Falls Chamber of Commerce and Industry. **Publications:** *Action Update*, periodic. Newsletter. **Price:** free.

18878 ■ United Association of Journeymen and Apprentices of the Plumbing and Pipe Fitting Industry of the United States and Canada - Local Union 183
W175 N5700 Tech. Dr.
Menomonee Falls, WI 53051
Ph: (262)252-0183
Fax: (262)252-7183
URL: http://sprinklerfitters183.org
Members: 200. **Local. Affiliated With:** United Association of Journeymen and Apprentices of the Plumbing, Pipe Fitting, Sprinkler Fitting Industry of the U.S. and Canada.

18879 ■ Wisconsin Society for Respiratory Care
c/o Brian Eisner, Pres.
Community Memorial Hosp.
W180 N8085 Town Hall Rd.
Menomonee Falls, WI 53051

Ph: (262)257-3088
E-mail: brianeisner@sbcglobal.net
URL: http://www.wsrconline.org
Contact: Brian Eisner, Pres.
State. Fosters the improvement of educational programs in respiratory care. Advocates research in the field of respiratory care. **Affiliated With:** American Association for Respiratory Care.

Menomonie

18880 ■ American Legion, Hosford-Chase Post 32
800 Wilson Ave.
Menomonie, WI 54751
Ph: (608)745-1090
Fax: (608)745-0179
URL: National Affiliate–www.legion.org
Local. Affiliated With: American Legion.

18881 ■ Greater Menomonie Area Chamber of Commerce (GMACC)
342 E Main St.
Menomonie, WI 54751
Ph: (715)235-9087
Fax: (715)235-2824
Free: (800)283-1862
E-mail: info@menomoniechamber.org
URL: http://www.menomoniechamber.org
Contact: Linda McIntyre, Exec.Dir.
Founded: 1937. **Local**. Promotes business and community development in the Menomonie, WI area. Holds summer and winter festivals. **Committees:** Ambassadors; Budget and Finance; Business Development; Community Events; Education; Public Affairs; Retail. **Councils:** Agri-Business. **Affiliated With:** U.S. Chamber of Commerce. **Publications:** Directory, periodic • Newsletter, monthly.

18882 ■ United Way of Dunn County
PO Box 3266
Menomonie, WI 54751
Ph: (715)235-3800
URL: National Affiliate–national.unitedway.org
Local. Affiliated With: United Way of America.

Mequon

18883 ■ American Association of Physicians of Indian Origin, Wisconsin
c/o Ashok Krishnaneny, MD
12078 N Lake Shore Dr., No. 5 W
Mequon, WI 53092
Ph: (414)647-5000
URL: National Affiliate–www.aapiusa.org
Contact: Ashok Krishnaneny MD, Contact
State. Represents Indian American physicians. Promotes excellence in patient care, teaching and research. Serves as a forum for scientific, educational and social interaction among members and other medical scientists of Indian heritage. Fosters the availability of medical assistance to indigent people in the United States. **Affiliated With:** American Association of Physicians of Indian Origin.

18884 ■ Associated Landscape Contractors of America, Milwaukee Area Technical College
c/o Mike Wendt, Faculty Advisor
Horticulture Club
5555 W Highland
Mequon, WI 53092-1199
Ph: (262)238-2332
Fax: (262)238-2346
URL: National Affiliate–www.alca.org
Contact: Mike Wendth, Faculty Advisor
Local. Affiliated With: Professional Landcare Network.

18885 ■ Association of Lutheran Secondary Schools
c/o Ross Stueber, Exec.Dir.
12800 N Lake Shore Dr.
Mequon, WI 53097-2418
Ph: (262)243-4519
Free: (262)243-4428
E-mail: ross.stueber@cuw.edu
URL: http://www.alss.org
Regional.

18886 ■ Health Care Public Relations and Marketing Society for Southeastern Wisconsin
c/o Anne Becker, Pres.
The Highlands at Newcastle Pl.
Admissions & Marketing Dir.
12600 N Port Washington Rd., No. 300
Mequon, WI 53092
Ph: (262)387-8883
Fax: (262)387-8881
E-mail: abecker@newcastleplace.com
URL: http://www.hcprms.org
Contact: Anne Becker, Pres.
Regional. Affiliated With: Society for Healthcare Strategy and Market Development of the American Hospital Association.

18887 ■ National Alliance for the Mentally Ill - Ozaukee
c/o Bobbie Hoffman, Pres.
10606 N Port Washington Rd.
Mequon, WI 53092
Ph: (262)241-3929 (262)241-8979
URL: http://www.namiwisconsin.org/library/directory
Contact: Bobbie Hoffman, Pres.
Local. Strives to improve the quality of life of children and adults with severe mental illness through support, education, research and advocacy. **Affiliated With:** National Alliance for the Mentally Ill.

18888 ■ Phi Theta Kappa, Sigma Theta Chapter - Milwaukee Area Technical College
c/o Jim Groff, Advisor
700 W State St.
Mequon, WI 53092-1199
Ph: (414)297-6058
E-mail: groffj@matc.edu
URL: http://www.ptk.org/directories/chapters/WI/342-1.htm
Contact: Jim Groff, Advisor
Founded: 1968. **Members:** 100. **Membership Dues:** student, $60 (annual). **Local Groups:** 1. **Local**.

18889 ■ Southeast Wisconsin FreeThinkers
PO Box 3
Mequon, WI 53092
E-mail: swift@humanists.net
URL: http://swift.humanists.net
Local. Affiliated With: American Atheists.

18890 ■ Wisconsin Arborist Association
c/o Bob Gansemer, Pres.
10352 N Cedarburg Rd.
Mequon, WI 53092
Ph: (262)242-2040
Fax: (262)242-9142
URL: http://www.arborist.com
State.

18891 ■ Wisconsin Curling Association - Milwaukee Curling Club (MCC)
c/o Ozaukee Country Club
10823 N River Rd.
Mequon, WI 53092
E-mail: info@milwaukeecurlingclub.com
URL: http://www.milwaukeecurlingclub.com
Contact: Bert Fredericksen, Pres.
Local. Affiliated With: United States Curling Association.

18892 ■ Wisconsin Orchid Society (WOS)
c/o Joe Gardner, Treas.
10127 N Rangline Rd.
Mequon, WI 53092-5434
Ph: (262)512-9476
E-mail: treasurer@wisconsinorchidsociety.com
URL: http://www.wisconsinorchidsociety.com
Contact: Joe Gardner, Treas.
Founded: 1961. **Members:** 100. **Membership Dues:** individual, $18 (annual) • family, $27 (annual) • junior, $9 (annual). **Local Groups:** 1. **State**. Professional growers, botanists, hobbyists, and others interested in extending the knowledge, production, use, and appreciation of orchids. **Libraries: Type:** not open to the public. **Holdings:** 250; audio recordings, books, periodicals, video recordings. **Awards:** Dusnick Award. **Frequency:** annual. **Type:** trophy. **Recipient:** for the best specimen plant at monthly meeting • Grower of the Year. **Frequency:** annual. **Type:** trophy. **Recipient:** for total points from all ribbon judging • Martha Schmidt Award. **Frequency:** annual. **Type:** trophy. **Recipient:** for the best specimen plant by a society member. **Telecommunication Services:** electronic mail, questions@wisconsinorchidsociety.com. **Affiliated With:** American Orchid Society; Orchid Digest. **Publications:** Newsletter, monthly. Contains information interesting to members, meeting dates and activities. **Price:** included in membership dues. **Circulation:** 100. **Advertising:** accepted. Alternate Formats: online; CD-ROM.

Mercer

18893 ■ Mercer Area Chamber of Commerce
5150 N Hwy. 51
Mercer, WI 54547
Ph: (715)476-2389
Fax: (715)476-2389
E-mail: info@mercercc.com
URL: http://www.mercercc.com
Contact: Tina Brunell, Office Mgr.
Membership Dues: business (base), $125 (annual) • lodging, rental, $150 (annual) • individual, non-profit organization, $25 (annual). **Local**. Promotes business and community development in Mercer, WI area. **Publications:** Newsletter, monthly. Contains information about the events and happenings in the chamber.

Merrill

18894 ■ American Legion, Wisconsin Post 46
c/o Edward Burns
PO Box 98
Merrill, WI 54452
Ph: (608)745-1090
Fax: (608)745-0179
URL: National Affiliate–www.legion.org
Contact: Edward Burns, Contact
Local. Affiliated With: American Legion.

18895 ■ Lincoln County Economic Development Corp.
c/o Jack L. Sroka, Exec.Dir.
1106 E 8th St.
Merrill, WI 54452-1100
Ph: (715)536-0383
E-mail: jsroka@co.lincoln.wi.us
URL: http://www.co.lincoln.wi.us
Contact: Jack L. Sroka, Exec.Dir.
Founded: 1999. **Members:** 3. **Staff:** 2. **Local**. Promotes county-wide economic development efforts.

18896 ■ Merrill Area Chamber of Commerce (MACC)
120 S Mill St.
Merrill, WI 54452
Ph: (715)536-9474
Fax: (715)539-2043
Free: (877)90P-ARKS
E-mail: info@merrillchamber.com
URL: http://www.merrillchamber.com
Contact: Jane Ann Savaske, Exec.Dir.
Founded: 1911. **Local**. Promotes business and community development in the Merrill, WI area. **Publications:** *Merrill City Directory*, periodic. **Price:** $14.00/copy • *Merrill, Wisconsin, A City of Progress and*

Promise. Booklet. **Price:** $2.00/copy • Booklets • Books • Brochures • Directories.

18897 ■ Merrill Area United Way
418 W Main St.
Merrill, WI 54452-2223
Ph: (715)536-2016
URL: National Affiliate–national.unitedway.org
Local. Affiliated With: United Way of America.

18898 ■ United Food and Commercial Workers, Local 688, Northcentral Region
PO Box 573
Merrill, WI 54452
Ph: (715)536-2444
URL: National Affiliate–www.ufcw.org
Local. Affiliated With: United Food and Commercial Workers International Union.

18899 ■ United Way of Merrill
418 W Main St.
Merrill, WI 54452-2223
Ph: (715)536-2016
Contact: Sharon Thatcher, Exec.Dir.
Founded: 1947. **Members:** 28. **Staff:** 1. **Budget:** $115,000. **Local.** Provides assistance in fundraising by conducting company-wide employee campaigns and by encouraging corporate contributions.

18900 ■ Wisconsin Maple Syrup Producers Association
N602 Leafy Grove Rd.
Merrill, WI 54452
Ph: (715)536-3114
E-mail: melander@dwave.net
Contact: Ray Melander, Exec.Dir.
Founded: 1948. **Members:** 200. **Staff:** 1. **State.** Members are pure maple syrup producers. Promotes the production and marketing of pure WI maple syrup. Sponsors a maple festival, elects a WI maple queen, holds a maple syrup judging contest, holds an annual maple tour, has a WI State Fair exhibit and conducts a series of educational institutes annually. Also sponsors a state promotion board. **Awards:** Wisconsin Maple Syrup Maker of the Year. **Frequency:** annual. **Type:** recognition. **Recipient:** to member of association. **Publications:** *WI Maple News*, semiannual. Newsletter. Educational and informational news. **Price:** $6.00/year. **Advertising:** accepted.

Merrillan

18901 ■ American Legion, Davis-Porter Post 140
PO Box 103
Merrillan, WI 54754
Ph: (608)745-1090
Fax: (608)745-0179
URL: National Affiliate–www.legion.org
Local. Affiliated With: American Legion.

Middleton

18902 ■ American Legion, Middleton Post 275
PO Box 620161
Middleton, WI 53562
Ph: (608)745-1090
Fax: (608)745-0179
URL: National Affiliate–www.legion.org
Local. Affiliated With: American Legion.

18903 ■ American Volkssport Association, North Central Region
c/o Bruce Dewey
2809 Meadowbrook Rd.
Middleton, WI 53562
Ph: (608)836-8576
E-mail: nc_rd@ava.org
URL: National Affiliate–www.ava.org
Contact: Bruce Dewey, Contact
Regional.

18904 ■ American Water Resources Association, Wisconsin Section
c/o James T. Krohelski
8505 Res. Way
Middleton, WI 53562-3586
Ph: (608)288-8004
E-mail: wri_info@wri.wisc.edu
URL: National Affiliate–www.awra.org
Contact: Paul McGinley, Pres.
State.

18905 ■ Democratic Socialists of America, Madison (DSA)
c/o Marc Silberman
DSA
PO Box 628313
Middleton, WI 53562
E-mail: mdsilber@wisc.edu
URL: National Affiliate–www.dsausa.org
Contact: Marc Silberman, Contact
Local. Affiliated With: Democratic Socialists of America.

18906 ■ Friends of the Kettle Ponds
c/o Robert Conhaim, Co-Pres.
7501 Voss Pkwy.
Middleton, WI 53562
Fax: (415)727-3813
E-mail: kettleponds@yahoo.com
URL: http://www.geocities.com/kettleponds
Contact: Robert Conhaim, Co-Pres.
Local.

18907 ■ Madison Bead Society
PO Box 620383
Middleton, WI 53562-0383
Ph: (608)831-3242
E-mail: madisonbeadsoc@hotmail.com
URL: http://www.madisonbeadsociety.org
Contact: Ms. Pat Helgerson, Pres.
Founded: 1992. **Members:** 80. **Membership Dues:** single, $20 (annual) • family, business, $30 (annual). **Local.** Provides a forum for the enjoyment and study of beads and related ornament; disseminates the knowledge acquired through this research. **Conventions/Meetings:** monthly meeting - September-May • semiannual show, with sales • periodic workshop.

18908 ■ Media Communications Association International, Kansas City
7600 Terrace Ave., Ste.203
Middleton, WI 53562
E-mail: info@mcai.org
URL: http://www.mca-i.org
Contact: Dan Nelson, Pres.
Local. Provides networking and education opportunities to media communications professionals. Facilitates effective communication using new technology and with sound communication principles. **Affiliated With:** Chemical Coaters Association International.

18909 ■ Middleton Chamber of Commerce (MCC)
7507 Hubbard Ave.
Middleton, WI 53562
Ph: (608)827-5797
Fax: (608)831-7765
E-mail: chamber@middletonchamber.com
URL: http://www.middletonchamber.com
Contact: Mr. Van Nutt, Exec.Dir.
Founded: 1952. **Members:** 330. **Membership Dues:** general business, financial institution, real estate agency, local media, $210 • real estate agent, $60 • sole proprietor, $160 • nonprofit, $55 • individual, $105. **Staff:** 2. **Local.** Represents businesses in Middleton, WI united to promote economic development. Aims to act as a liaison for business people and the community, and to provide governmental advocacy. **Committees:** Ambassadors; Annual Celebration; Economic Development; Education; Fall Seminar Series; Good Neighbor Festival; Retail/Restaurant; Silent Auction. **Affiliated With:** U.S. Chamber of Commerce. **Publications:** Newsletter, monthly. **Circulation:** 575. Alternate Formats: online. **Conventions/Meetings:** monthly Get Moving Middleton - breakfast - every 1st Thursday in Middleton, WI • annual meeting • periodic seminar.

18910 ■ Middleton Key Club
2100 Bristol St.
Middleton, WI 53562
Ph: (608)829-9660
E-mail: middletonkeyclub@yahoo.com
URL: http://www.middletonkeyclub.org
Contact: Courtney Miller, Pres.
Local.

18911 ■ National Active and Retired Federal Employees Association - Madison 120
6401 Cooper St.
Middleton, WI 53562-3346
Ph: (608)831-9623
URL: National Affiliate–www.narfe.org
Contact: Norman O. Everson, Contact
Local. Protects the retirement future of employees through education. Informs members on issues affecting the retirement. **Affiliated With:** National Association of Retired Federal Employees.

18912 ■ Wisconsin Amusement and Music Operators Association (WAMO)
c/o Maxine O'Brien, Exec.Dir.
PO Box 620830
Middleton, WI 53562-0830
Ph: (608)836-6090
Fax: (608)836-3890
Free: (800)827-8011
E-mail: wamomax@aol.com
URL: http://www.wamo.net
Contact: Maxine O'Brien, Exec.Dir.
State. Aims to further the interests of those engaged in the sales, marketing, distribution and manufacturing of coin operated equipment. Fosters and promotes goodwill, mutual respect and fair dealing among those engaged in the business of coin-operated amusement devices. **Affiliated With:** Amusement and Music Operators Association.

18913 ■ Wisconsin Auctioneers Association
c/o Maxine D. O'Brien
PO Box 620830
Middleton, WI 53562-0830
Ph: (608)836-6542
Fax: (608)836-3890
E-mail: waamaxine@aol.com
URL: http://www.wisconsinauctioneers.org
Contact: Maxine D. O'Brien, Exec.Dir.
Founded: 1952. **Members:** 283. **Membership Dues:** auctioneer, auction company, $100 (annual) • trade, vendor, $200 (annual). **Staff:** 2. **State Groups:** 1. **State.** Works to promote and protect the Wisconsin auction industry. **Awards:** Hall of Fame. **Frequency:** annual. **Type:** recognition. **Recipient:** by nomination of members • State Champion Bid-Caller. **Frequency:** annual. **Type:** trophy. **Publications:** *Wisconsin Auctioneer*, semiannual. **Advertising:** accepted. Alternate Formats: CD-ROM; online. **Conventions/Meetings:** annual conference, membership meeting, election (exhibits).

18914 ■ Wisconsin Dairy Products Association (WDPA)
8383 Greenway Blvd.
Middleton, WI 53562
Ph: (608)836-3336
Fax: (608)836-3334
E-mail: info@wdpa.net
URL: http://www.wdpa.net
Contact: Brad Legreid, Exec.Dir.
Founded: 1973. **Members:** 190. **Staff:** 2. Represents dairy processors united to promote legislation favorable to the dairy industry of Wisconsin. **Formed by Merger of:** Wisconsin Creameries Association; Wisconsin Dairy Foods Association. **Publications:**

Membership Directory, monthly. Includes newsletter covering legislative and regulatory issues affecting the industry. Contains calendar of events and research reports. **Conventions/Meetings:** annual meeting.

18915 ■ Wisconsin Federation of Stamp Clubs (WFSC)
c/o Karen L. Weigt, Sec.
4184 Rose Ct.
Middleton, WI 53562-4339
Ph: (608)836-1509
E-mail: karenweigt@earthlink.net
URL: http://www.WFSCstamps.org/
Contact: Karen L. Weigt, Sec.
State. Affiliated With: American Philatelic Society.

18916 ■ Wisconsin Retired Educators' Association (WREA)
2564 Br. St.
Middleton, WI 53562
Ph: (608)831-5115
Fax: (608)831-1694
E-mail: jelmer@wrea.net
Contact: Jane Elmer, Exec.Dir.
Founded: 1951. **Members:** 11,500. **Membership Dues:** individual, $40 (annual). **Staff:** 3. **Budget:** $300,000. **Local Groups:** 71. **State.** Retired educators in the state of Wisconsin; committed to monitoring and improving the benefits for retired educators and other members of the Wisconsin Retirement System (WRS); seeks to inform members about and advocates for educational and other relevant societal issues; structures opportunities for volunteer members to collaborate with one another and with organizations sharing similar goals. Provides intergenerational community services for members and the public. **Publications:** *Leadership News*, quarterly. Newsletter. **Price:** free for members • *WREA News*, quarterly. Newsletter. **Price:** free for members. **Conventions/Meetings:** annual Convention - usually April or May • annual District Meeting - always October.

Milladore

18917 ■ American Legion, Hinek-Hertel-Krupka Post 468
442 West St.
Milladore, WI 54454
Ph: (608)745-1090
Fax: (608)745-0179
URL: National Affiliate–www.legion.org
Local. Affiliated With: American Legion.

Milltown

18918 ■ American Legion, Wisconsin Post 254
c/o George W. Melby
305 2nd Ave. SW, Apt. 1
Milltown, WI 54858
Ph: (608)745-1090
Fax: (608)745-0179
URL: National Affiliate–www.legion.org
Contact: George W. Melby, Contact
Local. Affiliated With: American Legion.

Milton

18919 ■ American Legion, Randolph-West-Kelly Post 367
PO Box 183
Milton, WI 53563
Ph: (608)745-1090
Fax: (608)745-0179
URL: National Affiliate–www.legion.org
Local. Affiliated With: American Legion.

18920 ■ Milton Area Chamber of Commerce (MACC)
508 Campus St.
PO Box 222
Milton, WI 53563
Ph: (608)868-6222
E-mail: macc2@charter.net
URL: http://www.miltonareachamber.com
Contact: Mary J. Roehl, Exec.Dir.
Local. Promotes a strong business community in Milton, WI, resulting in a better quality of life for all.

18921 ■ Milton Historical Society (MHS)
PO Box 245
Milton, WI 53563
Ph: (608)868-7772
Fax: (608)868-1698
E-mail: miltonhouse@miltonhouse.org
URL: http://www.miltonhouse.org
Contact: Rob Christlieb, Pres.
Founded: 1948. **Members:** 300. **Membership Dues:** family, $15 (annual) • business, $25 (annual) • station master, $100-$249 (annual) • abolitionist, $250-$499 (annual) • North Star friend, $500 (annual). **Staff:** 2. **Budget:** $80,000. **State Groups:** 1. **Local Groups:** 1. **Local.** Individuals interested in the history of the Underground Railroad in Wisconsin. Operates the Milton House Museum. Sponsors annual arts and crafts fair. Pioneer history of Wisconsin. **Libraries: Type:** not open to the public; reference. **Holdings:** 2,500. **Subjects:** local and state history, underground railroad, historic preservation. **Affiliated With:** Wisconsin Historical Society. **Publications:** *The Herald*, quarterly. Newsletter. **Price:** included in membership dues • Pamphlets. **Conventions/Meetings:** annual meeting.

Milwaukee

18922 ■ 9to5 Poverty Network
c/o Mildred Navedo
207 E Buffalo St., No. 211
Milwaukee, WI 53202
Fax: (800)920-9925
Free: (800)920-9925
URL: National Affiliate–www.9to5.org
Contact: Mildred Navedo, Contact
Local. Affiliated With: 9 to 5, National Association of Working Women.

18923 ■ ACF Alterra Chapter
10000 Innovation Dr.
Milwaukee, WI 53226
Ph: (414)918-5348
E-mail: vzala@assisted.com
URL: National Affiliate–www.acfchefs.org
Contact: Vaishali Zala, Contact
Local. Promotes the culinary profession and provides on-going educational training and networking for members. Provides opportunities for competition, professional recognition, and access to educational forums with other culinarians at local, regional, national, and international events.

18924 ■ ACLU of Wisconsin
c/o Chris Ahmuty, Exec.Dir.
207 E Buffalo St., Ste.325
Milwaukee, WI 53202-5774
Ph: (414)272-4032
Fax: (414)272-0182
E-mail: liberty@aclu-wi.org
URL: http://www.aclu-wi.org
Contact: Chris Ahmuty, Exec.Dir.
State.

18925 ■ Adoption Resources of Wisconsin (ARW)
6682 W Greenfield, Ste.310
Milwaukee, WI 53214
Ph: (414)475-1246
Fax: (414)475-7007
Free: (800)762-8063
E-mail: info@wiadopt.org
URL: http://www.wiadopt.org
Contact: Ms. Colleen Ellingson, Exec.Dir.
State. "Finds permanence for all children who need a family and to help support and sustain healthy families." Conducts child specific recruitment on behalf of waiting children, operates the Adoption Information Center of Wisconsin, the Foster Care and Adoption Resource Center of Wisconsin, and the Post Adoption Resource Center for Milwaukee County and Southeastern Wisconsin. **Libraries: Type:** lending; open to the public. **Holdings:** 2,000; articles, audio recordings, books, periodicals, reports, video recordings. **Subjects:** adoption, foster care, post adoption, out of home care issues.

18926 ■ Alverno College Students In Free Enterprise
PO Box 343922
Milwaukee, WI 53234-3922
Ph: (414)382-6000
E-mail: alvernosife@aol.com
URL: http://www.geocities.com/alvernosife
Local.

18927 ■ Alzheimer's Association, Southeastern Wisconsin Chapter
6130 W Natl. Ave., Ste.200
Milwaukee, WI 53214
Ph: (414)479-8800
Fax: (414)479-8819
Free: (800)272-3900
E-mail: kristen.forman@alz.org
URL: http://www.alzheimers-sewi.org
Contact: Ms. Kristen Forman, Communications Specialist
Founded: 1983. **Staff;** 16. **Budget:** $1,376,845. **Nonmembership. Regional.** Works to eliminate Alzheimer's disease through the advancement of research and enhance care and support for individuals, their families and caregivers. **Libraries: Type:** lending; open to the public. **Holdings:** audiovisuals, books, periodicals, video recordings. **Subjects:** Alzheimer's disease and related disorders, and caregiving strategies. **Awards:** Alzheimers Practitioner Award. **Frequency:** annual. **Type:** recognition. **Recipient:** to an outstanding practitioner • Alzheimer's Research Award. **Frequency:** annual. **Type:** recognition. **Recipient:** to an outstanding researcher • Funders Award. **Frequency:** annual. **Type:** recognition. **Recipient:** for an outstanding support for the Alzheimer's association and its mission. **Affiliated With:** Alzheimer's Association.

18928 ■ American Association of Blacks in Energy, Wisconsin
c/o Sandra Camberos
1035 W Canal St.
Milwaukee, WI 53233
Ph: (414)221-3518
Fax: (414)221-3799
E-mail: sandracamberos@we-energies.com
URL: http://aabe.org
State. Affiliated With: American Association of Blacks in Energy.

18929 ■ American Association of Candy Technologists - Milwaukee Section
c/o Susan Hough, Sec.
PO Box 691
Milwaukee, WI 53201
Ph: (414)902-2203
Fax: (414)647-1170
E-mail: susan.hough@mastersoncompany.com
URL: National Affiliate–www.aactcandy.org
Contact: Dr. Richard Hartel PhD, Chm.
Local. Seeks to further the education of the technical community of the confectionery industry. Promotes the application of science and engineering to the manufacturing, handling and distribution of confectionery products. **Affiliated With:** American Association of Candy Technologists.

18930 ■ American Board of Trial Advocates - Wisconsin
735 N Water St. No. 630
Milwaukee, WI 53202-4104
Ph: (414)271-0054
Fax: (414)271-7131
E-mail: kenan@kerstenlaw.com
Contact: Kenan J. Kersten, Pres.
Local. Improves the ethical and technical standards of practice in the field of advocacy. Elevates the

standards of integrity, honor and courtesy in the legal profession. Promotes the efficient administration of justice and improvement of the law. **Affiliated With:** American Board of Trial Advocates.

18931 ■ American Civil Liberties Union, Wisconsin
c/o Christopher Ahmuty, Exec.Dir.
207 E Buffalo St., Ste.325
Milwaukee, WI 53202-5774
Ph: (414)272-4032
Fax: (414)272-0182
E-mail: liberty@aclu-wi.org
URL: http://www.aclu-wi.org
Contact: Christopher Ahmuty, Exec.Dir.
State. Champions the rights set forth in the Bill of Rights of the U.S. Constitution: freedom of speech, press, assembly, and religion; due process of law and fair trial; equality before the law regardless of race, color, sexual orientation, national origin, political opinion, or religious belief. Activities include litigation, advocacy, and public education. **Affiliated With:** American Civil Liberties Union.

18932 ■ American College of Cardiology - Wisconsin Chapter (WCACC)
c/o Martin B. Tirado, Chapter Admin.
1123 N Water St.
Milwaukee, WI 53202
Ph: (414)276-8788
Fax: (414)276-7704
E-mail: info@wcacc.org
URL: http://wcacc.org
Contact: Mr. Martin B. Tirado, Contact
State. **Affiliated With:** American College of Cardiology.

18933 ■ American Federation of State, County and Municipal Employees, AFL-CIO - Milwaukee Wisconsin District Council 48
3427 W St. Paul Ave.
Milwaukee, WI 53208
Ph: (414)344-6868
E-mail: afscme48@hotmail.com
URL: http://www.afscme48.org
Contact: Richard Abelson, Exec.Dir.
Members: 9,903. **Local**. Represents the interests of workers coming from different areas of government, health, education and other services, both public and private. **Affiliated With:** American Federation of State, County and Municipal Employees.

18934 ■ American Hiking Society - Ice Age Park and Trail Foundation (IAPTF)
207 E Buffalo St., Ste.515
Milwaukee, WI 53202
Ph: (414)278-8518
Fax: (414)278-8665
E-mail: christine@iceagetrail.org
URL: http://www.iceagetrail.org
Contact: Christine Thisted, Exec.Dir.
Local.

18935 ■ American Institute of Architects Southeast Wisconsin
335 E Chicago St.
Milwaukee, WI 53202-5809
Ph: (414)291-8172
Fax: (414)298-2254
E-mail: stuartl@eppsteinuhen.com
URL: National Affiliate–www.aia.org
Contact: William Babcock, Exec.Dir.
Local. **Affiliated With:** American Institute of Architects.

18936 ■ American Legion, Bay View Post 180
2860 S Kinnickinnic Ave.
Milwaukee, WI 53207
Ph: (608)745-1090
Fax: (608)745-0179
URL: National Affiliate–www.legion.org
Local. **Affiliated With:** American Legion.

18937 ■ American Legion, Electric Post 228
5177 N 62nd St.
Milwaukee, WI 53218
Ph: (608)745-1090
Fax: (608)745-0179
URL: National Affiliate–www.legion.org
Local. **Affiliated With:** American Legion.

18938 ■ American Legion, Federal Post 203
PO Box 864
Milwaukee, WI 53201
Ph: (608)745-1090
Fax: (608)745-0179
URL: National Affiliate–www.legion.org
Local. **Affiliated With:** American Legion.

18939 ■ American Legion, Gold Star Post 505
PO Box 340204
Milwaukee, WI 53234
Ph: (608)745-1090
Fax: (608)745-0179
URL: National Affiliate–www.legion.org
Local. **Affiliated With:** American Legion.

18940 ■ American Legion, Lakeshore Post 474
600 E Henry Clay St., Ste.A
Milwaukee, WI 53217
Ph: (414)466-6079
Fax: (608)745-0179
URL: National Affiliate–www.legion.org
Local. **Affiliated With:** American Legion.

18941 ■ American Legion, Luitink-Weishan Post 495
750 N Lincoln Memorial Dr.
Milwaukee, WI 53202
Ph: (414)871-6216
Fax: (608)745-0179
URL: National Affiliate–www.legion.org
Local. **Affiliated With:** American Legion.

18942 ■ American Legion, Milwaukee Fire Fighters Post 426
5625 W Wisconsin Ave.
Milwaukee, WI 53213
Ph: (608)745-1090
Fax: (608)745-0179
URL: National Affiliate–www.legion.org
Local. **Affiliated With:** American Legion.

18943 ■ American Legion, Milwaukee Police Post 415
PO Box 1491
Milwaukee, WI 53201
Ph: (608)745-1090
Fax: (608)745-0179
URL: National Affiliate–www.legion.org
Local. **Affiliated With:** American Legion.

18944 ■ American Legion, Milwaukee Post 18
PO Box 04545
Milwaukee, WI 53204
Ph: (608)745-1090
Fax: (608)745-0179
E-mail: alpost@yahoo.com
URL: National Affiliate–www.legion.org
Local. **Affiliated With:** American Legion.

18945 ■ American Legion, Milwaukee Womens Post 448
PO Box 371311
Milwaukee, WI 53237
Ph: (608)745-1090
Fax: (608)745-0179
URL: National Affiliate–www.legion.org
Local. **Affiliated With:** American Legion.

18946 ■ American Legion, Neville-Dunn Post 489
PO Box 1976
Milwaukee, WI 53201
Ph: (608)745-1090
Fax: (608)745-0179
URL: National Affiliate–www.legion.org
Local. **Affiliated With:** American Legion.

18947 ■ American Legion, Stoddard-Heinle Post 500
PO Box 13801
Milwaukee, WI 53213
Ph: (608)745-1090
Fax: (608)745-0179
URL: National Affiliate–www.legion.org
Local. **Affiliated With:** American Legion.

18948 ■ American Legion, Wisconsin Post 23
c/o Alonzo Cudworth
600 E Henry Clay St., Ste.A
750 N Lincoln Memorial Dr.
Milwaukee, WI 53217
Ph: (414)964-6480
Fax: (608)745-0179
URL: National Affiliate–www.legion.org
Contact: Alonzo Cudworth, Contact
Local. **Affiliated With:** American Legion.

18949 ■ American Legion, Wisconsin Post 406
c/o Gen. Charles King
5473 N Dexter Ave.
Milwaukee, WI 53209
Ph: (608)745-1090
Fax: (608)745-0179
URL: National Affiliate–www.legion.org
Contact: Gen. Charles King, Contact
Local. **Affiliated With:** American Legion.

18950 ■ American Legion, Wisconsin Post 408
c/o Jane Delano
1418 W Arthur Ave.
Milwaukee, WI 53215
Ph: (608)745-1090
Fax: (608)745-0179
URL: National Affiliate–www.legion.org
Contact: Jane Delano, Contact
Local. **Affiliated With:** American Legion.

18951 ■ American Legion, Wisconsin Post 411
c/o Erwin C. Uihlein
PO Box 250242
Milwaukee, WI 53225
Ph: (608)745-1090
Fax: (608)745-0179
URL: National Affiliate–www.legion.org
Contact: Erwin C. Uihlein, Contact
Local. **Affiliated With:** American Legion.

18952 ■ American Legion, Wisconsin Post 444
3577 S 13th St.
Milwaukee, WI 53221
Ph: (608)745-1090
Fax: (608)745-0179
URL: National Affiliate–www.legion.org
Local. **Affiliated With:** American Legion.

18953 ■ American Legion, Wisconsin Post 455
c/o Corporal Cornice D. Grace
PO Box 12864
Milwaukee, WI 53212
Ph: (608)745-1090
Fax: (608)745-0179
URL: National Affiliate–www.legion.org
Contact: Corporal Cornice D. Grace, Contact
Local. **Affiliated With:** American Legion.

18954 ■ American Legion, Wisconsin Post 498
c/o Rev. Raphael Heinz
5000 W Natl. Ave., Bldg. 1
Milwaukee, WI 53214
Ph: (608)745-1090
Fax: (608)745-0179
URL: National Affiliate–www.legion.org
Contact: Rev. Raphael Heinz, Contact
Local. Affiliated With: American Legion.

18955 ■ American Legion, Wisconsin Post 529
c/o David Valdes
PO Box 64055
Milwaukee, WI 53204
Ph: (608)745-1090
Fax: (608)745-0179
URL: National Affiliate–www.legion.org
Contact: David Valdes, Contact
Local. Affiliated With: American Legion.

18956 ■ American Red Cross - Greater Milwaukee Chapter
2600 W Wisconsin Ave.
Milwaukee, WI 53233
Ph: (414)342-8680
Fax: (414)342-7802
Free: (800)236-8680
E-mail: cr@redcrossinsewis.org
URL: http://www.redcrossinsewis.org
Contact: Bud Mckonly, CEO
Founded: 1916. **Staff:** 7. **Local**. Provides relief to victims of disaster and help people prevent, prepare for and respond to emergencies. **Publications:** *CrossRoads*, monthly. Newsletter. Alternate Formats: online.

18957 ■ American Society of Heating, Refrigerating and Air-Conditioning Engineers - Wisconsin Chapter
c/o Maggie Roll
10101 Innovation Dr., Ste.200
Milwaukee, WI 53226
Ph: (414)778-1700
E-mail: mroll@ringdu.com
URL: http://www.ashrae-wi.org
Contact: Sam Badani, Pres.
State. Advances the arts and sciences of heating, ventilation, air-conditioning and refrigeration. Provides a source of technical and educational information, standards and guidelines. Conducts seminars for professional growth. **Affiliated With:** American Society of Heating, Refrigerating and Air-Conditioning Engineers.

18958 ■ American Society of Interior Designers, Wisconsin
11801 W Silver Spring Dr., Ste.200
Milwaukee, WI 53225-3092
Ph: (414)755-3366
Fax: (414)464-0850
E-mail: heather@wamllc.net
URL: http://www.asidwi.org
Contact: Sandra Weber ASID, Pres.
State. Represents practicing professional interior designers, students and industry partners. Strives to advance the interior design profession. Aims to demonstrate and celebrate the power of design to positively change people's lives. **Affiliated With:** American Society of Interior Designers.

18959 ■ American Society of Mechanical Engineers, Milwaukee Section
PO Box 1881
Milwaukee, WI 53201
Ph: (414)645-0068
E-mail: milwaukee@asme.org
URL: http://sections.asme.org/milwaukee
Contact: Clifton Sanders, Chm.
Local. Promotes the art, science and practice of Mechanical Engineering and allied arts and sciences. Encourages original research and fosters engineering education. Promotes the technical and societal contribution of engineers. **Affiliated With:** American Society of Mechanical Engineers.

18960 ■ American Society for Quality, Milwaukee Section 1202
c/o Chuck Wasserman, Sec.
PO Box 1202
Milwaukee, WI 53201-1202
Ph: (414)762-3330
E-mail: chuckw@northwestcoatings.com
URL: http://www.asqmilwaukee.org
Contact: Chuck Wasserman, Sec.
Local. Advances learning, quality improvement and knowledge exchange to improve business results and to create better workplaces and communities worldwide. Provides a forum for information exchange, professional development and continuous learning in the science of quality. **Affiliated With:** American Society for Quality.

18961 ■ American Society for Training and Development, Southeast Wisconsin Chapter
6949 N 100th St.
Milwaukee, WI 53224
Ph: (414)358-3303
Fax: (414)358-9261
E-mail: administrator@sewi-astd.org
URL: http://www.sewi-astd.org
Contact: Patrice McGuire, Pres.
Founded: 1944. **Membership Dues:** regular, $145 (annual). **Local**. Represents professionals engaged in the training and development of business, industry, education, and government employees. **Affiliated With:** ASTD.

18962 ■ American Subcontractors Association of Greater Milwaukee
PO Box 26753
Milwaukee, WI 53226
Ph: (414)276-1743
Fax: (414)276-4420
E-mail: info@asamilwaukee.org
URL: http://www.asamilwaukee.org
Contact: Steve Garrison, Pres.
Local. Subcontractors, suppliers and service providers to the construction industry. Educates and informs about fair business practices. **Affiliated With:** American Subcontractors Association. **Publications:** *Subtalk*, quarterly. Newsletter.

18963 ■ Ancient Order of Hibernians - Milwaukee Division
c/o Irish Cultural and Heritage Center
2133 W Wisconsin Ave.
Milwaukee, WI 53233-1910
E-mail: webmaster@aohmilwaukee.com
URL: http://www.aohmilwaukee.com
Contact: Tom Callen, Pres.
Local. Affiliated With: Ancient Order of Hibernians in America.

18964 ■ Appraisal Institute, Wisconsin Chapter
c/o Chris Ruditys
223 N Water St., Ste.300
Milwaukee, WI 53202
Ph: (414)271-6858
Fax: (414)271-6868
E-mail: info@wamllc.net
URL: http://www.wisai.com
Contact: Chris Ruditys, Exec.Dir.
State. Affiliated With: Appraisal Institute.

18965 ■ Arthritis Foundation, Milwaukee
1650 S. 108th St.
Milwaukee, WI 53224
Ph: (414)321-3933
Fax: (414)321-0365
URL: http://www.arthritis.org
Founded: 1948. **Staff:** 17. **Budget:** $2,500,000. **State**. Group of medical professionals and caregivers that provides services and disease management to children and adults with arthritis. **Affiliated With:** Arthritis Foundation.

18966 ■ Associated General Contractors of Greater Milwaukee
10400 Innovation Dr., Ste.210
Milwaukee, WI 53226
Ph: (414)778-4100
Fax: (414)778-4119
E-mail: info@agc-gm.org
URL: http://www.agc-gm.org
Contact: Lisa Zarda, Contact
Regional.

18967 ■ Association of Clinical Research Professionals - Southern Wisconsin Chapter
c/o Mary Zimmerman, Sec.-Treas.
Aurora Hea. Care
2901 W KK River Pkwy., No. 516
Milwaukee, WI 53215
Ph: (414)649-6093
E-mail: mary.zimmerman@aurora.org
URL: http://www.acrpnet.org/chapters/sowi/index.html
Contact: Kathy Siech, Pres.
Local. Promotes professional growth in the field of clinical research. Provides networking opportunities for members. Advocates for the enhancement of education and knowledge in the field of clinical research. **Affiliated With:** Association of Clinical Research Professionals.

18968 ■ Association of Community Organizations for Reform Now, Milwaukee
152 W Wisconsin Ave., No. 731
Milwaukee, WI 53203
Ph: (414)276-8181
E-mail: wiacorn@acorn.org
URL: National Affiliate–www.acorn.org
Local. Affiliated With: Association of Community Organizations for Reform Now.

18969 ■ Association for Computing Machinery, Marquette University
c/o Dr. Edwin Yaz, Department Chm.
Elecl. and Cmpt. Engg. Dept.
PO Box 1881
Milwaukee, WI 53201-1881
Ph: (414)288-6820
Fax: (414)288-5579
E-mail: acm@mu.edu
URL: http://www.eng.mu.edu/acm
Contact: Dr. Edwin Yaz, Department Chm.
Local. Biological, medical, behavioral, and computer scientists; hospital administrators; programmers and others interested in application of computer methods to biological, behavioral, and medical problems. Stimulates understanding of the use and potential of computers in the Biosciences. **Affiliated With:** Association for Computing Machinery.

18970 ■ Association for Computing Machinery, Milwaukee School of Engineering
c/o John Ratke, Chair
Student Life
1025 N. Broadway
Milwaukee, WI 53202-3109
Ph: (414)277-6950
E-mail: ratkej@msoe.edu
URL: http://www.msoe.edu/st_orgs/acm
Biological, medical, behavioral, and computer scientists; hospital administrators; programmers and others interested in application of computer methods to biological, behavioral, and medical problems. Stimulates understanding of the use and potential of computers in the Biosciences. **Affiliated With:** Association for Computing Machinery.

18971 ■ Association for Computing Machinery, University of Wisconsin/Milwaukee (ACM)
c/o Michael Leonard, Pres.
3200 N Cramer
Dept. of EE & CS
Milwaukee, WI 53211

Ph: (414)229-4801
Free: (800)342-6626
E-mail: acm@miller.cs.uwm.edu
URL: http://www.cs.uwm.edu/public/acm
Contact: Michael Leonard, Pres.
Local. Biological, medical, behavioral, and computer scientists; hospital administrators; programmers and others interested in application of computer methods to biological, behavioral, and medical problems. Stimulates understanding of the use and potential of computers in the Biosciences. **Affiliated With:** Association for Computing Machinery.

18972 ■ Association of the United States Army, Milwaukee
c/o Gerald Brettschneider
3053 S 45th St.
Milwaukee, WI 53219
Ph: (414)545-0020
E-mail: ausamilwaukee@wi.rr.com
URL: National Affiliate–www.ausa.org
Local. Represents the interests and concerns of American Soldiers. Fosters public support of the Army's role in national security. Provides professional education and information programs.

18973 ■ Association of Wisconsin Cleaning Contractors
c/o Jeff Pintor, Pres.
1123 N Water St.
Milwaukee, WI 53202
Ph: (414)276-9799
Fax: (414)276-7704
Free: (800)236-7200
Contact: Kelly Wagner, Coor.
State.

18974 ■ Automobile Dealers Association of Mega Milwaukee (ADAMM)
c/o Mr. Don Hansen, Pres.
10810 W Liberty Dr.
Milwaukee, WI 53224
Ph: (414)359-9000
E-mail: adamm@adamm.org
URL: http://www.adamm.org
Contact: Mr. Don Hansen, Pres.
Local. **Affiliated With:** National Automobile Dealers Association.

18975 ■ Bach Babes
c/o Harry Drake
835 W Dean Rd.
Milwaukee, WI 53217-2528
Ph: (414)961-2357 (262)421-7153
URL: http://bachbabes.org
Contact: Harry L. Drake, Pres.
Founded: 2001. **Budget:** $20,000. **Local**. Promotes appreciation of the beauty and joy of Baroque music and culture. Conducts series of concerts and performs at Milwaukee area schools.

18976 ■ Badger Association of the Blind and Visually Impaired
912 N Hawley Rd.
Milwaukee, WI 53213
Ph: (414)258-9200
Fax: (414)256-8748
Free: (877)258-9200
E-mail: info@badgerassoc.org
URL: http://www.badgerassoc.org
Contact: Patrick Brown, Exec.Dir.
Local. Strives to improve the well-being of all blind and visually impaired individuals. Seeks to elevate the social, economic and cultural levels of blind people. Improves educational and rehabilitation facilities and opportunities for the visually impaired. **Affiliated With:** American Council of the Blind.

18977 ■ Badger State Rottweiler Fanciers
c/o Marylou Stott
4517 W Vliet St.
Milwaukee, WI 53208-2771
Ph: (414)342-6974
E-mail: mstott@aol.com
URL: National Affiliate–www.amrottclub.org
Contact: Marylou Stott, Contact
State. **Affiliated With:** American Rottweiler Club.

18978 ■ BASICS in Milwaukee
2224 W Kilbourn Ave., Ste.206
Milwaukee, WI 53233
Ph: (414)372-7200
E-mail: arn@quakkelaar.com
URL: http://www.basicsinmke.org
Contact: Arn Quakkelaar, Pres./CEO
Founded: 1995. **Members:** 500. **Staff:** 12. **Budget:** $107,000. **Local Groups:** 120. **Local**. Strives to seek out and support community-based Urban Ministries that deal with the spiritual as well as the physical condition of citizens. **Awards:** Ministry Support. **Frequency:** periodic. **Type:** monetary. **Recipient:** to Christian nonprofit organizations serving impoverished people in the Milwaukee, WI area.

18979 ■ Beta Beta Beta, Theta Alpha Chapter
c/o Sr. Rose Bast, PhD
Biology Dept.
2900 N Menomonee River Pkwy.
Mt. Mary Coll.
Milwaukee, WI 53222-4545
Ph: (414)258-4810
Fax: (414)256-1205
E-mail: bastr@mtmary.edu
Contact: Sr. Rose Bast PhD, Adv., Prof. and VP of North Central Reg.
Founded: 1961. **Members:** 10. **Membership Dues:** active (one-time fee), $30. **Regional Groups:** 1. **Regional**. Honorary society for undergraduate biology majors at Mount Mary College; interested individuals. Promotes research and interest in the biological sciences. **Affiliated With:** Beta Beta Beta. **Publications:** *BIOS*, quarterly. Journal. Original research by undergraduates and honor society information. **Price:** $15.00/year. **Advertising:** accepted. **Conventions/Meetings:** biennial convention, with oral and poster presentation of students' original research; also with science-related field trips - always early summer • monthly meeting • annual regional meeting - always spring.

18980 ■ Bethel Community Development Corp.
2014 W North Ave.
Milwaukee, WI 53205-1131
Ph: (414)342-0588
Contact: Joan Harris, CEO
Local.

18981 ■ Better Business Bureau of Wisconsin
10101 W Greenfield Ave., No. 125
Milwaukee, WI 53214
Ph: (414)847-6000
Fax: (414)302-0355
Free: (800)273-1002
E-mail: info@wisconsin.bbb.org
URL: http://www.wisconsin.bbb.org
Contact: Randall Hoth, Pres.
State. Seeks to promote and foster the highest ethical relationship between businesses and the public through voluntary self-regulation, consumer and business education, and service excellence. Provides information to help consumers and businesses make informed purchasing decisions and avoid costly scams and frauds; settles consumer complaints through arbitration and other means. **Affiliated With:** BBB Wise Giving Alliance.

18982 ■ Big Brothers Big Sisters for Milwaukee and Waukesha Counties
c/o Bob Dunn
8415 W Greenfield Ave.
Milwaukee, WI 53214-4473
Ph: (414)258-4778
Fax: (414)607-0156
E-mail: volunteer@bbbsmilwaukee.org
URL: http://www.bbbsmagic.org
Local.

18983 ■ BMW Car Club of America, Badger Bimmers Chapter
c/o Paul Szedziewski, Membership Chm.
PO Box 71139
Milwaukee, WI 53211
Ph: (414)264-4343
E-mail: membership@badgerbimmers.org
URL: http://www.badgerbimmers.org/main/index.shtml
Contact: Jeff Joy, Pres.
Local. **Affiliated With:** BMW Car Club of America.

18984 ■ Building and Construction Trades Department AFL-CIO, Milwaukee
c/o Lyle A. Balistreri, Pres.
5941 W Blue Mound Rd.
Milwaukee, WI 53213
Ph: (414)475-5580
Fax: (414)475-5590
E-mail: bldgtrds@execpc.com
URL: http://www.milwbuildingtrades.org
Contact: Lyle A. Balistreri, Pres.
Members: 10,339. **Local**. Represents all working men and women in the building and construction trades in the Greater Milwaukee area. Wants to achieve the goals of justice on the job, the highest possible wages and fringe benefits and quality work for the customer. **Affiliated With:** Building and Construction Trades Department - AFL-CIO.

18985 ■ Building Owners and Managers
710 N Plankinton Ave., No. 207
Milwaukee, WI 53203
Ph: (414)278-7557
Contact: John Periard, Exec.Dir.
Local.

18986 ■ Business Council, Milwaukee
c/o Devon R. Turner
756 N Milwaukee St., 4th Fl.
Milwaukee, WI 53202-3719
Ph: (414)287-4142
E-mail: tbcinfo@tbc.mmac.org
Contact: Ms. Devon R. Turner, Exec.Dir.
Local.

18987 ■ Caliburn Fencing Club
Plymouth Church Gym
2717 E Hampshire
Milwaukee, WI 53211
Ph: (414)270-1885
E-mail: neevel@execpc.com
URL: http://my.execpc.com/02/7A/neevel/caliburn
Contact: Dave Neevel, Contact
Local. Amateur fencers. **Affiliated With:** United States Fencing Association.

18988 ■ Catholics United for the Faith - St. Gregory VII Chapter
c/o Al and Margo Szews
PO Box 370302
Milwaukee, WI 53237
Ph: (414)321-9377
E-mail: almargo@mymailstation.com
URL: National Affiliate–www.cuf.org
Contact: Al Szews, Contact
Local.

18989 ■ Cedar Lakes Conservation Foundation
5555 N Port Washington Rd., Ste.210
Milwaukee, WI 53217
Ph: (414)962-3670
Fax: (414)962-3671
E-mail: askclcf@aol.com
URL: http://www.clcf.info
Contact: Geoffrey G. Maclay, Pres.
Founded: 1974. **Local**. Committed to the preservation of wetlands and woodlands within the tri-lakes region of Washington County, Wisconsin.

18990 ■ Center for Consumer Affairs, University of Wisconsin-Milwaukee (CCA-UWM)
c/o UWM School of Continuing Education
161 W Wisconsin Ave., Ste.6000
Milwaukee, WI 53203-2602
Ph: (414)227-3200 (414)227-3252
Fax: (414)227-3146
Free: (800)222-3623
E-mail: jbrown@uwm.edu
URL: http://cfprod.imt.uwm.edu/sce/dci_long.cfm?id=7
Contact: Prof. James L. Brown, Dir.
Founded: 1964. **Staff:** 4. **Budget:** $500,000. Develops consumer leadership skills through adult education programs. Provides referral service to appropriate agencies for the handling of consumer complaints. Makes available lecturers and resource persons for community group meetings and programs. Holds conferences, seminars, institutes, and meetings. Conducts extensive research on consumer issues. **Convention/Meeting:** none. **Committees:** Advisory. **Publications:** *Wisconsin Funeral Service: A Consumer's Guide* • Booklets • Manuals • Pamphlets.

18991 ■ Central Society for Clinical Research, Milwaukee
555 E Wells St., Ste.1100
Milwaukee, WI 53202-3823
Ph: (414)273-2209
Fax: (414)276-2146
E-mail: cscr@execinc.com
URL: http://www.cscr.com
Contact: David W. Kamp MD, Pres.
Local.

18992 ■ Citizens for a Better Environment - Wisconsin
152 W. Wisconsin Ave., Ste.510
Milwaukee, WI 53203
Ph: (414)271-7280
Fax: (414)271-5904
E-mail: cbewi@cbemw.org
Contact: Susan Mudd, State Dir.

18993 ■ Civil Trial Counsel of Wisconsin (CTCW)
1123 N Water St.
Milwaukee, WI 53202
Ph: (414)276-1881
Fax: (414)276-7704
E-mail: ctcw@ctcw.org
URL: http://www.ctcw.org
Contact: Jane Svinicki, Exec.Dir.
Founded: 1962. **Members:** 650. **Membership Dues:** regular, $140 (annual). **Staff:** 3. **Budget:** $110,000. **State**. Attorneys engaged in the defense of civil litigation. Maintains state advocacy and educational programs. **Formerly:** Insurance Trial Counsel of Wisconsin. **Publications:** *CTCW News*, quarterly. Newsletter • Membership Directory, annual. **Conventions/Meetings:** quarterly conference (exhibits).

18994 ■ Commercial Association of Realtors - Wisconsin
710 N Plankinton Ave., Ste.207
Milwaukee, WI 53203
Ph: (414)271-2021
Fax: (414)271-6126
E-mail: shawn@carw.com
URL: http://www.carw.com
Contact: Scott Revolinski, Pres.
Local. Strives to develop real estate business practices. Advocates the right to own, use and transfer real property. Provides a facility for professional development, research and exchange of information among members and to the general public. **Affiliated With:** National Association of Realtors.

18995 ■ Community Associations Institute - Wisconsin Chapter
223 N Water St., Ste.300
Milwaukee, WI 53202
Ph: (414)271-9456
Fax: (414)271-6868
E-mail: ruditys@wamllc.net
URL: http://www.wamllc.net/cai.htm
Contact: Christopher Ruditys, Exec.Dir.
State.

18996 ■ Comprehensive Health Education
c/o Carol J. Calvin
1100 W. Wells St., Ste.1801
Milwaukee, WI 53233-2342

18997 ■ Corporation for National and Community Service - Wisconsin
c/o Linda Sunde
310 W Wisconsin Ave., Rm. 1240
Milwaukee, WI 53203-2211
Ph: (414)297-1118
Fax: (414)297-1863
E-mail: wi@cns.gov
URL: http://www.nationalservice.gov/about/role_impact/state_profiles_detail.asp?tbl_profiles_state=WI
Contact: Linda Sunde, Contact
State.

18998 ■ Council of Small Business Executives (COSBE)
Metropolitan Milwaukee Assn. of Commerce
756 N Milwaukee St., Ste.400
Milwaukee, WI 53202
Ph: (414)287-4100
Fax: (414)271-7753
E-mail: info@mmac.org
URL: http://www.mmac.org
Contact: Gary Zimmerman, Pres.
Founded: 1861. **Members:** 2,000. **Staff:** 35. **Local.** Serves as an advocate for metropolitan businesses to encourage business development, capital investment and job creation. **Affiliated With:** National Small Business Association.

18999 ■ Dairyland Theatre Organ Society (DTOS)
c/o Gary Hanson, Pres.
4353 S 108th St.
Milwaukee, WI 53228-2502
Ph: (414)529-1177
E-mail: orgnpipr@aol.com
URL: http://theatreorgans.com/DTOS
Contact: Gary Hanson, Pres.
Local. Aims to restore, preserve and promote the theatre pipe organ and its music. Encourages the youth to learn the instrument. Operates a committee that gathers history and old music from silent film days and information on theatre organists, theaters and organ installations of the silent film era. **Affiliated With:** American Theatre Organ Society.

19000 ■ Donors Forum of Wisconsin (DFW)
c/o Deborah Fugenschuh, Pres.
759 N Milwaukee St., Ste.515
Milwaukee, WI 53202
Ph: (414)270-1978
Fax: (414)270-1979
Free: (877)783-6786
E-mail: admin@dfwonline.org
URL: http://dfwonline.org
Contact: Deborah Fugenschuh, Pres.
Founded: 1978. **Members:** 140. **Staff:** 3. **Budget:** $450,000. **State Groups:** 1. **For-Profit. State**. Serves as a resource for philanthropy in Wisconsin. Provides opportunities for exchange of information between service providers, funders and other sectors involved in philanthropy. **Libraries: Type:** reference. **Holdings:** 400; books, periodicals, reports. **Subjects:** philanthropy, grantmaking, foundations, technical assistance for grantmakers, nonprofit organizations. **Awards:** Good Grant Award. **Frequency:** annual. **Type:** recognition. **Recipient:** for creative partnership between a founder and a grantee. **Publications:** *DFW Capital Report* • *DFW Philanthropy Index*. Directory • *Wisconsin Foundation Directory* • *Wisconsin Giving Report* • *Wisconsin Philanthropy News*. Newsletter. **Conventions/Meetings:** annual New Frontiers in Philanthropy - conference - always April.

19001 ■ Down Syndrome Association of Wisconsin (DSAW)
c/o Ellen Mayer, Office Mgr.
9401 W Beloit Rd., Ste.311
Milwaukee, WI 53227
Ph: (414)327-3729
Fax: (414)327-1329
Free: (866)327-DSAW
E-mail: info@dsaw.org
URL: http://www.dsaw.org
Contact: Ellen Mayer, Office Mgr.
Founded: 1990. **Members:** 1,100. **Membership Dues:** basic, $15 (annual) • individual, $25 (biennial). **Staff:** 3. **Languages:** English, Spanish. **State**. Provides support to families and individuals with Down Syndrome through education, information, and the exchange of ideas and experiences. Offers many programs including newsletter, new parent information packets, parent match services, community education, and special events. **Affiliated With:** National Down Syndrome Congress; National Down Syndrome Society. **Publications:** *On the Up with Down Syndrome*, quarterly. Newsletter. Alternate Formats: online. **Conventions/Meetings:** annual Buddy Walk - assembly • monthly meeting - except December and May; always second Thursday.

19002 ■ East Town Association
770 N Jefferson St.
Milwaukee, WI 53202
Ph: (414)271-1416
Fax: (414)271-6401
E-mail: info1@easttown.com
URL: http://www.easttown.com
Contact: E. Kate Mohle, Exec.Dir.
Local.

19003 ■ Ebony Ice Ski Club
PO Box 136
Milwaukee, WI 53210-1701
Ph: (414)871-1170
E-mail: gricebb@mail.milwaukee.k12.wi.us
URL: National Affiliate–www.nbs.org
Contact: Bama Grice, Pres.
Local. Affiliated With: National Brotherhood of Skiers.

19004 ■ Electrical Contractors Association - Milwaukee Chapter - NECA
Two Honey Creek Corporate Center
115 S 84th St., Ste.110
Milwaukee, WI 53214
Ph: (414)778-0305
Fax: (414)778-0224
E-mail: rayburn@neca-milw.org
URL: http://www.neca-milw.org
Contact: Robert D. Rayburn, Exec.VP
Local. Contractors erecting, installing, repairing, servicing, and maintaining electric wiring, equipment, and appliances. **Affiliated With:** National Electrical Contractors Association.

19005 ■ Endometriosis Association
c/o Mary Lou Ballweg, Pres./Exec.Dir.
8585 N 76th Pl.
Milwaukee, WI 53223
Ph: (414)355-2200
Fax: (414)355-6065
Free: (800)992-3636
E-mail: endo@endometriosisassn.org
URL: http://www.killercramps.org
Contact: Mary Lou Ballweg, Pres./Exec.Dir.
Local. Aims to help women and girls suffering from endometriosis. Funds research on the disease, promotes education to the public and medical communities and offers support groups, counseling, crisis assistance and education to those dealing with the disease. Volunteer Programme. Products: Free brochures, newsletter for members (6 times annually), books, videotapes, audiotapes, CDs.

19006 ■ Executive Women International, Milwaukee Chapter
c/o Cindy Kunze
Frank F. Haack & Associates, Inc.
2323 N Mayfair Rd., Ste.No. 600
Milwaukee, WI 53226
Ph: (414)259-8802
Fax: (414)475-9366
E-mail: cindy.kunze@haack.com
URL: http://milwaukee-ewi.org
Contact: Cindy Kunze, Pres.
Founded: 1966. **Members:** 43. **Local**. Works to promote member firms and improve their communities. Provides opportunities for business and personal growth. **Committees:** Auction; Budget; Historian; Nomination; Program; Public Relations; Publication; Ways & Means. **Affiliated With:** Executive Women International. **Publications:** *Pulse*. Newsletter. **Advertising:** accepted. Alternate Formats: online. **Conventions/Meetings:** monthly meeting - 1st Tuesday of each month.

19007 ■ Federalist Society for Law and Public Policy Studies - Milwaukee Chapter
c/o Mr. Gordon Peter Giampietro, Pres.
517 E Wisconsin Ave.
Milwaukee, WI 53202
E-mail: gordon.giampietro@usdoj.gov
URL: National Affiliate–www.fed-soc.org
Contact: Mr. Gordon Peter Giampietro, Pres.
Local. Seeks to bring about a reordering of priorities within the U.S. legal system that will emphasize individual liberty, traditional values, and the rule of law. **Affiliated With:** Federalist Society for Law and Public Policy Studies.

19008 ■ Financial Executives International, Milwaukee Chapter
c/o Ms. Mary Alberte, Administrator
Blue Cross Blue Shield of Wisconsin
401 W Michigan
Milwaukee, WI 53203
Ph: (414)226-6975
Fax: (414)226-2996
E-mail: mary.alberte@bcbswi.com
URL: http://fei.org/chapter/milwaukee
Contact: Mr. Jay McKenna, Pres.
Founded: 1938. **Members:** 207. **Local**. Promotes personal and professional development of financial executives. Provides peer networking opportunities and advocacy services. **Committees:** Academic Relations; Career Services; Meeting Arrangements; Professional Development; Programs; Retention. **Affiliated With:** Financial Executives International. **Publications:** Newsletter. Alternate Formats: online. **Conventions/Meetings:** monthly meeting, with speakers - every 2nd Tuesday; September through April.

19009 ■ Financial Planning Association of Southern Wisconsin
6949 N 100th St.
Milwaukee, WI 53224
Ph: (414)358-9260
Fax: (414)358-9261
E-mail: info@fpasw.org
URL: http://www.fpasw.org
Contact: Michael Dubis CFP, Pres.
State. Promotes financial planning profession through education, networking, and mentoring. Enhances public awareness of the value of the financial planning process. Provides forum for education and career development for its members. **Affiliated With:** Financial Planning Association.

19010 ■ First Catholic Slovak Ladies Association - Milwaukee Senior Branch 376
2465 S Howell Ave.
Milwaukee, WI 53207-1638
Ph: (414)744-3496
URL: National Affiliate–www.fcsla.com
Local. Affiliated With: First Catholic Slovak Ladies Association.

19011 ■ Friends of Havenwoods
6141 N. Hopkins St.
Milwaukee, WI 53209
Ph: (414)527-0232
Fax: (414)527-0761
Contact: Glen Weiermann, Contact
Raises funds to purchase needed equipment and supplies for Havenwoods State Forest. Offer support to the staff to help maintain the quality of their programs and grounds.

19012 ■ Gathering of Southeast Wisconsin
c/o Virginia R. Schrag, Exec.Dir.
804 E Juneau Ave.
Milwaukee, WI 53202
Ph: (414)272-4122
Fax: (414)272-7790
E-mail: soulfood@thegatheringwis.org
URL: http://thegatheringwis.org
Contact: Virginia R. Schrag, Exec.Dir.
Founded: 1982. **Budget:** $350,000. **Regional**. Respects the dignity and values of every individual. Acts and addresses the root causes and related problems associated with hunger. Provides services to volunteers. **Awards:** Volunteer Awards. **Frequency:** annual. **Type:** recognition. **Conventions/Meetings:** monthly board meeting.

19013 ■ German-American Chamber of Commerce of the Midwest - Wisconsin Chapter
c/o John D. Gatto
PO Box 1099
Milwaukee, WI 53201
Ph: (262)695-3856
Contact: Dr. John Gatto, Contact
Founded: 2000. **Members:** 23. **Languages:** English, German. **State**.

19014 ■ Girl Scouts of Milwaukee Area
PO Box 14999
Milwaukee, WI 53214-0999
Ph: (414)476-1050
Fax: (414)476-5958
E-mail: gsma@girlscoutsmilwaukee.org
URL: http://www.girlscoutsmilwaukee.org
Contact: Mary Beth Malm, Exec.Dir./CEO
Local. Young girls and adult volunteers, corporate, government and individual supporters. Strives to develop potential and leadership skills among its members. Conducts trainings, educational programs and outdoor activities.

19015 ■ Graphic Communications International Union, AFL-CIO, CLC - Local Union 577
c/o Michael Sippy, VP
633 S Hawley Rd., Ste.100
Milwaukee, WI 53214
Ph: (414)476-1577
Free: (888)477-6331
E-mail: gciu577m@gciu577m.org
URL: http://www.gciu577m.org/public
Contact: Christopher J. Yatchak, Pres.
Members: 1,380. **Local. Affiliated With:** Graphic Communications Conference of the International Brotherhood of Teamsters.

19016 ■ Great Lakes Hemophilia Foundation (GLHF)
PO Box 704
Milwaukee, WI 53201-0704
Ph: (414)257-0200
Fax: (414)257-1225
Free: (888)797-4543
E-mail: info@glhf.org
URL: http://www.glhf.org
Contact: Brian K. Andrew CFA, Pres.
State. Affiliated With: National Hemophilia Foundation.

19017 ■ Greater Greenfield Lions Club
PO Box 270065
Milwaukee, WI 53227
Ph: (414)525-0061
E-mail: club@gglions.org
URL: http://www.gglions.org
Contact: Brian Manley, Pres.
Local. Affiliated With: Lions Clubs International.

19018 ■ Greater Milwaukee Association of Realtors
12300 W Center St.
Milwaukee, WI 53222
Ph: (414)778-4929
Fax: (414)778-4920
URL: http://www.gmar.ws
Contact: Mike Ruzicka, Pres.
Local. Strives to develop real estate business practices. Advocates the right to own, use and transfer real property. Provides a facility for professional development, research and exchange of information among members and to the general public. **Affiliated With:** National Association of Realtors.

19019 ■ Greater Milwaukee Bowling Association
9312 W. Natl. Ave.
Milwaukee, WI 53227
Ph: (414)541-7200

19020 ■ Greater Milwaukee Chapter of the American Payroll Association
PO BOX 240115
Milwaukee, WI 53224
E-mail: info@milwaukeeapa.com
URL: http://www.milwaukeeapa.com
Contact: Rick Mayer, Pres.
Local. Aims to increase the Payroll Professional's skill level through education and mutual support. Represents the Payroll Professional before legislative bodies. Administers the certified payroll professional program of recognition. Provides public service education on payroll and employment issues. **Affiliated With:** American Payroll Association.

19021 ■ Greater Mitchell Street Association
1717 S 12th St., No. 206
Milwaukee, WI 53204
Ph: (414)383-6601
Contact: Judy Keller, Exec.Dir.
Local.

19022 ■ Habitat For Humanity Milwaukee
2233 N 30th St.
Milwaukee, WI 53208
Ph: (414)562-6100
E-mail: skierzek@milwaukeehabitat.org
URL: http://www.milwaukeehabitat.org
Contact: Sara Kierzek, Exec.Dir.
Local. Affiliated With: Habitat for Humanity International.

19023 ■ Historic Third Ward Association (HTW)
219 N Milwaukee St.
Milwaukee, WI 53202
Ph: (414)273-1173
Fax: (414)273-2205
E-mail: okeefe@historicthirdward.org
URL: http://www.historicthirdward.org
Contact: Nancy O'Keefe, Exec.Dir.
Founded: 1976. **Members:** 287. **Membership Dues:** corporate, $250 (annual) • business, $100 (annual) • individual, $50 (annual) • resident, $25 (annual). **Staff:** 5. **Budget:** $252,454. **Local**. Represents the latest trend in Milwaukee's economic development efforts toward professional and white-collar business. Maintains its heritage in the retention of several businesses with great longevity. **Publications:** *Streetscapes*, quarterly. Newsletter. Contains membership and neighborhood information. **Price:** included in membership dues. **Circulation:** 294. **Advertising:** accepted.

19024 ■ Ice Age Park and Trail Foundation (IAPTF)
207 E Buffalo St., Ste.515
Milwaukee, WI 53202-5712
Ph: (414)278-8518
Fax: (414)278-8665
Free: (800)227-0046
E-mail: iat@iceagetrail.org
URL: http://www.iceagetrail.org
Contact: Christine Thisted, Exec.
Founded: 1958. **Local**. Works to create, support, and protect a thousand-mile-foot trail tracing Ice Age formations across Wisconsin. **Affiliated With:** American Hiking Society.

19025 ■ IndependenceFirst
c/o Carol Pritzlaff Voss
600 W. Virginia St., 4th Fl.
Milwaukee, WI 53204
Ph: (414)291-7520
Fax: (414)291-7525
E-mail: cvoss@independencefirst.org
URL: http://www.independencefirst.org
Contact: Mr. Lee Schulz, Exec.Dir.
Founded: 1979. **Staff:** 1,035. **Nonmembership**. **Local**. Works to provide nonprofit resource on access and independent living for people with all kinds of disabilities, in all age groups. **Libraries: Type:** open to the public; reference; lending. **Holdings:** books, periodicals, video recordings. **Subjects:** specific disabilities; programs and services with respect to access and independent living for people with disabilities. **Publications:** *Breaking Away*, quarterly. Newsletter. Features news about advocacy, programs and events sponsored by Independence First or other community providers. **Circulation:** 5,000.

19026 ■ Information Systems Audit and Control Association, Kettle Moraine Chapter
c/o Dan Buckley, CISA, Pres.
Marshall & Ilsley Corp.
770 N Water St.
Milwaukee, WI 53202
Ph: (414)765-8030
E-mail: dbuckley@isaca-km.org
URL: http://www.isaca-km.org
Contact: Dan Buckley CISA, Pres.
Local. **Affiliated With:** Information Systems Audit and Control Association and Foundation.

19027 ■ Institute of Real Estate Management - Milwaukee Chapter No. 13
c/o Angela Fullerton, Pres.
710 N Plankinton Ave., Ste.207
Milwaukee, WI 53203
Ph: (414)476-4736
Fax: (414)271-6126
E-mail: afullerton@mlgmanagement.com
Contact: Angela Fullerton CPM, Pres.
Local. Represents real property and asset management professionals. Works to promote professional ethics and standards in the field of property management. Strives to keep its members informed on the latest legislative activities and current industry trends. Provides classroom training, continuing education seminars, job referral service and candidate assistance services to enhance the effectiveness and professionalism of its members. **Affiliated With:** Institute of Real Estate Management.

19028 ■ International Association of Gay/Lesbian Country Western Dance Clubs, Shoreline-Milwaukee
2809 E Oklahoma Ave.
Milwaukee, WI 53207
Ph: (414)747-0388
E-mail: info@shoreline-milw.org
URL: http://www.shoreline-milw.org
Local. **Affiliated With:** International Association of Gay/Lesbian Country Western Dance Clubs.

19029 ■ International Association of Machinists and Aerospace Workers, AFL-CIO, CLC - Lodge 516
1650 S 38th St.
Milwaukee, WI 53215-1726
Ph: (414)643-4334
Fax: (414)643-4715
E-mail: presiam516@lakefield.net
URL: http://www.iamlodge516.org
Contact: Michael L. Glaser, Pres.
Founded: 1917. **Members:** 577. **Local**. Seeks for the dignity and equality of the workers. Strives to provide contractors with well-trained, productive employees. **Affiliated With:** International Association of Machinists and Aerospace Workers.

19030 ■ International Association of Machinists and Aerospace Workers, AFL-CIO, CLC - Lodge 2110
1650 S 38th St.
Milwaukee, WI 53215
Ph: (262)495-4802
E-mail: luv2write22000@yahoo.com
URL: http://www.iamaw2110.com
Contact: Joe Nicosia, Pres.
Members: 105. **Local**. **Affiliated With:** International Association of Machinists and Aerospace Workers.

19031 ■ International Association of Machinists and Aerospace Workers, AFL-CIO, CLC - United Lodge 66
2611 W Oklahoma Ave.
Milwaukee, WI 53215
Ph: (414)671-3800
Fax: (414)671-3800
E-mail: smjzer6471@sbcglobal.net
URL: http://www.unitedlodge66.org
Contact: Benito Elizondo, Pres.
Members: 2,407. **Local**. **Affiliated With:** International Association of Machinists and Aerospace Workers.

19032 ■ International Association of Machinists and Aerospace Workers, District Lodge 10
1650 S 38th St.
Milwaukee, WI 53215
Ph: (414)643-4334
Fax: (414)643-4715
URL: http://www.iamawd10.org
Contact: Michael H. Hornby, Directing Business Representative
Members: 10,374. **Local**. Represents workers. Strives to provide contractors with well-trained and productive employees. **Affiliated With:** International Association of Machinists and Aerospace Workers.

19033 ■ International Association of Ministers Wives and Ministers Widows, Wisconsin
4247 N 21st St.
Milwaukee, WI 53209
Ph: (414)873-3131
URL: National Affiliate–www.iamwmw.org
Contact: Mrs. Gloria Games, Pres.
State. **Affiliated With:** International Association of Ministers Wives and Ministers Widows.

19034 ■ International Brotherhood of Teamsters, Chauffeurs, Warehousemen and Helpers of America, AFL-CIO - Local Union 200
6200 Bluemound Rd.
Milwaukee, WI 53213
Ph: (414)771-6363
E-mail: team200@execpc.com
URL: http://www.teamsterslocal200.com
Contact: Sebastian Busalacchi, Contact
Members: 5,461. **Local**. **Affiliated With:** International Brotherhood of Teamsters.

19035 ■ International Institute of Wisconsin
1110 N Old World 3rd St., Ste.420
Milwaukee, WI 53203
Ph: (414)225-6220
Fax: (414)225-6235
E-mail: iiw@execpc.com
URL: http://www.IIWisconsin.org
Contact: Alexander P. Durtka Jr., Pres.
Founded: 1936. **Members:** 950. **Membership Dues:** individual, $15 (annual) • family, $25 (annual). **Staff:** 12. **Budget:** $600,000. **Regional Groups:** 100. **Languages:** Albanian, Croatian, English, French, German, Italian, Laotian, Polish, Russian, Spanish. **State**. Groups, families, and individuals dedicated to promoting the interests and understanding of foreign-born individuals. **Libraries: Type:** reference. **Holdings:** 500; books. **Subjects:** ethnic information. **Awards:** World Citizen. **Frequency:** annual. **Type:** recognition. **Recipient:** those making significant contributions in cultural diversity; one native born citizen, the other a foreign born, naturalized citizen. **Affiliated With:** Immigration and Refugee Services of America. **Publications:** *Communique*, quarterly. Newsletter. Contains information and update for members. **Price:** included in membership dues. **Circulation:** 1,000. **Advertising:** accepted • *Folk Fair Fan Fare*, quarterly. Newsletter. **Price:** free; free • *Viltis*, bimonthly. Magazine. **Price:** $20.00/year. **Conventions/Meetings:** annual Holiday Folk Fair International - festival, multi-ethnic festival (exhibits) - always weekend before Thanksgiving • monthly workshop.

19036 ■ International Union of Operating Engineers, Local 317
3152 S 27th St.
Milwaukee, WI 53215-4399
Ph: (414)671-0317
Fax: (414)671-3259
E-mail: office@iuoelocal317.org
URL: http://www.317.org
Contact: Mark Maierle, Business Mgr.
Founded: 1939. **Members:** 550. **Staff:** 3. **Local**. Works to bring economic justice to the workplace and to improve the lives of working families. **Affiliated With:** International Union of Operating Engineers.

19037 ■ International Union of Operating Engineers, Local 950
3271 N 94th St.
Milwaukee, WI 53222
Ph: (414)507-4538
URL: http://www.iuoelocal950.org
Contact: Dennis Daze, VP
Local. AFL-CIO. **Affiliated With:** International Union of Operating Engineers.

19038 ■ Izaak Walton League of America, Labudde Memorial Chapter
c/o Miriam Dahl
1700 W Bender Rd., Apt. 162
Milwaukee, WI 53209-3845
Ph: (414)228-0181
URL: National Affiliate–www.iwla.org
Local. Works to educate the public to conserve, maintain, protect, and restore the soil, forest, water, and other natural resources of the U.S; promotes the enjoyment and wholesome utilization of these resources. **Affiliated With:** Izaak Walton League of America.

19039 ■ Junior Achievement of Wisconsin
6924 N Port Washington Rd.
Milwaukee, WI 53217
Ph: (414)352-5350
Fax: (414)352-5614
E-mail: jamilw@jawis.org
URL: http://milwaukee.ja.org
Contact: Tim Greinert, Pres.
State. Aims to educate and inspire young people to value free enterprise and understand business and economics to improve the quality of their lives. **Affiliated With:** Junior Achievement.

19040 ■ Junior League of Milwaukee
1060 E Juneau Ave.
Milwaukee, WI 53202
Ph: (414)289-9242
Fax: (414)289-9066
E-mail: info@jlmilw.org
URL: http://www.jlmilw.org
Contact: Julie K. Gilpin, Pres.
Local.

19041 ■ Kiwanis Club of Milwaukee
750 N Lincoln Memorial Dr.
Milwaukee, WI 53202-4095
Ph: (414)276-1331
Fax: (414)276-1559
E-mail: kiwanismke@sbcglobal.net
URL: http://www.kiwanismilwaukee.org
Contact: Robo B. Brumder, Pres.
Local.

19042 ■ Library Council of Southeastern Wisconsin
814 W Wisconsin Ave.
Milwaukee, WI 53233
Ph: (414)271-8470
Fax: (414)286-2798
E-mail: libco@execpc.com
URL: http://www.mcfls.org/librarycouncil/default.htm
Contact: Susie Just, Exec.Dir.
Founded: 1973. **Members:** 160. **Membership Dues:** personal, $20 (annual) • associate, $100 (annual) • regular/institution (based on annual combined salaries and library materials budget), $76-$459 (annual) • benefactor, $650 (annual) • supporting benefactor, $900 (annual) • sustaining benefactor, $1,395 (annual). **Staff:** 2. **Budget:** $44,000. **Regional Groups:** 1. **Local.** Information centers (120) and individuals (40) in southeastern Wisconsin involved in or interested in the library field. Facilitates multi-type library cooperation; provides continuing education; acts as a clearinghouse for library related information. **Formerly:** (2003) Library Council of Metropolitan Milwaukee. **Publications:** *CD-ROM Directory of LCOMM Libraries*. Book. **Price:** $15.00 for members; $18.00 for nonmembers • *Guide to Genealogical Collections in the Milwaukee Metro Area*. Book. **Price:** $28.00 for members institutions; $35.00 for nonmembers institutions; $12.00 personal members; $15.00 for nonmembers • *LCOMM News*, 11/year. Newsletter. **Price:** free for members • *Library Catalogs in the Milwaukee Metro Area: A Guide to On-Line Computer Access*. Book. **Price:** $15.00 for 10 copies for members plus shipping; $18.00 for 10 copies for nonmembers plus shipping • *Library Directory of Metropolitan Milwaukee*, biennial. **Price:** $15.00 for members; $25.00 for nonmembers • *Union List of Currently Received Newspapers*. Book. **Price:** $10.00 for members; $13.00 for nonmembers • *Union List of Standards Held in Wisconsin Collections*. Book. **Price:** $30.00 for members plus shipping; $36.00 for nonmembers plus shipping. **Conventions/Meetings:** annual general assembly - always May in Milwaukee, WI.

19043 ■ Literacy Services of Wisconsin
2724 W Wells St.
Milwaukee, WI 53208
Ph: (414)344-5878
Fax: (414)344-1061
E-mail: info@literacyservices.org
URL: http://www.literacyservices.org
Contact: Barbara Felix, Exec.Dir.
State. Provides literacy education to motivated adults through the efforts of dedicated volunteers. Services offered include Adult Basic Education, preparation for GED-HSED and English as a Second Language; all services are free, students pay for books only. **Affiliated With:** ProLiteracy Worldwide.

19044 ■ Lunar Reclamation Society
PO Box 2102
Milwaukee, WI 53201-2102
Ph: (414)342-0705
E-mail: kokhmmm@aol.com
URL: http://www.lunar-reclamation.org
Contact: Peter Kokh, Contact
Local. Works for the creation of a spacefaring civilization. Encourages the establishment of self-sustaining human settlements in space. Promotes large-scale industrialization and private enterprise in space.

19045 ■ Manchester Village Owners Association
2260 W Good Hope Rd.
Milwaukee, WI 53209
Ph: (414)352-5054
Local.

19046 ■ Media Communications Association-International, Milwaukee Chapter
c/o Mike Brown
Rockwell Automation Studios
1201 S Second St.
Milwaukee, WI 53204
Ph: (414)382-2875
E-mail: mabrown2@ra.rockwell.com
URL: http://mcai-milwaukee.com
Contact: Mike Brown, Contact
Local. Serves individuals engaged in multimedia communications. Seeks to advance the benefits and image of media communications professionals. **Affiliated With:** Media Communications Association International. **Publications:** *Milwaukee Screening*, quarterly. Newsletter. **Advertising:** accepted. Alternate Formats: online • Directory, annual. Contains listings of independent contractors and companies categorized according to the services they provide. **Advertising:** accepted. Alternate Formats: online.

19047 ■ Medical Society of Milwaukee County (MSMC)
1126 S 70th St., Ste.N101A
Milwaukee, WI 53214-3104
Ph: (414)475-4750
Fax: (414)475-4799
E-mail: msmc@district-1.org
URL: http://www.milwaukeemedicalsociety.org
Contact: Eleanore R. Kirsch, Exec.VP
Founded: 1846. **Members:** 2,000. **Membership Dues:** individual, $249 (annual). **Staff:** 6. **Local.** Represents and promotes the medical profession and the patients it serves. **Affiliated With:** Wisconsin Medical Society. **Publications:** *MSMC News*, monthly. Newsletter.

19048 ■ Mental Health Association in Milwaukee County
734 N 4th St., Ste.200
Milwaukee, WI 53203-2102
Ph: (414)276-3122
Fax: (414)276-3124
Free: (877)642-4630
E-mail: info@mhamilw.org
URL: http://www.mhamilw.org
Contact: Martha Rasmus, Pres./CEO
Local. Seeks to promote mental health and prevent mental health disorders. Improves mental health of Americans through advocacy, public education, research and service. **Affiliated With:** National Mental Health Association.

19049 ■ Metropolitan Milwaukee Association of Commerce (MMAC)
756 N Milwaukee St., Ste.400
Milwaukee, WI 53202
Ph: (414)287-4100
Fax: (414)271-7753
E-mail: info@mmac.org
URL: http://www.mmac.org
Contact: Timothy Sheehy, Pres.
Founded: 1861. **Members:** 2,200. **Local.** Works to serve as advocate for metro Milwaukee companies to encourage business development, capital investment and job creation.

19050 ■ Midwest Physiological Society
c/o Allen W. Cowley, Jr.
PO Box 26509
Milwaukee, WI 53226-0509
Ph: (414)456-8266
Fax: (414)266-8705
E-mail: cowley@mcw.edu
URL: http://www.the-aps.org/chapters/midwest/index.htm
Contact: Allen W. Cowley Jr., Contact
Regional. Fosters education, scientific research and dissemination of information in the Physiological sciences. **Affiliated With:** American Physiological Society.

19051 ■ Milwaukee 9to5
c/o Donna Skenadore, Chair
207 E Buffalo St., No. 211
Milwaukee, WI 53202
Ph: (414)274-0925
URL: National Affiliate–www.9to5.org
Contact: Donna Skenadore, Chair
Local. Affiliated With: 9 to 5, National Association of Working Women.

19052 ■ Milwaukee Achiever Literacy Services
1512 W Pierce St.
Milwaukee, WI 53204
Ph: (414)643-5108
Fax: (414)643-8804
E-mail: ppalmer@milwaukeeachiever.org
URL: http://www.milwaukeeachiever.org
Contact: Peg Palmer, Exec.Dir.
Local. Works to inspire and empower adult learners to gain the skills necessary to enrich their lives through education and training in an atmosphere of mutual acceptance and respect. **Affiliated With:** Pro-Literacy Worldwide.

19053 ■ Milwaukee Aging Consortium
c/o Cunningham Hall, Rm. 441
PO Box 413
Milwaukee, WI 53201-0413
Ph: (414)229-2734
Fax: (414)229-2713
E-mail: milwagingconsortium@uwm.edu
URL: http://www.uwm.edu/org/milwaging
Contact: Amy Ambrose, Exec.Dir.
Local.

19054 ■ Milwaukee Association for Computing Machinery SIGCHI
c/o Amii Lapointe
Northwestern Mutual
720 East Wisconsin Ave.,
Milwaukee, WI 53202-4797
Ph: (414)665-3426
Fax: (414)665-4000
E-mail: chi-milwau-chi@acm.org
URL: http://www.acm.org/chapters/milwauchi
Contact: Amii Lapointe, Pres.
Founded: 1999. **Members:** 40. **Membership Dues:** annual membership, includes all meetings, $20 (bimonthly). **Regional Groups:** 1. **Local.** Strives to promote technical awareness and professionalism in the computing community of Milwaukee and Southeastern Wisconsin. Stimulates understanding for those who work or do research in computer-human interaction and related concepts. **Affiliated With:** Association for Computing Machinery.

19055 ■ Milwaukee Bar Association (MBA)
c/o Pamela Pepper, Pres.
424 E Wells St.
Milwaukee, WI 53202
Ph: (414)274-6760
Fax: (414)274-6765
E-mail: info@milwbar.org
URL: http://www.milwbar.org
Contact: Pamela Pepper, Pres.
Founded: 1858. **Members:** 2,500. **Membership Dues:** individual - active (more than 3 years licensed), $190 (annual) • associate (full-time judicial officer), $100 (annual) • less than 3 years licensed, $90 (annual) • senior (70 years and older), $90 (annual) • full-time law student, $20 (annual). **Staff:** 9. **Budget:** $700,000. **Local.** Attorneys in the metropolitan Milwaukee, WI area. Aids in the administration of justice. Promotes professional conduct. Works to

improve delivery of quality legal services. Provides lawyer referral and information services. Provides continuing legal education. **Publications:** *MBA Messenger*, monthly. Newsletter. **Circulation:** 2,600. **Advertising:** accepted • *Milwaukee Trial Judges Directory*, biennial • *Pro Bono Directory*, periodic. **Conventions/Meetings:** annual Bench/Bar Reception - meeting • annual Judges Night - meeting • monthly meeting.

19056 ■ Milwaukee Black Nurses Association (21)
PO Box 16649
Milwaukee, WI 53216-0649
Ph: (414)219-7862
E-mail: info@mcnbna.org
URL: http://www.mcnbna.org
Contact: Dessie Levy RN, Pres.
Local. Represents registered nurses, licensed practical nurses, licensed vocational nurses, and student nurses. Builds consumer knowledge and understanding of health care issues. Facilitates the professional development and career advancement of nurses in emerging healthcare systems. Promotes economic development of nurses through entrepreneurial and other business initiatives. **Affiliated With:** National Black Nurses Association.

19057 ■ Milwaukee Chapter of the National Electrical Contractors Association
Two Honey Creek Corporate Center
115 S 84th St., Ste.110
Milwaukee, WI 53214
Ph: (414)778-0305
Fax: (414)778-0224
E-mail: neca@neca-milw.org
URL: http://www.neca-milw.org
Contact: John Stoker, Pres.
Founded: 1916. **Local**. **Affiliated With:** National Electrical Contractors Association.

19058 ■ Milwaukee Chapter of the Society of Financial Service Professionals
c/o Martin B. Tirado, Exec.Dir.
Svinicki Assn. Mgt., Inc.
6737 W Washington St., Ste.1420
Milwaukee, WI 53214
Ph: (414)276-7340
Fax: (414)276-7704
E-mail: tirado@svinicki.com
URL: http://www.sfsp.net/Milwaukee
Contact: Martin B. Tirado, Exec.Dir.
Local. Represents the interests of financial advisers. Fosters the development of professional responsibility. Helps clients achieve their personal and business-related financial goals. **Affiliated With:** Society of Financial Service Professionals.

19059 ■ Milwaukee District Nurses Association - No. 4
7201 W Wabash Ave.
Milwaukee, WI 53223
Ph: (414)288-3727 (414)354-5204
Fax: (414)288-1939
E-mail: judith.kowatsch@marquette.edu
URL: http://www.milwaukeedistrictnurses.org
Contact: Judy Kowatsch, Pres.
Local. Works to advance the nursing profession. Seeks to meet the needs of nurses and health care consumers. Fosters high standards of nursing practice. Promotes the economic and general welfare of nurses in the workplace. **Affiliated With:** American Nurses Association; Wisconsin Nurses' Association.

19060 ■ Milwaukee Dog Training Club (MDTC)
PO Box 763
Milwaukee, WI 53201-0763
Ph: (414)961-6163
E-mail: info@milwaukeedog.com
URL: http://milwaukeedog.com
Contact: Mari Pavleje, Asst.Dir.
Founded: 1929. **Members:** 160. **Staff:** 20. **Local**. Dog obedience club. Offers training programs to dog owners in order to train their dog. **Affiliated With:** American Kennel Club. **Publications:** *Obedience Views*, monthly. Newsletter. **Price:** included in membership dues.

19061 ■ Milwaukee Gamma
PO Box 1900
Milwaukee, WI 53201-1900
Ph: (414)530-1886
E-mail: gamma@milwaukeegamma.com
URL: http://www.milwaukeegamma.com
Contact: Kyle Paskey, Pres.
Founded: 1978. **Members:** 140. **Membership Dues:** single, $30 (annual) • couple, $48 (annual). **Local**. Outdoor, social, and sports group for gay individuals from the Milwaukee, WI area. **Awards:** Volunteer of the Year. **Frequency:** annual. **Type:** recognition. **Publications:** *Gamma Rays*, monthly. Newsletter. **Price:** included in membership dues. **Conventions/Meetings:** annual banquet - always November.

19062 ■ Milwaukee Jewish Federation
1360 N Prospect Ave.
Milwaukee, WI 53202-3094
Ph: (414)390-5700
E-mail: info@milwaukeejewish.org
URL: http://www.milwaukeejewish.org
Contact: Evy Garfinkel, Contact
Local. Works to improve the quality of Jewish life; aims to unify Jewish community in Milwaukee, in Israel, and throughout the world.

19063 ■ Milwaukee Lake and Stream Fly Fishers (MLSFF)
PO Box 370668
Milwaukee, WI 53237
E-mail: mlsff@speakeasy.org
URL: http://www.speakeasy.org/~mlsff
Local. **Affiliated With:** Federation of Fly Fishers.

19064 ■ Milwaukee Minority Chamber of Commerce (MMCC)
PO Box 1662
Milwaukee, WI 53201-1662
Ph: (414)226-4105
Fax: (414)277-4152
Contact: J. Paul Jordan, Pres.
Founded: 1980. **Members:** 350. **Local**. Minority business organizations in the metropolitan Milwaukee, WI area. Facilitates communication among members; provides advocacy for concerns of minority businesses; trains aspiring minority executives. **Conventions/Meetings:** annual symposium.

19065 ■ Milwaukee Numismatic Society
c/o Bruce Benoit
PO Box 210064
Milwaukee, WI 53221
Ph: (414)282-8128
E-mail: benwab@sbcglobal.net
URL: National Affiliate–www.money.org
Contact: Bruce Benoit, Contact
Local. **Affiliated With:** American Numismatic Association.

19066 ■ Milwaukee Police Association (MPA)
1840 N Farwell Ave., Ste.400
Milwaukee, WI 53202-1716
Ph: (414)273-2515
Fax: (414)273-7237
URL: http://www.milwaukeepoliceassoc.com
Contact: Bradley DeBraska, Pres.
Local.

19067 ■ Milwaukee RSVP
c/o Linn K. Woodard, Dir.
600 W Virginia St., Ste.300
Milwaukee, WI 53204
Ph: (414)291-7500
Fax: (414)291-7510
E-mail: lwoodard@interfaithmilw.org
URL: http://www.seniorcorps.gov/about/programs/rsvp_state.asp?usestateabbr=wi&Search4.x=0&Search4.y=0
Contact: Linn K. Woodard, Dir.
Local. **Affiliated With:** Retired and Senior Volunteer Program.

19068 ■ Milwaukee School of Engineering, National Electrical Contractors Association
AEBC Dept.
1025 N Broadway
Milwaukee, WI 53202-3109
Ph: (414)277-7301
Fax: (414)277-7415
URL: National Affiliate–www.necanet.org
Local. **Affiliated With:** National Electrical Contractors Association.

19069 ■ Milwaukee Urban League
2800 W Wright St.
Milwaukee, WI 53210
Ph: (414)374-5850
Fax: (414)374-1995
E-mail: rhollmon@tmul.org
URL: http://www.tmul.org
Contact: Ralph E. Hollmon, Pres./CEO
Local. **Affiliated With:** National Urban League.

19070 ■ National Active and Retired Federal Employees Association - Greater Milwaukee 94
6524 W Carpenter Ave.
Milwaukee, WI 53220-4551
Ph: (414)282-2451
URL: National Affiliate–www.narfe.org
Contact: Thomas P. Kelnhofer, Contact
Local. Protects the retirement future of employees through education. Informs members on issues affecting the retirement. **Affiliated With:** National Association of Retired Federal Employees.

19071 ■ National Alliance for the Mentally Ill - Greater Milwaukee
3732 W Wisconsin Ave.
Milwaukee, WI 53208
Ph: (414)344-0447
Fax: (414)344-0450
E-mail: namigrm@execpc.com
URL: http://www.namigrm.org
Contact: Sandra Pasch MSN, Pres.
Local. Strives to improve the quality of life of children and adults with severe mental illness through support, education, research and advocacy. **Affiliated With:** National Alliance for the Mentally Ill.

19072 ■ National Association of Fleet Administrators, Wisconsin Chapter
c/o Sheryl Grossman , Chair
GE Healthcare
PO Box 414
Milwaukee, WI 53201
Ph: (262)524-5657
Fax: (262)896-4241
E-mail: sheryl.grossman@med.ge.com
URL: National Affiliate–www.nafa.org
Contact: Sheryl Grossman, Chair
State. Promotes the professional management of vehicles through education, government and industry relations and services to members. **Affiliated With:** National Association of Fleet Administrators.

19073 ■ National Association For Uniformed Services - Southern Wisconsin, Chapter 2
c/o Floyd S. Jack
2468 N 12th St.
Milwaukee, WI 53206-2503
Ph: (404)651-1425
URL: National Affiliate–www.naus.org
Contact: Floyd S. Jack, Contact
Local. Provides assistance and support to active or retired military uniformed service officers. Protects and improves the compensation, entitlements and benefits earned by members of the uniformed services for themselves, their families and survivors and all American citizens with common interests. **Affiliated With:** National Association for Uniformed Services.

19074 ■ National Association of Professional Organizers, Wisconsin Chapter
PO Box 170135
Milwaukee, WI 53217
Ph: (414)327-6171
URL: National Affiliate–www.napo.net
State. Promotes the profession of professional organizing. Educates the public about the field of professional organizing. Supports, educates, and provides a networking forum for members.

19075 ■ National Association of Watch and Clock Collectors, Menomonee Valley Chapter 47
c/o Lois Thomas, Sec.
5649 N 86th St.
Milwaukee, WI 53225
Ph: (262)539-4000 (414)466-8303
E-mail: james@clockbug.com
URL: http://www.nawcc47.com
Contact: Jim Mirek, Pres.
Local.

19076 ■ National Association of Women in Construction, Milwaukee Chapter
c/o Betty Kroll, Membership Chair
Walsh Constr.
2202 W Clybourn Ave.
Milwaukee, WI 53233
E-mail: bakroll@hotmail.com
URL: http://www.nawicmilwaukee.org
Contact: Betty Kroll, Membership Chair
Founded: 1965. **Local**. Serves as the voice of women in the construction industry. Contributes to the development of the industry. Encourages women to pursue and establish career in construction. Promotes cooperation, fellowship and understanding among members of the association. **Affiliated With:** National Association of Women in Construction. **Publications:** *Nuts and Bolts*, monthly. Newsletter. Alternate Formats: online. **Conventions/Meetings:** monthly meeting - every second Monday of the month.

19077 ■ National Black United Front, Milwaukee Chapter
PO Box 16482
Milwaukee, WI 53216
Ph: (414)445-2289
URL: http://www.nbufront.org/html/Chapters/NBUF-Milwaukee.html
Contact: Oshiyemi Adelabu, Chm.
Local. Affiliated With: National Black United Front.

19078 ■ National Model Railroad Association, Midwest Region
c/o Richard Cecil, Pres.
3131 N Cramer St.
Milwaukee, WI 53211-3004
Ph: (414)332-3729
E-mail: mwrprez@hq.nmra.org
URL: http://www.mwr-nmra.org
Contact: Richard Cecil, Pres.
Regional. Aims to promote model railroading throughout the Midwest area. **Affiliated With:** National Model Railroad Association.

19079 ■ National Organization for Women-Milwaukee
207 E. Buffalo, No. 544
Milwaukee, WI 53202
Ph: (414)276-3112
E-mail: now@milwaukeenow.org
URL: http://www.milwaukeenow.org
Founded: 1971. **Members:** 150. **Membership Dues:** individual, $35 (annual) • low income, students, $15-$34 (annual). **Local Groups:** 1. **Local**. Provides feminist activism covering multi-issue and multi-tactical subjects in order to take action and achieve full equality for all women. **Publications:** Newsletter, quarterly. **Price:** included in membership dues. **Circulation:** 250. **Advertising:** accepted. Alternate Formats: online. **Conventions/Meetings:** monthly meeting.

19080 ■ National Society of Black Engineers - University of Wisconsin, Milwaukee (NSBE-UWM)
PO Box 413
Milwaukee, WI 53201
Ph: (414)229-3216
E-mail: sajames@uwm.edu
URL: http://www.uwm.edu/StudentOrg/NSBE
Contact: Shawn James, Pres.
Local. Strives to increase the number of culturally responsible Black engineers who excel academically, succeed professionally and positively impact the community. **Affiliated With:** National Society of Black Engineers.

19081 ■ National Sojourners, Milwaukee No. 27
c/o Lt.Col. Charles N. Wallens
611 E Glencoe Pl.
Milwaukee, WI 53217-1838
Ph: (414)352-9965
E-mail: cwallens@execpc.com
URL: National Affiliate–www.nationalsojourners.org
Contact: Lt.Col. Charles N. Wallens, Contact
Local.

19082 ■ National Spinal Cord Injury Association - Greater Milwaukee Area Chapter
c/o John Dziewa, Pres.
1545 S Layton Blvd., Rm. 320
Milwaukee, WI 53215
Ph: (414)384-4022
Fax: (414)384-7820
URL: National Affiliate–www.spinalcord.org
Contact: John Dziewa, Pres.
Local. Empowers individuals who are suffering from spinal cord injury. Provides information on the causes and prevention of spinal cord injuries. **Affiliated With:** National Spinal Cord Injury Association.

19083 ■ National Technical Honor Society - Wisconsin Lutheran High School Wisconsin (WLHS)
330 N Glenview Ave.
Milwaukee, WI 53213-3379
Ph: (414)453-4567
Fax: (414)453-3001
E-mail: nhgoede@wlhs.k12.wi.us
URL: http://www.wlhs.org
Contact: Ned Goede, Contact
Local.

19084 ■ North Shore Philatelic Society of Milwaukee
PO Box 170832
Milwaukee, WI 53217
E-mail: henak@execpc.com
URL: http://www.virtualstampclub.com/apsnorthshore.html
Contact: Mr. Robert R. Henak, VP
Local. Aims to promote stamp collecting for people of all ages. **Affiliated With:** American Philatelic Society. **Also Known As:** (2006) North Shore Philatelic Society APS Chapter No. 623.

19085 ■ Ozaukee-Washington County ALU
c/o Tim Krull
1233 N Mayfair Rd., Ste.204
Milwaukee, WI 53226
Ph: (414)607-6082
Fax: (414)607-6088
URL: National Affiliate–www.naifa.org
Local. Represents the interest of insurance and financial advisors. Advocates for a positive legislative and regulatory environment. Enhances business and professional skills of members. **Affiliated With:** National Association of Insurance and Financial Advisors.

19086 ■ Paper, Allied-Industrial, Chemical and Energy Workers International Union, AFL-CIO, CLC Local Union 2-232
8500 W Capitol Dr.
Milwaukee, WI 53222
Ph: (414)463-7425
Fax: (414)463-7638
E-mail: office@pace7232.org
URL: http://www.pace7232.org
Contact: Scott Godshaw, Pres.
Members: 2,110. **Local. Affiliated With:** Pace International Union.

19087 ■ Park People of Milwaukee County (PPMC)
1845 N Farwell Ave., Ste.100
Milwaukee, WI 53202
Ph: (414)273-7275
E-mail: info@theparkpeople-milwaukee.org
URL: http://www.theparkpeople-milwaukee.org
Contact: Jim Price, Chm.
Founded: 1977. **Members:** 500. **Membership Dues:** individual, $20 (annual) • family, $30 (annual) • contributor, $50 (annual) • sponsor, $100 (annual) • benefactor, $250 (annual) • corporation or donor, $500 (annual). **Staff:** 2. **Budget:** $150,000. **Local**. Individuals in Milwaukee County, WI and surrounding counties interested in promoting and preserving county parks. Supports park use, safety, and appreciation. Advocates park improvement and opposes sale of park land. Has restored Triborn Farm and Will and Cava Ross Overnight Lodge. Sponsors recreational, cultural, and educational activities and tours; offers discounts on park events; accepts donations for living memorials through Park Market Program. Holds picnics, parties, talks, and treks. **Publications:** *Park People News*, bimonthly. Newsletter. **Price:** free. **Circulation:** 500 • Brochures, periodic. **Conventions/Meetings:** annual Antique Show and Sale • annual Harvest of Arts and Crafts - festival (exhibits) • annual meeting.

19088 ■ Pathfinders
1614 E Kane Pl.
Milwaukee, WI 53202
Ph: (414)271-1560 (414)271-9523
Fax: (414)271-1831
E-mail: jbock@tccmilw.org
URL: http://www.tccmilw.org
Contact: Ms Julie Bock, Dir.
Founded: 1970. **Staff:** 20. **Budget:** $700,000. **Nonmembership. Local**. Sponsors runaway group home for teenagers in the Milwaukee, WI area; provides counseling for runaway teens and their families. **Affiliated With:** National Network for Youth.

19089 ■ Peace Action Wisconsin
1001 E Keefe Ave.
Milwaukee, WI 53212
Ph: (414)964-5158
E-mail: website@peaceactionwi.org
URL: http://www.peaceactionwi.org
Contact: George Martin, Program Dir.
Founded: 1977. **Members:** 800. **Membership Dues:** individual, $30 (annual) • family, $40 (annual) • life, $1,000. **Staff:** 2. **Local**. Aims to: abolish nuclear weapons and power; end military intervention; save the environment; and meet human needs. Sponsors music benefits, earth day educational, lectures, and workshops. **Libraries: Type:** open to the public. **Holdings:** 300; books, video recordings. **Subjects:** nuclear disarmament/power, biographies of peacemakers, alternatives to war, Hiroshima/Nagasaki topics. **Committees:** Disarmament; Peaceful Alternative to Recruitment; Study Circles; Wisconsin Anti Violence Effort. **Affiliated With:** Peace Action. **Absorbed:** Women's Peace Presence to Stop Project Elf. **Formerly:** Mobilization for Survival. **Publications:** *Milwaukee Mobilizer*, monthly. Newsletter. **Price:** free for members. **Circulation:** 1,300.

19090 ■ People and Paws Search and Rescue
c/o Geoff Gardiner
3887 N 93rd St.
Milwaukee, WI 53222-2507

Ph: (414)531-4098
E-mail: info@peopleandpaws.org
URL: http://www.PeopleandPaws.org
Contact: Geoff Gardiner, Pres.

Founded: 2000. **Local**. Volunteer search and rescue team based in Milwaukee, WI, serving Wisconsin and the Midwest anywhere trained personnel and dogs can help locate lost or missing persons.

19091 ■ Personality Disorder Awareness Network (PDAN)
c/o Randi Kreger
3120 S Pennsylvania Ave.
Milwaukee, WI 53207-2914
E-mail: info@pdan.org
URL: http://www.pdan.org
Contact: Randi Kreger, Contact

Local.

19092 ■ PFLAG Milwaukee
315 W Court St., No. 101
Milwaukee, WI 53213
Ph: (414)299-9198
E-mail: pflagmilwaukee@hotmail.com
URL: http://www.pflagmilwaukee.org

Local. **Affiliated With:** Parents, Families, and Friends of Lesbians and Gays.

19093 ■ Planned Giving Council of Eastern Wisconsin
c/o Kathleen B. Schrader, Dir. of Financial & Estate Planning
Greater Milwaukee Found.
1020 N Broadway, Ste.112
Milwaukee, WI 53202
Ph: (414)272-5805
Fax: (414)272-6235
E-mail: kschrader@greatermkefdn.org
URL: National Affiliate–www.ncpg.org
Contact: Kathleen B. Schrader, Dir. of Financial & Estate Planning

Local. Comprised of approximately 150 charitable gift planning professionals and advisors. Works to increase gift planning to benefit the community. Hosts educational opportunities for members. **Affiliated With:** National Committee on Planned Giving.

19094 ■ Planned Parenthood of Wisconsin
c/o Public Affairs
302 N Jackson St.
Milwaukee, WI 53202
Free: (800)261-2464
E-mail: action.alert@ppwi.org
URL: http://www.ppwi.org

State.

19095 ■ Plumbing-Heating-Cooling Contractors Wisconsin Association
c/o Jane Svinicki, State Exec.Dir.
1123 N Water St.
Milwaukee, WI 53202
Ph: (414)276-0108
Fax: (414)276-7704
Free: (800)369-7422
E-mail: info@phcc-mpawi.com
URL: http://www.phcc-mpawi.com

State. Represents the interests of plumbing, heating and & cooling contractors in Wisconsin. **Affiliated With:** Plumbing-Heating-Cooling Contractors Association.

19096 ■ Polish Falcons of America, Nest 725
801 E Clark St.
Milwaukee, WI 53212
Ph: (414)264-0680
URL: http://www.polishfalcons.org/nest/725/index.html
Contact: Marian E. Hansen, Pres.

Local. **Affiliated With:** Polish Falcons of America.

19097 ■ Post-Polio Resource Group of Southeastern Wisconsin (PPRG)
PO Box 13841
Milwaukee, WI 53213-0841
Ph: (414)297-9093
E-mail: together@pprg.com
URL: http://www.pprg.org
Contact: Gerald DeLeeuw, Pres.

Founded: 1985. **Members:** 350. **Membership Dues:** individual, family, $10 (annual) • institution, $25 (annual). **Regional**. Serves as a support group for polio survivors. Provides medical, emotional, social and spiritual support to its members. **Libraries: Type:** open to the public. **Publications:** *Spirit*, quarterly. Newsletter. Contains news updates. **Price:** included in membership dues. **Circulation:** 350. **Conventions/Meetings:** meeting, with speakers, demonstrations - 6/year; March, April, May, September, October, November in Milwaukee, WI.

19098 ■ Prevent Blindness Wisconsin
759 N Milwaukee St., Ste.305
Milwaukee, WI 53202
Ph: (414)765-0505
Fax: (414)765-0377
E-mail: info@preventblindnesswisconsin.org
URL: http://www.preventblindness.org/wi/
Contact: Donna Brady, Exec.Dir.

Founded: 1958. **State**. **Affiliated With:** Prevent Blindness America.

19099 ■ Professional Golfers Association of America - Wisconsin (PGA)
c/o Joseph Stadler, Exec.Dir.
8989 N Port Washington Rd., Ste.203
Milwaukee, WI 53217
Ph: (414)540-3820
Fax: (414)540-3821
E-mail: wisc@pgahq.com
URL: http://www.wisconsin.pga.com
Contact: Joseph Stadler, Exec.Dir.

State.

19100 ■ Psi Chi, National Honor Society in Psychology - Alverno College
c/o Dept. of Psychology
PO Box 343922
Milwaukee, WI 53234-3922
Ph: (414)382-6053 (414)382-6182
Fax: (414)382-6354
E-mail: kris.vasquez@alverno.edu
URL: National Affiliate–www.psichi.org

Local. **Affiliated With:** Psi Chi, National Honor Society in Psychology.

19101 ■ Psi Chi, National Honor Society in Psychology - Cardinal Stritch University
c/o Dept. of Psychology
Box 102
6801 N Yates Rd.
Milwaukee, WI 53217
Ph: (414)410-4472 (414)410-4473
Fax: (414)410-4239
E-mail: kamarkell@stritch.edu
URL: National Affiliate–www.psichi.org

Local. **Affiliated With:** Psi Chi, National Honor Society in Psychology.

19102 ■ Psi Chi, National Honor Society in Psychology - Marquette University
c/o Dept. of Psychology
PO Box 1881
Milwaukee, WI 53201-1881
Ph: (414)288-7218 (414)288-3720
Fax: (414)288-5333
E-mail: debra.oswald@mu.edu
URL: National Affiliate–www.psichi.org

Local. **Affiliated With:** Psi Chi, National Honor Society in Psychology.

19103 ■ Psi Chi, National Honor Society in Psychology - Mary Mount College
c/o Behavioral Sciences
2900 N Menomonee River Pkwy.
Milwaukee, WI 53222
Ph: (414)258-4810
Fax: (414)256-0171
E-mail: endl@mtmary.edu
URL: National Affiliate–www.psichi.org

Local. **Affiliated With:** Psi Chi, National Honor Society in Psychology.

19104 ■ Psi Chi, National Honor Society in Psychology - Wisconsin Lutheran College
c/o Dept. of Psychology
8800 W Bluemound Rd.
Milwaukee, WI 53226
Ph: (414)443-8843
Fax: (414)443-8533
E-mail: leanne_olson@wlc.edu
URL: National Affiliate–www.psichi.org

Local. **Affiliated With:** Psi Chi, National Honor Society in Psychology.

19105 ■ Public Allies
c/o Paul Schmitz, Pres./CEO
633 W Wisconsin Ave., Ste.610
Milwaukee, WI 53203
Ph: (414)273-0533
Fax: (414)273-0543
E-mail: info@publicallies.org
URL: http://www.publicallies.org

Regional.

19106 ■ Public Policy Forum
633 W Wisconsin Ave., Ste.406
Milwaukee, WI 53203
Ph: (414)276-8240
Fax: (414)276-9962
E-mail: ppf@publicpolicyforum.org
URL: http://www.publicpolicyforum.org
Contact: Jeffrey Browne, Pres.

Local.

19107 ■ Racine Geological Society
c/o John Krolikowski, Pres.
1554 S 56th St.
Milwaukee, WI 53214
E-mail: candkiss2@yahoo.com
URL: National Affiliate–www.amfed.org
Contact: Bonnie Wozniak, Sec.

Local. Aims to further the study of Earth Sciences and the practice of lapidary arts and mineralogy. **Affiliated With:** American Federation of Mineralogical Societies.

19108 ■ RAINBOWS, Milwaukee
c/o Adult and Family Ministry
PO Box 070912
Milwaukee, WI 53207-0912
Ph: (414)769-3440 (414)769-3444
Fax: (414)769-3408
E-mail: nohlr@archmil.org
URL: http://www.rainbows.org
Contact: Randy Nohl, Associate Dir.

Local. Provides small support groups for children who have experienced a significant loss in their life, especially due to divorce or death. **Affiliated With:** RAINBOWS.

19109 ■ Residential Services Association of Wisconsin (RSA)
6737 W Washington Ave., Ste.1420
Milwaukee, WI 53214
Ph: (414)276-9273
Fax: (414)276-7704
E-mail: info@rsawisconsin.org
URL: http://www.rsawisconsin.org
Contact: Thomas Nowak, Pres.

State.

19110 ■ Risk and Insurance Management Society, Wisconsin Chapter
c/o Christopher Ksobiech
231 W Michigan St., M/S P387
Milwaukee, WI 53203

Ph: (414)221-3336
Fax: (414)221-2594
E-mail: chris.ksobiech@we-energies.com
URL: http://wisconsin.rims.org
Contact: Sheila Liebergen, Pres.
State. Seeks to promote the discipline of risk management and enhance the image of professional risk managers. Fosters the educational and professional development of risk managers and others involved in the risk management and insurance industry. **Affiliated With:** Risk and Insurance Management Society.

19111 ■ Ruffed Grouse Society, David V. Uihlein Chapter
c/o Haskell Noyes
6229 N Bay Ridge
Milwaukee, WI 53217
Ph: (414)964-4846
URL: National Affiliate–www.ruffedgrousesociety.org
Contact: Haskell Noyes, Contact
Local. **Affiliated With:** Ruffed Grouse Society.

19112 ■ SAGE/Milwaukee
c/o Eldon E. Murray, Founder, Chm. Board of Directors
1845 N Farwell, Ste.220
Milwaukee, WI 53202
Ph: (414)224-0517
Fax: (414)487-0432
E-mail: sage@sagemilwaukee.org
URL: http://www.sagemilwaukee.org
Local.

19113 ■ Sales and Marketing Executives International, Greater Milwaukee
3747 S Howell Ave.
Milwaukee, WI 53207
Ph: (414)744-1550
URL: National Affiliate–www.smei.org
Contact: Dean LePoidevin, Pres.
Local. Works to serve the sales and marketing community. Provides knowledge, growth, leadership and connections between peers in both sales and marketing. Conducts career education programs. **Affiliated With:** Sales and Marketing Executives International.

19114 ■ SCORE Chapter 28, Milwaukee, WI
c/o Chapter Chm.
310 W Wisconsin Ave., No. 425
Milwaukee, WI 53203
Ph: (414)297-3942
Fax: (414)297-1377
E-mail: score28@sbcglobal.net
URL: http://www.scoremilwaukee.org
Local. Provides counseling, workshops, and seminars to help entrepreneurs start and operate small businesses. **Affiliated With:** SCORE.

19115 ■ SER - Jobs for Progress, Milwaukee
c/o Abel R. Ortiz, Exec.Dir.
1020-30 W Mitchell St.
Milwaukee, WI 53204
Ph: (414)649-2640
Fax: (414)649-2644
E-mail: ortiz@serwisconsin.org
URL: National Affiliate–www.ser-national.org
Contact: Abel R. Ortiz, Exec.Dir.
Local. **Affiliated With:** SER - Jobs for Progress National.

19116 ■ Shamrock Club of Wisconsin
2133 W Wisconsin Ave.
Milwaukee, WI 53233
E-mail: club@shamrockclubwis.com
URL: http://shamrockclubwis.com
State.

19117 ■ Sheet Metal and Air Conditioning Contractors Association (SMACCA)
c/o Peter Lentz, Exec.VP
10427 W Lincoln Ave., Ste.1600
Milwaukee, WI 53227-1201
Ph: (414)543-7622
Fax: (414)543-7626
E-mail: peter@pmsmca.com
URL: http://www.pmsmca.com
Contact: Peter Lentz, Exec.VP
Local. Ventilating, air handling, warm air heating, architectural and industrial sheet metal, kitchen equipment, testing and balancing, siding, and decking and specialty fabrication contractors. **Affiliated With:** Sheet Metal and Air Conditioning Contractors' National Association.

19118 ■ Sierra Club - John Muir Chapter - Great Waters Group
8112 W Bluemound Rd., Ste.108
Milwaukee, WI 53213
Ph: (414)297-9846 (414)453-3127
Fax: (414)476-3970
E-mail: jimv@wi.rr.com
URL: http://www.sierraclub.org/chapters/wi/gwg
Contact: Jim Kerler, Conservation Chm.
Local.

19119 ■ Society of Architectural Historians - Wisconsin Chapter
c/o Carlen I. Hatala
5008 W Blue Mound Rd.
Milwaukee, WI 53208-3652
Ph: (414)286-5722 (414)453-9739
URL: National Affiliate–www.sah.org
Contact: Carlen I. Hatala, Contact
State. Promotes the preservation of buildings of historical and aesthetic significance. Encourages scholarly research in the field of architectural history. **Affiliated With:** Society of Architectural Historians.

19120 ■ Society of Broadcast Engineers, Chapter 28 Milwaukee
10010 W Schlinger Ave.
Milwaukee, WI 53214-1129
Free: (800)322-5348
E-mail: sbe-mil@broadcast.net
URL: http://www.broadcast.net/~sbe28/index.html
Contact: Todd Boettcher, Chm.
Local. Serves the interests of broadcast engineers. Promotes the profession and related fields for both theoretical and practical applications. Advocates for technical advancement of the industry. **Affiliated With:** Society of Broadcast Engineers. **Publications:** *The Broadcast*, monthly. Newsletter. **Conventions/Meetings:** monthly meeting - every third Tuesday.

19121 ■ Society of Manufacturing Engineers - University of Wisconsin - Milwaukee S152
PO Box 784
Milwaukee, WI 53201-0784
Ph: (414)229-2668
E-mail: seifoddi@uwm.edu
URL: National Affiliate–www.sme.org
Contact: Hamid Seiffodini, Contact
Local. Advances manufacturing knowledge to gain competitive advantage. Improves skills and manufacturing solutions for the growth of economy. Provides resources and opportunities for manufacturing professionals. **Affiliated With:** Pattern Recognition Society.

19122 ■ Sons of Norway, Fosselyngen Lodge 5-82
c/o Milton A. Sande, Pres.
7507 W Oklahoma Ave.
Milwaukee, WI 53219
Ph: (414)421-0859
E-mail: bardaboo37@sbcglobal.net
URL: http://www.norwayhouse-milw.org
Contact: Milton A. Sande, Pres.
Local. **Affiliated With:** Sons of Norway.

19123 ■ South Eastern Wisconsin Helicopter Association
8667 W Medford Ave.
Milwaukee, WI 53225-2844
URL: http://torchs.org/clubs/clubs.htm
Contact: Kirk Rawling, Contact
Local.

19124 ■ South Shore Coin Club
c/o Bruce Benoit
PO Box 241174
Milwaukee, WI 53223
Ph: (414)282-8128
E-mail: benwab@sbcglobal.net
URL: National Affiliate–www.money.org
Contact: Bruce Benoit, Contact
Local. **Affiliated With:** American Numismatic Association.

19125 ■ South Town Points
c/o Hispanic Chamber of Commerce of WI (HCCW)
816 W Natl. Ave.
Milwaukee, WI 53204-1359
Ph: (414)643-6963
Fax: (414)643-6994
E-mail: mcameron@hccw.org
Contact: Maria Monreal-Cameron, Pres./CEO
Founded: 1997. **Members:** 25. **Languages:** English, Spanish. **Local**. Promotes tourism in Milwaukee's predominantly Hispanic near south side. **Formerly:** (1999) Milwaukee International Tourism and Trade District Association.

19126 ■ South Wisconsin District, The Lutheran Church-Missouri Synod
8100 W Capitol Dr.
Milwaukee, WI 53222-1981
Ph: (414)464-8100
Fax: (414)464-0602
E-mail: swd@swd.lcms.org
URL: http://swd.lcms.org
Contact: Dr. Ronald Meyer, Pres.
Local.

19127 ■ Southeastern Sheet Metal Contractors Association of Wisconsin
10427 W Lincoln Ave., Ste.1600
Milwaukee, WI 53227-1200
Ph: (414)543-7622
Fax: (414)543-7626
URL: National Affiliate–www.smacna.org
State. Ventilating, air handling, warm air heating, architectural and industrial sheet metal, kitchen equipment, testing and balancing, siding, and decking and specialty fabrication contractors. **Affiliated With:** Sheet Metal and Air Conditioning Contractors' National Association.

19128 ■ Southeastern Wisconsin Association of Diabetes Educators (SWADE)
c/o Pat Shapiro, RN
2940 S 52nd St.
Milwaukee, WI 53219
Ph: (414)649-6640
URL: http://www.swade.org
Contact: Pat Shapiro RN, Contact
Local. Promotes the development of quality diabetes education for the diabetic consumer. Fosters communication and cooperation among individuals and organizations involved in diabetes patient education. Provides educational opportunities for the professional growth and development of members. **Affiliated With:** American Association of Diabetes Educators.

19129 ■ Southeastern Wisconsin Chapter - MOAA
c/o Maj. Charles McCormick
5260 N Santa Monica Blvd.
Milwaukee, WI 53217-5120
Ph: (262)335-1748
E-mail: mmccormick@core.com
URL: National Affiliate–www.moaa.org
Contact: Maj. Charles McCormick, Contact
Local. **Affiliated With:** Military Officers Association of America.

19130 ■ Special Kids
Anything's Possible Inc.
Special Kids Speech & Skill Dev. Rsrcs.
1863 N Farwell Ave.
Milwaukee, WI 53202
Fax: (414)226-4901
Free: (800)KIDS-153
E-mail: info@special-kids.com
URL: http://www.specialkids1.com
Local.

19131 ■ Sweet Adelines International, Crosstown Harmony Chorus
PO Box 210052
Milwaukee, WI 53221
E-mail: crosstownharmony@yahoo.com
URL: http://www.crosstownharmony.org
Contact: Brad Charles, Dir.
Local. Advances the musical art form of barbershop harmony through education and performances. Provides education, training and coaching in the development of women's four-part barbershop harmony. **Affiliated With:** Sweet Adelines International.

19132 ■ Sweet Adelines International, Milwaukee Showcase Chorus
Redemption Lutheran Church
4057 N Mayfair Rd.
Milwaukee, WI 53222-1101
E-mail: info@milwaukeeshowcasechorus.com
URL: http://www.milwaukeeshowcasechorus.com
Contact: Frank Marzocco, Dir.
Local. Advances the musical art form of barbershop harmony through education and performances. Provides education, training and coaching in the development of women's four-part barbershop harmony. **Affiliated With:** Sweet Adelines International.

19133 ■ Table Tennis Club at UWM
UWM Union
2200 E Kenwood Blvd.
Milwaukee, WI 53223
Ph: (414)791-6230
E-mail: bernhard@uwm.edu
URL: http://www.uwm.edu/StudentOrg/pingpong
Contact: Michael Bernhard, Contact
Local. Affiliated With: U.S.A. Table Tennis.

19134 ■ Tall Club of Milwaukee
c/o Barry Umbs
PO Box 1122
Milwaukee, WI 53201-1122
Ph: (414)321-8142
E-mail: milwaukee@tall.org
URL: National Affiliate–www.tall.org
Contact: Barry Umbs, Contact
Local. Affiliated With: Tall Clubs International.

19135 ■ Tax Club
c/o Robert E. Dallman
1000 N Water St., Ste.2100
Milwaukee, WI 53202-3197
Free: (877)829-2582
URL: http://www.thetaxclub.com
Contact: Robert E. Dallman, Contact
Local.

19136 ■ Theosophical Society - Milwaukee Branch
c/o Susan Miller
1718 E Geneva Pl.
Milwaukee, WI 53211
Ph: (414)962-4322
URL: National Affiliate–www.theosophical.org
Contact: Susan Miller, Contact
Local. Affiliated With: Theosophical Society in America.

19137 ■ Tripoli Shriners
c/o Robert E. Manske, P.P.
3000 W Wisconsin Ave.
Milwaukee, WI 53208-3999
Ph: (414)933-4700
Fax: (414)933-1591
URL: National Affiliate–www.shrinershq.org
Contact: Robert E. Manske P.P., Contact
Local. Affiliated With: Imperial Council of the Ancient Arabic Order of the Nobles of the Mystic Shrine for North America.

19138 ■ Trout Unlimited - Southeastern Wisconsin Chapter
c/o Mr. Rich Vetrano, Pres.
2731 N 91st St.
Milwaukee, WI 53222
Ph: (414)291-0912
E-mail: rich@corecreative.com
URL: http://www.tu.org
Contact: Mr. Rich Vetrano, Pres.
Regional. Conserves, protects and restores North America's trout and salmon fisheries and their watersheds. Publishes a quarterly magazine, intervenes in federal legal proceedings, and works with the organization's 142,000 volunteers in 450 chapters nationwide to keep them active and involved in conservation issues.

19139 ■ United Association of Journeymen and Apprentices of the Plumbing and Pipe Fitting Industry of the United States and Canada - Steamfitters Local Union 601
3300 S 103rd St.
Milwaukee, WI 53227
Ph: (414)543-0601
Fax: (414)543-7721
Free: (888)543-0601
URL: http://www.steam601.com
Contact: Doug Edwards, Pres.
Members: 2,245. **Local. Affiliated With:** United Association of Journeymen and Apprentices of the Plumbing, Pipe Fitting, Sprinkler Fitting Industry of the U.S. and Canada.

19140 ■ United Cerebral Palsy of Southeastern Wisconsin
7519 W Oklahoma Ave.
Milwaukee, WI 53219
Ph: (414)329-4500 (414)329-4511
Fax: (414)329-4510
E-mail: info@ucpsew.org
URL: http://www.ucpsew.org
Contact: Fred R. Hesselbein, Exec.Dir.
Founded: 1954. **Local.** Works to aid persons with cerebral palsy and other disabilities, and their families. Seeks to advance the independence, productivity, and full citizenship of people with cerebral palsy and other disabilities. **Affiliated With:** United Cerebral Palsy Associations. **Publications:** *UCP Profiles*, 3/year. Newsletter. **Conventions/Meetings:** bimonthly board meeting • annual meeting.

19141 ■ United Electrical, Radio and Machine Workers of America, Local 1111
939 S 2nd St.
Milwaukee, WI 53204-1824
Ph: (414)645-2769
Fax: (414)645-4709
E-mail: ue1111@execpc.com
URL: http://www.ue1111.org
Contact: Bob Rudek, Pres.
Local. Telecommunication Services: electronic mail, ue1111@sbcglobal.net. **Affiliated With:** United Electrical, Radio and Machine Workers of America.

19142 ■ United Food and Commercial Workers, Local 1444, Northcentral Region
2001 N Mayfair Rd.
Milwaukee, WI 53226
Ph: (414)476-1444
URL: http://www.ufcw1444.org
Local. Affiliated With: United Food and Commercial Workers International Union.

19143 ■ United Way of Greater Milwaukee (UWGM)
225 W Vine St.
Milwaukee, WI 53212
Ph: (414)263-8100
Fax: (414)263-8128
E-mail: caringworks@unitedwaymilwaukee.org
URL: http://www.unitedwaymilwaukee.org
Contact: Sue Dragisic, Pres.
Founded: 1909. **Members:** 120. **Staff:** 45. **Local.** Strives to support the community to have strong families and successful children who live in healthy, vibrant neighborhoods, Provides education and job skills needed to be self-supporting. **Affiliated With:** United Way of America; United Way of Wisconsin. **Publications:** *Impact Matters*, quarterly. Newsletter. **Price:** free. **Circulation:** 8,000.

19144 ■ University of Wisconsin, Milwaukee - Student Environmental Action Coalition
UMW Union, Rm. E386
Box 35
Milwaukee, WI 53201
Ph: (414)229-6522
Fax: (414)229-3958
E-mail: seac@uwm.edu
Contact: William E Gump, Contact
Local.

19145 ■ U.S.A. Volleyball Badger Region
c/o Chris Haworth, Commissioner
2931 N 73rd St.
Milwaukee, WI 53210
Ph: (414)443-1011
Fax: (414)443-1125
E-mail: jennyhahn@wi.rr.com
URL: http://www.badgerregionvolleyball.org
Contact: Chris Haworth, Commissioner
Regional. Affiliated With: United States Volleyball Association/United States Volleyball Association.

19146 ■ Variety of Wisconsin
PO Box 1997
Milwaukee, WI 53201-1997
Ph: (414)266-3812
Fax: (414)266-2671
E-mail: varietywisconsin@usvariety.org
URL: National Affiliate–www.usvariety.org
State. Affiliated With: Variety International - The Children's Charity.

19147 ■ Vintage Chevrolet Club of America, Wisconsin Region No. 4
c/o Tom Griepentrog, Dir.
8222 N 106th St.
Milwaukee, WI 53224
Ph: (414)354-2929
URL: National Affiliate–www.vcca.org
Contact: Tom Griepentrog, Dir.
State. Affiliated With: Vintage Chevrolet Club of America.

19148 ■ VISIT Milwaukee
648 N Plankinton Ave., Ste.425
Milwaukee, WI 53203-2917
Ph: (414)273-7222
Fax: (414)273-5596
Free: (800)554-1448
E-mail: visitor@milwaukee.org
URL: http://www.milwaukee.org
Contact: Doug Neilson, Pres./CEO
Local. Formerly: (2005) Greater Milwaukee Convention and Visitors Bureau.

19149 ■ Wheelmen, Wisconsin
7321 N Green Bay Ave.
Milwaukee, WI 53209-2020
Ph: (414)351-1565
URL: National Affiliate–www.thewheelmen.org
State.

19150 ■ Whitefish Bay Young Life
4530 N Oakland Ave.
Milwaukee, WI 53211
Ph: (414)967-0645
URL: http://sites.younglife.org/sites/WhitefishBayYL/default.aspx
Local. Affiliated With: Young Life.

19151 ■ Wisconsin Art Therapy Association (WATA)
PO Box 1765
Milwaukee, WI 53201-1765
E-mail: wiarttx@execpc.com
URL: http://my.execpc.com/~wiarttx
Contact: Michele Burnie, Pres.
State. Represents professionals using art as a creative process in healing and life enhancement. Supports the progressive development of the therapeutic uses of art, advancement in its research, and improvements in the standards of practice. **Affiliated With:** American Art Therapy Association.

19152 ■ Wisconsin Association of Academic Librarians (WAAL)
c/o Alberto Herrera, Jr., Chm.
PO Box 3141
Milwaukee, WI 53201-3141
Ph: (414)228-2140
Fax: (414)288-8821
E-mail: alberto.herrera@marquette.edu
URL: http://www.wla.lib.wi.us/waal
Contact: Alberto Herrera Jr., Chm.
State. Enhances the ability of academic library and information professionals to serve the information needs of the higher education community and to improve learning, teaching and research. **Affiliated With:** Association of College and Research Libraries.

19153 ■ Wisconsin Association African-American Attorneys
c/o Roy Love Williams, Pres.
PO Box 519
Milwaukee, WI 53201-0519
Ph: (414)223-4800
E-mail: roy@mfhupy.com
URL: National Affiliate–www.nationalbar.org
Contact: Roy Love Williams, Pres.
Local. Professional association of minority (predominantly African-American) attorneys, members of the judiciary, law students, and law faculty. Represents the interests of members and the communities they serve. **Affiliated With:** National Bar Association.

19154 ■ Wisconsin Association for Biomedical Research and Education (WABRE)
c/o Ms. Gale Davy, Exec.Dir.
PO Box 390
Milwaukee, WI 53201
Ph: (414)899-9246
Fax: (414)933-9500
E-mail: wabre@execpc.com
URL: http://www.wabre.org
Contact: Ms. Gale Davy, Exec.Dir.
Founded: 1986. **Membership Dues:** individual, $25-$100 • institutional, $5,000-$50,000. **Budget:** $130,000. **State.** Represents the bioscience research community in Wisconsin. Promotes excellence in science education. Provides public education on the role and purpose of biomedical research, education, testing and bioscience in general. **Publications:** *Bioscience Wisconsin 2004*, biennial. Report. Reports about bioscience research, development and industry in Wisconsin. • *Bioscience Wisconsin 2006*, biennial. Reports. Contains comprehensive report on bioscience in Wisconsin including economic data on academic and industry research and development. Alternate Formats: online.

19155 ■ Wisconsin Association of Educational Opportunity Program Personnel (WAEOPP)
c/o Don Campbell, Pres.-Elect
PO Box 413
Milwaukee, WI 53201
Ph: (414)229-3783
Fax: (414)229-5758
E-mail: dsbell@uwm.edu
URL: http://www.waeopp.org
Contact: Don Campbell, Pres.-Elect
State. Works to advance educational opportunities for disadvantaged students in colleges and universities. Provides professional development and continuing education. Monitors federal legislation designed to serve disadvantaged students. **Affiliated With:** Council for Opportunity in Education.

19156 ■ Wisconsin Association for Identification (WAI)
c/o Melissa Graf, Pres.
Wisconsin State Crime Lab
1578 S 11th St.
Milwaukee, WI 53204-2860
Ph: (414)382-7500
E-mail: secretary@thewai.org
URL: http://www.thewai.org
Contact: Melissa Graf, Pres.
Founded: 1966. **Members:** 236. **Membership Dues:** active, associate, student, $20 (annual). **Staff:** 20. **State.** Individuals actively employed in the business of identification, investigation, and scientific crime detection. Works to standardize the profession. **Libraries: Type:** reference. **Holdings:** 240; books, periodicals. **Subjects:** identification, investigation, scientific crime detection, photography. **Affiliated With:** International Association for Identification. **Publications:** *WAI Newsletter*, quarterly. Contains meeting minutes, related articles, etc. **Price:** $5.00/year. **Circulation:** 260. **Advertising:** accepted. **Conventions/Meetings:** annual Educational Conference, with vendors of various types-photography, fingerprint devices, etc (exhibits).

19157 ■ Wisconsin Association of Manufacturers' Agents (WAMA)
1504 N 68th St.
Milwaukee, WI 53213
Ph: (414)778-0640
Fax: (414)778-0640
E-mail: wama@wama.org
URL: http://www.wama.org
Contact: Carole J. Bluem, Exec.Dir.
State. Professional representatives of industrial firms. Holds monthly luncheon meetings with a speaker and one educational seminar per year. Provides a place for representatives to network; provides educational information; and assists the representatives in improving their own agency and skills. Seeks to promote the use of representatives as a means of providing field sales.

19158 ■ Wisconsin Association of Scholars (WAS)
c/o David Mulroy, Pres.
Dept. of Foreign Languages & Linguistics
Univ. of Wisconsin
Milwaukee, WI 53201-0413
Ph: (414)229-4711
Fax: (414)229-2741
E-mail: dmulroy@uwm.edu
URL: http://www.nas.org
Contact: David Mulroy, Pres.
State. Works to enrich the substance and to strengthen the integrity of scholarship and teaching. Provides a forum for the discussion of curricular issues and trends in higher education.

19159 ■ Wisconsin Bakers Association
c/o David J. Schmidt, CMB, Exec.Dir.
8112 W Bluemound Rd.
Milwaukee, WI 53213-3356
Ph: (414)258-5552
Fax: (414)258-5582
Free: (800)542-2688
E-mail: information@umwba.org
URL: http://www.umwba.org
Contact: David J. Schmidt CMB, Exec.Dir.
Founded: 1905. **Members:** 300. **Staff:** 4. **Budget:** $300,000. **Regional.** Serves the baking industry by fostering the education of future bakers through scholarship programs and workshops. **Awards:** WBA Scholarship. **Frequency:** annual. **Type:** scholarship. **Affiliated With:** Retailer's Bakery Association. **Publications:** *Beyond Baking*, monthly. Newsletter. **Circulation:** 1,200. **Advertising:** accepted.

19160 ■ Wisconsin Black Media Association
PO Box 100619
Milwaukee, WI 53210
Ph: (414)231-5555
E-mail: vivianking@msn.com
URL: National Affiliate–www.nabj.org
Contact: Vivian King, Pres.
State. Advocates the rights of black journalists. Provides informational and training services and professional development to black journalists and to the general public. **Affiliated With:** National Association of Black Journalists.

19161 ■ Wisconsin Chapter of the American College of Cardiology (WCACC)
6737 W Washington Ave., Ste.1420
Milwaukee, WI 53214
Ph: (414)276-8788
Fax: (414)276-7704
E-mail: info@wcacc.org
URL: http://www.wcacc.org
Contact: Kenneth W. Wallmeyer MD, Sec.-Treas.
State. Affiliated With: American College of Cardiology.

19162 ■ Wisconsin Chapter of the International Society for Performance Improvement (WISPI)
PO Box 400
Milwaukee, WI 53201-0400
Ph: (262)703-4830
E-mail: wi_ispi@yahoo.com
URL: http://www.wispi.org
Contact: Laura Dolnik, Pres.
State. Performance technologists, training directors, human resource managers, instructional designers, human factors practitioners, and organizational development consultants who work in a variety of industries such as automotive, communications and telecommunications, computer, financial services, government agencies, health services, manufacturing, the military, travel/hospitality, and education. Dedicated to improving productivity and performance in the workplace through the application of performance and instructional technologies.

19163 ■ Wisconsin Chapter of the National Alliance of Methadone Advocates (WI NAMA)
c/o Greg Keller, Pres.
3237 N Dousman
Milwaukee, WI 53212
Ph: (414)263-6904
E-mail: gkeller654@aol.com
Contact: Greg Keller, Pres.
State. Promotes quality methadone maintenance treatment. Eliminates discrimination toward methadone patients. **Affiliated With:** National Alliance of Methadone Advocates.

19164 ■ Wisconsin City/County Management Association (WCMA)
115 S 84th St., Ste.400
Milwaukee, WI 53214
Ph: (414)777-5382
Fax: (414)777-5555
E-mail: ehenschel@virchowkrause.com
URL: http://www.wcma-wi.org
Contact: Edmund Henschel, Exec.Dir.
Members: 135. **Membership Dues:** individual, $50 (annual). **Budget:** $25,000. **State.** Municipal managers and administrators. Promotes professional municipal management and provides professional development activities for members. **Publications:** *WCMA News and Notes*, quarterly. Newsletter. **Conventions/Meetings:** annual conference • annual seminar.

19165 ■ Wisconsin Concrete Masonry Association (WCMA)
6737 W Washington Ave., Ste.1420
Milwaukee, WI 53214
Ph: (414)276-0667
Fax: (414)276-7704
Free: (800)377-0667
E-mail: info@concretemasonry.org
URL: http://www.concretemasonry.org
Contact: Pat Winger, Pres.
State.

19166 ■ Wisconsin Dental Association (WDA)
111 E Wisconsin Ave., Ste.1300
Milwaukee, WI 53202
Ph: (414)276-4520
Fax: (414)276-8431
Free: (800)364-7646
E-mail: info@wda.org
URL: http://www.wda.org
Contact: Dennis J. McGuire CAE, Exec.Dir.
State.

19167 ■ Wisconsin Direct Marketing Association (WDMA)
c/o Kelly Gardner, Pres.
1123 N Water St.
Milwaukee, WI 53202
Ph: (414)277-9362
Fax: (414)276-7704
E-mail: info@wdma.org
URL: http://www.wdma.org
Contact: Kelly Gardner, Pres.
Membership Dues: individual, $150 (annual) • corporate, for up to 10 people ($25 per additional member), $500 (annual) • educator/student, $50 (annual). **State**. Works to encourage professional standards and further education in all aspects of direct marketing. **Awards:** Direct Marketer of the Year. **Frequency:** annual. **Type:** recognition. **Recipient:** for individual with contributions to the direct marketing industry in Wisconsin. **Affiliated With:** Direct Marketing Association. **Publications:** Newsletter, quarterly. **Price:** included in membership dues.

19168 ■ Wisconsin Environmental Balancing Bureau
c/o SMACCA of Milwaukee, Inc.
10427 W Lincoln Ave., Ste.1600
Milwaukee, WI 53227
Ph: (414)543-7622
Fax: (414)543-7626
E-mail: peter@pmsmca.com
URL: National Affiliate–www.nebb.org
Contact: Peter Lentz, Chapter Coor.
State. Works to help architects, engineers, building owners, and contractors produce buildings with HVAC systems. Establishes and maintains industry standards, procedures, and specifications for testing, adjusting, and balancing work. **Affiliated With:** National Environmental Balancing Bureau.

19169 ■ Wisconsin Figure Skating Club (WFSC)
PO Box 170385
Milwaukee, WI 53217
Ph: (414)228-7553
E-mail: wfsc@wisconsinfsc.org
URL: http://www.wisconsinfsc.org
Contact: Lisa M. Rivero, Contact
State. Provides programs to encourage participation and achievement in the sport of figure skating on ice. Defines and maintains uniform standards of skating proficiency. Organizes and sponsors competitions and exhibitions for the purpose of stimulating interest in figure skating. **Affiliated With:** United States Figure Skating Association.

19170 ■ Wisconsin Healthcare Engineering Association (WHEA)
c/o James L. Hildebrand, Pres.
Luther Manor
4545 N 92nd St.
Milwaukee, WI 53225
Ph: (414)464-3880
Fax: (414)464-1045
E-mail: jhildebrand@luthermanor.org
URL: http://www.whea.com
Contact: James L. Hildebrand, Pres.
State. Promotes better patient care by encouraging members to develop their knowledge and increase their competence in the field of facilities management. Cooperates with hospitals and allied associations in matters pertaining to facilities management. **Affiliated With:** American Society for Healthcare Engineering of the American Hospital Association.

19171 ■ Wisconsin Healthcare Purchasing and Materials Management Association
c/o Dave Skinner, Materials Mgr./Surgery
Columbia St. Mary's
2025 E Newport Ave.
Milwaukee, WI 53211
Ph: (414)961-4604
Fax: (414)961-3498
E-mail: dskinner@columbia-stmarys.org
URL: National Affiliate–www.ahrmm.org
Contact: Dave Skinner, Materials Mgr./Surgery
State. Represents purchasing agents and materials managers active in the field of purchasing, inventory, distribution and materials management as performed in hospitals, related patient care institutions and government and voluntary health organizations. Provides networking and educational opportunities for members. Develops new business ventures that ensure the financial stability of members. **Affiliated With:** Association for Healthcare Resource and Materials Management.

19172 ■ Wisconsin Humane Society
c/o Wendy Randall
4500 W Wisconsin Ave.
Milwaukee, WI 53208-3156
Ph: (414)264-6257
Fax: (414)431-6200
E-mail: wrandall@wihumane.org
URL: http://www.wihumane.org
Contact: Wendy Randall, Volunteer Coor.
State. Seeks to build a community that values animals and treats them with respect and kindness.

19173 ■ Wisconsin Marine Historical Society (WMHS)
814 W Wisconsin Ave.
Milwaukee, WI 53233
Ph: (414)286-3074
Fax: (414)286-2126
E-mail: suzette@wmhs.org
URL: http://www.wmhs.org
Contact: Suzette Lopez, Exec.Dir.
Founded: 1959. **Members:** 350. **Membership Dues:** $35 (annual). **Staff:** 1. **Budget:** $32,000. **State**. Researchers, writers, divers, sailors, and marine enthusiasts. Promotes interest in discovering, collecting, recording, preserving, disseminating charts, plans, prints, pictures, and other artifacts relating to the Great Lakes area. Sponsors exhibits at maritime festivals and museum and library events. **Libraries: Type:** open to the public. **Subjects:** Great Lakes marine history. **Committees:** Program. **Affiliated With:** Wisconsin Historical Society. **Publications:** *Pictorial Marine History*. Book • *Six Fitzgerald Brothers - Lake Captains All*. Book • *Soundings*, quarterly. Newsletter. **Conventions/Meetings:** annual dinner (exhibits) • bimonthly dinner, with film showings (exhibits) • annual meeting (exhibits) - always in January.

19174 ■ Wisconsin Parking Association (WisPA)
c/o Mike Kenney, Pres.
CPS Parking
100 E Wisconsin Ave.
Milwaukee, WI 53202
Ph: (414)223-4722
Fax: (414)223-4173
E-mail: mkenney@parking.com
URL: http://www.wisconsinparkingassociation.com
Contact: Mike Kenney, Pres.
Founded: 1991. **Members:** 100. **Membership Dues:** individual, $15 (annual). **State**. Seeks to aid persons involved in providing parking services; to provide educational services to members; and to promote and support legislation important to the parking field. **Affiliated With:** International Parking Institute. **Publications:** Newsletter, semiannual. **Conventions/ Meetings:** annual conference - every fall • annual workshop - always spring.

19175 ■ Wisconsin Parkinson Association (WPA)
c/o Aurora Sinai Medical Center
945 N 12th St., Ste.4602
Milwaukee, WI 53233
Ph: (414)219-7061
Fax: (414)871-7942
Free: (800)972-5455
E-mail: jackie.hoeft@aurora.org
URL: http://www.wiparkinson.org
Contact: Jackie Hoeft, Contact
Founded: 1982. **Membership Dues:** regular, $15 (annual). **Regional Groups:** 20. **State Groups:** 50. **Local Groups:** 10. **State**. Provides information about Parkinson's Disease to families, health professionals and community agencies. **Libraries: Type:** open to the public. **Holdings:** articles, books, video recordings. **Subjects:** chronic illnesses, emotional issues, Parkinson's disease. **Awards:** Clinical Center of Excellence. **Frequency:** annual. **Type:** grant. **Recipient:** for advocacy, education and clinical expertise. **Publications:** *Network*, quarterly. Newsletter. Contains educational information. **Price:** free. **Circulation:** 5,000. Alternate Formats: online. **Conventions/Meetings:** annual conference.

19176 ■ Wisconsin Procurement Institute Education and Training Services
756 N Milwaukee St.
Milwaukee, WI 53202-3719
Ph: (414)270-3600
Fax: (414)270-3610
E-mail: info@wispro.org
URL: http://www.wispro.org
Contact: Mary Herrera, Contact
State.

19177 ■ Wisconsin Psychoanalytic Society
2025 E Newport Ave., 4th Fl.
Milwaukee, WI 53211-2906
Ph: (414)961-8107
Fax: (414)961-8074
E-mail: admin@wisconsinpsa.org
URL: http://www.wisconsinpsa.org
Contact: Dr. Robert Walker, Pres.
Founded: 1983. **Members:** 20. **Membership Dues:** individual, $200 (annual). **State**. Disseminates psychoanalytic information that help improve the mental health. Supports outreach programs and research. **Conventions/Meetings:** monthly Scientific Meeting - held 1st Saturday.

19178 ■ Wisconsin Radiological Society (WRS)
c/o Paul A. Larson, Pres.
6737 W Washington St., Ste.1420
Milwaukee, WI 53214
Ph: (414)755-6293
Fax: (414)276-7704
URL: http://www.wi-rad.org
Contact: Paul A. Larson, Pres.
State. Promotes the value of radiology, radiation oncology, nuclear medicine, medical physics and other related fields. Seeks to improve the quality of patient care and influence the socio-economics of the practice of radiology. Provides continuing education for radiology and allied health professionals. **Affiliated With:** American College of Radiology.

19179 ■ Wisconsin Right to Life
10625 W North Ave., Ste.LL
Milwaukee, WI 53226
Ph: (414)778-5780
E-mail: blyons@wrtl.org
URL: http://www.wrtl.org
Contact: Barbara L. Lyons, Exec.Dir.
State. Affiliated With: National Right to Life Committee.

19180 ■ Wisconsin Scholars
c/o Rachel Hampton, Program Dir.
PO Box 170733
Milwaukee, WI 53217
Ph: (262)236-1610
E-mail: kbearden@wi.rr.com
URL: http://www.wisconsinscholars.com
Contact: Keith Bearden, Pres.
State.

19181 ■ Wisconsin Self Storage Association (WSSA)
c/o Chris Ruditys
223 N Water St., Ste.300
Milwaukee, WI 53202
Ph: (414)271-9456
Fax: (414)271-6868
E-mail: ruditys@wamllc.net
URL: http://www.wiselfstorage.org
Contact: Chris Ruditys, Contact
State. Represents owners and operators of self storage facilities. Works to improve the quality of management, customer service and facilities. Promotes public awareness of the self storage industry. Conducts educational meetings on management, marketing, security, and related topics. Lobbies for state legislation protecting and recognizing self storage owners and operators. **Affiliated With:** Self Storage Association.

19182 ■ Wisconsin Society of Association Executives
c/o Jane A. Svinicki, CAE, Exec.VP
Wisconsin Soc. of Assn. Executives
Milwaukee, WI 53202
Ph: (414)277-9723
Fax: (414)276-7704
E-mail: jane@svinicki.com
URL: http://www.wsae.org
Contact: Ms. Jen H., Coor.
State. Affiliated With: American Society of Association Executives.

19183 ■ Wisconsin State AFL-CIO
c/o David Newby, Pres.
6333 W Blue Mound Rd.
Milwaukee, WI 53213
Ph: (414)771-0700
Fax: (414)771-1715
E-mail: solidarity@wisaflcio.org
URL: http://www.wisaflcio.org
Contact: David Newby, Pres.
State. Provides services for hundreds of local unions and trade councils throughout Wisconsin state. **Affiliated With:** AFL-CIO.

19184 ■ Wisconsin Supreme Court Historical Society
c/o Paul E. Benson, Chm.
100 E Wisconsin Ave., Ste.3300
Milwaukee, WI 53202
Ph: (414)225-2757
Fax: (414)277-0656
E-mail: pebenson@mbf-law.com
URL: National Affiliate–www.supremecourthistory.org
Contact: Paul E. Benson, Chm.
State. Collects and preserves the history of the Supreme Court of the United States. Conducts educational programs and supports historical research. Collects antiques and artifacts related to the Court's history. Increases public awareness of the Court's contributions to the nation's constitutional heritage. **Affiliated With:** Supreme Court Historical Society.

19185 ■ Wisconsin Toy Fox Terrier Association
c/o Myles Notaro, Pres.
2925 S 10th St.
Milwaukee, WI 53215
Ph: (414)482-1633
E-mail: myleswi@aol.com
URL: National Affiliate–www.ntfta.netfirms.com
Contact: Myles Notaro, Pres.
State. Affiliated With: National Toy Fox Terrier Association.

19186 ■ Wisconsin Underground Contractors Association (WUCA)
c/o Richard W. Wanta, Exec.Dir.
2835 N Mayfair Rd., Ste.35
Milwaukee, WI 53222-4483
Ph: (414)778-1050
Fax: (414)778-0647
E-mail: rwanta@wuca.org
URL: http://www.wuca.org
Founded: 1937. **Members:** 190. **Membership Dues:** contractor, $850 (annual) • affiliate contractor, $459 (annual) • associate, $350 (annual). **Budget:** $330,000. **State. Publications:** *Standard Specifications for the Sewer and Water Construction in Wisconsin*. Book • *Trenches*, quarterly. Newsletter. **Conventions/Meetings:** annual conference - midwinter.

19187 ■ Wisconsin User Group of Applied Systems
c/o WDA Insurance Programs Inc.
111 E Wisconsin Ave., No. 1300
Milwaukee, WI 53202
Ph: (414)277-7727
Fax: (414)277-1124
E-mail: sdurand@insuranceformembers.net
URL: National Affiliate–www.ascnet.org
Contact: Stacey Durand, Pres.
State. Represents insurance agents and brokers using the Agency Manager software. Promotes successful automation and business practices through communication, education, and advocacy. **Affiliated With:** Applied Systems Client Network.

19188 ■ Wisconsin Women in Higher Education Leadership (WWHEL)
c/o Sonia Andrews
PO Box 413
Milwaukee, WI 53201-0413
URL: http://www.uwosh.edu/wwhel
Contact: Sonia Andrews, Contact
Local.

19189 ■ WyldLife - Whitefish Bay
4530 N Oakland Ave.
Milwaukee, WI 53211
Ph: (414)967-0645
E-mail: rbender@milwaukee.younglife.org
URL: http://sites.younglife.org/sites/WyldLife-WFB/default.aspx
Contact: Rebekah Bender, Team Leader
Local. Affiliated With: Young Life.

19190 ■ Young Life Milwaukee North Shore
4530 N Oakland Ave.
Milwaukee, WI 53211
Ph: (414)967-0645
E-mail: rbender@milwaukee.younglife.org
URL: http://sites.younglife.org/sites/Milwaukee/default.aspx
Contact: Rebekah Bender, Area Dir.
Local. Affiliated With: Young Life.

19191 ■ Zoological Society of Milwaukee (ZSM)
10005 W Blue Mound Rd.
Milwaukee, WI 53226
Ph: (414)258-2333
E-mail: membership@zoosociety.org
URL: http://www.zoosociety.org
Contact: Gil Boese PhD, Pres.
Founded: 1910. **Members:** 52,000. **Membership Dues:** individual, $40-$45 • family, single adult family, $54-$110 • affiliate, $200 • advocate, $300 • benefactor, $400. **Staff:** 61. **Languages:** English, Spanish. **Local. Formerly:** (2005) Zoological Society of Milwaukee County. **Publications:** *Alive*, 3/year, published in January, April and October. Magazine. **Price:** included in membership dues. Alternate Formats: online • *Wild Things*. Newsletter. **Price:** included in membership dues. Alternate Formats: online.

Mindoro

19192 ■ American Legion, Gunderson and Gilbertson Post 507
PO Box 195
Mindoro, WI 54644
Ph: (608)745-1090
Fax: (608)745-0179
URL: National Affiliate–www.legion.org
Local. Affiliated With: American Legion.

19193 ■ Mindoro Lions Club
c/o Todd Baumer, Pres.
N8128 Hwy. 108
Mindoro, WI 54644
Ph: (608)857-3591
URL: http://www.md27d2.org
Contact: Todd Baumer, Pres.
Local. Affiliated With: Lions Clubs International.

Mineral Point

19194 ■ American Legion, Homer and Lee Parkinson Post 170
c/o Lawrence Schaaf
416 N Chestnut St.
Mineral Point, WI 53565
Ph: (608)745-1090
Fax: (608)745-0179
URL: National Affiliate–www.legion.org
Contact: Lawrence Schaaf, Contact
Local. Affiliated With: American Legion.

19195 ■ Mineral Point Chamber of Commerce (MPCCMS)
225 High St.
Mineral Point, WI 53565
Ph: (608)987-3201
Fax: (608)987-4425
Free: (888)POI-NTWI
E-mail: info@mineralpoint.com
URL: http://www.mineralpoint.com
Contact: Joy Gieseke, Dir.
Founded: 1945. **Members:** 90. **Membership Dues:** personal, $50 • organization, $100 • business (based on number of employees), $165-$2,500. **Local.** Business owners. Strives to enrich the economic well being and supports local business and industry Mineral Point, WI. **Committees:** Cornish Festival; Design; Economic Development; Fourth of July; Organization; Promotions; Retail. **Publications:** *Community Resource Guide*, periodic • *Visitor's Guide*, annual. **Conventions/Meetings:** monthly board meeting.

19196 ■ Southwestern Wisconsin AIFA
c/o Dan Wiegman, Sec.
911 Fountain St.
Mineral Point, WI 53565-1313
Ph: (608)987-2604
Fax: (608)987-9984
E-mail: wiegmanrd@yahoo.com
URL: National Affiliate–naifa.org
Contact: Dan Wiegman, Sec.
Local. Represents the interests of insurance and financial advisors. Advocates for a positive legislative and regulatory environment. Enhances business and professional skills of members. **Affiliated With:** National Association of Insurance and Financial Advisors.

Minocqua

19197 ■ American Legion, Madsen-Empey Post 89
121 Front St.
Minocqua, WI 54548
Ph: (608)745-1090
Fax: (608)745-0179
URL: National Affiliate–www.legion.org
Local. Affiliated With: American Legion.

19198 ■ Environmentally Concerned Citizens of Lakeland Area (ECCOLA)
PO Box 537
Minocqua, WI 54548
Ph: (715)453-6015
Fax: (715)356-2850
E-mail: eccola@newnorth.net
URL: http://www.eccola.org
Contact: John Schwarzmann, Sec.-Treas.
Founded: 1992. **Members:** 366. **Membership Dues:** individual, $25 (annual). **Staff:** 1. **Budget:** $10,000. **Local.** Educates citizens on environmental issues and provides solutions to environmental problems.

19199 ■ Minocqua - Arbor Vitae - Woodruff Chamber of Commerce
PO Box 1006
Minocqua, WI 54548
Ph: (715)356-5266
Fax: (715)358-2446
Free: (800)446-6784
E-mail: mavwacc@minocqua.org
URL: http://www.minocqua.org
Contact: Cambria Mares, Exec.Dir.
Founded: 1993. **Members:** 453. **Staff:** 6. **Budget:** $509,000. **State Groups:** 1. **Local.** Works to develop, promote and maintain a positive economic climate which supports the community. **Publications:** *Northwoods News*, monthly. **Price:** included in membership dues. **Circulation:** 525.

19200 ■ Northern Lakes District Nurses Association - No. 14
8361 Doolittle Rd.
Minocqua, WI 54548
Ph: (715)356-6540
E-mail: hauerj@newnorth.net
URL: http://www.wisconsinnurses.org
Contact: Joan Hauer, Pres.
Local. Works to advance the nursing profession. Seeks to meet the needs of nurses and health care consumers. Fosters high standards of nursing practice. Promotes the economic and general welfare of nurses in the workplace. **Affiliated With:** American Nurses Association; Wisconsin Nurses' Association.

Minong

19201 ■ American Legion, Wisconsin Post 465
c/o Harold A. Smith
PO Box 56
Minong, WI 54859
Ph: (608)745-1090
Fax: (608)745-0179
URL: National Affiliate–www.legion.org
Contact: Harold A. Smith, Contact
Local. Affiliated With: American Legion.

Mishicot

19202 ■ Door County REACT
15719 Becker Rd.
Mishicot, WI 54228-0207
Ph: (920)755-2800
E-mail: kb9eme@milwpc.com
URL: http://www.reactintl.org/teaminfo/usa_teams/teams-uswi.htm
Local. Trained communication experts and professional volunteers. Provides volunteer public service and emergency communications through the use of radios (Citizen Band, General Mobile Radio Service, UHF and HAM). Coordinates with radio industries and government on safety communication matters and supports charitable activities and community organizations.

19203 ■ Mishicot Area Growth and Improvement Committee (MAGIC)
PO Box 237
Mishicot, WI 54228
Ph: (920)755-3411
Fax: (920)755-2525
E-mail: mishicot@milwpc.com
URL: http://mishicot.org
Contact: Kathy Lindsey, Mgr.
Founded: 1847. **Local.** Promotes business and community development in Mishicot, WI area.

Mondovi

19204 ■ American Legion, Dillon-Johnson-Anderson Post 154
239 E Hudson St.
Mondovi, WI 54755
Ph: (608)745-1090
Fax: (608)745-0179
URL: National Affiliate–www.legion.org
Local. Affiliated With: American Legion.

19205 ■ Sons of Norway, Viking Lodge 5-625
c/o Joanne M. Erickson, Pres.
149 N Harrison St.
Mondovi, WI 54755-1007
Ph: (715)926-5132
URL: National Affiliate–www.sofn.com
Contact: Joanne M. Erickson, Pres.
Local. Affiliated With: Sons of Norway.

Monona

19206 ■ American Legion, Monona Grove Post 429
6006 Bridge Rd.
Monona, WI 53716
Ph: (608)745-1090
Fax: (608)745-0179
URL: National Affiliate–www.legion.org
Local. Affiliated With: American Legion.

19207 ■ Madison Bowling Association
6213 Monona Dr.
Monona, WI 53716-3934
Ph: (608)221-0300
Fax: (608)221-2126
E-mail: mbassoc@execpc.com
URL: http://mba.bowlweb.com
Founded: 1913. **Members:** 9,000. **Staff:** 2. **Local.**

19208 ■ Madison Women's Bowling Association (MWBA)
6213 Monona Dr.
Monona, WI 53716
Ph: (608)221-0300
E-mail: mwba@execpc.com
URL: http://mwba.bowlweb.com
Contact: Marge Pursell, Sec.
Local.

19209 ■ Monona Chamber of Commerce
6320 Monona Dr.
Monona, WI 53716-3952
Ph: (608)222-8565
Fax: (608)222-8596
E-mail: chamber@monona.com
URL: http://monona.com
Contact: Terri Groves, Exec.Dir.
Founded: 1990. **Members:** 209. **Membership Dues:** basic, $50-$1,500 (annual). **Staff:** 1. **Budget:** $63,800. **Local Groups:** 1. **Local.** Promotes business and community development in Monona, WI area. **Publications:** Newsletter. **Price:** included in membership dues.

19210 ■ Sales and Marketing Executives of Madison
PO Box 6452
Monona, WI 53716-6452
Ph: (608)531-7636
E-mail: info@smemadison.com
URL: http://www.smemadison.com
Contact: Christin Miller, Pres.
Local. Works to serve the sales and marketing community. Provides knowledge, growth, leadership and connections between peers in both sales and marketing. Conducts career education programs. **Affiliated With:** Sales and Marketing Executives International.

19211 ■ Wisconsin Association of Criminal Defense Lawyers (WACDL)
PO Box 6706
Monona, WI 53716-6706
Ph: (608)223-1275
Fax: (608)223-9329
E-mail: info@wacdl.com
URL: http://www.wacdl.com
Contact: Peter McKeever, Exec.Dir.
State.

Monroe

19212 ■ Alpine Curling Club
1319 31st Ave.
Monroe, WI 53566
Ph: (608)325-9987
E-mail: bonsplr@sbcglobal.net
URL: http://www.alpinecurlingclub.com
Contact: Harold Marzolf, Pres.
Local. Affiliated With: United States Curling Association.

19213 ■ Big Brothers Big Sisters of Green County
1505 9th St.
Monroe, WI 53566-0563
Ph: (608)325-7855
Fax: (608)328-2241
E-mail: bbbsgreen@tds.net
URL: National Affiliate–www.bbbsa.org
Local. Affiliated With: Big Brothers Big Sisters of America.

19214 ■ Green County Historical Society (GCHS)
c/o Virginia V. Irvin
2109 20th Ave.
Monroe, WI 53566
Ph: (608)325-2609
E-mail: md2609@tds.net
Contact: Virginia V. Irvin, Treas.
Founded: 1937. **Members:** 110. **Membership Dues:** $5 (annual). **Local.** Individuals interested in preserving the history of the region. Maintains Green County Historical Society Museum; and Little Red Schoolhouse and antique cheese making equipment. **Conventions/Meetings:** annual meeting, with business reports.

19215 ■ Monroe Chamber of Commerce and Industry (MCCI)
1505 9th St.
Monroe, WI 53566
Ph: (608)325-7648
Fax: (608)325-7710
E-mail: contactus@monroechamber.org
URL: http://www.monroechamber.org
Contact: Matthew Urban, Exec.Dir.
Members: 220. **Staff:** 2. **Local.** Promotes business, industry, and tourism in the Monroe, WI area. Sponsors Balloon Rally. **Affiliated With:** U.S. Chamber of Commerce. **Publications:** *Issues*, monthly. Newsletter • *Visitor Guide*, annual. Directory.

19216 ■ Realtors Association of Southwest Wisconsin
2036 Lincoln Ave.
Monroe, WI 53566
Ph: (608)328-1907
Fax: (608)328-1909
E-mail: clutchi@charter.net
URL: National Affiliate–www.realtor.org
Contact: Christine Luchi, Exec. Officer
Local. Strives to develop real estate business practices. Advocates the right to own, use and transfer real property. Provides a facility for professional development, research and exchange of information among members and to the general public. **Affiliated With:** National Association of Realtors.

19217 ■ Society for Healthcare Consumer Advocacy of the American Hospital Association, Wisconsin
c/o Cathy Stouffer, Pres.
The Monroe Clinic
515 22nd Ave.
Monroe, WI 53566-1598
Ph: (608)324-1400
Fax: (608)324-1114
E-mail: cathy_stouffer@themonroeclinic.org
URL: National Affiliate–www.shca-aha.org
State. Affiliated With: Society for Healthcare Consumer Advocacy of the American Hospital Association.

19218 ■ Sons of Norway, Ostestaden Lodge 5-642
c/o Lois C. Gordee, Pres.
2820 6th St.
Monroe, WI 53566-1901
Ph: (608)328-2262
E-mail: elsiegor@tds.net
URL: National Affiliate–www.sofn.com
Contact: Lois C. Gordee, Pres.
Local. Affiliated With: Sons of Norway.

19219 ■ United Way of Green County
PO Box 511
Monroe, WI 53566-0511
Ph: (608)325-7747
E-mail: unitedway@wekz.com
URL: National Affiliate–national.unitedway.org
Contact: Staci Marrese-Wheeler, Exec.Dir.
Founded: 1956. **Members:** 32. **Staff:** 3. **State Groups:** 1. **Local.** Members of business community working to raise money for service organizations in the Green County, WI area. Provides community leadership to improve the quality of life for the people of Green County through developing and distributing resources that address human service needs. **Affiliated With:** United Way of America.

Montello

19220 ■ Adams Marquette Waushara Board of Realtors
PO Box 515
Montello, WI 53949
Ph: (608)297-7734
Fax: (608)297-7181
E-mail: lori_paczkowski@hotmail.com
URL: National Affiliate–www.realtor.org
Contact: Jennifer Dillman, Exec. Officer
Local. Strives to develop real estate business practices. Advocates the right to own, use and transfer real property. Provides a facility for professional development, research and exchange of information among members and to the general public. **Affiliated With:** National Association of Realtors.

19221 ■ Montello Area Chamber of Commerce (MCC)
PO Box 325
Montello, WI 53949
Ph: (608)297-7420
Free: (800)684-7199
E-mail: montellochamber@hotmail.com
URL: http://www.montellowi.com
Contact: Susanne Kufahl, Exec.Sec.
Founded: 1946. **Members:** 118. **Local.** Promotes business and community development in the Montello, WI area. Sponsors annual Father Marquette Days festival. **Convention/Meeting:** none. **Publications:** Newsletter, annual • Brochures.

19222 ■ Wisconsin Concrete Pipe Association (WCPA)
N3486 Indian Echoes Ln.
Montello, WI 53949
Ph: (608)297-7070
Fax: (608)297-7070
E-mail: wcpa@palacenet.net
URL: http://www.wcpa.com
Contact: Dennis Seigle, Exec.Dir.
State.

Montfort

19223 ■ Trout Unlimited - Harry and Laura Nohr Chapter
c/o David Fritz, Treas.
13528 Old County G
Montfort, WI 53569
Ph: (608)943-8454
E-mail: kayndave@mhtc.net
URL: http://www.nohrtu.org
Contact: David Fritz, Treas.
Local.

Monticello

19224 ■ 101st Airborne Division Association, Old Abe Chapter
c/o William Hustad, Pres.
W 4489 Exeter Crossing Rd.
Monticello, WI 53570
Ph: (608)527-2942
E-mail: wfhus1@tds.net
URL: National Affiliate–www.screamingeagle.org
Contact: William Hustad, Pres.
Local. Affiliated With: 101st Airborne Division Association.

19225 ■ American Legion, Amstutz-Marty Post 256
PO Box 145
Monticello, WI 53570
Ph: (608)325-3486
Fax: (608)745-0179
URL: National Affiliate–www.legion.org
Local. Affiliated With: American Legion.

19226 ■ Wisconsin Chihuahua Rescue
c/o Kim Rauen Eichorst
N7163 County Rd. N.
Monticello, WI 53570-9527
Ph: (608)219-4044
E-mail: ike@wekz.net
URL: http://www.wischirescue.org
Contact: Kim Eichorst, Pres.
Founded: 2000. **Members:** 9. **State Groups:** 1. **State.** Seeks homes for abandoned and surrendered Chihuahuas in WI. **Libraries: Type:** open to the public. **Computer Services:** database • mailing lists • online services. **Formerly:** (2004) Lucky Dogs Chihuahua Rescue of Wisconsin.

19227 ■ Wisconsin Morgan Horse Club
c/o Debbie Fairbanks, Sec.
N7655 County Rd. J
Monticello, WI 53570
Ph: (608)527-6064
E-mail: minglwd@tds.net
URL: http://www.wisconsinmorganhorseclub.org
Contact: Debbie Fairbanks, Sec.
State. Affiliated With: American Morgan Horse Association.

Mosinee

19228 ■ Innovative Minds of Wisconsin
1215 Norway Dr.
Mosinee, WI 54455
Ph: (715)693-3235
E-mail: innovativemindswisconsin@yahoo.com
URL: National Affiliate–www.uiausa.org
Contact: Craig Brown, Contact
State. Represents inventors' organizations and providers of services to inventors. Seeks to facilitate the development of innovation conceived by independent inventors. Provides leadership and support services to inventors and inventors' organizations. **Affiliated With:** United Inventors Association of the U.S.A.

19229 ■ Mosinee Area Chamber of Commerce
301 Main St., Ste.102
Mosinee, WI 54455
Ph: (715)693-4330
Fax: (715)693-9555
E-mail: macoc@mtc.net
URL: http://www.mosineechamber.org
Contact: Michelle Ringhoffer, Exec.Dir.
Membership Dues: business (based on number of full time employees), $110-$605 (annual) • agricultural, $110 (annual) • non-profit, $80 (annual) • associate, $75 (annual) • retired associate, $45 (annual). **Local.** Strives to serve as a resource in order to promote the interests of area businesses and the community of Mosinee. **Committees:** Events. **Subgroups:** Ambassadors. **Publications:** *Chamber News*, monthly. Newsletter.

19230 ■ Mosinee Sportsmen's Alliance
PO Box 71
Mosinee, WI 54455
Ph: (715)693-2111
URL: National Affiliate–www.mynssa.com
Local. Affiliated With: National Skeet Shooting Association.

19231 ■ Plumbers AFL-CIO, LU 434
912 View Dr.
Mosinee, WI 54455
Ph: (715)842-3012
Fax: (715)692-4344
Free: (800)413-0655
E-mail: info@ualocal434.net
URL: http://www.ualocal434.net
Contact: Richard Hintze, Bus.Mgr.
Founded: 1997. **Members:** 1,120. **Staff:** 7. **Local. Affiliated With:** AFL-CIO. **Formerly:** (1998) Plumbers AFL-CIO, LU 557.

19232 ■ United Association of Journeymen and Apprentices of the Plumbing and Pipe Fitting Industry of the United States and Canada - Local Union 434
912 N View Dr.
Mosinee, WI 54455
Ph: (715)692-4341
Fax: (715)692-4344
E-mail: info@ualocal434.org
URL: http://www.ualocal434.org
Contact: Terry Hayden, Business Mgr.
Members: 1,170. **Local. Affiliated With:** United Association of Journeymen and Apprentices of the Plumbing, Pipe Fitting, Sprinkler Fitting Industry of the U.S. and Canada.

Mount Calvary

19233 ■ American Legion, Wisconsin Post 454
c/o Abler Engel
107 Fond Du Lac St.
Mount Calvary, WI 53057
Ph: (608)745-1090
Fax: (608)745-0179
URL: National Affiliate–www.legion.org
Contact: Abler Engel, Contact
Local. Affiliated With: American Legion.

Mount Hope

19234 ■ American Legion, Gray-Wachter-Murphy Post 229
7949 Pleasant Valley Rd.
Mount Hope, WI 53816
Ph: (608)745-1090
Fax: (608)745-0179
URL: National Affiliate–www.legion.org
Local. Affiliated With: American Legion.

Mount Horeb

19235 ■ American Legion, Wisconsin Post 113
c/o Frank E. Malone
102 S 3rd St.
Mount Horeb, WI 53572
Ph: (608)745-1090
Fax: (608)745-0179
URL: National Affiliate–www.legion.org
Contact: Frank E. Malone, Contact
Local. Affiliated With: American Legion.

19236 ■ Greater Madison Young Life
PO Box 323
Mount Horeb, WI 53572
Ph: (608)437-7116
Fax: (608)437-4104
URL: http://sites.younglife.org/sites/madison/default.aspx
Local. Affiliated With: Young Life.

19237 ■ Madison Central City - Young Life
PO Box 323
Mount Horeb, WI 53572
Ph: (608)437-7116
URL: http://sites.younglife.org/sites/MadisonCentralCity/default.aspx
Local. Affiliated With: Young Life.

19238 ■ Mount Horeb Area Chamber of Commerce
c/o AMCORE Bank
100 S 1st St.
PO Box 84
Mount Horeb, WI 53572
Ph: (608)437-5914
Fax: (608)437-1427
Free: (888)765-5929
E-mail: info@trollway.com
URL: http://www.trollway.com
Contact: Melissa Theisen, Exec.Dir.
Membership Dues: business (based on number of employees), $220-$590 • nonprofit organization, $110 • affiliate, $40. **Local.** Promotes business and community development in Mount Horeb, WI. **Committees:** Ambassador Club; Community Promotions; Economic Development; Festival and Event. **Councils:** Retail.

19239 ■ Mt. Horeb Jr. High - Wyldlife
PO Box 323
Mount Horeb, WI 53572
Ph: (608)437-7113
URL: http://sites.younglife.org/sites/Mt.HorebMiddleSchool/default.aspx
Local. Affiliated With: Young Life.

19240 ■ Mt. Horeb Sr. High - Young Life
PO Box 323
Mount Horeb, WI 53572
Ph: (608)437-7113
URL: http://sites.younglife.org/sites/Mt.HorebHighschool/default.aspx
Local. Affiliated With: Young Life.

19241 ■ Newfoundland Club of America (NCA)
c/o Mary L. Price, Treas.
1004 State Hwy. 78
Mount Horeb, WI 53572
Ph: (608)437-4553
E-mail: mlprice@mhtc.net
URL: http://www.newfdogclub.org
Contact: Mary L. Price, Treas.
State. Affiliated With: American Kennel Club.

19242 ■ Sun Prairie Wyldlife
PO Box 323
Mount Horeb, WI 53572
Ph: (608)437-7116
URL: http://sites.younglife.org/sites/SunPrairieWyldlife/default.aspx
Local. Affiliated With: Young Life.

19243 ■ Sun Prairie Young Life
PO Box 323
Mount Horeb, WI 53572
Ph: (608)437-7116
URL: http://sites.younglife.org/sites/sunprairie/default.aspx
Local. Affiliated With: Young Life.

19244 ■ Upper Sugar River Watershed Association (USRWA)
207 E Main St.
PO Box 314
Mount Horeb, WI 53572
Ph: (608)437-7707
E-mail: execdr@usrwa.org
URL: http://www.usrwa.org
Contact: Frank Fetter, Exec.Dir.
Founded: 2000. **Members:** 100. **Membership Dues:** individual, $20 (annual) • family, $35 (annual) • business/municipal, $150 (annual). **Staff:** 1. **Budget:** $50,000. **Local Groups:** 1. **Local.**

19245 ■ West Madison/Verona Young Life
PO Box 323
Mount Horeb, WI 53572
Ph: (608)437-7116
URL: http://sites.younglife.org/sites/WestMadison/default.aspx
Local. Affiliated With: Young Life.

19246 ■ Young Life Heartland Region
PO Box 323
Mount Horeb, WI 53572
Ph: (608)437-7116
Fax: (608)437-4104
URL: http://sites.younglife.org/sites/HeartlandRegion/default.aspx
Regional. Affiliated With: Young Life.

19247 ■ Young Life Mt. Horeb
PO Box 323
Mount Horeb, WI 53572
Ph: (608)437-7113
Fax: (608)437-4104
URL: http://sites.younglife.org/sites/MtHoreb/default.aspx
Local. Affiliated With: Young Life.

Mukwonago

19248 ■ American Ex-Prisoners of War, Milwaukee Barb Wire Chapter
c/o John G. Maher
PO Box 317
Mukwonago, WI 53149-0317
Ph: (262)363-3242
URL: National Affiliate–www.axpow.org
Contact: John G. Maher, Contact
Local. Affiliated With: American Ex-Prisoners of War.

19249 ■ American Legion, Community Post 375
PO Box 152
Mukwonago, WI 53149
Ph: (608)745-1090
Fax: (608)745-0179
URL: National Affiliate–www.legion.org
Local. Affiliated With: American Legion.

19250 ■ Bikers Against Child Abuse, Southeast Wisconsin Chapter
PO Box 297
Mukwonago, WI 53149
Ph: (414)999-2222
E-mail: bacawiinfo@yahoo.com
URL: National Affiliate–www.bacausa.com
Local.

19251 ■ Greater Milwaukee Figure Skating Club
S 90 W27045 Norway Dr.
Mukwonago, WI 53149
E-mail: karens2p@yahoo.com
URL: National Affiliate–www.usfigureskating.org
Contact: Karen Peterson, Contact
Local. Provides programs to encourage participation and achievement in the sport of figure skating on ice. Defines and maintains uniform standards of skating proficiency. Organizes and sponsors competitions and exhibitions for the purpose of stimulating interest in figure skating. **Affiliated With:** United States Figure Skating Association.

19252 ■ Milwaukee Beagle Club
c/o Harry Erbs
S71W32817 Tower Hill Dr.
Mukwonago, WI 53149-9357
URL: National Affiliate–clubs.akc.org
Contact: Harry Erbs, Contact
Local.

19253 ■ Mukwonago Area Chamber of Commerce and Tourism Center
121 Wolf Run, Ste.4
Mukwonago, WI 53149
Ph: (262)363-7758
Fax: (262)363-7730
E-mail: director@mukwonagochamber.org
Contact: Barbara Cowsert, Exec.Dir.
Founded: 1985. **Members:** 329. **Membership Dues:** retail/service, $155 (annual). **Staff:** 2. **Local.** Promotes business and community development in Mukwonago, WI. **Libraries: Type:** open to the public. **Holdings:** 150; articles, books, video recordings. **Subjects:** Mukwonago, tourism information. **Awards:** Business of the Year. **Frequency:** annual. **Type:** recognition • Entrepreneur of the Year. **Frequency:** annual. **Type:** recognition • Executive Director Award. **Type:** recognition • President Award. **Type:** recognition • Volunteer of the Year. **Frequency:** annual. **Type:** recognition. **Computer Services:** database • mailing lists. **Boards:** Executive; Personnel. **Committees:** Economic Development; Fall Fest; Golf Outing; Job Fair; Midnight Magic; Spring Fling. **Affiliated With:** United Way. **Formerly:** (1999) Mukwonago Chamber of Commerce; (2004) Mukwonago Area Chamber of Commerce. **Publications:** *Bear Tracks*, 5/year. Newspaper. **Price:** free. **Circulation:** 10,500. **Advertising:** accepted • *Paw Prints*, bimonthly. Newsletter. **Price:** free. **Circulation:** 370. **Advertising:** accepted. Alternate Formats: online • Directory. **Circulation:** 10,000. **Advertising:** accepted.

19254 ■ Phantom Lake Young Men's Christian Association
S110 W30240 YMCA Camp Rd.
Mukwonago, WI 53149

Ph: (262)363-4386
Fax: (262)363-4351
E-mail: office@phantomlakeymca.com
URL: http://phantomlakeymca.com
Contact: Michael Rule, Exec.Dir.
Founded: 1896. **For-Profit**. **Regional**. Seeks to develop and improve the spiritual, social, mental, and physical well-being of young people and adults. **Publications:** *Phantom Crier*, semiannual. Newsletter.

19255 ■ Southeastern Wisconsin Alpine Team Racing
c/o George E. Loomans
W327 S8068 Oak Tree Dr.
Mukwonago, WI 53149-9246
Ph: (262)363-4951
E-mail: s.w.ateam@voyager.net
Contact: George E. Loomans, Exec.Dir.
Founded: 2001. **Members:** 50. **Staff:** 6. **Local**.

Muscoda

19256 ■ American Legion, Wisconsin Post 85
c/o Leslie J. Lee
PO Box 485
Muscoda, WI 53573
Ph: (608)745-1090
Fax: (608)745-0179
URL: National Affiliate–www.legion.org
Contact: Leslie J. Lee, Contact
Local. **Affiliated With:** American Legion.

19257 ■ Lower Wisconsin State Riverway Board (LWSRB)
PO Box 187
Muscoda, WI 53573
Ph: (608)739-3188
Fax: (608)739-4263
Free: (800)221-3792
E-mail: mark.cupp@lwr.state.wi.us
URL: http://lwr.state.wi.us
Contact: Mark E. Cupp, Exec.Dir.
State.

19258 ■ Ruffed Grouse Society, Southwest Wisconsin Chapter
c/o David J. Duffey
PO Box 595
Muscoda, WI 53573
Ph: (608)588-7613
E-mail: dduffey@rush-creek.com
URL: http://ruffedgrousehunt.tripod.com
Contact: David J. Duffey, Contact
Local. **Affiliated With:** Ruffed Grouse Society.

Muskego

19259 ■ American Legion, Muskego Post 356
PO Box 92
Muskego, WI 53150
Ph: (608)745-1090
Fax: (608)745-0179
URL: National Affiliate–www.legion.org
Local. **Affiliated With:** American Legion.

19260 ■ First Catholic Slovak Ladies Association - Milwaukee Junior Branch 130
7404 W Ohio Ave.
Muskego, WI 53150
Ph: (414)543-8586
URL: National Affiliate–www.fcsla.com
Local. **Affiliated With:** First Catholic Slovak Ladies Association.

19261 ■ First Catholic Slovak Ladies Association - Milwaukee Senior Branch 023
W 173 S 7996 Scenic Dr.
Muskego, WI 53150
Ph: (262)679-1145
URL: National Affiliate–www.fcsla.com
Local. **Affiliated With:** First Catholic Slovak Ladies Association.

19262 ■ Muskego Area Chamber of Commerce
W182 S8200 Racine Ave.
Muskego, WI 53150
Ph: (262)679-2550
Fax: (262)679-5592
E-mail: info@muskego.org
URL: http://www.muskego.org
Contact: Kathy Chiaverotti, Exec.Dir.
Founded: 1957. **Members:** 200. **Staff:** 2. **Budget:** $58,000. **State Groups:** 2. **Local**. Promotes business and community development in Muskego, WI area. **Publications:** Newsletter, bimonthly. **Circulation:** 700. **Advertising:** accepted.

Necedah

19263 ■ American Legion, Coughlin-Sanford Post 277
PO Box 322
Necedah, WI 54646
Ph: (608)745-1090
Fax: (608)745-0179
URL: National Affiliate–www.legion.org
Local. **Affiliated With:** American Legion.

19264 ■ Necedah Lions Club
c/o Duane Weed, Pres.
W10096 Hwy. 80
Necedah, WI 54646
Ph: (608)565-7888
URL: http://www.md27d2.org
Contact: Duane Weed, Pres.
Local. **Affiliated With:** Lions Clubs International.

Neenah

19265 ■ American Legion, Hawley-Dieckhoff Post 33
PO Box 632
Neenah, WI 54957
Ph: (608)745-1090
Fax: (608)745-0179
URL: National Affiliate–www.legion.org
Local. **Affiliated With:** American Legion.

19266 ■ American Red Cross, Neenah-Menasha Chapter
181 E North Water St., Ste.204
Neenah, WI 54956
Ph: (920)722-2871
Fax: (920)722-2146
URL: http://www.nmredcross.com
Local.

19267 ■ American Statistical Association, Milwaukee Chapter
c/o Eric T. Ashbrenner
PO Box 349
Neenah, WI 54957-0349
Ph: (920)721-6845
E-mail: eashbren@kcc.com
URL: National Affiliate–www.amstat.org
Contact: Eric T. Ashbrenner, Contact
Local. Promotes statistical practice, applications and research. Works for the improvement of statistical education at all levels. Seeks opportunities to advance the statistics profession. **Affiliated With:** American Statistical Association.

19268 ■ Appleton Young Life
991 Ehlers Rd.
Neenah, WI 54956
Ph: (920)722-2320
URL: http://sites.younglife.org/sites/Appleton/default.aspx
Contact: Noelle Coenen, Leader
Local. **Affiliated With:** Young Life.

19269 ■ Briard Club of America (BCA)
c/o Bill Weber, Pres.
7455 Sunwood Dr.
Neenah, WI 54956
Ph: (920)967-1785
E-mail: bweber@new.rr.com
URL: http://www.briardclubofamerica.org
Contact: Bill Weber, Pres.
State. **Affiliated With:** American Kennel Club.

19270 ■ Fox Valley WyldLife
991 Ehlers Rd.
Neenah, WI 54956
Ph: (920)722-2320
URL: http://sites.younglife.org/sites/FoxValleyWyldLife/default.aspx
Local. **Affiliated With:** Young Life.

19271 ■ Fox Valley Young Life
991 Ehlers Rd.
Neenah, WI 54956
Ph: (920)722-2320
Fax: (920)722-2776
E-mail: ylfoxvalley@sbcglobal.net
URL: http://sites.younglife.org/sites/FoxValley/default.aspx
Contact: Katie Lullo, Area Dir.
Local. **Affiliated With:** Young Life.

19272 ■ Hearing Loss Association of America, Wisconsin
c/o Julie Olson, Pres.
970 Manor Dr., Apt. 69
Neenah, WI 54956-5106
Ph: (920)969-3857
E-mail: julieo@athenet.net
URL: National Affiliate–www.hearingloss.org
Contact: Julie Olson, Pres.
State. Promotes understanding of the nature, causes, complications and remedies of hearing loss. Raises public awareness of the special needs of people who are hard of hearing through information, education, advocacy and support. **Affiliated With:** Hearing Loss Association of America.

19273 ■ Military Order of the Purple Heart - Winnebagoland Chapter No. 162 (MOPH)
742 Millbrook Dr.
Neenah, WI 54956
Ph: (920)725-2780
E-mail: leedar@athenet.net
URL: National Affiliate–www.purpleheart.org
Contact: LeRoy E. Schuff, Adj.
Local. **Affiliated With:** Military Order of the Purple Heart of the United States of America.

19274 ■ Neenah Young Life
991 Ehlers Rd.
Neenah, WI 54956
Ph: (920)722-2320
URL: http://sites.younglife.org/sites/Neenah/default.aspx
Contact: Sue Bere, Contact
Local. **Affiliated With:** Young Life.

19275 ■ Society of Consumer Affairs Professionals in Business, Wisconsin Chapter
c/o Jean Herres, Program Dir.
Alta Resources
One Neenah Ctr.
Neenah, WI 54956
Ph: (920)751-5800
Fax: (920)751-5850
URL: National Affiliate–www.socap.org
Contact: Jean Herres, Program Dir.
State. Works to provide the tools needed for corporations to reach their goal of maximum customer loyalty, excellent customer service and value-added innovations. **Affiliated With:** Society of Consumer Affairs Professionals in Business.

19276 ■ USA Diving - Fox Valley Dive Team
1122 Nuthatch Ln.
Neenah, WI 54956
Ph: (920)725-0316
E-mail: tfoulks@new.rr.com
URL: National Affiliate–www.usdiving.org
Contact: Tim Foulks, Contact
Local. Affiliated With: USA Diving.

19277 ■ Wisconsin 4WD Association (W4WDA)
203 Gruenwald Ave.
Neenah, WI 54956
Ph: (920)722-3777
E-mail: 9erscruiser@centurytel.net
URL: http://www.w4wda.org
Contact: Chris Hannis, Pres.
State. Affiliated With: United Four-Wheel Drive Associations.

19278 ■ Wisconsin Ice Arena Management Association
700 E Shady Ln.
Neenah, WI 54956
Ph: (920)882-0807
Fax: (920)882-0807
E-mail: randd3@tds.net
URL: http://wiama.com
Contact: Nancy Hacker, Sec.-Treas.
Members: 125. **State. Conventions/Meetings:** annual convention.

19279 ■ Wisconsin Shoreline Skippers No. 102
c/o Jeff Hallett
408 Peckham St.
Neenah, WI 54956
Ph: (920)720-9094
URL: http://home.new.rr.com/wss
Contact: Jeff Hallett, Contact
State.

Neillsville

19280 ■ Neillsville Area Chamber of Commerce (NACC)
PO Box 52
Neillsville, WI 54456-0052
Ph: (715)743-6444
Fax: (715)743-8262
E-mail: nacc@tds.net
URL: http://www.neillsville.org
Contact: Cindy Schwanz, Contact
Members: 103. **Membership Dues:** business (based on number of employees including owners), $100-$250 (annual) • church, service club, individual, $30 (annual) • new, $50. **Staff:** 1. **Local.** Retail and business owners; clubs and organizations. Promotes business and community development in the Neillsville, WI area. Conducts charitable activities. Sponsors annual Harvest Festival. **Programs:** Gift Certificate. **Publications:** *Teamwork for a Prosperous Community*, monthly. Newsletter. **Price:** free. **Conventions/Meetings:** quarterly Chamber Dinner Meeting • annual Golf Outing and Hole-in-One Contest - competition • annual Howdy Neighbor Banquet • annual June Dairy Breakfast - always in June • annual Neillsville Winter Carnival - festival - always in winter.

19281 ■ Ruffed Grouse Society, West Central Wisconsin Chapter
c/o Frank Vazquez
N5020 Sidney Ave.
Neillsville, WI 54456
Ph: (715)743-4289
URL: National Affiliate–www.ruffedgrousesociety.org
Contact: Frank Vazquez, Contact
Local. Affiliated With: Ruffed Grouse Society.

Nekoosa

19282 ■ American Legion, Wisconsin Post 322
c/o James Knutson
1023 W 3rd St.
Nekoosa, WI 54457
Ph: (608)745-1090
Fax: (608)745-0179
URL: National Affiliate–www.legion.org
Contact: James Knutson, Contact
Local. Affiliated With: American Legion.

19283 ■ Sons of Norway, Elvedal Lodge 5-556
c/o Thomas M. Boudreau, Pres.
8845 Holz Ln.
Nekoosa, WI 54457
Ph: (715)886-4514
E-mail: tsboud@hotmail.com
URL: National Affiliate–www.sofn.com
Contact: Thomas M. Boudreau, Pres.
Local. Affiliated With: Sons of Norway.

Neosho

19284 ■ Neosho-Rubicon Lions Club
PO Box 146
Neosho, WI 53059
Ph: (262)224-1309
E-mail: qualityrocker@hotmail.com
URL: http://www.lionwap.org/neoshorubiconwi
Contact: Keith Neu, Sec.
Local. Affiliated With: Lions Clubs International.

New Auburn

19285 ■ American Legion, Slining-Caulkins Post 267
10040 270th Ave.
New Auburn, WI 54757
Ph: (608)745-1090
Fax: (608)745-0179
URL: National Affiliate–www.legion.org
Local. Affiliated With: American Legion.

New Berlin

19286 ■ Electrical Maintenance Engineers of Milwaukee
4126 S Katherine Dr.
New Berlin, WI 53151
Ph: (262)789-9025
Local.

19287 ■ German Shepherd Dog Club of Wisconsin (GSDC)
c/o Nancy Bertsch, Board Member
13825 W Pleasant View Dr.
New Berlin, WI 53151
Ph: (262)782-5238
E-mail: karenlacosse@aol.com
URL: http://www.gsdcw.com
Contact: Nancy Bertsch, Board Member
State.

19288 ■ Healthcare Financial Management Association, Wisconsin Chapter
3000 S 132nd St.
New Berlin, WI 53151
Ph: (608)751-5651
E-mail: cmay@mhsjvl.org
URL: http://www.hfmawi.com
Contact: Carol J. May CPA, Pres.
State. Provides education, analysis and guidance to healthcare finance professionals. Helps members and other individuals in advancing the financial management of health care and in improving the business performance of organizations serving the healthcare field. **Affiliated With:** Healthcare Financial Management Association.

19289 ■ IEEE Milwaukee Section
13125 W Wilbur Dr.
New Berlin, WI 53151
Ph: (262)547-0121
E-mail: sec.milwaukee@ieee.org
URL: http://ewh.ieee.org/r4/milwaukee
Contact: Bill Henning, Contact
Local. Engineers and scientists in electrical engineering, electronics, and allied fields. Promotes creating, developing, integrating, sharing, and applying knowledge about electro and information technologies and sciences for the benefit of humanity and the profession. Conducts lectures on current engineering and scientific topics.

19290 ■ International Union of Bricklayers and Allied Craftworkers, AFL-CIO-CLC Wisconsin District Council
PO Box 510617
New Berlin, WI 53151
Ph: (262)827-4080
Fax: (262)827-4090
Free: (800)862-2294
E-mail: bacoffice@bacwi.org
URL: http://www.bacwi.org
Contact: Timothy Inlenfeld, Contact
Members: 3,587. **State. Affiliated With:** International Union of Bricklayers and Allied Craftworkers.

19291 ■ Milwaukee Astronomical Society
MAS Observatory
18850 W Observatory Rd.
New Berlin, WI 53146
Ph: (414)542-9071
E-mail: masmemb@aol.com
URL: http://www.milwaukeeastro.org
Contact: Neil Simmons, Contact
Local. Promotes the science of astronomy. Works to encourage and coordinate activities of amateur astronomical societies. Fosters observational and computational work and craftsmanship in various fields of astronomy. **Affiliated With:** Astronomical League.

19292 ■ Milwaukee Rookie Cricket Club
14826 W Hidden Creek Ct.
New Berlin, WI 53151
URL: http://www.usaca.org/Clubs.htm
Contact: Ajith Wijenayake, Contact
Local.

19293 ■ New Berlin Chamber of Commerce and Visitors Bureau (NBCC/VB)
2140 S Calhoun Rd.
New Berlin, WI 53151
Ph: (262)786-5280
Fax: (262)786-9165
E-mail: nbcadmin@nb-chamber.org
URL: http://www.nb-chamber.org
Contact: Jeff Seidl, Pres.
Founded: 1959. **Membership Dues:** business, $150 (annual) • non-profit, $50 (annual). **Local.** Promotes business and community development in New Berlin, WI. **Publications:** *Hilites*, periodic. Newsletter.

19294 ■ New Berlin Industrial Lions Club
PO Box 510646
New Berlin, WI 53151-0646
Ph: (262)251-1782
E-mail: louwee@execpc.com
URL: http://wilion.net/md27a1/nbi
Contact: Bob Fellenz, Pres.
Local. Affiliated With: Lions Clubs International.

19295 ■ New Berlin Lions Club
PO Box 510254
New Berlin, WI 53151-0024
Ph: (262)784-0352
E-mail: atatera@wi.rr.com
URL: http://www.wilions.org/newberlin
Contact: Al Tatera, Pres.
Local. Affiliated With: Lions Clubs International.

19296 ■ New Berlin Table Tennis Club
Hickory Grove Ctr.
Sunny Slope and Cleveland Ave.
New Berlin, WI 53151
Ph: (262)782-0126
E-mail: donw@execpc.com
URL: National Affiliate–www.usatt.org
Contact: Donald Winze, Contact
Local. Affiliated With: U.S.A. Table Tennis.

19297 ■ Pheasants Forever Southeastern Wisconsin Chapter
13617 W Milton Ct.
New Berlin, WI 53151
Ph: (262)789-0838
E-mail: dstrube@sewipf.org
URL: http://sewipf.org
Contact: Dallas Strube, Pres.
Local. Affiliated With: Pheasants Forever.

19298 ■ Wisconsin Association of Legal Administrators
c/o Michele A. Dretzka
Schober, Schober & Mitchell, S.C.
16845 W Cleveland Ave.
New Berlin, WI 53151
Ph: (262)785-1820
URL: http://www.wi-ala.org
Contact: Michele A. Dretzka, Contact
State. Affiliated With: Association of Legal Administrators.

19299 ■ Wisconsin Credit Association (WCA)
PO Box 510157
New Berlin, WI 53151-0157
Ph: (262)827-2880
Fax: (262)827-2899
E-mail: info@wcacredit.org
URL: http://www.nacmwi.org
Contact: Darryl M. Rowinski CCE, Pres./COO
State. Affiliated With: National Association of Credit Management. **Formerly:** (2005) National Association of Credit Management Wisconsin, Madison.

19300 ■ Wisconsin Mycological Society (WMS)
c/o Peter L. Vachuska
5315 S Sunnyslope Rd.
New Berlin, WI 53151-8077
E-mail: pvachusk@nconnect.net
URL: http://www.geocities.com/Yosemite/Trails/7331
Contact: Peter L. Vachuska, Contact
State. Amateur and professional mycologists, mycophagists, devotees of mushroom lore, students, and botanists. Promotes amateur mycology (the study of fungi, such as mushrooms, puffballs, molds, rusts, and smuts). **Affiliated With:** North American Mycological Association.

19301 ■ Wisconsin Woodland Owners Association, Phoenix Falls Chapter
c/o Randy Cooper, Chm.
3895 S Woelfel Rd.
New Berlin, WI 53146-3123
Ph: (262)542-7906
E-mail: rkcooper@genevaonline.com
URL: http://www.wisconsinwoodlands.org
Contact: Randy Cooper, Chm.
Local. Affiliated With: Wisconsin Woodland Owners Association.

New Glarus

19302 ■ American Legion, Stuessy-Kuenzi Post 141
PO Box 682
New Glarus, WI 53574
Ph: (608)745-1090
Fax: (608)745-0179
URL: National Affiliate–www.legion.org
Local. Affiliated With: American Legion.

19303 ■ Friends of the New Glarus Public Library
c/o Denise Anton Wright, Dir.
PO Box 35
New Glarus, WI 53574-0035
Ph: (608)527-2003
Fax: (608)527-5126
E-mail: ngpl@scls.lib.wi.us
URL: http://www.scls.lib.wi.us/ngl/friends.html
Contact: Dennis Anton Wright, Dir.
Local.

19304 ■ New Glarus Chamber of Commerce
418 Railroad St.
PO Box 713
New Glarus, WI 53574-0713
Ph: (608)527-2095
Fax: (608)527-4991
Free: (800)527-6838
E-mail: info@swisstown.com
URL: http://www.swisstown.com
Contact: Susie Weiss, Office Mgr.
Local. Promotes business and community development in New Glarus, WI. **Publications:** *America's Little Switzerland*, weekly. Brochure. **Price:** free. **Conventions/Meetings:** monthly meeting - always second Monday.

19305 ■ Society of Otorhinolaryngology and Head/Neck Nurses - Wisconsin Chapter
PO Box 250
New Glarus, WI 53574
Ph: (608)262-8016
Fax: (608)263-6199
E-mail: thayer@surgery.wisc.edu
URL: National Affiliate–www.sohnnurse.com
Contact: Sherrill J. Thayer MS, Contact
State. Advances the professional growth and development of nurses dedicated to the specialty of Otorhinolaryngology nursing through education and research. Promotes innovations in practice, research and healthcare policy initiatives. **Affiliated With:** Society of Otorhinolaryngology and Head/Neck Nurses.

19306 ■ Wisconsin Beef Improvement Association (WBIA)
PO Box 955
New Glarus, WI 53574
Ph: (608)527-5747
Fax: (608)527-3010
Free: (800)297-5747
E-mail: wisconsinbeefbulls@utelco.tds.net
URL: http://wisconsinbeef.com
Contact: John W. Freitag, Exec.Dir.
Founded: 1956. **Members:** 80. **Membership Dues:** $20 (annual). **Staff:** 1. **State. Formerly:** (2005) Wisconsin Beef Improvement.

New Holstein

19307 ■ Mid-Shores Home Builders Association
PO Box 125
New Holstein, WI 53061-0125
URL: National Affiliate–www.nahb.org
Contact: Tena Hartwig, Contact
Local. Single and multifamily home builders, commercial builders, and others associated with the building industry. **Affiliated With:** National Association of Home Builders.

19308 ■ New Holstein Area Chamber of Commerce
PO Box 17
New Holstein, WI 53061
Ph: (920)898-9095
E-mail: nhsecretary@newholstein.org
URL: http://www.newholstein.org
Contact: Samantha Ploor, Sec.
Local.

19309 ■ Wisconsin Quarter Horse Association (WQHA)
W2056 Tecumseh Rd.
New Holstein, WI 53061
E-mail: timz@wqha.com
URL: http://www.wqha.com
Contact: Ron Miller, Pres.
State. Affiliated With: American Quarter Horse Association.

New Lisbon

19310 ■ American Legion, D. W. K. Post 110
PO Box 113
New Lisbon, WI 53950
Ph: (608)745-1090
Fax: (608)745-0179
URL: National Affiliate–www.legion.org
Local. Affiliated With: American Legion.

19311 ■ New Lisbon Area Chamber of Commerce
PO Box 79
New Lisbon, WI 53950
Ph: (608)562-3555
Fax: (608)562-5625
E-mail: nlchambr@mwt.net
URL: http://www.homestead.com/newlisbonchamber
Contact: Tina Brounacker, Exec.Sec.
Local. Strives to promote economy and provide leadership that could influence public policy for the benefit of members. **Publications:** Newsletter.

19312 ■ New Lisbon Lions Club
c/o Levine Wetley, Pres.
218 S Leer St.
New Lisbon, WI 53950
Ph: (608)562-3663
URL: http://www.md27d2.org
Contact: Levine Wetley, Pres.
Local. Affiliated With: Lions Clubs International.

New London

19313 ■ American Legion, Norris-Spencer Post 263
PO Box 42
New London, WI 54961
Ph: (608)745-1090
Fax: (608)745-0179
URL: National Affiliate–www.legion.org
Local. Affiliated With: American Legion.

19314 ■ English Springer Spaniel Field Trial Association (ESSFTA)
c/o Mary Parszewski, Corresponding Sec.
E9538 Kanaman Rd.
New London, WI 54961
E-mail: admin@essfta.org
URL: http://www.essfta.org
Contact: Dean Reinke, Pres.
Local. Affiliated With: American Kennel Club.

19315 ■ New London Area Chamber of Commerce (NLACC)
301 E Beacon Ave.
New London, WI 54961
Ph: (920)982-5822
Fax: (920)982-6344
E-mail: chamber@newlondonwi.org
URL: http://www.newlondonchamber.com
Contact: Deborah Lederhaus, Exec.Dir.
Founded: 1932. **Members:** 150. **Staff:** 2. **Budget:** $40,000. **State Groups:** 3. **Local.** Represents businesses and individuals organized to promote economic and community development in the New London, WI area. **Awards:** Ambassador of the Year Award. **Frequency:** annual. **Type:** recognition. **Recipient:** to ambassadors for recruiting new members and attending meeting and chamber events • Business and Industry Awards. **Frequency:** annual. **Type:** recognition • Chamber Service Award. **Frequency:**

annual. **Type:** recognition. **Recipient:** to individuals for optimum service given to the chamber • Community Service Award. **Frequency:** annual. **Type:** recognition. **Recipient:** for service club, civic organization or individual with sincere service for the needy, handicapped, and youth in the community • Excellence in Industry Award. **Frequency:** annual. **Type:** recognition. **Recipient:** to individuals for showing innovation in the field of operation • New Business of the Year Award. **Frequency:** annual. **Type:** recognition. **Recipient:** to a business less than two years old that shows longevity • President's Award. **Frequency:** annual. **Type:** recognition. **Recipient:** to individuals for significant contribution to the community • Quality of Life Award. **Frequency:** annual. **Type:** recognition. **Recipient:** for service club, civic organization, business or individual who helps to improve New London. **Committees:** Ambassador/ Membership; Executive; Festival; Finance. **Councils:** Business and Industry; Community Development Corporation; Public Relations; Revitalization. **Affiliated With:** U.S. Chamber of Commerce. **Publications:** *Everybody's Business*, monthly. Newsletter. **Circulation:** 225. **Advertising:** accepted. Alternate Formats: CD-ROM. **Conventions/Meetings:** annual Expo - trade show (exhibits) • bimonthly Meet Your Business Neighbors - meeting • bimonthly workshop.

19316 ■ United Way of New London
500 W Washington St.
New London, WI 54961-1969
Ph: (920)982-4089
URL: National Affiliate–national.unitedway.org
Local. Affiliated With: United Way of America.

New Richmond

19317 ■ Catholics United for the Faith - Christ the King Chapter
c/o Theresa Livingston
Rte. 2, Box 117
New Richmond, WI 54017-5703
Ph: (612)280-8991
E-mail: acebilling@integrity.com
URL: National Affiliate–www.cuf.org
Contact: Theresa Livingston, Contact
Local.

19318 ■ National Alliance for the Mentally Ill - St. Croix
c/o Therese Wick
1140 Circle Pine Dr.
New Richmond, WI 54017
Ph: (715)246-7818
E-mail: tjwick@pressenter.com
URL: http://www.namiwisconsin.org/library/directory
Contact: Therese Wick, Contact
Local. Strives to improve the quality of life of children and adults with severe mental illness through support, education, research and advocacy. **Affiliated With:** National Alliance for the Mentally Ill.

19319 ■ National Association of Home Builders of the U.S., St. Croix Valley Home Builders Association
c/o Jill Larson, Exec. Officer
150 W 1st St., Ste.110
New Richmond, WI 54017
Ph: (715)246-5829
Fax: (715)246-5879
E-mail: info@scvhba.com
URL: http://www.scvhba.com
Contact: Jeff Hielkema, Pres.
Local. Represents single and multifamily home builders, commercial builders, and others associated with the building industry. **Affiliated With:** National Association of Home Builders.

19320 ■ New Richmond Area Chamber of Commerce and Visitors Bureau
235 S Knowles Ave.
New Richmond, WI 54017
Ph: (715)246-2900
Fax: (715)246-7100
Free: (800)654-6380
E-mail: info@newrichmondchamber.com
URL: http://www.newrichmondchamber.com
Contact: Russ Korpela, Exec.Dir.
Founded: 1947. **Members:** 329. **Membership Dues:** community club, service club, church, $78 • retired business person, community booster (no business connections), $50 • hospital, nursing home, school, government, $335 • financial institution, professional, retail trade and service, $232. **Staff:** 2. **Budget:** $174,000. **Regional Groups:** 1. **State Groups:** 2. **Local Groups:** 4. **Local.** Promotes economic and community development in the New Richmond, WI area. Conducts business, industry, community, and education partnership program. Sponsors annual Park Art Fair and Fun Festival. **Committees:** Events; Fun Fest. **Affiliated With:** U.S. Chamber of Commerce. **Formerly:** (2000) New Richmond Area Chamber of Commerce. **Publications:** *Chamber Connection*, monthly. Newsletter. **Price:** included in membership dues. **Circulation:** 450. **Advertising:** accepted. Alternate Formats: online. **Conventions/ Meetings:** monthly Ambassadors - meeting, welcomes new businesses; obtains new membership - every 2nd Wednesday (noon) • bimonthly BICEP: Business, Industry, Community, Education, Parents - meeting, exchange of knowledge and resources between schools, business, and industry - every 3rd Thursday of January, March, May, July, September, and November, 7:15 AM • monthly Business Recruitment Team - meeting - every 4th Tuesday, 8:00 AM • monthly Community Planning and Resource: CPR - Reviving the Business Community - meeting - every 2nd Tuesday, 8:00 AM.

19321 ■ St. Croix Valley Angus Association
c/o Karol Simon, Sec.-Treas.
1492 Hwy. 65
New Richmond, WI 54017
Ph: (715)246-4784
E-mail: kkangusfarm@frontiernet.net
URL: National Affiliate–www.angus.org
Contact: Brad Fagerland, Pres.
Local. Affiliated With: American Angus Association.

Niagara

19322 ■ American Legion, Cretton-Tutas Post 136
532 Washington Ave.
Niagara, WI 54151
Ph: (608)745-1090
Fax: (608)745-0179
URL: National Affiliate–www.legion.org
Local. Affiliated With: American Legion.

North Fond Du Lac

19323 ■ American Legion, Dreier-Bushee-Vanderboom Post 156
812 Wisconsin Ave.
North Fond Du Lac, WI 54937
Ph: (608)745-1090
Fax: (608)745-0179
URL: National Affiliate–www.legion.org
Local. Affiliated With: American Legion.

North Freedom

19324 ■ American Legion, Freedom Post 172
106 E Walnut St.
North Freedom, WI 53951
Ph: (608)745-1090
Fax: (608)745-0179
URL: National Affiliate–www.legion.org
Local. Affiliated With: American Legion.

North Prairie

19325 ■ Greater Milwaukee St. Bernard Club (GMSBC)
c/o Penny Janz
33400 Red Fox Way
North Prairie, WI 53153
Ph: (262)392-2852
Fax: (262)392-2852
E-mail: pmjanz@globaldialog.com
URL: National Affiliate–www.akc.org
Contact: Penny Janz, Sec.
Founded: 1966. **Members:** 30. **Membership Dues:** first family, $15 (annual) • each additional, $5 (annual). **Local.** Individuals interested in St. Bernard dogs. Promotes the betterment of the breed; conducts licensed specialty show. **Libraries: Type:** not open to the public. **Affiliated With:** American Kennel Club; Saint Bernard Club of America. **Publications:** *Snoop*, bimonthly. Bulletin. **Price:** $10.00 per year; free to members. **Conventions/Meetings:** bimonthly dinner - 2nd Saturday of odd numbered months.

Norwalk

19326 ■ American Legion, Norwalk Memorial Post 438
PO Box 98
Norwalk, WI 54648
Ph: (608)745-1090
Fax: (608)745-0179
URL: National Affiliate–www.legion.org
Local. Affiliated With: American Legion.

19327 ■ Norwalk Lions Club - Wisconsin
c/o Greg Weibel, Pres.
17556 Lasso Ave.
Norwalk, WI 54648
Ph: (608)823-7805
URL: http://www.md27d2.org
Contact: Greg Weibel, Pres.
Local. Affiliated With: Lions Clubs International.

Oak Creek

19328 ■ American Association for Medical Transcription, Greater Milwaukee Chapter
c/o Denise Luke, Pres.
8170 S Wilding Dr.
Oak Creek, WI 53154
E-mail: deeluke824@hotmail.com
URL: http://www.aamt.org/ca/milwaukee
Contact: Denise Luke, Pres.
Local. Works to represent and advance the profession of medical transcription and its practitioners. **Affiliated With:** American Association for Medical Transcription.

19329 ■ American Legion, Oelschlaeger-Dallmann Post 434
9327 S Shepard Ave.
Oak Creek, WI 53154
Ph: (608)745-1090
Fax: (608)745-0179
URL: National Affiliate–www.legion.org
Local. Affiliated With: American Legion.

19330 ■ American Truck Historical Society, Beer City Chapter
c/o Dan Durand
10030 S McGraw Dr.
Oak Creek, WI 53154
Ph: (414)762-0448
URL: National Affiliate–www.aths.org
Contact: Dan Durand, Contact
Local.

19331 ■ AMVETS, Oak Creek Post 60
Classic Lanes Oak Creek
7501 S Howell Ave.
Oak Creek, WI 53154

Ph: (414)764-3637
E-mail: jeansr@wans.net
URL: http://www.amvets-wi.org/post60
Contact: Jean Ruka, Commander
Local. Affiliated With: AMVETS - American Veterans.

19332 ■ Midwest Twisters Gymnastics Booster Club
600 E Rawson Ave.
Oak Creek, WI 53154-1512
Ph: (414)764-6540
Fax: (414)764-3199
URL: http://www.midwesttwisters.com
Contact: Rick Nelson, Owner
Founded: 1983. **Regional.** Provides a complete range of instructional classes, like gymnastics and cheerleading, and a large variety of special events.

19333 ■ National Association of Church Business Administrators, Wisconsin Chapter
c/o Richard J. McMaster
Harvest Community Church
6612 S Howell Ave.
Oak Creek, WI 53154-1135
Ph: (414)571-5040
Fax: (414)571-5064
E-mail: office@harvestcommunity.org
URL: http://www.harvestcommunity.org
Contact: Ms. Patty Sneesty, Admin. Asst.
State. Business administrators and managers employed by local churches or institutions of the Christian church. Provides a program of study, service, fellowship, training, information exchange, and problem discussion. **Affiliated With:** National Association of Church Business Administration.

19334 ■ Racine County Line Rifle Club
PO Box 71
Oak Creek, WI 53154
Ph: (414)762-7774
E-mail: rclrc@juno.com
URL: National Affiliate–www.mynssa.com
Local. Affiliated With: National Skeet Shooting Association.

19335 ■ South Eastern Chamber United in Business (SEACUB)
8580 S Howell Ave.
Oak Creek, WI 53154
Ph: (414)768-5845
Fax: (414)570-0461
E-mail: jenny@secub.com
URL: National Affiliate–www.uschamber.com
Contact: Jenny Polachowski, Exec.Dir.
Founded: 1959. **Local.** Promotes business and community development in Oak Creek, WI. Sponsors business and industry fair. **Affiliated With:** U.S. Chamber of Commerce. **Publications:** Newsletter, monthly. **Conventions/Meetings:** periodic Business After Hours - meeting • annual Health Fair - trade show.

19336 ■ Wisconsin Athletic Trainers' Association, Southeast
c/o Jeff Sischo
3121 E Diane Dr.
Oak Creek, WI 53154
Ph: (414)852-4022
Fax: (414)570-1451
E-mail: jsischo@wi.rr.com
URL: http://www.watainc.org
Contact: Jeff Sischo, Contact
Local. Affiliated With: National Athletic Trainers' Association.

Oakfield

19337 ■ Wisconsin Suffolk Sheep Association
c/o Etta J. Held, Sec.-Treas.
PO Box 56
Oakfield, WI 53065
Ph: (920)583-3084
URL: National Affiliate–www.u-s-s-a.org
Contact: Etta J. Held, Sec.-Treas.
State. Affiliated With: United Suffolk Sheep Association.

Oconomowoc

19338 ■ American Legion, Wisconsin Post 91
c/o Edwin L. Jones
128 W Wisconsin Ave.
Oconomowoc, WI 53066
Ph: (608)745-1090
Fax: (608)745-0179
URL: National Affiliate–www.legion.org
Contact: Edwin L. Jones, Contact
Local. Affiliated With: American Legion.

19339 ■ Oconomowoc Area Chamber of Commerce (OACC)
152 E Wisconsin Ave.
Oconomowoc, WI 53066
Ph: (262)567-2666
Fax: (262)567-3477
E-mail: chamber@oconomowoc.org
URL: http://www.oconomowoc.org
Contact: Stephanie Phillips, Exec.Dir.
Founded: 1969. **Members:** 300. **Membership Dues:** business (based on number of full time employees), $196-$1,185 (annual) • individual, civic, independent realtor, $103 (annual). **Staff:** 3. **Budget:** $95,000. **State Groups:** 2. **Local.** Promotes business and community development in the Oconomowoc, WI area. Offers numerous networking and advertising opportunities. **Programs:** Gift Certificate; Leadership. **Affiliated With:** U.S. Chamber of Commerce. **Publications:** *Oconomowoc Talk*, monthly. Newsletter. **Advertising:** accepted • *Oconomowoc Visitor's Guide*, annual. Booklet • Newsletter, periodic • Membership Directory. **Conventions/Meetings:** annual meeting • seminar, educational.

19340 ■ Oconomowoc Junior Woman's Club
PO Box 946
Oconomowoc, WI 53066-0946
Ph: (262)569-0074
E-mail: labracke@sbcglobal.net
URL: http://www.ojwc.org
Founded: 1971. **Members:** 23. **Membership Dues:** $35 (annual). **Local. Publications:** *OJWC Newsletter*, monthly. Features GFWC, club news, activities. **Price:** free via email. **Advertising:** accepted. Alternate Formats: online. **Conventions/Meetings:** monthly General Meetings - every first Tuesday.

19341 ■ Oconomowoc Lions Club
N54 W35718 Hill Rd.
Oconomowoc, WI 53066-3260
Ph: (262)567-3861
E-mail: dwille12@yahoo.com
URL: http://www.orgsites.com/wi/oconomowoclionsclub
Contact: Dan Wille, Pres.
Local. Affiliated With: Lions Clubs International.

19342 ■ Saluki Club of America (SCOA)
1203 N Coolidge Rd.
Oconomowoc, WI 53066
Ph: (920)474-4765
E-mail: secretary@salukiclub.org
URL: http://www.salukiclub.org
Contact: Lois-Ann Snyder, Sec.
Regional. Affiliated With: American Kennel Club.

19343 ■ Town and Country Beagle Club
c/o Mary Ellen Keeling
W2101 Washington Rd.
Oconomowoc, WI 53066-9536
URL: National Affiliate–clubs.akc.org
Contact: Mary Ellen Keeling, Contact
Local.

19344 ■ United States Naval Sea Cadet Corps - Battleship Wisconsin Division
WING Armory
1215 Wall St.
Oconomowoc, WI 53066
E-mail: stevenpotter@charter.net
URL: http://dolphin.seacadets.org/US_units/UnitDetails.asp?UnitID=091BAS
Contact: LTJG Steven Potter NSCC, Commanding Officer
Membership Dues: regular (initial sign up fee, after that there is an annual fee of $75), $250 (annual). **State.** Works to instill good citizenship and patriotism in youth. Encourages qualities such as personal neatness, loyalty, obedience, dependability, and responsibility to others. Offers courses in physical fitness and military drill, first aid, water safety, basic seamanship, and naval history and traditions. **Affiliated With:** Naval Sea Cadet Corps.

19345 ■ USA Weightlifting - Town and Country Lifting Club
c/o Sal Sorrentino
W360 N9049 Brown St.
Oconomowoc, WI 53066-9605
Ph: (920)474-4469
URL: National Affiliate–www.usaweightlifting.org
Contact: Sal Sorrentino, Contact
Local. Affiliated With: USA Weightlifting.

19346 ■ Waukesha District Nurses Association - No. 16
N53W35748 Hillview Ct.
Oconomowoc, WI 53066
Ph: (262)567-7131
E-mail: ppborg@core.com
URL: http://www.wisconsinnurses.org
Contact: Pat Borgman, Pres.
Local. Works to advance the nursing profession. Seeks to meet the needs of nurses and health care consumers. Fosters high standards of nursing practice. Promotes the economic and general welfare of nurses in the workplace. **Affiliated With:** American Nurses Association; Wisconsin Nurses' Association.

Oconto

19347 ■ American Legion, Jones-Modrow-Young Post 74
532 Jefferson St.
Oconto, WI 54153
Ph: (414)834-4619
Fax: (608)745-0179
URL: National Affiliate–www.legion.org
Local. Affiliated With: American Legion.

19348 ■ Oconto Area Chamber of Commerce (OACC)
PO Box 174
110 Brazeau Ave.
Oconto, WI 54153
Ph: (920)834-6254
Fax: (920)834-6254
E-mail: ocontocmbr@aol.com
Contact: Nancy Rhode, Sec.
Founded: 1917. **Members:** 120. **Budget:** $5,000. **Local.** Promotes business and community development in the Oconto, WI area. **Publications:** Newsletter, monthly. **Circulation:** 200.

19349 ■ Oconto Elementary School Parent Teacher Organization
c/o Sheryl Hendricks
810 Scherer Ave.
Oconto, WI 54153-1110
Local.

Oconto Falls

19350 ■ American Legion, Eick-Sankey Post 302
PO Box 15
Oconto Falls, WI 54154

Ph: (608)745-1090
Fax: (608)745-0179
URL: National Affiliate–www.legion.org
Local. Affiliated With: American Legion.

19351 ■ Oconto Falls Area Chamber of Commerce
251 N Main St.
Oconto Falls, WI 54154
Ph: (920)846-8306
Contact: Austin Caves, Pres.
Local.

19352 ■ Oconto Falls Lions Club
PO Box 145
Oconto Falls, WI 54154
Ph: (920)842-4048
E-mail: info@ocontofallslions.com
URL: http://www.ocontofallslions.com
Contact: Dave Polashek, Pres.
Local. Affiliated With: Lions Clubs International.

Odanah

19353 ■ Great Lakes Indian Fish and Wildlife Commission (GLIFWC)
PO Box 9
Odanah, WI 54861
Ph: (715)682-6619
Fax: (715)682-9294
E-mail: sue@glifwc.org
URL: http://www.glifwc.org
Contact: James Zorn, Exec. Administrator
Founded: 1983. **Members:** 11. **Staff:** 61. **Regional Groups:** 11. Chippewa tribes concerned with wildlife conservation in the Great Lakes region. Assists member tribes in the conservation and management of fish, wildlife, and natural resources. Promotes tribal self-government; encourages ecosystem protection. Sponsors educational and research programs. **Publications:** *A Guide to Understanding Ojibwe Treaty Rights*. Booklet. **Price:** $3.00. Alternate Formats: online • *BIZHIBAYASH: Circle of Flight*. Booklet. **Price:** free • *Chippewa Treaties Understanding and Impact*. Booklet. **Price:** $2.00 • *Chippewa Treaty Rights • Fishery Status Update*. Booklet. **Price:** free • *MAZINA'IGAN*, quarterly. Newspaper. **Price:** free • *Ojibwe Treaty Rights and Resource Management*. Brochure • *Poisoning the Circle: Mercury In Our Ecosystem*. Video. **Price:** $5.00 • *Seasons of the Ojibwe*. Booklet. **Price:** $3.00 • *Spearfishing Coverage Compilation*. Video. **Price:** $5.00 • *Sulfide Mining: The Process and The Price*. Booklet. **Price:** free • *With an Eagle's Eyes: Protecting Ojibwe Off-Reservation Treaty Rights and Resources*. Video. **Price:** $8.00 • Annual Report, annual • Manuals • Reports.

19354 ■ Midwest Regional Chapter of the Society of Environmental Toxicology and Chemistry
c/o Matt Hudson, VP
PO Box 9
Odanah, WI 54861
Ph: (715)685-2109
Fax: (715)682-9294
E-mail: jaweeks@scj.com
URL: http://www.midwestsetac.org
Contact: Matt Hudson, VP
Regional. Supports the development of principles and practices for protection, enhancement and management of sustainable environmental quality and ecosystem integrity. Promotes research, education, communication and training in the environmental sciences. Provides a forum for individuals and institutions engaged in the study of environmental issues, management and conservation of natural resources, and environmental research and development. **Affiliated With:** Society of Environmental Toxicology and Chemistry.

Ogema

19355 ■ American Legion, Spirit Post 452
W 710 State Hwy. 86
Ogema, WI 54459
Ph: (608)745-1090
Fax: (608)745-0179
URL: National Affiliate–www.legion.org
Local. Affiliated With: American Legion.

Omro

19356 ■ Lake Winnebago Optometric Society
c/o Ruth Weber, OD, Pres.
3779 City Rd. FF
Omro, WI 54963
Ph: (920)236-3541
Fax: (920)236-3546
E-mail: eyedoc35@aol.com
URL: http://www.woa-eyes.org
Contact: Ruth Weber OD, Pres.
Local. Aims to improve the quality, availability and accessibility of eye and vision care. Promotes high standards of patient care. Monitors and promotes legislation concerning the scope of optometric practice and other issues relevant to eye/vision care. **Affiliated With:** American Optometric Association; Wisconsin Optometric Association.

19357 ■ Omro Area Chamber of Commerce
PO Box 91
Omro, WI 54963
Ph: (920)685-6960
Fax: (920)685-6942
E-mail: omrochamber@charterinternet.net
URL: http://www.omro-wi.com
Contact: Ms. Jamie Kiesling, Dir.
Founded: 1986. **Members:** 120. **Membership Dues:** associate, non-profit and club, $65 (annual) • home business, $95 (annual) • small business (1-6 full time employees), $175 (annual) • medium business (7-15 full time employees), $250 (annual) • large business (16 or more full time employees), $325 (annual). **Staff:** 1. **Budget:** $20,000. **Local.** Promotes business and community development in Omro, WI. **Libraries: Type:** open to the public; lending; reference. **Holdings:** articles, books. **Subjects:** sales, marketing, customer service, advertisement. **Computer Services:** Information services • mailing lists. **Publications:** *The Communicator*, monthly. Newsletter. **Price:** free for members. **Advertising:** accepted. Alternate Formats: online. **Conventions/Meetings:** monthly meeting, working meeting of board of directors to review finances and operations - every first Thursday.

19358 ■ Oshkosh Violet Society
c/o Cathy Heider
4132 S Spring Rd.
Omro, WI 54963
Ph: (920)685-5262
URL: National Affiliate–www.avsa.org
Contact: Cathy Heider, Contact
Local. Affiliated With: African Violet Society of America.

Onalaska

19359 ■ American Cancer Society, La Crosse
1285 Rudy St., Ste.103
Onalaska, WI 54650
Ph: (608)783-5000
Fax: (608)783-5005
URL: http://www.cancer.org
Local. Affiliated With: American Cancer Society.

19360 ■ American Cancer Society, Onalaska
1285 Rudy St., Ste.103
Onalaska, WI 54650
Ph: (608)783-5000
Fax: (608)783-5005
Free: (877)423-9125
URL: http://www.cancer.org
Local. Affiliated With: American Cancer Society.

19361 ■ American Legion, Struck-Klandrud Post 336
731 Sand Lake Rd.
Onalaska, WI 54650
Ph: (608)745-1090
Fax: (608)745-0179
URL: National Affiliate–www.legion.org
Local. Affiliated With: American Legion.

19362 ■ Brice Prairie Lions Club
c/o Joe Pitsch, Pres.
W7053 Pineview Dr.
Onalaska, WI 54650
Ph: (608)526-9782
E-mail: jmpitsch@juno.com
URL: http://www.md27d2.org
Contact: Joe Pitsch, Pres.
Local. Affiliated With: Lions Clubs International.

19363 ■ Coulee Region Woodturners (CRW)
c/o Mr. Duane Hill, Pres.
808 Quincy
Onalaska, WI 54650
Ph: (608)783-0883
E-mail: wisawdust@centurytel.net
URL: http://www.crwoodturner.com
Contact: Mr. Duane Hill, Pres.
Regional. Represents amateur and professional woodturners, gallery owners, wood and equipment suppliers, and collectors. **Affiliated With:** American Association of Woodturners.

19364 ■ Holmen Lions Club
c/o Anthony Krueger, Pres.
711 Country Club Ln.
Onalaska, WI 54650
Ph: (608)783-6326
E-mail: krutony5@charter.net
URL: http://www.md27d2.org
Contact: Anthony Krueger, Pres.
Local. Affiliated With: Lions Clubs International.

19365 ■ La Crosse Area Builders Association
625 Main St.
Onalaska, WI 54650
Ph: (608)781-5242
Local. Formerly: (2005) La Crosse Area Home Builders.

19366 ■ National Association of Home Builders of the U.S., La Crosse Area Builders Association (LABA)
c/o Vicki Markussen
Local No. 5126
816 2nd Ave. S
PO Box 477
Onalaska, WI 54650-0477
Ph: (608)781-5242
Fax: (608)781-5221
E-mail: vicki@labaonline.com
URL: http://www.labaonline.com
Contact: Vicki Markussen, Exec. Officer
Founded: 1971. **Local.** Single and multifamily home builders, commercial builders, and others associated with the building industry. **Affiliated With:** National Association of Home Builders.

19367 ■ Onalaska Lions Club
c/o Jeffrey Powell, Pres.
W8376 Woodview Dr.
Onalaska, WI 54650
Ph: (608)783-3163
URL: http://www.md27d2.org
Contact: Jeffrey Powell, Pres.
Local. Affiliated With: Lions Clubs International.

19368 ■ Onalaska - Young Life
9534 E 16 Frontage Rd.
Onalaska, WI 54650
Ph: (608)786-3777
URL: http://sites.younglife.org/_layouts/ylext/default.aspx?ID=C-3559
Local. Affiliated With: Young Life.

19369 ■ St. Joseph's Ridge Lions Club
c/o Christopher Clements, Sec.
1207 Johnson St.
Onalaska, WI 54650
Ph: (608)781-1641
E-mail: clemy30@earthlink.net
URL: http://www.md27d2.org
Contact: Christopher Clements, Sec.
Local. Affiliated With: Lions Clubs International.

19370 ■ Sons of Norway, Wergeland Lodge 5-28
c/o Blyden J. Skogen, Pres.
818 Madison St.
Onalaska, WI 54650-2632
Ph: (608)783-2158
E-mail: cbskogen@centurytel.net
URL: National Affiliate–www.sofn.com
Contact: Blyden J. Skogen, Pres.
Local. Affiliated With: Sons of Norway.

19371 ■ United Way of the La Crosse Area
1855 E Main St.
Onalaska, WI 54650
Ph: (608)796-1400
Fax: (608)796-1410
E-mail: greatriversunitedway@centurytel.net
URL: http://www.greatriversunitedway.org
Contact: Rose Mary Boesen, Chief Professional Officer
Founded: 1949. **Local. Affiliated With:** United Way of America.

19372 ■ Wisconsin Chapter of National Association of Tax Professionals
c/o Linda Lueck, EA, Pres.
1115 Green St.
Onalaska, WI 54650-3018
Ph: (608)783-7135
E-mail: lueckl@wwtc.edu
URL: National Affiliate–www.natptax.com
Contact: Linda Lueck EA, Pres.
State. Affiliated With: National Association of Tax Professionals.

19373 ■ Wisconsin Woodland Owners Association, Chippewa Valley Chapter
c/o Carl Mueller, Chm.
1391 County Hwy., SS
Onalaska, WI 54650
Ph: (608)783-3070
E-mail: smschend@wwt.net
URL: http://www.wisconsinwoodlands.org
Contact: Carl Mueller, Chm.
Local. Affiliated With: Wisconsin Woodland Owners Association.

19374 ■ Young Life LaCrosse
9534 E 16 Frontage Rd.
Onalaska, WI 54650
Ph: (608)786-3777
URL: http://sites.younglife.org/sites/YoungLifeLaCrosse/default.aspx
Local. Affiliated With: Young Life.

Ontario

19375 ■ American Legion, Bredlow-Ewing Post 467
PO Box 214
Ontario, WI 54651
Ph: (608)745-1090
Fax: (608)745-0179
URL: National Affiliate–www.legion.org
Local. Affiliated With: American Legion.

Oostburg

19376 ■ American Legion, Hartman-Lammers Post 286
PO Box 501
Oostburg, WI 53070
Ph: (608)745-1090
Fax: (608)745-0179
URL: National Affiliate–www.legion.org
Local. Affiliated With: American Legion.

19377 ■ Center for Commerce Tourism
PO Box 700227
Oostburg, WI 53070-0227
Ph: (920)564-2336 (920)564-3214
Fax: (920)564-3596
E-mail: oostburg@wi.rr.com
URL: http://www.oostburg.org
Contact: Terry Katsma, Sec.-Treas.
Local. Enhances the economic prosperity of the members and promotes free enterprise and growth in Oostburg.

19378 ■ Sheboygan Astronomical Society
W3133 County Rd. W
Oostburg, WI 53070
Ph: (920)564-6688
E-mail: kiph@dotnet.net
URL: http://www.shebastro.org
Contact: Kip Hoffman, Contact
Local. Promotes the science of astronomy. Works to encourage and coordinate activities of amateur astronomical societies. Fosters observational and computational work and craftsmanship in various fields of astronomy. **Affiliated With:** Astronomical League.

19379 ■ Wisconsin Woodland Owners Association, Winnebagoland Chapter
c/o Larry Baer, Chm.
W1467 E Van Ess Rd.
Oostburg, WI 53070
Ph: (920)564-3189
E-mail: redoak99@aol.com
URL: http://www.wisconsinwoodlands.org
Contact: Larry Baer, Chm.
Local. Affiliated With: Wisconsin Woodland Owners Association.

Oregon

19380 ■ American Chesapeake Club, Wisconsin
c/o Patti Maye
955 Harding St.
Oregon, WI 53575
Ph: (608)835-2652
E-mail: baydogs@charter.net
URL: National Affiliate–www.amchessieclub.org
Contact: Patti Maye, Contact
State. Affiliated With: American Chesapeake Club.

19381 ■ Badger Lapidary And Geological Society (BLGS)
c/o Teri Macche, Pres.
5415 Lost Woods Ct.
Oregon, WI 53575
E-mail: badger_rock_club@yahoo.com
URL: http://www.angelfire.com/wi2/BLGS
Contact: Steve Holmes, Sec.
Local. Aims to further the study of Earth Sciences and the practice of lapidary arts and mineralogy. **Affiliated With:** American Federation of Mineralogical Societies.

Orfordville

19382 ■ American Legion, Wisconsin Post 209
c/o Kenneth S. Wells
PO Box 356
Orfordville, WI 53576
Ph: (608)745-1090
Fax: (608)745-0179
URL: National Affiliate–www.legion.org
Contact: Kenneth S. Wells, Contact
Local. Affiliated With: American Legion.

Osceola

19383 ■ Osceola Area Chamber of Commerce
310 Chieftain St.
Osceola, WI 54020
Ph: (715)755-3300
E-mail: chamber@vil.osceola.wi.us
URL: http://www.osceolachamber.org
Contact: Aaron Mork, Pres.
Members: 100. **Local.** Seeks to unite area businesses, industry, and services into a unified voice to promote, preserve, and protect Osceola and the surrounding area for the present and future.

Oshkosh

19384 ■ ACCA Northeast Wisconsin
c/o Wendi Hintz, Exec.Dir.
PO Box 2882
Oshkosh, WI 54903
Ph: (920)232-0436
Fax: (920)232-0436
E-mail: newacca@prodigy.net
URL: National Affiliate–www.acca.org
Contact: Wendi Hintz, Exec.Dir.
Local. Contractors involved in installation and service of heating, air conditioning, and refrigeration systems. **Affiliated With:** Air Conditioning Contractors of America. **Also Known As:** (2005) Air Conditioning Contractors of America, Region 3.

19385 ■ Advocap
2929 Harrison St.
Oshkosh, WI 54901
Ph: (920)426-0150
Fax: (920)426-3071
Free: (800)323-0150
E-mail: mikeb@advocap.org
URL: http://www.advocap.org
Contact: Michael Bonertz, Exec.Dir.
Founded: 1966. **Staff:** 250. **Budget:** $7,500,000. **Local.** Dedicated to helping low income individuals in Fond du Lac, Green Lake, and Winnebago counties in Wisconsin.

19386 ■ Air Conditioning Contractors of America, Northeast Wisconsin Chapter
c/o Wendi Hintz, Exec.Dir.
PO Box 2882
Oshkosh, WI 54903
Ph: (920)232-0436
Fax: (920)232-0436
E-mail: newacca@prodigy.net
URL: National Affiliate–www.acca.org
Contact: Wendi Hintz, Exec.Dir.
Local. Works to represent contractors involved in installation and service of heating, air conditioning, and refrigeration systems. **Affiliated With:** Air Conditioning Contractors of America.

19387 ■ American Association of University Women - Wisconsin (AAUW-WI)
1759 Lake Breeze Rd.
Oshkosh, WI 54904
Ph: (920)233-7991
E-mail: aauw.marge@charter.net
URL: http://www.aauw-wi.org
Contact: Marge Mueller, Pres.
Members: 2,000. **Membership Dues:** national, $43 • state, $10. **Budget:** $24,000. **Local Groups:** 40. **State.** Promotes equity for all women and girls, lifelong education and positive societal change. Membership is open to anyone with an associate or higher degree from an accredited college or university. **Publications:** *Badger Briefs*, 3-4 times per year. Newsletter. **Price:** included in membership dues.

19388 ■ American Legion, Cook-Fuller Post 70
1393 Washington Ave.
Oshkosh, WI 54901
Ph: (414)235-7007
Fax: (608)745-0179
URL: National Affiliate–www.legion.org
Local. Affiliated With: American Legion.

19389 ■ American Red Cross, East Central Wisconsin Chapter
36 Broad St., Ste.150
Oshkosh, WI 54901
Ph: (920)231-3590
Fax: (920)231-2016
URL: http://www.ecw-redcross.org
Regional.

19390 ■ Big Brothers Big Sisters of the Oshkosh Area
36 Broad St., Ste.130
Oshkosh, WI 54901
Ph: (920)231-2442
Fax: (920)235-8582
E-mail: bigbros1@northnet.net
URL: http://bigbros.oshkosh.net
Contact: Sue Steinhilber, Exec.Dir.
Local. Affiliated With: Big Brothers Big Sisters of America. **Formerly:** (2005) Big Brothers Big Sisters of America of the Oshkosh Area.

19391 ■ Community for Hope of Greater Oshkosh
c/o Steve Sobojinski, Pres.
PO Box 2744
Oshkosh, WI 54903-2744
Ph: (920)230-4840
E-mail: pahrens_60@yahoo.com
URL: http://www.communityforhope.org
Contact: Steve Sobojinski, Pres.
Local.

19392 ■ Fox Valley Chapter of Associated Locksmiths of America
c/o Eric Baier
Lockworks, Inc.
Oshkosh, WI 54902
Ph: (920)235-5625
E-mail: info@elockworks.com
URL: National Affiliate–www.aloa.org
Contact: Eric Baier, Contact
Local. Affiliated With: Associated Locksmiths of America.

19393 ■ Habitat for Humanity of Oshkosh
PO Box 1021
Oshkosh, WI 54903-1021
Ph: (920)235-3535
Fax: (920)303-2912
E-mail: habitat@northnet.net
URL: National Affiliate–www.habitat.org
Local. Committees: Building/Site Selection; Church Relations; Family Support/Selection; PR. **Affiliated With:** Habitat for Humanity International.

19394 ■ International Alliance of Theatrical Stage Employees, Moving Picture Technicians, Artists, M 470
PO Box 3351
Oshkosh, WI 54903
Ph: (920)688-3272
Fax: (920)688-3226
Free: (866)426-4707
E-mail: iatse470@hotmail.com
URL: http://www.ia470.com
Contact: Mr. Steve Dedow, Business Agent
Members: 80. **Local. Affiliated With:** International Alliance of Theatrical Stage Employees, Moving Picture Technicians, Artists and Allied Crafts of the United States, Its Territories and Canada.

19395 ■ National Active and Retired Federal Employees Association Oshkosh-Winnebagoland 416
739 Oak St.
Oshkosh, WI 54901-4670
Ph: (920)235-3731
URL: National Affiliate–www.narfe.org
Contact: Edmund W. Spanbauer, Contact
Local. Protects the retirement future of employees through education. Informs members on issues affecting the retirement. **Affiliated With:** National Association of Retired Federal Employees.

19396 ■ National Alliance for the Mentally Ill - Oshkosh
c/o Eugene Bengel, Pres.
Hope and Care Ctr.
525 Main St.
Oshkosh, WI 54902
Ph: (920)235-3041
URL: http://www.namiwisconsin.org/library/directory
Contact: Eugene Bengel, Pres.
Local. Strives to improve the quality of life of children and adults with severe mental illness through support, education, research and advocacy. **Affiliated With:** National Alliance for the Mentally Ill.

19397 ■ National Association of Housing and Redevelopment Officials, Wisconsin Chapter
c/o Brad J. Masterson, PHM, Exec.Dir.
Oshkosh Housing Authority
PO Box 397
Oshkosh, WI 54903-0397
Ph: (920)424-1474
Fax: (920)424-1450
E-mail: bradm@ohawcha.org
URL: National Affiliate–www.nahro.org
State. Strives to provide affordable housing and safe, viable communities that enhance the quality of life, especially those of low and moderate income. Enhances the professional development and effectiveness of its members through its comprehensive professional development curriculum, conferences and publications. **Affiliated With:** National Association of Housing and Redevelopment Officials.

19398 ■ North East Wisconsin Corvair Club
2251 Vinland Rd.
Oshkosh, WI 54901-1853
Ph: (920)427-8635
E-mail: markow2@earthlink.net
URL: http://www.geocities.com/MotorCity/Downs/6668
Contact: Jim Nirchl, Pres.
Founded: 1980. **Members:** 100. **Membership Dues:** family, $12 (annual). **Local.** Enthusiasts of Corvair automobiles. **Libraries: Type:** not open to the public. **Holdings:** books, periodicals. **Subjects:** corvair automobile. **Awards:** Service Award. **Frequency:** annual. **Type:** recognition. **Recipient:** for regular service at board meeting. **Affiliated With:** Corvair Society of America. **Also Known As:** N.E.W.C.C. **Publications:** *The Spyder Web*, monthly. Newsletter. **Price:** included in membership dues. **Circulation:** 100. **Advertising:** accepted. **Conventions/Meetings:** monthly show, with Club Library, Corvair Models (exhibits) - always 4th Sunday, Appleton, WI.

19399 ■ Northeast Wisconsin Stargazers
514 Union Ave., Apt. E
Oshkosh, WI 54901
Ph: (920)426-2286
E-mail: tbecker2@new.rr.com
URL: http://www.new-star.org
Contact: Terry Becker, Contact
Local. Promotes the science of astronomy. Works to encourage and coordinate activities of amateur astronomical societies. Fosters observational and computational work and craftsmanship in various fields of astronomy. **Affiliated With:** Astronomical League.

19400 ■ Oshkosh Area United Way
36 Broad St., Ste.100
Oshkosh, WI 54901
Ph: (920)235-8560
Fax: (920)235-8582
E-mail: oauw@oshkoshunitedway.org
URL: http://oshkoshunitedway.org
Contact: Susan M. Panek, Exec.Dir.
Local. Affiliated With: United Way of America.

19401 ■ Oshkosh Chamber of Commerce
120 Jackson St.
Oshkosh, WI 54901
Ph: (920)303-2266
Fax: (920)303-2263
E-mail: john@oshkoshchamber.com
URL: http://www.oshkoshchamber.com
Contact: John A. Casper, Pres./CEO
Founded: 1907. **Members:** 1,100. **Membership Dues:** business, $205 (annual). **Staff:** 13. **Budget:** $900,000. **State Groups:** 1. **Local.** Promotes business and community development in Oshkosh area. **Awards:** Ambassador of the Year. **Frequency:** annual. **Type:** recognition • Community Service. **Frequency:** annual. **Type:** recognition • Distinguished Service. **Frequency:** annual. **Type:** recognition • Small Business Person of the Year. **Frequency:** annual. **Type:** recognition • Volunteer of the Year. **Frequency:** annual. **Type:** recognition. **Computer Services:** Mailing lists, of members • online services, internet dialup services and website design. **Telecommunication Services:** information service, helps determine competitive wages, develop sales leads, attract new employees, and more • phone referral service, (920)426-9192. **Committees:** Career Fair Committee; School to Work Steering Committee. **Councils:** PALs Council. **Affiliated With:** U.S. Chamber of Commerce. **Formerly:** Oshkosh Association of Manufacturers and Commence. **Publications:** *Member Matters*, bimonthly. Newsletter • *Newswave*, bimonthly. Magazine. **Conventions/Meetings:** annual meeting • annual trade show (exhibits).

19402 ■ Oshkosh Table Tennis Organization
Downtown Oshkosh YMCA
324 Washington Ave.
Oshkosh, WI 54901
Ph: (920)589-4652
URL: http://www.usatt.org/clubs
Contact: Dick Dorsey, Contact
Local. Affiliated With: U.S.A. Table Tennis.

19403 ■ Pheasants Forever Fox River Valley Chapter
115 Overland Trail
Oshkosh, WI 54904
Ph: (920)722-6473
E-mail: pheasants@charter.net
URL: http://www.foxvalleypheasants.com
Contact: Scott Christie, Contact
Local. Affiliated With: Pheasants Forever.

19404 ■ Ruffed Grouse Society, Winnebago Land Chapter
c/o Jerry Davis
131 W 21st Ave.
Oshkosh, WI 54901
Ph: (920)233-0450
URL: National Affiliate–www.ruffedgrousesociety.org
Contact: Jerry Davis, Contact
Local. Affiliated With: Ruffed Grouse Society.

19405 ■ United Brotherhood of Carpenters and Joiners of America, Midwestern Council of Industrial Workers 4021
404 N Main St., Ste.103
Oshkosh, WI 54901
Ph: (920)426-2700
Fax: (920)426-2727
E-mail: mciw@mciw.org
URL: http://www.mciw.org
Contact: Dan Walbrun, Exec.Sec.-Treas.
Regional. Affiliated With: United Brotherhood of Carpenters and Joiners of America.

19406 ■ Winnebago Audubon Society
c/o Lisa Zeman, Pres.
PO Box 184
Oshkosh, WI 54902
E-mail: wiss@northnet.net
URL: National Affiliate–www.audubon.org
Contact: Janet Wissink, Ed.
Local. Works to conserve and restore natural ecosystems, focusing on birds and other wildlife for the benefit of humanity and the earth's biological diversity. **Affiliated With:** National Audubon Society.

19407 ■ Winnebago Home Builders Association
4041 State Rd. 91, Ste.A
Oshkosh, WI 54904
Ph: (920)253-2962
Fax: (920)235-1461
E-mail: whba@ntd.net
URL: National Affiliate–www.nahb.org
Contact: Don Glays, Contact
Founded: 1990. **Members:** 250. **Membership Dues:** builder and associate, $405 (annual) • affiliate, $80 (annual). **Staff:** 2. **State Groups:** 1. **Local Groups:** 24. **For-Profit**. **Local**. Works to ensure availability of affordable new housing. Sponsors community projects such as annual auction, casino night, holiday party, and white-tails banquet. **Awards:** Scholarship Award. **Frequency:** annual. **Type:** monetary. **Recipient:** to African American medical students for special achievements, academic excellence, and leadership. **Computer Services:** Mailing lists, of members. **Committees:** Ambassador Club; Arbitration; Associate Advisory; Auction; Governmental Affairs; Home and Garden Show; Parade of Homes; Programs/Education; Public Relations; Safety; Scholarship; Strategic Plan. **Affiliated With:** National Association of Home Builders; Oshkosh Chamber of Commerce. **Publications:** Newsletter, monthly. **Price:** free for members. **Circulation:** 290. **Advertising:** accepted. **Conventions/Meetings:** annual Golf Outing - meeting • annual Home Show - meeting (exhibits) • monthly meeting (exhibits) - always second Wednesday • annual Parade of Homes - meeting • annual picnic • annual Sporting Clay Shoot - meeting.

19408 ■ Wisconsin Association of Alcohol and Drug Abuse Counselors
c/o Michael Kemp
1545 Arboretum Dr., No. 427
Oshkosh, WI 54901
URL: National Affiliate–www.naadac.org
Contact: Michael Kemp, Contact
State. **Affiliated With:** NAADAC The Association for Addiction Professionals.

19409 ■ Wisconsin Association of College Stores (WACS)
c/o Kathy Kaltenbach, Pres.
Univ. Books & More
Univ. of Wisconsin-Oshkosh
748 Algoma Blvd.
Oshkosh, WI 54901-8685
Ph: (920)424-2381
Fax: (920)424-1082
E-mail: kaltenba@suwosh.edu
URL: National Affiliate–www.nacs.org
Contact: Kathy Kaltenbach, Pres.
State. Promotes the collegiate retailing industry. Enhances the college store industry through service, education and research. Promotes high standards of business practices and ethics within the industry. **Affiliated With:** National Association of College Stores.

19410 ■ Wisconsin Council of African Violet Clubs
c/o Kevin Degner
1741 Iowa St.
Oshkosh, WI 54901
Ph: (920)426-3764
URL: National Affiliate–www.avsa.org
Contact: Kevin Degner, Contact
State. **Affiliated With:** African Violet Society of America.

19411 ■ Wisconsin Society of Science Teachers (WSST)
Univ. of Wisconsin - Oshkosh
Off. of Sci. Outreach
800 Algoma Blvd.
Oshkosh, WI 54901
Ph: (920)424-0287
Fax: (920)424-7076
E-mail: office@wsst.org
URL: http://www.wsst.org
Contact: Dale Basler, Pres.
State. Promotes excellence and innovation in science teaching and learning for all. Serves as the voice for excellence and innovation in science teaching and learning, curriculum and instruction, and assessment. Promotes interest and support for science education. **Affiliated With:** National Science Teachers Association.

Osseo

19412 ■ American Legion, Wisconsin Post 324
c/o Carl Nelson
13519 Park Ave.
Osseo, WI 54758
Ph: (608)745-1090
Fax: (608)745-0179
URL: National Affiliate–www.legion.org
Contact: Carl Nelson, Contact
Local. **Affiliated With:** American Legion.

19413 ■ Sons of Norway, Trygvason Lodge 5-220
c/o Craig S. Vold, Pres.
N43255 County Rd. O
Osseo, WI 54758-8635
Ph: (715)694-2177
E-mail: cvold@triwest.net
URL: National Affiliate–www.sofn.com
Contact: Craig S. Vold, Pres.
Local. **Affiliated With:** Sons of Norway.

Owen

19414 ■ American Legion, Van-Huizen-Fritz Post 123
118 Central Ave.
Owen, WI 54460
Ph: (608)745-1090
Fax: (608)745-0179
URL: National Affiliate–www.legion.org
Local. **Affiliated With:** American Legion.

19415 ■ Black River Country United Way
PO Box 255
Owen, WI 54460-0255
Ph: (715)210-0071
URL: National Affiliate–national.unitedway.org
Local. **Affiliated With:** United Way of America.

Palmyra

19416 ■ American Legion, Thomas-Holcomb Post 304
115 N 3rd St.
Box 173
Palmyra, WI 53156
Ph: (608)745-1090
Fax: (608)745-0179
URL: National Affiliate–www.legion.org
Local. **Affiliated With:** American Legion.

19417 ■ Beemer Hill Riders, No. 317
c/o Sue Rihn-Manke
Beemer Hill, N1669 Hwy. H
Palmyra, WI 53156
Ph: (262)495-4163
E-mail: sue@beemerhill.com
URL: http://www.beemerhill.com
Contact: Sue Rihn-Manke, Pres.
Local.

19418 ■ Palmyra Area Chamber of Commerce
PO Box 139
Palmyra, WI 53156-0139
Ph: (262)495-2611 (262)495-8316
Fax: (262)495-8775
E-mail: cleanmats@hotmail.com
URL: http://www.palmyrawi.com
Contact: Rick Ball, Acting Pres.
Local.

19419 ■ Wisconsin BMW Motorcycle Club No. 10
c/o Sue Rihn-Manke
N1669 Hwy. H
Palmyra, WI 53156
Ph: (920)414-4163
E-mail: sue@wiscbmwclub.com
URL: http://www.wiscbmwclub.com
Contact: Sue Rihn-Manke, Contact
State. BMW motorcycle owners organized for pleasure, recreation, safety, and dissemination of information concerning BMW motorcycles. **Affiliated With:** BMW Motorcycle Owners of America.

19420 ■ Wisconsin Corn Growers Association
c/o Robert Oleson, Exec.Dir.
W1360 Hwy. 106
Palmyra, WI 53156
Ph: (262)495-2232
Fax: (262)495-3178
E-mail: wicorn@idcnet.com
URL: National Affiliate–www.ncga.com/
State. **Affiliated With:** National Corn Growers Association.

19421 ■ Wisconsin Corn Promotion Board
c/o Robert Oleson, Exec.Dir.
W1360 Hwy. 106
Palmyra, WI 53156
Ph: (262)495-2232
Fax: (262)495-3178
E-mail: wicorn@idcnet.com
URL: National Affiliate–www.ncga.com/
State. **Affiliated With:** National Corn Growers Association.

Pardeeville

19422 ■ American Legion, Wisconsin Post 215
c/o Harry D. Jerred
326 S Main St., No. 6
Pardeeville, WI 53954
Ph: (608)745-1090
Fax: (608)745-0179
URL: National Affiliate–www.legion.org
Contact: Harry D. Jerred, Contact
Local. **Affiliated With:** American Legion.

19423 ■ Pardeeville Area Business Association
PO Box 337
Pardeeville, WI 53954
Ph: (608)429-3121 (608)429-3976
Contact: Sue Schlapman, Sec.
Local.

Park Falls

19424 ■ American Legion, Wisconsin Post 182
c/o Frank Dirrigl
274 3rd Ave. N
Park Falls, WI 54552

Ph: (608)745-1090
Fax: (608)745-0179
URL: National Affiliate–www.legion.org
Contact: Frank Dirrigl, Contact
Local. Affiliated With: American Legion.

19425 ■ Park Falls Area Chamber of Commerce (PFACC)
400 4th Ave. S
Park Falls, WI 54552
Ph: (715)762-2703
Free: (800)762-2709
E-mail: chamber@parkfalls.com
URL: http://www.parkfalls.com
Contact: Jane Bentz, Exec.Dir.
Founded: 1947. **Members:** 160. **Membership Dues:** basic, $160 (annual). **Budget:** $115,000. **Local.** Resorts, industries, retailers, and service organizations in Ashland, Iron, Price, and Sawyer counties, WI. Promotes community and economic development; provides information; sponsors promotions and events. **Publications:** *Chamber Chatter*, weekly. Article • *Park Falls - Gateway to the Good Life*, annual. **Conventions/Meetings:** annual Flambeau Rama Celebration - festival - always in August.

19426 ■ Ruffed Grouse Society, Flambeau River Chapter
c/o Richard Wojcieszak
N15355 East Rd.
Park Falls, WI 54552
Ph: (715)762-2178
E-mail: sportsmn@pctcnet.net
URL: National Affiliate–www.ruffedgrousesociety.org
Contact: Richard Wojcieszak, Contact
Local. Affiliated With: Ruffed Grouse Society.

19427 ■ Wildlife Society - Wisconsin Chapter
c/o Adrian Wydeven, Pres.
PO Box 220
Park Falls, WI 54552
Ph: (715)762-4684
Contact: Adrian Wydeven, Pres.
Members: 9,000. **Membership Dues:** $10 (annual). **Local. Publications:** *Intelligent Tinkering*. Newsletter. Alternate Formats: online.

Patch Grove

19428 ■ American Legion, Hanley-Ariss-Millin Post 5
PO Box 136
Patch Grove, WI 53817
Ph: (608)745-1090
Fax: (608)745-0179
URL: National Affiliate–www.legion.org
Local. Affiliated With: American Legion.

Pelican Lake

19429 ■ Pelican Lake Chamber of Commerce (PLCC)
PO Box 45
Pelican Lake, WI 54463
Ph: (715)487-5222
URL: http://www.pelicanlakewi.org
Contact: Susan Welch, Sec.
Founded: 1962. **Members:** 19. **Local.** Businesses. Promotes business and community development in the Pelican Lake, WI area. Sponsors annual Ice Fishing Jamboree. **Publications:** Newsletter, monthly. **Conventions/Meetings:** monthly meeting.

Pembine

19430 ■ American Legion, Wisconsin Post 461
c/o James G. Delaney
PO Box 343
Pembine, WI 54156
Ph: (608)745-1090
Fax: (608)745-0179
URL: National Affiliate–www.legion.org
Contact: James G. Delaney, Contact
Local. Affiliated With: American Legion.

Pence

19431 ■ Wisconsin Woodland Owners Association, Penokee Chapter
c/o Charles Zinsmaster, Chm.
301 Birch St.
Pence, WI 54550
Ph: (715)561-5623
URL: http://www.wisconsinwoodlands.org
Contact: Charles Zinsmaster, Chm.
Local. Affiliated With: Wisconsin Woodland Owners Association.

Peshtigo

19432 ■ American Legion, Carlson-Alguire-Hougland Post 312
W 4358 County Trunk B
Peshtigo, WI 54157
Ph: (608)745-1090
Fax: (608)745-0179
URL: National Affiliate–www.legion.org
Local. Affiliated With: American Legion.

19433 ■ Wisconsin Polygraph Association
346 S Emery Ave.
Peshtigo, WI 54157
Ph: (715)732-7621
E-mail: wiscpoly@new.rr.com
URL: National Affiliate–www.polygraph.org
Contact: Anthony J. O'Neill, Contact
State. Represents individuals dedicated to providing a valid and reliable means to verify the truth and establish the highest standards of moral, ethical, and professional conduct in the polygraph field. Establishes standards of ethical practices, techniques, instrumentation, research, advanced training and continuing educational programs. Provides a forum for the presentation and exchange of information derived from such research, training and education. **Affiliated With:** American Polygraph Association.

Pewaukee

19434 ■ American Legion, Pewaukee Post 71
PO Box 132
Pewaukee, WI 53072
Ph: (608)745-1090
Fax: (608)745-0179
URL: National Affiliate–www.legion.org
Local. Affiliated With: American Legion.

19435 ■ Bowling Proprietors Association of Wisconsin
c/o Gary Hartel, Dir.
N35-W21140 Capitol Dr., Ste.5
Pewaukee, WI 53072
Ph: (262)783-4292
Fax: (262)783-4590
Contact: Gary Hartel, Dir.
State.

19436 ■ Business Marketing Association, Milwaukee Chapter
c/o Ilka Hoffins, Exec. Administrator
1028 Quietwood Ct.
Pewaukee, WI 53072
Ph: (262)746-9686
E-mail: ilka@bma-milwaukee.org
URL: http://www.bma-milwaukee.org
Contact: Susan Riese, Pres.
Local. Promotes the development of business-to-business marketing and communications professionals through education, training and networking. **Affiliated With:** Business Marketing Association.

19437 ■ International Union of Operating Engineers, Local 139
N27 W23233 Roundy Dr.
PO Box 130
Pewaukee, WI 53072
Ph: (262)896-0139
Fax: (262)896-0758
Free: (800)280-0139
E-mail: tmcgowan@iuoe139.org
URL: http://www.iuoe139.com
Contact: Terrance E. McGowan, Business Mgr.
Local. Works to bring economic justice to the workplace and to improve the lives of working families. **Affiliated With:** International Union of Operating Engineers.

19438 ■ MannaFest Dimensions
c/o Martin and Robyn Green
N26 W24160 River Park Dr., No. B
Pewaukee, WI 53072-5852
E-mail: info@mannafestdimensions.org
URL: http://www.mannafestdimensions.org
Contact: Robyn Green, Contact
Founded: 2002. **Members:** 3. **Budget:** $5,000. **Local.**

19439 ■ MRA - The Management Association
c/o Susan Fronk, Pres./CEO
PO Box 911
Pewaukee, WI 53072-0911
Ph: (262)523-9090
Fax: (262)523-9091
Free: (800)488-4845
E-mail: infonow@mranet.org
URL: http://www.mranet.org
Contact: Susan Fronk, Pres./CEO
Founded: 1901. **Regional.**

19440 ■ Pewaukee Chamber of Commerce
214 Oakton Ave.
Pewaukee, WI 53072-3430
Ph: (262)691-8851
Fax: (262)691-0922
E-mail: pewaukeecc@core.com
URL: http://www.pewaukeechamber.org
Contact: Stephanie Banning, Contact
Local. Works to serve the needs of business community.

19441 ■ Phi Theta Kappa, Alpha Rho Zeta Chapter - Waukesha County Technical College
c/o Kathleen Kaufelt
800 Main St., Rm. BO-206
Pewaukee, WI 53072
Ph: (262)691-5285
E-mail: kkaufelt@wctc.edu
URL: http://www.ptk.org/directories/chapters/WI/8972-1.htm
Contact: Kathleen Kaufelt, Advisor
Local.

19442 ■ Points of Light Foundation - Volunteer Center of Waukesha County
2220 Silvernail Rd.
Pewaukee, WI 53072-5529
Ph: (262)544-0150
Fax: (262)544-9657
E-mail: anneb@volunteerwaukesha.com
URL: National Affiliate–www.pointsoflight.org
Contact: Anne Borg, Contact
Local. Affiliated With: Points of Light Foundation.

19443 ■ Positively Pewaukee
120 W Wisconsin Ave.
Pewaukee, WI 53072
Ph: (262)695-9735
Fax: (262)695-9795
URL: http://www.positivelypewaukee.com
Local.

19444 ■ Printing Industries of Wisconsin (PIW)
800 Main St., I-201
Pewaukee, WI 53072
Ph: (262)695-6250
Fax: (262)695-6254
E-mail: admin@piw.org
URL: http://www.piw.org
Contact: N. Niall Power, Pres./CEO
Founded: 1886. **Members:** 200. **Staff:** 5. **Local Groups:** 3. **State**. Graphic arts firms and related suppliers. **Affiliated With:** Printing Industries of America. **Publications:** *Graphic Impressions*, monthly. Magazine • Directory, annual. **Advertising:** accepted. **Conventions/Meetings:** monthly meeting.

19445 ■ Waukesha County Fair Association
2417 Silvernail Rd.
Pewaukee, WI 53072-5406
Ph: (262)544-5922
Local.

19446 ■ Waukesha County Medical Society
PO Box 636
Pewaukee, WI 53072-0636
Ph: (262)695-7412
Fax: (262)695-7442
E-mail: wcms@wi.rr.com
URL: http://www.wisconsinmedicalsociety.org
Contact: Dawn Maerker, Exec.Dir.
Local. Advances the art and science of medicine. Promotes patient care and the betterment of public health.

19447 ■ Wisconsin Credit Union League (WCUL)
c/o Brett Thompson, Pres./CEO
N25 W23131 Paul Rd.
Pewaukee, WI 53072-5779
Ph: (262)549-0200
Fax: (262)549-7722
Free: (800)242-0833
E-mail: bthompson@theleague.coop
URL: http://www.wcul.org
Contact: Brett Thompson, Pres./CEO
State.

19448 ■ Wisconsin Racquetball Association
N 34 W 28338 Taylors Woods Dr.
Pewaukee, WI 53072
Ph: (414)695-0904 (414)321-2500
E-mail: pelftman@wi.rr.com
URL: http://wiracquetball.org
Contact: Trish Elftman, Contact
State. **Affiliated With:** United States Racquetball Association.

Phelps

19449 ■ American Legion, Albertson Esque Post 548
PO Box 225
Phelps, WI 54554
Ph: (608)745-1090
Fax: (608)745-0179
URL: National Affiliate–www.legion.org
Local. **Affiliated With:** American Legion.

19450 ■ Phelps Chamber of Commerce (PCC)
PO Box 217
Phelps, WI 54554
Ph: (715)545-3800
Free: (877)669-7077
E-mail: pcoc@nnex.net
URL: http://www.phelpswi.org
Contact: Debbie Vold, Pres.
Members: 355. **Local**. Promotes business and community development in Phelps, WI. Sponsors annual Colorama Brunch. **Conventions/Meetings:** annual meeting • monthly meeting.

19451 ■ Wisconsin Health Care Association, District 11
c/o Nancy Ellis, Pres.
Aspirus Lillian Kerr Hea. Care
2383 State Hwy. 17
Phelps, WI 54554
Ph: (715)545-2313
URL: http://www.whca.com
Contact: Nancy Ellis, Pres.
Local. Promotes professionalism and ethical behavior of individuals providing long-term care delivery for patients and for the general public. Provides information, education and administrative tools to enhance the quality of long-term care. Improves the standards of service and administration of member nursing homes. **Affiliated With:** American Health Care Association; Wisconsin Health Care Association.

Phillips

19452 ■ American Legion, Wisconsin Post 122
c/o Lyle N. Lane
PO Box 114
Phillips, WI 54555
Ph: (608)745-1090
Fax: (608)745-0179
URL: National Affiliate–www.legion.org
Contact: Lyle N. Lane, Contact
Local. **Affiliated With:** American Legion.

19453 ■ Phillips Area Chamber of Commerce (PACC)
305 S Lake Ave.
Phillips, WI 54555
Ph: (715)339-4100
Fax: (715)339-4190
Free: (888)408-4800
E-mail: pacc@pctcnet.net
Contact: Angela Hahn, Exec.Dir.
Members: 170. **Staff:** 6. **Budget:** $60,000. **Local**. Businesses and individuals interested in promoting business, industrial, agricultural, civic, recreational, tourist, and educational development in the Phillips, WI area. Sponsors 4th of July festivities, Winter Festival, Fall Harvest Festival, and the Home and Craft Show. **Publications:** *Promotional Book*, periodic. Journal • Newsletter, quarterly.

Phlox

19454 ■ American Legion, Devine-Menting Post 525
PO Box 93
Phlox, WI 54464
Ph: (608)745-1090
Fax: (608)745-0179
URL: National Affiliate–www.legion.org
Local. **Affiliated With:** American Legion.

Pine River

19455 ■ Creation Education Association (CEA)
W2228 Badger Ave.
Pine River, WI 54965
Ph: (920)987-5979
Fax: (920)987-5979
E-mail: sattlere1@juno.com
Contact: Eugene A. Sattler, Exec.Dir.
Founded: 1983. **Members:** 20. **Regional**. Individuals interested in creation-science. Conducts lectures and programs on creation versus evolution. Provides videos, books, and other materials to schools and churches. **Libraries: Type:** not open to the public. **Publications:** *CEA Update*, quarterly. Newsletter. Contains articles about creation vs. evolution. **Price:** free. **Circulation:** 3,000. **Conventions/Meetings:** annual meeting.

19456 ■ East Central Wisconsin Astronomers
N3714 30th Dr.
Pine River, WI 54965
Ph: (920)987-5325
E-mail: deepspacedave@centurytel.net
URL: http://ecwastronomers.org
Contact: Dave Schliepp, Contact
Local. Promotes the science of astronomy. Works to encourage and coordinate activities of amateur astronomical societies. Fosters observational and computational work and craftsmanship in various fields of astronomy. **Affiliated With:** Astronomical League.

Pittsville

19457 ■ American Legion, Palmer-Ritchie-Thomas Post 153
PO Box 99
Pittsville, WI 54466
Ph: (608)745-1090
Fax: (608)745-0179
URL: National Affiliate–www.legion.org
Local. **Affiliated With:** American Legion.

19458 ■ American Rabbit Breeders Association, Central Wisconsin
c/o Connie Burant, Sec.
8538 Hwy. E W
Pittsville, WI 54466
URL: http://www.geocities.com/wisconsin_state_rba/Local_Clubs.html
Contact: Connie Burant, Sec.
Local. **Affiliated With:** American Rabbit Breeders Association.

Plain

19459 ■ American Legion, Jennings-Kraemer-Gruber Post 398
PO Box 175
Plain, WI 53577
Ph: (608)745-1090
Fax: (608)745-0179
URL: National Affiliate–www.legion.org
Local. **Affiliated With:** American Legion.

19460 ■ Friends of the Kraemer Library and Community Center
c/o Sharon K. Bettinger, Pres.
PO Box 282
Plain, WI 53577-0282
Ph: (608)546-3781
E-mail: betto@charter.net
Contact: Sharon K. Bettinger, Pres.
Founded: 2001. **Membership Dues:** student (K-12), senior (62), $2 (annual) • individual, $5 (annual) • family, $10 (annual) • business, $25 (annual) • life (individual, family), $100 • life (business), $250. **Local**. Volunteers supporting the library programs through fundraising activities. **Libraries: Type:** open to the public. **Holdings:** audio recordings, books, periodicals, video recordings. **Committees:** Family and Local History; Fundraising; Program; Public Relation; Volunteer. **Publications:** Newsletter, annual. **Price:** free.

19461 ■ Plain Lions Club
c/o Patrick Mahoney, Pres.
940 Westbrook Dr.
Plain, WI 53577
Ph: (608)546-2623
URL: http://www.md27d2.org
Contact: Patrick Mahoney, Pres.
Local. **Affiliated With:** Lions Clubs International.

Platteville

19462 ■ American Legion, Wisconsin Post 42
c/o Leo M. Kane
PO Box 431
Platteville, WI 53818

Ph: (608)745-1090
Fax: (608)745-0179
URL: National Affiliate–www.legion.org
Contact: Leo M. Kane, Contact
Local. Affiliated With: American Legion.

19463 ■ Association for Computing Machinery, University of Wisconsin/Platteville
c/o Tom Scanlan, Prof., Sponsor
1 Univ. Plaza
421 Pioneer Tower
Dept. of Cmpt. Sci.
Platteville, WI 53818
Ph: (608)342-1401
Fax: (608)348-1254
E-mail: acm@uwplatt.edu
Biological, medical, behavioral, and computer scientists; hospital administrators; programmers and others interested in application of computer methods to biological, behavioral, and medical problems. Stimulates understanding of the use and potential of computers in the Biosciences. **Affiliated With:** Association for Computing Machinery.

19464 ■ FarmHouse Fraternity - University of Wisconsin Platteville
340 W Mineral
Platteville, WI 53818
Ph: (608)348-7872
E-mail: uwpfarmhouse@yahoo.com
URL: http://www.uwplatt.edu/org/farmhouse
Local. Promotes good fellowship and studiousness. Encourages members to seek the best in their chosen lines of study as well as in life. Works for the intellectual, spiritual, social, moral and physical development of members. **Affiliated With:** Farmhouse.

19465 ■ National Alliance for the Mentally Ill - Southwest Wisconsin
c/o Elissa Kinch, Pres.
PO Box 341
Platteville, WI 53818
Ph: (608)348-6136
URL: http://www.namiwisconsin.org/library/directory
Contact: Elissa Kinch, Pres.
Local. Strives to improve the quality of life of children and adults with severe mental illness through support, education, research and advocacy. **Affiliated With:** National Alliance for the Mentally Ill.

19466 ■ Platteville Chamber of Commerce
PO Box 16
Platteville, WI 53818
Ph: (608)348-8888
Fax: (608)348-8890
E-mail: chamber@platteville.com
URL: http://www.platteville.com
Contact: Kathy Kopp, Exec.Dir.
Membership Dues: base (general business, professional, financial institution), $205 • utility (including cooperative), $575 • cottage industry, $130 • associate (church, nonprofit organization, service club, governmental agency), $100 • individual/farmer, greeter service, $40. **Local.** Promotes business and community development in Platteville, WI. **Affiliated With:** U.S. Chamber of Commerce; Wisconsin Manufacturers and Commerce.

19467 ■ Platteville Main Street Prog.
55 S Bonson St.
Platteville, WI 53818
Ph: (608)348-4505
Fax: (608)348-8426
E-mail: pvmainst@yahoo.com
URL: http://www.plattevillemainstreet.com
Contact: Cheryl Zmina, Program Mgr.
Local.

19468 ■ Psi Chi, National Honor Society in Psychology - University of Wisconsin-Platteville
c/o Dept. of Psychology
228 Warner Hall
1 Univ. Plz.
Platteville, WI 53818-3099
Ph: (608)342-1723 (608)342-1724
Fax: (608)342-1429
E-mail: gatese@uwplatt.edu
URL: National Affiliate–www.psichi.org
Local. Affiliated With: Psi Chi, National Honor Society in Psychology.

19469 ■ Public Relations Society of America, Greater Dubuque
c/o Laura J. Bertjens, APR, Pres.
SW Hea. Ctr.
250 Camp St.
Platteville, WI 53818
Ph: (608)342-4779
Fax: (608)342-5044
E-mail: bertjens@southwesthealth.org
URL: National Affiliate–www.prsa.org
Contact: Laura J. Bertjens APR, Pres.
Local. Affiliated With: Public Relations Society of America.

19470 ■ Society of Physics Students - University of Wisconsin-Platteville Chapter No. 8316
1 Univ. Plaza
Platteville, WI 53818
Ph: (608)342-1651
Fax: (608)342-1566
E-mail: wilson@uwplatt.edu
URL: National Affiliate–www.spsnational.org
Local. Offers opportunities for the students to enrich their experiences and skills about physics. Helps students to become professional in the field of physics. **Affiliated With:** Society of Physics Students.

19471 ■ Southwest Badger Resource Conservation and Development Council
PO Box 751
Platteville, WI 53818
Ph: (608)348-3235
Fax: (608)348-4088
E-mail: steve.bertjens@wi.usda.gov
URL: http://www.swbadger.com
Contact: Steven Bertjens, Coor.
Local. Affiliated With: National Association of Resource Conservation and Development Councils.

19472 ■ Southwestern Wisconsin Regional Planning Commission (SWWRPC)
719 Pioneer Tower
1 Univ. Plz.
Platteville, WI 53818
Ph: (608)342-1214
Fax: (608)342-1220
E-mail: swwrpc@uwplatt.edu
URL: http://www.swwrpc.org
Contact: Lawrence T. Ward, Exec.Dir.
Founded: 1970. **Members:** 15. **Staff:** 6. **Budget:** $350,000. **Regional.** Serves the five counties of Grant, Green, Iowa, Lafayette and Richland. Provides intergovernmental planning and coordination for the physical, social and economic development of the region. **Publications:** *Comprehensive Economic Development Strategy*, annual. Report • Annual Report, annual. **Conventions/Meetings:** semimonthly executive committee meeting • annual meeting.

19473 ■ United Way of Platteville
PO Box 227
Platteville, WI 53818-0227
Ph: (608)348-2727
URL: National Affiliate–national.unitedway.org
Local. Affiliated With: United Way of America.

19474 ■ Wisconsin Nurses Association, Southwest District - No. 2
21870 Sand Hill Rd.
Platteville, WI 53818
Ph: (608)762-5388
URL: http://www.wisconsinnurses.org
Contact: Judy Pearce, Pres.
Local. Works to advance the nursing profession. Seeks to meet the needs of nurses and health care consumers. Fosters high standards of nursing practice. Promotes the economic and general welfare of nurses in the workplace. **Affiliated With:** American Nurses Association; Wisconsin Nurses' Association.

Pleasant Prairie

19475 ■ American Hellenic Educational Progressive Association - Racine, Chapter 377
c/o Peter Kyriazes, Pres.
3581 124th St.
Pleasant Prairie, WI 53158
Ph: (262)653-1811
URL: http://www.ahepafamily.org/d13
Contact: Peter Kyriazes, Pres.
Local. Affiliated With: American Hellenic Educational Progressive Association.

19476 ■ PFLAG Kenosha/Racine
PO Box 580058
Pleasant Prairie, WI 53158
Ph: (262)694-2729
E-mail: pflagkenosha@aol.com
URL: http://www.hometown.aol.com/pflagkenosha
Local. Affiliated With: Parents, Families, and Friends of Lesbians and Gays.

19477 ■ South East Wisconsin Optometric Society
c/o Debra Barnett, OD, Pres.
10314 83rd Pl.
Pleasant Prairie, WI 53158
Ph: (262)653-0100
Fax: (262)653-0200
E-mail: eyedocdeb@yahoo.com
URL: http://www.woa-eyes.org
Contact: Debra Barnett OD, Pres.
Local. Aims to improve the quality, availability and accessibility of eye and vision care. Promotes high standards of patient care. Monitors and promotes legislation concerning the scope of optometric practice and other issues relevant to eye/vision care. **Affiliated With:** American Optometric Association; Wisconsin Optometric Association.

Plover

19478 ■ American Legion, Palash-Platt Post 543
2021 Washington Ave.
Plover, WI 54467
Ph: (608)745-1090
Fax: (608)745-0179
URL: National Affiliate–www.legion.org
Local. Affiliated With: American Legion.

19479 ■ Associated Recyclers of Wisconsin (AROW)
c/o Recycling Connections Corp.
600 Moore Rd.
Plover, WI 54467
Ph: (715)343-6311
Fax: (715)345-5971
E-mail: execdirector@arow-online.org
URL: http://www.arow-online.org
Contact: Joe Van Rossum, Pres.
State. Advocates the use of recycled materials for environment conservation. Provides technical information on recycling methods, composting and reuse. Serves as a means of communication for recycling coordinators, environmental educators and other people advocating the importance of waste management. **Affiliated With:** National Recycling Coalition.

19480 ■ Bluebird Restoration Association of Wisconsin (BRAW)
c/o Sue Schultz, Membership Chair
5221 Cheryls Dr.
Plover, WI 54467

Ph: (608)873-1703
E-mail: joeschultz@coredcs.com
URL: http://www.braw.org
Contact: Joe Schultz, Pres.
State. Affiliated With: North American Bluebird Society.

19481 ■ Central Wisconsin Saints Hockey Association
c/o Joseph J. Zuniga
PO Box 604
Plover, WI 54467
Ph: (715)343-8997
E-mail: dzuniga@g2a.net
URL: http://www.saintshockey.org
Contact: Joe Zuniga, Pres.
Local.

19482 ■ Golden Sands Home Builders Association
1001 Theater Dr.
Plover, WI 54467-2637
Ph: (715)341-3536
Fax: (715)341-9899
E-mail: gshba@gza.net
URL: National Affiliate–www.nahb.org
Contact: Pam Jewell, Pres.
Local. Single and multifamily home builders, commercial builders, and others associated with the building industry. **Affiliated With:** National Association of Home Builders.

19483 ■ Izaak Walton League of America - Wisconsin Division
811 4th St.
Plover, WI 54467-2253
Ph: (715)344-4668
E-mail: jernst@pointonline.net
URL: National Affiliate–www.iwla.org
Contact: Gerald Ernst, Pres.
State. Educates the public to conserve, maintain, protect and restore the soil, forest, water and other natural resources of the U.S. and other lands.

19484 ■ Kiwanis Club of Plover
PO Box 183
Plover, WI 54467-0183
Ph: (715)341-3620
E-mail: ploverkiwanis@yahoo.com
URL: http://www.geocities.com/ploverkiwanis
Contact: Ron Odejewski, Pres.
Local.

19485 ■ Wisconsin Rural Water Association (WRWA)
350 Water Way
Plover, WI 54467
Ph: (715)344-7778
Fax: (715)344-5555
E-mail: wrwa@wrwa.org
URL: http://www.wrwa.org
Contact: Ken Blomberg, Exec.Dir.
State.

Plum City

19486 ■ American Legion, Wisconsin Post 365
c/o Frank Gilles
130 Pine Ave.
Plum City, WI 54761
Ph: (608)745-1090
Fax: (608)745-0179
URL: National Affiliate–www.legion.org
Contact: Frank Gilles, Contact
Local. Affiliated With: American Legion.

Plymouth

19487 ■ American Legion, Kupfahl-Meyer-Scheib Post 387
N 8139 Franklin Rd.
Plymouth, WI 53073
Ph: (608)745-1090
Fax: (608)745-0179
URL: National Affiliate–www.legion.org
Local. Affiliated With: American Legion.

19488 ■ American Legion, Ladewig-Zinkgraf Post 243
40 Stafford St.
Plymouth, WI 53073
Ph: (608)745-1090
Fax: (608)745-0179
URL: National Affiliate–www.legion.org
Local. Affiliated With: American Legion.

19489 ■ American Legion, Wisconsin Post 484
c/o Walter Gilles
W6632 Sandstone Ln.
Plymouth, WI 53073
Ph: (608)745-1090
Fax: (608)745-0179
URL: National Affiliate–www.legion.org
Contact: Walter Gilles, Contact
Local. Affiliated With: American Legion.

19490 ■ Boys and Girls Clubs of Sheboygan County Foundation
c/o John Grey
N5531 City Road S.
Plymouth, WI 53073-3814
Ph: (920)565-4114
Local.

19491 ■ National Association of Home Builders of the United States, Sheboygan County Home Builders Association (SCHBA)
435 E Mill St.
Plymouth, WI 53073
Ph: (920)892-6280
Fax: (920)893-9405
E-mail: mbinder@schba.org
URL: http://www.schba.org
Contact: Marsha Binder, Exec. Officer
Membership Dues: general, $455 (annual). **Local.** Single and multifamily home builders, commercial builders, and others associated with the building industry. **Computer Services:** Information services, member's directory. **Affiliated With:** National Association of Home Builders. **Publications:** *The Building Block*, monthly. Newsletter. Alternate Formats: online.

19492 ■ Plymouth Chamber of Commerce
PO Box 584
Plymouth, WI 53073
Ph: (920)893-0079
Fax: (920)893-8473
Free: (888)693-8263
E-mail: plymouthchamber@excel.net
URL: http://www.plymouthwisconsin.com
Contact: Lisa Hurley, Exec.Dir.
Founded: 1921. **Members:** 300. **Staff:** 1. **Local.** Promotes business and community development in Plymouth, WI. **Awards:** Business of the Year. **Frequency:** annual. **Type:** recognition • Family of the Year. **Frequency:** annual. **Type:** recognition. **Committees:** Community Development; Economic Development; Festival/Promotion; Membership; Tourism. **Programs:** Chamber Dollars Gift Certificate. **Publications:** *The Chamber Link*, monthly. Newsletter. Contains member news and chamber programs and meeting. **Circulation:** 300. **Advertising:** accepted.

19493 ■ Plymouth Junior Womans' Club (PJWC)
PO Box 185
Plymouth, WI 53073
E-mail: csedlacek@wi.rr.com
URL: http://home.wi.rr.com/gfwcplyjuniors
Contact: Clare Sedlacek, Pres.
Local.

Poplar

19494 ■ American Legion, Bong-Hofstedt-Douglas-County Post 409
PO Box 18
Poplar, WI 54864
Ph: (608)745-1090
Fax: (608)745-0179
URL: National Affiliate–www.legion.org
Local. Affiliated With: American Legion.

19495 ■ Brule River Riders Snowmobile Club
PO Box 107
Poplar, WI 54864-0107
Ph: (715)364-2590
E-mail: jmdeterl@pressenter.com
Local.

Port Edwards

19496 ■ American Society of Dowsers, The Heart of Wisconsin Dowsers Chapter
c/o Don Nolan
1631 Fourth St.
Port Edwards, WI 54469
Ph: (715)887-2693
E-mail: donnol@tznet.com
URL: National Affiliate–dowsers.new-hampshire.net
Local. Affiliated With: American Society of Dowsers.

19497 ■ Wisconsin Rapids Kennel Club (WRKC)
150 Market Ave.
Port Edwards, WI 54469
URL: http://www.wrkc.homestead.com/home.html
Contact: Lori Whitney, Sec.
State. Affiliated With: American Kennel Club.

Port Washington

19498 ■ American Legion, Wisconsin Post 82
c/o Andrew Van Ells
435 N Lake St., No. 482
Port Washington, WI 53074
Ph: (608)745-1090
Fax: (608)745-0179
URL: National Affiliate–www.legion.org
Contact: Andrew Van Ells, Contact
Local. Affiliated With: American Legion.

19499 ■ Classic Thunderbird Club of Wisconsin
1007 Fairview Dr.
Port Washington, WI 53074
Ph: (262)284-5321
E-mail: dws@smimail.com
URL: National Affiliate–www.vintagethunderbirdclub.org
State. Affiliated With: Vintage Thunderbird Club International.

19500 ■ Northeast Wisconsin Appaloosa Horse Club
c/o Tiffany Kindschy
148 E Prospect St.
Port Washington, WI 53074
Ph: (414)477-0676
E-mail: tiffanykindschy@yahoo.com
URL: National Affiliate–www.appaloosa.com
Contact: Tiffany Kindschy, Contact
Regional. Affiliated With: Appaloosa Horse Club.

19501 ■ Port Washington BMW Motorcycle Club No. 116
PO Box 94
Port Washington, WI 53074
Ph: (414)272-6907
E-mail: maraletaswenson@wi.rr.com
URL: http://www.portbmwclub.com
Contact: Dan Wundrock, Pres.
Local. Affiliated With: BMW Motorcycle Owners of America.

19502 ■ Port Washington Chamber of Commerce
PO Box 514
126 E Grand Ave.
Port Washington, WI 53074-0514
Ph: (262)284-0900
Fax: (262)284-0591
Free: (800)719-4881
E-mail: mary@portwashingtonchamber.com
URL: http://www.portwashingtonchamber.com
Contact: Mary Monday, Exec.Dir.
Local. Promotes business, community development, and tourism in Port Washington area.

19503 ■ United Way of Northern Ozaukee County
PO Box 39
Port Washington, WI 53074-0039
Ph: (262)284-8098
URL: National Affiliate–national.unitedway.org
Local. Affiliated With: United Way of America.

Port Wing

19504 ■ American Legion, Korppas-Johnson Post 531
PO Box 133
Port Wing, WI 54865
Ph: (715)372-5772
Fax: (608)745-0179
URL: National Affiliate–www.legion.org
Local. Affiliated With: American Legion.

Portage

19505 ■ American Legion Auxiliary of Wisconsin
c/o Kathy Wollmer, Sec.-Treas.
PO Box 140
Portage, WI 53901
Ph: (608)745-0124
Fax: (608)745-1947
E-mail: deptsec@amlegionauxwi.org
URL: http://www.amlegionauxwi.org
Contact: Kathy Wollmer, Sec.-Treas.
State. Affiliated With: American Legion Auxiliary.

19506 ■ American Legion Department of Wisconsin
c/o William R. West, Adj.
PO Box 388
2930 Amer. Legion Dr.
Portage, WI 53901-0388
Ph: (608)745-1090
Fax: (608)745-0179
E-mail: info@wilegion.org
Contact: Teddy L. Duckworth, Commander
Local. Affiliated With: American Legion. **Formerly:** (2005) American Legion of Wisconsin.

19507 ■ American Legion, Wisconsin Post 47
c/o Richard W. Mulcahy
PO Box 656
Portage, WI 53901
Ph: (608)745-1090
Fax: (608)745-0179
URL: National Affiliate–www.legion.org
Contact: Richard W. Mulcahy, Contact
Local. Affiliated With: American Legion.

19508 ■ Civic League
506 W Edgewater St.
Portage, WI 53901
Ph: (608)742-7744
Contact: Ms. Beverly Hoffman, Pres.
Founded: 1931. **Members:** 150. **Membership Dues:** $15 (annual). **Local.** Women in the Portage, WI area interested in raising funds for area civic needs. **Awards:** Four Year and Two Year Scholarship. **Frequency:** annual. **Type:** scholarship. **Recipient:** to a deserving high school student.

19509 ■ National Association of Home Builders of the U.S., Mid Wisconsin Home Builders Association
c/o Judy Shortreed
Local No. 5181
PO Box 865
Portage, WI 53901-0865
Ph: (608)742-1424
Fax: (608)742-1494
E-mail: mwhba@dwave.net
URL: http://www.mwhba.org
Contact: Judy Shortreed, Exec.Officer
Local. Single and multifamily home builders, commercial builders, and others associated with the building industry. **Affiliated With:** National Association of Home Builders.

19510 ■ Pony of the Americas Club, Wisconsin - Southern
c/o Amber Dreyer, Pres.
N7948 Hwy. EE
Portage, WI 53901
Ph: (608)697-1483
E-mail: kreierkountry@hotmail.com
URL: National Affiliate–www.poac.org
Contact: Amber Dreyer, Pres.
Regional. Affiliated With: Pony of the Americas Club.

19511 ■ Portage Area Chamber of Commerce (PACC)
132 W Cook St.
Portage, WI 53901
Ph: (608)742-6242
Fax: (608)742-3799
Free: (800)474-2525
E-mail: pacc@portagewi.com
URL: http://www.portagewi.com
Contact: Ken Jahn, Exec.Dir.
Founded: 1929. **Members:** 330. **Staff:** 2. **Budget:** $120,000. **Local.** Individuals and businesses working to enhance the quality of life and improve business in the Portage, WI area. Sponsors Taste of Portage. **Computer Services:** database, business directory. **Affiliated With:** U.S. Chamber of Commerce. **Formerly:** (1985) Greater Portage Area +Chamber of Commerce. **Publications:** *Chamber Inc.*, monthly. Newsletter. Includes business topics and membership updates. • *Portage Visitor Guides.* Brochures. **Conventions/Meetings:** annual meeting.

19512 ■ Portage Area REACT
PO Box 422
Portage, WI 53901-0422
Ph: (608)742-6603
E-mail: 4879@wireact.org
URL: http://www.reactintl.org/teaminfo/usa_teams/teams-uswi.htm
Local. Trained communication experts and professional volunteers. Provides volunteer public service and emergency communications through the use of radios (Citizen Band, General Mobile Radio Service, UHF and HAM). Coordinates with radio industries and government on safety communication matters and supports charitable activities and community organizations.

19513 ■ Portage Area United Way
PO Box 354
Portage, WI 53901-0354
Ph: (608)742-1919
URL: National Affiliate–national.unitedway.org
Local. Affiliated With: United Way of America.

19514 ■ Portage Curling Club
107 W Albert St.
Portage, WI 53901
Ph: (608)742-3237
E-mail: jjjpostman@charter.net
URL: http://www.portagecurling.com
Contact: Jim Jordan, Pres.
Local. Affiliated With: United States Curling Association.

19515 ■ Sons of Norway, Vakkertland Lodge 5-570
c/o Jeffery A. Levake, Pres.
N4655 Allan Rd.
Portage, WI 53901-8945
Ph: (608)742-3263
E-mail: levakefm@merr.com
URL: National Affiliate–www.sofn.com
Contact: Jeffery A. Levake, Pres.
Local. Affiliated With: Sons of Norway.

19516 ■ Wisconsin Christmas Tree Producers Association
c/o Cheryl Nicholson, Exec.Sec.
W9833 Hogan Rd.
Portage, WI 53901
Ph: (608)742-8663
Fax: (608)742-8667
E-mail: info@christmastrees-wi.org
URL: http://www.christmastrees-wi.org
Contact: Ms. Cheryl Nicholson, Exec.Sec.
Founded: 1954. **Members:** 300. **State.** Strives to educate and provide the latest information on current issues to members; sponsors two annual conventions and a summer farm tour to provide networking with other growers; publishes three journals a year.

19517 ■ Wisconsin Curling Association
c/o Chris Daly, Pres.
640 Morningstar Dr.
Portage, WI 53901
Ph: (608)742-8026
E-mail: dalyrjandcr@hotmail.com
Contact: Chris Daly, Pres.
State. Affiliated With: United States Curling Association.

19518 ■ Wisconsin Curling Association - Portage Curling Club
107 W Albert St.
Portage, WI 53901
Ph: (608)742-3237
URL: http://www.angelfire.com/hi5/bibby/main.html
Contact: Jim Jordan, Pres.
Local. Affiliated With: United States Curling Association.

Porterfield

19519 ■ American Legion, Schwartz-Loll-Richards Post 476
PO Box 36
Porterfield, WI 54159
Ph: (608)745-1090
Fax: (608)745-0179
URL: National Affiliate–www.legion.org
Local. Affiliated With: American Legion.

19520 ■ Sons of Norway, F.M. Christiansen Lodge 5-624
c/o John A. Berg, Pres.
W3614 County Rd. G
Porterfield, WI 54159-9732
Ph: (715)789-2453
E-mail: john.berg@centurytel.net
URL: National Affiliate–www.sofn.com
Contact: John A. Berg, Pres.
Local. Affiliated With: Sons of Norway.

Potosi

19521 ■ American Legion, Uppena-Kroepfle Post 473
105 Cross St.
Potosi, WI 53820
Ph: (608)745-1090
Fax: (608)745-0179
URL: National Affiliate–www.legion.org
Local. Affiliated With: American Legion.

19522 ■ Potosi - Tennyson Area Chamber of Commerce
PO Box 11
Potosi, WI 53820
Ph: (608)763-2261
Fax: (608)763-2537
Contact: Marilyn Hauth, Pres.
Local.

Poynette

19523 ■ American Legion, Wisconsin Post 271
c/o Clyde Sheppard
PO Box 132
Poynette, WI 53955
Ph: (608)745-1090
Fax: (608)745-0179
URL: National Affiliate–www.legion.org
Contact: Clyde Sheppard, Contact
Local. Affiliated With: American Legion.

19524 ■ Lake Wisconsin Chamber of Commerce
PO Box 441
Poynette, WI 53955
Ph: (608)635-8070
E-mail: info@lakewisconsin.org
URL: http://www.lakewisconsin.org
Contact: Denise Miller, Sec.
Local. Promotes business and community development in the Lake Wisconsin area.

19525 ■ Poynette Bowhunters Association
W2737 Hwy. Q
Poynette, WI 53955
Ph: (608)635-9852
E-mail: info@poynettebowhunters.com
URL: http://www.poynettebowhunters.com
Contact: Robert Nowak, Contact
Founded: 1975. **Members:** 307. **Staff:** 15. **Local.** Promotes the sport of archery. Seeks to make bowhunters better shooters; generate camaraderie with other sports; and help protect bowhunting. **Affiliated With:** Wisconsin Bowhunters Association.

19526 ■ Poynette Chamber of Commerce
PO Box 625
Poynette, WI 53955
Ph: (608)635-2425
E-mail: humblehost@tds.net
URL: http://www.poynettechamber.com/index.html
Contact: Garry Gill, Pres.
Local. Promotes business and community development in Poynette, WI.

Prairie Du Chien

19527 ■ American Legion, Caya-Bunders Post 68
PO Box 375
Prairie Du Chien, WI 53821
Ph: (608)745-1090
Fax: (608)745-0179
URL: National Affiliate–www.legion.org
Local. Affiliated With: American Legion.

19528 ■ Prairie du Chien Lions Club
c/o Jerome Lester, Pres.
402 N Beaumont Rd.
Prairie Du Chien, WI 53821
Ph: (608)326-1464
E-mail: jllpdc@hotmail.com
URL: http://www.md27d2.org
Contact: Jerome Lester, Pres.
Local. Affiliated With: Lions Clubs International.

19529 ■ Prairie Du Chien Area Chamber of Commerce (PDCACC)
211 S Main
PO Box 326
Prairie Du Chien, WI 53821
Ph: (608)326-8555
Fax: (608)326-7744
Free: (800)732-1673
E-mail: info@prairieduchien.org
URL: http://www.prairieduchien.org
Contact: Sharon Dearborn, Exec.Dir.
Founded: 1950. **Members:** 210. **Membership Dues:** business (3 FTE employees), $145 (annual) • business (2 or less FTE employees), $100 (annual) • individual, organization, $53 (annual) • associate, church, retired, $40 (annual). **Local.** Promotes business and community development in the Prairie du Chien, WI area. **Convention/Meeting:** none. **Telecommunication Services:** electronic mail, pdccoc@mhtc.net. **Affiliated With:** U.S. Chamber of Commerce.

19530 ■ Prairie Du Chien Industrial Development Corp.
c/o Sharon Cuchna, Sec.
211 S Main
PO Box 326
Prairie Du Chien, WI 53821
Ph: (608)326-8555
Fax: (608)326-7744
E-mail: pdccoc@mhtc.net
URL: http://www.prairieduchien.org
Contact: Sharon Cuchna, Sec.
Local.

19531 ■ United Way of the Prairie Du Chien Area
PO Box 181
Prairie Du Chien, WI 53821-0181
Ph: (608)326-0909
URL: National Affiliate–national.unitedway.org
Local. Affiliated With: United Way of America.

Prairie Du Sac

19532 ■ Sauk Prairie Area Chamber of Commerce (SPACC)
421 Water St., Ste.105
Prairie Du Sac, WI 53578
Ph: (608)643-4168
Fax: (608)643-3544
Free: (800)68-EAGLE
E-mail: saukprairie@verizon.net
URL: http://www.saukprairie.com
Contact: Leslie McFarlane, Exec.Dir.
Founded: 1956. **Members:** 173. **Local.** Promotes business and community development in the Sauk City and Prairie du Sac, WI area. **Publications:** *Sauk Prairie Area Chamber of Commerce Business/Membership Directory*, periodic • Newsletter, monthly. **Conventions/Meetings:** monthly meeting.

19533 ■ Sauk Prairie Lions Club
c/o Nancy Passehl, Sec.
1015 Eagle View Ct.
Prairie Du Sac, WI 53578
Ph: (608)643-3008
E-mail: nnbpass@charter.net
URL: http://www.md27d2.org
Contact: Nancy Passehl, Sec.
Local. Affiliated With: Lions Clubs International.

19534 ■ Sauk Prairie Trap and Skeet
E 11102 Sauk Prairie Rd.
Prairie Du Sac, WI 53578
Ph: (608)643-4844
URL: National Affiliate–www.mynssa.com
Local. Affiliated With: National Skeet Shooting Association.

19535 ■ Sauk-Prairie United Way
PO Box 122
Prairie Du Sac, WI 53578-0122
Ph: (608)643-8591
URL: National Affiliate–national.unitedway.org
Local. Affiliated With: United Way of America.

Prentice

19536 ■ American Legion, Johnson-Hallberg Post 407
N 5033 Hwy. A
Prentice, WI 54556
Ph: (608)745-1090
Fax: (608)745-0179
URL: National Affiliate–www.legion.org
Local. Affiliated With: American Legion.

19537 ■ Prentice Industrial Development Corporation
c/o Dale Heikkinen, Pres.
PO Box 78
Prentice, WI 54556
Ph: (715)428-2000 (715)428-2746
Fax: (715)428-2700
E-mail: daleh@pctcnet.net
URL: http://www.co.price.wi.us
Contact: Dale Heikkinen, Pres.
Founded: 1950. **Members:** 58. **Staff:** 7. **Local.**

Prescott

19538 ■ Prescott Area Chamber of Commerce (PACC)
237 Broad St. N
Prescott, WI 54021
Ph: (715)262-3284
Fax: (715)262-5943
E-mail: info@prescottwi.com
URL: http://www.prescottwi.com
Contact: Trisha Huber, Coor.
Founded: 1979. **Members:** 115. **Local.** Promotes business and community development in the Prescott, WI area. Assists with local festivals. **Publications:** *Prescott Visitor and New Residents Guide*, annual. Directory. **Conventions/Meetings:** monthly meeting - usually 2nd Thursday of the month.

19539 ■ Wisconsin Wildlife Federation (WWF)
PO Box 68
Prescott, WI 54021-0068
Ph: (715)262-9279
Fax: (715)262-5856
Free: (800)897-4161
E-mail: office@wiwf.org
URL: http://www.wiwf.org
Contact: George Meyer, Exec.Dir.
Founded: 1949. **State.** Aims for a stronger, more effective and recognized force for the sustainable use and protection of natural resources.

Presque Isle

19540 ■ American Legion, Winegar Post 480
11632 County Trunk W
Presque Isle, WI 54557
Ph: (608)745-1090
Fax: (608)745-0179
URL: National Affiliate–www.legion.org
Local. Affiliated With: American Legion.

19541 ■ Presque Isle Chamber of Commerce (PICC)
PO Box 135
Presque Isle, WI 54557
Ph: (715)686-2910
Fax: (715)686-2913
Free: (888)835-6508
E-mail: presqueisle@centurytel.net
URL: http://www.presqueislewi.org
Contact: George Nelson, Dir.
Members: 166. **Membership Dues:** base, $95 (annual). **Staff:** 1. **Local.** Promotes business and community development in Presque Isle, WI.

Princeton

19542 ■ American Legion, Kasierski-Kozlowski Post 366
853 W Main St.
Princeton, WI 54968
Ph: (608)745-1090
Fax: (608)745-0179
URL: National Affiliate–www.legion.org
Local. Affiliated With: American Legion.

19543 ■ Greater Princeton Area Chamber of Commerce (GPACC)
PO Box 45
Princeton, WI 54968
Ph: (920)295-3877
Fax: (920)295-4375
E-mail: chamber@princetonwi.com
URL: http://www.princetonwi.com
Contact: Vikki D. Van Buren, Chamber Dir.
Members: 161. **Membership Dues:** business, $90 (annual) • sevice organization, $35 (annual). **Staff:** 2. **Local.** Promotes business and community development in Princeton, WI. Makes charitable contributions; sponsors annual summer flea market. **Awards: Type:** scholarship. **Recipient:** enrollment in higher education. **Formerly:** (1999) Princeton Chamber of Commerce. **Publications:** Directory, periodic. **Conventions/Meetings:** monthly Chamber Meeting.

Pulaski

19544 ■ American Legion, Mixtacki-Johnson Post 337
PO Box 746
Pulaski, WI 54162
Ph: (608)745-1090
Fax: (608)745-0179
URL: National Affiliate–www.legion.org
Local. Affiliated With: American Legion.

19545 ■ American Rabbit Breeders Association, Fox Valley Rabbit Club
c/o Lisa Mossholder, Sec.
W1734 County Rd. S
Pulaski, WI 54162
URL: http://www.geocities.com/wisconsin_state_rba/Local_Clubs.html
Contact: Lisa Mossholder, Sec.
Local. Affiliated With: American Rabbit Breeders Association.

19546 ■ Organic Crop Improvement Association, Wisconsin- Chapter 1
c/o Dale Johnson
5381 Norway Dr.
Pulaski, WI 54162
Ph: (920)822-2629
Fax: (920)822-1261
E-mail: johnsonsorganics@hotmail.com
URL: National Affiliate–www.ocia.org
Contact: Dale Johnson, Contact
State. Affiliated With: Organic Crop Improvement Association.

19547 ■ Pulaski Area Chamber of Commerce
159 W Pulaski St.
PO Box 401
Pulaski, WI 54162-0401
Ph: (920)822-4400
Fax: (920)822-4455
E-mail: pacc@netnet.net
URL: http://www.pulaskichamber.org
Contact: Mr. Doug Prentice, Chamber Board Pres.
Members: 90. **Membership Dues:** associate, $77 • retired business person, $36. **Local.** Promotes business and community development in the Pulaski, WI area. **Programs:** Welcome. **Conventions/Meetings:** monthly meeting - every 2nd Monday.

Racine

19548 ■ Alcoholics Anonymous World Services, Racine Area Central Office
3701 Durand Ave., No. LL225B
Racine, WI 53405-4458
Ph: (262)554-6611 (262)554-7788
URL: National Affiliate–www.aa.org
Local. Individuals recovering from alcoholism. AA maintains that members can solve their common problem and help others achieve sobriety through a twelve step program that includes sharing their experience, strength, and hope with each other. **Affiliated With:** Alcoholics Anonymous World Services.

19549 ■ American Legion, Wisconsin Post 310
c/o Harvey R. Hansen
PO Box 044032
Racine, WI 53402
Ph: (608)745-1090
Fax: (608)745-0179
URL: National Affiliate–www.legion.org
Contact: Harvey R. Hansen, Contact
Local. Affiliated With: American Legion.

19550 ■ American Legion, Wisconsin Post 546
c/o Dorie Miller
1234 Douglas Ave.
Racine, WI 53402
Ph: (608)745-1090
Fax: (608)745-0179
URL: National Affiliate–www.legion.org
Contact: Dorie Miller, Contact
Local. Affiliated With: American Legion.

19551 ■ American Red Cross Southeast Wisconsin Tri-County Chapter
c/o Craig Husch
4521 Taylor Ave.
Racine, WI 53405
Ph: (262)554-9997
Fax: (262)554-9691
Free: (800)566-4060
E-mail: huschc@usa.redcross.org
URL: http://sewisconsin.redcross.org
Contact: Ms. Tressa Stein, Dir., Health and Safety Services
Local. Publications: *CrossRoads*. Newsletter.

19552 ■ APICS, The Association for Operations Management - Racine/Kenosha Chapter
PO Box 081302
Racine, WI 53408-1302
Ph: (262)898-6317
E-mail: information@rakeapics.org
URL: http://www.rakeapics.org
Contact: Rosemary Van Treeck CPIM, Pres.
Local. Provides information and services in production and inventory management and related areas to enable members, enterprises and individuals to add value to their business performance. **Affiliated With:** APICS - The Association for Operations Management.

19553 ■ Carwash Owner and Suppliers
1822 S. St.
Racine, WI 53404
Ph: (262)639-4393

19554 ■ Dress for Success Racine
YWCA of Racine
740 Coll. Ave.
Racine, WI 53403
Ph: (262)633-3503
E-mail: racine@dressforsuccess.org
URL: National Affiliate–www.dressforsuccess.org
Local.

19555 ■ Greater Racine Kennel Club (GRKC)
6320 6 Mile Rd.
Racine, WI 53402
Ph: (262)681-0700 (262)835-4166
E-mail: grkcobedience@grkc.org
URL: http://www.grkc.org
Contact: Ellen Hauerwas, Pres.
Local.

19556 ■ Hoy Audubon Society
c/o Eric Howe, Pres.
PO Box 044626
Racine, WI 53404
E-mail: info@hoyaudubon.org
URL: National Affiliate–www.audubon.org
Contact: Eric Howe, Pres.
Local. Works to conserve and restore natural ecosystems, focusing on birds and other wildlife for the benefit of humanity and the earth's biological diversity. **Affiliated With:** National Audubon Society.

19557 ■ Junior Achievement of Racine
c/o Lori Bastian, District Dir.
PO Box 1721
Racine, WI 53401
Ph: (262)638-4338
Fax: (262)638-4486
E-mail: director@jaracine.org
URL: http://wisconsin.ja.org
Contact: Lori Bastian, District Dir.
Local.

19558 ■ Milwaukee Corvair Club (MCC)
c/o Dave Schneider
3400 3 Mile Rd.
Racine, WI 53404
E-mail: milwaukeecorvairclub@yahoo.com
URL: http://www.milwaukeecorvairclub.com
Contact: Dave Schneider, Contact
Local. Affiliated With: Corvair Society of America.

19559 ■ Musicians' Union - Local 42, American Federation of Musicians
2803 Brentwood Dr.
Racine, WI 53403
Ph: (262)930-0468
Fax: (262)835-9677
E-mail: local42@afm.org
URL: http://www.afm.org/42
Contact: Byron Heusdens, Pres.
Local. AFL-CIO. Musicians. Seeks to improve the wages and working conditions of professional musicians. **Affiliated With:** American Federation of Musicians of the United States and Canada.

19560 ■ National Active and Retired Federal Employees Association - Racine 346
1726 Charles St.
Racine, WI 53404-2302
Ph: (262)633-8034
URL: National Affiliate–www.narfe.org
Contact: Robert C. Wemmert, Contact
Local. Protects the retirement future of employees through education. Informs members on issues affecting the retirement. **Affiliated With:** National Association of Retired Federal Employees.

19561 ■ National Alliance for the Mentally Ill - Racine County
2300 DeKoven Ave.
Racine, WI 53403
Ph: (262)637-0582
Fax: (262)637-0376
E-mail: info@namiracine.org
URL: http://www.namiracine.org
Contact: Debby Ganaway, Exec.Dir.

Local. Strives to improve the quality of life of children and adults with severe mental illness through support, education, research and advocacy. **Affiliated With:** National Alliance for the Mentally Ill.

19562 ■ National Association of Rocketry - Wisconsin Organization of Spacemodeling Hobbyists (WOOSH)
c/o Scott T. Goebel, Pres.
3423 Pierce Blvd.
Racine, WI 53405
Ph: (262)634-3971
E-mail: zapjolt@wi.rr.com
URL: http://www.wooshrocketry.org
Contact: Scott T. Goebel, Pres.

State.

19563 ■ Navy Club of Racine - Ship No. 60
1020 Coronado Dr.
Racine, WI 53402
Ph: (414)639-2250
URL: National Affiliate–www.navyclubusa.org
Contact: Rick Browne, Commander

Local. Represents individuals who are, or have been, in the active service of the U.S. Navy, Naval Reserve, Marine Corps, Marine Corps Reserve, and Coast Guard. Promotes and encourages further public interest in the U.S. Navy and its history. Upholds the spirit and ideals of the U.S. Navy. Acts as a public forum for members' views on national defense. Assists the Navy Recruiting Command whenever and wherever possible. Conducts charitable activities. **Affiliated With:** Navy Club of the United States of America.

19564 ■ Navy League of the United States, Milwaukee
c/o Richard T. Vallin
17 Sandalwood Ct.
Racine, WI 53402-2846
Ph: (262)375-5514
Fax: (262)375-3680
E-mail: amt@amt-wi.com
URL: National Affiliate–www.navyleague.org
Contact: Richard T. Vallin, Pres.

Local. Civilian organization that supports U.S. capability to keep the sea lanes open through a strong, viable Navy, Marine Corps, Coast Guard, and Merchant Marine. Seeks to awaken interest and cooperation of U.S. citizens in matters serving to aid, improve, and develop the efficiency of U.S. naval and maritime forces and equipment. **Affiliated With:** Navy League of the United States.

19565 ■ Racine Area Manufacturers and Commerce (RAMAC)
300 5th St.
Racine, WI 53403
Ph: (262)634-1931
Fax: (262)634-7422
E-mail: ramac@racinechamber.com
URL: http://www.racinechamber.com
Contact: Roger Caron, Pres.

Founded: 1982. **Members:** 750. **Local**. Strives to strengthen the economic and business community of Racine area. **Libraries: Type:** reference. **Telecommunication Services:** electronic mail, rcaron@racinechamber.com. **Committees:** Career Connections; Education; Environmental Quality/Energy; Legislative; Police and Fire; Racine Ambassadors; Safety. **Programs:** Mentor. **Formerly:** (1999) Racine Chamber of Commerce. **Publications:** Newsletter. **Advertising:** accepted. Alternate Formats: online.

19566 ■ Racine Astronomical Society
PO Box 085694
Racine, WI 53408
Ph: (404)634-7701
E-mail: rasastro@wi.net
URL: http://www.iwc.net/~rasastro
Contact: Webb Temple, Contact

Local. Promotes the science of astronomy. Works to encourage and coordinate activities of amateur astronomical societies. Fosters observational and computational work and craftsmanship in various fields of astronomy. **Affiliated With:** Astronomical League.

19567 ■ Racine Council on Alcohol and Other Drug Abuse
1220 Mound Ave., Ste.307
Racine, WI 53404
Ph: (262)632-6200
E-mail: racine.wi@ncadd.org
URL: National Affiliate–www.ncadd.org

Local. **Affiliated With:** National Council on Alcoholism and Drug Dependence.

19568 ■ Racine Curling Club
1914 Melvin Ave.
Racine, WI 53404
Ph: (262)639-9990
E-mail: info@racinecurlingclub.com
URL: http://www.racinecurlingclub.com
Contact: Chris Kelly, Pres.

Founded: 1954. **Local**. **Affiliated With:** United States Curling Association.

19569 ■ Racine Habitat for Humanity
1501 Villa St.
Racine, WI 53403
Ph: (262)637-9176
E-mail: ccc1501@root.com.net
Contact: Nora Grosse, Exec.Dir.

Founded: 1988. **Local**. Individuals interested in providing affordable housing to people in need. **Affiliated With:** Habitat for Humanity International.

19570 ■ Racine Numismatic Society
c/o Bill Spencer
4625 Washington Ave.
Racine, WI 53405
Ph: (262)637-7766
URL: National Affiliate–www.money.org
Contact: Bill Spencer, Contact

Local. **Affiliated With:** American Numismatic Association.

19571 ■ Racine Yacht Club
1 Barker St.
Racine, WI 53402
Ph: (262)634-8587
E-mail: office@racineyachtclub.org
URL: http://www.racineyachtclub.org

Local.

19572 ■ Retired and Senior Volunteer Program of Racine (RSVP)
c/o Cheryl Christensen, Dir.
6216 Washington Ave., Ste.G
Racine, WI 53406
Ph: (262)886-9612
Fax: (262)886-9632
E-mail: cchristensen@volunteercenterofracine.org
URL: http://www.seniorcorps.gov/about/programs/rsvp_state.asp?usestateabbr=wi&Search4.x=0&Search4.y=0
Contact: Cheryl Christensen, Dir.

Local. Works to promote volunteerism. Recruits individuals (55 and over) to share their life experience and skills to help in the community. **Affiliated With:** Retired and Senior Volunteer Program.

19573 ■ Sons of Norway, Nordlyset Lodge 5-183
c/o John W. Graham, Pres.
3306 Michigan Blvd.
Racine, WI 53402-3822
Ph: (262)752-9456
E-mail: graham-wi@tds.net
URL: National Affiliate–www.sofn.com
Contact: John W. Graham, Pres.

Local. **Affiliated With:** Sons of Norway.

19574 ■ Southeastern Wisconsin Youth for Christ
PO Box 081041
Racine, WI 53408
Ph: (262)633-9016
Fax: (262)633-9026
URL: http://www.youthforchrist.ws

Local. **Affiliated With:** Youth for Christ/U.S.A.

19575 ■ Sustainable Racine
413 S Main St.
Racine, WI 53403-1030
Ph: (262)632-6440
Fax: (262)632-6408
E-mail: bonnie@sustainable.org
URL: http://www.sustainableracine.org
Contact: Bonnie Prochaska, Exec.Dir.

Founded: 1997. **Staff:** 4. **Budget:** $500,000. **Local**.

19576 ■ Sweet Adelines International, Opus 2000 Chapter
Our Savior's Lutheran Church
2219 Washington Ave.
Racine, WI 53405-3551
Ph: (262)878-1947
E-mail: llameer@wi.rr.com
URL: National Affiliate–www.sweetadelineintl.org
Contact: Lucretia LaMeer, Contact

Local. Advances the musical art form of barbershop harmony through education and performances. Provides education, training and coaching in the development of women's four-part barbershop harmony. **Affiliated With:** Sweet Adelines International.

19577 ■ Tech Corps Wisconsin (TCW)
c/o Mr. Michael F. Pitsch, Exec.Dir.
1220 Mound Ave., Ste.205
Racine, WI 53404
Ph: (262)619-0931
Fax: (262)898-1560
E-mail: info@tcw.org
URL: http://www.tcw.org
Contact: Mr. Michael F. Pitsch, Exec.Dir.

Founded: 1996. **Members:** 50. **Staff:** 5. **Budget:** $150,000. **State Groups:** 1. **For-Profit**. **Local**. Works to bridge the digital divide by providing access to technology for children. **Computer Services:** Online services, refurbished computer systems and components, software and hardware skills training, technical support and repair of computer systems. **Telecommunication Services:** information service, Internet service provider (Racine local area). **Affiliated With:** TECH CORPS.

19578 ■ Tri-County Contractors Association (TCCA)
300 5th St.
Racine, WI 53403
Ph: (262)634-5231
Fax: (262)634-7422
E-mail: jacque@racinechamber.com
URL: http://www.tccaonline.com
Contact: Jacqueline Boudreau, Exec.Dir.

Membership Dues: regular, $350 (annual) • associate, $250 (annual). **Local**. Promotes construction in the Tri-County area. Fosters cooperation and understanding between general contractors, subcontractors, and suppliers, for their mutual benefit.

19579 ■ United Way of Racine County
2000 Domanik Dr.
Racine, WI 53404-2910
Ph: (262)632-5186
Fax: (262)632-1156
E-mail: unitedway@unitedwayracine.org
URL: http://www.unitedwayracine.org

Local. **Affiliated With:** United Way of America.

19580 ■ Urban League of Racine and Kenosha
c/o Honey Reneau, Pres.
718-22 N Memorial Dr.
Racine, WI 53404
Ph: (262)637-8532
E-mail: yethoney@prodigy.net
URL: National Affiliate–www.nul.org
Contact: Honey Reneau, Pres.
Local. Affiliated With: National Urban League.

19581 ■ Wisconsin Edsel Club
7529 Old Spring Rd.
Racine, WI 53406
E-mail: edseldave60@yahoo.com
URL: National Affiliate–www.internationaledsel.com
State. Affiliated With: International Edsel Club.

19582 ■ Wisconsin Society of Radiologic Technologists (WSRT)
c/o Kelley Grant, RT, Pres.
3801 Spring St.
Racine, WI 53405-1667
Ph: (262)687-4588 (262)835-1780
E-mail: kelley.grant@wfhc.org
URL: http://www.wsrt.net
Contact: Kelley Grant RT, Pres.
State. Represents the professional society of radiologic technologists. Advances education and research in the radiologic sciences. Evaluates quality patient care. Improves the welfare and socioeconomics of radiologic technologists. **Affiliated With:** American Society of Radiologic Technologists.

19583 ■ Wisillin Winds Radio Controlled Yacht Club No. 80
c/o Robert T. Maleske
2004 Esquire Ln.
Racine, WI 53406-2394
Ph: (262)886-4328
URL: National Affiliate–www.amya.org
Contact: Robert T. Maleske, Contact
Local.

Radisson

19584 ■ American Legion, Wisconsin Post 297
c/o Dave De Rosia
RR 1, Box 27c
Radisson, WI 54867
Ph: (608)745-1090
Fax: (608)745-0179
URL: National Affiliate–www.legion.org
Contact: Dave De Rosia, Contact
Local. Affiliated With: American Legion.

Randolph

19585 ■ Madison Area Miniature Enthusiasts
c/o Nancy L. Woudstra
W1607 Cemetery Rd.
Randolph, WI 53956
Ph: (920)348-5621
E-mail: mnwoudstra@centurytel.net
URL: http://www.miniatures.org/states/WI.html
Contact: Nancy L. Woudstra, Contact
Local. Affiliated With: National Association of Miniature Enthusiasts.

19586 ■ Randolph Chamber of Commerce (RCC)
349 Stark St.
Randolph, WI 53956
Ph: (920)326-4769
Fax: (920)326-4129
E-mail: ken.hillman@centurytel.com
URL: http://www.randolphwi.net
Contact: Harold De Vries, Sec.-Treas.
Members: 48. **Local.** Promotes business and community development in Randolph, WI. Sponsors annual Maxwell Street Festival. **Publications:** *Business Directory*, periodic • *Randolph: A Great Place to Grow*. Brochure. **Conventions/Meetings:** quarterly dinner - always 1st Wednesday of January, April, July, and October • meeting - 6/year; always first Wednesday of February, March, June, August, September, and December.

19587 ■ Wisconsin State Reading Association (WSRA)
c/o Sue Bradley, Admin.Asst.
N7902 E Friesland Rd.
Randolph, WI 53956
Ph: (920)326-6280
Fax: (920)326-6280
E-mail: wsra@centurytel.net
URL: http://www.wsra.org
Contact: Sue Bradley, Admin.Asst.
Founded: 1956. **Members:** 3,000. **Membership Dues:** $18 (annual). **Local Groups:** 20. **State.** Individuals involved in the teaching or supervising of reading united to improve the quality of reading instruction at all educational levels and to promote the lifetime reading habit. **Affiliated With:** International Reading Association. **Publications:** *Wisconsin Reading Update*, quarterly. Newsletter • *WSRA Journal*, 3/year. **Conventions/Meetings:** annual conference - always February.

Random Lake

19588 ■ Lake Shore Optometric Society
c/o Nichole M. Cruz, OD, Pres.
PO Box 2
Random Lake, WI 53075
Ph: (920)994-8500
Fax: (920)994-8550
E-mail: ncruznjot@hotmail.com
URL: http://www.woa-eyes.org
Contact: Nichole M. Cruz OD, Pres.
Local. Aims to improve the quality, availability and accessibility of eye and vision care. Promotes high standards of patient care. Monitors and promotes legislation concerning the scope of optometric practice and other issues relevant to eye/vision care. **Affiliated With:** American Optometric Association; Wisconsin Optometric Association.

Reedsburg

19589 ■ American Legion, Fuhrman-Finnegan Post 350
PO Box 354
Reedsburg, WI 53959
Ph: (608)745-1090
Fax: (608)745-0179
URL: National Affiliate–www.legion.org
Local. Affiliated With: American Legion.

19590 ■ Mothers Against Drunk Driving, Sauk County
E 10104 Buckhorn Rd.
Reedsburg, WI 53959
Ph: (608)355-6233 (608)356-1124
Fax: (608)356-4069
E-mail: graupman@midplains.net
URL: National Affiliate–www.madd.org
Contact: Marjorie Smith, Pres.
Local. Victims of drunk driving crashes; concerned citizens. Encourages citizen participation in working towards reform of the drunk driving problem and the prevention of underage drinking. Acts as the voice of victims of drunk driving crashes by speaking on their behalf to communities, businesses, and educational groups. **Affiliated With:** Mothers Against Drunk Driving.

19591 ■ Peaceways-Young General Assembly
c/o Ellen Brogren, Secretariat Coor.
1950 Sunset Dr.
Reedsburg, WI 53959
Ph: (608)524-4608
Fax: (608)524-4608
E-mail: peaceways@igc.org
URL: http://Young-GA.org
Contact: Ellen Brogren, Secretariat Coor.
Founded: 1989. **Members:** 2,500,000. **Regional.** Strives to promote peace and child rights by serving as a voice in international affairs for people under 18.

19592 ■ Reedsburg Area Chamber of Commerce (RACC)
PO Box 142
Reedsburg, WI 53959
Ph: (608)524-2850
Fax: (608)524-5392
Free: (800)844-3507
E-mail: webmaster@reedsburg.org
URL: http://www.reedsburg.org/
Contact: Jan Wirth, Exec.Dir.
Founded: 1921. **Members:** 222. **Staff:** 1. **Budget:** $45,000. **Local.** Promotes business and community development in the Reedsburg, WI area. **Publications:** *Chamber News*, monthly. Newsletter.

Reedsville

19593 ■ American Legion, Gosz-Novak Post 199
c/o Cletus Ratrichek
213 S 5th St.
Reedsville, WI 54230
Ph: (608)745-1090
Fax: (608)745-0179
URL: National Affiliate–www.legion.org
Contact: Cletus Ratrichek, Contact
Local. Affiliated With: American Legion.

Reeseville

19594 ■ American Legion, Reeseville Post 190
PO Box 175
Reeseville, WI 53579
Ph: (608)745-1090
Fax: (608)745-0179
URL: National Affiliate–www.legion.org
Local. Affiliated With: American Legion.

Rhinelander

19595 ■ American Association of Healthcare Administrative Management, Wisconsin Chapter
c/o Judy Waydick, Pres.
Sacred Heart/St. Mary's Americollect, Inc.
2251 N Shore Dr., No. 100
Rhinelander, WI 54501
Ph: (715)361-2856
E-mail: info@aaham-wi.org
URL: National Affiliate–www.aaham.org
Contact: Judy Waydick, Pres.
State. Represents the interests of healthcare administrative management professionals. Seeks proper recognition for the financial aspect of hospital and clinic management. Provides member services and leadership in the areas of education, communication, representation, professional standards and certification. **Affiliated With:** American Association of Healthcare Administrative Management.

19596 ■ American Legion, Dahlberg-Makris Post 7
1002 Coon St.
Rhinelander, WI 54501
Ph: (608)745-1090
Fax: (608)745-0179
URL: National Affiliate–www.legion.org
Local. Affiliated With: American Legion.

19597 ■ Camp Fire USA Oneida Council
City Hall
Rhinelander, WI 54501
Ph: (715)362-3513
Fax: (715)369-1932
E-mail: cfusaoneida@frontiernet.net
URL: http://www.gototomahawk.com/campfire
Contact: Traci Wehrman, Exec.Dir.

Founded: 1961. **Members:** 1,000. **Membership Dues:** youth, $7 (annual) • adult, $10 (annual) • family, $25 (annual). **Staff:** 3. **Budget:** $60,000. **Local.** Works to develop leadership and good citizenship in children and youth through informal educational and recreational programs, such as camp, club, self-reliance programs, workshops, and community services. **Boards:** Board of Directors. **Committees:** Camp; Finance; Fund Raising; Long Range Planning; Nomination; Program; Property; Self-reliance. **Affiliated With:** Camp Fire USA. **Formerly:** (1995) Oneida Council of Camp Fire. **Publications:** *Camp Fire Flame*, periodic. Newsletter. Contains activities offered by Council and information about the state of the Council. **Price:** included in membership dues. **Conventions/Meetings:** annual meeting - always last Monday of January in Rhinelander, WI.

19598 ■ Lumberjack Resource Conservation and Development Council
639 W Kemp St.
Rhinelander, WI 54501
Ph: (715)362-3690
Fax: (715)362-3694
E-mail: kim.goerg@wi.usda.gov
URL: http://www.wi.nrcs.usda.gov/partnerships/lumberjack/what.html
Contact: Kim Goerg, Coor.

Local. Affiliated With: National Association of Resource Conservation and Development Councils.

19599 ■ Midwest Association of Fish and Wildlife Agencies (MAFWA)
c/o Ollie Torgerson, Coor.
Wisconsin Dept. of Natural Resources
107 Sutliff Ave.
Rhinelander, WI 54501
Ph: (715)365-8924
Fax: (715)365-8932
E-mail: ollie.torgerson@dnr.state.wi.us
URL: http://www.mafwa.iafwa.org
Contact: Joe Kramer, Sec.-Treas.

Founded: 1934. **Members:** 17. **Membership Dues:** state, $300 (annual) • province, $100 (annual). **Staff:** 1. **State Groups:** 14. Fish and game commissioners and directors of 14 Midwestern states and three Canadian provinces. Promotes conservation of wildlife and outdoor recreation. **Libraries: Type:** open to the public. **Holdings:** 64. **Awards:** Resource Contribution Awards. **Frequency:** annual. **Type:** recognition. **Committees:** Auditing; By-Laws; Legal; National Conservation Needs; Nominating/Awards; Public Land Management; Resolutions; Wildlife and Fish Health. **Working Groups:** Private Lands. **Affiliated With:** International Association of Fish and Wildlife Agencies; Western Association of Fish and Wildlife Agencies. **Formerly:** (1975) Association of Midwest Fish and Game Commissioners; (1977) Association of Midwest Fish and Wildlife Commissioners; (2002) Association of Midwest Fish and Wildlife Agencies. **Publications:** Proceedings, annual. **Conventions/Meetings:** annual Director's Meeting - conference (exhibits).

19600 ■ Northeastern Wisconsin RSVP
c/o Lori J. Bushong, Dir.
1835 N Stevens St.
Rhinelander, WI 54501-0284
Ph: (715)369-1919
Fax: (715)369-3686
E-mail: lorijays@hotmail.com
URL: http://www.seniorcorps.gov/about/programs/rsvp_state.asp?usestateabbr=wi&Search4.x=0&Search4.y=0
Contact: Lori J. Bushong, Dir.

Local. Affiliated With: Retired and Senior Volunteer Program.

19601 ■ Northwoods United Way
PO Box 177
Rhinelander, WI 54501-0177
Ph: (715)369-0440
E-mail: nwuway@newnorth.net
URL: National Affiliate–national.unitedway.org
Contact: Tracy Beckman, Dir.

Founded: 1973. **Members:** 24. **Staff:** 1. **Budget:** $207,500. **State Groups:** 1. **Local.** Provides funding to 52 non-profit agencies that in turn provide human care services. **Affiliated With:** United Way of America. **Conventions/Meetings:** quarterly board meeting.

19602 ■ Oneida County Economic Development Corporation (OCEDC)
PO Box 682
Rhinelander, WI 54501-0682
Ph: (715)369-9110 (715)356-5590
Fax: (715)369-5758
E-mail: information@ocedc.org
URL: http://www.ocedc.org
Contact: James Kumbera, Exec.Dir.

Founded: 1989. **Staff:** 2. **Local.** Promotes economic and community development in Oneida County, WI.

19603 ■ Phi Theta Kappa, Alpha Nu Iota Chapter - Nicolet Area Technical College
c/o Mark Nebgen
PO Box 518
Rhinelander, WI 54501
Ph: (715)365-4628
E-mail: mnebgen@nicolet.tec.wi.us
URL: http://www.ptk.org/directories/chapters/WI/2061-1.htm
Contact: Mark Nebgen, Advisor

Local.

19604 ■ Rhinelander Area Chamber of Commerce (RACC)
PO Box 795
Rhinelander, WI 54501
Ph: (715)365-7464
Fax: (715)365-7467
Free: (800)236-4386
E-mail: info@rhinelanderchamber.com
URL: http://www.rhinelanderchamber.com
Contact: Crystal Lake Johnson, Exec.Dir.

Founded: 1928. **Members:** 371. **Membership Dues:** business base, $200 (annual). **Local.** Promotes business and community development in the Rhinelander, WI area. **Committees:** Advertising and Promotion,; Annual Golf Outing; Boom Lake Muskie Challenge; Business; Oktoberfest; Professional and Industrial; Salmo Hodag Muskie Challenge; Tourism and Convention. **Affiliated With:** American Chamber of Commerce Executives; Oneida County Economic Development Corporation; U.S. Chamber of Commerce; Wisconsin Innkeepers Association; Wisconsin Manufacturers and Commerce. **Publications:** Newsletter, monthly • Book, annual. Guidebook of region. • Brochure, periodic. **Conventions/Meetings:** monthly board meeting • monthly Event Committees Meeting • monthly executive committee meeting.

19605 ■ Rhinelander Figure Skating Club
c/o Rhinelander Ice Association
2021 E Timber Dr.
Rhinelander, WI 54501
Ph: (715)369-1416
E-mail: pizza@newnorth.net
URL: http://www.rhinelanderice.com
Contact: Gigi Wissbroecker, Pres.

Local. Provides programs to encourage participation and achievement in the sport of figure skating on ice. Defines and maintains uniform standards of skating proficiency. Organizes and sponsors competitions and exhibitions for the purpose of stimulating interest in figure skating. **Affiliated With:** United States Figure Skating Association.

19606 ■ Rhinelander Northwoods Quilters
c/o Sarah Bruso
4077 Cty. W
Rhinelander, WI 54501-2110
Contact: Sarah Bruso, Contact

Founded: 1984. **Members:** 43. **Membership Dues:** $18 (annual). **Local Groups:** 1. **Local.** Quilters of any age interested in furthering the art of quilting; works to educate the public; donates quilts to the needy. **Publications:** Newsletter, monthly. Informs members of minutes and events. **Price:** free. **Advertising:** not accepted. **Conventions/Meetings:** monthly meeting.

19607 ■ Timber Producers Association of Michigan and Wisconsin (TPA)
c/o Holly Peitsch, Admin.Asst.
PO Box 1278
Rhinelander, WI 54501
Ph: (715)282-5828
Fax: (715)282-4941
E-mail: holly@timberpa.com
URL: http://www.timberpa.com
Contact: Holly Peitsch, Admin.Asst.

State.

19608 ■ Tri-County Council on Domestic Violence and Sexual Assault
PO Box 233
Rhinelander, WI 54501
Ph: (715)362-6841
Fax: (715)362-9650
Free: (800)236-1222

19609 ■ Trout Unlimited, Northwoods 256
c/o Brian Hegge
2898 Oak Ridge Cir.
Rhinelander, WI 54501-8939
Ph: (715)282-5076 (715)362-3244
E-mail: bhegge@newworth.net
URL: National Affiliate–www.tu.org/
Contact: Brian Hegge, Pres.

Local. Affiliated With: Trout Unlimited.

19610 ■ Wisconsin Forest Productivity Council
c/o Geary Searfoss
PO Box 1375
Rhinelander, WI 54501-1375
Ph: (715)369-3475
E-mail: wfpc@newnorsh.net

Founded: 1986. **State.** Imparts the benefits of good forest management to forest landowners as well as to general public.

Rib Lake

19611 ■ American Legion, Lehman-Clenndenning Post 274
PO Box 311
Rib Lake, WI 54470
Ph: (608)745-1090
Fax: (608)745-0179
URL: National Affiliate–www.legion.org

Local. Affiliated With: American Legion.

Rice Lake

19612 ■ American Legion, Eubanks-Arneson Post 87
1404 Macauley Ave.
Rice Lake, WI 54868
Ph: (608)745-1090
Fax: (608)745-0179
URL: National Affiliate–www.legion.org

Local. Affiliated With: American Legion.

19613 ■ National Alliance for the Mentally Ill - Barron County
c/o Beverly Norelius, Pres.
119 W Humbird St.
Rice Lake, WI 54868

Ph: (715)736-0089
E-mail: namibc@chibardum.net
URL: http://www.namiwisconsin.org/library/directory
Contact: Beverly Norelius, Pres.
Local. Strives to improve the quality of life of children and adults with severe mental illness through support, education, research and advocacy. **Affiliated With:** National Alliance for the Mentally Ill.

19614 ■ Northwestern Wisconsin AIFA
215 E Saint Patrick St.
Rice Lake, WI 54868-0252
Ph: (715)434-3675
Fax: (715)434-5608
URL: National Affiliate–www.naifa.org
Local. Represents the interest of insurance and financial advisors. Advocates for a positive legislative and regulatory environment. Enhances business and professional skills of members. **Affiliated With:** National Association of Insurance and Financial Advisors.

19615 ■ Phi Theta Kappa, Alpha Theta Pi Chapter - University of Wisconsin-Barron
c/o Cary Komoto
Barron Campus
1800 Coll. Dr.
Rice Lake, WI 54868-2497
Ph: (715)234-8176
E-mail: ckomoto@uwc.edu
URL: http://www.ptk.org/directories/chapters/WI/343-1.htm
Contact: Cary Komoto, Advisor
Local.

19616 ■ Rice Lake Area Chamber of Commerce (RLACC)
37 S Main St.
Rice Lake, WI 54868-2299
Ph: (715)234-2126
Fax: (715)234-2085
Free: (800)523-6318
E-mail: chamber@rice-lake.com
URL: http://www.rice-lake.com
Contact: Marlene Arnold, Exec.Dir.
Founded: 1941. **Members:** 310. **Staff:** 2. **Budget:** $85,000. **Local.** Businesses. Promotes business and community development in the Rice Lake, WI area. **Publications:** *Chamber News*, monthly. Newsletter. **Conventions/Meetings:** Salute to Industry - convention, with local business & industry displays (exhibits).

19617 ■ Rice Lake Main Street Association
PO Box 167
Rice Lake, WI 54868
Ph: (715)234-5117
E-mail: rlmainst@chibardun.net
URL: http://www.ricelakemainstreet.com
Local.

19618 ■ United Way of Rice Lake
PO Box 325
Rice Lake, WI 54868-0325
Ph: (715)234-4777
URL: National Affiliate–national.unitedway.org
Local. Affiliated With: United Way of America.

19619 ■ Wisconsin Curling Association - Rice Lake Curling Club (RLCC)
PO Box 45
Rice Lake, WI 54868
Ph: (715)234-9812
E-mail: rlcurl@chibardun.net
URL: http://www.ricelakecurling.org
Contact: Ron Parker, Pres.-Elect
Local. Affiliated With: United States Curling Association.

Richfield

19620 ■ National Association of Miniature Enthusiasts - Mini Diversions
c/o Barbara J. Engel
3820 Cora Ln.
Richfield, WI 53076
Ph: (262)628-0110
E-mail: barbnminis@charter.net
URL: http://www.miniatures.org/states/WI.html
Contact: Barbara J. Engel, Contact
Local. Affiliated With: National Association of Miniature Enthusiasts.

Richland Center

19621 ■ American Legion, Bayard De Hart Post 13
900 Flag Park Dr.
Richland Center, WI 53581
Ph: (608)745-1090
Fax: (608)745-0179
URL: National Affiliate–www.legion.org
Local. Affiliated With: American Legion.

19622 ■ Boaz Area Lions Club
c/o Edward O'Hara, Sec.
785 E 2nd St.
Richland Center, WI 53581
Ph: (608)647-7544
E-mail: eao65@yahoo.com
URL: http://www.md27d2.org
Contact: Edward O'Hara, Sec.
Local. Affiliated With: Lions Clubs International.

19623 ■ National Alliance for the Mentally Ill - Richland County
c/o Faye Burghagen
PO Box 641
Richland Center, WI 53581
Ph: (608)647-8231
URL: http://www.namiwisconsin.org/library/directory
Contact: Faye Burghagen, Contact
Local. Strives to improve the quality of life of children and adults with severe mental illness through support, education, research and advocacy. **Affiliated With:** National Alliance for the Mentally Ill.

19624 ■ Phi Theta Kappa, Phi Mu Chapter - University of Wisconsin-Richland
c/o Aharon Zorea
1200 Hwy. 14 W
Richland Center, WI 53581
Ph: (608)647-6186
E-mail: azorea@uwc.edu
URL: http://www.ptk.org/directories/chapters/WI/344-1.htm
Contact: Aharon Zorea, Advisor
Local.

19625 ■ Richland Area Chamber of Commerce/Main Street Partnership (RACC)
397 W Seminary
PO Box 128
Richland Center, WI 53581-0128
Ph: (608)647-6205
Fax: (608)647-5449
Free: (800)422-1318
E-mail: info@richlandchamber.com
URL: http://www.richlandchamber.com
Contact: Susan Price, Exec.Dir.
Founded: 1936. **Members:** 180. **Membership Dues:** first year, $50 (annual) • gross business volume ($249,999), $100 (annual) • gross business volume ($499,999), $250 (annual) • gross business volume ($999,999), $500 (annual) • gross business volume ($1,000,000), $750 (annual) • patron, $1,000 (annual). **Staff:** 1. **Budget:** $90,000. **Local.** Promotes business and community development in the Richland Center, WI area. Sponsors celebration on Frank Lloyd Wright's birthday, Centerfest, and June Dairy Days. **Awards:** Certificates of Appreciation. **Frequency:** annual. **Type:** recognition. **Recipient:** for volunteer service throughout the year. **Computer Services:** Online services, lists of company name, addresses, phones, and e-mails in the website. **Subgroups:** Ambassador's Club. **Formerly:** (2004) Richland Area Chamber of Commerce. **Publications:** *Chamber Business*, semiannual. Directory. List of Chamber of Commerce members. **Circulation:** 300 • Newsletter, bimonthly. Features news updates, local businesses, leaders and volunteers. **Circulation:** 300. **Advertising:** accepted. **Conventions/Meetings:** monthly Board Meeting - always first Wednesday of the month.

19626 ■ Richland Center Lions Club
c/o Virgil Kanable, Pres.
691 E Haseltine St.
Richland Center, WI 53581
Ph: (608)647-3228
E-mail: vvkret@mwt.net
URL: http://www.md27d2.org
Contact: Virgil Kanable, Pres.
Local. Affiliated With: Lions Clubs International.

19627 ■ Sons of Norway, Gjemtedal Lodge 5-639
c/o Buena R. Anderson, Pres.
411 S Ira St.
Richland Center, WI 53581-2617
E-mail: buena@mwt.net
URL: National Affiliate–www.sofn.com
Contact: Buena R. Anderson, Pres.
Local. Affiliated With: Sons of Norway.

19628 ■ Wisconsin Woodland Owners Association, Bad Axe Chapter
c/o David Weigandt, Chm.
22880 Fancy Creek Ln.
Richland Center, WI 53581
Ph: (608)647-7614
E-mail: weigandt@mwt.net
URL: http://www.wisconsinwoodlands.org
Contact: David Weigandt, Chm.
Local. Affiliated With: Wisconsin Woodland Owners Association.

Ridgeland

19629 ■ American Legion, Wisconsin Post 511
c/o Willard L. Hinzman
PO Box 117
Ridgeland, WI 54763
Ph: (715)949-1943
Fax: (608)745-0179
URL: National Affiliate–www.legion.org
Contact: Willard L. Hinzman, Contact
Local. Affiliated With: American Legion.

19630 ■ Sons of Norway, Dovre Lodge 5-353
c/o Ann E. Lee, Sec.
E6696 County Rd. W
Ridgeland, WI 54763-9465
Ph: (715)658-1189
E-mail: results@winbright.net
URL: National Affiliate–www.sofn.com
Contact: Ann E. Lee, Sec.
Local. Affiliated With: Sons of Norway.

Ridgeway

19631 ■ American Legion, Beckett-Kurth Post 257
PO Box 207
Ridgeway, WI 53582
Ph: (608)745-1090
Fax: (608)745-0179
URL: National Affiliate–www.legion.org
Local. Affiliated With: American Legion.

Rio

19632 ■ American Legion, Wisconsin Post 208
c/o Francis Cuff
PO Box 91
Rio, WI 53960

Ph: (608)745-1090
Fax: (608)745-0179
URL: National Affiliate–www.legion.org
Contact: Francis Cuff, Contact
Local. Affiliated With: American Legion.

Ripon

19633 ■ American Legion, Brown-Parfitt Post 43
133 E Fond Du Lac St.
Ripon, WI 54971
Ph: (608)745-1090
Fax: (608)745-0179
URL: National Affiliate–www.legion.org
Local. Affiliated With: American Legion.

19634 ■ Phi Beta Kappa, Ripon College
c/o Dr. Marry Williams-Norton, Advisor
PO Box 248
Ripon, WI 54971-0248
Ph: (920)748-8132
E-mail: nortonm@ripon.edu
URL: http://www.ripon.edu/students/Orgs/PhiBetaKappa
Contact: Dr. Marry Williams-Norton, Advisor
Founded: 1776. **Local. Affiliated With:** Phi Beta Kappa.

19635 ■ Psi Chi, National Honor Society in Psychology - Ripon College
c/o Dept. of Psychology
PO Box 248
Ripon, WI 54971-0248
Ph: (920)748-8134
E-mail: petersikt@ripon.edu
URL: National Affiliate–www.psichi.org
Local. Affiliated With: Psi Chi, National Honor Society in Psychology.

19636 ■ Ripon Area Chamber of Commerce (RACC)
214 Jefferson St.
PO Box 305
Ripon, WI 54971-0305
Ph: (920)748-6764
Fax: (920)748-6784
E-mail: chamber@ripon-wi.com
URL: http://www.ripon-wi.com
Contact: Paula Price, Exec.Dir.
Founded: 1940. **Members:** 220. **Staff:** 2. **Local.** Promotes business and community development in the Ripon, WI area. Sponsors Dickens of A Christmas festival, Cookie Daze, Maxwell Street Day and Ducktona $500 Rubber Duck Race. **Awards:** Community Service. **Frequency:** annual. **Type:** recognition. **Recipient:** for community service • Distinguished Service. **Frequency:** annual. **Type:** recognition • Outstanding Business/Industry. **Frequency:** annual. **Type:** recognition. **Recipient:** to an outstanding community. **Affiliated With:** American Chamber of Commerce Executives. **Publications:** *Horn Blower*, bimonthly. Newsletter. Contains news of Chamber of Commerce happenings/events. **Price:** no charge. **Circulation:** 350 • *The Ripon Guide*, annual. Directory.

19637 ■ Ripon Rifle and Pistol Club (RRPC)
PO Box 543
Ripon, WI 54971-0543
Ph: (920)748-3453 (920)921-3353
E-mail: g.trepanier@sbcglobal.net
URL: http://www.riponqunclub.com
Contact: Gay Trepanier, Pres.
Founded: 1932. **Members:** 100. **Membership Dues:** young adult, $20 (annual) • regular, $40 (annual) • life, $750. **Staff:** 10. **Local.** Promotes shooting sports for competition and fun. Teaches hunter education. Competes in pistol matches, rifle shooting, trap shooting, and sporting clays. Sponsors single action shooting club and International Defense Pistol Shooting. **Publications:** Newsletter, quarterly. **Advertising:** accepted. **Conventions/Meetings:** monthly general assembly.

19638 ■ Ripon United Way
PO Box 71
Ripon, WI 54971-0071
Ph: (920)748-6695
URL: National Affiliate–national.unitedway.org
Local. Affiliated With: United Way of America.

River Falls

19639 ■ American Legion, Fletcher-Pechacek Post 121
701 N Main St.
River Falls, WI 54022
Ph: (608)745-1090
Fax: (608)745-0179
URL: National Affiliate–www.legion.org
Local. Affiliated With: American Legion.

19640 ■ Association for Computing Machinery, University of Wisconsin/River Falls
c/o Anthony Varghese, Advisor
Coll. of Bus. & Economics
207 S Hall
410 S 3rd St.
River Falls, WI 54022
Ph: (715)425-3335
Fax: (715)425-0707
E-mail: acm-support@uwrf.edu
URL: http://www.uwrf.edu/acm-chapter
Contact: Anthony Varghese, Advisor
Local. Promotes computer and information technology related activities at University of Wisconsin River Falls. **Affiliated With:** Association for Computing Machinery.

19641 ■ Korean War Veterans Association, Minnesota No. 1 Chapter
c/o Edward R. Valle
1410 Foster St.
River Falls, WI 54022
Ph: (715)425-8992
URL: National Affiliate–www.kwva.org
Contact: Edward R. Valle, Contact
Local. Affiliated With: Korean War Veterans Association.

19642 ■ North Central Conference on Summer Schools (NCCSS)
c/o Dr. Roger Swanson
Univ. of Wisconsin - River Falls
Summer Sessions
River Falls, WI 54022
Ph: (715)425-3851
Fax: (715)425-3785
E-mail: roger.a.swanson@uwrf.edu
Contact: Dr. Roger Swanson, Sec.-Treas.
Founded: 1949. **Members:** 150. **Membership Dues:** institution, $100 (annual). **Budget:** $15,000. College and university summer session representatives from the north central states of the U.S. Provides opportunities for members to review pertinent phases of summer school operations, review investigative reports, and exchange information. **Awards:** Honorary Membership Research. **Frequency:** annual. **Type:** recognition. **Committees:** Public Relations; Research, Development, and Statistics. **Publications:** Directory, annual • Proceedings. Provides information on annual meeting. • Report, annual. Provides statistical information. **Conventions/Meetings:** annual meeting (exhibits).

19643 ■ Protective Animal Welfare Society of Western Wisconsin
c/o Karen K. Zacharias
PO Box 254
River Falls, WI 54022-0254
Ph: (715)273-4306
Contact: Karen Zacharias, Pres.
Founded: 2000. **Local.** Promotes animal welfare, especially spay-neuter initiatives for domestic pets.

19644 ■ River Falls Area Chamber of Commerce and Tourism Bureau
214 N Main St.
River Falls, WI 54022
Ph: (715)425-2533
Fax: (715)425-2305
E-mail: info@rfchamber.com
URL: http://www.rfchamber.com
Contact: Rossane Bump, CEO
Founded: 1955. **Members:** 220. **Membership Dues:** general business and industry, professional office, financial institution, hotel, motel, apartment, and building (base), $190 (annual) • home based industry/outside sales representative (base), $136 (annual) • non-profit organization, $79 (annual). **Local.** Works to improve economic development and quality of life in the community through education, promotion and leadership. Sponsors River Falls Days, Town N' Country Day, Ambassadors Golf Outing, Business Show Case, Family Fair and many more events. **Awards:** Ambassador of the Year. **Frequency:** annual. **Type:** recognition • Business of the Year. **Frequency:** annual. **Type:** recognition • Citizen of the Year. **Frequency:** annual. **Type:** recognition • Small Business of the Year. **Frequency:** annual. **Type:** recognition. **Committees:** Ambassadors; Annual Golf Outing; Award and Recognition Banquet; Business Breakfast; Made in River Falls Day; Marketing Communications; Town and Country Day. **Programs:** Leadership River Falls. **Formerly:** (2004) River Falls Area Chamber of Commerce. **Publications:** *Chamber Newsletter*, monthly. Includes information about chamber events and activities. **Advertising:** accepted • Membership Directory. **Circulation:** 800. **Advertising:** accepted.

19645 ■ United Way of River Falls
PO Box 52
River Falls, WI 54022-0052
Ph: (715)425-8206
URL: http://www.pressenter.com/~uwayrf
Contact: Brad Caskey, Pres.
Local. Affiliated With: United Way of America.

19646 ■ Wisconsin Association of Accountants (WAA)
PO Box 356
River Falls, WI 54022
Ph: (715)425-7521
Free: (800)237-4080
E-mail: nolakay@sbcglobal.net
URL: http://www.wiassociationofaccountants.com
Contact: Byron L. Dopkins, Exec.Dir.
State. Promotes high professional and ethical standards; seeks to safeguard and defend the professional and legal rights of attorney-CPAs. Conducts research on dual licensing and dual practice; maintains speakers' bureau, placement service, and a collection of published and unpublished articles on these subjects. **Affiliated With:** National Society of Accountants.

19647 ■ Wisconsin Wrestling Federation (WWF)
626 N Winter St.
River Falls, WI 54022
Ph: (715)425-7946
Fax: (715)425-6439
E-mail: dave@leitchinsurance.com
URL: http://www.wiwrestling.com/WWF
Contact: Dave Black, State Dir.
State. Affiliated With: U.S.A. Wrestling.

Roberts

19648 ■ Roberts Lions Club
PO Box 295
Roberts, WI 54023
E-mail: president@robertslions.com
URL: http://www.robertslions.com
Contact: Joe Kaner, Pres.
Local. Affiliated With: Lions Clubs International.

Rosendale

19649 ■ Rosendale Historical Society
c/o Emajean Westphal
PO Box 254
Rosendale, WI 54974-0254
Ph: (920)872-2131 (920)872-2558
Fax: (920)872-2134
Contact: Emajean Westphal, Pres.
Founded: 2001. **Members:** 45. **Membership Dues:** family, $10 (annual). **Local**. Works to preserve the history and collect memorabilia of the Village of Rosendale.

Rosholt

19650 ■ Wisconsin Club Lamb Association
c/o Dan Smerchek
1813 Birch Rd.
Rosholt, WI 54473
Ph: (715)342-0306
URL: http://www.wisconsinclublambassociation.com
Contact: Dan Smerchek, Contact
State. **Affiliated With:** American Sheep Industry Association.

Rothschild

19651 ■ American Legion, Wisconsin Post 492
c/o Roy L. Drew
PO Box 82
Rothschild, WI 54474
Ph: (608)745-1090
Fax: (608)745-0179
URL: National Affiliate–www.legion.org
Contact: Roy L. Drew, Contact
Local. **Affiliated With:** American Legion.

Rudolph

19652 ■ American Legion, Wisconsin Post 485
c/o Elmer Blonien
1584 Main St.
Rudolph, WI 54475
Ph: (608)745-1090
Fax: (608)745-0179
URL: National Affiliate–www.legion.org
Contact: Elmer Blonien, Contact
Local. **Affiliated With:** American Legion.

19653 ■ Rudolph Volunteer Fire Department
1559 Main St.
Rudolph, WI 54475-0101
Ph: (715)435-3740
Contact: Tony Kankol, Chief
Local.

St. Cloud

19654 ■ American Legion, Wisconsin Post 478
c/o Harvey Blonigen
222 Gordon St.
St. Cloud, WI 53079
Ph: (608)745-1090
Fax: (608)745-0179
URL: National Affiliate–www.legion.org
Contact: Harvey Blonigen, Contact
Local. **Affiliated With:** American Legion.

St. Croix Falls

19655 ■ American Legion, Wisconsin Post 143
c/o Amherst I. Hansen
PO Box 462
St. Croix Falls, WI 54024
Ph: (608)745-1090
Fax: (608)745-0179
URL: National Affiliate–www.legion.org
Contact: Amherst I. Hansen, Contact
Local. **Affiliated With:** American Legion.

19656 ■ St. Croix Falls Chamber of Commerce
106 S Washington St.
St. Croix Falls, WI 54024
Ph: (715)483-3580
Fax: (715)483-0022
E-mail: ann@scfwi.com
URL: http://www.scfwi.com
Contact: Ann Perszyk, Exec.Dir.
Membership Dues: basic, $100 (annual) • bronze, $250 (annual) • silver, $500 (annual) • gold, $750 (annual) • platinum, $1,000 (annual) • new (initial), $350. **Local**. Promotes business and community development in the city of St. Croix Falls and its trade area. **Publications:** *Chamber News*. Newsletter. **Conventions/Meetings:** monthly meeting, with networking opportunities - every 2nd Thursday.

St. Francis

19657 ■ Cudahy Kennel Club (CKC)
3820 S Pennsylvania Ave.
St. Francis, WI 53235
Ph: (414)769-0758
URL: http://www.cudahykennelclub.org
Contact: Ms. Christel Sparks, Corresponding Sec.
Local.

St. Germain

19658 ■ Ruffed Grouse Society, Lakeland Area Chapter
c/o Russell Rydin
PO Box 218
St. Germain, WI 54558
Ph: (920)467-0682
E-mail: dave.lukaszewsk@kohler.com
URL: National Affiliate–www.ruffedgrousesociety.org
Contact: Russell Rydin, Contact
Local. **Affiliated With:** Ruffed Grouse Society.

19659 ■ St. Germain Chamber of Commerce
PO Box 155
St. Germain, WI 54558-0155
Ph: (715)477-2205
Fax: (715)542-3423
Free: (800)727-7203
E-mail: info@st-germain.com
Contact: Jim Anderson, Pres.
Local. Promotes business and community development in St. Germain, WI.

19660 ■ St. Germain PrimeTimers
c/o Doug Knapp
PO Box 281
St. Germain, WI 54558
Ph: (715)542-2538
E-mail: wuffman@nnex.net
URL: http://pages.zdnet.com/stgermainptimers
Contact: Fred Radtke, Pres.
Founded: 1998. **Members:** 205. **Membership Dues:** individual, $5 (annual). **Local**.

St. Nazianz

19661 ■ American Legion, Wagner-Eberle-Sukowaty Post 477
113 W Court St.
St. Nazianz, WI 54232
Ph: (608)745-1090
Fax: (608)745-0179
URL: National Affiliate–www.legion.org
Local. **Affiliated With:** American Legion.

Sarona

19662 ■ Association of the United States Army, GEN John W. Vessey Jr. - Minnesota
c/o Paul E. Amacher
N2904 Hagen Dr.
Sarona, WI 54870-9138
Ph: (612)713-3065
E-mail: c5401@ausa.org
URL: National Affiliate–www.ausa.org
State. Represents the interests and concerns of American Soldiers. Fosters public support of the Army's role in national security. Provides professional education and information programs.

19663 ■ National Audubon Society - Hunt Hill Audubon Sanctuary
N2384 Hunt Hill Rd.
Sarona, WI 54870
Ph: (715)635-6543
Fax: (715)635-3043
E-mail: info@hunthill.org
URL: http://www.wisconline.com/attractions/camps/hunthill.html
Contact: Mr. Storme Nelson, Exec.Dir.
Founded: 1954. **Members:** 476. **Membership Dues:** individual/senior, $25 (annual) • founder member, $1,000 (annual). **Staff:** 5. **Budget:** $200,000. **Regional**. Works to promote education and appreciation of nature. **Libraries: Type:** reference. **Holdings:** audiovisuals, books, clippings, periodicals, photographs. **Additional Websites:** http://www.hunthill.org. **Publications:** *Hunt Hill Almanac*, quarterly. Newsletter. **Circulation:** 476.

Sauk City

19664 ■ American Legion, Sauk Prairie Kuoni Reuter Post 167
PO Box 34
Sauk City, WI 53583
Ph: (608)745-1090
Fax: (608)745-0179
URL: National Affiliate–www.legion.org
Local. **Affiliated With:** American Legion.

19665 ■ Wisconsin Health Care Association, District 3
c/o Tom Graves, Pres.
Maplewood of Sauk Prairie
245 Sycamore St.
Sauk City, WI 53583
Ph: (608)643-3383
URL: http://www.whca.com
Contact: Tom Graves, Pres.
Local. Promotes professionalism and ethical behavior of individuals providing long-term care delivery for patients and for the general public. Provides information, education and administrative tools to enhance the quality of long-term care. Improves the standards of service and administration of member nursing homes. **Affiliated With:** American Health Care Association; Wisconsin Health Care Association.

Saukville

19666 ■ American Legion, Landt-Thiel Post 470
601 W Dekora St.
Saukville, WI 53080
Ph: (608)745-1090
Fax: (608)745-0179
URL: National Affiliate–www.legion.org
Local. **Affiliated With:** American Legion.

19667 ■ Saukville Chamber of Commerce
PO Box 80238
Saukville, WI 53080
Ph: (262)268-1970
E-mail: saukvillechamber@earthlink.net
URL: http://www.village.saukville.wi.us
Contact: Stacey Frey, Exec.Dir.
Membership Dues: regular (based on number of full time employees), $75-$250 (annual) • associate, $25

(annual). **Local**. Promotes business and community development in the Saukville, WI area. **Affiliated With:** U.S. Chamber of Commerce; Wisconsin Manufacturers and Commerce. **Publications:** Newsletter, monthly. **Advertising:** accepted.

19668 ■ Saukville Lions Club
PO Box 80208
Saukville, WI 53080
E-mail: lemons@execpc.com
URL: http://www.saukvillelions.com
Contact: Mike Krocka, Pres.
Local. Affiliated With: Lions Clubs International.

Sayner

19669 ■ Sayner-Starlake Chamber of Commerce (SSLCC)
PO Box 191
Sayner, WI 54560
Ph: (715)542-3789
Fax: (715)542-4363
Free: (888)722-3789
E-mail: bonbehling@nnex.net
URL: http://www.sayner-starlake.org
Contact: Marcia Kittleson, Pres.
Founded: 1980. **Members:** 55. **Local**. Promotes business and community development in the Sayner, WI area. **Publications:** Directory, annual. **Conventions/Meetings:** monthly meeting.

Schofield

19670 ■ ACF Middle Wisconsin Chefs
PO Box 319
Schofield, WI 54476
Ph: (715)359-1017 (715)846-3979
Fax: (715)845-3726
E-mail: randychef03@msn.com
URL: National Affiliate–www.acfchefs.org
Contact: Randal A. Adams, Pres.
Local. Promotes the culinary profession and provides on-going educational training and networking for members. Provides opportunities for competition, professional recognition, and access to educational forums with other culinarians at local, regional, national, and international events.

19671 ■ Media Communications Association-International, Greater Wisconsin Chapter (GW-MCA-I)
c/o Mr. Bryan Piepenburg, Past Pres.
5303 E Jelinek Ave.
PO Box 500
Schofield, WI 54476
Ph: (715)359-6133
Fax: (715)359-9159
E-mail: info@gwmcai.org
URL: http://www.gwmcai.org
Contact: Mr. Bryan Piepenburg, Past Pres.
Membership Dues: individual, $160 (annual) • organizational (3 members), $455 (annual). **Local**. Graphics artists, animators, videographers, editors, web designers, actors, writers, lighting specialists, and others. Fosters the interest of individuals working in the visual communications field. **Awards:** CameoFest. **Frequency:** annual. **Type:** recognition • Member of the Year. **Frequency:** annual. **Type:** recognition. **Recipient:** active corporate or individual member. **Affiliated With:** Media Communications Association International. **Formerly:** (2005) International Television Association. **Publications:** *The Monitor*, bimonthly. Newsletter. **Advertising:** accepted. Alternate Formats: online.

19672 ■ Wisconsin Elks Association
c/o Ken Johnson, Sec.
1602 FootHill Ave.
Schofield, WI 54476
Ph: (715)355-0758
Fax: (715)355-0758
E-mail: elksbugle@aol.com
URL: http://www.wielks.org
Contact: Ronald Bertrand, Pres.
State. Promotes the principles of charity, justice, brotherhood and loyalty among members. Fosters the spirit of American Patriotism. Seeks to stimulate pride and respect toward patriotism. **Affiliated With:** Benevolent and Protective Order of Elks.

Seneca

19673 ■ Seneca Lions Club - Wisconsin
c/o Mark Kramer, Sec.
PO Box 8
Seneca, WI 54654
Ph: (608)734-3651
E-mail: markkramer@webtv.net
URL: http://www.md27d2.org
Contact: Mark Kramer, Sec.
Local. Affiliated With: Lions Clubs International.

Seymour

19674 ■ American Legion, Krause-Kraft Post 106
Box 224
Seymour, WI 54165
Ph: (608)745-1090
Fax: (608)745-0179
URL: National Affiliate–www.legion.org
Local. Affiliated With: American Legion.

19675 ■ Fox Valley Professional Photographers Association
c/o Randy Peterson, Merit Supervisor
835 S Main St.
Seymour, WI 54165-1642
Ph: (920)833-6357 (920)336-6700
E-mail: apeter8733@aol.com
URL: National Affiliate–ppa.com
Local. Professional society of portrait, wedding, commercial, and industrial, and specialized photographers. **Affiliated With:** Professional Photographers of America.

19676 ■ United Food and Commercial Workers, Local 245, Northcentral Region
1013 Lincoln St.
Seymour, WI 54165
Ph: (920)497-7131
URL: National Affiliate–www.ufcw.org
Local. Affiliated With: United Food and Commercial Workers International Union.

Sharon

19677 ■ American Legion, Moser-Ortmann Post 130
PO Box 488
Sharon, WI 53585
Ph: (608)745-1090
Fax: (608)745-0179
URL: National Affiliate–www.legion.org
Local. Affiliated With: American Legion.

Shawano

19678 ■ American Legion, Elefson-Zeuske Post 117
PO Box 233
Shawano, WI 54166
Ph: (608)745-1090
Fax: (608)745-0179
URL: National Affiliate–www.legion.org
Local. Affiliated With: American Legion.

19679 ■ Genex Cooperative
100 MBC Dr.
Shawano, WI 54166
Ph: (715)526-2141
Fax: (715)526-4511
E-mail: info@crinet.com
URL: http://www.crinet.com
Contact: Donald Jensen, Pres.
Budget: $19,000. **Languages:** English, Spanish. **For-Profit. Regional.**

19680 ■ Masonic Lodge
201 1/2 S Main St.
Shawano, WI 54166
Ph: (715)526-3920
E-mail: s170@athenet.net
Local. Formerly: (2004) Masonic Temple.

19681 ■ National Active and Retired Federal Employees Association - Green Bay 403
277 Schrader Ave.
Shawano, WI 54166-3382
Ph: (715)524-8747
URL: National Affiliate–www.narfe.org
Contact: Charles C. Anderson, Contact
Local. Protects the retirement future of employees through education. Informs members on issues affecting the retirement. **Affiliated With:** National Association of Retired Federal Employees.

19682 ■ Ruffed Grouse Society, Shawano Area Chapter
c/o Pat Staniforth
908 S Evergreen St.
Shawano, WI 54166
Ph: (715)524-2435
URL: National Affiliate–www.ruffedgrousesociety.org
Contact: Pat Staniforth, Contact
Local. Affiliated With: Ruffed Grouse Society.

19683 ■ Shawano Area Chamber of Commerce (SACC)
c/o Donna M. Gueths
PO Box 38
Shawano, WI 54166-0038
Ph: (715)524-2139
Fax: (715)524-3127
Free: (800)235-8528
E-mail: nsmith@shawano.com
URL: http://www.shawanocountry.com
Contact: Nancy Smith, Exec.Dir.
Founded: 1926. **Members:** 345. **Membership Dues:** general business (basic), $203 (annual) • associate (basic), $80 (annual) • elected official, person at least 55 years old, $40 (annual). **Local**. Promotes business and community development in the Shawano, WI area. Acts as civic clearinghouse, public relations counselor, and legislative representative. **Committees:** Ambassador; Business; Education; Government Affairs; Manufacturing/Industrial. **Councils:** Shawano County Tourism. **Publications:** Newsletter, periodic.

19684 ■ Sweet Adelines International, Shawano Wolf River Harmony Chapter
Shawano Senior (Civic) Ctr.
225 S Main St.
Shawano, WI 54166-2745
Ph: (715)823-3498
URL: National Affiliate–www.sweetadelineintl.org
Contact: Mary Rades, Contact
Local. Advances the musical art form of barbershop harmony through education and performances. Provides education, training and coaching in the development of women's four-part barbershop harmony. **Affiliated With:** Sweet Adelines International.

19685 ■ United Way of Shawano County
PO Box 31
Shawano, WI 54166-0031
Ph: (715)524-9166 (715)853-9264
URL: National Affiliate–national.unitedway.org
Local. Affiliated With: United Way of America.

19686 ■ Wisconsin School Psychologists Association (WSPA)
N4212 Townline Rd.
Shawano, WI 54166
E-mail: wspa@execpc.com
URL: http://my.execpc.com/~wspa/
Contact: Milt Dehn, Pres.
State.

19687 ■ Wisconsin Towns Association (WTA)
c/o Richard J. Stadelman, Exec.Dir.
W 7686 County Rd. MMM
Shawano, WI 54166-6086
Ph: (715)526-3157
Fax: (715)524-3917
E-mail: wtastaff@wisctowns.com
URL: http://www.wisctowns.com
State.

Sheboygan

19688 ■ American Cancer Society, Sheboygan
515 Superior Ave.
Sheboygan, WI 53081
Ph: (920)457-5661
Fax: (920)457-8760
URL: National Affiliate–www.cancer.org
Local. Affiliated With: American Cancer Society.

19689 ■ American Legion, Prescott-Bayens Post 83
PO Box 1428
Sheboygan, WI 53082
Ph: (608)745-1090
Fax: (608)745-0179
URL: National Affiliate–www.legion.org
Local. Affiliated With: American Legion.

19690 ■ American Legion, Sheboygan Memorial Post 555
1642 N 12th St.
Sheboygan, WI 53081
Ph: (608)745-1090
Fax: (608)745-0179
URL: National Affiliate–www.legion.org
Local. Affiliated With: American Legion.

19691 ■ American Red Cross, Sheboygan County Chapter
2032 Erie Ave.
Sheboygan, WI 53081
Ph: (920)457-7739
Fax: (920)457-5504
E-mail: chapter@redcrosssheboygan.org
URL: http://www.redcrosssheboygan.org
Local.

19692 ■ APICS, The Association for Operations Management - Shoreline Chapter
PO Box 805
Sheboygan, WI 53082-0805
Ph: (414)875-4772
Fax: (414)875-4712
E-mail: brucegbalthazor@drs-pct.com
URL: http://www.shorelineapics.org
Contact: Bruce Balthazor CPM, Pres.
Local. Provides information and services in production and inventory management and related areas to enable members, enterprises and individuals to add value to their business performance. **Affiliated With:** APICS - The Association for Operations Management.

19693 ■ East Central Wisconsin Sheet Metal Contractors Association
c/o Alan Dvorak
Aldag/Honold Mech.
PO Box 1265
Sheboygan, WI 53082-1265
Ph: (920)458-5558
Fax: (920)458-3750
E-mail: alan_d@aldaghonold.com
URL: National Affiliate–www.smacna.org
Contact: Alan Dvorak, Contact
Local. Affiliated With: Sheet Metal and Air Conditioning Contractors' National Association.

19694 ■ Family Connections
2508 S 8th St.
Sheboygan, WI 53081
Ph: (920)457-1999
Fax: (920)451-0043
Free: (800)322-2046
E-mail: kristenfamilyconnections@yahoo.com
URL: http://www.familyconnectionscc.org
Contact: Kristen Radke, Exec.Dir.
Local. A childcare resource and referral agency.

19695 ■ Girl Scouts of Manitou Council
5212 Windward Ct.
Sheboygan, WI 53083
Ph: (920)565-4575
Fax: (920)565-4583
Free: (877)738-7014
E-mail: growstrong@gsmanitou.org
URL: http://www.gsmanitou.org
Local. Young girls and adult volunteers, corporate, government and individual supporters. Strives to develop potential and leadership skills among its members. Conducts trainings, educational programs and outdoor activities.

19696 ■ Insurance Accounting and Systems Association, Wisconsin
c/o Jim Keal, Pres.
2800 S Taylor Dr.
Sheboygan, WI 53081
Ph: (920)458-9131
Fax: (920)458-7843
Free: (800)242-7666
E-mail: jkeal@acuity.com
URL: National Affiliate–www.iasa.org
Contact: Jim Keal, Pres.
State. Accounting, financing, auditing, and technology professionals representing property-casualty, life-health, and public accounting firms. Education is the main objective and is accomplished through presenting professional and personal development sessions as well as a wide variety of technical sessions in the areas of accounting, finance, regulation, and technology. **Affiliated With:** Insurance Accounting and Systems Association. **Conventions/Meetings:** semiannual conference - always last week of March and September.

19697 ■ Izaak Walton League of America, Sheboygan County Chapter
2324 Lakeshore Dr.
Sheboygan, WI 53081-6346
Ph: (920)452-9937
URL: National Affiliate–www.iwla.org
Contact: Jim Baumgart, Pres.
Local. Works to educate the public to conserve, maintain, protect, and restore the soil, forest, water, and other natural resources of the U.S; promotes the enjoyment and wholesome utilization of these resources. **Affiliated With:** Izaak Walton League of America.

19698 ■ Kettle Moraine Corvette Club (KMCC)
PO Box 621
Sheboygan, WI 53082-0621
E-mail: jsrische@excel.net
URL: http://www.oopcd.com/kmcc
Contact: John Rische, Pres.
Local. Affiliated With: National Council of Corvette Clubs.

19699 ■ Literacy Council of Sheboygan County
926 Broughton Dr.
Sheboygan, WI 53081-4166
Ph: (920)457-1888
E-mail: execdirop@sheboyganliteracy.com
URL: National Affiliate–www.proliteracy.org
Contact: Ms. Mirta Cabrera, Exec.Dir.
Local. Affiliated With: ProLiteracy Worldwide.

19700 ■ Mental Health Association in Sheboygan County
2020 Erie Ave.
Sheboygan, WI 53081
Ph: (920)458-3951
Fax: (920)458-3441
E-mail: mhasheb@bytehead.com
URL: http://www.mhasheboygan.org
Contact: Beverly Randall MS, Exec.Dir.
Local. Seeks to promote mental health and prevent mental health disorders. Improves mental health of Americans through advocacy, public education, research and service. **Affiliated With:** National Mental Health Association.

19701 ■ National Alliance for the Mentally Ill - Sheboygan
c/o Susan Kilton, Pres.
2321 S 16th St.
Sheboygan, WI 53081
Ph: (920)458-4563
URL: http://www.namiwisconsin.org/library/directory
Contact: Susan Kilton, Pres.
Local. Strives to improve the quality of life of children and adults with severe mental illness through support, education, research and advocacy. **Affiliated With:** National Alliance for the Mentally Ill.

19702 ■ National Association of Miniature Enthusiasts - Lakeshore Miniature Makers
c/o Elaine R. Dunisch
2809-A Wilgus Ave.
Sheboygan, WI 53081
Ph: (920)452-4798 (920)803-3177
E-mail: dunische@schencksolutions.com
URL: http://www.miniatures.org/states/WI.html
Contact: Elaine R. Dunisch, Contact
Local. Affiliated With: National Association of Miniature Enthusiasts.

19703 ■ PFLAG Sheboygan/Lakeshore
829 Union Ave.
Sheboygan, WI 53081
Ph: (920)458-4889
URL: http://www.pflag.org/Wisconsin.246.0.html
Local. Affiliated With: Parents, Families, and Friends of Lesbians and Gays.

19704 ■ Phi Theta Kappa, Alpha Mu Omega Chapter - University of Wisconsin-Sheboygan
c/o Mary Beth Emmerichs
Sheboygan Center
One Univ. Dr.
Sheboygan, WI 53081-4789
Ph: (920)459-4422
E-mail: memmeric@uwc.edu
URL: http://www.ptk.org/directories/chapters/WI/2009-1.htm
Contact: Mary Beth Emmerichs, Advisor
Local.

19705 ■ Power Flour Action Network
c/o Thomas H. Hartzell
1717 Pheasant Ln.
Sheboygan, WI 53081-7724
Ph: (920)458-0244
Fax: (920)458-1729
E-mail: thartzel@excel.net
URL: http://www.powerflour.org
Contact: Tom Hartzell, Pres.
Founded: 1997. **Budget:** $9,000. **Languages:** English, French, Spanish. **Nonmembership. Local.** Works to distribute and evaluate Power Flour in developing countries that experience high infant child mortality. Power Flour is a food ingredient that turns

corn, rice and other staples into liquid, making them suitable for use as weaning foods. **Publications:** *Flour Power*. Brochure. **Conventions/Meetings:** quarterly board meeting (exhibits) • annual meeting - June, in Wisconsin.

19706 ■ Sheboygan AIFA
PO Box 565
Sheboygan, WI 53082-0565
Ph: (608)244-3131
Fax: (920)467-4941
URL: National Affiliate–www.naifa.org
Local. Represents the interest of insurance and financial advisors. Advocates for a positive legislative and regulatory environment. Enhances business and professional skills of members. **Affiliated With:** National Association of Insurance and Financial Advisors.

19707 ■ Sheboygan Area Chapter of the Society for Human Resource Management
PO Box 145
Sheboygan, WI 53082
E-mail: spattow@seekcareers.com
URL: http://www.wishrm.org/chapter/sheb/index.html
Contact: Sara Pattow, Pres.
Local. Represents the interests of human resource and industrial relations professionals and executives. Promotes the advancement of human resource management.

19708 ■ Sheboygan Area United Way (SAUW)
2020 Erie Ave.
Sheboygan, WI 53081-3711
Ph: (920)458-3425
Fax: (920)458-3426
E-mail: sauw@sauw.org
URL: http://www.sauw.org
Contact: William L. Weissert, Exec.Dir.
Staff: 2. **Local**. Aims to create a better life for the people of Sheboygan County by building a stronger community. Works to bring people together to focus on human needs. **Affiliated With:** United Way of America. **Formerly:** United Way of the Sheboygan Area.

19709 ■ Sheboygan Coin Club
c/o Carey Fenerer
1949 N 7th St.
Sheboygan, WI 53081
E-mail: cfederer@sbcglobal.net
URL: National Affiliate–www.money.org
Contact: Carey Fenerer, Contact
Local. **Affiliated With:** American Numismatic Association.

19710 ■ Sheboygan County Chamber of Commerce and Convention and Visitors Bureau
712 Riverfront Dr., Ste.101
Sheboygan, WI 53081
Ph: (920)457-9491 (920)457-9495
Fax: (920)457-6269
Free: (800)457-9497
E-mail: chamber@sheboygan.org
URL: http://www.sheboygan.org
Contact: Delores Olsen, Exce.Dir.
Local. Improves the economic, social and political conditions of Sheboygan County. Advances the status of the county by engaging in forums, addressing the needs of the community and developing beneficial programs for the members. **Committees:** Economic Development; Government and Public Policy; Members Services; Workforce Development. **Departments:** Convention and Visitors.

19711 ■ Sheboygan County Estate Planning Council
c/o Dennis R. Seipel
PO Box 726
Sheboygan, WI 53082
Ph: (920)458-3591
Fax: (920)458-4560
E-mail: drseipel@dandacpa.com
URL: National Affiliate–councils.naepc.org
Contact: Dennis R. Seipel, Contact
Local. Fosters understanding of the proper relationship between the functions of various professions in the field of estate planning including CPAs, attorneys, trust officers, life underwriters and other parties having to do with estate planning. Encourages cooperation among members. **Affiliated With:** National Association of Estate Planners and Councils.

19712 ■ Sheboygan County Historical Society (SCHS)
3110 Erie Ave.
Sheboygan, WI 53081
Ph: (920)458-1103
Fax: (920)458-5152
E-mail: koeppnlk@co.sheboygan.wi.us
URL: http://www.co.sheboygan.wi.us/html/d_museum.html
Contact: Robert Harker, Museum Exec.Dir.
Founded: 1923. **Members:** 850. **Membership Dues:** individual, $15 (annual) • family, $25 (annual). **Staff:** 7. **Budget:** $148,000. **Local**. Discovers, collects, and preserves records and artifacts relating to the history of Sheboygan County, WI; disseminates information about local history. Promotes artifact preservation and building restoration. Conducts workshops and tours. Sponsors history adventure weekend, Holiday Memories exhibit, and fundraising initiatives. **Affiliated With:** Wisconsin Historical Society. **Publications:** *Sheboygan County Historical Society Newsletter*, bimonthly. **Conventions/Meetings:** annual meeting - always November, Sheboygan, WI • quarterly meeting.

19713 ■ Sheboygan Noon Lions Club
PO Box 585
Sheboygan, WI 53082
Ph: (920)457-9451 (920)452-2845
E-mail: rkuehl@yahoo.com
URL: http://md27b1.org/sheboygannoon/index.html
Contact: Bob Kuehl, Pres.
Local. **Affiliated With:** Lions Clubs International.

19714 ■ Sons of Norway, Vennskap Lodge 5-622
c/o Burton A. Cooley, Sec.
3006 N 25th St.
Sheboygan, WI 53083-2767
Ph: (920)783-0041
E-mail: buracoo@yahoo.com
URL: National Affiliate–www.sofn.com
Contact: Burton A. Cooley, Sec.
Local. **Affiliated With:** Sons of Norway.

19715 ■ Wisconsin Amateur Field Trial Club
c/o Jim Powers, Sec.
N8110 Brookdale Rd.
Sheboygan, WI 53083
Ph: (920)565-3441
URL: http://my.voyager.net/waftc
Contact: Jim Powers, Sec.
State. **Affiliated With:** American Kennel Club.

19716 ■ Wisconsin School Bus Association (WSBA)
c/o Robert W. Christian, Exec.Dir.
PO Box 168
Sheboygan, WI 53082-0168
Ph: (920)457-7008
Fax: (920)457-5758
E-mail: dirbob@dirwsba.com
URL: http://www.dirwsba.com
State.

19717 ■ Wisconsin Speleological Society (WSS)
c/o Andy Ebenhoe
1520 S 26th St.
Sheboygan, WI 53081
E-mail: ae1216@hotmail.com
URL: http://www.caves.org/grotto/wss
Contact: Andy Ebenhoe, Contact
State. Seeks to study, explore and conserve cave and karst resources. Protects access to caves and promotes responsible caving. Encourages responsible management of caves and their unique environments. **Affiliated With:** National Speleological Society.

Sheboygan Falls

19718 ■ Muskies Between the Lakes Chapter
PO Box 61
Sheboygan Falls, WI 53085-0061
Ph: (920)564-3226
E-mail: tedscharl@aol.com
URL: National Affiliate–www.muskiesinc.org
Contact: Ted A. Scharl, Pres.
Local.

19719 ■ Sheboygan Falls Chamber Main Street
c/o Nancy L. Verstrate
504 Broadway
Sheboygan Falls, WI 53085-1358
Ph: (920)467-6206
Fax: (920)467-9571
E-mail: chambermnst@sheboyganfalls.org
URL: http://www.sheboyganfalls.org
Contact: Nancy Verstrate, Exec.Dir.
Founded: 1988. **Members:** 160. **Membership Dues:** $125 (annual). **Staff:** 2. **Budget:** $104,000. **Local**. Promotes commerce and redevelopment of downtown Sheboygan Falls.

19720 ■ Sheboygan Kennel Club
c/o Karen Winkel
415 Richmond Ave.
Sheboygan Falls, WI 53085
URL: http://sheboygankennelclub.com
Contact: Karen Winkel, Contact
Local.

19721 ■ United Way of Sheboygan Falls
PO Box 73
Sheboygan Falls, WI 53085-0073
Ph: (920)467-6768
URL: National Affiliate–national.unitedway.org
Local. **Affiliated With:** United Way of America.

Sheldon

19722 ■ American Legion, York-Kolar Post 316
PO Box 151
Sheldon, WI 54766
Ph: (608)745-1090
Fax: (608)745-0179
URL: National Affiliate–www.legion.org
Local. **Affiliated With:** American Legion.

Shell Lake

19723 ■ American Legion, Francis-Bergin-Paul-Nieman Post 225
PO Box 115
Shell Lake, WI 54871
Ph: (608)745-1090
Fax: (608)745-0179
URL: National Affiliate–www.legion.org
Local. **Affiliated With:** American Legion.

19724 ■ Northwoods Figure Skating Club
PO Box 20
Shell Lake, WI 54871
Ph: (715)468-7289
E-mail: cookie1family@centurytel.net
URL: National Affiliate–www.usfigureskating.org
Contact: Tom Schultz, Contact
Local. Provides programs to encourage participation and achievement in the sport of figure skating on ice. Defines and maintains uniform standards of skating proficiency. Organizes and sponsors competitions and exhibitions for the purpose of stimulating interest

in figure skating. **Affiliated With:** United States Figure Skating Association.

19725 ■ Shell Lake Chamber of Commerce (SLCC)
PO Box 121
Shell Lake, WI 54871
Ph: (715)468-4435
Contact: Louis Steele, Pres.
Members: 35. **Local**. Promotes business and community development in Shell Lake, WI. Sponsors Town and Country Days. **Publications:** none.

Sherwood

19726 ■ American Legion, Wisconsin Post 496
c/o Thomas E. Kees
W489 Clifton Rd.
Sherwood, WI 54169
Ph: (608)745-1090
Fax: (608)745-0179
URL: National Affiliate–www.legion.org
Contact: Thomas E. Kees, Contact
Local. Affiliated With: American Legion.

19727 ■ Fox Cities Optometric Society
c/o Bradley Jorgensen, OD, Pres.
N7807 Lake Shore Dr.
Sherwood, WI 54169
Ph: (920)731-2020
Fax: (920)731-2117
E-mail: bjorgensen@new.rr.com
URL: http://www.woa-eyes.org
Contact: Bradley Jorgensen OD, Pres.
Local. Aims to improve the quality, availability and accessibility of eye and vision care. Promotes high standards of patient care. Monitors and promotes legislation concerning the scope of optometric practice and other issues relevant to eye/vision care. **Affiliated With:** American Optometric Association; Wisconsin Optometric Association.

Shiocton

19728 ■ American Legion, Shiocton Post 512
N 5851 State Hwy. 76
Shiocton, WI 54170
Ph: (608)745-1090
Fax: (608)745-0179
URL: National Affiliate–www.legion.org
Local. Affiliated With: American Legion.

19729 ■ Miss Rodeo Wisconsin Pageant Association
c/o Wendy Vandenboom, Sec.-Treas.
W6775 County Rd. A
Shiocton, WI 54170
Ph: (920)986-3950
E-mail: wisrodeo@peoplepc.com
URL: http://www.missrodeowisconsin.com
Contact: Jill Kreklow, Pres.
Local.

Shorewood

19730 ■ American Legion, North Shore Post 331
4121 N Wilson Dr.
Shorewood, WI 53211
Ph: (608)745-1090
Fax: (608)745-0179
URL: National Affiliate–www.legion.org
Local. Affiliated With: American Legion.

19731 ■ Atwater School PTA
2100 E Capitol Dr.
Shorewood, WI 53211
E-mail: shorewoodinfo@shorewood.k12.wi.us
URL: http://familyeducation.com/WI/AtwaterPTA
Contact: Melissa Nelsen, Pres.
Local. Parents, teachers, students, and others interested in uniting the forces of home, school, and community. Promotes the welfare of children and youth. **Additional Websites:** http://www.shorewoodschools.org/sch_Atwater/atw_PTA/atw_PTA.htm.

19732 ■ Milwaukee Area Resources For Vegetarians
c/o Louise & Chuck Quigley
2201 E Jarvis St.
Shorewood, WI 53211
Ph: (414)962-2703
E-mail: chuckgyver@aol.com
URL: http://marveg.tripod.com/
Contact: Chuck Quigley, Contact
Local. Affiliated With: North American Vegetarian Society.

19733 ■ Shorewood Table Tennis Club
Shorewood Intermediate School
3830 N Morris Blvd.
Shorewood, WI 53211
Ph: (414)444-3143 (414)281-3123
E-mail: leaflin2@naspa.net
URL: http://www.usatt.org/clubs
Contact: Linda Leaf, Contact
Local. Affiliated With: U.S.A. Table Tennis.

Shullsburg

19734 ■ American Legion, Mc-Cann-Richards Post 105
PO Box 12
Shullsburg, WI 53586
Ph: (608)745-1090
Fax: (608)745-0179
URL: National Affiliate–www.legion.org
Local. Affiliated With: American Legion.

Silver Lake

19735 ■ American Legion, Schultz-Hahn Post 293
PO Box 537
Silver Lake, WI 53170
Ph: (608)745-1090
Fax: (608)745-0179
URL: National Affiliate–www.legion.org
Local. Affiliated With: American Legion.

Siren

19736 ■ American Legion, Lund-Brown Post 132
24049 1st Ave.
Siren, WI 54872
Ph: (608)745-1090
Fax: (608)745-0179
URL: National Affiliate–www.legion.org
Local. Affiliated With: American Legion.

19737 ■ Plumbing-Heating-Cooling Contractors Association, Western Wisconsin
c/o Dayton Daniels
24056 State Rd. 35, Box 316
Siren, WI 54872-8005
Ph: (715)349-5533
Fax: (715)349-7353
E-mail: danphvac@sirentel.net
URL: National Affiliate–www.phccweb.org
Contact: Dayton Daniels, Contact
Local. Represents the plumbing, heating and cooling contractors. Promotes the construction industry. Protects the environment, health, safety and comfort of society. **Affiliated With:** Plumbing-Heating-Cooling Contractors Association.

Sister Bay

19738 ■ American Legion, Wisconsin Post 527
c/o Billy Weiss
PO Box 554
Sister Bay, WI 54234
Ph: (608)745-1090
Fax: (608)745-0179
URL: National Affiliate–www.legion.org
Contact: Billy Weiss, Contact
Local. Affiliated With: American Legion.

Slinger

19739 ■ Federation of Environmental Technologists (FET)
PO Box 624
Slinger, WI 53086
Ph: (262)644-0070
Fax: (262)644-7106
E-mail: info@fetinc.org
URL: http://www.fetinc.org
Local. Conventions/Meetings: annual Environment - conference, 30 concurrent sessions to update and inform of environmental regulations (exhibits).

19740 ■ Professional Dairy Producers of Wisconsin (PDPW)
c/o Shelly Mayer, Exec.Dir.
4965 Hwy. E
Slinger, WI 53086
Ph: (262)644-0855
Fax: (262)644-1802
Free: (800)947-7379
E-mail: smayer@pdpw.org
URL: http://www.pdpw.org
Contact: Shelly Mayer, Exec.Dir.
State.

Soldiers Grove

19741 ■ American Legion, Wisconsin Post 220
c/o William Schoville
PO Box 37
Soldiers Grove, WI 54655
Ph: (608)745-1090
Fax: (608)745-0179
URL: National Affiliate–www.legion.org
Contact: William Schoville, Contact
Local. Affiliated With: American Legion.

Solon Springs

19742 ■ Minnesota Fire Service Certification Board
c/o James K. Heim, Exec.Sec.
10983 S Jackson Dr.
Solon Springs, WI 54873-8434
Ph: (715)378-2077
Fax: (715)378-2217
Free: (866)566-0911
E-mail: jheim@centurytel.net
URL: http://mfscb.org
Contact: James K. Heim, Exec.Sec.
Founded: 1989. **Members:** 15. **Staff:** 2. **State**. Certifies fire service members in Minnesota to the National Standards put forth by the National Fire Protection Association and are accredited by the International Fire Service Accreditation Congress (IFSAC).

19743 ■ National Alliance for the Mentally Ill - Douglas County
c/o Gina Rochon, Pres.
10900 S Stone Rd.
Solon Springs, WI 54873-8405
Ph: (715)378-2772
URL: http://www.namiwisconsin.org/library/directory
Contact: Gina Rochon, Pres.
Local. Strives to improve the quality of life of children and adults with severe mental illness through support, education, research and advocacy. **Affiliated With:** National Alliance for the Mentally Ill.

Somers

19744 ■ American Legion, Wisconsin Post 552
c/o David Leet
PO Box 31
Somers, WI 53171
Ph: (608)745-1090
Fax: (608)745-0179
URL: National Affiliate–www.legion.org
Contact: David Leet, Contact
Local. Affiliated With: American Legion.

Somerset

19745 ■ American Legion, Phaneuf-Vanasse Post 111
464 Hwy. 35 64
Somerset, WI 54025
Ph: (608)745-1090
Fax: (608)745-0179
URL: National Affiliate–www.legion.org
Local. Affiliated With: American Legion.

19746 ■ Somerset Area Chamber of Commerce (SACC)
PO Box 357
Somerset, WI 54025-0357
Ph: (715)247-3366
Fax: (715)247-2408
E-mail: schamber@somtel.net
Founded: 1950. **Members:** 40. **Local**. Promotes business and community development in the Somerset, WI area. **Conventions/Meetings:** quarterly meeting.

South Milwaukee

19747 ■ Easter Seals Southeastern Wisconsin
1016 Milwaukee Ave.
South Milwaukee, WI 53172
Ph: (414)571-5566
Fax: (414)571-5568
E-mail: agency@easterseals-sewi.org
URL: http://wi-se.easterseals.com
Contact: Bob Glowacki, CEO
Members: 12. **Local Groups:** 6. **State**. Provides services for children and adults with disabilities and their families. **Affiliated With:** Easter Seals.

South Range

19748 ■ American Legion, Wisconsin Post 418
PO Box 147
South Range, WI 54874
Ph: (608)745-1090
Fax: (608)745-0179
URL: National Affiliate–www.legion.org
Local. Affiliated With: American Legion.

19749 ■ Sons of Norway, Norrona Lodge 5-27
c/o Roy V. Peterson, Pres.
6288 S Pine Grove Rd.
South Range, WI 54874
Ph: (715)399-2338
E-mail: marpet6288@aol.com
URL: National Affiliate–www.sofn.com
Contact: Roy V. Peterson, Pres.
Local. Affiliated With: Sons of Norway.

Sparta

19750 ■ American Legion, O.-L.-Arnold-D.-K.-Slayton Post 100
1116 Angelo Rd.
Sparta, WI 54656
Ph: (608)745-1090
Fax: (608)745-0179
URL: National Affiliate–www.legion.org
Local. Affiliated With: American Legion.

19751 ■ Association of the United States Army, MG Robert D. McCoy
c/o Bob Woodburn
926 John St.
Sparta, WI 54656
Ph: (608)269-7713
URL: National Affiliate–www.ausa.org
Local. Represents the interests and concerns of American Soldiers. Fosters public support of the Army's role in national security. Provides professional education and information programs.

19752 ■ Kiwanis Club of Sparta
PO Box 405
Sparta, WI 54656
URL: http://www.wi.centuryinter.net/kiwanis
Contact: Duane R. McClain, Pres.
Local.

19753 ■ Monroe County Historical Society (MCHS)
PO Box 422
Sparta, WI 54656
Ph: (608)269-8630 (608)269-8680
URL: http://home.wi.rr.com/genealogywis/histsocs.htm
Contact: Carolyn Habelman, Pres.
Founded: 1972. **Members:** 220. **Staff:** 1. **Local**. Genealogists, family researchers, and preservationists who seek to preserve birth and death records and cemeteries in West Central Wisconsin. Sponsors educational programs, arts and crafts shows, and bus tours. Maintains Wegner Grotto. **Affiliated With:** Wisconsin Historical Society. **Publications:** *Heritage Book, Monroe County, WI* • *The Portals of Time*, quarterly. Newsletter • Books. **Conventions/Meetings:** periodic symposium.

19754 ■ Reserve Officers Association - Department of Wisconsin, Readiness Chapter 43
PO Box 451
Sparta, WI 54656-0451
E-mail: jonathan.pontius@us.army.mil
URL: http://www.geocities.com/Pentagon/Barracks/1272/roa43.html
Contact: Capt. Jonathan Pontius, Pres.
Local. Promotes and supports the development and execution of a military policy for the United States. Provides professional development seminars, workshops and programs for its members. **Affiliated With:** Reserve Officers Association of the United States.

19755 ■ Sparta Area Chamber of Commerce
111 Milwaukee Ave.
Sparta, WI 54656
Ph: (608)269-4123
Fax: (608)269-3350
E-mail: spartachamber@centurytel.net
URL: http://www.spartachamber.org
Contact: Todd Hammond, Pres.
Founded: 1940. **Members:** 350. **Membership Dues:** business, financial institution, motel/hotel/bed and breakfast, and utility (base), $160 (annual). **Staff:** 3. **Budget:** $130,000. **Local**. Fosters community prosperity and improvement of quality of life in the Sparta, WI area through cooperation, education, and active leadership. **Committees:** Ambassadors; Education; Promotion; Tourism. **Publications:** *The Ambassador*, monthly. Newsletter. Contains information about chamber events and activities. **Circulation:** 350. Alternate Formats: online • Membership Directory, biennial. **Conventions/Meetings:** annual Board and Executive Committee Meeting • monthly executive committee meeting • quarterly seminar.

19756 ■ Sparta Lions Club - Wisconsin
c/o Sheldon Lamson, Sec.
418 W Main St.
Sparta, WI 54656
Ph: (608)269-0115
E-mail: toonan@charter.net
URL: http://www.md27d2.org
Contact: Sheldon Lamson, Sec.
Local. Affiliated With: Lions Clubs International.

19757 ■ U.S. Army Warrant Officers Association, Fort McCoy Chapter
c/o Dennie C. Goss, Pres., CW4
PO Box 6093
Sparta, WI 54656-6093
Ph: (608)372-3962
E-mail: dennie.goss@us.army.mil
URL: http://www.geocities.com/Pentagon/Barracks/1272/mccoy.html
Local. Active duty, National Guard, Reserve, and retired U.S. Army warrant officers. Works to promote the technical and social welfare of warrant officers. **Affiliated With:** United States Army Warrant Officers Association.

19758 ■ Wisconsin Dietetic Association (WDA)
1411 W Montgomery St.
Sparta, WI 54656-1003
Ph: (608)269-0042
Fax: (608)269-0043
Free: (888)232-8631
E-mail: wda@centurytel.net
URL: http://www.eatrightwisc.org
Contact: Ms. Lynn Edwards, Exec.Coor.
Founded: 1936. **Members:** 1,550. **Membership Dues:** $0. **Staff:** 1. **Regional Groups:** 3. **State**. Promotes optimal nutrition and well-being for all people. **Affiliated With:** American Dietetic Association. **Publications:** *WDA Communique*, semiannual. Newsletter. **Advertising:** accepted. **Conventions/Meetings:** annual conference (exhibits).

Spencer

19759 ■ Spencer Area Chamber of Commerce
105 Park St.
Spencer, WI 54479
Ph: (715)659-5423
Contact: Mike Endreas, Pres.
Local.

Spooner

19760 ■ American Legion, Moe-Miller Post 12
PO Box 352
Spooner, WI 54801
Ph: (608)745-1090
Fax: (608)745-0179
URL: National Affiliate–www.legion.org
Local. Affiliated With: American Legion.

19761 ■ Forestry Conservation Communications Association, Region III
c/o Thomas Tesky, Chm.
Wisconsin Dept. of Trans., State Patrol
W7102 Green Valley Rd.
Spooner, WI 54801

Ph: (715)635-8173
Fax: (715)635-6373
E-mail: thomas.tesky@dot.state.wi.us
URL: National Affiliate–www.fcca-usa.org
Contact: Thomas Tesky, Chm.
Regional. Affiliated With: Forestry Conservation Communications Association.

19762 ■ Northwest Regional Planning Commission (NWRPC)
1400 S River St.
Spooner, WI 54801
Ph: (715)635-2197
Fax: (715)635-7262
E-mail: info@nwrpc.com
URL: http://www.nwrpc.com
Contact: Sheldon Johnson, Deputy Dir.
Local.

19763 ■ Spooner Area Chamber of Commerce (SACC)
122 N River St.
Spooner, WI 54801
Ph: (715)635-2168
Fax: (715)635-5170
Free: (800)367-3306
E-mail: chamber@spooneronline.com
URL: http://chamber.spooneronline.com/
Contact: Katherine Speare, Pres.
Founded: 1936. **Members:** 95. **Local.** Promotes business and community development in the Spooner, WI area. Sponsors Jack Pine Savage Days; Jack's A Hack Golf Tournament; Old Fashioned Saturday Night Woman's Day; conducts promotional activities. **Awards:** Business Person of the Year. **Frequency:** annual. **Type:** recognition. **Recipient:** for contributions to community through business • Chamber Member of the Year. **Frequency:** annual. **Type:** recognition. **Recipient:** for efforts to enhance chamber • Citizen of the Year. **Frequency:** annual. **Type:** recognition • Educator of the Year. **Frequency:** annual. **Type:** recognition. **Recipient:** for contributions to education and students. **Conventions/Meetings:** monthly general assembly.

19764 ■ Wisconsin Nurses Association, Northwest District - No. 11
1116 Elm St.
Spooner, WI 54801
Ph: (715)635-3331
E-mail: klkiss@centurytel.net
URL: http://www.wisconsinnurses.org
Contact: Jean Kissack, Pres.
Local. Works to advance the nursing profession. Seeks to meet the needs of nurses and health care consumers. Fosters high standards of nursing practice. Promotes the economic and general welfare of nurses in the workplace. **Affiliated With:** American Nurses Association; Wisconsin Nurses' Association.

Spring Green

19765 ■ American Legion, Spring Green Post 253
PO Box 482
Spring Green, WI 53588
Ph: (608)745-1090
Fax: (608)745-0179
URL: National Affiliate–www.legion.org
Local. Affiliated With: American Legion.

19766 ■ Bike Wisconsin Education and Action Coalition (BWEAC)
c/o Bill Hauda
PO Box 310
Spring Green, WI 53588-0310
Ph: (608)935-7433
Fax: (608)935-5816
Free: (888)575-3640
E-mail: wisbike@mhtc.net
URL: http://www.bikewisconsin.org
Contact: Bill Hauda, Contact
State.

19767 ■ River Valley Youth for Christ
Box 36
Spring Green, WI 53588
Ph: (608)341-9510
URL: National Affiliate–www.yfc.net
Local. Affiliated With: Youth for Christ/U.S.A.

19768 ■ Spring Green Area Chamber of Commerce (SGACC)
PO Box 3
Spring Green, WI 53588
Ph: (608)588-2054
Fax: (608)588-2054
Free: (800)588-2042
E-mail: info@springgreen.com
URL: http://www.springgreen.com
Contact: Jean Porter, Contact
Founded: 1968. **Membership Dues:** class A (based on number of employees), $150-$600 • associate, $100 • home based, $75 • not for profit, $50 • friend of the chamber, $25. **Local.** Promotes business and community development in the Spring Green, WI area. Sponsors Arts and Crafts Fair and Country Christmas Festival. Conducts charitable activities. **Committees:** Arts and Craft Fair; The Chamber News; Country Christmas; Marketing; Retail. **Publications:** *The Chamber News*. Newsletter • Directory, annual. **Conventions/Meetings:** monthly meeting.

19769 ■ Spring Green Lions Club
c/o Howard Orcutt, Pres.
553 N Baltimore St.
Spring Green, WI 53588
Ph: (608)588-7398
E-mail: hmorcutt@charter.net
URL: http://www.md27d2.org
Contact: Howard Orcutt, Pres.
Local. Affiliated With: Lions Clubs International.

Spring Valley

19770 ■ American Legion, Rickerd-Danielson Post 227
N 343 Sabin Ave.
Spring Valley, WI 54767
Ph: (608)745-1090
Fax: (608)745-0179
URL: National Affiliate–www.legion.org
Local. Affiliated With: American Legion.

19771 ■ Izaak Walton League of America, Western Wisconsin Chapter
N7626 U.S. Hwy. 63
Spring Valley, WI 54767
Ph: (715)273-4442
URL: National Affiliate–www.iwla.org
Local. Works to educate the public to conserve, maintain, protect, and restore the soil, forest, water, and other natural resources of the U.S; promotes the enjoyment and wholesome utilization of these resources. **Affiliated With:** Izaak Walton League of America.

Springbrook

19772 ■ American Legion, Sizer-Buchman Post 328
W 3399 Hwy. 63
Springbrook, WI 54875
Ph: (608)745-1090
Fax: (608)745-0179
URL: National Affiliate–www.legion.org
Local. Affiliated With: American Legion.

Stanley

19773 ■ American Legion, Victory Post 112
323 E 1st Ave.
Stanley, WI 54768
Ph: (608)745-1090
Fax: (608)745-0179
URL: National Affiliate–www.legion.org
Local. Affiliated With: American Legion.

19774 ■ Chippewa County Fire Chief Association
c/o Ronald Zais
945 No. Broadway
Stanley, WI 54768
Ph: (715)644-5564
Fax: (715)644-2950
E-mail: fire2@ecol.net
Founded: 1967. **Members:** 25. **Membership Dues:** $10 (annual). **Local.** Promotes fire safety throughout Chippewa County.

Star Prairie

19775 ■ Star Prairie Lions Club
PO Box 198
Star Prairie, WI 54026
E-mail: rbensen@frontiernet.net
URL: http://www.starprairielions.org/index.htm
Contact: Robert Bensen, Pres.
Local. Affiliated With: Lions Clubs International.

Steuben

19776 ■ American Legion, Daugherty-Larsen Post 446
PO Box 88
Steuben, WI 54657
Ph: (608)745-1090
Fax: (608)745-0179
URL: National Affiliate–www.legion.org
Local. Affiliated With: American Legion.

Stevens Point

19777 ■ Aldo Leopold Audubon Society
c/o Tom Overholt, Pres.
PO Box 928
Stevens Point, WI 54481-0928
Ph: (715)341-7631
URL: National Affiliate–www.audubon.org
Local. Works to conserve and restore natural ecosystems, focusing on birds and other wildlife for the benefit of humanity and the earth's biological diversity. **Affiliated With:** National Audubon Society.

19778 ■ American Association of Critical Care Nurses, North Central Wisconsin Chapter (NCWC)
c/o Kimberly Kuphal, Pres.
1400 4th Ave.
Stevens Point, WI 54481
E-mail: ncwc.info@aacn.org
URL: National Affiliate–www.aacn.org
Contact: Kimberly Kuphal, Pres.
Local. Professional critical care nurses. Established to provide continuing education programs for nurses specializing in critical care and to develop standards of nursing care of critically ill patients. **Affiliated With:** American Association of Critical-Care Nurses.

19779 ■ American Chemical Society, Central Wisconsin Section
c/o Dr. Laura Jane Cole, Chair
UWSP, Dept. of Chemistry
2100 Main St.
Stevens Point, WI 54481-3871
Ph: (715)346-4302
Fax: (715)346-2640
E-mail: lcole@uwsp.edu
URL: National Affiliate–acswebcontent.acs.org
Contact: Dr. Laura Jane Cole, Chair
Local. Represents the interests of individuals dedicated to the advancement of chemistry in all its branches. Provides opportunities for peer interaction and career development. **Affiliated With:** American Chemical Society.

19780 ■ American Legion, Berens-Scribner Post 6
PO Box 322
Stevens Point, WI 54481
Ph: (608)745-1090
Fax: (608)745-0179
URL: National Affiliate–www.legion.org
Local. Affiliated With: American Legion.

19781 ■ American Red Cross, Portage County Chapter
3057 Michigan Ave.
Stevens Point, WI 54481
Ph: (715)344-4052
Fax: (715)344-3059
Free: (800)939-4052
E-mail: pcarc@charter.net
URL: http://portagewi.redcross.org
Local.

19782 ■ American Water Resources Association - UWSP Student Chapter (AWRA)
Univ. of Wisconsin
Stevens Point
Coll. of Natural Rsrcs.
Stevens Point, WI 54481
Ph: (715)346-4613
E-mail: awra@uwsp.edu
URL: http://www.uwsp.edu/stuorg/awra/
Contact: N. Earl Spangenberg, Advisor
Local.

19783 ■ American Water Resources Association Wisconsin State Section
c/o Mike Penn, Pres.
Dept. of Geography/Geology
UW-Stevens Point
Stevens Point, WI 54481
Ph: (715)346-2287
Fax: (715)346-3372
E-mail: mrpenn@uwplatt.edu
URL: http://www.awra.org/state/wisconsin/index.html
Contact: Mike Penn, Pres.
Founded: 1977. **Members:** 250. **Membership Dues:** individual, $2 (annual). **Budget:** $8,500. **State.** Provides an interdisciplinary forum for people involved in all aspects of water resources research and management. **Affiliated With:** American Water Resources Association. **Publications:** Newsletter, annual. **Conventions/Meetings:** annual conference.

19784 ■ Bernese Mountain Dog Club of America (BMDCA)
c/o Stephanie Sotiros, Membership Chair
3109 Leahey
Stevens Point, WI 54481
E-mail: admin@bmdca.org
URL: http://www.bmdca.org
Contact: Alison Jaskiewicz, Pres.
State. Affiliated With: American Kennel Club.

19785 ■ Big Brothers Big Sisters of Portage County (BBBS)
3262 Church St., Ste.2
Stevens Point, WI 54481
Ph: (715)341-0661
Fax: (715)341-9508
E-mail: bbbs@bigimpact.org
URL: http://www.bigimpact.org
Contact: Sue Martens, Exec.Dir.
Local. Affiliated With: Big Brothers Big Sisters of America.

19786 ■ Central Wisconsin Habitat for Humanity
1314 Main St.
Stevens Point, WI 54481-2865
Ph: (715)345-2726
Fax: (715)342-0595
E-mail: tom@centralwisconsinhabitat.org
URL: National Affiliate–www.habitat.org
Local. Affiliated With: Habitat for Humanity International.

19787 ■ Crystal Ice Figure Skating Club (CIFSC)
PO Box 400
Stevens Point, WI 54481
E-mail: skate@cifsc.net
URL: http://www.cifsc.net
Local. Provides programs to encourage participation and achievement in the sport of figure skating on ice. Defines and maintains uniform standards of skating proficiency. Organizes and sponsors competitions and exhibitions for the purpose of stimulating interest in figure skating. **Affiliated With:** United States Figure Skating Association.

19788 ■ Environmental Council
Univ. of Wisconsin-Stevens Point
Univ. Centers
SIEO No. 38
Stevens Point, WI 54481
Ph: (715)346-4718
Fax: (715)346-3025
E-mail: chass940@uwsp.edu
URL: http://www.uwsp.edu/stuorg/envcon/index.htm
Contact: Katie Hassemer, Sec.
Local.

19789 ■ Epilepsy Foundation of Central and Northeast Wisconsin
1004 1st St., Ste.5
Stevens Point, WI 54481
Ph: (715)341-5811
Fax: (715)341-5713
Free: (800)924-9932
E-mail: efcnw@efcnw.com
URL: http://www.epilepsyfoundation.org/local/cnewisconsin
Contact: Cindy Piotrowski, Exec.Dir.
Founded: 1980. **Members:** 100. **Membership Dues:** full, $25 (annual). **Staff:** 7. **Budget:** $200,000. **Local.** People with epilepsy and interested persons in 22 Wisconsin counties. Provides direct services to people with epilepsy and educational services to the community. **Libraries: Type:** lending. **Holdings:** books, video recordings. **Subjects:** epilepsy issues. **Boards:** Board of Directors; Professional Advisory. **Programs:** Counseling and Case Management; Emergency Funding; Individual Advocacy; Living-Skills Training; Parent Network; Support Groups. **Affiliated With:** Epilepsy Foundation. **Formerly:** (1999) Midstate Epilepsy Association. **Publications:** *Currents*, quarterly. Newsletter. Focuses on epilepsy issues. **Conventions/Meetings:** annual Conference on Advances in Epilepsy Treatment, national speakers focus on advances in treatment; designed for professionals and public.

19790 ■ Golden Sands Resource Conservation and Development Council
1462 Strongs Ave.
Stevens Point, WI 54481
Ph: (715)343-6215
Contact: William Ebert, Project Mgr.

19791 ■ Interfaith Volunteer Caregivers of Portage County (IVCPC)
1100 Centerpoint Dr., Ste.301
Stevens Point, WI 54481-0847
Ph: (715)342-4084
E-mail: volunteer@unitedwaypoco.org
Contact: Sasha Vieth, Dir.
Staff: 1. **Local.** Coordinates volunteers through local churches to provide assistance to elderly and disabled. Works to provide respite care.

19792 ■ Izaak Walton League of America, Bill Cook Chapter
5245 Ann Marie Ct.
Stevens Point, WI 54481
Ph: (715)342-4602 (715)344-0166
URL: National Affiliate–www.iwla.org
Contact: Luke Carpenter, Contact
Local. Works to educate the public to conserve, maintain, protect, and restore the soil, forest, water, and other natural resources of the U.S; promotes the enjoyment and wholesome utilization of these resources. **Affiliated With:** Izaak Walton League of America.

19793 ■ Midwest Hardware Association (MHA)
c/o John J. Haka, Managing Dir.
PO Box 8033
2801 Dixon St.
Stevens Point, WI 54481-8033
Ph: (715)341-7100
Fax: (715)341-4080
Free: (800)888-1817
E-mail: mha@midwesthardware.com
URL: http://www.midwesthardware.com
Contact: John J. Haka, Managing Dir.
Founded: 1896. **Members:** 650. **Regional.** Provides services and benefits to independent retail hardware stores throughout the U.S. Services including accounting, payroll, and tax preparation.

19794 ■ Mothers Against Drunk Driving, Marathon/Portage
3209 Lindbergh Ave.
Stevens Point, WI 54481
Ph: (715)345-0509
E-mail: jacobs@coredcs.com
URL: National Affiliate–www.madd.org
Contact: Christine Jacobs, Contact
Founded: 1984. **Members:** 50. **Local.** Victims of drunk drivers and other interested individuals in Marathon and Portage counties, WI, seeking to eliminate drunk driving. Works to emphasize unacceptability and criminality of drunk driving, and to promote preventive policies and programs. **Affiliated With:** Mothers Against Drunk Driving. **Conventions/Meetings:** quarterly meeting.

19795 ■ NAIFA-Central Wisconsin
2615 Post Rd.
Stevens Point, WI 54481
Ph: (920)884-0282
Fax: (920)884-0282
URL: National Affiliate–www.naifa.org
Local. Represents the interest of insurance and financial advisors. Advocates for a positive legislative and regulatory environment. Enhances business and professional skills of members. **Affiliated With:** National Association of Insurance and Financial Advisors.

19796 ■ National Alliance for the Mentally Ill - Portage/Wood Counties
c/o Marvin Lutz, Pres.
6617 Old Hwy. 18
Stevens Point, WI 54481
Ph: (715)592-4522
URL: http://www.namiwisconsin.org/library/directory
Contact: Marvin Lutz, Pres.
Local. Strives to improve the quality of life of children and adults with severe mental illness through support, education, research and advocacy. **Affiliated With:** National Alliance for the Mentally Ill.

19797 ■ National Association of Student Personnel Administrators, Wisconsin
c/o Robert Tomlinson, Coor.
Univ. of Wisconsin-Stevens Point
2100 Main St.
Stevens Point, WI 54481
Ph: (715)346-2481
Fax: (715)346-2651
E-mail: btomlins@uwsp.edu
URL: National Affiliate–www.naspa.org
Contact: Robert Tomlinson, Coor.
State. Provides professional development and advocacy for student affairs educators and administrators. Seeks to promote, assess and support student learning through leadership. **Affiliated With:** National Association of Student Personnel Administrators.

19798 ■ Plumbing-Heating-Cooling Contractors Association, Wisconsin Valley
c/o Mr. Peter Laskowski, Pres.
3001 Hoover Rd.
Stevens Point, WI 54481-5670
Ph: (715)341-9530
Fax: (715)341-9529
E-mail: chets@chets.net
URL: National Affiliate–www.phccweb.org
Contact: Mr. Peter Laskowski, Pres.
Local. Represents the plumbing, heating and cooling contractors. Promotes the construction industry. Protects the environment, health, safety and comfort of society. **Affiliated With:** Plumbing-Heating-Cooling Contractors Association.

19799 ■ Pony of the Americas Club, Wisconsin - North Central
c/o Ginger Houck, Pres.
1816 Jordan Rd.
Stevens Point, WI 54481
Ph: (715)341-2520
E-mail: haymeadow81@hotmail.com
URL: National Affiliate–www.poac.org
Contact: Ginger Houck, Pres.
State. Affiliated With: Pony of the Americas Club.

19800 ■ Portage County Business Council
5501 Vern Holmes Dr.
Stevens Point, WI 54481
Ph: (715)344-1940
Fax: (715)344-4473
E-mail: info@portagecountybiz.com
URL: http://www.portagecountybiz.com
Contact: Jeff Landin, Exec.Dir.
Local. Represents over 500 Portage County businesses. Strengthens Portage County's quality of life by promoting a business climate that encourages growth and stability. **Publications:** *Active Voice*, monthly. Newsletter. **Advertising:** accepted.

19801 ■ Portage County Crime Stoppers
c/o Sgt.Mike Lukas
1500 Strongs Ave.
Stevens Point, WI 54481-3542
Free: (888)346-6600
Founded: 1994. **Local**.

19802 ■ Portage County Humane Society
PO Box 512
Stevens Point, WI 54481
Ph: (715)344-6012
E-mail: info@hspcwi.org
URL: http://www.hspcwi.org
Contact: Dolores Glytas, Pres.
Founded: 1969. **Membership Dues:** single, $15 (annual). **Local**. Provides animal control, humane animal care and humane education. **Libraries: Type:** open to the public. **Holdings:** 55. **Subjects:** pet information including pet overpopulation and spaying/neutering data. **Publications:** *Humane News*, quarterly. Newsletter. Contains pet Information, current events, and kids corner. **Price:** included in membership dues.

19803 ■ Portage County Literacy Council (PCLC)
1052 Main St., Ste.104
Stevens Point, WI 54481-2848
Ph: (715)345-5341
E-mail: pclc@pocolit.org
URL: http://www.pocolit.org
Contact: Thomas D. Parker PhD, Exec.Dir.
Founded: 1986. **Local**. Provides individual tutoring in reading, writing, English as a second language, and basic math for adults as well as a computer-based learning system for basic skills. **Convention/Meeting:** none. **Publications:** Newsletters, 3/year. **Price:** free. Alternate Formats: online.

19804 ■ Portage County RSVP
c/o Marti Sowka, Dir.
1519 Water St.
Stevens Point, WI 54481-3548
Ph: (715)346-1401
Fax: (715)346-1418
E-mail: rsvp@co.portage.wi.us
URL: http://www.seniorcorps.gov/about/programs/rsvp_state.asp?usestateabbr=wi&Search4.x=0&Search4.y=0
Contact: Marti Sowka, Dir.
Local. Additional Websites: http://www.co.portage.wi.us/Aging/page20.html. **Affiliated With:** Retired and Senior Volunteer Program.

19805 ■ Sentry Cares
c/o Ron Cook
1800 N Point Dr.
Stevens Point, WI 54481
Ph: (715)346-7450
Fax: (715)346-6330
E-mail: ron.cook@sentry.com
Contact: Ron Cook, Contact
Founded: 1990. **Budget:** $1,500. **Local**. Employee association which devotes its net earnings exclusively to charitable or educational purposes. Works to improve the quality of life for the less fortunate of Portage County, WI as identified by local social agencies, by distributing its proceeds to these needy individuals.

19806 ■ Soil and Water Conservation Society of America (SWCS)
Univ. of Wisconsin
Stevens Point
282 Coll. of Natural Resources
1900 Franklin St.
Stevens Point, WI 54481
Ph: (715)346-4180
E-mail: rhensler@uwsp.edu
Contact: Ronald Hensler, Prof. of Soils, Club Advisor
Regional. Natural resource students. Provides information about soil conservation. Activities include weekly meetings, hosting speakers, "adopt-a-highway" clean-up and the Horicon Marsh Project.

19807 ■ Sons of Norway, Vennligfolk Lodge 5-627
c/o Milo I. Harpstead, Pres.
612 Fieldcrest Ave.
Stevens Point, WI 54481-4317
Ph: (715)341-3145
E-mail: milohrp@voyager.net
URL: National Affiliate–www.sofn.com
Contact: Milo I. Harpstead, Pres.
Local. Affiliated With: Sons of Norway.

19808 ■ Stevens Point Area Genealogical Society
c/o Portage County Library
1001 Main St.
Stevens Point, WI 54481
Ph: (715)346-1548
E-mail: pointgen@yahoo.com
Contact: Ruth Steffen, Contact
Founded: 1975. **Membership Dues:** individual, $10 • family, $12. **Local**. Individuals interested in genealogy. Maintains obituary index and updates newspaper file in public library. **Publications:** *Pedigree Pointers*, quarterly. Newsletter. **Price:** included in membership dues. **Conventions/Meetings:** biennial workshop.

19809 ■ Stevens Point Area Human Resource Association
c/o Lisa Sobczak
ABR Employment Sers.
2813 Post Rd.
Stevens Point, WI 54481
E-mail: doris.mcallister@mstc.edu
URL: http://www.wishrm.org/chapter/stpoint/index.html
Contact: Dorris McAllister, Pres.
Local. Represents the interests of human resource and industrial relations professionals and executives. Promotes the advancement of human resource management.

19810 ■ Stevens Point PTSA
c/o Bill Hettler, Pres.
718 Linwood Ave.
Stevens Point, WI 54481
E-mail: pres@ptsa.org
URL: http://www.ptsa.org/index.htm
Contact: Bill Hettler, Pres.
Local. Parents, teachers, students, and others interested in uniting the forces of home, school, and community. Promotes the welfare of children and youth.

19811 ■ Sweet Adelines International, Center Point Chapter
Harmony Hall
3500 Harmony Ln.
Stevens Point, WI 54481-1315
Ph: (715)359-7975
E-mail: sltang@aol.com
URL: National Affiliate–www.sweetadelineintl.org
Contact: Sheila Tang, Contact
Local. Advances the musical art form of barbershop harmony through education and performances. Provides education, training and coaching in the development of women's four-part barbershop harmony. **Affiliated With:** Sweet Adelines International.

19812 ■ Trout Unlimited, Frank Hornberg 624
c/o Michael Mather, Pres.
PO Box 393
Stevens Point, WI 54481-0393
Ph: (715)824-2530
E-mail: friedpike@yahoo.com
URL: http://www.hornbergtu.org
Contact: Michael Mather, Pres.
Founded: 1992. **Local. Affiliated With:** Trout Unlimited.

19813 ■ United Way of Portage County
1100 Centerpoint Dr., Ste.302
Stevens Point, WI 54481-2849
Ph: (715)341-6740
Fax: (715)341-3717
E-mail: uway@unitedwaypoco.org
URL: http://www.unitedwaypoco.org
Contact: Susan Wilcox, Exec.Dir.
Founded: 1945. **Staff:** 5. **Budget:** $1,110,000. **Local**. Assists in fundraising by conducting company-wide employee campaigns and by encouraging corporate contributions. **Publications:** *At Work*, periodic. Newsletter. **Price:** free.

19814 ■ University of Wisconsin, Stevens Point - Wildlife Society - Student Chapter
359A CNR UWSP
Stevens Point, WI 54481
Ph: (715)346-2016
E-mail: wildsoc@uwsp.edu
URL: http://www.uwsp.edu/stuorg/wildlife
Contact: Matt Schuler, Pres.
Local. Seeks to provide opportunities for better liaison among members, other chapters, sections, and the Society. Evaluates and responds to proposed or enacted societal actions that could affect wildlife or wildlife habitats. Encourages professionalism and high standards of scholarship. Focuses aims and objectives to professional wildlife needs. Promotes communication to improve understanding of resource management sciences.

19815 ■ University of Wisconsin, Stevens Point - Wisconsin Parks and Recreation Association
Coll. of Natural Rsrcs.
Stevens Point, WI 54481
Ph: (715)346-4160
E-mail: rgeesey@uwsp.edu
Contact: Richard Geesey, Advisor
Local.

19816 ■ Wisconsin Association of Collegiate Registrars and Admissions Officers (WACRAO)
c/o Catherine Glennon
Off. of Admissions
Park Student Services Bldg.
UW-Stevens Point
Stevens Point, WI 54481
Ph: (715)346-2441
E-mail: cglennon@uwsp.edu
URL: http://www.wacrao.org
Founded: 1927. **State**. Postsecondary educational institutions in Wisconsin. Seeks to provide the dissemination of information and the interchange of ideas on problems of mutual interest to the individual participants of the member institutions; to foster a better understanding of the activities of member institutions and to develop a spirit of cooperativeness, helpfulness and unity in the solution of mutual problems; to advance and professionalize the activities of the offices of admissions, registration, records and student statistics through encouraging increased effectiveness and efficiency of the functions of these offices; and to contribute to the advancement of education in Wisconsin. **Affiliated With:** American Association of Collegiate Registrars and Admissions Officers. **Publications:** *Committee Handbook and Bylaws* • Newsletter, quarterly • Membership Directory. **Conventions/Meetings:** annual conference (exhibits) • Professional Development - workshop.

19817 ■ Wisconsin Association for Environmental Education (WAEE)
8 Nelson Hall
Univ. of Wisconsin-Stevens Point
Stevens Point, WI 54481
Ph: (715)346-2796
Fax: (715)346-3835
E-mail: waee@uwsp.edu
URL: http://www.uwsp.edu/cnr/waee
Contact: Carol Weston, Admin.Asst.
State.

19818 ■ Wisconsin Environmental Education Board (WEEB)
110 Coll. of Natural Resources
Univ. of Wisconsin
Stevens Point, WI 54481
Ph: (715)346-3805
Fax: (715)346-3025
E-mail: weeb@uwsp.edu
URL: http://www.uwsp.edu/cnr/weeb
Contact: Ginny Carlton, Admin. Specialist
State. Administers a state-wide environmental education grant program and sets policy for environmental education within Wisconsin.

19819 ■ Wisconsin Intramural Recreational Sports Association
c/o Mr. Ed Richmond, Station Dir.
Univ. of Wisconsin-Stevens Point
1015 Reserve St.
Stevens Point, WI 54481
Ph: (715)346-4343
Fax: (715)346-4365
E-mail: erichmn@uwsp.edu
URL: http://www.nirsa.org/administration/state/wisconsin.htm
Contact: Mr. Ed Richmond, Station Dir.
Founded: 2001. **Members:** 100. **Membership Dues:** professional/student, $10 (annual). **Staff:** 100. **Budget:** $500. **State Groups:** 1. **State**. **Awards:** Scholarship. **Frequency:** annual. **Type:** monetary. **Recipient:** to student members for National Conferences. **Affiliated With:** National Intramural-Recreational Sports Association. **Conventions/Meetings:** annual WIRSA State Workshop.

19820 ■ Wisconsin/Nicaragua Partners of the Americas
c/o Michael Dougherty, Exec.Dir.
Nelson Hall, Rm. 129
1209 Fremont St.
Stevens Point, WI 54481
Ph: (715)346-4702
Fax: (715)346-4703
E-mail: wnp@uwsp.edu
URL: http://wnp.uwsp.edu
State.

19821 ■ Wisconsin Woodland Owners Association, Kettle Moraine Chapter
PO Box 285
Stevens Point, WI 54481
Ph: (715)346-4798
E-mail: nbozek@uwsp.edu
URL: http://www.wisconsinwoodlands.org
Local. Affiliated With: Wisconsin Woodland Owners Association.

19822 ■ Xi Sigma Pi - Natural Resources Honor Society
University of Wisconsin
Stevens Point
College Natural Resources
Stevens Point, WI 54481
Ph: (715)346-2372
E-mail: espangen@uwsp.edu
Contact: N. Earl Spangenberg, Advisor

19823 ■ Young Life Stevens Point
PO Box 662
Stevens Point, WI 54481
Ph: (715)342-4138
URL: http://sites.younglife.org/_layouts/ylext/default.aspx?ID=A-WI103
Local. Affiliated With: Young Life.

Stockbridge

19824 ■ American Legion, Wisconsin Post 128
c/o William D. Hostettler
PO Box 211
Stockbridge, WI 53088
Ph: (608)745-1090
Fax: (608)745-0179
URL: National Affiliate–www.legion.org
Contact: William D. Hostettler, Contact
Local. Affiliated With: American Legion.

Stoddard

19825 ■ Genoa Lions Club - Wisconsin
c/o Alan Hammes, Pres.
146 N Cottage St.
Stoddard, WI 54658
Ph: (608)457-2790
URL: http://www.md27d2.org
Contact: Alan Hammes, Pres.
Local. Affiliated With: Lions Clubs International.

19826 ■ National Active and Retired Federal Employees Association - La Crosse 370
N 3000 Pebble Vally Rd.
Stoddard, WI 54658-9018
Ph: (608)787-5652
URL: National Affiliate–www.narfe.org
Contact: Ronald A. Willis, Contact
Local. Protects the retirement future of employees through education. Informs members on issues affecting the retirement. **Affiliated With:** National Association of Retired Federal Employees.

19827 ■ Stoddard Lions Club
c/o Lester Levendoski, Sec.
W1331 Skyline Ln.
Stoddard, WI 54658
Ph: (608)457-2238
E-mail: mrleven@mwt.net
URL: http://www.md27d2.org
Contact: Lester Levendoski, Sec.
Local. Affiliated With: Lions Clubs International.

Stoughton

19828 ■ American Legion, Otis Sampson Post 59
PO Box 16
Stoughton, WI 53589
Ph: (608)745-1090
Fax: (608)745-0179
URL: National Affiliate–www.legion.org
Local. Affiliated With: American Legion.

19829 ■ National Corvette Restorers Society, Wisconsin Chapter
c/o Jeff Zarth
PO Box 135
Stoughton, WI 53589
Ph: (608)873-0703
Fax: (608)873-7023
E-mail: trailer@zarthtrailer.com
URL: http://www.ncrs.org
Contact: Jeff Zarth, Chm.
State. Promotes restoration and preservation of Corvettes. **Affiliated With:** National Corvette Restorers Society.

19830 ■ Sons of Norway, Norsemen Of Lakes Lodge 5-650
c/o Roger A. Odalen, Pres.
1109 Sundt Ln.
Stoughton, WI 53589
Ph: (608)873-0890
E-mail: nancy.odalen@icecube.wisc.edu
URL: National Affiliate–www.sofn.com
Contact: Roger A. Odalen, Pres.
Local. Affiliated With: Sons of Norway.

19831 ■ Stoughton Chamber of Commerce
532 E Main St.
Stoughton, WI 53589
Ph: (608)873-7912
Fax: (608)873-7743
Free: (888)873-7912
E-mail: info@stoughtonwi.com
URL: http://www.stoughtonwi.com
Contact: Mickey McCormick, Asst.
Membership Dues: business, $190-$610 (annual) • second and subsequent business (plus $20 per full time contractor), $120 (annual) • city, public utility, $190 (annual) • civic/charitable organization, $190 (annual) • individual (non-business), $65 (annual). **Local. Publications:** Newsletter, monthly. Alternate Formats: online.

19832 ■ Wisconsin Capital Model T Ford Club
c/o David P. DeYoung, Pres.
972 County Rd. 'N'
Stoughton, WI 53589
Ph: (608)873-4579
E-mail: dgrmdey@charter.net
URL: National Affiliate–www.mtfca.com
Contact: David P. DeYoung, Pres.
Local. Affiliated With: Model "T" Ford Club of America. **Publications:** *Three Pedal Press*, monthly. Newsletters. 12-page booklet covering the workings of the club, Presidents message, special interest stories, and up-coming events. **Price:** included in membership dues. **Circulation:** 95. **Advertising:** accepted. Also Cited As: *3PP*.

19833 ■ World Future Society, Madison
c/o Hollie Hollister
H Cubed Gp., LLC
1108 Moline St.
Stoughton, WI 53589
Ph: (608)873-7981
E-mail: info@hcubedgroup.com
URL: http://www.wfsmadison.org
Contact: Hollie Hollister, Contact
Local. Affiliated With: World Future Society.

Stratford

19834 ■ Stratford Area Chamber of Commerce
PO Box 312
Stratford, WI 54484-0312
Ph: (715)687-4466
Contact: Jill Mielke, Sec.
Local.

Sturgeon Bay

19835 ■ American Legion, Wisconsin Post 72
c/o Archie Lackshire
428 N 7th Pl.
Sturgeon Bay, WI 54235
Ph: (608)745-1090
Fax: (608)745-0179
URL: National Affiliate–www.legion.org
Contact: Archie Lackshire, Contact
Local. Affiliated With: American Legion.

19836 ■ Door County Chamber of Commerce
1015 Green Bay Rd.
PO Box 406
Sturgeon Bay, WI 54235-0406
Ph: (920)743-4456
Fax: (920)743-7873
Free: (800)52R-ELAX
E-mail: info@doorcounty.com
URL: http://www.doorcountyvacations.com
Contact: Karen Raymore, CEO
Membership Dues: business (minimum dues), $350 (annual) • individual associate, $68 (annual) • home-based business, $170 (annual). **Local.** Promotes the civic and commercial progress of the Door community.

19837 ■ Door Peninsula Astronomical Society
2041 Michigan St.
Sturgeon Bay, WI 54235
Ph: (920)746-0428
E-mail: alcor@doorastronomy.org
URL: http://www.doorastronomy.org
Contact: Raymond Nancoz, Contact
Local. Promotes the science of astronomy. Works to encourage and coordinate activities of amateur astronomical societies. Fosters observational and computational work and craftsmanship in various fields of astronomy. **Affiliated With:** Astronomical League.

19838 ■ National Active and Retired Federal Employees Association Door-Kewaunee 1110
214 N Fulton
Sturgeon Bay, WI 54235-3330
Ph: (920)743-6020
URL: National Affiliate–www.narfe.org
Contact: Marilyn I. Grose, Contact
Local. Protects the retirement future of employees through education. Informs members on issues affecting the retirement. **Affiliated With:** National Association of Retired Federal Employees.

19839 ■ National Alliance for the Mentally Ill - Door County
c/o Marlys Trunkhill, Pres.
PO Box 273
Sturgeon Bay, WI 54235
Ph: (920)743-8818
E-mail: andrewbrown@greenbaynet.com
URL: http://www.namiwisconsin.org/library/directory
Contact: Marlys Trunkhill, Pres.
Local. Strives to improve the quality of life of children and adults with severe mental illness through support, education, research and advocacy. **Affiliated With:** National Alliance for the Mentally Ill.

19840 ■ National Association of Home Builders of the U.S., Door County Home Builders Association
c/o Larry Shefchik
810 S Lansing Ave.
Sturgeon Bay, WI 54235
Ph: (920)746-1092
Fax: (920)746-1099
E-mail: sturgeonbay@portside-properties.com
URL: http://www.dchba.org
Contact: Larry Shefchik, Contact
Local. Single and multifamily home builders, commercial builders, and others associated with the building industry. **Affiliated With:** National Association of Home Builders.

19841 ■ North East Wisconsin Optometric Society
c/o Paul Filar, OD, Pres.
50 S Madison Ave.
Sturgeon Bay, WI 54235
Ph: (920)743-5053
Fax: (920)743-8802
E-mail: docfilar@yahoo.com
URL: http://www.woa-eyes.org
Contact: Paul Filar OD, Pres.
Local. Aims to improve the quality, availability and accessibility of eye and vision care. Promotes high standards of patient care. Monitors and promotes legislation concerning the scope of optometric practice and other issues relevant to eye/vision care. **Affiliated With:** American Optometric Association; Wisconsin Optometric Association.

19842 ■ PFLAG Sturgeon Bay/Door County
PO Box 213
Sturgeon Bay, WI 54235
Ph: (920)743-8146
E-mail: sbrown@itol.com
URL: http://www.pflag.org/Wisconsin.246.0.html
Local. Affiliated With: Parents, Families, and Friends of Lesbians and Gays.

19843 ■ Points of Light Foundation - Volunteer Center of Door County
67 E Maple St.
Sturgeon Bay, WI 54235-3417
Ph: (920)746-7704
Fax: (920)746-7703
E-mail: volctrdc@doorpi.net
URL: http://volunteerdoorcounty.com
Contact: Chris Henkel, Contact
Founded: 2002. **Local. Affiliated With:** Points of Light Foundation.

19844 ■ Sons of Norway, H R Holand Lodge 5-549
c/o Donald J. Berns, Pres.
6347 Bay Shore Dr.
Sturgeon Bay, WI 54235-8104
Ph: (920)746-8925
E-mail: bernze@doorpi.net
URL: National Affiliate–www.sofn.com
Contact: Donald J. Berns, Pres.
Local. Affiliated With: Sons of Norway.

19845 ■ TSCA of Wisconsin
c/o James R. Kowall
Door County Maritime Museum
120 N Madison Ave.
Sturgeon Bay, WI 54235
Ph: (920)743-4631
URL: http://www.tsca.net/puget/index.htm
Contact: James R. Kowall, Contact
State.

19846 ■ United Way of Door County
PO Box 223
Sturgeon Bay, WI 54235-0223
Ph: (920)746-9645
Fax: (920)746-4693
E-mail: help@unitedwaydc.com
URL: http://www.unitedwaydc.com
Contact: Amy Kohnle, Exec.Dir.
Local. Affiliated With: United Way of America.

19847 ■ Wisconsin Council for the Social Studies (WCSS)
c/o Jim Adams, Pres.
School District of Sevastopol
4550 Hwy. 57
Sturgeon Bay, WI 54235
E-mail: jadams@dcwis.com
URL: http://www.wcss-wi.org
Contact: Jim Adams, Pres.
State. Represents teachers of elementary and secondary social studies, including instructors of civics, geography, history, law, economics, political science, psychology, sociology, and anthropology. Promotes the teaching of social studies. Provides members with opportunities to share strategies, have access to new material, and keep abreast of the national education scene. **Affiliated With:** National Council for the Social Studies.

Sturtevant

19848 ■ Racine/Kenosha Builders' Association (RKBA)
c/o Michelle Dawson, Exec. Officer
PO Box 706
Sturtevant, WI 53177
Ph: (262)886-5901 (262)554-7070
Fax: (262)886-5902
E-mail: info@rkbabuilders.com
URL: http://www.rkbabuilders.com
Contact: Michelle Dawson, Exec. Officer
Members: 110. **Membership Dues:** regular, $480 (annual). **Staff:** 1. **Budget:** $100,000. **State Groups:** 1. **Local.** Network of trade professionals dedicated to the creation and preservation of safe, affordable, quality housing.

Suamico

19849 ■ Beer Belly
c/o Kim M. Viduski
PO Box 22
Suamico, WI 54173
Ph: (920)432-6685
E-mail: kimski@etkg.com
URL: http://www.gbit.com/beerbelly
Contact: Kim M. Viduski, Event Dir.
Founded: 1999. **Members:** 8. **Local.** Organizes annual run/walk to raise money for Northeastern Wisconsin charities including Paul's Pantry, Families of Children with Cancer, the Family Violence Center, and The Ecumenical Partnership for Housing.

19850 ■ Howard/Suamico Storm Breakers
c/o Steven R. Thuerwachter
PO Box 266
Suamico, WI 54173-0266
URL: http://www.hssb-wi.org
Contact: Steven R. Thuerwachter, Contact
Local.

19851 ■ Mit Liebe German Shepherd Dog Rescue
2765 Longview Ln.
Suamico, WI 54173
Ph: (920)434-4274 (920)465-7796
E-mail: ccsgsds@aol.com
URL: http://www.shepherd-rescue.com
Contact: Anita Delzer, Contact
Local.

19852 ■ Windjammers Sailing Club
PO Box 11
Suamico, WI 54173
Ph: (920)434-6850
E-mail: inform@windjammerssailingclub.com
URL: http://www.windjammerssailingclub.com
Contact: Mark Zellner, Commodore
Local.

Sullivan

19853 ■ American Legion, Wenzel-Longley Post 349
767 Palmyra St.
Sullivan, WI 53178
Ph: (608)745-1090
Fax: (608)745-0179
URL: National Affiliate–www.legion.org
Local. Affiliated With: American Legion.

19854 ■ Bernese Mountain Dog Club of Southeastern Wisconsin (BMDCSEW)
c/o Jane Haefner, Pres.
W 1945 Elder Dr.
Sullivan, WI 53178
Ph: (262)593-8985
E-mail: admin@bmdcsew.org
URL: http://www.bmdcsew.org
Contact: Jane Haefner, Pres.
Regional.

Summit Lake

19855 ■ American Legion, Noetzelman-Boodry Post 377
W 10787 Rasmussen St.
Summit Lake, WI 54485
Ph: (608)745-1090
Fax: (608)745-0179
URL: National Affiliate–www.legion.org
Local. Affiliated With: American Legion.

Sun Prairie

19856 ■ American Legion, Wisconsin Post 333
c/o Elmer Peterson
137 S Bristol St.
Sun Prairie, WI 53590
Ph: (608)837-5828
Fax: (608)745-0179
URL: National Affiliate–www.legion.org
Contact: Elmer Peterson, Contact
Local. Affiliated With: American Legion.

19857 ■ ESOP Association, Wisconsin Chapter
c/o Ms. Pamela Klute, Pres.
Trachte Building Systems, Inc.
314 Wilburn Rd.
Sun Prairie, WI 53590-1474
Ph: (608)327-3156
Fax: (608)825-2606
E-mail: pklute@trachte.com
URL: National Affiliate–www.esopassociation.org
Contact: Ms. Pamela Klute, Pres.
State. Affiliated With: ESOP Association.

19858 ■ International Association of Machinists and Aerospace Workers, AFL-CIO, CLC - Badger Lodge Local 1406
1210 Emerald Terr.
Sun Prairie, WI 53590
E-mail: webmaster@iamlocal1406.net
URL: http://www.iamlocal1406.net
Contact: Michael Klemp, Pres.
Members: 659. **Local.** Seeks for the dignity and equality of the workers. Strives to provide contractors with well-trained, productive employees. **Affiliated With:** International Association of Machinists and Aerospace Workers. **Also Known As:** (2005) International Association of Machinists and Aerospace Workers, AFL-CIO, CLC - Lodge 1406.

19859 ■ International Association of Machinists and Aerospace Workers, District Lodge 121
1210 Emerald Terr.
Sun Prairie, WI 53590
Ph: (608)837-4088
Fax: (608)837-5031
URL: http://iamdl121.org
Contact: Dan Hilbert, Contact
Founded: 1967. **Members:** 3,573. **Local. Affiliated With:** International Association of Machinists and Aerospace Workers.

19860 ■ Madison Drum and Bugle Corps Association (MDBCA)
c/o Martin Redmann, Pres.
1475 W Main St.
Sun Prairie, WI 53590
Ph: (608)837-0707
Fax: (608)834-8909
E-mail: office@madisoncorps.org
URL: http://madisoncorps.org
Contact: Martin Redmann, Pres.
Founded: 1938. **Members:** 1,200. **Staff:** 100. **Budget:** $1,250,000. **Local.** Performers; teaching, support, and management staff. Provides musical organization in order to help develop musical, physical, social, and leadership talents in young men and women, ages 14-21. Sponsors Madison Scouts, Southwind and Capital Sound; sponsors and participates in performances and clinics before live audiences and through recorded media. **Affiliated With:** Drum Corps International. **Publications:** *Fleur-de-Lis*, bimonthly. Newsletter. **Conventions/Meetings:** periodic board meeting.

19861 ■ Municipal Electric Utilities of Wisconsin (MEUW)
c/o David J. Benforado, Exec.Dir.
725 Lois Dr.
Sun Prairie, WI 53590
Ph: (608)837-2263
Fax: (608)837-0206
E-mail: dbenforado@meuw.org
URL: http://www.meuw.org
Contact: David J. Benforado, Exec.Dir.
Founded: 1928. **Members:** 81. **State.**

19862 ■ North Bristol Sportsman's Club
7229 N Greenway Rd.
Box 202
Sun Prairie, WI 53590
Ph: (608)837-6048
URL: http://www.shootatnbsc.com
Local. Affiliated With: National Skeet Shooting Association.

19863 ■ Sons of Norway, Idun Lodge 5-74
c/o Mary Jane Bennett, Pres.
359 Sherbrooke Dr.
Sun Prairie, WI 53590-4204
Ph: (608)837-8335
E-mail: mjbenn@chorus.net
URL: National Affiliate–www.sofn.com
Contact: Mary Jane Bennett, Pres.
Local. Affiliated With: Sons of Norway.

19864 ■ Southern Wisconsin Chapter - MOAA
c/o Lt.Col. Edwin Addison
2130 Michigan Ave.
Sun Prairie, WI 53590-1608
Ph: (608)837-7844
E-mail: esaddison3@aol.com
URL: National Affiliate–www.moaa.org
Contact: Lt.Col. Edwin Addison, Contact
Local. Affiliated With: Military Officers Association of America.

19865 ■ Square Dance Association of Wisconsin
c/o Marilyn Kittle
320 Maynard Dr.
Sun Prairie, WI 53590
Ph: (608)837-6958
E-mail: skittle@merr.com
State. Conventions/Meetings: annual convention - 2004 Aug. 8.

19866 ■ United Federation of Doll Clubs - Region 10
194 Kroncke Dr.
Sun Prairie, WI 53590-2932
E-mail: beckers@mailbag.com
URL: http://www.ufdc.org/ufdcregion10.htm
Contact: Dodi Becker, Dir.
Regional. Affiliated With: United Federation of Doll Clubs.

19867 ■ Wisconsin Association for Food Protection (WAFP)
PO Box 329
Sun Prairie, WI 53590
Ph: (608)833-6181
E-mail: info@wafp-wi.org
URL: http://www.wafp-wi.org
Contact: Matt Mathison, Pres.-Elect
State. Provides food safety professionals with a forum to exchange information on protecting the food supply. Promotes sanitary methods and procedures for the development, production, processing, distribution, preparation and serving of food. **Affiliated With:** International Association for Food Protection.

19868 ■ Wisconsin Health Care Association, District 2
c/o Lars Rogeberg, Pres.
Sun Prairie Hea. Care Ctr.
228 W Main St.
Sun Prairie, WI 53590
Ph: (608)837-5959
URL: http://www.whca.com
Contact: Lars Rogeberg, Pres.
Local. Promotes professionalism and ethical behavior of individuals providing long-term care delivery for patients and for the general public. Provides information, education and administrative tools to enhance the quality of long-term care. Improves the standards of service and administration of member nursing homes. **Affiliated With:** American Health Care Association; Wisconsin Health Care Association.

19869 ■ Wisconsin Rottweiler Performance Club
c/o Bill Crawley
6060 Keller Dr.
Sun Prairie, WI 53590
Ph: (608)825-9509
E-mail: bill@ausbreitung.com
URL: National Affiliate–www.usrconline.org
Contact: Bill Crawley, Contact
State.

19870 ■ Wisconsin Society of PeriAnesthesia Nurses (WISPAN)
1579 Sunfield St.
Sun Prairie, WI 53590-2651
Ph: (608)837-8212
E-mail: carroll_peeper@msn.com
URL: http://www.slingshotrally.com/wispan
Contact: Cyndi Siebel-Mohler, Pres.
State. Promotes quality and cost effective care for patients, their families and the community through public and professional education, research and standards of practice. **Affiliated With:** American Society of PeriAnesthesia Nurses.

Superior

19871 ■ American Legion, Wisconsin Post 435
c/o Richard I. Bong
PO Box 34
Superior, WI 54880
Ph: (608)745-1090
Fax: (608)745-0179
URL: National Affiliate–www.legion.org
Contact: Richard I. Bong, Contact
Local. Affiliated With: American Legion.

19872 ■ American Rabbit Breeders Association, Northern Exposure Rabbit and Cavy
c/o Ashley Moe, Sec.
217 48th Ave. E
Superior, WI 54880
URL: http://www.geocities.com/wisconsin_state_rba/Local_Clubs.html
Contact: Ashley Moe, Sec.
Local. Affiliated With: American Rabbit Breeders Association.

19873 ■ National Active and Retired Federal Employees Association - Superior 2119
5423 Banks Ave.
Superior, WI 54880-5741
Ph: (715)392-5383
URL: National Affiliate–www.narfe.org
Contact: Robert V. Herubin, Contact
Local. Protects the retirement future of employees through education. Informs members on issues affecting the retirement. **Affiliated With:** National Association of Retired Federal Employees.

19874 ■ Retired Enlisted Association, 119
c/o Butch Liebaert
4222 E 2nd St.
Superior, WI 54880
Ph: (715)398-3152
URL: National Affiliate–www.trea.org
Contact: Butch Liebaert, Pres.
Local. Affiliated With: The Retired Enlisted Association.

19875 ■ Ruffed Grouse Society, Duluth/Superior Chapter
c/o Patricia Kukull
1705 Winter St.
Superior, WI 54880
Ph: (715)394-4982
URL: National Affiliate–www.ruffedgrousesociety.org
Contact: Patricia Kukull, Contact
Regional. Affiliated With: Ruffed Grouse Society.

19876 ■ Ruffed Grouse Society, Wisconsin Chapter
c/o Mark Fouts
8154 S Dowling Lake Rd. W
Superior, WI 54880
Ph: (715)399-2270
URL: National Affiliate–www.ruffedgrousesociety.org
Contact: Mark Fouts, Contact
State. Affiliated With: Ruffed Grouse Society.

19877 ■ SCORE Superior
c/o Clyde Eilo, CHR
1423 N. Eight St.
Superior, WI 54880
Ph: (715)394-7388
Fax: (715)394-7414
URL: http://www.score.org
Affiliated With: SCORE.

19878 ■ Superior Curling Club
4700 Tower Ave.
Superior, WI 54880
Ph: (715)392-2022
E-mail: rbergq@charter.net
URL: http://www.superiorcurlingclub.com
Contact: Roberta Bergquist, Pres.
Local. Affiliated With: United States Curling Association.

19879 ■ Superior - Douglas County Chamber of Commerce
205 Belknap St.
Superior, WI 54880
Ph: (715)394-7716
Fax: (715)394-3810
Free: (800)942-5313
E-mail: dm@superiorchamber.org
URL: http://www.superiorchamber.org
Contact: David W. Minor, Pres./CEO
Membership Dues: business, professional, lodging property, non-profit organization, and individual, home-based business, and church (base), $195 • financial institution (per million in assets), $30. **Local.** Business people. Works to improve the economic, civic, and cultural welfare of the area through community development programs. **Additional Websites:** http://www.superiorwi.com. **Committees:** Ambassadors; Convention and Visitors Bureau; Executive; Marketing and Communications; Public and Government Affairs; Retention; Youth Leadership.

19880 ■ Superior/Douglas RSVP
c/o Kendra-Sue Rohde, Dir.
PO Box 594
Superior, WI 54880
Ph: (715)394-4425
Fax: (715)394-9724
E-mail: rsvp@ccbsuperior.com
URL: http://www.seniorcorps.gov
Contact: Kendra-Sue Rohde, Dir.
Local. Affiliated With: Retired and Senior Volunteer Program.

19881 ■ Superior Figure Skating Club (SFSC)
PO Box 536
Superior, WI 54880
E-mail: dmccall@prodigy.net
URL: http://www.superiorfsc.org
Contact: Dean McCall, Contact
Local. Provides programs to encourage participation and achievement in the sport of figure skating on ice. Defines and maintains uniform standards of skating proficiency. Organizes and sponsors competitions and exhibitions for the purpose of stimulating interest in figure skating. **Affiliated With:** United States Figure Skating Association.

19882 ■ United Way of Superior-Douglas County
1507 Tower Ave., Ste.215
Superior, WI 54880-2554
Ph: (715)394-2733
URL: National Affiliate–national.unitedway.org
Local. Affiliated With: United Way of America.

Suring

19883 ■ American Legion, Wisconsin Post 283
c/o Harold C. Anderson
PO Box 403
Suring, WI 54174
Ph: (608)745-1090
Fax: (608)745-0179
URL: National Affiliate–www.legion.org
Contact: Harold C. Anderson, Contact
Local. Affiliated With: American Legion.

Sussex

19884 ■ Friends of Wisconsin Libraries (FOWL)
c/o Joanne Smith
W264-N7130 Thousands Oak Dr.
Sussex, WI 53089
Ph: (262)246-6250
E-mail: dbeine@wi.rr.com
URL: http://www.cheesestate.com/friends
Contact: David Beine, Pres.
State. Works to provide training, consultation and resources to further the development of support for libraries. **Affiliated With:** Friends of Libraries U.S.A.

19885 ■ Sussex Area Chamber of Commerce
N64 W24050 Main St., Ste.201
PO Box 24
Sussex, WI 53089-0024
Ph: (262)246-4940
Fax: (262)246-7350
E-mail: info@sussexareachamber.org
URL: http://www.sussexareachamber.org
Contact: Denise Schwid, Admin.
Membership Dues: business (depends upon the number of employees), $180-$310 (annual) • church, civic organization, non-profit, school, village, $105 (annual) • citizen, $50 (annual). **Local.** Works to advance the economic well-being of the community through commercial, civic, cultural, industrial and educational interest. **Publications:** Newsletter, monthly. Contains information on events and community activities. **Advertising:** accepted • Membership Directory, annual.

19886 ■ Sussex Lions Club
PO Box 22
Sussex, WI 53089
E-mail: contactlions@sussexlions.org
URL: http://www.sussexlions.org
Contact: Ralph Modjeska, Pres.
Local. Affiliated With: Lions Clubs International.

19887 ■ Wisconsin Skeet Shooting Association
N 82 W 22530 Scott
Sussex, WI 53089
Ph: (920)333-0129
E-mail: behrgott@ticon.net
URL: National Affiliate–www.mynssa.com
State. Affiliated With: National Skeet Shooting Association.

Theresa

19888 ■ American Legion, Miller-Justman-Guelig Post 270
PO Box 9
Theresa, WI 53091
Ph: (608)745-1090
Fax: (608)745-0179
URL: National Affiliate–www.legion.org
Local. Affiliated With: American Legion.

19889 ■ Milwaukee African Violet Society
c/o Joan Wilson
W 534 Zion Church Rd.
Theresa, WI 53091
Ph: (920)488-4020
E-mail: jklwilson@dotnet.com
URL: National Affiliate–www.avsa.org
Contact: Joan Wilson, Contact
Local. Affiliated With: African Violet Society of America.

19890 ■ Wisconsin Amateur Field Trial Club
c/o Raymond Muth
1626 Mountain Rd.
Theresa, WI 53091
URL: National Affiliate–www.akc.org
Contact: James Powers, Corresponding Sec.
Local. Affiliated With: American Kennel Club.

Thiensville

19891 ■ Human Resource Management Association of Southeastern Wisconsin
142 N Main St.
Thiensville, WI 53092
Ph: (262)242-9566
Fax: (262)242-1862
E-mail: office@hrma.org
URL: http://www.hrma.org
Contact: Vicky Wakefield, Pres.
Local. Represents the interests of human resource and industrial relations professionals and executives. Promotes the advancement of human resource management.

19892 ■ Mequon-Thiensville Area Chamber of Commerce (MTACC)
250 S Main St.
Thiensville, WI 53092
Ph: (262)512-9358
Fax: (262)512-9359
E-mail: info@mtchamber.org
URL: http://www.mtchamber.org
Contact: Linda Oakes, Exec.Dir.
Founded: 1980. **Members:** 450. **Membership Dues:** business (based on number of employees), $75-$275 (annual) • non-profit (based on number of employees), $42-$142 (annual) • community associate, $25 (annual). **Budget:** $93,000. **Local**. Promotes business and community development in Mequon and Thiensville, WI and its surrounding area. **Affiliated With:** U.S. Chamber of Commerce. **Formerly:** Mequon-Thiensville Area Chamber of Commerce. **Publications:** *Chamber News*, monthly. Newsletter. Alternate Formats: online • *Community Profile*, biennial, always even-numbered years • *Street Map*, biennial, always odd-numbered years • Directory, annual. **Conventions/Meetings:** monthly luncheon, with lecture • annual meeting.

19893 ■ Thiensville Mequon Lions Club
PO Box 131
Thiensville, WI 53092
E-mail: jdoornek@wi.rr.com
URL: http://www.tmlions.org
Local. Affiliated With: Lions Clubs International.

19894 ■ Wisconsin Academy of Family Physicians (WAFP)
c/o Larry Pheifer, Exec.Dir.
142 N Main St.
Thiensville, WI 53092
Ph: (262)512-0606
Fax: (262)242-1862
Free: (800)272-WAFP
E-mail: academy@wafp.org
URL: http://www.wafp.org
Contact: Larry Pheifer, Exec.Dir.
State. Affiliated With: American Academy of Family Physicians.

19895 ■ Wisconsin Association for Supervision and Curriculum Development (WASCD)
142 N Main St.
Thiensville, WI 53092
Ph: (262)242-3771
Fax: (262)242-1862
E-mail: office@wascd.org
URL: http://www.wascd.org
Contact: Peter Gust, Exec.Dir.
State. Strives to promote quality programs and practices, advocate continual professional growth and influence decisions that improves learning. **Affiliated With:** Association for Supervision and Curriculum Development.

Thorp

19896 ■ American Legion, Wisconsin Post 118
c/o Cecil Tormey
PO Box 120
Thorp, WI 54771
Ph: (608)745-1090
Fax: (608)745-0179
URL: National Affiliate–www.legion.org
Contact: Cecil Tormey, Contact
Local. Affiliated With: American Legion.

19897 ■ National Association of Rocketry - Thorp Apogee Heights
c/o Judy Smriga
500 S Lincoln, Box 362
Thorp, WI 54771
Ph: (715)669-7052
E-mail: cozmosinwi@hotmail.com
URL: National Affiliate–www.nar.org
Contact: Judy Smriga, Contact
Local.

Three Lakes

19898 ■ American Legion, Three Lakes Post 431
1795 Superior St.
Three Lakes, WI 54562
Ph: (608)745-1090
Fax: (608)745-0179
URL: National Affiliate–www.legion.org
Local. Affiliated With: American Legion.

19899 ■ Three Lakes Information Bureau (TLIB)
PO Box 268
Three Lakes, WI 54562
Ph: (715)546-3344
Free: (800)972-6103
E-mail: vacation@threelakes.com
Founded: 1988. **Members:** 94. **Staff:** 2. **State Groups:** 1. **Local Groups:** 2. **Local**. Promotes business and community development in Three Lakes, WI. Holds wine and loon festivals. **Conventions/Meetings:** monthly board meeting - always second Thursday of the month.

Tigerton

19900 ■ American Legion, Schlender-Polley Post 239
PO Box 325
Tigerton, WI 54486
Ph: (608)745-1090
Fax: (608)745-0179
URL: National Affiliate–www.legion.org
Local. Affiliated With: American Legion.

Tisch Mills

19901 ■ American Legion, Carlton Post 538
PO Box 212
Tisch Mills, WI 54240
Ph: (608)745-1090
Fax: (608)745-0179
URL: National Affiliate–www.legion.org
Local. Affiliated With: American Legion.

Tomah

19902 ■ American Legion, Wisconsin Post 129
c/o Andrew Blackhawk
PO Box 445
Tomah, WI 54660
Ph: (608)745-1090
Fax: (608)745-0179
URL: National Affiliate–www.legion.org
Contact: Andrew Blackhawk, Contact
Local. Affiliated With: American Legion.

19903 ■ Driftless Area Gem and Mineral Club
c/o Robert Crook
PO Box 273
Tomah, WI 54660
E-mail: chansen@mwt.net
URL: National Affiliate–www.amfed.org
Contact: Virginia Zietlow, Pres.
Local. Aims to further the study of Earth Sciences and the practice of lapidary arts and mineralogy. **Affiliated With:** American Federation of Mineralogical Societies.

19904 ■ Greater Tomah Area Chamber of Commerce
c/o Christopher Hanson, Exec.Dir.
805 Superior Ave.
Tomah, WI 54660-0625
Ph: (608)372-2166
Fax: (608)372-2167
Free: (800)94-TOMAH
E-mail: tchamber@mwt.net
URL: http://www.tomahwisconsin.com
Contact: Christopher Hanson, Exec.Dir.
Local. Works to foster a cohesive environment where businesses, families, and community can prosper.

19905 ■ Oakdale Lions Club
c/o Kathleen Friske, Sec.
7634 Dixie Rd.
Tomah, WI 54660
Ph: (608)372-2192
E-mail: friske@mwt.net
URL: http://www.md27d2.org
Contact: Kathleen Friske, Sec.
Local. Affiliated With: Lions Clubs International.

19906 ■ Tomah Lions Club
c/o Jerry Zuhlsdorf, Sec.
816 Lake St.
Tomah, WI 54660
Ph: (608)372-4937
E-mail: g.zuhls@smallbytes.net
URL: http://www.md27d2.org
Contact: Jerry Zuhlsdorf, Sec.
Local. Affiliated With: Lions Clubs International.

19907 ■ Wisconsin Rodeo Cowboys Association
c/o Carmilla J. Schneider
31503 Excelsior Ave.
Tomah, WI 54660-6505
Ph: (608)372-9169
Fax: (608)372-9169
E-mail: wrca@mwt.net
Contact: Carm Schneider, Sec.-Treas.
Founded: 2000. **Members:** 334. **Membership Dues:** individual, $75 (annual). **Staff:** 1. **State. Conventions/Meetings:** monthly meeting - 2nd Thursday.

Tomahawk

19908 ■ American Legion, Bronsted-Searl Post 93
PO Box 303
Tomahawk, WI 54487
Ph: (608)745-1090
Fax: (608)745-0179
URL: National Affiliate–www.legion.org
Local. Affiliated With: American Legion.

19909 ■ Association for Education and Rehabilitation of the Blind and Visually Impaired, Wisconsin Chapter
c/o Kay Glodowski
2060 Point Rd. W
Tomahawk, WI 54487
E-mail: kglodowski@cesa9.k12.wi.us
URL: National Affiliate–www.aerbvi.org
Contact: Kay Glodowski, Contact
Membership Dues: $120 (annual). **State. Affiliated With:** Association for Education and Rehabilitation of the Blind and Visually Impaired.

19910 ■ Ruffed Grouse Society, Lincoln County Chapter
c/o Patti Hilgendorf
W5193 Bruno Dr.
Tomahawk, WI 54487
Ph: (715)453-4702
URL: National Affiliate–www.ruffedgrousesociety.org
Contact: Patti Hilgendorf, Contact
Local. Affiliated With: Ruffed Grouse Society.

19911 ■ Tomahawk Regional Chamber of Commerce (TRCC)
PO Box 412
Tomahawk, WI 54487-0412
Ph: (715)453-5334
Fax: (715)453-1178
Free: (800)569-2160
E-mail: chambert@gototomahawk.com
URL: http://www.gototomahawk.com
Contact: Christine S. Brown, Exec.VP
Founded: 1949. **Members:** 220. **Staff:** 2. **Budget:** $90,000. **Local.** Promotes business and community development in the Tomahawk, WI area. **Committees:** Chamber's Annual Dinner; Hunter's Feed; Promotions; Taste of Tomahawk; Tomahawk Ambassadors. **Councils:** Tomahawk Downtown Business. **Programs:** Chamber Buck. **Task Forces:** Marketing. **Publications:** *Toma-Talk*, bimonthly. Newsletter • *Visitor Vacation Guide and Membership Directory*, annual. **Conventions/Meetings:** annual meeting - always in Tomahawk, WI.

19912 ■ Woodland Lakes Association of Realtors
PO Box 551
Tomahawk, WI 54487
Ph: (715)453-5566
Fax: (715)453-7003
E-mail: regmpg@newnorth.net
URL: National Affiliate–www.realtor.org
Contact: Rodney Greil, Exec. Officer
Local. Strives to develop real estate business practices. Advocates the right to own, use and transfer real property. Provides a facility for professional development, research and exchange of information among members and to the general public. **Affiliated With:** National Association of Realtors.

Trempealeau

19913 ■ Centerville Curling Club
Rte. 1, Hwy. 54/93
Trempealeau, WI 54661
Ph: (608)539-3651 (608)539-3923
E-mail: cntrvlnews@aol.com
URL: http://www.centervillecurlingclub.com
Contact: Ron Severson, Pres.
Founded: 1949. **Local. Affiliated With:** United States Curling Association.

Trevor

19914 ■ Quail Unlimited, Southeast Wisconsin Chapter
PO Box 253
Trevor, WI 53179
Ph: (262)862-2602
E-mail: widssquchairman@aol.com
URL: National Affiliate–www.qu.org
Local. Affiliated With: Quail Unlimited.

Turtle Lake

19915 ■ American Legion, Howard-Donalds-Richard-Hylkema Post 137
PO Box 235
Turtle Lake, WI 54889
Ph: (608)745-1090
Fax: (608)745-0179
URL: National Affiliate–www.legion.org
Local. Affiliated With: American Legion.

Twin Lakes

19916 ■ American Legion, Twin Lakes Post 544
989 Legion Dr.
Twin Lakes, WI 53181
Ph: (608)745-1090
Fax: (608)745-0179
URL: National Affiliate–www.legion.org
Local. Affiliated With: American Legion.

19917 ■ International Brotherhood of Magicians, Ring 41
1930 Esch Rd.
Twin Lakes, WI 53181
Ph: (262)279-5726
E-mail: dwightferg@charter.net
URL: http://www.ibmring.com
Contact: Dwight Ferguson, Pres.
Local. Professional and semi-professional magicians; suppliers, assistants, agents, and others interested in magic. Seeks to advance the art of magic in the field of amusement, entertainment, and culture. Promotes proper means of discouraging false or misleading advertising of effects, tricks, literature, merchandise, or actions appertaining to the magical arts; opposes exposures of principles of the art of magic, except in books on magic and magazines devoted to such art for the exclusive use of magicians and devotees of the art; encourages humane treatment and care of live animals whenever employed in magical performances. **Affiliated With:** International Brotherhood of Magicians.

19918 ■ Lakeland Audubon Society
124 W School St.
Twin Lakes, WI 53181
Ph: (262)763-6033
E-mail: edms_email@yahoo.com
URL: http://www.audubon.org/chapter/wi/index.html
Contact: Edwin Meixner, Pres.
Local. Formerly: (2005) National Audubon Society - Lakeland Chapter.

Two Rivers

19919 ■ American Legion, Wisconsin Post 165
c/o Robert E. Burns
PO Box 11
Two Rivers, WI 54241
Ph: (608)745-1090
Fax: (608)745-0179
URL: National Affiliate–www.legion.org
Contact: Robert E. Burns, Contact
Local. Affiliated With: American Legion.

19920 ■ Two Rivers Historical Society
1622 Jefferson St.
Two Rivers, WI 54241
Ph: (920)793-2490 (920)793-1103
Free: (888)857-3529
URL: http://www.lhinn.com/history.html
Contact: Gerald Schultz, Pres.
Founded: 1962. **Members:** 650. **Membership Dues:** single, $8 (annual) • family, $10 (annual) • contributing, $30 (annual). **Budget:** $50,000. **Regional Groups:** 1. **State Groups:** 1. **Local Groups:** 3. **Local.** Individuals interested in preserving, protecting and presenting the history of Two Rivers, WI. **Affiliated With:** Wisconsin Historical Society. **Publications:** Newsletter, quarterly. Contains pictures and events of old and present Two Rivers. **Price:** included in membership dues. **Circulation:** 600. **Conventions/Meetings:** quarterly meeting (exhibits).

19921 ■ Two Rivers Main Street
PO Box 417
Two Rivers, WI 54241
Ph: (920)794-1482
Fax: (920)793-4586
E-mail: mainstreet@lakefield.net
URL: http://www.trmainstreet.org
Local.

19922 ■ United Food and Commercial Workers AFL-CIO, LU 665T
2104 Madison St.
Two Rivers, WI 54241
Ph: (920)793-2217
URL: http://www.ufcw.org
Contact: Karen Hynek, Financial Sec.
Members: 33. **Local. Affiliated With:** AFL-CIO.

19923 ■ United Food and Commercial Workers, Local 236T, Northcentral Region
1731 28th St.
Two Rivers, WI 54241
Ph: (920)793-3951
URL: National Affiliate–www.ufcw.org
Local. Affiliated With: United Food and Commercial Workers International Union.

Union Grove

19924 ■ American Legion, Bixby and Hansen Post 171
PO Box 171
Union Grove, WI 53182
Ph: (608)745-1090
Fax: (608)745-0179
URL: National Affiliate–www.legion.org
Local. Affiliated With: American Legion.

19925 ■ Children's Rights Council of Wisconsin
640 12th Ave.
Union Grove, WI 53182
E-mail: bobeis@execpc.com
URL: National Affiliate–www.gocrc.com
State. Affiliated With: Children's Rights Council.

19926 ■ Greater Union Grove Area Chamber of Commerce (GUGACC)
PO Box 44
Union Grove, WI 53182-0044
Ph: (262)878-4606
Fax: (262)878-9125
E-mail: ugchambr@wi.net
URL: http://www.uniongrovechamber.org
Contact: Carol Knight, Exec.Dir.
Founded: 1986. **Members:** 100. **Staff:** 1. **Local.** Promotes business and community development in the Union Grove, WI area. Conducts Fourth of July Parade, Christmas Cookie Walk, and other community gatherings. Sponsors political candidate forums. **Committees:** Economic Development. **Subgroups:** Business Breakfast Alliance. **Formerly:** (1986) Union Grove Chamber of Commerce. **Publications:** Newsletter, monthly. **Price:** free for members. **Conventions/Meetings:** quarterly breakfast - always 2nd Tuesday in February, May, August, and November • monthly luncheon, with speaker - always second Monday; except February, May, August, and November.

Unity

19927 ■ American Legion, Wisconsin Post 358
c/o Otto H. Kops
233 2nd St.
Unity, WI 54488
Ph: (608)745-1090
Fax: (608)745-0179
URL: National Affiliate–www.legion.org
Contact: Otto H. Kops, Contact
Local. Affiliated With: American Legion.

Valders

19928 ■ American Legion, Thompson-Burkhard Post 28
c/o Gorman Lex
PO Box 156
Valders, WI 54245

Ph: (608)745-1090
Fax: (608)745-0179
URL: National Affiliate–www.legion.org
Contact: Gorman Lex, Contact
Local. Affiliated With: American Legion.

19929 ■ Lakeshore District Nurses Association - No. 12
14421 N Shore Dr.
Valders, WI 54245
Ph: (920)758-3103
E-mail: anne.neeb.cfnp@aurora.org
URL: http://www.wisconsinnurses.org
Contact: Anne Neeb, Pres.
Local. Works to advance the nursing profession. Seeks to meet the needs of nurses and health care consumers. Fosters high standards of nursing practice. Promotes the economic and general welfare of nurses in the workplace. **Affiliated With:** American Nurses Association; Wisconsin Nurses' Association.

Van Dyne

19930 ■ Van Dyne Sportsmen's Club
PO Box 8
Van Dyne, WI 54979
Ph: (920)688-2433
Fax: (920)688-2433
URL: National Affiliate–www.mynssa.com
Local. Affiliated With: National Skeet Shooting Association.

Verona

19931 ■ American Institute of Architects Southwest Wisconsin
c/o Paul Grzeszczak
509 Commerce Pkwy.
Verona, WI 53593-1377
Ph: (608)845-6501
E-mail: paulg@newcombbuilds.com
URL: National Affiliate–www.aia.org
Local. Affiliated With: American Institute of Architects.

19932 ■ Association of Certified Fraud Examiners, Wisconsin Area Chapter No. 32
c/o Casey S. Reilly, CFE, Pres.
Fidelitic, LLC
245 Horizon Dr., Ste.107
Verona, WI 53593
Ph: (608)848-9900
Fax: (608)848-9902
E-mail: casey.reilly@fidelitec.com
URL: National Affiliate–www.acfe.com
Contact: Casey S. Reilly CFE, Pres.
State. Works to reduce the incidence of fraud and white-collar crime and to assist the members in its detection and deterrence. Sponsors training seminars on fraud and loss prevention. Administers credentialing programs for Certified Fraud Examiners. **Affiliated With:** Association of Certified Fraud Examiners.

19933 ■ Madison Area Model Yacht Club No. 139
c/o Fred Foster
538 Linden Ct.
Verona, WI 53593
Ph: (608)209-2630
URL: http://www.madisonrcboats.org
Contact: Fred Foster, Contact
Local.

19934 ■ Sons of Norway, Vennelag Lodge 5-513
c/o Duane S. Kittleson, Pres.
7447 Rolling Meadow Rd.
Verona, WI 53593-9731
Ph: (608)845-9423
E-mail: dkitt@yahoo.com
URL: National Affiliate–www.sofn.com
Contact: Duane S. Kittleson, Pres.
Local. Affiliated With: Sons of Norway.

19935 ■ Sundowners African Violet Club
c/o Alice Peterson
3611 Mathias Way
Verona, WI 53593
Ph: (608)833-5552
URL: National Affiliate–www.avsa.org
Contact: Alice Peterson, Contact
Local. Affiliated With: African Violet Society of America.

19936 ■ Verona Area Chamber of Commerce
205 S Main St.
PO Box 930003
Verona, WI 53593-0003
Ph: (608)845-5777
Fax: (608)845-2519
E-mail: info@veronawi.com
URL: http://veronawi.com
Contact: David Phillips, Exec.Dir.
Members: 200. **Membership Dues:** basic, $160 (annual) • financial, utility, $400 (annual) • not-for-profit, individual, $90 (annual). **Staff:** 2. **Budget:** $125,000. **Local.**

Vesper

19937 ■ American Legion, Vesper Post 520
4231 County Rd. C
Vesper, WI 54489
Ph: (608)745-1090
Fax: (608)745-0179
URL: National Affiliate–www.legion.org
Local. Affiliated With: American Legion.

19938 ■ Central Wisconsin Beagle Club
c/o Jere Hamel
5490 Poplar Ln.
Vesper, WI 54489-9656
URL: National Affiliate–clubs.akc.org
Contact: Jere Hamel, Contact
Local.

19939 ■ Wisconsin Pony of the Americas Club (WPOAC)
c/o Judy Katzenberger, Pres.
5896 State Hwy. 186
Vesper, WI 54489
Ph: (715)569-4763
E-mail: jnfarm@wctc.net
URL: http://www.wpoac.com
Contact: Judy Katzenberger, Pres.
Membership Dues: individual, $15 (annual). **State. Affiliated With:** Pony of the Americas Club.

Viola

19940 ■ American Legion, Hamilton-Harris Post 447
PO Box 15
Viola, WI 54664
Ph: (608)745-1090
Fax: (608)745-0179
URL: National Affiliate–www.legion.org
Local. Affiliated With: American Legion.

Viroqua

19941 ■ American Legion, Wm-A.-Jacobson-Errett-B.-Olson Post 138
PO Box 254
Viroqua, WI 54665
Ph: (608)745-1090
Fax: (608)745-0179
URL: National Affiliate–www.legion.org
Local. Affiliated With: American Legion.

19942 ■ Sons of Norway, Jotunheimen Lodge 5-286
c/o Pauline A. Buckland, Sec.
PO Box 174
Viroqua, WI 54665-0174
Ph: (608)637-3397
E-mail: pjabuck@frontiernet.net
URL: National Affiliate–www.sofn.com
Contact: Pauline A. Buckland, Sec.
Local. Affiliated With: Sons of Norway.

19943 ■ Viroqua Lions Club
c/o James P. Stalsberg, Sec.
129 Greenhill Dr.
Viroqua, WI 54665
Ph: (608)637-7782
E-mail: paulines@mwt.net
URL: http://www.md27d2.org
Contact: James P. Stalsberg, Sec.
Local. Affiliated With: Lions Clubs International.

Wabeno

19944 ■ American Legion, Sylvan Post 44
PO Box 363
Wabeno, WI 54566
Ph: (608)745-1090
Fax: (608)745-0179
URL: National Affiliate–www.legion.org
Local. Affiliated With: American Legion.

Wales

19945 ■ Foster Grandparent Program of Ethan Allen School
PO Box 900
Wales, WI 53183-0900
Ph: (262)646-3341
Fax: (262)646-3761
E-mail: barbara.kresse@doc.state.wi.us
URL: National Affiliate–www.seniorcorps.org
Contact: Barbara Kresse, Dir.
Local. Serves as mentors, tutors and caregivers for at-risk children and youth with special needs. Provides older Americans the opportunity to put their life experiences to work for local communities.

Walworth

19946 ■ American Legion, Ingalls-Koeppen Post 102
W 6460 Brick Church Rd.
Walworth, WI 53184
Ph: (608)745-1090
Fax: (608)745-0179
URL: National Affiliate–www.legion.org
Local. Affiliated With: American Legion.

Warrens

19947 ■ Ruffed Grouse Society, Woods/Meadow Chapter
c/o Kris Goetzka
N4835 Potter Rd.
Warrens, WI 54666
Ph: (608)378-4223
URL: National Affiliate–www.ruffedgrousesociety.org
Contact: Kris Goetzka, Contact
Local. Affiliated With: Ruffed Grouse Society.

19948 ■ Warrens Lions Club
c/o Gerald J. Schaller, Sec.
PO Box 14
Warrens, WI 54666
Ph: (608)378-4644
URL: http://www.md27d2.org
Contact: Gerald J. Schaller, Sec.
Local. Affiliated With: Lions Clubs International.

Washburn

19949 ■ American Legion, Bodin-Finstad-Guski Post 86
201 Peterson Rd.
Washburn, WI 54891
Ph: (608)745-1090
Fax: (608)745-0179
URL: National Affiliate–www.legion.org
Local. Affiliated With: American Legion.

19950 ■ Inland Sea Society (ISS)
PO Box 145
Washburn, WI 54891
Ph: (715)682-8188
Fax: (715)682-8117
E-mail: iss@inlandsea.org
URL: http://www.inlandsea.org
Contact: Mike Gardner, Pres.
Founded: 1988. **Local.** Works to promote environmental stewardship through education and recreation, sustainable communities, and watershed-based organizing.

19951 ■ Washburn Area Chamber of Commerce (WACC)
PO Box 74
Washburn, WI 54891-0074
Ph: (715)373-5017
Fax: (715)373-0240
Free: (800)253-4495
E-mail: washburn@cheqnet.net
URL: http://www.washburnchamber.com
Contact: Bruce Hanson, Exec.Dir.
Founded: 1975. **Members:** 90. **Membership Dues:** business, $150 (annual) • associate/link, $50 (annual). **Staff:** 1. **Budget:** $58,000. **Local.** Promotes business and community development in Washburn, WI. Coordinates annual Summerfest. **Awards: Type:** scholarship. **Recipient:** education associated with background in tourism/marketing/economic development. **Computer Services:** Information services • online services. **Publications:** *Chamber News*, monthly. **Conventions/Meetings:** monthly meeting.

Washington Island

19952 ■ American Legion, Gislason-Richter Post 402
1254 Main Rd.
Washington Island, WI 54246
Ph: (608)745-1090
Fax: (608)745-0179
URL: National Affiliate–www.legion.org
Local. Affiliated With: American Legion.

19953 ■ Washington Island Chamber of Commerce
Rte. 1, Box 222
Washington Island, WI 54246-9768
Ph: (920)847-2179
E-mail: info@washingtonislandwi.org
URL: http://washingtonislandwi.org
Contact: Marianna Gibson, Sec.-Treas.
Local.

Waterford

19954 ■ American Industrial Hygiene Association, Wisconsin Section
c/o Kay Rowntree, Sec.
602 Fox Knoll Dr.
Waterford, WI 53185
E-mail: president@aihawi.org
URL: http://www.aihawi.org
Contact: Kay Rowntree, Sec.
State. Promotes the study and control of environmental factors affecting the health and well being of workers. Sponsors continuing education courses in industrial hygiene, government affairs, and public relations. Conducts educational and research programs. **Affiliated With:** American Industrial Hygiene Association.

19955 ■ American Legion, Essman-Schroeder Post 20
PO Box 65
Waterford, WI 53185
Ph: (608)745-1090
Fax: (608)745-0179
URL: National Affiliate–www.legion.org
Local. Affiliated With: American Legion.

19956 ■ Waterford Area Chamber of Commerce
102 E Main St.
Waterford, WI 53185
Ph: (262)534-5911
Fax: (262)534-6507
E-mail: chamber@waterford-wi.org
URL: http://www.waterford-wi.org
Contact: Raegan Dexter, Exec.Dir.
Membership Dues: business (based on number of employees), $115-$350 (annual) • individual (non-business owner and retiree), $25 (annual) • nonprofit organization (club, church, school), $75 (annual). **Local.** Strives to promote business, tourism and community of the Waterford area through services and representation of the business community. **Publications:** *Business to Business*, quarterly. Newsletter.

19957 ■ Waterford Lions Club - Wisconsin
PO Box 84
Waterford, WI 53185
E-mail: cstoes77@hotmail.com
URL: http://www.wilions.org/waterford/index.shtml
Contact: Cheryl Trovillion, Sec.
Local. Affiliated With: Lions Clubs International.

Waterloo

19958 ■ American Legion, Humphrey-Wilsey Post 233
360 Riverside Dr.
Waterloo, WI 53594
Ph: (608)745-1090
Fax: (608)745-0179
URL: National Affiliate–www.legion.org
Local. Affiliated With: American Legion.

19959 ■ Madison AIFA
211 Canal Rd.
Waterloo, WI 53594
Fax: (920)478-9586
Free: (800)784-3852
URL: National Affiliate–www.naifa.org
Local. Represents the interest of insurance and financial advisors. Advocates for a positive legislative and regulatory environment. Enhances business and professional skills of members. **Affiliated With:** National Association of Insurance and Financial Advisors.

19960 ■ Madison Chapter of the Society of Financial Service Professionals
211 Canal Rd.
Waterloo, WI 53594
Ph: (920)478-3852
Fax: (920)478-9586
E-mail: acminc@verizon.net
URL: http://www.sfsp.net/Madison
Contact: Anna M. Maenner, Chapter Exec.
Local. Represents the interests of financial advisers. Fosters the development of professional responsibility. Helps clients achieve their personal and business-related financial goals. **Affiliated With:** Society of Financial Service Professionals.

19961 ■ Waterloo Chamber of Commerce (WCC)
PO Box 1
Waterloo, WI 53594
Ph: (920)478-2500
E-mail: wchamber@hurleycomputers.com
URL: http://www.waterloowis.com
Contact: Kristen Klein, Sec.
Local. Promotes business and community development in Waterloo, WI.

19962 ■ Wisconsin Apple Growers Association (WAGA)
c/o Anna M. Maenner, Exec.Dir.
211 Canal Rd.
Waterloo, WI 53594
Ph: (920)478-4277
Fax: (920)478-9586
E-mail: office@waga.org
URL: http://www.waga.org
Contact: Anna M. Maenner, Exec.Dir.
State.

19963 ■ Wisconsin Berry Growers Association (WBGA)
211 Canal Rd.
Waterloo, WI 53594
Ph: (920)478-3852
Fax: (920)478-9586
E-mail: info@wiberries.org
URL: http://www.wiberries.org
Contact: Anna Maenner, Exec.Dir.
State. Works with dedication to the production and promotion of Wisconsin strawberries, raspberries and blueberries.

Watersmeet

19964 ■ Eagle River Figure Skating Club
PO Box 394
Watersmeet, WI 49969
E-mail: dzelinski@goisd.k12.mi.us
URL: National Affiliate–www.usfigureskating.org
Contact: Deb Zelinski, Contact
Local. Provides programs to encourage participation and achievement in the sport of figure skating on ice. Defines and maintains uniform standards of skating proficiency. Organizes and sponsors competitions and exhibitions for the purpose of stimulating interest in figure skating. **Affiliated With:** United States Figure Skating Association.

Watertown

19965 ■ American Legion, Pitterle-Beaudoin Post 189
PO Box 22
Watertown, WI 53094
Ph: (608)745-1090
Fax: (608)745-0179
URL: National Affiliate–www.legion.org
Local. Affiliated With: American Legion.

19966 ■ HIPAA - Collaborative of Wisconsin (HIPAA COW)
c/o Marjean Griggs
PO Box 372
Watertown, WI 53094
Ph: (920)206-1265
Fax: (920)261-8742
E-mail: marjean@griggsmanagement.com
URL: http://www.hipaacow.org
Contact: Catherine Boerner JD, Pres.
State.

19967 ■ Izaak Walton League of America, Watertown Chapter
c/o Herschel Wickert
430 Janet Ln.
Watertown, WI 53094-6728
Ph: (920)261-7224
URL: National Affiliate–www.iwla.org
Local. Works to educate the public to conserve, maintain, protect, and restore the soil, forest, water, and other natural resources of the U.S; promotes the enjoyment and wholesome utilization of these resources. **Affiliated With:** Izaak Walton League of America.

19968 ■ Jefferson County Human Resource Management Association
c/o Theresa Galewski
PO Box 307
Watertown, WI 53094
E-mail: sheryllhopkins@eaton.com
URL: http://www.wishrm.org/chapter/jeffcnty/index.html
Contact: Sheryl Hopkins, Pres.
Local. Represents the interests of human resource and industrial relations professionals and executives. Promotes the advancement of human resource management.

19969 ■ Rock River AIFA
c/o Jeff King
PO Box 497
Watertown, WI 53094
Ph: (920)261-6144
Fax: (920)261-6798
E-mail: qig1@gdinet.com
URL: National Affiliate–naifa.org
Contact: Jeff King, Contact
Local. Represents the interests of insurance and financial advisors. Advocates for a positive legislative and regulatory environment. Enhances business and professional skills of members. **Affiliated With:** National Association of Insurance and Financial Advisors.

19970 ■ United Way of Watertown
PO Box 114
Watertown, WI 53094
Ph: (920)262-7886
URL: National Affiliate–national.unitedway.org
Local. Affiliated With: United Way of America.

19971 ■ Watertown Area Chamber of Commerce
519 E Main St.
Watertown, WI 53094
Ph: (920)261-6320
Fax: (920)261-6434
E-mail: watncofc@powercom.net
URL: http://www.watertownchamber.com
Contact: Randy Roeseler, Exec.Dir.
Founded: 1920. **Local.** Promotes business and community development in Watertown, WI.

19972 ■ Watertown Historical Society (WHS)
919 Charles St.
Watertown, WI 53094
Ph: (920)261-2796 (920)261-5433
URL: http://www.watertownhistory.org
Contact: Linda Werth, Mgr.
Founded: 1933. **Members:** 600. **Membership Dues:** family, $27 (annual) • individual, $12 (annual) • patron, $50 (annual) • benefactor, $100 • couple, $18 (annual). **Staff:** 5. **Budget:** $40,000. **Local.** Individuals and business groups. Maintains two museums: Octagon House and First Kindergarten in America. Holds Victorian open house and ice cream social with Civil War band. Sponsors festival. **Libraries: Type:** open to the public. **Holdings:** 100; books. **Subjects:** local/state history. **Publications:** *Biography of Margarethe Meyer Schurz*, quarterly. Newsletter. **Price:** included in membership dues • *Froebel Gifts* • *Handi and Pussy go to Kindergarten* • *The Hill and the Mill* • *History of America's 1st Kindergarten* • *History of Jefferson County* • *History of Watertown* • *Watertown Then and Now.* **Conventions/Meetings:** quarterly board meeting.

19973 ■ Wisconsin NFA Shooters (WINS)
c/o Ron Albanese
203 S Church St.
Watertown, WI 53094-4303
URL: http://www.joinme.net/brkdnc/wins.html
State.

19974 ■ Wisconsin Society of Podiatric Medicine
c/o Victor Soderstrom, DPM, Pres.
101 Oakridge Ct.
Watertown, WI 53094
Ph: (920)261-9610
Fax: (920)261-9671
URL: http://www.wisconsinpodiatrist.com
Contact: Dr. Victor Soderscrom, Pres.
State. Affiliated With: American Podiatric Medical Association.

Waukesha

19975 ■ Addiction Resource Council
W228 N683 Westmound Dr.
Waukesha, WI 53186
Ph: (262)524-7921
E-mail: waukesha.wi@ncadd.org
URL: National Affiliate–www.ncadd.org
Founded: 1971. **Members:** 25. **Budget:** $650,000. **Local.** Works for the prevention and treatment of alcoholism and other drug dependence through programs of public education, information, and public policy advocacy. **Affiliated With:** National Council on Alcoholism and Drug Dependence. **Formerly:** (2001) Addiction Resources. **Publications:** *The Advocate*, 3/year. Newsletter. **Conventions/Meetings:** annual Women and Special Topics in Addiction - meeting.

19976 ■ American Cancer Society, Waukesha
N19w24350 Riverwood Dr.
Waukesha, WI 53188
Ph: (262)523-5500
Fax: (262)523-9433
Free: (800)947-0487
URL: http://www.cancer.org
Local. Affiliated With: American Cancer Society.

19977 ■ American Chemical Society, Milwaukee Section
c/o Dr. Joseph Piatt, Chm.
Carroll Coll., Dept. of Chemistry
100 N East Ave.
Waukesha, WI 53186-3103
Ph: (262)524-7156
Fax: (262)524-7112
E-mail: jpiatt@cc.edu
URL: National Affiliate–acswebcontent.acs.org
Contact: Dr. Joseph Piatt, Chm.
Local. Represents the interests of individuals dedicated to the advancement of chemistry in all its branches. Provides opportunities for peer interaction and career development. **Affiliated With:** American Chemical Society.

19978 ■ American Choral Directors Association - North Central Division (NCACDA)
c/o Greg Carpenter, Pres.
2226 Woodfield Cir.
Waukesha, WI 53188-4716
Ph: (262)547-0339
E-mail: grcarp@sbcglobal.net
URL: http://www.ncacda.org
Contact: Greg Carpenter, Pres.
Membership Dues: associate/active, $75 (annual) • student, $30 (annual) • life, $2,000. **Regional.** Promotes excellence in choral music through performance, composition, publication, research and teaching. Elevates choral music's position in American society. **Subgroups:** Repertoire and Standards. **Affiliated With:** American Choral Directors Association. **Publications:** *Melisma*, quarterly. Newsletter. Alternate Formats: online. **Conventions/Meetings:** biennial convention.

19979 ■ American Legion, Wisconsin Post 8
c/o Daniel J. Martin
PO Box 111
Waukesha, WI 53187
Ph: (608)745-1090
Fax: (608)745-0179
URL: National Affiliate–www.legion.org
Contact: Daniel J. Martin, Contact
Local. Affiliated With: American Legion.

19980 ■ American Legion, Wisconsin Post 219
c/o F. Bernie Schmitz
1102 Aspen Dr.
Waukesha, WI 53188
Ph: (608)745-1090
Fax: (608)745-0179
URL: National Affiliate–www.legion.org
Contact: F. Bernie Schmitz, Contact
Local. Affiliated With: American Legion.

19981 ■ American Meteorological Society, Greater Milwaukee
c/o James M. Frederick, Pres.
2108 Butler Dr.
Waukesha, WI 53186
Ph: (262)547-6954
E-mail: jmf@uwm.edu
URL: http://www.uwm.edu/~daj/amspage.html
Contact: James M. Frederick, Pres.
Regional. Affiliated With: American Meteorological Society.

19982 ■ American Saddlebred Association of Wisconsin (ASAW)
c/o Dee Dee Mackie
2230 Stony Ridge Dr.
Waukesha, WI 53189
Ph: (262)896-9669
E-mail: putney@wi.rr.com
URL: http://www.asaw.org
Contact: Dee Dee Mackie, Contact
State. Affiliated With: American Saddlebred Horse Association.

19983 ■ Financial Managers Society, Wisconsin Chapter
c/o John Udvare
Sunset Bank
521 W Sunset Dr.
Waukesha, WI 53189
Ph: (262)970-9000
E-mail: johnu@sunsetbank.net
URL: National Affiliate–www.fmsinc.org
Contact: John Udvare, VP
State. Provides technical information exchange for financial personnel within financial institutions. **Affiliated With:** Financial Managers Society.

19984 ■ Girl Scouts - Great Blue Heron Council
PO Box 1510
Waukesha, WI 53187-1510
Ph: (262)544-8777
Fax: (262)544-8770
Free: (800)565-GIRL
E-mail: mcharles@girlscoutsgbh.org
URL: http://www.girlscoutsgbh.org
Contact: Mary Charles, Exec.Dir.
Local. Young girls and adult volunteers, corporate, government and individual supporters. Strives to develop potential and leadership skills among its members. Conducts trainings, educational programs and outdoor activities.

19985 ■ Hospitality Financial and Technology Professionals - Greater Milwaukee Chapter
c/o Scott Saeger, CHAE, Pres.
Marriott Hotel Services, Inc.
N16W22419 Watertown Rd.
GE Healthcare Inst.
Waukesha, WI 53186-1118
Ph: (262)574-8922
Fax: (262)574-8808
E-mail: scott.saeger@marriott.com
URL: http://www.hftp.org/milwaukee
Contact: Scott Saeger CHAE, Pres.
Local. Provides opportunities to members through professional and educational development. **Affiliated With:** Hospitality Financial and Technology Professionals. **Publications:** Newsletter. **Conventions/Meetings:** monthly meeting - every fourth Wednesday.

19986 ■ Humane Animal Welfare Society - Waukesha County (HAWS)
701 Northview Rd.
Waukesha, WI 53188
Ph: (262)542-8851
E-mail: office@hawspets.org
URL: http://www.hawspets.org
Contact: Stewart Wangard, Pres.

Founded: 1969. **Members:** 112. **Membership Dues:** friend, $25-$49 (annual) • companion, $50-$99 (annual) • advocate, $100-$249 (annual) • rescuer, $250-$499 (annual) • protector, $500-$999 (annual) • guardian, $1,000 (annual). **Staff:** 28. **Budget:** $525,000. **Local.** Humane organization representing individuals seeking to prevent cruelty to animals. Offers education and promotes care and responsible ownership of animals. Conducts pet adoptions; stray animal care and control; wildlife rehabilitation. **Libraries: Type:** open to the public. **Holdings:** periodicals. **Subjects:** animals, humane issues. **Publications:** *Tattle Tails*, 3/year. Newsletter. Contains short stories, info on fund raising events, memorials, society needs. **Price:** free. **Conventions/Meetings:** annual meeting - second Wednesday in September.

19987 ■ Junior Woman's Club of Waukesha (JWCW)
PO Box 1535
Waukesha, WI 53187-1535
E-mail: president@jwcw.org
URL: http://www.jwcw.org

Local.

19988 ■ Kettle Moraine Optometric Society
c/o John McDaniel, OD, Pres.
2426D N Grand View Blvd.
Waukesha, WI 53188
Ph: (262)549-2020
E-mail: johnmacu2@aol.com
URL: http://www.woa-eyes.org
Contact: John McDaniel OD, Pres.

Local. Aims to improve the quality, availability and accessibility of eye and vision care. Promotes high standards of patient care. Monitors and promotes legislation concerning the scope of optometric practice and other issues relevant to eye/vision care. **Affiliated With:** American Optometric Association; Wisconsin Optometric Association.

19989 ■ Literacy Council of Greater Waukesha
217 Wisconsion Ave., Ste.No. 16
Waukesha, WI 53186-4946
Ph: (262)547-7323 (262)547-6284
Fax: (262)547-1820
E-mail: drunning@waukeshaliteracy.org
URL: http://www.waukeshaliteracy.org
Contact: Ms. Debra Running, Exec.Dir.

Founded: 1986. **Membership Dues:** student (initial materials fee), $10 • student (per tutoring session), $7. **Staff:** 3. **Budget:** $140,000. **State Groups:** 1. **Languages:** English, Spanish. **Nonmembership. Local.** Dedicated to providing and advocating basic literacy skills and services to improve the quality of lives of learners. Provides training to volunteers to tutor adults and children. **Libraries: Type:** not open to the public; by appointment only; lending. **Holdings:** books, periodicals, video recordings. **Subjects:** basic skills, learning disabled, English as a second language. **Affiliated With:** ProLiteracy Worldwide. **Publications:** *Open Page*, quarterly. Newsletter. Features information for public. **Circulation:** 2,000. **Advertising:** accepted • *Tutor Talk*, quarterly. Newsletter. Features information for tutors. **Circulation:** 200. **Advertising:** accepted.

19990 ■ Milwaukee Sail and Power Squadron (MSPS)
c/o Lt. Mary Ann R. Wolf
W 305 S 4095 Brookhill Rd.
Waukesha, WI 53189
Ph: (262)968-3828
E-mail: deckwatch@earthlink.net
URL: http://www.usps.org/localusps/mps
Contact: Lt. Mary Ann R. Wolf, Contact

Local. Affiliated With: United States Power Squadrons.

19991 ■ Mothers Against Drunk Driving, Waukesha County
S32 W27786 Dale View Dr.
Waukesha, WI 53189
Ph: (262)968-4437
E-mail: marmom@net-email.com
URL: National Affiliate–www.madd.org/
Contact: Marlene Williams, Co-Coor.

Local. Victims of drunk driving crashes; concerned citizens. Encourages citizen participation in working towards reform of the drunk driving problem and the prevention of underage drinking. Acts as the voice of victims of drunk driving crashes by speaking on their behalf to communities, businesses, and educational groups. **Affiliated With:** Mothers Against Drunk Driving.

19992 ■ National Active and Retired Federal Employees Association - Waukesha 490
W270n326 Arrowhead Trails
Waukesha, WI 53188-1939
Ph: (262)542-8528
URL: National Affiliate–www.narfe.org
Contact: Walter E. Dable, Contact

Local. Protects the retirement future of employees through education. Informs members on issues affecting the retirement. **Affiliated With:** National Association of Retired Federal Employees.

19993 ■ National Alliance for the Mentally Ill - Waukesha
c/o Ann Day, Exec.Dir.
217 Wisconsin Ave., Ste.311
Waukesha, WI 53186
Ph: (262)524-8886
Fax: (262)547-1321
E-mail: namiwauk@aol.com
URL: http://www.namiwisconsin.org/library/directory
Contact: Ann Day, Exec.Dir.

Local. Strives to improve the quality of life of children and adults with severe mental illness through support, education, research and advocacy. **Affiliated With:** National Alliance for the Mentally Ill.

19994 ■ National Association of Industrial and Office Properties, Wisconsin Chapter
c/o Gina Hansen
N16W23321 Stone Bridge Dr.
Waukesha, WI 53188
Ph: (262)436-1122
Fax: (262)436-1110
E-mail: ghansen@mbaonline.org
URL: National Affiliate–www.naiop.org
Contact: Ms. Gina Hansen, Exec.Dir.

State. Represents the interests of developers and owners of industrial, office and related commercial estate. Provides communication, networking, business opportunities and a forum to its members. Promotes effective public policy to create, protect and enhance property values. **Committees:** Public Affairs. **Affiliated With:** National Association of Industrial and Office Properties. **Conventions/Meetings:** annual meeting.

19995 ■ National Association of Rocketry - Waukesha County 4H Rocketeers (WACO4HRS)
c/o Flash Gordon
1115 Millwood Ave.
Waukesha, WI 53188
Ph: (262)544-0405
E-mail: flash_rescue31@hotmail.com
URL: National Affiliate–www.nar.org
Contact: Flash Gordon, Contact

Local.

19996 ■ PFLAG Waukesha
2016 Center Rd.
Waukesha, WI 53189
Ph: (414)299-9198
E-mail: office@christtheservant.org
URL: http://www.pflag.org/Wisconsin.246.0.html

Local. Affiliated With: Parents, Families, and Friends of Lesbians and Gays.

19997 ■ Phi Theta Kappa, Alpha Chi Rho Chapter - University of Wisconsin-Waukesha
c/o Sue Kalinka
Waukesha Campus
1500 Univ. Dr.
Waukesha, WI 53188
Ph: (262)521-5043
E-mail: skalinka@uwc.edu
URL: http://www.ptk.org/directories/chapters/WI/20575-1.htm
Contact: Sue Kalinka, Advisor

Local.

19998 ■ Retired and Senior Volunteer Program of Waukesha County
c/o Judith Goodrich, Exec.Dir.
310 South St.
Waukesha, WI 53186
Ph: (262)544-9559
Fax: (262)544-5307
E-mail: mail@rsvpwaukesha.org
URL: http://www.rsvpwaukesha.org
Contact: Judith Goodrich, Exec.Dir.

Local. Affiliated With: Retired and Senior Volunteer Program.

19999 ■ Society for Technical Communication, Wisconsin Chapter
c/o Jesse Kieck, Newsletter Ed.
421 N Moreland Blvd., No. 1
Waukesha, WI 53188
Ph: (414)299-0048
E-mail: president@stc-wi.org
URL: http://www.stc-wi.org
Contact: Mollye Barrett, Pres.

State. Seeks to advance the theory and practice of technical communication in all media. Enhances the professionalism of the members and the status of the profession. Promotes the education of members and supports research activities in the field. **Affiliated With:** Society for Technical Communication.

20000 ■ United Way in Waukesha County
1717 Paramount Dr.
Waukesha, WI 53186
Ph: (262)547-8459
Fax: (262)548-8945
E-mail: jayne@unitedwaywaukesha.org
URL: http://www.unitedwaywaukesha.org
Contact: Jayne Thoma, Exec.Dir.

Local. Affiliated With: United Way of America.

20001 ■ Waukesha Area REACT
PO Box 1825
Waukesha, WI 53187-1825
Ph: (262)524-2641
E-mail: react4089@wi.rr.com
URL: http://www.reactintl.org/teaminfo/usa_teams/teams-uswi.htm
Contact: Mark Kirschling, Pres.

Local. Trained communication experts and professional volunteers. Provides volunteer public service and emergency communications through the use of radios (Citizen Band, General Mobile Radio Service, UHF and HAM). Coordinates with radio industries and government on safety communication matters and supports charitable activities and community organizations.

20002 ■ Waukesha Coin Club
c/o Forrest Schumaker
2300 Avalon Dr.
Waukesha, WI 53186

Ph: (262)542-3934
URL: National Affiliate–www.money.org
Contact: Forrest Schumaker, Contact
Local. Affiliated With: American Numismatic Association.

20003 ■ Waukesha County Chamber of Commerce (WCCC)
223 Wisconsin Ave.
Waukesha, WI 53186
Ph: (262)542-4249
Fax: (262)542-8068
E-mail: pwallner@waukesha.org
URL: http://www.waukesha.org
Contact: Patti Wallner, Pres.
Membership Dues: business (based on number of full time employees), $285-$335. **Local.** Strives to enhance the business community of Waukesha County. **Formerly:** (2005) Waukesha Area Chamber of Commerce. **Publications:** *The Link.* Newsletter.

20004 ■ Waukesha County Historical Society (WCHS)
101 W Main St.
Waukesha, WI 53186-4811
Ph: (262)521-2859
Fax: (262)521-2865
E-mail: sbaker@wchsm.org
URL: http://www.waukeshacountymuseum.org
Contact: Susan K. Baker, Exec.Dir.
Founded: 1906. **Members:** 475. **Membership Dues:** preservationist, $30-$49 (annual) • builder, $50-$99 (annual) • educator, $100-$249 (annual) • visionary, $250-$499 (annual) • bronze director's circle, $500-$749 (annual) • silver director's circle, $750-$999 (annual) • gold director's circle, $1,000 (annual). **Staff:** 18. **Local.** Aims to preserve and promote the history of Waukesha County. Maintains museum and research center; provides educational programs, tours and historical markers. **Libraries: Type:** open to the public. **Holdings:** archival material, clippings. **Subjects:** county history. **Affiliated With:** Wisconsin Historical Society. **Publications:** *From Farmland to Freeways: A History of Waukesha County, Wisconsin.* Book. **Price:** $15.00. ISSN: 0961-3624 • *Historical Markers of Waukesha County.* Directory. **Price:** free with SASE • *Landmark*, quarterly. Magazine • *Museum Store Catalog.* **Price:** free with SASE • *Timeline*, quarterly. Newsletter. **Conventions/Meetings:** annual A Taste of History Social Fundraiser - meeting • annual Holiday Fair - festival, crafts, holiday music, children's activities, bake sale, and silent auction (exhibits) - November.

20005 ■ Waukesha County Philatelic Society (WCPS)
c/o MaryAnn J. Bowman
PO Box 1451
Waukesha, WI 53187
URL: http://www.stamps.org
Contact: Mrs. MaryAnn J. Bowman, Contact
Founded: 1969. **Members:** 45. **Membership Dues:** $10 (annual). **Local.** Stamp collectors seeking to promote stamp collecting through educational programs and activities. **Affiliated With:** American Philatelic Society. **Publications:** *Mail Chute*, monthly. Newsletter • *Tattler*, monthly. Bulletin.

20006 ■ Waukesha Gun Club
N 22 W 23170, Watertown Rd.
Waukesha, WI 53188
Ph: (262)547-9785
Fax: (262)547-9786
URL: http://www.waukeshagunclub.org
Local. Affiliated With: National Skeet Shooting Association.

20007 ■ Waukesha Noon Lions Club
PO Box 1004
Waukesha, WI 53189
Ph: (262)521-2945
URL: http://www.wilions.org/WaukeshaNoon/index.htm
Contact: Ken Hauser, Contact
Local. Affiliated With: Lions Clubs International.

20008 ■ Wisconsin Auto Collision Technicians Association (WACTAL)
c/o Sue Paterson
W 226 S1742 State Rd. 164S
Waukesha, WI 53186
Fax: (262)542-0906
Free: (800)366-9472
E-mail: wactal@execpc.com
URL: http://www.wactal.com
Contact: Sue Paterson, Contact
State. Seeks to raise the professional image of the collision repair specialist. Works to educate, inform and represent the collision repair professional in all aspects of the industry. **Affiliated With:** Society of Collision Repair Specialists.

20009 ■ Wisconsin Curling Association - Waukesha Curling Club
911 E Roberta Ave.
Waukesha, WI 53186
Ph: (414)542-3002
URL: http://www.goodcurling.net/basics/U.S.%20clubs/wisconsin.html
Contact: Bill Hoppenjan, Pres.
Local. Affiliated With: United States Curling Association.

20010 ■ Wisconsin Division of the International Association of Administrative Professionals
Red Prairie
20700 Swenson Dr., No. 200
Waukesha, WI 53186
Ph: (262)317-2313
Fax: (262)317-2624
E-mail: suea@itis.com
URL: http://www.iaapwisconsin.com
Contact: Sue Richtemeyer, Pres.
State. Professionals, corporations, academic institutions and students. Develops research and educational projects for administrative professionals. Provides training, seminars, conferences and educational programs.

20011 ■ Wisconsin Federation of Republican Women (WFRW)
260 Rip Van Winkle Dr.
Waukesha, WI 53186
Ph: (262)784-1247
Fax: (262)784-5288
E-mail: gmarschman@aol.com
URL: http://www.wifrw.org
Contact: Ginny Marschman, Pres.
Founded: 1940. **Members:** 1,025. **Local Groups:** 22. **For-Profit. State.**

20012 ■ Wisconsin Landscape Contractors Association (WLCA)
c/o Barbara Scheibe, Exec.Dir.
21620 Belgren Rd.
Waukesha, WI 53186
Ph: (262)782-9522
Fax: (262)786-2424
Free: (800)933-9522
E-mail: bscheibe@execpc.com
URL: http://www.findalandscaper.org
Contact: Barbara Scheibe, Exec.Dir.
Local. Strives to promote and improve the image of "professional landscaping", to encourage a high standard of professional ethics as well as quality workmanship in the landscape contracting industry, to support legislation that is beneficial to landscape contractors, the general public, and the environment. **Affiliated With:** Professional Landcare Network. **Also Known As:** (2006) Wisconsin Landscape Contractors Association of Metro-Milwaukee.

20013 ■ Wisconsin Society of Land Surveyors (WSLS)
c/o Harold Charlier, WSLS, Exec.Dir.
2935 Coventry Ln.
Waukesha, WI 53188
Ph: (262)549-1533
Fax: (262)549-1656
E-mail: hscwsls@aol.com
URL: http://www.wsls.org
Founded: 1952. **State.** Represents the interests of members. **Affiliated With:** National Society of Professional Surveyors.

Waunakee

20014 ■ American Legion, Wisconsin Post 360
c/o William Lansing
417 E Main St.
Waunakee, WI 53597
Ph: (608)745-1090
Fax: (608)745-0179
URL: National Affiliate–www.legion.org
Contact: William Lansing, Contact
Local. Affiliated With: American Legion.

20015 ■ American Legion, Wisconsin Post 481
c/o Robert M. Coakley
5337 River Rd.
Waunakee, WI 53597
Ph: (608)745-1090
Fax: (608)745-0179
URL: National Affiliate–www.legion.org
Contact: Robert M. Coakley, Contact
Local. Affiliated With: American Legion.

20016 ■ Friends of Governor Nelson State Park
5140 County Track M
Waunakee, WI 53597-0000
Ph: (608)831-3005
Contact: Rene Lee, Park Mgr.
Local.

20017 ■ Madison Advertising Federation (MAF)
7185 Hickory Run
Waunakee, WI 53597
Ph: (608)831-9242
Fax: (608)836-0722
E-mail: lois@madadfed.com
URL: http://www.madadfed.com
Contact: Lois Weiland, Exec.Dir.
Founded: 1947. **Members:** 173. **Membership Dues:** active, $240 (annual) • corporate, $355 (annual) • affiliate, $105 (annual). **For-Profit. Local.** Represents the interests of advertising individuals. Serves as a networking resource and strives to keep members updated to industry changes.

20018 ■ Madison Area Optometric Society
c/o David May, OD, Pres.
1200 Spahn Dr.
Waunakee, WI 53597
Ph: (608)644-3830
Fax: (608)644-3852
E-mail: dmayod@tds.net
URL: http://www.woa-eyes.org
Contact: David May OD, Pres.
Local. Aims to improve the quality, availability and accessibility of eye and vision care. Promotes high standards of patient care. Monitors and promotes legislation concerning the scope of optometric practice and other issues relevant to eye/vision care. **Affiliated With:** American Optometric Association; Wisconsin Optometric Association.

20019 ■ Waunakee/Westport Chamber of Commerce
100 E Main St.
PO Box 41
Waunakee, WI 53597

Ph: (608)849-5977
Fax: (608)849-9825
E-mail: wchamber@tds.net
URL: http://www.waunakee.com
Contact: Lisa Pertzborn-Whiting, Exec.Dir.
Founded: 1979. **Local**. Promotes business and community development in the Waunakee, WI area. **Formerly:** (1999) Waunakee Area Chamber of Commerce; (2006) Greater Waunakee Area Chamber of Commerce. **Publications:** *Greater Waunakee Area Chamber of Commerce News*, monthly. Newsletter. **Conventions/Meetings:** annual dinner.

20020 ■ Wisconsin Music Educators Association (WMEA)
c/o Eric Runestad, Exec.Dir.
1005 Quinn Dr.
Waunakee, WI 53597
Ph: (608)850-3566
Fax: (608)850-3515
Free: (800)589-9762
E-mail: erunestad@wsmamusic.org
URL: http://www.wmea.com
Contact: Eric Runestad, Exec.Dir.
State. **Affiliated With:** MENC: The National Association for Music Education.

Waupaca

20021 ■ American Rabbit Breeders Association, Wisconsin (WSRBA)
c/o Dennis Roloff, Sec.-Treas.
E1198 Haase Rd.
Waupaca, WI 54981
URL: http://www.geocities.com/wisconsin_state_rba
Contact: Dennis Roloff, Sec.-Treas.
Founded: 1945. **State**. **Affiliated With:** American Rabbit Breeders Association.

20022 ■ Vietnam Veterans of America, Region 6
c/o Steve House, Dir.
N 2566 County Rd. K
Waupaca, WI 54981
E-mail: shouse@vva.org
URL: National Affiliate–www.vva.org
Contact: Steve House, Dir.
Regional. **Affiliated With:** Vietnam Veterans of America.

20023 ■ Waupaca Area Chamber of Commerce (WACC)
221 S Main St.
Waupaca, WI 54981-1522
Ph: (715)258-7343
Fax: (715)258-7868
Free: (888)417-4040
E-mail: discoverwaupaca@waupacaareachamber.com
URL: http://www.WaupacaAreaChamber.com
Contact: Terri Schulz, Pres.
Founded: 1931. **Members:** 320. **Staff:** 3. **Budget:** $199,000. **Local**. Retailers, manufacturers, professionals, and service and community organizations united to promote economic and community development in the Waupaca, WI area. **Formerly:** Waupaca Area Association of Commerce. **Publications:** *Map Brochure*, semiannual • *Waupaca Area Chamber of Commerce Newsline*, monthly. Newsletter. **Price:** free • *Waupaca Area Chamber of Commerce Progress Report*, annual.

20024 ■ Waupaca Conservation League (WCL)
c/o John W. Woodliff, Pres.
PO Box 293
Waupaca, WI 54981
Ph: (715)258-7660
E-mail: woodliffentp@voyager.net
URL: http://www.unregisteredshoot.com/ClubPages/wi-waupacaCL.htm
Contact: John W. Woodliff, Pres.
Founded: 1934. **Members:** 365. **Membership Dues:** family, $35 (annual) • life, $250. **Staff:** 10. **Budget:** $755,000. **Local**. Individuals working to protect natural resources. Holds monthly programs; maintains trap, skeet, handgun, rifle, and sporting clay ranges; conducts seminars; provides free use of facilities to specific organizations; sponsors shooting events and recycling programs. **Publications:** Newsletter, quarterly. Contains calendar of events and membership activities. **Price:** free. **Circulation:** 385. **Conventions/Meetings:** monthly meeting - usually last Tuesday.

20025 ■ Waupaca Curling Club
216 S Franklin
PO Box 22
Waupaca, WI 54981
Ph: (715)258-8935
E-mail: mmuch@sbcglobal.net
URL: National Affiliate–www.usacurl.org
Contact: Miralee Much, Pres.
Local. **Affiliated With:** United States Curling Association.

20026 ■ Waupaca Historical Society
c/o Julie Hintz, Dir.
321 S Main St.
Waupaca, WI 54981-1745
Ph: (715)256-9980
E-mail: wauphistsoc@charter.net
URL: http://www.waupacahistory.org
Founded: 1953. **Members:** 200. **Membership Dues:** individual, $10 (annual) • couple, $20 (annual) • family, $25 (annual). **Staff:** 1. **Budget:** $35,000. **Local Groups:** 1. **Local**. Preserves and disseminates knowledge of the Waupaca Area and its history through education, artifact preservation and special programs and events. **Libraries: Type:** open to the public. **Holdings:** 2,000; archival material, books, clippings, periodicals, photographs. **Subjects:** Waupaca city history, Waupaca county history, family histories, Victorian artifacts. **Computer Services:** Record retrieval services, research, genealogical inquiries, internet access. **Publications:** *The Reporter*, quarterly. Newsletter. Contains listing of upcoming exhibits, events and other topics of interest. **Price:** free to members. **Circulation:** 200. **Conventions/Meetings:** annual Fall-O-Rama in South Park - festival - every third Saturday of September. Waupaca, WI • annual History Bee/Living History Festival - every first weekend of June. Waupaca, WI • annual Holiday Open House - meet - every December. Waupaca, WI.

Waupun

20027 ■ American Legion, Getchel-Nelson Post 210
130 N State St.
Waupun, WI 53963
Ph: (608)745-1090
Fax: (608)745-0179
URL: National Affiliate–www.legion.org
Local. **Affiliated With:** American Legion.

20028 ■ Waupun Area Chamber of Commerce
16 S Mill St.
Waupun, WI 53963
Ph: (920)324-3491
Fax: (920)324-4357
E-mail: info@waupunchamber.com
URL: http://www.waupunchamber.com
Contact: Ginger Kieltyka, Exec.Dir./Exec.VP
Local. Aims to provide business leadership, promote its members' interests and encourage the long-term sustainable development, quality of life and prosperity of the area.

20029 ■ Waupun Figure Skating Club
502 Grace St.
Waupun, WI 53963
E-mail: golden@powerweb.net
URL: National Affiliate–www.usfigureskating.org
Contact: Kathleen Decker, Contact
Local. Provides programs to encourage participation and achievement in the sport of figure skating on ice. Defines and maintains uniform standards of skating proficiency. Organizes and sponsors competitions and exhibitions for the purpose of stimulating interest in figure skating. **Affiliated With:** United States Figure Skating Association.

Wausau

20030 ■ American Cancer Society, Wausau
903 S 17th Ave., Ste.B
Wausau, WI 54401
Ph: (715)848-2881
Fax: (715)848-3797
Free: (877)423-9128
URL: http://www.cancer.org
Contact: Steve Carlton, Income Development Mgr.
Local. **Affiliated With:** American Cancer Society.

20031 ■ American Legion, Montgomery-Plant Post 10
1001 Golf Club Rd.
Wausau, WI 54403
Ph: (715)675-3663
Fax: (608)745-0179
URL: National Affiliate–www.legion.org
Local. **Affiliated With:** American Legion.

20032 ■ Boys and Girls Clubs
1710 N Second St.
Wausau, WI 54403
Ph: (715)845-2582
E-mail: brian@bgclub.com
URL: http://www.bgclub.com
Contact: Brian Stezenski-Williams PhD, Exec.Dir.
Membership Dues: individual, $15 (annual) • family, $40 (annual). **Local**.

20033 ■ Central Wisconsin Sail and Power Squadron
1022 Jackson St.
Wausau, WI 54403
Ph: (715)223-6939
E-mail: stannss100@verizon.net
URL: http://webpages.charter.net/billdohr/cwps
Contact: Stanley Dale, Exec. Officer
Local. **Affiliated With:** United States Power Squadrons.

20034 ■ Central Wisconsin Society for Human Resources (CWSHRM)
PO Box 2013
Wausau, WI 54402
E-mail: karenb@balancinglives.org
URL: http://www.wishrm.org/chapter/cenwis/index.html
Contact: Karen Brzezinski, Pres.
Local. Represents the interests of human resource and industrial relations professionals and executives. Promotes the advancement of human resource management.

20035 ■ Ginseng Board of Wisconsin
7575 Bombardier Ct., Ste.300
Wausau, WI 54401
Ph: (715)845-7300
Fax: (715)845-8006
Free: (800)950-7303
E-mail: ginseng@ginsengboard.com
Contact: Diane Zimmerman, Admin.Asst.
Founded: 1986. **Members:** 1,476. **Staff:** 2. **Budget:** $300,000. **State**. Promotes and expands the sale of Wisconsin ginseng. Works to improve product quality and educate growers and consumers as to the benefits of Wisconsin ginseng. Health benefits include Type II Diabetes research at University of Chicago medical school and Wisconsin Medical Foundation-a human study. **Publications:** *GRIA Bibliography and Supplement*. **Conventions/Meetings:** annual WGGA and GBW - meeting; Avg. Attendance: 200.

20036 ■ Junior Achievement of Wisconsin, Marathon County District Office
720 Third St.
Wausau, WI 54403
Ph: (715)842-1056
Fax: (715)845-1738
E-mail: jawausau@g2a.net
URL: http://marathonco.ja.org
Contact: Ms. Gina Zacho, Dir.
Local. Affiliated With: Junior Achievement. **Formerly:** (2005) Junior Achievement North Central.

20037 ■ Main Street Wausau
c/o Amy Altenburgh, Mgr.
426 Third St.
Wausau, WI 54403
Ph: (715)845-1328
Fax: (715)843-0938
E-mail: mainstreetwausau@g2a.net
URL: National Affiliate–www.commerce.state.wi.us
Contact: Amy Altenburgh, Mgr.
Local.

20038 ■ Marathon County Historical Society (MCHS)
410 McIndoe St.
Wausau, WI 54403
Ph: (715)842-5750 (715)848-6143
Fax: (715)848-0576
E-mail: research@marathoncountyhistory.org
URL: http://www.marathoncountyhistory.org
Contact: Mary Jane Hettinga, Exec.Dir.
Founded: 1952. **Members:** 800. **Membership Dues:** $25 (annual). **Staff:** 6. **Budget:** $120,000. **Local.** Strives to collect, advance and disseminate the knowledge of the History of Marathon County and the State of Wisconsin. This mission is carried out through the Yawkey House Museum, rotating exhibit in the Woodson, educational programs and the library. **Libraries: Type:** open to the public. **Holdings:** 8,000; clippings, periodicals, photographs, reports. **Subjects:** logging, Indians, history of Marathon County, genealogical research. **Affiliated With:** American Association of Museums; Wisconsin Historical Society. **Publications:** *The Wanigan*, quarterly. Newsletter. **Price:** free. **Circulation:** 800.

20039 ■ Marathon County REACT
PO Box 2073
Wausau, WI 54402-2073
Ph: (715)843-7256
E-mail: 4730@wireact.org
URL: http://www.reactintl.org/teaminfo/usa_teams/teams-uswi.htm
Local. Trained communication experts and professional volunteers. Provides volunteer public service and emergency communications through the use of radios (Citizen Band, General Mobile Radio Service, UHF and HAM). Coordinates with radio industries and government on safety communication matters and supports charitable activities and community organizations.

20040 ■ March of Dimes
308 Grand Ave.
Wausau, WI 54403-6278
Ph: (715)849-9444
Local.

20041 ■ National Association of Home Builders of the United States, Wausau Area Builders Association (WABA)
230 Reservoir Ave.
Wausau, WI 54401-4267
Ph: (715)842-9510
Fax: (715)848-3815
E-mail: info@wausauareabuilders.com
URL: http://wausauareabuilders.com
Contact: Jerry Draxler, Pres.
Founded: 1967. **Local.** Single and multifamily home builders, commercial builders, and others associated with the building industry. **Committees:** Home Show; Parade of Homes. **Affiliated With:** National Association of Home Builders.

20042 ■ Navy Club of Central Wisconsin - Ship No. 64
400 River Dr., Apt. 385
Wausau, WI 54403
Ph: (715)848-0384
URL: National Affiliate–www.navyclubusa.org
Contact: Harry Alvay, Commander
Local. Represents individuals who are, or have been, in the active service of the U.S. Navy, Naval Reserve, Marine Corps, Marine Corps Reserve, and Coast Guard. Promotes and encourages further public interest in the U.S. Navy and its history. Upholds the spirit and ideals of the U.S. Navy. Acts as a public forum for members' views on national defense. Assists the Navy Recruiting Command whenever and wherever possible. Conducts charitable activities. **Affiliated With:** Navy Club of the United States of America.

20043 ■ North Wisconsin District, The Lutheran Church-Missouri Synod
PO Box 8064
Wausau, WI 54402-8064
Ph: (715)845-8241
Fax: (715)845-3836
Free: (800)333-2421
E-mail: nwd@nwdlcms.org
URL: http://www.nwdlcms.org
Contact: Dr. Arleigh Lutz, Pres.
Regional.

20044 ■ Phi Theta Kappa, Beta Kappa Kappa Chapter - University of Wisconsin-Marathon County
c/o Laura Polum
Marathon County Campus
518 S 7th Ave.
Wausau, WI 54401
Ph: (715)261-6100
E-mail: lpolum@uwc.edu
URL: http://www.ptk.org/directories/chapters/WI/21675-1.htm
Contact: Laura Polum, Advisor
Local.

20045 ■ Ruffed Grouse Society, Rib Mountain Chapter
c/o David Boehm
4650 Rib Mountain Dr.
Wausau, WI 54401
Ph: (715)355-7776
URL: National Affiliate–www.ruffedgrousesociety.org
Contact: David Boehm, Contact
Local. Affiliated With: Ruffed Grouse Society.

20046 ■ SCORE Wausau
200 Washington St., Ste.200
Wausau, WI 54403
Ph: (715)845-6231
URL: National Affiliate–www.score.org
Local. Provides professional guidance, mentoring services and financial assistance to maximize the success of existing and emerging small businesses. **Affiliated With:** SCORE.

20047 ■ Society of Manufacturing Engineers - Northcentral Technical College S237
1000 W Campus Dr.
Wausau, WI 54401-1899
Ph: (715)675-3331
E-mail: schulzl@ntc.edu
URL: National Affiliate–www.sme.org
Contact: Laurie Schulz, Contact
Local. Advances manufacturing knowledge to gain competitive advantage. Improves skills and manufacturing solutions for the growth of economy. Provides resources and opportunities for manufacturing professionals.

20048 ■ Sons of Norway, Rib Fjell Lodge 5-496
c/o Gary E. Klofstad, Pres.
1202 Eastview Dr.
Wausau, WI 54403-9313
Ph: (715)843-7754
E-mail: geklofstad@charter.net
URL: National Affiliate–www.sofn.com
Contact: Gary E. Klofstad, Pres.
Local. Affiliated With: Sons of Norway.

20049 ■ Timberline Skating Club (TFSC)
PO Box 2082
Wausau, WI 54402
E-mail: info@timberlinefsc.org
URL: http://www.timberlinefsc.org
Contact: Tammy Steckling, Sec.
Local. Provides programs to encourage participation and achievement in the sport of figure skating on ice. Defines and maintains uniform standards of skating proficiency. Organizes and sponsors competitions and exhibitions for the purpose of stimulating interest in figure skating. **Affiliated With:** United States Figure Skating Association.

20050 ■ Trout Unlimited - Wisconsin River Valley Chapter
629 Hamilton St.
Wausau, WI 54403-3513
Ph: (715)842-1365
URL: http://www.tu.org
Contact: Herbert Hintze, Pres.
Local.

20051 ■ United Way of Marathon County
137 River Dr.
Wausau, WI 54403-5474
Ph: (715)848-2927
Fax: (715)848-2929
E-mail: uway@dwave.net
URL: http://www.unitedwaymc.org
Contact: Hugh Jones, Pres.
Local. Affiliated With: United Way of America.

20052 ■ Upland Chapter of Pheasants Forever (UCPF)
c/o Keith Koskey
H13971 School Rd.
Wausau, WI 54403
Ph: (715)849-3734
E-mail: f1pheasant@aol.com
URL: http://www.uplandchapterpf.freeservers.com
Contact: Steve Gasper, Sec.
Local. Affiliated With: Pheasants Forever.

20053 ■ Wausau Area Apartment Association
c/o John H. Fischer, Assn.Exec.
PO Box 723
Wausau, WI 54402-0723
Ph: (715)359-1500
Fax: (715)355-0028
E-mail: helprent@helprent.com
URL: National Affiliate–www.naahq.org
Contact: John H. Fischer, Assn.Exec.
Local. Affiliated With: National Apartment Association.

20054 ■ Wausau Curling Club
PO Box 627
Wausau, WI 54402-0627
Ph: (715)842-3614
E-mail: ringledogs@msn.com
URL: http://www.wausaucurling.org
Contact: Jodi Olmstead, Pres.
Local. Affiliated With: United States Curling Association.

20055 ■ Wausau/Marathon County Chamber of Commerce (WACC)
300 3rd St., No. 200
PO Box 6190
Wausau, WI 54402-6190
Ph: (715)845-6231
Fax: (715)845-6235
E-mail: info@wausauchamber.com
URL: http://www.wausauchamber.com
Contact: Roger A. Luce, Exec.Dir.
Membership Dues: general business (based on number of full time employees), $260-$1,040 (annual) • professional (plus $75 per associate), $260

(annual) • real estate individual agent, $150 (annual) • investment/security (plus $75 per broker), $260 (annual) • financial institution (per million in deposits), $40 (annual) • associate, $130 (annual). **Local**. Promotes business and community development in the Wausau, WI area. **Subgroups:** Business Advocacy; Economic Development; Small Business; Workforce Development. **Publications:** *Businessmatters*, quarterly. Magazine. Alternate Formats: online • *Membermatters*, monthly. Newsletter. Includes information about the chamber and its members. • *Speakers Bureau Booklet* • *Wausau Book* • Newsletters, monthly. Alternate Formats: online.

20056 ■ Wausau Skeet and Trap Club
PO Box 2154
Wausau, WI 54402
Ph: (715)675-7227
URL: National Affiliate–www.mynssa.com
Local. Affiliated With: National Skeet Shooting Association.

20057 ■ Wausau Table Tennis Club
Marathon Park - Youth Bldg.
1201 Stewart Ave.
Wausau, WI 54401
Ph: (715)847-1143
E-mail: ghlt@charter.net
URL: http://webpages.charter.net/lehoang/WebWTTC/index.htm
Contact: Long H. Le, Contact
Local. Affiliated With: U.S.A. Table Tennis.

20058 ■ Wisconsin Art Education Association (WAEA)
c/o Stephen Loftus
1243 Sunset Dr.
Wausau, WI 54401
Ph: (715)261-2350 (715)261-3939
Fax: (715)261-2355
E-mail: stephen.loftus@verizon.net
URL: http://www.wiarted.org
Contact: Julie Adams, Sec.
State. Promotes art education through professional development, service, advancement of knowledge, and leadership.

20059 ■ Wisconsin Automotive and Truck Education Association (WATEA)
c/o Tina L. Miller, Project Coor.
PO Box 1542
Wausau, WI 54402-1542
Ph: (715)536-3167
Fax: (715)536-3167
E-mail: ctrykin@aol.com
URL: http://www.watea.org
Contact: Tina L. Miller, Proj.Coor.
Founded: 2000. **Members:** 60. **State Groups:** 1. **State**. Dedicated to improving awareness of career paths and opportunities in the automotive/truck industry; promotes technical and continuing training, educational development, and certification of workers in the automotive/truck industry. **Publications:** *Your Quarterly Connection*. Newsletter. **Advertising:** accepted. Alternate Formats: online.

20060 ■ Wisconsin Valley Optometric Society
c/o R. Chris Marquardt, OD, Pres.
515 N 17th Ave.
Wausau, WI 54401
Ph: (715)848-1246
Fax: (715)842-1660
E-mail: cmarq@charter.net
URL: http://www.woa-eyes.org
Contact: R. Chris Marquardt OD, Pres.
Local. Aims to improve the quality, availability and accessibility of eye and vision care. Promotes high standards of patient care. Monitors and promotes legislation concerning the scope of optometric practice and other issues relevant to eye/vision care. **Affiliated With:** American Optometric Association; Wisconsin Optometric Association.

Wausaukee

20061 ■ American Legion, Polomis-Tahlier Post 150
PO Box 50
Wausaukee, WI 54177
Ph: (608)745-1090
Fax: (608)745-0179
URL: National Affiliate–www.legion.org
Local. Affiliated With: American Legion.

20062 ■ Wausaukee Area Business Association
502 Main St.
PO Box 254
Wausaukee, WI 54177-0254
Ph: (715)856-5627
Fax: (715)856-6209
Free: (888)856-5164
E-mail: waba@wausaukee.com
URL: http://www.wausaukee.com
Contact: Brian Hartnell, Pres.
Local. Local businesses and community members. Strives to promote the Wausaukee area and its businesses.

Wautoma

20063 ■ American Legion, Dakota-Richford Post 163
W 9432 Czech Rd.
Wautoma, WI 54982
Ph: (608)745-1090
Fax: (608)745-0179
URL: National Affiliate–www.legion.org
Local. Affiliated With: American Legion.

20064 ■ American Legion, Wolman-Minskey Post 317
PO Box 564
Wautoma, WI 54982
Ph: (608)745-1090
Fax: (608)745-0179
URL: National Affiliate–www.legion.org
Local. Affiliated With: American Legion.

20065 ■ Waushara Area Chamber of Commerce (WACC)
440 W Main St.
PO Box 65
Wautoma, WI 54982-0065
Ph: (920)787-3488
Fax: (920)787-3788
Free: (877)WAU-TOMA
E-mail: wacc@centurytel.net
URL: http://www.wausharachamber.com
Contact: Lisa Larson, Co-Pres.
Members: 162. **Membership Dues:** business with 1-10 employees, government agency, church, and non-profit organization, $165 (annual) • business with 11-40 employees, $230 (annual) • business with over 40 employees, $360 (annual). **Staff:** 1. **Budget:** $25,000. **Local**. Promotes business and community development in Waushara County, WI. **Awards:** Business Person of the Year. **Frequency:** annual. **Type:** recognition • Citizen of the Year. **Frequency:** annual. **Type:** recognition. **Recipient:** for community service. **Publications:** *WACC News*, monthly. Newsletter. Contains two pages of pertinent information. **Circulation:** 170. **Advertising:** accepted. Alternate Formats: online.

Wauwatosa

20066 ■ ALS Association Southeast Wisconsin Chapter
2421 N Mayfair Rd., Ste.212
Wauwatosa, WI 53226
Ph: (414)771-9400
Fax: (414)771-9503
E-mail: gehrigse@execpc.com
URL: http://www.se-wis-als.org
Contact: Cindy Gray, Office Mgr.
Regional. Affiliated With: Amyotrophic Lateral Sclerosis Association.

20067 ■ American Diabetes Association (ADA)
2323 N Mayfair Rd., Ste.502
Wauwatosa, WI 53226
Ph: (414)778-5500
Fax: (414)778-5511
Free: (888)342-2383
URL: National Affiliate–www.diabetes.org
Local.

20068 ■ American Legion, Craig-Schlosser Post 31
PO Box 26096
Wauwatosa, WI 53226
Ph: (608)745-1090
Fax: (608)745-0179
URL: National Affiliate–www.legion.org
Local. Affiliated With: American Legion.

20069 ■ American Legion, Harley-Davidson Post 400
11700 W Capitol Dr.
Wauwatosa, WI 53222
Ph: (608)745-1090
Fax: (608)745-0179
URL: National Affiliate–www.legion.org
Local. Affiliated With: American Legion.

20070 ■ APICS, The Association for Operations Management - Milwaukee Chapter
PO Box 26001
Wauwatosa, WI 53226-0001
Ph: (414)299-0945 (262)544-4811
E-mail: apicsmilw@yahoo.com
URL: http://www.apicsmilw.org
Contact: John Cotter, Pres.
Local. Provides information and services in production and inventory management and related areas to enable members, enterprises and individuals to add value to their business performance. **Affiliated With:** APICS - The Association for Operations Management.

20071 ■ Brain Injury Association of Wisconsin (BIAW)
2900 N 117th St., Ste.100
Wauwatosa, WI 53222
Ph: (414)778-4144
Fax: (414)778-0276
Free: (800)882-9282
E-mail: biaw@execpc.com
URL: http://www.biaw.org
Contact: Caroline Feller MS, Exec.Dir.
Founded: 1980. **Membership Dues:** individual, $35 (annual) • professional, $50 (annual) • patron, $100 (annual) • corporate, $200 (annual) • benefactor, $500 (annual) • founder, $1,000 (annual). **State**. Dedicated to serving over 50,000 individuals with brain injury and their families living in Wisconsin. **Libraries: Type:** open to the public. **Holdings:** articles, books, periodicals, video recordings. **Subjects:** brain injury, pediatric brain injury, prevention, safety tips, sports and concussion, information on coma, legal issues, family adjustment. **Affiliated With:** Brain Injury Association of America.

20072 ■ Citizens for a Scenic Wisconsin
7525 Oakhill Ave.
Wauwatosa, WI 53213
Ph: (414)258-8604
Fax: (414)258-9672
E-mail: mail@scenicwisconsin.org
URL: http://www.scenicwisconsin.org
Contact: Vernie Smith, Pres.
Founded: 2000. **Members:** 225. **Membership Dues:** supporting, $25 (annual) • regular, $10 (annual) • scenic leader, organization, corporation, $50 (annual) • scenic steward, $100 (annual) • scenic conservationist, $250 (annual) • scenic investor, $500 (annual) • scenic visionary, $1,000 (annual). **Staff:** 1. **State Groups:** 1. **State**. Individuals in the state of Wisconsin interested in the preservation of scenery and character of the state's cities and towns.

20073 ■ East Town Business and Merchant's Association
c/o Lisa Fohey, Pres.
7251 W N Ave., Ste.6
Wauwatosa, WI 53213-1851
Ph: (414)698-9846
URL: National Affiliate–www.wedc.net
Contact: Lisa Fohey, Pres.
Local.

20074 ■ Great Dane Club of Milwaukee (GDCM)
c/o Matt Mueller, Board Member
8356 Currie Ave.
Wauwatosa, WI 53213
Ph: (414)479-7134
E-mail: dmue721308@aol.com
URL: http://www.greatdaneclubmilwaukee.com
Contact: Matt Mueller, Board Member
Local.

20075 ■ Huntington's Disease Society of American, Wisconsin Chapter
c/o Sean Lanphier, Pres.
2041 N 107th St.
Wauwatosa, WI 53226
Ph: (414)257-9499
Free: (877)330-2699
E-mail: slanphier@mzmilw.com
URL: http://www.hdsa-wi.org
Contact: Sean Lanpier, Pres.
State. Dedicated to caring for those suffering from Huntington's disease and their families; provides public and professional education about Huntington's disease and supports research through the national organization. **Affiliated With:** Huntington's Disease Society of America.

20076 ■ Juvenile Diabetes Research Foundation, Southeastern Wisconsin Chapter
2825 N Mayfair Rd., Ste.9
Wauwatosa, WI 53222
Ph: (414)453-4673
Fax: (414)453-4919
E-mail: southeastwi@jdrf.org
URL: National Affiliate–www.jdrf.org
Contact: Wendy Hanisch, Exec.Dir.
Local. Supports diabetes research. Aims to find a cure for diabetes and its complications through the support of research. **Affiliated With:** Juvenile Diabetes Research Foundation International.

20077 ■ Milwaukee Marauders
c/o Matt Kufahl
2569 N 74th St.
Wauwatosa, WI 53213
Ph: (414)559-0434
E-mail: info@milwaukeemarauders.com
URL: http://www.milwaukeemarauders.com
Founded: 2000. **Local**.

20078 ■ Milwaukee/National Association of the Remodeling Industry Home Improvement Council
11815 W Dearbourn Ave.
Wauwatosa, WI 53226
Ph: (414)771-4071
Fax: (414)771-4077
E-mail: info@milwaukeenari.com
URL: http://www.milwaukeenari.com
Contact: Mary Fox-Hagner, Exec.Dir.
Founded: 1961. **Local**. **Affiliated With:** National Association of the Remodeling Industry.

20079 ■ Nightingale Alliance
c/o Brendan Doherty
PO Box 26674
Wauwatosa, WI 53226-0674
URL: http://www.nightingalealliance.org
Local.

20080 ■ Spina Bifida Association of Wisconsin, Inc. (SBAWI)
830 N 109th St., Ste.6
Wauwatosa, WI 53226
Ph: (414)607-9061
Fax: (414)607-9602
E-mail: sbawi@sbawi.org
URL: http://www.sbawi.org
Contact: Mary Person RN, Pres.
Founded: 1984. **Members:** 130. **Membership Dues:** family or individual, $25 (annual) • professional, $40 (annual). **Staff:** 1. **Regional Groups:** 3. **State Groups:** 1. **Local Groups:** 1. **State**. Families and professionals. Provides education, social, and emotional support. **Libraries: Type:** reference. **Holdings:** articles, books. **Subjects:** Spina Bifida and related materials. **Telecommunication Services:** electronic mail, sbawi_website@hotmail.com. **Affiliated With:** Spina Bifida Association of America. **Publications:** *SB Wins, Spina Bifida - WI Information, Network and Support*, bimonthly. Newsletter. Contains medical and educational information, sports, and family information. **Price:** free. **Circulation:** 500. **Conventions/Meetings:** annual convention (exhibits) • quarterly meeting.

20081 ■ Wauwatosa Curling Club (WCC)
7300 Chestnut St.
Wauwatosa, WI 53213
Ph: (414)453-2875
E-mail: info@curltosa.com
URL: http://www.curltosa.com
Contact: Rebecca Nguyen, Pres.
Local. **Affiliated With:** United States Curling Association.

20082 ■ Wauwatosa Lions Club
7336 St. James St.
Wauwatosa, WI 53213
Ph: (414)257-9582
E-mail: pamela.j.tatarowicz@jci.com
URL: http://www.1dynamicplace.com/Lions/default.htm
Contact: Pam Tatarowicz, Pres.
Local. **Affiliated With:** Lions Clubs International.

20083 ■ Wauwatosa Neighborhood Watch Steering Committee
c/o Dale Weiss
1700 N. 116th St.
Wauwatosa, WI 53226-3004
Local.

20084 ■ Wauwatosa West PTA
11400 W Ctr. St.
Wauwatosa, WI 53222
Ph: (414)773-3000
URL: http://familyeducation.com/WI/Wauwatosa_West_PTA1
Local. Parents, teachers, students, and others interested in uniting the forces of home, school, and community. Promotes the welfare of children and youth.

20085 ■ Wauwatosa Woman's Club
1626 Wauwatosa Ave.
Wauwatosa, WI 53213
Ph: (414)257-9935 (414)475-1836
URL: http://www.geocities.com/wwcrentals
Contact: Janet Chandler, Pres.
Founded: 1894. **Members:** 125. **Membership Dues:** woman, $55 (annual). **Staff:** 1. **Budget:** $46,100. **Local**. Provides social, educational and philanthropic opportunities for its members and the community. **Awards: Type:** scholarship. **Recipient:** to high school seniors.

20086 ■ West Suburban Chamber of Commerce (WSCC)
2421 N Mayfair Rd., Ste.17
Wauwatosa, WI 53226
Ph: (414)453-2330
Fax: (414)453-2336
E-mail: info@westsuburbanchamber.com
URL: http://www.westsuburbanchamber.com
Contact: Sharon Scaccia, Exec.Dir.
Members: 650. **Local**. Promotes business and community development in Wauwatosa, WI. **Committees:** Ambassador Club; Annual Golf Outing; Business and Education; Civic Appreciation Awards; Community Relations; Government Relations and Business Advocacy; Marketing and Communication; Tourism and Visitors. **Publications:** *Chamber Review*, monthly. Newsletter. Contains activities, events, and news of special interests. Alternate Formats: online • *Suburban Visitor Guide*. Booklet. Includes information about places to visit, stay, and dine. • Membership Directory. Alternate Formats: online.

20087 ■ Wisconsin Chapter of American Society of Plumbing Engineers
PO Box 13362
Wauwatosa, WI 53213-0362
Ph: (414)778-1700
Fax: (414)778-2360
E-mail: dherbert@ringdu.com
URL: http://www.aspewisconsin.com/index.htm
Contact: David E. Herbert CPD, Pres.
State. Represents the interests of individuals dedicated to the advancement of the science of plumbing engineering. Seeks to resolve professional problems in plumbing engineering. Advocates greater cooperation among members and plumbing officials, contractors, laborers and the public. **Affiliated With:** American Society of Plumbing Engineers.

20088 ■ Wisconsin Chapter of RESOLVE
PO Box 13842
Wauwatosa, WI 53213-0842
Ph: (262)521-4590
E-mail: info@resolvewi.org
URL: http://www.resolvewi.org
Contact: Julie Givens, Pres.
Membership Dues: basic, $55 (annual) • contributing, $65 (annual) • supporting, $75 (annual) • circle of friend, $100 (annual) • professional, $150 (annual). **State**. Provides support and information to people experiencing infertility and to increase awareness and access to treatment and resolution options, as well as to increase public support of infertility issues through public education an advocacy. Services include Journey to Resolution, a chapter newsletter, monthly educational and support group meetings in Milwaukee and Madison, a lending library, telephone HelpLine, and access to a Physician Referral List. **Affiliated With:** Resolve, The National Infertility Association.

20089 ■ Wisconsin Funeral Directors Association (WFDA)
c/o Mark Paget, Exec.Dir.
2300 N Mayfair Rd., Ste.595
Wauwatosa, WI 53226-1508
Ph: (414)453-3060
Fax: (414)453-9860
Free: (800)648-5580
E-mail: info@wfda.org
URL: http://www.wfda.org
Contact: Mark S. Paget, Exec.Dir.
Founded: 1881. **State**. Members adhere to a code of ethics to insure that the highest standards of professionalism are maintained. Dedicated to enhancing the funeral service profession and serving the public interest. **Affiliated With:** National Funeral Directors Association.

20090 ■ Wisconsin Soaring Society
c/o Pete Gaveras
1244 N 86th St.
Wauwatosa, WI 53226
Ph: (414)476-9390
E-mail: lavajava@aol.com
URL: http://www.wss.org
Contact: Pete Gaveras, Pres.
State. **Affiliated With:** Soaring Society of America.

Wauzeka

20091 ■ American Legion, Seely-Onstine Post 458
503 E Main St.
Wauzeka, WI 53826

Ph: (608)745-1090
Fax: (608)745-0179
URL: National Affiliate–www.legion.org
Local. Affiliated With: American Legion.

20092 ■ Wauzeka Lions Club
c/o Karen Burgis, Pres.
1201 Sandy Canyon Dr.
Wauzeka, WI 53826
Ph: (608)875-6008
URL: http://www.md27d2.org
Contact: Karen Burgis, Pres.
Local. Affiliated With: Lions Clubs International.

Webb Lake

20093 ■ American Legion, Webb Lake A and H Post 403
29836 Long Lake Rd.
Webb Lake, WI 54830
Ph: (608)745-1090
Fax: (608)745-0179
URL: National Affiliate–www.legion.org
Local. Affiliated With: American Legion.

20094 ■ Turf and Tundra Trails Association
c/o Harry Patneaude, Treas.
29836 Long Lake Rd.
Webb Lake, WI 54830-9580
Ph: (715)259-7775 (715)259-4361
Fax: (715)259-7776
Contact: Carl Hansen, Pres.
Local Groups: 1. **Local. Awards: Frequency:** annual. **Type:** recognition. **Conventions/Meetings:** meeting - 7/year.

Webster

20095 ■ American Legion, Wisconsin Post 96
c/o Otis Taylor
PO Box 148
Webster, WI 54893
Ph: (608)745-1090
Fax: (608)745-0179
URL: National Affiliate–www.legion.org
Contact: Otis Taylor, Contact
Local. Affiliated With: American Legion.

20096 ■ Webster Area Chamber of Commerce
PO Box 48
Webster, WI 54893
Ph: (715)349-7411 (715)866-4211
Contact: Angie Gibbs, Pres.
Local.

West Allis

20097 ■ American Legion, Bell Telephone Post 427
2169 S 64th St.
West Allis, WI 53219
Ph: (608)745-1090
Fax: (608)745-0179
URL: National Affiliate–www.legion.org
Local. Affiliated With: American Legion.

20098 ■ American Legion, Tanner-Paull Post 120
6922 W Orchard St.
West Allis, WI 53214
Ph: (608)745-1090
Fax: (608)745-0179
URL: National Affiliate–www.legion.org
Local. Affiliated With: American Legion.

20099 ■ Arthritis Foundation, Wisconsin Chapter
1650 S 108th St.
West Allis, WI 53214
Ph: (414)321-3933
Fax: (414)321-0365
Free: (800)242-9945
E-mail: info.wi@arthritis.org
URL: http://www.arthritis.org/Communities/Chapters/Chapter.asp?chapid=57
Contact: Maureen Blattner, Contact
Founded: 1948. **Membership Dues:** individual/business, $20 (annual). **Staff:** 21. **Budget:** $2,000,000. **Languages:** English, Spanish. **For-Profit. State.** Seeks to: discover the cause and improve the methods for the treatment and prevention of arthritis and other rheumatic diseases; increase the number of scientists investigating rheumatic diseases; provide training in rheumatic diseases for more doctors; extend knowledge of arthritis and other rheumatic diseases to the lay public, emphasizing the socioeconomic as well as medical aspects of these diseases. **Libraries: Type:** reference. **Holdings:** 300; articles, books, periodicals, video recordings. **Subjects:** treatments, medical information, disease management, general education on specific types of arthritis. **Awards:** Corporate Recognition. **Frequency:** annual. **Type:** recognition. **Recipient:** for service • Research Mentor. **Frequency:** annual. **Type:** scholarship. **Recipient:** for service • Volunteer Recognition. **Frequency:** annual. **Type:** recognition. **Recipient:** for service. **Affiliated With:** Arthritis Foundation; National Arthritis Foundation; Public Relations Society of America, Alabama; Public Relations Society of America, Alaska; Public Relations Society of America, Arkansas; Public Relations Society of America, California Capital Chapter; Public Relations Society of America, California Inland Empire; Public Relations Society of America, Central California Chapter; Public Relations Society of America, Los Angeles; Public Relations Society of America, Memphis Chapter; Public Relations Society of America, Miami Chapter; Public Relations Society of America, Orlando Regional Chapter; Public Relations Society of America, Phoenix Chapter; Public Relations Society of America, Southern Arizona; Public Relations Society of America, Sunshine District; Public Relations Society of America, West Virginia Chapter. **Publications:** *Educational Resource*, annual. Magazine. **Circulation:** 15,000. **Conventions/Meetings:** annual meeting, educational forum and awards.

20100 ■ Crohn's and Colitis Foundation of America, Wisconsin Chapter
1126 S 70th St., Ste.S210A
West Allis, WI 53214
Ph: (414)475-5520
Fax: (414)475-5502
Free: (877)586-5588
E-mail: wisconsin@ccfa.org
URL: National Affiliate–www.ccfa.org
Contact: Jan Lenz, Exec.Dir.
State. Works to cure and prevent Crohn's disease and ulcerative colitis through research, and to improve the quality of life of children and adults affected by these digestive diseases through education and support. **Affiliated With:** Crohn's and Colitis Foundation of America.

20101 ■ Greater Milwaukee Dental Association
6737 W Washington St., Ste.2360
West Allis, WI 53214
Ph: (414)755-4196
Fax: (414)276-8431
E-mail: gmda@execpc.com
URL: National Affiliate–www.ada.org
Contact: Ms. Nanci Dabareiner, Exec.Dir.
Local. Represents professional association of dentists committed to the public's oral health, ethics, science and professional advancement. Promotes the art and science of dentistry through advocacy, education, research and the development of standards. **Affiliated With:** American Dental Association; Wisconsin Dental Association.

20102 ■ March of Dimes of Southeastern Wisconsin
1126 S 70th St., Ste.S221A
West Allis, WI 53214-3124
Ph: (414)778-3500
Fax: (414)778-3503
E-mail: wi657@marchofdimes.com
URL: http://www.marchofdimes.com/wisconsin
Contact: Karon Szyszkiewicz, Office Mgr.
Local. Helps to improve the health of babies by preventing birth defects, premature birth and infant mortality.

20103 ■ Milwaukee County REACT
7902 W Natl. Ave., Apt.2
West Allis, WI 53214-4559
Ph: (414)476-9333
E-mail: 4712@wireact.org
URL: http://www.reactintl.org/teaminfo/usa_teams/teams-uswi.htm
Local. Trained communication experts and professional volunteers. Provides volunteer public service and emergency communications through the use of radios (Citizen Band, General Mobile Radio Service, UHF and HAM). Coordinates with radio industries and government on safety communication matters and supports charitable activities and community organizations.

20104 ■ Southeastern Wisconsin Professional Photographers Association (SEWPPA)
c/o Karen Verley
709 S 100 St.
West Allis, WI 53214
Ph: (414)771-9779
E-mail: president@sewppa.org
URL: http://www.sewppa.org
Contact: Karen Verley, Pres.
Local. Professional society of portrait, wedding, commercial, and industrial, and specialized photographers. **Affiliated With:** Professional Photographers of America.

20105 ■ University of Oklahoma Association - OU Club of Wisconsin
c/o Christopher Stockdale
1435 S 73rd St.
West Allis, WI 53214
E-mail: president@ouclubofwisconsin.org
URL: National Affiliate–alumni.ou.edu
Contact: Christopher Stockdale, Contact
State. Affiliated With: Oklahoma University Alumni Association.

20106 ■ West Allis/West Milwaukee Chamber of Commerce (WACC)
7149 W Greenfield Ave.
West Allis, WI 53214
Ph: (414)302-9901
Fax: (414)302-9918
E-mail: sue@westallis.org
URL: http://westallis.org
Contact: Jim Mejchar, Exec.Dir.
Founded: 1958. **Members:** 425. **Staff:** 2. **Local.** Promotes business and community development in West Allis and West Milwaukee. **Formerly:** (2004) West Allis Chamber of Commerce. **Publications:** *The Chamber Connection*, monthly. Newsletter • Directory, annual. **Conventions/Meetings:** annual meeting.

20107 ■ Wisconsin Burglar and Fire Alarm Association
c/o Marsha Kopan, Exec.Dir.
PO Box 14188
West Allis, WI 53214
Ph: (414)276-9232
Fax: (414)453-0030
Free: (877)230-5110
E-mail: information@wbfaa.org
URL: http://www.wbfaa.org
State. Affiliated With: National Burglar and Fire Alarm Association.

20108 ■ Wisconsin Chapter of the Myasthenia Gravis Foundation
2474 S 96th St.
West Allis, WI 53227-2204
Ph: (262)938-9800
E-mail: wiscmg@yahoo.com
URL: http://www.myasthenia.org/chapters/Wisconsin
Contact: Kristine Laufer, Chair

Founded: 1947. **Members:** 1,400. **Membership Dues:** $15 (annual). **Local**. Myasthenia gravis patients and their families and friends; health care professionals; interested individuals. Provides support groups and medical discounts. Conducts community education. Holds annual fundraising event. **Affiliated With:** Myasthenia Gravis Foundation of America. **Publications:** Newsletter, quarterly. **Conventions/Meetings:** annual meeting.

20109 ■ Wisconsin Healthy Mothers, Healthy Babies Coalition
March of Dimes
1126 S 70th St., Ste.S221A
West Allis, WI 53214-3151
Ph: (414)778-3500
Fax: (414)778-3503
E-mail: mcrist@marchofdimes.com
URL: http://www.marchofdimes.com
Contact: Ms. Marie Crist, Contact

State. Improves the health and safety of mothers, babies and families through education and collaborative partnerships of public and private organizations. **Affiliated With:** National Healthy Mothers, Healthy Babies Coalition.

20110 ■ Wisconsin Paralyzed Veterans of America
c/o Donald R. Fell, Exec.Dir.
2311 S 108th St.
West Allis, WI 53227
Ph: (414)328-8910
Fax: (414)328-8948
E-mail: info@wisconsinpva.org
URL: http://www.wisconsinpva.org
Contact: Donald R. Fell, Exec.Dir.

Founded: 1980. **Staff:** 3. **Budget:** $1,034,066. **State**. Dedicated solely for the benefit and representation of individuals with spinal cord injury or disease. **Libraries: Type:** open to the public; reference; by appointment only. **Holdings:** 30; books, periodicals. **Subjects:** spinal cord injuries, MS, sports and recreation for those with spinal cord injuries. **Awards:** Kathy Welter Nursing Scholarship. **Frequency:** annual. **Type:** scholarship. **Recipient:** for continuing education for nursing and medical staff of Spinal Cord Injury • Occupational Therapist Scholarship. **Frequency:** annual. **Type:** scholarship. **Recipient:** for continuing education for nursing and medical staff of Spinal Cord Injury • Pat Wiseman Award. **Frequency:** annual. **Type:** recognition. **Recipient:** for service to WPVA's members • Physical Therapy Scholarship. **Frequency:** annual. **Type:** scholarship. **Recipient:** for continuing education for nursing and medical staff of Spinal Cord Injury • President's Award. **Frequency:** annual. **Type:** recognition. **Recipient:** for service to WPVA's members • Ron Falkner Award. **Frequency:** annual. **Type:** recognition. **Recipient:** for service to WPVA's members • Schmidt Sportsman of the Year. **Frequency:** annual. **Type:** recognition. **Recipient:** for service to WPVA's members • Virginia Bea Root Nursing Scholarship. **Frequency:** annual. **Type:** scholarship. **Recipient:** for continuing education for nursing and medical staff of Spinal Cord Injury. **Computer Services:** database, membership database for PVA. **Affiliated With:** Paralyzed Veterans of America. **Formerly:** (2000) Paralyzed Veterans of America, Wisconsin Chapter. **Publications:** *Dairyland News*, MON. Newsletter. **Price:** $25.00. **Circulation:** 20,000 • *Paraplegic News*, monthly. Magazine. **Price:** $25. 00. **Circulation:** 20,000 • *Sports & Spokes*, monthly. Magazine. **Conventions/Meetings:** monthly board meeting • monthly Committee Meeting • monthly Membership Meeting.

20111 ■ Wisconsin Scottish
PO Box 270292
West Allis, WI 53227
Ph: (414)774-2044
Fax: (414)774-2044
E-mail: info@wisconsinscottish.org
URL: http://www.wisconsinscottish.org
State.

20112 ■ Wisconsin Youth Soccer Association (WYSA)
10708 W Hayes Ave.
West Allis, WI 53227
Ph: (414)545-7227
Fax: (414)545-7249
Free: (800)937-7778
E-mail: kross@wiyouthsoccer.com
URL: http://www.wiyouthsoccer.com
Contact: Kelly Ross, Exec.Dir.

Founded: 1914. **Members:** 56,000. **Staff:** 3. **Budget:** $800,000. **Regional Groups:** 1. **State**. Seeks to develop and promote the game of soccer for young people. Conducts tournaments. **Awards:** Coach of the Year. **Frequency:** annual. **Type:** scholarship • Parent of the Year. **Frequency:** annual. **Type:** scholarship • Young Referee. **Frequency:** annual. **Type:** scholarship. **Affiliated With:** United States Youth Soccer Association. **Publications:** *Wisconsin Soccer Post*, quarterly. Newspaper. **Price:** $7.95/ year; $2.00/issue. **Circulation:** 48,000. **Advertising:** accepted. Alternate Formats: CD-ROM; diskette. **Conventions/Meetings:** annual meeting (exhibits) - always 1st weekend of March.

20113 ■ Women in the Wind, Milwaukee Area
c/o Judy Schiel
PO Box 270512
West Allis, WI 53227
E-mail: witw@womeninthewind-milwaukee.org
URL: http://www.womeninthewind-milwaukee.org
Contact: Judy Schiel, Contact

Local. **Affiliated With:** Women in the Wind.

West Bend

20114 ■ American Sewing Guild, Milwaukee Chapter
c/o Jan Loomis
4920 Birchwood Trail
West Bend, WI 53095
Ph: (262)675-6109
E-mail: justjan-1@charter.net
URL: http://www.geocities.com/asgmilw
Contact: Jan Loomis, Contact

Local. **Affiliated With:** American Sewing Guild.

20115 ■ American Society of Women Accountants, Milwaukee No. 041
c/o Catherine Yekenevicz, CPA, Pres.
Benevolent Corp. Cedar Community
2330 Chestnut St., Apt. 35
West Bend, WI 53095-2989
Ph: (262)306-2100 (262)335-3304
Fax: (262)306-2126
E-mail: president@aswamilwaukee.org
URL: http://www.aswamilwaukee.org
Contact: Catherine Yekenevicz CPA, Pres.

Local. **Affiliated With:** American Society of Women Accountants.

20116 ■ Badger Orienteering Club (BGR)
c/o Catherine Ann Yekenevicz
2330 Chestnut St., No. 35
West Bend, WI 53095
Ph: (262)335-3304
E-mail: kevin@chorus.net
URL: http://userpages.chorus.net/kevin
Contact: Catherine Ann Yekenevicz, Contact

Local. **Affiliated With:** United States Orienteering Federation.

20117 ■ Council on Alcohol and Other Drug Abuse of Washington County
1625 E Washington St., No. 300
West Bend, WI 53095-2617
Ph: (262)335-6888
Fax: (262)335-6899
E-mail: info@councilonaoda.org
Contact: Mary Simon, Contact

Founded: 1972. **Members:** 15. **Budget:** $425,000. **Local**. Works for the prevention and treatment of alcoholism and other drug dependence through programs of public education, information, and public policy advocacy. **Libraries: Type:** reference. **Holdings:** books, video recordings. **Subjects:** alcohol and other drugs. **Affiliated With:** National Council on Alcoholism and Drug Dependence.

20118 ■ Downtown West Bend Association
128 S Sixth Ave., Ste.1
West Bend, WI 53095
Ph: (262)338-3909
Fax: (262)338-0635
E-mail: theresa@downtownwestbend.com
URL: http://www.downtownwestbend.com
Contact: Theresa Fuerbringer, Exec.Dir.
Local.

20119 ■ Friends of Burlington Northern Railroad (FOBNR)
PO Box 271
West Bend, WI 53095-0271
E-mail: info@fobnr.org
URL: http://www.fobnr.org
Contact: Dave Poplawski, Pres.

Founded: 1993. **Members:** 300. **Membership Dues:** regular, $25 (annual) • sustaining, $50 (annual) • youth (16 and under), $10 (annual). **Budget:** $5,000. **Regional**. Seeks to preserve and share the information about the history of the Burlington Northern Railroad and the current operations of the Burlington Northern and Santa Fe Railway. **Publications:** *The BN Expeditor*, quarterly. Newsletter. **Conventions/ Meetings:** annual convention, with tours, banquets, and presentations.

20120 ■ Kettle Moraine Figure Skating Club (KMFSC)
PO Box 314
West Bend, WI 53095
Ph: (262)335-0383
E-mail: info@kettlemorainefsc.org
URL: http://www.kettlemorainefsc.org
Contact: Sandy Knutson, Contact

Local. Provides programs to encourage participation and achievement in the sport of figure skating on ice. Defines and maintains uniform standards of skating proficiency. Organizes and sponsors competitions and exhibitions for the purpose of stimulating interest in figure skating. **Affiliated With:** United States Figure Skating Association.

20121 ■ Korean War Veterans Association, Cpl. Richard A. Bell Chapter
c/o Harry C. Waldeck
2205 Sylvan Way, No. 1
West Bend, WI 53095-5244
Ph: (262)338-3750
URL: National Affiliate–www.kwva.org
Contact: Harry C. Waldeck, Contact

Local. **Affiliated With:** Korean War Veterans Association.

20122 ■ Lac Lawrann Conservancy of West Bend, WI
c/o Kate Peterman
W Bend Park Sys.
1115 S Main St.
West Bend, WI 53095
Ph: (262)335-5085
Fax: (262)335-5092
E-mail: laclawrann@ci.west-bend.wi.us
Contact: Kate Peterman, Naturalist

Founded: 1979. **Membership Dues:** friend of LLC, $25. **Staff:** 1. **Budget:** $6,000. **Local Groups:** 1. **Local**. Seeks to preserve, enhance, and experience the natural world of Lac Lawrann Conservancy. **Libraries: Type:** open to the public. **Holdings:** 300; audio recordings, books, periodicals, video recordings. **Subjects:** nature, education. **Also Known As:** (2004) Friends of Lac Lawrann Conservancy. **Publications:** *Lac Lawrann Conservancy News Among Friends*, quarterly. Newsletter. **Price:** $25.00. **Circulation:** 350.

20123 ■ Mothers Against Drunk Driving, Washington County
1607 Williams Ct.
West Bend, WI 53090
Ph: (262)338-0418
URL: National Affiliate–www.madd.org
Local. Victims of drunk driving crashes; concerned citizens. Encourages citizen participation in working towards reform of the drunk driving problem and the prevention of underage drinking. Acts as the voice of victims of drunk driving crashes by speaking on their behalf to communities, businesses, and educational groups. **Affiliated With:** Mothers Against Drunk Driving.

20124 ■ National Alliance for the Mentally Ill - Washington County
c/o Debra Reak, Pres.
PO Box 1074
West Bend, WI 53095
Ph: (262)338-2393
URL: http://www.namiwisconsin.org/library/directory
Contact: Debra Reak, Pres.
Local. Strives to improve the quality of life of children and adults with severe mental illness through support, education, research and advocacy. **Affiliated With:** National Alliance for the Mentally Ill.

20125 ■ Paper, Allied-Industrial, Chemical and Energy Workers International Union, AFL-CIO, CLC - Local Union 369
1650 Curtis Ln.
West Bend, WI 53090
E-mail: kenai@pace8369.org
URL: http://www.pace8369.org/kenai
Contact: Allen Wallis, Pres.
Members: 208. **Regional**. **Affiliated With:** Pace International Union.

20126 ■ Parents Anonymous of Washington County, Wisconsin
139 N Main St., Ste.111
West Bend, WI 53095
Ph: (262)338-1661
Fax: (262)338-7761
E-mail: jwargolet@excel.net
URL: http://www.youthandfamilyproject.org
Contact: Jill Wargolet, Program Dir.
Local.

20127 ■ Phi Theta Kappa, Chi Chi Chapter - University of Wisconsin-Washington
c/o Daniel Cibrario, Advisor
Washington County
400 Univ. Dr.
West Bend, WI 53095
Ph: (262)335-5212
E-mail: dcibrari@uwc.edu
URL: http://www.ptk.org/directories/chapters/WI/346-1.htm
Contact: Daniel Cibrario, Advisor
Local.

20128 ■ Town and Country Resource Conservation and Development Council
333 E Washington St., Ste.3200
West Bend, WI 53095
Ph: (262)335-4855
Fax: (262)335-4171
E-mail: diane.georgetta@wi.usda.gov
URL: http://www.townandcountryrcd.org
Contact: Diane Georgetta, Coor.
Local. **Affiliated With:** National Association of Resource Conservation and Development Councils.

20129 ■ Washington County Convention and Visitors Bureau
3000 Hwy. PV
West Bend, WI 53095
Ph: (262)677-5069
Fax: (262)677-5077
Free: (888)974-8687
E-mail: info@visitwashingtoncounty.com
URL: http://www.visitwashingtoncounty.com
Contact: Linda Naumann, Contact
Founded: 2000. **Members:** 45. **Staff:** 2. **Regional Groups:** 1. **Local**. Promotes Washington County, WI as a destination for visitors and tourism. **Publications:** *Washington County Visitors Guide*, annual. Contains local destinations such as restaurants, hotels, attractions, and events. **Price:** free. **Advertising:** accepted.

20130 ■ West Bend Area Chamber of Commerce (WBACC)
735 S Main St.
West Bend, WI 53095
Ph: (262)338-2666
Fax: (262)338-1771
Free: (888)338-8666
E-mail: info@wbachamber.org
URL: http://www.wbchamber.org
Contact: Kim Swisher, Exec.VP
Founded: 1970. **Members:** 575. **Membership Dues:** general business (based on number of full time employees), $200-$2,127 (annual) • affiliate, $100 (annual). **Local**. Businesses and individuals organized to promote economic and community development in the West Bend, WI area. **Committees:** Ambassadors; Executive and Personnel; Golf Outing; Home Improvement Exposition; Smart Community; Tourism. **Programs:** Leadership Greater West Bend. **Publications:** *Comment*, monthly. Newsletter.

20131 ■ West Bend Noon Kiwanis Club (Wisconsin)
c/o Paul Albinger, Sec.
246 S 5th Ave.
West Bend, WI 53095
Ph: (262)334-9163
E-mail: bikeko@yahoo.com
URL: http://kc_westbendnoon.tripod.com
Contact: Doug Hall, Pres.
Local.

20132 ■ Wisconsin Dressage and Combined Training Association (WDCTA)
c/o Nicole Trapp
1145 Paradise Dr.
West Bend, WI 53095
Ph: (920)960-6930
E-mail: touchstn@chorus.net
URL: http://www.wdcta.org
Contact: Caryn Vesperman, Pres.
State. **Affiliated With:** United States Dressage Federation.

20133 ■ Wisconsin Jaguars
c/o Deb Korneli
6236 Gilbert Cir.
West Bend, WI 53095
Ph: (262)629-5314 (262)338-6312
Fax: (262)338-1158
E-mail: korneli@nconnect.net
URL: http://www.wisconsinjaguars.org
Contact: Mike Korneli, VP
State. **Affiliated With:** Jaguar Clubs of North America.

West Milwaukee

20134 ■ MEL - Milwaukee Evolution League
c/o Eric Hildeman, Pres.
PO Box 341121
West Milwaukee, WI 53219
Ph: (414)217-2876
E-mail: carlsaganjr@aol.com
URL: http://members.aol.com/GoEvolution
Contact: Eric Hildeman, Founder
Local. Works to counter the activities of creationist organizations in Milwaukee and all Southeastern Wisconsin. Hosts meetings, lectures, outings, and counter-protests, networks via the Internet. **Affiliated With:** American Humanist Association.

West Salem

20135 ■ American Legion, Berg-Hemker-Olson Post 51
148 S Leonard St.
West Salem, WI 54669
Ph: (608)745-1090
Fax: (608)745-0179
URL: National Affiliate–www.legion.org
Local. **Affiliated With:** American Legion.

20136 ■ Barre-Coed Lions Club
c/o Mark Gaethke, Pres.
N3305 County Hwy. M
West Salem, WI 54669
Ph: (608)786-2067
URL: http://www.md27d2.org
Contact: Mark Gaethke, Pres.
Local. **Affiliated With:** Lions Clubs International.

20137 ■ Institute of Management Accountants, LaCrosse-Winona Chapter
c/o Mary T. Hirsch-Justice, Pres.
PO Box 883
West Salem, WI 54669-0883
Ph: (608)786-2366 (608)781-8784
Fax: (608)786-2944
E-mail: maryh@housingdatasystems.com
URL: http://www.ima-northernlights.imanet.org
Contact: Mary T. Hirsch-Justice, Pres.
Local. Promotes professional and ethical standards. Equips members and students with knowledge and training required for the accounting profession. **Affiliated With:** Institute of Management Accountants.

20138 ■ Sparta Area Figure Skating Club
N5152 Shady Birch Ln.
West Salem, WI 54669
E-mail: staberg92@aol.com
URL: National Affiliate–www.usfigureskating.org
Contact: Jane Egan Staberg, Contact
Local. Provides programs to encourage participation and achievement in the sport of figure skating on ice. Defines and maintains uniform standards of skating proficiency. Organizes and sponsors competitions and exhibitions for the purpose of stimulating interest in figure skating. **Affiliated With:** United States Figure Skating Association.

20139 ■ West Salem Lions Club
c/o Darrel Talcott, Pres.
141 W Hamlin St.
West Salem, WI 54669
Ph: (608)786-4362
E-mail: dtalcott@execpc.com
URL: http://www.md27d2.org
Contact: Darrel Talcott, Pres.
Local. **Affiliated With:** Lions Clubs International.

20140 ■ Wisconsin Land Title Association (WLTA)
PO Box 873
West Salem, WI 54669
Ph: (608)786-2336
Fax: (608)786-2356
Free: (800)589-WLTA
E-mail: kgilster@wlta.org
URL: http://www.wlta.org
Contact: Karen Gilster, Exec.Dir.
State. Represents the interests of abstracters, title insurance companies and attorneys specializing in real property law. Improves the skills and knowledge of providers in real property transactions.

Westby

20141 ■ American Legion, Syverson-Funk Post 155
105 W State St.
Westby, WI 54667
Ph: (608)745-1090
Fax: (608)745-0179
URL: National Affiliate–www.legion.org
Local. Affiliated With: American Legion.

20142 ■ Christian Camp and Conference Association, Wisconsin
c/o Dennis Siler, Pres.-Elect
Living Waters Bible Camp
E8932 Rio Ave.
Westby, WI 54667
Ph: (608)634-4373
URL: National Affiliate–www.ccca-us.org
Contact: Dennis Siler, Pres.-Elect
State. Affiliated With: Christian Camping International/U.S.A.

20143 ■ Sons of Norway, Solvang Lodge 5-457
c/o Bertha M. Johnson, Sec.
S1314 Hwy. 27 N
Westby, WI 54667-9723
Ph: (608)634-3156
E-mail: nutriwis@mwt.net
URL: National Affiliate–www.sofn.com
Contact: Bertha M. Johnson, Sec.
Local. Affiliated With: Sons of Norway.

20144 ■ Westby Lions Club
c/o Tom Iverson, Sec.
S1605A State Hwy. 27
Westby, WI 54667
Ph: (608)634-3583
E-mail: tiverson@westbycu.org
URL: http://www.md27d2.org
Contact: Tom Iverson, Sec.
Local. Affiliated With: Lions Clubs International.

Westfield

20145 ■ American Legion, Metz-Mosher Post 244
PO Box 74
Westfield, WI 53964
Ph: (608)745-1090
Fax: (608)745-0179
URL: National Affiliate–www.legion.org
Local. Affiliated With: American Legion.

20146 ■ Marquette County Historical Society
PO Box 172
Westfield, WI 53964
Ph: (608)296-2618 (608)296-4700
E-mail: mchs@co.marquette.wi.us
URL: http://co.marquette.wi.us/MCHS
Contact: John Robinson, Treas.
Founded: 1969. **Members:** 100. **Membership Dues:** individual, $10 (annual) • sustaining, $25 (annual) • life (individual), $200. **Local.** Preserves, records and maintains the historical information and artifacts of Marquette County. **Publications:** *Imprints on Sands of Marquette County*, 3/year. Newsletter. **Conventions/Meetings:** monthly meeting - always March through December.

20147 ■ National Alliance for the Mentally Ill - Mid Central WI
PO Box 158
Westfield, WI 53964
Ph: (608)408-0177 (608)296-3373
Fax: (608)296-4631
E-mail: info@namimidcentralwi.org
URL: http://www.namimidcentralwi.org
Contact: Joann Stephens, Pres.
Local. Strives to improve the quality of life of children and adults with severe mental illness through support, education, research and advocacy. **Affiliated With:** National Alliance for the Mentally Ill.

20148 ■ Westfield Chamber of Commerce
PO Box 393
Westfield, WI 53964
Ph: (608)296-2363
URL: http://www.westfieldwi.com
Contact: Bob Kohel, Pres.
Local. Promotes business and community development in Westfield, WI.

Weston

20149 ■ Wisconsin State B.A.S.S. Federation
c/o Mike Hofmann
6111 Birchwood Ln.
Weston, WI 54476
Ph: (715)355-5669
E-mail: mike@wisconsinbass.com
URL: http://www.wisconsinbass.com
Contact: Ray Loendorf, Sec.
State.

Weyauwega

20150 ■ American Legion, Arndt-Bruley Post 176
PO Box 542
Weyauwega, WI 54983
Ph: (608)745-1090
Fax: (608)745-0179
URL: National Affiliate–www.legion.org
Local. Affiliated With: American Legion.

20151 ■ Weyauwega Area Chamber of Commerce
PO Box 531
Weyauwega, WI 54983
Ph: (920)867-2500
E-mail: bruce.ulbrich@centurytel.net
URL: http://www.weyauwegachamber.com
Contact: Eunice Kempf, Pres.
Local. Promotes business and community development in Weyauwega, WI.

Wheeler

20152 ■ American Legion, Lee-Ranney Post 235
PO Box 24
Wheeler, WI 54772
Ph: (608)745-1090
Fax: (608)745-0179
URL: National Affiliate–www.legion.org
Local. Affiliated With: American Legion.

White Lake

20153 ■ American Legion, Anderson-Sather Post 524
PO Box 217
White Lake, WI 54491
Ph: (608)745-1090
Fax: (608)745-0179
URL: National Affiliate–www.legion.org
Local. Affiliated With: American Legion.

20154 ■ Trout Unlimited, Wolf River
c/o Herb Buettner
N4297 Buettner Rd.
White Lake, WI 54491
Ph: (715)882-8610 (715)882-8611
URL: National Affiliate–www.tu.org/
Contact: Herb Buettner, Contact
Founded: 1964. **Members:** 60. **Membership Dues:** $20 (annual). **Budget:** $3,000. **Local.** Works with the DNR to protect and enhance the upper Wolf River Watershed and maintain its trout population by maintaining the quality and quantity of river water. Tries to improve the habitat through beaver control, stream improvement, and trout stocking. **Affiliated With:** Trout Unlimited. **Publications:** Newsletter, annual. **Price:** free; to membership and Wis. Trout. **Conventions/Meetings:** annual banquet (exhibits) - White Lake, WI • bimonthly meeting.

Whitefish Bay

20155 ■ Chemical Coaters Association International, Wisconsin
4865 N Larkin St.
Whitefish Bay, WI 53217
Ph: (414)333-8528
Fax: (414)964-0526
E-mail: jimglghr@execpc.com
URL: National Affiliate–www.ccaiweb.com
Contact: Jim Gallagher, Pres.
State. Provides information and training on surface coating technologies. Raises the standards of finishing operations through educational meetings and seminars, training manuals, certification programs, and outreach programs with colleges and universities. **Affiliated With:** Chemical Coaters Association International.

20156 ■ Physicians for Social Responsibility, Southeast Wisconsin
c/o Charles Baynton, MD, Exec.Dir.
4745 N Diversey Blvd.
Whitefish Bay, WI 53211
Ph: (414)961-1467
E-mail: cbaynton@earthlink.net
URL: http://www.wpsr.org
Contact: Charles Baynton MD, Exec.Dir.
Local. Affiliated With: Physicians for Social Responsibility.

Whitehall

20157 ■ American Legion, Hutchins-Stendahl Post 191
PO Box 385
Whitehall, WI 54773
Ph: (608)745-1090
Fax: (608)745-0179
URL: National Affiliate–www.legion.org
Local. Affiliated With: American Legion.

20158 ■ Whitehall Area Chamber of Commerce
PO Box 281
Whitehall, WI 54773
Ph: (715)538-4353
Fax: (715)538-2301
E-mail: kwitte@wppisys.org
URL: http://whitehall-chamber.com
Contact: Bernard Ziegeweid, Pres.
Local. Promotes business and community development in Whitehall, WI.

Whitewater

20159 ■ American Legion, Wisconsin Post 173
c/o William Graham
292 S Wisconsin St.
Whitewater, WI 53190
Ph: (608)745-1090
Fax: (608)745-0179
URL: National Affiliate–www.legion.org
Contact: William Graham, Contact
Local. Affiliated With: American Legion.

20160 ■ National Association of Student Personnel Administrators, NASPA Region IV-East
c/o Barbara Jones, Asst. Chancellor for Student Affairs
Univ. of Wisconsin-Whitewater
Hyer Hall 200
800 W. Main St.
Whitewater, WI 53190

Ph: (262)472-1051
Fax: (262)472-1275
E-mail: jonesb@mail.uww.edu
URL: http://www.naspa.org/communities/rc/community.cfm?rcid=41
Contact: Barbara Jones, Past VP

Regional. Student affairs professionals from OH, MI, IN, IL, WI, IA, and MN and Ontario, Canada. Provides professional development activities and information for student affairs professionals. **Affiliated With:** National Association of Student Personnel Administrators.

20161 ■ Rock Valley Innovators and Entrepreneurs Group
402 McCutchan Hall
Univ. of Wisconsin at Whitewater
Whitewater, WI 53190
Ph: (262)472-3217
E-mail: ask-sbdc@uww.edu
URL: National Affiliate–www.uiausa.org
Contact: Jeff Herman, Contact

Local. Represents inventors' organizations and providers of services to inventors. Seeks to facilitate the development of innovation conceived by independent inventors. Provides leadership and support services to inventors and inventors' organizations. **Affiliated With:** United Inventors Association of the U.S.A.

20162 ■ Southern Wisconsin Sporting Spaniel Club (SWSSC)
c/o Deb Schoene, Sec.
3706 N Wall Rd.
Whitewater, WI 53190-3538
E-mail: swssc@internetwi.com
URL: http://www.internetwi.com/swssc
Contact: Deb Schoene, Sec.

Regional. **Affiliated With:** American Kennel Club.

20163 ■ Walworth County RSVP
c/o Patti O'Brien, Dir.
162 W Main St., Ste.H
Whitewater, WI 53190
Ph: (262)472-9632
Fax: (262)472-9636
E-mail: arcrsvp@genevaonline.com
URL: http://www.seniorcorps.gov
Contact: Patti O'Brien, Dir.

Local. **Affiliated With:** Retired and Senior Volunteer Program.

20164 ■ Whitewater Area Chamber of Commerce (WACC)
402 W Main St.
PO Box 34
Whitewater, WI 53190-0034
Ph: (262)473-4005
Fax: (262)473-0529
Free: (866)4WW-TOUR
E-mail: wacc@idcnet.com
URL: http://www.whitewaterchamber.com
Contact: Betsy Gasper, Exec.Dir.

Founded: 1941. **Members:** 225. **Staff:** 2. **Local**. Promotes business and community development in the Whitewater, WI area. **Publications:** *Solutions*, monthly. Newsletter. Contains information on chamber activities, business, and news. **Price:** free for members. **Conventions/Meetings:** annual Badger State Games - Summer - competition - always summer • monthly board meeting - always last Wednesday of the month.

Wild Rose

20165 ■ American Legion, Wisconsin Post 370
c/o Daniel Dopp
PO Box 38
Wild Rose, WI 54984
Ph: (608)745-1090
Fax: (608)745-0179
URL: National Affiliate–www.legion.org
Contact: Daniel Dopp, Contact

Local. **Affiliated With:** American Legion.

Williams Bay

20166 ■ Williams Bay Lions Club
PO Box 550
Williams Bay, WI 53191
E-mail: wblions@charter.net
URL: http://www.wilions.org/WBLions
Contact: Stacy Maynard, Pres.

Local. **Affiliated With:** Lions Clubs International.

Wilmot

20167 ■ American Legion, Semrau-Scott Post 361
PO Box 25
Wilmot, WI 53192
Ph: (608)745-1090
Fax: (608)745-0179
URL: National Affiliate–www.legion.org

Local. **Affiliated With:** American Legion.

Wilson

20168 ■ Wisconsin National Barrel Horse Association
141 320th St.
Wilson, WI 54027
Ph: (715)772-4901
URL: National Affiliate–www.nbha.com
Contact: Lynette Beckman, Dir.

State. Promotes the sport of barrel horse racing. Conducts barrel racing competitions. Establishes standard rules for the sport. **Affiliated With:** National Barrel Horse Association.

Wilton

20169 ■ Ontario Area Lions Club
c/o Bob Streeter, Pres.
26712 Midge Rd.
Wilton, WI 54670
Ph: (608)435-6937
URL: http://www.md27d2.org
Contact: Bob Streeter, Pres.

Local. **Affiliated With:** Lions Clubs International.

20170 ■ Wilton Lions Club - Wisconsin
c/o Chuck Johansen, Pres.
PO Box 157
Wilton, WI 54670
Ph: (608)435-6817
E-mail: johansen@centurytel.net
URL: http://www.md27d2.org
Contact: Chuck Johansen, Pres.

Local. **Affiliated With:** Lions Clubs International.

Wind Lake

20171 ■ Wind Lake Lions Club
25502 Portsmouth Rd.
Wind Lake, WI 53185
Ph: (262)895-7750
E-mail: tswimmer@ticon.net
URL: http://windlakelionswi.lionwap.org
Contact: Jerry Schmechel, Sec.

Local. **Affiliated With:** Lions Clubs International.

Winneconne

20172 ■ American Legion, Giles-Luce Post 364
PO Box 131
Winneconne, WI 54986
Ph: (608)745-1090
Fax: (608)745-0179
URL: National Affiliate–www.legion.org

Local. **Affiliated With:** American Legion.

20173 ■ Mothers Against Drunk Driving, Winnebago County
8480 Shirley Ct.
Winneconne, WI 54986
Ph: (920)582-4379
URL: National Affiliate–www.madd.org

Local. Victims of drunk driving crashes; concerned citizens. Encourages citizen participation in working towards reform of the drunk driving problem and the prevention of underage drinking. Acts as the voice of victims of drunk driving crashes by speaking on their behalf to communities, businesses, and educational groups. **Affiliated With:** Mothers Against Drunk Driving.

20174 ■ Trout Unlimited - Central Wisconsin Chapter (CWTU)
c/o John Gremmer, Pres.
5935 Hiawatha Dr.
Winneconne, WI 54986
Ph: (920)582-7802
E-mail: jhg@vbe.com
URL: http://www.cwtu.org
Contact: John Gremmer, Pres.

Membership Dues: regular, $15 (annual). **Regional**. **Publications:** *Brookie News*, monthly. Newsletter. **Price:** included in membership dues. Alternate Formats: online.

Winter

20175 ■ American Legion, Adolph-Wacek-Patrick-Slattery Post 303
PO Box 394
Winter, WI 54896
Ph: (608)745-1090
Fax: (608)745-0179
URL: National Affiliate–www.legion.org

Local. **Affiliated With:** American Legion.

Wisconsin Dells

20176 ■ American Legion, Wisconsin Post 187
c/o Harold B. Larkin
609 Wisconsin Ave.
Wisconsin Dells, WI 53965
Ph: (608)745-1090
Fax: (608)745-0179
URL: National Affiliate–www.legion.org
Contact: Harold B. Larkin, Contact

Local. **Affiliated With:** American Legion.

20177 ■ Lake Delton Lions Club
c/o Rick Plouffe, Pres.
N656 Meadow Point Rd.
Wisconsin Dells, WI 53965
Ph: (608)253-7364
URL: http://www.md27d2.org
Contact: Rick Plouffe, Pres.

Local. **Affiliated With:** Lions Clubs International.

20178 ■ Riverside Skeet Club
12299 Cth 0
Wisconsin Dells, WI 53965
Ph: (608)742-2794
Fax: (608)742-5349
URL: National Affiliate–www.mynssa.com
Local. Affiliated With: National Skeet Shooting Association.

20179 ■ Sauk County Personnel Association (SCPA)
c/o Molly Toenjes, Membership Chair
PO Box 490
Wisconsin Dells, WI 53965
E-mail: trinas@qstaff.com
URL: http://www.wishrm.org/chapter/saukCo/index.html
Contact: Trina Sarbacker, Pres.
Local. Represents the interests of human resource and industrial relations professionals and executives. Promotes the advancement of human resource management.

20180 ■ Wally Byam Caravan Club International, Region 7
c/o Ellen McGaughey, Membership Chair
286 Mariealain Dr.
Wisconsin Dells, WI 53965
Ph: (608)254-7146 (608)345-5849
E-mail: ejmcg@merr.com
URL: http://www.wbcciregion7.net
Contact: Ellen McGaughey, Membership Chair
Regional. Affiliated With: Wally Byam Caravan Club International.

20181 ■ Wisconsin Dells Visitor and Convention Bureau (WDVCB)
PO Box 390
Wisconsin Dells, WI 53965
Ph: (608)254-8088 (608)254-4636
Fax: (608)254-4293
Free: (800)223-3557
E-mail: info@wisdells.com
URL: http://www.wisdells.com
Contact: Romy A. Snyder, Exec.Dir.
Founded: 1949. **Members:** 550. **Staff:** 18. **Budget:** $5,250,000. **Regional Groups:** 1. **Local.** Businesses involved in tourism. Seeks to promote the Wisconsin Dells, WI area as a major vacation destination. **Formerly:** (1983) Wisconsin Dells Regional Chamber of Commerce. **Publications:** *WDVCB Tourism News*, bimonthly. Newsletter • *Wisconsin Dells Group Tour Planner*, annual. Directory • *Wisconsin Dells Meeting & Planners Guide*, annual. Directory • *Wisconsin Dells Travel and Attraction Guide*, periodic. Directory.

Wisconsin Rapids

20182 ■ American Rabbit Breeders Association, Southwest Wisconsin Rabbit Club
c/o Deanna MacMillan, Sec.
6320 80th St. S
Wisconsin Rapids, WI 54494
URL: http://www.geocities.com/wisconsin_state_rba/Local_Clubs.html
Contact: Deanna MacMillan, Sec.
Local. Affiliated With: American Rabbit Breeders Association.

20183 ■ Elks Lodge
240 2nd St. S
Wisconsin Rapids, WI 54494-4165
Ph: (715)423-1930
E-mail: admin@bpoe693.com
URL: http://www.bpoe693.com
Contact: Bob Berg, Sec.
Members: 233. **Local. Publications:** *The Voice*, monthly. Newsletter. **Price:** free to members.

20184 ■ Girl Scouts of Woodland Council - Central Wisconsin
c/o Ann Saris, Exec.Dir./CEO
3910 Chestnut St.
Wisconsin Rapids, WI 54494
Ph: (715)423-6360
Fax: (715)423-6362
Free: (800)472-0073
E-mail: woodland@woodgsc.org
URL: http://woodgsc.org
Contact: Ann Saris, Exec.Dir./CEO
Regional.

20185 ■ Grand Rapids Lions Club
PO Box 97
Wisconsin Rapids, WI 54495-0097
Ph: (715)421-1888 (715)697-9797
E-mail: blewslb@wctc.net
URL: http://grandrapidswi.lionwap.org
Contact: Keith Luebke, 1st VP
Local. Affiliated With: Lions Clubs International.

20186 ■ Heart of Wisconsin Business and Economic Alliance
c/o Connie Coley Loden, Exec.Dir.
1120 Lincoln St.
Wisconsin Rapids, WI 54494-5229
Ph: (715)423-1830
Fax: (715)423-1865
E-mail: info@heartofwi.com
URL: http://www.heartofwi.com
Contact: Connie Coley Loden, Exec.Dir.
Founded: 1993. **Members:** 25. **Staff:** 1. **Budget:** $100,000. **Languages:** English, French, Italian. **Local.** Area wide (Central Wisconsin) economic development organization that includes area events coordination and convention and visitors' bureau activities. **Formerly:** (1994) Wisconsin Rapids Independent Development Committee; (2002) Wisconsin Rapids River Cities Development Corporation.

20187 ■ Heart of Wisconsin District Nurses Association - No. 5
4001 Downing St.
Wisconsin Rapids, WI 54494
E-mail: jonna.kronholm@mstc.edu
URL: http://www.wisconsinnurses.org
Contact: Jonna Kronholm, Pres.
Local. Works to advance the nursing profession. Seeks to meet the needs of nurses and health care consumers. Fosters high standards of nursing practice. Promotes the economic and general welfare of nurses in the workplace. **Affiliated With:** American Nurses Association; Wisconsin Nurses' Association.

20188 ■ National Association of Home Builders of the United States, Central Wisconsin Home Builders Association (CWHBA)
2135 8th St. S
Wisconsin Rapids, WI 54494
Ph: (715)424-5060
Fax: (715)424-6938
Free: (800)552-9422
E-mail: cwhba@charterinternet.com
URL: http://www.cwhba.com
Contact: Alice Franz, Pres.
Founded: 1969. **Members:** 200. **Membership Dues:** general, $365 (annual). **Local.** Single and multifamily home builders, commercial builders, and others associated with the building industry. **Affiliated With:** National Association of Home Builders. **Publications:** Directory, annual. Contains list of members.

20189 ■ Plumbing-Heating-Cooling Contractors Association, Central Wisconsin
c/o Debra Eron
1111 Alton St.
Wisconsin Rapids, WI 54495-3322
Ph: (715)423-7430
Fax: (715)423-4724
URL: National Affiliate–www.phccweb.org
Contact: Debra Eron, Contact
Local. Represents the plumbing, heating and cooling contractors. Promotes the construction industry. Protects the environment, health, safety and comfort of society. **Affiliated With:** Plumbing-Heating-Cooling Contractors Association.

20190 ■ Points of Light Foundation - Volunteer Center of South Wood County
351 Oak St.
Wisconsin Rapids, WI 54494-4362
Ph: (715)421-0390
Fax: (715)421-3740
E-mail: darlene@uwswc.org
URL: National Affiliate–www.pointsoflight.org
Contact: Darlene Rause, Contact
Local. Affiliated With: Points of Light Foundation.

20191 ■ River Cities African Violet Club
c/o JoAnn Marti
6621 Lenox Ave.
Wisconsin Rapids, WI 54494
Ph: (715)421-0087
E-mail: jmm@wctc.net
URL: National Affiliate–www.avsa.org
Contact: JoAnn Marti, Contact
Local. Affiliated With: African Violet Society of America.

20192 ■ Thimble Collectors International, Dairyland
c/o Rachael Lent
5511 37th St. S
Wisconsin Rapids, WI 54494
Ph: (715)423-6355
E-mail: rlent@wctc.net
URL: National Affiliate–www.thimblecollectors.com
Contact: Rachael Lent, Contact
Local. Affiliated With: Thimble Collectors International.

20193 ■ Tri-City Curling Club (TCCC)
PO Box 751
Hurley St., 2nd Ave. S
Wisconsin Rapids, WI 54495
Ph: (715)421-0201
E-mail: hrfishy@wctc.net
URL: http://www.tri-citycurlingclub.com
Contact: Jon Neidhold, Pres.
Local. Affiliated With: United States Curling Association.

20194 ■ United Way of South Wood County
351 Oak St.
Wisconsin Rapids, WI 54494
Ph: (715)421-0390
Fax: (715)421-3740
E-mail: info@uwswc.org
URL: http://www.uwswc.org
Contact: Bruce Trimble, Exec.Dir.
Staff: 3. **Local. Affiliated With:** United Way of America; United Way of Wisconsin.

20195 ■ Wisconsin Checkered Giant Rabbit Club
3410-48th St. N
Wisconsin Rapids, WI 54494
URL: http://www.arba.net
Contact: Mary Bronk, Sec.
Membership Dues: $5 (annual). **State.** Breeders of rabbits. **Affiliated With:** American Rabbit Breeders Association.

20196 ■ Wisconsin Healthcare Public Relations and Marketing Society (WHPRMS)
c/o Dave Mueller, Pres.
410 Dewey St.
PO Box 8080
Wisconsin Rapids, WI 54495-8080
Ph: (715)421-7577
Fax: (715)421-7551
E-mail: rha@rhahealthcare.org
URL: http://www.whprms.org
Contact: Dave Mueller, Pres.
State. Persons in hospitals, health systems and networks, managed care plans, and physician groups who are engaged in strategic planning, business development, marketing, or public relations activities.

Affiliated With: Society for Healthcare Strategy and Market Development of the American Hospital Association.

20197 ■ Wisconsin Rapids Area Convention and Visitors Bureau
c/o Lonnie Selje
2507 8th St.
Wisconsin Rapids, WI 54494-5229
Ph: (715)422-4650
Free: (800)554-4484
E-mail: info@visitwisrapids.com
URL: http://visitwisrapids.com
Contact: Lonnie Selje, Exec.Dir.
Staff: 2. **Budget:** $120,000. **Local.**

20198 ■ Wisconsin Rapids Figure Skating Club (WRFSC)
PO Box 32
Wisconsin Rapids, WI 54494
Ph: (715)421-1456
E-mail: kathyv@wrfsc.com
URL: http://www.wrfsc.com
Contact: Kathy Volz, Sec.
Local. Provides programs to encourage participation and achievement in the sport of figure skating on ice. Defines and maintains uniform standards of skating proficiency. Organizes and sponsors competitions and exhibitions for the purpose of stimulating interest in figure skating. **Affiliated With:** United States Figure Skating Association.

20199 ■ Wisconsin State Cranberry Growers Association
c/o Thomas H. Lochner, Exec.Dir.
PO Box 365
Wisconsin Rapids, WI 54494-0365
Ph: (715)423-2070
Fax: (715)423-0275
E-mail: wiscran@wctc.net
URL: http://www.wiscran.org
Contact: Mr. Tom Lochner, Exec.Dir.
Founded: 1887. **Members:** 250. **Membership Dues:** grower (varies by size of farm), $1,000 (annual) • associate, $275 (annual). **Staff:** 2. **Budget:** $400,000. **State.** Strives to promote cranberry agriculture in Wisconsin. Conducts various activities including education conferences, programs, publications, promotions and lobbying. **Publications:** *WSCGA News*, monthly. Newsletter. **Price:** $100.00 subscription fee; included in membership dues. **Circulation:** 500. **Advertising:** accepted. Alternate Formats: online. **Conventions/Meetings:** monthly board meeting • annual meeting - winter • annual meeting - summer.

Withee

20200 ■ American Legion, Boxrucker-Berry Post 519
W 11624 State Hwy. 64
Withee, WI 54498
Ph: (608)745-1090
Fax: (608)745-0179
URL: National Affiliate–www.legion.org
Local. Affiliated With: American Legion.

20201 ■ National Active and Retired Federal Employees Association - Neillsville 933
PO Box 71
Withee, WI 54498
Ph: (715)229-2090
URL: National Affiliate–www.narfe.org
Contact: George C. Sorensen, Contact
Local. Protects the retirement future of employees through education. Informs members on issues affecting the retirement. **Affiliated With:** National Association of Retired Federal Employees.

Wittenberg

20202 ■ Wisconsin Woodland Owners Association, North Central Chapter
c/o John Czerwonka, Chm.
565 S State Rd. 49
Wittenberg, WI 54499
Ph: (715)454-6440
URL: http://www.wisconsinwoodlands.org
Contact: John Czerwonka, Chm.
Local. Affiliated With: Wisconsin Woodland Owners Association.

20203 ■ Wittenberg Area Chamber of Commerce (WACC)
PO Box 284
Wittenberg, WI 54499
Ph: (715)253-3525
E-mail: wittcham@wittenbergchamber.org
URL: http://wittenbergchamber.org
Contact: Benell Thomas, Pres.
Members: 110. **Local.** Promotes business and community development in the Wittenberg, WI area. **Formerly:** (1999) Wittenberg Chamber of Commerce.

Wonewoc

20204 ■ American Legion, Clark-Gurgel Post 206
PO Box 277
Wonewoc, WI 53968
Ph: (608)745-1090
Fax: (608)745-0179
URL: National Affiliate–www.legion.org
Local. Affiliated With: American Legion.

Woodbury

20205 ■ Wisconsin Woodland Owners Association, West Central Chapter
c/o Stan Peskar, Chm.
8098 Somerset Knoll
Woodbury, WI 55125
Ph: (651)735-9098
E-mail: suepeskar@yahoo.com
URL: http://www.wisconsinwoodlands.org
Contact: Stan Peskar, Chm.
Local. Affiliated With: Wisconsin Woodland Owners Association.

Woodruff

20206 ■ Northwoods Association of Realtors
PO Box 377
Woodruff, WI 54568
Ph: (715)356-3400
Fax: (715)358-2338
E-mail: nwar@dwave.net
URL: National Affiliate–www.realtor.org
Contact: Dawn Kennedy, Exec. Officer
Local. Strives to develop real estate business practices. Advocates the right to own, use and transfer real property. Provides a facility for professional development, research and exchange of information among members and to the general public. **Affiliated With:** National Association of Realtors.

Woodville

20207 ■ American Legion, Woodville Post 301
PO Box 301
Woodville, WI 54028
Ph: (608)745-1090
Fax: (608)745-0179
URL: National Affiliate–www.legion.org
Local. Affiliated With: American Legion.

20208 ■ Sons of Norway, Valkyrien Lodge 5-53
c/o Carmen D. Peterson, Pres.
247 S Church St.
Woodville, WI 54028-9785
Ph: (715)698-2468
E-mail: car1vir@mymailstation.com
URL: National Affiliate–www.sofn.com
Contact: Carmen D. Peterson, Pres.
Local. Affiliated With: Sons of Norway.

Wrightstown

20209 ■ American Legion, Urban Klister Post 436
PO Box 26
Wrightstown, WI 54180
Ph: (608)745-1090
Fax: (608)745-0179
URL: National Affiliate–www.legion.org
Local. Affiliated With: American Legion.

Alphabetic Index to Organization Names and Keywords

Association names are listed alphabetically by name, by keywords appearing in the name, and by additional assigned keywords (subheadings in bold). Index numbers refer to entry numbers, not to page numbers. A star ★ before an entry number signifies that the name is not listed separately, but is mentioned or described within the entry indicated by the entry number.

NUMERIC

1st Capital Fed. of Families for Children's Mental Hea. **[13655]**, Chillicothe, OH
1st Chicago Bottle Club **[1487]**, Dolton, IL
3-M Stamp Club **[12342]**, St. Paul, MN
3 Rivers Velo Sport **[4617]**, Fort Wayne, IN
3M Trap and Skeet Club **[11925]**, Oakdale, MN
4-H Coun; La Porte County **[5597]**, La Porte, IN
4-H Coun; Vanderburgh County **[4586]**, Evansville, IN
4 Wheel Drive Assn; East Coast **[14252]**, Cleves, OH
4 Wheels to Freedom 4WD Club **[6189]**, Shelbyville, IN
9to5 Poverty Network **[18922]**, Milwaukee, WI
21st Century Leadership, Posey County **[5844]**, Mount Vernon, IN
100 Black Men of Alton **[34]**, Alton, IL
100 Black Men of Central Illinois **[251]**, Bloomington, IL
100 Black Men of Central Ohio **[14262]**, Columbus, OH
100 Black Men of Chicago **[590]**, Chicago, IL
100 Black Men of Gary **[4769]**, Gary, IN
100 Black Men of Greater Cleveland **[14039]**, Cleveland, OH
100 Black Men of Greater Detroit **[7291]**, Detroit, MI
100 Black Men of Indianapolis **[4960]**, Indianapolis, IN
100 Black Men of the Quad Cities, Davenport **[2512]**, Moline, IL
101st Airborne Div. Assn., Michigan Chap. **[9562]**, Roseville, MI
101st Airborne Div. Assn., Old Abe Chap. **[19224]**, Monticello, WI
1000 Friends of Wisconsin **[18441]**, Madison, WI
5600 South Paulina Block Club **[591]**, Chicago, IL

A

AAA Akron Auto Club **[13014]**, Akron, OH
AAA Akron Auto. Club **[13015]**, Akron, OH
AAA Akron Auto. Club **[14816]**, Cuyahoga Falls, OH
AAA Akron Auto. Club **[15177]**, Fairlawn, OH
AAA Akron Auto. Club **[15479]**, Hudson, OH
AAA Ashland County **[13157]**, Ashland, OH
AAA Barberton Auto. Club **[13251]**, Barberton, OH
AAA-Chicago Motor Club **[1448]**, Des Plaines, IL
AAA Cincinnati **[13681]**, Cincinnati, OH
AAA Cincinnati **[13682]**, Cincinnati, OH
AAA Cincinnati **[13684]**, Cincinnati, OH
AAA Cincinnati **[13683]**, Cincinnati, OH
AAA Cincinnati **[13686]**, Cincinnati, OH
AAA Cincinnati **[13685]**, Cincinnati, OH
AAA Cincinnati **[13687]**, Cincinnati, OH
AAA Cincinnati **[15616]**, Lebanon, OH
AAA Cincinnati **[16428]**, Piqua, OH
AAA Cincinnati **[16995]**, Troy, OH
AAA Columbiana County **[15074]**, East Liverpool, OH
AAA Hoosier Motor Club **[4961]**, Indianapolis, IN
AAA Hoosier Motor Club **[5859]**, Muncie, IN
AAA Hoosier Motor Club **[6302]**, Terre Haute, IN
AAA Massillon Auto. Club **[15879]**, Massillon, OH
AAA Miami Valley **[15555]**, Kettering, OH
AAA Michigan **[★6607]**
AAA Michigan **[7004]**, Brighton, MI
AAA Michigan **[7242]**, Dearborn, MI
AAA Michigan **[7877]**, Grand Rapids, MI
AAA Michigan **[8091]**, Grosse Pointe Woods, MI
AAA Michigan **[8186]**, Holland, MI
AAA Michigan **[8353]**, Jackson, MI
AAA Michigan **[8485]**, Kentwood, MI
AAA Michigan **[8525]**, Lansing, MI
AAA Michigan **[8929]**, Marquette, MI
AAA Michigan **[9359]**, Petoskey, MI
AAA Michigan **[9427]**, Port Huron, MI
AAA Michigan **[9767]**, South Lyon, MI
AAA Michigan, Allen Park Off. **[6607]**, Allen Park, MI
AAA Minneapolis **[10457]**, Bloomington, MN
AAA Minneapolis **[11473]**, Minneapolis, MN
AAA Minnesota/Iowa **[10583]**, Burnsville, MN
AAA Minnesota/Iowa **[10793]**, Duluth, MN
AAA Minnesota/Iowa **[11080]**, Grand Rapids, MN
AAA Minnesota/Iowa **[11372]**, Mankato, MN
AAA Minnesota/Iowa **[12121]**, Rochester, MN
AAA Missouri **[35]**, Alton, IL
AAA Missouri **[197]**, Belleville, IL
AAA Missouri **[408]**, Carbondale, IL
AAA Northwest Ohio **[15898]**, Maumee, OH
AAA Northwest Ohio **[16300]**, Oregon, OH
AAA Northwest Ohio **[16823]**, Sylvania, OH
AAA Ohio Auto Club **[16568]**, St. Clairsville, OH
AAA Ohio Auto. Club **[13318]**, Bellefontaine, OH
AAA Ohio Auto. Club **[14264]**, Columbus, OH
AAA Ohio Auto. Club **[14263]**, Columbus, OH
AAA Ohio Auto. Club **[14265]**, Columbus, OH
AAA Ohio Auto. Club **[15376]**, Hamilton, OH
AAA Ohio Auto. Club **[15423]**, Hilliard, OH
AAA Ohio Auto. Club **[15641]**, Lima, OH
AAA Ohio Auto. Club **[15758]**, Mansfield, OH
AAA Ohio Auto. Club **[16598]**, Sandusky, OH
AAA Shelby County **[16662]**, Sidney, OH
AAA South Central Ohio **[15510]**, Jackson, OH
AAA South Central Ohio **[16465]**, Portsmouth, OH
AAA South Central Ohio **[16757]**, Steubenville, OH
AAA Tuscarawas County **[16144]**, New Philadelphia, OH
Aad Shriners **[11148]**, Hermantown, MN
AARP Illinois **[592]**, Chicago, IL
AARP Michigan **[8526]**, Lansing, MI
AARP Minnesota **[12343]**, St. Paul, MN
AARP, Ohio **[14266]**, Columbus, OH
Abingdon Chamber of Commerce **[1]**, Abingdon, IL
Abortion; People Taking Action Against **[★8856]**
Abraham Lincoln Tourism Bur. of Logan County **[2270]**, Lincoln, IL
Abuse Council; Dearborn and Ohio County Prevent Child **[5658]**, Lawrenceburg, IN
Abuse Now; Stopping Woman **[2862]**, Olney, IL
Abuse Prevention Council; Dearborn and Ohio County Child **[★5658]**
Abuse Wisconsin; Prevent Child **[18599]**, Madison, WI
Acacia, Indiana Chap. **[4194]**, Bloomington, IN
Acacia, St. Cloud State Chap. **[12269]**, St. Cloud, MN
Acacia, Wisconsin Chap. **[18442]**, Madison, WI
Academic Freedom
Community Volunteers for Intl. Progs. **[7514]**, East Lansing, MI
Junior Achievement of Central Illinois **[3070]**, Peoria Heights, IL
Academic Lib. Assn. of Ohio **[14267]**, Columbus, OH
Academic Promoters; St. Henry **[16576]**, St. Henry, OH
Acadian Genealogists of Wisconsin; French Canadian- **[18170]**, Hales Corners, WI
ACCA Northeast Wisconsin **[19384]**, Oshkosh, WI
Access Living **[593]**, Chicago, IL
Access Services of Northern Illinois **[2348]**, Loves Park, IL
Accountants
Accounting Aid Soc. **[7292]**, Detroit, MI
Amer. Soc. of Women Accountants, Anderson/Muncie Chap. No. 077 **[5933]**, New Castle, IN
Amer. Soc. of Women Accountants, Louisville Chap. No. 018 **[5916]**, New Albany, IN
Illinois CPA Soc. **[938]**, Chicago, IL
Independent Accountants Assn. of Michigan **[6837]**, Bath, MI
Indiana CPA Soc. **[5221]**, Indianapolis, IN
Wisconsin Assn. of Accountants **[19646]**, River Falls, WI
Accountants, Anderson/Muncie Chap. No. 077; Amer. Soc. of Women **[5933]**, New Castle, IN
Accountants Assn. of Illinois; Independent **[1775]**, Galesburg, IL
Accountants, Cleveland Chap. No. 013; Amer. Soc. of Women **[16356]**, Parma, OH
Accountants, Indianapolis Chap. No. 001; Amer. Soc. of Women **[5025]**, Indianapolis, IN
Accounting
Accounting for Kids **[13688]**, Cincinnati, OH
Amer. Accounting Assn., Midwest Region **[11482]**, Minneapolis, MN
Amer. Accounting Assn., Ohio Region **[17023]**, University Heights, OH
Amer. Soc. of Women Accountants, Chicago Chap. No. 002 **[2960]**, Park Ridge, IL
Amer. Soc. of Women Accountants, Cleveland Chap. No. 013 **[16356]**, Parma, OH
Amer. Soc. of Women Accountants, Columbus Chap. No. 016 **[15258]**, Gahanna, OH
Amer. Soc. of Women Accountants, Flint Chap. No. 054 **[7715]**, Flint, MI
Amer. Soc. of Women Accountants, Fort Wayne Chap. No. 046 **[4636]**, Fort Wayne, IN
Amer. Soc. of Women Accountants, Grand Rapids Chap. No. 010 **[7903]**, Grand Rapids, MI
Amer. Soc. of Women Accountants, Indianapolis Chap. No. 001 **[5025]**, Indianapolis, IN
Amer. Soc. of Women Accountants, Marion Chap. No. 108 **[5726]**, Marion, IN
Amer. Soc. of Women Accountants, Milwaukee No. 041 **[20115]**, West Bend, WI
Amer. Soc. of Women Accountants, Minnesota/St. Paul Chap. No. 068 **[12975]**, Woodbury, MN
Amer. Soc. of Women Accountants, Saginaw/Midland/Bay Chap. No. 034 **[6877]**, Bay City, MI
Amer. Soc. of Women Accountants, Terre Haute Chap. No. 008 **[6313]**, Terre Haute, IN
Amer. Soc. of Women Accountants, Youngstown Chap. No. 072 **[13528]**, Canfield, OH
Amer. Woman's Soc. of Certified Public Accountants, Madison **[18475]**, Madison, WI

Assn. for Accounting Admin., Illinois Chap. **[1541]**, East Peoria, IL
Assn. for Accounting Admin., Indiana Chap. **[4166]**, Bedford, IN
Assn. for Accounting Admin., Michigan Chap. **[9265]**, Okemos, MI
Assn. for Accounting Admin., Minn Dak Chap. **[11785]**, Minnetonka, MN
Assn. for Accounting Admin., Ohio Chap. **[13039]**, Akron, OH
Assn. of Govt. Accountants - Central Ohio Chap. **[14324]**, Columbus, OH
Assn. of Govt. Accountants - Chicago Chap. **[750]**, Chicago, IL
Assn. of Govt. Accountants - Cleveland Chap. **[14078]**, Cleveland, OH
Assn. of Govt. Accountants - Indianapolis Chap. **[5046]**, Indianapolis, IN
Assn. of Govt. Accountants - Southern Wisconsin Chap. **[18483]**, Madison, WI
Hospitality Financial and Tech. Professionals - Chicago Chap. **[918]**, Chicago, IL
Hosp.ity Financial and Tech. Professionals - Cleveland/Akron Chap. **[16679]**, Solon, OH
Hosp.ity Financial and Tech. Professionals - Greater Detroit Chap. **[6985]**, Bloomfield Hills, MI
Hospitality Financial and Tech. Professionals - Greater Milwaukee Chap. **[19985]**, Waukesha, WI
Hosp.ity Financial and Tech. Professionals - Minneapolis/St. Paul Chap. **[12422]**, St. Paul, MN
Hosp.ity Financial and Tech. Professionals - West Michigan Chap. **[9487]**, Richland, MI
Independent Accountants Assn. of Illinois **[1775]**, Galesburg, IL
Indiana Soc. of Public Accountants **[4327]**, Carmel, IN
Inst. of Internal Auditors, Central Ohio Chap. **[17344]**, Worthington, OH
Inst. of Internal Auditors, Chicago Chap. **[149]**, Barrington, IL
Inst. of Internal Auditors, Detroit Chap. **[7662]**, Farmington Hills, MI
Inst. of Internal Auditors, Fort Wayne Chap. **[4680]**, Fort Wayne, IN
Inst. of Internal Auditors, Fox Valley/Central Wisconsin Chap. **[18108]**, Green Bay, WI
Inst. of Internal Auditors, Indianapolis Chap. **[4160]**, Batesville, IN
Inst. of Internal Auditors, Lake Superior Chap. **[10826]**, Duluth, MN
Inst. of Internal Auditors, Lansing Chap. **[8577]**, Lansing, MI
Inst. of Internal Auditors, Madison Chap. **[18525]**, Madison, WI
Inst. of Internal Auditors, Michiana Chap. **[6004]**, Notre Dame, IN
Inst. of Internal Auditors, Northwest Metro Chicago Chap. **[2036]**, Hoffman Estates, IL
Inst. of Internal Auditors, Springfield Chap. **[3646]**, Springfield, IL
Inst. of Internal Auditors, Tri-State Chap. **[4555]**, Evansville, IN
Inst. of Internal Auditors, Twin Cities Chap. **[10468]**, Bloomington, MN
Inst. of Internal Auditors, Western Michigan Chap. **[7967]**, Grand Rapids, MI
Inst. of Mgt. Accountants, Akron Chap. **[13058]**, Akron, OH
Inst. of Mgt. Accountants, Ann Arbor Chap. **[6708]**, Ann Arbor, MI
Inst. of Mgt. Accountants, Central Minnesota **[12287]**, St. Cloud, MN
Inst. of Mgt. Accountants, Chippewa Valley **[17880]**, Eau Claire, WI
Inst. of Mgt. Accountants, Cincinnati North Chap. **[17174]**, West Chester, OH
Inst. of Mgt. Accountants, Cleveland Chap. **[13428]**, Broadview Heights, OH
Inst. of Mgt. Accountants, Cleveland East Chap. **[16790]**, Strongsville, OH
Inst. of Mgt. Accountants, Dayton Chap. **[17001]**, Troy, OH
Inst. of Mgt. Accountants, Detroit Metro Chap. **[6612]**, Allen Park, MI
Inst. of Mgt. Accountants, Evansville Chap. **[4556]**, Evansville, IN
Inst. of Mgt. Accountants, Illinois State Univ. Chap. **[2722]**, Normal, IL
Inst. of Mgt. Accountants, Indianapolis Chap. **[5975]**, Noblesville, IN
Inst. of Mgt. Accountants, LaCrosse-Winona Chap. **[20137]**, West Salem, WI
Inst. of Mgt. Accountants, Lake Superior Chap. **[10827]**, Duluth, MN
Inst. of Mgt. Accountants, Minneapolis Chap. **[11788]**, Minnetonka, MN
Inst. of Mgt. Accountants, Saint Paul **[11223]**, Inver Grove Heights, MN
Inst. of Mgt. Accountants, Sangamon Valley Chap. **[1396]**, Decatur, IL
Inst. of Mgt. Accountants, South Central Minnesota **[11380]**, Mankato, MN
Inst. of Mgt. Accountants, Southern Minnesota **[12151]**, Rochester, MN
Inst. of Mgt. Accountants, Wabash Valley Chap. **[6331]**, Terre Haute, IN
Michigan Assn. of Certified Public Accountants **[9996]**, Troy, MI
Minnesota Assn. of Public Accountants **[12235]**, Roseville, MN
Minnesota Soc. of Certified Public Accountants **[10482]**, Bloomington, MN
Natl. Assn. of Black Accountants, Indianapolis Chap. **[5415]**, Indianapolis, IN
Natl. Assn. of Black Accountants, Lansing **[9298]**, Okemos, MI
Ohio Assn. of Independent Accountants **[16228]**, North Hampton, OH
Wisconsin Inst. of Certified Public Accountants **[17684]**, Brookfield, WI
Accounting Aid Soc. **[7292]**, Detroit, MI
Accounting for Kids **[13688]**, Cincinnati, OH
Accounting and Syss. Assn., Wisconsin; Insurance **[19696]**, Sheboygan, WI
Accreditation
Chicago Accreditation Partnership **[780]**, Chicago, IL
ACF Alterra Chap. **[18923]**, Milwaukee, WI
ACF Ann Arbor Culinary Assn. **[7005]**, Brighton, MI
ACF Arrowhead Professional Chefs Assn. **[10794]**, Duluth, MN
ACF Blue Water Chefs Assn. **[6797]**, Armada, MI
ACF Capitol Area Professional Chefs and Cooks Assn. **[7497]**, East Lansing, MI
ACF Central Illinois Culinary Arts Assn. **[2072]**, Jacksonville, IL
ACF Chefs 200 Club Detroit Michigan **[6596]**, Algonac, MI
ACF Chefs of Milwaukee **[18036]**, Germantown, WI
ACF Chefs of Northwest Indiana **[5780]**, Michigan City, IN
ACF Chicago Chefs of Cuisine **[3454]**, Schiller Park, IL
ACF Flint/Saginaw Valley Chap. **[9890]**, Swartz Creek, MI
ACF Fort Wayne Professional Chefs Assn. **[4618]**, Fort Wayne, IN
ACF Fox Valley Chap. **[17481]**, Appleton, WI
ACF Great Lakes Thumb Chap. **[7840]**, Grand Blanc, MI
ACF Greater Dayton Chap. **[14835]**, Dayton, OH
ACF Greater Geneva Lakes Professional Chefs Assn. **[18394]**, Lake Geneva, WI
ACF Greater Grand Rapids Chefs Assn. **[7878]**, Grand Rapids, MI
ACF Heart of Illinois Professional Chefs Assn. **[2998]**, Peoria, IL
ACF of Kalamazoo/Battle Creek **[6840]**, Battle Creek, MI
ACF Louis Joliet Chap. **[1309]**, Crest Hill, IL
ACF Middle Wisconsin Chefs **[19670]**, Schofield, WI
ACF Minneapolis Chap. **[10906]**, Edina, MN
ACF of Northwestern Michigan **[7783]**, Frankfort, MI
ACF St. Paul Chefs Assn. **[11456]**, Mendota Heights, MN
ACF Sandusky Bay Area Chefs Chap. **[16599]**, Sandusky, OH
ACF South Bend Chefs and Cooks Assn. **[6206]**, South Bend, IN
ACF Southeastern Minnesota Culinarian Chap. **[11806]**, Montgomery, MN
ACF Southwestern Minnesota Chap. **[12669]**, Slayton, MN
ACF Tri-State Chefs and Cooks Chap. **[4515]**, Evansville, IN
ACF Upper Michigan Chap. **[7484]**, Drummond Island, MI
ACF West Michigan Lakeshore Chap. **[9134]**, Muskegon, MI
ACF Windy City Professional Culinarians **[594]**, Chicago, IL
Achieva Rsrcs. Center Plant 3 - Franklin County **[4295]**, Brookville, IN
Achieva Rsrcs. Corp. - Wayne County **[6083]**, Richmond, IN
Achieva Rsrcs. First Steps - Madison County **[4088]**, Alexandria, IN
Achieva Rsrcs. - Hea.y Families and Employment Sers. - Fayette County **[4409]**, Connersville, IN
Achieva Rsrcs. Hea.y Families - Union County **[5677]**, Liberty, IN
ACI Greater Michigan Chap. **[7650]**, Farmington Hills, MI
ACLU of Wisconsin **[18924]**, Milwaukee, WI
ACM Siggraph Purdue Univ. Chap. **[6468]**, West Lafayette, IN
Acme Lodge 83 Free and Accepted Masons **[5781]**, Michigan City, IN
Acoustical Soc. of Am. - Central Ohio Chap. **[15424]**, Hilliard, OH
Acoustical Soc. of Am. - Cincinnati Chap. **[13689]**, Cincinnati, OH
Acoustics
Acoustical Soc. of Am. - Central Ohio Chap. **[15424]**, Hilliard, OH
Acoustical Soc. of Am. - Cincinnati Chap. **[13689]**, Cincinnati, OH
Upper Midwest Chap. of the Acoustical Soc. of Am. **[11771]**, Minneapolis, MN
ACRES, Inc. **[★4619]**
Acres Land Trust **[4619]**, Fort Wayne, IN
ACS club **[★2710]**
Action Agency Found; Cincinnati-Hamilton County Community **[13787]**, Cincinnati, OH
Action for Children **[595]**, Chicago, IL
Action Ohio Coalition For Battered Women **[14268]**, Columbus, OH
Actors
Monroe Actors Stage Company **[3900]**, Waterloo, IL
Actors' Fund of Am., Midwestern Region **[596]**, Chicago, IL
Actors Stage Company; Monroe **[3900]**, Waterloo, IL
Ada Chamber of Commerce **[10234]**, Ada, MN
Ada Lions Club - Minnesota **[10235]**, Ada, MN
Adams County Beagle Club **[13690]**, Cincinnati, OH
Adams County Chamber of Commerce **[17193]**, West Union, OH
Adams County Chamber of Commerce and Tourism **[17452]**, Adams, WI
Adams County Pork Producers **[3144]**, Quincy, IL
Adams County RSVP **[3145]**, Quincy, IL
Adams-Friendship Chamber of Commerce **[★17452]**
Adams, Jay and Wells County Youth for Christ **[4267]**, Bluffton, IN
Adams Lions Club **[10238]**, Adams, MN
Adams Marquette Waushara Bd. of Realtors **[19220]**, Montello, WI
Adams - Young Life **[6207]**, South Bend, IN
Adaptive Adventure Sports Coalition **[14269]**, Columbus, OH
Adcraft Club of Detroit **[7293]**, Detroit, MI
Addiction Medicine, Michigan; Amer. Soc. of **[7505]**, East Lansing, MI
Addiction Rsrc. Coun. **[19975]**, Waukesha, WI
Addiction Rsrcs. **[★19975]**
Addison Chamber of Commerce **[★3]**
Addison Chamber of Commerce and Indus. **[3]**, Addison, IL
Addison Indus. Assn. **[★3]**
ADEC Rsrcs. for Independence **[4290]**, Bristol, IN
Adena Lions Club **[13011]**, Adena, OH
Administration
Buckeye Assn. of School Administrators **[14341]**, Columbus, OH
Illinois Assn. of School Administrators **[3579]**, Springfield, IL
Illinois Assn. of School Bus. Officials **[1434]**, DeKalb, IL

Indiana Assn. of Public School Superintendents **[5181]**, Indianapolis, IN
Minnesota Assn. of School Administrators **[12457]**, St. Paul, MN
Natl. Assn. of Student Personnel Administrators, Illinois **[3038]**, Peoria, IL
Natl. Assn. of Student Personnel Administrators, Indiana **[4823]**, Greencastle, IN
Natl. Assn. of Student Personnel Administrators, Michigan **[8213]**, Holland, MI
Natl. Assn. of Student Personnel Administrators, Minnesota **[12547]**, St. Paul, MN
Natl. Assn. of Student Personnel Administrators, NASPA Region IV-East **[20160]**, Whitewater, WI
Natl. Assn. of Student Personnel Administrators, Ohio **[13119]**, Alliance, OH
Natl. Assn. of Student Personnel Administrators, Wisconsin **[19797]**, Stevens Point, WI
Ohio Assn. of School Bus. Officials **[14565]**, Columbus, OH
Wisconsin Assn. of School Bus. Officials **[18664]**, Madison, WI
Admin., Central Illinois Chap; Amer. Soc. for Public **[3530]**, Springfield, IL
Administrative Services
Executive Suite Assn., Cincinnati Local Member Network **[13822]**, Cincinnati, OH
Executive Women Intl., Chicago Chap. **[1863]**, Glenview, IL
Executive Women Intl., Cincinnati/Northern Kentucky Chap. **[13823]**, Cincinnati, OH
Executive Women Intl./Cleveland **[14118]**, Cleveland, OH
Executive Women Intl., Detroit-Windsor Chap. **[7361]**, Detroit, MI
Executive Women Intl., Indianapolis Chap. **[5113]**, Indianapolis, IN
Executive Women Intl., Milwaukee Chap. **[19006]**, Milwaukee, WI
Executive Women Intl., Minneapolis Chap. **[12410]**, St. Paul, MN
Executive Women Intl., Rochester Chap. **[12139]**, Rochester, MN
Executive Women Intl., Saint Paul Chap. **[12411]**, St. Paul, MN
Indiana Div. - IAAP **[4498]**, Elkhart, IN
Info. Systems Audit and Control Assn., Central Indiana Chap. **[5366]**, Indianapolis, IN
Info. Systems Audit and Control Assn., Central Ohio Chap. **[14469]**, Columbus, OH
Info. Systems Audit and Control Assn., Detroit Chap. **[9992]**, Troy, MI
Info. Syss. Audit and Control Assn. and Found., Michiana Chap. **[6232]**, South Bend, IN
Info. Systems Audit and Control Assn. and Found., Minnesota Chap. **[12230]**, Roseville, MN
Info. Syss. Audit and Control Assn. and Found., Quad Cities Chap. **[1538]**, East Moline, IL
Info. Syss. Audit and Control Assn., Kettle Moraine Chap. **[19026]**, Milwaukee, WI
Info. Syss. Audit and Control Assn., Northeast Ohio Chap. **[14141]**, Cleveland, OH
Intl. Assn. of Administrative Professionals - Minnesota-North Dakota-South Dakota Div. **[12852]**, Watertown, MN
Intl. Assn. of Administrative Professionals, River Park Chap. **[9836]**, Southgate, MI
Katoland Chap. IAAP **[11382]**, Mankato, MN
Legal Secretaries of Indiana **[5391]**, Indianapolis, IN
Minneapolis Chap. of Intl. Assn. of Administrative Professionals **[11611]**, Minneapolis, MN
Off. and Professional Employees Intl. Union, AFL-CIO, CLC -Local Union 39 **[18589]**, Madison, WI
Off. and Professional Employees Intl. Union, AFL-CIO, CLC - Local Union 512 **[8748]**, Lansing, MI
Saint Paul Chap. IAAP **[12577]**, St. Paul, MN
Wisconsin Division of the Intl. Assn. of Administrative Professionals **[20010]**, Waukesha, WI
Administrators Assn; Govt. **[7366]**, Detroit, MI
Administrators Assn; Michigan Interscholastic Athletic **[8851]**, Livonia, MI
Administrators; Michigan Assn. of School **[8626]**, Lansing, MI
Administrators, NASPA Region IV-East; Natl. Assn. of Student Personnel **[20160]**, Whitewater, WI
Administrators; Ohio Assn. of Elementary School **[14552]**, Columbus, OH
Administrators; Ohio Assn. of Secondary School **[14566]**, Columbus, OH
Admirals No. 144 **[4597]**, Fishers, IN
Admissions
Amer. Assn. of Collegiate Registrars and Admissions Officers, Indiana **[6084]**, Richmond, IN
Amer. Assn. of Collegiate Registrars and Admissions Officers, Michigan **[7298]**, Detroit, MI
Illinois Assn. for Coll. Admissions Counseling **[281]**, Bloomington, IL
Illinois Assn. of Collegiate Registrars and Admissions Officers **[3437]**, Schaumburg, IL
Michigan Assn. of Collegiate Registrars and Admissions Officers **[9108]**, Mount Pleasant, MI
Ohio Assn. of Collegiate Registrars and Admissions Officers **[14548]**, Columbus, OH
Wisconsin Assn. of Collegiate Registrars and Admissions Officers **[19816]**, Stevens Point, WI
Admissions Officers; Michigan Assn. of Collegiate Registrars and **[9108]**, Mount Pleasant, MI
Adopt-A-Child-Size and Support Services **[7294]**, Detroit, MI
Adoption
Adopt-A-Child-Size and Support Services **[7294]**, Detroit, MI
Adoption Identity Movement of Michigan **[8160]**, Hazel Park, MI
Adoption Network Cleveland **[14040]**, Cleveland, OH
Adoption Resources of Wisconsin **[18925]**, Milwaukee, WI
Adoption Support of Indianapolis **[4962]**, Indianapolis, IN
Adoptive Families Today **[138]**, Barrington, IL
African-American Adoption Agency **[12346]**, St. Paul, MN
Adoption Identity Movement of Michigan **[8160]**, Hazel Park, MI
Adoption Network Cleveland **[14040]**, Cleveland, OH
Adoption Resources of Wisconsin **[18925]**, Milwaukee, WI
Adoption Support of Indianapolis **[4962]**, Indianapolis, IN
Adoptive Families Today **[138]**, Barrington, IL
Adoptive Family Support Network **[7879]**, Grand Rapids, MI
Adrian Breakfast Lions Club **[6560]**, Adrian, MI
Adrian Evening Lions Club **[6561]**, Adrian, MI
Adrian - Young Life **[6562]**, Adrian, MI
Advertising
Adcraft Club of Detroit **[7293]**, Detroit, MI
Advt. Club of Cincinnati **[13691]**, Cincinnati, OH
Advt. Fed. of Minnesota **[12344]**, St. Paul, MN
Assn. of Independent Commercial Producers/Midwest **[751]**, Chicago, IL
Assn. of Independent Commercial Producers/Minnesota **[11528]**, Minneapolis, MN
Bus. Marketing Assn., Chicago Chap. **[773]**, Chicago, IL
Bus. Marketing Assn., Detroit Chap. **[9979]**, Troy, MI
Bus. Marketing Assn., Indianapolis Chap. **[5065]**, Indianapolis, IN
Bus. Marketing Assn., Milwaukee Chap. **[19436]**, Pewaukee, WI
Madison Advt. Fed. **[20017]**, Waunakee, WI
Michigan Advt. Indus. Alliance **[7391]**, Detroit, MI
Outdoor Advt. Assn. of Michigan **[7416]**, Detroit, MI
Outdoor Advt. Assn. of Wisconsin **[18593]**, Madison, WI
Advt. Club of Cincinnati **[13691]**, Cincinnati, OH
Advt. Fed. of Minnesota **[12344]**, St. Paul, MN
Advt. Indus. Alliance; Michigan **[7391]**, Detroit, MI
Advisors; Indy South Assn. of Insurance and Financial **[5361]**, Indianapolis, IN
Advisors, Southern Illinois Chap; Natl. Assn. of Insurance and Financial **[424]**, Carbondale, IL
Advocacy Centers; Ohio Network of Children's **[14644]**, Columbus, OH
Advocacy Ser; Michigan Protection and **[8700]**, Lansing, MI
Advocacy Services for Kids **[8411]**, Kalamazoo, MI
Advocap **[19385]**, Oshkosh, WI
Advocates for Colorectal Educ. **[12345]**, St. Paul, MN
Advocates of Indiana; Autism **[4602]**, Fishers, IN
Aeronautics and Astronautics, Case Western Reserve Univ; Amer. Inst. of **[14051]**, Cleveland, OH
Aerospace
Amer. Inst. of Aeronautics and Astronautics, Case Western Reserve Univ. **[14051]**, Cleveland, OH
Amer. Inst. of Aeronautics and Astronautics, Columbus Sect. **[14285]**, Columbus, OH
Amer. Inst. of Aeronautics and Astronautics, Illinois **[3802]**, Urbana, IL
Amer. Inst. of Aeronautics and Astronautics, Indiana **[4986]**, Indianapolis, IN
Amer. Inst. of Aeronautics and Astronautics, Michigan **[8190]**, Holland, MI
American Institute of Aeronautics and Astronautics, Northern ohio **[15993]**, Middleburg Heights, OH
Amer. Inst. of Aeronautics and Astronautics, Twin Cities **[11490]**, Minneapolis, MN
Central Indiana Soaring Soc. **[5081]**, Indianapolis, IN
Chap. 81 - Mentone Aero Club **[5807]**, Mishawaka, IN
Chicago Glider Club **[2501]**, Minooka, IL
Cloudbase Flyers **[18340]**, La Crosse, WI
Experimental Aircraft Assn., Chap. 5 **[15999]**, Middlefield, OH
Frontenac Flyer Assn. **[11280]**, Lake Elmo, MN
Greater Midwest Rotorcraft - Popular Rotocraft Assn. Chap. 18 **[2218]**, Lansing, IL
Green Point Flyers Assn. **[8505]**, Lake City, MI
Illinois Agricultural Aviation Assn. **[2441]**, Mattoon, IL
Illinois Pilots Assn. **[3423]**, Savoy, IL
Ohio Flyers Hang Gliding Assn. **[14611]**, Columbus, OH
Red Wing Soaring Assn. **[12899]**, White Bear Lake, MN
Reel Hang Glider Pilots Assn. **[1613]**, Elk Grove Village, IL
Sandhill Soaring Club **[6763]**, Ann Arbor, MI
School of Missionary Aviation Tech. **[8866]**, Lowell, MI
Silvercreek Glider Club **[2683]**, New Douglas, IL
Soc. of Antique Modelers - Flyers 79 **[16574]**, St. Clairsville, OH
Soc. of Antique Modelers - Heart of Ohio Chap. **[17029]**, Upper Arlington, OH
Soc. of Antique Modelers - Illinois 117 **[3107]**, Plainfield, IL
Soc. of Antique Modelers - Indiana 112, Hoosier Bombers **[4175]**, Bedford, IN
Soc. of Antique Modelers - Michigan 4 **[10193]**, Wyoming, MI
Soc. of Antique Modelers - Michigan 40 **[6766]**, Ann Arbor, MI
Soc. of Antique Modelers - Ohio 6 **[14732]**, Columbus, OH
Soc. of Antique Modelers - Ohio 39 **[16620]**, Sandusky, OH
Soc. of Antique Modelers - Old Fort Flyers **[4715]**, Fort Wayne, IN
Soc. of Antique Modelers - Springfield Antique Modelers **[15137]**, Enon, OH
Soc. of Antique Modelers - Variety Gp. **[4176]**, Bedford, IN
Soc. of Antique Modelers - Western Ohio Oldtimers **[14954]**, Dayton, OH
Western Lake Superior Flying and Hiking Soc. **[10694]**, Cloquet, MN
Windy City Soaring Assn. **[2010]**, Hinckley, IL
Wisconsin Soaring Soc. **[20090]**, Wauwatosa, WI
Wisconsin Space Inst. **[18754]**, Madison, WI
Aerospace; Central Illinois **[504]**, Champaign, IL
Aerospace Medicine
Natl. Assn. of Air Medical Commun. Specialists, Region 5 **[5414]**, Indianapolis, IN
Affordable Housing Alliance **[9017]**, Midland, MI
AFL-CIO
Quad City Illinois and Iowa Fed. of Labor **[3255]**, Rock Island, IL
Traverse Bay Area Central Labor Coun. **[9957]**, Traverse City, MI

AFL-CIO Coun; Youngstown **[17421]**, Youngstown, OH
AFL-CIO; South Central Fed. of Labor, **[18619]**, Madison, WI
Africa
Christian Leaders for Africa **[5085]**, Indianapolis, IN
African
Friends of Africa Educ. **[12878]**, West St. Paul, MN
Natl. Black United Front, Chicago Chap. **[396]**, Calumet Park, IL
Natl. Black United Front, Detroit Chap. **[7410]**, Detroit, MI
Natl. Black United Front, Milwaukee Chap. **[19077]**, Milwaukee, WI
African-American
100 Black Men of Alton **[34]**, Alton, IL
100 Black Men of Central Illinois **[251]**, Bloomington, IL
100 Black Men of Central Ohio **[14262]**, Columbus, OH
100 Black Men of Chicago **[590]**, Chicago, IL
100 Black Men of Gary **[4769]**, Gary, IN
100 Black Men of Greater Cleveland **[14039]**, Cleveland, OH
100 Black Men of Greater Detroit **[7291]**, Detroit, MI
100 Black Men of Indianapolis **[4960]**, Indianapolis, IN
100 Black Men of the Quad Cities, Davenport **[2512]**, Moline, IL
Concerned Black Men of Cook County Chicago **[1710]**, Forest Park, IL
Concerned Black Men of Mansfield **[15766]**, Mansfield, OH
Greater Detroit Michigan Chap. of Concerned Black Men **[7369]**, Detroit, MI
Indiana Black Expo **[5197]**, Indianapolis, IN
African-American Adoption Agency **[12346]**, St. Paul, MN
African-Amer. Genealogy and History Gp; Oberlin **[16287]**, Oberlin, OH
African Amer. Women Evolving **[597]**, Chicago, IL
African Univ. Found. **[4963]**, Indianapolis, IN
African Violet Soc. of Dayton **[17167]**, West Chester, OH
African Violet Soc. of Minnesota **[11031]**, Fridley, MN
African Violet Soc. of Northern Illinois **[2736]**, Norridge, IL
AFSME Coun. 31 **[598]**, Chicago, IL
AFT-Wisconsin **[18443]**, Madison, WI
Aga Khan Gymkhana Cricket Club **[3966]**, Westmont, IL
Agassiz Audubon Soc. **[12839]**, Warren, MN
AGC of The Quad Cities **[3237]**, Rock Island, IL
Aged; Citizens for Better Care in Nursing Homes for the **[★7334]**
Agency Manager of Illinois **[1413]**, Deerfield, IL
Agents
Michigan Assn. of Insurance Agents **[8619]**, Lansing, MI
Wisconsin Assn. of Manufacturers' Agents **[19157]**, Milwaukee, WI
Wisconsin Soc. of Enrolled Agents **[18794]**, Manitowoc, WI
Agents' Assn; Minnesota Bur. of Criminal Apprehension **[12461]**, St. Paul, MN
Agents Assn. of Ohio; Professional Insurance **[15271]**, Gahanna, OH
Agents of Wisconsin; Professional Insurance **[18600]**, Madison, WI
Aggregate Producers of Wisconsin **[18444]**, Madison, WI
Aggregate Ready Mix Assn. of Minnesota **[10584]**, Burnsville, MN
Aggregates and Indus. Minerals Assn; Ohio **[15268]**, Gahanna, OH
Agile Alliance **[10888]**, Eden Prairie, MN
Aging
Area Agencies on Aging Assn. of Michigan **[8548]**, Lansing, MI
Assn. of Ohio Philanthropic Homes and Housing and Services for the Aging **[14330]**, Columbus, OH
Central Minnesota Coun. on Aging **[12280]**, St. Cloud, MN
Coalition of Wisconsin Aging Groups **[18498]**, Madison, WI
Coun. For Jewish Elderly **[863]**, Chicago, IL
DARTS of Minnesota **[12877]**, West St. Paul, MN
DuPage Senior Citizens Coun. **[2331]**, Lombard, IL
Gerontology Network **[7939]**, Grand Rapids, MI
Gray Panthers, Metro Detroit **[9257]**, Oak Park, MI
Gray Panthers, Twin Cities **[11569]**, Minneapolis, MN
Indiana Assn. of Homes and Services for the Aging **[5174]**, Indianapolis, IN
Life Sers. Network of Illinois - Springfield **[3647]**, Springfield, IL
Little Bros. Friends of the Elderly, Minneapolis/St. Paul, Minnesota **[11597]**, Minneapolis, MN
Milwaukee Aging Consortium **[19053]**, Milwaukee, WI
Minnesota Hea. and Housing Alliance **[12487]**, St. Paul, MN
Minnesota Senior Fed., Heartland Region **[10516]**, Brainerd, MN
Minnesota Senior Fed. - Metropolitan Region **[12519]**, St. Paul, MN
Minnesota Senior Fed., Midwest Region **[12921]**, Willmar, MN
Minnesota Senior Fed., Minnesota Valley Region **[12922]**, Willmar, MN
Minnesota Senior Fed., North Star Region **[12798]**, Virginia, MN
Minnesota Senior Fed., Northwest Region **[12744]**, Thief River Falls, MN
Minnesota Senior Fed., South Central Region **[11389]**, Mankato, MN
Minnesota Senior Fed., Southwest Region **[12923]**, Willmar, MN
Ohio Assn. of Area Agencies on Aging **[14542]**, Columbus, OH
St. Germain PrimeTimers **[19660]**, St. Germain, WI
The Senior Alliance (Area Agency on Aging 1-C in Michigan) **[10101]**, Wayne, MI
Wisconsin Assn. of Homes and Services for the Aging **[18656]**, Madison, WI
Aging Consortium; Milwaukee **[19053]**, Milwaukee, WI
Aging Groups; Coalition of Wisconsin **[18498]**, Madison, WI
Agnostic
Skeptics and Agnostics for Christian Culture **[14729]**, Columbus, OH
Agri-Dealers Assn; Michigan **[★7531]**
Agri-Dealers Assn; Michigan Grain and **[★7531]**
Agribusiness
Illinois Specialty Growers Assn. **[289]**, Bloomington, IL
Indiana Plant Food and Agricultural Chems. Assn. **[5278]**, Indianapolis, IN
Mid-America Intl. Agri-Trade Coun. **[1048]**, Chicago, IL
Wisconsin Agribusiness Coun. **[18642]**, Madison, WI
Agricultural Development
Indiana Crop Improvement Assn. **[5615]**, Lafayette, IN
Minnesota Agri-Growth Coun. **[12451]**, St. Paul, MN
Agricultural Education
Illinois Assn. of Vocational Agriculture Teachers **[3582]**, Springfield, IL
Indiana Assn. of Agricultural Educators **[5849]**, Mount Vernon, IN
Michigan Assn. of Agriscience Educators **[7039]**, Byron, MI
Minnesota Assn. of Agricultural Educators **[12656]**, Sherburn, MN
Ohio Assn. of Agricultural Educators **[15447]**, Hillsboro, OH
Wisconsin Assn. of Agricultural Educators **[18004]**, Fox Lake, WI
Agricultural Educ. Partnership; Sangamon - Menard County **[3673]**, Springfield, IL
Agricultural Engineering
Amer. Soc. of Agricultural and Biological Engineers, District 3 - Central Illinois **[3805]**, Urbana, IL
Amer. Soc. of Agricultural and Biological Engineers, District 3 - Chicago **[4048]**, Woodridge, IL
Amer. Soc. of Agricultural and Biological Engineers, District 3 - Wisconsin **[18214]**, Horicon, WI
Agricultural Equipment
Ohio-Michigan Equip. Dealers Assn. **[15059]**, Dublin, OH
Agricultural Science
Amer. Soc. for Enology and Viticulture - Eastern Sect. **[6474]**, West Lafayette, IN
Illinois Coun. on Food and Agricultural Res. **[3822]**, Urbana, IL
North Central Weed Sci. Soc. **[541]**, Champaign, IL
Agricultural Soc; Wilkin County **[10527]**, Breckenridge, MN
Agriculture
FFA - Michigan Assn. **[7520]**, East Lansing, MI
Gardeners of Am./Men's Garden Clubs of Am. - Akron Men's Garden Club **[16842]**, Tallmadge, OH
Gardeners of Am./Men's Garden Clubs of Am. - Boone County Gardeners of Am. **[3278]**, Rockford, IL
Gardeners of Am./Men's Garden Clubs of Am. - Dixon Men's Garden Club **[1478]**, Dixon, IL
Gardeners of Am./Men's Garden Clubs of Am. - Elgin Gardeners of Am. **[1590]**, Elgin, IL
Gardeners of Am./Men's Garden Clubs of Am. - Erie County Men's Garden Club **[16612]**, Sandusky, OH
Gardeners of Am./Men's Garden Clubs of Am. - Findlay Men and Women's Garden Club **[15202]**, Findlay, OH
Gardeners of Am./Men's Garden Clubs of Am. - Forget-Me-Not Garden Club **[16918]**, Toledo, OH
Gardeners of Am./Men's Garden Clubs of Am. - Fulton County Garden Club **[17140]**, Wauseon, OH
Gardeners of Am./Men's Garden Clubs of Am. - Garden Club of Kent **[16497]**, Ravenna, OH
Gardeners of Am./Men's Garden Clubs of Am. - Gardeners of Am. Fort Wayne **[4665]**, Fort Wayne, IN
Gardeners of Am./Men's Garden Clubs of Am. - Gardeners of Central Lake County **[2258]**, Libertyville, IL
Gardeners of Am./Men's Garden Clubs of Am. - Gardeners Club of Bluffton-Pandora Area **[14776]**, Columbus Grove, OH
Gardeners of America/Men's Garden Clubs of Am. - Gardeners Club of Green Bay **[18099]**, Green Bay, WI
Gardeners of Am./Men's Garden Clubs of Am. - Gardeners Club of Mendota **[3734]**, Sublette, IL
Gardeners of Am./Men's Garden Clubs of Am. - Gardeners of Lima **[15652]**, Lima, OH
Gardeners of Am./Men's Garden Clubs of Am. - Gardeners of Van Wert County **[17049]**, Van Wert, OH
Gardeners of Am./Men's Garden Clubs of Am. - Greater Cleveland Men's Garden Club **[15583]**, Lakewood, OH
Gardeners of Am./Men's Garden Clubs of Am. - Maple City Men's Garden Club **[6568]**, Adrian, MI
Gardeners of Am./Men's Garden Clubs of Am. - Men's Garden Club of Grosse Pointe **[8081]**, Grosse Pointe, MI
Gardeners of Am./Men's Garden Clubs of Am. - Men's Garden Club of Youngstown **[17401]**, Youngstown, OH
Gardeners of Am./Men's Garden Clubs of Am. - Rochelle Gardeners of Am. **[3224]**, Rochelle, IL
Gardeners of Am./Men's Garden Clubs of Am. - Rockford Area Gardeners of Am. **[3279]**, Rockford, IL
Gardeners of Am./Men's Garden Clubs of Am. - St. Marys Gardeners of Am. **[16578]**, St. Marys, OH
Gardeners of Am./Men's Garden Clubs of Am. - Stow Community Garden Club **[16775]**, Stow, OH
Groundswell Inc. of Minnesota **[12836]**, Wanda, MN

Illinois Crop Improvement Assn. **[526]**, Champaign, IL
Minnesota Crop Production Retailers **[10895]**, Eden Prairie, MN
Ohio AgriBus. Assn. **[14537]**, Columbus, OH
Ohio Farmers Union **[14607]**, Columbus, OH
Perry County Agriculture Soc. **[16133]**, New Lexington, OH
Southeast Minnesota Agriculture Alliance **[12015]**, Plainview, MN
Wilkin County Agricultural Soc. **[10527]**, Breckenridge, MN
Wisconsin Crop Improvement Assn. **[18695]**, Madison, WI
Wisconsin Potato and Vegetable Growers Association **[17480]**, Antigo, WI
Agriculture Alliance; Southeast Minnesota **[12015]**, Plainview, MN
Agriculture; Morris Area Chamber of Commerce and **[11838]**, Morris, MN
AHEPA 127 **[13692]**, Cincinnati, OH
Ahmed Shriners **[8930]**, Marquette, MI
AIDS
AIDS Legal Coun. of Chicago **[599]**, Chicago, IL
AIDS Network **[18445]**, Madison, WI
AIDS Partnership Michigan **[7295]**, Detroit, MI
Alexian Bros. The Harbor **[3917]**, Waukegan, IL
Aliveness Proj. **[11475]**, Minneapolis, MN
Assn. of Nurses in AIDS Care **[13043]**, Akron, OH
Columbus AIDS Task Force **[14369]**, Columbus, OH
Community AIDS Rsrc. and Educ. Services of Southwest Michigan **[8424]**, Kalamazoo, MI
Indiana Chap. of the Names Proj. Found. **[5209]**, Indianapolis, IN
Intl. Assn. of Physicians in AIDS Care **[983]**, Chicago, IL
Lansing Area AIDS Network **[8587]**, Lansing, MI
Midwest AIDS Prevention Proj. **[7696]**, Ferndale, MI
NAMES Proj. Chicago **[1065]**, Chicago, IL
NAMES Proj. Michigan **[7697]**, Ferndale, MI
AIDS Legal Coun. of Chicago **[599]**, Chicago, IL
AIDS Network **[18445]**, Madison, WI
AIDS Partnership Michigan **[7295]**, Detroit, MI
AIDS Prevention Proj; Midwest **[7696]**, Ferndale, MI
AIDS Rsrc. and Educ. Services of Southwest Michigan; Community **[8424]**, Kalamazoo, MI
AIDS Task Force; Columbus **[14369]**, Columbus, OH
Aikido
Aikido of Cincinnati **[13693]**, Cincinnati, OH
Aikido of Cleveland **[15960]**, Mentor, OH
Aikido of Columbus **[14270]**, Columbus, OH
Aikido of Harvard **[1947]**, Harvard, IL
Aikido of Indianapolis **[4964]**, Indianapolis, IN
Central Illinois Aikikai **[3808]**, Urbana, IL
East Lansing Aikikai **[7515]**, East Lansing, MI
Fox Valley Aikikai **[2636]**, Naperville, IL
Grand Marais Aikikai **[11074]**, Grand Marais, MN
Great Lakes Aikikai **[6699]**, Ann Arbor, MI
Kenosha Aikikai **[18299]**, Kenosha, WI
McHenry County Aikido Club **[1327]**, Crystal Lake, IL
Mid-Michigan Aikikai **[7554]**, East Lansing, MI
Midwest Aikido Center **[1051]**, Chicago, IL
Midwest Aikido Fed. **[1052]**, Chicago, IL
Raisin River Aikikai **[10214]**, Ypsilanti, MI
River Dojo **[13977]**, Cincinnati, OH
Rockford Aikikai **[3304]**, Rockford, IL
Univ. of Wisconsin Aikido **[18634]**, Madison, WI
Youngstown Aikikai **[17422]**, Youngstown, OH
Aikido of Cincinnati **[13693]**, Cincinnati, OH
Aikido of Cleveland **[15960]**, Mentor, OH
Aikido of Columbus **[14270]**, Columbus, OH
Aikido of Harvard **[1947]**, Harvard, IL
Aikido of Indianapolis **[4964]**, Indianapolis, IN
Ainad Shriners **[1547]**, East St. Louis, IL
Air Conditioning Contractors of Am., Akron Canton Chap. **[16645]**, Sharon Center, OH
Air Conditioning Contractors of Am; Central Ohio **[15043]**, Dublin, OH
Air Conditioning Contractors of Am., Greater Cincinnati Chap. **[13694]**, Cincinnati, OH
Air Conditioning Contractors of Am., Greater Cleveland Chap. **[15742]**, Macedonia, OH
Air Conditioning Contractors of Am., Greater Dayton Chap. **[15040]**, Dublin, OH
Air Conditioning Contractors of Am., Indiana Chap. **[4965]**, Indianapolis, IN
Air Conditioning Contractors of Am., Northeast Wisconsin Chap. **[19386]**, Oshkosh, WI
Air Conditioning Contractors of Am. - Ohio Chap. **[13627]**, Chagrin Falls, OH
Air Conditioning Contractors of Am., Region 3 **[★19384]**
Air Conditioning Contractors of Am., Southern Illinois Chap. **[3869]**, Virden, IL
Air Conditioning Contractors of Am., Wabash Valley Chap. **[6303]**, Terre Haute, IN
Air Conditioning Contractors of Am., West Michigan Chap. **[9192]**, Newaygo, MI
Air Conditioning Contractors' Natl. Assn. of North Central Ohio; Sheet Metal and **[14216]**, Cleveland, OH
Air Force Assn., Columbus-Bakalar Chap. No. 288 **[4387]**, Columbus, IN
Air Force Assn., Gen. E.W. Rawlings Chap. **[12347]**, St. Paul, MN
Air Force Assn., Wright Memorial Chap. No. 212 **[17364]**, Xenia, OH
Air Vair Gp. **[15276]**, Galion, OH
Air and Waste Mgt. Assn. - East Michigan Chap. **[9187]**, New Haven, MI
Air and Waste Mgt. Assn., Indiana Chap. **[4966]**, Indianapolis, IN
Air and Waste Mgt. Assn. - North Ohio Chap. **[14041]**, Cleveland, OH
Air and Waste Mgt. Assn. - Upper Midwest Sect. **[10942]**, Elk River, MN
Air and Waste Mgt. Assn. - West Michigan Chap. **[6556]**, Ada, MI
Airborne Brigade, Midwest Chapter XVII; Society of the 173D **[14730]**, Columbus, OH
Aircraft
Natl. Assn. of Rocketry - A Method of Reaching Extreme Altitudes **[4732]**, Fortville, IN
Natl. Assn. of Rocketry - Central Illinois Aerospace **[3425]**, Savoy, IL
Natl. Assn. of Rocketry - Columbus Soc. for the Advancement of Rocketry **[14517]**, Columbus, OH
Natl. Assn. of Rocketry - Fermilab Assn. of Rocketry **[184]**, Batavia, IL
Natl. Assn. of Rocketry - Huron Valley Rocket Soc. **[8101]**, Hamburg, MI
Natl. Assn. of Rocketry - Jackson Model Rocketry Club **[8390]**, Jackson, MI
Natl. Assn. of Rocketry - Kalkaska Aerospace Club **[8906]**, Mancelona, MI
Natl. Assn. of Rocketry - Launch Crue **[4934]**, Holland, IN
Natl. Assn. of Rocketry - Mantua Township Missile Agency **[16777]**, Stow, OH
Natl. Assn. of Rocketry - Medford Assn. of Rocket Sci. **[18847]**, Medford, WI
Natl. Assn. of Rocketry - Minnesota Amateur Spacemodelers Assn. **[10604]**, Burnsville, MN
Natl. Assn. of Rocketry - NARScouts **[15708]**, Lorain, OH
Natl. Assn. of Rocketry - Northern Illinois Rocketry Assn. **[1506]**, Downers Grove, IL
Natl. Assn. of Rocketry - Queen City Area Rocket Club **[16029]**, Milford, OH
Natl. Assn. of Rocketry - Rocketeers of Central Indiana **[5422]**, Indianapolis, IN
Natl. Assn. of Rocketry - Southwest Michigan Assn. of Spacemodeling Hobbyists **[10053]**, Walker, MI
Natl. Assn. of Rocketry - Summit City Aerospace Modelers **[4699]**, Fort Wayne, IN
Natl. Assn. of Rocketry - Thorp Apogee Heights **[19897]**, Thorp, WI
Natl. Assn. of Rocketry - Toledo Area Rocket Soc. **[16935]**, Toledo, OH
Natl. Assn. of Rocketry - Tri-City Sky Busters **[14173]**, Cleveland, OH
Natl. Assn. of Rocketry - US Aerospace Challenge **[8212]**, Holland, MI
Natl. Assn. of Rocketry - Waukesha County 4H Rocketeers **[19995]**, Waukesha, WI
Natl. Assn. of Rocketry - Willow Hill Rocketry Gp. **[1544]**, East Peoria, IL
Natl. Assn. of Rocketry - Wisconsin Org. of Spacemodeling Hobbyists **[19562]**, Racine, WI
Aitkin Area Chamber of Commerce **[10243]**, Aitkin, MN
Aitkin-Carlton County RSVP **[10685]**, Cloquet, MN
Akron AIFA **[16773]**, Stow, OH
Akron Area Bd. of Realtors **[13016]**, Akron, OH
Akron Auto. Dealers Assn. **[13017]**, Akron, OH
Akron; Better Bus. Bur. of **[13046]**, Akron, OH
Akron Black Nurses Assn. (16) **[16836]**, Tallmadge, OH
Akron BMW Motorcycle Club **[13018]**, Akron, OH
Akron - Canton Area Cooks and Chefs Assn. **[16630]**, Seville, OH
Akron-Canton Bonsai Soc. **[16837]**, Tallmadge, OH
Akron-Canton Boxer Rescue of Ohio **[16212]**, North Canton, OH
Akron-Canton Muskie Maniacs **[14254]**, Clinton, OH
Akron-Canton Soc. of Radiologic Technologists **[13252]**, Barberton, OH
Akron Character Counts **[13019]**, Akron, OH
Akron Coun. of Engg. and Sci. Societies **[13020]**, Akron, OH
Akron Dental Soc. **[13021]**, Akron, OH
Akron Jewish Community Fed. **[13022]**, Akron, OH
Akron Mineral Soc. **[14817]**, Cuyahoga Falls, OH
Akron Soc. of Professional Photographers **[13023]**, Akron, OH
Akron Summit Convention and Visitors Bur. **[13024]**, Akron, OH
Akron Turner Club **[16838]**, Tallmadge, OH
Akron Urban League **[13025]**, Akron, OH
Al-Anon/Alateen of Central Oakland County **[10079]**, Waterford, MI
Al-Anon Family Gp. **[1370]**, Decatur, IL
Al-Anon Family Groups of the Detroit Area **[★9474]**
Al-Anon Family Groups of Metro Detroit **[9474]**, Redford, MI
Al Koran Shriners **[13422]**, Broadview Heights, OH
Aladdin Shriners **[14271]**, Columbus, OH
Alateen of Central Oakland County; Al-Anon/ **[10079]**, Waterford, MI
Albany Chamber of Commerce **[10249]**, Albany, MN
Albany Park Chamber of Commerce **[600]**, Chicago, IL
Albany Park Neighborhood Coun. **[601]**, Chicago, IL
Albany Sportsmen's Club **[10250]**, Albany, MN
Albert Lea-Austin AIFA **[10349]**, Austin, MN
Albert Lea Convention and Visitors Bur. **[10252]**, Albert Lea, MN
Albert Lea Figure Skating Club **[10253]**, Albert Lea, MN
Albert Lea - Freeborn County Chamber of Commerce **[10254]**, Albert Lea, MN
Albertville Lions Club **[10269]**, Albertville, MN
Albion-Homer United Way **[6587]**, Albion, MI
Albion Volunteer Ser. Org. **[6588]**, Albion, MI
Alcohol Abuse
Alcoholics Anonymous **[10975]**, Fairmont, MN
Alcoholics Anonymous **[12674]**, South St. Paul, MN
Alcoholics Anonymous-Alano Society of Minneapolis **[11474]**, Minneapolis, MN
West Suburban ALANO Club **[3973]**, Westmont, IL
Alcohol and Addictions Rsrc. Center **[6208]**, South Bend, IN
Alcohol and Drug Abuse Self-Help Network, d.b.a. SMART Recovery **[15961]**, Mentor, OH
Alcohol and Other Drug Abuse; Wisconsin Assn. on **[18649]**, Madison, WI
Alcohol and Other Drugs Coun. of Kenosha County **[18293]**, Kenosha, WI
Alcoholic Beverages
Assoc. Beer Distributors of Illinois **[3533]**, Springfield, IL
Green Bay Rackers Homebrewing Club **[18319]**, Kewaunee, WI
Illinois Licensed Beverage Assn. **[3611]**, Springfield, IL
Indiana Beverage Alliance **[5195]**, Indianapolis, IN
Indiana Licensed Beverage Assn. **[5255]**, Indianapolis, IN
Michigan Beer and Wine Wholesalers Assn. **[8635]**, Lansing, MI
Michigan Licensed Beverage Assn. **[7541]**, East Lansing, MI
Minnesota Beer Wholesalers Assn. **[11630]**, Minneapolis, MN

Minnesota Licensed Beverage Assn. [12494], St. Paul, MN
Ohio Licensed Beverage Assn. [14634], Columbus, OH
Tasters Guild Intl. - Akron, Chap. No. 079 [16257], Norton, OH
Tasters Guild Intl. - Ann Arbor, Chap. No. 037 [6773], Ann Arbor, MI
Tasters Guild Intl. - Cleveland, Chap. No. 070 [14250], Cleveland Heights, OH
Tasters Guild Intl. - Grand Rapids, Chap. No. 007 [8014], Grand Rapids, MI
Tasters Guild Intl. - Grand Traverse, Chap. No. 018 [9954], Traverse City, MI
Tasters Guild Intl. - Harbor Springs/Petoskey, Chap. No. 096 [8119], Harbor Springs, MI
Tasters Guild Intl. - Kalamazoo, Chap. No. 038 [10051], Vicksburg, MI
Tasters Guild Intl. - Lansing, Chap. No. 039 [7467], DeWitt, MI
Tasters Guild Intl. - Lapeer, Chap. No. 076 [8783], Lapeer, MI
Tasters Guild Intl. - Michigan Lakeshore, Chap. No. 057 [9216], North Muskegon, MI
Tasters Guild Intl. - Milwaukee, Chap. No. 017 [17678], Brookfield, WI
Tasters Guild Intl. - Oakland County, Chap. No. 040 [7675], Farmington Hills, MI
Tavern League of Wisconsin [18626], Madison, WI
Wholesale Beer and Wine Assn. of Ohio [14765], Columbus, OH
Alcoholics Anonymous [10975], Fairmont, MN
Alcoholics Anonymous [12674], South St. Paul, MN
Alcoholics Anonymous-Alano Society of Minneapolis [11474], Minneapolis, MN
Alcoholics Anonymous, Cincinnati Intergroup Off. [13695], Cincinnati, OH
Alcoholics Anonymous, Indianapolis Intergroup [4967], Indianapolis, IN
Alcoholics Anonymous, Intergroup Assn. of Minneapolis and Suburban Area [12329], St. Louis Park, MN
Alcoholics Anonymous, Kent County Central Off. [7880], Grand Rapids, MI
Alcoholics Anonymous, Michiana Central Ser. Off. [6209], South Bend, IN
Alcoholics Anonymous, Southwestern Indiana Central Off. [4516], Evansville, IN
Alcoholics Anonymous, Wabash Valley Intergroup [6304], Terre Haute, IN
Alcoholics Anonymous World Services, Akron Intergroup Coun. [13026], Akron, OH
Alcoholics Anonymous World Sers., Bloomington/Normal Intergroup [252], Bloomington, IL
Alcoholics Anonymous World Services, Canton Area Intergroup Coun. [13539], Canton, OH
Alcoholics Anonymous World Services, Central Ohio Fellowship Intergroup [14272], Columbus, OH
Alcoholics Anonymous World Services, Chicago Area Ser. Off. [602], Chicago, IL
Alcoholics Anonymous World Services, Cleveland District Off. [14042], Cleveland, OH
Alcoholics Anonymous World Sers., Comite De Intergrupos [603], Chicago, IL
Alcoholics Anonymous World Sers., Detroit and Wayne County Off. [7296], Detroit, MI
Alcoholics Anonymous World Sers., District 11 Central Off. [9920], Traverse City, MI
Alcoholics Anonymous World Sers., District 91 Central Off. [1766], Galesburg, IL
Alcoholics Anonymous World Sers., East Central Illinois Intergroup [494], Champaign, IL
Alcoholics Anonymous World Sers., Fort Wayne Area Intergroup [4620], Fort Wayne, IN
Alcoholics Anonymous World Sers., Fox Valley Central Off. [18854], Menasha, WI
Alcoholics Anonymous World Services, Huron Valley Intergroup [★10207]
Alcoholics Anonymous World Services, Illowa Intergroup [2513], Moline, IL
Alcoholics Anonymous World Sers., Intergroup Off. [16164], Newark, OH
Alcoholics Anonymous World Services, Lansing Central Off. [8527], Lansing, MI
Alcoholics Anonymous World Sers., Lorain County Central Off. [15698], Lorain, OH
Alcoholics Anonymous World Sers., Madison Area Intergroup/Central Off. [18446], Madison, WI
Alcoholics Anonymous World Sers., Madison County Intergroup [4094], Anderson, IN
Alcoholics Anonymous World Services, Midland Area Unity Coun. Intergroup [9018], Midland, MI
Alcoholics Anonymous World Sers., North Central Ohio Area Intergroup [16600], Sandusky, OH
Alcoholics Anonymous World Sers., Northwest Ohio and Southeastern Michigan Central Off. [16873], Toledo, OH
Alcoholics Anonymous World Sers., Original Recipe Intergroup [5953], New Paris, IN
Alcoholics Anonymous World Sers., Peoria Area Intergroup Assn. [2999], Peoria, IL
Alcoholics Anonymous World Sers., Racine Area Central Off. [19548], Racine, WI
Alcoholics Anonymous World Sers., Rockford Area Intergroup [3261], Rockford, IL
Alcoholics Anonymous World Services, Springfield Intergroup [3520], Springfield, IL
Alcoholics Anonymous World Sers., Twin Ports Area Intergroup [10795], Duluth, MN
Alcoholics Anonymous World Sers., Winnebago Land Central Off. [17967], Fond du Lac, WI
Alcoholics Anonymous World Sers., Youngstown Area Intergroup [17384], Youngstown, OH
Alcoholism Coun. of the Cincinnati Area, Natl. Coun. on Alcoholism and Drug Dependence [13696], Cincinnati, OH
Alcoholism and Drug Abuse Counselors; Ohio Assn. of [14541], Columbus, OH
Alcoholism and Drug Coun; Central East [564], Charleston, IL
Alcoholism and Drug Dependence of Michigan; Natl. Coun. on [8739], Lansing, MI
Alcoholism/Lansing Regional Area; Natl. Coun. on [8740], Lansing, MI
Alcona County Habitat for Humanity [8810], Lincoln, MI
Alcona Habitat [★8810]
Aldo Leopold Audubon Soc. [19777], Stevens Point, WI
Aledo Area Chamber of Commerce [17], Aledo, IL
Aledo Main St. [18], Aledo, IL
Alexander High School - Young Life [13192], Athens, OH
Alexandria Lakes Area Chamber of Commerce [10271], Alexandria, MN
Alexandria - Monroe Chamber of Commerce [4089], Alexandria, IN
Alexian Bros. The Harbor [3917], Waukegan, IL
Alfordsville-Reeve Township Schools Organization [5701], Loogootee, IN
Alger Chamber of Commerce [9129], Munising, MI
Algoma Area Chamber of Commerce [17459], Algoma, WI
Algoma Township Historical Soc. [9522], Rockford, MI
Algonac Firefighters Assn. [6597], Algonac, MI
Algonquin - Lake in the Hills Chamber of Commerce [24], Algonquin, IL
Aliveness Proj. [11475], Minneapolis, MN
All Amer. City Chorus of Sweet Adelines [15518], Jackson Center, OH
All Breed Training Club of Akron [16839], Tallmadge, OH
All Ohio Scanner Club [16120], New Carlisle, OH
All Stars Cricket Club [12348], St. Paul, MN
Allegan Area Chamber of Commerce [6600], Allegan, MI
Allegan County United Way [6601], Allegan, MI
Allegan Rsrc. Center [6602], Allegan, MI
Allen County Genealogical Soc. of Indiana [4621], Fort Wayne, IN
Allen County REACT [15642], Lima, OH
Allen Park Lions Club [7243], Dearborn, MI
Allendale Chamber of Commerce [6617], Allendale, MI
Allendale Middle School - Wyldlife [6618], Allendale, MI
Allergy
Asthma and Allergy Found. of Am. Michigan State Chap. [9789], Southfield, MI
Allergy Found. of Am. Michigan State Chap; Asthma and [9789], Southfield, MI
Alliance for Animals, Madison [18447], Madison, WI
Alliance Area Chamber of Commerce [13107], Alliance, OH
Alliance of Automotive Ser. Providers, Illinois [3521], Springfield, IL
Alliance of Automotive Ser. Providers of Minnesota [11476], Minneapolis, MN
Alliance of Constr. Mgt. Professionals, Detroit Area Chap. [9569], Royal Oak, MI
Alliance of Early Childhood Professionals [11477], Minneapolis, MN
The Alliance Genealogical Soc. [13108], Alliance, OH
Alliance for the Great Lakes [604], Chicago, IL
Alliance for the Great Lakes [7851], Grand Haven, MI
Alliance of Guardian Angels, Cincinnati [13697], Cincinnati, OH
Alliance of Guardian Angels, Fostoria [15227], Fostoria, OH
Alliance of Guardian Angels, Green Bay [18073], Green Bay, WI
Alliance for Hea. [7881], Grand Rapids, MI
Alliance for the Mentally Ill of Antrim/Kalkaska Counties [8903], Mancelona, MI
Alliance for the Mentally Ill of Delta County [7827], Gladstone, MI
Alliance for the Mentally Ill - Downtown Detroit [7297], Detroit, MI
Alliance for the Mentally Ill of Jackson/Hillsdale Counties [8354], Jackson, MI
Alliance for the Mentally Ill of Macomb County [10057], Warren, MI
Alliance for the Mentally Ill of Mecosta County [8995], Mecosta, MI
Alliance for the Mentally Ill of Northeast Michigan [9538], Rogers City, MI
Alliance for the Mentally Ill of Northern Lower Michigan [9360], Petoskey, MI
Alliance for the Mentally Ill, Rochester Area [★12163]
Alliance for the Mentally Ill - Share of Grand Rapids [7882], Grand Rapids, MI
Alliance for the Mentally Ill of Suburban West [8826], Livonia, MI
Alliance for Responsible Pet Ownership [4598], Fishers, IN
Alliance-Salem ALU [13109], Alliance, OH
Alliance of the St. [11478], Minneapolis, MN
Alliance for Sustainability - Intl. Alliance for Sustainable Agriculture [11479], Minneapolis, MN
Alma Area Chamber of Commerce [★6632]
Almena Commercial Club [17463], Almena, WI
Alpena Alcona Presque Isle Bd. of Realtors [6638], Alpena, MI
Alpena Area Convention and Visitors Bur. [6639], Alpena, MI
Alpena Tourist Assn. [★6639]
Alpena Youth Sailing Club [6640], Alpena, MI
Alpha Chi Chap. of Sigma Tau Gamma Alumni [495], Champaign, IL
Alpha Iota Delta, Pi Chap. [14836], Dayton, OH
Alpha Kappa Alpha, Alpha Mu Omega [4968], Indianapolis, IN
Alpha Kappa Alpha, Theta Lambda Omega [10110], West Bloomfield, MI
Alpha Parent Support Group [4622], Fort Wayne, IN
Alpine Curling Club [19212], Monroe, WI
Alpine Kiwanis of Rockford, Illinois [585], Cherry Valley, IL
Alpine Team Racing; Southeastern Wisconsin [19255], Mukwonago, WI
ALS Assn. of Indiana [4969], Indianapolis, IN
ALS Assn., Minnesota Chap. [11480], Minneapolis, MN
ALS Assn. Southeast Wisconsin Chap. [20066], Wauwatosa, WI
ALS Assn., West Michigan Chap. [7883], Grand Rapids, MI
ALS Assn., Western Ohio [14273], Columbus, OH
ALS of Michigan [★9783]
Alsip Chamber of Commerce and Economic Development [30], Alsip, IL
Altamont Chamber of Commerce [32], Altamont, IL
Alternative Medicine
Minnesota Natural Hea. Coalition [12215], Rosemount, MN
Alton Market Place Assn. [36], Alton, IL

Alton Regional Convention and Visitors Bur. **[37]**, Alton, IL
Altura Lions Club **[10288]**, Altura, MN
Alumni
Alpha Chi Chap. of Sigma Tau Gamma Alumni **[495]**, Champaign, IL
Bellaire High School Alumni Assn. **[13310]**, Bellaire, OH
Catholic Alumni Club of Detroit **[6689]**, Ann Arbor, MI
Catholic Alumni Club of Mississippi and Missouri River Valleys **[200]**, Belleville, IL
Catholic Single Adults Club of the Twin Cities **[11539]**, Minneapolis, MN
Chief Logan Reservation Staff Alumni Assn. **[13663]**, Chillicothe, OH
Columbus Ohio Catholic Alumni Club **[14398]**, Columbus, OH
Euclid Public Schools Alumni Assn. **[15142]**, Euclid, OH
Mayo School of Hea.-Related Scis. Alumni Assn. **[12154]**, Rochester, MN
North Royalton Alumni Assn. **[13413]**, Brecksville, OH
Orange Alumni Assn. **[16397]**, Pepper Pike, OH
Penn State Alumni Assn., Central Indiana Chap. **[4852]**, Greenwood, IN
Penn State Alumni Assn., Greater Chicago Chap. **[1838]**, Glen Ellyn, IL
Penn State Alumni Assn., Michigan **[9773]**, South Lyon, MI
Penn State Alumni Assn., Minnesota Chap. **[12661]**, Shoreview, MN
Quincy Citizens Police Acad. Alumni Assn. **[3164]**, Quincy, IL
Univ. of Oklahoma Assn. - OU Club of Wisconsin **[20105]**, West Allis, WI
West Lafayette High School Alumni Assn. **[6505]**, West Lafayette, IN
Alumni Assn; Bellaire High School **[13310]**, Bellaire, OH
Alumni Assn; Bellevue High School **[13328]**, Bellevue, OH
Alumni Assn., Central Illinois; Penn State **[2729]**, Normal, IL
Alumni Assn; Chief Logan Reservation Staff **[13663]**, Chillicothe, OH
Alumni Assn; Euclid Public Schools **[15142]**, Euclid, OH
Alumni Assn; Mayo School of Hea.-Related Scis. **[12154]**, Rochester, MN
Alumni Assn; North Royalton **[13413]**, Brecksville, OH
Alumni Assn; Orange **[16397]**, Pepper Pike, OH
Alumni Assn; Quincy Citizens Police Acad. **[3164]**, Quincy, IL
Alumni Assn; West Lafayette High School **[6505]**, West Lafayette, IN
Alumni Athletic Boosters; Female **[10184]**, Wyandotte, MI
Alvarado Lions Club **[10289]**, Alvarado, MN
Alverno Coll. Students In Free Enterprise **[18926]**, Milwaukee, WI
Alzheimer's Association, Akron Tri-County Chapter **[13027]**, Akron, OH
Alzheimer's Assn., Bloomington/Normal Illinois Chap. **[253]**, Bloomington, IL
Alzheimer's Assn., Central Illinois Chap. **[3000]**, Peoria, IL
Alzheimer's Assn., Central Indiana Chap. **[4970]**, Indianapolis, IN
Alzheimer's Assn., Cleveland Area Chap. **[14043]**, Cleveland, OH
Alzheimer's Assn., Detroit Area Chap. **[★9777]**
Alzheimer's Assn.-Duluth Center **[10796]**, Duluth, MN
Alzheimer's Assn., East Central Illinois Chap. **[★253]**
Alzheimer's Assn.-Fergus Falls Center **[10993]**, Fergus Falls, MN
Alzheimer's Assn. - Greater Cincinnati Chap. **[13698]**, Cincinnati, OH
Alzheimer's Assn., Greater East Ohio Area Chap., Canton Off. **[13540]**, Canton, OH
Alzheimer's Assn., Greater Illinois Chap. **[3522]**, Springfield, IL
Alzheimer's Assn. - Greater Illinois Chap., Rockford Regional Prog. Center **[3262]**, Rockford, IL
Alzheimer's Assn., Greater Michigan Chap. **[9777]**, Southfield, MI
Alzheimer's Assn., Greater Michigan Chap., Upper Peninsula Region **[8931]**, Marquette, MI
Alzheimer's Assn. of Greater WI, LaCrosse Regional Off. **[18331]**, La Crosse, WI
Alzheimer's Assn. of Greater Wisconsin **[18074]**, Green Bay, WI
Alzheimer's Assn., Miami Valley Chap. **[14837]**, Dayton, OH
Alzheimer's Assn., Michigan Great Lakes Chap. **[6653]**, Ann Arbor, MI
Alzheimer's Assn., Michigan Great Lakes Chap., Southwest Region **[8412]**, Kalamazoo, MI
Alzheimer's Assn., Minnesota Lakes **[11481]**, Minneapolis, MN
Alzheimer's Assn., Northwest Ohio Chap. **[16874]**, Toledo, OH
Alzheimer's Assn., Northwest Ohio Chap., Lima Off. **[15643]**, Lima, OH
Alzheimer's Assn.-Rochester Center **[12122]**, Rochester, MN
Alzheimer's Assn., South Central Michigan Chap. **[★6653]**
Alzheimer's Assn., South Central Wisconsin Chap. **[18448]**, Madison, WI
Alzheimer's Assn., Southeastern Wisconsin Chap. **[18927]**, Milwaukee, WI
Alzheimer's Association, West Michigan **[8187]**, Holland, MI
Alzheimer's Disease
Alzheimer's Association, Akron Tri-County Chapter **[13027]**, Akron, OH
Alzheimer's Assn., Bloomington/Normal Illinois Chap. **[253]**, Bloomington, IL
Alzheimer's Assn., Central Illinois Chap. **[3000]**, Peoria, IL
Alzheimer's Assn., Central Indiana Chap. **[4970]**, Indianapolis, IN
Alzheimer's Assn., Cleveland Area Chap. **[14043]**, Cleveland, OH
Alzheimer's Assn.-Duluth Center **[10796]**, Duluth, MN
Alzheimer's Assn.-Fergus Falls Center **[10993]**, Fergus Falls, MN
Alzheimer's Assn. - Greater Cincinnati Chap. **[13698]**, Cincinnati, OH
Alzheimer's Assn., Greater East Ohio Area Chap., Canton Off. **[13540]**, Canton, OH
Alzheimer's Assn., Greater Illinois Chap. **[3522]**, Springfield, IL
Alzheimer's Assn. - Greater Illinois Chap., Rockford Regional Prog. Center **[3262]**, Rockford, IL
Alzheimer's Assn., Greater Michigan Chap. **[9777]**, Southfield, MI
Alzheimer's Assn., Greater Michigan Chap., Upper Peninsula Region **[8931]**, Marquette, MI
Alzheimer's Assn. of Greater WI, LaCrosse Regional Off. **[18331]**, La Crosse, WI
Alzheimer's Assn. of Greater Wisconsin **[18074]**, Green Bay, WI
Alzheimer's Assn., Miami Valley Chap. **[14837]**, Dayton, OH
Alzheimer's Assn., Michigan Great Lakes Chap. **[6653]**, Ann Arbor, MI
Alzheimer's Assn., Michigan Great Lakes Chap., Southwest Region **[8412]**, Kalamazoo, MI
Alzheimer's Assn., Minnesota Lakes **[11481]**, Minneapolis, MN
Alzheimer's Assn., Northwest Ohio Chap. **[16874]**, Toledo, OH
Alzheimer's Assn., Northwest Ohio Chap., Lima Off. **[15643]**, Lima, OH
Alzheimer's Assn.-Rochester Center **[12122]**, Rochester, MN
Alzheimer's Assn., South Central Wisconsin Chap. **[18448]**, Madison, WI
Alzheimer's Assn., Southeastern Wisconsin Chap. **[18927]**, Milwaukee, WI
Alzheimer's Association, West Michigan **[8187]**, Holland, MI
Alzheimer's Family Support Gp. **[3801]**, Urbana, IL
Alzheimer's Services of Northern Indiana **[6210]**, South Bend, IN
Alzheimer's Disease and Related Disorders Assn. **[★6653]**
Alzheimer's Disease and Related Disorders Assn., Southfield Chap. **[★9777]**
Alzheimer's Family Support Gp. **[3801]**, Urbana, IL
Alzheimer's Services of Northern Indiana **[6210]**, South Bend, IN
Amateur Astronomers of Jackson **[8355]**, Jackson, MI
Amateur Hockey Assn; Wisconsin **[17851]**, Eagle River, WI
Amateur Radio
Western Reserve Amateur Radio Association **[16201]**, Newton Falls, OH
Amateur Radio Association; Western Reserve **[16201]**, Newton Falls, OH
Amateur Skating Union - Mid-Am. Club **[★2756]**
Amateur Softball Assn. of Am., Michigan **[★9029]**
Amazon Africa Aid Org. **[6654]**, Ann Arbor, MI
Amboy Area Chamber of Commerce **[48]**, Amboy, IL
AMBUCS - Alive After Five **[9731]**, Schoolcraft, MI
AMBUCS - Greater Twin Cities **[12657]**, Shoreview, MN
AMBUCS, Pekin Club **[2982]**, Pekin, IL
Ambulance Services; Michigan Assn. of **[8605]**, Lansing, MI
Ambulatory Care
Indiana Fed. of Ambulatory Surgical Centers **[4325]**, Carmel, IN
Amelia - Young Life **[13124]**, Amelia, OH
America Soc. of Greater Cincinnati; Japan- **[13874]**, Cincinnati, OH
Amer. Acad. of Pediatrics, Illinois Chap. **[605]**, Chicago, IL
Amer. Acad. of Pediatrics, Indiana Chap. **[4971]**, Indianapolis, IN
Amer. Acad. of Pediatrics, Minnesota Chap. **[12349]**, St. Paul, MN
Amer. Acad. of Pediatrics, Ohio Chap. **[17338]**, Worthington, OH
Amer. Acad. of Pediatrics, Wisconsin Chap. **[18449]**, Madison, WI
Amer. Accounting Assn., Midwest Region **[11482]**, Minneapolis, MN
Amer. Accounting Assn., Ohio Region **[17023]**, University Heights, OH
Amer. Alcohol and Drug Info. Found. **[8528]**, Lansing, MI
Amer. Arbitration Assn., Michigan **[9778]**, Southfield, MI
Amer. Arbitration Assn., Minnesota **[11483]**, Minneapolis, MN
Amer. Arbitration Assn., Ohio **[13699]**, Cincinnati, OH
Amer. Associates of Blacks in Energy, Chicago **[2623]**, Naperville, IL
Amer. Assn. of Airport Executives, Illinois **[606]**, Chicago, IL
Amer. Assn. of Airport Executives, Indiana **[4517]**, Evansville, IN
Amer. Assn. of Airport Executives, Michigan **[7884]**, Grand Rapids, MI
Amer. Assn. of Airport Executives, Ohio **[14274]**, Columbus, OH
Amer. Assn. of Airport Executives, Wisconsin **[18450]**, Madison, WI
Amer. Assn. of Blacks in Energy, Cincinnati **[13700]**, Cincinnati, OH
Amer. Assn. of Blacks in Energy, Indiana **[4623]**, Fort Wayne, IN
Amer. Assn. of Blacks in Energy, Michigan **[8356]**, Jackson, MI
Amer. Assn. of Blacks in Energy, Michigan State Univ. **[7498]**, East Lansing, MI
Amer. Assn. of Blacks in Energy, Wisconsin **[18928]**, Milwaukee, WI
Amer. Assn. of Bovine Practitioners, District 4 **[17308]**, Wooster, OH
Amer. Assn. of Bovine Practitioners, District 5 **[17769]**, Clintonville, WI
Amer. Assn. of Candy Technologists - Chicago Sect. **[2831]**, Oakbrook Terrace, IL
Amer. Assn. of Candy Technologists - Milwaukee Sect. **[18929]**, Milwaukee, WI
Amer. Assn. for Clinical Chemistry, Chicago Sect. **[18451]**, Madison, WI
Amer. Assn. for Clinical Chemistry, Michigan Sect. **[6811]**, Auburn Hills, MI
Amer. Assn. for Clinical Chemistry, Northeast Ohio Sect. **[14044]**, Cleveland, OH

Amer. Assn. for Clinical Chemistry, Ohio Valley Sect. [13701], Cincinnati, OH
Amer. Assn. of Collegiate Registrars and Admission Officers, Ohio [★14548]
Amer. Assn. of Collegiate Registrars and Admissions Officers, Indiana [6084], Richmond, IN
Amer. Assn. of Collegiate Registrars and Admissions Officers, Michigan [7298], Detroit, MI
Amer. Assn. of Critical Care Nurses, Greater Akron Area Chap. [13511], Canal Fulton, OH
Amer. Assn. of Critical Care Nurses, Greater Chicago Area Chap. [607], Chicago, IL
Amer. Assn. of Critical Care Nurses, Greater Cincinnati Chap. [13702], Cincinnati, OH
Amer. Assn. of Critical-Care Nurses, Greater Toledo Area Chap. [16875], Toledo, OH
Amer. Assn. of Critical-Care Nurses, Lake Superior Chap. [9176], Negaunee, MI
Amer. Assn. of Critical Care Nurses, North Central Wisconsin Chap. [19778], Stevens Point, WI
Amer. Assn. of Critical Care Nurses, Northeast Indiana Chap. [4624], Fort Wayne, IN
Amer. Assn. of Critical Care Nurses, West Michigan Chap. [6914], Belmont, MI
Amer. Assn. of Healthcare Administrative Mgt., Gopher Chap. [11974], Park Rapids, MN
Amer. Assn. of Healthcare Administrative Mgt., Western Reserve Chap. No. 18 [15493], Independence, OH
Amer. Assn. of Healthcare Administrative Mgt., Wisconsin Chap. [19595], Rhinelander, WI
Amer. Assn. for Lab. Animal Sci. - Chicago [608], Chicago, IL
Amer. Assn. for Lab. Animal Sci. - Indiana [4972], Indianapolis, IN
Amer. Assn. for Lab. Animal Sci. - Michigan [10196], Ypsilanti, MI
Amer. Assn. for Lab. Animal Sci. - Minnesota [12350], St. Paul, MN
Amer. Assn. for Lab. Animal Sci. - Southern Ohio [13703], Cincinnati, OH
Amer. Assn. of Legal Nurse Consultants, Cleveland/NEO Chap. [13239], Avon, OH
Amer. Assn. of Legal Nurse Consultants, Greater Chicago Chap. [609], Chicago, IL
Amer. Assn. of Legal Nurse Consultants, Greater Detroit Chap. [8827], Livonia, MI
Amer. Assn. of Legal Nurse Consultants, Greater Indianapolis Chap. [4973], Indianapolis, IN
Amer. Assn. for Medical Transcription, 500 Central Indiana Chap. [5931], New Castle, IN
Amer. Assn. for Medical Transcription, Bay Area Chap. [9595], Saginaw, MI
Amer. Assn. for Medical Transcription, Buckeye Area Chap. [16429], Piqua, OH
Amer. Assn. for Medical Transcription, Four Lakes Chap. [17482], Appleton, WI
Amer. Assn. for Medical Transcription, Greater Milwaukee Chap. [19328], Oak Creek, WI
Amer. Assn. for Medical Transcription, Mid-Michigan Chap. [8232], Holly, MI
Amer. Assn. for Medical Transcription, Red Cedar Chap. [8144], Haslett, MI
Amer. Assn. for Medical Transcription, Southeast Michigan Chap. [7213], Commerce Township, MI
Amer. Assn. for Medical Transcription, Twin Cities Chap. [12865], Welch, MN
Amer. Assn. for Medical Transcription, West Michigan Chap. [9008], Mesick, MI
Amer. Assn. of Neuroscience Nurses, Kentuckiana Chap. [4363], Clarksville, IN
Amer. Assn. of Pharmaceutical Scientists, Univ. of Michigan Student Chap. [6655], Ann Arbor, MI
Amer. Assn. of Physicians of Indian Origin, Downstate Illinois [485], Centralia, IL
Amer. Assn. of Physicians of Indian Origin, Northern Ohio [17226], Westlake, OH
Amer. Assn. of Physicians of Indian Origin, Wisconsin [18883], Mequon, WI
Amer. Assn. of Physics Teachers, Chicago Sect. [610], Chicago, IL
Amer. Assn. of Physics Teachers, Indiana Sect. [4974], Indianapolis, IN
Amer. Assn. of Physics Teachers, Michigan Sect. [9497], Rochester, MI
Amer. Assn. of Physics Teachers, Minnesota Sect. [11815], Moorhead, MN
Amer. Assn. of Physics Teachers, Ohio Sect. [16542], Rocky River, OH
Amer. Assn. of Physics Teachers, Puerto Rico Sect. [9498], Rochester, MI
Amer. Assn. of Physics Teachers, Southern Ohio Sect. [13704], Cincinnati, OH
Amer. Assn. of Physics Teachers, Wisconsin Sect. [17861], Eau Claire, WI
Amer. Assn. of Retired Persons, Chicago [611], Chicago, IL
American Association of Retired Persons, Indiana [4975], Indianapolis, IN
Amer. Assn. of Retired Persons, Michigan [8529], Lansing, MI
Amer. Assn. of Retired Persons, Wisconsin [18452], Madison, WI
Amer. Assn. of Teachers of German - Indiana Chap. [6002], Notre Dame, IN
Amer. Assn. of Teachers of German - Minnesota Chap. [12351], St. Paul, MN
Amer. Assn. of Teachers of German - Northern Illinois Chap. [1583], Elgin, IL
Amer. Assn. of Teachers of German - Southern Illinois Chap. [2222], Latham, IL
Amer. Assn. of Teachers of Spanish and Portuguese - Chicago Chap. [612], Chicago, IL
Amer. Assn. of Univ. Professors; Michigan Conf. of the [8649], Lansing, MI
Amer. Assn. of Univ. Women, Grand Rapids Br. [7885], Grand Rapids, MI
Amer. Assn. of Univ. Women - Illinois [1414], Deerfield, IL
Amer. Assn. of Univ. Women - Minnesota State [12075], Red Wing, MN
Amer. Assn. of Univ. Women - Wisconsin [19387], Oshkosh, WI
Amer. Assn. for Women in Community Colleges, Coll. of DuPage [1824], Glen Ellyn, IL
Amer. Assn. for Women in Community Colleges, Region V [2095], Joliet, IL
Amer. Baptist Churches of Michigan [7499], East Lansing, MI
Amer. Baptist Churches of Ohio [15340], Granville, OH
Amer. Bear Assn. - Minnesota [11941], Orr, MN
Amer. Begonia Soc., Greater Chicago Area Chap. [613], Chicago, IL
Amer. Bd. of Trial Advocates - Cincinnati [13705], Cincinnati, OH
Amer. Bd. of Trial Advocates - Illinois [3377], St. Charles, IL
Amer. Bd. of Trial Advocates - Indiana [4195], Bloomington, IN
Amer. Bd. of Trial Advocates - Michigan [7886], Grand Rapids, MI
Amer. Bd. of Trial Advocates - Minnesota [11484], Minneapolis, MN
Amer. Bd. of Trial Advocates - Ohio [14275], Columbus, OH
Amer. Bd. of Trial Advocates - Wisconsin [18930], Milwaukee, WI
Amer. Boer Goat Assn. - Region 10 [15593], Lancaster, OH
Amer. Brittany Club, Badger [18453], Madison, WI
Amer. Brittany Club - Directors Chap. [459], Carterville, IL
Amer. Brush Manufacturers Assn. [106], Aurora, IL
Amer. Camp Assn. Indiana [5998], North Webster, IN
Amer. Camp Assn. Michigan [7887], Grand Rapids, MI
Amer. Camp Assn. Northland [10662], Circle Pines, MN
Amer. Camp Assn. Ohio [15041], Dublin, OH
Amer. Camp Assn., Wisconsin [18454], Madison, WI
Amer. Camping Assn. - Illinois Sect. [614], Chicago, IL
Amer. Camping Assn. - Ohio Sect. [★15041]
Amer. Camping Assn., Wisconsin Sect. [★18454]
Amer. Cancer Soc. [6656], Ann Arbor, MI
Amer. Cancer Soc., Altoona [17466], Altoona, WI
Amer. Cancer Soc., Batavia - Fox Valley Regional [171], Batavia, IL
Amer. Cancer Soc., Bay Area Ser. Center [7621], Essexville, MI
Amer. Cancer Soc., Brainerd [10504], Brainerd, MN
Amer. Cancer Soc., Capital Area Ser. Center [7500], East Lansing, MI
Amer. Cancer Soc. - Central Indiana Area Ser. Center [4976], Indianapolis, IN
Amer. Cancer Soc., Champaign - Eastern Regional [496], Champaign, IL
Amer. Cancer Soc. Chicago Region [615], Chicago, IL
Amer. Cancer Soc., Clark/Miami Area [16712], Springfield, OH
Amer. Cancer Soc., Cuyahoga County [14045], Cleveland, OH
Amer. Cancer Soc., Defiance Area [14980], Defiance, OH
Amer. Cancer Soc., East Metro Unit [12352], St. Paul, MN
Amer. Cancer Soc., East Michigan Area Ser. Center [7707], Flint, MI
Amer. Cancer Soc., Eau Claire [17467], Altoona, WI
Amer. Cancer Soc., Evanston - North Shore Regional [1646], Evanston, IL
Amer. Cancer Soc., Fairfield Area [15594], Lancaster, OH
Amer. Cancer Soc., Franklin [18007], Franklin, WI
Amer. Cancer Soc., Franklin County [14276], Columbus, OH
Amer. Cancer Soc., Geauga Area [14777], Concord Township, OH
Amer. Cancer Soc., Geauga, Lake Ashtabula Area Off. [16330], Painesville, OH
Amer. Cancer Soc., Gladwin County [7622], Essexville, MI
Amer. Cancer Soc., Glen Ellyn - Du Page County Regional [2832], Oakbrook Terrace, IL
Amer. Cancer Soc., Green Bay [17811], De Pere, WI
Amer. Cancer Soc., Hamilton County [13706], Cincinnati, OH
Amer. Cancer Soc., Hancock [15191], Findlay, OH
Amer. Cancer Soc., Henry County Unit [14981], Defiance, OH
Amer. Cancer Soc., Highland Park - Lake County Regional [2282], Lincolnshire, IL
Amer. Cancer Soc., La Crosse [19359], Onalaska, WI
Amer. Cancer Soc., Lakeshore Area Ser. Center [8188], Holland, MI
Amer. Cancer Soc., Livingston County [7006], Brighton, MI
Amer. Cancer Soc., Lorain Area [15103], Elyria, OH
Amer. Cancer Soc., Lucas County [15899], Maumee, OH
Amer. Cancer Soc., Macomb County Unit [★9779]
Amer. Cancer Soc., Madison [18455], Madison, WI
Amer. Cancer Soc., Mahoning County [13525], Canfield, OH
Amer. Cancer Soc., Marion Area [15833], Marion, OH
Amer. Cancer Soc., Marion - Southern Regional [2399], Marion, IL
Amer. Cancer Soc., Mercer Area [15644], Lima, OH
Amer. Cancer Soc., Metro Detroit Area Ser. Center [9779], Southfield, MI
Amer. Cancer Soc., Mid-Indiana Area Ser. Center [4095], Anderson, IN
Amer. Cancer Soc., Mid-Indiana Area Ser. Center [5723], Marion, IN
Amer. Cancer Soc., Mid-Southwestern Area Ser. Center [5523], Jasper, IN
Amer. Cancer Soc., MidSouthwestern Area Ser. Center [6407], Vincennes, IN
Amer. Cancer Soc., Montgomery Area [14838], Dayton, OH
Amer. Cancer Soc., Moorhead [11816], Moorhead, MN
Amer. Cancer Soc., Muskingum Area [17434], Zanesville, OH
Amer. Cancer Soc., Northeast Indiana Area Ser. Center [4625], Fort Wayne, IN
Amer. Cancer Soc., Northwest Indiana Area Ser. Center [5762], Merrillville, IN
Amer. Cancer Soc., Onalaska [19360], Onalaska, WI
Amer. Cancer Soc., Palatine - Northwest Suburban Regional [2903], Palatine, IL
Amer. Cancer Soc., Peoria - West Central Regional [3001], Peoria, IL
Amer. Cancer Soc., Pickaway Area [15595], Lancaster, OH

Amer. Cancer Soc., Porter County Unit **[6375]**, Valparaiso, IN
Amer. Cancer Soc., Riverside Regional Off. **[3213]**, Riverside, IL
Amer. Cancer Soc., Rochester **[12123]**, Rochester, MN
Amer. Cancer Soc., Rock Island - Northwest Regional **[3238]**, Rock Island, IL
Amer. Cancer Soc., Rockford - Northern Regional **[3263]**, Rockford, IL
Amer. Cancer Soc., Ross Area **[13656]**, Chillicothe, OH
Amer. Cancer Soc., St. Cloud **[12270]**, St. Cloud, MN
Amer. Cancer Soc., Sheboygan **[19688]**, Sheboygan, WI
Amer. Cancer Soc., South Central Michigan Ser. Center **[9012]**, Michigan Center, MI
Amer. Cancer Soc., Southeast Indiana Area Ser. Center **[4364]**, Clarksville, IN
Amer. Cancer Soc., Southeast Michigan Rsrc. Center **[★9779]**
Amer. Cancer Soc., Southwest Ohio Area **[15870]**, Mason, OH
Amer. Cancer Soc., Springfield - Western Regional **[3523]**, Springfield, IL
Amer. Cancer Soc., Stark Area **[16213]**, North Canton, OH
Amer. Cancer Soc., Summit Area **[13028]**, Akron, OH
Amer. Cancer Soc., Tinley Park - Prairie Land Regional **[3765]**, Tinley Park, IL
Amer. Cancer Soc., Trumbull Area **[13526]**, Canfield, OH
Amer. Cancer Soc., Tuscarawas Area **[15025]**, Dover, OH
Amer. Cancer Soc., Vanderburgh County Unit **[4518]**, Evansville, IN
Amer. Cancer Soc., Wabash Valley Indiana Area Ser. Center **[6305]**, Terre Haute, IN
Amer. Cancer Soc., Washington Area **[15812]**, Marietta, OH
Amer. Cancer Soc., Waukesha **[19976]**, Waukesha, WI
Amer. Cancer Soc., Wausau **[20030]**, Wausau, WI
Amer. Cancer Soc., West Michigan Area Ser. Center **[7888]**, Grand Rapids, MI
Amer. Cancer Soc., Willmar **[12911]**, Willmar, MN
Amer. Cancer Soc., Wood Area **[13380]**, Bowling Green, OH
Amer. Chem. Soc., Akron Sect. **[16214]**, North Canton, OH
Amer. Chem. Soc., Central Wisconsin Sect. **[19779]**, Stevens Point, WI
Amer. Chem. Soc., Chicago Sect. **[2700]**, Niles, IL
Amer. Chem. Soc., Cincinnati Sect. **[13707]**, Cincinnati, OH
Amer. Chem. Soc., Cleveland Sect. **[14046]**, Cleveland, OH
Amer. Chem. Soc., Columbus Sect. **[14277]**, Columbus, OH
Amer. Chem. Soc., Dayton Sect. **[17354]**, Wright-Patterson AFB, OH
Amer. Chem. Soc., Decatur-Springfield Sect. **[1371]**, Decatur, IL
Amer. Chem. Soc., Detroit Sect. **[7299]**, Detroit, MI
Amer. Chem. Soc., East Central Illinois Sect. **[497]**, Champaign, IL
Amer. Chem. Soc., Huron Valley Sect. **[6657]**, Ann Arbor, MI
Amer. Chem. Soc., Indiana-Kentucky Border Sect. **[4519]**, Evansville, IN
Amer. Chem. Soc., Indiana Sect. **[4977]**, Indianapolis, IN
Amer. Chem. Soc., Joliet Sect. **[3097]**, Plainfield, IL
Amer. Chem. Soc., Kalamazoo Sect. **[8413]**, Kalamazoo, MI
Amer. Chem. Soc., Lacrosse-Winona Sect. **[18332]**, La Crosse, WI
Amer. Chem. Soc., Lake Superior Sect. **[12766]**, Two Harbors, MN
Amer. Chem. Soc., Louisiana Sect. **[15180]**, Fairview Park, OH
Amer. Chem. Soc., Mark Twain Sect. **[2365]**, Macomb, IL
Amer. Chem. Soc., Michigan State Univ. Sect. **[7501]**, East Lansing, MI
Amer. Chem. Soc., Midland Sect. **[9019]**, Midland, MI
Amer. Chem. Soc., Milwaukee Sect. **[19977]**, Waukesha, WI
Amer. Chem. Soc., Minnesota Sect. **[12888]**, White Bear Lake, MN
Amer. Chem. Soc., Northeast Wisconsin Sect. **[18855]**, Menasha, WI
Amer. Chem. Soc., Northeastern Indiana Sect. **[4626]**, Fort Wayne, IN
Amer. Chem. Soc., Northeastern Ohio Sect. **[17270]**, Willoughby, OH
Amer. Chem. Soc., Northwest Central Ohio Sect. **[13007]**, Ada, OH
Amer. Chem. Soc., Purdue Sect. **[6469]**, West Lafayette, IN
Amer. Chem. Soc., Red River Valley Sect. **[11817]**, Moorhead, MN
Amer. Chem. Soc., Rock River Sect. **[1424]**, DeKalb, IL
Amer. Chem. Soc., St. Joseph Valley Sect. **[9202]**, Niles, MI
Amer. Chem. Soc., Southern Illinois Sect. **[409]**, Carbondale, IL
Amer. Chem. Soc., Southern Indiana Sect. **[4196]**, Bloomington, IN
Amer. Chem. Soc., Toledo Sect. **[15455]**, Holland, OH
Amer. Chem. Soc., Upper Peninsula Sect. **[8248]**, Houghton, MI
Amer. Chem. Soc., Wabash Valley Sect. **[6306]**, Terre Haute, IN
Amer. Chem. Soc., Western Michigan Sect. **[9135]**, Muskegon, MI
Amer. Chem. Soc., Wisconsin Sect. **[18456]**, Madison, WI
Amer. Chem. Soc., Wooster Sect. **[13158]**, Ashland, OH
Amer. Chesapeake Club, Illinois **[2192]**, Lake Forest, IL
Amer. Chesapeake Club, Indiana **[5748]**, Martinsville, IN
Amer. Chesapeake Club, Michigan **[10016]**, Tustin, MI
Amer. Chesapeake Club, Minnesota **[11154]**, Hibbing, MN
Amer. Chesapeake Club, Wisconsin **[19380]**, Oregon, WI
Amer. Choral Directors Assn. - Central Div. **[616]**, Chicago, IL
Amer. Choral Directors Assn. - Illinois Chap. **[1425]**, DeKalb, IL
Amer. Choral Directors Assn. - Michigan Chap. **[7889]**, Grand Rapids, MI
Amer. Choral Directors Assn. - Minnesota Chap. **[11910]**, Northfield, MN
Amer. Choral Directors Assn. - North Central Div. **[19978]**, Waukesha, WI
Amer. Civil Liberties Union of Illinois **[617]**, Chicago, IL
Amer. Civil Liberties Union of Michigan **[7300]**, Detroit, MI
Amer. Civil Liberties Union of Minnesota **[12353]**, St. Paul, MN
Amer. Civil Liberties Union, Ohio Affl. **[14047]**, Cleveland, OH
Amer. Civil Liberties Union, Wisconsin **[18931]**, Milwaukee, WI
Amer. Coll. of Cardiology - Michigan Chap. **[7577]**, Eaton Rapids, MI
Amer. Coll. of Cardiology - Wisconsin Chap. **[18932]**, Milwaukee, WI
Amer. Coll. of Emergency Physicians Michigan Chap. **[★8644]**
Amer. Coll. of Emergency Physicians - Minnesota Chap. **[11485]**, Minneapolis, MN
Amer. Coll. of Obstetricians and Gynecologists-Minnesota **[11486]**, Minneapolis, MN
Amer. Coll. of Physicians - Ohio Chap. **[14048]**, Cleveland, OH
Amer. Coll. of Surgeons - Michigan Chap. **[7502]**, East Lansing, MI
Amer. Concrete Inst., Central Ohio Chap. **[14278]**, Columbus, OH
Amer. Consulting Engineers Coun. of Michigan **[★8530]**
Amer. Coun. of the Blind of Indiana **[4978]**, Indianapolis, IN
Amer. Coun. of the Blind of Minnesota **[11487]**, Minneapolis, MN
Amer. Coun. of the Blind of Ohio **[14279]**, Columbus, OH
Amer. Coun. of the Blind of Ohio **[14280]**, Columbus, OH
Amer. Coun. of Engg. Companies of Indiana **[4979]**, Indianapolis, IN
Amer. Coun. of Engg. Companies of Michigan **[8530]**, Lansing, MI
Amer. Coun. of Engg. Companies of Minnesota **[11784]**, Minnetonka, MN
Amer. Coun. of Engg. Companies of Ohio **[14281]**, Columbus, OH
Amer. Coun. of Engg. Companies of Wisconsin **[18457]**, Madison, WI
Amer. Coun. on Gift Annuities **[4980]**, Indianapolis, IN
Amer. Counseling Assn., Illinois **[1473]**, Dixon, IL
Amer. Counseling Assn., Indiana **[4981]**, Indianapolis, IN
Amer. Counseling Assn., Ohio **[13514]**, Canal Winchester, OH
Amer. Culinary Fed. Cleveland Chap. **[17281]**, Willowick, OH
Amer. Culinary Fed. Columbus Chap. **[14282]**, Columbus, OH
Amer. Culinary Fed. - Greater Indianapolis Chap. **[4846]**, Greenwood, IN
Amer. Dairy Assn. of Indiana **[4982]**, Indianapolis, IN
Amer. Dairy Sci. Assn. - Illinois State Univ. Dairy Club **[2707]**, Normal, IL
Amer. Dairy Sci. Assn. - Michigan State Univ. Dairy Sci. Club **[7503]**, East Lansing, MI
Amer. Dairy Sci. Assn. - Midwest Br. **[4828]**, Greenfield, IN
Amer. Dairy Sci. Assn. - Ohio State Univ. - Ag Tech Inst. **[17309]**, Wooster, OH
Amer. Diabetes Assn. **[7890]**, Grand Rapids, MI
Amer. Diabetes Assn. **[20067]**, Wauwatosa, WI
Amer. Diabetes Assn., Central Indiana Area **[4983]**, Indianapolis, IN
Amer. Diabetes Assn. - Northern Illinois **[618]**, Chicago, IL
Amer. Diabetes Assn., Southwest Ohio/Northern Kentucky Area **[17168]**, West Chester, OH
Amer. Ex-Prisoners of War, Badger Chap. **[18458]**, Madison, WI
Amer. Ex-Prisoners of War, Dayton Area Chap. **[15556]**, Kettering, OH
Amer. Ex-Prisoners of War, Greater Chicago Chap. **[4067]**, Worth, IL
Amer. Ex-Prisoners of War, Kickapoo Chap. **[2697]**, Newton, IL
Amer. Ex-Prisoners of War, Lakes Region Chap. **[11975]**, Park Rapids, MN
Amer. Ex-Prisoners of War, Milwaukee Barb Wire Chap. **[19248]**, Mukwonago, WI
Amer. Ex-Prisoners of War, Northeastern Wisconsin Chap. **[18284]**, Kaukauna, WI
Amer. Ex-Prisoners of War, Northern Indiana Chap. **[4867]**, Hammond, IN
Amer. Ex-Prisoners of War, Okaw Chap. **[1528]**, East Alton, IL
Amer. Ex-Prisoners of War, Prairieland Chap. **[12694]**, Springfield, MN
Amer. Ex-Prisoners of War, Southern Indiana Chap. **[4272]**, Boonville, IN
Amer. Ex-Prisoners of War, Southern Wisconsin Chap. **[17604]**, Beloit, WI
Amer. Ex-Prisoners of War, Western Illinois Chap. **[2514]**, Moline, IL
Amer. Family Assn. of Indiana **[4984]**, Indianapolis, IN
Amer. Family Assn. of Michigan **[9020]**, Midland, MI
Amer. Fed. of Govt. Employees, AFL-CIO - Coun. 164 **[17084]**, Walbridge, OH
Amer. Fed. of Govt. Employees, AFL-CIO - DOD Local Union 1138 **[14839]**, Dayton, OH
Amer. Fed. of Govt. Employees, AFL-CIO - DOD Local Union 1626 **[6841]**, Battle Creek, MI
Amer. Fed. of Govt. Employees, AFL-CIO - DOD Local Union 1658 **[10058]**, Warren, MI
Amer. Fed. of Govt. Employees, AFL-CIO - DOJ Local Union 1741 **[9046]**, Milan, MI
Amer. Fed. of Govt. Employees, AFL-CIO - Local Union 607 **[15099]**, Elkton, OH

Amer. Fed. of Govt. Employees, AFL-CIO - Veterans' Affairs Local Union 1629 **[6842]**, Battle Creek, MI
Amer. Fed. of Govt. Employees, District 6 **[4985]**, Indianapolis, IN
Amer. Fed. of Govt. Employees, District 7 **[619]**, Chicago, IL
Amer. Fed. of Govt. Employees, District 8 **[10458]**, Bloomington, MN
Amer. Fed. of Musicians, Local 101-473 **[14840]**, Dayton, OH
Amer. Fed. of State, County and Municipal Employees, AFL-CIO - Civil Ser. Employees Assn. Local Union 11 **[17202]**, Westerville, OH
Amer. Fed. of State, County and Municipal Employees, AFL-CIO - Michigan Coun. 25 **[8531]**, Lansing, MI
Amer. Fed. of State, County and Municipal Employees, AFL-CIO - Milwaukee Wisconsin District Coun. 48 **[18933]**, Milwaukee, WI
Amer. Fed. of State, County and Municipal Employees Coun. 8 Ohio **[17339]**, Worthington, OH
Amer. Fed. of Teachers, AFL-CIO - Professional Guild of Ohio Local Union 1960 **[14283]**, Columbus, OH
Amer. Fisheries Soc., Indiana Chap. Pres. **[6373]**, Vallonia, IN
Amer. Fisheries Soc., Michigan Chap. Pres. **[8803]**, Lewiston, MI
Amer. Fisheries Soc. - Minnesota Chap. **[★12832]**
Amer. Fisheries Soc., Minnesota Chap. Pres. **[10686]**, Cloquet, MN
Amer. Fisheries Soc., Ohio Chap. **[15414]**, Hebron, OH
Amer. Found. for Suicide Prevention of Northeast Ohio **[14049]**, Cleveland, OH
Amer. Friends Ser. Comm., Ann Arbor **[6658]**, Ann Arbor, MI
Amer. Friends Ser. Comm., Chicago **[620]**, Chicago, IL
Amer. Friends Ser. Comm. - Dayton, Ohio **[14841]**, Dayton, OH
Amer. Friends Ser. Comm., Michigan Area Off. **[6659]**, Ann Arbor, MI
Amer. Friends Ser. Comm., Northeast Ohio **[13029]**, Akron, OH
Amer. Guild of Organists, Ann Arbor (531) **[7301]**, Detroit, MI
Amer. Guild of Organists, Detroit Chap. **[10059]**, Warren, MI
Amer. Guild of Organists, Holland Area C556 **[8189]**, Holland, MI
Amer. Guild of Organists, Madison (644) **[18459]**, Madison, WI
Amer. Guild of Organists, Moody Bible Inst. (595) **[4079]**, Zion, IL
Amer. Guild of Organists, Muskegon-Lakeshore (538) **[9136]**, Muskegon, MI
American Guild of Organists, Twin Cities (628) **[12639]**, Savage, MN
Amer. Guild of Organists, Univ. of Evansville C592 **[5524]**, Jasper, IN
Amer. Guild of Organists, Wabash Valley (527) **[6307]**, Terre Haute, IN
Amer. Heart Assn. **[11488]**, Minneapolis, MN
Amer. Heart Assn., Cincinnati **[13708]**, Cincinnati, OH
Amer. Heart Assn., Madison **[18460]**, Madison, WI
Amer. Heart Assn., Michigan Affl. **[★9780]**
Amer. Heart Assn., Midwest Affl. **[9780]**, Southfield, MI
Amer. Hellenic Educational Progressive Assn. - Alton, Chap. 304 **[38]**, Alton, IL
Amer. Hellenic Educational Progressive Assn. - Beverly Hills, Chap. 350 **[2874]**, Orland Park, IL
Amer. Hellenic Educational Progressive Assn. - Chicago, Chap. 46 **[2582]**, Mount Prospect, IL
Amer. Hellenic Educational Progressive Assn. - Chicago/Logan, Chap. 260 **[1854]**, Glenview, IL
Amer. Hellenic Educational Progressive Assn. - Decatur, Chap. 457 **[1372]**, Decatur, IL
Amer. Hellenic Educational Progressive Assn. - District 11 **[17169]**, West Chester, OH
Amer. Hellenic Educational Progressive Assn. - DuPage, Chap. 423 **[4]**, Addison, IL
Amer. Hellenic Educational Progressive Assn. - Evanston, Chap. 204 **[621]**, Chicago, IL
Amer. Hellenic Educational Progressive Assn. - Garfield, Chap. 203 **[3198]**, River Forest, IL
Amer. Hellenic Educational Progressive Assn. - Joliet, Chap. 131 **[3098]**, Plainfield, IL
Amer. Hellenic Educational Progressive Assn. - Kankakee, Chap. 345 **[332]**, Bradley, IL
Amer. Hellenic Educational Progressive Assn. - Lincolnwood, Chap. 396 **[3480]**, Skokie, IL
Amer. Hellenic Educational Progressive Assn. - Madison, Chap. 369 **[18461]**, Madison, WI
Amer. Hellenic Educational Progressive Assn. - Milo, Chap. 348 **[622]**, Chicago, IL
Amer. Hellenic Educational Progressive Assn. - Milwaukee, Chap. 43 **[17662]**, Brookfield, WI
Amer. Hellenic Educational Progressive Assn. - Northshore, Chap. 94 **[623]**, Chicago, IL
Amer. Hellenic Educational Progressive Assn. - Northwestern, Chap. 388 **[624]**, Chicago, IL
Amer. Hellenic Educational Progressive Assn. - Oaklawn-Englewood, Chap. 323 **[367]**, Burbank, IL
Amer. Hellenic Educational Progressive Assn. - Racine, Chap. 377 **[19475]**, Pleasant Prairie, WI
Amer. Hellenic Educational Progressive Assn. - Shoreline, Chap. 380 **[625]**, Chicago, IL
Amer. Hellenic Educational Progressive Assn. - South Chicago, Chap. 351 **[2234]**, Lemont, IL
Amer. Hellenic Educational Progressive Assn. - Waukegan, Chap. 218 **[2255]**, Libertyville, IL
Amer. Hellenic Educational Progressive Assn. - West Suburban, Chap. 202 **[1357]**, Darien, IL
Amer. Hellenic Educational Progressive Assn. - Woodlawn, Chap. 93 **[2934]**, Palos Heights, IL
Amer. Hiking Soc. - Atwood Outdoor Educ. Center - Rockford Park District **[3264]**, Rockford, IL
Amer. Hiking Soc. - Buckeye Trail Assn. **[17340]**, Worthington, OH
Amer. Hiking Soc. - Camp Tuscazoar Found. **[16673]**, Smithville, OH
Amer. Hiking Soc. - Cleveland Hiking Club **[14050]**, Cleveland, OH
Amer. Hiking Soc. - Cuyahoga Valley Trails Coun. **[16565]**, Sagamore Hills, OH
Amer. Hiking Soc. - Delaware Greenways **[5860]**, Muncie, IN
Amer. Hiking Soc. - DuBois Center **[1515]**, Du Bois, IL
Amer. Hiking Soc. - Hoosiers Hikers Coun. **[5749]**, Martinsville, IN
Amer. Hiking Soc. - Ice Age Park and Trail Found. **[18934]**, Milwaukee, WI
Amer. Hiking Soc. - Indianapolis Hiking Club **[4847]**, Greenwood, IN
Amer. Hiking Soc. - Kekekabic Trail Club **[11489]**, Minneapolis, MN
Amer. Hiking Soc. - North Country Trail Assn. **[8860]**, Lowell, MI
Amer. Hiking Soc. - Parks and Trails Coun. of Minnesota **[12354]**, St. Paul, MN
Amer. Hiking Soc. - Preble County Historical Soc. **[15086]**, Eaton, OH
Amer. Hiking Soc. - River to River Trail Soc. **[1936]**, Harrisburg, IL
Amer. Hiking Soc. - Superior Hiking Trail Assn. **[12767]**, Two Harbors, MN
Amer. Hiking Soc. - Youth Conservation Corps **[3918]**, Waukegan, IL
Amer. Historical Soc. of Germans from Russia, Northern Illinois Chap. **[2803]**, Oak Park, IL
Amer. Historical Soc. of Germans from Russia, Saginaw Valley Chap. **[9596]**, Saginaw, MI
American Indian
Minnesota Amer. Indian Chamber of Commerce **[11623]**, Minneapolis, MN
Amer. Indus. Hygiene Assn., Central Ohio Sect. **[14284]**, Columbus, OH
Amer. Indus. Hygiene Assn. - Chicago Local Sect. **[1493]**, Downers Grove, IL
Amer. Indus. Hygiene Assn., Chicago Sect. **[2504]**, Mokena, IL
Amer. Indus. Hygiene Assn., Ohio Valley Sect. **[13709]**, Cincinnati, OH
Amer. Indus. Hygiene Assn. - Prairie Local Sect. **[254]**, Bloomington, IL
Amer. Indus. Hygiene Assn., Prairie Sect. **[255]**, Bloomington, IL
Amer. Indus. Hygiene Assn. - Upper Midwest Sect. **[12355]**, St. Paul, MN
Amer. Indus. Hygiene Assn., Wisconsin Sect. **[19954]**, Waterford, WI
Amer. Inst. of Aeronautics and Astronautics, Case Western Reserve Univ. **[14051]**, Cleveland, OH
Amer. Inst. of Aeronautics and Astronautics, Columbus Sect. **[14285]**, Columbus, OH
Amer. Inst. of Aeronautics and Astronautics, Illinois **[3802]**, Urbana, IL
Amer. Inst. of Aeronautics and Astronautics, Indiana **[4986]**, Indianapolis, IN
Amer. Inst. of Aeronautics and Astronautics, Michigan **[8190]**, Holland, MI
American Institute of Aeronautics and Astronautics, Northern ohio **[15993]**, Middleburg Heights, OH
Amer. Inst. of Aeronautics and Astronautics, Twin Cities **[11490]**, Minneapolis, MN
Amer. Inst. of Architects Akron **[16050]**, Mogadore, OH
Amer. Inst. of Architects Central/Southern Indiana **[5605]**, Lafayette, IN
Amer. Inst. of Architects Chicago **[626]**, Chicago, IL
Amer. Inst. of Architects Cincinnati **[13710]**, Cincinnati, OH
Amer. Inst. of Architects, Cleveland **[14052]**, Cleveland, OH
American Institute of Architects Columbus **[14286]**, Columbus, OH
Amer. Inst. of Architects Dayton **[14842]**, Dayton, OH
Amer. Inst. of Architects Eastern Illinois **[2894]**, Ottawa, IL
American Institute of Architects Eastern Ohio **[17385]**, Youngstown, OH
Amer. Inst. of Architects, Huron Valley Chap. **[6660]**, Ann Arbor, MI
Amer. Inst. of Architects - Illinois **[3524]**, Springfield, IL
Amer. Inst. of Architects Indiana **[4987]**, Indianapolis, IN
Amer. Inst. of Architects, Michigan **[7302]**, Detroit, MI
Amer. Inst. of Architects - Minnesota **[11491]**, Minneapolis, MN
Amer. Inst. of Architects Northeast Illinois **[2624]**, Naperville, IL
Amer. Inst. of Architects Ohio **[14287]**, Columbus, OH
Amer. Inst. of Architects Southeast Wisconsin **[18935]**, Milwaukee, WI
Amer. Inst. of Architects Southern Illinois **[410]**, Carbondale, IL
Amer. Inst. of Architects Southwest Wisconsin **[19931]**, Verona, WI
Amer. Inst. of Architects, Wisconsin **[18462]**, Madison, WI
Amer. Inst. of Chem. Engineers - Akron Sect. **[13541]**, Canton, OH
Amer. Inst. of Chem. Engineers - Chicago Sect. **[1449]**, Des Plaines, IL
Amer. Inst. of Chem. Engineers - Cleveland Sect. **[15419]**, Highland Heights, OH
Amer. Inst. of Chem. Engineers - Ohio Valley Sect. **[13711]**, Cincinnati, OH
Amer. Inst. of Chem. Engineers - Upper Midwest Sect. **[11013]**, Forest Lake, MN
American Legion
Amer. Legion, 3 M Post 599 **[12356]**, St. Paul, MN
Amer. Legion, A. E. E. E. W. Post 373 **[15015]**, Delta, OH
Amer. Legion, Aaron Post 788 **[444]**, Carol Stream, IL
Amer. Legion, Aaron Scisinger Post 178 **[4767]**, Garrett, IN
Amer. Legion, Aarvig-Campbell Post 78 **[3118]**, Pontiac, IL
Amer. Legion, Abe Lincoln Post 444 **[4439]**, Dale, IN
Amer. Legion, Abendroth-Connolly Post 282 **[18809]**, Markesan, WI
Amer. Legion, Abner Rude Post 481 **[12675]**, South St. Paul, MN
Amer. Legion, Abraham-Hickok-Wetmore Post 148 **[17555]**, Bagley, WI
Amer. Legion, Abramowicz-Kaczmarczyk-Cwikla Post 547 **[18433]**, Lublin, WI
Amer. Legion, A.C. of Flint Post 366 **[7708]**, Flint, MI

Amer. Legion, A.C. Hansen Post 185 **[12777]**, Tyler, MN
Amer. Legion, Acton-Bunker-Hill Post 220 **[4988]**, Indianapolis, IN
Amer. Legion, Adams-Helwig-Randles Post 162 **[17462]**, Alma Center, WI
Amer. Legion, Adams Post 43 **[4450]**, Decatur, IN
Amer. Legion, Adams Post 146 **[10239]**, Adams, MN
Amer. Legion, Adams Township Post 553 **[16876]**, Toledo, OH
Amer. Legion, Adamson-Norman Post 30 **[10994]**, Fergus Falls, MN
Amer. Legion, Adolph Oiseth Post 333 **[11243]**, Kasson, MN
Amer. Legion, Adolph-Wacek-Patrick-Slattery Post 303 **[20175]**, Winter, WI
Amer. Legion, Advt. Mens Post 38 **[627]**, Chicago, IL
Amer. Legion, Adwell-Garvey Post 180 **[12100]**, Renville, MN
Amer. Legion, Agnew-Shinabarger Post 307 **[16426]**, Pioneer, OH
Amer. Legion, Ahlberg-Weigelt Post 470 **[11248]**, Kelliher, MN
Amer. Legion, Aitkin-Lee Post 86 **[10244]**, Aitkin, MN
Amer. Legion, Akron Post 209 **[13030]**, Akron, OH
Amer. Legion, Al Besemann Post 482 **[10251]**, Albany, MN
Amer. Legion, Al Sirat Grotto Post 392 **[16351]**, Parma, OH
Amer. Legion, Albany Post 167 **[4083]**, Albany, IN
Amer. Legion, Albert Dennis Connell Post 422 **[10671]**, Claremont, MN
Amer. Legion, Albert-Shelby Post 298 **[59]**, Apple River, IL
Amer. Legion, Albert Williams Post 131 **[5560]**, Knox, IN
Amer. Legion, Albertson Esque Post 548 **[19449]**, Phelps, WI
Amer. Legion, Albin Johnson Post 244 **[11853]**, Mountain Lake, MN
Amer. Legion, Albion-Browns Post 590 **[14]**, Albion, IL
Amer. Legion, Albion Post 246 **[4084]**, Albion, IN
Amer. Legion, Alden Post 404 **[10270]**, Alden, MN
Amer. Legion, Alderman-Luce Post 259 **[7027]**, Bronson, MI
Amer. Legion, Alexander Bright Post 87 **[4090]**, Alexandria, IN
Amer. Legion, Alexandria Post 87 **[10272]**, Alexandria, MN
Amer. Legion, Algonac Post 278 **[6598]**, Algonac, MI
Amer. Legion, Algonquin Post 670 **[25]**, Algonquin, IL
Amer. Legion, Algot Johnson Post 69 **[10162]**, Whitehall, MI
Amer. Legion, Alhambra Post 1147 **[28]**, Alhambra, IL
Amer. Legion, All Amer. Post 1776 **[628]**, Chicago, IL
Amer. Legion, Allen-Bevnue Post 354 **[39]**, Alton, IL
Amer. Legion, Allen County Post 499 **[4627]**, Fort Wayne, IN
Amer. Legion, Allen-Myers-Hohn Post 176 **[16689]**, South Charleston, OH
Amer. Legion, Allen Park Post 409 **[6608]**, Allen Park, MI
Amer. Legion, Allen Post 538 **[6606]**, Allen, MI
Amer. Legion, Alliance Post 166 **[13110]**, Alliance, OH
Amer. Legion, Almont Post 479 **[6637]**, Almont, MI
Amer. Legion, Altenberg Post 497 **[1733]**, Franklin Grove, IL
Amer. Legion, Alto Post 528 **[6652]**, Alto, MI
Amer. Legion, Alton Post 126 **[40]**, Alton, IL
Amer. Legion, Alva Courier Post 487 **[588]**, Chester, IL
Amer. Legion, Ambelang-Ebelt-Lau Post 386 **[17718]**, Cascade, WI
Amer. Legion, Amboy Post 429 **[4093]**, Amboy, IN
Amer. Legion, Amer. Slovak Post 367 **[4770]**, Gary, IN
Amer. Legion, Amstutz-Marty Post 256 **[19225]**, Monticello, WI
Amer. Legion, Ancil Geiger Post 226 **[5799]**, Milford, IN
Amer. Legion, And-Quist Post 218 **[12357]**, St. Paul, MN
Amer. Legion, Anderson-Black Post 462 **[11304]**, Laporte, MN
Amer. Legion, Anderson-Claffy Post 109 **[12768]**, Two Harbors, MN
Amer. Legion, Anderson-Good Post 40 **[17565]**, Bangor, WI
Amer. Legion, Anderson Post 318 **[13712]**, Cincinnati, OH
Amer. Legion, Anderson-Sather Post 524 **[20153]**, White Lake, WI
Amer. Legion, Anderson-scroggins Post 460 **[3176]**, Ramsey, IL
Amer. Legion, Anderson-Tongen Post 559 **[11138]**, Hazel Run, MN
Amer. Legion, Andover Post 465 **[50]**, Andover, IL
Amer. Legion, Andrew Borgen Post 75 **[11880]**, New Richland, MN
Amer. Legion, Angola Post 31 **[4123]**, Angola, IN
Amer. Legion, Annandale Post 176 **[10299]**, Annandale, MN
Amer. Legion, Antioch Post 748 **[55]**, Antioch, IL
Amer. Legion, Antrim Post 461 **[13491]**, Cambridge, OH
Amer. Legion, Apple Valley Post 1776 **[10314]**, Apple Valley, MN
Amer. Legion, Arcade-Phalen Post 577 **[12358]**, St. Paul, MN
Amer. Legion, Arch Post 477 **[16128]**, New Holland, OH
Amer. Legion, Archer-Highland Post 698 **[629]**, Chicago, IL
Amer. Legion, Archview Post 1265 **[1532]**, East Carondelet, IL
Amer. Legion, Arcola Post 639 **[60]**, Arcola, IL
Amer. Legion, Arenzville Post 604 **[62]**, Arenzville, IL
Amer. Legion, Argo-Summit Post 735 **[3742]**, Summit, IL
Amer. Legion, Argonne Forest Post 278 **[10524]**, Brandon, MN
Amer. Legion, Argonne Post 32 **[10241]**, Adrian, MN
Amer. Legion, Argonne Post 33 **[16758]**, Steubenville, OH
Amer. Legion, Argonne Post 545 **[16877]**, Toledo, OH
Amer. Legion, Argyle Post 251 **[17536]**, Argyle, WI
Amer. Legion, Armenian Vartan Post 307 **[7244]**, Dearborn, MI
Amer. Legion, Army-Navy-Shaker Post 54 **[14053]**, Cleveland, OH
Amer. Legion, Arndt-Bruley Post 176 **[20150]**, Weyauwega, WI
Amer. Legion, Arnet-Sheldon Post 423 **[11197]**, Houston, MN
Amer. Legion, Arnold-B.-Moll-John-W.-Hazard Post 385 **[9652]**, St. Clair Shores, MI
Amer. Legion, Aroma Park Post 1019 **[85]**, Aroma Park, IL
Amer. Legion, Arthur and Leonard Falldin Post 555 **[11492]**, Minneapolis, MN
Amer. Legion, Arthur Post 479 **[87]**, Arthur, IL
Amer. Legion, Ashton Post 345 **[92]**, Ashton, IL
Amer. Legion, Ashville Community Post 730 **[13190]**, Ashville, OH
Amer. Legion, Astoria Post 25 **[95]**, Astoria, IL
Amer. Legion, Atkins Saw Post 355 **[4989]**, Indianapolis, IN
Amer. Legion, Atlanta Post 201 **[6801]**, Atlanta, MI
Amer. Legion, Attica Post 52 **[4135]**, Attica, IN
Amer. Legion, Attucks-Brooks Post 606 **[12359]**, St. Paul, MN
Amer. Legion, Atwood-Mauck Post 459 **[13469]**, Burton, OH
Amer. Legion, Auburn Post 277 **[102]**, Auburn, IL
Amer. Legion, Audie Johnson Post 211 **[7573]**, East Tawas, MI
Amer. Legion, Audubon Amer. Legion Post 339 **[10346]**, Audubon, MN
Amer. Legion, Auglaize Post 330 **[17088]**, Wapakoneta, OH
Amer. Legion, August Altheide Post 302 **[10394]**, Beardsley, MN
Amer. Legion, August Donner Post 309 **[10402]**, Belview, MN
Amer. Legion, August Mattson Post 71 **[7828]**, Gladstone, MI
Amer. Legion, Austin-Moore Post 415 **[8141]**, Hartland, MI
Amer. Legion, Austin Post 91 **[10350]**, Austin, MN
Amer. Legion, Austintown Memorial Post 301 **[13235]**, Austintown, OH
Amer. Legion Auxiliary of Michigan **[8532]**, Lansing, MI
Amer. Legion Auxiliary of Ohio **[17435]**, Zanesville, OH
Amer. Legion Auxiliary of Wisconsin **[19505]**, Portage, WI
Amer. Legion, Aviation Post 651 **[2875]**, Orland Park, IL
Amer. Legion, Avilla Post 240 **[4150]**, Avilla, IN
Amer. Legion, Avon Lake Post 211 **[13243]**, Avon Lake, OH
Amer. Legion, Avon Post 145 **[4443]**, Danville, IN
Amer. Legion, Avon Post 538 **[10366]**, Avon, MN
Amer. Legion, Baccarat Post 40 **[16527]**, Richwood, OH
Amer. Legion, Bad Axe Post 318 **[6819]**, Bad Axe, MI
Amer. Legion, Bailey-Frey Post 125 **[16713]**, Springfield, OH
Amer. Legion, Bailey-Kinnear Post 197 **[10655]**, Chatfield, MN
Amer. Legion, Bailey-Throne Post 596 **[10963]**, Erskine, MN
Amer. Legion, Bainbridge Post 355 **[10533]**, Brooklyn Center, MN
Amer. Legion, Baltimore Ohio Post 466 **[4990]**, Indianapolis, IN
Amer. Legion, Bank of Am. Post 383 **[1720]**, Fox River Grove, IL
Amer. Legion, Baraboo Post 26 **[17569]**, Baraboo, WI
Amer. Legion, Barberton Post 271 **[13253]**, Barberton, OH
Amer. Legion, Barnesville Post 168 **[13258]**, Barnesville, OH
Amer. Legion, Baroda Community Post 345 **[6831]**, Baroda, MI
Amer. Legion, Barrington Post 158 **[139]**, Barrington, IL
Amer. Legion, Barrus-Mc-Culligh-Stewart Post 393 **[8294]**, Hulbert, MI
Amer. Legion, Barry Post 222 **[155]**, Barry, IL
Amer. Legion, Bartholomew-Whetsel Post 212 **[5651]**, Lapel, IN
Amer. Legion, Bartlett Post 1212 **[158]**, Bartlett, IL
Amer. Legion, Bartley-Johnson-Bentley Post 437 **[13713]**, Cincinnati, OH
Amer. Legion, Bashaw-Roth Post 106 **[6546]**, Worthington, IN
Amer. Legion, Basil Grimes Post 222 **[14814]**, Crooksville, OH
Amer. Legion, Batavia Post 504 **[172]**, Batavia, IL
Amer. Legion, Bates-O'Brien-Howe-Wiegel Post 214 **[17805]**, Darlington, WI
Amer. Legion, Bates Post 560 **[3460]**, Sesser, IL
Amer. Legion, Bay View Post 180 **[18936]**, Milwaukee, WI
Amer. Legion, Bay Village Post 385 **[17227]**, Westlake, OH
Amer. Legion, Bayard Brown Post 337 **[1803]**, Genoa, IL
Amer. Legion, Bayard De Hart Post 13 **[19621]**, Richland Center, WI
Amer. Legion, Baylor Post 152 **[15524]**, Jefferson, OH
Amer. Legion, Beack-Thompson Post 126 **[10722]**, Cosmos, MN
Amer. Legion, Beallsville Post 768 **[13292]**, Beallsville, OH
Amer. Legion, Bear Creek Post 823 **[2474]**, Mendon, IL
Amer. Legion, Bearcat Post 504 **[12106]**, Richfield, MN
Amer. Legion, Beardstown Post 605 **[187]**, Beardstown, IL
Amer. Legion, Beasley-Zalesny Post 112 **[9390]**, Plymouth, MI
Amer. Legion, Beatty-Humphries Post 323 **[10677]**, Clearwater, MN

Amer. Legion, Beaver Post 578 **[16491]**, Quaker City, OH
Amer. Legion, Beavercreek Memorial Post 763 **[13294]**, Beavercreek, OH
Amer. Legion, Beaverville Post 877 **[192]**, Beaverville, IL
Amer. Legion, Becker-Reding Post 702 **[2398]**, Marine, IL
Amer. Legion, Beckett-Kurth Post 257 **[19631]**, Ridgeway, WI
Amer. Legion, Bedford Post 350 **[13303]**, Bedford, OH
Amer. Legion, Beech Grove Post 276 **[4181]**, Beech Grove, IN
Amer. Legion, Behling-Kutchera Post 296 **[17663]**, Brookfield, WI
Amer. Legion, Beisner-Brueggemann-Knop Post 480 **[3699]**, Steeleville, IL
Amer. Legion, Belgium Memorial Post 412 **[17600]**, Belgium, WI
Amer. Legion, Bell Telephone Post 427 **[20097]**, West Allis, WI
Amer. Legion, Bellaire Post 52 **[13308]**, Bellaire, OH
Amer. Legion, Bellaire Post 247 **[6903]**, Bellaire, MI
Amer. Legion, Belle Valley Post 641 **[13317]**, Belle Valley, OH
Amer. Legion, Bellechester Post 598 **[10398]**, Bellchester, MN
Amer. Legion, Belleville Post 58 **[7058]**, Canton, MI
Amer. Legion, Bellevue Post 280 **[6911]**, Bellevue, MI
Amer. Legion, Ben Krueger Post 49 **[11990]**, Pequot Lakes, MN
Amer. Legion, Bendix Aviation Post 284 **[6211]**, South Bend, IN
Amer. Legion, Benson Post 62 **[10432]**, Benson, MN
Amer. Legion, Benson Post 454 **[229]**, Benson, IL
Amer. Legion, Benton Harbor Post 105 **[6916]**, Benton Harbor, MI
Amer. Legion, Berens-Scribner Post 6 **[19780]**, Stevens Point, WI
Amer. Legion, Berg-Hemker-Olson Post 51 **[20135]**, West Salem, WI
Amer. Legion, Berg-Nylund Post 456 **[12647]**, Sebeka, MN
Amer. Legion, Berkeley Post 1016 **[2000]**, Hillside, IL
Amer. Legion, Berkley Post 374 **[6929]**, Berkley, MI
Amer. Legion, Berlin Heights Post 659 **[13352]**, Berlin Heights, OH
Amer. Legion, Bernard A. Bendle Post 294 **[9891]**, Swartz Creek, MI
Amer. Legion, Berne Post 468 **[4186]**, Berne, IN
Amer. Legion, Bernheisel and Riley Post 313 **[9850]**, Springport, MI
Amer. Legion, Berryhill Post 165 **[9021]**, Midland, MI
Amer. Legion, Berwyn Post 422 **[235]**, Berwyn, IL
Amer. Legion, Bethalto Post 214 **[241]**, Bethalto, IL
Amer. Legion, Bethany Post 507 **[242]**, Bethany, IL
Amer. Legion, Bevelhymer-Gilliland Post 400 **[15753]**, Malinta, OH
Amer. Legion, Bever Post 550 **[17950]**, Fall Creek, WI
Amer. Legion, Beverly Hills Post 407 **[2876]**, Orland Park, IL
Amer. Legion, Bexley Post 430 **[14288]**, Columbus, OH
Amer. Legion, Big Four Railway Post 116 **[4991]**, Indianapolis, IN
Amer. Legion, Big Red One Post 1111 **[10240]**, Adams, MN
Amer. Legion, Big Rock Post 529 **[243]**, Big Rock, IL
Amer. Legion, Biggsville Memorial Post 1176 **[244]**, Biggsville, IL
Amer. Legion, Bintzler-Waehler Post 347 **[18426]**, Lomira, WI
Amer. Legion, Birch Run Post 125 **[6956]**, Birch Run, MI
Amer. Legion, Bird Mc Ginnis Post 162 **[15834]**, Marion, OH
Amer. Legion, Bishop Post 1 **[2249]**, Lewistown, IL
Amer. Legion, Bivens-Bonner Post 285 **[8310]**, Inkster, MI
Amer. Legion, Bixby and Hansen Post 171 **[19924]**, Union Grove, WI
Amer. Legion, Black Oak Post 393 **[4771]**, Gary, IN
Amer. Legion, Blackduck Post 372 **[10445]**, Blackduck, MN
Amer. Legion, Blackhawk Post 553 **[18463]**, Madison, WI
Amer. Legion, Blake-Semrad Post 134 **[17647]**, Boscobel, WI
Amer. Legion, Blashe-Peters-Tober Post 456 **[17717]**, Caroline, WI
Amer. Legion, Blennerhassett Post 495 **[13340]**, Belpre, OH
Amer. Legion, Blentlinger-Tournear Post 640 **[2254]**, Liberty, IL
Amer. Legion, Bloedorn-Becker-Jensen Post 126 **[17657]**, Brillion, WI
Amer. Legion, Blue Earth Post 89 **[10495]**, Blue Earth, MN
Amer. Legion, Blue Island Post 50 **[314]**, Blue Island, IL
Amer. Legion, Bluffton Post 382 **[13365]**, Bluffton, OH
Amer. Legion, Bluford Post 1193 **[320]**, Bluford, IL
Amer. Legion, Blumfield Post 229 **[9597]**, Saginaw, MI
Amer. Legion, Blythe-Williams Post 789 **[16002]**, Middletown, OH
Amer. Legion, Bd. of Educ. Post 471 **[359]**, Buffalo Grove, IL
Amer. Legion, Bd. of Trade Post 304 **[630]**, Chicago, IL
Amer. Legion, Boardman Memorial Post 565 **[13370]**, Boardman, OH
Amer. Legion, Bodin-Finstad-Guski Post 86 **[19949]**, Washburn, WI
Amer. Legion, Bolingbrook Post 1288 **[321]**, Bolingbrook, IL
Amer. Legion, Bomsta-Johnson Post 615 **[11284]**, Lake Lillian, MN
Amer. Legion, Bond-Hill-Roselawn Post 427 **[13714]**, Cincinnati, OH
Amer. Legion, Bone Gap Post 1041 **[323]**, Bone Gap, IL
Amer. Legion, Bong-Hofstedt-Douglas-County Post 409 **[19494]**, Poplar, WI
Amer. Legion, Boone Post 77 **[218]**, Belvidere, IL
Amer. Legion, Boswell Post 476 **[4279]**, Boswell, IN
Amer. Legion, Bourbon Post 424 **[4280]**, Bourbon, IN
Amer. Legion, Bowen-Holliday Post 35 **[9921]**, Traverse City, MI
Amer. Legion, Bowen Post 1087 **[330]**, Bowen, IL
Amer. Legion, Bowers-Slusser Post 516 **[14775]**, Columbus Grove, OH
Amer. Legion, Bowling Green Post 45 **[13381]**, Bowling Green, OH
Amer. Legion, Boxrucker-Berry Post 519 **[20200]**, Withee, WI
Amer. Legion, Boyce-Carpenter-Bunce Post 195 **[8409]**, Jonesville, MI
Amer. Legion, Boyle-Hoy Post 379 **[3462]**, Shannon, IL
Amer. Legion, Bradford Post 445 **[331]**, Bradford, IL
Amer. Legion, Bradley-Maberry Post 736 **[1341]**, Danville, IL
Amer. Legion, Bradley Post 766 **[333]**, Bradley, IL
Amer. Legion, Brakeman-King Post 336 **[16331]**, Painesville, OH
Amer. Legion, Brask-Fossum-Janke Post 185 **[18070]**, Grantsburg, WI
Amer. Legion, Brecksville-Excelsior Post 196 **[13407]**, Brecksville, OH
Amer. Legion, Bredlow-Ewing Post 467 **[19375]**, Ontario, WI
Amer. Legion, Brenden-Johnson Post 223 **[11257]**, Kerkhoven, MN
Amer. Legion, Brewer-Tarasco Post 7 **[17253]**, Wickliffe, OH
Amer. Legion, Brewster Post 464 **[10530]**, Brewster, MN
Amer. Legion, Bridgeport Post 62 **[339]**, Bridgeport, IL
Amer. Legion, Bridgeport Post 227 **[13418]**, Bridgeport, OH
Amer. Legion, Bridgman Post 331 **[7002]**, Bridgman, MI
Amer. Legion, Brighton Post 476 **[343]**, Brighton, IL
Amer. Legion, Brilliant Post 573 **[13420]**, Brilliant, OH
Amer. Legion, Brimfield Post 452 **[345]**, Brimfield, IL
Amer. Legion, Broad Ripple Post 3 **[4992]**, Indianapolis, IN
Amer. Legion, Broadview-Hillside Post 626 **[2001]**, Hillside, IL
Amer. Legion, Bronsted-Searl Post 93 **[19908]**, Tomahawk, WI
Amer. Legion, Brook Park Post 610 **[13433]**, Brook Park, OH
Amer. Legion, Brook Post 364 **[4293]**, Brook, IN
Amer. Legion, Brooklyn Post 233 **[16352]**, Parma, OH
Amer. Legion, Brooklyn Post 657 **[1299]**, Compton, IL
Amer. Legion, Broome-Wood Post 292 **[16137]**, New London, OH
Amer. Legion, Browerville Post 293 **[10564]**, Browerville, MN
Amer. Legion, Brown-Dolson Post 113 **[5665]**, Lebanon, IN
Amer. Legion, Brown-Doyle Post 368 **[6396]**, Van Buren, IN
Amer. Legion, Brown-Miller Post 181 **[3415]**, Sandwich, IL
Amer. Legion, Brown-Parfitt Post 43 **[19633]**, Ripon, WI
Amer. Legion, Brown-Selvig Post 212 **[17582]**, Barron, WI
Amer. Legion, Brown Township Post 247 **[4765]**, Friendship, IN
Amer. Legion, Brown and Vernon Post 312 **[6957]**, Birch Run, MI
Amer. Legion, Brown-Webb Post 209 **[9761]**, South Haven, MI
Amer. Legion, Browne-Cavender Post 148 **[8976]**, Mason, MI
Amer. Legion, Brownsburg Lincoln Post 331 **[4302]**, Brownsburg, IN
Amer. Legion, Brunclik-Konop Post 540 **[18192]**, Haugen, WI
Amer. Legion, Bruner-Frehse Post 137 **[9714]**, Saugatuck, MI
Amer. Legion, Brunswick Post 485 **[6162]**, Schererville, IN
Amer. Legion, Buck-Reasoner Post 238 **[8239]**, Holt, MI
Amer. Legion, Buckeye Post 174 **[16253]**, North Star, OH
Amer. Legion, Buckeye Road Post 559 **[16783]**, Strongsville, OH
Amer. Legion, Buckingham-Dermer Post 514 **[17263]**, Willard, OH
Amer. Legion, Budlong District Post 837 **[631]**, Chicago, IL
Amer. Legion, Buehler-Bruggeman-Mantel Post 205 **[10973]**, Fairfax, MN
Amer. Legion, Buehrer-Lauber-Weckesser Post 311 **[13150]**, Archbold, OH
Amer. Legion, Buffalo Post 270 **[10570]**, Buffalo, MN
Amer. Legion, Buffalo Soldier Memorial Post 241 **[2096]**, Joliet, IL
Amer. Legion, Buick Liberty Motor Post 310 **[9892]**, Swartz Creek, MI
Amer. Legion, Burch-Wood Post 121 **[6456]**, Washington, IN
Amer. Legion, Burelbach Post 61 **[11991]**, Perham, MN
Amer. Legion, Burger-Benedict Post 573 **[2453]**, Mc Lean, IL
Amer. Legion, Burhans-Hagedon Post 197 **[8114]**, Harbor Beach, MI
Amer. Legion, Burlington Post 414 **[4307]**, Burlington, IN

Amer. Legion, Burlington Route Post 387 **[4047]**, Woodridge, IL
Amer. Legion, Burriss-Smith Post 396 **[16672]**, Smithfield, OH
Amer. Legion, Burton-Koppang Post 81 **[18828]**, Mauston, WI
Amer. Legion, Burton Post 130 **[7234]**, Davison, MI
Amer. Legion, Burton Woolery Post 18 **[4197]**, Bloomington, IN
Amer. Legion, Buseth-Tusow Post 18 **[11144]**, Henning, MN
Amer. Legion, Bushnell-Prairie-City Post 2004 **[2418]**, Marseilles, IL
Amer. Legion, Bus. and Professional Mens Post 332 **[11493]**, Minneapolis, MN
Amer. Legion, Bus. and Professional Mens Post 372 **[9389]**, Pleasant Ridge, MI
Amer. Legion, Bus. and Professional Mens Post 450 **[10544]**, Brooklyn Park, MN
Amer. Legion, Bus. and Professional Post 530 **[8533]**, Lansing, MI
Amer. Legion, Buss Waters Post 299 **[5861]**, Muncie, IN
Amer. Legion, Bussong-Mersinger Post 665 **[3398]**, St. Jacob, IL
Amer. Legion, Butler-Lindner Post 218 **[18194]**, Hayward, WI
Amer. Legion, Byesville Post 116 **[13477]**, Byesville, OH
Amer. Legion, Byron Center Post 292 **[7040]**, Byron Center, MI
Amer. Legion, Byron Cox Post 72 **[4424]**, Crawfordsville, IN
Amer. Legion, C.-Adams-R-Stierlen Post 311 **[10961]**, Elysian, MN
Amer. Legion, C. Walter Larson Post 378 **[11145]**, Herman, MN
Amer. Legion, Cadillac Post 333 **[8092]**, Grosse Pointe Woods, MI
Amer. Legion, Cadiz Post 34 **[13479]**, Cadiz, OH
Amer. Legion, Cahokia Memorial Post 784 **[385]**, Cahokia, IL
Amer. Legion, Caledonia Memorial Post 305 **[7053]**, Caledonia, MI
Amer. Legion, Caledonia Post 401 **[13487]**, Caledonia, OH
Amer. Legion, Calhoun Post 231 **[11494]**, Minneapolis, MN
Amer. Legion, Calhoun Post 636 **[1935]**, Hardin, IL
Amer. Legion, Call-Payton Post 285 **[6280]**, Spencer, IN
Amer. Legion, Calumet Memorial Post 330 **[391]**, Calumet City, IL
Amer. Legion, Calumet Park Post 1156 **[395]**, Calumet Park, IL
Amer. Legion, Calumet Post 99 **[4772]**, Gary, IN
Amer. Legion, Calvary Post 276 **[9570]**, Royal Oak, MI
Amer. Legion, Calvin-Knuth Post 5 **[12990]**, Worthington, MN
Amer. Legion, Cambria Post 401 **[17708]**, Cambria, WI
Amer. Legion, Cambridge Post 84 **[13492]**, Cambridge, OH
Amer. Legion, Cambridge Post 417 **[397]**, Cambridge, IL
Amer. Legion, Camden Post 413 **[4311]**, Camden, IN
Amer. Legion, Cameron-Butler Post 130 **[2737]**, Norridge, IL
Amer. Legion, Cameron-Ellis Post 242 **[17296]**, Winchester, OH
Amer. Legion, Cammack Post 327 **[5862]**, Muncie, IN
Amer. Legion, Camp Chase Post 98 **[14289]**, Columbus, OH
Amer. Legion, Camp Jackson Post 112 **[4305]**, Brownstown, IN
Amer. Legion, Camp Point Post 238 **[398]**, Camp Point, IL
Amer. Legion, Campbell Hill Post 1096 **[399]**, Campbell Hill, IL
Amer. Legion, Campbell-Richmond Post 63 **[7158]**, Clarkston, MI
Amer. Legion, Campbell-Williams Post 258 **[10682]**, Clinton, MN
Amer. Legion, Canfield Post 177 **[13527]**, Canfield, OH
Amer. Legion, Cannata-Mcdonough-Curcuru Post 994 **[1450]**, Des Plaines, IL
Amer. Legion, Canton Post 44 **[13542]**, Canton, OH
Amer. Legion, Canton Post 188 **[7059]**, Canton, MI
Amer. Legion, Capital City Post 12 **[8534]**, Lansing, MI
Amer. Legion, Carl Mount Post 104 **[6308]**, Terre Haute, IN
Amer. Legion, Carleton Mc Nicholas Post 523 **[8924]**, Marenisco, MI
Amer. Legion, Carleton Post 66 **[7077]**, Carleton, MI
Amer. Legion, Carlson-Alguire-Hougland Post 312 **[19432]**, Peshtigo, WI
Amer. Legion, Carlton Post 538 **[19901]**, Tisch Mills, WI
Amer. Legion, Carmel Post 155 **[4315]**, Carmel, IN
Amer. Legion, Carmi Post 224 **[442]**, Carmi, IL
Amer. Legion, Carney-Nadeau Post 487 **[7078]**, Carney, MI
Amer. Legion, Carpenter-Clash Post 363 **[8492]**, Kingsford, MI
Amer. Legion, Carr-Bailey Post 519 **[16041]**, Mineral City, OH
Amer. Legion, Carrier Mills Post 1140 **[1937]**, Harrisburg, IL
Amer. Legion, Carroll Post 428 **[13603]**, Carrollton, OH
Amer. Legion, Carrollton Post 114 **[457]**, Carrollton, IL
Amer. Legion, Carson City Post 380 **[7088]**, Carson City, MI
Amer. Legion, Casimer Pulaski Post 78 **[4471]**, East Chicago, IN
Amer. Legion, Cass County Post 60 **[5687]**, Logansport, IN
Amer. Legion, Cassel Post 257 **[4760]**, Fremont, IN
Amer. Legion, Castle Williams Post 105 **[1373]**, Decatur, IL
Amer. Legion, Caufield Post 434 **[13364]**, Bloomville, OH
Amer. Legion, Cave-Dahl Post 240 **[17558]**, Baldwin, WI
Amer. Legion, Caya-Bunders Post 68 **[19527]**, Prairie Du Chien, WI
Amer. Legion, C.C. Upton Post 91 **[7794]**, Fremont, MI
Amer. Legion, C.D. Burton Post 808 **[632]**, Chicago, IL
Amer. Legion, Cecil Ser. Post 255 **[7228]**, Croswell, MI
Amer. Legion, Cedar Lake Post 261 **[4335]**, Cedar Lake, IN
Amer. Legion, Cedarville Memorial Post 1224 **[484]**, Cedarville, IL
Amer. Legion, Celina Post 210 **[13609]**, Celina, OH
Amer. Legion, Celtic Post 372 **[4993]**, Indianapolis, IN
Amer. Legion, Central Park Post 1028 **[633]**, Chicago, IL
Amer. Legion, Central Post 132 **[4994]**, Indianapolis, IN
Amer. Legion, Cerro Gordo Post 117 **[492]**, Cerro Gordo, IL
Amer. Legion, Chadwick Post 739 **[493]**, Chadwick, IL
Amer. Legion, Chagrin Falls Post 383 **[13628]**, Chagrin Falls, OH
Amer. Legion, Challenger Post 521 **[12875]**, West St. Paul, MN
Amer. Legion, Chalmers Post 268 **[4343]**, Chalmers, IN
Amer. Legion, Chambers-Hautman-Budde Post 534 **[13715]**, Cincinnati, OH
Amer. Legion, Champaign Post 24 **[498]**, Champaign, IL
Amer. Legion, Champlin Post 600 **[10641]**, Champlin, MN
Amer. Legion, Chandler Post 694 **[559]**, Chandlerville, IL
Amer. Legion, Chanhassen Post 580 **[10645]**, Chanhassen, MN
Amer. Legion, Chapin Post 878 **[562]**, Chapin, IL
Amer. Legion, Chapman-Belter Post 4 **[17550]**, Athens, WI
Amer. Legion, Chardon Post 167 **[13640]**, Chardon, OH
Amer. Legion, Charles Andrews Post 460 **[13618]**, Centerburg, OH
Amer. Legion, Charles Claessens Post 305 **[12856]**, Waverly, MN
Amer. Legion, Charles De Crane Post 724 **[99]**, Atkinson, IL
Amer. Legion, Charles Forrest Post 288 **[6398]**, Veedersburg, IN
Amer. Legion, Charles Foster Blaker Post 202 **[4309]**, Butler, IN
Amer. Legion, Charles Harker Post 143 **[4291]**, Bristol, IN
Amer. Legion, Charles Hofer Post 522 **[16779]**, Strasburg, OH
Amer. Legion, Charles Mundell Post 216 **[5796]**, Middletown, IN
Amer. Legion, Charles Sturdevant Post 46 **[6356]**, Tipton, IN
Amer. Legion, Charles Walter Reid Post 258 **[3872]**, Virginia, IL
Amer. Legion, Charleston Memorial Post 1999 **[563]**, Charleston, IL
Amer. Legion, Charlton-Polan Post 233 **[8515]**, Lake Orion, MI
Amer. Legion, Chaseburg Post 202 **[17735]**, Chaseburg, WI
Amer. Legion, Chatham Post 759 **[577]**, Chatham, IL
Amer. Legion, Chauncey-Barr-Rex-Boyer Post 192 **[4483]**, Edwardsport, IN
Amer. Legion, Chauncey Curtis Smith Post 118 **[6559]**, Addison, MI
Amer. Legion, Chesaning Post 212 **[7144]**, Chesaning, MI
Amer. Legion, Chesapeake Memorial Post 640 **[13647]**, Chesapeake, OH
Amer. Legion, Chester Bird Post 523 **[11058]**, Golden Valley, MN
Amer. Legion, Chesterfield Post 695 **[634]**, Chicago, IL
Amer. Legion, Chesterland Post 780 **[16332]**, Painesville, OH
Amer. Legion, Chesterton Post 170 **[4349]**, Chesterton, IN
Amer. Legion, Chestnut-Beason Post 848 **[191]**, Beason, IL
Amer. Legion, Chicago Firemen's Post 667 **[635]**, Chicago, IL
Amer. Legion, Chicago Heights Post 131 **[1247]**, Chicago Heights, IL
Amer. Legion, Chicago Nisei Post 1183 **[636]**, Chicago, IL
Amer. Legion, Chicago Police Post 207 **[2935]**, Palos Heights, IL
Amer. Legion, Chicago Post 170 **[637]**, Chicago, IL
Amer. Legion, Chief Okemos Post 269 **[8145]**, Haslett, MI
Amer. Legion, Chief Pontiac Post 377 **[9414]**, Pontiac, MI
Amer. Legion, Childs-Demeray Post 222 **[10044]**, Vermontville, MI
Amer. Legion, Chillicothe Post 9 **[1254]**, Chillicothe, IL
Amer. Legion, Chinatown Post 1003 **[638]**, Chicago, IL
Amer. Legion, Chipilly-131st-Infantry Post 310 **[159]**, Bartlett, IL
Amer. Legion, Chisago City Post 272 **[10658]**, Chisago City, MN
Amer. Legion, Chrisman Post 477 **[1257]**, Chrisman, IL
Amer. Legion, Christie-De-Parcq Post 406 **[12360]**, St. Paul, MN
Amer. Legion, Christopher Columbus Post 354 **[8890]**, Madison Heights, MI
Amer. Legion, Christopher Post 528 **[1258]**, Christopher, IL
Amer. Legion, Chrysler A.B.D. Post 242 **[8103]**, Hamtramck, MI

Amer. Legion, Cicero Post 96 **[1259]**, Cicero, IL
Amer. Legion, Cincinnati Gas and Elec. Post 410 **[13716]**, Cincinnati, OH
Amer. Legion, Cissna Park Post 527 **[1265]**, Cissna Park, IL
Amer. Legion, Clara City Post 485 **[10668]**, Clara City, MN
Amer. Legion, Clare Burt Post 248 **[8496]**, Laingsburg, MI
Amer. Legion, Clare-Farwell Post 558 **[7678]**, Farwell, MI
Amer. Legion, Clarence-Bean-Warren-George Post 67 **[18402]**, Lake Mills, WI
Amer. Legion, Clarence Clofer Post 259 **[12664]**, Shorewood, MN
Amer. Legion, Clarence Wiles Post 222 **[4613]**, Flora, IN
Amer. Legion, Clarissa Post 213 **[10672]**, Clarissa, MN
Amer. Legion, Clark-Carrington Post 1031 **[2497]**, Mineral, IL
Amer. Legion, Clark County Post 90 **[2423]**, Marshall, IL
Amer. Legion, Clark-Ellis Post 152 **[8861]**, Lowell, MI
Amer. Legion, Clark-Gurgel Post 206 **[20204]**, Wonewoc, WI
Amer. Legion, Clark Post 362 **[16714]**, Springfield, OH
Amer. Legion, Claude Earl Post 887 **[2052]**, Hoyleton, IL
Amer. Legion, Claude Robinson Post 899 **[389]**, Cairo, IL
Amer. Legion, Clay City Post 225 **[4370]**, Clay City, IN
Amer. Legion, Clay City Post 840 **[1267]**, Clay City, IL
Amer. Legion, Clay County Post 2 **[4282]**, Brazil, IN
Amer. Legion, Clay County Post 14 **[1705]**, Flora, IL
Amer. Legion, Clayton Murray Post 159 **[8887]**, Mackinaw City, MI
Amer. Legion, Clayton Post 286 **[1268]**, Clayton, IL
Amer. Legion, Clearing Post 600 **[639]**, Chicago, IL
Amer. Legion, Cleary-Miller Post 115 **[17937]**, Elroy, WI
Amer. Legion, Cleveland Police Post 438 **[14054]**, Cleveland, OH
Amer. Legion, Cleveland Post 2 **[14055]**, Cleveland, OH
Amer. Legion, Clifford Garbison Post 356 **[4866]**, Hamlet, IN
Amer. Legion, Clifton Post 385 **[1269]**, Clifton, IL
Amer. Legion, Clifton Post 421 **[15181]**, Fairview Park, OH
Amer. Legion, Climaxscotts Post 465 **[7169]**, Climax, MI
Amer. Legion, Clinton Post 140 **[4371]**, Clinton, IN
Amer. Legion, Clough-Lambrix Post 389 **[9494]**, Riverview, MI
Amer. Legion, Cloverland Post 82 **[7607]**, Escanaba, MI
Amer. Legion, Clyde Johnston Post 230 **[9057]**, Mohawk, MI
Amer. Legion, Coal City Post 796 **[1275]**, Coal City, IL
Amer. Legion, Coal Valley Post 1248 **[1278]**, Coal Valley, IL
Amer. Legion, Cobb-Trygstad-Anderson Post 397 **[8245]**, Holton, MI
Amer. Legion, Cobb-Williams-Nehiba Post 222 **[11155]**, Hibbing, MN
Amer. Legion, Cobden Post 259 **[1281]**, Cobden, IL
Amer. Legion, Coe-Lamb Post 421 **[3126]**, Port Byron, IL
Amer. Legion, Cokato Post 209 **[10695]**, Cokato, MN
Amer. Legion, Col. A.L. Brodie Post 1437 **[3953]**, Westchester, IL
Amer. Legion, Colburn Post 286 **[12622]**, Sanborn, MN
Amer. Legion, Coldwater Post 52 **[7195]**, Coldwater, MI
Amer. Legion, Cole-Briggs Post 48 **[7870]**, Grand Ledge, MI
Amer. Legion, Colfax Post 439 **[4377]**, Colfax, IN
Amer. Legion, Collins-Tasch Post 399 **[5821]**, Monterey, IN
Amer. Legion, Collinwood Post 759 **[16675]**, Solon, OH
Amer. Legion, Coloma Post 362 **[7204]**, Coloma, MI
Amer. Legion, Colonel Crawford Post 181 **[13460]**, Bucyrus, OH
Amer. Legion, Colonel Jennings Post 715 **[15221]**, Fort Jennings, OH
Amer. Legion, Columbia City Post 98 **[4378]**, Columbia City, IN
Amer. Legion, Columbia Post 581 **[1297]**, Columbia, IL
Amer. Legion, Columbus Post 24 **[4388]**, Columbus, IN
Amer. Legion, Columbus Post 82 **[14290]**, Columbus, OH
Amer. Legion, Colvin-Dale Post 527 **[16020]**, Milan, OH
Amer. Legion, Commemorative Post 268 **[15013]**, Delphos, OH
Amer. Legion, Commodore Barry Post 256 **[236]**, Berwyn, IL
Amer. Legion, Commodore Denig Post 83 **[16601]**, Sandusky, OH
Amer. Legion, Commonwealth Edison Post 118 **[640]**, Chicago, IL
Amer. Legion, Community Memorial Post 635 **[15530]**, Jewell, OH
Amer. Legion, Community Post 279 **[15100]**, Elmore, OH
Amer. Legion, Community Post 375 **[19249]**, Mukwonago, WI
Amer. Legion, Community Post 403 **[16295]**, Olmsted Falls, OH
Amer. Legion, Community Post 429 **[2356]**, Lovington, IL
Amer. Legion, Community Post 666 **[15924]**, Maynard, OH
Amer. Legion, Community Post 1166 **[3188]**, Reynolds, IL
Amer. Legion, Comrade Whitehall Post 490 **[14291]**, Columbus, OH
Amer. Legion, Concord-Pulaski-Memorial Post 81 **[7216]**, Concord, MI
Amer. Legion, Conn-Weissenberger Post 587 **[16878]**, Toledo, OH
Amer. Legion, Conrad Post 179 **[6035]**, Petersburg, IN
Amer. Legion, Conrad-Wager-Keene Post 164 **[9054]**, Millington, MI
Amer. Legion, Constitution Post 224 **[10178]**, Wixom, MI
Amer. Legion, Constitution Post 326 **[214]**, Bellwood, IL
Amer. Legion, Cook-Fuller Post 70 **[19388]**, Oshkosh, WI
Amer. Legion, Cook-Nelson Post 20 **[9415]**, Pontiac, MI
Amer. Legion, Coon Valley Post 116 **[17784]**, Coon Valley, WI
Amer. Legion, Coral Hall Post 539 **[2145]**, Kansas, IL
Amer. Legion, Cordova Post 1033 **[1300]**, Cordova, IL
Amer. Legion, Cornell Post 928 **[2235]**, Lemont, IL
Amer. Legion, Cornell-Syverson Post 17 **[11984]**, Pel Rapids, MN
Amer. Legion, Corning Post 327 **[14788]**, Corning, OH
Amer. Legion, Cossette-Woitkielewicz Post 58 **[18229]**, Hurley, WI
Amer. Legion, Cottonwood Post 503 **[10730]**, Cottonwood, MN
Amer. Legion, Cottrell-Boylan Post 253 **[13146]**, Antwerp, OH
Amer. Legion, Coughlin-Sanford Post 277 **[19263]**, Necedah, WI
Amer. Legion, Courthouse Post 310 **[11495]**, Minneapolis, MN
Amer. Legion, Courtney-Carr-Milner Post 19 **[18176]**, Hartford, WI
Amer. Legion, Courtney Lawrence Post 202 **[15938]**, Medina, OH
Amer. Legion, Courts-Fussnecker Post 367 **[16535]**, Ripley, OH
Amer. Legion, Cowle Post 151 **[14780]**, Conneaut, OH
Amer. Legion, Craig-Bennett Post 103 **[1270]**, Clinton, IL
Amer. Legion, Craig-Reed Post 1181 **[1263]**, Cisco, IL
Amer. Legion, Craig-Schlosser Post 31 **[20068]**, Wauwatosa, WI
Amer. Legion, Crain and Ottman Post 207 **[17935]**, Elmwood, WI
Amer. Legion, Crawford County Post 84 **[5722]**, Marengo, IN
Amer. Legion, Crawford-Hale Post 95 **[3846]**, Vandalia, IL
Amer. Legion, Crawford Post 1038 **[2127]**, Kane, IL
Amer. Legion, Creston Post 497 **[14812]**, Creston, OH
Amer. Legion, Cretton-Tutas Post 136 **[19322]**, Niagara, WI
Amer. Legion, Creve Coeur Post 1234 **[1539]**, East Peoria, IL
Amer. Legion, Crispus Attucks Post 59 **[8486]**, Kentwood, MI
Amer. Legion, Crispus Attucks Post 1268 **[641]**, Chicago, IL
Amer. Legion, Crouse-Engles Post 357 **[2213]**, Lanark, IL
Amer. Legion, Cuff-Patricki Post 174 **[18193]**, Hawkins, WI
Amer. Legion, Cultice-Ward Post 6 **[16715]**, Springfield, OH
Amer. Legion, Curry-Ainsworth Post 168 **[18056]**, Glenwood City, WI
Amer. Legion, D. W. K. Post 110 **[19310]**, New Lisbon, WI
Amer. Legion, D. W. M. D. Post 407 **[15035]**, Doylestown, OH
Amer. Legion, Daffron-Presswood Post 2504 **[3089]**, Pinckneyville, IL
Amer. Legion, Dahlberg-Makris Post 7 **[19596]**, Rhinelander, WI
Amer. Legion, Dahlgren-Ettestad Post 499 **[11921]**, Northome, MN
Amer. Legion, Dakota-Richford Post 163 **[20063]**, Wautoma, WI
Amer. Legion, Dale L. Binkley Memorial Post 289 **[13439]**, Brookville, OH
Amer. Legion, Dan Patch Post 643 **[12640]**, Savage, MN
Amer. Legion, Danforth Post 367 **[1340]**, Danforth, IL
Amer. Legion, Daniel Post 864 **[3265]**, Rockford, IL
Amer. Legion, Daniel Waters Cassard Post 208 **[7891]**, Grand Rapids, MI
Amer. Legion, Danner-Madsen Post 663 **[1785]**, Gardner, IL
Amer. Legion, Darius-Girenas Post 271 **[642]**, Chicago, IL
Amer. Legion, Darling-Gunderson Post 341 **[17627]**, Birnamwood, WI
Amer. Legion, Darlington Post 302 **[4448]**, Darlington, IN
Amer. Legion, Dary-Paulsen Post 440 **[17768]**, Clinton, WI
Amer. Legion, Daugherty-Larsen Post 446 **[19776]**, Steuben, WI
Amer. Legion, Davenport-Lang Post 414 **[17651]**, Bowler, WI
Amer. Legion, David Humphrey Daniel Post 427 **[3427]**, Saybrook, IL
Amer. Legion, David Johnston Memorial Post 283 **[16417]**, Pickerington, OH
Amer. Legion, David Parrish Post 296 **[4628]**, Fort Wayne, IN
Amer. Legion, David-Wisted-Zenith-City Post 28 **[10797]**, Duluth, MN
Amer. Legion, Davis-Busby Post 776 **[483]**, Catlin, IL
Amer. Legion, Davis-Darrow-Meyer Post 112 **[10943]**, Elk River, MN
Amer. Legion, Davis-Kerber Post 653 **[1283]**, Colfax, IL

Amer. Legion, Davis-Porter Post 140 **[18901]**, Merrillan, WI
Amer. Legion, Dayton Post 5 **[14843]**, Dayton, OH
Amer. Legion, Dayton Rogers Post 531 **[10757]**, Dayton, MN
Amer. Legion, Daytons Bluff Post 515 **[10758]**, Dayton, MN
Amer. Legion, De-Gree-Fleisch Post 125 **[12711]**, Stewart, MN
Amer. Legion, De Kalb Post 66 **[1426]**, DeKalb, IL
Amer. Legion, De Kalb Post 97 **[4136]**, Auburn, IN
Amer. Legion, De Witt Post 379 **[7460]**, DeWitt, MI
Amer. Legion, Deal-Ridgeway Post 289 **[10167]**, Williamsburg, MI
Amer. Legion, Dean Horton Navy Post 108 **[16879]**, Toledo, OH
Amer. Legion, Deceased Veterans Post 975 **[1492]**, Dowell, IL
Amer. Legion, Deer Creek Post 1276 **[1411]**, Deer Creek, IL
Amer. Legion, Deerfield **[1415]**, Deerfield, IL
Amer. Legion, Deerfield Post 392 **[7289]**, Deerfield, MI
Amer. Legion, Deerfield Post 713 **[14977]**, Deerfield, OH
Amer. Legion, Delafield Post 196 **[17821]**, Delafield, WI
Amer. Legion, Delano Post 377 **[10768]**, Delano, MN
Amer. Legion, Delavan Post 382 **[1446]**, Delavan, IL
Amer. Legion, Delaware Post 19 **[5863]**, Muncie, IN
Amer. Legion, Dell-Hogan Post 123 **[11354]**, Luverne, MN
Amer. Legion, Dellroy Post 475 **[16656]**, Sherrodsville, OH
Amer. Legion, Demotte Post 440 **[4457]**, Demotte, IN
Amer. Legion, Deneen-Mc-Cabe Post 432 **[18173]**, Hammond, WI
Amer. Legion, Denton-Schreiner Post 582 **[1641]**, Erie, IL
Amer. Legion Dept. Of Illinois **[256]**, Bloomington, IL
Amer. Legion, Dept. of St. Railways Post 394 **[7212]**, Columbus, MI
Amer. Legion Dept. of Wisconsin **[19506]**, Portage, WI
Amer. Legion, Des Plaines Post 36 **[1451]**, Des Plaines, IL
Amer. Legion, Deshler Post 316 **[15020]**, Deshler, OH
Amer. Legion, Desrosier-Windnagle Post 562 **[6926]**, Bergland, MI
Amer. Legion, Detroit News Post 519 **[7279]**, Dearborn Heights, MI
Amer. Legion, Detroit Police Post 161 **[7172]**, Clinton Township, MI
Amer. Legion, Deutschle-Annick-Memorial Post 888 **[14995]**, Delaware, OH
Amer. Legion, Devereaux Post 141 **[8269]**, Howell, MI
Amer. Legion, Devine-Menting Post 525 **[19454]**, Phlox, WI
Amer. Legion, Devins-Teehan Post 237 **[17995]**, Footville, WI
Amer. Legion, Dewey Mc Glynn Post 280 **[6075]**, Remington, IN
Amer. Legion, Dewitt McConnell Post 235 **[15320]**, Girard, OH
Amer. Legion, Dexter Post 557 **[7470]**, Dexter, MI
Amer. Legion, Diamond Island Post 335 **[7097]**, Cassopolis, MI
Amer. Legion, Diemer-Dobmeyer Post 172 **[16033]**, Miller City, OH
Amer. Legion, Diesen-Winkler Post 325 **[1807]**, Germantown, IL
Amer. Legion, Dieterich Post 628 **[1472]**, Dieterich, IL
Amer. Legion, Dignam-Whitmore Post 526 **[15146]**, Fairborn, OH
Amer. Legion, Dillon-Johnson-Anderson Post 154 **[19204]**, Mondovi, WI
Amer. Legion, Dimondale Potterville Post 272 **[9458]**, Potterville, MI
Amer. Legion, Dixon Post 12 **[1474]**, Dixon, IL
Amer. Legion, Dobson-Johnson Post 142 **[17640]**, Blanchardville, WI
Amer. Legion, Doe-Wah-Jack Post 563 **[7477]**, Dowagiac, MI
Amer. Legion, Dolven-Wilcox Post 313 **[12735]**, Swanville, MN
Amer. Legion, Don Gentile Post 532 **[14292]**, Columbus, OH
Amer. Legion, Don Varnas Post 986 **[2792]**, Oak Lawn, IL
Amer. Legion, Doney-Degrave Post 342 **[18416]**, Lena, WI
Amer. Legion, Donovan Post 633 **[1491]**, Donovan, IL
Amer. Legion, Dorchester Chaplains Post 387 **[7303]**, Detroit, MI
Amer. Legion, Dorman-Dunn Post 547 **[643]**, Chicago, IL
Amer. Legion, Dornblaser Post 203 **[1806]**, Georgetown, IL
Amer. Legion, Doss-Malone Post 1200 **[2539]**, Monee, IL
Amer. Legion, Douglas County Post 27 **[3791]**, Tuscola, IL
Amer. Legion, Dover Post 205 **[15026]**, Dover, OH
Amer. Legion, Dovray Post 632 **[10364]**, Avoca, MN
Amer. Legion, Downey-Pogue-Scott Post 590 **[15507]**, Ironton, OH
Amer. Legion, Downing Winterling Post 232 **[17843]**, Downing, WI
Amer. Legion, Draeger-Fencil Post 260 **[17820]**, Deerfield, WI
Amer. Legion, Draza Mihailovich Post 1946 **[644]**, Chicago, IL
Amer. Legion, Dreier-Bushee-Vanderboom Post 156 **[19323]**, North Fond Du Lac, WI
Amer. Legion, Drew Webster Post 39 **[16454]**, Pomeroy, OH
Amer. Legion, Drews-Bleser Post 88 **[18774]**, Manitowoc, WI
Amer. Legion, Dublin Post 800 **[17203]**, Westerville, OH
Amer. Legion, Dubois County Post 147 **[5525]**, Jasper, IN
Amer. Legion, Duggar Post 553 **[2494]**, Milledgeville, IL
Amer. Legion, Duhm-Masch Post 332 **[17629]**, Black Creek, WI
Amer. Legion, Dundee-Carpentersville Post 679 **[1518]**, Dundee, IL
Amer. Legion, Duoos Bros. Post 630 **[10534]**, Brooklyn Center, MN
Amer. Legion, Duppler-Smith Post 460 **[17601]**, Belleville, WI
Amer. Legion, Durand Post 124 **[7489]**, Durand, MI
Amer. Legion, Durkee-Seager Post 550 **[9307]**, Onsted, MI
Amer. Legion, Durwin-Schantz Post 138 **[15377]**, Hamilton, OH
Amer. Legion, Dwight Post 486 **[1525]**, Dwight, IL
Amer. Legion, Dyrdal-Prolow Post 249 **[12688]**, Spring Grove, MN
Amer. Legion, Eagan Post 594 **[10863]**, Eagan, MN
Amer. Legion, Eagle Lake Post 617 **[10878]**, Eagle Lake, MN
Amer. Legion, Eagle Post 509 **[11177]**, Hopkins, MN
Amer. Legion, Eagletown Post 120 **[9885]**, Suttons Bay, MI
Amer. Legion, Earl Foust Post 73 **[15228]**, Fostoria, OH
Amer. Legion, Earl Gladfelter Post 268 **[9047]**, Milan, MI
Amer. Legion, Earl Green Post 344 **[13598]**, Carey, OH
Amer. Legion, Earl James Howe Post 298 **[11012]**, Foley, MN
Amer. Legion, Earl Park Post 455 **[4470]**, Earl Park, IN
Amer. Legion, Earle Ray Post 173 **[12756]**, Tracy, MN
Amer. Legion, East Alton Post 794 **[1529]**, East Alton, IL
Amer. Legion, East Chicago Allied Post 369 **[4472]**, East Chicago, IN
Amer. Legion, East Detroit Roseville Post 261 **[9563]**, Roseville, MI
Amer. Legion, East Dubuque Post 787 **[1533]**, East Dubuque, IL
Amer. Legion, East Grand Forks Post 157 **[10881]**, East Grand Forks, MN
Amer. Legion, East Hazel Crest Post 1139 **[2043]**, Homewood, IL
Amer. Legion, East Moline Post 227 **[1536]**, East Moline, IL
Amer. Legion, East Peoria Post 983 **[1540]**, East Peoria, IL
Amer. Legion, East St. Louis Post 53 **[480]**, Caseyville, IL
Amer. Legion, East St. Louis Post 2505 **[1548]**, East St. Louis, IL
Amer. Legion, Easton Post 569 **[10886]**, Easton, MN
Amer. Legion, Eau Claire Post 353 **[7585]**, Eau Claire, MI
Amer. Legion, E.B. Rinehart Post 754 **[16649]**, Shauck, OH
Amer. Legion, Ebert-Wunrow Post 475 **[17540]**, Arpin, WI
Amer. Legion, Eck-Ary-Douglas-Dickey Post 353 **[13145]**, Ansonia, OH
Amer. Legion, Ecklund-Holmstrom Post 117 **[12740]**, Thief River Falls, MN
Amer. Legion, Ecorse-Roy-B.-Salliotte Post 319 **[7588]**, Ecorse, MI
Amer. Legion, Eden Valley Post 381 **[10903]**, Eden Valley, MN
Amer. Legion, Edina Post 471 **[11178]**, Hopkins, MN
Amer. Legion, Edinburg Post 233 **[4479]**, Edinburgh, IN
Amer. Legion, Edison Park Post 541 **[645]**, Chicago, IL
Amer. Legion, Edon Post 662 **[15095]**, Edon, OH
Amer. Legion, Edward Born Post 343 **[11923]**, Norwood, MN
Amer. Legion, Edward Gill Post 204 **[10887]**, Echo, MN
Amer. Legion, Edward Schultz Post 697 **[2214]**, Lansing, IL
Amer. Legion, Edwards-Foye Post 534 **[18838]**, McFarland, WI
Amer. Legion, Edwardsburg Post 365 **[7589]**, Edwardsburg, MI
Amer. Legion, Edwardsville Post 199 **[1556]**, Edwardsville, IL
Amer. Legion, Edwin Corpin Post 905 **[2162]**, Kincaid, IL
Amer. Legion, Eel River Post 286 **[5986]**, North Manchester, IN
Amer. Legion, Effingham Post 120 **[1569]**, Effingham, IL
Amer. Legion, Efton James Post 206 **[7098]**, Cassopolis, MI
Amer. Legion, Ehret-Parsel Post 447 **[16448]**, Plymouth, OH
Amer. Legion, Eick-Sankey Post 302 **[19350]**, Oconto Falls, WI
Amer. Legion, Eiffert-Kirchenbauer Post 354 **[10674]**, Clear Lake, MN
Amer. Legion, E.J. Stover and A.D. Wagner Post 85 **[6934]**, Berrien Springs, MI
Amer. Legion, Ekstedt-Hurr Post 390 **[45]**, Altona, IL
Amer. Legion, El Paso Post 59 **[1575]**, El Paso, IL
Amer. Legion, Elberfeld Post 351 **[4484]**, Elberfeld, IN
Amer. Legion, Elburn Post 630 **[1578]**, Elburn, IL
Amer. Legion, Eldorado Post 169 **[1581]**, Eldorado, IL
Amer. Legion, Eldred Post 1135 **[1582]**, Eldred, IL
Amer. Legion, Elec. Post 228 **[18937]**, Milwaukee, WI
Amer. Legion, Elec. Post 769 **[646]**, Chicago, IL
Amer. Legion, Electro-Motive-Diesel Post 992 **[2031]**, Hodgkins, IL
Amer. Legion, Elefson-Zeuske Post 117 **[19678]**, Shawano, WI
Amer. Legion, Elgin Post 57 **[1584]**, Elgin, IL
Amer. Legion, Elgin Post 573 **[10940]**, Elgin, MN

Amer. Legion, Eli Denison Post 467 **[16564]**, Rutland, OH
Amer. Legion, Eli Lilly Post 374 **[4995]**, Indianapolis, IN
Amer. Legion, Eliza Post 1971 **[2681]**, New Boston, IL
Amer. Legion, Elk Grove Village Memorial Post 216 **[1605]**, Elk Grove Village, IL
Amer. Legion, Elkhart Post 616 **[1616]**, Elkhart, IL
Amer. Legion, Ellet Post 794 **[13031]**, Akron, OH
Amer. Legion, Ellingson-Brenden Post 376 **[12251]**, Rothsay, MN
Amer. Legion, Elliott Keller Post 1078 **[1520]**, Dunlap, IL
Amer. Legion, Ellsworth Meinke Post 1983 **[3429]**, Schaumburg, IL
Amer. Legion, Ellsworth Post 1244 **[1617]**, Ellsworth, IL
Amer. Legion, Elmer Dade Memorial Post 699 **[15615]**, Leavittsburg, OH
Amer. Legion, Elmer Johnson Post 118 **[13130]**, Amherst, OH
Amer. Legion, Elmwood Post 638 **[1629]**, Elmwood, IL
Amer. Legion, Elwood Monroe Swenson Post 445 **[11240]**, Karlstad, MN
Amer. Legion, Elyria Post 12 **[15104]**, Elyria, OH
Amer. Legion, Emden Post 506 **[1636]**, Emden, IL
Amer. Legion, Emery Whisler Post 607 **[2363]**, Mackinaw, IL
Amer. Legion, Emil Jacob Post 117 **[8907]**, Manchester, MI
Amer. Legion, Emil King Post 318 **[11037]**, Fulda, MN
Amer. Legion, Emmet Mannix Post 345 **[15224]**, Fort Recovery, OH
Amer. Legion, Engels-Wilson Post 564 **[11042]**, Ghent, MN
Amer. Legion, Enrico Fermi Post 1266 **[647]**, Chicago, IL
Amer. Legion, Epworth Post 90 **[13354]**, Bethesda, OH
Amer. Legion, Erickson-Rose Post 637 **[12883]**, Whalan, MN
Amer. Legion, Erickson-Strom Post 186 **[11935]**, Olivia, MN
Amer. Legion, Erk Cottrell Post 140 **[15355]**, Greenville, OH
Amer. Legion, Ernest Aselton Post 118 **[12857]**, Wayzata, MN
Amer. Legion, Erwin March Post 64 **[12670]**, Slayton, MN
Amer. Legion, Erwin Martensen Post 164 **[1284]**, Colfax, IL
Amer. Legion, Erwin Prieskorn Post 46 **[6661]**, Ann Arbor, MI
Amer. Legion, Escanaba River Post 115 **[7829]**, Gladstone, MI
Amer. Legion, Eshelman-Talley-Doye Post 1191 **[3139]**, Prophetstown, IL
Amer. Legion, Essexville-Hampton Post 249 **[7623]**, Essexville, MI
Amer. Legion, Essman-Schroeder Post 20 **[19955]**, Waterford, WI
Amer. Legion, Eubanks-Arneson Post 87 **[19612]**, Rice Lake, WI
Amer. Legion, Euclid Post 343 **[15138]**, Euclid, OH
Amer. Legion, Euclid Post 539 **[10966]**, Euclid, MN
Amer. Legion, Eugene Drill Post 606 **[1965]**, Hebron, IL
Amer. Legion, Eugene Hughes Post 319 **[5817]**, Monon, IN
Amer. Legion, Eugene Pate Post 265 **[4520]**, Evansville, IN
Amer. Legion, Eugene Wilson Post 346 **[12099]**, Remer, MN
Amer. Legion, Eureka Post 466 **[1642]**, Eureka, IL
Amer. Legion, Eva Casstevens Post 535 **[196]**, Beecher City, IL
Amer. Legion, Evans Post 329 **[11881]**, New Ulm, MN
Amer. Legion, Evans-Swanson Post 123 **[8484]**, Kent City, MI
Amer. Legion, Evanston Post 42 **[1647]**, Evanston, IL
Amer. Legion, Evansville Post 1172 **[1677]**, Evansville, IL
Amer. Legion, Eveland-Trainor Post 433 **[17581]**, Barneveld, WI
Amer. Legion, Everett H. Hale Post 68 **[12693]**, Spring Valley, MN
Amer. Legion, Everette Burdette Post 187 **[4521]**, Evansville, IN
Amer. Legion, Evergreen Park Post 854 **[1678]**, Evergreen Park, IL
Amer. Legion, Evzones Post 1039 **[2002]**, Hillside, IL
Amer. Legion, Ewen Post 41 **[7630]**, Ewen, MI
Amer. Legion, Ewert-Kline Post 720 **[2865]**, Orangeville, IL
Amer. Legion, Ex-Cell-O Post 440 **[8828]**, Livonia, MI
Amer. Legion, Eyota Post 551 **[10972]**, Eyota, MN
Amer. Legion, Ezra Barrows Post 338 **[11286]**, Lake Wilson, MN
Amer. Legion, Fairfax Post 554 **[13717]**, Cincinnati, OH
Amer. Legion, Fairfield Post 11 **[15596]**, Lancaster, OH
Amer. Legion, Fairmont City Post 961 **[1690]**, Fairmont City, IL
Amer. Legion, Fairmount Post 313 **[4592]**, Fairmount, IN
Amer. Legion, Fairview Heights Post 978 **[1693]**, Fairview Heights, IL
Amer. Legion, Fairview Post 738 **[15182]**, Fairview Park, OH
Amer. Legion, Fallerans Post 121 **[19]**, Aledo, IL
Amer. Legion, Farina Post 411 **[1699]**, Farina, IL
Amer. Legion, Farmer Post 137 **[15186]**, Farmer, OH
Amer. Legion, Farmington Post 140 **[1701]**, Farmington, IL
Amer. Legion, Fed. Employees Post 496 **[7709]**, Flint, MI
Amer. Legion, Fed. Post 203 **[18938]**, Milwaukee, WI
Amer. Legion, Feeney-Bennett Post 128 **[16001]**, Middleport, OH
Amer. Legion, Fellenzer Post 48 **[6130]**, Rockville, IN
Amer. Legion, Feneley-Mcneil-Nesbit Post 290 **[7605]**, Engadine, MI
Amer. Legion, Fengestad-Solie Post 200 **[12941]**, Winger, MN
Amer. Legion, Fennville Post 434 **[7680]**, Fennville, MI
Amer. Legion, Ferdinand Post 124 **[4595]**, Ferdinand, IN
Amer. Legion, Fertile Post 238 **[11007]**, Fertile, MN
Amer. Legion, Fickbohm-Hissem Post 193 **[1760]**, Galena, IL
Amer. Legion, Fidelity Post 296 **[10950]**, Ellendale, MN
Amer. Legion, Fiebirch Post 397 **[17063]**, Vermilion, OH
Amer. Legion, Fields-Myers-Smith-Dittenber Post 256 **[9696]**, St. Louis, MI
Amer. Legion, Fife Lake Post 219 **[7699]**, Fife Lake, MI
Amer. Legion, Fifield Post 532 **[17961]**, Fifield, WI
Amer. Legion, Fifteen Grand Post 583 **[12218]**, Roseville, MN
Amer. Legion, Filipino Post 509 **[648]**, Chicago, IL
Amer. Legion, Fingerson-Rule Post 463 **[17773]**, Cobb, WI
Amer. Legion, Fire Fighters Post 339 **[14056]**, Cleveland, OH
Amer. Legion, Firelands Memorial Post 706 **[16225]**, North Fairfield, OH
Amer. Legion, Firestone Memorial Post 449 **[13032]**, Akron, OH
Amer. Legion, First Div. Cantigny Post 556 **[3978]**, Wheaton, IL
Amer. Legion, First Natl. Post 985 **[2293]**, Lisle, IL
Amer. Legion, First United Methodist Church Post 38 **[6470]**, West Lafayette, IN
Amer. Legion, Fischer-Sollis Post 137 **[2767]**, O Fallon, IL
Amer. Legion, Fisher Body Lansing Post 183 **[8535]**, Lansing, MI
Amer. Legion, Fisher Body Post 342 **[7710]**, Flint, MI
Amer. Legion, Fisher-Lechnir-Wall Post 252 **[17860]**, Eastman, WI
Amer. Legion, Fitchville Memorial Post 729 **[16226]**, North Fairfield, OH
Amer. Legion, Fitzsimmons Post 225 **[1902]**, Greenfield, IL
Amer. Legion, Flanagan-Dorn Post 294 **[18180]**, Hartland, WI
Amer. Legion, Flanagan Post 456 **[1703]**, Flanagan, IL
Amer. Legion, Fletcher-Pechacek Post 121 **[19639]**, River Falls, WI
Amer. Legion, Floriano-Stecker Post 340 **[8163]**, Hermansville, MI
Amer. Legion, Floyd Becker Post 209 **[5832]**, Moores Hill, IN
Amer. Legion, Floyd Marshall Post 412 **[6147]**, Russiaville, IN
Amer. Legion, Flushing Amer. Legion Post 283 **[7762]**, Flushing, MI
Amer. Legion, Flushing Post 366 **[15219]**, Flushing, OH
Amer. Legion, Flynn Brown Post 455 **[1308]**, Cowden, IL
Amer. Legion, Flynn-Eick Post 451 **[1637]**, Emington, IL
Amer. Legion, Fohl-Martin Post 483 **[17461]**, Allenton, WI
Amer. Legion, Foody-Cornwell Post 95 **[17365]**, Xenia, OH
Amer. Legion, Ford Motor Company Post 173 **[7245]**, Dearborn, MI
Amer. Legion, Ford Wagar Memorial Post 447 **[10183]**, Wyandotte, MI
Amer. Legion, Forest Lake Post 225 **[11014]**, Forest Lake, MN
Amer. Legion, Forest Park Post 414 **[1709]**, Forest Park, IL
Amer. Legion, Forest Post 67 **[16660]**, Shreve, OH
Amer. Legion, Forrest Ballard Post 723 **[2492]**, Milford, IL
Amer. Legion, Forrest-Gunderson-Klevgard Post 264 **[18051]**, Gilmanton, WI
Amer. Legion, Forrest Lewis Post 266 **[10097]**, Wayland, MI
Amer. Legion, Forreston Post 308 **[1716]**, Forreston, IL
Amer. Legion, Fort Custer Post 257 **[6843]**, Battle Creek, MI
Amer. Legion, Fort Dearborn Post 364 **[7246]**, Dearborn, MI
Amer. Legion, Fort Harrison Post 40 **[6309]**, Terre Haute, IN
Amer. Legion, Fort Laurens Post 190 **[13376]**, Bolivar, OH
Amer. Legion, Fort Loramie Post 355 **[15223]**, Fort Loramie, OH
Amer. Legion, Fort Mc Kinley Memorial Post 613 **[16992]**, Trotwood, OH
Amer. Legion, Fort Wayne Post 47 **[4629]**, Fort Wayne, IN
Amer. Legion, Fortville Post 391 **[4731]**, Fortville, IN
Amer. Legion, Foss-Agin-Meyer Post 185 **[13008]**, Ada, OH
Amer. Legion, Foster-Bernhardt Post 373 **[12758]**, Trimont, MN
Amer. Legion, Foucault-Funke Post 444 **[6829]**, Baraga, MI
Amer. Legion, Fountain City Post 56 **[18002]**, Fountain City, WI
Amer. Legion, Fowler Post 57 **[4734]**, Fowler, IN
Amer. Legion, Fox-River-Geneva Post 75 **[1791]**, Geneva, IL
Amer. Legion, Francis-Bergin-Paul-Nieman Post 225 **[19723]**, Shell Lake, WI
Amer. Legion, Francis Pohlman Post 685 **[356]**, Brussels, IL
Amer. Legion, Frank Courtney Post 22 **[5682]**, Linton, IN
Amer. Legion, Frank Feia Post 211 **[11175]**, Holdingford, MN
Amer. Legion, Frank Heinzel Post 254 **[12635]**, Sauk Rapids, MN

Amer. Legion, Frank Horetski Post 499 **[9425]**, Port Austin, MI
Amer. Legion, Frank Kray Post 455 **[10698]**, Cold Spring, MN
Amer. Legion, Frank Lund Post 159 **[11934]**, Oklee, MN
Amer. Legion, Frankenmuth Post 150 **[7778]**, Frankenmuth, MI
Amer. Legion, Frankfort-Mokena Post 2000 **[2505]**, Mokena, IL
Amer. Legion, Franklin D. Roosevelt Post 560 **[13507]**, Campbell, OH
Amer. Legion, Franklin D. Roosevelt Post 923 **[649]**, Chicago, IL
Amer. Legion, Franklin Park Post 974 **[1735]**, Franklin Park, IL
Amer. Legion, Franklin Post 1 **[13191]**, Ashville, OH
Amer. Legion, Franklin Post 205 **[4746]**, Franklin, IN
Amer. Legion, Franklin Post 1089 **[1732]**, Franklin, IL
Amer. Legion, Fraser-Nelson Post 613 **[12006]**, Pine River, MN
Amer. Legion, Fraser Post 243 **[9743]**, Shelby Township, MI
Amer. Legion, Fred-W.-Strong-Donald-W.-Wolf Post 234 **[8135]**, Hart, MI
Amer. Legion, Fred Zeplin Post 1005 **[650]**, Chicago, IL
Amer. Legion, Fredericksburg Memorial Post 651 **[15241]**, Fredericksburg, OH
Amer. Legion, Freedom Post 172 **[19324]**, North Freedom, WI
Amer. Legion, Freedom Post 183 **[16393]**, Pemberville, OH
Amer. Legion, Freeman Spur Post 1273 **[1743]**, Freeman Spur, IL
Amer. Legion, Freeport Post 139 **[1744]**, Freeport, IL
Amer. Legion, Friedrichs-Mueller-Norgaard Post 149 **[17924]**, Elkhart Lake, WI
Amer. Legion, Fuhrman-Finnegan Post 350 **[19589]**, Reedsburg, WI
Amer. Legion, Fulton-Banta Post 291 **[4420]**, Covington, IN
Amer. Legion, Fulton Post 402 **[1757]**, Fulton, IL
Amer. Legion, Funkhouser Post 8 **[4522]**, Evansville, IN
Amer. Legion, Furniture City Post 258 **[7892]**, Grand Rapids, MI
Amer. Legion, Furo-Heinen Post 281 **[18278]**, Junction City, WI
Amer. Legion, G. Chandler Bond Post 275 **[6563]**, Adrian, MI
Amer. Legion, G.A. Leonard Norberg Post 63 **[11107]**, Hallock, MN
Amer. Legion, Gage Park Post 959 **[651]**, Chicago, IL
Amer. Legion, Gahanna Post 797 **[15257]**, Gahanna, OH
Amer. Legion, Galloway Post 799 **[14293]**, Columbus, OH
Amer. Legion, Galvin-Struckmeyer Post 248 **[17788]**, Cottage Grove, WI
Amer. Legion, Garden Post 545 **[7808]**, Garden, MI
Amer. Legion, Gardnerneihardt Post 463 **[9759]**, South Boardman, MI
Amer. Legion, Garfield Heights **[15301]**, Garfield Heights, OH
Amer. Legion, Garfield Heights Post 304 **[15801]**, Maple Heights, OH
Amer. Legion, Garfield Memorial Post 566 **[13033]**, Akron, OH
Amer. Legion, Garfield Park Post 88 **[4996]**, Indianapolis, IN
Amer. Legion, Garland-Tompkins Post 399 **[9300]**, Old Mission, MI
Amer. Legion, Garnett-Foch Post 684 **[1889]**, Grayslake, IL
Amer. Legion, Garrett-Baldridge Post 725 **[4029]**, Windsor, IL
Amer. Legion, Garrett-Riest Post 503 **[16658]**, Shiloh, OH
Amer. Legion, Garrettsville Post 32 **[16495]**, Ravenna, OH
Amer. Legion, Gary Post 505 **[11039]**, Gary, MN
Amer. Legion, Gaston Post 387 **[4789]**, Gaston, IN
Amer. Legion, Gateway Post 421 **[10023]**, Unionville, MI
Amer. Legion, Gedig Post 314 **[12970]**, Winthrop, MN
Amer. Legion, Gem Post 937 **[3491]**, Smithton, IL
Amer. Legion, Gen. Ike Eisenhower Post 98 **[652]**, Chicago, IL
Amer. Legion, Gen. C. Pulaski Post 86 **[1452]**, Des Plaines, IL
Amer. Legion, General-Schwengel-Seagram Post 807 **[2957]**, Park Ridge, IL
Amer. Legion, Genoa-De-Soto Post 246 **[18033]**, Genoa, WI
Amer. Legion, Genoa Post 324 **[15311]**, Genoa, OH
Amer. Legion, George Bergem Post 489 **[12780]**, Underwood, MN
Amer. Legion, George Call Post 124 **[15307]**, Geneva, OH
Amer. Legion, George Puckett Post 264 **[8904]**, Mancelona, MI
Amer. Legion, George Washington Post 88 **[7634]**, Farmington, MI
Amer. Legion, George William Benjamin Post 791 **[2749]**, Northbrook, IL
Amer. Legion, Gerald Pitts Post 473 **[6833]**, Barryton, MI
Amer. Legion, Germantown, Post 1 **[18037]**, Germantown, WI
Amer. Legion, Geroux Post 11 **[10052]**, Wakefield, MI
Amer. Legion, Getchel-Nelson Post 210 **[20027]**, Waupun, WI
Amer. Legion, Gibb Post 588 **[3092]**, Piper City, IL
Amer. Legion, Gilbert Davis Post 157 **[4356]**, Churubusco, IN
Amer. Legion, Gilbertson-Rude Post 526 **[11996]**, Peterson, MN
Amer. Legion, Giles-Luce Post 364 **[20172]**, Winneconne, WI
Amer. Legion, Gillen Post 33 **[4164]**, Bedford, IN
Amer. Legion, Gilmore-Stensrud Post 552 **[11030]**, Freeborn, MN
Amer. Legion, Giltz-Brown Post 341 **[16276]**, Oakwood, OH
Amer. Legion, Gingrich-Poince Post 487 **[17188]**, West Milton, OH
Amer. Legion, Girard-Horrocks Post 37 **[8314]**, Ionia, MI
Amer. Legion, Gislason-Richter Post 402 **[19952]**, Washington Island, WI
Amer. Legion, Gittens-Leidel Post 595 **[11262]**, La Crescent, MN
Amer. Legion, Gittings-Sandine Post 297 **[1338]**, Dallas City, IL
Amer. Legion, Gladstone Post 777 **[653]**, Chicago, IL
Amer. Legion, Gladwin County Post 171 **[7832]**, Gladwin, MI
Amer. Legion, Glen Ellyn Post 3 **[1825]**, Glen Ellyn, IL
Amer. Legion, Glen Hill Post 287 **[7104]**, Cedar Springs, MI
Amer. Legion, Glen Owens Post 14 **[6030]**, Peru, IN
Amer. Legion, Glen Park Post 214 **[5763]**, Merrillville, IN
Amer. Legion, Glencoe Post 95 **[11047]**, Glencoe, MN
Amer. Legion, Glencoe Post 632 **[15325]**, Glencoe, OH
Amer. Legion, Glendale Post 805 **[654]**, Chicago, IL
Amer. Legion, Glenmoor Post 736 **[15075]**, East Liverpool, OH
Amer. Legion, Glenn Maker Post 1160 **[1252]**, Chicago Ridge, IL
Amer. Legion, Glenville Post 264 **[11050]**, Glenville, MN
Amer. Legion, Glidewell-Yelton Post 1230 **[1964]**, Hazel Dell, IL
Amer. Legion, Gnadenhutten Post 154 **[15328]**, Gnadenhutten, OH
Amer. Legion, Godfrey Anderson Post 43 **[9859]**, Stephenson, MI
Amer. Legion, Godfrey Post 2506 **[1873]**, Godfrey, IL
Amer. Legion, Goetz St. Louis Post 522 **[18220]**, Hubertus, WI
Amer. Legion, Gold Star Post 505 **[18939]**, Milwaukee, WI
Amer. Legion, Gold Star Post 676 **[1524]**, Durand, IL
Amer. Legion, Gold Star Post 1102 **[3766]**, Tinley Park, IL
Amer. Legion, Goldstrand-Beadle Post 371 **[12207]**, Roosevelt, MN
Amer. Legion, Gonvick Post 304 **[11067]**, Gonvick, MN
Amer. Legion, Gopher Post 440 **[11496]**, Minneapolis, MN
Amer. Legion, Goshen Post 30 **[4792]**, Goshen, IN
Amer. Legion, Gosz-Novak Post 199 **[19593]**, Reedsville, WI
Amer. Legion, Granada Post 319 **[11072]**, Granada, MN
Amer. Legion, Grand Blanc Post 413 **[7841]**, Grand Blanc, MI
Amer. Legion, Grand Marais Post 413 **[11073]**, Grand Marais, MN
Amer. Legion, Granger Post 151 **[4807]**, Granger, IN
Amer. Legion, Grant Park Star Post 295 **[1887]**, Grant Park, IL
Amer. Legion, Grant Post 202 **[213]**, Bellflower, IL
Amer. Legion, Granville Post 180 **[1888]**, Granville, IL
Amer. Legion, Granville Post 398 **[15341]**, Granville, OH
Amer. Legion, Grassold-Schmidlkofer Post 125 **[17740]**, Chilton, WI
Amer. Legion, Gray-Wachter-Murphy Post 229 **[19234]**, Mount Hope, WI
Amer. Legion, Grayling Post 106 **[8057]**, Grayling, MI
Amer. Legion, Grayslake Post 659 **[1890]**, Grayslake, IL
Amer. Legion, Green-Hill Post 397 **[10786]**, Dilworth, MN
Amer. Legion, Green Isle Post 408 **[11097]**, Green Isle, MN
Amer. Legion, Green Oak Post 757 **[2793]**, Oak Lawn, IL
Amer. Legion, Green-Rock-Colona Post 1233 **[1293]**, Colona, IL
Amer. Legion, Greenawalt-Flaherty Post 42 **[7117]**, Charlotte, MI
Amer. Legion, Greendale Post 416 **[18149]**, Greendale, WI
Amer. Legion, Greening-Buelow Post 437 **[18835]**, Mazomanie, WI
Amer. Legion, Greenville Post 282 **[1905]**, Greenville, IL
Amer. Legion, Greenwood Post 252 **[4848]**, Greenwood, IN
Amer. Legion, Gresham-Crutchley Post 341 **[100]**, Atlanta, IL
Amer. Legion, Gresham Post 390 **[18166]**, Gresham, WI
Amer. Legion, Gresham Post 603 **[1264]**, Cisne, IL
Amer. Legion, Gridley Post 218 **[1910]**, Gridley, IL
Amer. Legion, Griggsville Post 213 **[1912]**, Griggsville, IL
Amer. Legion, Grobengieser-Fischer Post 512 **[33]**, Altamont, IL
Amer. Legion, Grosse Ile Post 75 **[8073]**, Grosse Ile, MI
Amer. Legion, Grosse Pointe Post 303 **[7304]**, Detroit, MI
Amer. Legion, Grover Sheets Post 111 **[4268]**, Bluffton, IN
Amer. Legion, Groves-Walker Post 346 **[7635]**, Farmington, MI
Amer. Legion, Gully Post 603 **[11104]**, Gully, MN
Amer. Legion, Gunder Austad Post 22 **[12070]**, Red Lake Falls, MN
Amer. Legion, Gunderson and Gilbertson Post 507 **[19192]**, Mindoro, WI
Amer. Legion, Gurnee Post 771 **[1913]**, Gurnee, IL

Amer. Legion, Gustav Berg Post 81 **[11118]**, Harmony, MN
Amer. Legion, Guth Bros. Post 111 **[13718]**, Cincinnati, OH
Amer. Legion, Guy Baird Post 554 **[437]**, Carlinville, IL
Amer. Legion, Guy Stanton Post 240 **[6969]**, Blanchard, MI
Amer. Legion, Haack-Good Post 496 **[10441]**, Bigelow, MN
Amer. Legion, Hackensack Post 202 **[11106]**, Hackensack, MN
Amer. Legion, Hacker-Gebke Post 976 **[157]**, Bartelso, IL
Amer. Legion, Haderer-Eineke Post 680 **[1929]**, Hampshire, IL
Amer. Legion, Hagberg-Hamlin Post 45 **[1784]**, Galva, IL
Amer. Legion, Hales Corners Memorial Post 299 **[18168]**, Hales Corners, WI
Amer. Legion, Halker-Flege Post 69 **[16506]**, Reading, OH
Amer. Legion, Hall-Adkins Post 134 **[14030]**, Circleville, OH
Amer. Legion, Hall-Dewinter Post 145 **[9230]**, Norway, MI
Amer. Legion, Ham Lake Post 2000 **[10294]**, Andover, MN
Amer. Legion, Hamilton-Harris Post 447 **[19940]**, Viola, WI
Amer. Legion, Hamilton Post 629 **[1927]**, Hamilton, IL
Amer. Legion, Hamline Post 418 **[12361]**, St. Paul, MN
Amer. Legion, Hamm-Miller Post 145 **[18020]**, Fredonia, WI
Amer. Legion, Hammond Post 16 **[4868]**, Hammond, IN
Amer. Legion, Hammond-Schmit Post 55 **[18217]**, Hortonville, WI
Amer. Legion Hammond Victory Post 168 **[4869]**, Hammond, IN
Amer. Legion, Hammondsville Post 742 **[15404]**, Hammondsville, OH
Amer. Legion, Hamon Gray Post 83 **[5594]**, La Porte, IN
Amer. Legion, Hamtramck Falcon Post 455 **[8104]**, Hamtramck, MI
Amer. Legion, Hancock Post 119 **[4829]**, Greenfield, IN
Amer. Legion, Hanley-Ariss-Millin Post 5 **[19428]**, Patch Grove, WI
Amer. Legion, Hanna Post 472 **[6365]**, Union Mills, IN
Amer. Legion, Hannahville Potawatomi Post 116 **[8124]**, Harris, MI
Amer. Legion, Hannan-Colvin Post 180 **[8288]**, Hudson, MI
Amer. Legion, Hanover-Horton Post 270 **[8113]**, Hanover, MI
Amer. Legion, Hanover Post 764 **[16165]**, Newark, OH
Amer. Legion, Hansel Roberts Post 248 **[5643]**, Lagro, IN
Amer. Legion, Hansen-Hayes Post 178 **[11464]**, Milaca, MN
Amer. Legion, Hanson-Anderson Post 361 **[12935]**, Willow River, MN
Amer. Legion, Hanson-Hatlestad Post 544 **[11954]**, Ostrander, MN
Amer. Legion, Hanson-Kennedy Post 1079 **[11]**, Albany, IL
Amer. Legion, Hanson-Lien Post 368 **[18209]**, Hixton, WI
Amer. Legion, Hanson-Maki Post 506 **[18238]**, Iron River, WI
Amer. Legion, Hanson Mc Fee Post 61 **[6200]**, Shoals, IN
Amer. Legion, Hanson Park Post 1177 **[655]**, Chicago, IL
Amer. Legion, Harding-Hall-Darrington Post 357 **[17583]**, Bay City, WI
Amer. Legion, Harding-Olk-Craidge Post 18 **[6875]**, Bay City, MI
Amer. Legion, Harley-Davidson Post 400 **[20069]**, Wauwatosa, WI
Amer. Legion, Harmeyer Post 343 **[4933]**, Holland, IN
Amer. Legion, Harmon-Harris Post 314 **[17652]**, Boyceville, WI
Amer. Legion, Harold Kripisch Post 96 **[5758]**, Medaryville, IN
Amer. Legion, Harold Washington Post 1987 **[656]**, Chicago, IL
Amer. Legion, Harper Woods Post 99 **[8120]**, Harper Woods, MI
Amer. Legion, Harr-Reese Post 160 **[13416]**, Brewster, OH
Amer. Legion, Harris Post 139 **[11121]**, Harris, MN
Amer. Legion, Harrison-Jones Post 223 **[18206]**, Hillsboro, WI
Amer. Legion, Harrison Post 123 **[4417]**, Corydon, IN
Amer. Legion, Harrison Post 404 **[8125]**, Harrison, MI
Amer. Legion, Harry Carpenter Post 428 **[3128]**, Potomac, IL
Amer. Legion, Harry Fogle Post 274 **[3228]**, Rochester, IL
Amer. Legion, Harry Ray Post 65 **[6085]**, Richmond, IN
Amer. Legion, Harry Riddle Post 448 **[2498]**, Minier, IL
Amer. Legion, Harter-Williams Post 536 **[15319]**, Gilboa, OH
Amer. Legion, Hartman-Lammers Post 286 **[19376]**, Oostburg, WI
Amer. Legion, Hartsburg Post 1146 **[1944]**, Hartsburg, IL
Amer. Legion, Harvey Stunkard Post 530 **[3475]**, Sidell, IL
Amer. Legion, Harwood Post 5 **[2097]**, Joliet, IL
Amer. Legion, Haslee-Doebert-Schmidt Post 261 **[18148]**, Greenbush, WI
Amer. Legion, Hassel Briese Post 473 **[12104]**, Rice, MN
Amer. Legion, Hatley Post 471 **[18191]**, Hatley, WI
Amer. Legion, Haubstadt Post 194 **[4905]**, Haubstadt, IN
Amer. Legion, Haug-Hammer Post 508 **[10747]**, Dalton, MN
Amer. Legion, Havana Post 138 **[1958]**, Havana, IL
Amer. Legion, Havlik-Koltes-Thaden Post 503 **[17803]**, Dane, WI
Amer. Legion, Hawley-Dieckhoff Post 33 **[19265]**, Neenah, WI
Amer. Legion, Hazel Crest Post 398 **[1962]**, Hazel Crest, IL
Amer. Legion, Heath-Perkins Post 51 **[12001]**, Pine City, MN
Amer. Legion, Heath Post 771 **[16166]**, Newark, OH
Amer. Legion, Hebron Post 285 **[15415]**, Hebron, OH
Amer. Legion, Hedrick-Brandt Post 23 **[5552]**, Kentland, IN
Amer. Legion, Heesaker-Brown Post 230 **[17812]**, De Pere, WI
Amer. Legion, Heightshillcrest Post 104 **[16690]**, South Euclid, OH
Amer. Legion, Heiland Post 446 **[13143]**, Anna, OH
Amer. Legion, Hellenic Post 100 **[9744]**, Shelby Township, MI
Amer. Legion, Hellenic Post 129 **[11497]**, Minneapolis, MN
Amer. Legion, Hellenic Post 343 **[2738]**, Norridge, IL
Amer. Legion, Hellenic Post 453 **[15183]**, Fairview Park, OH
Amer. Legion, Heminger-Jones Post 504 **[9329]**, Otter Lake, MI
Amer. Legion, Henderson County Post 765 **[2322]**, Lomax, IL
Amer. Legion, Henderson-Lewis Post 545 **[12686]**, Spicer, MN
Amer. Legion, Hendricks County Post 118 **[4444]**, Danville, IN
Amer. Legion, Henrizi-Schneider Post 382 **[18868]**, Menomonee Falls, WI
Amer. Legion, Henry M. Guttormson Post 40 **[11301]**, Lanesboro, MN
Amer. Legion, Henry Post 323 **[1968]**, Henry, IL
Amer. Legion, Henry Sollie Post 10 **[11269]**, Lake Benton, MN
Amer. Legion, Henryville Post 105 **[4908]**, Henryville, IN
Amer. Legion, Herbert K. Kellam Post 224 **[11152]**, Heron Lake, MN
Amer. Legion, Herrin Prairie Post 645 **[1972]**, Herrin, IL
Amer. Legion, Herscher Post 795 **[1975]**, Herscher, IL
Amer. Legion, Hesley Jensen Post 491 **[10391]**, Bayport, MN
Amer. Legion, Hess-Eastman Post 174 **[8791]**, Lawrence, MI
Amer. Legion, H.F. Hortz Post 415 **[3464]**, Sheffield, IL
Amer. Legion, Hice-Shutes Post 170 **[9913]**, Three Rivers, MI
Amer. Legion, Hickerson Post 432 **[357]**, Buckley, IL
Amer. Legion, Hicks-Olson Post 424 **[245]**, Blandinsville, IL
Amer. Legion, Higby-Oglan-Soerens Post 345 **[18208]**, Hingham, WI
Amer. Legion, Highland Memorial Post 180 **[4910]**, Highland, IN
Amer. Legion, Highland Park Post 145 **[1986]**, Highland Park, IL
Amer. Legion, Highwood Post 501 **[1994]**, Highwood, IL
Amer. Legion, Hill-Gazette Post 143 **[6812]**, Auburn Hills, MI
Amer. Legion, Hill-Palmer Post 561 **[2385]**, Manito, IL
Amer. Legion, Hillestad-Borgeson Post 410 **[11146]**, Herman, MN
Amer. Legion, Hills Post 399 **[11168]**, Hills, MN
Amer. Legion, Hillsdale Post 1144 **[1999]**, Hillsdale, IL
Amer. Legion, Hillside Post 863 **[2003]**, Hillside, IL
Amer. Legion, Hinek-Hertel-Krupka Post 468 **[18917]**, Milladore, WI
Amer. Legion, Hinkins-Moody Post 453 **[17603]**, Belmont, WI
Amer. Legion, Hinsdale Post 250 **[2012]**, Hinsdale, IL
Amer. Legion, Hiter-Wene Post 1049 **[3936]**, Weldon, IL
Amer. Legion, Hochstedler Post 318 **[6509]**, Westfield, IN
Amer. Legion, Hoffman Post 393 **[11173]**, Hoffman, MN
Amer. Legion, Hogaj-Francisco Post 516 **[18826]**, Mason, WI
Amer. Legion, Hogberg-Gerszewski Post 353 **[10333]**, Argyle, MN
Amer. Legion, Hokah Post 498 **[11174]**, Hokah, MN
Amer. Legion, Holien-Thompson Post 252 **[11443]**, Maynard, MN
Amer. Legion, Holland Post 646 **[15456]**, Holland, OH
Amer. Legion, Holland-Swenson Post 434 **[11143]**, Hendrum, MN
Amer. Legion, Hollandale Post 510 **[18212]**, Hollandale, WI
Amer. Legion, Holmes Post 192 **[16034]**, Millersburg, OH
Amer. Legion, Holte-Grygla-Fourtown Post 162 **[11102]**, Grygla, MN
Amer. Legion, Holthaus-Kampwerth Post 1227 **[193]**, Beckemeyer, IL
Amer. Legion, Holtz-Hirst Post 288 **[3495]**, South Beloit, IL
Amer. Legion, Homer Cameron Post 342 **[6141]**, Rossville, IN
Amer. Legion, Homer Dahringer Post 281 **[3919]**, Waukegan, IL
Amer. Legion, Homer Lawson Post 653 **[17125]**, Washington Court House, OH
Amer. Legion, Homer and Lee Parkinson Post 170 **[19194]**, Mineral Point, WI
Amer. Legion, Homer Post 290 **[2040]**, Homer, IL
Amer. Legion, Homer Weiss Post 494 **[16804]**, Sugarcreek, OH
Amer. Legion, Homer Wing Post 172 **[9499]**, Rochester, MI

Amer. Legion, Homewood Post 483 **[2044]**, Homewood, IL
Amer. Legion, Honored Seven Post 740 **[16524]**, Richmond, OH
Amer. Legion, Hope Post 229 **[4935]**, Hope, IN
Amer. Legion, Hopedale Post 682 **[15466]**, Hopedale, OH
Amer. Legion, Hopedale Post 1157 **[2051]**, Hopedale, IL
Amer. Legion, Hopland-Moen Post 459 **[17920]**, Eleva, WI
Amer. Legion, Horicon Post 157 **[18213]**, Horicon, WI
Amer. Legion, Hornickel Post 379 **[4486]**, Elizabeth, IN
Amer. Legion, Hosford-Chase Post 32 **[18880]**, Menomonie, WI
Amer. Legion, Houghton-Higgins-Lake Post 245 **[9463]**, Prudenville, MI
Amer. Legion, Houghton Post 80 **[8985]**, Mass City, MI
Amer. Legion, Howard-Donalds-Richard-Hylkema Post 137 **[19915]**, Turtle Lake, WI
Amer. Legion, Howard Post 145 **[11199]**, Howard Lake, MN
Amer. Legion, Howe-Paff Post 37 **[17921]**, Elk Mound, WI
Amer. Legion, Howland Post 700 **[17095]**, Warren, OH
Amer. Legion, Hubbard Post 51 **[15469]**, Hubbard, OH
Amer. Legion, Hubbard Post 336 **[11895]**, Nielsville, MN
Amer. Legion, Huber Heights Post 200 **[15472]**, Huber Heights, OH
Amer. Legion, Hudson Motor Post 357 **[9564]**, Roseville, MI
Amer. Legion, Hudsonville Post 329 **[8402]**, Jenison, MI
Amer. Legion, Huerter-Wilmette Post 46 **[4016]**, Wilmette, IL
Amer. Legion, Huffman-Hammond-Rando Post 502 **[7598]**, Elsie, MI
Amer. Legion, Hugh Allen Mc Innes Post 74 **[9195]**, Newberry, MI
Amer. Legion, Hugh Watson Post 190 **[12266]**, St. Charles, MN
Amer. Legion, Hugh Watson Post 530 **[13719]**, Cincinnati, OH
Amer. Legion, Hughes-Mc-Cormick Post 362 **[10760]**, De Graff, MN
Amer. Legion, Hugo Fales Post 203 **[6902]**, Belding, MI
Amer. Legion, Hugo Post 620 **[11202]**, Hugo, MN
Amer. Legion, Humphrey-Wilsey Post 233 **[19958]**, Waterloo, WI
Amer. Legion, Hunt-Trouse Post 287 **[4339]**, Centerville, IN
Amer. Legion, Huntley Post 673 **[2053]**, Huntley, IL
Amer. Legion, Hurlbut-Ziemer Post 476 **[10498]**, Bovey, MN
Amer. Legion, Huron Valley Post 231 **[7031]**, Brownstown, MI
Amer. Legion, Hurst-Collins Post 281 **[4373]**, Cloverdale, IN
Amer. Legion, Hustisford Memorial Post 420 **[18279]**, Juneau, WI
Amer. Legion, Hutchins-Stendahl Post 191 **[20157]**, Whitehall, WI
Amer. Legion, Hutchinson Post 96 **[11203]**, Hutchinson, MN
Amer. Legion, Hutton-Avery-Sherry Post 262 **[8407]**, Jones, MI
Amer. Legion, Hyatt-Allen Post 538 **[16880]**, Toledo, OH
Amer. Legion, Hyde-Park-Mt-Lookout Post 744 **[13720]**, Cincinnati, OH
Amer. Legion, Idlewild Amer. Legion Post 263 **[8304]**, Idlewild, MI
Amer. Legion, Illiana Post 220 **[657]**, Chicago, IL
Amer. Legion, Illini Post 254 **[2378]**, Magnolia, IL
Amer. Legion, Illinois Dept. of Employment Sec Post 815 **[658]**, Chicago, IL
Amer. Legion, Illinois HQ Post 2910 **[257]**, Bloomington, IL
Amer. Legion, Illinois Post 16 **[400]**, Canton, IL
Amer. Legion, Illinois Post 17 **[2065]**, Ipava, IL
Amer. Legion, Illinois Post 18 **[2309]**, Lockport, IL
Amer. Legion, Illinois Post 26 **[3851]**, Vermont, IL
Amer. Legion, Illinois Post 35 **[1815]**, Glasford, IL
Amer. Legion, Illinois Post 41 **[1304]**, Countryside, IL
Amer. Legion, Illinois Post 47 **[659]**, Chicago, IL
Amer. Legion, Illinois Post 51 **[3975]**, Westville, IL
Amer. Legion, Illinois Post 54 **[1684]**, Fairbury, IL
Amer. Legion, Illinois Post 55 **[1700]**, Farmer City, IL
Amer. Legion, Illinois Post 56 **[258]**, Bloomington, IL
Amer. Legion, Illinois Post 58 **[198]**, Belleville, IL
Amer. Legion, Illinois Post 60 **[2362]**, Machesney Park, IL
Amer. Legion, Illinois Post 69 **[3218]**, Robinson, IL
Amer. Legion, Illinois Post 74 **[464]**, Carthage, IL
Amer. Legion, Illinois Post 80 **[1494]**, Downers Grove, IL
Amer. Legion, Illinois Post 83 **[3116]**, Polo, IL
Amer. Legion, Illinois Post 87 **[660]**, Chicago, IL
Amer. Legion, Illinois Post 89 **[2478]**, Metamora, IL
Amer. Legion, Illinois Post 106 **[2465]**, McLeansboro, IL
Amer. Legion, Illinois Post 110 **[2670]**, Nashville, IL
Amer. Legion, Illinois Post 115 **[1813]**, Girard, IL
Amer. Legion, Illinois Post 119 **[1721]**, Fox River Grove, IL
Amer. Legion, Illinois Post 123 **[2310]**, Lockport, IL
Amer. Legion, Illinois Post 128 **[3407]**, Salem, IL
Amer. Legion, Illinois Post 129 **[97]**, Athens, IL
Amer. Legion, Illinois Post 132 **[1704]**, Flat Rock, IL
Amer. Legion, Illinois Post 135 **[2323]**, Lombard, IL
Amer. Legion, Illinois Post 136 **[2540]**, Monmouth, IL
Amer. Legion, Illinois Post 166 **[1855]**, Glenview, IL
Amer. Legion, Illinois Post 167 **[1938]**, Harrisburg, IL
Amer. Legion, Illinois Post 172 **[2414]**, Marissa, IL
Amer. Legion, Illinois Post 176 **[1686]**, Fairfield, IL
Amer. Legion, Illinois Post 177 **[4078]**, Zeigler, IL
Amer. Legion, Illinois Post 178 **[2857]**, Olmsted, IL
Amer. Legion, Illinois Post 182 **[3517]**, Spring Valley, IL
Amer. Legion, Illinois Post 189 **[21]**, Alexis, IL
Amer. Legion, Illinois Post 190 **[347]**, Brookfield, IL
Amer. Legion, Illinois Post 191 **[4025]**, Wilmington, IL
Amer. Legion, Illinois Post 194 **[2011]**, Hindsboro, IL
Amer. Legion, Illinois Post 197 **[2981]**, Pecatonica, IL
Amer. Legion, Illinois Post 209 **[381]**, Byron, IL
Amer. Legion, Illinois Post 210 **[1342]**, Danville, IL
Amer. Legion, Illinois Post 217 **[3724]**, Streator, IL
Amer. Legion, Illinois Post 233 **[2855]**, Okawville, IL
Amer. Legion, Illinois Post 234 **[584]**, Chenoa, IL
Amer. Legion, Illinois Post 236 **[1648]**, Evanston, IL
Amer. Legion, Illinois Post 237 **[2852]**, Oglesby, IL
Amer. Legion, Illinois Post 244 **[3474]**, Sibley, IL
Amer. Legion, Illinois Post 247 **[2958]**, Park Ridge, IL
Amer. Legion, Illinois Post 249 **[4052]**, Woodson, IL
Amer. Legion, Illinois Post 253 **[3190]**, Richmond, IL
Amer. Legion, Illinois Post 261 **[358]**, Buda, IL
Amer. Legion, Illinois Post 265 **[1948]**, Harvard, IL
Amer. Legion, Illinois Post 272 **[661]**, Chicago, IL
Amer. Legion, Illinois Post 276 **[468]**, Cary, IL
Amer. Legion, Illinois Post 279 **[2073]**, Jacksonville, IL
Amer. Legion, Illinois Post 284 **[94]**, Assumption, IL
Amer. Legion, Illinois Post 285 **[1767]**, Galesburg, IL
Amer. Legion, Illinois Post 291 **[2251]**, Lexington, IL
Amer. Legion, Illinois Post 292 **[2430]**, Mascoutah, IL
Amer. Legion, Illinois Post 303 **[3209]**, Riverdale, IL
Amer. Legion, Illinois Post 306 **[2481]**, Metropolis, IL
Amer. Legion, Illinois Post 327 **[1447]**, Depue, IL
Amer. Legion, Illinois Post 344 **[51]**, Anna, IL
Amer. Legion, Illinois Post 347 **[460]**, Carterville, IL
Amer. Legion, Illinois Post 362 **[3695]**, Staunton, IL
Amer. Legion, Illinois Post 363 **[662]**, Chicago, IL
Amer. Legion, Illinois Post 370 **[2607]**, Moweaqua, IL
Amer. Legion, Illinois Post 381 **[2]**, Abingdon, IL
Amer. Legion, Illinois Post 386 **[3870]**, Virden, IL
Amer. Legion, Illinois Post 396 **[3513]**, Sparta, IL
Amer. Legion, Illinois Post 410 **[1248]**, Chicago Heights, IL
Amer. Legion, Illinois Post 419 **[663]**, Chicago, IL
Amer. Legion, Illinois Post 435 **[1818]**, Glen Carbon, IL
Amer. Legion, Illinois Post 437 **[664]**, Chicago, IL
Amer. Legion, Illinois Post 440 **[3777]**, Toluca, IL
Amer. Legion, Illinois Post 441 **[319]**, Bluffs, IL
Amer. Legion, Illinois Post 442 **[4027]**, Winchester, IL
Amer. Legion, Illinois Post 446 **[486]**, Centralia, IL
Amer. Legion, Illinois Post 475 **[1339]**, Dalton City, IL
Amer. Legion, Illinois Post 482 **[3798]**, Union, IL
Amer. Legion, Illinois Post 495 **[1631]**, Elmwood Park, IL
Amer. Legion, Illinois Post 498 **[90]**, Ashland, IL
Amer. Legion, Illinois Post 500 **[2004]**, Hillside, IL
Amer. Legion, Illinois Post 514 **[411]**, Carbondale, IL
Amer. Legion, Illinois Post 524 **[3184]**, Red Bud, IL
Amer. Legion, Illinois Post 533 **[1335]**, Cuba, IL
Amer. Legion, Illinois Post 536 **[3858]**, Vienna, IL
Amer. Legion, Illinois Post 543 **[2966]**, Patoka, IL
Amer. Legion, Illinois Post 546 **[4046]**, Woodhull, IL
Amer. Legion, Illinois Post 549 **[1527]**, Earlville, IL
Amer. Legion, Illinois Post 559 **[499]**, Champaign, IL
Amer. Legion, Illinois Post 563 **[2094]**, Johnston City, IL
Amer. Legion, Illinois Post 565 **[2676]**, New Athens, IL
Amer. Legion, Illinois Post 571 **[3362]**, Rosiclare, IL
Amer. Legion, Illinois Post 572 **[2704]**, Noble, IL
Amer. Legion, Illinois Post 591 **[3239]**, Rock Island, IL
Amer. Legion, Illinois Post 619 **[137]**, Baldwin, IL
Amer. Legion, Illinois Post 620 **[224]**, Bement, IL
Amer. Legion, Illinois Post 622 **[3130]**, Prairie Du Rocher, IL
Amer. Legion, Illinois Post 624 **[1977]**, Heyworth, IL
Amer. Legion, Illinois Post 635 **[2708]**, Normal, IL
Amer. Legion, Illinois Post 647 **[1516]**, Du Quoin, IL
Amer. Legion, Illinois Post 650 **[2388]**, Mansfield, IL
Amer. Legion, Illinois Post 683 **[3402]**, St. Libory, IL
Amer. Legion, Illinois Post 692 **[2804]**, Oak Park, IL
Amer. Legion, Illinois Post 696 **[1898]**, Grayville, IL
Amer. Legion, Illinois Post 699 **[2360]**, Lyons, IL
Amer. Legion, Illinois Post 700 **[3759]**, Thawville, IL
Amer. Legion, Illinois Post 701 **[3873]**, Waggoner, IL
Amer. Legion, Illinois Post 716 **[665]**, Chicago, IL
Amer. Legion, Illinois Post 726 **[3857]**, Victoria, IL
Amer. Legion, Illinois Post 729 **[3469]**, Sheridan, IL
Amer. Legion, Illinois Post 746 **[666]**, Chicago, IL
Amer. Legion, Illinois Post 749 **[2165]**, Knoxville, IL

Amer. Legion, Illinois Post 752 **[1301]**, Cornell, IL
Amer. Legion, Illinois Post 768 **[469]**, Cary, IL
Amer. Legion, Illinois Post 802 **[667]**, Chicago, IL
Amer. Legion, Illinois Post 806 **[668]**, Chicago, IL
Amer. Legion, Illinois Post 809 **[3525]**, Springfield, IL
Amer. Legion, Illinois Post 829 **[669]**, Chicago, IL
Amer. Legion, Illinois Post 832 **[4010]**, Willow Springs, IL
Amer. Legion, Illinois Post 838 **[2448]**, Maywood, IL
Amer. Legion, Illinois Post 888 **[2764]**, Northlake, IL
Amer. Legion, Illinois Post 904 **[3266]**, Rockford, IL
Amer. Legion, Illinois Post 915 **[670]**, Chicago, IL
Amer. Legion, Illinois Post 917 **[2427]**, Maryville, IL
Amer. Legion, Illinois Post 938 **[2185]**, Ladd, IL
Amer. Legion, Illinois Post 948 **[2167]**, La Fayette, IL
Amer. Legion, Illinois Post 957 **[1495]**, Downers Grove, IL
Amer. Legion, Illinois Post 958 **[671]**, Chicago, IL
Amer. Legion, Illinois Post 963 **[3368]**, Royalton, IL
Amer. Legion, Illinois Post 977 **[346]**, Brocton, IL
Amer. Legion, Illinois Post 984 **[672]**, Chicago, IL
Amer. Legion, Illinois Post 1009 **[1856]**, Glenview, IL
Amer. Legion, Illinois Post 1010 **[2163]**, Kingston, IL
Amer. Legion, Illinois Post 1017 **[673]**, Chicago, IL
Amer. Legion, Illinois Post 1025 **[3760]**, Thomson, IL
Amer. Legion, Illinois Post 1056 **[2186]**, Ladd, IL
Amer. Legion, Illinois Post 1072 **[3712]**, Stillman Valley, IL
Amer. Legion, Illinois Post 1105 **[107]**, Aurora, IL
Amer. Legion, Illinois Post 1109 **[2747]**, North Riverside, IL
Amer. Legion, Illinois Post 1119 **[674]**, Chicago, IL
Amer. Legion, Illinois Post 1130 **[3952]**, West Union, IL
Amer. Legion, Illinois Post 1164 **[324]**, Bourbonnais, IL
Amer. Legion, Illinois Post 1205 **[4043]**, Wood Dale, IL
Amer. Legion, Illinois Post 1207 **[3267]**, Rockford, IL
Amer. Legion, Illinois Post 1531 **[3767]**, Tinley Park, IL
Amer. Legion, Illinois Post 1941 **[2168]**, La Grange, IL
Amer. Legion, Illinois Post 1960 **[2571]**, Mounds, IL
Amer. Legion, Illinois Post 1969 **[5]**, Addison, IL
Amer. Legion, Illinois Post 1974 **[1496]**, Downers Grove, IL
Amer. Legion, Illinois Post 1976 **[2787]**, Oak Forest, IL
Amer. Legion, Illinois Post 1977 **[2687]**, New Lenox, IL
Amer. Legion, Illinois Post 1984 **[2308]**, Livingston, IL
Amer. Legion, Illinois Post 1990 **[675]**, Chicago, IL
Amer. Legion, Illiopolis Post 508 **[2058]**, Illiopolis, IL
Amer. Legion, Indian Creek Post 109 **[2741]**, Norris City, IL
Amer. Legion, Indiana Post 10 **[5724]**, Marion, IN
Amer. Legion, Indiana Post 12 **[4738]**, Frankfort, IN
Amer. Legion, Indiana Post 13 **[5909]**, Nashville, IN
Amer. Legion, Indiana Post 15 **[6423]**, Wabash, IN
Amer. Legion, Indiana Post 20 **[4429]**, Crown Point, IN
Amer. Legion, Indiana Post 26 **[4998]**, Indianapolis, IN
Amer. Legion, Indiana Post 27 **[6045]**, Plymouth, IN
Amer. Legion, Indiana Post 28 **[5915]**, New Albany, IN
Amer. Legion, Indiana Post 29 **[6076]**, Rensselaer, IN
Amer. Legion, Indiana Post 32 **[4189]**, Bicknell, IN
Amer. Legion, Indiana Post 34 **[4999]**, Indianapolis, IN
Amer. Legion, Indiana Post 36 **[6121]**, Rochester, IN
Amer. Legion, Indiana Post 37 **[5782]**, Michigan City, IN
Amer. Legion, Indiana Post 41 **[6157]**, Salem, IN
Amer. Legion, Indiana Post 45 **[5968]**, Noblesville, IN
Amer. Legion, Indiana Post 49 **[6440]**, Warsaw, IN
Amer. Legion, Indiana Post 58 **[4814]**, Greencastle, IN
Amer. Legion, Indiana Post 63 **[6019]**, Paoli, IN
Amer. Legion, Indiana Post 67 **[6198]**, Sheridan, IN
Amer. Legion, Indiana Post 74 **[4488]**, Elkhart, IN
Amer. Legion, Indiana Post 75 **[4453]**, Delphi, IN
Amer. Legion, Indiana Post 76 **[4762]**, French Lick, IN
Amer. Legion, Indiana Post 77 **[4296]**, Brookville, IN
Amer. Legion, Indiana Post 79 **[6548]**, Zionsville, IN
Amer. Legion, Indiana Post 81 **[5822]**, Monticello, IN
Amer. Legion, Indiana Post 85 **[4943]**, Huntington, IN
Amer. Legion, Indiana Post 92 **[5982]**, North Judson, IN
Amer. Legion, Indiana Post 93 **[4489]**, Elkhart, IN
Amer. Legion, Indiana Post 94 **[6376]**, Valparaiso, IN
Amer. Legion, Indiana Post 102 **[5843]**, Morristown, IN
Amer. Legion, Indiana Post 125 **[6017]**, Otterbein, IN
Amer. Legion, Indiana Post 127 **[4096]**, Anderson, IN
Amer. Legion, Indiana Post 133 **[5663]**, Leavenworth, IN
Amer. Legion, Indiana Post 137 **[5932]**, New Castle, IN
Amer. Legion, Indiana Post 142 **[4313]**, Cannelton, IN
Amer. Legion, Indiana Post 148 **[4630]**, Fort Wayne, IN
Amer. Legion, Indiana Post 150 **[6142]**, Rushville, IN
Amer. Legion, Indiana Post 158 **[6360]**, Union City, IN
Amer. Legion, Indiana Post 160 **[6120]**, Roanoke, IN
Amer. Legion, Indiana Post 169 **[4310]**, Cambridge City, IN
Amer. Legion, Indiana Post 175 **[6372]**, Urbana, IN
Amer. Legion, Indiana Post 177 **[5563]**, Kokomo, IN
Amer. Legion, Indiana Post 185 **[6405]**, Vevay, IN
Amer. Legion, Indiana Post 186 **[5000]**, Indianapolis, IN
Amer. Legion, Indiana Post 191 **[4286]**, Bremen, IN
Amer. Legion, Indiana Post 199 **[5993]**, North Vernon, IN
Amer. Legion, Indiana Post 204 **[6175]**, Sellersburg, IN
Amer. Legion, Indiana Post 210 **[5795]**, Middlebury, IN
Amer. Legion, Indiana Post 211 **[6062]**, Portland, IN
Amer. Legion, Indiana Post 227 **[4465]**, Dunkirk, IN
Amer. Legion, Indiana Post 228 **[4737]**, Francesville, IN
Amer. Legion, Indiana Post 231 **[4145]**, Aurora, IN
Amer. Legion, Indiana Post 239 **[5652]**, Lawrenceburg, IN
Amer. Legion, Indiana Post 245 **[4511]**, Elnora, IN
Amer. Legion, Indiana Post 249 **[5001]**, Indianapolis, IN
Amer. Legion, Indiana Post 250 **[5814]**, Mitchell, IN
Amer. Legion, Indiana Post 251 **[4294]**, Brookston, IN
Amer. Legion, Indiana Post 253 **[5999]**, North Webster, IN
Amer. Legion, Indiana Post 255 **[6146]**, Russellville, IN
Amer. Legion, Indiana Post 267 **[6016]**, Osgood, IN
Amer. Legion, Indiana Post 274 **[5707]**, Lynn, IN
Amer. Legion, Indiana Post 278 **[6067]**, Poseyville, IN
Amer. Legion, Indiana Post 279 **[4773]**, Gary, IN
Amer. Legion, Indiana Post 301 **[5590]**, Kouts, IN
Amer. Legion, Indiana Post 307 **[6429]**, Wakarusa, IN
Amer. Legion, Indiana Post 309 **[6212]**, South Bend, IN
Amer. Legion, Indiana Post 310 **[5557]**, Kirklin, IN
Amer. Legion, Indiana Post 315 **[6086]**, Richmond, IN
Amer. Legion, Indiana Post 317 **[4844]**, Greentown, IN
Amer. Legion, Indiana Post 328 **[6116]**, Riley, IN
Amer. Legion, Indiana Post 333 **[4862]**, Hagerstown, IN
Amer. Legion, Indiana Post 337 **[6288]**, Sunman, IN
Amer. Legion, Indiana Post 344 **[4133]**, Arcadia, IN
Amer. Legion, Indiana Post 365 **[5984]**, North Liberty, IN
Amer. Legion, Indiana Post 381 **[6137]**, Rome City, IN
Amer. Legion, Indiana Post 408 **[4348]**, Chesterfield, IN
Amer. Legion, Indiana Post 410 **[6521]**, Whitestown, IN
Amer. Legion, Indiana Post 419 **[6119]**, Roann, IN
Amer. Legion, Indiana Post 428 **[4870]**, Hammond, IN
Amer. Legion, Indiana Post 438 **[5002]**, Indianapolis, IN
Amer. Legion, Indiana Post 446 **[4440]**, Daleville, IN
Amer. Legion, Indiana Post 451 **[5783]**, Michigan City, IN
Amer. Legion, Indiana Post 495 **[5003]**, Indianapolis, IN
Amer. Legion, Indiana Post 498 **[4774]**, Gary, IN
Amer. Legion, Indiana Post 501 **[6507]**, West Terre Haute, IN
Amer. Legion, Indiana Post 507 **[6115]**, Ridgeville, IN
Amer. Legion, Indiana Post 508 **[4473]**, East Chicago, IN
Amer. Legion, Indiana Post 510 **[4599]**, Fishers, IN
Amer. Legion, Indiana Post 911 **[5004]**, Indianapolis, IN
Amer. Legion, Indianapolis Power Light Post 300 **[5005]**, Indianapolis, IN
Amer. Legion, Ingalls-Koeppen Post 102 **[19946]**, Walworth, WI
Amer. Legion, Inspiration Peak Post 527 **[10273]**, Alexandria, MN
Amer. Legion, Inver Grove Heights Post 424 **[11222]**, Inver Grove Heights, MN
Amer. Legion, Ira Owen Kreager Post 384 **[2049]**, Hoopeston, IL
Amer. Legion, Ironton Post 433 **[15508]**, Ironton, OH
Amer. Legion, Ironwood Post 5 **[8335]**, Ironwood, MI
Amer. Legion, Iroquois Post 503 **[2320]**, Loda, IL
Amer. Legion, Irvin Blix Post 16 **[10372]**, Bagley, MN
Amer. Legion, Irvin Lee Terrey Post 229 **[3868]**, Viola, IL
Amer. Legion, Irwin Knudson Post 459 **[2695]**, Newark, IL
Amer. Legion, Isaac Harrison Lyons Post 326 **[12783]**, Verndale, MN
Amer. Legion, Isaacson-Bjorge Post 31 **[11370]**, Mahnomen, MN
Amer. Legion, Ishpemingnegaunee Post 136 **[8344]**, Ishpeming, MI
Amer. Legion, Ithaca Post 334 **[8351]**, Ithaca, MI
Amer. Legion, Ivan Stringer Post 164 **[12712]**, Stewartville, MN
Amer. Legion, Ivan V. Sarff Post 70 **[12702]**, Staples, MN

Amer. Legion, Iwaszuk-Cetwinski Post 943 **[2469]**, Melrose Park, IL
Amer. Legion, J. Ivan Dappert Post 73 **[3754]**, Taylorville, IL
Amer. Legion, Jack Brinker Post 409 **[5674]**, Leo, IN
Amer. Legion, Jackson-Keen Post 496 **[2433]**, Mason City, IL
Amer. Legion, Jackson-Koster-Gray Post 300 **[8503]**, Lake City, MI
Amer. Legion, Jackson Liberty Post 130 **[11233]**, Jackson, MN
Amer. Legion, Jackson-O-Meara Post 90 **[11313]**, Lewiston, MN
Amer. Legion, Jackson Park Post 555 **[2794]**, Oak Lawn, IL
Amer. Legion, Jacobsen Memorial Post 487 **[12658]**, Shoreview, MN
Amer. Legion, James De Armond Golliday Post 6 **[5564]**, Kokomo, IN
Amer. Legion, James De Witt Post 38 **[7681]**, Fenton, MI
Amer. Legion, James Evans Post 341 **[4358]**, Cicero, IN
Amer. Legion, James Gastineau Post 479 **[5709]**, Lyons, IN
Amer. Legion, James Lowell Corey Post 68 **[4134]**, Argos, IN
Amer. Legion, James Reeder Post 770 **[101]**, Atwood, IL
Amer. Legion, Jamestown Post 395 **[5519]**, Jamestown, IN
Amer. Legion, Janesville Post 281 **[11235]**, Janesville, MN
Amer. Legion, Jansen-Richardson Post 488 **[7597]**, Ellsworth, MI
Amer. Legion, Jasonville Post 172 **[5521]**, Jasonville, IN
Amer. Legion, Jasper Post 20 **[2698]**, Newton, IL
Amer. Legion, Jastrzemski-Lelo Post 439 **[9598]**, Saginaw, MI
Amer. Legion, Jay H. Findley Memorial Post 1994 **[2161]**, Keyesport, IL
Amer. Legion, J.C. Trigg Memorial Post 328 **[14844]**, Dayton, OH
Amer. Legion, J.D. Smith Memorial Post 10 **[15092]**, Edgerton, OH
Amer. Legion, Jean Post 543 **[7091]**, Caseville, MI
Amer. Legion, Jeep Gabrys Post 388 **[7305]**, Detroit, MI
Amer. Legion, Jefferson-Horton Post 340 **[3268]**, Rockford, IL
Amer. Legion, Jefferson Post 9 **[5710]**, Madison, IN
Amer. Legion, Jefferson Post 141 **[2593]**, Mount Vernon, IL
Amer. Legion, Jefferson Post 201 **[17181]**, West Jefferson, OH
Amer. Legion, Jenkins Post 254 **[6127]**, Rockport, IN
Amer. Legion, Jenkins-Vaughan Post 97 **[13596]**, Cardington, OH
Amer. Legion, Jennings-Kraemer-Gruber Post 398 **[19459]**, Plain, WI
Amer. Legion, Jennings Post 276 **[10291]**, Amboy, MN
Amer. Legion, Jensen-Hansen Post 394 **[18431]**, Loretta, WI
Amer. Legion, Jerome Post 749 **[15527]**, Jeromesville, OH
Amer. Legion, Jerry Wickham Post 1148 **[2229]**, Leaf River, IL
Amer. Legion, Jesse Poole Post 297 **[11238]**, Johnson, MN
Amer. Legion, Jesse Rogers Post 483 **[6539]**, Windfall, IN
Amer. Legion, Jfb Post 610 **[12753]**, Tintah, MN
Amer. Legion, Jim Falls Post 276 **[18770]**, Manawa, WI
Amer. Legion, John B. Lotz Memorial Post 91 **[5864]**, Muncie, IN
Amer. Legion, John Bridges Post 15 **[10772]**, Detroit Lakes, MN
Amer. Legion, John Ericsson Post 1042 **[676]**, Chicago, IL
Amer. Legion, John Poor Post 717 **[1554]**, Edinburg, IL
Amer. Legion, John-Rheaume-Fred-Knauf Post 438 **[6830]**, Bark River, MI
Amer. Legion, John Vessey Post 44 **[11293]**, Lakeville, MN
Amer. Legion, Johnson Curd Post 256 **[6009]**, Oakland City, IN
Amer. Legion, Johnson Day Post 104 **[9852]**, Standish, MI
Amer. Legion, Johnson-Hallberg Post 407 **[19536]**, Prentice, WI
Amer. Legion, Johnson-Hershman Post 363 **[17831]**, Denmark, WI
Amer. Legion, Johnson-Kelly Post 483 **[10752]**, Dassel, MN
Amer. Legion, Johnson-Miner Post 618 **[17269]**, Williamsport, OH
Amer. Legion, Johnson-Nicoles-Kuhlman-Olson Post 53 **[17862]**, Eau Claire, WI
Amer. Legion, Johnson-Olson Post 494 **[10437]**, Big Falls, MN
Amer. Legion, Johnson Post 382 **[11133]**, Hawley, MN
Amer. Legion, Johnson-Roll-Dougherty Post 187 **[11051]**, Glenwood, MN
Amer. Legion, Johnson-Whistler Post 323 **[18174]**, Hammond, WI
Amer. Legion, Johnstown Post 254 **[15531]**, Johnstown, OH
Amer. Legion, Joliet Post 1284 **[2098]**, Joliet, IL
Amer. Legion, Jones-Mehltretter Post 405 **[17841]**, Dousman, WI
Amer. Legion, Jones-Modrow-Young Post 74 **[19347]**, Oconto, WI
Amer. Legion, Joseph A. Gates Post 78 **[11253]**, Kenyon, MN
Amer. Legion, Joseph Viken Post 229 **[12262]**, Sacred Heart, MN
Amer. Legion, Juneau Post 15 **[18280]**, Juneau, WI
Amer. Legion, Justice-Leibolt Post 377 **[13503]**, Camden, OH
Amer. Legion, J.W. Roth Post 294 **[11277]**, Lake Crystal, MN
Amer. Legion, Kalamazoo Post 134 **[8414]**, Kalamazoo, MI
Amer. Legion, Kalamazoo Post 332 **[9203]**, Niles, MI
Amer. Legion, Kalbes-Seewald Post 280 **[17777]**, Coleman, WI
Amer. Legion, Kampsville Post 1083 **[2126]**, Kampsville, IL
Amer. Legion, Kankakee Post 85 **[2128]**, Kankakee, IL
Amer. Legion, Kanthak-Matthies Post 441 **[10400]**, Bellingham, MN
Amer. Legion, Kapperman Post 44 **[5959]**, Newburgh, IN
Amer. Legion, Kasal Post 457 **[3459]**, Seneca, IL
Amer. Legion, Kasierski-Kozlowski Post 366 **[19542]**, Princeton, WI
Amer. Legion, Kasota Post 348 **[11242]**, Kasota, MN
Amer. Legion, Kaukauna Post 41 **[18285]**, Kaukauna, WI
Amer. Legion, Keeler-Adams Post 1168 **[1553]**, Edgewood, IL
Amer. Legion, Keith Brown Post 420 **[5819]**, Monroeville, IN
Amer. Legion, Kelley-Gardner-Katzman-Stoflet Post 45 **[17926]**, Elkhorn, WI
Amer. Legion, Kellogg Post 546 **[11249]**, Kellogg, MN
Amer. Legion, Kelly-Johnson Post 90 **[17541]**, Ashland, WI
Amer. Legion, Kelly-Ward-Varley-Memorial Post 732 **[17386]**, Youngstown, OH
Amer. Legion, Ken-Bur-Bel Post 41 **[16258]**, Norwalk, OH
Amer. Legion, Kendallville Post 86 **[5549]**, Kendallville, IN
Amer. Legion, Kenney-Hallsville Post 1133 **[2153]**, Kenney, IL
Amer. Legion, Kenosha-Paul-Herrick Post 21 **[18294]**, Kenosha, WI
Amer. Legion, Kent-Metzler Post 261 **[16275]**, Oak Hill, OH
Amer. Legion, Kent Voyls Post 322 **[4487]**, Elizabethtown, IN
Amer. Legion, Kenton Post 198 **[15552]**, Kenton, OH
Amer. Legion, Kerl-Endres-Brannan Post 245 **[17792]**, Cross Plains, WI
Amer. Legion, Kerlin Farina Post 16 **[17797]**, Cudahy, WI
Amer. Legion, Kerner-Slusser Post 63 **[16315]**, Ottawa, OH
Amer. Legion, Kerr-Mize Post 168 **[2944]**, Pana, IL
Amer. Legion, Kessinger Post 713 **[3494]**, Sorento, IL
Amer. Legion, Kettering Post 598 **[15557]**, Kettering, OH
Amer. Legion, Kettle River Post 360 **[11259]**, Kettle River, MN
Amer. Legion, Kewanee Post 31 **[2154]**, Kewanee, IL
Amer. Legion, Kewaunee Post 29 **[18318]**, Kewaunee, WI
Amer. Legion, Kiester Post 454 **[11260]**, Kiester, MN
Amer. Legion, Kingman Post 384 **[5555]**, Kingman, IN
Amer. Legion, Kingston Post 291 **[15568]**, Kingston, OH
Amer. Legion, Kinmundy Post 519 **[2164]**, Kinmundy, IL
Amer. Legion, Kinne-Engelhart Post 204 **[17932]**, Ellsworth, WI
Amer. Legion, Kirby-Watkins Post 198 **[3084]**, Petersburg, IL
Amer. Legion, Kishwaukee Post 192 **[2396]**, Marengo, IL
Amer. Legion, K.M.B.B. Post 400 **[2902]**, Ozark, IL
Amer. Legion, Kneil-Lawrentz Post 255 **[16840]**, Tallmadge, OH
Amer. Legion, Kniery-Knagg Post 436 **[2305]**, Litchfield, IL
Amer. Legion, Knightstown Post 152 **[5558]**, Knightstown, IN
Amer. Legion, Knox-Helms Post 554 **[9083]**, Morley, MI
Amer. Legion, Knudtson-Mattison Post 231 **[17636]**, Blair, WI
Amer. Legion, Koca Post 39 **[335]**, Braidwood, IL
Amer. Legion, Korppas-Johnson Post 531 **[19504]**, Port Wing, WI
Amer. Legion, Kosciuszko Post 712 **[677]**, Chicago, IL
Amer. Legion, Koselke Mayfield Post 403 **[6439]**, Wanatah, IN
Amer. Legion, Kraft-Ostrom-American-Legion Post 142 **[10630]**, Cannon Falls, MN
Amer. Legion, Kramer-Berg Post 507 **[12909]**, Willernie, MN
Amer. Legion, Krause-Kraft Post 106 **[19674]**, Seymour, WI
Amer. Legion, Krause-Simpson Post 300 **[18047]**, Gillett, WI
Amer. Legion, Kriesel-Jacobsen Post 560 **[12998]**, Zimmerman, MN
Amer. Legion, Kropp-Braund Post 242 **[18386]**, La Valle, WI
Amer. Legion, K.T. Crossen Post 21 **[13193]**, Athens, OH
Amer. Legion, Kupfahl-Meyer-Scheib Post 387 **[19487]**, Plymouth, WI
Amer. Legion, Kupsh-Brockmann Post 127 **[18204]**, Hilbert, WI
Amer. Legion, Kurdel-Cigoi Post 1110 **[678]**, Chicago, IL
Amer. Legion, Kurtz-Booker Post 217 **[5992]**, North Salem, IN
Amer. Legion, La Fayette Post 159 **[679]**, Chicago, IL
Amer. Legion, La Grange Post 215 **[5638]**, Lagrange, IN
Amer. Legion, La Harpe Post 301 **[2178]**, La Harpe, IL
Amer. Legion, La Moille Post 1043 **[2179]**, La Moille, IL
Amer. Legion, La Porte, County Post 130 **[5784]**, Michigan City, IN
Amer. Legion, Lac Qui Parle Post 158 **[11365]**, Madison, MN

Amer. Legion, Ladewig-Zinkgraf Post 243 **[19488]**, Plymouth, WI
Amer. Legion, Lafayette Post 11 **[5606]**, Lafayette, IN
Amer. Legion, Lafayette Post 27 **[15289]**, Gallipolis, OH
Amer. Legion, Lafayette Post 300 **[11268]**, Lafayette, MN
Amer. Legion, Lake Bluff Post 510 **[2187]**, Lake Bluff, IL
Amer. Legion, Lake County Post 1122 **[3920]**, Waukegan, IL
Amer. Legion, Lake in the Hills Post 1231 **[2206]**, Lake in the Hills, IL
Amer. Legion, Lake Post 737 **[15578]**, Lake Milton, OH
Amer. Legion, Lake Region Post 703 **[1718]**, Fox Lake, IL
Amer. Legion, Lake Villa Township Post 1219 **[2290]**, Lindenhurst, IL
Amer. Legion, Lake Village Post 375 **[5646]**, Lake Village, IN
Amer. Legion, Lake Zurich Post 964 **[2208]**, Lake Zurich, IL
Amer. Legion, Lakeshore Post 474 **[18940]**, Milwaukee, WI
Amer. Legion, Lakeview Post 342 **[10798]**, Duluth, MN
Amer. Legion, Lakeville Community Post 363 **[5648]**, Lakeville, IN
Amer. Legion, Lakewood Post 571 **[10799]**, Duluth, MN
Amer. Legion, Lambertville Post 191 **[9327]**, Ottawa Lake, MI
Amer. Legion, Lamond-Frank Post 478 **[9833]**, Southgate, MI
Amer. Legion, Landt-Thiel Post 470 **[19666]**, Saukville, WI
Amer. Legion, Landua-Jensen Post 147 **[18843]**, Medford, WI
Amer. Legion, Lange-Ostrander-Hurd Post 62 **[17782]**, Columbus, WI
Amer. Legion, Langemo Post 295 **[12872]**, West Concord, MN
Amer. Legion, Lansing Post 336 **[8536]**, Lansing, MI
Amer. Legion, Lapaz Post 385 **[5650]**, Lapaz, IN
Amer. Legion, Lapeer Post 16 **[8774]**, Lapeer, MI
Amer. Legion, Laroy Farst Post 245 **[16139]**, New Madison, OH
Amer. Legion, Larson-Torgerson Post 169 **[17471]**, Amery, WI
Amer. Legion, Larue Messenger Post 26 **[9204]**, Niles, MI
Amer. Legion, Lauridsen Post 408 **[583]**, Chebanse, IL
Amer. Legion, Lawrence Capehart Post 35 **[5538]**, Jeffersonville, IN
Amer. Legion, Lawrence Post 28 **[2223]**, Lawrenceville, IL
Amer. Legion, Lawrence Rayburn Post 116 **[1904]**, Greenview, IL
Amer. Legion, Lawrence Riddle Post 88 **[2440]**, Mattoon, IL
Amer. Legion, Lawson Babbitt Post 614 **[3361]**, Roseville, IL
Amer. Legion, Le Center Post 108 **[11305]**, Le Center, MN
Amer. Legion, Leach-Benson Post 220 **[13515]**, Canal Winchester, OH
Amer. Legion, Leach-Paulson Post 517 **[17840]**, Dorchester, WI
Amer. Legion, Leasure-Blackston Post 239 **[17341]**, Worthington, OH
Amer. Legion, Lee-Bishop Post 464 **[15480]**, Hudson, OH
Amer. Legion, Lee C. Prentice Post 36 **[10976]**, Fairmont, MN
Amer. Legion, Lee Goldsmith Post 201 **[11831]**, Mora, MN
Amer. Legion, Lee Iten Post 439 **[1984]**, Highland, IL
Amer. Legion, Lee Lowery Post 568 **[1808]**, Gibson City, IL
Amer. Legion, Lee Post 1253 **[2232]**, Lee, IL
Amer. Legion, Lee-Ranney Post 235 **[20152]**, Wheeler, WI
Amer. Legion, Leech Lake Post 2001 **[10431]**, Bena, MN
Amer. Legion, Leelanau County Post 199 **[7602]**, Empire, MI
Amer. Legion, Leesburg Post 568 **[15629]**, Leesburg, OH
Amer. Legion, Legion Villa Post 210 **[6844]**, Battle Creek, MI
Amer. Legion, Lehman-Clenndenning Post 274 **[19611]**, Rib Lake, WI
Amer. Legion, Lehman-Zimmerman Post 259 **[15220]**, Forest, OH
Amer. Legion, Leighton Evatt Post 365 **[1286]**, Collinsville, IL
Amer. Legion, Lekstrum-Burnett Post 107 **[9845]**, Sparta, MI
Amer. Legion, Leland Post 570 **[2233]**, Leland, IL
Amer. Legion, Lemont Post 243 **[2236]**, Lemont, IL
Amer. Legion, Lenz-Gazecki Post 152 **[18856]**, Menasha, WI
Amer. Legion, Leo Carey Post 56 **[10255]**, Albert Lea, MN
Amer. Legion, Leon Burson Post 395 **[3108]**, Plano, IL
Amer. Legion, Leon J. Wetzel Post 9 **[12944]**, Winona, MN
Amer. Legion, Leora Weare Post 173 **[6401]**, Versailles, IN
Amer. Legion, Leroy Tout Post 338 **[4463]**, Dublin, IN
Amer. Legion, Leslie-Reddick Post 721 **[2561]**, Morrisonville, IL
Amer. Legion, Lester Newton Hensley Post 55 **[5865]**, Muncie, IN
Amer. Legion, Lester Reynolds Post 523 **[355]**, Brookport, IL
Amer. Legion, Lester Tjernlund Post 451 **[12362]**, St. Paul, MN
Amer. Legion, Lewis Post 208 **[14784]**, Convoy, OH
Amer. Legion, Lewis-Whitaker Post 520 **[15378]**, Hamilton, OH
Amer. Legion, Lewiston Post 198 **[8804]**, Lewiston, MI
Amer. Legion, Lewisville Post 561 **[11315]**, Lewisville, MN
Amer. Legion, Lexington Post 352 **[5760]**, Memphis, IN
Amer. Legion, Liberty Post 46 **[13327]**, Bellevue, OH
Amer. Legion, Liberty Post 289 **[3716]**, Strasburg, IL
Amer. Legion, Libertyville Post 329 **[2256]**, Libertyville, IL
Amer. Legion, Limestone Post 979 **[167]**, Bartonville, IL
Amer. Legion, Lincoln Post 82 **[4631]**, Fort Wayne, IN
Amer. Legion, Lincoln Post 102 **[1369]**, De Land, IL
Amer. Legion, Lincoln Square Post 473 **[680]**, Chicago, IL
Amer. Legion, Lincolnwood Post 1226 **[2287]**, Lincolnwood, IL
Amer. Legion, Lind-Gordon-Berg Post 106 **[12057]**, Proctor, MN
Amer. Legion, Linden Post 119 **[8816]**, Linden, MI
Amer. Legion, Linden Post 493 **[18419]**, Linden, WI
Amer. Legion, Lindstrom Post 83 **[11316]**, Lindstrom, MN
Amer. Legion, Lino Lakes Post 566 **[11319]**, Lino Lakes, MN
Amer. Legion, Linwood Laughy Post 217 **[10385]**, Baudette, MN
Amer. Legion, Lionel Boudreau Post 322 **[10746]**, Currie, MN
Amer. Legion, Liscum Bros. Post 482 **[17556]**, Bagley, WI
Amer. Legion, Littlefork Post 490 **[11341]**, Littlefork, MN
Amer. Legion, Lloyd Fleischer Post 1150 **[1513]**, Downs, IL
Amer. Legion, Locklar-Smith Post 550 **[1740]**, Freeburg, IL
Amer. Legion, Lockman-Jensen Post 499 **[18059]**, Gordon, WI
Amer. Legion, Lodi Post 523 **[15685]**, Lodi, OH
Amer. Legion, Loftness-Bandow Post 226 **[11043]**, Gibbon, MN
Amer. Legion, Logan Post 263 **[2271]**, Lincoln, IL
Amer. Legion, Logan Square Post 405 **[681]**, Chicago, IL
Amer. Legion, Lombard Post 391 **[2324]**, Lombard, IL
Amer. Legion, London Mills Post 470 **[2342]**, London Mills, IL
Amer. Legion, Long Point Post 1217 **[2345]**, Long Point, IL
Amer. Legion, Longton Post 618 **[11498]**, Minneapolis, MN
Amer. Legion, Lonsdale Post 586 **[11348]**, Lonsdale, MN
Amer. Legion, Loogootee Post 120 **[5702]**, Loogootee, IN
Amer. Legion, Loomis-Martin Post 188 **[17852]**, East Troy, WI
Amer. Legion, Lorain Post 30 **[15699]**, Lorain, OH
Amer. Legion, Lorentz Post 11 **[11373]**, Mankato, MN
Amer. Legion, Lost Five Post 444 **[3178]**, Rankin, IL
Amer. Legion, Lostant Post 173 **[2346]**, Lostant, IL
Amer. Legion, Loud Merkel La Plante Post 274 **[9315]**, Oscoda, MI
Amer. Legion, Loudon Post 257 **[15713]**, Loudonville, OH
Amer. Legion, Louis Monroe Post 53 **[4512]**, Elwood, IN
Amer. Legion, Louis Teistler Post 47 **[7214]**, Comstock Park, MI
Amer. Legion, Louis Tveite Post 317 **[10962]**, Emmons, MN
Amer. Legion, Louisville Post 914 **[2347]**, Louisville, IL
Amer. Legion, Loveland Post 256 **[15721]**, Loveland, OH
Amer. Legion, Loveless-Eikens Post 191 **[10616]**, Caledonia, MN
Amer. Legion, Lowell Beaver Post 470 **[4600]**, Fishers, IN
Amer. Legion, Lowell Post 101 **[5704]**, Lowell, IN
Amer. Legion, Lowell Post 750 **[15732]**, Lowell, OH
Amer. Legion, Lowell Stender Post 601 **[11865]**, New Germany, MN
Amer. Legion, Lowellville Post 247 **[15733]**, Lowellville, OH
Amer. Legion, Lozar-Mrace-Loushin Post 248 **[10953]**, Ely, MN
Amer. Legion, Lucas Vaughn Post 219 **[16267]**, Nova, OH
Amer. Legion, Ludlow Post 518 **[2357]**, Ludlow, IL
Amer. Legion, Luitink-Weishan Post 495 **[18941]**, Milwaukee, WI
Amer. Legion, Lulich-Ogrizovich Post 1001 **[682]**, Chicago, IL
Amer. Legion, Lund-Brown Post 132 **[19736]**, Siren, WI
Amer. Legion, Lundberg-Lee Post 266 **[11122]**, Hartland, MN
Amer. Legion, Luther-Hamshire-Pearsall Post 279 **[18813]**, Marshall, WI
Amer. Legion, Lybarger-Grimm Post 441 **[16987]**, Tontogany, OH
Amer. Legion, Lyle Post 105 **[11357]**, Lyle, MN
Amer. Legion, Machickanee Post 523 **[17450]**, Abrams, WI
Amer. Legion, Mackinac Island Post 299 **[8885]**, Mackinac Island, MI
Amer. Legion, Mackinder-Glenn Post 510 **[9876]**, Stockbridge, MI
Amer. Legion, Madden-Nottingham Post 348 **[5006]**, Indianapolis, IN
Amer. Legion, Madelia Post 19 **[11363]**, Madelia, MN
Amer. Legion, Madison Lake Post 269 **[11369]**, Madison Lake, MN
Amer. Legion, Madison Memorial Post 105 **[15692]**, London, OH
Amer. Legion, Madsen-Empey Post 89 **[19197]**, Minocqua, WI
Amer. Legion, Magnus Grondahl Post 325 **[12706]**, Starbuck, MN

Amer. Legion, Mahomet Post 1015 **[2379]**, Mahomet, IL
Amer. Legion, Mahoning Valley Post 15 **[16449]**, Poland, OH
Amer. Legion, Maki-Pinola Post 535 **[10367]**, Babbitt, MN
Amer. Legion, Malconta Post 24 **[15932]**, McConnelsville, OH
Amer. Legion, Manhattan Post 935 **[2383]**, Manhattan, IL
Amer. Legion, Manistee Post 10 **[8911]**, Manistee, MI
Amer. Legion, Manistique Post 83 **[7222]**, Cooks, MI
Amer. Legion, Manteno Post 755 **[2390]**, Manteno, IL
Amer. Legion, Manthey-Asmus Post 433 **[11041]**, Gaylord, MN
Amer. Legion, Mantua Post 193 **[15798]**, Mantua, OH
Amer. Legion, Mapes-Cathelyn Post 309 **[54]**, Annawan, IL
Amer. Legion, Maple Heights Post 309 **[15802]**, Maple Heights, OH
Amer. Legion, Maple Lake Post 131 **[11414]**, Maple Lake, MN
Amer. Legion, Maple Park Post 312 **[2391]**, Maple Park, IL
Amer. Legion, Maquon Post 1099 **[2395]**, Maquon, IL
Amer. Legion, Marengo Memorial Post 710 **[15809]**, Marengo, OH
Amer. Legion, Marietta Post 64 **[15813]**, Marietta, OH
Amer. Legion, Marine Post 273 **[683]**, Chicago, IL
Amer. Legion, Marion G.I. Post 584 **[15835]**, Marion, OH
Amer. Legion, Marion Lee Miller Post 931 **[3782]**, Towanda, IL
Amer. Legion, Marion Oshel Post 364 **[456]**, Carrier Mills, IL
Amer. Legion, Marion Post 179 **[13361]**, Blanchester, OH
Amer. Legion, Mark Hamilton Post 232 **[11499]**, Minneapolis, MN
Amer. Legion, Markham Manor Post 828 **[2416]**, Markham, IL
Amer. Legion, Marne Post 13 **[3099]**, Plainfield, IL
Amer. Legion, Marne Post 376 **[8928]**, Marne, MI
Amer. Legion, Marrs-Meyer Post 991 **[4068]**, Worth, IL
Amer. Legion, Marseilles Post 235 **[2419]**, Marseilles, IL
Amer. Legion, Marshallville Post 718 **[15859]**, Marshallville, OH
Amer. Legion, Martell-Musiaw Post 325 **[18058]**, Goodman, WI
Amer. Legion, Martin-Jensen Post 308 **[11026]**, Franklin, MN
Amer. Legion, Martin Krueger Post 407 **[12969]**, Winsted, MN
Amer. Legion, Martinez-Garcia-Nerio-Reyes Post 500 **[9599]**, Saginaw, MI
Amer. Legion, Martinsville Post 230 **[5750]**, Martinsville, IN
Amer. Legion, Martinsville Post 515 **[2425]**, Martinsville, IL
Amer. Legion, Marvin Seemann Garfield Ridge Post 1112 **[684]**, Chicago, IL
Amer. Legion, Mary P. Klaser Memorial Post 727 **[17387]**, Youngstown, OH
Amer. Legion, Marysville Post 449 **[8973]**, Marysville, MI
Amer. Legion, Massillon Post 221 **[15880]**, Massillon, OH
Amer. Legion, Matt Urban Post 40 **[9058]**, Monroe, MI
Amer. Legion, Matthews-Carter Post 325 **[15756]**, Manchester, OH
Amer. Legion, Mattox-Henslin Post 378 **[17655]**, Brandon, WI
Amer. Legion, Maumee Post 320 **[15900]**, Maumee, OH
Amer. Legion, Maxson-Van-Eps Post 368 **[10370]**, Backus, MN
Amer. Legion, May Berry Post 469 **[4758]**, Frankton, IN
Amer. Legion, Mayfield Heights Post 163 **[13641]**, Chardon, OH
Amer. Legion, Maynard-Schulgen Post 216 **[18421]**, Lodi, WI
Amer. Legion, Maywood Post 126 **[4871]**, Hammond, IN
Amer. Legion, Maywood Post 133 **[2470]**, Melrose Park, IL
Amer. Legion, Mazeppa Post 588 **[11445]**, Mazeppa, MN
Amer. Legion, Mazon Post 352 **[2450]**, Mazon, IL
Amer. Legion, Mc-Cann-Frederick Post 414 **[15326]**, Glouster, OH
Amer. Legion, Mc-Cann-Richards Post 105 **[19734]**, Shullsburg, WI
Amer. Legion, Mc Clure Post 900 **[2451]**, Mc Clure, IL
Amer. Legion, Mc Connell Post 1225 **[2452]**, Mc Connell, IL
Amer. Legion, Mc Cormack Post 658 **[3951]**, West Salem, IL
Amer. Legion, Mc-Cormick-Rose Post 308 **[18030]**, Gays Mills, WI
Amer. Legion, Mc-Dermott-Steindorf Post 144 **[17458]**, Albany, WI
Amer. Legion, Mc-Donald-Osmer Post 451 **[7893]**, Grand Rapids, MI
Amer. Legion, Mc Donough County Post 6 **[2366]**, Macomb, IL
Amer. Legion, Mc-Gowan-Johnson Post 68 **[9345]**, Paw Paw, MI
Amer. Legion, Mc Henry Post 491 **[2455]**, McHenry, IL
Amer. Legion, Mc-Ilvaine-Kothe Post 153 **[5007]**, Indianapolis, IN
Amer. Legion, Mc Kinley Post 76 **[16624]**, Sebring, OH
Amer. Legion, Mc Kinlock Post 264 **[2193]**, Lake Forest, IL
Amer. Legion, Mc-Kinney-Hatlevig Post 35 **[17945]**, Evansville, WI
Amer. Legion, Mc-Lain-Chandler Post 153 **[1996]**, Hillsboro, IL
Amer. Legion, Mc-Lain-Glover Post 595 **[1639]**, Equality, IL
Amer. Legion, Mc Nabb Post 1242 **[2454]**, Mc Nabb, IL
Amer. Legion, Mc-Veigh-Dunn Post 60 **[11081]**, Grand Rapids, MN
Amer. Legion, Mc Whirter Post 488 **[14807]**, Crestline, OH
Amer. Legion, Mead-Rath-Gutke Post 339 **[17465]**, Almond, WI
Amer. Legion, Medora Post 399 **[2468]**, Medora, IL
Amer. Legion, Medora Post 453 **[5759]**, Medora, IN
Amer. Legion, Meighen-Thompson Post 161 **[11308]**, Le Roy, MN
Amer. Legion, Melcher-Matti Post 320 **[18228]**, Humbird, WI
Amer. Legion, Melrose Post 101 **[11450]**, Melrose, MN
Amer. Legion, Melvin Post 642 **[2473]**, Melvin, IL
Amer. Legion, Melvindale Post 472 **[8997]**, Melvindale, MI
Amer. Legion, Memorial Post 188 **[4920]**, Hillsboro, IN
Amer. Legion, Memorial Post 196 **[4190]**, Bloomfield, IN
Amer. Legion, Memorial Post 320 **[10195]**, Yale, MI
Amer. Legion, Memorial Post 614 **[15425]**, Hilliard, OH
Amer. Legion, Memorial-Square Post 61 **[17064]**, Vermilion, OH
Amer. Legion, Mendota Post 540 **[2475]**, Mendota, IL
Amer. Legion, Menominee Post 146 **[9001]**, Menominee, MI
Amer. Legion, Menominee Post 497 **[18315]**, Keshena, WI
Amer. Legion, Mentor Post 352 **[15962]**, Mentor, OH
Amer. Legion, Menzie-Reece Post 258 **[6040]**, Pierceton, IN
Amer. Legion, Mercier-Kero Post 371 **[18167]**, Gurney, WI
Amer. Legion, Meredith Low Post 134 **[6514]**, Westport, IN
Amer. Legion, Meredosia Post 516 **[2477]**, Meredosia, IL
Amer. Legion, Merle Guild Post 208 **[63]**, Arlington Heights, IL
Amer. Legion, Merrick Potter Post 566 **[8999]**, Memphis, MI
Amer. Legion, Merrillville Post 430 **[5764]**, Merrillville, IN
Amer. Legion, Merritt Lamb Post 9 **[9137]**, Muskegon, MI
Amer. Legion, Merritt Lamb Post 102 **[9523]**, Rockford, MI
Amer. Legion, Merritt Post 142 **[17144]**, Waverly, OH
Amer. Legion, Merton-Dale Post 80 **[12884]**, Wheaton, MN
Amer. Legion, Metz-Mosher Post 244 **[20145]**, Westfield, WI
Amer. Legion, Meuli-Kelean-Kramer-Dannenberg Post 77 **[17742]**, Chippewa Falls, WI
Amer. Legion, Mexican-American Post 505 **[7306]**, Detroit, MI
Amer. Legion, Meyer-Thompson Post 536 **[11857]**, Nassau, MN
Amer. Legion, Meyers-Youngell Post 211 **[17965]**, Florence, WI
Amer. Legion, Miami Valley Post 652 **[14976]**, De Graff, OH
Amer. Legion, Miamisburg Post 165 **[15983]**, Miamisburg, OH
Amer. Legion, Michael-Boock Post 6 **[12009]**, Pipestone, MN
Amer. Legion-Michigan Dept. **[8537]**, Lansing, MI
Amer. Legion, Michigan Post 1 **[10060]**, Warren, MI
Amer. Legion, Michigan Post 2 **[7894]**, Grand Rapids, MI
Amer. Legion, Michigan Post 3 **[9717]**, Sault Ste. Marie, MI
Amer. Legion, Michigan Post 4 **[9085]**, Mount Clemens, MI
Amer. Legion, Michigan Post 6 **[8191]**, Holland, MI
Amer. Legion, Michigan Post 7 **[7080]**, Caro, MI
Amer. Legion, Michigan Post 8 **[9428]**, Port Huron, MI
Amer. Legion, Michigan Post 14 **[9969]**, Troy, MI
Amer. Legion, Michigan Post 15 **[7578]**, Eaton Rapids, MI
Amer. Legion, Michigan Post 17 **[8330]**, Iron River, MI
Amer. Legion, Michigan Post 25 **[9571]**, Royal Oak, MI
Amer. Legion, Michigan Post 28 **[7852]**, Grand Haven, MI
Amer. Legion, Michigan Post 29 **[8357]**, Jackson, MI
Amer. Legion, Michigan Post 30 **[9742]**, Shelby, MI
Amer. Legion, Michigan Post 31 **[7137]**, Chelsea, MI
Amer. Legion, Michigan Post 32 **[8829]**, Livonia, MI
Amer. Legion, Michigan Post 33 **[10223]**, Zeeland, MI
Amer. Legion, Michigan Post 36 **[8415]**, Kalamazoo, MI
Amer. Legion, Michigan Post 44 **[8932]**, Marquette, MI
Amer. Legion, Michigan Post 45 **[8153]**, Hastings, MI
Amer. Legion, Michigan Post 49 **[9762]**, South Haven, MI
Amer. Legion, Michigan Post 53 **[8174]**, Hillsdale, MI
Amer. Legion, Michigan Post 54 **[6845]**, Battle Creek, MI
Amer. Legion, Michigan Post 55 **[6589]**, Albion, MI
Amer. Legion, Michigan Post 56 **[7307]**, Detroit, MI
Amer. Legion, Michigan Post 60 **[9059]**, Monroe, MI
Amer. Legion, Michigan Post 61 **[8790]**, Laurium, MI
Amer. Legion, Michigan Post 62 **[9668]**, St. Ignace, MI

Amer. Legion, Michigan Post 65 **[6641]**, Alpena, MI
Amer. Legion, Michigan Post 67 **[8811]**, Lincoln Park, MI
Amer. Legion, Michigan Post 72 **[7488]**, Dundee, MI
Amer. Legion, Michigan Post 76 **[8869]**, Ludington, MI
Amer. Legion, Michigan Post 77 **[7308]**, Detroit, MI
Amer. Legion, Michigan Post 78 **[9480]**, Reed City, MI
Amer. Legion, Michigan Post 79 **[8965]**, Marshall, MI
Amer. Legion, Michigan Post 86 **[7280]**, Dearborn Heights, MI
Amer. Legion, Michigan Post 87 **[7231]**, Crystal Falls, MI
Amer. Legion, Michigan Post 89 **[6603]**, Allegan, MI
Amer. Legion, Michigan Post 92 **[9534]**, Rockland, MI
Amer. Legion, Michigan Post 94 **[7042]**, Cadillac, MI
Amer. Legion, Michigan Post 95 **[7129]**, Cheboygan, MI
Amer. Legion, Michigan Post 97 **[6564]**, Adrian, MI
Amer. Legion, Michigan Post 98 **[6939]**, Big Rapids, MI
Amer. Legion, Michigan Post 101 **[8065]**, Greenville, MI
Amer. Legion, Michigan Post 114 **[8345]**, Ishpeming, MI
Amer. Legion, Michigan Post 121 **[9539]**, Rogers City, MI
Amer. Legion, Michigan Post 122 **[10181]**, Wolverine, MI
Amer. Legion, Michigan Post 126 **[7309]**, Detroit, MI
Amer. Legion, Michigan Post 127 **[7475]**, Dorr, MI
Amer. Legion, Michigan Post 128 **[7310]**, Detroit, MI
Amer. Legion, Michigan Post 129 **[9456]**, Portland, MI
Amer. Legion, Michigan Post 132 **[8170]**, Highland Park, MI
Amer. Legion, Michigan Post 133 **[6822]**, Baldwin, MI
Amer. Legion, Michigan Post 135 **[8306]**, Imlay City, MI
Amer. Legion, Michigan Post 142 **[7074]**, Capac, MI
Amer. Legion, Michigan Post 144 **[8524]**, Lanse, MI
Amer. Legion, Michigan Post 147 **[9220]**, Northville, MI
Amer. Legion, Michigan Post 149 **[8233]**, Holly, MI
Amer. Legion, Michigan Post 151 **[7711]**, Flint, MI
Amer. Legion, Michigan Post 153 **[9673]**, St. Johns, MI
Amer. Legion, Michigan Post 155 **[7025]**, Britton, MI
Amer. Legion, Michigan Post 167 **[7166]**, Clawson, MI
Amer. Legion, Michigan Post 169 **[9185]**, New Buffalo, MI
Amer. Legion, Michigan Post 175 **[9713]**, Saranac, MI
Amer. Legion, Michigan Post 178 **[8538]**, Lansing, MI
Amer. Legion, Michigan Post 179 **[7895]**, Grand Rapids, MI
Amer. Legion, Michigan Post 182 **[8286]**, Hubbardston, MI
Amer. Legion, Michigan Post 184 **[7311]**, Detroit, MI
Amer. Legion, Michigan Post 185 **[9138]**, Muskegon, MI
Amer. Legion, Michigan Post 186 **[8106]**, Hancock, MI
Amer. Legion, Michigan Post 187 **[9572]**, Royal Oak, MI
Amer. Legion, Michigan Post 192 **[9910]**, Temperance, MI
Amer. Legion, Michigan Post 193 **[8880]**, Luna Pier, MI
Amer. Legion, Michigan Post 194 **[9361]**, Petoskey, MI
Amer. Legion, Michigan Post 202 **[7312]**, Detroit, MI
Amer. Legion, Michigan Post 214 **[7313]**, Detroit, MI
Amer. Legion, Michigan Post 215 **[7777]**, Fowlerville, MI
Amer. Legion, Michigan Post 216 **[9049]**, Milford, MI
Amer. Legion, Michigan Post 217 **[9060]**, Monroe, MI
Amer. Legion, Michigan Post 218 **[7127]**, Chassell, MI
Amer. Legion, Michigan Post 221 **[7784]**, Frankfort, MI
Amer. Legion, Michigan Post 223 **[7219]**, Constantine, MI
Amer. Legion, Michigan Post 225 **[8539]**, Lansing, MI
Amer. Legion, Michigan Post 226 **[7113]**, Charlevoix, MI
Amer. Legion, Michigan Post 228 **[6995]**, Boyne City, MI
Amer. Legion, Michigan Post 232 **[7281]**, Dearborn Heights, MI
Amer. Legion, Michigan Post 235 **[7007]**, Brighton, MI
Amer. Legion, Michigan Post 236 **[7627]**, Evart, MI
Amer. Legion, Michigan Post 239 **[8821]**, Linwood, MI
Amer. Legion, Michigan Post 250 **[9385]**, Plainwell, MI
Amer. Legion, Michigan Post 252 **[8053]**, Grass Lake, MI
Amer. Legion, Michigan Post 253 **[9573]**, Royal Oak, MI
Amer. Legion, Michigan Post 260 **[8416]**, Kalamazoo, MI
Amer. Legion, Michigan Post 267 **[7235]**, Davison, MI
Amer. Legion, Michigan Post 279 **[8823]**, Litchfield, MI
Amer. Legion, Michigan Post 297 **[9471]**, Ravenna, MI
Amer. Legion, Michigan Post 298 **[6846]**, Battle Creek, MI
Amer. Legion, Michigan Post 301 **[9469]**, Rapid River, MI
Amer. Legion, Michigan Post 304 **[9775]**, South Range, MI
Amer. Legion, Michigan Post 306 **[7712]**, Flint, MI
Amer. Legion, Michigan Post 317 **[9304]**, Onaway, MI
Amer. Legion, Michigan Post 322 **[9698]**, Saline, MI
Amer. Legion, Michigan Post 326 **[9861]**, Sterling Heights, MI
Amer. Legion, Michigan Post 330 **[7692]**, Ferndale, MI
Amer. Legion, Michigan Post 343 **[9221]**, Northville, MI
Amer. Legion, Michigan Post 344 **[7807]**, Galien, MI
Amer. Legion, Michigan Post 348 **[9056]**, Mio, MI
Amer. Legion, Michigan Post 351 **[10033]**, Utica, MI
Amer. Legion, Michigan Post 367 **[9077]**, Montrose, MI
Amer. Legion, Michigan Post 369 **[9707]**, Sandusky, MI
Amer. Legion, Michigan Post 375 **[7314]**, Detroit, MI
Amer. Legion, Michigan Post 381 **[7229]**, Croton, MI
Amer. Legion, Michigan Post 382 **[9651]**, St. Clair, MI
Amer. Legion, Michigan Post 386 **[7574]**, Eastpointe, MI
Amer. Legion, Michigan Post 396 **[7809]**, Garden City, MI
Amer. Legion, Michigan Post 400 **[9491]**, Richville, MI
Amer. Legion, Michigan Post 410 **[6917]**, Benton Harbor, MI
Amer. Legion, Michigan Post 411 **[8165]**, Hesperia, MI
Amer. Legion, Michigan Post 412 **[6834]**, Bath, MI
Amer. Legion, Michigan Post 422 **[8097]**, Hale, MI
Amer. Legion, Michigan Post 426 **[9965]**, Trenton, MI
Amer. Legion, Michigan Post 430 **[7896]**, Grand Rapids, MI
Amer. Legion, Michigan Post 458 **[7815]**, Gaylord, MI
Amer. Legion, Michigan Post 480 **[8475]**, Kalkaska, MI
Amer. Legion, Michigan Post 483 **[7636]**, Farmington, MI
Amer. Legion, Michigan Post 491 **[8800]**, Leslie, MI
Amer. Legion, Michigan Post 514 **[8298]**, Ida, MI
Amer. Legion, Michigan Post 526 **[9132]**, Munith, MI
Amer. Legion, Michigan Post 537 **[7218]**, Conklin, MI
Amer. Legion, Michigan Post 555 **[7247]**, Dearborn, MI
Amer. Legion, Mickelsons-Martin Post 313 **[17630]**, Black Earth, WI
Amer. Legion, Middleton Post 275 **[18902]**, Middleton, WI
Amer. Legion, Middletown Post 218 **[16003]**, Middletown, OH
Amer. Legion, Middleville Post 140 **[9015]**, Middleville, MI
Amer. Legion, Mikado Post 254 **[9045]**, Mikado, MI
Amer. Legion, Mike and George Bustos Post 7 **[4944]**, Huntington, IN
Amer. Legion, Mike-Militello-Joseph Post 570 **[8079]**, Grosse Pointe, MI
Amer. Legion, Mil-Bow-Mar Post 280 **[15365]**, Greenwich, OH
Amer. Legion, Milan Post 359 **[11467]**, Milan, MN
Amer. Legion, Milan Post 569 **[2488]**, Milan, IL
Amer. Legion, Miles-Hagen Post 200 **[17631]**, Black River Falls, WI
Amer. Legion, Millard-Brown Post 156 **[5831]**, Montpelier, IN
Amer. Legion, Miller-Justman-Guelig Post 270 **[19888]**, Theresa, WI
Amer. Legion, Miller-Manning Post 418 **[1490]**, Dongola, IL
Amer. Legion, Miller-Stockum Post 485 **[14251]**, Cleves, OH
Amer. Legion, Millersport Post 637 **[16039]**, Millersport, OH
Amer. Legion, Millstadt Post 502 **[2496]**, Millstadt, IL
Amer. Legion, Milltown Post 332 **[5804]**, Milltown, IN
Amer. Legion, Millville Valley Post 579 **[11469]**, Millville, MN
Amer. Legion, Milton Olive Post 1932 **[685]**, Chicago, IL
Amer. Legion, Milton W. Mager Memorial Post 691 **[2486]**, Midlothian, IL
Amer. Legion, Milwaukee Fire Fighters Post 426 **[18942]**, Milwaukee, WI
Amer. Legion, Milwaukee Police Post 415 **[18943]**, Milwaukee, WI
Amer. Legion, Milwaukee Post 18 **[18944]**, Milwaukee, WI
Amer. Legion, Milwaukee Womens Post 448 **[18945]**, Milwaukee, WI
Amer. Legion, Minford Post 622 **[16047]**, Minford, OH
Amer. Legion, Mingo Junction Post 351 **[16048]**, Mingo Junction, OH
Amer. Legion, Minneapolis Fire and Police Post 396 **[11500]**, Minneapolis, MN
Amer. Legion, Minneapolis Post 1 **[11501]**, Minneapolis, MN
Amer. Legion, Minneapolis Post office Post 540 **[12107]**, Richfield, MN
Amer. Legion, Minneapolis-Richfield Post 435 **[12108]**, Richfield, MN
Amer. Legion, Minneota Post 199 **[11782]**, Minneota, MN
Amer. Legion of Minnesota **[12363]**, St. Paul, MN
Amer. Legion, Minnesota At Large Post 1982 **[12364]**, St. Paul, MN
Amer. Legion, Minnesota Post 7 **[12672]**, Sleepy Eye, MN

Amer. Legion, Minnesota Post 12 **[11345]**, Long Prairie, MN
Amer. Legion, Minnesota Post 13 **[11171]**, Hitterdal, MN
Amer. Legion, Minnesota Post 20 **[10732]**, Crookston, MN
Amer. Legion, Minnesota Post 21 **[11818]**, Moorhead, MN
Amer. Legion, Minnesota Post 23 **[11447]**, Mcgregor, MN
Amer. Legion, Minnesota Post 24 **[12208]**, Roseau, MN
Amer. Legion, Minnesota Post 25 **[12843]**, Warroad, MN
Amer. Legion, Minnesota Post 35 **[10290]**, Alvarado, MN
Amer. Legion, Minnesota Post 37 **[12612]**, St. Peter, MN
Amer. Legion, Minnesota Post 38 **[12093]**, Redwood Falls, MN
Amer. Legion, Minnesota Post 39 **[11909]**, North St. Paul, MN
Amer. Legion, Minnesota Post 41 **[11298]**, Lamberton, MN
Amer. Legion, Minnesota Post 43 **[10982]**, Faribault, MN
Amer. Legion, Minnesota Post 45 **[11876]**, New Prague, MN
Amer. Legion, Minnesota Post 46 **[11333]**, Little Falls, MN
Amer. Legion, Minnesota Post 47 **[11124]**, Hastings, MN
Amer. Legion, Minnesota Post 50 **[12810]**, Wabasha, MN
Amer. Legion, Minnesota Post 53 **[10526]**, Breckenridge, MN
Amer. Legion, Minnesota Post 54 **[12076]**, Red Wing, MN
Amer. Legion, Minnesota Post 55 **[11309]**, Le Sueur, MN
Amer. Legion, Minnesota Post 57 **[10649]**, Chaska, MN
Amer. Legion, Minnesota Post 59 **[11799]**, Montevideo, MN
Amer. Legion, Minnesota Post 69 **[11095]**, Granite Falls, MN
Amer. Legion, Minnesota Post 71 **[10800]**, Duluth, MN
Amer. Legion, Minnesota Post 74 **[11141]**, Henderson, MN
Amer. Legion, Minnesota Post 76 **[12271]**, St. Cloud, MN
Amer. Legion, Minnesota Post 77 **[11956]**, Owatonna, MN
Amer. Legion, Minnesota Post 79 **[11807]**, Montgomery, MN
Amer. Legion, Minnesota Post 93 **[12254]**, Rush City, MN
Amer. Legion, Minnesota Post 99 **[11502]**, Minneapolis, MN
Amer. Legion, Minnesota Post 102 **[10301]**, Anoka, MN
Amer. Legion, Minnesota Post 110 **[11273]**, Lake City, MN
Amer. Legion, Minnesota Post 111 **[11948]**, Osakis, MN
Amer. Legion, Minnesota Post 113 **[11431]**, Marshall, MN
Amer. Legion, Minnesota Post 119 **[10613]**, Byron, MN
Amer. Legion, Minnesota Post 121 **[12851]**, Watertown, MN
Amer. Legion, Minnesota Post 122 **[10763]**, Deer River, MN
Amer. Legion, Minnesota Post 135 **[11139]**, Hector, MN
Amer. Legion, Minnesota Post 136 **[11010]**, Flensburg, MN
Amer. Legion, Minnesota Post 137 **[12253]**, Royalton, MN
Amer. Legion, Minnesota Post 140 **[11079]**, Grand Meadow, MN
Amer. Legion, Minnesota Post 143 **[10567]**, Brownton, MN
Amer. Legion, Minnesota Post 144 **[10399]**, Belle Plaine, MN
Amer. Legion, Minnesota Post 147 **[10440]**, Big Lake, MN
Amer. Legion, Minnesota Post 149 **[11843]**, Morristown, MN
Amer. Legion, Minnesota Post 151 **[12624]**, Sandstone, MN
Amer. Legion, Minnesota Post 153 **[10377]**, Barnesville, MN
Amer. Legion, Minnesota Post 156 **[11429]**, Marietta, MN
Amer. Legion, Minnesota Post 167 **[12912]**, Willmar, MN
Amer. Legion, Minnesota Post 169 **[10502]**, Boyd, MN
Amer. Legion, Minnesota Post 175 **[12788]**, Villard, MN
Amer. Legion, Minnesota Post 181 **[11285]**, Lake Park, MN
Amer. Legion, Minnesota Post 184 **[12004]**, Pine Island, MN
Amer. Legion, Minnesota Post 189 **[10989]**, Farmington, MN
Amer. Legion, Minnesota Post 193 **[10395]**, Becker, MN
Amer. Legion, Minnesota Post 194 **[11232]**, Ivanhoe, MN
Amer. Legion, Minnesota Post 195 **[11142]**, Hendricks, MN
Amer. Legion, Minnesota Post 196 **[10951]**, Ellsworth, MN
Amer. Legion, Minnesota Post 214 **[11299]**, Lancaster, MN
Amer. Legion, Minnesota Post 227 **[10748]**, Danube, MN
Amer. Legion, Minnesota Post 234 **[11503]**, Minneapolis, MN
Amer. Legion, Minnesota Post 243 **[10343]**, Askov, MN
Amer. Legion, Minnesota Post 253 **[11350]**, Lowry, MN
Amer. Legion, Minnesota Post 255 **[10505]**, Brainerd, MN
Amer. Legion, Minnesota Post 256 **[10676]**, Clearbrook, MN
Amer. Legion, Minnesota Post 257 **[12695]**, Springfield, MN
Amer. Legion, Minnesota Post 261 **[11261]**, Kimball, MN
Amer. Legion, Minnesota Post 262 **[10687]**, Cloquet, MN
Amer. Legion, Minnesota Post 263 **[12814]**, Wabasso, MN
Amer. Legion, Minnesota Post 267 **[12834]**, Walnut Grove, MN
Amer. Legion, Minnesota Post 271 **[11982]**, Paynesville, MN
Amer. Legion, Minnesota Post 273 **[11038]**, Garvin, MN
Amer. Legion, Minnesota Post 274 **[11470]**, Milroy, MN
Amer. Legion, Minnesota Post 275 **[12646]**, Seaforth, MN
Amer. Legion, Minnesota Post 277 **[12628]**, Sartell, MN
Amer. Legion, Minnesota Post 280 **[10877]**, Eagle Bend, MN
Amer. Legion, Minnesota Post 282 **[12330]**, St. Louis Park, MN
Amer. Legion, Minnesota Post 283 **[10762]**, Deer Creek, MN
Amer. Legion, Minnesota Post 284 **[10637]**, Cass Lake, MN
Amer. Legion, Minnesota Post 285 **[11287]**, Lake Wilson, MN
Amer. Legion, Minnesota Post 287 **[11783]**, Minnesota Lake, MN
Amer. Legion, Minnesota Post 289 **[10383]**, Battle Lake, MN
Amer. Legion, Minnesota Post 290 **[10617]**, Cambridge, MN
Amer. Legion, Minnesota Post 291 **[11504]**, Minneapolis, MN
Amer. Legion, Minnesota Post 299 **[11360]**, Mabel, MN
Amer. Legion, Minnesota Post 306 **[12786]**, Vesta, MN
Amer. Legion, Minnesota Post 320 **[11179]**, Hopkins, MN
Amer. Legion, Minnesota Post 321 **[10934]**, Elbow Lake, MN
Amer. Legion, Minnesota Post 328 **[12324]**, St. Joseph, MN
Amer. Legion, Minnesota Post 331 **[11950]**, Oslo, MN
Amer. Legion, Minnesota Post 340 **[11164]**, Hill City, MN
Amer. Legion, Minnesota Post 347 **[11169]**, Hinckley, MN
Amer. Legion, Minnesota Post 356 **[12655]**, Sherburn, MN
Amer. Legion, Minnesota Post 363 **[10248]**, Akeley, MN
Amer. Legion, Minnesota Post 365 **[11116]**, Hanska, MN
Amer. Legion, Minnesota Post 366 **[10436]**, Bertha, MN
Amer. Legion, Minnesota Post 386 **[10862]**, Dundee, MN
Amer. Legion, Minnesota Post 391 **[12732]**, Storden, MN
Amer. Legion, Minnesota Post 392 **[12649]**, Shafer, MN
Amer. Legion, Minnesota Post 394 **[11113]**, Hamel, MN
Amer. Legion, Minnesota Post 402 **[11109]**, Halstad, MN
Amer. Legion, Minnesota Post 412 **[12778]**, Ulen, MN
Amer. Legion, Minnesota Post 437 **[11505]**, Minneapolis, MN
Amer. Legion, Minnesota Post 438 **[12008]**, Pinewood, MN
Amer. Legion, Minnesota Post 444 **[11463]**, Middle River, MN
Amer. Legion, Minnesota Post 458 **[10501]**, Boy River, MN
Amer. Legion, Minnesota Post 460 **[12259]**, Russell, MN
Amer. Legion, Minnesota Post 461 **[12252]**, Round Lake, MN
Amer. Legion, Minnesota Post 466 **[12733]**, Strandquist, MN
Amer. Legion, Minnesota Post 467 **[11352]**, Lucan, MN
Amer. Legion, Minnesota Post 468 **[11506]**, Minneapolis, MN
Amer. Legion, Minnesota Post 469 **[10581]**, Buffalo Lake, MN
Amer. Legion, Minnesota Post 478 **[11117]**, Hardwick, MN
Amer. Legion, Minnesota Post 484 **[12365]**, St. Paul, MN
Amer. Legion, Minnesota Post 486 **[10771]**, Delavan, MN
Amer. Legion, Minnesota Post 511 **[11507]**, Minneapolis, MN
Amer. Legion, Minnesota Post 514 **[11415]**, Maple Plain, MN
Amer. Legion, Minnesota Post 519 **[10679]**, Clements, MN
Amer. Legion, Minnesota Post 534 **[11176]**, Holland, MN
Amer. Legion, Minnesota Post 550 **[10459]**, Bloomington, MN
Amer. Legion, Minnesota Post 558 **[10801]**, Duluth, MN
Amer. Legion, Minnesota Post 563 **[10568]**, Bruno, MN
Amer. Legion, Minnesota Post 572 **[12366]**, St. Paul, MN
Amer. Legion, Minnesota Post 576 **[10365]**, Avoca, MN
Amer. Legion, Minnesota Post 582 **[12103]**, Revere, MN
Amer. Legion, Minnesota Post 587 **[12829]**, Waldorf, MN
Amer. Legion, Minnesota Post 597 **[12264]**, St. Bonifacius, MN
Amer. Legion, Minnesota Post 616 **[10292]**, Amboy, MN
Amer. Legion, Minnesota Post 622 **[12319]**, St. Francis, MN
Amer. Legion, Minnesota Post 626 **[10401]**, Beltrami, MN
Amer. Legion, Minnesota Post 627 **[11896]**, Nisswa, MN
Amer. Legion, Minnesota Post 628 **[12201]**, Rockford, MN

Amer. Legion, Minnesota Post 634 **[12367]**, St. Paul, MN
Amer. Legion, Minnesota Post 642 **[10500]**, Bowlus, MN
Amer. Legion, Minnesota Post 1700 **[10585]**, Burnsville, MN
Amer. Legion, Minnesota Post 4444 **[12368]**, St. Paul, MN
Amer. Legion, Minnesota Veterans Home Post 581 **[11508]**, Minneapolis, MN
Amer. Legion, Minnetonka Post 398 **[11847]**, Mound, MN
Amer. Legion, Minonk Post 142 **[2499]**, Minonk, IL
Amer. Legion, Minooka Post 1188 **[2500]**, Minooka, IL
Amer. Legion, Minster Post 387 **[16049]**, Minster, OH
Amer. Legion, Mishawaka Post 161 **[5806]**, Mishawaka, IN
Amer. Legion, Mississinewa Post 95 **[5545]**, Jonesboro, IN
Amer. Legion, Mittlestat-Smith Post 337 **[7702]**, Flat Rock, MI
Amer. Legion, Mixtacki-Johnson Post 337 **[19544]**, Pulaski, WI
Amer. Legion, Moe-Indihar Post 138 **[11045]**, Gilbert, MN
Amer. Legion, Moe-Miller Post 12 **[19760]**, Spooner, WI
Amer. Legion, Moen-Zimek Post 88 **[11098]**, Greenbush, MN
Amer. Legion, Moline **[2515]**, Moline, IL
Amer. Legion, Momence-Ganeer Post 40 **[2537]**, Momence, IL
Amer. Legion, Moncravie Post 425 **[1997]**, Hillsboro, IL
Amer. Legion, Mondt-Lampe Post 1239 **[136]**, Aviston, IL
Amer. Legion, Monnier-Duplain Post 548 **[15716]**, Louisville, OH
Amer. Legion, Monona Grove Post 429 **[19206]**, Monona, WI
Amer. Legion, Monroe Post 87 **[17305]**, Woodsfield, OH
Amer. Legion, Montgomery-Plant Post 10 **[20031]**, Wausau, WI
Amer. Legion, Monticello Post 260 **[11809]**, Monticello, MN
Amer. Legion, Montpelier Post 109 **[16059]**, Montpelier, OH
Amer. Legion, Moore-Irvin Post 359 **[6087]**, Richmond, IN
Amer. Legion, Moore-Long Post 64 **[18390]**, Ladysmith, WI
Amer. Legion, Mooresville Post 103 **[5834]**, Mooresville, IN
Amer. Legion, Morenci Post 368 **[9082]**, Morenci, MI
Amer. Legion, Morris-Baldridge Post 583 **[13646]**, Cherry Fork, OH
Amer. Legion, Morris Post 294 **[2551]**, Morris, IL
Amer. Legion, Morrison-Mead Post 181 **[8988]**, Mayville, MI
Amer. Legion, Morrison Post 328 **[2556]**, Morrison, IL
Amer. Legion, Morton Grove Post 134 **[2565]**, Morton Grove, IL
Amer. Legion, Morton-Guntley Post 349 **[8825]**, Little Lake, MI
Amer. Legion, Morton Post 318 **[2562]**, Morton, IL
Amer. Legion, Moser-Ortmann Post 130 **[19677]**, Sharon, WI
Amer. Legion, Moss-Walton Post 953 **[2074]**, Jacksonville, IL
Amer. Legion, Mt. Auburn Post 1057 **[318]**, Blue Mound, IL
Amer. Legion, Mt. Carroll Post 67 **[2576]**, Mount Carroll, IL
Amer. Legion, Mt. Greenwood Post 844 **[4069]**, Worth, IL
Amer. Legion, Mount Moriah Post 460 **[8540]**, Lansing, MI
Amer. Legion, Mount Morris Post 143 **[2578]**, Mount Morris, IL
Amer. Legion, Mount Prospect Post 525 **[2583]**, Mount Prospect, IL
Amer. Legion, Mt. Sterling Post 374 **[2591]**, Mount Sterling, IL
Amer. Legion, Mt. Sterling Post 417 **[16077]**, Mount Sterling, OH
Amer. Legion, Mt. Washington Post 484 **[13721]**, Cincinnati, OH
Amer. Legion, Mount-Wilson Post 473 **[6171]**, Scottsburg, IN
Amer. Legion, Mountain Lake Post 389 **[11854]**, Mountain Lake, MN
Amer. Legion, Moyer-Pooler Post 159 **[4899]**, Hartford City, IN
Amer. Legion, M.R.L. Post 772 **[3492]**, Somonauk, IL
Amer. Legion, Mulberry Grove Post 1180 **[2608]**, Mulberry Grove, IL
Amer. Legion, Mulford-Butler Post 511 **[15930]**, McComb, OH
Amer. Legion, Mullaney-Mc-Trusty Post 428 **[17470]**, Amberg, WI
Amer. Legion, Mumm-Welsh Post 352 **[17723]**, Cassville, WI
Amer. Legion, Mundelein Post 867 **[2610]**, Mundelein, IL
Amer. Legion, Murbach-Siefert Post 479 **[16816]**, Swanton, OH
Amer. Legion, Murphy-Johnson Post 94 **[12255]**, Rushford, MN
Amer. Legion, Murray Post 420 **[16095]**, Murray City, OH
Amer. Legion, Murrayville Post 311 **[2622]**, Murrayville, IL
Amer. Legion, Muskego Post 356 **[19259]**, Muskego, WI
Amer. Legion, Myrin-James Post 443 **[11229]**, Ironton, MN
Amer. Legion, Naperville Post 43 **[2625]**, Naperville, IL
Amer. Legion, Nappanee Post 154 **[5907]**, Nappanee, IN
Amer. Legion, Nassen-Detert Post 529 **[10640]**, Ceylon, MN
Amer. Legion, Natl. Defense Employees Post 792 **[16112]**, New Albany, OH
Amer. Legion, National-Guard-Iron-Fist Post 70 **[8121]**, Harper Woods, MI
Amer. Legion, Natl. Trail Post 756 **[15348]**, Gratiot, OH
Amer. Legion, Nauvoo Post 711 **[2671]**, Nauvoo, IL
Amer. Legion, Naval Post 372 **[2795]**, Oak Lawn, IL
Amer. Legion, Navy-Marine Post 276 **[14294]**, Columbus, OH
Amer. Legion, Neal Post 743 **[15569]**, Kingsville, OH
Amer. Legion, Neeley La Bar Post 158 **[7188]**, Clio, MI
Amer. Legion, Neer-Goudie-Teamsters Post 846 **[686]**, Chicago, IL
Amer. Legion, Neffs Post 77 **[16106]**, Neffs, OH
Amer. Legion, Nels Lee Post 165 **[10531]**, Bricelyn, MN
Amer. Legion, Nelsan-Horton Post 104 **[11325]**, Litchfield, MN
Amer. Legion, Nelson-Jackson Post 245 **[12754]**, Tower, MN
Amer. Legion, Nelson-Otteson Post 370 **[12972]**, Wolverton, MN
Amer. Legion, Neponset Post 875 **[2675]**, Neponset, IL
Amer. Legion, Nesseth-Lien Post 431 **[12762]**, Twin Valley, MN
Amer. Legion, Netzel-Zenz Post 413 **[17791]**, Crivitz, WI
Amer. Legion, Neuman-Mc-Gaver Post 466 **[17949]**, Fairchild, WI
Amer. Legion, Neuman-Wenzel Post 73 **[9879]**, Sturgis, MI
Amer. Legion, Neville-Dunn Post 489 **[18946]**, Milwaukee, WI
Amer. Legion, New Boston Post 48 **[2682]**, New Boston, IL
Amer. Legion, New Bremen Post 241 **[16116]**, New Bremen, OH
Amer. Legion, New Carlisle Post 286 **[15959]**, Medway, OH
Amer. Legion, New Carlisle Post 297 **[5930]**, New Carlisle, IN
Amer. Legion, New Directions Post 511 **[5008]**, Indianapolis, IN
Amer. Legion, New Harmony Post 370 **[5943]**, New Harmony, IN
Amer. Legion, New Haven Post 330 **[5945]**, New Haven, IN
Amer. Legion, New Haven Post 1141 **[2684]**, New Haven, IL
Amer. Legion, New Indianapolis Post 4 **[5009]**, Indianapolis, IN
Amer. Legion, New Lebanon Post 762 **[16130]**, New Lebanon, OH
Amer. Legion, New Matamoras Post 378 **[16140]**, New Matamoras, OH
Amer. Legion, New Palestine Post 182 **[5949]**, New Palestine, IN
Amer. Legion, Newburgh Heights Post 627 **[16189]**, Newburgh Heights, OH
Amer. Legion, Newbury Post 663 **[16190]**, Newbury, OH
Amer. Legion, Newton Post 236 **[16199]**, Newton Falls, OH
Amer. Legion, Newton Post 726 **[15072]**, East Fultonham, OH
Amer. Legion, Ney Community Post 680 **[16203]**, Ney, OH
Amer. Legion, Nicely-Brindle Post 201 **[4082]**, Advance, IN
Amer. Legion, Nichols-Goleman-Boggs Post 566 **[1903]**, Greenup, IL
Amer. Legion, Nicollet Post 510 **[11894]**, Nicollet, MN
Amer. Legion, Niles-Northtown Post 29 **[2566]**, Morton Grove, IL
Amer. Legion, Noah O'bannion Post 59 **[6118]**, Rising Sun, IN
Amer. Legion, Noble Post 252 **[13485]**, Caldwell, OH
Amer. Legion, Noel Robison Post 664 **[2057]**, Hurst, IL
Amer. Legion, Noetzelman-Boodry Post 377 **[19855]**, Summit Lake, WI
Amer. Legion, Nonesuch Post 462 **[10161]**, White Pine, MI
Amer. Legion, Norcross-Meyers Post 305 **[17242]**, Weston, OH
Amer. Legion, Nordonia Hills Post 801 **[15743]**, Macedonia, OH
Amer. Legion, Norman Schulte Post 549 **[10750]**, Darfur, MN
Amer. Legion, Norridge Post 1263 **[2739]**, Norridge, IL
Amer. Legion, Norris-Spencer Post 263 **[19313]**, New London, WI
Amer. Legion, North Baltimore Post 539 **[16210]**, North Baltimore, OH
Amer. Legion, North Boone Post 205 **[3124]**, Poplar Grove, IL
Amer. Legion, North Br. Post 85 **[11899]**, North Branch, MN
Amer. Legion, North Br. Post 457 **[9215]**, North Branch, MI
Amer. Legion, North Dearborn Post 452 **[6289]**, Sunman, IN
Amer. Legion, North Eastern Post 459 **[7897]**, Grand Rapids, MI
Amer. Legion, North End Post 474 **[12369]**, St. Paul, MN
Amer. Legion, North End Post 576 **[16881]**, Toledo, OH
Amer. Legion, North Loop Post 949 **[687]**, Chicago, IL
Amer. Legion, North Madison Memorial Post 601 **[15745]**, Madison, OH
Amer. Legion, North Mankato Post 518 **[11902]**, North Mankato, MN
Amer. Legion, North Park Post 401 **[10187]**, Wyoming, MI
Amer. Legion, North Ridgeville Post 802 **[15105]**, Elyria, OH
Amer. Legion, North Shore Post 21 **[688]**, Chicago, IL
Amer. Legion, North Shore Post 331 **[19730]**, Shorewood, WI
Amer. Legion, North Side Post 230 **[11509]**, Minneapolis, MN
Amer. Legion, Northcutt-Laaker Post 292 **[4460]**, Dillsboro, IN

Amer. Legion, Northeast Post 630 **[13722]**, Cincinnati, OH
Amer. Legion, Northfield Post 84 **[11911]**, Northfield, MN
Amer. Legion, Northridge Memorial Post 746 **[14845]**, Dayton, OH
Amer. Legion, Northwest Detroit Post 302 **[7315]**, Detroit, MI
Amer. Legion, Northwest Du Page Post 1084 **[3352]**, Roselle, IL
Amer. Legion, Northwest Post 443 **[14295]**, Columbus, OH
Amer. Legion, Northwest Post 497 **[5010]**, Indianapolis, IN
Amer. Legion, Norwalk Memorial Post 438 **[19326]**, Norwalk, WI
Amer. Legion, Norwood Post 740 **[689]**, Chicago, IL
Amer. Legion, Novi Post 19 **[9231]**, Novi, MI
Amer. Legion, Nuwarine Post 535 **[8977]**, Mason, MI
Amer. Legion, Nysewander-Bayliff Post 329 **[6042]**, Plainfield, IN
Amer. Legion, O.-Connor-Chiers Post 340 **[17623]**, Berlin, WI
Amer. Legion, O-Donnell-Eddy-Floss Post 714 **[690]**, Chicago, IL
Amer. Legion, O.-L.-Arnold-D.-K.-Slayton Post 100 **[19750]**, Sparta, WI
Amer. Legion, O Leara Quirk Post 90 **[4476]**, Eaton, IN
Amer. Legion, Oakley Traynor Post 64 **[7713]**, Flint, MI
Amer. Legion, Oblong Post 219 **[2841]**, Oblong, IL
Amer. Legion, O'Brien Post 326 **[16653]**, Shelby, OH
Amer. Legion, Odegaard-Quade Post 401 **[11237]**, Jeffers, MN
Amer. Legion, Odell Post 666 **[2843]**, Odell, IL
Amer. Legion, Odessa Post 520 **[11930]**, Odessa, MN
Amer. Legion, Odon Post 293 **[6010]**, Odon, IN
Amer. Legion, Oelschlaeger-Dallmann Post 434 **[19329]**, Oak Creek, WI
Amer. Legion, Ogden Post 998 **[2851]**, Ogden, IL
Amer. Legion, Ogemaw Post 103 **[10127]**, West Branch, MI
Amer. Legion, Ogilvie Post 640 **[11932]**, Ogilvie, MN
Amer. Legion, Ogmar Post 268 **[11251]**, Kensington, MN
Amer. Legion of Ohio **[14996]**, Delaware, OH
Amer. Legion, Ohio Post 3 **[15192]**, Findlay, OH
Amer. Legion, Ohio Post 9 **[16447]**, Pleasantville, OH
Amer. Legion, Ohio Post 14 **[13247]**, Bainbridge, OH
Amer. Legion, Ohio Post 16 **[15759]**, Mansfield, OH
Amer. Legion, Ohio Post 18 **[16882]**, Toledo, OH
Amer. Legion, Ohio Post 20 **[13414]**, Bremen, OH
Amer. Legion, Ohio Post 22 **[15803]**, Maple Heights, OH
Amer. Legion, Ohio Post 23 **[16466]**, Portsmouth, OH
Amer. Legion, Ohio Post 25 **[17126]**, Washington Court House, OH
Amer. Legion, Ohio Post 31 **[15083]**, East Palestine, OH
Amer. Legion, Ohio Post 36 **[13405]**, Bradner, OH
Amer. Legion, Ohio Post 37 **[13723]**, Cincinnati, OH
Amer. Legion, Ohio Post 43 **[16996]**, Troy, OH
Amer. Legion, Ohio Post 56 **[16584]**, Salem, OH
Amer. Legion, Ohio Post 57 **[13122]**, Amanda, OH
Amer. Legion, Ohio Post 58 **[16687]**, Somerset, OH
Amer. Legion, Ohio Post 65 **[14793]**, Coshocton, OH
Amer. Legion, Ohio Post 71 **[16554]**, Roseville, OH
Amer. Legion, Ohio Post 72 **[13724]**, Cincinnati, OH
Amer. Legion, Ohio Post 78 **[15688]**, Logan, OH
Amer. Legion, Ohio Post 80 **[14806]**, Covington, OH
Amer. Legion, Ohio Post 81 **[15511]**, Jackson, OH
Amer. Legion, Ohio Post 85 **[16167]**, Newark, OH
Amer. Legion, Ohio Post 88 **[13159]**, Ashland, OH
Amer. Legion, Ohio Post 91 **[13343]**, Berea, OH
Amer. Legion, Ohio Post 92 **[17044]**, Utica, OH
Amer. Legion, Ohio Post 94 **[13306]**, Bedford Heights, OH
Amer. Legion, Ohio Post 96 **[15645]**, Lima, OH
Amer. Legion, Ohio Post 99 **[16883]**, Toledo, OH
Amer. Legion, Ohio Post 102 **[16278]**, Oberlin, OH
Amer. Legion, Ohio Post 103 **[13176]**, Ashtabula, OH
Amer. Legion, Ohio Post 106 **[16204]**, Niles, OH
Amer. Legion, Ohio Post 107 **[15571]**, Kirkersville, OH
Amer. Legion, Ohio Post 112 **[15746]**, Madison, OH
Amer. Legion, Ohio Post 113 **[16457]**, Port Clinton, OH
Amer. Legion, Ohio Post 114 **[16269]**, Oak Harbor, OH
Amer. Legion, Ohio Post 115 **[14997]**, Delaware, OH
Amer. Legion, Ohio Post 117 **[14982]**, Defiance, OH
Amer. Legion, Ohio Post 122 **[14255]**, Clyde, OH
Amer. Legion, Ohio Post 123 **[16265]**, Norwood, OH
Amer. Legion, Ohio Post 126 **[13657]**, Chillicothe, OH
Amer. Legion, Ohio Post 129 **[15442]**, Hillsboro, OH
Amer. Legion, Ohio Post 131 **[15630]**, Leetonia, OH
Amer. Legion, Ohio Post 132 **[16884]**, Toledo, OH
Amer. Legion, Ohio Post 135 **[16885]**, Toledo, OH
Amer. Legion, Ohio Post 136 **[16078]**, Mount Vernon, OH
Amer. Legion, Ohio Post 143 **[15187]**, Fayette, OH
Amer. Legion, Ohio Post 147 **[13149]**, Apple Creek, OH
Amer. Legion, Ohio Post 148 **[16583]**, St. Paris, OH
Amer. Legion, Ohio Post 149 **[15236]**, Franklin, OH
Amer. Legion, Ohio Post 155 **[15523]**, Jamestown, OH
Amer. Legion, Ohio Post 157 **[14296]**, Columbus, OH
Amer. Legion, Ohio Post 173 **[13319]**, Bellefontaine, OH
Amer. Legion, Ohio Post 175 **[16774]**, Stow, OH
Amer. Legion, Ohio Post 178 **[17047]**, Van Wert, OH
Amer. Legion, Ohio Post 180 **[15312]**, Georgetown, OH
Amer. Legion, Ohio Post 182 **[14297]**, Columbus, OH
Amer. Legion, Ohio Post 186 **[15617]**, Lebanon, OH
Amer. Legion, Ohio Post 188 **[16132]**, New Lexington, OH
Amer. Legion, Ohio Post 191 **[16702]**, Spencerville, OH
Amer. Legion, Ohio Post 194 **[15871]**, Mason, OH
Amer. Legion, Ohio Post 199 **[15406]**, Harrison, OH
Amer. Legion, Ohio Post 204 **[13543]**, Canton, OH
Amer. Legion, Ohio Post 207 **[17285]**, Willshire, OH
Amer. Legion, Ohio Post 212 **[16353]**, Parma, OH
Amer. Legion, Ohio Post 223 **[15417]**, Hicksville, OH
Amer. Legion, Ohio Post 224 **[15189]**, Felicity, OH
Amer. Legion, Ohio Post 226 **[13142]**, Andover, OH
Amer. Legion, Ohio Post 229 **[16107]**, Nelsonville, OH
Amer. Legion, Ohio Post 232 **[15337]**, Grand Rapids, OH
Amer. Legion, Ohio Post 234 **[13444]**, Brunswick, OH
Amer. Legion, Ohio Post 237 **[13265]**, Batavia, OH
Amer. Legion, Ohio Post 238 **[15937]**, Mechanicsburg, OH
Amer. Legion, Ohio Post 244 **[15084]**, East Sparta, OH
Amer. Legion, Ohio Post 246 **[15069]**, Duncan Falls, OH
Amer. Legion, Ohio Post 258 **[16233]**, North Lewisburg, OH
Amer. Legion, Ohio Post 262 **[15403]**, Hamler, OH
Amer. Legion, Ohio Post 266 **[13316]**, Belle Center, OH
Amer. Legion, Ohio Post 272 **[13034]**, Akron, OH
Amer. Legion, Ohio Post 274 **[16759]**, Steubenville, OH
Amer. Legion, Ohio Post 275 **[15676]**, Lisbon, OH
Amer. Legion, Ohio Post 278 **[17096]**, Warren, OH
Amer. Legion, Ohio Post 281 **[14818]**, Cuyahoga Falls, OH
Amer. Legion, Ohio Post 282 **[16307]**, Orrville, OH
Amer. Legion, Ohio Post 284 **[13453]**, Bryan, OH
Amer. Legion, Ohio Post 287 **[15632]**, Leipsic, OH
Amer. Legion, Ohio Post 290 **[14259]**, Columbiana, OH
Amer. Legion, Ohio Post 295 **[15351]**, Green Springs, OH
Amer. Legion, Ohio Post 297 **[16389]**, Payne, OH
Amer. Legion, Ohio Post 300 **[16097]**, Napoleon, OH
Amer. Legion, Ohio Post 303 **[15925]**, McArthur, OH
Amer. Legion, Ohio Post 322 **[17163]**, West Alexandria, OH
Amer. Legion, Ohio Post 334 **[16886]**, Toledo, OH
Amer. Legion, Ohio Post 337 **[16492]**, Quaker City, OH
Amer. Legion, Ohio Post 338 **[13406]**, Bradner, OH
Amer. Legion, Ohio Post 342 **[16849]**, Thornville, OH
Amer. Legion, Ohio Post 346 **[16293]**, Ohio City, OH
Amer. Legion, Ohio Post 354 **[16160]**, New Riegel, OH
Amer. Legion, Ohio Post 357 **[16044]**, Minerva, OH
Amer. Legion, Ohio Post 360 **[16143]**, New Paris, OH
Amer. Legion, Ohio Post 368 **[16484]**, Prospect, OH
Amer. Legion, Ohio Post 374 **[15076]**, East Liverpool, OH
Amer. Legion, Ohio Post 376 **[15534]**, Junction City, OH
Amer. Legion, Ohio Post 381 **[15489]**, Huntsville, OH
Amer. Legion, Ohio Post 389 **[13356]**, Beverly, OH
Amer. Legion, Ohio Post 399 **[15038]**, Dresden, OH
Amer. Legion, Ohio Post 405 **[16161]**, New Washington, OH
Amer. Legion, Ohio Post 406 **[13353]**, Bethel, OH
Amer. Legion, Ohio Post 423 **[16536]**, Rittman, OH
Amer. Legion, Ohio Post 431 **[16195]**, Newcomerstown, OH
Amer. Legion, Ohio Post 436 **[15354]**, Greentown, OH
Amer. Legion, Ohio Post 440 **[13544]**, Canton, OH
Amer. Legion, Ohio Post 442 **[16595]**, Salineville, OH
Amer. Legion, Ohio Post 450 **[16023]**, Milford, OH
Amer. Legion, Ohio Post 454 **[16531]**, Ridgeville Corners, OH
Amer. Legion, Ohio Post 457 **[16810]**, Sunbury, OH
Amer. Legion, Ohio Post 462 **[16110]**, Nevada, OH
Amer. Legion, Ohio Post 465 **[14298]**, Columbus, OH
Amer. Legion, Ohio Post 468 **[16824]**, Sylvania, OH
Amer. Legion, Ohio Post 471 **[16467]**, Portsmouth, OH
Amer. Legion, Ohio Post 473 **[14787]**, Copley, OH

Amer. Legion, Ohio Post 476 **[17262]**, Wilkesville, OH
Amer. Legion, Ohio Post 483 **[15235]**, Frankfort, OH
Amer. Legion, Ohio Post 486 **[14299]**, Columbus, OH
Amer. Legion, Ohio Post 491 **[15018]**, Dennison, OH
Amer. Legion, Ohio Post 492 **[15639]**, Liberty Center, OH
Amer. Legion, Ohio Post 499 **[17190]**, West Salem, OH
Amer. Legion, Ohio Post 500 **[15242]**, Fredericktown, OH
Amer. Legion, Ohio Post 504 **[17388]**, Youngstown, OH
Amer. Legion, Ohio Post 506 **[15570]**, Kinsman, OH
Amer. Legion, Ohio Post 508 **[16541]**, Rockford, OH
Amer. Legion, Ohio Post 517 **[17366]**, Xenia, OH
Amer. Legion, Ohio Post 518 **[13175]**, Ashley, OH
Amer. Legion, Ohio Post 525 **[13012]**, Adena, OH
Amer. Legion, Ohio Post 535 **[13334]**, Bellville, OH
Amer. Legion, Ohio Post 537 **[16301]**, Oregon, OH
Amer. Legion, Ohio Post 540 **[17097]**, Warren, OH
Amer. Legion, Ohio Post 544 **[13607]**, Cedarville, OH
Amer. Legion, Ohio Post 550 **[16159]**, New Richmond, OH
Amer. Legion, Ohio Post 551 **[15462]**, Holmesville, OH
Amer. Legion, Ohio Post 555 **[15805]**, Marblehead, OH
Amer. Legion, Ohio Post 564 **[17098]**, Warren, OH
Amer. Legion, Ohio Post 569 **[15804]**, Maple Heights, OH
Amer. Legion, Ohio Post 571 **[15811]**, Maria Stein, OH
Amer. Legion, Ohio Post 572 **[16354]**, Parma, OH
Amer. Legion, Ohio Post 574 **[13338]**, Beloit, OH
Amer. Legion, Ohio Post 581 **[13378]**, Bowerston, OH
Amer. Legion, Ohio Post 586 **[16868]**, Tipp City, OH
Amer. Legion, Ohio Post 609 **[15572]**, Kirtland, OH
Amer. Legion, Ohio Post 619 **[14846]**, Dayton, OH
Amer. Legion, Ohio Post 631 **[13725]**, Cincinnati, OH
Amer. Legion, Ohio Post 633 **[17194]**, West Union, OH
Amer. Legion, Ohio Post 650 **[17086]**, Walhonding, OH
Amer. Legion, Ohio Post 656 **[16279]**, Oberlin, OH
Amer. Legion, Ohio Post 660 **[16657]**, Sherrodsville, OH
Amer. Legion, Ohio Post 667 **[15070]**, East Canton, OH
Amer. Legion, Ohio Post 670 **[13726]**, Cincinnati, OH
Amer. Legion, Ohio Post 676 **[15760]**, Mansfield, OH
Amer. Legion, Ohio Post 679 **[13248]**, Baltic, OH
Amer. Legion, Ohio Post 681 **[15379]**, Hamilton, OH
Amer. Legion, Ohio Post 694 **[16092]**, Mowrystown, OH
Amer. Legion, Ohio Post 708 **[15461]**, Hollansburg, OH
Amer. Legion, Ohio Post 733 **[13355]**, Bettsville, OH
Amer. Legion, Ohio Post 735 **[16425]**, Piney Fork, OH
Amer. Legion, Ohio Post 755 **[16622]**, Sardinia, OH
Amer. Legion, Ohio Post 757 **[13658]**, Chillicothe, OH
Amer. Legion, Ohio Post 758 **[15277]**, Galion, OH
Amer. Legion, Ohio Post 770 **[14300]**, Columbus, OH
Amer. Legion, Ohio Post 773 **[13125]**, Amelia, OH
Amer. Legion, Ohio Post 776 **[14847]**, Dayton, OH
Amer. Legion, Ohio Post 777 **[15036]**, Doylestown, OH
Amer. Legion, Ohio Post 786 **[16887]**, Toledo, OH
Amer. Legion, Ohio Post 787 **[16716]**, Springfield, OH
Amer. Legion, Ohio Post 790 **[16647]**, Sharonville, OH
Amer. Legion, Ohio Post 791 **[13111]**, Alliance, OH
Amer. Legion, Ohio Valley Post 760 **[15405]**, Hannibal, OH
Amer. Legion, Oien-Horgen Post 198 **[10503]**, Boyd, MN
Amer. Legion, Olaf Locken Post 315 **[11271]**, Lake Bronson, MN
Amer. Legion, Old Town Chicago Post 184 **[691]**, Chicago, IL
Amer. Legion, Oldsmobile Post 237 **[7504]**, East Lansing, MI
Amer. Legion, Oles-Reader-Bosshart Post 115 **[12760]**, Truman, MN
Amer. Legion, Olson-Bute-Malone Post 737 **[2147]**, Kempton, IL
Amer. Legion, Olson-Graminske Post 426 **[12870]**, Wendell, MN
Amer. Legion, Olson-Grinde Post 348 **[17808]**, De Forest, WI
Amer. Legion, Olson-Stitzel Post 219 **[11471]**, Miltona, MN
Amer. Legion, Onarga Post 551 **[2863]**, Onarga, IL
Amer. Legion, Oney-Johnston-Edward-Blessman Post 38 **[17483]**, Appleton, WI
Amer. Legion, Ontonagon Post 288 **[9308]**, Ontonagon, MI
Amer. Legion, Oola Khan Post 372 **[13727]**, Cincinnati, OH
Amer. Legion, Ophiem Post 1077 **[2359]**, Lynn Center, IL
Amer. Legion, Oregon Post 97 **[2866]**, Oregon, IL
Amer. Legion, Orion Post 255 **[2872]**, Orion, IL
Amer. Legion, Orland Memorial Post 111 **[2877]**, Orland Park, IL
Amer. Legion, Orland Post 423 **[6012]**, Orland, IN
Amer. Legion, Orr Post 480 **[11942]**, Orr, MN
Amer. Legion, Orville Bidwell Post 138 **[6369]**, Upland, IN
Amer. Legion, Orville Easterday Post 189 **[6432]**, Walkerton, IN
Amer. Legion, Orwell Memorial Post 719 **[16313]**, Orwell, OH
Amer. Legion, Osborn Post 108 **[6150]**, St. Bernice, IN
Amer. Legion, Oscar Iverson Post 133 **[11236]**, Jasper, MN
Amer. Legion, Oscar Jacobson Post 417 **[12881]**, West Union, MN
Amer. Legion, Oscar Lee Post 177 **[10755]**, Dawson, MN
Amer. Legion, Oscar-Lee-Thomas-Moran Post 674 **[3179]**, Ransom, IL
Amer. Legion, Oscar Wellnitz Post 344 **[11844]**, Morton, MN
Amer. Legion, Osceola Post 308 **[6015]**, Osceola, IN
Amer. Legion, Osgood Post 588 **[16314]**, Osgood, OH
Amer. Legion, Oswego Post 675 **[2888]**, Oswego, IL
Amer. Legion, Othmar Braun Post 612 **[11451]**, Melrose, MN
Amer. Legion, Otis Sampson Post 59 **[19828]**, Stoughton, WI
Amer. Legion, Otis Stone Post 354 **[4523]**, Evansville, IN
Amer. Legion, Otsego Post 84 **[9324]**, Otsego, MI
Amer. Legion, Ottawa Post 33 **[2895]**, Ottawa, IL
Amer. Legion, Otto Hendrickson Post 212 **[11976]**, Park Rapids, MN
Amer. Legion, Otto Knutson Post 427 **[11892]**, Newfolden, MN
Amer. Legion, Otto T. Lund Post 52 **[10455]**, Blooming Prairie, MN
Amer. Legion, Ours For Victory Post 971 **[1980]**, Hickory Hills, IL
Amer. Legion, Owen Barrett Post 110 **[9096]**, Mount Pleasant, MI
Amer. Legion, Owen Dunn Post 5 **[5845]**, Mount Vernon, IN
Amer. Legion, Owensville Post 51 **[6018]**, Owensville, IN
Amer. Legion, Oxford Post 1197 **[29]**, Alpha, IL
Amer. Legion, Palash-Platt Post 543 **[19478]**, Plover, WI
Amer. Legion, Palatine Post 690 **[2904]**, Palatine, IL
Amer. Legion, Palmer Post 65 **[2701]**, Niles, IL
Amer. Legion, Palmer-Ritchie-Thomas Post 153 **[19457]**, Pittsville, WI
Amer. Legion, Palmer-Roberts Post 214 **[17271]**, Willoughby, OH
Amer. Legion, Palmyra Post 1034 **[2933]**, Palmyra, IL
Amer. Legion, Palos Memorial Post 1993 **[2943]**, Palos Park, IL
Amer. Legion, Pandora Post 616 **[16349]**, Pandora, OH
Amer. Legion, Paradise Valley Post 436 **[8494]**, Kingsley, MI
Amer. Legion, Park Etter Post 452 **[16051]**, Mogadore, OH
Amer. Legion, Park Forest Post 1198 **[1249]**, Chicago Heights, IL
Amer. Legion, Parker-Jose-Stockwell Post 66 **[17549]**, Athelstane, WI
Amer. Legion, Parma Heights Post 703 **[16355]**, Parma, OH
Amer. Legion, Partridge Post 578 **[365]**, Bunker Hill, IL
Amer. Legion, Paschall Post 164 **[15366]**, Grove City, OH
Amer. Legion, Passage-Gayde Post 391 **[9391]**, Plymouth, MI
Amer. Legion, Pat Petrone Post 885 **[246]**, Bloomingdale, IL
Amer. Legion, Patriotism Post 470 **[14257]**, Coldwater, OH
Amer. Legion, Patterson-Dawson Post 57 **[9332]**, Owosso, MI
Amer. Legion, Patton-Chastain Post 195 **[4312]**, Campbellsburg, IN
Amer. Legion, Paul Blagen Post 400 **[10635]**, Canton, MN
Amer. Legion, Paul F. Dille Post 364 **[10753]**, Dassel, MN
Amer. Legion, Paul Leon Wolek Memorial Post 454 **[4922]**, Hobart, IN
Amer. Legion, Paul Revere Post 623 **[692]**, Chicago, IL
Amer. Legion, Paul Robert Strange Post 502 **[6377]**, Valparaiso, IN
Amer. Legion, Paul Sodder Post 213 **[15636]**, Lewisburg, OH
Amer. Legion, Paul Stout Post 127 **[2617]**, Murphysboro, IL
Amer. Legion, Pawnee Post 586 **[2970]**, Pawnee, IL
Amer. Legion, P.E. Post 650 **[12623]**, Sanborn, MN
Amer. Legion, Pearce-Kerns Post 120 **[17036]**, Urbana, OH
Amer. Legion, Pearl City Post 1014 **[2979]**, Pearl City, IL
Amer. Legion, Peck Post 489 **[9349]**, Peck, MI
Amer. Legion, Pedersen Maunula Post 379 **[11829]**, Moose Lake, MN
Amer. Legion, Pederson-Tripp Post 357 **[10341]**, Ashby, MN
Amer. Legion, Pekin Post 203 **[6021]**, Pekin, IN
Amer. Legion, Pendleton Post 117 **[6023]**, Pendleton, IN
Amer. Legion, Penfield-Gifford-Memorial Post 1153 **[2997]**, Penfield, IL
Amer. Legion, Pennville Post 482 **[6028]**, Pennville, IN
Amer. Legion, Pentwater Post 327 **[9350]**, Pentwater, MI
Amer. Legion, Peoples Gas Post 336 **[693]**, Chicago, IL
Amer. Legion, Peoria Post 2 **[3002]**, Peoria, IL
Amer. Legion, Peoria Post 1151 **[3003]**, Peoria, IL
Amer. Legion, Peotone Post 392 **[3071]**, Peotone, IL

Amer. Legion, Percy Post 1145 **[3073]**, Percy, IL
Amer. Legion, Perkins Post 540 **[9353]**, Perkins, MI
Amer. Legion, Perrottet-Nickerson Post 76 **[3979]**, Wheaton, IL
Amer. Legion, Perry County Post 213 **[6295]**, Tell City, IN
Amer. Legion, Perry Memorial Post 697 **[16399]**, Perry, OH
Amer. Legion, Perry Post 1040 **[3074]**, Perry, IL
Amer. Legion, Perrysburg Post 28 **[16401]**, Perrysburg, OH
Amer. Legion, Peru Post 375 **[3075]**, Peru, IL
Amer. Legion, Pesotum Post 580 **[3083]**, Pesotum, IL
Amer. Legion, Peter-Gedda-Francis-Cychosz Post 27 **[6937]**, Bessemer, MI
Amer. Legion, Peter Leuze Post 420 **[12068]**, Raymond, MN
Amer. Legion, Peter Umathum Post 412 **[4053]**, Woodstock, IL
Amer. Legion, Peters Post 643 **[89]**, Ashkum, IL
Amer. Legion, Peterson-Lofquist-Bronczyk Post 160 **[10444]**, Biwabik, MN
Amer. Legion, Peterson and Waller Post 312 **[12699]**, Stacy, MN
Amer. Legion, Peterson-Westerberg Post 415 **[10380]**, Barnum, MN
Amer. Legion, Pettisville Post 445 **[16416]**, Pettisville, OH
Amer. Legion, Pewaukee Post 71 **[19434]**, Pewaukee, WI
Amer. Legion, Phaneuf-Vanasse Post 111 **[19745]**, Somerset, WI
Amer. Legion, Philip Whiteside Post 1961 **[2871]**, Orient, IL
Amer. Legion, Philippine-American-Veterans Post 1995 **[694]**, Chicago, IL
Amer. Legion, Phillippi-Clement Post 101 **[15575]**, La Rue, OH
Amer. Legion, Phillips-Elliott-Hodges Post 22 **[9600]**, Saginaw, MI
Amer. Legion, Phillips-Grigsby Post 149 **[6465]**, West Baden Springs, IN
Amer. Legion, Philo Post 1171 **[3087]**, Philo, IL
Amer. Legion, Phoenix Post 309 **[7284]**, Decatur, MI
Amer. Legion, Phoenix Post 1254 **[1953]**, Harvey, IL
Amer. Legion, Pickford Post 323 **[9375]**, Pickford, MI
Amer. Legion, Pieper-Hull-Sparks Post 176 **[7170]**, Clinton, MI
Amer. Legion, Pieper-Marsh Post 194 **[17712]**, Cameron, WI
Amer. Legion, Pierce-Davis Post 731 **[3841]**, Utica, IL
Amer. Legion, Pillager Post 100 **[11999]**, Pillager, MN
Amer. Legion, Pilsen Post 825 **[695]**, Chicago, IL
Amer. Legion, Pinckney Memorial Post 419 **[9380]**, Pinckney, MI
Amer. Legion, Pine Tree Post 448 **[11453]**, Menahga, MN
Amer. Legion, Pioneer Post 340 **[6310]**, Terre Haute, IN
Amer. Legion, Pitterle-Beaudoin Post 189 **[19965]**, Watertown, WI
Amer. Legion, Pittsboro Post 426 **[6041]**, Pittsboro, IN
Amer. Legion, Pittsfield Post 152 **[3093]**, Pittsfield, IL
Amer. Legion, Plain City Post 248 **[16442]**, Plain City, OH
Amer. Legion, Plato Post 641 **[12016]**, Plato, MN
Amer. Legion, Pleasant Hill Post 1048 **[3112]**, Pleasant Hill, IL
Amer. Legion, Pleasant Plains Post 599 **[3113]**, Pleasant Plains, IL
Amer. Legion, Pletcher-Chutich-Skrbich Post 575 **[11069]**, Goodland, MN
Amer. Legion, Plummer Post 623 **[12017]**, Plummer, MN
Amer. Legion, Plymouth Post 912 **[3114]**, Plymouth, IL
Amer. Legion, Pocahontas Memorial Post 1104 **[3115]**, Pocahontas, IL
Amer. Legion, Poelker Post 321 **[2677]**, New Baden, IL
Amer. Legion, Point Place Post 110 **[16888]**, Toledo, OH
Amer. Legion, Police Post 56 **[5011]**, Indianapolis, IN
Amer. Legion, Polomis-Tahlier Post 150 **[20061]**, Wausaukee, WI
Amer. Legion, Pope County Post 719 **[1877]**, Golconda, IL
Amer. Legion, Popek-Kostecky Post 163 **[12936]**, Willow River, MN
Amer. Legion, Poppe-Smuk-Appelget Post 327 **[11426]**, Marble, MN
Amer. Legion, Port City Post 260 **[6055]**, Portage, IN
Amer. Legion, Portage Memorial Post 725 **[16464]**, Portage, OH
Amer. Legion, Portage Park Post 183 **[696]**, Chicago, IL
Amer. Legion, Portage Post 207 **[9444]**, Portage, MI
Amer. Legion, Portage Post 496 **[15537]**, Kent, OH
Amer. Legion, Porter Bell Post 715 **[2685]**, New Holland, IL
Amer. Legion, Porter Post 457 **[12042]**, Porter, MN
Amer. Legion, Porter-Snyder Post 605 **[17085]**, Waldo, OH
Amer. Legion, Posen Post 990 **[3127]**, Posen, IL
Amer. Legion Post 66 **[4853]**, Griffith, IN
Amer. Legion Post 80 **[6524]**, Whiting, IN
Amer. Legion Post 232 **[4872]**, Hammond, IN
Amer. Legion, Post 545 Altoona **[17468]**, Altoona, WI
Amer. Legion, Post 556 Sanford White Eagle **[17570]**, Baraboo, WI
Amer. Legion, Poths-Lavelle Post 453 **[49]**, Amboy, IL
Amer. Legion, Potz Heartland Post 500 **[10741]**, Crosslake, MN
Amer. Legion, Prairie Creek Post 404 **[6311]**, Terre Haute, IN
Amer. Legion, Prairie Du Pont Post 485 **[1523]**, Dupo, IL
Amer. Legion, Prairie Post 150 **[2972]**, Paxton, IL
Amer. Legion, Prairie Post 1998 **[10328]**, Appleton, MN
Amer. Legion, Pratt-Volden-Mickelson Post 239 **[12791]**, Virginia, MN
Amer. Legion, Prell Bland Post 271 **[4156]**, Batesville, IN
Amer. Legion, Prescott-Bayens Post 83 **[19689]**, Sheboygan, WI
Amer. Legion, Press-Lloyd Post 247 **[10659]**, Chisholm, MN
Amer. Legion, Priddy-Walters Post 665 **[17186]**, West Manchester, OH
Amer. Legion, Princeton Post 25 **[6068]**, Princeton, IN
Amer. Legion, Princeton Post 125 **[3133]**, Princeton, IL
Amer. Legion, Princeville Post 248 **[3138]**, Princeville, IL
Amer. Legion, Prior Lake Post 447 **[12048]**, Prior Lake, MN
Amer. Legion, Private Ralph Kline Post 262 **[18435]**, Luxemburg, WI
Amer. Legion, Prophetstown Post 522 **[3140]**, Prophetstown, IL
Amer. Legion, Prosser-Curtis-Kubley Post 247 **[18057]**, Glidden, WI
Amer. Legion, Prudent Van Risseghem Post 395 **[11939]**, Onamia, MN
Amer. Legion, Przybylski Post 642 **[16889]**, Toledo, OH
Amer. Legion, Public Safety Post 449 **[11417]**, Maplewood, MN
Amer. Legion, Pulaski County Post 71 **[6531]**, Winamac, IN
Amer. Legion, Pulaski Post 357 **[6213]**, South Bend, IN
Amer. Legion, Putnam County Seat Post 1044 **[1966]**, Hennepin, IL
Amer. Legion, Putoff-Lautenschlager Post 141 **[4759]**, Freedom, IN
Amer. Legion, Quayle-Shuster-Truman-Muhich Post 241 **[10347]**, Aurora, MN
Amer. Legion, Quigle-Palin Post 394 **[6399]**, Veedersburg, IN
Amer. Legion, Quincy Post 37 **[3146]**, Quincy, IL
Amer. Legion, Racine Post 602 **[16493]**, Racine, OH
Amer. Legion, Railroad Post 416 **[12370]**, St. Paul, MN
Amer. Legion, Railroad Retirement Bd. Post 856 **[697]**, Chicago, IL
Amer. Legion, Rainbow Post 263 **[4334]**, Cayuga, IN
Amer. Legion, Ralph Gracie Post 14 **[10403]**, Bemidji, MN
Amer. Legion, Ralph Rumbaugh Post 51 **[7034]**, Buchanan, MI
Amer. Legion, Ralph Test Post 269 **[6283]**, Spiceland, IN
Amer. Legion, Randall Couchman Post 204 **[9912]**, Three Oaks, MI
Amer. Legion, Randolph Post 39 **[6535]**, Winchester, IN
Amer. Legion, Randolph Post 707 **[15129]**, Englewood, OH
Amer. Legion, Randolph-West-Kelly Post 367 **[18919]**, Milton, WI
Amer. Legion, Ranten-Sundflot Post 288 **[10563]**, Brooten, MN
Amer. Legion, Rantoul Post 287 **[3180]**, Rantoul, IL
Amer. Legion, Ravenna Post 331 **[16496]**, Ravenna, OH
Amer. Legion, Ray Keenan Post 207 **[10680]**, Cleveland, MN
Amer. Legion, Ray Kirkpatrick Post 463 **[11312]**, Lester Prairie, MN
Amer. Legion, Ray-S.-Neilson-John-H.-Winter Post 362 **[18292]**, Kennan, WI
Amer. Legion, Raymond Rankins Post 308 **[8541]**, Lansing, MI
Amer. Legion, Raymond Todd Post 323 **[6462]**, Waveland, IN
Amer. Legion, Read-Osborne Post 531 **[7225]**, Copemish, MI
Amer. Legion, Rebec-Hosler-Sweet Post 227 **[7495]**, East Jordan, MI
Amer. Legion, Red Arrow 32nd Div. Post 361 **[8093]**, Grosse Pointe Woods, MI
Amer. Legion, Red Cloud Post 250 **[17453]**, Adams, WI
Amer. Legion, Red Greissel Post 335 **[4346]**, Charlestown, IN
Amer. Legion, Redford-Township-Tansey-Weil Post 271 **[7810]**, Garden City, MI
Amer. Legion, Reese Post 139 **[9485]**, Reese, MI
Amer. Legion, Reeseville Post 190 **[19594]**, Reeseville, WI
Amer. Legion, Reginald Fisher Post 1 **[4410]**, Connersville, IN
Amer. Legion, Rehfeldt-Meyer Post 474 **[2435]**, Matteson, IL
Amer. Legion, Reinhardt-Windl Post 164 **[18270]**, Jefferson, WI
Amer. Legion, Reino Post 21 **[8331]**, Iron River, MI
Amer. Legion, Renault Post 1215 **[3187]**, Renault, IL
Amer. Legion, Reveille Post 184 **[5967]**, Newport, IN
Amer. Legion, Rexford Ballard Post 224 **[4464]**, Dugger, IN
Amer. Legion, Reynoldsburg Post 798 **[16512]**, Reynoldsburg, OH
Amer. Legion, Rheault-Cavis-Moilanen Post 291 **[8287]**, Hubbell, MI
Amer. Legion, Rhen Hilkert Post 21 **[6515]**, Westville, IN
Amer. Legion, Rice-Lemmerhart-Smith Post 327 **[18440]**, Lyons, WI
Amer. Legion, Rich Prairie Post 341 **[11997]**, Pierz, MN
Amer. Legion, Richard Dingle Post 98 **[12611]**, St. Paul Park, MN
Amer. Legion, Richard Hoffman Post 484 **[5802]**, Millersburg, IN
Amer. Legion, Richland Post 30 **[2858]**, Olney, IL

Amer. Legion, Richmond Heights Post 775 **[15963]**, Mentor, OH
Amer. Legion, Richmond Post 292 **[12115]**, Richmond, MN
Amer. Legion, Rickerd-Danielson Post 227 **[19770]**, Spring Valley, WI
Amer. Legion, Riders Memorial Post 17 **[4873]**, Hammond, IN
Amer. Legion, Ridgway Post 596 **[3195]**, Ridgway, IL
Amer. Legion, River Grove Post 335 **[3206]**, River Grove, IL
Amer. Legion, River Park Post 303 **[6214]**, South Bend, IN
Amer. Legion, Riverside Post 488 **[2325]**, Lombard, IL
Amer. Legion, Road of Remembrance Post 472 **[17389]**, Youngstown, OH
Amer. Legion, Roanoke Post 463 **[3216]**, Roanoke, IL
Amer. Legion, Robert Ihlang Post 537 **[11871]**, New London, MN
Amer. Legion, Robert Meachen Post 325 **[6972]**, Blissfield, MI
Amer. Legion, Robert Patterson Post 3 **[11239]**, Jordan, MN
Amer. Legion, Robert Turner Post 427 **[5957]**, New Ross, IN
Amer. Legion, Robert Woodburn Post 1037 **[2584]**, Mount Prospect, IL
Amer. Legion, Roberts-Mc-Millen Post 332 **[15929]**, McClure, OH
Amer. Legion, Robinson-Gibbs Post 265 **[17137]**, Wauseon, OH
Amer. Legion, Robinson and Starks Post 1972 **[1374]**, Decatur, IL
Amer. Legion, Rochelle Post 403 **[3222]**, Rochelle, IL
Amer. Legion, Rochester Post 446 **[12124]**, Rochester, MN
Amer. Legion, Rock Falls Post 902 **[3233]**, Rock Falls, IL
Amer. Legion, Rock Island Post 200 **[3240]**, Rock Island, IL
Amer. Legion, Rock Post 559 **[9521]**, Rock, MI
Amer. Legion, Rockwood Post 441 **[9535]**, Rockwood, MI
Amer. Legion, Rocky River Post 451 **[16543]**, Rocky River, OH
Amer. Legion, Roderick Prato Post 131 **[9130]**, Munising, MI
Amer. Legion, Roger B. Chaffee Post 154 **[10188]**, Wyoming, MI
Amer. Legion, Roger-Oestrich-Hancock-Coloma Post 343 **[18175]**, Hancock, WI
Amer. Legion, Rogers Park Post 108 **[698]**, Chicago, IL
Amer. Legion, Rolling Meadows Post 1251 **[3337]**, Rolling Meadows, IL
Amer. Legion, Rome Post 1 **[699]**, Chicago, IL
Amer. Legion, Romeo Post 109 **[10034]**, Utica, MI
Amer. Legion, Romsos-Malia Post 492 **[11025]**, Fountain, MN
Amer. Legion, Romulus Meehan Post 426 **[2180]**, La Salle, IL
Amer. Legion, Roodhouse Post 373 **[3349]**, Roodhouse, IL
Amer. Legion, Roose-Vanker Post 286 **[9862]**, Sterling Heights, MI
Amer. Legion, Roosevelt-Aurora Post 84 **[108]**, Aurora, IL
Amer. Legion, Roscommon Post 96 **[9553]**, Roscommon, MI
Amer. Legion, Rose City Post 324 **[8358]**, Jackson, MI
Amer. Legion, Rose-Harms Post 355 **[18061]**, Grafton, WI
Amer. Legion, Rosedale Park Post 390 **[9475]**, Redford, MI
Amer. Legion, Roseland Post 49 **[3762]**, Thornton, IL
Amer. Legion, Roselawn Post 238 **[6139]**, Roselawn, IN
Amer. Legion, Rosemount Post 65 **[12213]**, Rosemount, MN
Amer. Legion, Rosetown Memorial Post 542 **[12219]**, Roseville, MN
Amer. Legion, Ross County Post 62 **[13659]**, Chillicothe, OH
Amer. Legion, Rossford Post 533 **[16556]**, Rossford, OH
Amer. Legion, Rothie Post 330 **[11136]**, Hayfield, MN
Amer. Legion, Round Lake Post 1170 **[3366]**, Round Lake Park, IL
Amer. Legion, Roy Canavan Post 213 **[10048]**, Vicksburg, MI
Amer. Legion, Roy-Hamm-Robert-Burke Post 101 **[2546]**, Monticello, IL
Amer. Legion, Roy Ireland Post 317 **[2842]**, Oconee, IL
Amer. Legion, Roy Miller Post 644 **[1692]**, Fairview, IL
Amer. Legion, Roy P. Benavidez Memorial Post 226 **[700]**, Chicago, IL
Amer. Legion, Roy Vanderpool Post 81 **[3465]**, Shelbyville, IL
Amer. Legion, Royal Post 996 **[3367]**, Royal, IL
Amer. Legion, Rudolph Priebe Post 172 **[11952]**, Osseo, MN
Amer. Legion, Ruel Neal Post 79 **[2228]**, Le Roy, IL
Amer. Legion, Ruf-Marcham Post 404 **[440]**, Carlyle, IL
Amer. Legion, Runnestrand-Pederson Post 354 **[17943]**, Ettrick, WI
Amer. Legion, Russell Johnson Post 72 **[10329]**, Appleton, MN
Amer. Legion, Russell Square Post 1006 **[2215]**, Lansing, IL
Amer. Legion, Russell-Toycen Post 131 **[17778]**, Colfax, WI
Amer. Legion, Russell Weaver Post 166 **[5725]**, Marion, IN
Amer. Legion, Russell-Zenor Post 260 **[3778]**, Tonica, IL
Amer. Legion, Rutland Memorial Post 1121 **[3374]**, Rutland, IL
Amer. Legion, Rutledge-Boviall Post 95 **[17826]**, Delavan, WI
Amer. Legion, Rylander-Milroy Post 727 **[2864]**, Oneida, IL
Amer. Legion, Sahara Grotto Post 264 **[5012]**, Indianapolis, IN
Amer. Legion, Sailor Springs Post 230 **[3375]**, Sailor Springs, IL
Amer. Legion, St. Anne Post 842 **[3376]**, St. Anne, IL
Amer. Legion, St. Anthony Post 493 **[6149]**, St. Anthony, IN
Amer. Legion, St. Augusta Post 621 **[12272]**, St. Cloud, MN
Amer. Legion, St. Charles Post 342 **[3378]**, St. Charles, IL
Amer. Legion, St. Charles Post 468 **[9649]**, St. Charles, MI
Amer. Legion, St. Clair Post 215 **[15087]**, Eaton, OH
Amer. Legion, St. Clairsville Post 159 **[16569]**, St. Clairsville, OH
Amer. Legion, St. Francisville Post 947 **[3397]**, St. Francisville, IL
Amer. Legion, St. Helen Post 416 **[9667]**, St. Helen, MI
Amer. Legion, St. Henry Post 648 **[16575]**, St. Henry, OH
Amer. Legion, St. James Post 33 **[12322]**, St. James, MN
Amer. Legion, St. Joseph Post 163 **[9756]**, Sodus, MI
Amer. Legion, St. Joseph Post 464 **[4297]**, Brookville, IN
Amer. Legion, St. Joseph Post 634 **[3400]**, St. Joseph, IL
Amer. Legion, St. Josephs Park Post 1080 **[2099]**, Joliet, IL
Amer. Legion, St. Leo Post 524 **[12328]**, St. Leo, MN
Amer. Legion, St. Marys Post 323 **[16577]**, St. Marys, OH
Amer. Legion, St. Meinrad Post 366 **[6154]**, St. Meinrad, IN
Amer. Legion, St. Michael Post 567 **[12340]**, St. Michael, MN
Amer. Legion, St. Mihiel Post 86 **[16988]**, Toronto, OH
Amer. Legion, St. Mihiel Post 585 **[3463]**, Shawneetown, IL
Amer. Legion, St. Paul Memorial Post 533 **[12371]**, St. Paul, MN
Amer. Legion, St. Paul Post 8 **[12372]**, St. Paul, MN
Amer. Legion, St. Stephen Post 221 **[12325]**, St. Joseph, MN
Amer. Legion, Sainte Marie Post 932 **[3404]**, Ste. Marie, IL
Amer. Legion, Sam Mason Post 690 **[14301]**, Columbus, OH
Amer. Legion, Samstad-Jensen Post 375 **[10344]**, Atwater, MN
Amer. Legion, San Jose Memorial Post 1269 **[3414]**, San Jose, IL
Amer. Legion, Sandberg-Carlson Post 351 **[10382]**, Barrett, MN
Amer. Legion, Sandy Valley Post 432 **[17149]**, Waynesburg, OH
Amer. Legion, Saner Post 228 **[16482]**, Powhatan Point, OH
Amer. Legion, Sanford Post 192 **[10952]**, Elmore, MN
Amer. Legion, Santa Claus Post 242 **[6159]**, Santa Claus, IN
Amer. Legion, Sarlo-Sharp Post 368 **[2471]**, Melrose Park, IL
Amer. Legion, Sarver-Guthrie Post 839 **[1971]**, Herrick, IL
Amer. Legion, Sauk Centre Post 67 **[12632]**, Sauk Centre, MN
Amer. Legion, Sauk Prairie Kuoni Reuter Post 167 **[19664]**, Sauk City, WI
Amer. Legion, Sauk Trail Post 246 **[8359]**, Jackson, MI
Amer. Legion, Sauk Village Post 1259 **[3417]**, Sauk Village, IL
Amer. Legion, Saunemin Verdun Post 531 **[3418]**, Saunemin, IL
Amer. Legion, Sauvola Post 265 **[7128]**, Chassell, MI
Amer. Legion, Sawyer-Drumm Post 393 **[17914]**, Edgar, WI
Amer. Legion, Scarbrough Post 243 **[15278]**, Galion, OH
Amer. Legion, Sch-Loe-Man Post 547 **[16057]**, Monroeville, OH
Amer. Legion, Schaap-Galagan Post 636 **[11324]**, Lismore, MN
Amer. Legion, Scharmer-Berger Post 250 **[10336]**, Arlington, MN
Amer. Legion, Scheible-Downing Post 542 **[16489]**, Put In Bay, OH
Amer. Legion, Scherer Post 493 **[15519]**, Jackson Center, OH
Amer. Legion, Schiller Park Post 104 **[3455]**, Schiller Park, IL
Amer. Legion, Schlender-Polley Post 239 **[19900]**, Tigerton, WI
Amer. Legion, Schnell-Westfall Post 184 **[16430]**, Piqua, OH
Amer. Legion, Schuetz-Hermann Post 283 **[2230]**, Lebanon, IL
Amer. Legion, Schultz-Hahn Post 293 **[19735]**, Silver Lake, WI
Amer. Legion, Schuster-Stahl Post 370 **[9462]**, Prescott, MI
Amer. Legion, Schuyler Post 4 **[3369]**, Rushville, IL
Amer. Legion, Schwab-Bailey Post 425 **[13654]**, Cheviot, OH
Amer. Legion, Schwartz-Loll-Richards Post 476 **[19519]**, Porterfield, WI
Amer. Legion, Schwieger Kahler Post 522 **[11922]**, Northrop, MN
Amer. Legion, Scio Post 482 **[16623]**, Scio, OH
Amer. Legion, Scott-Lambert Post 415 **[4766]**, Galveston, IN
Amer. Legion, Scott Post 234 **[6172]**, Scottsburg, IN
Amer. Legion, S.C.S. Post 707 **[1933]**, Hanover, IL
Amer. Legion, Scudiero Post 1978 **[701]**, Chicago, IL

Amer. Legion, Security Post 284 **[7316]**, Detroit, MI
Amer. Legion, Seely-Onstine Post 458 **[20091]**, Wauzeka, WI
Amer. Legion, Seifert-Bianchi Post 132 **[11882]**, New Ulm, MN
Amer. Legion, Selma Post 437 **[6179]**, Selma, IN
Amer. Legion, Semrau-Scott Post 361 **[20167]**, Wilmot, WI
Amer. Legion, Ser. Post 128 **[5013]**, Indianapolis, IN
Amer. Legion, Seymour Post 89 **[6180]**, Seymour, IN
Amer. Legion, Seymour Post 1256 **[3461]**, Seymour, IL
Amer. Legion, Shaddrick and La Beau Post 303 **[11032]**, Fridley, MN
Amer. Legion, Shadyside Post 521 **[16633]**, Shadyside, OH
Amer. Legion, Shakopee Post 2 **[12650]**, Shakopee, MN
Amer. Legion, Sharpsville Post 443 **[6187]**, Sharpsville, IN
Amer. Legion, Sharvin Post 397 **[2745]**, North Chicago, IL
Amer. Legion, Shearer Post 350 **[1787]**, Geneseo, IL
Amer. Legion, Sheboygan Memorial Post 555 **[19690]**, Sheboygan, WI
Amer. Legion, Sheldon Post 393 **[3468]**, Sheldon, IL
Amer. Legion, Shepherd-Russell Post 298 **[4957]**, Hymera, IN
Amer. Legion, Sherman-Rice-Demorest Post 157 **[9464]**, Quincy, MI
Amer. Legion, Sheveland-Taylor Post 14 **[18233]**, Iola, WI
Amer. Legion, Shields Post 314 **[9601]**, Saginaw, MI
Amer. Legion, Shiocton Post 512 **[19728]**, Shiocton, WI
Amer. Legion, Shipley-Robinson-Moen-Will Post 161 **[18326]**, King, WI
Amer. Legion, Sickles-Arnold Post 516 **[7288]**, Deckerville, MI
Amer. Legion, Sidney Post 217 **[16663]**, Sidney, OH
Amer. Legion, Sidney Post 433 **[3476]**, Sidney, IL
Amer. Legion, Sievert-Peterson Post 608 **[11933]**, Okabena, MN
Amer. Legion, Sigel Post 1134 **[3478]**, Sigel, IL
Amer. Legion, Silver Lake Post 141 **[12668]**, Silver Lake, MN
Amer. Legion, Silver Lake Post 431 **[6202]**, Silver Lake, IN
Amer. Legion, Silver Star Post 428 **[12825]**, Waite Park, MN
Amer. Legion, Simmonds-Williams Post 484 **[8169]**, Hickory Corners, MI
Amer. Legion, Simon Ethelbert Snyder Post 122 **[5678]**, Liberty, IN
Amer. Legion, Simonson Betcher Post 26 **[10236]**, Ada, MN
Amer. Legion, Sioux Valley Post 614 **[11288]**, Lakefield, MN
Amer. Legion, Six Gold Star Post 672 **[2485]**, Middletown, IL
Amer. Legion, Sizer-Buchman Post 328 **[19772]**, Springbrook, WI
Amer. Legion, Skinner-Trost Post 122 **[1336]**, Cullom, IL
Amer. Legion, Skokie Post 320 **[3481]**, Skokie, IL
Amer. Legion, Slining-Caulkins Post 267 **[19285]**, New Auburn, WI
Amer. Legion, Smith-Ashcraft-Kissell Post 235 **[5797]**, Milan, IN
Amer. Legion, Smith-Hoover Post 281 **[8116]**, Harbor Springs, MI
Amer. Legion, Smith-Reynolds Post 511 **[2968]**, Paw Paw, IL
Amer. Legion, Smiths Creek Post 525 **[9755]**, Smiths Creek, MI
Amer. Legion, Smithville Post 711 **[16674]**, Smithville, OH
Amer. Legion, Snider-Richardson Post 273 **[18068]**, Grand Marsh, WI
Amer. Legion, Snyder-Lewis-Welty Post 454 **[7210]**, Colon, MI
Amer. Legion, Snyder-Turner Post 1163 **[370]**, Burnside, IL
Amer. Legion, Solsberry Post 450 **[6203]**, Solsberry, IN
Amer. Legion, Soquist-Binder-Kirk Post 464 **[18414]**, Land O' Lakes, WI
Amer. Legion, South Amherst Post 197 **[16688]**, South Amherst, OH
Amer. Legion, South Bend Post 50 **[6215]**, South Bend, IN
Amer. Legion, South Chicago Post 493 **[702]**, Chicago, IL
Amer. Legion, South Deering Post 1238 **[703]**, Chicago, IL
Amer. Legion, South Holland Post 883 **[3501]**, South Holland, IL
Amer. Legion, South Lyon Post 338 **[9768]**, South Lyon, MI
Amer. Legion, South Park Memorial Post 675 **[14848]**, Dayton, OH
Amer. Legion, South Roxana Post 1167 **[3512]**, South Roxana, IL
Amer. Legion, South Scott County Post 751 **[2382]**, Manchester, IL
Amer. Legion, South Shore Post 388 **[704]**, Chicago, IL
Amer. Legion, South Side Post 531 **[16890]**, Toledo, OH
Amer. Legion, South Suburban Post 1291 **[1313]**, Crete, IL
Amer. Legion, Southern Todd County Post 547 **[11100]**, Grey Eagle, MN
Amer. Legion, Southfield Post 328 **[8542]**, Lansing, MI
Amer. Legion, Southington Post 751 **[16699]**, Southington, OH
Amer. Legion, Southway Post 144 **[14302]**, Columbus, OH
Amer. Legion, Spam Post 570 **[10351]**, Austin, MN
Amer. Legion, Sparks-Doernenburg Post 3 **[17473]**, Antigo, WI
Amer. Legion, Spears-Dukes Post 733 **[3364]**, Rossville, IL
Amer. Legion, Speedway Post 500 **[6277]**, Speedway, IN
Amer. Legion, Speicher Post 499 **[1811]**, Gilman, IL
Amer. Legion, Spencer Post 608 **[16701]**, Spencer, OH
Amer. Legion, Spencer-Ross Post 134 **[12830]**, Walker, MN
Amer. Legion, Spink-Dobak Post 97 **[11944]**, Ortonville, MN
Amer. Legion, Spirit of 76 Post 8 **[17155]**, Wellington, OH
Amer. Legion, Spirit Post 452 **[19355]**, Ogema, WI
Amer. Legion, Spondley Post 291 **[17552]**, Augusta, WI
Amer. Legion, Sponholtz-Deignan Post 183 **[18034]**, Genoa City, WI
Amer. Legion, Sprague-Inman Post 577 **[2248]**, Lena, IL
Amer. Legion, Spring Bay Post 1115 **[3515]**, Spring Bay, IL
Amer. Legion, Spring Green Post 253 **[19765]**, Spring Green, WI
Amer. Legion, Springerton Post 1126 **[3519]**, Springerton, IL
Amer. Legion, Springfield Post 32 **[3526]**, Springfield, IL
Amer. Legion, Square Post 232 **[2936]**, Palos Heights, IL
Amer. Legion, Stahl-Linnemeyer Post 369 **[12995]**, Wykoff, MN
Amer. Legion, Stahl Post 778 **[3784]**, Trenton, IL
Amer. Legion, Stamnitz-Lindeman Post 293 **[9737]**, Sebewaing, MI
Amer. Legion, Stanley Mc Collum Post 280 **[230]**, Benton, IL
Amer. Legion, Stanton Burgett Post 201 **[2696]**, Newman, IL
Amer. Legion, Stanton Post 452 **[9854]**, Stanton, MI
Amer. Legion, Steele-Lambert Post 533 **[6899]**, Bay Port, MI
Amer. Legion, Steger Post 521 **[3701]**, Steger, IL
Amer. Legion, Stenmark-Farnsworth Post 388 **[11170]**, Hinckley, MN
Amer. Legion, Stenz-Griesell-Smith Post 449 **[17664]**, Brookfield, WI
Amer. Legion, Stephen Post 390 **[12709]**, Stephen, MN
Amer. Legion, Sterling Post 296 **[3702]**, Sterling, IL
Amer. Legion, Stevens-Christian-Memorial Post 557 **[17300]**, Wintersville, OH
Amer. Legion, Stevensville Post 568 **[9874]**, Stevensville, MI
Amer. Legion, Stewart-Norris Post 197 **[6188]**, Shelburn, IN
Amer. Legion, Stewart-Schneider Post 592 **[4041]**, Winslow, IL
Amer. Legion, Stickney Post 687 **[3710]**, Stickney, IL
Amer. Legion, Stillwater Post 48 **[12716]**, Stillwater, MN
Amer. Legion, Stinar-Sturdevant-Stoltz Post 116 **[11889]**, New York Mills, MN
Amer. Legion, Stockton Post 449 **[3713]**, Stockton, IL
Amer. Legion, Stoddard-Heinle Post 500 **[18947]**, Milwaukee, WI
Amer. Legion, Stoddard Post 93 **[8138]**, Hartford, MI
Amer. Legion, Stokes-Liebman Post 487 **[17702]**, Cable, WI
Amer. Legion, Stone Groeneweg Post 237 **[10376]**, Balaton, MN
Amer. Legion, Stookey Post 1255 **[199]**, Belleville, IL
Amer. Legion, Stout-Nesbit Post 156 **[9075]**, Montgomery, MI
Amer. Legion, Stover-Harrod Post 133 **[15646]**, Lima, OH
Amer. Legion, Streetsboro Post 685 **[16781]**, Streetsboro, OH
Amer. Legion, Strongsville Post 795 **[16296]**, Olmsted Falls, OH
Amer. Legion, Struck-Klandrud Post 336 **[19361]**, Onalaska, WI
Amer. Legion, Struthers Post 158 **[16801]**, Struthers, OH
Amer. Legion, Stuessy-Kuenzi Post 141 **[19302]**, New Glarus, WI
Amer. Legion, Stukenberg-Eilermann Post 1026 **[13]**, Albers, IL
Amer. Legion, Suburban Green Bay Post 518 **[18075]**, Green Bay, WI
Amer. Legion, Sugar Grove Post 1271 **[3735]**, Sugar Grove, IL
Amer. Legion, Sullivan Post 68 **[3738]**, Sullivan, IL
Amer. Legion, Sullivan Post 139 **[6286]**, Sullivan, IN
Amer. Legion, Sullivan-Wallen Post 11 **[18076]**, Green Bay, WI
Amer. Legion, Summerfield Post 415 **[16808]**, Summerfield, OH
Amer. Legion, Sunset Post 402 **[5647]**, Laketon, IN
Amer. Legion, Sura-Wiersgalla Post 186 **[18232]**, Independence, WI
Amer. Legion, Swann-Gehr Post 197 **[17660]**, Brodhead, WI
Amer. Legion, Swartz-Van-Fleet Post 138 **[10159]**, White Pigeon, MI
Amer. Legion, Swen Rasmussen Post 4 **[11289]**, Lakefield, MN
Amer. Legion, Sycamore Post 99 **[3745]**, Sycamore, IL
Amer. Legion, Sycamore Post 250 **[16821]**, Sycamore, OH
Amer. Legion, Sylvan Post 44 **[19944]**, Wabeno, WI
Amer. Legion, Sylvester Lyczynski Post 420 **[10155]**, White Lake, MI
Amer. Legion, Syverson-Funk Post 155 **[20141]**, Westby, WI
Amer. Legion, Table Grove Post 413 **[3749]**, Table Grove, IL
Amer. Legion, Tadeusz Kosciuszko Post 207 **[5765]**, Merrillville, IN
Amer. Legion, Tamaroa Memorial Post 1277 **[3751]**, Tamaroa, IL

Amer. Legion, Tampico Post 574 **[3753]**, Tampico, IL
Amer. Legion, Tangen-Walstrom Post 114 **[11022]**, Fosston, MN
Amer. Legion, Tanner-Paull Post 120 **[20098]**, West Allis, WI
Amer. Legion, Tattler Post 973 **[705]**, Chicago, IL
Amer. Legion, Taunton Post 604 **[12738]**, Taunton, MN
Amer. Legion, Taylor-Eckhardt Post 913 **[84]**, Armington, IL
Amer. Legion, Taylor Post 200 **[9899]**, Taylor, MI
Amer. Legion, Teddy-Budlong-Robert-Smith Post 39 **[18797]**, Marinette, WI
Amer. Legion, Temperly-Duncan Post 526 **[18200]**, Hazel Green, WI
Amer. Legion, Temple Post 273 **[8543]**, Lansing, MI
Amer. Legion, Tennyson Post 463 **[6301]**, Tennyson, IN
Amer. Legion, Tester-Niemi Post 562 **[10562]**, Brookston, MN
Amer. Legion, Teutopolis Post 924 **[3758]**, Teutopolis, IL
Amer. Legion, T.H.B. Post 187 **[1618]**, Elmhurst, IL
Amer. Legion, Theodore Roosevelt Post 469 **[14057]**, Cleveland, OH
Amer. Legion, Theodore Roosevelt Post 627 **[706]**, Chicago, IL
Amer. Legion, Theodore Stalemo Post 242 **[11009]**, Fisher, MN
Amer. Legion, Thibadeau-Drossart Post 319 **[17719]**, Casco, WI
Amer. Legion, Thomas-Daniels-Hand Post 443 **[9708]**, Sanford, MI
Amer. Legion, Thomas-Devaney-Collier Post 430 **[10442]**, Bird Island, MN
Amer. Legion, Thomas-Holcomb Post 304 **[19416]**, Palmyra, WI
Amer. Legion, Thomas and Leonard Johnson Post 541 **[18210]**, Hixton, WI
Amer. Legion, Thompson-Burkhard Post 28 **[19928]**, Valders, WI
Amer. Legion, Thompson-Wallingford Post 594 **[16392]**, Peebles, OH
Amer. Legion, Thornton Post 1070 **[3763]**, Thornton, IL
Amer. Legion, Thorntown Post 218 **[6355]**, Thorntown, IN
Amer. Legion, Thorpe-Taylor Post 551 **[17599]**, Beetown, WI
Amer. Legion, Three Lakes Post 431 **[19898]**, Three Lakes, WI
Amer. Legion, Thrush-Parry Post 212 **[1932]**, Hanna City, IL
Amer. Legion, Thurston-Zwir Post 121 **[15245]**, Fremont, OH
Amer. Legion, Tickfer-Erickson Post 17 **[17534]**, Arcadia, WI
Amer. Legion, Tiffin Post 169 **[16850]**, Tiffin, OH
Amer. Legion, Timewell Post 1059 **[3764]**, Timewell, IL
Amer. Legion, Timmermann-Benhoff Post 252 **[336]**, Breese, IL
Amer. Legion, Tinley Park Post 615 **[3768]**, Tinley Park, IL
Amer. Legion, Tiskilwa Post 346 **[3775]**, Tiskilwa, IL
Amer. Legion, Toledo Police Post 512 **[16891]**, Toledo, OH
Amer. Legion, Toledo Post 335 **[16892]**, Toledo, OH
Amer. Legion, Tolleston Post 270 **[4775]**, Gary, IN
Amer. Legion, Tony Kashon Post 290 **[6138]**, Rosedale, IN
Amer. Legion, Tony Rivord Post 244 **[9461]**, Powers, MI
Amer. Legion, Toulon Post 416 **[3779]**, Toulon, IL
Amer. Legion, Toutloff-Saunders-Duffy Post 49 **[17584]**, Bayfield, WI
Amer. Legion, Trafalgar Post 416 **[6359]**, Trafalgar, IN
Amer. Legion, Tremont Post 1236 **[3783]**, Tremont, IL
Amer. Legion, Tri-City Post 113 **[1881]**, Granite City, IL
Amer. Legion, Tri-City Post 513 **[11860]**, New Brighton, MN
Amer. Legion, Tri-County Post 124 **[11846]**, Motley, MN
Amer. Legion, Triangle B Post 193 **[17455]**, Adell, WI
Amer. Legion, Triangle Post 933 **[1253]**, Chicago Ridge, IL
Amer. Legion, Trier-Puddy Post 75 **[17968]**, Fond du Lac, WI
Amer. Legion, Triple Six Post 666 **[12373]**, St. Paul, MN
Amer. Legion, Triple Star Post 299 **[3183]**, Raymond, IL
Amer. Legion, Trombley-Polkas Post 494 **[9968]**, Trout Creek, MI
Amer. Legion, Troska Post 210 **[12867]**, Wells, MN
Amer. Legion, Troy Post 708 **[3786]**, Troy, IL
Amer. Legion, Troy-Webster Post 240 **[15738]**, Luckey, OH
Amer. Legion, Truman Blakesley Post 432 **[12838]**, Warba, MN
Amer. Legion, Tuscarawas Post 139 **[16145]**, New Philadelphia, OH
Amer. Legion, Tuttle-Miller Post 761 **[13313]**, Bellbrook, OH
Amer. Legion, Twin Cities Amer. Indian Post 419 **[12374]**, St. Paul, MN
Amer. Legion, Twin City Ford Post 439 **[11510]**, Minneapolis, MN
Amer. Legion, Twin City Post 266 **[4474]**, East Chicago, IN
Amer. Legion, Twin Lakes Post 544 **[19916]**, Twin Lakes, WI
Amer. Legion, Underwood-Orr Post 34 **[9906]**, Tecumseh, MI
Amer. Legion, Union City Post 196 **[10019]**, Union City, MI
Amer. Legion, Union League Post 758 **[707]**, Chicago, IL
Amer. Legion, Union Mills Post 295 **[6366]**, Union Mills, IN
Amer. Legion, Union Post 79 **[15862]**, Marysville, OH
Amer. Legion, Univ. of Minnesota Post 548 **[12375]**, St. Paul, MN
Amer. Legion, Uppena-Kroepfle Post 473 **[19521]**, Potosi, WI
Amer. Legion, Upsala Post 350 **[12781]**, Upsala, MN
Amer. Legion, Urban Klister Post 436 **[20209]**, Wrightstown, WI
Amer. Legion, Urbana Post 71 **[3803]**, Urbana, IL
Amer. Legion, Urbana Post 741 **[17037]**, Urbana, OH
Amer. Legion, Uren-Cooper-Johnson Post 50 **[8319]**, Iron Mountain, MI
Amer. Legion, Valier Post 82 **[3843]**, Valier, IL
Amer. Legion, Valley City Post 356 **[7898]**, Grand Rapids, MI
Amer. Legion, Valley Post 375 **[15754]**, Malvern, OH
Amer. Legion, Valmeyer Post 901 **[3845]**, Valmeyer, IL
Amer. Legion, Van-Bibber-Hansen Post 148 **[3419]**, Savanna, IL
Amer. Legion, Van Buren Post 401 **[708]**, Chicago, IL
Amer. Legion, Van-Der-Jagt-De-Bruine Post 338 **[17726]**, Cedar Grove, WI
Amer. Legion, Van-Huizen-Fritz Post 123 **[19414]**, Owen, WI
Amer. Legion, Vandalia Memorial Post 668 **[17057]**, Vandalia, OH
Amer. Legion, Vandercook Lake Post 166 **[8360]**, Jackson, MI
Amer. Legion, Vanderwaal-Lusty Post 421 **[11461]**, Mentor, MN
Amer. Legion, Varga-Fall Post 383 **[9559]**, Rosebush, MI
Amer. Legion, Venice-Madison Post 307 **[3123]**, Pontoon Beach, IL
Amer. Legion, Venier-Molea Post 452 **[11247]**, Keewatin, MN
Amer. Legion, Verhulst-Willmarth-Paulsen Post 311 **[18211]**, Holcombe, WI
Amer. Legion, Verner Hanes Post 110 **[6544]**, Wolcottville, IN
Amer. Legion, Vernon Post 1247 **[3852]**, Vernon Hills, IL
Amer. Legion, Versailles Post 435 **[17068]**, Versailles, OH
Amer. Legion, Vesper Post 520 **[19937]**, Vesper, WI
Amer. Legion, Veterans Memorial Post 63 **[17770]**, Clintonville, WI
Amer. Legion, Viall Post 166 **[12043]**, Preston, MN
Amer. Legion, Victor Hill Post 534 **[478]**, Casey, IL
Amer. Legion, Victor Post 255 **[18434]**, Luck, WI
Amer. Legion, Victoria Post 1995 **[12787]**, Victoria, MN
Amer. Legion, Victory Post 7 **[709]**, Chicago, IL
Amer. Legion, Victory Post 70 **[6190]**, Shelbyville, IN
Amer. Legion, Victory Post 112 **[19773]**, Stanley, WI
Amer. Legion, Victory Post 260 **[13223]**, Attica, OH
Amer. Legion, Viking Memorial Post 611 **[13035]**, Akron, OH
Amer. Legion, Viking Post 493 **[10460]**, Bloomington, MN
Amer. Legion, Villa Grove Post 215 **[259]**, Bloomington, IL
Amer. Legion, Villa Park Post 652 **[3862]**, Villa Park, IL
Amer. Legion, Vincennes Post 73 **[6408]**, Vincennes, IN
Amer. Legion, Vincent Hays Post 610 **[2839]**, Oakwood, IL
Amer. Legion, Vinton Post 161 **[17072]**, Vinton, OH
Amer. Legion, Voight Post 376 **[17951]**, Fall Creek, WI
Amer. Legion, Votaw-Swank Post 458 **[2673]**, Neoga, IL
Amer. Legion, Vytautas Post 289 **[5766]**, Merrillville, IN
Amer. Legion, W.-Grams-R-Schmidt Post 475 **[12268]**, St. Clair, MN
Amer. Legion, Wabash Post 423 **[2572]**, Mount Carmel, IL
Amer. Legion, Waconia Post 150 **[12815]**, Waconia, MN
Amer. Legion, Wade Benfer Post 404 **[16509]**, Republic, OH
Amer. Legion, Wade Post 598 **[2008]**, Hinckley, IL
Amer. Legion, Wadena Post 171 **[12820]**, Wadena, MN
Amer. Legion, Wadsworth Post 170 **[17073]**, Wadsworth, OH
Amer. Legion, Wagner-Eberle-Sukowaty Post 477 **[19661]**, St. Nazianz, WI
Amer. Legion, Wakeman Post 689 **[17082]**, Wakeman, OH
Amer. Legion, Waldron-Flaat Post 182 **[10930]**, Effie, MN
Amer. Legion, Walhonding Valley Post 634 **[17124]**, Warsaw, OH
Amer. Legion, Walker-Hecox-Hickle Post 677 **[15683]**, Lithopolis, OH
Amer. Legion, Wallace Sniffin Post 506 **[5830]**, Montmorenci, IN
Amer. Legion, Wally Bartley Post 162 **[8882]**, Luzerne, MI
Amer. Legion, Walnut Post 179 **[3874]**, Walnut, IL
Amer. Legion, Walter Clemons Post 613 **[581]**, Chatsworth, IL
Amer. Legion, Walter Durkee Post 311 **[7899]**, Grand Rapids, MI
Amer. Legion, Walter Fraser Post 108 **[9339]**, Oxford, MI
Amer. Legion, Walter Graham Post 332 **[3334]**, Rockton, IL
Amer. Legion, Walter Guede Post 593 **[2184]**, Lacon, IL
Amer. Legion, Walter Hoyt Post 350 **[6029]**, Perrysville, IN
Amer. Legion, Walter Miller Post 394 **[16563]**, Russellville, OH
Amer. Legion, Walter Riley Post 307 **[11856]**, Nashwauk, MN

Amer. Legion, Walter Scott Erickson Post 557 **[10767]**, Deerwood, MN
Amer. Legion, Walter Stelmaszek Post 792 **[392]**, Calumet City, IL
Amer. Legion, Walter Tripp Post 29 **[11836]**, Morris, MN
Amer. Legion, Walton Post 418 **[6438]**, Walton, IN
Amer. Legion, Wanda Post 385 **[12835]**, Wanda, MN
Amer. Legion, Waples-Bauer Post 94 **[2706]**, Nokomis, IL
Amer. Legion, Warren Brock Post 69 **[6013]**, Orleans, IN
Amer. Legion, Warren Post 27 **[12840]**, Warren, MN
Amer. Legion, Warren Post 259 **[6528]**, Williamsport, IN
Amer. Legion, Warren Post 490 **[7651]**, Farmington Hills, MI
Amer. Legion, Warrick Post 200 **[4273]**, Boonville, IN
Amer. Legion, Waseca Post 228 **[12846]**, Waseca, MN
Amer. Legion, Washburn Post 661 **[3884]**, Washburn, IL
Amer. Legion, Washington Post 100 **[3885]**, Washington, IL
Amer. Legion, Washington Post 444 **[16129]**, New Knoxville, OH
Amer. Legion, Waterford Post 24 **[8142]**, Hartland, MI
Amer. Legion, Waterford Post 230 **[17019]**, Uhrichsville, OH
Amer. Legion, Waterloo Post 747 **[3898]**, Waterloo, IL
Amer. Legion, Waterman Post 654 **[3905]**, Waterman, IL
Amer. Legion, Waters-Hackenberg Post 220 **[8792]**, Lawton, MI
Amer. Legion, Waterville Post 463 **[17135]**, Waterville, OH
Amer. Legion, Watkins Post 453 **[12854]**, Watkins, MN
Amer. Legion, Watseka Post 23 **[3907]**, Watseka, IL
Amer. Legion, Wauconda Post 911 **[3912]**, Wauconda, IL
Amer. Legion, Wave Post 988 **[710]**, Chicago, IL
Amer. Legion, Waverly Post 262 **[3933]**, Waverly, IL
Amer. Legion, Wawasee Post 223 **[6290]**, Syracuse, IN
Amer. Legion, Wayne City Post 1132 **[3934]**, Wayne City, IL
Amer. Legion, Wayne Newton Post 346 **[6312]**, Terre Haute, IN
Amer. Legion, Wayne Post 64 **[5014]**, Indianapolis, IN
Amer. Legion, Wayne Post 111 **[10099]**, Wayne, MI
Amer. Legion, Wayne Post 395 **[17150]**, Waynesfield, OH
Amer. Legion, Wayne Township Veterans Post 615 **[17151]**, Waynesville, OH
Amer. Legion, Wayne-Wright Post 1052 **[711]**, Chicago, IL
Amer. Legion, Waynedale Post 241 **[4632]**, Fort Wayne, IN
Amer. Legion, Waynesville Post 1189 **[3935]**, Waynesville, IL
Amer. Legion, Waynetown Post 445 **[6463]**, Waynetown, IN
Amer. Legion, Weakly-Rowland Post 420 **[3396]**, St. Elmo, IL
Amer. Legion, Weatherford-Vander-Hoeven Post 552 **[9653]**, St. Clair Shores, MI
Amer. Legion, Webb Lake A and H Post 403 **[20093]**, Webb Lake, WI
Amer. Legion, Wee-Chick Post 518 **[9191]**, New Troy, MI
Amer. Legion, Weeden-Zeller Post 609 **[3965]**, Westfield, IL
Amer. Legion, Weilepp-Cramer Post 660 **[2417]**, Maroa, IL
Amer. Legion, Weimer-Widder Post 549 **[13279]**, Beach City, OH
Amer. Legion, Weinsch-Gilbert-Patten-Gillett Post 353 **[17786]**, Cornell, WI
Amer. Legion, Welcome Post 553 **[12866]**, Welcome, MN
Amer. Legion, Welker-Smith Post 17 **[15318]**, Gibsonburg, OH
Amer. Legion, Wells-Peterson Post 384 **[10789]**, Dodge Center, MN
Amer. Legion, Wellston Post 371 **[17159]**, Wellston, OH
Amer. Legion, Wellsville Post 70 **[17161]**, Wellsville, OH
Amer. Legion, Welsh-Crawley-Kramer Post 129 **[4839]**, Greensburg, IN
Amer. Legion, Wenona Post 8 **[3937]**, Wenona, IL
Amer. Legion, Wenzel-Longley Post 349 **[19853]**, Sullivan, WI
Amer. Legion, Wesley Johnson Memorial Post 1195 **[3881]**, Wasco, IL
Amer. Legion, Wesley Werner Post 513 **[13728]**, Cincinnati, OH
Amer. Legion, West Chicago Post 300 **[3938]**, West Chicago, IL
Amer. Legion, West Douglas County Post 188 **[10967]**, Evansville, MN
Amer. Legion, West End Post 414 **[12889]**, White Bear Lake, MN
Amer. Legion, West-Field Post 48 **[17605]**, Beloit, WI
Amer. Legion, West Lafayette Post 466 **[17182]**, West Lafayette, OH
Amer. Legion, West Lafayette Post 492 **[6471]**, West Lafayette, IN
Amer. Legion, West Mansfield Post 603 **[17187]**, West Mansfield, OH
Amer. Legion, West Noble Post 243 **[5680]**, Ligonier, IN
Amer. Legion, West Randolph Post 353 **[4594]**, Farmland, IN
Amer. Legion, West Sangamon Post 743 **[2679]**, New Berlin, IL
Amer. Legion, West Side Memorial Post 151 **[18464]**, Madison, WI
Amer. Legion, West Unity Post 669 **[17200]**, West Unity, OH
Amer. Legion, Westbrook Post 152 **[12882]**, Westbrook, MN
Amer. Legion, Western Reserve Post 315 **[14058]**, Cleveland, OH
Amer. Legion, Western Taylor County Post 359 **[18050]**, Gilman, WI
Amer. Legion, Westland Post 251 **[9392]**, Plymouth, MI
Amer. Legion, Westmont Post 338 **[3967]**, Westmont, IL
Amer. Legion, Weston Post 409 **[17243]**, Weston, OH
Amer. Legion, Westphal Post 251 **[12116]**, Robbinsdale, MN
Amer. Legion, Westport Post 638 **[12789]**, Villard, MN
Amer. Legion, Whalen-Hill Post 648 **[1880]**, Grafton, IL
Amer. Legion, Wheatfield Post 406 **[6519]**, Wheatfield, IN
Amer. Legion, Wheeling Memorial Post 221 **[4004]**, Wheeling, IL
Amer. Legion, White Bear Lake Post 168 **[12890]**, White Bear Lake, MN
Amer. Legion, White Earth Indian Nation Post 625 **[11931]**, Ogema, MN
Amer. Legion, White Hall Post 70 **[4007]**, White Hall, IL
Amer. Legion, White River Post 114 **[4907]**, Hazleton, IN
Amer. Legion, Whitehouse Post 384 **[17250]**, Whitehouse, OH
Amer. Legion, Whitish-Funk Post 184 **[17956]**, Fennimore, WI
Amer. Legion, Whitmore Lake Post 359 **[8100]**, Hamburg, MI
Amer. Legion, Whittey Bennett Post 301 **[12737]**, Taconite, MN
Amer. Legion, Wickler-Copeland Post 464 **[3876]**, Warren, IL
Amer. Legion, Wilber-Bartlett Post 315 **[7029]**, Brooklyn, MI
Amer. Legion, Wilbur Braughton Post 611 **[3709]**, Stewardson, IL
Amer. Legion, Wilbur Bud Crane Post 400 **[6433]**, Walkerton, IN
Amer. Legion, Wilcox-Eastman-Salinas Post 160 **[6826]**, Bangor, MI
Amer. Legion, Wiley-Mumford Post 764 **[3776]**, Toledo, IL
Amer. Legion, Wileykoon Post 475 **[9732]**, Schoolcraft, MI
Amer. Legion, Wilkins-Kelly Post 450 **[17804]**, Darien, WI
Amer. Legion, Willey-Herda Post 192 **[18008]**, Franklin, WI
Amer. Legion, William Allen Post 179 **[12013]**, Plainview, MN
Amer. Legion, William-B.-Cairns-Victory Post 57 **[18465]**, Madison, WI
Amer. Legion, William C. Lee Memorial Post 503 **[4350]**, Chesterton, IN
Amer. Legion, William Chandler Peterson Post 171 **[1317]**, Crystal Lake, IL
Amer. Legion, William Chizum Post 146 **[5842]**, Morocco, IN
Amer. Legion, William Hall Post 282 **[4097]**, Anderson, IN
Amer. Legion, William Krensing Post 58 **[10565]**, Browns Valley, MN
Amer. Legion, William Mc Kinley Post 231 **[712]**, Chicago, IL
Amer. Legion, William Riker Johnson Post 205 **[8544]**, Lansing, MI
Amer. Legion, William Robideau Post 66 **[11214]**, International Falls, MN
Amer. Legion, William Schaefer Post 44 **[2983]**, Pekin, IL
Amer. Legion, William T. Mc Coy Post 92 **[12125]**, Rochester, MN
Amer. Legion, William Zeb Longest Post 42 **[4615]**, Floyds Knobs, IN
Amer. Legion, Williams-Giroux Post 90 **[8510]**, Lake Linden, MI
Amer. Legion, Williamsburg Post 288 **[17268]**, Williamsburg, OH
Amer. Legion, Williamsburg Post 442 **[6527]**, Williamsburg, IN
Amer. Legion, Williamsfield Post 371 **[4009]**, Williamsfield, IL
Amer. Legion, Williamson Post 147 **[2400]**, Marion, IL
Amer. Legion, Williamson-Smiley Post 401 **[6074]**, Redkey, IN
Amer. Legion, Willis-Chapel Post 306 **[18144]**, Green Lake, WI
Amer. Legion, Willis Hunter Post 378 **[1549]**, East St. Louis, IL
Amer. Legion, Willowick-Eastlake Post 678 **[17282]**, Willowick, OH
Amer. Legion, Wilmington Veterans Post 49 **[17286]**, Wilmington, OH
Amer. Legion, Wilson-Oliver-Riley Post 462 **[6205]**, Somerville, IN
Amer. Legion, Windham Post 674 **[17298]**, Windham, OH
Amer. Legion, Windom Post 206 **[12938]**, Windom, MN
Amer. Legion, Winegar Post 480 **[19540]**, Presque Isle, WI
Amer. Legion, Wingate Post 174 **[6540]**, Wingate, IN
Amer. Legion, Winifred Fairfax Warder Post 406 **[3752]**, Tamms, IL
Amer. Legion, Winnebago Post 82 **[12943]**, Winnebago, MN
Amer. Legion, Winnetka Post 10 **[3921]**, Waukegan, IL
Amer. Legion, Winnow-Arn Post 541 **[14783]**, Continental, OH
Amer. Legion, Winslow Post 115 **[6542]**, Winslow, IN
Amer. Legion, Wisconsin Post 8 **[19979]**, Waukesha, WI
Amer. Legion, Wisconsin Post 22 **[17472]**, Amherst, WI
Amer. Legion, Wisconsin Post 23 **[18948]**, Milwaukee, WI
Amer. Legion, Wisconsin Post 24 **[18395]**, Lake Geneva, WI
Amer. Legion, Wisconsin Post 30 **[17915]**, Edgerton, WI

Amer. Legion, Wisconsin Post 42 **[19462]**, Platteville, WI
Amer. Legion, Wisconsin Post 46 **[18894]**, Merrill, WI
Amer. Legion, Wisconsin Post 47 **[19507]**, Portage, WI
Amer. Legion, Wisconsin Post 50 **[18222]**, Hudson, WI
Amer. Legion, Wisconsin Post 52 **[18333]**, La Crosse, WI
Amer. Legion, Wisconsin Post 60 **[18324]**, Kimberly, WI
Amer. Legion, Wisconsin Post 72 **[19835]**, Sturgeon Bay, WI
Amer. Legion, Wisconsin Post 79 **[17695]**, Burlington, WI
Amer. Legion, Wisconsin Post 82 **[19498]**, Port Washington, WI
Amer. Legion, Wisconsin Post 85 **[19256]**, Muscoda, WI
Amer. Legion, Wisconsin Post 91 **[19338]**, Oconomowoc, WI
Amer. Legion, Wisconsin Post 96 **[20095]**, Webster, WI
Amer. Legion, Wisconsin Post 97 **[17834]**, Dodgeville, WI
Amer. Legion, Wisconsin Post 104 **[17794]**, Cuba City, WI
Amer. Legion, Wisconsin Post 108 **[17761]**, Clear Lake, WI
Amer. Legion, Wisconsin Post 109 **[18409]**, Lancaster, WI
Amer. Legion, Wisconsin Post 113 **[19235]**, Mount Horeb, WI
Amer. Legion, Wisconsin Post 114 **[17846]**, Eagle River, WI
Amer. Legion, Wisconsin Post 118 **[19896]**, Thorp, WI
Amer. Legion, Wisconsin Post 122 **[19452]**, Phillips, WI
Amer. Legion, Wisconsin Post 128 **[19824]**, Stockbridge, WI
Amer. Legion, Wisconsin Post 129 **[19902]**, Tomah, WI
Amer. Legion, Wisconsin Post 133 **[17713]**, Camp Douglas, WI
Amer. Legion, Wisconsin Post 143 **[19655]**, St. Croix Falls, WI
Amer. Legion, Wisconsin Post 146 **[17589]**, Beaver Dam, WI
Amer. Legion, Wisconsin Post 158 **[18769]**, Maiden Rock, WI
Amer. Legion, Wisconsin Post 159 **[17706]**, Cadott, WI
Amer. Legion, Wisconsin Post 160 **[17689]**, Brooklyn, WI
Amer. Legion, Wisconsin Post 165 **[19919]**, Two Rivers, WI
Amer. Legion, Wisconsin Post 173 **[20159]**, Whitewater, WI
Amer. Legion, Wisconsin Post 177 **[18072]**, Gratiot, WI
Amer. Legion, Wisconsin Post 181 **[17844]**, Durand, WI
Amer. Legion, Wisconsin Post 182 **[19424]**, Park Falls, WI
Amer. Legion, Wisconsin Post 187 **[20176]**, Wisc Dells, WI
Amer. Legion, Wisconsin Post 195 **[17709]**, Cambridge, WI
Amer. Legion, Wisconsin Post 198 **[18807]**, Marion, WI
Amer. Legion, Wisconsin Post 205 **[18242]**, Janesville, WI
Amer. Legion, Wisconsin Post 208 **[19632]**, Rio, WI
Amer. Legion, Wisconsin Post 209 **[19382]**, Orfordville, WI
Amer. Legion, Wisconsin Post 213 **[17817]**, Deer Park, WI
Amer. Legion, Wisconsin Post 215 **[19422]**, Pardeeville, WI
Amer. Legion, Wisconsin Post 219 **[19980]**, Waukesha, WI
Amer. Legion, Wisconsin Post 220 **[19741]**, Soldiers Grove, WI
Amer. Legion, Wisconsin Post 236 **[17460]**, Algoma, WI
Amer. Legion, Wisconsin Post 249 **[18018]**, Frederic, WI
Amer. Legion, Wisconsin Post 254 **[18918]**, Milltown, WI
Amer. Legion, Wisconsin Post 258 **[18420]**, Little Chute, WI
Amer. Legion, Wisconsin Post 265 **[17484]**, Appleton, WI
Amer. Legion, Wisconsin Post 266 **[17774]**, Colby, WI
Amer. Legion, Wisconsin Post 268 **[17694]**, Bruce, WI
Amer. Legion, Wisconsin Post 269 **[17801]**, Cushing, WI
Amer. Legion, Wisconsin Post 271 **[19523]**, Poynette, WI
Amer. Legion, Wisconsin Post 272 **[17701]**, Butternut, WI
Amer. Legion, Wisconsin Post 278 **[17562]**, Balsam Lake, WI
Amer. Legion, Wisconsin Post 283 **[19883]**, Suring, WI
Amer. Legion, Wisconsin Post 287 **[18827]**, Mattoon, WI
Amer. Legion, Wisconsin Post 290 **[17620]**, Benton, WI
Amer. Legion, Wisconsin Post 295 **[17641]**, Bloomer, WI
Amer. Legion, Wisconsin Post 297 **[19584]**, Radisson, WI
Amer. Legion, Wisconsin Post 309 **[18290]**, Kendall, WI
Amer. Legion, Wisconsin Post 310 **[19549]**, Racine, WI
Amer. Legion, Wisconsin Post 318 **[18407]**, Lake Tomahawk, WI
Amer. Legion, Wisconsin Post 322 **[19282]**, Nekoosa, WI
Amer. Legion, Wisconsin Post 324 **[19412]**, Osseo, WI
Amer. Legion, Wisconsin Post 326 **[17654]**, Boyd, WI
Amer. Legion, Wisconsin Post 329 **[17656]**, Briggsville, WI
Amer. Legion, Wisconsin Post 333 **[19856]**, Sun Prairie, WI
Amer. Legion, Wisconsin Post 335 **[17553]**, Avoca, WI
Amer. Legion, Wisconsin Post 346 **[17734]**, Centuria, WI
Amer. Legion, Wisconsin Post 358 **[19927]**, Unity, WI
Amer. Legion, Wisconsin Post 360 **[20014]**, Waunakee, WI
Amer. Legion, Wisconsin Post 365 **[19486]**, Plum City, WI
Amer. Legion, Wisconsin Post 370 **[20165]**, Wild Rose, WI
Amer. Legion, Wisconsin Post 372 **[17997]**, Forestville, WI
Amer. Legion, Wisconsin Post 383 **[18428]**, Lone Rock, WI
Amer. Legion, Wisconsin Post 384 **[18316]**, Kewaskum, WI
Amer. Legion, Wisconsin Post 392 **[17645]**, Bonduel, WI
Amer. Legion, Wisconsin Post 395 **[18327]**, Kingston, WI
Amer. Legion, Wisconsin Post 404 **[17942]**, Emerald, WI
Amer. Legion, Wisconsin Post 406 **[18949]**, Milwaukee, WI
Amer. Legion, Wisconsin Post 408 **[18950]**, Milwaukee, WI
Amer. Legion, Wisconsin Post 410 **[18021]**, Fredonia, WI
Amer. Legion, Wisconsin Post 411 **[18951]**, Milwaukee, WI
Amer. Legion, Wisconsin Post 418 **[19748]**, South Range, WI
Amer. Legion, Wisconsin Post 422 **[18203]**, Highland, WI
Amer. Legion, Wisconsin Post 435 **[19871]**, Superior, WI
Amer. Legion, Wisconsin Post 439 **[18853]**, Melrose, WI
Amer. Legion, Wisconsin Post 443 **[17644]**, Blue River, WI
Amer. Legion, Wisconsin Post 444 **[18952]**, Milwaukee, WI
Amer. Legion, Wisconsin Post 445 **[17720]**, Cashton, WI
Amer. Legion, Wisconsin Post 454 **[19233]**, Mount Calvary, WI
Amer. Legion, Wisconsin Post 455 **[18953]**, Milwaukee, WI
Amer. Legion, Wisconsin Post 461 **[19430]**, Pembine, WI
Amer. Legion, Wisconsin Post 462 **[17456]**, Adell, WI
Amer. Legion, Wisconsin Post 465 **[19201]**, Minong, WI
Amer. Legion, Wisconsin Post 469 **[18796]**, Marathon, WI
Amer. Legion, Wisconsin Post 478 **[19654]**, St. Cloud, WI
Amer. Legion, Wisconsin Post 481 **[20015]**, Waunakee, WI
Amer. Legion, Wisconsin Post 484 **[19489]**, Plymouth, WI
Amer. Legion, Wisconsin Post 485 **[19652]**, Rudolph, WI
Amer. Legion, Wisconsin Post 486 **[18241]**, Jackson, WI
Amer. Legion, Wisconsin Post 492 **[19651]**, Rothschild, WI
Amer. Legion, Wisconsin Post 494 **[18015]**, Franksville, WI
Amer. Legion, Wisconsin Post 496 **[19726]**, Sherwood, WI
Amer. Legion, Wisconsin Post 498 **[18954]**, Milwaukee, WI
Amer. Legion, Wisconsin Post 501 **[18466]**, Madison, WI
Amer. Legion, Wisconsin Post 504 **[17938]**, Elroy, WI
Amer. Legion, Wisconsin Post 511 **[19629]**, Ridgeland, WI
Amer. Legion, Wisconsin Post 527 **[19738]**, Sister Bay, WI
Amer. Legion, Wisconsin Post 529 **[18955]**, Milwaukee, WI
Amer. Legion, Wisconsin Post 539 **[18077]**, Green Bay, WI
Amer. Legion, Wisconsin Post 546 **[19550]**, Racine, WI
Amer. Legion, Wisconsin Post 552 **[19744]**, Somers, WI
Amer. Legion, Witt-Webber-Carrell Post 617 **[86]**, Arrowsmith, IL
Amer. Legion, Wittstein-Middleman Post 524 **[13729]**, Cincinnati, OH
Amer. Legion, Wm. A. Baker Post 363 **[15736]**, Lucasville, OH
Amer. Legion, Wm-A.-Jacobson-Errett-B.-Olson Post 138 **[19941]**, Viroqua, WI
Amer. Legion, Wm. F. Helmke Post 340 **[15454]**, Holgate, OH
Amer. Legion, Wodtka-Rothe-Reiss Post 380 **[3405]**, St. Peter, IL
Amer. Legion, Wojciak-Talberg Post 602 **[11165]**, Hillman, MN
Amer. Legion, Wolcott Post 294 **[6543]**, Wolcott, IN
Amer. Legion, Wolf River Post 391 **[18023]**, Fremont, WI
Amer. Legion, Wolman-Minskey Post 317 **[20064]**, Wautoma, WI
Amer. Legion, Wolverine Post 360 **[9473]**, Reading, MI
Amer. Legion, Wolverton-Sawvel-Falor Post 295 **[7000]**, Breckenridge, MI
Amer. Legion, Women Veterans Post 919 **[2796]**, Oak Lawn, IL
Amer. Legion, Wood-Gasteyer Post 542 **[17913]**, Eau Galle, WI
Amer. Legion, Wood-Hill Post 39 **[8923]**, Marcellus, MI
Amer. Legion, Wood Lake Post 556 **[12973]**, Wood Lake, MN
Amer. Legion, Wood River Post 204 **[4045]**, Wood River, IL
Amer. Legion, Wood-Rosebrook Post 745 **[15073]**, East Liberty, OH
Amer. Legion, Woodard-Mc-Govern Post 426 **[17183]**, West Liberty, OH

Amer. Legion, Woodburn Post 377 **[6545]**, Woodburn, IN
Amer. Legion, Woodbury Post 501 **[12974]**, Woodbury, MN
Amer. Legion, Woodcock-Herbst Post 216 **[12044]**, Princeton, MN
Amer. Legion, Woodrow Wilson Post 347 **[10061]**, Warren, MI
Amer. Legion, Woodrow Wilson Post 506 **[12260]**, Ruthton, MN
Amer. Legion, Woodville Post 301 **[20207]**, Woodville, WI
Amer. Legion, Wooster Post 68 **[17310]**, Wooster, OH
Amer. Legion, Worden Post 564 **[4066]**, Worden, IL
Amer. Legion, Worthey Post 492 **[2088]**, Jerseyville, IL
Amer. Legion, Wyandot Post 225 **[17031]**, Upper Sandusky, OH
Amer. Legion, Wycoff Post 296 **[10171]**, Williamston, MI
Amer. Legion, Wyoming Post 91 **[4072]**, Wyoming, IL
Amer. Legion, Y. T. R. Post 153 **[16867]**, Tiltonsville, OH
Amer. Legion, Yackee-Strong-Memorial Post 60 **[16802]**, Stryker, OH
Amer. Legion, Yoki-Bergman Post 220 **[11851]**, Mountain Iron, MN
Amer. Legion, Yonke-Christenson Post 533 **[17564]**, Bancroft, WI
Amer. Legion, York-Kolar Post 316 **[19722]**, Sheldon, WI
Amer. Legion, Yorktown Post 321 **[6547]**, Yorktown, IN
Amer. Legion, Yorkville Post 489 **[4073]**, Yorkville, IL
Amer. Legion, Young-Budd Post 171 **[15273]**, Galena, OH
Amer. Legion, Young-Moore Post 100 **[17195]**, West Union, OH
Amer. Legion, Ypsilanti Post 282 **[10197]**, Ypsilanti, MI
Amer. Legion, Yurkovich-Beck Post 594 **[2579]**, Mount Olive, IL
Amer. Legion, Zanesville Post 29 **[17436]**, Zanesville, OH
Amer. Legion, Zernicke-Wegner Post 217 **[17646]**, Bonduel, WI
Amer. Legion, Zion-Benton Post 865 **[4080]**, Zion, IL
Amer. Legion, Zook-Farrington Post 434 **[5556]**, Kingsford Heights, IN
Amer. Legion, Zook-Scott Post 325 **[5835]**, Mooresville, IN
Amer. Legion, Zue-Vandeveer Post 257 **[3715]**, Stonington, IL
Amer. Legion, Zumbrota Post 183 **[13004]**, Zumbrota, MN
Forty and Eight: Voiture 957 **[10205]**, Ypsilanti, MI
Sons of the Amer. Legion, Post 44 **[13583]**, Canton, OH
Amer. Legion, 3 M Post 599 **[12356]**, St. Paul, MN
Amer. Legion, A. E. E. E. W. Post 373 **[15015]**, Delta, OH
Amer. Legion, Aaron Post 788 **[444]**, Carol Stream, IL
Amer. Legion, Aaron Scisinger Post 178 **[4767]**, Garrett, IN
Amer. Legion, Aarvig-Campbell Post 78 **[3118]**, Pontiac, IL
Amer. Legion, Abe Lincoln Post 444 **[4439]**, Dale, IN
Amer. Legion, Abendroth-Connolly Post 282 **[18809]**, Markesan, WI
Amer. Legion, Abner Rude Post 481 **[12675]**, South St. Paul, MN
Amer. Legion, Abraham-Hickok-Wetmore Post 148 **[17555]**, Bagley, WI
Amer. Legion, Abramowicz-Kaczmarczyk-Cwikla Post 547 **[18433]**, Lublin, WI
Amer. Legion, A.C. of Flint Post 366 **[7708]**, Flint, MI
Amer. Legion, A.C. Hansen Post 185 **[12777]**, Tyler, MN
Amer. Legion, Acton-Bunker-Hill Post 220 **[4988]**, Indianapolis, IN
Amer. Legion, Adams-Helwig-Randles Post 162 **[17462]**, Alma Center, WI
Amer. Legion, Adams Post 43 **[4450]**, Decatur, IN
Amer. Legion, Adams Post 146 **[10239]**, Adams, MN
Amer. Legion, Adams Township Post 553 **[16876]**, Toledo, OH
Amer. Legion, Adamson-Norman Post 30 **[10994]**, Fergus Falls, MN
Amer. Legion, Adolph Oiseth Post 333 **[11243]**, Kasson, MN
Amer. Legion, Adolph-Wacek-Patrick-Slattery Post 303 **[20175]**, Winter, WI
Amer. Legion, Advt. Mens Post 38 **[627]**, Chicago, IL
Amer. Legion, Adwell-Garvey Post 180 **[12100]**, Renville, MN
Amer. Legion, Agnew-Shinabarger Post 307 **[16426]**, Pioneer, OH
Amer. Legion, Ahlberg-Weigelt Post 470 **[11248]**, Kelliher, MN
Amer. Legion, Aitkin-Lee Post 86 **[10244]**, Aitkin, MN
Amer. Legion, Akron Post 209 **[13030]**, Akron, OH
Amer. Legion, Al Besemann Post 482 **[10251]**, Albany, MN
Amer. Legion, Al Sirat Grotto Post 392 **[16351]**, Parma, OH
Amer. Legion, Albany Post 167 **[4083]**, Albany, IN
Amer. Legion, Albert Dennis Connell Post 422 **[10671]**, Claremont, MN
Amer. Legion, Albert-Shelby Post 298 **[59]**, Apple River, IL
Amer. Legion, Albert Williams Post 131 **[5560]**, Knox, IN
Amer. Legion, Albertson Esque Post 548 **[19449]**, Phelps, WI
Amer. Legion, Albin Johnson Post 244 **[11853]**, Mountain Lake, MN
Amer. Legion, Albion-Browns Post 590 **[14]**, Albion, IL
Amer. Legion, Albion Post 246 **[4084]**, Albion, IN
Amer. Legion, Alden Post 404 **[10270]**, Alden, MN
Amer. Legion, Alderman-Luce Post 259 **[7027]**, Bronson, MI
Amer. Legion, Alexander Bright Post 87 **[4090]**, Alexandria, IN
Amer. Legion, Alexandria Post 87 **[10272]**, Alexandria, MN
Amer. Legion, Algonac Post 278 **[6598]**, Algonac, MI
Amer. Legion, Algonquin Post 670 **[25]**, Algonquin, IL
Amer. Legion, Algot Johnson Post 69 **[10162]**, Whitehall, MI
Amer. Legion, Alhambra Post 1147 **[28]**, Alhambra, IL
Amer. Legion, All Amer. Post 1776 **[628]**, Chicago, IL
Amer. Legion, Allen-Bevnue Post 354 **[39]**, Alton, IL
Amer. Legion, Allen County Post 499 **[4627]**, Fort Wayne, IN
Amer. Legion, Allen-Myers-Hohn Post 176 **[16689]**, South Charleston, OH
Amer. Legion, Allen Park Post 409 **[6608]**, Allen Park, MI
Amer. Legion, Allen Post 538 **[6606]**, Allen, MI
Amer. Legion, Alliance Post 166 **[13110]**, Alliance, OH
Amer. Legion, Almont Post 479 **[6637]**, Almont, MI
Amer. Legion, Altenberg Post 497 **[1733]**, Franklin Grove, IL
Amer. Legion, Alto Post 528 **[6652]**, Alto, MI
Amer. Legion, Alton Post 126 **[40]**, Alton, IL
Amer. Legion, Alva Courier Post 487 **[588]**, Chester, IL
Amer. Legion, Ambelang-Ebelt-Lau Post 386 **[17718]**, Cascade, WI
Amer. Legion, Amboy Post 429 **[4093]**, Amboy, IN
Amer. Legion, Amer. Slovak Post 367 **[4770]**, Gary, IN
Amer. Legion, Amstutz-Marty Post 256 **[19225]**, Monticello, WI
Amer. Legion, Ancil Geiger Post 226 **[5799]**, Milford, IN
Amer. Legion, And-Quist Post 218 **[12357]**, St. Paul, MN
Amer. Legion, Anderson-Black Post 462 **[11304]**, Laporte, MN
Amer. Legion, Anderson-Claffy Post 109 **[12768]**, Two Harbors, MN
Amer. Legion, Anderson-Good Post 40 **[17565]**, Bangor, WI
Amer. Legion, Anderson Post 318 **[13712]**, Cincinnati, OH
Amer. Legion, Anderson-Sather Post 524 **[20153]**, White Lake, WI
Amer. Legion, Anderson-scroggins Post 460 **[3176]**, Ramsey, IL
Amer. Legion, Anderson-Tongen Post 559 **[11138]**, Hazel Run, MN
Amer. Legion, Andover Post 465 **[50]**, Andover, IL
Amer. Legion, Andrew Borgen Post 75 **[11880]**, New Richland, MN
Amer. Legion, Angola Post 31 **[4123]**, Angola, IN
Amer. Legion, Annandale Post 176 **[10299]**, Annandale, MN
Amer. Legion, Antioch Post 748 **[55]**, Antioch, IL
Amer. Legion, Antrim Post 461 **[13491]**, Cambridge, OH
Amer. Legion, Apple Valley Post 1776 **[10314]**, Apple Valley, MN
Amer. Legion, Arcade-Phalen Post 577 **[12358]**, St. Paul, MN
Amer. Legion, Arch Post 477 **[16128]**, New Holland, OH
Amer. Legion, Archer-Highland Post 698 **[629]**, Chicago, IL
Amer. Legion, Archview Post 1265 **[1532]**, East Carondelet, IL
Amer. Legion, Arcola Post 639 **[60]**, Arcola, IL
Amer. Legion, Arenzville Post 604 **[62]**, Arenzville, IL
Amer. Legion, Argo-Summit Post 735 **[3742]**, Summit, IL
Amer. Legion, Argonne Forest Post 278 **[10524]**, Brandon, MN
Amer. Legion, Argonne Post 32 **[10241]**, Adrian, MN
Amer. Legion, Argonne Post 33 **[16758]**, Steubenville, OH
Amer. Legion, Argonne Post 545 **[16877]**, Toledo, OH
Amer. Legion, Argyle Post 251 **[17536]**, Argyle, WI
Amer. Legion, Armenian Vartan Post 307 **[7244]**, Dearborn, MI
Amer. Legion, Army-Navy-Shaker Post 54 **[14053]**, Cleveland, OH
Amer. Legion, Arndt-Bruley Post 176 **[20150]**, Weyauwega, WI
Amer. Legion, Arnet-Sheldon Post 423 **[11197]**, Houston, MN
Amer. Legion, Arnold-B.-Moll-John-W.-Hazard Post 385 **[9652]**, St. Clair Shores, MI
Amer. Legion, Aroma Park Post 1019 **[85]**, Aroma Park, IL
Amer. Legion, Arthur and Leonard Falldin Post 555 **[11492]**, Minneapolis, MN
Amer. Legion, Arthur Post 479 **[87]**, Arthur, IL
Amer. Legion, Ashton Post 345 **[92]**, Ashton, IL
Amer. Legion, Ashville Community Post 730 **[13190]**, Ashville, OH
Amer. Legion, Astoria Post 25 **[95]**, Astoria, IL
Amer. Legion, Atkins Saw Post 355 **[4989]**, Indianapolis, IN
Amer. Legion, Atlanta Post 201 **[6801]**, Atlanta, MI
Amer. Legion, Attica Post 52 **[4135]**, Attica, IN
Amer. Legion, Attucks-Brooks Post 606 **[12359]**, St. Paul, MN
Amer. Legion, Atwood-Mauck Post 459 **[13469]**, Burton, OH
Amer. Legion, Auburn Post 277 **[102]**, Auburn, IL
Amer. Legion, Audie Johnson Post 211 **[7573]**, East Tawas, MI
Amer. Legion, Audubon Amer. Legion Post 339 **[10346]**, Audubon, MN
Amer. Legion, Auglaize Post 330 **[17088]**, Wapakoneta, OH
Amer. Legion, August Altheide Post 302 **[10394]**, Beardsley, MN
Amer. Legion, August Donner Post 309 **[10402]**, Belview, MN
Amer. Legion, August Mattson Post 71 **[7828]**, Gladstone, MI
Amer. Legion, Austin-Moore Post 415 **[8141]**, Hartland, MI
Amer. Legion, Austin Post 91 **[10350]**, Austin, MN
Amer. Legion, Austintown Memorial Post 301 **[13235]**, Austintown, OH
Amer. Legion Auxiliary of Michigan **[8532]**, Lansing, MI
Amer. Legion Auxiliary of Ohio **[17435]**, Zanesville, OH

Amer. Legion Auxiliary of Wisconsin **[19505]**, Portage, WI
Amer. Legion, Aviation Post 651 **[2875]**, Orland Park, IL
Amer. Legion, Avilla Post 240 **[4150]**, Avilla, IN
Amer. Legion, Avon Lake Post 211 **[13243]**, Avon Lake, OH
Amer. Legion, Avon Post 145 **[4443]**, Danville, IN
Amer. Legion, Avon Post 538 **[10366]**, Avon, MN
Amer. Legion, Baccarat Post 40 **[16527]**, Richwood, OH
Amer. Legion, Bad Axe Post 318 **[6819]**, Bad Axe, MI
Amer. Legion, Bailey-Frey Post 125 **[16713]**, Springfield, OH
Amer. Legion, Bailey-Kinnear Post 197 **[10655]**, Chatfield, MN
Amer. Legion, Bailey-Throne Post 596 **[10963]**, Erskine, MN
Amer. Legion, Bainbridge Post 355 **[10533]**, Brooklyn Center, MN
Amer. Legion, Baltimore Ohio Post 466 **[4990]**, Indianapolis, IN
Amer. Legion, Bank of Am. Post 383 **[1720]**, Fox River Grove, IL
Amer. Legion, Baraboo Post 26 **[17569]**, Baraboo, WI
Amer. Legion, Barberton Post 271 **[13253]**, Barberton, OH
Amer. Legion, Barnesville Post 168 **[13258]**, Barnesville, OH
Amer. Legion, Baroda Community Post 345 **[6831]**, Baroda, MI
Amer. Legion, Barrington Post 158 **[139]**, Barrington, IL
Amer. Legion, Barrus-Mc-Culligh-Stewart Post 393 **[8294]**, Hulbert, MI
Amer. Legion, Barry Post 222 **[155]**, Barry, IL
Amer. Legion, Bartholomew-Whetsel Post 212 **[5651]**, Lapel, IN
Amer. Legion, Bartlett Post 1212 **[158]**, Bartlett, IL
Amer. Legion, Bartley-Johnson-Bentley Post 437 **[13713]**, Cincinnati, OH
Amer. Legion, Bashaw-Roth Post 106 **[6546]**, Worthington, IN
Amer. Legion, Basil Grimes Post 222 **[14814]**, Crooksville, OH
Amer. Legion, Batavia Post 504 **[172]**, Batavia, IL
Amer. Legion, Bates-O'Brien-Howe-Wiegel Post 214 **[17805]**, Darlington, WI
Amer. Legion, Bates Post 560 **[3460]**, Sesser, IL
Amer. Legion, Bay View Post 180 **[18936]**, Milwaukee, WI
Amer. Legion, Bay Village Post 385 **[17227]**, Westlake, OH
Amer. Legion, Bayard Brown Post 337 **[1803]**, Genoa, IL
Amer. Legion, Bayard De Hart Post 13 **[19621]**, Richland Center, WI
Amer. Legion, Baylor Post 152 **[15524]**, Jefferson, OH
Amer. Legion, Beack-Thompson Post 126 **[10722]**, Cosmos, MN
Amer. Legion, Beallsville Post 768 **[13292]**, Beallsville, OH
Amer. Legion, Bear Creek Post 823 **[2474]**, Mendon, IL
Amer. Legion, Bearcat Post 504 **[12106]**, Richfield, MN
Amer. Legion, Beardstown Post 605 **[187]**, Beardstown, IL
Amer. Legion, Beasley-Zalesny Post 112 **[9390]**, Plymouth, MI
Amer. Legion, Beatty-Humphries Post 323 **[10677]**, Clearwater, MN
Amer. Legion, Beaver Post 578 **[16491]**, Quaker City, OH
Amer. Legion, Beavercreek Memorial Post 763 **[13294]**, Beavercreek, OH
Amer. Legion, Beaverville Post 877 **[192]**, Beaverville, IL
Amer. Legion, Becker-Reding Post 702 **[2398]**, Marine, IL
Amer. Legion, Beckett-Kurth Post 257 **[19631]**, Ridgeway, WI
Amer. Legion, Bedford Post 350 **[13303]**, Bedford, OH
Amer. Legion, Beech Grove Post 276 **[4181]**, Beech Grove, IN
Amer. Legion, Behling-Kutchera Post 296 **[17663]**, Brookfield, WI
Amer. Legion, Beisner-Brueggemann-Knop Post 480 **[3699]**, Steeleville, IL
Amer. Legion, Belgium Memorial Post 412 **[17600]**, Belgium, WI
Amer. Legion, Bell Telephone Post 427 **[20097]**, West Allis, WI
Amer. Legion, Bellaire Post 52 **[13308]**, Bellaire, OH
Amer. Legion, Bellaire Post 247 **[6903]**, Bellaire, MI
Amer. Legion, Belle Valley Post 641 **[13317]**, Belle Valley, OH
Amer. Legion, Bellechester Post 598 **[10398]**, Bellchester, MN
Amer. Legion, Belleville Post 58 **[7058]**, Canton, MI
Amer. Legion, Bellevue Post 280 **[6911]**, Bellevue, MI
Amer. Legion, Ben Krueger Post 49 **[11990]**, Pequot Lakes, MN
Amer. Legion, Bendix Aviation Post 284 **[6211]**, South Bend, IN
Amer. Legion, Benson Post 62 **[10432]**, Benson, MN
Amer. Legion, Benson Post 454 **[229]**, Benson, IL
Amer. Legion, Benton Harbor Post 105 **[6916]**, Benton Harbor, MI
Amer. Legion, Berens-Scribner Post 6 **[19780]**, Stevens Point, WI
Amer. Legion, Berg-Hemker-Olson Post 51 **[20135]**, West Salem, WI
Amer. Legion, Berg-Nylund Post 456 **[12647]**, Sebeka, MN
Amer. Legion, Berkeley Post 1016 **[2000]**, Hillside, IL
Amer. Legion, Berkley Post 374 **[6929]**, Berkley, MI
Amer. Legion, Berlin Heights Post 659 **[13352]**, Berlin Heights, OH
Amer. Legion, Bernard A. Bendle Post 294 **[9891]**, Swartz Creek, MI
Amer. Legion, Berne Post 468 **[4186]**, Berne, IN
Amer. Legion, Bernheisel and Riley Post 313 **[9850]**, Springport, MI
Amer. Legion, Berryhill Post 165 **[9021]**, Midland, MI
Amer. Legion, Berwyn Post 422 **[235]**, Berwyn, IL
Amer. Legion, Bethalto Post 214 **[241]**, Bethalto, IL
Amer. Legion, Bethany Post 507 **[242]**, Bethany, IL
Amer. Legion, Bevelhymer-Gilliland Post 400 **[15753]**, Malinta, OH
Amer. Legion, Bever Post 550 **[17950]**, Fall Creek, WI
Amer. Legion, Beverly Hills Post 407 **[2876]**, Orland Park, IL
Amer. Legion, Bexley Post 430 **[14288]**, Columbus, OH
Amer. Legion, Big Four Railway Post 116 **[4991]**, Indianapolis, IN
Amer. Legion, Big Red One Post 1111 **[10240]**, Adams, MN
Amer. Legion, Big Rock Post 529 **[243]**, Big Rock, IL
Amer. Legion, Biggsville Memorial Post 1176 **[244]**, Biggsville, IL
Amer. Legion, Bintzler-Waehler Post 347 **[18426]**, Lomira, WI
Amer. Legion, Birch Run Post 125 **[6956]**, Birch Run, MI
Amer. Legion, Bird Mc Ginnis Post 162 **[15834]**, Marion, OH
Amer. Legion, Bishop Post 1 **[2249]**, Lewistown, IL
Amer. Legion, Bivens-Bonner Post 285 **[8310]**, Inkster, MI
Amer. Legion, Bixby and Hansen Post 171 **[19924]**, Union Grove, WI
Amer. Legion, Black Oak Post 393 **[4771]**, Gary, IN
Amer. Legion, Blackduck Post 372 **[10445]**, Blackduck, MN
Amer. Legion, Blackhawk Post 553 **[18463]**, Madison, WI
Amer. Legion, Blake-Semrad Post 134 **[17647]**, Boscobel, WI
Amer. Legion, Blashe-Peters-Tober Post 456 **[17717]**, Caroline, WI
Amer. Legion, Blennerhassett Post 495 **[13340]**, Belpre, OH
Amer. Legion, Blentlinger-Tournear Post 640 **[2254]**, Liberty, IL
Amer. Legion, Bloedorn-Becker-Jensen Post 126 **[17657]**, Brillion, WI
Amer. Legion, Blue Earth Post 89 **[10495]**, Blue Earth, MN
Amer. Legion, Blue Island Post 50 **[314]**, Blue Island, IL
Amer. Legion, Bluffton Post 382 **[13365]**, Bluffton, OH
Amer. Legion, Bluford Post 1193 **[320]**, Bluford, IL
Amer. Legion, Blumfield Post 229 **[9597]**, Saginaw, MI
Amer. Legion, Blythe-Williams Post 789 **[16002]**, Middletown, OH
Amer. Legion, Bd. of Educ. Post 471 **[359]**, Buffalo Grove, IL
Amer. Legion, Bd. of Trade Post 304 **[630]**, Chicago, IL
Amer. Legion, Boardman Memorial Post 565 **[13370]**, Boardman, OH
Amer. Legion, Bodin-Finstad-Guski Post 86 **[19949]**, Washburn, WI
Amer. Legion, Bolingbrook Post 1288 **[321]**, Bolingbrook, IL
Amer. Legion, Bomsta-Johnson Post 615 **[11284]**, Lake Lillian, MN
Amer. Legion, Bond-Hill-Roselawn Post 427 **[13714]**, Cincinnati, OH
Amer. Legion, Bone Gap Post 1041 **[323]**, Bone Gap, IL
Amer. Legion, Bong-Hofstedt-Douglas-County Post 409 **[19494]**, Poplar, WI
Amer. Legion, Boone Post 77 **[218]**, Belvidere, IL
Amer. Legion, Boswell Post 476 **[4279]**, Boswell, IN
Amer. Legion, Bourbon Post 424 **[4280]**, Bourbon, IN
Amer. Legion, Bowen-Holliday Post 35 **[9921]**, Traverse City, MI
Amer. Legion, Bowen Post 1087 **[330]**, Bowen, IL
Amer. Legion, Bowers-Slusser Post 516 **[14775]**, Columbus Grove, OH
Amer. Legion, Bowling Green Post 45 **[13381]**, Bowling Green, OH
Amer. Legion, Boxrucker-Berry Post 519 **[20200]**, Withee, WI
Amer. Legion, Boyce-Carpenter-Bunce Post 195 **[8409]**, Jonesville, MI
Amer. Legion, Boyle-Hoy Post 379 **[3462]**, Shannon, IL
Amer. Legion, Bradford Post 445 **[331]**, Bradford, IL
Amer. Legion, Bradley-Maberry Post 736 **[1341]**, Danville, IL
Amer. Legion, Bradley Post 766 **[333]**, Bradley, IL
Amer. Legion, Brakeman-King Post 336 **[16331]**, Painesville, OH
Amer. Legion, Brask-Fossum-Janke Post 185 **[18070]**, Grantsburg, WI
Amer. Legion, Brecksville-Excelsior Post 196 **[13407]**, Brecksville, OH
Amer. Legion, Bredlow-Ewing Post 467 **[19375]**, Ontario, WI
Amer. Legion, Brenden-Johnson Post 223 **[11257]**, Kerkhoven, MN
Amer. Legion, Brewer-Tarasco Post 7 **[17253]**, Wickliffe, OH
Amer. Legion, Brewster Post 464 **[10530]**, Brewster, MN
Amer. Legion, Bridgeport Post 62 **[339]**, Bridgeport, IL
Amer. Legion, Bridgeport Post 227 **[13418]**, Bridgeport, OH
Amer. Legion, Bridgman Post 331 **[7002]**, Bridgman, MI
Amer. Legion, Brighton Post 476 **[343]**, Brighton, IL
Amer. Legion, Brilliant Post 573 **[13420]**, Brilliant, OH
Amer. Legion, Brimfield Post 452 **[345]**, Brimfield, IL
Amer. Legion, Broad Ripple Post 3 **[4992]**, Indianapolis, IN
Amer. Legion, Broadview-Hillside Post 626 **[2001]**, Hillside, IL
Amer. Legion, Bronsted-Searl Post 93 **[19908]**, Tomahawk, WI
Amer. Legion, Brook Park Post 610 **[13433]**, Brook Park, OH
Amer. Legion, Brook Post 364 **[4293]**, Brook, IN
Amer. Legion, Brooklyn Post 233 **[16352]**, Parma, OH
Amer. Legion, Brooklyn Post 657 **[1299]**, Compton, IL

Amer. Legion, Broome-Wood Post 292 **[16137]**, New London, OH
Amer. Legion, Browerville Post 293 **[10564]**, Browerville, MN
Amer. Legion, Brown-Dolson Post 113 **[5665]**, Lebanon, IN
Amer. Legion, Brown-Doyle Post 368 **[6396]**, Van Buren, IN
Amer. Legion, Brown-Miller Post 181 **[3415]**, Sandwich, IL
Amer. Legion, Brown-Parfitt Post 43 **[19633]**, Ripon, WI
Amer. Legion, Brown-Selvig Post 212 **[17582]**, Barron, WI
Amer. Legion, Brown Township Post 247 **[4765]**, Friendship, IN
Amer. Legion, Brown and Vernon Post 312 **[6957]**, Birch Run, MI
Amer. Legion, Brown-Webb Post 209 **[9761]**, South Haven, MI
Amer. Legion, Browne-Cavender Post 148 **[8976]**, Mason, MI
Amer. Legion, Brownsburg Lincoln Post 331 **[4302]**, Brownsburg, IN
Amer. Legion, Brunclik-Konop Post 540 **[18192]**, Haugen, WI
Amer. Legion, Bruner-Frehse Post 137 **[9714]**, Saugatuck, MI
Amer. Legion, Brunswick Post 485 **[6162]**, Schererville, IN
Amer. Legion, Buck-Reasoner Post 238 **[8239]**, Holt, MI
Amer. Legion, Buckeye Post 174 **[16253]**, North Star, OH
Amer. Legion, Buckeye Road Post 559 **[16783]**, Strongsville, OH
Amer. Legion, Buckingham-Dermer Post 514 **[17263]**, Willard, OH
Amer. Legion, Budlong District Post 837 **[631]**, Chicago, IL
Amer. Legion, Buehler-Bruggeman-Mantel Post 205 **[10973]**, Fairfax, MN
Amer. Legion, Buehrer-Lauber-Weckesser Post 311 **[13150]**, Archbold, OH
Amer. Legion, Buffalo Post 270 **[10570]**, Buffalo, MN
Amer. Legion, Buffalo Soldier Memorial Post 241 **[2096]**, Joliet, IL
Amer. Legion, Buick Liberty Motor Post 310 **[9892]**, Swartz Creek, MI
Amer. Legion, Burch-Wood Post 121 **[6456]**, Washington, IN
Amer. Legion, Burelbach Post 61 **[11991]**, Perham, MN
Amer. Legion, Burger-Benedict Post 573 **[2453]**, Mc Lean, IL
Amer. Legion, Burhans-Hagedon Post 197 **[8114]**, Harbor Beach, MI
Amer. Legion, Burlington Post 414 **[4307]**, Burlington, IN
Amer. Legion, Burlington Route Post 387 **[4047]**, Woodridge, IL
Amer. Legion, Burriss-Smith Post 396 **[16672]**, Smithfield, OH
Amer. Legion, Burton-Koppang Post 81 **[18828]**, Mauston, WI
Amer. Legion, Burton Post 130 **[7234]**, Davison, MI
Amer. Legion, Burton Woolery Post 18 **[4197]**, Bloomington, IN
Amer. Legion, Buseth-Tusow Post 18 **[11144]**, Henning, MN
Amer. Legion, Bushnell-Prairie-City Post 2004 **[2418]**, Marseilles, IL
Amer. Legion, Bus. and Professional Mens Post 332 **[11493]**, Minneapolis, MN
Amer. Legion, Bus. and Professional Mens Post 372 **[9389]**, Pleasant Ridge, MI
Amer. Legion, Bus. and Professional Mens Post 450 **[10544]**, Brooklyn Park, MN
Amer. Legion, Bus. and Professional Post 530 **[8533]**, Lansing, MI
Amer. Legion, Buss Waters Post 299 **[5861]**, Muncie, IN
Amer. Legion, Bussong-Mersinger Post 665 **[3398]**, St. Jacob, IL
Amer. Legion, Butler-Lindner Post 218 **[18194]**, Hayward, WI
Amer. Legion, Byesville Post 116 **[13477]**, Byesville, OH
Amer. Legion, Byron Center Post 292 **[7040]**, Byron Center, MI
Amer. Legion, Byron Cox Post 72 **[4424]**, Crawfordsville, IN
Amer. Legion, C.-Adams-R-Stierlen Post 311 **[10961]**, Elysian, MN
Amer. Legion, C. Walter Larson Post 378 **[11145]**, Herman, MN
Amer. Legion, Cadillac Post 333 **[8092]**, Grosse Pointe Woods, MI
Amer. Legion, Cadiz Post 34 **[13479]**, Cadiz, OH
Amer. Legion, Cahokia Memorial Post 784 **[385]**, Cahokia, IL
Amer. Legion, Caledonia Memorial Post 305 **[7053]**, Caledonia, MI
Amer. Legion, Caledonia Post 401 **[13487]**, Caledonia, OH
Amer. Legion, Calhoun Post 231 **[11494]**, Minneapolis, MN
Amer. Legion, Calhoun Post 636 **[1935]**, Hardin, IL
Amer. Legion, Call-Payton Post 285 **[6280]**, Spencer, IN
Amer. Legion, Calumet Memorial Post 330 **[391]**, Calumet City, IL
Amer. Legion, Calumet Park Post 1156 **[395]**, Calumet Park, IL
Amer. Legion, Calumet Post 99 **[4772]**, Gary, IN
Amer. Legion, Calvary Post 276 **[9570]**, Royal Oak, MI
Amer. Legion, Calvin-Knuth Post 5 **[12990]**, Worthington, MN
Amer. Legion, Cambria Post 401 **[17708]**, Cambria, WI
Amer. Legion, Cambridge Post 84 **[13492]**, Cambridge, OH
Amer. Legion, Cambridge Post 417 **[397]**, Cambridge, IL
Amer. Legion, Camden Post 413 **[4311]**, Camden, IN
Amer. Legion, Cameron-Butler Post 130 **[2737]**, Norridge, IL
Amer. Legion, Cameron-Ellis Post 242 **[17296]**, Winchester, OH
Amer. Legion, Cammack Post 327 **[5862]**, Muncie, IN
Amer. Legion, Camp Chase Post 98 **[14289]**, Columbus, OH
Amer. Legion, Camp Jackson Post 112 **[4305]**, Brownstown, IN
Amer. Legion, Camp Point Post 238 **[398]**, Camp Point, IL
Amer. Legion, Campbell Hill Post 1096 **[399]**, Campbell Hill, IL
Amer. Legion, Campbell-Richmond Post 63 **[7158]**, Clarkston, MI
Amer. Legion, Campbell-Williams Post 258 **[10682]**, Clinton, MN
Amer. Legion, Canfield Post 177 **[13527]**, Canfield, OH
Amer. Legion, Cannata-Mcdonough-Curcuru Post 994 **[1450]**, Des Plaines, IL
Amer. Legion, Canton Post 44 **[13542]**, Canton, OH
Amer. Legion, Canton Post 188 **[7059]**, Canton, MI
Amer. Legion, Capital City Post 12 **[8534]**, Lansing, MI
Amer. Legion, Carl Mount Post 104 **[6308]**, Terre Haute, IN
Amer. Legion, Carleton Mc Nicholas Post 523 **[8924]**, Marenisco, MI
Amer. Legion, Carleton Post 66 **[7077]**, Carleton, MI
Amer. Legion, Carlson-Alguire-Hougland Post 312 **[19432]**, Peshtigo, WI
Amer. Legion, Carlton Post 538 **[19901]**, Tisch Mills, WI
Amer. Legion, Carmel Post 155 **[4315]**, Carmel, IN
Amer. Legion, Carmi Post 224 **[442]**, Carmi, IL
Amer. Legion, Carney-Nadeau Post 487 **[7078]**, Carney, MI
Amer. Legion, Carpenter-Clash Post 363 **[8492]**, Kingsford, MI
Amer. Legion, Carr-Bailey Post 519 **[16041]**, Mineral City, OH
Amer. Legion, Carrier Mills Post 1140 **[1937]**, Harrisburg, IL
Amer. Legion, Carroll Post 428 **[13603]**, Carrollton, OH
Amer. Legion, Carrollton Post 114 **[457]**, Carrollton, IL
Amer. Legion, Carson City Post 380 **[7088]**, Carson City, MI
Amer. Legion, Casimer Pulaski Post 78 **[4471]**, East Chicago, IN
Amer. Legion, Cass County Post 60 **[5687]**, Logansport, IN
Amer. Legion, Cassel Post 257 **[4760]**, Fremont, IN
Amer. Legion, Castle Williams Post 105 **[1373]**, Decatur, IL
Amer. Legion, Caufield Post 434 **[13364]**, Bloomville, OH
Amer. Legion, Cave-Dahl Post 240 **[17558]**, Baldwin, WI
Amer. Legion, Caya-Bunders Post 68 **[19527]**, Prairie Du Chien, WI
Amer. Legion, C.C. Upton Post 91 **[7794]**, Fremont, MI
Amer. Legion, C.D. Burton Post 808 **[632]**, Chicago, IL
Amer. Legion, Cecil Ser. Post 255 **[7228]**, Croswell, MI
Amer. Legion, Cedar Lake Post 261 **[4335]**, Cedar Lake, IN
Amer. Legion, Cedarville Memorial Post 1224 **[484]**, Cedarville, IL
Amer. Legion, Celina Post 210 **[13609]**, Celina, OH
Amer. Legion, Celtic Post 372 **[4993]**, Indianapolis, IN
Amer. Legion, Central Park Post 1028 **[633]**, Chicago, IL
Amer. Legion, Central Post 132 **[4994]**, Indianapolis, IN
Amer. Legion, Cerro Gordo Post 117 **[492]**, Cerro Gordo, IL
Amer. Legion, Chadwick Post 739 **[493]**, Chadwick, IL
Amer. Legion, Chagrin Falls Post 383 **[13628]**, Chagrin Falls, OH
Amer. Legion, Challenger Post 521 **[12875]**, West St. Paul, MN
Amer. Legion, Chalmers Post 268 **[4343]**, Chalmers, IN
Amer. Legion, Chambers-Hautman-Budde Post 534 **[13715]**, Cincinnati, OH
Amer. Legion, Champaign Post 24 **[498]**, Champaign, IL
Amer. Legion, Champlin Post 600 **[10641]**, Champlin, MN
Amer. Legion, Chandler Post 694 **[559]**, Chandlerville, IL
Amer. Legion, Chanhassen Post 580 **[10645]**, Chanhassen, MN
Amer. Legion, Chapin Post 878 **[562]**, Chapin, IL
Amer. Legion, Chapman-Belter Post 4 **[17550]**, Athens, WI
Amer. Legion, Chardon Post 167 **[13640]**, Chardon, OH
Amer. Legion, Charles Andrews Post 460 **[13618]**, Centerburg, OH
Amer. Legion, Charles Claessens Post 305 **[12856]**, Waverly, MN
Amer. Legion, Charles De Crane Post 724 **[99]**, Atkinson, IL
Amer. Legion, Charles Forrest Post 288 **[6398]**, Veedersburg, IN
Amer. Legion, Charles Foster Blaker Post 202 **[4309]**, Butler, IN
Amer. Legion, Charles Harker Post 143 **[4291]**, Bristol, IN
Amer. Legion, Charles Hofer Post 522 **[16779]**, Strasburg, OH
Amer. Legion, Charles Mundell Post 216 **[5796]**, Middletown, IN
Amer. Legion, Charles Sturdevant Post 46 **[6356]**, Tipton, IN
Amer. Legion, Charles Walter Reid Post 258 **[3872]**, Virginia, IL
Amer. Legion, Charleston Memorial Post 1999 **[563]**, Charleston, IL
Amer. Legion, Charlton-Polan Post 233 **[8515]**, Lake Orion, MI
Amer. Legion, Chaseburg Post 202 **[17735]**, Chaseburg, WI
Amer. Legion, Chatham Post 759 **[577]**, Chatham, IL
Amer. Legion, Chauncey-Barr-Rex-Boyer Post 192 **[4483]**, Edwardsport, IN
Amer. Legion, Chauncey Curtis Smith Post 118 **[6559]**, Addison, MI

Amer. Legion, Chesaning Post 212 **[7144]**, Chesaning, MI
Amer. Legion, Chesapeake Memorial Post 640 **[13647]**, Chesapeake, OH
Amer. Legion, Chester Bird Post 523 **[11058]**, Golden Valley, MN
Amer. Legion, Chesterfield Post 695 **[634]**, Chicago, IL
Amer. Legion, Chesterland Post 780 **[16332]**, Painesville, OH
Amer. Legion, Chesterton Post 170 **[4349]**, Chesterton, IN
Amer. Legion, Chestnut-Beason Post 848 **[191]**, Beason, IL
Amer. Legion, Chicago Firemen's Post 667 **[635]**, Chicago, IL
Amer. Legion, Chicago Heights Post 131 **[1247]**, Chicago Heights, IL
Amer. Legion, Chicago Nisei Post 1183 **[636]**, Chicago, IL
Amer. Legion, Chicago Police Post 207 **[2935]**, Palos Heights, IL
Amer. Legion, Chicago Post 170 **[637]**, Chicago, IL
Amer. Legion, Chief Okemos Post 269 **[8145]**, Haslett, MI
Amer. Legion, Chief Pontiac Post 377 **[9414]**, Pontiac, MI
Amer. Legion, Childs-Demeray Post 222 **[10044]**, Vermontville, MI
Amer. Legion, Chillicothe Post 9 **[1254]**, Chillicothe, IL
Amer. Legion, Chinatown Post 1003 **[638]**, Chicago, IL
Amer. Legion, Chipilly-131st-Infantry Post 310 **[159]**, Bartlett, IL
Amer. Legion, Chisago City Post 272 **[10658]**, Chisago City, MN
Amer. Legion, Chrisman Post 477 **[1257]**, Chrisman, IL
Amer. Legion, Christie-De-Parcq Post 406 **[12360]**, St. Paul, MN
Amer. Legion, Christopher Columbus Post 354 **[8890]**, Madison Heights, MI
Amer. Legion, Christopher Post 528 **[1258]**, Christopher, IL
Amer. Legion, Chrysler A.B.D. Post 242 **[8103]**, Hamtramck, MI
Amer. Legion, Cicero Post 96 **[1259]**, Cicero, IL
Amer. Legion, Cincinnati Gas and Elec. Post 410 **[13716]**, Cincinnati, OH
Amer. Legion, Cissna Park Post 527 **[1265]**, Cissna Park, IL
Amer. Legion, Clara City Post 485 **[10668]**, Clara City, MN
Amer. Legion, Clare Burt Post 248 **[8496]**, Laingsburg, MI
Amer. Legion, Clare-Farwell Post 558 **[7678]**, Farwell, MI
Amer. Legion, Clarence-Bean-Warren-George Post 67 **[18402]**, Lake Mills, WI
Amer. Legion, Clarence Clofer Post 259 **[12664]**, Shorewood, MN
Amer. Legion, Clarence Wiles Post 222 **[4613]**, Flora, IN
Amer. Legion, Clarissa Post 213 **[10672]**, Clarissa, MN
Amer. Legion, Clark-Carrington Post 1031 **[2497]**, Mineral, IL
Amer. Legion, Clark County Post 90 **[2423]**, Marshall, IL
Amer. Legion, Clark-Ellis Post 152 **[8861]**, Lowell, MI
Amer. Legion, Clark-Gurgel Post 206 **[20204]**, Wonewoc, WI
Amer. Legion, Clark Post 362 **[16714]**, Springfield, OH
Amer. Legion, Claude Earl Post 887 **[2052]**, Hoyleton, IL
Amer. Legion, Claude Robinson Post 899 **[389]**, Cairo, IL
Amer. Legion, Clay City Post 225 **[4370]**, Clay City, IN
Amer. Legion, Clay City Post 840 **[1267]**, Clay City, IL
Amer. Legion, Clay County Post 2 **[4282]**, Brazil, IN
Amer. Legion, Clay County Post 14 **[1705]**, Flora, IL
Amer. Legion, Clayton Murray Post 159 **[8887]**, Mackinaw City, MI
Amer. Legion, Clayton Post 286 **[1268]**, Clayton, IL
Amer. Legion, Clearing Post 600 **[639]**, Chicago, IL
Amer. Legion, Cleary-Miller Post 115 **[17937]**, Elroy, WI
Amer. Legion, Cleveland Police Post 438 **[14054]**, Cleveland, OH
Amer. Legion, Cleveland Post 2 **[14055]**, Cleveland, OH
Amer. Legion, Clifford Garbison Post 356 **[4866]**, Hamlet, IN
Amer. Legion, Clifton Post 385 **[1269]**, Clifton, IL
Amer. Legion, Clifton Post 421 **[15181]**, Fairview Park, OH
Amer. Legion, Climaxscotts Post 465 **[7169]**, Climax, MI
Amer. Legion, Clinton Post 140 **[4371]**, Clinton, IN
Amer. Legion, Clough-Lambrix Post 389 **[9494]**, Riverview, MI
Amer. Legion, Cloverland Post 82 **[7607]**, Escanaba, MI
Amer. Legion, Clyde Johnston Post 230 **[9057]**, Mohawk, MI
Amer. Legion, Coal City Post 796 **[1275]**, Coal City, IL
Amer. Legion, Coal Valley Post 1248 **[1278]**, Coal Valley, IL
Amer. Legion, Cobb-Trygstad-Anderson Post 397 **[8245]**, Holton, MI
Amer. Legion, Cobb-Williams-Nehiba Post 222 **[11155]**, Hibbing, MN
Amer. Legion, Cobden Post 259 **[1281]**, Cobden, IL
Amer. Legion, Coe-Lamb Post 421 **[3126]**, Port Byron, IL
Amer. Legion, Cokato Post 209 **[10695]**, Cokato, MN
Amer. Legion, Col. A.L. Brodie Post 1437 **[3953]**, Westchester, IL
Amer. Legion, Colburn Post 286 **[12622]**, Sanborn, MN
Amer. Legion, Coldwater Post 52 **[7195]**, Coldwater, MI
Amer. Legion, Cole-Briggs Post 48 **[7870]**, Grand Ledge, MI
Amer. Legion, Colfax Post 439 **[4377]**, Colfax, IN
Amer. Legion, Collins-Tasch Post 399 **[5821]**, Monterey, IN
Amer. Legion, Collinwood Post 759 **[16675]**, Solon, OH
Amer. Legion, Coloma Post 362 **[7204]**, Coloma, MI
Amer. Legion, Colonel Crawford Post 181 **[13460]**, Bucyrus, OH
Amer. Legion, Colonel Jennings Post 715 **[15221]**, Fort Jennings, OH
Amer. Legion, Columbia City Post 98 **[4378]**, Columbia City, IN
Amer. Legion, Columbia Post 581 **[1297]**, Columbia, IL
Amer. Legion, Columbus Post 24 **[4388]**, Columbus, IN
Amer. Legion, Columbus Post 82 **[14290]**, Columbus, OH
Amer. Legion, Colvin-Dale Post 527 **[16020]**, Milan, OH
Amer. Legion, Commemorative Post 268 **[15013]**, Delphos, OH
Amer. Legion, Commodore Barry Post 256 **[236]**, Berwyn, IL
Amer. Legion, Commodore Denig Post 83 **[16601]**, Sandusky, OH
Amer. Legion, Commonwealth Edison Post 118 **[640]**, Chicago, IL
Amer. Legion, Community Memorial Post 635 **[15530]**, Jewell, OH
Amer. Legion, Community Post 279 **[15100]**, Elmore, OH
Amer. Legion, Community Post 375 **[19249]**, Mukwonago, WI
Amer. Legion, Community Post 403 **[16295]**, Olmsted Falls, OH
Amer. Legion, Community Post 429 **[2356]**, Lovington, IL
Amer. Legion, Community Post 666 **[15924]**, Maynard, OH
Amer. Legion, Community Post 1166 **[3188]**, Reynolds, IL
Amer. Legion, Comrade Whitehall Post 490 **[14291]**, Columbus, OH
Amer. Legion, Concord-Pulaski-Memorial Post 81 **[7216]**, Concord, MI
Amer. Legion, Conn-Weissenberger Post 587 **[16878]**, Toledo, OH
Amer. Legion, Conrad Post 179 **[6035]**, Petersburg, IN
Amer. Legion, Conrad-Wager-Keene Post 164 **[9054]**, Millington, MI
Amer. Legion, Constitution Post 224 **[10178]**, Wixom, MI
Amer. Legion, Constitution Post 326 **[214]**, Bellwood, IL
Amer. Legion, Cook-Fuller Post 70 **[19388]**, Oshkosh, WI
Amer. Legion, Cook-Nelson Post 20 **[9415]**, Pontiac, MI
Amer. Legion, Coon Rapids Post No. 334 Social Club **[10707]**, Coon Rapids, MN
Amer. Legion, Coon Valley Post 116 **[17784]**, Coon Valley, WI
Amer. Legion, Coral Hall Post 539 **[2145]**, Kansas, IL
Amer. Legion, Cordova Post 1033 **[1300]**, Cordova, IL
Amer. Legion, Cornell Post 928 **[2235]**, Lemont, IL
Amer. Legion, Cornell-Syverson Post 17 **[11984]**, Pel Rapids, MN
Amer. Legion, Corning Post 327 **[14788]**, Corning, OH
Amer. Legion, Cossette-Woitkielewicz Post 58 **[18229]**, Hurley, WI
Amer. Legion, Cottonwood Post 503 **[10730]**, Cottonwood, MN
Amer. Legion, Cottrell-Boylan Post 253 **[13146]**, Antwerp, OH
Amer. Legion, Coughlin-Sanford Post 277 **[19263]**, Necedah, WI
Amer. Legion, Courthouse Post 310 **[11495]**, Minneapolis, MN
Amer. Legion, Courtney-Carr-Milner Post 19 **[18176]**, Hartford, WI
Amer. Legion, Courtney Lawrence Post 202 **[15938]**, Medina, OH
Amer. Legion, Courts-Fussnecker Post 367 **[16535]**, Ripley, OH
Amer. Legion, Cowle Post 151 **[14780]**, Conneaut, OH
Amer. Legion, Craig-Bennett Post 103 **[1270]**, Clinton, IL
Amer. Legion, Craig-Reed Post 1181 **[1263]**, Cisco, IL
Amer. Legion, Craig-Schlosser Post 31 **[20068]**, Wauwatosa, WI
Amer. Legion, Crain and Ottman Post 207 **[17935]**, Elmwood, WI
Amer. Legion, Crawford County Post 84 **[5722]**, Marengo, IN
Amer. Legion, Crawford-Hale Post 95 **[3846]**, Vandalia, IL
Amer. Legion, Crawford Post 1038 **[2127]**, Kane, IL
Amer. Legion, Creston Post 497 **[14812]**, Creston, OH
Amer. Legion, Cretton-Tutas Post 136 **[19322]**, Niagara, WI
Amer. Legion, Creve Coeur Post 1234 **[1539]**, East Peoria, IL
Amer. Legion, Crispus Attucks Post 59 **[8486]**, Kentwood, MI
Amer. Legion, Crispus Attucks Post 1268 **[641]**, Chicago, IL
Amer. Legion, Crouse-Engles Post 357 **[2213]**, Lanark, IL
Amer. Legion, Cuff-Patricki Post 174 **[18193]**, Hawkins, WI
Amer. Legion, Cultice-Ward Post 6 **[16715]**, Springfield, OH
Amer. Legion, Curry-Ainsworth Post 168 **[18056]**, Glenwood City, WI
Amer. Legion, D. W. K. Post 110 **[19310]**, New Lisbon, WI
Amer. Legion, D. W. M. D. Post 407 **[15035]**, Doylestown, OH
Amer. Legion, Daffron-Presswood Post 2504 **[3089]**, Pinckneyville, IL
Amer. Legion, Dahlberg-Makris Post 7 **[19596]**, Rhinelander, WI
Amer. Legion, Dahlgren-Ettestad Post 499 **[11921]**, Northome, MN
Amer. Legion, Dakota-Richford Post 163 **[20063]**, Wautoma, WI

Amer. Legion, Dale L. Binkley Memorial Post 289 [13439], Brookville, OH
Amer. Legion, Dan Patch Post 643 [12640], Savage, MN
Amer. Legion, Danforth Post 367 [1340], Danforth, IL
Amer. Legion, Daniel Post 864 [3265], Rockford, IL
Amer. Legion, Daniel Waters Cassard Post 208 [7891], Grand Rapids, MI
Amer. Legion, Danner-Madsen Post 663 [1785], Gardner, IL
Amer. Legion, Darius-Girenas Post 271 [642], Chicago, IL
Amer. Legion, Darling-Gunderson Post 341 [17627], Birnamwood, WI
Amer. Legion, Darlington Post 302 [4448], Darlington, IN
Amer. Legion, Dary-Paulsen Post 440 [17768], Clinton, WI
Amer. Legion, Daugherty-Larsen Post 446 [19776], Steuben, WI
Amer. Legion, Davenport-Lang Post 414 [17651], Bowler, WI
Amer. Legion, David Humphrey Daniel Post 427 [3427], Saybrook, IL
Amer. Legion, David Johnston Memorial Post 283 [16417], Pickerington, OH
Amer. Legion, David Parrish Post 296 [4628], Fort Wayne, IN
Amer. Legion, David-Wisted-Zenith-City Post 28 [10797], Duluth, MN
Amer. Legion, Davis-Busby Post 776 [483], Catlin, IL
Amer. Legion, Davis-Darrow-Meyer Post 112 [10943], Elk River, MN
Amer. Legion, Davis-Kerber Post 653 [1283], Colfax, IL
Amer. Legion, Davis-Porter Post 140 [18901], Merrillan, WI
Amer. Legion, Dayton Post 5 [14843], Dayton, OH
Amer. Legion, Dayton Rogers Post 531 [10757], Dayton, MN
Amer. Legion, Daytons Bluff Post 515 [10758], Dayton, MN
Amer. Legion, De-Gree-Fleisch Post 125 [12711], Stewart, MN
Amer. Legion, De Kalb Post 66 [1426], DeKalb, IL
Amer. Legion, De Kalb Post 97 [4136], Auburn, IN
Amer. Legion, De Witt Post 379 [7460], DeWitt, MI
Amer. Legion, Deal-Ridgeway Post 289 [10167], Williamsburg, MI
Amer. Legion, Dean Horton Navy Post 108 [16879], Toledo, OH
Amer. Legion, Deceased Veterans Post 975 [1492], Dowell, IL
Amer. Legion, Deer Creek Post 1276 [1411], Deer Creek, IL
Amer. Legion, Deerfield [1415], Deerfield, IL
Amer. Legion, Deerfield Post 392 [7289], Deerfield, MI
Amer. Legion, Deerfield Post 713 [14977], Deerfield, OH
Amer. Legion, Delafield Post 196 [17821], Delafield, WI
Amer. Legion, Delano Post 377 [10768], Delano, MN
Amer. Legion, Delavan Post 382 [1446], Delavan, IL
Amer. Legion, Delaware Post 19 [5863], Muncie, IN
Amer. Legion, Dell-Hogan Post 123 [11354], Luverne, MN
Amer. Legion, Dellroy Post 475 [16656], Sherrodsville, OH
Amer. Legion, Demotte Post 440 [4457], Demotte, IN
Amer. Legion, Deneen-Mc-Cabe Post 432 [18173], Hammond, WI
Amer. Legion, Denton-Schreiner Post 582 [1641], Erie, IL
Amer. Legion Dept. Of Illinois [256], Bloomington, IL
Amer. Legion, Dept. of St. Railways Post 394 [7212], Columbus, MI
Amer. Legion Dept. of Wisconsin [19506], Portage, WI
Amer. Legion, Des Plaines Post 36 [1451], Des Plaines, IL
Amer. Legion, Deshler Post 316 [15020], Deshler, OH
Amer. Legion, Desrosier-Windnagle Post 562 [6926], Bergland, MI
Amer. Legion, Detroit News Post 519 [7279], Dearborn Heights, MI
Amer. Legion, Detroit Police Post 161 [7172], Clinton Township, MI
Amer. Legion, Deutschle-Annick-Memorial Post 888 [14995], Delaware, OH
Amer. Legion, Devereaux Post 141 [8269], Howell, MI
Amer. Legion, Devine-Menting Post 525 [19454], Phlox, WI
Amer. Legion, Devins-Teehan Post 237 [17995], Footville, WI
Amer. Legion, Dewey Mc Glynn Post 280 [6075], Remington, IN
Amer. Legion, Dewitt McConnell Post 235 [15320], Girard, OH
Amer. Legion, Dexter Post 557 [7470], Dexter, MI
Amer. Legion, Diamond Island Post 335 [7097], Cassopolis, MI
Amer. Legion, Diemer-Dobmeyer Post 172 [16033], Miller City, OH
Amer. Legion, Diesen-Winkler Post 325 [1807], Germantown, IL
Amer. Legion, Dieterich Post 628 [1472], Dieterich, IL
Amer. Legion, Dignam-Whitmore Post 526 [15146], Fairborn, OH
Amer. Legion, Dillon-Johnson-Anderson Post 154 [19204], Mondovi, WI
Amer. Legion, Dimondale Potterville Post 272 [9458], Potterville, MI
Amer. Legion, Dixon Post 12 [1474], Dixon, IL
Amer. Legion, Dobson-Johnson Post 142 [17640], Blanchardville, WI
Amer. Legion, Doe-Wah-Jack Post 563 [7477], Dowagiac, MI
Amer. Legion, Dolven-Wilcox Post 313 [12735], Swanville, MN
Amer. Legion, Don Gentile Post 532 [14292], Columbus, OH
Amer. Legion, Don Varnas Post 986 [2792], Oak Lawn, IL
Amer. Legion, Doney-Degrave Post 342 [18416], Lena, WI
Amer. Legion, Donovan Post 633 [1491], Donovan, IL
Amer. Legion, Dorchester Chaplains Post 387 [7303], Detroit, MI
Amer. Legion, Dorman-Dunn Post 547 [643], Chicago, IL
Amer. Legion, Dornblaser Post 203 [1806], Georgetown, IL
Amer. Legion, Doss-Malone Post 1200 [2539], Monee, IL
Amer. Legion, Douglas County Post 27 [3791], Tuscola, IL
Amer. Legion, Dover Post 205 [15026], Dover, OH
Amer. Legion, Dovray Post 632 [10364], Avoca, MN
Amer. Legion, Downey-Pogue-Scott Post 590 [15507], Ironton, OH
Amer. Legion, Downing Winterling Post 232 [17843], Downing, WI
Amer. Legion, Draeger-Fencil Post 260 [17820], Deerfield, WI
Amer. Legion, Draza Mihailovich Post 1946 [644], Chicago, IL
Amer. Legion, Dreier-Bushee-Vanderboom Post 156 [19323], North Fond Du Lac, WI
Amer. Legion, Drew Webster Post 39 [16454], Pomeroy, OH
Amer. Legion, Drews-Bleser Post 88 [18774], Manitowoc, WI
Amer. Legion, Dublin Post 800 [17203], Westerville, OH
Amer. Legion, Dubois County Post 147 [5525], Jasper, IN
Amer. Legion, Duggar Post 553 [2494], Milledgeville, IL
Amer. Legion, Duhm-Masch Post 332 [17629], Black Creek, WI
Amer. Legion, Dundee-Carpentersville Post 679 [1518], Dundee, IL
Amer. Legion, Duoos Bros. Post 630 [10534], Brooklyn Center, MN
Amer. Legion, Duppler-Smith Post 460 [17601], Belleville, WI
Amer. Legion, Durand Post 124 [7489], Durand, MI
Amer. Legion, Durkee-Seager Post 550 [9307], Onsted, MI
Amer. Legion, Durwin-Schantz Post 138 [15377], Hamilton, OH
Amer. Legion, Dwight Post 486 [1525], Dwight, IL
Amer. Legion, Dyrdal-Prolow Post 249 [12688], Spring Grove, MN
Amer. Legion, Eagan Post 594 [10863], Eagan, MN
Amer. Legion, Eagle Lake Post 617 [10878], Eagle Lake, MN
Amer. Legion, Eagle Post 509 [11177], Hopkins, MN
Amer. Legion, Eagletown Post 120 [9885], Suttons Bay, MI
Amer. Legion, Earl Foust Post 73 [15228], Fostoria, OH
Amer. Legion, Earl Gladfelter Post 268 [9047], Milan, MI
Amer. Legion, Earl Green Post 344 [13598], Carey, OH
Amer. Legion, Earl James Howe Post 298 [11012], Foley, MN
Amer. Legion, Earl Park Post 455 [4470], Earl Park, IN
Amer. Legion, Earle Ray Post 173 [12756], Tracy, MN
Amer. Legion, East Alton Post 794 [1529], East Alton, IL
Amer. Legion, East Chicago Allied Post 369 [4472], East Chicago, IN
Amer. Legion, East Detroit Roseville Post 261 [9563], Roseville, MI
Amer. Legion, East Dubuque Post 787 [1533], East Dubuque, IL
Amer. Legion, East Grand Forks Post 157 [10881], East Grand Forks, MN
Amer. Legion, East Hazel Crest Post 1139 [2043], Homewood, IL
Amer. Legion, East Moline Post 227 [1536], East Moline, IL
Amer. Legion, East Peoria Post 983 [1540], East Peoria, IL
Amer. Legion, East St. Louis Post 53 [480], Caseyville, IL
Amer. Legion, East St. Louis Post 2505 [1548], East St. Louis, IL
Amer. Legion, Easton Post 569 [10886], Easton, MN
Amer. Legion, Eau Claire Post 353 [7585], Eau Claire, MI
Amer. Legion, E.B. Rinehart Post 754 [16649], Shauck, OH
Amer. Legion, Ebert-Wunrow Post 475 [17540], Arpin, WI
Amer. Legion, Eck-Ary-Douglas-Dickey Post 353 [13145], Ansonia, OH
Amer. Legion, Ecklund-Holmstrom Post 117 [12740], Thief River Falls, MN
Amer. Legion, Ecorse-Roy-B.-Salliotte Post 319 [7588], Ecorse, MI
Amer. Legion, Eden Valley Post 381 [10903], Eden Valley, MN
Amer. Legion, Edina Post 471 [11178], Hopkins, MN
Amer. Legion, Edinburg Post 233 [4479], Edinburgh, IN
Amer. Legion, Edison Park Post 541 [645], Chicago, IL
Amer. Legion, Edon Post 662 [15095], Edon, OH
Amer. Legion, Edward Born Post 343 [11923], Norwood, MN
Amer. Legion, Edward Gill Post 204 [10887], Echo, MN
Amer. Legion, Edward Schultz Post 697 [2214], Lansing, IL
Amer. Legion, Edwards-Foye Post 534 [18838], McFarland, WI
Amer. Legion, Edwardsburg Post 365 [7589], Edwardsburg, MI
Amer. Legion, Edwardsville Post 199 [1556], Edwardsville, IL
Amer. Legion, Edwin Corpin Post 905 [2162], Kincaid, IL
Amer. Legion, Eel River Post 286 [5986], North Manchester, IN
Amer. Legion, Effingham Post 120 [1569], Effingham, IL
Amer. Legion, Efton James Post 206 [7098], Cassopolis, MI
Amer. Legion, Ehret-Parsel Post 447 [16448], Plymouth, OH

Amer. Legion, Eick-Sankey Post 302 **[19350]**, Oconto Falls, WI
Amer. Legion, Eiffert-Kirchenbauer Post 354 **[10674]**, Clear Lake, MN
Amer. Legion, E.J. Stover and A.D. Wagner Post 85 **[6934]**, Berrien Springs, MI
Amer. Legion, Ekstedt-Hurr Post 390 **[45]**, Altona, IL
Amer. Legion, El Paso Post 59 **[1575]**, El Paso, IL
Amer. Legion, Elberfeld Post 351 **[4484]**, Elberfeld, IN
Amer. Legion, Elburn Post 630 **[1578]**, Elburn, IL
Amer. Legion, Eldorado Post 169 **[1581]**, Eldorado, IL
Amer. Legion, Eldred Post 1135 **[1582]**, Eldred, IL
Amer. Legion, Elec. Post 228 **[18937]**, Milwaukee, WI
Amer. Legion, Elec. Post 769 **[646]**, Chicago, IL
Amer. Legion, Electro-Motive-Diesel Post 992 **[2031]**, Hodgkins, IL
Amer. Legion, Elefson-Zeuske Post 117 **[19678]**, Shawano, WI
Amer. Legion, Elgin Post 57 **[1584]**, Elgin, IL
Amer. Legion, Elgin Post 573 **[10940]**, Elgin, MN
Amer. Legion, Eli Denison Post 467 **[16564]**, Rutland, OH
Amer. Legion, Eli Lilly Post 374 **[4995]**, Indianapolis, IN
Amer. Legion, Eliza Post 1971 **[2681]**, New Boston, IL
Amer. Legion, Elk Grove Village Memorial Post 216 **[1605]**, Elk Grove Village, IL
Amer. Legion, Elkhart Post 616 **[1616]**, Elkhart, IL
Amer. Legion, Ellet Post 794 **[13031]**, Akron, OH
Amer. Legion, Ellingson-Brenden Post 376 **[12251]**, Rothsay, MN
Amer. Legion, Elliott Keller Post 1078 **[1520]**, Dunlap, IL
Amer. Legion, Ellsworth Meinke Post 1983 **[3429]**, Schaumburg, IL
Amer. Legion, Ellsworth Post 1244 **[1617]**, Ellsworth, IL
Amer. Legion, Elmer Dade Memorial Post 699 **[15615]**, Leavittsburg, OH
Amer. Legion, Elmer Johnson Post 118 **[13130]**, Amherst, OH
Amer. Legion, Elmwood Post 638 **[1629]**, Elmwood, IL
Amer. Legion, Elwood Monroe Swenson Post 445 **[11240]**, Karlstad, MN
Amer. Legion, Elyria Post 12 **[15104]**, Elyria, OH
Amer. Legion, Emden Post 506 **[1636]**, Emden, IL
Amer. Legion, Emery Whisler Post 607 **[2363]**, Mackinaw, IL
Amer. Legion, Emil Jacob Post 117 **[8907]**, Manchester, MI
Amer. Legion, Emil King Post 318 **[11037]**, Fulda, MN
Amer. Legion, Emmet Mannix Post 345 **[15224]**, Fort Recovery, OH
Amer. Legion, Engels-Wilson Post 564 **[11042]**, Ghent, MN
Amer. Legion, Enrico Fermi Post 1266 **[647]**, Chicago, IL
Amer. Legion, Epworth Post 90 **[13354]**, Bethesda, OH
Amer. Legion, Erickson-Rose Post 637 **[12883]**, Whalan, MN
Amer. Legion, Erickson-Strom Post 186 **[11935]**, Olivia, MN
Amer. Legion, Erk Cottrell Post 140 **[15355]**, Greenville, OH
Amer. Legion, Ernest Aselton Post 118 **[12857]**, Wayzata, MN
Amer. Legion, Erwin March Post 64 **[12670]**, Slayton, MN
Amer. Legion, Erwin Martensen Post 164 **[1284]**, Colfax, IL
Amer. Legion, Erwin Prieskorn Post 46 **[6661]**, Ann Arbor, MI
Amer. Legion, Escanaba River Post 115 **[7829]**, Gladstone, MI
Amer. Legion, Eshelman-Talley-Doye Post 1191 **[3139]**, Prophetstown, IL
Amer. Legion, Essexville-Hampton Post 249 **[7623]**, Essexville, MI
Amer. Legion, Essman-Schroeder Post 20 **[19955]**, Waterford, WI
Amer. Legion, Eubanks-Arneson Post 87 **[19612]**, Rice Lake, WI
Amer. Legion, Euclid Post 343 **[15138]**, Euclid, OH
Amer. Legion, Euclid Post 539 **[10966]**, Euclid, MN
Amer. Legion, Eugene Drill Post 606 **[1965]**, Hebron, IL
Amer. Legion, Eugene Hughes Post 319 **[5817]**, Monon, IN
Amer. Legion, Eugene Pate Post 265 **[4520]**, Evansville, IN
Amer. Legion, Eugene Wilson Post 346 **[12099]**, Remer, MN
Amer. Legion, Eureka Post 466 **[1642]**, Eureka, IL
Amer. Legion, Eva Casstevens Post 535 **[196]**, Beecher City, IL
Amer. Legion, Evans Post 329 **[11881]**, New Ulm, MN
Amer. Legion, Evans-Swanson Post 123 **[8484]**, Kent City, MI
Amer. Legion, Evanston Post 42 **[1647]**, Evanston, IL
Amer. Legion, Evansville Post 1172 **[1677]**, Evansville, IL
Amer. Legion, Eveland-Trainor Post 433 **[17581]**, Barneveld, WI
Amer. Legion, Everett H. Hale Post 68 **[12693]**, Spring Valley, MN
Amer. Legion, Everette Burdette Post 187 **[4521]**, Evansville, IN
Amer. Legion, Evergreen Park Post 854 **[1678]**, Evergreen Park, IL
Amer. Legion, Evzones Post 1039 **[2002]**, Hillside, IL
Amer. Legion, Ewen Post 41 **[7630]**, Ewen, MI
Amer. Legion, Ewert-Kline Post 720 **[2865]**, Orangeville, IL
Amer. Legion, Ex-Cell-O Post 440 **[8828]**, Livonia, MI
Amer. Legion, Eyota Post 551 **[10972]**, Eyota, MN
Amer. Legion, Ezra Barrows Post 338 **[11286]**, Lake Wilson, MN
Amer. Legion, Fairfax Post 554 **[13717]**, Cincinnati, OH
Amer. Legion, Fairfield Post 11 **[15596]**, Lancaster, OH
Amer. Legion, Fairmont City Post 961 **[1690]**, Fairmont City, IL
Amer. Legion, Fairmount Post 313 **[4592]**, Fairmount, IN
Amer. Legion, Fairview Heights Post 978 **[1693]**, Fairview Heights, IL
Amer. Legion, Fairview Post 738 **[15182]**, Fairview Park, OH
Amer. Legion, Fallerans Post 121 **[19]**, Aledo, IL
Amer. Legion, Farina Post 411 **[1699]**, Farina, IL
Amer. Legion, Farmer Post 137 **[15186]**, Farmer, OH
Amer. Legion, Farmington Post 140 **[1701]**, Farmington, IL
Amer. Legion, Fed. Employees Post 496 **[7709]**, Flint, MI
Amer. Legion, Fed. Post 203 **[18938]**, Milwaukee, WI
Amer. Legion, Feeney-Bennett Post 128 **[16001]**, Middleport, OH
Amer. Legion, Fellenzer Post 48 **[6130]**, Rockville, IN
Amer. Legion, Feneley-Mcneil-Nesbit Post 290 **[7605]**, Engadine, MI
Amer. Legion, Fengestad-Solie Post 200 **[12941]**, Winger, MN
Amer. Legion, Fennville Post 434 **[7680]**, Fennville, MI
Amer. Legion, Ferdinand Post 124 **[4595]**, Ferdinand, IN
Amer. Legion, Fertile Post 238 **[11007]**, Fertile, MN
Amer. Legion, Fickbohm-Hissem Post 193 **[1760]**, Galena, IL
Amer. Legion, Fidelity Post 296 **[10950]**, Ellendale, MN
Amer. Legion, Fiebirch Post 397 **[17063]**, Vermilion, OH
Amer. Legion, Fields-Myers-Smith-Dittenber Post 256 **[9696]**, St. Louis, MI
Amer. Legion, Fife Lake Post 219 **[7699]**, Fife Lake, MI
Amer. Legion, Fifield Post 532 **[17961]**, Fifield, WI
Amer. Legion, Fifteen Grand Post 583 **[12218]**, Roseville, MN
Amer. Legion, Filipino Post 509 **[648]**, Chicago, IL
Amer. Legion, Fingerson-Rule Post 463 **[17773]**, Cobb, WI
Amer. Legion, Fire Fighters Post 339 **[14056]**, Cleveland, OH
Amer. Legion, Firelands Memorial Post 706 **[16225]**, North Fairfield, OH
Amer. Legion, Firestone Memorial Post 449 **[13032]**, Akron, OH
Amer. Legion, First Div. Cantigny Post 556 **[3978]**, Wheaton, IL
Amer. Legion, First Natl. Post 985 **[2293]**, Lisle, IL
Amer. Legion, First United Methodist Church Post 38 **[6470]**, West Lafayette, IN
Amer. Legion, Fischer-Sollis Post 137 **[2767]**, O Fallon, IL
Amer. Legion, Fisher Body Lansing Post 183 **[8535]**, Lansing, MI
Amer. Legion, Fisher Body Post 342 **[7710]**, Flint, MI
Amer. Legion, Fisher-Lechnir-Wall Post 252 **[17860]**, Eastman, WI
Amer. Legion, Fitchville Memorial Post 729 **[16226]**, North Fairfield, OH
Amer. Legion, Fitzsimmons Post 225 **[1902]**, Greenfield, IL
Amer. Legion, Flanagan-Dorn Post 294 **[18180]**, Hartland, WI
Amer. Legion, Flanagan Post 456 **[1703]**, Flanagan, IL
Amer. Legion, Fletcher-Pechacek Post 121 **[19639]**, River Falls, WI
Amer. Legion, Floriano-Stecker Post 340 **[8163]**, Hermansville, MI
Amer. Legion, Floyd Becker Post 209 **[5832]**, Moores Hill, IN
Amer. Legion, Floyd Marshall Post 412 **[6147]**, Russiaville, IN
Amer. Legion, Flushing Amer. Legion Post 283 **[7762]**, Flushing, MI
Amer. Legion, Flushing Post 366 **[15219]**, Flushing, OH
Amer. Legion, Flynn Brown Post 455 **[1308]**, Cowden, IL
Amer. Legion, Flynn-Eick Post 451 **[1637]**, Emington, IL
Amer. Legion, Fohl-Martin Post 483 **[17461]**, Allenton, WI
Amer. Legion, Foody-Cornwell Post 95 **[17365]**, Xenia, OH
Amer. Legion, Ford Motor Company Post 173 **[7245]**, Dearborn, MI
Amer. Legion, Ford Wagar Memorial Post 447 **[10183]**, Wyandotte, MI
Amer. Legion, Forest Lake Post 225 **[11014]**, Forest Lake, MN
Amer. Legion, Forest Park Post 414 **[1709]**, Forest Park, IL
Amer. Legion, Forest Post 67 **[16660]**, Shreve, OH
Amer. Legion, Forrest Ballard Post 723 **[2492]**, Milford, IL
Amer. Legion, Forrest-Gunderson-Klevgard Post 264 **[18051]**, Gilmanton, WI
Amer. Legion, Forrest Lewis Post 266 **[10097]**, Wayland, MI
Amer. Legion, Forreston Post 308 **[1716]**, Forreston, IL
Amer. Legion, Fort Custer Post 257 **[6843]**, Battle Creek, MI
Amer. Legion, Fort Dearborn Post 364 **[7246]**, Dearborn, MI
Amer. Legion, Fort Harrison Post 40 **[6309]**, Terre Haute, IN
Amer. Legion, Fort Laurens Post 190 **[13376]**, Bolivar, OH
Amer. Legion, Fort Loramie Post 355 **[15223]**, Fort Loramie, OH
Amer. Legion, Fort Mc Kinley Memorial Post 613 **[16992]**, Trotwood, OH
Amer. Legion, Fort Wayne Post 47 **[4629]**, Fort Wayne, IN
Amer. Legion, Fortville Post 391 **[4731]**, Fortville, IN
Amer. Legion, Foss-Agin-Meyer Post 185 **[13008]**, Ada, OH
Amer. Legion, Foster-Bernhardt Post 373 **[12758]**, Trimont, MN
Amer. Legion, Foucault-Funke Post 444 **[6829]**, Baraga, MI

Amer. Legion, Fountain City Post 56 **[18002]**, Fountain City, WI
Amer. Legion, Fowler Post 57 **[4734]**, Fowler, IN
Amer. Legion, Fox-River-Geneva Post 75 **[1791]**, Geneva, IL
Amer. Legion, Francis-Bergin-Paul-Nieman Post 225 **[19723]**, Shell Lake, WI
Amer. Legion, Francis Pohlman Post 685 **[356]**, Brussels, IL
Amer. Legion, Frank Courtney Post 22 **[5682]**, Linton, IN
Amer. Legion, Frank Feia Post 211 **[11175]**, Holdingford, MN
Amer. Legion, Frank Heinzel Post 254 **[12635]**, Sauk Rapids, MN
Amer. Legion, Frank Horetski Post 499 **[9425]**, Port Austin, MI
Amer. Legion, Frank Kray Post 455 **[10698]**, Cold Spring, MN
Amer. Legion, Frank Lund Post 159 **[11934]**, Oklee, MN
Amer. Legion, Frankenmuth Post 150 **[7778]**, Frankenmuth, MI
Amer. Legion, Frankfort-Mokena Post 2000 **[2505]**, Mokena, IL
Amer. Legion, Franklin D. Roosevelt Post 560 **[13507]**, Campbell, OH
Amer. Legion, Franklin D. Roosevelt Post 923 **[649]**, Chicago, IL
Amer. Legion, Franklin Park Post 974 **[1735]**, Franklin Park, IL
Amer. Legion, Franklin Post 1 **[13191]**, Ashville, OH
Amer. Legion, Franklin Post 205 **[4746]**, Franklin, IN
Amer. Legion, Franklin Post 1089 **[1732]**, Franklin, IL
Amer. Legion, Fraser-Nelson Post 613 **[12006]**, Pine River, MN
Amer. Legion, Fraser Post 243 **[9743]**, Shelby Township, MI
Amer. Legion, Fred-W.-Strong-Donald-W.-Wolf Post 234 **[8135]**, Hart, MI
Amer. Legion, Fred Zeplin Post 1005 **[650]**, Chicago, IL
Amer. Legion, Fredericksburg Memorial Post 651 **[15241]**, Fredericksburg, OH
Amer. Legion, Freedom Post 172 **[19324]**, North Freedom, WI
Amer. Legion, Freedom Post 183 **[16393]**, Pemberville, OH
Amer. Legion, Freeman Spur Post 1273 **[1743]**, Freeman Spur, IL
Amer. Legion, Freeport Post 139 **[1744]**, Freeport, IL
Amer. Legion, Friedrichs-Mueller-Norgaard Post 149 **[17924]**, Elkhart Lake, WI
Amer. Legion, Fuhrman-Finnegan Post 350 **[19589]**, Reedsburg, WI
Amer. Legion, Fulton-Banta Post 291 **[4420]**, Covington, IN
Amer. Legion, Fulton Post 402 **[1757]**, Fulton, IL
Amer. Legion, Funkhouser Post 8 **[4522]**, Evansville, IN
Amer. Legion, Furniture City Post 258 **[7892]**, Grand Rapids, MI
Amer. Legion, Furo-Heinen Post 281 **[18278]**, Junction City, WI
Amer. Legion, G. Chandler Bond Post 275 **[6563]**, Adrian, MI
Amer. Legion, G.A. Leonard Norberg Post 63 **[11107]**, Hallock, MN
Amer. Legion, Gage Park Post 959 **[651]**, Chicago, IL
Amer. Legion, Gahanna Post 797 **[15257]**, Gahanna, OH
Amer. Legion, Galloway Post 799 **[14293]**, Columbus, OH
Amer. Legion, Galvin-Struckmeyer Post 248 **[17788]**, Cottage Grove, WI
Amer. Legion, Garden Post 545 **[7808]**, Garden, MI
Amer. Legion, Gardnerneihardt Post 463 **[9759]**, South Boardman, MI
Amer. Legion, Garfield Heights **[15301]**, Garfield Heights, OH
Amer. Legion, Garfield Heights Post 304 **[15801]**, Maple Heights, OH
Amer. Legion, Garfield Memorial Post 566 **[13033]**, Akron, OH
Amer. Legion, Garfield Park Post 88 **[4996]**, Indianapolis, IN
Amer. Legion, Garland-Tompkins Post 399 **[9300]**, Old Mission, MI
Amer. Legion, Garnett-Foch Post 684 **[1889]**, Grayslake, IL
Amer. Legion, Garrett-Baldridge Post 725 **[4029]**, Windsor, IL
Amer. Legion, Garrett-Riest Post 503 **[16658]**, Shiloh, OH
Amer. Legion, Garrettsville Post 32 **[16495]**, Ravenna, OH
Amer. Legion, Gary Post 505 **[11039]**, Gary, MN
Amer. Legion, Gaston Post 387 **[4789]**, Gaston, IN
Amer. Legion, Gateway Post 421 **[10023]**, Unionville, MI
Amer. Legion, Gedig Post 314 **[12970]**, Winthrop, MN
Amer. Legion, Gem Post 937 **[3491]**, Smithton, IL
Amer. Legion, Gen. Ike Eisenhower Post 98 **[652]**, Chicago, IL
Amer. Legion, Gen. C. Pulaski Post 86 **[1452]**, Des Plaines, IL
Amer. Legion, General-Schwengel-Seagram Post 807 **[2957]**, Park Ridge, IL
Amer. Legion, Genoa-De-Soto Post 246 **[18033]**, Genoa, WI
Amer. Legion, Genoa Post 324 **[15311]**, Genoa, OH
Amer. Legion, George Bergem Post 489 **[12780]**, Underwood, MN
Amer. Legion, George Call Post 124 **[15307]**, Geneva, OH
Amer. Legion, George Puckett Post 264 **[8904]**, Mancelona, MI
Amer. Legion, George Washington Post 88 **[7634]**, Farmington, MI
Amer. Legion, George William Benjamin Post 791 **[2749]**, Northbrook, IL
Amer. Legion, Gerald Pitts Post 473 **[6833]**, Barryton, MI
Amer. Legion, Germantown, Post 1 **[18037]**, Germantown, WI
Amer. Legion, Geroux Post 11 **[10052]**, Wakefield, MI
Amer. Legion, Getchel-Nelson Post 210 **[20027]**, Waupun, WI
Amer. Legion, Gibb Post 588 **[3092]**, Piper City, IL
Amer. Legion, Gilbert Davis Post 157 **[4356]**, Churubusco, IN
Amer. Legion, Gilbertson-Rude Post 526 **[11996]**, Peterson, MN
Amer. Legion, Giles-Luce Post 364 **[20172]**, Winneconne, WI
Amer. Legion, Gillen Post 33 **[4164]**, Bedford, IN
Amer. Legion, Gilmore-Stensrud Post 552 **[11030]**, Freeborn, MN
Amer. Legion, Giltz-Brown Post 341 **[16276]**, Oakwood, OH
Amer. Legion, Gingrich-Poince Post 487 **[17188]**, West Milton, OH
Amer. Legion, Girard-Horrocks Post 37 **[8314]**, Ionia, MI
Amer. Legion, Gislason-Richter Post 402 **[19952]**, Washington Island, WI
Amer. Legion, Gittens-Leidel Post 595 **[11262]**, La Crescent, MN
Amer. Legion, Gittings-Sandine Post 297 **[1338]**, Dallas City, IL
Amer. Legion, Gladstone Post 777 **[653]**, Chicago, IL
Amer. Legion, Gladwin County Post 171 **[7832]**, Gladwin, MI
Amer. Legion, Glen Ellyn Post 3 **[1825]**, Glen Ellyn, IL
Amer. Legion, Glen Hill Post 287 **[7104]**, Cedar Springs, MI
Amer. Legion, Glen Owens Post 14 **[6030]**, Peru, IN
Amer. Legion, Glen Park Post 214 **[5763]**, Merrillville, IN
Amer. Legion, Glencoe Post 95 **[11047]**, Glencoe, MN
Amer. Legion, Glencoe Post 632 **[15325]**, Glencoe, OH
Amer. Legion, Glendale Post 805 **[654]**, Chicago, IL
Amer. Legion, Glenmoor Post 736 **[15075]**, East Liverpool, OH
Amer. Legion, Glenn Maker Post 1160 **[1252]**, Chicago Ridge, IL
Amer. Legion, Glenville Post 264 **[11050]**, Glenville, MN
Amer. Legion, Glidewell-Yelton Post 1230 **[1964]**, Hazel Dell, IL
Amer. Legion, Gnadenhutten Post 154 **[15328]**, Gnadenhutten, OH
Amer. Legion, Godfrey Anderson Post 43 **[9859]**, Stephenson, MI
Amer. Legion, Godfrey Post 2506 **[1873]**, Godfrey, IL
Amer. Legion, Goetz St. Louis Post 522 **[18220]**, Hubertus, WI
Amer. Legion, Gold Star Post 505 **[18939]**, Milwaukee, WI
Amer. Legion, Gold Star Post 676 **[1524]**, Durand, IL
Amer. Legion, Gold Star Post 1102 **[3766]**, Tinley Park, IL
Amer. Legion, Goldstrand-Beadle Post 371 **[12207]**, Roosevelt, MN
Amer. Legion, Gonvick Post 304 **[11067]**, Gonvick, MN
Amer. Legion, Gopher Post 440 **[11496]**, Minneapolis, MN
Amer. Legion, Goshen Post 30 **[4792]**, Goshen, IN
Amer. Legion, Gosz-Novak Post 199 **[19593]**, Reedsville, WI
Amer. Legion, Granada Post 319 **[11072]**, Granada, MN
Amer. Legion, Grand Blanc Post 413 **[7841]**, Grand Blanc, MI
Amer. Legion, Grand Marais Post 413 **[11073]**, Grand Marais, MN
Amer. Legion, Granger Post 151 **[4807]**, Granger, IN
Amer. Legion, Grant Park Star Post 295 **[1887]**, Grant Park, IL
Amer. Legion, Grant Post 202 **[213]**, Bellflower, IL
Amer. Legion, Granville Post 180 **[1888]**, Granville, IL
Amer. Legion, Granville Post 398 **[15341]**, Granville, OH
Amer. Legion, Grassold-Schmidlkofer Post 125 **[17740]**, Chilton, WI
Amer. Legion, Gray-Wachter-Murphy Post 229 **[19234]**, Mount Hope, WI
Amer. Legion, Grayling Post 106 **[8057]**, Grayling, MI
Amer. Legion, Grayslake Post 659 **[1890]**, Grayslake, IL
Amer. Legion, Green-Hill Post 397 **[10786]**, Dilworth, MN
Amer. Legion, Green Isle Post 408 **[11097]**, Green Isle, MN
Amer. Legion, Green Oak Post 757 **[2793]**, Oak Lawn, IL
Amer. Legion, Green-Rock-Colona Post 1233 **[1293]**, Colona, IL
Amer. Legion, Greenawalt-Flaherty Post 42 **[7117]**, Charlotte, MI
Amer. Legion, Greendale Post 416 **[18149]**, Greendale, WI
Amer. Legion, Greening-Buelow Post 437 **[18835]**, Mazomanie, WI
Amer. Legion, Greenville Post 282 **[1905]**, Greenville, IL
Amer. Legion, Greenwood Post 252 **[4848]**, Greenwood, IN
Amer. Legion, Gresham-Crutchley Post 341 **[100]**, Atlanta, IL
Amer. Legion, Gresham Post 390 **[18166]**, Gresham, WI
Amer. Legion, Gresham Post 603 **[1264]**, Cisne, IL
Amer. Legion, Gridley Post 218 **[1910]**, Gridley, IL
Amer. Legion, Griggsville Post 213 **[1912]**, Griggsville, IL
Amer. Legion, Grobengieser-Fischer Post 512 **[33]**, Altamont, IL
Amer. Legion, Grosse Ile Post 75 **[8073]**, Grosse Ile, MI
Amer. Legion, Grosse Pointe Post 303 **[7304]**, Detroit, MI
Amer. Legion, Grover Sheets Post 111 **[4268]**, Bluffton, IN
Amer. Legion, Groves-Walker Post 346 **[7635]**, Farmington, MI
Amer. Legion, Gully Post 603 **[11104]**, Gully, MN
Amer. Legion, Gunder Austad Post 22 **[12070]**, Red Lake Falls, MN
Amer. Legion, Gunderson and Gilbertson Post 507 **[19192]**, Mindoro, WI
Amer. Legion, Gurnee Post 771 **[1913]**, Gurnee, IL

Amer. Legion, Gustav Berg Post 81 **[11118]**, Harmony, MN
Amer. Legion, Guth Bros. Post 111 **[13718]**, Cincinnati, OH
Amer. Legion, Guy Baird Post 554 **[437]**, Carlinville, IL
Amer. Legion, Guy Stanton Post 240 **[6969]**, Blanchard, MI
Amer. Legion, Haack-Good Post 496 **[10441]**, Bigelow, MN
Amer. Legion, Hackensack Post 202 **[11106]**, Hackensack, MN
Amer. Legion, Hacker-Gebke Post 976 **[157]**, Bartelso, IL
Amer. Legion, Haderer-Eineke Post 680 **[1929]**, Hampshire, IL
Amer. Legion, Hagberg-Hamlin Post 45 **[1784]**, Galva, IL
Amer. Legion, Hales Corners Memorial Post 299 **[18168]**, Hales Corners, WI
Amer. Legion, Halker-Flege Post 69 **[16506]**, Reading, OH
Amer. Legion, Hall-Adkins Post 134 **[14030]**, Circleville, OH
Amer. Legion, Hall-Dewinter Post 145 **[9230]**, Norway, MI
Amer. Legion, Ham Lake Post 2000 **[10294]**, Andover, MN
Amer. Legion, Hamilton-Harris Post 447 **[19940]**, Viola, WI
Amer. Legion, Hamilton Post 629 **[1927]**, Hamilton, IL
Amer. Legion, Hamline Post 418 **[12361]**, St. Paul, MN
Amer. Legion, Hamm-Miller Post 145 **[18020]**, Fredonia, WI
Amer. Legion, Hammond Post 16 **[4868]**, Hammond, IN
Amer. Legion, Hammond-Schmit Post 55 **[18217]**, Hortonville, WI
Amer. Legion Hammond Victory Post 168 **[4869]**, Hammond, IN
Amer. Legion, Hammondsville Post 742 **[15404]**, Hammondsville, OH
Amer. Legion, Hamon Gray Post 83 **[5594]**, La Porte, IN
Amer. Legion, Hamtramck Falcon Post 455 **[8104]**, Hamtramck, MI
Amer. Legion, Hancock Post 119 **[4829]**, Greenfield, IN
Amer. Legion, Hanley-Ariss-Millin Post 5 **[19428]**, Patch Grove, WI
Amer. Legion, Hanna Post 472 **[6365]**, Union Mills, IN
Amer. Legion, Hannahville Potawatomi Post 116 **[8124]**, Harris, MI
Amer. Legion, Hannan-Colvin Post 180 **[8288]**, Hudson, MI
Amer. Legion, Hanover-Horton Post 270 **[8113]**, Hanover, MI
Amer. Legion, Hanover Post 764 **[16165]**, Newark, OH
Amer. Legion, Hansel Roberts Post 248 **[5643]**, Lagro, IN
Amer. Legion, Hansen-Hayes Post 178 **[11464]**, Milaca, MN
Amer. Legion, Hanson-Anderson Post 361 **[12935]**, Willow River, MN
Amer. Legion, Hanson-Hatlestad Post 544 **[11954]**, Ostrander, MN
Amer. Legion, Hanson-Kennedy Post 1079 **[11]**, Albany, IL
Amer. Legion, Hanson-Lien Post 368 **[18209]**, Hixton, WI
Amer. Legion, Hanson-Maki Post 506 **[18238]**, Iron River, WI
Amer. Legion, Hanson Mc Fee Post 61 **[6200]**, Shoals, IN
Amer. Legion, Hanson Park Post 1177 **[655]**, Chicago, IL
Amer. Legion, Harding-Hall-Darrington Post 357 **[17583]**, Bay City, WI
Amer. Legion, Harding-Olk-Craidge Post 18 **[6875]**, Bay City, MI
Amer. Legion, Harley-Davidson Post 400 **[20069]**, Wauwatosa, WI
Amer. Legion, Harmeyer Post 343 **[4933]**, Holland, IN
Amer. Legion, Harmon-Harris Post 314 **[17652]**, Boyceville, WI
Amer. Legion, Harold Kripisch Post 96 **[5758]**, Medaryville, IN
Amer. Legion, Harold Washington Post 1987 **[656]**, Chicago, IL
Amer. Legion, Harper Woods Post 99 **[8120]**, Harper Woods, MI
Amer. Legion, Harr-Reese Post 160 **[13416]**, Brewster, OH
Amer. Legion, Harris Post 139 **[11121]**, Harris, MN
Amer. Legion, Harrison-Jones Post 223 **[18206]**, Hillsboro, WI
Amer. Legion, Harrison Post 123 **[4417]**, Corydon, IN
Amer. Legion, Harrison Post 404 **[8125]**, Harrison, MI
Amer. Legion, Harry Carpenter Post 428 **[3128]**, Potomac, IL
Amer. Legion, Harry Fogle Post 274 **[3228]**, Rochester, IL
Amer. Legion, Harry Ray Post 65 **[6085]**, Richmond, IN
Amer. Legion, Harry Riddle Post 448 **[2498]**, Minier, IL
Amer. Legion, Harter-Williams Post 536 **[15319]**, Gilboa, OH
Amer. Legion, Hartman-Lammers Post 286 **[19376]**, Oostburg, WI
Amer. Legion, Hartsburg Post 1146 **[1944]**, Hartsburg, IL
Amer. Legion, Harvey Stunkard Post 530 **[3475]**, Sidell, IL
Amer. Legion, Harwood Post 5 **[2097]**, Joliet, IL
Amer. Legion, Haslee-Doebert-Schmidt Post 261 **[18148]**, Greenbush, WI
Amer. Legion, Hassel Briese Post 473 **[12104]**, Rice, MN
Amer. Legion, Hatley Post 471 **[18191]**, Hatley, WI
Amer. Legion, Haubstadt Post 194 **[4905]**, Haubstadt, IN
Amer. Legion, Haug-Hammer Post 508 **[10747]**, Dalton, MN
Amer. Legion, Havana Post 138 **[1958]**, Havana, IL
Amer. Legion, Havlik-Koltes-Thaden Post 503 **[17803]**, Dane, WI
Amer. Legion, Hawley-Dieckhoff Post 33 **[19265]**, Neenah, WI
Amer. Legion, Hazel Crest Post 398 **[1962]**, Hazel Crest, IL
Amer. Legion, Heath-Perkins Post 51 **[12001]**, Pine City, MN
Amer. Legion, Heath Post 771 **[16166]**, Newark, OH
Amer. Legion, Hebron Post 285 **[15415]**, Hebron, OH
Amer. Legion, Hedrick-Brandt Post 23 **[5552]**, Kentland, IN
Amer. Legion, Heesaker-Brown Post 230 **[17812]**, De Pere, WI
Amer. Legion, Heightshillcrest Post 104 **[16690]**, South Euclid, OH
Amer. Legion, Heiland Post 446 **[13143]**, Anna, OH
Amer. Legion, Hellenic Post 100 **[9744]**, Shelby Township, MI
Amer. Legion, Hellenic Post 129 **[11497]**, Minneapolis, MN
Amer. Legion, Hellenic Post 343 **[2738]**, Norridge, IL
Amer. Legion, Hellenic Post 453 **[15183]**, Fairview Park, OH
Amer. Legion, Heminger-Jones Post 504 **[9329]**, Otter Lake, MI
Amer. Legion, Henderson County Post 765 **[2322]**, Lomax, IL
Amer. Legion, Henderson-Lewis Post 545 **[12686]**, Spicer, MN
Amer. Legion, Hendricks County Post 118 **[4444]**, Danville, IN
Amer. Legion, Henrizi-Schneider Post 382 **[18868]**, Menomonee Falls, WI
Amer. Legion, Henry M. Guttormson Post 40 **[11301]**, Lanesboro, MN
Amer. Legion, Henry Post 323 **[1968]**, Henry, IL
Amer. Legion, Henry Sollie Post 10 **[11269]**, Lake Benton, MN
Amer. Legion, Henryville Post 105 **[4908]**, Henryville, IN
Amer. Legion, Herbert K. Kellam Post 224 **[11152]**, Heron Lake, MN
Amer. Legion, Herrin Prairie Post 645 **[1972]**, Herrin, IL
Amer. Legion, Herscher Post 795 **[1975]**, Herscher, IL
Amer. Legion, Hesley Jensen Post 491 **[10391]**, Bayport, MN
Amer. Legion, Hess-Eastman Post 174 **[8791]**, Lawrence, MI
Amer. Legion, H.F. Hortz Post 415 **[3464]**, Sheffield, IL
Amer. Legion, Hice-Shutes Post 170 **[9913]**, Three Rivers, MI
Amer. Legion, Hickerson Post 432 **[357]**, Buckley, IL
Amer. Legion, Hicks-Olson Post 424 **[245]**, Blandinsville, IL
Amer. Legion, Higby-Oglan-Soerens Post 345 **[18208]**, Hingham, WI
Amer. Legion, Highland Memorial Post 180 **[4910]**, Highland, IN
Amer. Legion, Highland Park Post 145 **[1986]**, Highland Park, IL
Amer. Legion, Highwood Post 501 **[1994]**, Highwood, IL
Amer. Legion, Hill-Gazette Post 143 **[6812]**, Auburn Hills, MI
Amer. Legion, Hill-Palmer Post 561 **[2385]**, Manito, IL
Amer. Legion, Hillestad-Borgeson Post 410 **[11146]**, Herman, MN
Amer. Legion, Hills Post 399 **[11168]**, Hills, MN
Amer. Legion, Hillsdale Post 1144 **[1999]**, Hillsdale, IL
Amer. Legion, Hillside Post 863 **[2003]**, Hillside, IL
Amer. Legion, Hinek-Hertel-Krupka Post 468 **[18917]**, Milladore, WI
Amer. Legion, Hinkins-Moody Post 453 **[17603]**, Belmont, WI
Amer. Legion, Hinsdale Post 250 **[2012]**, Hinsdale, IL
Amer. Legion, Hiter-Wene Post 1049 **[3936]**, Weldon, IL
Amer. Legion, Hochstedler Post 318 **[6509]**, Westfield, IN
Amer. Legion, Hoffman Post 393 **[11173]**, Hoffman, MN
Amer. Legion, Hogaj-Francisco Post 516 **[18826]**, Mason, WI
Amer. Legion, Hogberg-Gerszewski Post 353 **[10333]**, Argyle, MN
Amer. Legion, Hokah Post 498 **[11174]**, Hokah, MN
Amer. Legion, Holien-Thompson Post 252 **[11443]**, Maynard, MN
Amer. Legion, Holland Post 646 **[15456]**, Holland, OH
Amer. Legion, Holland-Swenson Post 434 **[11143]**, Hendrum, MN
Amer. Legion, Hollandale Post 510 **[18212]**, Hollandale, WI
Amer. Legion, Holmes Post 192 **[16034]**, Millersburg, OH
Amer. Legion, Holte-Grygla-Fourtown Post 162 **[11102]**, Grygla, MN
Amer. Legion, Holthaus-Kampwerth Post 1227 **[193]**, Beckemeyer, IL
Amer. Legion, Holtz-Hirst Post 288 **[3495]**, South Beloit, IL
Amer. Legion, Homer Cameron Post 342 **[6141]**, Rossville, IN
Amer. Legion, Homer Dahringer Post 281 **[3919]**, Waukegan, IL
Amer. Legion, Homer Lawson Post 653 **[17125]**, Washington Court House, OH
Amer. Legion, Homer and Lee Parkinson Post 170 **[19194]**, Mineral Point, WI
Amer. Legion, Homer Post 290 **[2040]**, Homer, IL
Amer. Legion, Homer Weiss Post 494 **[16804]**, Sugarcreek, OH
Amer. Legion, Homer Wing Post 172 **[9499]**, Rochester, MI
Amer. Legion, Homewood Post 483 **[2044]**, Homewood, IL
Amer. Legion, Honored Seven Post 740 **[16524]**, Richmond, OH
Amer. Legion, Hope Post 229 **[4935]**, Hope, IN
Amer. Legion, Hopedale Post 682 **[15466]**, Hopedale, OH
Amer. Legion, Hopedale Post 1157 **[2051]**, Hopedale, IL

Amer. Legion, Hopland-Moen Post 459 **[17920]**, Eleva, WI
Amer. Legion, Horicon Post 157 **[18213]**, Horicon, WI
Amer. Legion, Hornickel Post 379 **[4486]**, Elizabeth, IN
Amer. Legion, Hosford-Chase Post 32 **[18880]**, Menomonie, WI
Amer. Legion, Houghton-Higgins-Lake Post 245 **[9463]**, Prudenville, MI
Amer. Legion, Houghton Post 80 **[8985]**, Mass City, MI
Amer. Legion, Howard-Donalds-Richard-Hylkema Post 137 **[19915]**, Turtle Lake, WI
Amer. Legion, Howard Post 145 **[11199]**, Howard Lake, MN
Amer. Legion, Howe-Paff Post 37 **[17921]**, Elk Mound, WI
Amer. Legion, Howland Post 700 **[17095]**, Warren, OH
Amer. Legion, Hubbard Post 51 **[15469]**, Hubbard, OH
Amer. Legion, Hubbard Post 336 **[11895]**, Nielsville, MN
Amer. Legion, Huber Heights Post 200 **[15472]**, Huber Heights, OH
Amer. Legion, Hudson Motor Post 357 **[9564]**, Roseville, MI
Amer. Legion, Hudsonville Post 329 **[8402]**, Jenison, MI
Amer. Legion, Huerter-Wilmette Post 46 **[4016]**, Wilmette, IL
Amer. Legion, Huffman-Hammond-Rando Post 502 **[7598]**, Elsie, MI
Amer. Legion, Hugh Allen Mc Innes Post 74 **[9195]**, Newberry, MI
Amer. Legion, Hugh Watson Post 190 **[12266]**, St. Charles, MN
Amer. Legion, Hugh Watson Post 530 **[13719]**, Cincinnati, OH
Amer. Legion, Hughes-Mc-Cormick Post 362 **[10760]**, De Graff, MN
Amer. Legion, Hugo Fales Post 203 **[6902]**, Belding, MI
Amer. Legion, Hugo Post 620 **[11202]**, Hugo, MN
Amer. Legion, Humphrey-Wilsey Post 233 **[19958]**, Waterloo, WI
Amer. Legion, Hunt-Trouse Post 287 **[4339]**, Centerville, IN
Amer. Legion, Huntley Post 673 **[2053]**, Huntley, IL
Amer. Legion, Hurlbut-Ziemer Post 476 **[10498]**, Bovey, MN
Amer. Legion, Huron Valley Post 231 **[7031]**, Brownstown, MI
Amer. Legion, Hurst-Collins Post 281 **[4373]**, Cloverdale, IN
Amer. Legion, Hustisford Memorial Post 420 **[18279]**, Juneau, WI
Amer. Legion, Hutchins-Stendahl Post 191 **[20157]**, Whitehall, WI
Amer. Legion, Hutchinson Post 96 **[11203]**, Hutchinson, MN
Amer. Legion, Hutton-Avery-Sherry Post 262 **[8407]**, Jones, MI
Amer. Legion, Hyatt-Allen Post 538 **[16880]**, Toledo, OH
Amer. Legion, Hyde-Park-Mt-Lookout Post 744 **[13720]**, Cincinnati, OH
Amer. Legion, Idlewild Amer. Legion Post 263 **[8304]**, Idlewild, MI
Amer. Legion, Illiana Post 220 **[657]**, Chicago, IL
Amer. Legion, Illini Post 254 **[2378]**, Magnolia, IL
Amer. Legion Illinois **[★256]**
Amer. Legion, Illinois Dept. of Employment Sec Post 815 **[658]**, Chicago, IL
Amer. Legion, Illinois HQ Post 2910 **[257]**, Bloomington, IL
Amer. Legion, Illinois Post 16 **[400]**, Canton, IL
Amer. Legion, Illinois Post 17 **[2065]**, Ipava, IL
Amer. Legion, Illinois Post 18 **[2309]**, Lockport, IL
Amer. Legion, Illinois Post 26 **[3851]**, Vermont, IL
Amer. Legion, Illinois Post 35 **[1815]**, Glasford, IL
Amer. Legion, Illinois Post 41 **[1304]**, Countryside, IL
Amer. Legion, Illinois Post 47 **[659]**, Chicago, IL
Amer. Legion, Illinois Post 51 **[3975]**, Westville, IL
Amer. Legion, Illinois Post 54 **[1684]**, Fairbury, IL
Amer. Legion, Illinois Post 55 **[1700]**, Farmer City, IL
Amer. Legion, Illinois Post 56 **[258]**, Bloomington, IL
Amer. Legion, Illinois Post 58 **[198]**, Belleville, IL
Amer. Legion, Illinois Post 60 **[2362]**, Machesney Park, IL
Amer. Legion, Illinois Post 69 **[3218]**, Robinson, IL
Amer. Legion, Illinois Post 74 **[464]**, Carthage, IL
Amer. Legion, Illinois Post 80 **[1494]**, Downers Grove, IL
Amer. Legion, Illinois Post 83 **[3116]**, Polo, IL
Amer. Legion, Illinois Post 87 **[660]**, Chicago, IL
Amer. Legion, Illinois Post 89 **[2478]**, Metamora, IL
Amer. Legion, Illinois Post 106 **[2465]**, McLeansboro, IL
Amer. Legion, Illinois Post 110 **[2670]**, Nashville, IL
Amer. Legion, Illinois Post 115 **[1813]**, Girard, IL
Amer. Legion, Illinois Post 119 **[1721]**, Fox River Grove, IL
Amer. Legion, Illinois Post 123 **[2310]**, Lockport, IL
Amer. Legion, Illinois Post 128 **[3407]**, Salem, IL
Amer. Legion, Illinois Post 129 **[97]**, Athens, IL
Amer. Legion, Illinois Post 132 **[1704]**, Flat Rock, IL
Amer. Legion, Illinois Post 135 **[2323]**, Lombard, IL
Amer. Legion, Illinois Post 136 **[2540]**, Monmouth, IL
Amer. Legion, Illinois Post 166 **[1855]**, Glenview, IL
Amer. Legion, Illinois Post 167 **[1938]**, Harrisburg, IL
Amer. Legion, Illinois Post 172 **[2414]**, Marissa, IL
Amer. Legion, Illinois Post 176 **[1686]**, Fairfield, IL
Amer. Legion, Illinois Post 177 **[4078]**, Zeigler, IL
Amer. Legion, Illinois Post 178 **[2857]**, Olmsted, IL
Amer. Legion, Illinois Post 182 **[3517]**, Spring Valley, IL
Amer. Legion, Illinois Post 189 **[21]**, Alexis, IL
Amer. Legion, Illinois Post 190 **[347]**, Brookfield, IL
Amer. Legion, Illinois Post 191 **[4025]**, Wilmington, IL
Amer. Legion, Illinois Post 194 **[2011]**, Hindsboro, IL
Amer. Legion, Illinois Post 197 **[2981]**, Pecatonica, IL
Amer. Legion, Illinois Post 209 **[381]**, Byron, IL
Amer. Legion, Illinois Post 210 **[1342]**, Danville, IL
Amer. Legion, Illinois Post 217 **[3724]**, Streator, IL
Amer. Legion, Illinois Post 233 **[2855]**, Okawville, IL
Amer. Legion, Illinois Post 234 **[584]**, Chenoa, IL
Amer. Legion, Illinois Post 236 **[1648]**, Evanston, IL
Amer. Legion, Illinois Post 237 **[2852]**, Oglesby, IL
Amer. Legion, Illinois Post 244 **[3474]**, Sibley, IL
Amer. Legion, Illinois Post 247 **[2958]**, Park Ridge, IL
Amer. Legion, Illinois Post 249 **[4052]**, Woodson, IL
Amer. Legion, Illinois Post 253 **[3190]**, Richmond, IL
Amer. Legion, Illinois Post 261 **[358]**, Buda, IL
Amer. Legion, Illinois Post 265 **[1948]**, Harvard, IL
Amer. Legion, Illinois Post 272 **[661]**, Chicago, IL
Amer. Legion, Illinois Post 276 **[468]**, Cary, IL
Amer. Legion, Illinois Post 279 **[2073]**, Jacksonville, IL
Amer. Legion, Illinois Post 284 **[94]**, Assumption, IL
Amer. Legion, Illinois Post 285 **[1767]**, Galesburg, IL
Amer. Legion, Illinois Post 291 **[2251]**, Lexington, IL
Amer. Legion, Illinois Post 292 **[2430]**, Mascoutah, IL
Amer. Legion, Illinois Post 303 **[3209]**, Riverdale, IL
Amer. Legion, Illinois Post 306 **[2481]**, Metropolis, IL
Amer. Legion, Illinois Post 327 **[1447]**, Depue, IL
Amer. Legion, Illinois Post 344 **[51]**, Anna, IL
Amer. Legion, Illinois Post 347 **[460]**, Carterville, IL
Amer. Legion, Illinois Post 362 **[3695]**, Staunton, IL
Amer. Legion, Illinois Post 363 **[662]**, Chicago, IL
Amer. Legion, Illinois Post 370 **[2607]**, Moweaqua, IL
Amer. Legion, Illinois Post 381 **[2]**, Abingdon, IL
Amer. Legion, Illinois Post 386 **[3870]**, Virden, IL
Amer. Legion, Illinois Post 396 **[3513]**, Sparta, IL
Amer. Legion, Illinois Post 410 **[1248]**, Chicago Heights, IL
Amer. Legion, Illinois Post 419 **[663]**, Chicago, IL
Amer. Legion, Illinois Post 435 **[1818]**, Glen Carbon, IL
Amer. Legion, Illinois Post 437 **[664]**, Chicago, IL
Amer. Legion, Illinois Post 440 **[3777]**, Toluca, IL
Amer. Legion, Illinois Post 441 **[319]**, Bluffs, IL
Amer. Legion, Illinois Post 442 **[4027]**, Winchester, IL
Amer. Legion, Illinois Post 446 **[486]**, Centralia, IL
Amer. Legion, Illinois Post 475 **[1339]**, Dalton City, IL
Amer. Legion, Illinois Post 482 **[3798]**, Union, IL
Amer. Legion, Illinois Post 495 **[1631]**, Elmwood Park, IL
Amer. Legion, Illinois Post 498 **[90]**, Ashland, IL
Amer. Legion, Illinois Post 500 **[2004]**, Hillside, IL
Amer. Legion, Illinois Post 514 **[411]**, Carbondale, IL
Amer. Legion, Illinois Post 524 **[3184]**, Red Bud, IL
Amer. Legion, Illinois Post 533 **[1335]**, Cuba, IL
Amer. Legion, Illinois Post 536 **[3858]**, Vienna, IL
Amer. Legion, Illinois Post 543 **[2966]**, Patoka, IL
Amer. Legion, Illinois Post 546 **[4046]**, Woodhull, IL
Amer. Legion, Illinois Post 549 **[1527]**, Earlville, IL
Amer. Legion, Illinois Post 559 **[499]**, Champaign, IL
Amer. Legion, Illinois Post 563 **[2094]**, Johnston City, IL
Amer. Legion, Illinois Post 565 **[2676]**, New Athens, IL
Amer. Legion, Illinois Post 571 **[3362]**, Rosiclare, IL
Amer. Legion, Illinois Post 572 **[2704]**, Noble, IL
Amer. Legion, Illinois Post 591 **[3239]**, Rock Island, IL
Amer. Legion, Illinois Post 619 **[137]**, Baldwin, IL
Amer. Legion, Illinois Post 620 **[224]**, Bement, IL
Amer. Legion, Illinois Post 622 **[3130]**, Prairie Du Rocher, IL
Amer. Legion, Illinois Post 624 **[1977]**, Heyworth, IL
Amer. Legion, Illinois Post 635 **[2708]**, Normal, IL
Amer. Legion, Illinois Post 647 **[1516]**, Du Quoin, IL
Amer. Legion, Illinois Post 650 **[2388]**, Mansfield, IL
Amer. Legion, Illinois Post 683 **[3402]**, St. Libory, IL
Amer. Legion, Illinois Post 692 **[2804]**, Oak Park, IL
Amer. Legion, Illinois Post 696 **[1898]**, Grayville, IL
Amer. Legion, Illinois Post 699 **[2360]**, Lyons, IL
Amer. Legion, Illinois Post 700 **[3759]**, Thawville, IL
Amer. Legion, Illinois Post 701 **[3873]**, Waggoner, IL
Amer. Legion, Illinois Post 716 **[665]**, Chicago, IL
Amer. Legion, Illinois Post 726 **[3857]**, Victoria, IL
Amer. Legion, Illinois Post 729 **[3469]**, Sheridan, IL
Amer. Legion, Illinois Post 746 **[666]**, Chicago, IL
Amer. Legion, Illinois Post 749 **[2165]**, Knoxville, IL
Amer. Legion, Illinois Post 752 **[1301]**, Cornell, IL
Amer. Legion, Illinois Post 768 **[469]**, Cary, IL
Amer. Legion, Illinois Post 802 **[667]**, Chicago, IL
Amer. Legion, Illinois Post 806 **[668]**, Chicago, IL
Amer. Legion, Illinois Post 809 **[3525]**, Springfield, IL
Amer. Legion, Illinois Post 829 **[669]**, Chicago, IL
Amer. Legion, Illinois Post 832 **[4010]**, Willow Springs, IL
Amer. Legion, Illinois Post 838 **[2448]**, Maywood, IL
Amer. Legion, Illinois Post 888 **[2764]**, Northlake, IL
Amer. Legion, Illinois Post 904 **[3266]**, Rockford, IL
Amer. Legion, Illinois Post 915 **[670]**, Chicago, IL
Amer. Legion, Illinois Post 917 **[2427]**, Maryville, IL
Amer. Legion, Illinois Post 938 **[2185]**, Ladd, IL
Amer. Legion, Illinois Post 948 **[2167]**, La Fayette, IL
Amer. Legion, Illinois Post 957 **[1495]**, Downers Grove, IL
Amer. Legion, Illinois Post 958 **[671]**, Chicago, IL
Amer. Legion, Illinois Post 963 **[3368]**, Royalton, IL
Amer. Legion, Illinois Post 977 **[346]**, Brocton, IL
Amer. Legion, Illinois Post 984 **[672]**, Chicago, IL
Amer. Legion, Illinois Post 1009 **[1856]**, Glenview, IL
Amer. Legion, Illinois Post 1010 **[2163]**, Kingston, IL
Amer. Legion, Illinois Post 1017 **[673]**, Chicago, IL
Amer. Legion, Illinois Post 1025 **[3760]**, Thomson, IL
Amer. Legion, Illinois Post 1056 **[2186]**, Ladd, IL
Amer. Legion, Illinois Post 1072 **[3712]**, Stillman Valley, IL
Amer. Legion, Illinois Post 1105 **[107]**, Aurora, IL
Amer. Legion, Illinois Post 1109 **[2747]**, North Riverside, IL
Amer. Legion, Illinois Post 1119 **[674]**, Chicago, IL
Amer. Legion, Illinois Post 1130 **[3952]**, West Union, IL
Amer. Legion, Illinois Post 1164 **[324]**, Bourbonnais, IL
Amer. Legion, Illinois Post 1205 **[4043]**, Wood Dale, IL
Amer. Legion, Illinois Post 1207 **[3267]**, Rockford, IL
Amer. Legion, Illinois Post 1531 **[3767]**, Tinley Park, IL
Amer. Legion, Illinois Post 1941 **[2168]**, La Grange, IL
Amer. Legion, Illinois Post 1960 **[2571]**, Mounds, IL
Amer. Legion, Illinois Post 1969 **[5]**, Addison, IL
Amer. Legion, Illinois Post 1974 **[1496]**, Downers Grove, IL
Amer. Legion, Illinois Post 1976 **[2787]**, Oak Forest, IL

Amer. Legion, Illinois Post 1977 **[2687]**, New Lenox, IL
Amer. Legion, Illinois Post 1984 **[2308]**, Livingston, IL
Amer. Legion, Illinois Post 1990 **[675]**, Chicago, IL
Amer. Legion, Illiopolis Post 508 **[2058]**, Illiopolis, IL
Amer. Legion, Indian Creek Post 109 **[2741]**, Norris City, IL
Amer. Legion of Indiana **[4997]**, Indianapolis, IN
Amer. Legion, Indiana Post 10 **[5724]**, Marion, IN
Amer. Legion, Indiana Post 12 **[4738]**, Frankfort, IN
Amer. Legion, Indiana Post 13 **[5909]**, Nashville, IN
Amer. Legion, Indiana Post 15 **[6423]**, Wabash, IN
Amer. Legion, Indiana Post 20 **[4429]**, Crown Point, IN
Amer. Legion, Indiana Post 26 **[4998]**, Indianapolis, IN
Amer. Legion, Indiana Post 27 **[6045]**, Plymouth, IN
Amer. Legion, Indiana Post 28 **[5915]**, New Albany, IN
Amer. Legion, Indiana Post 29 **[6076]**, Rensselaer, IN
Amer. Legion, Indiana Post 32 **[4189]**, Bicknell, IN
Amer. Legion, Indiana Post 34 **[4999]**, Indianapolis, IN
Amer. Legion, Indiana Post 36 **[6121]**, Rochester, IN
Amer. Legion, Indiana Post 37 **[5782]**, Michigan City, IN
Amer. Legion, Indiana Post 41 **[6157]**, Salem, IN
Amer. Legion, Indiana Post 45 **[5968]**, Noblesville, IN
Amer. Legion, Indiana Post 49 **[6440]**, Warsaw, IN
Amer. Legion, Indiana Post 58 **[4814]**, Greencastle, IN
Amer. Legion, Indiana Post 63 **[6019]**, Paoli, IN
Amer. Legion, Indiana Post 67 **[6198]**, Sheridan, IN
Amer. Legion, Indiana Post 74 **[4488]**, Elkhart, IN
Amer. Legion, Indiana Post 75 **[4453]**, Delphi, IN
Amer. Legion, Indiana Post 76 **[4762]**, French Lick, IN
Amer. Legion, Indiana Post 77 **[4296]**, Brookville, IN
Amer. Legion, Indiana Post 79 **[6548]**, Zionsville, IN
Amer. Legion, Indiana Post 81 **[5822]**, Monticello, IN
Amer. Legion, Indiana Post 85 **[4943]**, Huntington, IN
Amer. Legion, Indiana Post 92 **[5982]**, North Judson, IN
Amer. Legion, Indiana Post 93 **[4489]**, Elkhart, IN
Amer. Legion, Indiana Post 94 **[6376]**, Valparaiso, IN
Amer. Legion, Indiana Post 102 **[5843]**, Morristown, IN
Amer. Legion, Indiana Post 125 **[6017]**, Otterbein, IN
Amer. Legion, Indiana Post 127 **[4096]**, Anderson, IN
Amer. Legion, Indiana Post 133 **[5663]**, Leavenworth, IN
Amer. Legion, Indiana Post 137 **[5932]**, New Castle, IN
Amer. Legion, Indiana Post 142 **[4313]**, Cannelton, IN
Amer. Legion, Indiana Post 148 **[4630]**, Fort Wayne, IN
Amer. Legion, Indiana Post 150 **[6142]**, Rushville, IN
Amer. Legion, Indiana Post 158 **[6360]**, Union City, IN
Amer. Legion, Indiana Post 160 **[6120]**, Roanoke, IN
Amer. Legion, Indiana Post 169 **[4310]**, Cambridge City, IN
Amer. Legion, Indiana Post 175 **[6372]**, Urbana, IN
Amer. Legion, Indiana Post 177 **[5563]**, Kokomo, IN
Amer. Legion, Indiana Post 185 **[6405]**, Vevay, IN
Amer. Legion, Indiana Post 186 **[5000]**, Indianapolis, IN
Amer. Legion, Indiana Post 191 **[4286]**, Bremen, IN
Amer. Legion, Indiana Post 199 **[5993]**, North Vernon, IN
Amer. Legion, Indiana Post 204 **[6175]**, Sellersburg, IN
Amer. Legion, Indiana Post 210 **[5795]**, Middlebury, IN
Amer. Legion, Indiana Post 211 **[6062]**, Portland, IN
Amer. Legion, Indiana Post 227 **[4465]**, Dunkirk, IN
Amer. Legion, Indiana Post 228 **[4737]**, Francesville, IN
Amer. Legion, Indiana Post 231 **[4145]**, Aurora, IN
Amer. Legion, Indiana Post 239 **[5652]**, Lawrenceburg, IN
Amer. Legion, Indiana Post 245 **[4511]**, Elnora, IN
Amer. Legion, Indiana Post 249 **[5001]**, Indianapolis, IN
Amer. Legion, Indiana Post 250 **[5814]**, Mitchell, IN
Amer. Legion, Indiana Post 251 **[4294]**, Brookston, IN
Amer. Legion, Indiana Post 253 **[5999]**, North Webster, IN
Amer. Legion, Indiana Post 255 **[6146]**, Russellville, IN
Amer. Legion, Indiana Post 267 **[6016]**, Osgood, IN
Amer. Legion, Indiana Post 274 **[5707]**, Lynn, IN
Amer. Legion, Indiana Post 278 **[6067]**, Poseyville, IN
Amer. Legion, Indiana Post 279 **[4773]**, Gary, IN
Amer. Legion, Indiana Post 301 **[5590]**, Kouts, IN
Amer. Legion, Indiana Post 307 **[6429]**, Wakarusa, IN
Amer. Legion, Indiana Post 309 **[6212]**, South Bend, IN
Amer. Legion, Indiana Post 310 **[5557]**, Kirklin, IN
Amer. Legion, Indiana Post 315 **[6086]**, Richmond, IN
Amer. Legion, Indiana Post 317 **[4844]**, Greentown, IN
Amer. Legion, Indiana Post 328 **[6116]**, Riley, IN
Amer. Legion, Indiana Post 333 **[4862]**, Hagerstown, IN
Amer. Legion, Indiana Post 337 **[6288]**, Sunman, IN
Amer. Legion, Indiana Post 344 **[4133]**, Arcadia, IN
Amer. Legion, Indiana Post 365 **[5984]**, North Liberty, IN
Amer. Legion, Indiana Post 381 **[6137]**, Rome City, IN
Amer. Legion, Indiana Post 408 **[4348]**, Chesterfield, IN
Amer. Legion, Indiana Post 410 **[6521]**, Whitestown, IN
Amer. Legion, Indiana Post 419 **[6119]**, Roann, IN
Amer. Legion, Indiana Post 428 **[4870]**, Hammond, IN
Amer. Legion, Indiana Post 438 **[5002]**, Indianapolis, IN
Amer. Legion, Indiana Post 446 **[4440]**, Daleville, IN
Amer. Legion, Indiana Post 451 **[5783]**, Michigan City, IN
Amer. Legion, Indiana Post 495 **[5003]**, Indianapolis, IN
Amer. Legion, Indiana Post 498 **[4774]**, Gary, IN
Amer. Legion, Indiana Post 501 **[6507]**, West Terre Haute, IN
Amer. Legion, Indiana Post 507 **[6115]**, Ridgeville, IN
Amer. Legion, Indiana Post 508 **[4473]**, East Chicago, IN
Amer. Legion, Indiana Post 510 **[4599]**, Fishers, IN
Amer. Legion, Indiana Post 911 **[5004]**, Indianapolis, IN
Amer. Legion, Indianapolis Power Light Post 300 **[5005]**, Indianapolis, IN
Amer. Legion, Ingalls-Koeppen Post 102 **[19946]**, Walworth, WI
Amer. Legion, Inspiration Peak Post 527 **[10273]**, Alexandria, MN
Amer. Legion, Inver Grove Heights Post 424 **[11222]**, Inver Grove Heights, MN
Amer. Legion, Ira Owen Kreager Post 384 **[2049]**, Hoopeston, IL
Amer. Legion, Ironton Post 433 **[15508]**, Ironton, OH
Amer. Legion, Ironwood Post 5 **[8335]**, Ironwood, MI
Amer. Legion, Iroquois Post 503 **[2320]**, Loda, IL
Amer. Legion, Irvin Blix Post 16 **[10372]**, Bagley, MN
Amer. Legion, Irvin Lee Terrey Post 229 **[3868]**, Viola, IL
Amer. Legion, Irwin Knudson Post 459 **[2695]**, Newark, IL
Amer. Legion, Isaac Harrison Lyons Post 326 **[12783]**, Verndale, MN
Amer. Legion, Isaacson-Bjorge Post 31 **[11370]**, Mahnomen, MN
Amer. Legion, Ishpemingnegaunee Post 136 **[8344]**, Ishpeming, MI
Amer. Legion, Ithaca Post 334 **[8351]**, Ithaca, MI
Amer. Legion, Ivan Stringer Post 164 **[12712]**, Stewartville, MN
Amer. Legion, Ivan V. Sarff Post 70 **[12702]**, Staples, MN
Amer. Legion, Iwaszuk-Cetwinski Post 943 **[2469]**, Melrose Park, IL
Amer. Legion, J. Ivan Dappert Post 73 **[3754]**, Taylorville, IL
Amer. Legion, Jack Brinker Post 409 **[5674]**, Leo, IN
Amer. Legion, Jackson-Keen Post 496 **[2433]**, Mason City, IL
Amer. Legion, Jackson-Koster-Gray Post 300 **[8503]**, Lake City, MI
Amer. Legion, Jackson Liberty Post 130 **[11233]**, Jackson, MN
Amer. Legion, Jackson-O-Meara Post 90 **[11313]**, Lewiston, MN
Amer. Legion, Jackson Park Post 555 **[2794]**, Oak Lawn, IL
Amer. Legion, Jacobsen Memorial Post 487 **[12658]**, Shoreview, MN
Amer. Legion, James De Armond Golliday Post 6 **[5564]**, Kokomo, IN
Amer. Legion, James De Witt Post 38 **[7681]**, Fenton, MI
Amer. Legion, James Evans Post 341 **[4358]**, Cicero, IN
Amer. Legion, James Gastineau Post 479 **[5709]**, Lyons, IN
Amer. Legion, James Lowell Corey Post 68 **[4134]**, Argos, IN
Amer. Legion, James Reeder Post 770 **[101]**, Atwood, IL
Amer. Legion, Jamestown Post 395 **[5519]**, Jamestown, IN
Amer. Legion, Janesville Post 281 **[11235]**, Janesville, MN
Amer. Legion, Jansen-Richardson Post 488 **[7597]**, Ellsworth, MI
Amer. Legion, Jasonville Post 172 **[5521]**, Jasonville, IN
Amer. Legion, Jasper Post 20 **[2698]**, Newton, IL
Amer. Legion, Jastrzemski-Lelo Post 439 **[9598]**, Saginaw, MI
Amer. Legion, Jay H. Findley Memorial Post 1994 **[2161]**, Keyesport, IL
Amer. Legion, J.C. Trigg Memorial Post 328 **[14844]**, Dayton, OH
Amer. Legion, J.D. Smith Memorial Post 10 **[15092]**, Edgerton, OH
Amer. Legion, Jean Post 543 **[7091]**, Caseville, MI
Amer. Legion, Jeep Gabrys Post 388 **[7305]**, Detroit, MI
Amer. Legion, Jefferson-Horton Post 340 **[3268]**, Rockford, IL
Amer. Legion, Jefferson Post 9 **[5710]**, Madison, IN
Amer. Legion, Jefferson Post 141 **[2593]**, Mount Vernon, IL
Amer. Legion, Jefferson Post 201 **[17181]**, West Jefferson, OH
Amer. Legion, Jenkins Post 254 **[6127]**, Rockport, IN
Amer. Legion, Jenkins-Vaughan Post 97 **[13596]**, Cardington, OH
Amer. Legion, Jennings-Kraemer-Gruber Post 398 **[19459]**, Plain, WI
Amer. Legion, Jennings Post 276 **[10291]**, Amboy, MN
Amer. Legion, Jensen-Hansen Post 394 **[18431]**, Loretta, WI
Amer. Legion, Jerome Post 749 **[15527]**, Jeromesville, OH
Amer. Legion, Jerry Wickham Post 1148 **[2229]**, Leaf River, IL
Amer. Legion, Jesse Poole Post 297 **[11238]**, Johnson, MN
Amer. Legion, Jesse Rogers Post 483 **[6539]**, Windfall, IN
Amer. Legion, Jfb Post 610 **[12753]**, Tintah, MN
Amer. Legion, Jim Falls Post 276 **[18770]**, Manawa, WI
Amer. Legion, John B. Lotz Memorial Post 91 **[5864]**, Muncie, IN
Amer. Legion, John Bridges Post 15 **[10772]**, Detroit Lakes, MN
Amer. Legion, John Ericsson Post 1042 **[676]**, Chicago, IL
Amer. Legion, John Poor Post 717 **[1554]**, Edinburg, IL
Amer. Legion, John-Rheaume-Fred-Knauf Post 438 **[6830]**, Bark River, MI
Amer. Legion, John Vessey Post 44 **[11293]**, Lakeville, MN

Amer. Legion, Johnson Curd Post 256 **[6009]**, Oakland City, IN
Amer. Legion, Johnson Day Post 104 **[9852]**, Standish, MI
Amer. Legion, Johnson-Hallberg Post 407 **[19536]**, Prentice, WI
Amer. Legion, Johnson-Hershman Post 363 **[17831]**, Denmark, WI
Amer. Legion, Johnson-Kelly Post 483 **[10752]**, Dassel, MN
Amer. Legion, Johnson-Miner Post 618 **[17269]**, Williamsport, OH
Amer. Legion, Johnson-Nicoles-Kuhlman-Olson Post 53 **[17862]**, Eau Claire, WI
Amer. Legion, Johnson-Olson Post 494 **[10437]**, Big Falls, MN
Amer. Legion, Johnson Post 382 **[11133]**, Hawley, MN
Amer. Legion, Johnson-Roll-Dougherty Post 187 **[11051]**, Glenwood, MN
Amer. Legion, Johnson-Whistler Post 323 **[18174]**, Hammond, WI
Amer. Legion, Johnstown Post 254 **[15531]**, Johnstown, OH
Amer. Legion, Joliet Post 1284 **[2098]**, Joliet, IL
Amer. Legion, Jones-Mehltretter Post 405 **[17841]**, Dousman, WI
Amer. Legion, Jones-Modrow-Young Post 74 **[19347]**, Oconto, WI
Amer. Legion, Joseph A. Gates Post 78 **[11253]**, Kenyon, MN
Amer. Legion, Joseph Viken Post 229 **[12262]**, Sacred Heart, MN
Amer. Legion, Juneau Post 15 **[18280]**, Juneau, WI
Amer. Legion, Justice-Leibolt Post 377 **[13503]**, Camden, OH
Amer. Legion, J.W. Roth Post 294 **[11277]**, Lake Crystal, MN
Amer. Legion, Kalamazoo Post 134 **[8414]**, Kalamazoo, MI
Amer. Legion, Kalamazoo Post 332 **[9203]**, Niles, MI
Amer. Legion, Kalbes-Seewald Post 280 **[17777]**, Coleman, WI
Amer. Legion, Kampsville Post 1083 **[2126]**, Kampsville, IL
Amer. Legion, Kankakee Post 85 **[2128]**, Kankakee, IL
Amer. Legion, Kanthak-Matthies Post 441 **[10400]**, Bellingham, MN
Amer. Legion, Kapperman Post 44 **[5959]**, Newburgh, IN
Amer. Legion, Kasal Post 457 **[3459]**, Seneca, IL
Amer. Legion, Kasierski-Kozlowski Post 366 **[19542]**, Princeton, WI
Amer. Legion, Kasota Post 348 **[11242]**, Kasota, MN
Amer. Legion, Kaukauna Post 41 **[18285]**, Kaukauna, WI
Amer. Legion, Keeler-Adams Post 1168 **[1553]**, Edgewood, IL
Amer. Legion, Keith Brown Post 420 **[5819]**, Monroeville, IN
Amer. Legion, Kelley-Gardner-Katzman-Stoflet Post 45 **[17926]**, Elkhorn, WI
Amer. Legion, Kellogg Post 546 **[11249]**, Kellogg, MN
Amer. Legion, Kelly-Johnson Post 90 **[17541]**, Ashland, WI
Amer. Legion, Kelly-Ward-Varley-Memorial Post 732 **[17386]**, Youngstown, OH
Amer. Legion, Ken-Bur-Bel Post 41 **[16258]**, Norwalk, OH
Amer. Legion, Kendallville Post 86 **[5549]**, Kendallville, IN
Amer. Legion, Kenney-Hallsville Post 1133 **[2153]**, Kenney, IL
Amer. Legion, Kenosha-Paul-Herrick Post 21 **[18294]**, Kenosha, WI
Amer. Legion, Kent-Metzler Post 261 **[16275]**, Oak Hill, OH
Amer. Legion, Kent Voyls Post 322 **[4487]**, Elizabethtown, IN
Amer. Legion, Kenton Post 198 **[15552]**, Kenton, OH
Amer. Legion, Kerl-Endres-Brannan Post 245 **[17792]**, Cross Plains, WI
Amer. Legion, Kerlin Farina Post 16 **[17797]**, Cudahy, WI
Amer. Legion, Kerner-Slusser Post 63 **[16315]**, Ottawa, OH
Amer. Legion, Kerr-Mize Post 168 **[2944]**, Pana, IL
Amer. Legion, Kessinger Post 713 **[3494]**, Sorento, IL
Amer. Legion, Kettering Post 598 **[15557]**, Kettering, OH
Amer. Legion, Kettle River Post 360 **[11259]**, Kettle River, MN
Amer. Legion, Kewanee Post 31 **[2154]**, Kewanee, IL
Amer. Legion, Kewaunee Post 29 **[18318]**, Kewaunee, WI
Amer. Legion, Kiester Post 454 **[11260]**, Kiester, MN
Amer. Legion, Kingman Post 384 **[5555]**, Kingman, IN
Amer. Legion, Kingston Post 291 **[15568]**, Kingston, OH
Amer. Legion, Kinmundy Post 519 **[2164]**, Kinmundy, IL
Amer. Legion, Kinne-Engelhart Post 204 **[17932]**, Ellsworth, WI
Amer. Legion, Kirby-Watkins Post 198 **[3084]**, Petersburg, IL
Amer. Legion, Kishwaukee Post 192 **[2396]**, Marengo, IL
Amer. Legion, K.M.B.B. Post 400 **[2902]**, Ozark, IL
Amer. Legion, Kneil-Lawrentz Post 255 **[16840]**, Tallmadge, OH
Amer. Legion, Kniery-Knagg Post 436 **[2305]**, Litchfield, IL
Amer. Legion, Knightstown Post 152 **[5558]**, Knightstown, IN
Amer. Legion, Knox-Helms Post 554 **[9083]**, Morley, MI
Amer. Legion, Knudtson-Mattison Post 231 **[17636]**, Blair, WI
Amer. Legion, Koca Post 39 **[335]**, Braidwood, IL
Amer. Legion, Korppas-Johnson Post 531 **[19504]**, Port Wing, WI
Amer. Legion, Kosciuszko Post 712 **[677]**, Chicago, IL
Amer. Legion, Koselke Mayfield Post 403 **[6439]**, Wanatah, IN
Amer. Legion, Kraft-Ostrom-American-Legion Post 142 **[10630]**, Cannon Falls, MN
Amer. Legion, Kramer-Berg Post 507 **[12909]**, Willernie, MN
Amer. Legion, Krause-Kraft Post 106 **[19674]**, Seymour, WI
Amer. Legion, Krause-Simpson Post 300 **[18047]**, Gillett, WI
Amer. Legion, Kriesel-Jacobsen Post 560 **[12998]**, Zimmerman, MN
Amer. Legion, Kropp-Braund Post 242 **[18386]**, La Valle, WI
Amer. Legion, K.T. Crossen Post 21 **[13193]**, Athens, OH
Amer. Legion, Kupfahl-Meyer-Scheib Post 387 **[19487]**, Plymouth, WI
Amer. Legion, Kupsh-Brockmann Post 127 **[18204]**, Hilbert, WI
Amer. Legion, Kurdel-Cigoi Post 1110 **[678]**, Chicago, IL
Amer. Legion, Kurtz-Booker Post 217 **[5992]**, North Salem, IN
Amer. Legion, La Fayette Post 159 **[679]**, Chicago, IL
Amer. Legion, La Grange Post 215 **[5638]**, Lagrange, IN
Amer. Legion, La Harpe Post 301 **[2178]**, La Harpe, IL
Amer. Legion, La Moille Post 1043 **[2179]**, La Moille, IL
Amer. Legion, La Porte, County Post 130 **[5784]**, Michigan City, IN
Amer. Legion, Lac Qui Parle Post 158 **[11365]**, Madison, MN
Amer. Legion, Ladewig-Zinkgraf Post 243 **[19488]**, Plymouth, WI
Amer. Legion, Lafayette Post 11 **[5606]**, Lafayette, IN
Amer. Legion, Lafayette Post 27 **[15289]**, Gallipolis, OH
Amer. Legion, Lafayette Post 300 **[11268]**, Lafayette, MN
Amer. Legion, Lake Bluff Post 510 **[2187]**, Lake Bluff, IL
Amer. Legion, Lake County Post 1122 **[3920]**, Waukegan, IL
Amer. Legion, Lake in the Hills Post 1231 **[2206]**, Lake in the Hills, IL
Amer. Legion, Lake Post 737 **[15578]**, Lake Milton, OH
Amer. Legion, Lake Region Post 703 **[1718]**, Fox Lake, IL
Amer. Legion, Lake Villa Township Post 1219 **[2290]**, Lindenhurst, IL
Amer. Legion, Lake Village Post 375 **[5646]**, Lake Village, IN
Amer. Legion, Lake Zurich Post 964 **[2208]**, Lake Zurich, IL
Amer. Legion, Lakeshore Post 474 **[18940]**, Milwaukee, WI
Amer. Legion, Lakeview Post 342 **[10798]**, Duluth, MN
Amer. Legion, Lakeville Community Post 363 **[5648]**, Lakeville, IN
Amer. Legion, Lakewood Post 571 **[10799]**, Duluth, MN
Amer. Legion, Lambertville Post 191 **[9327]**, Ottawa Lake, MI
Amer. Legion, Lamond-Frank Post 478 **[9833]**, Southgate, MI
Amer. Legion, Landt-Thiel Post 470 **[19666]**, Saukville, WI
Amer. Legion, Landua-Jensen Post 147 **[18843]**, Medford, WI
Amer. Legion, Lange-Ostrander-Hurd Post 62 **[17782]**, Columbus, WI
Amer. Legion, Langemo Post 295 **[12872]**, West Concord, MN
Amer. Legion, Lansing Post 336 **[8536]**, Lansing, MI
Amer. Legion, Lapaz Post 385 **[5650]**, Lapaz, IN
Amer. Legion, Lapeer Post 16 **[8774]**, Lapeer, MI
Amer. Legion, Laroy Farst Post 245 **[16139]**, New Madison, OH
Amer. Legion, Larson-Torgerson Post 169 **[17471]**, Amery, WI
Amer. Legion, Larue Messenger Post 26 **[9204]**, Niles, MI
Amer. Legion, Lauridsen Post 408 **[583]**, Chebanse, IL
Amer. Legion, Lawrence Capehart Post 35 **[5538]**, Jeffersonville, IN
Amer. Legion, Lawrence Post 28 **[2223]**, Lawrenceville, IL
Amer. Legion, Lawrence Rayburn Post 116 **[1904]**, Greenview, IL
Amer. Legion, Lawrence Riddle Post 88 **[2440]**, Mattoon, IL
Amer. Legion, Lawson Babbitt Post 614 **[3361]**, Roseville, IL
Amer. Legion, Le Center Post 108 **[11305]**, Le Center, MN
Amer. Legion, Leach-Benson Post 220 **[13515]**, Canal Winchester, OH
Amer. Legion, Leach-Paulson Post 517 **[17840]**, Dorchester, WI
Amer. Legion, Leasure-Blackston Post 239 **[17341]**, Worthington, OH
Amer. Legion, Lee-Bishop Post 464 **[15480]**, Hudson, OH
Amer. Legion, Lee C. Prentice Post 36 **[10976]**, Fairmont, MN
Amer. Legion, Lee Goldsmith Post 201 **[11831]**, Mora, MN
Amer. Legion, Lee Iten Post 439 **[1984]**, Highland, IL
Amer. Legion, Lee Lowery Post 568 **[1808]**, Gibson City, IL
Amer. Legion, Lee Post 1253 **[2232]**, Lee, IL
Amer. Legion, Lee-Ranney Post 235 **[20152]**, Wheeler, WI
Amer. Legion, Leech Lake Post 2001 **[10431]**, Bena, MN
Amer. Legion, Leelanau County Post 199 **[7602]**, Empire, MI
Amer. Legion, Leesburg Post 568 **[15629]**, Leesburg, OH
Amer. Legion, Legion Villa Post 210 **[6844]**, Battle Creek, MI
Amer. Legion, Lehman-Clenndenning Post 274 **[19611]**, Rib Lake, WI
Amer. Legion, Lehman-Zimmerman Post 259 **[15220]**, Forest, OH
Amer. Legion, Leighton Evatt Post 365 **[1286]**, Collinsville, IL

Amer. Legion, Lekstrum-Burnett Post 107 **[9845]**, Sparta, MI
Amer. Legion, Leland Post 570 **[2233]**, Leland, IL
Amer. Legion, Lemont Post 243 **[2236]**, Lemont, IL
Amer. Legion, Lenz-Gazecki Post 152 **[18856]**, Menasha, WI
Amer. Legion, Leo Carey Post 56 **[10255]**, Albert Lea, MN
Amer. Legion, Leon Burson Post 395 **[3108]**, Plano, IL
Amer. Legion, Leon J. Wetzel Post 9 **[12944]**, Winona, MN
Amer. Legion, Leora Weare Post 173 **[6401]**, Versailles, IN
Amer. Legion, Leroy Tout Post 338 **[4463]**, Dublin, IN
Amer. Legion, Leslie-Reddick Post 721 **[2561]**, Morrisonville, IL
Amer. Legion, Lester Newton Hensley Post 55 **[5865]**, Muncie, IN
Amer. Legion, Lester Reynolds Post 523 **[355]**, Brookport, IL
Amer. Legion, Lester Tjernlund Post 451 **[12362]**, St. Paul, MN
Amer. Legion, Lewis Post 208 **[14784]**, Convoy, OH
Amer. Legion, Lewis-Whitaker Post 520 **[15378]**, Hamilton, OH
Amer. Legion, Lewiston Post 198 **[8804]**, Lewiston, MI
Amer. Legion, Lewisville Post 561 **[11315]**, Lewisville, MN
Amer. Legion, Lexington Post 352 **[5760]**, Memphis, IN
Amer. Legion, Liberty Post 46 **[13327]**, Bellevue, OH
Amer. Legion, Liberty Post 289 **[3716]**, Strasburg, IL
Amer. Legion, Libertyville Post 329 **[2256]**, Libertyville, IL
Amer. Legion, Limestone Post 979 **[167]**, Bartonville, IL
Amer. Legion, Lincoln Post 82 **[4631]**, Fort Wayne, IN
Amer. Legion, Lincoln Post 102 **[1369]**, De Land, IL
Amer. Legion, Lincoln Square Post 473 **[680]**, Chicago, IL
Amer. Legion, Lincolnwood Post 1226 **[2287]**, Lincolnwood, IL
Amer. Legion, Lind-Gordon-Berg Post 106 **[12057]**, Proctor, MN
Amer. Legion, Linden Post 119 **[8816]**, Linden, MI
Amer. Legion, Linden Post 493 **[18419]**, Linden, WI
Amer. Legion, Lindstrom Post 83 **[11316]**, Lindstrom, MN
Amer. Legion, Lino Lakes Post 566 **[11319]**, Lino Lakes, MN
Amer. Legion, Linwood Laughy Post 217 **[10385]**, Baudette, MN
Amer. Legion, Lionel Boudreau Post 322 **[10746]**, Currie, MN
Amer. Legion, Liscum Bros. Post 482 **[17556]**, Bagley, WI
Amer. Legion, Littlefork Post 490 **[11341]**, Littlefork, MN
Amer. Legion, Lloyd Fleischer Post 1150 **[1513]**, Downs, IL
Amer. Legion, Locklar-Smith Post 550 **[1740]**, Freeburg, IL
Amer. Legion, Lockman-Jensen Post 499 **[18059]**, Gordon, WI
Amer. Legion, Lodi Post 523 **[15685]**, Lodi, OH
Amer. Legion, Loftness-Bandow Post 226 **[11043]**, Gibbon, MN
Amer. Legion, Logan Post 263 **[2271]**, Lincoln, IL
Amer. Legion, Logan Square Post 405 **[681]**, Chicago, IL
Amer. Legion, Lombard Post 391 **[2324]**, Lombard, IL
Amer. Legion, London Mills Post 470 **[2342]**, London Mills, IL
Amer. Legion, Long Point Post 1217 **[2345]**, Long Point, IL
Amer. Legion, Longton Post 618 **[11498]**, Minneapolis, MN
Amer. Legion, Lonsdale Post 586 **[11348]**, Lonsdale, MN
Amer. Legion, Loogootee Post 120 **[5702]**, Loogootee, IN
Amer. Legion, Loomis-Martin Post 188 **[17852]**, East Troy, WI
Amer. Legion, Lorain Post 30 **[15699]**, Lorain, OH
Amer. Legion, Lorentz Post 11 **[11373]**, Mankato, MN
Amer. Legion, Lost Five Post 444 **[3178]**, Rankin, IL
Amer. Legion, Lostant Post 173 **[2346]**, Lostant, IL
Amer. Legion, Loud Merkel La Plante Post 274 **[9315]**, Oscoda, MI
Amer. Legion, Loudon Post 257 **[15713]**, Loudonville, OH
Amer. Legion, Louis Monroe Post 53 **[4512]**, Elwood, IN
Amer. Legion, Louis Teistler Post 47 **[7214]**, Comstock Park, MI
Amer. Legion, Louis Tveite Post 317 **[10962]**, Emmons, MN
Amer. Legion, Louisville Post 914 **[2347]**, Louisville, IL
Amer. Legion, Loveland Post 256 **[15721]**, Loveland, OH
Amer. Legion, Loveless-Eikens Post 191 **[10616]**, Caledonia, MN
Amer. Legion, Lowell Beaver Post 470 **[4600]**, Fishers, IN
Amer. Legion, Lowell Post 101 **[5704]**, Lowell, IN
Amer. Legion, Lowell Post 750 **[15732]**, Lowell, OH
Amer. Legion, Lowell Stender Post 601 **[11865]**, New Germany, MN
Amer. Legion, Lowellville Post 247 **[15733]**, Lowellville, OH
Amer. Legion, Lozar-Mrace-Loushin Post 248 **[10953]**, Ely, MN
Amer. Legion, Lucas Vaughn Post 219 **[16267]**, Nova, OH
Amer. Legion, Ludlow Post 518 **[2357]**, Ludlow, IL
Amer. Legion, Luitink-Weishan Post 495 **[18941]**, Milwaukee, WI
Amer. Legion, Lulich-Ogrizovich Post 1001 **[682]**, Chicago, IL
Amer. Legion, Lund-Brown Post 132 **[19736]**, Siren, WI
Amer. Legion, Lundberg-Lee Post 266 **[11122]**, Hartland, MN
Amer. Legion, Luther-Hamshire-Pearsall Post 279 **[18813]**, Marshall, WI
Amer. Legion, Lybarger-Grimm Post 441 **[16987]**, Tontogany, OH
Amer. Legion, Lyle Post 105 **[11357]**, Lyle, MN
Amer. Legion, Machickanee Post 523 **[17450]**, Abrams, WI
Amer. Legion, Mackinac Island Post 299 **[8885]**, Mackinac Island, MI
Amer. Legion, Mackinder-Glenn Post 510 **[9876]**, Stockbridge, MI
Amer. Legion, Madden-Nottingham Post 348 **[5006]**, Indianapolis, IN
Amer. Legion, Madelia Post 19 **[11363]**, Madelia, MN
Amer. Legion, Madison Lake Post 269 **[11369]**, Madison Lake, MN
Amer. Legion, Madison Memorial Post 105 **[15692]**, London, OH
Amer. Legion, Madsen-Empey Post 89 **[19197]**, Minocqua, WI
Amer. Legion, Magnus Grondahl Post 325 **[12706]**, Starbuck, MN
Amer. Legion, Mahomet Post 1015 **[2379]**, Mahomet, IL
Amer. Legion, Mahoning Valley Post 15 **[16449]**, Poland, OH
Amer. Legion, Maki-Pinola Post 535 **[10367]**, Babbitt, MN
Amer. Legion, Malconta Post 24 **[15932]**, McConnelsville, OH
Amer. Legion, Manhattan Post 935 **[2383]**, Manhattan, IL
Amer. Legion, Manistee Post 10 **[8911]**, Manistee, MI
Amer. Legion, Manistique Post 83 **[7222]**, Cooks, MI
Amer. Legion, Manteno Post 755 **[2390]**, Manteno, IL
Amer. Legion, Manthey-Asmus Post 433 **[11041]**, Gaylord, MN
Amer. Legion, Mantua Post 193 **[15798]**, Mantua, OH
Amer. Legion, Mapes-Cathelyn Post 309 **[54]**, Annawan, IL
Amer. Legion, Maple Heights Post 309 **[15802]**, Maple Heights, OH
Amer. Legion, Maple Lake Post 131 **[11414]**, Maple Lake, MN
Amer. Legion, Maple Park Post 312 **[2391]**, Maple Park, IL
Amer. Legion, Maquon Post 1099 **[2395]**, Maquon, IL
Amer. Legion, Marengo Memorial Post 710 **[15809]**, Marengo, OH
Amer. Legion, Marietta Post 64 **[15813]**, Marietta, OH
Amer. Legion, Marine Post 273 **[683]**, Chicago, IL
Amer. Legion, Marion G.I. Post 584 **[15835]**, Marion, OH
Amer. Legion, Marion Lee Miller Post 931 **[3782]**, Towanda, IL
Amer. Legion, Marion Oshel Post 364 **[456]**, Carrier Mills, IL
Amer. Legion, Marion Post 179 **[13361]**, Blanchester, OH
Amer. Legion, Mark Hamilton Post 232 **[11499]**, Minneapolis, MN
Amer. Legion, Markham Manor Post 828 **[2416]**, Markham, IL
Amer. Legion, Marne Post 13 **[3099]**, Plainfield, IL
Amer. Legion, Marne Post 376 **[8928]**, Marne, MI
Amer. Legion, Marrs-Meyer Post 991 **[4068]**, Worth, IL
Amer. Legion, Marseilles Post 235 **[2419]**, Marseilles, IL
Amer. Legion, Marshallville Post 718 **[15859]**, Marshallville, OH
Amer. Legion, Martell-Musiaw Post 325 **[18058]**, Goodman, WI
Amer. Legion, Martin-Jensen Post 308 **[11026]**, Franklin, MN
Amer. Legion, Martin Krueger Post 407 **[12969]**, Winsted, MN
Amer. Legion, Martinez-Garcia-Nerio-Reyes Post 500 **[9599]**, Saginaw, MI
Amer. Legion, Martinsville Post 230 **[5750]**, Martinsville, IN
Amer. Legion, Martinsville Post 515 **[2425]**, Martinsville, IL
Amer. Legion, Marvin Seemann Garfield Ridge Post 1112 **[684]**, Chicago, IL
Amer. Legion, Mary P. Klaser Memorial Post 727 **[17387]**, Youngstown, OH
Amer. Legion, Marysville Post 449 **[8973]**, Marysville, MI
Amer. Legion, Massillon Post 221 **[15880]**, Massillon, OH
Amer. Legion, Matt Urban Post 40 **[9058]**, Monroe, MI
Amer. Legion, Matthews-Carter Post 325 **[15756]**, Manchester, OH
Amer. Legion, Mattox-Henslin Post 378 **[17655]**, Brandon, WI
Amer. Legion, Maumee Post 320 **[15900]**, Maumee, OH
Amer. Legion, Maxson-Van-Eps Post 368 **[10370]**, Backus, MN
Amer. Legion, May Berry Post 469 **[4758]**, Frankton, IN
Amer. Legion, Mayfield Heights Post 163 **[13641]**, Chardon, OH
Amer. Legion, Maynard-Schulgen Post 216 **[18421]**, Lodi, WI
Amer. Legion, Maywood Post 126 **[4871]**, Hammond, IN
Amer. Legion, Maywood Post 133 **[2470]**, Melrose Park, IL
Amer. Legion, Mazeppa Post 588 **[11445]**, Mazeppa, MN
Amer. Legion, Mazon Post 352 **[2450]**, Mazon, IL
Amer. Legion, Mc-Cann-Frederick Post 414 **[15326]**, Glouster, OH
Amer. Legion, Mc-Cann-Richards Post 105 **[19734]**, Shullsburg, WI
Amer. Legion, Mc Clure Post 900 **[2451]**, Mc Clure, IL
Amer. Legion, Mc Connell Post 1225 **[2452]**, Mc Connell, IL
Amer. Legion, Mc Cormack Post 658 **[3951]**, West Salem, IL
Amer. Legion, Mc-Cormick-Rose Post 308 **[18030]**, Gays Mills, WI
Amer. Legion, Mc-Dermott-Steindorf Post 144 **[17458]**, Albany, WI

Amer. Legion, Mc-Donald-Osmer Post 451 **[7893]**, Grand Rapids, MI
Amer. Legion, Mc Donough County Post 6 **[2366]**, Macomb, IL
Amer. Legion, Mc-Gowan-Johnson Post 68 **[9345]**, Paw Paw, MI
Amer. Legion, Mc Henry Post 491 **[2455]**, McHenry, IL
Amer. Legion, Mc-Ilvaine-Kothe Post 153 **[5007]**, Indianapolis, IN
Amer. Legion, Mc Kinley Post 76 **[16624]**, Sebring, OH
Amer. Legion, Mc Kinlock Post 264 **[2193]**, Lake Forest, IL
Amer. Legion, Mc-Kinney-Hatlevig Post 35 **[17945]**, Evansville, WI
Amer. Legion, Mc-Lain-Chandler Post 153 **[1996]**, Hillsboro, IL
Amer. Legion, Mc-Lain-Glover Post 595 **[1639]**, Equality, IL
Amer. Legion, Mc Nabb Post 1242 **[2454]**, Mc Nabb, IL
Amer. Legion, Mc-Veigh-Dunn Post 60 **[11081]**, Grand Rapids, MN
Amer. Legion, Mc Whirter Post 488 **[14807]**, Crestline, OH
Amer. Legion, Mead-Rath-Gutke Post 339 **[17465]**, Almond, WI
Amer. Legion, Medora Post 399 **[2468]**, Medora, IL
Amer. Legion, Medora Post 453 **[5759]**, Medora, IN
Amer. Legion, Meighen-Thompson Post 161 **[11308]**, Le Roy, MN
Amer. Legion, Melcher-Matti Post 320 **[18228]**, Humbird, WI
Amer. Legion, Melrose Post 101 **[11450]**, Melrose, MN
Amer. Legion, Melvin Post 642 **[2473]**, Melvin, IL
Amer. Legion, Melvindale Post 472 **[8997]**, Melvindale, MI
Amer. Legion, Memorial Post 188 **[4920]**, Hillsboro, IN
Amer. Legion, Memorial Post 196 **[4190]**, Bloomfield, IN
Amer. Legion, Memorial Post 320 **[10195]**, Yale, MI
Amer. Legion, Memorial Post 614 **[15425]**, Hilliard, OH
Amer. Legion, Memorial-Square Post 61 **[17064]**, Vermilion, OH
Amer. Legion, Mendota Post 540 **[2475]**, Mendota, IL
Amer. Legion, Menominee Post 146 **[9001]**, Menominee, MI
Amer. Legion, Menominee Post 497 **[18315]**, Keshena, WI
Amer. Legion, Mentor Post 352 **[15962]**, Mentor, OH
Amer. Legion, Menzie-Reece Post 258 **[6040]**, Pierceton, IN
Amer. Legion, Mercier-Kero Post 371 **[18167]**, Gurney, WI
Amer. Legion, Meredith Low Post 134 **[6514]**, Westport, IN
Amer. Legion, Meredosia Post 516 **[2477]**, Meredosia, IL
Amer. Legion, Merle Guild Post 208 **[63]**, Arlington Heights, IL
Amer. Legion, Merrick Potter Post 566 **[8999]**, Memphis, MI
Amer. Legion, Merrillville Post 430 **[5764]**, Merrillville, IN
Amer. Legion, Merritt Lamb Post 9 **[9137]**, Muskegon, MI
Amer. Legion, Merritt Lamb Post 102 **[9523]**, Rockford, MI
Amer. Legion, Merritt Post 142 **[17144]**, Waverly, OH
Amer. Legion, Merton-Dale Post 80 **[12884]**, Wheaton, MN
Amer. Legion, Metz-Mosher Post 244 **[20145]**, Westfield, WI
Amer. Legion, Meuli-Kelean-Kramer-Dannenberg Post 77 **[17742]**, Chippewa Falls, WI
Amer. Legion, Mexican-American Post 505 **[7306]**, Detroit, MI
Amer. Legion, Meyer-Thompson Post 536 **[11857]**, Nassau, MN
Amer. Legion, Meyers-Youngell Post 211 **[17965]**, Florence, WI
Amer. Legion, Miami Valley Post 652 **[14976]**, De Graff, OH
Amer. Legion, Miamisburg Post 165 **[15983]**, Miamisburg, OH
Amer. Legion, Michael-Boock Post 6 **[12009]**, Pipestone, MN
Amer. Legion-Michigan Dept. **[8537]**, Lansing, MI
Amer. Legion, Michigan Post 1 **[10060]**, Warren, MI
Amer. Legion, Michigan Post 2 **[7894]**, Grand Rapids, MI
Amer. Legion, Michigan Post 3 **[9717]**, Sault Ste. Marie, MI
Amer. Legion, Michigan Post 4 **[9085]**, Mount Clemens, MI
Amer. Legion, Michigan Post 6 **[8191]**, Holland, MI
Amer. Legion, Michigan Post 7 **[7080]**, Caro, MI
Amer. Legion, Michigan Post 8 **[9428]**, Port Huron, MI
Amer. Legion, Michigan Post 14 **[9969]**, Troy, MI
Amer. Legion, Michigan Post 15 **[7578]**, Eaton Rapids, MI
Amer. Legion, Michigan Post 17 **[8330]**, Iron River, MI
Amer. Legion, Michigan Post 25 **[9571]**, Royal Oak, MI
Amer. Legion, Michigan Post 28 **[7852]**, Grand Haven, MI
Amer. Legion, Michigan Post 29 **[8357]**, Jackson, MI
Amer. Legion, Michigan Post 30 **[9742]**, Shelby, MI
Amer. Legion, Michigan Post 31 **[7137]**, Chelsea, MI
Amer. Legion, Michigan Post 32 **[8829]**, Livonia, MI
Amer. Legion, Michigan Post 33 **[10223]**, Zeeland, MI
Amer. Legion, Michigan Post 36 **[8415]**, Kalamazoo, MI
Amer. Legion, Michigan Post 44 **[8932]**, Marquette, MI
Amer. Legion, Michigan Post 45 **[8153]**, Hastings, MI
Amer. Legion, Michigan Post 49 **[9762]**, South Haven, MI
Amer. Legion, Michigan Post 53 **[8174]**, Hillsdale, MI
Amer. Legion, Michigan Post 54 **[6845]**, Battle Creek, MI
Amer. Legion, Michigan Post 55 **[6589]**, Albion, MI
Amer. Legion, Michigan Post 56 **[7307]**, Detroit, MI
Amer. Legion, Michigan Post 60 **[9059]**, Monroe, MI
Amer. Legion, Michigan Post 61 **[8790]**, Laurium, MI
Amer. Legion, Michigan Post 62 **[9668]**, St. Ignace, MI
Amer. Legion, Michigan Post 65 **[6641]**, Alpena, MI
Amer. Legion, Michigan Post 67 **[8811]**, Lincoln Park, MI
Amer. Legion, Michigan Post 72 **[7488]**, Dundee, MI
Amer. Legion, Michigan Post 76 **[8869]**, Ludington, MI
Amer. Legion, Michigan Post 77 **[7308]**, Detroit, MI
Amer. Legion, Michigan Post 78 **[9480]**, Reed City, MI
Amer. Legion, Michigan Post 79 **[8965]**, Marshall, MI
Amer. Legion, Michigan Post 86 **[7280]**, Dearborn Heights, MI
Amer. Legion, Michigan Post 87 **[7231]**, Crystal Falls, MI
Amer. Legion, Michigan Post 89 **[6603]**, Allegan, MI
Amer. Legion, Michigan Post 92 **[9534]**, Rockland, MI
Amer. Legion, Michigan Post 94 **[7042]**, Cadillac, MI
Amer. Legion, Michigan Post 95 **[7129]**, Cheboygan, MI
Amer. Legion, Michigan Post 97 **[6564]**, Adrian, MI
Amer. Legion, Michigan Post 98 **[6939]**, Big Rapids, MI
Amer. Legion, Michigan Post 101 **[8065]**, Greenville, MI
Amer. Legion, Michigan Post 114 **[8345]**, Ishpeming, MI
Amer. Legion, Michigan Post 121 **[9539]**, Rogers City, MI
Amer. Legion, Michigan Post 122 **[10181]**, Wolverine, MI
Amer. Legion, Michigan Post 126 **[7309]**, Detroit, MI
Amer. Legion, Michigan Post 127 **[7475]**, Dorr, MI
Amer. Legion, Michigan Post 128 **[7310]**, Detroit, MI
Amer. Legion, Michigan Post 129 **[9456]**, Portland, MI
Amer. Legion, Michigan Post 132 **[8170]**, Highland Park, MI
Amer. Legion, Michigan Post 133 **[6822]**, Baldwin, MI
Amer. Legion, Michigan Post 135 **[8306]**, Imlay City, MI
Amer. Legion, Michigan Post 142 **[7074]**, Capac, MI
Amer. Legion, Michigan Post 144 **[8524]**, Lanse, MI
Amer. Legion, Michigan Post 147 **[9220]**, Northville, MI
Amer. Legion, Michigan Post 149 **[8233]**, Holly, MI
Amer. Legion, Michigan Post 151 **[7711]**, Flint, MI
Amer. Legion, Michigan Post 153 **[9673]**, St. Johns, MI
Amer. Legion, Michigan Post 155 **[7025]**, Britton, MI
Amer. Legion, Michigan Post 167 **[7166]**, Clawson, MI
Amer. Legion, Michigan Post 169 **[9185]**, New Buffalo, MI
Amer. Legion, Michigan Post 175 **[9713]**, Saranac, MI
Amer. Legion, Michigan Post 178 **[8538]**, Lansing, MI
Amer. Legion, Michigan Post 179 **[7895]**, Grand Rapids, MI
Amer. Legion, Michigan Post 182 **[8286]**, Hubbardston, MI
Amer. Legion, Michigan Post 184 **[7311]**, Detroit, MI
Amer. Legion, Michigan Post 185 **[9138]**, Muskegon, MI
Amer. Legion, Michigan Post 186 **[8106]**, Hancock, MI
Amer. Legion, Michigan Post 187 **[9572]**, Royal Oak, MI
Amer. Legion, Michigan Post 192 **[9910]**, Temperance, MI
Amer. Legion, Michigan Post 193 **[8880]**, Luna Pier, MI
Amer. Legion, Michigan Post 194 **[9361]**, Petoskey, MI
Amer. Legion, Michigan Post 202 **[7312]**, Detroit, MI
Amer. Legion, Michigan Post 214 **[7313]**, Detroit, MI
Amer. Legion, Michigan Post 215 **[7777]**, Fowlerville, MI
Amer. Legion, Michigan Post 216 **[9049]**, Milford, MI
Amer. Legion, Michigan Post 217 **[9060]**, Monroe, MI
Amer. Legion, Michigan Post 218 **[7127]**, Chassell, MI
Amer. Legion, Michigan Post 221 **[7784]**, Frankfort, MI
Amer. Legion, Michigan Post 223 **[7219]**, Constantine, MI
Amer. Legion, Michigan Post 225 **[8539]**, Lansing, MI
Amer. Legion, Michigan Post 226 **[7113]**, Charlevoix, MI
Amer. Legion, Michigan Post 228 **[6995]**, Boyne City, MI
Amer. Legion, Michigan Post 232 **[7281]**, Dearborn Heights, MI
Amer. Legion, Michigan Post 235 **[7007]**, Brighton, MI
Amer. Legion, Michigan Post 236 **[7627]**, Evart, MI
Amer. Legion, Michigan Post 239 **[8821]**, Linwood, MI
Amer. Legion, Michigan Post 250 **[9385]**, Plainwell, MI
Amer. Legion, Michigan Post 252 **[8053]**, Grass Lake, MI
Amer. Legion, Michigan Post 253 **[9573]**, Royal Oak, MI
Amer. Legion, Michigan Post 260 **[8416]**, Kalamazoo, MI
Amer. Legion, Michigan Post 267 **[7235]**, Davison, MI
Amer. Legion, Michigan Post 279 **[8823]**, Litchfield, MI
Amer. Legion, Michigan Post 297 **[9471]**, Ravenna, MI
Amer. Legion, Michigan Post 298 **[6846]**, Battle Creek, MI
Amer. Legion, Michigan Post 301 **[9469]**, Rapid River, MI
Amer. Legion, Michigan Post 304 **[9775]**, South Range, MI
Amer. Legion, Michigan Post 306 **[7712]**, Flint, MI
Amer. Legion, Michigan Post 317 **[9304]**, Onaway, MI
Amer. Legion, Michigan Post 322 **[9698]**, Saline, MI
Amer. Legion, Michigan Post 326 **[9861]**, Sterling Heights, MI

Amer. Legion, Michigan Post 330 **[7692]**, Ferndale, MI
Amer. Legion, Michigan Post 343 **[9221]**, Northville, MI
Amer. Legion, Michigan Post 344 **[7807]**, Galien, MI
Amer. Legion, Michigan Post 348 **[9056]**, Mio, MI
Amer. Legion, Michigan Post 351 **[10033]**, Utica, MI
Amer. Legion, Michigan Post 367 **[9077]**, Montrose, MI
Amer. Legion, Michigan Post 369 **[9707]**, Sandusky, MI
Amer. Legion, Michigan Post 375 **[7314]**, Detroit, MI
Amer. Legion, Michigan Post 381 **[7229]**, Croton, MI
Amer. Legion, Michigan Post 382 **[9651]**, St. Clair, MI
Amer. Legion, Michigan Post 386 **[7574]**, Eastpointe, MI
Amer. Legion, Michigan Post 396 **[7809]**, Garden City, MI
Amer. Legion, Michigan Post 400 **[9491]**, Richville, MI
Amer. Legion, Michigan Post 410 **[6917]**, Benton Harbor, MI
Amer. Legion, Michigan Post 411 **[8165]**, Hesperia, MI
Amer. Legion, Michigan Post 412 **[6834]**, Bath, MI
Amer. Legion, Michigan Post 422 **[8097]**, Hale, MI
Amer. Legion, Michigan Post 426 **[9965]**, Trenton, MI
Amer. Legion, Michigan Post 430 **[7896]**, Grand Rapids, MI
Amer. Legion, Michigan Post 458 **[7815]**, Gaylord, MI
Amer. Legion, Michigan Post 480 **[8475]**, Kalkaska, MI
Amer. Legion, Michigan Post 483 **[7636]**, Farmington, MI
Amer. Legion, Michigan Post 491 **[8800]**, Leslie, MI
Amer. Legion, Michigan Post 514 **[8298]**, Ida, MI
Amer. Legion, Michigan Post 526 **[9132]**, Munith, MI
Amer. Legion, Michigan Post 537 **[7218]**, Conklin, MI
Amer. Legion, Michigan Post 555 **[7247]**, Dearborn, MI
Amer. Legion, Mickelsons-Martin Post 313 **[17630]**, Black Earth, WI
Amer. Legion, Middleton Post 275 **[18902]**, Middleton, WI
Amer. Legion, Middletown Post 218 **[16003]**, Middletown, OH
Amer. Legion, Middleville Post 140 **[9015]**, Middleville, MI
Amer. Legion, Mikado Post 254 **[9045]**, Mikado, MI
Amer. Legion, Mike and George Bustos Post 7 **[4944]**, Huntington, IN
Amer. Legion, Mike-Militello-Joseph Post 570 **[8079]**, Grosse Pointe, MI
Amer. Legion, Mil-Bow-Mar Post 280 **[15365]**, Greenwich, OH
Amer. Legion, Milan Post 359 **[11467]**, Milan, MN
Amer. Legion, Milan Post 569 **[2488]**, Milan, IL
Amer. Legion, Miles-Hagen Post 200 **[17631]**, Black River Falls, WI
Amer. Legion, Millard-Brown Post 156 **[5831]**, Montpelier, IN
Amer. Legion, Miller-Justman-Guelig Post 270 **[19888]**, Theresa, WI
Amer. Legion, Miller-Manning Post 418 **[1490]**, Dongola, IL
Amer. Legion, Miller-Stockum Post 485 **[14251]**, Cleves, OH
Amer. Legion, Millersport Post 637 **[16039]**, Millersport, OH
Amer. Legion, Millstadt Post 502 **[2496]**, Millstadt, IL
Amer. Legion, Milltown Post 332 **[5804]**, Milltown, IN
Amer. Legion, Millville Valley Post 579 **[11469]**, Millville, MN
Amer. Legion, Milton Olive Post 1932 **[685]**, Chicago, IL
Amer. Legion, Milton W. Mager Memorial Post 691 **[2486]**, Midlothian, IL
Amer. Legion, Milwaukee Fire Fighters Post 426 **[18942]**, Milwaukee, WI
Amer. Legion, Milwaukee Police Post 415 **[18943]**, Milwaukee, WI
Amer. Legion, Milwaukee Post 18 **[18944]**, Milwaukee, WI
Amer. Legion, Milwaukee Womens Post 448 **[18945]**, Milwaukee, WI
Amer. Legion, Minford Post 622 **[16047]**, Minford, OH
Amer. Legion, Mingo Junction Post 351 **[16048]**, Mingo Junction, OH
Amer. Legion, Minneapolis Fire and Police Post 396 **[11500]**, Minneapolis, MN
Amer. Legion, Minneapolis Post 1 **[11501]**, Minneapolis, MN
Amer. Legion, Minneapolis Post office Post 540 **[12107]**, Richfield, MN
Amer. Legion, Minneapolis-Richfield Post 435 **[12108]**, Richfield, MN
Amer. Legion, Minneota Post 199 **[11782]**, Minneota, MN
Amer. Legion of Minnesota **[12363]**, St. Paul, MN
Amer. Legion, Minnesota At Large Post 1982 **[12364]**, St. Paul, MN
Amer. Legion, Minnesota Post 7 **[12672]**, Sleepy Eye, MN
Amer. Legion, Minnesota Post 12 **[11345]**, Long Prairie, MN
Amer. Legion, Minnesota Post 13 **[11171]**, Hitterdal, MN
Amer. Legion, Minnesota Post 20 **[10732]**, Crookston, MN
Amer. Legion, Minnesota Post 21 **[11818]**, Moorhead, MN
Amer. Legion, Minnesota Post 23 **[11447]**, Mcgregor, MN
Amer. Legion, Minnesota Post 24 **[12208]**, Roseau, MN
Amer. Legion, Minnesota Post 25 **[12843]**, Warroad, MN
Amer. Legion, Minnesota Post 35 **[10290]**, Alvarado, MN
Amer. Legion, Minnesota Post 37 **[12612]**, St. Peter, MN
Amer. Legion, Minnesota Post 38 **[12093]**, Redwood Falls, MN
Amer. Legion, Minnesota Post 39 **[11909]**, North St. Paul, MN
Amer. Legion, Minnesota Post 41 **[11298]**, Lamberton, MN
Amer. Legion, Minnesota Post 43 **[10982]**, Faribault, MN
Amer. Legion, Minnesota Post 45 **[11876]**, New Prague, MN
Amer. Legion, Minnesota Post 46 **[11333]**, Little Falls, MN
Amer. Legion, Minnesota Post 47 **[11124]**, Hastings, MN
Amer. Legion, Minnesota Post 50 **[12810]**, Wabasha, MN
Amer. Legion, Minnesota Post 53 **[10526]**, Breckenridge, MN
Amer. Legion, Minnesota Post 54 **[12076]**, Red Wing, MN
Amer. Legion, Minnesota Post 55 **[11309]**, Le Sueur, MN
Amer. Legion, Minnesota Post 57 **[10649]**, Chaska, MN
Amer. Legion, Minnesota Post 59 **[11799]**, Montevideo, MN
Amer. Legion, Minnesota Post 69 **[11095]**, Granite Falls, MN
Amer. Legion, Minnesota Post 71 **[10800]**, Duluth, MN
Amer. Legion, Minnesota Post 74 **[11141]**, Henderson, MN
Amer. Legion, Minnesota Post 76 **[12271]**, St. Cloud, MN
Amer. Legion, Minnesota Post 77 **[11956]**, Owatonna, MN
Amer. Legion, Minnesota Post 79 **[11807]**, Montgomery, MN
Amer. Legion, Minnesota Post 93 **[12254]**, Rush City, MN
Amer. Legion, Minnesota Post 99 **[11502]**, Minneapolis, MN
Amer. Legion, Minnesota Post 102 **[10301]**, Anoka, MN
Amer. Legion, Minnesota Post 110 **[11273]**, Lake City, MN
Amer. Legion, Minnesota Post 111 **[11948]**, Osakis, MN
Amer. Legion, Minnesota Post 113 **[11431]**, Marshall, MN
Amer. Legion, Minnesota Post 119 **[10613]**, Byron, MN
Amer. Legion, Minnesota Post 121 **[12851]**, Watertown, MN
Amer. Legion, Minnesota Post 122 **[10763]**, Deer River, MN
Amer. Legion, Minnesota Post 135 **[11139]**, Hector, MN
Amer. Legion, Minnesota Post 136 **[11010]**, Flensburg, MN
Amer. Legion, Minnesota Post 137 **[12253]**, Royalton, MN
Amer. Legion, Minnesota Post 140 **[11079]**, Grand Meadow, MN
Amer. Legion, Minnesota Post 143 **[10567]**, Browntoin, MN
Amer. Legion, Minnesota Post 144 **[10399]**, Belle Plaine, MN
Amer. Legion, Minnesota Post 147 **[10440]**, Big Lake, MN
Amer. Legion, Minnesota Post 149 **[11843]**, Morristown, MN
Amer. Legion, Minnesota Post 151 **[12624]**, Sandstone, MN
Amer. Legion, Minnesota Post 153 **[10377]**, Barnesville, MN
Amer. Legion, Minnesota Post 156 **[11429]**, Marietta, MN
Amer. Legion, Minnesota Post 167 **[12912]**, Willmar, MN
Amer. Legion, Minnesota Post 169 **[10502]**, Boyd, MN
Amer. Legion, Minnesota Post 175 **[12788]**, Villard, MN
Amer. Legion, Minnesota Post 181 **[11285]**, Lake Park, MN
Amer. Legion, Minnesota Post 184 **[12004]**, Pine Island, MN
Amer. Legion, Minnesota Post 189 **[10989]**, Farmington, MN
Amer. Legion, Minnesota Post 193 **[10395]**, Becker, MN
Amer. Legion, Minnesota Post 194 **[11232]**, Ivanhoe, MN
Amer. Legion, Minnesota Post 195 **[11142]**, Hendricks, MN
Amer. Legion, Minnesota Post 196 **[10951]**, Ellsworth, MN
Amer. Legion, Minnesota Post 214 **[11299]**, Lancaster, MN
Amer. Legion, Minnesota Post 227 **[10748]**, Danube, MN
Amer. Legion, Minnesota Post 234 **[11503]**, Minneapolis, MN
Amer. Legion, Minnesota Post 243 **[10343]**, Askov, MN
Amer. Legion, Minnesota Post 253 **[11350]**, Lowry, MN
Amer. Legion, Minnesota Post 255 **[10505]**, Brainerd, MN
Amer. Legion, Minnesota Post 256 **[10676]**, Clearbrook, MN
Amer. Legion, Minnesota Post 257 **[12695]**, Springfield, MN
Amer. Legion, Minnesota Post 261 **[11261]**, Kimball, MN
Amer. Legion, Minnesota Post 262 **[10687]**, Cloquet, MN
Amer. Legion, Minnesota Post 263 **[12814]**, Wabasso, MN
Amer. Legion, Minnesota Post 267 **[12834]**, Walnut Grove, MN
Amer. Legion, Minnesota Post 271 **[11982]**, Paynesville, MN
Amer. Legion, Minnesota Post 273 **[11038]**, Garvin, MN
Amer. Legion, Minnesota Post 274 **[11470]**, Milroy, MN
Amer. Legion, Minnesota Post 275 **[12646]**, Seaforth, MN
Amer. Legion, Minnesota Post 277 **[12628]**, Sartell, MN
Amer. Legion, Minnesota Post 280 **[10877]**, Eagle Bend, MN
Amer. Legion, Minnesota Post 282 **[12330]**, St. Louis Park, MN
Amer. Legion, Minnesota Post 283 **[10762]**, Deer Creek, MN

Amer. Legion, Minnesota Post 284 **[10637]**, Cass Lake, MN
Amer. Legion, Minnesota Post 285 **[11287]**, Lake Wilson, MN
Amer. Legion, Minnesota Post 287 **[11783]**, Minnesota Lake, MN
Amer. Legion, Minnesota Post 289 **[10383]**, Battle Lake, MN
Amer. Legion, Minnesota Post 290 **[10617]**, Cambridge, MN
Amer. Legion, Minnesota Post 291 **[11504]**, Minneapolis, MN
Amer. Legion, Minnesota Post 299 **[11360]**, Mabel, MN
Amer. Legion, Minnesota Post 306 **[12786]**, Vesta, MN
Amer. Legion, Minnesota Post 320 **[11179]**, Hopkins, MN
Amer. Legion, Minnesota Post 321 **[10934]**, Elbow Lake, MN
Amer. Legion, Minnesota Post 328 **[12324]**, St. Joseph, MN
Amer. Legion, Minnesota Post 331 **[11950]**, Oslo, MN
Amer. Legion, Minnesota Post 340 **[11164]**, Hill City, MN
Amer. Legion, Minnesota Post 347 **[11169]**, Hinckley, MN
Amer. Legion, Minnesota Post 356 **[12655]**, Sherburn, MN
Amer. Legion, Minnesota Post 363 **[10248]**, Akeley, MN
Amer. Legion, Minnesota Post 365 **[11116]**, Hanska, MN
Amer. Legion, Minnesota Post 366 **[10436]**, Bertha, MN
Amer. Legion, Minnesota Post 386 **[10862]**, Dundee, MN
Amer. Legion, Minnesota Post 391 **[12732]**, Storden, MN
Amer. Legion, Minnesota Post 392 **[12649]**, Shafer, MN
Amer. Legion, Minnesota Post 394 **[11113]**, Hamel, MN
Amer. Legion, Minnesota Post 402 **[11109]**, Halstad, MN
Amer. Legion, Minnesota Post 412 **[12778]**, Ulen, MN
Amer. Legion, Minnesota Post 437 **[11505]**, Minneapolis, MN
Amer. Legion, Minnesota Post 438 **[12008]**, Pinewood, MN
Amer. Legion, Minnesota Post 444 **[11463]**, Middle River, MN
Amer. Legion, Minnesota Post 458 **[10501]**, Boy River, MN
Amer. Legion, Minnesota Post 460 **[12259]**, Russell, MN
Amer. Legion, Minnesota Post 461 **[12252]**, Round Lake, MN
Amer. Legion, Minnesota Post 466 **[12733]**, Strandquist, MN
Amer. Legion, Minnesota Post 467 **[11352]**, Lucan, MN
Amer. Legion, Minnesota Post 468 **[11506]**, Minneapolis, MN
Amer. Legion, Minnesota Post 469 **[10581]**, Buffalo Lake, MN
Amer. Legion, Minnesota Post 478 **[11117]**, Hardwick, MN
Amer. Legion, Minnesota Post 484 **[12365]**, St. Paul, MN
Amer. Legion, Minnesota Post 486 **[10771]**, Delavan, MN
Amer. Legion, Minnesota Post 511 **[11507]**, Minneapolis, MN
Amer. Legion, Minnesota Post 514 **[11415]**, Maple Plain, MN
Amer. Legion, Minnesota Post 519 **[10679]**, Clements, MN
Amer. Legion, Minnesota Post 534 **[11176]**, Holland, MN
Amer. Legion, Minnesota Post 550 **[10459]**, Bloomington, MN
Amer. Legion, Minnesota Post 558 **[10801]**, Duluth, MN
Amer. Legion, Minnesota Post 563 **[10568]**, Bruno, MN
Amer. Legion, Minnesota Post 572 **[12366]**, St. Paul, MN
Amer. Legion, Minnesota Post 576 **[10365]**, Avoca, MN
Amer. Legion, Minnesota Post 582 **[12103]**, Revere, MN
Amer. Legion, Minnesota Post 587 **[12829]**, Waldorf, MN
Amer. Legion, Minnesota Post 597 **[12264]**, St. Bonifacius, MN
Amer. Legion, Minnesota Post 616 **[10292]**, Amboy, MN
Amer. Legion, Minnesota Post 622 **[12319]**, St. Francis, MN
Amer. Legion, Minnesota Post 626 **[10401]**, Beltrami, MN
Amer. Legion, Minnesota Post 627 **[11896]**, Nisswa, MN
Amer. Legion, Minnesota Post 628 **[12201]**, Rockford, MN
Amer. Legion, Minnesota Post 634 **[12367]**, St. Paul, MN
Amer. Legion, Minnesota Post 642 **[10500]**, Bowlus, MN
Amer. Legion, Minnesota Post 1700 **[10585]**, Burnsville, MN
Amer. Legion, Minnesota Post 4444 **[12368]**, St. Paul, MN
Amer. Legion, Minnesota Veterans Home Post 581 **[11508]**, Minneapolis, MN
Amer. Legion, Minnetonka Post 398 **[11847]**, Mound, MN
Amer. Legion, Minonk Post 142 **[2499]**, Minonk, IL
Amer. Legion, Minooka Post 1188 **[2500]**, Minooka, IL
Amer. Legion, Minster Post 387 **[16049]**, Minster, OH
Amer. Legion, Mishawaka Post 161 **[5806]**, Mishawaka, IN
Amer. Legion, Mississinewa Post 95 **[5545]**, Jonesboro, IN
Amer. Legion, Mittlestat-Smith Post 337 **[7702]**, Flat Rock, MI
Amer. Legion, Mixtacki-Johnson Post 337 **[19544]**, Pulaski, WI
Amer. Legion, Moe-Indihar Post 138 **[11045]**, Gilbert, MN
Amer. Legion, Moe-Miller Post 12 **[19760]**, Spooner, WI
Amer. Legion, Moen-Zimek Post 88 **[11098]**, Greenbush, MN
Amer. Legion, Moline **[2515]**, Moline, IL
Amer. Legion, Momence-Ganeer Post 40 **[2537]**, Momence, IL
Amer. Legion, Moncravie Post 425 **[1997]**, Hillsboro, IL
Amer. Legion, Mondt-Lampe Post 1239 **[136]**, Aviston, IL
Amer. Legion, Monnier-Duplain Post 548 **[15716]**, Louisville, OH
Amer. Legion, Monona Grove Post 429 **[19206]**, Monona, WI
Amer. Legion, Monroe Post 87 **[17305]**, Woodsfield, OH
Amer. Legion, Montgomery-Plant Post 10 **[20031]**, Wausau, WI
Amer. Legion, Monticello Post 260 **[11809]**, Monticello, MN
Amer. Legion, Montpelier Post 109 **[16059]**, Montpelier, OH
Amer. Legion, Moore-Irvin Post 359 **[6087]**, Richmond, IN
Amer. Legion, Moore-Long Post 64 **[18390]**, Ladysmith, WI
Amer. Legion, Mooresville Post 103 **[5834]**, Mooresville, IN
Amer. Legion, Morenci Post 368 **[9082]**, Morenci, MI
Amer. Legion, Morris-Baldridge Post 583 **[13646]**, Cherry Fork, OH
Amer. Legion, Morris Post 294 **[2551]**, Morris, IL
Amer. Legion, Morrison-Mead Post 181 **[8988]**, Mayville, MI
Amer. Legion, Morrison Post 328 **[2556]**, Morrison, IL
Amer. Legion, Morton Grove Post 134 **[2565]**, Morton Grove, IL
Amer. Legion, Morton-Guntley Post 349 **[8825]**, Little Lake, MI
Amer. Legion, Morton Post 318 **[2562]**, Morton, IL
Amer. Legion, Moser-Ortmann Post 130 **[19677]**, Sharon, WI
Amer. Legion, Moss-Walton Post 953 **[2074]**, Jacksonville, IL
Amer. Legion, Mt. Auburn Post 1057 **[318]**, Blue Mound, IL
Amer. Legion, Mt. Carroll Post 67 **[2576]**, Mount Carroll, IL
Amer. Legion, Mt. Greenwood Post 844 **[4069]**, Worth, IL
Amer. Legion, Mount Moriah Post 460 **[8540]**, Lansing, MI
Amer. Legion, Mount Morris Post 143 **[2578]**, Mount Morris, IL
Amer. Legion, Mount Prospect Post 525 **[2583]**, Mount Prospect, IL
Amer. Legion, Mt. Sterling Post 374 **[2591]**, Mount Sterling, IL
Amer. Legion, Mt. Sterling Post 417 **[16077]**, Mount Sterling, OH
Amer. Legion, Mt. Washington Post 484 **[13721]**, Cincinnati, OH
Amer. Legion, Mount-Wilson Post 473 **[6171]**, Scottsburg, IN
Amer. Legion, Mountain Lake Post 389 **[11854]**, Mountain Lake, MN
Amer. Legion, Moyer-Pooler Post 159 **[4899]**, Hartford City, IN
Amer. Legion, M.R.L. Post 772 **[3492]**, Somonauk, IL
Amer. Legion, Mulberry Grove Post 1180 **[2608]**, Mulberry Grove, IL
Amer. Legion, Mulford-Butler Post 511 **[15930]**, McComb, OH
Amer. Legion, Mullaney-Mc-Trusty Post 428 **[17470]**, Amberg, WI
Amer. Legion, Mumm-Welsh Post 352 **[17723]**, Cassville, WI
Amer. Legion, Mundelein Post 867 **[2610]**, Mundelein, IL
Amer. Legion, Murbach-Siefert Post 479 **[16816]**, Swanton, OH
Amer. Legion, Murphy-Johnson Post 94 **[12255]**, Rushford, MN
Amer. Legion, Murray Post 420 **[16095]**, Murray City, OH
Amer. Legion, Murrayville Post 311 **[2622]**, Murrayville, IL
Amer. Legion, Muskego Post 356 **[19259]**, Muskego, WI
Amer. Legion, Myrin-James Post 443 **[11229]**, Ironton, MN
Amer. Legion, Naperville Post 43 **[2625]**, Naperville, IL
Amer. Legion, Nappanee Post 154 **[5907]**, Nappanee, IN
Amer. Legion, Nassen-Detert Post 529 **[10640]**, Ceylon, MN
Amer. Legion, Natl. Defense Employees Post 792 **[16112]**, New Albany, OH
Amer. Legion, National-Guard-Iron-Fist Post 70 **[8121]**, Harper Woods, MI
Amer. Legion, Natl. Trail Post 756 **[15348]**, Gratiot, OH
Amer. Legion, Nauvoo Post 711 **[2671]**, Nauvoo, IL
Amer. Legion, Naval Post 372 **[2795]**, Oak Lawn, IL
Amer. Legion, Navy-Marine Post 276 **[14294]**, Columbus, OH
Amer. Legion, Neal Post 743 **[15569]**, Kingsville, OH
Amer. Legion, Neeley La Bar Post 158 **[7188]**, Clio, MI
Amer. Legion, Neer-Goudie-Teamsters Post 846 **[686]**, Chicago, IL
Amer. Legion, Neffs Post 77 **[16106]**, Neffs, OH
Amer. Legion, Nels Lee Post 165 **[10531]**, Bricelyn, MN
Amer. Legion, Nelsan-Horton Post 104 **[11325]**, Litchfield, MN
Amer. Legion, Nelson-Jackson Post 245 **[12754]**, Tower, MN
Amer. Legion, Nelson-Otteson Post 370 **[12972]**, Wolverton, MN
Amer. Legion, Neponset Post 875 **[2675]**, Neponset, IL
Amer. Legion, Nesseth-Lien Post 431 **[12762]**, Twin Valley, MN

Amer. Legion, Netzel-Zenz Post 413 **[17791]**, Crivitz, WI
Amer. Legion, Neuman-Mc-Gaver Post 466 **[17949]**, Fairchild, WI
Amer. Legion, Neuman-Wenzel Post 73 **[9879]**, Sturgis, MI
Amer. Legion, Neville-Dunn Post 489 **[18946]**, Milwaukee, WI
Amer. Legion, New Boston Post 48 **[2682]**, New Boston, IL
Amer. Legion, New Bremen Post 241 **[16116]**, New Bremen, OH
Amer. Legion, New Carlisle Post 286 **[15959]**, Medway, OH
Amer. Legion, New Carlisle Post 297 **[5930]**, New Carlisle, IN
Amer. Legion, New Directions Post 511 **[5008]**, Indianapolis, IN
Amer. Legion, New Harmony Post 370 **[5943]**, New Harmony, IN
Amer. Legion, New Haven Post 330 **[5945]**, New Haven, IN
Amer. Legion, New Haven Post 1141 **[2684]**, New Haven, IL
Amer. Legion, New Indianapolis Post 4 **[5009]**, Indianapolis, IN
Amer. Legion, New Lebanon Post 762 **[16130]**, New Lebanon, OH
Amer. Legion, New Matamoras Post 378 **[16140]**, New Matamoras, OH
Amer. Legion, New Palestine Post 182 **[5949]**, New Palestine, IN
Amer. Legion, Newburgh Heights Post 627 **[16189]**, Newburgh Heights, OH
Amer. Legion, Newbury Post 663 **[16190]**, Newbury, OH
Amer. Legion, Newton Post 236 **[16199]**, Newton Falls, OH
Amer. Legion, Newton Post 726 **[15072]**, East Fultonham, OH
Amer. Legion, Ney Community Post 680 **[16203]**, Ney, OH
Amer. Legion, Nicely-Brindle Post 201 **[4082]**, Advance, IN
Amer. Legion, Nichols-Goleman-Boggs Post 566 **[1903]**, Greenup, IL
Amer. Legion, Nicollet Post 510 **[11894]**, Nicollet, MN
Amer. Legion, Niles-Northtown Post 29 **[2566]**, Morton Grove, IL
Amer. Legion, Noah O'bannion Post 59 **[6118]**, Rising Sun, IN
Amer. Legion, Noble Post 252 **[13485]**, Caldwell, OH
Amer. Legion, Noel Robison Post 664 **[2057]**, Hurst, IL
Amer. Legion, Noetzelman-Boodry Post 377 **[19855]**, Summit Lake, WI
Amer. Legion, Nonesuch Post 462 **[10161]**, White Pine, MI
Amer. Legion, Norcross-Meyers Post 305 **[17242]**, Weston, OH
Amer. Legion, Nordonia Hills Post 801 **[15743]**, Macedonia, OH
Amer. Legion, Norman Schulte Post 549 **[10750]**, Darfur, MN
Amer. Legion, Norridge Post 1263 **[2739]**, Norridge, IL
Amer. Legion, Norris-Spencer Post 263 **[19313]**, New London, WI
Amer. Legion, North Baltimore Post 539 **[16210]**, North Baltimore, OH
Amer. Legion, North Boone Post 205 **[3124]**, Poplar Grove, IL
Amer. Legion, North Br. Post 85 **[11899]**, North Branch, MN
Amer. Legion, North Br. Post 457 **[9215]**, North Branch, MI
Amer. Legion, North Dearborn Post 452 **[6289]**, Sunman, IN
Amer. Legion, North Eastern Post 459 **[7897]**, Grand Rapids, MI
Amer. Legion, North End Post 474 **[12369]**, St. Paul, MN
Amer. Legion, North End Post 576 **[16881]**, Toledo, OH
Amer. Legion, North Loop Post 949 **[687]**, Chicago, IL
Amer. Legion, North Madison Memorial Post 601 **[15745]**, Madison, OH
Amer. Legion, North Mankato Post 518 **[11902]**, North Mankato, MN
Amer. Legion, North Park Post 401 **[10187]**, Wyoming, MI
Amer. Legion, North Ridgeville Post 802 **[15105]**, Elyria, OH
Amer. Legion, North Shore Post 21 **[688]**, Chicago, IL
Amer. Legion, North Shore Post 331 **[19730]**, Shorewood, WI
Amer. Legion, North Side Post 230 **[11509]**, Minneapolis, MN
Amer. Legion, Northcutt-Laaker Post 292 **[4460]**, Dillsboro, IN
Amer. Legion, Northeast Post 630 **[13722]**, Cincinnati, OH
Amer. Legion, Northfield Post 84 **[11911]**, Northfield, MN
Amer. Legion, Northridge Memorial Post 746 **[14845]**, Dayton, OH
Amer. Legion, Northwest Detroit Post 302 **[7315]**, Detroit, MI
Amer. Legion, Northwest Du Page Post 1084 **[3352]**, Roselle, IL
Amer. Legion, Northwest Post 443 **[14295]**, Columbus, OH
Amer. Legion, Northwest Post 497 **[5010]**, Indianapolis, IN
Amer. Legion, Norwalk Memorial Post 438 **[19326]**, Norwalk, WI
Amer. Legion, Norwood Post 740 **[689]**, Chicago, IL
Amer. Legion, Novi Post 19 **[9231]**, Novi, MI
Amer. Legion, Nuwarine Post 535 **[8977]**, Mason, MI
Amer. Legion, Nysewander-Bayliff Post 329 **[6042]**, Plainfield, IN
Amer. Legion, O.-Connor-Chiers Post 340 **[17623]**, Berlin, WI
Amer. Legion, O-Donnell-Eddy-Floss Post 714 **[690]**, Chicago, IL
Amer. Legion, O.-L.-Arnold-D.-K.-Slayton Post 100 **[19750]**, Sparta, WI
Amer. Legion, O Leara Quirk Post 90 **[4476]**, Eaton, IN
Amer. Legion, Oakley Traynor Post 64 **[7713]**, Flint, MI
Amer. Legion, Oblong Post 219 **[2841]**, Oblong, IL
Amer. Legion, O'Brien Post 326 **[16653]**, Shelby, OH
Amer. Legion, Odegaard-Quade Post 401 **[11237]**, Jeffers, MN
Amer. Legion, Odell Post 666 **[2843]**, Odell, IL
Amer. Legion, Odessa Post 520 **[11930]**, Odessa, MN
Amer. Legion, Odon Post 293 **[6010]**, Odon, IN
Amer. Legion, Oelschlaeger-Dallmann Post 434 **[19329]**, Oak Creek, WI
Amer. Legion, Ogden Post 998 **[2851]**, Ogden, IL
Amer. Legion, Ogemaw Post 103 **[10127]**, West Branch, MI
Amer. Legion, Ogilvie Post 640 **[11932]**, Ogilvie, MN
Amer. Legion, Ogmar Post 268 **[11251]**, Kensington, MN
Amer. Legion of Ohio **[14996]**, Delaware, OH
Amer. Legion, Ohio Post 3 **[15192]**, Findlay, OH
Amer. Legion, Ohio Post 9 **[16447]**, Pleasantville, OH
Amer. Legion, Ohio Post 14 **[13247]**, Bainbridge, OH
Amer. Legion, Ohio Post 16 **[15759]**, Mansfield, OH
Amer. Legion, Ohio Post 18 **[16882]**, Toledo, OH
Amer. Legion, Ohio Post 20 **[13414]**, Bremen, OH
Amer. Legion, Ohio Post 22 **[15803]**, Maple Heights, OH
Amer. Legion, Ohio Post 23 **[16466]**, Portsmouth, OH
Amer. Legion, Ohio Post 25 **[17126]**, Washington Court House, OH
Amer. Legion, Ohio Post 31 **[15083]**, East Palestine, OH
Amer. Legion, Ohio Post 36 **[13405]**, Bradner, OH
Amer. Legion, Ohio Post 37 **[13723]**, Cincinnati, OH
Amer. Legion, Ohio Post 43 **[16996]**, Troy, OH
Amer. Legion, Ohio Post 56 **[16584]**, Salem, OH
Amer. Legion, Ohio Post 57 **[13122]**, Amanda, OH
Amer. Legion, Ohio Post 58 **[16687]**, Somerset, OH
Amer. Legion, Ohio Post 65 **[14793]**, Coshocton, OH
Amer. Legion, Ohio Post 71 **[16554]**, Roseville, OH
Amer. Legion, Ohio Post 72 **[13724]**, Cincinnati, OH
Amer. Legion, Ohio Post 78 **[15688]**, Logan, OH
Amer. Legion, Ohio Post 80 **[14806]**, Covington, OH
Amer. Legion, Ohio Post 81 **[15511]**, Jackson, OH
Amer. Legion, Ohio Post 85 **[16167]**, Newark, OH
Amer. Legion, Ohio Post 88 **[13159]**, Ashland, OH
Amer. Legion, Ohio Post 91 **[13343]**, Berea, OH
Amer. Legion, Ohio Post 92 **[17044]**, Utica, OH
Amer. Legion, Ohio Post 94 **[13306]**, Bedford Heights, OH
Amer. Legion, Ohio Post 96 **[15645]**, Lima, OH
Amer. Legion, Ohio Post 99 **[16883]**, Toledo, OH
Amer. Legion, Ohio Post 102 **[16278]**, Oberlin, OH
Amer. Legion, Ohio Post 103 **[13176]**, Ashtabula, OH
Amer. Legion, Ohio Post 106 **[16204]**, Niles, OH
Amer. Legion, Ohio Post 107 **[15571]**, Kirkersville, OH
Amer. Legion, Ohio Post 112 **[15746]**, Madison, OH
Amer. Legion, Ohio Post 113 **[16457]**, Port Clinton, OH
Amer. Legion, Ohio Post 114 **[16269]**, Oak Harbor, OH
Amer. Legion, Ohio Post 115 **[14997]**, Delaware, OH
Amer. Legion, Ohio Post 117 **[14982]**, Defiance, OH
Amer. Legion, Ohio Post 122 **[14255]**, Clyde, OH
Amer. Legion, Ohio Post 123 **[16265]**, Norwood, OH
Amer. Legion, Ohio Post 126 **[13657]**, Chillicothe, OH
Amer. Legion, Ohio Post 129 **[15442]**, Hillsboro, OH
Amer. Legion, Ohio Post 131 **[15630]**, Leetonia, OH
Amer. Legion, Ohio Post 132 **[16884]**, Toledo, OH
Amer. Legion, Ohio Post 135 **[16885]**, Toledo, OH
Amer. Legion, Ohio Post 136 **[16078]**, Mount Vernon, OH
Amer. Legion, Ohio Post 143 **[15187]**, Fayette, OH
Amer. Legion, Ohio Post 147 **[13149]**, Apple Creek, OH
Amer. Legion, Ohio Post 148 **[16583]**, St. Paris, OH
Amer. Legion, Ohio Post 149 **[15236]**, Franklin, OH
Amer. Legion, Ohio Post 155 **[15523]**, Jamestown, OH
Amer. Legion, Ohio Post 157 **[14296]**, Columbus, OH
Amer. Legion, Ohio Post 173 **[13319]**, Bellefontaine, OH
Amer. Legion, Ohio Post 175 **[16774]**, Stow, OH
Amer. Legion, Ohio Post 178 **[17047]**, Van Wert, OH
Amer. Legion, Ohio Post 180 **[15312]**, Georgetown, OH
Amer. Legion, Ohio Post 182 **[14297]**, Columbus, OH
Amer. Legion, Ohio Post 186 **[15617]**, Lebanon, OH
Amer. Legion, Ohio Post 188 **[16132]**, New Lexington, OH
Amer. Legion, Ohio Post 191 **[16702]**, Spencerville, OH
Amer. Legion, Ohio Post 194 **[15871]**, Mason, OH
Amer. Legion, Ohio Post 199 **[15406]**, Harrison, OH
Amer. Legion, Ohio Post 204 **[13543]**, Canton, OH
Amer. Legion, Ohio Post 207 **[17285]**, Willshire, OH
Amer. Legion, Ohio Post 212 **[16353]**, Parma, OH
Amer. Legion, Ohio Post 223 **[15417]**, Hicksville, OH
Amer. Legion, Ohio Post 224 **[15189]**, Felicity, OH
Amer. Legion, Ohio Post 226 **[13142]**, Andover, OH
Amer. Legion, Ohio Post 229 **[16107]**, Nelsonville, OH
Amer. Legion, Ohio Post 232 **[15337]**, Grand Rapids, OH
Amer. Legion, Ohio Post 234 **[13444]**, Brunswick, OH
Amer. Legion, Ohio Post 237 **[13265]**, Batavia, OH
Amer. Legion, Ohio Post 238 **[15937]**, Mechanicsburg, OH
Amer. Legion, Ohio Post 244 **[15084]**, East Sparta, OH
Amer. Legion, Ohio Post 246 **[15069]**, Duncan Falls, OH
Amer. Legion, Ohio Post 258 **[16233]**, North Lewisburg, OH
Amer. Legion, Ohio Post 262 **[15403]**, Hamler, OH
Amer. Legion, Ohio Post 266 **[13316]**, Belle Center, OH
Amer. Legion, Ohio Post 272 **[13034]**, Akron, OH
Amer. Legion, Ohio Post 274 **[16759]**, Steubenville, OH
Amer. Legion, Ohio Post 275 **[15676]**, Lisbon, OH

Amer. Legion, Ohio Post 278 **[17096]**, Warren, OH
Amer. Legion, Ohio Post 281 **[14818]**, Cuyahoga Falls, OH
Amer. Legion, Ohio Post 282 **[16307]**, Orrville, OH
Amer. Legion, Ohio Post 284 **[13453]**, Bryan, OH
Amer. Legion, Ohio Post 287 **[15632]**, Leipsic, OH
Amer. Legion, Ohio Post 290 **[14259]**, Columbiana, OH
Amer. Legion, Ohio Post 295 **[15351]**, Green Springs, OH
Amer. Legion, Ohio Post 297 **[16389]**, Payne, OH
Amer. Legion, Ohio Post 300 **[16097]**, Napoleon, OH
Amer. Legion, Ohio Post 303 **[15925]**, McArthur, OH
Amer. Legion, Ohio Post 322 **[17163]**, West Alexandria, OH
Amer. Legion, Ohio Post 334 **[16886]**, Toledo, OH
Amer. Legion, Ohio Post 337 **[16492]**, Quaker City, OH
Amer. Legion, Ohio Post 338 **[13406]**, Bradner, OH
Amer. Legion, Ohio Post 342 **[16849]**, Thornville, OH
Amer. Legion, Ohio Post 346 **[16293]**, Ohio City, OH
Amer. Legion, Ohio Post 354 **[16160]**, New Riegel, OH
Amer. Legion, Ohio Post 357 **[16044]**, Minerva, OH
Amer. Legion, Ohio Post 360 **[16143]**, New Paris, OH
Amer. Legion, Ohio Post 368 **[16484]**, Prospect, OH
Amer. Legion, Ohio Post 374 **[15076]**, East Liverpool, OH
Amer. Legion, Ohio Post 376 **[15534]**, Junction City, OH
Amer. Legion, Ohio Post 381 **[15489]**, Huntsville, OH
Amer. Legion, Ohio Post 389 **[13356]**, Beverly, OH
Amer. Legion, Ohio Post 399 **[15038]**, Dresden, OH
Amer. Legion, Ohio Post 405 **[16161]**, New Washington, OH
Amer. Legion, Ohio Post 406 **[13353]**, Bethel, OH
Amer. Legion, Ohio Post 423 **[16536]**, Rittman, OH
Amer. Legion, Ohio Post 431 **[16195]**, Newcomerstown, OH
Amer. Legion, Ohio Post 436 **[15354]**, Greentown, OH
Amer. Legion, Ohio Post 440 **[13544]**, Canton, OH
Amer. Legion, Ohio Post 442 **[16595]**, Salineville, OH
Amer. Legion, Ohio Post 450 **[16023]**, Milford, OH
Amer. Legion, Ohio Post 454 **[16531]**, Ridgeville Corners, OH
Amer. Legion, Ohio Post 457 **[16810]**, Sunbury, OH
Amer. Legion, Ohio Post 462 **[16110]**, Nevada, OH
Amer. Legion, Ohio Post 465 **[14298]**, Columbus, OH
Amer. Legion, Ohio Post 468 **[16824]**, Sylvania, OH
Amer. Legion, Ohio Post 471 **[16467]**, Portsmouth, OH
Amer. Legion, Ohio Post 473 **[14787]**, Copley, OH
Amer. Legion, Ohio Post 476 **[17262]**, Wilkesville, OH
Amer. Legion, Ohio Post 483 **[15235]**, Frankfort, OH
Amer. Legion, Ohio Post 486 **[14299]**, Columbus, OH
Amer. Legion, Ohio Post 491 **[15018]**, Dennison, OH
Amer. Legion, Ohio Post 492 **[15639]**, Liberty Center, OH
Amer. Legion, Ohio Post 499 **[17190]**, West Salem, OH
Amer. Legion, Ohio Post 500 **[15242]**, Fredericktown, OH
Amer. Legion, Ohio Post 504 **[17388]**, Youngstown, OH
Amer. Legion, Ohio Post 506 **[15570]**, Kinsman, OH
Amer. Legion, Ohio Post 508 **[16541]**, Rockford, OH
Amer. Legion, Ohio Post 517 **[17366]**, Xenia, OH
Amer. Legion, Ohio Post 518 **[13175]**, Ashley, OH
Amer. Legion, Ohio Post 525 **[13012]**, Adena, OH
Amer. Legion, Ohio Post 535 **[13334]**, Bellville, OH
Amer. Legion, Ohio Post 537 **[16301]**, Oregon, OH
Amer. Legion, Ohio Post 540 **[17097]**, Warren, OH
Amer. Legion, Ohio Post 544 **[13607]**, Cedarville, OH
Amer. Legion, Ohio Post 550 **[16159]**, New Richmond, OH
Amer. Legion, Ohio Post 551 **[15462]**, Holmesville, OH
Amer. Legion, Ohio Post 555 **[15805]**, Marblehead, OH
Amer. Legion, Ohio Post 564 **[17098]**, Warren, OH
Amer. Legion, Ohio Post 569 **[15804]**, Maple Heights, OH
Amer. Legion, Ohio Post 571 **[15811]**, Maria Stein, OH
Amer. Legion, Ohio Post 572 **[16354]**, Parma, OH
Amer. Legion, Ohio Post 574 **[13338]**, Beloit, OH
Amer. Legion, Ohio Post 581 **[13378]**, Bowerston, OH
Amer. Legion, Ohio Post 586 **[16868]**, Tipp City, OH
Amer. Legion, Ohio Post 609 **[15572]**, Kirtland, OH
Amer. Legion, Ohio Post 619 **[14846]**, Dayton, OH
Amer. Legion, Ohio Post 631 **[13725]**, Cincinnati, OH
Amer. Legion, Ohio Post 633 **[17194]**, West Union, OH
Amer. Legion, Ohio Post 650 **[17086]**, Walhonding, OH
Amer. Legion, Ohio Post 656 **[16279]**, Oberlin, OH
Amer. Legion, Ohio Post 660 **[16657]**, Sherrodsville, OH
Amer. Legion, Ohio Post 667 **[15070]**, East Canton, OH
Amer. Legion, Ohio Post 670 **[13726]**, Cincinnati, OH
Amer. Legion, Ohio Post 676 **[15760]**, Mansfield, OH
Amer. Legion, Ohio Post 679 **[13248]**, Baltic, OH
Amer. Legion, Ohio Post 681 **[15379]**, Hamilton, OH
Amer. Legion, Ohio Post 694 **[16092]**, Mowrystown, OH
Amer. Legion, Ohio Post 708 **[15461]**, Hollansburg, OH
Amer. Legion, Ohio Post 733 **[13355]**, Bettsville, OH
Amer. Legion, Ohio Post 735 **[16425]**, Piney Fork, OH
Amer. Legion, Ohio Post 755 **[16622]**, Sardinia, OH
Amer. Legion, Ohio Post 757 **[13658]**, Chillicothe, OH
Amer. Legion, Ohio Post 758 **[15277]**, Galion, OH
Amer. Legion, Ohio Post 770 **[14300]**, Columbus, OH
Amer. Legion, Ohio Post 773 **[13125]**, Amelia, OH
Amer. Legion, Ohio Post 776 **[14847]**, Dayton, OH
Amer. Legion, Ohio Post 777 **[15036]**, Doylestown, OH
Amer. Legion, Ohio Post 786 **[16887]**, Toledo, OH
Amer. Legion, Ohio Post 787 **[16716]**, Springfield, OH
Amer. Legion, Ohio Post 790 **[16647]**, Sharonville, OH
Amer. Legion, Ohio Post 791 **[13111]**, Alliance, OH
Amer. Legion, Ohio Valley Post 760 **[15405]**, Hannibal, OH
Amer. Legion, Oien-Horgen Post 198 **[10503]**, Boyd, MN
Amer. Legion, Olaf Locken Post 315 **[11271]**, Lake Bronson, MN
Amer. Legion, Old Town Chicago Post 184 **[691]**, Chicago, IL
Amer. Legion, Oldsmobile Post 237 **[7504]**, East Lansing, MI
Amer. Legion, Oles-Reader-Bosshart Post 115 **[12760]**, Truman, MN
Amer. Legion, Olson-Bute-Malone Post 737 **[2147]**, Kempton, IL
Amer. Legion, Olson-Graminske Post 426 **[12870]**, Wendell, MN
Amer. Legion, Olson-Grinde Post 348 **[17808]**, De Forest, WI
Amer. Legion, Olson-Stitzel Post 219 **[11471]**, Miltona, MN
Amer. Legion, Onarga Post 551 **[2863]**, Onarga, IL
Amer. Legion, Oney-Johnston-Edward-Blessman Post 38 **[17483]**, Appleton, WI
Amer. Legion, Ontonagon Post 288 **[9308]**, Ontonagon, MI
Amer. Legion, Oola Khan Post 372 **[13727]**, Cincinnati, OH
Amer. Legion, Ophiem Post 1077 **[2359]**, Lynn Center, IL
Amer. Legion, Oregon Post 97 **[2866]**, Oregon, IL
Amer. Legion, Orion Post 255 **[2872]**, Orion, IL
Amer. Legion, Orland Memorial Post 111 **[2877]**, Orland Park, IL
Amer. Legion, Orland Post 423 **[6012]**, Orland, IN
Amer. Legion, Orr Post 480 **[11942]**, Orr, MN
Amer. Legion, Orville Bidwell Post 138 **[6369]**, Upland, IN
Amer. Legion, Orville Easterday Post 189 **[6432]**, Walkerton, IN
Amer. Legion, Orwell Memorial Post 719 **[16313]**, Orwell, OH
Amer. Legion, Osborn Post 108 **[6150]**, St. Bernice, IN
Amer. Legion, Oscar Iverson Post 133 **[11236]**, Jasper, MN
Amer. Legion, Oscar Jacobson Post 417 **[12881]**, West Union, MN
Amer. Legion, Oscar Lee Post 177 **[10755]**, Dawson, MN
Amer. Legion, Oscar-Lee-Thomas-Moran Post 674 **[3179]**, Ransom, IL
Amer. Legion, Oscar Wellnitz Post 344 **[11844]**, Morton, MN
Amer. Legion, Osceola Post 308 **[6015]**, Osceola, IN
Amer. Legion, Osgood Post 588 **[16314]**, Osgood, OH
Amer. Legion, Oswego Post 675 **[2888]**, Oswego, IL
Amer. Legion, Othmar Braun Post 612 **[11451]**, Melrose, MN
Amer. Legion, Otis Sampson Post 59 **[19828]**, Stoughton, WI
Amer. Legion, Otis Stone Post 354 **[4523]**, Evansville, IN
Amer. Legion, Otsego Post 84 **[9324]**, Otsego, MI
Amer. Legion, Ottawa Post 33 **[2895]**, Ottawa, IL
Amer. Legion, Otto Hendrickson Post 212 **[11976]**, Park Rapids, MN
Amer. Legion, Otto Knutson Post 427 **[11892]**, Newfolden, MN
Amer. Legion, Otto T. Lund Post 52 **[10455]**, Blooming Prairie, MN
Amer. Legion, Ours For Victory Post 971 **[1980]**, Hickory Hills, IL
Amer. Legion, Owen Barrett Post 110 **[9096]**, Mount Pleasant, MI
Amer. Legion, Owen Dunn Post 5 **[5845]**, Mount Vernon, IN
Amer. Legion, Owensville Post 51 **[6018]**, Owensville, IN
Amer. Legion, Oxford Post 1197 **[29]**, Alpha, IL
Amer. Legion, Palash-Platt Post 543 **[19478]**, Plover, WI
Amer. Legion, Palatine Post 690 **[2904]**, Palatine, IL
Amer. Legion, Palmer Post 65 **[2701]**, Niles, IL
Amer. Legion, Palmer-Ritchie-Thomas Post 153 **[19457]**, Pittsville, WI
Amer. Legion, Palmer-Roberts Post 214 **[17271]**, Willoughby, OH
Amer. Legion, Palmyra Post 1034 **[2933]**, Palmyra, IL
Amer. Legion, Palos Memorial Post 1993 **[2943]**, Palos Park, IL
Amer. Legion, Pandora Post 616 **[16349]**, Pandora, OH
Amer. Legion, Paradise Valley Post 436 **[8494]**, Kingsley, MI
Amer. Legion, Park Etter Post 452 **[16051]**, Mogadore, OH
Amer. Legion, Park Forest Post 1198 **[1249]**, Chicago Heights, IL
Amer. Legion, Parker-Jose-Stockwell Post 66 **[17549]**, Athelstane, WI
Amer. Legion, Parma Heights Post 703 **[16355]**, Parma, OH
Amer. Legion, Partridge Post 578 **[365]**, Bunker Hill, IL
Amer. Legion, Paschall Post 164 **[15366]**, Grove City, OH
Amer. Legion, Passage-Gayde Post 391 **[9391]**, Plymouth, MI
Amer. Legion, Pat Petrone Post 885 **[246]**, Bloomingdale, IL
Amer. Legion, Patriotism Post 470 **[14257]**, Coldwater, OH
Amer. Legion, Patterson-Dawson Post 57 **[9332]**, Owosso, MI
Amer. Legion, Patton-Chastain Post 195 **[4312]**, Campbellsburg, IN
Amer. Legion, Paul Blagen Post 400 **[10635]**, Canton, MN
Amer. Legion, Paul F. Dille Post 364 **[10753]**, Dassel, MN
Amer. Legion, Paul Leon Wolek Memorial Post 454 **[4922]**, Hobart, IN

Amer. Legion, Paul Revere Post 623 **[692]**, Chicago, IL
Amer. Legion, Paul Robert Strange Post 502 **[6377]**, Valparaiso, IN
Amer. Legion, Paul Sodder Post 213 **[15636]**, Lewisburg, OH
Amer. Legion, Paul Stout Post 127 **[2617]**, Murphysboro, IL
Amer. Legion, Pawnee Post 586 **[2970]**, Pawnee, IL
Amer. Legion, P.E. Post 650 **[12623]**, Sanborn, MN
Amer. Legion, Pearce-Kerns Post 120 **[17036]**, Urbana, OH
Amer. Legion, Pearl City Post 1014 **[2979]**, Pearl City, IL
Amer. Legion, Peck Post 489 **[9349]**, Peck, MI
Amer. Legion, Pedersen Maunula Post 379 **[11829]**, Moose Lake, MN
Amer. Legion, Pederson-Tripp Post 357 **[10341]**, Ashby, MN
Amer. Legion, Pekin Post 203 **[6021]**, Pekin, IN
Amer. Legion, Pendleton Post 117 **[6023]**, Pendleton, IN
Amer. Legion, Penfield-Gifford-Memorial Post 1153 **[2997]**, Penfield, IL
Amer. Legion, Pennville Post 482 **[6028]**, Pennville, IN
Amer. Legion, Pentwater Post 327 **[9350]**, Pentwater, MI
Amer. Legion, Peoples Gas Post 336 **[693]**, Chicago, IL
Amer. Legion, Peoria Post 2 **[3002]**, Peoria, IL
Amer. Legion, Peoria Post 1151 **[3003]**, Peoria, IL
Amer. Legion, Peotone Post 392 **[3071]**, Peotone, IL
Amer. Legion, Percy Post 1145 **[3073]**, Percy, IL
Amer. Legion, Perkins Post 540 **[9353]**, Perkins, MI
Amer. Legion, Perrottet-Nickerson Post 76 **[3979]**, Wheaton, IL
Amer. Legion, Perry County Post 213 **[6295]**, Tell City, IN
Amer. Legion, Perry Memorial Post 697 **[16399]**, Perry, OH
Amer. Legion, Perry Post 1040 **[3074]**, Perry, IL
Amer. Legion, Perrysburg Post 28 **[16401]**, Perrysburg, OH
Amer. Legion, Peru Post 375 **[3075]**, Peru, IL
Amer. Legion, Pesotum Post 580 **[3083]**, Pesotum, IL
Amer. Legion, Peter-Gedda-Francis-Cychosz Post 27 **[6937]**, Bessemer, MI
Amer. Legion, Peter Leuze Post 420 **[12068]**, Raymond, MN
Amer. Legion, Peter Umathum Post 412 **[4053]**, Woodstock, IL
Amer. Legion, Peters Post 643 **[89]**, Ashkum, IL
Amer. Legion, Peterson-Lofquist-Bronczyk Post 160 **[10444]**, Biwabik, MN
Amer. Legion, Peterson and Waller Post 312 **[12699]**, Stacy, MN
Amer. Legion, Peterson-Westerberg Post 415 **[10380]**, Barnum, MN
Amer. Legion, Pettisville Post 445 **[16416]**, Pettisville, OH
Amer. Legion, Pewaukee Post 71 **[19434]**, Pewaukee, WI
Amer. Legion, Phaneuf-Vanasse Post 111 **[19745]**, Somerset, WI
Amer. Legion, Philip Whiteside Post 1961 **[2871]**, Orient, IL
Amer. Legion, Philippine-American-Veterans Post 1995 **[694]**, Chicago, IL
Amer. Legion, Phillippi-Clement Post 101 **[15575]**, La Rue, OH
Amer. Legion, Phillips-Elliott-Hodges Post 22 **[9600]**, Saginaw, MI
Amer. Legion, Phillips-Grigsby Post 149 **[6465]**, West Baden Springs, IN
Amer. Legion, Philo Post 1171 **[3087]**, Philo, IL
Amer. Legion, Phoenix Post 309 **[7284]**, Decatur, MI
Amer. Legion, Phoenix Post 1254 **[1953]**, Harvey, IL
Amer. Legion, Pickford Post 323 **[9375]**, Pickford, MI
Amer. Legion, Pieper-Hull-Sparks Post 176 **[7170]**, Clinton, MI
Amer. Legion, Pieper-Marsh Post 194 **[17712]**, Cameron, WI
Amer. Legion, Pierce-Davis Post 731 **[3841]**, Utica, IL
Amer. Legion, Pillager Post 100 **[11999]**, Pillager, MN
Amer. Legion, Pilsen Post 825 **[695]**, Chicago, IL
Amer. Legion, Pinckney Memorial Post 419 **[9380]**, Pinckney, MI
Amer. Legion, Pine Tree Post 448 **[11453]**, Menahga, MN
Amer. Legion, Pioneer Post 340 **[6310]**, Terre Haute, IN
Amer. Legion, Pitterle-Beaudoin Post 189 **[19965]**, Watertown, WI
Amer. Legion, Pittsboro Post 426 **[6041]**, Pittsboro, IN
Amer. Legion, Pittsfield Post 152 **[3093]**, Pittsfield, IL
Amer. Legion, Plain City Post 248 **[16442]**, Plain City, OH
Amer. Legion, Plato Post 641 **[12016]**, Plato, MN
Amer. Legion, Pleasant Hill Post 1048 **[3112]**, Pleasant Hill, IL
Amer. Legion, Pleasant Plains Post 599 **[3113]**, Pleasant Plains, IL
Amer. Legion, Pletcher-Chutich-Skrbich Post 575 **[11069]**, Goodland, MN
Amer. Legion, Plummer Post 623 **[12017]**, Plummer, MN
Amer. Legion, Plymouth Post 912 **[3114]**, Plymouth, IL
Amer. Legion, Pocahontas Memorial Post 1104 **[3115]**, Pocahontas, IL
Amer. Legion, Poelker Post 321 **[2677]**, New Baden, IL
Amer. Legion, Point Place Post 110 **[16888]**, Toledo, OH
Amer. Legion, Police Post 56 **[5011]**, Indianapolis, IN
Amer. Legion, Polomis-Tahlier Post 150 **[20061]**, Wausaukee, WI
Amer. Legion, Pope County Post 719 **[1877]**, Golconda, IL
Amer. Legion, Popek-Kostecky Post 163 **[12936]**, Willow River, MN
Amer. Legion, Poppe-Smuk-Appelget Post 327 **[11426]**, Marble, MN
Amer. Legion, Port City Post 260 **[6055]**, Portage, IN
Amer. Legion, Portage Memorial Post 725 **[16464]**, Portage, OH
Amer. Legion, Portage Park Post 183 **[696]**, Chicago, IL
Amer. Legion, Portage Post 207 **[9444]**, Portage, MI
Amer. Legion, Portage Post 496 **[15537]**, Kent, OH
Amer. Legion, Porter Bell Post 715 **[2685]**, New Holland, IL
Amer. Legion, Porter Post 457 **[12042]**, Porter, MN
Amer. Legion, Porter-Snyder Post 605 **[17085]**, Waldo, OH
Amer. Legion, Posen Post 990 **[3127]**, Posen, IL
Amer. Legion Post 66 **[4853]**, Griffith, IN
Amer. Legion Post 80 **[6524]**, Whiting, IN
Amer. Legion Post 232 **[4872]**, Hammond, IN
Amer. Legion, Post 545 Altoona **[17468]**, Altoona, WI
Amer. Legion, Post 556 Sanford White Eagle **[17570]**, Baraboo, WI
Amer. Legion, Poths-Lavelle Post 453 **[49]**, Amboy, IL
Amer. Legion, Potz Heartland Post 500 **[10741]**, Crosslake, MN
Amer. Legion, Prairie Creek Post 404 **[6311]**, Terre Haute, IN
Amer. Legion, Prairie Du Pont Post 485 **[1523]**, Dupo, IL
Amer. Legion, Prairie Post 150 **[2972]**, Paxton, IL
Amer. Legion, Prairie Post 1998 **[10328]**, Appleton, MN
Amer. Legion, Pratt-Volden-Mickelson Post 239 **[12791]**, Virginia, MN
Amer. Legion, Prell Bland Post 271 **[4156]**, Batesville, IN
Amer. Legion, Prescott-Bayens Post 83 **[19689]**, Sheboygan, WI
Amer. Legion, Press-Lloyd Post 247 **[10659]**, Chisholm, MN
Amer. Legion, Priddy-Walters Post 665 **[17186]**, West Manchester, OH
Amer. Legion, Princeton Post 25 **[6068]**, Princeton, IN
Amer. Legion, Princeton Post 125 **[3133]**, Princeton, IL
Amer. Legion, Princeville Post 248 **[3138]**, Princeville, IL
Amer. Legion, Prior Lake Post 447 **[12048]**, Prior Lake, MN
Amer. Legion, Private Ralph Kline Post 262 **[18435]**, Luxemburg, WI
Amer. Legion, Prophetstown Post 522 **[3140]**, Prophetstown, IL
Amer. Legion, Prosser-Curtis-Kubley Post 247 **[18057]**, Glidden, WI
Amer. Legion, Prudent Van Risseghem Post 395 **[11939]**, Onamia, MN
Amer. Legion, Przybylski Post 642 **[16889]**, Toledo, OH
Amer. Legion, Public Safety Post 449 **[11417]**, Maplewood, MN
Amer. Legion, Pulaski County Post 71 **[6531]**, Winamac, IN
Amer. Legion, Pulaski Post 357 **[6213]**, South Bend, IN
Amer. Legion, Putnam County Seat Post 1044 **[1966]**, Hennepin, IL
Amer. Legion, Putoff-Lautenschlager Post 141 **[4759]**, Freedom, IN
Amer. Legion, Quayle-Shuster-Truman-Muhich Post 241 **[10347]**, Aurora, MN
Amer. Legion, Quigle-Palin Post 394 **[6399]**, Veedersburg, IN
Amer. Legion, Quincy Post 37 **[3146]**, Quincy, IL
Amer. Legion, Racine Post 602 **[16493]**, Racine, OH
Amer. Legion, Railroad Post 416 **[12370]**, St. Paul, MN
Amer. Legion, Railroad Retirement Bd. Post 856 **[697]**, Chicago, IL
Amer. Legion, Rainbow Post 263 **[4334]**, Cayuga, IN
Amer. Legion, Ralph Gracie Post 14 **[10403]**, Bemidji, MN
Amer. Legion, Ralph Rumbaugh Post 51 **[7034]**, Buchanan, MI
Amer. Legion, Ralph Test Post 269 **[6283]**, Spiceland, IN
Amer. Legion, Randall Couchman Post 204 **[9912]**, Three Oaks, MI
Amer. Legion, Randolph Post 39 **[6535]**, Winchester, IN
Amer. Legion, Randolph Post 707 **[15129]**, Englewood, OH
Amer. Legion, Randolph-West-Kelly Post 367 **[18919]**, Milton, WI
Amer. Legion, Ranten-Sundflot Post 288 **[10563]**, Brooten, MN
Amer. Legion, Rantoul Post 287 **[3180]**, Rantoul, IL
Amer. Legion, Ravenna Post 331 **[16496]**, Ravenna, OH
Amer. Legion, Ray Keenan Post 207 **[10680]**, Cleveland, MN
Amer. Legion, Ray Kirkpatrick Post 463 **[11312]**, Lester Prairie, MN
Amer. Legion, Ray-S.-Neilson-John-H.-Winter Post 362 **[18292]**, Kennan, WI
Amer. Legion, Raymond Rankins Post 308 **[8541]**, Lansing, MI
Amer. Legion, Raymond Todd Post 323 **[6462]**, Waveland, IN
Amer. Legion, Read-Osborne Post 531 **[7225]**, Copemish, MI
Amer. Legion, Rebec-Hosler-Sweet Post 227 **[7495]**, East Jordan, MI
Amer. Legion, Red Arrow 32nd Div. Post 361 **[8093]**, Grosse Pointe Woods, MI
Amer. Legion, Red Cloud Post 250 **[17453]**, Adams, WI
Amer. Legion, Red Greissel Post 335 **[4346]**, Charlestown, IN
Amer. Legion, Redford-Township-Tansey-Weil Post 271 **[7810]**, Garden City, MI
Amer. Legion, Reese Post 139 **[9485]**, Reese, MI
Amer. Legion, Reeseville Post 190 **[19594]**, Reeseville, WI
Amer. Legion, Reginald Fisher Post 1 **[4410]**, Connersville, IN
Amer. Legion, Rehfeldt-Meyer Post 474 **[2435]**, Matteson, IL
Amer. Legion, Reinhardt-Windl Post 164 **[18270]**, Jefferson, WI
Amer. Legion, Reino Post 21 **[8331]**, Iron River, MI
Amer. Legion, Renault Post 1215 **[3187]**, Renault, IL
Amer. Legion, Reveille Post 184 **[5967]**, Newport, IN
Amer. Legion, Rexford Ballard Post 224 **[4464]**, Dugger, IN

Amer. Legion, Reynoldsburg Post 798 **[16512]**, Reynoldsburg, OH
Amer. Legion, Rheault-Cavis-Moilanen Post 291 **[8287]**, Hubbell, MI
Amer. Legion, Rhen Hilkert Post 21 **[6515]**, Westville, IN
Amer. Legion, Rice-Lemmerhart-Smith Post 327 **[18440]**, Lyons, WI
Amer. Legion, Rich Prairie Post 341 **[11997]**, Pierz, MN
Amer. Legion, Richard Dingle Post 98 **[12611]**, St. Paul Park, MN
Amer. Legion, Richard Hoffman Post 484 **[5802]**, Millersburg, IN
Amer. Legion, Richland Post 30 **[2858]**, Olney, IL
Amer. Legion, Richmond Heights Post 775 **[15963]**, Mentor, OH
Amer. Legion, Richmond Post 292 **[12115]**, Richmond, MN
Amer. Legion, Rickerd-Danielson Post 227 **[19770]**, Spring Valley, WI
Amer. Legion, Riders Memorial Post 17 **[4873]**, Hammond, IN
Amer. Legion, Ridgway Post 596 **[3195]**, Ridgway, IL
Amer. Legion, River Grove Post 335 **[3206]**, River Grove, IL
Amer. Legion, River Park Post 303 **[6214]**, South Bend, IN
Amer. Legion, Riverside Post 488 **[2325]**, Lombard, IL
Amer. Legion, Road of Remembrance Post 472 **[17389]**, Youngstown, OH
Amer. Legion, Roanoke Post 463 **[3216]**, Roanoke, IL
Amer. Legion, Robert Ihlang Post 537 **[11871]**, New London, MN
Amer. Legion, Robert Meachen Post 325 **[6972]**, Blissfield, MI
Amer. Legion, Robert Patterson Post 3 **[11239]**, Jordan, MN
Amer. Legion, Robert Turner Post 427 **[5957]**, New Ross, IN
Amer. Legion, Robert Woodburn Post 1037 **[2584]**, Mount Prospect, IL
Amer. Legion, Roberts-Mc-Millen Post 332 **[15929]**, McClure, OH
Amer. Legion, Robinson-Gibbs Post 265 **[17137]**, Wauseon, OH
Amer. Legion, Robinson and Starks Post 1972 **[1374]**, Decatur, IL
Amer. Legion, Rochelle Post 403 **[3222]**, Rochelle, IL
Amer. Legion, Rochester Post 446 **[12124]**, Rochester, MN
Amer. Legion, Rock Falls Post 902 **[3233]**, Rock Falls, IL
Amer. Legion, Rock Island Post 200 **[3240]**, Rock Island, IL
Amer. Legion, Rock Post 559 **[9521]**, Rock, MI
Amer. Legion, Rockwood Post 441 **[9535]**, Rockwood, MI
Amer. Legion, Rocky River Post 451 **[16543]**, Rocky River, OH
Amer. Legion, Roderick Prato Post 131 **[9130]**, Munising, MI
Amer. Legion, Roger B. Chaffee Post 154 **[10188]**, Wyoming, MI
Amer. Legion, Roger-Oestrich-Hancock-Coloma Post 343 **[18175]**, Hancock, WI
Amer. Legion, Rogers Park Post 108 **[698]**, Chicago, IL
Amer. Legion, Rolling Meadows Post 1251 **[3337]**, Rolling Meadows, IL
Amer. Legion, Rome Post 1 **[699]**, Chicago, IL
Amer. Legion, Romeo Post 109 **[10034]**, Utica, MI
Amer. Legion, Romsos-Malia Post 492 **[11025]**, Fountain, MN
Amer. Legion, Romulus Meehan Post 426 **[2180]**, La Salle, IL
Amer. Legion, Roodhouse Post 373 **[3349]**, Roodhouse, IL
Amer. Legion, Roose-Vanker Post 286 **[9862]**, Sterling Heights, MI
Amer. Legion, Roosevelt-Aurora Post 84 **[108]**, Aurora, IL
Amer. Legion, Roscommon Post 96 **[9553]**, Roscommon, MI
Amer. Legion, Rose City Post 324 **[8358]**, Jackson, MI
Amer. Legion, Rose-Harms Post 355 **[18061]**, Grafton, WI
Amer. Legion, Rosedale Park Post 390 **[9475]**, Redford, MI
Amer. Legion, Roseland Post 49 **[3762]**, Thornton, IL
Amer. Legion, Roselawn Post 238 **[6139]**, Roselawn, IN
Amer. Legion, Rosemount Post 65 **[12213]**, Rosemount, MN
Amer. Legion, Rosetown Memorial Post 542 **[12219]**, Roseville, MN
Amer. Legion, Ross County Post 62 **[13659]**, Chillicothe, OH
Amer. Legion, Rossford Post 533 **[16556]**, Rossford, OH
Amer. Legion, Rothie Post 330 **[11136]**, Hayfield, MN
Amer. Legion, Round Lake Post 1170 **[3366]**, Round Lake Park, IL
Amer. Legion, Roy Canavan Post 213 **[10048]**, Vicksburg, MI
Amer. Legion, Roy-Hamm-Robert-Burke Post 101 **[2546]**, Monticello, IL
Amer. Legion, Roy Ireland Post 317 **[2842]**, Oconee, IL
Amer. Legion, Roy Miller Post 644 **[1692]**, Fairview, IL
Amer. Legion, Roy P. Benavidez Memorial Post 226 **[700]**, Chicago, IL
Amer. Legion, Roy Vanderpool Post 81 **[3465]**, Shelbyville, IL
Amer. Legion, Royal Post 996 **[3367]**, Royal, IL
Amer. Legion, Rudolph Priebe Post 172 **[11952]**, Osseo, MN
Amer. Legion, Ruel Neal Post 79 **[2228]**, Le Roy, IL
Amer. Legion, Ruf-Marcham Post 404 **[440]**, Carlyle, IL
Amer. Legion, Runnestrand-Pederson Post 354 **[17943]**, Ettrick, WI
Amer. Legion, Russell Johnson Post 72 **[10329]**, Appleton, MN
Amer. Legion, Russell Square Post 1006 **[2215]**, Lansing, IL
Amer. Legion, Russell-Toycen Post 131 **[17778]**, Colfax, WI
Amer. Legion, Russell Weaver Post 166 **[5725]**, Marion, IN
Amer. Legion, Russell-Zenor Post 260 **[3778]**, Tonica, IL
Amer. Legion, Rutland Memorial Post 1121 **[3374]**, Rutland, IL
Amer. Legion, Rutledge-Boviall Post 95 **[17826]**, Delavan, WI
Amer. Legion, Rylander-Milroy Post 727 **[2864]**, Oneida, IL
Amer. Legion, Sahara Grotto Post 264 **[5012]**, Indianapolis, IN
Amer. Legion, Sailor Springs Post 230 **[3375]**, Sailor Springs, IL
Amer. Legion, St. Anne Post 842 **[3376]**, St. Anne, IL
Amer. Legion, St. Anthony Post 493 **[6149]**, St. Anthony, IN
Amer. Legion, St. Augusta Post 621 **[12272]**, St. Cloud, MN
Amer. Legion, St. Charles Post 342 **[3378]**, St. Charles, IL
Amer. Legion, St. Charles Post 468 **[9649]**, St. Charles, MI
Amer. Legion, St. Clair Post 215 **[15087]**, Eaton, OH
Amer. Legion, St. Clairsville Post 159 **[16569]**, St. Clairsville, OH
Amer. Legion, St. Francisville Post 947 **[3397]**, St. Francisville, IL
Amer. Legion, St. Helen Post 416 **[9667]**, St. Helen, MI
Amer. Legion, St. Henry Post 648 **[16575]**, St. Henry, OH
Amer. Legion, St. James Post 33 **[12322]**, St. James, MN
Amer. Legion, St. Joseph Post 163 **[9756]**, Sodus, MI
Amer. Legion, St. Joseph Post 464 **[4297]**, Brookville, IN
Amer. Legion, St. Joseph Post 634 **[3400]**, St. Joseph, IL
Amer. Legion, St. Josephs Park Post 1080 **[2099]**, Joliet, IL
Amer. Legion, St. Leo Post 524 **[12328]**, St. Leo, MN
Amer. Legion, St. Marys Post 323 **[16577]**, St. Marys, OH
Amer. Legion, St. Meinrad Post 366 **[6154]**, St. Meinrad, IN
Amer. Legion, St. Michael Post 567 **[12340]**, St. Michael, MN
Amer. Legion, St. Mihiel Post 86 **[16988]**, Toronto, OH
Amer. Legion, St. Mihiel Post 585 **[3463]**, Shawneetown, IL
Amer. Legion, St. Paul Memorial Post 533 **[12371]**, St. Paul, MN
Amer. Legion, St. Paul Post 8 **[12372]**, St. Paul, MN
Amer. Legion, St. Stephen Post 221 **[12325]**, St. Joseph, MN
Amer. Legion, Sainte Marie Post 932 **[3404]**, Ste. Marie, IL
Amer. Legion, Sam Mason Post 690 **[14301]**, Columbus, OH
Amer. Legion, Samstad-Jensen Post 375 **[10344]**, Atwater, MN
Amer. Legion, San Jose Memorial Post 1269 **[3414]**, San Jose, IL
Amer. Legion, Sandberg-Carlson Post 351 **[10382]**, Barrett, MN
Amer. Legion, Sandy Valley Post 432 **[17149]**, Waynesburg, OH
Amer. Legion, Saner Post 228 **[16482]**, Powhatan Point, OH
Amer. Legion, Sanford Post 192 **[10952]**, Elmore, MN
Amer. Legion, Santa Claus Post 242 **[6159]**, Santa Claus, IN
Amer. Legion, Sarlo-Sharp Post 368 **[2471]**, Melrose Park, IL
Amer. Legion, Sarver-Guthrie Post 839 **[1971]**, Herrick, IL
Amer. Legion, Sauk Centre Post 67 **[12632]**, Sauk Centre, MN
Amer. Legion, Sauk Prairie Kuoni Reuter Post 167 **[19664]**, Sauk City, WI
Amer. Legion, Sauk Trail Post 246 **[8359]**, Jackson, MI
Amer. Legion, Sauk Village Post 1259 **[3417]**, Sauk Village, IL
Amer. Legion, Saunemin Verdun Post 531 **[3418]**, Saunemin, IL
Amer. Legion, Sauvola Post 265 **[7128]**, Chassell, MI
Amer. Legion, Sawyer-Drumm Post 393 **[17914]**, Edgar, WI
Amer. Legion, Scarbrough Post 243 **[15278]**, Galion, OH
Amer. Legion, Sch-Loe-Man Post 547 **[16057]**, Monroeville, OH
Amer. Legion, Schaap-Galagan Post 636 **[11324]**, Lismore, MN
Amer. Legion, Scharmer-Berger Post 250 **[10336]**, Arlington, MN
Amer. Legion, Scheible-Downing Post 542 **[16489]**, Put In Bay, OH
Amer. Legion, Scherer Post 493 **[15519]**, Jackson Center, OH
Amer. Legion, Schiller Park Post 104 **[3455]**, Schiller Park, IL
Amer. Legion, Schlender-Polley Post 239 **[19900]**, Tigerton, WI
Amer. Legion, Schnell-Westfall Post 184 **[16430]**, Piqua, OH
Amer. Legion, Schuetz-Hermann Post 283 **[2230]**, Lebanon, IL
Amer. Legion, Schultz-Hahn Post 293 **[19735]**, Silver Lake, WI
Amer. Legion, Schuster-Stahl Post 370 **[9462]**, Prescott, MI
Amer. Legion, Schuyler Post 4 **[3369]**, Rushville, IL
Amer. Legion, Schwab-Bailey Post 425 **[13654]**, Cheviot, OH
Amer. Legion, Schwartz-Loll-Richards Post 476 **[19519]**, Porterfield, WI
Amer. Legion, Schwieger Kahler Post 522 **[11922]**, Northrop, MN

Amer. Legion, Scio Post 482 **[16623]**, Scio, OH
Amer. Legion, Scott-Lambert Post 415 **[4766]**, Galveston, IN
Amer. Legion, Scott Post 234 **[6172]**, Scottsburg, IN
Amer. Legion, S.C.S. Post 707 **[1933]**, Hanover, IL
Amer. Legion, Scudiero Post 1978 **[701]**, Chicago, IL
Amer. Legion, Security Post 284 **[7316]**, Detroit, MI
Amer. Legion, Seely-Onstine Post 458 **[20091]**, Wauzeka, WI
Amer. Legion, Seifert-Bianchi Post 132 **[11882]**, New Ulm, MN
Amer. Legion, Selma Post 437 **[6179]**, Selma, IN
Amer. Legion, Semrau-Scott Post 361 **[20167]**, Wilmot, WI
Amer. Legion, Ser. Post 128 **[5013]**, Indianapolis, IN
Amer. Legion, Seymour Post 89 **[6180]**, Seymour, IN
Amer. Legion, Seymour Post 1256 **[3461]**, Seymour, IL
Amer. Legion, Shaddrick and La Beau Post 303 **[11032]**, Fridley, MN
Amer. Legion, Shadyside Post 521 **[16633]**, Shadyside, OH
Amer. Legion, Shakopee Post 2 **[12650]**, Shakopee, MN
Amer. Legion, Sharpsville Post 443 **[6187]**, Sharpsville, IN
Amer. Legion, Sharvin Post 397 **[2745]**, North Chicago, IL
Amer. Legion, Shearer Post 350 **[1787]**, Geneseo, IL
Amer. Legion, Sheboygan Memorial Post 555 **[19690]**, Sheboygan, WI
Amer. Legion, Sheldon Post 393 **[3468]**, Sheldon, IL
Amer. Legion, Shepherd-Russell Post 298 **[4957]**, Hymera, IN
Amer. Legion, Sherman-Rice-Demorest Post 157 **[9464]**, Quincy, MI
Amer. Legion, Sheveland-Taylor Post 14 **[18233]**, Iola, WI
Amer. Legion, Shields Post 314 **[9601]**, Saginaw, MI
Amer. Legion, Shiocton Post 512 **[19728]**, Shiocton, WI
Amer. Legion, Shipley-Robinson-Moen-Will Post 161 **[18326]**, King, WI
Amer. Legion, Sickles-Arnold Post 516 **[7288]**, Deckerville, MI
Amer. Legion, Sidney Post 217 **[16663]**, Sidney, OH
Amer. Legion, Sidney Post 433 **[3476]**, Sidney, IL
Amer. Legion, Sievert-Peterson Post 608 **[11933]**, Okabena, MN
Amer. Legion, Sigel Post 1134 **[3478]**, Sigel, IL
Amer. Legion, Silver Lake Post 141 **[12668]**, Silver Lake, MN
Amer. Legion, Silver Lake Post 431 **[6202]**, Silver Lake, IN
Amer. Legion, Silver Star Post 428 **[12825]**, Waite Park, MN
Amer. Legion, Simmonds-Williams Post 484 **[8169]**, Hickory Corners, MI
Amer. Legion, Simon Ethelbert Snyder Post 122 **[5678]**, Liberty, IN
Amer. Legion, Simonson Betcher Post 26 **[10236]**, Ada, MN
Amer. Legion, Sioux Valley Post 614 **[11288]**, Lakefield, MN
Amer. Legion, Six Gold Star Post 672 **[2485]**, Middletown, IL
Amer. Legion, Sizer-Buchman Post 328 **[19772]**, Springbrook, WI
Amer. Legion, Skinner-Trost Post 122 **[1336]**, Cullom, IL
Amer. Legion, Skokie Post 320 **[3481]**, Skokie, IL
Amer. Legion, Slining-Caulkins Post 267 **[19285]**, New Auburn, WI
Amer. Legion, Smith-Ashcraft-Kissell Post 235 **[5797]**, Milan, IN
Amer. Legion, Smith-Hoover Post 281 **[8116]**, Harbor Springs, MI
Amer. Legion, Smith-Reynolds Post 511 **[2968]**, Paw Paw, IL
Amer. Legion, Smiths Creek Post 525 **[9755]**, Smiths Creek, MI
Amer. Legion, Smithville Post 711 **[16674]**, Smithville, OH
Amer. Legion, Snider-Richardson Post 273 **[18068]**, Grand Marsh, WI
Amer. Legion, Snyder-Lewis-Welty Post 454 **[7210]**, Colon, MI
Amer. Legion, Snyder-Turner Post 1163 **[370]**, Burnside, IL
Amer. Legion, Solsberry Post 450 **[6203]**, Solsberry, IN
Amer. Legion, Soquist-Binder-Kirk Post 464 **[18414]**, Land O' Lakes, WI
Amer. Legion, South Amherst Post 197 **[16688]**, South Amherst, OH
Amer. Legion, South Bend Post 50 **[6215]**, South Bend, IN
Amer. Legion, South Chicago Post 493 **[702]**, Chicago, IL
Amer. Legion, South Deering Post 1238 **[703]**, Chicago, IL
Amer. Legion, South Holland Post 883 **[3501]**, South Holland, IL
Amer. Legion, South Lyon Post 338 **[9768]**, South Lyon, MI
Amer. Legion, South Park Memorial Post 675 **[14848]**, Dayton, OH
Amer. Legion, South Roxana Post 1167 **[3512]**, South Roxana, IL
Amer. Legion, South Scott County Post 751 **[2382]**, Manchester, IL
Amer. Legion, South Shore Post 388 **[704]**, Chicago, IL
Amer. Legion, South Side Post 531 **[16890]**, Toledo, OH
Amer. Legion, South Suburban Post 1291 **[1313]**, Crete, IL
Amer. Legion, Southern Todd County Post 547 **[11100]**, Grey Eagle, MN
Amer. Legion, Southfield Post 328 **[8542]**, Lansing, MI
Amer. Legion, Southington Post 751 **[16699]**, Southington, OH
Amer. Legion, Southway Post 144 **[14302]**, Columbus, OH
Amer. Legion, Spam Post 570 **[10351]**, Austin, MN
Amer. Legion, Sparks-Doernenburg Post 3 **[17473]**, Antigo, WI
Amer. Legion, Spears-Dukes Post 733 **[3364]**, Rossville, IL
Amer. Legion, Speedway Post 500 **[6277]**, Speedway, IN
Amer. Legion, Speicher Post 499 **[1811]**, Gilman, IL
Amer. Legion, Spencer Post 608 **[16701]**, Spencer, OH
Amer. Legion, Spencer-Ross Post 134 **[12830]**, Walker, MN
Amer. Legion, Spink-Dobak Post 97 **[11944]**, Ortonville, MN
Amer. Legion, Spirit of 76 Post 8 **[17155]**, Wellington, OH
Amer. Legion, Spirit Post 452 **[19355]**, Ogema, WI
Amer. Legion, Spondley Post 291 **[17552]**, Augusta, WI
Amer. Legion, Sponholtz-Deignan Post 183 **[18034]**, Genoa City, WI
Amer. Legion, Sprague-Inman Post 577 **[2248]**, Lena, IL
Amer. Legion, Spring Bay Post 1115 **[3515]**, Spring Bay, IL
Amer. Legion, Spring Green Post 253 **[19765]**, Spring Green, WI
Amer. Legion, Springerton Post 1126 **[3519]**, Springerton, IL
Amer. Legion, Springfield Post 32 **[3526]**, Springfield, IL
Amer. Legion, Square Post 232 **[2936]**, Palos Heights, IL
Amer. Legion, Stahl-Linnemeyer Post 369 **[12995]**, Wykoff, MN
Amer. Legion, Stahl Post 778 **[3784]**, Trenton, IL
Amer. Legion, Stamnitz-Lindeman Post 293 **[9737]**, Sebewaing, MI
Amer. Legion, Stanley Mc Collum Post 280 **[230]**, Benton, IL
Amer. Legion, Stanton Burgett Post 201 **[2696]**, Newman, IL
Amer. Legion, Stanton Post 452 **[9854]**, Stanton, MI
Amer. Legion, Steele-Lambert Post 533 **[6899]**, Bay Port, MI
Amer. Legion, Steger Post 521 **[3701]**, Steger, IL
Amer. Legion, Stenmark-Farnsworth Post 388 **[11170]**, Hinckley, MN
Amer. Legion, Stenz-Griesell-Smith Post 449 **[17664]**, Brookfield, WI
Amer. Legion, Stephen Post 390 **[12709]**, Stephen, MN
Amer. Legion, Sterling Post 296 **[3702]**, Sterling, IL
Amer. Legion, Stevens-Christian-Memorial Post 557 **[17300]**, Wintersville, OH
Amer. Legion, Stevensville Post 568 **[9874]**, Stevensville, MI
Amer. Legion, Stewart-Norris Post 197 **[6188]**, Shelburn, IN
Amer. Legion, Stewart-Schneider Post 592 **[4041]**, Winslow, IL
Amer. Legion, Stickney Post 687 **[3710]**, Stickney, IL
Amer. Legion, Stillwater Post 48 **[12716]**, Stillwater, MN
Amer. Legion, Stinar-Sturdevant-Stoltz Post 116 **[11889]**, New York Mills, MN
Amer. Legion, Stockton Post 449 **[3713]**, Stockton, IL
Amer. Legion, Stoddard-Heinle Post 500 **[18947]**, Milwaukee, WI
Amer. Legion, Stoddard Post 93 **[8138]**, Hartford, MI
Amer. Legion, Stokes-Liebman Post 487 **[17702]**, Cable, WI
Amer. Legion, Stone Groeneweg Post 237 **[10376]**, Balaton, MN
Amer. Legion, Stookey Post 1255 **[199]**, Belleville, IL
Amer. Legion, Stout-Nesbit Post 156 **[9075]**, Montgomery, MI
Amer. Legion, Stover-Harrod Post 133 **[15646]**, Lima, OH
Amer. Legion, Streetsboro Post 685 **[16781]**, Streetsboro, OH
Amer. Legion, Strongsville Post 795 **[16296]**, Olmsted Falls, OH
Amer. Legion, Struck-Klandrud Post 336 **[19361]**, Onalaska, WI
Amer. Legion, Struthers Post 158 **[16801]**, Struthers, OH
Amer. Legion, Stuessy-Kuenzi Post 141 **[19302]**, New Glarus, WI
Amer. Legion, Stukenberg-Eilermann Post 1026 **[13]**, Albers, IL
Amer. Legion, Suburban Green Bay Post 518 **[18075]**, Green Bay, WI
Amer. Legion, Sugar Grove Post 1271 **[3735]**, Sugar Grove, IL
Amer. Legion, Sullivan Post 68 **[3738]**, Sullivan, IL
Amer. Legion, Sullivan Post 139 **[6286]**, Sullivan, IN
Amer. Legion, Sullivan-Wallen Post 11 **[18076]**, Green Bay, WI
Amer. Legion, Summerfield Post 415 **[16808]**, Summerfield, OH
Amer. Legion, Sunset Post 402 **[5647]**, Laketon, IN
Amer. Legion, Sura-Wiersgalla Post 186 **[18232]**, Independence, WI
Amer. Legion, Swann-Gehr Post 197 **[17660]**, Brodhead, WI
Amer. Legion, Swartz-Van-Fleet Post 138 **[10159]**, White Pigeon, MI
Amer. Legion, Swen Rasmussen Post 4 **[11289]**, Lakefield, MN
Amer. Legion, Sycamore Post 99 **[3745]**, Sycamore, IL
Amer. Legion, Sycamore Post 250 **[16821]**, Sycamore, OH
Amer. Legion, Sylvan Post 44 **[19944]**, Wabeno, WI
Amer. Legion, Sylvester Lyczynski Post 420 **[10155]**, White Lake, MI
Amer. Legion, Syverson-Funk Post 155 **[20141]**, Westby, WI
Amer. Legion, Table Grove Post 413 **[3749]**, Table Grove, IL
Amer. Legion, Tadeusz Kosciuszko Post 207 **[5765]**, Merrillville, IN
Amer. Legion, Tamaroa Memorial Post 1277 **[3751]**, Tamaroa, IL
Amer. Legion, Tampico Post 574 **[3753]**, Tampico, IL
Amer. Legion, Tangen-Walstrom Post 114 **[11022]**, Fosston, MN
Amer. Legion, Tanner-Paull Post 120 **[20098]**, West Allis, WI
Amer. Legion, Tattler Post 973 **[705]**, Chicago, IL
Amer. Legion, Taunton Post 604 **[12738]**, Taunton, MN
Amer. Legion, Taylor-Eckhardt Post 913 **[84]**, Armington, IL
Amer. Legion, Taylor Post 200 **[9899]**, Taylor, MI

Amer. Legion, Teddy-Budlong-Robert-Smith Post 39 **[18797]**, Marinette, WI
Amer. Legion, Temperly-Duncan Post 526 **[18200]**, Hazel Green, WI
Amer. Legion, Temple Post 273 **[8543]**, Lansing, MI
Amer. Legion, Tennyson Post 463 **[6301]**, Tennyson, IN
Amer. Legion, Tester-Niemi Post 562 **[10562]**, Brookston, MN
Amer. Legion, Teutopolis Post 924 **[3758]**, Teutopolis, IL
Amer. Legion, T.H.B. Post 187 **[1618]**, Elmhurst, IL
Amer. Legion, Theodore Roosevelt Post 469 **[14057]**, Cleveland, OH
Amer. Legion, Theodore Roosevelt Post 627 **[706]**, Chicago, IL
Amer. Legion, Theodore Stalemo Post 242 **[11009]**, Fisher, MN
Amer. Legion, Thibadeau-Drossart Post 319 **[17719]**, Casco, WI
Amer. Legion, Thomas-Daniels-Hand Post 443 **[9708]**, Sanford, MI
Amer. Legion, Thomas-Devaney-Collier Post 430 **[10442]**, Bird Island, MN
Amer. Legion, Thomas-Holcomb Post 304 **[19416]**, Palmyra, WI
Amer. Legion, Thomas and Leonard Johnson Post 541 **[18210]**, Hixton, WI
Amer. Legion, Thompson-Burkhard Post 28 **[19928]**, Valders, WI
Amer. Legion, Thompson-Wallingford Post 594 **[16392]**, Peebles, OH
Amer. Legion, Thornton Post 1070 **[3763]**, Thornton, IL
Amer. Legion, Thorntown Post 218 **[6355]**, Thorntown, IN
Amer. Legion, Thorpe-Taylor Post 551 **[17599]**, Beetown, WI
Amer. Legion, Three Lakes Post 431 **[19898]**, Three Lakes, WI
Amer. Legion, Thrush-Parry Post 212 **[1932]**, Hanna City, IL
Amer. Legion, Thurston-Zwir Post 121 **[15245]**, Fremont, OH
Amer. Legion, Tickfer-Erickson Post 17 **[17534]**, Arcadia, WI
Amer. Legion, Tiffin Post 169 **[16850]**, Tiffin, OH
Amer. Legion, Timewell Post 1059 **[3764]**, Timewell, IL
Amer. Legion, Timmermann-Benhoff Post 252 **[336]**, Breese, IL
Amer. Legion, Tinley Park Post 615 **[3768]**, Tinley Park, IL
Amer. Legion, Tiskilwa Post 346 **[3775]**, Tiskilwa, IL
Amer. Legion, Toledo Police Post 512 **[16891]**, Toledo, OH
Amer. Legion, Toledo Post 335 **[16892]**, Toledo, OH
Amer. Legion, Tolleston Post 270 **[4775]**, Gary, IN
Amer. Legion, Tony Kashon Post 290 **[6138]**, Rosedale, IN
Amer. Legion, Tony Rivord Post 244 **[9461]**, Powers, MI
Amer. Legion, Toulon Post 416 **[3779]**, Toulon, IL
Amer. Legion, Toutloff-Saunders-Duffy Post 49 **[17584]**, Bayfield, WI
Amer. Legion, Trafalgar Post 416 **[6359]**, Trafalgar, IN
Amer. Legion, Tremont Post 1236 **[3783]**, Tremont, IL
Amer. Legion, Tri-City Post 113 **[1881]**, Granite City, IL
Amer. Legion, Tri-City Post 513 **[11860]**, New Brighton, MN
Amer. Legion, Tri-County Post 124 **[11846]**, Motley, MN
Amer. Legion, Triangle B Post 193 **[17455]**, Adell, WI
Amer. Legion, Triangle Post 933 **[1253]**, Chicago Ridge, IL
Amer. Legion, Trier-Puddy Post 75 **[17968]**, Fond du Lac, WI
Amer. Legion, Triple Six Post 666 **[12373]**, St. Paul, MN
Amer. Legion, Triple Star Post 299 **[3183]**, Raymond, IL
Amer. Legion, Trombley-Polkas Post 494 **[9968]**, Trout Creek, MI
Amer. Legion, Troska Post 210 **[12867]**, Wells, MN
Amer. Legion, Troy Post 708 **[3786]**, Troy, IL
Amer. Legion, Troy-Webster Post 240 **[15738]**, Luckey, OH
Amer. Legion, Truman Blakesley Post 432 **[12838]**, Warba, MN
Amer. Legion, Tuscarawas Post 139 **[16145]**, New Philadelphia, OH
Amer. Legion, Tuttle-Miller Post 761 **[13313]**, Bellbrook, OH
Amer. Legion, Twin Cities Amer. Indian Post 419 **[12374]**, St. Paul, MN
Amer. Legion, Twin City Ford Post 439 **[11510]**, Minneapolis, MN
Amer. Legion, Twin City Post 266 **[4474]**, East Chicago, IN
Amer. Legion, Twin Lakes Post 544 **[19916]**, Twin Lakes, WI
Amer. Legion, Underwood-Orr Post 34 **[9906]**, Tecumseh, MI
Amer. Legion, Union City Post 196 **[10019]**, Union City, MI
Amer. Legion, Union League Post 758 **[707]**, Chicago, IL
Amer. Legion, Union Mills Post 295 **[6366]**, Union Mills, IN
Amer. Legion, Union Post 79 **[15862]**, Marysville, OH
Amer. Legion, Univ. of Minnesota Post 548 **[12375]**, St. Paul, MN
Amer. Legion, Uppena-Kroepfle Post 473 **[19521]**, Potosi, WI
Amer. Legion, Upsala Post 350 **[12781]**, Upsala, MN
Amer. Legion, Urban Klister Post 436 **[20209]**, Wrightstown, WI
Amer. Legion, Urbana Post 71 **[3803]**, Urbana, IL
Amer. Legion, Urbana Post 741 **[17037]**, Urbana, OH
Amer. Legion, Uren-Cooper-Johnson Post 50 **[8319]**, Iron Mountain, MI
Amer. Legion, Valier Post 82 **[3843]**, Valier, IL
Amer. Legion, Valley City Post 356 **[7898]**, Grand Rapids, MI
Amer. Legion, Valley Post 375 **[15754]**, Malvern, OH
Amer. Legion, Valmeyer Post 901 **[3845]**, Valmeyer, IL
Amer. Legion, Van-Bibber-Hansen Post 148 **[3419]**, Savanna, IL
Amer. Legion, Van Buren Post 401 **[708]**, Chicago, IL
Amer. Legion, Van-Der-Jagt-De-Bruine Post 338 **[17726]**, Cedar Grove, WI
Amer. Legion, Van-Huizen-Fritz Post 123 **[19414]**, Owen, WI
Amer. Legion, Vandalia Memorial Post 668 **[17057]**, Vandalia, OH
Amer. Legion, Vandercook Lake Post 166 **[8360]**, Jackson, MI
Amer. Legion, Vanderwaal-Lusty Post 421 **[11461]**, Mentor, MN
Amer. Legion, Varga-Fall Post 383 **[9559]**, Rosebush, MI
Amer. Legion, Venice-Madison Post 307 **[3123]**, Pontoon Beach, IL
Amer. Legion, Venier-Molea Post 452 **[11247]**, Keewatin, MN
Amer. Legion, Verhulst-Willmarth-Paulsen Post 311 **[18211]**, Holcombe, WI
Amer. Legion, Verner Hanes Post 110 **[6544]**, Wolcottville, IN
Amer. Legion, Vernon Post 1247 **[3852]**, Vernon Hills, IL
Amer. Legion, Versailles Post 435 **[17068]**, Versailles, OH
Amer. Legion, Vesper Post 520 **[19937]**, Vesper, WI
Amer. Legion, Veterans Memorial Post 63 **[17770]**, Clintonville, WI
Amer. Legion, Viall Post 166 **[12043]**, Preston, MN
Amer. Legion, Victor Hill Post 534 **[478]**, Casey, IL
Amer. Legion, Victor Post 255 **[18434]**, Luck, WI
Amer. Legion, Victoria Post 1995 **[12787]**, Victoria, MN
Amer. Legion, Victory Post 7 **[709]**, Chicago, IL
Amer. Legion, Victory Post 70 **[6190]**, Shelbyville, IN
Amer. Legion, Victory Post 112 **[19773]**, Stanley, WI
Amer. Legion, Victory Post 260 **[13223]**, Attica, OH
Amer. Legion, Viking Memorial Post 611 **[13035]**, Akron, OH
Amer. Legion, Viking Post 493 **[10460]**, Bloomington, MN
Amer. Legion, Villa Grove Post 215 **[259]**, Bloomington, IL
Amer. Legion, Villa Park Post 652 **[3862]**, Villa Park, IL
Amer. Legion, Vincennes Post 73 **[6408]**, Vincennes, IN
Amer. Legion, Vincent Hays Post 610 **[2839]**, Oakwood, IL
Amer. Legion, Vinton Post 161 **[17072]**, Vinton, OH
Amer. Legion, Voight Post 376 **[17951]**, Fall Creek, WI
Amer. Legion, Votaw-Swank Post 458 **[2673]**, Neoga, IL
Amer. Legion, Vytautas Post 289 **[5766]**, Merrillville, IN
Amer. Legion, W.-Grams-R-Schmidt Post 475 **[12268]**, St. Clair, MN
Amer. Legion, Wabash Post 423 **[2572]**, Mount Carmel, IL
Amer. Legion, Waconia Post 150 **[12815]**, Waconia, MN
Amer. Legion, Wade Benfer Post 404 **[16509]**, Republic, OH
Amer. Legion, Wade Post 598 **[2008]**, Hinckley, IL
Amer. Legion, Wadena Post 171 **[12820]**, Wadena, MN
Amer. Legion, Wadsworth Post 170 **[17073]**, Wadsworth, OH
Amer. Legion, Wagner-Eberle-Sukowaty Post 477 **[19661]**, St. Nazianz, WI
Amer. Legion, Wakeman Post 689 **[17082]**, Wakeman, OH
Amer. Legion, Waldron-Flaat Post 182 **[10930]**, Effie, MN
Amer. Legion, Walhonding Valley Post 634 **[17124]**, Warsaw, OH
Amer. Legion, Walker-Hecox-Hickle Post 677 **[15683]**, Lithopolis, OH
Amer. Legion, Wallace Sniffin Post 506 **[5830]**, Montmorenci, IN
Amer. Legion, Wally Bartley Post 162 **[8882]**, Luzerne, MI
Amer. Legion, Walnut Post 179 **[3874]**, Walnut, IL
Amer. Legion, Walter Clemons Post 613 **[581]**, Chatsworth, IL
Amer. Legion, Walter Durkee Post 311 **[7899]**, Grand Rapids, MI
Amer. Legion, Walter Fraser Post 108 **[9339]**, Oxford, MI
Amer. Legion, Walter Graham Post 332 **[3334]**, Rockton, IL
Amer. Legion, Walter Guede Post 593 **[2184]**, Lacon, IL
Amer. Legion, Walter Hoyt Post 350 **[6029]**, Perrysville, IN
Amer. Legion, Walter Miller Post 394 **[16563]**, Russellville, OH
Amer. Legion, Walter Riley Post 307 **[11856]**, Nashwauk, MN
Amer. Legion, Walter Scott Erickson Post 557 **[10767]**, Deerwood, MN
Amer. Legion, Walter Stelmaszek Post 792 **[392]**, Calumet City, IL
Amer. Legion, Walter Tripp Post 29 **[11836]**, Morris, MN
Amer. Legion, Walton Post 418 **[6438]**, Walton, IN
Amer. Legion, Wanda Post 385 **[12835]**, Wanda, MN
Amer. Legion, Waples-Bauer Post 94 **[2706]**, Nokomis, IL
Amer. Legion, Warren Brock Post 69 **[6013]**, Orleans, IN
Amer. Legion, Warren Post 27 **[12840]**, Warren, MN
Amer. Legion, Warren Post 259 **[6528]**, Williamsport, IN
Amer. Legion, Warren Post 490 **[7651]**, Farmington Hills, MI
Amer. Legion, Warrick Post 200 **[4273]**, Boonville, IN
Amer. Legion, Waseca Post 228 **[12846]**, Waseca, MN
Amer. Legion, Washburn Post 661 **[3884]**, Washburn, IL
Amer. Legion, Washington Post 100 **[3885]**, Washington, IL
Amer. Legion, Washington Post 444 **[16129]**, New Knoxville, OH

Amer. Legion, Waterford Post 24 **[8142]**, Hartland, MI
Amer. Legion, Waterford Post 230 **[17019]**, Uhrichsville, OH
Amer. Legion, Waterloo Post 747 **[3898]**, Waterloo, IL
Amer. Legion, Waterman Post 654 **[3905]**, Waterman, IL
Amer. Legion, Waters-Hackenberg Post 220 **[8792]**, Lawton, MI
Amer. Legion, Waterville Post 463 **[17135]**, Waterville, OH
Amer. Legion, Watkins Post 453 **[12854]**, Watkins, MN
Amer. Legion, Watseka Post 23 **[3907]**, Watseka, IL
Amer. Legion, Wauconda Post 911 **[3912]**, Wauconda, IL
Amer. Legion, Wave Post 988 **[710]**, Chicago, IL
Amer. Legion, Waverly Post 262 **[3933]**, Waverly, IL
Amer. Legion, Wawasee Post 223 **[6290]**, Syracuse, IN
Amer. Legion, Wayne City Post 1132 **[3934]**, Wayne City, IL
Amer. Legion, Wayne Newton Post 346 **[6312]**, Terre Haute, IN
Amer. Legion, Wayne Post 64 **[5014]**, Indianapolis, IN
Amer. Legion, Wayne Post 111 **[10099]**, Wayne, MI
Amer. Legion, Wayne Post 395 **[17150]**, Waynesfield, OH
Amer. Legion, Wayne Township Veterans Post 615 **[17151]**, Waynesville, OH
Amer. Legion, Wayne-Wright Post 1052 **[711]**, Chicago, IL
Amer. Legion, Waynedale Post 241 **[4632]**, Fort Wayne, IN
Amer. Legion, Waynesville Post 1189 **[3935]**, Waynesville, IL
Amer. Legion, Waynetown Post 445 **[6463]**, Waynetown, IN
Amer. Legion, Weakly-Rowland Post 420 **[3396]**, St. Elmo, IL
Amer. Legion, Weatherford-Vander-Hoeven Post 552 **[9653]**, St. Clair Shores, MI
Amer. Legion, Webb Lake A and H Post 403 **[20093]**, Webb Lake, WI
Amer. Legion, Wee-Chick Post 518 **[9191]**, New Troy, MI
Amer. Legion, Weeden-Zeller Post 609 **[3965]**, Westfield, IL
Amer. Legion, Weilepp-Cramer Post 660 **[2417]**, Maroa, IL
Amer. Legion, Weimer-Widder Post 549 **[13279]**, Beach City, OH
Amer. Legion, Weinsch-Gilbert-Patten-Gillett Post 353 **[17786]**, Cornell, WI
Amer. Legion, Welcome Post 553 **[12866]**, Welcome, MN
Amer. Legion, Welker-Smith Post 17 **[15318]**, Gibsonburg, OH
Amer. Legion, Wells-Peterson Post 384 **[10789]**, Dodge Center, MN
Amer. Legion, Wellston Post 371 **[17159]**, Wellston, OH
Amer. Legion, Wellsville Post 70 **[17161]**, Wellsville, OH
Amer. Legion, Welsh-Crawley-Kramer Post 129 **[4839]**, Greensburg, IN
Amer. Legion, Wenona Post 8 **[3937]**, Wenona, IL
Amer. Legion, Wenzel-Longley Post 349 **[19853]**, Sullivan, WI
Amer. Legion, Wesley Johnson Memorial Post 1195 **[3881]**, Wasco, IL
Amer. Legion, Wesley Werner Post 513 **[13728]**, Cincinnati, OH
Amer. Legion, West Chicago Post 300 **[3938]**, West Chicago, IL
Amer. Legion, West Douglas County Post 188 **[10967]**, Evansville, MN
Amer. Legion, West End Post 414 **[12889]**, White Bear Lake, MN
Amer. Legion, West-Field Post 48 **[17605]**, Beloit, WI
Amer. Legion, West Lafayette Post 466 **[17182]**, West Lafayette, OH
Amer. Legion, West Lafayette Post 492 **[6471]**, West Lafayette, IN
Amer. Legion, West Mansfield Post 603 **[17187]**, West Mansfield, OH
Amer. Legion, West Noble Post 243 **[5680]**, Ligonier, IN
Amer. Legion, West Randolph Post 353 **[4594]**, Farmland, IN
Amer. Legion, West Sangamon Post 743 **[2679]**, New Berlin, IL
Amer. Legion, West Side Memorial Post 151 **[18464]**, Madison, WI
Amer. Legion, West Unity Post 669 **[17200]**, West Unity, OH
Amer. Legion, Westbrook Post 152 **[12882]**, Westbrook, MN
Amer. Legion, Western Reserve Post 315 **[14058]**, Cleveland, OH
Amer. Legion, Western Taylor County Post 359 **[18050]**, Gilman, WI
Amer. Legion, Westland Post 251 **[9392]**, Plymouth, MI
Amer. Legion, Westmont Post 338 **[3967]**, Westmont, IL
Amer. Legion, Weston Post 409 **[17243]**, Weston, OH
Amer. Legion, Westphal Post 251 **[12116]**, Robbinsdale, MN
Amer. Legion, Westport Post 638 **[12789]**, Villard, MN
Amer. Legion, Whalen-Hill Post 648 **[1880]**, Grafton, IL
Amer. Legion, Wheatfield Post 406 **[6519]**, Wheatfield, IN
Amer. Legion, Wheeling Memorial Post 221 **[4004]**, Wheeling, IL
Amer. Legion, White Bear Lake Post 168 **[12890]**, White Bear Lake, MN
Amer. Legion, White Earth Indian Nation Post 625 **[11931]**, Ogema, MN
Amer. Legion, White Hall Post 70 **[4007]**, White Hall, IL
Amer. Legion, White River Post 114 **[4907]**, Hazleton, IN
Amer. Legion, Whitehouse Post 384 **[17250]**, Whitehouse, OH
Amer. Legion, Whitish-Funk Post 184 **[17956]**, Fennimore, WI
Amer. Legion, Whitmore Lake Post 359 **[8100]**, Hamburg, MI
Amer. Legion, Whittey Bennett Post 301 **[12737]**, Taconite, MN
Amer. Legion, Wickler-Copeland Post 464 **[3876]**, Warren, IL
Amer. Legion, Wilber-Bartlett Post 315 **[7029]**, Brooklyn, MI
Amer. Legion, Wilbur Braughton Post 611 **[3709]**, Stewardson, IL
Amer. Legion, Wilbur Bud Crane Post 400 **[6433]**, Walkerton, IN
Amer. Legion, Wilcox-Eastman-Salinas Post 160 **[6826]**, Bangor, MI
Amer. Legion, Wiley-Mumford Post 764 **[3776]**, Toledo, IL
Amer. Legion, Wileykoon Post 475 **[9732]**, Schoolcraft, MI
Amer. Legion, Wilkins-Kelly Post 450 **[17804]**, Darien, WI
Amer. Legion, Willey-Herda Post 192 **[18008]**, Franklin, WI
Amer. Legion, William Allen Post 179 **[12013]**, Plainview, MN
Amer. Legion, William-B.-Cairns-Victory Post 57 **[18465]**, Madison, WI
Amer. Legion, William C. Lee Memorial Post 503 **[4350]**, Chesterton, IN
Amer. Legion, William Chandler Peterson Post 171 **[1317]**, Crystal Lake, IL
Amer. Legion, William Chizum Post 146 **[5842]**, Morocco, IN
Amer. Legion, William Hall Post 282 **[4097]**, Anderson, IN
Amer. Legion, William Krensing Post 58 **[10565]**, Browns Valley, MN
Amer. Legion, William Mc Kinley Post 231 **[712]**, Chicago, IL
Amer. Legion, William Riker Johnson Post 205 **[8544]**, Lansing, MI
Amer. Legion, William Robideau Post 66 **[11214]**, International Falls, MN
Amer. Legion, William Schaefer Post 44 **[2983]**, Pekin, IL
Amer. Legion, William T. Mc Coy Post 92 **[12125]**, Rochester, MN
Amer. Legion, William Zeb Longest Post 42 **[4615]**, Floyds Knobs, IN
Amer. Legion, Williams-Giroux Post 90 **[8510]**, Lake Linden, MI
Amer. Legion, Williamsburg Post 288 **[17268]**, Williamsburg, OH
Amer. Legion, Williamsburg Post 442 **[6527]**, Williamsburg, IN
Amer. Legion, Williamsfield Post 371 **[4009]**, Williamsfield, IL
Amer. Legion, Williamson Post 147 **[2400]**, Marion, IL
Amer. Legion, Williamson-Smiley Post 401 **[6074]**, Redkey, IN
Amer. Legion, Willis-Chapel Post 306 **[18144]**, Green Lake, WI
Amer. Legion, Willis Hunter Post 378 **[1549]**, East St. Louis, IL
Amer. Legion, Willowick-Eastlake Post 678 **[17282]**, Willowick, OH
Amer. Legion, Wilmington Veterans Post 49 **[17286]**, Wilmington, OH
Amer. Legion, Wilson-Oliver-Riley Post 462 **[6205]**, Somerville, IN
Amer. Legion, Windham Post 674 **[17298]**, Windham, OH
Amer. Legion, Windom Post 206 **[12938]**, Windom, MN
Amer. Legion, Winegar Post 480 **[19540]**, Presque Isle, WI
Amer. Legion, Wingate Post 174 **[6540]**, Wingate, IN
Amer. Legion, Winifred Fairfax Warder Post 406 **[3752]**, Tamms, IL
Amer. Legion, Winnebago Post 82 **[12943]**, Winnebago, MN
Amer. Legion, Winnetka Post 10 **[3921]**, Waukegan, IL
Amer. Legion, Winnow-Arn Post 541 **[14783]**, Continental, OH
Amer. Legion, Winslow Post 115 **[6542]**, Winslow, IN
Amer. Legion of Wisconsin **[★19506]**
Amer. Legion, Wisconsin Post 8 **[19979]**, Waukesha, WI
Amer. Legion, Wisconsin Post 22 **[17472]**, Amherst, WI
Amer. Legion, Wisconsin Post 23 **[18948]**, Milwaukee, WI
Amer. Legion, Wisconsin Post 24 **[18395]**, Lake Geneva, WI
Amer. Legion, Wisconsin Post 30 **[17915]**, Edgerton, WI
Amer. Legion, Wisconsin Post 42 **[19462]**, Platteville, WI
Amer. Legion, Wisconsin Post 46 **[18894]**, Merrill, WI
Amer. Legion, Wisconsin Post 47 **[19507]**, Portage, WI
Amer. Legion, Wisconsin Post 50 **[18222]**, Hudson, WI
Amer. Legion, Wisconsin Post 52 **[18333]**, La Crosse, WI
Amer. Legion, Wisconsin Post 60 **[18324]**, Kimberly, WI
Amer. Legion, Wisconsin Post 72 **[19835]**, Sturgeon Bay, WI
Amer. Legion, Wisconsin Post 79 **[17695]**, Burlington, WI
Amer. Legion, Wisconsin Post 82 **[19498]**, Port Washington, WI
Amer. Legion, Wisconsin Post 85 **[19256]**, Muscoda, WI
Amer. Legion, Wisconsin Post 91 **[19338]**, Oconomowoc, WI
Amer. Legion, Wisconsin Post 96 **[20095]**, Webster, WI
Amer. Legion, Wisconsin Post 97 **[17834]**, Dodgeville, WI
Amer. Legion, Wisconsin Post 104 **[17794]**, Cuba City, WI
Amer. Legion, Wisconsin Post 108 **[17761]**, Clear Lake, WI
Amer. Legion, Wisconsin Post 109 **[18409]**, Lancaster, WI

Amer. Legion, Wisconsin Post 113 **[19235]**, Mount Horeb, WI
Amer. Legion, Wisconsin Post 114 **[17846]**, Eagle River, WI
Amer. Legion, Wisconsin Post 118 **[19896]**, Thorp, WI
Amer. Legion, Wisconsin Post 122 **[19452]**, Phillips, WI
Amer. Legion, Wisconsin Post 128 **[19824]**, Stockbridge, WI
Amer. Legion, Wisconsin Post 129 **[19902]**, Tomah, WI
Amer. Legion, Wisconsin Post 133 **[17713]**, Camp Douglas, WI
Amer. Legion, Wisconsin Post 143 **[19655]**, St. Croix Falls, WI
Amer. Legion, Wisconsin Post 146 **[17589]**, Beaver Dam, WI
Amer. Legion, Wisconsin Post 158 **[18769]**, Maiden Rock, WI
Amer. Legion, Wisconsin Post 159 **[17706]**, Cadott, WI
Amer. Legion, Wisconsin Post 160 **[17689]**, Brooklyn, WI
Amer. Legion, Wisconsin Post 165 **[19919]**, Two Rivers, WI
Amer. Legion, Wisconsin Post 173 **[20159]**, Whitewater, WI
Amer. Legion, Wisconsin Post 177 **[18072]**, Gratiot, WI
Amer. Legion, Wisconsin Post 181 **[17844]**, Durand, WI
Amer. Legion, Wisconsin Post 182 **[19424]**, Park Falls, WI
Amer. Legion, Wisconsin Post 187 **[20176]**, Wisc Dells, WI
Amer. Legion, Wisconsin Post 195 **[17709]**, Cambridge, WI
Amer. Legion, Wisconsin Post 198 **[18807]**, Marion, WI
Amer. Legion, Wisconsin Post 205 **[18242]**, Janesville, WI
Amer. Legion, Wisconsin Post 208 **[19632]**, Rio, WI
Amer. Legion, Wisconsin Post 209 **[19382]**, Orfordville, WI
Amer. Legion, Wisconsin Post 213 **[17817]**, Deer Park, WI
Amer. Legion, Wisconsin Post 215 **[19422]**, Pardeeville, WI
Amer. Legion, Wisconsin Post 219 **[19980]**, Waukesha, WI
Amer. Legion, Wisconsin Post 220 **[19741]**, Soldiers Grove, WI
Amer. Legion, Wisconsin Post 236 **[17460]**, Algoma, WI
Amer. Legion, Wisconsin Post 249 **[18018]**, Frederic, WI
Amer. Legion, Wisconsin Post 254 **[18918]**, Milltown, WI
Amer. Legion, Wisconsin Post 258 **[18420]**, Little Chute, WI
Amer. Legion, Wisconsin Post 265 **[17484]**, Appleton, WI
Amer. Legion, Wisconsin Post 266 **[17774]**, Colby, WI
Amer. Legion, Wisconsin Post 268 **[17694]**, Bruce, WI
Amer. Legion, Wisconsin Post 269 **[17801]**, Cushing, WI
Amer. Legion, Wisconsin Post 271 **[19523]**, Poynette, WI
Amer. Legion, Wisconsin Post 272 **[17701]**, Butternut, WI
Amer. Legion, Wisconsin Post 278 **[17562]**, Balsam Lake, WI
Amer. Legion, Wisconsin Post 283 **[19883]**, Suring, WI
Amer. Legion, Wisconsin Post 287 **[18827]**, Mattoon, WI
Amer. Legion, Wisconsin Post 290 **[17620]**, Benton, WI
Amer. Legion, Wisconsin Post 295 **[17641]**, Bloomer, WI
Amer. Legion, Wisconsin Post 297 **[19584]**, Radisson, WI
Amer. Legion, Wisconsin Post 309 **[18290]**, Kendall, WI
Amer. Legion, Wisconsin Post 310 **[19549]**, Racine, WI
Amer. Legion, Wisconsin Post 318 **[18407]**, Lake Tomahawk, WI
Amer. Legion, Wisconsin Post 322 **[19282]**, Nekoosa, WI
Amer. Legion, Wisconsin Post 324 **[19412]**, Osseo, WI
Amer. Legion, Wisconsin Post 326 **[17654]**, Boyd, WI
Amer. Legion, Wisconsin Post 329 **[17656]**, Briggsville, WI
Amer. Legion, Wisconsin Post 333 **[19856]**, Sun Prairie, WI
Amer. Legion, Wisconsin Post 335 **[17553]**, Avoca, WI
Amer. Legion, Wisconsin Post 346 **[17734]**, Centuria, WI
Amer. Legion, Wisconsin Post 358 **[19927]**, Unity, WI
Amer. Legion, Wisconsin Post 360 **[20014]**, Waunakee, WI
Amer. Legion, Wisconsin Post 365 **[19486]**, Plum City, WI
Amer. Legion, Wisconsin Post 370 **[20165]**, Wild Rose, WI
Amer. Legion, Wisconsin Post 372 **[17997]**, Forestville, WI
Amer. Legion, Wisconsin Post 383 **[18428]**, Lone Rock, WI
Amer. Legion, Wisconsin Post 384 **[18316]**, Kewaskum, WI
Amer. Legion, Wisconsin Post 392 **[17645]**, Bonduel, WI
Amer. Legion, Wisconsin Post 395 **[18327]**, Kingston, WI
Amer. Legion, Wisconsin Post 404 **[17942]**, Emerald, WI
Amer. Legion, Wisconsin Post 406 **[18949]**, Milwaukee, WI
Amer. Legion, Wisconsin Post 408 **[18950]**, Milwaukee, WI
Amer. Legion, Wisconsin Post 410 **[18021]**, Fredonia, WI
Amer. Legion, Wisconsin Post 411 **[18951]**, Milwaukee, WI
Amer. Legion, Wisconsin Post 418 **[19748]**, South Range, WI
Amer. Legion, Wisconsin Post 422 **[18203]**, Highland, WI
Amer. Legion, Wisconsin Post 435 **[19871]**, Superior, WI
Amer. Legion, Wisconsin Post 439 **[18853]**, Melrose, WI
Amer. Legion, Wisconsin Post 443 **[17644]**, Blue River, WI
Amer. Legion, Wisconsin Post 444 **[18952]**, Milwaukee, WI
Amer. Legion, Wisconsin Post 445 **[17720]**, Cashton, WI
Amer. Legion, Wisconsin Post 454 **[19233]**, Mount Calvary, WI
Amer. Legion, Wisconsin Post 455 **[18953]**, Milwaukee, WI
Amer. Legion, Wisconsin Post 461 **[19430]**, Pembine, WI
Amer. Legion, Wisconsin Post 462 **[17456]**, Adell, WI
Amer. Legion, Wisconsin Post 465 **[19201]**, Minong, WI
Amer. Legion, Wisconsin Post 469 **[18796]**, Marathon, WI
Amer. Legion, Wisconsin Post 478 **[19654]**, St. Cloud, WI
Amer. Legion, Wisconsin Post 481 **[20015]**, Waunakee, WI
Amer. Legion, Wisconsin Post 484 **[19489]**, Plymouth, WI
Amer. Legion, Wisconsin Post 485 **[19652]**, Rudolph, WI
Amer. Legion, Wisconsin Post 486 **[18241]**, Jackson, WI
Amer. Legion, Wisconsin Post 492 **[19651]**, Rothschild, WI
Amer. Legion, Wisconsin Post 494 **[18015]**, Franksville, WI
Amer. Legion, Wisconsin Post 496 **[19726]**, Sherwood, WI
Amer. Legion, Wisconsin Post 498 **[18954]**, Milwaukee, WI
Amer. Legion, Wisconsin Post 501 **[18466]**, Madison, WI
Amer. Legion, Wisconsin Post 504 **[17938]**, Elroy, WI
Amer. Legion, Wisconsin Post 511 **[19629]**, Ridgeland, WI
Amer. Legion, Wisconsin Post 527 **[19738]**, Sister Bay, WI
Amer. Legion, Wisconsin Post 529 **[18955]**, Milwaukee, WI
Amer. Legion, Wisconsin Post 539 **[18077]**, Green Bay, WI
Amer. Legion, Wisconsin Post 546 **[19550]**, Racine, WI
Amer. Legion, Wisconsin Post 552 **[19744]**, Somers, WI
Amer. Legion, Witt-Webber-Carrell Post 617 **[86]**, Arrowsmith, IL
Amer. Legion, Wittstein-Middleman Post 524 **[13729]**, Cincinnati, OH
Amer. Legion, Wm. A. Baker Post 363 **[15736]**, Lucasville, OH
Amer. Legion, Wm-A.-Jacobson-Errett-B.-Olson Post 138 **[19941]**, Viroqua, WI
Amer. Legion, Wm. F. Helmke Post 340 **[15454]**, Holgate, OH
Amer. Legion, Wodtka-Rothe-Reiss Post 380 **[3405]**, St. Peter, IL
Amer. Legion, Wojciak-Talberg Post 602 **[11165]**, Hillman, MN
Amer. Legion, Wolcott Post 294 **[6543]**, Wolcott, IN
Amer. Legion, Wolf River Post 391 **[18023]**, Fremont, WI
Amer. Legion, Wolman-Minskey Post 317 **[20064]**, Wautoma, WI
Amer. Legion, Wolverine Post 360 **[9473]**, Reading, MI
Amer. Legion, Wolverton-Sawvel-Falor Post 295 **[7000]**, Breckenridge, MI
Amer. Legion, Women Veterans Post 919 **[2796]**, Oak Lawn, IL
Amer. Legion, Wood-Gasteyer Post 542 **[17913]**, Eau Galle, WI
Amer. Legion, Wood-Hill Post 39 **[8923]**, Marcellus, MI
Amer. Legion, Wood Lake Post 556 **[12973]**, Wood Lake, MN
Amer. Legion, Wood River Post 204 **[4045]**, Wood River, IL
Amer. Legion, Wood-Rosebrook Post 745 **[15073]**, East Liberty, OH
Amer. Legion, Woodard-Mc-Govern Post 426 **[17183]**, West Liberty, OH
Amer. Legion, Woodburn Post 377 **[6545]**, Woodburn, IN
Amer. Legion, Woodbury Post 501 **[12974]**, Woodbury, MN
Amer. Legion, Woodcock-Herbst Post 216 **[12044]**, Princeton, MN
Amer. Legion, Woodrow Wilson Post 347 **[10061]**, Warren, MI
Amer. Legion, Woodrow Wilson Post 506 **[12260]**, Ruthton, MN
Amer. Legion, Woodville Post 301 **[20207]**, Woodville, WI
Amer. Legion, Wooster Post 68 **[17310]**, Wooster, OH
Amer. Legion, Worden Post 564 **[4066]**, Worden, IL
Amer. Legion, Worthey Post 492 **[2088]**, Jerseyville, IL
Amer. Legion, Wyandot Post 225 **[17031]**, Upper Sandusky, OH
Amer. Legion, Wycoff Post 296 **[10171]**, Williamston, MI
Amer. Legion, Wyoming Post 91 **[4072]**, Wyoming, IL
Amer. Legion, Y. T. R. Post 153 **[16867]**, Tiltonsville, OH
Amer. Legion, Yackee-Strong-Memorial Post 60 **[16802]**, Stryker, OH
Amer. Legion, Yoki-Bergman Post 220 **[11851]**, Mountain Iron, MN
Amer. Legion, Yonke-Christenson Post 533 **[17564]**, Bancroft, WI
Amer. Legion, York-Kolar Post 316 **[19722]**, Sheldon, WI

Amer. Legion, Yorktown Post 321 **[6547]**, Yorktown, IN
Amer. Legion, Yorkville Post 489 **[4073]**, Yorkville, IL
Amer. Legion, Young-Budd Post 171 **[15273]**, Galena, OH
Amer. Legion, Young-Moore Post 100 **[17195]**, West Union, OH
Amer. Legion, Ypsilanti Post 282 **[10197]**, Ypsilanti, MI
Amer. Legion, Yurkovich-Beck Post 594 **[2579]**, Mount Olive, IL
Amer. Legion, Zanesville Post 29 **[17436]**, Zanesville, OH
Amer. Legion, Zernicke-Wegner Post 217 **[17646]**, Bonduel, WI
Amer. Legion, Zion-Benton Post 865 **[4080]**, Zion, IL
Amer. Legion, Zook-Farrington Post 434 **[5556]**, Kingsford Heights, IN
Amer. Legion, Zook-Scott Post 325 **[5835]**, Mooresville, IN
Amer. Legion, Zue-Vandeveer Post 257 **[3715]**, Stonington, IL
Amer. Legion, Zumbrota Post 183 **[13004]**, Zumbrota, MN
Amer. Lib. Assn./Assoc. Lib. Sci. Students of Ohio, Kent State Univ. **[15538]**, Kent, OH
Amer. Lib. Assn., Dominican Univ. **[3199]**, River Forest, IL
Amer. Lib. Assn. Student Chap., Indiana Univ. **[4198]**, Bloomington, IN
Amer. Lib. Assn., Student Chap., Univ. of Michigan at Ann Arbor **[★6662]**
Amer. Lib. Assn., Student Chap., Univ. of Michigan School of Info. **[6662]**, Ann Arbor, MI
Amer. Lib. Assn., Wayne State Univ. **[7317]**, Detroit, MI
Amer. Line Builders Chap. Natl. Elecl. Contractors Assn. **[17058]**, Vandalia, OH
Amer. Liver Found. - Illinois Chap. **[713]**, Chicago, IL
Amer. Lung Assn. of Illinois **[3527]**, Springfield, IL
Amer. Lung Assn. of Illinois, Southern Illinois Region **[2401]**, Marion, IL
Amer. Lung Assn. of Indiana **[5015]**, Indianapolis, IN
Amer. Lung Assn. of Indiana, Northern **[4633]**, Fort Wayne, IN
Amer. Lung Assn. of Metropolitan Chicago **[714]**, Chicago, IL
Amer. Lung Assn. of Michigan **[9255]**, Oak Park, MI
Amer. Lung Assn. of Minnesota **[12376]**, St. Paul, MN
Amer. Lung Assn. of Ohio **[14303]**, Columbus, OH
Amer. Lung Assn. of Ohio, Northwest Br. **[16259]**, Norwalk, OH
Amer. Lung Assn. of Ohio, South Shore Br. **[★16259]**
Amer. Lung Assn. of Ohio, Southwest Br. **[13730]**, Cincinnati, OH
Amer. Lung Assn. of Wisconsin **[17665]**, Brookfield, WI
Amer. Maltese Assn. **[7159]**, Clarkston, MI
Amer. Marketing Assn. - Minnesota Chap. **[12377]**, St. Paul, MN
Amer. Meteorological Soc., Central Illinois **[2272]**, Lincoln, IL
Amer. Meteorological Soc., Central Michigan Univ. **[9097]**, Mount Pleasant, MI
Amer. Meteorological Soc., Central Ohio **[15618]**, Lebanon, OH
Amer. Meteorological Soc., Chicago **[3717]**, Streamwood, IL
Amer. Meteorological Soc., Greater Milwaukee **[19981]**, Waukesha, WI
Amer. Meteorological Soc., Greater St. Louis **[3456]**, Scott AFB, IL
Amer. Meteorological Soc., Northeast Ohio **[13036]**, Akron, OH
Amer. Meteorological Soc., Northern Illinois Univ. **[1427]**, DeKalb, IL
Amer. Meteorological Soc., Northland Coll. **[17542]**, Ashland, WI
Amer. Meteorological Soc., Packerland Chap. **[18078]**, Green Bay, WI
Amer. Meteorological Soc., Purdue Univ. **[★6498]**
Amer. Meteorological Soc., Twin Cities **[10331]**, Arden Hills, MN
Amer. Meteorological Soc., Univ. of Michigan - Ann Arbor **[8117]**, Harbor Springs, MI
Amer. Meteorological Soc., Wright Memorial **[17355]**, Wright-Patterson AFB, OH
Amer. Mold Builders Assn., Northern Ohio Chap. **[17013]**, Twinsburg, OH
Amer. Morgan Horse Assn., Region 3 **[6199]**, Sheridan, IN
Amer. Morgan Horse Assn., Region 5 **[715]**, Chicago, IL
Amer. Mothers - Illinois Chap. **[578]**, Chatham, IL
Amer. Mothers - Indiana Chap. **[4945]**, Huntington, IN
Amer. Mothers - Minnesota Chap. **[10681]**, Climax, MN
Amer. Mothers - Ohio Chap. **[14304]**, Columbus, OH
Amer. Musicological Soc. - Midwest Chap. **[6630]**, Alma, MI
Amer. Nuclear Soc., Central Illinois Sect. **[1271]**, Clinton, IL
Amer. Nuclear Soc., Ohio Sect. **[16402]**, Perrysburg, OH
Amer. Nuclear Soc., Wisconsin **[18467]**, Madison, WI
Amer. Nurses Assn. - Bay Area Medical Center, Prof LSC **[18798]**, Marinette, WI
Amer. Optometric Assn. - Ohio Chap. **[★17350]**
Amer. Orff-Schulwerk Assn., Greater Cleveland Chap. No. 1 **[16700]**, Southington, OH
Amer. Orff-Schulwerk Assn., West Michigan Chap. No. 32 **[9098]**, Mount Pleasant, MI
Amer. ORT Chicago Chap. **[716]**, Chicago, IL
Amer. ORT, Cleveland Chap. **[13282]**, Beachwood, OH
Amer. Ostrich Assn., Minnesota **[11511]**, Minneapolis, MN
Amer. Parkinson Disease Assn., Midwest Chap. **[1857]**, Glenview, IL
Amer. Parkinson Disease Assn. Minnesota Chap. **[11512]**, Minneapolis, MN
Amer. Parkinson Disease Assn., Tri-State Parkinson's Wellness Chap. **[13731]**, Cincinnati, OH
Amer. Payroll Assn., Chicago Chap. **[717]**, Chicago, IL
Amer. Payroll Assn., Columbus Area Chap. **[14305]**, Columbus, OH
Amer. Payroll Assn., Greater Cleveland Chap. **[13423]**, Broadview Heights, OH
Amer. Payroll Assn., Greater Lafayette Chap. **[6472]**, West Lafayette, IN
Amer. Payroll Assn., Hall of Fame Chap. **[16052]**, Mogadore, OH
Amer. Payroll Assn., Miami Valley Chap. **[14849]**, Dayton, OH
Amer. Payroll Assn., Northeast Indiana Chap. **[6441]**, Warsaw, IN
Amer. Payroll Assn., Northstar Chap. **[12378]**, St. Paul, MN
Amer. Payroll Assn., Toledo Area Chap. **[16893]**, Toledo, OH
Amer. Payroll Assn., Youngstown, Ohio Chap. **[17390]**, Youngstown, OH
Amer. Physical Therapy Assn., Illinois **[★2780]**
Amer. Physical Therapy Assn., Indiana Chap. **[5016]**, Indianapolis, IN
Amer. Physical Therapy Assn., Minnesota Chap. **[12220]**, Roseville, MN
Amer. Physical Therapy Assn. - Ohio Chap. **[★15269]**
Amer. Planning Assn. Chicago Chap. **[718]**, Chicago, IL
Amer. Planning Assn. - Ohio Chap. **[14059]**, Cleveland, OH
Amer. Postal Workers Union, AFL-CIO - Crystal Lake Local Union 1879 **[1519]**, Dundee, IL
Amer. Postal Workers Union, AFL-CIO - Indianapolis Local Union 130 **[5017]**, Indianapolis, IN
Amer. Postal Workers Union, AFL-CIO - Local Union 1701 **[3076]**, Peru, IL
Amer. Postal Workers Union, AFL-CIO - Minneapolis Area Local Union 125 **[11513]**, Minneapolis, MN
Amer. Postal Workers Union, AFL-CIO - Quincy Area Local Union 77 **[3147]**, Quincy, IL
Amer. Postal Workers Union, AFL-CIO - Twin Cities Postal Data Center Local Union 7019 **[10864]**, Eagan, MN
Amer. Postal Workers Union, AFL-CIO - Youngstown Local Union 443 **[17391]**, Youngstown, OH
Amer. Public Works Assn., Chicago Metro Chap. **[140]**, Barrington, IL
Amer. Public Works Assn., Illinois Chap. **[1694]**, Fairview Heights, IL
Amer. Public Works Assn., Indiana Chap. **[5018]**, Indianapolis, IN
Amer. Public Works Assn., Michigan Chap. **[8830]**, Livonia, MI
Amer. Public Works Assn., Minnesota Chap. **[11059]**, Golden Valley, MN
Amer. Public Works Assn., Ohio Chap. **[14060]**, Cleveland, OH
Amer. Public Works Assn., Wisconsin Chap. **[18079]**, Green Bay, WI
Amer. Purchasing Soc. of Illinois **[109]**, Aurora, IL
Amer. Rabbit Breeders Assn. **[260]**, Bloomington, IL
Amer. Rabbit Breeders Assn., Badger Rabbit Breeders **[17946]**, Evansville, WI
Amer. Rabbit Breeders Assn., Californian Rabbit Specialty Club of Illinois **[1945]**, Hartsburg, IL
Amer. Rabbit Breeders Assn., Central States Flemish Giant Rabbit Breeders **[1555]**, Edwards, IL
Amer. Rabbit Breeders Assn., Central Wisconsin **[19458]**, Pittsville, WI
Amer. Rabbit Breeders Assn., District 5 **[3792]**, Tuscola, IL
Amer. Rabbit Breeders Assn., District 8 **[5746]**, Markle, IN
Amer. Rabbit Breeders Assn., Fox Valley Rabbit Club **[19545]**, Pulaski, WI
Amer. Rabbit Breeders Assn., Friendly Rabbit of Trempealeau **[18334]**, La Crosse, WI
Amer. Rabbit Breeders Assn., Illinois Checkered Giant Rabbit Club **[1978]**, Heyworth, IL
Amer. Rabbit Breeders Assn., Illinois Dutch Rabbit Club **[1276]**, Coal City, IL
Amer. Rabbit Breeders Assn., Illinois Florida White Specialty Club **[2557]**, Morrison, IL
Amer. Rabbit Breeders Assn., Illinois Mini Lop Club **[2844]**, Odell, IL
Amer. Rabbit Breeders Assn., Illinois Mini Rex Rabbit Club **[2680]**, New Berlin, IL
Amer. Rabbit Breeders Assn., Illinois Netherland Dwarf Specialty Club **[1946]**, Hartsburg, IL
Amer. Rabbit Breeders Assn., Illinois New Zealand Rabbit Breeders Specialty Club **[2075]**, Jacksonville, IL
Amer. Rabbit Breeders Assn., Illinois Standard Chinchilla RC **[1816]**, Glasford, IL
Amer. Rabbit Breeders Assn., Indiana **[5607]**, Lafayette, IN
Amer. Rabbit Breeders Assn., Indianhead **[17743]**, Chippewa Falls, WI
Amer. Rabbit Breeders Assn., Lakeland **[18396]**, Lake Geneva, WI
Amer. Rabbit Breeders Assn., Land of Lincoln Satin Rabbit Breeders Assn. **[1277]**, Coal City, IL
Amer. Rabbit Breeders Assn., Lumberjack Rabbit Club **[17703]**, Cable, WI
Amer. Rabbit Breeders Assn., Michigan **[8514]**, Lake Odessa, MI
Amer. Rabbit Breeders Assn., Midwest Champagn D'Argent Rabbit Club **[2984]**, Pekin, IL
Amer. Rabbit Breeders Assn., Midwest Holland Lop Club **[3223]**, Rochelle, IL
Amer. Rabbit Breeders Assn., Minnesota **[10461]**, Bloomington, MN
Amer. Rabbit Breeders Assn., Misty Hills Rabbit Club **[17554]**, Avoca, WI
Amer. Rabbit Breeders Assn., Northern Exposure Rabbit and Cavy **[19872]**, Superior, WI
Amer. Rabbit Breeders Assn., Red Cedar **[17744]**, Chippewa Falls, WI
Amer. Rabbit Breeders Assn., Southern Lakes Rabbit Club **[18016]**, Franksville, WI
Amer. Rabbit Breeders Assn., Southwest Wisconsin Rabbit Club **[20182]**, Wisconsin Rapids, WI
Amer. Rabbit Breeders Assn., Tri-County Rabbit Breeders **[17998]**, Fort Atkinson, WI
Amer. Rabbit Breeders Assn., Wisconsin **[20021]**, Waupaca, WI
American Red Cross **[17745]**, Chippewa Falls, WI
Amer. Red Cross, Allen County Chap. **[15647]**, Lima, OH
Amer. Red Cross Amateur Radio Club **[5019]**, Indianapolis, IN
Amer. Red Cross, Athens County Chap. **[13194]**, Athens, OH
Amer. Red Cross, Badger Chap. **[18468]**, Madison, WI

Amer. Red Cross Badger-Hawkeye Blood Sers. Region **[18469]**, Madison, WI
Amer. Red Cross, Barberton Chap. **[13254]**, Barberton, OH
Amer. Red Cross, Berrien County Chap. **[6918]**, Benton Harbor, MI
Amer. Red Cross Blood Sers. Indiana-Ohio Region **[4634]**, Fort Wayne, IN
Amer. Red Cross, Butler County Chap. **[16004]**, Middletown, OH
Amer. Red Cross, Calhoun County Chap. **[6847]**, Battle Creek, MI
Amer. Red Cross, Central Illinois Chap. **[3004]**, Peoria, IL
Amer. Red Cross, Central Michigan Chap. **[9099]**, Mount Pleasant, MI
Amer. Red Cross, Central Ohio Blood Services Region **[14306]**, Columbus, OH
Amer. Red Cross, Champaign County Chap. **[17038]**, Urbana, OH
Amer. Red Cross, Chippewa Valley Chap. **[17863]**, Eau Claire, WI
Amer. Red Cross, Cincinnati Area Chap. **[13732]**, Cincinnati, OH
Amer. Red Cross, Clark County Chap. **[16717]**, Springfield, OH
Amer. Red Cross, Coshocton County Chap. **[14794]**, Coshocton, OH
Amer. Red Cross, Crawford County Chap. **[13461]**, Bucyrus, OH
Amer. Red Cross, Dayton Area Chap. **[14850]**, Dayton, OH
Amer. Red Cross, Defiance County Chap. **[14983]**, Defiance, OH
Amer. Red Cross, DeKalb County Chap. **[1428]**, DeKalb, IL
Amer. Red Cross, Delaware County Chap. **[14998]**, Delaware, OH
Amer. Red Cross, East Central Wisconsin Chap. **[19389]**, Oshkosh, WI
Amer. Red Cross, East Shoreline Chap. **[6876]**, Bay City, MI
Amer. Red Cross, Firelands Chap. **[16602]**, Sandusky, OH
Amer. Red Cross, First Capital District Chap. **[13660]**, Chillicothe, OH
Amer. Red Cross, Fond du Lac County Chap. **[17969]**, Fond du Lac, WI
Amer. Red Cross, Fox River Chap. **[3379]**, St. Charles, IL
Amer. Red Cross, Fulton County Ohio **[17138]**, Wauseon, OH
Amer. Red Cross, Galion Area Chap. **[15279]**, Galion, OH
Amer. Red Cross - Genesee/Lapeer Chap. **[7714]**, Flint, MI
Amer. Red Cross, Goodhue County Chap. **[12077]**, Red Wing, MN
Amer. Red Cross of Greater Chicago **[719]**, Chicago, IL
Amer. Red Cross, Greater Cleveland Chap. **[14061]**, Cleveland, OH
Amer. Red Cross of Greater Columbus **[14307]**, Columbus, OH
Amer. Red Cross of Greater Indianapolis **[5020]**, Indianapolis, IN
Amer. Red Cross, Greater Kalamazoo Area Chap. **[8417]**, Kalamazoo, MI
Amer. Red Cross - Greater Milwaukee Chap. **[18956]**, Milwaukee, WI
Amer. Red Cross, Greater Toledo Area Chap. **[16894]**, Toledo, OH
Amer. Red Cross, Grundy County Chap. **[2552]**, Morris, IL
Amer. Red Cross, Hamilton County Ser. Center **[5969]**, Noblesville, IN
Amer. Red Cross, Hancock County **[4830]**, Greenfield, IN
Amer. Red Cross, Hancock County Chap. **[15193]**, Findlay, OH
Amer. Red Cross Hoosier Hills Chap. **[4165]**, Bedford, IN
Amer. Red Cross, Illini Prairie Chap. **[3804]**, Urbana, IL
Amer. Red Cross, Illinois Capital Area Chap. **[3528]**, Springfield, IL
Amer. Red Cross, Johnson County Off. **[6520]**, Whiteland, IN
Amer. Red Cross, Kankakee County Chap. **[2129]**, Kankakee, IL
Amer. Red Cross, Knox County Chap. **[16079]**, Mount Vernon, OH
Amer. Red Cross, Lake County Chap. **[16333]**, Painesville, OH
Amer. Red Cross, Lakeland Chap. **[18080]**, Green Bay, WI
Amer. Red Cross, Lawrence County Chap. **[★4165]**
Amer. Red Cross of Lawrence County, Hoosier Hills Chap. **[★4165]**
Amer. Red Cross of Lawrence and Orange Counties **[★4165]**
Amer. Red Cross, Lee County Chap. **[1475]**, Dixon, IL
Amer. Red Cross, Lenawee County Chap. **[6565]**, Adrian, MI
Amer. Red Cross, Licking County Chap. **[16168]**, Newark, OH
Amer. Red Cross of Livingston County **[8270]**, Howell, MI
Amer. Red Cross, Lorain County Chap. **[15106]**, Elyria, OH
Amer. Red Cross, Madison County Chap. **[4098]**, Anderson, IN
Amer. Red Cross, Mahoning Chap. **[13371]**, Boardman, OH
Amer. Red Cross, Manitowoc/Calumet Chap. **[18775]**, Manitowoc, WI
Amer. Red Cross, Marion County Chap. **[15836]**, Marion, OH
Amer. Red Cross, McHenry County Chap. **[★719]**
Amer. Red Cross, McLean County Chap., Bloomington **[261]**, Bloomington, IL
Amer. Red Cross, Medina County Chap. **[15939]**, Medina, OH
Amer. Red Cross, Menard County Chap. **[★3529]**
Amer. Red Cross, Mercer County Chap. **[13610]**, Celina, OH
Amer. Red Cross, Mid-Illinois Chap. **[1375]**, Decatur, IL
Amer. Red Cross - Mid-Michigan Chap. **[8545]**, Lansing, MI
Amer. Red Cross, Midland/Gladwin Chap. **[9022]**, Midland, MI
Amer. Red Cross - Minneapolis Area Chap. **[11514]**, Minneapolis, MN
Amer. Red Cross of Monroe County **[9061]**, Monroe, MI
Amer. Red Cross, Morrow County Chap. **[16068]**, Mount Gilead, OH
Amer. Red Cross, Mower County Chap. **[10352]**, Austin, MN
Amer. Red Cross, Muskegon - Oceana Chap. **[9139]**, Muskegon, MI
Amer. Red Cross, Muskingum Lakes Chap. **[16146]**, New Philadelphia, OH
Amer. Red Cross, Neenah-Menasha Chap. **[19266]**, Neenah, WI
Amer. Red Cross, Norfolk Chap. **[★4098]**
Amer. Red Cross North Central Blood Sers. Region **[12379]**, St. Paul, MN
Amer. Red Cross, Northern Lower Michigan Chap. **[9362]**, Petoskey, MI
Amer. Red Cross of the Northern Miami Valley **[16997]**, Troy, OH
Amer. Red Cross Northern Ohio Blood Sers. Region **[14062]**, Cleveland, OH
Amer. Red Cross, Northland Chap. **[10802]**, Duluth, MN
Amer. Red Cross, Northwest Illinois Chap. **[1745]**, Freeport, IL
Amer. Red Cross of Northwest Indiana **[5767]**, Merrillville, IN
Amer. Red Cross, Northwest Michigan Chap. **[9922]**, Traverse City, MI
Amer. Red Cross, Ohio River Valley Chap. **[16468]**, Portsmouth, OH
Amer. Red Cross of Ottawa County **[8192]**, Holland, MI
Amer. Red Cross, Pickaway County Chap. **[14031]**, Circleville, OH
Amer. Red Cross, Portage County Chap. **[19781]**, Stevens Point, WI
Amer. Red Cross, Porter County Chap. **[6378]**, Valparaiso, IN
Amer. Red Cross, Posey County Chap. **[5846]**, Mount Vernon, IN
Amer. Red Cross of the Quad Cities Area **[2516]**, Moline, IL
Amer. Red Cross, Rice-LeSueur Counties Chap. **[10983]**, Faribault, MN
Amer. Red Cross, Richland County Chap. **[15761]**, Mansfield, OH
Amer. Red Cross, Rock River Chap. **[3269]**, Rockford, IL
Amer. Red Cross, Saginaw County Chap. **[9602]**, Saginaw, MI
Amer. Red Cross, St. Clair County Chap. **[9429]**, Port Huron, MI
Amer. Red Cross, St. Croix Valley Chap. **[10392]**, Bayport, MN
Amer. Red Cross of the St. Paul Area **[12380]**, St. Paul, MN
Amer. Red Cross, Sandusky County Chap. **[15246]**, Fremont, OH
Amer. Red Cross, Sangamon County Chap. **[★3529]**
Amer. Red Cross, Sangamon Valley Chap. **[3529]**, Springfield, IL
Amer. Red Cross-Scenic Bluffs Chap. **[18335]**, La Crosse, WI
Amer. Red Cross, Sheboygan County Chap. **[19691]**, Sheboygan, WI
Amer. Red Cross, South Central Michigan Chap. **[8361]**, Jackson, MI
Amer. Red Cross, South Central Minnesota Chap. **[11374]**, Mankato, MN
Amer. Red Cross, South Central Wisconsin Chap. **[18243]**, Janesville, WI
Amer. Red Cross, Southeast Minnesota Chap. **[12126]**, Rochester, MN
Amer. Red Cross Southeast Wisconsin Tri-County Chap. **[19551]**, Racine, WI
Amer. Red Cross Southeastern Michigan Blood Region **[7318]**, Detroit, MI
Amer. Red Cross, Southeastern Michigan Chap. **[7319]**, Detroit, MI
Amer. Red Cross, Southwestern Illinois Chap. **[41]**, Alton, IL
Amer. Red Cross, Steele County Chap. **[11957]**, Owatonna, MN
Amer. Red Cross, Streator Chap. **[3725]**, Streator, IL
Amer. Red Cross, Summit County Chap. **[13037]**, Akron, OH
Amer. Red Cross, Washington County Chap. **[15814]**, Marietta, OH
Amer. Red Cross, Washtenaw County Chap. **[6663]**, Ann Arbor, MI
Amer. Red Cross, Wayne County Chap. **[17311]**, Wooster, OH
Amer. Red Cross of West Central Michigan **[7900]**, Grand Rapids, MI
Amer. Red Cross, Western Stark County Chap. **[15881]**, Massillon, OH
Amer. Red Cross, Winona County Chap. **[12945]**, Winona, MN
American Revolution
Daughters of the Amer. Revolution, Sarah Winston Henry Chap. **[5934]**, New Castle, IN
Indiana Soc., Sons of the Amer. Revolution, Continental Chap. **[5881]**, Muncie, IN
Indiana Soc., Sons of the Amer. Revolution, Gen. Thomas Posey Chap. **[5851]**, Mount Vernon, IN
Indiana Soc., Sons of the Amer. Revolution, George Rogers Clark Chap. **[6410]**, Vincennes, IN
Indiana Soc., Sons of the Amer. Revolution, John Martin Chap. **[6329]**, Terre Haute, IN
Indiana Soc., Sons of the Amer. Revolution, Simon Kenton Chap. **[6079]**, Rensselaer, IN
Indiana Soc., Sons of the Amer. Revolution, William Knight Chap. **[4820]**, Greencastle, IN
Indiana Soc., Sons of the Amer. Revolution, William Van Gordon Chap. **[4915]**, Highland, IN
Ohio Soc., Sons of the Amer. Revolution, Samuel Huntington Chap. **[16341]**, Painesville, OH
Sons of the Amer. Revolution, Illinois Soc. **[3322]**, Rockford, IL
Sons of the Amer. Revolution - Ohio Soc. **[16345]**, Painesville, OH
Amer. Revolution, Sarah Winston Henry Chap; Daughters of the **[5934]**, New Castle, IN
Amer. Rose Soc., Buckeye District **[13462]**, Bucyrus, OH
Amer. Rose Soc., Great Lakes District **[6961]**, Birmingham, MI

Amer. Rose Soc., North Central District **[10315]**, Apple Valley, MN
Amer. Rottweiler Club **[3109]**, Plano, IL
Amer. Saddlebred Assn. of Wisconsin **[19982]**, Waukesha, WI
Amer. Saddlebred Horse Assn. of Michigan **[7763]**, Flushing, MI
Amer. Saddlebred Horse Assn. of Ohio **[15464]**, Homerville, OH
Amer. School Food Ser. Assn. - Mideast Regional Chap. **[★9040]**
Amer. Schools Assn. **[720]**, Chicago, IL
Amer. Sewing Guild, Chicago Chap. **[1914]**, Gurnee, IL
Amer. Sewing Guild, Cincinnati Chap. **[15353]**, Greenhills, OH
Amer. Sewing Guild, Detroit Chap. **[9970]**, Troy, MI
Amer. Sewing Guild, Evansville Chap. **[4524]**, Evansville, IN
Amer. Sewing Guild, Grand Rapids Chap. **[9016]**, Middleville, MI
Amer. Sewing Guild, Indianapolis Chap. **[5604]**, Ladoga, IN
Amer. Sewing Guild, Lansing Chap. **[9262]**, Okemos, MI
Amer. Sewing Guild, Milwaukee Chap. **[20114]**, West Bend, WI
Amer. Sewing Guild, Minneapolis/St. Paul Chap. **[11515]**, Minneapolis, MN
Amer. Sewing Guild, North Olmsted Chap. **[13344]**, Berea, OH
Amer. Shetland Sheepdog Assn. Sheltie Rescue Network **[2688]**, New Lenox, IL
Amer. Soc. of Addiction Medicine, Michigan **[7505]**, East Lansing, MI
Amer. Soc. of Agricultural and Biological Engineers, District 3 - Central Illinois **[3805]**, Urbana, IL
Amer. Soc. of Agricultural and Biological Engineers, District 3 - Chicago **[4048]**, Woodridge, IL
Amer. Soc. of Agricultural and Biological Engineers, District 3 - Wisconsin **[18214]**, Horicon, WI
Amer. Soc. of Appraisers, Akron - Cleveland Chap. **[16234]**, North Olmsted, OH
Amer. Soc. of Appraisers, Chicago Chap. **[2959]**, Park Ridge, IL
Amer. Soc. of Appraisers, Columbus Chap. **[17204]**, Westerville, OH
Amer. Soc. of Appraisers, Dayton - Cincinnati Chap. **[15619]**, Lebanon, OH
Amer. Soc. of Appraisers, Detroit Chap. **[9971]**, Troy, MI
Amer. Soc. of Appraisers, Greater Michigan Chap. **[7901]**, Grand Rapids, MI
Amer. Soc. of Appraisers, Indiana Chap. **[6473]**, West Lafayette, IN
Amer. Soc. of Appraisers, Toledo Chap. **[16895]**, Toledo, OH
Amer. Soc. of Appraisers, Twin Cities Chap. **[11449]**, Medina, MN
Amer. Soc. of Appraisers, Wisconsin Chap. **[17666]**, Brookfield, WI
Amer. Soc. of Bus. Press Editors, Cleveland Chap. **[★14063]**
Amer. Soc. of Bus. Publication Editors - Chicago Chap. **[721]**, Chicago, IL
Amer. Soc. of Bus. Publication Editors, Cleveland Chap. **[14063]**, Cleveland, OH
Amer. Soc. of Bus. Publication Editors - Michigan Chap. **[6664]**, Ann Arbor, MI
Amer. Soc. of Bus. Publication Editors - Twin Cities Chap. **[11516]**, Minneapolis, MN
Amer. Soc. of Civil Engineers - Illinois Sect. **[722]**, Chicago, IL
Amer. Soc. of Directors of Volunteer Ser. **[723]**, Chicago, IL
Amer. Soc. of Dowsers, Central Illiana Dowsers **[2674]**, Neoga, IL
Amer. Soc. of Dowsers, Great Serpent Mound Chap. **[17196]**, West Union, OH
Amer. Soc. of Dowsers, Northern Illinois Chap. **[3482]**, Skokie, IL
Amer. Soc. of Dowsers, Southwestern Ohio Dowsers **[16718]**, Springfield, OH
American Society of Dowsers, The Heart of Wisconsin Dowsers Chapter **[19496]**, Port Edwards, WI
Amer. Soc. of Employers **[9781]**, Southfield, MI
Amer. Soc. for Enology and Viticulture - Eastern Sect. **[6474]**, West Lafayette, IN
Amer. Soc. of Farm Managers and Rural Appraisers Illinois Chap. **[★18874]**
Amer. Soc. of Farm Managers and Rural Appraisers Indiana Chap. **[★6424]**
Amer. Soc. of Farm Managers and Rural Appraisers Michigan Chap. **[8480]**, Kawkawlin, MI
Amer. Soc. of Farm Managers and Rural Appraisers Minnesota Chap. **[11432]**, Marshall, MN
Amer. Soc. of Farm Managers and Rural Appraisers Ohio Chap. **[16270]**, Oak Harbor, OH
Amer. Soc. of Farm Managers and Rural Appraisers Wisconsin Chap. **[18470]**, Madison, WI
Amer. Soc. of Golf Course Architects **[17667]**, Brookfield, WI
Amer. Soc. for Healthcare Food Ser. Administrators, Central Minnesota Chap. **[11517]**, Minneapolis, MN
Amer. Soc. for Healthcare Food Ser. Administrators, Chicago Midwest Chap. **[2905]**, Palatine, IL
Amer. Soc. for Healthcare Food Ser. Administrators, Hoosier Chap. **[5751]**, Martinsville, IN
Amer. Soc. for Hea.care Food Ser. Administrators, Wisconsin Chap. **[18471]**, Madison, WI
Amer. Soc. of Heating, Refrigerating and Air-Conditioning Engineers Central Indiana Chap. **[5021]**, Indianapolis, IN
Amer. Soc. of Heating, Refrigerating and Air-Conditioning Engineers - Dayton **[14851]**, Dayton, OH
Amer. Soc. of Heating, Refrigerating and Air-Conditioning Engineers Detroit **[7320]**, Detroit, MI
Amer. Soc. of Heating, Refrigerating and Air-Conditioning Engineers Eastern Michigan **[7001]**, Bridgeport, MI
Amer. Soc. of Heating, Refrigerating and Air-Conditioning Engineers Evansville **[4525]**, Evansville, IN
Amer. Soc. of Heating, Refrigerating and Air-Conditioning Engineers - Illinois Chap. **[1679]**, Evergreen Park, IL
Amer. Soc. of Heating, Refrigerating and Air-Conditioning Engineers La Crosse Area Chap. **[18336]**, La Crosse, WI
Amer. Soc. of Heating, Refrigerating and Air-Conditioning Engineers Madison Chap. **[18472]**, Madison, WI
Amer. Soc. of Heating, Refrigerating and Air-Conditioning Engineers - Minnesota Chap. **[11866]**, New Hope, MN
Amer. Soc. of Heating, Refrigerating and Air-Conditioning Engineers Northern Indiana Chap. **[6216]**, South Bend, IN
Amer. Soc. of Heating, Refrigerating and Air-Conditioning Engineers Region 5 **[4316]**, Carmel, IN
Amer. Soc. of Heating, Refrigerating and Air-Conditioning Engineers - West Michigan Chap. **[7902]**, Grand Rapids, MI
Amer. Soc. of Heating, Refrigerating and Air-Conditioning Engineers - Wisconsin Chap. **[18957]**, Milwaukee, WI
Amer. Soc. of Interior Designers - Illinois Chap. **[724]**, Chicago, IL
Amer. Soc. of Interior Designers, Indiana **[5022]**, Indianapolis, IN
Amer. Soc. of Interior Designers - Michigan Chap. **[9972]**, Troy, MI
Amer. Soc. of Interior Designers, Minnesota **[★11518]**
Amer. Soc. of Interior Designers, Minnesota Chap. **[11518]**, Minneapolis, MN
Amer. Soc. of Interior Designers, Ohio North Chap. **[9263]**, Okemos, MI
Amer. Soc. of Interior Designers, Ohio South/ Kentucky **[13733]**, Cincinnati, OH
Amer. Soc. of Interior Designers, Wisconsin **[18958]**, Milwaukee, WI
Amer. Soc. of Mech. Engineers, Akron Sect. **[13038]**, Akron, OH
Amer. Soc. of Mech. Engineers, Chicago Sect. **[64]**, Arlington Heights, IL
Amer. Soc. of Mech. Engineers, Cleveland Sect. **[14064]**, Cleveland, OH
Amer. Soc. of Mech. Engineers, Metro Detroit Sect. **[7652]**, Farmington Hills, MI
Amer. Soc. of Mech. Engineers, Milwaukee Sect. **[18959]**, Milwaukee, WI
Amer. Soc. of Mech. Engineers, Minnesota Sect. **[12876]**, West St. Paul, MN
Amer. Soc. of Mech. Engineers, Northwest Ohio Sect. **[16896]**, Toledo, OH
Amer. Soc. of Media Photographers, Chicago/ Midwest **[725]**, Chicago, IL
Amer. Soc. of Media Photographers, Michigan **[9769]**, South Lyon, MI
Amer. Soc. of Media Photographers, Minneapolis/St. Paul **[12331]**, St. Louis Park, MN
Amer. Soc. of Media Photographers, Ohio/North Coast Chap. **[16096]**, N Canton, OH
Amer. Soc. of Media Photographers, Ohio Valley Chap. **[15620]**, Lebanon, OH
Amer. Soc. for Microbiology - Illinois Br. **[2788]**, Oak Forest, IL
Amer. Soc. for Microbiology - Indiana Br. **[5565]**, Kokomo, IN
Amer. Soc. for Microbiology - Michigan Br. **[7321]**, Detroit, MI
Amer. Soc. for Microbiology - Ohio Br. **[14999]**, Delaware, OH
Amer. Soc. of Professional Estimators, Chicago Chap. **[3863]**, Villa Park, IL
Amer. Soc. of Professional Estimators, Cleveland/ North Ohio Chap. **[14065]**, Cleveland, OH
Amer. Soc. for Public Admin., Central Illinois Chap. **[3530]**, Springfield, IL
Amer. Soc. for Quality, Akron-Canton Sect. 0810 **[16841]**, Tallmadge, OH
Amer. Soc. for Quality, Battle Creek-Kalamazoo Sect. 1003 **[8418]**, Kalamazoo, MI
Amer. Soc. for Quality, Chicago Sect. 1201 **[2750]**, Northbrook, IL
Amer. Soc. for Quality, Cincinnati Sect. 0900 **[13734]**, Cincinnati, OH
Amer. Soc. for Quality, Columbus Sect. 0801 **[14308]**, Columbus, OH
Amer. Soc. for Quality, East Central Indiana Sect. 0904 **[5866]**, Muncie, IN
Amer. Soc. for Quality, Evansville-Owensboro Sect. 0915 **[4526]**, Evansville, IN
Amer. Soc. for Quality, Fox Valley Sect. 1208 **[173]**, Batavia, IL
Amer. Soc. for Quality, Grand Rapids Sect. 1001 **[8862]**, Lowell, MI
Amer. Soc. for Quality, Greater Detroit Sect. 1000 **[8786]**, Lathrup Village, MI
Amer. Soc. for Quality, Illiana Sect. 1213 **[3502]**, South Holland, IL
Amer. Soc. for Quality, Indianapolis Sect. 0903 **[5023]**, Indianapolis, IN
Amer. Soc. for Quality, Lafayette Sect. 0917 **[5608]**, Lafayette, IN
Amer. Soc. for Quality, Lansing-Jackson Sect. 1008 **[7118]**, Charlotte, MI
Amer. Soc. for Quality, Louisville Sect. 0912 **[5539]**, Jeffersonville, IN
Amer. Soc. for Quality, Mansfield Sect. 0811 **[15762]**, Mansfield, OH
Amer. Soc. for Quality, Milwaukee Sect. 1202 **[18960]**, Milwaukee, WI
Amer. Soc. for Quality, Minnesota Sect. 1203 **[12381]**, St. Paul, MN
Amer. Soc. for Quality, Northeastern Illinois Sect. 1212 **[2257]**, Libertyville, IL
Amer. Soc. for Quality, Northeastern Indiana Sect. 0905 **[4635]**, Fort Wayne, IN
Amer. Soc. for Quality, Northwest Indiana Sect. 1011 **[5901]**, Munster, IN
Amer. Soc. for Quality, Racine-Kenosha-Walworth Sect. 1204 **[18295]**, Kenosha, WI
Amer. Soc. for Quality, Saginaw Valley Sect. 1004 **[9603]**, Saginaw, MI
Amer. Soc. for Quality, St. Joseph-Benton Harbor Sect. 1007 **[9680]**, St. Joseph, MI
Amer. Soc. for Quality, Scioto Valley Sect. 0815 **[13661]**, Chillicothe, OH
Amer. Soc. for Quality, South Central Indiana Sect. 0920 **[4389]**, Columbus, IN
Amer. Soc. for Quality, Toledo Sect. 1006 **[16897]**, Toledo, OH
Amer. Soc. for Quality, Wabash Valley Sect. 0919 **[6508]**, West Terre Haute, IN
Amer. Soc. for Quality, Winnebago Sect. 1206 **[18328]**, Kohler, WI
Amer. Soc. of Safety Engineers, Central Ohio Chap. **[14309]**, Columbus, OH

Amer. Soc. of Safety Engineers, Greater Detroit Chap. **[9782]**, Southfield, MI
Amer. Soc. of Safety Engineers, Kitty Hawk Chap. **[15237]**, Franklin, OH
Amer. Soc. of Safety Engineers, Nicolet Chap. **[18081]**, Green Bay, WI
Amer. Soc. of Safety Engineers, Northeastern Illinois Chap. **[3353]**, Roselle, IL
Amer. Soc. of Safety Engineers, Northern Ohio **[14066]**, Cleveland, OH
Amer. Soc. of Sanitary Engg., Central Ohio Chap. **[14310]**, Columbus, OH
Amer. Soc. of Sanitary Engg., Illinois Chap. **[2194]**, Lake Forest, IL
Amer. Soc. of Sanitary Engg., Michigan Chap. **[7322]**, Detroit, MI
Amer. Soc. of Sanitary Engg., Minnesota Chap. **[11519]**, Minneapolis, MN
Amer. Soc. of Sanitary Engg., Northern Ohio Chap. **[13649]**, Chesterland, OH
Amer. Soc. of Sanitary Engg., Region No. 2 - North Central **[10462]**, Bloomington, MN
Amer. Soc. of Sanitary Engg., Region No. 6 - East **[15494]**, Independence, OH
Amer. Soc. for Technion-Israel Inst. of Tech., West Central Region **[726]**, Chicago, IL
Amer. Soc. for Training and Development - Ann Arbor, Michigan Chap. **[6665]**, Ann Arbor, MI
Amer. Soc. for Training and Development, Central Indiana Chap. **[5024]**, Indianapolis, IN
Amer. Soc. for Training and Development - Central Ohio Chap. **[14311]**, Columbus, OH
Amer. Soc. for Training and Development, Chicagoland Chap. **[727]**, Chicago, IL
Amer. Soc. for Training and Development, Greater Cincinnati Chap. **[13735]**, Cincinnati, OH
Amer. Soc. for Training and Development - Greater Cleveland Chap. **[14067]**, Cleveland, OH
Amer. Soc. for Training and Development - Greater Detroit Chap. **[7637]**, Farmington, MI
Amer. Soc. for Training and Development - Lake Superior Chap. **[10803]**, Duluth, MN
Amer. Soc. for Training and Development - Michiana Chap. **[6217]**, South Bend, IN
Amer. Soc. for Training and Development, River Cities Chap. **[4527]**, Evansville, IN
Amer. Soc. for Training and Development, Rock Valley Chap. **[1476]**, Dixon, IL
Amer. Soc. for Training and Development - South Central Michigan **[8546]**, Lansing, MI
Amer. Soc. for Training and Development - South Central Wisconsin **[18473]**, Madison, WI
Amer. Soc. for Training and Development, Southeast Wisconsin Chap. **[18961]**, Milwaukee, WI
Amer. Soc. for Training and Development, Southern Minnesota Chap. **[★12382]**
Amer. Soc. for Training and Development, Twin Cities Chap. **[12382]**, St. Paul, MN
Amer. Soc. for Training and Development - Western Ohio Chap. **[14852]**, Dayton, OH
Amer. Soc. of Women Accountants, Anderson/Muncie Chap. No. 077 **[5933]**, New Castle, IN
Amer. Soc. of Women Accountants, Chicago Chap. No. 002 **[2960]**, Park Ridge, IL
Amer. Soc. of Women Accountants, Cleveland Chap. No. 013 **[16356]**, Parma, OH
Amer. Soc. of Women Accountants, Columbus Chap. No. 016 **[15258]**, Gahanna, OH
Amer. Soc. of Women Accountants, Flint Chap. No. 054 **[7715]**, Flint, MI
Amer. Soc. of Women Accountants, Fort Wayne Chap. No. 046 **[4636]**, Fort Wayne, IN
Amer. Soc. of Women Accountants, Grand Rapids Chap. No. 010 **[7903]**, Grand Rapids, MI
Amer. Soc. of Women Accountants, Indianapolis Chap. No. 001 **[5025]**, Indianapolis, IN
Amer. Soc. of Women Accountants, Louisville Chap. No. 018 **[5916]**, New Albany, IN
Amer. Soc. of Women Accountants, Marion Chap. No. 108 **[5726]**, Marion, IN
Amer. Soc. of Women Accountants, Milwaukee No. 041 **[20115]**, West Bend, WI
Amer. Soc. of Women Accountants, Minnesota/St. Paul Chap. No. 068 **[12975]**, Woodbury, MN
Amer. Soc. of Women Accountants, Saginaw/Midland/Bay Chap. No. 034 **[6877]**, Bay City, MI
Amer. Soc. of Women Accountants, Terre Haute Chap. No. 008 **[6313]**, Terre Haute, IN
Amer. Soc. of Women Accountants, Youngstown Chap. No. 072 **[13528]**, Canfield, OH
Amer. Statistical Assn., Ann Arbor Chap. **[6666]**, Ann Arbor, MI
Amer. Statistical Assn., Central Indiana Chap. **[5026]**, Indianapolis, IN
Amer. Statistical Assn., Chicago Chap. **[2906]**, Palatine, IL
Amer. Statistical Assn., Cincinnati Chap. **[13736]**, Cincinnati, OH
Amer. Statistical Assn., Cleveland Chap. **[14068]**, Cleveland, OH
Amer. Statistical Assn., Columbus Chap. **[14312]**, Columbus, OH
Amer. Statistical Assn., Dayton Chap. **[16719]**, Springfield, OH
Amer. Statistical Assn., Detroit Chap. **[9500]**, Rochester, MI
Amer. Statistical Assn., Milwaukee Chap. **[19267]**, Neenah, WI
Amer. Statistical Assn., Northeastern Illinois Chap. **[2283]**, Lincolnshire, IL
Amer. Statistical Assn., Northwest Ohio Chap. **[13382]**, Bowling Green, OH
Amer. Statistical Assn., Southwest Michigan Chap. **[8419]**, Kalamazoo, MI
Amer. Statistical Assn., Twin Cities Minnesota Chap. **[11015]**, Forest Lake, MN
Amer. String Teachers Assn., Michigan Chap. **[10111]**, West Bloomfield, MI
Amer. Subcontractors Assn.-Central Ohio Chap. **[16383]**, Pataskala, OH
Amer. Subcontractors Assn. of Cincinnati **[13737]**, Cincinnati, OH
Amer. Subcontractors Assn. of Greater Milwaukee **[18962]**, Milwaukee, WI
Amer. Subcontractors Assn. of Minnesota **[10302]**, Anoka, MN
Amer. Subcontractors Assn. of SE Michigan **[7693]**, Ferndale, MI
Amer. Theater Organ Soc., Joliet **[3954]**, Westchester, IL
Amer. Theater Organ Soc., Red River **[11056]**, Glyndon, MN
Amer. Theatre Organ Soc., Central Indiana Chap. **[5027]**, Indianapolis, IN
Amer. Theatre Organ Soc., Central Minnesota Chap. **[10995]**, Fergus Falls, MN
Amer. Theatre Organ Soc., Chicagoland Chap. **[728]**, Chicago, IL
Amer. Theatre Organ Soc., Heart Of Ohio Chap. **[16485]**, Prospect, OH
Amer. Theatre Organ Soc., Land O' Lakes **[12221]**, Roseville, MN
Amer. Theatre Organ Soc., Motor City Chap. **[7323]**, Detroit, MI
Amer. Theatre Organ Soc., Northern Michigan Chap. **[10168]**, Williamsburg, MI
Amer. Theatre Organ Soc., Ohio Valley Chap. **[13738]**, Cincinnati, OH
Amer. Theatre Organ Soc., Quad Cities Chap. **[2517]**, Moline, IL
Amer. Theatre Organ Soc., Southwest Michigan Chap. **[8420]**, Kalamazoo, MI
Amer. Theatre Organ Soc., Western Reserve Chap. **[13283]**, Beachwood, OH
Amer. Trail Horse Assn. **[1302]**, Cortland, IL
Amer. Trauma Soc., Wisconsin **[18474]**, Madison, WI
Amer. Truck Historical Soc., Auburn Heritage Truck Chap. **[4137]**, Auburn, IN
Amer. Truck Historical Soc., Beer City Chap. **[19330]**, Oak Creek, WI
Amer. Truck Historical Soc., Black Swamp Chap. **[16510]**, Republic, OH
Amer. Truck Historical Soc., Buckeye Vintage Haulers **[16384]**, Pataskala, OH
Amer. Truck Historical Soc., Central Illinois Chap. **[1817]**, Glasford, IL
Amer. Truck Historical Soc., Greater Cincinnati Chap. **[13739]**, Cincinnati, OH
Amer. Truck Historical Soc., Hiawathaland Chap. **[10256]**, Albert Lea, MN
Amer. Truck Historical Soc., Lincoln Trail Chap. **[1368]**, Dawson, IL
Amer. Truck Historical Soc., Mark Twain Chap. **[156]**, Barry, IL
Amer. Truck Historical Soc., Minnesota Metro Chap. **[12891]**, White Bear Lake, MN
Amer. Truck Historical Soc., Motor City Chap. **[9261]**, Oakland, MI
Amer. Truck Historical Soc., Northeast Ohio Chap. **[13240]**, Avon, OH
Amer. Truck Historical Soc., Northwest Illinois Chap. **[93]**, Ashton, IL
Amer. Truck Historical Soc., Northwest Indiana Chap. **[6218]**, South Bend, IN
Amer. Truck Historical Soc., Southeast Michigan Chap. **[6667]**, Ann Arbor, MI
Amer. Truck Historical Soc., Wabash Valley Chap. **[5944]**, New Harmony, IN
Amer. Truck Historical Soc., West Michigan Chap. **[7853]**, Grand Haven, MI
Amer. Truck Historical Soc., Windy City Chap. **[3959]**, Western Springs, IL
Amer. Vacuum Soc., Prairie Chap. **[2237]**, Lemont, IL
Amer. Vaulting Assn. - Agape Vaulters **[7586]**, Eau Claire, MI
Amer. Vaulting Assn. - Blue Moon Vaulters **[7160]**, Clarkston, MI
Amer. Vaulting Assn. - Diamond E Vaulters **[9914]**, Three Rivers, MI
Amer. Vaulting Assn. - MSU Vaulters **[7161]**, Clarkston, MI
Amer. Vaulting Assn. - Sunshine Vaulters **[9222]**, Northville, MI
Amer. Vaulting Assn. - Univ. of Findlay Vaulters **[15194]**, Findlay, OH
Amer. Vaulting Assn. - Victory Vaulters **[9776]**, South Rockwood, MI
Amer. Volkssport Assn., Mid-Am. Region **[13740]**, Cincinnati, OH
Amer. Volkssport Assn., North Central Region **[18903]**, Middleton, WI
Amer. Water Resources Assn., Michigan State Sect. **[8547]**, Lansing, MI
Amer. Water Rsrcs. Assn. - UWSP Student Chap. **[19782]**, Stevens Point, WI
Amer. Water Rsrcs. Assn., Wisconsin Sect. **[18904]**, Middleton, WI
Amer. Water Resources Assn. Wisconsin State Sect. **[19783]**, Stevens Point, WI
Amer. Welding Soc., Arrowhead **[12792]**, Virginia, MN
Amer. Welding Soc., Blackhawk Sect. 113 **[3270]**, Rockford, IL
Amer. Welding Soc., Central Michigan **[7506]**, East Lansing, MI
Amer. Welding Soc., Chicago Sect. **[4188]**, Beverly Shores, IN
Amer. Welding Soc., Chicago Sect. 002 **[2311]**, Lockport, IL
Amer. Welding Soc., Cleveland Sect. 006 **[14069]**, Cleveland, OH
Amer. Welding Soc., Columbus Sect. 036 **[14313]**, Columbus, OH
Amer. Welding Soc., Dayton **[17166]**, West Carrollton, OH
Amer. Welding Soc., Detroit Sect. 011 **[9863]**, Sterling Heights, MI
Amer. Welding Soc., Fox Valley Sect. **[17485]**, Appleton, WI
Amer. Welding Soc., J.A.K. Sect. **[2130]**, Kankakee, IL
Amer. Welding Soc., Johnny Appleseed Sect. 191 **[17048]**, Van Wert, OH
Amer. Welding Soc., Milwaukee Sect. **[18009]**, Franklin, WI
Amer. Welding Soc., Mississippi Valley Sect. 194 **[3148]**, Quincy, IL
Amer. Welding Soc., Northern Michigan Sect. 158 **[7700]**, Fife Lake, MI
Amer. Welding Soc., Northwest Ohio Sect. 046 **[15349]**, Graytown, OH
Amer. Welding Soc., Racine Kenosha Sect. 132 **[18296]**, Kenosha, WI
Amer. Welding Soc., Sangamon Valley Sect. 070 **[2273]**, Lincoln, IL
Amer. Welding Soc., Stark Central Sect. 085 **[15409]**, Hartville, OH
Amer. Welding Soc., Tri-River Sect. 107 **[4528]**, Evansville, IN
Amer. Welding Soc., Western Michigan **[7854]**, Grand Haven, MI

Amer. Welding Soc., Whitmer Career and Tech. Center **[16898]**, Toledo, OH
Amer. Wine Soc. - Bloomington-Normal **[262]**, Bloomington, IL
Amer. Wine Soc. - Cincinnati **[13741]**, Cincinnati, OH
Amer. Wine Soc. - Cleveland **[14779]**, Concord Twp, OH
Amer. Wine Soc. - Columbus **[15042]**, Dublin, OH
Amer. Wine Soc. - Cork Club Chicago **[2207]**, Lake in the Hills, IL
Amer. Wine Soc. - Covered Bridge **[15747]**, Madison, OH
Amer. Wine Soc. - Dayton **[13295]**, Beavercreek, OH
Amer. Wine Soc. - Metropolitan Detroit **[9548]**, Romulus, MI
Amer. Wine Soc. - Springfield **[16720]**, Springfield, OH
Amer. Wine Soc. - Suburban Cook County **[2013]**, Hinsdale, IL
Amer. Wine Soc. - Tippie Tasters **[6475]**, West Lafayette, IN
American Wine Society - Wabash Valley Chapter **[6131]**, Rockville, IN
Amer. Woman's Soc. of Certified Public Accountants, Madison **[18475]**, Madison, WI
Amer. Women in Radio and TV, Buckeye of Central Ohio **[14314]**, Columbus, OH
Amer. Women in Radio and TV, Chicago **[729]**, Chicago, IL
Amer. Women in Radio and TV, Indiana **[5028]**, Indianapolis, IN
Amer. Women in Radio and TV, Twin Cities Media Network **[12020]**, Plymouth, MN
Amer. Women in Radio and TV Western Michigan **[7904]**, Grand Rapids, MI
Amer. Youth Hostels-Northeast Ohio Coun. **[★16394]**
Amer. Youth Soccer Org., Region 115 **[586]**, Cherry Valley, IL
Amer. Youth Soccer Org., Region 163 **[2195]**, Lake Forest, IL
Amer. Youth Soccer Org., Region 190 **[9864]**, Sterling Heights, MI
Amer. Youth Soccer Org., Region 300 **[3960]**, Western Springs, IL
Amer. Youth Soccer Org., Region 362 **[1858]**, Glenview, IL
Amer. Youth Soccer Org., Region 372 **[2611]**, Mundelein, IL
Amer. Youth Soccer Org., Region 418 **[730]**, Chicago, IL
Amer. Youth Soccer Org., Region 425 **[4033]**, Winnetka, IL
Amer. Youth Soccer Org., Region 458 **[2238]**, Lemont, IL
Amer. Youth Soccer Org., Region 726 **[4054]**, Woodstock, IL
Amer. Youth Soccer Org., Region 1007 **[1416]**, Deerfield, IL
Amer. Youth Soccer Org., Region 1196 **[8154]**, Hastings, MI
Americans United for Separation of Church and State, Central Ohio **[14315]**, Columbus, OH
Americans United for Separation of Church and State, Greater Indianapolis Chap. **[5029]**, Indianapolis, IN
Amherst Historical Soc. **[13131]**, Amherst, OH
Amherst Lions Club - Ohio **[13132]**, Amherst, OH
Amnesty Intl. of the U.S.A., Midwest Regional Off. **[731]**, Chicago, IL
Amos W. Butler Audubon Soc. **[5030]**, Indianapolis, IN
AMVETS, Big Rapids **[6940]**, Big Rapids, MI
AMVETS, Bloomington Post 2000 **[4199]**, Bloomington, IN
AMVETS, Cadillac Post 110 **[7043]**, Cadillac, MI
AMVETS, Celina Post 91 **[13611]**, Celina, OH
AMVETS, Elyria Post 32 **[15107]**, Elyria, OH
AMVETS, Fisher Post 52 **[1702]**, Fisher, IL
AMVETS, Knoxville Post 8 **[2166]**, Knoxville, IL
AMVETS, Manitowoc Post 99 **[18776]**, Manitowoc, WI
AMVETS, Marion Post 5 **[5727]**, Marion, IN
AMVETS, Mount Vernon Post 4 **[2594]**, Mount Vernon, IL
AMVETS, Muncie Post 12 **[5867]**, Muncie, IN
AMVETS, Oak Creek Post 60 **[19331]**, Oak Creek, WI
AMVETS, Ottawa Post 30 **[2896]**, Ottawa, IL
AMVETS, Richfield Post 176 **[16521]**, Richfield, OH
AMVETS, Rockville Post 61 **[6132]**, Rockville, IN
AMVETS, Toledo Post 222 **[16899]**, Toledo, OH
AMVETS, Waverly Post 58 **[17145]**, Waverly, OH
AMVETS, West Harrison Post 13 **[6466]**, West Harrison, IN

Amyotrophic Lateral Sclerosis
ALS Assn., Minnesota Chap. **[11480]**, Minneapolis, MN
Amyotrophic Lateral Sclerosis Assn., Northeast Ohio Chap. **[14070]**, Cleveland, OH
Amyotrophic Lateral Sclerosis Assn., Northeast Ohio Chap. **[14070]**, Cleveland, OH
Amyotrophic Lateral Sclerosis Assn., West Michigan Chap. **[★7883]**
Amyotrophic Lateral Sclerosis of Michigan **[9783]**, Southfield, MI
Amyotrophic Lateral Sclerosis of Michigan, Inc. **[★9783]**
Anaconda Cricket Club **[10535]**, Brooklyn Center, MN
Anchor Bay Chamber of Commerce **[9180]**, New Baltimore, MI
Ancient Coin Club of Chicago **[732]**, Chicago, IL
Ancient Order of Hibernians of Bay County - Robert Shea Div. **[6878]**, Bay City, MI
Ancient Order of Hibernians of Genesee County - Sullivan and O'Sullivan Div. **[9093]**, Mount Morris, MI
Ancient Order of Hibernians of Grand Traverse County - Bun Brady Div. **[9923]**, Traverse City, MI
Ancient Order of Hibernians - John P. Kelly, Div. 1, Toledo, OH **[16900]**, Toledo, OH
Ancient Order of Hibernians of Kent County - Fr. John Whalen McGee Div. **[7905]**, Grand Rapids, MI
Ancient Order of Hibernians - Kevin Barry, Div. No. 3 **[5031]**, Indianapolis, IN
Ancient Order of Hibernians of Lenawee County - St. Patrick, Div. No. 1 **[6566]**, Adrian, MI
Ancient Order of Hibernians of Macomb County - Fr. Solanus Casey Div. **[9654]**, St. Clair Shores, MI
Ancient Order of Hibernians - Michigan State Bd. **[6567]**, Adrian, MI
Ancient Order of Hibernians - Milwaukee Div. **[18963]**, Milwaukee, WI
Ancient Order of Hibernians of Oakland County - James O. Flynn Div. **[6976]**, Bloomfield, MI
Ancient Order of Hibernians of Oakland County - Norman O'Brien, Div. 1 **[9574]**, Royal Oak, MI
Ancient Order of Hibernians of Otsego County - Hogan Div. **[7816]**, Gaylord, MI
Ancient Order of Hibernians of Wayne County - O' Brian Div. **[9575]**, Royal Oak, MI
Ancient Order of Hibernians of Wayne County - Patrick Ryan Div. **[9223]**, Northville, MI
Ancient Order of Hibernians of Wayne County - Stephen Walsh Div. **[10182]**, Wolverine Lake, MI
Ancient Order of Hibernians of Wayne County - Thomas Dunleavy Div. **[9393]**, Plymouth, MI
Anderson Area Chamber of Commerce **[13742]**, Cincinnati, OH
Anderson/Madison County Assn. of Realtors **[4099]**, Anderson, IN
Anderson/Madison County Visitors and Convention Bur. **[4100]**, Anderson, IN
Anderson Univ. Students In Free Enterprise **[4101]**, Anderson, IN
Anderson - Young Life **[13126]**, Amelia, OH
Andover Lions Club **[10295]**, Andover, MN

Anesthesiology
Michigan Assn. of Nurse Anesthetists **[6720]**, Ann Arbor, MI
Michigan Soc. of Anesthesiologists **[8714]**, Lansing, MI
Ohio Soc. of Anesthesiologists **[14673]**, Columbus, OH
Anglers of the Au Sable **[8058]**, Grayling, MI
Angola Area Chamber of Commerce **[4124]**, Angola, IN
Animal Allies Humane Soc. of Duluth, Minnesota **[10804]**, Duluth, MN

Animal Breeding
Amer. Ostrich Assn., Minnesota **[11511]**, Minneapolis, MN
East Central Dairy Goat Club **[12645]**, Scandia, MN
Genex Cooperative **[19679]**, Shawano, WI
Goat Lovers of Michigan **[9330]**, Ovid, MI
Heartland Dairy Goat Club **[3780]**, Toulon, IL
Helping Hands Dairy Goat Club **[4958]**, Idaville, IN
Illinois Alpaca Owners and Breeders Assn. **[3842]**, Utica, IL
Illinois Dairy Goat Assn. **[3428]**, Saybrook, IL
Indiana Dairy Goat Assn. **[4959]**, Idaville, IN
Just Kidding 4-H Dairy Goat Club **[7631]**, Ewen, MI
Michigan Dairy Goat Soc. **[8883]**, Lyons, MI
Michigan Sheep Breeders Assn. **[7125]**, Charlotte, MI
Midstates Mule and Donkey Show Society **[16427]**, Pioneer, OH
North East Ohio Dairy Goat Assn. **[16631]**, Seville, OH
Northern Illinois Dairy Goat Assn. **[1751]**, Freeport, IL
Northern Lights Goat Assn. **[7632]**, Ewen, MI
Ohio Alpaca Breeders Assn. **[13233]**, Aurora, OH
Ohio Dairy Goat Assn. **[13608]**, Cedarville, OH
Ohio Valley Dairy Goat Assn. **[15327]**, Glouster, OH
South Western Ohio Dairy Goat Assn. **[15861]**, Martinsville, OH
Southeastern Ohio Dairy Goat Assn. **[16184]**, Newark, OH
Western Reserve Dairy Goat Assn. **[13474]**, Burton, OH
Animal Liberation League **[★11548]**
Animal Love and Loss Network **[11082]**, Grand Rapids, MN

Animal Research
Amer. Assn. for Lab. Animal Sci. - Chicago **[608]**, Chicago, IL
Amer. Assn. for Lab. Animal Sci. - Indiana **[4972]**, Indianapolis, IN
Amer. Assn. for Lab. Animal Sci. - Michigan **[10196]**, Ypsilanti, MI
Amer. Assn. for Lab. Animal Sci. - Minnesota **[12350]**, St. Paul, MN
Amer. Assn. for Lab. Animal Sci. - Southern Ohio **[13703]**, Cincinnati, OH
Michigan Soc. for Medical Res. **[6736]**, Ann Arbor, MI
Animal Rights; Citizens for **[3014]**, Peoria, IL
Animal Shelter; Friends of Ingham County **[8569]**, Lansing, MI
Animal Treatment Soc; Humane **[10107]**, Weidman, MI

Animal Welfare
Akron-Canton Boxer Rescue of Ohio **[16212]**, North Canton, OH
Alliance for Animals, Madison **[18447]**, Madison, WI
Alliance for Responsible Pet Ownership **[4598]**, Fishers, IN
Animal Allies Humane Soc. of Duluth, Minnesota **[10804]**, Duluth, MN
Animal Love and Loss Network **[11082]**, Grand Rapids, MN
Animal Welfare Soc. of Southeastern Michigan **[8891]**, Madison Heights, MI
Anti-Cruelty Soc. **[733]**, Chicago, IL
CATNAP from the Heart **[2175]**, La Grange Park, IL
Champaign County Humane Soc. **[3812]**, Urbana, IL
Chinese Shar-Pei Rescue of Michigan **[6909]**, Belleville, MI
Chippewa County Humane Assn. **[17747]**, Chippewa Falls, WI
Citizens for Animal Rights **[3014]**, Peoria, IL
Columbus House Rabbit Soc. **[14388]**, Columbus, OH
Communication Alliance to Network Thoroughbred Ex-Racehorses **[249]**, Bloomingdale, IL
Compassionate Action for Animals **[11548]**, Minneapolis, MN
Dalmatians Off the Streets Rescue Gp. **[16787]**, Strongsville, OH
Dane County Humane Soc. **[18503]**, Madison, WI
For Animals **[9929]**, Traverse City, MI

For the Love of Rotts, The Michigan Connection [7487], Dryden, MI
Free Spirit Siberian Rescue [1949], Harvard, IL
Friends of Ingham County Animal Shelter [8569], Lansing, MI
Geauga Humane Soc. / Rescue Village [16561], Russell Township, OH
German Shepherd Rescue Alliance of Wisconsin [18514], Madison, WI
Golden Years Alaskan Malamute Rescue [9144], Muskegon, MI
Great Dane Rescue [9398], Plymouth, MI
Holmes County Humane Soc. [16037], Millersburg, OH
Hooved Animal Humane Soc. [4056], Woodstock, IL
House Rabbit Soc., Indiana Chap. [5149], Indianapolis, IN
Hugs for Homeless Animals [18011], Franklin, WI
Humane Animal Treatment Soc. [10107], Weidman, MI
Humane Animal Welfare Soc. - Waukesha County [19986], Waukesha, WI
Humane Ohio [16406], Perrysburg, OH
Humane Soc. of Br. County [9465], Quincy, MI
Humane Soc. for Hamilton County [5974], Noblesville, IN
Humane Soc. of Kent County [7964], Grand Rapids, MI
Humane Soc. of Rock Island County [2489], Milan, IL
Humane Soc. of Schoolcraft County [8917], Manistique, MI
Humane Soc. of Swift County [10434], Benson, MN
Humane Soc. of Tuscola County [7084], Caro, MI
Humane Soc. of the U.S., Central State Regional Off. [2637], Naperville, IL
Kalamazoo Animal Liberation League [8433], Kalamazoo, MI
Lakeshore Humane Soc. [18781], Manitowoc, WI
Marquette County Humane Soc. [9178], Negaunee, MI
Metro East Humane Soc. [1564], Edwardsville, IL
Miami Valley Vizsla Club [14502], Columbus, OH
Michigan Humane Soc. [9807], Southfield, MI
Michigan Humane Soc. - Westland [10139], Westland, MI
Mit Liebe German Shepherd Dog Rescue [19851], Suamico, WI
Naperville Area Humane Soc. [2648], Naperville, IL
Noah's Lost Ark [13351], Berlin Center, OH
Northwoods Humane Soc. [11019], Forest Lake, MN
Nuzzled Network [3995], Wheaton, IL
Outreach for Animals [14944], Dayton, OH
Ozaukee Humane Soc. [18065], Grafton, WI
PACT Humane Society [1507], Downers Grove, IL
Paws with a Cause NH Chap. [10098], Wayland, MI
PetSafe Rescue Alliance [9944], Traverse City, MI
Portage County Humane Soc. [19802], Stevens Point, WI
Safe Haven Humane Soc. for Jo Daviess County [1604], Elizabeth, IL
Save the Animals Found. [13979], Cincinnati, OH
Second Chance Animal Rescue [12901], White Bear Lake, MN
Spring Lake Animal Shelter [8326], Iron Mountain, MI
Tails a' Waggin' Rescue [6522], Whitestown, IN
Watonwan County Humane Soc. [12323], St. James, MN
White River Humane Soc. [4179], Bedford, IN
Wisconsin Chihuahua Rescue [19226], Monticello, WI
Wisconsin Humane Soc. [19172], Milwaukee, WI
Wyandot County Humane Soc. [17035], Upper Sandusky, OH
Animal Welfare Soc. of Southeastern Michigan [8891], Madison Heights, MI
Animal Welfare Soc. - Waukesha County; Humane [19986], Waukesha, WI
Animal Welfare Soc. of Western Wisconsin; Protective [19643], River Falls, WI
Animals
United Coalition for Animals [14015], Cincinnati, OH
Animals; Compassionate Action for [11548], Minneapolis, MN
Animals, Madison; Alliance for [18447], Madison, WI
Animals; United Coalition for [14015], Cincinnati, OH
Anjuman Cricket Club [2740], Norridge, IL
Ann Arbor Area Chamber of Commerce [6668], Ann Arbor, MI
Ann Arbor Area Convention and Visitors Bur. [6669], Ann Arbor, MI
Ann Arbor Chap. of Optical Soc. of Am. [6670], Ann Arbor, MI
Ann Arbor Coun. for Traditional Music and Dance [6671], Ann Arbor, MI
Ann Arbor Dueling Soc. [6906], Belleville, MI
Ann Arbor Evening Lions Club [6672], Ann Arbor, MI
Ann Arbor Fed. of Musicians - Local 625, Amer. Fed. of Musicians [6673], Ann Arbor, MI
Ann Arbor Figure Skating Club [6674], Ann Arbor, MI
Ann Arbor Garden Club [6675], Ann Arbor, MI
Ann Arbor Host Lions Club [7138], Chelsea, MI
Ann Arbor Huron Highschool Skating Club [6676], Ann Arbor, MI
Ann Arbor Mayor's Task Force [★6785]
Ann Arbor Model Yacht Club No. 138 [9224], Northville, MI
Ann Arbor Orchid Soc. [6677], Ann Arbor, MI
Ann Arbor Space Soc. [6678], Ann Arbor, MI
Ann Arbor Tenants Union [6679], Ann Arbor, MI
Anna-Jonesboro Area Chamber of Commerce [★53]
Anoka Area Chamber of Commerce [10303], Anoka, MN
Anoka County Chap. of Pheasants Forever [11320], Lino Lakes, MN
Anoka County Gem and Mineral Club [10723], Cottage Grove, MN
Anoka County Historical Soc. [10304], Anoka, MN
Anoka County RSVP [10305], Anoka, MN
Ansar Shriners [3531], Springfield, IL
Anthony Wayne HS - Young Life [15901], Maumee, OH
Anthony Wayne Stamp Soc. [4637], Fort Wayne, IN
Anthony Wayne Wyldlife [15902], Maumee, OH
Anti-Cruelty Soc. [733], Chicago, IL
Antigo Area Chamber of Commerce [17474], Antigo, WI
Antioch Chamber of Commerce and Indus. [56], Antioch, IL
Antioch Shriners [14853], Dayton, OH
Antioch Woman's Club [57], Antioch, IL
Antique Auto. Club of Am., Illinois Region [348], Brookfield, IL
Antique Auto. Club of Am., Illinois Region - Des Plaines Valley Chap. [2312], Lockport, IL
Antique Auto. Club of Am., Illinois Region - Fox Valley Chap. [1534], East Dundee, IL
Antique Auto. Club of Am., Illinois Region - Momence Chap. [325], Bourbonnais, IL
Antique Auto. Club of Am., Illinois Region - North Shore Chap. [1987], Highland Park, IL
Antique Auto. Club of Am., Illinois Region - Silver Springs Chap. [3493], Somonauk, IL
Antique Auto. Club of Am., Lower Ohio Valley Evansville Region [4274], Boonville, IN
Antique Auto. Club of Am., Minnesota Region - Capitol City Chap. [10545], Brooklyn Park, MN
Antique Auto. Club of Am., Minnesota Region - Hiawatha Chap. [12127], Rochester, MN
Antique Auto. Club of Am., Northwestern Michigan Region [9924], Traverse City, MI
Antique Auto. Club of Am., Ohio Region [15882], Massillon, OH
Antique Auto. Club of Am., Ohio Region - Canton Chap. [16104], Navarre, OH
Antique Auto. Club of Am., Ohio Region - Commodore Perry Chap. [15108], Elyria, OH
Antique Auto. Club of Am., Ohio Region - Meander Chap. [16141], New Middletown, OH
Antique Auto. Club of Am., Ohio Region - Northern Chap. [16522], Richfield, OH
Antique Auto. Club of Am., Ohio Region - Southern Chap. [15473], Huber Heights, OH
Antique Auto. Club of Am., Ohio Region - Western Reserve Chap. [16540], Rock Creek, OH
Antique Auto. Club of Am., Southern Illinois Region - Ohio Valley Chap. [2482], Metropolis, IL
Antique Auto. Club of Am., Wisconsin Region [18869], Menomonee Falls, WI
Antique Auto. Club of Am., Wolverine State Region [6907], Belleville, MI
Antique Bottle Club of Northern Illinois [3922], Waukegan, IL
Antique and Classic Boat Soc; Bob Speltz Land O' Lakes Chap. of the [10761], Deephaven, MN
Antiques
Chicago Map Soc. [815], Chicago, IL
Antrim County Habitat for Humanity [7594], Elk Rapids, MI
Antwerp Chamber of Commerce [13147], Antwerp, OH
Antwerp Preservation Soc. [13148], Antwerp, OH
Apartment Assn. of Fort Wayne-Northeast Indiana [4638], Fort Wayne, IN
Apartment Assn. of Michigan [7653], Farmington Hills, MI
Apartment Assn; Ohio [14538], Columbus, OH
Apartment Assn. of Southern Indiana [4529], Evansville, IN
Apartment Assn; Wisconsin [18645], Madison, WI
Apartment and Condominiums Assn; Ohio [★14538]
APICS, The Assn. for Operations Mgt. - Canton Area Chap. [13545], Canton, OH
APICS, The Assn. for Operations Mgt. - Central Indiana Chap. [5032], Indianapolis, IN
APICS, The Assn. for Operations Mgt. - Central Minnesota Chap. [12273], St. Cloud, MN
APICS, The Assn. for Operations Mgt. - Chicago Chap. [1859], Glenview, IL
APICS, The Assn. for Operations Mgt. - Cincinnati Chap. [13743], Cincinnati, OH
APICS, The Assn. for Operations Mgt. - Cleveland Chap. [14071], Cleveland, OH
APICS, The Assn. for Operations Mgt. - Columbus Chap. No. 99 [17205], Westerville, OH
APICS, The Assn. for Operations Mgt. - Dayton Chap. No. 64 [13619], Centerville, OH
APICS, The Assn. for Operations Mgt. - Fort Wayne Chap. 139 [4639], Fort Wayne, IN
APICS, The Assn. for Operations Mgt. - Fox River Chap. No. 207 [174], Batavia, IL
APICS, The Assn. for Operations Mgt. - Grand Rapids Chap. [7906], Grand Rapids, MI
APICS, The Assn. for Operations Mgt. - Highlands Chap. 261 [1318], Crystal Lake, IL
APICS, The Assn. for Operations Mgt. - Lima Area Chap. No. 290 [15356], Greenville, OH
APICS, The Assn. for Operations Mgt. - Michiana Chap. No. 57 [6219], South Bend, IN
APICS, The Assn. for Operations Mgt. - Mid Michigan Chap. [7579], Eaton Rapids, MI
APICS, The Assn. for Operations Mgt. - Milwaukee Chap. [20070], Wauwatosa, WI
APICS, The Assn. for Operations Mgt. - Racine/Kenosha Chap. [19552], Racine, WI
APICS, The Assn. for Operations Mgt. - Rock Valley Chap. [3271], Rockford, IL
APICS, The Assn. for Operations Mgt. - Shoreline Chap. [19692], Sheboygan, WI
APICS, The Assn. for Operations Mgt. - Southern Minnesota Chap. [11958], Owatonna, MN
APICS, The Assn. for Operations Mgt. - The Greater Detroit Chap. [8787], Lathrup Village, MI
APICS, The Assn. for Operations Mgt. - Toledo Chap. [16901], Toledo, OH
APICS, The Assn. for Operations Mgt. - Twin Cities Chap. [10463], Bloomington, MN
APMI Cleveland Chap. [14072], Cleveland, OH
APMI Dayton [5033], Indianapolis, IN
APMI Michigan [8271], Howell, MI
Apollo Educ. Assn. [15648], Lima, OH
Apollo VII REACT [1417], Deerfield, IL
Appalachian
IT Alliance of Appalachian Ohio [13205], Athens, OH
Appalachian Appaloosa Assn. [15443], Hillsboro, OH
Appalachian Peace and Justice Network [13195], Athens, OH
Apparel
Michigan Clothiers Assn. [8643], Lansing, MI
Professional Assn. of Clothiers, Chicago Chap. [1441], DeKalb, IL
Apple Comm; Michigan [7462], DeWitt, MI
Apple Creek Lions Club [17312], Wooster, OH
Apple Siders of Cincinnati [13744], Cincinnati, OH
Apple Valley Chamber of Commerce [10316], Apple Valley, MN

Apple Valley Lions Club **[10317]**, Apple Valley, MN
Apple Valley - Young Life **[10586]**, Burnsville, MN
Appleton Chamber of Commerce **[★17490]**
Appleton Curling Club **[17486]**, Appleton, WI
Appleton Lions Club **[10330]**, Appleton, MN
Appleton Noon Lions Club **[17487]**, Appleton, WI
Appleton Young Life **[19268]**, Neenah, WI
Appraisal Inst; Chicago Chap. of the **[799]**, Chicago, IL
Appraisal Inst., Metro/Minnesota Chap. **[12128]**, Rochester, MN
Appraisal Inst., Wisconsin Chap. **[18964]**, Milwaukee, WI

Appraisers
- Amer. Soc. of Appraisers, Akron - Cleveland Chap. **[16234]**, North Olmsted, OH
- Amer. Soc. of Appraisers, Chicago Chap. **[2959]**, Park Ridge, IL
- Amer. Soc. of Appraisers, Columbus Chap. **[17204]**, Westerville, OH
- Amer. Soc. of Appraisers, Dayton - Cincinnati Chap. **[15619]**, Lebanon, OH
- Amer. Soc. of Appraisers, Detroit Chap. **[9971]**, Troy, MI
- Amer. Soc. of Appraisers, Greater Michigan Chap. **[7901]**, Grand Rapids, MI
- Amer. Soc. of Appraisers, Indiana Chap. **[6473]**, West Lafayette, IN
- Amer. Soc. of Appraisers, Toledo Chap. **[16895]**, Toledo, OH
- Amer. Soc. of Appraisers, Twin Cities Chap. **[11449]**, Medina, MN
- Amer. Soc. of Appraisers, Wisconsin Chap. **[17666]**, Brookfield, WI
- Amer. Soc. of Farm Managers and Rural Appraisers Michigan Chap. **[8480]**, Kawkawlin, MI
- Amer. Soc. of Farm Managers and Rural Appraisers Minnesota Chap. **[11432]**, Marshall, MN
- Amer. Soc. of Farm Managers and Rural Appraisers Ohio Chap. **[16270]**, Oak Harbor, OH
- Amer. Soc. of Farm Managers and Rural Appraisers Wisconsin Chap. **[18470]**, Madison, WI
- Appraisal Inst., Metro/Minnesota Chap. **[12128]**, Rochester, MN
- Appraisal Inst., Wisconsin Chap. **[18964]**, Milwaukee, WI
- Chicago Chap. of the Appraisal Inst. **[799]**, Chicago, IL
- Halderman Real Estate Services - Halderman Farm Mgt. **[6424]**, Wabash, IN
- Illinois Soc. of Professional Farm Managers and Rural Appraisers **[18874]**, Menomonee Falls, WI

Aquaculture
- Akron-Canton Muskie Maniacs **[14254]**, Clinton, OH
- Bemidji/Cass Lake Chap. of Muskies **[10406]**, Bemidji, MN
- Central Illinois Muskie Hunters **[2547]**, Monticello, IL
- Central Ohio Chap. of Muskies **[14357]**, Columbus, OH
- Chicagoland Muskie Hunters **[3483]**, Skokie, IL
- Fox River Valley Chap. of Muskies **[27]**, Algonquin, IL
- Hoosier Muskie Hunters **[5144]**, Indianapolis, IN
- Michigan Muskie Alliance **[7055]**, Caledonia, MI
- Muskies Arrowhead Chap. **[12800]**, Virginia, MN
- Muskies Between the Lakes Chap. **[19718]**, Sheboygan Falls, WI
- Muskies Brainerd Lakes Chap. **[10517]**, Brainerd, MN
- Muskies Capital City Chap. **[18568]**, Madison, WI
- Muskies Central Wisconsin Chap. **[18846]**, Medford, WI
- Muskies Cleveland Chap. 23 **[16500]**, Ravenna, OH
- Muskies First Wisconsin Chap. **[17756]**, Chippewa Falls, WI
- Muskies Flatlanders Chap. **[3496]**, South Beloit, IL
- Muskies God's Country Chap. **[18371]**, La Crosse, WI
- Muskies Hayward Lakes Chap. **[18197]**, Hayward, WI
- Muskies Headwaters Chap. **[17848]**, Eagle River, WI
- Muskies Hopedale Chap. **[15024]**, Dillonvale, OH
- Muskies Lake Superior **[10691]**, Cloquet, MN
- Muskies Milwaukee Chap. **[18158]**, Greenfield, WI
- Muskies Mississippi Valley Chap. **[1931]**, Hampton, IL
- Muskies St. Cloud Chap. **[10701]**, Coleraine, MN
- Muskies Vikingland Chap. **[11981]**, Parkers Prairie, MN
- Muskies West Virginia Chap. 9 **[15684]**, Little Hocking, OH
- North Metro Muskies **[12031]**, Plymouth, MN
- Ohio Valley Muskie Hunters **[13379]**, Bowerston, OH
- Quad County Hawg Hunters **[3111]**, Plano, IL
- Shawnee Muskie Hunters **[1443]**, DeKalb, IL
- South of the Border Chap. of Muskies **[2463]**, McHenry, IL
- South Side Muskie Hawks **[369]**, Burbank, IL
- Twin Cities Chap. of Muskies **[11757]**, Minneapolis, MN
- Webster Musky Club **[6001]**, North Webster, IN

Aquatics
- Miami Valley Water Garden Soc. **[14919]**, Dayton, OH

Arab-American Alliance for the Mentally Ill **[7248]**, Dearborn, MI
Arabian Horse Assn. of Michigan **[10105]**, Webberville, MI
Arbitration Assn., Ohio; Amer. **[13699]**, Cincinnati, OH

Arbitration and Mediation
- Amer. Arbitration Assn., Michigan **[9778]**, Southfield, MI
- Amer. Arbitration Assn., Minnesota **[11483]**, Minneapolis, MN
- Amer. Arbitration Assn., Ohio **[13699]**, Cincinnati, OH
- Assn. for Conflict Resolution, Chicago Area Chap. **[3746]**, Sycamore, IL
- Mediation Council of Illinois **[1044]**, Chicago, IL

Arc Allegan **[★6602]**
Arc/Allegan County **[6604]**, Allegan, MI
Arc of Allen County **[15649]**, Lima, OH
Arc of Carroll County **[4614]**, Flora, IN
Arc of Dearborn County **[5653]**, Lawrenceburg, IN
Arc Eau Claire **[17864]**, Eau Claire, WI
Arc of Erie County **[16603]**, Sandusky, OH
Arc of Fairfield County **[16418]**, Pickerington, OH
ARC, Hennepin-Carver **[11520]**, Minneapolis, MN
ARC of Illinois **[2045]**, Homewood, IL
Arc of Indiana **[5034]**, Indianapolis, IN
Arc Kandiyohi County **[12913]**, Willmar, MN
Arc Kent County **[7907]**, Grand Rapids, MI
Arc Livingston **[8272]**, Howell, MI
Arc Minnesota **[12383]**, St. Paul, MN
Arc of Monroe County **[9062]**, Monroe, MI
Arc/Muskegon **[9140]**, Muskegon, MI
Arc of Neenah-Menasha **[18857]**, Menasha, WI
The Arc/Newaygo County **[7795]**, Fremont, MI
Arc of Oakland County **[9973]**, Troy, MI
ARC of Ohio **[14316]**, Columbus, OH
Arc Olmsted County **[★12129]**
ARC Opportunities - Lagrance County **[4936]**, Howe, IN
Arc of Owen County **[6281]**, Spencer, IN
ARC Rehab Sers. **[5666]**, Lebanon, IN
Arc St. Cloud **[12274]**, St. Cloud, MN
ARC Services of Macomb **[7173]**, Clinton Township, MI
Arc Southeastern Minnesota **[12129]**, Rochester, MN
ARC; Spencer County **[6128]**, Rockport, IN
Arc of Stark County **[13546]**, Canton, OH
Arc of Vigo County **[6314]**, Terre Haute, IN
Arc of Western Wayne County **[10137]**, Westland, MI
Arc of Winnebago, Boone and Ogle **[3272]**, Rockford, IL
Arc-Wisconsin Disability Assn. **[18476]**, Madison, WI
Arcade Park Garden Club **[734]**, Chicago, IL
Arcadia Chamber of Commerce **[17535]**, Arcadia, WI
Arcadia Lions Club **[6796]**, Arcadia, MI
Archaeological and Historical Soc; Logan County **[★13321]**

Archaeology
- Soc. for Indus. Archeology **[8261]**, Houghton, MI
- Soc. of Indus. Archeology, Northern Ohio Chap. **[17414]**, Youngstown, OH

Archbold Area Chamber of Commerce **[13151]**, Archbold, OH

Archery
- Joliet Archery Club **[2314]**, Lockport, IL
- Poynette Bowhunters Assn. **[19525]**, Poynette, WI

Archery Club; Joliet **[2314]**, Lockport, IL
Architects Eastern Illinois; Amer. Inst. of **[2894]**, Ottawa, IL
Architects, Michigan; Amer. Inst. of **[7302]**, Detroit, MI
Architects Northeast Illinois; Amer. Inst. of **[2624]**, Naperville, IL
Architects Southeast Wisconsin; Amer. Inst. of **[18935]**, Milwaukee, WI
Architects Southwest Wisconsin; Amer. Inst. of **[19931]**, Verona, WI
Architectural Found; Michigan **[7392]**, Detroit, MI

Architecture
- Amer. Inst. of Architects Akron **[16050]**, Mogadore, OH
- Amer. Inst. of Architects Central/Southern Indiana **[5605]**, Lafayette, IN
- Amer. Inst. of Architects Chicago **[626]**, Chicago, IL
- Amer. Inst. of Architects Cincinnati **[13710]**, Cincinnati, OH
- Amer. Inst. of Architects, Cleveland **[14052]**, Cleveland, OH
- American Institute of Architects Columbus **[14286]**, Columbus, OH
- Amer. Inst. of Architects Dayton **[14842]**, Dayton, OH
- Amer. Inst. of Architects Eastern Illinois **[2894]**, Ottawa, IL
- American Institute of Architects Eastern Ohio **[17385]**, Youngstown, OH
- Amer. Inst. of Architects, Huron Valley Chap. **[6660]**, Ann Arbor, MI
- Amer. Inst. of Architects - Illinois **[3524]**, Springfield, IL
- Amer. Inst. of Architects Indiana **[4987]**, Indianapolis, IN
- Amer. Inst. of Architects, Michigan **[7302]**, Detroit, MI
- Amer. Inst. of Architects - Minnesota **[11491]**, Minneapolis, MN
- Amer. Inst. of Architects Northeast Illinois **[2624]**, Naperville, IL
- Amer. Inst. of Architects Ohio **[14287]**, Columbus, OH
- Amer. Inst. of Architects Southeast Wisconsin **[18935]**, Milwaukee, WI
- Amer. Inst. of Architects Southern Illinois **[410]**, Carbondale, IL
- Amer. Inst. of Architects Southwest Wisconsin **[19931]**, Verona, WI
- Amer. Inst. of Architects, Wisconsin **[18462]**, Madison, WI
- Michigan Architectural Found. **[7392]**, Detroit, MI
- Soc. of Amer. Registered Architects - Minnesota Coun. **[10854]**, Duluth, MN
- Soc. of Amer. Registered Architects - Northern Ohio Chap. **[14218]**, Cleveland, OH

Archives
- Irish Amer. Archival Soc. **[13533]**, Canfield, OH
- Midwest Archives Conf. **[15151]**, Fairborn, OH

Arcola Chamber of Commerce **[61]**, Arcola, IL
Arctic Figure Skating Club **[7060]**, Canton, MI
Area Agencies on Aging Assn. of Michigan **[8548]**, Lansing, MI
Argyle Lions Club **[10334]**, Argyle, MN
Arlington Area Chamber of Commerce **[10337]**, Arlington, MN
Arlington Heights Chamber of Commerce **[65]**, Arlington Heights, IL
Arlington Heights Lions Club **[66]**, Arlington Heights, IL
Arlington Lions Club - Minnesota **[10338]**, Arlington, MN
ARMA, Greater Cincinnati Chapter **[13745]**, Cincinnati, OH
ARMA International - Fox Valley/Green Bay Chapter - The Information Management Professionals **[17813]**, De Pere, WI
ARMA Intl. - Info. Mgt. Professionals, Greater Dayton Chap. **[15984]**, Miamisburg, OH
ARMA Intl. - The Info. Mgt. Professionals, Greater Columbus Ohio Chap. **[15259]**, Gahanna, OH

ARMA Intl. - The Info. Mgt. Professionals, Twin Cities Chap. **[10464]**, Bloomington, MN
ARMA, Madison Chap. **[18477]**, Madison, WI
ARMA, Western Michigan Chap. **[7908]**, Grand Rapids, MI
Armed Forces
USO of Central Ohio **[17248]**, Whitehall, OH
USO of Northern Ohio **[13432]**, Broadview Heights, OH
Army
101st Airborne Div. Assn., Michigan Chap. **[9562]**, Roseville, MI
101st Airborne Div. Assn., Old Abe Chap. **[19224]**, Monticello, WI
Army and Navy Club of Grand Rapids **[8403]**, Jenison, MI
Arrowhead Country Rsrc. Conservation and Development Coun. **[6532]**, Winamac, IN
Arrowhead Hea. Care Engineers Assn. **[10805]**, Duluth, MN
Arrowhead Regional Development Commn. **[10806]**, Duluth, MN
Arrowhead RSVP **[12793]**, Virginia, MN
Arrowhead Young Life **[18181]**, Hartland, WI
Art
Art's Coun. of Greater Grand Rapids **[7909]**, Grand Rapids, MI
Colored Pencil Soc. of Am., Chicago, Illinois Chap. 103 **[851]**, Chicago, IL
Art Assn. of Randolph County **[6361]**, Union City, IN
Art Club; Saugatuck-Douglas **[9716]**, Saugatuck, MI
Art Educ. Assn. of Indiana **[5035]**, Indianapolis, IN
Art Guild; Brighton **[7010]**, Brighton, MI
Art League; Columbus **[★14539]**
Art League; Ohio **[14539]**, Columbus, OH
Art Libraries Soc. of North Am. - Midstates Chap. **[4601]**, Fishers, IN
Art Libraries Soc. of North Am. - Ohio Valley **[13196]**, Athens, OH
Art Libraries Soc. of North Am. - Twin Cities Chap. **[11521]**, Minneapolis, MN
Art Therapy
Michigan Assn. of Art Therapy **[10117]**, West Bloomfield, MI
Wisconsin Art Therapy Assn. **[19151]**, Milwaukee, WI
ArtBridge **[9232]**, Novi, MI
Arthritis Found., Adams County Br. **[3149]**, Quincy, IL
Arthritis Found., Central Ohio Chap. **[15426]**, Hilliard, OH
Arthritis Found., Champaign County Br. **[3806]**, Urbana, IL
Arthritis Found., Dayton Br. **[15558]**, Kettering, OH
Arthritis Found., Greater Chicago Chap. **[735]**, Chicago, IL
Arthritis Found., Greater Illinois Chap. **[3005]**, Peoria, IL
Arthritis Found., Illinois Valley Br. **[3077]**, Peru, IL
Arthritis Found., Indiana Chap. **[5036]**, Indianapolis, IN
Arthritis Found., Kankakee County Br. **[2131]**, Kankakee, IL
Arthritis Found., Livingston County Br. **[3119]**, Pontiac, IL
Arthritis Found., Macon County Br. **[1376]**, Decatur, IL
Arthritis Found., McLean County Br. **[2709]**, Normal, IL
Arthritis Found., Michigan Chap. **[9974]**, Troy, MI
Arthritis Foundation, Milwaukee **[18965]**, Milwaukee, WI
Arthritis Found., Minnesota Chap. **[★12384]**
Arthritis Found., North Central Chap. **[12384]**, St. Paul, MN
Arthritis Found., Northeast Indiana Br. **[4640]**, Fort Wayne, IN
Arthritis Found., Northeastern District Off. **[18082]**, Green Bay, WI
Arthritis Found. Northeastern Ohio Chap. **[14073]**, Cleveland, OH
Arthritis Found., Northern Indiana Br. **[6220]**, South Bend, IN
Arthritis Found., Northwestern Ohio **[16902]**, Toledo, OH
Arthritis Found., Ohio River Valley Chap. **[13746]**, Cincinnati, OH
Arthritis Found., Sangamon County Br. **[3532]**, Springfield, IL
Arthritis Found., Scioto Valley Br. **[16469]**, Portsmouth, OH
Arthritis Found., Southern Illinois Br. **[2402]**, Marion, IL
Arthritis Found., Southern Indiana Br. **[4530]**, Evansville, IN
Arthritis Found., Tri-County Br. **[3006]**, Peoria, IL
Arthritis Found., Winnebago County Br. **[3273]**, Rockford, IL
Arthritis Found., Wisconsin Chap. **[20099]**, West Allis, WI
Arthur Assn. of Commerce **[88]**, Arthur, IL
Artists
Colored Pencil Society of America, Detroit Chapter No. 104 **[9745]**, Shelby Township, MI
Michigan Guild of Artists and Artisans **[6727]**, Ann Arbor, MI
National Association of Artists' Organizations, Midwest **[1071]**, Chicago, IL
Artists and Craftsmen of Porter County; Assn. of **[4351]**, Chesterton, IN
Artists' Organizations, Midwest; National Association of **[1071]**, Chicago, IL
Arts
Art Assn. of Randolph County **[6361]**, Union City, IN
Art Educ. Assn. of Indiana **[5035]**, Indianapolis, IN
Arts Coun. of Indianapolis **[5037]**, Indianapolis, IN
Arts Midwest **[11522]**, Minneapolis, MN
ArtServe Michigan **[9784]**, Southfield, MI
Assn. of Artists and Craftsmen of Porter County **[4351]**, Chesterton, IN
Ballet Arts Minnesota **[11530]**, Minneapolis, MN
Brighton Art Guild **[7010]**, Brighton, MI
Cityfolk **[14866]**, Dayton, OH
Columbus Area Arts Coun. **[4391]**, Columbus, IN
Community Worship Arts **[4537]**, Evansville, IN
Copper Country Community Arts Coun. **[8107]**, Hancock, MI
Creative Arts Repertoire Ensemble **[7922]**, Grand Rapids, MI
Dearborn Community Arts Coun. **[7254]**, Dearborn, MI
Dillman's Creative Arts Found. **[18388]**, Lac Du Flambeau, WI
Downriver Coun. for the Arts **[9901]**, Taylor, MI
Eastern Upper Peninsula Fine Arts Coun. **[7240]**, De Tour Village, MI
Five Wings Arts Coun. **[12703]**, Staples, MN
Free Arts for Abused Children of Minnesota **[11563]**, Minneapolis, MN
Great Lakes Pastel Soc. **[7957]**, Grand Rapids, MI
Greater Cincinnati Tall Stacks Commn. **[13854]**, Cincinnati, OH
Heidelberg Proj. **[7374]**, Detroit, MI
Illinois Art Educ. Assn. **[3384]**, St. Charles, IL
Illinois Arts Alliance **[925]**, Chicago, IL
Indiana Arts Commn. **[5163]**, Indianapolis, IN
Lock One Community Arts **[16118]**, New Bremen, OH
Maumee Coun. for the Arts **[15910]**, Maumee, OH
Michigan Art Educ. Assn. **[9107]**, Mount Pleasant, MI
Michigan Assn. of Community Arts Agencies **[8609]**, Lansing, MI
Near NorthWest Arts Coun. **[1093]**, Chicago, IL
Northern Indiana Arts Assn. **[5905]**, Munster, IN
Ohio Art Educ. Assn. **[15606]**, Lancaster, OH
Ohio Art League **[14539]**, Columbus, OH
Owatonna Arts Center **[11963]**, Owatonna, MN
Paint a Miracle **[9508]**, Rochester, MI
Plymouth Community Arts Coun. **[9404]**, Plymouth, MI
Prairie Art Alliance **[3663]**, Springfield, IL
Rabbit Run Community Arts Assn. **[15750]**, Madison, OH
Ring Around the Arts **[10323]**, Apple Valley, MN
Sault Area Arts Coun. **[9724]**, Sault Ste. Marie, MI
Scarab Club **[7429]**, Detroit, MI
Short North Bus. Assn. **[14727]**, Columbus, OH
Springboard for the Arts **[12593]**, St. Paul, MN
VSA Arts of Ohio/Cleveland Area Ser. Div. **[14236]**, Cleveland, OH
Wayne County Coun. for Arts, History, and Humanities **[8085]**, Grosse Pointe, MI
Wisconsin Art Educ. Assn. **[20058]**, Wausau, WI
Wisconsin Arts Bd. **[18646]**, Madison, WI
Women in the Director's Chair of Chicago **[1235]**, Chicago, IL
Women's Art Registry of Minnesota **[12606]**, St. Paul, MN
Young Audiences of Greater Cleveland **[14241]**, Cleveland, OH
Young Audiences of Indiana **[5505]**, Indianapolis, IN
Young Audiences of Michigan **[7457]**, Detroit, MI
Young Audiences of Minnesota **[12609]**, St. Paul, MN
Arts Assn; Rabbit Run Community **[15750]**, Madison, OH
Arts; Community Worship **[4537]**, Evansville, IN
Arts Coun; Bay **[6883]**, Bay City, MI
Arts Coun; Columbus Area **[4391]**, Columbus, IN
Arts Coun; Copper Country Community **[8107]**, Hancock, MI
Arts Coun; Eastern Upper Peninsula Fine **[7240]**, De Tour Village, MI
Arts Coun; Five Wings **[12703]**, Staples, MN
Art's Coun. of Greater Grand Rapids **[7909]**, Grand Rapids, MI
Arts Coun. of Indianapolis **[5037]**, Indianapolis, IN
Arts Coun; Plymouth Community **[9404]**, Plymouth, MI
Arts Coun; Sault Area **[9724]**, Sault Ste. Marie, MI
Arts and Crafts
Hoosier Salon Patrons Assn. and Galleries **[5146]**, Indianapolis, IN
Ten Thousand Villages of Cincinnati **[14008]**, Cincinnati, OH
Zeitgeist Detroit **[7459]**, Detroit, MI
Arts and Cultural Assn; Fairborn Performing **[15149]**, Fairborn, OH
Arts; Harrison St. Cooperative of Performing and Fine **[2811]**, Oak Park, IL
Arts, History, and Humanities; Wayne County Coun. for **[8085]**, Grosse Pointe, MI
Arts, and Letters; Michigan Acad. of Sci., **[6633]**, Alma, MI
Arts; Lock One Community **[16118]**, New Bremen, OH
Arts; Maumee Coun. for the **[15910]**, Maumee, OH
Arts Midwest **[11522]**, Minneapolis, MN
Arts Minnesota; Ballet **[11530]**, Minneapolis, MN
Arts Repertoire Ensemble; Creative **[7922]**, Grand Rapids, MI
Arts; Resources and Counseling for the **[★12593]**
Arts and Sciences
ArtBridge **[9232]**, Novi, MI
Phi Beta Kappa, Hope Coll. **[8217]**, Holland, MI
Phi Beta Kappa, Ohio Univ. **[13215]**, Athens, OH
Phi Beta Kappa, Ripon Coll. **[19634]**, Ripon, WI
Phi Beta Kappa, Univ. of Illinois (Chicago) **[1126]**, Chicago, IL
Arts Soc; Eastern Howard Performing **[4845]**, Greentown, IN
Arts; Springboard for the **[12593]**, St. Paul, MN
ArtServe Michigan **[9784]**, Southfield, MI
Asbestos
Intl. Assn. of Heat and Frost Insulators and Asbestos Workers, Asbestos Abatement Workers Regional Local 207 **[9903]**, Taylor, MI
Intl. Assn. of Heat and Frost Insulators and Asbestos Workers, Local 18 **[5373]**, Indianapolis, IN
ASCnet Chap. of Southwest Ohio **[13747]**, Cincinnati, OH
Ash YL club - Young Life **[17313]**, Wooster, OH
Ashby Lions Club **[10342]**, Ashby, MN
Ashland Area Chamber of Commerce **[13160]**, Ashland, OH
Ashland Area Chamber of Commerce **[17543]**, Ashland, WI
Ashland Bd. of Realtors - Kentucky **[13161]**, Ashland, OH
Ashland Evening Lions Club **[13162]**, Ashland, OH
Ashland Lions Club - Wisconsin **[17544]**, Ashland, WI
Ashland Noon Lions Club **[13163]**, Ashland, OH
Ashley Lions Club **[6799]**, Ashley, MI
Ashtabula Area Chamber of Commerce **[13177]**, Ashtabula, OH
Ashtabula County AIFA **[13178]**, Ashtabula, OH

Ashtabula County Bd. of Realtors **[13179]**, Ashtabula, OH
Ashtabula County Genealogical Soc. **[15308]**, Geneva, OH
Ashtabula County Soc. for Human Rsrc. Mgt. **[13180]**, Ashtabula, OH
Ashtabula Lighthouse Restoration and Preservation Soc. **[16231]**, North Kingsville, OH
Ashtabula River Partnership **[13181]**, Ashtabula, OH
Ashtabula Yacht Club **[13182]**, Ashtabula, OH
Asian-American
Natl. Assn. of Asian Amer. Professionals, Chicago Chap. **[1072]**, Chicago, IL
Natl. Assn. of Asian Amer. Professionals, Minnesota Chap. **[11693]**, Minneapolis, MN
Asian Amer. Bar Assn. of the Greater Chicago Area **[736]**, Chicago, IL
Asian Amer. Bar Assn. of Michigan **[7324]**, Detroit, MI
Asian Amer. Bar Assn. of Ohio **[14074]**, Cleveland, OH
Asian Amer. Journalists Assn. - Chicago Chap. **[737]**, Chicago, IL
Asian Women United of Minnesota **[12385]**, St. Paul, MN
Asia's Hope **[17314]**, Wooster, OH
ASIS Intl., Central Illinois Chap. 158 **[4421]**, Covington, IN
ASIS Intl., Chicago Chap. **[31]**, Alsip, IL
ASIS Intl., Columbus Ohio Chap. 27 **[15427]**, Hilliard, OH
ASIS Intl., Detroit Chap. **[9785]**, Southfield, MI
ASIS Intl., Illinois North Shore Chap. **[2907]**, Palatine, IL
ASIS Intl., Lansing Chap. 120 **[7507]**, East Lansing, MI
ASIS Intl., Minnesota Chap. No. 25 **[11407]**, Maple Grove, MN
ASIS Intl., Toledo Chap. No. 56 **[16903]**, Toledo, OH
ASM Intl. - Detroit Chap. **[10062]**, Warren, MI
Asphalt Pavement Assn. of Indiana **[5038]**, Indianapolis, IN
Asphalt Pavement Assn; Wisconsin **[18647]**, Madison, WI
Assistance League of Chicagoland West **[2014]**, Hinsdale, IL
Assistance League of Fort Wayne **[4641]**, Fort Wayne, IN
Assistance League of Greater Cincinnati **[13748]**, Cincinnati, OH
Assistance League of Indianapolis **[5039]**, Indianapolis, IN
Assistance League of Metro Columbus **[14317]**, Columbus, OH
Assistance League of Minneapolis/St. Paul **[11523]**, Minneapolis, MN
Assistance League of Southeastern Michigan **[9512]**, Rochester Hills, MI
Assistants; Minnesota Acad. of Physician **[11620]**, Minneapolis, MN
Assisted Living Fed. of Am; Indiana **[5164]**, Indianapolis, IN
Assoc. Beer Distributors of Illinois **[3533]**, Springfield, IL
Assoc. Builders and Contractors, Central Michigan Chap. **[8549]**, Lansing, MI
Assoc. Builders and Contractors Illinois Chap. **[1606]**, Elk Grove Village, IL
Assoc. Builders and Contractors of Indiana **[5040]**, Indianapolis, IN
Assoc. Builders and Contractors of Michigan **[8550]**, Lansing, MI
Assoc. Builders and Contractors Minnesota Chap. **[10889]**, Eden Prairie, MN
Assoc. Builders and Contractors Northern Michigan Chap. **[7817]**, Gaylord, MI
Assoc. Builders and Contractors-Northern Ohio Chap. **[13424]**, Broadview Heights, OH
Assoc. Builders and Contractors-Ohio Valley Chap. **[16704]**, Springboro, OH
Assoc. Builders and Contractors, Saginaw Valley Chap. **[9023]**, Midland, MI
Assoc. Builders and Contractors-Southeastern Michigan Chap. **[8892]**, Madison Heights, MI
Assoc. Builders and Contractors, Western Michigan Chap. **[7910]**, Grand Rapids, MI
Assoc. Builders and Contractors of Wisconsin **[18478]**, Madison, WI
Assoc. Colleges of the Midwest **[738]**, Chicago, IL
Assoc. Concrete Contractors of Michigan **[8893]**, Madison Heights, MI
Assoc. Contract Loggers and Truckers of Minnesota **[12769]**, Two Harbors, MN
Assoc. Employers of Illinois **[★1505]**
Assoc. Firefighters of Illinois **[3534]**, Springfield, IL
Assoc. Food Dealers of Michigan **[7654]**, Farmington Hills, MI
Assoc. Gen. Contractors of Am., Greater Detroit Chap. **[9786]**, Southfield, MI
Assoc. Gen. Contractors of Am. - Michigan Chap. **[8551]**, Lansing, MI
Assoc. Gen. Contractors - Central Illinois Chap. **[3535]**, Springfield, IL
Assoc. Gen. Contractors of Greater Milwaukee **[18966]**, Milwaukee, WI
Assoc. Gen. Contractors of Illinois **[3536]**, Springfield, IL
Assoc. Gen. Contractors of Indiana **[5041]**, Indianapolis, IN
Assoc. Gen. Contractors of Minnesota **[12386]**, St. Paul, MN
Assoc. Gen. Contractors of Ohio **[14318]**, Columbus, OH
Assoc. Gen. Contractors of Wisconsin **[18479]**, Madison, WI
Assoc. Illinois Milk, Food and Environmental Sanitarians **[2626]**, Naperville, IL
Assoc. Landscape Contractors of Am., Cincinnati State Tech. and Community Coll. **[13749]**, Cincinnati, OH
Assoc. Landscape Contractors of Am., Columbus State Community Coll. **[14319]**, Columbus, OH
Assoc. Landscape Contractors of Am., Cuyahoga Community Coll. **[15420]**, Highland Hills, OH
Assoc. Landscape Contractors of Am., Dakota County Tech. Coll. **[12214]**, Rosemount, MN
Assoc. Landscape Contractors of Am., Illinois Central Coll. **[3007]**, Peoria, IL
Assoc. Landscape Contractors of Am., Joliet Junior Coll. **[2100]**, Joliet, IL
Assoc. Landscape Contractors of Am., Michigan State Univ. Horticulture Club **[7508]**, East Lansing, MI
Assoc. Landscape Contractors of Am., Milwaukee Area Tech. Coll. **[18884]**, Mequon, WI
Assoc. Landscape Contractors of Am., Ohio State Univ. **[14320]**, Columbus, OH
Assoc. Landscape Contractors of Am., Ohio State Univ./Agricultural Tech. Inst. **[17315]**, Wooster, OH
Assoc. Landscape Contractors of Am., Parkland Coll. **[500]**, Champaign, IL
Assoc. Landscape Contractors of Am., Purdue Univ. **[6476]**, West Lafayette, IN
Assoc. Recyclers of Wisconsin **[19479]**, Plover, WI
Assoc. Risk Managers of Ohio **[16478]**, Powell, OH
Assoc. Roofing Contractors of Maryland **[3359]**, Rosemont, IL
Assoc. Students of Madison **[18480]**, Madison, WI
Assoc. Students of Madison, the Student Govt. at the Univ. of Wisconsin - Madison **[★18480]**
Assoc. Underground Contractors-West Michigan Region **[9264]**, Okemos, MI
Assn. for Accounting Admin., Illinois Chap. **[1541]**, East Peoria, IL
Assn. for Accounting Admin., Indiana Chap. **[4166]**, Bedford, IN
Assn. for Accounting Admin., Michigan Chap. **[9265]**, Okemos, MI
Assn. for Accounting Admin., Minn Dak Chap. **[11785]**, Minnetonka, MN
Assn. for Accounting Admin., Ohio Chap. **[13039]**, Akron, OH
Assn. for the Advancement of Arts Educ. **[★13855]**
Assn. for the Advancement of Hmong Women in Minnesota **[11524]**, Minneapolis, MN
Assn. of Artists and Craftsmen of Porter County **[4351]**, Chesterton, IN
Assn. of Black Psychologists, Mid-West Region **[739]**, Chicago, IL
Assn. of Certified Fraud Examiners, Central Indiana Chap. No. 52 **[5042]**, Indianapolis, IN
Assn. of Certified Fraud Examiners, Central Ohio Chap. No. 39 **[15260]**, Gahanna, OH
Assn. of Certified Fraud Examiners, Cleveland Area Chap. No. 13 **[13040]**, Akron, OH
Assn. of Certified Fraud Examiners - Greater Chicago Chap. **[2506]**, Mokena, IL
Assn. of Certified Fraud Examiners, Northern Indiana Chap. No. 79 **[6379]**, Valparaiso, IN
Assn. of Certified Fraud Examiners, Southeast Michigan Area Chap., No. 37 **[9975]**, Troy, MI
Assn. of Certified Fraud Examiners, Southwest Ohio Chap. No. 46 **[15153]**, Fairfield, OH
Assn. of Certified Fraud Examiners, Toledo Chap. No. 122 **[15903]**, Maumee, OH
Assn. of Certified Fraud Examiners, Twin Cities Chap. No. 47 **[11525]**, Minneapolis, MN
Assn. of Certified Fraud Examiners, Wisconsin Area Chap. No. 32 **[19932]**, Verona, WI
Assn. for Children's Mental Hea. **[8552]**, Lansing, MI
Assn. of Christian Schools Intl., Ohio River Valley Region **[13547]**, Canton, OH
Assn. of Church Musicians **[★18459]**
Assn. of Clinical Res. Professionals - Circle City **[5043]**, Indianapolis, IN
Assn. of Clinical Res. Professionals - Northeastern Ohio Chap. **[15700]**, Lorain, OH
Assn. of Clinical Res. Professionals - Southern Wisconsin Chap. **[18967]**, Milwaukee, WI
Assn. of Colombians of Michigan **[9787]**, Southfield, MI
Assn. of Commerce and Indus. **[★7855]**
Assn. for Community Advocacy **[6680]**, Ann Arbor, MI
Assn. for Community Org. and Social Admin., Midwest Region **[14321]**, Columbus, OH
Assn. of Community Organizations for Reform Now, Akron **[13041]**, Akron, OH
Assn. of Community Organizations for Reform Now, Chicago **[740]**, Chicago, IL
Assn. of Community Organizations for Reform Now, Cincinnati **[13750]**, Cincinnati, OH
Assn. of Community Organizations for Reform Now, Cleveland **[14075]**, Cleveland, OH
Assn. of Community Organizations for Reform Now, Columbus **[14322]**, Columbus, OH
Assn. of Community Organizations for Reform Now, Dayton **[14854]**, Dayton, OH
Assn. of Community Organizations for Reform Now, Detroit **[7325]**, Detroit, MI
Assn. of Community Organizations for Reform Now, Flint **[7716]**, Flint, MI
Assn. of Community Organizations for Reform Now, Indianapolis **[5044]**, Indianapolis, IN
Assn. of Community Organizations for Reform Now, Lansing **[7509]**, East Lansing, MI
Assn. of Community Organizations for Reform Now, Madison **[18481]**, Madison, WI
Assn. of Community Organizations for Reform Now, Milwaukee **[18968]**, Milwaukee, WI
Assn. of Community Organizations for Reform Now, Minnesota **[12387]**, St. Paul, MN
Assn. of Community Organizations for Reform Now, Springfield, Illinois **[3537]**, Springfield, IL
Assn. of Community Organizations for Reform Now, Toledo **[16904]**, Toledo, OH
Assn. for Computing Machinery, Anderson Univ. **[4102]**, Anderson, IN
Assn. for Computing Machinery, Ashland Univ. **[13164]**, Ashland, OH
Assn. for Computing Machinery, Ball State Univ. Chap. **[5868]**, Muncie, IN
Assn. for Computing Machinery, Bryant and Stratton Parma Campus **[16357]**, Parma, OH
Assn. for Computing Machinery, Butler Univ. **[5045]**, Indianapolis, IN
Assn. for Computing Machinery, Carleton Coll. **[11912]**, Northfield, MN
Assn. for Computing Machinery, Case Western Reserve Univ. **[14076]**, Cleveland, OH
Assn. for Computing Machinery, Central Indiana Assn. for Computing Machinery-W Student Chap. **[4815]**, Greencastle, IN
Assn. for Computing Machinery, Central Michigan Univ. **[9100]**, Mount Pleasant, MI
Assn. for Computing Machinery, Chicago Military Acad.-Bronzville **[741]**, Chicago, IL
Assn. for Computing Machinery, Columbia Coll./Chicago **[742]**, Chicago, IL
Assn. for Computing Machinery, Concordia Coll. **[11819]**, Moorhead, MN
Assn. for Computing Machinery, Depauw Univ. **[4816]**, Greencastle, IN

Assn. for Computing Machinery, Eastern Michigan Univ. [10198], Ypsilanti, MI
Assn. for Computing Machinery, Franciscan Univ. of Steubenville [16760], Steubenville, OH
Assn. for Computing Machinery, Gustavus Adolphus Coll. [12613], St. Peter, MN
Assn. for Computing Machinery, Hope Coll. [8193], Holland, MI
Assn. for Computing Machinery, Illinois Inst. of Tech. [743], Chicago, IL
Assn. for Computing Machinery, Illinois State Univ. [2710], Normal, IL
Assn. for Computing Machinery, Illinois Wesleyan Univ. [263], Bloomington, IL
Assn. for Computing Machinery, Indiana Inst. of Tech. [4642], Fort Wayne, IN
Assn. for Computing Machinery, Indiana Univ. [4200], Bloomington, IN
Assn. for Computing Machinery, Indiana Univ. South Bend [6221], South Bend, IN
Assn. for Computing Machinery, John Carroll Univ. [17024], University Heights, OH
Assn. for Computing Machinery, Kent State Univ. [15539], Kent, OH
Assn. for Computing Machinery, Lawrence Technological Univ. [9788], Southfield, MI
Assn. for Computing Machinery, Macalester Coll. [12388], St. Paul, MN
Assn. for Computing Machinery, Marquette Univ. [18969], Milwaukee, WI
Assn. for Computing Machinery, Miami Univ. at Ohio [16323], Oxford, OH
Assn. for Computing Machinery, Michigan State Univ. [7510], East Lansing, MI
Assn. for Computing Machinery, Michigan Technological Univ. [8249], Houghton, MI
Assn. for Computing Machinery, Milwaukee School of Engg. [18970], Milwaukee, WI
Assn. for Computing Machinery, Minnesota State Univ. [★11375]
Assn. for Computing Machinery, Minnesota State Univ., Mankato [11375], Mankato, MN
Assn. for Computing Machinery, Minnesota State University/Moorhead [11820], Moorhead, MN
Assn. for Computing Machinery, Mount Vernon Nazarene Univ. [16080], Mount Vernon, OH
Assn. for Computing Machinery, Muskingum Coll. [16124], New Concord, OH
Assn. for Computing Machinery, Northern Chicago Student Chap. [1649], Evanston, IL
Assn. for Computing Machinery, Northern Michigan Univ. [8933], Marquette, MI
Assn. for Computing Machinery, Oberlin Coll. [16280], Oberlin, OH
Assn. for Computing Machinery, Ohio Northern Univ. [13009], Ada, OH
Assn. for Computing Machinery, Ohio State Univ. [14323], Columbus, OH
Assn. for Computing Machinery; Ohio Univ. Chap. of the [13213], Athens, OH
Assn. for Computing Machinery, Ohio Wesleyan Univ. [15000], Delaware, OH
Assn. for Computing Machinery, Olivet Coll. [9301], Olivet, MI
Assn. for Computing Machinery, Purdue Univ. Chap. [6477], West Lafayette, IN
Assn. for Computing Machinery, Rose-Hulman Inst. of Tech. [6315], Terre Haute, IN
Assn. for Computing Machinery, Saginaw Valley State Univ. [10026], University Center, MI
Assn. for Computing Machinery, St. Cloud State Univ. [12275], St. Cloud, MN
Assn. for Computing Machinery, St. Mary's Univ. of Minnesota [12946], Winona, MN
Assn. for Computing Machinery, Southern Illinois Univ. Carbondale [412], Carbondale, IL
Assn. for Computing Machinery, Southern Illinois Univ./Edwardsville [1557], Edwardsville, IL
Assn. for Computing Machinery, Univ. of Akron [13042], Akron, OH
Assn. for Computing Machinery, Univ. of Chicago [744], Chicago, IL
Assn. for Computing Machinery, Univ. of Detroit-Mercy [★7448]
Assn. for Computing Machinery, Univ. of Evansville [4531], Evansville, IN
Assn. for Computing Machinery, Univ. of ILL/Urbana-Champaign [3807], Urbana, IL
Assn. for Computing Machinery, Univ. of Illinois/Chicago [745], Chicago, IL
Assn. for Computing Machinery, Univ. of Michigan [6681], Ann Arbor, MI
Assn. for Computing Machinery, Univ. of Michigan-Dearborn [7249], Dearborn, MI
Assn. for Computing Machinery, Univ. of Michigan/Flint [7717], Flint, MI
Assn. for Computing Machinery, Univ. of Minnesota/Duluth [10807], Duluth, MN
Assn. for Computing Machinery, Univ. of Minnesota/Minneapolis [★11526]
Assn. for Computing Machinery, Univ. of Minnesota/Morris [11837], Morris, MN
Assn. for Computing Machinery, Univ. of Minnesota Student Chap. [11526], Minneapolis, MN
Assn. for Computing Machinery, Univ. of Notre Dame [6003], Notre Dame, IN
Assn. for Computing Machinery, Univ. of Toledo [16905], Toledo, OH
Assn. for Computing Machinery, Univ. of Wisconsin/Eau Claire [17865], Eau Claire, WI
Assn. for Computing Machinery, Univ. of Wisconsin/Madison [18482], Madison, WI
Assn. for Computing Machinery, Univ. of Wisconsin/Milwaukee [18971], Milwaukee, WI
Assn. for Computing Machinery, Univ. of Wisconsin/Platteville [19463], Platteville, WI
Assn. for Computing Machinery, Univ. of Wisconsin/River Falls [19640], River Falls, WI
Assn. for Computing Machinery, Walsh Coll. [9976], Troy, MI
Assn. for Computing Machinery, Wayne State Univ. [7326], Detroit, MI
Assn. for Computing Machinery, Western Illinois Univ. [2367], Macomb, IL
Assn. for Computing Machinery, Wilmington Coll. [17287], Wilmington, OH
Assn. for Computing Machinery, Winona State Univ. [12947], Winona, MN
Association for Computing Machinery, Wittenberg University [16721], Springfield, OH
Assn. for Computing Machinery, Wright State Univ. [14855], Dayton, OH
Assn. for Computing Machinery, Xavier Univ. [13751], Cincinnati, OH
Assn. for Conflict Resolution, Chicago Area Chap. [3746], Sycamore, IL
Assn. of Consultants to Nonprofits [746], Chicago, IL
Assn. for Corporate Growth, Chicago Chap. [3968], Westmont, IL
Assn. for Corporate Growth, Detroit Chap. [★6682]
Assn. for Corporate Growth, Greater Cincinnati Chap. [13752], Cincinnati, OH
Assn. for Corporate Growth, Minnesota Chap. [10880], East Bethel, MN
Assn. for Corporate Growth, Southeast Michigan Chap. [6682], Ann Arbor, MI
Assn. for Corporate Growth, Western Michigan Chap. [7911], Grand Rapids, MI
Assn. for Corporate Growth, Wisconsin Chap. [18038], Germantown, WI
Assn. of Descendents of the Shoah - Illinois [747], Chicago, IL
Assn. for the Developmentally Disabled in Woodford County [1643], Eureka, IL
Assn. for Educ. and Rehabilitation of the Blind and Visually Impaired, Wisconsin Chap. [19909], Tomahawk, WI
Assn. of Energy Engineers, Illinois/Chicago [748], Chicago, IL
Assn. of Energy Engineers, Michigan/East Michigan [9256], Oak Park, MI
Assn. of Energy Engineers, Minnesota/Twin Cities Chap. [11527], Minneapolis, MN
Assn. of Energy Engineers, Ohio/Northern - Cleveland/Akron [14077], Cleveland, OH
Assn. of Energy Engineers, Ohio/West Central Ohio [14856], Dayton, OH
Assn. of Energy Engineers, West Michigan Chap. [7912], Grand Rapids, MI
Assn. of Engg. Geologists - North Central Sect. [1650], Evanston, IL
Assn. of Eritreans and their Friends in Michigan [7511], East Lansing, MI
Assn. Executives Forum of Chicago [★749]
Assn. Forum [★749]
Assn. Forum of Chicagoland [749], Chicago, IL
Assn. of Fundraising Professionals - Greater Detroit [7638], Farmington, MI
Assn. of Govt. Accountants - Central Ohio Chap. [14324], Columbus, OH
Assn. of Govt. Accountants - Chicago Chap. [750], Chicago, IL
Assn. of Govt. Accountants - Cleveland Chap. [14078], Cleveland, OH
Assn. of Govt. Accountants - Indianapolis Chap. [5046], Indianapolis, IN
Assn. of Govt. Accountants - Southern Wisconsin Chap. [18483], Madison, WI
Assn. of HMOs in Michigan [★8617]
Assn. of Illinois Middle-Level Schools [501], Champaign, IL
Assn. of Illinois Soil and Water Conservation Districts [3538], Springfield, IL
Assn. of Independent Colls. and Universities of Ohio [14325], Columbus, OH
Assn. of Independent Commercial Producers/Midwest [751], Chicago, IL
Assn. of Independent Commercial Producers/Minnesota [11528], Minneapolis, MN
Assn. of Indiana Coll. Stores [6088], Richmond, IN
Assn. of Indiana Counties [5047], Indianapolis, IN
Assn. for Indiana Media Educators [5728], Marion, IN
Assn. of Indiana Museums [5048], Indianapolis, IN
Assn. for Individual Development of Aurora, IL [110], Aurora, IL
Assn. for Institutional Res. in the Upper Midwest [18484], Madison, WI
Assn. of Insurance Compliance Professionals, Great Lakes Chap. [1860], Glenview, IL
Assn. for Investment Mgt. and Res., Cleveland Soc. [★14104]
Assn. for Iron and Steel Tech. Midwest Chap. [3503], South Holland, IL
Assn. for Iron and Steel Tech. Northeastern Ohio Chap. [13112], Alliance, OH
Assn. for Iron and Steel Tech. Ohio Valley Chap. [13753], Cincinnati, OH
Assn. of Jewish Libraries - Cleveland (Greater Cleveland) [14244], Cleveland Heights, OH
Assn. of Late-Deafened Adults - Chicago [194], Bedford Park, IL
Assn. of Late-Deafened Adults - Freeport [1337], Dakota, IL
Assn. of Late-Deafened Adults - Midwest [14326], Columbus, OH
Assn. of Legal Administrators, Cleveland Chap. [14079], Cleveland, OH
Assn. of Legal Administrators, Columbus Chap. [14327], Columbus, OH
Assn. of Legal Administrators, Cyber Chap. [3008], Peoria, IL
Assn. of Lutheran Secondary Schools [18885], Mequon, WI
Assn. of Medical School Microbiology and Immunology Chairs [7327], Detroit, MI
Assn. of Midwest Fish and Game Commissioners [★19599]
Assn. of Midwest Fish and Wildlife Agencies [★19599]
Assn. of Midwest Fish and Wildlife Commissioners [★19599]
Assn. of Minnesota Counties [12389], St. Paul, MN
Assn. of Municipal Contractors [★3536]
Assn. of Nurses in AIDS Care [13043], Akron, OH
Assn. of Ohio Hea. Commissioners [14328], Columbus, OH
Assn. of Ohio Life Insurance Companies [14329], Columbus, OH
Assn. of Ohio Philanthropic Homes and Housing and Services for the Aging [14330], Columbus, OH
Assn. of Old Crows, Crane Roost [4423], Crane, IN
Assn. of Old Crows, Windy City Chap. [3338], Rolling Meadows, IL
Assn. of Pool and Spa Professionals [3980], Wheaton, IL
Assn. for Preservation Tech. Intl., Ohio Valley Chap. [13754], Cincinnati, OH
Assn. of Professional Researchers for Advancement, Illinois Chap. [752], Chicago, IL
Assn. for Professionals in Infection Control and Epidemiology, Chicago [753], Chicago, IL

Assn. for Professionals in Infection Control and Epidemiology, Greater Detroit **[7167]**, Clawson, MI
Assn. for Professionals in Infection Control and Epidemiology, Indiana Chap. **[4946]**, Huntington, IN
Assn. for Professionals in Infection Control and Epidemiology, Minnesota Chap. **[12390]**, St. Paul, MN
Assn. for Professionals in Infection Control and Epidemiology, Northwest Ohio **[16906]**, Toledo, OH
Assn. for Psychological Type - Chicago **[754]**, Chicago, IL
Assn. for Psychological Type - Columbus **[14331]**, Columbus, OH
Assn. for Psychological Type - Detroit **[7008]**, Brighton, MI
Assn. for Psychological Type - Greater Cincinnati **[16024]**, Milford, OH
Assn. for Psychological Type - Indiana **[5049]**, Indianapolis, IN
Assn. for Psychological Type - Interest Gp., Fox River Valley **[17970]**, Fond du Lac, WI
Assn. for Psychological Type - LaCrosse **[18337]**, La Crosse, WI
Assn. for Psychological Type - Madison **[18485]**, Madison, WI
Assn. for Psychological Type - Twin Cities **[11448]**, Medicine Lake, MN
Assn. of Realtors; Greater Lansing **[8572]**, Lansing, MI
Assn. of Residential Resources in Minnesota **[12676]**, South St. Paul, MN
Assn. for Retarded Citizens **[★18476]**
Assn. for Retarded Citizens/Allegan County **[★6604]**
Assn. for Retarded Citizens of Illinois **[★2045]**
Assn. for Retarded Citizens, Minnesota Off. **[★12383]**
Assn. of Retarded Citizens of Ohio **[★14316]**
Assn. for Retarded Citizens - Vanderburgh County **[4532]**, Evansville, IN
Assn. of the U.S. Army, 19th Star Chap. **[6191]**, Shelbyville, IN
Assn. of the U.S. Army, Buckeye Landpower **[13044]**, Akron, OH
Assn. of the U.S. Army, Central Ohio **[14332]**, Columbus, OH
Assn. of the U.S. Army, Detroit **[8831]**, Livonia, MI
Assn. of the U.S. Army, Fort Sheridan - Chicago **[4034]**, Winnetka, IL
Assn. of the U.S. Army, GEN John W. Vessey Jr. - Minnesota **[19662]**, Sarona, WI
Assn. of the U.S. Army, Indiana **[5050]**, Indianapolis, IN
Assn. of the U.S. Army, Major Samuel Woodfill - Cincinnati **[13620]**, Centerville, OH
Assn. of the U.S. Army, MG Robert D. McCoy **[19751]**, Sparta, WI
Assn. of the U.S. Army, Milwaukee **[18972]**, Milwaukee, WI
Assn. of the U.S. Army, Newton D. Baker **[16784]**, Strongsville, OH
Assn. of the U.S. Army, South Bend **[5688]**, Logansport, IN
Assn. of the U.S. Army, Southwestern Michigan **[6848]**, Battle Creek, MI
Assn. for Unmanned Vehicle Syss. Intl., Wright Kettering Chap. **[17356]**, Wright-Patterson AFB, OH
Assn. of Wisconsin Cleaning Contractors **[18973]**, Milwaukee, WI
Assn. of Wisconsin Hea. Maintenance Organizations **[★18653]**
Assn. of Wisconsin School Administrators **[18486]**, Madison, WI
Assn. of Wisconsin Snowmobile Clubs **[17488]**, Appleton, WI
Assn. for Women in Computing - Twin Cities Chap. **[12222]**, Roseville, MN
Assn. for Women in Sci., Bloomington **[4201]**, Bloomington, IN
Assn. for Women in Sci., Central Ohio **[14333]**, Columbus, OH
Assn. for Women in Sci., Detroit **[6683]**, Ann Arbor, MI
Assn. for Women in Sci., Heart of Illinois **[264]**, Bloomington, IL
Association for Women in Science, Indianapolis **[5051]**, Indianapolis, IN
Assn. for Women in Sci., Miami Valley **[14857]**, Dayton, OH
Assn. for Women in Sci., Univ. of Michigan-Ann Arbor **[6684]**, Ann Arbor, MI
Assn. for Women in Sci., Washtenaw Community Coll. **[6685]**, Ann Arbor, MI
Assn. of Women's Hea., Obstetric and Neonatal Nurses - Bloomington Chap. **[4202]**, Bloomington, IN
Assn. of Women's Hea., Obstetric and Neonatal Nurses - Evansville Chap. **[6316]**, Terre Haute, IN
Assn. of Women's Hea., Obstetric and Neonatal Nurses, Illinois Sect. **[2878]**, Orland Park, IL
Assn. of Women's Hea., Obstetric and Neonatal Nurses, Indiana Sect. **[5052]**, Indianapolis, IN
Assn. of Women's Hea., Obstetric and Neonatal Nurses - Indianapolis Chap. **[5053]**, Indianapolis, IN
Assn. of Women's Hea., Obstetric and Neonatal Nurses - Lafayette/ Sagamore Chap. **[6478]**, West Lafayette, IN
Assn. of Women's Hea., Obstetric and Neonatal Nurses - Marian/ Anderson/Muncie Chap. **[5869]**, Muncie, IN
Assn. of Women's Hea., Obstetric and Neonatal Nurses - Michiana Chap. **[4808]**, Granger, IN
Assn. of Women's Hea., Obstetric and Neonatal Nurses - Michigan Sect. **[6879]**, Bay City, MI
Assn. of Women's Hea., Obstetric and Neonatal Nurses - Northeast Chap. **[5675]**, Leo, IN
Assn. of Women's Hea., Obstetric and Neonatal Nurses - Northwest Chap. **[6061]**, Porter, IN
Assn. of Women's Hea., Obstetric and Neonatal Nurses - Ohio Sect. **[13621]**, Centerville, OH
Assn. of Women's Hea., Obstetric and Neonatal Nurses, Southern Illinois Chap. **[2768]**, O Fallon, IL
Assn. of Women's Hea., Obstetric and Neonatal Nurses - West Central Illiana Chap. **[6317]**, Terre Haute, IN

Associations
Amer. Soc. of Golf Course Architects **[17667]**, Brookfield, WI
Assn. of Descendents of the Shoah - Illinois **[747]**, Chicago, IL
Assn. Forum of Chicagoland **[749]**, Chicago, IL
Chicago District Golf Assn. **[2239]**, Lemont, IL
Cincinnati Soc. of Assn. Executives **[13799]**, Cincinnati, OH
Columbus District Golf Assn. **[14382]**, Columbus, OH
Greater Cincinnati Golf Assn. **[13846]**, Cincinnati, OH
Greater Cleveland Soc. of Assn. Executives **[13447]**, Brunswick, OH
Hermantown Arena Bd. **[11149]**, Hermantown, MN
Illinois Junior Golf Assn. **[2241]**, Lemont, IL
Illinois Movers' and Warehousemen's Assn. **[3617]**, Springfield, IL
Illinois Soc. of Assn. Executives **[3635]**, Springfield, IL
Indiana Assn. of Nonprofit Orgs. **[5178]**, Indianapolis, IN
Indiana Golf Assn. **[4749]**, Franklin, IN
Indiana Junior Golf Assn. **[5616]**, Lafayette, IN
Indiana Soc. of Assn. Executives **[5301]**, Indianapolis, IN
Invasive Plants Assn. of Wisconsin **[18534]**, Madison, WI
Little Creek Special Equestrians **[4337]**, Centerpoint, IN
Main St. Wausau **[20037]**, Wausau, WI
Miami Valley Golf Assn. **[14911]**, Dayton, OH
Michigan Soc. of Assn. Executives **[7548]**, East Lansing, MI
Midwest Soc. of Assn. Executives **[12445]**, St. Paul, MN
Minnesota Coun. of Nonprofits **[12472]**, St. Paul, MN
Northern Ohio Golf Assn. **[16237]**, North Olmsted, OH
OCIA Michigan, Chap. 2 **[9560]**, Rosebush, MI
Ohio Assn. of Nonprofit Organizations **[14560]**, Columbus, OH
Ohio Golf Assn. **[14617]**, Columbus, OH
Ohio Soc. of Assn. Executives **[17351]**, Worthington, OH
Rosenwald Harlanites **[8789]**, Lathrup Village, MI
Wisconsin NFA Shooters **[19973]**, Watertown, WI
Wisconsin Soc. of Assn. Executives **[19182]**, Milwaukee, WI
Wisconsin State Golf Assn. **[17687]**, Brookfield, WI

ASTD, South Central Wisconsin Chap. **[3430]**, Schaumburg, IL
Asthma and Allergy Found. of Am. Michigan State Chap. **[9789]**, Southfield, MI
Asthma Consortium; Chicago **[791]**, Chicago, IL
Astoria Lions Club **[96]**, Astoria, IL
Astronautics, Case Western Reserve Univ; Amer. Inst. of Aeronautics and **[14051]**, Cleveland, OH
Astronomical Assn. of Southern Illinois **[413]**, Carbondale, IL
Astronomical Soc; Chicago **[792]**, Chicago, IL
Astronomical Soc; La Crosse Area **[18351]**, La Crosse, WI
Astronomical Soc. of Michigan **[9394]**, Plymouth, MI

Astronomy
Amateur Astronomers of Jackson **[8355]**, Jackson, MI
Astronomical Assn. of Southern Illinois **[413]**, Carbondale, IL
Astronomical Soc. of Michigan **[9394]**, Plymouth, MI
Astronomy for Youth **[15763]**, Mansfield, OH
Calumet Astronomical Soc. **[4854]**, Griffith, IN
Capital Area Astronomy Assn. **[9459]**, Potterville, MI
Capital Area Astronomy Club **[7580]**, Eaton Rapids, MI
Champaign-Urbana Astronomical Soc. **[511]**, Champaign, IL
Chicago Astronomical Soc. **[792]**, Chicago, IL
Chippewa Valley Astronomical Soc. **[17952]**, Fall Creek, WI
Cincinnati Astronomical Soc. **[15874]**, Mason, OH
Door Peninsula Astronomical Soc. **[19837]**, Sturgeon Bay, WI
East Central Wisconsin Astronomers **[19456]**, Pine River, WI
Fort Wayne Astronomical Soc. **[4654]**, Fort Wayne, IN
Fox Valley Astronomical Soc. **[3883]**, Wasco, IL
Indiana Coun. on Outdoor Lightning Educ. **[5219]**, Indianapolis, IN
Kalamazoo Astronomical Soc. **[8435]**, Kalamazoo, MI
Kankakee Valley Astronomical Soc. **[5983]**, North Judson, IN
La Crosse Area Astronomical Soc. **[18351]**, La Crosse, WI
Marquette Astronomical Soc. **[8939]**, Marquette, MI
Miami Valley Astronomical Soc. **[16011]**, Middletown, OH
Michiana Astronomical Soc. **[6238]**, South Bend, IN
Milwaukee Astronomical Soc. **[19291]**, New Berlin, WI
Naperville Astronomical Association **[2649]**, Naperville, IL
Near Earth Object Search Soc. **[14529]**, Columbus, OH
Neville Public Museum Astronomical Soc. **[18119]**, Green Bay, WI
North Central Region of the Astronomical League **[17509]**, Appleton, WI
Northeast Wisconsin Stargazers **[19399]**, Oshkosh, WI
Northern Ohio Valley Astronomy Educators **[16571]**, St. Clairsville, OH
Northwest Suburban Astronomers **[3441]**, Schaumburg, IL
Oakland Astronomy Club **[8516]**, Lake Orion, MI
Peoria Astronomical Soc. **[1522]**, Dunlap, IL
Popular Astronomy Club **[3249]**, Rock Island, IL
Racine Astronomical Soc. **[19566]**, Racine, WI
River Bend Astronomy Club **[3399]**, St. Jacob, IL
Rochester Astronomy Club **[12173]**, Rochester, MN
Sandusky Valley Amateur Astronomy Club **[16860]**, Tiffin, OH
Sangamon Astronomical Soc. **[3671]**, Springfield, IL

Sheboygan Astronomical Soc. **[19378]**, Oostburg, WI
Shoreline Amateur Astronomy Assn. **[8220]**, Holland, MI
Skokie Valley Astronomers **[3879]**, Warrenville, IL
Steele County Astronomical Soc. **[11970]**, Owatonna, MN
Stillwater Stargazers **[17007]**, Troy, OH
Stonebelt Stargazers **[4177]**, Bedford, IN
Twin City Amateur Astronomers **[2734]**, Normal, IL
Wabash Valley Astronomical Soc. **[6503]**, West Lafayette, IN
Warren Astronomical Soc. **[10074]**, Warren, MI
Warsaw Astronomical Soc. **[6541]**, Winona Lake, IN
Wehr Astronomical Soc. **[18013]**, Franklin, WI
Astronomy for Youth **[15763]**, Mansfield, OH
Atheist
Campus Atheists and Secular Humanists **[11538]**, Minneapolis, MN
Fellowship of Freethinkers, Bradley Univ. **[3017]**, Peoria, IL
Madison Atheists, Univ. of Wisconsin **[18550]**, Madison, WI
Michigan Atheists **[9051]**, Milford, MI
Minnesota Atheists **[11628]**, Minneapolis, MN
Southeast Wisconsin FreeThinkers **[18889]**, Mequon, WI
ATHENA Found. **[★755]**
ATHENA Intl. **[755]**, Chicago, IL
Athens Bicycle Club **[13197]**, Athens, OH
Athens County Bd. of Realtors **[13198]**, Athens, OH
Athens County Historical Soc. and Museum **[★13212]**
Athens High School - Young Life **[13199]**, Athens, OH
Athens Middle School - YoungLife **[13200]**, Athens, OH
Athens-Union City Lions Club **[10020]**, Union City, MI
Athletes
Step 1 All-Stars **[14742]**, Columbus, OH
Athletes United for Spiritual Empowerment; Christian **[11543]**, Minneapolis, MN
Athletic Activities League; Rochester Police **[12181]**, Rochester, MN
Athletic Administrators Assn; Michigan Interscholastic **[8851]**, Livonia, MI
Athletic Association; Byron Area **[8817]**, Linden, MI
Athletic Boosters; Female Alumni **[10184]**, Wyandotte, MI
Athletic Boosters; Hilliard Davidson **[15434]**, Hilliard, OH
Athletic Club; Birmingham **[6978]**, Bloomfield Hills, MI
Athletic Conf; Great Rivers **[2059]**, Ina, IL
Athletic League; East Lansing Police **[7516]**, East Lansing, MI
Athletics
Athletics Directors Assn., Div. I-AAA **[14080]**, Cleveland, OH
Central Illinois District Amateur Athletic Union **[5914]**, Nashville, IN
Female Alumni Athletic Boosters **[10184]**, Wyandotte, MI
Great Rivers Athletic Conf. **[2059]**, Ina, IL
Hilliard Davidson Athletic Boosters **[15434]**, Hilliard, OH
Indiana District Amateur Athletic Union **[5227]**, Indianapolis, IN
Lake Erie District Amateur Athletic Union **[16680]**, Solon, OH
Michigan Amateur Athletic Union **[9565]**, Roseville, MI
Minnesota Amateur Athletic Union **[11188]**, Hopkins, MN
Ohio District Amateur Athletic Union **[13936]**, Cincinnati, OH
Tri-State Athletics **[14010]**, Cincinnati, OH
Athletics Directors Assn., Div. I-AAA **[14080]**, Cleveland, OH
Athletics and Recreation; Rochester Area Disabled **[12172]**, Rochester, MN
Athletics; Tri-State **[14010]**, Cincinnati, OH
Atlanta Area Chamber of Commerce **[6802]**, Atlanta, MI
Attica Lions Club **[13224]**, Attica, OH
Attorneys
Bay Arts Coun. **[6883]**, Bay City, MI
Cincinnati Bar Assn. **[13777]**, Cincinnati, OH
Civil Trial Counsel of Wisconsin **[18993]**, Milwaukee, WI
Cook County Bar Assn. **[856]**, Chicago, IL
D. Augustus Straker Bar Assn. **[9980]**, Troy, MI
Defense Trial Counsel of Indiana **[5100]**, Indianapolis, IN
Fed. Bar Assn., Columbus Chap. **[14432]**, Columbus, OH
Fed. Bar Assn., Western Michigan 869/06 **[7929]**, Grand Rapids, MI
Genesee County Bar Assn. **[7736]**, Flint, MI
Grand Rapids Bar Assn. **[7945]**, Grand Rapids, MI
Illinois State Bar Assn. **[3638]**, Springfield, IL
Illinois Trial Lawyers Assn. **[3645]**, Springfield, IL
Indiana State Bar Assn. **[5313]**, Indianapolis, IN
James Kimbrough Law Assn. **[4782]**, Gary, IN
Kane County Bar Assn. **[1796]**, Geneva, IL
Lake County Bar Assn. **[4432]**, Crown Point, IN
Lansing Black Lawyers Assn. **[8588]**, Lansing, MI
Lorain County Bar Assn. **[15117]**, Elyria, OH
Macomb County Bar Assn. **[9087]**, Mount Clemens, MI
Michigan Assn. of Municipal Attorneys **[6719]**, Ann Arbor, MI
Michigan Lawyers Auxiliary **[8680]**, Lansing, MI
Michigan Trial Lawyers Assn. **[8723]**, Lansing, MI
Milwaukee Bar Assn. **[19055]**, Milwaukee, WI
Minnesota Assn. of Black Lawyers **[11624]**, Minneapolis, MN
Minnesota Trial Lawyers Assn. **[11677]**, Minneapolis, MN
Minnesota Women Lawyers **[11683]**, Minneapolis, MN
Oakland County Bar Assn. **[6990]**, Bloomfield Hills, MI
Ohio Acad. of Trial Lawyers **[14535]**, Columbus, OH
Ohio Assn. of Civil Trial Attorneys **[14547]**, Columbus, OH
Ohio Prosecuting Attorneys Assn. **[14660]**, Columbus, OH
Ohio State Bar Assn. **[14680]**, Columbus, OH
Prosecuting Attorneys Coordinating Coun. **[8755]**, Lansing, MI
State Bar of Michigan **[8762]**, Lansing, MI
State Bar of Wisconsin **[18623]**, Madison, WI
Toledo Bar Assn. **[16968]**, Toledo, OH
Trumbull County Bar Assn. **[17111]**, Warren, OH
Vanezetti Hamilton Bar Assn. **[6780]**, Ann Arbor, MI
Washtenaw County Bar Assn. **[6784]**, Ann Arbor, MI
West Suburban Bar Assn. **[1715]**, Forest Park, IL
Wisconsin Acad. of Trial Lawyers **[18640]**, Madison, WI
Wisconsin Assn. African-Amer. Attorneys **[19153]**, Milwaukee, WI
Wolverine Bar Assn. **[7455]**, Detroit, MI
Women's Bar Assn. of Illinois **[1238]**, Chicago, IL
Attorneys; Michigan Assn. of Municipal **[6719]**, Ann Arbor, MI
Attorneys; Ohio Assn. of Civil Trial **[14547]**, Columbus, OH
Atwater Lions Club **[10345]**, Atwater, MN
Atwater Lions Club - Ohio **[13227]**, Atwater, OH
Atwater School PTA **[19731]**, Shorewood, WI
Au Gres Chamber of Commerce **[6805]**, Au Gres, MI
Auburn Area Chamber of Commerce **[6807]**, Auburn, MI
Auburn Chamber of Commerce **[4138]**, Auburn, IN
Auburn Duesey Walkers **[4937]**, Huntertown, IN
Auburn Lions Club - Michigan **[6808]**, Auburn, MI
Auctions
Indiana Auctioneers Assn. **[6484]**, West Lafayette, IN
Michigan State Auctioneers Assn. **[7984]**, Grand Rapids, MI
Ohio Auctioneers Assn. **[14570]**, Columbus, OH
Wisconsin Auctioneers Assn. **[18913]**, Middleton, WI
Audio Engg. Soc., Ball State Univ. Sect. **[5870]**, Muncie, IN
Audio Engg. Soc., Cincinnati Sect. **[15872]**, Mason, OH
Audio Engg. Soc., Columbia Coll. Sect. **[756]**, Chicago, IL
Audio Engg. Soc., Detroit Sect. **[9790]**, Southfield, MI
Audio Engg. Soc., Music Tech Coll. Sect. **[12391]**, St. Paul, MN
Audio Engg. Soc., Ohio Univ. Sect. **[13201]**, Athens, OH
Audio Engg. Soc., Ridgewater Coll., Hutchinson Campus Sect. **[11204]**, Hutchinson, MN
Audio Engg. Soc., Univ. of Cincinnati Sect. **[13755]**, Cincinnati, OH
Audio Engg. Soc., Upper Midwest Sect. **[10650]**, Chaska, MN
Audio Engg. Soc., West Michigan Sect. **[6849]**, Battle Creek, MI
Audiovisual Assn; Wisconsin **[★17649]**
Audubon Aullwood Center; Natl. **[★14858]**
Audubon Chap. of Minneapolis **[11529]**, Minneapolis, MN
Audubon Coun. of Illinois **[382]**, Byron, IL
Audubon Ohio **[14334]**, Columbus, OH
Audubon Soc., Dayton Chap; Natl. **[★14858]**
Audubon Soc; Illinois **[1349]**, Danville, IL
Audubon Soc., Illinois - McHenry County **[★4060]**
Audubon Soc; Michigan **[8632]**, Lansing, MI
Audubon Soc. of Ohio - Cincinnati Chap. **[13756]**, Cincinnati, OH
Audubon Soc; Oxford **[16325]**, Oxford, OH
Auglaize County Arc **[16117]**, New Bremen, OH
Auglaize County Genealogical Soc. **[17089]**, Wapakoneta, OH
Aullwood Audubon Center and Farm **[14858]**, Dayton, OH
Aurora Area Chamber of Commerce **[13230]**, Aurora, OH
Aurora Area Convention and Tourism Coun. **[111]**, Aurora, IL
Aurora Community Stud. Circles **[112]**, Aurora, IL
Aurora Lions Club **[10348]**, Aurora, MN
Aurora Tri-County Assn. of Realtors **[113]**, Aurora, IL
Aurora Univ. Biology Club **[114]**, Aurora, IL
Austin Area Chamber of Commerce **[10353]**, Austin, MN
Austin-Bailey Hea. and Wellness Found. **[13548]**, Canton, OH
Austin Childcare Providers Network **[757]**, Chicago, IL
Austin Lions Club **[10354]**, Austin, MN
Austin Philatelic Club **[1680]**, Evergreen Park, IL
Austintown Lions Club **[13236]**, Austintown, OH
Authors
Intl. Thomas Merton Soc. - Chicago, IL **[992]**, Chicago, IL
Intl. Thomas Merton Soc. - Cincinnati, OH **[14253]**, Cleves, OH
Jane Austen Soc. of North Am., Greater Chicago Region **[1002]**, Chicago, IL
Jane Austen Soc. of North Am., Ohio, Dayton **[14900]**, Dayton, OH
Jane Austen Soc. of North Am., Wisconsin **[18536]**, Madison, WI
Autism
Autism Advocates of Indiana **[4602]**, Fishers, IN
Autism Soc. of Am., Madison Area Chap. **[18487]**, Madison, WI
Autism Soc. of Am., Northwest Suburban Chap. **[3431]**, Schaumburg, IL
Autism Soc. of Am., Ohio Chap. **[13045]**, Akron, OH
Autism Soc. of Indiana **[5054]**, Indianapolis, IN
Autism Soc. of Michigan **[8553]**, Lansing, MI
Autism Advocates of Indiana **[4602]**, Fishers, IN
Autism Soc. of Am., Madison Area Chap. **[18487]**, Madison, WI
Autism Soc. of Am., Northwest Suburban Chap. **[3431]**, Schaumburg, IL
Autism Soc. of Am., Ohio Chap. **[13045]**, Akron, OH
Autism Soc. of Indiana **[5054]**, Indianapolis, IN
Autism Soc. of Michigan **[8553]**, Lansing, MI
Automatic Laundry and Cleaning Coun; Midwest **[★1500]**
Automatic Transmission Rebuilders Assn., Midwest Chap. **[18338]**, La Crosse, WI
Automobile
4 Wheels to Freedom 4WD Club **[6189]**, Shelbyville, IN

AAA Akron Auto Club **[13014]**, Akron, OH
AAA Akron Auto. Club **[13015]**, Akron, OH
AAA Akron Auto. Club **[14816]**, Cuyahoga Falls, OH
AAA Akron Auto. Club **[15177]**, Fairlawn, OH
AAA Akron Auto. Club **[15479]**, Hudson, OH
AAA Ashland County **[13157]**, Ashland, OH
AAA Barberton Auto. Club **[13251]**, Barberton, OH
AAA-Chicago Motor Club **[1448]**, Des Plaines, IL
AAA Cincinnati **[13681]**, Cincinnati, OH
AAA Cincinnati **[13682]**, Cincinnati, OH
AAA Cincinnati **[13684]**, Cincinnati, OH
AAA Cincinnati **[13683]**, Cincinnati, OH
AAA Cincinnati **[13686]**, Cincinnati, OH
AAA Cincinnati **[13685]**, Cincinnati, OH
AAA Cincinnati **[13687]**, Cincinnati, OH
AAA Cincinnati **[15616]**, Lebanon, OH
AAA Cincinnati **[16428]**, Piqua, OH
AAA Cincinnati **[16995]**, Troy, OH
AAA Columbiana County **[15074]**, East Liverpool, OH
AAA Hoosier Motor Club **[5859]**, Muncie, IN
AAA Hoosier Motor Club **[6302]**, Terre Haute, IN
AAA Massillon Auto. Club **[15879]**, Massillon, OH
AAA Miami Valley **[15555]**, Kettering, OH
AAA Michigan **[7004]**, Brighton, MI
AAA Michigan **[7242]**, Dearborn, MI
AAA Michigan **[7877]**, Grand Rapids, MI
AAA Michigan **[8091]**, Grosse Pointe Woods, MI
AAA Michigan **[8186]**, Holland, MI
AAA Michigan **[8353]**, Jackson, MI
AAA Michigan **[8485]**, Kentwood, MI
AAA Michigan **[8525]**, Lansing, MI
AAA Michigan **[8929]**, Marquette, MI
AAA Michigan **[9359]**, Petoskey, MI
AAA Michigan **[9427]**, Port Huron, MI
AAA Michigan **[9767]**, South Lyon, MI
AAA Michigan, Allen Park Off. **[6607]**, Allen Park, MI
AAA Minneapolis **[10457]**, Bloomington, MN
AAA Minneapolis **[11473]**, Minneapolis, MN
AAA Minnesota/Iowa **[10583]**, Burnsville, MN
AAA Minnesota/Iowa **[10793]**, Duluth, MN
AAA Minnesota/Iowa **[11080]**, Grand Rapids, MN
AAA Minnesota/Iowa **[11372]**, Mankato, MN
AAA Minnesota/Iowa **[12121]**, Rochester, MN
AAA Missouri **[35]**, Alton, IL
AAA Missouri **[197]**, Belleville, IL
AAA Missouri **[408]**, Carbondale, IL
AAA Northwest Ohio **[15898]**, Maumee, OH
AAA Northwest Ohio **[16300]**, Oregon, OH
AAA Northwest Ohio **[16823]**, Sylvania, OH
AAA Ohio Auto Club **[16568]**, St. Clairsville, OH
AAA Ohio Auto. Club **[13318]**, Bellefontaine, OH
AAA Ohio Auto. Club **[14264]**, Columbus, OH
AAA Ohio Auto. Club **[14263]**, Columbus, OH
AAA Ohio Auto. Club **[14265]**, Columbus, OH
AAA Ohio Auto. Club **[15376]**, Hamilton, OH
AAA Ohio Auto. Club **[15423]**, Hilliard, OH
AAA Ohio Auto. Club **[15641]**, Lima, OH
AAA Ohio Auto. Club **[15758]**, Mansfield, OH
AAA Ohio Auto. Club **[16598]**, Sandusky, OH
AAA Shelby County **[16662]**, Sidney, OH
AAA South Central Ohio **[15510]**, Jackson, OH
AAA South Central Ohio **[16465]**, Portsmouth, OH
AAA South Central Ohio **[16757]**, Steubenville, OH
AAA Tuscarawas County **[16144]**, New Philadelphia, OH
Air Vair Gp. **[15276]**, Galion, OH
Antique Auto. Club of Am., Illinois Region **[348]**, Brookfield, IL
Antique Auto. Club of Am., Illinois Region - Des Plaines Valley Chap. **[2312]**, Lockport, IL
Antique Auto. Club of Am., Illinois Region - Fox Valley Chap. **[1534]**, East Dundee, IL
Antique Auto. Club of Am., Illinois Region - Momence Chap. **[325]**, Bourbonnais, IL
Antique Auto. Club of Am., Illinois Region - North Shore Chap. **[1987]**, Highland Park, IL
Antique Auto. Club of Am., Illinois Region - Silver Springs Chap. **[3493]**, Somonauk, IL
Antique Auto. Club of Am., Lower Ohio Valley Evansville Region **[4274]**, Boonville, IN
Antique Auto. Club of Am., Minnesota Region - Capitol City Chap. **[10545]**, Brooklyn Park, MN
Antique Auto. Club of Am., Minnesota Region - Hiawatha Chap. **[12127]**, Rochester, MN
Antique Auto. Club of Am., Northwestern Michigan Region **[9924]**, Traverse City, MI
Antique Auto. Club of Am., Ohio Region **[15882]**, Massillon, OH
Antique Auto. Club of Am., Ohio Region - Canton Chap. **[16104]**, Navarre, OH
Antique Auto. Club of Am., Ohio Region - Commodore Perry Chap. **[15108]**, Elyria, OH
Antique Auto. Club of Am., Ohio Region - Meander Chap. **[16141]**, New Middletown, OH
Antique Auto. Club of Am., Ohio Region - Northern Chap. **[16522]**, Richfield, OH
Antique Auto. Club of Am., Ohio Region - Southern Chap. **[15473]**, Huber Heights, OH
Antique Auto. Club of Am., Ohio Region - Western Reserve Chap. **[16540]**, Rock Creek, OH
Antique Auto. Club of Am., Southern Illinois Region - Ohio Valley Chap. **[2482]**, Metropolis, IL
Antique Auto. Club of Am., Wisconsin Region **[18869]**, Menomonee Falls, WI
Antique Auto. Club of Am., Wolverine State Region **[6907]**, Belleville, MI
Auto. Dealers Alliance of Ohio **[13417]**, Brice, OH
Auto. Dealer's Assn. of Indiana **[5055]**, Indianapolis, IN
Avanti Owners Assn. Intl., Indiana Chap. **[4831]**, Greenfield, IN
Bedrock Jeepers **[7036]**, Burton, MI
BMW Car Club of Am., Badger Bimmers Chap. **[18983]**, Milwaukee, WI
BMW Car Club of Am., Buckeye Chap. **[14338]**, Columbus, OH
BMW Car Club of Am., Hoosier Chap. **[5059]**, Indianapolis, IN
BMW Car Club of Am., Illini Chap. **[2274]**, Lincoln, IL
BMW Car Club of Am., Michiana Chap. **[9445]**, Portage, MI
BMW Car Club of Am., Motor City Chap. **[7655]**, Farmington Hills, MI
BMW Car Club of Am., North Star Chap. **[11533]**, Minneapolis, MN
BMW Car Club of Am., Northern Ohio Chap. **[14819]**, Cuyahoga Falls, OH
BMW Car Club of Am., Windy City Chap. **[1861]**, Glenview, IL
Buckeye Corvettes **[13550]**, Canton, OH
Buckeye Triumphs **[15532]**, Johnstown, OH
Buckeye Vintage Thunderbird Club of Ohio **[16244]**, North Royalton, OH
Buick Club of Am. - Chicagoland Chap. **[3865]**, Villa Park, IL
Buick Club of Am. - Gopher State Chap. **[10725]**, Cottage Grove, MN
Capital City Corvair Club **[18495]**, Madison, WI
Capital City Corvette Club **[8558]**, Lansing, MI
Central Illinois Corvette Club **[3543]**, Springfield, IL
Central Illinois Jeep Club **[273]**, Bloomington, IL
Chicagoland Chap. of Avanti Owners Assn. Intl. **[3191]**, Richmond, IL
Chicagoland Sect. of the Mercedes-Benz Club of Am. **[374]**, Burr Ridge, IL
Chicagoland Thunderbirds **[2329]**, Lombard, IL
Cincinnati Corvette Club **[13782]**, Cincinnati, OH
Circle City Corvairs **[5088]**, Indianapolis, IN
Circle City Corvette Club **[5089]**, Indianapolis, IN
Classic Thunderbird Club of Wisconsin **[19499]**, Port Washington, WI
Competition Corvette Assn. **[15965]**, Mentor, OH
Corvair Minnesota **[12332]**, St. Louis Park, MN
Corvette Club of Michigan **[9513]**, Rochester Hills, MI
Corvette Troy **[16999]**, Troy, OH
Dayton-Buckeye Model 'A' Club **[15130]**, Englewood, OH
Detroit Area Corvair Club **[9893]**, Swartz Creek, MI
Detroit Auto Dealers Assn. **[9982]**, Troy, MI
Detroit Triumph Sportscar Club **[9655]**, St. Clair Shores, MI
Firewalker Four Wheel Drive Club **[1918]**, Gurnee, IL
Flint Corvette Club **[7729]**, Flint, MI
Fort Wayne Corvette Club **[4656]**, Fort Wayne, IN
Glass City Corvette Club **[17251]**, Whitehouse, OH
Glass Menagerie Corvette Club **[5123]**, Indianapolis, IN
Grand Valley Corvette Assn. **[8037]**, Grandville, MI
Great Lakes Four Wheel Drive Assn. **[9026]**, Midland, MI
Great Lakes SAAB Club **[8197]**, Holland, MI
Greater Dayton Corvette Club **[14891]**, Dayton, OH
Greater Metropolitan Auto. Dealers Assn. of Minnesota **[10910]**, Edina, MN
Hoosier Corvette Club **[5138]**, Indianapolis, IN
Hoosier Vintage Thunderbird Club **[4670]**, Fort Wayne, IN
Horseless Carriage Club of Am., Grand Rapids **[7054]**, Caledonia, MI
Illinois Auto. Dealers Assn. **[3584]**, Springfield, IL
Illinois Chap. Natl. Corvette Restorers Soc. **[226]**, Bensenville, IL
Illinois Four Wheel Drive Assn. **[2487]**, Midlothian, IL
Illinois Jaguar Club **[1662]**, Evanston, IL
Illinois Sports Owners Assn. **[1325]**, Crystal Lake, IL
Indiana Four Wheel Drive Assn. **[6092]**, Richmond, IN
Indiana Triumph Cars **[5331]**, Indianapolis, IN
Indianapolis Corvette Club **[5345]**, Indianapolis, IN
Indy Z Car Club **[5364]**, Indianapolis, IN
Intl. Edsel Club, Illinois Chap. **[3030]**, Peoria, IL
Intl. Edsel Club, Indiana Chap. **[5756]**, Martinsville, IN
Jackson Corvette Club **[8374]**, Jackson, MI
Jaguar Club of Greater Cincinnati **[15161]**, Fairfield, OH
Kalamazoo Corvette Club **[8438]**, Kalamazoo, MI
Kettle Moraine Corvette Club **[19698]**, Sheboygan, WI
Lake Shore Corvette Club **[16615]**, Sandusky, OH
Lakeshore Corvette Club **[10227]**, Zeeland, MI
Lambda Car Club, Detroit Region **[9585]**, Royal Oak, MI
Land of Lincoln Thunderbirds **[2083]**, Jacksonville, IL
Mad Anthony Corvair Club **[4691]**, Fort Wayne, IN
MBCA - Intl. Stars Sect. **[9237]**, Novi, MI
Medina Corvette Club **[17045]**, Valley City, OH
Mercedes Benz Club of Am. - 500 Sect. **[5404]**, Indianapolis, IN
Mercedes-Benz Club of Am. of the Western Michigan Sect. **[8291]**, Hudsonville, MI
Metro Detroit Chap. of Falcon Club of Am. **[6614]**, Allen Park, MI
Miami Valley Triumphs **[13315]**, Bellbrook, OH
Michiana Corvette Club **[6240]**, South Bend, IN
Michigan Towing Assn. **[9225]**, Northville, MI
Mid-Ohio Vair Force **[15435]**, Hilliard, OH
Midwest Corvette Club **[2491]**, Milan, IL
Midwest Sunbeam Registry **[12051]**, Prior Lake, MN
Milwaukee Corvair Club **[19558]**, Racine, WI
Minnesota Oldsmobile Club **[11323]**, Lino Lakes, MN
Minnesota SAAB Club **[11864]**, New Brighton, MN
Minnesota Triumphs **[11678]**, Minneapolis, MN
Model A Restorers Club, Calumet Region **[3771]**, Tinley Park, IL
Model A Restorers Club, Floral City A Region **[9065]**, Monroe, MI
Model A Restorers Club, Illinois Region **[2757]**, Northbrook, IL
Model T Ford Club of Northwest Ohio **[13367]**, Bluffton, OH
Motor City Viper Owners **[6988]**, Bloomfield Hills, MI
Mudchuggers Four Wheel Drive Club **[10089]**, Waterford, MI
Mudslingers 4x4 Club **[3972]**, Westmont, IL
Natl. Corvette Restorers Soc., Indiana Chap. **[4154]**, Avon, IN
Natl. Corvette Restorers Soc., Michigan Chap. **[10077]**, Washington, MI
Natl. Corvette Restorers Soc., North Central Chap. **[11343]**, Long Lake, MN
Natl. Corvette Restorers Soc., Queen City Chap. **[13924]**, Cincinnati, OH
Natl. Corvette Restorers Soc., Wisconsin Chap. **[19829]**, Stoughton, WI

Natl. Hot Rod Assn., Div. 3 **[4306]**, Bunker Hill, IN
North Coast Corvair Enthusiasts **[16338]**, Painesville, OH
North Coast Triumph Assn. **[16501]**, Ravenna, OH
North East Ohio Vette Club **[13232]**, Aurora, OH
North East Wisconsin Corvair Club **[19398]**, Oshkosh, WI
Northern Illinois Corvette Club **[3295]**, Rockford, IL
Northern Illinois Fiero Enthusiasts **[2659]**, Naperville, IL
Northern Ohio Model "A" Club **[13185]**, Ashtabula, OH
Northland Chap. of Falcon Club of Am. **[10322]**, Apple Valley, MN
Ohio Motorists Assn. **[13653]**, Chesterland, OH
Ohio Motorists Assn. **[17264]**, Willard, OH
Oldsmobile Club of Am., Gem City Rockets **[16706]**, Springboro, OH
Oldsmobile Club of Am., Illinois Valley Oldsmobile Chap. **[1113]**, Chicago, IL
Oldsmobile Club of Am., Motor City Rockets **[7672]**, Farmington Hills, MI
Oldsmobile Club of Am., Northern Ohio Chap. **[16223]**, North Canton, OH
Original Circle City Corvette Club **[5445]**, Indianapolis, IN
Pontiac-Oakland Club Intl., Illinois Chap. **[2318]**, Lockport, IL
Pontiac-Oakland Club Intl., Michigan WideTrackers **[10092]**, Waterford, MI
Pontiac-Oakland Club Intl., Northwest Ohio Chap. **[16950]**, Toledo, OH
Pontiac-Oakland Club Intl., Tomahawk Chap. 13 **[10925]**, Edina, MN
Pontiac-Oakland Club Intl., West Michigan Chap. **[10230]**, Zeeland, MI
Prairie Capital Corvair Assn. **[3664]**, Springfield, IL
Quad Cities British Auto Club **[1280]**, Coal Valley, IL
Rod Warriors Cruisin' Club **[13524]**, Canal Winchester, OH
Rolling Prairie Corvette Club **[1406]**, Decatur, IL
Rough Rangers Off Road club **[16255]**, Northfield, OH
Rustbelt 4x4 Trailriders Assn. **[15465]**, Homerville, OH
Secrets of Speed Soc. **[13271]**, Batavia, OH
Soc. of Automotive Engineers - Indiana State Univ.-Terre Haute **[6343]**, Terre Haute, IN
Soc. of Automotive Engineers - Northern Michigan Univ. **[9511]**, Rochester, MI
Soc. of Automotive Engineers - Univ. of Illinois-Chicago **[1187]**, Chicago, IL
Soc. of Automotive Engineers - Univ. of Michigan-Dearborn **[7269]**, Dearborn, MI
South Central Indiana Corvette Club **[6196]**, Shelbyville, IN
Studebaker Driver's Club, Black Hawk Chap. **[1204]**, Chicago, IL
Studebakers Driver's Club, Big Six River Bend Chap. **[2535]**, Moline, IL
Studebakers Driver's Club, Crossroads Zone **[9848]**, Spring Lake, MI
Studebakers Driver's Club, Indy Chap. **[5838]**, Mooresville, IN
Studebakers Driver's Club, North Star Chap. **[10332]**, Arden Hills, MN
Suburban Corvettes of Minnesota **[12594]**, St. Paul, MN
Sunburst Corvette Club **[1334]**, Crystal Lake, IL
Thunderbird Midwest **[12038]**, Plymouth, MN
Tri-State Corvette Club **[5964]**, Newburgh, IN
Two Rivers Jeep Club **[4028]**, Winchester, IL
Two Trackers Four Wheel Drive Club **[8490]**, Kentwood, MI
Vacationland Corvairs **[16347]**, Painesville, OH
Veteran Motor Car Club of Am. - Battle Creek Chap. **[6874]**, Battle Creek, MI
Veteran Motor Car Club of Am. - Black Swamp Chap. **[17252]**, Whitehouse, OH
Veteran Motor Car Club of Am. - Blue Water Chap. **[9443]**, Port Huron, MI
Veteran Motor Car Club of Am. - Brass and Gas Chap. **[6798]**, Armada, MI
Veteran Motor Car Club of Am. - Brighton Chap. **[12828]**, Waite Park, MN
Veteran Motor Car Club of Am. - Buckeye-Keystone Region **[16780]**, Strasburg, OH
Veteran Motor Car Club of Am. - Coulee Chap. **[18028]**, Galesville, WI
Veteran Motor Car Club of Am. - Defiance Chap. **[14994]**, Defiance, OH
Veteran Motor Car Club of Am. - Detroit Chap. **[9873]**, Sterling Heights, MI
Veteran Motor Car Club of Am. - Great Lakes Region **[16413]**, Perrysburg, OH
Veteran Motor Car Club of Am. - Hall of Fame Chap. **[13513]**, Canal Fulton, OH
Veteran Motor Car Club of Am. - Huron Valley Chap. **[9313]**, Orchard Lake, MI
Veteran Motor Car Club of Am. - Jackson Cascades Chap. **[6593]**, Albion, MI
Veteran Motor Car Club of Am. - Lakeshore Chap. **[9666]**, St. Clair Shores, MI
Veteran Motor Car Club of Am. - Lansing Chap. **[8984]**, Mason, MI
Veteran Motor Car Club of Am. - Nickel Age Touring Chap. **[16594]**, Salem, OH
Veteran Motor Car Club of Am. - Reagan Country Classics Chap. **[1486]**, Dixon, IL
Veteran Motor Car Club of Am. - Steel Valley Chap. **[17304]**, Wintersville, OH
Veteran Motor Car Club of Am. - Toledo Chap. **[16414]**, Perrysburg, OH
Veteran Motor Car Club of Am. - Tri-State Region **[16770]**, Steubenville, OH
Veteran Motor Car Club of Am. - Upper Mississippi Region **[18029]**, Galesville, WI
Vintage Thunderbird Club of Indiana **[4304]**, Brownsburg, IN
Vintage Triumphs of Wisconsin **[18187]**, Hartland, WI
Water Wonderland Thunderbirds **[6616]**, Allen Park, MI
West Michigan Corvair Club **[9472]**, Ravenna, MI
Western Michigan Thunderbird Club **[8048]**, Grandville, MI
Windy City Corvettes **[2887]**, Orland Park, IL
Windy City Z Club **[2665]**, Naperville, IL
Wisconsin 4WD Assn. **[19277]**, Neenah, WI
Wisconsin Capital Model T Ford Club **[19832]**, Stoughton, WI
Wisconsin Edsel Club **[19581]**, Racine, WI
Wisconsin Jaguars **[20133]**, West Bend, WI
Z Assn. of Cleveland, Ohio **[16686]**, Solon, OH
Z Car Club of Ohio **[15176]**, Fairfield, OH
Z Car and Roadster Owner Club **[14774]**, Columbus, OH
Z Owners of Minnesota **[12864]**, Wayzata, MN
Auto. Dealers Alliance of Ohio **[13417]**, Brice, OH
Auto. Dealers Assn. of Eastern Ohio **[17392]**, Youngstown, OH
Auto. Dealer's Assn. of Indiana **[5055]**, Indianapolis, IN
Auto. Dealers Assn. of Mega Milwaukee **[18974]**, Milwaukee, WI
Auto. Dealers Assn; Michigan **[7536]**, East Lansing, MI

Automotive

Automatic Transmission Rebuilders Assn., Midwest Chap. **[18338]**, La Crosse, WI
Automotive Ser. Couns. of Michigan **[9395]**, Plymouth, MI
Automotive Wholesalers of Illinois **[3539]**, Springfield, IL
Detroit Motorcity Chap. Elec. Auto Assn. **[9834]**, Southgate, MI
Fox Valley Elec. Auto Assn. **[3986]**, Wheaton, IL
Intl. Union, United Auto., Aerospace and Agricultural Implement Workers of Am., AFL-CIO - Local Union 12 **[16924]**, Toledo, OH
Intl. Union, United Auto., Aerospace and Agricultural Implement Workers of Am., AFL-CIO - Local Union 14 **[16925]**, Toledo, OH
Intl. Union, United Auto., Aerospace and Agricultural Implement Workers of Am., AFL-CIO - Local Union 22 **[7381]**, Detroit, MI
Intl. Union, United Auto., Aerospace and Agricultural Implement Workers of Am., AFL-CIO - Local Union 36 **[10179]**, Wixom, MI
Intl. Union, United Auto., Aerospace and Agricultural Implement Workers of Am., AFL-CIO - Local Union 160 **[10065]**, Warren, MI
Intl. Union, United Auto., Aerospace and Agricultural Implement Workers of Am., AFL-CIO - Local Union 211 **[14989]**, Defiance, OH
Intl. Union, United Auto., Aerospace and Agricultural Implement Workers of Am., AFL-CIO - Local Union 228 **[9866]**, Sterling Heights, MI
Intl. Union, United Auto., Aerospace and Agricultural Implement Workers of Am., AFL-CIO - Local Union 245 **[7262]**, Dearborn, MI
Intl. Union, United Auto., Aerospace and Agricultural Implement Workers of Am., AFL-CIO - Local Union 387 **[7704]**, Flat Rock, MI
Intl. Union, United Auto., Aerospace and Agricultural Implement Workers of Am., AFL-CIO - Local Union 402 **[16731]**, Springfield, OH
Intl. Union, United Auto., Aerospace and Agricultural Implement Workers of Am., AFL-CIO - Local Union 412 **[10066]**, Warren, MI
Intl. Union, United Auto., Aerospace and Agricultural Implement Workers of Am., AFL-CIO - Local Union 594 **[9419]**, Pontiac, MI
Intl. Union, United Auto., Aerospace and Agricultural Implement Workers of Am., AFL-CIO - Local Union 598 **[7743]**, Flint, MI
Intl. Union, United Auto., Aerospace and Agricultural Implement Workers of Am., AFL-CIO - Local Union 652 **[8581]**, Lansing, MI
Intl. Union, United Auto., Aerospace and Agricultural Implement Workers of Am., AFL-CIO - Local Union 663 **[4109]**, Anderson, IN
Intl. Union, United Auto., Aerospace and Agricultural Implement Workers of Am., AFL-CIO - Local Union 685 **[5570]**, Kokomo, IN
Intl. Union, United Auto., Aerospace and Agricultural Implement Workers of Am., AFL-CIO - Local Union 696 **[14898]**, Dayton, OH
Intl. Union, United Auto., Aerospace and Agricultural Implement Workers of Am., AFL-CIO - Local Union 699 **[9611]**, Saginaw, MI
Intl. Union, United Auto., Aerospace and Agricultural Implement Workers of Am., AFL-CIO - Local Union 730 **[7969]**, Grand Rapids, MI
Intl. Union, United Auto., Aerospace and Agricultural Implement Workers of Am., AFL-CIO - Local Union 735 **[7065]**, Canton, MI
Intl. Union, United Auto., Aerospace and Agricultural Implement Workers of Am., AFL-CIO - Local Union 845 **[7066]**, Canton, MI
Intl. Union, United Auto., Aerospace and Agricultural Implement Workers of Am., AFL-CIO - Local Union 863 **[13872]**, Cincinnati, OH
Intl. Union, United Auto., Aerospace and Agricultural Implement Workers of Am., AFL-CIO - Local Union 879 **[12430]**, St. Paul, MN
Intl. Union, United Auto., Aerospace and Agricultural Implement Workers of Am., AFL-CIO - Local Union 892 **[9700]**, Saline, MI
Intl. Union, United Auto., Aerospace and Agricultural Implement Workers of Am., AFL-CIO - Local Union 898 **[10209]**, Ypsilanti, MI
Intl. Union, United Auto., Aerospace and Agricultural Implement Workers of Am., AFL-CIO - Local Union 909 **[10067]**, Warren, MI
Intl. Union, United Auto., Aerospace and Agricultural Implement Workers of Am., AFL-CIO - Local Union 1111 **[5379]**, Indianapolis, IN
Intl. Union, United Auto., Aerospace and Agricultural Implement Workers of Am., AFL-CIO - Local Union 1112 **[17103]**, Warren, OH
Intl. Union, United Auto., Aerospace and Agricultural Implement Workers of Am., AFL-CIO - Local Union 1250 **[13435]**, Brook Park, OH
Intl. Union, United Auto., Aerospace and Agricultural Implement Workers of Am., AFL-CIO - Local Union 1292 **[7847]**, Grand Blanc, MI
Intl. Union, United Auto., Aerospace and Agricultural Implement Workers of Am., AFL-CIO - Local Union 1714 **[17104]**, Warren, OH
Intl. Union, United Auto., Aerospace and Agricultural Implement Workers of Am., AFL-CIO - Local Union 2000 **[16650]**, Sheffield Village, OH
Intl. Union, United Auto., Aerospace and Agricultural Implement Workers of Am., AFL-CIO - Local Union 2075 **[15656]**, Lima, OH

Intl. Union, United Auto., Aerospace and Agricultural Implement Workers of Am., AFL-CIO - Local Union 2093 **[9915]**, Three Rivers, MI
Intl. Union, United Auto., Aerospace and Agricultural Implement Workers of Am., AFL-CIO - Local Union 2151 **[7224]**, Coopersville, MI
Intl. Union, United Auto., Aerospace and Agricultural Implement Workers of Am., AFL-CIO - Local Union 2269 **[16528]**, Richwood, OH
Intl. Union, United Auto., Aerospace and Agricultural Implement Workers of Am., AFL-CIO - Local Union 2280 **[10035]**, Utica, MI
Intl. Union, United Auto., Aerospace and Agricultural Implement Workers of Am., AFL-CIO - Local Union 2488 **[292]**, Bloomington, IL
Intl. Union, United Auto., Aerospace and Agricultural Implement Workers of Am., AFL-CIO - Local Union 3206 **[1882]**, Granite City, IL
Intl. Union, United Auto., Aerospace and Agricultural Implement Workers of Am., AFL-CIO - Lorain County CAP Coun. Local 2000 **[16651]**, Sheffield Village, OH
Intl. Union, United Auto., Aerospace and Agricultural Implement Workers of Am., AFL-CIO - Mt. Clemens-Highland Park Local Union 400 **[10036]**, Utica, MI
Intl. Union, United Auto., Aerospace and Agricultural Implement Workers of Am., AFL-CIO - Pontiac Local Local Union 653 **[9420]**, Pontiac, MI
Automotive Education
Wisconsin Automotive and Truck Educ. Assn. **[20059]**, Wausau, WI
Automotive Industries
Alliance of Automotive Ser. Providers, Illinois **[3521]**, Springfield, IL
Alliance of Automotive Ser. Providers of Minnesota **[11476]**, Minneapolis, MN
Indiana Auto Body Assn. **[5191]**, Indianapolis, IN
Natl. Assn. of Fleet Administrators, Central Region **[2836]**, Oakbrook Terrace, IL
Natl. Assn. of Fleet Administrators, Michigan Chap. **[10002]**, Troy, MI
Natl. Assn. of Fleet Administrators, North Central Chap. **[10393]**, Bayport, MN
Natl. Assn. of Fleet Administrators, Tri-State **[14513]**, Columbus, OH
Natl. Assn. of Fleet Administrators, Western Reserve Chap. **[13139]**, Amherst, OH
Natl. Assn. of Fleet Administrators, Wisconsin Chap. **[19072]**, Milwaukee, WI
Automotive Parts and Ser. Assn. of Illinois **[★3539]**
Automotive Recyclers of Michigan **[7842]**, Grand Blanc, MI
Automotive Ser. Assn. of Minnesota **[★11476]**
Automotive Ser. Assn. of Ohio **[15634]**, Lewis Center, OH
Automotive Ser. Couns. of Michigan **[9395]**, Plymouth, MI
Automotive Ser. Professionals of Minnesota **[★11476]**
Automotive Ser. Providers of Minnesota; Alliance of **[11476]**, Minneapolis, MN
Automotive Services
Akron Auto. Dealers Assn. **[13017]**, Akron, OH
Auto. Dealers Assn. of Eastern Ohio **[17392]**, Youngstown, OH
Auto. Dealers Assn. of Mega Milwaukee **[18974]**, Milwaukee, WI
Automotive Ser. Assn. of Ohio **[15634]**, Lewis Center, OH
Chicago Auto. Trade Assn. **[2833]**, Oakbrook Terrace, IL
Dayton Area Auto Dealers Assn. **[14867]**, Dayton, OH
Greater Cincinnati Auto. Dealers Assn. **[13837]**, Cincinnati, OH
Greater Cincinnati Gas Dealers **[13845]**, Cincinnati, OH
Michigan Auto. Dealers Assn. **[7536]**, East Lansing, MI
Minnesota Ser. Sta. Assn. **[12243]**, Roseville, MN
Professional Towing and Recovery Operators of Illinois **[2992]**, Pekin, IL
Ser. Sta. Dealers Assn. of Indiana **[5471]**, Indianapolis, IN
Ser. Sta. Dealers Assn. of Michigan **[8758]**, Lansing, MI
Stark County Auto. Dealers Assn. **[13585]**, Canton, OH
Toledo Auto. Dealers Assn. **[16967]**, Toledo, OH
Wisconsin Auto Collision Technicians Assn. **[20008]**, Waukesha, WI
Wisconsin Auto. and Truck Dealers Assn. **[18671]**, Madison, WI
Automotive and Truck Educ. Assn; Wisconsin **[20059]**, Wausau, WI
Automotive Wholesalers of Illinois **[3539]**, Springfield, IL
Autonomy Party **[11926]**, Oakdale, MN
Auxiliary; Grant Regional Hea. Center **[18410]**, Lancaster, WI
Avanti Owners Assn. Intl., Indiana Chap. **[4831]**, Greenfield, IN
Avenues to Independence **[2961]**, Park Ridge, IL
Aviation
Amer. Assn. of Airport Executives, Illinois **[606]**, Chicago, IL
Amer. Assn. of Airport Executives, Indiana **[4517]**, Evansville, IN
Amer. Assn. of Airport Executives, Michigan **[7884]**, Grand Rapids, MI
Amer. Assn. of Airport Executives, Ohio **[14274]**, Columbus, OH
Amer. Assn. of Airport Executives, Wisconsin **[18450]**, Madison, WI
Intl. Assn. of Machinists and Aerospace Workers, AFL-CIO, CLC - Badger Lodge Local 1406 **[19858]**, Sun Prairie, WI
Intl. Assn. of Machinists and Aerospace Workers, AFL-CIO, CLC - District Lodge 90 **[5374]**, Indianapolis, IN
Intl. Assn. of Machinists and Aerospace Workers, AFL-CIO, CLC - District Lodge 141 **[1611]**, Elk Grove Village, IL
Intl. Assn. of Machinists and Aerospace Workers, AFL-CIO, CLC - District Lodge 143 **[11459]**, Mendota Heights, MN
Intl. Assn. of Machinists and Aerospace Workers, AFL-CIO, CLC - Local Lodge 46 **[6859]**, Battle Creek, MI
Intl. Assn. of Machinists and Aerospace Workers, AFL-CIO, CLC - Local Lodge 924 **[11903]**, North Mankato, MN
Intl. Assn. of Machinists and Aerospace Workers, AFL-CIO, CLC - Local Lodge 1217 **[17763]**, Clear Lake, WI
Intl. Assn. of Machinists and Aerospace Workers, AFL-CIO, CLC - Local Lodge 1487 **[1461]**, Des Plaines, IL
Intl. Assn. of Machinists and Aerospace Workers, AFL-CIO, CLC - Local Lodge 2484 **[15418]**, Hicksville, OH
Intl. Assn. of Machinists and Aerospace Workers, AFL-CIO, CLC - Local Lodge 2575 **[17501]**, Appleton, WI
Intl. Assn. of Machinists and Aerospace Workers, AFL-CIO, CLC - Lodge 225 **[14896]**, Dayton, OH
Intl. Assn. of Machinists and Aerospace Workers, AFL-CIO, CLC - Lodge 516 **[19029]**, Milwaukee, WI
Intl. Assn. of Machinists and Aerospace Workers, AFL-CIO, CLC - Lodge 1771 **[17568]**, Bangor, WI
Intl. Assn. of Machinists and Aerospace Workers, AFL-CIO, CLC - Lodge 2110 **[19030]**, Milwaukee, WI
Intl. Assn. of Machinists and Aerospace Workers, AFL-CIO, CLC - Lodge 2269 **[18438]**, Lyndon Station, WI
Intl. Assn. of Machinists and Aerospace Workers, AFL-CIO, CLC - United Lodge 66 **[19031]**, Milwaukee, WI
Intl. Assn. of Machinists and Aerospace Workers, District Lodge 10 **[19032]**, Milwaukee, WI
Intl. Assn. of Machinists and Aerospace Workers, District Lodge 55 **[2109]**, Joliet, IL
Intl. Assn. of Machinists and Aerospace Workers, District Lodge 66 **[18347]**, La Crosse, WI
Intl. Assn. of Machinists and Aerospace Workers, District Lodge 121 **[19859]**, Sun Prairie, WI
Intl. Assn. of Machinists and Aerospace Workers, District Lodge 165 **[12288]**, St. Cloud, MN
Intl. Assn. of Machinists and Aerospace Workers, LL-737 **[12429]**, St. Paul, MN
Intl. Assn. of Machinists and Aerospace Workers, LL-873 **[18216]**, Horicon, WI
Intl. Assn. of Machinists and Aerospace Workers, LL-1553 **[3282]**, Rockford, IL
Intl. Assn. of Machinists and Aerospace Workers, LL-2903 **[6517]**, Westville, IN
Intl. Assn. of Machinists and Aerospace Workers, Local Lodge 21 **[18348]**, La Crosse, WI
Intl. Assn. of Machinists and Aerospace Workers, Local Lodge 60 **[1530]**, East Alton, IL
Intl. Assn. of Machinists and Aerospace Workers, Local Lodge 1115 **[18349]**, La Crosse, WI
Intl. Assn. of Machinists and Aerospace Workers, Local Lodge 2458 **[2244]**, Lemont, IL
Southeastern Minnesota Flying Club **[12192]**, Rochester, MN
Tri-State Pilots Assn. **[16697]**, South Point, OH
Avon Lake - Avon Chamber of Commerce **[★13244]**
Avon Lions Club - Ohio **[13241]**, Avon, OH
Awana Clubs Intl. **[3718]**, Streamwood, IL
Awards
Military Order of the Purple Heart - Capital City Chap. 37 **[8151]**, Haslett, MI
Military Order of the Purple Heart - Winnebagoland Chap. No. 162 **[19273]**, Neenah, WI
Ayla's Originals Intl. Bead Bazaar **[1651]**, Evanston, IL
Azalea Soc. of Am., Lake Michigan Chap. **[2879]**, Orland Park, IL
Azalea Soc. of Am., Tri-State Chap. **[4533]**, Evansville, IN

B

Babbit Lions Club **[10368]**, Babbitt, MN
Babbitt Figure Skating Club **[10369]**, Babbitt, MN
Babies Coalition; Hea.y Mothers/Hea.y **[★8167]**
Bach Babes **[18975]**, Milwaukee, WI
Bach Collegium- Fort Wayne **[4643]**, Fort Wayne, IN
Back Country Horsemen of Illinois **[1640]**, Equality, IL
Back of the Yards Bus. Assn. **[758]**, Chicago, IL
BACnet Mfrs. Assn. **[759]**, Chicago, IL
Bad Axe Chamber of Commerce **[6820]**, Bad Axe, MI
Badger Assn. of the Blind and Visually Impaired **[18976]**, Milwaukee, WI
Badger Bonsai Soc. **[18488]**, Madison, WI
Badger Kennel Club **[17809]**, De Forest, WI
Badger Lapidary And Geological Soc. **[19381]**, Oregon, WI
Badger Orienteering Club **[20116]**, West Bend, WI
Badger Stamp Club **[18489]**, Madison, WI
Badger State Matchcover Club **[17853]**, East Troy, WI
Badger State Morgan Horse Club **[17854]**, East Troy, WI
Badger State Rottweiler Fanciers **[18977]**, Milwaukee, WI
Badgerland Gordon Setter Club **[17746]**, Chippewa Falls, WI
Badin ROKS **[15380]**, Hamilton, OH
Bagley Lions Club **[10373]**, Bagley, MN
Baileys Harbor Community Assn. **[17557]**, Baileys Harbor, WI
Bakery
Bakery, Confectionery, Tobacco Workers and Grain Millers Intl. Union, AFL-CIO, CLC - Local Union 19 **[14081]**, Cleveland, OH
Bakery, Confectionery, Tobacco Workers and Grain Millers Intl. Union, AFL-CIO, CLC - Local Union 19 **[14081]**, Cleveland, OH
Baking
Wisconsin Bakers Assn. **[19159]**, Milwaukee, WI
Bald Eagle Sportsmen's Assn. **[12892]**, White Bear Lake, MN
Baldwin Area Chamber of Commerce **[17559]**, Baldwin, WI
Baldwin Lions Club - Michigan **[6823]**, Baldwin, MI
Baldwin St. MS - Wyldlife **[6619]**, Allendale, MI
Ballet Arts Minnesota **[11530]**, Minneapolis, MN
Ballet Tech Ohio Performing Arts Assn. **[15752]**, Maineville, OH

Baltic Lions Club **[13249]**, Baltic, OH
Baltimore Area Chamber of Commerce **[13250]**, Baltimore, OH
Bancroft Lions Club **[6824]**, Bancroft, MI
Band Assn; Michigan Competing **[9078]**, Montrose, MI
Band; Chicago Highlanders Pipe **[2807]**, Oak Park, IL
Band and Orchestra Assn; Michigan School **[9291]**, Okemos, MI
Bands
Celtic Cross Pipes and Drums **[1770]**, Galesburg, IL
Bangor Bus. Club **[17566]**, Bangor, WI
Bangor Lions Club **[6827]**, Bangor, MI
Bangor Lions Club - Wisconsin **[17567]**, Bangor, WI
Bankers Assn; Indiana **[5192]**, Indianapolis, IN
Bankers Assn; Ohio Mortgage **[14639]**, Columbus, OH
Bankers Assn; Wisconsin Mortgage **[18729]**, Madison, WI
Bankers Club **[13757]**, Cincinnati, OH
Banking
Columbus Mortgage Bankers Assn. **[14394]**, Columbus, OH
Community Bankers Assn. of Illinois **[3545]**, Springfield, IL
Community Bankers Assn. of Indiana **[5094]**, Indianapolis, IN
Community Bankers Assn. of Ohio **[14409]**, Columbus, OH
Community Bankers of Wisconsin **[18501]**, Madison, WI
Eastern Michigan Mortgage Lenders Assn. **[9234]**, Novi, MI
Greater Cincinnati Mortgage Bankers Assn. **[13850]**, Cincinnati, OH
Greater Cleveland Mortgage Bankers Assn. **[17229]**, Westlake, OH
Illinois Bankers Assn. **[3585]**, Springfield, IL
Independent Community Bankers of Minnesota **[10867]**, Eagan, MN
Indiana Bankers Assn. **[5192]**, Indianapolis, IN
Indiana Mortgage Bankers Assn. **[5261]**, Indianapolis, IN
Indiana Mortgage Bankers Assn., Duneland Chap. **[6164]**, Schererville, IN
Indiana Mortgage Bankers Assn., Greater Indianapolis Chap. **[5262]**, Indianapolis, IN
Indiana Mortgage Bankers Assn., Northeast Chap. **[4678]**, Fort Wayne, IN
Indiana Mortgage Bankers Assn., South Central Chap. **[4228]**, Bloomington, IN
Indiana Mortgage Bankers Assn., Southwest Chap. **[4553]**, Evansville, IN
Indiana Mortgage Bankers Assn., Wabash Valley Chap. **[6327]**, Terre Haute, IN
MACU Assn. Gp. **[6890]**, Bay City, MI
Michigan Assn. of Community Bankers **[7533]**, East Lansing, MI
Michigan Bankers Assn. **[8633]**, Lansing, MI
Michigan Mortgage Brokers Assn. **[6729]**, Ann Arbor, MI
Mid-Michigan Mortgage Lenders Assn. **[9295]**, Okemos, MI
Minnesota Bankers Assn. **[10920]**, Edina, MN
Mortgage Bankers Assn. Of Northwest Ohio (Toledo) **[16930]**, Toledo, OH
Natl. Assn. of Professional Mortgage Women - Chicagoland **[2820]**, Oak Park, IL
Natl. Assn. of Professional Mortgage Women - Southeastern Michigan **[9812]**, Southfield, MI
Ohio Bankers League **[14572]**, Columbus, OH
Ohio Mortgage Bankers Assn. **[14639]**, Columbus, OH
Payments Authority **[10005]**, Troy, MI
Payments Central **[14708]**, Columbus, OH
Southeastern Michigan Mortgage Lenders Assn. **[8084]**, Grosse Pointe, MI
Upper Midwest ACH Assn. **[10560]**, Brooklyn Park, MN
Upper Midwest Automated CH Assn. **[10561]**, Brooklyn Park, MN
WACHA - The Premier Payments Rsrc. **[18044]**, Germantown, WI
Western Michigan Mortgage Lenders Assn. **[8029]**, Grand Rapids, MI
Wisconsin Assn. of Mortgage Brokers **[18660]**, Madison, WI
Wisconsin Bankers Assn. **[18672]**, Madison, WI
Wisconsin Mortgage Bankers Assn. **[18729]**, Madison, WI
Baptist
Amer. Baptist Churches of Michigan **[7499]**, East Lansing, MI
Baptist Churches of Ohio; Amer. **[15340]**, Granville, OH
Bar Assn; Genesee County **[7736]**, Flint, MI
Bar Assn; Grand Rapids **[7945]**, Grand Rapids, MI
Bar Assn; Kane County **[1796]**, Geneva, IL
Bar Assn; Macomb County **[9087]**, Mount Clemens, MI
Bar Assn; Michigan State **[★8762]**
Bar Assn; Milwaukee **[19055]**, Milwaukee, WI
Bar Assn; Oakland County **[6990]**, Bloomfield Hills, MI
Bar Assn; Peoria County **[3050]**, Peoria, IL
Bar Assn; Toledo **[16968]**, Toledo, OH
Bar Assn; Trumbull County **[17111]**, Warren, OH
Bar Assn; West Suburban **[1715]**, Forest Park, IL
Bar of Michigan; State **[8762]**, Lansing, MI
Bar of Wisconsin; State **[18623]**, Madison, WI
Baraboo Area Chamber of Commerce **[17571]**, Baraboo, WI
Baraboo Area United Way **[17572]**, Baraboo, WI
Baraboo Lions Club **[17573]**, Baraboo, WI
Baraga County Tourist and Recreation Assn. **[6795]**, L'Anse, MI
Barbershop Harmony Soc. - Illinois District **[2558]**, Morrison, IL
Barbershop Harmony Soc. - Pioneer District **[8421]**, Kalamazoo, MI
Barberton Community Found. **[13255]**, Barberton, OH
Barefoot Connections **[9495]**, Riverview, MI
Barnard Elementary School Parent Teacher Org. **[9977]**, Troy, MI
Barnes Area Development Corporation **[17580]**, Barnes, WI
Barnesville Area Chamber of Commerce **[13259]**, Barnesville, OH
Barnesville Area Chamber of Commerce and Development Coun. **[★13259]**
Barnesville Lions Club **[10378]**, Barnesville, MN
Barnesville Lions Club - Ohio **[13260]**, Barnesville, OH
Barnesville Thursday Nite Lions Club **[10379]**, Barnesville, MN
Baroda Lions Club **[6832]**, Baroda, MI
Barre-Coed Lions Club **[20136]**, West Salem, WI
Barrington Area Chamber of Commerce **[141]**, Barrington, IL
Barrington Area Character Counts **[142]**, Barrington, IL
Barrington Area United Way **[143]**, Barrington, IL
Barrington Bloomers African Violet Soc. **[3913]**, Wauconda, IL
Barrington Community Unit School District 220 **[144]**, Barrington, IL
Barrington Swim Club **[145]**, Barrington, IL
Barrington Women's Club **[146]**, Barrington, IL
Barry County Area Chamber of Commerce **[8155]**, Hastings, MI
Barry County United Way **[8156]**, Hastings, MI
Barryton Lions Club **[8500]**, Lake, MI
Bartlett Chamber of Commerce **[160]**, Bartlett, IL
Bartlett Character Counts **[161]**, Bartlett, IL
Bartlett Lions Club **[162]**, Bartlett, IL
Bartonville Lions Club **[168]**, Bartonville, IL
Bascom Lions Club **[15229]**, Fostoria, OH
Baseball
Minnesota Amer. Legion Baseball **[10647]**, Chanhassen, MN
Baseball Backers; Irish **[15049]**, Dublin, OH
Baseball and Softball; Hartford Youth **[15408]**, Hartford, OH
BASICS in Milwaukee **[18978]**, Milwaukee, WI
Basketball
Cary Basketball Assn. **[470]**, Cary, IL
Hopkins Royals Boys Basketball Assn. **[12333]**, St. Louis Park, MN
Howard Pulleys Pro-Am Basketball League **[11580]**, Minneapolis, MN
Lakota Thunderbird Youth Basketball **[13882]**, Cincinnati, OH
Queens of the Court **[4118]**, Anderson, IN
Rogers Area Youth Basketball Assn. **[12205]**, Rogers, MN
Basketball Assn; Cary **[470]**, Cary, IL
Basketball Assn; Hopkins Royals Boys **[12333]**, St. Louis Park, MN
Basketball Assn; Rogers Area Youth **[12205]**, Rogers, MN
Basketball; Lakota Thunderbird Youth **[13882]**, Cincinnati, OH
Basketball League; Howard Pulleys Pro-Am **[11580]**, Minneapolis, MN
Bat/Arenac Alliance for the Mentally Ill **[6880]**, Bay City, MI
Batavia Chamber of Commerce **[175]**, Batavia, IL
Batavia Community Chest/United Way **[176]**, Batavia, IL
Batavia Mothers Club **[★177]**
Batavia Mothers Club Found. **[177]**, Batavia, IL
Batesville Area Chamber of Commerce **[4157]**, Batesville, IN
Batesville - Wyld Life **[4158]**, Batesville, IN
Batesville - Young Life **[4159]**, Batesville, IN
Bath Township Lions Club **[6835]**, Bath, MI
Battle Creek Area Assn. of Realtors **[6850]**, Battle Creek, MI
Battle Creek Area Chamber of Commerce **[6851]**, Battle Creek, MI
Battle Creek Area Habitat for Humanity **[6852]**, Battle Creek, MI
Battle Creek Host Lions Club **[6853]**, Battle Creek, MI
Battle Creek Lakeview Lions Club **[6854]**, Battle Creek, MI
Battle Lake Lions Club **[10384]**, Battle Lake, MN
Baudette-Lake of the Woods Chamber of Commerce **[10386]**, Baudette, MN
Baxter Snowmobile Club **[12000]**, Pillager, MN
Bay Area Chamber of Commerce **[6881]**, Bay City, MI
Bay Area Convention and Visitors Bur. **[6882]**, Bay City, MI
Bay Area Music Teachers Assn. **[7081]**, Caro, MI
Bay Arts Coun. **[6883]**, Bay City, MI
Bay City Lions Club **[6884]**, Bay City, MI
Bay City Yacht Club **[6885]**, Bay City, MI
Bay County Conservation Club **[8822]**, Linwood, MI
Bay County Genealogical Soc. of Michigan **[6886]**, Bay City, MI
Bay County Medical Soc. **[7512]**, East Lansing, MI
Bay County REACT **[6887]**, Bay City, MI
Bay County Realtor Assn., Michigan **[6888]**, Bay City, MI
Bay De Noc Gem and Mineral Club **[9470]**, Rapid River, MI
Bay-Lake Regional Planning Commn. **[18083]**, Green Bay, WI
Bay de Noc Kiwanis Golden K of Escanaba **[7608]**, Escanaba, MI
Bay Point Yacht Club **[15806]**, Marblehead, OH
Bay Port High School - Young Life **[18084]**, Green Bay, WI
Bayfield Chamber of Commerce **[17585]**, Bayfield, WI
Bayview Yacht Club **[7328]**, Detroit, MI
Beach City Lions Club **[13280]**, Beach City, OH
Beachwood Chamber of Commerce **[13284]**, Beachwood, OH
Bead Soc. of Greater Chicago **[4017]**, Wilmette, IL
Bead Soc; Madison **[18907]**, Middleton, WI
Bear Lake Lions Club **[6900]**, Bear Lake, MI
Beardstown Chamber of Commerce **[188]**, Beardstown, IL
Bears Cricket Club **[2789]**, Oak Forest, IL
Beaver Creek Area Assn. of Realtors **[15077]**, East Liverpool, OH
Beaver Dam Area Chamber of Commerce **[17590]**, Beaver Dam, WI
Beavercreek Chamber of Commerce **[13296]**, Beavercreek, OH
Beavercreek - Young Life **[14859]**, Dayton, OH
Becca's Karing Individuals for Disabilities **[1768]**, Galesburg, IL
Bedford Area Chamber of Commerce **[4167]**, Bedford, IN
Bedford Bd. of Realtors **[4168]**, Bedford, IN
Bedford Chamber of Commerce **[13304]**, Bedford, OH

Bedford Heights Chamber of Commerce **[13307]**, Bedford Heights, OH
Bedford Hiking Club **[4169]**, Bedford, IN
Bedford Lions Club **[7483]**, Dowling, MI
Bedford Township Lions Club **[8523]**, Lambertville, MI
Bedford - Young Life **[8299]**, Ida, MI
Bedrock Jeepers **[7036]**, Burton, MI
Beecher Chamber of Commerce **[195]**, Beecher, IL
Beecher Lions Club **[9321]**, Otisville, MI
Beemer Hill Riders, No. 317 **[19417]**, Palmyra, WI
Beer
Beer Belly **[19849]**, Suamico, WI
Beer Assn. of Executives of Am; State **[★11630]**
Beer Assn. Executives of Am; Wholesale **[★11630]**
Beer Assn. Secretaries; Natl. Assn. of State **[★11630]**
Beer Belly **[19849]**, Suamico, WI
Beer Distributors Secretaries of Am. **[★11630]**
Beer Wholesalers Assn; Minnesota **[11630]**, Minneapolis, MN
Beer Wholesalers Secretaries; State **[★11630]**
Behavior Anal. Assn. of Michigan **[10199]**, Ypsilanti, MI
Behavior Anal. Soc. of Illinois **[3914]**, Wauconda, IL
Behavioral Sciences
Behavior Anal. Assn. of Michigan **[10199]**, Ypsilanti, MI
Behavior Anal. Soc. of Illinois **[3914]**, Wauconda, IL
Mid-American Assn. for Behavior Anal. **[17884]**, Eau Claire, WI
Beja Shriners **[18085]**, Green Bay, WI
Belclair Beagle Club **[2415]**, Marissa, IL
Bellaire Area Chamber of Commerce **[6904]**, Bellaire, MI
Bellaire Area Chamber of Commerce **[13309]**, Bellaire, OH
Bellaire High School Alumni Assn. **[13310]**, Bellaire, OH
Bellaire Lions Club **[13311]**, Bellaire, OH
Bellbrook - Sugarcreek Area Chamber of Commerce **[13314]**, Bellbrook, OH
Bellbrook - Young Life **[14860]**, Dayton, OH
Belle City Beemers 20/20 Riders No. 201 **[18297]**, Kenosha, WI
Bellefontaine ALU **[17184]**, West Liberty, OH
Belleville Area Chamber of Commerce **[6908]**, Belleville, MI
Belleville Community Club **[17602]**, Belleville, WI
Belleville Economic Progress **[★202]**
Bellevue High School Alumni Assn. **[13328]**, Bellevue, OH
Bellevue Lions Club **[13329]**, Bellevue, OH
Bellevue Lions Club - Michigan **[6912]**, Bellevue, MI
Bellville Chamber of Commerce **[13335]**, Bellville, OH
Bellville-Jefferson Township Historical Society **[13336]**, Bellville, OH
Bellville Lions Club - Ohio **[13337]**, Bellville, OH
Bellwood Chamber of Commerce and Indus. **[215]**, Bellwood, IL
Belmont-Central Chamber of Commerce **[760]**, Chicago, IL
Belmont County Bd. of Realtors **[17301]**, Wintersville, OH
Belmont County Chap. of the Ohio Genealogical Soc. **[13261]**, Barnesville, OH
Belmont County - Young Life **[15520]**, Jacobsburg, OH
Beloit Fencing Club **[17606]**, Beloit, WI
Belpre Area Chamber of Commerce **[13341]**, Belpre, OH
Belpre Lions Club **[13342]**, Belpre, OH
Belvidere Area Chamber of Commerce **[219]**, Belvidere, IL
Belvidere Bd. of Realtors **[220]**, Belvidere, IL
Belvidere Chamber of Commerce **[★219]**
Belvidere Lions Club **[221]**, Belvidere, IL
Bemidji Area Chamber of Commerce **[10404]**, Bemidji, MN
Bemidji Area Youth for Christ **[10405]**, Bemidji, MN
Bemidji/Cass Lake Chap. of Muskies **[10406]**, Bemidji, MN
Bemidji Curling Club **[10407]**, Bemidji, MN
Bemidji Figure Skating Club **[10408]**, Bemidji, MN
Bemidji First City Lions Club **[10409]**, Bemidji, MN
Bemidji Jaycees **[10410]**, Bemidji, MN
Bemidji Lions Club **[10411]**, Bemidji, MN
Bemidji Trap and Skeet Club **[10412]**, Bemidji, MN
Bemidji Visitors and Convention Bureau **[10413]**, Bemidji, MN
Ben Davis High School Key Club **[5056]**, Indianapolis, IN
Ben Franklin Parent Teacher Assn. **[1826]**, Glen Ellyn, IL
Benevolent and Protective Order of Elks Lodge 2243 **[★770]**
Benevolent Soc; Maltese-Amer. **[7388]**, Detroit, MI
Bennie PTA **[6609]**, Allen Park, MI
Bensenville Chamber of Commerce **[225]**, Bensenville, IL
Benson Lions Club **[10433]**, Benson, MN
Benton County Assn. for Retarded Citizens **[4735]**, Fowler, IN
Benton Kiwanis Club Found. **[231]**, Benton, IL
Benton Township of Monroe County Volunteer Fire Department **[6367]**, Unionville, IN
Benton-West City Area Chamber of Commerce **[232]**, Benton, IL
Benton-West City Economic Development Corp. **[233]**, Benton, IL
Benzie County Chamber of Commerce **[6925]**, Benzonia, MI
Berea Chamber of Commerce **[13345]**, Berea, OH
Berea Power Squadron **[16785]**, Strongsville, OH
Bereaved Parents of the USA, Hinsdale Chap. **[3864]**, Villa Park, IL
Bereaved Parents of the USA, Jacksonville Chap. **[2076]**, Jacksonville, IL
Bereaved Parents of the USA, Marion Chap. - Ohio **[15837]**, Marion, OH
Bereaved Parents of the USA, Saginaw Chap. **[9128]**, Munger, MI
Bereaved Parents of the USA, Southeastern (Ann Arbor) Michigan **[6686]**, Ann Arbor, MI
Bereaved Parents of the USA, Southern Illinois **[2595]**, Mount Vernon, IL
Bereaved Parents of the USA, Springfield Chap. **[3540]**, Springfield, IL
Bereaved Parents of the USA, Wayne County Illinois **[2093]**, Johnsonville, IL
Bereaved Parents of the USA, Woodfield Chap. **[2032]**, Hoffman Estates, IL
Bereavement
Bereaved Parents of the USA, Hinsdale Chap. **[3864]**, Villa Park, IL
Bereaved Parents of the USA, Jacksonville Chap. **[2076]**, Jacksonville, IL
Bereaved Parents of the USA, Marion Chap. - Ohio **[15837]**, Marion, OH
Bereaved Parents of the USA, Saginaw Chap. **[9128]**, Munger, MI
Bereaved Parents of the USA, Southeastern (Ann Arbor) Michigan **[6686]**, Ann Arbor, MI
Bereaved Parents of the USA, Southern Illinois **[2595]**, Mount Vernon, IL
Bereaved Parents of the USA, Springfield Chap. **[3540]**, Springfield, IL
Bereaved Parents of the USA, Wayne County Illinois **[2093]**, Johnsonville, IL
Bereaved Parents of the USA, Woodfield Chap. **[2032]**, Hoffman Estates, IL
Berlin Chamber of Commerce **[17624]**, Berlin, WI
Berlin Community Development Corp. **[17625]**, Berlin, WI
Berne Chamber of Commerce **[4187]**, Berne, IN
Bernese Mountain Dog
Bernese Mountain Dog Club of Northeastern Illinois **[2553]**, Morris, IL
Bernese Mountain Dog Club of Southeastern Wisconsin **[19854]**, Sullivan, WI
Bernese Mountain Dog Club of Am. **[19784]**, Stevens Point, WI
Bernese Mountain Dog Club of Northeastern Illinois **[2553]**, Morris, IL
Bernese Mountain Dog Club of Southeastern Wisconsin **[19854]**, Sullivan, WI
Berrien County Alliance for the Mentally Ill **[9757]**, Sodus, MI
Berrien County Chap. of Pheasants Forever **[7205]**, Coloma, MI
Berrien County Medical Soc. **[9681]**, St. Joseph, MI
Berrien Lib. Consortium **[6935]**, Berrien Springs, MI
Berry Growers Assn; Wisconsin **[19963]**, Waterloo, WI
Berwyn Chamber of Commerce **[★237]**
Berwyn Development Corp. **[237]**, Berwyn, IL
Best Buddies Illinois **[761]**, Chicago, IL
Beta Beta Beta, Gamma Gamma Chap. **[1906]**, Greenville, IL
Beta Beta Beta, Theta Alpha Chap. **[18979]**, Milwaukee, WI
Beta Gamma Sigma, Eastern Michigan Univ. Chap. **[10200]**, Ypsilanti, MI
Bethel Community Development Corp. **[18980]**, Milwaukee, WI
Bethel New Life **[762]**, Chicago, IL
Bethphage **[★2374]**
Better Bus. Bur. **[★5057]**
Better Bus. Bur. of Akron **[13046]**, Akron, OH
Better Bus. Bureau/Canton Regional **[★13549]**
Better Bus. Bureau/Canton Regional and Greater West Virginia **[13549]**, Canton, OH
Better Bus. Bur. of Central Illinois **[3009]**, Peoria, IL
Better Bus. Bur. of Central Indiana **[5057]**, Indianapolis, IN
Better Bus. Bur. of Central Ohio **[14335]**, Columbus, OH
Better Bus. Bur. of Chicago and Northern Illinois **[763]**, Chicago, IL
Better Bus. Bur., Cleveland **[14082]**, Cleveland, OH
Better Bus. Bur. serving Columbus and Central Ohio **[★14335]**
Better Bus. Bur. of Dayton/Miami Valley **[14861]**, Dayton, OH
Better Bus. Bur. of Detroit and Eastern Michigan **[9791]**, Southfield, MI
Better Bus. Bur. of Elkhart County **[4490]**, Elkhart, IN
Better Bus. Bur. of Mahoning Valley **[17393]**, Youngstown, OH
Better Bus. Bur. of Northeastern Indiana **[4644]**, Fort Wayne, IN
Better Bus. Bur. of Northwest Indiana **[5768]**, Merrillville, IN
Better Bus. Bur., Northwest Ohio and Southeastern Michigan **[16907]**, Toledo, OH
Better Bus. Bur. of St. Paul **[★12392]**
Better Bus. Bur. Serving Minnesota and North Dakota **[12392]**, St. Paul, MN
Better Bus. Bur. of West Central Ohio **[15650]**, Lima, OH
Better Bus. Bur. of Western Michigan **[7913]**, Grand Rapids, MI
Better Bus. Bur. of Wisconsin **[18981]**, Milwaukee, WI
Between the Bays Dance Camps **[9925]**, Traverse City, MI
Between Friends **[764]**, Chicago, IL
Beverage Assn; Indiana Licensed **[5255]**, Indianapolis, IN
Beverage Assn; Minnesota Licensed **[12494]**, St. Paul, MN
Beverage Retailers; Indiana Assn. of **[5165]**, Indianapolis, IN
Beverages
License Beverage Assn. **[13887]**, Cincinnati, OH
Michigan Soft Drink Assn. **[8718]**, Lansing, MI
Minnesota Municipal Beverage Assn. **[11657]**, Minneapolis, MN
Minnesota Soft Drink Assn. **[12524]**, St. Paul, MN
Ohio Soft Drink Association **[14675]**, Columbus, OH
Bexley Area Chamber of Commerce **[13358]**, Bexley, OH
Bexley Lions Club **[15261]**, Gahanna, OH
Bhakta Cricket Club **[10724]**, Cottage Grove, MN
Bi-State Regional Commn. **[3241]**, Rock Island, IL
Bi-State Sportsman's Assn. **[1294]**, Colona, IL
Bible
Amer. Family Assn. of Indiana **[4984]**, Indianapolis, IN
Amer. Family Assn. of Michigan **[9020]**, Midland, MI
LISTEN for Life **[16098]**, Napoleon, OH
Minnesota Family Assn. **[12482]**, St. Paul, MN
Wycliffe Bible Translators, North Central **[3944]**, West Chicago, IL
Bible Translators, North Central; Wycliffe **[3944]**, West Chicago, IL
Bickerdike Redevelopment Corp. **[765]**, Chicago, IL

Bicycle
Brighton BMX **[344]**, Brighton, IL
Chicagoland Bicycle Fed. **[840]**, Chicago, IL
Hill BMX Elgin Assn. **[1834]**, Glen Ellyn, IL
Indiana Bicycle Coalition **[5196]**, Indianapolis, IN
League of Michigan Bicyclists **[8595]**, Lansing, MI
Bicycle Fed. of Wisconsin **[18490]**, Madison, WI
Bicyclists; League of Michigan **[8595]**, Lansing, MI
Big Bend-Vernon Lions Club **[17626]**, Big Bend, WI
Big Brother/Big Sisters of Miami/Fulton Counties **[★5566]**
Big Bros. Big Sisters, A Community of Caring **[8422]**, Kalamazoo, MI
Big Brothers Big Sisters of America Association of Cincinnati **[13758]**, Cincinnati, OH
Big Brothers Big Sisters of America of Erie County **[16604]**, Sandusky, OH
Big Bros. Big Sisters of Am. of Lapeer County **[8775]**, Lapeer, MI
Big Bros. Big Sisters of Am. of Lorain County **[15701]**, Lorain, OH
Big Bros. Big Sisters of Am. of Mahoning Valley **[★15321]**
Big Bros. Big Sisters of Am. of Marquette County **[★9177]**
Big Bros. Big Sisters of Am. of Massillon **[15883]**, Massillon, OH
Big Bros. Big Sisters of Am. of McHenry County **[★2456]**
Big Bros. Big Sisters of Am. of Metropolitan Chicago **[★766]**
Big Bros. Big Sisters of Am. of North Central Indiana **[5566]**, Kokomo, IN
Big Bros. Big Sisters of Am. of Northeast Indiana **[4645]**, Fort Wayne, IN
Big Bros. Big Sisters of Am. of Northeastern Wisconsin **[18086]**, Green Bay, WI
Big Bros. Big Sisters of Am. of the Oshkosh Area **[★19390]**
Big Bros. Big Sisters of Am. of Wabash Valley **[★5609]**
Big Bros. Big Sisters Assn. of Central Ohio **[★14336]**
Big Bros. Big Sisters of Athens County **[13202]**, Athens, OH
Big Bros. Big Sisters of Central Indiana **[5058]**, Indianapolis, IN
Big Bros. Big Sisters of Central Minnesota **[12276]**, St. Cloud, MN
Big Bros. Big Sisters of Central Ohio **[14336]**, Columbus, OH
Big Bros. Big Sisters of Coshocton County **[14795]**, Coshocton, OH
Big Bros. Big Sisters of Dane County **[18491]**, Madison, WI
Big Bros. Big Sisters of Dickinson County and Surrounding Areas **[8320]**, Iron Mountain, MI
Big Bros. Big Sisters of East Central Ohio **[16147]**, New Philadelphia, OH
Big Brothers Big Sisters of the Fox Valley Region **[17489]**, Appleton, WI
Big Bros. Big Sisters of the Greater Twin Cities **[12393]**, St. Paul, MN
Big Bros. Big Sisters of Green County **[19213]**, Monroe, WI
Big Bros. Big Sisters of Isabella County **[9101]**, Mount Pleasant, MI
Big Bros. Big Sisters of Lake County **[1915]**, Gurnee, IL
Big Bros. Big Sisters of the Lakeshore **[9141]**, Muskegon, MI
Big Bros. Big Sisters of Livingston County **[8273]**, Howell, MI
Big Bros. Big Sisters of Mahoning Valley **[15321]**, Girard, OH
Big Bros. Big Sisters of Marquette County **[9177]**, Negaunee, MI
Big Bros. Big Sisters of McHenry County **[2456]**, McHenry, IL
Big Bros. Big Sisters of Metropolitan Chicago **[766]**, Chicago, IL
Big Bros. and Big Sisters of Metropolitan Detroit **[9792]**, Southfield, MI
Big Bros. Big Sisters for Milwaukee and Waukesha Counties **[18982]**, Milwaukee, WI
Big Bros. Big Sisters Northwestern Ohio **[16908]**, Toledo, OH
Big Bros. Big Sisters of Northwestern Wisconsin **[17866]**, Eau Claire, WI
Big Bros. Big Sisters of the Ohio Valley **[4534]**, Evansville, IN
Big Bros. Big Sisters of the Oshkosh Area **[19390]**, Oshkosh, WI
Big Bros. Big Sisters of Portage County **[19785]**, Stevens Point, WI
Big Bros. Big Sisters of Shelby and Darke County **[16664]**, Sidney, OH
Big Bros. Big Sisters of Tuscarawas, Carroll and Harrison Counties, and also serving Holmes County **[★16147]**
Big Bros. Big Sisters of Wabash Valley **[5609]**, Lafayette, IN
Big Bros. Big Sisters of West Central Illinois **[2077]**, Jacksonville, IL
Big Bros. Big Sisters of Will and Grundy Counties **[2101]**, Joliet, IL
Big Bros. and Sisters of Ozaukee County **[18062]**, Grafton, WI
Big Falls Lions Club **[10438]**, Big Falls, MN
Big Family of Michigan **[8832]**, Livonia, MI
Big Fork Lions Club **[10931]**, Effie, MN
Big Rapids Chamber of Commerce **[★6947]**
Big Rapids Lions Club **[6941]**, Big Rapids, MI
Big Rapids - Wyldlife **[6942]**, Big Rapids, MI
Big Rapids - Young Life **[6943]**, Big Rapids, MI
Big Ring Adventure Team **[5711]**, Madison, IN
Big River Appaloosa Horse club **[414]**, Carbondale, IL
Big River Bend Appaloosa Horse Club **[5847]**, Mount Vernon, IN
Big Rivers AIFA **[17867]**, Eau Claire, WI
Big Sisters of Metropolitan Detroit; Big Bros. and **[9792]**, Southfield, MI
Big Stone Lake Area Chamber of Commerce **[11945]**, Ortonville, MN
Big Walnut Breakfast Lions Club **[16811]**, Sunbury, OH
Bighorn Area Chamber of Commerce **[★17927]**
Bike Psychos Cycling Club **[2797]**, Oak Lawn, IL
Bike Wisconsin **[17835]**, Dodgeville, WI
Bike Wisconsin Educ. and Action Coalition **[19766]**, Spring Green, WI
Bikeline of Naperville **[2627]**, Naperville, IL
Bikers Against Child Abuse, Maritime Chap. **[18777]**, Manitowoc, WI
Bikers Against Child Abuse, Minnesota Chap. **[12394]**, St. Paul, MN
Bikers Against Child Abuse, Ohio Chap. **[13759]**, Cincinnati, OH
Bikers Against Child Abuse, Southeast Wisconsin Chap. **[19250]**, Mukwonago, WI
Bilingualism
Illinois Assn. for Mulitcultural Multilingual Educ. **[930]**, Chicago, IL
Biltmore Country Club Scholarship Found. **[2744]**, North Barrington, IL
Bio-Diversity Proj. **[18492]**, Madison, WI
Biology
Amer. Soc. for Microbiology - Illinois Br. **[2788]**, Oak Forest, IL
Amer. Soc. for Microbiology - Indiana Br. **[5565]**, Kokomo, IN
Amer. Soc. for Microbiology - Michigan Br. **[7321]**, Detroit, MI
Amer. Soc. for Microbiology - Ohio Br. **[14999]**, Delaware, OH
Beta Beta Beta, Gamma Gamma Chap. **[1906]**, Greenville, IL
Beta Beta Beta, Theta Alpha Chap. **[18979]**, Milwaukee, WI
Bioprocessing Professionals; Society of **[5474]**, Indianapolis, IN
Biotechnology
MichBio **[6718]**, Ann Arbor, MI
Wisconsin Assn. for Biomedical Res. and Educ. **[19154]**, Milwaukee, WI
Bipolar Support Alliance Fox Valley; Depression and **[3736]**, Sugar Grove, IL
Birch Run Area Chamber of Commerce **[6958]**, Birch Run, MI
Birch Run Lions Club **[6959]**, Birch Run, MI
Bird
Bird Strike Comm., U.S.A. **[16605]**, Sandusky, OH
Central Indiana Cage Bird Club **[5073]**, Indianapolis, IN
Chicago Audubon Soc. **[793]**, Chicago, IL
Coulee Region Audubon Soc. **[18341]**, La Crosse, WI
Dayton Audubon Soc. **[14871]**, Dayton, OH
Greater Cincinnati Bird Club **[13838]**, Cincinnati, OH
Hoosier Bird Buddies **[4669]**, Fort Wayne, IN
Michigan Audubon Soc. - Grand Traverse Audubon Club **[9938]**, Traverse City, MI
Natl. Audubon Soc. - Blackbrook **[15973]**, Mentor, OH
Natl. Audubon Soc. - Champaign County **[3829]**, Urbana, IL
Natl. Audubon Soc. - Columbus **[14520]**, Columbus, OH
Natl. Audubon Soc. - Greater Akron **[13069]**, Akron, OH
Natl. Audubon Soc.- Prairie Woods **[72]**, Arlington Heights, IL
Sycamore Audubon Soc. **[6500]**, West Lafayette, IN
Bird Island Lions Club **[10443]**, Bird Island, MN
Bird Strike Comm., U.S.A. **[16605]**, Sandusky, OH
Birmingham Athletic Club **[6978]**, Bloomfield Hills, MI
Birmingham-Bloomfield Chamber of Commerce **[6962]**, Birmingham, MI
Birmingham Bloomfield Families in Action **[6963]**, Birmingham, MI
Birth Defects
March of Dimes Birth Defects Found., Indiana Chap. **[5397]**, Indianapolis, IN
March of Dimes Birth Defects Found., Marquette Div. **[8936]**, Marquette, MI
March of Dimes Birth Defects Found., Southeast Minnesota Div. **[12153]**, Rochester, MN
March of Dimes/Michigan **[9803]**, Southfield, MI
March of Dimes Minnesota Chap. **[10915]**, Edina, MN
March of Dimes of Southeastern Wisconsin **[20102]**, West Allis, WI
Birth Defects Found., Marquette Div; March of Dimes **[8936]**, Marquette, MI
Birth Defects Found., Southeast Minnesota Div; March of Dimes **[12153]**, Rochester, MN
Birth Defects Found., Southeastern Minnesota Div; March of Dimes **[★12153]**
Birthright of Rensselaer **[6077]**, Rensselaer, IN
BKS Iyengar Yoga Assn. of the Midwest Bioregions **[6687]**, Ann Arbor, MI
BKS Iyengar Yoga Assn. Minnesota **[11531]**, Minneapolis, MN
Black Bear Yacht Racing Assn. **[12893]**, White Bear Lake, MN
Black Data Processing Associates - Detroit Chap. **[7329]**, Detroit, MI
Black Lake Chap. of Sturgeon for Tomorrow **[7130]**, Cheboygan, MI
Black Law Enforcement Executives, Northern Indiana Chap; Natl. Org. of **[4783]**, Gary, IN
Black Lawyers Assn. of Cincinnati **[13760]**, Cincinnati, OH
Black Nurses Assn. of Greater Cincinnati (18) **[13761]**, Cincinnati, OH
Black Physicians; Minnesota Assn. of **[11625]**, Minneapolis, MN
Black River Audubon Soc. **[15109]**, Elyria, OH
Black River Country United Way **[19415]**, Owen, WI
Black River Falls Figure Skating Club **[17632]**, Black River Falls, WI
Black Shield Police Assn. **[14083]**, Cleveland, OH
Black Social Workers; Chicago Chap. of the Natl. Assn. of **[801]**, Chicago, IL
Black Swamp Air Force **[16403]**, Perrysburg, OH
Black Swamp Angus Assn. **[16271]**, Oak Harbor, OH
Black Swamp Conservancy **[16404]**, Perrysburg, OH
Blackbrook Audubon Soc. **[15964]**, Mentor, OH
Blackduck Lions Club **[10446]**, Blackduck, MN
Blackford County Civil War Re-enactment Club **[4900]**, Hartford City, IN
Blackford County Historical Soc. **[4901]**, Hartford City, IN
Blackford Historical Museum **[★4901]**
Blackford United Way **[4902]**, Hartford City, IN
Blackhawk Appaloosa Horse Club **[3739]**, Sullivan, IL
Blackhawk Bicycle and Ski Club **[3274]**, Rockford, IL
Blackhawk Curling Club **[18244]**, Janesville, WI

Blackhawk Hills Rsrc. Conservation and Development Coun. **[3234]**, Rock Falls, IL
Blackhawk Human Rsrc. Assn. **[18245]**, Janesville, WI
Blackhawk Orchid Soc. **[1746]**, Freeport, IL
Blackhawk Retriever Club **[18339]**, La Crosse, WI
Blacks In Govt., Greater Cleveland Chap. **[14084]**, Cleveland, OH
Blacks In Govt., Greater Dayton Chap. **[14862]**, Dayton, OH
Blacksmiths
Farrier Indus. Assn. No. 37 **[2253]**, Lexington, IL
Indiana Farrier's Assn. No. 15 **[6442]**, Warsaw, IN
Land of Lincoln Horseshoer's Assn. No. 30 **[2389]**, Mansfield, IL
Michigan Horseshoer's Assn. No. 4 **[8401]**, Jeddo, MI
Mideastern Farrier's Assn. No. 17 **[15533]**, Johnstown, OH
Minnesota Farrier's Assn. No. 14 **[12239]**, Roseville, MN
Upper Midwest Horseshoer's Assn. No. 21 **[3196]**, Ringwood, IL
Blaine Jaycees **[10448]**, Blaine, MN
Blair Chamber of Commerce **[17637]**, Blair, WI
Blaisdell YMCA **[11532]**, Minneapolis, MN
Blanchard Valley AIFA **[15195]**, Findlay, OH
Blanchard Valley Volkssporters **[15196]**, Findlay, OH
Blanchester Area Chamber of Commerce **[13362]**, Blanchester, OH
Blind
Recording for the Blind and Dyslexic Illinois Unit **[1164]**, Chicago, IL
Blindness; Illinois Soc. for the Prevention of **[967]**, Chicago, IL
Blissfield Area Chamber of Commerce **[6973]**, Blissfield, MI
Blissfield Area Lions Club **[6974]**, Blissfield, MI
Blocks Together **[767]**, Chicago, IL
Blood
Michigan Assn. of Blood Banks **[7105]**, Center Line, MI
Blood Banks; Michigan Assn. of **[7105]**, Center Line, MI
Bloom Carroll Lions Club **[13602]**, Carroll, OH
Bloom-Carroll - Young Life **[14337]**, Columbus, OH
Bloomer Chamber of Commerce **[17642]**, Bloomer, WI
Bloomfield Chamber of Commerce **[4191]**, Bloomfield, IN
Blooming Prairie Chamber of Commerce **[10456]**, Blooming Prairie, MN
Bloomingdale Chamber of Commerce **[247]**, Bloomingdale, IL
Bloomingdale Character Counts **[248]**, Bloomingdale, IL
Bloomingdale/Gobles (KalHaven Trail) Lions Club **[6994]**, Bloomingdale, MI
Bloomington Bicycle Club **[4203]**, Bloomington, IN
Bloomington Bd. of Realtors **[4204]**, Bloomington, IN
Bloomington Bonsai Club **[6368]**, Unionville, IN
Bloomington Community Park and Recreation Found. **[4205]**, Bloomington, IN
Bloomington Convention and Visitors Bur. **[4206]**, Bloomington, IN
Bloomington Convention and Visitors Bur. **[10465]**, Bloomington, MN
Bloomington Flying Fish Volkssports **[★4207]**
Bloomington FlyingFish Walking Club **[4207]**, Bloomington, IN
Bloomington Lions Club, IL **[265]**, Bloomington, IL
Bloomington Lions Club - Minnesota **[11408]**, Maple Grove, MN
Bloomington Meals on Wheels **[4208]**, Bloomington, IN
Bloomington Normal Assn. of Realtors **[266]**, Bloomington, IL
Bloomington Normal Human Rsrc. Coun. **[267]**, Bloomington, IL
Bloomington Obedience Training Club **[10466]**, Bloomington, MN
Bloomington Old Time Music and Dance Gp. **[4209]**, Bloomington, IN
Bloomington Volunteer Network **[4210]**, Bloomington, IN
Bloomington - Wyldlife **[4211]**, Bloomington, IN
Bloomington Wyldlife **[11180]**, Hopkins, MN
Bloomington Wyldlife - Wyldlife **[2711]**, Normal, IL
Bloomington - Young Life **[2712]**, Normal, IL
Bloomington Young Life **[11181]**, Hopkins, MN
Bloomville Lions Club **[16851]**, Tiffin, OH
Blossomland Chap. of the United Way **[★6923]**
Blue Devil Swim Club **[1916]**, Gurnee, IL
Blue Earth Area Chamber of Commerce **[10496]**, Blue Earth, MN
Blue Earth Area Mentors **[10497]**, Blue Earth, MN
Blue Earth County Chap. of Pheasants Forever **[11376]**, Mankato, MN
Blue Island Area Chamber of Commerce and Indus. **[315]**, Blue Island, IL
Blue Island Citizens For Developmental Disabilities **[316]**, Blue Island, IL
Blue Water Area Convention and Visitors Bur. **[9430]**, Port Huron, MI
Blue Water Area Tourist Bureau **[★9439]**
Blue Water Beagle Club **[7601]**, Emmett, MI
Blue Water Habitat for Humanity **[9431]**, Port Huron, MI
Bluebird Restoration Assn. of Wisconsin **[19480]**, Plover, WI
Blues Alliance; Columbus **[14373]**, Columbus, OH
Bluewater Area Woodturners **[8799]**, Lenox, MI
Bluewater Michigan Chap., Natl. Railway Historical Soc. **[9576]**, Royal Oak, MI
Bluewater Thumb Youth for Christ **[9376]**, Pigeon, MI
Bluffton Area Chamber of Commerce **[13366]**, Bluffton, OH
Bluffton Bus.men Assn. **[★13366]**
Bluffton Chamber of Commerce **[★4271]**
Bluffview Montessori PTA **[12948]**, Winona, MN
BMW Car Club of Am., Badger Bimmers Chap. **[18983]**, Milwaukee, WI
BMW Car Club of Am., Buckeye Chap. **[14338]**, Columbus, OH
BMW Car Club of Am., Hoosier Chap. **[5059]**, Indianapolis, IN
BMW Car Club of Am., Illini Chap. **[2274]**, Lincoln, IL
BMW Car Club of Am., Michiana Chap. **[9445]**, Portage, MI
BMW Car Club of Am., Motor City Chap. **[7655]**, Farmington Hills, MI
BMW Car Club of Am., North Star Chap. **[11533]**, Minneapolis, MN
BMW Car Club of Am., Northern Ohio Chap. **[14819]**, Cuyahoga Falls, OH
BMW Car Club of Am., Windy City Chap. **[1861]**, Glenview, IL
BMW Motorcycle Owners of Cleveland No. 196 **[13629]**, Chagrin Falls, OH
BMW Motorcycle Owners Club of Minnesota No. 49 **[11867]**, New Hope, MN
BMW Of Battle Creek No. 14 **[6855]**, Battle Creek, MI
BMW Riders of Toledo No. 16 **[16557]**, Rossford, OH
BMW Touring Club of Detroit No. 1 **[9793]**, Southfield, MI
BMX; Brighton **[344]**, Brighton, IL
Bd. of Realtors; Dearborn Area **[7252]**, Dearborn, MI
Bd. of Trade of the City of Chicago **[★795]**
Boardman Lions Club **[13372]**, Boardman, OH
Bds. Assn; Ohio School **[14670]**, Columbus, OH
Boat Assn; Michigan Charter **[9550]**, Romulus, MI
Boating
Admirals No. 144 **[4597]**, Fishers, IN
Ann Arbor Model Yacht Club No. 138 **[9224]**, Northville, MI
Ashtabula Yacht Club **[13182]**, Ashtabula, OH
Bay City Yacht Club **[6885]**, Bay City, MI
Bay Point Yacht Club **[15806]**, Marblehead, OH
Bayview Yacht Club **[7328]**, Detroit, MI
Berea Power Squadron **[16785]**, Strongsville, OH
Black Bear Yacht Racing Assn. **[12893]**, White Bear Lake, MN
Bob Speltz Land O' Lakes Chap. of the Antique and Classic Boat Soc. **[10761]**, Deephaven, MN
Buckeye Model Yachtsmen No. 188 **[14343]**, Columbus, OH
Catalina 22 Fleet 158, Lafayette, Indiana **[6479]**, West Lafayette, IN
Catalina 22 Natl. Sailing Assn., Fleet 131 Atwood Lake, Ohio **[14820]**, Cuyahoga Falls, OH
Central Wisconsin Sail and Power Squadron **[20033]**, Wausau, WI
Chain-O-Lakes Sail and Power Squadron **[1891]**, Grayslake, IL
Chicago Model Yacht Club No. 7 **[2291]**, Lindenhurst, IL
Chicago Radio Controlled Sailing Club No. 181 **[826]**, Chicago, IL
Cincinnati Model Yacht Club No. 191 **[17171]**, West Chester, OH
Cleveland Model Boat Club No. 31 **[13410]**, Brecksville, OH
Columbia Yacht Club **[852]**, Chicago, IL
Detroit Model Yacht Club No. 88 **[7175]**, Clinton Township, MI
Doublehanded Sailing Assn. **[8087]**, Grosse Pointe Farms, MI
DuPage Power Squadron **[3969]**, Westmont, IL
Edgewater Yacht Club **[14112]**, Cleveland, OH
Edina Model Yacht Club No. 192 **[10969]**, Excelsior, MN
Four Lakes Ice Yacht Club **[18510]**, Madison, WI
Great Lakes Yacht Club **[9656]**, St. Clair Shores, MI
Hiawatha Valley Sail and Power Squadron **[10911]**, Edina, MN
Hoosier Sail and Power Squadron **[4320]**, Carmel, IN
Jackson Park Yacht Club of Chicago **[1001]**, Chicago, IL
Lake City Yacht Club **[12437]**, St. Paul, MN
Lake Shore Sail Club **[9660]**, St. Clair Shores, MI
LHV Model Yacht Club No. 168 **[4013]**, Willowbrook, IL
Madison Area Model Yacht Club No. 139 **[19933]**, Verona, WI
Madison Lakes Yacht Club **[18555]**, Madison, WI
Miami Valley Model Yacht Assn. No. 73 **[14914]**, Dayton, OH
Michigan Boating Indus. Assn. **[8849]**, Livonia, MI
Michigan Charter Boat Assn. **[9550]**, Romulus, MI
Michigan Model Sailing Club No. 70 **[9615]**, Saginaw, MI
Middle Bass Island Yacht Club **[15991]**, Middle Bass, OH
Milwaukee Sail and Power Squadron **[19990]**, Waukesha, WI
Muncie Sailing Club **[5889]**, Muncie, IN
North Cape Yacht Club **[8785]**, Lasalle, MI
North Coast Women's Sailing Assn. **[15589]**, Lakewood, OH
North Point Charter Boat Assn. **[4042]**, Winthrop Harbor, IL
North West Sailing Assn. **[75]**, Arlington Heights, IL
Pike's Creek Keel Club **[17587]**, Bayfield, WI
Pine Lake Small Craft Assn. **[7563]**, East Lansing, MI
Pontiac Yacht Club **[9424]**, Pontiac, MI
R/C Sailing Club of Cincinnati No. 217 **[13972]**, Cincinnati, OH
Racine Yacht Club **[19571]**, Racine, WI
Red Witch R/C Yacht Club No. 152 **[2160]**, Kewanee, IL
Rockford Sail and Power Squadron **[3311]**, Rockford, IL
Rocky River Power Squadron **[13277]**, Bay Village, OH
St. Paul Sail and Power Squadron **[11422]**, Maplewood, MN
Sassafras Star Sailing Soc. No. 160 **[14950]**, Dayton, OH
SE Michigan TSCA **[9519]**, Rochester Hills, MI
Secret Victoria's No. 190 **[16958]**, Toledo, OH
Toledo Power Squadron **[16975]**, Toledo, OH
TSCA of Wisconsin **[19845]**, Sturgeon Bay, WI
U.S. Power Squadrons - District 10 **[12862]**, Wayzata, MN
U.S. Power Squadrons - District 20 **[2056]**, Huntley, IL
U.S. Power Squadrons - District 29 **[14751]**, Columbus, OH
Western Michigan Model Yacht Assn No. 103 **[8406]**, Jenison, MI
Windjammers Sailing Club **[19852]**, Suamico, WI
Wisconsin Shoreline Skippers No. 102 **[19279]**, Neenah, WI

Wisillin Winds Radio Controlled Yacht Club No. 80 [19583], Racine, WI
Boaz Area Lions Club [19622], Richland Center, WI
Bob Speltz Land O' Lakes Chap. of the Antique and Classic Boat Soc. [10761], Deephaven, MN
Bocce
Club Corvo [2042], Homer Glen, IL
Dickinson Area Bocce Assn. [8321], Iron Mountain, MI
Kalamazoo Michigan Bocce Club [9448], Portage, MI
Sylvan Lake Bocce Club [9897], Sylvan Lake, MI
Bolingbrook Area Chamber of Commerce [322], Bolingbrook, IL
Bolingbrook Chamber of Commerce and Indus. [★322]
Bolivar Lions Club [13377], Bolivar, OH
Bonsai Club; West Michigan [8072], Greenville, MI
Bonsai Soc. of Greater Cincinnati [13762], Cincinnati, OH
Book Worm Angels [768], Chicago, IL
Booker T. Washington Bus. Assn. [7330], Detroit, MI
Books
Book Worm Angels [768], Chicago, IL
Midwest Antiquarian Booksellers Assn. [1053], Chicago, IL
Upper Midwest Booksellers Assn. [11770], Minneapolis, MN
Women's Natl. Book Assn., Detroit Chap. [10151], Westland, MI
Books, Brushes, and Bands for Education, LLC [4874], Hammond, IN
Booksellers Assn; Great Lakes [7860], Grand Haven, MI
Boone County Cancer Soc. [5667], Lebanon, IN
Boone County Chamber of Commerce [5668], Lebanon, IN
Booster Club; Loyola [11904], North Mankato, MN
Booster Club; Midwest Twisters Gymnastics [19332], Oak Creek, WI
Booster Club; People Who Care [11721], Minneapolis, MN
Boosters Club; South Gibson Wrestling [★6072]
Boosters; Female Alumni Athletic [10184], Wyandotte, MI
Boosters; Hilliard Davidson Athletic [15434], Hilliard, OH
Boosters; Independence Music [15498], Independence, OH
Boosters; Ohio Browns [15936], McDonald, OH
Boosters; Willoughby South High Instrumental Music [17279], Willoughby, OH
Boosters; Willoughby South Instrumental Music [★17279]
Boot and Shoe Workers Union [★17754]
Border Beagle Club [7233], Davisburg, MI
Borup Lions Club [10237], Ada, MN
Boscobel Chamber of Commerce [17648], Boscobel, WI
Botany
Ann Arbor Orchid Soc. [6677], Ann Arbor, MI
Blackhawk Orchid Soc. [1746], Freeport, IL
Central Ohio Orchid Soc. [14361], Columbus, OH
Coulee Region Orchid Guild [18342], La Crosse, WI
Dunes-Kalamazoo Orchid Soc. [10049], Vicksburg, MI
Grand Valley Orchid Soc. [8196], Holland, MI
Greater Akron Orchid Soc. [13055], Akron, OH
Greater Cincinnati Orchid Soc. [13852], Cincinnati, OH
Greater Lansing Orchid Soc. [9269], Okemos, MI
Greater Toledo Orchid Soc. [16771], Stony Ridge, OH
Hoosier Orchid Soc. [5145], Indianapolis, IN
Illinois Native Plant Soc., Central Chap. [579], Chatham, IL
Illinois Native Plant Soc., Forest Glen Chap. [1691], Fairmount, IL
Illinois Native Plant Soc., Northeast Chap. [2106], Joliet, IL
Illinois Native Plant Soc., Quad City Chap. [1480], Dixon, IL
Illinois Native Plant Soc., Southern Chap. [2125], Jonesboro, IL
Illinois Orchid Soc. [1622], Elmhurst, IL
Indiana Native Plant and Wildflower Soc. [5265], Indianapolis, IN
Indiana Orchid Soc. [4375], Cloverdale, IN
Kingwood Orchid Soc. [15838], Marion, OH
Lorain County Tropical Greenhouse and Museum Assn. [15706], Lorain, OH
Miami Valley Orchid Soc. [13901], Cincinnati, OH
Michiana Orchid Soc. [6490], West Lafayette, IN
Michigan Orchid Soc. [6987], Bloomfield Hills, MI
Northeastern Wisconsin Orchid Soc. [17725], Cecil, WI
Northwestern Michigan Orchid Soc. [8478], Kalkaska, MI
Ohio Native Plant Soc., Central Ohio Chap. [14643], Columbus, OH
Ohio Native Plant Soc., Miami Valley Chap. [14938], Dayton, OH
Ohio Native Plant Soc., Mohican Chap. [15784], Mansfield, OH
Ohio Native Plant Soc., Northeastern Ohio Chap. [16193], Newbury, OH
Olbrich Botanical Soc. [18590], Madison, WI
Orchid Growers Guild [18592], Madison, WI
Orchid Soc. of Minnesota [11128], Hastings, MN
Peoria Orchid Soc. [1545], East Peoria, IL
Prairie State Orchid Soc. [3665], Springfield, IL
Saginaw Valley Orchid Soc. [7203], Coleman, MI
Three Rivers Orchid Society, Fort Wayne [4724], Fort Wayne, IN
West Shore Orchid Soc. [15591], Lakewood, OH
Wisconsin Orchid Soc. [18892], Mequon, WI
Bottles
1st Chicago Bottle Club [1487], Dolton, IL
Antique Bottle Club of Northern Illinois [3922], Waukegan, IL
Findlay Antique Bottle Club [13390], Bowling Green, OH
Flint Antique Bottle and Collectibles Club [7803], Gaines, MI
Jelly Jammers [8181], Hillsdale, MI
Kalamazoo Antique Bottle Club [9446], Portage, MI
Metropolitan Detroit Antique Bottle Club [9995], Troy, MI
Midwest Antique Fruit Jar and Bottle Club [4612], Flat Rock, IN
Minnesota 1st Antique Bottle Club [11619], Minneapolis, MN
North Star Historical Bottle Assn. [11713], Minneapolis, MN
Ohio Bottle Club [13256], Barberton, OH
Wabash Valley Antique Glass and Pottery Club [4593], Farmersburg, IN
Boulder Junction Chamber of Commerce [17650], Boulder Junction, WI
Bourbannais Chamber of Commerce [★326]
Bourbon Lions Club [4281], Bourbon, IN
Bowling
Bowling Centers Assn. of Ohio [14863], Dayton, OH
Bowling Proprietors Assn. of Minnesota [11418], Maplewood, MN
Bowling Proprietors Assn. of Wisconsin [19435], Pewaukee, WI
Centennial Lakes Lawn Bowling Club [10908], Edina, MN
Chicago Lakeside Lawn Bowling Club [4049], Woodridge, IL
Flint Lawn Bowling Club [7732], Flint, MI
Forest Hill Lawn Bowling Club [16525], Richmond Heights, OH
Greater Cincinnati Bowling Proprietors [13839], Cincinnati, OH
Greater Detroit Bowling Assn. [9657], St. Clair Shores, MI
Illinois State Bowling Proprietors Assn. [2288], Lincolnwood, IL
Indiana Bowling Centers Assn. [5198], Indianapolis, IN
Lorain Lawn Bowling Club [13137], Amherst, OH
Madison Bowling Assn. [19207], Monbna, WI
Madison Women's Bowling Assn. [19208], Monona, WI
Michigan State Bowling Assn. [7836], Gladwin, MI
Waverly Lawn Bowling Club [17148], Waverly, OH
Westland Lawn Bowling Club [10148], Westland, MI
Bowling Assn; Greater Detroit [9657], St. Clair Shores, MI
Bowling Assn; Madison [19207], Monona, WI
Bowling Assn; Madison Women's [19208], Monona, WI
Bowling Assn; Michigan State [7836], Gladwin, MI
Bowling Assn; Michigan Women's [8386], Jackson, MI
Bowling Centers Assn. of Ohio [14863], Dayton, OH
Bowling Green Skating Club [13383], Bowling Green, OH
Bowling Green State Univ. Coun. of Teachers of Mathematics [13384], Bowling Green, OH
Bowling Green Woman's Club [13385], Bowling Green, OH
Bowling Green - Young Life [13386], Bowling Green, OH
Bowling Green Youth Hockey Assn. [13387], Bowling Green, OH
Bowling Proprietors Assn. of Minnesota [11418], Maplewood, MN
Bowling Proprietors Assn. of Wisconsin [19435], Pewaukee, WI
Bowsher HS - Young Life [15904], Maumee, OH
Box 15 Club [14339], Columbus, OH
Boxer Rescue of Ohio; Akron-Canton [16212], North Canton, OH
Boxing
Traverse City At-Risk Boxing [9959], Traverse City, MI
Boxing; Traverse City At-Risk [9959], Traverse City, MI
Boy Scouts of Am., Chippewa Valley Coun. [17868], Eau Claire, WI
Boy Scouts of Am. - Dan Beard Coun. [13763], Cincinnati, OH
Boy Scouts of Am., Eau Claire [★17868]
Boy Scouts of Am., Four Lakes Coun. [★18493]
Boy Scouts of Am., Gamehaven Coun. [12130], Rochester, MN
Boy Scouts of Am., Glacier's Edge Coun. [18493], Madison, WI
Boy Scouts of Am.-Great Sauk Trail Coun. [6688], Ann Arbor, MI
Boy Scouts of Am., Madison [★18493]
Boychoir; Rochester [12174], Rochester, MN
Boyne Area City Chamber of Commerce [6996], Boyne City, MI
Boyne Country Convention and Visitors Bur. [★9367]
Boys Basketball Assn; Hopkins Royals [12333], St. Louis Park, MN
Boys and Girls Club of Cass County [7099], Cassopolis, MI
Boys and Girls Club of Greater Holland [8194], Holland, MI
Boys and Girls Club of Hancock County [4832], Greenfield, IN
Boys and Girls Club of Indianapolis [5060], Indianapolis, IN
Boys and Girls Club of Lansing [8554], Lansing, MI
Boys and Girls Club; Neighborhood [1097], Chicago, IL
Boys and Girls Club of Sandusky [16606], Sandusky, OH
Boys and Girls Club of South Oakland County [9577], Royal Oak, MI
Boys and Girls Club of Troy [9978], Troy, MI
Boys and Girls Club of Zionsville [6549], Zionsville, IN
Boys and Girls Clubs [20032], Wausau, WI
Boys and Girls Clubs of Chicago [769], Chicago, IL
Boys and Girls Clubs of Northwest Indiana [4776], Gary, IN
Boys and Girls Clubs of Porter County [6380], Valparaiso, IN
Boys and Girls Clubs of Sheboygan County Found. [19490], Plymouth, WI
Boys Hope Girls Hope of Chicago [4018], Wilmette, IL
Boys Hope Girls Hope of Cleveland [17254], Wickliffe, OH
Boys Hope Girls Hope of Detroit [7331], Detroit, MI
Boys' Village - Young Life [17316], Wooster, OH
BPO Elks of the USA [770], Chicago, IL
Bradley Assn. of Commerce and Indus. [★326]
Bradley-Bourbonnais Chamber of Commerce [326], Bourbonnais, IL
Bradley Univ. Students In Free Enterprise [3010], Peoria, IL

Braemar-City of Lakes Figure Skating Club **[10907]**, Edina, MN
Brahma Samaj of Greater Chicago **[1497]**, Downers Grove, IL
Brain Injury Assn. of Illinois **[771]**, Chicago, IL
Brain Injury Assn. of Indiana **[5061]**, Indianapolis, IN
Brain Injury Assn. of Michigan **[7009]**, Brighton, MI
Brain Injury Assn. of Minnesota **[11534]**, Minneapolis, MN
Brain Injury Assn. of Ohio **[14340]**, Columbus, OH
Brain Injury Assn. of Wisconsin **[20071]**, Wauwatosa, WI
Brainerd Area Sertoma Club **[10506]**, Brainerd, MN
Brainerd Genealogical Soc. **[★10510]**
Brainerd Lakes Area Audubon Soc. **[10507]**, Brainerd, MN
Brainerd Lakes Area Chamber of Commerce and Convention/Visitors Bur. **[★10508]**
Brainerd Lakes Area Chamber of Commerce and Convention and Visitors Bur. **[★10508]**
Brainerd Lakes Area Chambers of Commerce **[10508]**, Brainerd, MN
Brainerd Lakes Area Development Corp. **[10509]**, Brainerd, MN
Br. County Area Chamber of Commerce **[7196]**, Coldwater, MI
Br. County Assn. of Realtors **[7197]**, Coldwater, MI
Br. County Literacy Coun. **[7198]**, Coldwater, MI
Br. County Tourism Bur. **[7199]**, Coldwater, MI
Br. County United Way **[7200]**, Coldwater, MI
Brandon Lions Club - Minnesota **[10525]**, Brandon, MN
Breakfast Discipleship - Young Life **[16431]**, Piqua, OH
Breastfeeding
La Leche League Northside of Evansville **[4558]**, Evansville, IN
Breastfeeding Coalition; Howard County **[5567]**, Kokomo, IN
Brebeuf - Young Life **[5062]**, Indianapolis, IN
Brecksville Chamber of Commerce **[13408]**, Brecksville, OH
Brecksville Historical Assn. **[13409]**, Brecksville, OH
Breese Chamber of Commerce **[337]**, Breese, IL
Bremen Chamber of Commerce **[4287]**, Bremen, IN
Bremen Chamber of Commerce **[13415]**, Bremen, OH
Bretton Woods Lions Club **[8555]**, Lansing, MI
Briar Patch Beagle Club **[16196]**, Newcomerstown, OH
Briard Club of Am. **[19269]**, Neenah, WI
Brice Prairie Lions Club **[19362]**, Onalaska, WI
Brick Distributors of Minnesota **[11535]**, Minneapolis, MN
Bricklayers AFL-CIO, LU 8 **[★502]**
Bricklayers and Allied Craftworkers Local No. 8 **[502]**, Champaign, IL
Brickyard Boogie Dancers **[5063]**, Indianapolis, IN
Bridge Syndicate **[10808]**, Duluth, MN
Bridgeport Area Chamber of Commerce **[13419]**, Bridgeport, OH
Bridgeport Lions Club - Michigan **[9604]**, Saginaw, MI
Bridgeview Chamber of Commerce **[340]**, Bridgeview, IL
Bridgeview Lions Club **[341]**, Bridgeview, IL
Bridgman Lions Club **[7003]**, Bridgman, MI
Bridgman - Young Life **[9682]**, St. Joseph, MI
Brigade, Midwest Chapter XVII; Society of the 173D Airborne **[14730]**, Columbus, OH
Brighton Art Guild **[7010]**, Brighton, MI
Brighton BMX **[344]**, Brighton, IL
Brighton Lions Club **[7011]**, Brighton, MI
Brilliant Lions Club **[13421]**, Brilliant, OH
Brillion Area Chamber of Commerce **[17658]**, Brillion, WI
Brimfield Area Chamber of Commerce **[15540]**, Kent, OH
Brimfield Lions Club **[16053]**, Mogadore, OH
Brittany Club - Directors Chap; Amer. **[459]**, Carterville, IL
Broadcasters
Indiana Broadcasters Assn. **[5199]**, Indianapolis, IN
Broadcasters' Assn; Illinois **[1638]**, Energy, IL
Broadcasters; Michigan Assn. of **[8606]**, Lansing, MI
Broadcasters; Ohio Assn. of **[14543]**, Columbus, OH
Broadcasting
Amer. Women in Radio and TV, Buckeye of Central Ohio **[14314]**, Columbus, OH
Amer. Women in Radio and TV, Chicago **[729]**, Chicago, IL
Amer. Women in Radio and TV, Indiana **[5028]**, Indianapolis, IN
Amer. Women in Radio and TV, Twin Cities Media Network **[12020]**, Plymouth, MN
Amer. Women in Radio and TV Western Michigan **[7904]**, Grand Rapids, MI
Cable and Telecommunications Assn. for Marketing, Ohio Chap. **[13047]**, Akron, OH
Communs. Workers of Am., AFL-CIO, CLC - Local Union 34001 **[14106]**, Cleveland, OH
Friends of WVON **[900]**, Chicago, IL
Illinois Broadcasters' Assn. **[1638]**, Energy, IL
Jewish Broadcasting Network Corp. **[1004]**, Chicago, IL
Michigan Assn. of Broadcasters **[8606]**, Lansing, MI
Minnesota Broadcasters Assn. **[11634]**, Minneapolis, MN
Natl. Acad. of TV Arts and Sciences, Chicago/ Midwest Chap. **[1066]**, Chicago, IL
Natl. Acad. of TV Arts and Sciences, Cleveland Regional Chap. **[13451]**, Brunswick, OH
Natl. Acad. of TV Arts and Sciences, Michigan Chap. **[10120]**, West Bloomfield, MI
Natl. Acad. of TV Arts and Sciences, Ohio Valley **[13914]**, Cincinnati, OH
Natl. Acad. of TV Arts and Sciences, Upper Midwest Chap. **[12665]**, Shorewood, MN
Ohio Assn. of Broadcasters **[14543]**, Columbus, OH
Soc. of Broadcast Engineers, Chap. 24 Madison Wisconsin **[18617]**, Madison, WI
Soc. of Broadcast Engineers, Chap. 25, Indianapolis **[5475]**, Indianapolis, IN
Soc. of Broadcast Engineers, Chap. 28 Milwaukee **[19120]**, Milwaukee, WI
Soc. of Broadcast Engineers, Chap. 33 - Southwest Ohio **[13992]**, Cincinnati, OH
Soc. of Broadcast Engineers, Chap. 35 - Kentucky **[5924]**, New Albany, IN
Soc. of Broadcast Engineers, Chap. 70 - Northeast Ohio **[13305]**, Bedford, OH
Soc. of Broadcast Engineers, Chap. 112 - Western Wisconsin **[17897]**, Eau Claire, WI
Wisconsin Broadcasters Assn. **[18674]**, Madison, WI
Broadview Heights Chamber of Commerce **[13425]**, Broadview Heights, OH
Broadview Heights Lions Club **[13426]**, Broadview Heights, OH
Brodhead Chamber of Commerce **[17661]**, Brodhead, WI
Broiler and Egg Assn. of Minnesota **[10571]**, Buffalo, MN
Broken Bird Rod and Gun Club **[13156]**, Arlington, OH
Brokers and Foreign Freight Forwarders Assn. of Chicago; Customs **[865]**, Chicago, IL
Bromeliad Soc. of Greater Chicago **[1319]**, Crystal Lake, IL
Brooke-Hancock-Jefferson Metropolitan Planning Commn. **[16761]**, Steubenville, OH
Brooke-Hancock Planning & Development Coun; WV Region XI **[★16761]**
Brookfield Chamber of Commerce **[349]**, Brookfield, IL
Brookfield Chamber of Commerce **[★17668]**
Brookfield Village Homeowners Assn. **[15428]**, Hilliard, OH
Brookfield Zoo/Chicago Zoological Soc. **[350]**, Brookfield, IL
Brooklyn Area Chamber of Commerce **[17690]**, Brooklyn, WI
Brooklyn Center Lions Club **[10546]**, Brooklyn Park, MN
Brooklyn - Irish Hills Chamber of Commerce **[7030]**, Brooklyn, MI
Brooklyn Park Figure Skating Club **[10547]**, Brooklyn Park, MN
Brooklyn Park Lady Lions Club **[10548]**, Brooklyn Park, MN
Brooklyn Park Lions Club **[10549]**, Brooklyn Park, MN
Brookville Fire Dept. Assn. **[13440]**, Brookville, OH
Brookville-Franklin County Chamber of Commerce **[4298]**, Brookville, IN
Brotherhood of Locomotive Engineers and Trainmen, AFL-CIO - Div. 333 **[11536]**, Minneapolis, MN
Brotherhood of Locomotive Engineers and Trainmen, AFL-CIO - Div. 724 **[3408]**, Salem, IL
Brotherhood of Maintenance of Way Employees, AFL-CIO, CLC - Chicago and Northwestern Sys. Fed. **[3235]**, Rock Falls, IL
Bros. and Sisters of Ozaukee County; Big **[18062]**, Grafton, WI
Brown County 4-H and Youth Prog. **[18087]**, Green Bay, WI
Brown County Assn. for Retarded Citizens **[18088]**, Green Bay, WI
Brown County Bluebird Soc. **[5910]**, Nashville, IN
Brown County Chamber of Commerce **[5911]**, Nashville, IN
Brown County Chamber of Commerce **[15313]**, Georgetown, OH
Brown County Civic Music Assn. **[18089]**, Green Bay, WI
Brown County Convention and Visitors Bur. **[5912]**, Nashville, IN
Brown County Historical Soc. **[11883]**, New Ulm, MN
Brown County Historical Soc. **[18090]**, Green Bay, WI
Brown County Lions Club **[5913]**, Nashville, IN
Brown County Sportsmen's Club **[18091]**, Green Bay, WI
Brown Deer Chamber of Commerce **[17691]**, Brown Deer, WI
Brownsburg Chamber of Commerce **[4303]**, Brownsburg, IN
Brownstown Lions Club **[7032]**, Brownstown, MI
Brownsville Lions Club **[10566]**, Brownsville, MN
Brukner Gem and Mineral Club **[16998]**, Troy, OH
Brule River Riders Snowmobile Club **[19495]**, Poplar, WI
Brunswick Area Chamber of Commerce **[13445]**, Brunswick, OH
Brunswick Chamber of Commerce **[★13445]**
Bryan Area Chamber of Commerce **[13454]**, Bryan, OH
Buchanan Area Chamber of Commerce **[7035]**, Buchanan, MI
Buckeye Appaloosa Horse Club **[13360]**, Big Prairie, OH
Buckeye Assn. of School Administrators **[14341]**, Columbus, OH
Buckeye Beagle Club **[16148]**, New Philadelphia, OH
Buckeye Beemers No. 99 **[14342]**, Columbus, OH
Buckeye Bop Club **[17206]**, Westerville, OH
Buckeye Chap. Paralyzed Veterans of Am. **[15139]**, Euclid, OH
Buckeye Corvettes **[13550]**, Canton, OH
Buckeye Forest Coun. **[13203]**, Athens, OH
Buckeye Fox Trotter Assn. **[13446]**, Brunswick, OH
Buckeye Hills-Hocking Valley Regional Development District **[15815]**, Marietta, OH
Buckeye Military Vehicle Collectors **[16065]**, Montville, OH
Buckeye Model Yachtsmen No. 188 **[14343]**, Columbus, OH
Buckeye SCORE **[13551]**, Canton, OH
Buckeye Sertoma Club **[14344]**, Columbus, OH
Buckeye State Sheriff's Assn. **[14345]**, Columbus, OH
Buckeye Trail Assn. **[17342]**, Worthington, OH
Buckeye Triumphs **[15532]**, Johnstown, OH
Buckeye United Fly Fishers **[13764]**, Cincinnati, OH
Buckeye Vintage Thunderbird Club of Ohio **[16244]**, North Royalton, OH
Buckeye Wander Freunde **[14346]**, Columbus, OH
Buckeye Woodworkers and Turners **[16549]**, Rootstown, OH
Bucks of Michigan; Commemorative **[7486]**, Dryden, MI
Bucyrus Area Bd. of Realtors **[13463]**, Bucyrus, OH
Bucyrus Area Chamber of Commerce **[13464]**, Bucyrus, OH
Bucyrus Area United Way **[13465]**, Bucyrus, OH
Bucyrus Lions Club **[13466]**, Bucyrus, OH
Buena Vista Lions Club - Michigan **[9605]**, Saginaw, MI

Buffalo Area Chamber of Commerce **[10572]**, Buffalo, MN
Buffalo Assn; Minnesota **[12953]**, Winona, MN
Buffalo Grove Area Chamber of Commerce **[360]**, Buffalo Grove, IL
Buffalo Grove Chamber of Commerce **[★360]**
Buffalo Lake Lions Club **[10582]**, Buffalo Lake, MN
Buffet - Wyldlife **[12717]**, Stillwater, MN
Bugle Corps Assn; Madison Drum and **[19860]**, Sun Prairie, WI
Buick Club of Am. - Chicagoland Chap. **[3865]**, Villa Park, IL
Buick Club of Am. - Gopher State Chap. **[10725]**, Cottage Grove, MN
Builders Assn. of Eastern Ohio and Western Pennsylvania **[17069]**, Vienna, OH
Builders Assn. of Fort Wayne; Home **[4668]**, Fort Wayne, IN
Builders Assn. of Greater Cleveland; Home **[15497]**, Independence, OH
Builders Assn. of Illinois; Home **[3559]**, Springfield, IL
Builders Assn; Illinois Road and Trans. **[2067]**, Itasca, IL
Builders Assn; Lakes Area **[10774]**, Detroit Lakes, MN
Builders Assn., Northern Ohio Chap; Amer. Mold **[17013]**, Twinsburg, OH
Builders Assn; Quad City **[★3237]**
Builders' Assn; Racine/Kenosha **[19848]**, Sturtevant, WI
Builders Assn. of Saginaw; Home **[9609]**, Saginaw, MI
Builders Assn; Suburban Northwest **[10949]**, Elk River, MN
Builders Assn. of the Twin Cities, Natl. Assn. of Home Building **[12223]**, Roseville, MN
Builders Assn. of Wayne and Holmes Counties; Home **[17319]**, Wooster, OH
Builders Assn; West Central **[11875]**, New London, MN
Builders and Contractors of Michigan; Assoc. **[8550]**, Lansing, MI
Builders and Contractors-Ohio Valley Chap; Assoc. **[16704]**, Springboro, OH
Builders Exchange of Central Ohio **[14347]**, Columbus, OH
Builders Exchange; Dayton **[14872]**, Dayton, OH
Builders Exchange of East Central Ohio **[13552]**, Canton, OH
Builders Exchange Foundation **[14348]**, Columbus, OH
Builders Exchange of Grand Rapids **[7914]**, Grand Rapids, MI
Builders Exchange of Lansing and Central Michigan **[8556]**, Lansing, MI
Builders Exchange of Rochester **[12131]**, Rochester, MN
Builders Exchange of St. Paul **[12395]**, St. Paul, MN
Builders of the U.S., Central Wisconsin Home Builders Assn; Natl. Assn. of Home **[20188]**, Wisconsin Rapids, WI
Builders of the U.S., Sheboygan County Home Builders Assn; Natl. Assn. of Home **[19491]**, Plymouth, WI
Builders of the U.S., Wausau Area Builders Assn; Natl. Assn. of Home **[20041]**, Wausau, WI
Builders of the U.S., Anderson Home Builders Assn; Natl. Assn. of Home **[★4114]**
Builders of the U.S., Building Indus. Assn. of Northwest Indiana; Natl. Assn. of Home **[4436]**, Crown Point, IN
Builders of the U.S., Central Minnesota Builders Assn; Natl. Assn. of Home **[12294]**, St. Cloud, MN
Builders of the U.S., Chippewa Valley Home Builders Assn; Natl. Assn. of Home **[17889]**, Eau Claire, WI
Builders of the U.S., Door County Home Builders Assn; Natl. Assn. of Home **[19840]**, Sturgeon Bay, WI
Builders of the U.S., Dubois County Builders Assn; Natl. Assn. of Home **[5531]**, Jasper, IN
Builders of the U.S., Hancock County Home Builders Assn; Natl. Assn. of Home **[15210]**, Findlay, OH
Builders of the U.S., Headwaters Builders Assn; Natl. Assn. of Home **[10422]**, Bemidji, MN
Builders of the U.S., Home Builders Assn. of Bloomington-Normal; Natl. Assn. of Home **[300]**, Bloomington, IL
Builders of the U.S., Home Builders Assn. of Greater Cincinnati; Natl. Assn. of Home **[13920]**, Cincinnati, OH
Builders of the U.S., Home Builders Assn. of Lawrence County; Natl. Assn. of Home **[6011]**, Oolitic, IN
Builders of the U.S., Home Builders Assn. of Miami County; Natl. Assn. of Home **[★17000]**
Builders of the U.S., Home Builders Assn. of the Upper Penninsula; Natl. Assn. of Home **[8954]**, Marquette, MI
Builders of the U.S., Home and Building Assn. of Greater Grand Rapids; Natl. Assn. of Home **[7989]**, Grand Rapids, MI
Builders of the U.S., La Crosse Area Builders Assn; Natl. Assn. of Home **[19366]**, Onalaska, WI
Builders of the U.S., Madison County Home Builders Assn; Natl. Assn. of Home **[4114]**, Anderson, IN
Builders of the U.S., Manitowoc County Home Builders Assn; Natl. Assn. of Home **[18789]**, Manitowoc, WI
Builders of the U.S., Mid Wisconsin Home Builders Assn; Natl. Assn. of Home **[19509]**, Portage, WI
Builders of the U.S., Monroe County Builders Assn; Natl. Assn. of Home **[4247]**, Bloomington, IN
Builders of the U.S., Northern Illinois Home Builders Assn; Natl. Assn. of Home **[3877]**, Warrenville, IL
Builders of the U.S., St. Croix Valley Home Builders Assn; Natl. Assn. of Home **[19319]**, New Richmond, WI
Builders of the U.S., South Central Home Builders Assn; Natl. Assn. of Home **[2602]**, Mount Vernon, IL
Builders of the U.S., Valley Home Builders Assn; Natl. Assn. of Home **[17506]**, Appleton, WI
Building Assn; West Union Firemens' **[17199]**, West Union, OH
Building and Constr. Trades Dept. AFL-CIO, Chicago and Cook County **[772]**, Chicago, IL
Building and Constr. Trades Dept. AFL-CIO, Decatur **[1377]**, Decatur, IL
Building and Constr. Trades Dept., AFL-CIO - Livingston and Mclean Counties Building and Constr. Trades Coun. **[268]**, Bloomington, IL
Building and Constr. Trades Dept. AFL-CIO, Milwaukee **[18984]**, Milwaukee, WI
Building and Constr. Trades Dept. AFL-CIO, Northeastern Indiana, BCTC **[★4702]**
Building Corp; Syracuse Municipal **[6292]**, Syracuse, IN
Building Industries
Aggregate Ready Mix Assn. of Minnesota **[10584]**, Burnsville, MN
Assoc. Roofing Contractors of Maryland **[3359]**, Rosemont, IL
Brick Distributors of Minnesota **[11535]**, Minneapolis, MN
Builders Exchange of Central Ohio **[14347]**, Columbus, OH
Builders Exchange of East Central Ohio **[13552]**, Canton, OH
Builders Exchange Foundation **[14348]**, Columbus, OH
Builders Exchange of Grand Rapids **[7914]**, Grand Rapids, MI
Builders Exchange of Rochester **[12131]**, Rochester, MN
Building Owners and Managers **[18985]**, Milwaukee, WI
Chicago Roofing Distributors Assn. **[828]**, Chicago, IL
Constr. Assn. of Michigan **[6981]**, Bloomfield Hills, MI
Design-Build Inst. of Am. - Great Lakes Chap. **[869]**, Chicago, IL
Design-Build Inst. of Am. - Upper Midwest Chap. **[11553]**, Minneapolis, MN
Duluth Builders Exchange **[10815]**, Duluth, MN
Fed. of Women Contractors **[891]**, Chicago, IL
Fox Valley Natl. Assn. of The Remodeling Indus. **[17493]**, Appleton, WI
Greater Peoria Contractors and Suppliers Assn. **[3022]**, Peoria, IL
Illinois Asphalt Pavement Assn. **[3563]**, Springfield, IL
Illinois Lumber and Materials Dealers Assn. **[3613]**, Springfield, IL
Indiana Ready-Mixed Concrete Assn. **[5288]**, Indianapolis, IN
Intl. Assn. for the Retractable Awning Indus., Michigan Chap. **[6613]**, Allen Park, MI
Kalamazoo Builders Exchange **[8436]**, Kalamazoo, MI
La Crosse Builders Exchange **[18356]**, La Crosse, WI
Lake County Contractors Assn. **[3927]**, Waukegan, IL
Lawrence County Homebuilders Association **[4173]**, Bedford, IN
Masonry Inst. of Michigan **[8846]**, Livonia, MI
Miami Valley NARI **[14915]**, Dayton, OH
Michigan Carpentry Contractors Assn. **[8850]**, Livonia, MI
Michigan Concrete Assn. **[8648]**, Lansing, MI
Michigan Concrete Paving Assn. **[9276]**, Okemos, MI
Michigan Lumber and Building Materials Assn. **[8684]**, Lansing, MI
Milwaukee/Natl. Assn. of the Remodeling Indus. Home Improvement Coun. **[20078]**, Wauwatosa, WI
Minneapolis Builders Exchange **[11610]**, Minneapolis, MN
Minnesota Asphalt Pavement Assn. **[11862]**, New Brighton, MN
Minnesota Concrete and Masonry Contractors Assn. **[12470]**, St. Paul, MN
Minnesota Lath and Plaster Bur. **[12492]**, St. Paul, MN
Minnesota Truss Manufacturers Assn. **[11814]**, Montrose, MN
Natl. Assn. of the Remodeling Indus. of Central Indiana **[5421]**, Indianapolis, IN
Natl. Assn. of the Remodeling Indus. of Central Ohio **[17216]**, Westerville, OH
Natl. Assn. of the Remodeling Indus. East Central Ohio **[17078]**, Wadsworth, OH
Natl. Assn. of the Remodeling Indus. of Greater Chicagoland **[1464]**, Des Plaines, IL
Natl. Assn. of the Remodeling Indus. of Michiana Chap. **[4811]**, Granger, IN
Natl. Assn. of the Remodeling Indus. of Southeast Michigan **[6744]**, Ann Arbor, MI
Natl. Assn. of the Remodeling Indus. of Wabash Valley **[5627]**, Lafayette, IN
Natl. Assn. of The Remodeling Indus. of Madison **[18577]**, Madison, WI
Northwest Regional Builders Exchange **[17890]**, Eau Claire, WI
Ohio Valley NARI **[14943]**, Dayton, OH
Professional Remodelers of Ohio **[15504]**, Independence, OH
Racine/Kenosha Builders' Assn. **[19848]**, Sturtevant, WI
St. Cloud Builders Exchange **[12300]**, St. Cloud, MN
Tri-County Natl. Assn. of The Remodeling Indus. **[13100]**, Akron, OH
Tri-Lakes Home Builders Assn. **[9558]**, Roscommon, MI
West Central Builders Assn. **[11875]**, New London, MN
Wisconsin Asphalt Pavement Assn. **[18647]**, Madison, WI
Wood Truss Coun. of Am. **[18767]**, Madison, WI
Wood Truss Coun. of Am. - Illinois **[3331]**, Rockford, IL
Wood Truss Coun. of Am. Ohio Chap. Assn. **[13595]**, Canton, OH
Wood Truss Coun. of Michigan **[9647]**, Saginaw, MI
Building Indus. Assn. of North Central Ohio **[15764]**, Mansfield, OH
Building Indus. Assn. of South Central Ohio **[13662]**, Chillicothe, OH
Building Industry Association of Southeastern Michigan **[7656]**, Farmington Hills, MI
Building Indus. Assn. of Stark County **[16215]**, North Canton, OH
Building Owners and Managers **[18985]**, Milwaukee, WI
Building Owners and Managers Assn. of Metropolitan Detroit **[7657]**, Farmington Hills, MI
Building Trades
Building and Constr. Trades Dept., AFL-CIO - Livingston and Mclean Counties Building and Constr. Trades Coun. **[268]**, Bloomington, IL

Greater Cincinnati Building and Constr. Trades Coun. **[13840]**, Cincinnati, OH
Indiana Building and Constr. Trades Coun. **[5201]**, Indianapolis, IN
Intl. Brotherhood of Painters and Allied Trades of the United States and Canada AFL-CIO-CFL - District Coun. 6 **[16791]**, Strongsville, OH
Intl. Brotherhood of Painters and Allied Trades of the United States and Canada AFL-CIO-CFL - District Coun. 14 **[985]**, Chicago, IL
Intl. Brotherhood of Painters and Allied Trades of the U.S. and Canada AFL-CIO-CFL - District Coun. 30 **[3386]**, St. Charles, IL
Intl. Union of Bricklayers and Allied Craftworkers, AFL-CIO-CLC Indiana and Kentucky Local Union 4 **[4108]**, Anderson, IN
Intl. Union of Bricklayers and Allied Craftworkers, AFL-CIO-CLC Local Union 6 **[3283]**, Rockford, IL
Intl. Union of Bricklayers and Allied Craftworkers, AFL-CIO-CLC Local Union 9 **[8580]**, Lansing, MI
Intl. Union of Bricklayers and Allied Craftworkers, AFL-CIO-CLC Local Union 20 **[3925]**, Waukegan, IL
Intl. Union of Bricklayers and Allied Craftworkers, AFL-CIO-CLC Local Union 36 **[14147]**, Cleveland, OH
Intl. Union of Bricklayers and Allied Craftworkers, AFL-CIO-CLC Local Union 43 **[17102]**, Warren, OH
Intl. Union of Bricklayers and Allied Craftworkers, AFL-CIO-CLC Michigan Local Union 1 **[10064]**, Warren, MI
Intl. Union of Bricklayers and Allied Craftworkers, AFL-CIO-CLC Wisconsin District Coun. **[19290]**, New Berlin, WI
Intl. Union of Operating Engineers, Local 018 **[14148]**, Cleveland, OH
Intl. Union of Operating Engineers, Local 049 **[11590]**, Minneapolis, MN
Intl. Union of Operating Engineers, Local 139 **[19437]**, Pewaukee, WI
Intl. Union of Operating Engineers, Local 143 **[995]**, Chicago, IL
Intl. Union of Operating Engineers, Local 148 **[2429]**, Maryville, IL
Intl. Union of Operating Engineers, Local 150 **[1306]**, Countryside, IL
Intl. Union of Operating Engineers, Local 310 **[18110]**, Green Bay, WI
Intl. Union of Operating Engineers, Local 317 **[19036]**, Milwaukee, WI
Intl. Union of Operating Engineers, Local 324 **[8841]**, Livonia, MI
Intl. Union of Operating Engineers, Local 399 **[996]**, Chicago, IL
Intl. Union of Operating Engineers, Local 547 **[7380]**, Detroit, MI
Intl. Union of Operating Engineers, Local 649 **[3031]**, Peoria, IL
Intl. Union of Operating Engineers, Local 950 **[19037]**, Milwaukee, WI
Michigan State Building and Constr. Trades Coun. **[8720]**, Lansing, MI
Northeast Wisconsin Building and Constr. Trades Coun. **[17510]**, Appleton, WI
Northwestern Lumber Assn. **[11716]**, Minneapolis, MN
Sheet Metal Workers' Local Union 33 Cleveland District **[14217]**, Cleveland, OH
United Brotherhood of Carpenters and Joiners of Am., Chicago Local Union No. 1185 **[2025]**, Hinsdale, IL
United Brotherhood of Carpenters and Joiners of Am., Chicago Local Union No. 9074 **[2026]**, Hinsdale, IL
United Brotherhood of Carpenters and Joiners of Am., Chicago Regional Coun. of Carpenters **[1214]**, Chicago, IL
United Brotherhood of Carpenters and Joiners of Am., Cleveland Local Union No. 21 **[14223]**, Cleveland, OH
United Brotherhood of Carpenters and Joiners of Am., Cleveland Local Union No. 509 **[14224]**, Cleveland, OH
United Brotherhood of Carpenters and Joiners of Am., Heartland Regional Coun. of Carpenters 4274 **[3705]**, Sterling, IL
United Brotherhood of Carpenters and Joiners of Am., Hobart Local Union No. 1005 **[4931]**, Hobart, IN
United Brotherhood of Carpenters and Joiners of Am., Lakes and Plains Regional Coun. 4020 **[12601]**, St. Paul, MN
United Brotherhood of Carpenters and Joiners of Am., Mankato Local Union No. 464 **[11405]**, Mankato, MN
United Brotherhood of Carpenters and Joiners of Am., Marshfield Local Union No. 2958 **[17551]**, Auburndale, WI
United Brotherhood of Carpenters and Joiners of Am., Michigan Regional Coun. of Carpenters and Millwrights **[7445]**, Detroit, MI
United Brotherhood of Carpenters and Joiners of Am., Mid-Central Illinois Regional Coun. of Carpenters **[3691]**, Springfield, IL
United Brotherhood of Carpenters and Joiners of Am., Midwestern Coun. of Indus. Workers 4021 **[19405]**, Oshkosh, WI
United Brotherhood of Carpenters and Joiners of Am., Northern Wisconsin Regional Coun. of Carpenters 4183 **[18289]**, Kaukauna, WI
United Brotherhood of Carpenters and Joiners of Am., Ohio and Vicinity Regional Coun. of Carpenters **[14225]**, Cleveland, OH
United Brotherhood of Carpenters and Joiners of Am., Toledo Local Union No. 248 **[16559]**, Rossford, OH
United Brotherhood of Carpenters and Joiners of Am., Youngstown Local Union No. 171 **[17418]**, Youngstown, OH
United Union Roofers, Waterproofers and Allied Workers, 96 **[11768]**, Minneapolis, MN
Bulls Run Ramblers **[16005]**, Middletown, OH
Bungalow Initiative; Historic Chicago **[915]**, Chicago, IL
Burbank Chamber of Commerce **[368]**, Burbank, IL
Bur. County Angus Assn. **[3733]**, Sublette, IL
Bur. County Historical Soc. **[3134]**, Princeton, IL
Bur. County United Way **[3135]**, Princeton, IL
Bur. of Criminal Apprehension Agents' Assn; Minnesota **[12461]**, St. Paul, MN
Burlington Area Chamber of Commerce **[17696]**, Burlington, WI
Burlington Lions Club **[17697]**, Burlington, WI
Burn Survivors Support Gp. **[5064]**, Indianapolis, IN
Burnham Astronomical Soc. **[★792]**
Burns
Phoenix Soc. for Burn Survivors **[7494]**, East Grand Rapids, MI
Burnsville Chamber of Commerce **[10587]**, Burnsville, MN
Burnsville Convention and Visitors Bur. **[10588]**, Burnsville, MN
Burnsville-Minnesota Valley Figure Skating Club **[10589]**, Burnsville, MN
Burnsville Young Life **[10590]**, Burnsville, MN
Bus
Wisconsin School Bus Assn. **[19716]**, Sheboygan, WI
Bushnell Chamber of Commerce **[379]**, Bushnell, IL
Business
Abraham Lincoln Tourism Bur. of Logan County **[2270]**, Lincoln, IL
Addison Chamber of Commerce and Indus. **[3]**, Addison, IL
Albert Lea Convention and Visitors Bur. **[10252]**, Albert Lea, MN
Alliance of the St. **[11478]**, Minneapolis, MN
Alpena Area Convention and Visitors Bur. **[6639]**, Alpena, MI
Alpha Iota Delta, Pi Chap. **[14836]**, Dayton, OH
Amer. Mold Builders Assn., Northern Ohio Chap. **[17013]**, Twinsburg, OH
Anderson/Madison County Visitors and Convention Bur. **[4100]**, Anderson, IN
Assn. for Corporate Growth, Chicago Chap. **[3968]**, Westmont, IL
Assn. for Corporate Growth, Greater Cincinnati Chap. **[13752]**, Cincinnati, OH
Assn. for Corporate Growth, Minnesota Chap. **[10880]**, East Bethel, MN
Assn. for Corporate Growth, Southeast Michigan Chap. **[6682]**, Ann Arbor, MI
Assn. for Corporate Growth, Western Michigan Chap. **[7911]**, Grand Rapids, MI
Assn. for Corporate Growth, Wisconsin Chap. **[18038]**, Germantown, WI
Back of the Yards Bus. Assn. **[758]**, Chicago, IL
Baraga County Tourist and Recreation Assn. **[6795]**, L'Anse, MI
Bay Area Convention and Visitors Bur. **[6882]**, Bay City, MI
Bemidji Visitors and Convention Bureau **[10413]**, Bemidji, MN
Berlin Community Development Corp. **[17625]**, Berlin, WI
Beta Gamma Sigma, Eastern Michigan Univ. Chap. **[10200]**, Ypsilanti, MI
Bloomington Convention and Visitors Bur. **[4206]**, Bloomington, IN
Bloomington Convention and Visitors Bur. **[10465]**, Bloomington, MN
Booker T. Washington Bus. Assn. **[7330]**, Detroit, MI
Brainerd Lakes Area Development Corp. **[10509]**, Brainerd, MN
Burnsville Convention and Visitors Bur. **[10588]**, Burnsville, MN
Bus. Coun., Milwaukee **[18986]**, Milwaukee, WI
Cadillac Area Visitors Bur. **[7045]**, Cadillac, MI
Carbondale Convention and Tourism Bur. **[416]**, Carbondale, IL
Cashton Development Corp. **[17721]**, Cashton, WI
Chicago Area Gay and Lesbian Chamber of Commerce **[783]**, Chicago, IL
Chicago Natl. Assn. of Women Bus. Owners **[822]**, Chicago, IL
Chicagoland Chamber of Commerce **[841]**, Chicago, IL
Chippewa Falls Main St. **[17751]**, Chippewa Falls, WI
Cincinnati Bus. and Professional Women's Club **[13779]**, Cincinnati, OH
Clark - Floyd Counties Convention and Tourism Bur. **[5541]**, Jeffersonville, IN
Clyde Bus. and Professional Assn. **[14256]**, Clyde, OH
Columbia Club **[5092]**, Indianapolis, IN
Cook Area Chamber of Commerce **[10705]**, Cook, MN
Cuba City Community Development Corp. **[17796]**, Cuba City, WI
Delta Solutions **[1420]**, Deerfield, IL
Detroit Metro Convention and Visitors Bur. **[7350]**, Detroit, MI
Detroit Regional Economic Partnership **[7355]**, Detroit, MI
Dickinson Area Partnership **[8322]**, Iron Mountain, MI
DKY Developers Association **[2507]**, Mokena, IL
East Side Bus. Men's Assn. **[18506]**, Madison, WI
East Town Bus. and Merchant's Assn. **[20073]**, Wauwatosa, WI
Eau Claire Area Economic Development Corp. **[17874]**, Eau Claire, WI
Elgin Area Convention and Visitors Bur. **[1588]**, Elgin, IL
Evansville Convention and Visitors Bur. **[4546]**, Evansville, IN
Executive Ser. Corps of Chicago **[888]**, Chicago, IL
Fairbury Chamber of Commerce **[1685]**, Fairbury, IL
Four Flags Area Coun. on Tourism **[9207]**, Niles, MI
Foxview Alliance for Corp. Enhancement **[453]**, Carpentersville, IL
Galesburg Area Convention and Visitors Bur. **[1772]**, Galesburg, IL
Gaylord Area Convention and Tourism Bur. **[7818]**, Gaylord, MI
Grand Haven-Spring Lake Convention and Visitors Bureau **[7858]**, Grand Haven, MI
Grand Rapids/Kent County Convention and Visitors Bur. **[7950]**, Grand Rapids, MI
Grayling Area Visitors Council **[8060]**, Grayling, MI
Greater Cincinnati Venture Association **[13856]**, Cincinnati, OH
Greater Erie County Marketing Gp. **[16613]**, Sandusky, OH

Greater Hamilton Convention and Visitors Bur. **[15385]**, Hamilton, OH
Greater Harlan Bus. Assn. **[4898]**, Harlan, IN
Greater Lansing Convention and Visitors Bur. **[8573]**, Lansing, MI
Greater Mankato Chamber of Commerce **[11378]**, Mankato, MN
Greater Minneapolis Convention and Visitors Assn. **[11570]**, Minneapolis, MN
Greater Mitchell St. Assn. **[19021]**, Milwaukee, WI
Growth Assn. of Southwestern Illinois **[1874]**, Godfrey, IL
Harbor Country Chamber of Commerce **[9186]**, New Buffalo, MI
Heart of Wisconsin Bus. and Economic Alliance **[20186]**, Wisconsin Rapids, WI
HIPAA - Collaborative of Wisconsin **[19966]**, Watertown, WI
Holland Convention and Visitor's Bur. **[8202]**, Holland, MI
Howard County Convention and Visitors Commission **[5568]**, Kokomo, IN
Huntington County Visitor and Convention Bur. **[4951]**, Huntington, IN
Illinois Assn. of Aggregate Producers **[3564]**, Springfield, IL
Illinois Mini Storage Assn. **[3615]**, Springfield, IL
Illinois Sign Assn. **[18156]**, Greenfield, WI
Independent Bus. Assn. of Wisconsin **[18522]**, Madison, WI
Indiana Northeast Development **[4679]**, Fort Wayne, IN
Indiana Self Storage Assn. **[5296]**, Indianapolis, IN
Indianapolis Convention and Visitors Assn. **[5344]**, Indianapolis, IN
Inforum **[7377]**, Detroit, MI
Jackson Convention and Tourist Bur. **[8373]**, Jackson, MI
Kokomo Howard County Development Corp. **[5575]**, Kokomo, IN
Korean Amer. Merchants Assn. of Chicago **[1014]**, Chicago, IL
Kosciusko County Convention and Visitors Bur. **[6446]**, Warsaw, IN
La Crosse Area Development Corp. **[18354]**, La Crosse, WI
Lafayette - West Lafayette Convention and Visitors Bur. **[5623]**, Lafayette, IN
Lafayette - West Lafayette Economic Development Corp. **[5624]**, Lafayette, IN
Lake County Convention and Visitors Bur. **[4885]**, Hammond, IN
Lansing Neighborhood Coun. **[8591]**, Lansing, MI
LaPorte County Convention and Visitors Bur. **[5785]**, Michigan City, IN
Lenawee County Chamber of Found. **[6575]**, Adrian, MI
Lenawee County Conf. and Visitors Bur. **[6577]**, Adrian, MI
Livingston County Convention and Visitors Bur. **[8280]**, Howell, MI
Madison Area Quality Improvement Network **[18547]**, Madison, WI
Marion-Grant County Convention and Visitors Bur. **[5739]**, Marion, IN
Marquette County Convention and Visitors Bur. **[8940]**, Marquette, MI
Marshall County Convention and Visitors Bur. **[6048]**, Plymouth, IN
Mecosta County Convention and Visitors Bur. **[6948]**, Big Rapids, MI
Michigan Bus. and Professional Assn. **[10069]**, Warren, MI
Michigan Fed. of Bus. and Professional Women's Clubs **[8970]**, Marshall, MI
Michigan's Sunrise Side Travel Assn. **[9175]**, National City, MI
Middletown Convention and Visitors Bur. **[16014]**, Middletown, OH
MidTown Cleveland **[14165]**, Cleveland, OH
Midwest Bus. Brokers and Intermediaries **[3439]**, Schaumburg, IL
Minneapolis Metro North Convention and Visitors Bur. **[11615]**, Minneapolis, MN
Minnesota Self Storage Assn. **[11063]**, Golden Valley, MN
Minocqua - Arbor Vitae - Woodruff Chamber of Commerce **[19199]**, Minocqua, WI
Montpelier Indus. Development Comm. **[16062]**, Montpelier, OH
Muskegon County Convention and Visitors Bur. **[9152]**, Muskegon, MI
Natl. Assn. of Women Bus. Owners, Greater Detroit Chap. **[7408]**, Detroit, MI
Natl. Assn. of Women Bus. Owners, Indianapolis **[5425]**, Indianapolis, IN
Natl. Assn. of Women Bus. Owners - Minnesota Chap. **[12548]**, St. Paul, MN
Natl. Fed. of Independent Bus. - Michigan **[8743]**, Lansing, MI
Newberry Area Tourism Assn. **[9199]**, Newberry, MI
North Ridgeville Chamber of Commerce/Visitors Bur. **[16242]**, North Ridgeville, OH
Northwest Ohio Mayors and Managers Assn. **[16943]**, Toledo, OH
Oak Park Area Convention and Visitors Bur. **[2821]**, Oak Park, IL
Ohio Storage Owner's Soc. **[14686]**, Columbus, OH
Ohio Venture Assn. **[14202]**, Cleveland, OH
Old Orchard Unit Owners Assn. **[13948]**, Cincinnati, OH
Old Village Business Alliance **[10072]**, Warren, MI
Oneida County Economic Development Corp. **[19602]**, Rhinelander, WI
Petoskey-Harbor Springs-Boyne Country Visitors Bur. **[9367]**, Petoskey, MI
Prairie Du Chien Indus. Development Corp. **[19530]**, Prairie Du Chien, WI
Prentice Indus. Development Corp. **[19537]**, Prentice, WI
Quad City Development Gp. **[3253]**, Rock Island, IL
Red Wing Visitors and Convention Bur. **[12084]**, Red Wing, MN
River Country Tourism Bur. **[9880]**, Sturgis, MI
Rochester Convention and Visitors Bur. **[12176]**, Rochester, MN
Roseland Bus. Development Coun. **[1170]**, Chicago, IL
Saginaw Future **[9633]**, Saginaw, MI
St. Clair County Convention and Visitors Bureau **[9439]**, Port Huron, MI
St. Ignace Area Convention and Visitors Bur. **[9671]**, St. Ignace, MI
Sault Ste. Marie Convention and Visitors Bur. **[9726]**, Sault Ste. Marie, MI
Schaumburg Bus. Assn. **[3445]**, Schaumburg, IL
Scioto Soc. **[13674]**, Chillicothe, OH
Shakopee Chamber of Commerce **[12652]**, Shakopee, MN
SHRM Ohio State Coun. **[13986]**, Cincinnati, OH
Small Bus. Development Center Network **[6108]**, Richmond, IN
South Bend/Mishawaka Convention and Visitors Bur. **[6268]**, South Bend, IN
South Haven Visitors Bur. **[9766]**, South Haven, MI
South Holland Bus. Assn. **[3507]**, South Holland, IL
South Suburban Mayors and Managers Assn. **[1535]**, East Hazel Crest, IL
Southern Indiana, Natl. Assn. of Women Bus. Owners **[5481]**, Indianapolis, IN
Southern Ohio Growth Partnership **[16476]**, Portsmouth, OH
Southwestern Michigan Tourist Coun. **[6922]**, Benton Harbor, MI
Verona Area Chamber of Commerce **[19936]**, Verona, WI
Warehouse District Bus. Assn. **[11777]**, Minneapolis, MN
West Branch-Ogemaw County Travel and Visitors Bur. **[10136]**, West Branch, MI
West Central Association **[1227]**, Chicago, IL
West Michigan Tourist Assn. **[8024]**, Grand Rapids, MI
West Ohio Development Coun. **[16671]**, Sidney, OH
Western U.P. Convention and Visitors Bur. **[8343]**, Ironwood, MI
Westerville Area Chamber of Commerce **[17223]**, Westerville, OH
Westridge Chamber of Commerce **[1231]**, Chicago, IL
Wisconsin Bus. Women's Coalition **[18675]**, Madison, WI
Wisconsin Dells Visitor and Convention Bur. **[20181]**, Wisconsin Dells, WI
Wisconsin Self Storage Assn. **[19181]**, Milwaukee, WI
Women's Entrepreneurial Network **[15920]**, Maumee, OH
Works in Progress **[12638]**, Sauk Rapids, MN
Ypsilanti Convention and Visitors Bur. **[10221]**, Ypsilanti, MI
Business Alliance; Old Village **[10072]**, Warren, MI
Business Alliance of Southwest Michigan; Minority **[8452]**, Kalamazoo, MI
Bus. Assn; Central Ohio Minority **[14360]**, Columbus, OH
Bus. Assn; Detroit Chinese **[7258]**, Dearborn, MI
Bus. Assn; Freedom **[18286]**, Kaukauna, WI
Bus. Assn. of Michigan; Small **[8760]**, Lansing, MI
Bus. Assn; Schaumburg **[3445]**, Schaumburg, IL
Bus. Assn; Wausaukee Area **[20062]**, Wausaukee, WI
Bus. Assn. of Wisconsin; Independent **[18522]**, Madison, WI
Bus. Assn; Young Men's **[★3160]**
Bus. Bureau/Canton Regional; Better **[★13549]**
Bus. Bureau/Canton Regional and Greater West Virginia; Better **[13549]**, Canton, OH
Bus. Bur. of Western Michigan; Better **[7913]**, Grand Rapids, MI

Business and Commerce
Allendale Chamber of Commerce **[6617]**, Allendale, MI
Better Bus. Bur. of Central Indiana **[5057]**, Indianapolis, IN
Bickerdike Redevelopment Corp. **[765]**, Chicago, IL
Brooklyn Area Chamber of Commerce **[17690]**, Brooklyn, WI
Detroit Chinese Bus. Assn. **[7258]**, Dearborn, MI
Detroit Downtown **[7343]**, Detroit, MI
Hispanic Chamber of Commerce of Minnesota **[11578]**, Minneapolis, MN
Illinois Assn. of Mortgage Brokers **[2332]**, Lombard, IL
Illinois Mortgage Bankers Assn. **[951]**, Chicago, IL
Near North Development Corp. **[1092]**, Chicago, IL
Shaker Square Area Development **[14215]**, Cleveland, OH
Sussex Area Chamber of Commerce **[19885]**, Sussex, WI
Bus. Coun; Intl. **[★993]**
Bus. Coun. Midamerica; Intl. **[★993]**
Bus. Coun., Milwaukee **[18986]**, Milwaukee, WI
Bus. Development Center; Illinois Small **[3634]**, Springfield, IL
Bus. Development Center; Indiana Small **[5300]**, Indianapolis, IN
Bus. Development Center; Minnesota Small **[12520]**, St. Paul, MN
Bus. Development Center; Small **[★13612]**
Bus. Development Coun; Michigan Minority **[7397]**, Detroit, MI

Business Education
Amer. Soc. for Training and Development, Central Indiana Chap. **[5024]**, Indianapolis, IN
Amer. Soc. for Training and Development, Chicagoland Chap. **[727]**, Chicago, IL
Amer. Soc. for Training and Development, Greater Cincinnati Chap. **[13735]**, Cincinnati, OH
Amer. Soc. for Training and Development, River Cities Chap. **[4527]**, Evansville, IN
Amer. Soc. for Training and Development, Rock Valley Chap. **[1476]**, Dixon, IL
Amer. Soc. for Training and Development, Southeast Wisconsin Chap. **[18961]**, Milwaukee, WI
Amer. Soc. for Training and Development, Twin Cities Chap. **[12382]**, St. Paul, MN
ASTD, South Central Wisconsin Chap. **[3430]**, Schaumburg, IL
Consortium for Entrepreneurship Educ. **[14413]**, Columbus, OH
Junior Achievement Akron **[13061]**, Akron, OH

Junior Achievement of Brown County **[18113]**, Green Bay, WI
Junior Achievement of Central Indiana **[5383]**, Indianapolis, IN
Junior Achievement of Chicago **[1010]**, Chicago, IL
Junior Achievement of East Central Illinois **[1397]**, Decatur, IL
Junior Achievement of East Central Ohio **[13570]**, Canton, OH
Junior Achievement of Eastern Indiana **[6095]**, Richmond, IN
Junior Achievement of Elkhart County **[4499]**, Elkhart, IN
Junior Achievement of Greater Genesee Valley **[7744]**, Flint, MI
Junior Achievement of Kalamazoo and Van Buren Counties **[8432]**, Kalamazoo, MI
Junior Achievement of Mahoning Valley **[15324]**, Girard, OH
Junior Achievement, Mankato Area **[11381]**, Mankato, MN
Junior Achievement, Michigan Edge **[8383]**, Jackson, MI
Junior Achievement of the Michigan Great Lakes **[7970]**, Grand Rapids, MI
Junior Achievement of the Michigan Great Lakes, Northern Ser. Off. **[6997]**, Boyne City, MI
Junior Achievement OKI Partners **[17175]**, West Chester, OH
Junior Achievement, Quad-Cities Area **[2522]**, Moline, IL
Junior Achievement of Racine **[19557]**, Racine, WI
Junior Achievement, Rochester Area **[12152]**, Rochester, MN
Junior Achievement, Rock County **[18254]**, Janesville, WI
Junior Achievement, Rock River Valley **[3284]**, Rockford, IL
Junior Achievement, South Central Michigan **[6860]**, Battle Creek, MI
Junior Achievement, Southeastern Michigan **[7385]**, Detroit, MI
Junior Achievement of the Wabash Valley **[6332]**, Terre Haute, IN
Junior Achievement West Michigan Lakeshore **[7861]**, Grand Haven, MI
Junior Achievement of Wisconsin **[19039]**, Milwaukee, WI
Junior Achievement of Wisconsin, Marathon County District Off. **[20036]**, Wausau, WI
Junior Achievement of Wisconsin Northwest District **[17882]**, Eau Claire, WI
Minnesota Bus. Educators Inc. **[12954]**, Winona, MN
Natl. Black MBA Assn., Cleveland Chap. **[13290]**, Beachwood, OH
Natl. Black MBA Assn., Detroit Chap. **[7409]**, Detroit, MI
Natl. Black MBA Assn., Twin Cities **[11699]**, Minneapolis, MN
Bus. Marketing Assn., Chicago Chap. **[773]**, Chicago, IL
Bus. Marketing Assn., Detroit Chap. **[9979]**, Troy, MI
Bus. Marketing Assn., Indianapolis Chap. **[5065]**, Indianapolis, IN
Bus. Marketing Assn., Milwaukee Chap. **[19436]**, Pewaukee, WI
Bus. Officials; Illinois Assn. of School **[1434]**, DeKalb, IL
Bus. Owners, Wisconsin; Natl. Assn. of Women **[17508]**, Appleton, WI
Bus. Press Editors, Cleveland Chap; Amer. Soc. of **[★14063]**
Business Products
Indiana Lumber and Builders' Supply Assn. **[5257]**, Indianapolis, IN
Bus. and Professional Assn; Clyde **[14256]**, Clyde, OH
Bus. and Professional Women Clubs; Illinois Fed. of **[3604]**, Springfield, IL
Bus. Professionals of Am., Michigan Assn. **[10201]**, Ypsilanti, MI
Bus. Publication Editors, Cleveland Chap; Amer. Soc. of **[14063]**, Cleveland, OH
Business Tourism
Chicago's North Suburbs, Prospect Heights CVB **[3143]**, Prospect Heights, IL
Perry County Convention and Visitor's Bureau **[6298]**, Tell City, IN
Sandusky County Convention and Visitors Bureau **[15253]**, Fremont, OH
Wisconsin Rapids Area Convention and Visitors Bureau **[20197]**, Wisconsin Rapids, WI
Bus. Volunteers Unlimited **[14085]**, Cleveland, OH
Bus. Women's Coalition; Wisconsin **[18675]**, Madison, WI
Businessmen's Assn; North Olmsted **[★16236]**
Butler Area Chamber of Commerce **[17698]**, Butler, WI
Butler County Chap. of Ohio Genealogical Soc. **[16006]**, Middletown, OH
Butler County Historical Soc. **[15381]**, Hamilton, OH
Butler County United Way **[15382]**, Hamilton, OH
Butler Lions Club **[13475]**, Butler, OH
Butler Lions Club - Wisconsin **[17699]**, Butler, WI
Butler/Warren County Soc. for Human Rsrc. Mgt. **[14864]**, Dayton, OH
Butter and Egg Bd; Chicago **[★818]**
Byesville Bd. of Trade **[13478]**, Byesville, OH
Byron Area Athletic Association **[8817]**, Linden, MI
Byron Area Chamber of Commerce **[383]**, Byron, IL
Byron Area Lions Club **[7038]**, Byron, MI
Byron Lions Club, IL **[384]**, Byron, IL

C

Caballo Norte **[18417]**, Lena, WI
Cabaret Professionals; Chicago **[796]**, Chicago, IL
Cable Area Chamber of Commerce **[17704]**, Cable, WI
Cable and Telecommunications Assn. for Marketing, Ohio Chap. **[13047]**, Akron, OH
Cable TV and Communs. Assn. of Illinois **[1453]**, Des Plaines, IL
Cadillac Area Chamber of Commerce **[7044]**, Cadillac, MI
Cadillac Area Visitors Bur. **[7045]**, Cadillac, MI
Cadillac Lions Club **[7046]**, Cadillac, MI
Cadillac Squares **[9476]**, Redford, MI
Cadillac - Young Life **[8504]**, Lake City, MI
Cadiz Lions Club **[13480]**, Cadiz, OH
Cadott Area Chamber of Commerce **[17707]**, Cadott, WI
Cahokia Area Chamber of Commerce **[386]**, Cahokia, IL
Cahokia Beagle Club **[1810]**, Gillespie, IL
Cairn Terrier Club of Greater Detroit **[7682]**, Fenton, MI
Cairo Chamber of Commerce **[390]**, Cairo, IL
Calcutta Area Chamber of Commerce **[13483]**, Calcutta, OH
Calcutta Lions Club **[13484]**, Calcutta, OH
Caldwell Elementary School PTA **[4875]**, Hammond, IN
Caledonia Lions Club **[11361]**, Mabel, MN
Caledonia - Young Life **[7915]**, Grand Rapids, MI
Calhoun County Genealogical Soc. **[8966]**, Marshall, MI
Calhoun County Medical Soc. - Michigan **[6856]**, Battle Creek, MI
Calhoun County Michigan Chap. of Pheasants Forever **[8967]**, Marshall, MI
Caliburn Fencing Club **[18987]**, Milwaukee, WI
Call to Action Chicagoland **[2805]**, Oak Park, IL
Call to Action of Michigan **[8105]**, Hamtramck, MI
Calumet Area Literacy Coun. **[4876]**, Hammond, IN
Calumet Astronomical Soc. **[4854]**, Griffith, IN
Calumet City Chamber of Commerce **[393]**, Calumet City, IL
Calumet Corner Chorus of Sweet Adelines Intl. **[4877]**, Hammond, IN
Calumet Stamp Club **[4855]**, Griffith, IN
Calvin Christian High School - Young Life **[8035]**, Grandville, MI
Calvin Christian Middle School - Wyldlife **[8036]**, Grandville, MI
Cambodian Assn. of Illinois **[774]**, Chicago, IL
Cambridge Area Chamber of Commerce **[10618]**, Cambridge, MN
Cambridge Area Chamber of Commerce **[13493]**, Cambridge, OH
Cambridge Bd. of Realtors **[13494]**, Cambridge, OH
Cambridge Chamber of Commerce **[17710]**, Cambridge, WI
Cambridge-Isanti - Young Life **[10619]**, Cambridge, MN
Cambridge Lioness Club **[13495]**, Cambridge, OH
Cambridge Lions Club - Ohio **[13496]**, Cambridge, OH
Cambridge - Young Life **[13497]**, Cambridge, OH
Camden Area Chamber of Commerce **[13504]**, Camden, OH
Camden Lions Club **[11537]**, Minneapolis, MN
Camden Lions Club - Ohio **[13505]**, Camden, OH
Camp Assn. Michigan; Amer. **[7887]**, Grand Rapids, MI
Camp Douglas Lions Club **[17714]**, Camp Douglas, WI
Camp Fire Boys & Girls, Minnesota Coun. **[★12396]**
Camp Fire Boys & Girls, Minnesota Lakes Coun. **[★12396]**
Camp Fire Boys and Girls Tayanoka Coun. **[16585]**, Salem, OH
Camp Fire Coun; Northern Star **[★11821]**
Camp Fire-North Oakland Coun. **[★10080]**
Camp Fire; Oneida Coun. of **[★19597]**
Camp Fire USA Greater Dayton Area Coun. **[14865]**, Dayton, OH
Camp Fire USA Illinois Prairie Coun. **[2326]**, Lombard, IL
Camp Fire USA Indiana Heartland Coun. **[5066]**, Indianapolis, IN
Camp Fire USA Metropolitan Chicago Coun. **[775]**, Chicago, IL
Camp Fire USA Minnesota Coun. **[12396]**, St. Paul, MN
Camp Fire USA North Oakland Coun. **[10080]**, Waterford, MI
Camp Fire USA Northeast Ohio Coun. **[13529]**, Canfield, OH
Camp Fire USA Northern Star Coun. **[11821]**, Moorhead, MN
Camp Fire USA Northwest Ohio Coun. **[15197]**, Findlay, OH
Camp Fire USA Oneida Coun. **[19597]**, Rhinelander, WI
Camp Fire USA River Bend Coun. **[6222]**, South Bend, IN
Camp Fire U.S.A. Tayanoka Coun. **[★16585]**
Camp Fire USA Wathana Coun. **[9794]**, Southfield, MI
Camp Fire USA West Michigan Coun. **[7916]**, Grand Rapids, MI
Camp Perry Shooting Club **[16458]**, Port Clinton, OH
Camp Randall Rowing Club **[18494]**, Madison, WI
Campgrounds; Michigan Assn. of Recreational Vehicles and **[9273]**, Okemos, MI
Camping
Amer. Camp Assn. Indiana **[5998]**, North Webster, IN
Amer. Camp Assn. Michigan **[7887]**, Grand Rapids, MI
Amer. Camp Assn. Northland **[10662]**, Circle Pines, MN
Amer. Camp Assn. Ohio **[15041]**, Dublin, OH
Amer. Camping Assn. - Illinois Sect. **[614]**, Chicago, IL
Camp Fire USA Minnesota Coun. **[12396]**, St. Paul, MN
Christian Camp and Conf. Assn., Great Lakes Region **[8408]**, Jones, MI
Christian Camp and Conf. Assn., Illinois **[402]**, Canton, IL
Christian Camp and Conf. Assn., Indiana **[5839]**, Morgantown, IN
Christian Camp and Conf. Assn., Michigan **[9537]**, Rodney, MI
Christian Camp and Conf. Assn., Minn-E-Dakotas Sect. **[12007]**, Pine River, MN
Christian Camp and Conf. Assn., North Central Region **[10683]**, Clitherall, MN
Christian Camp and Conf. Assn., Ohio Sect. **[17433]**, Zanesfield, OH
Christian Camp and Conf. Assn., Wisconsin **[20142]**, Westby, WI
Tourette Syndrome Camping Org. **[1208]**, Chicago, IL
Camping Org; Tourette Syndrome **[1208]**, Chicago, IL
Campus Atheists and Secular Humanists **[11538]**, Minneapolis, MN

Canal Fulton Lions Club **[13512]**, Canal Fulton, OH
Canal Soc. of Indiana **[4646]**, Fort Wayne, IN
Canal Winchester Area Chamber of Commerce **[13516]**, Canal Winchester, OH
Canal Winchester Lions Club **[13517]**, Canal Winchester, OH
Canal Winchester - Young Life **[14349]**, Columbus, OH
Canby Area Chamber of Commerce **[10627]**, Canby, MN
Cancer
Amer. Cancer Soc. **[6656]**, Ann Arbor, MI
Amer. Cancer Soc., Altoona **[17466]**, Altoona, WI
Amer. Cancer Soc., Batavia - Fox Valley Regional **[171]**, Batavia, IL
Amer. Cancer Soc., Bay Area Ser. Center **[7621]**, Essexville, MI
Amer. Cancer Soc., Brainerd **[10504]**, Brainerd, MN
Amer. Cancer Soc., Capital Area Ser. Center **[7500]**, East Lansing, MI
Amer. Cancer Soc. - Central Indiana Area Ser. Center **[4976]**, Indianapolis, IN
Amer. Cancer Soc., Champaign - Eastern Regional **[496]**, Champaign, IL
Amer. Cancer Soc. Chicago Region **[615]**, Chicago, IL
Amer. Cancer Soc., Clark/Miami Area **[16712]**, Springfield, OH
Amer. Cancer Soc., Cuyahoga County **[14045]**, Cleveland, OH
Amer. Cancer Soc., Defiance Area **[14980]**, Defiance, OH
Amer. Cancer Soc., East Michigan Area Ser. Center **[7707]**, Flint, MI
Amer. Cancer Soc., Eau Claire **[17467]**, Altoona, WI
Amer. Cancer Soc., Evanston - North Shore Regional **[1646]**, Evanston, IL
Amer. Cancer Soc., Fairfield Area **[15594]**, Lancaster, OH
Amer. Cancer Soc., Franklin **[18007]**, Franklin, WI
Amer. Cancer Soc., Franklin County **[14276]**, Columbus, OH
Amer. Cancer Soc., Geauga Area **[14777]**, Concord Township, OH
Amer. Cancer Soc., Geauga, Lake Ashtabula Area Off. **[16330]**, Painesville, OH
Amer. Cancer Soc., Gladwin County **[7622]**, Essexville, MI
Amer. Cancer Soc., Glen Ellyn - Du Page County Regional **[2832]**, Oakbrook Terrace, IL
Amer. Cancer Soc., Green Bay **[17811]**, De Pere, WI
Amer. Cancer Soc., Hamilton County **[13706]**, Cincinnati, OH
Amer. Cancer Soc., Hancock **[15191]**, Findlay, OH
Amer. Cancer Soc., Highland Park - Lake County Regional **[2282]**, Lincolnshire, IL
Amer. Cancer Soc., La Crosse **[19359]**, Onalaska, WI
Amer. Cancer Soc., Lakeshore Area Ser. Center **[8188]**, Holland, MI
Amer. Cancer Soc., Livingston County **[7006]**, Brighton, MI
Amer. Cancer Soc., Lorain Area **[15103]**, Elyria, OH
Amer. Cancer Soc., Lucas County **[15899]**, Maumee, OH
Amer. Cancer Soc., Madison **[18455]**, Madison, WI
Amer. Cancer Soc., Mahoning County **[13525]**, Canfield, OH
Amer. Cancer Soc., Marion Area **[15833]**, Marion, OH
Amer. Cancer Soc., Marion - Southern Regional **[2399]**, Marion, IL
Amer. Cancer Soc., Mercer Area **[15644]**, Lima, OH
Amer. Cancer Soc., Metro Detroit Area Ser. Center **[9779]**, Southfield, MI
Amer. Cancer Soc., Mid-Indiana Area Ser. Center **[4095]**, Anderson, IN
Amer. Cancer Soc., Mid-Indiana Area Ser. Center **[5723]**, Marion, IN
Amer. Cancer Soc., Mid-Southwestern Area Ser. Center **[5523]**, Jasper, IN
Amer. Cancer Soc., MidSouthwestern Area Ser. Center **[6407]**, Vincennes, IN
Amer. Cancer Soc., Montgomery Area **[14838]**, Dayton, OH
Amer. Cancer Soc., Moorhead **[11816]**, Moorhead, MN
Amer. Cancer Soc., Muskingum Area **[17434]**, Zanesville, OH
Amer. Cancer Soc., Northeast Indiana Area Ser. Center **[4625]**, Fort Wayne, IN
Amer. Cancer Soc., Northwest Indiana Area Ser. Center **[5762]**, Merrillville, IN
Amer. Cancer Soc., Onalaska **[19360]**, Onalaska, WI
Amer. Cancer Soc., Palatine - Northwest Suburban Regional **[2903]**, Palatine, IL
Amer. Cancer Soc., Peoria - West Central Regional **[3001]**, Peoria, IL
Amer. Cancer Soc., Pickaway Area **[15595]**, Lancaster, OH
Amer. Cancer Soc., Porter County Unit **[6375]**, Valparaiso, IN
Amer. Cancer Soc., Riverside Regional Off. **[3213]**, Riverside, IL
Amer. Cancer Soc., Rochester **[12123]**, Rochester, MN
Amer. Cancer Soc., Rock Island - Northwest Regional **[3238]**, Rock Island, IL
Amer. Cancer Soc., Rockford - Northern Regional **[3263]**, Rockford, IL
Amer. Cancer Soc., Ross Area **[13656]**, Chillicothe, OH
Amer. Cancer Soc., St. Cloud **[12270]**, St. Cloud, MN
Amer. Cancer Soc., Sheboygan **[19688]**, Sheboygan, WI
Amer. Cancer Soc., South Central Michigan Ser. Center **[9012]**, Michigan Center, MI
Amer. Cancer Soc., Southeast Indiana Area Ser. Center **[4364]**, Clarksville, IN
Amer. Cancer Soc., Southwest Ohio Area **[15870]**, Mason, OH
Amer. Cancer Soc., Springfield - Western Regional **[3523]**, Springfield, IL
Amer. Cancer Soc., Stark Area **[16213]**, North Canton, OH
Amer. Cancer Soc., Summit Area **[13028]**, Akron, OH
Amer. Cancer Soc., Tinley Park - Prairie Land Regional **[3765]**, Tinley Park, IL
Amer. Cancer Soc., Trumbull Area **[13526]**, Canfield, OH
Amer. Cancer Soc., Tuscarawas Area **[15025]**, Dover, OH
Amer. Cancer Soc., Vanderburgh County Unit **[4518]**, Evansville, IN
Amer. Cancer Soc., Wabash Valley Indiana Area Ser. Center **[6305]**, Terre Haute, IN
Amer. Cancer Soc., Washington Area **[15812]**, Marietta, OH
Amer. Cancer Soc., Waukesha **[19976]**, Waukesha, WI
Amer. Cancer Soc., Wausau **[20030]**, Wausau, WI
Amer. Cancer Soc., West Michigan Area Ser. Center **[7888]**, Grand Rapids, MI
Amer. Cancer Soc., Willmar **[12911]**, Willmar, MN
Amer. Cancer Soc., Wood Area **[13380]**, Bowling Green, OH
Coalition on Abortion/Breast Cancer **[2033]**, Hoffman Estates, IL
Creating Hope **[4603]**, Fishers, IN
Gilda's Club Grand Rapids **[7940]**, Grand Rapids, MI
Kidney Cancer Assn. **[1664]**, Evanston, IL
Leukemia and Lymphoma Soc. of Am., Northern Ohio **[14158]**, Cleveland, OH
Leukemia and Lymphoma Soc., Indiana Chap. **[5392]**, Indianapolis, IN
Leukemia and Lymphoma Soc., Southern Ohio Chap. **[13886]**, Cincinnati, OH
Little Red Door Cancer Agency **[5394]**, Indianapolis, IN
Teens Aiding the Cancer Community **[9245]**, Novi, MI
Walk and Roll Chicago - Amer. Cancer Soc. **[1225]**, Chicago, IL
Wisconsin Chap., Leukemia and Lymphoma Soc. **[17681]**, Brookfield, WI
Cancer Community; Teens Aiding the **[9245]**, Novi, MI
Cancer Soc., Geauga, Lake Ashtabula Area Off; Amer. **[16330]**, Painesville, OH
Cancer Soc., Henry County Unit; Amer. **[14981]**, Defiance, OH
Cancer Soc; Lagrange County **[5640]**, Lagrange, IN
Cancer Soc., Porter County Unit; Amer. **[6375]**, Valparaiso, IN
Cancer Soc., Southeast Michigan Rsrc. Center; Amer. **[★9779]**
Cancer Soc., Vanderburgh County Unit; Amer. **[4518]**, Evansville, IN
Candy Distributors; Ohio Assn. of Tobacco and **[★14698]**
Canfield Lions Club **[13530]**, Canfield, OH
Canine Rsrc. Development **[13630]**, Chagrin Falls, OH
Canned Vegetable Coun. **[18422]**, Lodi, WI
Cannon Falls Area Chamber of Commerce **[10631]**, Cannon Falls, MN
Cannonsburg Challenged Ski Assn. **[6557]**, Ada, MI
Canoeing
Chicago Whitewater Assn. **[2327]**, Lombard, IL
Northwest Passage Outing Club **[4021]**, Wilmette, IL
Wooden Canoe Heritage Assn., Illinois **[477]**, Cary, IL
Wooden Canoe Heritage Assn., Indiana **[5502]**, Indianapolis, IN
Wooden Canoe Heritage Assn., Michigan **[7584]**, Eaton Rapids, MI
Wooden Canoe Heritage Assn., Minnesota **[11850]**, Mounds View, MN
Wooden Canoe Heritage Assn., Wisconsin **[18283]**, Juneau, WI
Canterbury - Wyldlife **[4647]**, Fort Wayne, IN
Canton ALU **[13553]**, Canton, OH
Canton Area Chamber of Commerce **[401]**, Canton, IL
Canton Area Chap. MOAA **[13554]**, Canton, OH
Canton Audubon Soc. **[13555]**, Canton, OH
Canton Chamber of Commerce **[7061]**, Canton, MI
Canton County Planning Commn. **[★16726]**
Canton Lions Club - Michigan **[7062]**, Canton, MI
Canton Lions Club - Ohio **[13556]**, Canton, OH
Canton/Plymouth/Salem - Young Life **[9396]**, Plymouth, MI
Canton Regional Chamber of Commerce **[13557]**, Canton, OH
Canton South Lions Club **[13558]**, Canton, OH
Canton and Stark County Convention and Visitors Bur. **[13559]**, Canton, OH
Canton Table Tennis Club **[13560]**, Canton, OH
Canton Urban League **[13561]**, Canton, OH
Capac Area Chamber of Commerce **[7075]**, Capac, MI
Capac Community Historical Soc. **[7076]**, Capac, MI
Capital Area Assn. of Realtors **[3541]**, Springfield, IL
Capital Area Astronomy Assn. **[9459]**, Potterville, MI
Capital Area Astronomy Club **[7580]**, Eaton Rapids, MI
Capital Area Literacy Coalition **[8557]**, Lansing, MI
Capital Area United Way **[7513]**, East Lansing, MI
Capital City Corvair Club **[18495]**, Madison, WI
Capital City Corvette Club **[8558]**, Lansing, MI
Capital City Organizational Development Network **[14350]**, Columbus, OH
Capital Punishment
Illinois Coalition Against the Death Penalty **[933]**, Chicago, IL
Minnesotans Against the Death Penalty **[11684]**, Minneapolis, MN
Ohioans to Stop Executions **[14702]**, Columbus, OH
Carbondale Chamber of Commerce **[415]**, Carbondale, IL
Carbondale Convention and Tourism Bur. **[416]**, Carbondale, IL
Carbondale Main St. **[417]**, Carbondale, IL
Card Collectors; Chicago Playing **[2908]**, Palatine, IL
Cardiology
Amer. Coll. of Cardiology - Michigan Chap. **[7577]**, Eaton Rapids, MI
Amer. Coll. of Cardiology - Wisconsin Chap. **[18932]**, Milwaukee, WI
Amer. Heart Assn. **[11488]**, Minneapolis, MN

Amer. Heart Assn., Cincinnati **[13708]**, Cincinnati, OH
Amer. Heart Assn., Madison **[18460]**, Madison, WI
Amer. Heart Assn., Midwest Affl. **[9780]**, Southfield, MI
Illinois Chap. of the Amer. Coll. of Cardiology **[1868]**, Glenview, IL
Minnesota Chap. of the Amer. Coll. of Cardiology **[12464]**, St. Paul, MN
Pediatric Heart Res. Assn. **[17178]**, West Chester, OH
Soc. for Mitral Valve Prolapse Syndrome **[2069]**, Itasca, IL
Wisconsin Chap. of the Amer. Coll. of Cardiology **[19161]**, Milwaukee, WI
Cardiovascular and Pulmonary Rehabilitation; Ohio Assn. of **[16737]**, Springfield, OH
Care; Citizens for Better **[7334]**, Detroit, MI
Care Inst; Citizens for Better **[★7334]**
Care in Nursing Homes for the Aged; Citizens for Better **[★7334]**
Career Development Assn; Minnesota **[10320]**, Apple Valley, MN
Career Guidance Inst. **[★7726]**
Career Paths of Flint **[7718]**, Flint, MI
Career and Tech. Educ; Illinois Assn. for **[3565]**, Springfield, IL
Caregivers of Portage County; Interfaith Volunteer **[19791]**, Stevens Point, WI
Carey Area Chamber of Commerce **[13599]**, Carey, OH
Carey United Way **[13600]**, Carey, OH
Caring Rivers United Way **[10944]**, Elk River, MN
Carl Sanburg Coll. Literacy Coalition **[1769]**, Galesburg, IL
Carlinville Chamber of Commerce **[★438]**
Carlinville Community Chamber of Commerce **[438]**, Carlinville, IL
Carlinville Lions Club **[439]**, Carlinville, IL
Carlisle Lions Club - Ohio **[13601]**, Carlisle, OH
Carlos Lions Club **[10274]**, Alexandria, MN
Carlton County Gem and Mineral Club **[10688]**, Cloquet, MN
Carlton County Historical Soc. **[10689]**, Cloquet, MN
Carlton Lions Club **[10381]**, Barnum, MN
Carlyle Lake Chamber of Commerce **[441]**, Carlyle, IL
Carmel Clay Chamber of Commerce **[4317]**, Carmel, IN
Carmel Clay Veterans Memorial Corp. **[4318]**, Carmel, IN
Carmel High School - Young Life **[5067]**, Indianapolis, IN
Carmel - Wyldlife **[5068]**, Indianapolis, IN
Carmi Chamber of Commerce **[443]**, Carmi, IL
Caro Chamber of Commerce **[7082]**, Caro, MI
Caro Lions Club **[7083]**, Caro, MI
Carol Stream Chamber of Commerce **[445]**, Carol Stream, IL
Carol Stream Youth Cheerleading Assn. **[446]**, Carol Stream, IL
Carriers' Assn; Lake **[14153]**, Cleveland, OH
Carroll County Chamber of Commerce **[★13604]**
Carroll County Chamber of Commerce and Economic Development **[13604]**, Carrollton, OH
Carroll County Historical Soc. Museum **[4454]**, Delphi, IN
Carrollton Chamber of Commerce **[458]**, Carrollton, IL
Carrollton Chamber of Commerce **[★13604]**
Carrollton Lions Club **[13605]**, Carrollton, OH
Carrollton Lions Club - Michigan **[9606]**, Saginaw, MI
Carson City Lions Club **[7089]**, Carson City, MI
Carter Temple Community Development Corp. **[776]**, Chicago, IL
Carterville Chamber of Commerce **[461]**, Carterville, IL
Carthage Area Chamber of Commerce **[465]**, Carthage, IL
Carthage Chamber of Commerce **[★465]**
Carver County Chapter, American Red Cross **[11924]**, Norwood Young America, MN
Carver County Historical Soc. **[12816]**, Waconia, MN
Carver of Evansville Community Development Corp. **[4535]**, Evansville, IN
Carwash Owner and Suppliers **[19553]**, Racine, WI
Cary Basketball Assn. **[470]**, Cary, IL
Cary Character Counts **[471]**, Cary, IL
Cary/Grove Area Chamber of Commerce **[472]**, Cary, IL
Casa De Esperanza **[12397]**, St. Paul, MN
Caseyville Chamber of Commerce **[481]**, Caseyville, IL
Cashton Development Corp. **[17721]**, Cashton, WI
Cashton Lions Club **[17722]**, Cashton, WI
Casino Mgt. Assn. **[7332]**, Detroit, MI
Cass City Chamber of Commerce **[7093]**, Cass City, MI
Cass City Gun Club **[9377]**, Pigeon, MI
Cass City Lions Club **[7094]**, Cass City, MI
Cass County Bd. of Realtors **[5689]**, Logansport, IN
Cass County REACT Team **[5690]**, Logansport, IN
Cass County United Way, Michigan **[7478]**, Dowagiac, MI
Cass River Habitat for Humanity **[10040]**, Vassar, MI
Cassopolis (Central Cass) Lions Club **[7100]**, Cassopolis, MI
Cassville Lions Club **[17724]**, Cassville, WI
Cast Metals
Illinois Cast Metals Assn. **[3587]**, Springfield, IL
Indiana Cast Metals Assn. **[5204]**, Indianapolis, IN
Ohio Cast Metals Assn. **[14576]**, Columbus, OH
Castalia Lions Club **[13606]**, Castalia, OH
Cat
Cat Overpopulation Planned Endeavor **[561]**, Channahon, IL
Cat Overpopulation Planned Endeavor **[561]**, Channahon, IL
Catalina 22 Fleet 158, Lafayette, Indiana **[6479]**, West Lafayette, IN
Catalina 22 Natl. Sailing Assn., Fleet 131 Atwood Lake, Ohio **[14820]**, Cuyahoga Falls, OH
Catholic
Catholic League for Religious and Civil Rights, Ann Arbor Chap. **[6690]**, Ann Arbor, MI
Catholic League for Religious and Civil Rights, Chicago Chap. **[4035]**, Winnetka, IL
Catholic League for Religious and Civil Rights, Rockford, IL Chap. **[3275]**, Rockford, IL
Catholics United for the Faith - Abba, Father Chap. **[5069]**, Indianapolis, IN
Catholics United for the Faith - Blessed John XXIII Chap. **[2612]**, Mundelein, IL
Catholics United for the Faith - Cardinal Newman Chap. **[16852]**, Tiffin, OH
Catholics United for the Faith - Christ the King Chap. **[19317]**, New Richmond, WI
Catholics United for the Faith - Immaculate Heart of Mary Chap. **[7624]**, Essexville, MI
Catholics United for the Faith - Incarnate Word Chap. **[9674]**, St. Johns, MI
Catholics United for the Faith - Mary, Seat of Wisdom Chap. **[7917]**, Grand Rapids, MI
Catholics United for the Faith - Our Daily Bread Chap. **[9351]**, Pentwater, MI
Catholics United for the Faith - Our Lady of Good Help Chap. **[18092]**, Green Bay, WI
Catholics United for the Faith - Our Lady, Help of Christians Chap. **[15765]**, Mansfield, OH
Catholics United for the Faith - Our Lady of the Most Holy Eucharist Chap. **[13228]**, Atwater, OH
Catholics United for the Faith - St. Gregory VII Chap. **[18988]**, Milwaukee, WI
Catholics United for the Faith - St. John Vianney Chap. **[9540]**, Rogers City, MI
Catholics United for the Faith - St. Peter the Rock Chap. **[10984]**, Faribault, MN
Catholics United for the Faith - St. Therese of Lisieux Chap., Ohio **[13476]**, Butler, OH
Catholics United for the Faith - Servants of Christ Through Mary Chap. **[15807]**, Marblehead, OH
Central Ohio Assn. of Catholic Educators **[17207]**, Westerville, OH
Chicago Assn. of Holy Name Societies **[787]**, Chicago, IL
Knights of Columbus, Cleveland Coun. No. 733 **[14152]**, Cleveland, OH
Knights of Columbus, Columbus **[14487]**, Columbus, OH
Knights of Columbus, Coun. 1143 - Edwardsville **[1562]**, Edwardsville, IL
Knights of Columbus, Coun. 4400 **[2114]**, Joliet, IL
Knights of Columbus, Madison **[18538]**, Madison, WI
Knights of Columbus, Marshfield **[18816]**, Marshfield, WI
Minnesota St. Thomas More Chap. of the Catholics United for the Faith **[12516]**, St. Paul, MN
Youngstown Diocesan Confed. of Teachers **[13375]**, Boardman, OH
Catholic Alumni Club of Detroit **[6689]**, Ann Arbor, MI
Catholic Alumni Club of Mississippi and Missouri River Valleys **[200]**, Belleville, IL
Catholic Family Life Ministers, Region VI; Natl. Assn. of **[8457]**, Kalamazoo, MI
Catholic League for Religious and Civil Rights, Ann Arbor Chap. **[6690]**, Ann Arbor, MI
Catholic League for Religious and Civil Rights, Chicago Chap. **[4035]**, Winnetka, IL
Catholic League for Religious and Civil Rights, Rockford, IL Chap. **[3275]**, Rockford, IL
Catholic Men's Fellowship of Northeastern Ohio **[16191]**, Newbury, OH
Catholic Physicians' Guild of Chicago **[2806]**, Oak Park, IL
Catholic Single Adults Club of the Twin Cities **[11539]**, Minneapolis, MN
Catholics United for the Faith - Abba, Father Chap. **[5069]**, Indianapolis, IN
Catholics United for the Faith - Blessed John XXIII Chap. **[2612]**, Mundelein, IL
Catholics United for the Faith - Cardinal Newman Chap. **[16852]**, Tiffin, OH
Catholics United for the Faith - Christ the King Chap. **[19317]**, New Richmond, WI
Catholics United for the Faith - Immaculate Heart of Mary Chap. **[7624]**, Essexville, MI
Catholics United for the Faith - Incarnate Word Chap. **[9674]**, St. Johns, MI
Catholics United for the Faith - Mary, Seat of Wisdom Chap. **[7917]**, Grand Rapids, MI
Catholics United for the Faith - Our Daily Bread Chap. **[9351]**, Pentwater, MI
Catholics United for the Faith - Our Lady of Good Help Chap. **[18092]**, Green Bay, WI
Catholics United for the Faith - Our Lady, Help of Christians Chap. **[15765]**, Mansfield, OH
Catholics United for the Faith - Our Lady of the Most Holy Eucharist Chap. **[13228]**, Atwater, OH
Catholics United for the Faith - St. Gregory VII Chap. **[18988]**, Milwaukee, WI
Catholics United for the Faith - St. John Vianney Chap. **[9540]**, Rogers City, MI
Catholics United for the Faith - St. Peter the Rock Chap. **[10984]**, Faribault, MN
Catholics United for the Faith - St. Therese of Lisieux Chap., Ohio **[13476]**, Butler, OH
Catholics United for the Faith - Servants of Christ Through Mary Chap. **[15807]**, Marblehead, OH
CATNAP from the Heart **[2175]**, La Grange Park, IL
Cattle
Black Swamp Angus Assn. **[16271]**, Oak Harbor, OH
Bur. County Angus Assn. **[3733]**, Sublette, IL
Central Illinois Angus Assn. **[2252]**, Lexington, IL
Eastern Ohio Angus Assn. **[16626]**, Senecaville, OH
Great Lakes Belted Galloway Assn. **[17715]**, Camp Douglas, WI
Heart of Ohio Angus Assn. **[15244]**, Fredericktown, OH
Illinois Angus Assn. **[1285]**, Colfax, IL
Illinois Beef Assn. **[3586]**, Springfield, IL
Illinois Valley Angus Breeders Assn. **[3472]**, Shipman, IL
Indiana Angus Assn. **[4834]**, Greenfield, IN
Indiana Beef Cattle Assn. **[5193]**, Indianapolis, IN
Indiana Beef Coun. **[5194]**, Indianapolis, IN
Indiana Holstein Assn. **[4838]**, Greens Fork, IN
Lamoine Valley Angus Assn. **[3094]**, Pittsfield, IL
Logan County Angus Assn. **[2686]**, New Holland, IL
Mercer County Angus Assn. **[23]**, Alexis, IL
Miami Valley Angus Assn. **[15395]**, Hamilton, OH
Michigan Angus Assn. **[9701]**, Saline, MI
Michigan Beef Indus. Commn. **[9274]**, Okemos, MI
Minnesota Angus Assn. **[10339]**, Arlington, MN

Minnesota Beef Coun. [11629], Minneapolis, MN
Minnesota Dairy Herd Improvement Assn. [10575], Buffalo, MN
Minnesota Holstein Assn. [12827], Waite Park, MN
Minnesota State Cattlemen's Assn. [10704], Comfrey, MN
North Central Ohio Angus Assn. [13225], Attica, OH
Northeast Indiana Angus Assn. [5800], Milford, IN
Northeast Iowa Angus Breeders Assn. [11362], Mabel, MN
Northeastern Ohio Angus Assn. [16809], Summitville, OH
Northern Illinois Angus Assn. [2495], Milledgeville, IL
Northwest Indiana Angus Breeders Assn. [6436], Walkerton, IN
Ohio Angus Assn. [16103], Nashport, OH
Ohio Beef Coun. [15865], Marysville, OH
Ohio Simmental Assn. [17164], West Alexandria, OH
Red River Valley Angus Assn. [10335], Argyle, MN
St. Croix Valley Angus Assn. [19321], New Richmond, WI
South Central Ohio Angus Assn. [17132], Washington Court House, OH
South Eastern Minnesota Angus Assn. [12713], Stewartville, MN
Southeastern Indiana Angus Assn. [4837], Greenfield, IN
Southeastern Michigan Angus Assn. [9705], Saline, MI
Southeastern Ohio Angus Assn. [13359], Bidwell, OH
Southern Indiana Angus Assn. [6374], Vallonia, IN
Southwestern Illinois Angus Breeders Assn. [3132], Prairie du Rocher, IL
Southwestern Indiana Angus Assn. [4338], Centerpoint, IN
Southwestern Wisconsin Angus Assn. [17959], Fennimore, WI
Wabash Valley Angus Assn. [3743], Sumner, IL
West Central Indiana Angus Assn. [6523], Whitestown, IN
West Central Ohio Angus Assn. [15098], Elida, OH
West Michigan Angus Assn. [8867], Lowell, MI
Wisconsin Angus Assn. [18424], Lodi, WI
Wisconsin Beef Improvement Assn. [19306], New Glarus, WI
Wisconsin Jersey Breeders Assn. [18808], Marion, WI
CBMC Indiana [5070], Indianapolis, IN
CDIC Soc. for Coatings Tech. [13765], Cincinnati, OH
Cedar Lake Chamber of Commerce [4336], Cedar Lake, IN
Cedar Lake Park Assn. [11540], Minneapolis, MN
Cedar Lake Park Preservation and Development Assn. [★11540]
Cedar Lakes Conservation Found. [18989], Milwaukee, WI
Cedar-Maple City Lions Club [8921], Maple City, MI
Cedar Mills Lions Club [11205], Hutchinson, MN
Cedarburg Chamber of Commerce [17727], Cedarburg, WI
Cedarburg Lions Club [17728], Cedarburg, WI
Celiac Support Gp; Cincinnati [15383], Hamilton, OH
Celina Area Chamber of Commerce [★13612]
Celina-Mercer County Chamber of Commerce [13612], Celina, OH
Celtic Corner Miniature Club [8801], Leslie, MI
Celtic Cross Pipes and Drums [1770], Galesburg, IL
Cemetery Assn; Lake View [14154], Cleveland, OH
Cemetery Assn; Masonic [4953], Huntington, IN
Cemetery; Memorial Rifle Squad, Minnesota State Veterans [11167], Hillman, MN
Census
Southeast Michigan Census Coun. [9823], Southfield, MI
Census Advisory Comm; Detroit Regional [★9823]
Census Advisory Coun; Detroit Regional [★9823]
Census Coun; Southeast Michigan [9823], Southfield, MI
Centennial Lakes Lawn Bowling Club [10908], Edina, MN
Center for Child Abuse Prevention [★14712]
Center City Neighborhood Assn. [16722], Springfield, OH
Center for Commerce Tourism [19377], Oostburg, WI
Center for Consumer Affairs, Univ. of Wisconsin-Milwaukee [18990], Milwaukee, WI
Center for Effective Discipline [14351], Columbus, OH
Center Ice Skating Club [13562], Canton, OH
Center for Mental Retardation (Cayuhoga) [14086], Cleveland, OH
Center for Military Readiness [8833], Livonia, MI
Centerline Dressage [3542], Springfield, IL
Centerville Curling Club [19913], Trempealeau, WI
Centerville High School - Young Life [6089], Richmond, IN
Centerville Lions Club, IN [4340], Centerville, IN
Centreville Lions Club - Michigan [7108], Centreville, MI
Centerville Lions Club - Minnesota [10639], Centerville, MN
Centracare Found. [★12277]
Centracare Hea. Found. [12277], St. Cloud, MN
Central Chap. of the Soc. of Nuclear Medicine [372], Burr Ridge, IL
Central City Alliance [7333], Detroit, MI
Central District Dental Soc., Michigan [8559], Lansing, MI
Central East Alcoholism and Drug Coun. [564], Charleston, IL
Central Educational Network [1454], Des Plaines, IL
Central High School PTSA [503], Champaign, IL
Central Illinois Aerospace [504], Champaign, IL
Central Illinois Aikikai [3808], Urbana, IL
Central Illinois Angus Assn. [2252], Lexington, IL
Central Illinois Assn. for Computing Machinery Chap. [269], Bloomington, IL
Central Illinois Assn. of Diabetes Educators [3809], Urbana, IL
Central Illinois Bd. of Realtors [565], Charleston, IL
Central Illinois Chap. of Amer. Soc. of Plumbing Engineers [1979], Heyworth, IL
Central Illinois Chap., Amer. Soc. for Training and Development [270], Bloomington, IL
Central Illinois Chap. Natl. Elecl. Contractors Assn. [3011], Peoria, IL
Central Illinois Chap. of Sheet Metal and Air Conditioning Contractors' Natl. Assn. [3012], Peoria, IL
Central Illinois Chap. of the Soc. of Financial Ser. Professionals [271], Bloomington, IL
Central Illinois Club of Printing House Craftsmen [272], Bloomington, IL
Central Illinois Corvette Club [3543], Springfield, IL
Central Illinois District Amateur Athletic Union [5914], Nashville, IN
Central Illinois English Country Dancers [3810], Urbana, IL
Central Illinois Estate Planning Coun. [1378], Decatur, IL
Central Illinois Golf Course Superintendents Assn. [103], Auburn, IL
Central Illinois Hea. Info. Mgt. Assn. [1272], Clinton, IL
Central Illinois Human Rsrcs. Gp. [505], Champaign, IL
Central Illinois Jeep Club [273], Bloomington, IL
Central Illinois Mountain Bicycling Assn. [2985], Pekin, IL
Central Illinois Muskie Hunters [2547], Monticello, IL
Central Illinois Numismatic Assn. [1379], Decatur, IL
Central Illinois Paralegal Assn. [274], Bloomington, IL
Central Illinois Planned Giving Coun. [275], Bloomington, IL
Central Illinois TAM Users Gp. [3242], Rock Island, IL
Central Illinois Woodturners [3217], Roanoke, IL
Central Indiana Beagle Club [4806], Gosport, IN
Central Indiana Better Bus. Bur. [5071], Indianapolis, IN
Central Indiana Bicycling Assn. [5072], Indianapolis, IN
Central Indiana Cage Bird Club [5073], Indianapolis, IN
Central Indiana Chap. of the Assn. for Computing Machinery [5074], Indianapolis, IN
Central Indiana Chap. Natl. Elecl. Contractors Assn. [5075], Indianapolis, IN
Central Indiana Chap. of the Soc. of Financial Ser. Professionals [5076], Indianapolis, IN
Central Indiana Fellowship of Christian Athletes [5077], Indianapolis, IN
Central Indiana Natl. Space Soc. [5078], Indianapolis, IN
Central Indiana Pug Club [5079], Indianapolis, IN
Central Indiana Rotorwing Club [4103], Anderson, IN
Central Indiana Saint Bernard Club [5080], Indianapolis, IN
Central Indiana Soaring Soc. [5081], Indianapolis, IN
Central Indiana Youth for Christ [5082], Indianapolis, IN
Central Lake Chamber of Commerce [7107], Central Lake, MI
Central Lake Superior Watershed Partnership [8934], Marquette, MI
Central Livestock Assn. [12677], South St. Paul, MN
Central Macomb County Chamber of Commerce [9086], Mount Clemens, MI
Central Michigan Assn. of Realtors [9102], Mount Pleasant, MI
Central Michigan Youth for Christ [6631], Alma, MI
Central Mille Lacs United Way [11465], Milaca, MN
Central Minnesota Area Chap. of the Amer. Assn. of Critical Care Nurses [12278], St. Cloud, MN
Central Minnesota Audubon Soc. [12279], St. Cloud, MN
Central Minnesota Chap. 115, The Retired Enlisted Assn. [11810], Monticello, MN
Central Minnesota Coun. on Aging [12280], St. Cloud, MN
Central Minnesota Libraries Exchange [12281], St. Cloud, MN
Central Minnesota Self-Help for Hard of Hearing [12117], Robbinsdale, MN
Central Minnesota Soc. for Human Rsrc. Mgt. [12282], St. Cloud, MN
Central Minnesota Youth for Christ [12283], St. Cloud, MN
Central Ohio Air Conditioning Contractors of Am. [15043], Dublin, OH
Central Ohio Alpine Ski Troop [14352], Columbus, OH
Central Ohio Amer. Indus. Hygiene Assn. [15262], Gahanna, OH
Central Ohio ASCnet User Gp. [15001], Delaware, OH
Central Ohio Assn. of Catholic Educators [17207], Westerville, OH
Central Ohio Assn. for Computing Machinery SIGCHI (BuckCHI) [14353], Columbus, OH
Central Ohio Chap. of Amer. Soc. of Plumbing Engineers [14354], Columbus, OH
Central Ohio Chap. of the Human Factors and Ergonomics Soc. [14355], Columbus, OH
Central Ohio Chap. of Intl. Fac. Mgt. Assn. [14356], Columbus, OH
Central Ohio Chap. of Muskies [14357], Columbus, OH
Central Ohio Chap., Natl. Elecl. Contractors Assn. [14358], Columbus, OH
Central Ohio Coun. of Teachers of Mathematics [15429], Hilliard, OH
Central Ohio Diabetes Assn. [14359], Columbus, OH
Central Ohio Golf Course Superintendents Assn. [16102], Nashport, OH
Central Ohio Kennel Club [15044], Dublin, OH
Central Ohio Kennel Club [16419], Pickerington, OH
Central Ohio Minority Bus. Assn. [14360], Columbus, OH
Central Ohio Orchid Soc. [14361], Columbus, OH
Central Ohio Orienteering [16420], Pickerington, OH
Central Ohio Planned Giving Coun. [14362], Columbus, OH
Central Ohio Regional Organization Development Network [★14350]
Central Ohio Senior Olympics [14363], Columbus, OH
Central Ohio Shetland Sheepdog Assn. [17208], Westerville, OH
Central Ohio Theatre Organ Soc. [14815], Croton, OH
Central Ohio Theatre Organ Soc. [17039], Urbana, OH

Central Ohio Woodturners [17343], Worthington, OH
Central Ohio Youth for Christ [14364], Columbus, OH
Central Soc. for Clinical Res., Milwaukee [18991], Milwaukee, WI
Central State Univ. Assn. for Computing Machinery Student Chap. [17259], Wilberforce, OH
Central States Dressage and Eventing Assn. [12894], White Bear Lake, MN
Central States; Independent Schools Assn. of the [974], Chicago, IL
Central Upper Peninsula Planning and Development Regional Commn. [7609], Escanaba, MI
Central Wisconsin Beagle Club [19938], Vesper, WI
Central Wisconsin Habitat for Humanity [19786], Stevens Point, WI
Central Wisconsin Sail and Power Squadron [20033], Wausau, WI
Central Wisconsin Saints Hockey Assn. [19481], Plover, WI
Central Wisconsin Soc. for Human Rsrcs. [20034], Wausau, WI
Central Wisconsin Vizsla Club [17954], Fall River, WI
Centrill West LUA [2368], Macomb, IL
Ceramics
Wisconsin Pottery Assn. [18742], Madison, WI
Cereal City Lions Club [6857], Battle Creek, MI
Cerebral Palsy
Access Services of Northern Illinois [2348], Loves Park, IL
Peoria County Bar Assn. [3050], Peoria, IL
United Cerebral Palsy Assn. of Greater Cleveland [14226], Cleveland, OH
United Cerebral Palsy Assn. of Greater Indiana [5488], Indianapolis, IN
United Cerebral Palsy Assn., Michigan [8767], Lansing, MI
United Cerebral Palsy Assn. of Minnesota [12602], St. Paul, MN
United Cerebral Palsy of Illinois [3692], Springfield, IL
United Cerebral Palsy of Southeastern Wisconsin [19140], Milwaukee, WI
United Cerebral Palsy of Southern Illinois [2603], Mount Vernon, IL
United Cerebral Palsy of Will County [2121], Joliet, IL
Cerebral Palsy Assn. of Central Minnesota; United [12315], St. Cloud, MN
Cerebral Palsy Assn. of Greater Cleveland; United [14226], Cleveland, OH
Cerebral Palsy Assn. of Greater Indiana; United [5488], Indianapolis, IN
Cerebral Palsy Assn. of Metropolitan Detroit; United [9828], Southfield, MI
Cerebral Palsy Assn., Michigan; United [8767], Lansing, MI
Cerebral Palsy Assn. of Minnesota; United [12602], St. Paul, MN
Cerebral Palsy of Illinois; United [3692], Springfield, IL
Cerebral Palsy of Southern Illinois; United [2603], Mount Vernon, IL
Certified Fraud Examiners, Twin Cities Chap. No. 47; Assn. of [11525], Minneapolis, MN
Chagrin Falls Parent Teacher Org. [13631], Chagrin Falls, OH
Chagrin River Watershed Partners [17272], Willoughby, OH
Chagrin Valley Chamber of Commerce [13632], Chagrin Falls, OH
Chagrin Valley REACT [13633], Chagrin Falls, OH
Chagrin Valley Women's League [13634], Chagrin Falls, OH
Chain-O-Lakes Sail and Power Squadron [1891], Grayslake, IL
Chaldean Amers. Reaching and Encouraging [10112], West Bloomfield, MI
Chamber Collective; Cleveland [14095], Cleveland, OH
Chamber of Commerce [★1874]
Chamber of Commerce; Adams-Friendship [★17452]
Chamber of Commerce; Addison [★3]
Chamber of Commerce; Allendale [6617], Allendale, MI
Chamber of Commerce for Anderson and Madison County [4104], Anderson, IN
Chamber of Commerce; Ann Arbor Area [6668], Ann Arbor, MI
Chamber of Commerce; Anoka Area [10303], Anoka, MN
Chamber of Commerce; Appleton [★17490]
Chamber of Commerce; Baudette-Lake of the Woods [10386], Baudette, MN
Chamber of Commerce; Berwyn [★237]
Chamber of Commerce; Big Rapids [★6947]
Chamber of Commerce; Bighorn Area [★17927]
Chamber of Commerce; Bluffton [★4271]
Chamber of Commerce; Broadview Heights [13425], Broadview Heights, OH
Chamber of Commerce; Brookfield [★17668]
Chamber of Commerce; Brooklyn Area [17690], Brooklyn, WI
Chamber of Commerce; Brown County [5911], Nashville, IN
Chamber of Commerce; Brunswick [★13445]
Chamber of Commerce; Buffalo Grove [★360]
Chamber of Commerce; Carlinville [★438]
Chamber of Commerce; Carroll County [★13604]
Chamber of Commerce; Carthage [★465]
Chamber of Commerce; Chetek [★17738]
Chamber of Commerce; Chicago Negro [★859]
Chamber of Commerce; Circleville - Pickaway [14032], Circleville, OH
Chamber of Commerce; CLark County [★5927]
Chamber of Commerce and Convention and Visitors Bur; Brainerd Lakes Area [★10508]
Chamber of Commerce and Convention and Visitors Bur; Lake Benton Area [11270], Lake Benton, MN
Chamber of Commerce for Decatur and Macon County [1380], Decatur, IL
Chamber of Commerce; Deerfield [★1419]
Chamber of Commerce; Deerfield, Bannockburn, Riverwoods [1419], Deerfield, IL
Chamber of Commerce; Detroit Black [7341], Detroit, MI
Chamber of Commerce - Detroit Chapter; Swedish American [6968], Birmingham, MI
Chamber of Commerce; Dixon [★1477]
Chamber of Commerce; Du Quoin [1517], Du Quoin, IL
Chamber of Commerce; Dunkirk [★4466]
Chamber of Commerce; Eagle River Area [★17850]
Chamber of Commerce and Economic Development Commn; Mooresville [★5837]
Chamber of Commerce/Economic Development; Jennings County [★5995]
Chamber of Commerce; Elk River Area [10945], Elk River, MN
Chamber of Commerce; Evart [★7628]
Chamber of Commerce Executives; Illinois Assn. of [3566], Springfield, IL
Chamber of Commerce; Fairfield [★1688]
Chamber of Commerce of Fargo Moorhead [11822], Moorhead, MN
Chamber of Commerce; Farwell Area [7679], Farwell, MI
Chamber of Commerce; Floyd County [★5927]
Chamber of Commerce; Fox Lake [★18003]
Chamber of Commerce; Frankfort Area [★7785]
Chamber of Commerce; Frankfort - Elberta Area [7785], Frankfort, MI
Chamber of Commerce; Fridley [★11848]
Chamber of Commerce; Garrettsville Area [★15304]
Chamber of Commerce; Geneva Area [15309], Geneva, OH
Chamber of Commerce; Gibson [★1809]
Chamber of Commerce; Glenwood [★11052]
Chamber of Commerce; Goshen [4795], Goshen, IN
Chamber of Commerce; Greater Brighton Area [7012], Brighton, MI
Chamber of Commerce; Greater Clare Area [★7153]
Chamber of Commerce; Greater Decatur [7285], Decatur, MI
Chamber of Commerce; Greater Detroit [★7354]
Chamber of Commerce; Greater Durand Area [★7490]
Chamber of Commerce; Greater Gary [★4778]
Chamber of Commerce; Greater Greencastle [4817], Greencastle, IN
Chamber of Commerce; Greater Logan County Area [★13320]
Chamber of Commerce; Greater Lorain [★15705]
Chamber of Commerce; Greater Mackinaw Area [★8889]
Chamber of Commerce; Greater Mauston Area [★18829]
Chamber of Commerce; Greater Powell Area [★16480]
Chamber of Commerce; Green [15350], Green, OH
Chamber of Commerce; Greencastle [★4817]
Chamber of Commerce; Hampshire [★1930]
Chamber of Commerce of Harrison County [4418], Corydon, IN
Chamber of Commerce; Hermantown [11150], Hermantown, MN
Chamber of Commerce; Hibbing [★11157]
Chamber of Commerce; Hillsboro Area [★15446]
Chamber of Commerce; Huron Valley Area [★9050]
Chamber of Commerce; Hutchinson Area [11207], Hutchinson, MN
Chamber of Commerce and Indus; Darien [★1358]
Chamber of Commerce and Indus; Lombard Area [★2337]
Chamber of Commerce and Indus; Menomonee Falls [★18877]
Chamber of Commerce; Inkster [8311], Inkster, MI
Chamber of Commerce; Jefferson Area [15525], Jefferson, OH
Chamber of Commerce; Kettering [★15561]
Chamber of Commerce; La Crescent [11266], La Crescent, MN
Chamber of Commerce; Lakes Country [★18408]
Chamber of Commerce; Lakeview [★1017]
Chamber of Commerce; Lancaster [★18411]
Chamber of Commerce; Leelanau County [★9887]
Chamber of Commerce; Leetonia-Washingtonville Area [15631], Leetonia, OH
Chamber of Commerce; Lincoln Park [1030], Chicago, IL
Chamber of Commerce; Linton [★5684]
Chamber of Commerce; Livonia [8842], Livonia, MI
Chamber of Commerce; Loudonville-Greater Mohican Area [★15715]
Chamber of Commerce; Madison [★18517]
Chamber of Commerce; Manistee Area [8912], Manistee, MI
Chamber of Commerce; Marengo-Union [2397], Marengo, IL
Chamber of Commerce; Marion Area [15840], Marion, OH
Chamber of Commerce; Marquette Area [★8938]
Chamber of Commerce; Mequon-Thiensville Area [★19892]
Chamber of Commerce; Middleport [★16455]
Chamber of Commerce of the Midwest - Wisconsin Chapter; German-American [19013], Milwaukee, WI
Chamber of Commerce; Milton Area [18920], Milton, WI
Chamber of Commerce; Mineral Point [19195], Mineral Point, WI
Chamber of Commerce of Minnesota; Hispanic [11578], Minneapolis, MN
Chamber of Commerce; Mitchell [★5815]
Chamber of Commerce; Monticello [★11811]
Chamber of Commerce; Moorhead Area [★11822]
Chamber of Commerce; Morrow County [★16070]
Chamber of Commerce; Mount Gilead Area [★16070]
Chamber of Commerce; Mt. Vernon [★5855]
Chamber of Commerce; Mukwonago [★19253]
Chamber of Commerce; Muncie [★5887]
Chamber of Commerce; Neenah-Menasha [★17490]
Chamber of Commerce; New Castle Area [★5939]
Chamber of Commerce; North Br. Area [11900], North Branch, MN
Chamber of Commerce; Northwest Macomb [★9870]
Chamber of Commerce; Ohio-Israel [14197], Cleveland, OH
Chamber of Commerce; Ortonville Area [★11945]
Chamber of Commerce; Osceola Area [19383], Osceola, WI
Chamber of Commerce; Owatonna Area [★11962]
Chamber of Commerce; Palestine [2931], Palestine, IL
Chamber of Commerce; Parma Area [16376], Parma, OH

Chamber of Commerce; Paw Paw [★9346]
Chamber of Commerce in Pendleton [6024], Pendleton, IN
Chamber of Commerce; Pinconning [★9383]
Chamber of Commerce; Pomeroy [★16455]
Chamber of Commerce; Prescott Area [19538], Prescott, WI
Chamber of Commerce; Princeton [★19543]
Chamber of Commerce; Pulaski Area [19547], Pulaski, WI
Chamber of Commerce; Racine [★19565]
Chamber of Commerce; Redwood Falls Area [★12097]
Chamber of Commerce; Rockport [★6129]
Chamber of Commerce; Rogers-Dayton [★12203]
Chamber of Commerce; Rushville [★3371]
Chamber of Commerce of St. Joseph County [6223], South Bend, IN
Chamber of Commerce; St. Paul Area [12575], St. Paul, MN
Chamber of Commerce; Sauk Prairie Area [19532], Prairie Du Sac, WI
Chamber of Commerce Serving Middletown, Monroe and Trenton [★16012]
Chamber of Commerce; Sharonville [16648], Sharonville, OH
Chamber of Commerce; Silver Lake Sand Dunes Area [8994], Mears, MI
Chamber of Commerce; South St. Paul-Inver Grove Heights [★11227]
Chamber of Commerce; Spencer [★6282]
Chamber of Commerce; Spencer County Regional [6129], Rockport, IN
Chamber of Commerce; Spencer-Owen [★6282]
Chamber of Commerce; Strongsville Area [★16798]
Chamber of Commerce; Sussex Area [19885], Sussex, WI
Chamber of Commerce; Switzerland of Ohio [★17306]
Chamber of Commerce and Tourism Info; Harrison Regional [★13481]
Chamber of Commerce; Towersoudan [★12755]
Chamber of Commerce; TwinWest [11798], Minnetonka, MN
Chamber of Commerce; Union Grove [★19926]
Chamber of Commerce; Village of Mt. Zion [★2606]
Chamber of Commerce; Vincennes Area [★6413]
Chamber of Commerce; Virginia [★12795]
Chamber of Commerce; Walkerton [★6437]
Chamber of Commerce; Walled Lake [★10056]
Chamber of Commerce; Waukegan [★1921]
Chamber of Commerce; Waukegan-North Chicago [★1921]
Chamber of Commerce; Waukegan-North Chicago Area [★1921]
Chamber of Commerce; Waunakee Area [★20019]
Chamber of Commerce; West Chicago [★3943]
Chamber of Commerce; West Unity [★17201]
Chamber of Commerce; Wheaton [★12886]
Chamber of Commerce; Wisconsin Dells Regional [★20181]
Chamber of Commerce; Wittenberg [★20203]
Chamber; Detroit Regional [7354], Detroit, MI
Chamber Found; Greater Cincinnati Junior [13849], Cincinnati, OH
Chamber of Found; Lenawee County [6575], Adrian, MI
The Chamber - Grand Haven, Spring Lake, Ferrysburg [7855], Grand Haven, MI
Chamber of Northeast Cincinnati [15873], Mason, OH
Chambers of Commerce
Abingdon Chamber of Commerce [1], Abingdon, IL
Ada Chamber of Commerce [10234], Ada, MN
Adams County Chamber of Commerce [17193], West Union, OH
Adams County Chamber of Commerce and Tourism [17452], Adams, WI
Aitkin Area Chamber of Commerce [10243], Aitkin, MN
Albany Chamber of Commerce [10249], Albany, MN
Albany Park Chamber of Commerce [600], Chicago, IL
Albert Lea - Freeborn County Chamber of Commerce [10254], Albert Lea, MN
Aledo Area Chamber of Commerce [17], Aledo, IL
Alexandria Lakes Area Chamber of Commerce [10271], Alexandria, MN
Alexandria - Monroe Chamber of Commerce [4089], Alexandria, IN
Alger Chamber of Commerce [9129], Munising, MI
Algoma Area Chamber of Commerce [17459], Algoma, WI
Algonquin - Lake in the Hills Chamber of Commerce [24], Algonquin, IL
Allegan Area Chamber of Commerce [6600], Allegan, MI
Alliance Area Chamber of Commerce [13107], Alliance, OH
Almena Commercial Club [17463], Almena, WI
Alsip Chamber of Commerce and Economic Development [30], Alsip, IL
Altamont Chamber of Commerce [32], Altamont, IL
Amboy Area Chamber of Commerce [48], Amboy, IL
Anchor Bay Chamber of Commerce [9180], New Baltimore, MI
Anderson Area Chamber of Commerce [13742], Cincinnati, OH
Angola Area Chamber of Commerce [4124], Angola, IN
Ann Arbor Area Chamber of Commerce [6668], Ann Arbor, MI
Anoka Area Chamber of Commerce [10303], Anoka, MN
Antigo Area Chamber of Commerce [17474], Antigo, WI
Antioch Chamber of Commerce and Indus. [56], Antioch, IL
Antwerp Chamber of Commerce [13147], Antwerp, OH
Apple Valley Chamber of Commerce [10316], Apple Valley, MN
Arcadia Chamber of Commerce [17535], Arcadia, WI
Archbold Area Chamber of Commerce [13151], Archbold, OH
Arcola Chamber of Commerce [61], Arcola, IL
Arlington Area Chamber of Commerce [10337], Arlington, MN
Arlington Heights Chamber of Commerce [65], Arlington Heights, IL
Arthur Assn. of Commerce [88], Arthur, IL
Ashland Area Chamber of Commerce [13160], Ashland, OH
Ashland Area Chamber of Commerce [17543], Ashland, WI
Ashtabula Area Chamber of Commerce [13177], Ashtabula, OH
ATHENA Intl. [755], Chicago, IL
Atlanta Area Chamber of Commerce [6802], Atlanta, MI
Au Gres Chamber of Commerce [6805], Au Gres, MI
Auburn Area Chamber of Commerce [6807], Auburn, MI
Auburn Chamber of Commerce [4138], Auburn, IN
Aurora Area Chamber of Commerce [13230], Aurora, OH
Austin Area Chamber of Commerce [10353], Austin, MN
Bad Axe Chamber of Commerce [6820], Bad Axe, MI
Baileys Harbor Community Assn. [17557], Baileys Harbor, WI
Baldwin Area Chamber of Commerce [17559], Baldwin, WI
Baltimore Area Chamber of Commerce [13250], Baltimore, OH
Bangor Bus. Club [17566], Bangor, WI
Baraboo Area Chamber of Commerce [17571], Baraboo, WI
Barnesville Area Chamber of Commerce [13259], Barnesville, OH
Barrington Area Chamber of Commerce [141], Barrington, IL
Barry County Area Chamber of Commerce [8155], Hastings, MI
Bartlett Chamber of Commerce [160], Bartlett, IL
Batavia Chamber of Commerce [175], Batavia, IL
Batesville Area Chamber of Commerce [4157], Batesville, IN
Battle Creek Area Chamber of Commerce [6851], Battle Creek, MI
Baudette-Lake of the Woods Chamber of Commerce [10386], Baudette, MN
Bay Area Chamber of Commerce [6881], Bay City, MI
Bayfield Chamber of Commerce [17585], Bayfield, WI
Beachwood Chamber of Commerce [13284], Beachwood, OH
Beardstown Chamber of Commerce [188], Beardstown, IL
Beaver Dam Area Chamber of Commerce [17590], Beaver Dam, WI
Beavercreek Chamber of Commerce [13296], Beavercreek, OH
Bedford Area Chamber of Commerce [4167], Bedford, IN
Bedford Chamber of Commerce [13304], Bedford, OH
Bedford Heights Chamber of Commerce [13307], Bedford Heights, OH
Beecher Chamber of Commerce [195], Beecher, IL
Bellaire Area Chamber of Commerce [6904], Bellaire, MI
Bellaire Area Chamber of Commerce [13309], Bellaire, OH
Bellbrook - Sugarcreek Area Chamber of Commerce [13314], Bellbrook, OH
Belleville Area Chamber of Commerce [6908], Belleville, MI
Belleville Community Club [17602], Belleville, WI
Bellville Chamber of Commerce [13335], Bellville, OH
Bellwood Chamber of Commerce and Indus. [215], Bellwood, IL
Belmont-Central Chamber of Commerce [760], Chicago, IL
Belpre Area Chamber of Commerce [13341], Belpre, OH
Belvidere Area Chamber of Commerce [219], Belvidere, IL
Bemidji Area Chamber of Commerce [10404], Bemidji, MN
Bensenville Chamber of Commerce [225], Bensenville, IL
Benton-West City Area Chamber of Commerce [232], Benton, IL
Benzie County Chamber of Commerce [6925], Benzonia, MI
Berea Chamber of Commerce [13345], Berea, OH
Berlin Chamber of Commerce [17624], Berlin, WI
Berne Chamber of Commerce [4187], Berne, IN
Bexley Area Chamber of Commerce [13358], Bexley, OH
Big Stone Lake Area Chamber of Commerce [11945], Ortonville, MN
Birch Run Area Chamber of Commerce [6958], Birch Run, MI
Birmingham-Bloomfield Chamber of Commerce [6962], Birmingham, MI
Blair Chamber of Commerce [17637], Blair, WI
Blanchester Area Chamber of Commerce [13362], Blanchester, OH
Blissfield Area Chamber of Commerce [6973], Blissfield, MI
Bloomer Chamber of Commerce [17642], Bloomer, WI
Bloomfield Chamber of Commerce [4191], Bloomfield, IN
Blooming Prairie Chamber of Commerce [10456], Blooming Prairie, MN
Bloomingdale Chamber of Commerce [247], Bloomingdale, IL
Blue Earth Area Chamber of Commerce [10496], Blue Earth, MN
Blue Island Area Chamber of Commerce and Indus. [315], Blue Island, IL
Bluffton Area Chamber of Commerce [13366], Bluffton, OH
Bolingbrook Area Chamber of Commerce [322], Bolingbrook, IL

Boone County Chamber of Commerce **[5668]**, Lebanon, IN
Boscobel Chamber of Commerce **[17648]**, Boscobel, WI
Boulder Junction Chamber of Commerce **[17650]**, Boulder Junction, WI
Boyne Area City Chamber of Commerce **[6996]**, Boyne City, MI
Bradley-Bourbonnais Chamber of Commerce **[326]**, Bourbonnais, IL
Brainerd Lakes Area Chambers of Commerce **[10508]**, Brainerd, MN
Br. County Area Chamber of Commerce **[7196]**, Coldwater, MI
Brecksville Chamber of Commerce **[13408]**, Brecksville, OH
Breese Chamber of Commerce **[337]**, Breese, IL
Bremen Chamber of Commerce **[4287]**, Bremen, IN
Bremen Chamber of Commerce **[13415]**, Bremen, OH
Bridgeport Area Chamber of Commerce **[13419]**, Bridgeport, OH
Bridgeview Chamber of Commerce **[340]**, Bridgeview, IL
Brillion Area Chamber of Commerce **[17658]**, Brillion, WI
Brimfield Area Chamber of Commerce **[15540]**, Kent, OH
Broadview Heights Chamber of Commerce **[13425]**, Broadview Heights, OH
Brodhead Chamber of Commerce **[17661]**, Brodhead, WI
Brookfield Chamber of Commerce **[349]**, Brookfield, IL
Brooklyn - Irish Hills Chamber of Commerce **[7030]**, Brooklyn, MI
Brookville-Franklin County Chamber of Commerce **[4298]**, Brookville, IN
Brown County Chamber of Commerce **[5911]**, Nashville, IN
Brown County Chamber of Commerce **[15313]**, Georgetown, OH
Brown Deer Chamber of Commerce **[17691]**, Brown Deer, WI
Brownsburg Chamber of Commerce **[4303]**, Brownsburg, IN
Brunswick Area Chamber of Commerce **[13445]**, Brunswick, OH
Bryan Area Chamber of Commerce **[13454]**, Bryan, OH
Buchanan Area Chamber of Commerce **[7035]**, Buchanan, MI
Bucyrus Area Chamber of Commerce **[13464]**, Bucyrus, OH
Buffalo Area Chamber of Commerce **[10572]**, Buffalo, MN
Buffalo Grove Area Chamber of Commerce **[360]**, Buffalo Grove, IL
Burbank Chamber of Commerce **[368]**, Burbank, IL
Burlington Area Chamber of Commerce **[17696]**, Burlington, WI
Burnsville Chamber of Commerce **[10587]**, Burnsville, MN
Bushnell Chamber of Commerce **[379]**, Bushnell, IL
Butler Area Chamber of Commerce **[17698]**, Butler, WI
Byesville Bd. of Trade **[13478]**, Byesville, OH
Byron Area Chamber of Commerce **[383]**, Byron, IL
Cable Area Chamber of Commerce **[17704]**, Cable, WI
Cadillac Area Chamber of Commerce **[7044]**, Cadillac, MI
Cadott Area Chamber of Commerce **[17707]**, Cadott, WI
Cahokia Area Chamber of Commerce **[386]**, Cahokia, IL
Cairo Chamber of Commerce **[390]**, Cairo, IL
Calcutta Area Chamber of Commerce **[13483]**, Calcutta, OH
Calumet City Chamber of Commerce **[393]**, Calumet City, IL
Cambridge Area Chamber of Commerce **[10618]**, Cambridge, MN
Cambridge Area Chamber of Commerce **[13493]**, Cambridge, OH
Cambridge Chamber of Commerce **[17710]**, Cambridge, WI
Camden Area Chamber of Commerce **[13504]**, Camden, OH
Canal Winchester Area Chamber of Commerce **[13516]**, Canal Winchester, OH
Canby Area Chamber of Commerce **[10627]**, Canby, MN
Cannon Falls Area Chamber of Commerce **[10631]**, Cannon Falls, MN
Canton Area Chamber of Commerce **[401]**, Canton, IL
Canton Chamber of Commerce **[7061]**, Canton, MI
Canton Regional Chamber of Commerce **[13557]**, Canton, OH
Capac Area Chamber of Commerce **[7075]**, Capac, MI
Carbondale Chamber of Commerce **[415]**, Carbondale, IL
Carey Area Chamber of Commerce **[13599]**, Carey, OH
Carlinville Community Chamber of Commerce **[438]**, Carlinville, IL
Carlyle Lake Chamber of Commerce **[441]**, Carlyle, IL
Carmel Clay Chamber of Commerce **[4317]**, Carmel, IN
Carmi Chamber of Commerce **[443]**, Carmi, IL
Caro Chamber of Commerce **[7082]**, Caro, MI
Carol Stream Chamber of Commerce **[445]**, Carol Stream, IL
Carroll County Chamber of Commerce and Economic Development **[13604]**, Carrollton, OH
Carrollton Chamber of Commerce **[458]**, Carrollton, IL
Carterville Chamber of Commerce **[461]**, Carterville, IL
Carthage Area Chamber of Commerce **[465]**, Carthage, IL
Cary/Grove Area Chamber of Commerce **[472]**, Cary, IL
Caseyville Chamber of Commerce **[481]**, Caseyville, IL
Cass City Chamber of Commerce **[7093]**, Cass City, MI
Cedar Lake Chamber of Commerce **[4336]**, Cedar Lake, IN
Cedarburg Chamber of Commerce **[17727]**, Cedarburg, WI
Celina-Mercer County Chamber of Commerce **[13612]**, Celina, OH
Center for Commerce Tourism **[19377]**, Oostburg, WI
Central Lake Chamber of Commerce **[7107]**, Central Lake, MI
Central Macomb County Chamber of Commerce **[9086]**, Mount Clemens, MI
Chagrin Valley Chamber of Commerce **[13632]**, Chagrin Falls, OH
Chamber of Commerce for Anderson and Madison County **[4104]**, Anderson, IN
Chamber of Commerce for Decatur and Macon County **[1380]**, Decatur, IL
Chamber of Commerce of Fargo Moorhead **[11822]**, Moorhead, MN
Chamber of Commerce of Harrison County **[4418]**, Corydon, IN
Chamber of Commerce in Pendleton **[6024]**, Pendleton, IN
Chamber of Commerce of St. Joseph County **[6223]**, South Bend, IN
The Chamber - Grand Haven, Spring Lake, Ferrysburg **[7855]**, Grand Haven, MI
Chamber of Northeast Cincinnati **[15873]**, Mason, OH
Champaign County Chamber of Commerce **[508]**, Champaign, IL
Champaign County Chamber of Commerce **[17040]**, Urbana, OH
Chardon Area Chamber of Commerce **[13642]**, Chardon, OH
Charleston Area Chamber of Commerce **[566]**, Charleston, IL
Charlevoix Area Chamber of Commerce **[7115]**, Charlevoix, MI
Charlotte Chamber of Commerce **[7119]**, Charlotte, MI
Cheboygan Area Chamber of Commerce **[7131]**, Cheboygan, MI
Chelsea Area Chamber of Commerce **[7139]**, Chelsea, MI
Chesaning Chamber of Commerce **[7145]**, Chesaning, MI
Chester Chamber of Commerce **[589]**, Chester, IL
Chesterland Chamber of Commerce **[13650]**, Chesterland, OH
Chesterton and Duneland Chamber of Commerce **[4352]**, Chesterton, IN
Chetek Area Chamber of Commerce **[17738]**, Chetek, WI
Chicago Chinatown Chamber of Commerce **[802]**, Chicago, IL
Chicago Ridge - Worth Bus. Assn. **[4070]**, Worth, IL
Chillicothe Chamber of Commerce **[1255]**, Chillicothe, IL
Chillicothe Ross Chamber of Commerce **[13664]**, Chillicothe, OH
Chilton Chamber of Commerce **[17741]**, Chilton, WI
Chippewa Falls Area Chamber of Commerce **[17749]**, Chippewa Falls, WI
Chisholm Area Chamber of Commerce **[10660]**, Chisholm, MN
Cicero Area Chamber of Commerce **[4359]**, Cicero, IN
Cicero Chamber of Commerce and Indus. **[1260]**, Cicero, IL
Cincinnati USA Regional Chamber **[13801]**, Cincinnati, OH
Circleville - Pickaway Chamber of Commerce **[14032]**, Circleville, OH
Clare Area Chamber of Commerce **[7153]**, Clare, MI
Clarkston Area Chamber of Commerce **[7162]**, Clarkston, MI
Clay County Chamber of Commerce **[4283]**, Brazil, IN
Clear Community Club **[17762]**, Clear Lake, WI
Clermont County Chamber of Commerce **[16025]**, Milford, OH
Cleveland Chamber of Commerce **[17765]**, Cleveland, WI
Clinton Area Chamber of Commerce **[1273]**, Clinton, IL
Clinton County Chamber of Commerce **[4739]**, Frankfort, IN
Clintonville Area Chamber of Commerce **[17771]**, Clintonville, WI
Cloquet Carlton Area Chamber of Commerce **[10690]**, Cloquet, MN
Cloverdale Area Chamber of Commerce **[4374]**, Cloverdale, IN
Cokato Chamber of Commerce **[10696]**, Cokato, MN
Colby Chamber of Commerce **[17775]**, Colby, WI
Cold Spring Area Chamber of Commerce **[10699]**, Cold Spring, MN
Coldwater Area Chamber of Commerce **[14258]**, Coldwater, OH
Collinsville Chamber of Commerce **[1287]**, Collinsville, IL
Coloma-Watervliet Area Chamber of Commerce **[7207]**, Coloma, MI
Columbia City Area Chamber of Commerce **[4379]**, Columbia City, IN
Columbiana Area Chamber of Commerce **[14260]**, Columbiana, OH
Columbus Area Chamber of Commerce **[4392]**, Columbus, IN
Columbus Area Chamber of Commerce **[17783]**, Columbus, WI
Columbus Chamber **[14377]**, Columbus, OH
Conneaut Area Chamber of Commerce **[14781]**, Conneaut, OH
Connersville - Fayette County Chamber of Commerce **[4412]**, Connersville, IN
Cook County Chamber of Commerce **[3955]**, Westchester, IL
Coopersville Area Chamber of Commerce **[7223]**, Coopersville, MI
Coshocton County Chamber of Commerce **[14799]**, Coshocton, OH

Cosmopolitan Chamber of Commerce [859], Chicago, IL
Cottage Grove Area Chamber of Commerce [10726], Cottage Grove, MN
Crandon Area Chamber of Commerce [17789], Crandon, WI
Crawford County Chamber of Commerce [5664], Leavenworth, IN
Crawfordsville - Montgomery County Chamber of Commerce [4425], Crawfordsville, IN
Crete Area Chamber of Commerce [1314], Crete, IL
Crookston Convention and Visitors Bur. [10733], Crookston, MN
Crystal Lake Chamber of Commerce [1320], Crystal Lake, IL
Cuba City Chamber of Commerce [17795], Cuba City, WI
Culver Chamber of Commerce [4438], Culver, IN
Cumberland Chamber of Commerce [17799], Cumberland, WI
Cuyahoga Falls Chamber of Commerce [14821], Cuyahoga Falls, OH
Dalton Area Chamber of Commerce [14829], Dalton, OH
Darien Chamber of Commerce [1358], Darien, IL
Darke County Chamber of Commerce [15358], Greenville, OH
Darlington Chamber of Commerce [17806], Darlington, WI
Daviess County Chamber of Commerce [6457], Washington, IN
Davison Area Chamber of Commerce [7236], Davison, MI
Dayton Area Chamber of Commerce [14869], Dayton, OH
De Forest Area Chamber of Commerce [17810], De Forest, WI
Dearborn Chamber of Commerce [7253], Dearborn, MI
Dearborn County Chamber of Commerce [5655], Lawrenceburg, IN
Decatur Chamber of Commerce [4451], Decatur, IN
Deerfield, Bannockburn, Riverwoods Chamber of Commerce [1419], Deerfield, IL
Deerfield Chamber of Commerce [14978], Deerfield, OH
Defiance Area Chamber of Commerce [14984], Defiance, OH
DeKalb Chamber of Commerce [1431], DeKalb, IL
Delafield Chamber of Commerce [17822], Delafield, WI
Delano Area Chamber of Commerce [10769], Delano, MN
Delavan - Delavan Lake Area Chamber of Commerce [17827], Delavan, WI
Delaware Area Chamber of Commerce [15002], Delaware, OH
Delphos Area Chamber of Commerce [15014], Delphos, OH
Delta Chamber of Commerce [15016], Delta, OH
Delta County Area Chamber of Commerce [7611], Escanaba, MI
Demotte Chamber of Commerce [4458], Demotte, IN
Denmark Community Bus. Assn. [17832], Denmark, WI
Des Plaines Chamber of Commerce and Indus. [1457], Des Plaines, IL
Deshler Chamber of Commerce [15021], Deshler, OH
Detroit Black Chamber of Commerce [7341], Detroit, MI
Detroit Lakes Regional Chamber of Commerce [10773], Detroit Lakes, MN
Detroit Regional Chamber [7354], Detroit, MI
Dixon Area Chamber of Commerce and Indus. [1477], Dixon, IL
Dodgeville Area Chamber of Commerce [17836], Dodgeville, WI
Dolton Chamber of Commerce [1488], Dolton, IL
Door County Chamber of Commerce [19836], Sturgeon Bay, WI
Downers Grove Area Chamber of Commerce and Indus. [1501], Downers Grove, IL
Du Quoin Chamber of Commerce [1517], Du Quoin, IL
Duluth Area Chamber of Commerce [10813], Duluth, MN
Dunkirk Area Chamber of Commerce [4466], Dunkirk, IN
Durand Area Chamber of Commerce [7490], Durand, MI
Dwight Area Chamber of Commerce [1526], Dwight, IL
Dyer Chamber of Commerce [4467], Dyer, IN
East Grand Forks Chamber of Commerce [10882], East Grand Forks, MN
East Jordan Area Chamber of Commerce [7496], East Jordan, MI
East Lake County Chamber of Commerce [12770], Two Harbors, MN
East Liverpool Area Chamber of Commerce [15078], East Liverpool, OH
East Peoria Chamber of Commerce and Tourism [1542], East Peoria, IL
East Side Chamber of Commerce [879], Chicago, IL
East Troy Area Chamber of Commerce [17855], East Troy, WI
Eastern Maumee Bay Chamber of Commerce [16302], Oregon, OH
Eastpointe Chamber of Commerce [7576], Eastpointe, MI
Eaton - Preble County Chamber of Commerce [15088], Eaton, OH
Eau Claire Area Chamber of Commerce [17873], Eau Claire, WI
Eau Claire Lakes Bus. Assn. of Barnes and Gordon [18060], Gordon, WI
Eden Prairie Chamber of Commerce [10890], Eden Prairie, MN
Edgebrook Chamber of Commerce [881], Chicago, IL
Edgerton Area Chamber of Commerce [17917], Edgerton, WI
Edgerton Chamber of Commerce [15093], Edgerton, OH
Edwardsburg Area Chamber of Commerce [7590], Edwardsburg, MI
Edwardsville - Glen Carbon Chamber of Commerce [1558], Edwardsville, IL
El Paso Chamber of Commerce [1576], El Paso, IL
Elgin Area Chamber of Commerce [1587], Elgin, IL
Elizabeth Chamber of Commerce [1603], Elizabeth, IL
Elk Rapids Area Chamber of Commerce [7595], Elk Rapids, MI
Elk River Area Chamber of Commerce [10945], Elk River, MN
Elkhart Lake Area Chamber of Commerce [17925], Elkhart Lake, WI
Elkhorn Area Chamber of Commerce [17927], Elkhorn, WI
Ellsworth Chamber of Commerce [17933], Ellsworth, WI
Elmhurst Chamber of Commerce and Indus. [1619], Elmhurst, IL
Elroy Area Advancement Corp. [17940], Elroy, WI
Elwood Chamber of Commerce [4513], Elwood, IN
Ely Chamber of Commerce [10954], Ely, MN
Englewood-Northmont Chamber of Commerce [15131], Englewood, OH
Euclid Chamber of Commerce [15141], Euclid, OH
Evanston Chamber of Commerce [1655], Evanston, IL
Evansville Chamber of Commerce [17947], Evansville, WI
Evart Area Chamber of Commerce [7628], Evart, MI
Evergreen Park Chamber of Commerce [1682], Evergreen Park, IL
Fairborn Area Chamber of Commerce [15148], Fairborn, OH
Fairfield Chamber of Commerce [15155], Fairfield, OH
Fairmont Area Chamber of Commerce [10977], Fairmont, MN
Fairview Heights Chamber of Commerce [1696], Fairview Heights, IL
Faribault Area Chamber of Commerce [10985], Faribault, MN
Farmington Area Chamber of Commerce [10990], Farmington, MN
Farmington - Farmington Hills Chamber of Commerce [7659], Farmington Hills, MI
Farwell Area Chamber of Commerce [7679], Farwell, MI
Fayette County Chamber of Commerce [17127], Washington Court House, OH
Fennimore Area Chamber of Commerce [17957], Fennimore, WI
Fenton Area Chamber of Commerce [7683], Fenton, MI
Ferdinand Chamber of Commerce [4596], Ferdinand, IN
Fergus Falls Area Chamber of Commerce [10996], Fergus Falls, MN
Findlay-Hancock County Chamber of Commerce [15201], Findlay, OH
Fishers Chamber of Commerce [4604], Fishers, IN
Flint Area Chamber of Commerce [7726], Flint, MI
Flora Chamber of Commerce [1706], Flora, IL
Flushing Area Chamber of Commerce [7765], Flushing, MI
Fond du Lac Area Assn. of Commerce [17972], Fond du Lac, WI
Forest Lake Area Chamber of Commerce [11017], Forest Lake, MN
Forest Park Chamber of Commerce [1711], Forest Park, IL
Fort Atkinson Area Chamber of Commerce [17999], Fort Atkinson, WI
Fort Recovery Chamber of Commerce [15225], Fort Recovery, OH
Forward Janesville [18247], Janesville, WI
Fostoria Area Chamber of Commerce [15230], Fostoria, OH
Four Flags Area Chamber of Commerce [9206], Niles, MI
Fowler Chamber of Commerce [4736], Fowler, IN
Fox Cities Chamber of Commerce and Indus. [17490], Appleton, WI
Fox Lake Area Chamber of Commerce [18003], Fox Lake, WI
Fox Lake Area Chamber of Commerce and Indus. [1719], Fox Lake, IL
Frankenmuth Chamber of Commerce and Convention and Visitors Bur. [7779], Frankenmuth, MI
Frankfort Chamber of Commerce [1724], Frankfort, IL
Frankfort - Elberta Area Chamber of Commerce [7785], Frankfort, MI
Franklin Area Chamber of Commerce [15238], Franklin, OH
Franklin Chamber of Commerce [4747], Franklin, IN
Franklin Park/Schiller Park Chamber of Commerce [1739], Franklin Park, IL
Frederic Area Community Assn. [18019], Frederic, WI
Freeburg Chamber of Commerce [1742], Freeburg, IL
Freeport Area Chamber of Commerce [1747], Freeport, IL
Fremont Area Chamber of Commerce [4761], Fremont, IN
Fremont Area Chamber of Commerce [7796], Fremont, MI
Fremont Area Chamber of Commerce [18024], Fremont, WI
French Lick - West Baden Chamber of Commerce [4763], French Lick, IN
Friesland Chamber of Commerce [18025], Friesland, WI
Fulton Chamber of Commerce [1758], Fulton, IL
Gahanna Area Chamber of Commerce [15263], Gahanna, OH
Galena Area Chamber of Commerce [1761], Galena, IL
Galesburg Area Chamber of Commerce [1771], Galesburg, IL
Galesville Area Chamber of Commerce [18026], Galesville, WI

Galion Area Chamber of Commerce **[15280]**, Galion, OH
Gallia County Chamber of Commerce **[15290]**, Gallipolis, OH
Garden City Chamber of Commerce **[7811]**, Garden City, MI
Garfield Heights Chamber of Commerce **[15302]**, Garfield Heights, OH
Garrett Chamber of Commerce **[4768]**, Garrett, IN
Garrettsville - Hiram Area Chamber of Commerce **[15304]**, Garrettsville, OH
Gary Chamber of Commerce **[4778]**, Gary, IN
Gaylord - Otsego County Chamber of Commerce **[7819]**, Gaylord, MI
Geneseo Chamber of Commerce **[1788]**, Geneseo, IL
Geneva Area Chamber of Commerce **[15309]**, Geneva, OH
Geneva Chamber of Commerce **[1793]**, Geneva, IL
Geneva Lake Area Chamber of Commerce **[18397]**, Lake Geneva, WI
Geneva-on-the-Lake Chamber of Commerce **[15310]**, Geneva, OH
Genoa Chamber of Commerce **[1804]**, Genoa, IL
German-American Chamber of Commerce of the Midwest - Wisconsin Chapter **[19013]**, Milwaukee, WI
Germantown Area Chamber of Commerce **[18039]**, Germantown, WI
Gibson Area Chamber of Commerce **[1809]**, Gibson City, IL
Gilman Chamber of Commerce **[1812]**, Gilman, IL
Girard Chamber of Commerce **[1814]**, Girard, IL
Gladwin County Chamber of Commerce **[7835]**, Gladwin, MI
Glen Ellyn Chamber of Commerce **[1829]**, Glen Ellyn, IL
Glencoe Area Chamber of Commerce **[11048]**, Glencoe, MN
Glencoe Chamber of Commerce **[1849]**, Glencoe, IL
Glendale Assn. of Commerce **[18052]**, Glendale, WI
Glenview Chamber of Commerce **[1865]**, Glenview, IL
Glenwood Area Chamber of Commerce **[11052]**, Glenwood, MN
GLMV Area Chamber of Commerce **[2259]**, Libertyville, IL
Goshen Chamber of Commerce **[4795]**, Goshen, IN
Grafton Area Chamber of Commerce **[18063]**, Grafton, WI
Grand Blanc Chamber of Commerce **[7844]**, Grand Blanc, MI
Grand Ledge Area Chamber of Commerce **[7871]**, Grand Ledge, MI
Grand Marais Chamber of Commerce **[11075]**, Grand Marais, MN
Grand Rapids Area Chamber of Commerce **[7943]**, Grand Rapids, MI
Grand Rapids Area Chamber of Commerce **[11084]**, Grand Rapids, MN
Grand Rapids Area Chamber of Commerce **[15338]**, Grand Rapids, OH
Grandville Chamber of Commerce **[8038]**, Grandville, MI
Granite Falls Area Chamber of Commerce **[11096]**, Granite Falls, MN
Grantsburg Chamber of Commerce **[18071]**, Grantsburg, WI
Gratiot Area Chamber of Commerce **[6632]**, Alma, MI
Grayling Regional Chamber of Commerce **[8061]**, Grayling, MI
Grayslake Area Chamber of Commerce **[1893]**, Grayslake, IL
Grayville Chamber of Commerce **[1899]**, Grayville, IL
Greater Akron Chamber of Commerce **[13054]**, Akron, OH
Greater Albion Chamber of Commerce **[6590]**, Albion, MI
Greater Algonac Chamber of Commerce **[6599]**, Algonac, MI
Greater Aurora Chamber of Commerce **[118]**, Aurora, IL
Greater Avon Chamber of Commerce **[4152]**, Avon, IN
Greater Belleville Chamber of Commerce **[202]**, Belleville, IL
Greater Beloit Chamber of Commerce **[17609]**, Beloit, WI
Greater Berkley Chamber of Commerce **[6930]**, Berkley, MI
Greater Bloomington Chamber of Commerce **[4223]**, Bloomington, IN
Greater Brighton Area Chamber of Commerce **[7012]**, Brighton, MI
Greater Brookfield Chamber of Commerce **[17668]**, Brookfield, WI
Greater Buckeye Lake Chamber of Commerce **[13459]**, Buckeye Lake, OH
Greater Centralia Chamber of Commerce **[487]**, Centralia, IL
Greater Channahon-Minooka Area Chamber of Commerce **[2502]**, Minooka, IL
Greater Cincinnati Junior Chamber Found. **[13849]**, Cincinnati, OH
Greater Cincinnati and Northern Kentucky African-Amer. Chamber of Commerce **[13851]**, Cincinnati, OH
Greater Columbus Area Chamber of Commerce **[14446]**, Columbus, OH
Greater Croswell - Lexington Chamber of Commerce **[8808]**, Lexington, MI
Greater Danville Chamber of Commerce **[4445]**, Danville, IN
Greater Decatur Chamber of Commerce **[7285]**, Decatur, MI
Greater Dowagiac Area Chamber of Commerce **[7481]**, Dowagiac, MI
Greater East St. Louis Chamber of Commerce **[1550]**, East St. Louis, IL
Greater Edinburgh Community Chamber of Commerce **[4481]**, Edinburgh, IN
Greater Effingham Chamber of Commerce and Indus. **[1570]**, Effingham, IL
Greater Elkhart County Chamber of Commerce **[4497]**, Elkhart, IN
Greater Fairfield Area Chamber of Commerce **[1688]**, Fairfield, IL
Greater Fort Wayne Chamber of Commerce **[4667]**, Fort Wayne, IN
Greater Girard Area Chamber of Commerce **[15323]**, Girard, OH
Greater Greencastle Chamber of Commerce **[4817]**, Greencastle, IN
Greater Greenfield Chamber of Commerce **[4833]**, Greenfield, IN
Greater Greenwood Chamber of Commerce **[4849]**, Greenwood, IN
Greater Hamilton Chamber of Commerce **[15384]**, Hamilton, OH
Greater Harvard Area Chamber of Commerce **[1950]**, Harvard, IL
Greater Indianapolis Chamber of Commerce **[5128]**, Indianapolis, IN
Greater Jackson Chamber of Commerce **[8366]**, Jackson, MI
Greater La Porte Chamber of Commerce **[5596]**, La Porte, IN
Greater Lawrence County Area Chamber of Commerce **[16696]**, South Point, OH
Greater Lincolnshire Chamber of Commerce **[2284]**, Lincolnshire, IL
Greater Madison Chamber of Commerce **[18517]**, Madison, WI
Greater Martinsville Chamber of Commerce **[5752]**, Martinsville, IN
Greater Mauston Area Chamber of Commerce **[18829]**, Mauston, WI
Greater Menomonie Area Chamber of Commerce **[18881]**, Menomonie, WI
Greater Mitchell Chamber of Commerce **[5815]**, Mitchell, IN
Greater Monticello Chamber of Commerce and Visitors Bur. **[5823]**, Monticello, IN
Greater Paw Paw Chamber of Commerce **[9346]**, Paw Paw, MI
Greater Port Huron Area Chamber of Commerce **[9434]**, Port Huron, MI
Greater Portage Chamber of Commerce **[6056]**, Portage, IN
Greater Princeton Area Chamber of Commerce **[19543]**, Princeton, WI
Greater Romulus Chamber of Commerce **[9549]**, Romulus, MI
Greater Royal Oak Chamber of Commerce **[9582]**, Royal Oak, MI
Greater Salem Chamber of Commerce **[3409]**, Salem, IL
Greater Scott County Chamber of Commerce **[6173]**, Scottsburg, IN
Greater Seymour Chamber of Commerce **[6181]**, Seymour, IN
Greater South Haven Area Chamber of Commerce **[9763]**, South Haven, MI
Greater Springfield Chamber of Commerce **[3556]**, Springfield, IL
Greater Stillwater Chamber of Commerce **[12719]**, Stillwater, MN
Greater Terre Haute Chamber of Commerce **[6321]**, Terre Haute, IN
Greater Tomah Area Chamber of Commerce **[19904]**, Tomah, WI
Greater Union Grove Area Chamber of Commerce **[19926]**, Union Grove, WI
Greater Valparaiso Chamber of Commerce **[6383]**, Valparaiso, IN
Greater Wayzata Area Chamber of Commerce **[12860]**, Wayzata, MN
Greater West Bloomfield Chamber of Commerce **[10114]**, West Bloomfield, MI
Greater Zionsville Chamber of Commerce **[6550]**, Zionsville, IN
Green Bay Area Chamber of Commerce **[18102]**, Green Bay, WI
Green Lake Area Chamber of Commerce **[18146]**, Green Lake, WI
Greendale Chamber of Commerce **[18150]**, Greendale, WI
Greenfield Chamber of Commerce **[18155]**, Greenfield, WI
Greensburg Decatur County Chamber of Commerce **[4843]**, Greensburg, IN
Greenville Area Chamber of Commerce **[8067]**, Greenville, MI
Greenville Chamber of Commerce **[1907]**, Greenville, IL
Greenwood Chamber of Commerce **[18165]**, Greenwood, WI
Griffith Chamber of Commerce **[4857]**, Griffith, IN
Grove City Area Chamber of Commerce **[15368]**, Grove City, OH
Hamilton Area Chamber of Commerce **[4864]**, Hamilton, IN
Hamilton Chamber of Commerce **[4865]**, Hamilton, IN
Hamilton County Chamber of Commerce **[13859]**, Cincinnati, OH
Hamilton County Chamber of Commerce and Economic Development Commn. **[2466]**, McLeansboro, IL
Hampshire Area Chamber of Commerce **[1930]**, Hampshire, IL
Harbor Beach Chamber of Commerce **[8115]**, Harbor Beach, MI
Harbor Springs Chamber of Commerce **[8118]**, Harbor Springs, MI
Hardin County Chamber of Commerce **[15553]**, Kenton, OH
Harrison Chamber of Commerce **[8126]**, Harrison, MI
Harrison Regional Chamber of Commerce **[13481]**, Cadiz, OH
Hart - Silver Lake Mears Chamber of Commerce **[8137]**, Hart, MI
Hartford Area Chamber of Commerce **[18177]**, Hartford, WI
Hartford City Chamber of Commerce **[4903]**, Hartford City, IN
Hartland Area Chamber of Commerce **[18183]**, Hartland, WI
Hastings Area Chamber of Commerce and Tourism Bur. **[11125]**, Hastings, MN
Havana Area Chamber of Commerce **[1959]**, Havana, IL
Hayward Area Chamber of Commerce **[18195]**, Hayward, WI
Heart of the Valley Chamber of Commerce **[18287]**, Kaukauna, WI

Heights Regional Chamber of Commerce **[14247]**, Cleveland Heights, OH
Henry Area Chamber of Commerce **[1969]**, Henry, IL
Hermantown Chamber of Commerce **[11150]**, Hermantown, MN
Herrin Chamber of Commerce **[1974]**, Herrin, IL
Herscher Chamber of Commerce **[1976]**, Herscher, IL
Hibbing Area Chamber of Commerce **[11157]**, Hibbing, MN
Hickory Hills Chamber of Commerce **[1983]**, Hickory Hills, IL
Highland Chamber of Commerce **[1985]**, Highland, IL
Highland Chamber of Commerce **[4912]**, Highland, IN
Highland County Chamber of Commerce **[15446]**, Hillsboro, OH
Highland Park Chamber of Commerce **[1989]**, Highland Park, IL
Hilliard Area Chamber of Commerce **[15433]**, Hilliard, OH
Hillman Area Chamber of Commerce **[8173]**, Hillman, MI
Hillsboro Area Chamber of Commerce **[1998]**, Hillsboro, IL
Hillsdale County Chamber of Commerce **[8176]**, Hillsdale, MI
Hinsdale Chamber of Commerce **[2017]**, Hinsdale, IL
Hobart Chamber of Commerce **[4924]**, Hobart, IN
Hoffman Estates Chamber of Commerce **[2035]**, Hoffman Estates, IL
Holland Area Chamber of Commerce **[8200]**, Holland, MI
Holland - Springfield Chamber of Commerce **[15458]**, Holland, OH
Holly Area Chamber of Commerce **[8236]**, Holly, MI
Holmes County Chamber of Commerce **[16035]**, Millersburg, OH
Homewood Area Chamber of Commerce **[2048]**, Homewood, IL
Horicon Chamber of Commerce **[18215]**, Horicon, WI
Houghton Lake Chamber of Commerce **[8264]**, Houghton Lake, MI
Howell Area Chamber of Commerce **[8275]**, Howell, MI
Huber Heights Chamber of Commerce **[15476]**, Huber Heights, OH
Hudson Area Chamber of Commerce **[8289]**, Hudson, MI
Hudson Area Chamber of Commerce **[15481]**, Hudson, OH
Hudson Area Chamber of Commerce and Tourism Bur. **[18223]**, Hudson, WI
Hudsonville Area Chamber of Commerce **[8290]**, Hudsonville, MI
Huntingburg Chamber of Commerce **[4940]**, Huntingburg, IN
Huntington County Chamber of Commerce **[4949]**, Huntington, IN
Huntley Area Chamber of Commerce and Indus. **[2054]**, Huntley, IL
Hurley Area Chamber of Commerce **[18230]**, Hurley, WI
Huron Chamber of Commerce **[15491]**, Huron, OH
Huron Shores Chamber of Commerce **[8133]**, Harrisville, MI
Huron Township Chamber of Commerce **[9184]**, New Boston, MI
Huron Valley Chamber of Commerce **[9050]**, Milford, MI
Hutchinson Area Chamber of Commerce **[11207]**, Hutchinson, MN
Hyde Park Chamber of Commerce **[921]**, Chicago, IL
I-94 West Chamber of Commerce **[12203]**, Rogers, MN
Illinois Assn. of Chamber of Commerce Executives **[3566]**, Springfield, IL
Illinois Quad City Chamber of Commerce **[2521]**, Moline, IL
Illinois River Area Chamber of Commerce **[2420]**, Marseilles, IL
Illinois State Chamber of Commerce **[970]**, Chicago, IL
Illinois Valley Area Chamber of Commerce and Economic Development **[2182]**, La Salle, IL
Indian Lake Area Chamber of Commerce **[16562]**, Russells Point, OH
Indian River Resort Region Chamber of Commerce **[8308]**, Indian River, MI
Indiana Chamber of Commerce **[5206]**, Indianapolis, IN
Indiana State Hispanic Chamber of Commerce **[5316]**, Indianapolis, IN
Inkster Chamber of Commerce **[8311]**, Inkster, MI
Interlochen Area Chamber of Commerce **[8313]**, Interlochen, MI
Intl. Falls Area Chamber of Commerce **[11216]**, International Falls, MN
Iola - Scandinavia Area Chamber of Commerce **[18235]**, Iola, WI
Ionia Area Chamber of Commerce **[8315]**, Ionia, MI
Iron County Chamber of Commerce **[8332]**, Iron River, MI
Ironwood Area Chamber of Commerce **[8339]**, Ironwood, MI
Ishpeming Off. of Lake Superior Community Partnership **[8346]**, Ishpeming, MI
Jackson Area Chamber of Commerce **[11234]**, Jackson, MN
Jackson Area Chamber of Commerce **[15513]**, Jackson, OH
Jackson - Beldon Chamber of Commerce **[15884]**, Massillon, OH
Jacksonville Area Chamber of Commerce **[2080]**, Jacksonville, IL
Jasper Chamber of Commerce **[5528]**, Jasper, IN
Jasper County Chamber of Commerce **[2699]**, Newton, IL
Jefferson Area Chamber of Commerce **[15525]**, Jefferson, OH
Jefferson Chamber of Commerce **[18271]**, Jefferson, WI
Jefferson County Chamber of Commerce **[2599]**, Mount Vernon, IL
Jefferson County Chamber of Commerce **[16762]**, Steubenville, OH
Jefferson Park Chamber of Commerce **[1003]**, Chicago, IL
Jennings County Chamber of Commerce **[5995]**, North Vernon, IN
Jersey County Bus. Assn. **[2090]**, Jerseyville, IL
Johnson Creek Area Chamber of Commerce **[18277]**, Johnson Creek, WI
Joliet Region Chamber of Commerce and Indus. **[2113]**, Joliet, IL
Juneau Chamber of Commerce **[18282]**, Juneau, WI
Kalamazoo Regional Chamber of Commerce **[8443]**, Kalamazoo, MI
Kalkaska Area Chamber of Commerce **[8476]**, Kalkaska, MI
Kanabec Area Chamber of Commerce **[11833]**, Mora, MN
Kankakee River Valley Chamber of Commerce **[2137]**, Kankakee, IL
Kelleys Island Chamber of Commerce **[15535]**, Kelleys Island, OH
Kendallville Area Chamber of Commerce **[5550]**, Kendallville, IN
Kenosha Area Chamber of Commerce **[18300]**, Kenosha, WI
Kent Area Chamber of Commerce **[15541]**, Kent, OH
Kentland Area Chamber of Commerce **[5553]**, Kentland, IN
Kettering - Moraine - Oakwood Chamber of Commerce **[15561]**, Kettering, OH
Kewanee Chamber of Commerce **[2157]**, Kewanee, IL
Kewaunee Area Chamber of Commerce **[18320]**, Kewaunee, WI
Keweenaw Peninsula Chamber of Commerce **[8255]**, Houghton, MI
Kiel Area Assn. of Commerce **[18322]**, Kiel, WI
Knightstown Indiana Chamber of Commerce **[5559]**, Knightstown, IN
Knox County Chamber of Commerce **[6413]**, Vincennes, IN
Kokomo - Howard County Chamber of Commerce **[5574]**, Kokomo, IN
Kouts Chamber of Commerce **[5592]**, Kouts, IN
La Crescent Chamber of Commerce **[11266]**, La Crescent, MN
La Crosse Area Chamber of Commerce **[18352]**, La Crosse, WI
Lac Du Flambeau Chamber of Commerce **[18389]**, Lac Du Flambeau, WI
Lafayette - West Lafayette Chamber of Commerce **[5622]**, Lafayette, IN
Lagrange County Chamber of Commerce **[5641]**, Lagrange, IN
Lake Benton Area Chamber of Commerce and Convention and Visitors Bur. **[11270]**, Lake Benton, MN
Lake City Area Chamber of Commerce **[8506]**, Lake City, MI
Lake City Area Chamber of Commerce **[11275]**, Lake City, MN
Lake County Chamber of Commerce **[1921]**, Gurnee, IL
Lake Crystal Area Chamber of Commerce **[11278]**, Lake Crystal, MN
Lake Forest - Lake Bluff Chamber of Commerce **[2200]**, Lake Forest, IL
Lake Gogebic Area Chamber of Commerce **[6927]**, Bergland, MI
Lake Mills Area Chamber of Commerce **[18403]**, Lake Mills, WI
Lake Minnetonka Chamber of Commerce **[11858]**, Navarre, MN
Lake Sta. Chamber of Commerce **[5644]**, Lake Station, IN
Lake Township Chamber of Commerce **[15411]**, Hartville, OH
Lake Vermilion Area Chamber of Commerce **[12755]**, Tower, MN
Lake View East Chamber of Commerce **[1017]**, Chicago, IL
Lake Wisconsin Chamber of Commerce **[19524]**, Poynette, WI
Lake Zurich Area Chamber of Commerce **[2209]**, Lake Zurich, IL
Lakes Area Chamber of Commerce **[10056]**, Walled Lake, MI
Lakeshore Chamber of Commerce **[4887]**, Hammond, IN
Lakeshore Chamber of Commerce **[9875]**, Stevensville, MI
Lakeview Area Chamber of Commerce **[8518]**, Lakeview, MI
Lakewood Area Chamber of Commerce **[18408]**, Lakewood, WI
Lakewood Chamber of Commerce **[15586]**, Lakewood, OH
Lancaster Area Chamber of Commerce **[18411]**, Lancaster, WI
Lancaster Fairfield County Chamber of Commerce **[15604]**, Lancaster, OH
Land O'Lakes Chamber of Commerce **[18415]**, Land O' Lakes, WI
Lansing Chamber of Commerce **[2220]**, Lansing, IL
Lansing Regional Chamber of Commerce **[8593]**, Lansing, MI
Lapeer Area Chamber of Commerce **[8776]**, Lapeer, MI
Laurentian Chamber of Commerce **[12795]**, Virginia, MN
Lawrence County Chamber of Commerce **[2225]**, Lawrenceville, IL
Lebanon Area Chamber of Commerce **[15621]**, Lebanon, OH
Lebanon Chamber of Commerce **[2231]**, Lebanon, IL
Leech Lake Area Chamber of Commerce **[12831]**, Walker, MN
Leelanau Peninsula Chamber of Commerce **[9887]**, Suttons Bay, MI
Leetonia-Washingtonville Area Chamber of Commerce **[15631]**, Leetonia, OH
Leipsic Area Chamber of Commerce **[15633]**, Leipsic, OH
Lemont Area Chamber of Commerce **[2245]**, Lemont, IL
Lena Community Development Corp. **[18418]**, Lena, WI

Lenawee County Chamber of Commerce **[6574]**, Adrian, MI
Lewiston Area Chamber of Commerce **[8805]**, Lewiston, MI
Lewistown Chamber of Commerce **[2250]**, Lewistown, IL
Liberty - Union County Chamber of Commerce **[5679]**, Liberty, IN
Ligonier Chamber of Commerce **[5681]**, Ligonier, IN
Lima/Allen County Chamber of Commerce **[15658]**, Lima, OH
Limestone Area Chamber of Commerce **[169]**, Bartonville, IL
Lincoln - Logan County Chamber of Commerce **[2276]**, Lincoln, IL
Lincoln Park Chamber of Commerce **[1030]**, Chicago, IL
Lincoln Park Chamber of Commerce **[8813]**, Lincoln Park, MI
Lincolnwood Chamber of Commerce and Indus. **[2289]**, Lincolnwood, IL
Linden Argentine Chamber of Commerce **[8819]**, Linden, MI
Lindenhurst - Lake Villa Chamber of Commerce **[2292]**, Lindenhurst, IL
Linton-Stockton Chamber of Commerce **[5684]**, Linton, IN
Lisbon Area Chamber of Commerce **[15678]**, Lisbon, OH
Lisle Chamber of Commerce **[2299]**, Lisle, IL
Litchfield Chamber of Commerce **[2307]**, Litchfield, IL
Litchfield Chamber of Commerce **[8824]**, Litchfield, MI
Litchfield Chamber of Commerce **[11328]**, Litchfield, MN
Little Falls Area Chamber of Commerce **[11335]**, Little Falls, MN
Livonia Chamber of Commerce **[8842]**, Livonia, MI
Lockport Chamber of Commerce **[2316]**, Lockport, IL
Lodi Area Chamber of Commerce **[15686]**, Lodi, OH
Lodi Chamber of Commerce **[18423]**, Lodi, WI
Logan County Area Chamber of Commerce **[13320]**, Bellefontaine, OH
Logan - Hocking Chamber of Commerce **[15690]**, Logan, OH
Logansport - Cass County Chamber of Commerce **[5693]**, Logansport, IN
Lombard Area Chamber of Commerce and Indus. **[2337]**, Lombard, IL
Lomira Area Chamber of Commerce **[18427]**, Lomira, WI
Long Prairie Area Chamber of Commerce **[11346]**, Long Prairie, MN
Lorain County Chamber of Commerce **[15705]**, Lorain, OH
Loudonville - Mohican Area Convention and Visitor's Bur. **[15715]**, Loudonville, OH
Louisville Area Chamber of Commerce **[15718]**, Louisville, OH
Loveland Area Chamber of Commerce **[15728]**, Loveland, OH
Loves Park - Machesney Park Chamber of Commerce **[2351]**, Loves Park, IL
Lowell Area Chamber of Commerce **[8863]**, Lowell, MI
Lowell Chamber of Commerce **[5705]**, Lowell, IN
Ludington Area Chamber of Commerce **[8871]**, Ludington, MI
Luverne Area Chamber of Commerce **[11355]**, Luverne, MN
Luxemburg Chamber of Commerce **[18436]**, Luxemburg, WI
Mackinac Island Tourism Bur. **[8886]**, Mackinac Island, MI
Mackinaw City Chamber of Commerce **[8889]**, Mackinaw City, MI
Macomb Area Chamber of Commerce & Downtown Development Corporation **[2371]**, Macomb, IL
Macomb Chamber **[10068]**, Warren, MI
Madelia Area Chamber of Commerce **[11364]**, Madelia, MN
Madeline Island Chamber of Commerce **[18385]**, La Pointe, WI
Madison Area Chamber of Commerce **[5717]**, Madison, IN
Madison Area Chamber of Commerce **[11366]**, Madison, MN
Madison County Chamber of Commerce **[15695]**, London, OH
Madison Heights - Hazel Park Chamber of Commerce **[8896]**, Madison Heights, MI
Madison - Perry Area Chamber of Commerce **[15748]**, Madison, OH
Mahomet Chamber of Commerce **[2380]**, Mahomet, IL
Manawa Area Chamber of Commerce **[18771]**, Manawa, WI
Mancelona Area Chamber of Commerce **[8905]**, Mancelona, MI
Manchester Area Chamber of Commerce **[8908]**, Manchester, MI
Manhattan Chamber of Commerce **[2384]**, Manhattan, IL
Manistee Area Chamber of Commerce **[8912]**, Manistee, MI
Manito Area Chamber of Commerce **[2387]**, Manito, IL
Manitowish Waters Chamber of Commerce **[18773]**, Manitowish Waters, WI
Manitowoc/Two Rivers Area Chamber of Commerce **[18786]**, Manitowoc, WI
Mansfield-Richland Area Chamber of Commerce **[15776]**, Mansfield, OH
Marblehead Peninsula Chamber of Commerce **[15808]**, Marblehead, OH
Marengo-Union Chamber of Commerce **[2397]**, Marengo, IL
Marietta Area Chamber of Commerce **[15821]**, Marietta, OH
Marine City Chamber of Commerce **[8925]**, Marine City, MI
Marinette Area Chamber of Commerce **[18799]**, Marinette, WI
Marion Area Chamber of Commerce **[8926]**, Marion, MI
Marion Area Chamber of Commerce **[15840]**, Marion, OH
Marion Chamber of Commerce **[2405]**, Marion, IL
Marion-Grant County Chamber of Commerce **[5738]**, Marion, IN
Marquette Area Chamber of Commerce- Lake Superior Community Partnership **[8938]**, Marquette, MI
Marshall Area Chamber of Commerce **[2424]**, Marshall, IL
Marshall Area Chamber of Commerce **[8968]**, Marshall, MI
Marshall Area Chamber of Commerce **[11434]**, Marshall, MN
Marshfield Area Chamber of Commerce and Indus. **[18817]**, Marshfield, WI
Martin County Chamber of Commerce **[5703]**, Loogootee, IN
Martins Ferry Area Chamber of Commerce **[15860]**, Martins Ferry, OH
Martinsville Chamber of Commerce **[2426]**, Martinsville, IL
Marysville Chamber of Commerce **[8974]**, Marysville, MI
Mason Area Chamber of Commerce **[8978]**, Mason, MI
Massillon Area Chamber of Commerce **[15887]**, Massillon, OH
Matteson Area Chamber of Commerce **[2438]**, Matteson, IL
Mattoon Chamber of Commerce **[2443]**, Mattoon, IL
Maumee Chamber of Commerce **[15909]**, Maumee, OH
Mayville Area Chamber of Commerce **[18832]**, Mayville, WI
Maywood Chamber of Commerce **[2449]**, Maywood, IL
Mazomanie Chamber of Commerce **[18836]**, Mazomanie, WI
McBain Area Chamber of Commerce **[8991]**, McBain, MI
McFarland Chamber of Commerce **[18841]**, McFarland, WI
McHenry Area Chamber of Commerce **[2460]**, McHenry, IL
McLean County Chamber of Commerce **[295]**, Bloomington, IL
Mecosta County Area Chamber of Commerce **[6947]**, Big Rapids, MI
Medford Area Chamber of Commerce **[18844]**, Medford, WI
Medina Area Chamber of Commerce **[15944]**, Medina, OH
Meigs County Chamber of Commerce **[16455]**, Pomeroy, OH
Mellen Area Chamber of Commerce **[18851]**, Mellen, WI
Melrose Chamber of Commerce **[11452]**, Melrose, MN
Melrose Park Chamber of Commerce **[2472]**, Melrose Park, IL
Memphis Chamber of Commerce **[9000]**, Memphis, MI
Mendota Area Chamber of Commerce **[2476]**, Mendota, IL
Menomonee Falls Chamber of Commerce **[18877]**, Menomonee Falls, WI
Mentone Chamber of Commerce **[5761]**, Mentone, IN
Mentor Area Chamber of Commerce **[15970]**, Mentor, OH
Mequon-Thiensville Area Chamber of Commerce **[19892]**, Thiensville, WI
Mercer Area Chamber of Commerce **[18893]**, Mercer, WI
Merrill Area Chamber of Commerce **[18896]**, Merrill, WI
Merrillville Chamber of Commerce **[5774]**, Merrillville, IN
Mesick Area Chamber of Commerce **[9009]**, Mesick, MI
Metro East Chamber of Commerce **[9662]**, St. Clair Shores, MI
MetroNorth Chamber of Commerce **[10449]**, Blaine, MN
Metropolis Area Chamber of Commerce **[2484]**, Metropolis, IL
Metropolitan Evansville Chamber of Commerce **[4560]**, Evansville, IN
Metropolitan Milwaukee Assn. of Commerce **[19049]**, Milwaukee, WI
Michigan Chamber of Commerce **[8639]**, Lansing, MI
Michigan City Area Chamber of Commerce **[5786]**, Michigan City, IN
Mid-Miami Valley Chamber of Commerce **[16012]**, Middletown, OH
Middlefield Chamber of Commerce **[16000]**, Middlefield, OH
Middleton Chamber of Commerce **[18909]**, Middleton, WI
Midland Area Chamber of Commerce **[9033]**, Midland, MI
Milaca Chamber of Commerce **[11466]**, Milaca, MN
Milan Area Chamber of Commerce **[9048]**, Milan, MI
Milford - Miami Township Chamber of Commerce **[16027]**, Milford, OH
Milton Area Chamber of Commerce **[18920]**, Milton, WI
Milwaukee Minority Chamber of Commerce **[19064]**, Milwaukee, WI
Mineral Point Chamber of Commerce **[19195]**, Mineral Point, WI
Minerva Area Chamber of Commerce **[16045]**, Minerva, OH
Minneapolis Regional Chamber of Commerce **[11618]**, Minneapolis, MN
Minnesota State Chamber of Commerce **[12525]**, St. Paul, MN
Mishicot Area Growth and Improvement Comm. **[19203]**, Mishicot, WI
Mokena Chamber of Commerce **[2510]**, Mokena, IL
Momence Chamber of Commerce **[2538]**, Momence, IL
Monmouth Area Chamber of Commerce **[2541]**, Monmouth, IL
Monon Chamber of Commerce **[5818]**, Monon, IN

Monona Chamber of Commerce [19209], Monona, WI
Monroe Chamber of Commerce and Indus. [19215], Monroe, WI
Monroe County Chamber of Commerce [9068], Monroe, MI
Monroe County Chamber of Commerce [17306], Woodsfield, OH
Mont Clare - Elmwood Park Chamber of Commerce [1633], Elmwood Park, IL
Montello Area Chamber of Commerce [19221], Montello, WI
Montevideo Area Chamber of Commerce [11801], Montevideo, MN
Monticello Area Chamber of Commerce [11811], Monticello, MN
Monticello Chamber of Commerce [2548], Monticello, IL
Montpelier Area Chamber of Commerce [16061], Montpelier, OH
Mooresville Chamber of Commerce [5837], Mooresville, IN
Moose Lake Area Chamber of Commerce [11830], Moose Lake, MN
Morris Area Chamber of Commerce and Agriculture [11838], Morris, MN
Morrison Chamber of Commerce [2559], Morrison, IL
Morrow County Chamber of Commerce and Visitors' Bur. [16070], Mount Gilead, OH
Morton Chamber of Commerce [2564], Morton, IL
Morton Grove Chamber of Commerce and Indus. [2569], Morton Grove, IL
Mosinee Area Chamber of Commerce [19229], Mosinee, WI
Mount Carroll Chamber of Commerce [2577], Mount Carroll, IL
Mount Greenwood Chamber of Commerce [1059], Chicago, IL
Mount Horeb Area Chamber of Commerce [19238], Mount Horeb, WI
Mount Pleasant Area Chamber of Commerce [9115], Mount Pleasant, MI
Mount Prospect Chamber of Commerce [2589], Mount Prospect, IL
Mount Vernon - Knox County Chamber of Commerce [16086], Mount Vernon, OH
Mount Zion Chamber of Commerce [2606], Mount Zion, IL
Mukwonago Area Chamber of Commerce and Tourism Center [19253], Mukwonago, WI
Muncie-Delaware County Chamber of Commerce [5887], Muncie, IN
Munster Chamber of Commerce [5903], Munster, IN
Murphysboro Chamber of Commerce [2619], Murphysboro, IL
Muskego Area Chamber of Commerce [19262], Muskego, WI
Muskingum Valley Area Chamber of Commerce [13357], Beverly, OH
Naperville Area Chamber of Commerce [2647], Naperville, IL
Napoleon - Henry County Chamber of Commerce [16099], Napoleon, OH
Nappanee Area Chamber of Commerce [5908], Nappanee, IN
Nauvoo Chamber of Commerce [2672], Nauvoo, IL
Nebagamon Community Assn. [18406], Lake Nebagamon, WI
Neillsville Area Chamber of Commerce [19280], Neillsville, WI
New Berlin Chamber of Commerce and Visitors Bur. [19293], New Berlin, WI
New Castle-Henry County Chamber of Commerce [5939], New Castle, IN
New Glarus Chamber of Commerce [19304], New Glarus, WI
New Haven Chamber of Commerce [5948], New Haven, IN
New Holstein Area Chamber of Commerce [19308], New Holstein, WI
New Lenox Chamber of Commerce [2693], New Lenox, IL
New Lisbon Area Chamber of Commerce [19311], New Lisbon, WI
New London Area Chamber of Commerce [19315], New London, WI
New Palestine Area Chamber of Commerce [5951], New Palestine, IN
New Prague Chamber of Commerce [11878], New Prague, MN
New Richmond Area Chamber of Commerce and Visitors Bur. [19320], New Richmond, WI
New Ulm Area Chamber of Commerce [11885], New Ulm, MN
Newberry Area Chamber of Commerce [9198], Newberry, MI
Newcomerstown Chamber of Commerce [16197], Newcomerstown, OH
Niles Chamber of Chamber of Commerce and Indus. [2702], Niles, IL
Nisswa Chamber of Commerce [11898], Nisswa, MN
Noble County Chamber of Commerce [13486], Caldwell, OH
Noblesville Chamber of Commerce [5978], Noblesville, IN
Nordonia Hills Chamber of Commerce [16254], Northfield, OH
North Baltimore Area Chamber of Commerce [16211], North Baltimore, OH
North Br. Area Chamber of Commerce [11900], North Branch, MN
North Canton Area Chamber of Commerce [16219], North Canton, OH
North Coast Regional Chamber of Commerce [13244], Avon Lake, OH
North Hennepin Area Chamber of Commerce [11953], Osseo, MN
North Manchester Chamber of Commerce [5988], North Manchester, IN
North Newton Area Chamber of Commerce [6140], Roselawn, IN
North Olmsted Chamber of Commerce [16236], North Olmsted, OH
North Royalton Chamber of Commerce [16246], North Royalton, OH
North Webster - Tippecanoe Township Chamber of Commerce [6000], North Webster, IN
Northbrook Chamber of Commerce and Indus. [2761], Northbrook, IL
Northeast Cincinnati Chamber of Commerce [15877], Mason, OH
Northern Dakota County Chamber of Commerce [10872], Eagan, MN
Northfield Area Chamber of Commerce [11916], Northfield, MN
Northlake Chamber of Commerce [2766], Northlake, IL
Northville Chamber of Commerce [9226], Northville, MI
Northwest Suburban Chamber of Commerce [10721], Corcoran, MN
Norwalk Area Chamber of Commerce [16262], Norwalk, OH
Norwood Park Chamber of Commerce and Indus. [1110], Chicago, IL
Novi Chamber of Commerce [9241], Novi, MI
Oak Brook Area Assn. of Commerce and Indus. [2837], Oakbrook Terrace, IL
Oak Forest Chamber of Commerce [2790], Oak Forest, IL
Oak Harbor Area Chamber of Commerce [16273], Oak Harbor, OH
Oak Lawn Chamber of Commerce [2799], Oak Lawn, IL
Oak Park-River Forest Chamber of Commerce [2823], Oak Park, IL
Oberlin Area Chamber of Commerce [16288], Oberlin, OH
Oconomowoc Area Chamber of Commerce [19339], Oconomowoc, WI
Oconto Area Chamber of Commerce [19348], Oconto, WI
Oconto Falls Area Chamber of Commerce [19351], Oconto Falls, WI
O'Fallon Chamber of Commerce [2850], O'Fallon, IL
Ohio Chamber of Commerce [14577], Columbus, OH
Okawville Chamber of Commerce [2856], Okawville, IL
Olivia Area Chamber of Commerce [11936], Olivia, MN
Olney and the Greater Richland County Chamber of Commerce [2859], Olney, IL
Omro Area Chamber of Commerce [19357], Omro, WI
Ontonagon County Chamber of Commerce [9311], Ontonagon, MI
Oregon Chamber of Commerce [2869], Oregon, IL
Orion Area Chamber of Commerce [8517], Lake Orion, MI
Orland Park Area Chamber of Commerce [2883], Orland Park, IL
Orleans Chamber of Commerce [6014], Orleans, IN
Osceola Area Chamber of Commerce [19383], Osceola, WI
Oshkosh Chamber of Commerce [19401], Oshkosh, WI
Oswego Chamber of Commerce [2893], Oswego, IL
Otsego Area Chamber of Commerce [9325], Otsego, MI
Ottawa Area Chamber of Commerce [16318], Ottawa, OH
Ottawa Area Chamber of Commerce and Indus. [2899], Ottawa, IL
Over-The-Rhine Chamber of Commerce [13949], Cincinnati, OH
Owatonna Area Chamber of Commerce and Tourism [11962], Owatonna, MN
Owen County Chamber of Commerce and Economic Development Corp. [6282], Spencer, IN
Oxford Area Chamber of Commerce [9340], Oxford, MI
Oxford Chamber of Commerce [16326], Oxford, OH
Painesville Area Chamber of Commerce [16342], Painesville, OH
Palatine Area Chamber of Commerce [2921], Palatine, IL
Palestine Chamber of Commerce [2931], Palestine, IL
Palestine Development Assn. [2932], Palestine, IL
Palmyra Area Chamber of Commerce [19418], Palmyra, WI
Palos Hills Chamber of Commerce [2941], Palos Hills, IL
Pana Chamber of Commerce [2945], Pana, IL
Paoli Chamber of Commerce [6020], Paoli, IN
Pardeeville Area Bus. Assn. [19423], Pardeeville, WI
Paris Area Chamber of Commerce and Tourism [2950], Paris, IL
Park Falls Area Chamber of Commerce [19425], Park Falls, WI
Park Rapids Area Chamber of Commerce [11978], Park Rapids, MN
Park Ridge Chamber of Commerce [2964], Park Ridge, IL
Parke County Chamber of Commerce [6135], Rockville, IN
Parma Area Chamber of Commerce [16376], Parma, OH
Paxton Area Chamber of Commerce [2975], Paxton, IL
Paynesville Area Chamber of Commerce [11983], Paynesville, MN
Pekin Area Chamber of Commerce [2989], Pekin, IL
Pelican Lake Chamber of Commerce [19429], Pelican Lake, WI
Pelican Rapids Area Chamber of Commerce [11986], Pelican Rapids, MN
Pentwater Chamber of Commerce [9352], Pentwater, MI
Peoria Area Chamber of Commerce [3044], Peoria, IL
Peoria Heights Chamber of Commerce [3053], Peoria, IL
Perham Area Chamber of Commerce [11994], Perham, MN
Perry County Chamber of Commerce [6297], Tell City, IN
Perry County Chamber of Commerce [16134], New Lexington, OH

Perrysburg Area Chamber of Commerce **[16411]**, Perrysburg, OH
Peru - Miami County Chamber of Commerce **[6033]**, Peru, IN
Petersburg Chamber of Commerce **[3086]**, Petersburg, IL
Petoskey Regional Chamber of Commerce **[9368]**, Petoskey, MI
Pewaukee Chamber of Commerce **[19440]**, Pewaukee, WI
Phelps Chamber of Commerce **[19450]**, Phelps, WI
Phillips Area Chamber of Commerce **[19453]**, Phillips, WI
Pickerington Area Chamber of Commerce **[16424]**, Pickerington, OH
Pigeon Chamber of Commerce **[9378]**, Pigeon, MI
Pike County Chamber of Commerce **[3095]**, Pittsfield, IL
Pike County Chamber of Commerce **[6037]**, Petersburg, IN
Pike County Chamber of Commerce **[17147]**, Waverly, OH
Pinckneyville Chamber of Commerce **[3091]**, Pinckneyville, IL
Pinconning Area Chamber of Commerce **[9383]**, Pinconning, MI
Pine City Area Chamber of Commerce **[12003]**, Pine City, MN
Pipestone Area Chamber of Commerce **[12010]**, Pipestone, MN
Piqua Area Chamber of Commerce **[16437]**, Piqua, OH
Plainfield Area Chamber of Commerce **[3105]**, Plainfield, IL
Plainfield Chamber of Commerce **[6043]**, Plainfield, IN
Plainwell Chamber of Commerce **[9388]**, Plainwell, MI
Plano Commerce Assn. **[3110]**, Plano, IL
Platteville Chamber of Commerce **[19466]**, Platteville, WI
Plymouth Area Chamber of Commerce **[6052]**, Plymouth, IN
Plymouth Chamber of Commerce **[19492]**, Plymouth, WI
Plymouth Community Chamber of Commerce **[9405]**, Plymouth, MI
Polo Chamber of Commerce **[3117]**, Polo, IL
Pontiac Area Chamber of Commerce **[3120]**, Pontiac, IL
Pontiac Regional Chamber **[9423]**, Pontiac, MI
Port Washington Chamber of Commerce **[19502]**, Port Washington, WI
Portage Area Chamber of Commerce **[19511]**, Portage, WI
Portage County Bus. Coun. **[19800]**, Stevens Point, WI
Portage Park Chamber of Commerce **[1142]**, Chicago, IL
Portland Area Chamber of Commerce **[6064]**, Portland, IN
Portland Area Chamber of Commerce **[9457]**, Portland, MI
Portsmouth Area Chamber of Commerce **[16473]**, Portsmouth, OH
Posey County Chamber of Commerce **[5855]**, Mount Vernon, IN
Potosi - Tennyson Area Chamber of Commerce **[19522]**, Potosi, WI
Powell Area Chamber of Commerce **[16480]**, Powell, OH
Poynette Chamber of Commerce **[19526]**, Poynette, WI
Prairie Du Chien Area Chamber of Commerce **[19529]**, Prairie Du Chien, WI
Prescott Area Chamber of Commerce **[19538]**, Prescott, WI
Presque Isle Chamber of Commerce **[19541]**, Presque Isle, WI
Princeton Area Chamber of Commerce **[6071]**, Princeton, IN
Princeton Area Chamber of Commerce **[12046]**, Princeton, MN
Princeton Area Chamber of Commerce and Main St. **[3137]**, Princeton, IL
Prior Lake Area Chamber of Commerce **[12054]**, Prior Lake, MN
Prophetstown-Lyndon Area Chamber of Commerce **[3141]**, Prophetstown, IL
Pulaski Area Chamber of Commerce **[19547]**, Pulaski, WI
Put-in-Bay Chamber of Commerce **[16490]**, Put In Bay, OH
Quincy Area Chamber of Commerce **[3160]**, Quincy, IL
Quincy Chamber of Commerce **[9467]**, Quincy, MI
Racine Area Manufacturers and Commerce **[19565]**, Racine, WI
Randolph Chamber of Commerce **[19586]**, Randolph, WI
Rantoul Area Chamber of Commerce **[3182]**, Rantoul, IL
Ravenna Area Chamber of Commerce **[16504]**, Ravenna, OH
Reading Chamber of Commerce **[16507]**, Reading, OH
Red Wing Area Chamber of Commerce **[12081]**, Red Wing, MN
Redford Township Chamber of Commerce **[9479]**, Redford, MI
Redwood Area Chamber and Tourism **[12097]**, Redwood Falls, MN
Reed City Area Chamber of Commerce **[9483]**, Reed City, MI
Reedsburg Area Chamber of Commerce **[19592]**, Reedsburg, WI
Reese Chamber of Commerce **[9486]**, Reese, MI
Rensselaer - Remington Chamber of Commerce **[6081]**, Rensselaer, IN
Reynoldsburg Area Chamber of Commerce **[16519]**, Reynoldsburg, OH
Rhinelander Area Chamber of Commerce **[19604]**, Rhinelander, WI
Rice Lake Area Chamber of Commerce **[19616]**, Rice Lake, WI
Richfield Chamber of Commerce **[12113]**, Richfield, MN
Richland Area Chamber of Commerce/Main St. Partnership **[19625]**, Richland Center, WI
Richmond Area Chamber of Commerce **[9489]**, Richmond, MI
Richmond/Spring Grove Area Chamber of Commerce **[3192]**, Richmond, IL
Richmond-Wayne County Chamber of Commerce **[6106]**, Richmond, IN
Ripley County Chamber of Commerce **[6403]**, Versailles, IN
Ripon Area Chamber of Commerce **[19636]**, Ripon, WI
Rittman Area Chamber of Commerce **[16539]**, Rittman, OH
River Cities Regional Chamber of Commerce **[9004]**, Menominee, MI
River Falls Area Chamber of Commerce and Tourism Bur. **[19644]**, River Falls, WI
River Heights Chamber of Commerce **[11227]**, Inver Grove Heights, MN
Riverdale Chamber of Commerce **[3211]**, Riverdale, IL
Riverside Chamber of Commerce **[3214]**, Riverside, IL
Robbinsdale Chamber of Commerce **[12120]**, Robbinsdale, MN
Rochelle Area Chamber of Commerce **[3227]**, Rochelle, IL
Rochester Area Chamber of Commerce **[12171]**, Rochester, MN
Rochester and Lake Manitou Chamber of Commerce **[6125]**, Rochester, IN
Rock Falls Chamber of Commerce **[3236]**, Rock Falls, IL
Rockford Area Chamber of Commerce **[9528]**, Rockford, MI
Rockford Regional Chamber of Commerce **[3309]**, Rockford, IL
Rockford Regional Chamber of Commerce Bus. Women's Coun. **[3310]**, Rockford, IL
Rockton Chamber of Commerce **[3336]**, Rockton, IL
Rocky River Chamber of Commerce **[16548]**, Rocky River, OH
Rogers City Chamber of Commerce **[9543]**, Rogers City, MI
Rolling Meadows Chamber of Commerce **[3344]**, Rolling Meadows, IL
Romeo-Washington Chamber of Commerce **[9546]**, Romeo, MI
Romeoville Chamber of Commerce **[3347]**, Romeoville, IL
Rootstown Area Chamber of Commerce **[16551]**, Rootstown, OH
Roselle Chamber of Commerce and Indus. **[3355]**, Roselle, IL
Round Lake Area Chamber of Commerce and Indus. **[3365]**, Round Lake Beach, IL
Rush County Chamber of Commerce **[6145]**, Rushville, IN
Rushville Area Chamber of Commerce and Main St. **[3371]**, Rushville, IL
Saginaw County Chamber of Commerce **[9630]**, Saginaw, MI
St. Charles Area Chamber of Commerce **[3392]**, St. Charles, IL
St. Cloud Area Chamber of Commerce **[12298]**, St. Cloud, MN
St. Croix Falls Chamber of Commerce **[19656]**, St. Croix Falls, WI
St. Germain Chamber of Commerce **[19659]**, St. Germain, WI
St. Ignace Chamber of Commerce **[9672]**, St. Ignace, MI
St. John Chamber of Commerce **[6153]**, St. John, IN
St. Johns Area Chamber of Commerce **[9678]**, St. Johns, MI
St. Joseph Chamber of Commerce **[12327]**, St. Joseph, MN
St. Paul Area Chamber of Commerce **[12575]**, St. Paul, MN
St. Peter Area Chamber of Commerce **[12620]**, St. Peter, MN
Salem Area Chamber of Commerce **[16589]**, Salem, OH
Saline Area Chamber of Commerce **[9703]**, Saline, MI
Saline County Chamber of Commerce **[1940]**, Harrisburg, IL
Sandstone Chamber of Commerce **[12626]**, Sandstone, MN
Sandwich Chamber of Commerce **[3416]**, Sandwich, IL
Sauk Centre Area Chamber of Commerce **[12633]**, Sauk Centre, MN
Sauk Prairie Area Chamber of Commerce **[19532]**, Prairie Du Sac, WI
Sauk Valley Area Chamber of Commerce **[3703]**, Sterling, IL
Saukville Chamber of Commerce **[19667]**, Saukville, WI
Sault Area Chamber of Commerce **[9725]**, Sault Ste. Marie, MI
Savage Chamber of Commerce **[12643]**, Savage, MN
Savanna Chamber of Commerce **[3421]**, Savanna, IL
Sayner-Starlake Chamber of Commerce **[19669]**, Sayner, WI
Schererville Chamber of Commerce **[6168]**, Schererville, IN
Schoolcraft County Chamber of Commerce **[8919]**, Manistique, MI
Scottville Area Chamber of Commerce **[9736]**, Scottville, MI
Sebewaing Chamber of Commerce **[9740]**, Sebewaing, MI
Shakamak Chamber of Commerce **[5522]**, Jasonville, IN
Sharonville Chamber of Commerce **[16648]**, Sharonville, OH
Shawano Area Chamber of Commerce **[19683]**, Shawano, WI
Sheboygan Falls Chamber Main Street **[19719]**, Sheboygan Falls, WI
Shelby Chamber of Commerce **[16655]**, Shelby, OH
Shelby County Chamber of Commerce **[6195]**, Shelbyville, IN
Shelbyville Area Chamber of Commerce **[3467]**, Shelbyville, IL
Shell Lake Chamber of Commerce **[19725]**, Shell Lake, WI
Shiawassee Regional Chamber of Commerce **[9337]**, Owosso, MI

Silver Lake Sand Dunes Area Chamber of Commerce [8994], Mears, MI
Skokie Chamber of Commerce [3490], Skokie, IL
Slayton Area Chamber of Commerce [12671], Slayton, MN
Sleeping Bear Area Chamber of Commerce [7838], Glen Arbor, MI
Sleepy Eye Area Chamber of Commerce [12673], Sleepy Eye, MN
Solon Chamber of Commerce [16684], Solon, OH
Somerset Area Chamber of Commerce [19746], Somerset, WI
South Eastern Chamber United in Bus. [19335], Oak Creek, WI
South Lyon Area Chamber of Commerce [9774], South Lyon, MI
South Metro Regional Chamber of Commerce [14957], Dayton, OH
Southeastern Butler County Chamber of Commerce [17179], West Chester, OH
Southeastern Franklin County Chamber of Commerce [15374], Groveport, OH
Southern Indiana Chamber of Commerce [5927], New Albany, IN
Southern Wayne County Regional Chamber [9905], Taylor, MI
Southfield Area Chamber of Commerce [9825], Southfield, MI
Southwestern Auglaize County Chamber of Commerce [16119], New Bremen, OH
Southwestern Madison County Chamber of Commerce [1885], Granite City, IL
Sparta Area Chamber of Commerce [3514], Sparta, IL
Sparta Area Chamber of Commerce [19755], Sparta, WI
Spencer Area Chamber of Commerce [19759], Spencer, WI
Spencer County Regional Chamber of Commerce [6129], Rockport, IN
Spooner Area Chamber of Commerce [19763], Spooner, WI
Spring Green Area Chamber of Commerce [19768], Spring Green, WI
Spring Valley Area Chamber of Commerce [16703], Spring Valley, OH
Springboro Chamber of Commerce [16709], Springboro, OH
Springfield Area Chamber of Commerce [12697], Springfield, MN
Springfield-Clark County Chamber of Commerce [16747], Springfield, OH
Starke County Chamber of Commerce [5561], Knox, IN
Staunton Chamber of Commerce [3697], Staunton, IL
Sterling Heights Area Chamber of Commerce [9870], Sterling Heights, MI
Stewartville Chamber of Commerce [12714], Stewartville, MN
Stoughton Chamber of Commerce [19831], Stoughton, WI
Stow-Munroe Falls Chamber of Commerce [16778], Stow, OH
Stratford Area Chamber of Commerce [19834], Stratford, WI
Streamwood Chamber of Commerce [3721], Streamwood, IL
Streator Area Chamber of Commerce [3730], Streator, IL
Sts.boro Chamber of Commerce [16782], Streetsboro, OH
Strongsville Chamber of Commerce [16798], Strongsville, OH
Sturgis Area Chamber of Commerce [9883], Sturgis, MI
Le Sueur Area Chamber of Commerce [11310], Le Sueur, MN
Sullivan Chamber and Economic Development [3741], Sullivan, IL
Sullivan County Chamber of Commerce [6287], Sullivan, IN
Sunbury - Big Walnut Area Chamber of Commerce [16814], Sunbury, OH
Superior - Douglas County Chamber of Commerce [19879], Superior, WI
Suttons Bay Chamber of Commerce [9889], Suttons Bay, MI
Swansea Chamber of Commerce [3744], Swansea, IL
Swanton Area Chamber of Commerce [16819], Swanton, OH
Swedish American Chamber of Commerce - Detroit Chapter [6968], Birmingham, MI
Sycamore Chamber of Commerce [3748], Sycamore, IL
Sylvania Area Chamber of Commerce [16834], Sylvania, OH
Syracuse-Wawasee Chamber of Commerce [6293], Syracuse, IN
Tallmadge Chamber of Commerce [16844], Tallmadge, OH
Tawas Area Chamber of Commerce [9898], Tawas City, MI
Thief River Falls Chamber of Commerce [12751], Thief River Falls, MN
Three Rivers Area Chamber of Commerce [9918], Three Rivers, MI
Tiffin Area Chamber of Commerce [16864], Tiffin, OH
Tinley Park Chamber of Commerce [3774], Tinley Park, IL
Tipp City Area Chamber of Commerce [16870], Tipp City, OH
Tipton County Chamber of Commerce [6358], Tipton, IN
Toledo Area Chamber of Commerce [16962], Toledo, OH
Tomahawk Regional Chamber of Commerce [19911], Tomahawk, WI
Tracy Area Chamber of Commerce [12757], Tracy, MN
Traverse City Area Chamber of Commerce [9958], Traverse City, MI
Trotwood Chamber of Commerce [16993], Trotwood, OH
Troy Area Chamber of Commerce [3790], Troy, IL
Troy Area Chamber of Commerce [17008], Troy, OH
Troy Chamber of Commerce [10012], Troy, MI
Trufant Area Chamber of Commerce [10015], Trufant, MI
Turkish Amer. Chamber of Commerce [1210], Chicago, IL
Tuscarawas County Chamber of Commerce [16154], New Philadelphia, OH
Tuscola Chamber of Commerce [3796], Tuscola, IL
Twin Cities North Chamber of Commerce [11848], Mounds View, MN
Twin Cities Quorum [11762], Minneapolis, MN
Twin City Chamber of Commerce [17020], Uhrichsville, OH
Twinsburg Chamber of Commerce [17018], Twinsburg, OH
TwinWest Chamber of Commerce [11798], Minnetonka, MN
Two Harbors Area Chamber of Commerce [12775], Two Harbors, MN
Union City Chamber of Commerce [6364], Union City, IN
Union County Chamber of Commerce [53], Anna, IL
Union County Chamber of Commerce [15867], Marysville, OH
Upland Chamber of Commerce [6371], Upland, IN
Upper Arlington Area Chamber of Commerce [17030], Upper Arlington, OH
Upper Sandusky Area Chamber of Commerce [17033], Upper Sandusky, OH
Uptown Chamber of Commerce [1219], Chicago, IL
Valley City Chamber of Commerce [17046], Valley City, OH
Van Buren Chamber of Commerce [6397], Van Buren, IN
Van Wert Area County Chamber of Commerce [17054], Van Wert, OH
Vandalia Chamber of Commerce [3849], Vandalia, IL
Vermilion Advantage-Chamber of Commerce Div. [1354], Danville, IL
Vermilion Chamber of Commerce [17066], Vermilion, OH
Vermillion County Chamber of Commerce [4372], Clinton, IN
Vilas County Chamber of Commerce [17850], Eagle River, WI
Villa Park Chamber of Commerce [3866], Villa Park, IL
Village of Itasca Chamber of Commerce [2071], Itasca, IL
Vinton County Chamber of Commerce [15927], McArthur, OH
Wabash Area Chamber of Commerce [6426], Wabash, IN
Wabash County Chamber of Commerce [2575], Mount Carmel, IL
Wabasha-Kellogg Area Chamber of Commerce [12812], Wabasha, MN
Waconia Area Chamber of Commerce [12819], Waconia, MN
Wadsworth Area Chamber of Commerce [17079], Wadsworth, OH
Wakarusa Chamber of Commerce [6431], Wakarusa, IN
Walkerton Area Chamber of Commerce [6437], Walkerton, IN
Walnut Chamber of Commerce [3875], Walnut, IL
Wapakoneta Area Chamber of Commerce [17094], Wapakoneta, OH
Warrick County Chamber of Commerce [4276], Boonville, IN
Warsaw - Kosciusko County Chamber of Commerce [6455], Warsaw, IN
Waseca Area Chamber of Commerce [12847], Waseca, MN
Washburn Area Chamber of Commerce [19951], Washburn, WI
Washington Chamber of Commerce [3893], Washington, IL
Washington Island Chamber of Commerce [19953], Washington Island, WI
Waterford Area Chamber of Commerce [19956], Waterford, WI
Waterloo Chamber of Commerce [3903], Waterloo, IL
Waterloo Chamber of Commerce [19961], Waterloo, WI
Watertown Area Chamber of Commerce [19971], Watertown, WI
Waterville Area Chamber of Commerce [17136], Waterville, OH
Watseka Area Chamber of Commerce [3911], Watseka, IL
Wauconda Chamber of Commerce [3916], Wauconda, IL
Waukesha County Chamber of Commerce [20003], Waukesha, WI
Waunakee/Westport Chamber of Commerce [20019], Waunakee, WI
Waupaca Area Chamber of Commerce [20023], Waupaca, WI
Waupun Area Chamber of Commerce [20028], Waupun, WI
Wausau/Marathon County Chamber of Commerce [20055], Wausau, WI
Wausaukee Area Bus. Assn. [20062], Wausaukee, WI
Wauseon Chamber of Commerce [17143], Wauseon, OH
Waushara Area Chamber of Commerce [20065], Wautoma, WI
Wayne Chamber of Commerce [10102], Wayne, MI
Waynesville Area Chamber of Commerce [17152], Waynesville, OH
Webster Area Chamber of Commerce [20096], Webster, WI
Wellington Area Chamber of Commerce [17157], Wellington, OH
Wells Area Chamber of Commerce [12869], Wells, MN
Wells County Chamber of Commerce [4271], Bluffton, IN
West Allis/West Milwaukee Chamber of Commerce [20106], West Allis, WI
West Bend Area Chamber of Commerce [20130], West Bend, WI
West Br. Area Chamber of Commerce [10135], West Branch, MI
West Chicago Chamber of Commerce and Indus. [3943], West Chicago, IL

West Lawn Chamber of Commerce **[1229]**, Chicago, IL
West Shore Chamber of Commerce **[17238]**, Westlake, OH
West Suburban Chamber of Commerce **[20086]**, Wauwatosa, WI
West Suburban Chamber of Commerce and Indus. **[2173]**, La Grange, IL
West Unity Area Chamber of Commerce **[17201]**, West Unity, OH
Westchester Chamber of Commerce **[3958]**, Westchester, IL
Westfield Chamber of Commerce **[20148]**, Westfield, WI
Westfield Washington Chamber of Commerce **[6513]**, Westfield, IN
Westland Chamber of Commerce **[10144]**, Westland, MI
Westmont Chamber of Commerce and Tourism Bur. **[3974]**, Westmont, IL
Westville Area Chamber of Commerce **[6518]**, Westville, IN
Weyauwega Area Chamber of Commerce **[20151]**, Weyauwega, WI
Wheaton Area Chamber of Commerce **[12886]**, Wheaton, MN
Wheaton Chamber of Commerce **[4000]**, Wheaton, IL
Wheeling - Prospect Heights Area Chamber of Commerce and Indus. **[4006]**, Wheeling, IL
White Bear Area Chamber of Commerce **[12905]**, White Bear Lake, MN
White Cloud Area Chamber of Commerce **[10153]**, White Cloud, MI
White Lake Area Chamber of Commerce **[10165]**, Whitehall, MI
Whitehall Area Chamber of Commerce **[17249]**, Whitehall, OH
Whitehall Area Chamber of Commerce **[20158]**, Whitehall, WI
Whitewater Area Chamber of Commerce **[20164]**, Whitewater, WI
Whiting - Robertsdale Chamber of Commerce **[6526]**, Whiting, IN
Wickliffe Area Chamber of Commerce **[17258]**, Wickliffe, OH
Will County Center for Economic Development **[2123]**, Joliet, IL
Willard Area Chamber of Commerce **[17267]**, Willard, OH
Williamston Area Chamber of Commerce **[10175]**, Williamston, MI
Willmar Lakes Area Chamber of Commerce **[12932]**, Willmar, MN
Willoughby Area Chamber of Commerce **[17278]**, Willoughby, OH
Willowbrook - Burr Ridge Chamber of Commerce and Indus. **[378]**, Burr Ridge, IL
Willowick Chamber of Commerce **[17284]**, Willowick, OH
Wilmette Chamber of Commerce **[4023]**, Wilmette, IL
Wilmington Chamber of Commerce **[4026]**, Wilmington, IL
Wilmington - Clinton County Chamber of Commerce **[17295]**, Wilmington, OH
Winchester Area Chamber of Commerce **[6538]**, Winchester, IN
Windom Area Chamber of Commerce and Visitors Bur. **[12940]**, Windom, MN
Winfield Chamber of Commerce **[4031]**, Winfield, IL
Winnetka Chamber of Commerce **[4040]**, Winnetka, IL
Winona Area Chamber of Commerce **[12960]**, Winona, MN
Winthrop Area Chamber of Commerce **[12971]**, Winthrop, MN
Wisconsin Manufacturers and Commerce **[18723]**, Madison, WI
Wittenberg Area Chamber of Commerce **[20203]**, Wittenberg, WI
Women's Division of the Lancaster Chamber of Commerce **[15614]**, Lancaster, OH
Wood Dale Chamber of Commerce **[4044]**, Wood Dale, IL
Woodbury Chamber of Commerce **[12986]**, Woodbury, MN
Woodridge Area Chamber of Commerce **[4050]**, Woodridge, IL
Woodstock Chamber of Commerce and Indus. **[4065]**, Woodstock, IL
Wooster Area Chamber of Commerce **[17336]**, Wooster, OH
Worthington Area Chamber of Commerce **[12993]**, Worthington, MN
Worthington Area Chamber of Commerce **[17352]**, Worthington, OH
Wyanet Chamber of Commerce **[4071]**, Wyanet, IL
Wyoming Kentwood Area Chamber of Commerce **[10194]**, Wyoming, MI
Xenia Area Chamber of Commerce **[17378]**, Xenia, OH
Yellow Springs Chamber of Commerce **[17383]**, Yellow Springs, OH
Yorkville Area Chamber of Commerce **[4077]**, Yorkville, IL
Youngstown/Warren Regional Chamber of Commerce **[17432]**, Youngstown, OH
Ypsilanti Area Chamber of Commerce **[10220]**, Ypsilanti, MI
Zanesville - Muskingum County Chamber of Commerce **[17449]**, Zanesville, OH
Zeeland Chamber of Commerce **[10232]**, Zeeland, MI
Zion Chamber of Commerce **[4081]**, Zion, IL
Zumbrota Chamber of Commerce **[13005]**, Zumbrota, MN
Champaign Area AIFA **[506]**, Champaign, IL
Champaign Area Young Life **[507]**, Champaign, IL
Champaign County Assn. of Realtors **[3422]**, Savoy, IL
Champaign County Audubon Soc. **[3811]**, Urbana, IL
Champaign County Chamber of Commerce **[508]**, Champaign, IL
Champaign County Chamber of Commerce **[17040]**, Urbana, OH
Champaign County Humane Soc. **[3812]**, Urbana, IL
Champaign County REACT Team **[17041]**, Urbana, OH
Champaign/Douglas/Piatt RSVP **[509]**, Champaign, IL
Champaign PTA Coun. **[510]**, Champaign, IL
Champaign-Urbana Astronomical Soc. **[511]**, Champaign, IL
Champaign-Urbana Jewish Fed. **[512]**, Champaign, IL
Champaign-Urbana Junior Woman's Club **[513]**, Champaign, IL
Champaign-Urbana Stamp Club **[514]**, Champaign, IL
Champaign-Urbana Sweet Adelines **[515]**, Champaign, IL
Champaign WyldLife **[516]**, Champaign, IL
Champaign Young Life **[517]**, Champaign, IL
Champion Lions Club **[17099]**, Warren, OH
Champlin Lions Club **[10642]**, Champlin, MN
Chandler Kiwanis **[★4345]**
Chanhassen Lions Club **[10646]**, Chanhassen, MN
Chap. 81 - Mentone Aero Club **[5807]**, Mishawaka, IN
Character Coun. of Indiana **[5083]**, Indianapolis, IN
Chardon Area Chamber of Commerce **[13642]**, Chardon, OH
CharEm United Way **[7114]**, Charlevoix, MI
Charitable Classics **[3013]**, Peoria, IL
Charleston Area Chamber of Commerce **[566]**, Charleston, IL
Charlevoix Area Chamber of Commerce **[7115]**, Charlevoix, MI
Charlevoix Rod and Gun Club **[7116]**, Charlevoix, MI
Charlotte Chamber of Commerce **[7119]**, Charlotte, MI
Charlotte Lions Club **[7120]**, Charlotte, MI
Charter Comm. of Greater Cincinnati **[13766]**, Cincinnati, OH
Chaseburg Lions Club **[17736]**, Chaseburg, WI
Chaska Area Jaycees **[10651]**, Chaska, MN
Chaska Lions Club **[10652]**, Chaska, MN
Chatfield Lions Club **[10656]**, Chatfield, MN
CHCA Young Life **[13767]**, Cincinnati, OH
Cheboygan Area Chamber of Commerce **[7131]**, Cheboygan, MI
Cheboygan County Genealogical Soc. **[7132]**, Cheboygan, MI
Cheboygan County United Way **[7133]**, Cheboygan, MI
Cheerleaders; Laingsburg Pioneer **[8498]**, Laingsburg, MI
Cheerleading
Carol Stream Youth Cheerleading Assn. **[446]**, Carol Stream, IL
Cheerleading Assn; Carol Stream Youth **[446]**, Carol Stream, IL
Cheese Makers' Assn; Wisconsin **[18681]**, Madison, WI
Chefs
ACF Alterra Chap. **[18923]**, Milwaukee, WI
ACF Ann Arbor Culinary Assn. **[7005]**, Brighton, MI
ACF Arrowhead Professional Chefs Assn. **[10794]**, Duluth, MN
ACF Blue Water Chefs Assn. **[6797]**, Armada, MI
ACF Capitol Area Professional Chefs and Cooks Assn. **[7497]**, East Lansing, MI
ACF Central Illinois Culinary Arts Assn. **[2072]**, Jacksonville, IL
ACF Chefs 200 Club Detroit Michigan **[6596]**, Algonac, MI
ACF Chefs of Milwaukee **[18036]**, Germantown, WI
ACF Chefs of Northwest Indiana **[5780]**, Michigan City, IN
ACF Chicago Chefs of Cuisine **[3454]**, Schiller Park, IL
ACF Flint/Saginaw Valley Chap. **[9890]**, Swartz Creek, MI
ACF Fort Wayne Professional Chefs Assn. **[4618]**, Fort Wayne, IN
ACF Fox Valley Chap. **[17481]**, Appleton, WI
ACF Great Lakes Thumb Chap. **[7840]**, Grand Blanc, MI
ACF Greater Dayton Chap. **[14835]**, Dayton, OH
ACF Greater Geneva Lakes Professional Chefs Assn. **[18394]**, Lake Geneva, WI
ACF Greater Grand Rapids Chefs Assn. **[7878]**, Grand Rapids, MI
ACF Heart of Illinois Professional Chefs Assn. **[2998]**, Peoria, IL
ACF of Kalamazoo/Battle Creek **[6840]**, Battle Creek, MI
ACF Louis Joliet Chap. **[1309]**, Crest Hill, IL
ACF Middle Wisconsin Chefs **[19670]**, Schofield, WI
ACF Minneapolis Chap. **[10906]**, Edina, MN
ACF of Northwestern Michigan **[7783]**, Frankfort, MI
ACF St. Paul Chefs Assn. **[11456]**, Mendota Heights, MN
ACF Sandusky Bay Area Chefs Chap. **[16599]**, Sandusky, OH
ACF South Bend Chefs and Cooks Assn. **[6206]**, South Bend, IN
ACF Southeastern Minnesota Culinarian Chap. **[11806]**, Montgomery, MN
ACF Southwestern Minnesota Chap. **[12669]**, Slayton, MN
ACF Tri-State Chefs and Cooks Chap. **[4515]**, Evansville, IN
ACF Upper Michigan Chap. **[7484]**, Drummond Island, MI
ACF West Michigan Lakeshore Chap. **[9134]**, Muskegon, MI
ACF Windy City Professional Culinarians **[594]**, Chicago, IL
Akron - Canton Area Cooks and Chefs Assn. **[16630]**, Seville, OH
Amer. Culinary Fed. Cleveland Chap. **[17281]**, Willowick, OH
Amer. Culinary Fed. Columbus Chap. **[14282]**, Columbus, OH
Amer. Culinary Fed. - Greater Indianapolis Chap. **[4846]**, Greenwood, IN
Les Chefs de Cuisine of Greater Cincinnati **[13885]**, Cincinnati, OH
Maumee Valley Chefs Chap. ACF **[16825]**, Sylvania, OH
Michigan Chefs de Cuisine Assn. **[7667]**, Farmington Hills, MI
Chelsea Area Chamber of Commerce **[7139]**, Chelsea, MI
Chelsea Hockey Assn. **[7140]**, Chelsea, MI

Chelsea Lions Club **[7141]**, Chelsea, MI
Chelsea United Way **[7142]**, Chelsea, MI
Chem. Assn; Illinois Fertilizer and **[284]**, Bloomington, IL
Chem. Assn; Wisconsin Fertilizer and **[18705]**, Madison, WI
Chem. Coaters Assn. Intl., Northern Illinois **[115]**, Aurora, IL
Chem. Coaters Assn. Intl., Northern Ohio **[14087]**, Cleveland, OH
Chem. Coaters Assn. Intl., Quad Cities **[1537]**, East Moline, IL
Chem. Coaters Assn. Intl., Twin Cities **[12398]**, St. Paul, MN
Chem. Coaters Assn. Intl., West Michigan **[10224]**, Zeeland, MI
Chem. Coaters Assn. Intl., Wisconsin **[20155]**, Whitefish Bay, WI
Chem. Contamination; Citizens for Alternatives to **[8501]**, Lake, MI
Chem. Indus. Coun. of Illinois **[3544]**, Springfield, IL

Chemicals

Chem. Coaters Assn. Intl., Northern Illinois **[115]**, Aurora, IL
Chem. Coaters Assn. Intl., Northern Ohio **[14087]**, Cleveland, OH
Chem. Coaters Assn. Intl., Quad Cities **[1537]**, East Moline, IL
Chem. Coaters Assn. Intl., Twin Cities **[12398]**, St. Paul, MN
Chem. Coaters Assn. Intl., West Michigan **[10224]**, Zeeland, MI
Chem. Coaters Assn. Intl., Wisconsin **[20155]**, Whitefish Bay, WI
Chem. Indus. Coun. of Illinois **[3544]**, Springfield, IL
Michigan Chem. Coun. **[8641]**, Lansing, MI
Ohio Chemistry Tech. Coun. **[14580]**, Columbus, OH

Chemistry

Amer. Assn. for Clinical Chemistry, Chicago Sect. **[18451]**, Madison, WI
Amer. Assn. for Clinical Chemistry, Michigan Sect. **[6811]**, Auburn Hills, MI
Amer. Assn. for Clinical Chemistry, Northeast Ohio Sect. **[14044]**, Cleveland, OH
Amer. Assn. for Clinical Chemistry, Ohio Valley Sect. **[13701]**, Cincinnati, OH
Amer. Chem. Soc., Akron Sect. **[16214]**, North Canton, OH
Amer. Chem. Soc., Central Wisconsin Sect. **[19779]**, Stevens Point, WI
Amer. Chem. Soc., Chicago Sect. **[2700]**, Niles, IL
Amer. Chem. Soc., Cincinnati Sect. **[13707]**, Cincinnati, OH
Amer. Chem. Soc., Cleveland Sect. **[14046]**, Cleveland, OH
Amer. Chem. Soc., Columbus Sect. **[14277]**, Columbus, OH
Amer. Chem. Soc., Dayton Sect. **[17354]**, Wright-Patterson AFB, OH
Amer. Chem. Soc., Decatur-Springfield Sect. **[1371]**, Decatur, IL
Amer. Chem. Soc., Detroit Sect. **[7299]**, Detroit, MI
Amer. Chem. Soc., East Central Illinois Sect. **[497]**, Champaign, IL
Amer. Chem. Soc., Huron Valley Sect. **[6657]**, Ann Arbor, MI
Amer. Chem. Soc., Indiana-Kentucky Border Sect. **[4519]**, Evansville, IN
Amer. Chem. Soc., Indiana Sect. **[4977]**, Indianapolis, IN
Amer. Chem. Soc., Joliet Sect. **[3097]**, Plainfield, IL
Amer. Chem. Soc., Kalamazoo Sect. **[8413]**, Kalamazoo, MI
Amer. Chem. Soc., Lacrosse-Winona Sect. **[18332]**, La Crosse, WI
Amer. Chem. Soc., Lake Superior Sect. **[12766]**, Two Harbors, MN
Amer. Chem. Soc., Louisiana Sect. **[15180]**, Fairview Park, OH
Amer. Chem. Soc., Mark Twain Sect. **[2365]**, Macomb, IL
Amer. Chem. Soc., Michigan State Univ. Sect. **[7501]**, East Lansing, MI
Amer. Chem. Soc., Midland Sect. **[9019]**, Midland, MI
Amer. Chem. Soc., Milwaukee Sect. **[19977]**, Waukesha, WI
Amer. Chem. Soc., Minnesota Sect. **[12888]**, White Bear Lake, MN
Amer. Chem. Soc., Northeast Wisconsin Sect. **[18855]**, Menasha, WI
Amer. Chem. Soc., Northeastern Indiana Sect. **[4626]**, Fort Wayne, IN
Amer. Chem. Soc., Northeastern Ohio Sect. **[17270]**, Willoughby, OH
Amer. Chem. Soc., Northwest Central Ohio Sect. **[13007]**, Ada, OH
Amer. Chem. Soc., Purdue Sect. **[6469]**, West Lafayette, IN
Amer. Chem. Soc., Red River Valley Sect. **[11817]**, Moorhead, MN
Amer. Chem. Soc., Rock River Sect. **[1424]**, DeKalb, IL
Amer. Chem. Soc., St. Joseph Valley Sect. **[9202]**, Niles, MI
Amer. Chem. Soc., Southern Illinois Sect. **[409]**, Carbondale, IL
Amer. Chem. Soc., Southern Indiana Sect. **[4196]**, Bloomington, IN
Amer. Chem. Soc., Toledo Sect. **[15455]**, Holland, OH
Amer. Chem. Soc., Upper Peninsula Sect. **[8248]**, Houghton, MI
Amer. Chem. Soc., Wabash Valley Sect. **[6306]**, Terre Haute, IN
Amer. Chem. Soc., Western Michigan Sect. **[9135]**, Muskegon, MI
Amer. Chem. Soc., Wisconsin Sect. **[18456]**, Madison, WI
Amer. Chem. Soc., Wooster Sect. **[13158]**, Ashland, OH
Chlorine Free Prdts. Assn. **[26]**, Algonquin, IL
Particle Soc. of Minnesota **[12984]**, Woodbury, MN

Chequamegon Area Mountain Bike Assn. **[17705]**, Cable, WI
Chequamegon Audubon Soc. **[17586]**, Bayfield, WI
Cherry Marketing Inst. **[8560]**, Lansing, MI
Cherry Producers; Michigan Assn. of **[8607]**, Lansing, MI
Cherryland Beagle Club **[10128]**, West Branch, MI
Chesaning Chamber of Commerce **[7145]**, Chesaning, MI
Chesaning Lions Club **[7146]**, Chesaning, MI

Chess

Elkhart County Chess Club **[4493]**, Elkhart, IN
Green Bay Chess Assn. **[18104]**, Green Bay, WI
Michigan Chess Assn. **[9238]**, Novi, MI
North Boone High School Chess Club **[3125]**, Poplar Grove, IL

Chess Assn; Green Bay **[18104]**, Green Bay, WI
Chess Assn; Michigan **[9238]**, Novi, MI
Chess Club; Elkhart County **[4493]**, Elkhart, IN
Chess Club; North Boone High School **[3125]**, Poplar Grove, IL
Chessie Sys. Historical Soc. **[17170]**, West Chester, OH
Chester Chamber of Commerce **[589]**, Chester, IL
Chesterhill Lions Club **[13648]**, Chesterhill, OH
Chesterland Chamber of Commerce **[13650]**, Chesterland, OH
Chesterton and Duneland Chamber of Commerce **[4352]**, Chesterton, IN
Chetek Area Chamber of Commerce **[17738]**, Chetek, WI
Chetek Chamber of Commerce **[★17738]**
Cheviot Westwood Lions Club **[13768]**, Cincinnati, OH

Chevrolet

Vintage Chevrolet Club of Am., Central Illinois Region No. 7 **[3194]**, Ridge Farm, IL
Vintage Chevrolet Club of Am., Glass Capitol Region No. 7 **[16306]**, Oregon, OH
Vintage Chevrolet Club of Am., Great Lakes Region No. 7 **[2662]**, Naperville, IL
Vintage Chevrolet Club of Am., Indiana Region No. 7 **[5757]**, Martinsville, IN
Vintage Chevrolet Club of Am., Lake Erie (Ohio) Region No. 7 **[15638]**, Lexington, OH
Vintage Chevrolet Club of Am., Lower Michigan Region No. 7 **[8784]**, Lapeer, MI
Vintage Chevrolet Club of Am., Northern Illinois Region No. 7 **[153]**, Barrington, IL
Vintage Chevrolet Club of Am., Packerland Region No. 4 **[18793]**, Manitowoc, WI
Vintage Chevrolet Club of Am., Viking Region No. 4 **[10579]**, Buffalo, MN
Vintage Chevrolet Club of Am., Wisconsin Region No. 4 **[19147]**, Milwaukee, WI

Chi-Town Squares **[777]**, Chicago, IL
Chicago 1st Black Inventors/Entrepreneurs Org., NFP **[778]**, Chicago, IL
Chicago Abused Women Coalition **[779]**, Chicago, IL
Chicago Accreditation Partnership **[780]**, Chicago, IL
Chicago Action for Jews in the Former Soviet Union **[1988]**, Highland Park, IL
Chicago Ancient Hibernian Order - Div. No. 32 **[781]**, Chicago, IL
Chicago/ARC **[782]**, Chicago, IL
Chicago Area Assn. for Computing Machinery SIGCHI **[2628]**, Naperville, IL
Chicago Area Gay and Lesbian Chamber of Commerce **[783]**, Chicago, IL
Chicago Area Hea. Info. Mgt. Assn. **[784]**, Chicago, IL
Chicago Area Mountain Bikers **[3711]**, Stickney, IL
Chicago Area Orienteering Club **[3981]**, Wheaton, IL
Chicago Area Theatre Organ Enthusiasts **[3982]**, Wheaton, IL
Chicago Area Translators and Interpreters Assn. **[785]**, Chicago, IL
Chicago Area Vascular Assn. **[178]**, Batavia, IL
Chicago Assn. for Computing Machinery Chap. **[786]**, Chicago, IL
Chicago Assn. for Healthcare Central Ser. Professionals **[6]**, Addison, IL
Chicago Assn. of Holy Name Societies **[787]**, Chicago, IL
Chicago Assn. of Law Libraries **[788]**, Chicago, IL
Chicago Assn. of Litigation Support Managers **[789]**, Chicago, IL
Chicago Assn. of Realtors **[790]**, Chicago, IL
Chicago Asthma Consortium **[791]**, Chicago, IL
Chicago Astronomical Soc. **[792]**, Chicago, IL
Chicago Audubon Soc. **[793]**, Chicago, IL
Chicago Auto. Trade Assn. **[2833]**, Oakbrook Terrace, IL
Chicago Barn Dance Company **[1652]**, Evanston, IL
Chicago Beagle Club **[1786]**, Gardner, IL
Chicago Beverly Ridge Lions Club **[1681]**, Evergreen Park, IL
Chicago Bd. Options Exchange **[794]**, Chicago, IL
Chicago Bd. of Trade **[795]**, Chicago, IL
Chicago; Bd. of Trade of the City of **[★795]**
Chicago Br. Coast Guard Enlisted Assn. **[373]**, Burr Ridge, IL
Chicago Butter and Egg Bd. **[★818]**
Chicago Cabaret Professionals **[796]**, Chicago, IL
Chicago Catalysis Club **[1455]**, Des Plaines, IL
Chicago Chap. of the Amer. Recorder Soc. **[797]**, Chicago, IL
Chicago Chap. of Amer. Soc. of Plumbing Engineers **[798]**, Chicago, IL
Chicago Chap. of the Appraisal Inst. **[799]**, Chicago, IL
Chicago Chap. Black Nurses Assn. (09) **[800]**, Chicago, IL
Chicago Chap. of the Intl. Soc. for Performance Improvement **[2294]**, Lisle, IL
Chicago Chap. of the Natl. Assn. of Black Social Workers **[801]**, Chicago, IL
Chicago Chinatown Chamber of Commerce **[802]**, Chicago, IL
Chicago Coach Fed. **[1917]**, Gurnee, IL
Chicago Coin Club **[803]**, Chicago, IL
Chicago Compensation Assn. **[804]**, Chicago, IL
Chicago Convention and Tourism Bur. **[805]**, Chicago, IL
Chicago Coun. on Planned Giving **[2148]**, Kenilworth, IL
Chicago Curling Club **[2751]**, Northbrook, IL
Chicago Democratic Socialists of Am. **[806]**, Chicago, IL
Chicago Dental Soc. **[807]**, Chicago, IL
Chicago District Golf Assn. **[2239]**, Lemont, IL
Chicago Divorce Assn. **[3432]**, Schaumburg, IL
Chicago Electro-Platers Inst. **[★819]**
Chicago Elementary Teachers' Mathematics Club **[808]**, Chicago, IL

Chicago Fed. of Musicians [809], Chicago, IL
Chicago Fed. of Musicians - Local 10-208, Amer. Fed. of Musicians [★809]
Chicago Festival Assn. [810], Chicago, IL
Chicago Figure Skating Club [1607], Elk Grove Village, IL
Chicago Found. for Women [811], Chicago, IL
Chicago Glider Club [2501], Minooka, IL
Chicago Hea. Executives Forum [2149], Kenilworth, IL
Chicago Herpetological Soc. [812], Chicago, IL
Chicago Highlanders Pipe Band [2807], Oak Park, IL
Chicago; Intl. Kennel Club of [989], Chicago, IL
Chicago Jewish Historical Soc. [813], Chicago, IL
Chicago Lakeside Lawn Bowling Club [4049], Woodridge, IL
Chicago Local Sect. of the Amer. Nuclear Soc. [1498], Downers Grove, IL
Chicago Log Cabin Republicans [814], Chicago, IL
Chicago Map Soc. [815], Chicago, IL
Chicago Medical Soc. [816], Chicago, IL
Chicago Memorial Assn. [817], Chicago, IL
Chicago Mercantile Exchange [818], Chicago, IL
Chicago Metal Finishers Inst. [819], Chicago, IL
Chicago Metro AEYC [★820]
Chicago Metro Chap. of Assn. for Healthcare Rsrc. and Materials Mgt. [179], Batavia, IL
Chicago Metro REACT [4005], Wheeling, IL
Chicago Metropolitan Assn. for the Educ. of Young Children [820], Chicago, IL
Chicago - Midwest Chap. of the Turnaround Mgt. Assn. [★1722]
Chicago/Midwest Chap. of the Turnaround Mgt. Assn. [1722], Frankfort, IL
Chicago Military Acad. - Bronzeville Assn. [821], Chicago, IL
Chicago Model Yacht Club No. 7 [2291], Lindenhurst, IL
Chicago Natl. Assn. of Women Bus. Owners [822], Chicago, IL
Chicago Negro Chamber of Commerce [★859]
Chicago-North Romance Writers of Am. [67], Arlington Heights, IL
Chicago Philatelic Society [2769], Oak Brook, IL
Chicago Playing Card Collectors [2908], Palatine, IL
Chicago Police Women's Assn. [823], Chicago, IL
Chicago Pro Musica NFP [824], Chicago, IL
Chicago Psychoanalytic Soc. [825], Chicago, IL
Chicago Radio Controlled Sailing Club No. 181 [826], Chicago, IL
Chicago Radiological Soc. [68], Arlington Heights, IL
Chicago Region PTA [827], Chicago, IL
Chicago Regional Search and Rescue [2009], Hinckley, IL
Chicago Ridge - Worth Bus. Assn. [4070], Worth, IL
Chicago Rocks and Minerals Soc. [3433], Schaumburg, IL
Chicago Roofing Distributors Assn. [828], Chicago, IL
Chicago SCORES [829], Chicago, IL
Chicago Ski Twisters [830], Chicago, IL
Chicago Sno-Gophers Ski Club [831], Chicago, IL
Chicago Social Security Mgt. Assn. [3950], West Frankfort, IL
Chicago Soc. of Assn. Executives [★749]
Chicago Soc. of Clinical Hypnosis [1827], Glen Ellyn, IL
Chicago Soc. for Coatings Tech. [147], Barrington, IL
Chicago Soc. for Space Stud. [2748], North Riverside, IL
Chicago Southland Convention and Visitors Bur. [2216], Lansing, IL
Chicago Space Frontier L5 Soc. [180], Batavia, IL
Chicago (SPIE/OSC) Optical Gp. [1723], Frankfort, IL
Chicago Stock Exchange [832], Chicago, IL
Chicago Sun Club [3882], Wasco, IL
Chicago Table Tennis Club at Evanston [1653], Evanston, IL
Chicago Table Tennis Club at Franklin [1736], Franklin Park, IL
Chicago Table Tennis Club at Glenview [1862], Glenview, IL
Chicago Table Tennis Club at La Grange [2169], La Grange, IL
Chicago Table Tennis Club at Northern Illinois Univ. [1429], DeKalb, IL
Chicago Terminal Chap., Pennsylvania Railroad Tech. and Historical Soc. [2629], Naperville, IL
Chicago Thoracic Soc. [833], Chicago, IL
Chicago Trendsetters [834], Chicago, IL
Chicago Urban League [835], Chicago, IL
Chicago Vegetarian Soc. [1995], Highwood, IL
Chicago Whitewater Assn. [2327], Lombard, IL
Chicago Windy City Jitterbug Club [1737], Franklin Park, IL
Chicago Women in Bus. [836], Chicago, IL
Chicago Women in Publishing [837], Chicago, IL
Chicago Women in Trades [838], Chicago, IL
Chicago Women in Travel [839], Chicago, IL
Chicago Woodturners [2752], Northbrook, IL
Chicagoland Bearded Collie Club [18870], Menomonee Falls, WI
Chicagoland Bicycle Fed. [840], Chicago, IL
Chicagoland Chamber of Commerce [841], Chicago, IL
Chicagoland Chap. of Avanti Owners Assn. Intl. [3191], Richmond, IL
Chicagoland Environmental Network [351], Brookfield, IL
Chicagoland Evaluation Assn. [2328], Lombard, IL
Chicagoland Gerontological Advanced Practice Nurses [3200], River Forest, IL
Chicagoland Military Vehicle Club [2763], Northfield, IL
Chicagoland Muskie Hunters [3483], Skokie, IL
Chicagoland Region of Narcotics Anonymous [2808], Oak Park, IL
Chicagoland Rottweiler Club [842], Chicago, IL
Chicagoland Sect. of the Mercedes-Benz Club of Am. [374], Burr Ridge, IL
Chicagoland Sheet Metal Contractors Assn. [216], Bellwood, IL
Chicagoland Sky Liners [2630], Naperville, IL
Chicagoland Thunderbirds [2329], Lombard, IL
Chicagoland's Human Rsrc. Assn. [1499], Downers Grove, IL
Chicago's North Suburbs, Prospect Heights CVB [3143], Prospect Heights, IL
Chicanos Latinos Unidos En Servicio [12399], St. Paul, MN
Chief Logan Reservation Staff Alumni Assn. [13663], Chillicothe, OH
Chief Tarhe Beagle Club [15597], Lancaster, OH
Chiefs of Police; Michigan Assn. of [9272], Okemos, MI
Chiesa Nuova [843], Chicago, IL
Child Abuse
Bikers Against Child Abuse, Maritime Chap. [18777], Manitowoc, WI
Bikers Against Child Abuse, Minnesota Chap. [12394], St. Paul, MN
Bikers Against Child Abuse, Ohio Chap. [13759], Cincinnati, OH
Bikers Against Child Abuse, Southeast Wisconsin Chap. [19250], Mukwonago, WI
Ogemaw County Friends of Casa [10132], West Branch, MI
Child Abuse Coun. [2518], Moline, IL
Child Abuse Council; Dearborn and Ohio County Prevent [5658], Lawrenceburg, IN
Child Abuse Ohio; Prevent [14712], Columbus, OH
Child Abuse Prevention Council; Dearborn and Ohio County [★5658]
Child Abuse Wisconsin; Prevent [18599], Madison, WI
Child Care
Action for Children [595], Chicago, IL
Alliance of Early Childhood Professionals [11477], Minneapolis, MN
Austin Childcare Providers Network [757], Chicago, IL
Big Family of Michigan [8832], Livonia, MI
Childcare Works [11541], Minneapolis, MN
Children's Place Assn. [845], Chicago, IL
Children's Rsrc. Network 4-C [8195], Holland, MI
Evansville Area 4C [4540], Evansville, IN
Family Connections [19694], Sheboygan, WI
Illinois Assn. for Family Child Care [2813], Oak Park, IL
Illinois School-Age Child Care Network [287], Bloomington, IL
Indiana Assn. of Residential Child Care Agencies [5184], Indianapolis, IN
Minnesota School Age Care Alliance [12517], St. Paul, MN
Oakland County Child Care Coun. [8483], Keego Harbor, MI
Ohio Professionals for School-Age Children [14657], Columbus, OH
Child Care Agencies; Indiana Assn. of Residential [5184], Indianapolis, IN
Child Care Association of Morrison County; Licensed Family [12065], Randall, MN
Child Care Coalition of Lake County [2188], Lake Bluff, IL
Child Care Workers Alliance [★11477]
Child Caring Agencies; Ohio Assn. of [14546], Columbus, OH
Child Evangelism Ministries of St. Joseph County [★6224]
Child Evangelism of St. Joseph County [★6224]
Child Health
Aad Shriners [11148], Hermantown, MN
Ahmed Shriners [8930], Marquette, MI
Ainad Shriners [1547], East St. Louis, IL
Al Koran Shriners [13422], Broadview Heights, OH
Aladdin Shriners [14271], Columbus, OH
Ansar Shriners [3531], Springfield, IL
Antioch Shriners [14853], Dayton, OH
Beja Shriners [18085], Green Bay, WI
Elf Khurafeh Shriners [9608], Saginaw, MI
Hadi Shriners [4550], Evansville, IN
March of Dimes [20040], Wausau, WI
Medinah Shriners [2339], Lombard, IL
Mizpah Shriners [4695], Fort Wayne, IN
Mohammed Shriners [170], Bartonville, IL
Moslem Shriners [7401], Detroit, MI
Murat Shriners [5409], Indianapolis, IN
Orak Shriners [5791], Michigan City, IN
Osman Shriners [12558], St. Paul, MN
Saladin Shriners [8007], Grand Rapids, MI
Syrian Shriners [14007], Cincinnati, OH
Tadmor Shriners [13097], Akron, OH
Tebala Shriners [3325], Rockford, IL
Tripoli Shriners [19137], Milwaukee, WI
Zenobia Shriners [16986], Toledo, OH
Zor Shriners [18768], Madison, WI
Zorah Shriners [6354], Terre Haute, IN
Zuhrah Shriners [11781], Minneapolis, MN
Child Welfare
Big Bros. Big Sisters of Lake County [1915], Gurnee, IL
Boys Hope Girls Hope of Chicago [4018], Wilmette, IL
Child Abuse Coun. [2518], Moline, IL
Child Care Coalition of Lake County [2188], Lake Bluff, IL
Child Welfare League of Am., Mid-West Region [844], Chicago, IL
Children's Bur. of Indianapolis [5084], Indianapolis, IN
Christ Child Soc. of Akron [13048], Akron, OH
Christ Child Soc. of South Bend, Indiana [6225], South Bend, IN
Dearborn and Ohio County Prevent Child Abuse Council [5658], Lawrenceburg, IN
Jewish Children's Bur. of Chicago [1005], Chicago, IL
Michigan Community Coordinated Child Care Assn. [8647], Lansing, MI
Michigan's Children [8729], Lansing, MI
Ohio Assn. of Child Caring Agencies [14546], Columbus, OH
Parents Anonymous of Central and Southern Ohio [14707], Columbus, OH
Parents Anonymous of Chicago, Illinois [1122], Chicago, IL
Parents Anonymous of Marquette, Michigan [8956], Marquette, MI
Parents Anonymous of Stark County and Northern Ohio [13576], Canton, OH
Parents Anonymous of Washington County, Wisconsin [20126], West Bend, WI
Prevent Child Abuse Am. [1144], Chicago, IL
Prevent Child Abuse Illinois [3666], Springfield, IL
Prevent Child Abuse Indiana [5458], Indianapolis, IN

Prevent Child Abuse Minnesota [12561], St. Paul, MN
Prevent Child Abuse Ohio [14712], Columbus, OH
Prevent Child Abuse Wisconsin [18599], Madison, WI
Priority Children [7753], Flint, MI
Remember the Children [5980], Noblesville, IN
Teachers Saving Children [14834], Damascus, OH
Variety of Detroit [9829], Southfield, MI
Variety of Illinois [1221], Chicago, IL
Variety of Indiana [5492], Indianapolis, IN
Variety of Western Michigan [8047], Grandville, MI
Variety of Wisconsin [19146], Milwaukee, WI
Voices for Illinois Children [1223], Chicago, IL
Wisconsin Coun. on Children and Families [18688], Madison, WI

Child Welfare League of Am., Mid-West Region [844], Chicago, IL
Childbirth Educ. Assn. [13769], Cincinnati, OH
Childcare Providers Network; Austin [757], Chicago, IL
Childcare Works [11541], Minneapolis, MN
Childcare Works-Education Div. [★11541]

Childhood Education

Chicago Metropolitan Assn. for the Educ. of Young Children [820], Chicago, IL
Illinois Assn. for the Educ. of Young Children [3570], Springfield, IL
Indiana Assn. for the Educ. of Young Children [5170], Indianapolis, IN
Michigan Assn. for the Educ. of Young Children [7534], East Lansing, MI
Minnesota Assn. for the Educ. of Young Children [12455], St. Paul, MN
Ohio Assn. for the Educ. of Young Children [16072], Mount Gilead, OH
Parents are Important in Rochester [12167], Rochester, MN
Wisconsin Early Childhood Assn. [18696], Madison, WI

Children

Big Bros. Big Sisters, A Community of Caring [8422], Kalamazoo, MI
Big Brothers Big Sisters of America Association of Cincinnati [13758], Cincinnati, OH
Big Brothers Big Sisters of America of Erie County [16604], Sandusky, OH
Big Bros. Big Sisters of Am. of Lapeer County [8775], Lapeer, MI
Big Bros. Big Sisters of Am. of Lorain County [15701], Lorain, OH
Big Bros. Big Sisters of Am. of Massillon [15883], Massillon, OH
Big Bros. Big Sisters of Am. of North Central Indiana [5566], Kokomo, IN
Big Bros. Big Sisters of Am. of Northeast Indiana [4645], Fort Wayne, IN
Big Bros. Big Sisters of Am. of Northeastern Wisconsin [18086], Green Bay, WI
Big Bros. Big Sisters of Athens County [13202], Athens, OH
Big Bros. Big Sisters of Central Indiana [5058], Indianapolis, IN
Big Bros. Big Sisters of Central Minnesota [12276], St. Cloud, MN
Big Bros. Big Sisters of Central Ohio [14336], Columbus, OH
Big Bros. Big Sisters of Coshocton County [14795], Coshocton, OH
Big Bros. Big Sisters of Dane County [18491], Madison, WI
Big Bros. Big Sisters of Dickinson County and Surrounding Areas [8320], Iron Mountain, MI
Big Bros. Big Sisters of East Central Ohio [16147], New Philadelphia, OH
Big Brothers Big Sisters of the Fox Valley Region [17489], Appleton, WI
Big Bros. Big Sisters of the Greater Twin Cities [12393], St. Paul, MN
Big Bros. Big Sisters of Green County [19213], Monroe, WI
Big Bros. Big Sisters of Isabella County [9101], Mount Pleasant, MI
Big Bros. Big Sisters of the Lakeshore [9141], Muskegon, MI
Big Bros. Big Sisters of Livingston County [8273], Howell, MI
Big Bros. Big Sisters of Mahoning Valley [15321], Girard, OH
Big Bros. Big Sisters of Marquette County [9177], Negaunee, MI
Big Bros. Big Sisters of McHenry County [2456], McHenry, IL
Big Bros. Big Sisters of Metropolitan Chicago [766], Chicago, IL
Big Bros. Big Sisters Northwestern Ohio [16908], Toledo, OH
Big Bros. Big Sisters of Northwestern Wisconsin [17866], Eau Claire, WI
Big Bros. Big Sisters of the Ohio Valley [4534], Evansville, IN
Big Bros. Big Sisters of the Oshkosh Area [19390], Oshkosh, WI
Big Bros. Big Sisters of Portage County [19785], Stevens Point, WI
Big Bros. Big Sisters of Shelby and Darke County [16664], Sidney, OH
Big Bros. Big Sisters of Wabash Valley [5609], Lafayette, IN
Big Bros. Big Sisters of West Central Illinois [2077], Jacksonville, IL
Big Bros. Big Sisters of Will and Grundy Counties [2101], Joliet, IL
Big Bros. and Sisters of Ozaukee County [18062], Grafton, WI
Boys Hope Girls Hope of Cleveland [17254], Wickliffe, OH
Boys Hope Girls Hope of Detroit [7331], Detroit, MI
Children's Defense Fund, Cincinnati [13770], Cincinnati, OH
Children's Defense Fund, Minnesota [12400], St. Paul, MN
Children's Defense Fund, Ohio [14365], Columbus, OH
Children's Home and Aid Soc. of Illinois - Metropolitan Region [1654], Evanston, IL
Children's Home Soc. and Family Services [12401], St. Paul, MN
Crusaders for Kids [2479], Metamora, IL
Dakotas Children Auxiliary [10866], Eagan, MN
Dream Factory of Central Illinois [2986], Pekin, IL
Dream Factory of Southern Ohio [17197], West Union, OH
Foster Grandparent Prog. of Ethan Allen School [19945], Wales, WI
Foster Grandparent Prog. of Greater Dayton [14884], Dayton, OH
Foster Grandparent Prog. of Lincoln Hills School [18237], Irma, WI
Foster Grandparent Prog. of Peoria/Tazewell Counties [3020], Peoria, IL
Foster Grandparent Prog. of Suburban Cook County [895], Chicago, IL
Foster Grandparent Prog. of Summit County [13051], Akron, OH
Make-A-Wish Found. of Central Ohio [14496], Columbus, OH
Make-A-Wish Found. of Greater Ohio and Kentucky [14159], Cleveland, OH
Make-A-Wish Found. of Indiana [5395], Indianapolis, IN
Make-A-Wish Found. of Michigan [6715], Ann Arbor, MI
Make-A-Wish Found. of Michigan, Grand Rapids Off. [7976], Grand Rapids, MI
Make-A-Wish Found. of Michigan, Livonia Off. [8844], Livonia, MI
Make-A-Wish Found. of Minnesota [11599], Minneapolis, MN
Make-A-Wish Found. of Northeast Ohio [14160], Cleveland, OH
Make-A-Wish Found. of Northern Illinois [1037], Chicago, IL
Make-A-Wish Found. of Northwest Ohio [16928], Toledo, OH
Make-A-Wish Found. of Southern Ohio [13892], Cincinnati, OH
Make-A-Wish Found. of Wisconsin [17700], Butler, WI
Michigan Fed. for Children and Families [8665], Lansing, MI
Northeast Wisconsin Families with Children from China [18863], Menasha, WI
Ohio Network of Children's Advocacy Centers [14644], Columbus, OH
Partners in Play [1714], Forest Park, IL
Public Children Ser. Assn. of Ohio [14718], Columbus, OH
Rainbows, Cincinnati [13973], Cincinnati, OH
Rainbows, Illinois State Chap. [3343], Rolling Meadows, IL
Rainbows, Michigan Chap. [6615], Allen Park, MI
RAINBOWS, Milwaukee [19108], Milwaukee, WI
Special Kids [19130], Milwaukee, WI
Special Wish Found., Chicago Chap. [1199], Chicago, IL
Special Wish Found., Dayton [14959], Dayton, OH
Special Wish Found., Newark [16185], Newark, OH
Starlight Children's Found. Midwest [1200], Chicago, IL
UNICEF, Columbus Chap. [14748], Columbus, OH
World of Children [14767], Columbus, OH

Children from China; Northeast Wisconsin Families with [18863], Menasha, WI
Children of Lesbians and Gays Everywhere Minneapolis [11542], Minneapolis, MN
Children; Michigan Assn. for the Educ. of Young [7534], East Lansing, MI
Children Need the Lord [6224], South Bend, IN
Children; Remember the [5980], Noblesville, IN
Children; Teachers Saving [14834], Damascus, OH
Children's Advocacy Centers; Ohio Network of [14644], Columbus, OH
Children's Bur. of Indianapolis [5084], Indianapolis, IN
Children's Chorus; Elgin [1589], Elgin, IL
Children's Defense Fund, Cincinnati [13770], Cincinnati, OH
Children's Defense Fund, Minnesota [12400], St. Paul, MN
Children's Defense Fund, Ohio [14365], Columbus, OH
Children's Found. Midwest; Starlight [1200], Chicago, IL
Children's Home and Aid Soc. of Illinois - Metropolitan Region [1654], Evanston, IL
Children's Home Soc. and Family Services [12401], St. Paul, MN
Children's Home Soc. of Minnesota [★12401]
Children's Hunger Alliance [14366], Columbus, OH
Children's Leukemia Found. of Michigan [9795], Southfield, MI
Children's Literature Network [12021], Plymouth, MN
Children's Organ Transplant Assn. [4212], Bloomington, IN
Children's Place Assn. [845], Chicago, IL
Children's Rsrc. Network 4-C [8195], Holland, MI
Children's Rights Coun. of Cleveland [14088], Cleveland, OH
Children's Rights Coun. of Illinois [1418], Deerfield, IL
Children's Rights Coun. of Michigan [6979], Bloomfield Hills, MI
Children's Rights Coun. of Minnesota [12132], Rochester, MN
Children's Rights Coun. of Northeast Ohio [16232], North Kingsville, OH
Children's Rights Coun. of Ohio [16909], Toledo, OH
Children's Rights Coun. of South Ohio [13771], Cincinnati, OH
Children's Rights Coun. of Tri-county, Ohio [17394], Youngstown, OH
Children's Rights Coun. of Wisconsin [19925], Union Grove, WI
Chiller Figure Skating Club [15045], Dublin, OH
Chillicothe Chamber of Commerce [1255], Chillicothe, IL
Chillicothe Ross Chamber of Commerce [13664], Chillicothe, OH
Chillicothe Twin City REACT [1256], Chillicothe, IL
Chilton Chamber of Commerce [17741], Chilton, WI
Chinatown Chamber of Commerce [★802]
Chinese Amer. Ser. League [846], Chicago, IL
Chinese Bus. Assn; Detroit [7258], Dearborn, MI
Chinese Scholars and Students Association; United [1215], Chicago, IL

Chinese Shar-Pei Club of Am. **[2971]**, Pawnee, IL
Chinese Shar-Pei Rescue of Michigan **[6909]**, Belleville, MI
Chippewa County Fire Chief Association **[19774]**, Stanley, WI
Chippewa County Historical Soc. **[11800]**, Montevideo, MN
Chippewa County Humane Assn. **[17747]**, Chippewa Falls, WI
Chippewa County Humane Soc. **[★17747]**
Chippewa County Tourism Coun. **[17748]**, Chippewa Falls, WI
Chippewa Falls Area Chamber of Commerce **[17749]**, Chippewa Falls, WI
Chippewa Falls Humane Soc. **[★17747]**
Chippewa Falls Indus. Development Corp. **[17750]**, Chippewa Falls, WI
Chippewa Falls Main St. **[17751]**, Chippewa Falls, WI
Chippewa Lake Lions Club **[9536]**, Rodney, MI
Chippewa Valley Apartment Assn. **[17869]**, Eau Claire, WI
Chippewa Valley Astronomical Soc. **[17952]**, Fall Creek, WI
Chippewa Valley Convention and Visitors Bur. **[17870]**, Eau Claire, WI
Chippewa Valley Gem and Mineral Soc. **[17752]**, Chippewa Falls, WI
Chippewa Valley Young Life Club **[17871]**, Eau Claire, WI
Chippewa Wyldlife **[12224]**, Roseville, MN

Chiropractic

Illinois Chiropractic Soc. **[3589]**, Springfield, IL
Illinois Prairie State Chiropractic Assn. **[3245]**, Rock Island, IL
Indiana State Chiropractic Assn. **[5314]**, Indianapolis, IN
Intl. Chiropractors Assn. of Indiana **[6533]**, Winamac, IN
Michigan Chiropractic Soc. **[8642]**, Lansing, MI
Minnesota Chiropractic Assn. **[10596]**, Burnsville, MN
Ohio State Chiropractic Assn. **[14682]**, Columbus, OH
Wisconsin Chiropractic Assn. **[18682]**, Madison, WI

Chiropractic Assn; Indiana State **[5314]**, Indianapolis, IN
Chisholm Area Chamber of Commerce **[10660]**, Chisholm, MN
Chlorine Free Prdts. Assn. **[26]**, Algonquin, IL

Choirs

Amer. Choral Directors Assn. - Central Div. **[616]**, Chicago, IL
Amer. Choral Directors Assn. - Illinois Chap. **[1425]**, DeKalb, IL
Amer. Choral Directors Assn. - Michigan Chap. **[7889]**, Grand Rapids, MI
Amer. Choral Directors Assn. - Minnesota Chap. **[11910]**, Northfield, MN
Amer. Choral Directors Assn. - North Central Div. **[19978]**, Waukesha, WI
Barbershop Harmony Soc. - Illinois District **[2558]**, Morrison, IL
Barbershop Harmony Soc. - Pioneer District **[8421]**, Kalamazoo, MI
Elmhurst Choral Union **[1620]**, Elmhurst, IL
Indiana Choral Directors Assn. **[6551]**, Zionsville, IN
Ohio Choral Directors Assn. **[16858]**, Tiffin, OH
Wisconsin Choral Directors Assn. **[17451]**, Abrams, WI

Choral Union; Elmhurst **[1620]**, Elmhurst, IL
Chorus; Elgin Children's **[1589]**, Elgin, IL
Chorus; Grand Rapids Women's **[7953]**, Grand Rapids, MI
Christ Child Soc. of Akron **[13048]**, Akron, OH
Christ Child Soc. of South Bend, Indiana **[6225]**, South Bend, IN
Christ; Southwest Michigan Youth for **[9882]**, Sturgis, MI
Christ/West Central Ohio; Youth for **[17056]**, Van Wert, OH

Christian

Assn. of Christian Schools Intl., Ohio River Valley Region **[13547]**, Canton, OH
CBMC Indiana **[5070]**, Indianapolis, IN
Christian Athletes United for Spiritual Empowerment **[11543]**, Minneapolis, MN
Christians for Biblical Equality **[11544]**, Minneapolis, MN
Christians Golfers' Assn. - Hinsdale **[2015]**, Hinsdale, IL
Christians Golfers' Assn. - Kalamazoo **[8423]**, Kalamazoo, MI
Christians Golfers' Assn. - Lockport **[2313]**, Lockport, IL
Church Fed. of Greater Indianapolis **[5086]**, Indianapolis, IN
Concerned Women for Am. - Illinois **[2937]**, Palos Heights, IL
Connecting Bus. Men to Christ - Chicagoland **[2217]**, Lansing, IL
Connecting Bus. Men to Christ - Elkhart **[4491]**, Elkhart, IN
Connecting Bus. Men to Christ - Grand Rapids **[7921]**, Grand Rapids, MI
Connecting Bus. Men to Christ - Indiana **[5096]**, Indianapolis, IN
Connecting Bus. Men to Christ - Mid Michigan **[9266]**, Okemos, MI
Connecting Bus. Men to Christ - Northland **[12678]**, South St. Paul, MN
Connecting Bus. Men to Christ - Southeast Michigan **[9796]**, Southfield, MI
Inner City Christian Fed. **[7966]**, Grand Rapids, MI
Overseas Coun. Intl. **[5446]**, Indianapolis, IN
Southlake Young Men's Christian Association **[4437]**, Crown Point, IN
YMCA - Arthur Jordan **[5503]**, Indianapolis, IN
YMCA - Benjamin Harrison Br. **[5504]**, Indianapolis, IN

Christian Assn. for Psychological Stud., Midwest **[8834]**, Livonia, MI
Christian Athletes United for Spiritual Empowerment **[11543]**, Minneapolis, MN
Christian Camp and Conf. Assn., Great Lakes Region **[8408]**, Jones, MI
Christian Camp and Conf. Assn., Illinois **[402]**, Canton, IL
Christian Camp and Conf. Assn., Indiana **[5839]**, Morgantown, IN
Christian Camp and Conf. Assn., Michigan **[9537]**, Rodney, MI
Christian Camp and Conf. Assn., Minn-E-Dakotas Sect. **[12007]**, Pine River, MN
Christian Camp and Conf. Assn., North Central Region **[10683]**, Clitherall, MN
Christian Camp and Conf. Assn., Ohio Sect. **[17433]**, Zanesfield, OH
Christian Camp and Conf. Assn., Wisconsin **[20142]**, Westby, WI
Christian Coffee House Ministry; Overflowing Cup **[★17615]**
Christian Leaders for Africa **[5085]**, Indianapolis, IN
Christian Schools Intl., Ohio River Valley Region; Assn. of **[13547]**, Canton, OH

Christianity

InterVarsity Christian Fellowship in Downstate Illinois **[3032]**, Peoria, IL

Christians for Biblical Equality **[11544]**, Minneapolis, MN
Christians Golfers' Assn. - Hinsdale **[2015]**, Hinsdale, IL
Christians Golfers' Assn. - Kalamazoo **[8423]**, Kalamazoo, MI
Christians Golfers' Assn. - Lockport **[2313]**, Lockport, IL
Christians United in Service Focus; Fellowship of Orthodox **[4923]**, Hobart, IN
Christmas City REACT **[5546]**, Jonesboro, IN
Christmas Tree Assn., Illinois; Natl. **[★3403]**
Christmas Tree Assn., Indiana; Natl. **[★6284]**
Church Fed. of Greater Indianapolis **[5086]**, Indianapolis, IN

Church and State

Americans United for Separation of Church and State, Central Ohio **[14315]**, Columbus, OH
Americans United for Separation of Church and State, Greater Indianapolis Chap. **[5029]**, Indianapolis, IN

Church and Synagogue Lib. Assn., Hibbing Church Lib. Network **[11156]**, Hibbing, MN
Church and Synagogue Lib. Assn., Metro Detroit Chap. **[7250]**, Dearborn, MI
Church World Service/CROP, Indiana-Kentucky **[5087]**, Indianapolis, IN
Church World Service/CROP, Minn-Kota Region **[11545]**, Minneapolis, MN
Church World Ser./Crop, Wisconsin-Northern Illinois Region **[★18496]**
Church World Ser./CROP, Wisconsin Region **[18496]**, Madison, WI

Churches

Ohio Coun. of Churches **[14589]**, Columbus, OH

Churches; Illinois Conf. of **[3597]**, Springfield, IL
Churchill High School PTSA **[8835]**, Livonia, MI
Chusy Region United Synagogue Youth **[2753]**, Northbrook, IL
Cicero Area Chamber of Commerce **[4359]**, Cicero, IN
Cicero Chamber of Commerce and Indus. **[1260]**, Cicero, IL
Cincinnati 9to5 **[13772]**, Cincinnati, OH
Cincinnati African Violet Soc. **[13773]**, Cincinnati, OH
Cincinnati AIFA **[16846]**, Terrace Park, OH
Cincinnati Area Bd. of Realtors **[13774]**, Cincinnati, OH
Cincinnati Area RSVP **[13775]**, Cincinnati, OH
Cincinnati Assn. for the Blind and Visually Impaired **[13776]**, Cincinnati, OH
Cincinnati Astronomical Soc. **[15874]**, Mason, OH
Cincinnati Bar Assn. **[13777]**, Cincinnati, OH
Cincinnati Better Bus. Bur. **[13778]**, Cincinnati, OH
Cincinnati Bus. and Professional Women's Club **[13779]**, Cincinnati, OH
Cincinnati Celiac Support Gp. **[15383]**, Hamilton, OH
Cincinnati Chap. of the Soc. of Financial Ser. Professionals **[16847]**, Terrace Park, OH
Cincinnati Cmpt. Cooperative **[13780]**, Cincinnati, OH
Cincinnati Contra Dancers **[13781]**, Cincinnati, OH
Cincinnati Corvette Club **[13782]**, Cincinnati, OH
Cincinnati Dental Soc. **[13783]**, Cincinnati, OH
Cincinnati Estate Planning Coun. **[13784]**, Cincinnati, OH
Cincinnati Folk Life **[13785]**, Cincinnati, OH
Cincinnati Habitat for Humanity **[13786]**, Cincinnati, OH
Cincinnati-Hamilton County Community Action Agency Found. **[13787]**, Cincinnati, OH
Cincinnati Horticultural Soc. **[13788]**, Cincinnati, OH
Cincinnati Host Lions Club **[13789]**, Cincinnati, OH
Cincinnati Industrial Inst. **[★13820]**
Cincinnati-Kenwood Lions Club **[13790]**, Cincinnati, OH
Cincinnati Master Plumbers' Assn. **[13791]**, Cincinnati, OH
Cincinnati Mineral Soc. **[15330]**, Goshen, OH
Cincinnati Model Yacht Club No. 191 **[17171]**, West Chester, OH
Cincinnati Musicians' Assn. - Local 1, Amer. Fed. of Musicians **[13792]**, Cincinnati, OH
Cincinnati Numismatic Assn. **[13793]**, Cincinnati, OH
Cincinnati Off Road Alliance **[13794]**, Cincinnati, OH
Cincinnati Opera Assn. **[13795]**, Cincinnati, OH
Cincinnati Paralegal Assn. **[13796]**, Cincinnati, OH
Cincinnati Preservation Assn. **[13797]**, Cincinnati, OH
Cincinnati Psychoanalytic Soc. **[13798]**, Cincinnati, OH
Cincinnati Soc. of Assn. Executives **[13799]**, Cincinnati, OH
Cincinnati Table Tennis Club **[13800]**, Cincinnati, OH
Cincinnati USA Regional Chamber **[13801]**, Cincinnati, OH
Cincinnati-Western Hills Lions Club **[13802]**, Cincinnati, OH
Circle City Corvairs **[5088]**, Indianapolis, IN
Circle City Corvette Club **[5089]**, Indianapolis, IN
Circle City REACT **[5090]**, Indianapolis, IN
Circle Pines - Lexington Lions Club **[10663]**, Circle Pines, MN
Circleville - Pickaway Chamber of Commerce **[14032]**, Circleville, OH

Circumcision

Natl. Org. of Circumcision Info. Rsrc. Centers of Michigan **[6965]**, Birmingham, MI
Natl. Org. of Circumcision Info. Rsrc. Centers of Wisconsin - Madison **[18579]**, Madison, WI

NOCIRC of Michigan **[6966]**, Birmingham, MI
CISG Chap. of Northern Indiana and Southwestern Michigan **[4809]**, Granger, IN
Cities; League of Minnesota **[12440]**, St. Paul, MN
Cities and Towns; Indiana Assn. of **[5167]**, Indianapolis, IN
Citizen Action/Illinois **[847]**, Chicago, IL
Citizens Action Coalition **[★6226]**
Citizens Action Coalition of Indiana **[5091]**, Indianapolis, IN
Citizens Action Coalition of Indiana - North Off. **[6226]**, South Bend, IN
Citizens Against Domestic Violence **[16007]**, Middletown, OH
Citizens Against Repressive Zoning **[8146]**, Haslett, MI
Citizens for Alternatives to Chem. Contamination **[8501]**, Lake, MI
Citizens for Animal Rights **[3014]**, Peoria, IL
Citizens for Appropriate Rural Roads **[6285]**, Stanford, IN
Citizen's Assn. **[★1477]**
Citizens for Better Care **[7334]**, Detroit, MI
Citizens for Better Care Inst. **[★7334]**
Citizens for Better Care in Nursing Homes for the Aged **[★7334]**
Citizens for a Better Environment - Illinois **[848]**, Chicago, IL
Citizens for a Better Environment - Wisconsin **[18992]**, Milwaukee, WI
Citizens of Lakeland Area; Environmentally Concerned **[19198]**, Minocqua, WI
Citizens League **[12402]**, St. Paul, MN
Citizens for Legal Responsibility **[2567]**, Morton Grove, IL
Citizens Res. Coun. of Michigan **[8836]**, Livonia, MI
Citizens for a Scenic Wisconsin **[20072]**, Wauwatosa, WI
Citizens Utility Bd. **[18497]**, Madison, WI
Citizenship
The Ethic of Citizenship Soc. **[12718]**, Stillwater, MN
City Club of Chicago **[849]**, Chicago, IL
City Connect Detroit **[7335]**, Detroit, MI
City County Mgt. Assn; Illinois **[1435]**, DeKalb, IL
City of Greensburg Public Safety Facilities Building Corp. **[4840]**, Greensburg, IN
City High School - Young Life **[7918]**, Grand Rapids, MI
City of La Porte Urban Enterprise Zone **[5595]**, La Porte, IN
City of Lakes Sweet Adelines Chorus **[10865]**, Eagan, MN
City Limits Table Tennis Club **[16115]**, New Boston, OH
City News Community Development Corp. **[14089]**, Cleveland, OH
City Year Cleveland **[14090]**, Cleveland, OH
City Year Columbus **[14367]**, Columbus, OH
City Year Detroit **[7336]**, Detroit, MI
Cityfolk **[14866]**, Dayton, OH
Citywide Drag Racing Association **[2046]**, Homewood, IL
Civic League **[19508]**, Portage, WI
Civic Music Assn; Brown County **[18089]**, Green Bay, WI
Civics
City Year Columbus **[14367]**, Columbus, OH
Civil Engineering
Univ. of Minnesota - Civil Engg. Dept. - Enval. Engg. Soc. **[11769]**, Minneapolis, MN
Civil Law
Illinois Assn. of Defense Trial Counsel **[3569]**, Springfield, IL
Civil Liberties Union of Michigan; Amer. **[7300]**, Detroit, MI
Civil Liberties Union of Minnesota; Amer. **[12353]**, St. Paul, MN
Civil Liberties Union, Ohio Affl; Amer. **[14047]**, Cleveland, OH
Civil Liberties Union, Wisconsin; Amer. **[18931]**, Milwaukee, WI
Civil Rights and Liberties
ACLU of Wisconsin **[18924]**, Milwaukee, WI
Akron Urban League **[13025]**, Akron, OH
Amer. Civil Liberties Union of Illinois **[617]**, Chicago, IL
Amer. Civil Liberties Union of Michigan **[7300]**, Detroit, MI
Amer. Civil Liberties Union of Minnesota **[12353]**, St. Paul, MN
Amer. Civil Liberties Union, Ohio Affl. **[14047]**, Cleveland, OH
Amer. Civil Liberties Union, Wisconsin **[18931]**, Milwaukee, WI
Canton Urban League **[13561]**, Canton, OH
Chicago Urban League **[835]**, Chicago, IL
Citizens Against Domestic Violence **[16007]**, Middletown, OH
Columbus Urban League **[14405]**, Columbus, OH
Dayton Urban League **[14882]**, Dayton, OH
Detroit Urban League **[7357]**, Detroit, MI
Fort Wayne Urban League **[4661]**, Fort Wayne, IN
Grand Rapids Urban League **[7952]**, Grand Rapids, MI
Greater Toledo Urban League **[16920]**, Toledo, OH
Human Rights Commn. of Olmsted County **[12147]**, Rochester, MN
Illinois NORML **[952]**, Chicago, IL
Indiana Civil Liberties Union **[5211]**, Indianapolis, IN
Indiana Norml **[5268]**, Indianapolis, IN
Indianapolis Urban League **[5357]**, Indianapolis, IN
Lorain County Urban League **[15121]**, Elyria, OH
Massillon Urban League **[15890]**, Massillon, OH
Michigan Norml **[9478]**, Redford, MI
Michigan Technological Univ. Natl. Org. for the Reform of Marijuana Laws **[8256]**, Houghton, MI
Milwaukee Urban League **[19069]**, Milwaukee, WI
Natl. Assn. for the Advancement of Colored People, Chicago Southside Br. **[1070]**, Chicago, IL
Natl. Assn. for the Advancement of Colored People-Detroit Br. **[7406]**, Detroit, MI
Natl. Assn. for the Advancement of Colored People, Du Page County Br. **[3993]**, Wheaton, IL
Natl. Assn. for the Advancement of Colored People, East St. Louis, Illinois Br. **[1551]**, East St. Louis, IL
Natl. Assn. for the Advancement of Colored People, Indianapolis Br. **[5413]**, Indianapolis, IN
Natl. Assn. for the Advancement of Colored People, Lansing Br. **[8735]**, Lansing, MI
Natl. Assn. for the Advancement of Colored People, Minneapolis Br. **[11692]**, Minneapolis, MN
Natl. Assn. for the Advancement of Colored People, Monroe County Br. **[4246]**, Bloomington, IN
Natl. Assn. for the Advancement of Colored People, Rochester Br. 507 **[12164]**, Rochester, MN
Natl. Assn. for the Advancement of Colored People, Southern Oakland County **[9811]**, Southfield, MI
Natl. Assn. for the Advancement of Colored People, Western Michigan Univ. Chap. **[8456]**, Kalamazoo, MI
NORML of Macomb County **[9566]**, Roseville, MI
NORML at the Univ. of Minnesota **[11708]**, Minneapolis, MN
North Ohio Natl. Org. for the Reform of Marijuana Laws **[15687]**, Lodi, OH
Not In Your Name, Ohio - Cleveland **[14189]**, Cleveland, OH
Oberlin Coll. Natl. Org. for the Reform of Marijuana Laws **[16290]**, Oberlin, OH
People for the Amer. Way, Illinois **[1123]**, Chicago, IL
Purdue NORML **[6497]**, West Lafayette, IN
Quad County Urban League **[129]**, Aurora, IL
St. Cloud State Univ. Natl. Org. for the Reform of Marijuana Laws **[12305]**, St. Cloud, MN
St. Paul Urban League **[12585]**, St. Paul, MN
Southwestern Michigan Urban League **[6870]**, Battle Creek, MI
Univ. of Illinois Urbana Champaign Natl. Org. for the Reform of Marijuana Laws **[3839]**, Urbana, IL
Univ. of Wisconsin at Fox Valley Natl. Org. for the Reform of Marijuana Laws **[18867]**, Menasha, WI
Urban League of Champaign County **[557]**, Champaign, IL
Urban League of Flint **[7761]**, Flint, MI
Urban League of Greater Cincinnati **[14019]**, Cincinnati, OH
Urban League of Greater Cleveland **[14230]**, Cleveland, OH
Urban League of Greater Madison **[18635]**, Madison, WI
Urban League of Greater Muskegon **[9165]**, Muskegon, MI
Urban League of Madison County **[4122]**, Anderson, IN
Urban League of NW Indiana **[4787]**, Gary, IN
Urban League of Racine and Kenosha **[19580]**, Racine, WI
Urban League of South Bend and St. Joseph County **[6273]**, South Bend, IN
Warren - Trumbull Urban League **[17121]**, Warren, OH
Wisconsin Natl. Org. for the Reform of Marijuana Laws **[18141]**, Green Bay, WI
Civil Service
Blacks In Govt., Greater Cleveland Chap. **[14084]**, Cleveland, OH
Blacks In Govt., Greater Dayton Chap. **[14862]**, Dayton, OH
Civil Trial Attorneys; Ohio Assn. of **[14547]**, Columbus, OH
Civil Trial Counsel of Wisconsin **[18993]**, Milwaukee, WI
Civil War
Military Order of the Loyal Legion of the U.S., Michigan Commandery **[8243]**, Holt, MI
Military Order of the Loyal Legion of the U.S. Michigan Commandery **[8488]**, Kentwood, MI
Civil War Re-enactment Club; Blackford County **[4900]**, Hartford City, IN
Clague Middle School Parent-Teachers-Students Org. **[6691]**, Ann Arbor, MI
Clara City Lions Club **[10669]**, Clara City, MN
Clare Area Chamber of Commerce **[7153]**, Clare, MI
Clare County Visitor and Convention Bur. **[7154]**, Clare, MI
Clare Gladwin Bd. of Realtors **[7833]**, Gladwin, MI
Clarenceville - Young Life **[9397]**, Plymouth, MI
Clarendon Hills Lions Club **[1266]**, Clarendon Hills, IL
Clark County Audubon Soc. **[16723]**, Springfield, OH
Clark County Beagle Club **[15474]**, Huber Heights, OH
CLark County Chamber of Commerce **[★5927]**
Clark County Coin Club **[16724]**, Springfield, OH
Clark County Historical Society/Howard Steamboat Museum **[5540]**, Jeffersonville, IN
Clark County Literacy Coalition **[16725]**, Springfield, OH
Clark County Planning Commn. **[16726]**, Springfield, OH
Clark - Floyd Counties Convention and Tourism Bur. **[5541]**, Jeffersonville, IN
Clark Lake Found. **[7156]**, Clarklake, MI
Clark - YoungLife **[16727]**, Springfield, OH
Clarklake Lions Club **[7157]**, Clarklake, MI
Clarkston Area Chamber of Commerce **[7162]**, Clarkston, MI
Classic Boat Soc; Bob Speltz Land O' Lakes Chap. of the Antique and **[10761]**, Deephaven, MN
Classic Peruvian's Horse Club **[17916]**, Edgerton, WI
Classic Thunderbird Club of Wisconsin **[19499]**, Port Washington, WI
Classical Assn. of Illinois **[3197]**, Rio, IL
Classical Assn. of Indiana **[5848]**, Mount Vernon, IN
Classical Assn. of Michigan **[6620]**, Allendale, MI
Classical Assn. of the Middle West and South **[11913]**, Northfield, MN
Classical Assn. of Minnesota **[12133]**, Rochester, MN
Classical Assn. of Northern Plains Region **[11546]**, Minneapolis, MN
Classical Assn. of Ohio **[13803]**, Cincinnati, OH
Classical Assn. of Wisconsin **[17591]**, Beaver Dam, WI
Classical Attraction Dressage Soc. **[13437]**, Brooklyn, OH
Classical Studies
Classical Assn. of Illinois **[3197]**, Rio, IL

Classical Assn. of Indiana **[5848]**, Mount Vernon, IN
Classical Assn. of Michigan **[6620]**, Allendale, MI
Classical Assn. of the Middle West and South **[11913]**, Northfield, MN
Classical Assn. of Minnesota **[12133]**, Rochester, MN
Classical Assn. of Northern Plains Region **[11546]**, Minneapolis, MN
Classical Assn. of Ohio **[13803]**, Cincinnati, OH
Classical Assn. of Wisconsin **[17591]**, Beaver Dam, WI
Clay County Beagle Club **[4921]**, Hillsdale, IN
Clay County Chamber of Commerce **[4283]**, Brazil, IN
Clay County Historical Soc. **[11823]**, Moorhead, MN
Clay - Young Life **[6227]**, South Bend, IN
Clayland Lions Club **[15019]**, Dennison, OH
Clean Water Action of Clinton Township **[7174]**, Clinton Township, MI
Clean Water Action Coun. of Northeast Wisconsin **[18093]**, Green Bay, WI
Clean Water Action of Michigan **[7919]**, Grand Rapids, MI
Cleaning Coun; Midwest Automatic Laundry and **[★1500]**
Clear Community Club **[17762]**, Clear Lake, WI
Clear Lake Civic and Community Assn. **[★17762]**
Clearwater County Historical Soc. **[10374]**, Bagley, MN
Clermont County Bd. of Realtors **[★14000]**
Clermont County Chamber of Commerce **[16025]**, Milford, OH
Clermont County Genealogical Soc. **[13266]**, Batavia, OH
Clermont County Historical Soc. **[13267]**, Batavia, OH
Clermont County Kennel Club **[13804]**, Cincinnati, OH
Clermont County Stamp Club **[16445]**, Pleasant Plain, OH
Cleveland AIFA **[14091]**, Cleveland, OH
Cleveland/Akron 9to5 **[13049]**, Akron, OH
Cleveland-Akron Swing and Hustle Club **[15921]**, Mayfield Heights, OH
Cleveland All-Breed Training Club **[14092]**, Cleveland, OH
Cleveland Area Bd. of Realtors, Ohio **[15495]**, Independence, OH
Cleveland Area Mountain Bike Assn. **[14093]**, Cleveland, OH
Cleveland Assn. for Bus. Economics **[14094]**, Cleveland, OH
Cleveland Chamber Collective **[14095]**, Cleveland, OH
Cleveland Chamber of Commerce **[17765]**, Cleveland, WI
Cleveland Chap. of the Soc. of Financial Ser. Professionals **[14096]**, Cleveland, OH
Cleveland Coatings Soc. **[16786]**, Strongsville, OH
Cleveland Coun. Black Nurses Assn. (17) **[14097]**, Cleveland, OH
Cleveland Engg. Soc. **[14098]**, Cleveland, OH
Cleveland Fellowship of Christian Athletes **[14099]**, Cleveland, OH
Cleveland Hiking Club **[16395]**, Pepper Pike, OH
Cleveland Memorial Soc. **[14100]**, Cleveland, OH
Cleveland Model Boat Club No. 31 **[13410]**, Brecksville, OH
Cleveland Peace Action **[14101]**, Cleveland, OH
Cleveland Police Historical Soc., Inc. and Museum **[★14102]**
Cleveland Police Historical Soc. and Museum **[14102]**, Cleveland, OH
Cleveland Police Museum **[★14102]**
Cleveland Psychoanalytic Center **[14245]**, Cleveland Heights, OH
Cleveland Shetland Sheepdog Club **[13346]**, Berea, OH
Cleveland Skating Club **[16634]**, Shaker Heights, OH
Cleveland Soc. of Clinical Hypnosis **[13285]**, Beachwood, OH
Cleveland Soc. for Human Rsrc. Mgt. **[14103]**, Cleveland, OH
Cleveland Soc. of Security Analysts **[14104]**, Cleveland, OH
Cleveland Southeast Lions Club **[16544]**, Rocky River, OH
Cleveland Table Tennis Assn. **[14105]**, Cleveland, OH
Cleveland Vessel Owners Assn. **[★14153]**
Cleveland; YMCA of Greater **[14240]**, Cleveland, OH
Cleveland Young Men's Christian Association **[★14240]**
Clifton Heights Community Urban Redevelopment Corp. **[13805]**, Cincinnati, OH
Climax - Scotts PTA **[9734]**, Scotts, MI
Clinical Lab. Mgt. Assn., Chicago Chap. **[69]**, Arlington Heights, IL
Clinical Lab. Mgt. Assn., Greater Indiana Chap. **[5712]**, Madison, IN
Clinical Lab. Mgt. Assn., Minnesota Chap. **[11547]**, Minneapolis, MN
Clinical Lab. Mgt. Assn., Six Rivers Chap. **[15985]**, Miamisburg, OH
Clinical Lab. Mgt. Assn. of Wisconsin **[18094]**, Green Bay, WI
Clinical Lab. Sci; Michigan Soc. for **[6838]**, Bath, MI
Clinical Studies
Central Soc. for Clinical Res., Milwaukee **[18991]**, Milwaukee, WI
Clinton Area Chamber of Commerce **[1273]**, Clinton, IL
Clinton Chamber of Commerce **[★1273]**
Clinton Chamber of Commerce **[★4372]**
Clinton County Bd. of Realtors, Ohio **[17288]**, Wilmington, OH
Clinton County Chamber of Commerce **[4739]**, Frankfort, IN
Clinton County Chamber of Commerce **[★9678]**
Clinton County Farm Bur. Found. **[338]**, Breese, IL
Clinton County Farmers and Sportsman's Assn. **[17289]**, Wilmington, OH
Clinton County Historical Soc. **[17290]**, Wilmington, OH
Clinton County Historical Soc. and Historical Museum **[4740]**, Frankfort, IN
Clinton County Museum **[★4740]**
Clinton Rosette Middle School PTA **[1430]**, DeKalb, IL
Clinton Valley Trout Unlimited **[9501]**, Rochester, MI
Clintonville Area Chamber of Commerce **[17771]**, Clintonville, WI
Clio Lions Club **[7189]**, Clio, MI
Cloquet Carlton Area Chamber of Commerce **[10690]**, Cloquet, MN
Clothing
Jackets for Jobs Michigan WORKS **[7382]**, Detroit, MI
Cloudbase Flyers **[18340]**, La Crosse, WI
Cloverdale Area Chamber of Commerce **[4374]**, Cloverdale, IN
Cloverland District Dental Soc. **[7610]**, Escanaba, MI
Club Corvo **[2042]**, Homer Glen, IL
Club Managers Assn. of Am. - Greater Cleveland Chap. **[16635]**, Shaker Heights, OH
Club Managers Assn. of Am. - Purdue Univ. **[6480]**, West Lafayette, IN
Club; South Gibson Wrestling **[6072]**, Princeton, IN
Clubs
AAA Hoosier Motor Club **[4961]**, Indianapolis, IN
Club Managers Assn. of Am. - Greater Cleveland Chap. **[16635]**, Shaker Heights, OH
Club Managers Assn. of Am. - Purdue Univ. **[6480]**, West Lafayette, IN
Detroit Club Managers Assn. **[9770]**, South Lyon, MI
Clumber Spaniel Fanciers of Michigan **[9733]**, Schoolcraft, MI
Clyde Bus. and Professional Assn. **[14256]**, Clyde, OH
Coach Fed., Greater Indianapolis Chap; Intl. **[5375]**, Indianapolis, IN
Coaches Assn; Michigan High School **[8993]**, Mears, MI
Coaching
Chicago Coach Fed. **[1917]**, Gurnee, IL
Illinois Coaches Assn. **[22]**, Alexis, IL
Intl. Coach Fed., Greater Indianapolis Chap. **[5375]**, Indianapolis, IN
Michigan High School Coaches Assn. **[8993]**, Mears, MI
Minnesota State High School Coaches Assn. **[10779]**, Detroit Lakes, MN
Coal
Illinois Coal Assn. **[3590]**, Springfield, IL
Indiana Coal Coun. **[5212]**, Indianapolis, IN
Ohio Coal Assn. **[14583]**, Columbus, OH
Coal Valley Lions Club **[1279]**, Coal Valley, IL
Coalition on Abortion/Breast Cancer **[2033]**, Hoffman Estates, IL
Coalition of African, Asian, European and Latino Immigrants of Illinois **[850]**, Chicago, IL
Coalition for Fathers Rights **[★18703]**
Coalition on Homelessness and Housing in Ohio **[14368]**, Columbus, OH
Coalition of Reef Lovers **[7920]**, Grand Rapids, MI
Coalition of Wisconsin Aging Groups **[18498]**, Madison, WI
Coast Guard
Chicago Br. Coast Guard Enlisted Assn. **[373]**, Burr Ridge, IL
Greater Detroit Chap. Chief Petty Officers Assn. **[7368]**, Detroit, MI
Green Bay Chap. Chief Petty Officers Assn. **[18103]**, Green Bay, WI
North Coast Chief Petty Officers Assn. **[14179]**, Cleveland, OH
Coatings
CDIC Soc. for Coatings Tech. **[13765]**, Cincinnati, OH
Chicago Soc. for Coatings Tech. **[147]**, Barrington, IL
Cleveland Coatings Soc. **[16786]**, Strongsville, OH
Detroit Soc. for Coatings Tech. **[6813]**, Auburn Hills, MI
Northwestern Soc. for Coatings Tech. **[12557]**, St. Paul, MN
Cochlear Implant Club Minnesota **[12403]**, St. Paul, MN
Coin and Currency Club; Metro East **[207]**, Belleville, IL
Coin Laundry Assn. **[1500]**, Downers Grove, IL
Cokato Chamber of Commerce **[10696]**, Cokato, MN
Cokato Lions Club **[10697]**, Cokato, MN
Col. Crawford Lions Club **[16872]**, Tiro, OH
Colby Chamber of Commerce **[17775]**, Colby, WI
Colchester Lions Club **[1282]**, Colchester, IL
Cold Spring Area Chamber of Commerce **[10699]**, Cold Spring, MN
Cold Spring Home Pride Lions Club **[10700]**, Cold Spring, MN
Coldwater Area Chamber of Commerce **[14258]**, Coldwater, OH
Coldwater - Branch County Chamber of Commerce **[★7196]**
Coleman Lions Club **[7202]**, Coleman, MI
Colerain - Young Life **[15154]**, Fairfield, OH
Coles County Habitat for Humanity **[567]**, Charleston, IL
Coles County RSVP **[568]**, Charleston, IL
Colitis Found. of Am., Illinois Carol Fisher Chap; Crohn's and **[1456]**, Des Plaines, IL
Colitis Found. of Am., Wisconsin Chap; Crohn's and **[20100]**, West Allis, WI
Colitis, Midwest Regional; Natl. Found. for Ileitis and **[★1456]**
Collectors
Bead Soc. of Greater Chicago **[4017]**, Wilmette, IL
Celtic Corner Miniature Club **[8801]**, Leslie, MI
Chicago Playing Card Collectors **[2908]**, Palatine, IL
Columbus Area Miniature Enthusiasts **[4393]**, Columbus, IN
Columbus Miniature Soc. **[15431]**, Hilliard, OH
Dayton Miniature Soc. **[17367]**, Xenia, OH
Dollhouse and Miniature Soc. of Elkhart **[6291]**, Syracuse, IN
Glass City Miniatures Guild **[9328]**, Ottawa Lake, MI
Madison Area Miniature Enthusiasts **[19585]**, Randolph, WI
Madison Bead Soc. **[18907]**, Middleton, WI
Michiana Miniature Guild **[4288]**, Bremen, IN
Michigan Indiana Thimble Soc. **[5789]**, Michigan City, IN
Midwest Decoy Collectors Assn. **[1055]**, Chicago, IL
Miniature Soc. of Cincinnati **[13909]**, Cincinnati, OH

Natl. Assn. of Miniature Enthusiasts [4329], Carmel, IN
Natl. Assn. of Miniature Enthusiasts - A-3 Regional Miniaturists [17176], West Chester, OH
Natl. Assn. of Miniature Enthusiasts - A1 Minis R Us [2758], Northbrook, IL
Natl. Assn. of Miniature Enthusiasts - Crazy Eight's [1364], Darien, IL
Natl. Assn. of Miniature Enthusiasts - Dollhouse Divas [8297], Huntington Woods, MI
Natl. Assn. of Miniature Enthusiasts - Harbor Mini Crafters [7863], Grand Haven, MI
Natl. Assn. of Miniature Enthusiasts - Hoosier Mini-Mizers [5419], Indianapolis, IN
Natl. Assn. of Miniature Enthusiasts - Lakeshore Miniature Makers [19702], Sheboygan, WI
Natl. Assn. of Miniature Enthusiasts - Little Gems [7019], Brighton, MI
Natl. Assn. of Miniature Enthusiasts - Madison Avenue Miniaturists [5958], New Whiteland, IN
Natl. Assn. of Miniature Enthusiasts - Magic of Miniatures [7875], Grand Ledge, MI
Natl. Assn. of Miniature Enthusiasts - Mail-A-Mini Swappers [8990], Mayville, MI
Natl. Assn. of Miniature Enthusiasts - Married with Minis [17177], West Chester, OH
Natl. Assn. of Miniature Enthusiasts - Metro Mini Makers [2525], Moline, IL
Natl. Assn. of Miniature Enthusiasts - Metro Minis [4698], Fort Wayne, IN
Natl. Assn. of Miniature Enthusiasts - Midstate Minimakers of Illinois [2725], Normal, IL
Natl. Assn. of Miniature Enthusiasts - Mini Biddies [8782], Lapeer, MI
Natl. Assn. of Miniature Enthusiasts - Mini Constr. Company [5892], Muncie, IN
Natl. Assn. of Miniature Enthusiasts - Mini Diversions [19620], Richfield, WI
Natl. Assn. of Miniature Enthusiasts - Mini-Fingers of Kalamazoo [6862], Battle Creek, MI
Natl. Assn. of Miniature Enthusiasts - Mini-Magic Miniatures [15211], Findlay, OH
Natl. Assn. of Miniature Enthusiasts - Miniature Dream Builders [4610], Fishers, IN
Natl. Assn. of Miniature Enthusiasts - My Favorite Things [6247], South Bend, IN
Natl. Assn. of Miniature Enthusiasts - My Mini Friends [7265], Dearborn, MI
Natl. Assn. of Miniature Enthusiasts - Now and Again Club [4085], Albion, IN
Natl. Assn. of Miniature Enthusiasts - One More Time [6863], Battle Creek, MI
Natl. Assn. of Miniature Enthusiasts - People with Unfinished Projects [7069], Canton, MI
Natl. Assn. of Miniature Enthusiasts - Pinocchio's Mini Makers [7193], Clio, MI
Natl. Assn. of Miniature Enthusiasts - Quality Dreamers [9211], Niles, MI
Natl. Assn. of Miniature Enthusiasts - Retreat Into Miniatures [17507], Appleton, WI
Natl. Assn. of Miniature Enthusiasts - Soc. of Miniature Memories [16218], North Canton, OH
Natl. Assn. of Miniature Enthusiasts - Springfield Mini Ma'ams [16735], Springfield, OH
Natl. Assn. of Miniature Enthusiasts - Tiny Treasure Makers [11394], Mankato, MN
Natl. Assn. of Miniature Enthusiasts - Town Hall Minis [3104], Plainfield, IL
Natl. Assn. of Miniature Enthusiasts - Tri City Miniature Makers [9620], Saginaw, MI
Natl. Assn. of Miniature Enthusiasts - Wee Bee's of Birmingham [9515], Rochester Hills, MI
Natl. Assn. of Miniature Enthusiasts - Whole Fam Damily [9621], Saginaw, MI
Natl. Assn. of Miniature Enthusiasts - Wisconsin Wee World Soc. [18006], Fox Point, WI
Natl. Assn. of Watch and Clock Collectors, Chap. 3 [1307], Countryside, IL
Natl. Assn. of Watch and Clock Collectors, Chap. 18 [5424], Indianapolis, IN
Natl. Assn. of Watch and Clock Collectors, Chap. 66 [1412], Deer Creek, IL
Natl. Assn. of Watch and Clock Collectors, Chap. 171 [17964], Fitchburg, WI
Natl. Assn. of Watch and Clock Collectors, Great Lakes Chap. 6 [7070], Canton, MI
Natl. Assn. of Watch and Clock Collectors, Menomonee Valley Chap. 47 [19075], Milwaukee, WI
Natl. Novelty Salt and Pepper Shakers Club - Michigan [6864], Battle Creek, MI
Ohio Thimble Seekers [16423], Pickerington, OH
Peoria Area Miniature Soc. [3046], Peoria, IL
Thimble Collectors Intl., Dairyland [20192], Wisconsin Rapids, WI
Thimble Collectors Intl., Great Lakes [6775], Ann Arbor, MI
Thimble Collectors Intl., ILMO Thimblers [1879], Goreville, IL
Thimblefools of Northern Illinois [2545], Montgomery, IL
Troy Soldiers Miniatures Club [9594], Royal Oak, MI
Warren Area Miniature Club [17116], Warren, OH
Wee 'c' Mini Club [3131], Prairie Grove, IL
Western Reserve Carriage Assn. [14828], Cuyahoga Falls, OH
Windy City Miniature Club [1233], Chicago, IL
Wisconsin Collectors Assn. [18267], Janesville, WI
Coll. of Art and Design Student Assn. for Computing Machinery SIGGRAPH Center for Creative Stud. [7337], Detroit, MI
Coll. Assn; Michigan Community [8646], Lansing, MI
Coll. Democrats of Minnesota [12404], St. Paul, MN
Coll. Educ. Assn; Lake Michigan [6920], Benton Harbor, MI
Coll. Reading and Learning Assn., Minnesota/North Dakota/South Dakota [11786], Minnetonka, MN
Coll. Reading and Learning Assn., Ohio River Valley [15421], Highland Hills, OH
Coll. of St. Benedict and St. John's Univ. Students In Free Enterprise [10702], Collegeville, MN
Coll. of St. Scholastica Figure Skating Club [10809], Duluth, MN
Coll. Trustees Assn; Illinois Community [3595], Springfield, IL
Colls. Assn; Great Lakes [6700], Ann Arbor, MI
Colleges Found; Michigan [9806], Southfield, MI
Colleges of the Midwest; Assoc. [738], Chicago, IL
Colleges and Universities
African Univ. Found. [4963], Indianapolis, IN
Assoc. Colleges of the Midwest [738], Chicago, IL
Aurora Univ. Biology Club [114], Aurora, IL
Graduate Employees Org. [520], Champaign, IL
Great Lakes Colls. Assn. [6700], Ann Arbor, MI
Illinois Community Coll. Trustees Assn. [3595], Springfield, IL
Michigan Colleges Found. [9806], Southfield, MI
Ohio Assn. of Career Colls. and Schools [14544], Columbus, OH
Univ. of Minnesota-Duluth Literary Guild [10861], Duluth, MN
Wisconsin Assn. of Independent Colleges and Universities [18657], Madison, WI
Colleges and Universities; Wisconsin Assn. of Independent [18657], Madison, WI
Collegiate Registrars and Admission Officers, Ohio; Amer. Assn. of [★14548]
Collegiate Registrars and Admissions Officers; Michigan Assn. of [9108], Mount Pleasant, MI
Collegiate Registrars and Admissions Officers; Ohio Assn. of [14548], Columbus, OH
Collie Club of Am., Michigan [6595], Alger, MI
Collinsville Chamber of Commerce [1287], Collinsville, IL
Collinsville Convention and Visitors Bur. [1288], Collinsville, IL
Collinsville Memorial Public Lib. Found. [1289], Collinsville, IL
Coloma Area Chamber of Commerce [★7207]
Coloma Lions Club [7206], Coloma, MI
Coloma-Watervliet Area Chamber of Commerce [7207], Coloma, MI
Colombians of Michigan; Assn. of [9787], Southfield, MI
Colona-Green Rock-Orion United Way [1295], Colona, IL
Colorectal Educ; Advocates for [12345], St. Paul, MN
Colored Pencil Soc. of Am., Chicago, Illinois Chap. 103 [851], Chicago, IL
Colored Pencil Society of America, Detroit Chapter No. 104 [9745], Shelby Township, MI
Columbia City Area Chamber of Commerce [4379], Columbia City, IN
Columbia City Commercial Club [★4379]
Columbia Club [5092], Indianapolis, IN
Columbia Yacht Club [852], Chicago, IL
Columbiana Area Chamber of Commerce [14260], Columbiana, OH
Columbiana Area Lions Club [14261], Columbiana, OH
Columbiana County Chap. of the Ohio Genealogical Soc. [16586], Salem, OH
Columbus African Violet Soc. [15430], Hilliard, OH
Columbus AIDS Task Force [14369], Columbus, OH
Columbus Area AIFA [4390], Columbus, IN
Columbus Area Arts Coun. [4391], Columbus, IN
Columbus Area Chamber of Commerce [4392], Columbus, IN
Columbus Area Chamber of Commerce [17783], Columbus, WI
Columbus Area Miniature Enthusiasts [4393], Columbus, IN
Columbus Area Table Tennis Assn. [4394], Columbus, IN
Columbus Art League [★14539]
Columbus Assn. of Black Journalists [14370], Columbus, OH
Columbus Beagle Club [14371], Columbus, OH
Columbus Beechcroft Lions Club [17209], Westerville, OH
Columbus Black Nurses Assn. (82) [14372], Columbus, OH
Columbus Blues Alliance [14373], Columbus, OH
Columbus Bd. of Realtors [14374], Columbus, OH
Columbus Bd. of Realtors, Indiana [4395], Columbus, IN
Columbus Bonsai Soc. [14375], Columbus, OH
Columbus Campaign for Arms Control [14376], Columbus, OH
Columbus Chamber [14377], Columbus, OH
Columbus Chamber [★14446]
Columbus Chap. of the Natl. Stuttering Assn. [14378], Columbus, OH
Columbus Chorus of Sweet Adelines Intl. [14379], Columbus, OH
Columbus Compensation Assn. [14380], Columbus, OH
Columbus Coun. on World Affairs [14381], Columbus, OH
Columbus Dental Soc. [17210], Westerville, OH
Columbus District Golf Assn. [14382], Columbus, OH
Columbus Downtown Development Corp. [14383], Columbus, OH
Columbus Downtown Lions Club [14384], Columbus, OH
Columbus Evening Kiwanis Club [4396], Columbus, IN
Columbus Figure Skating Club [14385], Columbus, OH
Columbus High Soc. Tall Club [14386], Columbus, OH
Columbus Hilltop Lions Club [14387], Columbus, OH
Columbus House Rabbit Soc. [14388], Columbus, OH
Columbus Inner City Lions Club [14389], Columbus, OH
Columbus Jewish Fed. [14390], Columbus, OH
Columbus Jewish Historical Soc. [14391], Columbus, OH
Columbus Lions Club, IN [4397], Columbus, IN
Columbus Literacy Coun. [14392], Columbus, OH
Columbus Medical Assn. [14393], Columbus, OH
Columbus Miniature Soc. [15431], Hilliard, OH
Columbus Mortgage Bankers Assn. [14394], Columbus, OH
Columbus Northeast Lions Club [14395], Columbus, OH
Columbus Northern Lions Club [14396], Columbus, OH
Columbus Northland Lions Club [14397], Columbus, OH
Columbus Ohio Catholic Alumni Club [14398], Columbus, OH
Columbus Outdoor Club [★14399]
Columbus Outdoor Pursuits [14399], Columbus, OH
Columbus Parent Teacher Org. [11016], Forest Lake, MN

Columbus Philatelic Club [14400], Columbus, OH
Columbus Rotor Wing [15367], Grove City, OH
Columbus SCORE [14401], Columbus, OH
Columbus Softball Assn. [14402], Columbus, OH
Columbus Southeast Lions Club [15635], Lewis Center, OH
Columbus Southern Pines Lions Club [14403], Columbus, OH
Columbus Table Tennis Club [14404], Columbus, OH
Columbus Urban League [14405], Columbus, OH
Columbus Weightlifting Club [14406], Columbus, OH
Columbus Wellness Walkers [4398], Columbus, IN
Columbus West Indian Assn. [14407], Columbus, OH
Comfort House [5805], Milltown, IN
Commandery; Military Order of the Loyal Legion of the U.S., Michigan [8243], Holt, MI
Commemorative Bucks of Michigan [7486], Dryden, MI
Commerce; Arthur Assn. of [88], Arthur, IL
Commerce Assn; Plano [3110], Plano, IL
Commerce Club; Wauseon [★17143]
Commerce; Detroit Bd. of [★7354]
Commerce; Fond du Lac Area Assn. of [17972], Fond du Lac, WI
Commerce; Glendale Assn. of [18052], Glendale, WI
Commerce; Greater Channahon-Minooka Area Chamber of [2502], Minooka, IL
Commerce; Indiana State Hispanic Chamber of [5316], Indianapolis, IN
Commerce and Indus; Bradley Assn. of [★326]
Commerce; Kiel Area Assn. of [18322], Kiel, WI
Commerce; Metropolitan Milwaukee Assn. of [19049], Milwaukee, WI
Commerce; Racine Area Manufacturers and [19565], Racine, WI
Commerce; Turkish Amer. Chamber of [1210], Chicago, IL
Commerce; Wisconsin Manufacturers and [18723], Madison, WI
Commercial Assn. of Realtors - Wisconsin [18994], Milwaukee, WI
Commercial Club; Columbia City [★4379]
Commercial Club; Lake Zurich [★2209]
Commercial Club; Monmouth [★2541]
Commercial Finance Assn., Mid-West Chap. [853], Chicago, IL
Commercial Finance Assn., Ohio Chap. [13286], Beachwood, OH
Comm. on Gift Annuities [★4980]

Commodities

Illinois Corn Marketing Bd. [283], Bloomington, IL
Illinois Soybean Assn. [288], Bloomington, IL
Indiana Soybean Growers Assn. [5309], Indianapolis, IN
Michigan Soybean Assn. [7781], Frankenmuth, MI
Minnesota Corn Growers Assn. [12651], Shakopee, MN
Minnesota Cultivated Wild Rice Coun. [12475], St. Paul, MN
Minnesota Soybean Growers Assn. [11906], North Mankato, MN

Commodity Exchanges

Chicago Bd. of Trade [795], Chicago, IL
Chicago Mercantile Exchange [818], Chicago, IL
Common Cause of Michigan [8561], Lansing, MI
Common Cause - Ohio [14408], Columbus, OH
Common Cause Wisconsin [18499], Madison, WI
Common Good RSVP [12949], Winona, MN
Common Hope [12405], St. Paul, MN
Commonwealth Sportsmen's Club [17966], Florence, WI
Communication Alliance to Network Thoroughbred Ex-Racehorses [249], Bloomingdale, IL

Communications

BACnet Mfrs. Assn. [759], Chicago, IL
Cable TV and Communs. Assn. of Illinois [1453], Des Plaines, IL
Friends of WHA-TV [18513], Madison, WI
IABC/Columbus [14463], Columbus, OH
IABC/Indianapolis [5154], Indianapolis, IN
IABC/Madison [18520], Madison, WI
IABC Minnesota [12424], St. Paul, MN
IABC Southeastern Wisconsin [18053], Glendale, WI
Intl. Assn. of Bus. Communicators, Chicago Chap. [979], Chicago, IL
Intl. Assn. of Bus. Communicators, Cleveland Chap. [15499], Independence, OH
Intl. Assn. of Bus. Communicators, Columbus Chap. [14471], Columbus, OH
Intl. Assn. of Bus. Communicators, Dayton Chap. [14895], Dayton, OH
Intl. Assn. of Bus. Communicators, Detroit Chap. [8894], Madison Heights, MI
Intl. Assn. of Bus. Communicators, Greater Cincinnati Chap. [13869], Cincinnati, OH
Intl. Assn. of Bus. Communicators, Indianapolis Chap. [5372], Indianapolis, IN
Intl. Assn. of Bus. Communicators, Madison Chap. [18528], Madison, WI
Intl. Assn. of Bus. Communicators - Minnesota Chap. [12427], St. Paul, MN
Intl. Assn. of Bus. Communicators, Southeastern Wisconsin Chap. [18054], Glendale, WI
Lacrosse Area Communications Consortium [18365], La Crosse, WI
Minnesota Cable Communs. Assn. [12462], St. Paul, MN
Soc. for Tech. Commun., Central Illinois Chap. [3836], Urbana, IL
Soc. for Tech. Commun., Chicago Chap. [2928], Palatine, IL
Soc. for Tech. Commun., Quad Cities Chap. [2534], Moline, IL
Soc. for Tech. Commun., St. Joseph Valley Chap. [5955], New Paris, IN
Soc. for Tech. Commun., Southeastern Michigan Chap. [6768], Ann Arbor, MI
Soc. for Tech. Commun., Wisconsin Chap. [19999], Waukesha, WI
Wisconsin Cable Communs. Assn. [18676], Madison, WI
Communs. Workers of Am., AFL-CIO, CLC - Local Union 34001 [14106], Cleveland, OH
Communities Investing in Families [12739], Taylors Falls, MN
Communities United for Action [13806], Cincinnati, OH

Community

Asia's Hope [17314], Wooster, OH
Bankers Club [13757], Cincinnati, OH
Community Associations Inst. - Illinois Chap. [3354], Roselle, IL
Historic Irvington Community Coun. [5135], Indianapolis, IN
Jobs Partnership of Greater Indianapolis [5382], Indianapolis, IN
Michiana Emmaus Community [4501], Elkhart, IN
Midwest Crossroads Emmaus Community [6165], Schererville, IN
Pilsen Neighbors Community Coun. [1138], Chicago, IL
Quilting Stars of Ohio [13579], Canton, OH

Community Action

Albany Park Neighborhood Coun. [601], Chicago, IL
Assn. of Community Organizations for Reform Now, Akron [13041], Akron, OH
Assn. of Community Organizations for Reform Now, Chicago [740], Chicago, IL
Assn. of Community Organizations for Reform Now, Cincinnati [13750], Cincinnati, OH
Assn. of Community Organizations for Reform Now, Cleveland [14075], Cleveland, OH
Assn. of Community Organizations for Reform Now, Columbus [14322], Columbus, OH
Assn. of Community Organizations for Reform Now, Dayton [14854], Dayton, OH
Assn. of Community Organizations for Reform Now, Detroit [7325], Detroit, MI
Assn. of Community Organizations for Reform Now, Flint [7716], Flint, MI
Assn. of Community Organizations for Reform Now, Indianapolis [5044], Indianapolis, IN
Assn. of Community Organizations for Reform Now, Lansing [7509], East Lansing, MI
Assn. of Community Organizations for Reform Now, Madison [18481], Madison, WI
Assn. of Community Organizations for Reform Now, Milwaukee [18968], Milwaukee, WI
Assn. of Community Organizations for Reform Now, Minnesota [12387], St. Paul, MN
Assn. of Community Organizations for Reform Now, Springfield, Illinois [3537], Springfield, IL
Assn. of Community Organizations for Reform Now, Toledo [16904], Toledo, OH
Bethel New Life [762], Chicago, IL
Blocks Together [767], Chicago, IL
Chaldean Amers. Reaching and Encouraging [10112], West Bloomfield, MI
Citizen Action/Illinois [847], Chicago, IL
Citizens Res. Coun. of Michigan [8836], Livonia, MI
Communities United for Action [13806], Cincinnati, OH
Community Action Coun. [11294], Lakeville, MN
Detroit ACORN [7339], Detroit, MI
East Side Organizing Proj. [14111], Cleveland, OH
Edgewater Community Coun. [882], Chicago, IL
Highfields - Helping People Grow in Michigan [9306], Onondaga, MI
Illinois Community Action Assn. [3594], Springfield, IL
Indianhead Community Action [18391], Ladysmith, WI
Lakeview Action Coalition [1018], Chicago, IL
Michigan Citizen Action [8448], Kalamazoo, MI
Michigan Community Action Agency Assn. [8645], Lansing, MI
Mobilize Montgomery [11808], Montgomery, MN
Near Northwest Neighborhood Network [1095], Chicago, IL
Neighborhood Ser. Exchange [12723], Stillwater, MN
Nobel Neighbors [1101], Chicago, IL
Oak Park-River Forest Community Found. [2824], Oak Park, IL
Ohio Assn. of Community Action Agencies [14549], Columbus, OH
Ohio Citizen Action [14192], Cleveland, OH
Org. for a New Eastside [5444], Indianapolis, IN
River North Assn. [1167], Chicago, IL
Rogers Park Community Action Network [1168], Chicago, IL
Streeterville Org. of Active Residents [1203], Chicago, IL
Community Action Agency Found; Cincinnati-Hamilton County [13787], Cincinnati, OH
Community Action Coun. [11294], Lakeville, MN
Community AIDS Rsrc. and Educ. Services of Southwest Michigan [8424], Kalamazoo, MI
Community Alliance to Promote Educ. [5871], Muncie, IN
Community Anal. and Planning Div. [18500], Madison, WI
Community Arts Center [★8107]
Community Associations Inst., Central Indiana Chap. [5093], Indianapolis, IN
Community Associations Inst. - Illinois Chap. [3354], Roselle, IL
Community Associations Inst., Michigan Chap. [6980], Bloomfield Hills, MI
Community Associations Inst. - Minnesota Chap. [12406], St. Paul, MN
Community Associations Inst., Ohio Valley Chap. [15990], Miamitown, OH
Community Assns. Inst. - Wisconsin Chap. [18995], Milwaukee, WI
Community Bankers Assn. of Illinois [3545], Springfield, IL
Community Bankers Assn. of Indiana [5094], Indianapolis, IN
Community Bankers Assn. of Ohio [14409], Columbus, OH
Community Bankers of Wisconsin [18501], Madison, WI
Community Behavioral Healthcare Assn. of Illinois [3546], Springfield, IL
Community Center Assn; Salem [★16590]
Community Center; Friends of the Kraemer Lib. and [19460], Plain, WI
Community Center; Northwest Suburban Jewish [364], Buffalo Grove, IL
Community Centers Endowment Found; Jewish [1006], Chicago, IL
Community Chest/United Way of St. Charles [★3395]
Community Choice Fed. Credit Union, Indianapolis, Indiana [5095], Indianapolis, IN
Community Coll. Assn; Michigan [8646], Lansing, MI

Community Coll. Trustees Assn; Illinois **[3595]**, Springfield, IL
Community Colleges
Michigan Community Coll. Assn. **[8646]**, Lansing, MI
Ohio Assn. of Community Colleges **[14550]**, Columbus, OH
Community Cultivators **[1635]**, Elsah, IL
Community Development
Aledo Main St. **[18]**, Aledo, IL
Alton Market Place Assn. **[36]**, Alton, IL
Amer. Planning Assn. Chicago Chap. **[718]**, Chicago, IL
Amer. Planning Assn. - Ohio Chap. **[14059]**, Cleveland, OH
Arrowhead Regional Development Commn. **[10806]**, Duluth, MN
Barberton Community Found. **[13255]**, Barberton, OH
Batavia Mothers Club Found. **[177]**, Batavia, IL
Bay-Lake Regional Planning Commn. **[18083]**, Green Bay, WI
Berwyn Development Corp. **[237]**, Berwyn, IL
Bethel Community Development Corp. **[18980]**, Milwaukee, WI
Brahma Samaj of Greater Chicago **[1497]**, Downers Grove, IL
Brooke-Hancock-Jefferson Metropolitan Planning Commn. **[16761]**, Steubenville, OH
Brookfield Village Homeowners Assn. **[15428]**, Hilliard, OH
Carbondale Main St. **[417]**, Carbondale, IL
Carter Temple Community Development Corp. **[776]**, Chicago, IL
Carver of Evansville Community Development Corp. **[4535]**, Evansville, IN
Central City Alliance **[7333]**, Detroit, MI
Central Upper Peninsula Planning and Development Regional Commn. **[7609]**, Escanaba, MI
Cincinnati-Hamilton County Community Action Agency Found. **[13787]**, Cincinnati, OH
City Connect Detroit **[7335]**, Detroit, MI
City News Community Development Corp. **[14089]**, Cleveland, OH
Clark County Planning Commn. **[16726]**, Springfield, OH
Community Anal. and Planning Div. **[18500]**, Madison, WI
Community Associations Inst., Central Indiana Chap. **[5093]**, Indianapolis, IN
Community Associations Inst., Michigan Chap. **[6980]**, Bloomfield Hills, MI
Community Associations Inst. - Minnesota Chap. **[12406]**, St. Paul, MN
Community Associations Inst., Ohio Valley Chap. **[15990]**, Miamitown, OH
Community Assns. Inst. - Wisconsin Chap. **[18995]**, Milwaukee, WI
Community Development Corporations Assn. of Greater Cincinnati **[13807]**, Cincinnati, OH
Community Economic Development Assn. of Michigan **[8562]**, Lansing, MI
Community Economic Development and Info. Tech. **[9699]**, Saline, MI
County of Mecosta Development Corp. **[6944]**, Big Rapids, MI
Cuyahoga County Planning Commn. **[14108]**, Cleveland, OH
Daviess County Growth Coun. **[6458]**, Washington, IN
Downtown Bloomington Commn. **[4213]**, Bloomington, IN
Downtown Collinsville Main St. Prog. **[1290]**, Collinsville, IL
Downtown Evansville **[4539]**, Evansville, IN
Downtown Fond du Lac Partnership **[17971]**, Fond du Lac, WI
Downtown Lima **[15651]**, Lima, OH
Downtown Neighborhood Assn. of Elgin **[1586]**, Elgin, IL
Downtown St. Charles Partnership **[3380]**, St. Charles, IL
Downtown West Bend Assn. **[20118]**, West Bend, WI
Eau Claire Area Found. **[17875]**, Eau Claire, WI
Englewood Community Development Corp. **[5109]**, Indianapolis, IN
Enos Park Neighborhood Improvement Assn. **[3549]**, Springfield, IL
Forest Park Main St. **[1712]**, Forest Park, IL
Frankfort Main St. **[4742]**, Frankfort, IN
Freeburg Area Community Development Association **[1741]**, Freeburg, IL
Galesburg Downtown Coun. **[1773]**, Galesburg, IL
Global Volunteers **[12419]**, St. Paul, MN
Grand Boulevard Fed. **[904]**, Chicago, IL
Greater Cleveland Partnership **[14134]**, Cleveland, OH
Greater Lafayette Community Development Corp. **[5612]**, Lafayette, IN
Greater Mauston Area Development Corp. **[18830]**, Mauston, WI
Greater North Michigan Avenue Assn. **[908]**, Chicago, IL
Greater Wabash Regional Planning Commn. **[15]**, Albion, IL
Green Chamber of Commerce **[15350]**, Green, OH
Greening of Detroit **[7370]**, Detroit, MI
Gull Area Lakes Assn. **[11897]**, Nisswa, MN
Hamilton Community Development Coalition **[1928]**, Hamilton, IL
Heritage Community Development Corp. **[913]**, Chicago, IL
Heritage Hill Assn. **[7963]**, Grand Rapids, MI
Historic Newburgh **[5960]**, Newburgh, IN
Historic Quincy Bus. District **[3151]**, Quincy, IL
Indiana Assisted Living Fed. of Am. **[5164]**, Indianapolis, IN
Indus of Fox Valley **[17500]**, Appleton, WI
Jacksonville Main St. **[2081]**, Jacksonville, IL
Jeffersonville Main St. **[5542]**, Jeffersonville, IN
Joy-Southfield Community Development Corp. **[7384]**, Detroit, MI
Kankakee County Regional Planning Commn. **[2135]**, Kankakee, IL
Keep Indianapolis Beautiful **[5386]**, Indianapolis, IN
Kokomo Main St. Assn. **[5576]**, Kokomo, IN
Lake County Planning Commn. **[16335]**, Painesville, OH
Lawndale Christian Development Corp. **[1022]**, Chicago, IL
Life Services Network of Illinois **[2021]**, Hinsdale, IL
Lincoln and Logan County Development Partnership **[2277]**, Lincoln, IL
Logan's Landing **[5692]**, Logansport, IN
Macalester-Groveland Community Coun. **[12442]**, St. Paul, MN
Madison Hours **[18553]**, Madison, WI
Madison Main St. Prog. **[5718]**, Madison, IN
Main St. Amherst **[13138]**, Amherst, OH
Main St. Blue Island **[317]**, Blue Island, IL
Main St. Bowling Green **[13393]**, Bowling Green, OH
Main St. Elyria **[15122]**, Elyria, OH
Main St. Galion **[15286]**, Galion, OH
Main St. Libertyville **[2264]**, Libertyville, IL
Main St. Lincoln **[2279]**, Lincoln, IL
Main St. Oberlin **[16284]**, Oberlin, OH
Main St. O'Fallon **[2848]**, O'Fallon, IL
Main St. Orion **[2873]**, Orion, IL
Main St. Paris **[2949]**, Paris, IL
Main Street Piqua **[16433]**, Piqua, OH
Main St. Plainfield **[3101]**, Plainfield, IL
Main St. Richmond-Wayne County **[6096]**, Richmond, IN
Main Street Tuscola **[3794]**, Tuscola, IL
Main St. Wellington **[17156]**, Wellington, OH
Main St. Wooster **[17322]**, Wooster, OH
Marion Main St. **[2406]**, Marion, IL
McHenry County Regional Planning Commn. **[4062]**, Woodstock, IL
McLean County Regional Planning Commn. **[297]**, Bloomington, IL
Metropolitan Planning Coun. **[1047]**, Chicago, IL
Mexicantown Community Development Corp. **[7390]**, Detroit, MI
Miami Valley Regional Planning Commn. **[14917]**, Dayton, OH
Michigan Alliance of Cooperatives **[6971]**, Blanchard, MI
Mid-Ohio Regional Planning Commn. **[14505]**, Columbus, OH
Mid-South Planning and Development Commn. **[1049]**, Chicago, IL
Minneapolis Consortium of Community Developers **[11613]**, Minneapolis, MN
Mississippi River Regional Planning Commn. **[18367]**, La Crosse, WI
Monticello Main St. **[2550]**, Monticello, IL
Mundelein MainStreet **[2615]**, Mundelein, IL
Muskegon Area Chamber of Commerce **[9150]**, Muskegon, MI
Near West Side Community Development Corp. **[1096]**, Chicago, IL
Noblesville Main St. **[5979]**, Noblesville, IN
North Metro I-35W Corridor Coalition **[10555]**, Brooklyn Park, MN
Northeast Michigan Community Partnership **[6646]**, Alpena, MI
Northeastern Illinois Planning Commn. **[1106]**, Chicago, IL
Northwest Michigan Coun. of Governments **[9943]**, Traverse City, MI
Northwest Regional Planning Commn. **[19762]**, Spooner, WI
Ohio Community Development Corp. Assn. **[14586]**, Columbus, OH
Ohio Multi-County Development Corp. **[13078]**, Akron, OH
Ohio Rural Development Partnership **[16516]**, Reynoldsburg, OH
Olmsted County Govt. Center **[12165]**, Rochester, MN
Ottawa County Economic Development Off. **[6626]**, Allendale, MI
Pan-African Assn. **[1120]**, Chicago, IL
Pekin Main St. **[2991]**, Pekin, IL
Perry County Development Corp. **[6299]**, Tell City, IN
Platteville Main St. Prog. **[19467]**, Platteville, WI
Positively Pewaukee **[19443]**, Pewaukee, WI
Prevailing Community Development Corp. **[7423]**, Detroit, MI
Prophetstown's Main St. Prog. **[3142]**, Prophetstown, IL
Public Allies Cincinnati **[13965]**, Cincinnati, OH
Ravenswood Community Coun. **[1162]**, Chicago, IL
Rebuilding The Wall **[5466]**, Indianapolis, IN
Region 2 Planning Commn. **[8395]**, Jackson, MI
Region 5 Development Commn. **[12705]**, Staples, MN
Rice Lake Main St. Assn. **[19617]**, Rice Lake, WI
Richland County Regional Planning Commn. **[15792]**, Mansfield, OH
Rushville Area C.O.C. and Main St. **[3372]**, Rushville, IL
Sacred Heart-St. Elizabeth Community Development Corp. **[7427]**, Detroit, MI
St. Cloud Area Planning Org. **[12299]**, St. Cloud, MN
Sandusky Main St. Assn. **[16619]**, Sandusky, OH
Sheridan Neighborhood Org. **[11735]**, Minneapolis, MN
South Central Illinois Regional Planning and Development Commn. **[3412]**, Salem, IL
South Metropolitan Planning Coun. **[18620]**, Madison, WI
Southeast Chicago Commn. **[1193]**, Chicago, IL
Southeastern Illinois Regional Planning and Development Commn. **[1943]**, Harrisburg, IL
Southwestern Wisconsin Regional Planning Commn. **[19472]**, Platteville, WI
Springfield Jaycees **[3680]**, Springfield, IL
Staunton Main St. USA **[3698]**, Staunton, IL
Taylorville Main Street **[3756]**, Taylorville, IL
Three Lakes Info. Bur. **[19899]**, Three Lakes, WI
Tri-County Regional Planning Commn. **[3067]**, Peoria, IL
Troy Community Found. **[10013]**, Troy, MI
Troy Main St. **[17010]**, Troy, OH
Two Rivers Main St. **[19921]**, Two Rivers, WI
Urban Solutions Training and Development Corp. **[7449]**, Detroit, MI
Valparaiso Community Festivals and Events **[6393]**, Valparaiso, IN
Vandalia Main St. Prog. **[3850]**, Vandalia, IL
Vanderburgh County 4-H Coun. **[4586]**, Evansville, IN

Volunteers of Am. of Wisconsin [17679], Brookfield, WI
Wabash Marketplace [6428], Wabash, IN
Warren County Community Found. [6529], Williamsport, IN
Warren Jaycees [10075], Warren, MI
Waukegan Main St. [3932], Waukegan, IL
West Michigan Regional Planning Commn. [8022], Grand Rapids, MI
West Michigan Shoreline Regional Development Commn. [9168], Muskegon, MI
West Portage Park Neighborhood Improvement Assn. [1230], Chicago, IL
Williamson County Events Commission Corp. [2412], Marion, IL
Wisconsin Alliance of Cities [18643], Madison, WI
Wisconsin Chap. of the Amer. Planning Assn. [18678], Madison, WI
Wright Dunbar [14971], Dayton, OH
Community Development Corp; Carter Temple [776], Chicago, IL
Community Development Corp; Carver of Evansville [4535], Evansville, IN
Community Development Corp; Cos [13811], Cincinnati, OH
Community Development Corp; Heritage [913], Chicago, IL
Community Development Corp; Joy-Southfield [7384], Detroit, MI
Community Development Corp; Macedonia [14905], Dayton, OH
Community Development Corp; Prevailing [7423], Detroit, MI
Community Development Corp; Sacred Heart-St. Elizabeth [7427], Detroit, MI
Community Development Corp; St. Paul [★7428]
Community Development Corporations Assn. of Greater Cincinnati [13807], Cincinnati, OH
Community Economic Development Assn. of Michigan [8562], Lansing, MI
Community Economic Development and Info. Tech. [9699], Saline, MI
Community Education
Community Educ. Coalition [4411], Connersville, IN
Michigan Assn. of Community and Adult Educ. [8608], Lansing, MI
Community Educ. Coalition [4411], Connersville, IN
Community Financial Educ. [14410], Columbus, OH
Community Hea. Charities of Illinois [854], Chicago, IL
Community Hea. Info. Collaborative [10810], Duluth, MN
Community Hea. Partners of Ohio Consolidated [15702], Lorain, OH
Community for Hope of Greater Oshkosh [19391], Oshkosh, WI
Community Improvement
East Town Assn. [19002], Milwaukee, WI
Old Town Neighborhood Assn. [4804], Goshen, IN
Portage County Crime Stoppers [19801], Stevens Point, WI
Volunteer Impact [10125], West Bloomfield, MI
Community Marriage Builders [4536], Evansville, IN
Community Mental Health
Indiana Coun. of Community Mental Hea. Centers [5218], Indianapolis, IN
Michigan Assn. of Community Mental Hea. Boards [8610], Lansing, MI
Community Nutrition Network and Senior Services Assn. of Cook County [855], Chicago, IL
Community Organization
Center City Neighborhood Assn. [16722], Springfield, OH
Commonwealth Sportsmen's Club [17966], Florence, WI
Future Heights [14246], Cleveland Heights, OH
Indiana Township Assn. [4608], Fishers, IN
Jewish Community Centers Endowment Found. [1006], Chicago, IL
Northwest Neighborhood Fed. [1109], Chicago, IL
Community Organizing Center - For Mother Earth [14411], Columbus, OH
Community Partnership; Northeast Michigan [6646], Alpena, MI
Community Partnership for Prevention [★6646]
Community Service
1000 Friends of Wisconsin [18441], Madison, WI
Assn. of Residential Resources in Minnesota [12676], South St. Paul, MN
Call to Action Chicagoland [2805], Oak Park, IL
Call to Action of Michigan [8105], Hamtramck, MI
City Year Detroit [7336], Detroit, MI
Dearborn Community Found. [5654], Lawrenceburg, IN
E Angel Community [4036], Winnetka, IL
Echo Hills Kennel Club of Ohio [15739], Ludlow Falls, OH
Farmington Area Jaycees [7640], Farmington, MI
Hamilton County Alliance [5132], Indianapolis, IN
Horizon Community Sers., DBA Center on Halsted [916], Chicago, IL
Illinois Assn. of Community Care Prog. Homecare Providers [3201], River Forest, IL
Illinois Assn. of Rehabilitation Facilities [3578], Springfield, IL
Indiana Assn. of Rehabilitation Facilities [5183], Indianapolis, IN
Indianapolis Found. [5348], Indianapolis, IN
Land Info. Access Assn. [9936], Traverse City, MI
Near Northwest Civic Comm. [1094], Chicago, IL
Parkinson's Awareness Assn. of Central Indiana [5447], Indianapolis, IN
Residential Services Assn. of Wisconsin [19109], Milwaukee, WI
Rotary Club of Darien, Illinois [1365], Darien, IL
Streamwood Guns 'n Hoses Assn. [3722], Streamwood, IL
Transformation Cincinnati and Northern Kentucky [14009], Cincinnati, OH
Victorian Village Soc. [14757], Columbus, OH
Youth Ser. Bur. of Huntington County [4956], Huntington, IN
Community United; Madison [★18594]
Community Urban Redevelopment Corp; Clifton Heights [13805], Cincinnati, OH
Community Volunteers for Intl. Progs. [7514], East Lansing, MI
Community Worship Arts [4537], Evansville, IN
Companion Dog Training Club of Flint [★7719]
Companion Dog Training Club of Flint, Michigan [7719], Flint, MI
Compassionate Action for Animals [11548], Minneapolis, MN
Compassionate Friends - Central Ohio Chap. [14412], Columbus, OH
Compassionate Friends - Cuyahoga/Geauga Counties Chap. [13643], Chardon, OH
Compassionate Friends - East Central Indiana Chap. [4477], Economy, IN
Compassionate Friends - Flint, Michigan Chap. [7720], Flint, MI
Compassionate Friends - Greater Cincinnati-East Chap. [13808], Cincinnati, OH
Compassionate Friends - Lafayette, Indiana Chap. [5610], Lafayette, IN
Compassionate Friends - Lake Porter County Chap. [6525], Whiting, IN
Compassionate Friends - Lakes Area Chap. [10054], Walled Lake, MI
Compassionate Friends - Livonia, Michigan Chap. [10138], Westland, MI
The Compassionate Friends - Miami Valley, Ohio Chap. [15559], Kettering, OH
Compassionate Friends - Miami-WhiteWater Chap. [4478], Economy, IN
Compassionate Friends - Minneapolis Chap. [11549], Minneapolis, MN
Compassionate Friends - Northern Lake County Illinois Chap. [1901], Green Oaks, IL
Compassionate Friends - Pekin Area Chap. [2386], Manito, IL
Compassionate Friends - Southern Indiana Chap. [4538], Evansville, IN
The Compassionate Friends U.S.A. Natl. Org. [2770], Oak Brook, IL
Compensation and Benefits Professionals of Indiana [4319], Carmel, IN
Compensation Medicine
Natl. Assn. of Disability Examiners, Great Lakes [15436], Hilliard, OH
Compensation Network; Twin Cities [12597], St. Paul, MN
Competing Band Assn; Michigan [9078], Montrose, MI
Competition Corvette Assn. [15965], Mentor, OH
Composers
Midwestern Gilbert and Sullivan Soc. [2742], North Aurora, IL
Comprehensive Health Education [18996], Milwaukee, WI
Cmpt. Consultants Assn., Chicago; Independent [2913], Palatine, IL
Cmpt. Cooperative; Cincinnati [13780], Cincinnati, OH
Cmpt. Measurement Gp., Minneapolis-St. Paul [11321], Lino Lakes, MN
Computer Science
Cmpt. Measurement Gp., Minneapolis-St. Paul [11321], Lino Lakes, MN
Greater Dayton ACM Chap. [14888], Dayton, OH
IEEE Akron/Canton Sect. [13568], Canton, OH
IEEE Central Illinois Sect. [523], Champaign, IL
IEEE Central Indiana Sect. [5155], Indianapolis, IN
IEEE Chicago Sect. [924], Chicago, IL
IEEE Cmpt. Soc., Calumet [4882], Hammond, IN
IEEE Cmpt. Soc., Cleveland [16523], Richfield, OH
IEEE Computer Society, Columbus Chapter [14464], Columbus, OH
IEEE Cmpt. Soc., Milwaukee Chap. [18873], Menomonee Falls, WI
IEEE Cmpt. Soc., Ohio State Univ. [14465], Columbus, OH
IEEE Cmpt. Soc., Rock River Valley Chap. [3281], Rockford, IL
IEEE Cmpt. Soc., Southeastern Michigan Chap. [9504], Rochester, MI
IEEE Cmpt. Soc., Southern Minnesota Chap. [12149], Rochester, MN
IEEE Cmpt. Soc., Toledo Chap. [15908], Maumee, OH
IEEE Computer Soc., Twin Cities Chap. [11583], Minneapolis, MN
IEEE - Dayton Sect. [14893], Dayton, OH
IEEE Madison Sect. [18521], Madison, WI
IEEE Milwaukee Sect. [19289], New Berlin, WI
IEEE Southern Minnesota Sect. [12150], Rochester, MN
IEEE West Michigan Sect. [8430], Kalamazoo, MI
Illinois Computing Educators [8], Addison, IL
Michigan Assn. for Educ. Data Systems [7182], Clinton Township, MI
Midwest Cmpt. Measurement Gp. [1363], Darien, IL
Minneapolis-St. Paul Cmpt. Measurement Gp. [11322], Lino Lakes, MN
Computer Software
Agile Alliance [10888], Eden Prairie, MN
Computer Users
ACM Siggraph Purdue Univ. Chap. [6468], West Lafayette, IN
Assn. for Computing Machinery, Anderson Univ. [4102], Anderson, IN
Assn. for Computing Machinery, Ashland Univ. [13164], Ashland, OH
Assn. for Computing Machinery, Ball State Univ. Chap. [5868], Muncie, IN
Assn. for Computing Machinery, Bryant and Stratton Parma Campus [16357], Parma, OH
Assn. for Computing Machinery, Butler Univ. [5045], Indianapolis, IN
Assn. for Computing Machinery, Carleton Coll. [11912], Northfield, MN
Assn. for Computing Machinery, Case Western Reserve Univ. [14076], Cleveland, OH
Assn. for Computing Machinery, Central Indiana Assn. for Computing Machinery-W Student Chap. [4815], Greencastle, IN
Assn. for Computing Machinery, Central Michigan Univ. [9100], Mount Pleasant, MI
Assn. for Computing Machinery, Chicago Military Acad.-Bronzville [741], Chicago, IL
Assn. for Computing Machinery, Columbia Coll./Chicago [742], Chicago, IL
Assn. for Computing Machinery, Concordia Coll. [11819], Moorhead, MN
Assn. for Computing Machinery, Depauw Univ. [4816], Greencastle, IN
Assn. for Computing Machinery, Eastern Michigan Univ. [10198], Ypsilanti, MI

Assn. for Computing Machinery, Franciscan Univ. of Steubenville [16760], Steubenville, OH
Assn. for Computing Machinery, Gustavus Adolphus Coll. [12613], St. Peter, MN
Assn. for Computing Machinery, Hope Coll. [8193], Holland, MI
Assn. for Computing Machinery, Illinois Inst. of Tech. [743], Chicago, IL
Assn. for Computing Machinery, Illinois State Univ. [2710], Normal, IL
Assn. for Computing Machinery, Illinois Wesleyan Univ. [263], Bloomington, IL
Assn. for Computing Machinery, Indiana Inst. of Tech. [4642], Fort Wayne, IN
Assn. for Computing Machinery, Indiana Univ. [4200], Bloomington, IN
Assn. for Computing Machinery, Indiana Univ. South Bend [6221], South Bend, IN
Assn. for Computing Machinery, John Carroll Univ. [17024], University Heights, OH
Assn. for Computing Machinery, Kent State Univ. [15539], Kent, OH
Assn. for Computing Machinery, Lawrence Technological Univ. [9788], Southfield, MI
Assn. for Computing Machinery, Macalester Coll. [12388], St. Paul, MN
Assn. for Computing Machinery, Marquette Univ. [18969], Milwaukee, WI
Assn. for Computing Machinery, Miami Univ. at Ohio [16323], Oxford, OH
Assn. for Computing Machinery, Michigan State Univ. [7510], East Lansing, MI
Assn. for Computing Machinery, Michigan Technological Univ. [8249], Houghton, MI
Assn. for Computing Machinery, Milwaukee School of Engg. [18970], Milwaukee, WI
Assn. for Computing Machinery, Minnesota State Univ., Mankato [11375], Mankato, MN
Assn. for Computing Machinery, Minnesota State University/Moorhead [11820], Moorhead, MN
Assn. for Computing Machinery, Mount Vernon Nazarene Univ. [16080], Mount Vernon, OH
Assn. for Computing Machinery, Muskingum Coll. [16124], New Concord, OH
Assn. for Computing Machinery, Northern Chicago Student Chap. [1649], Evanston, IL
Assn. for Computing Machinery, Northern Michigan Univ. [8933], Marquette, MI
Assn. for Computing Machinery, Oberlin Coll. [16280], Oberlin, OH
Assn. for Computing Machinery, Ohio Northern Univ. [13009], Ada, OH
Assn. for Computing Machinery, Ohio State Univ. [14323], Columbus, OH
Assn. for Computing Machinery, Ohio Wesleyan Univ. [15000], Delaware, OH
Assn. for Computing Machinery, Olivet Coll. [9301], Olivet, MI
Assn. for Computing Machinery, Purdue Univ. Chap. [6477], West Lafayette, IN
Assn. for Computing Machinery, Rose-Hulman Inst. of Tech. [6315], Terre Haute, IN
Assn. for Computing Machinery, Saginaw Valley State Univ. [10026], University Center, MI
Assn. for Computing Machinery, St. Cloud State Univ. [12275], St. Cloud, MN
Assn. for Computing Machinery, St. Mary's Univ. of Minnesota [12946], Winona, MN
Assn. for Computing Machinery, Southern Illinois Univ. Carbondale [412], Carbondale, IL
Assn. for Computing Machinery, Southern Illinois Univ./Edwardsville [1557], Edwardsville, IL
Assn. for Computing Machinery, Univ. of Akron [13042], Akron, OH
Assn. for Computing Machinery, Univ. of Chicago [744], Chicago, IL
Assn. for Computing Machinery, Univ. of Evansville [4531], Evansville, IN
Assn. for Computing Machinery, Univ. of ILL/Urbana-Champaign [3807], Urbana, IL
Assn. for Computing Machinery, Univ. of Illinois/Chicago [745], Chicago, IL
Assn. for Computing Machinery, Univ. of Michigan [6681], Ann Arbor, MI
Assn. for Computing Machinery, Univ. of Michigan-Dearborn [7249], Dearborn, MI
Assn. for Computing Machinery, Univ. of Michigan/Flint [7717], Flint, MI
Assn. for Computing Machinery, Univ. of Minnesota/Duluth [10807], Duluth, MN
Assn. for Computing Machinery, Univ. of Minnesota/Morris [11837], Morris, MN
Assn. for Computing Machinery, Univ. of Minnesota Student Chap. [11526], Minneapolis, MN
Assn. for Computing Machinery, Univ. of Notre Dame [6003], Notre Dame, IN
Assn. for Computing Machinery, Univ. of Toledo [16905], Toledo, OH
Assn. for Computing Machinery, Univ. of Wisconsin/Eau Claire [17865], Eau Claire, WI
Assn. for Computing Machinery, Univ. of Wisconsin/Madison [18482], Madison, WI
Assn. for Computing Machinery, Univ. of Wisconsin/Milwaukee [18971], Milwaukee, WI
Assn. for Computing Machinery, Univ. of Wisconsin/Platteville [19463], Platteville, WI
Assn. for Computing Machinery, Univ. of Wisconsin/River Falls [19640], River Falls, WI
Assn. for Computing Machinery, Walsh Coll. [9976], Troy, MI
Assn. for Computing Machinery, Wayne State Univ. [7326], Detroit, MI
Assn. for Computing Machinery, Western Illinois Univ. [2367], Macomb, IL
Assn. for Computing Machinery, Wilmington Coll. [17287], Wilmington, OH
Assn. for Computing Machinery, Winona State Univ. [12947], Winona, MN
Association for Computing Machinery, Wittenberg University [16721], Springfield, OH
Assn. for Computing Machinery, Wright State Univ. [14855], Dayton, OH
Assn. for Computing Machinery, Xavier Univ. [13751], Cincinnati, OH
Central Illinois Assn. for Computing Machinery Chap. [269], Bloomington, IL
Central Indiana Chap. of the Assn. for Computing Machinery [5074], Indianapolis, IN
Central Ohio Assn. for Computing Machinery SIGCHI (BuckCHI) [14353], Columbus, OH
Central State Univ. Assn. for Computing Machinery Student Chap. [17259], Wilberforce, OH
Chicago Area Assn. for Computing Machinery SIGCHI [2628], Naperville, IL
Chicago Assn. for Computing Machinery Chap. [786], Chicago, IL
Coll. of Art and Design Student Assn. for Computing Machinery SIGGRAPH Center for Creative Stud. [7337], Detroit, MI
Indiana Univ. Purdue Univ. Assn. for Computing Machinery Student Siggraph [5332], Indianapolis, IN
Indiana Wesleyan Univ. Assn. for Computing Machinery Student Chap. [5734], Marion, IN
IUPUI Assn. for Computing Machinery Student SIGGRAPH [5380], Indianapolis, IN
Loyola Assn. for Computing Machinery [1035], Chicago, IL
Michiana Free-Net Soc. [6241], South Bend, IN
Milwaukee Association for Computing Machinery SIGCHI [19054], Milwaukee, WI
Minneapolis/St. Paul Assn. for Computing Machinery SIGGRAPH [12447], St. Paul, MN
Motown Assn. for Computing Machinery SIGGRAPH [7403], Detroit, MI
Mount Union Coll. Assn. for Computing Machinery Student Chap. [13118], Alliance, OH
Northeast Ohio Assn. for Computing Machinery SIGGRAPH [14184], Cleveland, OH
Ohio Univ. Chap. of the Assn. for Computing Machinery [13213], Athens, OH
Purdue Univ. Calumet Student Assn. for Computing Machinery SIGGRAPH [4894], Hammond, IN
Southern Michigan Northern Ohio Assn. for Computing Machinery SIGCHI [6770], Ann Arbor, MI
Sterling Heights Cmpt. Club [9871], Sterling Heights, MI
Twin Cities Assn. for Computing Machinery SIGAda [10493], Bloomington, MN
Univ. of Detroit-Mercy Assn. for Computing Machinery [7448], Detroit, MI
Univ. of Michigan ACM SIGGRAPH Student Chap. [6777], Ann Arbor, MI
Cmpt. Users in Learning; Michigan Assn. for [8241], Holt, MI
Computers
Assn. for Women in Computing - Twin Cities Chap. [12222], Roseville, MN
Cincinnati Cmpt. Cooperative [13780], Cincinnati, OH
Geospatial Info. and Tech. Assn. Minnesota Regional Chap. [12416], St. Paul, MN
Independent Cmpt. Consultants Assn., Chicago [2913], Palatine, IL
Independent Cmpt. Consultants Assn., Minnesota [12049], Prior Lake, MN
Michigan Assn. for Cmpt. Users in Learning [8241], Holt, MI
Perinatal Info. Syss. User Gp. [1509], Downers Grove, IL
Southeastern Michigan Cmpt. Org. [6991], Bloomfield Hills, MI
WAUG [6792], Ann Arbor, MI
Computing Machinery, Butler Univ; Assn. for [5045], Indianapolis, IN
Computing Machinery, Case Western Reserve Univ; Assn. for [14076], Cleveland, OH
Computing Machinery, Illinois Inst. of Tech; Assn. for [743], Chicago, IL
Computing Machinery, Macalester Coll; Assn. for [12388], St. Paul, MN
Computing Machinery, Mount Vernon Nazarene Univ; Assn. for [16080], Mount Vernon, OH
Computing Machinery, Northern Michigan Univ; Assn. for [8933], Marquette, MI
Computing Machinery, Oberlin Coll; Assn. for [16280], Oberlin, OH
Computing Machinery; Ohio Univ. Chap. of the Assn. for [13213], Athens, OH
Computing Machinery SIGCHI; Southern Michigan Northern Ohio Assn. for [6770], Ann Arbor, MI
Computing Machinery Student Siggraph; Indiana Univ. Purdue Univ. Assn. for [5332], Indianapolis, IN
Computing Machinery; Univ. of Detroit-Mercy Assn. for [7448], Detroit, MI
Computing Machinery, Univ. of Evansville; Assn. for [4531], Evansville, IN
Computing Machinery, Walsh Coll; Assn. for [9976], Troy, MI
Concerned Black Men of Cook County Chicago [1710], Forest Park, IL
Concerned Black Men of Mansfield [15766], Mansfield, OH
Concerned Parents for Literacy [9063], Monroe, MI
Concerned Women for Am. - Illinois [2937], Palos Heights, IL
Concerns of Police Survivors, Minnesota Chap. [12225], Roseville, MN
Concord Lions Club - Michigan [7217], Concord, MI
Concrete
Illinois Ready Mixed Concrete Assn. [2719], Normal, IL
Minnesota Concrete Masonry Assn. [10597], Burnsville, MN
Northeast Ohio Concrete Promotion Council [16627], Seven Hills, OH
Ohio Ready Mixed Concrete Assn. [14665], Columbus, OH
Precast/Prestressed Concrete Inst., Central Region [13442], Brookville, OH
Wisconsin Concrete Masonry Assn. [19165], Milwaukee, WI
Wisconsin Concrete Pipe Assn. [19222], Montello, WI
Wisconsin Ready Mixed Concrete Assn. [18749], Madison, WI
Concrete Assn; Indiana Ready-Mixed [5288], Indianapolis, IN
Concrete Contractors of Michigan; Assoc. [8893], Madison Heights, MI
Concrete Coun; Indiana [★5288]
Concrete Masonry Assn; Minnesota [10597], Burnsville, MN
Concrete Paving Assn; Michigan [9276], Okemos, MI
Concrete Promotion Council; Northeast Ohio [16627], Seven Hills, OH

Condominiums Assn; Ohio Apartment and [★14538]
Conf. on Geriatric Care [★12487]
Conf. and Visitors Bur; Lenawee County [6577], Adrian, MI
Conflict Resolution
Dispute Resolution Assn. of Michigan [8565], Lansing, MI
Congregation Kneseth Israel [1585], Elgin, IL
Cong. of Illinois Historical Societies and Museums [★3641]
Conneaut Area Chamber of Commerce [14781], Conneaut, OH
Conneaut Historical Society [14782], Conneaut, OH
Connecting Bus. Men to Christ - Chicagoland [2217], Lansing, IL
Connecting Bus. Men to Christ - Elkhart [4491], Elkhart, IN
Connecting Bus. Men to Christ - Grand Rapids [7921], Grand Rapids, MI
Connecting Bus. Men to Christ - Indiana [5096], Indianapolis, IN
Connecting Bus. Men to Christ - Mid Michigan [9266], Okemos, MI
Connecting Bus. Men to Christ - Northland [12678], South St. Paul, MN
Connecting Bus. Men to Christ - Southeast Michigan [9796], Southfield, MI
Connersville - Fayette County Chamber of Commerce [4412], Connersville, IN
Connersville Lions Club [4413], Connersville, IN
Conservancy, Indiana Field Office; Nature [5437], Indianapolis, IN
Conservancy, Michigan Chapter Office; Nature [8747], Lansing, MI
Conservancy; Milwaukee Area Land [18171], Hales Corners, WI
Conservancy of Minnesota; Nature [11706], Minneapolis, MN
Conservancy; Shaw Land [16046], Minerva, OH
Conservancy; Trillium Land [4507], Elkhart, IN
Conservancy; Walworth County Land [17931], Elkhorn, WI
Conservancy, Wisconsin Field Off; Nature [18583], Madison, WI
Conservation
Acres Land Trust [4619], Fort Wayne, IN
Agassiz Audubon Soc. [12839], Warren, MN
Aldo Leopold Audubon Soc. [19777], Stevens Point, WI
Alliance for the Great Lakes [604], Chicago, IL
Amos W. Butler Audubon Soc. [5030], Indianapolis, IN
Anglers of the Au Sable [8058], Grayling, MI
Arrowhead Country Rsrc. Conservation and Development Coun. [6532], Winamac, IN
Ashtabula River Partnership [13181], Ashtabula, OH
Assn. of Illinois Soil and Water Conservation Districts [3538], Springfield, IL
Audubon Chap. of Minneapolis [11529], Minneapolis, MN
Audubon Coun. of Illinois [382], Byron, IL
Audubon Ohio [14334], Columbus, OH
Audubon Soc. of Ohio - Cincinnati Chap. [13756], Cincinnati, OH
Aullwood Audubon Center and Farm [14858], Dayton, OH
Black River Audubon Soc. [15109], Elyria, OH
Black Swamp Conservancy [16404], Perrysburg, OH
Blackbrook Audubon Soc. [15964], Mentor, OH
Blackhawk Hills Rsrc. Conservation and Development Coun. [3234], Rock Falls, IL
Brainerd Lakes Area Audubon Soc. [10507], Brainerd, MN
Canton Audubon Soc. [13555], Canton, OH
Cedar Lake Park Assn. [11540], Minneapolis, MN
Central Lake Superior Watershed Partnership [8934], Marquette, MI
Central Minnesota Audubon Soc. [12279], St. Cloud, MN
Champaign County Audubon Soc. [3811], Urbana, IL
Chequamegon Audubon Soc. [17586], Bayfield, WI
Chicagoland Environmental Network [351], Brookfield, IL
Citizens for a Scenic Wisconsin [20072], Wauwatosa, WI
Clark County Audubon Soc. [16723], Springfield, OH
Clark Lake Found. [7156], Clarklake, MI
Conservation Rsrc. Alliance [9926], Traverse City, MI
Decatur Audubon Soc. [1386], Decatur, IL
DeKalb County Farmland Found. [1432], DeKalb, IL
Detroit Audubon Soc. [9579], Royal Oak, MI
Door County Enval. Coun. [17962], Fish Creek, WI
Dowagiac Conservation Club [7479], Dowagiac, MI
Duluth Audubon Soc. [10814], Duluth, MN
Dunes Calumet Audubon Soc. [4856], Griffith, IN
Environmentally Concerned Citizens of Lakeland Area [19198], Minocqua, WI
Evansville Audubon Soc. [4544], Evansville, IN
Fargo-Moorhead Audubon Soc. [11824], Moorhead, MN
Firelands Audubon Soc. [16611], Sandusky, OH
Fond du Lac County Audubon Soc. [17977], Fond du Lac, WI
Four Rivers Rsrc. Conservation and Development Coun. [6036], Petersburg, IN
Friends of the Boundary Waters Wilderness [11564], Minneapolis, MN
Friends of the Conservatory [14438], Columbus, OH
Friends of the Fox [17496], Appleton, WI
Friends of the Fox River [1324], Crystal Lake, IL
Friends of Harrison Lake State Park [15188], Fayette, OH
Friends of the Lower Olentangy Watershed [14439], Columbus, OH
Friends of the Oak Park Conservatory [2809], Oak Park, IL
Friends of the Upper Mississippi River Refuges [12950], Winona, MN
Friends of Volo Bog [2062], Ingleside, IL
Friends of Wetlands [15112], Elyria, OH
Giziibii Rsrc. Conservation and Development Coun. [10416], Bemidji, MN
Glacierland Rsrc. Conservation and Development Coun. [18100], Green Bay, WI
GRASLand Conservancy [17608], Beloit, WI
Grass River Natural Area [6905], Bellaire, MI
Great Lakes Fishery Commn. [6702], Ann Arbor, MI
Great River Greening [12421], St. Paul, MN
Great Rivers Land Preservation Assn. [42], Alton, IL
Greater Mohican Audubon Society [13165], Ashland, OH
Green-Rock Audubon Soc. [17610], Beloit, WI
Green-Rock Audubon Soc. [18249], Janesville, WI
Hiawatha Valley Rsrc. Conservation and Development Coun. [12144], Rochester, MN
Historic Hoosier Hills Rsrc. Conservation and Development Coun. [6402], Versailles, IN
Hoosier Heartland Rsrc. Conservation and Development Coun. [5140], Indianapolis, IN
Hoy Audubon Soc. [19556], Racine, WI
Huron Pines Rsrc. Conservation and Development Coun. [8063], Grayling, MI
Illinois Assn. of Conservation Districts [4057], Woodstock, IL
Illinois Assn. for Floodplain and Stormwater Mgt. [2952], Park Forest, IL
Illinois Audubon Soc. [1349], Danville, IL
Illinois Native Plant Soc. [3976], Westville, IL
Indian Village Historical Colls. [7375], Detroit, MI
Indiana Assn. for Floodplain and Stormwater Mgt. [5172], Indianapolis, IN
Indiana Karst Conservancy [5252], Indianapolis, IN
Indiana Wildlife Fed. [4328], Carmel, IN
Interstate Rsrc. Conservation and Development Coun. [2490], Milan, IL
Izaak Walton League of Am. - A.D. Sutherland Chap. [17984], Fond du Lac, WI
Izaak Walton League of Am., Alexandria Chap. [4092], Alexandria, IN
Izaak Walton League of Am., Anthony Wayne Chap. [15387], Hamilton, OH
Izaak Walton League of Am., Austin Chap. [10355], Austin, MN
Izaak Walton League of Am. - Beloit [17611], Beloit, WI
Izaak Walton League of Am., Bill Cook Chap. [19792], Stevens Point, WI
Izaak Walton League of Am. - Blackhawk Chap. [1789], Geneseo, IL
Izaak Walton League of Am., Buckeye All-State Chap. [15388], Hamilton, OH
Izaak Walton League of Am., Bush Lake Chap. [11591], Minneapolis, MN
Izaak Walton League of Am., Calumet Region Chap. [394], Calumet City, IL
Izaak Walton League of Am., Champaign County Chap. [3826], Urbana, IL
Izaak Walton League of Am. - Chicago Chap. No. 1 [2219], Lansing, IL
Izaak Walton League of Am., Cincinnati Chap. [15726], Loveland, OH
Izaak Walton League of Am., Clinton Chap. [6151], St. Bernice, IN
Izaak Walton League of America, DeKalb County Chapter [4139], Auburn, IN
Izaak Walton League of Am., Delta Chap. [15017], Delta, OH
Izaak Walton League of Am. - Des Plaines Chap. [2916], Palatine, IL
Izaak Walton League of Am., Dry Fork Chap. [15389], Hamilton, OH
Izaak Walton League of America, Dwight Lydell Chapter [9525], Rockford, MI
Izaak Walton League of Am., Elgin Chap. [1593], Elgin, IL
Izaak Walton League of Am. - Evansville [5961], Newburgh, IN
Izaak Walton League of Am., Fairfield Chap. [15390], Hamilton, OH
Izaak Walton League of Am. - Fenton [7849], Grand Blanc, MI
Izaak Walton League of Am., Fort Wayne Chap. [4939], Huntertown, IN
Izaak Walton League of Am., Fremont Chap. [15248], Fremont, OH
Izaak Walton League of Am., Grant County Chap. [5735], Marion, IN
Izaak Walton League of Am. - Griffith [4884], Hammond, IN
Izaak Walton League of Am., Hamilton Chap. [15391], Hamilton, OH
Izaak Walton League of Am., Howard County Chap. [5571], Kokomo, IN
Izaak Walton League of America, Illinois Division [163], Bartlett, IL
Izaak Walton League of Am., Indiana Div. [6058], Portage, IN
Izaak Walton League of Am., Kewanee Chap. [3781], Toulon, IL
Izaak Walton League of Am., Labudde Memorial Chap. [19038], Milwaukee, WI
Izaak Walton League of Am., Lawrence County Chap. [16391], Pedro, OH
Izaak Walton League of Am., Lock City Chap. [9720], Sault Ste. Marie, MI
Izaak Walton League of Am., Medina Chap. [15942], Medina, OH
Izaak Walton League of America, Miami Chapter [6032], Peru, IN
Izaak Walton League of Am., Michigan Div. [9526], Rockford, MI
Izaak Walton League of Am. Midwest Off. [12432], St. Paul, MN
Izaak Walton League of America, Minneapolis Chapter [10469], Bloomington, MN
Izaak Walton League of America, Minnesota Division [12433], St. Paul, MN
Izaak Walton League of Am., Natl. Youth Convention Chap. [15392], Hamilton, OH
Izaak Walton League of Am., New London Chap. [11872], New London, MN
Izaak Walton League of Am., Peoria Chap. [2480], Metamora, IL
Izaak Walton League of Am., Porter County Chap. [4353], Chesterton, IN
Izaak Walton League of Am., Rochester Chap. [10614], Byron, MN
Izaak Walton League of Am., Sheboygan County Chap. [19697], Sheboygan, WI

Izaak Walton League of Am. - Southern Brown Conservation **[18163]**, Greenleaf, WI
Izaak Walton League of Am., Southwestern Chap. **[17621]**, Benton, WI
Izaak Walton League of Am., Tiffin-Seneca County Chap. **[16853]**, Tiffin, OH
Izaak Walton League of Am., W. J. McCabe Chap. **[10829]**, Duluth, MN
Izaak Walton League of Am., Wabash Chap. **[6425]**, Wabash, IN
Izaak Walton League of Am., Wadsworth Chap. **[17076]**, Wadsworth, OH
Izaak Walton League of Am., Walter Sherry Memorial Chap. **[2110]**, Joliet, IL
Izaak Walton League of America, Wapashaw Chapter **[12811]**, Wabasha, MN
Izaak Walton League of Am., Watertown Chap. **[19967]**, Watertown, WI
Izaak Walton League of Am. - Waukesha County **[17824]**, Delafield, WI
Izaak Walton League of Am., Wayne County Chap. **[17320]**, Wooster, OH
Izaak Walton League of Am. - Western Reserve **[17273]**, Willoughby, OH
Izaak Walton League of Am., Western Wisconsin Chap. **[19771]**, Spring Valley, WI
Izaak Walton League of Am. - Wisconsin Div. **[19483]**, Plover, WI
Jackson Audubon Soc. **[8371]**, Jackson, MI
John Wesley Powell Audubon Soc. **[293]**, Bloomington, IL
Knob and Valley Audubon Soc. **[5917]**, New Albany, IN
Lac Lawrann Conservancy of West Bend, WI **[20122]**, West Bend, WI
Lake County Audubon Soc. **[2261]**, Libertyville, IL
Lake Traverse Assn. Corp. **[12885]**, Wheaton, MN
Lakeland Audubon Soc. **[19918]**, Twin Lakes, WI
Land Conservancy of West Michigan **[7974]**, Grand Rapids, MI
Laurentian Rsrc. Conservation and Development Coun. **[10832]**, Duluth, MN
Lincoln Hills Rsrc. Conservation and Development Coun. **[4314]**, Cannelton, IN
Little Village Enval. Justice Org. **[1034]**, Chicago, IL
Long Lake Assn. **[9450]**, Portage, MI
Lower Long Lake Found. **[17883]**, Eau Claire, WI
Lumberjack Rsrc. Conservation and Development Coun. **[19598]**, Rhinelander, WI
Macatawa Greenway Partnership **[8209]**, Holland, MI
Madison Audubon Soc. **[18551]**, Madison, WI
Mahoning Valley Audubon Soc. **[17404]**, Youngstown, OH
McHenry County Audubon Soc. **[4060]**, Woodstock, IL
McHenry County Defenders **[4061]**, Woodstock, IL
Medina Summit Land Conservancy **[15950]**, Medina, OH
Michigan Assn. of Conservation Districts **[7047]**, Cadillac, MI
Michigan Audubon Soc. **[8632]**, Lansing, MI
Michigan Forest Assn. **[6725]**, Ann Arbor, MI
Michigan Natural Areas Coun. **[6732]**, Ann Arbor, MI
Michigan United Conservation Clubs **[8726]**, Lansing, MI
Midwest Enval. Advocates **[18562]**, Madison, WI
Mill Creek Watershed Coun. **[13907]**, Cincinnati, OH
Milwaukee Audubon Soc. **[17781]**, Colgate, WI
Minnesota Conservation Fed. **[12471]**, St. Paul, MN
Minnesota Div. - Izaak Walton League of Am. **[12479]**, St. Paul, MN
Minnesota Native Plant Soc. **[12499]**, St. Paul, MN
Minnesota River Valley Audubon Chap. **[10479]**, Bloomington, MN
Minnesota Valley Action Coun. **[11391]**, Mankato, MN
Mississippi Headwaters Audubon Soc. **[10420]**, Bemidji, MN
Mississippi Headwaters Bd. **[12833]**, Walker, MN
Natl. Audubon Soc. - East Central Ohio **[16175]**, Newark, OH
Natl. Audubon Soc. - Hunt Hill Audubon Sanctuary **[19663]**, Sarona, WI
Natl. Audubon Soc. - Washtenaw **[6745]**, Ann Arbor, MI
Natural Heritage Land Trust **[18582]**, Madison, WI
Nature Conservancy, Indiana Field Office **[5437]**, Indianapolis, IN
Nature Conservancy Michigan Chap., Ives Rd. Fen Preserve **[8746]**, Lansing, MI
Nature Conservancy, Michigan Chapter Office **[8747]**, Lansing, MI
Nature Conservancy of Minnesota **[11706]**, Minneapolis, MN
Nature Conservancy, Ohio Chap. **[15052]**, Dublin, OH
Nature Conservancy, Wisconsin Field Off. **[18583]**, Madison, WI
Northwest Illinois Audubon Soc. **[2980]**, Pearl City, IL
Ohio Land Improvement Contractors Assn. **[14631]**, Columbus, OH
Ohio League of Conservation Voters **[14633]**, Columbus, OH
Ohio Prairie Assn. **[15785]**, Mansfield, OH
Onanegozie-Land Rsrc. Conservation and Development Coun. **[11835]**, Mora, MN
Oxford Audubon Soc. **[16325]**, Oxford, OH
Park People of Milwaukee County **[19087]**, Milwaukee, WI
Patton's Woods Nature Preserve Comm. **[542]**, Champaign, IL
Pembina Trail Rsrc. Conservation and Development Coun. **[12073]**, Red Lake Falls, MN
Post Oak Flats Rsrc. Conservation and Development Coun. **[2091]**, Jerseyville, IL
Potawatomi Audubon Soc. **[5602]**, La Porte, IN
Potawatomi Rsrc. Conservation and Development Coun. **[8972]**, Marshall, MI
Prairie Country Rsrc. Conservation and Development Coun. **[12926]**, Willmar, MN
Prairie Hills Rsrc. Conservation and Development Coun. **[2375]**, Macomb, IL
Prairie Woods Audubon Soc. **[77]**, Arlington Heights, IL
Preserve the Dunes **[9493]**, Riverside, MI
Pres. R.B. Hayes Audubon Soc. **[15251]**, Fremont, OH
Pri-Ru-Ta Rsrc. Conservation and Development Coun. **[18848]**, Medford, WI
Prior Lake Assn. **[12055]**, Prior Lake, MN
Quad City Conservation Alliance **[3252]**, Rock Island, IL
Recreation for Individuals Dedicated to the Env. **[1165]**, Chicago, IL
River Country Rsrc. Conservation and Development Coun. **[17469]**, Altoona, WI
Roscoe Village Found. **[14804]**, Coshocton, OH
Saginaw Bay Rsrc. Conservation and Development Coun. **[6895]**, Bay City, MI
St. Joseph River Basin Commn. **[6260]**, South Bend, IN
St. Paul Audubon Soc. **[12726]**, Stillwater, MN
Sassafras Audubon Soc. **[4255]**, Bloomington, IN
Sauk Trails Rsrc. Conservation and Development Coun. **[8466]**, Kalamazoo, MI
Save the Dunes Coun. **[5794]**, Michigan City, IN
Shawnee Rsrc. Conservation and Development Coun. **[2410]**, Marion, IL
Sierra Club - Hoosier Chapter - Dunelands Group **[4930]**, Hobart, IN
Sierra Club - Illinois Chap. - Blackhawk Gp. **[3319]**, Rockford, IL
Sierra Club - Illinois Chap. - Chicago Gp. **[1183]**, Chicago, IL
Sierra Club - John Muir Chap. - Chippewa Valley Gp. **[17896]**, Eau Claire, WI
Sierra Club, Ohio Chap. **[14728]**, Columbus, OH
Sinnissippi Audubon Soc. **[3320]**, Rockford, IL
Soil and Water Conservation Soc. of Am. **[19806]**, Stevens Point, WI
Sokaogon-Chippewa Comm. **[17790]**, Crandon, WI
South Bend-Elkhart Audubon Soc. **[5813]**, Mishawaka, IN
Southwest Badger Rsrc. Conservation and Development Coun. **[19471]**, Platteville, WI
Southwestern Illinois Rsrc. Conservation and Development Coun. **[2432]**, Mascoutah, IL
Sustainable Racine **[19575]**, Racine, WI
Sycamore Audubon Soc. **[5634]**, Lafayette, IN
Sycamore Trails Rsrc. Conservation and Development Coun. **[4826]**, Greencastle, IN
Thorn Creek Audubon Soc. **[2956]**, Park Forest, IL
Timberland Rsrc. Conservation and Development Coun. **[7215]**, Comstock Park, MI
Tinkers Creek Land Conservancy **[17017]**, Twinsburg, OH
Tip of the Mitt Watershed Coun. **[9373]**, Petoskey, MI
Tippecanoe Audubon Soc. **[5801]**, Milford, IN
Tippecanoe Audubon Soc. **[5991]**, North Manchester, IN
Town and Country Rsrc. Conservation and Development Coun. **[20128]**, West Bend, WI
Tri-Moraine Audubon Soc. **[15671]**, Lima, OH
Trillium Land Conservancy **[4507]**, Elkhart, IN
Trout Unlimited - Ann Arbor Chap. 127 **[6776]**, Ann Arbor, MI
Trout Unlimited - Headwaters Chap. **[10039]**, Vanderbilt, MI
Trout Unlimited - Menominee Range Chap. **[8334]**, Iron River, MI
Univ. of Wisconsin, Milwaukee - Student Enval. Action Coalition **[19144]**, Milwaukee, WI
Upper Mississippi River Conservation Comm. **[3260]**, Rock Island, IL
Upper Peninsula Rsrc. Conservation and Development Coun. **[8963]**, Marquette, MI
Wabash Valley Audubon Soc. **[6349]**, Terre Haute, IN
Wabash Valley Rsrc. Conservation and Development Coun. **[2227]**, Lawrenceville, IL
Waupaca Conservation League **[20024]**, Waupaca, WI
WesMin Rsrc. Conservation and Development Coun. **[10287]**, Alexandria, MN
West Creek Preservation Comm. **[16379]**, Parma, OH
Western Cuyahoga Audubon Soc. **[14237]**, Cleveland, OH
Western Reserve Historical Soc. **[14238]**, Cleveland, OH
White River Rsrc. Conservation and Development Coun. **[4180]**, Bedford, IN
Wild River Audubon Soc. **[10638]**, Center City, MN
Winnebago Audubon Soc. **[19406]**, Oshkosh, WI
Wisconsin Conservation Cong. **[18686]**, Madison, WI
Wisconsin Energy Conservation Corp. **[18700]**, Madison, WI
Wisconsin Land and Water Conservation Assn. **[18719]**, Madison, WI
Wisconsin Metro Audubon Soc. **[18014]**, Franklin, WI
Wisconsin Stewardship Network **[18757]**, Madison, WI
Wisconsin Waterfowl Assn. **[18189]**, Hartland, WI
Wood-Land-Lakes Rsrc. Conservation and Development Coun. **[4132]**, Angola, IN
Zumbro Valley Audubon Soc. **[12199]**, Rochester, MN

Conservation Club; Dowagiac **[7479]**, Dowagiac, MI
Conservation Clubs; Michigan United **[8726]**, Lansing, MI
Conservation Cong; Wisconsin **[18686]**, Madison, WI
Conservation Districts; Michigan Assn. of **[7047]**, Cadillac, MI
Conservation Fed; Minnesota **[12471]**, St. Paul, MN
Conservation League; Waupaca **[20024]**, Waupaca, WI
Conservation Rsrc. Alliance **[9926]**, Traverse City, MI
Conservatory Alliance; Garfield Park **[901]**, Chicago, IL
Consortium for Entrepreneurship Educ. **[14413]**, Columbus, OH
Consortium of Hea.y and Immunized Communities **[16358]**, Parma, OH

Constitutional Law
Indiana Trial Lawyers Assn. **[5330]**, Indianapolis, IN

Construction
ACI Greater Michigan Chap. **[7650]**, Farmington Hills, MI

Aggregate Producers of Wisconsin **[18444]**, Madison, WI
Alliance of Constr. Mgt. Professionals, Detroit Area Chap. **[9569]**, Royal Oak, MI
Amer. Concrete Inst., Central Ohio Chap. **[14278]**, Columbus, OH
Amer. Soc. of Professional Estimators, Chicago Chap. **[3863]**, Villa Park, IL
Amer. Soc. of Professional Estimators, Cleveland/North Ohio Chap. **[14065]**, Cleveland, OH
Builders Exchange of Lansing and Central Michigan **[8556]**, Lansing, MI
Independent Constr. Equip. Builders Union **[2155]**, Kewanee, IL
Indiana Chap. Amer. Concrete Inst. **[4606]**, Fishers, IN
Indiana Constructors **[5216]**, Indianapolis, IN
Michigan Asphalt Paving Assn. **[8604]**, Lansing, MI
Minnesota Constr. Assn. **[11643]**, Minneapolis, MN
Natl. Assn. of Women in Constr., Detroit Chap. **[7698]**, Ferndale, MI
Natl. Assn. of Women in Constr., Grand Rapids Chap. **[7992]**, Grand Rapids, MI
Natl. Assn. of Women in Constr., Milwaukee Chap. **[19076]**, Milwaukee, WI
Natl. Assn. of Women in Constr., Region 4 **[15997]**, Middleburg Heights, OH
Natl. Assn. of Women in Constr., Toledo Chap. **[16936]**, Toledo, OH
Ohio Equip. Distributors Assn. **[15056]**, Dublin, OH
Constr. Assn. of Michigan **[6981]**, Bloomfield Hills, MI
Constr. Educ. Found; Ohio Valley **[16705]**, Springboro, OH
Constr. Labor-Mgt. Assn. **[18502]**, Madison, WI
Constr. Safety Coun. **[2005]**, Hillside, IL
Consulting
Assn. of Consultants to Nonprofits **[746]**, Chicago, IL
Consulting Engineers Coun. of Illinois **[3547]**, Springfield, IL
Consulting Engineers Coun. of Michigan **[★8530]**
Consulting Engineers Coun. of Minnesota **[★11784]**
Consulting Engineers Coun. of Ohio **[★14281]**
Consumer Affairs Professionals in Bus., Ohio Chap; Soc. of **[13089]**, Akron, OH
Consumer Affairs Professionals in Bus., Wisconsin Chap; Soc. of **[19275]**, Neenah, WI
Consumers
Better Bus. Bur. of Akron **[13046]**, Akron, OH
Better Bus. Bureau/Canton Regional and Greater West Virginia **[13549]**, Canton, OH
Better Bus. Bur. of Central Illinois **[3009]**, Peoria, IL
Better Bus. Bur. of Central Ohio **[14335]**, Columbus, OH
Better Bus. Bur. of Chicago and Northern Illinois **[763]**, Chicago, IL
Better Bus. Bur., Cleveland **[14082]**, Cleveland, OH
Better Bus. Bur. of Dayton/Miami Valley **[14861]**, Dayton, OH
Better Bus. Bur. of Detroit and Eastern Michigan **[9791]**, Southfield, MI
Better Bus. Bur. of Elkhart County **[4490]**, Elkhart, IN
Better Bus. Bur. of Mahoning Valley **[17393]**, Youngstown, OH
Better Bus. Bur. of Northeastern Indiana **[4644]**, Fort Wayne, IN
Better Bus. Bur. of Northwest Indiana **[5768]**, Merrillville, IN
Better Bus. Bur., Northwest Ohio and Southeastern Michigan **[16907]**, Toledo, OH
Better Bus. Bur. Serving Minnesota and North Dakota **[12392]**, St. Paul, MN
Better Bus. Bur. of West Central Ohio **[15650]**, Lima, OH
Better Bus. Bur. of Western Michigan **[7913]**, Grand Rapids, MI
Better Bus. Bur. of Wisconsin **[18981]**, Milwaukee, WI
Center for Consumer Affairs, Univ. of Wisconsin-Milwaukee **[18990]**, Milwaukee, WI
Central Indiana Better Bus. Bur. **[5071]**, Indianapolis, IN
Cincinnati Better Bus. Bur. **[13778]**, Cincinnati, OH
Citizens Action Coalition of Indiana **[5091]**, Indianapolis, IN
Citizens Action Coalition of Indiana - North Off. **[6226]**, South Bend, IN
Family Ser. Rochester **[12140]**, Rochester, MN
Indiana Indus. Energy Consumers **[5251]**, Indianapolis, IN
Michigan Consumer Fed. **[7537]**, East Lansing, MI
Tri-State Better Bus. Bur. **[4583]**, Evansville, IN
Consumers Alliance of Bloomington, Indiana; Funeral **[4219]**, Bloomington, IN
Contamination; Citizens for Alternatives to Chem. **[8501]**, Lake, MI
Continental Cricket Club **[11409]**, Maple Grove, MN
Continental Trucking Assn. **[18276]**, Johnson Creek, WI
Contractors
AGC of The Quad Cities **[3237]**, Rock Island, IL
Amer. Camp Assn., Wisconsin **[18454]**, Madison, WI
Amer. Line Builders Chap. Natl. Elecl. Contractors Assn. **[17058]**, Vandalia, OH
Amer. Subcontractors Assn.-Central Ohio Chap. **[16383]**, Pataskala, OH
Amer. Subcontractors Assn. of Cincinnati **[13737]**, Cincinnati, OH
Amer. Subcontractors Assn. of Greater Milwaukee **[18962]**, Milwaukee, WI
Amer. Subcontractors Assn. of Minnesota **[10302]**, Anoka, MN
Amer. Subcontractors Assn. of SE Michigan **[7693]**, Ferndale, MI
Asphalt Pavement Assn. of Indiana **[5038]**, Indianapolis, IN
Assoc. Builders and Contractors, Central Michigan Chap. **[8549]**, Lansing, MI
Assoc. Builders and Contractors Illinois Chap. **[1606]**, Elk Grove Village, IL
Assoc. Builders and Contractors of Indiana **[5040]**, Indianapolis, IN
Assoc. Builders and Contractors of Michigan **[8550]**, Lansing, MI
Assoc. Builders and Contractors Minnesota Chap. **[10889]**, Eden Prairie, MN
Assoc. Builders and Contractors Northern Michigan Chap. **[7817]**, Gaylord, MI
Assoc. Builders and Contractors-Northern Ohio Chap. **[13424]**, Broadview Heights, OH
Assoc. Builders and Contractors-Ohio Valley Chap. **[16704]**, Springboro, OH
Assoc. Builders and Contractors, Saginaw Valley Chap. **[9023]**, Midland, MI
Assoc. Builders and Contractors-Southeastern Michigan Chap. **[8892]**, Madison Heights, MI
Assoc. Builders and Contractors, Western Michigan Chap. **[7910]**, Grand Rapids, MI
Assoc. Builders and Contractors of Wisconsin **[18478]**, Madison, WI
Assoc. Concrete Contractors of Michigan **[8893]**, Madison Heights, MI
Assoc. Gen. Contractors of Am., Greater Detroit Chap. **[9786]**, Southfield, MI
Assoc. Gen. Contractors of Am. - Michigan Chap. **[8551]**, Lansing, MI
Assoc. Gen. Contractors - Central Illinois Chap. **[3535]**, Springfield, IL
Assoc. Gen. Contractors of Greater Milwaukee **[18966]**, Milwaukee, WI
Assoc. Gen. Contractors of Illinois **[3536]**, Springfield, IL
Assoc. Gen. Contractors of Indiana **[5041]**, Indianapolis, IN
Assoc. Gen. Contractors of Minnesota **[12386]**, St. Paul, MN
Assoc. Gen. Contractors of Ohio **[14318]**, Columbus, OH
Assoc. Gen. Contractors of Wisconsin **[18479]**, Madison, WI
Assoc. Underground Contractors-West Michigan Region **[9264]**, Okemos, MI
Assn. of Wisconsin Cleaning Contractors **[18973]**, Milwaukee, WI
Builders Assn. of the Twin Cities, Natl. Assn. of Home Building **[12223]**, Roseville, MN
Builders Exchange of St. Paul **[12395]**, St. Paul, MN
Building Indus. Assn. of North Central Ohio **[15764]**, Mansfield, OH
Building Indus. Assn. of South Central Ohio **[13662]**, Chillicothe, OH
Building Industry Association of Southeastern Michigan **[7656]**, Farmington Hills, MI
Building Indus. Assn. of Stark County **[16215]**, North Canton, OH
Central Illinois Chap. Natl. Elecl. Contractors Assn. **[3011]**, Peoria, IL
Central Illinois Chap. of Sheet Metal and Air Conditioning Contractors' Natl. Assn. **[3012]**, Peoria, IL
Central Indiana Chap. Natl. Elecl. Contractors Assn. **[5075]**, Indianapolis, IN
Central Ohio Air Conditioning Contractors of Am. **[15043]**, Dublin, OH
Central Ohio Chap., Natl. Elecl. Contractors Assn. **[14358]**, Columbus, OH
Dayton Builders Exchange **[14872]**, Dayton, OH
Dearborn County Home Builders Assn. **[5656]**, Lawrenceburg, IN
Decatur Assn. of Builders **[1384]**, Decatur, IL
Democratic Party of Wisconsin **[18504]**, Madison, WI
East Central Ohio Home Building Industry Association **[16042]**, Mineral City, OH
Eastern Illinois Chap. Natl. Elecl. Contractors Assn. **[2104]**, Joliet, IL
Elecl. Contractors' Assn. of City of Chicago **[3956]**, Westchester, IL
Elecl. Contractors Assn. - Milwaukee Chap. - NECA **[19004]**, Milwaukee, WI
Fox Valley Gen. Contractors Assn. **[3382]**, St. Charles, IL
Glenview Area Historical Soc. **[1864]**, Glenview, IL
Golden Sands Home Builders Assn. **[19482]**, Plover, WI
Great Lakes Fabricators and Erectors Assn. **[7367]**, Detroit, MI
Greater Cleveland Chap. Natl. Elecl. Contractors Assn. **[14129]**, Cleveland, OH
Greater Lansing Home Builders Assn. **[8574]**, Lansing, MI
Greater Michigan MSCA Student Chap. **[6945]**, Big Rapids, MI
Highland Park Historical Soc. **[1990]**, Highland Park, IL
Home Builders Association of Bay County **[6889]**, Bay City, MI
Home Builders Assn. of Central Michigan **[9106]**, Mount Pleasant, MI
Home Builders Assn. of Central Ohio **[17214]**, Westerville, OH
Home Builders Assn. of Fort Wayne **[4668]**, Fort Wayne, IN
Home Builders Assn. of the Grand Traverse Area **[9933]**, Traverse City, MI
Home Builders Assn. of Greater Chicago **[7]**, Addison, IL
Home Builders Assn. of Greater Cleveland **[15497]**, Independence, OH
Home Builders Assn. of Greater Fox Valley **[3383]**, St. Charles, IL
Home Builders Association of Greater Southwest Illinois **[2428]**, Maryville, IL
Home Builders Association of Greater Terre Haute **[6323]**, Terre Haute, IN
Home Builders Assn. of Greater Toledo **[15907]**, Maumee, OH
Home Builders Assn. of Illinois **[3559]**, Springfield, IL
Home Builders Assn. of Kankakee **[2132]**, Kankakee, IL
Home Builders Assn. of Lenawee County **[6570]**, Adrian, MI
Home Builders Assn. of Livingston County **[7013]**, Brighton, MI
Home Builders Association of Mecosta County **[6946]**, Big Rapids, MI
Home Builders Association of Metro Flint **[7845]**, Grand Blanc, MI
Home Builders Assn. of Miami County **[17000]**, Troy, OH

Home Builders Assn. of Muncie **[5877]**, Muncie, IN
Home Builders Assn. of Northwestern Ohio **[14988]**, Defiance, OH
Home Builders Assn. of Portage and Summit Counties **[13057]**, Akron, OH
Home Builders Assn. of Saginaw **[9609]**, Saginaw, MI
Home Builders Assn. of St. Joseph Valley **[5808]**, Mishawaka, IN
Home Builders Assn. of Southern Indiana **[4365]**, Clarksville, IN
Home Builders Assn. of Washington County **[15819]**, Marietta, OH
Home Builders Assn. of Washtenaw County **[6705]**, Ann Arbor, MI
Home Builders Assn. of Wayne and Holmes Counties **[17319]**, Wooster, OH
Illinois Assn. of Plumbing-Heating-Cooling Contractors **[3576]**, Springfield, IL
Illinois Chap. Natl. Elecl. Contractors Assn. **[3588]**, Springfield, IL
Illinois Landscape Contractors Educational and Charitable Org. **[2778]**, Oak Brook, IL
Illinois Manufactured Housing Assn. **[3614]**, Springfield, IL
Illinois Regional Insulation Contractors Assn. **[3438]**, Schaumburg, IL
Independent Elecl. Contractors, Central Ohio **[14466]**, Columbus, OH
Independent Elecl. Contractors of Greater Cincinnati **[13863]**, Cincinnati, OH
Independent Elecl. Contractors, Southern Indiana/ Evansville Chap. **[4551]**, Evansville, IN
Independent Elecl. Contractors, Western Reserve **[13374]**, Boardman, OH
Indiana Assn. of Plumbing, Heating, Cooling Contractors **[5179]**, Indianapolis, IN
Indiana Builders Assn. **[5200]**, Indianapolis, IN
Indiana Land Improvement Contractors Assn. **[5956]**, New Richmond, IN
Indiana Subcontractors Assn. **[5326]**, Indianapolis, IN
Intl. Interior Design Assn., Illinois Chap. **[1726]**, Frankfort, IL
Intl. Interior Design Assn., Indiana Chap. **[5377]**, Indianapolis, IN
Intl. Interior Design Assn., Michigan Chap. **[9801]**, Southfield, MI
Intl. Interior Design Assn., Wisconsin Chap. **[18531]**, Madison, WI
Lake County Illinois Genealogical Soc. **[2614]**, Mundelein, IL
Lakes Area Builders Assn. **[10774]**, Detroit Lakes, MN
Little Egypt Independent Elecl. Contractors **[234]**, Benton, IL
Madison Area Builders Association **[18544]**, Madison, WI
Madison Assn. of Plumbing Contractors **[18549]**, Madison, WI
Mason Contractors Assn. **[8845]**, Livonia, MI
Mason Contractors Assns. of Akron and Vicinity **[13064]**, Akron, OH
Master Electrical Contractors Independent Electrical Contractors of Dayton **[14906]**, Dayton, OH
Master Insulation Assn. of Greater Detroit **[9993]**, Troy, MI
Mech. Contractors Assn. **[14161]**, Cleveland, OH
Mech. Contractors Assn. of Central Indiana **[5400]**, Indianapolis, IN
Mech. Contractors Assn. of Central Ohio **[14497]**, Columbus, OH
Mech. Contractors Assn. Chicago **[1042]**, Chicago, IL
Mech. Contractors Assn. of Cincinnati **[13895]**, Cincinnati, OH
Mech. Contractors Assn. of Greater Dayton **[14908]**, Dayton, OH
Mech. Contractors Assn. of Indiana **[5401]**, Indianapolis, IN
Mech. and Plumbing Indus. Coun. **[14162]**, Cleveland, OH
Medina County Home Builders Assn. **[15948]**, Medina, OH
Michigan Assn. of Home Builders **[8618]**, Lansing, MI
Michigan Infrastructure and Trans. Assn. **[9283]**, Okemos, MI
Michigan Optometric Assn. **[8692]**, Lansing, MI
Michigan Roofing Contractors Assn. **[10071]**, Warren, MI
Michigan State Police Troopers Assn. **[7551]**, East Lansing, MI
Mid-Michigan Mech. Contractors Assn. **[8732]**, Lansing, MI
Mid-Minnesota Home Builders Association **[10513]**, Brainerd, MN
Mid-Shores Home Builders Assn. **[19307]**, New Holstein, WI
Midwest Independent Elecl. Contractors **[6166]**, Schererville, IN
Milwaukee Chap. of the Natl. Elecl. Contractors Assn. **[19057]**, Milwaukee, WI
Milwaukee School of Engg., Natl. Elecl. Contractors Assn. **[19068]**, Milwaukee, WI
Minneapolis Chap. Natl. Elecl. Contractors Assn. **[11612]**, Minneapolis, MN
Minnesota Mech. Contractors Assn. **[12497]**, St. Paul, MN
Minnesota Utility Contractors Assn. **[12981]**, Woodbury, MN
MMCA **[12534]**, St. Paul, MN
Natl. Assn. of Home Builders, Arrowhead Builders Assn. **[10842]**, Duluth, MN
Natl. Assn. of Home Builders, Building Authority of Greater Indianapolis **[5416]**, Indianapolis, IN
Natl. Assn. of Home Builders, Building Authority of Kosciusko-Fulton County **[6450]**, Warsaw, IN
Natl. Assn. of Home Builders, Building Authority of Minnesota **[12543]**, St. Paul, MN
Natl. Assn. of Home Builders, Mercer County Building Authority **[15226]**, Fort Recovery, OH
Natl. Assn. of Home Builders, Minnesota River Building Authority **[11393]**, Mankato, MN
Natl. Assn. of Home Builders, Union County Building Authority **[15864]**, Marysville, OH
Natl. Assn. of Home Builders of the U.S., Central Wisconsin Home Builders Assn. **[20188]**, Wisconsin Rapids, WI
Natl. Assn. of Home Builders of the U.S., Sheboygan County Home Builders Assn. **[19491]**, Plymouth, WI
Natl. Assn. of Home Builders of the U.S., Wausau Area Builders Assn. **[20041]**, Wausau, WI
Natl. Assn. of Home Builders of the U.S., Building Indus. Assn. of Northwest Indiana **[4436]**, Crown Point, IN
Natl. Assn. of Home Builders of the U.S., Central Minnesota Builders Assn. **[12294]**, St. Cloud, MN
Natl. Assn. of Home Builders of the U.S., Door County Home Builders Assn. **[19840]**, Sturgeon Bay, WI
Natl. Assn. of Home Builders of the U.S., Dubois County Builders Assn. **[5531]**, Jasper, IN
Natl. Assn. of Home Builders of the U.S., Hancock County Home Builders Assn. **[15210]**, Findlay, OH
Natl. Assn. of Home Builders of the U.S., Headwaters Builders Assn. **[10422]**, Bemidji, MN
Natl. Assn. of Home Builders of the U.S., Home Builders Assn. of Bloomington-Normal **[300]**, Bloomington, IL
Natl. Assn. of Home Builders of the U.S., Home Builders Assn. of Greater Cincinnati **[13920]**, Cincinnati, OH
Natl. Assn. of Home Builders of the U.S., Home Builders Assn. of Lawrence County **[6011]**, Oolitic, IN
Natl. Assn. of Home Builders of the U.S., Home Builders Assn. of the Upper Penninsula **[8954]**, Marquette, MI
Natl. Assn. of Home Builders of the U.S., Home and Building Assn. of Greater Grand Rapids **[7989]**, Grand Rapids, MI
Natl. Assn. of Home Builders of the U.S., La Crosse Area Builders Assn. **[19366]**, Onalaska, WI
Natl. Assn. of Home Builders of the U.S., Madison County Home Builders Assn. **[4114]**, Anderson, IN
Natl. Assn. of Home Builders of the U.S., Manitowoc County Home Builders Assn. **[18789]**, Manitowoc, WI
Natl. Assn. of Home Builders of the U.S., Mid Wisconsin Home Builders Assn. **[19509]**, Portage, WI
Natl. Assn. of Home Builders of the U.S., Monroe County Builders Assn. **[4247]**, Bloomington, IN
Natl. Assn. of Home Builders of the U.S., Northern Illinois Home Builders Assn. **[3877]**, Warrenville, IL
Natl. Assn. of Home Builders of the U.S., St. Croix Valley Home Builders Assn. **[19319]**, New Richmond, WI
Natl. Assn. of Home Builders of the U.S., South Central Home Builders Assn. **[2602]**, Mount Vernon, IL
Natl. Assn. of Home Builders of the U.S., Valley Home Builders Assn. **[17506]**, Appleton, WI
Natl. Assn. of Home Builders, Western Illinois Building Authority **[1778]**, Galesburg, IL
Natl. Assn. of Minority Contractors, Central Ohio **[14516]**, Columbus, OH
Natl. Assn. of Minority Contractors, Minnesota **[12983]**, Woodbury, MN
Natl. Assn. of Minority Contractors of Upper Midwest **[11695]**, Minneapolis, MN
Natl. Elecl. Contractors Assn., Cincinnati **[13925]**, Cincinnati, OH
Natl. Elecl. Contractors Assn., Michigan Chap. **[8741]**, Lansing, MI
Natl. Elecl. Contractors Assn., North Central Ohio Chap. **[13070]**, Akron, OH
Natl. Elecl. Contractors Assn. - Penn-Ohio Chap. **[17405]**, Youngstown, OH
Natl. Utility Contractors Assn. of Indiana **[5436]**, Indianapolis, IN
North Coast Building Indus. Assn. **[16652]**, Sheffield Village, OH
Northeastern Illinois Chap., Natl. Elecl. Contractors Assn. **[3941]**, West Chicago, IL
Northern Illinois Building Contractors Assn. **[3293]**, Rockford, IL
Northern Illinois Chap. Natl. Elecl. Contractors Assn. **[3294]**, Rockford, IL
Northern Indiana Chap., Natl. Elecl. Contractors Assn. **[5790]**, Michigan City, IN
Northern Ohio Electrical Contractors Association **[15590]**, Lakewood, OH
Northern Ohio Painting and Taping Contractors Assn. **[15998]**, Middleburg Heights, OH
Northland Area Builders Assn. **[18198]**, Hayward, WI
Ohio Florists' Assn. **[14610]**, Columbus, OH
Ohio Home Builders Assn. **[14625]**, Columbus, OH
Ohio State Assn. of Plumbing, Heating and Cooling Contractors **[13637]**, Chagrin Falls, OH
Ohio Subcontractors Coun. **[14687]**, Columbus, OH
Penn-Ohio Chap. Natl. Elecl. Contractors Assn. **[17410]**, Youngstown, OH
Plumbing-Heating-Cooling Contractors Wisconsin Assn. **[19095]**, Milwaukee, WI
Plumbing and Mech. Contractors of Detroit **[7420]**, Detroit, MI
Porter County Home Builders Assn. **[6388]**, Valparaiso, IN
Professional Photographers of Am. of Northern Illinois **[78]**, Arlington Heights, IL
St. Paul Chap. Natl. Elecl. Contractors Assn. **[12578]**, St. Paul, MN
Seneca County Home Builders Assn. **[16862]**, Tiffin, OH
South Central Wisconsin Builders Assn. **[18264]**, Janesville, WI
South Macomb Assn. of Plumbing Contractors **[8522]**, Lakeville, MI
Southeastern Michigan Chap., Natl. Elecl. Contractors Assn. **[9824]**, Southfield, MI
Southern Indiana Chap. Natl. Elecl. Contractors Assn. **[4575]**, Evansville, IN
Springfield Home Builders Assn. **[3678]**, Springfield, IL
Stephenson County Historical Soc. **[1754]**, Freeport, IL
Straits Area Home Builders Assn. **[7136]**, Cheboygan, MI
Subcontractors Assn. of Northeast Ohio **[13092]**, Akron, OH

Suburban Northwest Builders Assn. **[10949]**, Elk River, MN
Toledo Chap. Natl. Elecl. Contractors Assn. **[16558]**, Rossford, OH
Tri-County Contractors Assn. **[19578]**, Racine, WI
Twin Ports-Arrowhead Chap. Natl. Elecl. Contractors Assn. **[10857]**, Duluth, MN
Two Rivers Historical Soc. **[19920]**, Two Rivers, WI
Underground Contractors Assn. **[2070]**, Itasca, IL
Washtenaw Contractors Assn. **[6783]**, Ann Arbor, MI
Western Ohio Chap., Natl. Elecl. Contractors Assn. **[14970]**, Dayton, OH
Will-Grundy Home Builders Association **[1311]**, Crest Hill, IL
Wisconsin Chap. Natl. Elecl. Contractors Assn. **[18679]**, Madison, WI
Wisconsin Medical Soc. **[18726]**, Madison, WI
Wisconsin Underground Contractors Assn. **[19186]**, Milwaukee, WI
Contractors of Am; Central Ohio Air Conditioning **[15043]**, Dublin, OH
Contractors of Am., Greater Detroit Chap; Assoc. Gen. **[9786]**, Southfield, MI
Contractors Assn; Central Illinois Chap. Natl. Elecl. **[3011]**, Peoria, IL
Contractors Assn; Central Indiana Chap. Natl. Elecl. **[5075]**, Indianapolis, IN
Contractors Assn. of Central Indiana; Mech. **[5400]**, Indianapolis, IN
Contractors Assn. of Central Ohio; Mech. **[14497]**, Columbus, OH
Contractors Assn. Chicago; Mech. **[1042]**, Chicago, IL
Contractors Assn. of Evansville; Sheet Metal **[4572]**, Evansville, IN
Contractors Assn; Greater Cleveland Chap. Natl. Elecl. **[14129]**, Cleveland, OH
Contractors Assn., Greater Cleveland Chap; Natl. Elecl. **[14174]**, Cleveland, OH
Contractors Assn; Illinois Chap. Natl. Elecl. **[3588]**, Springfield, IL
Contractors Assn; Metropolitan Detroit Plumbing and Mech. **[★7420]**
Contractors Assn; Michigan Roofing **[10071]**, Warren, MI
Contractors Assn. - Milwaukee Chap. - NECA; Elecl. **[19004]**, Milwaukee, WI
Contractors Assn; Milwaukee School of Engg., Natl. Elecl. **[19068]**, Milwaukee, WI
Contractors; Assn. of Municipal **[★3536]**
Contractors Assn., North Central Ohio Chap; Natl. Elecl. **[13070]**, Akron, OH
Contractors Assn; Northeastern Illinois Sheet Metal **[1598]**, Elgin, IL
Contractors Assn; Northern Illinois Chap. Natl. Elecl. **[3294]**, Rockford, IL
Contractors Assn; Northern Ohio Painting and Taping **[15998]**, Middleburg Heights, OH
Contractors Assn; Penn-Ohio Chap. Natl. Elecl. **[17410]**, Youngstown, OH
Contractors Assn; Toledo Chap. Natl. Elecl. **[16558]**, Rossford, OH
Contractors Educational and Charitable Org; Illinois Landscape **[2778]**, Oak Brook, IL
Contractors; Fed. of Women **[891]**, Chicago, IL
Contractors of Illinois; Assoc. Gen. **[3536]**, Springfield, IL
Contractors of Indiana; Assoc. Gen. **[5041]**, Indianapolis, IN
Contractors; Indiana Assn. of Plumbing, Heating, Cooling **[5179]**, Indianapolis, IN
Contractors; Madison Assn. of Plumbing **[18549]**, Madison, WI
Contractors of Michigan; Assoc. Builders and **[8550]**, Lansing, MI
Contractors of Michigan; Assoc. Concrete **[8893]**, Madison Heights, MI
Contractors' Natl. Assn. of North Central Ohio; Sheet Metal and Air Conditioning **[14216]**, Cleveland, OH
Contractors-Ohio Valley Chap; Assoc. Builders and **[16704]**, Springboro, OH
Contractors; South Macomb Assn. of Plumbing **[8522]**, Lakeville, MI
Contractors of Upper Midwest; Natl. Assn. of Minority **[11695]**, Minneapolis, MN
Convention Bur; Anderson/Madison County Visitors and **[4100]**, Anderson, IN
Convention Bur; Clare County Visitor and **[7154]**, Clare, MI
Convention Bur; Greater Grand Rapids **[★7950]**
Convention Bur; Red Wing Visitors and **[12084]**, Red Wing, MN
Convention Bur; Wisconsin Dells Visitor and **[20181]**, Wisconsin Dells, WI
Convention Mgt. Assn., Greater Midwest Chap; Professional **[377]**, Burr Ridge, IL
Convention and Tourism Bur; Southern Indiana, Clark-Floyd Counties **[★5541]**
Convention and Tourist Bur; Jackson **[8373]**, Jackson, MI
Convention and Visitor Bur., Charlotte Chicago, Illinois; Intl. Assn. of **[980]**, Chicago, IL
Convention and Visitor Burs., Kansas City - Palatine, Illinois; Intl. Assn. of **[2914]**, Palatine, IL
Convention and Visitors Assn; Indianapolis **[5344]**, Indianapolis, IN
Convention and Visitors Bur; Albert Lea **[10252]**, Albert Lea, MN
Convention and Visitors Bur; Ann Arbor Area **[6669]**, Ann Arbor, MI
Convention and Visitors Bur; Bay Area **[6882]**, Bay City, MI
Convention and Visitors Bur; Bloomington **[4206]**, Bloomington, IN
Convention and Visitors Bur; Bloomington **[10465]**, Bloomington, MN
Convention and Visitors Bur; Boyne Country **[★9367]**
Convention and Visitors Bur; Collinsville **[1288]**, Collinsville, IL
Convention and Visitors Bur; Decatur Area **[1382]**, Decatur, IL
Convention and Visitors Bur; Elgin Area **[1588]**, Elgin, IL
Convention and Visitors Bur; Evansville **[4546]**, Evansville, IN
Convention and Visitors Bur; Fairmont **[10978]**, Fairmont, MN
Convention and Visitors Bur; Fort Wayne/Allen County **[4651]**, Fort Wayne, IN
Convention and Visitors Bur; Galesburg Area **[1772]**, Galesburg, IL
Convention and Visitors Bureau; Grand Haven-Spring Lake **[7858]**, Grand Haven, MI
Convention and Visitors Bur; Grant County **[★5739]**
Convention and Visitors Bur. of Greater Cleveland **[14107]**, Cleveland, OH
Convention and Visitors Bur; Greater Hamilton **[15385]**, Hamilton, OH
Convention and Visitors Bur; Greater Lafayette **[★5623]**
Convention and Visitors Bur; Greater Lansing **[8573]**, Lansing, MI
Convention and Visitors Bur; Greater Milwaukee **[★19148]**
Convention and Visitors Bur; Knox County **[16083]**, Mount Vernon, OH
Convention and Visitors Bur; Kosciusko County **[6446]**, Warsaw, IN
Convention and Visitors Bur; Lake Benton Area Chamber of Commerce and **[11270]**, Lake Benton, MN
Convention and Visitors Bur; Lake County **[4885]**, Hammond, IN
Convention and Visitors Bur; Lakeshore **[★9766]**
Convention and Visitors Bur; LaPorte County **[5785]**, Michigan City, IN
Convention and Visitors Bur; Livingston County **[8280]**, Howell, MI
Convention and Visitors Bur; Ludington Area **[8872]**, Ludington, MI
Convention and Visitors Bur; Marion-Grant County **[5739]**, Marion, IN
Convention and Visitors Bur; Marshall County **[6048]**, Plymouth, IN
Convention and Visitors Bur; Mecosta County **[6948]**, Big Rapids, MI
Convention and Visitors Bur; Medina County **[15946]**, Medina, OH
Convention and Visitors Bur; Middletown **[16014]**, Middletown, OH
Convention and Visitors Bur; Minneapolis Metro North **[11615]**, Minneapolis, MN
Convention and Visitor's Bur; Orange County **[4764]**, French Lick, IN
Convention and Visitor's Bureau; Perry County **[6298]**, Tell City, IN
Convention and Visitors Bur; Rochester **[12176]**, Rochester, MN
Convention and Visitors Bur; Rockford Area **[3307]**, Rockford, IL
Convention and Visitors Bur; South Bend/Mishawaka **[6268]**, South Bend, IN
Convention and Visitors Bur. of the Thunder Bay Region **[★6639]**
Convention and Visitors Bur; Vinton County **[15928]**, McArthur, OH
Convention and Visitors Bur; Washington County **[20129]**, West Bend, WI
Convention and Visitors Bur; Western U.P. **[8343]**, Ironwood, MI
Convention and Visitors Bureau; Wisconsin Rapids Area **[20197]**, Wisconsin Rapids, WI
Convention and Visitors Commission; Howard County **[5568]**, Kokomo, IN
Cook Area Chamber of Commerce **[10705]**, Cook, MN
Cook County Bar Assn. **[856]**, Chicago, IL
Cook County Chamber of Commerce **[3955]**, Westchester, IL
Cook Lions Club **[10706]**, Cook, MN
Cooling Contractors; Indiana Assn. of Plumbing, Heating, **[5179]**, Indianapolis, IN
Coolville Lions Club **[14786]**, Coolville, OH
Coon Rapids Cardinal Lions Club **[10708]**, Coon Rapids, MN
Coon Rapids Lions Club **[10709]**, Coon Rapids, MN
Coon Valley Lions Club **[17785]**, Coon Valley, WI
Cooperative for Educ. **[13809]**, Cincinnati, OH
Cooperative for Educal. Development **[★13809]**
Cooperative Extension
Epsilon Sigma Phi, Alpha Lambda **[6381]**, Valparaiso, IN
Epsilon Sigma Phi, NC Alpha PSI - Michigan **[9433]**, Port Huron, MI
Cooperatives
Minnesota Assn. of Cooperatives **[12453]**, St. Paul, MN
Wisconsin Elec. Cooperative Assn. **[18699]**, Madison, WI
Wisconsin Fed. of Cooperatives **[18704]**, Madison, WI
Cooperatives; Michigan Alliance of **[6971]**, Blanchard, MI
Cooperatives; Wisconsin Fed. of **[18704]**, Madison, WI
Coopersville Area Chamber of Commerce **[7223]**, Coopersville, MI
Copley - Young Life **[17074]**, Wadsworth, OH
Copper Country Community Arts Coun. **[8107]**, Hancock, MI
Copper Country Cycling Club **[8250]**, Houghton, MI
Copper Country Habitat for Humanity **[8251]**, Houghton, MI
Copper Country Rock and Mineral Club **[8108]**, Hancock, MI
Copper Country United Way **[8252]**, Houghton, MI
Copper County District Dental Soc. **[8109]**, Hancock, MI
Corbeau Ski Club **[13810]**, Cincinnati, OH
Corcoran Lions Club **[10720]**, Corcoran, MN
Core Mfg. Credit Assn; Natl. Radiator **[★11688]**
CoreNet Global - Chicago Chap. **[857]**, Chicago, IL
Corn Belt Philatelic Soc. **[276]**, Bloomington, IL
Corn Growers Assn; Ohio **[15848]**, Marion, OH
Cornbelt Professional Photographers Assn. **[12134]**, Rochester, MN
Cornerstone Aviation Sers. **[★8866]**
Corp. for Natl. and Community Ser. - Kansas **[858]**, Chicago, IL
Corp. for Natl. and Community Ser. - Missouri **[11550]**, Minneapolis, MN
Corp. for Natl. and Community Ser. - Oklahoma **[14414]**, Columbus, OH
Corp. for Natl. and Community Ser. - Wisconsin **[18997]**, Milwaukee, WI
Corps Assn; Madison Drum and Bugle **[19860]**, Sun Prairie, WI
Correctional
Correctional Educ. Assn. - Region III **[15693]**, London, OH

Macomb County Deputies and Dispatchers Association [9088], Mount Clemens, MI
Michigan Corrections Org. [8651], Lansing, MI
Correctional Educ. Assn. - Region III [15693], London, OH
Cortland Lions Club [14789], Cortland, OH
Corvair Minnesota [12332], St. Louis Park, MN
Corvette Club of Michigan [9513], Rochester Hills, MI
Corvette Restorers Soc., Indiana Chap; Natl. [4154], Avon, IN
Corvette Restorers Soc., North Central Chap; Natl. [11343], Long Lake, MN
Corvette Restorers Soc., Wisconsin Chap; Natl. [19829], Stoughton, WI
Corvette Troy [16999], Troy, OH
Corydon Noon Lions Club [4419], Corydon, IN
Corydon Palmer Dental Soc. [17395], Youngstown, OH
Cos Community Development Corp. [13811], Cincinnati, OH
Coshocton Area Chamber of Commerce [★14799]
Coshocton Chamber of Commerce [★14799]
Coshocton Co REACT [14796], Coshocton, OH
Coshocton County ALU [14797], Coshocton, OH
Coshocton County Bd. of Realtors [14798], Coshocton, OH
Coshocton County Chamber of Commerce [14799], Coshocton, OH
Coshocton Friends of the Lib. [14800], Coshocton, OH
Coshocton Lions Club [14801], Coshocton, OH
Cosmetology
NCA of Illinois [1091], Chicago, IL
Cosmology
Nation Coun. for GeoCosmic Res., Madison Chap. [18571], Madison, WI
Nation Coun. for GeoCosmic Res., Ohio Valley Chap. [13913], Cincinnati, OH
Nation Coun. for GeoCosmic Res., Southwest Suburban Chicago Chap. [1963], Hazel Crest, IL
Natl. Coun. for Geocosmic Res., STARS Chap. [12549], St. Paul, MN
Cosmopolitan Chamber of Commerce [859], Chicago, IL
Cosmos Cricket Club [10318], Apple Valley, MN
Cosmos Lions Club [11326], Litchfield, MN
Cottage Grove Area Chamber of Commerce [10726], Cottage Grove, MN
Coulee Kennel Club [11263], La Crescent, MN
Coulee Region Audubon Soc. [18341], La Crosse, WI
Coulee Region Orchid Guild [18342], La Crosse, WI
Coulee Region RSVP [18343], La Crosse, WI
Coulee Region Woodturners [19363], Onalaska, WI
Coulee Rock Club Of Lacrosse [11264], La Crescent, MN
Coun. for Adult and Experiential Learning [860], Chicago, IL
Coun. Against Domestic Assault [★8566]
Coun. on Alcohol and Other Drug Abuse of Washington County [20117], West Bend, WI
Coun. on Crime and Justice [11551], Minneapolis, MN
Council for Disability Rights [861], Chicago, IL
Coun. for Exceptional Children, Illinois [862], Chicago, IL
Coun. for Exceptional Children, Indiana [4648], Fort Wayne, IN
Coun. for Exceptional Children, Ohio [14415], Columbus, OH
Coun. for Exceptional Children, Wisconsin [17872], Eau Claire, WI
Coun. For Jewish Elderly [863], Chicago, IL
Coun. of Govts; Madison County [4110], Anderson, IN
Coun. of Great Lakes Governors [864], Chicago, IL
Coun. of Michigan Foundations [7856], Grand Haven, MI
Coun. of Residential Specialists, Ohio Chap. [14416], Columbus, OH
Coun. of Small Bus. Executives [18998], Milwaukee, WI
Coun. of State Governments Midwestern Off. [2330], Lombard, IL
Coun. of Volunteers and Orgs. for Hoosiers with Disabilities [5097], Indianapolis, IN
Counseling
Amer. Counseling Assn., Illinois [1473], Dixon, IL
Amer. Counseling Assn., Indiana [4981], Indianapolis, IN
Amer. Counseling Assn., Ohio [13514], Canal Winchester, OH
Community Marriage Builders [4536], Evansville, IN
Michigan Counseling Assn. [8653], Lansing, MI
Counseling for the Arts; Resources and [★12593]
Counselors Assn; Michigan Mental Hea. [9506], Rochester, MI
Counselors; Ohio Assn. of Alcoholism and Drug Abuse [14541], Columbus, OH
Counselors of Real Estate, Chesapeake Chap. [2962], Park Ridge, IL
Counselors of Real Estate, Midwest Chap. [473], Cary, IL
Counselors of Real Estate, Minnesota Chap. [11552], Minneapolis, MN
Counselors of Real Estate, Ohio/Kentucky Chap. [14417], Columbus, OH
Counties; Assn. of Indiana [5047], Indianapolis, IN
Counties; Assn. of Minnesota [12389], St. Paul, MN
Counties Coun. of Illinois; Urban [★3693]
Country Dancing in Kalamazoo [8425], Kalamazoo, MI
Country Music
Urbana Country Dancers [558], Champaign, IL
Country Music Assn; Illinois [1514], Downs, IL
Country Quilters Society of McHenry [2457], McHenry, IL
Countryside Lions Club [1305], Countryside, IL
County Commissioners' Assn. of Ohio [14418], Columbus, OH
County Engineers Assn. of Ohio [14419], Columbus, OH
County Fair Assn; Waukesha [19445], Pewaukee, WI
County Government
Assn. of Indiana Counties [5047], Indianapolis, IN
Assn. of Minnesota Counties [12389], St. Paul, MN
County Commissioners' Assn. of Ohio [14418], Columbus, OH
Township Officials of Illinois [3689], Springfield, IL
United Counties Coun. of Illinois [3693], Springfield, IL
Wisconsin Counties Assn. [18693], Madison, WI
County Line - Wyldlife [17075], Wadsworth, OH
County of Mecosta Development Corp. [6944], Big Rapids, MI
County Road Assn. of Michigan [8563], Lansing, MI
County Treasurers Assn. of Ohio [14420], Columbus, OH
Court Appointed Special Advocates of Grant County [5729], Marion, IN
Court Employees
Illinois Court Reporters Assn. [2597], Mount Vernon, IL
Michigan Assn. of Professional Court Rpt.ers [7745], Flint, MI
Michigan Assn. of Professional Court Reporters [9381], Pinckney, MI
Minnesota Assn. of Verbatim Reporters and Captioners [11437], Marshall, MN
Ohio Court Reporters Assn. [15054], Dublin, OH
Wisconsin Court Reporters Assn. [18694], Madison, WI
Covered Bridge Girl Scout Coun. [6318], Terre Haute, IN
Covert Township Lions Club [7227], Covert, MI
Cowboys Association; Wisconsin Rodeo [19907], Tomah, WI
Crafts
Amer. Sewing Guild, Chicago Chap. [1914], Gurnee, IL
Amer. Sewing Guild, Cincinnati Chap. [15353], Greenhills, OH
Amer. Sewing Guild, Detroit Chap. [9970], Troy, MI
Amer. Sewing Guild, Evansville Chap. [4524], Evansville, IN
Amer. Sewing Guild, Grand Rapids Chap. [9016], Middleville, MI
Amer. Sewing Guild, Indianapolis Chap. [5604], Ladoga, IN
Amer. Sewing Guild, Lansing Chap. [9262], Okemos, MI
Amer. Sewing Guild, Milwaukee Chap. [20114], West Bend, WI
Amer. Sewing Guild, Minneapolis/St. Paul Chap. [11515], Minneapolis, MN
Amer. Sewing Guild, North Olmsted Chap. [13344], Berea, OH
Ayla's Originals Intl. Bead Bazaar [1651], Evanston, IL
Bluewater Area Woodturners [8799], Lenox, MI
Buckeye Woodworkers and Turners [16549], Rootstown, OH
Central Illinois Woodturners [3217], Roanoke, IL
Central Ohio Woodturners [17343], Worthington, OH
Chicago Woodturners [2752], Northbrook, IL
Coulee Region Woodturners [19363], Onalaska, WI
Michigan Assn. of Woodturners [7016], Brighton, MI
Michigan Detroit Area Woodturners [9997], Troy, MI
Minn-Dak Woodturners [11825], Moorhead, MN
Minnesota Woodturners Assn. [10297], Andover, MN
North Coast Woodturners [13074], Akron, OH
Northern Illinois Woodturners [3297], Rockford, IL
Ohio Designer Craftsmen [14595], Columbus, OH
Craftsmen of Porter County; Assn. of Artists and [4351], Chesterton, IN
Cranbrook Peace Found. [6982], Bloomfield Hills, MI
Crandon Area Chamber of Commerce [17789], Crandon, WI
Crawford County Chamber of Commerce [5664], Leavenworth, IN
Crawford County Genealogical Soc. [3219], Robinson, IL
Crawford County Habitat for Humanity [3220], Robinson, IL
Crawford County United Way, Michigan [8059], Grayling, MI
Crawford/Perry/Spencer RSVP [6296], Tell City, IN
Crawfordsville - Montgomery County Chamber of Commerce [4425], Crawfordsville, IN
Creameries Assn; Wisconsin [★18914]
Creating Hope [4603], Fishers, IN
Creation
Creation Educ. Assn. [19455], Pine River, WI
Creation Educ. Assn. [19455], Pine River, WI
Creative Arts Repertoire Ensemble [7922], Grand Rapids, MI
Creative Change Educal. Solutions [10202], Ypsilanti, MI
Creative Housing Alternative of Minnesota [12118], Robbinsdale, MN
Creative Network of West Michigan [9142], Muskegon, MI
Credit
Credit Professionals Intl. of Ann Arbor [6692], Ann Arbor, MI
Credit Professionals Intl., Goshen [4793], Goshen, IN
Credit Professionals Intl., Illiana [4777], Gary, IN
Credit Professionals Intl., West Central Illinois [2519], Moline, IL
Indiana Assn. of Credit Mgt. [5169], Indianapolis, IN
Michigan Credit Union League [9402], Plymouth, MI
Natl. Assn. of Credit Mgt. - Chicago/Midwest [3340], Rolling Meadows, IL
Ohio Credit Union League [15055], Dublin, OH
Credit Assn; Natl. Radiator Core Mfg. [★11688]
Credit Assn; Natl. Radiator Mfg. [★11688]
Credit Mgt. - Western Michigan; Natl. Assn. of [10191], Wyoming, MI
Credit Professionals Intl. of Ann Arbor [6692], Ann Arbor, MI
Credit Professionals Intl., Goshen [4793], Goshen, IN
Credit Professionals Intl., Illiana [4777], Gary, IN
Credit Professionals Intl., West Central Illinois [2519], Moline, IL
Credit Unions
Community Choice Fed. Credit Union, Indianapolis, Indiana [5095], Indianapolis, IN

Illinois Credit Union League [2640], Naperville, IL
Indiana Credit Union League [5222], Indianapolis, IN
Minnesota Credit Union Network [12473], St. Paul, MN
Wisconsin Credit Union League [19447], Pewaukee, WI
Crestline Area United Way [14808], Crestline, OH
Crestline Lions Club - Ohio [14809], Crestline, OH
Creston Lions Club [14813], Creston, OH
Crestwood Lions Club [15799], Mantua, OH
Crete Area Chamber of Commerce [1314], Crete, IL
Crete Lions Club [1315], Crete, IL
Cricket
Aga Khan Gymkhana Cricket Club [3966], Westmont, IL
All Stars Cricket Club [12348], St. Paul, MN
Anaconda Cricket Club [10535], Brooklyn Center, MN
Anjuman Cricket Club [2740], Norridge, IL
Bears Cricket Club [2789], Oak Forest, IL
Bhakta Cricket Club [10724], Cottage Grove, MN
Continental Cricket Club [11409], Maple Grove, MN
Cosmos Cricket Club [10318], Apple Valley, MN
Eagles Cricket Club [3434], Schaumburg, IL
Flames Cricket Club [894], Chicago, IL
Hyderabad Decan Cricket Club [923], Chicago, IL
Illinois Cricket Club [939], Chicago, IL
Jaguars Cricket Club [2817], Oak Park, IL
Kaiteur Sports Club [12641], Savage, MN
Lions Cricket Club [12110], Richfield, MN
Midwest Cricket Conf. [1669], Evanston, IL
Milwaukee Cricket Club [17692], Brown Deer, WI
Milwaukee Rookie Cricket Club [19292], New Berlin, WI
Minnesota Cricket Club [10476], Bloomington, MN
Minnesota Falcons Cricket Club [11648], Minneapolis, MN
Minnesota Gymkhana Cricket Club [10868], Eagan, MN
Minnesota Intl. Cricket Club [10553], Brooklyn Park, MN
Minnesota Lakers Cricket Club [10869], Eagan, MN
Minnesota Northstar Cricket Club [11793], Minnetonka, MN
Muslim Gymkhana [2570], Morton Grove, IL
North Shore Cricket Club [1103], Chicago, IL
Pak Gymkhana [1119], Chicago, IL
Polo Cricket Club [1853], Glendale Heights, IL
Rams Cricket Club [11730], Minneapolis, MN
Rogers Park Cricket Club [164], Bartlett, IL
Tiger Cricket Club [3451], Schaumburg, IL
United Cricket Club [3345], Rolling Meadows, IL
Wildcats Cricket Club [3453], Schaumburg, IL
Windians Cricket Club [10929], Edina, MN
Crime
Alliance of Guardian Angels, Cincinnati [13697], Cincinnati, OH
Alliance of Guardian Angels, Fostoria [15227], Fostoria, OH
Alliance of Guardian Angels, Green Bay [18073], Green Bay, WI
Blue Earth Area Mentors [10497], Blue Earth, MN
Coun. on Crime and Justice [11551], Minneapolis, MN
Indiana Crime Prevention Coalition [5223], Indianapolis, IN
Michigan Coun. on Crime and Delinquency [8652], Lansing, MI
Williams County Area Crime Stoppers [16064], Montpelier, OH
Crime and Delinquency; Michigan Coun. on [8652], Lansing, MI
Crime Stoppers; Portage County [19801], Stevens Point, WI
Crime Stoppers; Williams County Area [16064], Montpelier, OH
Criminal Apprehension Agents' Assn; Minnesota Bur. of [12461], St. Paul, MN
Criminal Defense Lawyers; Illinois Assn. of [927], Chicago, IL
Criminal Justice
Illinois Assn. of Criminal Defense Lawyers [927], Chicago, IL
Minnesota Bur. of Criminal Apprehension Agents' Assn. [12461], St. Paul, MN
Transition of Prisoners [7442], Detroit, MI
Wisconsin Assn. of Criminal Defense Lawyers [19211], Monona, WI
Critical Care
Amer. Assn. of Critical Care Nurses, Greater Chicago Area Chap. [607], Chicago, IL
Amer. Assn. of Critical Care Nurses, Greater Cincinnati Chap. [13702], Cincinnati, OH
Amer. Assn. of Critical-Care Nurses, Greater Toledo Area Chap. [16875], Toledo, OH
Amer. Assn. of Critical Care Nurses, Northeast Indiana Chap. [4624], Fort Wayne, IN
Critical-Care Nurses, Lake Superior Chap; Amer. Assn. of [9176], Negaunee, MI
Crohn's and Colitis Found. of Am., Central Ohio Chap. [14421], Columbus, OH
Crohn's and Colitis Found. of Am., Illinois Carol Fisher Chap. [1456], Des Plaines, IL
Crohn's and Colitis Found. of Am., Indiana Chap. [5098], Indianapolis, IN
Crohn's and Colitis Found. of Am., Michigan Chap. [7658], Farmington Hills, MI
Crohn's and Colitis Found. of Am. Midwest Region [★1456]
Crohn's and Colitis Found. of Am., Wisconsin Chap. [20100], West Allis, WI
Crohn's and Colitis Found. of Amer., Southwest Ohio Chap. [13812], Cincinnati, OH
Crooked Creek Conservation and Gun Club [5970], Noblesville, IN
Crookston Area Chamber of Commerce [★10733]
Crookston Convention and Visitors Bur. [10733], Crookston, MN
Crookston Dawn To Dusk Lions Club [10734], Crookston, MN
Crookston Figure Skating Club [10735], Crookston, MN
Crookston Lions Club [10736], Crookston, MN
Crop [★11545]
CROP, Indiana-Kentucky; Church World Service/ [5087], Indianapolis, IN
CROP, Minn-Kota Region; Church World Service/ [11545], Minneapolis, MN
Crop, Wisconsin-Northern Illinois Region; Church World Ser./ [★18496]
CROP, Wisconsin Region; Church World Ser./ [18496], Madison, WI
Crosby Township Historical Soc. [15407], Harrison, OH
Cross Plains Lions Club [17793], Cross Plains, WI
Cross; Waseca County Chap., Amer. Red [12849], Waseca, MN
Crosslake-Ideal Lions Club [10742], Crosslake, MN
Crossroads Donkey Rescue [9233], Novi, MI
Crosstown African Violet Club [17939], Elroy, WI
Crow River Area Youth for Christ [11327], Litchfield, MN
Crow River Habitat for Humanity [11206], Hutchinson, MN
Crow Wing County Genealogical Soc. [10510], Brainerd, MN
Crow Wing County United Way [10511], Brainerd, MN
Crusaders for Kids [2479], Metamora, IL
Crystal Ice Figure Skating Club [19787], Stevens Point, WI
Crystal Lake Chamber of Commerce [1320], Crystal Lake, IL
Crystal Lake Historical Soc. [1321], Crystal Lake, IL
Crystal Lake Lions Club [1322], Crystal Lake, IL
Crystal Lions Club [10573], Buffalo, MN
Crystal Lions Club - Michigan [7230], Crystal, MI
CSCI [★2005]
Cuba City Chamber of Commerce [17795], Cuba City, WI
Cuba City Community Development Corp. [17796], Cuba City, WI
Cuckoos, Metropolitan Detroit Tent of the Intl. Sons of the Desert; Dancing [7063], Canton, MI
Cudahy Historical Soc. [17798], Cudahy, WI
Cudahy Kennel Club [19657], St. Francis, WI
Cultivators; Community [1635], Elsah, IL
Cultural Alliance; Prairie Renaissance [11840], Morris, MN
Cultural Assn; Fairborn Performing Arts and [15149], Fairborn, OH
Cultural Center; Swedish Museum and [★1205]
Cultural Centers
Northwest Cultural Coun. [3341], Rolling Meadows, IL
Cultural Coun; Northwest [3341], Rolling Meadows, IL
Cultural Exchange
Assn. of Colombians of Michigan [9787], Southfield, MI
Sister Cities Assn. of Greater Cincinnati [13989], Cincinnati, OH
Cultural Resources
Illinois Heritage Assn. [527], Champaign, IL
Prairie Renaissance Cultural Alliance [11840], Morris, MN
Sheridan Chamber Players [1674], Evanston, IL
Culver Chamber of Commerce [4438], Culver, IN
Cumberland Chamber of Commerce [17799], Cumberland, WI
Cumberland PTA [17800], Cumberland, WI
Curl Mesabi [12794], Virginia, MN
Curling
Alpine Curling Club [19212], Monroe, WI
Appleton Curling Club [17486], Appleton, WI
Bemidji Curling Club [10407], Bemidji, MN
Blackhawk Curling Club [18244], Janesville, WI
Centerville Curling Club [19913], Trempealeau, WI
Chicago Curling Club [2751], Northbrook, IL
Cleveland Skating Club [16634], Shaker Heights, OH
Curl Mesabi [12794], Virginia, MN
Duluth Curling Club [10817], Duluth, MN
Eau Claire Curling Club [17876], Eau Claire, WI
Great Lakes Curling Assn. [13635], Chagrin Falls, OH
Great Lakes Curling Assn. - Bowling Green Curling Club [13391], Bowling Green, OH
Great Lakes Curling Assn. - Copper Country Curling Club [7056], Calumet, MI
Great Lakes Curling Assn. - Delta Rocks Curling Club [7830], Gladstone, MI
Great Lakes Curling Assn. - Detroit Curling Club [7694], Ferndale, MI
Great Lakes Curling Assn. - Lewiston Curling Club [6803], Atlanta, MI
Great Lakes Curling Assn. - Mayfield Curling Club [16691], South Euclid, OH
Great Lakes Curling Assn. - Midland Curling Club [9025], Midland, MI
Great Lakes Curling Assn. - Newark Curling Club [16169], Newark, OH
Green Bay Curling Club [18105], Green Bay, WI
Illinois Curling Assn. [2198], Lake Forest, IL
Illinois Curling Assn. - Exmoor Curling Club [1992], Highland Park, IL
Illinois Curling Assn. - Indian Hill Curling Club [4037], Winnetka, IL
Illinois Curling Assn. - North Shore Curling Club [1869], Glenview, IL
Illinois Curling Assn. - Oak Park Curling Club [3203], River Forest, IL
Illinois Curling Assn. - Waltham Curling Club [3785], Triumph, IL
Itasca Curling Club [11089], Grand Rapids, MN
Lakes Curling Club [10777], Detroit Lakes, MN
Madison Curling Club [18840], McFarland, WI
Medford Curling Club [18845], Medford, WI
Minnesota State Curling Assn. - Caledonian Curling Club [11390], Mankato, MN
Minnesota State Curling Assn. - Curl Mesabi [12799], Virginia, MN
Minnesota State Curling Assn. - St. Paul Curling Club [12526], St. Paul, MN
Minnesota State Curling Assn. - Two Harbors Curling Club [12772], Two Harbors, MN
Portage Curling Club [19514], Portage, WI
Racine Curling Club [19568], Racine, WI
Superior Curling Club [19878], Superior, WI
Tri-City Curling Club [20193], Wisconsin Rapids, WI
Waupaca Curling Club [20025], Waupaca, WI
Wausau Curling Club [20054], Wausau, WI
Wauwatosa Curling Club [20081], Wauwatosa, WI
Wisconsin Curling Assn. [19517], Portage, WI
Wisconsin Curling Assn. - Arlington Curling Club [17538], Arlington, WI
Wisconsin Curling Assn. - Clintonville Curling Club [17772], Clintonville, WI

Wisconsin Curling Assn. - Kettle Moraine Curling Club [18188], Hartland, WI
Wisconsin Curling Assn. - Loch Wissota Curling Club [17909], Eau Claire, WI
Wisconsin Curling Assn. - Lodi Curling Club [18425], Lodi, WI
Wisconsin Curling Assn. - Milwaukee Curling Club [18891], Mequon, WI
Wisconsin Curling Assn. - Portage Curling Club [19518], Portage, WI
Wisconsin Curling Assn. - Rice Lake Curling Club [19619], Rice Lake, WI
Wisconsin Curling Assn. - Waukesha Curling Club [20009], Waukesha, WI
Currency Club; Metro East Coin and [207], Belleville, IL
Curriculum
Illinois Assn. for Supervision and Curriculum Development [2715], Normal, IL
Indiana Assn. for Supervision and Curriculum Development [5188], Indianapolis, IN
Michigan Assn. for Supervision and Curriculum Development [8629], Lansing, MI
Minnesota Assn. for Supervision and Curriculum Development [10919], Edina, MN
Wisconsin Assn. for Supervision and Curriculum Development [19895], Thiensville, WI
Curriculum Development; Michigan Assn. for Supervision and [8629], Lansing, MI
Curriculum Development; Wisconsin Assn. for Supervision and [19895], Thiensville, WI
Customs Brokers and Foreign Freight Forwarders Assn. of Chicago [865], Chicago, IL
Cuy-Lor Stamp Club [17228], Westlake, OH
Cuyahoga County Planning Commn. [14108], Cleveland, OH
Cuyahoga Falls Chamber of Commerce [14821], Cuyahoga Falls, OH
Cuyahoga Valley Space Soc. [16359], Parma, OH
Cuyahoga Valley Spaziergangers [14822], Cuyahoga Falls, OH
Cuyahoga West Chap. of the Ohio Genealogical Soc. [★15184]
Cuyuna Rock, Gem and Mineral Soc. [10245], Aitkin, MN
Cycle Conservation Club of Michigan [9496], Rives Junction, MI
Cycling
3 Rivers Velo Sport [4617], Fort Wayne, IN
Athens Bicycle Club [13197], Athens, OH
Bicycle Fed. of Wisconsin [18490], Madison, WI
Big Ring Adventure Team [5711], Madison, IN
Bike Psychos Cycling Club [2797], Oak Lawn, IL
Bike Wisconsin [17835], Dodgeville, WI
Bike Wisconsin Educ. and Action Coalition [19766], Spring Green, WI
Bikeline of Naperville [2627], Naperville, IL
Blackhawk Bicycle and Ski Club [3274], Rockford, IL
Bloomington Bicycle Club [4203], Bloomington, IN
Central Illinois Mountain Bicycling Assn. [2985], Pekin, IL
Central Indiana Bicycling Assn. [5072], Indianapolis, IN
Chequamegon Area Mountain Bike Assn. [17705], Cable, WI
Chicago Area Mountain Bikers [3711], Stickney, IL
Cincinnati Off Road Alliance [13794], Cincinnati, OH
Cleveland Area Mountain Bike Assn. [14093], Cleveland, OH
Copper Country Cycling Club [8250], Houghton, MI
Cyclists of Gitchee Gumee Shores [10811], Duluth, MN
Dayton Cycling Club [14874], Dayton, OH
Diva Adventures [18095], Green Bay, WI
Folks on Spokes Bicycle Club [2436], Matteson, IL
Friends of Off-Road Cycling [3243], Rock Island, IL
Holly Flint MMBA [7695], Ferndale, MI
Hoosier Mountain Bike Assn. [5142], Indianapolis, IN
Hoosier Mountain Bike Club Assn. [5143], Indianapolis, IN
Illinois Mountain Bicyclists Coalition [3229], Rochester, IL
Intl. Brotherhood of Trail Workers [2915], Palatine, IL
Kickapoo Mountain Bike Club [2840], Oakwood, IL
La Crosse Velo Club [18364], La Crosse, WI
League of Illinois Bicyclists [123], Aurora, IL
Michigan Mountain Bike Assn. [10087], Waterford, MI
Mid State MMBA [8387], Jackson, MI
Minnesota Coalition of Bicyclists [12468], St. Paul, MN
Minnesota Off-Road Cyclists [10599], Burnsville, MN
North Central Mountain Bike Patrol [10665], Circle Pines, MN
Northeast MMBA [9038], Midland, MI
Northern Indiana Mountain Bicycling Assn. [6249], South Bend, IN
Ohio Bicycle Fed. [17376], Xenia, OH
Ohio Valley Bicycle Club [15294], Gallipolis, OH
Outback Trail Commn. [4929], Hobart, IN
Peoria Area Mountain Bike Assn. [3047], Peoria, IL
Pontiac MMBA [9189], New Hudson, MI
Potawatomi MMBA [6759], Ann Arbor, MI
Rock Cut Trail Crew [3301], Rockford, IL
Rum River Cycling Team [12047], Princeton, MN
Southeast MMBA [9411], Plymouth, MI
Southwest Chain Gang Bicycle Club [17839], Dodgeville, WI
Southwest MMBA [6818], Augusta, MI
Springfield Area Mountain Bike Assn. [3675], Springfield, IL
Trips for Kids-Fox Valley [3500], South Elgin, IL
Two Wheel View/Trips for Kids - Twin Cities [12600], St. Paul, MN
Upgrade Cycle [1218], Chicago, IL
Upper Peninsula Mountain Bike Club [8962], Marquette, MI
Village Cycle Sport MTB Club [1615], Elk Grove Village, IL
Washtenaw Bicycling and Walking Coalition [6782], Ann Arbor, MI
Western MMBA [8049], Grandville, MI
Wheel Fast Racing [2664], Naperville, IL
Wheelmen, Illinois [1232], Chicago, IL
Wheelmen, Indiana [6044], Plainfield, IN
Wheelmen, Michigan [10149], Westland, MI
Wheelmen, Minnesota [11778], Minneapolis, MN
Wheelmen, Ohio [15217], Findlay, OH
Wheelmen, Wisconsin [19149], Milwaukee, WI
Winona Area Mountain Bikers [12961], Winona, MN
Wisconsin Off-Road Bicycling Assn. [17934], Elm Grove, WI
Yellow Bike Coalition [12608], St. Paul, MN
Cyclists of Gitchee Gumee Shores [10811], Duluth, MN
Cystic Fibrosis Found., Greater Michigan Chap. - Eastern Region [9607], Saginaw, MI
Cystic Fibrosis Foundation, Mahoning County Chapter [13531], Canfield, OH

D

D. Augustus Straker Bar Assn. [9980], Troy, MI
Dachshund
Minnesota Dachshund Club [10835], Duluth, MN
Dachshund Club of Southwestern Ohio [17172], West Chester, OH
DADS Am., Ohio [15432], Hilliard, OH
Dads Club; St. Mary's Preparatory Moms and [9312], Orchard Lake, MI
Daguerre Club of Indiana [5526], Jasper, IN
Dairies
Amer. Dairy Sci. Assn. - Illinois State Univ. Dairy Club [2707], Normal, IL
Amer. Dairy Sci. Assn. - Michigan State Univ. Dairy Sci. Club [7503], East Lansing, MI
Amer. Dairy Sci. Assn. - Midwest Br. [4828], Greenfield, IN
Amer. Dairy Sci. Assn. - Ohio State Univ. - Ag Tech Inst. [17309], Wooster, OH
Midwest Dairy Foods Assn. [14507], Columbus, OH
Dairy Coun. of Michigan [9267], Okemos, MI
Dairy Foods Assn; Midwest [14507], Columbus, OH
Dairy Foods Assn; Wisconsin [★18914]
Dairy and Nutrition Coun., Inc. [5099], Indianapolis, IN
Dairy Producers of Wisconsin; Professional [19740], Slinger, WI
Dairy Products
Amer. Dairy Assn. of Indiana [4982], Indianapolis, IN
Dairy Coun. of Michigan [9267], Okemos, MI
Dodge County Dairy Testing [18281], Juneau, WI
Illinois Milk Producers' Assn. [286], Bloomington, IL
Indiana State Dairy Assn. [6486], West Lafayette, IN
Michigan Milk Producers Assn. [9239], Novi, MI
Midwest Dairy Assn. [12444], St. Paul, MN
Milk Promotion Services of Indiana [5408], Indianapolis, IN
Professional Dairy Producers of Wisconsin [19740], Slinger, WI
Wisconsin Cheese Makers' Assn. [18681], Madison, WI
Wisconsin Dairy Products Assn. [18914], Middleton, WI
Wisconsin Holstein Assn. [17579], Baraboo, WI
Dairyland Theatre Organ Soc. [18999], Milwaukee, WI
Dakota County Genealogical Soc. [12679], South St. Paul, MN
Dakota County Historical Soc. [12680], South St. Paul, MN
Dakota Genealogical Soc. [★12679]
Dakotas Children Auxiliary [10866], Eagan, MN
Daleville Skeet and Trap Club [6031], Peru, IN
Dalmatians Off the Streets Rescue Gp. [16787], Strongsville, OH
Dalton Area Chamber of Commerce [14829], Dalton, OH
Dalton Lions Club - Ohio [14830], Dalton, OH
DAMA-Michigan Chap. [9981], Troy, MI
Dance
Between the Bays Dance Camps [9925], Traverse City, MI
Bloomington Old Time Music and Dance Gp. [4209], Bloomington, IN
Brickyard Boogie Dancers [5063], Indianapolis, IN
Buckeye Bop Club [17206], Westerville, OH
Cadillac Squares [9476], Redford, MI
Central Illinois English Country Dancers [3810], Urbana, IL
Chi-Town Squares [777], Chicago, IL
Chicago Barn Dance Company [1652], Evanston, IL
Chicago Windy City Jitterbug Club [1737], Franklin Park, IL
Cincinnati Contra Dancers [13781], Cincinnati, OH
Cleveland-Akron Swing and Hustle Club [15921], Mayfield Heights, OH
Country Dancing in Kalamazoo [8425], Kalamazoo, MI
DanceCincinnati [13813], Cincinnati, OH
English Country Dancers of Columbus [14429], Columbus, OH
Folk Music Soc. of Midland [8481], Kawkawlin, MI
Goshen Old-Time Dancing [4380], Columbia City, IN
Grand River Folk Arts Soc. [7955], Grand Rapids, MI
Great Lakes Swing Dance Club [7037], Burton, MI
Greater Cleveland FEIS Soc. [16545], Rocky River, OH
Illinois Assn. for Hea., Physical Educ., Recreation, and Dance [2078], Jacksonville, IL
Indianapolis Traditional Music and Dance Gp. [5356], Indianapolis, IN
Indy Swing Dance Club [5362], Indianapolis, IN
Intl. Assn. of Gay/Lesbian Country Western Dance Clubs, Columbus Stompers [14472], Columbus, OH
Intl. Assn. of Gay/Lesbian Country Western Dance Clubs, Dairyland Cowboys and Cowgirls [18529], Madison, WI
Intl. Assn. of Gay/Lesbian Country Western Dance Clubs, Northern Lights [11588], Minneapolis, MN

Intl. Assn. of Gay/Lesbian Country Western Dance Clubs, Rainbow Wranglers [14143], Cleveland, OH
Intl. Assn. of Gay/Lesbian Country Western Dance Clubs, Shoreline-Milwaukee [19028], Milwaukee, WI
Intl. Assn. of Gay Square Dance Clubs - Chi-Town Squares [981], Chicago, IL
Intl. Assn. of Gay Square Dance Clubs - Cleveland City Country Dancers [14144], Cleveland, OH
Madcap Squares [18543], Madison, WI
Madison West Coast Swing Club [18556], Madison, WI
Mid-Michigan USA Dance [9031], Midland, MI
Midwestern U.S. Imperial Club [1291], Collinsville, IL
Minnesota West Coast Swing Dance Club [12910], Willernie, MN
Northern Lights Ballroom Dance Club [11985], Pelican Rapids, MN
Northwest Ohio Traditional Music and Dance [16829], Sylvania, OH
Oakland County Traditional Dance Soc. [10122], West Bloomfield, MI
Paint Creek Foklore Soc. [9516], Rochester Hills, MI
Tango Soc. of Minnesota [10927], Edina, MN
Tapestry Folkdance Center [11754], Minneapolis, MN
USA Dance - Central Michigan Chap. No. 2037 [8769], Lansing, MI
USA Dance - Chap. 2015 [17115], Warren, OH
USA Dance - Chicagoland Chap. [250], Bloomingdale, IL
USA Dance - Greater Fox Valley of Illinois Chap. No. 2042 [4064], Woodstock, IL
USA Dance - Heartland Chap. [4263], Bloomington, IN
USA Dance - North Coast Ohio [15982], Mentor, OH
USA Dance - Southern Minnesota Chap. No. 2017 [12197], Rochester, MN
USABDA Minnesota Chap. [12339], St. Louis Park, MN
Dance; Illinois Assn. for Hea., Physical Educ., Recreation, and [2078], Jacksonville, IL
Dance; Ohio Assn. for Hea., Physical Educ., Recreation and [13245], Avon Lake, OH
Dance Soc; Oakland County Traditional [10122], West Bloomfield, MI
DanceCincinnati [13813], Cincinnati, OH
Dancers; Central Illinois English Country [3810], Urbana, IL
Dancers; Urbana Country [558], Champaign, IL
Dancing Cuckoos, Metropolitan Detroit Tent of the Intl. Sons of the Desert [7063], Canton, MI
Dane County Humane Soc. [18503], Madison, WI
Dane County Labor Coun. [★18619]
Dane County Labor Coun. [★18619]
Dane County Natural Heritage Found. [★18582]
Danube Lions Club [10749], Danube, MN
Danville Area Bd. of Realtors [1343], Danville, IL
Danville Area Convention and Visitors Bur. [1344], Danville, IL
Danville District Dental Soc. [1345], Danville, IL
Danville Kiwanis' Clubs, Breakfast Club [1346], Danville, IL
Danville Kiwanis' Clubs, Golden K Club [1347], Danville, IL
Danville Kiwanis' Clubs, Noon Club [1348], Danville, IL
Darien Chamber of Commerce [1358], Darien, IL
Darien Chamber of Commerce and Indus. [★1358]
Darien Lions Club, IL [1359], Darien, IL
Darke County Assn. of Realtors [15357], Greenville, OH
Darke County Chamber of Commerce [15358], Greenville, OH
Darke County, Ohio Habitat for Humanity [15359], Greenville, OH
Darke County Pheasants Forever [16555], Rossburg, OH
Darke County United Way [15360], Greenville, OH
Darke County Youth for Christ [15361], Greenville, OH
Darlington Chamber of Commerce [17806], Darlington, WI
Dartford Historical Soc. [18145], Green Lake, WI
DARTS of Minnesota [12877], West St. Paul, MN
Darwin Lions Club [10751], Darwin, MN
Data Center Cooperative; Illinois State [3639], Springfield, IL
Data Processing
Black Data Processing Associates - Detroit Chap. [7329], Detroit, MI
Daughters of the Amer. Revolution, Sarah Winston Henry Chap. [5934], New Castle, IN
Daviess County Chamber of Commerce [6457], Washington, IN
Daviess County Growth Coun. [6458], Washington, IN
Davison Area Chamber of Commerce [7236], Davison, MI
Davison Athletic Club [7237], Davison, MI
Dawson Lions Club [10756], Dawson, MN
Day Care Action Coun. of Illinois [★595]
Daylily Soc; Southwestern Indiana [4578], Evansville, IN
Dayton Amateur Softball Assn. [15315], Germantown, OH
Dayton Area Auto Dealers Assn. [14867], Dayton, OH
Dayton Area Bd. of Realtors [14868], Dayton, OH
Dayton Area Chamber of Commerce [14869], Dayton, OH
Dayton Area Chamber of Commerce Economic Development Div. [★14869]
Dayton Area Chap. - MOAA [15147], Fairborn, OH
Dayton Assn. of Insurance and Financial Advisors [14870], Dayton, OH
Dayton Assn. of Life Underwriters [★14870]
Dayton Audubon Soc. [14871], Dayton, OH
Dayton-Buckeye Model 'A' Club [15130], Englewood, OH
Dayton Builders Exchange [14872], Dayton, OH
Dayton Chap. of the Intl. Fac. Mgt. Assn. [15986], Miamisburg, OH
Dayton Chap. of the Soc. of Financial Ser. Professionals [14873], Dayton, OH
Dayton Cycling Club [14874], Dayton, OH
Dayton Dental Soc. [14875], Dayton, OH
Dayton Dog Training Club [16066], Moraine, OH
Dayton Dog Training Club [17381], Yellow Springs, OH
Dayton Downtown Lions Club [14876], Dayton, OH
Dayton Gem and Mineral Soc. [14877], Dayton, OH
Dayton Lions Club [10759], Dayton, MN
Dayton/Miami Valley Safety Coun. [14878], Dayton, OH
Dayton Miniature Soc. [17367], Xenia, OH
Dayton and Montgomery County Convention and Visitors Bur. [14879], Dayton, OH
Dayton Ohio Habitat for Humanity [14880], Dayton, OH
Dayton Table Tennis Club [14881], Dayton, OH
Dayton Urban League [14882], Dayton, OH
De Forest Area Chamber of Commerce [17810], De Forest, WI
De Soto Area Lions Club [17816], De Soto, WI
Deaf
DeafArt Club [12976], Woodbury, MN
Northern Illinois Deaf Golf Assn. [1107], Chicago, IL
Deaf Golf Assn; Northern Illinois [1107], Chicago, IL
Deaf, Hearing and Speech Sers; Michigan Assn. for [8612], Lansing, MI
DeafArt Club [12976], Woodbury, MN
Dealers Assn; Rental Purchase [4253], Bloomington, IN
Dearborn Area Alliance for the Mentally Ill [7251], Dearborn, MI
Dearborn Area Bd. of Realtors [7252], Dearborn, MI
Dearborn Chamber of Commerce [7253], Dearborn, MI
Dearborn Community Arts Coun. [7254], Dearborn, MI
Dearborn Community Found. [5654], Lawrenceburg, IN
Dearborn County Beagle Club [6467], West Harrison, IN
Dearborn County Chamber of Commerce [5655], Lawrenceburg, IN
Dearborn County Home Builders Assn. [5656], Lawrenceburg, IN
Dearborn County RSVP [5657], Lawrenceburg, IN
Dearborn Figure Skating Club [7255], Dearborn, MI
Dearborn Heights Lions Club [7282], Dearborn Heights, MI
Dearborn Lions Club [7256], Dearborn, MI
Dearborn and Ohio County Child Abuse Prevention Council [★5658]
Dearborn and Ohio County Prevent Child Abuse Council [5658], Lawrenceburg, IN
Dearborn Realtist Bd. [866], Chicago, IL
Dearborn Soccer Club [7257], Dearborn, MI
DECA; Michigan [10210], Ypsilanti, MI
Decatur AIFA [1381], Decatur, IL
Decatur AMBUCS [2605], Mount Zion, IL
Decatur Area Convention and Visitors Bur. [1382], Decatur, IL
Decatur Area RSVP [1383], Decatur, IL
Decatur Assn. of Builders [1384], Decatur, IL
Decatur Assn. of Realtors [1385], Decatur, IL
Decatur Audubon Soc. [1386], Decatur, IL
Decatur Chamber of Commerce [4451], Decatur, IN
Decatur County Bd. of Realtors, Indiana [4841], Greensburg, IN
Decatur County Historical Soc. [4842], Greensburg, IN
Decatur County Historical Soc. Museum [★4842]
Decatur District Dental Soc. [1387], Decatur, IL
Decatur Gun Club [1388], Decatur, IL
Decatur Masonic Temple Assn. [1389], Decatur, IL
Decatur Sheet Metal Contractors Assn. [1390], Decatur, IL
Decatur Stamp Club [277], Bloomington, IL
Decoy Collectors Assn; Midwest [1055], Chicago, IL
Deer
Minnesota Official Measures [11314], Lewiston, MN
Deer River Avenue of Pines Lions Club [10764], Deer River, MN
Deer River Golden Age Club [10765], Deer River, MN
Deer River Lions Club [10766], Deer River, MN
Deerfield, Bannockburn, Riverwoods Chamber of Commerce [1419], Deerfield, IL
Deerfield Chamber of Commerce [★1419]
Deerfield Chamber of Commerce [14978], Deerfield, OH
Defense Lawyers; Illinois Assn. of Criminal [927], Chicago, IL
Defense Trial Counsel of Indiana [5100], Indianapolis, IN
Defiance Area Chamber of Commerce [14984], Defiance, OH
Defiance Area Young Men's Christian Association [14985], Defiance, OH
Defiance Area Youth for Christ [14986], Defiance, OH
Defiance County Chap. of the Ohio Genealogical Soc. [14987], Defiance, OH
DeKalb Area Assn. of Realtors, Illinois [3747], Sycamore, IL
DeKalb Chamber of Commerce [1431], DeKalb, IL
DeKalb County Farmland Found. [1432], DeKalb, IL
Del-Tone/Luth Gun Club [12284], St. Cloud, MN
Delafield Chamber of Commerce [17822], Delafield, WI
Delano Area Chamber of Commerce [10769], Delano, MN
Delano Loretto Area United Way [10770], Delano, MN
Delavan - Delavan Lake Area Chamber of Commerce [17827], Delavan, WI
Delaware Area Chamber of Commerce [15002], Delaware, OH
Delaware Community Lions Club [15003], Delaware, OH
Delaware County Bd. of Realtors [15004], Delaware, OH
Delaware County Chamber of Commerce [★15002]
Delaware County Genealogical Soc. [15005], Delaware, OH
Delaware County Habitat for Humanity [15006], Delaware, OH
Delaware County Historical Soc. [5872], Muncie, IN
Delaware County Historical Soc. [15007], Delaware, OH
Delaware Lions Club [17211], Westerville, OH
Delinquency; Michigan Coun. on Crime and [8652], Lansing, MI

Delphos Area Chamber of Commerce **[15014]**, Delphos, OH
Delta Chamber of Commerce **[15016]**, Delta, OH
Delta County Area Chamber of Commerce **[7611]**, Escanaba, MI
Delta County Genealogical Soc. **[7612]**, Escanaba, MI
Delta Sigma Phi Fraternity, SDSU **[5101]**, Indianapolis, IN
Delta Solutions **[1420]**, Deerfield, IL
Democratic Party
Minnesota Democratic Farmer Labor Party **[12476]**, St. Paul, MN
Democratic Party of Illinois **[3548]**, Springfield, IL
Democratic Party of Wisconsin **[18504]**, Madison, WI
Democratic Socialists of America, Columbus **[14422]**, Columbus, OH
Democratic Socialists of Am., Madison **[18905]**, Middleton, WI
Democratic Socialists of Am., Twin Cities **[12407]**, St. Paul, MN
Democratic Socialists of Central Ohio (DSCO) **[★14422]**
Demotte Chamber of Commerce **[4458]**, Demotte, IN
Denmark Community Bus. Assn. **[17832]**, Denmark, WI
Dennison Lions Club **[11859]**, Nerstrand, MN
Dental Assn; Indiana **[5225]**, Indianapolis, IN
Dental Hygiene
Illinois Dental Hygienists' Assn. **[3600]**, Springfield, IL
Dental Hygienists' Assn; Michigan **[9277]**, Okemos, MI
Dental Soc; Cincinnati **[13783]**, Cincinnati, OH
Dental Soc; Illinois State **[3640]**, Springfield, IL
Dentistry
Akron Dental Soc. **[13021]**, Akron, OH
Amer. Cancer Soc., Henry County Unit **[14981]**, Defiance, OH
Central District Dental Soc., Michigan **[8559]**, Lansing, MI
Chicago Dental Soc. **[807]**, Chicago, IL
Cincinnati Dental Soc. **[13783]**, Cincinnati, OH
Cloverland District Dental Soc. **[7610]**, Escanaba, MI
Columbus Dental Soc. **[17210]**, Westerville, OH
Copper County District Dental Soc. **[8109]**, Hancock, MI
Corydon Palmer Dental Soc. **[17395]**, Youngstown, OH
Danville District Dental Soc. **[1345]**, Danville, IL
Dayton Dental Soc. **[14875]**, Dayton, OH
Decatur District Dental Soc. **[1387]**, Decatur, IL
Detroit District Dental Soc. **[7342]**, Detroit, MI
Eastern Illinois Dental Soc. **[3793]**, Tuscola, IL
First District Dental Soc. **[4548]**, Evansville, IN
Fox River Valley Dental Soc. **[1792]**, Geneva, IL
Genesee District Dental Soc. **[7738]**, Flint, MI
Great Lakes Assn. of Orthodontists **[14445]**, Columbus, OH
Greater Cleveland Dental Soc. **[14130]**, Cleveland, OH
Greater Milwaukee Dental Assn. **[20101]**, West Allis, WI
G.V. Black District Dental Soc. **[3557]**, Springfield, IL
Illinois Dental Lab. Assn. **[2641]**, Naperville, IL
Illinois State Dental Soc. **[3640]**, Springfield, IL
Illinois Valley Dental Soc. **[2898]**, Ottawa, IL
Indiana Dental Assn. **[5225]**, Indianapolis, IN
Indianapolis District Dental Soc. **[5346]**, Indianapolis, IN
Isaac Knapp District Dental Soc. **[4684]**, Fort Wayne, IN
Jackson District Dental Soc. **[8378]**, Jackson, MI
Kalamazoo Valley District Dental Soc. **[8444]**, Kalamazoo, MI
Kankakee District Dental Soc. **[2136]**, Kankakee, IL
Lakeland Valley District Dental Soc. **[7209]**, Coloma, MI
Macomb Dental Soc. **[7150]**, Chesterfield, MI
Madison District Dental Soc. **[1531]**, East Alton, IL
Manistee-Mason District Dental Soc. **[8914]**, Manistee, MI
McHenry County Dental Soc. **[2055]**, Huntley, IL
McLean County Dental Soc. **[1911]**, Gridley, IL
Michigan Assn. of Commercial Dental Labs. **[7181]**, Clinton Township, MI
Michigan Dental Assn. **[8657]**, Lansing, MI
Michigan Dental Hygienists' Assn. **[9277]**, Okemos, MI
Minneapolis District Dental Soc. **[11861]**, New Brighton, MN
Minnesota Dental Assn. **[12477]**, St. Paul, MN
Minnesota Dental Hygienists' Assn. **[10477]**, Bloomington, MN
Muskegon District Dental Soc. **[9154]**, Muskegon, MI
Ninth District Dental Soc., MIC **[9121]**, Mount Pleasant, MI
North Central Dental Soc. **[6248]**, South Bend, IN
Northeastern District Dental Soc., Michigan **[6647]**, Alpena, MI
Northeastern District Dental Soc., Minnesota **[10845]**, Duluth, MN
Northern Thumb District Dental Soc. **[7095]**, Cass City, MI
Northwest Indiana Dental Soc. **[5778]**, Merrillville, IN
Northwestern District Dental Soc., Minnesota **[11024]**, Fosston, MN
Oakland County Dental Soc. **[6938]**, Beverly Hills, MI
Ohio Dental Assn. **[14594]**, Columbus, OH
Peoria District Dental Soc. **[3051]**, Peoria, IL
Prairie Valley District Dental Soc. **[1780]**, Galesburg, IL
Resort District Dental Soc. **[9948]**, Traverse City, MI
Rock Island District Dental Soc. **[2532]**, Moline, IL
Saginaw Valley District Dental Soc. **[9636]**, Saginaw, MI
St. Clair District Dental Soc. **[2431]**, Mascoutah, IL
St. Paul District Dental Soc. **[12580]**, St. Paul, MN
Sault Ste. Marie District Dental Soc. **[9727]**, Sault Ste. Marie, MI
Southeastern District Dental Soc., Minnesota **[10361]**, Austin, MN
Southern District Dental Soc., Minnesota **[11307]**, Le Center, MN
Southern Illinois Dental Soc. **[3861]**, Vienna, IL
Southwestern District Dental Soc., Michigan **[6869]**, Battle Creek, MI
Stark County Dental Soc. **[13586]**, Canton, OH
Superior District Dental Soc. **[8959]**, Marquette, MI
T.L. Gilmer Dental Soc. **[3373]**, Rushville, IL
Toledo Dental Soc. **[16970]**, Toledo, OH
U.S. Grant Dental Soc. **[1755]**, Freeport, IL
Vacationland District Dental Soc. **[9374]**, Petoskey, MI
Wabash River Dental Soc. **[3413]**, Salem, IL
Washtenaw District Dental Soc. **[6789]**, Ann Arbor, MI
West Central District Dental Soc., Minnesota **[10523]**, Brainerd, MN
West Michigan District Dental Soc. **[8020]**, Grand Rapids, MI
Whiteside-Lee County Dental Soc. **[3708]**, Sterling, IL
Will County Dental Soc. **[2124]**, Joliet, IL
Winnebago County Dental Soc. - Illinois **[3329]**, Rockford, IL
Wisconsin Dental Assn. **[19166]**, Milwaukee, WI
DePaul Univ. Students In Free Enterprise **[867]**, Chicago, IL
Depression and Bipolar Support Alliance **[868]**, Chicago, IL
Depression and Bipolar Support Alliance Fox Valley **[3736]**, Sugar Grove, IL
Depression and Bipolar Support Alliance Metropolitan Detroit **[7338]**, Detroit, MI
Depressive and Manic-Depressive Assn. Maine **[★868]**
Deputies and Dispatchers Association; Macomb County **[9088]**, Mount Clemens, MI
Deputy Corps; Hancock County Sheriff Reserve **[466]**, Carthage, IL
Des Plaines Chamber of Commerce and Indus. **[1457]**, Des Plaines, IL
Des Plaines Historical Soc. **[1458]**, Des Plaines, IL
Des Plaines History Center **[★1458]**
Deshler Chamber of Commerce **[15021]**, Deshler, OH
Design
Designers Without Borders **[9103]**, Mount Pleasant, MI
Ohio City Design Rev. Comm. **[14193]**, Cleveland, OH
Design-Build Inst. of Am. - Great Lakes Chap. **[869]**, Chicago, IL
Design-Build Inst. of Am. - Upper Midwest Chap. **[11553]**, Minneapolis, MN
Designers Without Borders **[9103]**, Mount Pleasant, MI
DeTour Reef Light Preservation Soc. **[7485]**, Drummond Island, MI
Detroit ACORN **[7339]**, Detroit, MI
Detroit Area Corvair Club **[9893]**, Swartz Creek, MI
Detroit Area Coun. of Teachers of Mathematics **[9578]**, Royal Oak, MI
Detroit Assn. of Realtors **[7340]**, Detroit, MI
Detroit Audubon Soc. **[9579]**, Royal Oak, MI
Detroit Auto Dealers Assn. **[9982]**, Troy, MI
Detroit Black Chamber of Commerce **[7341]**, Detroit, MI
Detroit Bd. of Commerce **[★7354]**
Detroit Chap. of Myasthenia Gravis Found. of Am. **[★9810]**
Detroit Chap. of the Soc. of Financial Ser. Professionals **[9983]**, Troy, MI
Detroit Chinese Bus. Assn. **[7258]**, Dearborn, MI
Detroit Club Managers Assn. **[9770]**, South Lyon, MI
Detroit District Dental Soc. **[7342]**, Detroit, MI
Detroit Downtown **[7343]**, Detroit, MI
Detroit Downtown Lions Club **[7344]**, Detroit, MI
Detroit East Area Narcotics Anonymous **[7345]**, Detroit, MI
Detroit, Eastern Michigan and Northern Ohio Chap., Pennsylvania Railroad Tech. and Historical Soc. **[8274]**, Howell, MI
Detroit Eastside-Friendship Lions Club **[9865]**, Sterling Heights, MI
Detroit Economic Club **[7346]**, Detroit, MI
Detroit Fed. of Musicians - Local 5, Amer. Fed. of Musicians **[9797]**, Southfield, MI
Detroit Guild of the Catholic Medical Assn. **[9984]**, Troy, MI
Detroit Gun Club **[10055]**, Walled Lake, MI
Detroit Heidelberg Community St. Art **[★7374]**
Detroit Hispanic Lions Club **[7259]**, Dearborn, MI
Detroit Historical Soc. **[7347]**, Detroit, MI
Detroit Inst. of Arts **[7348]**, Detroit, MI
Detroit Inst. of Arts Volunteer Comm. **[★7348]**
Detroit Jewish Coalition for Literacy **[6983]**, Bloomfield Hills, MI
Detroit Kiwanis Club No. 1, Michigan **[7349]**, Detroit, MI
Detroit Lakes Regional Chamber of Commerce **[10773]**, Detroit Lakes, MN
Detroit Lakes United Fund **[★10785]**
Detroit Medical Center Lions Club **[7787]**, Fraser, MI
Detroit Metro Convention and Visitors Bur. **[7350]**, Detroit, MI
Detroit Michigan of the Assn. of Occupational Hea. Nurses **[7351]**, Detroit, MI
Detroit Mid-City Lions Club **[8788]**, Lathrup Village, MI
Detroit Model Yacht Club No. 88 **[7175]**, Clinton Township, MI
Detroit Motorcity Chap. DMC-Electric Auto Assn. **[★9834]**
Detroit Motorcity Chap. Elec. Auto Assn. **[9834]**, Southgate, MI
Detroit New Center Lions Club **[7352]**, Detroit, MI
Detroit North Central Lions Club **[9798]**, Southfield, MI
Detroit Northwest Lions Club **[7353]**, Detroit, MI
Detroit Org. Network **[9985]**, Troy, MI
Detroit Regional Census Advisory Comm. **[★9823]**
Detroit Regional Census Advisory Coun. **[★9823]**
Detroit Regional Chamber **[7354]**, Detroit, MI
Detroit Regional Economic Partnership **[7355]**, Detroit, MI
Detroit Renaissance Lions Club **[7356]**, Detroit, MI
Detroit Rugby Football Club of Metropolitan Detroit **[9502]**, Rochester, MI
Detroit Soc. for Coatings Tech. **[6813]**, Auburn Hills, MI

Detroit Telugu Literary Club [6977], Bloomfield, MI
Detroit Tooling Assn. [★7671]
Detroit Triumph Sportscar Club [9655], St. Clair Shores, MI
Detroit University/New Gratiot Lions Club [8295], Huntington Woods, MI
Detroit Urban League [7357], Detroit, MI
Detroit Urban - Young Life [7358], Detroit, MI
Detroit Women's Rowing Assn. [8080], Grosse Pointe, MI
Detroit Youth for Christ [7359], Detroit, MI
Developers Association; DKY [2507], Mokena, IL
Development Bur; Upper Peninsula [★8328]
Development Coalition; Hamilton Community [1928], Hamilton, IL
Development Commn; Arrowhead Regional [10806], Duluth, MN
Development Commn; South Central Illinois Regional Planning and [3412], Salem, IL
Development Commn; Southeastern Illinois Regional Planning and [1943], Harrisburg, IL
Development Commn; West Michigan Shoreline Regional [9168], Muskegon, MI
Development Corporation; Barnes Area [17580], Barnes, WI
Development Corp; Benton-West City Economic [233], Benton, IL
Development Corp; Berwyn [237], Berwyn, IL
Development Corp; Carter Temple Community [776], Chicago, IL
Development Corp; Carver of Evansville Community [4535], Evansville, IN
Development Corp; City News Community [14089], Cleveland, OH
Development Corp; Cos Community [13811], Cincinnati, OH
Development Corp; Ekklesia [13818], Cincinnati, OH
Development Corp; Englewood Community [5109], Indianapolis, IN
Development Corp; Greater Lafayette Community [5612], Lafayette, IN
Development Corporation; Harvest Community [7373], Detroit, MI
Development Corp; Heritage Community [913], Chicago, IL
Development Corp; Joy-Southfield Community [7384], Detroit, MI
Development Corp; Lapeer [8779], Lapeer, MI
Development Corp; Lincoln County Economic [18895], Merrill, WI
Development Corp; Macedonia Community [14905], Dayton, OH
Development Corp; Ohio Multi-County [13078], Akron, OH
Development Corp; Perry County [6299], Tell City, IN
Development Corp; Portland Economic [6065], Portland, IN
Development Corp; Prevailing Community [7423], Detroit, MI
Development Corp; Regional Economic [2409], Marion, IL
Development Corp; Sacred Heart-St. Elizabeth Community [7427], Detroit, MI
Development Corp; St. Paul Community [★7428]
Development Corp; Urban Solutions Training and [7449], Detroit, MI
Development Corp; Youth [8773], Lansing, MI
Development District; Buckeye Hills-Hocking Valley Regional [15815], Marietta, OH
Development and Info. Tech; Community Economic [9699], Saline, MI
Development Org; Warren County Local Economic [6530], Williamsport, IN
Development, Rock Valley Chap; Amer. Soc. for Training and [1476], Dixon, IL
Development, Southeast Wisconsin Chap; Amer. Soc. for Training and [18961], Milwaukee, WI

Developmental Education

Illinois Learning Specialists and Developmental Educators [2133], Kankakee, IL
Indiana Assn. for Developmental Educ. [6516], Westville, IN
Junior Achievement of the Upper Midwest [11419], Maplewood, MN
Minnesota Assn. for Developmental Educ. [11626], Minneapolis, MN
Ohio Assn. for Developmental Educ. [16944], Toledo, OH

Devon North Town Bus. and Professional Assn. [★1231]
DeWitt Breakfast Lions Club [8564], Lansing, MI
DeWitt Host Lions Club [7461], DeWitt, MI
Dexter HS - Young Life [6693], Ann Arbor, MI
Dexter Lions Club [10166], Whitmore Lake, MI
Dexter - Wyldlife [6694], Ann Arbor, MI

Diabetes

Amer. Diabetes Assn. [7890], Grand Rapids, MI
Amer. Diabetes Assn. [20067], Wauwatosa, WI
Amer. Diabetes Assn., Central Indiana Area [4983], Indianapolis, IN
Amer. Diabetes Assn. - Northern Illinois [618], Chicago, IL
Amer. Diabetes Assn., Southwest Ohio/Northern Kentucky Area [17168], West Chester, OH
Central Illinois Assn. of Diabetes Educators [3809], Urbana, IL
Central Ohio Diabetes Assn. [14359], Columbus, OH
Diabetes Educators of Chicago Area Amer. Assn. of Diabetes Educators [3769], Tinley Park, IL
Indiana Central Assn. of Diabetes Educators [5205], Indianapolis, IN
Juvenile Diabetes Res. Found. Illinois [1011], Chicago, IL
Juvenile Diabetes Res. Found., Indiana State Chap. [5385], Indianapolis, IN
Juvenile Diabetes Res. Found. Intl., East Central Ohio Br. [15500], Independence, OH
Juvenile Diabetes Res. Found. Intl., Greater Cincinnati Chap. [13878], Cincinnati, OH
Juvenile Diabetes Res. Found. Intl., Greater Dayton Chap. [14902], Dayton, OH
Juvenile Diabetes Research Foundation International, Mid-Ohio Chapter [14482], Columbus, OH
Juvenile Diabetes Res. Found. Intl., Minnesota Chap. [10471], Bloomington, MN
Juvenile Diabetes Res. Foundation International, Northeast Ohio Chapter [14151], Cleveland, OH
Juvenile Diabetes Res. Found. Intl., Northwest Ohio Chap. [16408], Perrysburg, OH
Juvenile Diabetes Research Foundation International, Western Wisconsin Chapter [18537], Madison, WI
Juvenile Diabetes Res. Found., Metropolitan Detroit and Southeast Michigan Chap. [9802], Southfield, MI
Juvenile Diabetes Res. Found., Northeast Wisconsin Chap. [18860], Menasha, WI
Juvenile Diabetes Res. Found., Southeastern Wisconsin Chap. [20076], Wauwatosa, WI
Michigan Org. of Diabetes Educators [7151], Chesterfield, MI
North Eastern Ohio Amer. Assn. of Diabetes Educators [14180], Cleveland, OH
Southeastern Wisconsin Assn. of Diabetes Educators [19128], Milwaukee, WI

Diabetes Assn; Central Ohio [14359], Columbus, OH
Diabetes Assn., Southwest Ohio/Northern Kentucky Area; Amer. [17168], West Chester, OH
Diabetes Educators of Chicago Area Amer. Assn. of Diabetes Educators [3769], Tinley Park, IL
Diabetes Found., Chicago Metro Chap; Juvenile [★1011]
Diabetes Found. of Greater Chicago; Juvenile [★1011]
Diabetes Found. of Illinois; Juvenile [★1011]
Diabetes Res. Found. of Greater Chicago; Juvenile [★1011]
Diabetes Res. Found. Illinois; Juvenile [1011], Chicago, IL
Diabetes Res. Found., Indiana State Chap; Juvenile [5385], Indianapolis, IN
Diabetes Res. Found. Intl., East Central Ohio Br; Juvenile [15500], Independence, OH
Diabetes Res. Found. Intl., Greater Cincinnati Chap; Juvenile [13878], Cincinnati, OH
Diabetes Res. Found. Intl., Greater Dayton Chap; Juvenile [14902], Dayton, OH
Diabetes Research Foundation International, Mid-Ohio Chapter; Juvenile [14482], Columbus, OH
Diabetes Res. Found. Intl., Minnesota Chap; Juvenile [10471], Bloomington, MN
Diabetes Res. Foundation International, Northeast Ohio Chapter; Juvenile [14151], Cleveland, OH
Diabetes Res. Found. Intl., Northwest Ohio Chap; Juvenile [16408], Perrysburg, OH
Diabetes Res. Found., Metropolitan Detroit and Southeast Michigan Chap; Juvenile [9802], Southfield, MI
Diabetes Res. Found., Northeast Wisconsin Chap; Juvenile [18860], Menasha, WI
Diabetes Res. Found., Southeastern Wisconsin Chap; Juvenile [20076], Wauwatosa, WI
Dickinson Area Bocce Assn. [8321], Iron Mountain, MI
Dickinson Area Partnership [8322], Iron Mountain, MI
Dietetic Assn; Wisconsin [19758], Sparta, WI
Dignity - Chicago [870], Chicago, IL
Dignity - Dayton [14883], Dayton, OH
Dignity - Indianapolis [5102], Indianapolis, IN
Dignity - Toledo [16910], Toledo, OH
Dignity - Twin Cities [11554], Minneapolis, MN
Dignity - USA, Columbus Chap. [14423], Columbus, OH
Dillman's Creative Arts Found. [18388], Lac Du Flambeau, WI
Dillonvale-Mt. Pleasant Lions Club [16076], Mount Pleasant, OH
Dilworth Lions Club [10787], Dilworth, MN
Dimondale Lions Club [7472], Dimondale, MI
Direct Mail Club of Detroit [★7639]
Direct Marketing Assn. of Detroit [7639], Farmington, MI
Directors Assn., Div. I-AAA; Athletics [14080], Cleveland, OH
Directors Assn; Minnesota Medical [11656], Minneapolis, MN
Directors of Indiana; Independent Funeral [5755], Martinsville, IN

Disabilities

Assn. for Individual Development of Aurora, IL [110], Aurora, IL
Avenues to Independence [2961], Park Ridge, IL
Easter Seals Southeastern Wisconsin [19747], South Milwaukee, WI
Easter Seals Wisconsin [18507], Madison, WI
Friendship Ventures [10300], Annandale, MN
Goodwill Columbus [14443], Columbus, OH
Governor's Planning Coun. for People with Disabilities, Indiana [5126], Indianapolis, IN
Hamilton County First Steps Coun. [5971], Noblesville, IN
Illinois Coun. on Developmental Disabilities [935], Chicago, IL
IndependenceFirst [19025], Milwaukee, WI
Minnesota Governor's Coun. on Developmental Disabilities [12485], St. Paul, MN
Ohio Developmental Disabilities Planning Coun. [14596], Columbus, OH
Ray Graham Assn. for People with Disabilities [1510], Downers Grove, IL
Wisconsin Coun. on Developmental Disabilities [18690], Madison, WI

Disabilities Assn. of Illinois; Learning [2940], Palos Hills, IL
Disabilities; Becca's Karing Individuals for [1768], Galesburg, IL
Disabilities Coun; Michigan Developmental [8658], Lansing, MI
Disabilities; Illinois Coun. on Developmental [935], Chicago, IL
Disabilities Planning Coun; Ohio Developmental [14596], Columbus, OH
Disabilities; Wisconsin Coun. on Developmental [18690], Madison, WI
The Disability Network [7721], Flint, MI

Disabled

Access Living [593], Chicago, IL
Adaptive Adventure Sports Coalition [14269], Columbus, OH
Arc of Indiana [5034], Indianapolis, IN
Arc of Monroe County [9062], Monroe, MI
Cannonsburg Challenged Ski Assn. [6557], Ada, MI
Council for Disability Rights [861], Chicago, IL
The Disability Network [7721], Flint, MI
Dreams for Kids [873], Chicago, IL
Easter Seals ARC of Northeast Indiana [4649], Fort Wayne, IN

Easter Seals Central Illinois **[1391]**, Decatur, IL
Easter Seals Central and Southeast Ohio **[13665]**, Chillicothe, OH
Easter Seals Central and Southeast Ohio **[14427]**, Columbus, OH
Easter Seals Central and Southeast Ohio **[15816]**, Marietta, OH
Easter Seals Genesee County, Michigan **[7724]**, Flint, MI
Easter Seals-Joliet **[2103]**, Joliet, IL
Easter Seals of LaSalle and Bur. Counties, Illinois **[2897]**, Ottawa, IL
Easter Seals Metropolitan Chicago, Illinois **[880]**, Chicago, IL
Easter Seals Michigan **[9927]**, Traverse City, MI
Easter Seals Michigan **[10081]**, Waterford, MI
Easter Seals Minnesota - Rochester **[12136]**, Rochester, MN
Easter Seals Minnesota - Willmar **[12914]**, Willmar, MN
Easter Seals Northeast Ohio **[13050]**, Akron, OH
Easter Seals Northeast Ohio **[13427]**, Broadview Heights, OH
Easter Seals Northeast Ohio **[15580]**, Lakewood, OH
Easter Seals Northeast Ohio **[17025]**, University Heights, OH
Easter Seals Northeast Ohio, Canton **[13563]**, Canton, OH
Easter Seals Northwestern Ohio **[15703]**, Lorain, OH
Easter Seals Northwestern Ohio **[16260]**, Norwalk, OH
Easter Seals Northwestern Ohio **[16607]**, Sandusky, OH
Easter Seals Northwestern Ohio **[16911]**, Toledo, OH
Easter Seals St. Clairsville, Ohio **[16570]**, St. Clairsville, OH
Easter Seals Southwestern Ohio **[13817]**, Cincinnati, OH
Easter Seals Trumbull County, Ohio **[17101]**, Warren, OH
Easter Seals Wayne and Union Counties **[4341]**, Centerville, IN
Easter Seals Youngstown **[17396]**, Youngstown, OH
Goodwill Indus./Easter Seals - Minnesota **[12420]**, St. Paul, MN
Goodwill Indus. of the Miami Valley **[14887]**, Dayton, OH
Goodwill Indus. of Wayne County **[17317]**, Wooster, OH
Great Lakes Adaptive Sports Assn. **[2197]**, Lake Forest, IL
Great Lakes Disability and Bus. Tech. Assistance Center **[906]**, Chicago, IL
Indiana Assn. on Higher Educ. and Disability **[4226]**, Bloomington, IN
Indiana Canine Asst. and Adolescent Network **[5203]**, Indianapolis, IN
League for the Blind and Disabled **[4689]**, Fort Wayne, IN
Michigan Adaptive Sports **[8482]**, Keego Harbor, MI
Michigan Developmental Disabilities Coun. **[8658]**, Lansing, MI
Michigan Protection and Advocacy Ser. **[8700]**, Lansing, MI
Michigan Wheelchair Athletic Assn. **[10000]**, Troy, MI
Minnesota Assn. on Higher Educ. and Disability **[10474]**, Bloomington, MN
North Central Wheelchair Athletic Assn. **[11064]**, Golden Valley, MN
Open Doors Org. **[1114]**, Chicago, IL
People First of Illinois **[304]**, Bloomington, IL
People First of Ohio **[16088]**, Mount Vernon, OH
Rehabilitation for Wisconsin **[18606]**, Madison, WI
Rochester Area Disabled Athletics and Recreation **[12172]**, Rochester, MN
Share Found. with the Handicapped **[6136]**, Rolling Prairie, IN
Special Olympics Illinois **[2733]**, Normal, IL
Special Olympics Indiana **[5483]**, Indianapolis, IN
Special Olympics Michigan **[9124]**, Mount Pleasant, MI
Special Olympics Minnesota **[11752]**, Minneapolis, MN
Special Olympics, Ohio **[14740]**, Columbus, OH
Special Olympics Wisconsin **[18622]**, Madison, WI
Three Trackers of Ohio **[14222]**, Cleveland, OH
U.S. Elec. Wheelchair Hockey Assn. **[11765]**, Minneapolis, MN
VSA Arts of Michigan **[7452]**, Detroit, MI
VSA arts of Indiana **[5497]**, Indianapolis, IN
VSA arts of Minnesota **[11776]**, Minneapolis, MN
VSA arts of Wisconsin **[18637]**, Madison, WI
Disabled Amer. Veterans, Detroit **[7360]**, Detroit, MI
Disabled Athletics and Recreation; Rochester Area **[12172]**, Rochester, MN
Disabled Veterans
Buckeye Chap. Paralyzed Veterans of Am. **[15139]**, Euclid, OH
Disabled Amer. Veterans, Detroit **[7360]**, Detroit, MI
Michigan Disabled Amer. Veterans **[7395]**, Detroit, MI
Ohio Disabled Amer. Veterans **[14194]**, Cleveland, OH
Paralyzed Veterans of Am., Michigan Chap. **[9244]**, Novi, MI
Paralyzed Veterans of Am., Vaughan Chap. **[3957]**, Westchester, IL
Wisconsin Paralyzed Veterans of America **[20110]**, West Allis, WI
Disarmament
Educators for Social Responsibility, Grand Rapids Chap. **[7927]**, Grand Rapids, MI
Discipline
Center for Effective Discipline **[14351]**, Columbus, OH
Discover Golf on Michigan's Sunrise Side **[9174]**, National City, MI
Disease
Minnesota Chronic Fatigue Syndrome/Fibromyalgia Assn. **[11639]**, Minneapolis, MN
Disorder Awareness Network; Personality **[19091]**, Milwaukee, WI
Dispatchers Association; Macomb County Deputies and **[9088]**, Mount Clemens, MI
Dispute Resolution Assn. of Michigan **[8565]**, Lansing, MI
Distance Running
Road Runners Club of Am. - Calumet Region Striders **[4859]**, Griffith, IN
Road Runners Club of Am. - Island Road Runners **[8078]**, Grosse Ile, MI
Distributors Assn; Chicago Roofing **[828]**, Chicago, IL
Distributors; Ohio Assn. of Tobacco and Candy **[★14698]**
Distributors Secretaries of Am; Beer **[★11630]**
Distributors and Vendors Assn; Michigan **[8659]**, Lansing, MI
District 1199 Indiana/Iowa of Ser. Employees Intl. Union Local **[★1176]**
Diva Adventures **[18095]**, Green Bay, WI
Divine Praise **[871]**, Chicago, IL
Diving
Michigan Underwater Preserves Coun. **[9669]**, St. Ignace, MI
USA Diving - Dive Cincinnati **[16030]**, Milford, OH
USA Diving - Fox Valley Dive Team **[19276]**, Neenah, WI
USA Diving - Indiana Diving **[4264]**, Bloomington, IN
USA Diving - Jeff Arnold Diving Enterprises **[17277]**, Willoughby, OH
USA Diving - No. 19 Wisconsin **[17693]**, Brown Deer, WI
USA Diving - No. 21 Minnesota **[12692]**, Spring Lake Park, MN
USA Diving - Rock Solid Diving **[9532]**, Rockford, MI
Divorce
Chicago Divorce Assn. **[3432]**, Schaumburg, IL
Children's Rights Coun. of Cleveland **[14088]**, Cleveland, OH
Children's Rights Coun. of Illinois **[1418]**, Deerfield, IL
Children's Rights Coun. of Michigan **[6979]**, Bloomfield Hills, MI
Children's Rights Coun. of Minnesota **[12132]**, Rochester, MN
Children's Rights Coun. of Northeast Ohio **[16232]**, North Kingsville, OH
Children's Rights Coun. of Ohio **[16909]**, Toledo, OH
Children's Rights Coun. of South Ohio **[13771]**, Cincinnati, OH
Children's Rights Coun. of Tri-county, Ohio **[17394]**, Youngstown, OH
Children's Rights Coun. of Wisconsin **[19925]**, Union Grove, WI
Fathers For Equal Rights of America, Michigan **[9800]**, Southfield, MI
Parents And Children for Equality **[13951]**, Cincinnati, OH
Wisconsin Fathers for Children and Families **[18703]**, Madison, WI
Divorce Assn; Chicago **[3432]**, Schaumburg, IL
Dixon Area Chamber of Commerce and Indus. **[1477]**, Dixon, IL
Dixon Chamber of Commerce **[★1477]**
Dixon Coin Club **[1734]**, Franklin Grove, IL
DKY Developers Association **[2507]**, Mokena, IL
Doberman Pinscher
Doberman Pinscher Club of Greater Dayton **[16728]**, Springfield, OH
Doberman Pinscher Club of Greater Dayton **[16728]**, Springfield, OH
Dodge Center Lions Club **[10790]**, Dodge Center, MN
Dodge County Area District Nurses Assn. - No. 15 **[17592]**, Beaver Dam, WI
Dodge County Dairy Promotion **[★18281]**
Dodge County Dairy Testing **[18281]**, Juneau, WI
Dodge County Fair Assn. **[17593]**, Beaver Dam, WI
Dodge County Historical Soc. **[11406]**, Mantorville, MN
Dodgeville Area Chamber of Commerce **[17836]**, Dodgeville, WI
Dodgeville Chamber of Commerce **[★17836]**
Dog
Adams County Beagle Club **[13690]**, Cincinnati, OH
All Breed Training Club of Akron **[16839]**, Tallmadge, OH
Amer. Brittany Club, Badger **[18453]**, Madison, WI
Amer. Brittany Club - Directors Chap. **[459]**, Carterville, IL
Amer. Chesapeake Club, Illinois **[2192]**, Lake Forest, IL
Amer. Chesapeake Club, Indiana **[5748]**, Martinsville, IN
Amer. Chesapeake Club, Michigan **[10016]**, Tustin, MI
Amer. Chesapeake Club, Minnesota **[11154]**, Hibbing, MN
Amer. Chesapeake Club, Wisconsin **[19380]**, Oregon, WI
Amer. Maltese Assn. **[7159]**, Clarkston, MI
Amer. Rottweiler Club **[3109]**, Plano, IL
Badger Kennel Club **[17809]**, De Forest, WI
Badger State Rottweiler Fanciers **[18977]**, Milwaukee, WI
Badgerland Gordon Setter Club **[17746]**, Chippewa Falls, WI
Bernese Mountain Dog Club of Am. **[19784]**, Stevens Point, WI
Blackhawk Retriever Club **[18339]**, La Crosse, WI
Bloomington Obedience Training Club **[10466]**, Bloomington, MN
Border Beagle Club **[7233]**, Davisburg, MI
Briar Patch Beagle Club **[16196]**, Newcomerstown, OH
Briard Club of Am. **[19269]**, Neenah, WI
Buckeye Beagle Club **[16148]**, New Philadelphia, OH
Cairn Terrier Club of Greater Detroit **[7682]**, Fenton, MI
Canine Rsrc. Development **[13630]**, Chagrin Falls, OH
Central Indiana Pug Club **[5079]**, Indianapolis, IN
Central Indiana Saint Bernard Club **[5080]**, Indianapolis, IN
Central Ohio Kennel Club **[15044]**, Dublin, OH
Central Ohio Kennel Club **[16419]**, Pickerington, OH
Central Ohio Shetland Sheepdog Assn. **[17208]**, Westerville, OH

Central Wisconsin Vizsla Club **[17954]**, Fall River, WI
Cherryland Beagle Club **[10128]**, West Branch, MI
Chicagoland Bearded Collie Club **[18870]**, Menomonee Falls, WI
Chicagoland Rottweiler Club **[842]**, Chicago, IL
Chinese Shar-Pei Club of Am. **[2971]**, Pawnee, IL
Clay County Beagle Club **[4921]**, Hillsdale, IN
Clermont County Kennel Club **[13804]**, Cincinnati, OH
Cleveland All-Breed Training Club **[14092]**, Cleveland, OH
Cleveland Shetland Sheepdog Club **[13346]**, Berea, OH
Clumber Spaniel Fanciers of Michigan **[9733]**, Schoolcraft, MI
Collie Club of Am., Michigan **[6595]**, Alger, MI
Companion Dog Training Club of Flint, Michigan **[7719]**, Flint, MI
Coulee Kennel Club **[11263]**, La Crescent, MN
Cudahy Kennel Club **[19657]**, St. Francis, WI
Dachshund Club of Southwestern Ohio **[17172]**, West Chester, OH
Dayton Dog Training Club **[16066]**, Moraine, OH
Dayton Dog Training Club **[17381]**, Yellow Springs, OH
Dearborn County Beagle Club **[6467]**, West Harrison, IN
Eastern Indiana Beagle Club **[4342]**, Centerville, IN
Eastern Upper Peninsula Beagle Club **[9928]**, Traverse City, MI
Elkhart County Beagle Club **[7592]**, Edwardsburg, MI
Emerald Valley Rottweiler Club of Greater Cleveland, Ohio **[5108]**, Indianapolis, IN
English Cocker Spaniel Club of Am. **[18169]**, Hales Corners, WI
English Springer Spaniel Field Trial Assn. **[19314]**, New London, WI
Field Spaniel Soc. of Am. **[17856]**, East Troy, WI
Flat-Coated Retriever Club of Illinois **[148]**, Barrington, IL
Flat-Coated Retriever Soc. of Am. **[6320]**, Terre Haute, IN
Fond du Lac County Kennel Club **[17979]**, Fond du Lac, WI
Fort Detroit Golden Retriever Club **[9314]**, Ortonville, MI
Fox Valley Dog Training Club **[3381]**, St. Charles, IL
Fox Valley Retriever Club **[18022]**, Fredonia, WI
German Shepherd Dog Club of Minneapolis and St. Paul **[10664]**, Circle Pines, MN
German Shepherd Dog Club of Wisconsin **[18154]**, Greenfield, WI
German Shepherd Dog Club of Wisconsin **[19287]**, New Berlin, WI
Golden Retriever Club of Columbus, Ohio **[15047]**, Dublin, OH
Golden Retriever Club of Greater Toledo **[15906]**, Maumee, OH
Great Dane Club of Am. **[16729]**, Springfield, OH
Great Dane Club of Cleveland **[15941]**, Medina, OH
Great Dane Club of Milwaukee **[20074]**, Wauwatosa, WI
Great Lakes German Shorthaired Pointer Club and Rescue **[7572]**, East Leroy, MI
Great Lakes Rottweiler Club of Southeast Michigan **[9188]**, New Haven, MI
Great Pyrenees Rescue of Greater Chicago **[2063]**, Ingleside, IL
Greater Chicagoland Basenji Club **[2689]**, New Lenox, IL
Greater Cincinnati Rottweiler Club **[13127]**, Amelia, OH
Greater Cincinnati St. Bernard Club **[13853]**, Cincinnati, OH
Greater Cleveland Norwegian Elkhound Club **[16235]**, North Olmsted, OH
Greater Milwaukee St. Bernard Club **[19325]**, North Prairie, WI
Greater Minneapolis St. Paul Basset Hound Club **[11034]**, Fridley, MN
Greater Racine Kennel Club **[19555]**, Racine, WI
Greater Twin Cities Golden Retriever Club **[12859]**, Wayzata, MN
Greater Twin Cities St. Bernard Club **[10947]**, Elk River, MN
Greater Twin Cities Whippet Club **[12228]**, Roseville, MN
Hamilton Dog Training Club **[15158]**, Fairfield, OH
Heart of Am. Keeshond Club **[12896]**, White Bear Lake, MN
Heart of Am. Scottish Terrier Club **[10727]**, Cottage Grove, MN
Heart of Michigan English Cocker Spaniel **[7741]**, Flint, MI
Indiana Amer. Eskimo Dog Club **[4482]**, Edinburgh, IN
Indiana Collie Club **[5214]**, Indianapolis, IN
Interlocking Shetland Sheepdog Club of Monee **[2692]**, New Lenox, IL
Intl. Kennel Club of Chicago **[989]**, Chicago, IL
Jaxon Kennel Club **[10172]**, Williamston, MI
Jay County Beagle Club **[5882]**, Muncie, IN
K-9 Obedience Training Club of Menomonee Falls **[18875]**, Menomonee Falls, WI
Kalamazoo Dog Training Club **[8439]**, Kalamazoo, MI
Kalamazoo Kennel Club **[7290]**, Delton, MI
Labrador Retriever Club of the Twin Cities **[10472]**, Bloomington, MN
Lake Country Retriever Club **[12050]**, Prior Lake, MN
Lake Superior Pointing Dog Club **[12761]**, Twig, MN
Lakeshore Beagle Club **[17766]**, Cleveland, WI
Lakeshore Pembroke Welsh Corgi Club **[8094]**, Gwinn, MI
Loveland Beagle Club **[13888]**, Cincinnati, OH
Madison County Beagle Club **[388]**, Cahokia, IL
Manitowoc County Kennel Club **[18785]**, Manitowoc, WI
Marietta Beagle Club **[15822]**, Marietta, OH
Marshfield Area Kennel Club **[18818]**, Marshfield, WI
Maumee Valley St. Bernard Club **[4127]**, Angola, IN
Medallion Rottweiler Club **[2881]**, Orland Park, IL
Meigs County Beagle Club **[16494]**, Racine, OH
Miami Valley Boxer Club **[16854]**, Tiffin, OH
Miami Valley Doberman Pinscher Club **[13900]**, Cincinnati, OH
Michigan Amer. Eskimo Dog Assn. **[9753]**, Sherwood, MI
Michigan Boxer club **[7666]**, Farmington Hills, MI
Michigan Toy Fox Terrier Assn. **[6910]**, Belleville, MI
Mid Illinois Retriever Club **[1777]**, Galesburg, IL
Mid-Michigan Pug Club **[6932]**, Berkley, MI
Midland Michigan Kennel Club **[9711]**, Sanford, MI
Midwest Waterways Flat-coated Retriever Club **[4693]**, Fort Wayne, IN
Milwaukee Beagle Club **[19252]**, Mukwonago, WI
Milwaukee Dog Training Club **[19060]**, Milwaukee, WI
Miniature Pinscher Club of Greater Twin Cities **[17560]**, Baldwin, WI
Minnesota Boston Terrier Club **[11633]**, Minneapolis, MN
Minnesota Brittany Club **[10710]**, Coon Rapids, MN
Minnesota Brittany Club **[10711]**, Coon Rapids, MN
Minnesota Field Trial Assn. **[11018]**, Forest Lake, MN
Minnesota Iron Range Retriever Club **[12797]**, Virginia, MN
Minnesota Working Rottweiler Assn. **[12982]**, Woodbury, MN
Muncie Obedience Training Club **[5888]**, Muncie, IN
Newfoundland Club of Am. **[19241]**, Mount Horeb, WI
North Amer. Versatile Hunting Dog Assn. **[74]**, Arlington Heights, IL
North Shore Dog Training Club **[3489]**, Skokie, IL
Northeastern Indiana Kennel Club **[4704]**, Fort Wayne, IN
Northeastern Wisconsin Beagle Club **[18125]**, Green Bay, WI
Northern Flight Hunting Retriever Assn. **[12701]**, Stacy, MN
Northern Flyway Golden Retriever Club of Am. **[18821]**, Marshfield, WI
Northern Illinois Saint Bernard Club **[1951]**, Harvard, IL
Northern Lights Amer. Eskimo Dog Assn. **[12556]**, St. Paul, MN
Northern Ohio Beagle Club **[16277]**, Oakwood Village, OH
Norwegian Elkhound Assn. of Minnesota **[11430]**, Marine on St. Croix, MN
Oakland County Kennel Club **[9243]**, Novi, MI
Ohio St. Bernard Club **[16695]**, South Euclid, OH
Ohio Toy Fox Terrier Assn. **[17092]**, Wapakoneta, OH
Ohio Valley Pembroke Welsh Corgi Club **[14694]**, Columbus, OH
Ohio Valley Retriever Club **[15063]**, Dublin, OH
Okaw Valley Beagle Club **[1759]**, Fults, IL
Olentangy Beagle Club **[15786]**, Mansfield, OH
Packerland Kennel Club **[18127]**, Green Bay, WI
Pembroke Welsh Corgi Club of the Western Reserve **[13638]**, Chagrin Falls, OH
Peoria Obedience Training Club **[3056]**, Peoria, IL
Portuguese Water Dog Club of the Twin Cities **[10667]**, Circle Pines, MN
Prairie Creek Beagle Club **[6027]**, Pendleton, IN
Puli Club of Am. **[13967]**, Cincinnati, OH
Rand Park Dog Training Club **[4008]**, Wildwood, IL
Rescue A Shar-Pei **[4308]**, Burns Harbor, IN
Rice Creek Hunting Dog Club **[11338]**, Little Falls, MN
Richland County Illinois Beagle Club **[2705]**, Noble, IL
Rochester Dog Obedience Club **[12177]**, Rochester, MN
Rochester Minnesota Kennel Club **[12180]**, Rochester, MN
Saint Bernard Club of Greater Detroit **[10093]**, Waterford, MI
Saint Bernard Club of Greater St. Louis **[3063]**, Peoria, IL
St. Croix Valley Brittany Club **[12900]**, White Bear Lake, MN
St. Croix Valley Kennel Club **[10242]**, Afton, MN
St. Croix Valley Kennel Club **[12573]**, St. Paul, MN
St. Joseph Valley Beagle Club **[5985]**, North Liberty, IN
Saluki Club of Am. **[19342]**, Oconomowoc, WI
Samoyed Assn. of Minneapolis-St. Paul **[10486]**, Bloomington, MN
Scottish Terrier Club of Northern Ohio **[14833]**, Dalton, OH
Sheboygan Kennel Club **[19720]**, Sheboygan Falls, WI
Siberian Husky Club of Greater Cleveland **[13349]**, Berea, OH
Siberian Husky Club of Greater Detroit **[7021]**, Brighton, MI
Siberian Husky Club of the Twin Cities **[10675]**, Clear Lake, MN
Silver Creek Beagle Club **[4149]**, Austin, IN
Skokie Valley Kennel Club **[3358]**, Roselle, IL
Skokie Valley Kennel Club **[3773]**, Tinley Park, IL
Southeastern Illinois Beagle Club **[2041]**, Homer, IL
Southern Michigan Obedience Training Club **[9520]**, Rochester Hills, MI
Southern Wisconsin Sporting Spaniel Club **[20162]**, Whitewater, WI
Stittsville Beagle Club **[10134]**, West Branch, MI
Terre Haute Kennel Club **[4285]**, Brazil, IN
Toledo Kennel Club **[13363]**, Bloomdale, OH
Town and Country Beagle Club **[19343]**, Oconomowoc, WI
Tri-Cities Dog Training Club of Saginaw Michigan **[9640]**, Saginaw, MI
Tri State Beagle Club **[4582]**, Evansville, IN
Twin Cities Area Yorkshire Terrier Club **[12728]**, Stillwater, MN
Twin Cities Irish Water Spaniel Club **[12729]**, Stillwater, MN
Twin Cities Obedience Training Club **[11760]**, Minneapolis, MN
Twin Cities Poodle Club **[11761]**, Minneapolis, MN
Twin Cities Vizsla Club **[10327]**, Apple Valley, MN

Waukesha Kennel Club **[17680]**, Brookfield, WI
Weimaraner Club of Columbus **[15372]**, Grove City, OH
West Highland White Terrier Club of Northern Illinois **[2801]**, Oak Lawn, IL
West Highland White Terrier Club of Northern Ohio **[16224]**, North Canton, OH
West Highland White Terrier Club of Southeastern Michigan **[7471]**, Dexter, MI
West Michigan Beagle Club **[7600]**, Elwell, MI
Western Beagle Club **[5589]**, Kokomo, IN
Western Buckeye Rottweiler Club **[16754]**, Springfield, OH
Western Reserve Kennel Club **[16194]**, Newbury, OH
Western Waukesha County Dog Training Club **[18240]**, Ixonia, WI
Williana Clumber Spaniel Club **[2319]**, Lockport, IL
Wilmington Illinois Beagle Club **[2341]**, Lombard, IL
Wisconsin Amateur Field Trial Club **[19715]**, Sheboygan, WI
Wisconsin Amateur Field Trial Club **[19890]**, Theresa, WI
Wisconsin Rapids Kennel Club **[19497]**, Port Edwards, WI
Wisconsin Rottweiler Performance Club **[19869]**, Sun Prairie, WI
Wisconsin Toy Fox Terrier Assn. **[19185]**, Milwaukee, WI
Wolverine Beagle Club **[8158]**, Hastings, MI
Wright County Minnesota Kennel Club **[11813]**, Monticello, MN
Wrinkled Rescue/Chinese Shar-Pei Rescue **[13123]**, Amanda, OH
Youngstown All Breed Training Club **[16230]**, North Jackson, OH

Dog Racing
Warren County Kennel Club of Ohio **[15626]**, Lebanon, OH

Dog Rescue; Mit Liebe German Shepherd **[19851]**, Suamico, WI
Dollhouse and Miniature Soc. of Elkhart **[6291]**, Syracuse, IN

Dolls
United Fed. of Doll Clubs - Region 5 **[10429]**, Bemidji, MN
United Fed. of Doll Clubs - Region 10 **[19866]**, Sun Prairie, WI
United Fed. of Doll Clubs - Region 12 **[5489]**, Indianapolis, IN

Dolton Chamber of Commerce **[1488]**, Dolton, IL
Domestic Assault; Lapeer Area Citizens Against **[8777]**, Lapeer, MI

Domestic Violence
Action Ohio Coalition For Battered Women **[14268]**, Columbus, OH
Between Friends **[764]**, Chicago, IL
Illinois Coalition Against Domestic Violence **[3591]**, Springfield, IL
Indiana Coalition Against Domestic Violence **[5213]**, Indianapolis, IN
Lapeer Area Citizens Against Domestic Assault **[8777]**, Lapeer, MI
Minnesota Coalition for Battered Women **[12467]**, St. Paul, MN
Ohio Domestic Violence Network **[14598]**, Columbus, OH
Stopping Woman Abuse Now **[2862]**, Olney, IL
Wisconsin Coalition Against Domestic Violence **[18684]**, Madison, WI

Domestic Violence; Citizens Against **[16007]**, Middletown, OH
Domestic Violence; Indiana Coalition Against **[5213]**, Indianapolis, IN
Domestic Violence Task Force of Gibson County **[6069]**, Princeton, IN
Donkey Rescue; Crossroads **[9233]**, Novi, MI
Donkey Show Society; Midstates Mule and **[16427]**, Pioneer, OH
Donors Forum of Chicago **[872]**, Chicago, IL
Donors Forum of Wisconsin **[19000]**, Milwaukee, WI
Door County Chamber of Commerce **[19836]**, Sturgeon Bay, WI
Door County Enval. Coun. **[17962]**, Fish Creek, WI
Door County REACT **[19202]**, Mishicot, WI
Door Peninsula Astronomical Soc. **[19837]**, Sturgeon Bay, WI
Doublehanded Sailing Assn. **[8087]**, Grosse Pointe Farms, MI
Douglas County Historical Soc. **[10275]**, Alexandria, MN
Dover Historical Soc. **[15027]**, Dover, OH
Dover Lions Club - Ohio **[16149]**, New Philadelphia, OH
Dow/Midland - Young Life **[9024]**, Midland, MI
Dowagiac Conservation Club **[7479]**, Dowagiac, MI
Dowagiac Lions Club **[7480]**, Dowagiac, MI
Down River Assn. of Realtors **[9900]**, Taylor, MI
Down Syndrome Assn. of Greater Cincinnati **[13814]**, Cincinnati, OH
Down Syndrome Assn. of West Michigan **[7923]**, Grand Rapids, MI
Down Syndrome Assn. of Wisconsin **[19001]**, Milwaukee, WI
Downers Grove Area Chamber of Commerce and Indus. **[1501]**, Downers Grove, IL
Downers Grove South High School Parent Teacher Assn. **[1502]**, Downers Grove, IL
Downriver Coun. for the Arts **[9901]**, Taylor, MI
Downriver Genealogical Soc. **[8812]**, Lincoln Park, MI

Down's Syndrome
Down Syndrome Assn. of West Michigan **[7923]**, Grand Rapids, MI
Down Syndrome Assn. of Wisconsin **[19001]**, Milwaukee, WI

Downtown Bloomington Commn. **[4213]**, Bloomington, IN
Downtown Collinsville Main St. Prog. **[1290]**, Collinsville, IL
Downtown Evansville **[4539]**, Evansville, IN
Downtown Fond du Lac Partnership **[17971]**, Fond du Lac, WI
Downtown Kiwanis Club of Bloomington **[4214]**, Bloomington, IN
Downtown Kiwanis Club of Jackson, Michigan **[8362]**, Jackson, MI
Downtown Lima **[15651]**, Lima, OH
Downtown Minneapolis Trans. Mgt. Org. **[11555]**, Minneapolis, MN
Downtown Neighborhood Assn. of Elgin **[1586]**, Elgin, IL
Downtown Ohio **[★14453]**
Downtown Ohio Development Found. **[★14453]**
Downtown St. Charles Partnership **[3380]**, St. Charles, IL
Downtown West Bend Assn. **[20118]**, West Bend, WI
Doylestown Lions Club **[16537]**, Rittman, OH

Drag Racing
Citywide Drag Racing Association **[2046]**, Homewood, IL

Dream Factory of Central Illinois **[2986]**, Pekin, IL
Dream Factory of Southern Ohio **[17197]**, West Union, OH
Dreams for Kids **[873]**, Chicago, IL
Dresden REACT **[15039]**, Dresden, OH
Dress for Success Chicago **[874]**, Chicago, IL
Dress for Success Cincinnati **[13815]**, Cincinnati, OH
Dress for Success Cleveland **[14109]**, Cleveland, OH
Dress for Success Detroit **[8171]**, Highland Park, MI
Dress for Success Flint **[7722]**, Flint, MI
Dress for Success Indianapolis **[5103]**, Indianapolis, IN
Dress for Success Joliet **[2102]**, Joliet, IL
Dress for Success Michigan **[10203]**, Ypsilanti, MI
Dress for Success, Northwest Minnesota **[11134]**, Hawley, MN
Dress for Success Peoria **[3015]**, Peoria, IL
Dress for Success Racine **[19554]**, Racine, WI
Dress for Success Warren-Youngstown **[17100]**, Warren, OH
Drifting Dunes Girl Scout Coun. **[5769]**, Merrillville, IN
Driftless Area Gem and Mineral Club **[19903]**, Tomah, WI
Driftskippers Snowmobile Club **[7208]**, Coloma, MI
Drink Assn; Michigan Soft **[8718]**, Lansing, MI
Drug Abuse Counselors; Ohio Assn. of Alcoholism and **[14541]**, Columbus, OH
Drug Abuse; Wisconsin Assn. on Alcohol and Other **[18649]**, Madison, WI
Drug Coun; Central East Alcoholism and **[564]**, Charleston, IL
Drug-Free Marion County **[5104]**, Indianapolis, IN
Drug Info. Found; Amer. Alcohol and **[8528]**, Lansing, MI

Drug Rehabilitation
Natl. Alliance of Methadone Advocates of Chicago **[2616]**, Mundelein, IL
Natl. Alliance of Methadone Advocates of Indiana **[5593]**, La Crosse, IN
Wisconsin Chap. of the Natl. Alliance of Methadone Advocates **[19163]**, Milwaukee, WI

Drum and Bugle Corps Assn; Madison **[19860]**, Sun Prairie, WI
Drums; Celtic Cross Pipes and **[1770]**, Galesburg, IL

Drunk Driving
Indiana SADD **[6362]**, Union City, IN
Mothers Against Drunk Driving, Central Indiana **[4183]**, Beech Grove, IN
Ohio SADD **[15502]**, Independence, OH

Drunk Driving, Dupage County; Mothers Against **[2301]**, Lisle, IL
Drunk Driving, Heartland Chapter; Mothers Against **[1543]**, East Peoria, IL
Drunk Driving, Kent County Chap; Mothers Against **[7986]**, Grand Rapids, MI
Drunk Driving, Macomb County; Mothers Against **[9091]**, Mount Clemens, MI
Drunk Driving, Michigan State; Mothers Against **[8733]**, Lansing, MI
Drunk Driving, Oakland County; Mothers Against **[10088]**, Waterford, MI
Drunk Driving, Southwestern Ohio; Mothers Against **[13912]**, Cincinnati, OH
Drunk Driving, State Off; Mothers Against **[12538]**, St. Paul, MN
Drunk Driving, Wabash Valley Chap; Mothers Against **[6335]**, Terre Haute, IN
Drunk Driving, Waukesha County; Mothers Against **[19991]**, Waukesha, WI
Drunk Driving, Winona County; Mothers Against **[12956]**, Winona, MN
Drunk Driving, Wisconsin State; Mothers Against **[17503]**, Appleton, WI

Dry Cleaning
Ohio Cleaners Assn. **[14582]**, Columbus, OH
Wisconsin Fabricare Inst. **[18160]**, Greenfield, WI

Du Page County Historical Museum **[★3983]**
Du Page County Historical Soc. **[3983]**, Wheaton, IL
Du Page County (IL) Genealogical Soc. **[3984]**, Wheaton, IL
Du Page Genealogical Soc. **[★3984]**
Du Quoin Chamber of Commerce **[1517]**, Du Quoin, IL
Dublin Coffman/Jerome - Young Life **[14424]**, Columbus, OH
Dublin Lions Club - Ohio **[16032]**, Milford Center, OH
Dublin Scioto - Young Life **[14425]**, Columbus, OH
Dubois/Pike and Warrick County RSVP **[5527]**, Jasper, IN

Duck
Duckling Coun. **[875]**, Chicago, IL

Duckling Coun. **[875]**, Chicago, IL
DuKane A.B.A.T.E. **[3939]**, West Chicago, IL
Duluth Area Assn. of Realtors **[10812]**, Duluth, MN
Duluth Area Chamber of Commerce **[10813]**, Duluth, MN
Duluth Audubon Soc. **[10814]**, Duluth, MN
Duluth Builders Exchange **[10815]**, Duluth, MN
Duluth Chamber of Commerce **[★10813]**
Duluth Convention and Visitors Bur. **[10816]**, Duluth, MN
Duluth Curling Club **[10817]**, Duluth, MN
Duluth Figure Skating Club **[10818]**, Duluth, MN
Duluth Lions Club **[10819]**, Duluth, MN
Duluth Saddle Club **[10820]**, Duluth, MN
Duluth Spirit Valley Lions Club **[10821]**, Duluth, MN
Duncan Falls-Philo Lions Club **[17437]**, Zanesville, OH
Dunes Calumet Audubon Soc. **[4856]**, Griffith, IN
Dunes-Kalamazoo Orchid Soc. **[10049]**, Vicksburg, MI
Dunkirk Area Chamber of Commerce **[4466]**, Dunkirk, IN

Dunkirk Chamber of Commerce [★4466]
Dunlap - Central Illinois - Young Life [3886], Washington, IL
Dunlap Wyldlife - Wyldlife [3887], Washington, IL
Dupage Area AIFA [447], Carol Stream, IL
DuPage Convention and Visitors Bur. [2771], Oak Brook, IL
DuPage Figure Skating Club [2196], Lake Forest, IL
DuPage Habitat for Humanity [3985], Wheaton, IL
DuPage Libertarians [448], Carol Stream, IL
DuPage Power Squadron [3969], Westmont, IL
DuPage Senior Citizens Coun. [2331], Lombard, IL
DuPage Soc. for Human Rsrc. Mgt. [2631], Naperville, IL
DuPage Unitarian Universalist Church [2632], Naperville, IL
Dupo Coin Club [1695], Fairview Heights, IL
Durand Area Chamber of Commerce [7490], Durand, MI
Durand Lions Club [7491], Durand, MI
Durendal Fencing Club [18505], Madison, WI
Dutch
Public Relations Soc. of Am., West Michigan Chap. [8003], Grand Rapids, MI
Dwight Area Chamber of Commerce [1526], Dwight, IL
Dyer Chamber of Commerce [4467], Dyer, IN
Dyslexia
Dyslexia Inst. of Minnesota [12135], Rochester, MN
Northern Ohio Br. of the Intl. Dyslexia Assn. [16682], Solon, OH
Dyslexia Assn; Northern Ohio Br. of the Intl. [16682], Solon, OH
Dyslexia Inst. of Minnesota [12135], Rochester, MN
Dyslexia Soc; Northern Ohio Br. of the Orton [★16682]

E

E Angel Community [4036], Winnetka, IL
Eagan-Heights Figure Skating Club [10319], Apple Valley, MN
Eagle Creek Beagle Club [15722], Loveland, OH
Eagle Historical Soc. [17845], Eagle, WI
Eagle River Area Chamber of Commerce [★17850]
Eagle River Figure Skating Club [19964], Watersmeet, WI
Eagles
Fraternal Order of Eagles, Bedford No. 654 [4170], Bedford, IN
Fraternal Order of Eagles, Bemidji No. 351 [10415], Bemidji, MN
Fraternal Order of Eagles, Huron No. 2875 [15490], Huron, OH
Fraternal Order of Eagles, Waterford No. 2887 [10082], Waterford, MI
Eagles Cricket Club [3434], Schaumburg, IL
Early Settlers Assn. [★3134]
Early Settler's Assn. of Brecksville [★13409]
Earth Day Coalition [14110], Cleveland, OH
Earth First! Illinois / Last Wizards [876], Chicago, IL
Earth Share of Illinois [877], Chicago, IL
Earth Share of Michigan [6836], Bath, MI
Earth Share of Ohio [14426], Columbus, OH
EarthSave, Bloomington [4215], Bloomington, IN
EarthSave, Cincinnati [13816], Cincinnati, OH
Earthsave Intl., Chicago [878], Chicago, IL
Earthsave Intl., Minnesota [11556], Minneapolis, MN
EarthSave, Twin Cities [11557], Minneapolis, MN
East Aurora Young Life [2633], Naperville, IL
East Canton Lions Club [15071], East Canton, OH
East Central Coun. of Teachers of Mathematics [479], Casey, IL
East Central Dairy Goat Club [12645], Scandia, MN
East Central Illinois Bluebird Soc. [2946], Paris, IL
East Central Illinois MOAA [518], Champaign, IL
East Central Illinois Youth for Christ [519], Champaign, IL
East Central Indiana AIFA [5873], Muncie, IN
East Central Indiana Bd. of Realtors [4414], Connersville, IN
East Central Indiana Human Rsrcs. Assn. [5874], Muncie, IN
East Central Indiana Payroll Assn. [5875], Muncie, IN
East Central Indiana Youth for Christ [4105], Anderson, IN
East Central Michigan Soc. for Healthcare Engg. [9986], Troy, MI
East Central Minnesota Habitat for Humanity [10620], Cambridge, MN
East Central Minnesota RSVP [11832], Mora, MN
East Central Minnesota Young Life [10621], Cambridge, MN
East Central Ohio Home Building Industry Association [16042], Mineral City, OH
East Central Wisconsin Astronomers [19456], Pine River, WI
East Central Wisconsin Regional Planning Commn. [18858], Menasha, WI
East Central Wisconsin Sheet Metal Contractors Assn. [19693], Sheboygan, WI
East Central Wyldlife [10622], Cambridge, MN
East China Consolidated Parent Teacher Organization [7152], China, MI
East Coast 4 Wheel Drive Assn. [14252], Cleves, OH
East Detroit Historical Soc. [7575], Eastpointe, MI
East Flint Lions Club [7723], Flint, MI
East Grand Forks Chamber of Commerce [10882], East Grand Forks, MN
East Grand Forks Lions Club [10883], East Grand Forks, MN
East Grand Rapids High - Young Life [7924], Grand Rapids, MI
East Grand Rapids Middle School - Wyldlife [7925], Grand Rapids, MI
East Jackson Lions Club [8363], Jackson, MI
East Jordan Area Chamber of Commerce [7496], East Jordan, MI
East Knox Lions Club [15467], Howard, OH
East Lake County Chamber of Commerce [12770], Two Harbors, MN
East Lansing Aikikai [7515], East Lansing, MI
East Lansing-Meridian Lions Club [9268], Okemos, MI
East Lansing Police Athletic League [7516], East Lansing, MI
East Lansing - Young Life [7517], East Lansing, MI
East Liverpool Area Chamber of Commerce [15078], East Liverpool, OH
East Liverpool Beagle Club [15677], Lisbon, OH
East Liverpool Lions Club [15079], East Liverpool, OH
East Michigan District of Precision Metalforming Assn. [9987], Troy, MI
East Michigan Environmental Action Coun. [6984], Bloomfield Hills, MI
East Peoria Chamber of Commerce [★1542]
East Peoria Chamber of Commerce and Tourism [1542], East Peoria, IL
East Peoria - Young Life [3888], Washington, IL
East Prairie School Educal. Found. [3484], Skokie, IL
East Side AIFA [1819], Glen Carbon, IL
East Side Assn. of Insurance and Financial Advisors [2845], O'Fallon, IL
East Side Bus. Men's Assn. [18506], Madison, WI
East Side Chamber of Commerce [879], Chicago, IL
East Side Life Underwriters Assn. [★2845]
East Side Organizing Proj. [14111], Cleveland, OH
East Town Assn. [19002], Milwaukee, WI
East Town Bus. and Merchant's Assn. [20073], Wauwatosa, WI
East Troy Area Chamber of Commerce [17855], East Troy, WI
East View Rod and Gun Club [16360], Parma, OH
East West Corporate Corridor Assn. [2634], Naperville, IL
Easter Seals ARC of Northeast Indiana [4649], Fort Wayne, IN
Easter Seals Central Illinois [1391], Decatur, IL
Easter Seals Central and Southeast Ohio [13665], Chillicothe, OH
Easter Seals Central and Southeast Ohio [14427], Columbus, OH
Easter Seals Central and Southeast Ohio [15816], Marietta, OH
Easter Seals Genesee County, Michigan [7724], Flint, MI
Easter Seals-Joliet [2103], Joliet, IL
Easter Seals of LaSalle and Bur. Counties, Illinois [2897], Ottawa, IL
Easter Seals Metropolitan Chicago, Illinois [880], Chicago, IL
Easter Seals Michigan [9927], Traverse City, MI
Easter Seals Michigan [10081], Waterford, MI
Easter Seals - Minnesota; Goodwill Indus./ [12420], St. Paul, MN
Easter Seals Minnesota - Rochester [12136], Rochester, MN
Easter Seals Minnesota - Willmar [12914], Willmar, MN
Easter Seals Northeast Ohio [13050], Akron, OH
Easter Seals Northeast Ohio [13427], Broadview Heights, OH
Easter Seals Northeast Ohio [15580], Lakewood, OH
Easter Seals Northeast Ohio [17025], University Heights, OH
Easter Seals Northeast Ohio, Canton [13563], Canton, OH
Easter Seals Northwestern Ohio [15703], Lorain, OH
Easter Seals Northwestern Ohio [16260], Norwalk, OH
Easter Seals Northwestern Ohio [16607], Sandusky, OH
Easter Seals Northwestern Ohio [16911], Toledo, OH
Easter Seals St. Clairsville, Ohio [16570], St. Clairsville, OH
Easter Seals Southeastern Wisconsin [19747], South Milwaukee, WI
Easter Seals Southwestern Ohio [13817], Cincinnati, OH
Easter Seals Trumbull County, Ohio [17101], Warren, OH
Easter Seals Wayne and Union Counties [4341], Centerville, IN
Easter Seals Wisconsin [18507], Madison, WI
Easter Seals Youngstown [17396], Youngstown, OH
Eastern Europe
Chicago Action for Jews in the Former Soviet Union [1988], Highland Park, IL
Eastern (Greene) - Young Life [4216], Bloomington, IN
Eastern Howard Performing Arts Soc. [4845], Greentown, IN
Eastern Illinois AIFA [569], Charleston, IL
Eastern Illinois Chap. Natl. Elecl. Contractors Assn. [2104], Joliet, IL
Eastern Illinois Dental Soc. [3793], Tuscola, IL
Eastern Indiana Beagle Club [4342], Centerville, IN
Eastern Indiana Human Rsrc. Assn. [6090], Richmond, IN
Eastern Market Merchants Association [10063], Warren, MI
Eastern Maumee Bay Chamber of Commerce [16302], Oregon, OH
Eastern Michigan Chap. of Amer. Soc. of Plumbing Engineers [7283], Dearborn Heights, MI
Eastern Michigan Mortgage Lenders Assn. [9234], Novi, MI
Eastern Neuroradiological Soc. [2772], Oak Brook, IL
Eastern Ohio Angus Assn. [16626], Senecaville, OH
Eastern Ohio Coun. of Teachers of Mathematics [17397], Youngstown, OH
Eastern Ohio Hea. Info. Mgt. Assn. [17021], Uniontown, OH
Eastern Ottawa Young Life [6621], Allendale, MI
Eastern Star Minnesota Grand Chap; Order of the [11718], Minneapolis, MN
Eastern Thumb Assn. of Realtors [9432], Port Huron, MI
Eastern Upper Peninsula Beagle Club [9928], Traverse City, MI
Eastern Upper Peninsula Bd. of Realtors [9718], Sault Ste. Marie, MI
Eastern Upper Peninsula Fine Arts Coun. [7240], De Tour Village, MI
Eastern Upper Peninsula Search and Rescue [9196], Newberry, MI
Eastern - Young Life [4217], Bloomington, IN
Eastlake Coin Club [15966], Mentor, OH
Eastlake Women's Club [15085], Eastlake, OH
Eastland Disaster Historical Soc. [70], Arlington Heights, IL
Eastpointe Chamber of Commerce [7576], Eastpointe, MI
Eastwood - Wyldlife [5105], Indianapolis, IN
Eastwood - Young Life [13388], Bowling Green, OH

Eaton County Genealogical Soc. **[7121]**, Charlotte, MI
Eaton County United Way **[7122]**, Charlotte, MI
Eaton - Preble County Chamber of Commerce **[15088]**, Eaton, OH
Eaton Rapids Lions Club **[7581]**, Eaton Rapids, MI
Eaton Rapids Middle School - Wyldlife **[7926]**, Grand Rapids, MI
Eaton Rapids United Way **[★7122]**
Eaton Rapids - Young Life **[7518]**, East Lansing, MI
Eau Claire Area Chamber of Commerce **[17873]**, Eau Claire, WI
Eau Claire Area Economic Development Corp. **[17874]**, Eau Claire, WI
Eau Claire Area Found. **[17875]**, Eau Claire, WI
Eau Claire Area Indus. Development Corp. **[★17874]**
Eau Claire Curling Club **[17876]**, Eau Claire, WI
Eau Claire Figure Skating Club **[17877]**, Eau Claire, WI
Eau Claire Horseshoe Club **[17753]**, Chippewa Falls, WI
Eau Claire Lakes Bus. Assn. of Barnes and Gordon **[18060]**, Gordon, WI
Eau Claire Lions Club **[7587]**, Eau Claire, MI
Ebony Ice Ski Club **[19003]**, Milwaukee, WI
Echo Hills Kennel Club of Ohio **[15739]**, Ludlow Falls, OH
Ecology
EarthSave, Bloomington **[4215]**, Bloomington, IN
EarthSave, Cincinnati **[13816]**, Cincinnati, OH
Earthsave Intl., Chicago **[878]**, Chicago, IL
Earthsave Intl., Minnesota **[11556]**, Minneapolis, MN
EarthSave, Twin Cities **[11557]**, Minneapolis, MN
Greater Cleveland Ecology Association **[14131]**, Cleveland, OH
Michigan Sierra Club **[8713]**, Lansing, MI
Sierra Club - Illinois Chap. - Piasa Palisades Gp. **[44]**, Alton, IL
Sierra Club - John Muir Chap. **[18614]**, Madison, WI
Sierra Club - John Muir Chap. - Great Waters Gp. **[19118]**, Milwaukee, WI
Sierra Club - Mackinac Chap. **[8759]**, Lansing, MI
Sierra Club - Mackinac Chap. - Crossroads Gp. **[7022]**, Brighton, MI
Sierra Club - Mackinac Chap. - Huron Valley Gp. **[6765]**, Ann Arbor, MI
Sierra Club - Midwest Off. **[18615]**, Madison, WI
Washtenaw Sierra Club Inner City Outings **[6790]**, Ann Arbor, MI
Economic Alliance; Osceola **[9482]**, Reed City, MI
Economic Club; Women's **[★7377]**
Economic Development
Benton-West City Economic Development Corp. **[233]**, Benton, IL
Bridge Syndicate **[10808]**, Duluth, MN
Buckeye Hills-Hocking Valley Regional Development District **[15815]**, Marietta, OH
Chippewa Falls Indus. Development Corp. **[17750]**, Chippewa Falls, WI
City of La Porte Urban Enterprise Zone **[5595]**, La Porte, IN
Clifton Heights Community Urban Redevelopment Corp. **[13805]**, Cincinnati, OH
Columbus Downtown Development Corp. **[14383]**, Columbus, OH
Detroit Economic Club **[7346]**, Detroit, MI
East Central Wisconsin Regional Planning Commn. **[18858]**, Menasha, WI
Euclid-St. Clair Development Corp. **[14117]**, Cleveland, OH
Hammond Urban Enterprise Assn. **[4881]**, Hammond, IN
Indiana Assn. for Community Economic Development **[5168]**, Indianapolis, IN
Lapeer Development Corp. **[8779]**, Lapeer, MI
Lincoln County Economic Development Corp. **[18895]**, Merrill, WI
Newark Alliance **[16178]**, Newark, OH
Northwest Suburban Alliance for Commerce and Indus. **[3342]**, Rolling Meadows, IL
Osceola Economic Alliance **[9482]**, Reed City, MI
Portland Economic Development Corp. **[6065]**, Portland, IN
Regional Economic Development Corp. **[2409]**, Marion, IL
Southwest Detroit Business Association **[7439]**, Detroit, MI
Warren County Local Economic Development Org. **[6530]**, Williamsport, IN
Wisconsin Economic Development Assn. **[18697]**, Madison, WI
World Affairs Coun. of Greater Cincinnati **[14026]**, Cincinnati, OH
Economic Development; Alsip Chamber of Commerce and **[30]**, Alsip, IL
Economic Development; Carroll County Chamber of Commerce and **[13604]**, Carrollton, OH
Economic Development Commn; Hamilton County Chamber of Commerce and **[2466]**, McLeansboro, IL
Economic Development Corp; Benton-West City **[233]**, Benton, IL
Economic Development Corp; Lincoln County **[18895]**, Merrill, WI
Economic Development Corp; Oneida County **[19602]**, Rhinelander, WI
Economic Development Corp; Portland **[6065]**, Portland, IN
Economic Development Corp; Regional **[2409]**, Marion, IL
Economic Development; Illinois Valley Area Chamber of Commerce and **[2182]**, La Salle, IL
Economic Development and Info. Tech; Community **[9699]**, Saline, MI
Economic Development; Jennings County Chamber of Commerce/ **[★5995]**
Economic Development; Metropolis Area Chamber of Commerce, Tourism and **[★2484]**
Economic Development Off; Ottawa County **[6626]**, Allendale, MI
Economic Development Org. **[★1874]**
Economic Development Org; Warren County Local **[6530]**, Williamsport, IN
Economic Educ; Illinois Coun. on **[1436]**, DeKalb, IL
Economic Roundtable of the Ohio Valley **[15817]**, Marietta, OH
Economics
Cleveland Assn. for Bus. Economics **[14094]**, Cleveland, OH
Economic Roundtable of the Ohio Valley **[15817]**, Marietta, OH
Illinois Coun. on Economic Educ. **[1436]**, DeKalb, IL
Ecorse-River Rouge Lions Club **[9492]**, River Rouge, MI
Ecumenical
Evangelical Pastors Fellowship of Rochester **[12138]**, Rochester, MN
Illinois Conf. of Churches **[3597]**, Springfield, IL
Intl. Assn. of Ministers Wives and Ministers Widows, Illinois **[2335]**, Lombard, IL
Intl. Assn. of Ministers Wives and Ministers Widows, Michigan **[7379]**, Detroit, MI
Intl. Assn. of Ministers Wives and Ministers Widows, Ohio **[17122]**, Warrensville Heights, OH
Intl. Assn. of Ministers Wives and Ministers Widows, Wisconsin **[19033]**, Milwaukee, WI
Eden Prairie Chamber of Commerce **[10890]**, Eden Prairie, MN
Eden Prairie Coun. for the Gifted and Talented **[10891]**, Eden Prairie, MN
Eden Prairie Figure Skating Club **[10892]**, Eden Prairie, MN
Eden Prairie Lions Club **[10893]**, Eden Prairie, MN
Eden Prairie - Young Life **[11182]**, Hopkins, MN
Eden Valley Lions Club **[10904]**, Eden Valley, MN
Edgar County Genealogical Society **[2947]**, Paris, IL
Edgar County Sportsman's Club **[2948]**, Paris, IL
Edgebrook Chamber of Commerce **[881]**, Chicago, IL
Edgebrook-Sauganash Chamber of Commerce **[★881]**
Edgerton Area Chamber of Commerce **[17917]**, Edgerton, WI
Edgerton Chamber of Commerce **[15093]**, Edgerton, OH
Edgewater Community Coun. **[882]**, Chicago, IL
Edgewater Yacht Club **[14112]**, Cleveland, OH
Edgewood - Young Life **[4218]**, Bloomington, IN
Edina Lions Club **[10909]**, Edina, MN
Edina Model Yacht Club No. 192 **[10969]**, Excelsior, MN
Edina - Young Life **[11183]**, Hopkins, MN
Edinburgh Lions Club **[4480]**, Edinburgh, IN
Edison Birthplace Assn. **[16021]**, Milan, OH
Editors, Cleveland Chap; Amer. Soc. of Bus. Press **[★14063]**
Editors, Cleveland Chap; Amer. Soc. of Bus. Publication **[14063]**, Cleveland, OH
Edmore Lions Club **[6970]**, Blanchard, MI
Education
Advocates for Colorectal Educ. **[12345]**, St. Paul, MN
AFT-Wisconsin **[18443]**, Madison, WI
Amer. Fed. of Teachers, AFL-CIO - Professional Guild of Ohio Local Union 1960 **[14283]**, Columbus, OH
Apollo Educ. Assn. **[15648]**, Lima, OH
Assn. of Eritreans and their Friends in Michigan **[7511]**, East Lansing, MI
Assn. of Wisconsin School Administrators **[18486]**, Madison, WI
Clague Middle School Parent-Teachers-Students Org. **[6691]**, Ann Arbor, MI
Community Alliance to Promote Educ. **[5871]**, Muncie, IN
Cooperative for Educ. **[13809]**, Cincinnati, OH
Creative Change Educal. Solutions **[10202]**, Ypsilanti, MI
East Prairie School Educal. Found. **[3484]**, Skokie, IL
Educ. Minnesota **[12408]**, St. Paul, MN
Educ. Minnesota, Dilworth **[10788]**, Dilworth, MN
Educ. Minnesota, Osseo **[11410]**, Maple Grove, MN
Educ. Minnesota, Willmar **[12915]**, Willmar, MN
Educ. Minnesota, Windom **[12939]**, Windom, MN
Evanston-Skokie District 65 Educ. Found. **[1657]**, Evanston, IL
Fox Valley German Amer. Team of Educal. Sponsors **[449]**, Carol Stream, IL
Franklin Township Educ. Found. **[5118]**, Indianapolis, IN
Gift of Reading **[7365]**, Detroit, MI
Illinois Educ. Assn. **[3601]**, Springfield, IL
Illinois High School and Coll. Driver Educ. Assn. **[2189]**, Lake Bluff, IL
Indiana Student Public Interest Res. Gp. **[4230]**, Bloomington, IN
Lake Michigan Coll. Educ. Assn. **[6920]**, Benton Harbor, MI
Michigan Assn. of Educal. Representatives **[7862]**, Grand Haven, MI
Michigan Assn. of School Administrators **[8626]**, Lansing, MI
Michigan Coalition of Essential Schools **[8385]**, Jackson, MI
Michigan Educ. Assn. **[7539]**, East Lansing, MI
Michigan Educational Res. Assn. **[7746]**, Flint, MI
Michigan Fed. of Teachers and School Related Personnel **[7396]**, Detroit, MI
Michigan School Bus. Officials **[8709]**, Lansing, MI
Michigan School Investment Assn. **[8710]**, Lansing, MI
Middle Cities Educ. Assn. **[9296]**, Okemos, MI
Natl. Earth Sci. Teachers Assn., East Central Chap. **[15952]**, Medina, OH
Ohio Assn. of Elementary School Administrators **[14552]**, Columbus, OH
Ohio Assn. of Secondary School Administrators **[14566]**, Columbus, OH
Ohio Educ. Assn. **[14600]**, Columbus, OH
Ohio Educational Ser. Center Assn. **[14602]**, Columbus, OH
Ohio Middle School Assn. **[14638]**, Columbus, OH
Ohio School Bds. Assn. **[14670]**, Columbus, OH
Our Lady of Grace School Home and School Assn. **[4919]**, Highland, IN
Parents As Teachers of Hammond Lake County **[4890]**, Hammond, IN
Parents for Public Schools, Cincinnati Chap. **[13952]**, Cincinnati, OH
Parents for Public Schools, Oberlin Chap. **[16292]**, Oberlin, OH
Parents for Public Schools of Toledo **[16947]**, Toledo, OH
Professors Fund for Educational Issues **[8752]**, Lansing, MI

Springfield Parents for Public Schools **[3683]**, Springfield, IL
Tri-Rivers Educ. Assn. **[15855]**, Marion, OH
Warren Arts and Educ. Found. **[5498]**, Indianapolis, IN
West Bloomfield School District Parent Communications Network **[10126]**, West Bloomfield, MI
Wisconsin Educ. Assn. Coun. **[18698]**, Madison, WI
Wisconsin School-Age Care Alliance **[18268]**, Janesville, WI
Educ. Assn; Apollo **[15648]**, Lima, OH
Educ. Assn; Creation **[19455]**, Pine River, WI
Educ. Assn; Green Bay **[18106]**, Green Bay, WI
Educ. Assn; Illinois **[3601]**, Springfield, IL
Educ. Assn; Indiana Non-Public **[5266]**, Indianapolis, IN
Educ. Assn; Lake Michigan Coll. **[6920]**, Benton Harbor, MI
Educ. Assn; Middle Cities **[9296]**, Okemos, MI
Educ. Assn; Tri-Rivers **[15855]**, Marion, OH
Education Association; Wellington **[17158]**, Wellington, OH
Educ. Coalition; Community **[4411]**, Connersville, IN
Educ; Community Alliance to Promote **[5871]**, Muncie, IN
Educ; Community Financial **[14410]**, Columbus, OH
Education; Comprehensive Health **[18996]**, Milwaukee, WI
Educ. Coun; Holocaust **[14458]**, Columbus, OH
Education Div; Childcare Works- **[★11541]**
Education Fund; League of Women Voters of Illinois **[★1026]**
Educ; Illinois Assn. for Career and Tech. **[3565]**, Springfield, IL
Educ; Illinois Assn. for Media in **[★404]**
Educ; Illinois Coun. on Economic **[1436]**, DeKalb, IL
Educ. Leadership; Wisconsin Women in Higher **[19188]**, Milwaukee, WI
Educ. Minnesota **[12408]**, St. Paul, MN
Educ. Minnesota, Dilworth **[10788]**, Dilworth, MN
Educ. Minnesota, Osseo **[11410]**, Maple Grove, MN
Educ. Minnesota, Willmar **[12915]**, Willmar, MN
Educ. Minnesota, Windom **[12939]**, Windom, MN
Educ. Partnership; Sangamon - Menard County Agricultural **[3673]**, Springfield, IL
Educ., Recreation, and Dance; Illinois Assn. for Hea., Physical **[2078]**, Jacksonville, IL
Educ., Recreation and Dance; Ohio Assn. for Hea., Physical **[13245]**, Avon Lake, OH
Education, Special
Educational Teleconsortium of Michigan **[8837]**, Livonia, MI
Educ. and Training Sers; Wisconsin Procurement Inst. **[19176]**, Milwaukee, WI
Educ. of Young Children; Michigan Assn. for the **[7534]**, East Lansing, MI
Education Youth
Horizons for Youth **[917]**, Chicago, IL
Summit Educ. Initiative **[13096]**, Akron, OH
Wisconsin Assn. of School District Administrators **[18666]**, Madison, WI
Educational Advocacy
Common Cause - Ohio **[14408]**, Columbus, OH
Illinois Student Environment Network **[3825]**, Urbana, IL
Indiana Non-Public Educ. Assn. **[5266]**, Indianapolis, IN
Inner-City Teaching Corps **[976]**, Chicago, IL
IUB Latino Faculty and Staff Coun. **[4238]**, Bloomington, IN
Michigan Communities In Schools **[8210]**, Holland, MI
Wisconsin Assn. of Educational Opportunity Prog. Personnel **[19155]**, Milwaukee, WI
Educational Funding
Greater Cincinnati TV Educal. Found. **[13855]**, Cincinnati, OH
Indiana Student Financial Aid Assn. **[6330]**, Terre Haute, IN
Michigan Student Financial Aid Assn. **[10029]**, University Center, MI
Midwest Assn. of Student Financial Aid Administrators **[15208]**, Findlay, OH
Minnesota Assn. of Financial Aid Administrators **[11436]**, Marshall, MN
Ohio Assn. of Student Financial Aid Administrators **[13010]**, Ada, OH
Wisconsin Assn. of Student Financial Aid Administrators **[18667]**, Madison, WI
Educational Issues; Professors Fund for **[8752]**, Lansing, MI
Educational Media Assn; Wisconsin **[17649]**, Boscobel, WI
Educational Reform
BASICS in Milwaukee **[18978]**, Milwaukee, WI
Educational Res. Assn; Michigan **[7746]**, Flint, MI
Educal. Solutions; Creative Change **[10202]**, Ypsilanti, MI
Educal. Sponsors; Fox Valley German Amer. Team of **[449]**, Carol Stream, IL
Educational Teleconsortium of Michigan **[8837]**, Livonia, MI
Educators
Illinois Music Educators Assn. **[2509]**, Mokena, IL
Michigan Assn. of Middle School Educators **[9614]**, Saginaw, MI
Minnesota Music Educators Assn. **[10540]**, Brooklyn Center, MN
Educators; Assn. for Indiana Media **[5728]**, Marion, IN
Educators' Assn; Wisconsin Retired **[18916]**, Middleton, WI
Educators for Social Responsibility, Grand Rapids Chap. **[7927]**, Grand Rapids, MI
Edwards River Earth Sci. Club **[20]**, Aledo, IL
Edwardsburg Area Chamber of Commerce **[7590]**, Edwardsburg, MI
Edwardsburg Lions Club **[9205]**, Niles, MI
Edwardsburg Museum Gp. **[7591]**, Edwardsburg, MI
Edwardsville Glen Carbon Chamber of Commerce **[★1558]**
Edwardsville - Glen Carbon Chamber of Commerce **[1558]**, Edwardsville, IL
Egg Bd; Chicago Butter and **[★818]**
Eggers Middle School PTSA **[4878]**, Hammond, IN
Egyptian Beagle Club **[1303]**, Coulterville, IL
Egyptian Bd. of Realtors **[2596]**, Mount Vernon, IL
Eitzen Lions Club **[10933]**, Eitzen, MN
Ekklesia Development Corp. **[13818]**, Cincinnati, OH
El Paso Chamber of Commerce **[1576]**, El Paso, IL
Elbow Lake Lions Club **[10935]**, Elbow Lake, MN
Elburn Lions Club **[1579]**, Elburn, IL
Elder Network **[12137]**, Rochester, MN
Eldercircle RSVP **[11083]**, Grand Rapids, MN
Eldorado Lions Club **[15096]**, Eldorado, OH
Elec. Cooperatives; Indiana Statewide Assn. of Rural **[5325]**, Indianapolis, IN
Elec. and Gas Assn; Michigan **[8660]**, Lansing, MI
Elec. League of Indiana **[5106]**, Indianapolis, IN
Elec. Ser. Dealers Assn. of Illinois **[883]**, Chicago, IL
Electrical
Elecl. Indus. of Central Ohio Labor Mgt. Cooperation **[14428]**, Columbus, OH
Elecl. Maintenance Engineers of Milwaukee **[19286]**, New Berlin, WI
Minnesota Elecl. Assn. **[11645]**, Minneapolis, MN
Natl. Elecl. Contractors Assn., Greater Cleveland Chap. **[14174]**, Cleveland, OH
Ohio Rural Elec. Cooperatives **[14669]**, Columbus, OH
Elecl. Contractors Assn; Central Illinois Chap. Natl. **[3011]**, Peoria, IL
Elecl. Contractors Assn; Central Indiana Chap. Natl. **[5075]**, Indianapolis, IN
Elecl. Contractors' Assn. of City of Chicago **[3956]**, Westchester, IL
Elecl. Contractors Assn; Greater Cleveland Chap. Natl. **[14129]**, Cleveland, OH
Elecl. Contractors Assn., Greater Cleveland Chap; Natl. **[14174]**, Cleveland, OH
Elecl. Contractors Assn; Illinois Chap. Natl. **[3588]**, Springfield, IL
Elecl. Contractors Assn. - Milwaukee Chap. - NECA **[19004]**, Milwaukee, WI
Elecl. Contractors Assn; Milwaukee School of Engg., Natl. **[19068]**, Milwaukee, WI
Elecl. Contractors Assn., North Central Ohio Chap; Natl. **[13070]**, Akron, OH
Elecl. Contractors Assn; Northern Illinois Chap. Natl. **[3294]**, Rockford, IL
Elecl. Contractors Assn; Penn-Ohio Chap. Natl. **[17410]**, Youngstown, OH
Elecl. Contractors Assn; Toledo Chap. Natl. **[16558]**, Rossford, OH
Elecl. Indus. of Central Ohio Labor Mgt. Cooperation **[14428]**, Columbus, OH
Elecl. Inspectors, Ohio Chap; Intl. Assn. of **[16661]**, Shreve, OH
Elecl. Maintenance Engineers of Milwaukee **[19286]**, New Berlin, WI
Elecl., Radio and Machine Workers of Am., Local 1111; United **[19141]**, Milwaukee, WI
Elecl. Workers AFL-CIO, LU 983; Intl. Brotherhood of **[4952]**, Huntington, IN
Electrical Workers AFL-CIO, LU 1220; Radio and TV Broadcast Engineers Intl. Brotherhood of **[★984]**
Elecl. Workers IBEW AFL-CIO, LU 1220 **[★984]**
Electricity
Greater Chicago Insulator Club **[3940]**, West Chicago, IL
Huron Valley Bottle and Insulator Club **[10084]**, Waterford, MI
Municipal Elec. Utilities of Wisconsin **[19861]**, Sun Prairie, WI
North Western Insulator Club **[12642]**, Savage, MN
Western Reserve Insulator Club **[16251]**, North Royalton, OH
Electromagnetic Compatibility Soc. - Twin Cities Chap; IEEE **[11584]**, Minneapolis, MN
Electronic Ser. Assn; Indiana **[4818]**, Greencastle, IN
Electronic Ser. Assn., Indianhead Chap; Wisconsin **[17910]**, Eau Claire, WI
Electronics
Assn. of Old Crows, Crane Roost **[4423]**, Crane, IN
Assn. of Old Crows, Windy City Chap. **[3338]**, Rolling Meadows, IL
Audio Engg. Soc., Ball State Univ. Sect. **[5870]**, Muncie, IN
Audio Engg. Soc., Cincinnati Sect. **[15872]**, Mason, OH
Audio Engg. Soc., Columbia Coll. Sect. **[756]**, Chicago, IL
Audio Engg. Soc., Detroit Sect. **[9790]**, Southfield, MI
Audio Engg. Soc., Music Tech Coll. Sect. **[12391]**, St. Paul, MN
Audio Engg. Soc., Ohio Univ. Sect. **[13201]**, Athens, OH
Audio Engg. Soc., Ridgewater Coll., Hutchinson Campus Sect. **[11204]**, Hutchinson, MN
Audio Engg. Soc., Univ. of Cincinnati Sect. **[13755]**, Cincinnati, OH
Audio Engg. Soc., Upper Midwest Sect. **[10650]**, Chaska, MN
Audio Engg. Soc., West Michigan Sect. **[6849]**, Battle Creek, MI
Electronics Representatives Assn. - Indiana/Kentucky Chap. **[5107]**, Indianapolis, IN
IEEE Electromagnetic Compatibility Soc., Chicago **[1503]**, Downers Grove, IL
IEEE Electromagnetic Compatibility Soc., Milwaukee **[17729]**, Cedarburg, WI
IEEE Electromagnetic Compatibility Soc., Southeastern Michigan **[7064]**, Canton, MI
IEEE Electromagnetic Compatibility Soc. - Twin Cities Chap. **[11584]**, Minneapolis, MN
IEEE Lasers and Electro-Optics Soc., Cleveland **[14140]**, Cleveland, OH
Intl. Brotherhood of Elecl. Workers, AFL-CIO, CFL - Local Union 306 **[13059]**, Akron, OH
Intl. Brotherhood of Elecl. Workers, AFL-CIO, CFL - Local Union 557 **[9610]**, Saginaw, MI
Intl. Brotherhood of Elecl. Workers, AFL-CIO, CFL - Local Union 601 **[531]**, Champaign, IL
Intl. Brotherhood of Elecl. Workers, AFL-CIO, CFL - Local Union 723 **[4682]**, Fort Wayne, IN
Intl. Brotherhood of Elecl. Workers, AFL-CIO, CFL - Local Union 1347 **[13870]**, Cincinnati, OH
Intl. Brotherhood of Elecl. Workers AFL-CIO, LU 983 **[4952]**, Huntington, IN
Intl. Brotherhood of Elecl. Workers, Local 1220 **[984]**, Chicago, IL
Intl. Union of Electronic, Elecl., Salaried, Machine and Furniture Workers, AFL-CIO-CLC - Local Union 750 **[13114]**, Alliance, OH
Intl. Union of Electronic, Elecl., Salaried, Machine and Furniture Workers, AFL-CIO-CLC - Local Union 755 **[14897]**, Dayton, OH

Wisconsin Electronic Ser. Assn., Indianhead Chap. **[17910]**, Eau Claire, WI
Electronics Representatives Assn. - Indiana/ Kentucky Chap. **[5107]**, Indianapolis, IN
Elementary School Administrators; Ohio Assn. of **[14552]**, Columbus, OH
Elementary School Principals; Ohio Assn. of **[★14552]**
Elf Khurafeh Shriners **[9608]**, Saginaw, MI
Elgin AIFA **[2773]**, Oak Brook, IL
Elgin Area Chamber of Commerce **[1587]**, Elgin, IL
Elgin Area Convention and Visitors Bur. **[1588]**, Elgin, IL
Elgin Area United Jewish Appeal **[★1585]**
Elgin Children's Chorus **[1589]**, Elgin, IL
Elgin Coin Club **[3497]**, South Elgin, IL
Elgin Lions Club **[10941]**, Elgin, MN
Elizabeth Chamber of Commerce **[1603]**, Elizabeth, IL
Elk Rapids Area Chamber of Commerce **[7595]**, Elk Rapids, MI
Elk Rapids Chamber of Commerce **[★7595]**
Elk Rapids Sportsman's Club **[7596]**, Elk Rapids, MI
Elk River Area Chamber of Commerce **[10945]**, Elk River, MN
Elk River Lions Club **[10946]**, Elk River, MN
Elkhart County Beagle Club **[7592]**, Edwardsburg, MI
Elkhart County Bd. of Realtors **[4492]**, Elkhart, IN
Elkhart County Chess Club **[4493]**, Elkhart, IN
Elkhart County RSVP **[4494]**, Elkhart, IN
Elkhart County Youth for Christ **[4495]**, Elkhart, IN
Elkhart Lake Area Chamber of Commerce **[17925]**, Elkhart Lake, WI
Elkhart Lions Club **[4496]**, Elkhart, IN
Elkhorn Area Chamber of Commerce **[17927]**, Elkhorn, WI
Elks
BPO Elks of the USA **[770]**, Chicago, IL
Elks Lodge **[20183]**, Wisconsin Rapids, WI
Illinois Elks Assn. **[2598]**, Mount Vernon, IL
Indiana Elks Assn. **[6193]**, Shelbyville, IN
Michigan Elks Assn. **[7018]**, Brighton, MI
Minnesota Elks Assn. **[11211]**, Hutchinson, MN
Ohio/West Virginia State Assn. of Emblem Club **[15288]**, Galion, OH
Wisconsin Elks Assn. **[19672]**, Schofield, WI
Wisconsin-Illinois-Indiana-Michigan State Assn. of Emblem Club **[190]**, Beardstown, IL
Elks Lodge **[403]**, Canton, IL
Elks Lodge **[10414]**, Bemidji, MN
Elks Lodge **[13819]**, Cincinnati, OH
Elks Lodge **[15198]**, Findlay, OH
Elks Lodge **[16912]**, Toledo, OH
Elks Lodge **[20183]**, Wisconsin Rapids, WI
Elks Lodge 2243; Benevolent and Protective Order of **[★770]**
Ellettsville Main Street **[4510]**, Ellettsville, IN
Ellsworth Chamber of Commerce **[17933]**, Ellsworth, WI
Elmhurst Chamber of Commerce and Indus. **[1619]**, Elmhurst, IL
Elmhurst Choral Union **[1620]**, Elmhurst, IL
Elmore Lions Club **[15101]**, Elmore, OH
Elmwood - Young Life **[13389]**, Bowling Green, OH
Elroy Area Advancement Corp. **[17940]**, Elroy, WI
Elroy Lions Club **[17941]**, Elroy, WI
Elsie Lions Club **[7599]**, Elsie, MI
Elwood Chamber of Commerce **[4513]**, Elwood, IN
Ely Chamber of Commerce **[10954]**, Ely, MN
Ely Lions Club **[10955]**, Ely, MN
Elyria Evening Lions Club **[15110]**, Elyria, OH
Emerald Valley Rottweiler Club of Greater Cleveland, Ohio **[5108]**, Indianapolis, IN
Emergency Aid
Illinois Natl. Emergency Number Assn. **[3385]**, St. Charles, IL
Indiana Chap. of the Assn. of Air Medical Services **[4674]**, Fort Wayne, IN
Indiana Chap. of Natl. Emergency Number Assn. **[5713]**, Madison, IN
Michigan Assn. of Ambulance Services **[8605]**, Lansing, MI
Michigan Chap. of Natl. Emergency Number Assn. **[9030]**, Midland, MI
Wisconsin Chap. of the Natl. Emergency Number Assn. **[18382]**, La Crosse, WI
Emergency Medicine
Illinois Coll. of Emergency Physicians **[2834]**, Oakbrook Terrace, IL
Michigan Coll. of Emergency Physicians **[8644]**, Lansing, MI
Ohio Chap. Amer. Coll. of Emergency Physicians **[14578]**, Columbus, OH
Emergency Physicians Michigan Chap; Amer. Coll. of **[★8644]**
Emergency Physicians; Michigan Coll. of **[8644]**, Lansing, MI
Emergency Response Assn; Ohio Spill Planning Prevention and **[14677]**, Columbus, OH
Emergency Services
Amer. Red Cross - Minneapolis Area Chap. **[11514]**, Minneapolis, MN
Illinois Emergency Sers. Mgt. Assn. **[2260]**, Libertyville, IL
Minnesota Ambulance Assn. **[12290]**, St. Cloud, MN
Minnesota Ambulance Assn., Central **[12822]**, Wadena, MN
Minnesota Ambulance Assn., Metro **[11622]**, Minneapolis, MN
Minnesota Ambulance Assn., Northeast **[11077]**, Grand Marais, MN
Minnesota Ambulance Assn., Northwest **[10737]**, Crookston, MN
Minnesota Ambulance Assn., South Central **[11306]**, Le Center, MN
Minnesota Ambulance Assn., Southeast **[10657]**, Chatfield, MN
Minnesota Ambulance Assn., Southwest **[10731]**, Cottonwood, MN
Minnesota Ambulance Assn., West Central **[10281]**, Alexandria, MN
Ohio Assn. of Emergency Medical Sers. **[16666]**, Sidney, OH
Emmet Assn. of Realtors **[9363]**, Petoskey, MI
Empire Lions Club **[7603]**, Empire, MI
Employee Assistance Professionals Assn. - Central Illinois Chap. **[3813]**, Urbana, IL
Employee Assistance Professionals Assn. - Greater Toledo Chap. **[16913]**, Toledo, OH
Employee Assistance Professionals Assn. - Northern Illinois Chap. **[884]**, Chicago, IL
Employee Assistance Professionals Assn. - Northern Ohio Chap. **[14113]**, Cleveland, OH
Employee Assistance Professionals Assn. - South Central Wisconsin Chap. **[18508]**, Madison, WI
Employee Assistance Programs
Employee Assistance Professionals Assn. - Central Illinois Chap. **[3813]**, Urbana, IL
Employee Assistance Professionals Assn. - Greater Toledo Chap. **[16913]**, Toledo, OH
Employee Assistance Professionals Assn. - Northern Illinois Chap. **[884]**, Chicago, IL
Employee Assistance Professionals Assn. - Northern Ohio Chap. **[14113]**, Cleveland, OH
Employee Assistance Professionals Assn. - South Central Wisconsin Chap. **[18508]**, Madison, WI
Employee Benefits
Employers Assn. **[3016]**, Peoria, IL
Ohio Assn. of Public School Employees **[14563]**, Columbus, OH
Employee Ownership
Employee Stock Ownership Plan Assn., Michigan **[6858]**, Battle Creek, MI
Employee Stock Ownership Plan Assn., Wisconsin **[18234]**, Iola, WI
ESOP Assn., Executive Comm. of the State and Regional Chap. Coun. **[15744]**, Macedonia, OH
ESOP Assn., Illinois **[886]**, Chicago, IL
ESOP Assn., Indiana **[5110]**, Indianapolis, IN
ESOP Assn., Minnesota Chap. **[11558]**, Minneapolis, MN
ESOP Assn., Ohio **[17382]**, Yellow Springs, OH
ESOP Assn., Wisconsin Chap. **[19857]**, Sun Prairie, WI
Employee Services Coun; Toledo Indus. Recreation and **[16304]**, Oregon, OH
Employee Stock Ownership Plan Assn., Michigan **[6858]**, Battle Creek, MI
Employee Stock Ownership Plan Assn., Wisconsin **[18234]**, Iola, WI
Employees Assn; Indiana State **[5315]**, Indianapolis, IN
Employees Assn; Michigan State **[8721]**, Lansing, MI
Employer Labor Relations Assn; Ohio Public **[15397]**, Hamilton, OH
Employers
Amer. Soc. of Employers **[9781]**, Southfield, MI
Employers Assn., Plymouth **[12022]**, Plymouth, MN
Employers Workforce Development Network **[18096]**, Green Bay, WI
MRA - The Mgt. Assn. **[19439]**, Pewaukee, WI
Employers Assn. **[3016]**, Peoria, IL
The Employers' Assn. **[7928]**, Grand Rapids, MI
Employers Assn., Peoria **[★3016]**
Employers Assn., Plymouth **[12022]**, Plymouth, MN
Employers of Illinois; Assoc. **[★1505]**
Employers Inst; Greater Cincinnati **[★13820]**
Employers Rsrc. Assn. **[13820]**, Cincinnati, OH
Employers Workforce Development Network **[18096]**, Green Bay, WI
Employment
Amer. Payroll Assn., Chicago Chap. **[717]**, Chicago, IL
Amer. Payroll Assn., Columbus Area Chap. **[14305]**, Columbus, OH
Amer. Payroll Assn., Greater Cleveland Chap. **[13423]**, Broadview Heights, OH
Amer. Payroll Assn., Greater Lafayette Chap. **[6472]**, West Lafayette, IN
Amer. Payroll Assn., Hall of Fame Chap. **[16052]**, Mogadore, OH
Amer. Payroll Assn., Miami Valley Chap. **[14849]**, Dayton, OH
Amer. Payroll Assn., Northeast Indiana Chap. **[6441]**, Warsaw, IN
Amer. Payroll Assn., Northstar Chap. **[12378]**, St. Paul, MN
Amer. Payroll Assn., Toledo Area Chap. **[16893]**, Toledo, OH
Amer. Payroll Assn., Youngstown, Ohio Chap. **[17390]**, Youngstown, OH
Chicago Compensation Assn. **[804]**, Chicago, IL
Chicago Women in Trades **[838]**, Chicago, IL
Columbus Compensation Assn. **[14380]**, Columbus, OH
Compensation and Benefits Professionals of Indiana **[4319]**, Carmel, IN
East Central Indiana Payroll Assn. **[5875]**, Muncie, IN
The Employers' Assn. **[7928]**, Grand Rapids, MI
Fox Valley Payroll Assn. **[2554]**, Morris, IL
Greater Cincinnati Compensation and Benefits Assn. **[13841]**, Cincinnati, OH
Greater Milwaukee Chap. of the Amer. Payroll Assn. **[19020]**, Milwaukee, WI
Intl. Personnel Mgt. Assn., Chicago **[990]**, Chicago, IL
Intl. Personnel Mgt. Assn., Cleveland **[15584]**, Lakewood, OH
Intl. Personnel Mgt. Assn., Dayton, Ohio **[17357]**, Wright-Patterson AFB, OH
Intl. Personnel Mgt. Assn., Greater Illinois **[1571]**, Effingham, IL
Intl. Personnel Mgt. Assn., Greater St. Louis, Missouri **[991]**, Chicago, IL
Intl. Personnel Mgt. Assn., Minnesota **[10537]**, Brooklyn Center, MN
Intl. Personnel Mgt. Assn., Wisconsin **[18532]**, Madison, WI
IPMA-HR Chicago Chap. **[998]**, Chicago, IL
IPMA-HR Cleveland Chap. **[15585]**, Lakewood, OH
IPMA-HR Greater Illinois Chap. **[1572]**, Effingham, IL
IPMA-HR Greater St. Louis, Missouri Chap. **[999]**, Chicago, IL
IPMA-HR Michigan Chap. **[8582]**, Lansing, MI
IPMA-HR Minnesota Chap. **[10538]**, Brooklyn Center, MN
IPMA-HR Wisconsin Chap. **[18535]**, Madison, WI
Job Transition Support Gp. **[10913]**, Edina, MN
Jobs For Youth/Chicago **[1009]**, Chicago, IL
Jobs for Minnesota's Graduates **[11411]**, Maple Grove, MN
Jobs for Ohio's Graduates **[14479]**, Columbus, OH
Madison Area Compensation Network **[18545]**, Madison, WI

Michigan Ontario Compensation Assn. **[7646]**, Farmington, MI
Milwaukee Area Compensation Assn. **[18041]**, Germantown, WI
Minnesota Career Development Assn. **[10320]**, Apple Valley, MN
Northeast Wisconsin Chap. of the APA **[18122]**, Green Bay, WI
Rockford Area Chap. of the Amer. Payroll Assn. **[3306]**, Rockford, IL
SER - Jobs for Progress, Central States **[1177]**, Chicago, IL
SER - Jobs for Progress, Lake County **[3931]**, Waukegan, IL
SER - Jobs for Progress, Metro Detroit **[7431]**, Detroit, MI
SER - Jobs for Progress, Milwaukee **[19115]**, Milwaukee, WI
Southern Seven Workforce Investment Bd. **[5929]**, New Albany, IN
Twin Cities Compensation Network **[12597]**, St. Paul, MN
West Michigan Chap. of the APA **[8223]**, Holland, MI
Western Michigan Compensation Assn. **[8868]**, Lowell, MI
Workforce Opportunities Rsrc. Consortium **[576]**, Charleston, IL
YMCA Training Alliance **[1240]**, Chicago, IL
Employment and Training Assn; MARO **[8602]**, Lansing, MI
EMS Alliance; Miami Valley Fire- **[14910]**, Dayton, OH
End Violent Encounters **[8566]**, Lansing, MI
Endometriosis Assn. **[19005]**, Milwaukee, WI
Energy
Amer. Associates of Blacks in Energy, Chicago **[2623]**, Naperville, IL
Amer. Assn. of Blacks in Energy, Cincinnati **[13700]**, Cincinnati, OH
Amer. Assn. of Blacks in Energy, Indiana **[4623]**, Fort Wayne, IN
Amer. Assn. of Blacks in Energy, Michigan **[8356]**, Jackson, MI
Amer. Assn. of Blacks in Energy, Michigan State Univ. **[7498]**, East Lansing, MI
Amer. Assn. of Blacks in Energy, Wisconsin **[18928]**, Milwaukee, WI
Assn. of Energy Engineers, Illinois/Chicago **[748]**, Chicago, IL
Assn. of Energy Engineers, Michigan/East Michigan **[9256]**, Oak Park, MI
Assn. of Energy Engineers, Minnesota/Twin Cities Chap. **[11527]**, Minneapolis, MN
Assn. of Energy Engineers, Ohio/Northern - Cleveland/Akron **[14077]**, Cleveland, OH
Assn. of Energy Engineers, Ohio/West Central Ohio **[14856]**, Dayton, OH
Assn. of Energy Engineers, West Michigan Chap. **[7912]**, Grand Rapids, MI
Energy Indus. of Ohio **[15496]**, Independence, OH
Great Lakes Renewable Energy Assn. **[7473]**, Dimondale, MI
Green Energy Ohio **[14448]**, Columbus, OH
Illinois Renewable Energy Association **[2867]**, Oregon, IL
Indiana Energy Assn. **[5229]**, Indianapolis, IN
Indiana Gas Assn. **[5238]**, Indianapolis, IN
Midwest Energy Assn. **[11789]**, Minnetonka, MN
Midwest Energy Efficiency Alliance **[1056]**, Chicago, IL
Midwest Renewable Energy Assn. **[17802]**, Custer, WI
Minnesotans for an Energy-Efficient Economy **[12533]**, St. Paul, MN
Ohio Partners for Affordable Energy **[15213]**, Findlay, OH
Energy Association; Illinois Renewable **[2867]**, Oregon, IL
Energy Assn; Midwest Renewable **[17802]**, Custer, WI
Energy Efficiency Alliance; Midwest **[1056]**, Chicago, IL
Energy Indus. of Ohio **[15496]**, Independence, OH
Energy Ohio; Green **[14448]**, Columbus, OH
Energy; Ohio Partners for Affordable **[15213]**, Findlay, OH
Energy Users-Ohio; Indus. **[14468]**, Columbus, OH
Enforcement Executives, Northern Indiana Chap; Natl. Org. of Black Law **[4783]**, Gary, IN
Enforcement Firearms Instructors; Minnesota Assn. of Law **[12157]**, Rochester, MN
Engineering
Akron Coun. of Engg. and Sci. Societies **[13020]**, Akron, OH
Amer. Coun. of Engg. Companies of Indiana **[4979]**, Indianapolis, IN
Amer. Coun. of Engg. Companies of Michigan **[8530]**, Lansing, MI
Amer. Coun. of Engg. Companies of Minnesota **[11784]**, Minnetonka, MN
Amer. Coun. of Engg. Companies of Ohio **[14281]**, Columbus, OH
Amer. Coun. of Engg. Companies of Wisconsin **[18457]**, Madison, WI
Amer. Inst. of Chem. Engineers - Akron Sect. **[13541]**, Canton, OH
Amer. Inst. of Chem. Engineers - Chicago Sect. **[1449]**, Des Plaines, IL
Amer. Inst. of Chem. Engineers - Cleveland Sect. **[15419]**, Highland Heights, OH
Amer. Inst. of Chem. Engineers - Ohio Valley Sect. **[13711]**, Cincinnati, OH
Amer. Inst. of Chem. Engineers - Upper Midwest Sect. **[11013]**, Forest Lake, MN
Amer. Soc. of Civil Engineers - Illinois Sect. **[722]**, Chicago, IL
Amer. Soc. of Heating, Refrigerating and Air-Conditioning Engineers Central Indiana Chap. **[5021]**, Indianapolis, IN
Amer. Soc. of Heating, Refrigerating and Air-Conditioning Engineers - Dayton **[14851]**, Dayton, OH
Amer. Soc. of Heating, Refrigerating and Air-Conditioning Engineers Detroit **[7320]**, Detroit, MI
Amer. Soc. of Heating, Refrigerating and Air-Conditioning Engineers Eastern Michigan **[7001]**, Bridgeport, MI
Amer. Soc. of Heating, Refrigerating and Air-Conditioning Engineers Evansville **[4525]**, Evansville, IN
Amer. Soc. of Heating, Refrigerating and Air-Conditioning Engineers - Illinois Chap. **[1679]**, Evergreen Park, IL
Amer. Soc. of Heating, Refrigerating and Air-Conditioning Engineers La Crosse Area Chap. **[18336]**, La Crosse, WI
Amer. Soc. of Heating, Refrigerating and Air-Conditioning Engineers Madison Chap. **[18472]**, Madison, WI
Amer. Soc. of Heating, Refrigerating and Air-Conditioning Engineers - Minnesota Chap. **[11866]**, New Hope, MN
Amer. Soc. of Heating, Refrigerating and Air-Conditioning Engineers Northern Indiana Chap. **[6216]**, South Bend, IN
Amer. Soc. of Heating, Refrigerating and Air-Conditioning Engineers Region 5 **[4316]**, Carmel, IN
Amer. Soc. of Heating, Refrigerating and Air-Conditioning Engineers - West Michigan Chap. **[7902]**, Grand Rapids, MI
Amer. Soc. of Heating, Refrigerating and Air-Conditioning Engineers - Wisconsin Chap. **[18957]**, Milwaukee, WI
Amer. Soc. of Safety Engineers, Central Ohio Chap. **[14309]**, Columbus, OH
Amer. Soc. of Safety Engineers, Greater Detroit Chap. **[9782]**, Southfield, MI
Amer. Soc. of Safety Engineers, Kitty Hawk Chap. **[15237]**, Franklin, OH
Amer. Soc. of Safety Engineers, Nicolet Chap. **[18081]**, Green Bay, WI
Amer. Soc. of Safety Engineers, Northeastern Illinois Chap. **[3353]**, Roselle, IL
Amer. Soc. of Safety Engineers, Northern Ohio **[14066]**, Cleveland, OH
Central Illinois Chap. of Amer. Soc. of Plumbing Engineers **[1979]**, Heyworth, IL
Central Ohio Chap. of Amer. Soc. of Plumbing Engineers **[14354]**, Columbus, OH
Chicago Chap. of Amer. Soc. of Plumbing Engineers **[798]**, Chicago, IL
Cleveland Engg. Soc. **[14098]**, Cleveland, OH
Consulting Engineers Coun. of Illinois **[3547]**, Springfield, IL
County Engineers Assn. of Ohio **[14419]**, Columbus, OH
Eastern Michigan Chap. of Amer. Soc. of Plumbing Engineers **[7283]**, Dearborn Heights, MI
IEEE Engg. Mgt. Soc. - Twin Cities Sect. **[10550]**, Brooklyn Park, MN
Illinois Soc. of Professional Engineers **[3636]**, Springfield, IL
Indiana Soc. of Professional Engineers **[5306]**, Indianapolis, IN
Indiana Structural Engineers Assn. **[5771]**, Merrillville, IN
Intl. Fed. of Professional and Tech. Engineers Local 7 **[14475]**, Columbus, OH
Michigan Soc. of Professional Engineers **[8716]**, Lansing, MI
Minnesota Chap. of Amer. Soc. of Plumbing Engineers **[12465]**, St. Paul, MN
Minnesota Soc. of Professional Engineers **[12880]**, West St. Paul, MN
NACE Intl., Chicago Sect. **[1063]**, Chicago, IL
NACE Intl., Cleveland Sect. **[15951]**, Medina, OH
NACE Intl., Detroit Sect. **[9118]**, Mount Pleasant, MI
NACE Intl., Ohio Univ. Student Sect. **[13208]**, Athens, OH
NACE Intl., Southwest Ohio Sect. **[17189]**, West Milton, OH
NACE Intl., Twin Cities Sect. **[12539]**, St. Paul, MN
NACE Intl., Wisconsin Sect. **[18569]**, Madison, WI
Natl. Soc. of Black Engineers - Detroit Alumni Extension **[7414]**, Detroit, MI
Natl. Soc. of Black Engineers - Indianapolis Alumni Extension **[5431]**, Indianapolis, IN
Natl. Soc. of Black Engineers - Michigan State Univ. Chap. **[7560]**, East Lansing, MI
Natl. Soc. of Black Engineers - Purdue Univ. Chap. **[6494]**, West Lafayette, IN
Natl. Soc. of Black Engineers - Univ. of Cincinnati **[13932]**, Cincinnati, OH
Natl. Soc. of Black Engineers - Univ. of Illinois, Urbana-Champaign **[3831]**, Urbana, IL
Natl. Soc. of Black Engineers - Univ. of Michigan **[6747]**, Ann Arbor, MI
Natl. Soc. of Black Engineers - Univ. of Wisconsin, Milwaukee **[19080]**, Milwaukee, WI
Natl. Soc. of Black Engineers - Wisconsin Black Engg. Student Soc. **[18581]**, Madison, WI
Northeast Ohio Alumni Extension - Natl. Soc. of Black Engineers **[14182]**, Cleveland, OH
Ohio Soc. of Professional Engineers **[14674]**, Columbus, OH
Soc. of Amer. Military Engineers, Chicago Post **[1185]**, Chicago, IL
Soc. of Amer. Military Engineers, Cincinnati Post **[13990]**, Cincinnati, OH
Soc. of Amer. Military Engineers, Detroit Post **[7433]**, Detroit, MI
Soc. of Amer. Military Engineers, Rock Island Post **[3259]**, Rock Island, IL
Soc. of Mfg. Engineers, Henry Ford Community Coll. Student Chap. S-331 **[7270]**, Dearborn, MI
Soc. of Reliability Engineer, Southeastern Michigan Chap. **[10124]**, West Bloomfield, MI
Soc. of Tribologists and Lubrication Engineers - Canton Sect. **[13582]**, Canton, OH
Soc. of Tribologists and Lubrication Engineers - Central Illinois Sect. **[2364]**, Mackinaw, IL
Soc. of Tribologists and Lubrication Engineers - Chicago Sect. **[1628]**, Elmhurst, IL
Soc. of Tribologists and Lubrication Engineers - Cincinnati Sect. **[13996]**, Cincinnati, OH
Soc. of Tribologists and Lubrication Engineers - Cleveland Sect. **[16628]**, Seven Hills, OH
Soc. of Tribologists and Lubrication Engineers - Dayton Sect. **[17362]**, Wright-Patterson AFB, OH
Soc. of Tribologists and Lubrication Engineers - Detroit Sect. **[9822]**, Southfield, MI
Soc. of Tribologists and Lubrication Engineers - Twin Cities Sect. **[12589]**, St. Paul, MN
Western Michigan Chap. of Amer. Soc. of Plumbing Engineers **[8026]**, Grand Rapids, MI

Wisconsin Chap. of Amer. Soc. of Plumbing Engineers **[20087]**, Wauwatosa, WI
Engg. Companies of Ohio; Amer. Coun. of **[14281]**, Columbus, OH
Engg. and Sci. Societies; Akron Coun. of **[13020]**, Akron, OH
Engg. Soc; Cleveland **[14098]**, Cleveland, OH
Engg; Southern Illinois Chap. for Healthcare **[431]**, Carbondale, IL
Engg; Southern Illinois Chap. for Hosp. **[★431]**
Engineers Assn; Indiana Structural **[5771]**, Merrillville, IN
Engineers, Chicago Post; Soc. of Amer. Military **[1185]**, Chicago, IL
Engineers Coun. of Illinois; Consulting **[3547]**, Springfield, IL
Engineers Coun. of Michigan; Consulting **[★8530]**
Engineers, Henry Ford Community Coll. Student Chap. S-331; Soc. of Mfg. **[7270]**, Dearborn, MI
Engineers; Illinois Soc. of Professional **[3636]**, Springfield, IL
Engineers Intl. Brotherhood of Electrical Workers AFL-CIO, LU 1220; Radio and TV Broadcast **[★984]**
Engineers; Michigan Soc. of Professional **[8716]**, Lansing, MI
Engineers; Minnesota Soc. of Professional **[12880]**, West St. Paul, MN
Englewood Community Development Corp. **[5109]**, Indianapolis, IN
Englewood-Northmont Chamber of Commerce **[15131]**, Englewood, OH
English
Illinois Assn. of Teachers of English **[2716]**, Normal, IL
Indiana Coun. of Teachers of English **[4382]**, Columbia City, IN
Minnesota Coun. of Teachers of English **[10712]**, Coon Rapids, MN
Natl. Coun. of Teachers of English Student Affl. at Eastern Michigan State Univ. **[10211]**, Ypsilanti, MI
Natl. Coun. of Teachers of English Student Affiliate of Michigan State Univ. **[7557]**, East Lansing, MI
New Mexico Coun. of Teachers of English **[3832]**, Urbana, IL
Ohio Coun. of Teachers of English Language Arts **[14592]**, Columbus, OH
Southern Ohio Coun. of Teachers of English **[13219]**, Athens, OH
Western Reserve of Ohio Teachers of English **[13510]**, Campbell, OH
Wisconsin Coun. of Teachers of English Language Arts **[17908]**, Eau Claire, WI
English Cocker Spaniel Club of Am. **[18169]**, Hales Corners, WI
English Country Dancers of Columbus **[14429]**, Columbus, OH
English; Illinois Assn. of Teachers of **[2716]**, Normal, IL
English; Minnesota Coun. of Teachers of **[10712]**, Coon Rapids, MN
English; New Mexico Coun. of Teachers of **[3832]**, Urbana, IL
English Springer Spaniel Field Trial Assn. **[19314]**, New London, WI
English Toy Spaniel
Wisconsin English Springer Spaniel Assn. **[17858]**, East Troy, WI
Enology and Viticulture - Eastern Sect; Amer. Soc. for **[6474]**, West Lafayette, IN
Enon Community Historical Soc. **[15136]**, Enon, OH
Enos Park Neighborhood Improvement Assn. **[3549]**, Springfield, IL
Ensemble; Prairie **[547]**, Champaign, IL
Enterprise Zone; City of La Porte Urban **[5595]**, La Porte, IN
Entertainers
Actors' Fund of Am., Midwestern Region **[596]**, Chicago, IL
Entertainment
Chicago Festival Assn. **[810]**, Chicago, IL
Dodge County Fair Assn. **[17593]**, Beaver Dam, WI
Friends of Folklore Village **[17837]**, Dodgeville, WI
Indiana Amusement and Music Operators Assn. **[5161]**, Indianapolis, IN
League of Professionally Managed Theaters **[5390]**, Indianapolis, IN
Minnesota Festivals and Events Assn. **[11884]**, New Ulm, MN
Minnesota Operators of Music and Amusement **[11661]**, Minneapolis, MN
Ohio Festivals and Events Assn. **[15696]**, London, OH
Sophisticated Gents **[15711]**, Lorain, OH
Wisconsin Amusement and Music Operators Assn. **[18912]**, Middleton, WI
Entomology
Young Entomologists' Soc. **[8771]**, Lansing, MI
Entrepreneurship Educ; Consortium for **[14413]**, Columbus, OH
Environment
Buckeye Trail Assn. **[17342]**, Worthington, OH
Community Organizing Center - For Mother Earth **[14411]**, Columbus, OH
Coun. of Great Lakes Governors **[864]**, Chicago, IL
East Michigan Environmental Action Coun. **[6984]**, Bloomfield Hills, MI
Enval. Coun. **[19788]**, Stevens Point, WI
Hoosier Environmental Coun. **[5139]**, Indianapolis, IN
Illinois Assn. of Environmental Professionals **[928]**, Chicago, IL
Illinois Environmental Coun. **[3602]**, Springfield, IL
Indiana Electronic Ser. Assn. **[4818]**, Greencastle, IN
Mankato Area Environmentalists **[11384]**, Mankato, MN
Michigan Environmental Coun. **[8661]**, Lansing, MI
Mid-Michigan Enval. Action Coun. **[8730]**, Lansing, MI
Minnesota Environmental Initiative **[11646]**, Minneapolis, MN
Nature of Illinois Found. **[540]**, Champaign, IL
North Amer. Lake Mgt. Soc. **[18586]**, Madison, WI
North River Commn. **[1102]**, Chicago, IL
Northern Ohio Wellness Connection **[17087]**, Walton Hills, OH
Ohio Environmental Coun. **[14604]**, Columbus, OH
Pontiac Lake Horsemans Assn. **[10158]**, White Lake, MI
Rural Land Alliance **[16708]**, Springboro, OH
Scenic Illinois **[1468]**, Des Plaines, IL
Scenic Michigan **[9371]**, Petoskey, MI
Scenic Ohio **[13087]**, Akron, OH
Southwest Detroit Enval. Vision **[7440]**, Detroit, MI
United Auto Workers Local No. 599 Enval. Comm. **[7759]**, Flint, MI
Univ. of Michigan-Dearborn - Student Environmental Assn. **[7272]**, Dearborn, MI
Upper Peninsula Environmental Coalition **[8263]**, Houghton, MI
Walworth County Land Conservancy **[17931]**, Elkhorn, WI
West Michigan Enval. Action Coun. **[8021]**, Grand Rapids, MI
Wisconsin Assn. for Environmental Educ. **[19817]**, Stevens Point, WI
Environmental Action Coun; East Michigan **[6984]**, Bloomfield Hills, MI
Enval. Advocates; Midwest **[18562]**, Madison, WI
Environmental Assn. for Great Lakes Educ. **[10822]**, Duluth, MN
Enval. Coun. **[19788]**, Stevens Point, WI
Enval. Coun; Door County **[17962]**, Fish Creek, WI
Environmental Coun; Illinois **[3602]**, Springfield, IL
Environmental Education
Earth Day Coalition **[14110]**, Cleveland, OH
Earth Share of Illinois **[877]**, Chicago, IL
Earth Share of Michigan **[6836]**, Bath, MI
Earth Share of Ohio **[14426]**, Columbus, OH
Environmental Assn. for Great Lakes Educ. **[10822]**, Duluth, MN
Environmental Educ. Assn. of Indiana **[4794]**, Goshen, IN
Environmental Educ. Coun. of Ohio **[15598]**, Lancaster, OH
Fed. of Environmental Technologists **[19739]**, Slinger, WI
Kids for Saving Earth Worldwide **[11595]**, Minneapolis, MN
Ohio Alliance for the Env. **[13520]**, Canal Winchester, OH
Univ. of Illinois - Comm. on Natural Areas **[556]**, Champaign, IL
Wisconsin Environmental Educ. Bd. **[19818]**, Stevens Point, WI
Environmental Educ. Assn. of Indiana **[4794]**, Goshen, IN
Environmental Educ. Coun. of Ohio **[15598]**, Lancaster, OH
Environmental Health
Illinois Environmental Hea. Assn. **[3225]**, Rochelle, IL
Illinois Environmental Hea. Assn. - Central Chap. **[1774]**, Galesburg, IL
Illinois Environmental Hea. Assn. - North Chap. **[71]**, Arlington Heights, IL
Illinois Environmental Hea. Assn. - South Chap. **[2224]**, Lawrenceville, IL
Indiana Environmental Hea. Assn. **[5231]**, Indianapolis, IN
Michigan Environmental Hea. Assn. **[8662]**, Lansing, MI
Midwest Regional Chap. of the Soc. of Environmental Toxicology and Chemistry **[19354]**, Odanah, WI
Minnesota Environmental Hea. Assn. **[10306]**, Anoka, MN
Ohio Valley Regional Chap. of the Soc. of Environmental Toxicology and Chemistry **[14695]**, Columbus, OH
Environmental Hea. Assn; Indiana **[5231]**, Indianapolis, IN
Environmental Initiative; Minnesota **[11646]**, Minneapolis, MN
Enval. Justice Org; Little Village **[1034]**, Chicago, IL
Environmental Law
Indiana Univ. - Environmental Law Soc. **[4233]**, Bloomington, IN
Environmental Law Soc; Indiana Univ. - **[4233]**, Bloomington, IN
Environmental Quality
Friends of the Trolley Line Trail **[7190]**, Clio, MI
Green Party of Minnesota **[11572]**, Minneapolis, MN
Minnesota Pollution Control Agency **[12509]**, St. Paul, MN
Save the Valley **[5721]**, Madison, IN
Environmentalists; Mankato Area **[11384]**, Mankato, MN
Environmentally Concerned Citizens of Lakeland Area **[19198]**, Minocqua, WI
Epilepsy
Epilepsy Assn. **[14114]**, Cleveland, OH
Epilepsy Found. of Central and Northeast Wisconsin **[19789]**, Stevens Point, WI
Epilepsy Found. of Central Ohio **[14430]**, Columbus, OH
Epilepsy Found. of Greater Chicago **[885]**, Chicago, IL
Epilepsy Found. of Greater Cincinnati **[13821]**, Cincinnati, OH
Epilepsy Found. of Michigan **[9799]**, Southfield, MI
Epilepsy Found. of Minnesota **[12409]**, St. Paul, MN
Epilepsy Found. of North/Central Illinois **[3276]**, Rockford, IL
Epilepsy Found. of Northwest Ohio **[16914]**, Toledo, OH
Epilepsy Found. South Central Wisconsin **[18509]**, Madison, WI
Epilepsy Foundation of Southern Wisconsin **[18246]**, Janesville, WI
Epilepsy Found. of Southwestern Illinois **[201]**, Belleville, IL
Epilepsy Found. of Western Ohio **[15475]**, Huber Heights, OH
Epilepsy Found. of Western Wisconsin **[17878]**, Eau Claire, WI
Epilepsy Assn. **[14114]**, Cleveland, OH
Epilepsy Center and Assn; Michigan **[★9799]**
Epilepsy Center of Michigan **[★9799]**
Epilepsy Center; Michigan **[★9799]**
Epilepsy Center of Western Wisconsin **[★17878]**
Epilepsy Found. of Central and Northeast Wisconsin **[19789]**, Stevens Point, WI

Epilepsy Found. of Central Ohio [14430], Columbus, OH
Epilepsy Found. of Greater Chicago [885], Chicago, IL
Epilepsy Found. of Greater Cincinnati [13821], Cincinnati, OH
Epilepsy Found. of Michigan [9799], Southfield, MI
Epilepsy Found. of Minnesota [12409], St. Paul, MN
Epilepsy Found. of North/Central Illinois [3276], Rockford, IL
Epilepsy Found. of Northeast Ohio [★14114]
Epilepsy Found. of Northwest Ohio [16914], Toledo, OH
Epilepsy Found. South Central Wisconsin [18509], Madison, WI
Epilepsy Foundation of Southern Wisconsin [18246], Janesville, WI
Epilepsy Found. of Southwestern Illinois [201], Belleville, IL
Epilepsy Found. of Western Ohio [15475], Huber Heights, OH
Epilepsy Found. of Western Wisconsin [17878], Eau Claire, WI
Epilepsy; Michigan Assn. for [★9799]
Epsilon Sigma Phi, Alpha Lambda [6381], Valparaiso, IN
Epsilon Sigma Phi, NC Alpha PSI - Michigan [9433], Port Huron, MI
Equal Rights for Fathers [★9800]
Equestrians; Little Creek Special [4337], Centerpoint, IN
Equip. Services; Ohio Assn. of Medical [14558], Columbus, OH
Ergonomics
Central Ohio Chap. of the Human Factors and Ergonomics Soc. [14355], Columbus, OH
Southern Ohio Chap. of the Human Factors and Ergonomics Soc. [14958], Dayton, OH
Erie County Chap. of the Ohio Genealogical Soc. [16608], Sandusky, OH
Erie County MR-DD Employees Assn. [16609], Sandusky, OH
Erie Mason - Young Life [8300], Ida, MI
Erskine Lions Club [10964], Erskine, MN
Escanaba Areas Figure Skating Club [7613], Escanaba, MI
Escanaba Kiwanis Club [7614], Escanaba, MI
Esko Lions Club [10823], Duluth, MN
ESOP Assn., Executive Comm. of the State and Regional Chap. Coun. [15744], Macedonia, OH
ESOP Assn., Illinois [886], Chicago, IL
ESOP Assn., Indiana [5110], Indianapolis, IN
ESOP Assn., Minnesota Chap. [11558], Minneapolis, MN
ESOP Assn., Ohio [17382], Yellow Springs, OH
ESOP Assn., Wisconsin Chap. [19857], Sun Prairie, WI
Esperanto
Esperanto Soc. of Chicago [887], Chicago, IL
Esperanto Soc. of Michigan [9580], Royal Oak, MI
Esperanto Soc. of Chicago [887], Chicago, IL
Esperanto Soc. of Michigan [9580], Royal Oak, MI
Esprit The Ultimate Ski and Sports Club [14115], Cleveland, OH
Essex County Stamp Club [9235], Novi, MI
Essexville-Hampton Lions Club [7625], Essexville, MI
Estate Planning Coun. of Cleveland [14116], Cleveland, OH
Estate Planning Coun. of Lake County [3485], Skokie, IL
Estate Planning Coun. of Upper Ohio Valley [13262], Barnesville, OH
The Ethic of Citizenship Soc. [12718], Stillwater, MN
Ethical Humanist Soc. of Greater Chicago [3486], Skokie, IL
Ethics Rsrc. Network of Michigan; Medical [7529], East Lansing, MI
Euclid Blade and Edge Figure Skating Club [15140], Euclid, OH
Euclid Chamber of Commerce [15141], Euclid, OH
Euclid Public Schools Alumni Assn. [15142], Euclid, OH
Euclid-St. Clair Development Corp. [14117], Cleveland, OH
Euclid Stamp Club [15143], Euclid, OH
Evaluation
Chicagoland Evaluation Assn. [2328], Lombard, IL
Indiana Evaluation Assn. [5233], Indianapolis, IN
Michigan Assn. for Evaluation [7393], Detroit, MI
Minnesota Evaluation Assn. [11647], Minneapolis, MN
Ohio Prog. Evaluators' Gp. [14658], Columbus, OH
Evangelical Pastors Fellowship of Rochester [12138], Rochester, MN
Evangelism
Central Indiana Fellowship of Christian Athletes [5077], Indianapolis, IN
Children Need the Lord [6224], South Bend, IN
Cleveland Fellowship of Christian Athletes [14099], Cleveland, OH
Michigan FCA [8405], Jenison, MI
Midwest Region FCA [536], Champaign, IL
North Central Illinois FCA [2728], Normal, IL
Southern Illinois Fellowship of Christian Athletes [432], Carbondale, IL
Evans Scholars Foundation [★1878]
Evanston Chamber of Commerce [1655], Evanston, IL
Evanston Community Tennis Assn. [3487], Skokie, IL
Evanston Historical Soc. [1656], Evanston, IL
Evanston-Skokie District 65 Educ. Found. [1657], Evanston, IL
Evanston United Way/Community Ser. [1658], Evanston, IL
Evansville Area 4C [4540], Evansville, IN
Evansville Area Assn. of Realtors [4541], Evansville, IN
Evansville Area Coun. of Parent Teacher Assns. [4542], Evansville, IN
Evansville Area Human Rsrc. Assn. [4543], Evansville, IN
Evansville Audubon Soc. [4544], Evansville, IN
Evansville Chamber of Commerce [17947], Evansville, WI
Evansville Coin Club [4545], Evansville, IN
Evansville Convention and Visitors Bur. [4546], Evansville, IN
Evansville Gun Club [4906], Haubstadt, IN
Evansville Lapidary Soc. [4547], Evansville, IN
Evart Area Chamber of Commerce [7628], Evart, MI
Evart Chamber of Commerce [★7628]
Evart Lions Club [7629], Evart, MI
EVE-End Violent Encounters [★8566]
Eveleth Lions Club [10968], Eveleth, MN
Evergreen Park Chamber of Commerce [1682], Evergreen Park, IL
Evergreen Park Lions Club [1683], Evergreen Park, IL
Exchange Club of Detroit [9988], Troy, MI
Exchange Club of Grayslake [1892], Grayslake, IL
Exchange Club of Speedway [5111], Indianapolis, IN
Exchange Club of Terre Haute [6319], Terre Haute, IN
Executive Ser. Corps of Chicago [888], Chicago, IL
Executive Suite Assn., Cincinnati Local Member Network [13822], Cincinnati, OH
Executive Women in Hea.Care [5112], Indianapolis, IN
Executive Women Intl., Chicago Chap. [1863], Glenview, IL
Executive Women Intl., Cincinnati/Northern Kentucky Chap. [13823], Cincinnati, OH
Executive Women Intl./Cleveland [14118], Cleveland, OH
Executive Women Intl., Detroit-Windsor Chap. [7361], Detroit, MI
Executive Women Intl., Indianapolis Chap. [5113], Indianapolis, IN
Executive Women Intl., Milwaukee Chap. [19006], Milwaukee, WI
Executive Women Intl., Minneapolis Chap. [12410], St. Paul, MN
Executive Women Intl., Rochester Chap. [12139], Rochester, MN
Executive Women Intl., Saint Paul Chap. [12411], St. Paul, MN
Executives of Am; State Beer Assn. of [★11630]
Executives Forum of Chicago; Assn. [★749]
Executives; Illinois Assn. of Chamber of Commerce [3566], Springfield, IL
Executives; Ohio Trade Assn. [★17351]
Exhibitors
Michigan Assn. of Fairs and Exhibitions [8614], Lansing, MI
Ohio Fair Managers Assn. [16410], Perrysburg, OH
Experience Columbus [14431], Columbus, OH
Experiential Education
Coun. for Adult and Experiential Learning [860], Chicago, IL
Experimental Aircraft Assn., Chap. 5 [15999], Middlefield, OH
Exploration
Explorers Club - Chicago/Great Lakes Chap. [889], Chicago, IL
Explorers Club - George Rogers Clark Chap. [13622], Centerville, OH
Explorers Club - Chicago/Great Lakes Chap. [889], Chicago, IL
Explorers Club - George Rogers Clark Chap. [13622], Centerville, OH
Explosives
Indiana Fireworks Users Assn. [5879], Muncie, IN
Export Managers Club of Chicago [★993]

F

Fac. Mgt. Assn., Chicago; Intl. [1725], Frankfort, IL
Fac. Mgt. Assn; Dayton Chap. of the Intl. [15986], Miamisburg, OH
Facing History and Ourselves, Chicago [890], Chicago, IL
Facing History and Ourselves Natl. Found., Chicago [★890]
Faculty and Staff Coun; IUB Latino [4238], Bloomington, IN
Fair Agencies
Otsego County Fair Association [7821], Gaylord, MI
Waukesha County Fair Assn. [19445], Pewaukee, WI
Fair Association; Otsego County [7821], Gaylord, MI
Fairborn Area Chamber of Commerce [15148], Fairborn, OH
Fairborn Performing Arts and Cultural Assn. [15149], Fairborn, OH
Fairbury Assn. of Commerce [★1685]
Fairbury Chamber of Commerce [1685], Fairbury, IL
Fairfax Lions Club [10974], Fairfax, MN
Fairfield Chamber of Commerce [★1688]
Fairfield Chamber of Commerce [15155], Fairfield, OH
Fairfield County Genealogical Soc. [★15607]
Fairfield County Youth Football League [15599], Lancaster, OH
Fairfield Heritage Assn. [15600], Lancaster, OH
Fairfield Sportsmen's Assn. [13824], Cincinnati, OH
Fairgrove Lions Club [7633], Fairgrove, MI
Fairmont Area AIFA [12868], Wells, MN
Fairmont Area Chamber of Commerce [10977], Fairmont, MN
Fairmont Convention and Visitors Bur. [10978], Fairmont, MN
Fairport Harbor Historical Soc. [15178], Fairport Harbor, OH
Fairport Harbor Rod and Reel Assn. [15179], Fairport Harbor, OH
Fairport Marine Museum and Lighthouse [★15178]
Fairview Heights Chamber of Commerce [1696], Fairview Heights, IL
Faith in Action in Dodge County [11244], Kasson, MN
Faith in Action of McHenry County [1323], Crystal Lake, IL
Falcon Heights-Lauderdale Lions Club [12226], Roseville, MN
Families
Adoptive Family Support Network [7879], Grand Rapids, MI
Amer. Mothers - Illinois Chap. [578], Chatham, IL
Amer. Mothers - Indiana Chap. [4945], Huntington, IN
Amer. Mothers - Minnesota Chap. [10681], Climax, MN
Amer. Mothers - Ohio Chap. [14304], Columbus, OH
Birmingham Bloomfield Families in Action [6963], Birmingham, MI

Common Hope [12405], St. Paul, MN
Communities Investing in Families [12739], Taylors Falls, MN
Family, Career and Community Leaders of Am., Illinois [3550], Springfield, IL
Family, Career and Community Leaders of Am., Michigan [10204], Ypsilanti, MI
Family Ser. Assn. of Central Indiana [5115], Indianapolis, IN
Michigan Family Forum [8663], Lansing, MI
PACER Center [11719], Minneapolis, MN
Rainbow Families Wisconsin [18604], Madison, WI
Tomorrow's Hope [18274], Jefferson, WI
United Way of Porter County Indiana [6392], Valparaiso, IN
Wisconsin Assn. of Family and Children's Agencies [18652], Madison, WI
Families with Children from China; Northeast Wisconsin [18863], Menasha, WI
Families; Communities Investing in [12739], Taylors Falls, MN
Families Reaching for Rainbows Fed. of Families for Children's Mental Hea. [5114], Indianapolis, IN
Families Today; Adoptive [138], Barrington, IL
Family Action Network of Lake County [4879], Hammond, IN
Family, Career and Community Leaders of Am., Illinois [3550], Springfield, IL
Family, Career and Community Leaders of Am., Michigan [10204], Ypsilanti, MI
Family Child Care Association of Morrison County; Licensed [12065], Randall, MN
Family Connections [19694], Sheboygan, WI
Family Firm Inst., Cincinnati Study Group [13825], Cincinnati, OH
Family Firm Inst., Midwest (Chicago) Study Group [1421], Deerfield, IL
Family Hea. Partnership [★4055]
Family Hea. Partnership Clinic [4055], Woodstock, IL
Family Medicine
Indiana Acad. of Family Physicians [5159], Indianapolis, IN
Ohio Acad. of Family Physicians [14532], Columbus, OH
Wisconsin Acad. of Family Physicians [19894], Thiensville, WI
Family Motor Coach Assn. - Just Friends [13826], Cincinnati, OH
Family Physicians; Illinois Acad. of [2296], Lisle, IL
Family Planning
Planned Parenthood of Chicago Area [1139], Chicago, IL
Planned Parenthood of Decatur [1402], Decatur, IL
Planned Parenthood Fed. of Am. [2838], Oakbrook Terrace, IL
Planned Parenthood of Greater Cleveland [14205], Cleveland, OH
Planned Parenthood of Indiana [5453], Indianapolis, IN
Planned Parenthood of Mahoning Valley [17411], Youngstown, OH
Planned Parenthood of Northwest Ohio [16949], Toledo, OH
Planned Parenthood of Southeast Ohio [13216], Athens, OH
Planned Parenthood of Southwest Ohio Region [13960], Cincinnati, OH
Planned Parenthood of Springfield Area [3662], Springfield, IL
Planned Parenthood of Summit, Portage, and Medina Counties [13081], Akron, OH
Family Ser. Assn. of Central Indiana [5115], Indianapolis, IN
Family Ser. Rochester [12140], Rochester, MN
Far Northwest Suburban United Way [2034], Hoffman Estates, IL
Fargo-Moorhead Audubon Soc. [11824], Moorhead, MN
Faribault Area Chamber of Commerce [10985], Faribault, MN
Fariborn High School - Young Life [17368], Xenia, OH
Farm Bur. Fed; Ohio [14606], Columbus, OH
Farm Bur. Fed; Wisconsin [18702], Madison, WI
Farm Bur. Found; Clinton County [338], Breese, IL
Farm Bur. Found; Mason County [1960], Havana, IL
Farm Equipment
Midwest Equip. Dealers Assn. [18563], Madison, WI
Minnesota-South Dakota Equip. Dealers Assn. [11960], Owatonna, MN
Farm Equip. Assn. of Minnesota and South Dakota [★11960]
Farm Management
Indiana Farm Bur. [5235], Indianapolis, IN
Farm Managers and Rural Appraisers Indiana Chap; Amer. Soc. of [★6424]
Farmers Elevator Assn. of Minnesota [★11649]
Farmers' Market; Friends of the St. Paul [12659], Shoreview, MN
Farmers Union; Illinois [3603], Springfield, IL
Farmers Union, Indiana; Natl. [4754], Franklin, IN
Farmers Union; Ohio [16316], Ottawa, OH
FarmHouse Fraternity - Illinois FarmHouse [3814], Urbana, IL
FarmHouse Fraternity - Michigan State FarmHouse [7519], East Lansing, MI
FarmHouse Fraternity - Minnesota FarmHouse [12412], St. Paul, MN
FarmHouse Fraternity - Univ. of Wisconsin Platteville [19464], Platteville, WI
FarmHouse - Purdue Univ. Chap. [6481], West Lafayette, IN
Farming
Alliance for Sustainability - Intl. Alliance for Sustainable Agriculture [11479], Minneapolis, MN
Clinton County Farm Bur. Found. [338], Breese, IL
Fond du Lac County-Farm Bur. [17978], Fond du Lac, WI
Illinois Farmers Union [3603], Springfield, IL
Illinois State Grange [2846], O'Fallon, IL
Indiana State Grange [4800], Goshen, IN
Lorain County Farm Bur. [16283], Oberlin, OH
Mason County Farm Bur. Found. [1960], Havana, IL
Michigan Agri Bus. Assn. [7531], East Lansing, MI
Michigan Farm Bur. [8664], Lansing, MI
Michigan State Grange [8150], Haslett, MI
Minnesota Farm Bur. Fed. [12483], St. Paul, MN
Minnesota Farmers Union [12484], St. Paul, MN
Minnesota State Grange [10615], Byron, MN
Natl. Farmers Union, Indiana [4754], Franklin, IN
Natl. Farmers Union, Michigan [9846], Sparta, MI
Ohio Ecological Food and Farm Assn. [14599], Columbus, OH
Ohio Farm Bur. Fed. [14606], Columbus, OH
Ohio Farmers Union [16316], Ottawa, OH
Ohio Natl. Farmers Org. [13144], Anna, OH
Pickaway County Farm Bur. [14035], Circleville, OH
Stark County Farm Bur. [13587], Canton, OH
Sustainable Farming Assn. of Minnesota [12708], Starbuck, MN
Sustainable Farming Assn. of Minnesota - Cannon River [11256], Kenyon, MN
Sustainable Farming Assn. of Minnesota - South Central [10266], Albert Lea, MN
Wisconsin Farm Bur. Fed. [18702], Madison, WI
Wisconsin Farmers Union [17758], Chippewa Falls, WI
Wisconsin State Grange [18269], Janesville, WI
Farming Assn. of Minnesota; Sustainable [12708], Starbuck, MN
Farmington Area Chamber of Commerce [10990], Farmington, MN
Farmington Area Jaycees [7640], Farmington, MI
Farmington - Farmington Hills Chamber of Commerce [7659], Farmington Hills, MI
Farmington Hills Figure Skating Club [7641], Farmington, MI
Farmington Wyldlife [7642], Farmington, MI
Farmington Wyldlife [10591], Burnsville, MN
Farmington Young Life [7643], Farmington, MI
Farrier Indus. Assn. No. 37 [2253], Lexington, IL
Farwell Area Chamber of Commerce [7679], Farwell, MI
Fat Acceptance, Chicago Chap; Natl. Assn. to Advance [3772], Tinley Park, IL
Fat Acceptance, Northern Ohio Chap; Natl. Assn. to Advance [15996], Middleburg Heights, OH
Fathers for Children and Families; Wisconsin [18703], Madison, WI
Fathers For Equal Rights of America, Michigan [9800], Southfield, MI
Fathers Rights; Coalition for [★18703]
Fayette County Chamber of Commerce [17127], Washington Court House, OH
Fayette County Girl Scouts [★6091]
Fayette County Historical Soc. [17128], Washington Court House, OH
Fayette County Museum [★17128]
Fed. Bar Assn., Columbus Chap. [14432], Columbus, OH
Fed. Bar Assn., Western Michigan 869/06 [7929], Grand Rapids, MI
Fed. Hocking High School - Young Life [13204], Athens, OH
Federalist Soc. for Law and Public Policy Stud. - Cincinnati Chap. [13827], Cincinnati, OH
Federalist Soc. for Law and Public Policy Stud. - Cleveland Chap. [14119], Cleveland, OH
Federalist Soc. for Law and Public Policy Stud. - Columbus Chap. [14433], Columbus, OH
Federalist Soc. for Law and Public Policy Stud. - Grand Rapids Chap. [7930], Grand Rapids, MI
Federalist Soc. for Law and Public Policy Stud. - Indianapolis Chap. [5116], Indianapolis, IN
Federalist Soc. for Law and Public Policy Stud. - Michigan Chap. (Detroit) [7362], Detroit, MI
Federalist Soc. for Law and Public Policy Stud. - Milwaukee Chap. [19007], Milwaukee, WI
Federalist Soc. for Law and Public Policy Stud. - Minneapolis Chap. [12858], Wayzata, MN
Fed. of Environmental Technologists [19739], Slinger, WI
Fed. of Families for Children's Mental Hea. - First Ohio Chap. [13532], Canfield, OH
Fed. of Independent Illinois Colls. and Universities [3551], Springfield, IL
Fed. of Musicians - Local 5, Amer. Fed. of Musicians [★9797]
Fed. of Women Contractors [891], Chicago, IL
Feed
Minnesota Grain and Feed Assn. [11649], Minneapolis, MN
Northwest Agri-Dealers Assn. [11395], Mankato, MN
Wisconsin Agri-Service Assn. [18641], Madison, WI
Feed Testing Consortium; NIRS Forage and [18584], Madison, WI
Fellowship of Freethinkers, Bradley Univ. [3017], Peoria, IL
Fellowship of Orthodox Christians United in Service Focus [4923], Hobart, IN
Female Alumni Athletic Boosters [10184], Wyandotte, MI
Feminism
9to5 Poverty Network [18922], Milwaukee, WI
Cincinnati 9to5 [13772], Cincinnati, OH
Cleveland/Akron 9to5 [13049], Akron, OH
Illinois Fed. of Bus. and Professional Women Clubs [3604], Springfield, IL
Milwaukee 9to5 [19051], Milwaukee, WI
Moms Club of Apple Valley [10321], Apple Valley, MN
Natl. Hook-up of Black Women, Chicago Chap. [1082], Chicago, IL
Natl. Hook-up of Black Women, Joliet Chap. [2115], Joliet, IL
Natl. Org. for Women - Akron Area [13072], Akron, OH
Natl. Org. for Women - Ann Arbor/Washtenaw County [10212], Ypsilanti, MI
Natl. Org. for Women - Astabula [15526], Jefferson, OH
Natl. Org. for Women - Athens [13209], Athens, OH
Natl. Org. for Women - Cincinnati [13930], Cincinnati, OH
Natl. Org. for Women - Columbus [14525], Columbus, OH
Natl. Org. for Women - Dayton [13624], Centerville, OH
Natl. Org. for Women - Detroit [7413], Detroit, MI
Natl. Org. for Women - Downriver [8077], Grosse Ile, MI

Natl. Org. for Women - Fox Valley **[3390]**, St. Charles, IL
Natl. Org. for Women - Grand Traverse **[9942]**, Traverse City, MI
Natl. Org. for Women - Greater Cleveland **[15709]**, Lorain, OH
Natl. Org. for Women - Greater Kalamazoo Area **[8458]**, Kalamazoo, MI
Natl. Org. for Women - Greater Youngstown **[17406]**, Youngstown, OH
Natl. Org. for Women - Illinois **[3655]**, Springfield, IL
Natl. Org. for Women - Indiana **[5430]**, Indianapolis, IN
Natl. Org. for Women - Lake-to-Lake **[7831]**, Gladstone, MI
Natl. Org. for Women - Lansing **[7558]**, East Lansing, MI
Natl. Org. for Women - Livingston County **[7020]**, Brighton, MI
Natl. Org. for Women - Macomb County **[9092]**, Mount Clemens, MI
Natl. Org. for Women - Michigan **[7559]**, East Lansing, MI
Natl. Org. for Women - Minnesota **[12551]**, St. Paul, MN
Natl. Org. for Women - Mount Pleasant **[9119]**, Mount Pleasant, MI
Natl. Org. for Women - Muskegon-Ottawa **[9172]**, Muskegon Heights, MI
Natl. Org. for Women - Northwest Suburban (Chicago) **[73]**, Arlington Heights, IL
Natl. Org. for Women - Oakland County **[9587]**, Royal Oak, MI
Natl. Org. for Women - Oberlin **[16286]**, Oberlin, OH
Natl. Org. for Women - Ohio **[14526]**, Columbus, OH
Natl. Org. for Women - Port Clinton **[16459]**, Port Clinton, OH
Natl. Org. for Women - Toledo Area **[16937]**, Toledo, OH
Natl. Org. for Women - Twin Cities **[11703]**, Minneapolis, MN
Natl. Org. for Women - Wisconsin **[18580]**, Madison, WI
Natl. Org. for Women - Youngstown S **[17070]**, Vienna, OH
Natl. Org. for Women - Zanesville **[17440]**, Zanesville, OH
Warren, OH 9to5 **[17119]**, Warren, OH

Fencing
Ann Arbor Dueling Soc. **[6906]**, Belleville, MI
Beloit Fencing Club **[17606]**, Beloit, WI
Caliburn Fencing Club **[18987]**, Milwaukee, WI
Durendal Fencing Club **[18505]**, Madison, WI
Genesee Fencing Club **[7843]**, Grand Blanc, MI
Great Lakes Sword Club **[7582]**, Eaton Rapids, MI
Illinois Fencers Club **[2587]**, Mount Prospect, IL
Indianapolis Fencing Club **[5347]**, Indianapolis, IN
Kent Fencing Club **[15542]**, Kent, OH
Minnesota Sword Club **[11676]**, Minneapolis, MN
MTU Fencing Club **[8258]**, Houghton, MI
Northern Illinois Univ. Fencing Club **[1440]**, DeKalb, IL
Oberlin Coll. Flaming Blades **[16289]**, Oberlin, OH
Ohio State Univ. Fencing Club **[14683]**, Columbus, OH
Renaissance Fencing Club **[8900]**, Madison Heights, MI
Twin Cities Fencing Club **[12598]**, St. Paul, MN

Fencing Club; Caliburn **[18987]**, Milwaukee, WI
Fencing Club; Durendal **[18505]**, Madison, WI
Fencing Club; Genesee **[7843]**, Grand Blanc, MI
Fencing Club; Indianapolis **[5347]**, Indianapolis, IN
Fencing Club; Kent **[15542]**, Kent, OH
Fencing Club; MTU **[8258]**, Houghton, MI
Fencing Club; Northern Illinois Univ. **[1440]**, DeKalb, IL
Fencing Club; Oberlin Coll. **[★16289]**
Fencing Club; Ohio State Univ. **[14683]**, Columbus, OH
Fencing Club; Renaissance **[8900]**, Madison Heights, MI
Fencing Club; Twin Cities **[12598]**, St. Paul, MN
Fennimore Area Chamber of Commerce **[17957]**, Fennimore, WI
Fenton Area Chamber of Commerce **[7683]**, Fenton, MI
Fenton/Flint Table Tennis Club **[8818]**, Linden, MI
Fenton Lions Club **[7684]**, Fenton, MI
Ferdinand Chamber of Commerce **[4596]**, Ferdinand, IN
Fergus Falls Area Chamber of Commerce **[10996]**, Fergus Falls, MN
Fergus Falls Convention and Visitors Bur. **[10997]**, Fergus Falls, MN

Ferret
In the Company of Ferrets **[12720]**, Stillwater, MN

Ferrets; In the Company of **[12720]**, Stillwater, MN
Fertile Lions Club **[11008]**, Fertile, MN

Fertility
Resolve of Illinois Chap. **[2023]**, Hinsdale, IL
Resolve of Michigan **[9590]**, Royal Oak, MI
Resolve of Minnesota **[10926]**, Edina, MN
Resolve of Ohio **[14721]**, Columbus, OH
Wisconsin Chap. of RESOLVE **[20088]**, Wauwatosa, WI

Fertilizer
Illinois Fertilizer and Chem. Assn. **[284]**, Bloomington, IL
Wisconsin Fertilizer and Chem. Assn. **[18705]**, Madison, WI

Fertilizer and Chem. Assn; Illinois **[284]**, Bloomington, IL
Fertilizer and Chem. Assn; Wisconsin **[18705]**, Madison, WI
Festival Assn; Waseca Sleigh and Cutter **[12850]**, Waseca, MN
Festivals and Events Assn; Ohio **[15696]**, London, OH
FFA - Michigan Assn. **[7520]**, East Lansing, MI
Field Spaniel Soc. of Am. **[17856]**, East Troy, WI
Fiero Enthusiasts; Northern Illinois **[2659]**, Naperville, IL
Fighters Public Awareness Comm; Westland Fire **[10146]**, Westland, MI
Figure Skating Club of Bloomington **[10467]**, Bloomington, MN
Figure Skating Club of Cincinnati **[13828]**, Cincinnati, OH
Figure Skating Club of Minneapolis **[11559]**, Minneapolis, MN
Figure Skating Club of Rochester **[12141]**, Rochester, MN
Figure Skating Club of Rockford **[3277]**, Rockford, IL
Fil-Am Assn. of Mundelein, Illinois **[2613]**, Mundelein, IL
Filipino-Amer. Women's Network, Minnesota **[12413]**, St. Paul, MN

Film
Sons of the Desert, Tree in a Test Tube Soc. **[165]**, Bartlett, IL

Film Industry
Green Bay Film Soc. **[18107]**, Green Bay, WI
IFP Minnesota Center for Media Arts **[12425]**, St. Paul, MN
Media Communications Assn. Intl., Greater Cleveland Chap. **[13449]**, Brunswick, OH
Media Communications Assn.-Intl., Greater Wisconsin Chap. **[19671]**, Schofield, WI
Media Communications Assn.-Intl., Madison Chap. **[18560]**, Madison, WI
Media Communs. Assn.-Intl., Milwaukee Chap. **[19046]**, Milwaukee, WI
Women In Film Chicago **[1237]**, Chicago, IL

Film Soc. of Chicago; Silent **[1184]**, Chicago, IL
Film Soc; Green Bay **[18107]**, Green Bay, WI

Finance
Financial Executives Intl., Central Ohio Chap. **[17212]**, Westerville, OH
Financial Executives Intl., Chicago Chap. **[892]**, Chicago, IL
Financial Executives Intl., Cincinnati Chap. **[17173]**, West Chester, OH
Financial Executives Intl., Milwaukee Chap. **[19008]**, Milwaukee, WI
Financial Executives Intl., Northeast Ohio Chap. **[14120]**, Cleveland, OH
Financial Executives Intl., Northeast Wisconsin Chap. **[18097]**, Green Bay, WI
Financial Executives Intl., Toledo Chap. **[16915]**, Toledo, OH
Financial Executives Intl., Twin Cities Chap. **[11560]**, Minneapolis, MN
Financial Executives Intl., Western Michigan Chap. **[7931]**, Grand Rapids, MI
Financial Managers Soc., Chicago Chap. **[893]**, Chicago, IL
Financial Managers Soc., Ohio Chap. **[13829]**, Cincinnati, OH
Financial Managers Soc., Wisconsin Chap. **[19983]**, Waukesha, WI
Illinois League of Financial Institutions **[3610]**, Springfield, IL
Indiana Assn. of Mortgage Brokers **[5177]**, Indianapolis, IN
Indiana Consumer Finance Assn. **[5217]**, Indianapolis, IN
Michigan Campaign Finance Network **[8638]**, Lansing, MI
Minnesota Assn. of Mortgage Brokers **[10917]**, Edina, MN
NACM Hartland **[15468]**, Howard, OH
NACM North Central **[11688]**, Minneapolis, MN
Natl. Assn. of Credit Mgt. Great Lakes **[8898]**, Madison Heights, MI
Natl. Assn. of Credit Mgt. Greater Cleveland **[17231]**, Westlake, OH
Natl. Assn. of Credit Mgt. Ohio **[14928]**, Dayton, OH
Natl. Assn. of Credit Mgt. - Western Michigan **[10191]**, Wyoming, MI
Natl. Assn. of Credit Managers Ohio, Cincinnati **[13919]**, Cincinnati, OH
Ohio Assn. of Mortgage Brokers **[16221]**, North Canton, OH
Ohio Govt. Finance Officers Assn. **[14618]**, Columbus, OH
Wisconsin Credit Assn. **[19299]**, New Berlin, WI

Finance Network; Michigan Campaign **[8638]**, Lansing, MI
Financial Advisors; Dayton Assn. of Insurance and **[14870]**, Dayton, OH
Financial Advisors; Indiana Assn. of Insurance and **[5176]**, Indianapolis, IN
Financial Advisors; Indy South Assn. of Insurance and **[5361]**, Indianapolis, IN
Financial Advisors; Ohio Assn. of Insurance and **[14557]**, Columbus, OH
Financial Advisors, Southern Illinois Chap; Natl. Assn. of Insurance and **[424]**, Carbondale, IL
Financial Advisors; Western Michigan Assn. of Insurance and **[9169]**, Muskegon, MI

Financial Aid
Minnesota Dollars for Scholars **[12616]**, St. Peter, MN

Financial Educ; Community **[14410]**, Columbus, OH
Financial and Estate Planning Coun. of Metro Detroit **[9989]**, Troy, MI
Financial Executives Intl., Central Ohio Chap. **[17212]**, Westerville, OH
Financial Executives Intl., Chicago Chap. **[892]**, Chicago, IL
Financial Executives Intl., Cincinnati Chap. **[17173]**, West Chester, OH
Financial Executives Intl., Milwaukee Chap. **[19008]**, Milwaukee, WI
Financial Executives Intl., Northeast Ohio Chap. **[14120]**, Cleveland, OH
Financial Executives Intl., Northeast Wisconsin Chap. **[18097]**, Green Bay, WI
Financial Executives Intl., Toledo Chap. **[16915]**, Toledo, OH
Financial Executives Intl., Twin Cities Chap. **[11560]**, Minneapolis, MN
Financial Executives Intl., Western Michigan Chap. **[7931]**, Grand Rapids, MI
Financial Managers Soc., Chicago Chap. **[893]**, Chicago, IL
Financial Managers Soc., Ohio Chap. **[13829]**, Cincinnati, OH
Financial Managers Soc., Wisconsin Chap. **[19983]**, Waukesha, WI

Financial Planning
Central Illinois Estate Planning Coun. **[1378]**, Decatur, IL
Central Illinois Planned Giving Coun. **[275]**, Bloomington, IL
Cincinnati Estate Planning Coun. **[13784]**, Cincinnati, OH
Estate Planning Coun. of Cleveland **[14116]**, Cleveland, OH

Estate Planning Coun. of Lake County **[3485]**, Skokie, IL
Estate Planning Coun. of Upper Ohio Valley **[13262]**, Barnesville, OH
Financial and Estate Planning Coun. of Metro Detroit **[9989]**, Troy, MI
Financial Planning Assn. of Central Ohio **[15046]**, Dublin, OH
Financial Planning Assn. of Greater Hudson Valley **[11561]**, Minneapolis, MN
Financial Planning Assn. of Greater Indiana **[5117]**, Indianapolis, IN
Financial Planning Assn. of Greater Michigan **[7521]**, East Lansing, MI
Financial Planning Assn. of Illinois **[3018]**, Peoria, IL
Financial Planning Assn. of Michigan **[9771]**, South Lyon, MI
Financial Planning Assn. of Minnesota **[11562]**, Minneapolis, MN
Financial Planning Assn. of Northeast Ohio Chap. **[13273]**, Bay Village, OH
Financial Planning Assn. of Southern Wisconsin **[19009]**, Milwaukee, WI
Hoosier Hills Estate Planning Coun. **[4225]**, Bloomington, IN
Lakeshore Estate Planning Coun. **[18780]**, Manitowoc, WI
Minneapolis Estate Planning Coun. **[12446]**, St. Paul, MN
North Coast Estate Planning Coun. **[15249]**, Fremont, OH
Northeastern Michigan Estate Planning Coun. **[9623]**, Saginaw, MI
Northern Illinois Estate Planning Coun. **[3296]**, Rockford, IL
Quad City Estate Planning Coun. **[3254]**, Rock Island, IL
Sheboygan County Estate Planning Coun. **[19711]**, Sheboygan, WI
Southwestern Michigan Estate Planning Coun. **[9693]**, St. Joseph, MI
Toledo Estate Planning Coun. **[16972]**, Toledo, OH
Tri-County Estate Planning Coun. **[13501]**, Cambridge, OH
Western Michigan Estate Planning Coun. **[8027]**, Grand Rapids, MI
Financial Planning Assn. of Central Ohio **[15046]**, Dublin, OH
Financial Planning Assn. of Greater Hudson Valley **[11561]**, Minneapolis, MN
Financial Planning Assn. of Greater Indiana **[5117]**, Indianapolis, IN
Financial Planning Assn. of Greater Michigan **[7521]**, East Lansing, MI
Financial Planning Assn. of Illinois **[3018]**, Peoria, IL
Financial Planning Assn. of Michigan **[9771]**, South Lyon, MI
Financial Planning Assn. of Minnesota **[11562]**, Minneapolis, MN
Financial Planning Assn. of Northeast Ohio Chap. **[13273]**, Bay Village, OH
Financial Planning Assn. of Southern Wisconsin **[19009]**, Milwaukee, WI
Findlay Antique Bottle Club **[13390]**, Bowling Green, OH
Findlay Area Human Rsrc. Assn. **[15199]**, Findlay, OH
Findlay Area Youth for Christ **[15200]**, Findlay, OH
Findlay-Hancock County Chamber of Commerce **[15201]**, Findlay, OH
Finneytown - Young Life **[15156]**, Fairfield, OH
Finnish
Finnish Center Assn. **[7660]**, Farmington Hills, MI
Finnish Center Assn. **[7660]**, Farmington Hills, MI
Fire Chief Association; Chippewa County **[19774]**, Stanley, WI
Fire Dept. Assn; Brookville **[13440]**, Brookville, OH
Fire Dept; Prairie Township Volunteer **[15463]**, Holmesville, OH
Fire Fighters Public Awareness Comm; Westland **[10146]**, Westland, MI
Fire Fighting
Algonac Firefighters Assn. **[6597]**, Algonac, MI
Benton Township of Monroe County Volunteer Fire Department **[6367]**, Unionville, IN
Box 15 Club **[14339]**, Columbus, OH
Brookville Fire Dept. Assn. **[13440]**, Brookville, OH
Illinois Professional Firefighters Assn. **[1623]**, Elmhurst, IL
Miami Valley Fire-EMS Alliance **[14910]**, Dayton, OH
Michigan Assn. of Fire Chiefs **[8615]**, Lansing, MI
Michigan Professional Fire Fighters Union **[9966]**, Trenton, MI
Michigan State Firemen's Assn. **[9895]**, Swartz Creek, MI
New Waterford Fireman's Assn. **[16162]**, New Waterford, OH
Ohio Assn. of Professional Fire Fighters **[14562]**, Columbus, OH
Prairie Township Volunteer Fire Dept **[15463]**, Holmesville, OH
Ridgeway Township Firefighters Assn. **[7026]**, Britton, MI
Rudolph Volunteer Fire Dept. **[19653]**, Rudolph, WI
South Holland Professional Firefighters Assn. **[3509]**, South Holland, IL
Fire Protection
Chippewa County Fire Chief Association **[19774]**, Stanley, WI
Groveland Township Firefighters and Dive Team Assn. **[8235]**, Holly, MI
Illinois Assn. of Fire Protection Districts **[3571]**, Springfield, IL
Minnesota Fire Ser. Certification Bd. **[19742]**, Solon Springs, WI
Soc. of Fire Protection Engineers - Minnesota **[12036]**, Plymouth, MN
Soc. of Fire Protection Engineers - Northeast Ohio Chap. **[16382]**, Parma Heights, OH
Westland Fire Fighters Public Awareness Comm. **[10146]**, Westland, MI
Fire Ser. Certification Bd; Minnesota **[19742]**, Solon Springs, WI
Firearms
People's Rights Org. **[14709]**, Columbus, OH
Ripon Rifle and Pistol Club **[19637]**, Ripon, WI
Firearms Instructors; Minnesota Assn. of Law Enforcement **[12157]**, Rochester, MN
Firefighters Assn; Algonac **[6597]**, Algonac, MI
Firefighters Association; Marseilles Volunteer **[2422]**, Marseilles, IL
Firefighters Assn; Ridgeway Township **[7026]**, Britton, MI
Firefighters Assn; South Holland Professional **[3509]**, South Holland, IL
Firefighters and Dive Team Assn; Groveland Township **[8235]**, Holly, MI
Firelands Assn. of Realtors **[16610]**, Sandusky, OH
Firelands Audubon Soc. **[16611]**, Sandusky, OH
Firelands Fly Fishers **[13242]**, Avon, OH
Firelands Lions Club **[15111]**, Elyria, OH
Firemen's Assn; Michigan State **[9895]**, Swartz Creek, MI
Firemens' Building Assn; West Union **[17199]**, West Union, OH
Firewalker Four Wheel Drive Club **[1918]**, Gurnee, IL
First Call for Help **[4399]**, Columbus, IN
First Call for Help **[12285]**, St. Cloud, MN
First Catholic Slovak Ladies Assn. - Beachwood Junior Br. HO **[13287]**, Beachwood, OH
First Catholic Slovak Ladies Assn. - Beachwood Senior Br. ZJ **[13288]**, Beachwood, OH
First Catholic Slovak Ladies Assn. - Bedford Junior Br. 380 **[13470]**, Burton, OH
First Catholic Slovak Ladies Assn. - Bedford Senior Br. 475 **[13471]**, Burton, OH
First Catholic Slovak Ladies Assn. - Berwyn Junior Br. 426 **[1360]**, Darien, IL
First Catholic Slovak Ladies Assn. - Berwyn Senior Br. 503 **[1361]**, Darien, IL
First Catholic Slovak Ladies Assn. - Campbell Junior Br. 250 **[13508]**, Campbell, OH
First Catholic Slovak Ladies Assn. - Canton Junior Br. 143 **[13564]**, Canton, OH
First Catholic Slovak Ladies Assn. - Canton Senior Br. 301 **[13565]**, Canton, OH
First Catholic Slovak Ladies Assn. - Chicago Junior Br. 174 **[1316]**, Crete, IL
First Catholic Slovak Ladies Assn. - Chicago Junior Br. 308 **[2938]**, Palos Hills, IL
First Catholic Slovak Ladies Assn. - Chicago Junior Br. 370 **[1981]**, Hickory Hills, IL
First Catholic Slovak Ladies Assn. - Chicago Senior Br. 225 **[1982]**, Hickory Hills, IL
First Catholic Slovak Ladies Assn. - Chicago Senior Br. 352 **[2939]**, Palos Hills, IL
First Catholic Slovak Ladies Assn. - Chicago Senior Br. 421 **[4012]**, Willowbrook, IL
First Catholic Slovak Ladies Assn. - Cleveland Junior Br. 014 **[13434]**, Brook Park, OH
First Catholic Slovak Ladies Assn. - Cleveland Junior Br. 057 **[16361]**, Parma, OH
First Catholic Slovak Ladies Assn. - Cleveland Junior Br. 240 **[14121]**, Cleveland, OH
First Catholic Slovak Ladies Assn. - Cleveland Junior Br. 441 **[16362]**, Parma, OH
First Catholic Slovak Ladies Assn. - Cleveland Junior Br. 453 **[17255]**, Wickliffe, OH
First Catholic Slovak Ladies Assn. - Cleveland Junior Br. 461 **[15740]**, Lyndhurst, OH
First Catholic Slovak Ladies Assn. - Cleveland Junior Br. 481 **[16363]**, Parma, OH
First Catholic Slovak Ladies Assn. - Cleveland Junior Br. 483 **[16676]**, Solon, OH
First Catholic Slovak Ladies Assn. - Cleveland Junior Br. 485 **[16364]**, Parma, OH
First Catholic Slovak Ladies Assn. - Cleveland Junior Br. 503 **[15994]**, Middleburg Heights, OH
First Catholic Slovak Ladies Assn. - Cleveland Senior Br. 010 **[14122]**, Cleveland, OH
First Catholic Slovak Ladies Assn. - Cleveland Senior Br. 141 **[16365]**, Parma, OH
First Catholic Slovak Ladies Assn. - Cleveland Senior Br. 176 **[17014]**, Twinsburg, OH
First Catholic Slovak Ladies Assn. - Cleveland Senior Br. 221 **[16366]**, Parma, OH
First Catholic Slovak Ladies Assn. - Cleveland Senior Br. 238 **[16367]**, Parma, OH
First Catholic Slovak Ladies Assn. - Cleveland Senior Br. 360 **[14123]**, Cleveland, OH
First Catholic Slovak Ladies Assn. - Cleveland Senior Br. 378 **[15741]**, Lyndhurst, OH
First Catholic Slovak Ladies Assn. - Cleveland Senior Br. 517 **[16380]**, Parma Heights, OH
First Catholic Slovak Ladies Assn. - Cleveland Senior Br. 522 **[17256]**, Wickliffe, OH
First Catholic Slovak Ladies Assn. - Cleveland Senior Br. 530 **[14124]**, Cleveland, OH
First Catholic Slovak Ladies Assn. - Cleveland Senior Br. 555 **[16677]**, Solon, OH
First Catholic Slovak Ladies Assn. - Cleveland Senior Br. 557 **[16368]**, Parma, OH
First Catholic Slovak Ladies Assn. - Cleveland Senior Br. 578 **[15995]**, Middleburg Heights, OH
First Catholic Slovak Ladies Assn. - Detroit Junior Br. 232 **[6610]**, Allen Park, MI
First Catholic Slovak Ladies Assn. - Detroit Junior Br. 327 **[7788]**, Fraser, MI
First Catholic Slovak Ladies Assn. - Detroit Senior Br. 334 **[6611]**, Allen Park, MI
First Catholic Slovak Ladies Assn. - Detroit Senior Br. 403 **[7789]**, Fraser, MI
First Catholic Slovak Ladies Assn. - Elyria Junior Br. 478 **[16281]**, Oberlin, OH
First Catholic Slovak Ladies Assn. - Elyria Senior Br. 476 **[16282]**, Oberlin, OH
First Catholic Slovak Ladies Assn. - Joliet Senior Br. 053 **[2105]**, Joliet, IL
First Catholic Slovak Ladies Assn. - Lakewood Junior Br. 088 **[16788]**, Strongsville, OH
First Catholic Slovak Ladies Assn. - Lakewood Junior Br. 429 **[15581]**, Lakewood, OH
First Catholic Slovak Ladies Assn. - Lakewood Junior Br. 457 **[16369]**, Parma, OH
First Catholic Slovak Ladies Assn. - Lakewood Senior Br. 432 **[15582]**, Lakewood, OH
First Catholic Slovak Ladies Assn. - Lakewood Senior Br. 524 **[16370]**, Parma, OH
First Catholic Slovak Ladies Assn. - Lorain Senior Br. 114 **[15704]**, Lorain, OH
First Catholic Slovak Ladies Assn. - Milwaukee Junior Br. 130 **[19260]**, Muskego, WI
First Catholic Slovak Ladies Assn. - Milwaukee Senior Br. 023 **[19261]**, Muskego, WI
First Catholic Slovak Ladies Assn. - Milwaukee Senior Br. 376 **[19010]**, Milwaukee, WI

First Catholic Slovak Ladies Assn. - Mount Olive Junior Br. 140 **[2580]**, Mount Olive, IL
First Catholic Slovak Ladies Assn. - Mount Olive Senior Br. 049 **[2581]**, Mount Olive, IL
First Catholic Slovak Ladies Assn. - Muskegon Heights Senior Br. 445 **[9170]**, Muskegon Heights, MI
First Catholic Slovak Ladies Assn. - Muskegon Junior Br. 357 **[9171]**, Muskegon Heights, MI
First Catholic Slovak Ladies Assn. - North Olmsted Junior Br. 499 **[16297]**, Olmsted Falls, OH
First Catholic Slovak Ladies Assn. - North Olmsted Senior Br. 573 **[16298]**, Olmsted Falls, OH
First Catholic Slovak Ladies Assn. - Streator Junior Br. 077 **[3726]**, Streator, IL
First Catholic Slovak Ladies Assn. - Streator Senior Br. 007 **[3727]**, Streator, IL
First Catholic Slovak Ladies Assn. - Streator Senior Br. 066 **[3728]**, Streator, IL
First Catholic Slovak Ladies Assn. - Struthers Junior Br. 066 **[15470]**, Hubbard, OH
First Catholic Slovak Ladies Assn. - Toledo Junior Br. 149 **[16916]**, Toledo, OH
First Catholic Slovak Ladies Assn. - Youngstown Junior Br. 029 **[17398]**, Youngstown, OH
First Catholic Slovak Ladies Assn. - Youngstown Junior Br. 192 **[17399]**, Youngstown, OH
First Catholic Slovak Ladies Assn. - Youngstown Senior Br. 030 **[17400]**, Youngstown, OH
First District Dental Soc. **[4548]**, Evansville, IN
First Priority of Muskegon **[9143]**, Muskegon, MI

Fish

- Black Lake Chap. of Sturgeon for Tomorrow **[7130]**, Cheboygan, MI
- Minnesota Chap. of Amer. Fisheries Soc. **[12832]**, Walker, MN
- Trout Unlimited - Ottawa Chap. **[8342]**, Ironwood, MI

Fish and Game Commissioners; Assn. of Midwest **[★19599]**
Fish Point Wildlife Assn. **[10024]**, Unionville, MI
Fish and Wildlife Agencies; Assn. of Midwest **[★19599]**
Fish and Wildlife Agencies; Midwest Assn. of **[19599]**, Rhinelander, WI
Fish and Wildlife Commn; Great Lakes Indian **[19353]**, Odanah, WI
Fish and Wildlife Commissioners; Assn. of Midwest **[★19599]**
Fishers Chamber of Commerce **[4604]**, Fishers, IN
Fishery Commn; Great Lakes **[6702]**, Ann Arbor, MI

Fishing

- Buckeye United Fly Fishers **[13764]**, Cincinnati, OH
- Charlevoix Rod and Gun Club **[7116]**, Charlevoix, MI
- Fairport Harbor Rod and Reel Assn. **[15179]**, Fairport Harbor, OH
- Firelands Fly Fishers **[13242]**, Avon, OH
- Flygirls of Michigan **[9581]**, Royal Oak, MI
- Grand River Fly Tyers **[7954]**, Grand Rapids, MI
- Great Lakes Sport Fishing Coun. **[1621]**, Elmhurst, IL
- Illinois B.A.S.S. Fed. **[3085]**, Petersburg, IL
- Indiana B.A.S.S. Fed. **[5840]**, Morgantown, IN
- Let's Go Fishing of Minnesota **[12918]**, Willmar, MN
- Michigan Bass Chap. Fed. **[9013]**, Michigan Center, MI
- Milwaukee Lake and Stream Fly Fishers **[19063]**, Milwaukee, WI
- North Coast Fly Fishers **[16339]**, Painesville, OH
- Ohio BASS Chap. Fed. **[15293]**, Gallipolis, OH
- St. Joseph River Valley Fly Fishers **[6261]**, South Bend, IN
- Salmon Unlimited **[1172]**, Chicago, IL
- Three Rivers Fly Fishers **[4722]**, Fort Wayne, IN
- Wisconsin State B.A.S.S. Fed. **[20149]**, Weston, WI

Fishing Coun; Great Lakes Sport **[1621]**, Elmhurst, IL
Fishing of Minnesota; Let's Go **[12918]**, Willmar, MN
Five Cities Assn. of Michigan **[8986]**, Mattawan, MI
Five-Os Young Life - Oconomowoc **[18182]**, Hartland, WI
Five Wings Arts Coun. **[12703]**, Staples, MN
Flag City REACT **[17062]**, Vanlue, OH
Flames Cricket Club **[894]**, Chicago, IL
Flat-Coated Retriever Club of Illinois **[148]**, Barrington, IL
Flat-Coated Retriever Soc. of Am. **[6320]**, Terre Haute, IN
Flat River Historical Society and Museums **[8066]**, Greenville, MI
Flat Rock Kiwanis **[7703]**, Flat Rock, MI
Flint 4 Seasons Figure Skating Club **[9894]**, Swartz Creek, MI
Flint Antique Bottle and Collectibles Club **[7803]**, Gaines, MI
Flint Area Assn. of Realtors **[7725]**, Flint, MI
Flint Area Chamber of Commerce **[7726]**, Flint, MI
Flint Area Convention and Visitors Bur. **[7727]**, Flint, MI
Flint Area Narcotics Anonymous **[7728]**, Flint, MI
Flint Corvette Club **[7729]**, Flint, MI
Flint Downtown Host Lions Club **[9514]**, Rochester Hills, MI
Flint Flying Eagle Coin Club **[7685]**, Fenton, MI
Flint Inner City Lions Club **[7730]**, Flint, MI
Flint Jewish Fed. **[7731]**, Flint, MI
Flint Lawn Bowling Club **[7732]**, Flint, MI
Flint - North Central Weed and Seed **[7733]**, Flint, MI
Flint Rock and Gem Club **[6960]**, Birch Run, MI
Flint Snowbirds SkiClub **[7734]**, Flint, MI
Flint Table Tennis Club **[7735]**, Flint, MI
Flint Township Lions Club **[7764]**, Flushing, MI
Flom and Area Lions Club **[12763]**, Twin Valley, MN
Floodplain and Stormwater Mgt; Indiana Assn. for **[5172]**, Indianapolis, IN
Floodwood Area Lions Club **[11011]**, Floodwood, MN
Flora Chamber of Commerce **[1706]**, Flora, IL
Floral City Stamp Club **[9064]**, Monroe, MI
Florida Urological Soc. **[3435]**, Schaumburg, IL

Florists

- Michigan Floral Assn. **[8149]**, Haslett, MI
- State Florist Assn. of Indiana **[5820]**, Monrovia, IN

Florists' Assn; Ohio **[14610]**, Columbus, OH
Flossie Wiley Elementary School PTA **[3815]**, Urbana, IL

Flowers

- Minnesota Native Wildflower Grass Producers Assn. **[12955]**, Winona, MN

Floyd County Chamber of Commerce **[★5927]**
Flushing Area Chamber of Commerce **[7765]**, Flushing, MI
Flushing Area Historical Soc. **[7766]**, Flushing, MI
Flushing Lions Club **[7767]**, Flushing, MI
Flygirls of Michigan **[9581]**, Royal Oak, MI
Focus: HOPE **[7363]**, Detroit, MI

Folk

- Cincinnati Folk Life **[13785]**, Cincinnati, OH

Folk Music Soc. of Midland **[8481]**, Kawkawlin, MI
Folklore Village; Friends of **[17837]**, Dodgeville, WI
Folks on Spokes **[★123]**
Folks on Spokes **[★2436]**
Folks on Spokes Bicycle Club **[2436]**, Matteson, IL
Fond du Lac Area Assn. of Commerce **[17972]**, Fond du Lac, WI
Fond du Lac Area Chamber of Commerce **[★17972]**
Fond du Lac Area Convention and Visitors Bur. **[17973]**, Fond du Lac, WI
Fond du Lac Area United Way **[17974]**, Fond du Lac, WI
Fond du Lac Area Youth for Christ **[17975]**, Fond du Lac, WI
Fond du Lac Blue Line Figure Skating **[17976]**, Fond du Lac, WI
Fond du Lac County Audubon Soc. **[17977]**, Fond du Lac, WI
Fond du Lac County-Farm Bur. **[17978]**, Fond du Lac, WI
Fond du Lac County Kennel Club **[17979]**, Fond du Lac, WI
Fond du Lac County REACT **[17980]**, Fond du Lac, WI
Fond du Lac Home Builders **[17981]**, Fond du Lac, WI

Food

- Amer. Assn. of Candy Technologists - Chicago Sect. **[2831]**, Oakbrook Terrace, IL
- Amer. Assn. of Candy Technologists - Milwaukee Sect. **[18929]**, Milwaukee, WI
- Assoc. Food Dealers of Michigan **[7654]**, Farmington Hills, MI
- Friends of the St. Paul Farmers' Market **[12659]**, Shoreview, MN
- Greater Detroit Frozen Food Assn. **[9399]**, Plymouth, MI
- Illinois Food Retailers Assn. **[2333]**, Lombard, IL
- Illinois Stewardship Alliance **[3231]**, Rochester, IL
- Meals on Wheels of Rochester **[12155]**, Rochester, MN
- Michigan Celery Promotion Cooperative **[8292]**, Hudsonville, MI
- Michigan Distributors and Vendors Assn. **[8659]**, Lansing, MI
- Michigan Food and Beverage Assn. **[10070]**, Warren, MI
- Mother Hubbard's Cupboard **[4242]**, Bloomington, IN
- United Food and Commercial Workers Intl. Union, AFL-CIO, CLC - Local Union 6 **[10267]**, Albert Lea, MN
- United Food and Commercial Workers Intl. Union, AFL-CIO, CLC -Local Union 9 **[10362]**, Austin, MN
- United Food and Commercial Workers Intl. Union, AFL-CIO, CLC - Local Union 789 **[12685]**, South St. Paul, MN
- United Food and Commercial Workers Intl. Union, AFL-CIO, CLC - Local Union 880 **[14227]**, Cleveland, OH
- United Food and Commercial Workers Intl. Union, AFL-CIO, CLC -Local Union 881, Northcentral Region **[3360]**, Rosemont, IL
- Wisconsin Grocers Assn. **[18709]**, Madison, WI
- Wisconsin Maple Syrup Producers Assn. **[18900]**, Merrill, WI

Food Assn; Greater Detroit Frozen **[9399]**, Plymouth, MI
Food and Beverage Assn; Michigan **[10070]**, Warren, MI
Food and Commercial Workers AFL-CIO, LU 268 **[17754]**, Chippewa Falls, WI

Food and Drugs

- Assoc. Illinois Milk, Food and Environmental Sanitarians **[2626]**, Naperville, IL
- Ohio Assn. of Food and Environmental Sanitarians **[13521]**, Canal Winchester, OH
- Upper Midwest Dairy Indus. Assn. **[11849]**, Mounds View, MN
- Wisconsin Assn. for Food Protection **[19867]**, Sun Prairie, WI

Food Processors Assn; Midwest **[18564]**, Madison, WI

Food Service

- Meals on Wheels of Hamilton County **[5976]**, Noblesville, IN
- Midwest Food Processors Assn. **[18564]**, Madison, WI
- Power Flour Action Network **[19705]**, Sheboygan, WI

Food Trade Coun; Michigan **[★10070]**
Foods Assn; Wisconsin Dairy **[★18914]**

Football

- Fairfield County Youth Football League **[15599]**, Lancaster, OH
- Menasha Bluejay Football Club **[18861]**, Menasha, WI
- Middletown Pee Wee Football and Cheerleading **[16015]**, Middletown, OH
- Midland Area Youth Football League **[9034]**, Midland, MI
- Milwaukee Marauders **[20077]**, Wauwatosa, WI
- North End Club **[13184]**, Ashtabula, OH
- Oakland Highlanders Rugby Football Club **[9588]**, Royal Oak, MI

Football Club; Menasha Bluejay **[18861]**, Menasha, WI
Football Club of Metropolitan Detroit; Detroit Rugby **[9502]**, Rochester, MI
Football Club; Oakland Highlanders Rugby **[9588]**, Royal Oak, MI
Football League; Fairfield County Youth **[15599]**, Lancaster, OH
Football League; Midland Area Youth **[9034]**, Midland, MI
For Animals **[9929]**, Traverse City, MI
For the Love of Rotts, The Michigan Connection **[7487]**, Dryden, MI
Forada Lions Club **[10276]**, Alexandria, MN

Foreign Freight Forwarders Assn. of Chicago; Customs Brokers and **[865]**, Chicago, IL
Foreign Service
Illinois Restaurant Assn. **[962]**, Chicago, IL
Foreign Students
Minnesota Intl. Educators **[12491]**, St. Paul, MN
NAFSA: Assn. of Intl. Educators, Region IV **[11915]**, Northfield, MN
Foreign Trade
Customs Brokers and Foreign Freight Forwarders Assn. of Chicago **[865]**, Chicago, IL
Forensic Assn; Michigan Interscholastic **[6728]**, Ann Arbor, MI
Forensic Sciences
Illinois Division of the Intl. Assn. for Identification **[2642]**, Naperville, IL
Illinois Polygraph Soc. **[2107]**, Joliet, IL
Indiana Division of the Intl. Assn. for Identification **[4676]**, Fort Wayne, IN
Indiana Polygraph Assn. **[5280]**, Indianapolis, IN
Michigan-Ontario Identification Assn. **[7106]**, Center Line, MI
Minnesota Division of the Intl. Assn. for Identification **[12478]**, St. Paul, MN
Minnesota Polygraph Assn. **[11666]**, Minneapolis, MN
Ohio Assn. of Polygraph Examiners **[14561]**, Columbus, OH
Ohio Division of the Intl. Assn. for Identification **[16375]**, Parma, OH
Wisconsin Assn. for Identification **[19156]**, Milwaukee, WI
Wisconsin Polygraph Assn. **[19433]**, Peshtigo, WI
Forest Assn; Michigan **[6725]**, Ann Arbor, MI
Forest Hill Lawn Bowling Club **[16525]**, Richmond Heights, OH
Forest Hills Central High School - Young Life **[7932]**, Grand Rapids, MI
Forest Hills Central Middle School - Wyldlife **[7933]**, Grand Rapids, MI
Forest Hills Eastern High School - Young Life **[7934]**, Grand Rapids, MI
Forest Hills Eastern Middle School - Wyldlife **[7935]**, Grand Rapids, MI
Forest Hills Northern High School - Young Life **[7936]**, Grand Rapids, MI
Forest Hills Northern Middle School - Wyldlife **[7937]**, Grand Rapids, MI
Forest Industries
Assoc. Contract Loggers and Truckers of Minnesota **[12769]**, Two Harbors, MN
Minnesota Forest Indus. **[10836]**, Duluth, MN
Minnesota Timber Producers Assn. **[10839]**, Duluth, MN
Ohio Lumbermen's Assn. **[14636]**, Columbus, OH
Paper, Allied-Industrial, Chem. and Energy Workers Intl. Union, AFL-CIO, CLC Local Union 2-232 **[19086]**, Milwaukee, WI
Paper, Allied-Indus., Chem. and Energy Workers Intl. Union, AFL-CIO, CLC - Local Union 369 **[20125]**, West Bend, WI
Paper, Allied-Indus., Chem. and Energy Workers Intl. Union, AFL-CIO, CLC - Local Union 555 **[6419]**, Vincennes, IN
Paper, Allied-Indus., Chem. and Energy Workers Intl. Union, AFL-CIO, CLC - Local Union 609 **[13950]**, Cincinnati, OH
Paper, Allied-Indus., Chem. and Energy Workers Intl. Union, AFL-CIO, CLC - Local Union 801 **[16310]**, Orrville, OH
Forest Lake Area Chamber of Commerce **[11017]**, Forest Lake, MN
Forest Park Chamber of Commerce **[1711]**, Forest Park, IL
Forest Park Found. **[3019]**, Peoria, IL
Forest Park Main St. **[1712]**, Forest Park, IL
Forest Productivity Council; Wisconsin **[19610]**, Rhinelander, WI
Forest Products
Michigan Assn. of Timbermen **[8630]**, Lansing, MI
Michigan Assn. of Timbermen **[9197]**, Newberry, MI
Minnesota Maple Syrup Producers **[11353]**, Lutsen, MN
Wisconsin Retail Lumber Assn. **[18046]**, Germantown, WI
Forest Prdts. Soc., Great Lakes Sect. **[8426]**, Kalamazoo, MI
Forest Rsrc. Alliance; Michigan **[8666]**, Lansing, MI
Forestry
Buckeye Forest Coun. **[13203]**, Athens, OH
Forest Park Found. **[3019]**, Peoria, IL
Forest Prdts. Soc., Great Lakes Sect. **[8426]**, Kalamazoo, MI
Forestry Conservation Communications Assn., Region III **[19761]**, Spooner, WI
Indiana Hardwood Lumbermen's Assn. **[5243]**, Indianapolis, IN
Michigan Forest Rsrc. Alliance **[8666]**, Lansing, MI
Minnesota Forestry Assn. **[11091]**, Grand Rapids, MN
Natl. Assn. of State Foresters, Illinois **[3653]**, Springfield, IL
Natl. Assn. of State Foresters, Indiana **[5423]**, Indianapolis, IN
Natl. Assn. of State Foresters, Michigan **[8738]**, Lansing, MI
Natl. Assn. of State Foresters, Minnesota **[12546]**, St. Paul, MN
Natl. Assn. of State Foresters, Ohio **[14519]**, Columbus, OH
Natl. Assn. of State Foresters, Wisconsin **[18576]**, Madison, WI
Ohio Forestry Assn. **[14612]**, Columbus, OH
Soc. of Amer. Foresters, Headwaters Chap. **[11220]**, International Falls, MN
Soc. of Amer. Foresters, Illinois Chap. **[1941]**, Harrisburg, IL
Soc. of Amer. Foresters, Lake Superior Chap. **[12937]**, Willow River, MN
Soc. of Amer. Foresters, Minnesota **[10932]**, Effie, MN
Soc. of Amer. Foresters, Ohio **[14731]**, Columbus, OH
Soc. of Amer. Foresters, Southeast Illinois Student Chap. **[1942]**, Harrisburg, IL
Soc. of Amer. Foresters, Southern Chap. **[12188]**, Rochester, MN
Soc. of Amer. Foresters, Southern Illinois Univ. Student Chap. **[2621]**, Murphysboro, IL
Soc. of Amer. Foresters, Univ. of Illinois Student Chap. **[3833]**, Urbana, IL
Soc. of Amer. Foresters, Univ. of Minnesota Student Chap. **[12587]**, St. Paul, MN
Soc. of Amer. Foresters, Vermilion Community Coll. Student Chap. **[10958]**, Ely, MN
Walnut Coun. **[6504]**, West Lafayette, IN
Wisconsin Forest Productivity Council **[19610]**, Rhinelander, WI
Forestry Conservation Communications Assn., Region III **[19761]**, Spooner, WI
Forestwood Figure Skating Club of Parma Ohio **[16245]**, North Royalton, OH
Forgotten Eagles **[7241]**, De Tour Village, MI
Forsythe - Wyldlife **[6695]**, Ann Arbor, MI
Fort Atkinson Area Chamber of Commerce **[17999]**, Fort Atkinson, WI
Fort Detroit Golden Retriever Club **[9314]**, Ortonville, MI
Fort Recovery Chamber of Commerce **[15225]**, Fort Recovery, OH
Fort Thunder PSC **[11992]**, Perham, MN
Fort Wayne AIFA **[4650]**, Fort Wayne, IN
Fort Wayne/Allen County Convention and Visitors Bur. **[4651]**, Fort Wayne, IN
Fort Wayne Area Assn. of Realtors **[4652]**, Fort Wayne, IN
Fort Wayne Area Sheet Metal Contractors Assn. **[6054]**, Poneto, IN
Fort Wayne Area Youth for Christ **[4653]**, Fort Wayne, IN
Fort Wayne Astronomical Soc. **[4654]**, Fort Wayne, IN
Fort Wayne Beagle Club **[4655]**, Fort Wayne, IN
Fort Wayne Bonsai Club **[4938]**, Huntertown, IN
Fort Wayne Corvette Club **[4656]**, Fort Wayne, IN
Fort Wayne Habitat for Humanity **[4657]**, Fort Wayne, IN
Fort Wayne Hi-Lites **[4658]**, Fort Wayne, IN
Fort Wayne Medical Soc. **[4659]**, Fort Wayne, IN
Fort Wayne Table Tennis Club **[4660]**, Fort Wayne, IN
Fort Wayne Urban League **[4661]**, Fort Wayne, IN
Ft. Wayne Young Life Club **[4662]**, Fort Wayne, IN
Forty and Eight: Voiture 957 **[10205]**, Ypsilanti, MI
Forward Janesville **[18247]**, Janesville, WI
Forwarders Assn. of Chicago; Customs Brokers and Foreign Freight **[865]**, Chicago, IL
Fosston-Lengby Lions Club **[11023]**, Fosston, MN
Foster and Adoptive Care Assn. of Minnesota **[11279]**, Lake Elmo, MN
Foster Grandparent Prog. of Ethan Allen School **[19945]**, Wales, WI
Foster Grandparent Prog. of Greater Dayton **[14884]**, Dayton, OH
Foster Grandparent Prog. of Lincoln Hills School **[18237]**, Irma, WI
Foster Grandparent Prog. of Peoria/Tazewell Counties **[3020]**, Peoria, IL
Foster Grandparent Prog. of Suburban Cook County **[895]**, Chicago, IL
Foster Grandparent Prog. of Summit County **[13051]**, Akron, OH
Foster Parents
Foster Parents Mission Club **[7364]**, Detroit, MI
Foster Parents Mission Club **[7364]**, Detroit, MI
Fostoria Area Chamber of Commerce **[15230]**, Fostoria, OH
Fostoria Coin Club **[14434]**, Columbus, OH
Fostoria Lions Club **[15231]**, Fostoria, OH
Foundations; Coun. of Michigan **[7856]**, Grand Haven, MI
Fountain County Assn. for Retarded Citizens **[6400]**, Veedersburg, IN
Four Flags Area Chamber of Commerce **[9206]**, Niles, MI
Four Flags Area Coun. on Tourism **[9207]**, Niles, MI
Four Lakes Ice Yacht Club **[18510]**, Madison, WI
Four Rivers Rsrc. Conservation and Development Coun. **[6036]**, Petersburg, IN
Four Seasons Bonsai Club of Michigan **[8234]**, Holly, MI
Fowler Chamber of Commerce **[4736]**, Fowler, IN
Fowler Lions Club **[9675]**, St. Johns, MI
Fox Cities Chamber of Commerce and Indus. **[17490]**, Appleton, WI
Fox Cities Convention and Visitors Bur. **[17491]**, Appleton, WI
Fox Cities Optometric Soc. **[19727]**, Sherwood, WI
Fox Lake Area Chamber of Commerce **[18003]**, Fox Lake, WI
Fox Lake Area Chamber of Commerce and Indus. **[1719]**, Fox Lake, IL
Fox Lake Chamber of Commerce **[★18003]**
Fox River; Friends of the **[1324]**, Crystal Lake, IL
Fox River Valley Chap. of Muskies **[27]**, Algonquin, IL
Fox River Valley Dental Soc. **[1792]**, Geneva, IL
Fox Valley African Violet Soc. **[2635]**, Naperville, IL
Fox Valley Aikikai **[2636]**, Naperville, IL
Fox Valley Astronomical Soc. **[3883]**, Wasco, IL
Fox Valley Chap. of Assoc. Locksmiths of Am. **[19392]**, Oshkosh, WI
Fox Valley District Nurses Assn. - No. 6 **[18218]**, Hortonville, WI
Fox Valley Dog Training Club **[3381]**, St. Charles, IL
Fox Valley Elec. Auto Assn. **[3986]**, Wheaton, IL
Fox Valley Gen. Contractors Assn. **[3382]**, St. Charles, IL
Fox Valley German Amer. Team of Educal. Sponsors **[449]**, Carol Stream, IL
Fox Valley Literacy Coalition **[17492]**, Appleton, WI
Fox Valley Natl. Assn. of The Remodeling Indus. **[17493]**, Appleton, WI
Fox Valley Payroll Assn. **[2554]**, Morris, IL
Fox Valley Professional Photographers Assn. **[19675]**, Seymour, WI
Fox Valley Retriever Club **[18022]**, Fredonia, WI
Fox Valley United Way **[116]**, Aurora, IL
Fox Valley WyldLife **[19270]**, Neenah, WI
Fox Valley Young Life **[19271]**, Neenah, WI
Fox-Wolf Watershed Alliance **[17494]**, Appleton, WI
Foxview Alliance for Corp. Enhancement **[453]**, Carpentersville, IL
Franciscan Haircuts from the Heart **[13830]**, Cincinnati, OH
Franciscan Outreach Assn. **[896]**, Chicago, IL
Frank Bob Perrin - Lansing, Michigan Chap. of Trout Unlimited **[8567]**, Lansing, MI
Frankenmuth Chamber of Commerce **[★7779]**
Frankenmuth Chamber of Commerce and Convention and Visitors Bur. **[7779]**, Frankenmuth, MI

Frankenmuth Lions Club [7780], Frankenmuth, MI
Frankfort Area Chamber of Commerce [★7785]
Frankfort Bd. of Realtors, Indiana [4741], Frankfort, IN
Frankfort Chamber of Commerce [1724], Frankfort, IL
Frankfort - Elberta Area Chamber of Commerce [7785], Frankfort, MI
Frankfort Lions Club [7786], Frankfort, MI
Frankfort Main St. [4742], Frankfort, IN
Frankfort Sportsman Club [2508], Mokena, IL
Franklin Area Chamber of Commerce [15238], Franklin, OH
Franklin Chamber of Commerce [4747], Franklin, IN
Franklin County Beagle Club [3844], Valier, IL
Franklin County Genealogical and Historical Soc. [14435], Columbus, OH
Franklin Elementary School PTA [17495], Appleton, WI
Franklin Lions Club - Minnesota [11027], Franklin, MN
Franklin Park Chamber of Commerce and Indus. [★1739]
Franklin Park Manila Lions Club [1738], Franklin Park, IL
Franklin Park/Schiller Park Chamber of Commerce [1739], Franklin Park, IL
Franklin Township Educ. Found. [5118], Indianapolis, IN
Franklinton Bd. of Trade [14436], Columbus, OH
Fraser Figure Skating Club [7790], Fraser, MI
Fraternal Order of Eagles, Bedford No. 654 [4170], Bedford, IN
Fraternal Order of Eagles, Bemidji No. 351 [10415], Bemidji, MN
Fraternal Order of Eagles, Huron No. 2875 [15490], Huron, OH
Fraternal Order of Eagles, Waterford No. 2887 [10082], Waterford, MI
Fraternal Order of Police, Illinois State Lodge [3552], Springfield, IL
Fraternal Order of Police Lodge 86 [5119], Indianapolis, IN
Fraternal Order of Police, Michigan State Lodge [8568], Lansing, MI
Fraternal Order of Police, Minnesota State Lodge [11060], Golden Valley, MN
Fraternal Order of Police of Ohio, State Lodge [14437], Columbus, OH
Fraternal Order of Police, Wisconsin State Lodge [18098], Green Bay, WI
Fraternities, Service
Independent Order of Odd Fellows, Century Lodge No. 492 [454], Carpentersville, IL
Independent Order of Odd Fellows, Mad River Lodge 243 [15150], Fairborn, OH
Independent Order of Odd Fellows, Nankin Lodge No. 396 [10100], Wayne, MI
Troopers Lodge 41 [3690], Springfield, IL
Fraternities and Sororities
Zeta Beta Tau Fraternity [5517], Indianapolis, IN
Fraternity; Zeta Beta Tau [5517], Indianapolis, IN
Fraud Examiners, Southeast Michigan Area Chap., No. 37; Assn. of Certified [9975], Troy, MI
Frazeysburg Revitalization Association [15239], Frazeysburg, OH
Frederic Area Community Assn. [18019], Frederic, WI
Free Arts for Abused Children of Minnesota [11563], Minneapolis, MN
Free Enterprise
Alverno Coll. Students In Free Enterprise [18926], Milwaukee, WI
Anderson Univ. Students In Free Enterprise [4101], Anderson, IN
Bradley Univ. Students In Free Enterprise [3010], Peoria, IL
Coll. of St. Benedict and St. John's Univ. Students In Free Enterprise [10702], Collegeville, MN
DePaul Univ. Students In Free Enterprise [867], Chicago, IL
Frontier Community Coll. Students In Free Enterprise [1687], Fairfield, IL
Illinois Valley Community Coll. Students In Free Enterprise [2853], Oglesby, IL
John Carroll Univ. Students In Free Enterprise [17026], University Heights, OH
Quincy Univ. Students In Free Enterprise [3168], Quincy, IL
Rock Valley Coll. Students In Free Enterprise [3302], Rockford, IL
Southwest Minnesota State Univ. Students In Free Enterprise [11441], Marshall, MN
Youngstown State Univ. Students In Free Enterprise [17430], Youngstown, OH
Free Inquiry Gp. of Greater Cincinnati and Northern Kentucky [13831], Cincinnati, OH
Free Spirit Siberian Rescue [1949], Harvard, IL
Freeborn County Genealogical Soc. [10257], Albert Lea, MN
Freeborn County Historical Soc. [10258], Albert Lea, MN
Freeborn County Museum and Historical Village [★10258]
Freeburg Area Community Development Association [1741], Freeburg, IL
Freeburg Chamber of Commerce [1742], Freeburg, IL
Freedom
Friends of Freedom Soc. Ohio Underground Railroad Assn. [15922], Mayfield Heights, OH
Freedom Bus. Assn. [18286], Kaukauna, WI
Freeport Area Chamber of Commerce [1747], Freeport, IL
Freeport Galena Area Assn. of Realtors [1748], Freeport, IL
Freethought Assn. of West Michigan [6622], Allendale, MI
Freight Forwarders Assn. of Chicago; Customs Brokers and Foreign [865], Chicago, IL
Fremd - Young Life [2909], Palatine, IL
Fremont Area Chamber of Commerce [4761], Fremont, IN
Fremont Area Chamber of Commerce [7796], Fremont, MI
Fremont Area Chamber of Commerce [18024], Fremont, WI
Fremont Chamber of Commerce [★7796]
Fremont Lions Club - Michigan [7797], Fremont, MI
Fremont Noon Lions Club [15247], Fremont, OH
French Canadian-Acadian Genealogists of Wisconsin [18170], Hales Corners, WI
French Island Lions Club [18344], La Crosse, WI
French Lick - West Baden Chamber of Commerce [4763], French Lick, IN
Freshwater Soc. [10970], Excelsior, MN
Fridley Chamber of Commerce [★11848]
Fridley Lions Club [11033], Fridley, MN
Friends
Friends of WGUC [13832], Cincinnati, OH
Friends of Africa Educ. [12878], West St. Paul, MN
Friends of the Airport [8491], Kimball, MI
Friends of the Athens Municipal Lib. [98], Athens, IL
Friends of Battered Women and Their Children [★764]
Friends of Bears Mill [15362], Greenville, OH
Friends of the Boundary Waters Wilderness [11564], Minneapolis, MN
Friends of the Broadway [9104], Mount Pleasant, MI
Friends of Burlington Northern Railroad [20119], West Bend, WI
Friends of the Colonel Benjamin Stephenson House [1559], Edwardsville, IL
Friends of the Conservatory [14438], Columbus, OH
Friends of the Corunna Historical Village of Shiawassee County [7226], Corunna, MI
Friends of the Farnsworth House [897], Chicago, IL
Friends of Folklore Village [17837], Dodgeville, WI
Friends of the Fox [17496], Appleton, WI
Friends of the Fox River [1324], Crystal Lake, IL
Friends of the Franklin Public Lib. [18010], Franklin, WI
Friends of Freedom Soc. Ohio Underground Railroad Assn. [15922], Mayfield Heights, OH
Friends of Governor Dodge State Park [17838], Dodgeville, WI
Friends of Governor Nelson State Park [20016], Waunakee, WI
Friends of Harrison Lake State Park [15188], Fayette, OH
Friends of Havenwoods [19011], Milwaukee, WI
Friends of Ingham County Animal Shelter [8569], Lansing, MI
Friends of the Kettle Ponds [18906], Middleton, WI
Friends of the Kraemer Lib. and Community Center [19460], Plain, WI
Friends of Lac Lawrann Conservancy [★20122]
Friends of Lagrange Community Park [15577], Lagrange, OH
Friends of Lagrange County Lib. [5639], Lagrange, IN
Friends of Les Cheneaux Community Library [8168], Hessel, MI
Friends of Lexington Area Parks [12227], Roseville, MN
Friends of the Liberty Center Public Lib. [15640], Liberty Center, OH
Friends of the Lib. [18239], Iron River, WI
Friends of the Lower Olentangy Watershed [14439], Columbus, OH
Friends of the Lower Olentangy Watershed Flow [★14439]
Friends of Madison School and Community Recreation [18511], Madison, WI
Friends of Medina County Parks [15940], Medina, OH
Friends of Meigs Field [898], Chicago, IL
Friends of Michigan Libraries [8838], Livonia, MI
Friends of the Minneapolis Public Lib. [11565], Minneapolis, MN
Friends of the Minnesota Sinfonia [11566], Minneapolis, MN
Friends of the Mississippi River [12414], St. Paul, MN
Friends of the Mount Prospect Public Lib. [2585], Mount Prospect, IL
Friends of the New Glarus Public Lib. [19303], New Glarus, WI
Friends for a Non-Violent World [12415], St. Paul, MN
Friends of Novi Parks [9236], Novi, MI
Friends of the Oak Park Conservatory [2809], Oak Park, IL
Friends of Off-Road Cycling [3243], Rock Island, IL
Friends of the Park [3787], Troy, IL
Friends of the Parks [899], Chicago, IL
Friends of the Parks of Allen County, Indiana [4663], Fort Wayne, IN
Friends of the Paullin Lib. [15037], Doylestown, OH
Friends of Pontiac Lake Recreation Area [10083], Waterford, MI
Friends of the Pontiac Public Lib. [9416], Pontiac, MI
Friends of Reed Memorial Lib. [★16505]
Friends of the St. Joe River Assn. [6800], Athens, MI
Friends of the St. Paul Farmers' Market [12659], Shoreview, MN
Friends of Southern Illinois Regional Social Services [418], Carbondale, IL
Friends of Stark Parks [13566], Canton, OH
Friends of Sugar Creek [4449], Darlington, IN
Friends of the Third World [4664], Fort Wayne, IN
Friends of the Town and Country Public Lib. [1580], Elburn, IL
Friends of the Trolley Line Trail [7190], Clio, MI
Friends of Troy Gardens [18512], Madison, WI
Friends of the Upper Mississippi [★12950]
Friends of the Upper Mississippi River Refuges [12950], Winona, MN
Friends of Volo Bog [2062], Ingleside, IL
Friends of Voyageurs National Park [11215], International Falls, MN
Friends of Wetlands [15112], Elyria, OH
Friends of WGUC [13832], Cincinnati, OH
Friends of WHA-TV [18513], Madison, WI
Friends of the White River [5120], Indianapolis, IN
Friends of Wisconsin Libraries [19884], Sussex, WI
Friends of Women's Stud. [13833], Cincinnati, OH
Friends of WVON [900], Chicago, IL
Friendship Circle [10113], West Bloomfield, MI
Friendship Ventures [10300], Annandale, MN
Friesen Historical Soc. [10670], Clara City, MN
Friesland Chamber of Commerce [18025], Friesland, WI
From The Heart [★2175]
Frontenac Flyer Assn. [11280], Lake Elmo, MN
Frontier Community Coll. Students In Free Enterprise [1687], Fairfield, IL
Frozen Food Assn; Greater Detroit [9399], Plymouth, MI
Fruits and Vegetables
Illiana Watermelon Assn. [6409], Vincennes, IN

Michigan Apple Comm. **[7462]**, DeWitt, MI
Michigan Assn. of Cherry Producers **[8607]**, Lansing, MI
Minnesota Fruit and Vegetable Growers Assn. **[11112]**, Ham Lake, MN
Ohio Corn Growers Assn. **[15848]**, Marion, OH
Ohio Fruit Growers Soc. **[14613]**, Columbus, OH
Ohio Vegetable and Potato Growers Assn. **[14696]**, Columbus, OH
Wisconsin Apple Growers Assn. **[19962]**, Waterloo, WI
Wisconsin Berry Growers Assn. **[19963]**, Waterloo, WI
Wisconsin State Cranberry Growers Association **[20199]**, Wisconsin Rapids, WI
Fuel
Illinois Propane Gas Assn. **[3630]**, Springfield, IL
North Central Hearth, Patio and Barbecue Assn. **[18588]**, Madison, WI
Fulton Chamber of Commerce **[1758]**, Fulton, IL
Fulton County Chap., Ohio Genealogical Soc. **[16817]**, Swanton, OH
Fulton County Historical Soc. **[17139]**, Wauseon, OH
Fulton County United Way **[6122]**, Rochester, IN
Fundraising
Albion-Homer United Way **[6587]**, Albion, MI
Allegan County United Way **[6601]**, Allegan, MI
Amer. Coun. on Gift Annuities **[4980]**, Indianapolis, IN
Assn. of Fundraising Professionals - Greater Detroit **[7638]**, Farmington, MI
Baraboo Area United Way **[17572]**, Baraboo, WI
Barrington Area United Way **[143]**, Barrington, IL
Barry County United Way **[8156]**, Hastings, MI
Batavia Community Chest/United Way **[176]**, Batavia, IL
Black River Country United Way **[19415]**, Owen, WI
Blackford United Way **[4902]**, Hartford City, IN
Br. County United Way **[7200]**, Coldwater, MI
Bucyrus Area United Way **[13465]**, Bucyrus, OH
Bur. County United Way **[3135]**, Princeton, IL
Butler County United Way **[15382]**, Hamilton, OH
Capital Area United Way **[7513]**, East Lansing, MI
Carey United Way **[13600]**, Carey, OH
Caring Rivers United Way **[10944]**, Elk River, MN
Cass County United Way, Michigan **[7478]**, Dowagiac, MI
Central Mille Lacs United Way **[11465]**, Milaca, MN
Central Ohio Planned Giving Coun. **[14362]**, Columbus, OH
CharEm United Way **[7114]**, Charlevoix, MI
Charitable Classics **[3013]**, Peoria, IL
Cheboygan County United Way **[7133]**, Cheboygan, MI
Chelsea United Way **[7142]**, Chelsea, MI
Chicago Coun. on Planned Giving **[2148]**, Kenilworth, IL
Colona-Green Rock-Orion United Way **[1295]**, Colona, IL
Copper Country United Way **[8252]**, Houghton, MI
Crawford County United Way, Michigan **[8059]**, Grayling, MI
Crow Wing County United Way **[10511]**, Brainerd, MN
Darke County United Way **[15360]**, Greenville, OH
Delano Loretto Area United Way **[10770]**, Delano, MN
Eaton County United Way **[7122]**, Charlotte, MI
Evanston United Way/Community Ser. **[1658]**, Evanston, IL
Far Northwest Suburban United Way **[2034]**, Hoffman Estates, IL
Fond du Lac Area United Way **[17974]**, Fond du Lac, WI
Fox Valley United Way **[116]**, Aurora, IL
Fulton County United Way **[6122]**, Rochester, IN
Galion Area United Way **[15281]**, Galion, OH
Geneva Lakes Area United Way **[18398]**, Lake Geneva, WI
Genoa-Kingston United Way **[1805]**, Genoa, IL
Gogebic Range United Way **[8338]**, Ironwood, MI
Greater Dayton Planned Giving Coun. **[14892]**, Dayton, OH
Greater Huron County United Way **[6821]**, Bad Axe, MI
Greater Kalamazoo United Way **[8429]**, Kalamazoo, MI
Greater Mankato Area United Way **[11377]**, Mankato, MN
Greater Marietta United Way **[15818]**, Marietta, OH
Greater Marion Area United Way **[2403]**, Marion, IL
Greater Ottawa County United Way **[8198]**, Holland, MI
Greater Twin Cities United Way **[11571]**, Minneapolis, MN
Hands of Hope **[13056]**, Akron, OH
Heart of Illinois United Way **[3026]**, Peoria, IL
Heart of Lakes Chap. of the United Way **[10279]**, Alexandria, MN
Heart of West Michigan United Way **[7962]**, Grand Rapids, MI
Hillsdale County United Way **[8177]**, Hillsdale, MI
Illinois Agricultural Assn. Found. **[280]**, Bloomington, IL
Imperial Windy City Court of the Prairie State Empire **[973]**, Chicago, IL
Indiana Assn. of United Way **[5189]**, Indianapolis, IN
Indiana Nonprofit Rsrc. Network **[5267]**, Indianapolis, IN
Jackson County United Way, Indiana **[6183]**, Seymour, IN
Jefferson County United Way, Indiana **[5715]**, Madison, IN
Jennings County United Way **[5996]**, North Vernon, IN
Jewish United Fund/Jewish Fed. of Metropolitan Chicago **[1008]**, Chicago, IL
Kewanee Area United Way **[2156]**, Kewanee, IL
Kishwaukee United Way **[1438]**, DeKalb, IL
Lake Area United Way, Indiana **[4858]**, Griffith, IN
Lenawee United Way and Volunteer Center **[6579]**, Adrian, MI
Licking County United Way **[16171]**, Newark, OH
Marshall United Way, Michigan **[8969]**, Marshall, MI
Marshfield Area United Way **[18819]**, Marshfield, WI
Massac County United Way **[2483]**, Metropolis, IL
McDonough County United Way **[2373]**, Macomb, IL
Mecosta-Osceola United Way **[6950]**, Big Rapids, MI
Merrill Area United Way **[18897]**, Merrill, WI
Michigan Assn. of United Ways **[8631]**, Lansing, MI
Minnesota Planned Giving Coun. **[12508]**, St. Paul, MN
Montevideo Area United Way **[11802]**, Montevideo, MN
Morrison County United Way **[11337]**, Little Falls, MN
Motor City Striders **[8296]**, Huntington Woods, MI
Moultrie County United Way **[3740]**, Sullivan, IL
Naperville United Way **[2654]**, Naperville, IL
North Central Ohio Planned Giving Coun. **[13168]**, Ashland, OH
North Suburban United Way **[2760]**, Northbrook, IL
Northfield Area United Way **[11917]**, Northfield, MN
Northwest Suburban United Way **[2590]**, Mount Prospect, IL
Northwoods United Way **[19601]**, Rhinelander, WI
Ogemaw County United Way **[10133]**, West Branch, MI
Ohio United Way **[14693]**, Columbus, OH
Orrville Area United Way **[16309]**, Orrville, OH
Oscoda Area United Way **[9317]**, Oscoda, MI
Oshkosh Area United Way **[19400]**, Oshkosh, WI
Otsego County United Way **[7822]**, Gaylord, MI
Paulding County United Way **[16388]**, Paulding, OH
Pioneers Midwest Chap. 128 **[13959]**, Cincinnati, OH
Piqua Area United Way **[16438]**, Piqua, OH
Planned Giving Coun. of Eastern Wisconsin **[19093]**, Milwaukee, WI
Planned Giving Gp. of Indiana **[5452]**, Indianapolis, IN
Planned Giving Info. Consortium of East Central Illinois **[2446]**, Mattoon, IL
Plymouth Community United Way **[9406]**, Plymouth, MI
Portage Area United Way **[19513]**, Portage, WI
Prairieland United Way **[2085]**, Jacksonville, IL
Qwest Pioneers Minnesota Chap. 8 **[10542]**, Brooklyn Center, MN
Red Wing Area United Way **[12082]**, Red Wing, MN
Redwood Area United Way **[12098]**, Redwood Falls, MN
Ripon United Way **[19638]**, Ripon, WI
Roscommon County United Way **[9557]**, Roscommon, MI
St. Croix Area United Way **[12724]**, Stillwater, MN
St. Joseph County United Way, Michigan **[7111]**, Centreville, MI
Sauk-Prairie United Way **[19535]**, Prairie Du Sac, WI
SBC Pioneers Illinois Chap. **[1601]**, Elgin, IL
SBC Pioneers Ohio Chap. **[13431]**, Broadview Heights, OH
SBC Pioneers Wisconsin Chap. **[17894]**, Eau Claire, WI
Sheboygan Area United Way **[19708]**, Sheboygan, WI
Shelby County United Way **[16669]**, Sidney, OH
Shiawassee United Way **[9338]**, Owosso, MI
Southwest Suburban United Way **[2885]**, Orland Park, IL
Springfield Coun. of the Natl. Comm. on Planned Giving **[16748]**, Springfield, OH
Starfire Coun. of Greater Cincinnati **[14004]**, Cincinnati, OH
Stateline United Way **[17619]**, Beloit, WI
Steuben County United Way **[4130]**, Angola, IN
Streator Area United Way **[3731]**, Streator, IL
Suburban Chicago Planned Giving Coun. **[2151]**, Kenilworth, IL
Le Sueur Area United Way **[11311]**, Le Sueur, MN
Thief River Falls Area United Way **[12750]**, Thief River Falls, MN
Tiffin-Seneca United Way **[16866]**, Tiffin, OH
Tipp City Area United Way **[16871]**, Tipp City, OH
Toledo Area Planned Giving Coun. **[16965]**, Toledo, OH
Tri-City Area United Way **[18805]**, Marinette, WI
United Fund of Switzerland County **[6406]**, Vevay, IN
United Way of 1000 Lakes **[11094]**, Grand Rapids, MN
United Way of Adams County **[3173]**, Quincy, IL
United Way of Adams County, Indiana **[4452]**, Decatur, IN
United Way of Allen County **[4729]**, Fort Wayne, IN
United Way of Ashland County **[13174]**, Ashland, OH
United Way of Ashtabula County **[13188]**, Ashtabula, OH
United Way of Auglaize County **[16581]**, St. Marys, OH
United Way of Bartholomew County **[4407]**, Columbus, IN
United Way of Bay County **[6897]**, Bay City, MI
United Way of Becker County **[10785]**, Detroit Lakes, MN
United Way of Bemidji Area **[10430]**, Bemidji, MN
United Way of Bluffton, Beaverdam, and Richland Township **[13369]**, Bluffton, OH
United Way of Boone County, Illinois **[223]**, Belvidere, IL
United Way of Brown County, Illinois **[2592]**, Mount Sterling, IL
United Way of Carlton County **[10693]**, Cloquet, MN
United Way of Cass County **[5699]**, Logansport, IN
United Way of Central Illinois **[3694]**, Springfield, IL
United Way of Central Indiana **[5491]**, Indianapolis, IN
United Way of Central Minnesota **[12316]**, St. Cloud, MN
United Way of Central Ohio **[14753]**, Columbus, OH

United Way of Champaign County **[554]**, Champaign, IL
United Way of Chippewa County **[9730]**, Sault Ste. Marie, MI
United Way of Christian County **[3757]**, Taylorville, IL
United Way of Clark and Champaign Counties **[16753]**, Springfield, OH
United Way for Clinton County **[4745]**, Frankfort, IN
United Way of Clinton County **[17294]**, Wilmington, OH
United Way of Coles County **[2447]**, Mattoon, IL
United Way Community Ser. of Monroe County **[4262]**, Bloomington, IN
United Way of Coshocton County **[14805]**, Coshocton, OH
United Way of Crookston **[10740]**, Crookston, MN
United Way of Dane County **[18632]**, Madison, WI
United Way of the Danville Area **[1353]**, Danville, IL
United Way of Daviess County **[6461]**, Washington, IN
United Way of Decatur/Macon County **[1408]**, Decatur, IL
United Way of Decatur and Mid Illinois **[1409]**, Decatur, IL
United Way of Defiance County **[14993]**, Defiance, OH
United Way of DeKalb County **[4144]**, Auburn, IN
United Way of Delavan-Darien **[17829]**, Delavan, WI
United Way of Delaware County, Indiana **[5899]**, Muncie, IN
United Way of Delaware County, Ohio **[15012]**, Delaware, OH
United Way of Delta County **[7620]**, Escanaba, MI
United Way of Dickinson County **[8327]**, Iron Mountain, MI
United Way of Dodge County, Minnesota **[10791]**, Dodge Center, MN
United Way of Dodge County, Wisconsin **[17598]**, Beaver Dam, WI
United Way of Door County **[19846]**, Sturgeon Bay, WI
United Way of Dunn County **[18882]**, Menomonie, WI
United Way of the DuPage Area **[2785]**, Oak Brook, IL
United Way of Eastern La Salle County **[2901]**, Ottawa, IL
United Way of Edgar County **[2951]**, Paris, IL
United Way of Effingham County **[1574]**, Effingham, IL
United Way of Elgin **[1602]**, Elgin, IL
United Way of Elkhart County **[4508]**, Elkhart, IN
United Way of Erie County, Ohio **[16621]**, Sandusky, OH
United Way of Fairfield County, Ohio **[15613]**, Lancaster, OH
United Way of Fairmont **[10981]**, Fairmont, MN
United Way of Faribault **[10988]**, Faribault, MN
United Way of Fayette County, Indiana **[4416]**, Connersville, IN
United Way of Fayette County, Ohio **[17133]**, Washington Court House, OH
United Way of Fostoria **[15232]**, Fostoria, OH
United Way Fox Cities **[18866]**, Menasha, WI
United Way of Franklin County, Indiana **[4300]**, Brookville, IN
United Way of Freeborn County **[10268]**, Albert Lea, MN
United Way of Fulton County, Ohio **[17141]**, Wauseon, OH
United Way of Gallia County **[15296]**, Gallipolis, OH
United Way of Genesee County **[7760]**, Flint, MI
United Way of Gibson County **[6073]**, Princeton, IN
United Way of Gladwin County **[7837]**, Gladwin, MI
United Way of Grant County, Indiana **[5745]**, Marion, IN
United Way of Grant County, Wisconsin **[18412]**, Lancaster, WI
United Way of Gratiot County **[6636]**, Alma, MI
United Way of Greater Battle Creek **[6873]**, Battle Creek, MI
United Way of Greater Beardstown **[189]**, Beardstown, IL
United Way of Greater Cincinnati **[14018]**, Cincinnati, OH
United Way of the Greater Dayton Area **[14965]**, Dayton, OH
United Way of Greater Duluth **[10860]**, Duluth, MN
United Way of Greater Eau Claire **[17904]**, Eau Claire, WI
United Way of Greater La Porte County **[5603]**, La Porte, IN
United Way of Greater Lafayette **[5636]**, Lafayette, IN
United Way of Greater Lima **[15672]**, Lima, OH
United Way of Greater Lorain County **[15712]**, Lorain, OH
United Way of Greater Milwaukee **[19143]**, Milwaukee, WI
United Way of Greater Niles **[9213]**, Niles, MI
United Way of Greater Stark County **[13593]**, Canton, OH
United Way of Greater Toledo **[16979]**, Toledo, OH
United Way of Greater Toledo Ottawa County Off. **[16462]**, Port Clinton, OH
United Way of Greater Toledo Wood County Off. **[13400]**, Bowling Green, OH
United Way of the Greater Winona Area **[12959]**, Winona, MN
United Way of Green County **[19219]**, Monroe, WI
United Way of Grundy County, Illinois **[2555]**, Morris, IL
United Way of Guernsey and Noble County **[13502]**, Cambridge, OH
United Way of Hancock County **[15215]**, Findlay, OH
United Way of Hardin County **[15554]**, Kenton, OH
United Way of Hastings, Minnesota **[11132]**, Hastings, MN
United Way of Henry County **[16100]**, Napoleon, OH
United Way of Hibbing **[11163]**, Hibbing, MN
United Way of Hocking County **[15691]**, Logan, OH
United Way of Howard County **[5588]**, Kokomo, IN
United Way of Huntington County **[4955]**, Huntington, IN
United Way of the Hutchinson Area **[11213]**, Hutchinson, MN
United Way of Illinois **[2786]**, Oak Brook, IL
United Way of Illinois Valley **[2183]**, La Salle, IL
United Way of Ionia County **[8318]**, Ionia, MI
United Way of Isabella County **[9126]**, Mount Pleasant, MI
United Way of Jackson County **[8399]**, Jackson, MI
United Way of Jay County **[6066]**, Portland, IN
United Way of Jefferson County, Illinois **[2604]**, Mount Vernon, IL
United Way of Jefferson County, Ohio **[16769]**, Steubenville, OH
United Way of Jefferson and North Walworth Counties **[18001]**, Fort Atkinson, WI
United Way of Johnson County, Indiana **[4757]**, Franklin, IN
United Way of Kandiyohi County **[12928]**, Willmar, MN
United Way of Kankakee County **[2144]**, Kankakee, IL
United Way of Kenosha County **[18313]**, Kenosha, WI
United Way of Knox County, Illinois **[1782]**, Galesburg, IL
United Way of Knox County, Indiana **[6422]**, Vincennes, IN
United Way of Knox County, Ohio **[16090]**, Mount Vernon, OH
United Way of Kosciusko County **[6454]**, Warsaw, IN
United Way of the La Crosse Area **[19371]**, Onalaska, WI
United Way of Lake County, Illinois **[1926]**, Gurnee, IL
United Way of Lake County, Ohio **[15981]**, Mentor, OH
United Way of Langlade County **[17477]**, Antigo, WI
United Way of Lawrence County, Indiana **[4178]**, Bedford, IN
United Way of Lee County, Illinois **[1485]**, Dixon, IL
United Way of Licking County **[16187]**, Newark, OH
United Way of Livingston County **[7024]**, Brighton, MI
United Way of Logan County **[2281]**, Lincoln, IL
United Way of Logan County, Ohio **[13326]**, Bellefontaine, OH
United Way of Madison County **[4121]**, Anderson, IN
United Way of Manistee County **[8916]**, Manistee, MI
United Way of Manitowoc County **[18792]**, Manitowoc, WI
United Way of Marathon County **[20051]**, Wausau, WI
United Way Marion County **[15856]**, Marion, OH
United Way of Marquette County **[8960]**, Marquette, MI
United Way of Marshall County, Indiana **[6053]**, Plymouth, IN
United Way of Mason County **[8876]**, Ludington, MI
United Way of McHenry County **[2464]**, McHenry, IL
United Way of McLean County **[312]**, Bloomington, IL
United Way of Medina County **[15957]**, Medina, OH
United Way of Merrill **[18899]**, Merrill, WI
United Way of Metropolitan Chicago **[1217]**, Chicago, IL
United Way of Miami County **[6034]**, Peru, IN
United Way of Midland County **[9043]**, Midland, MI
United Way of Montcalm County **[8071]**, Greenville, MI
United Way of Morrow County **[16074]**, Mount Gilead, OH
United Way of Mower County **[10363]**, Austin, MN
United Way of Muskegon County **[9164]**, Muskegon, MI
United Way of Muskingum, Perry, and Morgan Counties **[17445]**, Zanesville, OH
United Way of New London **[19316]**, New London, WI
United Way of New Ulm **[11888]**, New Ulm, MN
United Way of Newaygo County **[7801]**, Fremont, MI
United Way of Noble County **[4087]**, Albion, IN
United Way of North Rock County **[18266]**, Janesville, WI
United Way of the North Shore **[2205]**, Lake Forest, IL
United Way of Northeast Michigan **[6651]**, Alpena, MI
United Way of Northeastern Minnesota **[10661]**, Chisholm, MN
United Way of Northern Ozaukee County **[19503]**, Port Washington, WI
United Way of Northwest Illinois **[1756]**, Freeport, IL
United Way of Northwest Michigan **[9963]**, Traverse City, MI
United Way of Oak Park, River Forest and Forest Park **[2827]**, Oak Park, IL
United Way of Olmsted County **[12196]**, Rochester, MN
United Way of Otter Tail County **[11005]**, Fergus Falls, MN
United Way of Oxford, Ohio and Vicinity **[16329]**, Oxford, OH
United Way of Pekin **[2995]**, Pekin, IL
United Way of Perry County **[6300]**, Tell City, IN
United Way of Pickaway County **[14038]**, Circleville, OH
United Way of Pike County, Indiana **[6039]**, Petersburg, IN
United Way - Pipestone, Ihlen, Woodstock, Holland, Ruthton **[12012]**, Pipestone, MN
United Way of Platteville **[19473]**, Platteville, WI
United Way of Pontiac **[3122]**, Pontiac, IL

United Way of Portage County [19813], Stevens Point, WI
United Way of Posey County [5858], Mount Vernon, IN
United Way of the Prairie Du Chien Area [19531], Prairie Du Chien, WI
United Way of Putnam County, Indiana [4827], Greencastle, IN
United Way of Putnam County, Ohio [16320], Ottawa, OH
United Way of Racine County [19579], Racine, WI
United Way of Randolph County [6537], Winchester, IN
United Way of Rice Lake [19618], Rice Lake, WI
United Way of Richland County [15795], Mansfield, OH
United Way of River Falls [19645], River Falls, WI
United Way of Rock River Valley [3327], Rockford, IL
United Way of Ross County [13677], Chillicothe, OH
United Way of Saginaw County [9645], Saginaw, MI
United Way of St. Charles and Elburn [3395], St. Charles, IL
United Way of St. Clair County [9442], Port Huron, MI
United Way of St. Croix County [18227], Hudson, WI
United Way of St. Joseph County [6272], South Bend, IN
United Way of St. Peter [12621], St. Peter, MN
United Way of Sandusky County [15255], Fremont, OH
United Way of Sanilac County [8809], Lexington, MI
United Way of Scioto County [16477], Portsmouth, OH
United Way of Scott County [6174], Scottsburg, IN
United Way Services of Geauga County [13645], Chardon, OH
United Way Services of Greater Cleveland [14229], Cleveland, OH
United Way Services of Northern Columbiana County [16593], Salem, OH
United Way of Shawano County [19685], Shawano, WI
United Way of Sheboygan Falls [19721], Sheboygan Falls, WI
United Way of South Wood County [20194], Wisconsin Rapids, WI
United Way for Southeastern Michigan [7447], Detroit, MI
United Way of Southern Columbiana County [15082], East Liverpool, OH
United Way of Southern Illinois [2411], Marion, IL
United Way of Southwest Michigan [6923], Benton Harbor, MI
United Way of Southwest Minnesota [11442], Marshall, MN
United Way of Southwestern Indiana [4585], Evansville, IN
United Way for Spoon River Country [407], Canton, IL
United Way of Steele County [11972], Owatonna, MN
United Way of Summit County [13101], Akron, OH
United Way of Superior-Douglas County [19882], Superior, WI
United Way of Taylor County [18849], Medford, WI
United Way of Troy, Ohio [17012], Troy, OH
United Way of Trumbull County [17114], Warren, OH
United Way of Tuscarawas County [16157], New Philadelphia, OH
United Way of Tuscola County [7096], Cass City, MI
United Way of Union County, Ohio [15868], Marysville, OH
United Way of Upper Sandusky and Pitt Township [17032], Upper Sandusky, OH
United Way of Van Wert County [17053], Van Wert, OH
United Way and Volunteer Center of Clare County [7155], Clare, MI
United Way of the Wabash Valley [6347], Terre Haute, IN
United Way of Wadena Area [12824], Wadena, MN
United Way of Watertown [19970], Watertown, WI
United Way in Waukesha County [20000], Waukesha, WI
United Way of Wayne and Holmes Counties [17327], Wooster, OH
United Way of Wells County [4270], Bluffton, IN
United Way of Wexford County [7050], Cadillac, MI
United Way of Whiteside County [3706], Sterling, IL
United Way of Whitewater Valley [6109], Richmond, IN
United Way of Whitley County [4385], Columbia City, IN
United Way of Will County [2122], Joliet, IL
United Way of Williams County [13458], Bryan, OH
United Way of Wisconsin [18633], Madison, WI
Van Buren County United Way [9348], Paw Paw, MI
Warren County United Way, Illinois [2543], Monmouth, IL
Warren County United Way, Ohio [15628], Lebanon, OH
Waseca Area United Way [12848], Waseca, MN
Washtenaw United Way [6791], Ann Arbor, MI
West Suburban United Way [2177], La Grange Park, IL
Western Michigan Planned Giving Gp. [8227], Holland, MI
White County United Way [5829], Monticello, IN
Windy City Women's Charity Club [1234], Chicago, IL
Wisconsin Planned Giving Coun. [18741], Madison, WI
Worthington Area United Way [12994], Worthington, MN
Wright County Area United Way [11812], Monticello, MN
Youngstown/Mahoning Valley United Way [17427], Youngstown, OH

Funeral
Funeral Consumers Alliance of Bloomington, Indiana [4219], Bloomington, IN
Memorial Societies of Wisconsin [17919], Egg Harbor, WI
Michigan Funeral Directors Assn. [9278], Okemos, MI

Funeral Consumers Alliance - Akron Region [13052], Akron, OH
Funeral Consumers Alliance of Bloomington, Indiana [4219], Bloomington, IN
Funeral Consumers Alliance of Central Ohio [14440], Columbus, OH
Funeral Consumers Alliance of Champaign County [3816], Urbana, IL
Funeral Consumers Alliance of the Fox Valley [17497], Appleton, WI
Funeral Consumers' Alliance of Northwest Ohio [16917], Toledo, OH
Funeral Directors Assn; Illinois [3605], Springfield, IL
Funeral Directors Assn; Minnesota [12025], Plymouth, MN
Funeral Directors of Indiana; Independent [5755], Martinsville, IN

Future
Greater Chicagoland Futurists [1713], Forest Park, IL
World Future Soc., Akron (Northeastern Ohio) [13105], Akron, OH
World Future Soc., Cincinnati [16031], Milford, OH
World Future Soc., Columbus [17225], Westerville, OH
World Future Soc., Detroit [8161], Hazel Park, MI
World Future Soc., Madison [19833], Stoughton, WI
World Future Soc., Minneapolis-St. Paul [11779], Minneapolis, MN
World Future Soc., Pekin [2996], Pekin, IL

Future Heights [14246], Cleveland Heights, OH
Future Homemakers of Am., Indiana Assn. [★5234]

G

Gahanna Area Chamber of Commerce [15263], Gahanna, OH
Gahanna Lions Club [15264], Gahanna, OH
Gahanna - Young Life [14441], Columbus, OH
Gaia Collective [11567], Minneapolis, MN
Gaines Area Lions Club [7804], Gaines, MI
Galena Area Chamber of Commerce [1761], Galena, IL
Galena and Jo Daviess County Convention and Visitors Bur. [1762], Galena, IL
Galena/Jo Daviess County Historical Soc. [1763], Galena, IL
Galesburg Area Chamber of Commerce [1771], Galesburg, IL
Galesburg Area Convention and Visitors Bur. [1772], Galesburg, IL
Galesburg Downtown Coun. [1773], Galesburg, IL
Galesburg Philatelic Soc. [46], Altona, IL
Galesville Area Chamber of Commerce [18026], Galesville, WI
Galion Area Chamber of Commerce [15280], Galion, OH
Galion Area United Way [15281], Galion, OH
Galion Bd. of Realtors [15282], Galion, OH
Galion Lions Club [15283], Galion, OH
Gallia County Chamber of Commerce [15290], Gallipolis, OH
Gallia County Genealogical Soc., Ohio Genealogical Chap. [15291], Gallipolis, OH
Gallia/Jackson/Vinton Counties RSVP [15512], Jackson, OH
Gallipolis Junior Woman's Club [15292], Gallipolis, OH

Gambling
Casino Mgt. Assn. [7332], Detroit, MI
Wisconsin Coun. on Problem Gambling [18139], Green Bay, WI

Game Commissioners; Assn. of Midwest Fish and [★19599]

Games
Barrington Community Unit School District 220 [144], Barrington, IL
Decatur County Historical Soc. [4842], Greensburg, IN
McHenry County Historical Soc. [3799], Union, IL
Michigan Assn. for Infant Mental Hea. [9837], Southgate, MI

Garaway Young Life [16805], Sugarcreek, OH
Garden City Chamber of Commerce [7811], Garden City, MI
Garden City Lions Club - Michigan [7812], Garden City, MI
Garden Club; Arcade Park [734], Chicago, IL
Garden Club of Marion [5730], Marion, IN
Gardener Assn; Marion County Master [5398], Indianapolis, IN
Gardener Assn; Southwestern Indiana Master [4579], Evansville, IN
Gardeners of Am./Men's Garden Clubs of Am. - Akron Men's Garden Club [16842], Tallmadge, OH
Gardeners of Am./Men's Garden Clubs of Am. - Boone County Gardeners of Am. [3278], Rockford, IL
Gardeners of Am./Men's Garden Clubs of Am. - Dixon Men's Garden Club [1478], Dixon, IL
Gardeners of Am./Men's Garden Clubs of Am. - Elgin Gardeners of Am. [1590], Elgin, IL
Gardeners of Am./Men's Garden Clubs of Am. - Erie County Men's Garden Club [16612], Sandusky, OH
Gardeners of Am./Men's Garden Clubs of Am. - Findlay Men and Women's Garden Club [15202], Findlay, OH
Gardeners of Am./Men's Garden Clubs of Am. - Forget-Me-Not Garden Club [16918], Toledo, OH
Gardeners of Am./Men's Garden Clubs of Am. - Fulton County Garden Club [17140], Wauseon, OH
Gardeners of Am./Men's Garden Clubs of Am. - Garden Club of Kent [16497], Ravenna, OH
Gardeners of Am./Men's Garden Clubs of Am. - Gardeners of Am. Fort Wayne [4665], Fort Wayne, IN
Gardeners of Am./Men's Garden Clubs of Am. - Gardeners of Central Lake County [2258], Libertyville, IL

Gardeners of Am./Men's Garden Clubs of Am. - Gardeners Club of Bluffton-Pandora Area **[14776]**, Columbus Grove, OH
Gardeners of America/Men's Garden Clubs of Am. - Gardeners Club of Green Bay **[18099]**, Green Bay, WI
Gardeners of Am./Men's Garden Clubs of Am. - Gardeners Club of Mendota **[3734]**, Sublette, IL
Gardeners of Am./Men's Garden Clubs of Am. - Gardeners of Lima **[15652]**, Lima, OH
Gardeners of Am./Men's Garden Clubs of Am. - Gardeners of Van Wert County **[17049]**, Van Wert, OH
Gardeners of Am./Men's Garden Clubs of Am. - Greater Cleveland Men's Garden Club **[15583]**, Lakewood, OH
Gardeners of Am./Men's Garden Clubs of Am. - Maple City Men's Garden Club **[6568]**, Adrian, MI
Gardeners of Am./Men's Garden Clubs of Am. - Men's Garden Club of Grosse Pointe **[8081]**, Grosse Pointe, MI
Gardeners of Am./Men's Garden Clubs of Am. - Men's Garden Club of Youngstown **[17401]**, Youngstown, OH
Gardeners of Am./Men's Garden Clubs of Am. - Rochelle Gardeners of Am. **[3224]**, Rochelle, IL
Gardeners of Am./Men's Garden Clubs of Am. - Rockford Area Gardeners of Am. **[3279]**, Rockford, IL
Gardeners of Am./Men's Garden Clubs of Am. - St. Marys Gardeners of Am. **[16578]**, St. Marys, OH
Gardeners of Am./Men's Garden Clubs of Am. - Stow Community Garden Club **[16775]**, Stow, OH
Gardening
African Violet Soc. of Dayton **[17167]**, West Chester, OH
African Violet Soc. of Minnesota **[11031]**, Fridley, MN
African Violet Soc. of Northern Illinois **[2736]**, Norridge, IL
Akron-Canton Bonsai Soc. **[16837]**, Tallmadge, OH
Amer. Begonia Soc., Greater Chicago Area Chap. **[613]**, Chicago, IL
Amer. Rose Soc., Buckeye District **[13462]**, Bucyrus, OH
Amer. Rose Soc., Great Lakes District **[6961]**, Birmingham, MI
Amer. Rose Soc., North Central District **[10315]**, Apple Valley, MN
Ann Arbor Garden Club **[6675]**, Ann Arbor, MI
Azalea Soc. of Am., Lake Michigan Chap. **[2879]**, Orland Park, IL
Azalea Soc. of Am., Tri-State Chap. **[4533]**, Evansville, IN
Badger Bonsai Soc. **[18488]**, Madison, WI
Barrington Bloomers African Violet Soc. **[3913]**, Wauconda, IL
Bloomington Bonsai Club **[6368]**, Unionville, IN
Bonsai Soc. of Greater Cincinnati **[13762]**, Cincinnati, OH
Bromeliad Soc. of Greater Chicago **[1319]**, Crystal Lake, IL
Cincinnati African Violet Soc. **[13773]**, Cincinnati, OH
Columbus African Violet Soc. **[15430]**, Hilliard, OH
Columbus Bonsai Soc. **[14375]**, Columbus, OH
Crosstown African Violet Club **[17939]**, Elroy, WI
Fort Wayne Bonsai Club **[4938]**, Huntertown, IN
Four Seasons Bonsai Club of Michigan **[8234]**, Holly, MI
Fox Valley African Violet Soc. **[2635]**, Naperville, IL
Friends of Troy Gardens **[18512]**, Madison, WI
Garden Club of Marion **[5730]**, Marion, IN
Glenview/North Shore African Violet Soc. **[1866]**, Glenview, IL
Greater Cincinnati Daylily and Hosta Soc. **[13844]**, Cincinnati, OH
Greater Evansville Bonsai Soc. **[5708]**, Lynnville, IN
Hoosier African Violet Soc. **[6057]**, Portage, IN
Illinois African Violet Soc. **[1659]**, Evanston, IL
Indy African Violet Club **[5359]**, Indianapolis, IN
Judges Coun. of Minnesota **[10470]**, Bloomington, MN
Lake Shore African Violet Soc. **[1666]**, Evanston, IL
Lakes Area Violet Growers **[12438]**, St. Paul, MN
Late Bloomers African Violet Soc. **[17996]**, Footville, WI
Marion County Master Gardener Assn. **[5398]**, Indianapolis, IN
Michiana Master Gardeners Assn. **[4802]**, Goshen, IN
Michigan Cactus and Succulent Soc. **[10119]**, West Bloomfield, MI
Michigan State African Violet Soc. **[9838]**, Southgate, MI
Midwest Daffodil Soc. **[2201]**, Lake Forest, IL
Milwaukee African Violet Soc. **[19889]**, Theresa, WI
Minnesota Bonsai Soc. **[11631]**, Minneapolis, MN
North Star African Violet Coun. **[10309]**, Anoka, MN
Ohio Gourd Soc. **[16182]**, Newark, OH
Ohio State African Violet Soc. **[16202]**, Newtown, OH
Oshkosh Violet Soc. **[19358]**, Omro, WI
Parmatown African Violet Club **[16239]**, North Olmsted, OH
Prairie State Bonsai Soc. **[1840]**, Glen Ellyn, IL
Quad Cities African Violet Soc. **[1790]**, Geneseo, IL
River Cities African Violet Club **[20191]**, Wisconsin Rapids, WI
South Eastern Michigan Bromeliad Soc. **[9229]**, Northville, MI
Southern Indiana Daylily, Hosta, Daffodil, and Iris Soc. **[4260]**, Bloomington, IN
Sundowners African Violet Club **[19935]**, Verona, WI
Town and Country African Violet Club **[6992]**, Bloomfield Hills, MI
Town and Country African Violet Soc. **[16346]**, Painesville, OH
Wisconsin Coun. of African Violet Clubs **[19410]**, Oshkosh, WI
Wisconsin Regional Lily Soc. **[17760]**, Chippewa Falls, WI
Garfield Heights Chamber of Commerce **[15302]**, Garfield Heights, OH
Garfield Heights Figure Skating Club **[13472]**, Burton, OH
Garfield Park Conservatory Alliance **[901]**, Chicago, IL
Garrett Chamber of Commerce **[4768]**, Garrett, IN
Garrettsville Area Chamber of Commerce **[★15304]**
Garrettsville - Hiram Area Chamber of Commerce **[15304]**, Garrettsville, OH
Garrettsville Lions Club **[15305]**, Garrettsville, OH
Gary Chamber of Commerce **[4778]**, Gary, IN
Gary-East Chicago-Hammond Empowerment Zone **[4779]**, Gary, IN
Gary Lions Club **[11040]**, Gary, MN
Gas Assn; Michigan Elec. and **[8660]**, Lansing, MI
Gas Task Force Assn; Midwest Regional **[11210]**, Hutchinson, MN
Gases
Michigan Propane Gas Assn. **[8699]**, Lansing, MI
Midwest Regional Gas Task Force Assn. **[11210]**, Hutchinson, MN
Ohio Oil and Gas Assn. **[15346]**, Granville, OH
Ohio Propane Gas Assn. **[14659]**, Columbus, OH
Gastroenterology
Crohn's and Colitis Found. of Am., Central Ohio Chap. **[14421]**, Columbus, OH
Crohn's and Colitis Found. of Am., Illinois Carol Fisher Chap. **[1456]**, Des Plaines, IL
Crohn's and Colitis Found. of Am., Indiana Chap. **[5098]**, Indianapolis, IN
Crohn's and Colitis Found. of Am., Michigan Chap. **[7658]**, Farmington Hills, MI
Crohn's and Colitis Found. of Am., Wisconsin Chap. **[20100]**, West Allis, WI
Crohn's and Colitis Found. of Amer., Southwest Ohio Chap. **[13812]**, Cincinnati, OH
Gateway Optometric Soc. **[18345]**, La Crosse, WI
Gateway Riders BMW Club No. 22 **[1697]**, Fairview Heights, IL
Gateway Sportsmen's Club **[10025]**, Unionville, MI
Gateway - Wyldlife **[15905]**, Maumee, OH
Gathering of Southeast Wisconsin **[19012]**, Milwaukee, WI
Gavit PTSA **[4880]**, Hammond, IN
Gay/Lesbian
Children of Lesbians and Gays Everywhere Minneapolis **[11542]**, Minneapolis, MN
Dignity - Chicago **[870]**, Chicago, IL
Dignity - Dayton **[14883]**, Dayton, OH
Dignity - Indianapolis **[5102]**, Indianapolis, IN
Dignity - Toledo **[16910]**, Toledo, OH
Dignity - Twin Cities **[11554]**, Minneapolis, MN
Dignity - USA, Columbus Chap. **[14423]**, Columbus, OH
Gay/Lesbian Community Services of Rochester **[12142]**, Rochester, MN
Indiana Youth Gp. **[5336]**, Indianapolis, IN
Kalamazoo Gay-Lesbian Rsrc. Center **[8442]**, Kalamazoo, MI
Milwaukee Gamma **[19061]**, Milwaukee, WI
North Suburban Gays **[4020]**, Wilmette, IL
OutReach **[18594]**, Madison, WI
PFLAG Alexandria **[11472]**, Miltona, MN
PFLAG Ann Arbor **[6753]**, Ann Arbor, MI
PFLAG Appleton/Fox Cities **[17514]**, Appleton, WI
PFLAG Aurora/Fox Valley **[127]**, Aurora, IL
PFLAG Bay City/Saginaw/Midland **[6893]**, Bay City, MI
PFLAG Bemidji **[10423]**, Bemidji, MN
PFLAG Bloomington **[4250]**, Bloomington, IN
PFLAG Bloomington/Normal **[305]**, Bloomington, IL
PFLAG Brainerd Lakes **[10390]**, Baxter, MN
PFLAG Carbondale/Southern Illinois **[428]**, Carbondale, IL
PFLAG Chicago/Hinsdale/West Suburban **[1124]**, Chicago, IL
PFLAG Chicago/Lakeview **[1125]**, Chicago, IL
PFLAG Detroit **[9589]**, Royal Oak, MI
PFLAG Downriver **[9840]**, Southgate, MI
PFLAG Duluth **[10848]**, Duluth, MN
PFLAG DuPage **[3996]**, Wheaton, IL
PFLAG Eau Claire/Greater Chippewa Valley **[17757]**, Chippewa Falls, WI
PFLAG Evansville/Tri-State **[5963]**, Newburgh, IN
PFLAG Family Reunion: People Of Color Chap. **[7417]**, Detroit, MI
PFLAG Flint/Genesee County **[7770]**, Flushing, MI
PFLAG Fort Wayne **[4708]**, Fort Wayne, IN
PFLAG Galesville/Western Wisconsin **[18027]**, Galesville, WI
PFLAG Glenview/North Suburban Chicago **[1872]**, Glenview, IL
PFLAG Grand Rapids **[7996]**, Grand Rapids, MI
PFLAG Grand Rapids/Itasca **[11092]**, Grand Rapids, MN
PFLAG Hammond **[4891]**, Hammond, IN
PFLAG Holland/Lakeshore **[8216]**, Holland, MI
PFLAG Huntington **[4954]**, Huntington, IN
PFLAG Indianapolis **[5448]**, Indianapolis, IN
PFLAG Kalamazoo/Southwest Michigan **[9452]**, Portage, MI
PFLAG Kenosha/Racine **[19476]**, Pleasant Prairie, WI
PFLAG Keweenaw **[8260]**, Houghton, MI
PFLAG La Crosse **[18374]**, La Crosse, WI
PFLAG Lafayette/Tippecanoe County **[4163]**, Battle Ground, IN
PFLAG Lansing **[9299]**, Okemos, MI
PFLAG Marshall/Buffalo Ridge **[11439]**, Marshall, MN
PFLAG Michigan City/Indiana Dunes **[5700]**, Long Beach, IN
PFLAG Milwaukee **[19092]**, Milwaukee, WI
PFLAG Moline **[2526]**, Moline, IL
PFLAG Mt. Pleasant **[9122]**, Mount Pleasant, MI
PFLAG Muncie **[5893]**, Muncie, IN
PFLAG Northfield **[11918]**, Northfield, MN
PFLAG Oak Park Area **[2826]**, Oak Park, IL
PFLAG Palatine **[2925]**, Palatine, IL
PFLAG Park Rapids **[11979]**, Park Rapids, MN
PFLAG Port Huron/Sarnia-Bluewater **[9436]**, Port Huron, MI
PFLAG Quincy **[3157]**, Quincy, IL
PFLAG Red Wing **[12080]**, Red Wing, MN
PFLAG Richmond/Whitewater Valley **[6099]**, Richmond, IN
PFLAG Rochester/Southern Minnesota **[12168]**, Rochester, MN
PFLAG Rock River Valley **[222]**, Belvidere, IL

PFLAG St. Cloud/Central Minnesota **[12295]**, St. Cloud, MN
PFLAG St. Joseph/Berrien County **[9688]**, St. Joseph, MI
PFLAG St. Paul/Minneapolis **[11722]**, Minneapolis, MN
PFLAG Seymour **[6185]**, Seymour, IN
PFLAG Sheboygan/Lakeshore **[19703]**, Sheboygan, WI
PFLAG South Bend/Michiana **[6252]**, South Bend, IN
PFLAG Sturgeon Bay/Door County **[19842]**, Sturgeon Bay, WI
PFLAG Traverse City **[9945]**, Traverse City, MI
PFLAG Urbana-Champaign **[544]**, Champaign, IL
PFLAG Waukesha **[19996]**, Waukesha, WI
PFLAG Woodstock/McHenry County **[4063]**, Woodstock, IL
Rainbow Families **[11729]**, Minneapolis, MN
SAGE/Milwaukee **[19112]**, Milwaukee, WI
Triangle Found. **[7444]**, Detroit, MI
Gay and Lesbian Chamber of Commerce; Chicago Area **[783]**, Chicago, IL
Gay/Lesbian Community Services of Rochester **[12142]**, Rochester, MN
Gay-Lesbian Rsrc. Center; Kalamazoo **[8442]**, Kalamazoo, MI
Gay, Lesbian and Straight Educ. Network, Ann Arbor-Ypsilanti Area **[6696]**, Ann Arbor, MI
Gaylord Area Convention and Tourism Bur. **[7818]**, Gaylord, MI
Gaylord - Otsego County Chamber of Commerce **[7819]**, Gaylord, MI
Gays Mills Lions Club **[18031]**, Gays Mills, WI
Gays; North Suburban **[4020]**, Wilmette, IL
Geauga County Historical Soc. **[13473]**, Burton, OH
Geauga Humane Soc. / Rescue Village **[16561]**, Russell Township, OH
Gelende Ski Club **[11568]**, Minneapolis, MN
Gem City Gliders Ski and Bike Club **[14885]**, Dayton, OH
Gemutlich Wanderers **[16538]**, Rittman, OH
Genealogical and Historical Soc; Tazewell County **[2993]**, Pekin, IL
Genealogical Soc., Ashland County Chap; Ohio **[13170]**, Ashland, OH
Genealogical Soc; Belmont County Chap. of the Ohio **[13261]**, Barnesville, OH
Genealogical Soc; Calhoun County **[8966]**, Marshall, MI
Genealogical Soc; Cheboygan County **[7132]**, Cheboygan, MI
Genealogical Soc; Columbiana County Chap. of the Ohio **[16586]**, Salem, OH
Genealogical Soc; Crawford County **[3219]**, Robinson, IL
Genealogical Soc; Crow Wing County **[10510]**, Brainerd, MN
Genealogical Soc; Dakota **[★12679]**
Genealogical Soc; Dakota County **[12679]**, South St. Paul, MN
Genealogical Soc; Delta County **[7612]**, Escanaba, MI
Genealogical Soc; Downriver **[8812]**, Lincoln Park, MI
Genealogical Soc; Du Page **[★3984]**
Genealogical Soc; Du Page County (IL) **[3984]**, Wheaton, IL
Genealogical Soc; Eaton County **[7121]**, Charlotte, MI
Genealogical Society; Edgar County **[2947]**, Paris, IL
Genealogical Soc., Fairfield County Chap; Ohio **[15607]**, Lancaster, OH
Genealogical Soc; Freeborn County **[10257]**, Albert Lea, MN
Genealogical Soc., Fulton County Chap; Ohio **[★16817]**
Genealogical Soc; Fulton County Chap., Ohio **[16817]**, Swanton, OH
Genealogical Soc; Grand Traverse Area **[9931]**, Traverse City, MI
Genealogical Soc., Hamilton County Chap; Ohio **[13938]**, Cincinnati, OH
Genealogical Soc., Holmes County Chap; Ohio **[16038]**, Millersburg, OH
Genealogical Soc; Howard County **[6008]**, Oakford, IN
Genealogical Soc., Hudson Chap; Ohio **[★15482]**
Genealogical Soc., Huron County Chap; Ohio **[16264]**, Norwalk, OH
Genealogical Soc; Illiana Jewish **[1708]**, Flossmoor, IL
Genealogical Soc. of Illinois; Jewish **[2755]**, Northbrook, IL
Genealogical Soc; Indiana **[4677]**, Fort Wayne, IN
Genealogical Soc. of Indiana; Allen County **[4621]**, Fort Wayne, IN
Genealogical Soc; Iroquois County **[3908]**, Watseka, IL
Genealogical Soc; Jackson County **[8375]**, Jackson, MI
Genealogical Soc; Knox County **[1776]**, Galesburg, IL
Genealogical Soc; Lake County Illinois **[2614]**, Mundelein, IL
Genealogical Soc; Lombard Suburban **[★3984]**
Genealogical Soc; Macoupin County **[3696]**, Staunton, IL
Genealogical Soc; Marquette County **[8942]**, Marquette, MI
Genealogical Soc. of Michigan; Bay County **[6886]**, Bay City, MI
Genealogical Soc; Mid-Michigan **[8731]**, Lansing, MI
Genealogical Soc; Montgomery County Chap., Ohio **[14921]**, Dayton, OH
Genealogical Soc., Morgan County Chap; Ohio **[15934]**, McConnelsville, OH
Genealogical Soc., Morrow County Chap; Ohio **[16073]**, Mount Gilead, OH
Genealogical Soc; Noble County **[4086]**, Albion, IN
Genealogical Soc., Ottawa County Chap; Ohio **[16460]**, Port Clinton, OH
Genealogical Soc; Preble County Chap. - Ohio **[15089]**, Eaton, OH
Genealogical Society; Ross County **[13673]**, Chillicothe, OH
Genealogical Soc; Stevens Point Area **[19808]**, Stevens Point, WI
Genealogical Soc; Van Buren Regional **[7287]**, Decatur, MI
Genealogical Soc; Walworth County **[17830]**, Delavan, WI
Genealogical Soc. of Washtenaw County **[6697]**, Ann Arbor, MI
Genealogical Soc; Wisconsin State **[18755]**, Madison, WI
Genealogical Study Group; Hudson **[15482]**, Hudson, OH
Genealogists of Wisconsin; French Canadian-Acadian **[18170]**, Hales Corners, WI
Genealogy
Allen County Genealogical Soc. of Indiana **[4621]**, Fort Wayne, IN
The Alliance Genealogical Soc. **[13108]**, Alliance, OH
Ashtabula County Genealogical Soc. **[15308]**, Geneva, OH
Auglaize County Genealogical Soc. **[17089]**, Wapakoneta, OH
Bay County Genealogical Soc. of Michigan **[6886]**, Bay City, MI
Belmont County Chap. of the Ohio Genealogical Soc. **[13261]**, Barnesville, OH
Butler County Chap. of Ohio Genealogical Soc. **[16006]**, Middletown, OH
Calhoun County Genealogical Soc. **[8966]**, Marshall, MI
Cheboygan County Genealogical Soc. **[7132]**, Cheboygan, MI
Clermont County Genealogical Soc. **[13266]**, Batavia, OH
Columbiana County Chap. of the Ohio Genealogical Soc. **[16586]**, Salem, OH
Crawford County Genealogical Soc. **[3219]**, Robinson, IL
Crow Wing County Genealogical Soc. **[10510]**, Brainerd, MN
Dakota County Genealogical Soc. **[12679]**, South St. Paul, MN
Defiance County Chap. of the Ohio Genealogical Soc. **[14987]**, Defiance, OH
Delaware County Genealogical Soc. **[15005]**, Delaware, OH
Delaware County Historical Soc. **[5872]**, Muncie, IN
Delta County Genealogical Soc. **[7612]**, Escanaba, MI
Downriver Genealogical Soc. **[8812]**, Lincoln Park, MI
Eaton County Genealogical Soc. **[7121]**, Charlotte, MI
Edgar County Genealogical Society **[2947]**, Paris, IL
Erie County Chap. of the Ohio Genealogical Soc. **[16608]**, Sandusky, OH
Franklin County Genealogical and Historical Soc. **[14435]**, Columbus, OH
Freeborn County Genealogical Soc. **[10257]**, Albert Lea, MN
French Canadian-Acadian Genealogists of Wisconsin **[18170]**, Hales Corners, WI
Fulton County Chap., Ohio Genealogical Soc. **[16817]**, Swanton, OH
Gallia County Genealogical Soc., Ohio Genealogical Chap. **[15291]**, Gallipolis, OH
Genealogical Soc. of Washtenaw County **[6697]**, Ann Arbor, MI
Gogebic Range Genealogy Soc. **[8337]**, Ironwood, MI
Grand Traverse Area Genealogical Soc. **[9931]**, Traverse City, MI
Greene County Chap. of the Ohio Genealogical Soc. **[17369]**, Xenia, OH
Howard County Genealogical Soc. **[6008]**, Oakford, IN
Hudson Genealogical Study Group **[15482]**, Hudson, OH
Illiana Jewish Genealogical Soc. **[1708]**, Flossmoor, IL
Indiana Genealogical Soc. **[4677]**, Fort Wayne, IN
Iroquois County Genealogical Soc. **[3908]**, Watseka, IL
Jackson County Genealogical Soc. **[8375]**, Jackson, MI
Jewish Genealogical Soc. of Illinois **[2755]**, Northbrook, IL
Knox County Genealogical Soc. **[1776]**, Galesburg, IL
Lawrence County Genealogical Soc., OGS Chap. 74 **[16483]**, Proctorville, OH
Lorain County Chap. of the Ohio Genealogical Soc. **[15118]**, Elyria, OH
Macomb County Genealogy Gp. **[9089]**, Mount Clemens, MI
Macoupin County Genealogical Soc. **[3696]**, Staunton, IL
Mahoning County Chap. of Ohio Genealogical Soc. **[17403]**, Youngstown, OH
Marquette County Genealogical Soc. **[8942]**, Marquette, MI
Mercer County Chap. of the Ohio Genealogical Soc. **[13614]**, Celina, OH
Mid-Michigan Genealogical Soc. **[8731]**, Lansing, MI
Minnesota Genealogical Soc. **[11062]**, Golden Valley, MN
Monroe County Chap. of the Ohio Genealogical Soc. **[17307]**, Woodsfield, OH
Montgomery County Chap., Ohio Genealogical Soc. **[14921]**, Dayton, OH
Noble County Genealogical Soc. **[4086]**, Albion, IN
Oberlin African-Amer. Genealogy and History Gp. **[16287]**, Oberlin, OH
Ohio Genealogical Soc. **[15782]**, Mansfield, OH
Ohio Genealogical Soc., Allen County **[15665]**, Lima, OH
Ohio Genealogical Soc., Ashland County Chap. **[13170]**, Ashland, OH
Ohio Genealogical Soc., Athens County Chap. **[13212]**, Athens, OH
Ohio Genealogical Soc., Brown County **[15314]**, Georgetown, OH
Ohio Genealogical Soc., Crawford County **[15287]**, Galion, OH
Ohio Genealogical Soc., Cuyahoga West Chap. **[15184]**, Fairview Park, OH
Ohio Genealogical Soc., Darke County **[15364]**, Greenville, OH
Ohio Genealogical Soc., Fairfield County Chap. **[15607]**, Lancaster, OH
Ohio Genealogical Soc., Fayette County **[17131]**, Washington Court House, OH

Ohio Genealogical Soc., Greater Cleveland **[14195]**, Cleveland, OH
Ohio Genealogical Soc., Hamilton County Chap. **[13938]**, Cincinnati, OH
Ohio Genealogical Soc., Harrison County **[13482]**, Cadiz, OH
Ohio Genealogical Soc., Henry County **[15022]**, Deshler, OH
Ohio Genealogical Soc., Holmes County Chap. **[16038]**, Millersburg, OH
Ohio Genealogical Soc., Hudson Genealogical Study Group **[15487]**, Hudson, OH
Ohio Genealogical Soc., Huron County Chap. **[16264]**, Norwalk, OH
Ohio Genealogical Soc., Jackson County Chap. **[15515]**, Jackson, OH
Ohio Genealogical Soc., Licking County **[16181]**, Newark, OH
Ohio Genealogical Soc., Logan County **[13323]**, Bellefontaine, OH
Ohio Genealogical Soc., Marion Area **[15849]**, Marion, OH
Ohio Genealogical Soc., Medina County **[15953]**, Medina, OH
Ohio Genealogical Soc., Morgan County Chap. **[15934]**, McConnelsville, OH
Ohio Genealogical Soc., Morrow County Chap. **[16073]**, Mount Gilead, OH
Ohio Genealogical Soc., Ottawa County Chap. **[16460]**, Port Clinton, OH
Ohio Genealogical Soc., Pickaway County Historical Soc. **[14033]**, Circleville, OH
Ohio Genealogical Soc., Pike County **[17146]**, Waverly, OH
Ohio Genealogical Soc., Putnam County **[16317]**, Ottawa, OH
Ohio Genealogical Soc., Richland County-Shelby Chap. **[16654]**, Shelby, OH
Ohio Genealogical Soc., Southwest Cuyahoga **[16794]**, Strongsville, OH
Ohio Genealogical Soc., Stark County Chap. **[13575]**, Canton, OH
Ohio Genealogical Soc., Tuscarawas County **[16152]**, New Philadelphia, OH
Ohio Genealogical Soc., Union County Chap. **[15866]**, Marysville, OH
Ohio Genealogical Soc., Van Wert County Ohio Chap. **[17052]**, Van Wert, OH
Ohio Genealogical Soc., Warren County Chap. **[15623]**, Lebanon, OH
Ohio Genealogical Soc., Williams County **[13457]**, Bryan, OH
Ohio Genealogical Soc., Wood County **[13396]**, Bowling Green, OH
Ohio Genealogy Soc., Jefferson County Chap. **[16765]**, Steubenville, OH
Pipestone County Historical Society **[12011]**, Pipestone, MN
Portage County Chap. of the Ohio Genealogical Soc. **[16503]**, Ravenna, OH
Preble County Chap. - Ohio Genealogical Soc. **[15089]**, Eaton, OH
Richland County Genealogical Soc. **[15790]**, Mansfield, OH
Ross County Genealogical Society **[13673]**, Chillicothe, OH
Scioto County Chap. of the Ohio Genealogical Soc. **[16475]**, Portsmouth, OH
Seneca County Genealogical Soc. **[16861]**, Tiffin, OH
Stevens Point Area Genealogical Soc. **[19808]**, Stevens Point, WI
Summit County Chap. of Ohio Genealogical Soc. **[13093]**, Akron, OH
Tazewell County Genealogical and Historical Soc. **[2993]**, Pekin, IL
Tippecanoe County Historical Assn. - Alameda McCollough Lib. **[5635]**, Lafayette, IN
Trumbull County Genealogical Soc. **[17112]**, Warren, OH
Van Buren Regional Genealogical Soc. **[7287]**, Decatur, MI
Versailles Area Genealogical and Historical Soc. **[3856]**, Versailles, IL
Walworth County Genealogical Soc. **[17830]**, Delavan, WI
Wayne County Genealogical Soc. **[17331]**, Wooster, OH
Wayne County Genealogical Soc. **[17330]**, Wooster, OH
Western Michigan Genealogical Soc. **[8028]**, Grand Rapids, MI
Wisconsin State Genealogical Soc. **[18755]**, Madison, WI
Genealogy Gp; Macomb County **[9089]**, Mount Clemens, MI
Genealogy and History Gp; Oberlin African-Amer. **[16287]**, Oberlin, OH
Genealogy Soc; Gogebic Range **[8337]**, Ironwood, MI
Genealogy Soc., Jefferson County Chap; Ohio **[16765]**, Steubenville, OH
Gen. Contractors of Am., Greater Detroit Chap; Assoc. **[9786]**, Southfield, MI
Gen. Contractors of Illinois; Assoc. **[3536]**, Springfield, IL
Genesee County Alliance for the Mentally Ill **[7191]**, Clio, MI
Genesee County Bar Assn. **[7736]**, Flint, MI
Genesee County Medical Soc. **[7737]**, Flint, MI
Genesee District Dental Soc. **[7738]**, Flint, MI
Genesee Fencing Club **[7843]**, Grand Blanc, MI
Genesee Lions Club **[7826]**, Genesee, MI
Genesee Sportsman's Club **[7768]**, Flushing, MI
Geneseo Chamber of Commerce **[1788]**, Geneseo, IL
Geneseo Development Group **[★1788]**
Genetic Disorders
Neurofibromatosis - Minnesota **[11707]**, Minneapolis, MN
Prader-Willi Michigan Assn. **[8865]**, Lowell, MI
Prader-Willi Syndrome Assn. Illinois **[2703]**, Niles, IL
Prader-Willi Syndrome Assn. of Minnesota **[10900]**, Eden Prairie, MN
Prader-Willi Syndrome Assn. of Ohio **[15955]**, Medina, OH
Sotos Syndrome Support Assn. **[3998]**, Wheaton, IL
Geneva Area Chamber of Commerce **[15309]**, Geneva, OH
Geneva Chamber of Commerce **[1793]**, Geneva, IL
Geneva Lake Area Chamber of Commerce **[18397]**, Lake Geneva, WI
Geneva Lakes Area United Way **[18398]**, Lake Geneva, WI
Geneva Lions Club **[1794]**, Geneva, IL
Geneva-on-the-Lake Chamber of Commerce **[15310]**, Geneva, OH
Geneva - Young Life **[1795]**, Geneva, IL
Genex Cooperative **[19679]**, Shawano, WI
Genoa Chamber of Commerce **[1804]**, Genoa, IL
Genoa City Lions Club **[18035]**, Genoa City, WI
Genoa-Kingston United Way **[1805]**, Genoa, IL
Genoa Lions Club - Wisconsin **[19825]**, Stoddard, WI
Geographical Soc; Illinois **[2717]**, Normal, IL
Geography
Illinois Geographical Soc. **[2717]**, Normal, IL
Geological Alliance **[15331]**, Goshen, OH
Geology
Assn. of Engg. Geologists - North Central Sect. **[1650]**, Evanston, IL
Great Lakes Sect. of the Soc. for Sedimentary Geology **[521]**, Champaign, IL
Michigan Basin Geological Soc. **[8634]**, Lansing, MI
Ohio Geological Soc. **[14616]**, Columbus, OH
Professional Geologists of Indiana **[5459]**, Indianapolis, IN
Sigma Gamma Epsilon, Zeta Sigma Chap., Western Michigan Univ. **[8467]**, Kalamazoo, MI
Wisconsin Geological and Natural History Survey **[18708]**, Madison, WI
George Wright Soc. **[8110]**, Hancock, MI
Geospatial Info. and Tech. Assn. Minnesota Regional Chap. **[12416]**, St. Paul, MN
Gerald R. Ford Found. **[7938]**, Grand Rapids, MI
Geriatric Care; Conf. on **[★12487]**
German
Amer. Assn. of Teachers of German - Indiana Chap. **[6002]**, Notre Dame, IN
Amer. Assn. of Teachers of German - Minnesota Chap. **[12351]**, St. Paul, MN
Amer. Assn. of Teachers of German - Northern Illinois Chap. **[1583]**, Elgin, IL
Amer. Assn. of Teachers of German - Southern Illinois Chap. **[2222]**, Latham, IL
Amer. Historical Soc. of Germans from Russia, Northern Illinois Chap. **[2803]**, Oak Park, IL
Amer. Historical Soc. of Germans from Russia, Saginaw Valley Chap. **[9596]**, Saginaw, MI
German-American Chamber of Commerce of the Midwest - Wisconsin Chapter **[19013]**, Milwaukee, WI
German Heritage Society; Indiana **[5239]**, Indianapolis, IN
German Pointer
German Shorthaired Pointer Club of Illinois **[1310]**, Crest Hill, IL
German Wirehaired Pointer Club of Am. **[8054]**, Grass Lake, MI
Twin Cities German Wirehair Pointer Club **[10875]**, Eagan, MN
German Shepherd
German Shepherd Dog Club of Central Ohio **[15243]**, Fredericktown, OH
German Shepherd Dog Training Club of Chicago **[1934]**, Hanover Park, IL
German Shepherd Dog Club of Central Ohio **[15243]**, Fredericktown, OH
German Shepherd Dog Club of Minneapolis and St. Paul **[10664]**, Circle Pines, MN
German Shepherd Dog Club of Toledo **[15203]**, Findlay, OH
German Shepherd Dog Club of Wisconsin **[18154]**, Greenfield, WI
German Shepherd Dog Club of Wisconsin **[19287]**, New Berlin, WI
German Shepherd Dog Training Club of Chicago **[1934]**, Hanover Park, IL
German Shepherd Rescue Alliance of Wisconsin **[18514]**, Madison, WI
German Shorthaired Pointer Club of Illinois **[1310]**, Crest Hill, IL
German Village Wander Volk **[15284]**, Galion, OH
German Wirehaired Pointer Club of Am. **[8054]**, Grass Lake, MI
Germania Volksmarch Gruppe **[13834]**, Cincinnati, OH
Germantown Area Chamber of Commerce **[18039]**, Germantown, WI
Germantown Junior Women's Club **[18040]**, Germantown, WI
Germantown Lions Club **[15316]**, Germantown, OH
Germany Philatelic Soc., Chap. 5 **[2810]**, Oak Park, IL
Germany Philatelic Soc., No. 19 Cleveland **[14125]**, Cleveland, OH
Gerontological Advanced Practice Nurses; Chicagoland **[3200]**, River Forest, IL
Gerontology Network **[7939]**, Grand Rapids, MI
GFWC Indiana **[4430]**, Crown Point, IN
GFWC of Minnesota **[11890]**, New York Mills, MN
GFWC/Ohio Fed. of Women's Clubs **[13835]**, Cincinnati, OH
GFWC Upper Peninsula District No. 5 **[8323]**, Iron Mountain, MI
Ghetto Grouse Gun Club **[5798]**, Milan, IN
GHHS PTSA **[7857]**, Grand Haven, MI
Gibson Area Chamber of Commerce **[1809]**, Gibson City, IL
Gibson Chamber of Commerce **[★1809]**
Gift of Reading **[7365]**, Detroit, MI
Gifted
Eden Prairie Coun. for the Gifted and Talented **[10891]**, Eden Prairie, MN
Illinois Assn. for Gifted Children **[2911]**, Palatine, IL
Indiana Assn. for the Gifted **[4323]**, Carmel, IN
Michigan Alliance for Gifted Educ. **[7978]**, Grand Rapids, MI
Minnesota Coun. for the Gifted and Talented **[10921]**, Edina, MN
Ohio Assn. for Gifted Children **[14553]**, Columbus, OH
Wisconsin Assn. for Talented and Gifted **[17531]**, Appleton, WI
Gilbert and Sullivan Soc; Midwestern **[2742]**, North Aurora, IL
Gilda's Club Grand Rapids **[7940]**, Grand Rapids, MI
Gilman Chamber of Commerce **[1812]**, Gilman, IL
Gilmour Acad. Figure Skating Club **[16678]**, Solon, OH

Ginseng Bd. of Wisconsin **[20035]**, Wausau, WI
Girard Chamber of Commerce **[1814]**, Girard, IL
Girard Lions Club **[15322]**, Girard, OH
Girl Scout Coun. of Cannon Valley **[11914]**, Northfield, MN
Girl Scout Coun. of Greater Minneapolis **[10536]**, Brooklyn Center, MN
Girl Scout Coun. of Kenosha County **[18298]**, Kenosha, WI
Girl Scout Coun; Michigan Metro **[9998]**, Troy, MI
Girl Scout Coun. of River Trails **[12143]**, Rochester, MN
Girl Scout Coun. of St. Croix Valley **[12417]**, St. Paul, MN
Girl Scouts of Appleseed Ridge **[15653]**, Lima, OH
Girl Scouts of Badger Coun. **[17607]**, Beloit, WI
Girl Scouts of Black Hawk Coun. **[18515]**, Madison, WI
Girl Scouts of Buckeye Trails Coun. **[14886]**, Dayton, OH
Girl Scouts of Chicago **[902]**, Chicago, IL
Girl Scouts of Crooked Tree **[9930]**, Traverse City, MI
Girl Scouts of DuPage County Coun. **[2295]**, Lisle, IL
Girl Scouts Fair Winds Coun. **[7739]**, Flint, MI
Girl Scouts; Fayette County **[★6091]**
Girl Scouts of the Fox River Area **[17498]**, Appleton, WI
Girl Scouts - Fox Valley Coun. **[117]**, Aurora, IL
Girl Scouts of Glowing Embers Coun. **[8427]**, Kalamazoo, MI
Girl Scouts - Great Blue Heron Coun. **[19984]**, Waukesha, WI
Girl Scouts-Great Rivers Coun. **[13836]**, Cincinnati, OH
Girl Scouts - Great Trail Coun. **[16216]**, North Canton, OH
Girl Scouts - Green Meadows Coun. **[3817]**, Urbana, IL
Girl Scouts - Heart of Ohio **[17438]**, Zanesville, OH
Girl Scouts of Heritage Trails Coun. **[15767]**, Mansfield, OH
Girl Scouts of Hoosier Capital Coun. **[5121]**, Indianapolis, IN
Girl Scouts - Illinois Crossroads Coun. **[3853]**, Vernon Hills, IL
Girl Scouts - Irish Hills Coun. **[8364]**, Jackson, MI
Girl Scouts-Kickapoo Coun. **[3021]**, Peoria, IL
Girl Scouts of Lake Erie Coun. **[14126]**, Cleveland, OH
Girl Scouts of Lake to River Coun. **[16205]**, Niles, OH
Girl Scouts - Land of Lakes Coun. **[12826]**, Waite Park, MN
Girl Scouts, Land of Lincoln Coun. **[3553]**, Springfield, IL
Girl Scouts of Limberlost Coun. **[4666]**, Fort Wayne, IN
Girl Scouts of Macomb County - Otsikita Coun. **[7176]**, Clinton Township, MI
Girl Scouts of Manitou Coun. **[19695]**, Sheboygan, WI
Girl Scouts of Michigan Trails **[7941]**, Grand Rapids, MI
Girl Scouts of Milwaukee Area **[19014]**, Milwaukee, WI
Girl Scouts Peacepipe Coun. **[12094]**, Redwood Falls, MN
Girl Scouts of River Bluff's Coun. **[1820]**, Glen Carbon, IL
Girl Scouts of Riverland Coun. **[18346]**, La Crosse, WI
Girl Scouts - Rock River Valley **[3280]**, Rockford, IL
Girl Scouts - Seal of Ohio Coun. **[14442]**, Columbus, OH
Girl Scouts of Shagbark Coun. **[1973]**, Herrin, IL
Girl Scouts of Singing Sands Coun. **[6228]**, South Bend, IN
Girl Scouts of South Cook County **[2047]**, Homewood, IL
Girl Scouts - Sybaquay Coun. **[1591]**, Elgin, IL
Girl Scouts of Sycamore Coun. **[5611]**, Lafayette, IN
Girl Scouts of The Calumet Coun. **[4911]**, Highland, IN
Girl Scouts of The Mississippi Valley **[3244]**, Rock Island, IL
Girl Scouts of The Western Reserve **[13053]**, Akron, OH
Girl Scouts of Treaty Line Coun. **[6091]**, Richmond, IN
Girl Scouts of Tulip Trace Coun. **[4220]**, Bloomington, IN
Girl Scouts of Two Rivers Coun. **[3150]**, Quincy, IL
Girl Scouts of Wapehani Coun. **[4441]**, Daleville, IN
Girl Scouts; Wayne County **[★6091]**
Girl Scouts of Whispering Oaks Coun. **[352]**, Brookfield, IL
Girl Scouts of Woodland Council - Central Wisconsin **[20184]**, Wisconsin Rapids, WI
Girls
  Girl Scouts of River Bluff's Coun. **[1820]**, Glen Carbon, IL
  Girls Incorporated of Indianapolis **[5122]**, Indianapolis, IN
Girls Club of Cass County; Boys and **[7099]**, Cassopolis, MI
Girls Club of Sandusky; Boys and **[16606]**, Sandusky, OH
Girls Clubs of Sheboygan County Found; Boys and **[19490]**, Plymouth, WI
Girls Incorporated of Indianapolis **[5122]**, Indianapolis, IN
Girls Incorporated of Monroe County **[4221]**, Bloomington, IN
Girls Incorporated of Shelbyville and Shelby County **[6192]**, Shelbyville, IN
Girls Sports League; Peoria **[3052]**, Peoria, IL
Giving Coun; Central Illinois Planned **[275]**, Bloomington, IL
Giving Coun; North Central Ohio Planned **[13168]**, Ashland, OH
Giziibii Rsrc. Conservation and Development Coun. **[10416]**, Bemidji, MN
GK Riverbottom Hunt Club **[16060]**, Montpelier, OH
Glacial Ridge AIFA **[10277]**, Alexandria, MN
Glacial Ridge Appaloosa Horse Club **[12614]**, St. Peter, MN
Glacierland Rsrc. Conservation and Development Coun. **[18100]**, Green Bay, WI
Gladwin Area Hockey Association **[7834]**, Gladwin, MI
Gladwin County Chamber of Commerce **[7835]**, Gladwin, MI
Glass
  Indiana Glass Assn. **[4362]**, Cicero, IN
  Michigan Glass Assn. **[8668]**, Lansing, MI
  Minnesota Glass Assn. **[10896]**, Eden Prairie, MN
  Ohio Glass Assn. **[14196]**, Cleveland, OH
Glass Center Coin Club **[15457]**, Holland, OH
Glass City Corvette Club **[17251]**, Whitehouse, OH
Glass City Miniatures Guild **[9328]**, Ottawa Lake, MI
Glass Menagerie Corvette Club **[5123]**, Indianapolis, IN
Glawe School Committee **[9053]**, Millersburg, MI
Glen Carbon Chamber of Commerce; Edwardsville - **[1558]**, Edwardsville, IL
Glen Crest Wyld Life - Wyldlife **[1828]**, Glen Ellyn, IL
Glen Ellyn Chamber of Commerce **[1829]**, Glen Ellyn, IL
Glen Ellyn Lions Club **[1830]**, Glen Ellyn, IL
Glen Ellyn Lions Found. **[1831]**, Glen Ellyn, IL
Glen Ellyn Philatelic Club **[1832]**, Glen Ellyn, IL
Glen Lake Chamber of Commerce **[★7838]**
Glen Lake/Sleeping Bear Area Chamber of Commerce **[★7838]**
Glenbard North PTSA **[450]**, Carol Stream, IL
Glencoe Area Chamber of Commerce **[11048]**, Glencoe, MN
Glencoe Chamber of Commerce **[1849]**, Glencoe, IL
Glencoe PTO **[1850]**, Glencoe, IL
Glendale Assn. of Commerce **[18052]**, Glendale, WI
Glendale Heights Barangay Lions Club **[1851]**, Glendale Heights, IL
Glendale Heights Junior Woman's Club **[1852]**, Glendale Heights, IL
Glenview Area Historical Soc. **[1864]**, Glenview, IL
Glenview Chamber of Commerce **[1865]**, Glenview, IL
Glenview/North Shore African Violet Soc. **[1866]**, Glenview, IL
Glenwood Area Chamber of Commerce **[11052]**, Glenwood, MN
Glenwood Chamber of Commerce **[★11052]**
Glenwood Figure Skating Club **[1707]**, Flossmoor, IL
Glenwood Lions Club - Minnesota **[11053]**, Glenwood, MN
GLMV Area Chamber of Commerce **[2259]**, Libertyville, IL
Global Citizens Network **[12418]**, St. Paul, MN
Global Grid Forum **[2240]**, Lemont, IL
Global Volunteers **[12419]**, St. Paul, MN
Glyndon Lions Club **[11057]**, Glyndon, MN
Gnadenhutten Historical Soc. **[15329]**, Gnadenhutten, OH
Gnadenhutten Historical Soc. Museum **[★15329]**
Go Veggie! **[903]**, Chicago, IL
Goat Lovers of Michigan **[9330]**, Ovid, MI
Goats
  Amer. Boer Goat Assn. - Region 10 **[15593]**, Lancaster, OH
  Illinois Boer Goat Assn. **[282]**, Bloomington, IL
  Illinois Meat Goat Producers **[3370]**, Rushville, IL
  Indiana Boer Goat Assn. **[4347]**, Charlestown, IN
  Michigan Boer Goat Assn. **[9853]**, Standish, MI
  Minnesota Boer Goat Assn. **[11020]**, Foreston, MN
  Ohio Boer Goat Assn. **[15858]**, Mark Center, OH
  Ohio Meat Goat Assn. **[16125]**, New Concord, OH
  Wisconsin Boer Goat Assn. **[18400]**, Lake Geneva, WI
Gogebic Range Beagle Club **[8336]**, Ironwood, MI
Gogebic Range Genealogy Soc. **[8337]**, Ironwood, MI
Gogebic Range United Way **[8338]**, Ironwood, MI
Gold Wing Touring Assn. **[5124]**, Indianapolis, IN
Golden K Kiwanis Club of Grand Rapids, Michigan **[7942]**, Grand Rapids, MI
Golden Retriever Club of Columbus, Ohio **[15047]**, Dublin, OH
Golden Retriever Club of Greater Toledo **[15906]**, Maumee, OH
Golden Sands Home Builders Assn. **[19482]**, Plover, WI
Golden Sands Resource Conservation and Development Council **[19790]**, Stevens Point, WI
Golden Valley Lions Club **[11868]**, New Hope, MN
Golden Years Alaskan Malamute Rescue **[9144]**, Muskegon, MI
Golden Years AMR **[★9144]**
Golf
  Central Illinois Golf Course Superintendents Assn. **[103]**, Auburn, IL
  Central Ohio Golf Course Superintendents Assn. **[16102]**, Nashport, OH
  Discover Golf on Michigan's Sunrise Side **[9174]**, National City, MI
  Golf Assn. of Michigan **[7661]**, Farmington Hills, MI
  Greater Cincinnati Golf Course Superintendents Assn. of Am. **[13847]**, Cincinnati, OH
  Greater Detroit Golf Course Superintendents Assn. **[8571]**, Lansing, MI
  Kentuckiana Golf Course Superintendents Assn. **[5543]**, Jeffersonville, IN
  Miami Valley Golf Course Superintendents Assn. **[14912]**, Dayton, OH
  Michigan Golf Course Owners Assn. **[8669]**, Lansing, MI
  Midwest Assn. Golf Course Superintendents **[2247]**, Lemont, IL
  Minnesota Golf Assn. **[10922]**, Edina, MN
  Minnesota Golf Course Superintendents Assn. **[11792]**, Minnetonka, MN
  Minnesota Sect. PGA of Am. **[10713]**, Coon Rapids, MN
  Northwestern Illinois Golf Course Superintendents Assn. **[186]**, Batavia, IL
  Northwestern Ohio Golf Course Superintendents Assn. **[15212]**, Findlay, OH
  Ohio Golf Course Owners Assn. **[16479]**, Powell, OH
  Professional Golfers Assn. of Am. - Michigan Sect. **[7564]**, East Lansing, MI
  Professional Golfers Assn. of Am. - Wisconsin **[19099]**, Milwaukee, WI
  Toledo District Golf Assn. **[16971]**, Toledo, OH
  West Michigan Golf Course Superintendents Assn. **[9533]**, Rockford, MI
  Western Golf Assn. **[1878]**, Golf, IL
  Wilmette Golf Club **[4024]**, Wilmette, IL

Wisconsin Golf Course Superintendents Assn. [17682], Brookfield, WI
Golf Assn. of Michigan [7661], Farmington Hills, MI
Golf Assn; Northern Illinois Deaf [1107], Chicago, IL
Golf Assn; Toledo District [16971], Toledo, OH
Golf Club; Wilmette [4024], Wilmette, IL
Golf on Michigan's Sunrise Side; Discover [9174], National City, MI
Golf School District 67 PTA [2568], Morton Grove, IL
Good Shepherd K-9 Rescue [18248], Janesville, WI
Goodhue County Habitat for Humanity [12078], Red Wing, MN
Goodhue County Historical Soc. [12079], Red Wing, MN
Goodhue Lions Club [11068], Goodhue, MN
Goodrich Lions Club [7238], Davison, MI
Goodridge Lion Tamers Club [11070], Goodridge, MN
Goodridge Lions Club [12741], Thief River Falls, MN
Goodtime Trailblazers [5125], Indianapolis, IN
Goodwill Columbus [14443], Columbus, OH
Goodwill Indus./Easter Seals - Minnesota [12420], St. Paul, MN
Goodwill Indus./Easter Seals Soc. of Minnesota [★12420]
Goodwill Indus. of the Miami Valley [14887], Dayton, OH
Goodwill Indus. of Wayne County [17317], Wooster, OH
Goshen Chamber of Commerce [4795], Goshen, IN
Goshen Historical Soc./Museum [4796], Goshen, IN
Goshen Lions Club [15332], Goshen, OH
Goshen Noon Kiwanis Club [4797], Goshen, IN
Goshen Old-Time Dancing [4380], Columbia City, IN
Goshen Trail Beagle Club [3363], Rosiclare, IL
Gospel Music
Divine Praise [871], Chicago, IL
Government
Southeast Michigan Coun. of Governments [7437], Detroit, MI
Govt. Administrators Assn. [7366], Detroit, MI
Government Employees
Amer. Fed. of Govt. Employees, AFL-CIO - Coun. 164 [17084], Walbridge, OH
Amer. Fed. of Govt. Employees, AFL-CIO - DOD Local Union 1138 [14839], Dayton, OH
Amer. Fed. of Govt. Employees, AFL-CIO - DOD Local Union 1626 [6841], Battle Creek, MI
Amer. Fed. of Govt. Employees, AFL-CIO - DOD Local Union 1658 [10058], Warren, MI
Amer. Fed. of Govt. Employees, AFL-CIO - DOJ Local Union 1741 [9046], Milan, MI
Amer. Fed. of Govt. Employees, AFL-CIO - Local Union 607 [15099], Elkton, OH
Amer. Fed. of Govt. Employees, AFL-CIO - Veterans' Affairs Local Union 1629 [6842], Battle Creek, MI
Amer. Fed. of Govt. Employees, District 6 [4985], Indianapolis, IN
Amer. Fed. of Govt. Employees, District 7 [619], Chicago, IL
Amer. Fed. of Govt. Employees, District 8 [10458], Bloomington, MN
Amer. Fed. of State, County and Municipal Employees, AFL-CIO - Civil Ser. Employees Assn. Local Union 11 [17202], Westerville, OH
Amer. Fed. of State, County and Municipal Employees, AFL-CIO - Michigan Coun. 25 [8531], Lansing, MI
Amer. Fed. of State, County and Municipal Employees, AFL-CIO - Milwaukee Wisconsin District Coun. 48 [18933], Milwaukee, WI
Amer. Fed. of State, County and Municipal Employees Coun. 8 Ohio [17339], Worthington, OH
Erie County MR-DD Employees Assn. [16609], Sandusky, OH
Govt. Administrators Assn. [7366], Detroit, MI
Illinois Govt. Finance Officers Assn. [3971], Westmont, IL
Indiana State Employees Assn. [5315], Indianapolis, IN
Michigan Assn. of Governmental Employees [8616], Lansing, MI
Governments; Southeast Michigan Coun. of [7437], Detroit, MI
Governor John Wood Mansion Museum [★3152]
Governor's Planning Coun. for People with Disabilities, Indiana [5126], Indianapolis, IN
Gr. Cleveland YoungLives - YoungLives [14127], Cleveland, OH
GR Lans Assn. of Realtors [★8572]
Graduate Employees Org. [520], Champaign, IL
Graduate Prog. in Neural Sci., Indiana Univ., Bloomington Chap. [4222], Bloomington, IN
Grafton Area Chamber of Commerce [18063], Grafton, WI
Grafton Lions Club - Wisconsin [18064], Grafton, WI
Grain
Grain and Feed Assn. of Illinois [3554], Springfield, IL
Michigan Corn Growers Assn. [7463], DeWitt, MI
Minnesota Assn. of Wheat Growers [12071], Red Lake Falls, MN
Wisconsin Corn Growers Assn. [19420], Palmyra, WI
Wisconsin Corn Promotion Bd. [19421], Palmyra, WI
Grain and Agri-Dealers Assn; Michigan [★7531]
Grain and Feed Assn. of Illinois [3554], Springfield, IL
Grand Blanc Chamber of Commerce [7844], Grand Blanc, MI
Grand Blanc Huntsman's Club [7839], Goodrich, MI
Grand Boulevard Fed. [904], Chicago, IL
Grand Haven-Spring Lake Convention and Visitors Bureau [7858], Grand Haven, MI
Grand Haven - Young Life [7859], Grand Haven, MI
Grand Lake Beagle Club [13613], Celina, OH
Grand Ledge Area Chamber of Commerce [7871], Grand Ledge, MI
Grand Ledge Lions Club [7872], Grand Ledge, MI
Grand Lodge Ancient Free and Accepted Masons Illinois [3555], Springfield, IL
Grand Marais Aikikai [11074], Grand Marais, MN
Grand Marais Chamber of Commerce [11075], Grand Marais, MN
Grand Marais Lions Club [11076], Grand Marais, MN
Grand Prairie Friends of Illinois [3818], Urbana, IL
Grand Rapids Area Chamber of Commerce [7943], Grand Rapids, MI
Grand Rapids Area Chamber of Commerce [11084], Grand Rapids, MN
Grand Rapids Area Chamber of Commerce [15338], Grand Rapids, OH
Grand Rapids Area Youth for Christ [8404], Jenison, MI
Grand Rapids Assn. of Realtors [7944], Grand Rapids, MI
Grand Rapids Bar Assn. [7945], Grand Rapids, MI
Grand Rapids Cap Baker Lions Club [11427], Marcell, MN
Grand Rapids Chorus of Sweet Adelines Intl. [7946], Grand Rapids, MI
Grand Rapids Christian High - Young Life [7947], Grand Rapids, MI
Grand Rapids Christian Middle School - Wyldlife [7948], Grand Rapids, MI
Grand Rapids Fed. of Musicians - Local 56, Amer. Fed. of Musicians [7949], Grand Rapids, MI
Grand Rapids Gun Club [11085], Grand Rapids, MN
Grand Rapids and Indiana Chap., Pennsylvania Railroad Tech. and Historical Soc. [10225], Zeeland, MI
Grand Rapids/Kent County Convention and Visitors Bur. [7950], Grand Rapids, MI
Grand Rapids Lions Club [20185], Wisconsin Rapids, WI
Grand Rapids Opportunities for Women [7951], Grand Rapids, MI
Grand Rapids Star of the North Lions Club [11086], Grand Rapids, MN
Grand Rapids Urban League [7952], Grand Rapids, MI
Grand Rapids Women's Chorus [7953], Grand Rapids, MI
Grand River Fly Tyers [7954], Grand Rapids, MI
Grand River Folk Arts Soc. [7955], Grand Rapids, MI
Grand River Partners, Inc. [16334], Painesville, OH
Grand Traverse Area Genealogical Soc. [9931], Traverse City, MI
Grand Traverse Chorus of Sweet Adelines Intl. [9932], Traverse City, MI
Grand Valley Corvette Assn. [8037], Grandville, MI
Grand Valley Orchid Soc. [8196], Holland, MI
Grandview High School - Young Life [14444], Columbus, OH
Grandville Chamber of Commerce [8038], Grandville, MI
Grandville High School - Young Life [8039], Grandville, MI
Grandville Middle School - Wyldlife [8040], Grandville, MI
Grange; Michigan State [8150], Haslett, MI
Granite Falls Area Chamber of Commerce [11096], Granite Falls, MN
Granite Falls Area Chamber of Commerce - Convention and Visitors Bur. [★11096]
Grant County Convention and Visitors Bur. [★5739]
Grant County Historical Soc. [10936], Elbow Lake, MN
Grant County Literacy [★5731]
Grant County Literacy Coun. [5731], Marion, IN
Grant County Museum [★10936]
Grant Lions Club [8051], Grant, MI
Grant Regional Hea. Center Auxiliary [18410], Lancaster, WI
Grantsburg Chamber of Commerce [18071], Grantsburg, WI
Granville - Young Life [15342], Granville, OH
Graphic Arts
Central Illinois Club of Printing House Craftsmen [272], Bloomington, IL
Graphic Communs. Intl. Union, AFL-CIO, CLC - Local Union 577 [19015], Milwaukee, WI
Intl. Graphic Arts Educ. Assn. - Region 1, North Central [2286], Lincolnshire, IL
Printing Indus. of Michigan [9817], Southfield, MI
Printing Indus. of Wisconsin [19444], Pewaukee, WI
Printing Indus. of Illinois-Indiana Assn. [1145], Chicago, IL
Printing Industry of Illinois/Indiana Association [4332], Carmel, IN
Printing Indus. of Minnesota [11726], Minneapolis, MN
Graphic Communs. Intl. Union, AFL-CIO, CLC - Local Union 577 [19015], Milwaukee, WI
Graphics
Printing Indus. Assn. [17220], Westerville, OH
GRASLand Conservancy [17608], Beloit, WI
Grass
Grand Prairie Friends of Illinois [3818], Urbana, IL
Illinois Turfgrass Found. [2243], Lemont, IL
Grass Lake Lions Club [8055], Grass Lake, MI
Grass Producers Assn; Minnesota Native Wildflower [12955], Winona, MN
Grass River Natural Area [6905], Bellaire, MI
Grassroots Collaborative of Chicago, Illinois [905], Chicago, IL
Gratiot Area Chamber of Commerce [6632], Alma, MI
Gray M. Sanborn PTA [2910], Palatine, IL
Gray Panthers of Huron Valley [6698], Ann Arbor, MI
Gray Panthers, Metro Detroit [9257], Oak Park, MI
Gray Panthers, Twin Cities [11569], Minneapolis, MN
Grayling Area Visitors Council [8060], Grayling, MI
Grayling Regional Chamber of Commerce [8061], Grayling, MI
Grayling Sportsmen's Club [8062], Grayling, MI
Grayslake Area Chamber of Commerce [1893], Grayslake, IL
Grayville Chamber of Commerce [1899], Grayville, IL
Great Dane Club of Am. [16729], Springfield, OH
Great Dane Club of Cleveland [15941], Medina, OH
Great Dane Club of Milwaukee [20074], Wauwatosa, WI
Great Dane Rescue [9398], Plymouth, MI
Great Lake Sound Chorus of Sweet Adelines Intl. [6382], Valparaiso, IN
Great Lakes
Intl. Assn. for Great Lakes Res. [6710], Ann Arbor, MI
Great Lakes ADA Center [★906]
Great Lakes Adaptive Sports Assn. [2197], Lake Forest, IL
Great Lakes Aikikai [6699], Ann Arbor, MI
Great Lakes Appaloosa Horse Club [15008], Delaware, OH

Great Lakes Area Show Series Educal. Dressage [7123], Charlotte, MI
Great Lakes Assn. of Orthodontists [14445], Columbus, OH
Great Lakes Athletic Trainers Assn. [8935], Marquette, MI
Great Lakes Belted Galloway Assn. [17715], Camp Douglas, WI
Great Lakes Booksellers Assn. [7860], Grand Haven, MI
Great Lakes Chap. of the Amer. Assn. of Physicists in Medicine [8839], Livonia, MI
Great Lakes Chap. of the Amer. Coll. of Healthcare Executives [7956], Grand Rapids, MI
Great Lakes Colls. Assn. [6700], Ann Arbor, MI
Great Lakes Commn. [6701], Ann Arbor, MI
Great Lakes Curling Assn. [13635], Chagrin Falls, OH
Great Lakes Curling Assn. - Bowling Green Curling Club [13391], Bowling Green, OH
Great Lakes Curling Assn. - Copper Country Curling Club [7056], Calumet, MI
Great Lakes Curling Assn. - Delta Rocks Curling Club [7830], Gladstone, MI
Great Lakes Curling Assn. - Detroit Curling Club [7694], Ferndale, MI
Great Lakes Curling Assn. - Lewiston Curling Club [6803], Atlanta, MI
Great Lakes Curling Assn. - Mayfield Curling Club [16691], South Euclid, OH
Great Lakes Curling Assn. - Midland Curling Club [9025], Midland, MI
Great Lakes Curling Assn. - Newark Curling Club [16169], Newark, OH
Great Lakes Disability and Bus. Tech. Assistance Center [906], Chicago, IL
Great Lakes Fabricators and Erectors Assn. [7367], Detroit, MI
Great Lakes Fishery Commn. [6702], Ann Arbor, MI
Great Lakes Four Wheel Drive Assn. [9026], Midland, MI
Great Lakes German Shorthaired Pointer Club and Rescue [7572], East Leroy, MI
Great Lakes GSP Rescue [★7572]
Great Lakes Hemophilia Found. [19016], Milwaukee, WI
Great Lakes Historical Soc. [17065], Vermilion, OH
Great Lakes Humanist Soc. [9105], Mount Pleasant, MI
Great Lakes Indian Fish and Wildlife Commn. [19353], Odanah, WI
Great Lakes Lighthouse Keepers Assn. [8888], Mackinaw City, MI
Great Lakes Maintenance Assn. [17499], Appleton, WI
Great Lakes Match Club [12895], White Bear Lake, MN
Great Lakes Military Vehicle Preservation Assn. [8365], Jackson, MI
Great Lakes Org. Development Network [13152], Archbold, OH
Great Lakes Pastel Soc. [7957], Grand Rapids, MI
Great Lakes Petroleum Retailers and Allied Trades Assn. [8570], Lansing, MI
Great Lakes REACT [14128], Cleveland, OH
Great Lakes Region Youth for Christ [5127], Indianapolis, IN
Great Lakes Renewable Energy Assn. [7473], Dimondale, MI
Great Lakes Rottweiler Club of Southeast Michigan [9188], New Haven, MI
Great Lakes SAAB Club [8197], Holland, MI
Great Lakes Sect. of the Soc. for Sedimentary Geology [521], Champaign, IL
Great Lakes Soc. of Orthodontists [★14445]
Great Lakes Sport Fishing Coun. [1621], Elmhurst, IL
Great Lakes Swing Dance Club [7037], Burton, MI
Great Lakes Sword Club [7582], Eaton Rapids, MI
Great Lakes Yacht Club [9656], St. Clair Shores, MI
Great Pyrenees Rescue of Greater Chicago [2063], Ingleside, IL
Great River Greening [12421], St. Paul, MN
Great River REACT [3899], Waterloo, IL
Great Rivers Athletic Conf. [2059], Ina, IL
Great Rivers Girl Scout Coun. [★13836]
Great Rivers Land Preservation Assn. [42], Alton, IL
Greater Akron Chamber of Commerce [13054], Akron, OH
Greater Akron Mathematics Educators' Soc. [16776], Stow, OH
Greater Akron Orchid Soc. [13055], Akron, OH
Greater Albion Chamber of Commerce [6590], Albion, MI
Greater Alexandria Area Assn. of Realtors [10278], Alexandria, MN
Greater Algonac Chamber of Commerce [6599], Algonac, MI
Greater/Alton Twin Rivers Convention and Visitors Bur. [★37]
Greater Ann Arbor Soc. for Human Rsrc. Mgt. [9990], Troy, MI
Greater Ashburn Planning Assn. [907], Chicago, IL
Greater Aurora Chamber of Commerce [118], Aurora, IL
Greater Avon Chamber of Commerce [4152], Avon, IN
Greater Belleville Chamber of Commerce [202], Belleville, IL
Greater Beloit Assn. [★17609]
Greater Beloit Chamber of Commerce [17609], Beloit, WI
Greater Berkley Chamber of Commerce [6930], Berkley, MI
Greater Bloomington Chamber of Commerce [4223], Bloomington, IN
Greater Brighton Area Chamber of Commerce [7012], Brighton, MI
Greater Brookfield Chamber of Commerce [17668], Brookfield, WI
Greater Buckeye Lake Chamber of Commerce [13459], Buckeye Lake, OH
Greater Centralia Chamber of Commerce [487], Centralia, IL
Greater Channahon-Minooka Area Chamber of Commerce [2502], Minooka, IL
Greater Chicago Amer. Orff-Schulwerk Assn. [119], Aurora, IL
Greater Chicago Chap. of the Assn. of Legal Administrators [3987], Wheaton, IL
Greater Chicago Chap. of the Soc. of Financial Ser. Professionals [2774], Oak Brook, IL
Greater Chicago Insulator Club [3940], West Chicago, IL
Greater Chicagoland Basenji Club [2689], New Lenox, IL
Greater Chicagoland Futurists [1713], Forest Park, IL
Greater Cincinnati Auto. Dealers Assn. [13837], Cincinnati, OH
Greater Cincinnati Bird Club [13838], Cincinnati, OH
Greater Cincinnati BMW Club No. 18 [15723], Loveland, OH
Greater Cincinnati Bowling Proprietors [13839], Cincinnati, OH
Greater Cincinnati Building and Constr. Trades Coun. [13840], Cincinnati, OH
Greater Cincinnati Chamber of Commerce [★13801]
Greater Cincinnati Chap. of Amer. Orff-Schulwerk Assn. [16026], Milford, OH
Greater Cincinnati Compensation and Benefits Assn. [13841], Cincinnati, OH
Greater Cincinnati Convention and Visitors Bur. [13842], Cincinnati, OH
Greater Cincinnati Coun. of Teachers of Mathematics [13843], Cincinnati, OH
Greater Cincinnati Daylily and Hosta Soc. [13844], Cincinnati, OH
Greater Cincinnati/Dayton Org. Development Network [15724], Loveland, OH
Greater Cincinnati Employers Inst. [★13820]
Greater Cincinnati Gas Dealers [13845], Cincinnati, OH
Greater Cincinnati Golf Assn. [13846], Cincinnati, OH
Greater Cincinnati Golf Course Superintendents Assn. of Am. [13847], Cincinnati, OH
Greater Cincinnati Hea. Coun. [13848], Cincinnati, OH
Greater Cincinnati Hea. Info. Mgt. Assn. [5833], Moores Hill, IN
Greater Cincinnati Junior Chamber Found. [13849], Cincinnati, OH
Greater Cincinnati Mortgage Bankers Assn. [13850], Cincinnati, OH
Greater Cincinnati and Northern Kentucky African-Amer. Chamber of Commerce [13851], Cincinnati, OH
Greater Cincinnati Orchid Soc. [13852], Cincinnati, OH
Greater Cincinnati Philatelic Soc. [15157], Fairfield, OH
Greater Cincinnati Rottweiler Club [13127], Amelia, OH
Greater Cincinnati St. Bernard Club [13853], Cincinnati, OH
Greater Cincinnati Tall Stacks Commn. [13854], Cincinnati, OH
Greater Cincinnati TV Educal. Found. [13855], Cincinnati, OH
Greater Cincinnati Venture Association [13856], Cincinnati, OH
Greater Cincinnati Weimaraner Club [13857], Cincinnati, OH
Greater Clare Area Chamber of Commerce [★7153]
Greater Cleveland Chap., MOAA [16636], Shaker Heights, OH
Greater Cleveland Chap. Natl. Elecl. Contractors Assn. [14129], Cleveland, OH
Greater Cleveland Chap. of Parents of Murdered Children [15967], Mentor, OH
Greater Cleveland Coun. Figure Skating Club [16241], North Ridgeville, OH
Greater Cleveland Coun. of Teachers of Mathematics [16789], Strongsville, OH
Greater Cleveland Dental Soc. [14130], Cleveland, OH
Greater Cleveland Ecology Association [14131], Cleveland, OH
Greater Cleveland FEIS Soc. [16545], Rocky River, OH
Greater Cleveland Film Commn. [★14133]
Greater Cleveland Habitat for Humanity [14132], Cleveland, OH
Greater Cleveland Media Development Corp. [14133], Cleveland, OH
Greater Cleveland Mortgage Bankers Assn. [17229], Westlake, OH
Greater Cleveland NARI [★15504]
Greater Cleveland Norwegian Elkhound Club [16235], North Olmsted, OH
Greater Cleveland Nurses Assn. [15113], Elyria, OH
Greater Cleveland Partnership [14134], Cleveland, OH
Greater Cleveland Soc. of Assn. Executives [13447], Brunswick, OH
Greater Cleveland Youth for Christ [14135], Cleveland, OH
Greater Columbus Area Chamber of Commerce [14446], Columbus, OH
Greater Columbus Chamber of Commerce [★14377]
Greater Columbus Habitat for Humanity [14447], Columbus, OH
Greater Croswell - Lexington Chamber of Commerce [8808], Lexington, MI
Greater Danville Chamber of Commerce [4445], Danville, IN
Greater Dayton ACM Chap. [14888], Dayton, OH
Greater Dayton Apartment Assn. [14889], Dayton, OH
Greater Dayton Assn. of Black Journalists [14890], Dayton, OH
Greater Dayton Assn. for Computing Machinery Chap. [★14888]
Greater Dayton Corvette Club [14891], Dayton, OH
Greater Dayton Planned Giving Coun. [14892], Dayton, OH
Greater Decatur Chamber of Commerce [7285], Decatur, MI
Greater Detroit Association of Life Underwriters [★10001]
Greater Detroit Bowling Assn. [9657], St. Clair Shores, MI
Greater Detroit Chamber of Commerce [★7354]
Greater Detroit Chap. Chief Petty Officers Assn. [7368], Detroit, MI
Greater Detroit Frozen Food Assn. [9399], Plymouth, MI
Greater Detroit Golf Course Superintendents Assn. [8571], Lansing, MI
Greater Detroit Michigan Chap. of Concerned Black Men [7369], Detroit, MI

Greater Detroit Romance Writers of Am. **[7163]**, Clarkston, MI
Greater Dowagiac Area Chamber of Commerce **[7481]**, Dowagiac, MI
Greater Durand Area Chamber of Commerce **[★7490]**
Greater East St. Louis Chamber of Commerce **[1550]**, East St. Louis, IL
Greater Edinburgh Community Chamber of Commerce **[4481]**, Edinburgh, IN
Greater Effingham Chamber of Commerce and Indus. **[1570]**, Effingham, IL
Greater Elkhart County Chamber of Commerce **[4497]**, Elkhart, IN
Greater Erie County Marketing Gp. **[16613]**, Sandusky, OH
Greater Evansville Bonsai Soc. **[5708]**, Lynnville, IN
Greater Evansville Figure Skating Club **[4549]**, Evansville, IN
Greater Fairfield Area Chamber of Commerce **[1688]**, Fairfield, IL
Greater Fort Wayne Chamber of Commerce **[4667]**, Fort Wayne, IN
Greater Fox Cities Area Habitat for Humanity **[18859]**, Menasha, WI
Greater Gary Chamber of Commerce **[★4778]**
Greater Gateway Assn. of Realtors **[1821]**, Glen Carbon, IL
Greater Girard Area Chamber of Commerce **[15323]**, Girard, OH
Greater Grand Rapids Assn. for Human Rsrc. Mgt. **[7958]**, Grand Rapids, MI
Greater Grand Rapids Convention Bur. **[★7950]**
Greater Grand Rapids Figure Skating Club **[7959]**, Grand Rapids, MI
Greater Green Bay Figure Skating Club **[18101]**, Green Bay, WI
Greater Greencastle Chamber of Commerce **[4817]**, Greencastle, IN
Greater Greenfield Chamber of Commerce **[4833]**, Greenfield, IN
Greater Greenfield Lions Club **[19017]**, Milwaukee, WI
Greater Greenwood Chamber of Commerce **[4849]**, Greenwood, IN
Greater Hamilton Chamber of Commerce **[15384]**, Hamilton, OH
Greater Hamilton Convention and Visitors Bur. **[15385]**, Hamilton, OH
Greater Harlan Bus. Assn. **[4898]**, Harlan, IN
Greater Harvard Area Chamber of Commerce **[1950]**, Harvard, IL
Greater Huron County United Way **[6821]**, Bad Axe, MI
Greater Indianapolis Chamber of Commerce **[5128]**, Indianapolis, IN
Greater Indianapolis Coun. on Alcoholism and Drug Dependence **[5129]**, Indianapolis, IN
Greater Indianapolis Literacy League - Indy Reads **[5130]**, Indianapolis, IN
Greater Intl. Falls Chamber of Commerce **[★11216]**
Greater Jackson Chamber of Commerce **[8366]**, Jackson, MI
Greater Kalamazoo Assn. of Realtors **[8428]**, Kalamazoo, MI
Greater Kalamazoo United Way **[8429]**, Kalamazoo, MI
Greater Knox Area Chamber of Commerce **[★5561]**
Greater La Porte Chamber of Commerce **[5596]**, La Porte, IN
Greater Lafayette Chamber of Commerce **[★5622]**
Greater Lafayette Community Development Corp. **[5612]**, Lafayette, IN
Greater Lafayette Convention and Visitors Bur. **[★5623]**
Greater Lafayette Progress **[★5624]**
Greater Lafayette Young Life **[6482]**, West Lafayette, IN
Greater Lakes Assn. of Realtors **[10388]**, Baxter, MN
Greater Lansing Assn. of Realtors **[8572]**, Lansing, MI
Greater Lansing Convention and Visitors Bur. **[8573]**, Lansing, MI
Greater Lansing Home Builders Assn. **[8574]**, Lansing, MI
Greater Lansing Orchid Soc. **[9269]**, Okemos, MI
Greater Lawrence County Area Chamber of Commerce **[16696]**, South Point, OH
Greater Lincolnshire Chamber of Commerce **[2284]**, Lincolnshire, IL
Greater Logan County Area Chamber of Commerce **[★13320]**
Greater Lorain Chamber of Commerce **[★15705]**
Greater Lorain County Chap. of the Soc. for Human Rsrc. Mgt. **[15114]**, Elyria, OH
Greater Loveland Historical Soc. **[15725]**, Loveland, OH
Greater Mackinaw Area Chamber of Commerce **[★8889]**
Greater Madison Area Soc. for Human Rsrc. Mgt. **[18516]**, Madison, WI
Greater Madison Chamber of Commerce **[18517]**, Madison, WI
Greater Madison Convention and Visitors Bur. **[18518]**, Madison, WI
Greater Madison Young Life **[19236]**, Mount Horeb, WI
Greater Mankato Area United Way **[11377]**, Mankato, MN
Greater Mankato Chamber of Commerce **[11378]**, Mankato, MN
Greater Marietta United Way **[15818]**, Marietta, OH
Greater Marion Area United Way **[2403]**, Marion, IL
Greater Martinsville Chamber of Commerce **[5752]**, Martinsville, IN
Greater Mauston Area Chamber of Commerce **[★18829]**
Greater Mauston Area Chamber of Commerce **[18829]**, Mauston, WI
Greater Mauston Area Development Corp. **[18830]**, Mauston, WI
Greater Menomonie Area Chamber of Commerce **[18881]**, Menomonie, WI
Greater Metropolitan Auto. Dealers Assn. of Minnesota **[10910]**, Edina, MN
Greater Michigan MSCA Student Chap. **[6945]**, Big Rapids, MI
Greater Midwest Rotorcraft - Popular Rotocraft Assn. Chap. 18 **[2218]**, Lansing, IL
Greater Milwaukee Assn. of Realtors **[19018]**, Milwaukee, WI
Greater Milwaukee Bowling Assn. **[19019]**, Milwaukee, WI
Greater Milwaukee Chap. of the Amer. Payroll Assn. **[19020]**, Milwaukee, WI
Greater Milwaukee Convention and Visitors Bur. **[★19148]**
Greater Milwaukee Dental Assn. **[20101]**, West Allis, WI
Greater Milwaukee Figure Skating Club **[19251]**, Mukwonago, WI
Greater Milwaukee St. Bernard Club **[19325]**, North Prairie, WI
Greater Minneapolis Convention and Visitors Assn. **[11570]**, Minneapolis, MN
Greater Minneapolis St. Paul Basset Hound Club **[11034]**, Fridley, MN
Greater Mitchell Chamber of Commerce **[5815]**, Mitchell, IN
Greater Mitchell St. Assn. **[19021]**, Milwaukee, WI
Greater Mohican Audubon Society **[13165]**, Ashland, OH
Greater Monticello Chamber of Commerce and Visitors Bur. **[5823]**, Monticello, IN
Greater Muncie Indiana Habitat for Humanity **[5876]**, Muncie, IN
Greater North Michigan Avenue Assn. **[908]**, Chicago, IL
Greater Northwest Indiana Assn. of Realtors **[5770]**, Merrillville, IN
Greater Ottawa County United Way **[8198]**, Holland, MI
Greater Palatine Chamber of Commerce and Indus. **[★2921]**
Greater Paw Paw Chamber of Commerce **[9346]**, Paw Paw, MI
Greater Peoria Contractors and Suppliers Assn. **[3022]**, Peoria, IL
Greater Pontiac Area Chamber of Commerce **[★9423]**
Greater Port Huron Area Chamber of Commerce **[9434]**, Port Huron, MI
Greater Portage Area Chamber of Commerce **[★19511]**
Greater Portage Chamber of Commerce **[6056]**, Portage, IN
Greater Portsmouth Area Bd. of Realtors **[17245]**, Wheelersburg, OH
Greater Powell Area Chamber of Commerce **[★16480]**
Greater Princeton Area Chamber of Commerce **[19543]**, Princeton, WI
Greater Racine Kennel Club **[19555]**, Racine, WI
Greater Romulus Chamber of Commerce **[9549]**, Romulus, MI
Greater Royal Oak Chamber of Commerce **[9582]**, Royal Oak, MI
Greater Saint Cloud RSVP **[12286]**, St. Cloud, MN
Greater Salem Chamber of Commerce **[3409]**, Salem, IL
Greater Scott County Chamber of Commerce **[6173]**, Scottsburg, IN
Greater Seymour Chamber of Commerce **[6181]**, Seymour, IN
Greater South Bend-Mishawaka Assn. of Realtors **[6229]**, South Bend, IN
Greater South Haven Area Chamber of Commerce **[9763]**, South Haven, MI
Greater Springfield Chamber of Commerce **[3556]**, Springfield, IL
Greater Stillwater Chamber of Commerce **[12719]**, Stillwater, MN
Greater Sycamore Chamber of Commerce **[★3748]**
Greater Terre Haute Chamber of Commerce **[6321]**, Terre Haute, IN
Greater Toledo Convention and Visitors Bur. **[16919]**, Toledo, OH
Greater Toledo Coun. of Teachers of Mathematics **[16405]**, Perrysburg, OH
Greater Toledo Orchid Soc. **[16771]**, Stony Ridge, OH
Greater Toledo Urban League **[16920]**, Toledo, OH
Greater Tomah Area Chamber of Commerce **[19904]**, Tomah, WI
Greater Twin Cities Golden Retriever Club **[12859]**, Wayzata, MN
Greater Twin Cities St. Bernard Club **[10947]**, Elk River, MN
Greater Twin Cities United Way **[11571]**, Minneapolis, MN
Greater Twin Cities Whippet Club **[12228]**, Roseville, MN
Greater Union Grove Area Chamber of Commerce **[19926]**, Union Grove, WI
Greater Valparaiso Chamber of Commerce **[6383]**, Valparaiso, IN
Greater Wabash Regional Planning Commn. **[15]**, Albion, IL
Greater Wabash Valley SCORE **[6322]**, Terre Haute, IN
Greater Waunakee Area Chamber of Commerce **[★20019]**
Greater Wayzata Area Chamber of Commerce **[12860]**, Wayzata, MN
Greater West Bloomfield Chamber of Commerce **[10114]**, West Bloomfield, MI
Greater Wheeling Area Youth Outreach **[2586]**, Mount Prospect, IL
Greater Woodfield Convention and Visitors Bur. **[3436]**, Schaumburg, IL
Greater Zionsville Chamber of Commerce **[6550]**, Zionsville, IN
Greek
Amer. Hellenic Educational Progressive Assn. - Alton, Chap. 304 **[38]**, Alton, IL
Amer. Hellenic Educational Progressive Assn. - Beverly Hills, Chap. 350 **[2874]**, Orland Park, IL
Amer. Hellenic Educational Progressive Assn. - Chicago, Chap. 46 **[2582]**, Mount Prospect, IL
Amer. Hellenic Educational Progressive Assn. - Chicago/Logan, Chap. 260 **[1854]**, Glenview, IL
Amer. Hellenic Educational Progressive Assn. - Decatur, Chap. 457 **[1372]**, Decatur, IL
Amer. Hellenic Educational Progressive Assn. - District 11 **[17169]**, West Chester, OH
Amer. Hellenic Educational Progressive Assn. - DuPage, Chap. 423 **[4]**, Addison, IL
Amer. Hellenic Educational Progressive Assn. - Evanston, Chap. 204 **[621]**, Chicago, IL
Amer. Hellenic Educational Progressive Assn. - Garfield, Chap. 203 **[3198]**, River Forest, IL
Amer. Hellenic Educational Progressive Assn. - Joliet, Chap. 131 **[3098]**, Plainfield, IL

Amer. Hellenic Educational Progressive Assn. - Kankakee, Chap. 345 **[332]**, Bradley, IL
Amer. Hellenic Educational Progressive Assn. - Lincolnwood, Chap. 396 **[3480]**, Skokie, IL
Amer. Hellenic Educational Progressive Assn. - Madison, Chap. 369 **[18461]**, Madison, WI
Amer. Hellenic Educational Progressive Assn. - Milo, Chap. 348 **[622]**, Chicago, IL
Amer. Hellenic Educational Progressive Assn. - Milwaukee, Chap. 43 **[17662]**, Brookfield, WI
Amer. Hellenic Educational Progressive Assn. - Northshore, Chap. 94 **[623]**, Chicago, IL
Amer. Hellenic Educational Progressive Assn. - Northwestern, Chap. 388 **[624]**, Chicago, IL
Amer. Hellenic Educational Progressive Assn. - Oaklawn-Englewood, Chap. 323 **[367]**, Burbank, IL
Amer. Hellenic Educational Progressive Assn. - Racine, Chap. 377 **[19475]**, Pleasant Prairie, WI
Amer. Hellenic Educational Progressive Assn. - Shoreline, Chap. 380 **[625]**, Chicago, IL
Amer. Hellenic Educational Progressive Assn. - South Chicago, Chap. 351 **[2234]**, Lemont, IL
Amer. Hellenic Educational Progressive Assn. - Waukegan, Chap. 218 **[2255]**, Libertyville, IL
Amer. Hellenic Educational Progressive Assn. - West Suburban, Chap. 202 **[1357]**, Darien, IL
Amer. Hellenic Educational Progressive Assn. - Woodlawn, Chap. 93 **[2934]**, Palos Heights, IL
Green Bay Area Chamber of Commerce **[18102]**, Green Bay, WI
Green Bay Chap. Chief Petty Officers Assn. **[18103]**, Green Bay, WI
Green Bay Chess Assn. **[18104]**, Green Bay, WI
Green Bay Curling Club **[18105]**, Green Bay, WI
Green Bay Educ. Assn. **[18106]**, Green Bay, WI
Green Bay Film Soc. **[18107]**, Green Bay, WI
Green Bay Rackers Homebrewing Club **[18319]**, Kewaunee, WI
Green Camp Lions Club **[16486]**, Prospect, OH
Green Chamber of Commerce **[15350]**, Green, OH
Green County Historical Soc. **[19214]**, Monroe, WI
Green Energy Ohio **[14448]**, Columbus, OH
Green Lake Area Chamber of Commerce **[18146]**, Green Lake, WI
Green Oaks - Libertyville - Mundelein - Vernon Hills Area Chamber of Commerce and Liberty **[★2259]**
Green Party of Minnesota **[11572]**, Minneapolis, MN
Green Point Flyers Assn. **[8505]**, Lake City, MI
Green-Rock Audubon Soc. **[17610]**, Beloit, WI
Green-Rock Audubon Soc. **[18249]**, Janesville, WI
Green Springs Lions Club **[15352]**, Green Springs, OH
Greenbush Lions Club **[11099]**, Greenbush, MN
Greencastle Chamber of Commerce **[★4817]**
Greendale Chamber of Commerce **[18150]**, Greendale, WI
Greendale Lions Club **[18151]**, Greendale, WI
Greene County Bd. of Realtors **[5683]**, Linton, IN
Greene County Chap. of the Ohio Genealogical Soc. **[17369]**, Xenia, OH
Greene County Coin Club **[4192]**, Bloomfield, IN
Greene County Convention and Visitors Bur. **[13297]**, Beavercreek, OH
Greene County Historical Soc. **[17370]**, Xenia, OH
Greene County Right To Life **[17371]**, Xenia, OH
Greenfield Chamber of Commerce **[18155]**, Greenfield, WI
Greenhouse and Museum Assn; Lorain County Tropical **[15706]**, Lorain, OH
Greening of Detroit **[7370]**, Detroit, MI
Greensburg Decatur County Chamber of Commerce **[4843]**, Greensburg, IN
Greenville Area Chamber of Commerce **[8067]**, Greenville, MI
Greenville Chamber of Commerce **[1907]**, Greenville, IL
Greenville Lions Club - Michigan **[8068]**, Greenville, MI
Greenville Lions Club - Wisconsin **[18164]**, Greenville, WI
Greenway Lions Club **[10499]**, Bovey, MN
Greenwood Chamber of Commerce **[18165]**, Greenwood, WI
Greyhound
Michigan Greyhound Connection **[6931]**, Berkley, MI
GriefNet **[6703]**, Ann Arbor, MI
Griefshare **[3819]**, Urbana, IL
Griffith Chamber of Commerce **[4857]**, Griffith, IN
Grocers Assn; Michigan **[8670]**, Lansing, MI
Grocers Assn; Youngstown Area **[17423]**, Youngstown, OH
Grosse Ile Lions Club **[8074]**, Grosse Ile, MI
Grosse Pointe Bd. of Realtors **[8082]**, Grosse Pointe, MI
Grosse Pointe Historical Soc. **[8088]**, Grosse Pointe Farms, MI
Grosse Pointe Lacrosse Assn. **[8089]**, Grosse Pointe Farms, MI
Grosse Pointe Lions Club **[8083]**, Grosse Pointe, MI
Grounds Management
Grounds Managers Assn. **[14136]**, Cleveland, OH
Professional Grounds Mgt. Soc., Greater Cincinnati **[13962]**, Cincinnati, OH
Professional Grounds Mgt. Soc., Midwest Region **[16312]**, Orrville, OH
Grounds Managers Assn. **[14136]**, Cleveland, OH
Groundswell Inc. of Minnesota **[12836]**, Wanda, MN
Grove City Area Chamber of Commerce **[15368]**, Grove City, OH
Grove City Lions Club **[11101]**, Grove City, MN
Grove City Lions Club - Ohio **[15369]**, Grove City, OH
Grove City Noon Lions Club **[17213]**, Westerville, OH
Grove City, OH - Young Life **[14449]**, Columbus, OH
Groveland Township Firefighters and Dive Team Assn. **[8235]**, Holly, MI
Groveport-Madison Area Chamber of Commerce **[★15374]**
Groveport Madison Lions Club **[13518]**, Canal Winchester, OH
Growers Association; Wisconsin Potato and Vegetable **[17480]**, Antigo, WI
Growth Assn. of Southwestern Illinois **[1874]**, Godfrey, IL
Growth Coun; Daviess County **[6458]**, Washington, IN
Grygla Lions Club **[11103]**, Grygla, MN
GT Corp. Empowerment Org. **[13509]**, Campbell, OH
Guernsey - Wyldlife **[13498]**, Cambridge, OH
Guild Incorporated **[12879]**, West St. Paul, MN
Gull Area Lakes Assn. **[11897]**, Nisswa, MN
Gull Lake Area Property Owners Assn. **[★11897]**
Gun Club; Charlevoix Rod and **[7116]**, Charlevoix, MI
Gun River Skeet and Trap **[9386]**, Plainwell, MI
Gun Violence; Hoosiers Concerned about **[5148]**, Indianapolis, IN
G.V. Black District Dental Soc. **[3557]**, Springfield, IL
Gymnastics
Midwest Twisters Gymnastics Booster Club **[19332]**, Oak Creek, WI
Gymnastics Booster Club; Midwest Twisters **[19332]**, Oak Creek, WI

H

Habitat Comm; Lake Chapeau **[10259]**, Albert Lea, MN
Habitat For Humanity Milwaukee **[19022]**, Milwaukee, WI
Habitat for Humanity Alpena Area **[6642]**, Alpena, MI
Habitat for Humanity of Ashland County **[13166]**, Ashland, OH
Habitat for Humanity Barry County **[8157]**, Hastings, MI
Habitat for Humanity of Boone County **[5669]**, Lebanon, IN
Habitat for Humanity of Champaign County **[522]**, Champaign, IL
Habitat for Humanity Cheboygan County **[7134]**, Cheboygan, MI
Habitat for Humanity Chicago South Suburbs **[1250]**, Chicago Heights, IL
Habitat for Humanity; Cincinnati **[13786]**, Cincinnati, OH
Habitat for Humanity in Crawford County, Ohio **[15285]**, Galion, OH
Habitat for Humanity of Dane County **[18519]**, Madison, WI
Habitat for Humanity Detroit **[7371]**, Detroit, MI
Habitat for Humanity of Dodge County, Wisconsin **[17594]**, Beaver Dam, WI
Habitat for Humanity of Fairfield County **[15601]**, Lancaster, OH
Habitat for Humanity of Fond du Lac County **[17982]**, Fond du Lac, WI
Habitat for Humanity of Geauga County **[16192]**, Newbury, OH
Habitat for Humanity of Genesee County **[7740]**, Flint, MI
Habitat for Humanity of Greater Canton **[13567]**, Canton, OH
Habitat for Humanity of Greater Indianapolis **[5131]**, Indianapolis, IN
Habitat for Humanity of the Greater Marion Area **[2404]**, Marion, IL
Habitat for Humanity of the Greater Peoria Area **[3023]**, Peoria, IL
Habitat for Humanity of Greene County **[17372]**, Xenia, OH
Habitat for Humanity Hamilton County **[6510]**, Westfield, IN
Habitat for Humanity of Huron Valley **[6704]**, Ann Arbor, MI
Habitat for Humanity of Illinois **[2889]**, Oswego, IL
Habitat for Humanity of Jo Daviess County **[1764]**, Galena, IL
Habitat for Humanity of Kent County **[7960]**, Grand Rapids, MI
Habitat for Humanity of La Salle, Bur., and Putnam Counties **[2181]**, La Salle, IL
Habitat for Humanity of Lafayette **[5613]**, Lafayette, IN
Habitat for Humanity Lake County, Illinois **[3923]**, Waukegan, IL
Habitat for Humanity of Lenawee County **[6569]**, Adrian, MI
Habitat for Humanity - Lima Area **[15654]**, Lima, OH
Habitat for Humanity of Lyon County, Minnesota **[11433]**, Marshall, MN
Habitat for Humanity Macomb County **[7177]**, Clinton Township, MI
Habitat for Humanity of Mahoning County **[17402]**, Youngstown, OH
Habitat for Humanity of Mason County, Michigan **[8870]**, Ludington, MI
Habitat for Humanity; Maumee Valley **[16929]**, Toledo, OH
Habitat for Humanity of Mc Lean County Illinois **[278]**, Bloomington, IL
Habitat for Humanity of Michigan **[8575]**, Lansing, MI
Habitat for Humanity - MidWest Region **[909]**, Chicago, IL
Habitat for Humanity of Minnesota **[11573]**, Minneapolis, MN
Habitat for Humanity of Monroe County, Indiana **[4224]**, Bloomington, IN
Habitat for Humanity of Morgan County, Indiana **[5753]**, Martinsville, IN
Habitat for Humanity of Morrison County **[11334]**, Little Falls, MN
Habitat for Humanity of Morrow County **[16069]**, Mount Gilead, OH
Habitat for Humanity of Niles-Buchanan Area **[9208]**, Niles, MI
Habitat for Humanity of Northern Columbiana County **[16587]**, Salem, OH
Habitat for Humanity of Northern Fox Valley **[3945]**, West Dundee, IL
Habitat for Humanity of Oakland County **[9417]**, Pontiac, MI
Habitat for Humanity of Oshkosh **[19393]**, Oshkosh, WI
Habitat for Humanity of Paulding County **[16387]**, Paulding, OH
Habitat for Humanity of Portage County **[16498]**, Ravenna, OH
Habitat for Humanity of Prairie Lakes **[11054]**, Glenwood, MN
Habitat for Humanity of Presque Isle County **[9541]**, Rogers City, MI
Habitat for Humanity; Racine **[19569]**, Racine, WI
Habitat for Humanity of St. Joseph County, IN **[6230]**, South Bend, IN
Habitat for Humanity Sangamon County **[3558]**, Springfield, IL
Habitat for Humanity of South Central Minnesota **[11379]**, Mankato, MN

Habitat for Humanity of Waukesha **[18871]**, Menomonee Falls, WI
Habitat for Humanity in Wayne County, Ohio **[17318]**, Wooster, OH
Habitat for Humanity of West Central Minnesota **[12916]**, Willmar, MN
Habitat for Humanity Western Wayne County **[9400]**, Plymouth, MI
Habitat for Humanity of Whitley County **[4381]**, Columbia City, IN
Habitat for Humanity Winona County, Minnesota **[12951]**, Winona, MN
Hadi Shriners **[4550]**, Evansville, IN
Hadley Wyld Life **[1833]**, Glen Ellyn, IL
Hagerstown Lions Club **[4863]**, Hagerstown, IN
Haigh PTA **[7260]**, Dearborn, MI
Haiti
Hearts for Haiti **[13113]**, Alliance, OH
Halderman Real Estate Services - Halderman Farm Mgt. **[6424]**, Wabash, IN
Hall of Fame and Women's Historical Center; Women's **[★8728]**
Hallock Lions Club **[11108]**, Hallock, MN
Halstad Lions Club **[11110]**, Halstad, MN
Hamel Lions Club **[11114]**, Hamel, MN
Hamilton Area Chamber of Commerce **[4864]**, Hamilton, IN
Hamilton Chamber of Commerce **[4865]**, Hamilton, IN
Hamilton Community Development Coalition **[1928]**, Hamilton, IL
Hamilton County Alliance **[5132]**, Indianapolis, IN
Hamilton County Bd. of Mental Retardation and Developmental Disabilities **[13858]**, Cincinnati, OH
Hamilton County Chamber of Commerce **[13859]**, Cincinnati, OH
Hamilton County Chamber of Commerce and Economic Development Commn. **[2466]**, McLeansboro, IL
Hamilton County Compeer **[13860]**, Cincinnati, OH
Hamilton County First Steps Coun. **[5971]**, Noblesville, IN
Hamilton County Sertoma Club **[5972]**, Noblesville, IN
Hamilton County Sheriffs Dept. Chaplaincy **[5973]**, Noblesville, IN
Hamilton Dog Training Club **[15158]**, Fairfield, OH
Hamilton Fairfield Oxford Bd. of Realtors **[15159]**, Fairfield, OH
Hamilton Middletown Beagle Club **[15317]**, Germantown, OH
Hamilton, Ohio City of Sculpture **[15386]**, Hamilton, OH
Hamilton Park Neighborhood Association **[3024]**, Peoria, IL
Hamilton - Young Life **[8199]**, Holland, MI
Hamilton - Young Life **[15160]**, Fairfield, OH
Hammon Chamber of Commerce **[★4887]**
Hammond Urban Enterprise Assn. **[4881]**, Hammond, IN
Hampshire Area Chamber of Commerce **[1930]**, Hampshire, IL
Hampshire Chamber of Commerce **[★1930]**
Hampton Elementary PTA **[7372]**, Detroit, MI
Hancock County Sheriff Reserve Deputy Corps **[466]**, Carthage, IL
Hancock Lions Club **[11115]**, Hancock, MN
Handicapped; Share Found. with the **[6136]**, Rolling Prairie, IN
Hands of Hope **[13056]**, Akron, OH
Handshake Beagle Club **[1894]**, Grayslake, IL
Hanover-Horton Lions Club **[8367]**, Jackson, MI
Harbor Beach Chamber of Commerce **[8115]**, Harbor Beach, MI
Harbor Country Chamber of Commerce **[9186]**, New Buffalo, MI
Harbor Habitat for Humanity **[6919]**, Benton Harbor, MI
Harbor Historical Soc; Fairport **[15178]**, Fairport Harbor, OH
Harbor Springs Chamber of Commerce **[8118]**, Harbor Springs, MI
Harcatus RSVP **[16150]**, New Philadelphia, OH
Hard of Hearing; Central Minnesota Self-Help for **[12117]**, Robbinsdale, MN
Hardin County Chamber of Commerce **[15553]**, Kenton, OH
Hardware
Fox Valley Chap. of Assoc. Locksmiths of Am. **[19392]**, Oshkosh, WI
Midwest Hardware Assn. **[19793]**, Stevens Point, WI
Minnesota Chap. of Assoc. Locksmiths of Am. **[10552]**, Brooklyn Park, MN
Northern Indiana Chap. of Assoc. Locksmiths of Am. **[4705]**, Fort Wayne, IN
Ohio North Coast Chap. of Assoc. Locksmiths of Am. **[16058]**, Monroeville, OH
Ohio Valley Chap. of Assoc. Locksmiths of Am. **[15563]**, Kettering, OH
Wisconsin Indianhead Chap. of Assoc. Locksmiths of Am. **[17759]**, Chippewa Falls, WI
Hardwood Country Sportsman's Club **[12256]**, Rushford, MN
Harmony Lions Club **[11119]**, Harmony, MN
Harper Woods Lions Club **[9658]**, St. Clair Shores, MI
Harrison Area Chamber of Commerce **[★8126]**
Harrison Chamber of Commerce **[8126]**, Harrison, MI
Harrison High School - Young Life **[6483]**, West Lafayette, IN
Harrison Lions Club - Michigan **[8127]**, Harrison, MI
Harrison Regional Chamber of Commerce **[13481]**, Cadiz, OH
Harrison Regional Chamber of Commerce and Tourism Info. **[★13481]**
Harrison St. Cooperative of Performing and Fine Arts **[2811]**, Oak Park, IL
Hart Lions Club **[8136]**, Hart, MI
Hart - Silver Lake Mears Chamber of Commerce **[8137]**, Hart, MI
Hartford Area Chamber of Commerce **[18177]**, Hartford, WI
Hartford City Chamber of Commerce **[4903]**, Hartford City, IN
Hartford Lions Club - Michigan **[8139]**, Hartford, MI
Hartford Youth Baseball and Softball **[15408]**, Hartford, OH
Hartland Area Chamber of Commerce **[18183]**, Hartland, WI
Hartland Lions Club **[8143]**, Hartland, MI
Hartville Lions Club **[15410]**, Hartville, OH
Harvest Community Development Corporation **[7373]**, Detroit, MI
Hastings Area Chamber of Commerce and Tourism Bur. **[11125]**, Hastings, MN
Havana Area Chamber of Commerce **[1959]**, Havana, IL
Hawks Inn Historical Soc. **[17823]**, Delafield, WI
Hawley Lions Club **[11135]**, Hawley, MN
Hawthorne Valley Skeet Club **[13231]**, Aurora, OH
Hayesville Lions Club **[16452]**, Polk, OH
Hayfield Lions Club **[11137]**, Hayfield, MN
Hayward Area Chamber of Commerce **[18195]**, Hayward, WI
Hayward Figure Skating Club **[18196]**, Hayward, WI
Hayward - YoungLife **[16730]**, Springfield, OH
Head Injury
Brain Injury Assn. of Illinois **[771]**, Chicago, IL
Brain Injury Assn. of Indiana **[5061]**, Indianapolis, IN
Brain Injury Assn. of Michigan **[7009]**, Brighton, MI
Brain Injury Assn. of Wisconsin **[20071]**, Wauwatosa, WI
Head Injury Found. - Indiana **[★5061]**
Head of the Lakes Youth for Christ **[10824]**, Duluth, MN
Headwaters AIFA **[10375]**, Bagley, MN
Headwaters Search and Rescue Dog Assn. **[17847]**, Eagle River, WI
Health
Assn. of Ohio Hea. Commissioners **[14328]**, Columbus, OH
Community Hea. Partners of Ohio Consolidated **[15702]**, Lorain, OH
Grant Regional Hea. Center Auxiliary **[18410]**, Lancaster, WI
Hea. and Medicine Policy Res. Gp. **[910]**, Chicago, IL
Hea. Partners **[11574]**, Minneapolis, MN
Indiana Hea. Care Assn. **[5244]**, Indianapolis, IN
Michigan Hea. Coun. **[9280]**, Okemos, MI
Michigan Hea. and Hosp. Assn. **[8671]**, Lansing, MI
Myasthenia Gravis Assn. **[9810]**, Southfield, MI
North Central Region Hea. Ministries Network **[11712]**, Minneapolis, MN
Ohio Hea. Care Assn., District 1 **[13939]**, Cincinnati, OH
Ohio Hea. Care Assn., District 2 **[14937]**, Dayton, OH
Ohio Hea. Care Assn., District 3 **[15666]**, Lima, OH
Ohio Hea. Care Assn., District 4 **[16830]**, Sylvania, OH
Ohio Hea. Care Assn., District 5 **[16291]**, Oberlin, OH
Ohio Hea. Care Assn., District 6 **[16087]**, Mount Vernon, OH
Ohio Hea. Care Assn., District 7 **[14622]**, Columbus, OH
Ohio Hea. Care Assn., District 8 **[15448]**, Hillsboro, OH
Ohio Hea. Care Assn., District 9 **[13670]**, Chillicothe, OH
Ohio Hea. Care Assn., District 10 **[15031]**, Dover, OH
Ohio Hea. Care Assn., District 11 **[15680]**, Lisbon, OH
Ohio Hea. Care Assn., District 12 **[13077]**, Akron, OH
Ohio Hea. Care Assn., District 13 **[13347]**, Berea, OH
Ohio Hea. Care Assn., District 14 **[15749]**, Madison, OH
Ohio Hea. Care Assn., District 15 **[16818]**, Swanton, OH
Wisconsin Hea. Care Assn. **[18710]**, Madison, WI
Wisconsin Hea. Care Assn., District 1 **[18314]**, Kenosha, WI
Wisconsin Hea. Care Assn., District 2 **[19868]**, Sun Prairie, WI
Wisconsin Hea. Care Assn., District 3 **[19665]**, Sauk City, WI
Wisconsin Hea. Care Assn., District 5 **[18172]**, Hales Corners, WI
Wisconsin Hea. Care Assn., District 6 **[17731]**, Cedarburg, WI
Wisconsin Hea. Care Assn., District 7 **[17478]**, Antigo, WI
Wisconsin Hea. Care Assn., District 8 **[18140]**, Green Bay, WI
Wisconsin Hea. Care Assn., District 9 **[17639]**, Blair, WI
Wisconsin Hea. Care Assn., District 10 **[17911]**, Eau Claire, WI
Wisconsin Hea. Care Assn., District 11 **[19451]**, Phelps, WI
Wisconsin Hea. Care Assn., District 12 **[18852]**, Mellen, WI
Women Hea. Executives Network **[2152]**, Kenilworth, IL
Hea. Agencies in Illinois; Natl. Voluntary **[★854]**
Hea. Assn; Indiana Environmental **[5231]**, Indianapolis, IN
Health Care
Alliance for Hea. **[7881]**, Grand Rapids, MI
Chicago Asthma Consortium **[791]**, Chicago, IL
Community Behavioral Healthcare Assn. of Illinois **[3546]**, Springfield, IL
Endometriosis Assn. **[19005]**, Milwaukee, WI
Executive Women in Hea.Care **[5112]**, Indianapolis, IN
Family Hea. Partnership Clinic **[4055]**, Woodstock, IL
Greater Cincinnati Hea. Coun. **[13848]**, Cincinnati, OH
Hospice Patients Alliance **[9524]**, Rockford, MI
Illinois Campaign for Better Hea. Care **[931]**, Chicago, IL
Illinois Primary Hea. Care Assn. **[958]**, Chicago, IL
Illinois Soc. for Respiratory Care **[3210]**, Riverdale, IL
Indiana Primary Hea. Care Assn. **[5281]**, Indianapolis, IN
LifeCare Alliance **[14493]**, Columbus, OH
Michigan Soc. for Respiratory Care **[6737]**, Ann Arbor, MI

Midwest Healthcare Marketing Assn. **[2646]**, Naperville, IL
Minnesota Soc. of Health-System Pharmacists **[11795]**, Minnetonka, MN
Minnesota Soc. for Respiratory Care **[12523]**, St. Paul, MN
Ohio Assn. of Hea. Plans **[14554]**, Columbus, OH
Ohio Hea. Info. Mgt. Assn. **[17349]**, Worthington, OH
SMA Support **[5587]**, Kokomo, IN
Special Needs Network **[3855]**, Vernon Hills, IL
Visiting Nurses Assn. **[3328]**, Rockford, IL
Wellness Coun. of Indiana **[5779]**, Merrillville, IN
Wisconsin Assn. for Perinatal Care **[18662]**, Madison, WI
Wisconsin Hosp. Assn. **[18713]**, Madison, WI
Wisconsin Primary Hea. Care Assn. **[18743]**, Madison, WI
Wisconsin Soc. for Respiratory Care **[18879]**, Menomonee Falls, WI
Hea. Care Assn; Illinois **[3606]**, Springfield, IL
Health Care Products
Indiana Medical Device Manufacturers Coun. **[5259]**, Indianapolis, IN
Michigan Medical Device Assn. **[8283]**, Howell, MI
Ohio Assn. of Medical Equip. Services **[14558]**, Columbus, OH
Hea. Care Public Relations and Marketing Soc. for Southeastern Wisconsin **[18886]**, Mequon, WI
Hea. Center Auxiliary; Grant Regional **[18410]**, Lancaster, WI
Hea. Charities of Illinois; Community **[854]**, Chicago, IL
Hea. Clinics Org; Michigan Rural **[7799]**, Fremont, MI
Hea. Counselors Assn; Michigan Mental **[9506]**, Rochester, MI
Health Education
Community Hea. Info. Collaborative **[10810]**, Duluth, MN
Health Education; Comprehensive **[18996]**, Milwaukee, WI
Hea. Found; Centracare **[12277]**, St. Cloud, MN
Hea. Info. Collaborative; Community **[10810]**, Duluth, MN
Hea. Info. Mgt. Assn; Indiana **[5518]**, Ireland, IN
Hea. Info. Mgt. Assn; Michigan **[9148]**, Muskegon, MI
Hea. Info. Mgt. Assn; Wisconsin **[18383]**, La Crosse, WI
Hea. and Medicine Policy Res. Gp. **[910]**, Chicago, IL
Hea; Michigan Assn. for Infant Mental **[9837]**, Southgate, MI
Hea; Michigan Assn. for Local Public **[8620]**, Lansing, MI
Hea. Ministries Network; North Central Region **[11712]**, Minneapolis, MN
Hea. Partners **[11574]**, Minneapolis, MN
Hea. Partners Select **[★17234]**
Hea., Physical Educ., Recreation, and Dance; Illinois Assn. for **[2078]**, Jacksonville, IL
Hea., Physical Educ., Recreation and Dance; Ohio Assn. for **[13245]**, Avon Lake, OH
Hea. Physics Soc., Northern Ohio Chap. **[16546]**, Rocky River, OH
Health Plans
Michigan Assn. of Hea. Plans **[8617]**, Lansing, MI
Wisconsin Assn. of Hea. Plans **[18653]**, Madison, WI
Hea. Practitioner Certification Bd; Public **[1159]**, Chicago, IL
Health Professionals
Illinois Coun. of Hea. Sys. Pharmacists **[2349]**, Loves Park, IL
Indiana Dental Hygienists' Assn. **[5226]**, Indianapolis, IN
Physicians for Social Responsibility, Chicago **[1137]**, Chicago, IL
Physicians for Social Responsibility, Madison **[18598]**, Madison, WI
Physicians for Social Responsibility, Northeast Ohio **[14248]**, Cleveland Heights, OH
Physicians for Social Responsibility, Southeast Wisconsin **[20156]**, Whitefish Bay, WI
Wisconsin Assn. of Hea. Underwriters **[18654]**, Madison, WI
Hea.-Related Scis. Alumni Assn; Mayo School of **[12154]**, Rochester, MN
Health Services
Austin-Bailey Hea. and Wellness Found. **[13548]**, Canton, OH
Centracare Hea. Found. **[12277]**, St. Cloud, MN
Community Nutrition Network and Senior Services Assn. of Cook County **[855]**, Chicago, IL
Consortium of Hea.y and Immunized Communities **[16358]**, Parma, OH
Illinois School Hea. Assn. **[2720]**, Normal, IL
Indiana Speech-Language-Hearing Assn. **[5310]**, Indianapolis, IN
Michigan Rural Hea. Clinics Org. **[7799]**, Fremont, MI
North Central Coll. Hea. Assn. **[18587]**, Madison, WI
Ohio Assn. of Ambulatory Surgery Centers **[17234]**, Westlake, OH
Ohio Primary Care Assn. **[14656]**, Columbus, OH
Hea. and Wellness Found; Austin-Bailey **[13548]**, Canton, OH
Healthcare Consumer Advocacy of the Amer. Hosp. Assn; Soc. for **[1189]**, Chicago, IL
Hea.care Engg; Indiana Soc. for **[5303]**, Indianapolis, IN
Hea.Care; Executive Women in **[5112]**, Indianapolis, IN
Healthcare Executives Assn. of Northeast Ohio **[13636]**, Chagrin Falls, OH
Healthcare Financial Mgt. Assn., Central Ohio Chap. **[14450]**, Columbus, OH
Healthcare Financial Mgt. Assn., Eastern Michigan Chap. **[10076]**, Washington, MI
Healthcare Financial Mgt. Assn., First Illinois Chap. **[1954]**, Harvey, IL
Healthcare Financial Mgt. Assn., Indiana Pressler Memorial Chap. **[5836]**, Mooresville, IN
Healthcare Financial Mgt. Assn., Minnesota Chap. **[11575]**, Minneapolis, MN
Healthcare Financial Mgt. Assn., Northeast Ohio Chap. **[14137]**, Cleveland, OH
Healthcare Financial Mgt. Assn., Northwest Ohio Chap. **[16921]**, Toledo, OH
Healthcare Financial Mgt. Assn., Southern Illinois Chap. **[2089]**, Jerseyville, IL
Healthcare Financial Mgt. Assn., Southwestern Ohio Chap. **[13861]**, Cincinnati, OH
Healthcare Financial Mgt. Assn., Western Michigan Chap. **[7961]**, Grand Rapids, MI
Healthcare Financial Mgt. Assn., Wisconsin Chap. **[19288]**, New Berlin, WI
Healthcare Marketing Assn; Midwest **[2646]**, Naperville, IL
Hea.y Babies Coalition; Hea.y Mothers/ **[★8167]**
Hea.y Communities Hea.y Youth **[1919]**, Gurnee, IL
Hea.y Mothers/Hea.y Babies Coalition **[★8167]**
Hearing Assn; Michigan Speech-Language- **[7549]**, East Lansing, MI
Hearing Assn; Minnesota Speech-Language- **[12337]**, St. Louis Park, MN
Hearing Impaired
Assn. of Late-Deafened Adults - Chicago **[194]**, Bedford Park, IL
Assn. of Late-Deafened Adults - Freeport **[1337]**, Dakota, IL
Assn. of Late-Deafened Adults - Midwest **[14326]**, Columbus, OH
Central Minnesota Self-Help for Hard of Hearing **[12117]**, Robbinsdale, MN
CISG Chap. of Northern Indiana and Southwestern Michigan **[4809]**, Granger, IN
Cochlear Implant Club Minnesota **[12403]**, St. Paul, MN
Hearing Loss Assn. of Am., Michigan **[9991]**, Troy, MI
Hearing Loss Assn. of Am., Ohio **[14451]**, Columbus, OH
Hearing Loss Assn. of Am., Wisconsin **[19272]**, Neenah, WI
Illinois Cochlear Implant Club **[1504]**, Downers Grove, IL
Michigan Assn. for Deaf, Hearing and Speech Sers. **[8612]**, Lansing, MI
Michigan Speech-Language-Hearing Assn. **[7549]**, East Lansing, MI
West Michigan Cochlear Implant Club **[8019]**, Grand Rapids, MI
Wisconsin Alliance of Hearing Professionals **[18644]**, Madison, WI
Hearing Loss Assn. of Am., Michigan **[9991]**, Troy, MI
Hearing Loss Assn. of Am., Ohio **[14451]**, Columbus, OH
Hearing Loss Assn. of Am., Wisconsin **[19272]**, Neenah, WI
Hearing Professionals; Wisconsin Alliance of **[18644]**, Madison, WI
Hearing and Speech Sers; Michigan Assn. for Deaf, **[8612]**, Lansing, MI
Heart of Am. Keeshond Club **[12896]**, White Bear Lake, MN
Heart of Am. Scottish Terrier Club **[10727]**, Cottage Grove, MN
Heart Disease
Lucky Hearts Support Gp. **[3910]**, Watseka, IL
Heart of Illinois Chap. - MOAA **[3025]**, Peoria, IL
Heart of Illinois United Way **[3026]**, Peoria, IL
Heart of Lakes Chap. of the United Way **[10279]**, Alexandria, MN
Heart of Michigan English Cocker Spaniel **[7741]**, Flint, MI
Heart of Ohio Angus Assn. **[15244]**, Fredericktown, OH
Heart of Ohio Hikers 522 **[14452]**, Columbus, OH
Heart Res. Assn; Pediatric **[17178]**, West Chester, OH
Heart and Scroll Romance Writers of Am. **[2713]**, Normal, IL
Heart of the Valley Chamber of Commerce **[18287]**, Kaukauna, WI
Heart of West Michigan United Way **[7962]**, Grand Rapids, MI
Heart of Wisconsin Bus. and Economic Alliance **[20186]**, Wisconsin Rapids, WI
Heart of Wisconsin District Nurses Assn. - No. 5 **[20187]**, Wisconsin Rapids, WI
Heartland Alliance for Human Needs and Human Rights **[911]**, Chicago, IL
Heartland Bd. of Realtors **[15204]**, Findlay, OH
Heartland Dairy Goat Club **[3780]**, Toulon, IL
Heartland Peruvian Horse Club **[5994]**, North Vernon, IN
Heartland Water Rsrcs. Coun. **[3027]**, Peoria, IL
Hearts At Home **[2714]**, Normal, IL
Hearts for Haiti **[13113]**, Alliance, OH
Hearts United Association **[2306]**, Litchfield, IL
Hearty Sole Walkers **[17983]**, Fond du Lac, WI
Heath High School - Young Life **[15343]**, Granville, OH
Heath Lions Club **[15413]**, Heath, OH
Heather McNally Milko **[14138]**, Cleveland, OH
Heating and Cooling
ACCA Northeast Wisconsin **[19384]**, Oshkosh, WI
Air Conditioning Contractors of Am., Akron Canton Chap. **[16645]**, Sharon Center, OH
Air Conditioning Contractors of Am., Greater Cincinnati Chap. **[13694]**, Cincinnati, OH
Air Conditioning Contractors of Am., Greater Cleveland Chap. **[15742]**, Macedonia, OH
Air Conditioning Contractors of Am., Greater Dayton Chap. **[15040]**, Dublin, OH
Air Conditioning Contractors of Am., Indiana Chap. **[4965]**, Indianapolis, IN
Air Conditioning Contractors of Am., Northeast Wisconsin Chap. **[19386]**, Oshkosh, WI
Air Conditioning Contractors of Am. - Ohio Chap. **[13627]**, Chagrin Falls, OH
Air Conditioning Contractors of Am., Southern Illinois Chap. **[3869]**, Virden, IL
Air Conditioning Contractors of Am., Wabash Valley Chap. **[6303]**, Terre Haute, IN
Air Conditioning Contractors of Am., West Michigan Chap. **[9192]**, Newaygo, MI
Builders Assn. of Eastern Ohio and Western Pennsylvania **[17069]**, Vienna, OH
Chicagoland Sheet Metal Contractors Assn. **[216]**, Bellwood, IL
Decatur Sheet Metal Contractors Assn. **[1390]**, Decatur, IL
East Central Wisconsin Sheet Metal Contractors Assn. **[19693]**, Sheboygan, WI
Five Cities Assn. of Michigan **[8986]**, Mattawan, MI
Fort Wayne Area Sheet Metal Contractors Assn. **[6054]**, Poneto, IN

Illinois Enval. Balancing Bur. **[940]**, Chicago, IL
Indiana Enval. Balancing Bur. **[5230]**, Indianapolis, IN
Intl. Assn. of Heat and Frost Insulators and Asbestos Workers, AFL-CIO, CFL - Local Union 17 **[982]**, Chicago, IL
Intl. Assn. of Heat and Frost Insulators and Asbestos Workers, AFL-CIO, CFL - Local Union 34 **[12428]**, St. Paul, MN
Intl. Assn. of Heat and Frost Insulators and Asbestos Workers, Local 44 **[14473]**, Columbus, OH
Joliet Area of Sheet Metal and Air Conditioning Contractors' Natl. Assn. **[1594]**, Elgin, IL
Michigan Chap. - Sheet Metal and Air Conditioning Contractors' Natl. Assn. **[8148]**, Haslett, MI
Michigan Enval. Balancing Bur. **[7769]**, Flushing, MI
Mid-State Sheet Metal and Air Conditioning Contractors Assn. **[3424]**, Savoy, IL
Minnesota Assn. of Plumbing-Heating-Cooling Contractors **[10539]**, Brooklyn Center, MN
North Central Environmental Balancing Bur. **[11711]**, Minneapolis, MN
Northeastern Illinois Sheet Metal Contractors Assn. **[1598]**, Elgin, IL
Northern Illinois Air Conditioning Contractors of Am. **[1466]**, Des Plaines, IL
Northern Indiana Sheet Metal Contractors Assn. **[4927]**, Hobart, IN
Plumbing-Heating-Cooling Contractors Assn., Akron **[15800]**, Mantua, OH
Plumbing-Heating-Cooling Contractors Assn., Bloomington/Normal **[306]**, Bloomington, IL
Plumbing-Heating-Cooling Contractors Assn., Central Ohio **[15609]**, Lancaster, OH
Plumbing-Heating-Cooling Contractors Assn., Central Wisconsin **[20189]**, Wisconsin Rapids, WI
Plumbing-Heating-Cooling Contractors Assn., Dayton Area **[14947]**, Dayton, OH
Plumbing-Heating-Cooling Contractors Assn., East Central Illinois **[546]**, Champaign, IL
Plumbing-Heating-Cooling Contractors Assn., Eastern Ohio **[13538]**, Canfield, OH
Plumbing-Heating-Cooling Contractors Assn., Egyptian **[2407]**, Marion, IL
Plumbing-Heating-Cooling Contractors Assn., Flint **[6757]**, Ann Arbor, MI
Plumbing-Heating-Cooling Contractors Assn., Fort Wayne **[4711]**, Fort Wayne, IN
Plumbing-Heating-Cooling Contractors Assn., Greater Indianapolis **[5454]**, Indianapolis, IN
Plumbing-Heating-Cooling Contractors Assn., Greater SW Illinois **[1698]**, Fairview Heights, IL
Plumbing-Heating-Cooling Contractors Assn., Lake and McHenry Counties **[1924]**, Gurnee, IL
Plumbing-Heating-Cooling Contractors Assn., Lakes Area **[11995]**, Perham, MN
Plumbing-Heating-Cooling Contractors Assn., Metro **[10541]**, Brooklyn Center, MN
Plumbing-Heating-Cooling Contractors Assn., Michigan **[8854]**, Livonia, MI
Plumbing-Heating-Cooling Contractors Assn., North Central **[6649]**, Alpena, MI
Plumbing-Heating-Cooling Contractors Assn., North Central Indiana **[6051]**, Plymouth, IN
Plumbing-Heating-Cooling Contractors Assn., North East Ohio **[16797]**, Strongsville, OH
Plumbing-Heating-Cooling Contractors Assn., Northern Wisconsin **[17849]**, Eagle River, WI
Plumbing-Heating-Cooling Contractors Assn., Northwest **[4468]**, Dyer, IN
Plumbing-Heating-Cooling Contractors Assn., Northwestern Michigan **[7103]**, Cedar, MI
Plumbing-Heating-Cooling Contractors Assn., Range **[12805]**, Virginia, MN
Plumbing-Heating-Cooling Contractors Assn., Rochester **[12170]**, Rochester, MN
Plumbing-Heating-Cooling Contractors Assn., Saginaw Valley **[9624]**, Saginaw, MI
Plumbing-Heating-Cooling Contractors Assn., St. Joseph Valley **[5812]**, Mishawaka, IN
Plumbing-Heating-Cooling Contractors Assn., Sheboygan County **[17457]**, Adell, WI
Plumbing-Heating-Cooling Contractors Assn., South Central Indiana **[5535]**, Jasper, IN
Plumbing-Heating-Cooling Contractors Assn., South Macomb **[8521]**, Lakeville, MI
Plumbing-Heating-Cooling Contractors Assn., Southeastern Michigan **[7419]**, Detroit, MI
Plumbing-Heating-Cooling Contractors Assn., Southwestern **[5853]**, Mount Vernon, IN
Plumbing-Heating-Cooling Contractors Assn., Stark **[13281]**, Beach City, OH
Plumbing-Heating-Cooling Contractors Assn., Thumb Area **[9379]**, Pigeon, MI
Plumbing-Heating-Cooling Contractors Assn., West Central Indiana **[5631]**, Lafayette, IN
Plumbing-Heating-Cooling Contractors Assn., West Michigan **[8045]**, Grandville, MI
Plumbing-Heating-Cooling Contractors Assn., West Suburban **[217]**, Bellwood, IL
Plumbing-Heating-Cooling Contractors Assn., Western Wayne County **[10141]**, Westland, MI
Plumbing-Heating-Cooling Contractors Assn., Western Wisconsin **[19737]**, Siren, WI
Plumbing-Heating-Cooling Contractors Assn., Wisconsin Valley **[19798]**, Stevens Point, WI
Sheet Metal and Air Conditioning Contractors Assn. **[19117]**, Milwaukee, WI
Sheet Metal and Air Conditioning Contractors' Natl. Assn. - Cleveland **[16250]**, North Royalton, OH
Sheet Metal and Air Conditioning Contractors Natl. Assn. Metropolitan Detroit Chap. **[10009]**, Troy, MI
Sheet Metal and Air Conditioning Contractors' Natl. Assn. of Michiana **[6264]**, South Bend, IN
Sheet Metal and Air Conditioning Contractors' Natl. Assn. of Minnesota **[11734]**, Minneapolis, MN
Sheet Metal and Air Conditioning Contractors' Natl. Assn. of North Central Ohio **[14216]**, Cleveland, OH
Sheet Metal and Air Conditioning Contractors' Natl. Assn. of Northern Illinois **[3318]**, Rockford, IL
Sheet Metal Contractors Assn. of Central Indiana **[5472]**, Indianapolis, IN
Sheet Metal Contractors Assn. of Evansville **[4572]**, Evansville, IN
Sheet Metal Contractors Assn. of Greater Cincinnati **[13983]**, Cincinnati, OH
Sheet Metal Contractors Assn. of Nortwest Ohio **[16959]**, Toledo, OH
Sheet Metal and Roofing Contractors Assn. of Miami Valley **[14952]**, Dayton, OH
Southeast Michigan Air Conditioning Contractors of Am. **[8857]**, Livonia, MI
Southeastern Sheet Metal Contractors Assn. of Wisconsin **[19127]**, Milwaukee, WI
Southern Illinois Sheet Metal Contractors Org. **[1568]**, Edwardsville, IL
Southwest Ohio Enval. Balancing Bur. **[14001]**, Cincinnati, OH
Springfield and Vicinity Sheet Metal Contractors' Assn. **[3684]**, Springfield, IL
Wisconsin Enval. Balancing Bur. **[19168]**, Milwaukee, WI
Wisconsin Fox Valley Sheet Metal Contractors Assn. **[17532]**, Appleton, WI
Heating, Cooling Contractors; Indiana Assn. of Plumbing, **[5179]**, Indianapolis, IN
Hector Lions Club - Minnesota **[11140]**, Hector, MN
Heidelberg Proj. **[7374]**, Detroit, MI
Heights Regional Chamber of Commerce **[14247]**, Cleveland Heights, OH
Helicopter
Central Indiana Rotorwing Club **[4103]**, Anderson, IN
Columbus Rotor Wing **[15367]**, Grove City, OH
Lake-Geauga Helicopter Assn. **[16526]**, Richmond Heights, OH
Michiana R/C Choppers **[4502]**, Elkhart, IN
Michigan Whirlybirds **[9869]**, Sterling Heights, MI
South Eastern Wisconsin Helicopter Assn. **[19123]**, Milwaukee, WI
Help Against Violent Encounters Now **[9418]**, Pontiac, MI
Helping Hands Dairy Goat Club **[4958]**, Idaville, IN
Helping Other People Prepare and Endure **[15768]**, Mansfield, OH
Hematology
Great Lakes Hemophilia Found. **[19016]**, Milwaukee, WI
Hemophilia Found. of Illinois **[912]**, Chicago, IL
Hemophilia Found. of Michigan **[10206]**, Ypsilanti, MI
Hemophilia Found. of Minnesota/Dakotas **[11457]**, Mendota Heights, MN
Hemophilia of Indiana **[5133]**, Indianapolis, IN
Northwest Ohio Hemophilia Found. **[16942]**, Toledo, OH
SCDAA - Ohio Sickle Cell and Hea. Assn. **[13980]**, Cincinnati, OH
Sickle Cell Awareness Gp. of Greater Cincinnati **[13988]**, Cincinnati, OH
Sickle Cell Disease Assn. of Am. - Michigan **[7432]**, Detroit, MI
Hemlock Lions Club **[8162]**, Hemlock, MI
Hemophilia Found. of Illinois **[912]**, Chicago, IL
Hemophilia Found. of Michigan **[10206]**, Ypsilanti, MI
Hemophilia Found. of Minnesota/Dakotas **[11457]**, Mendota Heights, MN
Hemophilia of Indiana **[5133]**, Indianapolis, IN
Hennepin Medical Soc. **[11576]**, Minneapolis, MN
Henry Area Chamber of Commerce **[1969]**, Henry, IL
Henry County Historical Soc. **[5935]**, New Castle, IN
Henry Sibley High School PTA **[11458]**, Mendota Heights, MN
Henryville Beagle Club **[5906]**, Nabb, IN
Herbs
Ginseng Bd. of Wisconsin **[20035]**, Wausau, WI
Wisconsin Mint Bd. **[17479]**, Antigo, WI
Heritage Assn; Illinois **[527]**, Champaign, IL
Heritage Community Development Corp. **[913]**, Chicago, IL
Heritage Hall **[★15843]**
Heritage Hill Assn. **[7963]**, Grand Rapids, MI
Heritage; Media **[13896]**, Cincinnati, OH
Heritage Ohio **[14453]**, Columbus, OH
Hermantown Arena Bd. **[11149]**, Hermantown, MN
Hermantown Chamber of Commerce **[11150]**, Hermantown, MN
Herpetology
Chicago Herpetological Soc. **[812]**, Chicago, IL
Herrin Chamber of Commerce **[1974]**, Herrin, IL
Herscher Chamber of Commerce **[1976]**, Herscher, IL
Hesperia Lions Club **[8166]**, Hesperia, MI
HI-USA, Central and Southern Ohio Coun. **[14454]**, Columbus, OH
Hiawatha Bicycling Club **[11577]**, Minneapolis, MN
Hiawatha Valley Rsrc. Conservation and Development Coun. **[12144]**, Rochester, MN
Hiawatha Valley Sail and Power Squadron **[10911]**, Edina, MN
Hibbing Area Chamber of Commerce **[11157]**, Hibbing, MN
Hibbing Chamber of Commerce **[★11157]**
Hibbing Figure Skating Club **[11158]**, Hibbing, MN
Hibbing Historical Soc. **[11159]**, Hibbing, MN
Hibbing Lions Club **[11160]**, Hibbing, MN
Hickory Hills Chamber of Commerce **[1983]**, Hickory Hills, IL
Hidden Victims Support Gp. **[1392]**, Decatur, IL
High Cincinnatians Tall Club **[13862]**, Cincinnati, OH
High School Alumni Assn; Bellaire **[13310]**, Bellaire, OH
High School Chess Club; North Boone **[3125]**, Poplar Grove, IL
High School Coaches Assn; Michigan **[8993]**, Mears, MI
High School Coun. PTSA **[914]**, Chicago, IL
High Tech. Crime Investigation Assn. - Minnesota **[11126]**, Hastings, MN
High Tech. Crime Investigation Assn. - Ohio **[14139]**, Cleveland, OH
Higher Education
Indiana Assn. of Scholars **[4227]**, Bloomington, IN
Minnesota Assn. of Scholars **[11627]**, Minneapolis, MN
Wisconsin Assn. of Scholars **[19158]**, Milwaukee, WI
Wisconsin Women in Higher Educ. Leadership **[19188]**, Milwaukee, WI
Highfields - Helping People Grow in Michigan **[9306]**, Onondaga, MI
Highland Beagle Club **[15444]**, Hillsboro, OH
Highland Chamber of Commerce **[1985]**, Highland, IL
Highland Chamber of Commerce **[4912]**, Highland, IN

Highland County Bd. of Realtors [15445], Hillsboro, OH
Highland County Chamber of Commerce [15446], Hillsboro, OH
Highland Park Chamber of Commerce [1989], Highland Park, IL
Highland Park Historical Soc. [1990], Highland Park, IL
Highland Park Lions Club - Michigan [8172], Highland Park, MI
Highland Park Public Lib. [1991], Highland Park, IL
Highland Soccer Club [4913], Highland, IN
Highland Table Tennis Club [4914], Highland, IN
Highview Wyldlife [12229], Roseville, MN
Highway Coalition; I-69 Mid-Continent [5153], Indianapolis, IN
Hikers 522; Heart of Ohio [14452], Columbus, OH
Hiking
Amer. Hiking Soc. - Atwood Outdoor Educ. Center - Rockford Park District [3264], Rockford, IL
Amer. Hiking Soc. - Buckeye Trail Assn. [17340], Worthington, OH
Amer. Hiking Soc. - Camp Tuscazoar Found. [16673], Smithville, OH
Amer. Hiking Soc. - Cleveland Hiking Club [14050], Cleveland, OH
Amer. Hiking Soc. - Cuyahoga Valley Trails Coun. [16565], Sagamore Hills, OH
Amer. Hiking Soc. - Delaware Greenways [5860], Muncie, IN
Amer. Hiking Soc. - DuBois Center [1515], Du Bois, IL
Amer. Hiking Soc. - Hoosiers Hikers Coun. [5749], Martinsville, IN
Amer. Hiking Soc. - Ice Age Park and Trail Found. [18934], Milwaukee, WI
Amer. Hiking Soc. - Indianapolis Hiking Club [4847], Greenwood, IN
Amer. Hiking Soc. - Kekekabic Trail Club [11489], Minneapolis, MN
Amer. Hiking Soc. - North Country Trail Assn. [8860], Lowell, MI
Amer. Hiking Soc. - Parks and Trails Coun. of Minnesota [12354], St. Paul, MN
Amer. Hiking Soc. - Preble County Historical Soc. [15086], Eaton, OH
Amer. Hiking Soc. - River to River Trail Soc. [1936], Harrisburg, IL
Amer. Hiking Soc. - Superior Hiking Trail Assn. [12767], Two Harbors, MN
Amer. Hiking Soc. - Youth Conservation Corps [3918], Waukegan, IL
Cleveland Hiking Club [16395], Pepper Pike, OH
Superior Hiking Trail Assn. [12774], Two Harbors, MN
Hill BMX Elgin Assn. [1834], Glen Ellyn, IL
Hillforest Historical Found. [4146], Aurora, IN
Hilliard Area Chamber of Commerce [15433], Hilliard, OH
Hilliard Darby - Young Life [14455], Columbus, OH
Hilliard Davidson Athletic Boosters [15434], Hilliard, OH
Hilliard Davidson - Young Life [14456], Columbus, OH
Hilliard Lions Club [14457], Columbus, OH
Hillman Adult Leisure Club [11166], Hillman, MN
Hillman Area Chamber of Commerce [8173], Hillman, MI
Hillsboro Area Chamber of Commerce [1998], Hillsboro, IL
Hillsboro Area Chamber of Commerce [★15446]
Hillsboro Lions Club - Wisconsin [18207], Hillsboro, WI
Hillsdale County Bd. of Realtors [8175], Hillsdale, MI
Hillsdale County Chamber of Commerce [8176], Hillsdale, MI
Hillsdale County United Way [8177], Hillsdale, MI
Hillsdale Lions Club [8178], Hillsdale, MI
Hillsdale - Wyldlife [8179], Hillsdale, MI
Hillsdale - Young Life [8180], Hillsdale, MI
Hillside Coin Club [2006], Hillside, IL
Hindu Temple of Central Indiana [5134], Indianapolis, IN
Hinduism
Hindu Temple of Central Indiana [5134], Indianapolis, IN
Hinsdale Central - Young Life [2016], Hinsdale, IL
Hinsdale Chamber of Commerce [2017], Hinsdale, IL
Hinsdale South - Young Life [2018], Hinsdale, IL
Hinsdale WyldLife [2019], Hinsdale, IL
HIPAA - Collaborative of Wisconsin [19966], Watertown, WI
Hispanic
Casa De Esperanza [12397], St. Paul, MN
Natl. Coun. of La Raza-Midwest [1079], Chicago, IL
United Hispanic-Americans [4728], Fort Wayne, IN
Hispanic-Americans; United [4728], Fort Wayne, IN
Hispanic Chamber of Commerce; Indiana State [5316], Indianapolis, IN
Hispanic Chamber of Commerce of Minnesota [11578], Minneapolis, MN
Historic Bluff Country; Southeastern Minnesota [11120], Harmony, MN
Historic Chicago Bungalow Initiative [915], Chicago, IL
Historic Hoosier Hills Rsrc. Conservation and Development Coun. [6402], Versailles, IN
Historic Irvington Community Coun. [5135], Indianapolis, IN
Historic Landmarks Found. of Indiana [5136], Indianapolis, IN
Historic Lyme Church Assn. [★13330]
Historic Lyme Village Assn. [13330], Bellevue, OH
Historic Newburgh [5960], Newburgh, IN
Historic Preservation
Ashtabula Lighthouse Restoration and Preservation Soc. [16231], North Kingsville, OH
Assn. for Preservation Tech. Intl., Ohio Valley Chap. [13754], Cincinnati, OH
Blackford County Civil War Re-enactment Club [4900], Hartford City, IN
Butler County Historical Soc. [15381], Hamilton, OH
Canal Soc. of Indiana [4646], Fort Wayne, IN
Cincinnati Preservation Assn. [13797], Cincinnati, OH
Crosby Township Historical Soc. [15407], Harrison, OH
DeTour Reef Light Preservation Soc. [7485], Drummond Island, MI
Dover Historical Soc. [15027], Dover, OH
Du Page County (IL) Genealogical Soc. [3984], Wheaton, IL
Eastland Disaster Historical Soc. [70], Arlington Heights, IL
Fairborn Performing Arts and Cultural Assn. [15149], Fairborn, OH
Fairfield Heritage Assn. [15600], Lancaster, OH
Friends of Bears Mill [15362], Greenville, OH
Friends of Burlington Northern Railroad [20119], West Bend, WI
Friends of the Colonel Benjamin Stephenson House [1559], Edwardsville, IL
Friends of the Farnsworth House [897], Chicago, IL
Friends of Meigs Field [898], Chicago, IL
Great Lakes Lighthouse Keepers Assn. [8888], Mackinaw City, MI
Greater Loveland Historical Soc. [15725], Loveland, OH
Hillforest Historical Found. [4146], Aurora, IN
Historic Chicago Bungalow Initiative [915], Chicago, IL
Historic Landmarks Found. of Indiana [5136], Indianapolis, IN
Historic Lyme Village Assn. [13330], Bellevue, OH
Houghton County Historical Museum Soc. [8511], Lake Linden, MI
Indiana German Heritage Society [5239], Indianapolis, IN
Indianapolis Historic Preservation Commn. [5350], Indianapolis, IN
Intl. Personnel Mgt. Assn., Michigan [7846], Grand Blanc, MI
Jackson Township Historical Soc. [5520], Jamestown, IN
Lake County Historical Soc. [15574], Kirtland Hills, OH
Lakewood Historical Soc. [15587], Lakewood, OH
Landmarks Preservation Coun. of Illinois [1019], Chicago, IL
Log Cabin Soc. of Michigan [9758], Sodus, MI
Mansfield Reformatory Preservation Soc. [15775], Mansfield, OH
Marquette County History Museum [8944], Marquette, MI
Maxwell St. Historic Preservation Coalition [1040], Chicago, IL
Michigan Hemingway Soc. [9365], Petoskey, MI
Michigan Historic Preservation Network [8672], Lansing, MI
Newton County Historical Soc. [5554], Kentland, IN
Ohio Historical Soc. - Cedar Bog Nature Preserve [17042], Urbana, OH
Pastways [7648], Farmington, MI
Preservation Wayne [7422], Detroit, MI
Preserve Historic Sleeping Bear [7604], Empire, MI
Revitalize Gillett [18048], Gillett, WI
Rogers Park/West Ridge Historical Soc. [1169], Chicago, IL
Route 66 Assn. of Illinois [3669], Springfield, IL
Shelby County Historical Soc. [16668], Sidney, OH
Soc. for the Preservation of Old Mills, Great Lakes Chap. [9531], Rockford, MI
Terrace Park Historical Soc. [16848], Terrace Park, OH
Van Wert County Historical Soc. [17055], Van Wert, OH
Vermilion County Museum Soc. [1356], Danville, IL
Waterford Township Historical Soc. [10096], Waterford, MI
Historic Preservation Network; Michigan [8672], Lansing, MI
Historic Quincy Bus. District [3151], Quincy, IL
Historic Third Ward Assn. [19023], Milwaukee, WI
Historical Assn. - Alameda McCollough Lib; Tippecanoe County [5635], Lafayette, IN
Historical Bur. Found; Indiana State Lib. and [5317], Indianapolis, IN
Historical Center; Women's Hall of Fame and Women's [★8728]
Historical Colls; Indian Village [7375], Detroit, MI
Historical Found; Hillforest [4146], Aurora, IN
Historical Found; Roselle [3356], Roselle, IL
Historical Museum; Blackford [★4901]
Historical Museum; Du Page County [★3983]
Historical Museum; Leelanau [★8796]
Historical Museum and Lib; Madison County [★1563]
Historical and Museum Soc; Iron County [7092], Caspian, MI
Historical Museum and Soc; Johnson County [4751], Franklin, IN
Historical Societies
Anoka County Historical Soc. [10304], Anoka, MN
Crystal Lake Historical Soc. [1321], Crystal Lake, IL
Douglas County Historical Soc. [10275], Alexandria, MN
Eagle Historical Soc. [17845], Eagle, WI
Hibbing Historical Soc. [11159], Hibbing, MN
Kankakee Valley Historical Soc. [5591], Kouts, IN
Lake County Historical Soc. [12771], Two Harbors, MN
Nicollet County Historical Soc. [12618], St. Peter, MN
Otsego Area Historical Soc. [9326], Otsego, MI
Pittsfield Township Historical Soc. [6756], Ann Arbor, MI
Virginia Area Historical Soc. [12808], Virginia, MN
Watrousville-Caro Area Historical Soc. [7087], Caro, MI
Historical Societies and Museums; Ohio Assn. of [14555], Columbus, OH
Historical Soc; Algoma Township [9522], Rockford, MI
Historical Soc; Amherst [13131], Amherst, OH
Historical Soc; Blackford County [4901], Hartford City, IN
Historical Soc; Bluewater Michigan Chap., Natl. Railway [9576], Royal Oak, MI
Historical Soc; Brown County [11883], New Ulm, MN
Historical Soc; Bur. County [3134], Princeton, IL
Historical Soc; Butler County [15381], Hamilton, OH

Historical Soc; Carlton County [10689], Cloquet, MN
Historical Soc; Chessie Sys. [17170], West Chester, OH
Historical Soc; Chippewa County [11800], Montevideo, MN
Historical Soc; Clay County [11823], Moorhead, MN
Historical Soc; Clearwater County [10374], Bagley, MN
Historical Soc; Clermont County [13267], Batavia, OH
Historical Soc; Clinton County [17290], Wilmington, OH
Historical Society; Conneaut [14782], Conneaut, OH
Historical Soc; Crosby Township [15407], Harrison, OH
Historical Soc; Crystal Lake [1321], Crystal Lake, IL
Historical Soc; Cudahy [17798], Cudahy, WI
Historical Soc; Dakota County [12680], South St. Paul, MN
Historical Soc; Dartford [18145], Green Lake, WI
Historical Soc; Decatur County [4842], Greensburg, IN
Historical Soc; Delaware County [5872], Muncie, IN
Historical Soc; Delaware County [15007], Delaware, OH
Historical Soc; Detroit [7347], Detroit, MI
Historical Soc; Dover [15027], Dover, OH
Historical Soc; Du Page County [3983], Wheaton, IL
Historical Soc; Eagle [17845], Eagle, WI
Historical Soc; East Detroit [7575], Eastpointe, MI
Historical Soc; Enon Community [15136], Enon, OH
Historical Soc; Evanston [1656], Evanston, IL
Historical Soc; Fairport Harbor [15178], Fairport Harbor, OH
Historical Soc; Fayette County [17128], Washington Court House, OH
Historical Soc; Freeborn County [10258], Albert Lea, MN
Historical Soc; Friesen [10670], Clara City, MN
Historical Soc; Fulton County [17139], Wauseon, OH
Historical Soc; Galena/Jo Daviess County [1763], Galena, IL
Historical Soc; Geauga County [13473], Burton, OH
Historical Soc; Glenview Area [1864], Glenview, IL
Historical Soc; Gnadenhutten [15329], Gnadenhutten, OH
Historical Soc; Goodhue County [12079], Red Wing, MN
Historical Soc; Grant County [10936], Elbow Lake, MN
Historical Soc; Great Lakes [17065], Vermilion, OH
Historical Soc; Green County [19214], Monroe, WI
Historical Soc; Greene County [17370], Xenia, OH
Historical Soc; Hawks Inn [17823], Delafield, WI
Historical Soc; Henry County [5935], New Castle, IN
Historical Soc; Highland Park [1990], Highland Park, IL
Historical Soc; Hobart [4925], Hobart, IN
Historical Society/Howard Steamboat Museum; Clark County [5540], Jeffersonville, IN
Historical Soc; Hudson Lib. and [15483], Hudson, OH
Historical Soc; Illinois State [3641], Springfield, IL
Historical Soc; Indian Hill [13864], Cincinnati, OH
Historical Society; Iron County [18231], Hurley, WI
Historical Soc; Isanti County [10623], Cambridge, MN
Historical Soc; Jackson County [2618], Murphysboro, IL
Historical Soc; Jackson County [11290], Lakefield, MN
Historical Soc; Jackson Township [5520], Jamestown, IN
Historical Soc; Kankakee Valley [5591], Kouts, IN
Historical Soc; Keweenaw [★7493]
Historical Soc; Keweenaw County [7493], Eagle Harbor, MI
Historical Soc; Kosciusko County [6447], Warsaw, IN
Historical Soc; La Crosse County [18357], La Crosse, WI
Historical Soc. of Lake County Ohio; Perry [16400], Perry, OH
Historical Soc; Libertyville-Mundelein [2263], Libertyville, IL
Historical Soc; Logan County [★13321]
Historical Soc; Logan County Archaeological and [★13321]
Historical Soc. and Logan County Museum; Logan County [13321], Bellefontaine, OH
Historical Soc; Manitowoc County [18784], Manitowoc, WI
Historical Soc; Marathon County [20038], Wausau, WI
Historical Soc; Marion County [15843], Marion, OH
Historical Soc; Marquette County [20146], Westfield, WI
Historical Soc; Marshall County [6049], Plymouth, IN
Historical Soc; Martin County [10979], Fairmont, MN
Historical Soc; Maumee Valley [15912], Maumee, OH
Historical Soc; Mayville [18833], Mayville, WI
Historical Soc; McHenry County [3799], Union, IL
Historical Soc; McLean County [296], Bloomington, IL
Historical Soc. of Michigan [7522], East Lansing, MI
Historical Soc; Michigan City [5788], Michigan City, IN
Historical Soc; Michigan Photographic [6964], Birmingham, MI
Historical Soc; Milford [9052], Milford, MI
Historical Soc; Milton [18921], Milton, WI
Historical Soc; Monroe County [19753], Sparta, WI
Historical Soc; Montgomery County [14922], Dayton, OH
Historical Soc. and Museum; Cleveland Police [14102], Cleveland, OH
Historical Soc. Museum; Decatur County [★4842]
Historical Soc. Museum; Gnadenhutten [★15329]
Historical Soc./Museum; Goshen [4796], Goshen, IN
Historical Soc. and Museum; Leelanau [8796], Leland, MI
Historical Soc. Museum and Lib; Madison County [1563], Edwardsville, IL
Historical Soc. Museum and Lib; McLean County [★296]
Historical Soc. and Museum; Madison County [★1563]
Historical Soc. Museum; Mayville [★18833]
Historical Society and Museums; Flat River [8066], Greenville, MI
Historical Soc; New Baltimore [9183], New Baltimore, MI
Historical Soc; Newton County [5554], Kentland, IN
Historical Soc; Northville [9227], Northville, MI
Historical Soc. of Oak Park and River Forest [2812], Oak Park, IL
Historical Soc; Oakland County Pioneer and [9422], Pontiac, MI
Historical Soc. of Olmsted County [★12166]
Historical Soc; Otsego Area [9326], Otsego, MI
Historical Soc; Outagamie County [17512], Appleton, WI
Historical Soc; Outagamie County Pioneer and [★17512]
Historical Soc; Palatine [2923], Palatine, IL
Historical Soc; Park Forest [2954], Park Forest, IL
Historical Soc; Perry County [3090], Pinckneyville, IL
Historical Soc; Pittsfield Township [6756], Ann Arbor, MI
Historical Soc; Plymouth [9407], Plymouth, MI
Historical Soc; Preble County [15091], Eaton, OH
Historical Soc; Putnam County [1967], Hennepin, IL
Historical Soc. of Quincy and Adams County [3152], Quincy, IL
Historical Soc; Ramsey County [12568], St. Paul, MN
Historical Soc; Ripley County, Indiana [6404], Versailles, IN
Historical Soc; Rock County [18260], Janesville, WI
Historical Soc; Roseau County [12209], Roseau, MN
Historical Soc; Roselle [★3356]
Historical Society; Rosendale [19649], Rosendale, WI
Historical Soc; St. Croix County [18226], Hudson, WI
Historical Soc; Sauk County [17577], Baraboo, WI
Historical Soc; Shaker [16641], Shaker Heights, OH
Historical Soc; Sheboygan County [19712], Sheboygan, WI
Historical Soc; Sherburne County [10397], Becker, MN
Historical Soc; South Holland [3508], South Holland, IL
Historical Society; Spring Valley Mine and [3518], Spring Valley, IL
Historical Soc; Stearns County [★12313]
Historical Soc; Stephenson County [1754], Freeport, IL
Historical Soc; Summit County [13094], Akron, OH
Historical Soc; Terrace Park [16848], Terrace Park, OH
Historical Soc; Two Rivers [19920], Two Rivers, WI
Historical Soc; Warren County [15625], Lebanon, OH
Historical Soc; Washington County [12730], Stillwater, MN
Historical Soc; Washtenaw County [6786], Ann Arbor, MI
Historical Soc; Watertown [19972], Watertown, WI
Historical Soc; Watrousville-Caro Area [7087], Caro, MI
Historical Soc; Waukesha County [20004], Waukesha, WI
Historical Society; Waupaca [20026], Waupaca, WI
Historical Soc; Wayne County [17332], Wooster, OH
Historical Soc; Wilkin County [10528], Breckenridge, MN
Historical Soc; Winona County [12962], Winona, MN
Historical Soc; Wisconsin [18711], Madison, WI
Historical Soc; Wisconsin Marine [19173], Milwaukee, WI
Historical Soc; Wood County [13402], Bowling Green, OH
Historical Village; Pinecrest [★18784]
Historical Village of Shiawassee County; Friends of the Corunna [7226], Corunna, MI
History
Algoma Township Historical Soc. [9522], Rockford, MI
Amherst Historical Soc. [13131], Amherst, OH
Bellville-Jefferson Township Historical Society [13336], Bellville, OH
Blackford County Historical Soc. [4901], Hartford City, IN
Brecksville Historical Assn. [13409], Brecksville, OH
Brown County Historical Soc. [11883], New Ulm, MN
Brown County Historical Soc. [18090], Green Bay, WI
Bur. County Historical Soc. [3134], Princeton, IL
Carlton County Historical Soc. [10689], Cloquet, MN
Carroll County Historical Soc. Museum [4454], Delphi, IN
Chippewa County Historical Soc. [11800], Montevideo, MN
Clark County Historical Society/Howard Steamboat Museum [5540], Jeffersonville, IN
Clay County Historical Soc. [11823], Moorhead, MN
Clearwater County Historical Soc. [10374], Bagley, MN
Clermont County Historical Soc. [13267], Batavia, OH
Cleveland Police Historical Soc. and Museum [14102], Cleveland, OH
Clinton County Historical Soc. [17290], Wilmington, OH
Clinton County Historical Soc. and Historical Museum [4740], Frankfort, IN
Cudahy Historical Soc. [17798], Cudahy, WI
Dakota County Historical Soc. [12680], South St. Paul, MN
Dartford Historical Soc. [18145], Green Lake, WI
Delaware County Historical Soc. [15007], Delaware, OH
Des Plaines Historical Soc. [1458], Des Plaines, IL
Dodge County Historical Soc. [11406], Mantorville, MN
Du Page County Historical Soc. [3983], Wheaton, IL
East Detroit Historical Soc. [7575], Eastpointe, MI
Enon Community Historical Soc. [15136], Enon, OH
Evanston Historical Soc. [1656], Evanston, IL
Facing History and Ourselves, Chicago [890], Chicago, IL
Fairport Harbor Historical Soc. [15178], Fairport Harbor, OH
Fayette County Historical Soc. [17128], Washington Court House, OH

Flat River Historical Society and Museums [8066], Greenville, MI
Flushing Area Historical Soc. [7766], Flushing, MI
Freeborn County Historical Soc. [10258], Albert Lea, MN
Fulton County Historical Soc. [17139], Wauseon, OH
Galena/Jo Daviess County Historical Soc. [1763], Galena, IL
Geauga County Historical Soc. [13473], Burton, OH
Gerald R. Ford Found. [7938], Grand Rapids, MI
Gnadenhutten Historical Soc. [15329], Gnadenhutten, OH
Goodhue County Historical Soc. [12079], Red Wing, MN
Goshen Historical Soc./Museum [4796], Goshen, IN
Grant County Historical Soc. [10936], Elbow Lake, MN
Green County Historical Soc. [19214], Monroe, WI
Greene County Historical Soc. [17370], Xenia, OH
Grosse Pointe Historical Soc. [8088], Grosse Pointe Farms, MI
Henry County Historical Soc. [5935], New Castle, IN
Historic Third Ward Assn. [19023], Milwaukee, WI
Historical Soc. of Oak Park and River Forest [2812], Oak Park, IL
Historical Soc. of Quincy and Adams County [3152], Quincy, IL
Hobart Historical Soc. [4925], Hobart, IN
Hudson Lib. and Historical Soc. [15483], Hudson, OH
Illinois Central Railroad Historical Soc. [2973], Paxton, IL
Illinois State Historical Soc. [3641], Springfield, IL
Illinois State Museum Soc. [3642], Springfield, IL
Indian Hill Historical Soc. [13864], Cincinnati, OH
Indiana Supreme Court Historical Soc. [5327], Indianapolis, IN
Iron County Historical and Museum Soc. [7092], Caspian, MI
Iron County Historical Society [18231], Hurley, WI
Isanti County Historical Soc. [10623], Cambridge, MN
Jackson County Historical Soc. [2618], Murphysboro, IL
Johnson County Historical Museum and Soc. [4751], Franklin, IN
Kenosha History Center [18302], Kenosha, WI
Keweenaw County Historical Soc. [7493], Eagle Harbor, MI
Kosciusko County Historical Soc. [6447], Warsaw, IN
La Crosse County Historical Soc. [18357], La Crosse, WI
Lake County Historical Soc. [4433], Crown Point, IN
Leelanau Historical Soc. and Museum [8796], Leland, MI
Libertyville-Mundelein Historical Soc. [2263], Libertyville, IL
Logan County Historical Soc. and Logan County Museum [13321], Bellefontaine, OH
Madison County Historical Soc. Museum and Lib. [1563], Edwardsville, IL
Manitowoc County Historical Soc. [18784], Manitowoc, WI
Marathon County Historical Soc. [20038], Wausau, WI
Marion County Historical Soc. [15843], Marion, OH
Marquette County Historical Soc. [20146], Westfield, WI
Marshall County Historical Soc. [6049], Plymouth, IN
Martin County Historical Soc. [10979], Fairmont, MN
Maumee Valley Historical Soc. [15912], Maumee, OH
Mayville Historical Soc. [18833], Mayville, WI
McLean County Historical Soc. [296], Bloomington, IL
Miami County Historical and Genealogical Soc., Chap. of OGS [17003], Troy, OH
Michigan City Historical Soc. [5788], Michigan City, IN
Michigan Oral History Assn. [8693], Lansing, MI
Michigan Photographic Historical Soc. [6964], Birmingham, MI
Michigan Supreme Court Historical Soc. [7400], Detroit, MI
Milford Historical Soc. [9052], Milford, MI
Milton Historical Soc. [18921], Milton, WI
Minnesota Chap. of the Soc. of Architectural Historians [11638], Minneapolis, MN
Minnesota Supreme Court Historical Soc. [11675], Minneapolis, MN
Monroe County Historical Soc. [19753], Sparta, WI
Montgomery County Historical Soc. [14922], Dayton, OH
New Baltimore Historical Soc. [9183], New Baltimore, MI
Oakland County Pioneer and Historical Soc. [9422], Pontiac, MI
Ohio Assn. of Historical Societies and Museums [14555], Columbus, OH
Ohio Genealogical Soc., Vinton County [15375], Hamden, OH
Ohio Historical Soc. [14624], Columbus, OH
Ohio Supreme Court Historical Soc. [14201], Cleveland, OH
Olmsted County Historical Soc. [12166], Rochester, MN
Outagamie County Historical Soc. [17512], Appleton, WI
Palatine Historical Soc. [2923], Palatine, IL
Park Forest Historical Soc. [2954], Park Forest, IL
Perry County Historical Soc. [3090], Pinckneyville, IL
Perry Historical Soc. of Lake County Ohio [16400], Perry, OH
Plymouth Historical Soc. [9407], Plymouth, MI
Preble County Historical Soc. [15091], Eaton, OH
Putnam County Historical Soc. [1967], Hennepin, IL
Ramsey County Historical Soc. [12568], St. Paul, MN
Ripley County, Indiana Historical Soc. [6404], Versailles, IN
Rock County Historical Soc. [18260], Janesville, WI
Roseau County Historical Soc. [12209], Roseau, MN
Roselle Historical Found. [3356], Roselle, IL
St. Croix County Historical Soc. [18226], Hudson, WI
Sauk County Historical Soc. [17577], Baraboo, WI
Shaker Historical Soc. [16641], Shaker Heights, OH
Sheboygan County Historical Soc. [19712], Sheboygan, WI
Sherburne County Historical Soc. [10397], Becker, MN
Soc. of Architectural Historians - Chicago Chap. [1186], Chicago, IL
Soc. of Architectural Historians - Wisconsin Chap. [19119], Milwaukee, WI
South Holland Historical Soc. [3508], South Holland, IL
Southeastern Minnesota Historic Bluff Country [11120], Harmony, MN
Stearns History Museum [12313], St. Cloud, MN
Summit County Historical Soc. [13094], Akron, OH
Trotwood-Madison Historical Soc. [16994], Trotwood, OH
Warren County Historical Soc. [15625], Lebanon, OH
Washington County Historical Soc. [12730], Stillwater, MN
Washtenaw County Historical Soc. [6786], Ann Arbor, MI
Watertown Historical Soc. [19972], Watertown, WI
Waukesha County Historical Soc. [20004], Waukesha, WI
Waupaca Historical Society [20026], Waupaca, WI
Wayne County Historical Soc. [17332], Wooster, OH
Waynesville Historical Preservation Bd. [17153], Waynesville, OH
Wilkin County Historical Soc. [10528], Breckenridge, MN
Winona County Historical Soc. [12962], Winona, MN
Wisconsin Historical Soc. [18711], Madison, WI
Wisconsin Marine Historical Soc. [19173], Milwaukee, WI
Wisconsin Supreme Court Historical Soc. [19184], Milwaukee, WI
Wood County Historical Soc. [13402], Bowling Green, OH
The History Center [★10374]
History Center; Kenosha [18302], Kenosha, WI
History Gp; Oberlin African-Amer. Genealogy and [16287], Oberlin, OH
History, and Humanities; Wayne County Coun. for Arts, [8085], Grosse Pointe, MI
History and Ourselves, Chicago; Facing [890], Chicago, IL
History and Ourselves Natl. Found., Chicago; Facing [★890]
Hitterdal Lions Club [11172], Hitterdal, MN
Hobart Chamber of Commerce [4924], Hobart, IN
Hobart Historical Soc. [4925], Hobart, IN
Hobbies
Jackson Model Rocketry Club [8381], Jackson, MI
Minnesota Quilters [11670], Minneapolis, MN
Hockey
Bowling Green Youth Hockey Assn. [13387], Bowling Green, OH
Central Wisconsin Saints Hockey Assn. [19481], Plover, WI
Chelsea Hockey Assn. [7140], Chelsea, MI
Marquette Junior Hockey [8947], Marquette, MI
Peoria Youth Hockey Assn. [3057], Peoria, IL
Port Huron Minor Hockey Assn. [9438], Port Huron, MI
Wisconsin Amateur Hockey Assn. [17851], Eagle River, WI
Hockey Assn; Bowling Green Youth [13387], Bowling Green, OH
Hockey Assn; Central Wisconsin Saints [19481], Plover, WI
Hockey Assn; Chelsea [7140], Chelsea, MI
Hockey Association; Gladwin Area [7834], Gladwin, MI
Hockey Assn; Port Huron Minor [9438], Port Huron, MI
Hockey Assn; Wisconsin Amateur [17851], Eagle River, WI
Hockey; Marquette Junior [8947], Marquette, MI
Hoffman Estates Chamber of Commerce [2035], Hoffman Estates, IL
Hoffman Lions Club [11147], Herman, MN
Hokah Lions Club [11265], La Crescent, MN
Holbrook Elementary School PTA [7873], Grand Ledge, MI
Holiday Rambler Recreational [★6430]
Holiday Rambler Recreational Vehicle Club [6430], Wakarusa, IN
Holistic Medicine
Mind-Body-Spirit Connected [13289], Beachwood, OH
Holland Area AGO [★8189]
Holland Area Chamber of Commerce [8200], Holland, MI
Holland Area Convention and Visitors Bur. [★8202]
Holland Christian - Young Life [8201], Holland, MI
Holland Convention and Visitor's Bur. [8202], Holland, MI
Holland High - Young Life [8203], Holland, MI
Holland Piano Teachers Forum [10226], Zeeland, MI
Holland - Springfield Chamber of Commerce [15458], Holland, OH
Holland - Wyldlife [8204], Holland, MI
Holly Area Chamber of Commerce [8236], Holly, MI
Holly Flint MMBA [7695], Ferndale, MI
Holmen Lions Club [19364], Onalaska, WI
Holmes County Chamber of Commerce [16035], Millersburg, OH
Holmes County Habitat for Humanity [16036], Millersburg, OH
Holmes County Humane Soc. [16037], Millersburg, OH
Holocaust
Holocaust Educ. Coun. [14458], Columbus, OH
Holocaust Educ. Coun. [14458], Columbus, OH

Holstein Assn; Indiana **[4838]**, Greens Fork, IN
Holstein Assn; Wisconsin **[17579]**, Baraboo, WI
Holt Lions Club **[8240]**, Holt, MI
Home
Natl. Assn. of Home Builders of the U.S., Chippewa Valley Home Builders Assn. **[17889]**, Eau Claire, WI
Home Builders Association of Bay County **[6889]**, Bay City, MI
Home Builders Assn. of Central Michigan **[9106]**, Mount Pleasant, MI
Home Builders Assn. of Central Ohio **[17214]**, Westerville, OH
Home Builders Assn. of Fort Wayne **[4668]**, Fort Wayne, IN
Home Builders Assn. of the Grand Traverse Area **[9933]**, Traverse City, MI
Home Builders Assn. of Greater Akron **[★13057]**
Home Builders Assn. of Greater Chicago **[7]**, Addison, IL
Home Builders Assn. of Greater Cleveland **[15497]**, Independence, OH
Home Builders Assn. of Greater Fox Valley **[3383]**, St. Charles, IL
Home Builders Association of Greater Southwest Illinois **[2428]**, Maryville, IL
Home Builders Association of Greater Terre Haute **[6323]**, Terre Haute, IN
Home Builders Assn. of Greater Toledo **[15907]**, Maumee, OH
Home Builders Assn. of Illinois **[3559]**, Springfield, IL
Home Builders Assn. of Kankakee **[2132]**, Kankakee, IL
Home Builders Assn. of Lenawee County **[6570]**, Adrian, MI
Home Builders Assn. of Livingston County **[7013]**, Brighton, MI
Home Builders Association of Mecosta County **[6946]**, Big Rapids, MI
Home Builders Association of Metro Flint **[7845]**, Grand Blanc, MI
Home Builders Assn. of Miami County **[17000]**, Troy, OH
Home Builders Assn. of Muncie **[5877]**, Muncie, IN
Home Builders Assn. of Northwestern Ohio **[14988]**, Defiance, OH
Home Builders Assn. of Portage and Summit Counties **[13057]**, Akron, OH
Home Builders Assn. of Saginaw **[9609]**, Saginaw, MI
Home Builders Assn. of St. Joseph Valley **[5808]**, Mishawaka, IN
Home Builders Assn. of Southern Indiana **[4365]**, Clarksville, IN
Home Builders Association of Southwest Illinois **[★2428]**
Home Builders Assn. of Washington County **[15819]**, Marietta, OH
Home Builders Assn. of Washtenaw County **[6705]**, Ann Arbor, MI
Home Builders Assn. of Wayne and Holmes Counties **[17319]**, Wooster, OH
Home Care
Bloomington Meals on Wheels **[4208]**, Bloomington, IN
Illinois Home Care Coun. **[1870]**, Glenview, IL
Indiana Assn. for Home and Hospice Care **[5173]**, Indianapolis, IN
Meals On Wheels of Northwest Indiana **[4434]**, Crown Point, IN
Meals on Wheels of Chicago **[1041]**, Chicago, IL
Meals on Wheels of Stark and Wayne Counties **[15891]**, Massillon, OH
Metro Meals on Wheels **[11602]**, Minneapolis, MN
Michigan Home Hea. Assn. **[9281]**, Okemos, MI
Michigan Hospice and Palliative Care Org. **[8673]**, Lansing, MI
Minnesota HomeCare Assn. **[12489]**, St. Paul, MN
Natl. Assn. for Home Care and Hospice, Region V **[3136]**, Princeton, IL
Nightingale Alliance **[20079]**, Wauwatosa, WI
Ohio Coun. for Home Care **[14590]**, Columbus, OH
Visiting Nurses Assn. First **[4015]**, Willowbrook, IL
Wisconsin Homecare Org. **[18712]**, Madison, WI
Home Care; Ohio Coun. for **[14590]**, Columbus, OH
Home Economics
Indiana Family, Career and Community Leaders of Am. **[5234]**, Indianapolis, IN
The Home Network Center **[14459]**, Columbus, OH
Home Repair
People Working Cooperatively - serving the Greater Cincinnati Community **[13956]**, Cincinnati, OH
Home and School Association; Nativity **[6059]**, Portage, IN
Home School Children's Club **[3181]**, Rantoul, IL
Homebrewing Club; Green Bay Rackers **[18319]**, Kewaunee, WI
Homebuilders Association; Lawrence County **[4173]**, Bedford, IN
Homeless
Illinois Coalition to End Homelessness **[1592]**, Elgin, IL
Minnesota Coalition for the Homeless **[11641]**, Minneapolis, MN
Northeast Ohio Coalition for the Homeless **[14185]**, Cleveland, OH
Homemakers of Am., Indiana Assn; Future **[★5234]**
Homeowners Assn; Brookfield Village **[15428]**, Hilliard, OH
Homer Lions Club - Michigan **[8246]**, Homer, MI
Homes Assn; Ohio Manufactured **[15058]**, Dublin, OH
Homewood Area Chamber of Commerce **[2048]**, Homewood, IL
Homewood-Flossmoor - Young Life **[3504]**, South Holland, IL
Homeworth Lions Club **[13339]**, Beloit, OH
Hononegah High School Key Club **[3335]**, Rockton, IL
Honor Lions Club **[8247]**, Honor, MI
Honor Societies
Phi Theta Kappa - Alpha Alpha Alpha Chap. **[17442]**, Zanesville, OH
Phi Theta Kappa, Alpha Alpha Gamma Chap. - Century Coll. **[12898]**, White Bear Lake, MN
Phi Theta Kappa, Alpha Alpha Omicron Chap. - Richland Community Coll. **[1401]**, Decatur, IL
Phi Theta Kappa, Alpha Alpha Pi Chap. - Coll. of Lake County **[1897]**, Grayslake, IL
Phi Theta Kappa - Alpha Alpha Psi Chap. **[13080]**, Akron, OH
Phi Theta Kappa, Alpha Chi Rho Chap. - Univ. of Wisconsin-Waukesha **[19997]**, Waukesha, WI
Phi Theta Kappa, Alpha Delta Alpha Chap. - Anoka-Ramsey Community Coll. **[10716]**, Coon Rapids, MN
Phi Theta Kappa, Alpha Delta Eta Chap. - Kankakee Community Coll. **[2142]**, Kankakee, IL
Phi Theta Kappa, Alpha Delta Omega Chap. - Glen Oaks Community Coll. **[7109]**, Centreville, MI
Phi Theta Kappa, Alpha Delta Upsilon Chap. - Anoka-Ramsey Community Coll. - Cambridge **[10625]**, Cambridge, MN
Phi Theta Kappa - Alpha Epsilon Eta Chap. **[15422]**, Highland Hills, OH
Phi Theta Kappa, Alpha Epsilon Kappa Chap. - Alpha Epsilon Kappa Chap. **[3660]**, Springfield, IL
Phi Theta Kappa, Alpha Epsilon Sigma Chap. - Minneapolis Community and Tech. Coll. **[11723]**, Minneapolis, MN
Phi Theta Kappa, Alpha Epsilon Theta Chap. - Univ. of Wisconsin-Marinette **[18802]**, Marinette, WI
Phi Theta Kappa, Alpha Eta Zeta Chap. - Ridgewater Coll. **[12925]**, Willmar, MN
Phi Theta Kappa, Alpha Iota Epsilon Chap. - Lincoln Trail Coll. **[3221]**, Robinson, IL
Phi Theta Kappa, Alpha Iota Lambda Chap. - Moraine Valley Community Coll. **[2942]**, Palos Hills, IL
Phi Theta Kappa, Alpha Iota Phi Chap. - Oakton Community Coll. **[1467]**, Des Plaines, IL
Phi Theta Kappa - Alpha Iota Theta Chap. **[13270]**, Batavia, OH
Phi Theta Kappa, Alpha Kappa Alpha Chap. - Normandale Community Coll. **[10485]**, Bloomington, MN
Phi Theta Kappa, Alpha Kappa Nu Chap. - Indiana Univ. - Purdue Univ. Fort Wayne **[4709]**, Fort Wayne, IN
Phi Theta Kappa, Alpha Kappa Rho Chap. - Southwestern Illinois Coll. **[1884]**, Granite City, IL
Phi Theta Kappa, Alpha Lambda Epsilon Chap. - Shawnee Community Coll. **[3797]**, Ullin, IL
Phi Theta Kappa - Alpha Lambda Eta Chap. **[16436]**, Piqua, OH
Phi Theta Kappa, Alpha Lambda Iota Chap. - Malcolm X Coll. **[1127]**, Chicago, IL
Phi Theta Kappa, Alpha Lambda Phi Chap. - Joliet Junior Coll. **[2117]**, Joliet, IL
Phi Theta Kappa - Alpha Mu Delta Chap. **[16108]**, Nelsonville, OH
Phi Theta Kappa - Alpha Mu Epsilon Chap. **[15250]**, Fremont, OH
Phi Theta Kappa, Alpha Mu Omega Chap. - Univ. of Wisconsin-Sheboygan **[19704]**, Sheboygan, WI
Phi Theta Kappa - Alpha Mu Xi Chap. **[17325]**, Wooster, OH
Phi Theta Kappa, Alpha Nu Eta Chap. - Kellogg Community Coll. **[6868]**, Battle Creek, MI
Phi Theta Kappa, Alpha Nu Iota Chap. - Nicolet Area Tech. Coll. **[19603]**, Rhinelander, WI
Phi Theta Kappa, Alpha Nu Kappa Chap. - Minnesota West Community and Tech. Coll. **[12991]**, Worthington, MN
Phi Theta Kappa - Alpha Nu Lambda Chap. **[16739]**, Springfield, OH
Phi Theta Kappa, Alpha Nu Theta Chap. - DeVry Univ. **[10]**, Addison, IL
Phi Theta Kappa, Alpha Omega Delta Chap. - Ivy Tech State Coll. **[4115]**, Anderson, IN
Phi Theta Kappa - Alpha Omega Pi Chap. **[16948]**, Toledo, OH
Phi Theta Kappa, Alpha Omega Xi Chap. - Heartland Community Coll. **[2730]**, Normal, IL
Phi Theta Kappa, Alpha Omicron Beta Chap. - Inver Hills Community Coll. **[11225]**, Inver Grove Heights, MN
Phi Theta Kappa - Alpha Omicron Eta Chap. **[15449]**, Hillsboro, OH
Phi Theta Kappa, Alpha Omicron Gamma Chap. - Kirtland Community Coll. **[9556]**, Roscommon, MI
Phi Theta Kappa, Alpha Omicron Iota Chap. - Mott Community Coll. **[7750]**, Flint, MI
Phi Theta Kappa, Alpha Omicron Kappa Chap. - Oakland Community Coll. **[10091]**, Waterford, MI
Phi Theta Kappa - Alpha Omicron Mu Chap. **[13155]**, Archbold, OH
Phi Theta Kappa - Alpha Omicron Nu Chap. **[16767]**, Steubenville, OH
Phi Theta Kappa, Alpha Omicron Omicron Chap. - Mid Michigan Community Coll. **[8130]**, Harrison, MI
Phi Theta Kappa, Alpha Omicron Psi Chap. - Oakland Community Coll. **[9816]**, Southfield, MI
Phi Theta Kappa, Alpha Omicron Rho Chap. - Oakland Community Coll. **[6815]**, Auburn Hills, MI
Phi Theta Kappa, Alpha Omicron Upsilon Chap. - North Central Michigan Coll. **[9369]**, Petoskey, MI
Phi Theta Kappa, Alpha Omicron Xi Chap. - Oakland Community Coll. **[7673]**, Farmington Hills, MI
Phi Theta Kappa, Alpha Phi Beta Chap. - Black Hawk Coll. **[2159]**, Kewanee, IL
Phi Theta Kappa, Alpha Phi Eta Chap. - Ivy Tech State Coll. **[6339]**, Terre Haute, IN
Phi Theta Kappa ,Alpha Phi Omega Chap. - Ivy Tech State Coll. **[4785]**, Gary, IN
Phi Theta Kappa, Alpha Phi Phi Chap. - West Shore Community Coll. **[9735]**, Scottville, MI
Phi Theta Kappa, Alpha Phi Pi Chap. - Ivy Tech State Coll. **[5581]**, Kokomo, IN
Phi Theta Kappa, Alpha Phi Theta Chap. - Ivy Tech State Coll. **[4565]**, Evansville, IN
Phi Theta Kappa, Alpha Phi Upsilon Chap. - Hennepin Tech. Coll. **[10692]**, Cloquet, MN
Phi Theta Kappa, Alpha Pi Phi Chap. - Alexandria Tech. Coll. **[10284]**, Alexandria, MN
Phi Theta Kappa, Alpha Psi Eta Chap. - Parkland Coll. **[545]**, Champaign, IL
Phi Theta Kappa, Alpha Psi Lambda Chap. - Ivy Tech State Coll. **[5719]**, Madison, IN

Phi Theta Kappa - Alpha Psi Phi Chap. [13671], Chillicothe, OH
Phi Theta Kappa - Alpha Psi Rho Chap. [15573], Kirtland, OH
Phi Theta Kappa, Alpha Rho Alpha Chap. - Rainy River Community Coll. [11218], International Falls, MN
Phi Theta Kappa, Alpha Rho Chi Chap. - Gogebic Community Coll. [8340], Ironwood, MI
Phi Theta Kappa - Alpha Rho Epsilon Chap. [14710], Columbus, OH
Phi Theta Kappa, Alpha Rho Eta Chap. - Kishwaukee Coll. [2381], Malta, IL
Phi Theta Kappa - Alpha Rho Gamma Chap. [15827], Marietta, OH
Phi Theta Kappa, Alpha Rho Lambda Chap. - Jackson Community Coll. [8393], Jackson, MI
Phi Theta Kappa, Alpha Rho Nu Chap. - Kalamazoo Valley Community Coll. [8460], Kalamazoo, MI
Phi Theta Kappa, Alpha Rho Pi Chap. - Northwestern Michigan Coll. [9946], Traverse City, MI
Phi Theta Kappa, Alpha Rho Sigma Chap. - Ivy Tech State Coll. [4251], Bloomington, IN
Phi Theta Kappa, Alpha Rho Tau Chap. - Ivy Tech State Coll. [4404], Columbus, IN
Phi Theta Kappa, Alpha Rho Zeta Chap. - Waukesha County Tech. Coll. [19441], Pewaukee, WI
Phi Theta Kappa, Alpha Sigma Kappa Chap. - Ivy Tech State Coll. [5630], Lafayette, IN
Phi Theta Kappa, Alpha Sigma Lambda Chap. - Univ. of Wisconsin-Manitowoc [18790], Manitowoc, WI
Phi Theta Kappa, Alpha Tau Alpha Chap. - Montcalm Community Coll. [9754], Sidney, MI
Phi Theta Kappa, Alpha Tau Gamma Chap. - John Wood Community Coll. [3158], Quincy, IL
Phi Theta Kappa - Alpha Tau Mu Chap. [15668], Lima, OH
Phi Theta Kappa, Alpha Tau Omicron Chap. - Ivy Tech State Coll. [6253], South Bend, IN
Phi Theta Kappa, Alpha Tau Sigma Chap. - Ivy Tech State Coll. [6178], Sellersburg, IN
Phi Theta Kappa ,Alpha Tau Xi Chap. - Ivy Tech State Coll. [4710], Fort Wayne, IN
Phi Theta Kappa, Alpha Theta Eta Chap. - Olney Central Coll. [2860], Olney, IL
Phi Theta Kappa, Alpha Theta Pi Chap. - Univ. of Wisconsin-Barron [19615], Rice Lake, WI
Phi Theta Kappa, Alpha Theta Psi Chap. - Lake Land Coll. [2445], Mattoon, IL
Phi Theta Kappa, Alpha Theta Tau Chap. - Univ. of Wisconsin-Fox Valley [18864], Menasha, WI
Phi Theta Kappa - Alpha Theta Zeta Chap. [16183], Newark, OH
Phi Theta Kappa, Alpha Upsilon Gamma Chap. - Lake Superior Coll. [10849], Duluth, MN
Phi Theta Kappa, Alpha Upsilon Kappa Chap. - Grand Rapids Community Coll. [7997], Grand Rapids, MI
Phi Theta Kappa, Alpha Upsilon Lambda Chap. - Ivy Tech State Coll. [5894], Muncie, IN
Phi Theta Kappa, Alpha Upsilon Omega Chap. - Ivy Tech State Coll. [6100], Richmond, IN
Phi Theta Kappa, Alpha Upsilon Tau Chap. - Ivy Tech State Coll. [5449], Indianapolis, IN
Phi Theta Kappa, Alpha Upsilon Zeta Chap. - Wayne County Community Coll. [7418], Detroit, MI
Phi Theta Kappa, Alpha Xi Delta Chap. - Bay de Noc Community Coll. [7617], Escanaba, MI
Phi Theta Kappa, Alpha Xi Iota Chap. - Gateway Tech. Coll. [18307], Kenosha, WI
Phi Theta Kappa, Alpha Xi Kappa Chap. - Univ. of Wisconsin-Marshfield/Wood County [18822], Marshfield, WI
Phi Theta Kappa, Alpha Xi Mu Chap. - Henry Ford Community Coll. [7266], Dearborn, MI
Phi Theta Kappa - Alpha Zeta Chi Chap. [16311], Orrville, OH
Phi Theta Kappa - Alpha Zeta Delta Chap. [14204], Cleveland, OH
Phi Theta Kappa, Beta Alpha Gamma Chap. - Sauk Valley Community Coll. [1482], Dixon, IL
Phi Theta Kappa, Beta Alpha Lambda Chap. - Frontier Community Coll. [1689], Fairfield, IL
Phi Theta Kappa, Beta Alpha Omega Chap. - Univ. of Indianapolis [5450], Indianapolis, IN
Phi Theta Kappa, Beta Beta Alpha Chap. - Ivy Tech State Coll. [4504], Elkhart, IN
Phi Theta Kappa, Beta Beta Beta Chap. - Ancilla Coll. [4462], Donaldson, IN
Phi Theta Kappa, Beta Beta Psi Chap. - Madison Area Tech. Coll. [18597], Madison, WI
Phi Theta Kappa - Beta Beta Theta Chap. [15608], Lancaster, OH
Phi Theta Kappa - Beta Epsilon Delta Chap. [16018], Middletown, OH
Phi Theta Kappa, Beta Epsilon Omicron Chap. - Fox Valley Tech. Coll. [17515], Appleton, WI
Phi Theta Kappa, Beta Epsilon Rho Chap. - Holy Cross Coll. [6005], Notre Dame, IN
Phi Theta Kappa, Beta Eta Chi Chap. - Ridgewater Coll. [11212], Hutchinson, MN
Phi Theta Kappa, Beta Gamma Alpha Chap. - Washtenaw Community Coll. [6754], Ann Arbor, MI
Phi Theta Kappa - Beta Gamma Epsilon Chap. [13578], Canton, OH
Phi Theta Kappa - Beta Gamma Sigma Chap. [13957], Cincinnati, OH
Phi Theta Kappa, Beta Gamma Tau Chap. - Ivy Tech State Coll. [5661], Lawrenceburg, IN
Phi Theta Kappa, Beta Gamma Zeta Chap. - Ivy Tech State Coll. [5696], Logansport, IN
Phi Theta Kappa, Beta Iota Iota Chap. - Southwestern Illinois Coll. [3186], Red Bud, IL
Phi Theta Kappa, Beta Kappa Eta Chap. - Univ. of Wisconsin-Baraboo/Sauk [17576], Baraboo, WI
Phi Theta Kappa, Beta Kappa Kappa Chap. - Univ. of Wisconsin-Marathon County [20044], Wausau, WI
Phi Theta Kappa, Beta Kappa Rho Chap. - Northwest Tech. Coll. [12002], Pine City, MN
Phi Theta Kappa, Beta Kappa Xi Chap. - Hennepin Tech. Coll. [10556], Brooklyn Park, MN
Phi Theta Kappa, Beta Lambda Kappa Chap. - Macomb Community Coll. [7186], Clinton Township, MI
Phi Theta Kappa - Beta Lambda Nu Chap. [16136], New Lexington, OH
Phi Theta Kappa, Beta Lambda Sigma Chap. - Lakeshore Tech. Coll. [17767], Cleveland, WI
Phi Theta Kappa, Beta Lambda Xi Chap. - Dunwood Coll. of Tech. [11724], Minneapolis, MN
Phi Theta Kappa, Beta Mu Chi Chap. - Univ. of Wisconsin-Rock County [18259], Janesville, WI
Phi Theta Kappa, Beta Mu Eta Chap. - South Central Tech. Coll. [11907], North Mankato, MN
Phi Theta Kappa, Beta Mu Kappa Chap. - Moraine Park Tech. Coll. [17990], Fond du Lac, WI
Phi Theta Kappa, Beta Nu Beta Chap. - South Central Tech. Coll. [10986], Faribault, MN
Phi Theta Kappa, Beta Nu Chi Chap. - Western Wisconsin Tech. Coll. [18375], La Crosse, WI
Phi Theta Kappa, Beta Nu Kappa Chap. - Northland Community and Tech. Coll. [10884], East Grand Forks, MN
Phi Theta Kappa, Beta Nu Omicron Chap. - Anoka Tech. Coll. [10310], Anoka, MN
Phi Theta Kappa - Beta Nu Phi Chap. [16533], Rio Grande, OH
Phi Theta Kappa - Beta Nu Pi Chap. [15851], Marion, OH
Phi Theta Kappa, Beta Nu Tau Chap. - Northwest Tech. Coll. [10424], Bemidji, MN
Phi Theta Kappa - Beta Theta Eta Chap. [15787], Mansfield, OH
Phi Theta Kappa - Beta Theta Mu Chap. [16572], St. Clairsville, OH
Phi Theta Kappa, Beta Theta Tau Chap. - Dakota County Tech. Coll. [12216], Rosemount, MN
Phi Theta Kappa, Beta Xi Alpha Chap. - Saint Paul Coll. [12559], St. Paul, MN
Phi Theta Kappa, Beta Zeta Beta Chap. - Trinity Coll. of Nursing [3248], Rock Island, IL
Phi Theta Kappa, Beta Zeta Kappa Chap. - Ivy Tech State Coll. [6453], Warsaw, IN
Phi Theta Kappa, Beta Zeta Rho Chap. - Vincennes Univ.-Jasper [5534], Jasper, IN
Phi Theta Kappa, Chi Chi Chap. - Univ. of Wisconsin-Washington [20127], West Bend, WI
Phi Theta Kappa, Chi Kappa Chap. - Carl Sandburg Coll. [1779], Galesburg, IL
Phi Theta Kappa - Chi Omega Chap. [16377], Parma, OH
Phi Theta Kappa, Chi Upsilon Chap. - McHenry County Coll. [1332], Crystal Lake, IL
Phi Theta Kappa, Chi Zeta Chap. - Triton Coll. [3207], River Grove, IL
Phi Theta Kappa, Delta Theta Chap. - Springfield Coll. [3661], Springfield, IL
Phi Theta Kappa, Eta Kappa Chap. - Black Hawk Coll. [2527], Moline, IL
Phi Theta Kappa, Eta Psi Chap. - Lewis and Clark Community Coll. [1875], Godfrey, IL
Phi Theta Kappa, Iota Chi Chap. - Lincoln Coll. [2280], Lincoln, IL
Phi Theta Kappa, Iota Omicron Chap. - Kaskaskia Coll. [491], Centralia, IL
Phi Theta Kappa, Kappa Beta Chap. - Kendall Coll. [1128], Chicago, IL
Phi Theta Kappa, Lambda Iota Chap. - Olive-Harvey Coll. [1129], Chicago, IL
Phi Theta Kappa, Lambda Mu Chap. - St. Clair County Community Coll. [9437], Port Huron, MI
Phi Theta Kappa, Lambda Rho Chap. - Kennedy-King Coll. [1130], Chicago, IL
Phi Theta Kappa, Mu Nu Chap. - Lake Michigan Coll. [6921], Benton Harbor, MI
Phi Theta Kappa, Mu Pi Chap. - Harold Washington Coll. [1131], Chicago, IL
Phi Theta Kappa, Mu Psi Chap. - Southeastern Illinois Coll. [1939], Harrisburg, IL
Phi Theta Kappa, Mu Tau Chap. - Lansing Community Coll. [8750], Lansing, MI
Phi Theta Kappa, Nu Delta Chap. - Spoon River Coll. [406], Canton, IL
Phi Theta Kappa, Nu Lambda Chap. - Harry S. Truman Coll. [1132], Chicago, IL
Phi Theta Kappa, Nu Mu Chap. - Highland Community Coll. [1752], Freeport, IL
Phi Theta Kappa, Nu Omicron Chap. - Alpena Community Coll. [6648], Alpena, MI
Phi Theta Kappa - Nu Pi Chap. [14946], Dayton, OH
Phi Theta Kappa, Nu Sigma Chap. - Prairie State Coll. [1251], Chicago Heights, IL
Phi Theta Kappa, Omicron Chap. - Rochester Community and Tech. Coll. [12169], Rochester, MN
Phi Theta Kappa, Omicron Eta Chap. - Rock Valley Coll. [3298], Rockford, IL
Phi Theta Kappa, Omicron Iota Chap. - Schoolcraft Coll. [8853], Livonia, MI
Phi Theta Kappa, Omicron Omicron Chap. - Minnesota State Community and Tech. Coll. [11002], Fergus Falls, MN
Phi Theta Kappa, Phi Beta Chap. - Coll. of DuPage [1839], Glen Ellyn, IL
Phi Theta Kappa, Phi Mu Chap. - Univ. of Wisconsin-Richland [19624], Richland Center, WI
Phi Theta Kappa, Phi Omicron Chap. - Waubonsee Community Coll. [3737], Sugar Grove, IL
Phi Theta Kappa, Phi Phi Chap. - William Rainey Harper Coll. [2926], Palatine, IL
Phi Theta Kappa - Phi Pi Chap. [15124], Elyria, OH
Phi Theta Kappa, Phi Xi Chap. - North Hennepin Community Coll. [10557], Brooklyn Park, MN
Phi Theta Kappa, Pi Omega Chap. - Danville Area Community Coll. [1350], Danville, IL
Phi Theta Kappa, Pi Rho Chap. - Richard J. Daley Coll. [1133], Chicago, IL
Phi Theta Kappa, Psi Pi Chap. - South Suburban Coll. of Cook County [3506], South Holland, IL
Phi Theta Kappa, Rho Kappa Chap. - Elgin Community Coll. [1599], Elgin, IL
Phi Theta Kappa, Rho Omega Chap. - Illinois Valley Community Coll. [2854], Oglesby, IL
Phi Theta Kappa, Rho Psi Chap. - Wabash Valley Coll. [2574], Mount Carmel, IL
Phi Theta Kappa, Rho Xi Chap. - Rend Lake Coll. [2060], Ina, IL
Phi Theta Kappa, Sigma Alpha Chap. - Northland Community and Tech. Coll. [12746], Thief River Falls, MN
Phi Theta Kappa, Sigma Psi Chap. - Southwestern Michigan Coll. [7482], Dowagiac, MI

Phi Theta Kappa, Sigma Theta Chap. - Milwaukee Area Tech. Coll. **[18888]**, Mequon, WI
Phi Theta Kappa, Tau Delta Chap. - MacCormac Coll. **[1134]**, Chicago, IL
Phi Theta Kappa, Tau Omicron Chap. - Monroe County Community Coll. **[9073]**, Monroe, MI
Phi Theta Kappa, Theta Epsilon Chap. - Southwestern Illinois Coll. **[209]**, Belleville, IL
Phi Theta Kappa, Theta Kappa Chap. - Hibbing Community Coll. **[11161]**, Hibbing, MN
Phi Theta Kappa, Theta Omega Chap. - Wilbur Wright Coll. **[1135]**, Chicago, IL
Phi Theta Kappa, Theta Omicron Chap. - Morton Coll. **[1261]**, Cicero, IL
Phi Theta Kappa, Upsilon Mu Chap. - Illinois Central Coll. **[3058]**, Peoria, IL
Phi Theta Kappa, Upsilon Omega Chap. - Central Lakes Coll. **[10518]**, Brainerd, MN
Phi Theta Kappa, Upsilon Pi Chap. - John A. Logan Coll. **[463]**, Carterville, IL
Phi Theta Kappa - Upsilon Psi Chap. **[13958]**, Cincinnati, OH
Phi Theta Kappa, Xi Delta Chap. - Delta Coll. **[10030]**, University Center, MI
Phi Theta Kappa, Zeta Eta Chap. - Riverland Community Coll. **[10357]**, Austin, MN
Phi Theta Kappa, Zeta Iota Chap. - Mesabi Range Community/Tech. Coll. **[12804]**, Virginia, MN
Phi Theta Kappa, Zeta Psi Chap. - Vincennes Univ. **[6420]**, Vincennes, IN
Hoosier African Violet Soc. **[6057]**, Portage, IN
Hoosier Appaloosas **[4376]**, Coatesville, IN
Hoosier Assn. of Sci. Teachers **[5137]**, Indianapolis, IN
Hoosier Back Country Horsemen, Indiana **[4748]**, Franklin, IN
Hoosier Bird Buddies **[4669]**, Fort Wayne, IN
Hoosier Corvette Club **[5138]**, Indianapolis, IN
Hoosier Environmental Coun. **[5139]**, Indianapolis, IN
Hoosier Heartland Rsrc. Conservation and Development Coun. **[5140]**, Indianapolis, IN
Hoosier Hikers Coun. **[5754]**, Martinsville, IN
Hoosier Hills Estate Planning Coun. **[4225]**, Bloomington, IN
Hoosier Kitefliers Soc. **[5141]**, Indianapolis, IN
Hoosier Mountain Bike Assn. **[5142]**, Indianapolis, IN
Hoosier Mountain Bike Club Assn. **[5143]**, Indianapolis, IN
Hoosier Muskie Hunters **[5144]**, Indianapolis, IN
Hoosier Orchid Soc. **[5145]**, Indianapolis, IN
Hoosier Praire ARC **[5824]**, Monticello, IN
Hoosier Sail and Power Squadron **[4320]**, Carmel, IN
Hoosier Salon Patrons Assn. and Galleries **[5146]**, Indianapolis, IN
Hoosier State Press Assn. **[5147]**, Indianapolis, IN
Hoosier Vintage Thunderbird Club **[4670]**, Fort Wayne, IN
Hoosiers Concerned about Gun Violence **[5148]**, Indianapolis, IN
Hooved Animal Humane Soc. **[4056]**, Woodstock, IL
Hoover-Wood Elementary School Parent Teacher Org. **[181]**, Batavia, IL
Hopkins Area Jaycees **[11184]**, Hopkins, MN
Hopkins Evening Lions Club **[11787]**, Minnetonka, MN
Hopkins Noontime Lions Club **[10948]**, Elk River, MN
The Hopkins Painters **[★7429]**
Hopkins Royals Boys Basketball Assn. **[12333]**, St. Louis Park, MN
Hopkins - Young Life **[8205]**, Holland, MI
Hopkins Young Life **[11185]**, Hopkins, MN
Horicon Chamber of Commerce **[18215]**, Horicon, WI
Horizon Community Sers., DBA Center on Halsted **[916]**, Chicago, IL
Horizons for Youth **[917]**, Chicago, IL
Horse Assn. of Ohio; Pinto **[13229]**, Atwater, OH
Horse Club; Mid Am. Miniature **[16812]**, Sunbury, OH

Horse Racing

Illinois Natl. Barrel Horse Assn. **[2978]**, Payson, IL
Indiana Natl. Barrel Horse Assn. **[6464]**, Waynetown, IN
Michigan Natl. Barrel Horse Assn. **[7041]**, Byron Center, MI
Minnesota Natl. Barrel Horse Assn. **[12066]**, Randolph, MN
Ohio Harness Horsemen's Assn. **[14621]**, Columbus, OH
Ohio Natl. Barrel Horse Assn. **[15256]**, Fresno, OH
U.S. Harness Writers Assn., Ohio Chap. **[14750]**, Columbus, OH
Wisconsin Natl. Barrel Horse Assn. **[20168]**, Wilson, WI

Horseback Riding

Back Country Horsemen of Illinois **[1640]**, Equality, IL
Centerline Dressage **[3542]**, Springfield, IL
Central States Dressage and Eventing Assn. **[12894]**, White Bear Lake, MN
Classical Attraction Dressage Soc. **[13437]**, Brooklyn, OH
Great Lakes Area Show Series Educal. Dressage **[7123]**, Charlotte, MI
Hoosier Back Country Horsemen, Indiana **[4748]**, Franklin, IN
Illinois Dressage and Combined Training Assn. **[3719]**, Streamwood, IL
Illinois Trail Riders **[1561]**, Edwardsville, IL
Indiana Dressage Soc. **[4361]**, Cicero, IN
Michiana Dressage Club **[7286]**, Decatur, MI
Mid-Ohio Dressage Assn. **[15274]**, Galena, OH
Midwest Dressage Assn. **[9618]**, Saginaw, MI
Northern Ohio Dressage Assn. **[16683]**, Solon, OH
Ohio Dressage Soc. **[16386]**, Pataskala, OH
Ottawa Back Country Horsemen, Michigan **[7033]**, Bruce Crossing, MI
West Wisconsin Dressage Assn. **[17923]**, Elk Mound, WI
Wisconsin Dressage and Combined Training Assn. **[20132]**, West Bend, WI
Horseless Carriage Club of Am., Grand Rapids **[7054]**, Caledonia, MI

Horses

Amer. Morgan Horse Assn., Region 3 **[6199]**, Sheridan, IN
Amer. Morgan Horse Assn., Region 5 **[715]**, Chicago, IL
Amer. Saddlebred Assn. of Wisconsin **[19982]**, Waukesha, WI
Amer. Saddlebred Horse Assn. of Michigan **[7763]**, Flushing, MI
Amer. Saddlebred Horse Assn. of Ohio **[15464]**, Homerville, OH
Amer. Trail Horse Assn. **[1302]**, Cortland, IL
Appalachian Appaloosa Assn. **[15443]**, Hillsboro, OH
Arabian Horse Assn. of Michigan **[10105]**, Webberville, MI
Badger State Morgan Horse Club **[17854]**, East Troy, WI
Big River Appaloosa Horse club **[414]**, Carbondale, IL
Big River Bend Appaloosa Horse Club **[5847]**, Mount Vernon, IN
Blackhawk Appaloosa Horse Club **[3739]**, Sullivan, IL
Buckeye Appaloosa Horse Club **[13360]**, Big Prairie, OH
Buckeye Fox Trotter Assn. **[13446]**, Brunswick, OH
Caballo Norte **[18417]**, Lena, WI
Classic Peruvian's Horse Club **[17916]**, Edgerton, WI
Glacial Ridge Appaloosa Horse Club **[12614]**, St. Peter, MN
Great Lakes Appaloosa Horse Club **[15008]**, Delaware, OH
Heartland Peruvian Horse Club **[5994]**, North Vernon, IN
Hoosier Appaloosas **[4376]**, Coatesville, IN
Illinois Amer. Saddlebred Horse Assn. **[1867]**, Glenview, IL
Illinois Appaloosa Assn. **[3750]**, Tallula, IL
Illinois Draft Horse and Mule Breeders Assn. **[3129]**, Prairie City, IL
Illinois Haflinger Assn. **[1717]**, Forreston, IL
Illinois Quarter Horse Assn. **[1610]**, Elk Grove Village, IL
Illinois Quarter Horse Assn., District No. 2 **[182]**, Batavia, IL
Illinois Quarter Horse Assn., District No. 3 **[1895]**, Grayslake, IL
Illinois Quarter Horse Assn., District No. 4 **[2343]**, London Mills, IL
Illinois Quarter Horse Assn., District No. 6 **[528]**, Champaign, IL
Illinois Quarter Horse Assn., District No. 7 **[560]**, Chandlerville, IL
Illinois Quarter Horse Assn., District No. 8 **[104]**, Auburn, IL
Illinois Quarter Horse Assn., District No. 9 **[2967]**, Patoka, IL
Illinois Quarter Horse Assn., District No. 11 **[3860]**, Vienna, IL
Illinois Quarter Horse Assn., District No. 12 **[2754]**, Northbrook, IL
Illinois Standardbred Owners and Breeders Assn. **[3637]**, Springfield, IL
Illinois Thoroughbred Breeders and Owners Found. **[482]**, Caseyville, IL
Indiana Amer. Saddlebred Horse Assn. **[4322]**, Carmel, IN
Indiana Appaloosa Assn. **[4151]**, Avilla, IN
Indiana Draft Horse Breeders **[4360]**, Cicero, IN
Indiana Fox Trotter Association **[6326]**, Terre Haute, IN
Indiana Haflinger Horse Assn. **[4798]**, Goshen, IN
Indiana Horse Coun. **[5246]**, Indianapolis, IN
Indiana Morgan Horse Club **[6046]**, Plymouth, IN
Indiana Quarter Horse Assn. **[6047]**, Plymouth, IN
Indianhead Appaloosa Horse Club **[11028]**, Franklin, MN
KYOVA Morgan Horse Assn. **[15727]**, Loveland, OH
Lagos Grandes Peruvian Horse Club **[7090]**, Carson City, MI
Michigan Appaloosa Horse Assn. **[9772]**, South Lyon, MI
Michigan Draft Horse Breeders Assn. **[6913]**, Bellevue, MI
Michigan Fox Trotter Assn. **[10157]**, White Lake, MI
Michigan Harness Horsemen's Assn. **[9279]**, Okemos, MI
Michigan Justin Morgan Horse Assn. **[7687]**, Fenton, MI
Michigan Quarter Horse Assn. **[8069]**, Greenville, MI
Michigan Trail Riders Assn. **[9877]**, Stockbridge, MI
Mid Am. Miniature Horse Club **[16812]**, Sunbury, OH
Mid-States Morgan Horse Club **[2211]**, Lake Zurich, IL
Midwest Natl. Show Horse Assn. **[15222]**, Fort Jennings, OH
Minnesota Fox Trotter Assn. **[13000]**, Zimmerman, MN
Minnesota Quarter Horse Assn. **[10632]**, Cannon Falls, MN
Minnesota Quarter Horse Assn., District 1 **[11438]**, Marshall, MN
Minnesota Quarter Horse Assn., District 2 **[10293]**, Amboy, MN
Minnesota Quarter Horse Assn., District 3 **[11246]**, Kasson, MN
Minnesota Quarter Horse Assn., District 4 **[12241]**, Roseville, MN
Minnesota Quarter Horse Assn., District 5 **[11200]**, Howard Lake, MN
Minnesota Quarter Horse Assn., District 6 **[12785]**, Verndale, MN
Minnesota Quarter Horse Assn., District 7 **[13001]**, Zimmerman, MN
Minnesota Quarter Horse Assn., District 8 **[10532]**, Brook Park, MN
Minnesota Quarter Horse Assn., District 9 **[10419]**, Bemidji, MN
Minnesota Saddlebred Horse Assn. **[10600]**, Burnsville, MN
Mississippi Valley Morgan Horse Club **[3650]**, Springfield, IL
Natl. Show Horse Assn. of Minnesota **[12338]**, St. Louis Park, MN
North Amer. Horse and Mule Loggers Assn. **[11359]**, Lyle, MN

North Central Morgan Horse Assn. **[10899]**, Eden Prairie, MN
North Country Appaloosa Horse Club **[12648]**, Sebeka, MN
Northeast Wisconsin Appaloosa Horse Club **[19500]**, Port Washington, WI
Northern Indiana Draft Horse Breeders **[5803]**, Millersburg, IN
Northern Lights Peruvian House Club **[17818]**, Deer Park, WI
Northern Michigan Appaloosa Horse Club **[8064]**, Grayling, MI
Northern Ohio Draft Pony Assn. **[13226]**, Attica, OH
Ohio Chap. of the MFTHBA **[15536]**, Kensington, OH
Ohio Haflinger Assn. **[17324]**, Wooster, OH
Ohio Morgan Horse Assn. **[15334]**, Grafton, OH
Ohio Quarter Horse Assn. **[16529]**, Richwood, OH
Ohio State Pony of the Americas Club **[15810]**, Marengo, OH
Ohio Thoroughbred Breeders and Owners **[13945]**, Cincinnati, OH
Pinto Horse Assn. of Ohio **[13229]**, Atwater, OH
Pony of the Americas Club, Minnesota **[11397]**, Mankato, MN
Pony of the Ams. Club, Wisconsin - North **[17922]**, Elk Mound, WI
Pony of the Ams. Club, Wisconsin - North Central **[19799]**, Stevens Point, WI
Pony of the Ams. Club, Wisconsin - Southern **[19510]**, Portage, WI
Red River Valley Appaloosa Horse Club **[12873]**, West Concord, MN
Shawnee Hills Appaloosa Horse Club **[3411]**, Salem, IL
Southern Illinois Haflinger Assn. **[3902]**, Waterloo, IL
Southern Ohio Draft Horse Assn. **[15451]**, Hillsboro, OH
Southern Wisconsin Appaloosa Horse Club **[17930]**, Elkhorn, WI
West Virginia Quarter Horse Assn. **[17247]**, Wheelersburg, OH
Western Michigan Appaloosa Horse Club **[7220]**, Constantine, MI
Wisconsin Draft Horse Breeders **[18205]**, Hilbert, WI
Wisconsin/Illinois Show Horse Soc. **[17859]**, East Troy, WI
Wisconsin Morgan Horse Club **[19227]**, Monticello, WI
Wisconsin Pony of the Americas Club **[19939]**, Vesper, WI
Wisconsin Quarter Horse Assn. **[19309]**, New Holstein, WI
Wissota Appaloosa Horse Club **[12874]**, West Concord, MN
Wolverine Morgan Horse Assn. **[8479]**, Kalkaska, MI
Horses Have Hope and Other Animals Too **[17842]**, Dousman, WI
Horseshoe Club; Eau Claire **[17753]**, Chippewa Falls, WI
Horseshoes
Eau Claire Horseshoe Club **[17753]**, Chippewa Falls, WI
Natl. Horseshoe Pitchers Assn. - Ohio **[14522]**, Columbus, OH
Horticultural Soc; Cincinnati **[13788]**, Cincinnati, OH
Horticultural Soc; Michigan State **[8140]**, Hartford, MI
Horticulture
Cincinnati Horticultural Soc. **[13788]**, Cincinnati, OH
Illinois State Horticultural Soc. **[290]**, Bloomington, IL
Michigan State Horticultural Soc. **[8140]**, Hartford, MI
Southwestern Indiana Master Gardener Assn. **[4579]**, Evansville, IN
West Michigan Bonsai Club **[8072]**, Greenville, MI
Hospice
Ohio Hospice and Palliative Care Org. **[15057]**, Dublin, OH
Palliative CareCenter and Hospice of the North Shore **[1672]**, Evanston, IL
Hospice Patients Alliance **[9524]**, Rockford, MI
Hospital
Amer. Soc. for Healthcare Food Ser. Administrators, Central Minnesota Chap. **[11517]**, Minneapolis, MN
Amer. Soc. for Healthcare Food Ser. Administrators, Chicago Midwest Chap. **[2905]**, Palatine, IL
Amer. Soc. for Healthcare Food Ser. Administrators, Hoosier Chap. **[5751]**, Martinsville, IN
Amer. Soc. for Hea.care Food Ser. Administrators, Wisconsin Chap. **[18471]**, Madison, WI
Arrowhead Hea. Care Engineers Assn. **[10805]**, Duluth, MN
Chicago Assn. for Healthcare Central Ser. Professionals **[6]**, Addison, IL
Chicago Hea. Executives Forum **[2149]**, Kenilworth, IL
Chicago Metro Chap. of Assn. for Healthcare Rsrc. and Materials Mgt. **[179]**, Batavia, IL
East Central Michigan Soc. for Healthcare Engg. **[9986]**, Troy, MI
Great Lakes Chap. of the Amer. Coll. of Healthcare Executives **[7956]**, Grand Rapids, MI
Hea. Care Public Relations and Marketing Soc. for Southeastern Wisconsin **[18886]**, Mequon, WI
Healthcare Executives Assn. of Northeast Ohio **[13636]**, Chagrin Falls, OH
Hosp. Engineers Soc. of Northern Illinois **[3078]**, Peru, IL
Illinois Hosp. Assn. **[2643]**, Naperville, IL
Indiana Healthcare Executives Network **[4607]**, Fishers, IN
Indiana Hosp. and Hea. Assn. **[5247]**, Indianapolis, IN
Indiana Hosp. Purchasing and Materials Mgt. Assn. **[5248]**, Indianapolis, IN
Indiana Soc. for Hea.care Engg. **[5303]**, Indianapolis, IN
Intl. Assn. for Healthcare Security and Safety - Michigan Chap. **[7378]**, Detroit, MI
Michigan Healthcare Executive Gp. and Associates **[9664]**, St. Clair Shores, MI
Michigan Healthcare Rsrc. and Materials Mgt. **[9090]**, Mount Clemens, MI
Michigan Soc. of Healthcare Risk Mgt. **[7263]**, Dearborn, MI
Mid-Ohio Central Ser. Professionals **[14503]**, Columbus, OH
Mid-Western Hea. Care Engg. Assn. **[11977]**, Park Rapids, MN
Midwest Central Ser. Assn. **[3479]**, Silvis, IL
Minnesota Chap. of the Assn. for Healthcare Rsrc. and Materials Mgt. **[12920]**, Willmar, MN
Mount Sinai Hosp. **[1060]**, Chicago, IL
Ohio Hosp. Assn. **[14626]**, Columbus, OH
Ohio Soc. for Healthcare Engg. **[16017]**, Middletown, OH
Ohio Valley Central Ser. Professionals **[4564]**, Evansville, IN
Southern Illinois Chap. for Healthcare Engg. **[431]**, Carbondale, IL
Southern Illinois Healthcare Materials Mgt. Assn. **[2092]**, Jerseyville, IL
Southern Minnesota Healthcare Engineers Assn. **[12193]**, Rochester, MN
Tri-State Soc. for Healthcare Engineerings **[14012]**, Cincinnati, OH
Tri-State Soc. for Healthcare Engineers **[14013]**, Cincinnati, OH
Twin City Healthcare Engg. Assn. **[10928]**, Edina, MN
West Michigan Soc. for Healthcare Engg. **[8023]**, Grand Rapids, MI
Wisconsin Assn. of Central Ser. Professionals **[18651]**, Madison, WI
Wisconsin Forum for Healthcare Strategy **[18707]**, Madison, WI
Wisconsin Healthcare Engg. Assn. **[19170]**, Milwaukee, WI
Wisconsin Hea.care Public Relations and Marketing Soc. **[20196]**, Wisconsin Rapids, WI
Wisconsin Healthcare Purchasing and Materials Mgt. Assn. **[19171]**, Milwaukee, WI
Hosp. Assn; Ohio **[14626]**, Columbus, OH
Hosp. Engineers Soc. of Northern Illinois **[3078]**, Peru, IL
Hospitality Financial and Tech. Professionals - Chicago Chap. **[918]**, Chicago, IL
Hosp.ity Financial and Tech. Professionals - Cleveland/Akron Chap. **[16679]**, Solon, OH
Hosp.ity Financial and Tech. Professionals - Greater Detroit Chap. **[6985]**, Bloomfield Hills, MI
Hospitality Financial and Tech. Professionals - Greater Milwaukee Chap. **[19985]**, Waukesha, WI
Hosp.ity Financial and Tech. Professionals - Minneapolis/St. Paul Chap. **[12422]**, St. Paul, MN
Hosp.ity Financial and Tech. Professionals - West Michigan Chap. **[9487]**, Richland, MI
Hospitality Industries
Hotel Employees and Restaurant Employees Intl. Union, AFL-CIO, CLC - Local Union 21 **[12145]**, Rochester, MN
Hotel Employees and Restaurant Employees Intl. Union, AFL-CIO, CLC - Minnesota State Coun. **[12146]**, Rochester, MN
Hotel Employees and Restaurant Employees Intl. Union Local 17 **[11579]**, Minneapolis, MN
Hotel Employees and Restaurant Employees Intl. Union, Local 99 Duluth **[10825]**, Duluth, MN
Michigan Hotel, Motel and Resort Assn. **[8674]**, Lansing, MI
Michigan Lake to Lake Bed and Breakfast Assn. **[8128]**, Harrison, MI
Michigan Restaurant Assn. **[8705]**, Lansing, MI
Ohio Bed and Breakfast Assn. **[14573]**, Columbus, OH
Ohio Hotel and Lodging Assn. **[14627]**, Columbus, OH
Ohio Restaurant Assn. **[14667]**, Columbus, OH
Wisconsin Innkeepers Assn. **[17683]**, Brookfield, WI
Hostelling Intl. - Amer. Youth Hostels, Metropolitan Chicago Coun. **[919]**, Chicago, IL
Hostelling Intl. - Amer. Youth Hostels; Wisconsin Coun. of **[18691]**, Madison, WI
Hostelling Intl., Michigan Coun. **[8840]**, Livonia, MI
Hostelling Intl., Minnesota AYH **[12423]**, St. Paul, MN
Hostelling International-Northeast Ohio Coun. **[16394]**, Peninsula, OH
Hostelling Intl. - Toledo Area Coun. **[16922]**, Toledo, OH
Hotel Employees and Restaurant Employees Intl. Union, AFL-CIO, CLC - Local Union 21 **[12145]**, Rochester, MN
Hotel Employees and Restaurant Employees Intl. Union, AFL-CIO, CLC - Minnesota State Coun. **[12146]**, Rochester, MN
Hotel Employees and Restaurant Employees Intl. Union Local 17 **[11579]**, Minneapolis, MN
Hotel Employees and Restaurant Employees Intl. Union, Local 99 Duluth **[10825]**, Duluth, MN
Hotel and Lodging Assn; Ohio **[14627]**, Columbus, OH
Hotel Management
Illinois Hotel and Lodging Assn. **[944]**, Chicago, IL
Indiana Hotel and Lodging Assn. **[5249]**, Indianapolis, IN
Hotel-Motel Assn. of Illinois **[★944]**
Houghton County Historical Museum Soc. **[8511]**, Lake Linden, MI
Houghton Lake Chamber of Commerce **[8264]**, Houghton Lake, MI
Houghton-Portage Township Highschool Skating Club **[8253]**, Houghton, MI
Hound
Belclair Beagle Club **[2415]**, Marissa, IL
Blue Water Beagle Club **[7601]**, Emmett, MI
Cahokia Beagle Club **[1810]**, Gillespie, IL
Central Indiana Beagle Club **[4806]**, Gosport, IN
Central Wisconsin Beagle Club **[19938]**, Vesper, WI
Chicago Beagle Club **[1786]**, Gardner, IL
Chief Tarhe Beagle Club **[15597]**, Lancaster, OH
Clark County Beagle Club **[15474]**, Huber Heights, OH
Columbus Beagle Club **[14371]**, Columbus, OH
Eagle Creek Beagle Club **[15722]**, Loveland, OH
East Liverpool Beagle Club **[15677]**, Lisbon, OH
Egyptian Beagle Club **[1303]**, Coulterville, IL
Fort Wayne Beagle Club **[4655]**, Fort Wayne, IN
Franklin County Beagle Club **[3844]**, Valier, IL
Gogebic Range Beagle Club **[8336]**, Ironwood, MI

Goshen Trail Beagle Club [3363], Rosiclare, IL
Grand Lake Beagle Club [13613], Celina, OH
Hamilton Middletown Beagle Club [15317], Germantown, OH
Handshake Beagle Club [1894], Grayslake, IL
Henryville Beagle Club [5906], Nabb, IN
Highland Beagle Club [15444], Hillsboro, OH
Huntington Beagle Club [17246], Wheelersburg, OH
Huron Valley Beagle Club [8277], Howell, MI
Indian Springs Beagle Club [16385], Pataskala, OH
Ishpeming Beagle Club [7112], Champion, MI
Jackson County Beagle Club [15514], Jackson, OH
King City Beagle Club [462], Carterville, IL
Lima Beagle Club [15660], Lima, OH
Marquette Beagle Club [8348], Ishpeming, MI
Miami Valley Beagle Club [13441], Brookville, OH
Michiana Beagle Club [7593], Edwardsburg, MI
Muskingum Valley Beagle Club [16173], Newark, OH
Northern Illinois Beagle Club [17614], Beloit, WI
Northwestern Indiana Beagle Club [5600], La Porte, IN
Ottawa County Beagle Club [8293], Hudsonville, MI
Ottawa River Beagle Club [16945], Toledo, OH
Pleasant Valley Beagle Club [15755], Malvern, OH
Port City Beagle Club [9159], Muskegon, MI
Portage County Beagle Club [15023], Diamond, OH
Red Cedar Beagle Club [10174], Williamston, MI
Salt Creek Beagle Club [17444], Zanesville, OH
Shenango Valley Beagle Club [16451], Poland, OH
Southern Indiana Beagle Club [4574], Evansville, IN
Southern Michigan Beagle Club [7171], Clinton, MI
Southern Ohio Beagle Club [15401], Hamilton, OH
Strait's of Mackinac Beagle Club [9081], Moran, MI
Sturgeon Creek Beagle Club [9860], Sterling, MI
Summit Beagle Club [17180], West Farmington, OH
Wisconsin Beagle Club [18837], Mazomanie, WI
Wisconsin Timberline Hare Beagle Club [18392], Ladysmith, WI
Wurtland Beagle Club [15509], Ironton, OH
House Rabbit Soc., Indiana Chap. [5149], Indianapolis, IN
Housing
Affordable Housing Alliance [9017], Midland, MI
Alcona County Habitat for Humanity [8810], Lincoln, MI
Antrim County Habitat for Humanity [7594], Elk Rapids, MI
Apartment Assn. of Michigan [7653], Farmington Hills, MI
Battle Creek Area Habitat for Humanity [6852], Battle Creek, MI
Blue Water Habitat for Humanity [9431], Port Huron, MI
Cass River Habitat for Humanity [10040], Vassar, MI
Central Wisconsin Habitat for Humanity [19786], Stevens Point, WI
Cincinnati Habitat for Humanity [13786], Cincinnati, OH
Coalition on Homelessness and Housing in Ohio [14368], Columbus, OH
Coles County Habitat for Humanity [567], Charleston, IL
Copper Country Habitat for Humanity [8251], Houghton, MI
Crawford County Habitat for Humanity [3220], Robinson, IL
Creative Housing Alternative of Minnesota [12118], Robbinsdale, MN
Crow River Habitat for Humanity [11206], Hutchinson, MN
Darke County, Ohio Habitat for Humanity [15359], Greenville, OH
Dayton Ohio Habitat for Humanity [14880], Dayton, OH
Delaware County Habitat for Humanity [15006], Delaware, OH
DuPage Habitat for Humanity [3985], Wheaton, IL
East Central Minnesota Habitat for Humanity [10620], Cambridge, MN
Fond du Lac Home Builders [17981], Fond du Lac, WI
Fort Wayne Habitat for Humanity [4657], Fort Wayne, IN
Goodhue County Habitat for Humanity [12078], Red Wing, MN
Greater Cleveland Habitat for Humanity [14132], Cleveland, OH
Greater Columbus Habitat for Humanity [14447], Columbus, OH
Greater Fox Cities Area Habitat for Humanity [18859], Menasha, WI
Greater Muncie Indiana Habitat for Humanity [5876], Muncie, IN
Habitat For Humanity Milwaukee [19022], Milwaukee, WI
Habitat for Humanity Alpena Area [6642], Alpena, MI
Habitat for Humanity of Ashland County [13166], Ashland, OH
Habitat for Humanity Barry County [8157], Hastings, MI
Habitat for Humanity of Boone County [5669], Lebanon, IN
Habitat for Humanity of Champaign County [522], Champaign, IL
Habitat for Humanity Cheboygan County [7134], Cheboygan, MI
Habitat for Humanity Chicago South Suburbs [1250], Chicago Heights, IL
Habitat for Humanity in Crawford County, Ohio [15285], Galion, OH
Habitat for Humanity of Dane County [18519], Madison, WI
Habitat for Humanity Detroit [7371], Detroit, MI
Habitat for Humanity of Dodge County, Wisconsin [17594], Beaver Dam, WI
Habitat for Humanity of Fairfield County [15601], Lancaster, OH
Habitat for Humanity of Fond du Lac County [17982], Fond du Lac, WI
Habitat for Humanity of Geauga County [16192], Newbury, OH
Habitat for Humanity of Genesee County [7740], Flint, MI
Habitat for Humanity of Greater Canton [13567], Canton, OH
Habitat for Humanity of Greater Indianapolis [5131], Indianapolis, IN
Habitat for Humanity of the Greater Marion Area [2404], Marion, IL
Habitat for Humanity of the Greater Peoria Area [3023], Peoria, IL
Habitat for Humanity of Greene County [17372], Xenia, OH
Habitat for Humanity Hamilton County [6510], Westfield, IN
Habitat for Humanity of Huron Valley [6704], Ann Arbor, MI
Habitat for Humanity of Illinois [2889], Oswego, IL
Habitat for Humanity of Jo Daviess County [1764], Galena, IL
Habitat for Humanity of Kent County [7960], Grand Rapids, MI
Habitat for Humanity of La Salle, Bur., and Putnam Counties [2181], La Salle, IL
Habitat for Humanity of Lafayette [5613], Lafayette, IN
Habitat for Humanity Lake County, Illinois [3923], Waukegan, IL
Habitat for Humanity of Lenawee County [6569], Adrian, MI
Habitat for Humanity - Lima Area [15654], Lima, OH
Habitat for Humanity of Lyon County, Minnesota [11433], Marshall, MN
Habitat for Humanity Macomb County [7177], Clinton Township, MI
Habitat for Humanity of Mahoning County [17402], Youngstown, OH
Habitat for Humanity of Mason County, Michigan [8870], Ludington, MI
Habitat for Humanity of Mc Lean County Illinois [278], Bloomington, IL
Habitat for Humanity of Michigan [8575], Lansing, MI
Habitat for Humanity - MidWest Region [909], Chicago, IL
Habitat for Humanity of Minnesota [11573], Minneapolis, MN
Habitat for Humanity of Monroe County, Indiana [4224], Bloomington, IN
Habitat for Humanity of Morgan County, Indiana [5753], Martinsville, IN
Habitat for Humanity of Morrison County [11334], Little Falls, MN
Habitat for Humanity of Morrow County [16069], Mount Gilead, OH
Habitat for Humanity of Niles-Buchanan Area [9208], Niles, MI
Habitat for Humanity of Northern Columbiana County [16587], Salem, OH
Habitat for Humanity of Northern Fox Valley [3945], West Dundee, IL
Habitat for Humanity of Oakland County [9417], Pontiac, MI
Habitat for Humanity of Oshkosh [19393], Oshkosh, WI
Habitat for Humanity of Paulding County [16387], Paulding, OH
Habitat for Humanity of Portage County [16498], Ravenna, OH
Habitat for Humanity of Prairie Lakes [11054], Glenwood, MN
Habitat for Humanity of Presque Isle County [9541], Rogers City, MI
Habitat for Humanity of St. Joseph County, IN [6230], South Bend, IN
Habitat for Humanity Sangamon County [3558], Springfield, IL
Habitat for Humanity of South Central Minnesota [11379], Mankato, MN
Habitat for Humanity of Waukesha [18871], Menomonee Falls, WI
Habitat for Humanity in Wayne County, Ohio [17318], Wooster, OH
Habitat for Humanity of West Central Minnesota [12916], Willmar, MN
Habitat for Humanity Western Wayne County [9400], Plymouth, MI
Habitat for Humanity of Whitley County [4381], Columbia City, IN
Habitat for Humanity Winona County, Minnesota [12951], Winona, MN
Harbor Habitat for Humanity [6919], Benton Harbor, MI
Holmes County Habitat for Humanity [16036], Millersburg, OH
Huntington County Habitat for Humanity [4950], Huntington, IN
Illinois Assn. of Housing Authorities [1394], Decatur, IL
Illinois Tenants Union [972], Chicago, IL
Inkster Housing and Redevelopment Commn. [8312], Inkster, MI
Itasca County Habitat for Humanity [11088], Grand Rapids, MN
Jackson Affordable Housing Corp. [8369], Jackson, MI
Jackson-Union County Habitat for Humanity [419], Carbondale, IL
Kalamazoo Valley Habitat for Humanity [8445], Kalamazoo, MI
Kishwaukee Valley Habitat for Humanity [1439], DeKalb, IL
Knox County Habitat for Humanity [16084], Mount Vernon, OH
La Crosse Area Builders Assn. [19365], Onalaska, WI
Lake Area Habitat for Humanity [10512], Brainerd, MN
Lawyers' Comm. for Better Housing [1023], Chicago, IL
Leaf River Area, Habitat For Humanity [12821], Wadena, MN
Livingston County Habitat for Humanity [7015], Brighton, MI
Manchester Village Owners Assn. [19045], Milwaukee, WI

Marquette County Habitat for Humanity **[8943]**, Marquette, MI
Maumee Valley Habitat for Humanity **[16929]**, Toledo, OH
Midwest Affordable Housing Mgt. Assn. **[14506]**, Columbus, OH
Midwest Assn. of Housing Cooperatives **[9551]**, Romulus, MI
Millcreek Valley Habitat for Humanity **[13908]**, Cincinnati, OH
Minnesota Housing Partnership **[12490]**, St. Paul, MN
Minnesota Multi Housing Assn. **[10478]**, Bloomington, MN
Montmorency County Habitat for Humanity **[8806]**, Lewiston, MI
NASCO Member Forums **[6741]**, Ann Arbor, MI
Natl. Assn. of Housing and Redevelopment Officials, Minnesota Chap. **[10870]**, Eagan, MN
Natl. Assn. of Housing and Redevelopment Officials, North Central Regional Coun. **[10871]**, Eagan, MN
Natl. Assn. of Housing and Redevelopment Officials, Wisconsin Chap. **[19397]**, Oshkosh, WI
Natl. Assn. of Housing and Redevopment Officials, Illinois Assn. **[2620]**, Murphysboro, IL
New Albany/Floyd County Habitat for Humanity **[5920]**, New Albany, IN
Newaygo County Habitat for Humanity **[7800]**, Fremont, MI
North St. Louis County Habitat for Humanity **[12802]**, Virginia, MN
North Star Habitat for Humanity **[9723]**, Sault Ste. Marie, MI
Northeast Ohio Apartment Assn. **[14183]**, Cleveland, OH
Northwest Indiana Habitat for Humanity **[4888]**, Hammond, IN
Northwest Minnesota Multi-County Housing and Redevelopment Authority **[11462]**, Mentor, MN
Ohio Apartment Assn. **[14538]**, Columbus, OH
Ohio Assisted Living Assn. **[14540]**, Columbus, OH
Ohio Housing Authorities Conf. **[15783]**, Mansfield, OH
Orange Community Homeowners Assn. **[13291]**, Beachwood, OH
Painesville Area Habitat for Humanity **[16343]**, Painesville, OH
Park River Estates Resident Coun. Found. **[10715]**, Coon Rapids, MN
Partners for Affordable Housing **[11396]**, Mankato, MN
Preble County Habitat for Humanity **[15090]**, Eaton, OH
Racine Habitat for Humanity **[19569]**, Racine, WI
Richland County Habitat for Humanity **[15791]**, Mansfield, OH
River Cities Habitat for Humanity, Wisconsin **[18803]**, Marinette, WI
Rockford Area Habitat for Humanity **[2353]**, Loves Park, IL
Rural Rental Housing Assn. of Indiana **[5469]**, Indianapolis, IN
Saginaw Habitat for Humanity **[9635]**, Saginaw, MI
Sandusky County Builders Assn. **[15252]**, Fremont, OH
Seneca Habitat for Humanity **[16863]**, Tiffin, OH
Three Meadows Home Owners Assn. **[16412]**, Perrysburg, OH
TriState Habitat for Humanity **[15402]**, Hamilton, OH
Twin Cities Habitat for Humanity **[11758]**, Minneapolis, MN
Washington County (Ohio) Habitat for Humanity **[15831]**, Marietta, OH
Wexford County Habitat for Humanity **[7051]**, Cadillac, MI
Wisconsin Assisted Living Assn. **[18648]**, Madison, WI
Housing Alliance; Affordable **[9017]**, Midland, MI
Housing Alliance; Wisconsin **[18715]**, Madison, WI
Housing Assn; Michigan Manufactured **[9285]**, Okemos, MI
Housing Authorities Conf; Ohio **[15783]**, Mansfield, OH
Housing Corp; Jackson Affordable **[8369]**, Jackson, MI
Housing Inst; Michigan Manufactured **[★9285]**
Houston Lions Club - Minnesota **[11198]**, Houston, MN
Howard City Lions Club **[8266]**, Howard City, MI
Howard County Breastfeeding Coalition **[5567]**, Kokomo, IN
Howard County Convention and Visitors Commission **[5568]**, Kokomo, IN
Howard County Genealogical Soc. **[6008]**, Oakford, IN
Howard Pulleys Pro-Am Basketball League **[11580]**, Minneapolis, MN
Howard Steamboat Museum **[★5540]**
Howard/Suamico Storm Breakers **[19850]**, Suamico, WI
Howell Area Chamber of Commerce **[8275]**, Howell, MI
Howell Lions Club **[8276]**, Howell, MI
Howell Shooting Club **[4074]**, Yorkville, IL
Hoy Audubon Soc. **[19556]**, Racine, WI
Hoyt Lakes Lions Club **[11201]**, Hoyt Lakes, MN
Hubbard Lions Club **[15471]**, Hubbard, OH
Huber Heights Chamber of Commerce **[15476]**, Huber Heights, OH
Hudson Area Chamber of Commerce **[8289]**, Hudson, MI
Hudson Area Chamber of Commerce **[15481]**, Hudson, OH
Hudson Area Chamber of Commerce and Tourism Bur. **[18223]**, Hudson, WI
Hudson Genealogical Study Group **[15482]**, Hudson, OH
Hudson Lib. and Historical Soc. **[15483]**, Hudson, OH
Hudson Lions Club - Wisconsin **[18224]**, Hudson, WI
Hudson Premier Table Tennis Club **[15484]**, Hudson, OH
Hudson - Young Life **[15485]**, Hudson, OH
Hudsonville Area Chamber of Commerce **[8290]**, Hudsonville, MI
Hudsonville High - Young Life **[6623]**, Allendale, MI
Huff Run Watershed Restoration Partnership **[16043]**, Mineral City, OH
Hugger Elementary PTA **[9503]**, Rochester, MI
Hugh O'Brian Youth Leadership of Michigan **[7261]**, Dearborn, MI
Hugs for Homeless Animals **[18011]**, Franklin, WI
Hull House Assn. **[920]**, Chicago, IL
Human Engineering
Natl. Assn. of Professional Organizers, Michigan Chap. **[7689]**, Fenton, MI
Natl. Assn. of Professional Organizers, Minnesota Chap. **[12029]**, Plymouth, MN
Natl. Assn. of Professional Organizers, Ohio Chap. **[15339]**, Grandview Heights, OH
Natl. Assn. of Professional Organizers, Wisconsin Chap. **[19074]**, Milwaukee, WI
Human Life Issues
Right to Life-Lifespan - Oakland Chap. **[10007]**, Troy, MI
Human Relations
News and Letters Comm., Chicago Chap. **[1100]**, Chicago, IL
Human Rsrc. Assn. of Central Indiana **[5150]**, Indianapolis, IN
Human Rsrc. Assn. of Greater Detroit **[7644]**, Farmington, MI
Human Rsrc. Assn. of Greater Oak Brook **[2775]**, Oak Brook, IL
Human Rsrc. Mgt. Assn. of Mid-Michigan **[8576]**, Lansing, MI
Human Rsrc. Mgt. Assn. of Southeastern Wisconsin **[19891]**, Thiensville, WI
Human Rsrc. Professional Development Assn. **[5151]**, Indianapolis, IN
Human Resources
Employers Rsrc. Assn. **[13820]**, Cincinnati, OH
Natl. Human Rsrcs. Assn., Cincinnati Chap. **[13927]**, Cincinnati, OH
South Central Human Rsrcs. Mgt. Assn. **[8398]**, Jackson, MI
Human Resources Assn. of Central Ohio **[15048]**, Dublin, OH
Human Rsrcs. Assn. of Western Ohio **[17291]**, Wilmington, OH
Human Rights
Amnesty Intl. of the U.S.A., Midwest Regional Off. **[731]**, Chicago, IL
Minnesota Advocates for Human Rights **[11621]**, Minneapolis, MN
Human Rights Commn. of Olmsted County **[12147]**, Rochester, MN
Human Rights Commn. of Rochester **[★12147]**
Human Rights Comm; Minnesota Lawyers Intl. **[★11621]**
Human Rights; Minnesota Advocates for **[11621]**, Minneapolis, MN
Human Services
Akron Character Counts **[13019]**, Akron, OH
Barrington Area Character Counts **[142]**, Barrington, IL
Bartlett Character Counts **[161]**, Bartlett, IL
Blaisdell YMCA **[11532]**, Minneapolis, MN
Bloomingdale Character Counts **[248]**, Bloomingdale, IL
Cary Character Counts **[471]**, Cary, IL
Dress for Success Chicago **[874]**, Chicago, IL
Dress for Success Cincinnati **[13815]**, Cincinnati, OH
Dress for Success Cleveland **[14109]**, Cleveland, OH
Dress for Success Detroit **[8171]**, Highland Park, MI
Dress for Success Flint **[7722]**, Flint, MI
Dress for Success Indianapolis **[5103]**, Indianapolis, IN
Dress for Success Joliet **[2102]**, Joliet, IL
Dress for Success Michigan **[10203]**, Ypsilanti, MI
Dress for Success, Northwest Minnesota **[11134]**, Hawley, MN
Dress for Success Peoria **[3015]**, Peoria, IL
Dress for Success Racine **[19554]**, Racine, WI
Dress for Success Warren-Youngstown **[17100]**, Warren, OH
Franciscan Haircuts from the Heart **[13830]**, Cincinnati, OH
Info. and Referral Network **[5365]**, Indianapolis, IN
The Littlest Heroes **[13652]**, Chesterland, OH
Meals on Wheels of Marion County **[5399]**, Indianapolis, IN
Michigan League for Human Services **[8681]**, Lansing, MI
Neighbors Helping Neighbors of Athens County **[13210]**, Athens, OH
Volunteer Guardianship Prog. of Lorain County **[15128]**, Elyria, OH
Humane Animal Treatment Soc. **[10107]**, Weidman, MI
Humane Animal Welfare Soc. - Waukesha County **[19986]**, Waukesha, WI
Humane Assn; Chippewa County **[17747]**, Chippewa Falls, WI
Humane Ohio **[16406]**, Perrysburg, OH
Humane Soc. of Br. County **[9465]**, Quincy, MI
Humane Soc; Chippewa County **[★17747]**
Humane Soc; Chippewa Falls **[★17747]**
Humane Soc. for Hamilton County **[5974]**, Noblesville, IN
Humane Soc; Holmes County **[16037]**, Millersburg, OH
Humane Soc. of Kent County **[7964]**, Grand Rapids, MI
Humane Soc; Lakeshore **[18781]**, Manitowoc, WI
Humane Soc; Lawrence County **[★4179]**
Humane Soc; Portage County **[19802]**, Stevens Point, WI
Humane Soc. of Rock Island County **[2489]**, Milan, IL
Humane Soc. of Schoolcraft County **[8917]**, Manistique, MI
Humane Soc. of Swift County **[10434]**, Benson, MN
Humane Soc. of Tuscola County **[7084]**, Caro, MI
Humane Soc. of the U.S., Central State Regional Off. **[2637]**, Naperville, IL
Humane Soc. of the U.S., Great Lakes Regional Off. 2 **[★2637]**
Humane Soc; Watonwan County **[12323]**, St. James, MN
Humane Soc; White River **[4179]**, Bedford, IN
Humane Soc; Wyandot County **[17035]**, Upper Sandusky, OH
Humanism
DuPage Unitarian Universalist Church **[2632]**, Naperville, IL

Ethical Humanist Soc. of Greater Chicago **[3486]**, Skokie, IL
Free Inquiry Gp. of Greater Cincinnati and Northern Kentucky **[13831]**, Cincinnati, OH
Freethought Assn. of West Michigan **[6622]**, Allendale, MI
Great Lakes Humanist Soc. **[9105]**, Mount Pleasant, MI
Humanist Community of Central Ohio **[14460]**, Columbus, OH
Humanist Friendship Gp. of Central Indiana **[4850]**, Greenwood, IN
Humanist Soc. of Columbus **[14461]**, Columbus, OH
Humanists of Minnesota **[11581]**, Minneapolis, MN
Humanists of North Eastern Illinois **[1920]**, Gurnee, IL
Humanists of Northwest Ohio **[13392]**, Bowling Green, OH
Humanists of Southeast Michigan **[9835]**, Southgate, MI
Humanists of West Suburban Chicagoland **[2890]**, Oswego, IL
Lucent Humanist League **[2300]**, Lisle, IL
MEL - Milwaukee Evolution League **[20134]**, West Milwaukee, WI
Secular Humanist Soc. of Chicago **[1175]**, Chicago, IL
Humanist Assn. of Minneapolis-Saint Paul **[★11581]**
Humanist Community of Central Ohio **[14460]**, Columbus, OH
Humanist Friendship Gp. of Central Indiana **[4850]**, Greenwood, IN
Humanist Soc. of Columbus **[14461]**, Columbus, OH
Humanists of Minnesota **[11581]**, Minneapolis, MN
Humanists of North Eastern Illinois **[1920]**, Gurnee, IL
Humanists of Northwest Ohio **[13392]**, Bowling Green, OH
Humanists of Southeast Michigan **[9835]**, Southgate, MI
Humanists of West Suburban Chicagoland **[2890]**, Oswego, IL
Humanities
Illinois Humanities Coun. **[945]**, Chicago, IL
Indiana Humanities Coun. **[5250]**, Indianapolis, IN
Mac-A-Cheek Found. for the Humanities **[17185]**, West Liberty, OH
Michigan Humanities Coun. **[8675]**, Lansing, MI
Ohio Humanities Coun. **[14628]**, Columbus, OH
Humanities; Wayne County Coun. for Arts, History, and **[8085]**, Grosse Pointe, MI
Hunger
Children's Hunger Alliance **[14366]**, Columbus, OH
Hunting
Commemorative Bucks of Michigan **[7486]**, Dryden, MI
Hunting Dogs
Minnesota Hunting Spaniel Assn. **[10728]**, Cottage Grove, MN
Southern Minnesota Hunting Retriever Assn. **[11969]**, Owatonna, MN
Hunting Valley Gun Club **[16396]**, Pepper Pike, OH
Huntingburg Chamber of Commerce **[4940]**, Huntingburg, IN
Huntington Area Assn. of Realtors **[4947]**, Huntington, IN
Huntington Beagle Club **[17246]**, Wheelersburg, OH
Huntington Chap. of the Amer. Red Cross **[4948]**, Huntington, IN
Huntington County Chamber of Commerce **[4949]**, Huntington, IN
Huntington County Habitat for Humanity **[4950]**, Huntington, IN
Huntington County Visitor and Convention Bur. **[4951]**, Huntington, IN
Huntington's Disease Soc. of Am., Central Ohio Chap. **[14462]**, Columbus, OH
Huntington's Disease Soc. of Am., Illinois Chap. **[3339]**, Rolling Meadows, IL
Huntington's Disease Soc. of Am., Indiana Chap. **[5152]**, Indianapolis, IN
Huntington's Disease Soc. of Am., Michigan Chap. **[7474]**, Dimondale, MI
Huntington's Disease Soc. of Am., Northeast Ohio Chap. **[13651]**, Chesterland, OH
Huntington's Disease Soc. of Amer., Wisconsin Chap. **[20075]**, Wauwatosa, WI
Huntley Area Chamber of Commerce and Indus. **[2054]**, Huntley, IL
Hurley Area Chamber of Commerce **[18230]**, Hurley, WI
Huron Chamber of Commerce **[15491]**, Huron, OH
Huron High - Young Life **[6706]**, Ann Arbor, MI
Huron Lions Club **[15492]**, Huron, OH
Huron Pines Rsrc. Conservation and Development Coun. **[8063]**, Grayling, MI
Huron River Watershed Coun. **[6707]**, Ann Arbor, MI
Huron Shores Chamber of Commerce **[8133]**, Harrisville, MI
Huron Township Chamber of Commerce **[9184]**, New Boston, MI
Huron Valley Area Chamber of Commerce **[★9050]**
Huron Valley Area Intergroup **[10207]**, Ypsilanti, MI
Huron Valley Beagle Club **[8277]**, Howell, MI
Huron Valley Bottle and Insulator Club **[10084]**, Waterford, MI
Huron Valley Chamber of Commerce **[9050]**, Milford, MI
Huron Valley Intergroup **[★10207]**
Huron Valley Sunrise Lions Club **[10208]**, Ypsilanti, MI
Hutchinson Area Chamber of Commerce **[11207]**, Hutchinson, MN
Hutchinson Area Convention and Visitors Bur. **[11208]**, Hutchinson, MN
Hutchinson Jaycees **[11209]**, Hutchinson, MN
Hyde Park Chamber of Commerce **[921]**, Chicago, IL
Hyde Park Young Life **[922]**, Chicago, IL
Hyderabad Decan Cricket Club **[923]**, Chicago, IL
Hygienists' Assn; Michigan Dental **[9277]**, Okemos, MI
Hypnosis
Chicago Soc. of Clinical Hypnosis **[1827]**, Glen Ellyn, IL
Cleveland Soc. of Clinical Hypnosis **[13285]**, Beachwood, OH
Michigan Soc. of Clinical Hypnosis **[7670]**, Farmington Hills, MI
Minnesota Soc. of Clinical Hypnosis **[12522]**, St. Paul, MN
Wisconsin Soc. of Clinical Hypnosis **[18753]**, Madison, WI

I

I-69 Mid-Continent Highway Coalition **[5153]**, Indianapolis, IN
I-94 West Chamber of Commerce **[12203]**, Rogers, MN
IABC/Columbus **[14463]**, Columbus, OH
IABC/Indianapolis **[5154]**, Indianapolis, IN
IABC/Madison **[18520]**, Madison, WI
IABC Minnesota **[12424]**, St. Paul, MN
IABC Southeastern Wisconsin **[18053]**, Glendale, WI
IAIFA Bloomington **[279]**, Bloomington, IL
IAMAW Air Transport District Lodge 141 **[1608]**, Elk Grove Village, IL
Ice Age Park and Trail Found. **[19024]**, Milwaukee, WI
Ice Arena Mgt. Assn; Wisconsin **[19278]**, Neenah, WI
Ice Skating Club of Indianapolis **[4321]**, Carmel, IN
Ice Zone Figure Skating Club **[13373]**, Boardman, OH
Ichthyology
Amer. Fisheries Soc., Indiana Chap. Pres. **[6373]**, Vallonia, IN
Amer. Fisheries Soc., Michigan Chap. Pres. **[8803]**, Lewiston, MI
Amer. Fisheries Soc., Minnesota Chap. Pres. **[10686]**, Cloquet, MN
Amer. Fisheries Soc., Ohio Chap. **[15414]**, Hebron, OH
Ida - Young Life **[8301]**, Ida, MI
IEEE Akron/Canton Sect. **[13568]**, Canton, OH
IEEE Central Illinois Sect. **[523]**, Champaign, IL
IEEE Central Indiana Sect. **[5155]**, Indianapolis, IN
IEEE Chicago Sect. **[924]**, Chicago, IL
IEEE Communications Soc., Chicago Chap. **[2638]**, Naperville, IL
IEEE Communs. Soc., Columbus Chap. **[16513]**, Reynoldsburg, OH
IEEE Communs. Soc., Milwaukee Chap. **[18872]**, Menomonee Falls, WI
IEEE Communs. Soc., Southeastern Michigan Chap. **[9401]**, Plymouth, MI
IEEE Communs. Soc., Southern Minnesota Chap. **[12148]**, Rochester, MN
IEEE Communs. Soc., Twin Cities Chap. **[11582]**, Minneapolis, MN
IEEE Cmpt. Soc., Calumet **[4882]**, Hammond, IN
IEEE Cmpt. Soc., Cleveland **[16523]**, Richfield, OH
IEEE Computer Society, Columbus Chapter **[14464]**, Columbus, OH
IEEE Cmpt. Soc., Milwaukee Chap. **[18873]**, Menomonee Falls, WI
IEEE Cmpt. Soc., Ohio State Univ. **[14465]**, Columbus, OH
IEEE Cmpt. Soc., Rock River Valley Chap. **[3281]**, Rockford, IL
IEEE Cmpt. Soc., Southeastern Michigan Chap. **[9504]**, Rochester, MI
IEEE Cmpt. Soc., Southern Minnesota Chap. **[12149]**, Rochester, MN
IEEE Cmpt. Soc., Toledo Chap. **[15908]**, Maumee, OH
IEEE Computer Soc., Twin Cities Chap. **[11583]**, Minneapolis, MN
IEEE - Dayton Sect. **[14893]**, Dayton, OH
IEEE Electromagnetic Compatibility Soc., Chicago **[1503]**, Downers Grove, IL
IEEE Electromagnetic Compatibility Soc., Milwaukee **[17729]**, Cedarburg, WI
IEEE Electromagnetic Compatibility Soc., Southeastern Michigan **[7064]**, Canton, MI
IEEE Electromagnetic Compatibility Soc. - Twin Cities Chap. **[11584]**, Minneapolis, MN
IEEE Engg. Mgt. Soc. - Twin Cities Sect. **[10550]**, Brooklyn Park, MN
IEEE Lasers and Electro-Optics Soc., Cleveland **[14140]**, Cleveland, OH
IEEE Madison Sect. **[18521]**, Madison, WI
IEEE Milwaukee Sect. **[19289]**, New Berlin, WI
IEEE Southern Minnesota Sect. **[12150]**, Rochester, MN
IEEE West Michigan Sect. **[8430]**, Kalamazoo, MI
IFP Minneapolis/St. Paul **[★12425]**
IFP Minnesota Center for Media Arts **[12425]**, St. Paul, MN
Ileitis and Colitis, Midwest Regional; Natl. Found. for **[★1456]**
Illiana Jewish Genealogical Soc. **[1708]**, Flossmoor, IL
Illiana Watermelon Assn. **[6409]**, Vincennes, IN
Illini Space Development Soc. **[3820]**, Urbana, IL
Illini Valley Assn. of Realtors **[3079]**, Peru, IL
Illinois Acad. of Family Physicians **[2296]**, Lisle, IL
Illinois Acad. of Physician Assistants **[3560]**, Springfield, IL
Illinois African Violet Soc. **[1659]**, Evanston, IL
Illinois Agricultural Assn. Found. **[280]**, Bloomington, IL
Illinois Agricultural Aviation Assn. **[2441]**, Mattoon, IL
Illinois AIFA **[3561]**, Springfield, IL
Illinois Alcoholism and Drug Dependence Assn. **[3562]**, Springfield, IL
Illinois Alpaca Owners and Breeders Assn. **[3842]**, Utica, IL
Illinois Amateur Softball Assn. **[1393]**, Decatur, IL
Illinois Amer. Saddlebred Horse Assn. **[1867]**, Glenview, IL
Illinois Angus Assn. **[1285]**, Colfax, IL
Illinois Appaloosa Assn. **[3750]**, Tallula, IL
Illinois Art Educ. Assn. **[3384]**, St. Charles, IL
Illinois Arts Alliance **[925]**, Chicago, IL
Illinois Asphalt Pavement Assn. **[3563]**, Springfield, IL
Illinois Assn. of Aggregate Producers **[3564]**, Springfield, IL
Illinois Assn. for Career and Tech. Educ. **[3565]**, Springfield, IL
Illinois Assn. of Chamber of Commerce Executives **[3566]**, Springfield, IL
Illinois Assn. of Chiefs of Police **[3567]**, Springfield, IL
Illinois Assn. for Coll. Admissions Counseling **[281]**, Bloomington, IL
Illinois Assn. of Coll. and Res. Libraries **[926]**, Chicago, IL

Illinois Assn. of Coll. Stores [524], Champaign, IL
Illinois Assn. of Collegiate Registrars and Admissions Officers [3437], Schaumburg, IL
Illinois Assn. of Collegiate Registrars and Admissions Off.rs [3821], Urbana, IL
Illinois Assn. of Community Care Prog. Homecare Providers [3201], River Forest, IL
Illinois Assn. of Conservation Districts [4057], Woodstock, IL
Illinois Assn. of County Engineers [3568], Springfield, IL
Illinois Assn. of Criminal Defense Lawyers [927], Chicago, IL
Illinois Assn. of Defense Trial Counsel [3569], Springfield, IL
Illinois Assn. for the Educ. of Young Children [3570], Springfield, IL
Illinois Assn. for Educal. Communs. and Tech. [1433], DeKalb, IL
Illinois Assn. of Environmental Professionals [928], Chicago, IL
Illinois Assn. for Family Child Care [2813], Oak Park, IL
Illinois Assn. of Fire Protection Districts [3571], Springfield, IL
Illinois Assn. for Floodplain and Stormwater Mgt. [2952], Park Forest, IL
Illinois Assn. for Gifted Children [2911], Palatine, IL
Illinois Assn. of Groundwater Professionals [3202], River Forest, IL
Illinois Assn. for Hea., Physical Educ., Recreation, and Dance [2078], Jacksonville, IL
Illinois Assn. for Hea.care Quality [2150], Kenilworth, IL
Illinois Assn. of Housing Authorities [1394], Decatur, IL
Illinois Assn. for Infant Mental Hea. [929], Chicago, IL
Illinois Assn. for Institutional Res. [525], Champaign, IL
Illinois Assn. of Learning Assistance Professionals [★2133]
Illinois Assn. for Marriage and Family Therapy [1835], Glen Ellyn, IL
Illinois Assn. of Meat Processors [1749], Freeport, IL
Illinois Assn. for Media in Educ. [★404]
Illinois Assn. for Medical Equip. Services [2639], Naperville, IL
Illinois Assn. of Mortgage Brokers [2332], Lombard, IL
Illinois Assn. for Mulitcultural Multilingual Educ. [930], Chicago, IL
Illinois Assn. of Museums [3572], Springfield, IL
Illinois Assn. of Mutual Insurance Companies [3573], Springfield, IL
Illinois Assn. of Occupational Hea. Nurses [2285], Lincolnshire, IL
Illinois Assn. for Parents of Children with Visual Impairments [3574], Springfield, IL
Illinois Assn. of Park Districts [3575], Springfield, IL
Illinois Assn. of Plumbing-Heating-Cooling Contractors [3576], Springfield, IL
Illinois Assn. of Realtors [3577], Springfield, IL
Illinois Assn. of Rehabilitation Facilities [3578], Springfield, IL
Illinois Assn. of School Administrators [3579], Springfield, IL
Illinois Assn. of School Bds. [3580], Springfield, IL
Illinois Assn. of School Bus. Officials [1434], DeKalb, IL
Illinois Assn. of School Nurses [1479], Dixon, IL
Illinois Assn. for Supervision and Curriculum Development [2715], Normal, IL
Illinois Assn. of Teachers of English [2716], Normal, IL
Illinois Assn. of Tobacco and Candy Distributors [3581], Springfield, IL
Illinois Assn. of Vocational Agriculture Teachers [3582], Springfield, IL
Illinois Assn. of Wastewater Agencies [3583], Springfield, IL
Illinois Athletic Trainers' Assn. [1660], Evanston, IL
Illinois Audubon Soc. [1349], Danville, IL
Illinois Auto. Dealers Assn. [3584], Springfield, IL
Illinois Bankers Assn. [3585], Springfield, IL
Illinois B.A.S.S. Fed. [3085], Petersburg, IL
Illinois Beef Assn. [3586], Springfield, IL
Illinois Boer Goat Assn. [282], Bloomington, IL
Illinois Broadcasters' Assn. [1638], Energy, IL
Illinois Campaign for Better Hea. Care [931], Chicago, IL
Illinois CASA [★3592]
Illinois Cast Metals Assn. [3587], Springfield, IL
Illinois Central Railroad Historical Soc. [2973], Paxton, IL
Illinois Chapter, American Academy of Pediatrics [932], Chicago, IL
Illinois Chap. of the Amer. Coll. of Cardiology [1868], Glenview, IL
Illinois Chap. of Amer. Medical Billing Assn. [1459], Des Plaines, IL
Illinois Chap. of the Amer. Soc. of Landscape Architects [2776], Oak Brook, IL
Illinois Chap. of Natl. Assn. of Tax Professionals [120], Aurora, IL
Illinois Chap. of the Natl. Assn. of Telecommunications Officers and Advisors [1661], Evanston, IL
Illinois Chap. Natl. Corvette Restorers Soc. [226], Bensenville, IL
Illinois Chap. Natl. Elecl. Contractors Assn. [3588], Springfield, IL
Illinois Chiropractic Soc. [3589], Springfield, IL
Illinois Christmas Tree Assn. [3403], St. Libory, IL
Illinois City County Mgt. Assn. [1435], DeKalb, IL
Illinois Coaches Assn. [22], Alexis, IL
Illinois Coal Assn. [3590], Springfield, IL
Illinois Coalition Against the Death Penalty [933], Chicago, IL
Illinois Coalition Against Domestic Violence [3591], Springfield, IL
Illinois Coalition Against Sexual Assault [3592], Springfield, IL
Illinois Coalition to End Homelessness [1592], Elgin, IL
Illinois Coalition for Immigrant and Refugee Rights [934], Chicago, IL
Illinois Cochlear Implant Club [1504], Downers Grove, IL
Illinois Coin Laundry Assn. [1609], Elk Grove Village, IL
Illinois Coin Machine Operators Assn. [3593], Springfield, IL
Illinois Coll. of Emergency Physicians [2834], Oakbrook Terrace, IL
Illinois Community Action Assn. [3594], Springfield, IL
Illinois Community Coll. Trustees Assn. [3595], Springfield, IL
Illinois Computing Educators [8], Addison, IL
Illinois Concrete Pipe Assn. [3596], Springfield, IL
Illinois Conf. of Churches [3597], Springfield, IL
Illinois Conservation Found. [3598], Springfield, IL
Illinois Corn Marketing Bd. [283], Bloomington, IL
Illinois Cosmetology Assn. [★1091]
Illinois Coun. of the Blind [3599], Springfield, IL
Illinois Coun. on Developmental Disabilities [935], Chicago, IL
Illinois Coun. on Economic Educ. [1436], DeKalb, IL
Illinois Coun. on Food and Agricultural Res. [3822], Urbana, IL
Illinois Coun. of Hea. Sys. Pharmacists [2349], Loves Park, IL
Illinois Coun. on Long Term Care [936], Chicago, IL
Illinois Coun. of Teachers of Mathematics [937], Chicago, IL
Illinois Country Music Assn. [1514], Downs, IL
Illinois Court Reporters Assn. [2597], Mount Vernon, IL
Illinois CPA Soc. [938], Chicago, IL
Illinois Credit Union League [2640], Naperville, IL
Illinois Cricket Club [939], Chicago, IL
Illinois Crop Improvement Assn. [526], Champaign, IL
Illinois Curling Assn. [2198], Lake Forest, IL
Illinois Curling Assn. - Exmoor Curling Club [1992], Highland Park, IL
Illinois Curling Assn. - Indian Hill Curling Club [4037], Winnetka, IL
Illinois Curling Assn. - North Shore Curling Club [1869], Glenview, IL
Illinois Curling Assn. - Oak Park Curling Club [3203], River Forest, IL
Illinois Curling Assn. - Waltham Curling Club [3785], Triumph, IL
Illinois Dairy Goat Assn. [3428], Saybrook, IL
Illinois Dental Hygienists' Assn. [3600], Springfield, IL
Illinois Dental Lab. Assn. [2641], Naperville, IL
Illinois Dietetic Assn. [1970], Henry, IL
Illinois Division of the Intl. Assn. for Identification [2642], Naperville, IL
Illinois Draft Horse and Mule Breeders Assn. [3129], Prairie City, IL
Illinois Dressage and Combined Training Assn. [3719], Streamwood, IL
Illinois Educ. Assn. [3601], Springfield, IL
Illinois Elks Assn. [2598], Mount Vernon, IL
Illinois Emergency Sers. Mgt. Assn. [2260], Libertyville, IL
Illinois Enval. Balancing Bur. [940], Chicago, IL
Illinois Environmental Coun. [3602], Springfield, IL
Illinois Environmental Hea. Assn. [3225], Rochelle, IL
Illinois Environmental Hea. Assn. - Central Chap. [1774], Galesburg, IL
Illinois Environmental Hea. Assn. - North Chap. [71], Arlington Heights, IL
Illinois Environmental Hea. Assn. - South Chap. [2224], Lawrenceville, IL
Illinois Fair Plan Assn. [941], Chicago, IL
Illinois Farmers Union [3603], Springfield, IL
Illinois Fed. of Bus. and Professional Women Clubs [3604], Springfield, IL
Illinois Fed. of Families [3859], Vienna, IL
Illinois Fed. of Republican Women [4075], Yorkville, IL
Illinois Fed. of Teachers [3970], Westmont, IL
Illinois Fencers Club [2587], Mount Prospect, IL
Illinois Fertilizer and Chem. Assn. [284], Bloomington, IL
Illinois Food Retailers Assn. [2333], Lombard, IL
Illinois Four Wheel Drive Assn. [2487], Midlothian, IL
Illinois Funeral Directors Assn. [3605], Springfield, IL
Illinois Gay Rodeo Association [942], Chicago, IL
Illinois Geographical Soc. [2717], Normal, IL
Illinois Govt. Finance Officers Assn. [3971], Westmont, IL
Illinois Groundwater Assn. [2369], Macomb, IL
Illinois Haflinger Assn. [1717], Forreston, IL
Illinois Hea. Care Assn. [3606], Springfield, IL
Illinois Hea. Info. Mgt. Assn. [943], Chicago, IL
Illinois Heritage Assn. [527], Champaign, IL
Illinois High School Assn. [285], Bloomington, IL
Illinois High School and Coll. Driver Educ. Assn. [2189], Lake Bluff, IL
Illinois Home Care Coun. [1870], Glenview, IL
Illinois Hosp. Assn. [2643], Naperville, IL
Illinois Hotel and Lodging Assn. [944], Chicago, IL
Illinois Humanities Coun. [945], Chicago, IL
Illinois Innovators and Inventors [1560], Edwardsville, IL
Illinois Jaguar Club [1662], Evanston, IL
Illinois Jewelers Assn. [3607], Springfield, IL
Illinois Junior Golf Assn. [2241], Lemont, IL
Illinois Lake Mgt. Assn. [3608], Springfield, IL
Illinois Lamb and Wool Producers [380], Bushnell, IL
Illinois Land Title Assn. [3609], Springfield, IL
Illinois Landscape Contractors Assn. [2777], Oak Brook, IL
Illinois Landscape Contractors Educational and Charitable Org. [2778], Oak Brook, IL
Illinois League of Financial Institutions [3610], Springfield, IL
Illinois Learning Specialists and Developmental Educators [2133], Kankakee, IL
Illinois Lib. Assn. [946], Chicago, IL
Illinois Licensed Beverage Assn. [3611], Springfield, IL
Illinois Life and Hea. Insurance Guaranty Assn. [947], Chicago, IL
Illinois Life Insurance Coun. [3612], Springfield, IL
Illinois Lumber and Materials Dealers Assn. [3613], Springfield, IL
Illinois Manufactured Housing Assn. [3614], Springfield, IL
Illinois Mfrs. Assn. [2779], Oak Brook, IL
Illinois Maternal and Child Hea. Coalition [948], Chicago, IL
Illinois Mathematics Assn. of Community Colleges [2912], Palatine, IL
Illinois Mathematics Teacher Educators [3477], Sidney, IL

Illinois Meat Goat Producers **[3370]**, Rushville, IL
Illinois Medical Gp. Mgt. Assn. **[949]**, Chicago, IL
Illinois Migrant Coun. **[950]**, Chicago, IL
Illinois Milk Producers' Assn. **[286]**, Bloomington, IL
Illinois Mini Storage Assn. **[3615]**, Springfield, IL
Illinois Mortgage Bankers Assn. **[951]**, Chicago, IL
Illinois Motorcycle Dealers Assn. **[3616]**, Springfield, IL
Illinois Mountain Bicyclists Coalition **[3229]**, Rochester, IL
Illinois Mountain Bike Assn. **[★2915]**
Illinois Movers' and Warehousemen's Assn. **[3617]**, Springfield, IL
Illinois Municipal League **[3618]**, Springfield, IL
Illinois Municipal Utilities Assn. **[3619]**, Springfield, IL
Illinois Music Educators Assn. **[2509]**, Mokena, IL
Illinois Mycological Assn. **[2242]**, Lemont, IL
Illinois Natl. Barrel Horse Assn. **[2978]**, Payson, IL
Illinois Natl. Cong. of Parents and Teachers **[3620]**, Springfield, IL
Illinois Natl. Emergency Number Assn. **[3385]**, St. Charles, IL
Illinois Native Plant Soc. **[3976]**, Westville, IL
Illinois Native Plant Soc., Central Chap. **[579]**, Chatham, IL
Illinois Native Plant Soc., Forest Glen Chap. **[1691]**, Fairmount, IL
Illinois Native Plant Soc., Northeast Chap. **[2106]**, Joliet, IL
Illinois Native Plant Soc., Quad City Chap. **[1480]**, Dixon, IL
Illinois Native Plant Soc., Southern Chap. **[2125]**, Jonesboro, IL
Illinois Neurofibromatosis **[2334]**, Lombard, IL
Illinois NORML **[952]**, Chicago, IL
Illinois North Shore North Shore Soc. **[4038]**, Winnetka, IL
Illinois Numismatic Assn. **[2520]**, Moline, IL
Illinois Nurserymen's Assn. **[3621]**, Springfield, IL
Illinois Occupational Therapy Assn. **[2814]**, Oak Park, IL
Illinois Optometric Assn. **[3622]**, Springfield, IL
Illinois Optometric Licensing and Disciplinary Bd. **[3623]**, Springfield, IL
Illinois Orchid Soc. **[1622]**, Elmhurst, IL
Illinois Osteopathic Medical Assn. **[953]**, Chicago, IL
Illinois Paralegal Assn. **[2690]**, New Lenox, IL
Illinois Parents of Blind Children **[954]**, Chicago, IL
Illinois Park and Recreation Assn. **[2835]**, Oakbrook Terrace, IL
Illinois Peace Action **[955]**, Chicago, IL
Illinois Petroleum Coun. **[3624]**, Springfield, IL
Illinois Petroleum Marketers Assn. **[3625]**, Springfield, IL
Illinois Pharmaceutical Assn. **[★3626]**
Illinois Pharmacists Assn. **[3626]**, Springfield, IL
Illinois Physical Therapy Assn. **[2780]**, Oak Brook, IL
Illinois Pilots Assn. **[3423]**, Savoy, IL
Illinois Planning Coun. on Developmental Disabilities **[★935]**
Illinois Podiatric Medical Assn. **[956]**, Chicago, IL
Illinois Police Assn. **[1632]**, Elmwood Park, IL
Illinois Pollution Control Bd. **[957]**, Chicago, IL
Illinois Polygraph Soc. **[2107]**, Joliet, IL
Illinois Pork Producers Assn. **[3627]**, Springfield, IL
Illinois Poultry Indus. Coun. **[3823]**, Urbana, IL
Illinois Prairie Coun. of Camp Fire **[★2326]**
Illinois Prairie State Chiropractic Assn. **[3245]**, Rock Island, IL
Illinois Press Assn. **[3628]**, Springfield, IL
Illinois Primary Hea. Care Assn. **[958]**, Chicago, IL
Illinois Principals Assn. **[3629]**, Springfield, IL
Illinois Professional Firefighters Assn. **[1623]**, Elmhurst, IL
Illinois Professional Land Surveyors Assn. **[3230]**, Rochester, IL
Illinois Propane Gas Assn. **[3630]**, Springfield, IL
Illinois Psychiatric Soc. **[959]**, Chicago, IL
Illinois Psychological Assn. **[960]**, Chicago, IL
Illinois Public Airports Assn. **[3631]**, Springfield, IL
Illinois Public Hea. Administrator Certification Bd. **[★1159]**
Illinois Public Hea. Assn. **[3632]**, Springfield, IL
Illinois Public Interest Res. Gp. **[961]**, Chicago, IL
Illinois Quad City Chamber of Commerce **[2521]**, Moline, IL
Illinois Quarter Horse Assn. **[1610]**, Elk Grove Village, IL
Illinois Quarter Horse Assn., District No. 2 **[182]**, Batavia, IL
Illinois Quarter Horse Assn., District No. 3 **[1895]**, Grayslake, IL
Illinois Quarter Horse Assn., District No. 4 **[2343]**, London Mills, IL
Illinois Quarter Horse Assn., District No. 6 **[528]**, Champaign, IL
Illinois Quarter Horse Assn., District No. 7 **[560]**, Chandlerville, IL
Illinois Quarter Horse Assn., District No. 8 **[104]**, Auburn, IL
Illinois Quarter Horse Assn., District No. 9 **[2967]**, Patoka, IL
Illinois Quarter Horse Assn., District No. 11 **[3860]**, Vienna, IL
Illinois Quarter Horse Assn., District No. 12 **[2754]**, Northbrook, IL
Illinois Radiological Soc. **[375]**, Burr Ridge, IL
Illinois Reading Coun. **[2718]**, Normal, IL
Illinois Ready Mixed Concrete Assn. **[2719]**, Normal, IL
Illinois Recycling Assn. **[2815]**, Oak Park, IL
Illinois Regional Insulation Contractors Assn. **[3438]**, Schaumburg, IL
Illinois Regional Planning and Development Commn; South Central **[3412]**, Salem, IL
Illinois Regional Planning and Development Commn; Southeastern **[1943]**, Harrisburg, IL
Illinois Renewable Energy Association **[2867]**, Oregon, IL
Illinois Restaurant Assn. **[962]**, Chicago, IL
Illinois Retail Merchants Assn. **[963]**, Chicago, IL
Illinois Right to Life Comm. **[964]**, Chicago, IL
Illinois River Area Chamber of Commerce **[2420]**, Marseilles, IL
Illinois River Valley Orienteering Club **[1521]**, Dunlap, IL
Illinois Road and Trans. Builders Assn. **[2067]**, Itasca, IL
Illinois Rural Hea. Assn. **[3633]**, Springfield, IL
Illinois School-Age Child Care Network **[287]**, Bloomington, IL
Illinois School Hea. Assn. **[2720]**, Normal, IL
Illinois School Lib. Media Assn. **[404]**, Canton, IL
Illinois School Psychologists Assn. **[3988]**, Wheaton, IL
Illinois School Trans. Assn. **[2437]**, Matteson, IL
Illinois Sci. Teachers Assn. **[121]**, Aurora, IL
Illinois Seed Trade Assn. **[529]**, Champaign, IL
Illinois Sheriffs Association **[3470]**, Sherman, IL
Illinois Sign Assn. **[18156]**, Greenfield, WI
Illinois Skeet Assn. **[1395]**, Decatur, IL
Illinois Small Bus. Development Center **[3634]**, Springfield, IL
Illinois Soc. of Assn. Executives **[3635]**, Springfield, IL
Illinois Soc. of Enrolled Agents **[2458]**, McHenry, IL
Illinois Soc. of Enrolled Agents - Northwest Chap. **[361]**, Buffalo Grove, IL
Illinois Soc. of Enrolled Agents - Southern Chap. **[488]**, Centralia, IL
Illinois Soc. of Enrolled Agents - Tri-Counties Chap. **[965]**, Chicago, IL
Illinois Soc. for Histotechnologists **[3824]**, Urbana, IL
Illinois Soc. of Pediatric Dentists **[966]**, Chicago, IL
Illinois Soc. for the Prevention of Blindness **[967]**, Chicago, IL
Illinois Soc. of Professional Engineers **[3636]**, Springfield, IL
Illinois Soc. of Professional Farm Managers and Rural Appraisers **[18874]**, Menomonee Falls, WI
Illinois Soc. for Respiratory Care **[3210]**, Riverdale, IL
Illinois Solar Energy Assn. **[3989]**, Wheaton, IL
Illinois Soybean Assn. **[288]**, Bloomington, IL
Illinois Special Olympics **[★2733]**
Illinois Specialty Growers Assn. **[289]**, Bloomington, IL
Illinois Speech-Language-Hearing Assn. **[968]**, Chicago, IL
Illinois Spina Bifida Assn. **[2297]**, Lisle, IL
Illinois Sporting Clay Assn. **[2691]**, New Lenox, IL
Illinois Sports Owners Assn. **[1325]**, Crystal Lake, IL
Illinois Standardbred Owners and Breeders Assn. **[3637]**, Springfield, IL
Illinois State Acupuncture Assn. **[969]**, Chicago, IL
Illinois State Bar Assn. **[3638]**, Springfield, IL
Illinois State Bowling Proprietors Assn. **[2288]**, Lincolnwood, IL
Illinois State Chamber of Commerce **[970]**, Chicago, IL
Illinois State Data Center Cooperative **[3639]**, Springfield, IL
Illinois State Dental Soc. **[3640]**, Springfield, IL
Illinois State Fabricare Assn. **[971]**, Chicago, IL
Illinois State Grange **[2846]**, O'Fallon, IL
Illinois State Historical Soc. **[3641]**, Springfield, IL
Illinois State Horticultural Soc. **[290]**, Bloomington, IL
Illinois State Museum Soc. **[3642]**, Springfield, IL
Illinois State Racquetball Assn. **[2020]**, Hinsdale, IL
Illinois State Rifle Assn. **[582]**, Chatsworth, IL
Illinois State Soc. of Amer. Medical Technologists **[2644]**, Naperville, IL
Illinois State Soc. of Radiologic Technologists **[291]**, Bloomington, IL
Illinois State Univ. FarmHouse Fraternity **[2721]**, Normal, IL
Illinois Stewardship Alliance **[3231]**, Rochester, IL
Illinois Student Environment Network **[3825]**, Urbana, IL
Illinois Suffolk Sheep Assn. **[2421]**, Marseilles, IL
Illinois Telecommunications Assn. **[3643]**, Springfield, IL
Illinois Tenants Union **[972]**, Chicago, IL
Illinois Thoracic Soc. **[3644]**, Springfield, IL
Illinois Thoroughbred Breeders and Owners Found. **[482]**, Caseyville, IL
Illinois Trail Riders **[1561]**, Edwardsville, IL
Illinois Trekkers Volkssport Club **[3457]**, Scott AFB, IL
Illinois Trial Lawyers Assn. **[3645]**, Springfield, IL
Illinois Turfgrass Found. **[2243]**, Lemont, IL
Illinois USA Wrestling **[451]**, Carol Stream, IL
Illinois Vaccine Awareness Coalition **[2816]**, Oak Park, IL
Illinois Valley AIFA **[3080]**, Peru, IL
Illinois Valley Angus Breeders Assn. **[3472]**, Shipman, IL
Illinois Valley Area Chamber of Commerce and Economic Development **[2182]**, La Salle, IL
Illinois Valley BMW MOA No. 70 **[2563]**, Morton, IL
Illinois Valley BMW No. 70 **[★2563]**
Illinois Valley Community Coll. Students In Free Enterprise **[2853]**, Oglesby, IL
Illinois Valley Dental Soc. **[2898]**, Ottawa, IL
Illinois Valley Figure Skating Club **[3028]**, Peoria, IL
Illinois Volkssport Assn. **[530]**, Champaign, IL
Illinois Walnut Council **[3977]**, Westville, IL
Illinois Young Democrats **[2544]**, Montgomery, IL
Immigration
  Coalition of African, Asian, European and Latino Immigrants of Illinois **[850]**, Chicago, IL
  Illinois Coalition for Immigrant and Refugee Rights **[934]**, Chicago, IL
  Intl. Inst. of Flint **[7742]**, Flint, MI
  Intl. Inst. of Wisconsin **[19035]**, Milwaukee, WI
Imperial Windy City Court of the Prairie State Empire **[973]**, Chicago, IL
In the Company of Ferrets **[12720]**, Stillwater, MN
In His Presence **[10912]**, Edina, MN
Independence Music Boosters **[15498]**, Independence, OH
IndependenceFirst **[19025]**, Milwaukee, WI
Independent Accountants Assn. of Illinois **[1775]**, Galesburg, IL
Independent Accountants Assn. of Michigan **[6837]**, Bath, MI
Independent Bus. Assn. of Wisconsin **[18522]**, Madison, WI
Independent Colleges of Indiana **[5156]**, Indianapolis, IN
Independent Colleges and Universities; Wisconsin Assn. of **[18657]**, Madison, WI
Independent Community Bankers of Minnesota **[10867]**, Eagan, MN
Independent Cmpt. Consultants Assn., Chicago **[2913]**, Palatine, IL
Independent Cmpt. Consultants Assn., Minnesota **[12049]**, Prior Lake, MN
Independent Constr. Equip. Builders Union **[2155]**, Kewanee, IL
Independent Elecl. Contractors, Central Ohio **[14466]**, Columbus, OH

Independent Elecl. Contractors of Greater Cincinnati [13863], Cincinnati, OH
Independent Electrical Contractors, Northern Ohio [★15590]
Independent Elecl. Contractors, Southern Indiana/ Evansville Chap. [4551], Evansville, IN
Independent Elecl. Contractors, Western Reserve [13374], Boardman, OH
Independent Funeral Directors of Indiana [5755], Martinsville, IN
Independent Insurance Agents Assn. of Ohio [14467], Columbus, OH
Independent Insurance Agents of Indiana [5157], Indianapolis, IN
Independent Order of Odd Fellows, Century Lodge No. 492 [454], Carpentersville, IL
Independent Order of Odd Fellows, Mad River Lodge 243 [15150], Fairborn, OH
Independent Order of Odd Fellows, Nankin Lodge No. 396 [10100], Wayne, MI
Independent Schools
Assn. of Independent Colls. and Universities of Ohio [14325], Columbus, OH
Fed. of Independent Illinois Colls. and Universities [3551], Springfield, IL
Independent Colleges of Indiana [5156], Indianapolis, IN
Independent Schools Assn. of the Central States [974], Chicago, IL
Minnesota Private Coll. Coun. [12510], St. Paul, MN
Independent Schools Assn. of the Central States [974], Chicago, IL
Indian Fish and Wildlife Commn; Great Lakes [19353], Odanah, WI
Indian Hill Historical Museum Assn. [★13864]
Indian Hill Historical Soc. [13864], Cincinnati, OH
Indian Hill Shooting Club [13865], Cincinnati, OH
Indian Hill Young Life [13866], Cincinnati, OH
Indian Lake Area Chamber of Commerce [16562], Russells Point, OH
Indian Mounds Rock and Mineral Club [10189], Wyoming, MI
Indian Physicians Assn. of Greater Canton [13569], Canton, OH
Indian River Resort Region Chamber of Commerce [8308], Indian River, MI
Indian Springs Beagle Club [16385], Pataskala, OH
Indian Village Historical Colls. [7375], Detroit, MI
Indiana 4-H Found. [5158], Indianapolis, IN
Indiana Acad. of Family Physicians [5159], Indianapolis, IN
Indiana Acad. of Ophthalmology [4605], Fishers, IN
Indiana Acad. of Osteopathy [5160], Indianapolis, IN
Indiana Amateur Softball Assn. [6324], Terre Haute, IN
Indiana Amateur Softball Assn., Region 1 [4431], Crown Point, IN
Indiana Amateur Softball Assn., Region 2 [4810], Granger, IN
Indiana Amateur Softball Assn., Region 3 [4671], Fort Wayne, IN
Indiana Amateur Softball Assn., Region 4 [4426], Crawfordsville, IN
Indiana Amateur Softball Assn., Region 5 [5691], Logansport, IN
Indiana Amateur Softball Assn., Region 6 [4091], Alexandria, IN
Indiana Amateur Softball Assn., Region 7 [6325], Terre Haute, IN
Indiana Amateur Softball Assn., Region 8 [4153], Avon, IN
Indiana Amateur Softball Assn., Region 9 [6156], St. Paul, IN
Indiana Amateur Softball Assn., Region 10 [5816], Mitchell, IN
Indiana Amateur Softball Assn., Region 11 [6170], Scipio, IN
Indiana Amateur Softball Assn., Region 12 [4552], Evansville, IN
Indiana Amer. Eskimo Dog Club [4482], Edinburgh, IN
Indiana Amer. Saddlebred Horse Assn. [4322], Carmel, IN
Indiana Amusement and Music Operators Assn. [5161], Indianapolis, IN
Indiana Angus Assn. [4834], Greenfield, IN
Indiana Apartment Assn. [5162], Indianapolis, IN
Indiana Appaloosa Assn. [4151], Avilla, IN
Indiana Applied Users Gp. [4672], Fort Wayne, IN
Indiana Arts Commn. [5163], Indianapolis, IN
Indiana Assisted Living Fed. of Am. [5164], Indianapolis, IN
Indiana Assn. of Agricultural Educators [5849], Mount Vernon, IN
Indiana Assn. of Beverage Retailers [5165], Indianapolis, IN
Indiana Assn. of Chiefs of Police [5166], Indianapolis, IN
Indiana Assn. of Cities and Towns [5167], Indianapolis, IN
Indiana Assn. of Coll. and Res. Libraries [6231], South Bend, IN
Indiana Assn. for Community Economic Development [5168], Indianapolis, IN
Indiana Assn. of Credit Mgt. [5169], Indianapolis, IN
Indiana Assn. for Developmental Educ. [6516], Westville, IN
Indiana Assn. for the Educ. of Young Children [5170], Indianapolis, IN
Indiana Assn. for Employment in Educ. [5171], Indianapolis, IN
Indiana Assn. for Floodplain and Stormwater Mgt. [5172], Indianapolis, IN
Indiana Assn. for the Gifted [4323], Carmel, IN
Indiana Assn. on Higher Educ. and Disability [4226], Bloomington, IN
Indiana Assn. for Home and Hospice Care [5173], Indianapolis, IN
Indiana Assn. of Homes and Services for the Aging [5174], Indianapolis, IN
Indiana Assn. for Infant and Toddler Mental Hea. [5175], Indianapolis, IN
Indiana Assn. for Institutional Res. [6384], Valparaiso, IN
Indiana Assn. of Insurance and Financial Advisors [5176], Indianapolis, IN
Indiana Assn. of Mortgage Brokers [5177], Indianapolis, IN
Indiana Assn. of Nonprofit Orgs. [5178], Indianapolis, IN
Indiana Assn. of Nurserymen [★5269]
Indiana Assn. of Plumbing, Heating, Cooling Contractors [5179], Indianapolis, IN
Indiana Assn. of Private Career Schools [5180], Indianapolis, IN
Indiana Assn. of Public School Superintendents [5181], Indianapolis, IN
Indiana Assn. of Realtors [5182], Indianapolis, IN
Indiana Assn. of Rehabilitation Facilities [5183], Indianapolis, IN
Indiana Assn. of Residential Child Care Agencies [5184], Indianapolis, IN
Indiana Assn. of Sanitarians [★5231]
Indiana Assn. of Scholars [4227], Bloomington, IN
Indiana Assn. of School Nurses [4673], Fort Wayne, IN
Indiana Assn. of School Principals [5185], Indianapolis, IN
Indiana Assn. of School Psychologists [5186], Indianapolis, IN
Indiana Assn. of Soil and Water Conservation Districts [5187], Indianapolis, IN
Indiana Assn. for Supervision and Curriculum Development [5188], Indianapolis, IN
Indiana Assn. of United Way [5189], Indianapolis, IN
Indiana Athletic Trainers' Assn. [5190], Indianapolis, IN
Indiana Auctioneers Assn. [6484], West Lafayette, IN
Indiana Auto Body Assn. [5191], Indianapolis, IN
Indiana Bankers Assn. [5192], Indianapolis, IN
Indiana B.A.S.S. Fed. [5840], Morgantown, IN
Indiana Beef Cattle Assn. [5193], Indianapolis, IN
Indiana Beef Coun. [5194], Indianapolis, IN
Indiana Beverage Alliance [5195], Indianapolis, IN
Indiana Bicycle Coalition [5196], Indianapolis, IN
Indiana Black Expo [5197], Indianapolis, IN
Indiana Bluebird Soc. [6078], Rensselaer, IN
Indiana Boer Goat Assn. [4347], Charlestown, IN
Indiana Bowling Centers Assn. [5198], Indianapolis, IN
Indiana Bowling Proprietors' Assn. [★5198]
Indiana Broadcasters Assn. [5199], Indianapolis, IN
Indiana Builders Assn. [5200], Indianapolis, IN
Indiana Building and Constr. Trades Coun. [5201], Indianapolis, IN
Indiana Cable Telecommunications Assn. [5202], Indianapolis, IN
Indiana Canine Asst. and Adolescent Network [5203], Indianapolis, IN
Indiana Cast Metals Assn. [5204], Indianapolis, IN
Indiana Central Assn. of Diabetes Educators [5205], Indianapolis, IN
Indiana Chamber of Commerce [5206], Indianapolis, IN
Indiana Chap. Amer. Concrete Inst. [4606], Fishers, IN
Indiana Chap. of Amer. Medical Billing Assn. [6163], Schererville, IN
Indiana Chap. of the Amer. Soc. of Landscape Architects [5207], Indianapolis, IN
Indiana Chap. of the Assn. of Air Medical Services [4674], Fort Wayne, IN
Indiana Chap., Assn. of Legal Administrators [5208], Indianapolis, IN
Indiana Chap. of the Names Proj. Found. [5209], Indianapolis, IN
Indiana Chap. of the Natl. Assn. of Drug Diversion Investigators [5210], Indianapolis, IN
Indiana Chap. of Natl. Assn. of Tax Professionals [6276], South Milford, IN
Indiana Chap. of Natl. Emergency Number Assn. [5713], Madison, IN
Indiana Choral Directors Assn. [6551], Zionsville, IN
Indiana Christmas Tree Growers Assn. [6284], Springport, IN
Indiana Civil Liberties Union [5211], Indianapolis, IN
Indiana Coal Coun. [5212], Indianapolis, IN
Indiana Coalition Against Domestic Violence [5213], Indianapolis, IN
Indiana Collie Club [5214], Indianapolis, IN
Indiana Commercial Bd. of Realtors [5215], Indianapolis, IN
Indiana Concrete Coun. [★5288]
Indiana Constructors [5216], Indianapolis, IN
Indiana Consumer Finance Assn. [5217], Indianapolis, IN
Indiana Coun. of Community Mental Hea. Centers [5218], Indianapolis, IN
Indiana Coun. on Outdoor Lightning Educ. [5219], Indianapolis, IN
Indiana Coun. of Teachers of English [4382], Columbia City, IN
Indiana Coun. of Teachers of Mathematics [5614], Lafayette, IN
Indiana Counselors Assn. on Alcohol and Drug Abuse [5220], Indianapolis, IN
Indiana County Assessors Assn. [6158], Salem, IN
Indiana CPA Soc. [5221], Indianapolis, IN
Indiana Credit Union League [5222], Indianapolis, IN
Indiana Crime Prevention Coalition [5223], Indianapolis, IN
Indiana Crop Improvement Assn. [5615], Lafayette, IN
Indiana Crossroads Orienteering [4324], Carmel, IN
Indiana Dairy Goat Assn. [4959], Idaville, IN
Indiana Democratic Party [5224], Indianapolis, IN
Indiana Dental Assn. [5225], Indianapolis, IN
Indiana Dental Hygienists' Assn. [5226], Indianapolis, IN
Indiana Dietary Managers Assn. [4171], Bedford, IN
Indiana Dietetic Assn. [4485], Elberfeld, IN
Indiana District Amateur Athletic Union [5227], Indianapolis, IN
Indiana District of Precision Metalforming Assn. [5228], Indianapolis, IN
Indiana District, The Lutheran Church-Missouri Synod [4675], Fort Wayne, IN
Indiana Div. - IAAP [4498], Elkhart, IN
Indiana Division of the Intl. Assn. for Identification [4676], Fort Wayne, IN
Indiana Donors Alliance [★5240]
Indiana Draft Horse Breeders [4360], Cicero, IN
Indiana Dressage Soc. [4361], Cicero, IN
Indiana Elec. Assn. [★5229]
Indiana Electronic Ser. Assn. [4818], Greencastle, IN
Indiana Elks Assn. [6193], Shelbyville, IN
Indiana Energy Assn. [5229], Indianapolis, IN
Indiana Enval. Balancing Bur. [5230], Indianapolis, IN
Indiana Environmental Hea. Assn. [5231], Indianapolis, IN

Indiana Equip. Distributors [5232], Indianapolis, IN
Indiana Evaluation Assn. [5233], Indianapolis, IN
Indiana Family, Career and Community Leaders of Am. [5234], Indianapolis, IN
Indiana Farm Bur. [5235], Indianapolis, IN
Indiana Farrier's Assn. No. 15 [6442], Warsaw, IN
Indiana Fed. of Ambulatory Surgical Centers [4325], Carmel, IN
Indiana Fed. of Families for Children's Mental Hea. [4106], Anderson, IN
Indiana Fed. of Republican Women [5236], Indianapolis, IN
Indiana Fireworks Distributors Assn. [5878], Muncie, IN
Indiana Fireworks Users Assn. [5879], Muncie, IN
Indiana First Judicial District Pro Bono Comm. [4926], Hobart, IN
Indiana Four Wheel Drive Assn. [6092], Richmond, IN
Indiana Fox Trotter Association [6326], Terre Haute, IN
Indiana Funeral Directors Assn. [5237], Indianapolis, IN
Indiana Gas Assn. [5238], Indianapolis, IN
Indiana Genealogical Soc. [4677], Fort Wayne, IN
Indiana German Heritage Society [5239], Indianapolis, IN
Indiana Glass Assn. [4362], Cicero, IN
Indiana Golf Assn. [4749], Franklin, IN
Indiana Grant Makers Alliance [5240], Indianapolis, IN
Indiana Grocery and Convenience Store Assn. [5241], Indianapolis, IN
Indiana Ground Water Assn. [5242], Indianapolis, IN
Indiana Haflinger Horse Assn. [4798], Goshen, IN
Indiana Hardwood Lumbermen's Assn. [5243], Indianapolis, IN
Indiana Hea. Care Assn. [5244], Indianapolis, IN
Indiana Hea. Info. Mgt. Assn. [5518], Ireland, IN
Indiana Healthcare Executives Network [4607], Fishers, IN
Indiana High School Athletic Assn. [5245], Indianapolis, IN
Indiana Holstein Assn. [4838], Greens Fork, IN
Indiana Horse Coun. [5246], Indianapolis, IN
Indiana Hosp. and Hea. Assn. [5247], Indianapolis, IN
Indiana Hosp. Purchasing and Material Mgt. Assn. [6093], Richmond, IN
Indiana Hosp. Purchasing and Materials Mgt. Assn. [5248], Indianapolis, IN
Indiana Hotel and Lodging Assn. [5249], Indianapolis, IN
Indiana Humanities Coun. [5250], Indianapolis, IN
Indiana Indus. Energy Consumers [5251], Indianapolis, IN
Indiana Inventors Assn. [5732], Marion, IN
Indiana Junior Golf Assn. [5616], Lafayette, IN
Indiana Karst Conservancy [5252], Indianapolis, IN
Indiana Lake Mgt. Soc. [4125], Angola, IN
Indiana Lakeland Girl Scout Coun. [4799], Goshen, IN
Indiana Lakes Area Youth for Christ [6443], Warsaw, IN
Indiana Land Improvement Contractors Assn. [5956], New Richmond, IN
Indiana Land Title Assn. [5253], Indianapolis, IN
Indiana Lib. Fed. [5254], Indianapolis, IN
Indiana Lib. Trustee Assn. [★5254]
Indiana Licensed Beverage Assn. [5255], Indianapolis, IN
Indiana Life and Hea. Insurance Guaranty Assn. [5256], Indianapolis, IN
Indiana Limestone Inst. of Am. [4172], Bedford, IN
Indiana Limestone; Natl. Assn. for [★4172]
Indiana Lumber and Builders' Supply Assn. [5257], Indianapolis, IN
Indiana Manufacturers Assn. [5258], Indianapolis, IN
Indiana Marine Trade Association [4126], Angola, IN
Indiana Mathematical Assn. of Two-Year Colleges [5617], Lafayette, IN
Indiana Medical Device Manufacturers Coun. [5259], Indianapolis, IN
Indiana Medical Gp. Mgt. Assn. [5260], Indianapolis, IN
Indiana Military Vehicle Preservation Assn. [6511], Westfield, IN
Indiana Mineral Aggregates Assn. [4326], Carmel, IN
Indiana Morgan Horse Club [6046], Plymouth, IN
Indiana Mortgage Bankers [★5261]
Indiana Mortgage Bankers Assn. [5261], Indianapolis, IN
Indiana Mortgage Bankers Assn., Duneland Chap. [6164], Schererville, IN
Indiana Mortgage Bankers Assn., Greater Indianapolis Chap. [5262], Indianapolis, IN
Indiana Mortgage Bankers Assn., Northeast Chap. [4678], Fort Wayne, IN
Indiana Mortgage Bankers Assn., South Central Chap. [4228], Bloomington, IN
Indiana Mortgage Bankers Assn., Southwest Chap. [4553], Evansville, IN
Indiana Mortgage Bankers Assn., Wabash Valley Chap. [6327], Terre Haute, IN
Indiana Motorcycle Dealers Assn. [5263], Indianapolis, IN
Indiana Municipal League [★5167]
Indiana Music Educators Assn. [5880], Muncie, IN
Indiana Natl. Barrel Horse Assn. [6464], Waynetown, IN
Indiana Natl. Cong. of Parents and Teachers [5264], Indianapolis, IN
Indiana Native Plant and Wildflower Soc. [5265], Indianapolis, IN
Indiana Non-Public Educ. Assn. [5266], Indianapolis, IN
Indiana Nonprofit Rsrc. Network [5267], Indianapolis, IN
Indiana Norml [5268], Indianapolis, IN
Indiana Northeast Development [4679], Fort Wayne, IN
Indiana Nursery and Landscape Assn. [5269], Indianapolis, IN
Indiana Occupational Therapy Assn. [6485], West Lafayette, IN
Indiana Optometric Assn. [5270], Indianapolis, IN
Indiana Optometric Assn., Central District [5936], New Castle, IN
Indiana Optometric Assn., Northwestern District [4780], Gary, IN
Indiana Optometric Assn., Southeastern District [4278], Borden, IN
Indiana Optometric Assn., West Central District [5618], Lafayette, IN
Indiana Optometric Assn., Western District [4819], Greencastle, IN
Indiana Optometry Bd. [5271], Indianapolis, IN
Indiana Orchid Soc. [4375], Cloverdale, IN
Indiana Org. of Nurse Executives [5272], Indianapolis, IN
Indiana Osteopathic Assn. [5273], Indianapolis, IN
Indiana Parents of Blind Children [5274], Indianapolis, IN
Indiana Perinatal Network [5275], Indianapolis, IN
Indiana Petroleum Marketers and Convenience Store Assn. [5276], Indianapolis, IN
Indiana Pharmacists Alliance [5277], Indianapolis, IN
Indiana Pioneers; Soc. of [5477], Indianapolis, IN
Indiana Plant Food and Agricultural Chems. Assn. [5278], Indianapolis, IN
Indiana Podiatric Medical Assn. [5279], Indianapolis, IN
Indiana Polygraph Assn. [5280], Indianapolis, IN
Indiana Pork Producers Assn. [6552], Zionsville, IN
Indiana Primary Hea. Care Assn. [5281], Indianapolis, IN
Indiana Professional Educators [5282], Indianapolis, IN
Indiana Psychiatric Soc. [5283], Indianapolis, IN
Indiana Psychological Assn. [5284], Indianapolis, IN
Indiana PTA [5285], Indianapolis, IN
Indiana Public Health Association [5286], Indianapolis, IN
Indiana Quarter Horse Assn. [6047], Plymouth, IN
Indiana Radiological Soc. [5287], Indianapolis, IN
Indiana Ready-Mixed Concrete Assn. [5288], Indianapolis, IN
Indiana Recycling Coalition [4229], Bloomington, IN
Indiana Retail Coun. [5289], Indianapolis, IN
Indiana Retired Teachers Assn. [5290], Indianapolis, IN
Indiana Right to Life [5291], Indianapolis, IN
Indiana Romance Writers of Am. [5292], Indianapolis, IN
Indiana Rural Hea. Assn. [6328], Terre Haute, IN
Indiana SADD [6362], Union City, IN
Indiana School-Age Consortium [5293], Indianapolis, IN
Indiana School Bds. Assn. [5294], Indianapolis, IN
Indiana Seed Trade Assn. [5295], Indianapolis, IN
Indiana Self Storage Assn. [5296], Indianapolis, IN
Indiana Sheriffs' Assn. [5297], Indianapolis, IN
Indiana Skeet Shooting Assn. [6148], Russiaville, IN
Indiana SkillsUSA [5298], Indianapolis, IN
Indiana Small Bus. Coun. [5299], Indianapolis, IN
Indiana Small Bus. Development Center [5300], Indianapolis, IN
Indiana Soc. of Assn. Executives [5301], Indianapolis, IN
Indiana Soc. of Enrolled Agents [4446], Danville, IN
Indiana Soc. of Health-System Pharmacists [5302], Indianapolis, IN
Indiana Soc. for Hea.care Consumer Advocacy [5733], Marion, IN
Indiana Soc. for Hea.care Engg. [5303], Indianapolis, IN
Indiana Soc. for Histotechnology [5304], Indianapolis, IN
Indiana Soc. of Internal Medicine [5305], Indianapolis, IN
Indiana Soc. of Professional Engineers [5306], Indianapolis, IN
Indiana Soc. of Professional Land Surveyors [5307], Indianapolis, IN
Indiana Soc. of Public Accountants [4327], Carmel, IN
Indiana Soc. of Radiologic Technologists [5308], Indianapolis, IN
Indiana Soc. of Radiologic Technologists, District 4 [5569], Kokomo, IN
Indiana Soc. of Radiologic Technologists, District 8 [5850], Mount Vernon, IN
Indiana Soc., Sons of the Amer. Revolution, Continental Chap. [5881], Muncie, IN
Indiana Soc., Sons of the Amer. Revolution, Gen. Thomas Posey Chap. [5851], Mount Vernon, IN
Indiana Soc., Sons of the Amer. Revolution, George Rogers Clark Chap. [6410], Vincennes, IN
Indiana Soc., Sons of the Amer. Revolution, John Martin Chap. [6329], Terre Haute, IN
Indiana Soc., Sons of the Amer. Revolution, Simon Kenton Chap. [6079], Rensselaer, IN
Indiana Soc., Sons of the Amer. Revolution, William Knight Chap. [4820], Greencastle, IN
Indiana Soc., Sons of the Amer. Revolution, William Van Gordon Chap. [4915], Highland, IN
Indiana Soybean Growers Assn. [5309], Indianapolis, IN
Indiana Speech-Language-Hearing Assn. [5310], Indianapolis, IN
Indiana Sporting Clays Assn. [4554], Evansville, IN
Indiana Stamp Club [5311], Indianapolis, IN
Indiana State Assembly of the Assn. of Surgical Technologists [5312], Indianapolis, IN
Indiana State Assn. of Life Underwriters [★5176]
Indiana State Bar Assn. [5313], Indianapolis, IN
Indiana State Chiropractic Assn. [5314], Indianapolis, IN
Indiana State Dairy Assn. [6486], West Lafayette, IN
Indiana State Employees Assn. [5315], Indianapolis, IN
Indiana State Grange [4800], Goshen, IN
Indiana State Hispanic Chamber of Commerce [5316], Indianapolis, IN
Indiana State Lib. and Historical Bur. Found. [5317], Indianapolis, IN
Indiana State Medical Assn. [5318], Indianapolis, IN
Indiana State Museum Found. [5319], Indianapolis, IN
Indiana State Museum Volunteers [5320], Indianapolis, IN
Indiana State Numismatic Assn. [4107], Anderson, IN
Indiana State Nurses Assn. [5321], Indianapolis, IN
Indiana State Podiatry Assn. [★5279]
Indiana State Poultry Assn. [6487], West Lafayette, IN
Indiana State Racquetball Assn. [5322], Indianapolis, IN
Indiana State Rifle and Pistol Assn. [5323], Indianapolis, IN

Indiana State Teachers Assn. [5324], Indianapolis, IN
Indiana State Trappers Assn. [5547], Kempton, IN
Indiana State Wrestling Assn. [4182], Beech Grove, IN
Indiana Statewide Assn. of Rural Elec. Cooperatives [5325], Indianapolis, IN
Indiana Structural Engineers Assn. [5771], Merrillville, IN
Indiana Student Financial Aid Assn. [6330], Terre Haute, IN
Indiana Student Public Interest Res. Gp. [4230], Bloomington, IN
Indiana Subcontractors Assn. [5326], Indianapolis, IN
Indiana Suffolk Sheep Assn. [6070], Princeton, IN
Indiana Supreme Court Historical Soc. [5327], Indianapolis, IN
Indiana Telecommunications Assn. [5328], Indianapolis, IN
Indiana Thoracic Soc. [5329], Indianapolis, IN
Indiana Township Assn. [4608], Fishers, IN
Indiana Trans. Assn. [4231], Bloomington, IN
Indiana Trial Lawyers Assn. [5330], Indianapolis, IN
Indiana Triumph Cars [5331], Indianapolis, IN
Indiana Univ. Coll. Democrats [4232], Bloomington, IN
Indiana Univ. - Environmental Law Soc. [4233], Bloomington, IN
Indiana Univ. Figure Skating Club [4234], Bloomington, IN
Indiana Univ. Northwest Student Nurses' Assn. [4781], Gary, IN
Indiana Univ. Purdue Univ. Assn. for Computing Machinery Student Siggraph [5332], Indianapolis, IN
Indiana Univ. Student Assn. [4235], Bloomington, IN
Indiana U.S.A. Track and Field [4590], Fairland, IN
Indiana Veterinary Medical Assn. [5333], Indianapolis, IN
Indiana Volkssport Assn. [4400], Columbus, IN
Indiana Water Resources Assn. [5334], Indianapolis, IN
Indiana Wesleyan Univ. Assn. for Computing Machinery Student Chap. [5734], Marion, IN
Indiana Wholesale Distributors [5335], Indianapolis, IN
Indiana Wildlife Fed. [4328], Carmel, IN
Indiana Young Democrats [4236], Bloomington, IN
Indiana Youth Gp. [5336], Indianapolis, IN
Indiana Youth Inst. [5337], Indianapolis, IN
Indianapolis Ambassadors [5338], Indianapolis, IN
Indianapolis Assn. of Black Journalists [5339], Indianapolis, IN
Indianapolis BMW Club No. 17 [5340], Indianapolis, IN
Indianapolis Chamber of Commerce [★5128]
Indianapolis Chapel Hill Lions Club [5341], Indianapolis, IN
Indianapolis Children's Choir [5342], Indianapolis, IN
Indianapolis Coin Club [5343], Indianapolis, IN
Indianapolis Convention and Visitors Assn. [5344], Indianapolis, IN
Indianapolis Corvette Club [5345], Indianapolis, IN
Indianapolis District Dental Soc. [5346], Indianapolis, IN
Indianapolis Fencing Club [5347], Indianapolis, IN
Indianapolis Found. [5348], Indianapolis, IN
Indianapolis Franklin Township Lions Club [5349], Indianapolis, IN
Indianapolis Historic Preservation Commn. [5350], Indianapolis, IN
Indianapolis Medical Soc. [5351], Indianapolis, IN
Indianapolis Memorial Soc. [5352], Indianapolis, IN
Indianapolis Musicians' Assn. - Local 3, Amer. Fed. of Musicians [★5353]
Indianapolis Musicians - Local 3, Amer. Fed. of Musicians [5353], Indianapolis, IN
Indianapolis Org. Development Network [5354], Indianapolis, IN
Indianapolis Professional Photographers Guild [5950], New Palestine, IN
Indianapolis RSVP [5355], Indianapolis, IN
Indianapolis Traditional Music and Dance Gp. [5356], Indianapolis, IN
Indianapolis Urban League [5357], Indianapolis, IN
Indianapolis Youth Gp. [★5336]
Indianapolis Zoo [5358], Indianapolis, IN
Indianhead Appaloosa Horse Club [11028], Franklin, MN
Indianhead Chap. MOAA [17787], Cornell, WI
Indianhead Community Action [18391], Ladysmith, WI
Indianhead Optometric Soc. [17755], Chippewa Falls, WI
Indianhead Professional Photographers Assn. [17879], Eau Claire, WI
Indus of Fox Valley [17500], Appleton, WI
Indus. Assn; Addison [★3]
Indus. Assn; North Eastern Michigan [10131], West Branch, MI

Industrial Development
21st Century Leadership, Posey County [5844], Mount Vernon, IN
Indus. Development Comm; Montpelier [16062], Montpelier, OH
Indus. Development Corp; Chippewa Falls [17750], Chippewa Falls, WI

Industrial Education
Indiana SkillsUSA [5298], Indianapolis, IN
Skills USA, Albert Lea High School [10261], Albert Lea, MN
Skills USA, Anoka-Hennepin Tech. Coll. [10311], Anoka, MN
Skills USA, Anoka High School [10312], Anoka, MN
Skills USA, Austin High School [10358], Austin, MN
Skills USA, Blaine High School [10452], Blaine, MN
Skills USA, Cambridge High School [10626], Cambridge, MN
Skills USA, Carver-Scott Educal. Cooperative [10654], Chaska, MN
Skills USA, Century High School [12185], Rochester, MN
Skills USA, Champlin Park High School [10644], Champlin, MN
Skills USA, Chisago Lakes High School [11317], Lindstrom, MN
Skills USA, Coon Rapids High School [10717], Coon Rapids, MN
Skills USA, Cottonwood River Cooperative Center [12696], Springfield, MN
Skills USA, Dakota County Tech. Center [12217], Rosemount, MN
Skills USA, Duluth Secondary Tech. Center [10853], Duluth, MN
Skills USA, East Grand Forks High School [10885], East Grand Forks, MN
Skills USA, Edison High School [11737], Minneapolis, MN
Skills USA, Fergus Falls High School [11003], Fergus Falls, MN
Skills USA, Hennepin Tech. Coll. [10559], Brooklyn Park, MN
Skills USA, Hopkins High School [11796], Minnetonka, MN
Skills USA, Independent District 287 [10901], Eden Prairie, MN
Skills USA, John F. Kennedy High School [10488], Bloomington, MN
Skills USA, John Marshall High School [12186], Rochester, MN
Skills USA, Lakeville High School [11296], Lakeville, MN
Skills USA, Mankato West High School [11399], Mankato, MN
Skills USA, Mayo High School [12187], Rochester, MN
Skills USA, Minneapolis Public Schools [11738], Minneapolis, MN
Skills USA, North Community High School [11739], Minneapolis, MN
Skills USA, Owatonna High School [11968], Owatonna, MN
Skills USA, Patrick Henry High School [11740], Minneapolis, MN
Skills USA, Proctor High School [12059], Proctor, MN
Skills USA, Red Wing Central High School [12085], Red Wing, MN
Skills USA, Roosevelt High School [11741], Minneapolis, MN
Skills USA, Roseau High School [12211], Roseau, MN
Skills USA, St. Francis High School [12321], St. Francis, MN
Skills USA, South High School [11742], Minneapolis, MN
Skills USA, Southwest High School [11743], Minneapolis, MN
Skills USA, S.T.E.P. - Secondary Tech. Educ. Prog. [10313], Anoka, MN
Skills USA, Tartan High School [11929], Oakdale, MN
Skills USA, Tech. High School [12308], St. Cloud, MN
Skills USA, Washburn High School [11744], Minneapolis, MN
Skills USA, Wayzata High School [12035], Plymouth, MN
Skills USA, Work Opportunity Center [11745], Minneapolis, MN
Skills USA, Wright Tech. Center [10578], Buffalo, MN
SkillsUSA Illinois [2511], Mokena, IL
SkillsUSA Michigan [9530], Rockford, MI
SkillsUSA Minnesota [11746], Minneapolis, MN
Tech. Student Assn., Illinois [2609], Mulberry Grove, IL
Indus. Energy Users-Ohio [14468], Columbus, OH

Industrial Engineering
APICS, The Assn. for Operations Mgt. - Canton Area Chap. [13545], Canton, OH
APICS, The Assn. for Operations Mgt. - Central Indiana Chap. [5032], Indianapolis, IN
APICS, The Assn. for Operations Mgt. - Central Minnesota Chap. [12273], St. Cloud, MN
APICS, The Assn. for Operations Mgt. - Chicago Chap. [1859], Glenview, IL
APICS, The Assn. for Operations Mgt. - Cincinnati Chap. [13743], Cincinnati, OH
APICS, The Assn. for Operations Mgt. - Cleveland Chap. [14071], Cleveland, OH
APICS, The Assn. for Operations Mgt. - Columbus Chap. No. 99 [17205], Westerville, OH
APICS, The Assn. for Operations Mgt. - Dayton Chap. No. 64 [13619], Centerville, OH
APICS, The Assn. for Operations Mgt. - Fort Wayne Chap. 139 [4639], Fort Wayne, IN
APICS, The Assn. for Operations Mgt. - Fox River Chap. No. 207 [174], Batavia, IL
APICS, The Assn. for Operations Mgt. - Grand Rapids Chap. [7906], Grand Rapids, MI
APICS, The Assn. for Operations Mgt. - Highlands Chap. 261 [1318], Crystal Lake, IL
APICS, The Assn. for Operations Mgt. - Lima Area Chap. No. 290 [15356], Greenville, OH
APICS, The Assn. for Operations Mgt. - Michiana Chap. No. 57 [6219], South Bend, IN
APICS, The Assn. for Operations Mgt. - Mid Michigan Chap. [7579], Eaton Rapids, MI
APICS, The Assn. for Operations Mgt. - Milwaukee Chap. [20070], Wauwatosa, WI
APICS, The Assn. for Operations Mgt. - Racine/Kenosha Chap. [19552], Racine, WI
APICS, The Assn. for Operations Mgt. - Rock Valley Chap. [3271], Rockford, IL
APICS, The Assn. for Operations Mgt. - Shoreline Chap. [19692], Sheboygan, WI
APICS, The Assn. for Operations Mgt. - Southern Minnesota Chap. [11958], Owatonna, MN
APICS, The Assn. for Operations Mgt. - The Greater Detroit Chap. [8787], Lathrup Village, MI
APICS, The Assn. for Operations Mgt. - Toledo Chap. [16901], Toledo, OH
APICS, The Assn. for Operations Mgt. - Twin Cities Chap. [10463], Bloomington, MN

Industrial Equipment
Indiana Equip. Distributors [5232], Indianapolis, IN
Michigan Equip. Distributors [9258], Oak Park, MI
Michigan Tooling Assn. [7671], Farmington Hills, MI
North Amer. Die Casting Assn. Southern Ohio Chap. 14 [14934], Dayton, OH
North Amer. Die Casting Assn. West Michigan Chap. 3 [7994], Grand Rapids, MI
Industrial Inst; Cincinnati [★13820]
Indus. Recreation and Employee Services Coun; Toledo [16304], Oregon, OH

Indus. Relations Res. Assn. - Northeast Ohio Chap. **[★15501]**
Indus. Sand Assn; Michigan **[8676]**, Lansing, MI
Industrial Security
ASIS Intl., Central Illinois Chap. 158 **[4421]**, Covington, IN
ASIS Intl., Chicago Chap. **[31]**, Alsip, IL
ASIS Intl., Columbus Ohio Chap. 27 **[15427]**, Hilliard, OH
ASIS Intl., Detroit Chap. **[9785]**, Southfield, MI
ASIS Intl., Illinois North Shore Chap. **[2907]**, Palatine, IL
ASIS Intl., Lansing Chap. 120 **[7507]**, East Lansing, MI
ASIS Intl., Minnesota Chap. No. 25 **[11407]**, Maple Grove, MN
ASIS Intl., Toledo Chap. No. 56 **[16903]**, Toledo, OH
Assn. of Certified Fraud Examiners, Central Indiana Chap. No. 52 **[5042]**, Indianapolis, IN
Assn. of Certified Fraud Examiners, Central Ohio Chap. No. 39 **[15260]**, Gahanna, OH
Assn. of Certified Fraud Examiners, Cleveland Area Chap. No. 13 **[13040]**, Akron, OH
Assn. of Certified Fraud Examiners - Greater Chicago Chap. **[2506]**, Mokena, IL
Assn. of Certified Fraud Examiners, Northern Indiana Chap. No. 79 **[6379]**, Valparaiso, IN
Assn. of Certified Fraud Examiners, Southeast Michigan Area Chap., No. 37 **[9975]**, Troy, MI
Assn. of Certified Fraud Examiners, Southwest Ohio Chap. No. 46 **[15153]**, Fairfield, OH
Assn. of Certified Fraud Examiners, Toledo Chap. No. 122 **[15903]**, Maumee, OH
Assn. of Certified Fraud Examiners, Twin Cities Chap. No. 47 **[11525]**, Minneapolis, MN
Assn. of Certified Fraud Examiners, Wisconsin Area Chap. No. 32 **[19932]**, Verona, WI
Info. Systems Security Assn., Central Indiana Chap. **[5367]**, Indianapolis, IN
Info. Systems Security Assn., Milwaukee Chap. **[17669]**, Brookfield, WI
Info. Systems Security Assn., Minnesota Chap. **[12109]**, Richfield, MN
Industrial Workers
Bricklayers and Allied Craftworkers Local No. 8 **[502]**, Champaign, IL
Building and Constr. Trades Dept. AFL-CIO, Chicago and Cook County **[772]**, Chicago, IL
Building and Constr. Trades Dept. AFL-CIO, Decatur **[1377]**, Decatur, IL
Building and Constr. Trades Dept. AFL-CIO, Milwaukee **[18984]**, Milwaukee, WI
Food and Commercial Workers AFL-CIO, LU 268 **[17754]**, Chippewa Falls, WI
Indus. Workers of the World - Chicago **[975]**, Chicago, IL
Indus. Workers of the World - Detroit **[7376]**, Detroit, MI
Indus. Workers of the World - Grand Rapids **[7965]**, Grand Rapids, MI
Indus. Workers of the World - Joliet **[2108]**, Joliet, IL
Indus. Workers of the World - Lakeside Press **[18523]**, Madison, WI
Indus. Workers of the World - Ohio Valley **[13867]**, Cincinnati, OH
Indus. Workers of the World - Railroad Workers **[18524]**, Madison, WI
Indus. Workers of the World - Twin Cities **[11585]**, Minneapolis, MN
Indus. Workers of the World - Waukegan **[3924]**, Waukegan, IL
Intl. Union of Elevator Constructors, Local 2 - Chicago, Illinois **[994]**, Chicago, IL
Intl. Union of Elevator Constructors, Local 9 - Minneapolis, Minnesota **[11332]**, Little Canada, MN
Intl. Union of Elevator Constructors, Local 34 - Indianapolis, Indiana **[5378]**, Indianapolis, IN
Intl. Union of Painters and Allied Trades AFL-CIO, Local 156 **[4557]**, Evansville, IN
Laborers AFL-CIO, LU 355 **[6861]**, Battle Creek, MI
Local 15C, Chem. Workers Coun. of the UFCW **[4366]**, Clarksville, IN
Local 20C, Chem. Workers Coun. of the UFCW **[16151]**, New Philadelphia, OH
Local 60C, Chem. Workers Coun. of the UFCW **[334]**, Bradley, IL
Local 70C, Chem. Workers Coun. of the UFCW **[10163]**, Whitehall, MI
Local 132C, Chem. Workers Coun. of the UFCW **[7975]**, Grand Rapids, MI
Local 228C, Chem. Workers Coun. of the UFCW **[12952]**, Winona, MN
Local 530, RWDSU District Coun. of the UFCW **[9147]**, Muskegon, MI
Local 705, RWDSU District Coun. of the UFCW **[8207]**, Holland, MI
Local 758C, Chem. Workers Coun. of the UFCW **[1481]**, Dixon, IL
Local 776C, Chem. Workers Coun. of the UFCW **[17129]**, Washington Court House, OH
Local 799C, Chem. Workers Coun. of the UFCW **[9721]**, Sault Ste. Marie, MI
Local 822, RWDSU District Coun. of the UFCW **[8208]**, Holland, MI
Local 825, RWDSU District Coun. of the UFCW **[8794]**, Lawton, MI
Local 871C, Chem. Workers Coun. of the UFCW **[387]**, Cahokia, IL
Local 872C, Chem. Workers Coun. of the UFCW **[2140]**, Kankakee, IL
Minnesota AFL-CIO **[12450]**, St. Paul, MN
Musicians AFL-CIO, LU 118 **[17106]**, Warren, OH
Northeast Indiana Constr. Alliance **[4702]**, Fort Wayne, IN
Ohio AFL-CIO **[14536]**, Columbus, OH
Plumbers AFL-CIO, LU 434 **[19231]**, Mosinee, WI
Sheet Metal Workers AFL-CIO, LU 80 **[9819]**, Southfield, MI
Sheet Metal Workers Intl. Assn. LU 183/AFL-CIO **[13984]**, Cincinnati, OH
Sheet Metal Workers' Union Local 73, AFL-CIO **[2007]**, Hillside, IL
South Central Fed. of Labor, AFL-CIO **[18619]**, Madison, WI
Teamsters Local 916 **[3687]**, Springfield, IL
Teamsters Local Union 563 **[17527]**, Appleton, WI
United Elecl., Radio and Machine Workers of Am., Local 1111 **[19141]**, Milwaukee, WI
United Food and Commercial Workers AFL-CIO, Local 951 **[8016]**, Grand Rapids, MI
United Food and Commercial Workers AFL-CIO, LU 665T **[19922]**, Two Rivers, WI
United Food and Commercial Workers, Local 12A, Northcentral Region **[10858]**, Duluth, MN
United Food and Commercial Workers, Local 78T, Northcentral Region **[17529]**, Appleton, WI
United Food and Commercial Workers, Local 200T, Northcentral Region **[3723]**, Streamwood, IL
United Food and Commercial Workers, Local 236T, Northcentral Region **[19923]**, Two Rivers, WI
United Food and Commercial Workers, Local 245, Northcentral Region **[19676]**, Seymour, WI
United Food and Commercial Workers, Local 335, Northcentral Region **[12089]**, Red Wing, MN
United Food and Commercial Workers, Local 527, Northcentral Region **[12090]**, Red Wing, MN
United Food and Commercial Workers, Local 536, Northcentral Region **[3068]**, Peoria, IL
United Food and Commercial Workers, Local 580T, Northcentral Region **[1470]**, Des Plaines, IL
United Food and Commercial Workers, Local 653, Northcentral Region **[12040]**, Plymouth, MN
United Food and Commercial Workers, Local 688, Northcentral Region **[18898]**, Merrill, WI
United Food and Commercial Workers, Local 717, Northcentral Region **[17739]**, Chili, WI
United Food and Commercial Workers, Local 876, Central Region **[8901]**, Madison Heights, MI
United Food and Commercial Workers, Local 911 **[15460]**, Holland, OH
United Food and Commercial Workers, Local 1059, Central Region **[14749]**, Columbus, OH
United Food and Commercial Workers, Local 1099, Central Region **[16056]**, Monroe, OH
United Food and Commercial Workers, Local 1116, Northcentral Region **[10859]**, Duluth, MN
United Food and Commercial Workers, Local 1281P, Northcentral Region **[2143]**, Kankakee, IL
United Food and Commercial Workers, Local 1444, Northcentral Region **[19142]**, Milwaukee, WI
Western Wisconsin AFL-CIO **[18381]**, La Crosse, WI
Wisconsin Coun. of County and Municipal Employees AFSCME, Coun. 40 AFL-CIO **[18689]**, Madison, WI
Wisconsin State AFL-CIO **[19183]**, Milwaukee, WI
Indus. Workers of the World - Chicago **[975]**, Chicago, IL
Indus. Workers of the World - Detroit **[7376]**, Detroit, MI
Indus. Workers of the World - Grand Rapids **[7965]**, Grand Rapids, MI
Indus. Workers of the World - Joliet **[2108]**, Joliet, IL
Indus. Workers of the World - Lakeside Press **[18523]**, Madison, WI
Indus. Workers of the World - Ohio Valley **[13867]**, Cincinnati, OH
Indus. Workers of the World - Railroad Workers **[18524]**, Madison, WI
Indus. Workers of the World - Twin Cities **[11585]**, Minneapolis, MN
Indus. Workers of the World - Waukegan **[3924]**, Waukegan, IL
Indus. of Ohio; Energy **[15496]**, Independence, OH
Indus; Antioch Chamber of Commerce and **[56]**, Antioch, IL
Indus; Bradley Assn. of Commerce and **[★326]**
Indus; Cicero Chamber of Commerce and **[1260]**, Cicero, IL
Indus; Darien Chamber of Commerce and **[★1358]**
Indus; Dixon Area Chamber of Commerce and **[1477]**, Dixon, IL
Indus; Fox Cities Chamber of Commerce and **[17490]**, Appleton, WI
Indus; Fox Lake Area Chamber of Commerce and **[1719]**, Fox Lake, IL
Indus; Greater Effingham Chamber of Commerce and **[1570]**, Effingham, IL
Indus; Lombard Area Chamber of Commerce and **[★2337]**
Indus; Marshfield Area Chamber of Commerce and **[18817]**, Marshfield, WI
Indus; Menomonee Falls Chamber of Commerce and **[★18877]**
Indus; Monroe Chamber of Commerce and **[19215]**, Monroe, WI
Indus; Morton Grove Chamber of Commerce and **[2569]**, Morton Grove, IL
Indus; Niles Chamber of Chamber of Commerce and **[2702]**, Niles, IL
Indus; Ottawa Area Chamber of Commerce and **[2899]**, Ottawa, IL
Indus; Round Lake Area Chamber of Commerce and **[3365]**, Round Lake Beach, IL
Indus; Wheeling - Prospect Heights Area Chamber of Commerce and **[4006]**, Wheeling, IL
Indus; Woodstock Chamber of Commerce and **[4065]**, Woodstock, IL
Indy African Violet Club **[5359]**, Indianapolis, IN
Indy 'G' Walkers **[5360]**, Indianapolis, IN
Indy South Assn. of Insurance and Financial Advisors **[5361]**, Indianapolis, IN
Indy Swing Dance Club **[5362]**, Indianapolis, IN
Indy West Daybreakers Kiwanis Club **[5363]**, Indianapolis, IN
Indy Z Car Club **[5364]**, Indianapolis, IN
Infant Mental Hea; Michigan Assn. for **[9837]**, Southgate, MI
Infants
Indiana Perinatal Network **[5275]**, Indianapolis, IN
Newborns In Need Indianapolis Chap. **[5438]**, Indianapolis, IN
Southeast Indiana Healthy Mothers, Healthy Babies Coalition **[5662]**, Lawrenceburg, IN
Wisconsin Healthy Mothers, Healthy Babies Coalition **[20109]**, West Allis, WI
Infectious Diseases
Assn. for Professionals in Infection Control and Epidemiology, Chicago **[753]**, Chicago, IL
Assn. for Professionals in Infection Control and Epidemiology, Greater Detroit **[7167]**, Clawson, MI
Assn. for Professionals in Infection Control and Epidemiology, Indiana Chap. **[4946]**, Huntington, IN

Assn. for Professionals in Infection Control and Epidemiology, Minnesota Chap. [12390], St. Paul, MN
Assn. for Professionals in Infection Control and Epidemiology, Northwest Ohio [16906], Toledo, OH
Michigan Infectious Diseases Soc. [9939], Traverse City, MI
North Central Chap., Infectious Diseases Soc. of Am. [12861], Wayzata, MN
Info. Bur; Three Lakes [19899], Three Lakes, WI

Information Management
ARMA, Greater Cincinnati Chapter [13745], Cincinnati, OH
ARMA International - Fox Valley/Green Bay Chapter - The Information Management Professionals [17813], De Pere, WI
ARMA Intl. - Info. Mgt. Professionals, Greater Dayton Chap. [15984], Miamisburg, OH
ARMA Intl. - The Info. Mgt. Professionals, Greater Columbus Ohio Chap. [15259], Gahanna, OH
ARMA Intl. - The Info. Mgt. Professionals, Twin Cities Chap. [10464], Bloomington, MN
ARMA, Madison Chap. [18477], Madison, WI
ARMA, Western Michigan Chap. [7908], Grand Rapids, MI
DAMA-Michigan Chap. [9981], Troy, MI
Illinois State Data Center Cooperative [3639], Springfield, IL
Info. Mgt. Assn; Indiana Hea. [5518], Ireland, IN
Info. Mgt. Assn; Michigan Hea. [9148], Muskegon, MI
Info. Mgt., Chicago; Soc. for [1191], Chicago, IL
Info. and Referral Coalition [★12285]
Info. and Referral Network [5365], Indianapolis, IN
Info. Systems Audit and Control Assn., Central Indiana Chap. [5366], Indianapolis, IN
Info. Systems Audit and Control Assn., Central Ohio Chap. [14469], Columbus, OH
Info. Systems Audit and Control Assn., Detroit Chap. [9992], Troy, MI
Info. Syss. Audit and Control Assn. and Found., Michiana Chap. [6232], South Bend, IN
Info. Systems Audit and Control Assn. and Found., Minnesota Chap. [12230], Roseville, MN
Info. Syss. Audit and Control Assn. and Found., Quad Cities Chap. [1538], East Moline, IL
Info. Syss. Audit and Control Assn., Kettle Moraine Chap. [19026], Milwaukee, WI
Info. Syss. Audit and Control Assn., Northeast Ohio Chap. [14141], Cleveland, OH
Info. Systems Security Assn., Central Indiana Chap. [5367], Indianapolis, IN
Info. Systems Security Assn., Milwaukee Chap. [17669], Brookfield, WI
Info. Systems Security Assn., Minnesota Chap. [12109], Richfield, MN
Info. Tech; Community Economic Development and [9699], Saline, MI
Info. Tech. Student Assn. [★2710]
Inforum [7377], Detroit, MI
Infusion Nurses Soc., Buckeye [14894], Dayton, OH
Infusion Nurses Soc., Capital [8147], Haslett, MI
Infusion Nurses Soc., Great Lakes [9902], Taylor, MI
Infusion Nurses Soc., Illinois [3990], Wheaton, IL
Infusion Nurses Soc., Mid-Michigan [6901], Beaverton, MI
Infusion Nurses Soc., Southern Wisconsin [17670], Brookfield, WI
Infusion Nurses Soc., Upper Midwest [10592], Burnsville, MN
Ingalls Stroke Club [1955], Harvey, IL
Ingham County Medical Soc. [7523], East Lansing, MI
Inkster Chamber of Commerce [8311], Inkster, MI
Inkster Housing and Redevelopment Commn. [8312], Inkster, MI
Inland Press Assn. [1460], Des Plaines, IL
Inland Sea Soc. [19950], Washburn, WI
Inland Seas Educ. Assn. [9886], Suttons Bay, MI
Inner City Christian Fed. [7966], Grand Rapids, MI
Inner-City Teaching Corps [976], Chicago, IL
Innovative Minds of Wisconsin [19228], Mosinee, WI
Inroads, Indiana [5368], Indianapolis, IN
INROADS, St. Paul, Minnesota [12426], St. Paul, MN
Inspectors, Ohio Chap; Intl. Assn. of Elecl. [16661], Shreve, OH
Inst. of Internal Auditors, Central Ohio Chap. [17344], Worthington, OH
Inst. of Internal Auditors, Chicago Chap. [149], Barrington, IL
Inst. of Internal Auditors, Detroit Chap. [7662], Farmington Hills, MI
Inst. of Internal Auditors, Fort Wayne Chap. [4680], Fort Wayne, IN
Inst. of Internal Auditors, Fox Valley/Central Wisconsin Chap. [18108], Green Bay, WI
Inst. of Internal Auditors, Indianapolis Chap. [4160], Batesville, IN
Inst. of Internal Auditors, Lake Superior Chap. [10826], Duluth, MN
Inst. of Internal Auditors, Lansing Chap. [8577], Lansing, MI
Inst. of Internal Auditors, Madison Chap. [18525], Madison, WI
Inst. of Internal Auditors, Michiana Chap. [6004], Notre Dame, IN
Inst. of Internal Auditors, Northwest Metro Chicago Chap. [2036], Hoffman Estates, IL
Inst. of Internal Auditors, Springfield Chap. [3646], Springfield, IL
Inst. of Internal Auditors, Tri-State Chap. [4555], Evansville, IN
Inst. of Internal Auditors, Twin Cities Chap. [10468], Bloomington, MN
Inst. of Internal Auditors, Western Michigan Chap. [7967], Grand Rapids, MI
Inst. of Mgt. Accountants, Akron Chap. [13058], Akron, OH
Inst. of Mgt. Accountants, Ann Arbor Chap. [6708], Ann Arbor, MI
Inst. of Mgt. Accountants, Central Minnesota [12287], St. Cloud, MN
Inst. of Mgt. Accountants, Chippewa Valley [17880], Eau Claire, WI
Inst. of Mgt. Accountants, Cincinnati North Chap. [17174], West Chester, OH
Inst. of Mgt. Accountants, Cleveland Chap. [13428], Broadview Heights, OH
Inst. of Mgt. Accountants, Cleveland East Chap. [16790], Strongsville, OH
Inst. of Mgt. Accountants, Dayton Chap. [17001], Troy, OH
Inst. of Mgt. Accountants, Detroit Metro Chap. [6612], Allen Park, MI
Inst. of Mgt. Accountants, Evansville Chap. [4556], Evansville, IN
Inst. of Mgt. Accountants, Illinois State Univ. Chap. [2722], Normal, IL
Inst. of Mgt. Accountants, Indianapolis Chap. [5975], Noblesville, IN
Inst. of Mgt. Accountants, LaCrosse-Winona Chap. [20137], West Salem, WI
Inst. of Mgt. Accountants, Lake Superior Chap. [10827], Duluth, MN
Inst. of Mgt. Accountants, Minneapolis Chap. [11788], Minnetonka, MN
Inst. of Mgt. Accountants, Saint Paul [11223], Inver Grove Heights, MN
Inst. of Mgt. Accountants, Sangamon Valley Chap. [1396], Decatur, IL
Inst. of Mgt. Accountants, South Central Minnesota [11380], Mankato, MN
Inst. of Mgt. Accountants, Southern Minnesota [12151], Rochester, MN
Inst. of Mgt. Accountants, Wabash Valley Chap. [6331], Terre Haute, IN
Inst. of Packaging Professionals, Central Indiana Chap. [5369], Indianapolis, IN
Inst. of Packaging Professionals, Michigan Chap. [9181], New Baltimore, MI
Institute of Packaging Professionals, West Michigan Chapter [8431], Kalamazoo, MI
Inst. of Real Estate Mgt. - Central Illinois Chap. No. 78 [3029], Peoria, IL
Inst. of Real Estate Mgt. - Chicago Chap. No. 23 [2298], Lisle, IL
Inst. of Real Estate Mgt. - Columbus Chap. No. 42 [16772], Stoutsville, OH
Inst. of Real Estate Mgt. - Greater Cincinnati Chap. No. 9 [13868], Cincinnati, OH
Inst. of Real Estate Mgt. - Indianapolis Chap. No. 24 [5370], Indianapolis, IN
Inst. of Real Estate Mgt. - Madison Chap. No. 82 [18526], Madison, WI
Inst. of Real Estate Mgt. - Michigan Chap. No. 5 [7645], Farmington, MI
Inst. of Real Estate Mgt. - Milwaukee Chap. No. 13 [19027], Milwaukee, WI
Inst. of Real Estate Mgt. - Minnesota Chap. No. 45 [11586], Minneapolis, MN
Inst. of Real Estate Mgt. - Northern Indiana Chap. No. 100 [6233], South Bend, IN
Inst. of Real Estate Mgt. - Northern Ohio Chap. No. 41 [13274], Bay Village, OH
Inst. of Real Estate Mgt., Region 9 [977], Chicago, IL
Inst. of Real Estate Mgt. - West Michigan Chap. No. 62 [7663], Farmington Hills, MI

Instructional Media
Assn. for Indiana Media Educators [5728], Marion, IN
Illinois Assn. for Educal. Communs. and Tech. [1433], DeKalb, IL
Minnesota Educational Media Org. [12238], Roseville, MN
Instructors; Minnesota Assn. of Law Enforcement Firearms [12157], Rochester, MN
Instrumental Music Boosters; Willoughby South [★17279]
Instrumental Music Boosters; Willoughby South High [17279], Willoughby, OH

Insurance
Agency Manager of Illinois [1413], Deerfield, IL
Akron AIFA [16773], Stow, OH
Albert Lea-Austin AIFA [10349], Austin, MN
Alliance-Salem ALU [13109], Alliance, OH
ASCnet Chap. of Southwest Ohio [13747], Cincinnati, OH
Ashtabula County AIFA [13178], Ashtabula, OH
Assoc. Risk Managers of Ohio [16478], Powell, OH
Assn. of Insurance Compliance Professionals, Great Lakes Chap. [1860], Glenview, IL
Assn. of Ohio Life Insurance Companies [14329], Columbus, OH
Bellefontaine ALU [17184], West Liberty, OH
Big Rivers AIFA [17867], Eau Claire, WI
Blanchard Valley AIFA [15195], Findlay, OH
Canton ALU [13553], Canton, OH
Central Illinois Chap. of the Soc. of Financial Ser. Professionals [271], Bloomington, IL
Central Illinois TAM Users Gp. [3242], Rock Island, IL
Central Indiana Chap. of the Soc. of Financial Ser. Professionals [5076], Indianapolis, IN
Central Ohio ASCnet User Gp. [15001], Delaware, OH
Centrill West LUA [2368], Macomb, IL
Champaign Area AIFA [506], Champaign, IL
Cincinnati AIFA [16846], Terrace Park, OH
Cincinnati Chap. of the Soc. of Financial Ser. Professionals [16847], Terrace Park, OH
Cleveland AIFA [14091], Cleveland, OH
Cleveland Chap. of the Soc. of Financial Ser. Professionals [14096], Cleveland, OH
Columbus Area AIFA [4390], Columbus, IN
Coshocton County ALU [14797], Coshocton, OH
Dayton Assn. of Insurance and Financial Advisors [14870], Dayton, OH
Dayton Chap. of the Soc. of Financial Ser. Professionals [14873], Dayton, OH
Decatur AIFA [1381], Decatur, IL
Detroit Chap. of the Soc. of Financial Ser. Professionals [9983], Troy, MI
Dupage Area AIFA [447], Carol Stream, IL
East Central Indiana AIFA [5873], Muncie, IN
East Side AIFA [1819], Glen Carbon, IL
East Side Assn. of Insurance and Financial Advisors [2845], O'Fallon, IL
Eastern Illinois AIFA [569], Charleston, IL
Elgin AIFA [2773], Oak Brook, IL
Fairmont Area AIFA [12868], Wells, MN
Fort Wayne AIFA [4650], Fort Wayne, IN
Glacial Ridge AIFA [10277], Alexandria, MN
Greater Chicago Chap. of the Soc. of Financial Ser. Professionals [2774], Oak Brook, IL
Headwaters AIFA [10375], Bagley, MN
IAIFA Bloomington [279], Bloomington, IL
Illinois AIFA [3561], Springfield, IL
Illinois Assn. of Mutual Insurance Companies [3573], Springfield, IL

Illinois Fair Plan Assn. **[941]**, Chicago, IL
Illinois Life and Hea. Insurance Guaranty Assn. **[947]**, Chicago, IL
Illinois Life Insurance Coun. **[3612]**, Springfield, IL
Illinois Valley AIFA **[3080]**, Peru, IL
Independent Insurance Agents of Indiana **[5157]**, Indianapolis, IN
Indiana Applied Users Gp. **[4672]**, Fort Wayne, IN
Indiana Assn. of Insurance and Financial Advisors **[5176]**, Indianapolis, IN
Indiana Life and Hea. Insurance Guaranty Assn. **[5256]**, Indianapolis, IN
Indy South Assn. of Insurance and Financial Advisors **[5361]**, Indianapolis, IN
Insurance Accounting and Syss. Assn., Wisconsin **[19696]**, Sheboygan, WI
Insurance Inst. of Indiana **[5371]**, Indianapolis, IN
Insurance Inst. of Michigan **[8578]**, Lansing, MI
Jacksonville Area AIFA **[3871]**, Virden, IL
Joliet ALU **[2111]**, Joliet, IL
Kankakee Valley AIFA **[2138]**, Kankakee, IL
Kokomo AIFA **[5572]**, Kokomo, IN
Kosciusko AIFA **[6444]**, Warsaw, IN
Lake Superior AIFA **[10830]**, Duluth, MN
Lakeshore AIFA **[18778]**, Manitowoc, WI
Licking-Knox AIFA **[16085]**, Mount Vernon, OH
Life Insurance Assn. of Michigan **[8600]**, Lansing, MI
Little Crow AIFA **[12919]**, Willmar, MN
Lorain County AIFA **[15116]**, Elyria, OH
Madison AIFA **[19959]**, Waterloo, WI
Madison Chap. of the Soc. of Financial Ser. Professionals **[19960]**, Waterloo, WI
Madison County AIFA **[4442]**, Daleville, IN
Mahoning Valley AIFA **[15185]**, Farmdale, OH
Mansfield Area AIFA **[15771]**, Mansfield, OH
Marietta AIFA **[15820]**, Marietta, OH
Marion Area AIFA **[15839]**, Marion, OH
Marion Area Independent Insurance Agents Assn. **[15841]**, Marion, OH
McHenry County AIFA **[1326]**, Crystal Lake, IL
Medina County ALU **[14163]**, Cleveland, OH
Miami Valley ALU **[17004]**, Troy, OH
Michigan Applied Systems User Gp. **[7532]**, East Lansing, MI
Middletown AIFA **[13902]**, Cincinnati, OH
Milwaukee Chap. of the Soc. of Financial Ser. Professionals **[19058]**, Milwaukee, WI
Minneapolis AIFA **[11607]**, Minneapolis, MN
Minnesota Assn. of Farm Mutual Insurance Companies **[12326]**, St. Joseph, MN
Minnesota Independent Insurance Agents and Brokers **[10897]**, Eden Prairie, MN
Minnesota Users Gp. of Applied Systems **[11680]**, Minneapolis, MN
Minnesota Workers' Compensation Insurers Assn. **[10924]**, Edina, MN
Mutual Insurance Companies Association of Indiana **[6512]**, Westfield, IN
NAIFA-Bloomington **[4244]**, Bloomington, IN
NAIFA-Central Minnesota **[12292]**, St. Cloud, MN
NAIFA-Central Wisconsin **[19795]**, Stevens Point, WI
NAIFA-Chicago Region **[2064]**, Ingleside, IL
NAIFA-Columbus (OH) **[15050]**, Dublin, OH
NAIFA-Fond du Lac **[17986]**, Fond du Lac, WI
NAIFA-Indianapolis **[5410]**, Indianapolis, IN
NAIFA-Lafayette Indiana **[5625]**, Lafayette, IN
NAIFA-Lake County **[2265]**, Libertyville, IL
NAIFA-Lima **[15992]**, Middle Point, OH
NAIFA-Minnesota **[11689]**, Minneapolis, MN
NAIFA-North Metro **[10450]**, Blaine, MN
NAIFA-Northeastern Wisconsin **[18116]**, Green Bay, WI
NAIFA-Rochester **[12162]**, Rochester, MN
NAIFA-St. Paul **[11690]**, Minneapolis, MN
NAIFA-Sioux Valley **[11804]**, Montevideo, MN
NAIFA-South Cook Region **[2953]**, Park Forest, IL
NAIFA-Southeast Wisconsin **[18405]**, Lake Mills, WI
NAIFA-Southern Minnesota **[11392]**, Mankato, MN
NAIFA-Terre Haute **[6336]**, Terre Haute, IN
NAIFA-Wayne Holmes **[16308]**, Orrville, OH
NAIFA-Western Wisconsin **[18372]**, La Crosse, WI
NAIFA-Wisconsin-Fox River Valley **[17504]**, Appleton, WI
Natl. Assn. of Insurance and Financial Advisors, Elkhart County Chap. **[4503]**, Elkhart, IN
Natl. Assn. of Insurance and Financial Advisors, Southern Illinois Chap. **[424]**, Carbondale, IL
Natl. Assn. of Professional Insurance Agents, Indiana **[15267]**, Gahanna, OH
Natl. Fraternal Cong. of Am. **[2781]**, Oak Brook, IL
Natl. Soc. of Professional Insurance Investigators, Michigan Chap. **[10003]**, Troy, MI
North Central Indiana AIFA **[5811]**, Mishawaka, IN
North Central LUGAS **[6581]**, Adrian, MI
North Central Ohio AIFA **[16616]**, Sandusky, OH
Northeast Ohio AIFA **[16340]**, Painesville, OH
Northeast Ohio Applied Systems Users Gp. **[16374]**, Parma, OH
Northern AIFA **[12803]**, Virginia, MN
Northern Indiana TAM Users Gp. **[4918]**, Highland, IN
Northwest Indiana AIFA **[5777]**, Merrillville, IN
Northwest Ohio Applied Systems Users Gp. **[16580]**, St. Marys, OH
Northwestern Wisconsin AIFA **[19614]**, Rice Lake, WI
Ohio Assn. of Insurance and Financial Advisors **[14557]**, Columbus, OH
Ohio Insurance Inst. **[14629]**, Columbus, OH
Ohio Self Insurers Assn. **[14671]**, Columbus, OH
Ozaukee-Washington County ALU **[19085]**, Milwaukee, WI
Paul Bunyan ALU **[10389]**, Baxter, MN
Peoria AIFA **[3042]**, Peoria, IL
Police and Firemen's Insurance Assn. - Alton Fire Dept. **[43]**, Alton, IL
Police and Firemen's Insurance Assn. - Anderson Fire Dept. **[4116]**, Anderson, IN
Police and Firemen's Insurance Assn. - Ann Arbor Fire and Police Dept. **[6758]**, Ann Arbor, MI
Police and Firemen's Insurance Assn. - Bloomington Fire and Police Dept. **[307]**, Bloomington, IL
Police and Firemen's Insurance Assn. - Chicago Fire Dept. **[1140]**, Chicago, IL
Police and Firemen's Insurance Assn. - Chicago Southern Suburbs **[3193]**, Richton Park, IL
Police and Firemen's Insurance Assn. - Columbus Fire Dept. **[4405]**, Columbus, IN
Police and Firemen's Insurance Assn. - Decatur Fire Dept. **[1403]**, Decatur, IL
Police and Firemen's Insurance Assn. - Detroit Police Dept. **[7421]**, Detroit, MI
Police and Firemen's Insurance Assn. - Evansville Fire Dept. **[4566]**, Evansville, IN
Police and Firemen's Insurance Assn. - Flint Police Dept. **[7751]**, Flint, MI
Police and Firemen's Insurance Assn. - Grand Rapids Fire Dept. **[8267]**, Howard City, MI
Police and Firemen's Insurance Assn. - Grand Traverse County Fire and Police Dept. **[9947]**, Traverse City, MI
Police and Firemen's Insurance Assn. - Hammond Fire Dept. **[4892]**, Hammond, IN
Police and Firemen's Insurance Assn. - Indianapolis Fire Dept. **[5952]**, New Palestine, IN
Police and Firemen's Insurance Assn. - Indianapolis Police Dept. **[5455]**, Indianapolis, IN
Police and Firemen's Insurance Assn. - Inghamn County Sheriff **[7126]**, Charlotte, MI
Police and Firemen's Insurance Assn. - Kokomo Fire Dept. **[5582]**, Kokomo, IN
Police and Firemen's Insurance Assn. - Lansing Fire Dept. **[7466]**, DeWitt, MI
Police and Firemen's Insurance Assn. - Logansport Fire and Police Dept. **[5697]**, Logansport, IN
Police and Firemen's Insurance Assn. - Marion County Fire Dept. **[4836]**, Greenfield, IN
Police and Firemen's Insurance Assn. - Marion County Sheriff **[5456]**, Indianapolis, IN
Police and Firemen's Insurance Assn. - Muncie Fire Dept. **[5895]**, Muncie, IN
Police and Firemen's Insurance Assn. - Muskegon Fire Dept. **[9157]**, Muskegon, MI
Police and Firemen's Insurance Assn. - Oakland County Sheriff **[7752]**, Flint, MI
Police and Firemen's Insurance Assn. - Peoria Fire Dept. **[3059]**, Peoria, IL
Police and Firemen's Insurance Assn. - Richmond Fire Dept. **[6101]**, Richmond, IN
Police and Firemen's Insurance Assn. - Rock Island Fire Dept. **[3189]**, Reynolds, IL
Police and Firemen's Insurance Assn. - Saginaw County Police Dept. **[9625]**, Saginaw, MI
Police and Firemen's Insurance Assn. - St. Cloud Fire and Police Dept. **[12105]**, Rice, MN
Police and Firemen's Insurance Assn. - St. Paul Fire Dept. **[12985]**, Woodbury, MN
Police and Firemen's Insurance Assn. - South Bend Fire and Police Dept. **[4813]**, Granger, IN
Police and Firemen's Insurance Assn. - Terre Haute Fire Dept. **[6340]**, Terre Haute, IN
Police and Firemen's Insurance Assn. - Urbana Fire Dept. **[3088]**, Philo, IL
Police and Firemen's Insurance Assn. - Vincennes Fire Dept. **[6421]**, Vincennes, IN
Police and Firemen's Insurance Assn. - Wayne County Sheriff **[9409]**, Plymouth, MI
Police and Firemen's Insurance Assn. - Western Wayne County Fire Dept. **[9410]**, Plymouth, MI
Portsmouth ALU **[16472]**, Portsmouth, OH
Professional Independent Insurance Agents of Illinois **[3667]**, Springfield, IL
Professional Insurance Agents Assn. of Ohio **[15271]**, Gahanna, OH
Professional Insurance Agents of Minnesota **[12034]**, Plymouth, MN
Professional Insurance Agents of Wisconsin **[18600]**, Madison, WI
Quad City Chap. of the Soc. of Financial Ser. Professionals **[3251]**, Rock Island, IL
Racine-Kenosha AIFA **[18310]**, Kenosha, WI
Richmond Area AIFA **[6104]**, Richmond, IN
Risk and Insurance Mgt. Soc., Central Ohio Chap. **[14722]**, Columbus, OH
Risk and Insurance Mgt. Soc., Chicago Chap. **[2204]**, Lake Forest, IL
Risk and Insurance Mgt. Soc., Detroit Chap. **[10008]**, Troy, MI
Risk and Insurance Mgt. Soc., Indiana Chap. **[6342]**, Terre Haute, IN
Risk and Insurance Mgt. Soc., Minnesota Chap. **[11732]**, Minneapolis, MN
Risk and Insurance Mgt. Soc., Northeast Ohio Chap. **[14211]**, Cleveland, OH
Risk and Insurance Mgt. Soc., Ohio River Valley Chap. **[13976]**, Cincinnati, OH
Risk and Insurance Mgt. Soc., Wisconsin Chap. **[19110]**, Milwaukee, WI
Rock River AIFA **[19969]**, Watertown, WI
Rockford AIFA **[3303]**, Rockford, IL
Salamonie AIFA **[5742]**, Marion, IN
Sandusky River Basin LUA **[15254]**, Fremont, OH
Self Insurers' Gp. of Ohio **[14214]**, Cleveland, OH
Sheboygan AIFA **[19706]**, Sheboygan, WI
Soc. of Financial Ser. Professionals - Columbus, Ohio Chap. **[14733]**, Columbus, OH
South Central Indiana AIFA **[5544]**, Jeffersonville, IN
South Central Ohio AIFA **[13675]**, Chillicothe, OH
South Central Wisconsin AIFA **[17578]**, Baraboo, WI
South Metro ALU **[12818]**, Waconia, MN
Southeastern Illinois AIFA **[2861]**, Olney, IL
Southern Wisconsin AIFA **[17828]**, Delavan, WI
Southwest Michigan Associates of Health Underwriters **[9319]**, Oshtemo, MI
Southwestern Indiana AIFA **[4577]**, Evansville, IN
Southwestern Minnesota AIFA **[11356]**, Luverne, MN
Southwestern Wisconsin AIFA **[19196]**, Mineral Point, WI
Steubenville AIFA **[17302]**, Wintersville, OH
Toledo AIFA **[16961]**, Toledo, OH
Tri-County AIFA **[6197]**, Shelbyville, IN
Tri County AIFA **[11971]**, Owatonna, MN
Tuscarawas County ALU **[15033]**, Dover, OH
Twin Cities Chap. of the Soc. of Financial Ser. Professionals **[12903]**, White Bear Lake, MN
Vermilion AIFA **[1355]**, Danville, IL
West Central Illinois AIFA **[3174]**, Quincy, IL
West Central Ohio ALU **[16582]**, St. Marys, OH
Western Michigan Assn. of Insurance and Financial Advisors **[9169]**, Muskegon, MI
Winona AIFA **[11071]**, Goodview, MN

Wisconsin Assn. of Insurance and Financial Advisors **[18658]**, Madison, WI
Wisconsin User Gp. of Applied Systems **[19187]**, Milwaukee, WI
Women in Insurance and Financial Sers., Cincinnati Chap. **[15731]**, Loveland, OH
Zanesville Area AIFA **[17448]**, Zanesville, OH
Insurance Accounting and Syss. Assn., Wisconsin **[19696]**, Sheboygan, WI
Insurance Agents Assn; Marion Area Independent **[15841]**, Marion, OH
Insurance Agents Assn. of Ohio; Professional **[15271]**, Gahanna, OH
Insurance Agents of Indiana; Independent **[5157]**, Indianapolis, IN
Insurance Agents; Ohio Assn. of Mutual **[★15271]**
Insurance Agents of Wisconsin; Professional **[18600]**, Madison, WI
Insurance Companies; Illinois Assn. of Mutual **[3573]**, Springfield, IL
Insurance and Financial Advisors; Dayton Assn. of **[14870]**, Dayton, OH
Insurance and Financial Advisors; Indiana Assn. of **[5176]**, Indianapolis, IN
Insurance and Financial Advisors; Indy South Assn. of **[5361]**, Indianapolis, IN
Insurance and Financial Advisors; Ohio Assn. of **[14557]**, Columbus, OH
Insurance and Financial Advisors, Southern Illinois Chap; Natl. Assn. of **[424]**, Carbondale, IL
Insurance and Financial Advisors; Western Michigan Assn. of **[9169]**, Muskegon, MI
Insurance Inst. of Indiana **[5371]**, Indianapolis, IN
Insurance Inst. of Michigan **[8578]**, Lansing, MI
Insurance Investigators, Michigan Chap; Natl. Soc. of Professional **[10003]**, Troy, MI
Insurance Trial Counsel of Wisconsin **[★18993]**
Insurers Assn; Ohio Self **[14671]**, Columbus, OH
Inter-Lakes Lions Club **[8368]**, Jackson, MI
Inter-Tribal Coun. of Michigan **[9719]**, Sault Ste. Marie, MI
Intercultural Studies
Natl. Assn. for Multicultural Educ., Indiana Chap. **[5420]**, Indianapolis, IN
Natl. Assn. for Multicultural Educ., Michigan Chap. **[6742]**, Ann Arbor, MI
Natl. Assn. for Multicultural Educ., Minnesota Chap. **[12544]**, St. Paul, MN
Natl. Assn. for Multicultural Educ., Ohio Chap. **[15437]**, Hilliard, OH
Natl. Assn. for Multicultural Educ., Region 5 **[6493]**, West Lafayette, IN
Interfaith Coun. for Peace and Justice **[6709]**, Ann Arbor, MI
Interfaith Volunteer Caregivers of Portage County **[19791]**, Stevens Point, WI
Interfaith Youth Core **[978]**, Chicago, IL
Interior Design
Amer. Soc. of Interior Designers - Illinois Chap. **[724]**, Chicago, IL
Amer. Soc. of Interior Designers, Indiana **[5022]**, Indianapolis, IN
Amer. Soc. of Interior Designers - Michigan Chap. **[9972]**, Troy, MI
Amer. Soc. of Interior Designers, Minnesota Chap. **[11518]**, Minneapolis, MN
Amer. Soc. of Interior Designers, Ohio North Chap. **[9263]**, Okemos, MI
Amer. Soc. of Interior Designers, Ohio South/Kentucky **[13733]**, Cincinnati, OH
Amer. Soc. of Interior Designers, Wisconsin **[18958]**, Milwaukee, WI
Natl. Assn. of the Remodeling Indus. of Minnesota **[11696]**, Minneapolis, MN
Interior Design Assn., Illinois Chap; Intl. **[1726]**, Frankfort, IL
Interior Design Assn., Indiana Chap; Intl. **[5377]**, Indianapolis, IN
Interior Design Assn., Michigan Chap; Intl. **[9801]**, Southfield, MI
Interlibrary Cooperation; Wayne Oakland Region of **[9831]**, Southfield, MI
Interlibrary Services; Wisconsin **[18717]**, Madison, WI
Interlochen Area Chamber of Commerce **[8313]**, Interlochen, MI
Interlocking Shetland Sheepdog Club of Monee **[2692]**, New Lenox, IL
Internal Medicine
Amer. Coll. of Physicians - Ohio Chap. **[14048]**, Cleveland, OH
Amer. Liver Found. - Illinois Chap. **[713]**, Chicago, IL
Indiana Soc. of Internal Medicine **[5305]**, Indianapolis, IN
International Affairs
Columbus Coun. on World Affairs **[14381]**, Columbus, OH
Intl. Alliance of Theatrical Stage Employees, Moving Picture Technicians, Artists, M 251 **[18527]**, Madison, WI
Intl. Alliance of Theatrical Stage Employees, Moving Picture Technicians, Artists, M 470 **[19394]**, Oshkosh, WI
Intl. Alliance of Theatrical Stage Employees, Moving Picture Technicians, Artists, M 618 **[4237]**, Bloomington, IN
Intl. Alliance of Theatrical Stage Employees, Moving Picture Technicians, Artists, MPP, OandVT 160 **[14142]**, Cleveland, OH
Intl. Alliance of Theatrical Stage Employees, Moving Picture Technicians, Artists, S 12 **[14470]**, Columbus, OH
Intl. Alliance of Theatrical Stage Employees, Moving Picture Technicians, Artists, S 13 **[11587]**, Minneapolis, MN
Intl. Alliance of Theatrical Stage Employees, Moving Picture Technicians, Artists, S 146 **[4681]**, Fort Wayne, IN
Intl. Assn. of Administrative Professionals - Minnesota-North Dakota-South Dakota Div. **[12852]**, Watertown, MN
Intl. Assn. of Administrative Professionals, River Park Chap. **[9836]**, Southgate, MI
Intl. Assn. of Bus. Communicators, Chicago Chap. **[979]**, Chicago, IL
Intl. Assn. of Bus. Communicators, Cleveland Chap. **[15499]**, Independence, OH
Intl. Assn. of Bus. Communicators, Columbus Chap. **[14471]**, Columbus, OH
Intl. Assn. of Bus. Communicators, Dayton Chap. **[14895]**, Dayton, OH
Intl. Assn. of Bus. Communicators, Detroit Chap. **[8894]**, Madison Heights, MI
Intl. Assn. of Bus. Communicators, Greater Cincinnati Chap. **[13869]**, Cincinnati, OH
Intl. Assn. of Bus. Communicators, Indianapolis Chap. **[5372]**, Indianapolis, IN
Intl. Assn. of Bus. Communicators, Madison Chap. **[18528]**, Madison, WI
Intl. Assn. of Bus. Communicators - Minnesota Chap. **[12427]**, St. Paul, MN
Intl. Assn. of Bus. Communicators, Southeastern Wisconsin Chap. **[18054]**, Glendale, WI
Intl. Assn. of Convention and Visitor Bur., Charlotte Chicago, Illinois **[980]**, Chicago, IL
Intl. Assn. of Convention and Visitor Burs., Kansas City - Palatine, Illinois **[2914]**, Palatine, IL
Intl. Assn. of Elecl. Inspectors, Ohio Chap. **[16661]**, Shreve, OH
Intl. Assn. of Gay/Lesbian Country Western Dance Clubs, Columbus Stompers **[14472]**, Columbus, OH
Intl. Assn. of Gay/Lesbian Country Western Dance Clubs, Dairyland Cowboys and Cowgirls **[18529]**, Madison, WI
Intl. Assn. of Gay/Lesbian Country Western Dance Clubs, Northern Lights **[11588]**, Minneapolis, MN
Intl. Assn. of Gay/Lesbian Country Western Dance Clubs, Rainbow Wranglers **[14143]**, Cleveland, OH
Intl. Assn. of Gay/Lesbian Country Western Dance Clubs, Shoreline-Milwaukee **[19028]**, Milwaukee, WI
Intl. Assn. of Gay Square Dance Clubs - Chi-Town Squares **[981]**, Chicago, IL
Intl. Assn. of Gay Square Dance Clubs - Cleveland City Country Dancers **[14144]**, Cleveland, OH
Intl. Assn. for Great Lakes Res. **[6710]**, Ann Arbor, MI
Intl. Assn. for Healthcare Security and Safety - Michigan Chap. **[7378]**, Detroit, MI
Intl. Assn. of Heat and Frost Insulators and Asbestos Workers, AFL-CIO, CFL - Local Union 17 **[982]**, Chicago, IL
Intl. Assn. of Heat and Frost Insulators and Asbestos Workers, AFL-CIO, CFL - Local Union 34 **[12428]**, St. Paul, MN
Intl. Assn. of Heat and Frost Insulators and Asbestos Workers, Asbestos Abatement Workers Regional Local 207 **[9903]**, Taylor, MI
Intl. Assn. of Heat and Frost Insulators and Asbestos Workers, Local 18 **[5373]**, Indianapolis, IN
Intl. Assn. of Heat and Frost Insulators and Asbestos Workers, Local 44 **[14473]**, Columbus, OH
Intl. Assn. of Machinists and Aerospace Workers, AFL-CIO, CLC - Badger Lodge Local 1406 **[19858]**, Sun Prairie, WI
Intl. Assn. of Machinists and Aerospace Workers, AFL-CIO, CLC - District Lodge 90 **[5374]**, Indianapolis, IN
Intl. Assn. of Machinists and Aerospace Workers, AFL-CIO, CLC - District Lodge 141 **[1611]**, Elk Grove Village, IL
Intl. Assn. of Machinists and Aerospace Workers, AFL-CIO, CLC - District Lodge 143 **[11459]**, Mendota Heights, MN
Intl. Assn. of Machinists and Aerospace Workers, AFL-CIO, CLC - Local Lodge 46 **[6859]**, Battle Creek, MI
Intl. Assn. of Machinists and Aerospace Workers, AFL-CIO, CLC - Local Lodge 924 **[11903]**, North Mankato, MN
Intl. Assn. of Machinists and Aerospace Workers, AFL-CIO, CLC - Local Lodge 1217 **[17763]**, Clear Lake, WI
Intl. Assn. of Machinists and Aerospace Workers, AFL-CIO, CLC - Local Lodge 1487 **[1461]**, Des Plaines, IL
Intl. Assn. of Machinists and Aerospace Workers, AFL-CIO, CLC - Local Lodge 2484 **[15418]**, Hicksville, OH
Intl. Assn. of Machinists and Aerospace Workers, AFL-CIO, CLC - Local Lodge 2575 **[17501]**, Appleton, WI
Intl. Assn. of Machinists and Aerospace Workers, AFL-CIO, CLC - Lodge 225 **[14896]**, Dayton, OH
Intl. Assn. of Machinists and Aerospace Workers, AFL-CIO, CLC - Lodge 516 **[19029]**, Milwaukee, WI
Intl. Assn. of Machinists and Aerospace Workers, AFL-CIO, CLC - Lodge 1406 **[★19858]**
Intl. Assn. of Machinists and Aerospace Workers, AFL-CIO, CLC - Lodge 1771 **[17568]**, Bangor, WI
Intl. Assn. of Machinists and Aerospace Workers, AFL-CIO, CLC - Lodge 2110 **[19030]**, Milwaukee, WI
Intl. Assn. of Machinists and Aerospace Workers, AFL-CIO, CLC - Lodge 2269 **[18438]**, Lyndon Station, WI
Intl. Assn. of Machinists and Aerospace Workers, AFL-CIO, CLC - United Lodge 66 **[19031]**, Milwaukee, WI
Intl. Assn. of Machinists and Aerospace Workers, District Lodge 10 **[19032]**, Milwaukee, WI
Intl. Assn. of Machinists and Aerospace Workers, District Lodge 55 **[2109]**, Joliet, IL
Intl. Assn. of Machinists and Aerospace Workers, District Lodge 66 **[18347]**, La Crosse, WI
Intl. Assn. of Machinists and Aerospace Workers, District Lodge 121 **[19859]**, Sun Prairie, WI
Intl. Assn. of Machinists and Aerospace Workers, District Lodge 165 **[12288]**, St. Cloud, MN
Intl. Assn. of Machinists and Aerospace Workers, LL-737 **[12429]**, St. Paul, MN
Intl. Assn. of Machinists and Aerospace Workers, LL-873 **[18216]**, Horicon, WI
Intl. Assn. of Machinists and Aerospace Workers, LL-1553 **[3282]**, Rockford, IL
Intl. Assn. of Machinists and Aerospace Workers, LL-2903 **[6517]**, Westville, IN
Intl. Assn. of Machinists and Aerospace Workers, Local Lodge 21 **[18348]**, La Crosse, WI
Intl. Assn. of Machinists and Aerospace Workers, Local Lodge 60 **[1530]**, East Alton, IL
Intl. Assn. of Machinists and Aerospace Workers, Local Lodge 1115 **[18349]**, La Crosse, WI
Intl. Assn. of Machinists and Aerospace Workers, Local Lodge 2458 **[2244]**, Lemont, IL
Intl. Assn. of Ministers Wives and Ministers Widows, Illinois **[2335]**, Lombard, IL
Intl. Assn. of Ministers Wives and Ministers Widows, Michigan **[7379]**, Detroit, MI
Intl. Assn. of Ministers Wives and Ministers Widows, Ohio **[17122]**, Warrensville Heights, OH

Intl. Assn. of Ministers Wives and Ministers Widows, Wisconsin **[19033]**, Milwaukee, WI
Intl. Assn. of Physicians in AIDS Care **[983]**, Chicago, IL
Intl. Assn. of Psychosocial Rehabilitation Services, Michigan Chap. **[7524]**, East Lansing, MI
Intl. Assn. for the Retractable Awning Indus., Michigan Chap. **[6613]**, Allen Park, MI
Intl. Assn. of Torch Clubs, Region 5 **[16637]**, Shaker Heights, OH
Intl. Assn. of Torch Clubs, Region 6 **[1624]**, Elmhurst, IL
Intl. Assn. of Women Police, Region 6 **[4883]**, Hammond, IN
Intl. Brotherhood of Elecl. Workers, AFL-CIO, CFL - Local Union 306 **[13059]**, Akron, OH
Intl. Brotherhood of Elecl. Workers, AFL-CIO, CFL - Local Union 557 **[9610]**, Saginaw, MI
Intl. Brotherhood of Elecl. Workers, AFL-CIO, CFL - Local Union 601 **[531]**, Champaign, IL
Intl. Brotherhood of Elecl. Workers, AFL-CIO, CFL - Local Union 723 **[4682]**, Fort Wayne, IN
Intl. Brotherhood of Elecl. Workers, AFL-CIO, CFL - Local Union 1347 **[13870]**, Cincinnati, OH
Intl. Brotherhood of Elecl. Workers AFL-CIO, LU 983 **[4952]**, Huntington, IN
Intl. Brotherhood of Elecl. Workers, Local 1220 **[984]**, Chicago, IL
Intl. Brotherhood of Locomotive Engineers, AFL-CIO - Div. 333 **[★11536]**
Intl. Brotherhood of Locomotive Engineers, AFL-CIO - Div. 724 **[★3408]**
Intl. Brotherhood of Magicians, Ring 2 **[16206]**, Niles, OH
Intl. Brotherhood of Magicians, Ring 7 **[15265]**, Gahanna, OH
Intl. Brotherhood of Magicians, Ring 19 **[12062]**, Ramsey, MN
Intl. Brotherhood of Magicians, Ring 22 **[10115]**, West Bloomfield, MI
Intl. Brotherhood of Magicians, Ring 23 **[14145]**, Cleveland, OH
Intl. Brotherhood of Magicians, Ring 41 **[19917]**, Twin Lakes, WI
Intl. Brotherhood of Magicians, Ring 56 **[4344]**, Chandler, IN
Intl. Brotherhood of Magicians, Ring 68 **[16407]**, Perrysburg, OH
Intl. Brotherhood of Magicians, Ring 71 **[16266]**, Norwood, OH
Intl. Brotherhood of Magicians, Ring 205 **[15655]**, Lima, OH
Intl. Brotherhood of Magicians, Ring 210 - Duke Stern **[8075]**, Grosse Ile, MI
Intl. Brotherhood of Magicians, Ring 211 - John DeVries Magic Club **[10190]**, Wyoming, MI
Intl. Brotherhood of Magicians, Ring 221 - A.H. Stoner Ring **[5946]**, New Haven, IN
Intl. Brotherhood of Magicians, Ring 236 - The Magic Wand Ring **[532]**, Champaign, IL
Intl. Brotherhood of Magicians, Ring 310 - Muncie Mystifiers **[6094]**, Richmond, IN
Intl. Brotherhood of Magicians, Ring 324 **[16008]**, Middletown, OH
Intl. Brotherhood of Magicians, Ring 336 **[4401]**, Columbus, IN
Intl. Brotherhood of Painters and Allied Trades of the United States and Canada AFL-CIO-CFL - District Coun. 6 **[16791]**, Strongsville, OH
Intl. Brotherhood of Painters and Allied Trades of the United States and Canada AFL-CIO-CFL - District Coun. 14 **[985]**, Chicago, IL
Intl. Brotherhood of Painters and Allied Trades of the U.S. and Canada AFL-CIO-CFL - District Coun. 30 **[3386]**, St. Charles, IL
Intl. Brotherhood of Teamsters, Chauffeurs, Warehousemen and Helpers of Am., AFL-CIO - Local Union 24 **[13060]**, Akron, OH
Intl. Brotherhood of Teamsters, Chauffeurs, Warehousemen and Helpers of Am., AFL-CIO - Local Union 200 **[19034]**, Milwaukee, WI
Intl. Brotherhood of Teamsters, Chauffeurs, Warehousemen and Helpers of Am., AFL-CIO - Local Union 580 **[8579]**, Lansing, MI
Intl. Brotherhood of Teamsters, Chauffeurs, Warehousemen and Helpers of Am., AFL-CIO - Local Union 637 **[17439]**, Zanesville, OH
Intl. Brotherhood of Teamsters, Chauffeurs, Warehousemen and Helpers of Am., AFL-CIO - Local Union 662 **[17881]**, Eau Claire, WI
Intl. Brotherhood of Teamsters, Chauffeurs, Warehousemen and Helpers of Am., AFL-CIO - Local Union 710 **[986]**, Chicago, IL
Intl. Brotherhood of Teamsters, Chauffeurs, Warehousemen and Helpers of Am., AFL-CIO - Local Union 714 **[238]**, Berwyn, IL
Intl. Brotherhood of Trail Workers **[2915]**, Palatine, IL
Intl. Bus. Coun. **[★993]**
Intl. Bus. Coun. Midamerica **[★993]**
Intl. Center for Dispute Resolution (ICDR) **[★9778]**
Intl. Chiropractors Assn. of Indiana **[6533]**, Winamac, IN
Intl. Coach Fed., Chicago Chap. **[★1917]**
Intl. Coach Fed., Greater Indianapolis Chap. **[5375]**, Indianapolis, IN
Intl. Customer Ser. Assn., Chicago **[987]**, Chicago, IL
Intl. Customer Ser. Assn., Cleveland/Northcoast **[14146]**, Cleveland, OH
Intl. Customer Ser. Assn., Greater Cincinnati **[15875]**, Mason, OH
Intl. Dark-Sky Assn. - Minnesota **[11274]**, Lake City, MN
Intl. Dark-Sky - Illinois At-Large Sect. **[2588]**, Mount Prospect, IL
Intl. Dark-Sky - Illinois-Central **[1644]**, Eureka, IL
Intl. Dark-Sky - Illinois-Chicago **[988]**, Chicago, IL
Intl. Dark-Sky - Illinois-Northwest **[1765]**, Galena, IL
International Development
Wisconsin/Nicaragua Partners of the Ams. **[19820]**, Stevens Point, WI
Intl. Dyslexia Assn; Northern Ohio Br. of the **[16682]**, Solon, OH
Intl. Edsel Club, Illinois Chap. **[3030]**, Peoria, IL
Intl. Edsel Club, Indiana Chap. **[5756]**, Martinsville, IN
Intl. Facilities Mgt. Assn. - Minneapolis/St. Paul Chap. **[12023]**, Plymouth, MN
Intl. Fac. Mgt. Assn., Central Illinois (Bloomington/Decatur/Champaign) **[1274]**, Clinton, IL
Intl. Fac. Mgt. Assn., Central Ohio Chap. **[14474]**, Columbus, OH
Intl. Fac. Mgt. Assn., Chicago **[1725]**, Frankfort, IL
Intl. Fac. Mgt. Assn., Cincinnati **[13871]**, Cincinnati, OH
Intl. Fac. Mgt. Assn., Columbus **[★14356]**
Intl. Fac. Mgt. Assn., Ferris State Univ. **[7968]**, Grand Rapids, MI
Intl. Fac. Mgt. Assn., Indianapolis **[5376]**, Indianapolis, IN
Intl. Fac. Mgt. Assn., Madison **[18530]**, Madison, WI
Intl. Fac. Mgt. Assn., Mid-Michigan **[9027]**, Midland, MI
Intl. Fac. Mgt. Assn., Minneapolis/St. Paul **[12024]**, Plymouth, MN
Intl. Fac. Mgt. Assn., North Indiana **[4683]**, Fort Wayne, IN
Intl. Fac. Mgt. Assn., Northeast Wisconsin Chap. **[18109]**, Green Bay, WI
Intl. Fac. Mgt. Assn., Northern Illinois (Suburban Chicago) **[362]**, Buffalo Grove, IL
Intl. Fac. Mgt. Assn., Northern Ohio (Cleveland) **[13275]**, Bay Village, OH
Intl. Fac. Mgt. Assn., Northwest Ohio Chap. **[16923]**, Toledo, OH
Intl. Fac. Mgt. Assn., Southeast Wisconsin (Milwaukee) **[17857]**, East Troy, WI
Intl. Fac. Mgt. Assn., Southeastern Michigan Chap. **[7014]**, Brighton, MI
International Facility Management Association, West Michigan **[8102]**, Hamilton, MI
Intl. Falls Area Chamber of Commerce **[11216]**, International Falls, MN
Intl. Falls Lions Club **[11217]**, International Falls, MN
Intl. Fed. of Professional and Tech. Engineers Local 7 **[14475]**, Columbus, OH
Intl. Graphic Arts Educ. Assn. - Region 1, North Central **[2286]**, Lincolnshire, IL
Intl. Inst. of Flint **[7742]**, Flint, MI
Intl. Inst. of Wisconsin **[19035]**, Milwaukee, WI
Intl. Interior Design Assn., Illinois Chap. **[1726]**, Frankfort, IL
Intl. Interior Design Assn., Indiana Chap. **[5377]**, Indianapolis, IN
Intl. Interior Design Assn., Michigan Chap. **[9801]**, Southfield, MI
Intl. Interior Design Assn., Wisconsin Chap. **[18531]**, Madison, WI
Intl. Kennel Club of Chicago **[989]**, Chicago, IL
International Law
Khmers Kampuchea-Krom Fed. **[14485]**, Columbus, OH
Intl. Masonry Inst., Minneapolis **[11589]**, Minneapolis, MN
Intl. Personnel Mgt. Assn., Chicago **[990]**, Chicago, IL
Intl. Personnel Mgt. Assn., Cleveland **[15584]**, Lakewood, OH
Intl. Personnel Mgt. Assn., Dayton, Ohio **[17357]**, Wright-Patterson AFB, OH
Intl. Personnel Mgt. Assn., Greater Illinois **[1571]**, Effingham, IL
Intl. Personnel Mgt. Assn., Greater St. Louis, Missouri **[991]**, Chicago, IL
Intl. Personnel Mgt. Assn., Michigan **[7846]**, Grand Blanc, MI
Intl. Personnel Mgt. Assn., Minnesota **[10537]**, Brooklyn Center, MN
Intl. Personnel Mgt. Assn., Wisconsin **[18532]**, Madison, WI
Intl. Physicians Commn. **[★1988]**
International Relations
Org. of Chinese Amers. - Columbus Chap. **[14706]**, Columbus, OH
Org. of Chinese Amers. - Greater Chicago Chap. **[1115]**, Chicago, IL
Intl. Sons of the Desert; Dancing Cuckoos, Metropolitan Detroit Tent of the **[7063]**, Canton, MI
International Standards
Wisconsin Coordinating Coun. on Nicaragua **[18687]**, Madison, WI
Intl. TV Assn. **[★19671]**
Intl. Thomas Merton Soc. - Chicago, IL **[992]**, Chicago, IL
Intl. Thomas Merton Soc. - Cincinnati, OH **[14253]**, Cleves, OH
International Trade
Intl. Trade Club of Chicago **[993]**, Chicago, IL
Intl. Trade Club of Chicago **[★993]**
Intl. Trade Club of Chicago **[993]**, Chicago, IL
Intl. Union of Bricklayers and Allied Craftworkers, AFL-CIO-CLC Indiana and Kentucky Local Union 4 **[4108]**, Anderson, IN
Intl. Union of Bricklayers and Allied Craftworkers, AFL-CIO-CLC Local Union 6 **[3283]**, Rockford, IL
Intl. Union of Bricklayers and Allied Craftworkers, AFL-CIO-CLC Local Union 9 **[8580]**, Lansing, MI
Intl. Union of Bricklayers and Allied Craftworkers, AFL-CIO-CLC Local Union 20 **[3925]**, Waukegan, IL
Intl. Union of Bricklayers and Allied Craftworkers, AFL-CIO-CLC Local Union 36 **[14147]**, Cleveland, OH
Intl. Union of Bricklayers and Allied Craftworkers, AFL-CIO-CLC Local Union 43 **[17102]**, Warren, OH
Intl. Union of Bricklayers and Allied Craftworkers, AFL-CIO-CLC Michigan Local Union 1 **[10064]**, Warren, MI
Intl. Union of Bricklayers and Allied Craftworkers, AFL-CIO-CLC Wisconsin District Coun. **[19290]**, New Berlin, WI
Intl. Union of Electronic, Elecl., Salaried, Machine and Furniture Workers, AFL-CIO-CLC - Local Union 750 **[13114]**, Alliance, OH
Intl. Union of Electronic, Elecl., Salaried, Machine and Furniture Workers, AFL-CIO-CLC - Local Union 755 **[14897]**, Dayton, OH
Intl. Union of Elevator Constructors, Local 2 - Chicago, Illinois **[994]**, Chicago, IL
Intl. Union of Elevator Constructors, Local 9 - Minneapolis, Minnesota **[11332]**, Little Canada, MN
Intl. Union of Elevator Constructors, Local 34 - Indianapolis, Indiana **[5378]**, Indianapolis, IN
Intl. Union of Operating Engineers, Local 018 **[14148]**, Cleveland, OH
Intl. Union of Operating Engineers, Local 049 **[11590]**, Minneapolis, MN
Intl. Union of Operating Engineers, Local 139 **[19437]**, Pewaukee, WI
Intl. Union of Operating Engineers, Local 143 **[995]**, Chicago, IL

Intl. Union of Operating Engineers, Local 148 **[2429]**, Maryville, IL
Intl. Union of Operating Engineers, Local 150 **[1306]**, Countryside, IL
Intl. Union of Operating Engineers, Local 310 **[18110]**, Green Bay, WI
Intl. Union of Operating Engineers, Local 317 **[19036]**, Milwaukee, WI
Intl. Union of Operating Engineers, Local 324 **[8841]**, Livonia, MI
Intl. Union of Operating Engineers, Local 399 **[996]**, Chicago, IL
Intl. Union of Operating Engineers, Local 547 **[7380]**, Detroit, MI
Intl. Union of Operating Engineers, Local 649 **[3031]**, Peoria, IL
Intl. Union of Operating Engineers, Local 950 **[19037]**, Milwaukee, WI
Intl. Union of Painters and Allied Trades AFL-CIO, Local 156 **[4557]**, Evansville, IN
Intl. Union of Police Assns., AFL-CIO - Illinois Coun. of Police and Sherif Local Union 7 **[1625]**, Elmhurst, IL
Intl. Union, United Auto., Aerospace and Agricultural Implement Workers of Am., AFL-CIO - Local Union 12 **[16924]**, Toledo, OH
Intl. Union, United Auto., Aerospace and Agricultural Implement Workers of Am., AFL-CIO - Local Union 14 **[16925]**, Toledo, OH
Intl. Union, United Auto., Aerospace and Agricultural Implement Workers of Am., AFL-CIO - Local Union 22 **[7381]**, Detroit, MI
Intl. Union, United Auto., Aerospace and Agricultural Implement Workers of Am., AFL-CIO - Local Union 36 **[10179]**, Wixom, MI
Intl. Union, United Auto., Aerospace and Agricultural Implement Workers of Am., AFL-CIO - Local Union 160 **[10065]**, Warren, MI
Intl. Union, United Auto., Aerospace and Agricultural Implement Workers of Am., AFL-CIO - Local Union 211 **[14989]**, Defiance, OH
Intl. Union, United Auto., Aerospace and Agricultural Implement Workers of Am., AFL-CIO - Local Union 228 **[9866]**, Sterling Heights, MI
Intl. Union, United Auto., Aerospace and Agricultural Implement Workers of Am., AFL-CIO - Local Union 245 **[7262]**, Dearborn, MI
Intl. Union, United Auto., Aerospace and Agricultural Implement Workers of Am., AFL-CIO - Local Union 387 **[7704]**, Flat Rock, MI
Intl. Union, United Auto., Aerospace and Agricultural Implement Workers of Am., AFL-CIO - Local Union 402 **[16731]**, Springfield, OH
Intl. Union, United Auto., Aerospace and Agricultural Implement Workers of Am., AFL-CIO - Local Union 412 **[10066]**, Warren, MI
Intl. Union, United Auto., Aerospace and Agricultural Implement Workers of Am., AFL-CIO - Local Union 594 **[9419]**, Pontiac, MI
Intl. Union, United Auto., Aerospace and Agricultural Implement Workers of Am., AFL-CIO - Local Union 598 **[7743]**, Flint, MI
Intl. Union, United Auto., Aerospace and Agricultural Implement Workers of Am., AFL-CIO - Local Union 652 **[8581]**, Lansing, MI
Intl. Union, United Auto., Aerospace and Agricultural Implement Workers of Am., AFL-CIO - Local Union 663 **[4109]**, Anderson, IN
Intl. Union, United Auto., Aerospace and Agricultural Implement Workers of Am., AFL-CIO - Local Union 685 **[5570]**, Kokomo, IN
Intl. Union, United Auto., Aerospace and Agricultural Implement Workers of Am., AFL-CIO - Local Union 696 **[14898]**, Dayton, OH
Intl. Union, United Auto., Aerospace and Agricultural Implement Workers of Am., AFL-CIO - Local Union 699 **[9611]**, Saginaw, MI
Intl. Union, United Auto., Aerospace and Agricultural Implement Workers of Am., AFL-CIO - Local Union 730 **[7969]**, Grand Rapids, MI
Intl. Union, United Auto., Aerospace and Agricultural Implement Workers of Am., AFL-CIO - Local Union 735 **[7065]**, Canton, MI
Intl. Union, United Auto., Aerospace and Agricultural Implement Workers of Am., AFL-CIO - Local Union 845 **[7066]**, Canton, MI
Intl. Union, United Auto., Aerospace and Agricultural Implement Workers of Am., AFL-CIO - Local Union 863 **[13872]**, Cincinnati, OH
Intl. Union, United Auto., Aerospace and Agricultural Implement Workers of Am., AFL-CIO - Local Union 879 **[12430]**, St. Paul, MN
Intl. Union, United Auto., Aerospace and Agricultural Implement Workers of Am., AFL-CIO - Local Union 892 **[9700]**, Saline, MI
Intl. Union, United Auto., Aerospace and Agricultural Implement Workers of Am., AFL-CIO - Local Union 898 **[10209]**, Ypsilanti, MI
Intl. Union, United Auto., Aerospace and Agricultural Implement Workers of Am., AFL-CIO - Local Union 909 **[10067]**, Warren, MI
Intl. Union, United Auto., Aerospace and Agricultural Implement Workers of Am., AFL-CIO - Local Union 1111 **[5379]**, Indianapolis, IN
Intl. Union, United Auto., Aerospace and Agricultural Implement Workers of Am., AFL-CIO - Local Union 1112 **[17103]**, Warren, OH
Intl. Union, United Auto., Aerospace and Agricultural Implement Workers of Am., AFL-CIO - Local Union 1250 **[13435]**, Brook Park, OH
Intl. Union, United Auto., Aerospace and Agricultural Implement Workers of Am., AFL-CIO - Local Union 1292 **[7847]**, Grand Blanc, MI
Intl. Union, United Auto., Aerospace and Agricultural Implement Workers of Am., AFL-CIO - Local Union 1714 **[17104]**, Warren, OH
Intl. Union, United Auto., Aerospace and Agricultural Implement Workers of Am., AFL-CIO - Local Union 2000 **[16650]**, Sheffield Village, OH
Intl. Union, United Auto., Aerospace and Agricultural Implement Workers of Am., AFL-CIO - Local Union 2075 **[15656]**, Lima, OH
Intl. Union, United Auto., Aerospace and Agricultural Implement Workers of Am., AFL-CIO - Local Union 2093 **[9915]**, Three Rivers, MI
Intl. Union, United Auto., Aerospace and Agricultural Implement Workers of Am., AFL-CIO - Local Union 2151 **[7224]**, Coopersville, MI
Intl. Union, United Auto., Aerospace and Agricultural Implement Workers of Am., AFL-CIO - Local Union 2269 **[16528]**, Richwood, OH
Intl. Union, United Auto., Aerospace and Agricultural Implement Workers of Am., AFL-CIO - Local Union 2280 **[10035]**, Utica, MI
Intl. Union, United Auto., Aerospace and Agricultural Implement Workers of Am., AFL-CIO - Local Union 2488 **[292]**, Bloomington, IL
Intl. Union, United Auto., Aerospace and Agricultural Implement Workers of Am., AFL-CIO - Local Union 3206 **[1882]**, Granite City, IL
Intl. Union, United Auto., Aerospace and Agricultural Implement Workers of Am., AFL-CIO - Lorain County CAP Coun. Local 2000 **[16651]**, Sheffield Village, OH
Intl. Union, United Auto., Aerospace and Agricultural Implement Workers of Am., AFL-CIO - Mt. Clemens-Highland Park Local Union 400 **[10036]**, Utica, MI
Intl. Union, United Auto., Aerospace and Agricultural Implement Workers of Am., AFL-CIO - Pontiac Local Local Union 653 **[9420]**, Pontiac, MI
Intl. Visitors Coun. - Columbus **[14476]**, Columbus, OH
Intl. Visitors Coun. of Metropolitan Detroit **[6814]**, Auburn Hills, MI
Interscholastic Athletic Administrators Assn; Michigan **[8851]**, Livonia, MI
Interscholastic Forensic Assn; Michigan **[6728]**, Ann Arbor, MI
Interstate Rsrc. Conservation and Development Coun. **[2490]**, Milan, IL
InterVarsity Christian Fellowship in Downstate Illinois **[3032]**, Peoria, IL
InterVarsity Christian Fellowship/USA **[18533]**, Madison, WI
Invasive Plants Assn. of Wisconsin **[18534]**, Madison, WI
InventorEd **[7848]**, Grand Blanc, MI
Inventors
Chicago 1st Black Inventors/Entrepreneurs Org., NFP **[778]**, Chicago, IL
Creative Network of West Michigan **[9142]**, Muskegon, MI
Illinois Innovators and Inventors **[1560]**, Edwardsville, IL
Indiana Inventors Assn. **[5732]**, Marion, IN
Innovative Minds of Wisconsin **[19228]**, Mosinee, WI
InventorEd **[7848]**, Grand Blanc, MI
Inventors Assn. of Metropolitan Detroit **[9659]**, St. Clair Shores, MI
Inventors Connection of Greater Cleveland **[16792]**, Strongsville, OH
Inventors Coun. of Canton **[16217]**, North Canton, OH
Inventor's Coun. of Cincinnati **[13873]**, Cincinnati, OH
Inventors Coun. of Dayton **[14899]**, Dayton, OH
Inventors Coun. of Mid-Michigan **[8797]**, Lennon, MI
Inventors and Entrepreneurs Club of Juneau County **[17716]**, Camp Douglas, WI
Inventors' Network **[12431]**, St. Paul, MN
Inventors Network **[14477]**, Columbus, OH
Inventors Network of Wisconsin **[18111]**, Green Bay, WI
Minnesota Inventors Cong. **[12095]**, Redwood Falls, MN
Rock Valley Innovators and Entrepreneurs Gp. **[20161]**, Whitewater, WI
Soc. of Minnesota Inventors **[10718]**, Coon Rapids, MN
Youngstown-Warren Inventors Assn. **[17431]**, Youngstown, OH
Inventors Assn. of Metropolitan Detroit **[9659]**, St. Clair Shores, MI
Inventors Connection of Greater Cleveland **[16792]**, Strongsville, OH
Inventors Coun. of Canton **[16217]**, North Canton, OH
Inventor's Coun. of Cincinnati **[13873]**, Cincinnati, OH
Inventors Coun. of Dayton **[14899]**, Dayton, OH
Inventors Coun. of Mid-Michigan **[8797]**, Lennon, MI
Inventors and Entrepreneurs Club of Juneau County **[17716]**, Camp Douglas, WI
Inventors' Network **[12431]**, St. Paul, MN
Inventors Network **[14477]**, Columbus, OH
Inventors Network of Wisconsin **[18111]**, Green Bay, WI
Investigation
High Tech. Crime Investigation Assn. - Minnesota **[11126]**, Hastings, MN
High Tech. Crime Investigation Assn. - Ohio **[14139]**, Cleveland, OH
Natl. Assn. of Legal Investigators, Mid-Eastern Region **[7991]**, Grand Rapids, MI
Investigators, Michigan Chap; Natl. Soc. of Professional Insurance **[10003]**, Troy, MI
Investment Analysts Soc. of Chicago **[997]**, Chicago, IL
Investment Assn; Michigan School **[8710]**, Lansing, MI
Investment Bd; Southern Seven Workforce **[5929]**, New Albany, IN
Investments
Cleveland Soc. of Security Analysts **[14104]**, Cleveland, OH
Investment Analysts Soc. of Chicago **[997]**, Chicago, IL
Natl. Assn. of Investors Corp. **[17346]**, Worthington, OH
Natl. Assn. of Investors Corp., Capital Area Chap. **[8736]**, Lansing, MI
Natl. Assn. of Investors Corp., Central Indiana Chap. **[5418]**, Indianapolis, IN
Natl. Assn. of Investors Corp., Chicago South Chap. **[1956]**, Harvey, IL
Natl. Assn. of Investors Corp., Evansville Tri-State Chap. **[4562]**, Evansville, IN
Natl. Assn. of Investors Corp., Greater North Suburban Chap. **[1076]**, Chicago, IL
Natl. Assn. of Investors Corp., Heart of Illinois Chap. **[2987]**, Pekin, IL
Natl. Assn. of Investors Corp., Mid-Michigan Chap. **[9095]**, Mount Morris, MI
Natl. Assn. of Investors Corp., Milwaukee Chap. **[17674]**, Brookfield, WI
Natl. Assn. of Investors Corp., Northeast Hoosier Chap. **[4697]**, Fort Wayne, IN
Natl. Assn. of Investors Corp., Northeast Ohio Chap. **[15923]**, Mayfield Heights, OH
Natl. Assn. of Investors Corp., Northern Michigan Chap. **[10170]**, Williamsburg, MI

Natl. Assn. of Investors Corp., Northwest Buckeye Chap. [16934], Toledo, OH
Natl. Assn. of Investors Corp., Northwest Indiana Chap. [5810], Mishawaka, IN
Natl. Assn. of Investors Corp., OKI Tri-State Chap. [13922], Cincinnati, OH
Natl. Assn. of Investors Corp., South Central Wisconsin Chap. [18574], Madison, WI
Natl. Assn. of Investors Corp., Southeastern Michigan Chap. [10121], West Bloomfield, MI
Natl. Assn. of Investors Corp., Western Michigan Chap. [7990], Grand Rapids, MI
West Union Firemens' Building Assn. [17199], West Union, OH
Investors Corp., Northeast Ohio Chap; Natl. Assn. of [15923], Mayfield Heights, OH
InWord Resources [16009], Middletown, OH
Iola - Scandinavia Area Chamber of Commerce [18235], Iola, WI
Ionia Area Chamber of Commerce [8315], Ionia, MI
Ionia County Bd. of Realtors [8316], Ionia, MI
Iowa Lumber Assn. [★11716]
IPMA-HR Chicago Chap. [998], Chicago, IL
IPMA-HR Cleveland Chap. [15585], Lakewood, OH
IPMA-HR Greater Illinois Chap. [1572], Effingham, IL
IPMA-HR Greater St. Louis, Missouri Chap. [999], Chicago, IL
IPMA-HR Michigan Chap. [8582], Lansing, MI
IPMA-HR Minnesota Chap. [10538], Brooklyn Center, MN
IPMA-HR Wisconsin Chap. [18535], Madison, WI
Iranian
Iranian Cultural Assn. of Greater Columbus [14478], Columbus, OH
Iranian Cultural Assn. [★14478]
Iranian Cultural Assn. of Greater Columbus [14478], Columbus, OH
Irish
Ancient Order of Hibernians of Bay County - Robert Shea Div. [6878], Bay City, MI
Ancient Order of Hibernians of Genesee County - Sullivan and O'Sullivan Div. [9093], Mount Morris, MI
Ancient Order of Hibernians of Grand Traverse County - Bun Brady Div. [9923], Traverse City, MI
Ancient Order of Hibernians - John P. Kelly, Div. 1, Toledo, OH [16900], Toledo, OH
Ancient Order of Hibernians of Kent County - Fr. John Whalen McGee Div. [7905], Grand Rapids, MI
Ancient Order of Hibernians - Kevin Barry, Div. No. 3 [5031], Indianapolis, IN
Ancient Order of Hibernians of Lenawee County - St. Patrick, Div. No. 1 [6566], Adrian, MI
Ancient Order of Hibernians of Macomb County - Fr. Solanus Casey Div. [9654], St. Clair Shores, MI
Ancient Order of Hibernians - Michigan State Bd. [6567], Adrian, MI
Ancient Order of Hibernians - Milwaukee Div. [18963], Milwaukee, WI
Ancient Order of Hibernians of Oakland County - James O. Flynn Div. [6976], Bloomfield, MI
Ancient Order of Hibernians of Oakland County - Norman O'Brien, Div. 1 [9574], Royal Oak, MI
Ancient Order of Hibernians of Otsego County - Hogan Div. [7816], Gaylord, MI
Ancient Order of Hibernians of Wayne County - O' Brian Div. [9575], Royal Oak, MI
Ancient Order of Hibernians of Wayne County - Patrick Ryan Div. [9223], Northville, MI
Ancient Order of Hibernians of Wayne County - Stephen Walsh Div. [10182], Wolverine Lake, MI
Ancient Order of Hibernians of Wayne County - Thomas Dunleavy Div. [9393], Plymouth, MI
Chicago Ancient Hibernian Order - Div. No. 32 [781], Chicago, IL
Irish-Am. Alliance [1000], Chicago, IL
Shamrock Club of Wisconsin [19116], Milwaukee, WI
Irish-Am. Alliance [1000], Chicago, IL
Irish Amer. Archival Soc. [13533], Canfield, OH
Irish Baseball Backers [15049], Dublin, OH
Irish Music Club; Murphy Roche [376], Burr Ridge, IL
Iron County Chamber of Commerce [8332], Iron River, MI
Iron County Historical and Museum Soc. [7092], Caspian, MI
Iron County Historical Society [18231], Hurley, WI
Iron Mining Assn. of Minnesota [10828], Duluth, MN
Irondale Young Life [12231], Roseville, MN
Ironwood Area Chamber of Commerce [8339], Ironwood, MI
Iroquois County Genealogical Soc. [3908], Watseka, IL
Iroquois Valley Youth for Christ [3909], Watseka, IL
Isaac Knapp District Dental Soc. [4684], Fort Wayne, IN
Isanti County Historical Soc. [10623], Cambridge, MN
Ishpeming Beagle Club [7112], Champion, MI
Ishpeming Off. of Lake Superior Community Partnership [8346], Ishpeming, MI
Ishpeming Rock and Mineral Club [8347], Ishpeming, MI
Islamic
Org. of Islamic Speakers, Midwest [2660], Naperville, IL
Islamic Soc. - Northern Illinois Univ. [1437], DeKalb, IL
Islamic Speakers, Midwest; Org. of [2660], Naperville, IL
Isle Royale Natural History Assn. [8254], Houghton, MI
ISPI Michigan Chap. [9583], Royal Oak, MI
Israel
Ohio-Israel Chamber of Commerce [14197], Cleveland, OH
Israeli
Amer. Soc. for Technion-Israel Inst. of Tech., West Central Region [726], Chicago, IL
IT Alliance of Appalachian Ohio [13205], Athens, OH
Itasca County Bd. of Realtors [11087], Grand Rapids, MN
Itasca County Habitat for Humanity [11088], Grand Rapids, MN
Itasca Curling Club [11089], Grand Rapids, MN
Itasca Youth for Christ [11090], Grand Rapids, MN
Ithaca Chamber [★6632]
Ithaca Lions Club - Michigan [8352], Ithaca, MI
Ithaca Lions Club - Wisconsin [18429], Lone Rock, WI
ITSA [★2710]
IUB Latino Faculty and Staff Coun. [4238], Bloomington, IN
IUPUI Assn. for Computing Machinery Student SIGGRAPH [5380], Indianapolis, IN
Izaak Walton League of Am. - A.D. Sutherland Chap. [17984], Fond du Lac, WI
Izaak Walton League of Am., Alexandria Chap. [4092], Alexandria, IN
Izaak Walton League of Am., Anthony Wayne Chap. [15387], Hamilton, OH
Izaak Walton League of Am., Austin Chap. [10355], Austin, MN
Izaak Walton League of Am. - Beloit [17611], Beloit, WI
Izaak Walton League of Am., Bill Cook Chap. [19792], Stevens Point, WI
Izaak Walton League of Am. - Blackhawk Chap. [1789], Geneseo, IL
Izaak Walton League of Am., Buckeye All-State Chap. [15388], Hamilton, OH
Izaak Walton League of Am., Bush Lake Chap. [11591], Minneapolis, MN
Izaak Walton League of Am., Calumet Region Chap. [394], Calumet City, IL
Izaak Walton League of Am., Champaign County Chap. [3826], Urbana, IL
Izaak Walton League of Am. - Chicago Chap. No. 1 [2219], Lansing, IL
Izaak Walton League of Am., Cincinnati Chap. [15726], Loveland, OH
Izaak Walton League of Am., Clinton Chap. [6151], St. Bernice, IN
Izaak Walton League of America, DeKalb County Chapter [4139], Auburn, IN
Izaak Walton League of Am., Delta Chap. [15017], Delta, OH
Izaak Walton League of Am. - Des Plaines Chap. [2916], Palatine, IL
Izaak Walton League of Am., Dry Fork Chap. [15389], Hamilton, OH
Izaak Walton League of America, Dwight Lydell Chapter [9525], Rockford, MI
Izaak Walton League of Am., Elgin Chap. [1593], Elgin, IL
Izaak Walton League of Am. - Evansville [5961], Newburgh, IN
Izaak Walton League of Am., Fairfield Chap. [15390], Hamilton, OH
Izaak Walton League of Am. - Fenton [7849], Grand Blanc, MI
Izaak Walton League of Am., Fort Wayne Chap. [4939], Huntertown, IN
Izaak Walton League of Am., Fremont Chap. [15248], Fremont, OH
Izaak Walton League of Am., Grant County Chap. [5735], Marion, IN
Izaak Walton League of Am. - Griffith [4884], Hammond, IN
Izaak Walton League of Am., Hamilton Chap. [15391], Hamilton, OH
Izaak Walton League of Am., Howard County Chap. [5571], Kokomo, IN
Izaak Walton League of America, Illinois Division [163], Bartlett, IL
Izaak Walton League of Am., Indiana Div. [6058], Portage, IN
Izaak Walton League of Am., Kewanee Chap. [3781], Toulon, IL
Izaak Walton League of Am., Labudde Memorial Chap. [19038], Milwaukee, WI
Izaak Walton League of Am., Lawrence County Chap. [16391], Pedro, OH
Izaak Walton League of Am., Lock City Chap. [9720], Sault Ste. Marie, MI
Izaak Walton League of Am., Medina Chap. [15942], Medina, OH
Izaak Walton League of America, Miami Chapter [6032], Peru, IN
Izaak Walton League of Am., Michigan Div. [9526], Rockford, MI
Izaak Walton League of Am. Midwest Off. [12432], St. Paul, MN
Izaak Walton League of America, Minneapolis Chapter [10469], Bloomington, MN
Izaak Walton League of America, Minnesota Division [12433], St. Paul, MN
Izaak Walton League of Am., Natl. Youth Convention Chap. [15392], Hamilton, OH
Izaak Walton League of Am., New London Chap. [11872], New London, MN
Izaak Walton League of Am. - Ohio Div. [15393], Hamilton, OH
Izaak Walton League of Am., Peoria Chap. [2480], Metamora, IL
Izaak Walton League of Am., Porter County Chap. [4353], Chesterton, IN
Izaak Walton League of Am., Rochester Chap. [10614], Byron, MN
Izaak Walton League of Am., Sheboygan County Chap. [19697], Sheboygan, WI
Izaak Walton League of Am. - Southern Brown Conservation [18163], Greenleaf, WI
Izaak Walton League of Am., Southwestern Chap. [17621], Benton, WI
Izaak Walton League of Am., Tiffin-Seneca County Chap. [16853], Tiffin, OH
Izaak Walton League of Am., W. J. McCabe Chap. [10829], Duluth, MN
Izaak Walton League of Am., Wabash Chap. [6425], Wabash, IN
Izaak Walton League of Am., Wadsworth Chap. [17076], Wadsworth, OH
Izaak Walton League of Am., Walter Sherry Memorial Chap. [2110], Joliet, IL
Izaak Walton League of America, Wapashaw Chapter [12811], Wabasha, MN
Izaak Walton League of Am., Watertown Chap. [19967], Watertown, WI
Izaak Walton League of Am. - Waukesha County [17824], Delafield, WI
Izaak Walton League of Am., Wayne County Chap. [17320], Wooster, OH
Izaak Walton League of Am. - Western Reserve [17273], Willoughby, OH
Izaak Walton League of Am., Western Wisconsin Chap. [19771], Spring Valley, WI

Izaak Walton League of Am. - Wisconsin Div. [19483], Plover, WI

J

J-Sak Snowboarding [13133], Amherst, OH
JA of the Wabash Valley [★6332]
Jackets for Jobs [★7382]
Jackets for Jobs Michigan WORKS [7382], Detroit, MI
Jackson Affordable Housing Corp. [8369], Jackson, MI
Jackson Area Assn. of Realtors [8370], Jackson, MI
Jackson Area Chamber of Commerce [11234], Jackson, MN
Jackson Area Chamber of Commerce [15513], Jackson, OH
Jackson Audubon Soc. [8371], Jackson, MI
Jackson - Beldon Chamber of Commerce [15884], Massillon, OH
Jackson Cascades Lions Club [8372], Jackson, MI
Jackson Company Hea. Center [★418]
Jackson Convention and Tourist Bur. [8373], Jackson, MI
Jackson Corvette Club [8374], Jackson, MI
Jackson County Beagle Club [15514], Jackson, OH
Jackson County Genealogical Soc. [8375], Jackson, MI
Jackson County Historical Soc. [2618], Murphysboro, IL
Jackson County Historical Soc. [11290], Lakefield, MN
Jackson County Medical Soc. - Michigan [8376], Jackson, MI
Jackson County Mental Hea. Assn. [6182], Seymour, IN
Jackson County United Way, Indiana [6183], Seymour, IN
Jackson County Wolverine REACT [8377], Jackson, MI
Jackson District Dental Soc. [8378], Jackson, MI
Jackson Eye Openers Lions Club [8379], Jackson, MI
Jackson Host Lions Club [8380], Jackson, MI
Jackson Model Rocketry Club [8381], Jackson, MI
Jackson Park Yacht Club of Chicago [1001], Chicago, IL
Jackson Township Historical Soc. [5520], Jamestown, IN
Jackson Township Lions Club [15885], Massillon, OH
Jackson-Union County Habitat for Humanity [419], Carbondale, IL
Jackson - Young Life [8382], Jackson, MI
Jacksonville Area AIFA [3871], Virden, IL
Jacksonville Area Assn. of Realtors [2079], Jacksonville, IL
Jacksonville Area Chamber of Commerce [2080], Jacksonville, IL
Jacksonville Main St. [2081], Jacksonville, IL
Jaguar Club of Greater Cincinnati [15161], Fairfield, OH
Jaguars Cricket Club [2817], Oak Park, IL
James Kimbrough Law Assn. [4782], Gary, IN
Jane Addams Middle School PTA [9584], Royal Oak, MI
Jane Austen Soc. of North Am., Greater Chicago Region [1002], Chicago, IL
Jane Austen Soc. of North Am., Illinois / Northern Indiana [★1002]
Jane Austen Soc. of North Am., Ohio, Dayton [14900], Dayton, OH
Jane Austen Soc. of North Am., Wisconsin [18536], Madison, WI
Janesville Area Apartment Assn. [★18250]
Janesville Area Rental Property Assn. [18250], Janesville, WI
Janesville Figure Skating Club [18251], Janesville, WI
Janesville Masonic Center [18252], Janesville, WI
Janesville Noon Kiwanis Club [18253], Janesville, WI
Japan-America Soc. of Greater Cincinnati [13874], Cincinnati, OH
Japan Soc. of Cincinnati [★13874]
Japanese
Japan-America Soc. of Greater Cincinnati [13874], Cincinnati, OH
Japanese Amer. Citizens League - Cleveland Chap. [14149], Cleveland, OH
Japanese Amer. Citizens League - Cleveland Chap. [14149], Cleveland, OH
Jasper Chamber of Commerce [5528], Jasper, IN
Jasper County Chamber of Commerce [2699], Newton, IL
Jasper County Improvement Assn. [★2699]
Jasper - Wyldlife [5529], Jasper, IN
Jaxon Kennel Club [10172], Williamston, MI
Jay County Beagle Club [5882], Muncie, IN
Jaycees
Michigan Jaycees [8678], Lansing, MI
Jayco Jafari Intl. Travel Club, Flight 3 Tri-State Jaybirds [4383], Columbia City, IN
Jayco Jafari Intl. Travel Club, Flight 5 Heart of Illinois Jaytrackers [2493], Milford, IL
Jayco Jafari Intl. Travel Club, Flight 9 Four Rivers Jaycos [420], Carbondale, IL
Jayco Jafari Intl. Travel Club, Flight 13 Ja Triskaideka [2917], Palatine, IL
Jayco Jafari Intl. Travel Club, Flight 32 Holi-Jays [2392], Maple Park, IL
Jayco Jafari Intl. Travel Club, Flight 41 Jay Pack [18112], Green Bay, WI
Jayco Jafari Intl. Travel Club, Flight 101 Jayco Big Birds [4058], Woodstock, IL
Jayco Jafari Intl. Travel Club, Flight 106 Jaybirds of Milwaukee [17780], Colgate, WI
Jayco Jafari Intl. Travel Club, Flight 117 Lake Jayco Jypsies [10156], White Lake, MI
Jazz
Toledo Jazz Soc. [16973], Toledo, OH
JDF [★18860]
Jean Butz James Museum [★1990]
Jefferson Area Chamber of Commerce [15525], Jefferson, OH
Jefferson Chamber of Commerce [18271], Jefferson, WI
Jefferson County Bd. of Realtors, Indiana [5714], Madison, IN
Jefferson County Chamber of Commerce [2599], Mount Vernon, IL
Jefferson County Chamber of Commerce [16762], Steubenville, OH
Jefferson County Human Rsrc. Mgt. Assn. [19968], Watertown, WI
Jefferson County Literacy Coun. [18272], Jefferson, WI
Jefferson County United Way, Indiana [5715], Madison, IN
Jefferson High School - Young Life [6488], West Lafayette, IN
Jefferson Park Chamber of Commerce [1003], Chicago, IL
Jefferson Switzerland Assn. for Retarded Citizens [5716], Madison, IN
Jeffersonville Main St. [5542], Jeffersonville, IN
Jelly Jammers [8181], Hillsdale, MI
Jenison High - Young Life [6624], Allendale, MI
Jenison Junior High - Wyldlife [6625], Allendale, MI
Jennings County Chamber of Commerce [5995], North Vernon, IN
Jennings County Chamber of Commerce/Economic Development [★5995]
Jennings County United Way [5996], North Vernon, IN
Jeromesville Lions Club [15528], Jeromesville, OH
Jersey County Bus. Assn. [2090], Jerseyville, IL
Jersey County Chamber of Commerce [★2090]
Jewelry
Illinois Jewelers Assn. [3607], Springfield, IL
Minnesota Jewelers Assn. [12291], St. Cloud, MN
Ohio Jewelers Assn. [14630], Columbus, OH
Wisconsin Jewelers Assn. [18718], Madison, WI
Jewish
Akron Jewish Community Fed. [13022], Akron, OH
Amer. ORT Chicago Chap. [716], Chicago, IL
Amer. ORT, Cleveland Chap. [13282], Beachwood, OH
Champaign-Urbana Jewish Fed. [512], Champaign, IL
Chicago Jewish Historical Soc. [813], Chicago, IL
Chusy Region United Synagogue Youth [2753], Northbrook, IL
Columbus Jewish Fed. [14390], Columbus, OH
Columbus Jewish Historical Soc. [14391], Columbus, OH
Flint Jewish Fed. [7731], Flint, MI
Jewish Community Action [12434], St. Paul, MN
Jewish Community Fed. of Cleveland [14150], Cleveland, OH
Jewish Coun. on Urban Affairs [1007], Chicago, IL
Jewish Fed. of Cincinnati [13875], Cincinnati, OH
Jewish Fed. of Greater Dayton [14901], Dayton, OH
Jewish Fed. of Greater Indianapolis [5381], Indianapolis, IN
Jewish Fed. of Metropolitan Detroit [6986], Bloomfield Hills, MI
Jewish Fed. Northwest Indiana [5902], Munster, IN
Jewish Fed. of St. Joseph Valley [6234], South Bend, IN
Jewish Fed. of Southern Illinois, Southeastern Missouri and Western Kentucky [203], Belleville, IL
Jewish Fed. of Washtenaw County [6711], Ann Arbor, MI
Madison Jewish Community Coun. [18554], Madison, WI
Milwaukee Jewish Fed. [19062], Milwaukee, WI
Minneapolis Jewish Fed. [11790], Minnetonka, MN
Na'amat U.S.A., Cleveland Coun. [14169], Cleveland, OH
Northwest Suburban Jewish Community Center [364], Buffalo Grove, IL
Or Emet Congregation, Humanistic Jews of Minnesota [12119], Robbinsdale, MN
Springfield Jewish Fed. [3681], Springfield, IL
United Jewish Fund and Coun. [12603], St. Paul, MN
United Synagogue of Conservative Judaism, Great Lakes and Rivers Region [16644], Shaker Heights, OH
United Synagogue of Conservative Judaism, Mid-Continent Region [11767], Minneapolis, MN
Women of Reform Judaism: Isaac M. Wise Temple Sisterhood [14024], Cincinnati, OH
Women of Reform Judaism: Temple Israel Sisterhood, Columbus [14766], Columbus, OH
Jewish Broadcasting Network Corp. [1004], Chicago, IL
Jewish Children's Bur. of Chicago [1005], Chicago, IL
Jewish Community Action [12434], St. Paul, MN
Jewish Community Center; Northwest Suburban [364], Buffalo Grove, IL
Jewish Community Centers Endowment Found. [1006], Chicago, IL
Jewish Community Fed. of Cleveland [14150], Cleveland, OH
Jewish Coun. on Urban Affairs [1007], Chicago, IL
Jewish Fed. [★18554]
Jewish Fed. of Cincinnati [13875], Cincinnati, OH
Jewish Fed. of Greater Dayton [14901], Dayton, OH
Jewish Fed. of Greater Indianapolis [5381], Indianapolis, IN
Jewish Fed. of Metropolitan Detroit [6986], Bloomfield Hills, MI
Jewish Fed. Northwest Indiana [5902], Munster, IN
Jewish Fed. of the Quad Cities [3246], Rock Island, IL
Jewish Fed. of St. Joseph Valley [6234], South Bend, IN
Jewish Fed. of Southern Illinois, Southeastern Missouri and Western Kentucky [203], Belleville, IL
Jewish Fed. of Washtenaw County [6711], Ann Arbor, MI
Jewish Genealogical Soc; Illiana [1708], Flossmoor, IL
Jewish Genealogical Soc. of Illinois [2755], Northbrook, IL
Jewish Historical Soc. of Michigan [10116], West Bloomfield, MI
Jewish United Fund/Jewish Fed. of Metropolitan Chicago [1008], Chicago, IL
Jim Dandy Ski Club [7383], Detroit, MI
Job Search Focus Gp. [13876], Cincinnati, OH
Job Transition Support Gp. [10913], Edina, MN
Jobs For Youth/Chicago [1009], Chicago, IL
Jobs for Minnesota's Graduates [11411], Maple Grove, MN

Jobs for Ohio's Graduates **[14479]**, Columbus, OH
Jobs Partnership of Greater Indianapolis **[5382]**, Indianapolis, IN
John Allen Parent Coun. **[6712]**, Ann Arbor, MI
John Carroll Univ. Students In Free Enterprise **[17026]**, University Heights, OH
John Mercer Langston Bar Assn. **[14480]**, Columbus, OH
John Muir PTA **[2037]**, Hoffman Estates, IL
John Wesley Powell Audubon Soc. **[293]**, Bloomington, IL
John Young - Wyldlife **[6235]**, South Bend, IN
Johnson County Assn. for Retarded Citizens **[4750]**, Franklin, IN
Johnson County Historical Museum and Soc. **[4751]**, Franklin, IN
Johnson County REACT **[4752]**, Franklin, IN
Johnson Creek Area Chamber of Commerce **[18277]**, Johnson Creek, WI
Johnson-Humrickhouse Museum **[14802]**, Coshocton, OH
Joint Religious Legislative Coalition **[11592]**, Minneapolis, MN
Joliet ALU **[2111]**, Joliet, IL
Joliet Archery Club **[2314]**, Lockport, IL
Joliet Area of Sheet Metal and Air Conditioning Contractors' Natl. Assn. **[1594]**, Elgin, IL
Joliet Area Theatre Organ Enthusiasts **[2112]**, Joliet, IL
Joliet Region Chamber of Commerce and Indus. **[2113]**, Joliet, IL
Jonathan Alder - Young Life **[14481]**, Columbus, OH
Jonesville Lions Club **[8410]**, Jonesville, MI
Jonesville Wyld Life - Wyldlife **[8182]**, Hillsdale, MI
Jordan Hall Research Associates **[3788]**, Troy, IL
Joseph Watts Philanthropic Golden Gloves Boxing Group **[8583]**, Lansing, MI
Journalism
Columbus Assn. of Black Journalists **[14370]**, Columbus, OH
Greater Dayton Assn. of Black Journalists **[14890]**, Dayton, OH
Indianapolis Assn. of Black Journalists **[5339]**, Indianapolis, IN
Minnesota News Coun. **[11659]**, Minneapolis, MN
Natl. Assn. of Black Journalists - Chicago Chap. **[1073]**, Chicago, IL
Natl. Assn. of Black Journalists - Cincinnati Chap. **[13917]**, Cincinnati, OH
Natl. Assn. of Black Journalists - Detroit Chap. **[7407]**, Detroit, MI
Northwest Ohio Black Media Assn. **[16939]**, Toledo, OH
Twin Cities Black Journalists **[11756]**, Minneapolis, MN
Wisconsin Black Media Assn. **[19160]**, Milwaukee, WI
Wisconsin Newspaper Assn. **[18736]**, Madison, WI
Joy-Southfield Community Development Corp. **[7384]**, Detroit, MI
Judges Coun. of Minnesota **[10470]**, Bloomington, MN
Judicial District Pro Bono Comm; Indiana First **[4926]**, Hobart, IN
Judiciary
Federalist Soc. for Law and Public Policy Stud. - Cincinnati Chap. **[13827]**, Cincinnati, OH
Federalist Soc. for Law and Public Policy Stud. - Cleveland Chap. **[14119]**, Cleveland, OH
Federalist Soc. for Law and Public Policy Stud. - Columbus Chap. **[14433]**, Columbus, OH
Federalist Soc. for Law and Public Policy Stud. - Grand Rapids Chap. **[7930]**, Grand Rapids, MI
Federalist Soc. for Law and Public Policy Stud. - Indianapolis Chap. **[5116]**, Indianapolis, IN
Federalist Soc. for Law and Public Policy Stud. - Michigan Chap. (Detroit) **[7362]**, Detroit, MI
Federalist Soc. for Law and Public Policy Stud. - Milwaukee Chap. **[19007]**, Milwaukee, WI
Federalist Soc. for Law and Public Policy Stud. - Minneapolis Chap. **[12858]**, Wayzata, MN
Michigan Acad. of Sci., Arts, and Letters **[6633]**, Alma, MI
Juneau Chamber of Commerce **[18282]**, Juneau, WI
Junior Achievement Akron **[13061]**, Akron, OH
Junior Achievement of Brown County **[18113]**, Green Bay, WI
Junior Achievement of Central Illinois **[3070]**, Peoria Heights, IL
Junior Achievement of Central Indiana **[5383]**, Indianapolis, IN
Junior Achievement of Chicago **[1010]**, Chicago, IL
Junior Achievement of East Central Illinois **[1397]**, Decatur, IL
Junior Achievement of East Central Ohio **[13570]**, Canton, OH
Junior Achievement of Eastern Indiana **[6095]**, Richmond, IN
Junior Achievement of Elkhart County **[4499]**, Elkhart, IN
Junior Achievement of Greater Genesee Valley **[7744]**, Flint, MI
Junior Achievement of Kalamazoo and Van Buren Counties **[8432]**, Kalamazoo, MI
Junior Achievement of Mahoning Valley **[15324]**, Girard, OH
Junior Achievement, Mankato Area **[11381]**, Mankato, MN
Junior Achievement, Michigan Edge **[8383]**, Jackson, MI
Junior Achievement of the Michigan Great Lakes **[7970]**, Grand Rapids, MI
Junior Achievement of the Michigan Great Lakes, Northern Ser. Off. **[6997]**, Boyne City, MI
Junior Achievement North Central **[★20036]**
Junior Achievement OKI Partners **[17175]**, West Chester, OH
Junior Achievement, Quad-Cities Area **[2522]**, Moline, IL
Junior Achievement of Racine **[19557]**, Racine, WI
Junior Achievement, Rochester Area **[12152]**, Rochester, MN
Junior Achievement, Rock County **[18254]**, Janesville, WI
Junior Achievement, Rock River Valley **[3284]**, Rockford, IL
Junior Achievement, South Central Michigan **[6860]**, Battle Creek, MI
Junior Achievement, Southeastern Michigan **[7385]**, Detroit, MI
Junior Achievement of the Upper Midwest **[11419]**, Maplewood, MN
Junior Achievement of the Wabash Valley **[6332]**, Terre Haute, IN
Junior Achievement West Michigan Lakeshore **[7861]**, Grand Haven, MI
Junior Achievement of Wisconsin **[19039]**, Milwaukee, WI
Junior Achievement of Wisconsin, Marathon County District Off. **[20036]**, Wausau, WI
Junior Achievement of Wisconsin Northwest District **[17882]**, Eau Claire, WI
Junior League of Cincinnati **[13877]**, Cincinnati, OH
Junior League of Detroit **[8090]**, Grosse Pointe Farms, MI
Junior League of Grand Rapids **[7971]**, Grand Rapids, MI
Junior League of Indianapolis **[5384]**, Indianapolis, IN
Junior League of Milwaukee **[19040]**, Milwaukee, WI
Junior League of St. Paul **[12435]**, St. Paul, MN
Junior Woman's Club of Des Plaines **[1462]**, Des Plaines, IL
Junior Woman's Club of Waukesha **[19987]**, Waukesha, WI
Just Kidding 4-H Dairy Goat Club **[7631]**, Ewen, MI
Justice In Mental Hea. Org. **[8584]**, Lansing, MI
Justice Initiative; Juvenile **[1663]**, Evanston, IL
Justice Network; Appalachian Peace and **[13195]**, Athens, OH
Justice Org; Little Village Enval. **[1034]**, Chicago, IL
Justice; Wisconsin Network for Peace and **[18734]**, Madison, WI
Juvenile
Juvenile Justice Initiative **[1663]**, Evanston, IL
Juvenile Diabetes Found., Chicago Metro Chap. **[★1011]**
Juvenile Diabetes Found. of Greater Chicago **[★1011]**
Juvenile Diabetes Found. of Illinois **[★1011]**
Juvenile Diabetes Found., Indiana State Chap. **[★5385]**
Juvenile Diabetes Found., Metropolitan Detroit Chap. **[★9802]**
Juvenile Diabetes Res. Found. of Greater Chicago **[★1011]**
Juvenile Diabetes Res. Found. Illinois **[1011]**, Chicago, IL
Juvenile Diabetes Res. Found., Indiana State Chap. **[5385]**, Indianapolis, IN
Juvenile Diabetes Res. Found. Intl., East Central Ohio Br. **[15500]**, Independence, OH
Juvenile Diabetes Res. Found. Intl., Greater Cincinnati Chap. **[13878]**, Cincinnati, OH
Juvenile Diabetes Res. Found. Intl., Greater Dayton Chap. **[14902]**, Dayton, OH
Juvenile Diabetes Research Foundation International, Mid-Ohio Chapter **[14482]**, Columbus, OH
Juvenile Diabetes Res. Found. Intl., Minnesota Chap. **[10471]**, Bloomington, MN
Juvenile Diabetes Res. Foundation International, Northeast Ohio Chapter **[14151]**, Cleveland, OH
Juvenile Diabetes Res. Found. Intl., Northwest Ohio Chap. **[16408]**, Perrysburg, OH
Juvenile Diabetes Research Foundation International, Western Wisconsin Chapter **[18537]**, Madison, WI
Juvenile Diabetes Res. Found., Metropolitan Detroit and Southeast Michigan Chap. **[9802]**, Southfield, MI
Juvenile Diabetes Res. Found., Northeast Wisconsin Chap. **[18860]**, Menasha, WI
Juvenile Diabetes Res. Found., Southeastern Wisconsin Chap. **[20076]**, Wauwatosa, WI
Juvenile Justice Initiative **[1663]**, Evanston, IL

K

K-9 Obedience Training Club of Menomonee Falls **[18875]**, Menomonee Falls, WI
K-9 Rescue; Good Shepherd **[18248]**, Janesville, WI
Kaiteur Sports Club **[12641]**, Savage, MN
Kalamazoo AIDS Rsrc. and Educ. Services **[★8424]**
Kalamazoo Animal Liberation League **[8433]**, Kalamazoo, MI
Kalamazoo Antique Bottle Club **[9446]**, Portage, MI
Kalamazoo Area Youth for Christ **[8434]**, Kalamazoo, MI
Kalamazoo Astronomical Soc. **[8435]**, Kalamazoo, MI
Kalamazoo Builders Exchange **[8436]**, Kalamazoo, MI
Kalamazoo Christian - Young Life **[8437]**, Kalamazoo, MI
Kalamazoo Corvette Club **[8438]**, Kalamazoo, MI
Kalamazoo Dog Training Club **[8439]**, Kalamazoo, MI
Kalamazoo Downtown Lions Club **[8440]**, Kalamazoo, MI
Kalamazoo Figure Skating Club **[8441]**, Kalamazoo, MI
Kalamazoo Gay-Lesbian Rsrc. Center **[8442]**, Kalamazoo, MI
Kalamazoo Human Rsrcs. Mgt. Assn. **[9447]**, Portage, MI
Kalamazoo Kennel Club **[7290]**, Delton, MI
Kalamazoo Michigan Bocce Club **[9448]**, Portage, MI
Kalamazoo Numismatic Club **[9449]**, Portage, MI
Kalamazoo Regional Associates of Health Underwriters **[★9319]**
Kalamazoo Regional Chamber of Commerce **[8443]**, Kalamazoo, MI
Kalamazoo Valley District Dental Soc. **[8444]**, Kalamazoo, MI
Kalamazoo Valley Habitat for Humanity **[8445]**, Kalamazoo, MI
Kalamazoo Valley Landscape and Nursery Assn. **[8446]**, Kalamazoo, MI
Kalamazoo West Side Lions Club **[9318]**, Oshtemo, MI
Kaleidoscope Youth Coalition **[14483]**, Columbus, OH
Kaleva Lions Club **[8474]**, Kaleva, MI
Kalkaska Area Chamber of Commerce **[8476]**, Kalkaska, MI
Kanabec Area Chamber of Commerce **[11833]**, Mora, MN
Kandiyohi County Pheasants Forever **[12917]**, Willmar, MN

Kane County Bar Assn. **[1796]**, Geneva, IL
Kane County Medical Soc. **[3387]**, St. Charles, IL
Kane/McHenry Counties RSVP **[2459]**, McHenry, IL
Kankakee Area Chamber of Commerce **[★2137]**
Kankakee Area Youth for Christ **[327]**, Bourbonnais, IL
Kankakee County Assn. of Realtors **[2134]**, Kankakee, IL
Kankakee County Regional Planning Commn. **[2135]**, Kankakee, IL
Kankakee District Dental Soc. **[2136]**, Kankakee, IL
Kankakee River Valley Chamber of Commerce **[2137]**, Kankakee, IL
Kankakee Valley AIFA **[2138]**, Kankakee, IL
Kankakee Valley Astronomical Soc. **[5983]**, North Judson, IN
Kankakee Valley Historical Soc. **[5591]**, Kouts, IN
Kankakee Valley REACT **[2139]**, Kankakee, IL
Karlstad Lions Club **[11241]**, Karlstad, MN
Karrer MS - Wyldlife **[14484]**, Columbus, OH
Kasson-Mantorville Lions Club **[11245]**, Kasson, MN
Katoland Chap. IAAP **[11382]**, Mankato, MN
Keep Indianapolis Beautiful **[5386]**, Indianapolis, IN
Kekekabic Trail Club **[11593]**, Minneapolis, MN
Kelleys Island Chamber of Commerce **[15535]**, Kelleys Island, OH
Kellogg Lions Club **[11250]**, Kellogg, MN
Kendall Lions Club **[18291]**, Kendall, WI
Kendallville Area Chamber of Commerce **[5550]**, Kendallville, IN
Kennel Club of Chicago; Intl. **[989]**, Chicago, IL
Kennel Club; St. Croix Valley **[10242]**, Afton, MN
Kenosha Aikikai **[18299]**, Kenosha, WI
Kenosha Area Chamber of Commerce **[18300]**, Kenosha, WI
Kenosha County RSVP **[18301]**, Kenosha, WI
Kenosha History Center **[18302]**, Kenosha, WI
Kenosha Realtors Assn. **[18303]**, Kenosha, WI
Kenowa Hills High School - Young Life **[8041]**, Grandville, MI
Kensington Lions Club **[11252]**, Kensington, MN
Kent Area Chamber of Commerce **[15541]**, Kent, OH
Kent Area Chamber of Commerce and Info. Center **[★15541]**
Kent County Conservation League **[6558]**, Ada, MI
Kent County Humane Soc. **[★7964]**
Kent County Literacy Coun. **[7972]**, Grand Rapids, MI
Kent Fencing Club **[15542]**, Kent, OH
Kent Figure Skating Club **[15486]**, Hudson, OH
Kent Lions Club **[15543]**, Kent, OH
Kentland Area Chamber of Commerce **[5553]**, Kentland, IN
Kenton Ridge - Young Life **[16732]**, Springfield, OH
Kentuckiana Golf Course Superintendents Assn. **[5543]**, Jeffersonville, IN
Kentwood - Young Life **[7973]**, Grand Rapids, MI
Kenwood Elementary PTA **[533]**, Champaign, IL
Kenyon Lions Club **[11254]**, Kenyon, MN
Kerkhoven Lions Club **[11258]**, Kerkhoven, MN
Kettering Chamber of Commerce **[★15561]**
Kettering Kilometer Climbers **[13623]**, Centerville, OH
Kettering Lions Club **[15560]**, Kettering, OH
Kettering - Moraine - Oakwood Chamber of Commerce **[15561]**, Kettering, OH
Kettering - Young Life **[14903]**, Dayton, OH
Kettle Moraine Corvette Club **[19698]**, Sheboygan, WI
Kettle Moraine Figure Skating Club **[20120]**, West Bend, WI
Kettle Moraine Optometric Soc. **[19988]**, Waukesha, WI
Kettle Moraine Young Life **[18184]**, Hartland, WI
Kewanee Area United Way **[2156]**, Kewanee, IL
Kewanee Chamber of Commerce **[2157]**, Kewanee, IL
Kewaskum Lions Club **[18317]**, Kewaskum, WI
Kewaunee Area Chamber of Commerce **[18320]**, Kewaunee, WI
Keweenaw County Historical Soc. **[7493]**, Eagle Harbor, MI
Keweenaw Historical Soc. **[★7493]**
Keweenaw Peninsula Chamber of Commerce **[8255]**, Houghton, MI
Keyhole Players **[1012]**, Chicago, IL
KFAI Fresh Air of Minnesota **[11594]**, Minneapolis, MN
Khmers Kampuchea-Krom Fed. **[14485]**, Columbus, OH
Kiap Tu Wish Chap. of Trout Unlimited **[12977]**, Woodbury, MN
Kickapoo Mountain Bike Club **[2840]**, Oakwood, IL
Kickers Soccer Club **[122]**, Aurora, IL
Kidney
  Kidney Found. of Medina County **[13448]**, Brunswick, OH
Kidney Cancer Assn. **[1664]**, Evanston, IL
Kidney Found. of Greater Cincinnati **[13879]**, Cincinnati, OH
Kidney Found. of Medina County **[13448]**, Brunswick, OH
Kidney Found. of Ohio; Natl. **[14523]**, Columbus, OH
Kids of the Kingdom **[5530]**, Jasper, IN
Kids for Saving Earth Worldwide **[11595]**, Minneapolis, MN
Kids; Special **[19130]**, Milwaukee, WI
Kiel Area Assn. of Commerce **[18322]**, Kiel, WI
Kilbourne - Young Life **[14486]**, Columbus, OH
Killerspin Multiplex Table Tennis Club **[1013]**, Chicago, IL
Kilroy Military Vehicle Preservation Assn. **[6176]**, Sellersburg, IN
King City Beagle Club **[462]**, Carterville, IL
Kings Young Life **[13880]**, Cincinnati, OH
Kingsley PTA **[1665]**, Evanston, IL
Kingston Lions Club - Michigan **[8495]**, Kingston, MI
Kingston Lions Club - Minnesota **[10754]**, Dassel, MN
Kingwood Orchid Soc. **[15838]**, Marion, OH
Kinship Youth Mentoring of Princeton **[12045]**, Princeton, MN
Kishwaukee United Way **[1438]**, DeKalb, IL
Kishwaukee Valley Habitat for Humanity **[1439]**, DeKalb, IL
Kite Flying
  Black Swamp Air Force **[16403]**, Perrysburg, OH
  Chicagoland Sky Liners **[2630]**, Naperville, IL
  Hoosier Kitefliers Soc. **[5141]**, Indianapolis, IN
  Minnesota Kite Soc. **[11653]**, Minneapolis, MN
  Ohio Soc. for the Elevation of Kites **[15145]**, Euclid, OH
Kitty Matchcover Club **[12436]**, St. Paul, MN
Kiwanis Club of Addison **[9]**, Addison, IL
Kiwanis Club of Adrian **[6571]**, Adrian, MI
Kiwanis Club of Ann Arbor **[6713]**, Ann Arbor, MI
Kiwanis Club of Baraboo **[17574]**, Baraboo, WI
Kiwanis Club of Beloit Stateline Golden K **[17612]**, Beloit, WI
Kiwanis Club of Bensenville-Wood Dale **[227]**, Bensenville, IL
Kiwanis Club of Bloomington, Illinois **[294]**, Bloomington, IL
Kiwanis Club of Brookfield, IL **[353]**, Brookfield, IL
Kiwanis Club of Brookfield, Wisconsin **[17671]**, Brookfield, WI
Kiwanis Club of Champaign-Urbana **[534]**, Champaign, IL
Kiwanis Club of Chandler **[4345]**, Chandler, IN
Kiwanis Club of Chatham **[580]**, Chatham, IL
Kiwanis Club of Chesaning, Michigan **[7147]**, Chesaning, MI
Kiwanis Club of Clinton Township, Michigan **[7178]**, Clinton Township, MI
Kiwanis Club of Columbia, Illinois **[1298]**, Columbia, IL
Kiwanis Club of Darien-Westmont **[1362]**, Darien, IL
Kiwanis Club Delphi Chap. **[4455]**, Delphi, IN
Kiwanis Club of Des Plaines, Illinois **[1463]**, Des Plaines, IL
Kiwanis Club of East Lansing **[7525]**, East Lansing, MI
Kiwanis Club of Elkhorn, Wisconsin **[17928]**, Elkhorn, WI
Kiwanis Club of Fishers Sta. **[4609]**, Fishers, IN
Kiwanis Club Found; Benton **[231]**, Benton, IL
Kiwanis Club of Glen Ellyn **[1836]**, Glen Ellyn, IL
Kiwanis Club of Holland **[8884]**, Macatawa, MI
Kiwanis Club of Indianapolis **[5387]**, Indianapolis, IN
Kiwanis Club of Jacksonville, Illinois **[2082]**, Jacksonville, IL
Kiwanis Club of Kaukauna **[18288]**, Kaukauna, WI
Kiwanis Club of La Grange, Illinois **[2170]**, La Grange, IL
Kiwanis Club of Lombard **[2336]**, Lombard, IL
Kiwanis Club of Menomonee Falls **[18876]**, Menomonee Falls, WI
Kiwanis Club of Milwaukee **[19041]**, Milwaukee, WI
Kiwanis Club of Mt. Vernon **[2600]**, Mount Vernon, IL
Kiwanis Club of Park Ridge - Noon **[2963]**, Park Ridge, IL
Kiwanis Club of Plainfield **[3100]**, Plainfield, IL
Kiwanis Club of Plover **[19484]**, Plover, WI
Kiwanis Club of Potowatomi-South Bend **[6236]**, South Bend, IN
Kiwanis Club of Rockford **[3285]**, Rockford, IL
Kiwanis Club of Shelbyville **[6194]**, Shelbyville, IN
Kiwanis Club; Shorewood **[9567]**, Roseville, MI
Kiwanis Club of Sparta **[19752]**, Sparta, WI
Kiwanis Club of Streamwood **[3720]**, Streamwood, IL
Kiwanis Club of Tinley Park **[3770]**, Tinley Park, IL
Kiwanis Club of Traverse City **[9934]**, Traverse City, MI
Kiwanis Intl; Michigan District of **[8980]**, Mason, MI
Knights of Columbus, Cleveland Coun. No. 733 **[14152]**, Cleveland, OH
Knights of Columbus, Columbus **[14487]**, Columbus, OH
Knights of Columbus, Coun. 1143 - Edwardsville **[1562]**, Edwardsville, IL
Knights of Columbus, Coun. 4400 **[2114]**, Joliet, IL
Knights of Columbus, Joliet **[★2114]**
Knights of Columbus, Madison **[18538]**, Madison, WI
Knights of Columbus, Marshfield **[18816]**, Marshfield, WI
Knightstown Area Chamber of Commerce **[★5559]**
Knightstown Indiana Chamber of Commerce **[5559]**, Knightstown, IN
Kno Ho County RSVP **[16081]**, Mount Vernon, OH
Knob and Valley Audubon Soc. **[5917]**, New Albany, IN
Knollwood Gun Club **[2891]**, Oswego, IL
Knox County Assn. for Retarded Citizens **[6411]**, Vincennes, IN
Knox County Bd. of Realtors **[6412]**, Vincennes, IN
Knox County Bd. of Realtors **[16082]**, Mount Vernon, OH
Knox County Chamber of Commerce **[6413]**, Vincennes, IN
Knox County Convention and Visitors Bur. **[16083]**, Mount Vernon, OH
Knox County Genealogical Soc. **[1776]**, Galesburg, IL
Knox County Habitat for Humanity **[16084]**, Mount Vernon, OH
Knox County RSVP **[6414]**, Vincennes, IN
Kochville Lions Club **[9612]**, Saginaw, MI
Kokomo AIFA **[5572]**, Kokomo, IN
Kokomo Area Chap. of the United Ostomy Assn. **[5573]**, Kokomo, IN
Kokomo - Howard County Chamber of Commerce **[5574]**, Kokomo, IN
Kokomo Howard County Development Corp. **[5575]**, Kokomo, IN
Kokomo Indiana Visitors Bureau **[★5568]**
Kokomo Main St. Assn. **[5576]**, Kokomo, IN
Kokomo Shrine Club **[5577]**, Kokomo, IN
Kokomo Table Tennis Club **[5578]**, Kokomo, IN
Kokomo Visitors Bureau **[★5568]**
Korean Amer. Merchants Assn. of Chicago **[1014]**, Chicago, IL
Korean War
  Korean War Veterans Assn., Akron Regional Chap. **[13062]**, Akron, OH
  Korean War Veterans Assn., Buckeye Chap. **[15717]**, Louisville, OH
  Korean War Veterans Assn., Central Indiana Chap. **[5388]**, Indianapolis, IN
  Korean War Veterans Assn., Central Ohio Chap. **[14488]**, Columbus, OH
  Korean War Veterans Assn., Charles Parlier Chap. **[1398]**, Decatur, IL
  Korean War Veterans Assn., Coshocton Chap. **[14803]**, Coshocton, OH
  Korean War Veterans Assn., Cpl. Richard A. Bell Chap. **[20121]**, West Bend, WI
  Korean War Veterans Assn., Dale H. Williams Post No. 1996 Chap. **[8920]**, Manton, MI
  Korean War Veterans Assn., Dept. of Illinois **[3033]**, Peoria, IL

Korean War Veterans Assn., Dept. of Indiana [6025], Pendleton, IN
Korean War Veterans Assn., Dept. of Ohio [14489], Columbus, OH
Korean War Veterans Assn., Fairmont Chap. [12759], Trimont, MN
Korean War Veterans Assn., Frozen Chosin Chap. [11383], Mankato, MN
Korean War Veterans Assn., Gene A. Sturgeon Memorial Chap. [4415], Connersville, IN
Korean War Veterans Assn., Greater Chicago Chap. [1015], Chicago, IL
Korean War Veterans Assn., Greater Cincinnati Chap. [13881], Cincinnati, OH
Korean War Veterans Assn., Greater Cleveland Chap. [16371], Parma, OH
Korean War Veterans Assn., Greater Rockford Chap. [3286], Rockford, IL
Korean War Veterans Assn., Greene County Chap. [17373], Xenia, OH
Korean War Veterans Assn., Hancock County Chap. [15931], McComb, OH
Korean War Veterans Assn., Hocking Valley Chap. [15689], Logan, OH
Korean War Veterans Assn., Imjin Chap. [2847], O'Fallon, IL
Korean War Veterans Assn., Indiana No. 1 Chap. [4685], Fort Wayne, IN
Korean War Veterans Assn., Indiana No. 2 Chap. [5619], Lafayette, IN
Korean War Veterans Assn., Johnny Johnson Chap. [15657], Lima, OH
Korean War Veterans Assn., Lake Erie Chap. [16692], South Euclid, OH
Korean War Veterans Assn., Lester Hammond Chap. [3153], Quincy, IL
Korean War Veterans Assn., Mahoning Valley Chap. [13237], Austintown, OH
Korean War Veterans Assn., Marion Chap. [16487], Prospect, OH
Korean War Veterans Assn., Mid-Michigan Chap. [10041], Vassar, MI
Korean War Veterans Assn., Minnesota No. 1 Chap. [19641], River Falls, WI
Korean War Veterans Assn., Northwest Illinois Chap. [1750], Freeport, IL
Korean War Veterans Assn., Northwest Michigan Chap. [9935], Traverse City, MI
Korean War Veterans Assn., Northwest Ohio Chap. [16926], Toledo, OH
Korean War Veterans Assn., Oakland, Macomb, Wayne Chap. [10085], Waterford, MI
Korean War Veterans Assn., Ohio Valley Chap. [13312], Bellaire, OH
Korean War Veterans Assn., Peoria Chap. [1630], Elmwood, IL
Korean War Veterans Assn., Quad Cities Chap. [3247], Rock Island, IL
Korean War Veterans Assn., Quiet Warrior Chap. [4686], Fort Wayne, IN
Korean War Veterans Assn., Richland County Chap. [15769], Mansfield, OH
Korean War Veterans Assn., Robert Wurtsbaugh Chap. [47], Alvin, IL
Korean War Veterans Assn., Saginaw/Frankenmuth Chap. [9613], Saginaw, MI
Korean War Veterans Assn., Sangamon County Chap. [3755], Taylorville, IL
Korean War Veterans Assn., Sgt. William E. Windrich No. 3 Chap. [4475], East Chicago, IN
Korean War Veterans Assn., South Central Wisconsin Chap. [18539], Madison, WI
Korean War Veterans Assn., South Suburban Chap. [2880], Orland Park, IL
Korean War Veterans Assn., Southeastern Indiana No. 4 Chap. [4147], Aurora, IN
Korean War Veterans Assn., Tri-State Chap. [15080], East Liverpool, OH
Korean War Veterans Assn., West Central Wisconsin Chap. [18350], La Crosse, WI
Korean War Veterans Assn., Western Ohio Chap. [16432], Piqua, OH
Korean War Veterans Assn., William J. Sanpozzi Chap. [16614], Sandusky, OH
Korean War Veterans Assn., Akron Regional Chap. [13062], Akron, OH
Korean War Veterans Assn., Buckeye Chap. [15717], Louisville, OH
Korean War Veterans Assn., Central Indiana Chap. [5388], Indianapolis, IN
Korean War Veterans Assn., Central Ohio Chap. [14488], Columbus, OH
Korean War Veterans Assn., Charles Parlier Chap. [1398], Decatur, IL
Korean War Veterans Assn., Coshocton Chap. [14803], Coshocton, OH
Korean War Veterans Assn., Cpl. Richard A. Bell Chap. [20121], West Bend, WI
Korean War Veterans Assn., Dale H. Williams Post No. 1996 Chap. [8920], Manton, MI
Korean War Veterans Assn., Dept. of Illinois [3033], Peoria, IL
Korean War Veterans Assn., Dept. of Indiana [6025], Pendleton, IN
Korean War Veterans Assn., Dept. of Ohio [14489], Columbus, OH
Korean War Veterans Assn., Fairmont Chap. [12759], Trimont, MN
Korean War Veterans Assn., Frozen Chosin Chap. [11383], Mankato, MN
Korean War Veterans Assn., Gene A. Sturgeon Memorial Chap. [4415], Connersville, IN
Korean War Veterans Assn., Greater Chicago Chap. [1015], Chicago, IL
Korean War Veterans Assn., Greater Cincinnati Chap. [13881], Cincinnati, OH
Korean War Veterans Assn., Greater Cleveland Chap. [16371], Parma, OH
Korean War Veterans Assn., Greater Rockford Chap. [3286], Rockford, IL
Korean War Veterans Assn., Greene County Chap. [17373], Xenia, OH
Korean War Veterans Assn., Hancock County Chap. [15931], McComb, OH
Korean War Veterans Assn., Hocking Valley Chap. [15689], Logan, OH
Korean War Veterans Assn., Imjin Chap. [2847], O'Fallon, IL
Korean War Veterans Assn., Indiana No. 1 Chap. [4685], Fort Wayne, IN
Korean War Veterans Assn., Indiana No. 2 Chap. [5619], Lafayette, IN
Korean War Veterans Assn., Johnny Johnson Chap. [15657], Lima, OH
Korean War Veterans Assn., Lake Erie Chap. [16692], South Euclid, OH
Korean War Veterans Assn., Lester Hammond Chap. [3153], Quincy, IL
Korean War Veterans Assn., Mahoning Valley Chap. [13237], Austintown, OH
Korean War Veterans Assn., Marion Chap. [16487], Prospect, OH
Korean War Veterans Assn., Mid-Michigan Chap. [10041], Vassar, MI
Korean War Veterans Assn., Minnesota No. 1 Chap. [19641], River Falls, WI
Korean War Veterans Assn., Northwest Illinois Chap. [1750], Freeport, IL
Korean War Veterans Assn., Northwest Michigan Chap. [9935], Traverse City, MI
Korean War Veterans Assn., Northwest Ohio Chap. [16926], Toledo, OH
Korean War Veterans Assn., Oakland, Macomb, Wayne Chap. [10085], Waterford, MI
Korean War Veterans Assn., Ohio Valley Chap. [13312], Bellaire, OH
Korean War Veterans Assn., Peoria Chap. [1630], Elmwood, IL
Korean War Veterans Assn., Quad Cities Chap. [3247], Rock Island, IL
Korean War Veterans Assn., Quiet Warrior Chap. [4686], Fort Wayne, IN
Korean War Veterans Assn., Richland County Chap. [15769], Mansfield, OH
Korean War Veterans Assn., Robert Wurtsbaugh Chap. [47], Alvin, IL
Korean War Veterans Assn., Saginaw/Frankenmuth Chap. [9613], Saginaw, MI
Korean War Veterans Assn., Sangamon County Chap. [3755], Taylorville, IL
Korean War Veterans Assn., Sgt. William E. Windrich No. 3 Chap. [4475], East Chicago, IN
Korean War Veterans Assn., South Central Wisconsin Chap. [18539], Madison, WI
Korean War Veterans Assn., South Suburban Chap. [2880], Orland Park, IL
Korean War Veterans Assn., Southeastern Indiana No. 4 Chap. [4147], Aurora, IN
Korean War Veterans Assn., Tri-State Chap. [15080], East Liverpool, OH
Korean War Veterans Assn., West Central Wisconsin Chap. [18350], La Crosse, WI
Korean War Veterans Assn., Western Ohio Chap. [16432], Piqua, OH
Korean War Veterans Assn., William J. Sanpozzi Chap. [16614], Sandusky, OH
Kosciusko AIFA [6444], Warsaw, IN
Kosciusko Bd. of Realtors [6445], Warsaw, IN
Kosciusko County Convention and Visitors Bur. [6446], Warsaw, IN
Kosciusko County Historical Soc. [6447], Warsaw, IN
Kosciusko County Jail Museum [★6447]
Kosko Conservation [6448], Warsaw, IN
Kouts Chamber of Commerce [5592], Kouts, IN
KYOVA Morgan Horse Assn. [15727], Loveland, OH

L

La Crescent Chamber of Commerce [11266], La Crescent, MN
La Crosse AFL-CIO Central Labor Coun. [★18381]
La Crosse AFL-CIO Coun. [★18381]
La Crosse Area Astronomical Soc. [18351], La Crosse, WI
La Crosse Area Builders Assn. [19365], Onalaska, WI
La Crosse Area Chamber of Commerce [18352], La Crosse, WI
La Crosse Area Convention and Visitors Bur. [18353], La Crosse, WI
La Crosse Area Development Corp. [18354], La Crosse, WI
La Crosse Area Home Builders [★19365]
La Crosse Area Realtors Assn. [18355], La Crosse, WI
La Crosse Builders Exchange [18356], La Crosse, WI
La Crosse County Historical Soc. [18357], La Crosse, WI
La Crosse District Nurses Assn. [17737], Chaseburg, WI
La Crosse Educ. Assn. [18358], La Crosse, WI
La Crosse Kiwanis Club [18359], La Crosse, WI
La Crosse Lions Club [18360], La Crosse, WI
La Crosse North Lions Club [18361], La Crosse, WI
La Crosse Scenic Bluffs Chap. of the Amer. Theatre Organ Soc. [18362], La Crosse, WI
La Crosse Scenic Bluffs Chap. of the Amer. Theatre Organ Soc. [18363], La Crosse, WI
La Crosse Velo Club [18364], La Crosse, WI
La Farge Lions Club [18384], La Farge, WI
La Leche League Northside of Evansville [4558], Evansville, IN
La Leche League of Warrick County [★4558]
La Porte County 4-H Coun. [5597], La Porte, IN
La Rue Lions Club [15576], La Rue, OH
Labor
  Ohio Public Employer Labor Relations Assn. [15397], Hamilton, OH
Labor, AFL-CIO; South Central Fed. of [18619], Madison, WI
Labor Coun; Dane County [★18619]
Labor Coun. for Latin Amer. Advancement - Oakland County Chap. [7386], Detroit, MI
Labor Coun; Traverse Bay Area Central [9957], Traverse City, MI
Labor and Employment Relations Assn. [535], Champaign, IL
Labor and Employment Relations Assn., Central Ohio [14490], Columbus, OH
Labor and Employment Relations Assn., Chicago [1016], Chicago, IL
Labor and Employment Relations Assn., Mid - Michigan [8585], Lansing, MI
Labor and Employment Relations Assn. - Northeast Ohio Chap. [15501], Independence, OH
Labor and Employment Relations Assn., Wisconsin [18005], Fox Point, WI
Labor; Madison Fed. of [★18619]
Labor Management
  Labor Coun. for Latin Amer. Advancement - Oakland County Chap. [7386], Detroit, MI

Labor Mgt. Partnership of Mid-Michigan [8586], Lansing, MI
Labor Mgt. Partnership of Mid-Michigan [8586], Lansing, MI
Labor; Quad City Illinois and Iowa Fed. of [3255], Rock Island, IL
Labor Relations Assn; Ohio Public Employer [15397], Hamilton, OH
Labor; Sauk County Fed. of [★18619]
Labor Studies
Labor and Employment Relations Assn., Central Ohio [14490], Columbus, OH
Labor and Employment Relations Assn., Chicago [1016], Chicago, IL
Labor and Employment Relations Assn., Mid - Michigan [8585], Lansing, MI
Labor and Employment Relations Assn. - Northeast Ohio Chap. [15501], Independence, OH
Labor and Employment Relations Assn., Wisconsin [18005], Fox Point, WI
Labor Unions
Assoc. Firefighters of Illinois [3534], Springfield, IL
Labor and Employment Relations Assn. [535], Champaign, IL
Michigan State AFL-CIO [8719], Lansing, MI
Michigan State Employees Assn. [8721], Lansing, MI
Milwaukee Police Assn. [19066], Milwaukee, WI
Musicians AFM, LU 166 - AFL-CIO [18567], Madison, WI
Teamsters for a Democratic Union [7441], Detroit, MI
Univ. of Toledo Police Patrolman's Assn. [16980], Toledo, OH
Laboratory
Clinical Lab. Mgt. Assn., Chicago Chap. [69], Arlington Heights, IL
Clinical Lab. Mgt. Assn., Greater Indiana Chap. [5712], Madison, IN
Clinical Lab. Mgt. Assn., Minnesota Chap. [11547], Minneapolis, MN
Clinical Lab. Mgt. Assn., Six Rivers Chap. [15985], Miamisburg, OH
Clinical Lab. Mgt. Assn. of Wisconsin [18094], Green Bay, WI
Michigan Soc. for Clinical Lab. Sci. [6838], Bath, MI
Lab. Sci; Michigan Soc. for Clinical [6838], Bath, MI
Laborers AFL-CIO, LU 355 [6861], Battle Creek, MI
Labrador Retriever Club of the Twin Cities [10472], Bloomington, MN
Lac Du Flambeau Chamber of Commerce [18389], Lac Du Flambeau, WI
Lac Lawrann Conservancy of West Bend, WI [20122], West Bend, WI
Lac Qui Parle County Ser. Unit, Amer. Red Cross [12289], St. Cloud, MN
LaCrescent Lions Club [11267], La Crescent, MN
Lacrosse
Grosse Pointe Lacrosse Assn. [8089], Grosse Pointe Farms, MI
Lacrosse Club of Pike Township [5389], Indianapolis, IN
Lacrosse Area Communications Consortium [18365], La Crosse, WI
Lacrosse Assn; Grosse Pointe [8089], Grosse Pointe Farms, MI
Lacrosse Club of Pike Township [5389], Indianapolis, IN
Lafayette Lions Club, IN [5620], Lafayette, IN
Lafayette Regional Assn. of Realtors [5621], Lafayette, IN
Lafayette - West Lafayette Chamber of Commerce [5622], Lafayette, IN
Lafayette - West Lafayette Convention and Visitors Bur. [5623], Lafayette, IN
Lafayette - West Lafayette Economic Development Corp. [5624], Lafayette, IN
Lagos Grandes Peruvian Horse Club [7090], Carson City, MI
Lagrange County Cancer Soc. [5640], Lagrange, IN
Lagrange County Chamber of Commerce [5641], Lagrange, IN
LaGrange Lions Club - Ohio [15115], Elyria, OH
LaGrange - Wyldlife [3961], Western Springs, IL
Laingsburg Lions Club [8497], Laingsburg, MI
Laingsburg Pioneer Cheerleaders [8498], Laingsburg, MI
Lake Ann Lions Club [8502], Lake Ann, MI
Lake Area Habitat for Humanity [10512], Brainerd, MN
Lake Area United Way, Indiana [4858], Griffith, IN
Lake Benton Area Chamber of Commerce and Convention and Visitors Bur. [11270], Lake Benton, MN
Lake Bronson Lions Club [11272], Lake Bronson, MN
Lake Carriers' Assn. [14153], Cleveland, OH
Lake Chapeau Habitat Comm. [10259], Albert Lea, MN
Lake City Area Chamber of Commerce [8506], Lake City, MI
Lake City Area Chamber of Commerce [11275], Lake City, MN
Lake City Lions Club [11276], Lake City, MN
Lake City Yacht Club [12437], St. Paul, MN
Lake Country Retriever Club [12050], Prior Lake, MN
Lake County Audubon Soc. [2261], Libertyville, IL
Lake County Bar Assn. [4432], Crown Point, IN
Lake County Chamber of Commerce [1921], Gurnee, IL
Lake County Coin Club [3926], Waukegan, IL
Lake County Contractors Assn. [3927], Waukegan, IL
Lake County Convention and Visitors Bur. [4885], Hammond, IN
Lake County Democratic Party [15968], Mentor, OH
Lake County Gem and Mineral Soc. [1900], Great Lakes, IL
Lake County Historical Soc. [4433], Crown Point, IN
Lake County Historical Soc. [12771], Two Harbors, MN
Lake County Historical Soc. [15574], Kirtland Hills, OH
Lake County Illinois Convention and Visitors Bur. [1922], Gurnee, IL
Lake County Illinois Genealogical Soc. [2614], Mundelein, IL
Lake County Medical Soc. - Illinois [2199], Lake Forest, IL
Lake County Medical Soc. - Indiana [5772], Merrillville, IN
Lake County Medical Soc. - Ohio [17257], Wickliffe, OH
Lake County Merry Makers [8305], Idlewild, MI
Lake County Philatelic Soc. [1923], Gurnee, IL
Lake County Planning Commn. [16335], Painesville, OH
Lake County Public Library Staff Association [5773], Merrillville, IN
Lake County REACT Team [4886], Hammond, IN
Lake County Right to Life [4916], Highland, IN
Lake County RSVP [3928], Waukegan, IL
Lake Crystal Area Chamber of Commerce [11278], Lake Crystal, MN
Lake Delton Lions Club [20177], Wisconsin Dells, WI
Lake Elmo Jaycees [11281], Lake Elmo, MN
Lake Elmo Minnesota Lions Club [11282], Lake Elmo, MN
Lake Erie Assn., USA Track and Field [16372], Parma, OH
Lake Erie District Amateur Athletic Union [16680], Solon, OH
Lake Forest - Lake Bluff Chamber of Commerce [2200], Lake Forest, IL
Lake and Geauga Area Assn. of Realtors [15969], Mentor, OH
Lake and Geauga County Fed. of Musicians - Local 657, Amer. Fed. of Musicians [17283], Willowick, OH
Lake-Geauga Helicopter Assn. [16526], Richmond Heights, OH
Lake Gogebic Area Chamber of Commerce [6927], Bergland, MI
Lake to Lake Bed and Breakfast Assn. [★8128]
Lake Mgt. Soc; Ohio [15544], Kent, OH
Lake Michigan Air and Waste Mgt. Assn. [2918], Palatine, IL
Lake Michigan Coll. Educ. Assn. [6920], Benton Harbor, MI
Lake Michigan Fed. [★604]
Lake Michigan Fed. [★7851]
Lake Mills Area Chamber of Commerce [18403], Lake Mills, WI
Lake Mills Lions Club [18404], Lake Mills, WI
Lake Minnetonka Chamber of Commerce [11858], Navarre, MN
Lake Region Assn. of Realtors [10998], Fergus Falls, MN
Lake Shore African Violet Soc. [1666], Evanston, IL
Lake Shore Corvette Club [16615], Sandusky, OH
Lake Shore Optometric Soc. [19588], Random Lake, WI
Lake Shore Sail Club [9660], St. Clair Shores, MI
Lake Sta. Chamber of Commerce [5644], Lake Station, IN
Lake Superior AIFA [10830], Duluth, MN
Lake Superior Community Partnership; Marquette Area Chamber of Commerce- [8938], Marquette, MI
Lake Superior Medical Soc. [10831], Duluth, MN
Lake Superior Pointing Dog Club [12761], Twig, MN
Lake Township Chamber of Commerce [15411], Hartville, OH
Lake Traverse Assn. Corp. [12885], Wheaton, MN
Lake Vermilion Area Chamber of Commerce [12755], Tower, MN
Lake View Cemetery Assn. [14154], Cleveland, OH
Lake View East Chamber of Commerce [1017], Chicago, IL
Lake Winnebago Optometric Soc. [19356], Omro, WI
Lake Wisconsin Chamber of Commerce [19524], Poynette, WI
Lake of the Woods Tourism [10387], Baudette, MN
Lake Zurich Area Chamber of Commerce [2209], Lake Zurich, IL
Lake Zurich Commercial Club [★2209]
Lakeland Audubon Soc. [19918], Twin Lakes, WI
Lakeland Valley District Dental Soc. [7209], Coloma, MI
Lakes
Alliance for the Great Lakes [7851], Grand Haven, MI
Cedar Lakes Conservation Found. [18989], Milwaukee, WI
Illinois Lake Mgt. Assn. [3608], Springfield, IL
Indiana Lake Mgt. Soc. [4125], Angola, IN
Michigan Chap. of NALMS [9684], St. Joseph, MI
Minnesota Lakes Assn. [10514], Brainerd, MN
Natl. Wildlife Fed. - Great Lakes Natural Rsrc. Center [6748], Ann Arbor, MI
Ohio Lake Mgt. Soc. [15544], Kent, OH
Wisconsin Assn. of Lakes [18659], Madison, WI
Lakes Area Builders Assn. [10774], Detroit Lakes, MN
Lakes Area Chamber of Commerce [10056], Walled Lake, MI
Lakes Area Chamber of Commerce; Alexandria [10271], Alexandria, MN
Lakes Area Realtors Assn. [17929], Elkhorn, WI
Lakes Area Violet Growers [12438], St. Paul, MN
Lakes Area Young Life [10775], Detroit Lakes, MN
Lakes Assn; Minnesota [10514], Brainerd, MN
Lakes Commn; Great [6701], Ann Arbor, MI
Lakes Country Assn. of Realtors [10776], Detroit Lakes, MN
Lakes Country Chamber of Commerce [★18408]
Lakes Curling Club [10777], Detroit Lakes, MN
Lakes Historical Soc; Great [17065], Vermilion, OH
Lakes Indian Fish and Wildlife Commn; Great [19353], Odanah, WI
Lakeshore AIFA [18778], Manitowoc, WI
Lakeshore Area Human Rsrcs. Assn. [18779], Manitowoc, WI
Lakeshore Beagle Club [17766], Cleveland, WI
Lakeshore Chamber of Commerce [4887], Hammond, IN
Lakeshore Chamber of Commerce [9875], Stevensville, MI
Lakeshore Convention and Visitors Bur. [★9766]
Lakeshore Corvette Club [10227], Zeeland, MI
Lakeshore District Nurses Assn. - No. 12 [19929], Valders, WI
Lakeshore Estate Planning Coun. [18780], Manitowoc, WI
Lakeshore Human Rsrcs. Mgt. Assn. [8206], Holland, MI

Lakeshore Humane Soc. **[18781]**, Manitowoc, WI
Lakeshore Lung Soc. **[9145]**, Muskegon, MI
Lakeshore Pembroke Welsh Corgi Club **[8094]**, Gwinn, MI
Lakeshore - Young Life **[9683]**, St. Joseph, MI
Lakeshore Youth for Christ **[9146]**, Muskegon, MI
Lakeview Action Coalition **[1018]**, Chicago, IL
Lakeview Area Chamber of Commerce **[8518]**, Lakeview, MI
Lakeview Chamber of Commerce **[★1017]**
Lakeview Chamber of Commerce **[★8518]**
Lakeview Lions Club - Michigan **[8519]**, Lakeview, MI
Lakeville HS - Young Life **[10593]**, Burnsville, MN
Lakewood Area Chamber of Commerce **[18408]**, Lakewood, WI
Lakewood Chamber of Commerce **[15586]**, Lakewood, OH
Lakewood Historical Soc. **[15587]**, Lakewood, OH
Lakewood Wyldlife **[17230]**, Westlake, OH
Lakota East - Young Life **[15162]**, Fairfield, OH
Lakota Thunderbird Youth Basketball **[13882]**, Cincinnati, OH
Lakota West - Young Life **[15163]**, Fairfield, OH
Lambda Car Club, Detroit Region **[9585]**, Royal Oak, MI
Lamoine Valley Angus Assn. **[3094]**, Pittsfield, IL
Lamoine Valley Assn. of Realtors **[2370]**, Macomb, IL
Lamplighter's Civic and Social Org. **[17321]**, Wooster, OH
Lancaster Area Chamber of Commerce **[18411]**, Lancaster, WI
Lancaster Area Soc. for Human Rsrc. Mgt. **[15602]**, Lancaster, OH
Lancaster Bd. of Realtors **[15603]**, Lancaster, OH
Lancaster Chamber of Commerce **[★18411]**
Lancaster Fairfield County Chamber of Commerce **[15604]**, Lancaster, OH
Lancaster Lions Club - Minnesota **[11300]**, Lancaster, MN
Lancaster Sertoma Club **[15605]**, Lancaster, OH
Land of Blackhawk Chap. of the United Way **[★18001]**
Land Conservancy; Trillium **[4507]**, Elkhart, IN
Land Conservancy; Walworth County **[17931]**, Elkhorn, WI
Land Conservancy of West Michigan **[7974]**, Grand Rapids, MI
Land Control
Milwaukee Area Land Conservancy **[18171]**, Hales Corners, WI
Orland Park Open Lands Corp. **[2884]**, Orland Park, IL
Shaw Land Conservancy **[16046]**, Minerva, OH
Land Info. Access Assn. **[9936]**, Traverse City, MI
Land of Lincoln Horseshoer's Assn. No. 30 **[2389]**, Mansfield, IL
Land of Lincoln Thunderbirds **[2083]**, Jacksonville, IL
Land O' Lakes Theatre Organ Soc. **[12232]**, Roseville, MN
Land O'Lakes Chamber of Commerce **[18415]**, Land O' Lakes, WI
Land Surveyors Assn; Illinois Professional **[3230]**, Rochester, IL
Land Trust; Acres **[4619]**, Fort Wayne, IN
Landlords; St. Paul Assn. of Responsible **[12576]**, St. Paul, MN
Landmarks Preservation Coun. of Illinois **[1019]**, Chicago, IL
Landscape Assn; Minnesota Nursery and **[12501]**, St. Paul, MN
Landscape Assn; Ohio Nursery and **[17217]**, Westerville, OH
Landscapers Assn; Ohio **[★13429]**
Landscaping
Assoc. Landscape Contractors of Am., Cincinnati State Tech. and Community Coll. **[13749]**, Cincinnati, OH
Assoc. Landscape Contractors of Am., Columbus State Community Coll. **[14319]**, Columbus, OH
Assoc. Landscape Contractors of Am., Cuyahoga Community Coll. **[15420]**, Highland Hills, OH
Assoc. Landscape Contractors of Am., Dakota County Tech. Coll. **[12214]**, Rosemount, MN
Assoc. Landscape Contractors of Am., Illinois Central Coll. **[3007]**, Peoria, IL
Assoc. Landscape Contractors of Am., Joliet Junior Coll. **[2100]**, Joliet, IL
Assoc. Landscape Contractors of Am., Michigan State Univ. Horticulture Club **[7508]**, East Lansing, MI
Assoc. Landscape Contractors of Am., Milwaukee Area Tech. Coll. **[18884]**, Mequon, WI
Assoc. Landscape Contractors of Am., Ohio State Univ. **[14320]**, Columbus, OH
Assoc. Landscape Contractors of Am., Ohio State Univ./Agricultural Tech. Inst. **[17315]**, Wooster, OH
Assoc. Landscape Contractors of Am., Parkland Coll. **[500]**, Champaign, IL
Assoc. Landscape Contractors of Am., Purdue Univ. **[6476]**, West Lafayette, IN
Illinois Chap. of the Amer. Soc. of Landscape Architects **[2776]**, Oak Brook, IL
Illinois Landscape Contractors Assn. **[2777]**, Oak Brook, IL
Indiana Chap. of the Amer. Soc. of Landscape Architects **[5207]**, Indianapolis, IN
Michigan Chap. of the Amer. Soc. of Landscape Architects **[8640]**, Lansing, MI
Michigan Nursery and Landscape Assn. **[9286]**, Okemos, MI
Minnesota Chap. of the Amer. Soc. of Landscape Architects **[11635]**, Minneapolis, MN
Ohio Landscape Assn. **[13429]**, Broadview Heights, OH
Ohio Nursery and Landscape Assn. **[17217]**, Westerville, OH
Wisconsin Landscape Contractors Assn. **[20012]**, Waukesha, WI
Wisconsin Landscape Federation **[18161]**, Greenfield, WI
Lane Middle School - Wyldlife **[4687]**, Fort Wayne, IN
Lane Tech - Young Life **[1020]**, Chicago, IL
Lanesboro Lions Club **[11302]**, Lanesboro, MN
Language
Amer. Assn. of Teachers of Spanish and Portuguese - Chicago Chap. **[612]**, Chicago, IL
Language-Hearing Assn; Michigan Speech- **[7549]**, East Lansing, MI
Language-Hearing Assn; Minnesota Speech- **[12337]**, St. Louis Park, MN
Lansing Area AIDS Network **[8587]**, Lansing, MI
Lansing Black Lawyers Assn. **[8588]**, Lansing, MI
Lansing Chamber of Commerce **[2220]**, Lansing, IL
Lansing Delta Lions Club **[8589]**, Lansing, MI
Lansing Host Lions Club **[8590]**, Lansing, MI
Lansing Junior Woman's Club **[2221]**, Lansing, IL
Lansing Neighborhood Coun. **[8591]**, Lansing, MI
Lansing REACT **[8592]**, Lansing, MI
Lansing Regional Chamber of Commerce **[8593]**, Lansing, MI
Lansing Skating Club **[7526]**, East Lansing, MI
Lansing Youth for Christ **[8594]**, Lansing, MI
Lapeer Area Chamber of Commerce **[8776]**, Lapeer, MI
Lapeer Area Citizens Against Domestic Assault **[8777]**, Lapeer, MI
Lapeer County Alliance for the Mentally Ill **[7211]**, Columbiaville, MI
Lapeer County Community Mental Hea. Sers. **[8778]**, Lapeer, MI
Lapeer Development Corp. **[8779]**, Lapeer, MI
Lapeer and Upper Thumb Assn. of Realtors **[8780]**, Lapeer, MI
LaPorte County Assn. of Realtors **[5598]**, La Porte, IN
LaPorte County Convention and Visitors Bur. **[5785]**, Michigan City, IN
LaSalle St. Young Lives - YoungLives **[1021]**, Chicago, IL
Late Bloomers African Violet Soc. **[17996]**, Footville, WI
Lathers Elementary School PTA **[7813]**, Garden City, MI
Latin
Latin Liturgy Assn. **[16547]**, Rocky River, OH
Latin American
New Latino Visions **[8459]**, Kalamazoo, MI
Latin Liturgy Assn. **[16547]**, Rocky River, OH
Latino Faculty and Staff Coun; IUB **[4238]**, Bloomington, IN
Latino Visions; New **[8459]**, Kalamazoo, MI
Lauj Youth Soc. of Minnesota **[12439]**, St. Paul, MN
Laundry
Illinois Coin Laundry Assn. **[1609]**, Elk Grove Village, IL
Michigan Coin Laundry Assn. **[8183]**, Hillsdale, MI
Michigan Inst. of Laundering and Drycleaning **[8677]**, Lansing, MI
Minnesota Coin Laundry Assn. **[12469]**, St. Paul, MN
Ohio Coin Laundry Assn. **[17108]**, Warren, OH
Wisconsin Self-Service Laundry Assn. **[17685]**, Brookfield, WI
Laundry Assn; Coin **[1500]**, Downers Grove, IL
Laundry and Cleaning Coun; Midwest Automatic **[★1500]**
Laurel and Hardy
Dancing Cuckoos, Metropolitan Detroit Tent of the Intl. Sons of the Desert **[7063]**, Canton, MI
Laurentian Chamber of Commerce **[12795]**, Virginia, MN
Laurentian Rsrc. Conservation and Development Coun. **[10832]**, Duluth, MN
Laurentian Shield Resources for Nonviolence **[18795]**, Maple, WI
Law
Asian Amer. Bar Assn. of the Greater Chicago Area **[736]**, Chicago, IL
Asian Amer. Bar Assn. of Michigan **[7324]**, Detroit, MI
Asian Amer. Bar Assn. of Ohio **[14074]**, Cleveland, OH
Assn. of Legal Administrators, Cleveland Chap. **[14079]**, Cleveland, OH
Assn. of Legal Administrators, Columbus Chap. **[14327]**, Columbus, OH
Assn. of Legal Administrators, Cyber Chap. **[3008]**, Peoria, IL
Black Lawyers Assn. of Cincinnati **[13760]**, Cincinnati, OH
Greater Chicago Chap. of the Assn. of Legal Administrators **[3987]**, Wheaton, IL
Indiana Chap., Assn. of Legal Administrators **[5208]**, Indianapolis, IN
John Mercer Langston Bar Assn. **[14480]**, Columbus, OH
Michigan Natl. Lawyers Guild **[7398]**, Detroit, MI
Minnesota Legal Administrators Assn. **[11654]**, Minneapolis, MN
Minnesota State Bar Assn. **[11674]**, Minneapolis, MN
Natl. Asian Pacific Amer. Bar Assn. - Minnesota Chap. **[11691]**, Minneapolis, MN
Norman S. Minor Bar Assn. **[14178]**, Cleveland, OH
Northwest Ohio Chap. of the Assn. of Legal Administrators **[16940]**, Toledo, OH
Thurgood Marshall Law Soc. **[14962]**, Dayton, OH
Wisconsin Assn. of Legal Administrators **[19298]**, New Berlin, WI
Law Enforcement
Buckeye State Sheriff's Assn. **[14345]**, Columbus, OH
Chicago Police Women's Assn. **[823]**, Chicago, IL
Fraternal Order of Police, Illinois State Lodge **[3552]**, Springfield, IL
Fraternal Order of Police Lodge 86 **[5119]**, Indianapolis, IN
Fraternal Order of Police, Michigan State Lodge **[8568]**, Lansing, MI
Fraternal Order of Police, Minnesota State Lodge **[11060]**, Golden Valley, MN
Fraternal Order of Police, Wisconsin State Lodge **[18098]**, Green Bay, WI
Hancock County Sheriff Reserve Deputy Corps **[466]**, Carthage, IL
Illinois Assn. of Chiefs of Police **[3567]**, Springfield, IL
Illinois Police Assn. **[1632]**, Elmwood Park, IL
Illinois Sheriffs Association **[3470]**, Sherman, IL
Indiana Assn. of Chiefs of Police **[5166]**, Indianapolis, IN
Indiana Chap. of the Natl. Assn. of Drug Diversion Investigators **[5210]**, Indianapolis, IN
Indiana Sheriffs' Assn. **[5297]**, Indianapolis, IN
Intl. Assn. of Women Police, Region 6 **[4883]**, Hammond, IN

Intl. Union of Police Assns., AFL-CIO - Illinois Coun. of Police and Sherif Local Union 7 **[1625]**, Elmhurst, IL
Marquette Professional Police Off.rs Assn. **[8948]**, Marquette, MI
Marshall County Mounted Posse **[12841]**, Warren, MN
Michigan Assn. of Chiefs of Police **[9272]**, Okemos, MI
Michigan Fraternal Order of Police **[8667]**, Lansing, MI
Michigan Sheriffs' Assn. **[8712]**, Lansing, MI
Midwest Enval. Enforcement Assn. **[3389]**, St. Charles, IL
Minnesota Assn. of Law Enforcement Firearms Instructors **[12157]**, Rochester, MN
Minnesota Assn. of Women Police **[12460]**, St. Paul, MN
Natl. Assn. of Drug Diversion Investigators of Ohio **[16514]**, Reynoldsburg, OH
Natl. Org. of Black Law Enforcement Executives, Central Illinois Land of Lincoln Chap. **[3830]**, Urbana, IL
Natl. Org. of Black Law Enforcement Executives, Chicago Metropolitan Chap. **[1086]**, Chicago, IL
Natl. Org. of Black Law Enforcement Executives, Greater Cincinnati Chap. **[13929]**, Cincinnati, OH
Natl. Org. of Black Law Enforcement Executives, Northern Illinois Chap. **[124]**, Aurora, IL
Natl. Org. of Black Law Enforcement Executives, Northern Indiana Chap. **[4783]**, Gary, IN
Natl. Org. of Black Law Enforcement Executives, Southern Indiana Chap. **[5429]**, Indianapolis, IN
Ohio Assn. of Chiefs of Police **[15053]**, Dublin, OH
Ohio Women's Law Enforcement Network **[14700]**, Columbus, OH
Warrenville Firemen **[3880]**, Warrenville, IL
Wisconsin Assn. of Women Police **[18668]**, Madison, WI
Wisconsin Professional Police Assn. **[18744]**, Madison, WI
Law Enforcement Administrators; Minnesota Chap. of Intl. Assn. of Campus **[12615]**, St. Peter, MN
Law Enforcement Executives, Northern Indiana Chap; Natl. Org. of Black **[4783]**, Gary, IN
Law Enforcement Firearms Instructors; Minnesota Assn. of **[12157]**, Rochester, MN
Law Libraries; Ohio Regional Assn. of **[14941]**, Dayton, OH
Law Soc; Indiana Univ. - Environmental **[4233]**, Bloomington, IN
Lawndale Christian Development Corp. **[1022]**, Chicago, IL
Lawrence County Chamber of Commerce **[2225]**, Lawrenceville, IL
Lawrence County Genealogical Soc., OGS Chap. 74 **[16483]**, Proctorville, OH
Lawrence County Homebuilders Association **[4173]**, Bedford, IN
Lawrence County Humane Soc. **[★4179]**
Lawrenceburg Lions Club **[5659]**, Lawrenceburg, IN
Laws, Illinois Chap; Natl. Org. for Reform of Marijuana **[1087]**, Chicago, IL
Lawton Lions Club **[8793]**, Lawton, MI
Lawyers Assn; Michigan Trial **[8723]**, Lansing, MI
Lawyers' Comm. for Better Housing **[1023]**, Chicago, IL
Lawyers; Illinois Assn. of Criminal Defense **[927]**, Chicago, IL
Lawyers Intl. Human Rights Comm; Minnesota **[★11621]**
Lawyers; Ohio Acad. of Trial **[14535]**, Columbus, OH
Leader Area Lions Club **[12784]**, Verndale, MN
Leadership
Hugh O'Brian Youth Leadership of Michigan **[7261]**, Dearborn, MI
Inroads, Indiana **[5368]**, Indianapolis, IN
INROADS, St. Paul, Minnesota **[12426]**, St. Paul, MN
Leadership Medina County **[15943]**, Medina, OH
Leadership Fort Wayne **[4688]**, Fort Wayne, IN
Leadership Medina County **[15943]**, Medina, OH
Leadership; Wisconsin Women in Higher Educ. **[19188]**, Milwaukee, WI
Leaf River Area, Habitat For Humanity **[12821]**, Wadena, MN
League for the Blind and Disabled **[4689]**, Fort Wayne, IN
League of Illinois Bicyclists **[123]**, Aurora, IL
League of Michigan Bicyclists **[8595]**, Lansing, MI
League of Minnesota Cities **[12440]**, St. Paul, MN
League of Professionally Managed Theaters **[5390]**, Indianapolis, IN
League of Wisconsin Municipalities **[18540]**, Madison, WI
League of Women Voters in the Akron Area **[13063]**, Akron, OH
League of Women Voters of Champaign County **[3827]**, Urbana, IL
League of Women Voters of Chicago **[1024]**, Chicago, IL
League of Women Voters of the Cincinnati Area **[13883]**, Cincinnati, OH
League of Women Voters of the Cleveland Area **[14155]**, Cleveland, OH
League of Women Voters of Cook County **[1025]**, Chicago, IL
League of Women Voters of Cuyahoga County **[14156]**, Cleveland, OH
League of Women Voters of the Elgin Area **[1595]**, Elgin, IL
League of Women Voters of Evanston **[1667]**, Evanston, IL
League of Women Voters of Glen Ellyn **[1837]**, Glen Ellyn, IL
League of Women Voters of the Greater Dayton Area **[14904]**, Dayton, OH
League of Women Voters of Highland Park **[1993]**, Highland Park, IL
League of Women Voters of Illinois **[1026]**, Chicago, IL
League of Women Voters of Illinois Education Fund **[★1026]**
League of Women Voters of Janesville **[18255]**, Janesville, WI
League of Women Voters - Lake Erie Basin Comm. **[17274]**, Willoughby, OH
League of Women Voters, Lansing Area **[★8596]**
League of Women Voters of the Lansing Area **[8596]**, Lansing, MI
League of Women Voters of Michigan **[8597]**, Lansing, MI
League of Women Voters of Minneapolis **[11596]**, Minneapolis, MN
League of Women Voters of Ohio **[14491]**, Columbus, OH
Learning Disabilities Assn. of Illinois **[2940]**, Palos Hills, IL
Learning Disabilities Assn. of Michigan **[8598]**, Lansing, MI
Learning Disabilities Assn. of Wisconsin **[17672]**, Brookfield, WI
Learning Disabled
Learning Disabilities Assn. of Illinois **[2940]**, Palos Hills, IL
Learning Disabilities Assn. of Michigan **[8598]**, Lansing, MI
Learning Disabilities Assn. of Wisconsin **[17672]**, Brookfield, WI
Learning Society of Elkhart **[★4805]**
Learning Society of Elkhart/Views on Learning **[★4805]**
Lebanon Area Chamber of Commerce **[15621]**, Lebanon, OH
Lebanon Cedar Cruisers **[2678]**, New Baden, IL
Lebanon Chamber of Commerce **[2231]**, Lebanon, IL
Lebanon Kiwanis **[5670]**, Lebanon, IN
Lebanon Lions Club - Ohio **[15622]**, Lebanon, OH
Lebanon - Young Life **[16010]**, Middletown, OH
Lee High School - Young Life **[8042]**, Grandville, MI
Leech Lake Area Chamber of Commerce **[12831]**, Walker, MN
Leelanau Conservancy **[8795]**, Leland, MI
Leelanau County Chamber of Commerce **[★9887]**
Leelanau Historical Museum **[★8796]**
Leelanau Historical Soc. and Museum **[8796]**, Leland, MI
Leelanau Peninsula Chamber of Commerce **[9887]**, Suttons Bay, MI
Leetonia-Washingtonville Area Chamber of Commerce **[15631]**, Leetonia, OH
Legal
Amer. Assn. of Legal Nurse Consultants, Cleveland/NEO Chap. **[13239]**, Avon, OH
Amer. Assn. of Legal Nurse Consultants, Greater Chicago Chap. **[609]**, Chicago, IL
Amer. Assn. of Legal Nurse Consultants, Greater Detroit Chap. **[8827]**, Livonia, MI
Amer. Assn. of Legal Nurse Consultants, Greater Indianapolis Chap. **[4973]**, Indianapolis, IN
Indiana Soc. for Hea.care Consumer Advocacy **[5733]**, Marion, IN
NALS of Michigan **[8453]**, Kalamazoo, MI
Soc. for Healthcare Consumer Advocacy of the Amer. Hosp. Assn. **[1189]**, Chicago, IL
Society for Healthcare Consumer Advocacy of the American Hospital Association **[4030]**, Winfield, IL
Soc. for Hea.care Consumer Advocacy of the Amer. Hosp. Assn., Wisconsin **[19217]**, Monroe, WI
Soc. for Hea.care Consumer Advocacy, Illinois **[3834]**, Urbana, IL
Soc. for Hea.care Consumer Advocacy, Indiana **[5744]**, Marion, IN
Legal Aid
Indiana First Judicial District Pro Bono Comm. **[4926]**, Hobart, IN
Legal Aid Soc. of Greater Cincinnati **[13884]**, Cincinnati, OH
Legal Aid Soc. of Greater Cincinnati **[13884]**, Cincinnati, OH
Legal Secretaries of Indiana **[5391]**, Indianapolis, IN
Legal Services
Legislative Reference Bur. - Wisconsin **[18541]**, Madison, WI
NALS of Illinois **[1064]**, Chicago, IL
Legion of the U.S., Michigan Commandery; Military Order of the Loyal **[8243]**, Holt, MI
Legislative Efforts for Animal Protection **[10914]**, Edina, MN
Legislative Reference Bur. - Wisconsin **[18541]**, Madison, WI
Leipsic Area Chamber of Commerce **[15633]**, Leipsic, OH
Lemont Area Chamber of Commerce **[2245]**, Lemont, IL
Lemont Junior Woman's Club **[2246]**, Lemont, IL
Lena Community Development Corp. **[18418]**, Lena, WI
Lenawee Community REACT **[6572]**, Adrian, MI
Lenawee County Assn. of Realtors **[6573]**, Adrian, MI
Lenawee County Chamber of Commerce **[6574]**, Adrian, MI
Lenawee County Chamber of Found. **[6575]**, Adrian, MI
Lenawee County Chap. of Natl. Alliance for the Mentally Ill **[6576]**, Adrian, MI
Lenawee County Conf. and Visitors Bur. **[6577]**, Adrian, MI
Lenawee County Medical Soc. **[9907]**, Tecumseh, MI
Lenawee Noon Lions Club **[6578]**, Adrian, MI
Lenawee United Way and Volunteer Center **[6579]**, Adrian, MI
Lending
Commercial Finance Assn., Mid-West Chap. **[853]**, Chicago, IL
Commercial Finance Assn., Ohio Chap. **[13286]**, Beachwood, OH
Wisconsin Financial Sers. Assn. **[18706]**, Madison, WI
Lennon Lions Club **[8798]**, Lennon, MI
Lepidopterology
North Amer. Butterfly Assn. - Northeastern Ohio **[15412]**, Hartville, OH
North Amer. Butterfly Association-Northern Crescents Chap. **[10844]**, Duluth, MN
Les Chefs de Cuisine of Greater Cincinnati **[13885]**, Cincinnati, OH
Lesbian Chamber of Commerce; Chicago Area Gay and **[783]**, Chicago, IL
Lesbian Community Services of Rochester; Gay/ **[12142]**, Rochester, MN
Lesbian/Gay Community Center of Greater Cleveland **[14157]**, Cleveland, OH
Lesbian Rsrc. Center; Kalamazoo Gay- **[8442]**, Kalamazoo, MI
Lesbian and Straight Educ. Network, Ann Arbor-Ypsilanti Area; Gay, **[6696]**, Ann Arbor, MI
Leslie Lions Club **[8802]**, Leslie, MI

Let Every Adult Read Now [★13082]
Let's Go Fishing of Minnesota [12918], Willmar, MN
Letters Comm., Chicago Chap; News and [1100], Chicago, IL
Letters; Michigan Acad. of Sci., Arts, and [6633], Alma, MI
Leukemia
Children's Leukemia Found. of Michigan [9795], Southfield, MI
Leukemia and Lymphoma Soc., Michigan Chap. [8895], Madison Heights, MI
Leukemia and Lymphoma Soc. of Am., Northern Ohio [14158], Cleveland, OH
Leukemia and Lymphoma Soc., Indiana Chap. [5392], Indianapolis, IN
Leukemia and Lymphoma Soc., Michigan Chap. [8895], Madison Heights, MI
Leukemia and Lymphoma Soc., Southern Ohio Chap. [13886], Cincinnati, OH
Leukemia Soc. of Am., Indiana [★5392]
Leukemia Soc. of Am. - Michigan Chap. [★8895]
Leukemia Soc. of Am., Northern Ohio [★14158]
Levy Cares [1027], Chicago, IL
Lewisburg Lions Club [15637], Lewisburg, OH
Lewiston Area Chamber of Commerce [8805], Lewiston, MI
Lewistown Chamber of Commerce [2250], Lewistown, IL
Lexington Lions Club - Ohio [15770], Mansfield, OH
LHS Key Club [5660], Lawrenceburg, IN
LHV Model Yacht Club No. 168 [4013], Willowbrook, IL
Libertarian Party of Chicago [1028], Chicago, IL
Libertarian Party of Illinois [1908], Greenville, IL
Libertarian Party of Indiana [5393], Indianapolis, IN
Libertarian Party of Lake County [2210], Lake Zurich, IL
Libertarian Party of Michigan [8599], Lansing, MI
Libertarian Party of Minnesota [12441], St. Paul, MN
Libertarian Party of Ohio [14492], Columbus, OH
Libertarian Party of Wisconsin [18157], Greenfield, WI
Liberty Benton Parent Teacher Org. [15205], Findlay, OH
Liberty - Union County Chamber of Commerce [5679], Liberty, IN
Libertyville Junior Woman's Club [2262], Libertyville, IL
Libertyville-Mundelein Historical Soc. [2263], Libertyville, IL
Libraries
Academic Lib. Assn. of Ohio [14267], Columbus, OH
Amer. Lib. Assn./Assoc. Lib. Sci. Students of Ohio, Kent State Univ. [15538], Kent, OH
Amer. Lib. Assn., Dominican Univ. [3199], River Forest, IL
Amer. Lib. Assn. Student Chap., Indiana Univ. [4198], Bloomington, IN
Amer. Lib. Assn., Student Chap., Univ. of Michigan School of Info. [6662], Ann Arbor, MI
Amer. Lib. Assn., Wayne State Univ. [7317], Detroit, MI
Art Libraries Soc. of North Am. - Midstates Chap. [4601], Fishers, IN
Art Libraries Soc. of North Am. - Ohio Valley [13196], Athens, OH
Art Libraries Soc. of North Am. - Twin Cities Chap. [11521], Minneapolis, MN
Assn. of Jewish Libraries - Cleveland (Greater Cleveland) [14244], Cleveland Heights, OH
Berrien Lib. Consortium [6935], Berrien Springs, MI
Central Minnesota Libraries Exchange [12281], St. Cloud, MN
Chicago Assn. of Law Libraries [788], Chicago, IL
Church and Synagogue Lib. Assn., Hibbing Church Lib. Network [11156], Hibbing, MN
Church and Synagogue Lib. Assn., Metro Detroit Chap. [7250], Dearborn, MI
Collinsville Memorial Public Lib. Found. [1289], Collinsville, IL
Coshocton Friends of the Lib. [14800], Coshocton, OH
Friends of the Athens Municipal Lib. [98], Athens, IL
Friends of the Franklin Public Lib. [18010], Franklin, WI
Friends of the Kraemer Lib. and Community Center [19460], Plain, WI
Friends of Lagrange County Lib. [5639], Lagrange, IN
Friends of the Liberty Center Public Lib. [15640], Liberty Center, OH
Friends of Michigan Libraries [8838], Livonia, MI
Friends of the Minneapolis Public Lib. [11565], Minneapolis, MN
Friends of the Mount Prospect Public Lib. [2585], Mount Prospect, IL
Friends of the New Glarus Public Lib. [19303], New Glarus, WI
Friends of the Paullin Lib. [15037], Doylestown, OH
Friends of the Town and Country Public Lib. [1580], Elburn, IL
Friends of Wisconsin Libraries [19884], Sussex, WI
Highland Park Public Lib. [1991], Highland Park, IL
Illinois Assn. of Coll. and Res. Libraries [926], Chicago, IL
Indiana Assn. of Coll. and Res. Libraries [6231], South Bend, IN
Indiana Lib. Fed. [5254], Indianapolis, IN
Indiana State Lib. and Historical Bur. Found. [5317], Indianapolis, IN
Michigan Lib. Assn. [8682], Lansing, MI
Minnesota Assn. of Lib. Friends [12456], St. Paul, MN
Minnesota Lib. Assn. [12493], St. Paul, MN
Mount Carmel Public Lib. Found. [2573], Mount Carmel, IL
North Country Lib. Cooperative [11852], Mountain Iron, MN
Northern Lights Lib. Network [10782], Detroit Lakes, MN
Ohio Educational Lib. Media Assn. [14601], Columbus, OH
Ohio Regional Assn. of Law Libraries [14941], Dayton, OH
Reed Memorial Lib. [16505], Ravenna, OH
Special Libraries Assn., Central Ohio Chap. [14739], Columbus, OH
Special Libraries Assn., Cincinnati Chap. [14003], Cincinnati, OH
Special Libraries Assn., Cleveland Chap. [13090], Akron, OH
Special Libraries Assn., Illinois Chap. [1198], Chicago, IL
Special Libraries Assn., Indiana Chap. [5482], Indianapolis, IN
Special Libraries Assn., Michigan Chap. [6772], Ann Arbor, MI
Special Libraries Assn., Michigan - Western/Upper Peninsula [476], Cary, IL
Special Libraries Assn., Minnesota Chap. [11751], Minneapolis, MN
Special Libraries Assn., Wisconsin Chap. [18621], Madison, WI
Urbana Free Lib. Found. [3840], Urbana, IL
Wayne Oakland Region of Interlibrary Cooperation [9831], Southfield, MI
Wisconsin Assn. of Academic Librarians [19152], Milwaukee, WI
Wisconsin Educational Media Assn. [17649], Boscobel, WI
Wisconsin Lib. Assn. [18720], Madison, WI
Wisconsin Lib. Services [18721], Madison, WI
Woodlands Lib. Cooperative [6594], Albion, MI
Libraries Exchange; Central Minnesota [12281], St. Cloud, MN
Libraries of Medicine, Greater Midwest Region; Natl. Network of [1085], Chicago, IL
Libraries; Ohio Regional Assn. of Law [14941], Dayton, OH
Lib. Assn; Illinois [946], Chicago, IL
Lib. Assn., Metro Detroit Chap; Church and Synagogue [7250], Dearborn, MI
Lib. Assn; Minnesota [12493], St. Paul, MN
Lib. and Community Center; Friends of the Kraemer [19460], Plain, WI
Lib. Consortium; Berrien [6935], Berrien Springs, MI
Library Cooperation; Wayne Oakland Region of Inter [9831], Southfield, MI
Lib. Cooperative; North Country [11852], Mountain Iron, MN
Lib. Cooperative; Woodlands [6594], Albion, MI
Lib. Coun. of Metropolitan Milwaukee [★19042]
Lib. Coun. of Southeastern Wisconsin [19042], Milwaukee, WI
Lib. Found; Mount Carmel Public [2573], Mount Carmel, IL
Lib; Friends of the [18239], Iron River, WI
Lib; Friends of the Franklin Public [18010], Franklin, WI
Lib; Friends of Lagrange County [5639], Lagrange, IN
Library; Friends of Les Cheneaux Community [8168], Hessel, MI
Lib; Friends of the Mount Prospect Public [2585], Mount Prospect, IL
Lib; Friends of the New Glarus Public [19303], New Glarus, WI
Lib; Friends of the Paullin [15037], Doylestown, OH
Lib; Friends of the Pontiac Public [9416], Pontiac, MI
Lib; Friends of Reed Memorial [★16505]
Lib; Friends of the Town and Country Public [1580], Elburn, IL
Lib; Highland Park Public [1991], Highland Park, IL
Lib. and Historical Bur. Found; Indiana State [5317], Indianapolis, IN
Lib. and Historical Soc; Hudson [15483], Hudson, OH
Lib; Madison County Historical Museum and [★1563]
Lib; McLean County Historical Soc. Museum and [★296]
Lib. Media Assn; Illinois School [404], Canton, IL
Lib. Network; Northern Lights [10782], Detroit Lakes, MN
Lib; Reed Memorial [16505], Ravenna, OH
Library Science
Illinois Lib. Assn. [946], Chicago, IL
Lake County Public Library Staff Association [5773], Merrillville, IN
Library Services; Wisconsin Inter [18717], Madison, WI
License Beverage Assn. [13887], Cincinnati, OH
Licensed Beverage Assn; Indiana [5255], Indianapolis, IN
Licensed Beverage Assn; Minnesota [12494], St. Paul, MN
Licensed Family Child Care Association of Morrison County [12065], Randall, MN
Licensed Practical Nurses Assn. of Illinois [1029], Chicago, IL
Licensed Practical Nurses Assn; Michigan [8683], Lansing, MI
Licking County Bd. of Realtors [16170], Newark, OH
Licking County Rock and Mineral Soc. [15344], Granville, OH
Licking County United Way [16171], Newark, OH
Licking-Knox AIFA [16085], Mount Vernon, OH
Life Center; Overflowing Cup Total [17615], Beloit, WI
Life Insurance Assn. of Michigan [8600], Lansing, MI
Life Services Network of Illinois [2021], Hinsdale, IL
Life Sers. Network of Illinois - Springfield [3647], Springfield, IL
Life Underwriters; Dayton Assn. of [★14870]
Life Underwriters; Indiana State Assn. of [★5176]
LifeCare Alliance [14493], Columbus, OH
Lighthouse Keepers Assn. [★8888]
Lighthouse Keepers Assn; Great Lakes [8888], Mackinaw City, MI
Lighthouse Restoration and Preservation Soc; Ashtabula [16231], North Kingsville, OH
Lighting
Intl. Dark-Sky Assn. - Minnesota [11274], Lake City, MN
Intl. Dark-Sky - Illinois At-Large Sect. [2588], Mount Prospect, IL
Intl. Dark-Sky - Illinois-Central [1644], Eureka, IL
Intl. Dark-Sky - Illinois-Chicago [988], Chicago, IL
Intl. Dark-Sky - Illinois-Northwest [1765], Galena, IL
Michigan Dark-Sky Assn. [8449], Kalamazoo, MI
Ligonier Chamber of Commerce [5681], Ligonier, IN
Lilies
Southwestern Indiana Daylily Soc. [4578], Evansville, IN
Lily Lake Elementary Parent Teacher Organization [12721], Stillwater, MN

Lima/Allen County Chamber of Commerce **[15658]**, Lima, OH
Lima Area Senior Olympics **[15659]**, Lima, OH
Lima Beagle Club **[15660]**, Lima, OH
Lima Exchange Club **[15661]**, Lima, OH
Lima Soc. for Human Rsrc. Mgt. **[15662]**, Lima, OH
Lima Soc. of Professional Photographers **[16579]**, St. Marys, OH
Limaville Lions Club **[13115]**, Alliance, OH
Lime City Development Corp. **[★4949]**
Limelight Players, Not-for-Profit **[204]**, Belleville, IL
Limestone Area Chamber of Commerce **[169]**, Bartonville, IL
Limestone Inst. of Am; Indiana **[4172]**, Bedford, IN
Limestone; Natl. Assn. for Indiana **[★4172]**
Lincoln Center Figure Skating Club **[4402]**, Columbus, IN
Lincoln County Economic Development Corp. **[18895]**, Merrill, WI
Lincoln High School Figure Skating Club **[12742]**, Thief River Falls, MN
Lincoln Hills Rsrc. Conservation and Development Coun. **[4314]**, Cannelton, IN
Lincoln Junior Woman's Club **[2275]**, Lincoln, IL
Lincoln - Logan County Chamber of Commerce **[2276]**, Lincoln, IL
Lincoln and Logan County Development Partnership **[2277]**, Lincoln, IL
Lincoln Orbit Earth Sci. Soc. **[3232]**, Rochester, IL
Lincoln Park Chamber of Commerce **[1030]**, Chicago, IL
Lincoln Park Chamber of Commerce **[8813]**, Lincoln Park, MI
Lincoln Park Lions Club - Michigan **[8814]**, Lincoln Park, MI
Lincoln Park Zoo **[1031]**, Chicago, IL
Lincoln Park Zoological Soc. **[★1031]**
Lincoln Prairie PTSA **[2038]**, Hoffman Estates, IL
Lincoln-Railsplitter REACT **[2278]**, Lincoln, IL
Lincolnwood Chamber of Commerce **[★2289]**
Lincolnwood Chamber of Commerce and Indus. **[2289]**, Lincolnwood, IL
Linden Argentine Chamber of Commerce **[8819]**, Linden, MI
Linden Lions Club - Michigan **[8820]**, Linden, MI
Lindenhurst - Lake Villa Chamber of Commerce **[2292]**, Lindenhurst, IL
Lindley Elementary PTA **[4690]**, Fort Wayne, IN
Lindsey Lions Club **[15675]**, Lindsey, OH
Lines West Buckeye Region Chap., Pennsylvania Railroad Tech. and Historical Soc. **[14494]**, Columbus, OH
Linton Chamber of Commerce **[★5684]**
Linton-Stockton Chamber of Commerce **[5684]**, Linton, IN
Lions Club of Alliance **[13116]**, Alliance, OH
Lions Club; Burlington **[17697]**, Burlington, WI
Lions Cricket Club **[12110]**, Richfield, MN
Lions Found; Glen Ellyn **[1831]**, Glen Ellyn, IL
Lisbon Area Chamber of Commerce **[15678]**, Lisbon, OH
Lisbon Lions Club - Ohio **[15679]**, Lisbon, OH
Lisle Chamber of Commerce **[2299]**, Lisle, IL
LISTEN for Life **[16098]**, Napoleon, OH
Litchfield Chamber of Commerce **[2307]**, Litchfield, IL
Litchfield Chamber of Commerce **[8824]**, Litchfield, MI
Litchfield Chamber of Commerce **[11328]**, Litchfield, MN
Litchfield Lions Club **[11329]**, Litchfield, MN
Literacy
  Br. County Literacy Coun. **[7198]**, Coldwater, MI
  Calumet Area Literacy Coun. **[4876]**, Hammond, IN
  Capital Area Literacy Coalition **[8557]**, Lansing, MI
  Carl Sanburg Coll. Literacy Coalition **[1769]**, Galesburg, IL
  Clark County Literacy Coalition **[16725]**, Springfield, OH
  Columbus Literacy Coun. **[14392]**, Columbus, OH
  Concerned Parents for Literacy **[9063]**, Monroe, MI
  Detroit Jewish Coalition for Literacy **[6983]**, Bloomfield Hills, MI
  Fox Valley Literacy Coalition **[17492]**, Appleton, WI
  Grant County Literacy Coun. **[5731]**, Marion, IN
  Greater Indianapolis Literacy League - Indy Reads **[5130]**, Indianapolis, IN
  Illinois Reading Coun. **[2718]**, Normal, IL
  Jefferson County Literacy Coun. **[18272]**, Jefferson, WI
  Kent County Literacy Coun. **[7972]**, Grand Rapids, MI
  Literacy Chicago **[1032]**, Chicago, IL
  Literacy Connection **[1596]**, Elgin, IL
  Literacy Coun. **[3287]**, Rockford, IL
  Literacy Council of Greater Waukesha **[19989]**, Waukesha, WI
  Literacy Coun. of Midland County **[9028]**, Midland, MI
  Literacy Coun. of Sheboygan County **[19699]**, Sheboygan, WI
  Literacy Services of Wisconsin **[19043]**, Milwaukee, WI
  Literacy Volunteers of Am.-Detroit **[7387]**, Detroit, MI
  Literacy Volunteers of DuPage **[2645]**, Naperville, IL
  Literacy Volunteers of Illinois **[1033]**, Chicago, IL
  Literacy Volunteers of Western Cook County **[2818]**, Oak Park, IL
  Macomb Literacy Partners **[7180]**, Clinton Township, MI
  Madison Area Literacy Coun. **[18546]**, Madison, WI
  Michigan Literacy **[9284]**, Okemos, MI
  Michigan Reading Assn. **[7982]**, Grand Rapids, MI
  Milwaukee Achiever Literacy Sers. **[19052]**, Milwaukee, WI
  Minnesota Literacy Coun. **[12495]**, St. Paul, MN
  Ohio Literacy Network **[14635]**, Columbus, OH
  Pickaway County Literacy Coun. **[14036]**, Circleville, OH
  Portage County Literacy Coun. **[19803]**, Stevens Point, WI
  Proj.: LEARN **[14207]**, Cleveland, OH
  Proj.: LEARN of Medina County **[15956]**, Medina, OH
  Proj.: LEARN of Summit County **[13082]**, Akron, OH
  Read To Learn **[79]**, Arlington Heights, IL
  Tazewell County S.T.A.R. (Student-Tutor-Adult Reading) **[2994]**, Pekin, IL
  Views on Learning/The Learning Society **[4805]**, Goshen, IN
  Washtenaw Literacy **[10218]**, Ypsilanti, MI
  Whitley County Literacy Coun. **[4386]**, Columbia City, IN
  Wisconsin State Reading Assn. **[19587]**, Randolph, WI
Literacy Chicago **[1032]**, Chicago, IL
Literacy Coalition; Clark County **[16725]**, Springfield, OH
Literacy; Concerned Parents for **[9063]**, Monroe, MI
Literacy Connection **[1596]**, Elgin, IL
Literacy Coun. **[3287]**, Rockford, IL
Literacy Coun; Calumet Area **[4876]**, Hammond, IN
Literacy Coun; Columbus **[14392]**, Columbus, OH
Literacy Council of Greater Waukesha **[19989]**, Waukesha, WI
Literacy Coun. of Medina County, Proj. Learn Prog. **[★15956]**
Literacy Coun. of Midland County **[9028]**, Midland, MI
Literacy Coun; Portage County **[19803]**, Stevens Point, WI
Literacy Coun. of Sheboygan County **[19699]**, Sheboygan, WI
Literacy; Grant County **[★5731]**
Literacy; Michigan **[9284]**, Okemos, MI
Literacy Services of Wisconsin **[19043]**, Milwaukee, WI
Literacy Volunteers of Am. - Central Du Page, Affl. **[★2645]**
Literacy Volunteers of Am., Chicago Chap. **[★1032]**
Literacy Volunteers of Am.-Detroit **[7387]**, Detroit, MI
Literacy Volunteers of Am. - Elgin Affl. **[★1596]**
Literacy Volunteers of DuPage **[2645]**, Naperville, IL
Literacy Volunteers of Illinois **[1033]**, Chicago, IL
Literacy Volunteers of Western Cook County **[2818]**, Oak Park, IL
Literacy; Washtenaw **[10218]**, Ypsilanti, MI
Literary Club; Detroit Telugu **[6977]**, Bloomfield, MI
Literary Guild; Univ. of Minnesota-Duluth **[10861]**, Duluth, MN
Literature
  Children's Literature Network **[12021]**, Plymouth, MN
  Detroit Telugu Literary Club **[6977]**, Bloomfield, MI
  Minnesota Center for the Book **[12463]**, St. Paul, MN
  Ohio Center for the Book **[14191]**, Cleveland, OH
  Wisconsin Center for the Book **[18677]**, Madison, WI
Literature Network; Children's **[12021]**, Plymouth, MN
Little Bros. Friends of the Elderly, Minneapolis/St. Paul, Minnesota **[11597]**, Minneapolis, MN
Little Creek Special Equestrians **[4337]**, Centerpoint, IN
Little Crow AIFA **[12919]**, Willmar, MN
Little Egypt Independent Elecl. Contractors **[234]**, Benton, IL
Little Falls Area Chamber of Commerce **[11335]**, Little Falls, MN
Little Falls Taekwondo **[11336]**, Little Falls, MN
Little Fork Lions Club **[11342]**, Littlefork, MN
Little Red Door Cancer Agency **[5394]**, Indianapolis, IN
Little Traverse Figure Skating Club **[9364]**, Petoskey, MI
Little Village Enval. Justice Org. **[1034]**, Chicago, IL
The Littlest Heroes **[13652]**, Chesterland, OH
Liturgy Assn; Latin **[16547]**, Rocky River, OH
Livestock
  Central Livestock Assn. **[12677]**, South St. Paul, MN
  Minnesota Buffalo Assn. **[12953]**, Winona, MN
Living Fed. of Am; Indiana Assisted **[5164]**, Indianapolis, IN
Livingston Assn. of Realtors **[8278]**, Howell, MI
Livingston County Assn. of Realtors **[8279]**, Howell, MI
Livingston County Convention and Visitors Bur. **[8280]**, Howell, MI
Livingston County Habitat for Humanity **[7015]**, Brighton, MI
Livingston County Pheasants Forever **[8281]**, Howell, MI
Livingston County Visitors Bur. **[★8280]**
Livingston Gem and Mineral Soc. **[7686]**, Fenton, MI
Livonia Chamber of Commerce **[8842]**, Livonia, MI
Livonia Hi-Nooners Lions Club **[8843]**, Livonia, MI
Livonia Lamplighter Lions Club **[9477]**, Redford, MI
Livonia Lions Club **[12999]**, Zimmerman, MN
Local 15C, Chem. Workers Coun. of the UFCW **[4366]**, Clarksville, IN
Local 20C, Chem. Workers Coun. of the UFCW **[16151]**, New Philadelphia, OH
Local 60C, Chem. Workers Coun. of the UFCW **[334]**, Bradley, IL
Local 70C, Chem. Workers Coun. of the UFCW **[10163]**, Whitehall, MI
Local 132C, Chem. Workers Coun. of the UFCW **[7975]**, Grand Rapids, MI
Local 228C, Chem. Workers Coun. of the UFCW **[12952]**, Winona, MN
Local 530, RWDSU District Coun. of the UFCW **[9147]**, Muskegon, MI
Local 705, RWDSU District Coun. of the UFCW **[8207]**, Holland, MI
Local 758C, Chem. Workers Coun. of the UFCW **[1481]**, Dixon, IL
Local 776C, Chem. Workers Coun. of the UFCW **[17129]**, Washington Court House, OH
Local 799C, Chem. Workers Coun. of the UFCW **[9721]**, Sault Ste. Marie, MI
Local 822, RWDSU District Coun. of the UFCW **[8208]**, Holland, MI
Local 825, RWDSU District Coun. of the UFCW **[8794]**, Lawton, MI
Local 871C, Chem. Workers Coun. of the UFCW **[387]**, Cahokia, IL
Local 872C, Chem. Workers Coun. of the UFCW **[2140]**, Kankakee, IL
Local Public Hea; Michigan Assn. for **[8620]**, Lansing, MI
Lock One Community Arts **[16118]**, New Bremen, OH

Lockport Area Exchange Club [2315], Lockport, IL
Lockport Chamber of Commerce [2316], Lockport, IL
Loda Lions Club [2321], Loda, IL
Loda Sportsmen's Club [2358], Ludlow, IL
Lodgings
Masonic Lodge [6415], Vincennes, IN
Masonic Lodge [19680], Shawano, WI
Lodi Area Chamber of Commerce [15686], Lodi, OH
Lodi Chamber of Commerce [18423], Lodi, WI
Log Cabin Republicans of Northwest Ohio [16927], Toledo, OH
Log Cabin Soc. of Michigan [9758], Sodus, MI
Logan County Angus Assn. [2686], New Holland, IL
Logan County Archaeological and Historical Soc. [★13321]
Logan County Area Chamber of Commerce [13320], Bellefontaine, OH
Logan County Historical Soc. [★13321]
Logan County Historical Soc. and Logan County Museum [13321], Bellefontaine, OH
Logan High School - Young Life [13206], Athens, OH
Logan - Hocking Chamber of Commerce [15690], Logan, OH
Logan's Landing [5692], Logansport, IN
Logansport - Cass County Chamber of Commerce [5693], Logansport, IN
Lombard Area Chamber of Commerce and Indus. [★2337]
Lombard Area Chamber of Commerce and Indus. [2337], Lombard, IL
Lombard Junior Woman's Club [2338], Lombard, IL
Lombard Suburban Genealogical Soc. [★3984]
Lomira Area Chamber of Commerce [18427], Lomira, WI
London Area Chamber of Commerce [★15695]
London Lions Club [15694], London, OH
Long Lake Assn. [9450], Portage, MI
Long Prairie Area Chamber of Commerce [11346], Long Prairie, MN
Long Track Club of USA; Mid-Am. Speed Skating - The [2756], Northbrook, IL
Longville Lakes Area Snowmobile Club [11347], Longville, MN
Lorain County AIFA [15116], Elyria, OH
Lorain County Assn. of Realtors [13134], Amherst, OH
Lorain County Bar Assn. [15117], Elyria, OH
Lorain County Chamber of Commerce [15705], Lorain, OH
Lorain County Chap. of the Ohio Genealogical Soc. [15118], Elyria, OH
Lorain County Farm Bur. [16283], Oberlin, OH
Lorain County Medical Soc. [15119], Elyria, OH
Lorain County RSVP [15120], Elyria, OH
Lorain County Tropical Greenhouse and Museum Assn. [15706], Lorain, OH
Lorain County Urban League [15121], Elyria, OH
Lorain County Visitors Bur. [13135], Amherst, OH
Lorain Harbor Lions Club [13136], Amherst, OH
Lorain Lawn Bowling Club [13137], Amherst, OH
Lorain Lions Club [15707], Lorain, OH
Lordstown Lions Club [17105], Warren, OH
Loretto Lions Club [11349], Loretto, MN
Loudonville-Greater Mohican Area Chamber of Commerce [★15715]
Loudonville Lions Club [15714], Loudonville, OH
Loudonville - Mohican Area Chamber of Commerce [★15715]
Loudonville - Mohican Area Convention and Visitor's Bur. [15715], Loudonville, OH
Louisville Area Chamber of Commerce [15718], Louisville, OH
Louisville Lions Club - Ohio [15719], Louisville, OH
Love Inc. of Ross County [13666], Chillicothe, OH
Loveland Area Chamber of Commerce [15728], Loveland, OH
Loveland Beagle Club [13888], Cincinnati, OH
Loves Park Lions Club [2350], Loves Park, IL
Loves Park - Machesney Park Chamber of Commerce [2351], Loves Park, IL
Lowell Area Chamber of Commerce [8863], Lowell, MI
Lowell Chamber of Commerce [5705], Lowell, IN
Lower Kaskaskia Stakeholders, Inc. [3185], Red Bud, IL
Lower Long Lake Found. [17883], Eau Claire, WI
Lower Wisconsin State Riverway Bd. [19257], Muscoda, WI
Lowry Lions Club [11351], Lowry, MN
Loyal Legion of the U.S. Michigan Commandery; Military Order of the [8488], Kentwood, MI
Loyola Assn. for Computing Machinery [1035], Chicago, IL
Loyola Booster Club [11904], North Mankato, MN
Lucas Lions Club [15734], Lucas, OH
Lucent Humanist League [2300], Lisle, IL
Lucky Dogs Chihuahua Rescue of Wisconsin [★19226]
Lucky Hearts Support Gp. [3910], Watseka, IL
Ludington Area Chamber of Commerce [8871], Ludington, MI
Ludington Area Convention and Visitors Bur. [8872], Ludington, MI
Ludington Coin Club [8873], Ludington, MI
Ludington Lions Club [8874], Ludington, MI
Lumberjack Rsrc. Conservation and Development Coun. [19598], Rhinelander, WI
Lumbermen's Assn; Ohio [14636], Columbus, OH
Lunar Reclamation Soc. [19044], Milwaukee, WI
Lung Assn. of Illinois; Amer. [3527], Springfield, IL
Lung Assn. of Illinois, Southern Illinois Region; Amer. [2401], Marion, IL
Lung Assn. of Ohio; Amer. [14303], Columbus, OH
Lung Assn. of Ohio, Northwest Br; Amer. [16259], Norwalk, OH
Lung Assn; South Shore [★16259]
Lung Assn. of Wisconsin; Amer. [17665], Brookfield, WI
Lupus Alliance of Am., Michigan/Indiana Affl. [9661], St. Clair Shores, MI
Lupus Erythematosus
Lupus Alliance of Am., Michigan/Indiana Affl. [9661], St. Clair Shores, MI
Lupus Found. of Am., Akron Area Chap. [14823], Cuyahoga Falls, OH
Lupus Found. of Am., Columbus, Marcy Zitron Chap. [14495], Columbus, OH
Lupus Found. of Am., Greater Cleveland Chap. [13411], Brecksville, OH
Lupus Found. of Am. Northwest Ohio Chap. [15206], Findlay, OH
Lupus Found. of Minnesota [10473], Bloomington, MN
Lupus Support Gp., Logan County [1036], Chicago, IL
Lupus Found. of Am., Akron Area Chap. [14823], Cuyahoga Falls, OH
Lupus Found. of Am., Columbus, Marcy Zitron Chap. [14495], Columbus, OH
Lupus Found. of Am., Greater Cleveland Chap. [13411], Brecksville, OH
Lupus Found. of Am., Northeast Indiana Chap. [★9661]
Lupus Found. of Am. Northwest Ohio Chap. [15206], Findlay, OH
Lupus Found. of Minnesota [10473], Bloomington, MN
Lupus Support Gp., Logan County [1036], Chicago, IL
Luther Lions Club [8881], Luther, MI
Lutheran
Assn. of Lutheran Secondary Schools [18885], Mequon, WI
Indiana District, The Lutheran Church-Missouri Synod [4675], Fort Wayne, IN
Michigan District, The Lutheran Church-Missouri Synod [6724], Ann Arbor, MI
Minnesota North District, The Lutheran Church-Missouri Synod [10515], Brainerd, MN
Minnesota South District, The Lutheran Church-Missouri Synod [10602], Burnsville, MN
North Wisconsin District, The Lutheran Church-Missouri Synod [20043], Wausau, WI
Ohio District, The Lutheran Church-Missouri Synod [16299], Olmsted Falls, OH
South Wisconsin District, The Lutheran Church-Missouri Synod [19126], Milwaukee, WI
Southern Illinois District, The Lutheran Church-Missouri Synod [211], Belleville, IL
Lutheran Secondary Schools; Assn. of [18885], Mequon, WI
Lutherans Concerned/Great Lakes [6714], Ann Arbor, MI
Luverne Area Chamber of Commerce [11355], Luverne, MN
Luxemburg Chamber of Commerce [18436], Luxemburg, WI
LVA Dupage [★2645]
LW Central - Young Life [1727], Frankfort, IL
LW East - Young Life [1728], Frankfort, IL
Lyle Lions Club [11358], Lyle, MN
Lymphoma Soc. of Am., Northern Ohio; Leukemia and [14158], Cleveland, OH
Lymphoma Soc; Wisconsin Chap., Leukemia and [17681], Brookfield, WI
Lyons Lions Club, IL [2361], Lyons, IL
Lyons Township Young Life [3962], Western Springs, IL

M

Mabel Lions Club [10636], Canton, MN
Mac-A-Cheek Found. for the Humanities [17185], West Liberty, OH
Macalester-Groveland Community Coun. [12442], St. Paul, MN
Macatawa Greenway Partnership [8209], Holland, MI
Macedonia Community Development Corp. [14905], Dayton, OH
Machine Workers of Am., Local 1111; United Elecl., Radio and [19141], Milwaukee, WI
Machinery; Univ. of Detroit-Mercy Assn. for Computing [7448], Detroit, MI
Mackinac Island Chamber of Commerce [★8886]
Mackinac Island Tourism Bur. [8886], Mackinac Island, MI
Mackinaw City Chamber of Commerce [8889], Mackinaw City, MI
Mackinaw Walkers Volkssport Club [205], Belleville, IL
Macomb Area Chamber of Commerce [★2371]
Macomb Area Chamber of Commerce & Downtown Development Corporation [2371], Macomb, IL
Macomb Chamber [10068], Warren, MI
Macomb County Bar Assn. [9087], Mount Clemens, MI
Macomb County Deputies and Dispatchers Association [9088], Mount Clemens, MI
Macomb County Genealogy Gp. [9089], Mount Clemens, MI
Macomb County Medical Soc. [7179], Clinton Township, MI
Macomb County Professional Deputy Association [★9088]
Macomb Dental Soc. [7150], Chesterfield, MI
Macomb Literacy Partners [7180], Clinton Township, MI
Macomb Literacy Proj. [★7180]
Macomb Reading Partners [★7180]
Macoupin County Genealogical Soc. [3696], Staunton, IL
MACU Assn. Gp. [6890], Bay City, MI
Mad Anthony Corvair Club [4691], Fort Wayne, IN
Mad River and NKP Railroad Soc. [13331], Bellevue, OH
Mad Town Talls [18542], Madison, WI
Madcap Squares [18543], Madison, WI
Madeira Woman's Club [13889], Cincinnati, OH
Madelia Area Chamber of Commerce [11364], Madelia, MN
Madeline Island Chamber of Commerce [18385], La Pointe, WI
Madiera Young Life [13890], Cincinnati, OH
Madison Advt. Fed. [20017], Waunakee, WI
Madison Aids Support [★18445]
Madison AIFA [19959], Waterloo, WI
Madison Area Builders Association [18544], Madison, WI
Madison Area Building Authority [★18544]
Madison Area Chamber of Commerce [5717], Madison, IN
Madison Area Chamber of Commerce [11366], Madison, MN
Madison Area Compensation Network [18545], Madison, WI
Madison Area Literacy Coun. [18546], Madison, WI
Madison Area Miniature Enthusiasts [19585], Randolph, WI
Madison Area Model Yacht Club No. 139 [19933], Verona, WI

Madison Area Musicians Assn. Local 166 [★18567]
Madison Area Optometric Soc. [20018], Waunakee, WI
Madison Area Quality Improvement Network [18547], Madison, WI
Madison Area Tech. Coll. Soc. for Electron Microscopy [★18548]
Madison Area Tech. College's Electron Microscopy [18548], Madison, WI
Madison Area Volkssport Assn. [18814], Marshall, WI
Madison Assn. of Plumbing Contractors [18549], Madison, WI
Madison Atheists, Univ. of Wisconsin [18550], Madison, WI
Madison Audubon Soc. [18551], Madison, WI
Madison Bead Soc. [18907], Middleton, WI
Madison BMW Club No. 7 [18839], McFarland, WI
Madison Bowling Assn. [19207], Monona, WI
Madison Central City - Young Life [19237], Mount Horeb, WI
Madison Chamber of Commerce [★18517]
Madison Chap. of the Soc. of Financial Ser. Professionals [19960], Waterloo, WI
Madison Community United [★18594]
Madison County AIFA [4442], Daleville, IN
Madison County Beagle Club [388], Cahokia, IL
Madison County Chamber of Commerce [15695], London, OH
Madison County Coun. of Govts. [4110], Anderson, IN
Madison County Historical Museum and Lib. [★1563]
Madison County Historical Soc. and Museum [★1563]
Madison County Historical Soc. Museum and Lib. [1563], Edwardsville, IL
Madison County REACT [4111], Anderson, IN
Madison Curling Club [18840], McFarland, WI
Madison District Dental Soc. [1531], East Alton, IL
Madison District Nurses Assn. - No. 3 [17963], Fitchburg, WI
Madison Drum and Bugle Corps Assn. [19860], Sun Prairie, WI
Madison Fed. of Labor [★18619]
Madison Gem and Mineral Club [18552], Madison, WI
Madison Heights Chamber of Commerce [★8896]
Madison Heights - Hazel Park Chamber of Commerce [8896], Madison Heights, MI
Madison Hours [18553], Madison, WI
Madison Jewish Community Coun. [18554], Madison, WI
Madison Jewish Welfare Fund [★18554]
Madison Lakes Yacht Club [18555], Madison, WI
Madison Lions Club - Minnesota [11367], Madison, MN
Madison Main St. Prog. [5718], Madison, IN
Madison - Perry Area Chamber of Commerce [15748], Madison, OH
Madison Township Lions Club [15735], Lucas, OH
Madison West Coast Swing Club [18556], Madison, WI
Madison West Kiwanis Club [18557], Madison, WI
Madison Women's Bowling Assn. [19208], Monona, WI
Magic
- Intl. Brotherhood of Magicians, Ring 2 [16206], Niles, OH
- Intl. Brotherhood of Magicians, Ring 7 [15265], Gahanna, OH
- Intl. Brotherhood of Magicians, Ring 19 [12062], Ramsey, MN
- Intl. Brotherhood of Magicians, Ring 22 [10115], West Bloomfield, MI
- Intl. Brotherhood of Magicians, Ring 23 [14145], Cleveland, OH
- Intl. Brotherhood of Magicians, Ring 41 [19917], Twin Lakes, WI
- Intl. Brotherhood of Magicians, Ring 56 [4344], Chandler, IN
- Intl. Brotherhood of Magicians, Ring 68 [16407], Perrysburg, OH
- Intl. Brotherhood of Magicians, Ring 71 [16266], Norwood, OH
- Intl. Brotherhood of Magicians, Ring 205 [15655], Lima, OH
- Intl. Brotherhood of Magicians, Ring 210 - Duke Stern [8075], Grosse Ile, MI
- Intl. Brotherhood of Magicians, Ring 211 - John DeVries Magic Club [10190], Wyoming, MI
- Intl. Brotherhood of Magicians, Ring 221 - A.H. Stoner Ring [5946], New Haven, IN
- Intl. Brotherhood of Magicians, Ring 236 - The Magic Wand Ring [532], Champaign, IL
- Intl. Brotherhood of Magicians, Ring 310 - Muncie Mystifiers [6094], Richmond, IN
- Intl. Brotherhood of Magicians, Ring 324 [16008], Middletown, OH
- Intl. Brotherhood of Magicians, Ring 336 [4401], Columbus, IN

Magic Soccer Club [18558], Madison, WI
Magnolia Lions Club - Ohio [15751], Magnolia, OH
Mahnomen Lions Club [11371], Mahnomen, MN
Mahomet Chamber of Commerce [2380], Mahomet, IL
Mahoning County Chap. of Ohio Genealogical Soc. [17403], Youngstown, OH
Mahoning County Medical Assn. [13534], Canfield, OH
Mahoning Valley AIFA [15185], Farmdale, OH
Mahoning Valley Audubon Soc. [17404], Youngstown, OH
Mahtomedi - Young Life [12897], White Bear Lake, MN
Mahube RSVP [10778], Detroit Lakes, MN
Mail Syss. Mgt. Assn., Chicago Chap. [3488], Skokie, IL
Mail Syss. Mgt. Assn., Minnesota Chap. [11598], Minneapolis, MN
Mail Syss. Mgt. Assn., Ohio Valley Chap. [13891], Cincinnati, OH
Mail Syss. Mgt. Assn., Wisconsin Chap. [17985], Fond du Lac, WI
Main St. Amherst [13138], Amherst, OH
Main St. Blue Island [317], Blue Island, IL
Main St. Bowling Green [13393], Bowling Green, OH
Main St. Elyria [15122], Elyria, OH
Main St. Galion [15286], Galion, OH
Main St. Libertyville [2264], Libertyville, IL
Main St. Lincoln [2279], Lincoln, IL
Main St. Oberlin [16284], Oberlin, OH
Main St. O'Fallon [2848], O'Fallon, IL
Main St. Orion [2873], Orion, IL
Main St. Paris [2949], Paris, IL
Main Street Piqua [16433], Piqua, OH
Main St. Plainfield [3101], Plainfield, IL
Main St. Richmond-Wayne County [6096], Richmond, IN
Main Street Romeo [9544], Romeo, MI
Main Street Tuscola [3794], Tuscola, IL
Main St. Wausau [20037], Wausau, WI
Main St. Wellington [17156], Wellington, OH
Main St. Wooster [17322], Wooster, OH
Maintenance
- Great Lakes Maintenance Assn. [17499], Appleton, WI
- Ohio Public Facilities Maintenance Assn. [16238], North Olmsted, OH

Make-A-Wish Found. of Central Ohio [14496], Columbus, OH
Make-A-Wish Found. of Greater Ohio and Kentucky [14159], Cleveland, OH
Make-A-Wish Found. of Indiana [5395], Indianapolis, IN
Make-A-Wish Found. of Michigan [6715], Ann Arbor, MI
Make-A-Wish Found. of Michigan, Grand Rapids Off. [7976], Grand Rapids, MI
Make-A-Wish Found. of Michigan, Livonia Off. [8844], Livonia, MI
Make-A-Wish Found. of Minnesota [11599], Minneapolis, MN
Make-A-Wish Found. of Northeast, Central, and Southern Ohio [★14159]
Make-A-Wish Found. of Northeast Ohio [14160], Cleveland, OH
Make-A-Wish Found. of Northern Illinois [1037], Chicago, IL
Make-A-Wish Found. of Northwest Ohio [16928], Toledo, OH
Make-A-Wish Found. of Southern Ohio [13892], Cincinnati, OH
Make-A-Wish Found. of Wisconsin [17700], Butler, WI
Malamute Rescue; Golden Years Alaskan [9144], Muskegon, MI
Maltese
- Maltese-Amer. Benevolent Soc. [7388], Detroit, MI

Maltese-Amer. Benevolent Soc. [7388], Detroit, MI
Management
- Air and Waste Mgt. Assn., Indiana Chap. [4966], Indianapolis, IN
- Chicago/Midwest Chap. of the Turnaround Mgt. Assn. [1722], Frankfort, IL
- Illinois City County Mgt. Assn. [1435], DeKalb, IL
- Intl. Facilities Mgt. Assn. - Minneapolis/St. Paul Chap. [12023], Plymouth, MN
- Mgt. Assn. of Illinois [1505], Downers Grove, IL
- Minnesota Chap. of the Natl. Assn. of Corporate Directors [11637], Minneapolis, MN
- Minnesota Chap. of the Proj. Mgt. Inst. [12466], St. Paul, MN
- Natl. Assn. of Corporate Directors, Chicago Chap. [1074], Chicago, IL
- Natl. Mgt. Assn., Argo-Tech Leadership Chap. [15144], Euclid, OH
- Natl. Mgt. Assn., Blue Cross and Blue Shield of Michigan [7412], Detroit, MI
- Natl. Mgt. Assn., Columbus Public Ser. Chap. [14524], Columbus, OH
- Natl. Mgt. Assn., Greater Dayton Leadership Assn. [14931], Dayton, OH
- Natl. Mgt. Assn., The Blues [8745], Lansing, MI
- Natl. Mgt. Assn., Van Kuren [17358], Wright-Patterson AFB, OH
- Natl. Mgt. Assn., Wright Chap. [17359], Wright-Patterson AFB, OH
- Northeast Ohio Chap. of Proj. Mgt. Inst. [15974], Mentor, OH
- Prdt. Development and Mgt. Assn., Great Lakes [10231], Zeeland, MI
- Prdt. Development and Mgt. Assn., Minnesota [11283], Lake Elmo, MN
- Prdt. Development and Mgt. Assn., Tri-State [13961], Cincinnati, OH
- Proj. Mgt. Inst., Calumet Chap. [6167], Schererville, IN
- Proj. Mgt. Inst., Central Illinois Chap. [308], Bloomington, IL
- Proj. Mgt. Inst., Central Indiana [5460], Indianapolis, IN
- Proj. Mgt. Inst., Central Ohio Chap. [14716], Columbus, OH
- Proj. Mgt. Inst., Chicagoland Chap. [2176], La Grange Park, IL
- Proj. Mgt. Inst. - Dayton/Miami Valley Chap. [14948], Dayton, OH
- Proj. Mgt. Inst., Great Lakes Chap. [10006], Troy, MI
- Proj. Mgt. Inst., Kentuckiana Chap. [4909], Henryville, IN
- Proj. Mgt. Inst., Madison/S. Central Wisconsin [18602], Madison, WI
- Proj. Mgt. Inst., Michigan Capital Area Chap. [8753], Lansing, MI
- Proj. Mgt. Inst., Michigan Huron Valley Chap. [9702], Saline, MI
- Project Mgt. Inst., Michigan Thumb [9011], Metamora, MI
- Proj. Mgt. Inst. - Milwaukee/SE WI Chap. [18043], Germantown, WI
- Proj. Mgt. Inst., Northeast Indiana Chap. [4712], Fort Wayne, IN
- Proj. Mgt. Inst., Northeast Ohio [15977], Mentor, OH
- Proj. Mgt. Inst., Northwest Ohio [15788], Mansfield, OH
- Proj. Mgt. Inst., Southwest Indiana Chap. [5857], Mount Vernon, IN
- Proj. Mgt. Inst., Western Lake Erie Chap. [16954], Toledo, OH
- Proj. Mgt. Inst., Western Michigan Chap. [7999], Grand Rapids, MI
- Soc. for Info. Mgt., Chicago [1191], Chicago, IL
- Soc. for Info. Mgt., Evansville Area [4573], Evansville, IN

Mgt. Assn; Casino [7332], Detroit, MI
Mgt. Assn., Chicago; Intl. Fac. [1725], Frankfort, IL
Mgt. Assn; Chicago - Midwest Chap. of the Turnaround [★1722]
Mgt. Assn; Chicago/Midwest Chap. of the Turnaround [1722], Frankfort, IL

Mgt. Assn; Dayton Chap. of the Intl. Fac. **[15986]**, Miamisburg, OH
Mgt. Assn. of Illinois **[1505]**, Downers Grove, IL
Mgt. Assn; Illinois City County **[1435]**, DeKalb, IL
Mgt. Assn; Indiana Hea. Info. **[5518]**, Ireland, IN
Mgt. Assn; Michigan Hea. Info. **[9148]**, Muskegon, MI
Mgt. Assn; MIMA, The **[★1505]**
Mgt. Assn; South Central Human Rsrcs. **[8398]**, Jackson, MI
Mgt. Assn; Wisconsin Ice Arena **[19278]**, Neenah, WI
Mgt. Org; Downtown Minneapolis Trans. **[11555]**, Minneapolis, MN
Mgt. Partnership of Mid-Michigan; Labor **[8586]**, Lansing, MI
Mgt. - Western Michigan; Natl. Assn. of Credit **[10191]**, Wyoming, MI
Managers
Chicago Assn. of Litigation Support Managers **[789]**, Chicago, IL
Professional Risk Managers Intl. Assn. **[11727]**, Minneapolis, MN
Teleprofessional Managers Assn. - Minnesota **[12595]**, St. Paul, MN
Managers Assn. of Metropolitan Detroit; Building Owners and **[7657]**, Farmington Hills, MI
Managers Assn; Northwest Ohio Mayors and **[16943]**, Toledo, OH
Managers Club of Chicago; Export **[★993]**
Managers Intl. Assn; Professional Risk **[11727]**, Minneapolis, MN
Managers and Rural Appraisers Indiana Chap; Amer. Soc. of Farm **[★6424]**
Manawa Area Chamber of Commerce **[18771]**, Manawa, WI
Mancelona Area Chamber of Commerce **[8905]**, Mancelona, MI
Manchester Area Chamber of Commerce **[8908]**, Manchester, MI
Manchester Village Owners Assn. **[19045]**, Milwaukee, WI
Manhattan Chamber of Commerce **[2384]**, Manhattan, IL
Manistee Area Chamber of Commerce **[8912]**, Manistee, MI
Manistee County Chamber of Commerce **[★8912]**
Manistee Lions Club **[8913]**, Manistee, MI
Manistee-Mason District Dental Soc. **[8914]**, Manistee, MI
Manistique Area Kiwanis Club **[8918]**, Manistique, MI
Manito Area Chamber of Commerce **[2387]**, Manito, IL
Manitowish Waters Chamber of Commerce **[18773]**, Manitowish Waters, WI
Manitowoc City Centre Assn. **[18782]**, Manitowoc, WI
Manitowoc County Figure Skating Club **[18783]**, Manitowoc, WI
Manitowoc County Historical Soc. **[18784]**, Manitowoc, WI
Manitowoc County Kennel Club **[18785]**, Manitowoc, WI
Manitowoc Humane Soc. **[★18781]**
Manitowoc/Two Rivers Area Chamber of Commerce **[18786]**, Manitowoc, WI
Mankato Area Environmentalists **[11384]**, Mankato, MN
Mankato Figure Skating Club **[11385]**, Mankato, MN
MannaFest Dimensions **[19438]**, Pewaukee, WI
Mansfield Area AIFA **[15771]**, Mansfield, OH
Mansfield Bd. of Realtors **[15772]**, Mansfield, OH
Mansfield Evening Lions Club **[15773]**, Mansfield, OH
Mansfield Noon Lions **[15774]**, Mansfield, OH
Mansfield Reformatory Preservation Soc. **[15775]**, Mansfield, OH
Mansfield-Richland Area Chamber of Commerce **[15776]**, Mansfield, OH
Mansfield and Richland County Convention and Visitors Bur. **[15777]**, Mansfield, OH
Manufactured Homes Assn; Ohio **[15058]**, Dublin, OH
Manufactured Housing
Michigan Manufactured Housing Assn. **[9285]**, Okemos, MI
Minnesota Manufactured Housing Assn. **[12496]**, St. Paul, MN
Wisconsin Housing Alliance **[18715]**, Madison, WI
Manufactured Housing Inst; Michigan **[★9285]**
Manufacturers' Agents; Wisconsin Assn. of **[19157]**, Milwaukee, WI
Mfrs. Assn; BACnet **[759]**, Chicago, IL
Manufacturers Assn; Michigan **[8685]**, Lansing, MI
Manufacturers' Assn; Midwest **[10937]**, Elbow Lake, MN
Manufacturers and Commerce; Racine Area **[19565]**, Racine, WI
Manufacturers and Commerce; Wisconsin **[18723]**, Madison, WI
Manufacturing
Amer. Brush Manufacturers Assn. **[106]**, Aurora, IL
Illinois Mfrs. Assn. **[2779]**, Oak Brook, IL
Indiana Manufacturers Assn. **[5258]**, Indianapolis, IN
Indus. Energy Users-Ohio **[14468]**, Columbus, OH
Michigan Manufacturers Assn. **[8685]**, Lansing, MI
Midwest Manufacturers' Assn. **[10937]**, Elbow Lake, MN
Minnesota Precision Mfg. Assn. **[12027]**, Plymouth, MN
North Eastern Michigan Indus. Assn. **[10131]**, West Branch, MI
Ohio Manufacturers' Assn. **[14637]**, Columbus, OH
Soc. of Mfg. Engineers - Baker Coll. U159 **[6816]**, Auburn Hills, MI
Soc. of Mfg. Engineers - Bemidji State Univ. S182 **[10426]**, Bemidji, MN
Soc. of Mfg. Engineers - Bowling Green State Univ. S102 **[13399]**, Bowling Green, OH
Soc. of Mfg. Engineers - Central State Univ. S307 **[17261]**, Wilberforce, OH
Soc. of Mfg. Engineers - Chippewa Valley Technological Coll. S170 **[17899]**, Eau Claire, WI
Soc. of Mfg. Engineers - Columbus State Community Coll. S092 **[14734]**, Columbus, OH
Soc. of Mfg. Engineers - Delta Coll. U185 **[10032]**, University Center, MI
Soc. of Mfg. Engineers - Eastern Illinois Univ. S151 **[572]**, Charleston, IL
Soc. of Mfg. Engineers - Eastern Michigan Univ. S111 **[10215]**, Ypsilanti, MI
Soc. of Mfg. Engineers - Ferris State Univ. S129 **[6952]**, Big Rapids, MI
Soc. of Mfg. Engineers - Focus-Hope Center for Advanced Technologies S279 **[7435]**, Detroit, MI
Soc. of Mfg. Engineers - Grand Valley State Univ. S283 **[8010]**, Grand Rapids, MI
Soc. of Mfg. Engineers - Illinois State Univ. S203 **[2732]**, Normal, IL
Soc. of Mfg. Engineers - Indiana Inst. of Tech. S345 **[4716]**, Fort Wayne, IN
Soc. of Mfg. Engineers - Indiana Purdue Univ.-Ft. Wayne S292 **[4717]**, Fort Wayne, IN
Soc. of Mfg. Engineers - ITT - Ft. Wayne S214 **[4718]**, Fort Wayne, IN
Soc. of Mfg. Engineers - ITT - Indianapolis S178 **[5478]**, Indianapolis, IN
Soc. of Mfg. Engineers - ITT Tech. Inst. S347 **[18133]**, Green Bay, WI
Soc. of Mfg. Engineers - Ivy Tech State Coll. S265 **[4719]**, Fort Wayne, IN
Soc. of Mfg. Engineers - James A. Rhodes State Coll. S226 **[15669]**, Lima, OH
Soc. of Mfg. Engineers - Kent State Univ. - Ashtabula U165 **[13186]**, Ashtabula, OH
Soc. of Mfg. Engineers - Kent State Univ. S050 **[15550]**, Kent, OH
Soc. of Mfg. Engineers - Kent State Univ. - Tuscarawas S180 **[16153]**, New Philadelphia, OH
Soc. of Mfg. Engineers - Kettering Univ. S041 **[7757]**, Flint, MI
Soc. of Mfg. Engineers - Lake Superior State Univ. S082 **[9728]**, Sault Ste. Marie, MI
Soc. of Mfg. Engineers - Lawrence Technological Univ. S011 **[9820]**, Southfield, MI
Soc. of Mfg. Engineers - Lorain County Community Coll. S254 **[15125]**, Elyria, OH
Soc. of Mfg. Engineers - Macomb Community Coll. S071 **[10073]**, Warren, MI
Soc. of Mfg. Engineers - Miami Univ. S076 **[16328]**, Oxford, OH
Soc. of Mfg. Engineers - Michigan State Univ. S329 **[7567]**, East Lansing, MI
Soc. of Mfg. Engineers - Michigan Technological Univ. S077 **[8262]**, Houghton, MI
Soc. of Mfg. Engineers - Minnesota State Univ. Moorhead S189 **[11828]**, Moorhead, MN
Soc. of Mfg. Engineers - Moraine Park Tech. Coll. S234 **[17993]**, Fond du Lac, WI
Soc. of Mfg. Engineers - Morrison Inst. of Tech. S321 **[2560]**, Morrison, IL
Soc. of Mfg. Engineers - Northcentral Tech. Coll. S237 **[20047]**, Wausau, WI
Soc. of Mfg. Engineers - Northern Illinois Univ. S210 **[1444]**, DeKalb, IL
Soc. of Mfg. Engineers - Oakland County Community Coll. S144 **[6817]**, Auburn Hills, MI
Soc. of Mfg. Engineers - Ohio State Univ. S205 **[14735]**, Columbus, OH
Soc. of Mfg. Engineers - Ohio Univ. S087 **[13218]**, Athens, OH
Soc. of Mfg. Engineers - Owens Community Coll. S217 **[15214]**, Findlay, OH
Soc. of Mfg. Engineers - Purdue Univ. - Calumet S161 **[4895]**, Hammond, IN
Soc. of Mfg. Engineers - Purdue Univ. - Indianapolis S098 **[5479]**, Indianapolis, IN
Soc. of Mfg. Engineers - Purdue Univ. - Lafayette S006 **[6499]**, West Lafayette, IN
Soc. of Mfg. Engineers - Purdue Univ. - New Albany S351 **[5925]**, New Albany, IN
Soc. of Mfg. Engineers - Riverland Community Coll. U164 **[10359]**, Austin, MN
Soc. of Mfg. Engineers - Rock Valley Coll. S269 **[3321]**, Rockford, IL
Soc. of Mfg. Engineers - St. Cloud State Univ. - S225 **[12309]**, St. Cloud, MN
Soc. of Mfg. Engineers - St. Paul Tech. Coll. S207 **[12588]**, St. Paul, MN
Soc. of Mfg. Engineers - Sinclair Community Coll. U156 **[14955]**, Dayton, OH
Soc. of Mfg. Engineers - Southern Illinois Univ. Edwardsville S349 **[1567]**, Edwardsville, IL
Soc. of Mfg. Engineers - Stark State Coll. U172 **[13581]**, Canton, OH
Soc. of Mfg. Engineers - Tri-State Univ. U173 **[4129]**, Angola, IN
Soc. of Mfg. Engineers - Trumbull Career and Tech. Center S301 **[17109]**, Warren, OH
Soc. of Mfg. Engineers - Univ. of Cincinnati S145 **[13993]**, Cincinnati, OH
Soc. of Mfg. Engineers - Univ. of Dayton S070 **[14956]**, Dayton, OH
Soc. of Mfg. Engineers - Univ. of Detroit - Mercy S081 **[7436]**, Detroit, MI
Soc. of Mfg. Engineers - Univ. of Illinois S219 **[3835]**, Urbana, IL
Soc. of Mfg. Engineers - Univ. of Michigan - Dearborn S326 **[7271]**, Dearborn, MI
Soc. of Mfg. Engineers - Univ. of Michigan S001 **[6767]**, Ann Arbor, MI
Soc. of Mfg. Engineers - Univ. of Toledo S319 **[16960]**, Toledo, OH
Soc. of Mfg. Engineers - Univ. of Wisconsin - Madison S133 **[18618]**, Madison, WI
Soc. of Mfg. Engineers - Univ. of Wisconsin - Milwaukee S152 **[19121]**, Milwaukee, WI
Tooling and Mfg. Assn. **[2965]**, Park Ridge, IL
Mfg. Assn; Minnesota Precision **[12027]**, Plymouth, MN
Mfg. Credit Assn; Natl. Radiator **[★11688]**
Mfg. Credit Assn; Natl. Radiator Core **[★11688]**
Mfg. Engineers, Henry Ford Community Coll. Student Chap. S-331; Soc. of **[7270]**, Dearborn, MI
Map Soc; Chicago **[815]**, Chicago, IL
Maple Grove Dande Lions Club **[11412]**, Maple Grove, MN
Maple Grove Lions Club **[11413]**, Maple Grove, MN
Maple Plain Lions Club **[11416]**, Maple Plain, MN
Maple Syrup Producers Assn; Wisconsin **[18900]**, Merrill, WI
Maple Valley Lions Club **[9354]**, Perrinton, MI
Mapleton-Fall Creek Neighborhood Assn./mid North Weed and Seed **[5396]**, Indianapolis, IN
Maplewood Figure Skating Club **[11927]**, Oakdale, MN
Maplewood-Oakdale Lions Club **[11928]**, Oakdale, MN

MARAL Pro-Choice Michigan **[8601]**, Lansing, MI
Marathon County Historical Soc. **[20038]**, Wausau, WI
Marathon County REACT **[20039]**, Wausau, WI
Marblehead Peninsula Chamber of Commerce **[15808]**, Marblehead, OH
Marblehead Peninsula Lions Club **[15579]**, Lakeside, OH
March of Dimes **[20040]**, Wausau, WI
March of Dimes Birth Defects Found., Indiana Chap. **[5397]**, Indianapolis, IN
March of Dimes Birth Defects Found., Marquette Div. **[8936]**, Marquette, MI
March of Dimes Birth Defects Found., Rochester Chap. **[★12153]**
March of Dimes Birth Defects Found., Southeast Minnesota Div. **[12153]**, Rochester, MN
March of Dimes Birth Defects Found., Southeastern Minnesota Div. **[★12153]**
March of Dimes Birth Defects Found., Upper Peninsula Div. **[★8936]**
March of Dimes/Michigan **[9803]**, Southfield, MI
March of Dimes Minnesota Chap. **[10915]**, Edina, MN
March of Dimes of Southeastern Wisconsin **[20102]**, West Allis, WI
Marengo-Union Chamber of Commerce **[2397]**, Marengo, IL
Mariemont Young Life **[13893]**, Cincinnati, OH
Marietta AIFA **[15820]**, Marietta, OH
Marietta Area Chamber of Commerce **[15821]**, Marietta, OH
Marietta Beagle Club **[15822]**, Marietta, OH
Marietta Bd. of Realtors **[15823]**, Marietta, OH
Marijuana
Natl. Org. for Reform of Marijuana Laws, Illinois Chap. **[1087]**, Chicago, IL
Marijuana Laws, Illinois Chap; Natl. Org. for Reform of **[1087]**, Chicago, IL
Marine
Coalition of Reef Lovers **[7920]**, Grand Rapids, MI
Great Lakes Historical Soc. **[17065]**, Vermilion, OH
Indiana Marine Trade Association **[4126]**, Angola, IN
Inland Seas Educ. Assn. **[9886]**, Suttons Bay, MI
Marine City Chamber of Commerce **[8925]**, Marine City, MI
Marine Corps
Marine Corps League Auxiliary - Sgt. Paul T. Varley Unit **[13535]**, Canfield, OH
Marine Corps League Auxiliary - Sgt. Paul T. Varley Unit **[13535]**, Canfield, OH
Marine Historical Soc; Wisconsin **[19173]**, Milwaukee, WI
Marine Industries
Lake Carriers' Assn. **[14153]**, Cleveland, OH
Marine Trade Association; Indiana **[4126]**, Angola, IN
Marinette Area Chamber of Commerce **[18799]**, Marinette, WI
Marinette and Menominee Counties Youth Suicide Prevention **[18800]**, Marinette, WI
Marion Area AIFA **[15839]**, Marion, OH
Marion Area Bd. of Realtors **[5736]**, Marion, IN
Marion Area Chamber of Commerce **[8926]**, Marion, MI
Marion Area Chamber of Commerce **[15840]**, Marion, OH
Marion Area Independent Insurance Agents Assn. **[15841]**, Marion, OH
Marion Bd. of Realtors **[15842]**, Marion, OH
Marion Chamber of Commerce **[2405]**, Marion, IL
Marion Coin Club **[5737]**, Marion, IN
Marion County Historical Soc. **[15843]**, Marion, OH
Marion County Master Gardener Assn. **[5398]**, Indianapolis, IN
Marion and Crawford Counties RSVP **[15844]**, Marion, OH
Marion Evening Lions Club **[15845]**, Marion, OH
Marion-Grant County Chamber of Commerce **[5738]**, Marion, IN
Marion-Grant County Convention and Visitors Bur. **[5739]**, Marion, IN
Marion Main St. **[2406]**, Marion, IL
Marion Noon Lions Club **[15846]**, Marion, OH
Market; Friends of the St. Paul Farmers' **[12659]**, Shoreview, MN
Marketers Assn; Illinois Petroleum **[3625]**, Springfield, IL
Marketers Assn; Ohio Petroleum **[★15060]**
Marketers Assn. of Wisconsin/Wisconsin Assn. of Convenience Stores; Petroleum **[18595]**, Madison, WI
Marketers and Convenience Store Assn; Ohio Petroleum **[15060]**, Dublin, OH
Marketing
Amer. Marketing Assn. - Minnesota Chap. **[12377]**, St. Paul, MN
Cherry Marketing Inst. **[8560]**, Lansing, MI
Direct Marketing Assn. of Detroit **[7639]**, Farmington, MI
Eastern Market Merchants Association **[10063]**, Warren, MI
Michigan DECA **[10210]**, Ypsilanti, MI
Midwest Direct Marketing Assn. **[11604]**, Minneapolis, MN
NAMD Cleveland **[16693]**, South Euclid, OH
Sales and Marketing Executives **[16093]**, Munroe Falls, OH
Soc. for Marketing Professional Services, Chicago Chap. **[1614]**, Elk Grove Village, IL
Soc. for Marketing Professional Sers./Columbus Chap. **[14736]**, Columbus, OH
Soc. for Marketing Professional Sers./Michigan **[9821]**, Southfield, MI
Soc. for Marketing Professional Services/ Northeast Ohio **[14219]**, Cleveland, OH
Soc. for Marketing Professional Services/Twin Cities Chap. **[11748]**, Minneapolis, MN
Wisconsin Direct Marketing Assn. **[19167]**, Milwaukee, WI
Women in Direct Marketing Intl., Chicago Chap. **[1634]**, Elmwood Park, IL
Marketing Assn. of Detroit; Direct **[7639]**, Farmington, MI
Marketing Assn; Midwest Healthcare **[2646]**, Naperville, IL
Marketing Executives, Minneapolis/St. Paul; Sales and **[10543]**, Brooklyn Center, MN
Marlboro Lions Club - Ohio **[15720]**, Louisville, OH
MARO Employment and Training Assn. **[8602]**, Lansing, MI
Marquette-Alger County Medical Soc. **[8937]**, Marquette, MI
Marquette Area Chamber of Commerce **[★8938]**
Marquette Area Chamber of Commerce - Lake Superior Community Partnership **[★8938]**
Marquette Area Chamber of Commerce- Lake Superior Community Partnership **[8938]**, Marquette, MI
Marquette Astronomical Soc. **[8939]**, Marquette, MI
Marquette Beagle Club **[8348]**, Ishpeming, MI
Marquette County Convention and Visitors Bur. **[8940]**, Marquette, MI
Marquette County Exchange Club **[8941]**, Marquette, MI
Marquette County Genealogical Soc. **[8942]**, Marquette, MI
Marquette County Habitat for Humanity **[8943]**, Marquette, MI
Marquette County Historical Soc. **[20146]**, Westfield, WI
Marquette County History Museum **[8944]**, Marquette, MI
Marquette County Humane Soc. **[9178]**, Negaunee, MI
Marquette County RSVP **[8945]**, Marquette, MI
Marquette Figure Skating Club **[8946]**, Marquette, MI
Marquette Junior Hockey **[8947]**, Marquette, MI
Marquette Professional Police Off.rs Assn. **[8948]**, Marquette, MI
Marriage
Illinois Assn. for Marriage and Family Therapy **[1835]**, Glen Ellyn, IL
Marriage Builders; Community **[4536]**, Evansville, IN
Marseilles Volunteer Firefighters Association **[2422]**, Marseilles, IL
Marshall Area Chamber of Commerce **[2424]**, Marshall, IL
Marshall Area Chamber of Commerce **[8968]**, Marshall, MI
Marshall Area Chamber of Commerce **[11434]**, Marshall, MN
Marshall Convention and Visitors Bur. **[11435]**, Marshall, MN
Marshall County Convention and Visitors Bur. **[6048]**, Plymouth, IN
Marshall County Historical Soc. **[6049]**, Plymouth, IN
Marshall County Mounted Posse **[12841]**, Warren, MN
Marshall Lions Club - Wisconsin **[18815]**, Marshall, WI
Marshall United Way, Michigan **[8969]**, Marshall, MI
Marshfield Area Chamber of Commerce and Indus. **[18817]**, Marshfield, WI
Marshfield Area Kennel Club **[18818]**, Marshfield, WI
Marshfield Area United Way **[18819]**, Marshfield, WI
Marshfield Lions Club - Wisconsin **[18820]**, Marshfield, WI
Martial Arts
Little Falls Taekwondo **[11336]**, Little Falls, MN
Martin County Chamber of Commerce **[5703]**, Loogootee, IN
Martin County Historical Soc. **[10979]**, Fairmont, MN
Martinism
Fairmont Convention and Visitors Bur. **[10978]**, Fairmont, MN
Martins Ferry Area Chamber of Commerce **[15860]**, Martins Ferry, OH
Martin's Ferry/Bridgeport - Young Life **[15521]**, Jacobsburg, OH
Martinsville Chamber of Commerce **[2426]**, Martinsville, IL
Marysville Assn. of Realtors **[15863]**, Marysville, OH
Marysville Chamber of Commerce **[8974]**, Marysville, MI
Mason Area Chamber of Commerce **[8978]**, Mason, MI
Mason Chamber of Commerce **[★15873]**
Mason Contractors Assn. **[8845]**, Livonia, MI
Mason Contractors Assns. of Akron and Vicinity **[13064]**, Akron, OH
Mason County Farm Bur. Found. **[1960]**, Havana, IL
Mason Landen Kings Chamber of Commerce **[★15877]**
Mason Lions Club **[15876]**, Mason, OH
Mason Lions Club - Michigan **[8979]**, Mason, MI
Mason Middle School - Wyldlife **[7527]**, East Lansing, MI
Mason-Oceana-Manistree Bd. of Realtors **[8875]**, Ludington, MI
Mason - Young Life **[7528]**, East Lansing, MI
Mason Young Life **[13894]**, Cincinnati, OH
Masonic Cemetery Assn. **[4953]**, Huntington, IN
Masonic Lodge **[★1389]**
Masonic Lodge **[1577]**, El Paso, IL
Masonic Lodge **[1668]**, Evanston, IL
Masonic Lodge **[2372]**, Macomb, IL
Masonic Lodge **[2442]**, Mattoon, IL
Masonic Lodge **[6415]**, Vincennes, IN
Masonic Lodge **[13667]**, Chillicothe, OH
Masonic Lodge **[15847]**, Marion, OH
Masonic Lodge **[15886]**, Massillon, OH
Masonic Lodge **[17077]**, Wadsworth, OH
Masonic Lodge **[17345]**, Worthington, OH
Masonic Lodge **[19680]**, Shawano, WI
Masonic Lodge No. 246 **[15306]**, Garrettsville, OH
Masonic Temple **[15081]**, East Liverpool, OH
Masonic Temple **[★19680]**
Masonry
Intl. Masonry Inst., Minneapolis **[11589]**, Minneapolis, MN
Masonic Lodge **[13667]**, Chillicothe, OH
Masonic Lodge **[17345]**, Worthington, OH
Masonry Inst. of Michigan **[8846]**, Livonia, MI
Masons
Decatur Masonic Temple Assn. **[1389]**, Decatur, IL
Janesville Masonic Center **[18252]**, Janesville, WI
Kokomo Shrine Club **[5577]**, Kokomo, IN
Masonic Lodge No. 246 **[15306]**, Garrettsville, OH
Natl. Sojourners, Charles A. Lindbergh No. 247 **[208]**, Belleville, IL
Natl. Sojourners, Chicago **[2656]**, Naperville, IL
Natl. Sojourners, Cleveland No. 23 **[16694]**, South Euclid, OH
Natl. Sojourners, Columbus No. 10 **[14527]**, Columbus, OH
Natl. Sojourners, Detroit No. 1 **[9904]**, Taylor, MI
Natl. Sojourners, Indiana - Fort Harrison No. 66 **[5433]**, Indianapolis, IN
Natl. Sojourners, Indiana Masonic Home No. 541 **[4755]**, Franklin, IN

Natl. Sojourners, John S. Bersey No. 316 [8982], Mason, MI
Natl. Sojourners, Lake Michigan No. 289 [2190], Lake Bluff, IL
Natl. Sojourners, Maumee Valley No. 518 [15094], Edgerton, OH
Natl. Sojourners, Milwaukee No. 27 [19081], Milwaukee, WI
Natl. Sojourners, Minnesota No. 25 [11460], Mendota Heights, MN
Natl. Sojourners, Northern Indiana No. 544 [6451], Warsaw, IN
Natl. Sojourners, Southern Indiana No. 328 [6201], Shoals, IN
Natl. Sojourners, Wayne W. Gatewood No. 536 [490], Centralia, IL
Order of the Eastern Star Minnesota Grand Chap. [11718], Minneapolis, MN
Philalethes Society, Logos Chapter [1136], Chicago, IL
Massac County United Way [2483], Metropolis, IL
Massachusetts Thoracic Soc. [8603], Lansing, MI
Massillon Area Chamber of Commerce [15887], Massillon, OH
Massillon HS - Young Life [13571], Canton, OH
Massillon Lions Club [15888], Massillon, OH
Massillon-Stark County REACT [15889], Massillon, OH
Massillon Urban League [15890], Massillon, OH
Master Electrical Contractors Independent Electrical Contractors of Dayton [14906], Dayton, OH
Master Insulation Assn. of Greater Detroit [9993], Troy, MI
Matchcover
Badger State Matchcover Club [17853], East Troy, WI
Great Lakes Match Club [12895], White Bear Lake, MN
Kitty Matchcover Club [12436], St. Paul, MN
Rathkamp Matchcover Soc., Vandalia [17059], Vandalia, OH
Windy City Matchcover Club [4003], Wheaton, IL
Materials
Soc. for the Advancement of Material and Process Engg., Chicago Chap. [1676], Evanston, IL
Soc. for the Advancement of Material and Process Engg., Michigan Chap. [7792], Fraser, MI
Soc. for the Advancement of Material and Process Engg., Midwest Chap. [14953], Dayton, OH
Soc. for the Advancement of Material and Process Engg., Northern Ohio Chap. [15549], Kent, OH
Math Energy Club of Eastern Illinois Univ. [1038], Chicago, IL
Mathematical Assn. of Am., Illinois Sect. [206], Belleville, IL
Mathematical Assn. of Am., Indiana Sect. [6370], Upland, IN
Mathematical Assn. of Am., Lawrence Tech. Univ. Student Chap. [9804], Southfield, MI
Mathematical Assn. of Am., Michigan Sect. [6716], Ann Arbor, MI
Mathematical Assn. of Am., Univ. of Dayton Student Chap. [14907], Dayton, OH
Mathematical Assn. of Am., Wisconsin Sect. [18559], Madison, WI
Mathematics
Bowling Green State Univ. Coun. of Teachers of Mathematics [13384], Bowling Green, OH
Central Ohio Coun. of Teachers of Mathematics [15429], Hilliard, OH
Chicago Elementary Teachers' Mathematics Club [808], Chicago, IL
Detroit Area Coun. of Teachers of Mathematics [9578], Royal Oak, MI
East Central Coun. of Teachers of Mathematics [479], Casey, IL
Eastern Ohio Coun. of Teachers of Mathematics [17397], Youngstown, OH
Greater Akron Mathematics Educators' Soc. [16776], Stow, OH
Greater Cincinnati Coun. of Teachers of Mathematics [13843], Cincinnati, OH
Greater Cleveland Coun. of Teachers of Mathematics [16789], Strongsville, OH
Greater Toledo Coun. of Teachers of Mathematics [16405], Perrysburg, OH
Illinois Mathematics Assn. of Community Colleges [2912], Palatine, IL
Illinois Mathematics Teacher Educators [3477], Sidney, IL
Indiana Coun. of Teachers of Mathematics [5614], Lafayette, IN
Indiana Mathematical Assn. of Two-Year Colleges [5617], Lafayette, IN
Math Energy Club of Eastern Illinois Univ. [1038], Chicago, IL
Mathematical Assn. of Am., Illinois Sect. [206], Belleville, IL
Mathematical Assn. of Am., Indiana Sect. [6370], Upland, IN
Mathematical Assn. of Am., Lawrence Tech. Univ. Student Chap. [9804], Southfield, MI
Mathematical Assn. of Am., Michigan Sect. [6716], Ann Arbor, MI
Mathematical Assn. of Am., Univ. of Dayton Student Chap. [14907], Dayton, OH
Mathematical Assn. of Am., Wisconsin Sect. [18559], Madison, WI
Mathematics Dept. Heads of Western Chicago Suburbs [3516], Spring Grove, IL
Mathematics Teachers' Assn. of Chicago and Vicinity [1039], Chicago, IL
Metropolitan Mathematics Club of Chicago [2819], Oak Park, IL
Miami Univ. Coun. of Teachers of Mathematics [16324], Oxford, OH
Michigan Mathematical Assn. of Two-Year Colleges [10028], University Center, MI
Minnesota Mathematical Assn. of Two-Year Colleges [11221], Inver Grove, MN
Northern Illinois Assn. of Teachers of Mathematics [3292], Rockford, IL
Ohio Coun. of Teachers of Mathematics [13644], Chardon, OH
Ohio Mathematics Assn. of Two-Year Colleges [16435], Piqua, OH
Ohio Univ. Coun. of Teachers of Mathematics [13214], Athens, OH
Southwest Indiana Coun. of Teachers of Mathematics [4576], Evansville, IN
Wisconsin Mathematical Assn. of Two-Year Colleges [18724], Madison, WI
Wisconsin Mathematics Coun. [18045], Germantown, WI
Wright State Univ. Area Coun. of Teachers of Mathematics [14972], Dayton, OH
Mathematics Dept. Heads of Western Chicago Suburbs [3516], Spring Grove, IL
Mathematics; Minnesota Coun. of Teachers of [11863], New Brighton, MN
Mathematics Teachers' Assn. of Chicago and Vicinity [1039], Chicago, IL
Mattawan Lions Club [8987], Mattawan, MI
Mattawan - Young Life [8447], Kalamazoo, MI
Matteson Area Chamber of Commerce [2438], Matteson, IL
Mattoon Area PADs Community Org. [★2444]
Mattoon Chamber of Commerce [2443], Mattoon, IL
Mattoon Public Action to Deliver Shelter [2444], Mattoon, IL
Maumee Chamber of Commerce [15909], Maumee, OH
Maumee Coun. for the Arts [15910], Maumee, OH
Maumee HS - Young Life [15911], Maumee, OH
Maumee Valley Acad. of Family Physicians [13153], Archbold, OH
Maumee Valley Chefs Chap. ACF [16825], Sylvania, OH
Maumee Valley Habitat for Humanity [16929], Toledo, OH
Maumee Valley Historical Soc. [15912], Maumee, OH
Maumee Valley St. Bernard Club [4127], Angola, IN
Maumee Valley Volkssporters [15913], Maumee, OH
Mauston Chamber of Commerce [★18829]
Mauston Lions Club [18439], Lyndon Station, WI
Maxwell St. Historic Preservation Coalition [1040], Chicago, IL
Maynard Lions Club [11444], Maynard, MN
Mayo School of Hea.-Related Scis. Alumni Assn. [12154], Rochester, MN
Mayors Caucus; Metropolitan [1046], Chicago, IL
Mayors and Managers Assn; Northwest Ohio [16943], Toledo, OH
Mayville Area Chamber of Commerce [18832], Mayville, WI
Mayville Historical Soc. [18833], Mayville, WI
Mayville Historical Soc. Museum [★18833]
Mayville Lions Club [8989], Mayville, MI
Maywood Chamber of Commerce [2449], Maywood, IL
Mazeppa Lions Club [11446], Mazeppa, MN
Mazomanie Chamber of Commerce [18836], Mazomanie, WI
MBCA - Intl. Stars Sect. [9237], Novi, MI
McBain Area Chamber of Commerce [8991], McBain, MI
McCutcheon High School - Young Life [6489], West Lafayette, IN
McDonald Lions Club [15935], McDonald, OH
McDonough County United Way [2373], Macomb, IL
McFarland Chamber of Commerce [18841], McFarland, WI
McHenry Area Chamber of Commerce [2460], McHenry, IL
McHenry County AIFA [1326], Crystal Lake, IL
McHenry County Aikido Club [1327], Crystal Lake, IL
McHenry County Assn. of Realtors [4059], Woodstock, IL
McHenry County Audubon Soc. [4060], Woodstock, IL
McHenry County Defenders [4061], Woodstock, IL
McHenry County Dental Soc. [2055], Huntley, IL
McHenry County Historical Soc. [3799], Union, IL
McHenry County Medical Soc. [3388], St. Charles, IL
McHenry County Regional Planning Commn. [4062], Woodstock, IL
McHenry County Table Tennis Club [2461], McHenry, IL
Mchenry Wyldlife [3946], West Dundee, IL
McKinley Jr. High - Wyldlife [3505], South Holland, IL
McLean County Chamber of Commerce [295], Bloomington, IL
McLean County Dental Soc. [1911], Gridley, IL
McLean County Historical Soc. [296], Bloomington, IL
McLean County Historical Soc. Museum and Lib. [★296]
McLean County Museum of History [★296]
McLean County Regional Planning Commn. [297], Bloomington, IL
McLean County RSVP [2723], Normal, IL
McNabb Magnolia Junior Woman's Club [2467], McNabb, IL
Mdewakanton Dakota Community; Mendota [11454], Mendota, MN
Meadowlawn Parent Teacher Org. [5825], Monticello, IN
Meals On Wheels of Northwest Indiana [4434], Crown Point, IN
Meals on Wheels of Chicago [1041], Chicago, IL
Meals on Wheels of Hamilton County [5976], Noblesville, IN
Meals on Wheels of Hendricks County [4447], Danville, IN
Meals on Wheels of Marion County [5399], Indianapolis, IN
Meals on Wheels of Rochester [12155], Rochester, MN
Meals on Wheels of Stark and Wayne Counties [15891], Massillon, OH
Meat
Adams County Pork Producers [3144], Quincy, IL
Illinois Assn. of Meat Processors [1749], Freeport, IL
Indiana Pork Producers Assn. [6552], Zionsville, IN
Michigan Veal Comm. [9292], Okemos, MI
Minnesota Pork Producers Assn. [11905], North Mankato, MN
Ohio Assn. of Meat Processors [15240], Frazeysburg, OH
Wisconsin Assn. of Meat Processors [17643], Bloomington, WI
Wisconsin Beef Coun. [18673], Madison, WI
Wisconsin Pork Assn. [18413], Lancaster, WI
Meat Processors; Illinois Assn. of [1749], Freeport, IL
Mech. Contractors Assn. [14161], Cleveland, OH
Mech. Contractors Assn. of Am. - Indiana Chap. [★5401]

Mech. Contractors Assn. of Central Indiana [5400], Indianapolis, IN
Mech. Contractors Assn. of Central Ohio [14497], Columbus, OH
Mech. Contractors Assn. Chicago [1042], Chicago, IL
Mech. Contractors Assn. of Cincinnati [13895], Cincinnati, OH
Mech. Contractors Assn. of Cleveland [★14162]
Mech. Contractors Assn. of Greater Dayton [14908], Dayton, OH
Mech. Contractors Assn. of Indiana [5401], Indianapolis, IN
Mech. Contractors Assn; Metropolitan Detroit Plumbing and [★7420]
Mech. Contractors Assn; Mid-Michigan [8732], Lansing, MI
Mech. and Plumbing Indus. Coun. [14162], Cleveland, OH

Mechanics

Amer. Soc. of Mech. Engineers, Akron Sect. [13038], Akron, OH
Amer. Soc. of Mech. Engineers, Chicago Sect. [64], Arlington Heights, IL
Amer. Soc. of Mech. Engineers, Cleveland Sect. [14064], Cleveland, OH
Amer. Soc. of Mech. Engineers, Metro Detroit Sect. [7652], Farmington Hills, MI
Amer. Soc. of Mech. Engineers, Milwaukee Sect. [18959], Milwaukee, WI
Amer. Soc. of Mech. Engineers, Minnesota Sect. [12876], West St. Paul, MN
Amer. Soc. of Mech. Engineers, Northwest Ohio Sect. [16896], Toledo, OH

Mecosta County Area Chamber of Commerce [6947], Big Rapids, MI
Mecosta County Convention and Visitors Bur. [6948], Big Rapids, MI
Mecosta County Support Gp. [6949], Big Rapids, MI
Mecosta Lions Club [8996], Mecosta, MI
Mecosta-Osceola United Way [6950], Big Rapids, MI
Medallion Rottweiler Club [2881], Orland Park, IL
Medford Area Chamber of Commerce [18844], Medford, WI
Medford Curling Club [18845], Medford, WI

Media

Greater Cleveland Media Development Corp. [14133], Cleveland, OH
KFAI Fresh Air of Minnesota [11594], Minneapolis, MN
Media Communications Assn. Intl., Ball State Univ. [5883], Muncie, IN
Media Communications Assn. Intl., Chicago [1043], Chicago, IL
Media Communications Assn. Intl., Kansas City [18908], Middleton, WI
Media Communs. Assn. Intl., Mid Michigan [7977], Grand Rapids, MI
Media Communications Assn. Intl., Minnesota [11600], Minneapolis, MN
Media Communications Assn. Intl., Ohio Valley Chap. [14909], Dayton, OH
Media Heritage [13896], Cincinnati, OH
Olinga Productions Association [4022], Wilmette, IL

Media Assn; Illinois School Lib. [404], Canton, IL
Media Assn; Wisconsin Educational [17649], Boscobel, WI
Media Communications Assn. Intl., Ball State Univ. [5883], Muncie, IN
Media Communications Assn. Intl., Chicago [1043], Chicago, IL
Media Communications Assn. Intl., Greater Cleveland Chap. [13449], Brunswick, OH
Media Communications Assn.-Intl., Greater Wisconsin Chap. [19671], Schofield, WI
Media Communications Assn. Intl., Kansas City [18908], Middleton, WI
Media Communications Assn.-Intl., Madison Chap. [18560], Madison, WI
Media Communs. Assn. Intl., Mid Michigan [7977], Grand Rapids, MI
Media Communs. Assn.-Intl., Milwaukee Chap. [19046], Milwaukee, WI
Media Communications Assn. Intl., Minnesota [11600], Minneapolis, MN
Media Communications Assn. Intl., Ohio Valley Chap. [14909], Dayton, OH
Media Development Corp; Greater Cleveland [14133], Cleveland, OH
Media in Educ; Illinois Assn. for [★404]
Media Educators; Assn. for Indiana [5728], Marion, IN
Media Heritage [13896], Cincinnati, OH
Mediation Council of Illinois [1044], Chicago, IL

Medical

Bay County Medical Soc. [7512], East Lansing, MI
Berrien County Medical Soc. [9681], St. Joseph, MI
Calhoun County Medical Soc. - Michigan [6856], Battle Creek, MI
Chicago Medical Soc. [816], Chicago, IL
Columbus Medical Assn. [14393], Columbus, OH
Fort Wayne Medical Soc. [4659], Fort Wayne, IN
Genesee County Medical Soc. [7737], Flint, MI
Hennepin Medical Soc. [11576], Minneapolis, MN
Illinois Assn. for Medical Equip. Services [2639], Naperville, IL
Indiana State Medical Assn. [5318], Indianapolis, IN
Ingham County Medical Soc. [7523], East Lansing, MI
Jackson County Medical Soc. - Michigan [8376], Jackson, MI
Kane County Medical Soc. [3387], St. Charles, IL
Lake County Medical Soc. - Illinois [2199], Lake Forest, IL
Lake County Medical Soc. - Indiana [5772], Merrillville, IN
Lake County Medical Soc. - Ohio [17257], Wickliffe, OH
Lake Superior Medical Soc. [10831], Duluth, MN
Lenawee County Medical Soc. [9907], Tecumseh, MI
Lorain County Medical Soc. [15119], Elyria, OH
Macomb County Medical Soc. [7179], Clinton Township, MI
Mahoning County Medical Assn. [13534], Canfield, OH
Marquette-Alger County Medical Soc. [8937], Marquette, MI
McHenry County Medical Soc. [3388], St. Charles, IL
Medical Soc. of Greater Akron [13065], Akron, OH
Michigan Assn. of Emergency Medical Technicians [8613], Lansing, MI
Michigan Medical Directors Assn. [7980], Grand Rapids, MI
Midland County Medical Soc. [9036], Midland, MI
Minnesota Medical Assn. [11655], Minneapolis, MN
Minnesota Medical Directors Assn. [11656], Minneapolis, MN
Montgomery County Medical Soc. - Ohio [14923], Dayton, OH
Muskegon County Medical Soc. [9153], Muskegon, MI
Oakland County Medical Soc. [6967], Birmingham, MI
Ohio State Medical Assn. [15441], Hilliard, OH
Ottawa County Medical Soc. [8215], Holland, MI
Peoria Medical Soc. [3055], Peoria, IL
Ramsey Medical Soc. [12569], St. Paul, MN
Rock Island County Medical Soc. [1366], Davenport, IL
Saginaw County Medical Soc. [9632], Saginaw, MI
St. Clair County Medical Soc. [210], Belleville, IL
St. Clair County Medical Soc. - Michigan [9440], Port Huron, MI
St. Joseph County Medical Soc. [6259], South Bend, IN
Sangamon County Medical Soc. [3672], Springfield, IL
Stark County Medical Soc. [13589], Canton, OH
Stearns-Benton County Medical Soc. [12312], St. Cloud, MN
Trumbull County Medical Soc. [17113], Warren, OH
Vanderburgh County Medical Soc. [4587], Evansville, IN
Vigo Parke Vermillion Medical Soc. [6348], Terre Haute, IN
Washtenaw County Medical Soc. [6787], Ann Arbor, MI
Waukesha County Medical Soc. [19446], Pewaukee, WI
Wayne County Medical Soc. of Southeast Michigan [7454], Detroit, MI
Winnebago County Medical Soc. [3330], Rockford, IL

Medical Administration

Amer. Assn. of Healthcare Administrative Mgt., Gopher Chap. [11974], Park Rapids, MN
Amer. Assn. of Healthcare Administrative Mgt., Western Reserve Chap. No. 18 [15493], Independence, OH
Amer. Assn. of Healthcare Administrative Mgt., Wisconsin Chap. [19595], Rhinelander, WI
Healthcare Financial Mgt. Assn., Central Ohio Chap. [14450], Columbus, OH
Healthcare Financial Mgt. Assn., Eastern Michigan Chap. [10076], Washington, MI
Healthcare Financial Mgt. Assn., First Illinois Chap. [1954], Harvey, IL
Healthcare Financial Mgt. Assn., Indiana Pressler Memorial Chap. [5836], Mooresville, IN
Healthcare Financial Mgt. Assn., Minnesota Chap. [11575], Minneapolis, MN
Healthcare Financial Mgt. Assn., Northeast Ohio Chap. [14137], Cleveland, OH
Healthcare Financial Mgt. Assn., Northwest Ohio Chap. [16921], Toledo, OH
Healthcare Financial Mgt. Assn., Southern Illinois Chap. [2089], Jerseyville, IL
Healthcare Financial Mgt. Assn., Southwestern Ohio Chap. [13861], Cincinnati, OH
Healthcare Financial Mgt. Assn., Western Michigan Chap. [7961], Grand Rapids, MI
Healthcare Financial Mgt. Assn., Wisconsin Chap. [19288], New Berlin, WI
Illinois Chap. of Amer. Medical Billing Assn. [1459], Des Plaines, IL
Illinois Medical Gp. Mgt. Assn. [949], Chicago, IL
Indiana Chap. of Amer. Medical Billing Assn. [6163], Schererville, IN
Indiana Medical Gp. Mgt. Assn. [5260], Indianapolis, IN
Medical Gp. Mgt. Assn. Ohio [14498], Columbus, OH
Michigan Medical Gp. Mgt. Assn. [7542], East Lansing, MI
Minnesota Medical Gp. Mgt. Assn. [12498], St. Paul, MN
Wisconsin Medical Gp. Mgt. Assn. [18725], Madison, WI

Medical Assistants

Amer. Assn. for Medical Transcription, 500 Central Indiana Chap. [5931], New Castle, IN
Amer. Assn. for Medical Transcription, Bay Area Chap. [9595], Saginaw, MI
Amer. Assn. for Medical Transcription, Buckeye Area Chap. [16429], Piqua, OH
Amer. Assn. for Medical Transcription, Four Lakes Chap. [17482], Appleton, WI
Amer. Assn. for Medical Transcription, Greater Milwaukee Chap. [19328], Oak Creek, WI
Amer. Assn. for Medical Transcription, Mid-Michigan Chap. [8232], Holly, MI
Amer. Assn. for Medical Transcription, Red Cedar Chap. [8144], Haslett, MI
Amer. Assn. for Medical Transcription, Southeast Michigan Chap. [7213], Commerce Township, MI
Amer. Assn. for Medical Transcription, Twin Cities Chap. [12865], Welch, MN
Amer. Assn. for Medical Transcription, West Michigan Chap. [9008], Mesick, MI
Natl. Network of Libraries of Medicine, Greater Midwest Region [1085], Chicago, IL
Wisconsin Interlibrary Services [18717], Madison, WI

Medical Assn; Indiana Podiatric [5279], Indianapolis, IN
Medical Assn; Michigan Veterinary [9293], Okemos, MI
Medical Device Assn; Michigan [8283], Howell, MI
Medical Device Manufacturers Coun; Indiana [5259], Indianapolis, IN
Medical Directors Assn; Minnesota [11656], Minneapolis, MN

Medical Education

Assn. of Medical School Microbiology and Immunology Chairs [7327], Detroit, MI

Michigan HOSA **[9282]**, Okemos, MI
Minnesota HOSA **[10648]**, Chanhassen, MN
Medical Equip. Services; Ohio Assn. of **[14558]**, Columbus, OH
Medical Ethics Rsrc. Network of Michigan **[7529]**, East Lansing, MI
Medical Gp. Mgt. Assn; Michigan **[7542]**, East Lansing, MI
Medical Gp. Mgt. Assn. Ohio **[14498]**, Columbus, OH
Medical Records
Central Illinois Hea. Info. Mgt. Assn. **[1272]**, Clinton, IL
Chicago Area Hea. Info. Mgt. Assn. **[784]**, Chicago, IL
Eastern Ohio Hea. Info. Mgt. Assn. **[17021]**, Uniontown, OH
Greater Cincinnati Hea. Info. Mgt. Assn. **[5833]**, Moores Hill, IN
Illinois Hea. Info. Mgt. Assn. **[943]**, Chicago, IL
Indiana Hea. Info. Mgt. Assn. **[5518]**, Ireland, IN
Miami Valley Hea. Info. Mgt. Assn. **[14913]**, Dayton, OH
Michigan Hea. Info. Mgt. Assn. **[9148]**, Muskegon, MI
Michigan Hea. Info. Mgt. Assn., Michiana **[5809]**, Mishawaka, IN
Michigan Hea. Info. Mgt. Assn., Mid-Michigan **[10173]**, Williamston, MI
Michigan Hea. Info. Mgt. Assn., North Central **[10129]**, West Branch, MI
Michigan Hea. Info. Mgt. Assn., Northwest **[9149]**, Muskegon, MI
Michigan Hea. Info. Mgt. Assn., Southeast **[7668]**, Farmington Hills, MI
Michigan Hea. Info. Mgt. Assn., Southwest **[8211]**, Holland, MI
Michigan Hea. Info. Mgt. Assn., Upper Peninsula **[8349]**, Ishpeming, MI
Minnesota Hea. Info. Mgt. Assn. **[12722]**, Stillwater, MN
Northeast Ohio Hea. Info. Mgt. Assn. **[14186]**, Cleveland, OH
Northwest Ohio Hea. Info. Mgt. Assn. **[16941]**, Toledo, OH
Southern Illinois Hea. Info. Mgt. Assn. **[3406]**, St. Peter, IL
West Central Hea. Info. Mgt. Assn. **[14785]**, Convoy, OH
Wisconsin Hea. Info. Mgt. Assn. **[18383]**, La Crosse, WI
Medical Res; Michigan Soc. for **[6736]**, Ann Arbor, MI
Medical School Microbiology and Immunology Chairs; Assn. of **[7327]**, Detroit, MI
Medical Soc; Chicago **[816]**, Chicago, IL
Medical Soc. of Greater Akron **[13065]**, Akron, OH
Medical Soc; Michigan State **[7550]**, East Lansing, MI
Medical Soc. of Milwaukee County **[19047]**, Milwaukee, WI
Medical Soc; Zumbro Valley **[12200]**, Rochester, MN
Medical Technology
Akron-Canton Soc. of Radiologic Technologists **[13252]**, Barberton, OH
Illinois Soc. for Histotechnologists **[3824]**, Urbana, IL
Illinois State Soc. of Amer. Medical Technologists **[2644]**, Naperville, IL
Illinois State Soc. of Radiologic Technologists **[291]**, Bloomington, IL
Indiana Soc. for Histotechnology **[5304]**, Indianapolis, IN
Indiana Soc. of Radiologic Technologists **[5308]**, Indianapolis, IN
Indiana Soc. of Radiologic Technologists, District 4 **[5569]**, Kokomo, IN
Indiana Soc. of Radiologic Technologists, District 8 **[5850]**, Mount Vernon, IN
Indiana State Assembly of the Assn. of Surgical Technologists **[5312]**, Indianapolis, IN
Michigan Soc. for Histotechnologists **[6644]**, Alpena, MI
Michigan Soc. of Radiologic Technologists **[7192]**, Clio, MI
Minnesota Assn. of Orthopaedic Technologists **[10894]**, Eden Prairie, MN
Ohio Assn. of Orthopaedic Technologists **[13573]**, Canton, OH
Ohio Soc. of Radiologic Technologists **[13079]**, Akron, OH
Ohio State Assembly of the Assn. of Surgical Technologists **[14678]**, Columbus, OH
Ohio State Soc. of Amer. Medical Technologists **[13332]**, Bellevue, OH
Orthopaedic Technologists Assn. of Illinois **[1118]**, Chicago, IL
Wisconsin Soc. of Radiologic Technologists **[19582]**, Racine, WI
Medical Tech; Michigan Soc. for **[★6838]**
Medicine
Illinois Vaccine Awareness Coalition **[2816]**, Oak Park, IL
Indianapolis Medical Soc. **[5351]**, Indianapolis, IN
Medical Ethics Rsrc. Network of Michigan **[7529]**, East Lansing, MI
Medical Soc. of Milwaukee County **[19047]**, Milwaukee, WI
Zumbro Valley Medical Soc. **[12200]**, Rochester, MN
Medicine; Central Chap. of the Soc. of Nuclear **[372]**, Burr Ridge, IL
Medicine, Greater Midwest Region; Natl. Network of Libraries of **[1085]**, Chicago, IL
Medicine, Michigan; Amer. Soc. of Addiction **[7505]**, East Lansing, MI
Medina Area Chamber of Commerce **[15944]**, Medina, OH
Medina Corvette Club **[17045]**, Valley City, OH
Medina County ALU **[14163]**, Cleveland, OH
Medina County Bd. of Realtors **[15945]**, Medina, OH
Medina County Convention and Visitors Bur. **[15946]**, Medina, OH
Medina County Dept. of Planning Services **[15947]**, Medina, OH
Medina County Home Builders Assn. **[15948]**, Medina, OH
Medina County Parks; Friends of **[15940]**, Medina, OH
Medina County REACT **[15949]**, Medina, OH
Medina County Youth for Christ **[13450]**, Brunswick, OH
Medina Summit Land Conservancy **[15950]**, Medina, OH
Medinah Shriners **[2339]**, Lombard, IL
Meeting Planners
Intl. Assn. of Convention and Visitor Bur., Charlotte Chicago, Illinois **[980]**, Chicago, IL
Intl. Assn. of Convention and Visitor Burs., Kansas City - Palatine, Illinois **[2914]**, Palatine, IL
Medina County Convention and Visitors Bur. **[15946]**, Medina, OH
Meeting Professionals Intl., Wisconsin Chap. **[18561]**, Madison, WI
Ohio Assn. of Convention and Visitor Bureaus **[14551]**, Columbus, OH
Professional Convention Mgt. Assn., Greater Midwest Chap. **[377]**, Burr Ridge, IL
Meeting Professionals Intl. - Minnesota Chap. **[12443]**, St. Paul, MN
Meeting Professionals Intl., Wisconsin Chap. **[18561]**, Madison, WI
Meigs County Beagle Club **[16494]**, Racine, OH
Meigs County Chamber of Commerce **[16455]**, Pomeroy, OH
Meigs Field; Friends of **[898]**, Chicago, IL
Meigs RSVP **[16456]**, Pomeroy, OH
MEL - Milwaukee Evolution League **[20134]**, West Milwaukee, WI
Mellen Area Chamber of Commerce **[18851]**, Mellen, WI
Melrose Chamber of Commerce **[11452]**, Melrose, MN
Melrose Park Chamber of Commerce **[2472]**, Melrose Park, IL
Melvindale Figure Skating Club **[8998]**, Melvindale, MI
Memorial Advisory and Planning Soc. **[6717]**, Ann Arbor, MI
Memorial Committee; Wayne County Veterans **[6112]**, Richmond, IN
Memorial Rifle Squad, Minnesota State Veterans Cemetery **[11167]**, Hillman, MN
Memorial Societies of Wisconsin **[17919]**, Egg Harbor, WI
Memphis Chamber of Commerce **[9000]**, Memphis, MI
Menasha Bluejay Football Club **[18861]**, Menasha, WI
Mendota Area Chamber of Commerce **[2476]**, Mendota, IL
Mendota Mdewakanton Dakota Community **[11454]**, Mendota, MN
Mennonite Nurses Assn. **[4801]**, Goshen, IN
Menominee Area Chamber of Commerce **[★9004]**
Menomonee Falls Chamber of Commerce **[18877]**, Menomonee Falls, WI
Menomonee Falls Chamber of Commerce and Indus. **[★18877]**
Men's Bus. Assn; Young **[★3160]**
Men's Fellowship of Northeastern Ohio; Catholic **[16191]**, Newbury, OH
Men's Rights
Natl. Coalition of Free Men **[11700]**, Minneapolis, MN
Mental Health
1st Capital Fed. of Families for Children's Mental Hea. **[13655]**, Chillicothe, OH
Advocacy Services for Kids **[8411]**, Kalamazoo, MI
Alliance for the Mentally Ill of Antrim/Kalkaska Counties **[8903]**, Mancelona, MI
Alliance for the Mentally Ill of Delta County **[7827]**, Gladstone, MI
Alliance for the Mentally Ill - Downtown Detroit **[7297]**, Detroit, MI
Alliance for the Mentally Ill of Jackson/Hillsdale Counties **[8354]**, Jackson, MI
Alliance for the Mentally Ill of Macomb County **[10057]**, Warren, MI
Alliance for the Mentally Ill of Mecosta County **[8995]**, Mecosta, MI
Alliance for the Mentally Ill of Northeast Michigan **[9538]**, Rogers City, MI
Alliance for the Mentally Ill of Northern Lower Michigan **[9360]**, Petoskey, MI
Alliance for the Mentally Ill - Share of Grand Rapids **[7882]**, Grand Rapids, MI
Alliance for the Mentally Ill of Suburban West **[8826]**, Livonia, MI
Arab-American Alliance for the Mentally Ill **[7248]**, Dearborn, MI
Assn. for Children's Mental Hea. **[8552]**, Lansing, MI
Bat/Arenac Alliance for the Mentally Ill **[6880]**, Bay City, MI
Berrien County Alliance for the Mentally Ill **[9757]**, Sodus, MI
Dearborn Area Alliance for the Mentally Ill **[7251]**, Dearborn, MI
Depression and Bipolar Support Alliance **[868]**, Chicago, IL
Depression and Bipolar Support Alliance Fox Valley **[3736]**, Sugar Grove, IL
Depression and Bipolar Support Alliance Metropolitan Detroit **[7338]**, Detroit, MI
Families Reaching for Rainbows Fed. of Families for Children's Mental Hea. **[5114]**, Indianapolis, IN
Family Action Network of Lake County **[4879]**, Hammond, IN
Fed. of Families for Children's Mental Hea. - First Ohio Chap. **[13532]**, Canfield, OH
Genesee County Alliance for the Mentally Ill **[7191]**, Clio, MI
Guild Incorporated **[12879]**, West St. Paul, MN
Hamilton County Compeer **[13860]**, Cincinnati, OH
Illinois Fed. of Families **[3859]**, Vienna, IL
Indiana Fed. of Families for Children's Mental Hea. **[4106]**, Anderson, IN
Jackson County Mental Hea. Assn. **[6182]**, Seymour, IN
Justice In Mental Hea. Org. **[8584]**, Lansing, MI
Lapeer County Alliance for the Mentally Ill **[7211]**, Columbiaville, MI
Lapeer County Community Mental Hea. Sers. **[8778]**, Lapeer, MI
Lenawee County Chap. of Natl. Alliance for the Mentally Ill **[6576]**, Adrian, MI

Mental Hea. Alliance of Monroe County **[4239]**, Bloomington, IN
Mental Hea. Assn. in Allen County **[4692]**, Fort Wayne, IN
Mental Hea. Assn. in Blackford County **[4904]**, Hartford City, IN
Mental Hea. Assn. in Boone County **[5671]**, Lebanon, IN
Mental Hea. Assn. in Cass County **[5694]**, Logansport, IN
Mental Hea. Assn. in Clark County **[6177]**, Sellersburg, IN
Mental Hea. Assn. in Clay County **[4284]**, Brazil, IN
Mental Hea. Assn. in Clinton County **[4743]**, Frankfort, IN
Mental Hea. Assn. in Daviess County **[6459]**, Washington, IN
Mental Hea. Assn. in Dekalb County **[4140]**, Auburn, IN
Mental Hea. Assn. in Delaware County **[5884]**, Muncie, IN
Mental Hea. Assn. in Dubois County **[4941]**, Huntingburg, IN
Mental Hea. Assn. in Elkhart County **[4500]**, Elkhart, IN
Mental Hea. Assn. in Floyd County **[5918]**, New Albany, IN
Mental Hea. Assn. of Franklin County **[14499]**, Columbus, OH
Mental Hea. Assn. in Franklin County, Indiana **[4299]**, Brookville, IN
Mental Hea. Assn. in Fulton County **[6123]**, Rochester, IN
Mental Hea. Assn. in Greene County **[6204]**, Solsberry, IN
Mental Hea. Assn. in Hancock County **[4835]**, Greenfield, IN
Mental Hea. Assn. in Henry County **[5937]**, New Castle, IN
Mental Hea. Assn. in Howard County **[5579]**, Kokomo, IN
Mental Hea. Assn. in Illinois **[1045]**, Chicago, IL
Mental Hea. Assn. of Illinois Valley **[3034]**, Peoria, IL
Mental Hea. Assn. in Indiana **[5402]**, Indianapolis, IN
Mental Hea. Assn. in Jay County **[6063]**, Portland, IN
Mental Hea. Assn. in Knox County **[6416]**, Vincennes, IN
Mental Hea. Assn. in Kosciusko County **[6449]**, Warsaw, IN
Mental Hea. Assn. in Lake County **[4917]**, Highland, IN
Mental Hea. Assn. of Licking County **[16172]**, Newark, OH
Mental Hea. Assn. in Marion County **[5403]**, Indianapolis, IN
Mental Hea. Assn. in Marshall County **[6434]**, Walkerton, IN
Mental Hea. Assn. of Miami County **[17002]**, Troy, OH
Mental Hea. Assn. in Michigan **[9805]**, Southfield, MI
Mental Hea. Assn. in Milwaukee County **[19048]**, Milwaukee, WI
Mental Hea. Assn. in Parke County **[6133]**, Rockville, IN
Mental Hea. Assn. in Porter County **[6385]**, Valparaiso, IN
Mental Hea. Assn. in Putnam County, Indiana **[4821]**, Greencastle, IN
Mental Hea. Assn. in Randolph County, Indiana **[6363]**, Union City, IN
Mental Hea. Assn. in Rush County **[6143]**, Rushville, IN
Mental Hea. Assn. in St. Joseph County **[6237]**, South Bend, IN
Mental Hea. Assn. in Sheboygan County **[19700]**, Sheboygan, WI
Mental Hea. Assn. of Southwest Ohio **[13897]**, Cincinnati, OH
Mental Hea. Assn. in Spencer County **[6155]**, St. Meinrad, IN
Mental Hea. Assn. in Steuben County **[4128]**, Angola, IN
Mental Hea. Assn. of Summit County **[14824]**, Cuyahoga Falls, OH
Mental Hea. Assn. in Vanderburgh County **[4559]**, Evansville, IN
Mental Hea. Assn. in Vigo County **[6333]**, Terre Haute, IN
Mental Hea. Assn. in Wabash County **[5987]**, North Manchester, IN
Mental Hea. Assn. in Wayne County, Indiana **[6097]**, Richmond, IN
Mental Hea. Assn. in Wells County **[4269]**, Bluffton, IN
Mental Hea. Assn. in White County **[5826]**, Monticello, IN
Michigan Assisted Living Assn. **[8847]**, Livonia, MI
Michigan Mental Hea. Counselors Assn. **[9506]**, Rochester, MI
Midland Alliance for the Mentally Ill **[9032]**, Midland, MI
Monroe Alliance for the Mentally Ill **[9066]**, Monroe, MI
NAMI Ohio **[14512]**, Columbus, OH
NAMI Olmsted County **[12163]**, Rochester, MN
NAMI, Richland County, Ohio **[15778]**, Mansfield, OH
NAMI Wisconsin **[18570]**, Madison, WI
Natl. Alliance on Mental Illness - Cook County North Suburban **[4039]**, Winnetka, IL
Natl. Alliance on Mental Illness - Fox Valley **[17505]**, Appleton, WI
Natl. Alliance for the Mentally Ill - Alger-Marquette County **[8953]**, Marquette, MI
Natl. Alliance for the Mentally Ill - Ba-Ho-Ke-On **[8512]**, Lake Linden, MI
Natl. Alliance for the Mentally Ill - Barron County **[19613]**, Rice Lake, WI
Natl. Alliance for the Mentally Ill - Belmont, Harrison, Monroe **[13264]**, Barnesville, OH
Natl. Alliance for the Mentally Ill - Brown County **[18117]**, Green Bay, WI
Natl. Alliance for the Mentally Ill - Champaign County **[538]**, Champaign, IL
Natl. Alliance for the Mentally Ill - Chequamegon Bay Area **[18202]**, High Bridge, WI
Natl. Alliance for the Mentally Ill, Clermont County **[13268]**, Batavia, OH
Natl. Alliance for the Mentally Ill - Dane County **[18573]**, Madison, WI
Natl. Alliance for the Mentally Ill - Door County **[19839]**, Sturgeon Bay, WI
Natl. Alliance for the Mentally Ill - Douglas County **[19743]**, Solon Springs, WI
Natl. Alliance for the Mentally Ill of DuPage County **[3992]**, Wheaton, IL
Natl. Alliance for the Mentally Ill - Eau Claire **[17888]**, Eau Claire, WI
Natl. Alliance for the Mentally Ill - Fond du Lac **[17988]**, Fond du Lac, WI
Natl. Alliance for the Mentally Ill of Greater Chicago **[1069]**, Chicago, IL
Natl. Alliance for the Mentally Ill - Greater Milwaukee **[19071]**, Milwaukee, WI
Natl. Alliance for the Mentally Ill Indiana **[5412]**, Indianapolis, IN
Natl. Alliance for the Mentally Ill - Jefferson County, Wisconsin **[18273]**, Jefferson, WI
Natl. Alliance for the Mentally Ill of Kalamazoo **[8455]**, Kalamazoo, MI
Natl. Alliance for the Mentally Ill - Kane County South **[1797]**, Geneva, IL
Natl. Alliance for the Mentally Ill - Kenosha **[18305]**, Kenosha, WI
Natl. Alliance for the Mentally Ill - La Crosse **[18373]**, La Crosse, WI
Natl. Alliance for the Mentally Ill - Lake County **[2266]**, Libertyville, IL
Natl. Alliance for the Mentally Ill - Lansing **[9297]**, Okemos, MI
Natl. Alliance for the Mentally Ill of Mackinac **[9080]**, Moran, MI
Natl. Alliance for the Mentally Ill - Madison County **[1883]**, Granite City, IL
Natl. Alliance for the Mentally Ill - Manitowoc **[18788]**, Manitowoc, WI
Natl. Alliance for the Mentally Ill - Marinette and Menominee **[9003]**, Menominee, MI
Natl. Alliance for the Mentally Ill - McHenry County **[1329]**, Crystal Lake, IL
Natl. Alliance for the Mentally Ill of Michigan **[8734]**, Lansing, MI
Natl. Alliance for the Mentally Ill - Mid Central WI **[20147]**, Westfield, WI
Natl. Alliance for the Mentally Ill - Newaygo **[9193]**, Newaygo, MI
Natl. Alliance for the Mentally Ill of Northwest Michigan **[9941]**, Traverse City, MI
Natl. Alliance for the Mentally Ill - Oshkosh **[19396]**, Oshkosh, WI
Natl. Alliance for the Mentally Ill - Ozaukee **[18887]**, Mequon, WI
Natl. Alliance for the Mentally Ill - Portage/Wood Counties **[19796]**, Stevens Point, WI
Natl. Alliance for the Mentally Ill - Racine County **[19561]**, Racine, WI
Natl. Alliance for the Mentally Ill - Richland County **[19623]**, Richland Center, WI
Natl. Alliance for the Mentally Ill - Rock County **[3351]**, Roscoe, IL
Natl. Alliance for the Mentally Ill - St. Croix **[19318]**, New Richmond, WI
Natl. Alliance for the Mentally Ill - Sheboygan **[19701]**, Sheboygan, WI
Natl. Alliance for the Mentally Ill - South Central **[17575]**, Baraboo, WI
Natl. Alliance for the Mentally Ill - Southwest Wisconsin **[19465]**, Platteville, WI
Natl. Alliance for the Mentally Ill - Tri-County **[3037]**, Peoria, IL
Natl. Alliance for the Mentally Ill - Tuscarawas County **[15029]**, Dover, OH
Natl. Alliance for the Mentally Ill - Washington County **[20124]**, West Bend, WI
Natl. Alliance for the Mentally Ill - Waukesha **[19993]**, Waukesha, WI
Natl. Alliance for the Mentally Ill - Wishigan **[17955]**, Fence, WI
Obsessive Compulsive Found. of Metropolitan Chicago **[1112]**, Chicago, IL
Ohio Coun. of Behavioral Hea.care Providers **[14588]**, Columbus, OH
Ohio Fed. of Families for Children's Mental Hea. - Summit Behavioral Hea. **[13937]**, Cincinnati, OH
Personality Disorder Awareness Network **[19091]**, Milwaukee, WI
Saginaw Alliance for the Mentally Ill **[7149]**, Chesaning, MI
Shiawassee Family and Friends Alliance for the Mentally Ill **[9335]**, Owosso, MI
Wayne-Westland Alliance for the Mentally Ill **[7278]**, Dearborn, MI
Wisconsin Family Ties **[18701]**, Madison, WI
Mental Hea. Alliance of Monroe County **[4239]**, Bloomington, IN
Mental Hea. Assn. in Allen County **[4692]**, Fort Wayne, IN
Mental Hea. Assn. in Blackford County **[4904]**, Hartford City, IN
Mental Hea. Assn. in Boone County **[5671]**, Lebanon, IN
Mental Hea. Assn. in Cass County **[5694]**, Logansport, IN
Mental Hea. Assn. in Clark County **[6177]**, Sellersburg, IN
Mental Hea. Assn. in Clay County **[4284]**, Brazil, IN
Mental Hea. Assn. in Clinton County **[4743]**, Frankfort, IN
Mental Hea. Assn. in Daviess County **[6459]**, Washington, IN
Mental Hea. Assn. in Dekalb County **[4140]**, Auburn, IN
Mental Hea. Assn. in Delaware County **[5884]**, Muncie, IN
Mental Hea. Assn. in Dubois County **[4941]**, Huntingburg, IN
Mental Hea. Assn. in Elkhart County **[4500]**, Elkhart, IN
Mental Hea. Assn. in Floyd County **[5918]**, New Albany, IN
Mental Hea. Assn. of Franklin County **[14499]**, Columbus, OH
Mental Hea. Assn. in Franklin County, Indiana **[4299]**, Brookville, IN
Mental Hea. Assn. in Fulton County **[6123]**, Rochester, IN

Mental Hea. Assn. in Greene County **[6204]**, Solsberry, IN
Mental Hea. Assn. in Hancock County **[4835]**, Greenfield, IN
Mental Hea. Assn. in Henry County **[5937]**, New Castle, IN
Mental Hea. Assn. in Howard County **[5579]**, Kokomo, IN
Mental Hea. Assn. in Illinois **[1045]**, Chicago, IL
Mental Hea. Assn. of Illinois Valley **[3034]**, Peoria, IL
Mental Hea. Assn. in Indiana **[5402]**, Indianapolis, IN
Mental Hea. Assn. in Jay County **[6063]**, Portland, IN
Mental Hea. Assn. in Knox County **[6416]**, Vincennes, IN
Mental Hea. Assn. in Kosciusko County **[6449]**, Warsaw, IN
Mental Hea. Assn. in Lake County **[4917]**, Highland, IN
Mental Hea. Assn. of Licking County **[16172]**, Newark, OH
Mental Hea. Assn. in Marion County **[5403]**, Indianapolis, IN
Mental Hea. Assn. in Marshall County **[6434]**, Walkerton, IN
Mental Hea. Assn. of Miami County **[17002]**, Troy, OH
Mental Hea. Assn. in Michigan **[9805]**, Southfield, MI
Mental Hea. Assn. in Milwaukee County **[19048]**, Milwaukee, WI
Mental Hea. Assn. in Parke County **[6133]**, Rockville, IN
Mental Hea. Assn. in Porter County **[6385]**, Valparaiso, IN
Mental Hea. Assn. in Putnam County, Indiana **[4821]**, Greencastle, IN
Mental Hea. Assn. in Randolph County, Indiana **[6363]**, Union City, IN
Mental Hea. Assn. in Rush County **[6143]**, Rushville, IN
Mental Hea. Assn. in St. Joseph County **[6237]**, South Bend, IN
Mental Hea. Assn. in Sheboygan County **[19700]**, Sheboygan, WI
Mental Hea. Assn. of Southwest Ohio **[13897]**, Cincinnati, OH
Mental Hea. Assn. in Spencer County **[6155]**, St. Meinrad, IN
Mental Hea. Assn. in Steuben County **[4128]**, Angola, IN
Mental Hea. Assn. of Summit County **[14824]**, Cuyahoga Falls, OH
Mental Hea. Assn. in Vanderburgh County **[4559]**, Evansville, IN
Mental Hea. Assn. in Vigo County **[6333]**, Terre Haute, IN
Mental Hea. Assn. in Wabash County **[5987]**, North Manchester, IN
Mental Hea. Assn. in Wayne County, Indiana **[6097]**, Richmond, IN
Mental Hea. Assn. in Wells County **[4269]**, Bluffton, IN
Mental Hea. Assn. in White County **[5826]**, Monticello, IN
Mental Hea. Counselors Assn; Michigan **[9506]**, Rochester, MI
Mental Hea; Michigan Assn. for Infant **[9837]**, Southgate, MI
Mental Hea. Sers; Lapeer County Community **[8778]**, Lapeer, MI
Mentally Disabled
Achieva Rsrcs. Center Plant 3 - Franklin County **[4295]**, Brookville, IN
Achieva Rsrcs. Corp. - Wayne County **[6083]**, Richmond, IN
Achieva Rsrcs. First Steps - Madison County **[4088]**, Alexandria, IN
Achieva Rsrcs. - Hea.y Families and Employment Sers. - Fayette County **[4409]**, Connersville, IN
Achieva Rsrcs. Hea.y Families - Union County **[5677]**, Liberty, IN
ADEC Rsrcs. for Independence **[4290]**, Bristol, IN
Allegan Rsrc. Center **[6602]**, Allegan, MI
Arc/Allegan County **[6604]**, Allegan, MI
Arc of Allen County **[15649]**, Lima, OH
Arc of Carroll County **[4614]**, Flora, IN
Arc of Dearborn County **[5653]**, Lawrenceburg, IN
Arc Eau Claire **[17864]**, Eau Claire, WI
Arc of Erie County **[16603]**, Sandusky, OH
Arc of Fairfield County **[16418]**, Pickerington, OH
ARC of Illinois **[2045]**, Homewood, IL
Arc Kandiyohi County **[12913]**, Willmar, MN
Arc Livingston **[8272]**, Howell, MI
Arc Minnesota **[12383]**, St. Paul, MN
Arc/Muskegon **[9140]**, Muskegon, MI
Arc of Neenah-Menasha **[18857]**, Menasha, WI
The Arc/Newaygo County **[7795]**, Fremont, MI
Arc of Oakland County **[9973]**, Troy, MI
ARC of Ohio **[14316]**, Columbus, OH
ARC Opportunities - Lagrance County **[4936]**, Howe, IN
Arc of Owen County **[6281]**, Spencer, IN
ARC Rehab Sers. **[5666]**, Lebanon, IN
Arc St. Cloud **[12274]**, St. Cloud, MN
ARC Services of Macomb **[7173]**, Clinton Township, MI
Arc Southeastern Minnesota **[12129]**, Rochester, MN
Arc of Stark County **[13546]**, Canton, OH
Arc of Vigo County **[6314]**, Terre Haute, IN
Arc of Western Wayne County **[10137]**, Westland, MI
Arc of Winnebago, Boone and Ogle **[3272]**, Rockford, IL
Arc-Wisconsin Disability Assn. **[18476]**, Madison, WI
Assn. for Community Advocacy **[6680]**, Ann Arbor, MI
Assn. for the Developmentally Disabled in Woodford County **[1643]**, Eureka, IL
Assn. for Retarded Citizens - Vanderburgh County **[4532]**, Evansville, IN
Auglaize County Arc **[16117]**, New Bremen, OH
Becca's Karing Individuals for Disabilities **[1768]**, Galesburg, IL
Benton County Assn. for Retarded Citizens **[4735]**, Fowler, IN
Best Buddies Illinois **[761]**, Chicago, IL
Blue Island Citizens For Developmental Disabilities **[316]**, Blue Island, IL
Brown County Assn. for Retarded Citizens **[18088]**, Green Bay, WI
Center for Mental Retardation (Cayuhoga) **[14086]**, Cleveland, OH
Chicago/ARC **[782]**, Chicago, IL
Down Syndrome Assn. of Greater Cincinnati **[13814]**, Cincinnati, OH
Elder Network **[12137]**, Rochester, MN
Fountain County Assn. for Retarded Citizens **[6400]**, Veedersburg, IN
Hoosier Praire ARC **[5824]**, Monticello, IN
Jefferson Switzerland Assn. for Retarded Citizens **[5716]**, Madison, IN
Knox County Assn. for Retarded Citizens **[6411]**, Vincennes, IN
Mosaic **[2374]**, Macomb, IL
Natl. Alliance for the Mentally Ill - Southwest **[2798]**, Oak Lawn, IL
New Hope Assn. **[1489]**, Dolton, IL
Noble Arc of Central Indiana - Hamilton, Howard, Marion, Shelby and Tipton Counties **[5439]**, Indianapolis, IN
Noble ARC of Greater Indianapolis **[5440]**, Indianapolis, IN
Ohio Assn. of County Boards of MRDD **[17347]**, Worthington, OH
Options and Advocacy for McHenry County **[1330]**, Crystal Lake, IL
Park Lawn Arc **[2800]**, Oak Lawn, IL
Peoria Assn. For Retarded Citizens **[3049]**, Peoria, IL
Posey County Assn. for Retarded Citizens **[5854]**, Mount Vernon, IN
Rock Island County Arc **[3256]**, Rock Island, IL
Seguin Retarded Citizens Assn. **[239]**, Berwyn, IL
Soc. For The Handicapped Of Medina County **[16632]**, Seville, OH
South Chicago Parents And Friends Of Retarded Children **[1192]**, Chicago, IL
Spencer County ARC **[6128]**, Rockport, IN
Springfield Assn. for Retarded Citizens **[3676]**, Springfield, IL
Stone Belt Arc - Monroe County **[4261]**, Bloomington, IN
Tri-County Community Advocates for People with Developmental Disabilities **[8765]**, Lansing, MI
Victor C Neumann Assn. **[1222]**, Chicago, IL
Voice of the Retarded, Illinois **[2735]**, Normal, IL
Voice of the Retarded, Michigan **[8770]**, Lansing, MI
Voice of the Retarded, Minnesota **[11773]**, Minneapolis, MN
Voice of the Retarded, Ohio **[17447]**, Zanesville, OH
Voice of the Retarded, Wisconsin **[18178]**, Hartford, WI
Mentally Ill, Clermont County; Natl. Alliance for the **[13268]**, Batavia, OH
Mentally Ill - Southwest; Natl. Alliance for the **[2798]**, Oak Lawn, IL
Mentone Chamber of Commerce **[5761]**, Mentone, IN
Mentor Area Chamber of Commerce **[15970]**, Mentor, OH
Mentor Figure Skating Club **[15971]**, Mentor, OH
Mentoring Moms **[18256]**, Janesville, WI
Mentoring Partnership of Minnesota **[11601]**, Minneapolis, MN
Mentoring of Princeton; Kinship Youth **[12045]**, Princeton, MN
Mequon-Thiensville Area Chamber of Commerce **[★19892]**
Mequon-Thiensville Area Chamber of Commerce **[19892]**, Thiensville, WI
Mercantile Exchange; Chicago **[818]**, Chicago, IL
Mercedes Benz Club of Am. - 500 Sect. **[5404]**, Indianapolis, IN
Mercedes-Benz Club of Am. of the Western Michigan Sect. **[8291]**, Hudsonville, MI
Mercer Area Chamber of Commerce **[18893]**, Mercer, WI
Mercer County Angus Assn. **[23]**, Alexis, IL
Mercer County Chap. of the Ohio Genealogical Soc. **[13614]**, Celina, OH
Merchant Assn; Oxford **[★9340]**
Merchants Assn. of Chicago; Korean Amer. **[1014]**, Chicago, IL
Merrill Area Chamber of Commerce **[18896]**, Merrill, WI
Merrill Area United Way **[18897]**, Merrill, WI
Merrill Lions Club **[9006]**, Merrill, MI
Merrillville Chamber of Commerce **[5774]**, Merrillville, IN
Merry Makers; Lake County **[8305]**, Idlewild, MI
Mesabi Range Youth for Christ **[12796]**, Virginia, MN
Mesick Area Chamber of Commerce **[9009]**, Mesick, MI
Mesick Lions Club **[9010]**, Mesick, MI
Metabolic Disorders
Wilson's Disease Assn. **[17334]**, Wooster, OH
Metal
Chicago Metal Finishers Inst. **[819]**, Chicago, IL
East Michigan District of Precision Metalforming Assn. **[9987]**, Troy, MI
Indiana District of Precision Metalforming Assn. **[5228]**, Indianapolis, IN
Northwest Ohio District of Precision Metalforming Assn. **[16828]**, Sylvania, OH
Ohio Valley District of Precision Metalforming Assn. **[16738]**, Springfield, OH
Precision Metalforming Assn. **[15503]**, Independence, OH
Sheet Metal Workers' Intl. Assn., AFL-CIO, CFL - Local Union 10 **[11423]**, Maplewood, MN
Sheet Metal Workers' Intl. Assn., Local Union 265 **[452]**, Carol Stream, IL
United Steelworkers of Am., Sub District Off. **[17123]**, Warrensville Heights, OH
West Michigan District of Precision Metalforming Assn. **[8224]**, Holland, MI
Wisconsin District of Precision Metalforming Assn. **[18834]**, Mayville, WI
Metal and Air Conditioning Contractors' Natl. Assn. of North Central Ohio; Sheet **[14216]**, Cleveland, OH
Metal Contractors Assn. of Evansville; Sheet **[4572]**, Evansville, IN
Metal Contractors Assn; Northeastern Illinois Sheet **[1598]**, Elgin, IL
Metal Workers' Local Union 33 Cleveland District; Sheet **[14217]**, Cleveland, OH

Metallurgy
APMI Cleveland Chap. **[14072]**, Cleveland, OH
APMI Dayton **[5033]**, Indianapolis, IN
APMI Michigan **[8271]**, Howell, MI
ASM Intl. - Detroit Chap. **[10062]**, Warren, MI
Assn. for Iron and Steel Tech. Midwest Chap. **[3503]**, South Holland, IL
Assn. for Iron and Steel Tech. Northeastern Ohio Chap. **[13112]**, Alliance, OH
Assn. for Iron and Steel Tech. Ohio Valley Chap. **[13753]**, Cincinnati, OH
Metals
Natl. Ornamental and Miscellaneous Metals Assn. Upper Midwest Chap. **[1612]**, Elk Grove Village, IL
Meteorological Soc., Greater St. Louis; Amer. **[3456]**, Scott AFB, IL
Meteorological Soc., Northeast Ohio; Amer. **[13036]**, Akron, OH
Meteorological Soc., Packerland Chap; Amer. **[18078]**, Green Bay, WI
Meteorological Soc., Purdue Univ; Amer. **[★6498]**
Meteorology
Amer. Meteorological Soc., Central Illinois **[2272]**, Lincoln, IL
Amer. Meteorological Soc., Central Michigan Univ. **[9097]**, Mount Pleasant, MI
Amer. Meteorological Soc., Central Ohio **[15618]**, Lebanon, OH
Amer. Meteorological Soc., Chicago **[3717]**, Streamwood, IL
Amer. Meteorological Soc., Greater Milwaukee **[19981]**, Waukesha, WI
Amer. Meteorological Soc., Greater St. Louis **[3456]**, Scott AFB, IL
Amer. Meteorological Soc., Northeast Ohio **[13036]**, Akron, OH
Amer. Meteorological Soc., Northern Illinois Univ. **[1427]**, DeKalb, IL
Amer. Meteorological Soc., Northland Coll. **[17542]**, Ashland, WI
Amer. Meteorological Soc., Packerland Chap. **[18078]**, Green Bay, WI
Amer. Meteorological Soc., Twin Cities **[10331]**, Arden Hills, MN
Amer. Meteorological Soc., Univ. of Michigan - Ann Arbor **[8117]**, Harbor Springs, MI
Amer. Meteorological Soc., Wright Memorial **[17355]**, Wright-Patterson AFB, OH
Purdue Univ. Meteorological Assn. **[6498]**, West Lafayette, IN
Metro Airport Lions Club **[7664]**, Farmington Hills, MI
Metro Chicago Youth for Christ **[3991]**, Wheaton, IL
Metro Cincinnati Amateur Softball Assn. **[13898]**, Cincinnati, OH
Metro Cleveland Amateur Softball Assn. **[14164]**, Cleveland, OH
Metro Columbus - Young Life **[14500]**, Columbus, OH
Metro Decatur Home Builders Assn. **[★1384]**
Metro Detroit Amateur Softball Assn. **[9270]**, Okemos, MI
Metro Detroit Chap. of Falcon Club of Am. **[6614]**, Allen Park, MI
Metro East Chamber of Commerce **[9662]**, St. Clair Shores, MI
Metro East Coin and Currency Club **[207]**, Belleville, IL
Metro East Humane Soc. **[1564]**, Edwardsville, IL
Metro Marines **[10643]**, Champlin, MN
Metro Meals on Wheels **[11602]**, Minneapolis, MN
Metrokids **[11603]**, Minneapolis, MN
MetroNorth Chamber of Commerce **[10449]**, Blaine, MN
MetroNorth Chamber of Commerce - Serving Anoka County and Surrounding Areas **[★10449]**
Metropolis Area Chamber of Commerce **[2484]**, Metropolis, IL
Metropolis Area Chamber of Commerce, Tourism and Economic Development **[★2484]**
Metropolitan Consolidated Assn. of Realtors **[9994]**, Troy, MI
Metropolitan Detroit Antique Bottle Club **[9995]**, Troy, MI
Metropolitan Detroit Landscaping Assn. **[★6955]**
Metropolitan Detroit Plumbing and Mech. Contractors Assn. **[★7420]**
Metropolitan Detroit Sci. Teachers Assn. **[7389]**, Detroit, MI
Metropolitan Evansville Chamber of Commerce **[4560]**, Evansville, IN
Metropolitan Indianapolis Bd. of Realtors **[5405]**, Indianapolis, IN
Metropolitan Mathematics Club of Chicago **[2819]**, Oak Park, IL
Metropolitan Mayors Caucus **[1046]**, Chicago, IL
Metropolitan Milwaukee Assn. of Commerce **[19049]**, Milwaukee, WI
Metropolitan Planning Coun. **[1047]**, Chicago, IL
Metropolitan Sewer District of Greater Cincinnati **[13899]**, Cincinnati, OH
Mexicantown Community Development Corp. **[7390]**, Detroit, MI
Miami County Historical and Genealogical Soc., Chap. of OGS **[17003]**, Troy, OH
Miami Indian Trekkers **[15394]**, Hamilton, OH
Miami Univ. Coun. of Teachers of Mathematics **[16324]**, Oxford, OH
Miami Valley ALU **[17004]**, Troy, OH
Miami Valley Angus Assn. **[15395]**, Hamilton, OH
Miami Valley Astronomical Soc. **[16011]**, Middletown, OH
Miami Valley Beagle Club **[13441]**, Brookville, OH
Miami Valley Boxer Club **[16854]**, Tiffin, OH
Miami Valley Doberman Pinscher Club **[13900]**, Cincinnati, OH
Miami Valley DX Club **[14501]**, Columbus, OH
Miami Valley Fire-EMS Alliance **[14910]**, Dayton, OH
Miami Valley Golf Assn. **[14911]**, Dayton, OH
Miami Valley Golf Course Superintendents Assn. **[14912]**, Dayton, OH
Miami Valley Hea. Info. Mgt. Assn. **[14913]**, Dayton, OH
Miami Valley Human Rsrc. Assn. **[15987]**, Miamisburg, OH
Miami Valley Mineral and Gem Club **[16733]**, Springfield, OH
Miami Valley Model Yacht Assn. No. 73 **[14914]**, Dayton, OH
Miami Valley NARI **[14915]**, Dayton, OH
Miami Valley Natl. Assn. of the Remodeling Indus. **[★14915]**
Miami Valley Orchid Soc. **[13901]**, Cincinnati, OH
Miami Valley Orienteering Club **[14916]**, Dayton, OH
Miami Valley Pheasants Forever **[13506]**, Camden, OH
Miami Valley Regional Planning Commn. **[14917]**, Dayton, OH
Miami Valley Restaurant Assn. **[14918]**, Dayton, OH
Miami Valley RSVP **[15363]**, Greenville, OH
Miami Valley Triumphs **[13315]**, Bellbrook, OH
Miami Valley Venture Assn. **[★14918]**
Miami Valley Vizsla Club **[14502]**, Columbus, OH
Miami Valley Water Garden Soc. **[14919]**, Dayton, OH
Miamisburg Lion Club **[15988]**, Miamisburg, OH
MichBio **[6718]**, Ann Arbor, MI
Michiana Astronomical Soc. **[6238]**, South Bend, IN
Michiana Beagle Club **[7593]**, Edwardsburg, MI
Michiana Chap. of Soc. for Human Rsrc. Mgt. **[6239]**, South Bend, IN
Michiana Corvette Club **[6240]**, South Bend, IN
Michiana Dressage Club **[7286]**, Decatur, MI
Michiana Emmaus Community **[4501]**, Elkhart, IN
Michiana Figure Skating Club **[9209]**, Niles, MI
Michiana Free-Net Soc. **[6241]**, South Bend, IN
Michiana Gem and Mineral Soc. **[6242]**, South Bend, IN
Michiana Master Gardeners Assn. **[4802]**, Goshen, IN
Michiana Miniature Guild **[4288]**, Bremen, IN
Michiana Orchid Soc. **[6490]**, West Lafayette, IN
Michiana Peace and Justice Coalition **[6243]**, South Bend, IN
Michiana Professional Photographers **[5775]**, Merrillville, IN
Michiana R/C Choppers **[4502]**, Elkhart, IN
Michiana War Resistors League **[★6243]**
Michigan 4-H Youth Programs **[★7552]**
Michigan Abortion and Reproductive Rights Action League **[★8601]**
Michigan Acad. of Family Physicians **[9271]**, Okemos, MI
Michigan Acad. of Physician Assistants **[7530]**, East Lansing, MI
Michigan Acad. of Sci., Arts, and Letters **[6633]**, Alma, MI
Michigan ACORN **[★7339]**
Michigan Adaptive Sports **[8482]**, Keego Harbor, MI
Michigan Advt. Indus. Alliance **[7391]**, Detroit, MI
Michigan AEYC, MIAEYC **[★7534]**
Michigan Agri Bus. Assn. **[7531]**, East Lansing, MI
Michigan Agri-Dealers Assn. **[★7531]**
Michigan Alcohol and Drug Info. **[★8528]**
Michigan Alliance of Cooperatives **[6971]**, Blanchard, MI
Michigan Alliance for Gifted Educ. **[7978]**, Grand Rapids, MI
Michigan Amateur Athletic Union **[9565]**, Roseville, MI
Michigan Amateur Softball Assn. **[9029]**, Midland, MI
Michigan Amer. Eskimo Dog Assn. **[9753]**, Sherwood, MI
Michigan Angus Assn. **[9701]**, Saline, MI
Michigan Appaloosa Horse Assn. **[9772]**, South Lyon, MI
Michigan Apple Comm. **[7462]**, DeWitt, MI
Michigan Applied Systems User Gp. **[7532]**, East Lansing, MI
Michigan Architectural Found. **[7392]**, Detroit, MI
Michigan Art Educ. Assn. **[9107]**, Mount Pleasant, MI
Michigan Asphalt Paving Assn. **[8604]**, Lansing, MI
Michigan Assisted Living Assn. **[8847]**, Livonia, MI
Michigan Assn. of Acupuncture and Oriental Medicine **[9451]**, Portage, MI
Michigan Assn. of Agriscience Educators **[7039]**, Byron, MI
Michigan Assn. of Alcoholism and Drug Abuse Counselors **[7067]**, Canton, MI
Michigan Assn. of Ambulance Services **[8605]**, Lansing, MI
Michigan Assn. of Art Therapy **[10117]**, West Bloomfield, MI
Michigan Assn. of Blood Banks **[7105]**, Center Line, MI
Michigan Assn. of Broadcasters **[8606]**, Lansing, MI
Michigan Assn. of Campus Law Enforcement Administrators **[10027]**, University Center, MI
Michigan Assn. of Certified Public Accountants **[9996]**, Troy, MI
Michigan Assn. of Cherry Producers **[8607]**, Lansing, MI
Michigan Assn. of Chiefs of Police **[9272]**, Okemos, MI
Michigan Assn. of Coll. Stores **[8949]**, Marquette, MI
Michigan Assn. of Collegiate Registrars and Admissions Officers **[9108]**, Mount Pleasant, MI
Michigan Assn. of Commercial Dental Labs. **[7181]**, Clinton Township, MI
Michigan Assn. of Community and Adult Educ. **[8608]**, Lansing, MI
Michigan Assn. of Community Arts Agencies **[8609]**, Lansing, MI
Michigan Assn. of Community Bankers **[7533]**, East Lansing, MI
Michigan Assn. of Community Mental Hea. Boards **[8610]**, Lansing, MI
Michigan Assn. for Cmpt. Users in Learning **[8241]**, Holt, MI
Michigan Assn. of Conservation Districts **[7047]**, Cadillac, MI
Michigan Assn. of Convenience Stores **[8611]**, Lansing, MI
Michigan Assn. for Deaf, Hearing and Speech Sers. **[8612]**, Lansing, MI
Michigan Assn. of Distributors **[13488]**, Caledonia, OH
Michigan Assn. for Educ. Data Systems **[7182]**, Clinton Township, MI
Michigan Assn. for the Educ. of Young Children **[7534]**, East Lansing, MI
Michigan Assn. of Educal. Representatives **[7862]**, Grand Haven, MI
Michigan Assn. of Emergency Medical Technicians **[8613]**, Lansing, MI
Michigan Assn. for Epilepsy **[★9799]**
Michigan Assn. for Evaluation **[7393]**, Detroit, MI
Michigan Assn. of Fairs and Exhibitions **[8614]**, Lansing, MI
Michigan Assn. of Fire Chiefs **[8615]**, Lansing, MI
Michigan Assn. of Governmental Employees **[8616]**, Lansing, MI

Michigan Assn. of Hea. Plans [8617], Lansing, MI
Michigan Assn. for Hea.care Quality [10118], West Bloomfield, MI
Michigan Assn. of Home Builders [8618], Lansing, MI
Michigan Assn. for Infant Mental Hea. [9837], Southgate, MI
Michigan Assn. for Institutional Res. [8950], Marquette, MI
Michigan Assn. of Insurance Agents [8619], Lansing, MI
Michigan Assn. for Local Public Hea. [8620], Lansing, MI
Michigan Assn. of Middle School Educators [9614], Saginaw, MI
Michigan Assn. of Municipal Attorneys [6719], Ann Arbor, MI
Michigan Assn. of Neurological Surgeons [7394], Detroit, MI
Michigan Assn. of Non-Public Schools [8621], Lansing, MI
Michigan Assn. of Nurse Anesthetists [6720], Ann Arbor, MI
Michigan Assn. of Occupational Hea. Nurses [8622], Lansing, MI
Michigan Assn. of Osteopathic Physicians and Surgeons [★9288]
Michigan Assn. of PeriAnesthesia Nurses [9545], Romeo, MI
Michigan Assn. of Physicians of Indian Origin [8848], Livonia, MI
Michigan Assn. of Planning [6721], Ann Arbor, MI
Michigan Assn. of Professional Court Rpt.ers [7745], Flint, MI
Michigan Assn. of Professional Court Reporters [9381], Pinckney, MI
Michigan Assn. of Professional Landmen [8623], Lansing, MI
Michigan Assn. of Professional Psychologists [7665], Farmington Hills, MI
Michigan Assn. for Pupil Trans. [8624], Lansing, MI
Michigan Assn. of Realtors [8625], Lansing, MI
Michigan Assn. of Recreational Vehicles and Campgrounds [9273], Okemos, MI
Michigan Assn. of Rehabilitation Organizations [★8602]
Michigan Assn. of School Administrators [8626], Lansing, MI
Michigan Assn. of School Bds. [8627], Lansing, MI
Michigan Assn. of School Psychologists [9937], Traverse City, MI
Michigan Assn. of Secondary School Principals [8628], Lansing, MI
Michigan Assn. of Substance Abuse Coordinating Agencies [7535], East Lansing, MI
Michigan Assn. of Substance Abuse Coordinators [★7535]
Michigan Assn. for Supervision and Curriculum Development [8629], Lansing, MI
Michigan Assn. of Timbermen [8630], Lansing, MI
Michigan Assn. of Timbermen [9197], Newberry, MI
Michigan Assn. of United Ways [8631], Lansing, MI
Michigan Assn. of Woodturners [7016], Brighton, MI
Michigan Atheists [9051], Milford, MI
Michigan Athletic Trainers' Soc. [6722], Ann Arbor, MI
Michigan Audubon Soc. [8632], Lansing, MI
Michigan Audubon Soc. - Grand Traverse Audubon Club [9938], Traverse City, MI
Michigan Auto. Dealers Assn. [7536], East Lansing, MI
Michigan Bankers Assn. [8633], Lansing, MI
Michigan Basin Geological Soc. [8634], Lansing, MI
Michigan Bass Chap. Fed. [9013], Michigan Center, MI
Michigan Bean Commn. [9676], St. Johns, MI
Michigan Beef Indus. Commn. [9274], Okemos, MI
Michigan Beer and Wine Wholesalers Assn. [8635], Lansing, MI
Michigan Biosciences Indus. Assn. [★6718]
Michigan Black Independent Publishers Assn. [8636], Lansing, MI
Michigan Bluebird Soc. [8384], Jackson, MI
Michigan Bd. of Optometry [8637], Lansing, MI
Michigan Boating Indus. Assn. [8849], Livonia, MI
Michigan Boer Goat Assn. [9853], Standish, MI
Michigan Bookmen's Club [★7862]
Michigan Boxer club [7666], Farmington Hills, MI
Michigan Bus. and Professional Assn. [10069], Warren, MI
Michigan Cactus and Succulent Soc. [10119], West Bloomfield, MI
Michigan Campaign Finance Network [8638], Lansing, MI
Michigan Capitol Girl Scout Coun. [8242], Holt, MI
Michigan Carpentry Contractors Assn. [8850], Livonia, MI
Michigan Catalysis Soc. [9746], Shelby Township, MI
Michigan Celery Promotion Cooperative [8292], Hudsonville, MI
Michigan Center Lions Club [9014], Michigan Center, MI
Michigan Chamber of Commerce [8639], Lansing, MI
Michigan Chap. of the Amer. Soc. of Landscape Architects [8640], Lansing, MI
Michigan Chap. of Assn. for Career and Tech. Educ. [10086], Waterford, MI
Michigan Chapter of the Assn. of Rehabilitation Nurses [8897], Madison Heights, MI
Michigan Chap. of IARP [7057], Cannonsburg, MI
Michigan Chap. of NALMS [9684], St. Joseph, MI
Michigan Chap. of Natl. Assn. of Tax Practitioners [8237], Holly, MI
Michigan Chap. of Natl. Emergency Number Assn. [9030], Midland, MI
Michigan Chap. of the Novelty Salt and Pepper Shakers Club [★6864]
Michigan Chap. - Sheet Metal and Air Conditioning Contractors' Natl. Assn. [8148], Haslett, MI
Michigan Charter Boat Assn. [9550], Romulus, MI
Michigan Chefs de Cuisine Assn. [7667], Farmington Hills, MI
Michigan Chem. Coun. [8641], Lansing, MI
Michigan Chess Assn. [9238], Novi, MI
Michigan Chiropractic Soc. [8642], Lansing, MI
Michigan Christmas Tree Assn. [8282], Howell, MI
Michigan Citizen Action [8448], Kalamazoo, MI
Michigan City Area Chamber of Commerce [5786], Michigan City, IN
Michigan City Exchange Club [5787], Michigan City, IN
Michigan City Historical Soc. [5788], Michigan City, IN
Michigan Clothiers Assn. [8643], Lansing, MI
Michigan Coalition Against Domestic and Sexual Violence [9275], Okemos, MI
Michigan Coalition of Essential Schools [8385], Jackson, MI
Michigan Coin Laundry Assn. [8183], Hillsdale, MI
Michigan Coll. of Emergency Physicians [8644], Lansing, MI
Michigan Colleges Found. [9806], Southfield, MI
Michigan Communities In Schools [8210], Holland, MI
Michigan Community Action Agency Assn. [8645], Lansing, MI
Michigan Community Coll. Assn. [8646], Lansing, MI
Michigan Community Coordinated Child Care Assn. [8647], Lansing, MI
Michigan Competing Band Assn. [9078], Montrose, MI
Michigan Concrete Assn. [8648], Lansing, MI
Michigan Concrete Paving Assn. [9276], Okemos, MI
Michigan Conf. of the Amer. Assn. of Univ. Professors [8649], Lansing, MI
Michigan Cong. of Parents, Teachers and Students [8650], Lansing, MI
Michigan Consumer Fed. [7537], East Lansing, MI
Michigan Corn Growers Assn. [7463], DeWitt, MI
Michigan Corrections Org. [8651], Lansing, MI
Michigan Coun. of the Blind and Visually Impaired [9435], Port Huron, MI
Michigan Coun. of Chapters of the MOAA [7017], Brighton, MI
Michigan Coun. on Crime and Delinquency [8652], Lansing, MI
Michigan Coun. for the Social Stud. [9109], Mount Pleasant, MI
Michigan Coun. of Teachers of English [9505], Rochester, MI
Michigan Coun. of Teachers of Mathematics [6723], Ann Arbor, MI
Michigan Coun. Trout Unlimited [7979], Grand Rapids, MI
Michigan Counseling Assn. [8653], Lansing, MI
Michigan County Social Ser. Assn. [8654], Lansing, MI
Michigan Credit Union League [9402], Plymouth, MI
Michigan Crop Improvement Assn. [8655], Lansing, MI
Michigan Dairy Goat Soc. [8883], Lyons, MI
Michigan Dark-Sky Assn. [8449], Kalamazoo, MI
Michigan DECA [10210], Ypsilanti, MI
Michigan Democratic Party [8656], Lansing, MI
Michigan Dental Assn. [8657], Lansing, MI
Michigan Dental Hygienists' Assn. [9277], Okemos, MI
Michigan Detroit Area Woodturners [9997], Troy, MI
Michigan Developmental Disabilities Coun. [8658], Lansing, MI
Michigan Dietetic Assn. [9663], St. Clair Shores, MI
Michigan Disability Sports Alliance [7538], East Lansing, MI
Michigan Disabled Amer. Veterans [7395], Detroit, MI
Michigan Distributors and Vendors Assn. [8659], Lansing, MI
Michigan District of Kiwanis Intl. [8980], Mason, MI
Michigan District, The Lutheran Church-Missouri Synod [6724], Ann Arbor, MI
Michigan Draft Horse Breeders Assn. [6913], Bellevue, MI
Michigan Educ. Assn. [7539], East Lansing, MI
Michigan Educational Res. Assn. [7746], Flint, MI
Michigan Elec. and Gas Assn. [8660], Lansing, MI
Michigan Elementary and Middle School Principals Assn. [8981], Mason, MI
Michigan Elks Assn. [7018], Brighton, MI
Michigan Enval. Balancing Bur. [7769], Flushing, MI
Michigan Environmental Coun. [8661], Lansing, MI
Michigan Environmental Hea. Assn. [8662], Lansing, MI
Michigan Epilepsy Center [★9799]
Michigan Epilepsy Center and Assn. [★9799]
Michigan Equip. Distributors [9258], Oak Park, MI
Michigan Family Forum [8663], Lansing, MI
Michigan Farm Bur. [8664], Lansing, MI
Michigan FCA [8405], Jenison, MI
Michigan Fed. of Bus. and Professional Women's Clubs [8970], Marshall, MI
Michigan Fed. for Children and Families [8665], Lansing, MI
Michigan Fed; Lake [★604]
Michigan Fed. of Private Child and Family Agencies [★8665]
Michigan Fed. of Teachers and School Related Personnel [7396], Detroit, MI
Michigan Floral Assn. [8149], Haslett, MI
Michigan Food and Beverage Assn. [10070], Warren, MI
Michigan Food Coun. [★10070]
Michigan Food Processors Assn. [9888], Suttons Bay, MI
Michigan Food Trade Coun. [★10070]
Michigan Forest Assn. [6725], Ann Arbor, MI
Michigan Forest Rsrc. Alliance [8666], Lansing, MI
Michigan Found. for Exceptional Children [6726], Ann Arbor, MI
Michigan Fox Trotter Assn. [10157], White Lake, MI
Michigan Fraternal Order of Police [8667], Lansing, MI
Michigan Funeral Directors Assn. [9278], Okemos, MI
Michigan Glass Assn. [8668], Lansing, MI
Michigan Golf Course Owners Assn. [8669], Lansing, MI
Michigan Grain and Agri-Dealers Assn. [★7531]
Michigan Green Indus. Assn. [6955], Bingham Farms, MI
Michigan Greyhound Connection [6931], Berkley, MI
Michigan Grocers Assn. [8670], Lansing, MI
Michigan Ground Water Assn. [8909], Manchester, MI
Michigan Guild of Artists and Artisans [6727], Ann Arbor, MI
Michigan Handicapped Sports and Recreation Assn. [★8482]
Michigan Harness Horsemen's Assn. [9279], Okemos, MI

Michigan Hea. Coun. **[9280]**, Okemos, MI
Michigan Hea. and Hosp. Assn. **[8671]**, Lansing, MI
Michigan Hea. Info. Mgt. Assn. **[9148]**, Muskegon, MI
Michigan Hea. Info. Mgt. Assn., Michiana **[5809]**, Mishawaka, IN
Michigan Hea. Info. Mgt. Assn., Mid-Michigan **[10173]**, Williamston, MI
Michigan Hea. Info. Mgt. Assn., North Central **[10129]**, West Branch, MI
Michigan Hea. Info. Mgt. Assn., Northwest **[9149]**, Muskegon, MI
Michigan Hea. Info. Mgt. Assn., Southeast **[7668]**, Farmington Hills, MI
Michigan Hea. Info. Mgt. Assn., Southwest **[8211]**, Holland, MI
Michigan Hea. Info. Mgt. Assn., Upper Peninsula **[8349]**, Ishpeming, MI
Michigan Healthcare Executive Gp. and Associates **[9664]**, St. Clair Shores, MI
Michigan Healthcare Rsrc. and Materials Mgt. **[9090]**, Mount Clemens, MI
Michigan Hemingway Soc. **[9365]**, Petoskey, MI
Michigan High School Athletic Assn. **[7540]**, East Lansing, MI
Michigan High School Coaches Assn. **[8993]**, Mears, MI
Michigan Historic Preservation Network **[8672]**, Lansing, MI
Michigan Home Hea. Assn. **[9281]**, Okemos, MI
Michigan Horseshoer's Assn. No. 4 **[8401]**, Jeddo, MI
Michigan HOSA **[9282]**, Okemos, MI
Michigan Hospice Org. **[★8673]**
Michigan Hospice and Palliative Care Org. **[8673]**, Lansing, MI
Michigan Hotel, Motel and Resort Assn. **[8674]**, Lansing, MI
Michigan Humane Soc. **[9807]**, Southfield, MI
Michigan Humane Soc. - Westland **[10139]**, Westland, MI
Michigan Humanities Coun. **[8675]**, Lansing, MI
Michigan Indiana Thimble Soc. **[5789]**, Michigan City, IN
Michigan Indus. Hygiene Soc. **[9182]**, New Baltimore, MI
Michigan Indus. Sand Assn. **[8676]**, Lansing, MI
Michigan Infectious Diseases Soc. **[9939]**, Traverse City, MI
Michigan Infrastructure and Trans. Assn. **[9283]**, Okemos, MI
Michigan Inst. of Laundering and Drycleaning **[8677]**, Lansing, MI
Michigan Insurance Fed. **[★8578]**
Michigan Interscholastic Athletic Administrators Assn. **[8851]**, Livonia, MI
Michigan Interscholastic Forensic Assn. **[6728]**, Ann Arbor, MI
Michigan Jaycees **[8678]**, Lansing, MI
Michigan Justin Morgan Horse Assn. **[7687]**, Fenton, MI
Michigan Lake to Lake Bed and Breakfast Assn. **[8128]**, Harrison, MI
Michigan Lake and Stream Associations **[9916]**, Three Rivers, MI
Michigan Land Title Assn. **[8679]**, Lansing, MI
Michigan Lawyers Auxiliary **[8680]**, Lansing, MI
Michigan League for Human Services **[8681]**, Lansing, MI
Michigan Lib. Assn. **[8682]**, Lansing, MI
Michigan Licensed Beverage Assn. **[7541]**, East Lansing, MI
Michigan Licensed Practical Nurses Assn. **[8683]**, Lansing, MI
Michigan Literacy **[9284]**, Okemos, MI
Michigan Loon Preservation Association/Michigan Loonwatch **[9749]**, Shepherd, MI
Michigan Lumber and Building Materials Assn. **[8684]**, Lansing, MI
Michigan Manufactured Housing Assn. **[9285]**, Okemos, MI
Michigan Manufactured Housing Inst. **[★9285]**
Michigan Manufacturers Assn. **[8685]**, Lansing, MI
Michigan Mathematical Assn. of Two-Year Colleges **[10028]**, University Center, MI
Michigan Medical Device Assn. **[8283]**, Howell, MI
Michigan Medical Device Manufacturers and Suppliers Assn. **[★8283]**
Michigan Medical Directors Assn. **[7980]**, Grand Rapids, MI
Michigan Medical Gp. Mgt. Assn. **[7542]**, East Lansing, MI
Michigan Mental Hea. Counselors Assn. **[9506]**, Rochester, MI
Michigan Metro Girl Scout Coun. **[9998]**, Troy, MI
Michigan Midwives Assn. **[8167]**, Hesperia, MI
Michigan Milk Producers Assn. **[9239]**, Novi, MI
Michigan Mineralogical Soc. **[8852]**, Livonia, MI
Michigan Minority Bus. Development Coun. **[7397]**, Detroit, MI
Michigan Model Sailing Club No. 70 **[9615]**, Saginaw, MI
Michigan Mortgage Brokers Assn. **[6729]**, Ann Arbor, MI
Michigan Mosquito Control Assn. **[6891]**, Bay City, MI
Michigan Motorcycle Dealers Assn. **[8686]**, Lansing, MI
Michigan Mountain Bike Assn. **[10087]**, Waterford, MI
Michigan Movers Assn. **[8687]**, Lansing, MI
Michigan Movers and Warehousemen's Assn. **[★8687]**
Michigan Municipal Elec. Assn. **[8688]**, Lansing, MI
Michigan Municipal League **[6730]**, Ann Arbor, MI
Michigan Museums Assn. **[8689]**, Lansing, MI
Michigan Mushroom Hunters Club **[6731]**, Ann Arbor, MI
Michigan Muskie Alliance **[7055]**, Caledonia, MI
Michigan Mutual UFO Network **[8487]**, Kentwood, MI
Michigan Natl. Barrel Horse Assn. **[7041]**, Byron Center, MI
Michigan Natl. Lawyers Guild **[7398]**, Detroit, MI
Michigan Natl. Wild Turkey Fed., Alpena Longbeards **[6643]**, Alpena, MI
Michigan Natl. Wild Turkey Fed., Arenac County **[6806]**, Au Gres, MI
Michigan Natl. Wild Turkey Fed., Bay De Noc Gobblers **[7615]**, Escanaba, MI
Michigan Natl. Wild Turkey Fed., Beards and Spurs Chap. **[9867]**, Sterling Heights, MI
Michigan Natl. Wild Turkey Fed., Beaver Creek Chap. **[9554]**, Roscommon, MI
Michigan Natl. Wild Turkey Fed., Berrien County **[9685]**, St. Joseph, MI
Michigan Natl. Wild Turkey Fed., Black Mountain Chap. **[8159]**, Hawks, MI
Michigan Natl. Wild Turkey Fed., Blue Water Chap. **[8307]**, Imlay City, MI
Michigan Natl. Wild Turkey Fed., Br. County Longbeards **[7028]**, Bronson, MI
Michigan Natl. Wild Turkey Fed., Cass River Chap. **[8927]**, Marlette, MI
Michigan Natl. Wild Turkey Fed., Clam River Gobblers **[8992]**, McBain, MI
Michigan Natl. Wild Turkey Fed., Dowagiac River Chap. **[9210]**, Niles, MI
Michigan Natl. Wild Turkey Fed., Dune Drummers Chap. **[10164]**, Whitehall, MI
Michigan Natl. Wild Turkey Fed., Elk Country Gobblers **[6804]**, Atlanta, MI
Michigan Natl. Wild Turkey Fed., Flat Rock Longbeards **[7705]**, Flat Rock, MI
Michigan Natl. Wild Turkey Fed., Flint River Chap. **[7747]**, Flint, MI
Michigan Natl. Wild Turkey Fed., Freemont Area Chap. **[7798]**, Fremont, MI
Michigan Natl. Wild Turkey Fed., Gateway Gobblers **[9709]**, Sanford, MI
Michigan Natl. Wild Turkey Fed., Grand River Longbeards **[10045]**, Vermontville, MI
Michigan Natl. Wild Turkey Fed., Grand Valley Chap. **[8043]**, Grandville, MI
Michigan Natl. Wild Turkey Fed., Grant Gobblers **[8052]**, Grant, MI
Michigan Natl. Wild Turkey Fed., Highbanks Chap. **[9387]**, Plainwell, MI
Michigan Natl. Wild Turkey Fed., Hillsdale Chap. **[9076]**, Montgomery, MI
Michigan Natl. Wild Turkey Fed., Houghton Lake Longbeards **[8265]**, Houghton Lake, MI
Michigan Natl. Wild Turkey Fed., Huron Valley Chap. **[7814]**, Garden City, MI
Michigan Natl. Wild Turkey Fed., Kalamazoo Chap. **[10169]**, Williamsburg, MI
Michigan Natl. Wild Turkey Fed., Kalkaska Gobblers **[8477]**, Kalkaska, MI
Michigan Natl. Wild Turkey Fed., Lapeer Longbeards **[8781]**, Lapeer, MI
Michigan Natl. Wild Turkey Fed., Lenawee Limbhangers **[6975]**, Blissfield, MI
Michigan Natl. Wild Turkey Fed., Little Traverse Bay Gobbler Chap. **[9366]**, Petoskey, MI
Michigan Natl. Wild Turkey Fed., Livingston Longbeards **[8284]**, Howell, MI
Michigan Natl. Wild Turkey Fed., Macomb Lost Gobblers **[8122]**, Harper Woods, MI
Michigan Natl. Wild Turkey Fed., Mecosta County Strutters Chap. **[9110]**, Mount Pleasant, MI
Michigan Natl. Wild Turkey Fed., Menominee Strutting Chap. **[7079]**, Carney, MI
Michigan Natl. Wild Turkey Fed., Mountain Top Gobblers **[9111]**, Mount Pleasant, MI
Michigan Natl. Wild Turkey Fed., Newaygo Valley Gobblers **[9857]**, Stanwood, MI
Michigan Natl. Wild Turkey Fed., North Kent Chap. **[9527]**, Rockford, MI
Michigan Natl. Wild Turkey Fed., North Oakland Gobblers **[8238]**, Holly, MI
Michigan Natl. Wild Turkey Fed., North Ottawa Toms Chap. **[10228]**, Zeeland, MI
Michigan Natl. Wild Turkey Fed., Northern Snow Shoe Toms Chap. **[7802]**, Gaastra, MI
Michigan Natl. Wild Turkey Fed., Ogemaw Hills Chap. **[10130]**, West Branch, MI
Michigan Natl. Wild Turkey Fed., Presque Isle Longbeards **[9542]**, Rogers City, MI
Michigan Natl. Wild Turkey Fed., Rabbit River Chap. **[7476]**, Dorr, MI
Michigan Natl. Wild Turkey Fed., River Raisin Chap. **[9908]**, Tecumseh, MI
Michigan Natl. Wild Turkey Fed., St. Joe Valley Limbhangers **[9917]**, Three Rivers, MI
Michigan Natl. Wild Turkey Fed., Sebawaing Gobblers **[9738]**, Sebewaing, MI
Michigan Natl. Wild Turkey Fed., Shiawasse River Strutters Chap. **[7148]**, Chesaning, MI
Michigan Natl. Wild Turkey Fed., Southwestern Michigan Chap. **[10050]**, Vicksburg, MI
Michigan Natl. Wild Turkey Fed., Superior Turkey Trackers Chap. **[8951]**, Marquette, MI
Michigan Natl. Wild Turkey Fed., Sycamore Creek Chap. **[7124]**, Charlotte, MI
Michigan Natl. Wild Turkey Fed., Tamarock Toms Chap. **[8520]**, Lakeview, MI
Michigan Natl. Wild Turkey Fed., Thornapple Valley Chap. **[9173]**, Nashville, MI
Michigan Natl. Wild Turkey Fed., Three Corners Habitat Chap. **[10017]**, Tustin, MI
Michigan Natl. Wild Turkey Fed., Timber Ghost Gobblers **[9355]**, Perry, MI
Michigan Natl. Wild Turkey Fed., Tri-Valley Gobblers **[9007]**, Merrill, MI
Michigan Natl. Wild Turkey Fed., Tuscola Longbeards **[9739]**, Sebewaing, MI
Michigan Natl. Wild Turkey Fed., U.P. Snow Gobblers **[7232]**, Curtis, MI
Michigan Natl. Wild Turkey Fed., Upper Thumb Gobblers **[7701]**, Filion, MI
Michigan Natl. Wild Turkey Fed., Vanburen Longbeards **[6828]**, Bangor, MI
Michigan Natl. Wild Turkey Fed., Washtenaw County Chap. **[8910]**, Manchester, MI
Michigan Natl. Wild Turkey Fed., Waterloo Longbeards **[8056]**, Grass Lake, MI
Michigan Natl. Wild Turkey Fed., Western U.P. Tommy Knockers Chap. **[6928]**, Bergland, MI
Michigan Natl. Wild Turkey Fed., White River Longbeards **[10152]**, White Cloud, MI
Michigan Natl. Wild Turkey Fed., Whiteford Valley Chap. **[9357]**, Petersburg, MI
Michigan Natural Areas Coun. **[6732]**, Ann Arbor, MI
Michigan Nonprofit Assn. **[8690]**, Lansing, MI
Michigan Norml **[9478]**, Redford, MI
Michigan/Northeast Indiana Lupus Found. **[★9661]**
Michigan Nursery and Landscape Assn. **[9286]**, Okemos, MI
Michigan Nurses Assn. **[9287]**, Okemos, MI
Michigan Occupational Therapy Assn. **[8691]**, Lansing, MI
Michigan Ontario Compensation Assn. **[7646]**, Farmington, MI

Michigan-Ontario Identification Assn. **[7106]**, Center Line, MI
Michigan Ophthalmological Soc. **[7543]**, East Lansing, MI
Michigan Optometric Assn. **[8692]**, Lansing, MI
Michigan Oral History Assn. **[8693]**, Lansing, MI
Michigan Orchid Soc. **[6987]**, Bloomfield Hills, MI
Michigan Org. of Diabetes Educators **[7151]**, Chesterfield, MI
Michigan Org. of Nurse Executives - District 1 **[8076]**, Grosse Ile, MI
Michigan Org. of Nurse Executives - District 2 **[8450]**, Kalamazoo, MI
Michigan Org. of Nurse Executives - District 3 **[7981]**, Grand Rapids, MI
Michigan Org. of Nurse Executives - District 4 **[8694]**, Lansing, MI
Michigan Org. of Nurse Executives - District 5 **[9616]**, Saginaw, MI
Michigan Org. of Nurse Executives - District 6 **[8915]**, Manistee, MI
Michigan Org. of Nurse Executives - District 7 **[8333]**, Iron River, MI
Michigan Osteopathic Assn. **[9288]**, Okemos, MI
Michigan Parents of Blind Children **[7102]**, Cedar, MI
Michigan Parking Assn. **[7399]**, Detroit, MI
Michigan Parkinson Found. **[9808]**, Southfield, MI
Michigan Pathfinders **[9868]**, Sterling Heights, MI
Michigan Personnel and Guidance Assn. **[★8653]**
Michigan Pest Control Assn. **[7791]**, Fraser, MI
Michigan Petroleum Assn. **[8695]**, Lansing, MI
Michigan Pharmacists Assn. **[8696]**, Lansing, MI
Michigan Photographic Historical Soc. **[6964]**, Birmingham, MI
Michigan Physical Therapy Assn. **[6733]**, Ann Arbor, MI
Michigan Podiatric Medical Assn. **[8697]**, Lansing, MI
Michigan Potato Indus. Commn. **[7464]**, DeWitt, MI
Michigan Press Assn. **[8698]**, Lansing, MI
Michigan Professional Fire Fighters Union **[9966]**, Trenton, MI
Michigan Propane Gas Assn. **[8699]**, Lansing, MI
Michigan Protection and Advocacy Ser. **[8700]**, Lansing, MI
Michigan Psychiatric Soc. **[7544]**, East Lansing, MI
Michigan Psychoanalytic Soc. **[7669]**, Farmington Hills, MI
Michigan Psychological Assn. **[9289]**, Okemos, MI
Michigan Public Hea. Assn. **[7545]**, East Lansing, MI
Michigan Public Transit Assn. **[7546]**, East Lansing, MI
Michigan Quarter Horse Assn. **[8069]**, Greenville, MI
Michigan Racing Assn. **[8701]**, Lansing, MI
Michigan Railroads Assn. **[8702]**, Lansing, MI
Michigan Reading Assn. **[7982]**, Grand Rapids, MI
Michigan Recreation and Park Assn. **[9290]**, Okemos, MI
Michigan Recycling Coalition **[8703]**, Lansing, MI
Michigan Rsrc. Center for Hea. and Safety **[8704]**, Lansing, MI
Michigan Restaurant Assn. **[8705]**, Lansing, MI
Michigan Retail Hardware Assn. **[8706]**, Lansing, MI
Michigan Retailers Assn. **[8707]**, Lansing, MI
Michigan Rifle and Pistol Assn. **[8971]**, Marshall, MI
Michigan Road Builders Assn. **[8708]**, Lansing, MI
Michigan Roofing Contractors Assn. **[10071]**, Warren, MI
Michigan Rural Hea. Assn. **[7547]**, East Lansing, MI
Michigan Rural Hea. Clinics Org. **[7799]**, Fremont, MI
Michigan Rural Water Assn. **[8129]**, Harrison, MI
Michigan Safety Conf. **[6591]**, Albion, MI
Michigan School Band and Orchestra Assn. **[9291]**, Okemos, MI
Michigan School Bus. Officials **[8709]**, Lansing, MI
Michigan School Food Ser. Assn. **[★9040]**
Michigan School Investment Assn. **[8710]**, Lansing, MI
Michigan School Public Relations Assn. **[8711]**, Lansing, MI
Michigan Sci. Teachers Assn. **[6734]**, Ann Arbor, MI
Michigan Sect. of the Amer. Nuclear Soc. **[6735]**, Ann Arbor, MI
Michigan Senior Olympics **[9507]**, Rochester, MI
Michigan Sheep Breeders Assn. **[7125]**, Charlotte, MI
Michigan Sheriffs' Assn. **[8712]**, Lansing, MI
Michigan Sheriffs' Assn. Educational Services **[★8712]**
Michigan Sierra Club **[8713]**, Lansing, MI
Michigan Skeet Assn. **[10042]**, Vassar, MI
Michigan Snowmobile Assn. **[7983]**, Grand Rapids, MI
Michigan Soc. of Anesthesiologists **[8714]**, Lansing, MI
Michigan Soc. of Assn. Executives **[7548]**, East Lansing, MI
Michigan Soc. of Clinical Hypnosis **[7670]**, Farmington Hills, MI
Michigan Soc. for Clinical Lab. Sci. **[6838]**, Bath, MI
Michigan Soc. of EAs **[9333]**, Owosso, MI
Michigan Soc. of Health-System Pharmacists **[8715]**, Lansing, MI
Michigan Soc. of Healthcare Risk Mgt. **[7263]**, Dearborn, MI
Michigan Soc. for Histotechnologists **[6644]**, Alpena, MI
Michigan Soc. for Medical Res. **[6736]**, Ann Arbor, MI
Michigan Soc. for Medical Tech. **[★6838]**
Michigan Soc. of Planning Officials **[★6721]**
Michigan Soc. of Professional Engineers **[8716]**, Lansing, MI
Michigan Soc. of Professional Surveyors **[8717]**, Lansing, MI
Michigan Soc. of Radiologic Technologists **[7192]**, Clio, MI
Michigan Soc. for Respiratory Care **[6737]**, Ann Arbor, MI
Michigan Soft Drink Assn. **[8718]**, Lansing, MI
Michigan Soybean Assn. **[7781]**, Frankenmuth, MI
Michigan Speech Coaches **[9999]**, Troy, MI
Michigan Speech-Language-Hearing Assn. **[7549]**, East Lansing, MI
Michigan Sports Unlimited **[9617]**, Saginaw, MI
Michigan State AFL-CIO **[8719]**, Lansing, MI
Michigan State African Violet Soc. **[9838]**, Southgate, MI
Michigan State Assn. of Parliamentarians **[9809]**, Southfield, MI
Michigan State Auctioneers Assn. **[7984]**, Grand Rapids, MI
Michigan State Bar Assn. **[★8762]**
Michigan State Bowling Assn. **[7836]**, Gladwin, MI
Michigan State Building and Constr. Trades Coun. **[8720]**, Lansing, MI
Michigan State Employees Assn. **[8721]**, Lansing, MI
Michigan State Firemen's Assn. **[9895]**, Swartz Creek, MI
Michigan State Grange **[8150]**, Haslett, MI
Michigan State Horticultural Soc. **[8140]**, Hartford, MI
Michigan State Medical Soc. **[7550]**, East Lansing, MI
Michigan State Numismatic Soc. **[7068]**, Canton, MI
Michigan State Police Troopers Assn. **[7551]**, East Lansing, MI
Michigan State Spiritualists Assn. **[9760]**, South Branch, MI
Michigan State Univ. Extension 4-H Youth Programs **[7552]**, East Lansing, MI
Michigan State Univ. Figure Skating Club **[7553]**, East Lansing, MI
Michigan Student Financial Aid Assn. **[10029]**, University Center, MI
Michigan Supreme Court Historical Soc. **[7400]**, Detroit, MI
Michigan Technological Univ. Natl. Org. for the Reform of Marijuana Laws **[8256]**, Houghton, MI
Michigan Technological Univ. Synchronized Skating Club **[8257]**, Houghton, MI
Michigan Tooling Assn. **[7671]**, Farmington Hills, MI
Michigan Towing Assn. **[9225]**, Northville, MI
Michigan Townships Assn. **[8722]**, Lansing, MI
Michigan Toy Fox Terrier Assn. **[6910]**, Belleville, MI
Michigan Trail Riders Assn. **[9877]**, Stockbridge, MI
Michigan Translators/Interpreters Network **[9240]**, Novi, MI
Michigan Trial Lawyers Assn. **[8723]**, Lansing, MI
Michigan Truck Stop Operators Assn. **[8724]**, Lansing, MI
Michigan Trucking Assn. **[8725]**, Lansing, MI
Michigan Underwater Preserves Coun. **[9669]**, St. Ignace, MI
Michigan United Conservation Clubs **[8726]**, Lansing, MI
Michigan Veal Comm. **[9292]**, Okemos, MI
Michigan Vegetable Coun. **[7606]**, Erie, MI
Michigan Veterinary Medical Assn. **[9293]**, Okemos, MI
Michigan Well Drillers Assn. **[★8909]**
Michigan Wheelchair Athletic Assn. **[10000]**, Troy, MI
Michigan Whirlybirds **[9869]**, Sterling Heights, MI
Michigan Wildlife Conservancy **[6839]**, Bath, MI
Michigan Wildlife Habitat Found. **[★6839]**
Michigan Women's Bowling Assn. **[8386]**, Jackson, MI
Michigan Women's Commn. **[8727]**, Lansing, MI
Michigan Women's Stud. Assn. **[8728]**, Lansing, MI
Michigan Wrestling Fed. **[7183]**, Clinton Township, MI
Michigan Youth in Govt. **[9466]**, Quincy, MI
Michigan's Children **[8729]**, Lansing, MI
Michigan's Heavy Constr. Assn. **[9294]**, Okemos, MI
Michigan's Sunrise Side Travel Assn. **[9175]**, National City, MI
Microbiology and Immunology Chairs; Assn. of Medical School **[7327]**, Detroit, MI
Microscopy
  Madison Area Tech. College's Electron Microscopy **[18548]**, Madison, WI
  Microscopy Soc. of Northeastern Ohio **[16550]**, Rootstown, OH
  Microscopy Soc. of the Ohio River Valley **[14920]**, Dayton, OH
  Minnesota Microscopy Soc. **[11869]**, New Hope, MN
Microscopy Soc. of Northeastern Ohio **[16550]**, Rootstown, OH
Microscopy Soc. of the Ohio River Valley **[14920]**, Dayton, OH
MiCTA **[9112]**, Mount Pleasant, MI
Mid-America Equip. Retailers Assn. **[5406]**, Indianapolis, IN
Mid-America Intl. Agri-Trade Coun. **[1048]**, Chicago, IL
Mid Am. Miniature Horse Club **[16812]**, Sunbury, OH
Mid-America Orthopaedic Assn. **[12156]**, Rochester, MN
Mid-Am. Speed Skating - The Long Track Club of USA **[2756]**, Northbrook, IL
Mid-American Assn. for Behavior Anal. **[17884]**, Eau Claire, WI
Mid-Eastern Indiana Assn. of Realtors **[5885]**, Muncie, IN
Mid Illinois Retriever Club **[1777]**, Galesburg, IL
Mid-Miami Valley Chamber of Commerce **[16012]**, Middletown, OH
Mid-Michigan Aikikai **[7554]**, East Lansing, MI
Mid-Michigan Chap. of Romance Writers of Am. **[8451]**, Kalamazoo, MI
Mid-Michigan Enval. Action Coun. **[8730]**, Lansing, MI
Mid-Michigan Genealogical Soc. **[8731]**, Lansing, MI
Mid Michigan Human Rsrc. Assn. **[9113]**, Mount Pleasant, MI
Mid-Michigan Mech. Contractors Assn. **[8732]**, Lansing, MI
Mid-Michigan Mortgage Lenders Assn. **[9295]**, Okemos, MI
Mid-Michigan Professional Photographers Assn. **[9114]**, Mount Pleasant, MI
Mid-Michigan Pug Club **[6932]**, Berkley, MI
Mid-Michigan USA Dance **[9031]**, Midland, MI
Mid-Minnesota Home Builders Association **[10513]**, Brainerd, MN
Mid-Ohio Central Ser. Professionals **[14503]**, Columbus, OH
Mid Ohio District Nurses Assn. **[14504]**, Columbus, OH
Mid-Ohio Dressage Assn. **[15274]**, Galena, OH
Mid-Ohio Regional Planning Commn. **[14505]**, Columbus, OH
Mid-Ohio Vair Force **[15435]**, Hilliard, OH
Mid-Shores Home Builders Assn. **[19307]**, New Holstein, WI
Mid-South Planning and Development Commn. **[1049]**, Chicago, IL
Mid State MMBA **[8387]**, Jackson, MI
Mid-State Sheet Metal and Air Conditioning Contractors Assn. **[3424]**, Savoy, IL

Mid-States Morgan Horse Club **[2211]**, Lake Zurich, IL
Mid-States Woolgrowers Cooperative Assn. **[13519]**, Canal Winchester, OH
Mid-up Shooters **[8095]**, Gwinn, MI
Mid Valley Assn. of Realtors **[2158]**, Kewanee, IL
Mid-West Truckers Assn. **[3648]**, Springfield, IL
Mid-Western Hea. Care Engg. Assn. **[11977]**, Park Rapids, MN
Middle-Atlantic Wholesalers Assn. **[1050]**, Chicago, IL
Middle Bass Island Yacht Club **[15991]**, Middle Bass, OH
Middle Channel Improvement Assn. **[8134]**, Harsens Island, MI
Middle Cities Educ. Assn. **[9296]**, Okemos, MI
Middle School Assn; Ohio **[14638]**, Columbus, OH
Middlefield Chamber of Commerce **[16000]**, Middlefield, OH
Middleport Chamber of Commerce **[★16455]**
Middleton Chamber of Commerce **[18909]**, Middleton, WI
Middleton Key Club **[18910]**, Middleton, WI
Middletown AIFA **[13902]**, Cincinnati, OH
Middletown Area Chamber of Commerce **[★16012]**
Middletown Bd. of Realtors **[16013]**, Middletown, OH
Middletown Convention and Visitors Bur. **[16014]**, Middletown, OH
Middletown Pee Wee Football and Cheerleading **[16015]**, Middletown, OH
Middletown - Young Life **[16016]**, Middletown, OH
Mideastern Farrier's Assn. No. 17 **[15533]**, Johnstown, OH
Midland Alliance for the Mentally Ill **[9032]**, Midland, MI
Midland Area Chamber of Commerce **[9033]**, Midland, MI
Midland Area Youth Football League **[9034]**, Midland, MI
Midland Bd. of Realtors **[9035]**, Midland, MI
Midland County Medical Soc. **[9036]**, Midland, MI
Midland Figure Skating Club **[9037]**, Midland, MI
Midland Lions Club **[9710]**, Sanford, MI
Midland Michigan Kennel Club **[9711]**, Sanford, MI
Midstate District Nurses Assn. - No. 8 **[17776]**, Colby, WI
Midstate Epilepsy Assn. **[★19789]**
Midstates Mule and Donkey Show Society **[16427]**, Pioneer, OH
MidTown Cleveland **[14165]**, Cleveland, OH
Midtown Corridor **[★14165]**
Midview High School Key Club **[15333]**, Grafton, OH
Midwest Affordable Housing Mgt. Assn. **[14506]**, Columbus, OH
Midwest AIDS Prevention Proj. **[7696]**, Ferndale, MI
Midwest Aikido Center **[1051]**, Chicago, IL
Midwest Aikido Fed. **[1052]**, Chicago, IL
Midwest Antiquarian Booksellers Assn. **[1053]**, Chicago, IL
Midwest Antique Fruit Jar and Bottle Club **[4612]**, Flat Rock, IN
Midwest Archives Conf. **[15151]**, Fairborn, OH
Midwest Assn. for Employment in Educ. **[3854]**, Vernon Hills, IL
Midwest Assn. of Fish and Wildlife Agencies **[19599]**, Rhinelander, WI
Midwest Assn. Golf Course Superintendents **[2247]**, Lemont, IL
Midwest Assn. of Housing Cooperatives **[9551]**, Romulus, MI
Midwest Assn. for Sickle Cell Anemia **[★1182]**
Midwest Assn. of Student Employment Administrators **[15207]**, Findlay, OH
Midwest Assn. of Student Financial Aid Administrators **[15208]**, Findlay, OH
Midwest Automatic Laundry and Cleaning Coun. **[★1500]**
Midwest Bookhunters **[★1053]**
Midwest Bus. Brokers and Intermediaries **[3439]**, Schaumburg, IL
Midwest Bus. Travel Assn. **[1054]**, Chicago, IL
Midwest Central Ser. Assn. **[3479]**, Silvis, IL
Midwest Cmpt. Measurement Gp. **[1363]**, Darien, IL
Midwest Corvette Club **[2491]**, Milan, IL
Midwest Cricket Conf. **[1669]**, Evanston, IL
Midwest Crossroad Chorus of Sweet Adelines Intl. **[2317]**, Lockport, IL
Midwest Crossroads Emmaus Community **[6165]**, Schererville, IN
Midwest Daffodil Soc. **[2201]**, Lake Forest, IL
Midwest Dairy Assn. **[12444]**, St. Paul, MN
Midwest Dairy Foods Assn. **[14507]**, Columbus, OH
Midwest Decoy Collectors Assn. **[1055]**, Chicago, IL
Midwest Direct Marketing Assn. **[11604]**, Minneapolis, MN
Midwest Dressage Assn. **[9618]**, Saginaw, MI
Midwest Energy Assn. **[11789]**, Minnetonka, MN
Midwest Energy Efficiency Alliance **[1056]**, Chicago, IL
Midwest Enval. Advocates **[18562]**, Madison, WI
Midwest Enval. Enforcement Assn. **[3389]**, St. Charles, IL
Midwest Equip. Dealers Assn. **[18563]**, Madison, WI
Midwest Fiction Writers **[11605]**, Minneapolis, MN
Midwest Fish and Game Commissioners; Assn. of **[★19599]**
Midwest Fish and Wildlife Commissioners; Assn. of **[★19599]**
Midwest Food Processors Assn. **[18564]**, Madison, WI
Midwest Gas Assn. **[★11789]**
Midwest Hardware Assn. **[19793]**, Stevens Point, WI
Midwest Healthcare Marketing Assn. **[2646]**, Naperville, IL
Midwest Independent Elecl. Contractors **[6166]**, Schererville, IN
Midwest Independent Publishers Assn. **[11606]**, Minneapolis, MN
Midwest Manufacturers' Assn. **[10937]**, Elbow Lake, MN
Midwest Mineralogical and Lapidary Soc. **[7264]**, Dearborn, MI
Midwest Minnesota Chapter, American Red Cross **[10999]**, Fergus Falls, MN
Midwest Natl. Show Horse Assn. **[15222]**, Fort Jennings, OH
Midwest Pain Soc. **[1871]**, Glenview, IL
Midwest Physiological Soc. **[19050]**, Milwaukee, WI
Midwest Poultry Fed. **[10574]**, Buffalo, MN
Midwest Region FCA **[536]**, Champaign, IL
Midwest Regional Chap. of the Soc. of Environmental Toxicology and Chemistry **[19354]**, Odanah, WI
Midwest Regional Gas Task Force Assn. **[11210]**, Hutchinson, MN
Midwest Renewable Energy Assn. **[17802]**, Custer, WI
Midwest Securities Transfer Assn. **[1057]**, Chicago, IL
Midwest Sign Assn. **[13903]**, Cincinnati, OH
Midwest Soc. of Assn. Executives **[12445]**, St. Paul, MN
Midwest Stamp Dealers Assn. **[363]**, Buffalo Grove, IL
Midwest Stock Exchange **[★832]**
Midwest Sunbeam Registry **[12051]**, Prior Lake, MN
Midwest Twisters Gymnastics Booster Club **[19332]**, Oak Creek, WI
Midwest Waterways Flat-coated Retriever Club **[4693]**, Fort Wayne, IN
Midwest Weightlifting **[4435]**, Crown Point, IN
Midwestern Gilbert and Sullivan Soc. **[2742]**, North Aurora, IL
Midwestern Governors Assn. **[2340]**, Lombard, IL
Midwestern Governors' Conf. of the Coun. of State Governments **[★2340]**
Midwestern Legislative Conf. of the Coun. of State Governments **[★2330]**
Midwestern Ohio Assn. of Realtors **[17005]**, Troy, OH
Midwestern Psychological Assn. **[4694]**, Fort Wayne, IN
Midwestern U.S. Imperial Club **[1291]**, Collinsville, IL
Midwives Assn; Michigan **[8167]**, Hesperia, MI
Mifflin Lions Club **[13167]**, Ashland, OH
Migrant Workers
Illinois Migrant Coun. **[950]**, Chicago, IL
Mikenauk Rock and Gem Club **[9555]**, Roscommon, MI
Milaca Chamber of Commerce **[11466]**, Milaca, MN
Milan Area Chamber of Commerce **[9048]**, Milan, MI
Milan Edison Lions Club **[16022]**, Milan, OH
Milan Lions Club - Minnesota **[11468]**, Milan, MN
Milford Gun Club **[13904]**, Cincinnati, OH
Milford Historical Soc. **[9052]**, Milford, MI
Milford - Miami Township Chamber of Commerce **[16027]**, Milford, OH
Milford Theatre Guilde **[16028]**, Milford, OH
Milford - Young Life **[13905]**, Cincinnati, OH
Military
Air Force Assn., Columbus-Bakalar Chap. No. 288 **[4387]**, Columbus, IN
Air Force Assn., Gen. E.W. Rawlings Chap. **[12347]**, St. Paul, MN
Air Force Assn., Wright Memorial Chap. No. 212 **[17364]**, Xenia, OH
Assn. of the U.S. Army, 19th Star Chap. **[6191]**, Shelbyville, IN
Assn. of the U.S. Army, Buckeye Landpower **[13044]**, Akron, OH
Assn. of the U.S. Army, Central Ohio **[14332]**, Columbus, OH
Assn. of the U.S. Army, Detroit **[8831]**, Livonia, MI
Assn. of the U.S. Army, Fort Sheridan - Chicago **[4034]**, Winnetka, IL
Assn. of the U.S. Army, GEN John W. Vessey Jr. - Minnesota **[19662]**, Sarona, WI
Assn. of the U.S. Army, Indiana **[5050]**, Indianapolis, IN
Assn. of the U.S. Army, Major Samuel Woodfill - Cincinnati **[13620]**, Centerville, OH
Assn. of the U.S. Army, MG Robert D. McCoy **[19751]**, Sparta, WI
Assn. of the U.S. Army, Milwaukee **[18972]**, Milwaukee, WI
Assn. of the U.S. Army, Newton D. Baker **[16784]**, Strongsville, OH
Assn. of the U.S. Army, South Bend **[5688]**, Logansport, IN
Assn. of the U.S. Army, Southwestern Michigan **[6848]**, Battle Creek, MI
Buckeye Military Vehicle Collectors **[16065]**, Montville, OH
Center for Military Readiness **[8833]**, Livonia, MI
Chicago Military Acad. - Bronzeville Assn. **[821]**, Chicago, IL
Chicagoland Military Vehicle Club **[2763]**, Northfield, IL
Great Lakes Military Vehicle Preservation Assn. **[8365]**, Jackson, MI
Indiana Military Vehicle Preservation Assn. **[6511]**, Westfield, IN
Kilroy Military Vehicle Preservation Assn. **[6176]**, Sellersburg, IN
Military Vehicle Collectors of Southern Illinois **[91]**, Ashley, IL
Minnesota National Guard Enlisted Association **[10729]**, Cottage Grove, MN
Natl. Assn. For Uniformed Services - Northern Wisconsin, Chap. 1 **[18801]**, Marinette, WI
Natl. Assn. For Uniformed Services - Southern Wisconsin, Chap. 2 **[19073]**, Milwaukee, WI
Natl. Guard Assn. of Michigan **[8744]**, Lansing, MI
Naval Reserve Assn., 4-218 Columbus Chap. **[16421]**, Pickerington, OH
Navy League of the U.S., Akron-Canton **[13073]**, Akron, OH
Navy League of the U.S., Aurora **[4076]**, Yorkville, IL
Navy League of the U.S., Champaign **[3426]**, Savoy, IL
Navy League of the U.S., Chicago **[2022]**, Hinsdale, IL
Navy League of the U.S., Cleveland **[15588]**, Lakewood, OH
Navy League of the U.S., Dayton **[13301]**, Beavercreek, OH
Navy League of the U.S., Glenview **[1465]**, Des Plaines, IL
Navy League of the U.S., Greater Columbus **[15373]**, Groveport, OH
Navy League of the U.S., Madison **[18000]**, Fort Atkinson, WI
Navy League of the U.S., Milwaukee **[19564]**, Racine, WI
Navy League of the U.S., Toledo-Erie Islands **[16938]**, Toledo, OH
Navy League of the U.S., Western Reserve **[17107]**, Warren, OH
Northern Illinois Chap. of the Military Vehicle Assn. **[2061]**, Indian Head Park, IL

Red Bull Historic Military Vehicle Assn. **[11940]**, Onamia, MN
Reserve Officers Assn. - Dept. of Illinois **[2927]**, Palatine, IL
Reserve Officers Assn. - Dept. of Illinois, Central Illinois Chap. 33 **[310]**, Bloomington, IL
Reserve Officers Assn. - Dept. of Illinois, Champaign Chap. 4 **[3795]**, Tuscola, IL
Reserve Officers Assn. - Dept. of Illinois, Cook County Chap. 6 **[2212]**, Lake Zurich, IL
Reserve Officers Assn. - Dept. of Illinois, Decatur Chap. 7 **[1405]**, Decatur, IL
Reserve Officers Assn. - Dept. of Illinois, DuPage County Chap. 11 **[3997]**, Wheaton, IL
Reserve Officers Assn. - Dept. of Illinois, Eastern Illinois Chap. 12 **[571]**, Charleston, IL
Reserve Officers Assn. - Dept. of Illinois, Fort Sheridan Chap. 48 **[3215]**, Riverwoods, IL
Reserve Officers Assn. - Dept. of Illinois, O'Hare Chap. 61 **[81]**, Arlington Heights, IL
Reserve Officers Assn. - Dept. of Illinois, Quincy Chap. 35 **[3171]**, Quincy, IL
Reserve Officers Assn. - Dept. of Illinois, Springfield Chap. 39 **[105]**, Auburn, IL
Reserve Officers Assn. - Dept. of Minnesota **[12572]**, St. Paul, MN
Reserve Officers Assn. - Dept. of Ohio **[13975]**, Cincinnati, OH
Reserve Officers Assn. - Dept. of Ohio, Alfred Gus Karger Chap. 7 **[16567]**, St. Bernard, OH
Reserve Officers Assn. - Dept. of Ohio, Anthony Wayne Chap. 4 **[17093]**, Wapakoneta, OH
Reserve Officers Assn. - Dept. of Ohio, Buckeye Chap. 5 **[16740]**, Springfield, OH
Reserve Officers Assn. - Dept. of Ohio, Cincinnati Navy Chap. 71 **[15730]**, Loveland, OH
Reserve Officers Assn. - Dept. of Ohio, Cleveland Coast Guard Chap. 10 **[13452]**, Brunswick, OH
Reserve Officers Assn. - Dept. of Ohio, Col. Coleman Todd Chap. 53 **[15789]**, Mansfield, OH
Reserve Officers Assn. - Dept. of Ohio, Col. Copeland Chap. 43 **[15853]**, Marion, OH
Reserve Officers Assn. - Dept. of Ohio, Col. John E. Coleman Chap. 16 **[16123]**, New Carlisle, OH
Reserve Officers Assn. - Dept. of Ohio, Columbus Navy Chap. 12 **[16518]**, Reynoldsburg, OH
Reserve Officers Assn. - Dept. of Ohio, Gen. Grant Chap. 28 **[15450]**, Hillsboro, OH
Reserve Officers Assn. - Dept. of Ohio, Gen. Orton Chap. 26 **[15272]**, Gahanna, OH
Reserve Officers Assn. - Dept. of Ohio, Gen. Patton Chap. 25 **[15303]**, Garfield Heights, OH
Reserve Officers Assn. - Dept. of Ohio, Kittyhawk Chap. 70 **[16707]**, Springboro, OH
Reserve Officers Assn. - Dept. of Ohio, Mahoning County Chap. 42 **[17412]**, Youngstown, OH
Reserve Officers Assn. - Dept. of Ohio, M.G. Geisman Chap. 46 **[16200]**, Newton Falls, OH
Reserve Officers Assn. - Dept. of Ohio, North Coast Cleveland Chap. 8 **[13430]**, Broadview Heights, OH
Reserve Officers Assn. - Dept. of Wisconsin, Readiness Chap. 43 **[19754]**, Sparta, WI
State Guard Assn. of the U.S., Indiana **[5484]**, Indianapolis, IN
State Guard Assn. of the U.S., Michigan **[7023]**, Brighton, MI
State Guard Assn. of the U.S., Ohio **[14960]**, Dayton, OH
U.S. Army Warrant Off.rs Assn., Fort McCoy Chap. **[19757]**, Sparta, WI
U.S. Army Warrant Officers Assn., St. Louis Gateway Chap. 0312/3312 **[1823]**, Glen Carbon, IL
U.S. Naval Sea Cadet Corps - Aurora Div. **[133]**, Aurora, IL
U.S. Naval Sea Cadet Corps - Badger Div. **[18630]**, Madison, WI
U.S. Naval Sea Cadet Corps - Battleship Wisconsin Div. **[19344]**, Oconomowoc, WI
U.S. Naval Sea Cadet Corps - Carl G. Stockholm Battalion **[1216]**, Chicago, IL
U.S. Naval Sea Cadet Corps - Chosin Div. **[9125]**, Mount Pleasant, MI
U.S. Naval Sea Cadet Corps - Cincinnati Div. **[14017]**, Cincinnati, OH
U.S. Naval Sea Cadet Corps - Cleveland Div. **[14228]**, Cleveland, OH
U.S. Naval Sea Cadet Corps - Cruiser Indianapolis (CA 35) Div. **[5490]**, Indianapolis, IN
U.S. Naval Sea Cadet Corps - Darter-Dace Div. **[8096]**, Gwinn, MI
U.S. Naval Sea Cadet Corps - Dayton Div. **[15478]**, Huber Heights, OH
U.S. Naval Sea Cadet Corps - Gen. Colin L. Powell Div. **[3212]**, Riverdale, IL
U.S. Naval Sea Cadet Corps - HR Doud Div. **[9644]**, Saginaw, MI
U.S. Naval Sea Cadet Corps - James M. Hannan Div. **[7446]**, Detroit, MI
U.S. Naval Sea Cadet Corps - Maj. Gen. John L. Borling Div. **[3326]**, Rockford, IL
U.S. Naval Sea Cadet Corps - Manatra Div. **[152]**, Barrington, IL
U.S. Naval Sea Cadet Corps - Michigan Sea Tigers Div. **[9729]**, Sault Ste. Marie, MI
U.S. Naval Sea Cadet Corps - Tomcat Squadron **[9741]**, Selfridge, MI
U.S. Naval Sea Cadet Corps - U.S. Div. **[8768]**, Lansing, MI
U.S. Naval Sea Cadet Corps - VADM James H. Flatley, Jr. Div. **[18138]**, Green Bay, WI
U.S. Naval Sea Cadet Corps - West Michigan Div. **[9163]**, Muskegon, MI
Wisconsin Natl. Guard Assn. **[18733]**, Madison, WI
Military Acad. - Bronzeville Assn; Chicago **[821]**, Chicago, IL
Military Engineers, Chicago Post; Soc. of Amer. **[1185]**, Chicago, IL
Military Officers Assn. of Am., Bloomington Area Chap. **[4240]**, Bloomington, IN
Military Officers Assn. of Am., Capitol Area Chap. **[7874]**, Grand Ledge, MI
Military Officers Assn. of Am., Ernie Pyle Chap. **[6334]**, Terre Haute, IN
Military Officers Assn. of Am., Greater Cincinnati Chap. **[13906]**, Cincinnati, OH
Military Officers Assn. of Am., Head O'The Lakes Chap. **[10833]**, Duluth, MN
Military Officers' Assn. of Am., Indianapolis Chap. **[5407]**, Indianapolis, IN
Military Officers Assn. of Am., La Crosse Chap. **[18366]**, La Crosse, WI
Military Officers Assn. of Am., Lafayette Chap. **[6491]**, West Lafayette, IN
Military Officers Assn. of Am., Lincolnland Chap. **[3649]**, Springfield, IL
Military Officers Assn. of Am., Little Egypt Chap. **[421]**, Carbondale, IL
Military Officers Assn. of Am., Michiana Chap. **[6244]**, South Bend, IN
Military Officers Assn. of Am., Northern Illinois Chap. **[3288]**, Rockford, IL
Military Officers Assn. of Am., Ohio Western Reserve Chap. **[13066]**, Akron, OH
Military Off.rs Assn. of Am., Quad Cities Chap. **[2523]**, Moline, IL
Military Officers Assn. of Am., Southwest Illinois Chap. **[3458]**, Scott AFB, IL
Military Officers Club of Central Ohio **[17215]**, Westerville, OH
Military Order of the Loyal Legion of the U.S., Michigan Commandery **[8243]**, Holt, MI
Military Order of the Loyal Legion of the U.S. Michigan Commandery **[8488]**, Kentwood, MI
Military Order of the Purple Heart - Capital City Chap. 37 **[8151]**, Haslett, MI
Military Order of the Purple Heart - Winnebagoland Chap. No. 162 **[19273]**, Neenah, WI
Military Vehicle Collectors of Southern Illinois **[91]**, Ashley, IL
Milk Promotion Services of Indiana **[5408]**, Indianapolis, IN
Mill Creek Watershed Coun. **[13907]**, Cincinnati, OH
Millcreek Valley Habitat for Humanity **[13908]**, Cincinnati, OH
Millington Lions Club - Michigan **[9055]**, Millington, MI
Milton Area Chamber of Commerce **[18920]**, Milton, WI
Milton Historical Soc. **[18921]**, Milton, WI
Miltona Lions Club **[10280]**, Alexandria, MN
Milwaukee 9to5 **[19051]**, Milwaukee, WI
Milwaukee Achiever Literacy Sers. **[19052]**, Milwaukee, WI
Milwaukee African Violet Soc. **[19889]**, Theresa, WI
Milwaukee Aging Consortium **[19053]**, Milwaukee, WI
Milwaukee Area Compensation Assn. **[18041]**, Germantown, WI
Milwaukee Area Land Conservancy **[18171]**, Hales Corners, WI
Milwaukee Area Rsrcs. For Vegetarians **[19732]**, Shorewood, WI
Milwaukee Association for Computing Machinery SIGCHI **[19054]**, Milwaukee, WI
Milwaukee Astronomical Soc. **[19291]**, New Berlin, WI
Milwaukee Audubon Soc. **[17781]**, Colgate, WI
Milwaukee Bar Assn. **[19055]**, Milwaukee, WI
Milwaukee Beagle Club **[19252]**, Mukwonago, WI
Milwaukee Black Nurses Assn. (21) **[19056]**, Milwaukee, WI
Milwaukee Chap. of the Natl. Elecl. Contractors Assn. **[19057]**, Milwaukee, WI
Milwaukee Chap. of the Soc. of Financial Ser. Professionals **[19058]**, Milwaukee, WI
Milwaukee Corvair Club **[19558]**, Racine, WI
Milwaukee County REACT **[20103]**, West Allis, WI
Milwaukee Cricket Club **[17692]**, Brown Deer, WI
Milwaukee District Nurses Assn. - No. 4 **[19059]**, Milwaukee, WI
Milwaukee Dog Training Club **[19060]**, Milwaukee, WI
Milwaukee Gamma **[19061]**, Milwaukee, WI
Milwaukee Intl. Tourism and Trade District Assn. **[★19125]**
Milwaukee Jewish Fed. **[19062]**, Milwaukee, WI
Milwaukee Lake and Stream Fly Fishers **[19063]**, Milwaukee, WI
Milwaukee Marauders **[20077]**, Wauwatosa, WI
Milwaukee Minority Chamber of Commerce **[19064]**, Milwaukee, WI
Milwaukee/Natl. Assn. of the Remodeling Indus. Home Improvement Coun. **[20078]**, Wauwatosa, WI
Milwaukee Numismatic Soc. **[19065]**, Milwaukee, WI
Milwaukee Optometric Soc. **[17673]**, Brookfield, WI
Milwaukee Police Assn. **[19066]**, Milwaukee, WI
Milwaukee Rookie Cricket Club **[19292]**, New Berlin, WI
Milwaukee RSVP **[19067]**, Milwaukee, WI
Milwaukee Sail and Power Squadron **[19990]**, Waukesha, WI
Milwaukee School of Engg., Natl. Elecl. Contractors Assn. **[19068]**, Milwaukee, WI
Milwaukee Urban League **[19069]**, Milwaukee, WI
MIMA, The Mgt. Assn. **[★1505]**
Mind-Body-Spirit Connected **[13289]**, Beachwood, OH
Mindoro Lions Club **[19193]**, Mindoro, WI
Mine and Historical Society; Spring Valley **[3518]**, Spring Valley, IL
Mineral Point Chamber of Commerce **[19195]**, Mineral Point, WI
Mineralogy
Akron Mineral Soc. **[14817]**, Cuyahoga Falls, OH
Anoka County Gem and Mineral Club **[10723]**, Cottage Grove, MN
Badger Lapidary And Geological Soc. **[19381]**, Oregon, WI
Bay De Noc Gem and Mineral Club **[9470]**, Rapid River, MI
Brukner Gem and Mineral Club **[16998]**, Troy, OH
Carlton County Gem and Mineral Club **[10688]**, Cloquet, MN
Chicago Rocks and Minerals Soc. **[3433]**, Schaumburg, IL
Chippewa Valley Gem and Mineral Soc. **[17752]**, Chippewa Falls, WI
Cincinnati Mineral Soc. **[15330]**, Goshen, OH
Copper Country Rock and Mineral Club **[8108]**, Hancock, MI
Coulee Rock Club Of Lacrosse **[11264]**, La Crescent, MN
Cuyuna Rock, Gem and Mineral Soc. **[10245]**, Aitkin, MN
Dayton Gem and Mineral Soc. **[14877]**, Dayton, OH

Driftless Area Gem and Mineral Club **[19903]**, Tomah, WI
Edwards River Earth Sci. Club **[20]**, Aledo, IL
Evansville Lapidary Soc. **[4547]**, Evansville, IN
Flint Rock and Gem Club **[6960]**, Birch Run, MI
Geological Alliance **[15331]**, Goshen, OH
Indian Mounds Rock and Mineral Club **[10189]**, Wyoming, MI
Ishpeming Rock and Mineral Club **[8347]**, Ishpeming, MI
Lake County Gem and Mineral Soc. **[1900]**, Great Lakes, IL
Licking County Rock and Mineral Soc. **[15344]**, Granville, OH
Lincoln Orbit Earth Sci. Soc. **[3232]**, Rochester, IL
Livingston Gem and Mineral Soc. **[7686]**, Fenton, MI
Madison Gem and Mineral Club **[18552]**, Madison, WI
Miami Valley Mineral and Gem Club **[16733]**, Springfield, OH
Michiana Gem and Mineral Soc. **[6242]**, South Bend, IN
Michigan Mineralogical Soc. **[8852]**, Livonia, MI
Midwest Mineralogical and Lapidary Soc. **[7264]**, Dearborn, MI
Mikenauk Rock and Gem Club **[9555]**, Roscommon, MI
Mount Clemens - Macomb County Gem and Lapidary Soc. **[7184]**, Clinton Township, MI
Neville Public Museum Geology Club **[18120]**, Green Bay, WI
North Coast Fossil Club **[15452]**, Hinckley, OH
Northwest Illinois Rock Club **[2868]**, Oregon, IL
Northwest Wisconsin Gem and Mineral Soc. **[17464]**, Almena, WI
Oshkosh Earth Sci. Club **[17511]**, Appleton, WI
Peoria Acad. Of Sci. - Geology Sect. **[3041]**, Peoria, IL
Racine Geological Soc. **[19107]**, Milwaukee, WI
Richland Lithic and Lapidary Soc. **[13467]**, Bucyrus, OH
Three Rivers Gem and Mineral Soc. **[4723]**, Fort Wayne, IN
Wabash Valley Gem and Mineral Soc. **[4456]**, Delphi, IN
West Shore Rock and Mineral Club **[8878]**, Ludington, MI
Minerals
Indiana Mineral Aggregates Assn. **[4326]**, Carmel, IN
Minerals Assn; Ohio Aggregates and Indus. **[15268]**, Gahanna, OH
Minerva Area Chamber of Commerce **[16045]**, Minerva, OH
Miniature Pinscher Club of Greater Twin Cities **[17560]**, Baldwin, WI
Miniature Soc. of Cincinnati **[13909]**, Cincinnati, OH
Mining
Iron Mining Assn. of Minnesota **[10828]**, Duluth, MN
Mining Impact Coalition of Wisconsin **[18565]**, Madison, WI
Ohio Aggregates and Indus. Minerals Assn. **[15268]**, Gahanna, OH
Mining Impact Coalition of Wisconsin **[18565]**, Madison, WI
Ministries Network; North Central Region Hea. **[11712]**, Minneapolis, MN
Ministry
MannaFest Dimensions **[19438]**, Pewaukee, WI
Natl. Assn. of Catholic Family Life Ministers **[14927]**, Dayton, OH
Natl. Assn. of Catholic Family Life Ministers, Region No. 7 **[3290]**, Rockford, IL
Natl. Assn. of Catholic Family Life Ministers, Region No. 8 **[12293]**, St. Cloud, MN
Natl. Assn. of Catholic Family Life Ministers, Region VI **[8457]**, Kalamazoo, MI
Ministry; Overflowing Cup Christian Coffee House **[★17615]**
Minn-Dak Woodturners **[11825]**, Moorhead, MN
Minneapolis AIFA **[11607]**, Minneapolis, MN
Minneapolis Amateur Softball Assn. **[11608]**, Minneapolis, MN
Minneapolis Ambassadores Lions Club **[11609]**, Minneapolis, MN
Minneapolis Area Assn. of Realtors **[10916]**, Edina, MN
Minneapolis Builders Exchange **[11610]**, Minneapolis, MN
Minneapolis Central Lions Club **[12978]**, Woodbury, MN
Minneapolis Chap. of Intl. Assn. of Administrative Professionals **[11611]**, Minneapolis, MN
Minneapolis Chap. Natl. Elecl. Contractors Assn. **[11612]**, Minneapolis, MN
Minneapolis Consortium of Community Developers **[11613]**, Minneapolis, MN
Minneapolis District Dental Soc. **[11861]**, New Brighton, MN
Minneapolis Estate Planning Coun. **[12446]**, St. Paul, MN
Minneapolis Fort Snelling Lions Club **[12334]**, St. Louis Park, MN
Minneapolis Gun Club **[12052]**, Prior Lake, MN
Minneapolis Hiawatha Lions Club **[11614]**, Minneapolis, MN
Minneapolis Jewish Fed. **[11790]**, Minnetonka, MN
Minneapolis Lyn Lake Lions Club **[12335]**, St. Louis Park, MN
Minneapolis Metro North Convention and Visitors Bur. **[11615]**, Minneapolis, MN
Minneapolis North Lions Club **[11616]**, Minneapolis, MN
Minneapolis Northeast Lions Club **[11617]**, Minneapolis, MN
Minneapolis Regional Chamber of Commerce **[11618]**, Minneapolis, MN
Minneapolis Riverview Lions Club **[10551]**, Brooklyn Park, MN
Minneapolis-St. Cloud Fencers Assn. **[★11676]**
Minneapolis/St. Paul Assn. for Computing Machinery SIGGRAPH **[12447]**, St. Paul, MN
Minneapolis-St. Paul Cmpt. Measurement Gp. **[11322]**, Lino Lakes, MN
Minneapolis South Young Life **[11186]**, Hopkins, MN
Minneapolis Southwest Lions Club **[10594]**, Burnsville, MN
Minneapolis Twin City Airport Lions Club **[12448]**, St. Paul, MN
Minnehaha Acad. - Wyldlife **[11187]**, Hopkins, MN
Minnesota 1st Antique Bottle Club **[11619]**, Minneapolis, MN
Minnesota Acad. of Family Physicians **[12336]**, St. Louis Park, MN
Minnesota Acad. of Physician Assistants **[11620]**, Minneapolis, MN
Minnesota ACORN **[12449]**, St. Paul, MN
Minnesota Advocates for Human Rights **[11621]**, Minneapolis, MN
Minnesota AFL-CIO **[12450]**, St. Paul, MN
Minnesota Agri-Growth Coun. **[12451]**, St. Paul, MN
Minnesota Alliance for Progressive Action **[12452]**, St. Paul, MN
Minnesota Amateur Athletic Union **[11188]**, Hopkins, MN
Minnesota Ambulance Assn. **[12290]**, St. Cloud, MN
Minnesota Ambulance Assn., Central **[12822]**, Wadena, MN
Minnesota Ambulance Assn., Metro **[11622]**, Minneapolis, MN
Minnesota Ambulance Assn., Northeast **[11077]**, Grand Marais, MN
Minnesota Ambulance Assn., Northwest **[10737]**, Crookston, MN
Minnesota Ambulance Assn., South Central **[11306]**, Le Center, MN
Minnesota Ambulance Assn., Southeast **[10657]**, Chatfield, MN
Minnesota Ambulance Assn., Southwest **[10731]**, Cottonwood, MN
Minnesota Ambulance Assn., West Central **[10281]**, Alexandria, MN
Minnesota Amer. Indian Chamber of Commerce **[11623]**, Minneapolis, MN
Minnesota Amer. Legion Baseball **[10647]**, Chanhassen, MN
Minnesota Angus Assn. **[10339]**, Arlington, MN
Minnesota Asphalt Pavement Assn. **[11862]**, New Brighton, MN
Minnesota Assn. of Agricultural Educators **[12656]**, Sherburn, MN
Minnesota Assn. of Black Lawyers **[11624]**, Minneapolis, MN
Minnesota Assn. of Black Physicians **[11625]**, Minneapolis, MN
Minnesota Assn. for Career and Tech. Educ. **[12233]**, Roseville, MN
Minnesota Assn. of Community Telecommunications Administrators **[12234]**, Roseville, MN
Minnesota Assn. of Cooperatives **[12453]**, St. Paul, MN
Minnesota Assn. of County Off.rs **[12454]**, St. Paul, MN
Minnesota Assn. for Developmental Educ. **[11626]**, Minneapolis, MN
Minnesota Assn. for the Educ. of Young Children **[12455]**, St. Paul, MN
Minnesota Assn. of Farm Mutual Insurance Companies **[12326]**, St. Joseph, MN
Minnesota Assn. of Financial Aid Administrators **[11436]**, Marshall, MN
Minnesota Assn. on Higher Educ. and Disability **[10474]**, Bloomington, MN
Minnesota Assn. of Law Enforcement Firearms Instructors **[12157]**, Rochester, MN
Minnesota Assn. of Lib. Friends **[12456]**, St. Paul, MN
Minnesota Assn. of Mortgage Brokers **[10917]**, Edina, MN
Minnesota Assn. of Occupational Hea. Nurses **[11791]**, Minnetonka, MN
Minnesota Assn. of Orthopaedic Technologists **[10894]**, Eden Prairie, MN
Minnesota Assn. of Plumbing-Heating-Cooling Contractors **[10539]**, Brooklyn Center, MN
Minnesota Assn. of Public Accountants **[12235]**, Roseville, MN
Minnesota Assn. of Realtors **[10918]**, Edina, MN
Minnesota Assn. of Rehabilitation Providers **[11061]**, Golden Valley, MN
Minnesota Assn. for Retarded Citizens **[★12383]**
Minnesota Assn. of Scholars **[11627]**, Minneapolis, MN
Minnesota Assn. of School Administrators **[12457]**, St. Paul, MN
Minnesota Assn. of Secondary School Principals **[12458]**, St. Paul, MN
Minnesota Assn. of Soil and Water Conservation Districts **[12459]**, St. Paul, MN
Minnesota Assn. for Supervision and Curriculum Development **[10919]**, Edina, MN
Minnesota Assn. of Townships **[12341]**, St. Michael, MN
Minnesota Assn. of Verbatim Reporters and Captioners **[11437]**, Marshall, MN
Minnesota Assn. for Volunteer Admin. **[11420]**, Maplewood, MN
Minnesota Assn. of Wheat Growers **[12071]**, Red Lake Falls, MN
Minnesota Assn. of Women Police **[12460]**, St. Paul, MN
Minnesota Atheists **[11628]**, Minneapolis, MN
Minnesota Athletic Trainers' Assn. **[10475]**, Bloomington, MN
Minnesota Bankers Assn. **[10920]**, Edina, MN
Minnesota Beef Coun. **[11629]**, Minneapolis, MN
Minnesota Beer Wholesalers Assn. **[11630]**, Minneapolis, MN
Minnesota Board of Water and Soil Resources **[10834]**, Duluth, MN
Minnesota Boer Goat Assn. **[11020]**, Foreston, MN
Minnesota Bonsai Soc. **[11631]**, Minneapolis, MN
Minnesota Book Publishers Roundtable **[11632]**, Minneapolis, MN
Minnesota Boston Terrier Club **[11633]**, Minneapolis, MN
Minnesota Brittany Club **[10710]**, Coon Rapids, MN
Minnesota Brittany Club **[10711]**, Coon Rapids, MN
Minnesota Broadcasters Assn. **[11634]**, Minneapolis, MN
Minnesota Buffalo Assn. **[12953]**, Winona, MN
Minnesota Bur. of Criminal Apprehension Agents' Assn. **[12461]**, St. Paul, MN
Minnesota Burglar and Fire Alarm Assn. **[★12480]**
Minnesota Bus. Educators Inc. **[12954]**, Winona, MN
Minnesota Cable Communs. Assn. **[12462]**, St. Paul, MN
Minnesota Career Development Assn. **[10320]**, Apple Valley, MN
Minnesota Cattlemen's Assn. **[★10704]**

Minnesota Center for the Book **[12463]**, St. Paul, MN
Minnesota Chap. of the Amer. Coll. of Cardiology **[12464]**, St. Paul, MN
Minnesota Chap. of Amer. Fisheries Soc. **[12832]**, Walker, MN
Minnesota Chap. of the Amer. Soc. of Landscape Architects **[11635]**, Minneapolis, MN
Minnesota Chap. of Amer. Soc. of Plumbing Engineers **[12465]**, St. Paul, MN
Minnesota Chap. of Assoc. Locksmiths of Am. **[10552]**, Brooklyn Park, MN
Minnesota Chap. of the Assn. for Healthcare Rsrc. and Materials Mgt. **[12920]**, Willmar, MN
Minnesota Chap. of Intl. Assn. of Campus Law Enforcement Administrators **[12615]**, St. Peter, MN
Minnesota Chap. of the Intl. Soc. for Performance Improvement **[11636]**, Minneapolis, MN
Minnesota Chap., MOAA **[10595]**, Burnsville, MN
Minnesota Chap. of Myasthenia Gravis Found. of Am. **[10529]**, Breezy Point, MN
Minnesota Chap. of the Natl. Assn. of Corporate Directors **[11637]**, Minneapolis, MN
Minnesota Chap. of Natl. Assn. of Tax Practitioners **[12158]**, Rochester, MN
Minnesota Chapter of National Association of Tax Professionals **[12159]**, Rochester, MN
Minnesota Chap. of the Proj. Mgt. Inst. **[12466]**, St. Paul, MN
Minnesota Chap. of the Soc. of Architectural Historians **[11638]**, Minneapolis, MN
Minnesota Chiefs of Police Assn. **[12979]**, Woodbury, MN
Minnesota Chiropractic Assn. **[10596]**, Burnsville, MN
Minnesota Chronic Fatigue Syndrome/Fibromyalgia Assn. **[11639]**, Minneapolis, MN
Minnesota Citizens Concerned for Life **[11640]**, Minneapolis, MN
Minnesota Coalition for Battered Women **[12467]**, St. Paul, MN
Minnesota Coalition of Bicyclists **[12468]**, St. Paul, MN
Minnesota Coalition for the Homeless **[11641]**, Minneapolis, MN
Minnesota Coin Laundry Assn. **[12469]**, St. Paul, MN
Minnesota Coll. Personnel Assn. **[11386]**, Mankato, MN
Minnesota Commercial Association of Realtors **[11642]**, Minneapolis, MN
Minnesota Concrete Masonry Assn. **[10597]**, Burnsville, MN
Minnesota Concrete and Masonry Contractors Assn. **[12470]**, St. Paul, MN
Minnesota Conservation Fed. **[12471]**, St. Paul, MN
Minnesota Consortium of Community Developers **[★11613]**
Minnesota Constr. Assn. **[11643]**, Minneapolis, MN
Minnesota Constr. Mgt. Assn. **[★11643]**
Minnesota Corn Growers Assn. **[12651]**, Shakopee, MN
Minnesota Coun. for Exceptional Children **[12160]**, Rochester, MN
Minnesota Coun. on Foundations **[11644]**, Minneapolis, MN
Minnesota Coun. for the Gifted and Talented **[10921]**, Edina, MN
Minnesota Coun. of Nonprofits **[12472]**, St. Paul, MN
Minnesota Coun. for the Social Stud. **[12236]**, Roseville, MN
Minnesota Coun. of Teachers of English **[10712]**, Coon Rapids, MN
Minnesota Coun. of Teachers of Mathematics **[11863]**, New Brighton, MN
Minnesota Credit Union Network **[12473]**, St. Paul, MN
Minnesota Cricket Club **[10476]**, Bloomington, MN
Minnesota Crop Improvement Assn. **[12474]**, St. Paul, MN
Minnesota Crop Production Retailers **[10895]**, Eden Prairie, MN
Minnesota Cultivated Wild Rice Coun. **[12475]**, St. Paul, MN
Minnesota Dachshund Club **[10835]**, Duluth, MN
Minnesota Dairy Herd Improvement Assn. **[10575]**, Buffalo, MN
Minnesota-Dakotas Soc. of PeriAnesthesia Nurses **[12629]**, Sartell, MN
Minnesota Democratic Farmer Labor Party **[12476]**, St. Paul, MN
Minnesota Dental Assn. **[12477]**, St. Paul, MN
Minnesota Dental Hygienists' Assn. **[10477]**, Bloomington, MN
Minnesota Dietary Managers Assn. **[11855]**, Mountain Lake, MN
Minnesota Dietetic Assn. **[12237]**, Roseville, MN
Minnesota Division of the Intl. Assn. for Identification **[12478]**, St. Paul, MN
Minnesota Div. - Izaak Walton League of Am. **[12479]**, St. Paul, MN
Minnesota Dollars for Scholars **[12616]**, St. Peter, MN
Minnesota Dry Edible Bean Res. and Promotion Coun. **[11993]**, Perham, MN
Minnesota Educational Media Org. **[12238]**, Roseville, MN
Minnesota Elecl. Assn. **[11645]**, Minneapolis, MN
Minnesota Electronic Security and Tech. Assn. **[12480]**, St. Paul, MN
Minnesota Elementary School Principals' Assn. **[12481]**, St. Paul, MN
Minnesota Elks Assn. **[11211]**, Hutchinson, MN
Minnesota Environmental Hea. Assn. **[10306]**, Anoka, MN
Minnesota Environmental Initiative **[11646]**, Minneapolis, MN
Minnesota Evaluation Assn. **[11647]**, Minneapolis, MN
Minnesota Falcons Cricket Club **[11648]**, Minneapolis, MN
Minnesota Family Assn. **[12482]**, St. Paul, MN
Minnesota Farm Bur. Fed. **[12483]**, St. Paul, MN
Minnesota Farmers Union **[12484]**, St. Paul, MN
Minnesota Farrier's Assn. No. 14 **[12239]**, Roseville, MN
Minnesota Festivals and Events Assn. **[11884]**, New Ulm, MN
Minnesota Field Trial Assn. **[11018]**, Forest Lake, MN
Minnesota Fire Ser. Certification Bd. **[19742]**, Solon Springs, WI
Minnesota Forest Indus. **[10836]**, Duluth, MN
Minnesota Forestry Assn. **[11091]**, Grand Rapids, MN
Minnesota Fox Trotter Assn. **[13000]**, Zimmerman, MN
Minnesota Fruit and Vegetable Growers Assn. **[11112]**, Ham Lake, MN
Minnesota Funeral Directors Assn. **[12025]**, Plymouth, MN
Minnesota Genealogical Soc. **[11062]**, Golden Valley, MN
Minnesota Glass Assn. **[10896]**, Eden Prairie, MN
Minnesota Golf Assn. **[10922]**, Edina, MN
Minnesota Golf Course Superintendents Assn. **[11792]**, Minnetonka, MN
Minnesota Governor's Coun. on Developmental Disabilities **[12485]**, St. Paul, MN
Minnesota Grain and Feed Assn. **[11649]**, Minneapolis, MN
Minnesota Grocers Assn. **[12486]**, St. Paul, MN
Minnesota Groundswell **[★12836]**
Minnesota Gymkhana Cricket Club **[10868]**, Eagan, MN
Minnesota Hea. and Housing Alliance **[12487]**, St. Paul, MN
Minnesota Hea. Info. Mgt. Assn. **[12722]**, Stillwater, MN
Minnesota Heartland Tall Soc. **[11650]**, Minneapolis, MN
Minnesota Herpetological Soc. **[11651]**, Minneapolis, MN
Minnesota Historical Soc. - Field Ser. Dept. **[12488]**, St. Paul, MN
Minnesota Holstein Assn. **[12827]**, Waite Park, MN
Minnesota HomeCare Assn. **[12489]**, St. Paul, MN
Minnesota HOSA **[10648]**, Chanhassen, MN
Minnesota Housing Partnership **[12490]**, St. Paul, MN
Minnesota Hunting Spaniel Assn. **[10728]**, Cottage Grove, MN
Minnesota Independent Insurance Agents **[★10897]**
Minnesota Independent Insurance Agents and Brokers **[10897]**, Eden Prairie, MN
Minnesota Intl. Cricket Club **[10553]**, Brooklyn Park, MN
Minnesota Intl. Educators **[12491]**, St. Paul, MN
Minnesota Inventors Cong. **[12095]**, Redwood Falls, MN
Minnesota Iron Range Retriever Club **[12797]**, Virginia, MN
Minnesota Jaycees **[10598]**, Burnsville, MN
Minnesota Jewelers Assn. **[12291]**, St. Cloud, MN
Minnesota Jung Association **[11652]**, Minneapolis, MN
Minnesota Kite Soc. **[11653]**, Minneapolis, MN
Minnesota Lakers Cricket Club **[10869]**, Eagan, MN
Minnesota Lakes Assn. **[10514]**, Brainerd, MN
Minnesota Lamb and Wool Producers Assn. **[11877]**, New Prague, MN
Minnesota Land Title Assn. **[11127]**, Hastings, MN
Minnesota Lath and Plaster Bur. **[12492]**, St. Paul, MN
Minnesota Lathing and Plastering Bur. **[★12492]**
Minnesota Lawyers Intl. Human Rights Comm. **[★11621]**
Minnesota Legal Administrators Assn. **[11654]**, Minneapolis, MN
Minnesota Lib. Assn. **[12493]**, St. Paul, MN
Minnesota Licensed Beverage Assn. **[12494]**, St. Paul, MN
Minnesota Literacy Coun. **[12495]**, St. Paul, MN
Minnesota Manufactured Housing Assn. **[12496]**, St. Paul, MN
Minnesota Maple Syrup Producers **[11353]**, Lutsen, MN
Minnesota Mathematical Assn. of Two-Year Colleges **[11221]**, Inver Grove, MN
Minnesota Mech. Contractors Assn. **[12497]**, St. Paul, MN
Minnesota Medical Assn. **[11655]**, Minneapolis, MN
Minnesota Medical Directors Assn. **[11656]**, Minneapolis, MN
Minnesota Medical Gp. Mgt. Assn. **[12498]**, St. Paul, MN
Minnesota Microscopy Soc. **[11869]**, New Hope, MN
Minnesota Multi Housing Assn. **[10478]**, Bloomington, MN
Minnesota Municipal Beverage Assn. **[11657]**, Minneapolis, MN
Minnesota Municipal Utilities Assn. **[12026]**, Plymouth, MN
Minnesota Music Educators Assn. **[10540]**, Brooklyn Center, MN
Minnesota Natl. Abortion and Reproductive Rights Action League **[★12540]**
Minnesota Natl. Barrel Horse Assn. **[12066]**, Randolph, MN
Minnesota National Guard Enlisted Association **[10729]**, Cottage Grove, MN
Minnesota Native Plant Soc. **[12499]**, St. Paul, MN
Minnesota Native Wildflower Grass Producers Assn. **[12955]**, Winona, MN
Minnesota Natural Hea. Coalition **[12215]**, Rosemount, MN
Minnesota Neuropathy Association **[11658]**, Minneapolis, MN
Minnesota Neurosurgical Soc. **[12500]**, St. Paul, MN
Minnesota News Coun. **[11659]**, Minneapolis, MN
Minnesota Newspaper Assn. **[11660]**, Minneapolis, MN
Minnesota North District, The Lutheran Church-Missouri Synod **[10515]**, Brainerd, MN
Minnesota Northstar Cricket Club **[11793]**, Minnetonka, MN
Minnesota Nursery and Landscape Assn. **[12501]**, St. Paul, MN
Minnesota Nurserymen's Assn. **[★12501]**
Minnesota Nurses Assn. **[12502]**, St. Paul, MN
Minnesota Nurses Assn. - District 1 **[12743]**, Thief River Falls, MN
Minnesota Nurses Assn. - District 2 **[10837]**, Duluth, MN
Minnesota Nurses Assn. - District 3 **[10923]**, Edina, MN
Minnesota Nurses Assn. - District 4 **[12503]**, St. Paul, MN
Minnesota Nurses Assn. - District 5 **[11387]**, Mankato, MN
Minnesota Nurses Assn. - District 6 **[12161]**, Rochester, MN

Minnesota Nurses Assn. - District 7 **[10684]**, Clitherall, MN
Minnesota Nurses Assn. - District 8 **[12101]**, Renville, MN
Minnesota Nurses Assn. - District 11 **[10417]**, Bemidji, MN
Minnesota Nurses Assn. - District 12 **[10624]**, Cambridge, MN
Minnesota Nurses Assn. - District 13 **[11959]**, Owatonna, MN
Minnesota Occupational Therapy Assn. **[12504]**, St. Paul, MN
Minnesota Off-Road Cyclists **[10599]**, Burnsville, MN
Minnesota Official Measures **[11314]**, Lewiston, MN
Minnesota Oldsmobile Club **[11323]**, Lino Lakes, MN
Minnesota Operators of Music and Amusement **[11661]**, Minneapolis, MN
Minnesota Optometric Assn. **[11662]**, Minneapolis, MN
Minnesota Org. Development Network **[12660]**, Shoreview, MN
Minnesota Org. of Leaders in Nursing **[12505]**, St. Paul, MN
Minnesota Org. Network **[★12660]**
Minnesota Orienteering Club **[11663]**, Minneapolis, MN
Minnesota Ornithologists' Union **[11664]**, Minneapolis, MN
Minnesota Osteopathic Medical Soc. **[11291]**, Lakeland, MN
Minnesota Parents of Blind Children **[11665]**, Minneapolis, MN
Minnesota Petroleum Marketers Assn. **[12506]**, St. Paul, MN
Minnesota Pharmacists Assn. **[12240]**, Roseville, MN
Minnesota Pharmacists Assn., Central District **[10282]**, Alexandria, MN
Minnesota Pharmacists Assn., East Metro District **[12507]**, St. Paul, MN
Minnesota Pharmacists Assn., Northeast District **[10838]**, Duluth, MN
Minnesota Pharmacists Assn., Northwest District **[10418]**, Bemidji, MN
Minnesota Pharmacists Assn., Southeast District **[10356]**, Austin, MN
Minnesota Pharmacists Assn., Southwest District **[10628]**, Canby, MN
Minnesota Pharmacists Assn., West Metro District **[10296]**, Andover, MN
Minnesota Planned Giving Coun. **[12508]**, St. Paul, MN
Minnesota Pollution Control Agency **[12509]**, St. Paul, MN
Minnesota Polygraph Assn. **[11666]**, Minneapolis, MN
Minnesota Pork Producers Assn. **[11905]**, North Mankato, MN
Minnesota Precision Mfg. Assn. **[12027]**, Plymouth, MN
Minnesota Private Coll. Coun. **[12510]**, St. Paul, MN
Minnesota Professional Photographers Assn. **[10980]**, Fairmont, MN
Minnesota Psychiatric Soc. **[12511]**, St. Paul, MN
Minnesota Psychoanalytic Soc. **[11667]**, Minneapolis, MN
Minnesota Psychological Assn. **[12512]**, St. Paul, MN
Minnesota PTA **[12513]**, St. Paul, MN
Minnesota PTSA **[★12513]**
Minnesota Public Hea. Assn. **[11668]**, Minneapolis, MN
Minnesota Public Interest Res. Gp. **[11669]**, Minneapolis, MN
Minnesota Quarter Horse Assn. **[10632]**, Cannon Falls, MN
Minnesota Quarter Horse Assn., District 1 **[11438]**, Marshall, MN
Minnesota Quarter Horse Assn., District 2 **[10293]**, Amboy, MN
Minnesota Quarter Horse Assn., District 3 **[11246]**, Kasson, MN
Minnesota Quarter Horse Assn., District 4 **[12241]**, Roseville, MN
Minnesota Quarter Horse Assn., District 5 **[11200]**, Howard Lake, MN
Minnesota Quarter Horse Assn., District 6 **[12785]**, Verndale, MN
Minnesota Quarter Horse Assn., District 7 **[13001]**, Zimmerman, MN
Minnesota Quarter Horse Assn., District 8 **[10532]**, Brook Park, MN
Minnesota Quarter Horse Assn., District 9 **[10419]**, Bemidji, MN
Minnesota Quilters **[11670]**, Minneapolis, MN
Minnesota Racquetball Assn. **[12028]**, Plymouth, MN
Minnesota Recreation and Park Assn. **[11035]**, Fridley, MN
Minnesota Region of Narcotics Anonymous **[11671]**, Minneapolis, MN
Minnesota Renewable Energy Soc. **[11672]**, Minneapolis, MN
Minnesota Retailers Assn. **[12514]**, St. Paul, MN
Minnesota Rifle and Revolver Assn. **[11794]**, Minnetonka, MN
Minnesota River Valley Audubon Chap. **[10479]**, Bloomington, MN
Minnesota Rural Hea. Assn. **[11388]**, Mankato, MN
Minnesota Rural Water Assn. **[10938]**, Elbow Lake, MN
Minnesota SAAB Club **[11864]**, New Brighton, MN
Minnesota Saddlebred Horse Assn. **[10600]**, Burnsville, MN
Minnesota Safety Coun. **[12515]**, St. Paul, MN
Minnesota St. Thomas More Chap. of the Catholics United for the Faith **[12516]**, St. Paul, MN
Minnesota School Age Care Alliance **[12517]**, St. Paul, MN
Minnesota School Bds. Assn. **[12617]**, St. Peter, MN
Minnesota School Public Relations Assn. **[12242]**, Roseville, MN
Minnesota Sci. Teachers Assn. **[12518]**, St. Paul, MN
Minnesota Sect. of Optical Soc. of Am. **[10480]**, Bloomington, MN
Minnesota Sect. PGA of Am. **[10713]**, Coon Rapids, MN
Minnesota Self Storage Assn. **[11063]**, Golden Valley, MN
Minnesota Senior Fed., Heartland Region **[10516]**, Brainerd, MN
Minnesota Senior Fed. - Metropolitan Region **[12519]**, St. Paul, MN
Minnesota Senior Fed., Midwest Region **[12921]**, Willmar, MN
Minnesota Senior Fed., Minnesota Valley Region **[12922]**, Willmar, MN
Minnesota Senior Fed., North Star Region **[12798]**, Virginia, MN
Minnesota Senior Fed., Northwest Region **[12744]**, Thief River Falls, MN
Minnesota Senior Fed., South Central Region **[11389]**, Mankato, MN
Minnesota Senior Fed., Southwest Region **[12923]**, Willmar, MN
Minnesota Ser. Sta. Assn. **[12243]**, Roseville, MN
Minnesota Ser. Sta. and Convenience Store Assn. **[★12243]**
Minnesota Sheriffs' Assn. **[12980]**, Woodbury, MN
Minnesota Shopping Center Assn. **[10481]**, Bloomington, MN
Minnesota Small Bus. Development Center **[12520]**, St. Paul, MN
Minnesota Social Ser. Assn. **[12521]**, St. Paul, MN
Minnesota Soc. of Certified Public Accountants **[10482]**, Bloomington, MN
Minnesota Soc. of Clinical Hypnosis **[12522]**, St. Paul, MN
Minnesota Soc. of Enrolled Agents **[10678]**, Clearwater, MN
Minnesota Soc. of Health-System Pharmacists **[11795]**, Minnetonka, MN
Minnesota Soc. of Professional Engineers **[12880]**, West St. Paul, MN
Minnesota Soc. of Professional Surveyors **[10601]**, Burnsville, MN
Minnesota Soc. for Respiratory Care **[12523]**, St. Paul, MN
Minnesota Soft Drink Assn. **[12524]**, St. Paul, MN
Minnesota-South Dakota Equip. Dealers Assn. **[11960]**, Owatonna, MN
Minnesota South District, The Lutheran Church-Missouri Synod **[10602]**, Burnsville, MN
Minnesota Soybean Growers Assn. **[11906]**, North Mankato, MN
Minnesota Space Frontier Soc. **[11673]**, Minneapolis, MN
Minnesota Speech-Language-Hearing Assn. **[12337]**, St. Louis Park, MN
Minnesota Sports Fed. Amateur Softball Assn. **[12691]**, Spring Lake Park, MN
Minnesota State Bar Assn. **[11674]**, Minneapolis, MN
Minnesota State Cattlemen's Assn. **[10704]**, Comfrey, MN
Minnesota State Chamber of Commerce **[12525]**, St. Paul, MN
Minnesota State Curling Assn. - Caledonian Curling Club **[11390]**, Mankato, MN
Minnesota State Curling Assn. - Curl Mesabi **[12799]**, Virginia, MN
Minnesota State Curling Assn. - St. Paul Curling Club **[12526]**, St. Paul, MN
Minnesota State Curling Assn. - Two Harbors Curling Club **[12772]**, Two Harbors, MN
Minnesota State Grange **[10615]**, Byron, MN
Minnesota State High School Coaches Assn. **[10779]**, Detroit Lakes, MN
Minnesota State Patrol Troopers Assn. **[12111]**, Richfield, MN
Minnesota State Univ. Student Assn. **[12527]**, St. Paul, MN
Minnesota State Volkssport Assn. **[★11682]**
Minnesota Supreme Court Historical Soc. **[11675]**, Minneapolis, MN
Minnesota Sword Club **[11676]**, Minneapolis, MN
Minnesota Table Tennis Fed. **[11295]**, Lakeville, MN
Minnesota Taxpayers Assn. **[12528]**, St. Paul, MN
Minnesota Telecom Alliance **[12529]**, St. Paul, MN
Minnesota Telephone Alliance **[★12529]**
Minnesota Timber Producers Assn. **[10839]**, Duluth, MN
Minnesota Tooling and Machining Assn. **[★12027]**
Minnesota Transport Services Assn. **[12530]**, St. Paul, MN
Minnesota Trappers Assn. **[10569]**, Bruno, MN
Minnesota Trial Lawyers Assn. **[11677]**, Minneapolis, MN
Minnesota Triumphs **[11678]**, Minneapolis, MN
Minnesota Trucking Assn. **[12244]**, Roseville, MN
Minnesota Truss Manufacturers Assn. **[11814]**, Montrose, MN
Minnesota Turkey Growers Assn. **[10576]**, Buffalo, MN
Minnesota Turkey Res. and Promotion Coun. **[10577]**, Buffalo, MN
Minnesota United Snowmobilers Assn. **[10554]**, Brooklyn Park, MN
Minnesota Urological Soc. **[11292]**, Lakeland, MN
Minnesota USA Wrestling **[11679]**, Minneapolis, MN
Minnesota Users Gp. of Applied Systems **[11680]**, Minneapolis, MN
Minnesota Utility Contractors Assn. **[12981]**, Woodbury, MN
Minnesota Valley Action Coun. **[11391]**, Mankato, MN
Minnesota Valley Young Life **[10603]**, Burnsville, MN
Minnesota Veterans for Peace - Chap. 27 **[11681]**, Minneapolis, MN
Minnesota Veterinary Medical Assn. **[12681]**, South St. Paul, MN
Minnesota Volkssport Assn. **[11682]**, Minneapolis, MN
Minnesota Water Well Assn. **[12531]**, St. Paul, MN
Minnesota West Coast Swing Dance Club **[12910]**, Willernie, MN
Minnesota Women Lawyers **[11683]**, Minneapolis, MN
Minnesota Women of Today **[10307]**, Anoka, MN
Minnesota Women's Consortium **[12532]**, St. Paul, MN
Minnesota Woodturners Assn. **[10297]**, Andover, MN
Minnesota Workers' Compensation Insurers Assn. **[10924]**, Edina, MN
Minnesota Working Rottweiler Assn. **[12982]**, Woodbury, MN
Minnesotans Against the Death Penalty **[11684]**, Minneapolis, MN
Minnesotans Against Terrorism **[11189]**, Hopkins, MN
Minnesotans for an Energy-Efficient Economy **[12533]**, St. Paul, MN
Minnesotans for Responsible Recreation **[10840]**, Duluth, MN

Minnetonka Game and Fish Club [10308], Anoka, MN
Minnetonka South Lions Club [11190], Hopkins, MN
Minocqua - Arbor Vitae - Woodruff Chamber of Commerce [19199], Minocqua, WI
Minority Business
Central Ohio Minority Bus. Assn. [14360], Columbus, OH
Michigan Minority Bus. Development Coun. [7397], Detroit, MI
Minority Business Alliance of Southwest Michigan [8452], Kalamazoo, MI
South Central Ohio Minority Bus. Coun. [13998], Cincinnati, OH
Minority Business Alliance of Southwest Michigan [8452], Kalamazoo, MI
Minority Bus. Assn; Central Ohio [14360], Columbus, OH
Minority Chamber of Commerce; Milwaukee [19064], Milwaukee, WI
Minority Contractors of Upper Midwest; Natl. Assn. of [11695], Minneapolis, MN
Mishawaka - Young Life [6245], South Bend, IN
Mishicot Area Growth and Improvement Comm. [19203], Mishicot, WI
Miss Rodeo Wisconsin Pageant Assn. [19729], Shiocton, WI
Missing-in-Action
Forgotten Eagles [7241], De Tour Village, MI
Mississippi Assn. for Psychology in the Schools [9940], Traverse City, MI
Mississippi Corridor Neighborhood Coalition [11685], Minneapolis, MN
Mississippi Headwaters Audubon Soc. [10420], Bemidji, MN
Mississippi Headwaters Bd. [12833], Walker, MN
Mississippi River Conservation Comm; Upper [3260], Rock Island, IL
Mississippi River Refuges; Friends of the Upper [12950], Winona, MN
Mississippi River Regional Planning Commn. [18367], La Crosse, WI
Mississippi Valley Morgan Horse Club [3650], Springfield, IL
Missouri Soc. of Health-System Pharmacists [2352], Loves Park, IL
Missouri Veterinary Medical Assn. [★12681]
MIT Enterprise Forum of Chicago [1058], Chicago, IL
MIT Enterprise Forum of the Great Lakes [6738], Ann Arbor, MI
Mit Liebe German Shepherd Dog Rescue [19851], Suamico, WI
Mitchell Chamber of Commerce [★5815]
Mitral Valve Prolapse Syndrome; Soc. for [2069], Itasca, IL
Mizpah Shriners [4695], Fort Wayne, IN
MMCA [12534], St. Paul, MN
MOAA Illinois Coun. of Chapters [3102], Plainfield, IL
MOAA Indiana Coun. of Chapters [5977], Noblesville, IN
MOAA Wisconsin Coun. of Chapters [18368], La Crosse, WI
Mobile Home and Recreational Vehicle Assn; Ohio [★15058]
Mobilization for Survival [★19089]
Mobilize Montgomery [11808], Montgomery, MN
MOC of Northeastern Wisconsin [18114], Green Bay, WI
Model A Restorers Club, Calumet Region [3771], Tinley Park, IL
Model A Restorers Club, Floral City A Region [9065], Monroe, MI
Model A Restorers Club, Illinois Region [2757], Northbrook, IL
Model T Ford Club of Northwest Ohio [13367], Bluffton, OH
Model Trains
Natl. Model Railroad Assn., Mid-Central Region [15370], Grove City, OH
Natl. Model Railroad Assn., Midwest Region [19078], Milwaukee, WI
National Model Railroad Association, Thousand Lakes Region [10605], Burnsville, MN
Models
Central Illinois Aerospace [504], Champaign, IL
Mohammed Shriners [170], Bartonville, IL
Mohawk Valley Rabbit Breeders Assn. [★260]
Mohawk Valley Rabbit and Cavy Breeders Assn. [★260]
Mokena Chamber of Commerce [2510], Mokena, IL
Moline - Young Life [2524], Moline, IL
Momence Chamber of Commerce [2538], Momence, IL
Moms Club [7985], Grand Rapids, MI
Moms Club [12053], Prior Lake, MN
Moms Club of Apple Valley [10321], Apple Valley, MN
Moms Club of Brooklyn Center/North Minneapolis [11686], Minneapolis, MN
Moms Club of Pendleton, IN [6026], Pendleton, IN
Moms and Dads Club; St. Mary's Preparatory [9312], Orchard Lake, MI
Monmouth Area Chamber of Commerce [2541], Monmouth, IL
Monmouth Commercial Club [★2541]
Monon Chamber of Commerce [5818], Monon, IN
Monona Chamber of Commerce [19209], Monona, WI
Monroe Actors Stage Company [3900], Waterloo, IL
Monroe Alliance for the Mentally Ill [9066], Monroe, MI
Monroe Chamber of Commerce and Indus. [19215], Monroe, WI
Monroe Coin Club [10185], Wyandotte, MI
Monroe County Apartment Assn. [4241], Bloomington, IN
Monroe County Assn. of Realtors [9067], Monroe, MI
Monroe County Chamber of Commerce [9068], Monroe, MI
Monroe County Chamber of Commerce [17306], Woodsfield, OH
Monroe County Chap. of the Ohio Genealogical Soc. [17307], Woodsfield, OH
Monroe County Historical Soc. [19753], Sparta, WI
Monroe County Planning Commn. [9069], Monroe, MI
Monroe County Young Life [8302], Ida, MI
Monroe Figure Skating Club [9070], Monroe, MI
Monroe Golden Lions Club [9071], Monroe, MI
Monroe Lions Club - Ohio [16055], Monroe, OH
Monroe - Young Life [8303], Ida, MI
Mont Clare - Elmwood Park Chamber of Commerce [1633], Elmwood Park, IL
Montcalm County Assn. of Realtors [8070], Greenville, MI
Montello Area Chamber of Commerce [19221], Montello, WI
Montevideo Area Chamber of Commerce [11801], Montevideo, MN
Montevideo Area United Way [11802], Montevideo, MN
Montevideo Lions Club [11803], Montevideo, MN
Montgomery County Chamber of Commerce [★4425]
Montgomery County Chap., Ohio Genealogical Soc. [14921], Dayton, OH
Montgomery County Historical Soc. [14922], Dayton, OH
Montgomery County Medical Soc. - Ohio [14923], Dayton, OH
Montgomery County, Ohio - Young Democrats [14924], Dayton, OH
Montgomery/Greene Counties RSVP [14925], Dayton, OH
Montgomery Women's Club [13910], Cincinnati, OH
Monticello Area Chamber of Commerce [11811], Monticello, MN
Monticello Chamber of Commerce [2548], Monticello, IL
Monticello Chamber of Commerce [★11811]
Monticello Lions Club, IL [2549], Monticello, IL
Monticello Main St. [2550], Monticello, IL
Montmorency County Habitat for Humanity [8806], Lewiston, MI
Montpelier Area Chamber of Commerce [16061], Montpelier, OH
Montpelier Independent Development Comm [★16062]
Montpelier Indus. Development Comm. [16062], Montpelier, OH
Montrose Lions Club - Michigan [9079], Montrose, MI
Mooresville Chamber of Commerce [5837], Mooresville, IN
Mooresville Chamber of Commerce and Economic Development Commn. [★5837]
Moorhead Area Chamber of Commerce [★11822]
Moorhead Midday-Central Lions Club [11826], Moorhead, MN
Moose
Moose Intl., Family Center 1408 - Eau Claire [17885], Eau Claire, WI
Moose Intl., Family Center 1408 - Eau Claire [17885], Eau Claire, WI
Moose Lake Area Chamber of Commerce [11830], Moose Lake, MN
Mora Area Chamber of Commerce [★11833]
Mora Lions Club [11834], Mora, MN
Morgenroth Baseball [13911], Cincinnati, OH
Mormon Coulee Lions Club [18369], La Crosse, WI
Morrice Lions Club [9084], Morrice, MI
Morris Area Chamber of Commerce and Agriculture [11838], Morris, MN
Morris Lions Club [11839], Morris, MN
Morrison Chamber of Commerce [2559], Morrison, IL
Morrison County United Way [11337], Little Falls, MN
Morrow County Chamber of Commerce [★16070]
Morrow County Chamber of Commerce and Visitors' Bur. [16070], Mount Gilead, OH
Mortgage Bankers Assn. Of Northwest Ohio (Toledo) [16930], Toledo, OH
Mortgage Bankers Assn; Wisconsin [18729], Madison, WI
Morton - Central Illinois - Young Life [3889], Washington, IL
Morton Chamber of Commerce [2564], Morton, IL
Morton Grove Chamber of Commerce and Indus. [2569], Morton Grove, IL
Morton Lions Club [11845], Morton, MN
Mortuary Services
Chicago Memorial Assn. [817], Chicago, IL
Cleveland Memorial Soc. [14100], Cleveland, OH
Funeral Consumers Alliance - Akron Region [13052], Akron, OH
Funeral Consumers Alliance of Central Ohio [14440], Columbus, OH
Funeral Consumers Alliance of Champaign County [3816], Urbana, IL
Funeral Consumers Alliance of the Fox Valley [17497], Appleton, WI
Funeral Consumers' Alliance of Northwest Ohio [16917], Toledo, OH
Illinois Funeral Directors Assn. [3605], Springfield, IL
Independent Funeral Directors of Indiana [5755], Martinsville, IN
Indiana Funeral Directors Assn. [5237], Indianapolis, IN
Indianapolis Memorial Soc. [5352], Indianapolis, IN
Memorial Advisory and Planning Soc. [6717], Ann Arbor, MI
Minnesota Funeral Directors Assn. [12025], Plymouth, MN
Nevada Funeral Directors Assn. [17676], Brookfield, WI
Ohio Funeral Directors Assn. [14614], Columbus, OH
Venice Cemetery Assn. [15172], Fairfield, OH
Wisconsin Funeral Directors Assn. [20089], Wauwatosa, WI
Mosaic [2374], Macomb, IL
Mosinee Area Chamber of Commerce [19229], Mosinee, WI
Mosinee Sportsmen's Alliance [19230], Mosinee, WI
Moslem Shriners [7401], Detroit, MI
Mosquito Beemers [14790], Cortland, OH
Mosquito Control Assn; Michigan [6891], Bay City, MI
Mother Earth/Ohio Peace March; Walkacross America for [★14411]
Mother Hubbard's Cupboard [4242], Bloomington, IN
Mothers Against Drunk Driving, Allen/Putnam Counties [15663], Lima, OH
Mothers Against Drunk Driving, Becker County [10780], Detroit Lakes, MN
Mothers Against Drunk Driving, Blue Earth/Nicollet [12535], St. Paul, MN

Mothers Against Drunk Driving, Brown/Marinette Counties **[18115]**, Green Bay, WI
Mothers Against Drunk Driving, Carver County **[12536]**, St. Paul, MN
Mothers Against Drunk Driving, Central Indiana **[4183]**, Beech Grove, IN
Mothers Against Drunk Driving, Chisago/Isanti Counties **[12700]**, Stacy, MN
Mothers Against Drunk Driving, Delaware County **[15009]**, Delaware, OH
Mothers Against Drunk Driving, Dupage County **[2301]**, Lisle, IL
Mothers Against Drunk Driving, East Central Indiana **[4112]**, Anderson, IN
Mothers Against Drunk Driving, Eau Claire County **[17886]**, Eau Claire, WI
Mothers Against Drunk Driving, Fayette County **[3847]**, Vandalia, IL
Mothers Against Drunk Driving, Fayette/Pickaway Counties **[17130]**, Washington Court House, OH
Mothers Against Drunk Driving, Franklin County **[14508]**, Columbus, OH
Mothers Against Drunk Driving, Freeborn County **[11123]**, Hartland, MN
Mothers Against Drunk Driving, Fulton County **[405]**, Canton, IL
Mothers Against Drunk Driving, Greater Toledo Area **[16826]**, Sylvania, OH
Mothers Against Drunk Driving, Greene County **[17374]**, Xenia, OH
Mothers Against Drunk Driving, Heartland Chapter **[1543]**, East Peoria, IL
Mothers Against Drunk Driving, Illinois State **[3651]**, Springfield, IL
Mothers Against Drunk Driving, Indiana State **[4184]**, Beech Grove, IN
Mothers Against Drunk Driving, Kane County **[183]**, Batavia, IL
Mothers Against Drunk Driving, Kent County Chap. **[7986]**, Grand Rapids, MI
Mothers Against Drunk Driving, La Crosse County **[18370]**, La Crosse, WI
Mothers Against Drunk Driving, Macomb County **[9091]**, Mount Clemens, MI
Mothers Against Drunk Driving, Marathon/Portage **[19794]**, Stevens Point, WI
Mothers Against Drunk Driving, McHenry County **[1328]**, Crystal Lake, IL
Mothers Against Drunk Driving, McLean County **[298]**, Bloomington, IL
Mothers Against Drunk Driving, Mercer County **[2434]**, Matherville, IL
Mothers Against Drunk Driving, Michigan State **[8733]**, Lansing, MI
Mothers Against Drunk Driving, North Coast Chap. **[14166]**, Cleveland, OH
Mothers Against Drunk Driving, Oakland County **[10088]**, Waterford, MI
Mothers Against Drunk Driving, Ohio **[14509]**, Columbus, OH
Mothers Against Drunk Driving, Ohio Valley Chap. **[16763]**, Steubenville, OH
Mothers Against Drunk Driving, Otter Tail County **[12537]**, St. Paul, MN
Mothers Against Drunk Driving, Portage County **[16499]**, Ravenna, OH
Mothers Against Drunk Driving, Quinsippi Chap. **[3154]**, Quincy, IL
Mothers Against Drunk Driving, Rock/Walworth Counties **[17613]**, Beloit, WI
Mothers Against Drunk Driving, St. Clair/Sanilac Counties **[8975]**, Marysville, MI
Mothers Against Drunk Driving, Sauk County **[19590]**, Reedsburg, WI
Mothers Against Drunk Driving, Shelby County **[3466]**, Shelbyville, IL
Mothers Against Drunk Driving, Southwestern Ohio **[13912]**, Cincinnati, OH
Mothers Against Drunk Driving, Stark County **[13117]**, Alliance, OH
Mothers Against Drunk Driving, State Off. **[12538]**, St. Paul, MN
Mothers Against Drunk Driving, Upper Fox Valley **[17502]**, Appleton, WI
Mothers Against Drunk Driving, Wabash Valley Chap. **[6335]**, Terre Haute, IN
Mothers Against Drunk Driving, Washington County **[20123]**, West Bend, WI
Mothers Against Drunk Driving, Washtenaw County **[6739]**, Ann Arbor, MI
Mothers Against Drunk Driving, Waukesha County **[19991]**, Waukesha, WI
Mothers Against Drunk Driving, Wayne County **[10140]**, Westland, MI
Mothers Against Drunk Driving, Western Reserve **[16336]**, Painesville, OH
Mothers Against Drunk Driving, Winnebago County **[20173]**, Winneconne, WI
Mothers Against Drunk Driving, Winona County **[12956]**, Winona, MN
Mothers Against Drunk Driving, Wisconsin State **[17503]**, Appleton, WI
Mothers' Center of Greater Toledo **[16931]**, Toledo, OH
Mothers Club; Batavia **[★177]**
Mothers Club Found; Batavia **[177]**, Batavia, IL
Mothers Connection PTA **[10898]**, Eden Prairie, MN
Mothers/Hea.y Babies Coalition; Hea.y **[★8167]**
Mothers from Hell 2 **[3081]**, Peru, IL
Motor City Striders **[8296]**, Huntington Woods, MI
Motor City Theatre Organ Soc. **[7402]**, Detroit, MI
Motor City Viper Owners **[6988]**, Bloomfield Hills, MI
Motorcycle
Akron BMW Motorcycle Club **[13018]**, Akron, OH
Beemer Hill Riders, No. 317 **[19417]**, Palmyra, WI
Belle City Beemers 20/20 Riders No. 201 **[18297]**, Kenosha, WI
BMW Motorcycle Owners of Cleveland No. 196 **[13629]**, Chagrin Falls, OH
BMW Motorcycle Owners Club of Minnesota No. 49 **[11867]**, New Hope, MN
BMW Of Battle Creek No. 14 **[6855]**, Battle Creek, MI
BMW Riders of Toledo No. 16 **[16557]**, Rossford, OH
BMW Touring Club of Detroit No. 1 **[9793]**, Southfield, MI
Buckeye Beemers No. 99 **[14342]**, Columbus, OH
DuKane A.B.A.T.E. **[3939]**, West Chicago, IL
Gateway Riders BMW Club No. 22 **[1697]**, Fairview Heights, IL
Gold Wing Touring Assn. **[5124]**, Indianapolis, IN
Greater Cincinnati BMW Club No. 18 **[15723]**, Loveland, OH
Illinois Motorcycle Dealers Assn. **[3616]**, Springfield, IL
Illinois Valley BMW MOA No. 70 **[2563]**, Morton, IL
Indiana Motorcycle Dealers Assn. **[5263]**, Indianapolis, IN
Indianapolis BMW Club No. 17 **[5340]**, Indianapolis, IN
Madison BMW Club No. 7 **[18839]**, McFarland, WI
Michigan Motorcycle Dealers Assn. **[8686]**, Lansing, MI
Mosquito Beemers **[14790]**, Cortland, OH
Natl. R90S Sport Owners Club No. 67 **[13140]**, Amherst, OH
Northern Illinois BMW Riders No. 271 **[3942]**, West Chicago, IL
Penton Owners Gp. **[13141]**, Amherst, OH
Port Washington BMW Motorcycle Club No. 116 **[19501]**, Port Washington, WI
Sisters of the Moon **[18616]**, Madison, WI
Springfield Milers BMW Motorcycle Club No. 121 **[3682]**, Springfield, IL
Wisconsin BMW Motorcycle Club No. 10 **[19419]**, Palmyra, WI
Women on Wheels **[12605]**, St. Paul, MN
Women in the Wind **[16985]**, Toledo, OH
Women in the Wind - Akron Chap. **[13103]**, Akron, OH
Women in the Wind, Milwaukee Area **[20113]**, West Allis, WI
Youngstown BMW No. 120 **[17424]**, Youngstown, OH
Motorcycle Dealers Assn; Illinois **[3616]**, Springfield, IL
Motown Assn. for Computing Machinery SIGGRAPH **[7403]**, Detroit, MI
Moultrie County United Way **[3740]**, Sullivan, IL
Moundsview - Young Life **[12245]**, Roseville, MN
Mount Carmel Public Lib. Found. **[2573]**, Mount Carmel, IL
Mount Carroll Chamber of Commerce **[2577]**, Mount Carroll, IL
Mount Clemens - Macomb County Gem and Lapidary Soc. **[7184]**, Clinton Township, MI
Mount Gilead Area Chamber of Commerce **[★16070]**
Mount Gilead Lions Club - Ohio **[16071]**, Mount Gilead, OH
Mount Greenwood Chamber of Commerce **[1059]**, Chicago, IL
Mt. Healthy - Young Life **[15164]**, Fairfield, OH
Mount Horeb Area Chamber of Commerce **[19238]**, Mount Horeb, WI
Mt. Horeb Jr. High - Wyldlife **[19239]**, Mount Horeb, WI
Mt. Horeb Sr. High - Young Life **[19240]**, Mount Horeb, WI
Mt. Morris Lions Club **[9094]**, Mount Morris, MI
Mount Pleasant Area Chamber of Commerce **[9115]**, Mount Pleasant, MI
Mt. Pleasant Figure Skating Club **[9116]**, Mount Pleasant, MI
Mount Pleasant Lions Club - Michigan **[9117]**, Mount Pleasant, MI
Mount Prospect Chamber of Commerce **[2589]**, Mount Prospect, IL
Mount Sinai Hosp. **[1060]**, Chicago, IL
Mount Sinai Medical Inst. Coun. **[★1060]**
Mount Union Coll. Assn. for Computing Machinery Student Chap. **[13118]**, Alliance, OH
Mt. Vernon Chamber of Commerce **[★5855]**
Mount Vernon - Knox County Chamber of Commerce **[16086]**, Mount Vernon, OH
Mt. Vernon - Young Life **[5852]**, Mount Vernon, IN
Mount Zion Chamber of Commerce **[2606]**, Mount Zion, IL
Mountain Iron Lions Club **[11228]**, Iron, MN
MRA - The Mgt. Assn. **[19439]**, Pewaukee, WI
MRPA **[★11035]**
MS Connection **[6825]**, Bancroft, MI
MTU Fencing Club **[8258]**, Houghton, MI
Mudchuggers Four Wheel Drive Club **[10089]**, Waterford, MI
Mudslingers 4x4 Club **[3972]**, Westmont, IL
Mukwonago Area Chamber of Commerce **[★19253]**
Mukwonago Area Chamber of Commerce and Tourism Center **[19253]**, Mukwonago, WI
Mukwonago Chamber of Commerce **[★19253]**
Mule and Donkey Show Society; Midstates **[16427]**, Pioneer, OH
Mulliken Lions Club **[9127]**, Mulliken, MI
Multiple Sclerosis Soc., Indiana State Chap; Natl. **[5428]**, Indianapolis, IN
Multiple Sclerosis Soc., Ohio Valley Chap; Natl. **[13928]**, Cincinnati, OH
Muncie Area Youth for Christ **[5886]**, Muncie, IN
Muncie Chamber of Commerce **[★5887]**
Muncie-Delaware County Chamber of Commerce **[5887]**, Muncie, IN
Muncie Obedience Training Club **[5888]**, Muncie, IN
Muncie Sailing Club **[5889]**, Muncie, IN
Muncie - Young Life **[5890]**, Muncie, IN
Mundelein MainStreet **[2615]**, Mundelein, IL
Municipal Attorneys; Michigan Assn. of **[6719]**, Ann Arbor, MI
Municipal Contractors; Assn. of **[★3536]**
Municipal Elec. Utilities of Wisconsin **[19861]**, Sun Prairie, WI
Municipal Government
Civic League **[19508]**, Portage, WI
Illinois Municipal League **[3618]**, Springfield, IL
Indiana Assn. of Cities and Towns **[5167]**, Indianapolis, IN
League of Minnesota Cities **[12440]**, St. Paul, MN
League of Wisconsin Municipalities **[18540]**, Madison, WI
Madison County Coun. of Govts. **[4110]**, Anderson, IN
Michigan Municipal League **[6730]**, Ann Arbor, MI
Michigan Townships Assn. **[8722]**, Lansing, MI
Minnesota Assn. of Townships **[12341]**, St. Michael, MN
Ohio-Kentucky-Indiana Regional Coun. of Governments **[13940]**, Cincinnati, OH
Ohio Mid-Eastern Govts. Assn. **[13499]**, Cambridge, OH
Ohio Municipal League **[14640]**, Columbus, OH

Ohio Township Assn. **[14690]**, Columbus, OH
Wisconsin City/County Mgt. Assn. **[19164]**, Milwaukee, WI
Wisconsin Towns Assn. **[19687]**, Shawano, WI
Municipal League; Indiana **[★5167]**
Munising Visitors Bur. **[★9129]**
Munith Lions Club **[9133]**, Munith, MI
Munster Chamber of Commerce **[5903]**, Munster, IN
Munster High School PTO **[5904]**, Munster, IN
Murat Shriners **[5409]**, Indianapolis, IN
Murphy Roche Irish Music Club **[376]**, Burr Ridge, IL
Murphysboro Chamber of Commerce **[2619]**, Murphysboro, IL
Muscatatuck Bd. of Realtors **[5997]**, North Vernon, IN
Muscular Dystrophy Assn. **[7748]**, Flint, MI
Muscular Dystrophy Association, Columbus **[14510]**, Columbus, OH
Muscular Dystrophy Assn., Dayton **[14926]**, Dayton, OH
Muscular Dystrophy Assn., Midpark **[★14167]**
Muscular Dystrophy Assn., Northeast Ohio **[14167]**, Cleveland, OH
Muscular Dystrophy Assn. of Southwestern Wisconsin **[18566]**, Madison, WI
Muscular Dystrophy Assn. Support Gps. **[3035]**, Peoria, IL
Museum Assn; Lorain County Tropical Greenhouse and **[15706]**, Lorain, OH
Museum; Blackford Historical **[★4901]**
Museum; Clark County Historical Society/Howard Steamboat **[5540]**, Jeffersonville, IN
Museum; Cleveland Police **[★14102]**
Museum; Cleveland Police Historical Soc. and **[14102]**, Cleveland, OH
Museum; Clinton County **[★4740]**
Museum and Cultural Center; Swedish **[★1205]**
Museum; Decatur County Historical Soc. **[★4842]**
Museum; Du Page County Historical **[★3983]**
Museum; Fayette County **[★17128]**
Museum; Gnadenhutten Historical Soc. **[★15329]**
Museum; Governor John Wood Mansion **[★3152]**
Museum Gp; Edwardsburg **[7591]**, Edwardsburg, MI
Museum; Howard Steamboat **[★5540]**
Museum; Jean Butz James **[★1990]**
Museum; Johnson-Humrickhouse **[14802]**, Coshocton, OH
Museum; Kosciusko County Jail **[★6447]**
Museum; Leelanau Historical **[★8796]**
Museum and Lib; Madison County Historical **[★1563]**
Museum and Lib; Madison County Historical Soc. **[1563]**, Edwardsville, IL
Museum and Lib; McLean County Historical Soc. **[★296]**
Museum; Logan County Historical Soc. and Logan County **[13321]**, Bellefontaine, OH
Museum; Madison County Historical Soc. and **[★1563]**
Museum; Mayville Historical Soc. **[★18833]**
Museum; Old Iron County Courthouse **[★18231]**
Museum; Outagamie **[★17512]**
Museum; Pound **[★6447]**
Museum Soc; Iron County Historical and **[7092]**, Caspian, MI
Museum and Soc; Johnson County Historical **[4751]**, Franklin, IN
Museum Soc; Vermilion County **[1356]**, Danville, IL
Museum; Walt Durbahn Tool **[★1990]**
Museums
Assn. of Indiana Museums **[5048]**, Indianapolis, IN
Detroit Inst. of Arts **[7348]**, Detroit, MI
Edwardsburg Museum Gp. **[7591]**, Edwardsburg, MI
Illinois Assn. of Museums **[3572]**, Springfield, IL
Indiana State Museum Found. **[5319]**, Indianapolis, IN
Indiana State Museum Volunteers **[5320]**, Indianapolis, IN
Johnson-Humrickhouse Museum **[14802]**, Coshocton, OH
Lake View Cemetery Assn. **[14154]**, Cleveland, OH
Michigan Museums Assn. **[8689]**, Lansing, MI
Ohio Museums Assn. **[14641]**, Columbus, OH
Public Museum of Grand Rapids **[8002]**, Grand Rapids, MI
Museums; Ohio Assn. of Historical Societies and **[14555]**, Columbus, OH
Music
All Amer. City Chorus of Sweet Adelines **[15518]**, Jackson Center, OH
Amer. Guild of Organists, Ann Arbor (531) **[7301]**, Detroit, MI
Amer. Guild of Organists, Detroit Chap. **[10059]**, Warren, MI
Amer. Guild of Organists, Holland Area C556 **[8189]**, Holland, MI
Amer. Guild of Organists, Madison (644) **[18459]**, Madison, WI
Amer. Guild of Organists, Moody Bible Inst. (595) **[4079]**, Zion, IL
Amer. Guild of Organists, Muskegon-Lakeshore (538) **[9136]**, Muskegon, MI
American Guild of Organists, Twin Cities (628) **[12639]**, Savage, MN
Amer. Guild of Organists, Univ. of Evansville C592 **[5524]**, Jasper, IN
Amer. Guild of Organists, Wabash Valley (527) **[6307]**, Terre Haute, IN
Amer. Musicological Soc. - Midwest Chap. **[6630]**, Alma, MI
Amer. Orff-Schulwerk Assn., Greater Cleveland Chap. No. 1 **[16700]**, Southington, OH
Amer. Orff-Schulwerk Assn., West Michigan Chap. No. 32 **[9098]**, Mount Pleasant, MI
Amer. String Teachers Assn., Michigan Chap. **[10111]**, West Bloomfield, MI
Amer. Theater Organ Soc., Joliet **[3954]**, Westchester, IL
Amer. Theater Organ Soc., Red River **[11056]**, Glyndon, MN
Amer. Theatre Organ Soc., Central Indiana Chap. **[5027]**, Indianapolis, IN
Amer. Theatre Organ Soc., Central Minnesota Chap. **[10995]**, Fergus Falls, MN
Amer. Theatre Organ Soc., Chicagoland Chap. **[728]**, Chicago, IL
Amer. Theatre Organ Soc., Heart Of Ohio Chap. **[16485]**, Prospect, OH
Amer. Theatre Organ Soc., Land O' Lakes **[12221]**, Roseville, MN
Amer. Theatre Organ Soc., Motor City Chap. **[7323]**, Detroit, MI
Amer. Theatre Organ Soc., Northern Michigan Chap. **[10168]**, Williamsburg, MI
Amer. Theatre Organ Soc., Ohio Valley Chap. **[13738]**, Cincinnati, OH
Amer. Theatre Organ Soc., Quad Cities Chap. **[2517]**, Moline, IL
Amer. Theatre Organ Soc., Southwest Michigan Chap. **[8420]**, Kalamazoo, MI
Amer. Theatre Organ Soc., Western Reserve Chap. **[13283]**, Beachwood, OH
Ann Arbor Coun. for Traditional Music and Dance **[6671]**, Ann Arbor, MI
Bach Babes **[18975]**, Milwaukee, WI
Bach Collegium- Fort Wayne **[4643]**, Fort Wayne, IN
Bay Area Music Teachers Assn. **[7081]**, Caro, MI
Brown County Civic Music Assn. **[18089]**, Green Bay, WI
Calumet Corner Chorus of Sweet Adelines Intl. **[4877]**, Hammond, IN
Central Ohio Theatre Organ Soc. **[14815]**, Croton, OH
Central Ohio Theatre Organ Soc. **[17039]**, Urbana, OH
Champaign-Urbana Sweet Adelines **[515]**, Champaign, IL
Chicago Area Theatre Organ Enthusiasts **[3982]**, Wheaton, IL
Chicago Chap. of the Amer. Recorder Soc. **[797]**, Chicago, IL
Chicago Highlanders Pipe Band **[2807]**, Oak Park, IL
City of Lakes Sweet Adelines Chorus **[10865]**, Eagan, MN
Columbus Blues Alliance **[14373]**, Columbus, OH
Columbus Chorus of Sweet Adelines Intl. **[14379]**, Columbus, OH
Dairyland Theatre Organ Soc. **[18999]**, Milwaukee, WI
Elgin Children's Chorus **[1589]**, Elgin, IL
Friends of the Minnesota Sinfonia **[11566]**, Minneapolis, MN
Grand Rapids Chorus of Sweet Adelines Intl. **[7946]**, Grand Rapids, MI
Grand Rapids Women's Chorus **[7953]**, Grand Rapids, MI
Grand Traverse Chorus of Sweet Adelines Intl. **[9932]**, Traverse City, MI
Great Lake Sound Chorus of Sweet Adelines Intl. **[6382]**, Valparaiso, IN
Greater Chicago Amer. Orff-Schulwerk Assn. **[119]**, Aurora, IL
Greater Cincinnati Chap. of Amer. Orff-Schulwerk Assn. **[16026]**, Milford, OH
Holland Piano Teachers Forum **[10226]**, Zeeland, MI
Illinois Country Music Assn. **[1514]**, Downs, IL
Independence Music Boosters **[15498]**, Independence, OH
Indiana Music Educators Assn. **[5880]**, Muncie, IN
Indianapolis Children's Choir **[5342]**, Indianapolis, IN
Joliet Area Theatre Organ Enthusiasts **[2112]**, Joliet, IL
La Crosse Scenic Bluffs Chap. of the Amer. Theatre Organ Soc. **[18362]**, La Crosse, WI
La Crosse Scenic Bluffs Chap. of the Amer. Theatre Organ Soc. **[18363]**, La Crosse, WI
Land O' Lakes Theatre Organ Soc. **[12232]**, Roseville, MN
Madison Drum and Bugle Corps Assn. **[19860]**, Sun Prairie, WI
Michigan Competing Band Assn. **[9078]**, Montrose, MI
Michigan School Band and Orchestra Assn. **[9291]**, Okemos, MI
Midwest Crossroad Chorus of Sweet Adelines Intl. **[2317]**, Lockport, IL
Motor City Theatre Organ Soc. **[7402]**, Detroit, MI
Murphy Roche Irish Music Club **[376]**, Burr Ridge, IL
Natl. Assn. of Pastoral Musicians, Cincinnati Chap. **[13923]**, Cincinnati, OH
Natl. Assn. of Pastoral Musicians, Cincinnati-Miami Valley **[13300]**, Beavercreek, OH
Natl. Assn. of Pastoral Musicians, Columbus **[15266]**, Gahanna, OH
Natl. Assn. of Pastoral Musicians, Kalamazoo **[9687]**, St. Joseph, MI
Natl. Assn. of Pastoral Musicians, Lansing **[6743]**, Ann Arbor, MI
Ohio Music Educ. Assn. **[15894]**, Massillon, OH
Packerland Theatre Organ Soc. **[17814]**, De Pere, WI
Prairie Brass Band Assn. **[76]**, Arlington Heights, IL
Pride of Toledo Chorus of Sweet Adelines Intl. **[16952]**, Toledo, OH
Riverside Chorus of Sweet Adelines Intl. **[3948]**, West Dundee, IL
Song of the Lakes Sweet Adelines Chorus **[7239]**, Davison, MI
Sweet Adelines Intl., Alexienne Chap. **[10286]**, Alexandria, MN
Sweet Adelines Intl., Battle Creek Chap. **[6871]**, Battle Creek, MI
Sweet Adelines Intl., Capital City Chorus **[5485]**, Indianapolis, IN
Sweet Adelines Intl., Capitol Showcase Chap. **[14743]**, Columbus, OH
Sweet Adelines Intl., Center Point Chap. **[19811]**, Stevens Point, WI
Sweet Adelines Intl., Chippewa Valley Chap. **[17902]**, Eau Claire, WI
Sweet Adelines Intl., Choral-Aires Chorus **[2782]**, Oak Brook, IL
Sweet Adelines Intl., City of Flags Chorus **[13591]**, Canton, OH
Sweet Adelines Intl., County Connection Chorus **[10216]**, Ypsilanti, MI
Sweet Adelines Intl., Crosstown Harmony Chorus **[19131]**, Milwaukee, WI
Sweet Adelines Intl., Danville Chap. **[1352]**, Danville, IL
Sweet Adelines Intl., Dogwood Blossoms Chap. **[16089]**, Mount Vernon, OH
Sweet Adelines Intl., Edge O' Town Chap. **[1206]**, Chicago, IL

Sweet Adelines Intl., Fenton Lakes Chorus **[7691]**, Fenton, MI
Sweet Adelines Intl., Fox Valley Chorus **[17526]**, Appleton, WI
Sweet Adelines Intl., French Colony Chap. **[15295]**, Gallipolis, OH
Sweet Adelines Intl., Friendship VII Chap. **[16127]**, New Concord, OH
Sweet Adelines Intl., Gem City Chorus **[13626]**, Centerville, OH
Sweet Adelines Intl., Granite City Sound Chap. **[12314]**, St. Cloud, MN
Sweet Adelines Intl., Great Lakes Chorus **[9872]**, Sterling Heights, MI
Sweet Adelines Intl., Greater Cleveland Chorus **[15506]**, Independence, OH
Sweet Adelines Intl., Harmony of the Hill Chap. **[18221]**, Hubertus, WI
Sweet Adelines Intl., Heart of Illinois Chorus **[3891]**, Washington, IL
Sweet Adelines Intl., Heart of Michigan Chap. **[9751]**, Shepherd, MI
Sweet Adelines Intl., Heart O' Wisconsin Chap. **[18825]**, Marshfield, WI
Sweet Adelines Intl., Heart of Ohio Show Chorus **[16094]**, Munroe Falls, OH
Sweet Adelines Intl., Hocking Valley Chap. **[13220]**, Athens, OH
Sweet Adelines Intl., Irish Hills Chap. **[6584]**, Adrian, MI
Sweet Adelines Intl., Lake Country Chorus **[12902]**, White Bear Lake, MN
Sweet Adelines Intl., Lake Ridge Chorus **[15127]**, Elyria, OH
Sweet Adelines Intl., Lakes Area Chap. **[12997]**, Wyoming, MN
Sweet Adelines Intl., Little River Chap. **[4131]**, Angola, IN
Sweet Adelines Intl., Maple Mountain Chap. **[15980]**, Mentor, OH
Sweet Adelines Intl., Melodeers Chorus **[2762]**, Northbrook, IL
Sweet Adelines Intl., Menominee River Chap. **[9005]**, Menominee, MI
Sweet Adelines Intl., Michigan Northern Lights Chap. **[7824]**, Gaylord, MI
Sweet Adelines Intl., Milwaukee Showcase Chorus **[19132]**, Milwaukee, WI
Sweet Adelines Intl., Minnesota Valley Chap. **[11403]**, Mankato, MN
Sweet Adelines Intl., Newark Chap. **[16186]**, Newark, OH
Sweet Adelines Intl., Northern Buckeye Chap. **[13333]**, Bellevue, OH
Sweet Adelines Intl., Ohio Heartland Chap. **[17222]**, Westerville, OH
Sweet Adelines Intl., Opus 2000 Chap. **[19576]**, Racine, WI
Sweet Adelines Intl., Prairie Echoes Chap. **[1445]**, DeKalb, IL
Sweet Adelines Intl., Queen City Chorus **[17363]**, Wyoming, OH
Sweet Adelines Intl., Red Cedar Sounds Chap. **[17779]**, Colfax, WI
Sweet Adelines Intl., Rhythm of the River Chap. **[17635]**, Black River Falls, WI
Sweet Adelines Intl., River Bend Chorus **[6271]**, South Bend, IN
Sweet Adelines Intl., River City Sound Chap. **[3324]**, Rockford, IL
Sweet Adelines Intl., Sauk Trail Sound Chap. **[7201]**, Coldwater, MI
Sweet Adelines Intl., Scioto Valley Chorus **[15066]**, Dublin, OH
Sweet Adelines Intl., Seven Hills Show Chorus **[14005]**, Cincinnati, OH
Sweet Adelines Intl., Shawano Wolf River Harmony Chap. **[19684]**, Shawano, WI
Sweet Adelines Intl., Shoreline Sound Chap. **[9592]**, Royal Oak, MI
Sweet Adelines Intl., Sisters in Song Chap. **[15670]**, Lima, OH
Sweet Adelines Intl., Sound Celebration Chorus **[3685]**, Springfield, IL
Sweet Adelines Intl., Sound of Madison Chap. **[18624]**, Madison, WI
Sweet Adelines Intl., Spirit of Detroit Chap. **[7674]**, Farmington Hills, MI
Sweet Adelines Intl., Spirit of Evansville Chap. **[4581]**, Evansville, IN
Sweet Adelines Intl., Spirit of the Lakes Chorus **[18399]**, Lake Geneva, WI
Sweet Adelines Intl., Spirit of the Valley Chap. **[17416]**, Youngstown, OH
Sweet Adelines Intl., Spring Valley Chorus **[166]**, Bartlett, IL
Sweet Adelines Intl., Towns of Harmony Chap. **[4721]**, Fort Wayne, IN
Sweet Adelines Intl., Tri-City Chap. **[6810]**, Auburn, MI
Sweet Adelines Intl., Twin Cities Show Chorus **[10610]**, Burnsville, MN
Sweet Adelines Intl., Vallee de Croix Chorus **[12727]**, Stillwater, MN
Sweet Adelines Intl., Vermillion Valley Show Chap. **[3121]**, Pontiac, IL
Sweet Adelines Intl., Westosha Lakes Chorus **[58]**, Antioch, IL
Sweet Adelines Intl., Yahara River Chap. **[18625]**, Madison, WI
Sweet Adelines Intl., Zumbro Valley Chorus **[12194]**, Rochester, MN
Toledo Area Theatre Organ Soc. **[16966]**, Toledo, OH
Univ. Musical Soc. **[6779]**, Ann Arbor, MI
West Shore Chorus of Sweet Adelines Intl. **[7868]**, Grand Haven, MI
Western Lights Chorus of Sweet Adelines Intl. **[2027]**, Hinsdale, IL
White River Sound Chorus of Sweet Adelines Intl. **[5499]**, Indianapolis, IN
Willoughby South High Instrumental Music Boosters **[17279]**, Willoughby, OH
Wisconsin Music Educators Assn. **[20020]**, Waunakee, WI
Music Assn; Brown County Civic **[18089]**, Green Bay, WI
Music Assn; Illinois Country **[1514]**, Downs, IL
Music Boosters; Independence **[15498]**, Independence, OH
Music Boosters; Willoughby South High Instrumental **[17279]**, Willoughby, OH
Music Boosters; Willoughby South Instrumental **[★17279]**
Music Club; Murphy Roche Irish **[376]**, Burr Ridge, IL
Musical Soc; Univ. **[6779]**, Ann Arbor, MI
Musicians
Twin Cities Musicians Union, Local 30-73 **[11759]**, Minneapolis, MN
Musicians AFL-CIO, LU 118 **[17106]**, Warren, OH
Musicians AFM, LU 166 - AFL-CIO **[18567]**, Madison, WI
Musicians Club; North Shore **[2920]**, Palatine, IL
Musicians' Union - Local 42, Amer. Fed. of Musicians **[19559]**, Racine, WI
Muskego Area Chamber of Commerce **[19262]**, Muskego, WI
Muskegon Area Chamber of Commerce **[9150]**, Muskegon, MI
Muskegon Co REACT **[9151]**, Muskegon, MI
Muskegon County Convention and Visitors Bur. **[9152]**, Muskegon, MI
Muskegon County Medical Soc. **[9153]**, Muskegon, MI
Muskegon District Dental Soc. **[9154]**, Muskegon, MI
Muskegon Lakeshore Figure Skating Club **[9155]**, Muskegon, MI
Muskies Arrowhead Chap. **[12800]**, Virginia, MN
Muskies Between the Lakes Chap. **[19718]**, Sheboygan Falls, WI
Muskies Brainerd Lakes Chap. **[10517]**, Brainerd, MN
Muskies Capital City Chap. **[18568]**, Madison, WI
Muskies Central Wisconsin Chap. **[18846]**, Medford, WI
Muskies Cleveland Chap. 23 **[16500]**, Ravenna, OH
Muskies First Wisconsin Chap. **[17756]**, Chippewa Falls, WI
Muskies Flatlanders Chap. **[3496]**, South Beloit, IL
Muskies God's Country Chap. **[18371]**, La Crosse, WI
Muskies Hayward Lakes Chap. **[18197]**, Hayward, WI
Muskies Headwaters Chap. **[17848]**, Eagle River, WI
Muskies Hopedale Chap. **[15024]**, Dillonvale, OH
Muskies Lake Superior **[10691]**, Cloquet, MN
Muskies Milwaukee Chap. **[18158]**, Greenfield, WI
Muskies Mississippi Valley Chap. **[1931]**, Hampton, IL
Muskies St. Cloud Chap. **[10701]**, Coleraine, MN
Muskies Vikingland Chap. **[11981]**, Parkers Prairie, MN
Muskies West Virginia Chap. 9 **[15684]**, Little Hocking, OH
Muskingum Co REACT **[16698]**, South Zanesville, OH
Muskingum Valley Area Chamber of Commerce **[13357]**, Beverly, OH
Muskingum Valley Beagle Club **[16173]**, Newark, OH
Muslim-cultural Students Assn. - Northwestern Univ. **[1670]**, Evanston, IL
Muslim Gymkhana **[2570]**, Morton Grove, IL
Muslim Student Assn. - Purdue Univ. **[6492]**, West Lafayette, IN
Muslim Student Assn. - Southern Illinois Univ. at Carbondale **[422]**, Carbondale, IL
Muslim Student Assn. - Univ. of Illinois - Chicago **[1957]**, Harwood Heights, IL
Muslim Student Assn., Univ. of Minnesota **[11687]**, Minneapolis, MN
Muslim Student Union - Indiana Univ., Bloomington **[4243]**, Bloomington, IN
Muslim Student's Assn. of Cleveland State Univ. **[14168]**, Cleveland, OH
Muslim Students' Assn. - Hiram Coll. **[15453]**, Hiram, OH
Muslim Students' Assn. - Indiana Univ., Bloomington **[★4243]**
Muslim Students' Assn. - Loyola Univ. of Chicago **[1061]**, Chicago, IL
Muslim Students' Assn. of Michigan State Univ. **[7555]**, East Lansing, MI
Muslim Students' Assn. - Northeastern Illinois Univ. **[1062]**, Chicago, IL
Muslim Students' Assn. - Ohio State Univ. **[14511]**, Columbus, OH
Muslim Students Assn. - Ohio Univ. at Athens **[13207]**, Athens, OH
Muslim Students' Assn. - Univ. of Akron **[13067]**, Akron, OH
Muslim Students Assn. - Univ. of Illinois at Urbana-Champaign **[3828]**, Urbana, IL
Muslim Students' Assn. - Univ. of Michigan - Ann Arbor **[6740]**, Ann Arbor, MI
Muslim Students' Assn. - Univ. of Toledo **[16932]**, Toledo, OH
Mutual Insurance Agents; Ohio Assn. of **[★15271]**
Mutual Insurance Companies Association of Indiana **[6512]**, Westfield, IN
Mutual UFO Network, Indiana **[6417]**, Vincennes, IN
Myasthenia Gravis Assn. **[9810]**, Southfield, MI
Myasthenia Gravis Found., Great Lakes Chap. **[7987]**, Grand Rapids, MI
Myasthenia Gravis Found; Ohio Chap. of the **[15893]**, Massillon, OH
Mycology
Illinois Mycological Assn. **[2242]**, Lemont, IL
Michigan Mushroom Hunters Club **[6731]**, Ann Arbor, MI
Ohio Mushroom Soc. **[15345]**, Granville, OH
West Michigan Mycological Soc. **[8877]**, Ludington, MI
Wisconsin Mycological Soc. **[19300]**, New Berlin, WI
Mystery Writers of Am., Midwest Chap. **[4019]**, Wilmette, IL

N

Na'amat U.S.A., Cleveland Coun. **[14169]**, Cleveland, OH
NACE Intl., Chicago Sect. **[1063]**, Chicago, IL
NACE Intl., Cleveland Sect. **[15951]**, Medina, OH
NACE Intl., Detroit Sect. **[9118]**, Mount Pleasant, MI
NACE Intl., Ohio Univ. Student Sect. **[13208]**, Athens, OH
NACE Intl., Southwest Ohio Sect. **[17189]**, West Milton, OH
NACE Intl., Twin Cities Sect. **[12539]**, St. Paul, MN
NACE Intl., Wisconsin Sect. **[18569]**, Madison, WI

NACM Hartland **[15468]**, Howard, OH
NACM North Central **[11688]**, Minneapolis, MN
NAFSA: Assn. of Intl. Educators, Region IV **[11915]**, Northfield, MN
NAIFA-Bloomington **[4244]**, Bloomington, IN
NAIFA-Central Minnesota **[12292]**, St. Cloud, MN
NAIFA-Central Wisconsin **[19795]**, Stevens Point, WI
NAIFA-Chicago Region **[2064]**, Ingleside, IL
NAIFA-Columbus (OH) **[15050]**, Dublin, OH
NAIFA-Fond du Lac **[17986]**, Fond du Lac, WI
NAIFA-Indianapolis **[5410]**, Indianapolis, IN
NAIFA-Lafayette Indiana **[5625]**, Lafayette, IN
NAIFA-Lake County **[2265]**, Libertyville, IL
NAIFA-Lima **[15992]**, Middle Point, OH
NAIFA-Minnesota **[11689]**, Minneapolis, MN
NAIFA-North Metro **[10450]**, Blaine, MN
NAIFA-Northeastern Wisconsin **[18116]**, Green Bay, WI
NAIFA-Rochester **[12162]**, Rochester, MN
NAIFA-St. Paul **[11690]**, Minneapolis, MN
NAIFA-Sioux Valley **[11804]**, Montevideo, MN
NAIFA-South Cook Region **[2953]**, Park Forest, IL
NAIFA Southeast Michigan **[10001]**, Troy, MI
NAIFA-Southeast Wisconsin **[18405]**, Lake Mills, WI
NAIFA-Southern Minnesota **[11392]**, Mankato, MN
NAIFA-Terre Haute **[6336]**, Terre Haute, IN
NAIFA-Wayne Holmes **[16308]**, Orrville, OH
NAIFA-Western Wisconsin **[18372]**, La Crosse, WI
NAIFA-Wisconsin-Fox River Valley **[17504]**, Appleton, WI
NALS of Illinois **[1064]**, Chicago, IL
NALS of Michigan **[8453]**, Kalamazoo, MI
NAMD Cleveland **[16693]**, South Euclid, OH
NAMES Proj. Chicago **[1065]**, Chicago, IL
NAMES Proj. Michigan **[7697]**, Ferndale, MI
NAMI Ohio **[14512]**, Columbus, OH
NAMI Olmsted County **[12163]**, Rochester, MN
NAMI, Richland County, Ohio **[15778]**, Mansfield, OH
NAMI Wisconsin **[18570]**, Madison, WI
Naperville Area Chamber of Commerce **[2647]**, Naperville, IL
Naperville Area Humane Soc. **[2648]**, Naperville, IL
Naperville Astronomical Association **[2649]**, Naperville, IL
Naperville Central Young Life **[2650]**, Naperville, IL
Naperville Junior Woman's Club **[2651]**, Naperville, IL
Naperville Noon Lions Club **[2652]**, Naperville, IL
Naperville North Young Life **[2653]**, Naperville, IL
Naperville United Way **[2654]**, Naperville, IL
Napoleon Area Chamber of Commerce **[★16099]**
Napoleon - Henry County Chamber of Commerce **[16099]**, Napoleon, OH
Napoleon Lions Club **[8388]**, Jackson, MI
Nappanee Area Chamber of Commerce **[5908]**, Nappanee, IN
NARAL Pro-Choice Minnesota **[12540]**, St. Paul, MN
NARAL Pro-Choice Ohio **[14170]**, Cleveland, OH
NASCO Member Forums **[6741]**, Ann Arbor, MI
Nation Coun. for GeoCosmic Res., Madison Chap. **[18571]**, Madison, WI
Nation Coun. for GeoCosmic Res., Ohio Valley Chap. **[13913]**, Cincinnati, OH
Nation Coun. for GeoCosmic Res., Southwest Suburban Chicago Chap. **[1963]**, Hazel Crest, IL
Natl. Abortion and Reproductive Action League of Wisconsin **[18572]**, Madison, WI
Natl. Abortion and Reproductive Rights Action League Ohio **[★14170]**
Natl. Acad. of TV Arts and Sciences, Chicago/ Midwest Chap. **[1066]**, Chicago, IL
Natl. Acad. of TV Arts and Sciences, Cleveland Regional Chap. **[13451]**, Brunswick, OH
Natl. Acad. of TV Arts and Sciences, Michigan Chap. **[10120]**, West Bloomfield, MI
Natl. Acad. of TV Arts and Sciences, Ohio Valley **[13914]**, Cincinnati, OH
Natl. Acad. of TV Arts and Sciences, Upper Midwest Chap. **[12665]**, Shorewood, MN
Natl. Active And Retired Fed. Employees Assn. - Alton 575 **[366]**, Bunker Hill, IL
Natl. Active And Retired Fed. Employees Assn. - Alvin G Bohley 1019 **[2849]**, O'Fallon, IL
Natl. Active And Retired Fed. Employees Assn. - Blackhawk 338 **[1296]**, Colona, IL
Natl. Active And Retired Fed. Employees Assn. Bloomington-Normal 2177 **[299]**, Bloomington, IL
Natl. Active And Retired Fed. Employees Assn. - Danville 332 **[4422]**, Covington, IN
Natl. Active And Retired Fed. Employees Assn. - Downtown 1878 **[1067]**, Chicago, IL
Natl. Active And Retired Fed. Employees Assn. - Dupage 1771 **[228]**, Bensenville, IL
Natl. Active And Retired Fed. Employees Assn. - East Central 854 **[2974]**, Paxton, IL
Natl. Active And Retired Fed. Employees Assn. - Edwards 399 **[1399]**, Decatur, IL
Natl. Active And Retired Fed. Employees Assn. - Effingham 849 **[3177]**, Ramsey, IL
Natl. Active And Retired Fed. Employees Assn. - Egyptian Gateway 2190 **[489]**, Centralia, IL
Natl. Active And Retired Fed. Employees Assn. - Granite 1067 **[3901]**, Waterloo, IL
Natl. Active And Retired Fed. Employees Assn. - Greater Egypt 1097 **[423]**, Carbondale, IL
Natl. Active And Retired Fed. Employees Assn. - Greater Fox Valley 2181 **[455]**, Carpentersville, IL
Natl. Active And Retired Fed. Employees Assn. - Greater Peoria 268 **[3036]**, Peoria, IL
Natl. Active And Retired Fed. Employees Assn. - Hardscrabble 2202 **[3729]**, Streator, IL
Natl. Active And Retired Fed. Employees Assn. - Illini 348 **[537]**, Champaign, IL
Natl. Active And Retired Fed. Employees Assn. - Jefferson 688 **[2601]**, Mount Vernon, IL
Natl. Active And Retired Fed. Employees Assn. - Joseph F.Gore 6 **[1068]**, Chicago, IL
Natl. Active And Retired Fed. Employees Assn. - Kankakee 1109 **[2141]**, Kankakee, IL
Natl. Active And Retired Fed. Employees Assn. - Lake County 441 **[3929]**, Waukegan, IL
Natl. Active And Retired Fed. Employees Assn. Lawrenceville 1041 **[2226]**, Lawrenceville, IL
Natl. Active And Retired Fed. Employees Assn. - Lincoln Home 402 **[3652]**, Springfield, IL
Natl. Active And Retired Fed. Employees Assn. - Little Egypt 1007 **[16]**, Albion, IL
Natl. Active And Retired Fed. Employees Assn. - Louis Joliet 655 **[3103]**, Plainfield, IL
Natl. Active And Retired Fed. Employees Assn. - Marion Payne 1309 **[2202]**, Lake Forest, IL
Natl. Active And Retired Fed. Employees Assn. - Michael C. Nave 1344 **[1312]**, Crestwood, IL
Natl. Active And Retired Fed. Employees Assn. - North West Chicago Area 852 **[1671]**, Evanston, IL
Natl. Active And Retired Fed. Employees Assn. - Palisades 604 **[3420]**, Savanna, IL
Natl. Active And Retired Fed. Employees Assn. - Prairie 2332 **[3761]**, Thomson, IL
Natl. Active And Retired Fed. Employees Assn. - Rockford 415 **[3289]**, Rockford, IL
Natl. Active And Retired Fed. Employees Assn. - Southwest Chicago Metro 1106 **[342]**, Bridgeview, IL
Natl. Active And Retired Fed. Employees Assn. - West Central Ill. 361 **[3155]**, Quincy, IL
Natl. Active and Retired Fed. Employees Assn. - Albert Lea-Austin 469 **[10260]**, Albert Lea, MN
Natl. Active and Retired Fed. Employees Assn. - Ann Arbor 304 **[9072]**, Monroe, MI
Natl. Active and Retired Fed. Employees Assn. - Arrowhead 106 **[10841]**, Duluth, MN
Natl. Active and Retired Fed. Employees Assn. - Ashtabula 624 **[13183]**, Ashtabula, OH
Natl. Active and Retired Fed. Employees Assn. Auglaize-Mercer 2170 **[17090]**, Wapakoneta, OH
Natl. Active and Retired Fed. Employees Assn. - Battle Creek 123 **[7805]**, Galesburg, MI
Natl. Active and Retired Fed. Employees Assn. - Bay City 165 **[6892]**, Bay City, MI
Natl. Active and Retired Fed. Employees Assn. - Beavercreek 2217 **[13298]**, Beavercreek, OH
Natl. Active and Retired Fed. Employees Assn. - Bedford 578 **[4174]**, Bedford, IN
Natl. Active and Retired Fed. Employees Assn. - Belmont County 2175 **[13263]**, Barnesville, OH
Natl. Active and Retired Fed. Employees Assn. - Belpre 865 **[15824]**, Marietta, OH
Natl. Active and Retired Fed. Employees Assn. - Bemidji 1049 **[10421]**, Bemidji, MN
Natl. Active and Retired Fed. Employees Assn. - Bloomfield 847 **[4193]**, Bloomfield, IN
Natl. Active and Retired Fed. Employees Assn. - Bloomington 580 **[4245]**, Bloomington, IN
Natl. Active and Retired Fed. Employees Assn. - Brainerd 738 **[12704]**, Staples, MN
Natl. Active and Retired Fed. Employees Assn. - Brecksville 2264 **[13412]**, Brecksville, OH
Natl. Active and Retired Fed. Employees Assn. - Bryan 1136 **[13455]**, Bryan, OH
Natl. Active and Retired Fed. Employees Assn. Butler/Warren Counties 569 **[15396]**, Hamilton, OH
Natl. Active and Retired Fed. Employees Assn. - Cadillac Area 1946 **[8123]**, Harrietta, MI
Natl. Active and Retired Fed. Employees Assn. - Campbell County 1760 **[13915]**, Cincinnati, OH
Natl. Active and Retired Fed. Employees Assn. - Charles Hogg 14 **[16229]**, North Jackson, OH
Natl. Active and Retired Fed. Employees Assn. - Chillicothe 315 **[13668]**, Chillicothe, OH
Natl. Active and Retired Fed. Employees Assn. - Cincinnati 265 **[13916]**, Cincinnati, OH
Natl. Active and Retired Fed. Employees Assn. - Cleveland 470 **[16373]**, Parma, OH
Natl. Active and Retired Fed. Employees Assn. - Cleveland East 2232 **[14171]**, Cleveland, OH
Natl. Active and Retired Fed. Employees Assn. - Clinton City 2204 **[17292]**, Wilmington, OH
Natl. Active and Retired Fed. Employees Assn. - Columbus 235 **[16813]**, Sunbury, OH
Natl. Active and Retired Fed. Employees Assn. - Columbus 1052 **[4403]**, Columbus, IN
Natl. Active and Retired Fed. Employees Assn. - Crow River 2019 **[11330]**, Litchfield, MN
Natl. Active and Retired Fed. Employees Assn. - Dayton 35 **[13299]**, Beavercreek, OH
Natl. Active and Retired Fed. Employees Assn. - Dearborn Area 1515 **[9839]**, Southgate, MI
Natl. Active and Retired Fed. Employees Assn. - Detroit 89 **[7404]**, Detroit, MI
Natl. Active and Retired Fed. Employees Assn. - Detroit Lakes 1842 **[10781]**, Detroit Lakes, MN
Natl. Active and Retired Fed. Employees Assn. Door-Kewaunee 1110 **[19838]**, Sturgeon Bay, WI
Natl. Active and Retired Fed. Employees Assn. - Eastside 2197 **[4185]**, Beech Grove, IN
Natl. Active and Retired Fed. Employees Assn. - Eau Claire 371 **[17887]**, Eau Claire, WI
Natl. Active and Retired Fed. Employees Assn. - Elkhart 539 **[4803]**, Goshen, IN
Natl. Active and Retired Fed. Employees Assn. - Escanaba 1389 **[7616]**, Escanaba, MI
Natl. Active and Retired Fed. Employees Assn. - Evansville 326 **[4561]**, Evansville, IN
Natl. Active and Retired Fed. Employees Assn. - Fairborn 610 **[15152]**, Fairborn, OH
Natl. Active and Retired Fed. Employees Assn. - Firelands 382 **[16261]**, Norwalk, OH
Natl. Active and Retired Fed. Employees Assn. - Flint 285 **[7688]**, Fenton, MI
Natl. Active and Retired Fed. Employees Assn. - Fond du Lac 708 **[17987]**, Fond du Lac, WI
Natl. Active and Retired Fed. Employees Assn. - Fort Steuben 2191 **[16764]**, Steubenville, OH
Natl. Active and Retired Fed. Employees Assn. - Fort Wayne 223 **[4696]**, Fort Wayne, IN
Natl. Active and Retired Fed. Employees Assn. - Fox Valley 437 **[18862]**, Menasha, WI
Natl. Active and Retired Fed. Employees Assn. - Frankfort 1989 **[4744]**, Frankfort, IN
Natl. Active and Retired Fed. Employees Assn. - Ft Defiance 1862 **[14990]**, Defiance, OH
Natl. Active and Retired Fed. Employees Assn. - Fulton-Henry County 1856 **[13154]**, Archbold, OH
Natl. Active and Retired Fed. Employees Assn. - Grand Rapids 234 **[7988]**, Grand Rapids, MI
Natl. Active and Retired Fed. Employees Assn. - Grand Traverse Bay Area 1215 **[8922]**, Maple City, MI
Natl. Active and Retired Fed. Employees Assn. - Grayling 2305 **[7820]**, Gaylord, MI
Natl. Active and Retired Fed. Employees Assn. - Greater Milwaukee 94 **[19070]**, Milwaukee, WI
Natl. Active and Retired Fed. Employees Assn. - Green Bay 403 **[19681]**, Shawano, WI
Natl. Active and Retired Fed. Employees Assn. - Greencastle 1024 **[4822]**, Greencastle, IN
Natl. Active and Retired Fed. Employees Assn. - Greenville 2227 **[9855]**, Stanton, MI
Natl. Active and Retired Fed. Employees Assn. Guernsey-Noble 2189 **[15567]**, Kimbolton, OH

Natl. Active and Retired Fed. Employees Assn. - Hammond 546 **[5776]**, Merrillville, IN
Natl. Active and Retired Fed. Employees Assn. - Hancock County 2278 **[15209]**, Findlay, OH
Natl. Active and Retired Fed. Employees Assn. - Herbert L. Gabel 565 **[6435]**, Walkerton, IN
Natl. Active and Retired Fed. Employees Assn. - Highland County 2230 **[17297]**, Winchester, OH
Natl. Active and Retired Fed. Employees Assn. - Holland 1243 **[10229]**, Zeeland, MI
Natl. Active and Retired Fed. Employees Assn. - Huber Heights 2238 **[15477]**, Huber Heights, OH
Natl. Active and Retired Fed. Employees Assn. - Indianapolis 151 **[5411]**, Indianapolis, IN
Natl. Active and Retired Fed. Employees Assn. - Indianhead 1581 **[17563]**, Balsam Lake, WI
Natl. Active and Retired Fed. Employees Assn. Intl. Falls 1582 **[12067]**, Ray, MN
Natl. Active and Retired Fed. Employees Assn. - Jackson 25 **[8389]**, Jackson, MI
Natl. Active and Retired Fed. Employees Assn. - Jackson County 944 **[6184]**, Seymour, IN
Natl. Active and Retired Fed. Employees Assn. - Janesville 44 **[3350]**, Roscoe, IL
Natl. Active and Retired Fed. Employees Assn. - Jefferson County 1677 **[5676]**, Lexington, IN
Natl. Active and Retired Fed. Employees Assn. Jeffersonville 381 **[4367]**, Clarksville, IN
Natl. Active and Retired Fed. Employees Assn. - John Folk 317 **[15097]**, Elida, OH
Natl. Active and Retired Fed. Employees Assn. - Johnny Appleseed 612 **[15779]**, Mansfield, OH
Natl. Active and Retired Fed. Employees Assn. - Johnson County 1612 **[4753]**, Franklin, IN
Natl. Active and Retired Fed. Employees Assn. - Kenosha 1436 **[18304]**, Kenosha, WI
Natl. Active and Retired Fed. Employees Assn. - Ket-Cent-Oak 1927 **[15562]**, Kettering, OH
Natl. Active and Retired Fed. Employees Assn. - Kokomo 562 **[5548]**, Kempton, IN
Natl. Active and Retired Fed. Employees Assn. - La Crosse 370 **[19826]**, Stoddard, WI
Natl. Active and Retired Fed. Employees Assn. - Lafayette 330 **[5626]**, Lafayette, IN
Natl. Active and Retired Fed. Employees Assn. - Lake County2182 **[17275]**, Willoughby, OH
Natl. Active and Retired Fed. Employees Assn. - Lake Region 1207 **[11000]**, Fergus Falls, MN
Natl. Active and Retired Fed. Employees Assn. - Lake Superior 1254 **[8259]**, Houghton, MI
Natl. Active and Retired Fed. Employees Assn. - Lansing Area 289 **[7556]**, East Lansing, MI
Natl. Active and Retired Fed. Employees Assn. - Lenawee 1953 **[6580]**, Adrian, MI
Natl. Active and Retired Fed. Employees Assn. - Licking County 310 **[16174]**, Newark, OH
Natl. Active and Retired Fed. Employees Assn. - Linton 1688 **[5685]**, Linton, IN
Natl. Active and Retired Fed. Employees Assn. - Little Traverse Bay Area 1483 **[8309]**, Indian River, MI
Natl. Active and Retired Fed. Employees Assn. - Livonia Area 1163 **[9259]**, Oak Park, MI
Natl. Active and Retired Fed. Employees Assn. - Lock City 477 **[9722]**, Sault Ste. Marie, MI
Natl. Active and Retired Fed. Employees Assn. - Logan County 2162 **[13322]**, Bellefontaine, OH
Natl. Active and Retired Fed. Employees Assn. - Logansport 1046 **[5695]**, Logansport, IN
Natl. Active and Retired Fed. Employees Assn. - Lorain Cnty 1592 **[15123]**, Elyria, OH
Natl. Active and Retired Fed. Employees Assn. - Macomb 1474 **[8131]**, Harrison Township, MI
Natl. Active and Retired Fed. Employees Assn. - Madison 120 **[18911]**, Middleton, WI
Natl. Active and Retired Fed. Employees Assn. - Madison County 36 **[4113]**, Anderson, IN
Natl. Active and Retired Fed. Employees Assn. - Manitowoc 710 **[18787]**, Manitowoc, WI
Natl. Active and Retired Fed. Employees Assn. - Mankato 282 **[10879]**, Eagle Lake, MN
Natl. Active and Retired Fed. Employees Assn. - Manley 1705 **[6809]**, Auburn, MI
Natl. Active and Retired Fed. Employees Assn. - Marion 503 **[4788]**, Gas City, IN
Natl. Active and Retired Fed. Employees Assn. - Marshall 1580 **[12096]**, Redwood Falls, MN
Natl. Active and Retired Fed. Employees Assn. - Mckinley 341 **[13572]**, Canton, OH
Natl. Active and Retired Fed. Employees Assn. - Menominee 2246 **[9002]**, Menominee, MI
Natl. Active and Retired Fed. Employees Assn. Michigan-Wisconsin Border 1673 **[8493]**, Kingsford, MI
Natl. Active and Retired Fed. Employees Assn. - Mid-Michigan 2103 **[10108]**, Weidman, MI
Natl. Active and Retired Fed. Employees Assn. - Minneapolis 150 **[12112]**, Richfield, MN
Natl. Active and Retired Fed. Employees Assn. - Monroe County 2193 **[15529]**, Jerusalem, OH
Natl. Active and Retired Fed. Employees Assn. - Muncie 125 **[5891]**, Muncie, IN
Natl. Active and Retired Fed. Employees Assn. - Muskegon 309 **[9156]**, Muskegon, MI
Natl. Active and Retired Fed. Employees Assn. - Muskegon River 1921 **[8164]**, Hersey, MI
Natl. Active and Retired Fed. Employees Assn. - Neillsville 933 **[20201]**, Withee, WI
Natl. Active and Retired Fed. Employees Assn. - New Albany 1777 **[5919]**, New Albany, IN
Natl. Active and Retired Fed. Employees Assn. - New Ulm 1444 **[11044]**, Gibbon, MN
Natl. Active and Retired Fed. Employees Assn. - North Central U.P. 1900 **[8952]**, Marquette, MI
Natl. Active and Retired Fed. Employees Assn. - North West Suburbia-Twin Cities 2243 **[10744]**, Crystal, MN
Natl. Active and Retired Fed. Employees Assn. Oconomowoc-Watertown 1112 **[18042]**, Germantown, WI
Natl. Active and Retired Fed. Employees Assn. - Oscoda 1955 **[9316]**, Oscoda, MI
Natl. Active and Retired Fed. Employees Assn. Oshkosh-Winnebagoland 416 **[19395]**, Oshkosh, WI
Natl. Active and Retired Fed. Employees Assn. - Owatonna 1975 **[11961]**, Owatonna, MN
Natl. Active and Retired Fed. Employees Assn. - Patoka Valley 1847 **[6160]**, Santa Claus, IN
Natl. Active and Retired Fed. Employees Assn. - Pine 1746 **[12625]**, Sandstone, MN
Natl. Active and Retired Fed. Employees Assn. - Plainfield 2141 **[5672]**, Lebanon, IN
Natl. Active and Retired Fed. Employees Assn. - Pokegama 1800 **[12736]**, Swatara, MN
Natl. Active and Retired Fed. Employees Assn. - Port Huron 12 **[7773]**, Fort Gratiot, MI
Natl. Active and Retired Fed. Employees Assn. - Portage Path 168 **[13068]**, Akron, OH
Natl. Active and Retired Fed. Employees Assn. - Portsmouth 2121 **[16470]**, Portsmouth, OH
Natl. Active and Retired Fed. Employees Assn. - Queen City 1963 **[12801]**, Virginia, MN
Natl. Active and Retired Fed. Employees Assn. - Racine 346 **[19560]**, Racine, WI
Natl. Active and Retired Fed. Employees Assn. - Red Wing 1661 **[10633]**, Cannon Falls, MN
Natl. Active and Retired Fed. Employees Assn. - Region IV **[16793]**, Strongsville, OH
Natl. Active and Retired Fed. Employees Assn. - Richmond 536 **[6098]**, Richmond, IN
Natl. Active and Retired Fed. Employees Assn. - Rochester 391 **[13002]**, Zumbro Falls, MN
Natl. Active and Retired Fed. Employees Assn. - Rochester 2179 **[10037]**, Utica, MI
Natl. Active and Retired Fed. Employees Assn. - Rockville 1660 **[6134]**, Rockville, IN
Natl. Active and Retired Fed. Employees Assn. - Royal Oak 1532 **[9586]**, Royal Oak, MI
Natl. Active and Retired Fed. Employees Assn. - Saginaw 376 **[9619]**, Saginaw, MI
Natl. Active and Retired Fed. Employees Assn. - St. Cloud 644 **[12630]**, Sartell, MN
Natl. Active and Retired Fed. Employees Assn. - St. Paul 140 **[12541]**, St. Paul, MN
Natl. Active and Retired Fed. Employees Assn. - Shelbyville 813 **[6144]**, Rushville, IN
Natl. Active and Retired Fed. Employees Assn. - South Bend-Mishawaka 145 **[6246]**, South Bend, IN
Natl. Active and Retired Fed. Employees Assn. - South West Michigan 572 **[9686]**, St. Joseph, MI
Natl. Active and Retired Fed. Employees Assn. - Southwest Michigan 173 **[8454]**, Kalamazoo, MI
Natl. Active and Retired Fed. Employees Assn. Springfield-Clark 187 **[16734]**, Springfield, OH
Natl. Active and Retired Fed. Employees Assn. - Superior 2119 **[19873]**, Superior, WI
Natl. Active and Retired Fed. Employees Assn. - Tarcom 1593 **[7405]**, Detroit, MI
Natl. Active and Retired Fed. Employees Assn. - Terre Haute 327 **[6337]**, Terre Haute, IN
Natl. Active and Retired Fed. Employees Assn. - Thief River Falls 2328 **[12745]**, Thief River Falls, MN
Natl. Active and Retired Fed. Employees Assn. - Three Rivers 1521 **[7101]**, Cassopolis, MI
Natl. Active and Retired Fed. Employees Assn. - Thunder Bay 1487 **[6645]**, Alpena, MI
Natl. Active and Retired Fed. Employees Assn. - Tiffin 504 **[16855]**, Tiffin, OH
Natl. Active and Retired Fed. Employees Assn. - Toledo 226 **[16933]**, Toledo, OH
Natl. Active and Retired Fed. Employees Assn. - Tri-County 1386 **[17633]**, Black River Falls, WI
Natl. Active and Retired Fed. Employees Assn. - Tuscarawas Valley 635 **[15028]**, Dover, OH
Natl. Active and Retired Fed. Employees Assn. - Upper Miami Valley 325 **[16665]**, Sidney, OH
Natl. Active and Retired Fed. Employees Assn. - Vacationland 1030 **[16272]**, Oak Harbor, OH
Natl. Active and Retired Fed. Employees Assn. - Van Wert-Paulding 630 **[16390]**, Payne, OH
Natl. Active and Retired Fed. Employees Assn. - Vermilion 1725 **[10956]**, Ely, MN
Natl. Active and Retired Fed. Employees Assn. - Vikingland 2213 **[10283]**, Alexandria, MN
Natl. Active and Retired Fed. Employees Assn. - Warren G Harding 329 **[13489]**, Caledonia, OH
Natl. Active and Retired Fed. Employees Assn. Washington/Vincennes 527 **[6418]**, Vincennes, IN
Natl. Active and Retired Fed. Employees Assn. - Waukesha 490 **[19992]**, Waukesha, WI
Natl. Active and Retired Fed. Employees Assn. - Wausau 689 **[17628]**, Birnamwood, WI
Natl. Active and Retired Fed. Employees Assn. - Wayne County 2218 **[14831]**, Dalton, OH
Natl. Active and Retired Fed. Employees Assn. - White Bear Lake 1232 **[12542]**, St. Paul, MN
Natl. Active and Retired Fed. Employees Assn. - Willmar 2280 **[12924]**, Willmar, MN
Natl. Active and Retired Fed. Employees Assn. - Wood County 1942 **[13394]**, Bowling Green, OH
Natl. Active and Retired Fed. Employees Assn. - Wright 1840 **[16121]**, New Carlisle, OH
Natl. Active and Retired Fed. Employees Assn. - Xenia 2163 **[17375]**, Xenia, OH
Natl. Active and Retired Fed. Employees Assn. - Yarb 2122 **[13536]**, Canfield, OH
Natl. Active and Retired Fed. Employees Assn. - Zanesville 648 **[15933]**, McConnelsville, OH
Natl. Alliance on Mental Illness - Cook County North Suburban **[4039]**, Winnetka, IL
Natl. Alliance on Mental Illness - Fox Valley **[17505]**, Appleton, WI
Natl. Alliance for the Mentally Ill - Alger-Marquette County **[8953]**, Marquette, MI
Natl. Alliance for the Mentally Ill - Ba-Ho-Ke-On **[8512]**, Lake Linden, MI
Natl. Alliance for the Mentally Ill - Barron County **[19613]**, Rice Lake, WI
Natl. Alliance for the Mentally Ill - Belmont, Harrison, Monroe **[13264]**, Barnesville, OH
Natl. Alliance for the Mentally Ill - Brown County **[18117]**, Green Bay, WI
Natl. Alliance for the Mentally Ill - Champaign County **[538]**, Champaign, IL
Natl. Alliance for the Mentally Ill - Chequamegon Bay Area **[18202]**, High Bridge, WI
Natl. Alliance for the Mentally Ill, Clermont County **[13268]**, Batavia, OH
Natl. Alliance for the Mentally Ill - Dane County **[18573]**, Madison, WI
Natl. Alliance for the Mentally Ill - Door County **[19839]**, Sturgeon Bay, WI
Natl. Alliance for the Mentally Ill - Douglas County **[19743]**, Solon Springs, WI
Natl. Alliance for the Mentally Ill of DuPage County **[3992]**, Wheaton, IL
Natl. Alliance for the Mentally Ill - Eau Claire **[17888]**, Eau Claire, WI

Natl. Alliance for the Mentally Ill - Fond du Lac [17988], Fond du Lac, WI
Natl. Alliance for the Mentally Ill of Greater Chicago [1069], Chicago, IL
Natl. Alliance for the Mentally Ill - Greater Milwaukee [19071], Milwaukee, WI
Natl. Alliance for the Mentally Ill Indiana [5412], Indianapolis, IN
Natl. Alliance for the Mentally Ill - Jefferson County, Wisconsin [18273], Jefferson, WI
Natl. Alliance for the Mentally Ill of Kalamazoo [8455], Kalamazoo, MI
Natl. Alliance for the Mentally Ill - Kane County South [1797], Geneva, IL
Natl. Alliance for the Mentally Ill - Kenosha [18305], Kenosha, WI
Natl. Alliance for the Mentally Ill - La Crosse [18373], La Crosse, WI
Natl. Alliance for the Mentally Ill - Lake County [2266], Libertyville, IL
Natl. Alliance for the Mentally Ill - Lansing [9297], Okemos, MI
Natl. Alliance for the Mentally Ill of Mackinac [9080], Moran, MI
Natl. Alliance for the Mentally Ill - Madison County [1883], Granite City, IL
Natl. Alliance for the Mentally Ill - Manitowoc [18788], Manitowoc, WI
Natl. Alliance for the Mentally Ill - Marinette and Menominee [9003], Menominee, MI
Natl. Alliance for the Mentally Ill - McHenry County [1329], Crystal Lake, IL
Natl. Alliance for the Mentally Ill of Michigan [8734], Lansing, MI
Natl. Alliance for the Mentally Ill - Mid Central WI [20147], Westfield, WI
Natl. Alliance for the Mentally Ill - Newaygo [9193], Newaygo, MI
Natl. Alliance for the Mentally Ill of Northwest Michigan [9941], Traverse City, MI
Natl. Alliance for the Mentally Ill - Oshkosh [19396], Oshkosh, WI
Natl. Alliance for the Mentally Ill - Ozaukee [18887], Mequon, WI
Natl. Alliance for the Mentally Ill - Portage/Wood Counties [19796], Stevens Point, WI
Natl. Alliance for the Mentally Ill - Racine County [19561], Racine, WI
Natl. Alliance for the Mentally Ill - Richland County [19623], Richland Center, WI
Natl. Alliance for the Mentally Ill - Rock County [3351], Roscoe, IL
Natl. Alliance for the Mentally Ill - St. Croix [19318], New Richmond, WI
Natl. Alliance for the Mentally Ill - Sheboygan [19701], Sheboygan, WI
Natl. Alliance for the Mentally Ill - South Central [17575], Baraboo, WI
Natl. Alliance for the Mentally Ill - Southwest [2798], Oak Lawn, IL
Natl. Alliance for the Mentally Ill - Southwest Wisconsin [19465], Platteville, WI
Natl. Alliance for the Mentally Ill - Tri-County [3037], Peoria, IL
Natl. Alliance for the Mentally Ill - Tuscarawas County [15029], Dover, OH
Natl. Alliance for the Mentally Ill - Washington County [20124], West Bend, WI
Natl. Alliance for the Mentally Ill - Waukesha [19993], Waukesha, WI
Natl. Alliance for the Mentally Ill - Wishigan [17955], Fence, WI
Natl. Alliance of Methadone Advocates of Chicago [2616], Mundelein, IL
Natl. Alliance of Methadone Advocates of Indiana [5593], La Crosse, IN
Natl. Asian Pacific Amer. Bar Assn. - Minnesota Chap. [11691], Minneapolis, MN
Natl. Assn. to Advance Fat Acceptance, Chicago Chap. [3772], Tinley Park, IL
Natl. Assn. to Advance Fat Acceptance, Northern Ohio Chap. [15996], Middleburg Heights, OH
Natl. Assn. for the Advancement of Colored People, Chicago Southside Br. [1070], Chicago, IL
Natl. Assn. for the Advancement of Colored People-Detroit Br. [7406], Detroit, MI
Natl. Assn. for the Advancement of Colored People, Du Page County Br. [3993], Wheaton, IL
Natl. Assn. for the Advancement of Colored People, East St. Louis, Illinois Br. [1551], East St. Louis, IL
Natl. Assn. for the Advancement of Colored People, Indianapolis Br. [5413], Indianapolis, IN
Natl. Assn. for the Advancement of Colored People, Lansing Br. [8735], Lansing, MI
Natl. Assn. for the Advancement of Colored People, Minneapolis Br. [11692], Minneapolis, MN
Natl. Assn. for the Advancement of Colored People, Monroe County Br. [4246], Bloomington, IN
Natl. Assn. for the Advancement of Colored People, Rochester Br. 507 [12164], Rochester, MN
Natl. Assn. for the Advancement of Colored People, Southern Oakland County [9811], Southfield, MI
Natl. Assn. for the Advancement of Colored People, Western Michigan Univ. Chap. [8456], Kalamazoo, MI
Natl. Assn. of Air Medical Commun. Specialists, Region 5 [5414], Indianapolis, IN
National Association of Artists' Organizations, Midwest [1071], Chicago, IL
Natl. Assn. of Asian Amer. Professionals, Chicago Chap. [1072], Chicago, IL
Natl. Assn. of Asian Amer. Professionals, Minnesota Chap. [11693], Minneapolis, MN
Natl. Assn. of Black Accountants, Indianapolis Chap. [5415], Indianapolis, IN
Natl. Assn. of Black Accountants, Lansing [9298], Okemos, MI
Natl. Assn. of Black Journalists - Chicago Chap. [1073], Chicago, IL
Natl. Assn. of Black Journalists - Cincinnati Chap. [13917], Cincinnati, OH
Natl. Assn. of Black Journalists - Detroit Chap. [7407], Detroit, MI
Natl. Assn. of Catholic Family Life Ministers [14927], Dayton, OH
Natl. Assn. of Catholic Family Life Ministers, Region No. 7 [3290], Rockford, IL
Natl. Assn. of Catholic Family Life Ministers, Region No. 8 [12293], St. Cloud, MN
Natl. Assn. of Catholic Family Life Ministers, Region VI [8457], Kalamazoo, MI
Natl. Assn. of Church Bus. Admin., Chicago Chap. [2655], Naperville, IL
Natl. Assn. of Church Bus. Admin., Greater Cincinnati Chap. [13918], Cincinnati, OH
Natl. Assn. of Church Bus. Administrators, Columbus Chap. [15298], Galloway, OH
Natl. Assn. of Church Bus. Administrators, Wisconsin Chap. [19333], Oak Creek, WI
Natl. Assn. of Coll. Auxiliary Services, Central [2724], Normal, IL
Natl. Assn. of Corporate Directors, Chicago Chap. [1074], Chicago, IL
Natl. Assn. of Credit Mgt. - Chicago/Midwest [3340], Rolling Meadows, IL
Natl. Assn. of Credit Mgt. Great Lakes [8898], Madison Heights, MI
Natl. Assn. of Credit Mgt. Greater Cleveland [17231], Westlake, OH
Natl. Assn. of Credit Mgt. Heartland Unit [★15468]
Natl. Assn. of Credit Mgt. North Central [★11688]
Natl. Assn. of Credit Mgt. Ohio [14928], Dayton, OH
Natl. Assn. of Credit Mgt. - Western Michigan [10191], Wyoming, MI
Natl. Assn. of Credit Mgt. Wisconsin, Madison [★19299]
Natl. Assn. of Credit Managers Great Lakes [★8898]
Natl. Assn. of Credit Managers Ohio [★14928]
Natl. Assn. of Credit Managers Ohio, Cincinnati [13919], Cincinnati, OH
Natl. Assn. of Disability Examiners, Great Lakes [15436], Hilliard, OH
Natl. Assn. of Drug Diversion Investigators of Ohio [16514], Reynoldsburg, OH
Natl. Assn. of Fleet Administrators, Central Region [2836], Oakbrook Terrace, IL
Natl. Assn. of Fleet Administrators, Michigan Chap. [10002], Troy, MI
Natl. Assn. of Fleet Administrators, North Central Chap. [10393], Bayport, MN
Natl. Assn. of Fleet Administrators, Tri-State [14513], Columbus, OH
Natl. Assn. of Fleet Administrators, Western Reserve Chap. [13139], Amherst, OH
Natl. Assn. of Fleet Administrators, Wisconsin Chap. [19072], Milwaukee, WI
Natl. Assn. For Uniformed Services - Northern Wisconsin, Chap. 1 [18801], Marinette, WI
Natl. Assn. For Uniformed Services - Southern Wisconsin, Chap. 2 [19073], Milwaukee, WI
Natl. Assn. of Home Builders, Arrowhead Builders Assn. [10842], Duluth, MN
Natl. Assn. of Home Builders, Building Authority of Greater Indianapolis [5416], Indianapolis, IN
Natl. Assn. of Home Builders, Building Authority of Kosciusko-Fulton County [6450], Warsaw, IN
Natl. Assn. of Home Builders, Building Authority of Minnesota [12543], St. Paul, MN
Natl. Assn. of Home Builders, Mercer County Building Authority [15226], Fort Recovery, OH
Natl. Assn. of Home Builders, Minnesota River Building Authority [11393], Mankato, MN
Natl. Assn. of Home Builders, Union County Building Authority [15864], Marysville, OH
Natl. Assn. of Home Builders of the U.S., Central Wisconsin Home Builders Assn. [20188], Wisconsin Rapids, WI
Natl. Assn. of Home Builders of the U.S., Sheboygan County Home Builders Assn. [19491], Plymouth, WI
Natl. Assn. of Home Builders of the U.S., Wausau Area Builders Assn. [20041], Wausau, WI
Natl. Assn. of Home Builders of the U.S., Anderson Home Builders Assn. [★4114]
Natl. Assn. of Home Builders of the U.S., Building Indus. Assn. of Northwest Indiana [4436], Crown Point, IN
Natl. Assn. of Home Builders of the U.S., Central Minnesota Builders Assn. [12294], St. Cloud, MN
Natl. Assn. of Home Builders of the U.S., Chippewa Valley Home Builders Assn. [17889], Eau Claire, WI
Natl. Assn. of Home Builders of the U.S., Door County Home Builders Assn. [19840], Sturgeon Bay, WI
Natl. Assn. of Home Builders of the U.S., Dubois County Builders Assn. [5531], Jasper, IN
Natl. Assn. of Home Builders of the U.S., Hancock County Home Builders Assn. [15210], Findlay, OH
Natl. Assn. of Home Builders of the U.S., Headwaters Builders Assn. [10422], Bemidji, MN
Natl. Assn. of Home Builders of the U.S., Home Builders Assn. of Bloomington-Normal [300], Bloomington, IL
Natl. Assn. of Home Builders of the U.S., Home Builders Assn. of Greater Cincinnati [13920], Cincinnati, OH
Natl. Assn. of Home Builders of the U.S., Home Builders Assn. of Lawrence County [6011], Oolitic, IN
Natl. Assn. of Home Builders of the U.S., Home Builders Assn. of Miami County [★17000]
Natl. Assn. of Home Builders of the U.S., Home Builders Assn. of the Upper Penninsula [8954], Marquette, MI
Natl. Assn. of Home Builders of the U.S., Home and Building Assn. of Greater Grand Rapids [7989], Grand Rapids, MI
Natl. Assn. of Home Builders of the U.S., La Crosse Area Builders Assn. [19366], Onalaska, WI
Natl. Assn. of Home Builders of the U.S., Madison County Home Builders Assn. [4114], Anderson, IN
Natl. Assn. of Home Builders of the U.S., Manitowoc County Home Builders Assn. [18789], Manitowoc, WI
Natl. Assn. of Home Builders of the U.S., Mid Wisconsin Home Builders Assn. [19509], Portage, WI
Natl. Assn. of Home Builders of the U.S., Monroe County Builders Assn. [4247], Bloomington, IN
Natl. Assn. of Home Builders of the U.S., Northern Illinois Home Builders Assn. [3877], Warrenville, IL
Natl. Assn. of Home Builders of the U.S., St. Croix Valley Home Builders Assn. [19319], New Richmond, WI
Natl. Assn. of Home Builders of the U.S., South Central Home Builders Assn. [2602], Mount Vernon, IL
Natl. Assn. of Home Builders of the U.S., Valley Home Builders Assn. [17506], Appleton, WI
Natl. Assn. of Home Builders, Western Illinois Building Authority [1778], Galesburg, IL
Natl. Assn. for Home Care and Hospice, Region V [3136], Princeton, IL

Natl. Assn. of Housing and Redevelopment Officials, Illinois [★1394]
Natl. Assn. of Housing and Redevelopment Officials, Minnesota Chap. [10870], Eagan, MN
Natl. Assn. of Housing and Redevelopment Officials, North Central Regional Coun. [10871], Eagan, MN
Natl. Assn. of Housing and Redevelopment Officials, Wisconsin Chap. [19397], Oshkosh, WI
Natl. Assn. of Housing and Redevopment Officials, Illinois Assn. [2620], Murphysboro, IL
Natl. Assn. for Indiana Limestone [★4172]
Natl. Assn. of Indus. and Off. Properties, Central Ohio Chap. [14514], Columbus, OH
Natl. Assn. of Indus. and Off. Properties, Chicago Chap. [1075], Chicago, IL
Natl. Assn. of Indus. and Off. Properties, Cincinnati-Northern Kentucky Chap. [13921], Cincinnati, OH
Natl. Assn. of Indus. and Off. Properties, Dayton Chap. [14929], Dayton, OH
Natl. Assn. of Indus. and Off. Properties, Michigan Chap. [6989], Bloomfield Hills, MI
Natl. Assn. of Indus. and Off. Properties Minnesota Chap. [11694], Minneapolis, MN
Natl. Assn. of Indus. and Off. Properties, Northern Ohio Chap. [14172], Cleveland, OH
Natl. Assn. of Indus. and Off. Properties, Ohio Chap. [14515], Columbus, OH
Natl. Assn. of Indus. and Off. Properties, Wisconsin Chap. [19994], Waukesha, WI
Natl. Assn. of Insurance and Financial Advisors, Elkhart County Chap. [4503], Elkhart, IN
Natl. Assn. of Insurance and Financial Advisors, Southern Illinois Chap. [424], Carbondale, IL
Natl. Assn. for Interpretation - Region 4 [5417], Indianapolis, IN
Natl. Assn. of Investors Corp. [17346], Worthington, OH
Natl. Assn. of Investors Corp., Capital Area Chap. [8736], Lansing, MI
Natl. Assn. of Investors Corp., Central Indiana Chap. [5418], Indianapolis, IN
Natl. Assn. of Investors Corp., Chicago South Chap. [1956], Harvey, IL
Natl. Assn. of Investors Corp., Evansville Tri-State Chap. [4562], Evansville, IN
Natl. Assn. of Investors Corp., Greater North Suburban Chap. [1076], Chicago, IL
Natl. Assn. of Investors Corp., Heart of Illinois Chap. [2987], Pekin, IL
Natl. Assn. of Investors Corp., Mid-Michigan Chap. [9095], Mount Morris, MI
Natl. Assn. of Investors Corp., Milwaukee Chap. [17674], Brookfield, WI
Natl. Assn. of Investors Corp., Northeast Hoosier Chap. [4697], Fort Wayne, IN
Natl. Assn. of Investors Corp., Northeast Ohio Chap. [15923], Mayfield Heights, OH
Natl. Assn. of Investors Corp., Northern Michigan Chap. [10170], Williamsburg, MI
Natl. Assn. of Investors Corp., Northwest Buckeye Chap. [16934], Toledo, OH
Natl. Assn. of Investors Corp., Northwest Indiana Chap. [5810], Mishawaka, IN
Natl. Assn. of Investors Corp., OKI Tri-State Chap. [13922], Cincinnati, OH
Natl. Assn. of Investors Corp., South Central Wisconsin Chap. [18574], Madison, WI
Natl. Assn. of Investors Corp., Southeastern Michigan Chap. [10121], West Bloomfield, MI
Natl. Assn. of Investors Corp., Western Michigan Chap. [7990], Grand Rapids, MI
Natl. Assn. of Legal Investigators, Mid-Eastern Region [7991], Grand Rapids, MI
Natl. Assn. of Miniature Enthusiasts [4329], Carmel, IN
Natl. Assn. of Miniature Enthusiasts - A-3 Regional Miniaturists [17176], West Chester, OH
Natl. Assn. of Miniature Enthusiasts - A1 Minis R Us [2758], Northbrook, IL
Natl. Assn. of Miniature Enthusiasts - Crazy Eight's [1364], Darien, IL
Natl. Assn. of Miniature Enthusiasts - Dollhouse Divas [8297], Huntington Woods, MI
Natl. Assn. of Miniature Enthusiasts - Harbor Mini Crafters [7863], Grand Haven, MI
Natl. Assn. of Miniature Enthusiasts - Hoosier Mini-Mizers [5419], Indianapolis, IN
Natl. Assn. of Miniature Enthusiasts - Lakeshore Miniature Makers [19702], Sheboygan, WI
Natl. Assn. of Miniature Enthusiasts - Little Gems [7019], Brighton, MI
Natl. Assn. of Miniature Enthusiasts - Madison Avenue Miniaturists [5958], New Whiteland, IN
Natl. Assn. of Miniature Enthusiasts - Magic of Miniatures [7875], Grand Ledge, MI
Natl. Assn. of Miniature Enthusiasts - Mail-A-Mini Swappers [8990], Mayville, MI
Natl. Assn. of Miniature Enthusiasts - Married with Minis [17177], West Chester, OH
Natl. Assn. of Miniature Enthusiasts - Metro Mini Makers [2525], Moline, IL
Natl. Assn. of Miniature Enthusiasts - Metro Minis [4698], Fort Wayne, IN
Natl. Assn. of Miniature Enthusiasts - Midstate Mini-makers of Illinois [2725], Normal, IL
Natl. Assn. of Miniature Enthusiasts - Mini Biddies [8782], Lapeer, MI
Natl. Assn. of Miniature Enthusiasts - Mini Constr. Company [5892], Muncie, IN
Natl. Assn. of Miniature Enthusiasts - Mini Diversions [19620], Richfield, WI
Natl. Assn. of Miniature Enthusiasts - Mini-Fingers of Kalamazoo [6862], Battle Creek, MI
Natl. Assn. of Miniature Enthusiasts - Mini-Magic Miniatures [15211], Findlay, OH
Natl. Assn. of Miniature Enthusiasts - Miniature Dream Builders [4610], Fishers, IN
Natl. Assn. of Miniature Enthusiasts - My Favorite Things [6247], South Bend, IN
Natl. Assn. of Miniature Enthusiasts - My Mini Friends [7265], Dearborn, MI
Natl. Assn. of Miniature Enthusiasts - Now and Again Club [4085], Albion, IN
Natl. Assn. of Miniature Enthusiasts - One More Time [6863], Battle Creek, MI
Natl. Assn. of Miniature Enthusiasts - People with Unfinished Projects [7069], Canton, MI
Natl. Assn. of Miniature Enthusiasts - Pinocchio's Mini Makers [7193], Clio, MI
Natl. Assn. of Miniature Enthusiasts - Quality Dreamers [9211], Niles, MI
Natl. Assn. of Miniature Enthusiasts - Retreat Into Miniatures [17507], Appleton, WI
Natl. Assn. of Miniature Enthusiasts - Soc. of Miniature Memories [16218], North Canton, OH
Natl. Assn. of Miniature Enthusiasts - Springfield Mini Ma'ams [16735], Springfield, OH
Natl. Assn. of Miniature Enthusiasts - Tiny Treasure Makers [11394], Mankato, MN
Natl. Assn. of Miniature Enthusiasts - Town Hall Minis [3104], Plainfield, IL
Natl. Assn. of Miniature Enthusiasts - Tri City Miniature Makers [9620], Saginaw, MI
Natl. Assn. of Miniature Enthusiasts - Wee Bee's of Birmingham [9515], Rochester Hills, MI
Natl. Assn. of Miniature Enthusiasts - Whole Fam Damily [9621], Saginaw, MI
Natl. Assn. of Miniature Enthusiasts - Wisconsin Wee World Soc. [18006], Fox Point, WI
Natl. Assn. of Minority Contractors, Central Ohio [14516], Columbus, OH
Natl. Assn. of Minority Contractors, Minnesota [12983], Woodbury, MN
Natl. Assn. of Minority Contractors of Upper Midwest [11695], Minneapolis, MN
Natl. Assn. for Multicultural Educ., Indiana Chap. [5420], Indianapolis, IN
Natl. Assn. for Multicultural Educ., Michigan Chap. [6742], Ann Arbor, MI
Natl. Assn. for Multicultural Educ., Minnesota Chap. [12544], St. Paul, MN
Natl. Assn. for Multicultural Educ., Ohio Chap. [15437], Hilliard, OH
Natl. Assn. for Multicultural Educ., Region 5 [6493], West Lafayette, IN
Natl. Assn. of Pastoral Musicians, Cincinnati Chap. [13923], Cincinnati, OH
Natl. Assn. of Pastoral Musicians, Cincinnati-Miami Valley [13300], Beavercreek, OH
Natl. Assn. of Pastoral Musicians, Columbus [15266], Gahanna, OH
Natl. Assn. of Pastoral Musicians, Kalamazoo [9687], St. Joseph, MI
Natl. Assn. of Pastoral Musicians, Lansing [6743], Ann Arbor, MI
Natl. Assn. of Professional Insurance Agents, Indiana [15267], Gahanna, OH
Natl. Assn. of Professional Mortgage Women - Chicagoland [2820], Oak Park, IL
Natl. Assn. of Professional Mortgage Women - Southeastern Michigan [9812], Southfield, MI
Natl. Assn. of Professional Organizers, Michigan Chap. [7689], Fenton, MI
Natl. Assn. of Professional Organizers, Minnesota Chap. [12029], Plymouth, MN
Natl. Assn. of Professional Organizers, Ohio Chap. [15339], Grandview Heights, OH
Natl. Assn. of Professional Organizers, Wisconsin Chap. [19074], Milwaukee, WI
Natl. Assn. of the Remodeling Indus. of Central Indiana [5421], Indianapolis, IN
Natl. Assn. of the Remodeling Indus. of Central Ohio [17216], Westerville, OH
Natl. Assn. of the Remodeling Indus. East Central Ohio [17078], Wadsworth, OH
Natl. Assn. of the Remodeling Indus. of Greater Chicagoland [1464], Des Plaines, IL
Natl. Assn. of the Remodeling Indus. of Michiana Chap. [4811], Granger, IN
Natl. Assn. of the Remodeling Indus. of Minnesota [11696], Minneapolis, MN
Natl. Assn. of the Remodeling Indus. of Southeast Michigan [6744], Ann Arbor, MI
Natl. Assn. of the Remodeling Indus. of Wabash Valley [5627], Lafayette, IN
Natl. Assn. of Rocketry - A Method of Reaching Extreme Altitudes [4732], Fortville, IN
Natl. Assn. of Rocketry - Central Illinois Aerospace [3425], Savoy, IL
Natl. Assn. of Rocketry - Columbus Soc. for the Advancement of Rocketry [14517], Columbus, OH
Natl. Assn. of Rocketry - Fermilab Assn. of Rocketry [184], Batavia, IL
Natl. Assn. of Rocketry - Huron Valley Rocket Soc. [8101], Hamburg, MI
Natl. Assn. of Rocketry - Jackson Model Rocketry Club [8390], Jackson, MI
Natl. Assn. of Rocketry - Kalkaska Aerospace Club [8906], Mancelona, MI
Natl. Assn. of Rocketry - Launch Crue [4934], Holland, IN
Natl. Assn. of Rocketry - Mantua Township Missile Agency [16777], Stow, OH
Natl. Assn. of Rocketry - Medford Assn. of Rocket Sci. [18847], Medford, WI
Natl. Assn. of Rocketry - Minnesota Amateur Spacemodelers Assn. [10604], Burnsville, MN
Natl. Assn. of Rocketry - NARScouts [15708], Lorain, OH
Natl. Assn. of Rocketry - Northern Illinois Rocketry Assn. [1506], Downers Grove, IL
Natl. Assn. of Rocketry - Queen City Area Rocket Club [16029], Milford, OH
Natl. Assn. of Rocketry - Rocketeers of Central Indiana [5422], Indianapolis, IN
Natl. Assn. of Rocketry - Southwest Michigan Assn. of Spacemodeling Hobbyists [10053], Walker, MI
Natl. Assn. of Rocketry - Summit City Aerospace Modelers [4699], Fort Wayne, IN
Natl. Assn. of Rocketry - Thorp Apogee Heights [19897], Thorp, WI
Natl. Assn. of Rocketry - Toledo Area Rocket Soc. [16935], Toledo, OH
Natl. Assn. of Rocketry - Tri-City Sky Busters [14173], Cleveland, OH
Natl. Assn. of Rocketry - US Aerospace Challenge [8212], Holland, MI
Natl. Assn. of Rocketry - Waukesha County 4H Rocketeers [19995], Waukesha, WI
Natl. Assn. of Rocketry - Willow Hill Rocketry Gp. [1544], East Peoria, IL
Natl. Assn. of Rocketry - Wisconsin Org. of Spacemodeling Hobbyists [19562], Racine, WI
Natl. Assn. of Social Workers, Illinois Chap. [1077], Chicago, IL
Natl. Assn. of Social Workers - Michigan Chap. [8737], Lansing, MI
Natl. Assn. of Social Workers, Minnesota Chap. [12545], St. Paul, MN
Natl. Assn. of Social Workers - Ohio Chap. [14518], Columbus, OH
Natl. Assn. of Social Workers - Wisconsin Chap. [18575], Madison, WI

Natl. Assn. of State Beer Assn. Secretaries [★11630]
Natl. Assn. of State Foresters, Illinois [3653], Springfield, IL
Natl. Assn. of State Foresters, Indiana [5423], Indianapolis, IN
Natl. Assn. of State Foresters, Michigan [8738], Lansing, MI
Natl. Assn. of State Foresters, Minnesota [12546], St. Paul, MN
Natl. Assn. of State Foresters, Ohio [14519], Columbus, OH
Natl. Assn. of State Foresters, Wisconsin [18576], Madison, WI
Natl. Assn. of Student Personnel Administrators, Illinois [3038], Peoria, IL
Natl. Assn. of Student Personnel Administrators, Indiana [4823], Greencastle, IN
Natl. Assn. of Student Personnel Administrators, Michigan [8213], Holland, MI
Natl. Assn. of Student Personnel Administrators, Minnesota [12547], St. Paul, MN
Natl. Assn. of Student Personnel Administrators, NASPA Region IV-East [20160], Whitewater, WI
Natl. Assn. of Student Personnel Administrators, Ohio [13119], Alliance, OH
Natl. Assn. of Student Personnel Administrators, Wisconsin [19797], Stevens Point, WI
Natl. Assn. of Telecommunications Off.rs and Advisors, Michigan [9813], Southfield, MI
Natl. Assn. of Telecommunications Off.rs and Advisors, Ohio [15972], Mentor, OH
Natl. Assn. of The Remodeling Indus. of Madison [18577], Madison, WI
Natl. Assn. of Urban Debate Leagues [1078], Chicago, IL
Natl. Assn. of Watch and Clock Collectors, Chap. 3 [1307], Countryside, IL
Natl. Assn. of Watch and Clock Collectors, Chap. 18 [5424], Indianapolis, IN
Natl. Assn. of Watch and Clock Collectors, Chap. 66 [1412], Deer Creek, IL
Natl. Assn. of Watch and Clock Collectors, Chap. 171 [17964], Fitchburg, WI
Natl. Assn. of Watch and Clock Collectors, Great Lakes Chap. 6 [7070], Canton, MI
Natl. Assn. of Watch and Clock Collectors, Menomonee Valley Chap. 47 [19075], Milwaukee, WI
Natl. Assn. of Women Bus. Owners, Greater Detroit Chap. [7408], Detroit, MI
Natl. Assn. of Women Bus. Owners, Indianapolis [5425], Indianapolis, IN
Natl. Assn. of Women Bus. Owners - Minnesota Chap. [12548], St. Paul, MN
Natl. Assn. of Women Bus. Owners, Wisconsin [17508], Appleton, WI
Natl. Assn. of Women in Constr., Detroit Chap. [7698], Ferndale, MI
Natl. Assn. of Women in Constr., Grand Rapids Chap. [7992], Grand Rapids, MI
Natl. Assn. of Women in Constr., Milwaukee Chap. [19076], Milwaukee, WI
Natl. Assn. of Women in Constr., Region 4 [15997], Middleburg Heights, OH
Natl. Assn. of Women in Constr., Toledo Chap. [16936], Toledo, OH
Natl. Ataxia Found., Mark A. Newell [11697], Minneapolis, MN
Natl. Ataxia Found., Minneapolis, Minnesota Support Gp. [11698], Minneapolis, MN
Natl. Audubon Aullwood Center [★14858]
Natl. Audubon Soc. - Audubon Soc. of Ohio - Cincinnati Chap. [★13756]
Natl. Audubon Soc. - Blackbrook [15973], Mentor, OH
Natl. Audubon Soc. - Canton [★13555]
Natl. Audubon Soc. - Central Minnesota [★12279]
Natl. Audubon Soc. - Champaign County [3829], Urbana, IL
Natl. Audubon Soc. - Chequamegon Chap. [★17586]
Natl. Audubon Soc. - Clark County [★16723]
Natl. Audubon Soc. - Columbus [14520], Columbus, OH
Natl. Audubon Soc. - Coulee Region [★18341]
Natl. Audubon Soc., Dayton Chap. [★14858]
Natl. Audubon Soc. - Decatur [★1386]
Natl. Audubon Soc. - East Central Ohio [16175], Newark, OH
Natl. Audubon Soc. - Firelands [★16611]
Natl. Audubon Soc. - Greater Akron [13069], Akron, OH
Natl. Audubon Soc. - Green Rock [★17610]
Natl. Audubon Soc. - Hunt Hill Audubon Sanctuary [19663], Sarona, WI
Natl. Audubon Soc. - Knob and Valley [★5917]
Natl. Audubon Soc. - Lake County [★2261]
Natl. Audubon Soc. - Lakeland Chap. [★19918]
Natl. Audubon Soc. - Milwaukee Chap. [★17781]
Natl. Audubon Soc. - Minnesota River Valley Audubon Chap. [10483], Bloomington, MN
Natl. Audubon Soc. - Minnesota River Valley Club [★10483]
Natl. Audubon Soc. - Mississippi Headwaters [★10420]
Natl. Audubon Soc. - Northwest Illinois [★2980]
Natl. Audubon Soc.- Prairie Woods [72], Arlington Heights, IL
Natl. Audubon Soc. - Pres. R.B. Hayes [★15251]
Natl. Audubon Soc. - St. Paul [★12726]
Natl. Audubon Soc. - South Bend [★5813]
Natl. Audubon Soc. - Sycamore [★6500]
Natl. Audubon Soc. - Thorn Creek [★2956]
Natl. Audubon Soc. - Tippecanoe [★5991]
Natl. Audubon Soc. - Tri-Moraine [★15671]
Natl. Audubon Soc. - Washtenaw [6745], Ann Arbor, MI
Natl. Audubon Soc. - Western Cuyahoga [★14237]
Natl. Audubon Soc. - Wild River [★10638]
Natl. Audubon Soc. - Wisconsin Metro [★18014]
Natl. Audubon Soc. - Zumbro Valley [★12199]
Natl. Black MBA Assn., Cleveland Chap. [13290], Beachwood, OH
Natl. Black MBA Assn., Detroit Chap. [7409], Detroit, MI
Natl. Black MBA Assn., Euclid [★13290]
Natl. Black MBA Assn., Twin Cities [11699], Minneapolis, MN
Natl. Black United Front, Chicago Chap. [396], Calumet Park, IL
Natl. Black United Front, Detroit Chap. [7410], Detroit, MI
Natl. Black United Front, Milwaukee Chap. [19077], Milwaukee, WI
Natl. Christmas Tree Assn., Illinois [★3403]
Natl. Christmas Tree Assn., Indiana [★6284]
Natl. Christmas Tree Assn., Michigan [★8282]
Natl. Christmas Tree Assn., Mid Am. [2066], Irving, IL
Natl. Coalition of Free Men [11700], Minneapolis, MN
Natl. Corvette Restorers Soc., Indiana Chap. [4154], Avon, IN
Natl. Corvette Restorers Soc., Michigan Chap. [10077], Washington, MI
Natl. Corvette Restorers Soc., North Central Chap. [11343], Long Lake, MN
Natl. Corvette Restorers Soc., Queen City Chap. [13924], Cincinnati, OH
Natl. Corvette Restorers Soc., Wisconsin Chap. [19829], Stoughton, WI
Natl. Coun. on Alcoholism and Addictions-Greater Flint Area [7749], Flint, MI
Natl. Coun. on Alcoholism and Drug Dependence, Greater Detroit Area [7411], Detroit, MI
Natl. Coun. on Alcoholism and Drug Dependence of Michigan [8739], Lansing, MI
Natl. Coun. on Alcoholism/Lansing Regional Area [8740], Lansing, MI
Natl. Coun. for Geocosmic Res., STARS Chap. [12549], St. Paul, MN
Natl. Coun. of La Raza-Midwest [1079], Chicago, IL
Natl. Coun. of Teachers of English Student Affl. at Eastern Michigan State Univ. [10211], Ypsilanti, MI
Natl. Coun. of Teachers of English Student Affiliate of Michigan State Univ. [7557], East Lansing, MI
Natl. Earth Sci. Teachers Assn., East Central Chap. [15952], Medina, OH
Natl. Elecl. Contractors Assn., Cincinnati [13925], Cincinnati, OH
Natl. Elecl. Contractors Assn., Greater Cleveland Chap. [14174], Cleveland, OH
Natl. Elecl. Contractors Assn., Michigan Chap. [8741], Lansing, MI
Natl. Elecl. Contractors Assn., North Central Ohio Chap. [13070], Akron, OH
Natl. Elecl. Contractors Assn. - Penn-Ohio Chap. [17405], Youngstown, OH
Natl. Exchange Carrier Assn., Midwest [1080], Chicago, IL
Natl. Farmers Union, Indiana [4754], Franklin, IN
Natl. Farmers Union, Michigan [9846], Sparta, MI
Natl. Fed. of the Blind, Greater Summit County [13071], Akron, OH
Natl. Fed. of the Blind of Illinois [2084], Jacksonville, IL
Natl. Fed. of the Blind of Michigan [8742], Lansing, MI
Natl. Fed. of the Blind of Ohio [16285], Oberlin, OH
Natl. Fed. of the Blind, Rock County Chap. [18257], Janesville, WI
Natl. Fed. of the Blind of Wisconsin [18258], Janesville, WI
Natl. Fed. of Independent Bus. - Illinois [3654], Springfield, IL
Natl. Fed. of Independent Bus. - Indiana [5426], Indianapolis, IN
Natl. Fed. of Independent Bus. - Michigan [8743], Lansing, MI
Natl. Fed. of Independent Bus. - Minnesota [12550], St. Paul, MN
Natl. Fed. of Independent Bus. - Ohio [14521], Columbus, OH
National Federation of Independent Business - Wisconsin [18578], Madison, WI
Natl. Forum for Black Public Administrators, Cincinnati Chap. [13926], Cincinnati, OH
Natl. Forum for Black Public Administrators, Cleveland Chap. [14175], Cleveland, OH
Natl. Forum for Black Public Administrators, Dayton Chap. [14930], Dayton, OH
Natl. Forum for Black Public Administrators, Illinois Chap. [1081], Chicago, IL
Natl. Found. for Ileitis and Colitis, Midwest Regional [★1456]
Natl. Fraternal Cong. of Am. [2781], Oak Brook, IL
Natl. Guard Assn. of Michigan [8744], Lansing, MI
Natl. Hook-up of Black Women, Chicago Chap. [1082], Chicago, IL
Natl. Hook-up of Black Women, Joliet Chap. [2115], Joliet, IL
Natl. Horseshoe Pitchers Assn. - Ohio [14522], Columbus, OH
Natl. Hot Rod Assn., Div. 3 [4306], Bunker Hill, IN
Natl. Human Rsrcs. Assn., Cincinnati Chap. [13927], Cincinnati, OH
Natl. Kidney Found. of Illinois [1083], Chicago, IL
Natl. Kidney Found. of Indiana [5427], Indianapolis, IN
National Kidney Foundation of Michigan [6746], Ann Arbor, MI
Natl. Kidney Found. of Minnesota [11701], Minneapolis, MN
Natl. Kidney Found. of Ohio [14523], Columbus, OH
Natl. Kidney Found. of Wisconsin [17675], Brookfield, WI
Natl. Lawyers Guild - Detroit Chap. [★7398]
Natl. Mgt. Assn., Argo-Tech Leadership Chap. [15144], Euclid, OH
Natl. Mgt. Assn., Blue Cross and Blue Shield of Michigan [7412], Detroit, MI
Natl. Mgt. Assn., Columbus Public Ser. Chap. [14524], Columbus, OH
Natl. Mgt. Assn., Greater Dayton Leadership Assn. [14931], Dayton, OH
Natl. Mgt. Assn., The Blues [8745], Lansing, MI
Natl. Mgt. Assn., Van Kuren [17358], Wright-Patterson AFB, OH
Natl. Mgt. Assn., Wright Chap. [17359], Wright-Patterson AFB, OH
Natl. Model Railroad Assn., Mid-Central Region [15370], Grove City, OH
Natl. Model Railroad Assn., Midwest Region [19078], Milwaukee, WI
National Model Railroad Association, Thousand Lakes Region [10605], Burnsville, MN
Natl. Multiple Sclerosis Soc. of Greater Illinois [1084], Chicago, IL
Natl. Multiple Sclerosis Soc., Indiana State Chap. [5428], Indianapolis, IN
Natl. Multiple Sclerosis Soc., Michigan Chap. [9814], Southfield, MI

Natl. Multiple Sclerosis Soc., Minnesota Chap. [11702], Minneapolis, MN
National Multiple Sclerosis Society, Ohio Buckeye [14176], Cleveland, OH
Natl. Multiple Sclerosis Soc., Ohio Valley Chap. [13928], Cincinnati, OH
Natl. Multiple Sclerosis Soc., Wisconsin [18185], Hartland, WI
Natl. Network of Libraries of Medicine, Greater Midwest Region [1085], Chicago, IL
Natl. Novelty Salt and Pepper Shakers Club - Michigan [6864], Battle Creek, MI
Natl. Nutritional Foods Association-Southwest [8152], Haslett, MI
Natl. Org. of Black Law Enforcement Executives, Central Illinois Land of Lincoln Chap. [3830], Urbana, IL
Natl. Org. of Black Law Enforcement Executives, Chicago Metropolitan Chap. [1086], Chicago, IL
Natl. Org. of Black Law Enforcement Executives, Greater Cincinnati Chap. [13929], Cincinnati, OH
Natl. Org. of Black Law Enforcement Executives, Northern Illinois Chap. [124], Aurora, IL
Natl. Org. of Black Law Enforcement Executives, Northern Indiana Chap. [4783], Gary, IN
Natl. Org. of Black Law Enforcement Executives, Southern Indiana Chap. [5429], Indianapolis, IN
Natl. Org. of Circumcision Info. Rsrc. Centers of Michigan [6965], Birmingham, MI
Natl. Org. of Circumcision Info. Rsrc. Centers (NoCirc) Michigan Chap. [★6965]
Natl. Org. of Circumcision Info. Rsrc. Centers of Wisconsin - Madison [18579], Madison, WI
Natl. Org. for Reform of Marijuana Laws, Illinois Chap. [1087], Chicago, IL
Natl. Org. for Women - Akron Area [13072], Akron, OH
Natl. Org. for Women - Ann Arbor/Washtenaw County [10212], Ypsilanti, MI
Natl. Org. for Women - Astabula [15526], Jefferson, OH
Natl. Org. for Women - Athens [13209], Athens, OH
Natl. Org. for Women - Chicago [1088], Chicago, IL
Natl. Org. for Women - Cincinnati [13930], Cincinnati, OH
Natl. Org. for Women - Columbus [14525], Columbus, OH
Natl. Org. for Women - Dayton [13624], Centerville, OH
Natl. Org. for Women - Detroit [7413], Detroit, MI
Natl. Org. for Women - Downriver [8077], Grosse Ile, MI
Natl. Org. for Women - Fox Valley [3390], St. Charles, IL
Natl. Org. for Women - Grand Traverse [9942], Traverse City, MI
Natl. Org. for Women - Greater Cleveland [15709], Lorain, OH
Natl. Org. for Women - Greater Kalamazoo Area [8458], Kalamazoo, MI
Natl. Org. for Women - Greater Youngstown [17406], Youngstown, OH
Natl. Org. for Women - Illinois [3655], Springfield, IL
Natl. Org. for Women - Indiana [5430], Indianapolis, IN
Natl. Org. for Women - Lake-to-Lake [7831], Gladstone, MI
Natl. Org. for Women - Lansing [7558], East Lansing, MI
Natl. Org. for Women - Livingston County [7020], Brighton, MI
Natl. Org. for Women - Macomb County [9092], Mount Clemens, MI
Natl. Org. for Women - Michigan [7559], East Lansing, MI
Natl. Org. for Women-Milwaukee [19079], Milwaukee, WI
Natl. Org. for Women - Minnesota [12551], St. Paul, MN
Natl. Org. for Women - Mount Pleasant [9119], Mount Pleasant, MI
Natl. Org. for Women - Muskegon-Ottawa [9172], Muskegon Heights, MI
Natl. Org. for Women - Northwest Suburban (Chicago) [73], Arlington Heights, IL
Natl. Org. for Women - Oakland County [9587], Royal Oak, MI
Natl. Org. for Women - Oberlin [16286], Oberlin, OH
Natl. Org. for Women - Ohio [14526], Columbus, OH
Natl. Org. for Women - Port Clinton [16459], Port Clinton, OH
Natl. Org. for Women - Toledo Area [16937], Toledo, OH
Natl. Org. for Women - Twin Cities [11703], Minneapolis, MN
Natl. Org. for Women - Wisconsin [18580], Madison, WI
Natl. Org. for Women - Youngstown S [17070], Vienna, OH
Natl. Org. for Women - Zanesville [17440], Zanesville, OH
Natl. Ornamental and Miscellaneous Metals Assn. Upper Midwest Chap. [1612], Elk Grove Village, IL
Natl. Postal Mail Handlers Union, Local 304 [13931], Cincinnati, OH
Natl. Press Photographers Assn., Region 4 [4563], Evansville, IN
Natl. R90S Sport Owners Club No. 67 [13140], Amherst, OH
Natl. Radiator Core Mfg. Credit Assn. [★11688]
Natl. Radiator Mfg. Credit Assn. [★11688]
Natl. Railway Historical Soc; Bluewater Michigan Chap., [9576], Royal Oak, MI
Natl. Recreation and Park Assn. - Central Region [2039], Hoffman Estates, IL
Natl. Results Coun. [12552], St. Paul, MN
Natl. Reye's Syndrome Found. - Support Gp. [13456], Bryan, OH
Natl. Safety Coun., Chicago Chap. [2068], Itasca, IL
Natl. Safety Coun., Northern Ohio Chap. [17407], Youngstown, OH
Natl. School Public Relations Assn., Illinois [1729], Frankfort, IL
Natl. School Public Relations Assn., Michigan [★8711]
Natl. School Public Relations Assn., Minnesota [★12242]
Natl. School Public Relations Assn., Ohio [16515], Reynoldsburg, OH
Natl. School Public Relations Assn., Wisconsin [★18751]
Natl. School Trans. Assn., Illinois Chap. [★2437]
Natl. Show Horse Assn. of Minnesota [12338], St. Louis Park, MN
Natl. Soc. of Black Engineers - Detroit Alumni Extension [7414], Detroit, MI
Natl. Soc. of Black Engineers - Indianapolis Alumni Extension [5431], Indianapolis, IN
Natl. Soc. of Black Engineers - Michigan State Univ. Chap. [7560], East Lansing, MI
Natl. Soc. of Black Engineers - Purdue Univ. Chap. [6494], West Lafayette, IN
Natl. Soc. of Black Engineers - Univ. of Cincinnati [13932], Cincinnati, OH
Natl. Soc. of Black Engineers - Univ. of Illinois, Urbana-Champaign [3831], Urbana, IL
Natl. Soc. of Black Engineers - Univ. of Michigan [6747], Ann Arbor, MI
Natl. Soc. of Black Engineers - Univ. of Wisconsin, Milwaukee [19080], Milwaukee, WI
Natl. Soc. of Black Engineers - Wisconsin Black Engg. Student Soc. [18581], Madison, WI
Natl. Soc. of Fund Raising Executives - Greater Detroit Chap. [★7638]
Natl. Soc. to Prevent Blindness-Ohio Affl. [★14711]
Natl. Soc. of Professional Insurance Investigators, Michigan Chap. [10003], Troy, MI
Natl. Softball Assn. - Illinois [539], Champaign, IL
Natl. Softball Assn. - Michigan [7690], Fenton, MI
Natl. Softball Assn. - Minnesota [12553], St. Paul, MN
Natl. Softball Assn. - Northern Indiana [5599], La Porte, IN
Natl. Softball Assn. - Ohio [13438], Brooklyn, OH
Natl. Softball Assn. - Southern Indiana [5432], Indianapolis, IN
Natl. Sojourners, Charles A. Lindbergh No. 247 [208], Belleville, IL
Natl. Sojourners, Chicago [2656], Naperville, IL
Natl. Sojourners, Cleveland No. 23 [16694], South Euclid, OH
Natl. Sojourners, Columbus No. 10 [14527], Columbus, OH
Natl. Sojourners, Detroit No. 1 [9904], Taylor, MI
Natl. Sojourners, Indiana - Fort Harrison No. 66 [5433], Indianapolis, IN
Natl. Sojourners, Indiana Masonic Home No. 541 [4755], Franklin, IN
Natl. Sojourners, John S. Bersey No. 316 [8982], Mason, MI
Natl. Sojourners, Lake Michigan No. 289 [2190], Lake Bluff, IL
Natl. Sojourners, Maumee Valley No. 518 [15094], Edgerton, OH
Natl. Sojourners, Milwaukee No. 27 [19081], Milwaukee, WI
Natl. Sojourners, Minnesota No. 25 [11460], Mendota Heights, MN
Natl. Sojourners, Northern Indiana No. 544 [6451], Warsaw, IN
Natl. Sojourners, Southern Indiana No. 328 [6201], Shoals, IN
Natl. Sojourners, Wayne W. Gatewood No. 536 [490], Centralia, IL
Natl. Spa and Pool Inst. Central Ohio Chap. [15438], Hilliard, OH
Natl. Spa and Pool Inst. Michigan Chap. [10004], Troy, MI
Natl. Spa and Pool Inst. Midwest Chap. [1089], Chicago, IL
Natl. Spa and Pool Inst. - Region V [★3980]
Natl. Spa and Pool Inst. Region VI [8044], Grandville, MI
Natl. Space Soc. Southwest Michigan Chap. [7806], Galesburg, MI
Natl. Speakers Association/Illinois Chap. [1798], Geneva, IL
Natl. Speakers Assn., Indiana [5673], Lebanon, IN
Natl. Speakers Association/Michigan [7647], Farmington, MI
Natl. Speakers Assn. - Minnesota Chap. [12030], Plymouth, MN
Natl. Speleological Soc., Bloomington, Indiana Grotto [4248], Bloomington, IN
Natl. Speleological Soc., Central Indiana Grotto [5434], Indianapolis, IN
Natl. Speleological Soc., Central Ohio Grotto [15275], Galena, OH
Natl. Speleological Soc., Cleveland Grotto [17232], Westlake, OH
Natl. Speleological Soc., Dayton Underground Grotto [14932], Dayton, OH
Natl. Speleological Soc., Detroit Urban Grotto [7143], Chelsea, MI
Natl. Speleological Soc., Eastern Indiana Grotto [4756], Franklin, IN
Natl. Speleological Soc., Evansville Metropolitan Grotto [5532], Jasper, IN
Natl. Speleological Soc., Greater Cincinnati Grotto [13269], Batavia, OH
Natl. Speleological Soc., Harrison-Crawford Grotto [4790], Georgetown, IN
Natl. Speleological Soc., Little Egypt Grotto [425], Carbondale, IL
Natl. Speleological Soc., Miami Valley Grotto [16075], Mount Orab, OH
Natl. Speleological Soc., Michigan Interlakes Grotto [10021], Union Lake, MI
Natl. Speleological Soc., Minnesota Speleological Survey [12682], South St. Paul, MN
Natl. Speleological Soc., Near Normal Grotto [2726], Normal, IL
Natl. Speleological Soc., Northern Indiana Grotto [4357], Churubusco, IN
Natl. Speleological Soc., Ohio Cavers and Climbers [17191], West Salem, OH
Natl. Speleological Soc., Pinckney Area Grotto [7492], Durand, MI
Natl. Speleological Soc., Red-Eye Karst Team [15729], Loveland, OH
Natl. Speleological Soc., St. Joseph Valley Grotto [4812], Granger, IN
Natl. Speleological Soc., Shady Grove Grotto [14528], Columbus, OH
Natl. Speleological Soc., Standing Stone Grotto [16803], Sugar Grove, OH
Natl. Speleological Soc., Sub-Urban Chicago Grotto [3878], Warrenville, IL
Natl. Speleological Soc., West Michigan Grotto [9481], Reed City, MI
Natl. Speleological Soc., Windy City Grotto [2919], Palatine, IL

Natl. Spinal Cord Injury Assn. - Calumet Region Chap. **[4784]**, Gary, IN
Natl. Spinal Cord Injury Assn. - Greater Milwaukee Area Chap. **[19082]**, Milwaukee, WI
Natl. Spinal Cord Injury Assn. - Northwest Ohio Chap. **[16409]**, Perrysburg, OH
Natl. Stroke Assn., Minnesota Chap. **[11704]**, Minneapolis, MN
Natl. Tech. Honor Soc. - Alma High School - Michigan **[6634]**, Alma, MI
Natl. Tech. Honor Soc. - Auburn Career Center - Ohio **[16337]**, Painesville, OH
Natl. Tech. Honor Soc. - Calhoun Area Tech. Center Michigan **[6865]**, Battle Creek, MI
Natl. Tech. Honor Soc. - Career Quest Cmpt. Learning Center and Staffing Ser. - Michigan **[7561]**, East Lansing, MI
Natl. Tech. Honor Soc. - Career and Tech. Educ. Centers - Ohio **[16176]**, Newark, OH
Natl. Tech. Honor Soc. - Central Nine Career Center - Indiana **[4851]**, Greenwood, IN
Natl. Tech. Honor Soc. - CTEC Satellite Progs. - Ohio **[16177]**, Newark, OH
Natl. Tech. Honor Soc. - Diamond Oaks - Ohio **[13933]**, Cincinnati, OH
Natl. Tech. Honor Soc. - ITT Tech. Inst. - Canton Michigan **[7071]**, Canton, MI
Natl. Tech. Honor Soc. - ITT Tech. Inst. - Dayton Ohio **[14933]**, Dayton, OH
Natl. Tech. Honor Soc. - ITT Tech. Inst. - Grand Rapids - Michigan **[7993]**, Grand Rapids, MI
Natl. Tech. Honor Soc. - ITT Tech. Inst. - Indiana **[5435]**, Indianapolis, IN
Natl. Tech. Honor Soc. - Jackson Area Career Center - Michigan **[8391]**, Jackson, MI
Natl. Tech. Honor Soc. - John H. Hinds Career Center - Indiana **[4514]**, Elwood, IN
Natl. Tech. Honor Soc. - Mt. Pleasant Area Tech. Center Michigan **[9120]**, Mount Pleasant, MI
Natl. Tech. Honor Soc. - Mt. Vernon High School - Indiana **[4733]**, Fortville, IN
Natl. Tech. Honor Soc. - Northwest Career Center - Ohio **[15051]**, Dublin, OH
Natl. Tech. Honor Soc. - Oakland Schools Tech Campus Northeast - Michigan **[9421]**, Pontiac, MI
Natl. Tech. Honor Soc. - Oakland Schools Tech Campus Northwest - Michigan **[7164]**, Clarkston, MI
Natl. Tech. Honor Soc. - Oakland Schools Tech Campus Soutwest - Michigan **[10180]**, Wixom, MI
Natl. Tech. Honor Soc. - Ohio Valley and Tech. Center Ohio **[17198]**, West Union, OH
Natl. Tech. Honor Soc. - Pankow Vocational Tech. Center Michigan **[7185]**, Clinton Township, MI
Natl. Tech. Honor Soc. - Pickaway-Ross Career and Tech. Center - Ohio **[13669]**, Chillicothe, OH
Natl. Tech. Honor Soc. - Remington Coll. - Cleveland Campus - Ohio **[14177]**, Cleveland, OH
Natl. Tech. Honor Soc. - Scioto County JVS - Ohio **[15737]**, Lucasville, OH
Natl. Tech. Honor Soc. - The Career Center - Ohio **[15825]**, Marietta, OH
Natl. Tech. Honor Soc. - Tuscola Tech. Center - Michigan **[7085]**, Caro, MI
Natl. Tech. Honor Soc. - Vanguard-Sentinel Career Centers Ohio **[16856]**, Tiffin, OH
Natl. Tech. Honor Soc. - Vantage Career Center - Ohio **[17050]**, Van Wert, OH
Natl. Tech. Honor Soc. - Wisconsin Lutheran High School Wisconsin **[19083]**, Milwaukee, WI
Natl. Tech. Honor Soc. - Wright State Univ. Lake Campus Ohio **[13615]**, Celina, OH
Natl. Technological Honor Soc. - Batavia High School - Illinois **[185]**, Batavia, IL
Natl. Technological Honor Soc. - Bloomington Area Vocational Center - Illinois **[301]**, Bloomington, IL
Natl. Technological Honor Soc. - Capital Area Career Center Illinois **[3656]**, Springfield, IL
Natl. Technological Honor Soc. - East Aurora High School - Illinois **[125]**, Aurora, IL
Natl. Technological Honor Soc. - Elgin High School - Illinois **[1597]**, Elgin, IL
Natl. Technological Honor Soc. - Fox Valley Career Center Illinois **[2393]**, Maple Park, IL
Natl. Technological Honor Soc. - Geneva Community High School Illinois **[1799]**, Geneva, IL
Natl. Technological Honor Soc. - Illinois Central Coll. Illinois **[3039]**, Peoria, IL
Natl. Technological Honor Soc. - Joliet Junior Coll. - Illinois **[2116]**, Joliet, IL
Natl. Technological Honor Soc. - Kaneland High School - Illinois **[2394]**, Maple Park, IL
Natl. Technological Honor Soc. - Oswego High School - Illinois **[2892]**, Oswego, IL
Natl. Technological Honor Soc. - Paw Paw High School - Illinois **[2969]**, Paw Paw, IL
Natl. Technological Honor Soc. - Vatterott Coll. - Quincy Illinois **[3156]**, Quincy, IL
Natl. Technological Honor Soc. - West Aurora High School - Illinois **[126]**, Aurora, IL
Natl. Technological Honor Soc. - West Leyden High School - Illinois **[2765]**, Northlake, IL
Natl. Utility Contractors Assn. of Indiana **[5436]**, Indianapolis, IN
Natl. Vocational-Technical Honor Soc., Mahoning County Career and Tech. Center **[13537]**, Canfield, OH
Natl. Voluntary Hea. Agencies in Illinois **[★854]**
Natl. Wildlife Fed. - Great Lakes Natural Rsrc. Center **[6748]**, Ann Arbor, MI
Natl. Writers Union - Chicago Chap. **[1090]**, Chicago, IL
Natl. Writers Union, Southeast Michigan **[7415]**, Detroit, MI
Natl. Writers Union, Twin Cities Chap. **[11705]**, Minneapolis, MN
Natl. Youth Leadership Coun. **[12554]**, St. Paul, MN
Native American
Inter-Tribal Coun. of Michigan **[9719]**, Sault Ste. Marie, MI
Mendota Mdewakanton Dakota Community **[11454]**, Mendota, MN
Nativity Home and School Association **[6059]**, Portage, IN
Natural Areas Coun; Michigan **[6732]**, Ann Arbor, MI
Natural Hea. Coalition; Minnesota **[12215]**, Rosemount, MN
Natural Heritage Land Trust **[18582]**, Madison, WI
Natural Resources
Grand River Partners, Inc. **[16334]**, Painesville, OH
Great Lakes Commn. **[6701]**, Ann Arbor, MI
Illinois Conservation Found. **[3598]**, Springfield, IL
Indiana Assn. of Soil and Water Conservation Districts **[5187]**, Indianapolis, IN
Leelanau Conservancy **[8795]**, Leland, MI
Ohio Fed. of Soil and Water Conservation Districts **[14608]**, Columbus, OH
Sand County Found. **[18612]**, Madison, WI
Timber Producers Assn. of Michigan and Wisconsin **[19607]**, Rhinelander, WI
Voyageurs Natl. Park Assn. **[11775]**, Minneapolis, MN
Natural Sciences
Natl. Assn. for Interpretation - Region 4 **[5417]**, Indianapolis, IN
Nature Conservancy, Indiana Field Office **[5437]**, Indianapolis, IN
Nature Conservancy Michigan Chap., Ives Rd. Fen Preserve **[8746]**, Lansing, MI
Nature Conservancy, Michigan Chapter Office **[8747]**, Lansing, MI
Nature Conservancy of Minnesota **[11706]**, Minneapolis, MN
The Nature Conservancy, Minnesota Field Off. **[★11706]**
Nature Conservancy, Ohio Chap. **[15052]**, Dublin, OH
Nature Conservancy, Wisconsin Field Off. **[18583]**, Madison, WI
Nature of Illinois Found. **[540]**, Champaign, IL
Nauvoo Chamber of Commerce **[2672]**, Nauvoo, IL
Naval Reserve Assn., 4-218 Columbus Chap. **[16421]**, Pickerington, OH
Navy
Navy Club of Adam G. Stelzer - Ship No. 9 **[15664]**, Lima, OH
Navy Club of Central Wisconsin - Ship No. 64 **[20042]**, Wausau, WI
Navy Club of Dubois County - Ship No. 90 **[5533]**, Jasper, IN
Navy Club of Fort Wayne - Ship No. 48 **[4700]**, Fort Wayne, IN
Navy Club of Green Bay - Ship No. 18 **[18118]**, Green Bay, WI
Navy Club of Kenosha - Ship No. 40 **[18306]**, Kenosha, WI
Navy Club of Lafayette - Ship No. 12 **[5628]**, Lafayette, IN
Navy Club of New Haven - Ship No. 245 **[5947]**, New Haven, IN
Navy Club of Racine - Ship No. 60 **[19563]**, Racine, WI
Navy Club of Rockford - Ship No. 1 **[3291]**, Rockford, IL
Navy Club of Sangamon - Ship No. 32 **[3657]**, Springfield, IL
Navy Club of Tippecanoe County - Ship No. 11 **[5629]**, Lafayette, IN
Navy Club of USS Indianapolis - Ship No. 35 **[4330]**, Carmel, IN
Navy Club of USS Meeker County - Ship No. 222 **[11331]**, Litchfield, MN
Navy Club of the USS Ohio - Ship No. 726 **[17051]**, Van Wert, OH
Navy Club of Warrick County - Ship No. 237 **[4275]**, Boonville, IN
U.S. Naval Sea Cadet Corps, Windward Div. **[6872]**, Battle Creek, MI
Navy Club of Adam G. Stelzer - Ship No. 9 **[15664]**, Lima, OH
Navy Club of Central Wisconsin - Ship No. 64 **[20042]**, Wausau, WI
Navy Club of Dubois County - Ship No. 90 **[5533]**, Jasper, IN
Navy Club of Fort Wayne - Ship No. 48 **[4700]**, Fort Wayne, IN
Navy Club of Green Bay - Ship No. 18 **[18118]**, Green Bay, WI
Navy Club of Kenosha - Ship No. 40 **[18306]**, Kenosha, WI
Navy Club of Lafayette - Ship No. 12 **[5628]**, Lafayette, IN
Navy Club of New Haven - Ship No. 245 **[5947]**, New Haven, IN
Navy Club of Racine - Ship No. 60 **[19563]**, Racine, WI
Navy Club of Rockford - Ship No. 1 **[3291]**, Rockford, IL
Navy Club of Sangamon - Ship No. 32 **[3657]**, Springfield, IL
Navy Club of Tippecanoe County - Ship No. 11 **[5629]**, Lafayette, IN
Navy Club of USS Indianapolis - Ship No. 35 **[4330]**, Carmel, IN
Navy Club of USS Meeker County - Ship No. 222 **[11331]**, Litchfield, MN
Navy Club of the USS Ohio - Ship No. 726 **[17051]**, Van Wert, OH
Navy Club of Warrick County - Ship No. 237 **[4275]**, Boonville, IN
Navy League of the U.S., Akron-Canton **[13073]**, Akron, OH
Navy League of the U.S., Aurora **[4076]**, Yorkville, IL
Navy League of the U.S., Champaign **[3426]**, Savoy, IL
Navy League of the U.S., Chicago **[2022]**, Hinsdale, IL
Navy League of the U.S., Cleveland **[15588]**, Lakewood, OH
Navy League of the U.S., Dayton **[13301]**, Beavercreek, OH
Navy League of the U.S., Glenview **[1465]**, Des Plaines, IL
Navy League of the U.S., Greater Columbus **[15373]**, Groveport, OH
Navy League of the U.S., Madison **[18000]**, Fort Atkinson, WI
Navy League of the U.S., Milwaukee **[19564]**, Racine, WI
Navy League of the U.S., Toledo-Erie Islands **[16938]**, Toledo, OH
Navy League of the U.S., Western Reserve **[17107]**, Warren, OH
NCA of Illinois **[1091]**, Chicago, IL
Near Earth Object Search Soc. **[14529]**, Columbus, OH
Near North Development Corp. **[1092]**, Chicago, IL
Near NorthWest Arts Coun. **[1093]**, Chicago, IL
Near Northwest Civic Comm. **[1094]**, Chicago, IL
Near Northwest Neighborhood Network **[1095]**, Chicago, IL

Near West Side Community Development Corp. [1096], Chicago, IL
Nebagamon Community Assn. [18406], Lake Nebagamon, WI
Necedah Lions Club [19264], Necedah, WI
Neenah-Menasha Chamber of Commerce [★17490]
Neenah Young Life [19274], Neenah, WI
Negro Chamber of Commerce; Chicago [★859]
Neighborhood Association; Hamilton Park [3024], Peoria, IL
Neighborhood Assn; Old Town [4804], Goshen, IN
Neighborhood Boys Club [★1097]
Neighborhood Boys and Girls Club [1097], Chicago, IL
Neighborhood Development Corporations Assn. of Cincinnati [★13807]
Neighborhood Improvement Assn; Enos Park [3549], Springfield, IL
Neighborhood Improvement Assn; West Portage Park [1230], Chicago, IL
Neighborhood Org; Sheridan [11735], Minneapolis, MN
Neighborhood Ser. Exchange [12723], Stillwater, MN
Neighborhood Watch Steering Comm; Wauwatosa [20083], Wauwatosa, WI
Neighbors Helping Neighbors of Athens County [13210], Athens, OH
Neillsville Area Chamber of Commerce [19280], Neillsville, WI
Nelsonville York - Young Life [13211], Athens, OH
Neosho-Rubicon Lions Club [19284], Neosho, WI
Nephrology
Kidney Found. of Greater Cincinnati [13879], Cincinnati, OH
Natl. Kidney Found. of Illinois [1083], Chicago, IL
Natl. Kidney Found. of Indiana [5427], Indianapolis, IN
National Kidney Foundation of Michigan [6746], Ann Arbor, MI
Natl. Kidney Found. of Minnesota [11701], Minneapolis, MN
Natl. Kidney Found. of Ohio [14523], Columbus, OH
Natl. Kidney Found. of Wisconsin [17675], Brookfield, WI
Net and Paddle Club [1098], Chicago, IL
Nettleton Magnet School PTA [10843], Duluth, MN
Network of Women Entrepreneurs [1099], Chicago, IL
Networking
The Home Network Center [14459], Columbus, OH
Neuqua Valley Young Life [2657], Naperville, IL
Neurofibromatosis; Illinois [2334], Lombard, IL
Neurofibromatosis - Minnesota [11707], Minneapolis, MN
Neurological Disorders
ALS Assn. of Indiana [4969], Indianapolis, IN
ALS Assn. Southeast Wisconsin Chap. [20066], Wauwatosa, WI
ALS Assn., West Michigan Chap. [7883], Grand Rapids, MI
ALS Assn., Western Ohio [14273], Columbus, OH
Amer. Parkinson Disease Assn., Midwest Chap. [1857], Glenview, IL
Amer. Parkinson Disease Assn. Minnesota Chap. [11512], Minneapolis, MN
Amer. Parkinson Disease Assn., Tri-State Parkinson's Wellness Chap. [13731], Cincinnati, OH
Amyotrophic Lateral Sclerosis of Michigan [9783], Southfield, MI
Huntington's Disease Soc. of Am., Central Ohio Chap. [14462], Columbus, OH
Huntington's Disease Soc. of Am., Illinois Chap. [3339], Rolling Meadows, IL
Huntington's Disease Soc. of Am., Indiana Chap. [5152], Indianapolis, IN
Huntington's Disease Soc. of Am., Michigan Chap. [7474], Dimondale, MI
Huntington's Disease Soc. of Am., Northeast Ohio Chap. [13651], Chesterland, OH
Huntington's Disease Soc. of Amer., Wisconsin Chap. [20075], Wauwatosa, WI
Illinois Neurofibromatosis [2334], Lombard, IL
Michigan Parkinson Found. [9808], Southfield, MI
Minnesota Chap. of Myasthenia Gravis Found. of Am. [10529], Breezy Point, MN
Minnesota Neuropathy Association [11658], Minneapolis, MN
MS Connection [6825], Bancroft, MI
Muscular Dystrophy Assn. [7748], Flint, MI
Muscular Dystrophy Association, Columbus [14510], Columbus, OH
Muscular Dystrophy Assn., Dayton [14926], Dayton, OH
Muscular Dystrophy Assn., Northeast Ohio [14167], Cleveland, OH
Muscular Dystrophy Assn. of Southwestern Wisconsin [18566], Madison, WI
Muscular Dystrophy Assn. Support Gps. [3035], Peoria, IL
Myasthenia Gravis Found., Great Lakes Chap. [7987], Grand Rapids, MI
Natl. Ataxia Found., Mark A. Newell [11697], Minneapolis, MN
Natl. Ataxia Found., Minneapolis, Minnesota Support Gp. [11698], Minneapolis, MN
Natl. Multiple Sclerosis Soc. of Greater Illinois [1084], Chicago, IL
Natl. Multiple Sclerosis Soc., Indiana State Chap. [5428], Indianapolis, IN
Natl. Multiple Sclerosis Soc., Michigan Chap. [9814], Southfield, MI
Natl. Multiple Sclerosis Soc., Minnesota Chap. [11702], Minneapolis, MN
National Multiple Sclerosis Society, Ohio Buckeye [14176], Cleveland, OH
Natl. Multiple Sclerosis Soc., Ohio Valley Chap. [13928], Cincinnati, OH
Natl. Multiple Sclerosis Soc., Wisconsin [18185], Hartland, WI
Ohio Chap. of the Myasthenia Gravis Found. [15893], Massillon, OH
Tourette Syndrome Assn. of Illinois [1842], Glen Ellyn, IL
Tourette Syndrome Assn. of Minnesota Chap. [11797], Minnetonka, MN
Tourette Syndrome Association of Ohio [14745], Columbus, OH
United Cerebral Palsy Assn. of Central Minnesota [12315], St. Cloud, MN
United Cerebral Palsy Assn. of Metropolitan Detroit [9828], Southfield, MI
Wisconsin Chap. of the Myasthenia Gravis Found. [20108], West Allis, WI
Wisconsin Chap. of the Tourette Syndrome Assn. [17994], Fond du Lac, WI
Wisconsin Parkinson Assn. [19175], Milwaukee, WI
Neurology
Brain Injury Assn. of Minnesota [11534], Minneapolis, MN
Brain Injury Assn. of Ohio [14340], Columbus, OH
Soc. for Neuroscience, Southern Minnesota Chap. [12189], Rochester, MN
Neuropathy Association; Minnesota [11658], Minneapolis, MN
Neuroscience
Graduate Prog. in Neural Sci., Indiana Univ., Bloomington Chap. [4222], Bloomington, IN
Soc. for Neuroscience, Chicago Chap. [2746], North Chicago, IL
Neurosurgery
Michigan Assn. of Neurological Surgeons [7394], Detroit, MI
Minnesota Neurosurgical Soc. [12500], St. Paul, MN
Ohio State Neurosurgical Soc. [14200], Cleveland, OH
Wisconsin Neurosurgical Soc. [18735], Madison, WI
Nevada Funeral Directors Assn. [17676], Brookfield, WI
Nevada Lions Club - Ohio [16111], Nevada, OH
Neville Public Museum Astronomical Soc. [18119], Green Bay, WI
Neville Public Museum Geology Club [18120], Green Bay, WI
New Albany/Floyd County Habitat for Humanity [5920], New Albany, IN
New Albany Lions Club [16113], New Albany, OH
New Albany - Young Life [14530], Columbus, OH
New Baltimore Historical Soc. [9183], New Baltimore, MI
New Berlin Chamber of Commerce and Visitors Bur. [19293], New Berlin, WI
New Berlin Indus. Lions Club [19294], New Berlin, WI
New Berlin Lions Club [19295], New Berlin, WI
New Berlin Table Tennis Club [19296], New Berlin, WI
New Buffalo Lions Club [10022], Union Pier, MI
New Castle Area Chamber of Commerce [★5939]
New Castle Area - Young Life [5938], New Castle, IN
New Castle-Henry County Chamber of Commerce [5939], New Castle, IN
New Glarus Chamber of Commerce [19304], New Glarus, WI
New Goshen-West Vigo Lions Club [5942], New Goshen, IN
New Haven Chamber of Commerce [5948], New Haven, IN
New Holstein Area Chamber of Commerce [19308], New Holstein, WI
New Hope Assn. [1489], Dolton, IL
New Hope Lions Club [11870], New Hope, MN
New Knoxville - Young Life [16434], Piqua, OH
New Latino Visions [8459], Kalamazoo, MI
New Lebanon Lions Club [16131], New Lebanon, OH
New Lenox Chamber of Commerce [2693], New Lenox, IL
New Lisbon Area Chamber of Commerce [19311], New Lisbon, WI
New Lisbon Lions Club [19312], New Lisbon, WI
New London Area Chamber of Commerce [19315], New London, WI
New London Lions Club [11873], New London, MN
New Lothrop Lions Club [9190], New Lothrop, MI
New Mexico Coun. of Teachers of English [3832], Urbana, IL
New Middletown Lions Club [16142], New Middletown, OH
New Palestine Area Chamber of Commerce [5951], New Palestine, IN
New Paris Lions Club [5954], New Paris, IN
New Prague Chamber of Commerce [11878], New Prague, MN
New Prague Figure Skating Club [11879], New Prague, MN
New Richmond Area Chamber of Commerce [★19320]
New Richmond Area Chamber of Commerce and Visitors Bur. [19320], New Richmond, WI
New Richmond - Young Life [13128], Amelia, OH
New Ulm Area Chamber of Commerce [11885], New Ulm, MN
New Ulm Figure Skating Club [11886], New Ulm, MN
New Waterford Fireman's Assn. [16162], New Waterford, OH
New Waterford Lions Club [16163], New Waterford, OH
Newark Alliance [16178], Newark, OH
Newark Downtown Assn. [★16178]
Newark Table Tennis Club [16179], Newark, OH
Newark Teacher's Assn. [16180], Newark, OH
Newaygo County Habitat for Humanity [7800], Fremont, MI
Newaygo Lions Club [9194], Newaygo, MI
Newberry Area Chamber of Commerce [9198], Newberry, MI
Newberry Area Tourism Assn. [9199], Newberry, MI
Newberry High School Key Club [9200], Newberry, MI
Newborn Lifeline Network [6022], Pekin, IN
Newborns In Need Indianapolis Chap. [5438], Indianapolis, IN
Newburgh - Wyldlife [5962], Newburgh, IN
N.E.W.C.C. [★19398]
Newcomers Club of Saginaw [9622], Saginaw, MI
Newcomerstown Chamber of Commerce [16197], Newcomerstown, OH
Newfolden Lions Club [11893], Newfolden, MN
Newfoundland Club of Am. [19241], Mount Horeb, WI
News and Letters Comm., Chicago Chap. [1100], Chicago, IL
Newspaper Assn; Minnesota [11660], Minneapolis, MN

Newspaper Assn; Wisconsin **[18736]**, Madison, WI
Newspapers
Minnesota Newspaper Assn. **[11660]**, Minneapolis, MN
Newton County Historical Soc. **[5554]**, Kentland, IN
Newton Falls Lions Club **[14791]**, Cortland, OH
Nicolet Coin Club **[18121]**, Green Bay, WI
Nicollet County Historical Soc. **[12618]**, St. Peter, MN
Nigerian Friendship Assn. of Greater Columbus, Ohio **[14531]**, Columbus, OH
Nightingale Alliance **[20079]**, Wauwatosa, WI
Niles Chamber of Chamber of Commerce and Indus. **[2702]**, Niles, IL
Niles Lions Club **[16207]**, Niles, OH
Niles Lions Club - Michigan **[9212]**, Niles, MI
Niles Soc. **[★9206]**
Ninth District Dental Soc., MIC **[9121]**, Mount Pleasant, MI
NIRS Forage and Feed Testing Consortium **[18584]**, Madison, WI
Nisswa Chamber of Commerce **[11898]**, Nisswa, MN
NO-WE-OH- Coun. of Campfire, Inc. **[★15197]**
Noah's Lost Ark **[13351]**, Berlin Center, OH
Nobel Neighbors **[1101]**, Chicago, IL
Noble Arc of Central Indiana - Hamilton, Howard, Marion, Shelby and Tipton Counties **[5439]**, Indianapolis, IN
Noble ARC of Greater Indianapolis **[5440]**, Indianapolis, IN
Noble County Chamber of Commerce **[13486]**, Caldwell, OH
Noble County Genealogical Soc. **[4086]**, Albion, IN
Noblesville Chamber of Commerce **[5978]**, Noblesville, IN
Noblesville Main St. **[5979]**, Noblesville, IN
NOCIRC of Michigan **[6966]**, Birmingham, MI
Non-Public Schools; Michigan Assn. of **[8621]**, Lansing, MI
Nonprofit Organizations
Michigan Nonprofit Assn. **[8690]**, Lansing, MI
Nonprofit Tech **[18585]**, Madison, WI
Soc. for Nonprofit Orgs. **[7073]**, Canton, MI
Nonprofit Tech **[18585]**, Madison, WI
Nonprofit Tech Association **[★18585]**
Nonviolence
Laurentian Shield Resources for Nonviolence **[18795]**, Maple, WI
Michiana Peace and Justice Coalition **[6243]**, South Bend, IN
Nordonia Hills Chamber of Commerce **[16254]**, Northfield, OH
Normal Wyldlife - Wyldlife **[2727]**, Normal, IL
Normal - Young Life **[302]**, Bloomington, IL
Norman S. Minor Bar Assn. **[14178]**, Cleveland, OH
NORML of Macomb County **[9566]**, Roseville, MI
NORML at the Univ. of Minnesota **[11708]**, Minneapolis, MN
North Adams Lions Club **[9214]**, North Adams, MI
North Amer. Butterfly Association-Duluth **[★10844]**
North Amer. Butterfly Assn. - Northeastern Ohio **[15412]**, Hartville, OH
North Amer. Butterfly Association-Northern Crescents Chap. **[10844]**, Duluth, MN
North Amer. Die Casting Assn. Southern Ohio Chap. 14 **[14934]**, Dayton, OH
North Amer. Die Casting Assn. West Michigan Chap. 3 **[7994]**, Grand Rapids, MI
North Amer. Horse and Mule Loggers Assn. **[11359]**, Lyle, MN
North Amer. Intl. Auto Show **[★9982]**
North Amer. Lake Mgt. Soc. **[18586]**, Madison, WI
North Amer. Naturists **[★3882]**
North Amer. Versatile Hunting Dog Assn. **[74]**, Arlington Heights, IL
North Aurora Lions Club **[2743]**, North Aurora, IL
North Baltimore Area Chamber of Commerce **[16211]**, North Baltimore, OH
North Bend Lions Club **[17944]**, Ettrick, WI
North Boone High School Chess Club **[3125]**, Poplar Grove, IL
North Br. Area Chamber of Commerce **[11900]**, North Branch, MN
North Br. Lions Club **[11901]**, North Branch, MN
North Bristol Sportsman's Club **[19862]**, Sun Prairie, WI
North Canton Area Chamber of Commerce **[16219]**, North Canton, OH
North Canton Lions Club **[16220]**, North Canton, OH
North Cape Yacht Club **[8785]**, Lasalle, MI
North Central Bus. Travel Assn. **[11709]**, Minneapolis, MN
North Central Chap. of the Amer. Assn. of Physicists in Medicine **[11710]**, Minneapolis, MN
North Central Chap., Infectious Diseases Soc. of Am. **[12861]**, Wayzata, MN
North Central Coll. Hea. Assn. **[18587]**, Madison, WI
North Central Conf. on Summer Schools **[19642]**, River Falls, WI
North Central Dental Soc. **[6248]**, South Bend, IN
North Central Elec. League **[10484]**, Bloomington, MN
North Central Environmental Balancing Bur. **[11711]**, Minneapolis, MN
North Central Hearth, Patio and Barbecue Assn. **[18588]**, Madison, WI
North Central Illinois FCA **[2728]**, Normal, IL
North Central Indiana AIFA **[5811]**, Mishawaka, IN
North Central Indiana Assn. of Realtors **[6050]**, Plymouth, IN
North Central Indiana Youth for Christ **[5740]**, Marion, IN
North Central LUGAS **[6581]**, Adrian, MI
North Central Morgan Horse Assn. **[10899]**, Eden Prairie, MN
North Central Mountain Bike Patrol **[10665]**, Circle Pines, MN
North Central Ohio AIFA **[16616]**, Sandusky, OH
North Central Ohio Angus Assn. **[13225]**, Attica, OH
North Central Ohio Planned Giving Coun. **[13168]**, Ashland, OH
North Central Ohio SCORE **[15780]**, Mansfield, OH
North Central Ohio Youth for Christ **[15781]**, Mansfield, OH
North Central Region of the Astronomical League **[17509]**, Appleton, WI
North Central Region Hea. Ministries Network **[11712]**, Minneapolis, MN
North Central Sect. of the Amer. Urological Assn. **[3440]**, Schaumburg, IL
North Central Weed Sci. Soc. **[541]**, Champaign, IL
North Central Wheelchair Athletic Assn. **[11064]**, Golden Valley, MN
North Central - Young Life **[5441]**, Indianapolis, IN
North Coast Building Indus. Assn. **[16652]**, Sheffield Village, OH
North Coast Chief Petty Officers Assn. **[14179]**, Cleveland, OH
North Coast Corvair Enthusiasts **[16338]**, Painesville, OH
North Coast Estate Planning Coun. **[15249]**, Fremont, OH
North Coast Fly Fishers **[16339]**, Painesville, OH
North Coast Fossil Club **[15452]**, Hinckley, OH
North Coast Lions Club **[17276]**, Willoughby, OH
North Coast Regional Chamber of Commerce **[13244]**, Avon Lake, OH
North Coast Triumph Assn. **[16501]**, Ravenna, OH
North Coast Women's Sailing Assn. **[15589]**, Lakewood, OH
North Coast Woodturners **[13074]**, Akron, OH
North Country Appaloosa Horse Club **[12648]**, Sebeka, MN
North Country Lib. Cooperative **[11852]**, Mountain Iron, MN
North Country Region USA Volleyball **[10653]**, Chaska, MN
North Country Trail Assn. **[8864]**, Lowell, MI
North East Ohio Dairy Goat Assn. **[16631]**, Seville, OH
North East Ohio Vette Club **[13232]**, Aurora, OH
North East Wisconsin Corvair Club **[19398]**, Oshkosh, WI
North East Wisconsin Optometric Soc. **[19841]**, Sturgeon Bay, WI
North Eastern Michigan Indus. Assn. **[10131]**, West Branch, MI
North Eastern Ohio Amer. Assn. of Diabetes Educators **[14180]**, Cleveland, OH
North Eastern Ohio Educ. Assn. **[16381]**, Parma Heights, OH
North Eastern Ohio Orienteering Club **[14181]**, Cleveland, OH
North End Club **[13184]**, Ashtabula, OH
North Fairfield Lions Club **[16227]**, North Fairfield, OH
North Hennepin Area Chamber of Commerce **[11953]**, Osseo, MN
North Jackson Lions Club **[8392]**, Jackson, MI
North Lansing Lions Club **[7562]**, East Lansing, MI
North Macomb Sportsman Club **[10078]**, Washington, MI
North Manchester Chamber of Commerce **[5988]**, North Manchester, IN
North Manchester Fellowship of Reconciliation **[5989]**, North Manchester, IN
North Metro I-35W Corridor Coalition **[10555]**, Brooklyn Park, MN
North Metro Muskies **[12031]**, Plymouth, MN
North Metro Realtors Assn. **[10714]**, Coon Rapids, MN
North Newton Area Chamber of Commerce **[6140]**, Roselawn, IN
North Oakland County Bd. of Realtors **[10090]**, Waterford, MI
North Ohio Natl. Org. for the Reform of Marijuana Laws **[15687]**, Lodi, OH
North Olmsted Businessmen's Assn. **[★16236]**
North Olmsted Chamber of Commerce **[16236]**, North Olmsted, OH
North Ottawa Rod and Gun Club **[7864]**, Grand Haven, MI
North Point Charter Boat Assn. **[4042]**, Winthrop Harbor, IL
North Ridgeville Chamber of Commerce/Visitors Bur. **[16242]**, North Ridgeville, OH
North Ridgeville Lions Club **[16243]**, North Ridgeville, OH
North River Commn. **[1102]**, Chicago, IL
North Royalton Alumni Assn. **[13413]**, Brecksville, OH
North Royalton Chamber of Commerce **[16246]**, North Royalton, OH
North Royalton Lions Club **[16247]**, North Royalton, OH
North Royalton - Young Life **[16248]**, North Royalton, OH
North St. Louis County Habitat for Humanity **[12802]**, Virginia, MN
North Shore-Barrington Assn. of Realtors **[2759]**, Northbrook, IL
North Shore and Chicago Chap. of the MOAA **[2267]**, Libertyville, IL
North Shore Cricket Club **[1103]**, Chicago, IL
North Shore Dog Training Club **[3489]**, Skokie, IL
North Shore Musicians Club **[2920]**, Palatine, IL
North Shore Philatelic Soc. **[1104]**, Chicago, IL
North Shore Philatelic Soc. APS Chap. No. 623 **[★19084]**
North Shore Philatelic Soc. of Milwaukee **[19084]**, Milwaukee, WI
North Star African Violet Coun. **[10309]**, Anoka, MN
North Star Figure Skating Assn. **[7135]**, Cheboygan, MI
North Star Gay Rodeo Assn. **[12555]**, St. Paul, MN
North Star Habitat for Humanity **[9723]**, Sault Ste. Marie, MI
North Star Historical Bottle Assn. **[11713]**, Minneapolis, MN
North Suburban Gays **[4020]**, Wilmette, IL
North Suburban United Way **[2760]**, Northbrook, IL
North Webster - Tippecanoe Township Chamber of Commerce **[6000]**, North Webster, IN
North West Sailing Assn. **[75]**, Arlington Heights, IL
North Western Insulator Club **[12642]**, Savage, MN
North Wisconsin District, The Lutheran Church-Missouri Synod **[20043]**, Wausau, WI
North - Young Life **[4249]**, Bloomington, IN
Northalsted Area Merchants Association **[1105]**, Chicago, IL
Northarvest Bean Growers Assn. **[11029]**, Frazee, MN
Northbrook Chamber of Commerce **[★2761]**
Northbrook Chamber of Commerce and Indus. **[2761]**, Northbrook, IL
Northbrook Sports Club **[1896]**, Grayslake, IL
Northcoast (Lake County-Cleveland) Senior Olympics **[14778]**, Concord Township, OH
Northcoast Naturists **[★14187]**
Northcrest Elementary School PTA **[4701]**, Fort Wayne, IN
Northeast Cincinnati Chamber of Commerce **[15877]**, Mason, OH

Northeast Grand Rapids Young Life [7995], Grand Rapids, MI
Northeast Indiana Angus Assn. [5800], Milford, IN
Northeast Indiana Constr. Alliance [4702], Fort Wayne, IN
Northeast Indiana Human Rsrc. Assn. [4703], Fort Wayne, IN
Northeast Indiana Youth for Christ [4141], Auburn, IN
Northeast Iowa Angus Breeders Assn. [11362], Mabel, MN
Northeast Michigan Community Partnership [6646], Alpena, MI
Northeast MMBA [9038], Midland, MI
Northeast Ohio AIFA [16340], Painesville, OH
Northeast Ohio Alumni Extension - Natl. Soc. of Black Engineers [14182], Cleveland, OH
Northeast Ohio Amer. Soc. for Training and Development [13075], Akron, OH
Northeast Ohio Apartment Assn. [14183], Cleveland, OH
Northeast Ohio Applied Systems Users Gp. [16374], Parma, OH
Northeast Ohio Assn. for Computing Machinery SIGGRAPH [14184], Cleveland, OH
Northeast Ohio Chap. of Proj. Mgt. Inst. [15974], Mentor, OH
Northeast Ohio Coalition for the Homeless [14185], Cleveland, OH
Northeast Ohio CoDA Community [17015], Twinsburg, OH
Northeast Ohio Coin Club [15975], Mentor, OH
Northeast Ohio Concrete Promotion Council [16627], Seven Hills, OH
Northeast Ohio Hea. Info. Mgt. Assn. [14186], Cleveland, OH
Northeast Ohio Romance Writers of Am. [17233], Westlake, OH
Northeast Ohio Translators Assn. [16681], Solon, OH
Northeast Ohio's Northcoast Naturists [14187], Cleveland, OH
Northeast Wisconsin Appaloosa Horse Club [19500], Port Washington, WI
Northeast Wisconsin Assn. for Career and Tech. Educ. [★18123]
Northeast Wisconsin Building and Constr. Trades Coun. [17510], Appleton, WI
Northeast Wisconsin Building and Trades Coun. [★17510]
Northeast Wisconsin Chap. of the APA [18122], Green Bay, WI
Northeast Wisconsin District Nurses Assn. - No. 9 [18330], Krakow, WI
Northeast Wisconsin Families with Children from China [18863], Menasha, WI
Northeast Wisconsin Stargazers [19399], Oshkosh, WI
Northeast Wisconsin Tech. Coll. [18123], Green Bay, WI
Northeast Wisconsin Vocational Assn. [★18123]
Northeastern District Dental Soc., Michigan [6647], Alpena, MI
Northeastern District Dental Soc., Minnesota [10845], Duluth, MN
Northeastern Illinois Chap., Natl. Elecl. Contractors Assn. [3941], West Chicago, IL
Northeastern Illinois Planning Commn. [1106], Chicago, IL
Northeastern Illinois Sheet Metal Contractors Assn. [1598], Elgin, IL
Northeastern Indiana Assn. of Realtors [5551], Kendallville, IN
Northeastern Indiana Kennel Club [4704], Fort Wayne, IN
Northeastern Lions Club [16321], Owensville, OH
Northeastern Michigan Bd. of Realtors [8098], Hale, MI
Northeastern Michigan Estate Planning Coun. [9623], Saginaw, MI
Northeastern Ohio Angus Assn. [16809], Summitville, OH
Northeastern Wisconsin Area Local Amer. Postal Workers Union [18124], Green Bay, WI
Northeastern Wisconsin Beagle Club [18125], Green Bay, WI
Northeastern Wisconsin Orchid Soc. [17725], Cecil, WI
Northeastern Wisconsin RSVP [19600], Rhinelander, WI
Northern AIFA [12803], Virginia, MN
Northern Blades Figure Skating Club [10451], Blaine, MN
Northern Dakota County Chamber of Commerce [10872], Eagan, MN
Northern Flight Hunting Retriever Assn. [12701], Stacy, MN
Northern Flyway Golden Retriever Club of Am. [18821], Marshfield, WI
Northern Ice Skating Club [2882], Orland Park, IL
Northern Illinois Air Conditioning Contractors of Am. [1466], Des Plaines, IL
Northern Illinois Angus Assn. [2495], Milledgeville, IL
Northern Illinois Assn. of Teachers of Mathematics [3292], Rockford, IL
Northern Illinois Beagle Club [17614], Beloit, WI
Northern Illinois BMW Riders No. 271 [3942], West Chicago, IL
Northern Illinois Building Contractors Assn. [3293], Rockford, IL
Northern Illinois Chap. Assn. of Rehabilitation Nurses [2658], Naperville, IL
Northern Illinois Chap. of the Military Vehicle Assn. [2061], Indian Head Park, IL
Northern Illinois Chap. Natl. Elecl. Contractors Assn. [3294], Rockford, IL
Northern Illinois Commercial Assn. of Realtors [3994], Wheaton, IL
Northern Illinois Corvette Club [3295], Rockford, IL
Northern Illinois Dairy Goat Assn. [1751], Freeport, IL
Northern Illinois Deaf Golf Assn. [1107], Chicago, IL
Northern Illinois Estate Planning Coun. [3296], Rockford, IL
Northern Illinois Fiero Enthusiasts [2659], Naperville, IL
Northern Illinois Orienteering Club [3714], Stockton, IL
Northern Illinois Saint Bernard Club [1951], Harvard, IL
Northern Illinois Univ. Fencing Club [1440], DeKalb, IL
Northern Illinois Woodturners [3297], Rockford, IL
Northern Indiana Arts Assn. [5905], Munster, IN
Northern Indiana Chap. of Assoc. Locksmiths of Am. [4705], Fort Wayne, IN
Northern Indiana Chap., Natl. Elecl. Contractors Assn. [5790], Michigan City, IN
Northern Indiana Draft Horse Breeders [5803], Millersburg, IN
Northern Indiana Mountain Bicycling Assn. [6249], South Bend, IN
Northern Indiana Sheet Metal Contractors Assn. [4927], Hobart, IN
Northern Indiana TAM Users Gp. [4918], Highland, IN
Northern Lakes District Nurses Assn. - No. 14 [19200], Minocqua, WI
Northern Lights Amer. Eskimo Dog Assn. [12556], St. Paul, MN
Northern Lights Ballroom Dance Club [11985], Pelican Rapids, MN
Northern Lights Goat Assn. [7632], Ewen, MI
Northern Lights Lib. Network [10782], Detroit Lakes, MN
Northern Lights Peruvian House Club [17818], Deer Park, WI
Northern Lights Sams [9309], Ontonagon, MI
Northern Metro Convention and Tourism Bur. [★11615]
Northern Michigan Appaloosa Horse Club [8064], Grayling, MI
Northern Michigan Univ. Figure Skating Club [8955], Marquette, MI
Northern Ohio Beagle Club [16277], Oakwood Village, OH
Northern Ohio Br. of the Intl. Dyslexia Assn. [16682], Solon, OH
Northern Ohio Br. of the Orton Dyslexia Soc. [★16682]
Northern Ohio Draft Pony Assn. [13226], Attica, OH
Northern Ohio Dressage Assn. [16683], Solon, OH
Northern Ohio Electrical Contractors Association [15590], Lakewood, OH
Northern Ohio Golf Assn. [16237], North Olmsted, OH
Northern Ohio Model "A" Club [13185], Ashtabula, OH
Northern Ohio Painting and Taping Contractors Assn. [15998], Middleburg Heights, OH
Northern Ohio Valley Astronomy Educators [16571], St. Clairsville, OH
Northern Ohio Vascular Assn. [14188], Cleveland, OH
Northern Ohio Wellness Connection [17087], Walton Hills, OH
Northern Star Camp Fire Coun. [★11821]
Northern Thumb District Dental Soc. [7095], Cass City, MI
Northfield Area Chamber of Commerce [11916], Northfield, MN
Northfield Area United Way [11917], Northfield, MN
Northlake Chamber of Commerce [2766], Northlake, IL
Northland Area Builders Assn. [18198], Hayward, WI
Northland Area Building Authority [★18198]
Northland Chap. of Falcon Club of Am. [10322], Apple Valley, MN
Northland Human Rsrc. Assn. [10846], Duluth, MN
Northland Senior Games [10847], Duluth, MN
Northmont Lions Club [15132], Englewood, OH
Northport Lions Club [9218], Northport, MI
Northside Wyldlife - Wyldlife [1108], Chicago, IL
NorthStar Trail Travelers [11714], Minneapolis, MN
Northstar Weimaraner Club [11224], Inver Grove Heights, MN
Northview - Wyldlife [5442], Indianapolis, IN
Northview - Young Life [16827], Sylvania, OH
Northville Chamber of Commerce [9226], Northville, MI
Northville Historical Soc. [9227], Northville, MI
Northville Lions Club [9228], Northville, MI
Northwest Agri-Dealers Assn. [11395], Mankato, MN
Northwest Coin Club [11715], Minneapolis, MN
Northwest Cultural Coun. [3341], Rolling Meadows, IL
Northwest Human Rsrcs. Coun. [474], Cary, IL
Northwest Illinois Audubon Soc. [2980], Pearl City, IL
Northwest Illinois Rock Club [2868], Oregon, IL
Northwest Indiana AIFA [5777], Merrillville, IN
Northwest Indiana Angus Breeders Assn. [6436], Walkerton, IN
Northwest Indiana Dental Soc. [5778], Merrillville, IN
Northwest Indiana Habitat for Humanity [4888], Hammond, IN
Northwest Indiana Independent Elecl. Contractors [★6166]
Northwest Indiana Youth for Christ [6386], Valparaiso, IN
Northwest Lions Club [15892], Massillon, OH
Northwest Macomb Chamber of Commerce [★9870]
Northwest Michigan Coun. of Governments [9943], Traverse City, MI
Northwest Minnesota Community Housing Development Org. [★11462]
Northwest Minnesota Multi-County Housing and Redevelopment Authority [11462], Mentor, MN
Northwest Neighborhood Fed. [1109], Chicago, IL
Northwest Ohio Amer. Indus. Hygiene Assn. [13395], Bowling Green, OH
Northwest Ohio Applied Systems Users Gp. [16580], St. Marys, OH
Northwest Ohio Black Media Assn. [16939], Toledo, OH
Northwest Ohio Chap. of the Assn. of Legal Administrators [16940], Toledo, OH
Northwest Ohio Dietary Managers Assn. [16303], Oregon, OH
Northwest Ohio District of Precision Metalforming Assn. [16828], Sylvania, OH
Northwest Ohio Hea. Info. Mgt. Assn. [16941], Toledo, OH
Northwest Ohio Hemophilia Found. [16942], Toledo, OH
Northwest Ohio Mayors and Managers Assn. [16943], Toledo, OH
Northwest Ohio Traditional Music and Dance [16829], Sylvania, OH
Northwest Passage Outing Club [4021], Wilmette, IL
Northwest Regional Builders Exchange [17890], Eau Claire, WI
Northwest Regional Planning Commn. [19762], Spooner, WI

Northwest RSVP **[17545]**, Ashland, WI
Northwest Suburban Alliance for Commerce and Indus. **[3342]**, Rolling Meadows, IL
Northwest Suburban Astronomers **[3441]**, Schaumburg, IL
Northwest Suburban Chamber of Commerce **[10721]**, Corcoran, MN
Northwest Suburban Jewish Community Center **[364]**, Buffalo Grove, IL
Northwest Suburban United Way **[2590]**, Mount Prospect, IL
Northwest Tonka Lions Club **[12666]**, Shorewood, MN
Northwest Wisconsin Gem and Mineral Soc. **[17464]**, Almena, WI
Northwestern District Dental Soc., Minnesota **[11024]**, Fosston, MN
Northwestern Illinois Golf Course Superintendents Assn. **[186]**, Batavia, IL
Northwestern Indiana Beagle Club **[5600]**, La Porte, IN
Northwestern Indiana Nurserymen's Assn. **[4928]**, Hobart, IN
Northwestern Lumber Assn. **[11716]**, Minneapolis, MN
Northwestern Michigan Orchid Soc. **[8478]**, Kalkaska, MI
Northwestern Ohio Bd. of Realtors **[14991]**, Defiance, OH
Northwestern Ohio Golf Course Superintendents Assn. **[15212]**, Findlay, OH
Northwestern Soc. for Coatings Tech. **[12557]**, St. Paul, MN
Northwestern Wisconsin AIFA **[19614]**, Rice Lake, WI
Northwestern - Young Life **[16736]**, Springfield, OH
Northwood Middle School PTSA **[4706]**, Fort Wayne, IN
Northwoods Area of Narcotics Anonymous **[7221]**, Conway, MI
Northwoods Assn. of Realtors **[20206]**, Woodruff, WI
Northwoods Figure Skating Club **[19724]**, Shell Lake, WI
Northwoods Humane Soc. **[11019]**, Forest Lake, MN
Northwoods United Way **[19601]**, Rhinelander, WI
Norwalk Area Chamber of Commerce **[16262]**, Norwalk, OH
Norwalk Lions Club **[16263]**, Norwalk, OH
Norwalk Lions Club - Wisconsin **[19327]**, Norwalk, WI
Norwayne - Young Life **[17323]**, Wooster, OH
Norwegian
Sons of Norway, Arctic Circle Lodge 5-662 **[13120]**, Alliance, OH
Sons of Norway, Askeladden Lodge 5-610 **[8468]**, Kalamazoo, MI
Sons of Norway, Bemidji Lodge 1-500 **[10427]**, Bemidji, MN
Sons of Norway, Birkebeiner Lodge 5-611 **[17588]**, Bayfield, WI
Sons of Norway, Bjorgvin Lodge 1-10 **[10435]**, Benson, MN
Sons of Norway, Christian Radich Lodge 5-568 **[9219]**, Northport, MI
Sons of Norway, Circle City Lodge 5-614 **[6553]**, Zionsville, IN
Sons of Norway, Cleng Peerson Lodge 5-525 **[2900]**, Ottawa, IL
Sons of Norway, Dovre Lodge 5-353 **[19630]**, Ridgeland, WI
Sons of Norway, Draxten Lodge 1-464 **[12590]**, St. Paul, MN
Sons of Norway, Edvard Grieg Lodge 5-657 **[16446]**, Pleasant Plain, OH
Sons of Norway, Elvedal Lodge 5-556 **[19283]**, Nekoosa, WI
Sons of Norway, Elvesund Lodge 5-593 **[3963]**, Western Springs, IL
Sons of Norway, Elvesvingen Lodge 1-582 **[11400]**, Mankato, MN
Sons of Norway, Elvidal Lodge 1-509 **[10673]**, Clarkfield, MN
Sons of Norway, Fagernes Lodge 5-616 **[17638]**, Blair, WI
Sons of Norway, Fedraheimen Lodge 1-59 **[12927]**, Willmar, MN
Sons of Norway, Fjell Syn Lodge 1-667 **[12591]**, St. Paul, MN
Sons of Norway, Fjordland Lodge 5-606 **[2462]**, McHenry, IL
Sons of Norway, F.M. Christiansen Lodge 5-624 **[19520]**, Porterfield, WI
Sons of Norway, Fosselyngen Lodge 5-82 **[19122]**, Milwaukee, WI
Sons of Norway, Fossen Lodge 5-534 **[17634]**, Black River Falls, WI
Sons of Norway, Gjemtedal Lodge 5-639 **[19627]**, Richland Center, WI
Sons of Norway, Granlund Lodge 1-240 **[11105]**, Gully, MN
Sons of Norway, Gronnvik Lodge 5-632 **[18135]**, Green Bay, WI
Sons of Norway, H R Holand Lodge 5-549 **[19844]**, Sturgeon Bay, WI
Sons of Norway, Haarfager Lodge 1-40 **[12807]**, Virginia, MN
Sons of Norway, Hafrsfjord Lodge 5-206 **[18312]**, Kenosha, WI
Sons of Norway, Heimbygda Lodge 1-376 **[11303]**, Lanesboro, MN
Sons of Norway, Heimskringla Lodge 1-12 **[11004]**, Fergus Falls, MN
Sons of Norway, Heimsyn Lodge 1-15 **[10965]**, Esko, MN
Sons of Norway, Henrik Ibsen Lodge 4-565 **[10792]**, Doran, MN
Sons of Norway, Hjemkomst Lodge 1-599 **[11130]**, Hastings, MN
Sons of Norway, Idun Lodge 5-74 **[19863]**, Sun Prairie, WI
Sons of Norway, Jaabaek Lodge 1-264 **[11805]**, Montevideo, MN
Sons of Norway, Jotunheimen Lodge 5-286 **[19942]**, Viroqua, WI
Sons of Norway, Kenyon Viking Lodge 1-487 **[11255]**, Kenyon, MN
Sons of Norway, Knute Rockne Lodge 5-634 **[6265]**, South Bend, IN
Sons of Norway, Kristiania Lodge 1-47 **[12190]**, Rochester, MN
Sons of Norway, Lauris Norstad Lodge 1-558 **[12086]**, Red Wing, MN
Sons of Norway, Leif Erikson Lodge 1-32 **[12790]**, Vining, MN
Sons of Norway, Leif Erikson Lodge 5-97 **[1512]**, Downers Grove, IL
Sons of Norway, Lin-Hans-Rud Lodge 1-479 **[11401]**, Mankato, MN
Sons of Norway, Lincolnland Lodge 5-598 **[3471]**, Sherman, IL
Sons of Norway, Loven Lodge 5-29 **[17901]**, Eau Claire, WI
Sons of Norway, Midnatsolen Lodge 1-58 **[11988]**, Pengilly, MN
Sons of Norway, Mjosen Lodge 1-175 **[11055]**, Glenwood, MN
Sons of Norway, Morgensol Lodge 1-458 **[10739]**, Crookston, MN
Sons of Norway, Myrmarken Lodge 5-609 **[18824]**, Marshfield, WI
Sons of Norway, Nidaros Lodge 1-1 **[10298]**, Andover, MN
Sons of Norway, Nor-Win Lodge 1-505 **[12958]**, Winona, MN
Sons of Norway, Nordkap Lodge 5-378 **[6769]**, Ann Arbor, MI
Sons of Norway, Nordland Lodge 1-492 **[12764]**, Twin Valley, MN
Sons of Norway, Nordlandet Lodge 5-620 **[18201]**, Hazelhurst, WI
Sons of Norway, Nordlys Lodge 1-498 **[12837]**, Wannaska, MN
Sons of Norway, Nordlyset Lodge 5-183 **[19573]**, Racine, WI
Sons of Norway, Nordmarka Lodge 1-585 **[10987]**, Faribault, MN
Sons of Norway, Nordskogen Lodge 1-626 **[11980]**, Park Rapids, MN
Sons of Norway, Nordstjernen Lodge 1-563 **[11428]**, Marcell, MN
Sons of Norway, Normanna Lodge 1-52 **[10263]**, Albert Lea, MN
Sons of Norway, Nornen Lodge 1-41 **[11368]**, Madison, MN
Sons of Norway, Norrona Lodge 5-27 **[19749]**, South Range, WI
Sons of Norway, Norse Valley Lodge 5-491 **[17525]**, Appleton, WI
Sons of Norway, Norsemen Of Lakes Lodge 5-650 **[19830]**, Stoughton, WI
Sons of Norway, Norskeland Lodge 5-580 **[18236]**, Iola, WI
Sons of Norway, Norskfodt Lodge 1-590 **[11842]**, Morris, MN
Sons of Norway, Norsota Lodge 1-602 **[12592]**, St. Paul, MN
Sons of Norway, Nortun Lodge 1-16 **[10855]**, Duluth, MN
Sons of Norway, Norumbega Lodge 1-217 **[10609]**, Burnsville, MN
Sons of Norway, Oslo Lodge 1-2 **[11750]**, Minneapolis, MN
Sons of Norway, Ostestaden Lodge 5-642 **[19218]**, Monroe, WI
Sons of Norway, Polar Star Lodge 5-472 **[131]**, Aurora, IL
Sons of Norway, Rib Fjell Lodge 5-496 **[20048]**, Wausau, WI
Sons of Norway, Runic Vennskap Lodge 1-530 **[10285]**, Alexandria, MN
Sons of Norway, Sagatun Lodge 1-18 **[10521]**, Brainerd, MN
Sons of Norway, Samhold Lodge 5-473 **[10094]**, Waterford, MI
Sons of Norway, Scandiana Lodge 5-600 **[6390]**, Valparaiso, IN
Sons of Norway, Sjoland Lodge 5-635 **[17764]**, Clear Lake, WI
Sons of Norway, Skjold Lodge 5-100 **[83]**, Arlington Heights, IL
Sons of Norway, Skogvannet Lodge 1-658 **[11021]**, Fort Benedict, MN
Sons of Norway, Snorre Lodge 1-70 **[12749]**, Thief River Falls, MN
Sons of Norway, Sognefjord Lodge 5-523 **[9162]**, Muskegon, MI
Sons of Norway, Solheim Lodge 5-278 **[17653]**, Boyceville, WI
Sons of Norway, Solvang Lodge 5-457 **[20143]**, Westby, WI
Sons of Norway, Sonja Henie Lodge 5-490 **[8761]**, Lansing, MI
Sons of Norway, Sor Vest Viskonsin Lodge 5-629 **[17958]**, Fennimore, WI
Sons of Norway, Stavanger Lodge 1-538 **[11153]**, Heron Lake, MN
Sons of Norway, Stenlandet Lodge 1-640 **[10905]**, Edgerton, MN
Sons of Norway, Storting Lodge 1-519 **[10360]**, Austin, MN
Sons of Norway, Synnove-Nordkap Lodge 1-8 **[12663]**, Shoreview, MN
Sons of Norway, Syttende Mai Lodge 1-517 **[12817]**, Waconia, MN
Sons of Norway, Terje Viken Lodge 1-17 **[12773]**, Two Harbors, MN
Sons of Norway, Tordenskjold Lodge 1-55 **[11111]**, Halstad, MN
Sons of Norway, Tre Elver Lodge 5-628 **[4720]**, Fort Wayne, IN
Sons of Norway, Trollhaugen Lodge 5-417 **[6391]**, Valparaiso, IN
Sons of Norway, Trollheim Lodge 1-511 **[11339]**, Little Falls, MN
Sons of Norway, Trygvason Lodge 5-220 **[19413]**, Osseo, WI
Sons of Norway, Tusenvann Lodge 1-659 **[11231]**, Isle, MN
Sons of Norway, Vakkertland Lodge 5-570 **[19515]**, Portage, WI
Sons of Norway, Valheim Lodge 1-364 **[12689]**, Spring Grove, MN
Sons of Norway, Valkyrien Lodge 5-53 **[20208]**, Woodville, WI
Sons of Norway, Vennekretsen Lodge 1-559 **[10719]**, Coon Rapids, MN
Sons of Norway, Vennelag Lodge 1-546 **[11318]**, Lindstrom, MN
Sons of Norway, Vennelag Lodge 5-513 **[19934]**, Verona, WI
Sons of Norway, Vennligfolk Lodge 5-627 **[19807]**, Stevens Point, WI
Sons of Norway, Vennskap Lodge 1-554 **[10629]**, Canby, MN

Sons of Norway, Vennskap Lodge 5-622 **[19714]**, Sheboygan, WI
Sons of Norway, Vestland Lodge 1-601 **[11193]**, Hopkins, MN
Sons of Norway, Viking Lodge 5-625 **[19205]**, Mondovi, WI
Sons of Norway, Vikingland Lodge 1-495 **[10784]**, Detroit Lakes, MN
Sons of Norway, Vinland Lodge 1-193 **[10439]**, Big Falls, MN
Sons of Norway, Vonheim Lodge 1-108 **[10873]**, Eagan, MN
Sons of Norway, Wergeland Lodge 5-28 **[19370]**, Onalaska, WI
Norwegian Elkhound Assn. of Minnesota **[11430]**, Marine on St. Croix, MN
Norwood Park Chamber of Commerce and Indus. **[1110]**, Chicago, IL
Not In Your Name, Ohio - Cleveland **[14189]**, Cleveland, OH
Nova Lions Club **[16268]**, Nova, OH
Novi Chamber of Commerce **[9241]**, Novi, MI
Novi High School Skating Club **[9242]**, Novi, MI
NPPA Region 5 **[11065]**, Golden Valley, MN
NSA-Minnesota Chap. **[★12030]**

Nuclear
Amer. Nuclear Soc., Central Illinois Sect. **[1271]**, Clinton, IL
Amer. Nuclear Soc., Ohio Sect. **[16402]**, Perrysburg, OH
Amer. Nuclear Soc., Wisconsin **[18467]**, Madison, WI
Chicago Local Sect. of the Amer. Nuclear Soc. **[1498]**, Downers Grove, IL
Michigan Sect. of the Amer. Nuclear Soc. **[6735]**, Ann Arbor, MI
Peace Action Wisconsin **[19089]**, Milwaukee, WI

Nuclear Medicine
Central Chap. of the Soc. of Nuclear Medicine **[372]**, Burr Ridge, IL
Soc. of Nuclear Medicine - Southeastern Chaps. **[13994]**, Cincinnati, OH
Nuclear Medicine; Central Chap. of the Soc. of **[372]**, Burr Ridge, IL

Nuclear War and Weapons
Columbus Campaign for Arms Control **[14376]**, Columbus, OH
Illinois Peace Action **[955]**, Chicago, IL

Nudism
Chicago Sun Club **[3882]**, Wasco, IL
Northeast Ohio's Northcoast Naturists **[14187]**, Cleveland, OH

Numismatic
Ancient Coin Club of Chicago **[732]**, Chicago, IL
Central Illinois Numismatic Assn. **[1379]**, Decatur, IL
Chicago Coin Club **[803]**, Chicago, IL
Cincinnati Numismatic Assn. **[13793]**, Cincinnati, OH
Clark County Coin Club **[16724]**, Springfield, OH
Dixon Coin Club **[1734]**, Franklin Grove, IL
Dupo Coin Club **[1695]**, Fairview Heights, IL
Eastlake Coin Club **[15966]**, Mentor, OH
Elgin Coin Club **[3497]**, South Elgin, IL
Evansville Coin Club **[4545]**, Evansville, IN
Flint Flying Eagle Coin Club **[7685]**, Fenton, MI
Fostoria Coin Club **[14434]**, Columbus, OH
Glass Center Coin Club **[15457]**, Holland, OH
Greene County Coin Club **[4192]**, Bloomfield, IN
Hillside Coin Club **[2006]**, Hillside, IL
Illinois Numismatic Assn. **[2520]**, Moline, IL
Indiana State Numismatic Assn. **[4107]**, Anderson, IN
Indianapolis Coin Club **[5343]**, Indianapolis, IN
Kalamazoo Numismatic Club **[9449]**, Portage, MI
Lake County Coin Club **[3926]**, Waukegan, IL
Ludington Coin Club **[8873]**, Ludington, MI
Marion Coin Club **[5737]**, Marion, IN
Metro East Coin and Currency Club **[207]**, Belleville, IL
Michigan State Numismatic Soc. **[7068]**, Canton, MI
Milwaukee Numismatic Soc. **[19065]**, Milwaukee, WI
Monroe Coin Club **[10185]**, Wyandotte, MI
Nicolet Coin Club **[18121]**, Green Bay, WI
Northeast Ohio Coin Club **[15975]**, Mentor, OH
Northwest Coin Club **[11715]**, Minneapolis, MN
Oak Forest Numismatic Soc. **[2791]**, Oak Forest, IL
Ohio State Numismatic Assn. **[17016]**, Twinsburg, OH
Ohio Valley Coin Assn. **[16766]**, Steubenville, OH
Old Fort Coin Club **[4707]**, Fort Wayne, IN
Paper Money Collectors of Michigan **[9341]**, Oxford, MI
Racine Numismatic Soc. **[19570]**, Racine, WI
Rochester Coin and Stamp Club **[12175]**, Rochester, MN
Rockford Area Coin Club **[587]**, Cherry Valley, IL
Royal Oak Coin Club **[9591]**, Royal Oak, MI
St. Paul Liberty Coin Club **[12583]**, St. Paul, MN
Sheboygan Coin Club **[19709]**, Sheboygan, WI
Shelby County Coin Club **[16667]**, Sidney, OH
South Shore Coin Club **[19124]**, Milwaukee, WI
Tazewell Numismatic Soc. **[3065]**, Peoria, IL
Tuscarawas County Coin Club **[15034]**, Dover, OH
Wabash Valley Coin Club **[6350]**, Terre Haute, IN
Warrensville Heights Coin Club **[16685]**, Solon, OH
Waukesha Coin Club **[20002]**, Waukesha, WI
Western Reserve Numismatic Club **[16629]**, Seven Hills, OH
Will County Coin Club **[2694]**, New Lenox, IL
Youngstown Numismatic Club **[17428]**, Youngstown, OH
Nurse Assn. of Greater Youngstown; Visiting **[17420]**, Youngstown, OH
Nurse Assn. of Ohio; Visiting **[★14234]**

Nurseries
Illinois Nurserymen's Assn. **[3621]**, Springfield, IL
Indiana Nursery and Landscape Assn. **[5269]**, Indianapolis, IN
Kalamazoo Valley Landscape and Nursery Assn. **[8446]**, Kalamazoo, MI
Michigan Green Indus. Assn. **[6955]**, Bingham Farms, MI
Minnesota Nursery and Landscape Assn. **[12501]**, St. Paul, MN
Northwestern Indiana Nurserymen's Assn. **[4928]**, Hobart, IN
Wisconsin Nursery Assn. **[18162]**, Greenfield, WI
Nursery and Landscape Assn; Minnesota **[12501]**, St. Paul, MN
Nursery and Landscape Assn; Ohio **[17217]**, Westerville, OH
Nurses Assn. of Illinois; Licensed Practical **[1029]**, Chicago, IL
Nurses Assn; Indiana State **[5321]**, Indianapolis, IN
Nurses Assn; Mennonite **[4801]**, Goshen, IN
Nurses Assn; Michigan **[9287]**, Okemos, MI
Nurses Assn; Michigan Licensed Practical **[8683]**, Lansing, MI
Nurses Assn; Minnesota **[12502]**, St. Paul, MN
Nurses Assn; Ohio **[14646]**, Columbus, OH
Nurses' Assn; Wisconsin **[18737]**, Madison, WI
Nurses; Chicagoland Gerontological Advanced Practice **[3200]**, River Forest, IL
Nurses, Greater Chicago Area Chap; Amer. Assn. of Critical Care **[607]**, Chicago, IL
Nurses, Greater Toledo Area Chap; Amer. Assn. of Critical-Care **[16875]**, Toledo, OH
Nurses, Lake Superior Chap; Amer. Assn. of Critical-Care **[9176]**, Negaunee, MI

Nursing
Akron Black Nurses Assn. (16) **[16836]**, Tallmadge, OH
Amer. Assn. of Critical Care Nurses, Greater Akron Area Chap. **[13511]**, Canal Fulton, OH
Amer. Assn. of Critical Care Nurses, North Central Wisconsin Chap. **[19778]**, Stevens Point, WI
Amer. Assn. of Critical Care Nurses, West Michigan Chap. **[6914]**, Belmont, MI
Amer. Assn. of Neuroscience Nurses, Kentuckiana Chap. **[4363]**, Clarksville, IN
Amer. Nurses Assn. - Bay Area Medical Center, Prof LSC **[18798]**, Marinette, WI
Assn. of Women's Hea., Obstetric and Neonatal Nurses - Bloomington Chap. **[4202]**, Bloomington, IN
Assn. of Women's Hea., Obstetric and Neonatal Nurses - Evansville Chap. **[6316]**, Terre Haute, IN
Assn. of Women's Hea., Obstetric and Neonatal Nurses, Illinois Sect. **[2878]**, Orland Park, IL
Assn. of Women's Hea., Obstetric and Neonatal Nurses, Indiana Sect. **[5052]**, Indianapolis, IN
Assn. of Women's Hea., Obstetric and Neonatal Nurses - Indianapolis Chap. **[5053]**, Indianapolis, IN
Assn. of Women's Hea., Obstetric and Neonatal Nurses - Lafayette/ Sagamore Chap. **[6478]**, West Lafayette, IN
Assn. of Women's Hea., Obstetric and Neonatal Nurses - Marian/ Anderson/Muncie Chap. **[5869]**, Muncie, IN
Assn. of Women's Hea., Obstetric and Neonatal Nurses - Michiana Chap. **[4808]**, Granger, IN
Assn. of Women's Hea., Obstetric and Neonatal Nurses - Michigan Sect. **[6879]**, Bay City, MI
Assn. of Women's Hea., Obstetric and Neonatal Nurses - Northeast Chap. **[5675]**, Leo, IN
Assn. of Women's Hea., Obstetric and Neonatal Nurses - Northwest Chap. **[6061]**, Porter, IN
Assn. of Women's Hea., Obstetric and Neonatal Nurses - Ohio Sect. **[13621]**, Centerville, OH
Assn. of Women's Hea., Obstetric and Neonatal Nurses, Southern Illinois Chap. **[2768]**, O Fallon, IL
Assn. of Women's Hea., Obstetric and Neonatal Nurses - West Central Illiana Chap. **[6317]**, Terre Haute, IN
Black Nurses Assn. of Greater Cincinnati (18) **[13761]**, Cincinnati, OH
Central Minnesota Area Chap. of the Amer. Assn. of Critical Care Nurses **[12278]**, St. Cloud, MN
Chicago Chap. Black Nurses Assn. (09) **[800]**, Chicago, IL
Chicagoland Gerontological Advanced Practice Nurses **[3200]**, River Forest, IL
Cleveland Coun. Black Nurses Assn. (17) **[14097]**, Cleveland, OH
Columbus Black Nurses Assn. (82) **[14372]**, Columbus, OH
Detroit Michigan of the Assn. of Occupational Hea. Nurses **[7351]**, Detroit, MI
Dodge County Area District Nurses Assn. - No. 15 **[17592]**, Beaver Dam, WI
Fox Valley District Nurses Assn. - No. 6 **[18218]**, Hortonville, WI
Greater Cleveland Nurses Assn. **[15113]**, Elyria, OH
Heart of Wisconsin District Nurses Assn. - No. 5 **[20187]**, Wisconsin Rapids, WI
Illinois Assn. of Occupational Hea. Nurses **[2285]**, Lincolnshire, IL
Illinois Assn. of School Nurses **[1479]**, Dixon, IL
Illinois Coun. on Long Term Care **[936]**, Chicago, IL
Indiana Assn. of School Nurses **[4673]**, Fort Wayne, IN
Indiana Org. of Nurse Executives **[5272]**, Indianapolis, IN
Indiana State Nurses Assn. **[5321]**, Indianapolis, IN
Indiana Univ. Northwest Student Nurses' Assn. **[4781]**, Gary, IN
La Crosse District Nurses Assn. **[17737]**, Chaseburg, WI
Lakeshore District Nurses Assn. - No. 12 **[19929]**, Valders, WI
Licensed Practical Nurses Assn. of Illinois **[1029]**, Chicago, IL
Madison District Nurses Assn. - No. 3 **[17963]**, Fitchburg, WI
Mennonite Nurses Assn. **[4801]**, Goshen, IN
Michigan Assn. of Occupational Hea. Nurses **[8622]**, Lansing, MI
Michigan Assn. of PeriAnesthesia Nurses **[9545]**, Romeo, MI
Michigan Chapter of the Assn. of Rehabilitation Nurses **[8897]**, Madison Heights, MI
Michigan Licensed Practical Nurses Assn. **[8683]**, Lansing, MI
Michigan Nurses Assn. **[9287]**, Okemos, MI
Michigan Org. of Nurse Executives - District 1 **[8076]**, Grosse Ile, MI
Michigan Org. of Nurse Executives - District 2 **[8450]**, Kalamazoo, MI
Michigan Org. of Nurse Executives - District 3 **[7981]**, Grand Rapids, MI

Michigan Org. of Nurse Executives - District 4 **[8694]**, Lansing, MI
Michigan Org. of Nurse Executives - District 5 **[9616]**, Saginaw, MI
Michigan Org. of Nurse Executives - District 6 **[8915]**, Manistee, MI
Michigan Org. of Nurse Executives - District 7 **[8333]**, Iron River, MI
Mid Ohio District Nurses Assn. **[14504]**, Columbus, OH
Midstate District Nurses Assn. - No. 8 **[17776]**, Colby, WI
Milwaukee Black Nurses Assn. (21) **[19056]**, Milwaukee, WI
Milwaukee District Nurses Assn. - No. 4 **[19059]**, Milwaukee, WI
Minnesota Assn. of Occupational Hea. Nurses **[11791]**, Minnetonka, MN
Minnesota-Dakotas Soc. of PeriAnesthesia Nurses **[12629]**, Sartell, MN
Minnesota Nurses Assn. **[12502]**, St. Paul, MN
Minnesota Nurses Assn. - District 1 **[12743]**, Thief River Falls, MN
Minnesota Nurses Assn. - District 2 **[10837]**, Duluth, MN
Minnesota Nurses Assn. - District 3 **[10923]**, Edina, MN
Minnesota Nurses Assn. - District 4 **[12503]**, St. Paul, MN
Minnesota Nurses Assn. - District 5 **[11387]**, Mankato, MN
Minnesota Nurses Assn. - District 6 **[12161]**, Rochester, MN
Minnesota Nurses Assn. - District 7 **[10684]**, Clitherall, MN
Minnesota Nurses Assn. - District 8 **[12101]**, Renville, MN
Minnesota Nurses Assn. - District 11 **[10417]**, Bemidji, MN
Minnesota Nurses Assn. - District 12 **[10624]**, Cambridge, MN
Minnesota Nurses Assn. - District 13 **[11959]**, Owatonna, MN
Minnesota Org. of Leaders in Nursing **[12505]**, St. Paul, MN
Northeast Wisconsin District Nurses Assn. - No. 9 **[18330]**, Krakow, WI
Northern Illinois Chap. Assn. of Rehabilitation Nurses **[2658]**, Naperville, IL
Northern Lakes District Nurses Assn. - No. 14 **[19200]**, Minocqua, WI
Ohio Assn. of School Nurses **[16869]**, Tipp City, OH
Ohio League for Nursing **[14198]**, Cleveland, OH
Ohio Nurses Assn. **[14646]**, Columbus, OH
Ohio Nurses Assn. - District Three **[17408]**, Youngstown, OH
Ohio Nursing Admin. in Long Term Care **[16638]**, Shaker Heights, OH
Ohio Nursing Students' Assn. **[14647]**, Columbus, OH
Ohio State Assn. of Nurse Anesthetists **[14679]**, Columbus, OH
St. Croix Valley District Nurses Assn. - No. 13 **[17561]**, Baldwin, WI
School Nurse Org. of Minnesota **[12064]**, Ramsey, MN
Sigma Theta Tau Intl. Honor Soc. of Nursing **[5473]**, Indianapolis, IN
Visiting Nurse Assn. Hea.Care and Partners of Ohio **[14234]**, Cleveland, OH
Waukesha District Nurses Assn. - No. 16 **[19346]**, Oconomowoc, WI
Wisconsin Assn. of School Nurses **[18325]**, Kimberly, WI
Wisconsin League for Nursing **[18430]**, Long Lake, WI
Wisconsin Nurses' Assn. **[18737]**, Madison, WI
Wisconsin Nurses Assn., Northwest District - No. 11 **[19764]**, Spooner, WI
Wisconsin Nurses Assn., Southwest District - No. 2 **[19474]**, Platteville, WI
Wisconsin Org. of Nurse Executives **[18142]**, Green Bay, WI
Wisconsin Soc. of PeriAnesthesia Nurses **[19870]**, Sun Prairie, WI
Nursing Homes
Citizens for Better Care **[7334]**, Detroit, MI
Illinois Hea. Care Assn. **[3606]**, Springfield, IL
Ohio Acad. of Nursing Homes **[14533]**, Columbus, OH
Nursing Homes for the Aged; Citizens for Better Care in **[★7334]**
Nutrition
Amer. Assn. of Critical-Care Nurses, Lake Superior Chap. **[9176]**, Negaunee, MI
Dairy and Nutrition Coun., Inc. **[5099]**, Indianapolis, IN
Illinois Dietetic Assn. **[1970]**, Henry, IL
Indiana Dietary Managers Assn. **[4171]**, Bedford, IN
Indiana Dietetic Assn. **[4485]**, Elberfeld, IN
Michigan Dietetic Assn. **[9663]**, St. Clair Shores, MI
Minnesota Dietary Managers Assn. **[11855]**, Mountain Lake, MN
Minnesota Dietetic Assn. **[12237]**, Roseville, MN
Northwest Ohio Dietary Managers Assn. **[16303]**, Oregon, OH
Ohio Dietetic Assn. **[16114]**, New Albany, OH
Visiting Nurse Assn. of Greater Youngstown **[17420]**, Youngstown, OH
Wisconsin Dietary Managers Assn. **[18017]**, Franksville, WI
Wisconsin Dietetic Assn. **[19758]**, Sparta, WI
Nutrition Network and Senior Services Assn. of Cook County; Community **[855]**, Chicago, IL
Nuts
Illinois Walnut Council **[3977]**, Westville, IL
Nuzzled Network **[3995]**, Wheaton, IL

O

O.A. Thorp Scholastic Acad. Parent-Teacher Assn. **[1111]**, Chicago, IL
Oak Brook Area Assn. of Commerce and Indus. **[2837]**, Oakbrook Terrace, IL
Oak Forest Chamber of Commerce **[2790]**, Oak Forest, IL
Oak Forest Numismatic Soc. **[2791]**, Oak Forest, IL
Oak Harbor Area Chamber of Commerce **[16273]**, Oak Harbor, OH
Oak Harbor Lions Club **[16274]**, Oak Harbor, OH
Oak Hills - Young Life **[15165]**, Fairfield, OH
Oak Lawn Chamber of Commerce **[2799]**, Oak Lawn, IL
Oak Park Area Convention and Visitors Bur. **[2821]**, Oak Park, IL
Oak Park Bd. of Realtors **[2822]**, Oak Park, IL
Oak Park-River Forest Chamber of Commerce **[2823]**, Oak Park, IL
Oak Park-River Forest Community Found. **[2824]**, Oak Park, IL
Oak Park/River Forest - Young Life **[2825]**, Oak Park, IL
Oak Park Visitors Bur. **[★2821]**
Oak Tree Corner **[14935]**, Dayton, OH
Oakdale Lions Club **[19905]**, Tomah, WI
Oakland Astronomy Club **[8516]**, Lake Orion, MI
Oakland County Bar Assn. **[6990]**, Bloomfield Hills, MI
Oakland County Child Care Coun. **[8483]**, Keego Harbor, MI
Oakland County Dental Soc. **[6938]**, Beverly Hills, MI
Oakland County Kennel Club **[9243]**, Novi, MI
Oakland County Medical Soc. **[6967]**, Birmingham, MI
Oakland County Pioneer and Historical Soc. **[9422]**, Pontiac, MI
Oakland County RSVP **[9815]**, Southfield, MI
Oakland County Traditional Dance Soc. **[10122]**, West Bloomfield, MI
Oakland Highlanders Rugby Football Club **[9588]**, Royal Oak, MI
Oberlin African-Amer. Genealogy and History Gp. **[16287]**, Oberlin, OH
Oberlin Area Chamber of Commerce **[16288]**, Oberlin, OH
Oberlin Coll. Fencing Club **[★16289]**
Oberlin Coll. Flaming Blades **[16289]**, Oberlin, OH
Oberlin Coll. Natl. Org. for the Reform of Marijuana Laws **[16290]**, Oberlin, OH
Obesity
Natl. Assn. to Advance Fat Acceptance, Chicago Chap. **[3772]**, Tinley Park, IL
Natl. Assn. to Advance Fat Acceptance, Northern Ohio Chap. **[15996]**, Middleburg Heights, OH
Obsessive Compulsive Found. of Metropolitan Chicago **[1112]**, Chicago, IL
Obstetrics and Gynecology
Amer. Coll. of Obstetricians and Gynecologists-Minnesota **[11486]**, Minneapolis, MN
Illinois Maternal and Child Hea. Coalition **[948]**, Chicago, IL
Michigan Midwives Assn. **[8167]**, Hesperia, MI
Occupational Medicine
Amer. Indus. Hygiene Assn., Central Ohio Sect. **[14284]**, Columbus, OH
Amer. Indus. Hygiene Assn. - Chicago Local Sect. **[1493]**, Downers Grove, IL
Amer. Indus. Hygiene Assn., Chicago Sect. **[2504]**, Mokena, IL
Amer. Indus. Hygiene Assn., Ohio Valley Sect. **[13709]**, Cincinnati, OH
Amer. Indus. Hygiene Assn. - Prairie Local Sect. **[254]**, Bloomington, IL
Amer. Indus. Hygiene Assn., Prairie Sect. **[255]**, Bloomington, IL
Amer. Indus. Hygiene Assn. - Upper Midwest Sect. **[12355]**, St. Paul, MN
Amer. Indus. Hygiene Assn., Wisconsin Sect. **[19954]**, Waterford, WI
Central Ohio Amer. Indus. Hygiene Assn. **[15262]**, Gahanna, OH
Michigan Indus. Hygiene Soc. **[9182]**, New Baltimore, MI
Michigan Occupational Therapy Assn. **[8691]**, Lansing, MI
Northwest Ohio Amer. Indus. Hygiene Assn. **[13395]**, Bowling Green, OH
Ohio Valley Sect. of the Amer. Indus. Hygiene Assn. **[13947]**, Cincinnati, OH
Occupational Therapy Assn; Michigan **[8691]**, Lansing, MI
Oceanography
West Michigan Artificial Reef Soc. **[9167]**, Muskegon, MI
OCF Chicago **[★1112]**
OCIA Michigan, Chap. 2 **[9560]**, Rosebush, MI
Oconomowoc Area Chamber of Commerce **[19339]**, Oconomowoc, WI
Oconomowoc Junior Woman's Club **[19340]**, Oconomowoc, WI
Oconomowoc Lions Club **[19341]**, Oconomowoc, WI
Oconto Area Chamber of Commerce **[19348]**, Oconto, WI
Oconto Elementary School Parent Teacher Organization **[19349]**, Oconto, WI
Oconto Falls Area Chamber of Commerce **[19351]**, Oconto Falls, WI
Oconto Falls Lions Club **[19352]**, Oconto Falls, WI
O'Fallon Chamber of Commerce **[2850]**, O'Fallon, IL
Off. and Professional Employees Intl. Union, AFL-CIO, CLC -Local Union 39 **[18589]**, Madison, WI
Off. and Professional Employees Intl. Union, AFL-CIO, CLC - Local Union 512 **[8748]**, Lansing, MI
Officers
Army and Navy Club of Grand Rapids **[8403]**, Jenison, MI
Canton Area Chap. MOAA **[13554]**, Canton, OH
Dayton Area Chap. - MOAA **[15147]**, Fairborn, OH
East Central Illinois MOAA **[518]**, Champaign, IL
Greater Cleveland Chap., MOAA **[16636]**, Shaker Heights, OH
Hamilton County Sheriffs Dept. Chaplaincy **[5973]**, Noblesville, IN
Heart of Illinois Chap. - MOAA **[3025]**, Peoria, IL
Indianhead Chap. MOAA **[17787]**, Cornell, WI
Michigan Coun. of Chapters of the MOAA **[7017]**, Brighton, MI
Military Officers Assn. of Am., Bloomington Area Chap. **[4240]**, Bloomington, IN
Military Officers Assn. of Am., Capitol Area Chap. **[7874]**, Grand Ledge, MI
Military Officers Assn. of Am., Ernie Pyle Chap. **[6334]**, Terre Haute, IN
Military Officers Assn. of Am., Greater Cincinnati Chap. **[13906]**, Cincinnati, OH
Military Officers Assn. of Am., Head O'The Lakes Chap. **[10833]**, Duluth, MN
Military Officers' Assn. of Am., Indianapolis Chap. **[5407]**, Indianapolis, IN

Military Officers Assn. of Am., La Crosse Chap. [18366], La Crosse, WI
Military Officers Assn. of Am., Lafayette Chap. [6491], West Lafayette, IN
Military Officers Assn. of Am., Lincolnland Chap. [3649], Springfield, IL
Military Officers Assn. of Am., Little Egypt Chap. [421], Carbondale, IL
Military Officers Assn. of Am., Michiana Chap. [6244], South Bend, IN
Military Officers Assn. of Am., Northern Illinois Chap. [3288], Rockford, IL
Military Officers Assn. of Am., Ohio Western Reserve Chap. [13066], Akron, OH
Military Off.rs Assn. of Am., Quad Cities Chap. [2523], Moline, IL
Military Officers Assn. of Am., Southwest Illinois Chap. [3458], Scott AFB, IL
Military Officers Club of Central Ohio [17215], Westerville, OH
Minnesota Assn. of County Off.rs [12454], St. Paul, MN
Minnesota Chap., MOAA [10595], Burnsville, MN
MOAA Illinois Coun. of Chapters [3102], Plainfield, IL
MOAA Indiana Coun. of Chapters [5977], Noblesville, IN
MOAA Wisconsin Coun. of Chapters [18368], La Crosse, WI
MOC of Northeastern Wisconsin [18114], Green Bay, WI
North Shore and Chicago Chap. of the MOAA [2267], Libertyville, IL
Ohio Coun. of Chapters, MOAA [15914], Maumee, OH
Reading Police Off.rs Assn. [16508], Reading, OH
Southeastern Michigan Chap., MOAA [8132], Harrison Township, MI
Southeastern Wisconsin Chap. - MOAA [19129], Milwaukee, WI
Southern Wisconsin Chap. - MOAA [19864], Sun Prairie, WI
Toledo Area Military Officers Assn. of Am. [16964], Toledo, OH
TROA Coun. of MN Chapters [11131], Hastings, MN
TROA Coun. of MN Chapters - Military Officers Assn. of Am. [10611], Burnsville, MN
Utica Police Off.rs Assn. [10038], Utica, MI
West Suburban Chicago Chap., MOAA [2174], La Grange, IL
White River Chap. MOAA [4333], Carmel, IN
Officers' Assn. of Am., Indianapolis Chap; Military [5407], Indianapolis, IN
Ogemaw County Friends of Casa [10132], West Branch, MI
Ogemaw County United Way [10133], West Branch, MI
Ohio Acad. of Family Physicians [14532], Columbus, OH
Ohio Acad. of Nursing Homes [14533], Columbus, OH
Ohio Acad. of Sci. [14534], Columbus, OH
Ohio Acad. of Trial Lawyers [14535], Columbus, OH
Ohio ACTE [★14545]
Ohio AFL-CIO [14536], Columbus, OH
Ohio Aggregates and Indus. Minerals Assn. [15268], Gahanna, OH
Ohio Agri-Women [14936], Dayton, OH
Ohio AgriBus. Assn. [14537], Columbus, OH
Ohio Alliance for the Env. [13520], Canal Winchester, OH
Ohio Alpaca Breeders Assn. [13233], Aurora, OH
Ohio Amateur Softball Assn. [13169], Ashland, OH
Ohio Angus Assn. [16103], Nashport, OH
Ohio Apartment Assn. [14538], Columbus, OH
Ohio Apartment and Condominiums Assn. [★14538]
Ohio Art Educ. Assn. [15606], Lancaster, OH
Ohio Art League [14539], Columbus, OH
Ohio Assisted Living Assn. [14540], Columbus, OH
Ohio Assn. of Agricultural Educators [15447], Hillsboro, OH
Ohio Assn. of Alcoholism and Drug Abuse Counselors [14541], Columbus, OH
Ohio Assn. of Ambulatory Surgery Centers [17234], Westlake, OH
Ohio Assn. of Area Agencies on Aging [14542], Columbus, OH
Ohio Assn. of Broadcasters [14543], Columbus, OH
Ohio Assn. of Cardiovascular and Pulmonary Rehabilitation [16737], Springfield, OH
Ohio Assn. of Career Colls. and Schools [14544], Columbus, OH
Ohio Assn. for Career and Tech. Educ. [14545], Columbus, OH
Ohio Assn. of Chiefs of Police [15053], Dublin, OH
Ohio Assn. of Child Caring Agencies [14546], Columbus, OH
Ohio Assn. of Civil Trial Attorneys [14547], Columbus, OH
Ohio Assn. of Civil Trial Lawyers [★14547]
Ohio Assn. of Coll. Stores [16532], Rio Grande, OH
Ohio Assn. of Coll. and Univ. Bus. Officers [★14202]
Ohio Assn. of Collegiate Registrars and Admissions Officers [14548], Columbus, OH
Ohio Assn. of Community Action Agencies [14549], Columbus, OH
Ohio Assn. of Community Colleges [14550], Columbus, OH
Ohio Assn. of Convention and Visitor Bureaus [14551], Columbus, OH
Ohio Assn. of County Boards of MRDD [17347], Worthington, OH
Ohio Assn. for Developmental Educ. [16944], Toledo, OH
Ohio Assn. of Durable Medical Equip. Companies [★14558]
Ohio Assn. for the Educ. of Young Children [16072], Mount Gilead, OH
Ohio Assn. of Elementary School Administrators [14552], Columbus, OH
Ohio Assn. of Elementary School Principals [★14552]
Ohio Assn. of Emergency Medical Sers. [16666], Sidney, OH
Ohio Assn. for Employment in Educ. [16857], Tiffin, OH
Ohio Assn. of Food and Environmental Sanitarians [13521], Canal Winchester, OH
Ohio Assn. for Gifted Children [14553], Columbus, OH
Ohio Assn. for Hea., Physical Educ., Recreation and Dance [13245], Avon Lake, OH
Ohio Assn. of Hea. Plans [14554], Columbus, OH
Ohio Assn. for Healthcare Quality [14190], Cleveland, OH
Ohio Assn. of Historical Societies and Museums [14555], Columbus, OH
Ohio Assn. of Independent Accountants [16228], North Hampton, OH
Ohio Assn. for Infant Mental Hea. [13934], Cincinnati, OH
Ohio Assn. of Institutional Res. and Planning [14556], Columbus, OH
Ohio Assn. of Insurance and Financial Advisors [14557], Columbus, OH
Ohio Assn. of Meat Processors [15240], Frazeysburg, OH
Ohio Assn. of Medical Equip. Services [14558], Columbus, OH
Ohio Assn. of Mortgage Brokers [16221], North Canton, OH
Ohio Assn. of Movers [14559], Columbus, OH
Ohio Assn. of Mutual Insurance Agents [★15271]
Ohio Assn. of Nonprofit Organizations [14560], Columbus, OH
Ohio Assn. of Orthopaedic Technologists [13573], Canton, OH
Ohio Assn. of Parliamentarians [16566], Sagamore Hills, OH
Ohio Assn. of Physician Assistants [17348], Worthington, OH
Ohio Assn. of Polygraph Examiners [14561], Columbus, OH
Ohio Assn. of Professional Fire Fighters [14562], Columbus, OH
Ohio Assn. of Public School Employees [14563], Columbus, OH
Ohio Assn. of Realtors [14564], Columbus, OH
Ohio Assn. of School Bus. Officials [14565], Columbus, OH
Ohio Assn. of School Nurses [16869], Tipp City, OH
Ohio Assn. of Secondary School Administrators [14566], Columbus, OH
Ohio Assn. of Security and Investigation Services [14567], Columbus, OH
Ohio Assn. of Student Financial Aid Administrators [13010], Ada, OH
Ohio Assn. of Textile Sers. [14568], Columbus, OH
Ohio Assn. of Tobacco and Candy Distributors [★14698]
Ohio Assn. of Wholesale Distributors [14569], Columbus, OH
Ohio Athletic Trainers' Assn. [15299], Galloway, OH
Ohio Auctioneers Assn. [14570], Columbus, OH
Ohio Automatic Merchandising Association [14571], Columbus, OH
Ohio Bankers Assn. [★14572]
Ohio Bankers League [14572], Columbus, OH
Ohio BASS Chap. Fed. [15293], Gallipolis, OH
Ohio Bed and Breakfast Assn. [14573], Columbus, OH
Ohio Beef Coun. [15865], Marysville, OH
Ohio Bicycle Fed. [17376], Xenia, OH
Ohio Bluebird Soc. [13935], Cincinnati, OH
Ohio Boer Goat Assn. [15858], Mark Center, OH
Ohio Bottle Club [13256], Barberton, OH
Ohio Browns Boosters [15936], McDonald, OH
Ohio Burglar and Fire Alarm Assn. [14574], Columbus, OH
Ohio Cable Telecommunications Assn. [14575], Columbus, OH
Ohio Car Wash Assn. [13574], Canton, OH
Ohio Cast Metals Assn. [14576], Columbus, OH
Ohio Center for the Book [14191], Cleveland, OH
Ohio Chamber of Commerce [14577], Columbus, OH
Ohio Chap. Amer. Coll. of Emergency Physicians [14578], Columbus, OH
Ohio Chap. of the Amer. Coll. of Surgeons [14579], Columbus, OH
Ohio Chap. of the MFTHBA [15536], Kensington, OH
Ohio Chap. of the Myasthenia Gravis Found. [15893], Massillon, OH
Ohio Chap. Natl. Assn. of Tax Professionals [15030], Dover, OH
Ohio Chemistry Tech. Coun. [14580], Columbus, OH
Ohio Choral Directors Assn. [16858], Tiffin, OH
Ohio Christmas Tree Assn. [14581], Columbus, OH
Ohio Citizen Action [14192], Cleveland, OH
Ohio City Design Rev. Comm. [14193], Cleveland, OH
Ohio Cleaners Assn. [14582], Columbus, OH
Ohio Coal Assn. [14583], Columbus, OH
Ohio Coalition for More Effective School Discipline [★14351]
Ohio Coin Laundry Assn. [17108], Warren, OH
Ohio Coin Machine Assn. [14584], Columbus, OH
Ohio Coll. Personnel Assn. [14585], Columbus, OH
Ohio Community Development Corp. Assn. [14586], Columbus, OH
Ohio Contractors Assn. [14587], Columbus, OH
Ohio Corn Growers Assn. [15848], Marion, OH
Ohio Coun. of Behavioral Hea.care Providers [14588], Columbus, OH
Ohio Coun. of Chapters, MOAA [15914], Maumee, OH
Ohio Coun. of Churches [14589], Columbus, OH
Ohio Coun. of Community Mental Hea. and Recovery Orgs. [★14588]
Ohio Coun. for Home Care [14590], Columbus, OH
Ohio Coun. of Retail Merchants [14591], Columbus, OH
Ohio Coun. for the Social Stud. [15439], Hilliard, OH
Ohio Coun. of Teachers of English Language Arts [14592], Columbus, OH
Ohio Coun. of Teachers of Mathematics [13644], Chardon, OH
Ohio Counseling Assn. [13522], Canal Winchester, OH
Ohio Court Reporters Assn. [15054], Dublin, OH
Ohio Credit Union League [15055], Dublin, OH
Ohio Dairy Goat Assn. [13608], Cedarville, OH
Ohio Democratic Party [14593], Columbus, OH
Ohio Dental Assn. [14594], Columbus, OH
Ohio Designer Craftsmen [14595], Columbus, OH
Ohio Developmental Disabilities Planning Coun. [14596], Columbus, OH
Ohio Dietetic Assn. [16114], New Albany, OH
Ohio Disabled Amer. Veterans [14194], Cleveland, OH
Ohio District Amateur Athletic Union [13936], Cincinnati, OH

Ohio District, The Lutheran Church-Missouri Synod [16299], Olmsted Falls, OH
Ohio Division of the Intl. Assn. for Identification [16375], Parma, OH
Ohio Division of Travel and Tourism [14597], Columbus, OH
Ohio Domestic Violence Network [14598], Columbus, OH
Ohio Dressage Soc. [16386], Pataskala, OH
Ohio Ecological Food and Farm Assn. [14599], Columbus, OH
Ohio Educ. Assn. [14600], Columbus, OH
Ohio Educational Lib. Media Assn. [14601], Columbus, OH
Ohio Educational Ser. Center Assn. [14602], Columbus, OH
Ohio Elec. Utility Inst. [14603], Columbus, OH
Ohio Environmental Coun. [14604], Columbus, OH
Ohio Equip. Distributors Assn. [15056], Dublin, OH
Ohio and Erie Canal Corridor Coalition [★13076]
Ohio and Erie Canalway Coalition [13076], Akron, OH
Ohio Fair Managers Assn. [16410], Perrysburg, OH
Ohio Family Care Assn. [14605], Columbus, OH
Ohio Farm Bur. Fed. [14606], Columbus, OH
Ohio Farmers Union [14607], Columbus, OH
Ohio Farmers Union [16316], Ottawa, OH
Ohio Fed. of Families for Children's Mental Hea. - Summit Behavioral Hea. [13937], Cincinnati, OH
Ohio Fed. of Soil and Water Conservation Districts [14608], Columbus, OH
Ohio Fed. of Soil and Water Conservation Districts Soil and Water [★14608]
Ohio Fed. of Teachers [14609], Columbus, OH
Ohio Festivals and Events Assn. [15696], London, OH
Ohio Florists' Assn. [14610], Columbus, OH
Ohio Flyers Hang Gliding Assn. [14611], Columbus, OH
Ohio Forestry Assn. [14612], Columbus, OH
Ohio Fruit Growers Soc. [14613], Columbus, OH
Ohio Funeral Directors Assn. [14614], Columbus, OH
Ohio Gas Assn. [14615], Columbus, OH
Ohio Genealogical Soc. [15782], Mansfield, OH
Ohio Genealogical Soc., Allen County [15665], Lima, OH
Ohio Genealogical Soc., Ashland County Chap. [13170], Ashland, OH
Ohio Genealogical Soc., Athens County Chap. [13212], Athens, OH
Ohio Genealogical Soc., Auglaize County Chap. [★17089]
Ohio Genealogical Soc., Brown County [15314], Georgetown, OH
Ohio Genealogical Soc., Crawford County [15287], Galion, OH
Ohio Genealogical Soc., Cuyahoga West Chap. [15184], Fairview Park, OH
Ohio Genealogical Soc., Darke County [15364], Greenville, OH
Ohio Genealogical Soc., Defiance County Chap. [★14987]
Ohio Genealogical Soc., Fairfield County Chap. [15607], Lancaster, OH
Ohio Genealogical Soc., Fayette County [17131], Washington Court House, OH
Ohio Genealogical Soc., Fulton County Chap. [★16817]
Ohio Genealogical Soc., Gallia County Chap. [★15291]
Ohio Genealogical Soc., Greater Cleveland [14195], Cleveland, OH
Ohio Genealogical Soc., Hamilton County Chap. [13938], Cincinnati, OH
Ohio Genealogical Soc., Harrison County [13482], Cadiz, OH
Ohio Genealogical Soc., Henry County [15022], Deshler, OH
Ohio Genealogical Soc., Holmes County Chap. [16038], Millersburg, OH
Ohio Genealogical Soc., Hudson Chap. [★15482]
Ohio Genealogical Soc., Hudson Genealogical Study Group [15487], Hudson, OH
Ohio Genealogical Soc., Huron County Chap. [16264], Norwalk, OH
Ohio Genealogical Soc., Jackson County Chap. [15515], Jackson, OH
Ohio Genealogical Soc., Licking County [16181], Newark, OH
Ohio Genealogical Soc., Logan County [13323], Bellefontaine, OH
Ohio Genealogical Soc., Marion Area [15849], Marion, OH
Ohio Genealogical Soc., Medina County [15953], Medina, OH
Ohio Genealogical Soc., Morgan County Chap. [15934], McConnelsville, OH
Ohio Genealogical Soc., Morrow County Chap. [16073], Mount Gilead, OH
Ohio Genealogical Soc., Ottawa County Chap. [16460], Port Clinton, OH
Ohio Genealogical Soc., Pickaway County Historical Soc. [14033], Circleville, OH
Ohio Genealogical Soc., Pike County [17146], Waverly, OH
Ohio Genealogical Soc., Putnam County [16317], Ottawa, OH
Ohio Genealogical Soc., Putnam County Chap. [★16317]
Ohio Genealogical Soc., Richland County-Shelby Chap. [16654], Shelby, OH
Ohio Genealogical Society, Ross County Chapter [★13673]
Ohio Genealogical Soc., Seneca County [★16861]
Ohio Genealogical Soc., Southwest Cuyahoga [16794], Strongsville, OH
Ohio Genealogical Soc., Stark County Chap. [13575], Canton, OH
Ohio Genealogical Soc., Tuscarawas County [16152], New Philadelphia, OH
Ohio Genealogical Soc., Union County Chap. [15866], Marysville, OH
Ohio Genealogical Soc., Van Wert County Ohio Chap. [17052], Van Wert, OH
Ohio Genealogical Soc., Vinton County [15375], Hamden, OH
Ohio Genealogical Soc., Warren County Chap. [15623], Lebanon, OH
Ohio Genealogical Soc., Williams County [13457], Bryan, OH
Ohio Genealogical Soc., Wood County [13396], Bowling Green, OH
Ohio Genealogy Soc., Jefferson County Chap. [16765], Steubenville, OH
Ohio Geological Soc. [14616], Columbus, OH
Ohio Glass Assn. [14196], Cleveland, OH
Ohio Golf Assn. [14617], Columbus, OH
Ohio Golf Course Owners Assn. [16479], Powell, OH
Ohio Gourd Soc. [16182], Newark, OH
Ohio Govt. Finance Officers Assn. [14618], Columbus, OH
Ohio Grantmakers Forum [14619], Columbus, OH
Ohio Grocers Assn. [14620], Columbus, OH
Ohio Grocers Assn. [17028], Upper Arlington, OH
Ohio Haflinger Assn. [17324], Wooster, OH
Ohio Harness Horsemen's Assn. [14621], Columbus, OH
Ohio Hea. Care Assn., District 1 [13939], Cincinnati, OH
Ohio Hea. Care Assn., District 2 [14937], Dayton, OH
Ohio Hea. Care Assn., District 3 [15666], Lima, OH
Ohio Hea. Care Assn., District 4 [16830], Sylvania, OH
Ohio Hea. Care Assn., District 5 [16291], Oberlin, OH
Ohio Hea. Care Assn., District 6 [16087], Mount Vernon, OH
Ohio Hea. Care Assn., District 7 [14622], Columbus, OH
Ohio Hea. Care Assn., District 8 [15448], Hillsboro, OH
Ohio Hea. Care Assn., District 9 [13670], Chillicothe, OH
Ohio Hea. Care Assn., District 10 [15031], Dover, OH
Ohio Hea. Care Assn., District 11 [15680], Lisbon, OH
Ohio Hea. Care Assn., District 12 [13077], Akron, OH
Ohio Hea. Care Assn., District 13 [13347], Berea, OH
Ohio Hea. Care Assn., District 14 [15749], Madison, OH
Ohio Hea. Care Assn., District 15 [16818], Swanton, OH
Ohio Hea. Info. Mgt. Assn. [17349], Worthington, OH
Ohio Heartland Chap. of the Intl. Soc. for Performance Improvement [13523], Canal Winchester, OH
Ohio High School Athletic Assn. [14623], Columbus, OH
Ohio Historical and Genealogical Soc., Miami County Chap. [★17003]
Ohio Historical Soc. [14624], Columbus, OH
Ohio Historical Soc. - Cedar Bog Nature Preserve [17042], Urbana, OH
Ohio HMO Assn. [★14554]
Ohio Home Builders Assn. [14625], Columbus, OH
Ohio Hospice Org. [★15057]
Ohio Hospice and Palliative Care Org. [15057], Dublin, OH
Ohio Hosp. Assn. [14626], Columbus, OH
Ohio Hotel and Lodging Assn. [14627], Columbus, OH
Ohio Hotel & Motel Assn. [★14627]
Ohio Housing Authorities Conf. [15783], Mansfield, OH
Ohio Humanities Coun. [14628], Columbus, OH
Ohio Independent Telephone Assn. [★14688]
Ohio Insurance Inst. [14629], Columbus, OH
Ohio-Israel Chamber of Commerce [14197], Cleveland, OH
Ohio Jewelers Assn. [14630], Columbus, OH
Ohio-Kentucky-Indiana Regional Coun. of Governments [13940], Cincinnati, OH
Ohio Lake Mgt. Soc. [15544], Kent, OH
Ohio Land Improvement Contractors Assn. [14631], Columbus, OH
Ohio Land Title Assn. [14632], Columbus, OH
Ohio Landscape Assn. [13429], Broadview Heights, OH
Ohio Landscapers Assn. [★13429]
Ohio League of Conservation Voters [14633], Columbus, OH
Ohio League of Conservation Voters Educ. Fund [★14633]
Ohio League for Nursing [14198], Cleveland, OH
Ohio Licensed Beverage Assn. [14634], Columbus, OH
Ohio Literacy Network [14635], Columbus, OH
Ohio Lumbermen's Assn. [14636], Columbus, OH
Ohio Manufactured Homes Assn. [15058], Dublin, OH
Ohio Manufacturers' Assn. [14637], Columbus, OH
Ohio Mathematics Assn. of Two-Year Colleges [16435], Piqua, OH
Ohio Meat Goat Assn. [16125], New Concord, OH
Ohio-Michigan Equip. Dealers Assn. [15059], Dublin, OH
Ohio Mid-Eastern Govts. Assn. [13499], Cambridge, OH
Ohio Middle School Assn. [14638], Columbus, OH
Ohio Mobile Home and Recreational Vehicle Assn. [★15058]
Ohio Morgan Horse Assn. [15334], Grafton, OH
Ohio Mortgage Bankers Assn. [14639], Columbus, OH
Ohio Motorists Assn. [13653], Chesterland, OH
Ohio Motorists Assn. [17264], Willard, OH
Ohio Multi-County Development Corp. [13078], Akron, OH
Ohio Municipal League [14640], Columbus, OH
Ohio Museums Assn. [14641], Columbus, OH
Ohio Mushroom Soc. [15345], Granville, OH
Ohio Music Educ. Assn. [15894], Massillon, OH
Ohio Natl. Barrel Horse Assn. [15256], Fresno, OH
Ohio Natl. Cong. of Parents and Teachers [14642], Columbus, OH
Ohio Natl. Farmers Org. [13144], Anna, OH
Ohio Native Plant Soc., Central Ohio Chap. [14643], Columbus, OH
Ohio Native Plant Soc., Miami Valley Chap. [14938], Dayton, OH
Ohio Native Plant Soc., Mohican Chap. [15784], Mansfield, OH
Ohio Native Plant Soc., Northeastern Ohio Chap. [16193], Newbury, OH
Ohio Network of Children's Advocacy Centers [14644], Columbus, OH
Ohio Newspaper Assn. [14645], Columbus, OH

Ohio North Coast Chap. of Assoc. Locksmiths of Am. [16058], Monroeville, OH
Ohio Northern Kentucky Indiana Vascular Technologists [13941], Cincinnati, OH
Ohio Nursery and Landscape Assn. [17217], Westerville, OH
Ohio Nurses Assn. [14646], Columbus, OH
Ohio Nurses Assn. - District Three [17408], Youngstown, OH
Ohio Nursing Admin. in Long Term Care [16638], Shaker Heights, OH
Ohio Nursing Students' Assn. [14647], Columbus, OH
Ohio Occupational Therapy Assn. [14648], Columbus, OH
Ohio Oil and Gas Assn. [15346], Granville, OH
Ohio Onsite Wastewater Assn. [15757], Manchester, OH
Ohio Ophthalmological Soc. [15440], Hilliard, OH
Ohio Optometric Assn. [17350], Worthington, OH
Ohio Osteopathic Assn. [14649], Columbus, OH
Ohio Parents of Blind Children [13324], Bellefontaine, OH
Ohio Parents of Children with Visual Impairments [15954], Medina, OH
Ohio Parks and Recreation Assn. [17218], Westerville, OH
Ohio Partners for Affordable Energy [15213], Findlay, OH
Ohio Peace March; Walkacross America for Mother Earth/ [★14411]
Ohio Petroleum Coun. [14650], Columbus, OH
Ohio Petroleum Gas Assn. [14651], Columbus, OH
Ohio Petroleum Marketers Assn. [★15060]
Ohio Petroleum Marketers and Convenience Store Assn. [15060], Dublin, OH
Ohio Petroleum Retailers and Repair Assn. and Ser. Sta. Dealers Assn. of Michigan [★8570]
Ohio Pharmacists Assn. [14652], Columbus, OH
Ohio Physical Therapy Assn. [15269], Gahanna, OH
Ohio Physiological Soc. [14939], Dayton, OH
Ohio Planning Conf. [14199], Cleveland, OH
Ohio Podiatric Medical Assn. [14653], Columbus, OH
Ohio Pork Producers Coun. [14654], Columbus, OH
Ohio Poultry Assn. [14655], Columbus, OH
Ohio Prairie Assn. [15785], Mansfield, OH
Ohio Primary Care Assn. [14656], Columbus, OH
Ohio Private Residential Assn. [★14661]
Ohio Professionals for School-Age Care [★14657]
Ohio Professionals for School-Age Children [14657], Columbus, OH
Ohio Prog. Evaluators' Gp. [14658], Columbus, OH
Ohio Propane Gas Assn. [14659], Columbus, OH
Ohio Prosecuting Attorneys Assn. [14660], Columbus, OH
Ohio Prospect Res. Network [14940], Dayton, OH
Ohio Provider Rsrc. Assn. [14661], Columbus, OH
Ohio Psychiatric Assn. [14662], Columbus, OH
Ohio Psychological Assn. [14663], Columbus, OH
Ohio PTA [★14642]
Ohio Public Employer Labor Relations Assn. [15397], Hamilton, OH
Ohio Public Facilities Maintenance Assn. [16238], North Olmsted, OH
Ohio Public Hea. Assn. [16422], Pickerington, OH
Ohio Public Interest Res. Gp. [14664], Columbus, OH
Ohio Quarter Horse Assn. [16529], Richwood, OH
Ohio Racquetball Assn. [17219], Westerville, OH
Ohio Ready Mixed Concrete Assn. [14665], Columbus, OH
Ohio Region of Narcotics Anonymous [14666], Columbus, OH
Ohio Regional Assn. of Law Libraries [14941], Dayton, OH
Ohio Restaurant Assn. [14667], Columbus, OH
Ohio Rifle and Pistol Assn. [13942], Cincinnati, OH
Ohio Rifle and Pistol Assn. [16138], New London, OH
Ohio Right to Life Soc. [14668], Columbus, OH
Ohio River REACT Team [16471], Portsmouth, OH
Ohio River Valley Water Sanitation Commn. [13943], Cincinnati, OH
Ohio Rural Development Partnership [16516], Reynoldsburg, OH
Ohio Rural Elec. Cooperatives [14669], Columbus, OH
Ohio Rural Partners [★16516]
Ohio SADD [15502], Independence, OH
Ohio St. Bernard Club [16695], South Euclid, OH
Ohio School Bds. Assn. [14670], Columbus, OH
Ohio School Psychologists Assn. [15270], Gahanna, OH
Ohio Sci. Educ. and Res. Assn. [15061], Dublin, OH
Ohio Sect. of the Amer. Physical Soc. [17360], Wright-Patterson AFB, OH
Ohio Seed Improvement Assn. [15062], Dublin, OH
Ohio Self Insurers Assn. [14671], Columbus, OH
Ohio Senior Olympics [17409], Youngstown, OH
Ohio Sheep Improvement Assn. [14672], Columbus, OH
Ohio Simmental Assn. [17164], West Alexandria, OH
Ohio Soc. of Anesthesiologists [14673], Columbus, OH
Ohio Soc. of Assn. Executives [17351], Worthington, OH
Ohio Soc. of Certified Public Accountants - Cincinnati Chap. [13944], Cincinnati, OH
Ohio Soc. for the Elevation of Kites [15145], Euclid, OH
Ohio Soc. of Health-System Pharmacists [15826], Marietta, OH
Ohio Soc. for Healthcare Engg. [16017], Middletown, OH
Ohio Soc. of Professional Engineers [14674], Columbus, OH
Ohio Soc. of Radiologic Technologists [13079], Akron, OH
Ohio Soc., Sons of the Amer. Revolution, Samuel Huntington Chap. [16341], Painesville, OH
Ohio Soft Drink Association [14675], Columbus, OH
Ohio Solar Energy Soc. [★14448]
Ohio Soybean Coun. [14676], Columbus, OH
Ohio Speedskating Assn. [17235], Westlake, OH
Ohio Spill Planning Prevention and Emergency Response Assn. [14677], Columbus, OH
Ohio State African Violet Soc. [16202], Newtown, OH
Ohio State Assembly of the Assn. of Surgical Technologists [14678], Columbus, OH
Ohio State Assn. of Nurse Anesthetists [14679], Columbus, OH
Ohio State Assn. of Plumbing, Heating and Cooling Contractors [13637], Chagrin Falls, OH
Ohio State Bar Assn. [14680], Columbus, OH
Ohio State Buckeye Univ. Lions Club [14681], Columbus, OH
Ohio State Chiropractic Assn. [14682], Columbus, OH
Ohio State Medical Assn. [15441], Hilliard, OH
Ohio State Neurosurgical Soc. [14200], Cleveland, OH
Ohio State Numismatic Assn. [17016], Twinsburg, OH
Ohio State Pony of the Americas Club [15810], Marengo, OH
Ohio State Reformatory Historic Site [★15775]
Ohio State Skeet Assn. [16222], North Canton, OH
Ohio State Soc. of Amer. Medical Technologists [13332], Bellevue, OH
Ohio State Soc. of Enrolled Agents - Greater Cleveland Chap. [16795], Strongsville, OH
Ohio State Soc. of Enrolled Agents - Greater Columbus Chap. [15300], Galloway, OH
Ohio State Soc. of Enrolled Agents - Greater Dayton Chap. [14942], Dayton, OH
Ohio State Trappers Assn. [14832], Dalton, OH
Ohio State Trapshooting Found. [15371], Grove City, OH
Ohio State Univ. Fencing Club [14683], Columbus, OH
Ohio State University - Great Lakes Aquatic Ecosystem Research Consortium [14684], Columbus, OH
Ohio State Univ. Lions Club [14685], Columbus, OH
Ohio Storage Owner's Soc. [14686], Columbus, OH
Ohio Subcontractors Coun. [14687], Columbus, OH
Ohio Suffolk Sheep Assn. [17091], Wapakoneta, OH
Ohio Supreme Court Historical Soc. [14201], Cleveland, OH
Ohio Telecom Assn. [14688], Columbus, OH
Ohio Telecommunications Indus. Assn. [★14688]
Ohio Telephone Assn. [★14688]
Ohio Thimble Seekers [16423], Pickerington, OH
Ohio Thoracic Soc. [15667], Lima, OH
Ohio Thoroughbred Breeders and Owners [13945], Cincinnati, OH
Ohio Tire Dealers and Retreaders [★14689]
Ohio Tire Dealers and Retreaders Assn. [14689], Columbus, OH
Ohio Township Assn. [14690], Columbus, OH
Ohio Toy Fox Terrier Assn. [17092], Wapakoneta, OH
Ohio Trade Assn. Executives [★17351]
Ohio Travel Assn. [14691], Columbus, OH
Ohio Trucking Assn. [14692], Columbus, OH
Ohio Turfgrass Found. [17441], Zanesville, OH
Ohio United Way [14693], Columbus, OH
Ohio Univ. Chap. of the Assn. for Computing Machinery [13213], Athens, OH
Ohio Univ. Coun. of Teachers of Mathematics [13214], Athens, OH
Ohio Urological Soc. [3442], Schaumburg, IL
Ohio Valley Bicycle Club [15294], Gallipolis, OH
Ohio Valley Bus. Travel Assn. [13946], Cincinnati, OH
Ohio Valley Central Ser. Professionals [4564], Evansville, IN
Ohio Valley Chap. of Assoc. Locksmiths of Am. [15563], Kettering, OH
Ohio Valley Coin Assn. [16766], Steubenville, OH
Ohio Valley Constr. Educ. Found. [16705], Springboro, OH
Ohio Valley Dairy Goat Assn. [15327], Glouster, OH
Ohio Valley District of Precision Metalforming Assn. [16738], Springfield, OH
Ohio Valley Muskie Hunters [13379], Bowerston, OH
Ohio Valley NARI [14943], Dayton, OH
Ohio Valley Natl. Assn. of the Remodeling Indus. [★14943]
Ohio Valley Pembroke Welsh Corgi Club [14694], Columbus, OH
Ohio Valley Regional Chap. of the Soc. of Environmental Toxicology and Chemistry [14695], Columbus, OH
Ohio Valley Retriever Club [15063], Dublin, OH
Ohio Valley Sect. of the Amer. Indus. Hygiene Assn. [13947], Cincinnati, OH
Ohio Vegetable and Potato Growers Assn. [14696], Columbus, OH
Ohio Vegetarian Advocates [16639], Shaker Heights, OH
Ohio Vehicle Leasing Assn. [15064], Dublin, OH
Ohio Venture Assn. [14202], Cleveland, OH
Ohio Veterinary Medical Assn. [14697], Columbus, OH
Ohio Vocational Assn. [★14545]
Ohio Volkssport Assn. [15133], Englewood, OH
Ohio Volkssports Assn. [17377], Xenia, OH
Ohio Water Well Assn. [15398], Hamilton, OH
Ohio/West Virginia State Assn. of Emblem Club [15288], Galion, OH
Ohio Wholesale Marketers Assn. [14698], Columbus, OH
Ohio Wine Producers Assn. [13234], Austinburg, OH
Ohio Women's Bus. Rsrc. Network [14699], Columbus, OH
Ohio Women's Law Enforcement Network [14700], Columbus, OH
Ohio Young Democrats [14701], Columbus, OH
Ohioans to Stop Executions [14702], Columbus, OH
Oil Jobbers of Wisconsin [★18595]
Okaw Valley Beagle Club [1759], Fults, IL
Okaw Valley Libertarians [3848], Vandalia, IL
Okawville Chamber of Commerce [2856], Okawville, IL
Olbrich Botanical Soc. [18590], Madison, WI
Old English Sheepdog Club of Am. [18055], Glendale, WI
Old Fort Coin Club [4707], Fort Wayne, IN
Old Fort Lions Club [16294], Old Fort, OH
Old Iron County Courthouse Museum [★18231]
Old Orchard Unit Owners Assn. [13948], Cincinnati, OH
Old Town Neighborhood Assn. [4804], Goshen, IN
Old Village Business Alliance [10072], Warren, MI
Oldsmobile Club of Am., Gem City Rockets [16706], Springboro, OH
Oldsmobile Club of Am., Illinois Valley Oldsmobile Chap. [1113], Chicago, IL
Oldsmobile Club of Am., Motor City Rockets [7672], Farmington Hills, MI

Oldsmobile Club of Am., Northern Ohio Chap. **[16223]**, North Canton, OH
Olentangy Beagle Club **[15786]**, Mansfield, OH
Olentangy Liberty - Young Life **[14703]**, Columbus, OH
Olentangy - Young Life **[14704]**, Columbus, OH
Olinga Productions Association **[4022]**, Wilmette, IL
Olive Br. Farm Skeet Club **[15065]**, Dublin, OH
Olivet Lions Club **[9302]**, Olivet, MI
Olivia Area Chamber of Commerce **[11936]**, Olivia, MN
Olivia Lions Club **[11937]**, Olivia, MN
Olmsted County Govt. Center **[12165]**, Rochester, MN
Olmsted County Historical Soc. **[12166]**, Rochester, MN
Olney and the Greater Richland County Chamber of Commerce **[2859]**, Olney, IL
Olympia Homeowners Assn. **[16796]**, Strongsville, OH
Omro Area Chamber of Commerce **[19357]**, Omro, WI
Onalaska Lions Club **[19367]**, Onalaska, WI
Onalaska - Young Life **[19368]**, Onalaska, WI
Onanegozie-Land Rsrc. Conservation and Development Coun. **[11835]**, Mora, MN
One by One Civic Club **[6387]**, Valparaiso, IN
Oneida Coun. of Camp Fire **[★19597]**
Oneida County Economic Development Corp. **[19602]**, Rhinelander, WI
Onekama Lions Club **[9305]**, Onekama, MI
Only One Promise Area of Narcotics Anonymous **[1400]**, Decatur, IL
Ontario Area Lions Club **[20169]**, Wilton, WI
Ontario Lions Club **[14810]**, Crestline, OH
Ontonagon Area High School Skating Club **[9310]**, Ontonagon, MI
Ontonagon County Chamber of Commerce **[9311]**, Ontonagon, MI
Ontonagon County Chamber of Commerce and Tourism Assn. **[★9311]**
Open Doors Org. **[1114]**, Chicago, IL
Open Lands Corp; Orland Park **[2884]**, Orland Park, IL
Opera
Cincinnati Opera Assn. **[13795]**, Cincinnati, OH
Oper. Lifesaver, Indiana **[5443]**, Indianapolis, IN
Oper. Lifesaver, Michigan **[8749]**, Lansing, MI
Oper. Lifesaver, Ohio **[14705]**, Columbus, OH
Operation Lifesaver, Wisconsin **[18591]**, Madison, WI
Ophthalmological Soc; Michigan **[7543]**, East Lansing, MI
Ophthalmology
Indiana Acad. of Ophthalmology **[4605]**, Fishers, IN
Michigan Ophthalmological Soc. **[7543]**, East Lansing, MI
Ohio Ophthalmological Soc. **[15440]**, Hilliard, OH
Optical Soc. of Am., Ann Arbor **[6749]**, Ann Arbor, MI
Optical Soc. of Am., Minnesota **[11717]**, Minneapolis, MN
Opticianry
Opticians Assn. of Michigan **[7465]**, DeWitt, MI
Opticians Assn. of Michigan **[7465]**, DeWitt, MI
Optics
Ann Arbor Chap. of Optical Soc. of Am. **[6670]**, Ann Arbor, MI
Chicago (SPIE/OSC) Optical Gp. **[1723]**, Frankfort, IL
Minnesota Sect. of Optical Soc. of Am. **[10480]**, Bloomington, MN
Optical Soc. of Am., Ann Arbor **[6749]**, Ann Arbor, MI
Optical Soc. of Am., Minnesota **[11717]**, Minneapolis, MN
Options and Advocacy for McHenry County **[1330]**, Crystal Lake, IL
Options Exchange; Chicago Bd. **[794]**, Chicago, IL
Optometric Assn; Ohio **[17350]**, Worthington, OH
Optometric Assn. - Ohio Chap; Amer. **[★17350]**
Optometry
Fox Cities Optometric Soc. **[19727]**, Sherwood, WI
Gateway Optometric Soc. **[18345]**, La Crosse, WI
Illinois Optometric Assn. **[3622]**, Springfield, IL
Illinois Optometric Licensing and Disciplinary Bd. **[3623]**, Springfield, IL
Indiana Optometric Assn. **[5270]**, Indianapolis, IN
Indiana Optometric Assn., Central District **[5936]**, New Castle, IN
Indiana Optometric Assn., Northwestern District **[4780]**, Gary, IN
Indiana Optometric Assn., Southeastern District **[4278]**, Borden, IN
Indiana Optometric Assn., West Central District **[5618]**, Lafayette, IN
Indiana Optometric Assn., Western District **[4819]**, Greencastle, IN
Indiana Optometry Bd. **[5271]**, Indianapolis, IN
Indianhead Optometric Soc. **[17755]**, Chippewa Falls, WI
Kettle Moraine Optometric Soc. **[19988]**, Waukesha, WI
Lake Shore Optometric Soc. **[19588]**, Random Lake, WI
Lake Winnebago Optometric Soc. **[19356]**, Omro, WI
Madison Area Optometric Soc. **[20018]**, Waunakee, WI
Michigan Bd. of Optometry **[8637]**, Lansing, MI
Milwaukee Optometric Soc. **[17673]**, Brookfield, WI
Minnesota Optometric Assn. **[11662]**, Minneapolis, MN
North East Wisconsin Optometric Soc. **[19841]**, Sturgeon Bay, WI
Ohio Optometric Assn. **[17350]**, Worthington, OH
South Central Wisconsin Optometric Soc. **[18831]**, Mauston, WI
South East Wisconsin Optometric Soc. **[19477]**, Pleasant Prairie, WI
South West Wisconsin Optometric Soc. **[17807]**, Darlington, WI
Wisconsin Optometric Assn. **[18739]**, Madison, WI
Wisconsin Valley Optometric Soc. **[20060]**, Wausau, WI
Or Emet Congregation, Humanistic Jews of Minnesota **[12119]**, Robbinsdale, MN
Orak Shriners **[5791]**, Michigan City, IN
Orange Alumni Assn. **[16397]**, Pepper Pike, OH
Orange Community Homeowners Assn. **[13291]**, Beachwood, OH
Orange County Convention and Visitor's Bur. **[4764]**, French Lick, IN
Orchard Drive PTA **[4889]**, Hammond, IN
Orchestra Assn; Michigan School Band and **[9291]**, Okemos, MI
Orchestra; Upper Arlington Community **[14754]**, Columbus, OH
Orchestras
Upper Arlington Community Orchestra **[14754]**, Columbus, OH
Orchid Growers Guild **[18592]**, Madison, WI
Orchid Society, Fort Wayne; Three Rivers **[4724]**, Fort Wayne, IN
Orchid Soc. of Minnesota **[11128]**, Hastings, MN
Order of the Eastern Star Minnesota Grand Chap. **[11718]**, Minneapolis, MN
Oregon Chamber of Commerce **[2869]**, Oregon, IL
Oregon Lions Club **[2870]**, Oregon, IL
Organ
Children's Organ Transplant Assn. **[4212]**, Bloomington, IN
Organic Consumers Assn. **[11340]**, Little Marais, MN
Organic Crop Improvement Assn., Michigan- Chap. 2 **[9561]**, Rosebush, MI
Organic Crop Improvement Assn., Minnesota **[12072]**, Red Lake Falls, MN
Organic Crop Improvement Assn., Northeast Wisconsin **[18321]**, Kewaunee, WI
Organic Crop Improvement Assn., Ohio- Chap. 1 **[17192]**, West Salem, OH
Organic Crop Improvement Assn., Ohio- Chap. 2 **[14811]**, Crestline, OH
Organic Crop Improvement Assn., Wisconsin- Chap. 1 **[19546]**, Pulaski, WI
Organic Farming
Community Cultivators **[1635]**, Elsah, IL
Organic Consumers Assn. **[11340]**, Little Marais, MN
Organic Crop Improvement Assn., Michigan- Chap. 2 **[9561]**, Rosebush, MI
Organic Crop Improvement Assn., Minnesota **[12072]**, Red Lake Falls, MN
Organic Crop Improvement Assn., Northeast Wisconsin **[18321]**, Kewaunee, WI
Organic Crop Improvement Assn., Ohio- Chap. 1 **[17192]**, West Salem, OH
Organic Crop Improvement Assn., Ohio- Chap. 2 **[14811]**, Crestline, OH
Organic Crop Improvement Assn., Wisconsin- Chap. 1 **[19546]**, Pulaski, WI
Organists, Detroit Chap; Amer. Guild of **[10059]**, Warren, MI
Organists, Holland Area C556; Amer. Guild of **[8189]**, Holland, MI
Org. of Chinese Amers. - Columbus Chap. **[14706]**, Columbus, OH
Org. of Chinese Amers. - Greater Chicago Chap. **[1115]**, Chicago, IL
Organization Development
Capital City Organizational Development Network **[14350]**, Columbus, OH
Detroit Org. Network **[9985]**, Troy, MI
Great Lakes Org. Development Network **[13152]**, Archbold, OH
Greater Cincinnati/Dayton Org. Development Network **[15724]**, Loveland, OH
Indianapolis Org. Development Network **[5354]**, Indianapolis, IN
Minnesota Org. Development Network **[12660]**, Shoreview, MN
Org. Development Connection of Northeast Ohio **[14203]**, Cleveland, OH
Org. Development Network of Chicago **[1116]**, Chicago, IL
Org. Development Connection of Northeast Ohio **[14203]**, Cleveland, OH
Org. Development Network of Chicago **[1116]**, Chicago, IL
Org. of Islamic Speakers, Midwest **[2660]**, Naperville, IL
Org. for a New Eastside **[5444]**, Indianapolis, IN
Org. of the North East **[1117]**, Chicago, IL
Organizations
Citizens Against Repressive Zoning **[8146]**, Haslett, MI
Coun. of Michigan Foundations **[7856]**, Grand Haven, MI
Lake Chapeau Habitat Comm. **[10259]**, Albert Lea, MN
Ten Thousand Villages-Minnesota **[12596]**, St. Paul, MN
Oriental Healing
Illinois State Acupuncture Assn. **[969]**, Chicago, IL
Michigan Assn. of Acupuncture and Oriental Medicine **[9451]**, Portage, MI
Orienteering
Badger Orienteering Club **[20116]**, West Bend, WI
Badin ROKS **[15380]**, Hamilton, OH
Central Ohio Orienteering **[16420]**, Pickerington, OH
Chicago Area Orienteering Club **[3981]**, Wheaton, IL
Illinois River Valley Orienteering Club **[1521]**, Dunlap, IL
Indiana Crossroads Orienteering **[4324]**, Carmel, IN
Miami Valley Orienteering Club **[14916]**, Dayton, OH
Minnesota Orienteering Club **[11663]**, Minneapolis, MN
North Eastern Ohio Orienteering Club **[14181]**, Cleveland, OH
Northern Illinois Orienteering Club **[3714]**, Stockton, IL
Orienteering Club of Cincinnati **[15399]**, Hamilton, OH
Orienteering Wilmington Coll. **[17293]**, Wilmington, OH
Southern Michigan Orienteering Club **[6771]**, Ann Arbor, MI
Steinmetz HS JROTC Pathfinders **[1201]**, Chicago, IL
Orienteering Club of Cincinnati **[15399]**, Hamilton, OH
Orienteering Club; Illinois River Valley **[1521]**, Dunlap, IL
Orienteering Wilmington Coll. **[17293]**, Wilmington, OH
Original Circle City Corvette Club **[5445]**, Indianapolis, IN

Orion Area Chamber of Commerce **[8517]**, Lake Orion, MI
Orland Park Area Chamber of Commerce **[2883]**, Orland Park, IL
Orland Park Open Lands Corp. **[2884]**, Orland Park, IL
Orleans Chamber of Commerce **[6014]**, Orleans, IN
Ornithology
Minnesota Ornithologists' Union **[11664]**, Minneapolis, MN
Orono District Lions Club **[11344]**, Long Lake, MN
Orr Lions Club **[11943]**, Orr, MN
Orrville Area United Way **[16309]**, Orrville, OH
Orthodontists; Great Lakes Assn. of **[14445]**, Columbus, OH
Orthodontists; Great Lakes Soc. of **[★14445]**
Orthodox Christians United in Service Focus; Fellowship of **[4923]**, Hobart, IN
Orthopaedic Technologists Assn. of Illinois **[1118]**, Chicago, IL
Orthopedics
Mid-America Orthopaedic Assn. **[12156]**, Rochester, MN
Orton Dyslexia Soc; Northern Ohio Br. of the **[★16682]**
Ortonville Area Chamber of Commerce **[★11945]**
Ortonville Lions Club **[11946]**, Ortonville, MN
Osakis Lions Club **[11949]**, Osakis, MN
Osceola Area Chamber of Commerce **[19383]**, Osceola, WI
Osceola Economic Alliance **[9482]**, Reed City, MI
Osceola Economic Development Corp. **[★9482]**
Oscoda Area United Way **[9317]**, Oscoda, MI
Oshkosh Area United Way **[19400]**, Oshkosh, WI
Oshkosh Assn. of Manufacturers and Commence **[★19401]**
Oshkosh Chamber of Commerce **[19401]**, Oshkosh, WI
Oshkosh Earth Sci. Club **[17511]**, Appleton, WI
Oshkosh Philatelic Society **[17989]**, Fond du Lac, WI
Oshkosh Table Tennis Org. **[19402]**, Oshkosh, WI
Oshkosh Violet Soc. **[19358]**, Omro, WI
Oslo Lions Club **[11951]**, Oslo, MN
Osman Shriners **[12558]**, St. Paul, MN
Osseo Lions Club **[12032]**, Plymouth, MN
Osteopathic Medicine
Illinois Osteopathic Medical Assn. **[953]**, Chicago, IL
Michigan Osteopathic Assn. **[9288]**, Okemos, MI
Minnesota Osteopathic Medical Soc. **[11291]**, Lakeland, MN
Ohio Osteopathic Assn. **[14649]**, Columbus, OH
Osteopathy
Indiana Acad. of Osteopathy **[5160]**, Indianapolis, IN
Indiana Osteopathic Assn. **[5273]**, Indianapolis, IN
Osteopathy; Indiana Acad. of **[5160]**, Indianapolis, IN
Ostomy
Kokomo Area Chap. of the United Ostomy Assn. **[5573]**, Kokomo, IN
St. Paul Ostomy Assn. **[12584]**, St. Paul, MN
Ostomy Assn; Kokomo Area Chap. of the United **[5573]**, Kokomo, IN
Ostomy Assn; St. Paul **[12584]**, St. Paul, MN
Ostrander Lions Club **[11955]**, Ostrander, MN
Oswego Chamber of Commerce **[2893]**, Oswego, IL
Otisville Lions Club **[9322]**, Otisville, MI
Otorhinolaryngology
Soc. of Otorhinolaryngology and Head/Neck Nurses - Chicago Chap. **[240]**, Berwyn, IL
Soc. of Otorhinolaryngology and Head/Neck Nurses - Grand Rapids Chap. **[8011]**, Grand Rapids, MI
Soc. of Otorhinolaryngology and Head/Neck Nurses - Greater Cleveland Area Chap. **[16398]**, Pepper Pike, OH
Soc. of Otorhinolaryngology and Head/Neck Nurses - Wisconsin Chap. **[19305]**, New Glarus, WI
Otsego Area Chamber of Commerce **[9325]**, Otsego, MI
Otsego Area Historical Soc. **[9326]**, Otsego, MI
Otsego County Fair Association **[7821]**, Gaylord, MI
Otsego County United Way **[7822]**, Gaylord, MI
Ottawa and Allegan Counties Youth for Christ **[8214]**, Holland, MI
Ottawa Area Chamber of Commerce **[16318]**, Ottawa, OH
Ottawa Area Chamber of Commerce and Indus. **[2899]**, Ottawa, IL
Ottawa Back Country Horsemen, Michigan **[7033]**, Bruce Crossing, MI
Ottawa County Beagle Club **[8293]**, Hudsonville, MI
Ottawa County Economic Development Off. **[6626]**, Allendale, MI
Ottawa County Medical Soc. **[8215]**, Holland, MI
Ottawa Lions Club **[16319]**, Ottawa, OH
Ottawa River Beagle Club **[16945]**, Toledo, OH
Ottertail County - Young Life **[11001]**, Fergus Falls, MN
Our Lady of Grace School Home and School Assn. **[4919]**, Highland, IN
Our Lady of the Rosary - Young Life **[15166]**, Fairfield, OH
Outagamie County Historical Soc. **[17512]**, Appleton, WI
Outagamie County Pioneer and Historical Soc. **[★17512]**
Outagamie Museum **[★17512]**
Outagamie Philatelic Soc. **[17513]**, Appleton, WI
Outback Trail Commn. **[4929]**, Hobart, IN
Outdoor Advt. Assn. of Michigan **[7416]**, Detroit, MI
Outdoor Advt. Assn. of Wisconsin **[18593]**, Madison, WI
Outdoor Pursuits; Columbus **[14399]**, Columbus, OH
Outdoor Recreation
Columbus Outdoor Pursuits **[14399]**, Columbus, OH
Prairie Club **[1626]**, Elmhurst, IL
Vinton County Convention and Visitors Bur. **[15928]**, McArthur, OH
Wisconsin Outdoor Access **[18275]**, Jefferson, WI
OutReach **[18594]**, Madison, WI
Outreach for Animals **[14944]**, Dayton, OH
Over-The-Rhine Chamber of Commerce **[13949]**, Cincinnati, OH
Overflowing Cup Christian Coffee House Ministry **[★17615]**
Overflowing Cup Total Life Center **[17615]**, Beloit, WI
Overseas Coun. **[★5446]**
Overseas Coun. Intl. **[5446]**, Indianapolis, IN
Ovid Lions Club **[9331]**, Ovid, MI
Owatonna Area Chamber of Commerce **[★11962]**
Owatonna Area Chamber of Commerce and Tourism **[11962]**, Owatonna, MN
Owatonna Arts Center **[11963]**, Owatonna, MN
Owatonna Arts Coun. **[★11963]**
Owatonna Bus. Incubator **[11964]**, Owatonna, MN
Owatonna Figure Skating Club **[11965]**, Owatonna, MN
Owatonna Incubator **[★11964]**
Owatonna Wyldlife **[11966]**, Owatonna, MN
Owatonna Young Life **[11967]**, Owatonna, MN
Owen County Chamber of Commerce and Economic Development Corp. **[6282]**, Spencer, IN
Owen Marsh Elementary School Parent Teacher Org. **[3658]**, Springfield, IL
Owners Assn; Cleveland Vessel **[★14153]**
Owners Assn; Village of Turner Trace Property **[★5495]**
Owners and Managers Assn. of Metropolitan Detroit; Building **[7657]**, Farmington Hills, MI
Owners; Motor City Viper **[6988]**, Bloomfield Hills, MI
Owosso-Corunna Area Chamber of Commerce **[★9337]**
Owosso/Corunna Lions Club **[9334]**, Owosso, MI
Oxford Area Chamber of Commerce **[9340]**, Oxford, MI
Oxford Audubon Soc. **[16325]**, Oxford, OH
Oxford Chamber of Commerce **[16326]**, Oxford, OH
Oxford Lions Club - Ohio **[16327]**, Oxford, OH
Oxford Merchant Assn. **[★9340]**
Ozaukee Humane Soc. **[18065]**, Grafton, WI
Ozaukee Realtors Assn. **[18066]**, Grafton, WI
Ozaukee-Washington County ALU **[19085]**, Milwaukee, WI

P

PACER Center **[11719]**, Minneapolis, MN
Packaging
Inst. of Packaging Professionals, Central Indiana Chap. **[5369]**, Indianapolis, IN
Inst. of Packaging Professionals, Michigan Chap. **[9181]**, New Baltimore, MI
Institute of Packaging Professionals, West Michigan Chapter **[8431]**, Kalamazoo, MI
Packaging Professionals, Michigan Chap; Inst. of **[9181]**, New Baltimore, MI
Packer Country Sports and Ports **[18126]**, Green Bay, WI
Packerland Kennel Club **[18127]**, Green Bay, WI
Packerland Theatre Organ Soc. **[17814]**, De Pere, WI
PACT Humane Society **[1507]**, Downers Grove, IL
Pageant Assn; Miss Rodeo Wisconsin **[19729]**, Shiocton, WI
Pain
Midwest Pain Soc. **[1871]**, Glenview, IL
Painesville Area Chamber of Commerce **[16342]**, Painesville, OH
Painesville Area Habitat for Humanity **[16343]**, Painesville, OH
Paint Creek Foklore Soc. **[9516]**, Rochester Hills, MI
Paint a Miracle **[9508]**, Rochester, MI
Painters AFL-CIO, LU 156 **[★4557]**
Painting and Taping Contractors Assn; Northern Ohio **[15998]**, Middleburg Heights, OH
Paints and Finishes
Soc. for Protective Coatings, North Central **[11749]**, Minneapolis, MN
Pak Gymkhana **[1119]**, Chicago, IL
Palace Cultural Arts Assn. **[15850]**, Marion, OH
Palatine Area Chamber of Commerce **[2921]**, Palatine, IL
Palatine/Fremd - Young Life **[2922]**, Palatine, IL
Palatine Historical Soc. **[2923]**, Palatine, IL
Palatine Lions Club **[2924]**, Palatine, IL
Palestine Chamber of Commerce **[2931]**, Palestine, IL
Palestine Development Assn. **[2932]**, Palestine, IL
Palliative CareCenter and Hospice of the North Shore **[1672]**, Evanston, IL
Palmyra Area Chamber of Commerce **[19418]**, Palmyra, WI
Palos Hills Chamber of Commerce **[2941]**, Palos Hills, IL
Palos Sportsman's Club **[1730]**, Frankfort, IL
Pan-African Assn. **[1120]**, Chicago, IL
Pana Chamber of Commerce **[2945]**, Pana, IL
Paoli Chamber of Commerce **[6020]**, Paoli, IN
Paper
Pulp and Paper Manufacturers Assn. **[17519]**, Appleton, WI
Tech. Assn. of the Pulp and Paper Indus. - Chicago Sect. **[4011]**, Willow Springs, IL
Tech. Assn. of the Pulp and Paper Indus. - Ohio Sect. **[14961]**, Dayton, OH
Paper, Allied-Industrial, Chem. and Energy Workers Intl. Union, AFL-CIO, CLC Local Union 2-232 **[19086]**, Milwaukee, WI
Paper, Allied-Indus., Chem. and Energy Workers Intl. Union, AFL-CIO, CLC - Local Union 369 **[20125]**, West Bend, WI
Paper, Allied-Indus., Chem. and Energy Workers Intl. Union, AFL-CIO, CLC - Local Union 555 **[6419]**, Vincennes, IN
Paper, Allied-Indus., Chem. and Energy Workers Intl. Union, AFL-CIO, CLC - Local Union 609 **[13950]**, Cincinnati, OH
Paper, Allied-Indus., Chem. and Energy Workers Intl. Union, AFL-CIO, CLC - Local Union 801 **[16310]**, Orrville, OH
Paper Money Collectors of Michigan **[9341]**, Oxford, MI
Paralegal Assn. of Northwest Ohio **[16946]**, Toledo, OH
Paralegals
Central Illinois Paralegal Assn. **[274]**, Bloomington, IL
Cincinnati Paralegal Assn. **[13796]**, Cincinnati, OH
Illinois Paralegal Assn. **[2690]**, New Lenox, IL
Paralegal Assn. of Northwest Ohio **[16946]**, Toledo, OH
Paralyzed Veterans of Am., Michigan Chap. **[9244]**, Novi, MI
Paralyzed Veterans of Am., Ohio; Buckeye Chap. **[★15139]**
Paralyzed Veterans of Am., Vaughan Chap. **[3957]**, Westchester, IL

Paralyzed Veterans of America, Wisconsin Chapter [★20110]
Paramount Tall Club of Chicago [1121], Chicago, IL
Parapsychology
St. Cloud Extraordinary Pseudoscience Teaching Investigations and Community Service [12301], St. Cloud, MN
Parasitology
Pennfield Parent Teacher and Student Org. [6867], Battle Creek, MI
Pardeeville Area Bus. Assn. [19423], Pardeeville, WI
Parent Coun; John Allen [6712], Ann Arbor, MI
Parent Teacher Org; Barnard Elementary School [9977], Troy, MI
Parent Teacher Org; Chagrin Falls [13631], Chagrin Falls, OH
Parent Teacher Org; Columbus [11016], Forest Lake, MN
Parent Teacher Organization; East China Consolidated [7152], China, MI
Parent Teacher Org; Hoover-Wood Elementary School [181], Batavia, IL
Parent Teacher Org; Liberty Benton [15205], Findlay, OH
Parent Teacher Organization; Lily Lake Elementary [12721], Stillwater, MN
Parent Teacher Org; Meadowlawn [5825], Monticello, IN
Parent Teacher Organization; Oconto Elementary School [19349], Oconto, WI
Parent Teacher Org; Owen Marsh Elementary School [3658], Springfield, IL
Parent Teacher Org; Troy Special Services [10014], Troy, MI
Parent Teacher Organization; University Avenue [10453], Blaine, MN
Parent Teacher and Student Org; Pennfield [6867], Battle Creek, MI
Parent Teacher Student Org; Plainfield South High School [3106], Plainfield, IL
Parent-Teachers-Students Org; Clague Middle School [6691], Ann Arbor, MI
Parenthood Assn. of Summit County; Planned [★13081]
Parenthood of Summit, Portage, and Medina Counties; Planned [13081], Akron, OH
Parents
Atwater School PTA [19731], Shorewood, WI
Barnard Elementary School Parent Teacher Org. [9977], Troy, MI
Ben Franklin Parent Teacher Assn. [1826], Glen Ellyn, IL
Bennie PTA [6609], Allen Park, MI
Bluffview Montessori PTA [12948], Winona, MN
Caldwell Elementary School PTA [4875], Hammond, IN
Central High School PTSA [503], Champaign, IL
Chagrin Falls Parent Teacher Org. [13631], Chagrin Falls, OH
Champaign PTA Coun. [510], Champaign, IL
Chicago Region PTA [827], Chicago, IL
Churchill High School PTSA [8835], Livonia, MI
Climax - Scotts PTA [9734], Scotts, MI
Clinton Rosette Middle School PTA [1430], DeKalb, IL
Cumberland PTA [17800], Cumberland, WI
DADS Am., Ohio [15432], Hilliard, OH
Downers Grove South High School Parent Teacher Assn. [1502], Downers Grove, IL
Eggers Middle School PTSA [4878], Hammond, IN
Evansville Area Coun. of Parent Teacher Assns. [4542], Evansville, IN
Flossie Wiley Elementary School PTA [3815], Urbana, IL
Foster and Adoptive Care Assn. of Minnesota [11279], Lake Elmo, MN
Franklin Elementary School PTA [17495], Appleton, WI
Gavit PTSA [4880], Hammond, IN
GHHS PTSA [7857], Grand Haven, MI
Glenbard North PTSA [450], Carol Stream, IL
Glencoe PTO [1850], Glencoe, IL
Golf School District 67 PTA [2568], Morton Grove, IL
Gray M. Sanborn PTA [2910], Palatine, IL
Greater Cleveland Chap. of Parents of Murdered Children [15967], Mentor, OH
Haigh PTA [7260], Dearborn, MI
Hampton Elementary PTA [7372], Detroit, MI
Hearts At Home [2714], Normal, IL
Henry Sibley High School PTA [11458], Mendota Heights, MN
High School Coun. PTSA [914], Chicago, IL
Holbrook Elementary School PTA [7873], Grand Ledge, MI
Hoover-Wood Elementary School Parent Teacher Org. [181], Batavia, IL
Hugger Elementary PTA [9503], Rochester, MI
Illinois Natl. Cong. of Parents and Teachers [3620], Springfield, IL
Indiana Natl. Cong. of Parents and Teachers [5264], Indianapolis, IN
Indiana PTA [5285], Indianapolis, IN
Jane Addams Middle School PTA [9584], Royal Oak, MI
John Allen Parent Coun. [6712], Ann Arbor, MI
John Muir PTA [2037], Hoffman Estates, IL
Kenwood Elementary PTA [533], Champaign, IL
Kingsley PTA [1665], Evanston, IL
Lathers Elementary School PTA [7813], Garden City, MI
Liberty Benton Parent Teacher Org. [15205], Findlay, OH
Lincoln Prairie PTSA [2038], Hoffman Estates, IL
Lindley Elementary PTA [4690], Fort Wayne, IN
Michigan Cong. of Parents, Teachers and Students [8650], Lansing, MI
Minnesota PTA [12513], St. Paul, MN
Mothers' Center of Greater Toledo [16931], Toledo, OH
Mothers Connection PTA [10898], Eden Prairie, MN
Mothers from Hell 2 [3081], Peru, IL
Munster High School PTO [5904], Munster, IN
Nettleton Magnet School PTA [10843], Duluth, MN
Northcrest Elementary School PTA [4701], Fort Wayne, IN
Northwood Middle School PTSA [4706], Fort Wayne, IN
O.A. Thorp Scholastic Acad. Parent-Teacher Assn. [1111], Chicago, IL
Ohio Family Care Assn. [14605], Columbus, OH
Ohio Natl. Cong. of Parents and Teachers [14642], Columbus, OH
Orchard Drive PTA [4889], Hammond, IN
Parents of Murdered Children Minnesota Hope Chap. [10666], Circle Pines, MN
Parents TV Coun. - Carbondale, Illinois/Paducah, Kentucky Chap. [426], Carbondale, IL
Parents TV Coun. - Central Illinois Chap. [3659], Springfield, IL
Parents TV Coun. - Chicago Illinois Chap. [150], Barrington, IL
Parents TV Coun. - Cincinnati, Ohio Chap. [13953], Cincinnati, OH
Parents TV Coun. - Minnesota Chap. [11455], Mendota, MN
Parents TV Coun. - South Bend, Indiana Chap. [6250], South Bend, IN
Parents TV Coun. - Southeast Michigan Chap. [6750], Ann Arbor, MI
Parents Without Partners, Ann Arbor Chap. 38 [6751], Ann Arbor, MI
Parents Without Partners, Cincinnati Chap. 203 [13954], Cincinnati, OH
Parents Without Partners, Dayton [14945], Dayton, OH
Parents Without Partners, Lake Geauga [15976], Mentor, OH
Parents Without Partners, Ogden Trails [1508], Downers Grove, IL
Plainfield South High School Parent Teacher Student Org. [3106], Plainfield, IL
Rochester High School PTSA [9518], Rochester Hills, MI
St. Mary's Preparatory Moms and Dads Club [9312], Orchard Lake, MI
Stevens Point PTSA [19810], Stevens Point, WI
Stone Acad. PTA [1202], Chicago, IL
Virginia Lake PTA [2929], Palatine, IL
Wadsworth School PTA [4861], Griffith, IN
Wauwatosa West PTA [20084], Wauwatosa, WI
Willow Ridge Elementary PTA [7876], Grand Ledge, MI
Winona Senior High School PTSA [12965], Winona, MN
Wisconsin Natl. Cong. of Parents and Teachers [18732], Madison, WI
Parents And Children for Equality [13951], Cincinnati, OH
Parents Anonymous of Central and Southern Ohio [14707], Columbus, OH
Parents Anonymous of Chicago, Illinois [1122], Chicago, IL
Parents Anonymous of Marquette, Michigan [8956], Marquette, MI
Parents Anonymous of Stark County and Northern Ohio [13576], Canton, OH
Parents Anonymous of Washington County, Wisconsin [20126], West Bend, WI
Parents As Teachers of Hammond Lake County [4890], Hammond, IN
Parents are Important in Rochester [12167], Rochester, MN
Parents for Literacy; Concerned [9063], Monroe, MI
Parents of Murdered Children Minnesota Hope Chap. [10666], Circle Pines, MN
Parents for Public Schools, Cincinnati Chap. [13952], Cincinnati, OH
Parents for Public Schools, Oberlin Chap. [16292], Oberlin, OH
Parents for Public Schools of Toledo [16947], Toledo, OH
Parents TV Coun. - Carbondale, Illinois/Paducah, Kentucky Chap. [426], Carbondale, IL
Parents TV Coun. - Central Illinois Chap. [3659], Springfield, IL
Parents TV Coun. - Chicago Illinois Chap. [150], Barrington, IL
Parents TV Coun. - Cincinnati, Ohio Chap. [13953], Cincinnati, OH
Parents TV Coun. - Minnesota Chap. [11455], Mendota, MN
Parents TV Coun. - South Bend, Indiana Chap. [6250], South Bend, IN
Parents TV Coun. - Southeast Michigan Chap. [6750], Ann Arbor, MI
Parents Without Partners, Ann Arbor Chap. 38 [6751], Ann Arbor, MI
Parents Without Partners, Cincinnati [★13954]
Parents Without Partners, Cincinnati Chap. 203 [13954], Cincinnati, OH
Parents Without Partners, Dayton [14945], Dayton, OH
Parents Without Partners, Lake Geauga [15976], Mentor, OH
Parents Without Partners, Ogden Trails [1508], Downers Grove, IL
Paris Area Chamber of Commerce [★2950]
Paris Area Chamber of Commerce and Tourism [2950], Paris, IL
Paris Lions Club - Ohio [16350], Paris, OH
Park Assn; Michigan Recreation and [9290], Okemos, MI
Park Assn; Minnesota Recreation and [11035], Fridley, MN
Park Falls Area Chamber of Commerce [19425], Park Falls, WI
Park Forest Historical Soc. [2954], Park Forest, IL
Park Forest Table Tennis Club [2955], Park Forest, IL
Park; Friends of the [3787], Troy, IL
Park; Friends of Lagrange Community [15577], Lagrange, OH
Park Lawn Arc [2800], Oak Lawn, IL
Park People of Milwaukee County [19087], Milwaukee, WI
Park Rapids Area Chamber of Commerce [11978], Park Rapids, MN
Park and Recreation Assn; Wisconsin [18153], Greendale, WI
Park and Recreation Found; Bloomington Community [4205], Bloomington, IN
Park Ridge Chamber of Commerce [2964], Park Ridge, IL
Park River Estates Resident Coun. Found. [10715], Coon Rapids, MN
Parke County Chamber of Commerce [6135], Rockville, IN
Parking
Michigan Parking Assn. [7399], Detroit, MI

Wisconsin Parking Assn. [19174], Milwaukee, WI
Parkinson Found; Michigan [9808], Southfield, MI
Parkinson's Awareness Assn. of Central Indiana [5447], Indianapolis, IN
ParkLands Found. [303], Bloomington, IL
Parks Chamber of Commerce [★2351]
Parks; Friends of Novi [9236], Novi, MI
Parks and Recreation
Arcade Park Garden Club [734], Chicago, IL
Bloomington Community Park and Recreation Found. [4205], Bloomington, IN
Friends of Governor Dodge State Park [17838], Dodgeville, WI
Friends of Governor Nelson State Park [20016], Waunakee, WI
Friends of Lagrange Community Park [15577], Lagrange, OH
Friends of Lexington Area Parks [12227], Roseville, MN
Friends of Medina County Parks [15940], Medina, OH
Friends of Novi Parks [9236], Novi, MI
Friends of the Parks [899], Chicago, IL
Friends of Pontiac Lake Recreation Area [10083], Waterford, MI
Friends of Stark Parks [13566], Canton, OH
Friends of Voyageurs National Park [11215], International Falls, MN
Garfield Park Conservatory Alliance [901], Chicago, IL
George Wright Soc. [8110], Hancock, MI
Illinois Assn. of Park Districts [3575], Springfield, IL
Illinois Park and Recreation Assn. [2835], Oakbrook Terrace, IL
Isle Royale Natural History Assn. [8254], Houghton, MI
Michigan Recreation and Park Assn. [9290], Okemos, MI
Minnesota Recreation and Park Assn. [11035], Fridley, MN
Natl. Recreation and Park Assn. - Central Region [2039], Hoffman Estates, IL
Ohio Parks and Recreation Assn. [17218], Westerville, OH
Univ. of Wisconsin, Stevens Point - Wisconsin Parks and Recreation Assn. [19815], Stevens Point, WI
Wisconsin Park and Recreation Assn. [18153], Greendale, WI
Parliamentarians; Ohio Assn. of [16566], Sagamore Hills, OH
Parliaments
Michigan State Assn. of Parliamentarians [9809], Southfield, MI
Ohio Assn. of Parliamentarians [16566], Sagamore Hills, OH
Wisconsin Assn. of Parliamentarians [18661], Madison, WI
Parma Area Chamber of Commerce [16376], Parma, OH
Parma-Spring Arbor Lions Club [9344], Parma, MI
Parmatown African Violet Club [16239], North Olmsted, OH
Particle Soc. of Minnesota [12984], Woodbury, MN
Partners for Affordable Housing [11396], Mankato, MN
Partners in Charity [3947], West Dundee, IL
Partners in Community and Collaboration [13955], Cincinnati, OH
Partners in Play [1714], Forest Park, IL
Pastors Fellowship of Rochester; Evangelical [12138], Rochester, MN
Pastways [7648], Farmington, MI
Pathfinders [19088], Milwaukee, WI
Pathfinders Ski Club [3040], Peoria, IL
Patients Alliance; Hospice [9524], Rockford, MI
Patton's Woods Nature Preserve Comm. [542], Champaign, IL
Paul Bunyan ALU [10389], Baxter, MN
Paul Bunyan Bd. of Realtors [7048], Cadillac, MI
Paulding County United Way [16388], Paulding, OH
Paullin Lib; Friends of the [15037], Doylestown, OH
Pavement Assn; Wisconsin Asphalt [18647], Madison, WI
Paving Assn; Michigan Concrete [9276], Okemos, MI
Paw Paw Chamber of Commerce [★9346]
Paw Paw Lions Club [9347], Paw Paw, MI
Paws [17454], Adams, WI
Paws with a Cause NH Chap. [10098], Wayland, MI
Paxton Area Chamber of Commerce [2975], Paxton, IL
Paxton Lions Club [2976], Paxton, IL
Payments Authority [10005], Troy, MI
Payments Central [14708], Columbus, OH
Paynesville Area Chamber of Commerce [11983], Paynesville, MN
PC - WyldLife [9403], Plymouth, MI
Peace
Amer. Friends Ser. Comm., Michigan Area Off. [6659], Ann Arbor, MI
Appalachian Peace and Justice Network [13195], Athens, OH
Cleveland Peace Action [14101], Cleveland, OH
Cranbrook Peace Found. [6982], Bloomfield Hills, MI
Friends for a Non-Violent World [12415], St. Paul, MN
Interfaith Coun. for Peace and Justice [6709], Ann Arbor, MI
Minnesota Veterans for Peace - Chap. 27 [11681], Minneapolis, MN
North Manchester Fellowship of Reconciliation [5989], North Manchester, IN
Peace Coalition of Southern Illinois Fellowship of Reconciliation [427], Carbondale, IL
Peaceways-Young General Assembly [19591], Reedsburg, WI
Veterans For Peace - Chap. 93 [10217], Ypsilanti, MI
Wisconsin Network for Peace and Justice [18734], Madison, WI
Women's Intl. League for Peace and Freedom - Ann Arbor/Ypsilanti [6793], Ann Arbor, MI
Peace Action Wisconsin [19089], Milwaukee, WI
Peace Coalition of Southern Illinois Fellowship of Reconciliation [427], Carbondale, IL
Peace Corps-Minneapolis [11720], Minneapolis, MN
Peace and Justice Network; Appalachian [13195], Athens, OH
Peace and Justice; Wisconsin Network for [18734], Madison, WI
Peace March; Walkacross America for Mother Earth/Ohio [★14411]
Peace Presence to Stop Proj. Elf; Women's [★19089]
Peaceways-Young General Assembly [19591], Reedsburg, WI
Pediatric Heart Res. Assn. [17178], West Chester, OH
Pediatrics
Amer. Acad. of Pediatrics, Illinois Chap. [605], Chicago, IL
Amer. Acad. of Pediatrics, Indiana Chap. [4971], Indianapolis, IN
Amer. Acad. of Pediatrics, Minnesota Chap. [12349], St. Paul, MN
Amer. Acad. of Pediatrics, Wisconsin Chap. [18449], Madison, WI
Illinois Chapter, American Academy of Pediatrics [932], Chicago, IL
Illinois Soc. of Pediatric Dentists [966], Chicago, IL
Pee Wee Football and Cheerleading; Middletown [16015], Middletown, OH
Pekin Area Bd. of Realtors [2988], Pekin, IL
Pekin Area Chamber of Commerce [2989], Pekin, IL
Pekin Lions Club [2990], Pekin, IL
Pekin Main St. [2991], Pekin, IL
Pelican Lake Chamber of Commerce [19429], Pelican Lake, WI
Pelican Rapids Area Chamber of Commerce [11986], Pelican Rapids, MN
Pelican Rapids CC Walking Club [11987], Pelican Rapids, MN
Pelican Rapids Chamber of Commerce [★11986]
Pembina Trail Rsrc. Conservation and Development Coun. [12073], Red Lake Falls, MN
Pembroke Welsh Corgi Club of the Western Reserve [13638], Chagrin Falls, OH
Pencil Society of America, Detroit Chapter No. 104; Colored [9745], Shelby Township, MI
Peninsula Chamber of Commerce [★15808]
Penn-Ohio Chap. Natl. Elecl. Contractors Assn. [17410], Youngstown, OH
Penn State Alumni Assn., Central Illinois [2729], Normal, IL
Penn State Alumni Assn., Central Indiana Chap. [4852], Greenwood, IN
Penn State Alumni Assn., Greater Chicago Chap. [1838], Glen Ellyn, IL
Penn State Alumni Assn., Michigan [9773], South Lyon, MI
Penn State Alumni Assn., Minnesota Chap. [12661], Shoreview, MN
Penn - Young Life [6251], South Bend, IN
Pennfield Lions Club [6866], Battle Creek, MI
Pennfield Parent Teacher and Student Org. [6867], Battle Creek, MI
Pennock Lions Club [11989], Pennock, MN
Penton Owners Gp. [13141], Amherst, OH
Pentwater Area Chamber of Commerce [★9352]
Pentwater Chamber of Commerce [9352], Pentwater, MI
People for the Amer. Way, Illinois [1123], Chicago, IL
People First of Illinois [304], Bloomington, IL
People First of Ohio [16088], Mount Vernon, OH
People and Paws Search and Rescue [19090], Milwaukee, WI
People Taking Action Against Abortion [★8856]
People Who Care Booster Club [11721], Minneapolis, MN
People Working Cooperatively - serving the Greater Cincinnati Community [13956], Cincinnati, OH
People's Rights Org. [14709], Columbus, OH
Peoria Acad. Of Sci. - Geology Sect. [3041], Peoria, IL
Peoria AIFA [3042], Peoria, IL
Peoria Area Assn. of Realtors [3043], Peoria, IL
Peoria Area Chamber of Commerce [3044], Peoria, IL
Peoria Area Convention and Visitors Bur. [3045], Peoria, IL
Peoria Area Miniature Soc. [3046], Peoria, IL
Peoria Area Mountain Bike Assn. [3047], Peoria, IL
Peoria Area Youth for Christ [3048], Peoria, IL
Peoria Assn. For Retarded Citizens [3049], Peoria, IL
Peoria Astronomical Soc. [1522], Dunlap, IL
Peoria Citizens Comm. for Economic Opportunity [★3020]
Peoria County Bar Assn. [3050], Peoria, IL
Peoria District Dental Soc. [3051], Peoria, IL
Peoria Girls Sports League [3052], Peoria, IL
Peoria Heights Chamber of Commerce [3053], Peoria, IL
Peoria Lions Club [3054], Peoria, IL
Peoria Medical Soc. [3055], Peoria, IL
Peoria Obedience Training Club [3056], Peoria, IL
Peoria Orchid Soc. [1545], East Peoria, IL
Peoria Sheet Metal, Air Conditioning and Roofing Contractors Assn. [★3012]
Peoria Skeet and Trap [1546], East Peoria, IL
Peoria Youth Hockey Assn. [3057], Peoria, IL
Peotone Woman's Club [3072], Peotone, IL
Performance Network Theatre [6752], Ann Arbor, MI
Performing Arts
Amer. Fed. of Musicians, Local 101-473 [14840], Dayton, OH
Ann Arbor Fed. of Musicians - Local 625, Amer. Fed. of Musicians [6673], Ann Arbor, MI
Ballet Tech Ohio Performing Arts Assn. [15752], Maineville, OH
Chicago Cabaret Professionals [796], Chicago, IL
Chicago Fed. of Musicians [809], Chicago, IL
Chiesa Nuova [843], Chicago, IL
Cincinnati Musicians' Assn. - Local 1, Amer. Fed. of Musicians [13792], Cincinnati, OH
Detroit Fed. of Musicians - Local 5, Amer. Fed. of Musicians [9797], Southfield, MI
Eastern Howard Performing Arts Soc. [4845], Greentown, IN
Gaia Collective [11567], Minneapolis, MN
Grand Rapids Fed. of Musicians - Local 56, Amer. Fed. of Musicians [7949], Grand Rapids, MI
Harrison St. Cooperative of Performing and Fine Arts [2811], Oak Park, IL
Indianapolis Musicians - Local 3, Amer. Fed. of Musicians [5353], Indianapolis, IN
Intl. Alliance of Theatrical Stage Employees, Moving Picture Technicians, Artists, M 251 [18527], Madison, WI

Intl. Alliance of Theatrical Stage Employees, Moving Picture Technicians, Artists, M 470 [19394], Oshkosh, WI
Intl. Alliance of Theatrical Stage Employees, Moving Picture Technicians, Artists, M 618 [4237], Bloomington, IN
Intl. Alliance of Theatrical Stage Employees, Moving Picture Technicians, Artists, MPP, OandVT 160 [14142], Cleveland, OH
Intl. Alliance of Theatrical Stage Employees, Moving Picture Technicians, Artists, S 12 [14470], Columbus, OH
Intl. Alliance of Theatrical Stage Employees, Moving Picture Technicians, Artists, S 13 [11587], Minneapolis, MN
Intl. Alliance of Theatrical Stage Employees, Moving Picture Technicians, Artists, S 146 [4681], Fort Wayne, IN
Lake and Geauga County Fed. of Musicians - Local 657, Amer. Fed. of Musicians [17283], Willowick, OH
Limelight Players, Not-for-Profit [204], Belleville, IL
Musicians' Union - Local 42, Amer. Fed. of Musicians [19559], Racine, WI
Professional Musicians of NW Ohio - Local No. 15-286, Amer. Fed. of Musicians [16953], Toledo, OH
South Bend Fed. of Musicians - Local 278, Amer. Fed. of Musicians [6266], South Bend, IN
Performing Arts Soc; Eastern Howard [4845], Greentown, IN
Performing and Fine Arts; Harrison St. Cooperative of [2811], Oak Park, IL
Perham Area Chamber of Commerce [11994], Perham, MN
Perinatal Info. Syss. User Gp. [1509], Downers Grove, IL
Perry County Agriculture Soc. [16133], New Lexington, OH
Perry County Chamber of Commerce [6297], Tell City, IN
Perry County Chamber of Commerce [16134], New Lexington, OH
Perry County Convention and Visitor's Bureau [6298], Tell City, IN
Perry County Development Corp. [6299], Tell City, IN
Perry County Historical Soc. [3090], Pinckneyville, IL
Perry County RSVP [16135], New Lexington, OH
Perry Historical Soc. of Lake County Ohio [16400], Perry, OH
Perry-Morrice Jr. Football Association [9356], Perry, MI
Perry Township Lions Club [13577], Canton, OH
Perrysburg Area Chamber of Commerce [16411], Perrysburg, OH
Perrysburg HS - Young Life [15915], Maumee, OH
Perrysburg - Wyldlife [15916], Maumee, OH
Perrysville Lions Club [16415], Perrysville, OH
Personality Disorder Awareness Network [19091], Milwaukee, WI
Personnel
Ashtabula County Soc. for Human Rsrc. Mgt. [13180], Ashtabula, OH
Blackhawk Human Rsrc. Assn. [18245], Janesville, WI
Bloomington Normal Human Rsrc. Coun. [267], Bloomington, IL
Butler/Warren County Soc. for Human Rsrc. Mgt. [14864], Dayton, OH
Central Illinois Human Rsrcs. Gp. [505], Champaign, IL
Central Minnesota Soc. for Human Rsrc. Mgt. [12282], St. Cloud, MN
Central Wisconsin Soc. for Human Rsrcs. [20034], Wausau, WI
Chicagoland's Human Rsrc. Assn. [1499], Downers Grove, IL
Cleveland Soc. for Human Rsrc. Mgt. [14103], Cleveland, OH
DuPage Soc. for Human Rsrc. Mgt. [2631], Naperville, IL
East Central Indiana Human Rsrcs. Assn. [5874], Muncie, IN
Eastern Indiana Human Rsrc. Assn. [6090], Richmond, IN
Evansville Area Human Rsrc. Assn. [4543], Evansville, IN
Findlay Area Human Rsrc. Assn. [15199], Findlay, OH
Greater Ann Arbor Soc. for Human Rsrc. Mgt. [9990], Troy, MI
Greater Grand Rapids Assn. for Human Rsrc. Mgt. [7958], Grand Rapids, MI
Greater Lorain County Chap. of the Soc. for Human Rsrc. Mgt. [15114], Elyria, OH
Greater Madison Area Soc. for Human Rsrc. Mgt. [18516], Madison, WI
Human Rsrc. Assn. of Central Indiana [5150], Indianapolis, IN
Human Rsrc. Assn. of Greater Detroit [7644], Farmington, MI
Human Rsrc. Assn. of Greater Oak Brook [2775], Oak Brook, IL
Human Rsrc. Mgt. Assn. of Mid-Michigan [8576], Lansing, MI
Human Rsrc. Mgt. Assn. of Southeastern Wisconsin [19891], Thiensville, WI
Human Rsrc. Professional Development Assn. [5151], Indianapolis, IN
Human Resources Assn. of Central Ohio [15048], Dublin, OH
Human Rsrcs. Assn. of Western Ohio [17291], Wilmington, OH
Jefferson County Human Rsrc. Mgt. Assn. [19968], Watertown, WI
Kalamazoo Human Rsrcs. Mgt. Assn. [9447], Portage, MI
Lakeshore Area Human Rsrcs. Assn. [18779], Manitowoc, WI
Lakeshore Human Rsrcs. Mgt. Assn. [8206], Holland, MI
Lancaster Area Soc. for Human Rsrc. Mgt. [15602], Lancaster, OH
Lima Soc. for Human Rsrc. Mgt. [15662], Lima, OH
Miami Valley Human Rsrc. Assn. [15987], Miamisburg, OH
Michiana Chap. of Soc. for Human Rsrc. Mgt. [6239], South Bend, IN
Mid Michigan Human Rsrc. Assn. [9113], Mount Pleasant, MI
Minnesota Coll. Personnel Assn. [11386], Mankato, MN
Northeast Indiana Human Rsrc. Assn. [4703], Fort Wayne, IN
Northland Human Rsrc. Assn. [10846], Duluth, MN
Northwest Human Rsrcs. Coun. [474], Cary, IL
Ohio Coll. Personnel Assn. [14585], Columbus, OH
Quincy Area Chap. of the Soc. for Human Rsrc. Mgt. [3161], Quincy, IL
RiverBend Soc. for Human Rsrc. Mgt. [16534], Rio Grande, OH
Rochester Human Rsrcs. Assn. [12179], Rochester, MN
Rock River Human Rsrcs. Professional Assn. [1483], Dixon, IL
Rockford Area Soc. for Human Rsrc. Mgt. [2354], Loves Park, IL
Sauk County Personnel Assn. [20179], Wisconsin Dells, WI
Sheboygan Area Chap. of the Soc. for Human Rsrc. Mgt. [19707], Sheboygan, WI
Soc. for Human Rsrc. Mgt. - Chippewa Valley Chap. [17898], Eau Claire, WI
Soc. for Human Rsrc. Mgt. - Dodge County Chap. [17595], Beaver Dam, WI
Soc. for Human Rsrc. Mgt. - Fond du Lac Chap. [17992], Fond du Lac, WI
Soc. for Human Rsrc. Mgt. - Fox Valley Chap. [17524], Appleton, WI
Soc. for Human Rsrc. Mgt. - Green Bay Area [18132], Green Bay, WI
Soc. for Human Rsrc. Mgt. - La Crosse Chap. [18378], La Crosse, WI
Soc. for Human Rsrc. Mgt. - Lake/Geauga Chap. [15979], Mentor, OH
Soc. for Human Rsrc. Mgt. - Northwest Indiana Chap. [6169], Schererville, IN
Soc. for Human Rsrc. Mgt. - Tuscora Chap. [15032], Dover, OH
Soc. of Human Rsrc. Professionals [1190], Chicago, IL
Southern Minnesota Area Human Rsrc. Assn. [11402], Mankato, MN
Springfield Human Resources Mgt. Assn. [16750], Springfield, OH
Stark County Human Rsrc. Assn. [13588], Canton, OH
Stateline Soc. for Human Rsrc. Mgt. [1333], Crystal Lake, IL
Stevens Point Area Human Rsrc. Assn. [19809], Stevens Point, WI
Superiorland Chap. of Human Rsrc. Professionals [10177], Wilson, MI
Toledo Area Human Rsrcs. Assn. [16963], Toledo, OH
Traverse Area Human Rsrcs. Assn. [9956], Traverse City, MI
Twin Cities Human Rsrc. Assn. [10326], Apple Valley, MN
Valley Soc. for Human Rsrc. Mgt. [9646], Saginaw, MI
Wayne Area Human Rsrcs. Assn. [17329], Wooster, OH
Winona Soc. for Human Rsrc. Mgt. [12966], Winona, MN
Wisconsin Coll. Personnel Assn. [18685], Madison, WI
Personnel and Guidance Assn; Michigan [★8653]
Peru - Miami County Chamber of Commerce [6033], Peru, IN
Pest Control
Michigan Mosquito Control Assn. [6891], Bay City, MI
Michigan Pest Control Assn. [7791], Fraser, MI
Pet Ownership; Alliance for Responsible [4598], Fishers, IN
Petersburg Chamber of Commerce [3086], Petersburg, IL
Petersburg-Summerfield Lions Club [9358], Petersburg, MI
Petoskey-Harbor Springs-Boyne Country Visitors Bur. [9367], Petoskey, MI
Petoskey Regional Chamber of Commerce [9368], Petoskey, MI
Petroleum
Great Lakes Petroleum Retailers and Allied Trades Assn. [8570], Lansing, MI
Illinois Petroleum Coun. [3624], Springfield, IL
Illinois Petroleum Marketers Assn. [3625], Springfield, IL
Indiana Petroleum Marketers and Convenience Store Assn. [5276], Indianapolis, IN
Michigan Assn. of Professional Landmen [8623], Lansing, MI
Michigan Petroleum Assn. [8695], Lansing, MI
Minnesota Petroleum Marketers Assn. [12506], St. Paul, MN
Ohio Gas Assn. [14615], Columbus, OH
Ohio Petroleum Gas Assn. [14651], Columbus, OH
Ohio Petroleum Marketers and Convenience Store Assn. [15060], Dublin, OH
Petroleum Marketers Assn. of Wisconsin/ Wisconsin Assn. of Convenience Stores [18595], Madison, WI
Petroleum Tech. Transfer Coun. Midwest Region [543], Champaign, IL
Soc. of Petrophysicists and Well Log Analysts - Ohio Chap. [14979], Deerfield, OH
Petroleum Marketers Assn; Illinois [3625], Springfield, IL
Petroleum Marketers Assn. of Wisconsin/Wisconsin Assn. of Convenience Stores [18595], Madison, WI
Petroleum Tech. Transfer Coun. Midwest Region [543], Champaign, IL
Pets
Pets Abandoned Wanting Support [12823], Wadena, MN
Tammy's Loyal Companions [8013], Grand Rapids, MI
Pets Abandoned Wanting Support [12823], Wadena, MN
PetSafe Rescue Alliance [9944], Traverse City, MI
Pewaukee Chamber of Commerce [19440], Pewaukee, WI

PFLAG Alexandria [11472], Miltona, MN
PFLAG Ann Arbor [6753], Ann Arbor, MI
PFLAG Appleton/Fox Cities [17514], Appleton, WI
PFLAG Aurora/Fox Valley [127], Aurora, IL
PFLAG Bay City/Saginaw/Midland [6893], Bay City, MI
PFLAG Bemidji [10423], Bemidji, MN
PFLAG Bloomington [4250], Bloomington, IN
PFLAG Bloomington/Normal [305], Bloomington, IL
PFLAG Brainerd Lakes [10390], Baxter, MN
PFLAG Carbondale/Southern Illinois [428], Carbondale, IL
PFLAG Chicago/Hinsdale/West Suburban [1124], Chicago, IL
PFLAG Chicago/Lakeview [1125], Chicago, IL
PFLAG Detroit [9589], Royal Oak, MI
PFLAG Downriver [9840], Southgate, MI
PFLAG Duluth [10848], Duluth, MN
PFLAG DuPage [3996], Wheaton, IL
PFLAG Eau Claire/Greater Chippewa Valley [17757], Chippewa Falls, WI
PFLAG Evansville/Tri-State [5963], Newburgh, IN
PFLAG Family Reunion: People Of Color Chap. [7417], Detroit, MI
PFLAG Flint/Genesee County [7770], Flushing, MI
PFLAG Fort Wayne [4708], Fort Wayne, IN
PFLAG Galesville/Western Wisconsin [18027], Galesville, WI
PFLAG Glenview/North Suburban Chicago [1872], Glenview, IL
PFLAG Grand Rapids [7996], Grand Rapids, MI
PFLAG Grand Rapids/Itasca [11092], Grand Rapids, MN
PFLAG Hammond [4891], Hammond, IN
PFLAG Holland/Lakeshore [8216], Holland, MI
PFLAG Huntington [4954], Huntington, IN
PFLAG Indianapolis [5448], Indianapolis, IN
PFLAG Kalamazoo/Southwest Michigan [9452], Portage, MI
PFLAG Kenosha/Racine [19476], Pleasant Prairie, WI
PFLAG Keweenaw [8260], Houghton, MI
PFLAG La Crosse [18374], La Crosse, WI
PFLAG Lafayette/Tippecanoe County [4163], Battle Ground, IN
PFLAG Lansing [9299], Okemos, MI
PFLAG Marshall/Buffalo Ridge [11439], Marshall, MN
PFLAG Michigan City/Indiana Dunes [5700], Long Beach, IN
PFLAG Milwaukee [19092], Milwaukee, WI
PFLAG Moline [2526], Moline, IL
PFLAG Mt. Pleasant [9122], Mount Pleasant, MI
PFLAG Muncie [5893], Muncie, IN
PFLAG Northfield [11918], Northfield, MN
PFLAG Oak Park Area [2826], Oak Park, IL
PFLAG Palatine [2925], Palatine, IL
PFLAG Park Rapids [11979], Park Rapids, MN
PFLAG Port Huron/Sarnia-Bluewater [9436], Port Huron, MI
PFLAG Quincy [3157], Quincy, IL
PFLAG Red Wing [12080], Red Wing, MN
PFLAG Richmond/Whitewater Valley [6099], Richmond, IN
PFLAG-Rochester [★12168]
PFLAG Rochester/Southern Minnesota [12168], Rochester, MN
PFLAG Rock River Valley [222], Belvidere, IL
PFLAG St. Cloud/Central Minnesota [12295], St. Cloud, MN
PFLAG St. Joseph/Berrien County [9688], St. Joseph, MI
PFLAG St. Paul/Minneapolis [11722], Minneapolis, MN
PFLAG Seymour [6185], Seymour, IN
PFLAG Sheboygan/Lakeshore [19703], Sheboygan, WI
PFLAG South Bend/Michiana [6252], South Bend, IN
PFLAG Sturgeon Bay/Door County [19842], Sturgeon Bay, WI
PFLAG Traverse City [9945], Traverse City, MI
PFLAG Urbana-Champaign [544], Champaign, IL
PFLAG Waukesha [19996], Waukesha, WI
PFLAG Woodstock/McHenry County [4063], Woodstock, IL
Phantom Lake Young Men's Christian Association [19254], Mukwonago, WI
Pharmaceutical Assn; Illinois [★3626]
Pharmaceuticals
Illinois Pharmacists Assn. [3626], Springfield, IL
Pharmacists Assn; Illinois [3626], Springfield, IL
Pharmacists; Minnesota Soc. of Health-System [11795], Minnetonka, MN
Pharmacy
Assn. of Clinical Res. Professionals - Circle City [5043], Indianapolis, IN
Assn. of Clinical Res. Professionals - Northeastern Ohio Chap. [15700], Lorain, OH
Assn. of Clinical Res. Professionals - Southern Wisconsin Chap. [18967], Milwaukee, WI
Indiana Pharmacists Alliance [5277], Indianapolis, IN
Indiana Soc. of Health-System Pharmacists [5302], Indianapolis, IN
Michigan Pharmacists Assn. [8696], Lansing, MI
Michigan Soc. of Health-System Pharmacists [8715], Lansing, MI
Minnesota Pharmacists Assn. [12240], Roseville, MN
Minnesota Pharmacists Assn., Central District [10282], Alexandria, MN
Minnesota Pharmacists Assn., East Metro District [12507], St. Paul, MN
Minnesota Pharmacists Assn., Northeast District [10838], Duluth, MN
Minnesota Pharmacists Assn., Northwest District [10418], Bemidji, MN
Minnesota Pharmacists Assn., Southeast District [10356], Austin, MN
Minnesota Pharmacists Assn., Southwest District [10628], Canby, MN
Minnesota Pharmacists Assn., West Metro District [10296], Andover, MN
Missouri Soc. of Health-System Pharmacists [2352], Loves Park, IL
Ohio Pharmacists Assn. [14652], Columbus, OH
Ohio Soc. of Health-System Pharmacists [15826], Marietta, OH
Pharmacy Soc. of Wisconsin [18596], Madison, WI
Southeastern Michigan Soc. of Health-System Pharmacists [9260], Oak Park, MI
Pharmacy Soc. of Wisconsin [18596], Madison, WI
Pheasants Forever of Ashland Ohio [13171], Ashland, OH
Pheasants Forever Bay/Midland Chap. of Michigan [9039], Midland, MI
Pheasants Forever Central Indiana Chap. [4331], Carmel, IN
Pheasants Forever Central Indiana, Clinton County [4616], Forest, IN
Pheasants Forever Central Indiana, Coal Greek [4427], Crawfordsville, IN
Pheasants Forever Central Indiana, Door Prairie [5601], La Porte, IN
Pheasants Forever Central Indiana, Eel River [4384], Columbia City, IN
Pheasants Forever Central Indiana, Elkhart County [4292], Bristol, IN
Pheasants Forever Central Indiana, Fulton County [6124], Rochester, IN
Pheasants Forever Central Indiana, Iroquois River [4459], Demotte, IN
Pheasants Forever Central Indiana, Lagrange County [5642], Lagrange, IN
Pheasants Forever Central Indiana, Marshall County [4289], Bremen, IN
Pheasants Forever Central Indiana, Northeast Indiana [5649], Laotto, IN
Pheasants Forever Central Indiana, Sagamore [6495], West Lafayette, IN
Pheasants Forever Central Indiana, Tippe River Basin [6452], Warsaw, IN
Pheasants Forever Central Indiana, Twin Lakes [5827], Monticello, IN
Pheasants Forever Central Indiana, Wabash Valley [6338], Terre Haute, IN
Pheasants Forever Central Indiana, Wildcat Creek [5580], Kokomo, IN
Pheasants Forever Fox River Valley Chap. [19403], Oshkosh, WI
Pheasants Forever Illinois Pioneer Chap. [2977], Paxton, IL
Pheasants Forever Ionia County Chap. 161 [8317], Ionia, MI
Pheasants Forever Lake Michigan Chap. 75 [9764], South Haven, MI
Pheasants Forever, Macomb County [9488], Richmond, MI
Pheasants Forever - Mchenry County Chap. [1331], Crystal Lake, IL
Pheasants Forever Northeast Indiana Chap. 182 [4142], Auburn, IN
Pheasants Forever Ozaukee County [18067], Grafton, WI
Pheasants Forever Southeastern Wisconsin Chap. [19297], New Berlin, WI
Phelps Chamber of Commerce [19450], Phelps, WI
Phenomena
Amer. Soc. of Dowsers, Central Illiana Dowsers [2674], Neoga, IL
Amer. Soc. of Dowsers, Great Serpent Mound Chap. [17196], West Union, OH
Amer. Soc. of Dowsers, Northern Illinois Chap. [3482], Skokie, IL
Amer. Soc. of Dowsers, Southwestern Ohio Dowsers [16718], Springfield, OH
American Society of Dowsers, The Heart of Wisconsin Dowsers Chapter [19496], Port Edwards, WI
Michigan Mutual UFO Network [8487], Kentwood, MI
Mutual UFO Network, Indiana [6417], Vincennes, IN
Phi Beta Kappa, Hope Coll. [8217], Holland, MI
Phi Beta Kappa, Ohio Univ. [13215], Athens, OH
Phi Beta Kappa, Ripon Coll. [19634], Ripon, WI
Phi Beta Kappa, Univ. of Illinois (Chicago) [1126], Chicago, IL
Phi Theta Kappa - Alpha Alpha Alpha Chap. [17442], Zanesville, OH
Phi Theta Kappa, Alpha Alpha Gamma Chap. - Century Coll. [12898], White Bear Lake, MN
Phi Theta Kappa, Alpha Alpha Omicron Chap. - Richland Community Coll. [1401], Decatur, IL
Phi Theta Kappa, Alpha Alpha Pi Chap. - Coll. of Lake County [1897], Grayslake, IL
Phi Theta Kappa - Alpha Alpha Psi Chap. [13080], Akron, OH
Phi Theta Kappa, Alpha Chi Rho Chap. - Univ. of Wisconsin-Waukesha [19997], Waukesha, WI
Phi Theta Kappa, Alpha Delta Alpha Chap. - Anoka-Ramsey Community Coll. [10716], Coon Rapids, MN
Phi Theta Kappa, Alpha Delta Eta Chap. - Kankakee Community Coll. [2142], Kankakee, IL
Phi Theta Kappa, Alpha Delta Omega Chap. - Glen Oaks Community Coll. [7109], Centreville, MI
Phi Theta Kappa, Alpha Delta Upsilon Chap. - Anoka-Ramsey Community Coll. - Cambridge [10625], Cambridge, MN
Phi Theta Kappa - Alpha Epsilon Eta Chap. [15422], Highland Hills, OH
Phi Theta Kappa, Alpha Epsilon Kappa Chap. - Alpha Epsilon Kappa Chap. [3660], Springfield, IL
Phi Theta Kappa, Alpha Epsilon Sigma Chap. - Minneapolis Community and Tech. Coll. [11723], Minneapolis, MN
Phi Theta Kappa, Alpha Epsilon Theta Chap. - Univ. of Wisconsin-Marinette [18802], Marinette, WI
Phi Theta Kappa, Alpha Eta Zeta Chap. - Ridgewater Coll. [12925], Willmar, MN
Phi Theta Kappa, Alpha Iota Epsilon Chap. - Lincoln Trail Coll. [3221], Robinson, IL
Phi Theta Kappa, Alpha Iota Lambda Chap. - Moraine Valley Community Coll. [2942], Palos Hills, IL
Phi Theta Kappa, Alpha Iota Phi Chap. - Oakton Community Coll. [1467], Des Plaines, IL
Phi Theta Kappa - Alpha Iota Theta Chap. [13270], Batavia, OH
Phi Theta Kappa, Alpha Kappa Alpha Chap. - Normandale Community Coll. [10485], Bloomington, MN
Phi Theta Kappa, Alpha Kappa Nu Chap. - Indiana Univ. - Purdue Univ. Fort Wayne [4709], Fort Wayne, IN
Phi Theta Kappa, Alpha Kappa Rho Chap. - Southwestern Illinois Coll. [1884], Granite City, IL
Phi Theta Kappa, Alpha Lambda Epsilon Chap. - Shawnee Community Coll. [3797], Ullin, IL
Phi Theta Kappa - Alpha Lambda Eta Chap. [16436], Piqua, OH

Phi Theta Kappa, Alpha Lambda Iota Chap. - Malcolm X Coll. **[1127]**, Chicago, IL
Phi Theta Kappa, Alpha Lambda Phi Chap. - Joliet Junior Coll. **[2117]**, Joliet, IL
Phi Theta Kappa - Alpha Mu Delta Chap. **[16108]**, Nelsonville, OH
Phi Theta Kappa - Alpha Mu Epsilon Chap. **[15250]**, Fremont, OH
Phi Theta Kappa, Alpha Mu Omega Chap. - Univ. of Wisconsin-Sheboygan **[19704]**, Sheboygan, WI
Phi Theta Kappa - Alpha Mu Xi Chap. **[17325]**, Wooster, OH
Phi Theta Kappa, Alpha Nu Eta Chap. - Kellogg Community Coll. **[6868]**, Battle Creek, MI
Phi Theta Kappa, Alpha Nu Iota Chap. - Nicolet Area Tech. Coll. **[19603]**, Rhinelander, WI
Phi Theta Kappa, Alpha Nu Kappa Chap. - Minnesota West Community and Tech. Coll. **[12991]**, Worthington, MN
Phi Theta Kappa - Alpha Nu Lambda Chap. **[16739]**, Springfield, OH
Phi Theta Kappa, Alpha Nu Theta Chap. - DeVry Univ. **[10]**, Addison, IL
Phi Theta Kappa, Alpha Omega Delta Chap. - Ivy Tech State Coll. **[4115]**, Anderson, IN
Phi Theta Kappa - Alpha Omega Pi Chap. **[16948]**, Toledo, OH
Phi Theta Kappa, Alpha Omega Xi Chap. - Heartland Community Coll. **[2730]**, Normal, IL
Phi Theta Kappa, Alpha Omicron Beta Chap. - Inver Hills Community Coll. **[11225]**, Inver Grove Heights, MN
Phi Theta Kappa - Alpha Omicron Eta Chap. **[15449]**, Hillsboro, OH
Phi Theta Kappa, Alpha Omicron Gamma Chap. - Kirtland Community Coll. **[9556]**, Roscommon, MI
Phi Theta Kappa, Alpha Omicron Iota Chap. - Mott Community Coll. **[7750]**, Flint, MI
Phi Theta Kappa, Alpha Omicron Kappa Chap. - Oakland Community Coll. **[10091]**, Waterford, MI
Phi Theta Kappa - Alpha Omicron Mu Chap. **[13155]**, Archbold, OH
Phi Theta Kappa - Alpha Omicron Nu Chap. **[16767]**, Steubenville, OH
Phi Theta Kappa, Alpha Omicron Omicron Chap. - Mid Michigan Community Coll. **[8130]**, Harrison, MI
Phi Theta Kappa, Alpha Omicron Psi Chap. - Oakland Community Coll. **[9816]**, Southfield, MI
Phi Theta Kappa, Alpha Omicron Rho Chap. - Oakland Community Coll. **[6815]**, Auburn Hills, MI
Phi Theta Kappa, Alpha Omicron Upsilon Chap. - North Central Michigan Coll. **[9369]**, Petoskey, MI
Phi Theta Kappa, Alpha Omicron Xi Chap. - Oakland Community Coll. **[7673]**, Farmington Hills, MI
Phi Theta Kappa, Alpha Phi Beta Chap. - Black Hawk Coll. **[2159]**, Kewanee, IL
Phi Theta Kappa, Alpha Phi Eta Chap. - Ivy Tech State Coll. **[6339]**, Terre Haute, IN
Phi Theta Kappa ,Alpha Phi Omega Chap. - Ivy Tech State Coll. **[4785]**, Gary, IN
Phi Theta Kappa, Alpha Phi Phi Chap. - West Shore Community Coll. **[9735]**, Scottville, MI
Phi Theta Kappa, Alpha Phi Pi Chap. - Ivy Tech State Coll. **[5581]**, Kokomo, IN
Phi Theta Kappa, Alpha Phi Theta Chap. - Ivy Tech State Coll. **[4565]**, Evansville, IN
Phi Theta Kappa, Alpha Phi Upsilon Chap. - Hennepin Tech. Coll. **[10692]**, Cloquet, MN
Phi Theta Kappa, Alpha Pi Phi Chap. - Alexandria Tech. Coll. **[10284]**, Alexandria, MN
Phi Theta Kappa, Alpha Psi Eta Chap. - Parkland Coll. **[545]**, Champaign, IL
Phi Theta Kappa, Alpha Psi Lambda Chap. - Ivy Tech State Coll. **[5719]**, Madison, IN
Phi Theta Kappa - Alpha Psi Phi Chap. **[13671]**, Chillicothe, OH
Phi Theta Kappa - Alpha Psi Rho Chap. **[15573]**, Kirtland, OH
Phi Theta Kappa, Alpha Rho Alpha Chap. - Rainy River Community Coll. **[11218]**, International Falls, MN
Phi Theta Kappa, Alpha Rho Chi Chap. - Gogebic Community Coll. **[8340]**, Ironwood, MI
Phi Theta Kappa - Alpha Rho Epsilon Chap. **[14710]**, Columbus, OH
Phi Theta Kappa, Alpha Rho Eta Chap. - Kishwaukee Coll. **[2381]**, Malta, IL
Phi Theta Kappa - Alpha Rho Gamma Chap. **[15827]**, Marietta, OH
Phi Theta Kappa, Alpha Rho Lambda Chap. - Jackson Community Coll. **[8393]**, Jackson, MI
Phi Theta Kappa, Alpha Rho Nu Chap. - Kalamazoo Valley Community Coll. **[8460]**, Kalamazoo, MI
Phi Theta Kappa, Alpha Rho Pi Chap. - Northwestern Michigan Coll. **[9946]**, Traverse City, MI
Phi Theta Kappa, Alpha Rho Sigma Chap. - Ivy Tech State Coll. **[4251]**, Bloomington, IN
Phi Theta Kappa, Alpha Rho Tau Chap. - Ivy Tech State Coll. **[4404]**, Columbus, IN
Phi Theta Kappa, Alpha Rho Zeta Chap. - Waukesha County Tech. Coll. **[19441]**, Pewaukee, WI
Phi Theta Kappa, Alpha Sigma Kappa Chap. - Ivy Tech State Coll. **[5630]**, Lafayette, IN
Phi Theta Kappa, Alpha Sigma Lambda Chap. - Univ. of Wisconsin-Manitowoc **[18790]**, Manitowoc, WI
Phi Theta Kappa, Alpha Tau Alpha Chap. - Montcalm Community Coll. **[9754]**, Sidney, MI
Phi Theta Kappa, Alpha Tau Gamma Chap. - John Wood Community Coll. **[3158]**, Quincy, IL
Phi Theta Kappa - Alpha Tau Mu Chap. **[15668]**, Lima, OH
Phi Theta Kappa, Alpha Tau Omicron Chap. - Ivy Tech State Coll. **[6253]**, South Bend, IN
Phi Theta Kappa, Alpha Tau Sigma Chap. - Ivy Tech State Coll. **[6178]**, Sellersburg, IN
Phi Theta Kappa ,Alpha Tau Xi Chap. - Ivy Tech State Coll. **[4710]**, Fort Wayne, IN
Phi Theta Kappa, Alpha Theta Eta Chap. - Olney Central Coll. **[2860]**, Olney, IL
Phi Theta Kappa, Alpha Theta Pi Chap. - Univ. of Wisconsin-Barron **[19615]**, Rice Lake, WI
Phi Theta Kappa, Alpha Theta Psi Chap. - Lake Land Coll. **[2445]**, Mattoon, IL
Phi Theta Kappa, Alpha Theta Tau Chap. - Univ. of Wisconsin-Fox Valley **[18864]**, Menasha, WI
Phi Theta Kappa - Alpha Theta Zeta Chap. **[16183]**, Newark, OH
Phi Theta Kappa, Alpha Upsilon Gamma Chap. - Lake Superior Coll. **[10849]**, Duluth, MN
Phi Theta Kappa, Alpha Upsilon Kappa Chap. - Grand Rapids Community Coll. **[7997]**, Grand Rapids, MI
Phi Theta Kappa, Alpha Upsilon Lambda Chap. - Ivy Tech State Coll. **[5894]**, Muncie, IN
Phi Theta Kappa, Alpha Upsilon Omega Chap. - Ivy Tech State Coll. **[6100]**, Richmond, IN
Phi Theta Kappa, Alpha Upsilon Tau Chap. - Ivy Tech State Coll. **[5449]**, Indianapolis, IN
Phi Theta Kappa, Alpha Upsilon Zeta Chap. - Wayne County Community Coll. **[7418]**, Detroit, MI
Phi Theta Kappa, Alpha Xi Delta Chap. - Bay de Noc Community Coll. **[7617]**, Escanaba, MI
Phi Theta Kappa, Alpha Xi Iota Chap. - Gateway Tech. Coll. **[18307]**, Kenosha, WI
Phi Theta Kappa, Alpha Xi Kappa Chap. - Univ. of Wisconsin-Marshfield/Wood County **[18822]**, Marshfield, WI
Phi Theta Kappa, Alpha Xi Mu Chap. - Henry Ford Community Coll. **[7266]**, Dearborn, MI
Phi Theta Kappa - Alpha Zeta Chi Chap. **[16311]**, Orrville, OH
Phi Theta Kappa - Alpha Zeta Delta Chap. **[14204]**, Cleveland, OH
Phi Theta Kappa, Beta Alpha Gamma Chap. - Sauk Valley Community Coll. **[1482]**, Dixon, IL
Phi Theta Kappa, Beta Alpha Lambda Chap. - Frontier Community Coll. **[1689]**, Fairfield, IL
Phi Theta Kappa, Beta Alpha Omega Chap. - Univ. of Indianapolis **[5450]**, Indianapolis, IN
Phi Theta Kappa, Beta Beta Alpha Chap. - Ivy Tech State Coll. **[4504]**, Elkhart, IN
Phi Theta Kappa, Beta Beta Beta Chap. - Ancilla Coll. **[4462]**, Donaldson, IN
Phi Theta Kappa, Beta Beta Psi Chap. - Madison Area Tech. Coll. **[18597]**, Madison, WI
Phi Theta Kappa - Beta Beta Theta Chap. **[15608]**, Lancaster, OH
Phi Theta Kappa - Beta Epsilon Delta Chap. **[16018]**, Middletown, OH
Phi Theta Kappa, Beta Epsilon Omicron Chap. - Fox Valley Tech. Coll. **[17515]**, Appleton, WI
Phi Theta Kappa, Beta Epsilon Rho Chap. - Holy Cross Coll. **[6005]**, Notre Dame, IN
Phi Theta Kappa, Beta Eta Chi Chap. - Ridgewater Coll. **[11212]**, Hutchinson, MN
Phi Theta Kappa, Beta Gamma Alpha Chap. - Washtenaw Community Coll. **[6754]**, Ann Arbor, MI
Phi Theta Kappa - Beta Gamma Epsilon Chap. **[13578]**, Canton, OH
Phi Theta Kappa - Beta Gamma Sigma Chap. **[13957]**, Cincinnati, OH
Phi Theta Kappa, Beta Gamma Tau Chap. - Ivy Tech State Coll. **[5661]**, Lawrenceburg, IN
Phi Theta Kappa, Beta Gamma Zeta Chap. - Ivy Tech State Coll. **[5696]**, Logansport, IN
Phi Theta Kappa, Beta Iota Iota Chap. - Southwestern Illinois Coll. **[3186]**, Red Bud, IL
Phi Theta Kappa, Beta Kappa Eta Chap. - Univ. of Wisconsin-Baraboo/Sauk **[17576]**, Baraboo, WI
Phi Theta Kappa, Beta Kappa Kappa Chap. - Univ. of Wisconsin-Marathon County **[20044]**, Wausau, WI
Phi Theta Kappa, Beta Kappa Rho Chap. - Northwest Tech. Coll. **[12002]**, Pine City, MN
Phi Theta Kappa, Beta Kappa Xi Chap. - Hennepin Tech. Coll. **[10556]**, Brooklyn Park, MN
Phi Theta Kappa, Beta Lambda Kappa Chap. - Macomb Community Coll. **[7186]**, Clinton Township, MI
Phi Theta Kappa - Beta Lambda Nu Chap. **[16136]**, New Lexington, OH
Phi Theta Kappa, Beta Lambda Sigma Chap. - Lakeshore Tech. Coll. **[17767]**, Cleveland, WI
Phi Theta Kappa, Beta Lambda Xi Chap. - Dunwood Coll. of Tech. **[11724]**, Minneapolis, MN
Phi Theta Kappa, Beta Mu Chi Chap. - Univ. of Wisconsin-Rock County **[18259]**, Janesville, WI
Phi Theta Kappa, Beta Mu Eta Chap. - South Central Tech. Coll. **[11907]**, North Mankato, MN
Phi Theta Kappa, Beta Mu Kappa Chap. - Moraine Park Tech. Coll. **[17990]**, Fond du Lac, WI
Phi Theta Kappa, Beta Nu Beta Chap. - South Central Tech. Coll. **[10986]**, Faribault, MN
Phi Theta Kappa, Beta Nu Chi Chap. - Western Wisconsin Tech. Coll. **[18375]**, La Crosse, WI
Phi Theta Kappa, Beta Nu Kappa Chap. - Northland Community and Tech. Coll. **[10884]**, East Grand Forks, MN
Phi Theta Kappa, Beta Nu Omicron Chap. - Anoka Tech. Coll. **[10310]**, Anoka, MN
Phi Theta Kappa - Beta Nu Phi Chap. **[16533]**, Rio Grande, OH
Phi Theta Kappa - Beta Nu Pi Chap. **[15851]**, Marion, OH
Phi Theta Kappa, Beta Nu Tau Chap. - Northwest Tech. Coll. **[10424]**, Bemidji, MN
Phi Theta Kappa - Beta Theta Eta Chap. **[15787]**, Mansfield, OH
Phi Theta Kappa - Beta Theta Mu Chap. **[16572]**, St. Clairsville, OH
Phi Theta Kappa, Beta Theta Tau Chap. - Dakota County Tech. Coll. **[12216]**, Rosemount, MN
Phi Theta Kappa, Beta Xi Alpha Chap. - Saint Paul Coll. **[12559]**, St. Paul, MN
Phi Theta Kappa, Beta Zeta Beta Chap. - Trinity Coll. of Nursing **[3248]**, Rock Island, IL
Phi Theta Kappa, Beta Zeta Kappa Chap. - Ivy Tech State Coll. **[6453]**, Warsaw, IN
Phi Theta Kappa, Beta Zeta Rho Chap. - Vincennes Univ.-Jasper **[5534]**, Jasper, IN
Phi Theta Kappa, Chi Chi Chap. - Univ. of Wisconsin-Washington **[20127]**, West Bend, WI
Phi Theta Kappa, Chi Kappa Chap. - Carl Sandburg Coll. **[1779]**, Galesburg, IL
Phi Theta Kappa - Chi Omega Chap. **[16377]**, Parma, OH
Phi Theta Kappa, Chi Upsilon Chap. - McHenry County Coll. **[1332]**, Crystal Lake, IL
Phi Theta Kappa, Chi Zeta Chap. - Triton Coll. **[3207]**, River Grove, IL
Phi Theta Kappa, Delta Theta Chap. - Springfield Coll. **[3661]**, Springfield, IL
Phi Theta Kappa, Eta Kappa Chap. - Black Hawk Coll. **[2527]**, Moline, IL
Phi Theta Kappa, Eta Psi Chap. - Lewis and Clark Community Coll. **[1875]**, Godfrey, IL
Phi Theta Kappa, Iota Chi Chap. - Lincoln Coll. **[2280]**, Lincoln, IL
Phi Theta Kappa, Iota Omicron Chap. - Kaskaskia Coll. **[491]**, Centralia, IL

Phi Theta Kappa, Kappa Beta Chap. - Kendall Coll. **[1128]**, Chicago, IL
Phi Theta Kappa, Lambda Iota Chap. - Olive-Harvey Coll. **[1129]**, Chicago, IL
Phi Theta Kappa, Lambda Mu Chap. - St. Clair County Community Coll. **[9437]**, Port Huron, MI
Phi Theta Kappa, Lambda Rho Chap. - Kennedy-King Coll. **[1130]**, Chicago, IL
Phi Theta Kappa, Mu Nu Chap. - Lake Michigan Coll. **[6921]**, Benton Harbor, MI
Phi Theta Kappa, Mu Pi Chap. - Harold Washington Coll. **[1131]**, Chicago, IL
Phi Theta Kappa, Mu Psi Chap. - Southeastern Illinois Coll. **[1939]**, Harrisburg, IL
Phi Theta Kappa, Mu Tau Chap. - Lansing Community Coll. **[8750]**, Lansing, MI
Phi Theta Kappa, Nu Delta Chap. - Spoon River Coll. **[406]**, Canton, IL
Phi Theta Kappa, Nu Lambda Chap. - Harry S. Truman Coll. **[1132]**, Chicago, IL
Phi Theta Kappa, Nu Mu Chap. - Highland Community Coll. **[1752]**, Freeport, IL
Phi Theta Kappa, Nu Omicron Chap. - Alpena Community Coll. **[6648]**, Alpena, MI
Phi Theta Kappa - Nu Pi Chap. **[14946]**, Dayton, OH
Phi Theta Kappa, Nu Sigma Chap. - Prairie State Coll. **[1251]**, Chicago Heights, IL
Phi Theta Kappa, Omicron Chap. - Rochester Community and Tech. Coll. **[12169]**, Rochester, MN
Phi Theta Kappa, Omicron Eta Chap. - Rock Valley Coll. **[3298]**, Rockford, IL
Phi Theta Kappa, Omicron Iota Chap. - Schoolcraft Coll. **[8853]**, Livonia, MI
Phi Theta Kappa, Omicron Omicron Chap. - Minnesota State Community and Tech. Coll. **[11002]**, Fergus Falls, MN
Phi Theta Kappa, Phi Beta Chap. - Coll. of DuPage **[1839]**, Glen Ellyn, IL
Phi Theta Kappa, Phi Mu Chap. - Univ. of Wisconsin-Richland **[19624]**, Richland Center, WI
Phi Theta Kappa, Phi Omicron Chap. - Waubonsee Community Coll. **[3737]**, Sugar Grove, IL
Phi Theta Kappa, Phi Phi Chap. - William Rainey Harper Coll. **[2926]**, Palatine, IL
Phi Theta Kappa - Phi Pi Chap. **[15124]**, Elyria, OH
Phi Theta Kappa, Phi Xi Chap. - North Hennepin Community Coll. **[10557]**, Brooklyn Park, MN
Phi Theta Kappa, Pi Omega Chap. - Danville Area Community Coll. **[1350]**, Danville, IL
Phi Theta Kappa, Pi Rho Chap. - Richard J. Daley Coll. **[1133]**, Chicago, IL
Phi Theta Kappa, Psi Pi Chap. - South Suburban Coll. of Cook County **[3506]**, South Holland, IL
Phi Theta Kappa, Rho Kappa Chap. - Elgin Community Coll. **[1599]**, Elgin, IL
Phi Theta Kappa, Rho Omega Chap. - Illinois Valley Community Coll. **[2854]**, Oglesby, IL
Phi Theta Kappa, Rho Psi Chap. - Wabash Valley Coll. **[2574]**, Mount Carmel, IL
Phi Theta Kappa, Rho Xi Chap. - Rend Lake Coll. **[2060]**, Ina, IL
Phi Theta Kappa, Sigma Alpha Chap. - Northland Community and Tech. Coll. **[12746]**, Thief River Falls, MN
Phi Theta Kappa, Sigma Psi Chap. - Southwestern Michigan Coll. **[7482]**, Dowagiac, MI
Phi Theta Kappa, Sigma Theta Chap. - Milwaukee Area Tech. Coll. **[18888]**, Mequon, WI
Phi Theta Kappa, Tau Delta Chap. - MacCormac Coll. **[1134]**, Chicago, IL
Phi Theta Kappa, Tau Omicron Chap. - Monroe County Community Coll. **[9073]**, Monroe, MI
Phi Theta Kappa, Theta Epsilon Chap. - Southwestern Illinois Coll. **[209]**, Belleville, IL
Phi Theta Kappa, Theta Kappa Chap. - Hibbing Community Coll. **[11161]**, Hibbing, MN
Phi Theta Kappa, Theta Omega Chap. - Wilbur Wright Coll. **[1135]**, Chicago, IL
Phi Theta Kappa, Theta Omicron Chap. - Morton Coll. **[1261]**, Cicero, IL
Phi Theta Kappa, Upsilon Mu Chap. - Illinois Central Coll. **[3058]**, Peoria, IL
Phi Theta Kappa, Upsilon Omega Chap. - Central Lakes Coll. **[10518]**, Brainerd, MN
Phi Theta Kappa, Upsilon Pi Chap. - John A. Logan Coll. **[463]**, Carterville, IL
Phi Theta Kappa - Upsilon Psi Chap. **[13958]**, Cincinnati, OH
Phi Theta Kappa, Xi Delta Chap. - Delta Coll. **[10030]**, University Center, MI
Phi Theta Kappa, Zeta Eta Chap. - Riverland Community Coll. **[10357]**, Austin, MN
Phi Theta Kappa, Zeta Iota Chap. - Mesabi Range Community/Tech. Coll. **[12804]**, Virginia, MN
Phi Theta Kappa, Zeta Psi Chap. - Vincennes Univ. **[6420]**, Vincennes, IN
Philalethes Society, Logos Chapter **[1136]**, Chicago, IL

Philanthropy
Crestline Area United Way **[14808]**, Crestline, OH
Donors Forum of Chicago **[872]**, Chicago, IL
Donors Forum of Wisconsin **[19000]**, Milwaukee, WI
Indiana Grant Makers Alliance **[5240]**, Indianapolis, IN
Minnesota Coun. on Foundations **[11644]**, Minneapolis, MN
Ohio Grantmakers Forum **[14619]**, Columbus, OH

Philatelic
3-M Stamp Club **[12342]**, St. Paul, MN
Anthony Wayne Stamp Soc. **[4637]**, Fort Wayne, IN
Austin Philatelic Club **[1680]**, Evergreen Park, IL
Badger Stamp Club **[18489]**, Madison, WI
Calumet Stamp Club **[4855]**, Griffith, IN
Champaign-Urbana Stamp Club **[514]**, Champaign, IL
Chicago Philatelic Society **[2769]**, Oak Brook, IL
Clermont County Stamp Club **[16445]**, Pleasant Plain, OH
Columbus Philatelic Club **[14400]**, Columbus, OH
Corn Belt Philatelic Soc. **[276]**, Bloomington, IL
Cuy-Lor Stamp Club **[17228]**, Westlake, OH
Decatur Stamp Club **[277]**, Bloomington, IL
Essex County Stamp Club **[9235]**, Novi, MI
Euclid Stamp Club **[15143]**, Euclid, OH
Floral City Stamp Club **[9064]**, Monroe, MI
Galesburg Philatelic Soc. **[46]**, Altona, IL
Germany Philatelic Soc., Chap. 5 **[2810]**, Oak Park, IL
Germany Philatelic Soc., No. 19 Cleveland **[14125]**, Cleveland, OH
Glen Ellyn Philatelic Club **[1832]**, Glen Ellyn, IL
Greater Cincinnati Philatelic Soc. **[15157]**, Fairfield, OH
Indiana Stamp Club **[5311]**, Indianapolis, IN
Lake County Philatelic Soc. **[1923]**, Gurnee, IL
Midwest Stamp Dealers Assn. **[363]**, Buffalo Grove, IL
North Shore Philatelic Soc. **[1104]**, Chicago, IL
North Shore Philatelic Soc. of Milwaukee **[19084]**, Milwaukee, WI
Oshkosh Philatelic Society **[17989]**, Fond du Lac, WI
Outagamie Philatelic Soc. **[17513]**, Appleton, WI
Quad City Stamp Club **[2531]**, Moline, IL
Southern Illinois Stamp Club **[434]**, Carbondale, IL
Warren Area Stamp Club **[17117]**, Warren, OH
Waukesha County Philatelic Soc. **[20005]**, Waukesha, WI
West Suburban Stamp Club **[9412]**, Plymouth, MI
Wisconsin Fed. of Stamp Clubs **[18915]**, Middleton, WI
Philatelic Soc., Chap. 5; Germany **[2810]**, Oak Park, IL
Philatelic Soc; Outagamie **[17513]**, Appleton, WI
Philatelic Soc; Waukesha County **[20005]**, Waukesha, WI
Phillips Area Chamber of Commerce **[19453]**, Phillips, WI
Phoenix Soc. for Burn Survivors **[7494]**, East Grand Rapids, MI
Photographers Assn; Indianhead Professional **[17879]**, Eau Claire, WI
Photographers, Chicago/Midwest; Amer. Soc. of Media **[725]**, Chicago, IL
Photographers; Lima Soc. of Professional **[16579]**, St. Marys, OH
Photographers of Michigan; Professional **[9747]**, Shelby Township, MI
Photographers, Minneapolis/St. Paul; Amer. Soc. of Media **[12331]**, St. Louis Park, MN
Photographers, Ohio/North Coast Chap; Amer. Soc. of Media **[16096]**, N Canton, OH
Photographers, Ohio Valley Chap; Amer. Soc. of Media **[15620]**, Lebanon, OH
Photographers of Western Michigan; Professional **[7865]**, Grand Haven, MI
Photographic Art Specialist of Ohio **[16122]**, New Carlisle, OH
Photographic Historical Soc; Michigan **[6964]**, Birmingham, MI

Photography
Akron Soc. of Professional Photographers **[13023]**, Akron, OH
Amer. Soc. of Media Photographers, Chicago/Midwest **[725]**, Chicago, IL
Amer. Soc. of Media Photographers, Michigan **[9769]**, South Lyon, MI
Amer. Soc. of Media Photographers, Minneapolis/St. Paul **[12331]**, St. Louis Park, MN
Amer. Soc. of Media Photographers, Ohio/North Coast Chap. **[16096]**, N Canton, OH
Amer. Soc. of Media Photographers, Ohio Valley Chap. **[15620]**, Lebanon, OH
Cornbelt Professional Photographers Assn. **[12134]**, Rochester, MN
Daguerre Club of Indiana **[5526]**, Jasper, IN
Fox Valley Professional Photographers Assn. **[19675]**, Seymour, WI
Indianapolis Professional Photographers Guild **[5950]**, New Palestine, IN
Indianhead Professional Photographers Assn. **[17879]**, Eau Claire, WI
Lima Soc. of Professional Photographers **[16579]**, St. Marys, OH
Michiana Professional Photographers **[5775]**, Merrillville, IN
Mid-Michigan Professional Photographers Assn. **[9114]**, Mount Pleasant, MI
Minnesota Professional Photographers Assn. **[10980]**, Fairmont, MN
Natl. Press Photographers Assn., Region 4 **[4563]**, Evansville, IN
NPPA Region 5 **[11065]**, Golden Valley, MN
Photographic Art Specialist of Ohio **[16122]**, New Carlisle, OH
Professional Photographers of Central Ohio **[14714]**, Columbus, OH
Professional Photographers of Greater Louisville **[5921]**, New Albany, IN
Professional Photographers of Indiana **[6038]**, Petersburg, IN
Professional Photographers of Michigan **[9747]**, Shelby Township, MI
Professional Photographers of Ohio **[14715]**, Columbus, OH
Professional Photographers of Southwest Ohio **[13625]**, Centerville, OH
Professional Photographers of Western Michigan **[7865]**, Grand Haven, MI
Professional Photographers of Western Michigan **[8489]**, Kentwood, MI
Soc. of Northern Ohio Professional Photographers **[14220]**, Cleveland, OH
South Central Professional Photographers Assn. **[17618]**, Beloit, WI
Southeastern Wisconsin Professional Photographers Assn. **[20104]**, West Allis, WI
Twin Cities Professional Photographers of Am. **[11194]**, Hopkins, MN

Physical Education
Michigan Interscholastic Athletic Administrators Assn. **[8851]**, Livonia, MI
Physical Educ., Recreation, and Dance; Illinois Assn. for Hea., **[2078]**, Jacksonville, IL
Physical Educ., Recreation and Dance; Ohio Assn. for Hea., **[13245]**, Avon Lake, OH

Physical Fitness
Central Ohio Senior Olympics **[14363]**, Columbus, OH
Lima Area Senior Olympics **[15659]**, Lima, OH
Michigan Senior Olympics **[9507]**, Rochester, MI
Northcoast (Lake County-Cleveland) Senior Olympics **[14778]**, Concord Township, OH
Northland Senior Games **[10847]**, Duluth, MN
Ohio Assn. for Hea., Physical Educ., Recreation and Dance **[13245]**, Avon Lake, OH
Ohio Senior Olympics **[17409]**, Youngstown, OH
Southwest Ohio Senior Olympics **[14002]**, Cincinnati, OH

Southwestern Indiana Regional Coun. on Aging **[4580]**, Evansville, IN
Toledo Senior Olympics **[16977]**, Toledo, OH
Wisconsin Senior Olympics **[17686]**, Brookfield, WI
Physical Therapy
Amer. Physical Therapy Assn., Indiana Chap. **[5016]**, Indianapolis, IN
Michigan Physical Therapy Assn. **[6733]**, Ann Arbor, MI
Wisconsin Physical Therapy Assn. **[18740]**, Madison, WI
Physical Therapy Assn., Indiana Chap; Amer. **[5016]**, Indianapolis, IN
Physical Therapy Assn., Minnesota Chap; Amer. **[12220]**, Roseville, MN
Physician Asst. Assn; Veterans Affairs **[8329]**, Iron Mountain, MI
Physician Assistants
Illinois Acad. of Physician Assistants **[3560]**, Springfield, IL
Michigan Acad. of Physician Assistants **[7530]**, East Lansing, MI
Minnesota Acad. of Physician Assistants **[11620]**, Minneapolis, MN
Ohio Assn. of Physician Assistants **[17348]**, Worthington, OH
Veterans Affairs Physician Asst. Assn. **[8329]**, Iron Mountain, MI
Wisconsin Acad. of Physician Assistants **[18639]**, Madison, WI
Physician Assistants; Minnesota Acad. of **[11620]**, Minneapolis, MN
Physician Assistants; Wisconsin Acad. of **[18639]**, Madison, WI
Physicians
Amer. Assn. of Physicians of Indian Origin, Downstate Illinois **[485]**, Centralia, IL
Amer. Assn. of Physicians of Indian Origin, Northern Ohio **[17226]**, Westlake, OH
Amer. Assn. of Physicians of Indian Origin, Wisconsin **[18883]**, Mequon, WI
Amer. Coll. of Emergency Physicians - Minnesota Chap. **[11485]**, Minneapolis, MN
Catholic Physicians' Guild of Chicago **[2806]**, Oak Park, IL
Detroit Guild of the Catholic Medical Assn. **[9984]**, Troy, MI
Illinois Acad. of Family Physicians **[2296]**, Lisle, IL
Indian Physicians Assn. of Greater Canton **[13569]**, Canton, OH
Michigan Acad. of Family Physicians **[9271]**, Okemos, MI
Michigan Assn. of Physicians of Indian Origin **[8848]**, Livonia, MI
Michigan State Medical Soc. **[7550]**, East Lansing, MI
Minnesota Acad. of Family Physicians **[12336]**, St. Louis Park, MN
Minnesota Assn. of Black Physicians **[11625]**, Minneapolis, MN
Southern Thoracic Surgical Assn. **[1194]**, Chicago, IL
Southwestern Surgical Cong. **[1197]**, Chicago, IL
Physicians Commn; Intl. **[★1988]**
Physicians; Illinois Acad. of Family **[2296]**, Lisle, IL
Physicians Michigan Chap; Amer. Coll. of Emergency **[★8644]**
Physicians; Michigan Coll. of Emergency **[8644]**, Lansing, MI
Physicians; Ohio Acad. of Family **[14532]**, Columbus, OH
Physicians for Social Responsibility, Chicago **[1137]**, Chicago, IL
Physicians for Social Responsibility, Madison **[18598]**, Madison, WI
Physicians for Social Responsibility, Northeast Ohio **[14248]**, Cleveland Heights, OH
Physicians for Social Responsibility, Southeast Wisconsin **[20156]**, Whitefish Bay, WI
Physics
Amer. Assn. of Physics Teachers, Chicago Sect. **[610]**, Chicago, IL
Amer. Assn. of Physics Teachers, Indiana Sect. **[4974]**, Indianapolis, IN
Amer. Assn. of Physics Teachers, Michigan Sect. **[9497]**, Rochester, MI
Amer. Assn. of Physics Teachers, Minnesota Sect. **[11815]**, Moorhead, MN
Amer. Assn. of Physics Teachers, Ohio Sect. **[16542]**, Rocky River, OH
Amer. Assn. of Physics Teachers, Puerto Rico Sect. **[9498]**, Rochester, MI
Amer. Assn. of Physics Teachers, Southern Ohio Sect. **[13704]**, Cincinnati, OH
Amer. Assn. of Physics Teachers, Wisconsin Sect. **[17861]**, Eau Claire, WI
Great Lakes Chap. of the Amer. Assn. of Physicists in Medicine **[8839]**, Livonia, MI
Hea. Physics Soc., Northern Ohio Chap. **[16546]**, Rocky River, OH
North Central Chap. of the Amer. Assn. of Physicists in Medicine **[11710]**, Minneapolis, MN
Ohio Sect. of the Amer. Physical Soc. **[17360]**, Wright-Patterson AFB, OH
Soc. of Physics Students - Carthage Coll. Chap. No. 1015 **[18311]**, Kenosha, WI
Soc. of Physics Students - Cleveland State Univ. Chap. No. 1247 **[14221]**, Cleveland, OH
Soc. of Physics Students - John Carroll Univ. Chap. No. 3329 **[17027]**, University Heights, OH
Soc. of Physics Students - Ohio State Univ. Chap. No. 5175 **[14737]**, Columbus, OH
Soc. of Physics Students - Otterbein Coll. Chap. No. 5413 **[17221]**, Westerville, OH
Soc. of Physics Students - St. Cloud State Univ. Chap. No. 6122 **[12310]**, St. Cloud, MN
Soc. of Physics Students - Sauk Valley Coll. Chap. No. 6390 **[1484]**, Dixon, IL
Soc. of Physics Students - Southwest Minnesota State Univ. Chap. No. 6666 **[11440]**, Marshall, MN
Soc. of Physics Students - Univ. of Wisconsin-Eau Claire Chap. No. 8289 **[17900]**, Eau Claire, WI
Soc. of Physics Students - Univ. of Wisconsin-Platteville Chap. No. 8316 **[19470]**, Platteville, WI
Soc. of Physics Students - Wittenberg Univ. Chap. No. 8379 **[16744]**, Springfield, OH
Physics Teachers, Wisconsin Sect; Amer. Assn. of **[17861]**, Eau Claire, WI
Physiology
Midwest Physiological Soc. **[19050]**, Milwaukee, WI
Ohio Physiological Soc. **[14939]**, Dayton, OH
Pickaway County Bd. of Realtors **[14034]**, Circleville, OH
Pickaway County Farm Bur. **[14035]**, Circleville, OH
Pickaway County Literacy Coun. **[14036]**, Circleville, OH
Pickaway County Visitors Bur. **[14037]**, Circleville, OH
Pickerington Area Chamber of Commerce **[16424]**, Pickerington, OH
Pierz Lions Club **[11998]**, Pierz, MN
Pigeon Chamber of Commerce **[9378]**, Pigeon, MI
Pike County Chamber of Commerce **[3095]**, Pittsfield, IL
Pike County Chamber of Commerce **[6037]**, Petersburg, IN
Pike County Chamber of Commerce **[17147]**, Waverly, OH
Pike - Young Life **[5451]**, Indianapolis, IN
Pike's Creek Keel Club **[17587]**, Bayfield, WI
Pilots Assn; Tri-State **[16697]**, South Point, OH
Pilsen Neighbors Community Coun. **[1138]**, Chicago, IL
Pinckney Lions Club **[9382]**, Pinckney, MI
Pinckneyville Chamber of Commerce **[3091]**, Pinckneyville, IL
Pinconning Area Chamber of Commerce **[9383]**, Pinconning, MI
Pinconning Chamber of Commerce **[★9383]**
Pinconning Lions Club **[9384]**, Pinconning, MI
Pine City Area Chamber of Commerce **[12003]**, Pine City, MN
Pine Island Lions Club **[12005]**, Pine Island, MN
Pine Lake Small Craft Assn. **[7563]**, East Lansing, MI
Pinecrest Historical Village **[★18784]**
Pinewood Middle - Wyldlife **[7998]**, Grand Rapids, MI
Pinto Horse Assn. of Ohio **[13229]**, Atwater, OH
Pioneer High - Young Life **[6755]**, Ann Arbor, MI
Pioneer and Historical Soc; Oakland County **[9422]**, Pontiac, MI
Pioneer and Historical Soc; Outagamie County **[★17512]**
Pioneers
Soc. of Indiana Pioneers **[5477]**, Indianapolis, IN
Pioneers Midwest Chap. 128 **[13959]**, Cincinnati, OH
Pioneers; Soc. of Indiana **[5477]**, Indianapolis, IN
Pipe Band; Chicago Highlanders **[2807]**, Oak Park, IL
Pipefitters Union, Local 370; Plumbers and **[7771]**, Flushing, MI
Pipes
Illinois Concrete Pipe Assn. **[3596]**, Springfield, IL
Pipes and Drums; Celtic Cross **[1770]**, Galesburg, IL
Pipestone Area Chamber of Commerce **[12010]**, Pipestone, MN
Pipestone Chamber of Commerce **[★12010]**
Pipestone County Historical Society **[12011]**, Pipestone, MN
Piqua Area Chamber of Commerce **[16437]**, Piqua, OH
Piqua Area United Way **[16438]**, Piqua, OH
Piqua Jr. High - Wyldlife **[16439]**, Piqua, OH
Piqua - Young Life **[16440]**, Piqua, OH
Pistol Club; Ripon Rifle and **[19637]**, Ripon, WI
Pittsfield Lions Club **[3096]**, Pittsfield, IL
Pittsfield Township Historical Soc. **[6756]**, Ann Arbor, MI
Pittsford Area Lions Club **[9320]**, Osseo, MI
Placement
Indiana Assn. for Employment in Educ. **[5171]**, Indianapolis, IN
Midwest Assn. for Employment in Educ. **[3854]**, Vernon Hills, IL
Midwest Assn. of Student Employment Administrators **[15207]**, Findlay, OH
Ohio Assn. for Employment in Educ. **[16857]**, Tiffin, OH
Plain City Lions Club **[16443]**, Plain City, OH
Plain Lions Club **[19461]**, Plain, WI
Plainfield Area Chamber of Commerce **[3105]**, Plainfield, IL
Plainfield Chamber of Commerce **[6043]**, Plainfield, IN
Plainfield South High School Parent Teacher Student Org. **[3106]**, Plainfield, IL
Plainview Lions Club **[12014]**, Plainview, MN
Plainwell Chamber of Commerce **[9388]**, Plainwell, MI
Planned Giving Coun. of Eastern Wisconsin **[19093]**, Milwaukee, WI
Planned Giving Gp. of Indiana **[5452]**, Indianapolis, IN
Planned Giving Info. Consortium of East Central Illinois **[2446]**, Mattoon, IL
Planned Parenthood Assn. of Summit County **[★13081]**
Planned Parenthood of Central and Southern Indiana **[★5453]**
Planned Parenthood of Chicago Area **[1139]**, Chicago, IL
Planned Parenthood of Decatur **[1402]**, Decatur, IL
Planned Parenthood Fed. of Am. **[2838]**, Oakbrook Terrace, IL
Planned Parenthood of Greater Cleveland **[14205]**, Cleveland, OH
Planned Parenthood of Indiana **[5453]**, Indianapolis, IN
Planned Parenthood of Mahoning Valley **[17411]**, Youngstown, OH
Planned Parenthood of Minnesota, North Dakota and South Dakota **[12560]**, St. Paul, MN
Planned Parenthood of Minnesota and South Dakota **[★12560]**
Planned Parenthood of Northwest Ohio **[16949]**, Toledo, OH
Planned Parenthood of Southeast Ohio **[13216]**, Athens, OH
Planned Parenthood of Southwest Ohio Region **[13960]**, Cincinnati, OH
Planned Parenthood of Springfield Area **[3662]**, Springfield, IL
Planned Parenthood of Summit, Portage, and Medina Counties **[13081]**, Akron, OH

Planned Parenthood of Wisconsin [19094], Milwaukee, WI
Planning
Assn. for Institutional Res. in the Upper Midwest [18484], Madison, WI
Greater Ashburn Planning Assn. [907], Chicago, IL
Illinois Assn. for Institutional Res. [525], Champaign, IL
Indiana Assn. for Institutional Res. [6384], Valparaiso, IN
Medina County Dept. of Planning Services [15947], Medina, OH
Michigan Assn. for Institutional Res. [8950], Marquette, MI
Michigan Assn. of Planning [6721], Ann Arbor, MI
Monroe County Planning Commn. [9069], Monroe, MI
Ohio Assn. of Institutional Res. and Planning [14556], Columbus, OH
Ohio Planning Conf. [14199], Cleveland, OH
Ohio Spill Planning Prevention and Emergency Response Assn. [14677], Columbus, OH
Soc. for Coll. and Univ. Planning, Illinois [1188], Chicago, IL
Planning Commn; Bay-Lake Regional [18083], Green Bay, WI
Planning Commn; Brooke-Hancock-Jefferson Metropolitan [16761], Steubenville, OH
Planning Commn; East Central Wisconsin Regional [18858], Menasha, WI
Planning Commn; Greater Wabash Regional [15], Albion, IL
Planning Commn; Kankakee County Regional [2135], Kankakee, IL
Planning Commn; McHenry County Regional [4062], Woodstock, IL
Planning Commn; Monroe County [9069], Monroe, MI
Planning Commn; Southwestern Wisconsin Regional [19472], Platteville, WI
Planning Coun; South Metropolitan [18620], Madison, WI
Planning and Development Commn; South Central Illinois Regional [3412], Salem, IL
Planning and Development Commn; Southeastern Illinois Regional [1943], Harrisburg, IL
Planning Prevention and Emergency Response Assn; Ohio Spill [14677], Columbus, OH
Plano Commerce Assn. [3110], Plano, IL
Plant Soc; Illinois Native [3976], Westville, IL
Plants Assn. of Wisconsin; Invasive [18534], Madison, WI
Platteville Chamber of Commerce [19466], Platteville, WI
Platteville Main St. Prog. [19467], Platteville, WI
Players, Not-for-Profit; Limelight [204], Belleville, IL
Players; Sheridan Chamber [1674], Evanston, IL
Players; Showbiz [13985], Cincinnati, OH
Playing Card Collectors; Chicago [2908], Palatine, IL
Pleasant Lions Club [15852], Marion, OH
Pleasant Valley Beagle Club [15755], Malvern, OH
Plumbers AFL-CIO, LU 434 [19231], Mosinee, WI
Plumbers AFL-CIO, LU 557 [★19231]
Plumbers' Assn; Cincinnati Master [13791], Cincinnati, OH
Plumbers and Pipefitters Union, Local 370 [7771], Flushing, MI
Plumbing
Plumbers and Pipefitters Union, Local 370 [7771], Flushing, MI
United Assn. of Journeymen and Apprentices of the Plumbing and Pipe Fitting Indus. of the U.S. and Canada - Local Union 15 [11764], Minneapolis, MN
United Assn. of Journeymen and Apprentices of the Plumbing and Pipe Fitting Indus. of the U.S. and Canada - Local Union 136 [4584], Evansville, IN
United Assn. of Journeymen and Apprentices of the Plumbing and Pipe Fitting Indus. of the U.S. and Canada - Local Union 183 [18878], Menomonee Falls, WI
United Assn. of Journeymen and Apprentices of the Plumbing and Pipe Fitting Indus. of the U.S. and Canada - Local Union 370 [7772], Flushing, MI
United Assn. of Journeymen and Apprentices of the Plumbing and Pipe Fitting Indus. of the U.S. and Canada - Local Union 392 [14014], Cincinnati, OH
United Assn. of Journeymen and Apprentices of the Plumbing and Pipe Fitting Indus. of the U.S. and Canada - Local Union 434 [19232], Mosinee, WI
United Assn. of Journeymen and Apprentices of the Plumbing and Pipe Fitting Indus. of the U.S. and Canada - Local Union 501 [132], Aurora, IL
United Assn. of Journeymen and Apprentices of the Plumbing and Pipe Fitting Indus. of the U.S. and Canada - Local Union 597 [1213], Chicago, IL
United Assn. of Journeymen and Apprentices of the Plumbing and Pipe Fitting Indus. of the U.S. and Canada - Local Union 636 [7677], Farmington Hills, MI
United Assn. of Journeymen and Apprentices of the Plumbing and Pipe Fitting Indus. of the U.S. and Canada - Steamfitters Local Union 601 [19139], Milwaukee, WI
Plumbing Contractors; Madison Assn. of [18549], Madison, WI
Plumbing Contractors; South Macomb Assn. of [8522], Lakeville, MI
Plumbing-Heating-Cooling Contractors Assn., Akron [15800], Mantua, OH
Plumbing-Heating-Cooling Contractors Assn., Bloomington/Normal [306], Bloomington, IL
Plumbing-Heating-Cooling Contractors Assn., Central Ohio [15609], Lancaster, OH
Plumbing-Heating-Cooling Contractors Assn., Central Wisconsin [20189], Wisconsin Rapids, WI
Plumbing-Heating-Cooling Contractors Assn., Dayton Area [14947], Dayton, OH
Plumbing-Heating-Cooling Contractors Assn., East Central Illinois [546], Champaign, IL
Plumbing-Heating-Cooling Contractors Assn., Eastern Ohio [13538], Canfield, OH
Plumbing-Heating-Cooling Contractors Assn., Egyptian [2407], Marion, IL
Plumbing-Heating-Cooling Contractors Assn., Flint [6757], Ann Arbor, MI
Plumbing-Heating-Cooling Contractors Assn., Fort Wayne [4711], Fort Wayne, IN
Plumbing-Heating-Cooling Contractors Assn., Greater Indianapolis [5454], Indianapolis, IN
Plumbing-Heating-Cooling Contractors Assn., Greater SW Illinois [1698], Fairview Heights, IL
Plumbing-Heating-Cooling Contractors Assn., Lake and McHenry Counties [1924], Gurnee, IL
Plumbing-Heating-Cooling Contractors Assn., Lakes Area [11995], Perham, MN
Plumbing-Heating-Cooling Contractors Assn., Metro [10541], Brooklyn Center, MN
Plumbing-Heating-Cooling Contractors Assn., Michigan [8854], Livonia, MI
Plumbing-Heating-Cooling Contractors Assn., North Central [6649], Alpena, MI
Plumbing-Heating-Cooling Contractors Assn., North Central Indiana [6051], Plymouth, IN
Plumbing-Heating-Cooling Contractors Assn., North East Ohio [16797], Strongsville, OH
Plumbing-Heating-Cooling Contractors Assn., Northern Wisconsin [17849], Eagle River, WI
Plumbing-Heating-Cooling Contractors Assn., Northwest [4468], Dyer, IN
Plumbing-Heating-Cooling Contractors Assn., Northwestern Michigan [7103], Cedar, MI
Plumbing-Heating-Cooling Contractors Assn., Range [12805], Virginia, MN
Plumbing-Heating-Cooling Contractors Assn., Rochester [12170], Rochester, MN
Plumbing-Heating-Cooling Contractors Assn., Saginaw Valley [9624], Saginaw, MI
Plumbing-Heating-Cooling Contractors Assn., St. Joseph Valley [5812], Mishawaka, IN
Plumbing-Heating-Cooling Contractors Assn., Sheboygan County [17457], Adell, WI
Plumbing-Heating-Cooling Contractors Assn., South Central Indiana [5535], Jasper, IN
Plumbing-Heating-Cooling Contractors Assn., South Macomb [8521], Lakeville, MI
Plumbing-Heating-Cooling Contractors Assn., Southeastern Michigan [7419], Detroit, MI
Plumbing-Heating-Cooling Contractors Assn., Southwestern [5853], Mount Vernon, IN
Plumbing-Heating-Cooling Contractors Assn., Stark [13281], Beach City, OH
Plumbing-Heating-Cooling Contractors Assn., Thumb Area [9379], Pigeon, MI
Plumbing-Heating-Cooling Contractors Assn., West Central Indiana [5631], Lafayette, IN
Plumbing-Heating-Cooling Contractors Assn., West Michigan [8045], Grandville, MI
Plumbing-Heating-Cooling Contractors Assn., West Suburban [217], Bellwood, IL
Plumbing-Heating-Cooling Contractors Assn., Western Wayne County [10141], Westland, MI
Plumbing-Heating-Cooling Contractors Assn., Western Wisconsin [19737], Siren, WI
Plumbing-Heating-Cooling Contractors Assn., Wisconsin Valley [19798], Stevens Point, WI
Plumbing, Heating, Cooling Contractors; Indiana Assn. of [5179], Indianapolis, IN
Plumbing-Heating-Cooling Contractors Wisconsin Assn. [19095], Milwaukee, WI
Plumbing and Mech. Contractors Assn; Metropolitan Detroit [★7420]
Plumbing and Mech. Contractors of Detroit [7420], Detroit, MI
Plummer Lions Club [12018], Plummer, MN
Plummers Lions Too Club [12019], Plummer, MN
Plymouth Area Chamber of Commerce [6052], Plymouth, IN
Plymouth Chamber of Commerce [19492], Plymouth, WI
Plymouth Community Arts Coun. [9404], Plymouth, MI
Plymouth Community Chamber of Commerce [9405], Plymouth, MI
Plymouth Community United Way [9406], Plymouth, MI
Plymouth Historical Museum [★9407]
Plymouth Historical Soc. [9407], Plymouth, MI
Plymouth Junior Womans' Club [19493], Plymouth, WI
Plymouth Lions Club - Michigan [9408], Plymouth, MI
Plymouth Lions Club - Minnesota [12033], Plymouth, MN
Plymouth Lions Club - Ohio [17265], Willard, OH
PMI Midwest Chap. [★2176]
Podiatric Medical Assn; Illinois [956], Chicago, IL
Podiatric Medical Assn; Indiana [5279], Indianapolis, IN
Podiatry
Illinois Podiatric Medical Assn. [956], Chicago, IL
Indiana Podiatric Medical Assn. [5279], Indianapolis, IN
Michigan Podiatric Medical Assn. [8697], Lansing, MI
Ohio Podiatric Medical Assn. [14653], Columbus, OH
Wisconsin Soc. of Podiatric Medicine [19974], Watertown, WI
Podiatry Assn; Indiana State [★5279]
Poets Critique; Songwriters and [14738], Columbus, OH
Points of Light Found. - Volunteer Center of Door County [19843], Sturgeon Bay, WI
Points of Light Found. - Volunteer Center of East Central Wisconsin [17516], Appleton, WI
Points of Light Found. - Volunteer Center of Fond du Lac County [17991], Fond du Lac, WI
Points of Light Found. - Volunteer Center Of Greater Kalamazoo [8461], Kalamazoo, MI
Points of Light Found. - Volunteer Center of South Wood County [20190], Wisconsin Rapids, WI
Points of Light Found. - Volunteer Center of Waukesha County [19442], Pewaukee, WI
Points of Light Found. - Volunteer Rsrc. Center [11725], Minneapolis, MN
Poland Lions Club [16450], Poland, OH
Police
Black Shield Police Assn. [14083], Cleveland, OH
Concerns of Police Survivors, Minnesota Chap. [12225], Roseville, MN
East Lansing Police Athletic League [7516], East Lansing, MI
Fraternal Order of Police of Ohio, State Lodge [14437], Columbus, OH

Minnesota Chiefs of Police Assn. **[12979]**, Woodbury, MN
Minnesota Sheriffs' Assn. **[12980]**, Woodbury, MN
Sentinel Police Assn. **[13981]**, Cincinnati, OH
Toledo Police Patrolman's Assn. **[16974]**, Toledo, OH
Police Acad. Alumni Assn; Quincy Citizens **[3164]**, Quincy, IL
Police Assn; Black Shield **[14083]**, Cleveland, OH
Police Assn; Wisconsin Professional **[18744]**, Madison, WI
Police Athletic Activities League; Rochester **[12181]**, Rochester, MN
Police Athletic League; East Lansing **[7516]**, East Lansing, MI
Police Color Guard; Warrensville Heights Reserve **[13639]**, Chagrin Falls, OH
Police and Firemen's Insurance Assn. - Alton Fire Dept. **[43]**, Alton, IL
Police and Firemen's Insurance Assn. - Anderson Fire Dept. **[4116]**, Anderson, IN
Police and Firemen's Insurance Assn. - Ann Arbor Fire and Police Dept. **[6758]**, Ann Arbor, MI
Police and Firemen's Insurance Assn. - Bloomington Fire and Police Dept. **[307]**, Bloomington, IL
Police and Firemen's Insurance Assn. - Chicago Fire Dept. **[1140]**, Chicago, IL
Police and Firemen's Insurance Assn. - Chicago Southern Suburbs **[3193]**, Richton Park, IL
Police and Firemen's Insurance Assn. - Columbus Fire Dept. **[4405]**, Columbus, IN
Police and Firemen's Insurance Assn. - Decatur Fire Dept. **[1403]**, Decatur, IL
Police and Firemen's Insurance Assn. - Detroit Police Dept. **[7421]**, Detroit, MI
Police and Firemen's Insurance Assn. - Evansville Fire Dept. **[4566]**, Evansville, IN
Police and Firemen's Insurance Assn. - Flint Police Dept. **[7751]**, Flint, MI
Police and Firemen's Insurance Assn. - Grand Rapids Fire Dept. **[8267]**, Howard City, MI
Police and Firemen's Insurance Assn. - Grand Traverse County Fire and Police Dept. **[9947]**, Traverse City, MI
Police and Firemen's Insurance Assn. - Hammond Fire Dept. **[4892]**, Hammond, IN
Police and Firemen's Insurance Assn. - Indianapolis Fire Dept. **[5952]**, New Palestine, IN
Police and Firemen's Insurance Assn. - Indianapolis Police Dept. **[5455]**, Indianapolis, IN
Police and Firemen's Insurance Assn. - Inghamn County Sheriff **[7126]**, Charlotte, MI
Police and Firemen's Insurance Assn. - Kokomo Fire Dept. **[5582]**, Kokomo, IN
Police and Firemen's Insurance Assn. - Lansing Fire Dept. **[7466]**, DeWitt, MI
Police and Firemen's Insurance Assn. - Logansport Fire and Police Dept. **[5697]**, Logansport, IN
Police and Firemen's Insurance Assn. - Marion County Fire Dept. **[4836]**, Greenfield, IN
Police and Firemen's Insurance Assn. - Marion County Sheriff **[5456]**, Indianapolis, IN
Police and Firemen's Insurance Assn. - Muncie Fire Dept. **[5895]**, Muncie, IN
Police and Firemen's Insurance Assn. - Muskegon Fire Dept. **[9157]**, Muskegon, MI
Police and Firemen's Insurance Assn. - Oakland County Sheriff **[7752]**, Flint, MI
Police and Firemen's Insurance Assn. - Peoria Fire Dept. **[3059]**, Peoria, IL
Police and Firemen's Insurance Assn. - Richmond Fire Dept. **[6101]**, Richmond, IN
Police and Firemen's Insurance Assn. - Rock Island Fire Dept. **[3189]**, Reynolds, IL
Police and Firemen's Insurance Assn. - Saginaw County Police Dept. **[9625]**, Saginaw, MI
Police and Firemen's Insurance Assn. - St. Cloud Fire and Police Dept. **[12105]**, Rice, MN
Police and Firemen's Insurance Assn. - St. Paul Fire Dept. **[12985]**, Woodbury, MN
Police and Firemen's Insurance Assn. - South Bend Fire and Police Dept. **[4813]**, Granger, IN
Police and Firemen's Insurance Assn. - Terre Haute Fire Dept. **[6340]**, Terre Haute, IN
Police and Firemen's Insurance Assn. - Urbana Fire Dept. **[3088]**, Philo, IL
Police and Firemen's Insurance Assn. - Vincennes Fire Dept. **[6421]**, Vincennes, IN
Police and Firemen's Insurance Assn. - Wayne County Sheriff **[9409]**, Plymouth, MI
Police and Firemen's Insurance Assn. - Western Wayne County Fire Dept. **[9410]**, Plymouth, MI
Police Historical Soc. and Museum; Cleveland **[14102]**, Cleveland, OH
Police Lodge 86; Fraternal Order of **[5119]**, Indianapolis, IN
Police; Michigan Assn. of Chiefs of **[9272]**, Okemos, MI
Police Museum; Cleveland **[★14102]**
Police Off.rs Assn; Marquette Professional **[8948]**, Marquette, MI
Police Off.rs Assn; Reading **[16508]**, Reading, OH
Police Off.rs Assn; Utica **[10038]**, Utica, MI
Police, Region 6; Intl. Assn. of Women **[4883]**, Hammond, IN
Police Troopers Assn; Michigan State **[7551]**, East Lansing, MI
Policemen's Assn; Wisconsin Professional **[★18744]**
Policy
Citizens for Appropriate Rural Roads **[6285]**, Stanford, IN
Policy Matters Ohio **[14206]**, Cleveland, OH
Polio
Post-Polio Rsrc. Gp. of Southeastern Wisconsin **[19097]**, Milwaukee, WI
Polish
Polish Amer. Cong., Illinois Div. **[1141]**, Chicago, IL
Polish Falcons of Am., Nest 4 **[6254]**, South Bend, IN
Polish Falcons of Am., Nest 79 **[9841]**, Southgate, MI
Polish Falcons of Am., Nest 80 **[6255]**, South Bend, IN
Polish Falcons of Am., Nest 124 **[9626]**, Saginaw, MI
Polish Falcons of Am., Nest 276 **[9158]**, Muskegon, MI
Polish Falcons of Am., Nest 336 **[8394]**, Jackson, MI
Polish Falcons of Am., Nest 507 **[3299]**, Rockford, IL
Polish Falcons of Am., Nest 652 **[8751]**, Lansing, MI
Polish Falcons of Am., Nest 725 **[19096]**, Milwaukee, WI
Polish Amer. Cong., Illinois Div. **[1141]**, Chicago, IL
Polish Falcons of Am., Nest 4 **[6254]**, South Bend, IN
Polish Falcons of Am., Nest 79 **[9841]**, Southgate, MI
Polish Falcons of Am., Nest 80 **[6255]**, South Bend, IN
Polish Falcons of Am., Nest 124 **[9626]**, Saginaw, MI
Polish Falcons of Am., Nest 276 **[9158]**, Muskegon, MI
Polish Falcons of Am., Nest 336 **[8394]**, Jackson, MI
Polish Falcons of Am., Nest 507 **[3299]**, Rockford, IL
Polish Falcons of Am., Nest 652 **[8751]**, Lansing, MI
Polish Falcons of Am., Nest 725 **[19096]**, Milwaukee, WI
Political Action
Common Cause of Michigan **[8561]**, Lansing, MI
Common Cause Wisconsin **[18499]**, Madison, WI
Wisconsin Taxpayers Alliance **[18758]**, Madison, WI
Political Parties
Autonomy Party **[11926]**, Oakdale, MN
Charter Comm. of Greater Cincinnati **[13766]**, Cincinnati, OH
Democratic Party of Illinois **[3548]**, Springfield, IL
DuPage Libertarians **[448]**, Carol Stream, IL
Indiana Democratic Party **[5224]**, Indianapolis, IN
Libertarian Party of Chicago **[1028]**, Chicago, IL
Libertarian Party of Illinois **[1908]**, Greenville, IL
Libertarian Party of Indiana **[5393]**, Indianapolis, IN
Libertarian Party of Lake County **[2210]**, Lake Zurich, IL
Libertarian Party of Michigan **[8599]**, Lansing, MI
Libertarian Party of Minnesota **[12441]**, St. Paul, MN
Libertarian Party of Ohio **[14492]**, Columbus, OH
Libertarian Party of Wisconsin **[18157]**, Greenfield, WI
Michigan Democratic Party **[8656]**, Lansing, MI
Ohio Democratic Party **[14593]**, Columbus, OH
Okaw Valley Libertarians **[3848]**, Vandalia, IL
Progressive Dane **[18601]**, Madison, WI
Progressive Minnesota **[12562]**, St. Paul, MN
Rockford Area Libertarians **[3308]**, Rockford, IL
Southern Illinois Libertarians **[433]**, Carbondale, IL
Students for Individual Liberty - Univ. of Illinois, Urbana/Champaign **[3838]**, Urbana, IL
Politics
League of Women Voters of Champaign County **[3827]**, Urbana, IL
League of Women Voters of Chicago **[1024]**, Chicago, IL
League of Women Voters of the Cincinnati Area **[13883]**, Cincinnati, OH
League of Women Voters of the Cleveland Area **[14155]**, Cleveland, OH
League of Women Voters of Cook County **[1025]**, Chicago, IL
League of Women Voters of Cuyahoga County **[14156]**, Cleveland, OH
League of Women Voters of the Elgin Area **[1595]**, Elgin, IL
League of Women Voters of Evanston **[1667]**, Evanston, IL
League of Women Voters of Glen Ellyn **[1837]**, Glen Ellyn, IL
League of Women Voters of the Greater Dayton Area **[14904]**, Dayton, OH
League of Women Voters of Highland Park **[1993]**, Highland Park, IL
League of Women Voters of Illinois **[1026]**, Chicago, IL
League of Women Voters of Janesville **[18255]**, Janesville, WI
League of Women Voters - Lake Erie Basin Comm. **[17274]**, Willoughby, OH
League of Women Voters of the Lansing Area **[8596]**, Lansing, MI
League of Women Voters of Michigan **[8597]**, Lansing, MI
League of Women Voters of Minneapolis **[11596]**, Minneapolis, MN
League of Women Voters of Ohio **[14491]**, Columbus, OH
Polk Lions Club **[16453]**, Polk, OH
Pollution Control
Air and Waste Mgt. Assn. - East Michigan Chap. **[9187]**, New Haven, MI
Air and Waste Mgt. Assn. - North Ohio Chap. **[14041]**, Cleveland, OH
Air and Waste Mgt. Assn. - Upper Midwest Sect. **[10942]**, Elk River, MN
Air and Waste Mgt. Assn. - West Michigan Chap. **[6556]**, Ada, MI
Citizens for Alternatives to Chem. Contamination **[8501]**, Lake, MI
Clean Water Action Coun. of Northeast Wisconsin **[18093]**, Green Bay, WI
Illinois Pollution Control Bd. **[957]**, Chicago, IL
Lake Michigan Air and Waste Mgt. Assn. **[2918]**, Palatine, IL
Pollution Control Agency; Minnesota **[12509]**, St. Paul, MN
Pollution Control Agency of Rochester **[★12509]**
Polo Chamber of Commerce **[3117]**, Polo, IL
Polo Cricket Club **[1853]**, Glendale Heights, IL
Pomeroy Area Chamber of Commerce **[★16455]**
Pomeroy Chamber of Commerce **[★16455]**
Pontiac Area Chamber of Commerce **[3120]**, Pontiac, IL
Pontiac Lake Horsemans Assn. **[10158]**, White Lake, MI
Pontiac MMBA **[9189]**, New Hudson, MI
Pontiac-Oakland Club Intl., Illinois Chap. **[2318]**, Lockport, IL
Pontiac-Oakland Club Intl., Michigan WideTrackers **[10092]**, Waterford, MI
Pontiac-Oakland Club Intl., Northwest Ohio Chap. **[16950]**, Toledo, OH
Pontiac-Oakland Club Intl., Tomahawk Chap. 13 **[10925]**, Edina, MN
Pontiac-Oakland Club Intl., West Michigan Chap. **[10230]**, Zeeland, MI
Pontiac Regional Chamber **[9423]**, Pontiac, MI
Pontiac Yacht Club **[9424]**, Pontiac, MI

Pony of the Americas Club, Minnesota **[11397]**, Mankato, MN
Pony of the Ams. Club, Wisconsin - North **[17922]**, Elk Mound, WI
Pony of the Ams. Club, Wisconsin - North Central **[19799]**, Stevens Point, WI
Pony of the Ams. Club, Wisconsin - Southern **[19510]**, Portage, WI
Popular Astronomy Club **[3249]**, Rock Island, IL
Pork Producers; Adams County **[3144]**, Quincy, IL
Pork Producers Assn; Illinois **[3627]**, Springfield, IL
Pork Producers Assn; Indiana **[6552]**, Zionsville, IN
Port Austin Reeflight Assn. **[9426]**, Port Austin, MI
Port City Beagle Club **[9159]**, Muskegon, MI
Port Clinton Lions Club **[16461]**, Port Clinton, OH
Port Huron Minor Hockey Assn. **[9438]**, Port Huron, MI
Port Huron Northern High School Skating Club **[7774]**, Fort Gratiot, MI
Port Washington BMW Motorcycle Club No. 116 **[19501]**, Port Washington, WI
Port Washington Chamber of Commerce **[19502]**, Port Washington, WI
Portage Area Chamber of Commerce **[19511]**, Portage, WI
Portage Area REACT **[19512]**, Portage, WI
Portage Area United Way **[19513]**, Portage, WI
Portage County Assn. of Realtors **[16502]**, Ravenna, OH
Portage County Beagle Club **[15023]**, Diamond, OH
Portage County Bus. Coun. **[19800]**, Stevens Point, WI
Portage County Chap. of the Ohio Genealogical Soc. **[16503]**, Ravenna, OH
Portage County Crime Stoppers **[19801]**, Stevens Point, WI
Portage County Humane Soc. **[19802]**, Stevens Point, WI
Portage County Literacy Coun. **[19803]**, Stevens Point, WI
Portage County RSVP **[19804]**, Stevens Point, WI
Portage Curling Club **[19514]**, Portage, WI
Portage Exchange Club **[6060]**, Portage, IN
Portage Lions Club **[13397]**, Bowling Green, OH
Portage Lions Club - Michigan **[9453]**, Portage, MI
Portage Park Chamber of Commerce **[1142]**, Chicago, IL
Portage River Basin Council **[16951]**, Toledo, OH
Portage - Young Life **[8462]**, Kalamazoo, MI
Porter County Convention Bur. **[4354]**, Chesterton, IN
Porter County Home Builders Assn. **[6388]**, Valparaiso, IN
Portland Area Chamber of Commerce **[6064]**, Portland, IN
Portland Area Chamber of Commerce **[9457]**, Portland, MI
Portland Economic Development Corp. **[6065]**, Portland, IN
Portsmouth ALU **[16472]**, Portsmouth, OH
Portsmouth Area Chamber of Commerce **[16473]**, Portsmouth, OH
Portuguese Water Dog Club of the Twin Cities **[10667]**, Circle Pines, MN
Posey County Assn. for Retarded Citizens **[5854]**, Mount Vernon, IN
Posey County Chamber of Commerce **[5855]**, Mount Vernon, IN
Posey County Young Life **[5856]**, Mount Vernon, IN
Positively Pewaukee **[19443]**, Pewaukee, WI
Post Oak Flats Rsrc. Conservation and Development Coun. **[2091]**, Jerseyville, IL
Post-Polio Rsrc. Gp. of Southeastern Wisconsin **[19097]**, Milwaukee, WI
Postal Service
Mail Syss. Mgt. Assn., Chicago Chap. **[3488]**, Skokie, IL
Mail Syss. Mgt. Assn., Minnesota Chap. **[11598]**, Minneapolis, MN
Mail Syss. Mgt. Assn., Ohio Valley Chap. **[13891]**, Cincinnati, OH
Mail Syss. Mgt. Assn., Wisconsin Chap. **[17985]**, Fond du Lac, WI
Postal Workers
Amer. Postal Workers Union, AFL-CIO - Crystal Lake Local Union 1879 **[1519]**, Dundee, IL
Amer. Postal Workers Union, AFL-CIO - Indianapolis Local Union 130 **[5017]**, Indianapolis, IN
Amer. Postal Workers Union, AFL-CIO - Local Union 1701 **[3076]**, Peru, IL
Amer. Postal Workers Union, AFL-CIO - Minneapolis Area Local Union 125 **[11513]**, Minneapolis, MN
Amer. Postal Workers Union, AFL-CIO - Quincy Area Local Union 77 **[3147]**, Quincy, IL
Amer. Postal Workers Union, AFL-CIO - Twin Cities Postal Data Center Local Union 7019 **[10864]**, Eagan, MN
Amer. Postal Workers Union, AFL-CIO - Youngstown Local Union 443 **[17391]**, Youngstown, OH
Natl. Postal Mail Handlers Union, Local 304 **[13931]**, Cincinnati, OH
Northeastern Wisconsin Area Local Amer. Postal Workers Union **[18124]**, Green Bay, WI
Postal Workers Union; Northeastern Wisconsin Area Local Amer. **[18124]**, Green Bay, WI
Potato and Vegetable Growers Association; Wisconsin **[17480]**, Antigo, WI
Potawatomi Audubon Soc. **[5602]**, La Porte, IN
Potawatomi MMBA **[6759]**, Ann Arbor, MI
Potawatomi Rsrc. Conservation and Development Coun. **[8972]**, Marshall, MI
Potosi - Tennyson Area Chamber of Commerce **[19522]**, Potosi, WI
Potterville Lions Club **[9460]**, Potterville, MI
Pottery Assn; Wisconsin **[18742]**, Madison, WI
Poultry
Broiler and Egg Assn. of Minnesota **[10571]**, Buffalo, MN
Illinois Poultry Indus. Coun. **[3823]**, Urbana, IL
Indiana State Poultry Assn. **[6487]**, West Lafayette, IN
Midwest Poultry Fed. **[10574]**, Buffalo, MN
Minnesota Turkey Growers Assn. **[10576]**, Buffalo, MN
Minnesota Turkey Res. and Promotion Coun. **[10577]**, Buffalo, MN
Ohio Poultry Assn. **[14655]**, Columbus, OH
Turkey Market Development Council **[6502]**, West Lafayette, IN
Poultry Assn; Ohio **[14655]**, Columbus, OH
Poultry Fed; Midwest **[10574]**, Buffalo, MN
Pound Museum **[★6447]**
Poverty
Advocap **[19385]**, Oshkosh, WI
Friends of the Third World **[4664]**, Fort Wayne, IN
Women in Community Ser., Midwest Region **[7456]**, Detroit, MI
Powell Area Chamber of Commerce **[16480]**, Powell, OH
Powell Sertoma Club **[16481]**, Powell, OH
Power Flour Action Network **[19705]**, Sheboygan, WI
Poynette Bowhunters Assn. **[19525]**, Poynette, WI
Poynette Chamber of Commerce **[19526]**, Poynette, WI
Practitioner Certification Bd; Public Hea. **[1159]**, Chicago, IL
Prader-Willi Michigan Assn. **[8865]**, Lowell, MI
Prader-Willi Syndrome Assn. Illinois **[2703]**, Niles, IL
Prader-Willi Syndrome Assn. of Minnesota **[10900]**, Eden Prairie, MN
Prader-Willi Syndrome Assn. of Ohio **[15955]**, Medina, OH
Prairie Art Alliance **[3663]**, Springfield, IL
Prairie Brass Band Assn. **[76]**, Arlington Heights, IL
Prairie Capital Corvair Assn. **[3664]**, Springfield, IL
Prairie du Chien Lions Club **[19528]**, Prairie Du Chien, WI
Prairie Club **[1626]**, Elmhurst, IL
Prairie Country Rsrc. Conservation and Development Coun. **[12926]**, Willmar, MN
Prairie Creek Beagle Club **[6027]**, Pendleton, IN
Prairie Du Chien Area Chamber of Commerce **[19529]**, Prairie Du Chien, WI
Prairie Du Chien Indus. Development Corp. **[19530]**, Prairie Du Chien, WI
Prairie Ensemble **[547]**, Champaign, IL
Prairie Hearts Romance Writers of Am. Chap. 43 **[3401]**, St. Joseph, IL
Prairie Hills Rsrc. Conservation and Development Coun. **[2375]**, Macomb, IL
Prairie Renaissance Cultural Alliance **[11840]**, Morris, MN
Prairie Rivers Network **[548]**, Champaign, IL
Prairie State Bonsai Soc. **[1840]**, Glen Ellyn, IL
Prairie State Orchid Soc. **[3665]**, Springfield, IL
Prairie Township Volunteer Fire Dept **[15463]**, Holmesville, OH
Prairie Valley District Dental Soc. **[1780]**, Galesburg, IL
Prairie Woods Audubon Soc. **[77]**, Arlington Heights, IL
Prairieland United Way **[2085]**, Jacksonville, IL
Preble County Chap. - Ohio Genealogical Soc. **[15089]**, Eaton, OH
Preble County Habitat for Humanity **[15090]**, Eaton, OH
Preble County Historical Soc. **[15091]**, Eaton, OH
Precast/Prestressed Concrete Inst., Central Region **[13442]**, Brookville, OH
Precision Metalforming Assn. **[15503]**, Independence, OH
Prentice Indus. Development Corp. **[19537]**, Prentice, WI
Preschool Education
Kids of the Kingdom **[5530]**, Jasper, IN
Prescott Area Chamber of Commerce **[19538]**, Prescott, WI
Preservation Comm; West Creek **[16379]**, Parma, OH
Preservation Network; Michigan Historic **[8672]**, Lansing, MI
Preservation Soc; Ashtabula Lighthouse Restoration and **[16231]**, North Kingsville, OH
Preservation Soc; DeTour Reef Light **[7485]**, Drummond Island, MI
Preservation Society; St. Leo **[14725]**, Columbus, OH
Preservation Wayne **[7422]**, Detroit, MI
Preserve the Dunes **[9493]**, Riverside, MI
Preserve Historic Sleeping Bear **[7604]**, Empire, MI
Pres. R.B. Hayes Audubon Soc. **[15251]**, Fremont, OH
Presque Isle Chamber of Commerce **[19541]**, Presque Isle, WI
Press
Amer. Soc. of Bus. Publication Editors - Chicago Chap. **[721]**, Chicago, IL
Amer. Soc. of Bus. Publication Editors - Michigan Chap. **[6664]**, Ann Arbor, MI
Amer. Soc. of Bus. Publication Editors - Twin Cities Chap. **[11516]**, Minneapolis, MN
Asian Amer. Journalists Assn. - Chicago Chap. **[737]**, Chicago, IL
Illinois Press Assn. **[3628]**, Springfield, IL
Inland Press Assn. **[1460]**, Des Plaines, IL
Michigan Press Assn. **[8698]**, Lansing, MI
Ohio Newspaper Assn. **[14645]**, Columbus, OH
Soc. of Professional Jour.ists **[5480]**, Indianapolis, IN
Press Editors, Cleveland Chap; Amer. Soc. of Bus. **[★14063]**
Prevailing Community Development Corp. **[7423]**, Detroit, MI
Prevent Blindness Am., Illinois Div. **[1143]**, Chicago, IL
Prevent Blindness Indiana **[5457]**, Indianapolis, IN
Prevent Blindness Ohio **[14711]**, Columbus, OH
Prevent Blindness Wisconsin **[19098]**, Milwaukee, WI
Prevent Child Abuse Am. **[1144]**, Chicago, IL
Prevent Child Abuse Illinois **[3666]**, Springfield, IL
Prevent Child Abuse Indiana **[5458]**, Indianapolis, IN
Prevent Child Abuse Minnesota **[12561]**, St. Paul, MN
Prevent Child Abuse Ohio **[14712]**, Columbus, OH
Prevent Child Abuse Wisconsin **[18599]**, Madison, WI
Prevention of Blindness; Illinois Soc. for the **[967]**, Chicago, IL
Pri-Ru-Ta Rsrc. Conservation and Development Coun. **[18848]**, Medford, WI
Pride-N-Living Housing Development Corp. **[★12118]**
Pride and Respect for Youth in a Sexual Minority **[★14157]**
Pride of Toledo Chorus of Sweet Adelines Intl. **[16952]**, Toledo, OH
Primary Purpose Area of Narcotics Anonymous **[549]**, Champaign, IL
Princeton Area Chamber of Commerce **[6071]**, Princeton, IN

Princeton Area Chamber of Commerce [★12046]
Princeton Area Chamber of Commerce [12046], Princeton, MN
Princeton Area Chamber of Commerce and Main St. [3137], Princeton, IL
Princeton Chamber of Commerce [★3137]
Princeton Chamber of Commerce [★19543]
Princeton - Young Life [15167], Fairfield, OH
Principals
Illinois Principals Assn. [3629], Springfield, IL
Indiana Assn. of School Principals [5185], Indianapolis, IN
Michigan Assn. of Secondary School Principals [8628], Lansing, MI
Michigan Elementary and Middle School Principals Assn. [8981], Mason, MI
Minnesota Assn. of Secondary School Principals [12458], St. Paul, MN
Minnesota Elementary School Principals' Assn. [12481], St. Paul, MN
Principals' Assn; Minnesota Elementary School [12481], St. Paul, MN
Principals; Michigan Assn. of Secondary School [8628], Lansing, MI
Principals; Ohio Assn. of Elementary School [★14552]
Printing Indus. Assn. [17220], Westerville, OH
Printing Indus. of Michigan [9817], Southfield, MI
Printing Indus. of Wisconsin [19444], Pewaukee, WI
Printing Indus. of Illinois-Indiana Assn. [1145], Chicago, IL
Printing Industry of Illinois/Indiana Association [4332], Carmel, IN
Printing Indus. of Minnesota [11726], Minneapolis, MN
Prior Lake Area Chamber of Commerce [12054], Prior Lake, MN
Prior Lake Assn. [12055], Prior Lake, MN
Prior Lake Lions Club [12056], Prior Lake, MN
Priority Children [7753], Flint, MI
Prisoners of War
Amer. Ex-Prisoners of War, Badger Chap. [18458], Madison, WI
Amer. Ex-Prisoners of War, Dayton Area Chap. [15556], Kettering, OH
Amer. Ex-Prisoners of War, Greater Chicago Chap. [4067], Worth, IL
Amer. Ex-Prisoners of War, Kickapoo Chap. [2697], Newton, IL
Amer. Ex-Prisoners of War, Lakes Region Chap. [11975], Park Rapids, MN
Amer. Ex-Prisoners of War, Milwaukee Barb Wire Chap. [19248], Mukwonago, WI
Amer. Ex-Prisoners of War, Northeastern Wisconsin Chap. [18284], Kaukauna, WI
Amer. Ex-Prisoners of War, Northern Indiana Chap. [4867], Hammond, IN
Amer. Ex-Prisoners of War, Okaw Chap. [1528], East Alton, IL
Amer. Ex-Prisoners of War, Prairieland Chap. [12694], Springfield, MN
Amer. Ex-Prisoners of War, Southern Indiana Chap. [4272], Boonville, IN
Amer. Ex-Prisoners of War, Southern Wisconsin Chap. [17604], Beloit, WI
Amer. Ex-Prisoners of War, Western Illinois Chap. [2514], Moline, IL
Private Radio
Allen County REACT [15642], Lima, OH
Apollo VII REACT [1417], Deerfield, IL
Bay County REACT [6887], Bay City, MI
Cass County REACT Team [5690], Logansport, IN
Chagrin Valley REACT [13633], Chagrin Falls, OH
Champaign County REACT Team [17041], Urbana, OH
Chicago Metro REACT [4005], Wheeling, IL
Chillicothe Twin City REACT [1256], Chillicothe, IL
Christmas City REACT [5546], Jonesboro, IN
Circle City REACT [5090], Indianapolis, IN
Coshocton Co REACT [14796], Coshocton, OH
Door County REACT [19202], Mishicot, WI
Dresden REACT [15039], Dresden, OH
Flag City REACT [17062], Vanlue, OH
Fond du Lac County REACT [17980], Fond du Lac, WI
Great Lakes REACT [14128], Cleveland, OH
Great River REACT [3899], Waterloo, IL
Jackson County Wolverine REACT [8377], Jackson, MI
Johnson County REACT [4752], Franklin, IN
Kankakee Valley REACT [2139], Kankakee, IL
Lake County REACT Team [4886], Hammond, IN
Lansing REACT [8592], Lansing, MI
Lenawee Community REACT [6572], Adrian, MI
Lincoln-Railsplitter REACT [2278], Lincoln, IL
Madison County REACT [4111], Anderson, IN
Marathon County REACT [20039], Wausau, WI
Massillon-Stark County REACT [15889], Massillon, OH
Medina County REACT [15949], Medina, OH
Milwaukee County REACT [20103], West Allis, WI
Muskegon Co REACT [9151], Muskegon, MI
Muskingum Co REACT [16698], South Zanesville, OH
Ohio River REACT Team [16471], Portsmouth, OH
Portage Area REACT [19512], Portage, WI
Pulaski County REACT [6534], Winamac, IN
Ramsey Co REACT [12567], St. Paul, MN
Ross Co. Radio Pat. Svr REACT [13672], Chillicothe, OH
St. Joseph Valley REACT [6262], South Bend, IN
So. Mn. Albert Lea REACT [10262], Albert Lea, MN
Spencer County REACT [4355], Chrisney, IN
St Cloud REACT [12311], St. Cloud, MN
Summit County REACT [13095], Akron, OH
Tri-City REACT [329], Bourbonnais, IL
Tri City REACT [18265], Janesville, WI
Tri-County REACT [4727], Fort Wayne, IN
Tuscarawas and Carroll REACT [13592], Canton, OH
Vanderburgh County REACT [4588], Evansville, IN
Wabash Valley REACT [6351], Terre Haute, IN
Waukesha Area REACT [20001], Waukesha, WI
West Suburbs REACT [2829], Oak Park, IL
Whiteside Co. Emergency REACT [3707], Sterling, IL
Private School B - Young Life [11191], Hopkins, MN
Private Schools
Michigan Assn. of Non-Public Schools [8621], Lansing, MI
Processors; Illinois Assn. of Meat [1749], Freeport, IL
Proctor Lions Club [12058], Proctor, MN
Producers of Wisconsin; Professional Dairy [19740], Slinger, WI
Prdt. Development and Mgt. Assn., Great Lakes [10231], Zeeland, MI
Prdt. Development and Mgt. Assn., Minnesota [11283], Lake Elmo, MN
Prdt. Development and Mgt. Assn., Tri-State [13961], Cincinnati, OH
Productivity Council; Wisconsin Forest [19610], Rhinelander, WI
Professional Assn. of Clothiers, Chicago Chap. [1441], DeKalb, IL
Professional Convention Mgt. Assn., Greater Midwest Chap. [377], Burr Ridge, IL
Professional Dairy Producers of Wisconsin [19740], Slinger, WI
Professional Engineers; Illinois Soc. of [3636], Springfield, IL
Professional Engineers; Michigan Soc. of [8716], Lansing, MI
Professional Geologists of Indiana [5459], Indianapolis, IN
Professional Golfers Assn. of Am. - Michigan Sect. [7564], East Lansing, MI
Professional Golfers Assn. of Am. - Minnesota Sect. [★10713]
Professional Golfers Assn. of Am. - Wisconsin [19099], Milwaukee, WI
Professional Grounds Mgt. Soc., Greater Cincinnati [13962], Cincinnati, OH
Professional Grounds Mgt. Soc., Midwest Region [16312], Orrville, OH
Professional Independent Insurance Agents of Illinois [3667], Springfield, IL
Professional Insurance Agents Assn. of Ohio [15271], Gahanna, OH
Professional Insurance Agents of Illinois [★3667]
Professional Insurance Agents of Minnesota [12034], Plymouth, MN
Professional Insurance Agents of Wisconsin [18600], Madison, WI
Professional Insurance Investigators, Michigan Chap; Natl. Soc. of [10003], Troy, MI
Professional Land Surveyors of Ohio [14713], Columbus, OH
Professional Musicians of NW Ohio - Local No. 15-286, Amer. Fed. of Musicians [16953], Toledo, OH
Professional Photographers of Am. of Northern Illinois [78], Arlington Heights, IL
Professional Photographers Assn; Indianhead [17879], Eau Claire, WI
Professional Photographers of Central Ohio [14714], Columbus, OH
Professional Photographers of Greater Louisville [5921], New Albany, IN
Professional Photographers of Indiana [6038], Petersburg, IN
Professional Photographers of Michigan [9747], Shelby Township, MI
Professional Photographers of Ohio [14715], Columbus, OH
Professional Photographers of Southwest Ohio [13625], Centerville, OH
Professional Photographers of Western Michigan [7865], Grand Haven, MI
Professional Photographers of Western Michigan [8489], Kentwood, MI
Professional Police Assn; Wisconsin [18744], Madison, WI
Professional Police Off.rs Assn; Marquette [8948], Marquette, MI
Professional Policemen's Assn; Wisconsin [★18744]
Professional Remodelers of Ohio [15504], Independence, OH
Professional Risk Managers Intl. Assn. [11727], Minneapolis, MN
Professional Secretaries Intl. - River Park Chap. [★9836]
Professional Towing and Recovery Operators of Illinois [2992], Pekin, IL
Professional Women Clubs; Illinois Fed. of Bus. and [3604], Springfield, IL
Professionally Managed Theaters; League of [5390], Indianapolis, IN
Professionals
Amer. Soc. for Training and Development - Ann Arbor, Michigan Chap. [6665], Ann Arbor, MI
Amer. Soc. for Training and Development - Central Ohio Chap. [14311], Columbus, OH
Amer. Soc. for Training and Development - Greater Cleveland Chap. [14067], Cleveland, OH
Amer. Soc. for Training and Development - Greater Detroit Chap. [7637], Farmington, MI
Amer. Soc. for Training and Development - Lake Superior Chap. [10803], Duluth, MN
Amer. Soc. for Training and Development - Michiana Chap. [6217], South Bend, IN
Amer. Soc. for Training and Development - South Central Michigan [8546], Lansing, MI
Amer. Soc. for Training and Development - South Central Wisconsin [18473], Madison, WI
Amer. Soc. for Training and Development - Western Ohio Chap. [14852], Dayton, OH
Central Illinois Chap., Amer. Soc. for Training and Development [270], Bloomington, IL
Illinois Assn. of Collegiate Registrars and Admissions Off.rs [3821], Urbana, IL
Meeting Professionals Intl. - Minnesota Chap. [12443], St. Paul, MN
Northeast Ohio Amer. Soc. for Training and Development [13075], Akron, OH
Professionals; Chicago Cabaret [796], Chicago, IL
Professionals; Society of Bioprocessing [5474], Indianapolis, IN
Professions
Intl. Assn. of Torch Clubs, Region 5 [16637], Shaker Heights, OH
Intl. Assn. of Torch Clubs, Region 6 [1624], Elmhurst, IL
Professors
Michigan Conf. of the Amer. Assn. of Univ. Professors [8649], Lansing, MI

Professors Fund for Educational Issues **[8752]**, Lansing, MI
Professors; Michigan Conf. of the Amer. Assn. of Univ. **[8649]**, Lansing, MI
Progressive Dane **[18601]**, Madison, WI
Progressive Minnesota **[12562]**, St. Paul, MN
Project Danztheatre Company **[1146]**, Chicago, IL
Proj.: LEARN **[14207]**, Cleveland, OH
Proj.: LEARN of Medina County **[15956]**, Medina, OH
Proj.: LEARN of Summit County **[13082]**, Akron, OH
Proj. Mgt. Inst., Calumet **[★6167]**
Proj. Mgt. Inst., Calumet Chap. **[6167]**, Schererville, IN
Proj. Mgt. Inst., Central Illinois Chap. **[308]**, Bloomington, IL
Proj. Mgt. Inst., Central Indiana **[5460]**, Indianapolis, IN
Proj. Mgt. Inst., Central Ohio Chap. **[14716]**, Columbus, OH
Proj. Mgt. Inst., Chicagoland Chap. **[2176]**, La Grange Park, IL
Proj. Mgt. Inst. - Dayton/Miami Valley Chap. **[14948]**, Dayton, OH
Proj. Mgt. Inst., Great Lakes Chap. **[10006]**, Troy, MI
Proj. Mgt. Inst., Kentuckiana Chap. **[4909]**, Henryville, IN
Proj. Mgt. Inst., Madison/S. Central Wisconsin **[18602]**, Madison, WI
Proj. Mgt. Inst., Michigan Capital Area Chap. **[8753]**, Lansing, MI
Proj. Mgt. Inst., Michigan Capitol Area **[★8753]**
Proj. Mgt. Inst., Michigan Huron Valley Chap. **[9702]**, Saline, MI
Project Mgt. Inst., Michigan Thumb **[9011]**, Metamora, MI
Proj. Mgt. Inst. - Milwaukee/SE WI Chap. **[18043]**, Germantown, WI
Proj. Mgt. Inst., Northeast Indiana Chap. **[4712]**, Fort Wayne, IN
Proj. Mgt. Inst., Northeast Ohio **[★15974]**
Proj. Mgt. Inst., Northeast Ohio **[15977]**, Mentor, OH
Proj. Mgt. Inst., Northwest Ohio **[15788]**, Mansfield, OH
Proj. Mgt. Inst., Southwest Indiana Chap. **[5857]**, Mount Vernon, IN
Proj. Mgt. Inst., Western Lake Erie Chap. **[16954]**, Toledo, OH
Proj. Mgt. Inst., Western Michigan Chap. **[7999]**, Grand Rapids, MI
Proj. Repair **[14249]**, Cleveland Heights, OH
Promotion Council; Northeast Ohio Concrete **[16627]**, Seven Hills, OH
Promotional Bureau; St. Louis County **[11046]**, Gilbert, MN
Property Management
Central Ohio Chap. of Intl. Fac. Mgt. Assn. **[14356]**, Columbus, OH
Dayton Chap. of the Intl. Fac. Mgt. Assn. **[15986]**, Miamisburg, OH
Intl. Fac. Mgt. Assn., Central Illinois (Bloomington/Decatur/Champaign) **[1274]**, Clinton, IL
Intl. Fac. Mgt. Assn., Central Ohio Chap. **[14474]**, Columbus, OH
Intl. Fac. Mgt. Assn., Chicago **[1725]**, Frankfort, IL
Intl. Fac. Mgt. Assn., Cincinnati **[13871]**, Cincinnati, OH
Intl. Fac. Mgt. Assn., Ferris State Univ. **[7968]**, Grand Rapids, MI
Intl. Fac. Mgt. Assn., Indianapolis **[5376]**, Indianapolis, IN
Intl. Fac. Mgt. Assn., Madison **[18530]**, Madison, WI
Intl. Fac. Mgt. Assn., Minneapolis/St. Paul **[12024]**, Plymouth, MN
Intl. Fac. Mgt. Assn., North Indiana **[4683]**, Fort Wayne, IN
Intl. Fac. Mgt. Assn., Northeast Wisconsin Chap. **[18109]**, Green Bay, WI
Intl. Fac. Mgt. Assn., Northern Illinois (Suburban Chicago) **[362]**, Buffalo Grove, IL
Intl. Fac. Mgt. Assn., Northern Ohio (Cleveland) **[13275]**, Bay Village, OH
Intl. Fac. Mgt. Assn., Northwest Ohio Chap. **[16923]**, Toledo, OH
Intl. Fac. Mgt. Assn., Southeast Wisconsin (Milwaukee) **[17857]**, East Troy, WI
Intl. Fac. Mgt. Assn., Southeastern Michigan Chap. **[7014]**, Brighton, MI
International Facility Management Association, West Michigan **[8102]**, Hamilton, MI
Sugar Creek Protection Society **[15102]**, Elmore, OH
Property Mgt. Assn. of Mid-Michigan **[8754]**, Lansing, MI
Property Mgt. Assn. of West Michigan **[10192]**, Wyoming, MI
Property Owners Assn; Gull Lake Area **[★11897]**
Property Owners Assn; Village of Turner Trace **[★5495]**
Property Rights
Ohio Provider Rsrc. Assn. **[14661]**, Columbus, OH
Prophetstown-Lyndon Area Chamber of Commerce **[3141]**, Prophetstown, IL
Prophetstown's Main St. Prog. **[3142]**, Prophetstown, IL
Prosecuting Attorneys Assn. of Michigan **[★8755]**
Prosecuting Attorneys Coordinating Coun. **[8755]**, Lansing, MI
Prospect Heights Convention and Visitors Bur. **[★3143]**
Prospect Lions Club - Ohio **[16488]**, Prospect, OH
Protection and Advocacy Ser; Michigan **[8700]**, Lansing, MI
Protective Animal Welfare Soc. of Western Wisconsin **[19643]**, River Falls, WI
Protestants for the Common Good **[1147]**, Chicago, IL
PRSA **[★17518]**
PRSA, Akron Area Chap. **[13083]**, Akron, OH
Psi Chi, Natl. Honor Soc. in Psychology - Adler School of Professional Psychology **[1148]**, Chicago, IL
Psi Chi, Natl. Honor Soc. in Psychology - Adrian Coll. **[6582]**, Adrian, MI
Psi Chi, Natl. Honor Soc. in Psychology - Albion Coll. **[6592]**, Albion, MI
Psi Chi, Natl. Honor Soc. in Psychology - Alma Coll. **[6635]**, Alma, MI
Psi Chi, Natl. Honor Soc. in Psychology - Alverno Coll. **[19100]**, Milwaukee, WI
Psi Chi, Natl. Honor Soc. in Psychology - Anderson Univ. **[4117]**, Anderson, IN
Psi Chi, Natl. Honor Soc. in Psychology - Andrews Univ. **[6936]**, Berrien Springs, MI
Psi Chi, Natl. Honor Soc. in Psychology - Aquinas Coll. **[8000]**, Grand Rapids, MI
Psi Chi, Natl. Honor Soc. in Psychology - Ashland Univ. **[13172]**, Ashland, OH
Psi Chi, Natl. Honor Soc. in Psychology - Augustana Coll. **[3250]**, Rock Island, IL
Psi Chi, Natl. Honor Soc. in Psychology - Aurora Univ. **[128]**, Aurora, IL
Psi Chi, Natl. Honor Soc. in Psychology - Baldwin-Wallace Coll. **[13348]**, Berea, OH
Psi Chi, Natl. Honor Soc. in Psychology - Ball State Univ. **[5896]**, Muncie, IN
Psi Chi, Natl. Honor Soc. in Psychology - Benedectine Univ. **[2302]**, Lisle, IL
Psi Chi, Natl. Honor Soc. in Psychology - Bluffton Univ. **[13368]**, Bluffton, OH
Psi Chi, Natl. Honor Soc. in Psychology - Bowling Green State Univ. **[13398]**, Bowling Green, OH
Psi Chi, Natl. Honor Soc. in Psychology - Bradley Univ. **[3060]**, Peoria, IL
Psi Chi, Natl. Honor Soc. in Psychology - Butler Univ. **[5461]**, Indianapolis, IN
Psi Chi, Natl. Honor Soc. in Psychology - Calvin Coll. **[8001]**, Grand Rapids, MI
Psi Chi, Natl. Honor Soc. in Psychology - Cardinal Stritch Univ. **[19101]**, Milwaukee, WI
Psi Chi, Natl. Honor Soc. in Psychology - Carthage Coll. **[18308]**, Kenosha, WI
Psi Chi, Natl. Honor Soc. in Psychology - Case Western Reserve Univ. **[14208]**, Cleveland, OH
Psi Chi, Natl. Honor Soc. in Psychology - Central Michigan Univ. **[9123]**, Mount Pleasant, MI
Psi Chi, Natl. Honor Soc. in Psychology - Central State Univ. **[17260]**, Wilberforce, OH
Psi Chi, Natl. Honor Soc. in Psychology - Chicago State Univ. **[1149]**, Chicago, IL
Psi Chi, Natl. Honor Soc. in Psychology - Coll. of Mount St. Joseph **[13963]**, Cincinnati, OH
Psi Chi, Natl. Honor Soc. in Psychology - Concordia Coll. **[11827]**, Moorhead, MN
Psi Chi, Natl. Honor Soc. in Psychology - Concordia Univ. **[3204]**, River Forest, IL
Psi Chi, Natl. Honor Soc. in Psychology - Defiance Coll. **[14992]**, Defiance, OH
Psi Chi, Natl. Honor Soc. in Psychology - DePaul Univ. **[1150]**, Chicago, IL
Psi Chi, Natl. Honor Soc. in Psychology - DePauw Univ. **[4824]**, Greencastle, IN
Psi Chi, Natl. Honor Soc. in Psychology - Dominican Univ. **[3205]**, River Forest, IL
Psi Chi, Natl. Honor Soc. in Psychology - Earlham Coll. **[6102]**, Richmond, IN
Psi Chi, Natl. Honor Soc. in Psychology - Eastern Illinois Univ. **[570]**, Charleston, IL
Psi Chi, Natl. Honor Soc. in Psychology - Eastern Michigan Univ. **[10213]**, Ypsilanti, MI
Psi Chi, Natl. Honor Soc. in Psychology - Elmhurst Coll. **[1627]**, Elmhurst, IL
Psi Chi, Natl. Honor Soc. in Psychology - Franciscan Univ. of Steubenville **[16768]**, Steubenville, OH
Psi Chi, Natl. Honor Soc. in Psychology - Governors State Univ. **[3800]**, University Park, IL
Psi Chi, Natl. Honor Soc. in Psychology - Grand Valley State Univ. **[6627]**, Allendale, MI
Psi Chi, Natl. Honor Soc. in Psychology - Greenville Coll. **[1909]**, Greenville, IL
Psi Chi, Natl. Honor Soc. in Psychology - Gustavus Adolphus Coll. **[12619]**, St. Peter, MN
Psi Chi, Natl. Honor Soc. in Psychology - Hanover Coll. **[4897]**, Hanover, IN
Psi Chi, Natl. Honor Soc. in Psychology - Heidelberg Coll. **[16859]**, Tiffin, OH
Psi Chi, Natl. Honor Soc. in Psychology - Hillsdale Coll. **[8184]**, Hillsdale, MI
Psi Chi, Natl. Honor Soc. in Psychology - Hope Coll. **[8218]**, Holland, MI
Psi Chi, Natl. Honor Soc. in Psychology - Illinois Coll. **[2086]**, Jacksonville, IL
Psi Chi, Natl. Honor Soc. in Psychology - Illinois Inst. of Tech. **[1151]**, Chicago, IL
Psi Chi, Natl. Honor Soc. in Psychology - Illinois School of Professional Psychology at Argosy University-Schaumburg **[3443]**, Schaumburg, IL
Psi Chi, Natl. Honor Soc. in Psychology - Illinois State Univ. **[2731]**, Normal, IL
Psi Chi, Natl. Honor Soc. in Psychology - Illinois Wesleyan Univ. **[309]**, Bloomington, IL
Psi Chi, Natl. Honor Soc. in Psychology - Indiana State Univ. **[6341]**, Terre Haute, IN
Psi Chi, Natl. Honor Soc. in Psychology - Indiana Univ. Bloomington **[4252]**, Bloomington, IN
Psi Chi, Natl. Honor Soc. in Psychology - Indiana Univ. East **[6103]**, Richmond, IN
Psi Chi, Natl. Honor Soc. in Psychology - Indiana Univ. Kokomo **[5583]**, Kokomo, IN
Psi Chi, Natl. Honor Soc. in Psychology - Indiana Univ. Northwest **[4786]**, Gary, IN
Psi Chi, Natl. Honor Soc. in Psychology - Indiana University-Purdue Univ. Fort Wayne **[4713]**, Fort Wayne, IN
Psi Chi, Natl. Honor Soc. in Psychology - Indiana University-Purdue Univ. Indianapolis **[5462]**, Indianapolis, IN
Psi Chi, Natl. Honor Soc. in Psychology - Indiana Univ. South Bend **[6256]**, South Bend, IN
Psi Chi, Natl. Honor Soc. in Psychology - Indiana Univ. Southeast **[5922]**, New Albany, IN
Psi Chi, Natl. Honor Soc. in Psychology - Indiana Wesleyan Univ. **[5741]**, Marion, IN
Psi Chi, Natl. Honor Soc. in Psychology - Judson Coll. **[1600]**, Elgin, IL
Psi Chi, Natl. Honor Soc. in Psychology - Kent State Univ. **[15545]**, Kent, OH
Psi Chi, Natl. Honor Soc. in Psychology - Knox Coll. **[1781]**, Galesburg, IL
Psi Chi, Natl. Honor Soc. in Psychology - Lake Erie Coll. **[16344]**, Painesville, OH
Psi Chi, Natl. Honor Soc. in Psychology - Lake Forest Coll. **[2203]**, Lake Forest, IL
Psi Chi, Natl. Honor Soc. in Psychology - Lawrence Univ. **[17517]**, Appleton, WI
Psi Chi, Natl. Honor Soc. in Psychology - Lewis Univ. **[3346]**, Romeoville, IL
Psi Chi, Natl. Honor Soc. in Psychology - Loyola Univ. Chicago **[1152]**, Chicago, IL
Psi Chi, Natl. Honor Soc. in Psychology - Macalester Coll. **[12563]**, St. Paul, MN

Psi Chi, Natl. Honor Soc. in Psychology - MacMurray Coll. **[2087]**, Jacksonville, IL
Psi Chi, Natl. Honor Soc. in Psychology - Madonna Univ. **[8855]**, Livonia, MI
Psi Chi, Natl. Honor Soc. in Psychology - Manchester Coll. **[5990]**, North Manchester, IN
Psi Chi, Natl. Honor Soc. in Psychology - Marian Coll. **[5463]**, Indianapolis, IN
Psi Chi, Natl. Honor Soc. in Psychology - Marietta Coll. **[15828]**, Marietta, OH
Psi Chi, Natl. Honor Soc. in Psychology - Marquette Univ. **[19102]**, Milwaukee, WI
Psi Chi, Natl. Honor Soc. in Psychology - Mary Mount Coll. **[19103]**, Milwaukee, WI
Psi Chi, Natl. Honor Soc. in Psychology - Marygrove Coll. **[7424]**, Detroit, MI
Psi Chi, Natl. Honor Soc. in Psychology - Metropolitan State Univ. **[12564]**, St. Paul, MN
Psi Chi, Natl. Honor Soc. in Psychology - Michigan State Univ. **[7565]**, East Lansing, MI
Psi Chi, Natl. Honor Soc. in Psychology - Monmouth Coll. **[2542]**, Monmouth, IL
Psi Chi, Natl. Honor Soc. in Psychology - Muskingum Coll. **[16126]**, New Concord, OH
Psi Chi, Natl. Honor Soc. in Psychology - North Central Coll. **[2661]**, Naperville, IL
Psi Chi, Natl. Honor Soc. in Psychology - North Central Univ. **[11728]**, Minneapolis, MN
Psi Chi, Natl. Honor Soc. in Psychology - North Park Univ. **[1153]**, Chicago, IL
Psi Chi, Natl. Honor Soc. in Psychology - Northeastern Illinois Univ. **[1154]**, Chicago, IL
Psi Chi, Natl. Honor Soc. in Psychology - Northern Illinois Univ. **[1442]**, DeKalb, IL
Psi Chi, Natl. Honor Soc. in Psychology - Northern Michigan Univ. **[8957]**, Marquette, MI
Psi Chi, Natl. Honor Soc. in Psychology - Northland Coll. **[17546]**, Ashland, WI
Psi Chi, Natl. Honor Soc. in Psychology - Oakland Univ. **[9509]**, Rochester, MI
Psi Chi, Natl. Honor Soc. in Psychology - Ohio Dominican Univ. **[14717]**, Columbus, OH
Psi Chi, Natl. Honor Soc. in Psychology - Ohio Wesleyan Univ. **[15010]**, Delaware, OH
Psi Chi, Natl. Honor Soc. in Psychology - Olivet Coll. **[9303]**, Olivet, MI
Psi Chi, Natl. Honor Soc. in Psychology - Olivet Nazarene Univ. **[328]**, Bourbonnais, IL
Psi Chi, Natl. Honor Soc. in Psychology - Purdue Univ. **[6496]**, West Lafayette, IN
Psi Chi, Natl. Honor Soc. in Psychology - Purdue Univ. Calumet **[4893]**, Hammond, IN
Psi Chi, Natl. Honor Soc. in Psychology - Quincy Univ. **[3159]**, Quincy, IL
Psi Chi, Natl. Honor Soc. in Psychology - Ripon Coll. **[19635]**, Ripon, WI
Psi Chi, Natl. Honor Soc. in Psychology - Rochester Coll. **[9517]**, Rochester Hills, MI
Psi Chi, Natl. Honor Soc. in Psychology - Rockford Coll. **[3300]**, Rockford, IL
Psi Chi, Natl. Honor Soc. in Psychology - Roosevelt Univ. **[1155]**, Chicago, IL
Psi Chi, Natl. Honor Soc. in Psychology - Roosevelt Univ. Albert A. Robin Campus **[3444]**, Schaumburg, IL
Psi Chi, Natl. Honor Soc. in Psychology - Saginaw Valley State Univ. **[10031]**, University Center, MI
Psi Chi, Natl. Honor Soc. in Psychology - Saint John's Univ. **[10703]**, Collegeville, MN
Psi Chi, Natl. Honor Soc. in Psychology - Saint Joseph's Coll. **[6080]**, Rensselaer, IN
Psi Chi, Natl. Honor Soc. in Psychology - Saint Mary's Coll. **[6006]**, Notre Dame, IN
Psi Chi, Natl. Honor Soc. in Psychology - Saint Mary's Univ. of Minnesota **[12957]**, Winona, MN
Psi Chi, Natl. Honor Soc. in Psychology - St. Olaf Coll. **[11919]**, Northfield, MN
Psi Chi, Natl. Honor Soc. in Psychology - Saint Xavier Univ. **[1156]**, Chicago, IL
Psi Chi, Natl. Honor Soc. in Psychology - Siena Heights Univ. **[6583]**, Adrian, MI
Psi Chi, Natl. Honor Soc. in Psychology - Southern Illinois Univ. at Carbondale **[429]**, Carbondale, IL
Psi Chi, Natl. Honor Soc. in Psychology - Southern Illinois Univ. Edwardsville **[1565]**, Edwardsville, IL
Psi Chi, Natl. Honor Soc. in Psychology - Spring Arbor Univ. **[9847]**, Spring Arbor, MI
Psi Chi, Natl. Honor Soc. in Psychology - Trinity Intl. Univ. **[1422]**, Deerfield, IL
Psi Chi, Natl. Honor Soc. in Psychology - Univ. of Akron **[13084]**, Akron, OH
Psi Chi, Natl. Honor Soc. in Psychology - Univ. of Chicago **[1157]**, Chicago, IL
Psi Chi, Natl. Honor Soc. in Psychology - Univ. of Evansville **[4567]**, Evansville, IN
Psi Chi, Natl. Honor Soc. in Psychology - Univ. of Illinois at Chicago **[1158]**, Chicago, IL
Psi Chi, Natl. Honor Soc. in Psychology - Univ. of Illinois at Springfield **[3668]**, Springfield, IL
Psi Chi, Natl. Honor Soc. in Psychology - Univ. of Illinois at Urbana-Champaign **[550]**, Champaign, IL
Psi Chi, Natl. Honor Soc. in Psychology - Univ. of Indianapolis **[5464]**, Indianapolis, IN
Psi Chi, Natl. Honor Soc. in Psychology - Univ. of Michigan **[6760]**, Ann Arbor, MI
Psi Chi, Natl. Honor Soc. in Psychology - Univ. of Michigan-Dearborn **[7267]**, Dearborn, MI
Psi Chi, Natl. Honor Soc. in Psychology - Univ. of Michigan-Flint **[7754]**, Flint, MI
Psi Chi, Natl. Honor Soc. in Psychology - Univ. of Minnesota, Duluth **[10850]**, Duluth, MN
Psi Chi, Natl. Honor Soc. in Psychology - Univ. of Minnesota, Morris **[11841]**, Morris, MN
Psi Chi, Natl. Honor Soc. in Psychology - Univ. of Notre Dame **[6007]**, Notre Dame, IN
Psi Chi, Natl. Honor Soc. in Psychology - Univ. of St. Francis **[2118]**, Joliet, IL
Psi Chi, Natl. Honor Soc. in Psychology - Univ. of Southern Indiana **[4568]**, Evansville, IN
Psi Chi, Natl. Honor Soc. in Psychology - Univ. of Wisconsin-Green Bay **[18128]**, Green Bay, WI
Psi Chi, Natl. Honor Soc. in Psychology - Univ. of Wisconsin-Parkside **[18309]**, Kenosha, WI
Psi Chi, Natl. Honor Soc. in Psychology - Univ. of Wisconsin-Platteville **[19468]**, Platteville, WI
Psi Chi, Natl. Honor Soc. in Psychology - Valparaiso Univ. **[6389]**, Valparaiso, IN
Psi Chi, Natl. Honor Soc. in Psychology - Wabash Coll. **[4428]**, Crawfordsville, IN
Psi Chi, Natl. Honor Soc. in Psychology - Wayne State Univ. **[7425]**, Detroit, MI
Psi Chi, Natl. Honor Soc. in Psychology - Western Illinois Univ. **[2376]**, Macomb, IL
Psi Chi, Natl. Honor Soc. in Psychology - Western Michigan Univ. **[8463]**, Kalamazoo, MI
Psi Chi, Natl. Honor Soc. in Psychology - Wisconsin Lutheran Coll. **[19104]**, Milwaukee, WI
Psi Chi, Natl. Honor Soc. in Psychology - Xavier Univ. **[13964]**, Cincinnati, OH
Psychiatric Assn; Wisconsin **[18745]**, Madison, WI

Psychiatry

Illinois Assn. for Infant Mental Hea. **[929]**, Chicago, IL
Illinois Psychiatric Soc. **[959]**, Chicago, IL
Indiana Assn. for Infant and Toddler Mental Hea. **[5175]**, Indianapolis, IN
Indiana Psychiatric Soc. **[5283]**, Indianapolis, IN
Michigan Psychiatric Soc. **[7544]**, East Lansing, MI
Minnesota Psychiatric Soc. **[12511]**, St. Paul, MN
Ohio Assn. for Infant Mental Hea. **[13934]**, Cincinnati, OH
Ohio Psychiatric Assn. **[14662]**, Columbus, OH
Wisconsin Psychiatric Assn. **[18745]**, Madison, WI

Psychoanalysis

Chicago Psychoanalytic Soc. **[825]**, Chicago, IL
Cincinnati Psychoanalytic Soc. **[13798]**, Cincinnati, OH
Cleveland Psychoanalytic Center **[14245]**, Cleveland Heights, OH
Michigan Psychoanalytic Soc. **[7669]**, Farmington Hills, MI
Minnesota Jung Association **[11652]**, Minneapolis, MN
Minnesota Psychoanalytic Soc. **[11667]**, Minneapolis, MN
Wisconsin Psychoanalytic Soc. **[19177]**, Milwaukee, WI

Psychoanalytic Soc; Chicago **[825]**, Chicago, IL
Psychological Assn; Minnesota **[12512]**, St. Paul, MN
Psychologists Assn; Ohio School **[15270]**, Gahanna, OH

Psychology

Assn. of Black Psychologists, Mid-West Region **[739]**, Chicago, IL
Assn. for Psychological Type - Chicago **[754]**, Chicago, IL
Assn. for Psychological Type - Columbus **[14331]**, Columbus, OH
Assn. for Psychological Type - Detroit **[7008]**, Brighton, MI
Assn. for Psychological Type - Greater Cincinnati **[16024]**, Milford, OH
Assn. for Psychological Type - Indiana **[5049]**, Indianapolis, IN
Assn. for Psychological Type - Interest Gp., Fox River Valley **[17970]**, Fond du Lac, WI
Assn. for Psychological Type - LaCrosse **[18337]**, La Crosse, WI
Assn. for Psychological Type - Madison **[18485]**, Madison, WI
Assn. for Psychological Type - Twin Cities **[11448]**, Medicine Lake, MN
Christian Assn. for Psychological Stud., Midwest **[8834]**, Livonia, MI
Illinois Psychological Assn. **[960]**, Chicago, IL
Illinois School Psychologists Assn. **[3988]**, Wheaton, IL
Indiana Assn. of School Psychologists **[5186]**, Indianapolis, IN
Indiana Psychological Assn. **[5284]**, Indianapolis, IN
Michigan Assn. of School Psychologists **[9937]**, Traverse City, MI
Michigan Psychological Assn. **[9289]**, Okemos, MI
Midwestern Psychological Assn. **[4694]**, Fort Wayne, IN
Minnesota Psychological Assn. **[12512]**, St. Paul, MN
Mississippi Assn. for Psychology in the Schools **[9940]**, Traverse City, MI
Ohio Psychological Assn. **[14663]**, Columbus, OH
Ohio School Psychologists Assn. **[15270]**, Gahanna, OH
Psi Chi, Natl. Honor Soc. in Psychology - Adler School of Professional Psychology **[1148]**, Chicago, IL
Psi Chi, Natl. Honor Soc. in Psychology - Adrian Coll. **[6582]**, Adrian, MI
Psi Chi, Natl. Honor Soc. in Psychology - Albion Coll. **[6592]**, Albion, MI
Psi Chi, Natl. Honor Soc. in Psychology - Alma Coll. **[6635]**, Alma, MI
Psi Chi, Natl. Honor Soc. in Psychology - Alverno Coll. **[19100]**, Milwaukee, WI
Psi Chi, Natl. Honor Soc. in Psychology - Anderson Univ. **[4117]**, Anderson, IN
Psi Chi, Natl. Honor Soc. in Psychology - Andrews Univ. **[6936]**, Berrien Springs, MI
Psi Chi, Natl. Honor Soc. in Psychology - Aquinas Coll. **[8000]**, Grand Rapids, MI
Psi Chi, Natl. Honor Soc. in Psychology - Ashland Univ. **[13172]**, Ashland, OH
Psi Chi, Natl. Honor Soc. in Psychology - Augustana Coll. **[3250]**, Rock Island, IL
Psi Chi, Natl. Honor Soc. in Psychology - Aurora Univ. **[128]**, Aurora, IL
Psi Chi, Natl. Honor Soc. in Psychology - Baldwin-Wallace Coll. **[13348]**, Berea, OH
Psi Chi, Natl. Honor Soc. in Psychology - Ball State Univ. **[5896]**, Muncie, IN
Psi Chi, Natl. Honor Soc. in Psychology - Benedectine Univ. **[2302]**, Lisle, IL
Psi Chi, Natl. Honor Soc. in Psychology - Bluffton Univ. **[13368]**, Bluffton, OH
Psi Chi, Natl. Honor Soc. in Psychology - Bowling Green State Univ. **[13398]**, Bowling Green, OH
Psi Chi, Natl. Honor Soc. in Psychology - Bradley Univ. **[3060]**, Peoria, IL
Psi Chi, Natl. Honor Soc. in Psychology - Butler Univ. **[5461]**, Indianapolis, IN
Psi Chi, Natl. Honor Soc. in Psychology - Calvin Coll. **[8001]**, Grand Rapids, MI
Psi Chi, Natl. Honor Soc. in Psychology - Cardinal Stritch Univ. **[19101]**, Milwaukee, WI
Psi Chi, Natl. Honor Soc. in Psychology - Carthage Coll. **[18308]**, Kenosha, WI
Psi Chi, Natl. Honor Soc. in Psychology - Case Western Reserve Univ. **[14208]**, Cleveland, OH
Psi Chi, Natl. Honor Soc. in Psychology - Central Michigan Univ. **[9123]**, Mount Pleasant, MI
Psi Chi, Natl. Honor Soc. in Psychology - Central State Univ. **[17260]**, Wilberforce, OH

Psi Chi, Natl. Honor Soc. in Psychology - Chicago State Univ. **[1149]**, Chicago, IL
Psi Chi, Natl. Honor Soc. in Psychology - Coll. of Mount St. Joseph **[13963]**, Cincinnati, OH
Psi Chi, Natl. Honor Soc. in Psychology - Concordia Coll. **[11827]**, Moorhead, MN
Psi Chi, Natl. Honor Soc. in Psychology - Concordia Univ. **[3204]**, River Forest, IL
Psi Chi, Natl. Honor Soc. in Psychology - Defiance Coll. **[14992]**, Defiance, OH
Psi Chi, Natl. Honor Soc. in Psychology - DePaul Univ. **[1150]**, Chicago, IL
Psi Chi, Natl. Honor Soc. in Psychology - DePauw Univ. **[4824]**, Greencastle, IN
Psi Chi, Natl. Honor Soc. in Psychology - Dominican Univ. **[3205]**, River Forest, IL
Psi Chi, Natl. Honor Soc. in Psychology - Earlham Coll. **[6102]**, Richmond, IN
Psi Chi, Natl. Honor Soc. in Psychology - Eastern Illinois Univ. **[570]**, Charleston, IL
Psi Chi, Natl. Honor Soc. in Psychology - Eastern Michigan Univ. **[10213]**, Ypsilanti, MI
Psi Chi, Natl. Honor Soc. in Psychology - Elmhurst Coll. **[1627]**, Elmhurst, IL
Psi Chi, Natl. Honor Soc. in Psychology - Franciscan Univ. of Steubenville **[16768]**, Steubenville, OH
Psi Chi, Natl. Honor Soc. in Psychology - Governors State Univ. **[3800]**, University Park, IL
Psi Chi, Natl. Honor Soc. in Psychology - Grand Valley State Univ. **[6627]**, Allendale, MI
Psi Chi, Natl. Honor Soc. in Psychology - Greenville Coll. **[1909]**, Greenville, IL
Psi Chi, Natl. Honor Soc. in Psychology - Gustavus Adolphus Coll. **[12619]**, St. Peter, MN
Psi Chi, Natl. Honor Soc. in Psychology - Hanover Coll. **[4897]**, Hanover, IN
Psi Chi, Natl. Honor Soc. in Psychology - Heidelberg Coll. **[16859]**, Tiffin, OH
Psi Chi, Natl. Honor Soc. in Psychology - Hillsdale Coll. **[8184]**, Hillsdale, MI
Psi Chi, Natl. Honor Soc. in Psychology - Hope Coll. **[8218]**, Holland, MI
Psi Chi, Natl. Honor Soc. in Psychology - Illinois Coll. **[2086]**, Jacksonville, IL
Psi Chi, Natl. Honor Soc. in Psychology - Illinois Inst. of Tech. **[1151]**, Chicago, IL
Psi Chi, Natl. Honor Soc. in Psychology - Illinois School of Professional Psychology at Argosy University-Schaumburg **[3443]**, Schaumburg, IL
Psi Chi, Natl. Honor Soc. in Psychology - Illinois State Univ. **[2731]**, Normal, IL
Psi Chi, Natl. Honor Soc. in Psychology - Illinois Wesleyan Univ. **[309]**, Bloomington, IL
Psi Chi, Natl. Honor Soc. in Psychology - Indiana State Univ. **[6341]**, Terre Haute, IN
Psi Chi, Natl. Honor Soc. in Psychology - Indiana Univ. Bloomington **[4252]**, Bloomington, IN
Psi Chi, Natl. Honor Soc. in Psychology - Indiana Univ. East **[6103]**, Richmond, IN
Psi Chi, Natl. Honor Soc. in Psychology - Indiana Univ. Kokomo **[5583]**, Kokomo, IN
Psi Chi, Natl. Honor Soc. in Psychology - Indiana Univ. Northwest **[4786]**, Gary, IN
Psi Chi, Natl. Honor Soc. in Psychology - Indiana University-Purdue Univ. Fort Wayne **[4713]**, Fort Wayne, IN
Psi Chi, Natl. Honor Soc. in Psychology - Indiana University-Purdue Univ. Indianapolis **[5462]**, Indianapolis, IN
Psi Chi, Natl. Honor Soc. in Psychology - Indiana Univ. South Bend **[6256]**, South Bend, IN
Psi Chi, Natl. Honor Soc. in Psychology - Indiana Univ. Southeast **[5922]**, New Albany, IN
Psi Chi, Natl. Honor Soc. in Psychology - Indiana Wesleyan Univ. **[5741]**, Marion, IN
Psi Chi, Natl. Honor Soc. in Psychology - Judson Coll. **[1600]**, Elgin, IL
Psi Chi, Natl. Honor Soc. in Psychology - Kent State Univ. **[15545]**, Kent, OH
Psi Chi, Natl. Honor Soc. in Psychology - Knox Coll. **[1781]**, Galesburg, IL
Psi Chi, Natl. Honor Soc. in Psychology - Lake Erie Coll. **[16344]**, Painesville, OH
Psi Chi, Natl. Honor Soc. in Psychology - Lake Forest Coll. **[2203]**, Lake Forest, IL
Psi Chi, Natl. Honor Soc. in Psychology - Lawrence Univ. **[17517]**, Appleton, WI
Psi Chi, Natl. Honor Soc. in Psychology - Lewis Univ. **[3346]**, Romeoville, IL
Psi Chi, Natl. Honor Soc. in Psychology - Loyola Univ. Chicago **[1152]**, Chicago, IL
Psi Chi, Natl. Honor Soc. in Psychology - Macalester Coll. **[12563]**, St. Paul, MN
Psi Chi, Natl. Honor Soc. in Psychology - MacMurray Coll. **[2087]**, Jacksonville, IL
Psi Chi, Natl. Honor Soc. in Psychology - Madonna Univ. **[8855]**, Livonia, MI
Psi Chi, Natl. Honor Soc. in Psychology - Manchester Coll. **[5990]**, North Manchester, IN
Psi Chi, Natl. Honor Soc. in Psychology - Marian Coll. **[5463]**, Indianapolis, IN
Psi Chi, Natl. Honor Soc. in Psychology - Marietta Coll. **[15828]**, Marietta, OH
Psi Chi, Natl. Honor Soc. in Psychology - Marquette Univ. **[19102]**, Milwaukee, WI
Psi Chi, Natl. Honor Soc. in Psychology - Mary Mount Coll. **[19103]**, Milwaukee, WI
Psi Chi, Natl. Honor Soc. in Psychology - Marygrove Coll. **[7424]**, Detroit, MI
Psi Chi, Natl. Honor Soc. in Psychology - Metropolitan State Univ. **[12564]**, St. Paul, MN
Psi Chi, Natl. Honor Soc. in Psychology - Michigan State Univ. **[7565]**, East Lansing, MI
Psi Chi, Natl. Honor Soc. in Psychology - Monmouth Coll. **[2542]**, Monmouth, IL
Psi Chi, Natl. Honor Soc. in Psychology - Muskingum Coll. **[16126]**, New Concord, OH
Psi Chi, Natl. Honor Soc. in Psychology - North Central Coll. **[2661]**, Naperville, IL
Psi Chi, Natl. Honor Soc. in Psychology - North Central Univ. **[11728]**, Minneapolis, MN
Psi Chi, Natl. Honor Soc. in Psychology - North Park Univ. **[1153]**, Chicago, IL
Psi Chi, Natl. Honor Soc. in Psychology - Northeastern Illinois Univ. **[1154]**, Chicago, IL
Psi Chi, Natl. Honor Soc. in Psychology - Northern Illinois Univ. **[1442]**, DeKalb, IL
Psi Chi, Natl. Honor Soc. in Psychology - Northern Michigan Univ. **[8957]**, Marquette, MI
Psi Chi, Natl. Honor Soc. in Psychology - Northland Coll. **[17546]**, Ashland, WI
Psi Chi, Natl. Honor Soc. in Psychology - Oakland Univ. **[9509]**, Rochester, MI
Psi Chi, Natl. Honor Soc. in Psychology - Ohio Dominican Univ. **[14717]**, Columbus, OH
Psi Chi, Natl. Honor Soc. in Psychology - Ohio Wesleyan Univ. **[15010]**, Delaware, OH
Psi Chi, Natl. Honor Soc. in Psychology - Olivet Coll. **[9303]**, Olivet, MI
Psi Chi, Natl. Honor Soc. in Psychology - Olivet Nazarene Univ. **[328]**, Bourbonnais, IL
Psi Chi, Natl. Honor Soc. in Psychology - Purdue Univ. **[6496]**, West Lafayette, IN
Psi Chi, Natl. Honor Soc. in Psychology - Purdue Univ. Calumet **[4893]**, Hammond, IN
Psi Chi, Natl. Honor Soc. in Psychology - Quincy Univ. **[3159]**, Quincy, IL
Psi Chi, Natl. Honor Soc. in Psychology - Ripon Coll. **[19635]**, Ripon, WI
Psi Chi, Natl. Honor Soc. in Psychology - Rochester Coll. **[9517]**, Rochester Hills, MI
Psi Chi, Natl. Honor Soc. in Psychology - Rockford Coll. **[3300]**, Rockford, IL
Psi Chi, Natl. Honor Soc. in Psychology - Roosevelt Univ. **[1155]**, Chicago, IL
Psi Chi, Natl. Honor Soc. in Psychology - Roosevelt Univ. Albert A. Robin Campus **[3444]**, Schaumburg, IL
Psi Chi, Natl. Honor Soc. in Psychology - Saginaw Valley State Univ. **[10031]**, University Center, MI
Psi Chi, Natl. Honor Soc. in Psychology - Saint John's Univ. **[10703]**, Collegeville, MN
Psi Chi, Natl. Honor Soc. in Psychology - Saint Joseph's Coll. **[6080]**, Rensselaer, IN
Psi Chi, Natl. Honor Soc. in Psychology - Saint Mary's Coll. **[6006]**, Notre Dame, IN
Psi Chi, Natl. Honor Soc. in Psychology - Saint Mary's Univ. of Minnesota **[12957]**, Winona, MN
Psi Chi, Natl. Honor Soc. in Psychology - St. Olaf Coll. **[11919]**, Northfield, MN
Psi Chi, Natl. Honor Soc. in Psychology - Saint Xavier Univ. **[1156]**, Chicago, IL
Psi Chi, Natl. Honor Soc. in Psychology - Siena Heights Univ. **[6583]**, Adrian, MI
Psi Chi, Natl. Honor Soc. in Psychology - Southern Illinois Univ. at Carbondale **[429]**, Carbondale, IL
Psi Chi, Natl. Honor Soc. in Psychology - Southern Illinois Univ. Edwardsville **[1565]**, Edwardsville, IL
Psi Chi, Natl. Honor Soc. in Psychology - Spring Arbor Univ. **[9847]**, Spring Arbor, MI
Psi Chi, Natl. Honor Soc. in Psychology - Trinity Intl. Univ. **[1422]**, Deerfield, IL
Psi Chi, Natl. Honor Soc. in Psychology - Univ. of Akron **[13084]**, Akron, OH
Psi Chi, Natl. Honor Soc. in Psychology - Univ. of Chicago **[1157]**, Chicago, IL
Psi Chi, Natl. Honor Soc. in Psychology - Univ. of Evansville **[4567]**, Evansville, IN
Psi Chi, Natl. Honor Soc. in Psychology - Univ. of Illinois at Chicago **[1158]**, Chicago, IL
Psi Chi, Natl. Honor Soc. in Psychology - Univ. of Illinois at Springfield **[3668]**, Springfield, IL
Psi Chi, Natl. Honor Soc. in Psychology - Univ. of Illinois at Urbana-Champaign **[550]**, Champaign, IL
Psi Chi, Natl. Honor Soc. in Psychology - Univ. of Indianapolis **[5464]**, Indianapolis, IN
Psi Chi, Natl. Honor Soc. in Psychology - Univ. of Michigan **[6760]**, Ann Arbor, MI
Psi Chi, Natl. Honor Soc. in Psychology - Univ. of Michigan-Dearborn **[7267]**, Dearborn, MI
Psi Chi, Natl. Honor Soc. in Psychology - Univ. of Michigan-Flint **[7754]**, Flint, MI
Psi Chi, Natl. Honor Soc. in Psychology - Univ. of Minnesota, Duluth **[10850]**, Duluth, MN
Psi Chi, Natl. Honor Soc. in Psychology - Univ. of Minnesota, Morris **[11841]**, Morris, MN
Psi Chi, Natl. Honor Soc. in Psychology - Univ. of Notre Dame **[6007]**, Notre Dame, IN
Psi Chi, Natl. Honor Soc. in Psychology - Univ. of St. Francis **[2118]**, Joliet, IL
Psi Chi, Natl. Honor Soc. in Psychology - Univ. of Southern Indiana **[4568]**, Evansville, IN
Psi Chi, Natl. Honor Soc. in Psychology - Univ. of Wisconsin-Green Bay **[18128]**, Green Bay, WI
Psi Chi, Natl. Honor Soc. in Psychology - Univ. of Wisconsin-Parkside **[18309]**, Kenosha, WI
Psi Chi, Natl. Honor Soc. in Psychology - Univ. of Wisconsin-Platteville **[19468]**, Platteville, WI
Psi Chi, Natl. Honor Soc. in Psychology - Valparaiso Univ. **[6389]**, Valparaiso, IN
Psi Chi, Natl. Honor Soc. in Psychology - Wabash Coll. **[4428]**, Crawfordsville, IN
Psi Chi, Natl. Honor Soc. in Psychology - Wayne State Univ. **[7425]**, Detroit, MI
Psi Chi, Natl. Honor Soc. in Psychology - Western Illinois Univ. **[2376]**, Macomb, IL
Psi Chi, Natl. Honor Soc. in Psychology - Western Michigan Univ. **[8463]**, Kalamazoo, MI
Psi Chi, Natl. Honor Soc. in Psychology - Wisconsin Lutheran Coll. **[19104]**, Milwaukee, WI
Psi Chi, Natl. Honor Soc. in Psychology - Xavier Univ. **[13964]**, Cincinnati, OH
Soc. of Stud. of Male Psychology **[16063]**, Montpelier, OH
Wisconsin Psychological Assn. **[18746]**, Madison, WI
Wisconsin School Psychologists Assn. **[19686]**, Shawano, WI

PTA; Minnesota **[12513]**, St. Paul, MN

Public Administration

Amer. Soc. for Public Admin., Central Illinois Chap. **[3530]**, Springfield, IL
Indiana County Assessors Assn. **[6158]**, Salem, IN
Natl. Forum for Black Public Administrators, Cincinnati Chap. **[13926]**, Cincinnati, OH
Natl. Forum for Black Public Administrators, Cleveland Chap. **[14175]**, Cleveland, OH
Natl. Forum for Black Public Administrators, Dayton Chap. **[14930]**, Dayton, OH
Natl. Forum for Black Public Administrators, Illinois Chap. **[1081]**, Chicago, IL
Syracuse Municipal Building Corp. **[6292]**, Syracuse, IN

Public Admin., Central Illinois Chap; Amer. Soc. for **[3530]**, Springfield, IL

Public Affairs
Bio-Diversity Proj. [18492], Madison, WI
City Club of Chicago [849], Chicago, IL
City Year Cleveland [14090], Cleveland, OH
Earth First! Illinois / Last Wizards [876], Chicago, IL
Metropolitan Mayors Caucus [1046], Chicago, IL
Minnesota Alliance for Progressive Action [12452], St. Paul, MN
Public Allies [19105], Milwaukee, WI
Rainbow/PUSH Coalition [1161], Chicago, IL
Public Allies [19105], Milwaukee, WI
Public Allies Cincinnati [13965], Cincinnati, OH
Public Children Ser. Assn. of Ohio [14718], Columbus, OH
Public Finance
County Treasurers Assn. of Ohio [14420], Columbus, OH
Public Health
Illinois Public Hea. Assn. [3632], Springfield, IL
Illinois Rural Hea. Assn. [3633], Springfield, IL
Indiana Public Health Association [5286], Indianapolis, IN
Indiana Rural Hea. Assn. [6328], Terre Haute, IN
Michigan Assn. for Local Public Hea. [8620], Lansing, MI
Michigan Public Hea. Assn. [7545], East Lansing, MI
Michigan Rural Hea. Assn. [7547], East Lansing, MI
Minnesota Public Hea. Assn. [11668], Minneapolis, MN
Minnesota Rural Hea. Assn. [11388], Mankato, MN
Ohio Public Hea. Assn. [16422], Pickerington, OH
Public Hea. Practitioner Certification Bd. [1159], Chicago, IL
Wisconsin Assn. of Local Hea. Dept. and Boards [18147], Green Lake, WI
Wisconsin Public Hea. Assn. [18747], Madison, WI
Public Hea; Michigan Assn. for Local [8620], Lansing, MI
Public Hea. Practitioner Certification Bd. [1159], Chicago, IL
Public Information
West Suburban Access News Assn. [2828], Oak Park, IL
Public Interest Res. Gp. - Ohio [14719], Columbus, OH
Public Museum of Grand Rapids [8002], Grand Rapids, MI
Public Policy
Citizens League [12402], St. Paul, MN
Citizens for Legal Responsibility [2567], Morton Grove, IL
Illinois Public Interest Res. Gp. [961], Chicago, IL
Joint Religious Legislative Coalition [11592], Minneapolis, MN
Lower Wisconsin State Riverway Bd. [19257], Muscoda, WI
Public Interest Res. Gp. - Ohio [14719], Columbus, OH
Public Policy Forum [19106], Milwaukee, WI
Wisconsin Public Interest Res. Gp. [18748], Madison, WI
Public Policy Forum [19106], Milwaukee, WI
Public Relations
Heather McNally Milko [14138], Cleveland, OH
Michigan School Public Relations Assn. [8711], Lansing, MI
Minnesota School Public Relations Assn. [12242], Roseville, MN
Natl. School Public Relations Assn., Illinois [1729], Frankfort, IL
Natl. School Public Relations Assn., Ohio [16515], Reynoldsburg, OH
PRSA, Akron Area Chap. [13083], Akron, OH
Public Relations Soc. of Am., Central Illinois [3061], Peoria, IL
Public Relations Society of America, Central Michigan Chapter [8983], Mason, MI
Public Relations Soc. of Am., Central Ohio [16517], Reynoldsburg, OH
Public Relations Soc. of Am., Chicago Chap. [3915], Wauconda, IL
Public Relations Soc. of Am., Cincinnati [13966], Cincinnati, OH
Public Relations Soc. of Am., Cleveland [13276], Bay Village, OH
Public Relations Soc. of Am., Dayton/Miami Valley [14949], Dayton, OH
Public Relations Soc. of Am., Detroit Chap. [8899], Madison Heights, MI
Public Relations Soc. of Am., Greater Dubuque [19469], Platteville, WI
Public Relations Soc. of Am., Hoosier [4155], Avon, IN
Public Relations Soc. of Am., Madison [18603], Madison, WI
Public Relations Soc. of Am., Minnesota [12565], St. Paul, MN
Public Relations Soc. of Am., Northeast Wisconsin Chap. [17518], Appleton, WI
Public Relations Soc. of Am., Northwest Ohio [16955], Toledo, OH
Public Relations Soc. of Am., Quad Cities [2528], Moline, IL
Public Relations Soc. of Am., Southeastern Wisconsin Chap. [17677], Brookfield, WI
Public Relations Soc. of Am., Suburban Chicagoland Chap. [3391], St. Charles, IL
Public Relations Soc. of Am., White Pine [7793], Freeland, MI
Public Relations Soc. of Am., White Pine [9627], Saginaw, MI
Soc. of Consumer Affairs Professionals in Bus., Chicago Chap. [3348], Romeoville, IL
Soc. of Consumer Affairs Professionals in Bus., Great Lakes Chap. [10010], Troy, MI
Soc. of Consumer Affairs Professionals in Bus., Indiana Chap. [5476], Indianapolis, IN
Soc. of Consumer Affairs Professionals in Bus., Minnesota Chap. [11747], Minneapolis, MN
Soc. of Consumer Affairs Professionals in Bus., Ohio Chap. [13089], Akron, OH
Soc. of Consumer Affairs Professionals in Bus., Wisconsin Chap. [17730], Cedarburg, WI
Soc. of Consumer Affairs Professionals in Bus., Wisconsin Chap. [19275], Neenah, WI
Wisconsin School Public Relations Assn. [18751], Madison, WI
Public Relations Assn., Michigan; Natl. School [★8711]
Public Relations Assn; Minnesota School [12242], Roseville, MN
Public Relations Soc. of Am., Central Illinois [3061], Peoria, IL
Public Relations Society of America, Central Michigan Chapter [8983], Mason, MI
Public Relations Soc. of Am., Central Ohio [16517], Reynoldsburg, OH
Public Relations Soc. of Am., Chicago Chap. [3915], Wauconda, IL
Public Relations Soc. of Am., Cincinnati [13966], Cincinnati, OH
Public Relations Soc. of Am., Cleveland [13276], Bay Village, OH
Public Relations Soc. of Am., Dayton/Miami Valley [14949], Dayton, OH
Public Relations Soc. of Am., Detroit Chap. [8899], Madison Heights, MI
Public Relations Soc. of Am., Greater Cleveland [★13276]
Public Relations Soc. of Am., Greater Dubuque [19469], Platteville, WI
Public Relations Soc. of Am., Hoosier [4155], Avon, IN
Public Relations Soc. of Am., Madison [18603], Madison, WI
Public Relations Soc. of Am., Minnesota [12565], St. Paul, MN
Public Relations Soc. of Am., Northeast Wisconsin Chap. [17518], Appleton, WI
Public Relations Soc. of Am., Northwest Ohio [16955], Toledo, OH
Public Relations Soc. of Am., Quad Cities [2528], Moline, IL
Public Relations Soc. of Am., Southeastern Wisconsin Chap. [17677], Brookfield, WI
Public Relations Soc. of Am., Suburban Chicagoland Chap. [3391], St. Charles, IL
Public Relations Soc. of Am., West Michigan [★8003]
Public Relations Soc. of Am., West Michigan Chap. [8003], Grand Rapids, MI
Public Relations Soc. of Am., White Pine [7793], Freeland, MI
Public Relations Soc. of Am., White Pine [9627], Saginaw, MI
Public Schools; Michigan Assn. of Non- [8621], Lansing, MI
Public Service
First Call for Help [12285], St. Cloud, MN
Partners in Charity [3947], West Dundee, IL
Public Speaking
Natl. Speakers Association/Illinois Chap. [1798], Geneva, IL
Natl. Speakers Assn., Indiana [5673], Lebanon, IN
Natl. Speakers Association/Michigan [7647], Farmington, MI
Natl. Speakers Assn. - Minnesota Chap. [12030], Plymouth, MN
Toastmasters Intl.-District 62 [8015], Grand Rapids, MI
Public Transit Assn; Michigan [7546], East Lansing, MI
Public Welfare
Hoosiers Concerned about Gun Violence [5148], Indianapolis, IN
Public Works
Amer. Public Works Assn., Chicago Metro Chap. [140], Barrington, IL
Amer. Public Works Assn., Illinois Chap. [1694], Fairview Heights, IL
Amer. Public Works Assn., Indiana Chap. [5018], Indianapolis, IN
Amer. Public Works Assn., Michigan Chap. [8830], Livonia, MI
Amer. Public Works Assn., Minnesota Chap. [11059], Golden Valley, MN
Amer. Public Works Assn., Ohio Chap. [14060], Cleveland, OH
Amer. Public Works Assn., Wisconsin Chap. [18079], Green Bay, WI
Publication Editors, Cleveland Chap; Amer. Soc. of Bus. [14063], Cleveland, OH
Publishers Roundtable; Minnesota Book [11632], Minneapolis, MN
Publishing
Amer. Soc. of Bus. Publication Editors, Cleveland Chap. [14063], Cleveland, OH
Chicago Women in Publishing [837], Chicago, IL
Great Lakes Booksellers Assn. [7860], Grand Haven, MI
Hoosier State Press Assn. [5147], Indianapolis, IN
Michigan Black Independent Publishers Assn. [8636], Lansing, MI
Midwest Independent Publishers Assn. [11606], Minneapolis, MN
Minnesota Book Publishers Roundtable [11632], Minneapolis, MN
Reformed Free Publishing Assn. [8046], Grandville, MI
Upper Peninsula Publishers and Authors Assn. [8513], Lake Linden, MI
Publishing Assn; Reformed Free [8046], Grandville, MI
Pulaski Area Chamber of Commerce [19547], Pulaski, WI
Pulaski County REACT [6534], Winamac, IN
Puli Club of Am. [13967], Cincinnati, OH
Pulmonary Rehabilitation; Ohio Assn. of Cardiovascular and [16737], Springfield, OH
Pulp and Paper Manufacturers Assn. [17519], Appleton, WI
Puppeteers of Am. - Central Illinois Puppetry Guild [551], Champaign, IL
Puppeteers of Am. - Chicagoland Puppetry Guild [1160], Chicago, IL
Puppeteers of Am. - Cincinnati Area Puppetry Guild [13968], Cincinnati, OH
Puppeteers of Am. - Columbus Puppetry Guild [13325], Bellefontaine, OH
Puppeteers of Am. - Detroit Puppeteers Guild [7165], Clarkston, MI
Puppeteers of Am. - Great Lakes Region [13969], Cincinnati, OH
Puppeteers of Am. - Great Plains Region [12566], St. Paul, MN
Puppeteers of Am. - Indiana Puppetry Guild [6357], Tipton, IN
Puppeteers of Am. - Puppetry Guild of Northeastern Ohio [14209], Cleveland, OH

Puppeteers of Am. - Twin Cities Puppeteers **[11226]**, Inver Grove Heights, MN
Puppeteers of Am. - West Michigan Puppetry Guild **[9715]**, Saugatuck, MI
Puppeteers of Am. - Wisconsin Puppetry Guild **[17622]**, Benton, WI
Puppetry
Puppeteers of Am. - Central Illinois Puppetry Guild **[551]**, Champaign, IL
Puppeteers of Am. - Chicagoland Puppetry Guild **[1160]**, Chicago, IL
Puppeteers of Am. - Cincinnati Area Puppetry Guild **[13968]**, Cincinnati, OH
Puppeteers of Am. - Columbus Puppetry Guild **[13325]**, Bellefontaine, OH
Puppeteers of Am. - Detroit Puppeteers Guild **[7165]**, Clarkston, MI
Puppeteers of Am. - Great Lakes Region **[13969]**, Cincinnati, OH
Puppeteers of Am. - Great Plains Region **[12566]**, St. Paul, MN
Puppeteers of Am. - Indiana Puppetry Guild **[6357]**, Tipton, IN
Puppeteers of Am. - Puppetry Guild of Northeastern Ohio **[14209]**, Cleveland, OH
Puppeteers of Am. - Twin Cities Puppeteers **[11226]**, Inver Grove Heights, MN
Puppeteers of Am. - West Michigan Puppetry Guild **[9715]**, Saugatuck, MI
Puppeteers of Am. - Wisconsin Puppetry Guild **[17622]**, Benton, WI
Purchasing
Amer. Purchasing Soc. of Illinois **[109]**, Aurora, IL
Indiana Hosp. Purchasing and Material Mgt. Assn. **[6093]**, Richmond, IN
Wisconsin Procurement Inst. Educ. and Training Sers. **[19176]**, Milwaukee, WI
Purdue NORML **[6497]**, West Lafayette, IN
Purdue Univ. Calumet Student Assn. for Computing Machinery SIGGRAPH **[4894]**, Hammond, IN
Purdue Univ. Meteorological Assn. **[6498]**, West Lafayette, IN
Purple Penquins **[13302]**, Beavercreek, OH
Put-in-Bay Chamber of Commerce **[16490]**, Put In Bay, OH
Putnam County Bd. of Realtors **[4825]**, Greencastle, IN
Putnam County Historical Soc. **[1967]**, Hennepin, IL

Q

Quad Cities African Violet Soc. **[1790]**, Geneseo, IL
Quad Cities British Auto Club **[1280]**, Coal Valley, IL
Quad Cities Convention and Visitors Bur., Illinois-Iowa **[2529]**, Moline, IL
Quad City Area Youth for Christ **[2530]**, Moline, IL
Quad City Builders Assn. **[★3237]**
Quad City Chap. of the Soc. of Financial Ser. Professionals **[3251]**, Rock Island, IL
Quad City Conservation Alliance **[3252]**, Rock Island, IL
Quad City Development Gp. **[3253]**, Rock Island, IL
Quad City Estate Planning Coun. **[3254]**, Rock Island, IL
Quad City Illinois and Iowa Fed. of Labor **[3255]**, Rock Island, IL
Quad City Stamp Club **[2531]**, Moline, IL
Quad County Hawg Hunters **[3111]**, Plano, IL
Quad County Urban League **[129]**, Aurora, IL
Quail Unlimited, Butler County Chap. **[15989]**, Miamisburg, OH
Quail Unlimited, Northern Indiana Chap. **[4505]**, Elkhart, IN
Quail Unlimited, Ohio Valley Chap. **[15610]**, Lancaster, OH
Quail Unlimited, Patoka Hills **[4942]**, Huntingburg, IN
Quail Unlimited, Quad County Chap. **[3473]**, Shipman, IL
Quail Unlimited, Shawnee Chap. **[2408]**, Marion, IL
Quail Unlimited, Skillet Fork Chap. **[3410]**, Salem, IL
Quail Unlimited, Southeast Wisconsin Chap. **[19914]**, Trevor, WI
Quail Unlimited, Southern Indiana Chap. **[4791]**, Georgetown, IN
Quail Unlimited, Sullivan County Chap. **[5686]**, Linton, IN
Quality Assurance
Illinois Assn. for Hea.care Quality **[2150]**, Kenilworth, IL
Michigan Assn. for Hea.care Quality **[10118]**, West Bloomfield, MI
Ohio Assn. for Healthcare Quality **[14190]**, Cleveland, OH
Wisconsin Assn. for Healthcare Quality **[18655]**, Madison, WI
Quality Control
Amer. Soc. for Quality, Akron-Canton Sect. 0810 **[16841]**, Tallmadge, OH
Amer. Soc. for Quality, Battle Creek-Kalamazoo Sect. 1003 **[8418]**, Kalamazoo, MI
Amer. Soc. for Quality, Chicago Sect. 1201 **[2750]**, Northbrook, IL
Amer. Soc. for Quality, Cincinnati Sect. 0900 **[13734]**, Cincinnati, OH
Amer. Soc. for Quality, Columbus Sect. 0801 **[14308]**, Columbus, OH
Amer. Soc. for Quality, East Central Indiana Sect. 0904 **[5866]**, Muncie, IN
Amer. Soc. for Quality, Evansville-Owensboro Sect. 0915 **[4526]**, Evansville, IN
Amer. Soc. for Quality, Fox Valley Sect. 1208 **[173]**, Batavia, IL
Amer. Soc. for Quality, Grand Rapids Sect. 1001 **[8862]**, Lowell, MI
Amer. Soc. for Quality, Greater Detroit Sect. 1000 **[8786]**, Lathrup Village, MI
Amer. Soc. for Quality, Illiana Sect. 1213 **[3502]**, South Holland, IL
Amer. Soc. for Quality, Indianapolis Sect. 0903 **[5023]**, Indianapolis, IN
Amer. Soc. for Quality, Lafayette Sect. 0917 **[5608]**, Lafayette, IN
Amer. Soc. for Quality, Lansing-Jackson Sect. 1008 **[7118]**, Charlotte, MI
Amer. Soc. for Quality, Louisville Sect. 0912 **[5539]**, Jeffersonville, IN
Amer. Soc. for Quality, Mansfield Sect. 0811 **[15762]**, Mansfield, OH
Amer. Soc. for Quality, Milwaukee Sect. 1202 **[18960]**, Milwaukee, WI
Amer. Soc. for Quality, Minnesota Sect. 1203 **[12381]**, St. Paul, MN
Amer. Soc. for Quality, Northeastern Illinois Sect. 1212 **[2257]**, Libertyville, IL
Amer. Soc. for Quality, Northeastern Indiana Sect. 0905 **[4635]**, Fort Wayne, IN
Amer. Soc. for Quality, Northwest Indiana Sect. 1011 **[5901]**, Munster, IN
Amer. Soc. for Quality, Racine-Kenosha-Walworth Sect. 1204 **[18295]**, Kenosha, WI
Amer. Soc. for Quality, Saginaw Valley Sect. 1004 **[9603]**, Saginaw, MI
Amer. Soc. for Quality, St. Joseph-Benton Harbor Sect. 1007 **[9680]**, St. Joseph, MI
Amer. Soc. for Quality, Scioto Valley Sect. 0815 **[13661]**, Chillicothe, OH
Amer. Soc. for Quality, South Central Indiana Sect. 0920 **[4389]**, Columbus, IN
Amer. Soc. for Quality, Toledo Sect. 1006 **[16897]**, Toledo, OH
Amer. Soc. for Quality, Wabash Valley Sect. 0919 **[6508]**, West Terre Haute, IN
Amer. Soc. for Quality, Winnebago Sect. 1206 **[18328]**, Kohler, WI
Quality for Indiana Taxpayers **[5465]**, Indianapolis, IN
Queen City Figure Skating Club **[13970]**, Cincinnati, OH
Queen City Skywalkers **[13971]**, Cincinnati, OH
Queens of the Court **[4118]**, Anderson, IN
Quilters; Minnesota **[11670]**, Minneapolis, MN
Quilters; Rhinelander Northwoods **[19606]**, Rhinelander, WI
Quilters Society of McHenry; Country **[2457]**, McHenry, IL
Quilting Stars of Ohio **[13579]**, Canton, OH
Quincy Area Chamber of Commerce **[3160]**, Quincy, IL
Quincy Area Chap. of the Soc. for Human Rsrc. Mgt. **[3161]**, Quincy, IL
Quincy Area Convention and Visitors Bur. **[3162]**, Quincy, IL
Quincy Assn. of Realtors **[3163]**, Quincy, IL
Quincy Chamber of Commerce **[9467]**, Quincy, MI
Quincy Citizens Police Acad. Alumni Assn. **[3164]**, Quincy, IL
Quincy Convention and Visitors Bur. **[★3162]**
Quincy Exchange Club **[3165]**, Quincy, IL
Quincy Gun Club **[3166]**, Quincy, IL
Quincy Lions Club - Michigan **[9468]**, Quincy, MI
Quincy Noon Kiwanis **[3167]**, Quincy, IL
Quincy Univ. Students In Free Enterprise **[3168]**, Quincy, IL
Quincy Wyldlife - Wyldlife **[3169]**, Quincy, IL
Quincy Young Lives - YoungLives **[3170]**, Quincy, IL
Qwest Pioneers Minnesota Chap. 8 **[10542]**, Brooklyn Center, MN

R

R/C Sailing Club of Cincinnati No. 217 **[13972]**, Cincinnati, OH
Rabbit Breeders Assn; Mohawk Valley **[★260]**
Rabbit Breeders Assn; Tuscarawas County **[16155]**, New Philadelphia, OH
Rabbit and Cavy Breeders Assn; Mohawk Valley **[★260]**
Rabbit Run Community Arts Assn. **[15750]**, Madison, OH
Rabbit Soc; Columbus House **[14388]**, Columbus, OH
Rabbits
Amer. Rabbit Breeders Assn. **[260]**, Bloomington, IL
Amer. Rabbit Breeders Assn., Badger Rabbit Breeders **[17946]**, Evansville, WI
Amer. Rabbit Breeders Assn., Californian Rabbit Specialty Club of Illinois **[1945]**, Hartsburg, IL
Amer. Rabbit Breeders Assn., Central States Flemish Giant Rabbit Breeders **[1555]**, Edwards, IL
Amer. Rabbit Breeders Assn., Central Wisconsin **[19458]**, Pittsville, WI
Amer. Rabbit Breeders Assn., District 5 **[3792]**, Tuscola, IL
Amer. Rabbit Breeders Assn., District 8 **[5746]**, Markle, IN
Amer. Rabbit Breeders Assn., Fox Valley Rabbit Club **[19545]**, Pulaski, WI
Amer. Rabbit Breeders Assn., Friendly Rabbit of Trempealeau **[18334]**, La Crosse, WI
Amer. Rabbit Breeders Assn., Illinois Checkered Giant Rabbit Club **[1978]**, Heyworth, IL
Amer. Rabbit Breeders Assn., Illinois Dutch Rabbit Club **[1276]**, Coal City, IL
Amer. Rabbit Breeders Assn., Illinois Florida White Specialty Club **[2557]**, Morrison, IL
Amer. Rabbit Breeders Assn., Illinois Mini Lop Club **[2844]**, Odell, IL
Amer. Rabbit Breeders Assn., Illinois Mini Rex Rabbit Club **[2680]**, New Berlin, IL
Amer. Rabbit Breeders Assn., Illinois Netherland Dwarf Specialty Club **[1946]**, Hartsburg, IL
Amer. Rabbit Breeders Assn., Illinois New Zealand Rabbit Breeders Specialty Club **[2075]**, Jacksonville, IL
Amer. Rabbit Breeders Assn., Illinois Standard Chinchilla RC **[1816]**, Glasford, IL
Amer. Rabbit Breeders Assn., Indiana **[5607]**, Lafayette, IN
Amer. Rabbit Breeders Assn., Indianhead **[17743]**, Chippewa Falls, WI
Amer. Rabbit Breeders Assn., Lakeland **[18396]**, Lake Geneva, WI
Amer. Rabbit Breeders Assn., Land of Lincoln Satin Rabbit Breeders Assn. **[1277]**, Coal City, IL
Amer. Rabbit Breeders Assn., Lumberjack Rabbit Club **[17703]**, Cable, WI
Amer. Rabbit Breeders Assn., Michigan **[8514]**, Lake Odessa, MI
Amer. Rabbit Breeders Assn., Midwest Champagn D'Argent Rabbit Club **[2984]**, Pekin, IL
Amer. Rabbit Breeders Assn., Midwest Holland Lop Club **[3223]**, Rochelle, IL
Amer. Rabbit Breeders Assn., Minnesota **[10461]**, Bloomington, MN
Amer. Rabbit Breeders Assn., Misty Hills Rabbit Club **[17554]**, Avoca, WI
Amer. Rabbit Breeders Assn., Northern Exposure Rabbit and Cavy **[19872]**, Superior, WI
Amer. Rabbit Breeders Assn., Red Cedar **[17744]**, Chippewa Falls, WI

Amer. Rabbit Breeders Assn., Southern Lakes Rabbit Club **[18016]**, Franksville, WI
Amer. Rabbit Breeders Assn., Southwest Wisconsin Rabbit Club **[20182]**, Wisconsin Rapids, WI
Amer. Rabbit Breeders Assn., Tri-County Rabbit Breeders **[17998]**, Fort Atkinson, WI
Amer. Rabbit Breeders Assn., Wisconsin **[20021]**, Waupaca, WI
Tuscarawas County Rabbit Breeders Assn. **[16155]**, New Philadelphia, OH
Wisconsin Checkered Giant Rabbit Club **[20195]**, Wisconsin Rapids, WI
Wisconsin House Rabbit Soc. **[18714]**, Madison, WI
Racine Area Manufacturers and Commerce **[19565]**, Racine, WI
Racine Astronomical Soc. **[19566]**, Racine, WI
Racine Chamber of Commerce **[★19565]**
Racine Coun. on Alcohol and Other Drug Abuse **[19567]**, Racine, WI
Racine County Line Rifle Club **[19334]**, Oak Creek, WI
Racine Curling Club **[19568]**, Racine, WI
Racine Geological Soc. **[19107]**, Milwaukee, WI
Racine Habitat for Humanity **[19569]**, Racine, WI
Racine-Kenosha AIFA **[18310]**, Kenosha, WI
Racine/Kenosha Builders' Assn. **[19848]**, Sturtevant, WI
Racine Lions Club **[12061]**, Racine, MN
Racine Numismatic Soc. **[19570]**, Racine, WI
Racine Yacht Club **[19571]**, Racine, WI
Racing
Michigan Racing Assn. **[8701]**, Lansing, MI
Racing Association; Citywide Drag **[2046]**, Homewood, IL
Racing Assn; Michigan **[8701]**, Lansing, MI
Racing for Recovery **[16831]**, Sylvania, OH
Racing; Southeastern Wisconsin Alpine Team **[19255]**, Mukwonago, WI
Racquetball
Illinois State Racquetball Assn. **[2020]**, Hinsdale, IL
Indiana State Racquetball Assn. **[5322]**, Indianapolis, IN
Minnesota Racquetball Assn. **[12028]**, Plymouth, MN
Ohio Racquetball Assn. **[17219]**, Westerville, OH
Racquetball Assn. of Michigan **[8004]**, Grand Rapids, MI
Wisconsin Racquetball Assn. **[19448]**, Pewaukee, WI
Racquetball Assn. of Michigan **[8004]**, Grand Rapids, MI
Radiator Core Mfg. Credit Assn; Natl. **[★11688]**
Radiator Mfg. Credit Assn; Natl. **[★11688]**
Radio
All Ohio Scanner Club **[16120]**, New Carlisle, OH
Miami Valley DX Club **[14501]**, Columbus, OH
Radio Association; Western Reserve Amateur **[16201]**, Newton Falls, OH
Radio and Machine Workers of Am., Local 1111; United Elecl., **[19141]**, Milwaukee, WI
Radio and TV Broadcast Engineers **[★984]**
Radio and TV Broadcast Engineers Intl. Brotherhood of Electrical Workers AFL-CIO, LU 1220 **[★984]**
Radiologic Technologists; Illinois State Soc. of **[291]**, Bloomington, IL
Radiology
Chicago Radiological Soc. **[68]**, Arlington Heights, IL
Eastern Neuroradiological Soc. **[2772]**, Oak Brook, IL
Illinois Radiological Soc. **[375]**, Burr Ridge, IL
Indiana Radiological Soc. **[5287]**, Indianapolis, IN
Wisconsin Radiological Soc. **[19178]**, Milwaukee, WI
Railroad Assn., Midwest Region; Natl. Model **[19078]**, Milwaukee, WI
Railroad; Friends of Burlington Northern **[20119]**, West Bend, WI
Railroad Historical Soc; Illinois Central **[2973]**, Paxton, IL
Railroad Soc; Mad River and NKP **[13331]**, Bellevue, OH
Railroads
Bluewater Michigan Chap., Natl. Railway Historical Soc. **[9576]**, Royal Oak, MI
Brotherhood of Locomotive Engineers and Trainmen, AFL-CIO - Div. 333 **[11536]**, Minneapolis, MN
Brotherhood of Locomotive Engineers and Trainmen, AFL-CIO - Div. 724 **[3408]**, Salem, IL
Brotherhood of Maintenance of Way Employees, AFL-CIO, CLC - Chicago and Northwestern Sys. Fed. **[3235]**, Rock Falls, IL
Chicago Terminal Chap., Pennsylvania Railroad Tech. and Historical Soc. **[2629]**, Naperville, IL
Detroit, Eastern Michigan and Northern Ohio Chap., Pennsylvania Railroad Tech. and Historical Soc. **[8274]**, Howell, MI
Grand Rapids and Indiana Chap., Pennsylvania Railroad Tech. and Historical Soc. **[10225]**, Zeeland, MI
Lines West Buckeye Region Chap., Pennsylvania Railroad Tech. and Historical Soc. **[14494]**, Columbus, OH
Mad River and NKP Railroad Soc. **[13331]**, Bellevue, OH
Michigan Railroads Assn. **[8702]**, Lansing, MI
Saginaw Valley Railroad Historical Soc. **[9637]**, Saginaw, MI
United Trans. Union, AFL-CIO - Local Union 322 **[18012]**, Franklin, WI
United Trans. Union, AFL-CIO - Local Union 469 **[1886]**, Granite City, IL
United Trans. Union, AFL-CIO - Local Union 1258 **[3452]**, Schaumburg, IL
United Trans. Union, AFL-CIO - Local Union 1397 **[14752]**, Columbus, OH
United Trans. Union, AFL-CIO - Wisconsin State Legislative Bd. 56 **[18631]**, Madison, WI
Railsplitter Wanderers **[1404]**, Decatur, IL
Railway Historical Soc; Bluewater Michigan Chap., Natl. **[9576]**, Royal Oak, MI
Rainbow Families **[11729]**, Minneapolis, MN
Rainbow Families Wisconsin **[18604]**, Madison, WI
Rainbow/PUSH Coalition **[1161]**, Chicago, IL
Rainbows, Cincinnati **[13973]**, Cincinnati, OH
Rainbows, Illinois State Chap. **[3343]**, Rolling Meadows, IL
Rainbows, Michigan Chap. **[6615]**, Allen Park, MI
RAINBOWS, Milwaukee **[19108]**, Milwaukee, WI
Raisin River Aikikai **[10214]**, Ypsilanti, MI
Rams Cricket Club **[11730]**, Minneapolis, MN
Ramsey Co REACT **[12567]**, St. Paul, MN
Ramsey County Historical Soc. **[12568]**, St. Paul, MN
Ramsey Lions Club **[12063]**, Ramsey, MN
Ramsey Medical Soc. **[12569]**, St. Paul, MN
Rand Park Dog Training Club **[4008]**, Wildwood, IL
Randolph Chamber of Commerce **[19586]**, Randolph, WI
Randolph County Bd. of Realtors **[6536]**, Winchester, IN
Randolph Lions Club - Ohio **[16054]**, Mogadore, OH
Rankin Lions Club - Michigan **[7850]**, Grand Blanc, MI
Rantoul Area Chamber of Commerce **[3182]**, Rantoul, IL
Rantoul Ridgewalkers **[★552]**
Rape
Chicanos Latinos Unidos En Servicio **[12399]**, St. Paul, MN
Illinois Coalition Against Sexual Assault **[3592]**, Springfield, IL
Michigan Coalition Against Domestic and Sexual Violence **[9275]**, Okemos, MI
Washtenaw County Coalition on Gender Violence and Safety **[6785]**, Ann Arbor, MI
YWCA of Metropolitan Chicago **[1246]**, Chicago, IL
Rasp, Chinese Shar-Pei Rescue Gp. **[★4308]**
Rathkamp Matchcover Soc., Vandalia **[17059]**, Vandalia, OH
Ravenna Area Chamber of Commerce **[16504]**, Ravenna, OH
Ravenna Lions Club **[15546]**, Kent, OH
Ravenswood Community Coun. **[1162]**, Chicago, IL
Ravenswood Conservation Commn. **[★1162]**
Ray Graham Assn. for People with Disabilities **[1510]**, Downers Grove, IL
Raymond Lions Club - Minnesota **[12069]**, Raymond, MN
Read Now; Let Every Adult **[★13082]**
Read To Learn **[79]**, Arlington Heights, IL
Read To Learn for a Brighter Future **[★79]**
Readiness; Center for Military **[8833]**, Livonia, MI
Reading
Coll. Reading and Learning Assn., Minnesota/North Dakota/South Dakota **[11786]**, Minnetonka, MN
Coll. Reading and Learning Assn., Ohio River Valley **[15421]**, Highland Hills, OH
Rolling Readers USA Mid-Michigan Chap. **[8499]**, Laingsburg, MI
Reading Assn; Michigan **[7982]**, Grand Rapids, MI
Reading Assn; Wisconsin State **[19587]**, Randolph, WI
The Reading Center **[★12135]**
Reading Chamber of Commerce **[16507]**, Reading, OH
Reading; Gift of **[7365]**, Detroit, MI
Reading Partners; Macomb **[★7180]**
Reading Police Off.rs Assn. **[16508]**, Reading, OH
Real Estate
Adams Marquette Waushara Bd. of Realtors **[19220]**, Montello, WI
Akron Area Bd. of Realtors **[13016]**, Akron, OH
Alpena Alcona Presque Isle Bd. of Realtors **[6638]**, Alpena, MI
Anderson/Madison County Assn. of Realtors **[4099]**, Anderson, IN
Apartment Assn. of Fort Wayne-Northeast Indiana **[4638]**, Fort Wayne, IN
Apartment Assn. of Southern Indiana **[4529]**, Evansville, IN
Ashland Bd. of Realtors - Kentucky **[13161]**, Ashland, OH
Ashtabula County Bd. of Realtors **[13179]**, Ashtabula, OH
Athens County Bd. of Realtors **[13198]**, Athens, OH
Aurora Tri-County Assn. of Realtors **[113]**, Aurora, IL
Battle Creek Area Assn. of Realtors **[6850]**, Battle Creek, MI
Bay County Realtor Assn., Michigan **[6888]**, Bay City, MI
Beaver Creek Area Assn. of Realtors **[15077]**, East Liverpool, OH
Bedford Bd. of Realtors **[4168]**, Bedford, IN
Belmont County Bd. of Realtors **[17301]**, Wintersville, OH
Belvidere Bd. of Realtors **[220]**, Belvidere, IL
Bloomington Bd. of Realtors **[4204]**, Bloomington, IN
Bloomington Normal Assn. of Realtors **[266]**, Bloomington, IL
Br. County Assn. of Realtors **[7197]**, Coldwater, MI
Bucyrus Area Bd. of Realtors **[13463]**, Bucyrus, OH
Building Owners and Managers Assn. of Metropolitan Detroit **[7657]**, Farmington Hills, MI
Cambridge Bd. of Realtors **[13494]**, Cambridge, OH
Capital Area Assn. of Realtors **[3541]**, Springfield, IL
Cass County Bd. of Realtors **[5689]**, Logansport, IN
Central Illinois Bd. of Realtors **[565]**, Charleston, IL
Central Michigan Assn. of Realtors **[9102]**, Mount Pleasant, MI
Champaign County Assn. of Realtors **[3422]**, Savoy, IL
Chicago Assn. of Realtors **[790]**, Chicago, IL
Chippewa Valley Apartment Assn. **[17869]**, Eau Claire, WI
Cincinnati Area Bd. of Realtors **[13774]**, Cincinnati, OH
Clare Gladwin Bd. of Realtors **[7833]**, Gladwin, MI
Cleveland Area Bd. of Realtors, Ohio **[15495]**, Independence, OH
Clinton County Bd. of Realtors, Ohio **[17288]**, Wilmington, OH
Columbus Bd. of Realtors **[14374]**, Columbus, OH
Columbus Bd. of Realtors, Indiana **[4395]**, Columbus, IN
Commercial Assn. of Realtors - Wisconsin **[18994]**, Milwaukee, WI

CoreNet Global - Chicago Chap. [857], Chicago, IL
Coshocton County Bd. of Realtors [14798], Coshocton, OH
Coun. of Residential Specialists, Ohio Chap. [14416], Columbus, OH
Counselors of Real Estate, Chesapeake Chap. [2962], Park Ridge, IL
Counselors of Real Estate, Midwest Chap. [473], Cary, IL
Counselors of Real Estate, Minnesota Chap. [11552], Minneapolis, MN
Counselors of Real Estate, Ohio/Kentucky Chap. [14417], Columbus, OH
Danville Area Bd. of Realtors [1343], Danville, IL
Darke County Assn. of Realtors [15357], Greenville, OH
Dayton Area Bd. of Realtors [14868], Dayton, OH
Dearborn Area Bd. of Realtors [7252], Dearborn, MI
Dearborn Realtist Bd. [866], Chicago, IL
Decatur Assn. of Realtors [1385], Decatur, IL
Decatur County Bd. of Realtors, Indiana [4841], Greensburg, IN
DeKalb Area Assn. of Realtors, Illinois [3747], Sycamore, IL
Delaware County Bd. of Realtors [15004], Delaware, OH
Detroit Assn. of Realtors [7340], Detroit, MI
Down River Assn. of Realtors [9900], Taylor, MI
Duluth Area Assn. of Realtors [10812], Duluth, MN
East Central Indiana Bd. of Realtors [4414], Connersville, IN
Eastern Thumb Assn. of Realtors [9432], Port Huron, MI
Eastern Upper Peninsula Bd. of Realtors [9718], Sault Ste. Marie, MI
Egyptian Bd. of Realtors [2596], Mount Vernon, IL
Elkhart County Bd. of Realtors [4492], Elkhart, IN
Emmet Assn. of Realtors [9363], Petoskey, MI
Evansville Area Assn. of Realtors [4541], Evansville, IN
Firelands Assn. of Realtors [16610], Sandusky, OH
Flint Area Assn. of Realtors [7725], Flint, MI
Fort Wayne Area Assn. of Realtors [4652], Fort Wayne, IN
Frankfort Bd. of Realtors, Indiana [4741], Frankfort, IN
Freeport Galena Area Assn. of Realtors [1748], Freeport, IL
Galion Bd. of Realtors [15282], Galion, OH
Grand Rapids Assn. of Realtors [7944], Grand Rapids, MI
Greater Alexandria Area Assn. of Realtors [10278], Alexandria, MN
Greater Dayton Apartment Assn. [14889], Dayton, OH
Greater Gateway Assn. of Realtors [1821], Glen Carbon, IL
Greater Kalamazoo Assn. of Realtors [8428], Kalamazoo, MI
Greater Lakes Assn. of Realtors [10388], Baxter, MN
Greater Lansing Assn. of Realtors [8572], Lansing, MI
Greater Milwaukee Assn. of Realtors [19018], Milwaukee, WI
Greater Northwest Indiana Assn. of Realtors [5770], Merrillville, IN
Greater Portsmouth Area Bd. of Realtors [17245], Wheelersburg, OH
Greater South Bend-Mishawaka Assn. of Realtors [6229], South Bend, IN
Greene County Bd. of Realtors [5683], Linton, IN
Grosse Pointe Bd. of Realtors [8082], Grosse Pointe, MI
Hamilton Fairfield Oxford Bd. of Realtors [15159], Fairfield, OH
Heartland Bd. of Realtors [15204], Findlay, OH
Highland County Bd. of Realtors [15445], Hillsboro, OH
Hillsdale County Bd. of Realtors [8175], Hillsdale, MI
Huntington Area Assn. of Realtors [4947], Huntington, IN
Illini Valley Assn. of Realtors [3079], Peru, IL
Illinois Assn. of Realtors [3577], Springfield, IL
Illinois Land Title Assn. [3609], Springfield, IL
Indiana Apartment Assn. [5162], Indianapolis, IN
Indiana Assn. of Realtors [5182], Indianapolis, IN
Indiana Commercial Bd. of Realtors [5215], Indianapolis, IN
Indiana Land Title Assn. [5253], Indianapolis, IN
Inst. of Real Estate Mgt. - Central Illinois Chap. No. 78 [3029], Peoria, IL
Inst. of Real Estate Mgt. - Chicago Chap. No. 23 [2298], Lisle, IL
Inst. of Real Estate Mgt. - Columbus Chap. No. 42 [16772], Stoutsville, OH
Inst. of Real Estate Mgt. - Greater Cincinnati Chap. No. 9 [13868], Cincinnati, OH
Inst. of Real Estate Mgt. - Indianapolis Chap. No. 24 [5370], Indianapolis, IN
Inst. of Real Estate Mgt. - Madison Chap. No. 82 [18526], Madison, WI
Inst. of Real Estate Mgt. - Michigan Chap. No. 5 [7645], Farmington, MI
Inst. of Real Estate Mgt. - Milwaukee Chap. No. 13 [19027], Milwaukee, WI
Inst. of Real Estate Mgt. - Minnesota Chap. No. 45 [11586], Minneapolis, MN
Inst. of Real Estate Mgt. - Northern Indiana Chap. No. 100 [6233], South Bend, IN
Inst. of Real Estate Mgt. - Northern Ohio Chap. No. 41 [13274], Bay Village, OH
Inst. of Real Estate Mgt., Region 9 [977], Chicago, IL
Inst. of Real Estate Mgt. - West Michigan Chap. No. 62 [7663], Farmington Hills, MI
Ionia County Bd. of Realtors [8316], Ionia, MI
Itasca County Bd. of Realtors [11087], Grand Rapids, MN
Jackson Area Assn. of Realtors [8370], Jackson, MI
Jacksonville Area Assn. of Realtors [2079], Jacksonville, IL
Janesville Area Rental Property Assn. [18250], Janesville, WI
Jefferson County Bd. of Realtors, Indiana [5714], Madison, IN
Kankakee County Assn. of Realtors [2134], Kankakee, IL
Kenosha Realtors Assn. [18303], Kenosha, WI
Knox County Bd. of Realtors [6412], Vincennes, IN
Knox County Bd. of Realtors [16082], Mount Vernon, OH
Kosciusko Bd. of Realtors [6445], Warsaw, IN
La Crosse Area Realtors Assn. [18355], La Crosse, WI
Lafayette Regional Assn. of Realtors [5621], Lafayette, IN
Lake and Geauga Area Assn. of Realtors [15969], Mentor, OH
Lake Region Assn. of Realtors [10998], Fergus Falls, MN
Lakes Area Realtors Assn. [17929], Elkhorn, WI
Lakes Country Assn. of Realtors [10776], Detroit Lakes, MN
Lamoine Valley Assn. of Realtors [2370], Macomb, IL
Lancaster Bd. of Realtors [15603], Lancaster, OH
Lapeer and Upper Thumb Assn. of Realtors [8780], Lapeer, MI
LaPorte County Assn. of Realtors [5598], La Porte, IN
Lenawee County Assn. of Realtors [6573], Adrian, MI
Licking County Bd. of Realtors [16170], Newark, OH
Livingston Assn. of Realtors [8278], Howell, MI
Livingston County Assn. of Realtors [8279], Howell, MI
Lorain County Assn. of Realtors [13134], Amherst, OH
Mansfield Bd. of Realtors [15772], Mansfield, OH
Marietta Bd. of Realtors [15823], Marietta, OH
Marion Area Bd. of Realtors [5736], Marion, IN
Marion Bd. of Realtors [15842], Marion, OH
Marysville Assn. of Realtors [15863], Marysville, OH
Mason-Oceana-Manistree Bd. of Realtors [8875], Ludington, MI
McHenry County Assn. of Realtors [4059], Woodstock, IL
Medina County Bd. of Realtors [15945], Medina, OH
Metropolitan Consolidated Assn. of Realtors [9994], Troy, MI
Metropolitan Indianapolis Bd. of Realtors [5405], Indianapolis, IN
Michigan Assn. of Realtors [8625], Lansing, MI
Michigan Land Title Assn. [8679], Lansing, MI
Mid-Eastern Indiana Assn. of Realtors [5885], Muncie, IN
Mid Valley Assn. of Realtors [2158], Kewanee, IL
Middletown Bd. of Realtors [16013], Middletown, OH
Midland Bd. of Realtors [9035], Midland, MI
Midwestern Ohio Assn. of Realtors [17005], Troy, OH
Minneapolis Area Assn. of Realtors [10916], Edina, MN
Minnesota Assn. of Realtors [10918], Edina, MN
Minnesota Commercial Association of Realtors [11642], Minneapolis, MN
Minnesota Land Title Assn. [11127], Hastings, MN
Monroe County Apartment Assn. [4241], Bloomington, IN
Monroe County Assn. of Realtors [9067], Monroe, MI
Montcalm County Assn. of Realtors [8070], Greenville, MI
Muscatatuck Bd. of Realtors [5997], North Vernon, IN
Natl. Assn. of Indus. and Off. Properties, Central Ohio Chap. [14514], Columbus, OH
Natl. Assn. of Indus. and Off. Properties, Chicago Chap. [1075], Chicago, IL
Natl. Assn. of Indus. and Off. Properties, Cincinnati-Northern Kentucky Chap. [13921], Cincinnati, OH
Natl. Assn. of Indus. and Off. Properties, Dayton Chap. [14929], Dayton, OH
Natl. Assn. of Indus. and Off. Properties, Michigan Chap. [6989], Bloomfield Hills, MI
Natl. Assn. of Indus. and Off. Properties Minnesota Chap. [11694], Minneapolis, MN
Natl. Assn. of Indus. and Off. Properties, Northern Ohio Chap. [14172], Cleveland, OH
Natl. Assn. of Indus. and Off. Properties, Ohio Chap. [14515], Columbus, OH
Natl. Assn. of Indus. and Off. Properties, Wisconsin Chap. [19994], Waukesha, WI
North Central Indiana Assn. of Realtors [6050], Plymouth, IN
North Metro Realtors Assn. [10714], Coon Rapids, MN
North Oakland County Bd. of Realtors [10090], Waterford, MI
North Shore-Barrington Assn. of Realtors [2759], Northbrook, IL
Northeastern Indiana Assn. of Realtors [5551], Kendallville, IN
Northeastern Michigan Bd. of Realtors [8098], Hale, MI
Northern Illinois Commercial Assn. of Realtors [3994], Wheaton, IL
Northwestern Ohio Bd. of Realtors [14991], Defiance, OH
Northwoods Assn. of Realtors [20206], Woodruff, WI
Oak Park Bd. of Realtors [2822], Oak Park, IL
Ohio Assn. of Realtors [14564], Columbus, OH
Ohio Land Title Assn. [14632], Columbus, OH
Ozaukee Realtors Assn. [18066], Grafton, WI
Paul Bunyan Bd. of Realtors [7048], Cadillac, MI
Pekin Area Bd. of Realtors [2988], Pekin, IL
Peoria Area Assn. of Realtors [3043], Peoria, IL
Pickaway County Bd. of Realtors [14034], Circleville, OH
Portage County Assn. of Realtors [16502], Ravenna, OH
Property Mgt. Assn. of Mid-Michigan [8754], Lansing, MI
Property Mgt. Assn. of West Michigan [10192], Wyoming, MI
Putnam County Bd. of Realtors [4825], Greencastle, IN
Quincy Assn. of Realtors [3163], Quincy, IL

Randolph County Bd. of Realtors [6536], Winchester, IN
Real Estate Investors Assn. [14210], Cleveland, OH
Realtor Assn. of NorthWest Chicagoland [80], Arlington Heights, IL
Realtor Assn. of West/South Suburban Chicagoland [1511], Downers Grove, IL
Realtors Assn. of Central Indiana [5584], Kokomo, IN
Realtors Assn. of Northeast Wisconsin [17520], Appleton, WI
Realtors Assn. of Northwestern Wisconsin [17891], Eau Claire, WI
Realtors Assn. of South Central Wisconsin [18605], Madison, WI
Realtors Assn. of Southwest Wisconsin [19216], Monroe, WI
Richmond Assn. of Realtors, Indiana [6105], Richmond, IN
Rock Green Realtors Assn. [18261], Janesville, WI
Rockford Area Assn. of Realtors [3305], Rockford, IL
Saginaw Bd. of Realtors [9629], Saginaw, MI
St. Joseph County Assn. of Realtors [7110], Centreville, MI
Saint Paul Area Assn. of Realtors [12574], St. Paul, MN
St. Paul Assn. of Responsible Landlords [12576], St. Paul, MN
Sauk Valley Assn. of Realtors [3704], Sterling, IL
Shiawassee Regional Bd. of Realtors [9336], Owosso, MI
Southeast Minnesota Assn. of Realtors [12191], Rochester, MN
Southeastern Indiana Bd. of Realtors [4148], Aurora, IN
Southern Indiana Realtors Assn. [4368], Clarksville, IN
Southern Ohio Assn. of Realtors [13999], Cincinnati, OH
Southern Ohio Bd. of Realtors [14000], Cincinnati, OH
Southern Twin Cities Assn. of Realtors [10874], Eagan, MN
Southwestern Michigan Assn. of Realtors [9692], St. Joseph, MI
Springfield Bd. of Realtors [16746], Springfield, OH
Stark County Assn. of Realtors Charitable Found. [13584], Canton, OH
Starke/Pulaski Bd. of Realtors [5562], Knox, IN
Steubenville Area Bd. of Realtors [17303], Wintersville, OH
Terre Haute Area Assn. of Realtors, Indiana [6344], Terre Haute, IN
Three Rivers Assn. of Realtors [2120], Joliet, IL
Toledo Bd. of Realtors [16969], Toledo, OH
Traverse Area Assn. of Realtors [9955], Traverse City, MI
Upper Peninsula Assn. of Realtors [8961], Marquette, MI
Village of Turner Trace [5495], Indianapolis, IN
Wabash County Bd. of Realtors [6427], Wabash, IN
Water Wonderland Bd. of Realtors [7825], Gaylord, MI
Wausau Area Apartment Assn. [20053], Wausau, WI
Wayne-Holmes Assn. of Realtors [17333], Wooster, OH
West Central Assn. of Realtors, Ohio [15674], Lima, OH
West Central Illinois Assn. of Realtors [1783], Galesburg, IL
West Michigan Lakeshore Assn. of Realtors [7867], Grand Haven, MI
West Towns Bd. of Realtors [1262], Cicero, IL
Western Wayne Oakland County Assn. of Realtors [7649], Farmington, MI
White County Assn. of Realtors [5828], Monticello, IN
Wisconsin Land Title Assn. [20140], West Salem, WI
Woodland Lakes Assn. of Realtors [19912], Tomahawk, WI
Youngstown Columbiana Assn. of Realtors [17425], Youngstown, OH
Real Estate Investors Assn. [14210], Cleveland, OH
Real Presence Assn. [1163], Chicago, IL
Realtor Assn. of NorthWest Chicagoland [80], Arlington Heights, IL
Realtor Assn. of West/South Suburban Chicagoland [1511], Downers Grove, IL
Realtors Assn. of Central Indiana [5584], Kokomo, IN
Realtors Assn. of Northeast Wisconsin [17520], Appleton, WI
Realtors Assn. of Northwestern Wisconsin [17891], Eau Claire, WI
Realtors Assn. of South Central Wisconsin [18605], Madison, WI
Realtors Assn. of Southwest Wisconsin [19216], Monroe, WI
Realtors; Battle Creek Area Assn. of [6850], Battle Creek, MI
Realtors Charitable Found; Stark County Assn. of [13584], Canton, OH
Realtors; Dearborn Area Bd. of [7252], Dearborn, MI
Realtors; Greater Kalamazoo Assn. of [8428], Kalamazoo, MI
Realtors; Greater Lansing Assn. of [8572], Lansing, MI
Realtors; Indiana Assn. of [5182], Indianapolis, IN
Realtors; Lake Region Assn. of [10998], Fergus Falls, MN
Realtors; Marion Bd. of [15842], Marion, OH
Realtors; Minnesota Commercial Association of [11642], Minneapolis, MN
Rebuilding The Wall [5466], Indianapolis, IN
Recording for the Blind and Dyslexic Illinois Unit [1164], Chicago, IL
Recovery Operators of Illinois; Professional Towing and [2992], Pekin, IL
Recreation
Assn. of Pool and Spa Professionals [3980], Wheaton, IL
Assn. of Wisconsin Snowmobile Clubs [17488], Appleton, WI
Cycle Conservation Club of Michigan [9496], Rives Junction, MI
East Coast 4 Wheel Drive Assn. [14252], Cleves, OH
Friends of Madison School and Community Recreation [18511], Madison, WI
HI-USA, Central and Southern Ohio Coun. [14454], Columbus, OH
Hostelling Intl. - Amer. Youth Hostels, Metropolitan Chicago Coun. [919], Chicago, IL
Hostelling Intl., Michigan Coun. [8840], Livonia, MI
Hostelling Intl., Minnesota AYH [12423], St. Paul, MN
Hostelling International-Northeast Ohio Coun. [16394], Peninsula, OH
Hostelling Intl. - Toledo Area Coun. [16922], Toledo, OH
Minnesota United Snowmobilers Assn. [10554], Brooklyn Park, MN
Minnesotans for Responsible Recreation [10840], Duluth, MN
Natl. Spa and Pool Inst. Central Ohio Chap. [15438], Hilliard, OH
Natl. Spa and Pool Inst. Michigan Chap. [10004], Troy, MI
Natl. Spa and Pool Inst. Midwest Chap. [1089], Chicago, IL
Natl. Spa and Pool Inst. Region VI [8044], Grandville, MI
Riverbend Benders Snowmobile Club [475], Cary, IL
Salem Community Center [16590], Salem, OH
Toledo Indus. Recreation and Employee Services Coun. [16304], Oregon, OH
Wisconsin Coun. of Hostelling Intl. - Amer. Youth Hostels [18691], Madison, WI
Wisconsin Intramural Recreational Sports Assn. [19819], Stevens Point, WI
Recreation Assn; Baraga County Tourist and [6795], L'Anse, MI
Recreation Assn; Upper Peninsula Travel and [8328], Iron Mountain, MI
Recreation Assn; Wisconsin [★18153]
Recreation Assn; Wisconsin Park and [18153], Greendale, WI
Recreation, and Dance; Illinois Assn. for Hea., Physical Educ., [2078], Jacksonville, IL
Recreation and Dance; Ohio Assn. for Hea., Physical Educ., [13245], Avon Lake, OH
Recreation and Employee Services Coun; Toledo Indus. [16304], Oregon, OH
Recreation Found; Bloomington Community Park and [4205], Bloomington, IN
Recreation; Friends of Madison School and Community [18511], Madison, WI
Recreation for Individuals Dedicated to the Env. [1165], Chicago, IL
Recreation; Minnesotans for Responsible [10840], Duluth, MN
Recreation and Park Assn; Michigan [9290], Okemos, MI
Recreation and Park Assn; Minnesota [11035], Fridley, MN
Recreation; Rochester Area Disabled Athletics and [12172], Rochester, MN
Recreational; Holiday Rambler [★6430]
Recreational Vehicle Assn; Ohio Mobile Home and [★15058]
Recreational Vehicle Club; Holiday Rambler [6430], Wakarusa, IN
Recreational Vehicles
Family Motor Coach Assn. - Just Friends [13826], Cincinnati, OH
Holiday Rambler Recreational Vehicle Club [6430], Wakarusa, IN
Jayco Jafari Intl. Travel Club, Flight 3 Tri-State Jaybirds [4383], Columbia City, IN
Jayco Jafari Intl. Travel Club, Flight 5 Heart of Illinois Jaytrackers [2493], Milford, IL
Jayco Jafari Intl. Travel Club, Flight 9 Four Rivers Jaycos [420], Carbondale, IL
Jayco Jafari Intl. Travel Club, Flight 13 Ja Triskaideka [2917], Palatine, IL
Jayco Jafari Intl. Travel Club, Flight 32 Holi-Jays [2392], Maple Park, IL
Jayco Jafari Intl. Travel Club, Flight 41 Jay Pack [18112], Green Bay, WI
Jayco Jafari Intl. Travel Club, Flight 101 Jayco Big Birds [4058], Woodstock, IL
Jayco Jafari Intl. Travel Club, Flight 106 Jaybirds of Milwaukee [17780], Colgate, WI
Jayco Jafari Intl. Travel Club, Flight 117 Lake Jayco Jypsies [10156], White Lake, MI
Michigan Assn. of Recreational Vehicles and Campgrounds [9273], Okemos, MI
Ohio Manufactured Homes Assn. [15058], Dublin, OH
Wally Byam Caravan Club Intl., Region 7 [20180], Wisconsin Dells, WI
Winnebago Home Builders Assn. [19407], Oshkosh, WI
Recreational Vehicles and Campgrounds; Michigan Assn. of [9273], Okemos, MI
Recycling
Assoc. Recyclers of Wisconsin [19479], Plover, WI
Automotive Recyclers of Michigan [7842], Grand Blanc, MI
Recycling Assn. of Minnesota [12570], St. Paul, MN
Recycling Assn; Illinois [2815], Oak Park, IL
Recycling Assn. of Minnesota [12570], St. Paul, MN
Recycling Coalition; Indiana [4229], Bloomington, IN
Recycling Coalition; Michigan [8703], Lansing, MI
Red Bull Historic Military Vehicle Assn. [11940], Onamia, MN
Red Cedar Beagle Club [10174], Williamston, MI
Red Cross
American Red Cross [17745], Chippewa Falls, WI
Amer. Red Cross, Allen County Chap. [15647], Lima, OH
Amer. Red Cross, Athens County Chap. [13194], Athens, OH
Amer. Red Cross, Badger Chap. [18468], Madison, WI
Amer. Red Cross Badger-Hawkeye Blood Sers. Region [18469], Madison, WI
Amer. Red Cross, Barberton Chap. [13254], Barberton, OH
Amer. Red Cross, Berrien County Chap. [6918], Benton Harbor, MI

Amer. Red Cross Blood Sers. Indiana-Ohio Region **[4634]**, Fort Wayne, IN
Amer. Red Cross, Butler County Chap. **[16004]**, Middletown, OH
Amer. Red Cross, Calhoun County Chap. **[6847]**, Battle Creek, MI
Amer. Red Cross, Central Illinois Chap. **[3004]**, Peoria, IL
Amer. Red Cross, Central Michigan Chap. **[9099]**, Mount Pleasant, MI
Amer. Red Cross, Champaign County Chap. **[17038]**, Urbana, OH
Amer. Red Cross, Chippewa Valley Chap. **[17863]**, Eau Claire, WI
Amer. Red Cross, Cincinnati Area Chap. **[13732]**, Cincinnati, OH
Amer. Red Cross, Clark County Chap. **[16717]**, Springfield, OH
Amer. Red Cross, Coshocton County Chap. **[14794]**, Coshocton, OH
Amer. Red Cross, Crawford County Chap. **[13461]**, Bucyrus, OH
Amer. Red Cross, Dayton Area Chap. **[14850]**, Dayton, OH
Amer. Red Cross, Defiance County Chap. **[14983]**, Defiance, OH
Amer. Red Cross, DeKalb County Chap. **[1428]**, DeKalb, IL
Amer. Red Cross, Delaware County Chap. **[14998]**, Delaware, OH
Amer. Red Cross, East Central Wisconsin Chap. **[19389]**, Oshkosh, WI
Amer. Red Cross, East Shoreline Chap. **[6876]**, Bay City, MI
Amer. Red Cross, Firelands Chap. **[16602]**, Sandusky, OH
Amer. Red Cross, First Capital District Chap. **[13660]**, Chillicothe, OH
Amer. Red Cross, Fond du Lac County Chap. **[17969]**, Fond du Lac, WI
Amer. Red Cross, Fox River Chap. **[3379]**, St. Charles, IL
Amer. Red Cross, Fulton County Ohio **[17138]**, Wauseon, OH
Amer. Red Cross, Galion Area Chap. **[15279]**, Galion, OH
Amer. Red Cross, Goodhue County Chap. **[12077]**, Red Wing, MN
Amer. Red Cross, Greater Cleveland Chap. **[14061]**, Cleveland, OH
Amer. Red Cross of Greater Columbus **[14307]**, Columbus, OH
Amer. Red Cross of Greater Indianapolis **[5020]**, Indianapolis, IN
Amer. Red Cross, Greater Kalamazoo Area Chap. **[8417]**, Kalamazoo, MI
Amer. Red Cross, Greater Toledo Area Chap. **[16894]**, Toledo, OH
Amer. Red Cross, Grundy County Chap. **[2552]**, Morris, IL
Amer. Red Cross, Hancock County Chap. **[15193]**, Findlay, OH
Amer. Red Cross, Illini Prairie Chap. **[3804]**, Urbana, IL
Amer. Red Cross, Illinois Capital Area Chap. **[3528]**, Springfield, IL
Amer. Red Cross, Kankakee County Chap. **[2129]**, Kankakee, IL
Amer. Red Cross, Knox County Chap. **[16079]**, Mount Vernon, OH
Amer. Red Cross, Lake County Chap. **[16333]**, Painesville, OH
Amer. Red Cross, Lakeland Chap. **[18080]**, Green Bay, WI
Amer. Red Cross, Lee County Chap. **[1475]**, Dixon, IL
Amer. Red Cross, Lenawee County Chap. **[6565]**, Adrian, MI
Amer. Red Cross, Licking County Chap. **[16168]**, Newark, OH
Amer. Red Cross of Livingston County **[8270]**, Howell, MI
Amer. Red Cross, Lorain County Chap. **[15106]**, Elyria, OH
Amer. Red Cross, Mahoning Chap. **[13371]**, Boardman, OH
Amer. Red Cross, Manitowoc/Calumet Chap. **[18775]**, Manitowoc, WI
Amer. Red Cross, Marion County Chap. **[15836]**, Marion, OH
Amer. Red Cross, McLean County Chap., Bloomington **[261]**, Bloomington, IL
Amer. Red Cross, Medina County Chap. **[15939]**, Medina, OH
Amer. Red Cross, Mercer County Chap. **[13610]**, Celina, OH
Amer. Red Cross, Mid-Illinois Chap. **[1375]**, Decatur, IL
Amer. Red Cross, Midland/Gladwin Chap. **[9022]**, Midland, MI
Amer. Red Cross of Monroe County **[9061]**, Monroe, MI
Amer. Red Cross, Morrow County Chap. **[16068]**, Mount Gilead, OH
Amer. Red Cross, Mower County Chap. **[10352]**, Austin, MN
Amer. Red Cross, Muskegon - Oceana Chap. **[9139]**, Muskegon, MI
Amer. Red Cross, Muskingum Lakes Chap. **[16146]**, New Philadelphia, OH
Amer. Red Cross, Neenah-Menasha Chap. **[19266]**, Neenah, WI
Amer. Red Cross North Central Blood Sers. Region **[12379]**, St. Paul, MN
Amer. Red Cross, Northern Lower Michigan Chap. **[9362]**, Petoskey, MI
Amer. Red Cross of the Northern Miami Valley **[16997]**, Troy, OH
Amer. Red Cross Northern Ohio Blood Sers. Region **[14062]**, Cleveland, OH
Amer. Red Cross, Northland Chap. **[10802]**, Duluth, MN
Amer. Red Cross, Northwest Illinois Chap. **[1745]**, Freeport, IL
Amer. Red Cross of Northwest Indiana **[5767]**, Merrillville, IN
Amer. Red Cross, Northwest Michigan Chap. **[9922]**, Traverse City, MI
Amer. Red Cross, Ohio River Valley Chap. **[16468]**, Portsmouth, OH
Amer. Red Cross, Pickaway County Chap. **[14031]**, Circleville, OH
Amer. Red Cross, Portage County Chap. **[19781]**, Stevens Point, WI
Amer. Red Cross, Posey County Chap. **[5846]**, Mount Vernon, IN
Amer. Red Cross of the Quad Cities Area **[2516]**, Moline, IL
Amer. Red Cross, Rice-LeSueur Counties Chap. **[10983]**, Faribault, MN
Amer. Red Cross, Richland County Chap. **[15761]**, Mansfield, OH
Amer. Red Cross, Rock River Chap. **[3269]**, Rockford, IL
Amer. Red Cross, Saginaw County Chap. **[9602]**, Saginaw, MI
Amer. Red Cross, St. Clair County Chap. **[9429]**, Port Huron, MI
Amer. Red Cross, St. Croix Valley Chap. **[10392]**, Bayport, MN
Amer. Red Cross, Sandusky County Chap. **[15246]**, Fremont, OH
Amer. Red Cross, Sheboygan County Chap. **[19691]**, Sheboygan, WI
Amer. Red Cross, South Central Michigan Chap. **[8361]**, Jackson, MI
Amer. Red Cross, South Central Minnesota Chap. **[11374]**, Mankato, MN
Amer. Red Cross, South Central Wisconsin Chap. **[18243]**, Janesville, WI
Amer. Red Cross, Southeast Minnesota Chap. **[12126]**, Rochester, MN
Amer. Red Cross Southeastern Michigan Blood Region **[7318]**, Detroit, MI
Amer. Red Cross, Southwestern Illinois Chap. **[41]**, Alton, IL
Amer. Red Cross, Steele County Chap. **[11957]**, Owatonna, MN
Amer. Red Cross, Streator Chap. **[3725]**, Streator, IL
Amer. Red Cross, Summit County Chap. **[13037]**, Akron, OH
Amer. Red Cross, Washington County Chap. **[15814]**, Marietta, OH
Amer. Red Cross, Washtenaw County Chap. **[6663]**, Ann Arbor, MI
Amer. Red Cross, Wayne County Chap. **[17311]**, Wooster, OH
Amer. Red Cross of West Central Michigan **[7900]**, Grand Rapids, MI
Amer. Red Cross, Winona County Chap. **[12945]**, Winona, MN
Red Cross of Greater Chicago; Amer. **[719]**, Chicago, IL
Red Cross of Lawrence and Orange Counties; Amer. **[★4165]**
Red Cross, Madison County Chap; Amer. **[4098]**, Anderson, IN
Red Cross, Menard County Chap; Amer. **[★3529]**
Red Cross, Norfolk Chap; Amer. **[★4098]**
Red Cross, Porter County Chap; Amer. **[6378]**, Valparaiso, IN
Red Cross, Posey County Chap; Amer. **[5846]**, Mount Vernon, IN
Red Cross, Sangamon County Chap; Amer. **[★3529]**
Red Cross, Sangamon Valley Chap; Amer. **[3529]**, Springfield, IL
Red Cross, Southeastern Michigan Chap; Amer. **[7319]**, Detroit, MI
Red Cross; Waseca County Chap., Amer. **[12849]**, Waseca, MN
Red Cross, Western Stark County Chap; Amer. **[15881]**, Massillon, OH
Red Lake Falls Lions Club **[12074]**, Red Lake Falls, MN
Red River Valley Angus Assn. **[10335]**, Argyle, MN
Red River Valley Appaloosa Horse Club **[12873]**, West Concord, MN
Red River Valley Fighter Pilot Assn. - Cincinnati, Ohio **[13974]**, Cincinnati, OH
Red River Valley Fighter Pilot Assn. - Michigan **[10123]**, West Bloomfield, MI
Red River Valley Fighter Pilot Assn. - Minnesota **[10606]**, Burnsville, MN
Red River Valley Fighter Pilot Assn. - Wright Patterson AFB/Dayton, Ohio **[15564]**, Kettering, OH
Red Wing Area Chamber of Commerce **[12081]**, Red Wing, MN
Red Wing Area United Way **[12082]**, Red Wing, MN
Red Wing High School - Young Life **[12083]**, Red Wing, MN
Red Wing Soaring Assn. **[12899]**, White Bear Lake, MN
Red Wing Visitors and Convention Bur. **[12084]**, Red Wing, MN
Red Witch R/C Yacht Club No. 152 **[2160]**, Kewanee, IL
Redevelopment Commn; Inkster Housing and **[8312]**, Inkster, MI
Redevelopment Corp; Clifton Heights Community Urban **[13805]**, Cincinnati, OH
Redford Township Chamber of Commerce **[9479]**, Redford, MI
Redford Township Lions Club **[7268]**, Dearborn, MI
Redwood Area Chamber and Tourism **[12097]**, Redwood Falls, MN
Redwood Area United Way **[12098]**, Redwood Falls, MN
Redwood Falls Area Chamber of Commerce **[★12097]**
Reed City Area Chamber of Commerce **[9483]**, Reed City, MI
Reed City Lions Club **[9484]**, Reed City, MI
Reed Memorial Lib. **[16505]**, Ravenna, OH
Reedsburg Area Chamber of Commerce **[19592]**, Reedsburg, WI
Reedsburg Lions Club **[18387]**, La Valle, WI
Reel Hang Glider Pilots Assn. **[1613]**, Elk Grove Village, IL
Reese Area Chamber of Commerce **[★9486]**
Reese Chamber of Commerce **[9486]**, Reese, MI
Reform
Minnesota ACORN **[12449]**, St. Paul, MN
Reform of Marijuana Laws, Illinois Chap; Natl. Org. for **[1087]**, Chicago, IL
Reformed Free Publishing Assn. **[8046]**, Grandville, MI
Refrigeration
Refrigeration Ser. Engineers Soc., Fox Valley Chap. **[3498]**, South Elgin, IL
Refrigeration Sers. Engineers **[16956]**, Toledo, OH
Refrigeration Ser. Engineers Soc., Fox Valley Chap. **[3498]**, South Elgin, IL

Refrigeration Sers. Engineers **[16956]**, Toledo, OH
Refugee Mentoring Prog. **[12571]**, St. Paul, MN
Refugee Women's Initiative **[★12571]**
Refugees
Refugee Mentoring Prog. **[12571]**, St. Paul, MN
Region 2 Planning Commn. **[8395]**, Jackson, MI
Region 5 Development Commn. **[12705]**, Staples, MN
Regional Development Commn; West Michigan Shoreline **[9168]**, Muskegon, MI
Regional Economic Development Corp. **[2409]**, Marion, IL
Regional Government
Bi-State Regional Commn. **[3241]**, Rock Island, IL
Regional Planning Commn; East Central Wisconsin **[18858]**, Menasha, WI
Rehabilitation
Intl. Assn. of Psychosocial Rehabilitation Services, Michigan Chap. **[7524]**, East Lansing, MI
MARO Employment and Training Assn. **[8602]**, Lansing, MI
Michigan Chap. of IARP **[7057]**, Cannonsburg, MI
Minnesota Assn. of Rehabilitation Providers **[11061]**, Golden Valley, MN
Ohio Assn. of Cardiovascular and Pulmonary Rehabilitation **[16737]**, Springfield, OH
U.S. Psychiatric Rehabilitation Assn. - Minnesota **[11766]**, Minneapolis, MN
U.S. Psychiatric Rehabilitation Assn. - Ohio Chap. **[15612]**, Lancaster, OH
Rehabilitation Center; White Pine Wildlife **[17953]**, Fall Creek, WI
Rehabilitation; Ohio Assn. of Cardiovascular and Pulmonary **[16737]**, Springfield, OH
Rehabilitation Providers; Minnesota Assn. of **[11061]**, Golden Valley, MN
Rehabilitation Services, Michigan Chap; Intl. Assn. of Psychosocial **[7524]**, East Lansing, MI
Rehabilitation for Wisconsin **[18606]**, Madison, WI
Relief
Amer. Red Cross Amateur Radio Club **[5019]**, Indianapolis, IN
Amer. Red Cross, Central Ohio Blood Services Region **[14306]**, Columbus, OH
Amer. Red Cross - Genesee/Lapeer Chap. **[7714]**, Flint, MI
Amer. Red Cross of Greater Chicago **[719]**, Chicago, IL
Amer. Red Cross - Greater Milwaukee Chap. **[18956]**, Milwaukee, WI
Amer. Red Cross, Hancock County **[4830]**, Greenfield, IN
Amer. Red Cross Hoosier Hills Chap. **[4165]**, Bedford, IN
Amer. Red Cross, Johnson County Off. **[6520]**, Whiteland, IN
Amer. Red Cross, Madison County Chap. **[4098]**, Anderson, IN
Amer. Red Cross, Porter County Chap. **[6378]**, Valparaiso, IN
Amer. Red Cross of the St. Paul Area **[12380]**, St. Paul, MN
Amer. Red Cross, Sangamon Valley Chap. **[3529]**, Springfield, IL
Amer. Red Cross-Scenic Bluffs Chap. **[18335]**, La Crosse, WI
Amer. Red Cross Southeast Wisconsin Tri-County Chap. **[19551]**, Racine, WI
Amer. Red Cross, Southeastern Michigan Chap. **[7319]**, Detroit, MI
Amer. Red Cross, Western Stark County Chap. **[15881]**, Massillon, OH
Carver County Chapter, American Red Cross **[11924]**, Norwood Young America, MN
Church World Service/CROP, Indiana-Kentucky **[5087]**, Indianapolis, IN
Church World Service/CROP, Minn-Kota Region **[11545]**, Minneapolis, MN
Church World Ser./CROP, Wisconsin Region **[18496]**, Madison, WI
Huntington Chap. of the Amer. Red Cross **[4948]**, Huntington, IN
Lac Qui Parle County Ser. Unit, Amer. Red Cross **[12289]**, St. Cloud, MN
Midwest Minnesota Chapter, American Red Cross **[10999]**, Fergus Falls, MN
Renville/Redwood Chap., Amer. Red Cross **[11938]**, Olivia, MN
Sentry Cares **[19805]**, Stevens Point, WI
Waseca County Chap., Amer. Red Cross **[12849]**, Waseca, MN
Wright County Chap., Amer. Red Cross **[10580]**, Buffalo, MN
Relief after Violent Encounter, Ionia-Montcalm **[9677]**, St. Johns, MI
Religion
Amer. Baptist Churches of Ohio **[15340]**, Granville, OH
Religious Administration
Congregation Kneseth Israel **[1585]**, Elgin, IL
Natl. Assn. of Church Bus. Admin., Chicago Chap. **[2655]**, Naperville, IL
Natl. Assn. of Church Bus. Admin., Greater Cincinnati Chap. **[13918]**, Cincinnati, OH
Natl. Assn. of Church Bus. Administrators, Columbus Chap. **[15298]**, Galloway, OH
Natl. Assn. of Church Bus. Administrators, Wisconsin Chap. **[19333]**, Oak Creek, WI
St. Paul African Methodist Episcopal Church **[7428]**, Detroit, MI
Religious and Civil Rights, Ann Arbor Chap; Catholic League for **[6690]**, Ann Arbor, MI
Religious and Civil Rights, Chicago Chap; Catholic League for **[4035]**, Winnetka, IL
Religious Coalition for Reproductive Choice - Illinois Chap. **[2171]**, La Grange, IL
Religious Coalition for Reproductive Choice - Indiana Chap. **[5632]**, Lafayette, IN
Religious Coalition for Reproductive Choice - Michigan Chap. **[7566]**, East Lansing, MI
Religious Coalition for Reproductive Choice - Minnesota Chap. **[11731]**, Minneapolis, MN
Religious Coalition for Reproductive Choice - Ohio Chap. **[14720]**, Columbus, OH
Religious Coalition for Reproductive Choice - Wisconsin Chap. **[18607]**, Madison, WI
Religious Studies
Catholic Men's Fellowship of Northeastern Ohio **[16191]**, Newbury, OH
First Priority of Muskegon **[9143]**, Muskegon, MI
Metrokids **[11603]**, Minneapolis, MN
Real Presence Assn. **[1163]**, Chicago, IL
Time Out 4 Youth **[6082]**, Richland, IN
Religious Understanding
InterVarsity Christian Fellowship/USA **[18533]**, Madison, WI
Remember the Children **[5980]**, Noblesville, IN
Remodeling Indus; Fox Valley Natl. Assn. of The **[17493]**, Appleton, WI
Remodeling Indus. of Madison; Natl. Assn. of The **[18577]**, Madison, WI
Remodeling Indus. of Minnesota; Natl. Assn. of the **[11696]**, Minneapolis, MN
Remodeling Indus; Tri-County Natl. Assn. of The **[13100]**, Akron, OH
Remus Lions Club **[9858]**, Stanwood, MI
Renaissance
Renaissance Initiative **[1351]**, Danville, IL
Renaissance Fencing Club **[8900]**, Madison Heights, MI
Renaissance Initiative **[1351]**, Danville, IL
Renewable Energy Assn; Midwest **[17802]**, Custer, WI
Reno Lions Club **[15829]**, Marietta, OH
Rensselaer - Remington Area Chamber of Commerce **[★6081]**
Rensselaer - Remington Chamber of Commerce **[6081]**, Rensselaer, IN
Rental Purchase Dealers Assn. **[4253]**, Bloomington, IN
Renting and Leasing
Ohio Vehicle Leasing Assn. **[15064]**, Dublin, OH
Rental Purchase Dealers Assn. **[4253]**, Bloomington, IN
Renville Lions Club **[12102]**, Renville, MN
Renville/Redwood Chap., Amer. Red Cross **[11938]**, Olivia, MN
Repair
Proj. Repair **[14249]**, Cleveland Heights, OH
Reproductive Health
Planned Parenthood of Minnesota, North Dakota and South Dakota **[12560]**, St. Paul, MN
Planned Parenthood of Wisconsin **[19094]**, Milwaukee, WI
Reproductive Rights
Greene County Right To Life **[17371]**, Xenia, OH
MARAL Pro-Choice Michigan **[8601]**, Lansing, MI
NARAL Pro-Choice Minnesota **[12540]**, St. Paul, MN
NARAL Pro-Choice Ohio **[14170]**, Cleveland, OH
Natl. Abortion and Reproductive Action League of Wisconsin **[18572]**, Madison, WI
Religious Coalition for Reproductive Choice - Illinois Chap. **[2171]**, La Grange, IL
Religious Coalition for Reproductive Choice - Indiana Chap. **[5632]**, Lafayette, IN
Religious Coalition for Reproductive Choice - Michigan Chap. **[7566]**, East Lansing, MI
Religious Coalition for Reproductive Choice - Minnesota Chap. **[11731]**, Minneapolis, MN
Religious Coalition for Reproductive Choice - Ohio Chap. **[14720]**, Columbus, OH
Religious Coalition for Reproductive Choice - Wisconsin Chap. **[18607]**, Madison, WI
Reptiles
Minnesota Herpetological Soc. **[11651]**, Minneapolis, MN
Republic Lions Club **[16511]**, Republic, OH
Republican Party
Chicago Log Cabin Republicans **[814]**, Chicago, IL
Illinois Fed. of Republican Women **[4075]**, Yorkville, IL
Indiana Fed. of Republican Women **[5236]**, Indianapolis, IN
Log Cabin Republicans of Northwest Ohio **[16927]**, Toledo, OH
Wisconsin Fed. of Republican Women **[20011]**, Waukesha, WI
Rescue
Amer. Shetland Sheepdog Assn. Sheltie Rescue Network **[2688]**, New Lenox, IL
Chicago Regional Search and Rescue **[2009]**, Hinckley, IL
Crossroads Donkey Rescue **[9233]**, Novi, MI
Headwaters Search and Rescue Dog Assn. **[17847]**, Eagle River, WI
People and Paws Search and Rescue **[19090]**, Milwaukee, WI
Rescue A Shar-Pei **[4308]**, Burns Harbor, IN
Rescue Alliance of Wisconsin; German Shepherd **[18514]**, Madison, WI
Rescue; Crossroads Donkey **[9233]**, Novi, MI
Rescue; Eastern Upper Peninsula Search and **[9196]**, Newberry, MI
Rescue of Greater Chicago; Great Pyrenees **[2063]**, Ingleside, IL
Research
Assn. of Professional Researchers for Advancement, Illinois Chap. **[752]**, Chicago, IL
Chessie Sys. Historical Soc. **[17170]**, West Chester, OH
Minnesota Public Interest Res. Gp. **[11669]**, Minneapolis, MN
Ohio Prospect Res. Network **[14940]**, Dayton, OH
Ohio Public Interest Res. Gp. **[14664]**, Columbus, OH
Research Associates; Jordan Hall **[3788]**, Troy, IL
Res. Assn; Michigan Educational **[7746]**, Flint, MI
Res. Assn; Pediatric Heart **[17178]**, West Chester, OH
Res. Coun. of Michigan; Citizens **[8836]**, Livonia, MI
Res; Michigan Soc. for Medical **[6736]**, Ann Arbor, MI
Reservation Staff Alumni Assn; Chief Logan **[13663]**, Chillicothe, OH
Reserve Officers Assn. - Dept. of Illinois **[2927]**, Palatine, IL
Reserve Officers Assn. - Dept. of Illinois, Central Illinois Chap. 33 **[310]**, Bloomington, IL
Reserve Officers Assn. - Dept. of Illinois, Champaign Chap. 4 **[3795]**, Tuscola, IL
Reserve Officers Assn. - Dept. of Illinois, Cook County Chap. 6 **[2212]**, Lake Zurich, IL
Reserve Officers Assn. - Dept. of Illinois, Decatur Chap. 7 **[1405]**, Decatur, IL
Reserve Officers Assn. - Dept. of Illinois, DuPage County Chap. 11 **[3997]**, Wheaton, IL
Reserve Officers Assn. - Dept. of Illinois, Eastern Illinois Chap. 12 **[571]**, Charleston, IL
Reserve Officers Assn. - Dept. of Illinois, Fort Sheridan Chap. 48 **[3215]**, Riverwoods, IL
Reserve Officers Assn. - Dept. of Illinois, O'Hare Chap. 61 **[81]**, Arlington Heights, IL

Reserve Officers Assn. - Dept. of Illinois, Quincy Chap. 35 **[3171]**, Quincy, IL
Reserve Officers Assn. - Dept. of Illinois, Springfield Chap. 39 **[105]**, Auburn, IL
Reserve Officers Assn. - Dept. of Minnesota **[12572]**, St. Paul, MN
Reserve Officers Assn. - Dept. of Ohio **[13975]**, Cincinnati, OH
Reserve Officers Assn. - Dept. of Ohio, Alfred Gus Karger Chap. 7 **[16567]**, St. Bernard, OH
Reserve Officers Assn. - Dept. of Ohio, Anthony Wayne Chap. 4 **[17093]**, Wapakoneta, OH
Reserve Officers Assn. - Dept. of Ohio, Buckeye Chap. 5 **[16740]**, Springfield, OH
Reserve Officers Assn. - Dept. of Ohio, Cincinnati Navy Chap. 71 **[15730]**, Loveland, OH
Reserve Officers Assn. - Dept. of Ohio, Cleveland Coast Guard Chap. 10 **[13452]**, Brunswick, OH
Reserve Officers Assn. - Dept. of Ohio, Col. Coleman Todd Chap. 53 **[15789]**, Mansfield, OH
Reserve Officers Assn. - Dept. of Ohio, Col. Copeland Chap. 43 **[15853]**, Marion, OH
Reserve Officers Assn. - Dept. of Ohio, Col. John E. Coleman Chap. 16 **[16123]**, New Carlisle, OH
Reserve Officers Assn. - Dept. of Ohio, Columbus Navy Chap. 12 **[16518]**, Reynoldsburg, OH
Reserve Officers Assn. - Dept. of Ohio, Gen. Grant Chap. 28 **[15450]**, Hillsboro, OH
Reserve Officers Assn. - Dept. of Ohio, Gen. Orton Chap. 26 **[15272]**, Gahanna, OH
Reserve Officers Assn. - Dept. of Ohio, Gen. Patton Chap. 25 **[15303]**, Garfield Heights, OH
Reserve Officers Assn. - Dept. of Ohio, Kittyhawk Chap. 70 **[16707]**, Springboro, OH
Reserve Officers Assn. - Dept. of Ohio, Mahoning County Chap. 42 **[17412]**, Youngstown, OH
Reserve Officers Assn. - Dept. of Ohio, M.G. Geisman Chap. 46 **[16200]**, Newton Falls, OH
Reserve Officers Assn. - Dept. of Ohio, North Coast Cleveland Chap. 8 **[13430]**, Broadview Heights, OH
Reserve Officers Assn. - Dept. of Wisconsin, Readiness Chap. 43 **[19754]**, Sparta, WI
Resident Coun. Found; Park River Estates **[10715]**, Coon Rapids, MN
Resident Coun; Warren West **[7453]**, Detroit, MI
Residential Services Assn. of Wisconsin **[19109]**, Milwaukee, WI
Residential Specialists, Ohio Chap; Coun. of **[14416]**, Columbus, OH
Resolve of Illinois **[★2023]**
Resolve of Illinois Chap. **[2023]**, Hinsdale, IL
Resolve of Michigan **[9590]**, Royal Oak, MI
Resolve of Minnesota **[10926]**, Edina, MN
Resolve of Minnesota, Minnesota **[★10926]**
Resolve of Ohio **[14721]**, Columbus, OH
Resort District Dental Soc. **[9948]**, Traverse City, MI
Rsrcs. Assn., Wisconsin Sect; Amer. Water **[18904]**, Middleton, WI
Resources and Counseling for the Arts **[★12593]**

Respiratory Diseases
Amer. Lung Assn. of Illinois **[3527]**, Springfield, IL
Amer. Lung Assn. of Illinois, Southern Illinois Region **[2401]**, Marion, IL
Amer. Lung Assn. of Indiana **[5015]**, Indianapolis, IN
Amer. Lung Assn. of Indiana, Northern **[4633]**, Fort Wayne, IN
Amer. Lung Assn. of Metropolitan Chicago **[714]**, Chicago, IL
Amer. Lung Assn. of Michigan **[9255]**, Oak Park, MI
Amer. Lung Assn. of Minnesota **[12376]**, St. Paul, MN
Amer. Lung Assn. of Ohio **[14303]**, Columbus, OH
Amer. Lung Assn. of Ohio, Northwest Br. **[16259]**, Norwalk, OH
Amer. Lung Assn. of Ohio, Southwest Br. **[13730]**, Cincinnati, OH
Amer. Lung Assn. of Wisconsin **[17665]**, Brookfield, WI
Cystic Fibrosis Found., Greater Michigan Chap. - Eastern Region **[9607]**, Saginaw, MI
Cystic Fibrosis Foundation, Mahoning County Chapter **[13531]**, Canfield, OH

Responsible Landlords; St. Paul Assn. of **[12576]**, St. Paul, MN
Responsible Pet Ownership; Alliance for **[4598]**, Fishers, IN

Restaurant
Miami Valley Restaurant Assn. **[14918]**, Dayton, OH
Wisconsin Restaurant Assn. **[18750]**, Madison, WI

Restoration and Preservation Soc; Ashtabula Lighthouse **[16231]**, North Kingsville, OH

Retail Hardware
Michigan Retail Hardware Assn. **[8706]**, Lansing, MI

Retail, Wholesale and Dept. Store Union District Coun., UFCW, AFL-CIO, CLC Local Union 17 **[3082]**, Peru, IL
Retail, Wholesale and Dept. Store Union District Coun., UFCW, AFL-CIO, CLC Local Union 578 **[3226]**, Rochelle, IL
Retailers Assn; Michigan **[8707]**, Lansing, MI
Retailers; Indiana Assn. of Beverage **[5165]**, Indianapolis, IN

Retailing
Assn. of Indiana Coll. Stores **[6088]**, Richmond, IN
Illinois Assn. of Coll. Stores **[524]**, Champaign, IL
Illinois Retail Merchants Assn. **[963]**, Chicago, IL
Indiana Retail Coun. **[5289]**, Indianapolis, IN
Michigan Assn. of Coll. Stores **[8949]**, Marquette, MI
Michigan Assn. of Convenience Stores **[8611]**, Lansing, MI
Michigan Grocers Assn. **[8670]**, Lansing, MI
Michigan Retailers Assn. **[8707]**, Lansing, MI
Mid-America Equip. Retailers Assn. **[5406]**, Indianapolis, IN
Minnesota Grocers Assn. **[12486]**, St. Paul, MN
Minnesota Retailers Assn. **[12514]**, St. Paul, MN
Minnesota Shopping Center Assn. **[10481]**, Bloomington, MN
Natl. Nutritional Foods Association-Southwest **[8152]**, Haslett, MI
Ohio Assn. of Coll. Stores **[16532]**, Rio Grande, OH
Ohio Coun. of Retail Merchants **[14591]**, Columbus, OH
Ohio Grocers Assn. **[14620]**, Columbus, OH
Ohio Grocers Assn. **[17028]**, Upper Arlington, OH
Retail, Wholesale and Dept. Store Union District Coun., UFCW, AFL-CIO, CLC Local Union 17 **[3082]**, Peru, IL
Retail, Wholesale and Dept. Store Union District Coun., UFCW, AFL-CIO, CLC Local Union 578 **[3226]**, Rochelle, IL
Wisconsin Assn. of Coll. Stores **[19409]**, Oshkosh, WI
Wisconsin Merchants Fed. **[18727]**, Madison, WI
Youngstown Area Grocers Assn. **[17423]**, Youngstown, OH

Retardation, Mental
ARC, Hennepin-Carver **[11520]**, Minneapolis, MN
Arc Kent County **[7907]**, Grand Rapids, MI
Hamilton County Bd. of Mental Retardation and Developmental Disabilities **[13858]**, Cincinnati, OH
Johnson County Assn. for Retarded Citizens **[4750]**, Franklin, IN

Retarded Citizens; Brown County Assn. for **[18088]**, Green Bay, WI
Retarded Citizens, Minnesota Off; Assn. for **[★12383]**
Retarded Citizens of Ohio; Assn. of **[★14316]**
Retarded Citizens; Springfield Assn. for **[3676]**, Springfield, IL
Retired Educators' Assn; Wisconsin **[18916]**, Middleton, WI
Retired Enlisted Assn., 77 **[17892]**, Eau Claire, WI
Retired Enlisted Assn., 90 **[3930]**, Waukegan, IL
Retired Enlisted Assn., 119 **[19874]**, Superior, WI
The Retired Enlisted Assn. Chap. 66 **[17521]**, Appleton, WI
The Retired Enlisted Assn. Chap. 96 **[11162]**, Hibbing, MN
The Retired Enlisted Assn., Chap., 115 **[12296]**, St. Cloud, MN
Retired and Senior Volunteer Prog. of Peoria and Tazewell Counties **[3062]**, Peoria, IL
Retired and Senior Volunteer Prog. of Racine **[19572]**, Racine, WI
Retired and Senior Volunteer Prog. of Rock County **[17616]**, Beloit, WI
Retired and Senior Volunteer Prog. of South Central Minnesota **[11398]**, Mankato, MN
Retired and Senior Volunteer Prog. of Waukesha County **[19998]**, Waukesha, WI

Retirees
Natl. Active And Retired Fed. Employees Assn. - Alton 575 **[366]**, Bunker Hill, IL
Natl. Active And Retired Fed. Employees Assn. - Alvin G Bohley 1019 **[2849]**, O'Fallon, IL
Natl. Active And Retired Fed. Employees Assn. - Blackhawk 338 **[1296]**, Colona, IL
Natl. Active And Retired Fed. Employees Assn. Bloomington-Normal 2177 **[299]**, Bloomington, IL
Natl. Active And Retired Fed. Employees Assn. - Danville 332 **[4422]**, Covington, IN
Natl. Active And Retired Fed. Employees Assn. - Downtown 1878 **[1067]**, Chicago, IL
Natl. Active And Retired Fed. Employees Assn. - Dupage 1771 **[228]**, Bensenville, IL
Natl. Active And Retired Fed. Employees Assn. - East Central 854 **[2974]**, Paxton, IL
Natl. Active And Retired Fed. Employees Assn. - Edwards 399 **[1399]**, Decatur, IL
Natl. Active And Retired Fed. Employees Assn. - Effingham 849 **[3177]**, Ramsey, IL
Natl. Active And Retired Fed. Employees Assn. - Egyptian Gateway 2190 **[489]**, Centralia, IL
Natl. Active And Retired Fed. Employees Assn. - Granite 1067 **[3901]**, Waterloo, IL
Natl. Active And Retired Fed. Employees Assn. - Greater Egypt 1097 **[423]**, Carbondale, IL
Natl. Active And Retired Fed. Employees Assn. - Greater Fox Valley 2181 **[455]**, Carpentersville, IL
Natl. Active And Retired Fed. Employees Assn. - Greater Peoria 268 **[3036]**, Peoria, IL
Natl. Active And Retired Fed. Employees Assn. - Hardscrabble 2202 **[3729]**, Streator, IL
Natl. Active And Retired Fed. Employees Assn. - Illini 348 **[537]**, Champaign, IL
Natl. Active And Retired Fed. Employees Assn. - Jefferson 688 **[2601]**, Mount Vernon, IL
Natl. Active And Retired Fed. Employees Assn. - Joseph F.Gore 6 **[1068]**, Chicago, IL
Natl. Active And Retired Fed. Employees Assn. - Kankakee 1109 **[2141]**, Kankakee, IL
Natl. Active And Retired Fed. Employees Assn. - Lake County 441 **[3929]**, Waukegan, IL
Natl. Active And Retired Fed. Employees Assn. Lawrenceville 1041 **[2226]**, Lawrenceville, IL
Natl. Active And Retired Fed. Employees Assn. - Lincoln Home 402 **[3652]**, Springfield, IL
Natl. Active And Retired Fed. Employees Assn. - Little Egypt 1007 **[16]**, Albion, IL
Natl. Active And Retired Fed. Employees Assn. - Louis Joliet 655 **[3103]**, Plainfield, IL
Natl. Active And Retired Fed. Employees Assn. - Marion Payne 1309 **[2202]**, Lake Forest, IL
Natl. Active And Retired Fed. Employees Assn. - Michael C. Nave 1344 **[1312]**, Crestwood, IL
Natl. Active And Retired Fed. Employees Assn. - North West Chicago Area 852 **[1671]**, Evanston, IL
Natl. Active And Retired Fed. Employees Assn. - Palisades 604 **[3420]**, Savanna, IL
Natl. Active And Retired Fed. Employees Assn. - Prairie 2332 **[3761]**, Thomson, IL
Natl. Active And Retired Fed. Employees Assn. - Rockford 415 **[3289]**, Rockford, IL
Natl. Active And Retired Fed. Employees Assn. - Southwest Chicago Metro 1106 **[342]**, Bridgeview, IL
Natl. Active And Retired Fed. Employees Assn. - West Central Ill. 361 **[3155]**, Quincy, IL
Natl. Active and Retired Fed. Employees Assn. - Albert Lea-Austin 469 **[10260]**, Albert Lea, MN
Natl. Active and Retired Fed. Employees Assn. - Ann Arbor 304 **[9072]**, Monroe, MI
Natl. Active and Retired Fed. Employees Assn. - Arrowhead 106 **[10841]**, Duluth, MN
Natl. Active and Retired Fed. Employees Assn. - Ashtabula 624 **[13183]**, Ashtabula, OH
Natl. Active and Retired Fed. Employees Assn. Auglaize-Mercer 2170 **[17090]**, Wapakoneta, OH

Natl. Active and Retired Fed. Employees Assn. - Battle Creek 123 **[7805]**, Galesburg, MI
Natl. Active and Retired Fed. Employees Assn. - Bay City 165 **[6892]**, Bay City, MI
Natl. Active and Retired Fed. Employees Assn. - Beavercreek 2217 **[13298]**, Beavercreek, OH
Natl. Active and Retired Fed. Employees Assn. - Bedford 578 **[4174]**, Bedford, IN
Natl. Active and Retired Fed. Employees Assn. - Belmont County 2175 **[13263]**, Barnesville, OH
Natl. Active and Retired Fed. Employees Assn. - Belpre 865 **[15824]**, Marietta, OH
Natl. Active and Retired Fed. Employees Assn. - Bemidji 1049 **[10421]**, Bemidji, MN
Natl. Active and Retired Fed. Employees Assn. - Bloomfield 847 **[4193]**, Bloomfield, IN
Natl. Active and Retired Fed. Employees Assn. - Bloomington 580 **[4245]**, Bloomington, IN
Natl. Active and Retired Fed. Employees Assn. - Brainerd 738 **[12704]**, Staples, MN
Natl. Active and Retired Fed. Employees Assn. - Brecksville 2264 **[13412]**, Brecksville, OH
Natl. Active and Retired Fed. Employees Assn. - Bryan 1136 **[13455]**, Bryan, OH
Natl. Active and Retired Fed. Employees Assn. Butler/Warren Counties 569 **[15396]**, Hamilton, OH
Natl. Active and Retired Fed. Employees Assn. - Cadillac Area 1946 **[8123]**, Harrietta, MI
Natl. Active and Retired Fed. Employees Assn. - Campbell County 1760 **[13915]**, Cincinnati, OH
Natl. Active and Retired Fed. Employees Assn. - Charles Hogg 14 **[16229]**, North Jackson, OH
Natl. Active and Retired Fed. Employees Assn. - Chillicothe 315 **[13668]**, Chillicothe, OH
Natl. Active and Retired Fed. Employees Assn. - Cincinnati 265 **[13916]**, Cincinnati, OH
Natl. Active and Retired Fed. Employees Assn. - Cleveland 470 **[16373]**, Parma, OH
Natl. Active and Retired Fed. Employees Assn. - Cleveland East 2232 **[14171]**, Cleveland, OH
Natl. Active and Retired Fed. Employees Assn. - Clinton City 2204 **[17292]**, Wilmington, OH
Natl. Active and Retired Fed. Employees Assn. - Columbus 235 **[16813]**, Sunbury, OH
Natl. Active and Retired Fed. Employees Assn. - Columbus 1052 **[4403]**, Columbus, IN
Natl. Active and Retired Fed. Employees Assn. - Crow River 2019 **[11330]**, Litchfield, MN
Natl. Active and Retired Fed. Employees Assn. - Dayton 35 **[13299]**, Beavercreek, OH
Natl. Active and Retired Fed. Employees Assn. - Dearborn Area 1515 **[9839]**, Southgate, MI
Natl. Active and Retired Fed. Employees Assn. - Detroit 89 **[7404]**, Detroit, MI
Natl. Active and Retired Fed. Employees Assn. - Detroit Lakes 1842 **[10781]**, Detroit Lakes, MN
Natl. Active and Retired Fed. Employees Assn. Door-Kewaunee 1110 **[19838]**, Sturgeon Bay, WI
Natl. Active and Retired Fed. Employees Assn. - Eastside 2197 **[4185]**, Beech Grove, IN
Natl. Active and Retired Fed. Employees Assn. - Eau Claire 371 **[17887]**, Eau Claire, WI
Natl. Active and Retired Fed. Employees Assn. - Elkhart 539 **[4803]**, Goshen, IN
Natl. Active and Retired Fed. Employees Assn. - Escanaba 1389 **[7616]**, Escanaba, MI
Natl. Active and Retired Fed. Employees Assn. - Evansville 326 **[4561]**, Evansville, IN
Natl. Active and Retired Fed. Employees Assn. - Fairborn 610 **[15152]**, Fairborn, OH
Natl. Active and Retired Fed. Employees Assn. - Firelands 382 **[16261]**, Norwalk, OH
Natl. Active and Retired Fed. Employees Assn. - Flint 285 **[7688]**, Fenton, MI
Natl. Active and Retired Fed. Employees Assn. - Fond du Lac 708 **[17987]**, Fond du Lac, WI
Natl. Active and Retired Fed. Employees Assn. - Fort Steuben 2191 **[16764]**, Steubenville, OH
Natl. Active and Retired Fed. Employees Assn. - Fort Wayne 223 **[4696]**, Fort Wayne, IN
Natl. Active and Retired Fed. Employees Assn. - Fox Valley 437 **[18862]**, Menasha, WI
Natl. Active and Retired Fed. Employees Assn. - Frankfort 1989 **[4744]**, Frankfort, IN
Natl. Active and Retired Fed. Employees Assn. - Ft Defiance 1862 **[14990]**, Defiance, OH
Natl. Active and Retired Fed. Employees Assn. - Fulton-Henry County 1856 **[13154]**, Archbold, OH
Natl. Active and Retired Fed. Employees Assn. - Grand Rapids 234 **[7988]**, Grand Rapids, MI
Natl. Active and Retired Fed. Employees Assn. - Grand Traverse Bay Area 1215 **[8922]**, Maple City, MI
Natl. Active and Retired Fed. Employees Assn. - Grayling 2305 **[7820]**, Gaylord, MI
Natl. Active and Retired Fed. Employees Assn. - Greater Milwaukee 94 **[19070]**, Milwaukee, WI
Natl. Active and Retired Fed. Employees Assn. - Green Bay 403 **[19681]**, Shawano, WI
Natl. Active and Retired Fed. Employees Assn. - Greencastle 1024 **[4822]**, Greencastle, IN
Natl. Active and Retired Fed. Employees Assn. - Greenville 2227 **[9855]**, Stanton, MI
Natl. Active and Retired Fed. Employees Assn. Guernsey-Noble 2189 **[15567]**, Kimbolton, OH
Natl. Active and Retired Fed. Employees Assn. - Hammond 546 **[5776]**, Merrillville, IN
Natl. Active and Retired Fed. Employees Assn. - Hancock County 2278 **[15209]**, Findlay, OH
Natl. Active and Retired Fed. Employees Assn. - Herbert L. Gabel 565 **[6435]**, Walkerton, IN
Natl. Active and Retired Fed. Employees Assn. - Highland County 2230 **[17297]**, Winchester, OH
Natl. Active and Retired Fed. Employees Assn. - Holland 1243 **[10229]**, Zeeland, MI
Natl. Active and Retired Fed. Employees Assn. - Huber Heights 2238 **[15477]**, Huber Heights, OH
Natl. Active and Retired Fed. Employees Assn. - Indianapolis 151 **[5411]**, Indianapolis, IN
Natl. Active and Retired Fed. Employees Assn. - Indianhead 1581 **[17563]**, Balsam Lake, WI
Natl. Active and Retired Fed. Employees Assn. Intl. Falls 1582 **[12067]**, Ray, MN
Natl. Active and Retired Fed. Employees Assn. - Jackson 25 **[8389]**, Jackson, MI
Natl. Active and Retired Fed. Employees Assn. - Jackson County 944 **[6184]**, Seymour, IN
Natl. Active and Retired Fed. Employees Assn. - Janesville 44 **[3350]**, Roscoe, IL
Natl. Active and Retired Fed. Employees Assn. - Jefferson County 1677 **[5676]**, Lexington, IN
Natl. Active and Retired Fed. Employees Assn. Jeffersonville 381 **[4367]**, Clarksville, IN
Natl. Active and Retired Fed. Employees Assn. - John Folk 317 **[15097]**, Elida, OH
Natl. Active and Retired Fed. Employees Assn. - Johnny Appleseed 612 **[15779]**, Mansfield, OH
Natl. Active and Retired Fed. Employees Assn. - Johnson County 1612 **[4753]**, Franklin, IN
Natl. Active and Retired Fed. Employees Assn. - Kenosha 1436 **[18304]**, Kenosha, WI
Natl. Active and Retired Fed. Employees Assn. - Ket-Cent-Oak 1927 **[15562]**, Kettering, OH
Natl. Active and Retired Fed. Employees Assn. - Kokomo 562 **[5548]**, Kempton, IN
Natl. Active and Retired Fed. Employees Assn. - La Crosse 370 **[19826]**, Stoddard, WI
Natl. Active and Retired Fed. Employees Assn. - Lafayette 330 **[5626]**, Lafayette, IN
Natl. Active and Retired Fed. Employees Assn. - Lake County2182 **[17275]**, Willoughby, OH
Natl. Active and Retired Fed. Employees Assn. - Lake Region 1207 **[11000]**, Fergus Falls, MN
Natl. Active and Retired Fed. Employees Assn. - Lake Superior 1254 **[8259]**, Houghton, MI
Natl. Active and Retired Fed. Employees Assn. - Lansing Area 289 **[7556]**, East Lansing, MI
Natl. Active and Retired Fed. Employees Assn. - Lenawee 1953 **[6580]**, Adrian, MI
Natl. Active and Retired Fed. Employees Assn. - Licking County 310 **[16174]**, Newark, OH
Natl. Active and Retired Fed. Employees Assn. - Linton 1688 **[5685]**, Linton, IN
Natl. Active and Retired Fed. Employees Assn. - Little Traverse Bay Area 1483 **[8309]**, Indian River, MI
Natl. Active and Retired Fed. Employees Assn. - Livonia Area 1163 **[9259]**, Oak Park, MI
Natl. Active and Retired Fed. Employees Assn. - Lock City 477 **[9722]**, Sault Ste. Marie, MI
Natl. Active and Retired Fed. Employees Assn. - Logan County 2162 **[13322]**, Bellefontaine, OH
Natl. Active and Retired Fed. Employees Assn. - Logansport 1046 **[5695]**, Logansport, IN
Natl. Active and Retired Fed. Employees Assn. - Lorain Cnty 1592 **[15123]**, Elyria, OH
Natl. Active and Retired Fed. Employees Assn. - Macomb 1474 **[8131]**, Harrison Township, MI
Natl. Active and Retired Fed. Employees Assn. - Madison 120 **[18911]**, Middleton, WI
Natl. Active and Retired Fed. Employees Assn. - Madison County 36 **[4113]**, Anderson, IN
Natl. Active and Retired Fed. Employees Assn. - Manitowoc 710 **[18787]**, Manitowoc, WI
Natl. Active and Retired Fed. Employees Assn. - Mankato 282 **[10879]**, Eagle Lake, MN
Natl. Active and Retired Fed. Employees Assn. - Manley 1705 **[6809]**, Auburn, MI
Natl. Active and Retired Fed. Employees Assn. - Marion 503 **[4788]**, Gas City, IN
Natl. Active and Retired Fed. Employees Assn. - Marshall 1580 **[12096]**, Redwood Falls, MN
Natl. Active and Retired Fed. Employees Assn. - Mckinley 341 **[13572]**, Canton, OH
Natl. Active and Retired Fed. Employees Assn. - Menominee 2246 **[9002]**, Menominee, MI
Natl. Active and Retired Fed. Employees Assn. Michigan-Wisconsin Border 1673 **[8493]**, Kingsford, MI
Natl. Active and Retired Fed. Employees Assn. - Mid-Michigan 2103 **[10108]**, Weidman, MI
Natl. Active and Retired Fed. Employees Assn. - Minneapolis 150 **[12112]**, Richfield, MN
Natl. Active and Retired Fed. Employees Assn. - Monroe County 2193 **[15529]**, Jerusalem, OH
Natl. Active and Retired Fed. Employees Assn. - Muncie 125 **[5891]**, Muncie, IN
Natl. Active and Retired Fed. Employees Assn. - Muskegon 309 **[9156]**, Muskegon, MI
Natl. Active and Retired Fed. Employees Assn. - Muskegon River 1921 **[8164]**, Hersey, MI
Natl. Active and Retired Fed. Employees Assn. - Neillsville 933 **[20201]**, Withee, WI
Natl. Active and Retired Fed. Employees Assn. - New Albany 1777 **[5919]**, New Albany, IN
Natl. Active and Retired Fed. Employees Assn. - New Ulm 1444 **[11044]**, Gibbon, MN
Natl. Active and Retired Fed. Employees Assn. - North Central U.P. 1900 **[8952]**, Marquette, MI
Natl. Active and Retired Fed. Employees Assn. - North West Suburbia-Twin Cities 2243 **[10744]**, Crystal, MN
Natl. Active and Retired Fed. Employees Assn. Oconomowoc-Watertown 1112 **[18042]**, Germantown, WI
Natl. Active and Retired Fed. Employees Assn. - Oscoda 1955 **[9316]**, Oscoda, MI
Natl. Active and Retired Fed. Employees Assn. Oshkosh-Winnebagoland 416 **[19395]**, Oshkosh, WI
Natl. Active and Retired Fed. Employees Assn. - Owatonna 1975 **[11961]**, Owatonna, MN
Natl. Active and Retired Fed. Employees Assn. - Patoka Valley 1847 **[6160]**, Santa Claus, IN
Natl. Active and Retired Fed. Employees Assn. - Pine 1746 **[12625]**, Sandstone, MN
Natl. Active and Retired Fed. Employees Assn. - Plainfield 2141 **[5672]**, Lebanon, IN
Natl. Active and Retired Fed. Employees Assn. - Pokegama 1800 **[12736]**, Swatara, MN
Natl. Active and Retired Fed. Employees Assn. - Port Huron 12 **[7773]**, Fort Gratiot, MI
Natl. Active and Retired Fed. Employees Assn. - Portage Path 168 **[13068]**, Akron, OH
Natl. Active and Retired Fed. Employees Assn. - Portsmouth 2121 **[16470]**, Portsmouth, OH
Natl. Active and Retired Fed. Employees Assn. - Queen City 1963 **[12801]**, Virginia, MN
Natl. Active and Retired Fed. Employees Assn. - Racine 346 **[19560]**, Racine, WI
Natl. Active and Retired Fed. Employees Assn. - Red Wing 1661 **[10633]**, Cannon Falls, MN
Natl. Active and Retired Fed. Employees Assn. - Region IV **[16793]**, Strongsville, OH
Natl. Active and Retired Fed. Employees Assn. - Richmond 536 **[6098]**, Richmond, IN
Natl. Active and Retired Fed. Employees Assn. - Rochester 391 **[13002]**, Zumbro Falls, MN
Natl. Active and Retired Fed. Employees Assn. - Rochester 2179 **[10037]**, Utica, MI

Natl. Active and Retired Fed. Employees Assn. - Rockville 1660 **[6134]**, Rockville, IN
Natl. Active and Retired Fed. Employees Assn. - Royal Oak 1532 **[9586]**, Royal Oak, MI
Natl. Active and Retired Fed. Employees Assn. - Saginaw 376 **[9619]**, Saginaw, MI
Natl. Active and Retired Fed. Employees Assn. - St. Cloud 644 **[12630]**, Sartell, MN
Natl. Active and Retired Fed. Employees Assn. - St. Paul 140 **[12541]**, St. Paul, MN
Natl. Active and Retired Fed. Employees Assn. - Shelbyville 813 **[6144]**, Rushville, IN
Natl. Active and Retired Fed. Employees Assn. - South Bend-Mishawaka 145 **[6246]**, South Bend, IN
Natl. Active and Retired Fed. Employees Assn. - South West Michigan 572 **[9686]**, St. Joseph, MI
Natl. Active and Retired Fed. Employees Assn. - Southwest Michigan 173 **[8454]**, Kalamazoo, MI
Natl. Active and Retired Fed. Employees Assn. Springfield-Clark 187 **[16734]**, Springfield, OH
Natl. Active and Retired Fed. Employees Assn. - Superior 2119 **[19873]**, Superior, WI
Natl. Active and Retired Fed. Employees Assn. - Tarcom 1593 **[7405]**, Detroit, MI
Natl. Active and Retired Fed. Employees Assn. - Terre Haute 327 **[6337]**, Terre Haute, IN
Natl. Active and Retired Fed. Employees Assn. - Thief River Falls 2328 **[12745]**, Thief River Falls, MN
Natl. Active and Retired Fed. Employees Assn. - Three Rivers 1521 **[7101]**, Cassopolis, MI
Natl. Active and Retired Fed. Employees Assn. - Thunder Bay 1487 **[6645]**, Alpena, MI
Natl. Active and Retired Fed. Employees Assn. - Tiffin 504 **[16855]**, Tiffin, OH
Natl. Active and Retired Fed. Employees Assn. - Toledo 226 **[16933]**, Toledo, OH
Natl. Active and Retired Fed. Employees Assn. - Tri-County 1386 **[17633]**, Black River Falls, WI
Natl. Active and Retired Fed. Employees Assn. - Tuscarawas Valley 635 **[15028]**, Dover, OH
Natl. Active and Retired Fed. Employees Assn. - Upper Miami Valley 325 **[16665]**, Sidney, OH
Natl. Active and Retired Fed. Employees Assn. - Vacationland 1030 **[16272]**, Oak Harbor, OH
Natl. Active and Retired Fed. Employees Assn. - Van Wert-Paulding 630 **[16390]**, Payne, OH
Natl. Active and Retired Fed. Employees Assn. - Vermilion 1725 **[10956]**, Ely, MN
Natl. Active and Retired Fed. Employees Assn. - Vikingland 2213 **[10283]**, Alexandria, MN
Natl. Active and Retired Fed. Employees Assn. - Warren G Harding 329 **[13489]**, Caledonia, OH
Natl. Active and Retired Fed. Employees Assn. Washington/Vincennes 527 **[6418]**, Vincennes, IN
Natl. Active and Retired Fed. Employees Assn. - Waukesha 490 **[19992]**, Waukesha, WI
Natl. Active and Retired Fed. Employees Assn. - Wausau 689 **[17628]**, Birnamwood, WI
Natl. Active and Retired Fed. Employees Assn. - Wayne County 2218 **[14831]**, Dalton, OH
Natl. Active and Retired Fed. Employees Assn. - White Bear Lake 1232 **[12542]**, St. Paul, MN
Natl. Active and Retired Fed. Employees Assn. - Willmar 2280 **[12924]**, Willmar, MN
Natl. Active and Retired Fed. Employees Assn. - Wood County 1942 **[13394]**, Bowling Green, OH
Natl. Active and Retired Fed. Employees Assn. - Wright 1840 **[16121]**, New Carlisle, OH
Natl. Active and Retired Fed. Employees Assn. - Xenia 2163 **[17375]**, Xenia, OH
Natl. Active and Retired Fed. Employees Assn. - Yarb 2122 **[13536]**, Canfield, OH
Natl. Active and Retired Fed. Employees Assn. - Zanesville 648 **[15933]**, McConnelsville, OH
Retirement
AARP Illinois **[592]**, Chicago, IL
AARP Michigan **[8526]**, Lansing, MI
AARP Minnesota **[12343]**, St. Paul, MN
AARP, Ohio **[14266]**, Columbus, OH
Amer. Assn. of Retired Persons, Chicago **[611]**, Chicago, IL
American Association of Retired Persons, Indiana **[4975]**, Indianapolis, IN
Amer. Assn. of Retired Persons, Michigan **[8529]**, Lansing, MI
Amer. Assn. of Retired Persons, Wisconsin **[18452]**, Madison, WI
Gray Panthers of Huron Valley **[6698]**, Ann Arbor, MI
Indiana Retired Teachers Assn. **[5290]**, Indianapolis, IN
Revitalization Association; Frazeysburg **[15239]**, Frazeysburg, OH
Revitalize Gillett **[18048]**, Gillett, WI
Revolution, Sarah Winston Henry Chap; Daughters of the Amer. **[5934]**, New Castle, IN
Reye's Syndrome
Natl. Reye's Syndrome Found. - Support Gp. **[13456]**, Bryan, OH
Reynoldsburg Area Chamber of Commerce **[16519]**, Reynoldsburg, OH
Reynoldsburg Lions Club **[15416]**, Hebron, OH
Rheumatic Diseases
Arthritis Found., Adams County Br. **[3149]**, Quincy, IL
Arthritis Found., Central Ohio Chap. **[15426]**, Hilliard, OH
Arthritis Found., Champaign County Br. **[3806]**, Urbana, IL
Arthritis Found., Dayton Br. **[15558]**, Kettering, OH
Arthritis Found., Greater Chicago Chap. **[735]**, Chicago, IL
Arthritis Found., Greater Illinois Chap. **[3005]**, Peoria, IL
Arthritis Found., Illinois Valley Br. **[3077]**, Peru, IL
Arthritis Found., Indiana Chap. **[5036]**, Indianapolis, IN
Arthritis Found., Kankakee County Br. **[2131]**, Kankakee, IL
Arthritis Found., Livingston County Br. **[3119]**, Pontiac, IL
Arthritis Found., Macon County Br. **[1376]**, Decatur, IL
Arthritis Found., McLean County Br. **[2709]**, Normal, IL
Arthritis Found., Michigan Chap. **[9974]**, Troy, MI
Arthritis Foundation, Milwaukee **[18965]**, Milwaukee, WI
Arthritis Found., North Central Chap. **[12384]**, St. Paul, MN
Arthritis Found., Northeast Indiana Br. **[4640]**, Fort Wayne, IN
Arthritis Found., Northeastern District Off. **[18082]**, Green Bay, WI
Arthritis Found. Northeastern Ohio Chap. **[14073]**, Cleveland, OH
Arthritis Found., Northern Indiana Br. **[6220]**, South Bend, IN
Arthritis Found., Northwestern Ohio **[16902]**, Toledo, OH
Arthritis Found., Ohio River Valley Chap. **[13746]**, Cincinnati, OH
Arthritis Found., Sangamon County Br. **[3532]**, Springfield, IL
Arthritis Found., Scioto Valley Br. **[16469]**, Portsmouth, OH
Arthritis Found., Southern Illinois Br. **[2402]**, Marion, IL
Arthritis Found., Southern Indiana Br. **[4530]**, Evansville, IN
Arthritis Found., Tri-County Br. **[3006]**, Peoria, IL
Arthritis Found., Winnebago County Br. **[3273]**, Rockford, IL
Arthritis Found., Wisconsin Chap. **[20099]**, West Allis, WI
Rhinelander Area Chamber of Commerce **[19604]**, Rhinelander, WI
Rhinelander Figure Skating Club **[19605]**, Rhinelander, WI
Rhinelander Northwoods Quilters **[19606]**, Rhinelander, WI
Rice Creek Hunting Dog Club **[11338]**, Little Falls, MN
Rice Lake Area Chamber of Commerce **[19616]**, Rice Lake, WI
Rice Lake Main St. Assn. **[19617]**, Rice Lake, WI
Rich Rattlers Wrestling Club **[2439]**, Matteson, IL
Richfield Chamber of Commerce **[12113]**, Richfield, MN
Richfield - Young Life **[11192]**, Hopkins, MN
Richland Area Chamber of Commerce **[★19625]**
Richland Area Chamber of Commerce/Main St. Partnership **[19625]**, Richland Center, WI
Richland Center Lions Club **[19626]**, Richland Center, WI
Richland County Chap. - Ohio Genealogical Soc. **[★15790]**
Richland County Genealogical Soc. **[15790]**, Mansfield, OH
Richland County Habitat for Humanity **[15791]**, Mansfield, OH
Richland County Illinois Beagle Club **[2705]**, Noble, IL
Richland County Regional Planning Commn. **[15792]**, Mansfield, OH
Richland Lithic and Lapidary Soc. **[13467]**, Bucyrus, OH
Richmond Area AIFA **[6104]**, Richmond, IN
Richmond Area Chamber of Commerce **[9489]**, Richmond, MI
Richmond Assn. of Realtors, Indiana **[6105]**, Richmond, IN
Richmond/Spring Grove Area Chamber of Commerce **[3192]**, Richmond, IL
Richmond-Wayne County Chamber of Commerce **[6106]**, Richmond, IN
Richmond - Young Life **[6107]**, Richmond, IN
Richwoods - Central Illinois - Young Life **[3890]**, Washington, IL
Riders Assn; Michigan Trail **[9877]**, Stockbridge, MI
Riders United; Trans. **[7443]**, Detroit, MI
Ridgedale Lions Club **[15854]**, Marion, OH
Ridgewalkers Walking Club **[552]**, Champaign, IL
Ridgeway Township Firefighters Assn. **[7026]**, Britton, MI
Rifle and Pistol Club; Ripon **[19637]**, Ripon, WI
Rifle Squad, Minnesota State Veterans Cemetery; Memorial **[11167]**, Hillman, MN
Rifles
Ohio Rifle and Pistol Assn. **[13942]**, Cincinnati, OH
Right to Life
Birthright of Rensselaer **[6077]**, Rensselaer, IN
Illinois Right to Life Comm. **[964]**, Chicago, IL
Indiana Right to Life **[5291]**, Indianapolis, IN
Lake County Right to Life **[4916]**, Highland, IN
Minnesota Citizens Concerned for Life **[11640]**, Minneapolis, MN
Ohio Right to Life Soc. **[14668]**, Columbus, OH
Right to Life of Indianapolis **[5467]**, Indianapolis, IN
Right to Life - Lifespan **[8856]**, Livonia, MI
Right to Life of Michigan **[8005]**, Grand Rapids, MI
Wisconsin Right to Life **[19179]**, Milwaukee, WI
Right to Life Comm; Illinois **[964]**, Chicago, IL
Right to Life of Indianapolis **[5467]**, Indianapolis, IN
Right to Life - Lifespan **[8856]**, Livonia, MI
Right to Life-Lifespan - Oakland Chap. **[10007]**, Troy, MI
Right to Life of Michigan **[8005]**, Grand Rapids, MI
Right To Life; Greene County **[17371]**, Xenia, OH
Right-to-Life Lifespan of Metro Detroit **[★8856]**
Rights Commn. of Olmsted County; Human **[12147]**, Rochester, MN
Riley St. MS - Wyldlife **[6628]**, Allendale, MI
Riley Township Lions Club **[6117]**, Riley, IN
Riley - Young Life **[6257]**, South Bend, IN
Ring Around the Arts **[10323]**, Apple Valley, MN
Ripley County Chamber of Commerce **[6403]**, Versailles, IN
Ripley County, Indiana Historical Soc. **[6404]**, Versailles, IN
Ripon Area Chamber of Commerce **[19636]**, Ripon, WI
Ripon Jr. High - Wyldlife **[18810]**, Markesan, WI
Ripon Rifle and Pistol Club **[19637]**, Ripon, WI
Ripon Sr. High - Young Life **[18811]**, Markesan, WI
Ripon United Way **[19638]**, Ripon, WI
Risk and Insurance Mgt. Soc., Central Ohio Chap. **[14722]**, Columbus, OH
Risk and Insurance Mgt. Soc., Chicago Chap. **[2204]**, Lake Forest, IL
Risk and Insurance Mgt. Soc., Detroit Chap. **[10008]**, Troy, MI

Risk and Insurance Mgt. Soc., Indiana Chap. **[6342]**, Terre Haute, IN
Risk and Insurance Mgt. Soc., Minnesota Chap. **[11732]**, Minneapolis, MN
Risk and Insurance Mgt. Soc., Northeast Ohio Chap. **[14211]**, Cleveland, OH
Risk and Insurance Mgt. Soc., Ohio River Valley Chap. **[13976]**, Cincinnati, OH
Risk and Insurance Mgt. Soc., Wisconsin Chap. **[19110]**, Milwaukee, WI
Risk Managers Intl. Assn; Professional **[11727]**, Minneapolis, MN
Rittman Area Chamber of Commerce **[16539]**, Rittman, OH
Rivendell Theatre Ensemble **[1166]**, Chicago, IL
River Bend Astronomy Club **[3399]**, St. Jacob, IL
River Bend Growth Assn. **[★1874]**
River Cities African Violet Club **[20191]**, Wisconsin Rapids, WI
River Cities Habitat for Humanity, Wisconsin **[18803]**, Marinette, WI
River Cities Regional Chamber of Commerce **[9004]**, Menominee, MI
River City Ramblers **[4569]**, Evansville, IN
River Conservation Comm; Upper Mississippi **[3260]**, Rock Island, IL
River Country Rsrc. Conservation and Development Coun. **[17469]**, Altoona, WI
River Country Tourism Bur. **[9880]**, Sturgis, MI
River Dojo **[13977]**, Cincinnati, OH
River Falls Area Chamber of Commerce **[★19644]**
River Falls Area Chamber of Commerce and Tourism Bur. **[19644]**, River Falls, WI
River; Friends of the Fox **[1324]**, Crystal Lake, IL
River Heights Chamber of Commerce **[11227]**, Inver Grove Heights, MN
River North Assn. **[1167]**, Chicago, IL
River Valley Lions Club **[13490]**, Caledonia, OH
River Valley Youth for Christ **[19767]**, Spring Green, WI
Riverbend Benders Snowmobile Club **[475]**, Cary, IL
Riverbend Skating Club **[1566]**, Edwardsville, IL
RiverBend Soc. for Human Rsrc. Mgt. **[16534]**, Rio Grande, OH
Riverbend Striders Volksmarch Club **[11908]**, North Mankato, MN
Rivercity High Soc. **[4570]**, Evansville, IN
Riverdale Chamber of Commerce **[3211]**, Riverdale, IL
Rivers Coun. of Minnesota **[12636]**, Sauk Rapids, MN
Riverside Chamber of Commerce **[3214]**, Riverside, IL
Riverside Chorus of Sweet Adelines Intl. **[3948]**, West Dundee, IL
Riverside Skeet Club **[20178]**, Wisconsin Dells, WI
Riverside Township Chamber of Commerce **[★3214]**
Riverview Lions Club **[8815]**, Lincoln Park, MI
Road Runners Club of Am. - Calumet Region Striders **[4859]**, Griffith, IN
Road Runners Club of Am. - Island Road Runners **[8078]**, Grosse Ile, MI
Road and Trans. Builders Assn; Illinois **[2067]**, Itasca, IL
Robbinsdale Chamber of Commerce **[12120]**, Robbinsdale, MN
Robbinsdale Lions Club **[10745]**, Crystal, MN
Roberts Lions Club **[19648]**, Roberts, WI
Robot Club of Traverse City, Michigan **[9949]**, Traverse City, MI
Robotics
  Assn. for Unmanned Vehicle Syss. Intl., Wright Kettering Chap. **[17356]**, Wright-Patterson AFB, OH
  Robot Club of Traverse City, Michigan **[9949]**, Traverse City, MI
Rochelle Area Chamber of Commerce **[3227]**, Rochelle, IL
Rochester Area Chamber of Commerce **[12171]**, Rochester, MN
Rochester Area Disabled Athletics and Recreation **[12172]**, Rochester, MN
Rochester Area Realtors Assn. **[★12191]**
Rochester Astronomy Club **[12173]**, Rochester, MN
Rochester Boychoir **[12174]**, Rochester, MN
Rochester Chamber of Commerce **[★6125]**
Rochester Coin and Stamp Club **[12175]**, Rochester, MN
Rochester Convention and Visitors Bur. **[12176]**, Rochester, MN
Rochester Dog Obedience Club **[12177]**, Rochester, MN
Rochester High School PTSA **[9518]**, Rochester Hills, MI
Rochester Host Lions Club **[12178]**, Rochester, MN
Rochester Human Rsrcs. Assn. **[12179]**, Rochester, MN
Rochester Junior Woman's Club **[9510]**, Rochester, MI
Rochester and Lake Manitou Chamber of Commerce **[6125]**, Rochester, IN
Rochester Minnesota Kennel Club **[12180]**, Rochester, MN
Rochester Police Athletic Activities League **[12181]**, Rochester, MN
Rochester Table Tennis Club **[12182]**, Rochester, MN
Rock County Historical Soc. **[18260]**, Janesville, WI
Rock Cut Trail Crew **[3301]**, Rockford, IL
Rock Falls Chamber of Commerce **[3236]**, Rock Falls, IL
Rock Green Realtors Assn. **[18261]**, Janesville, WI
Rock Island County Arc **[3256]**, Rock Island, IL
Rock Island County Chap. of Pheasants Forever **[3257]**, Rock Island, IL
Rock Island County Medical Soc. **[1366]**, Davenport, IL
Rock Island District Dental Soc. **[2532]**, Moline, IL
Rock Island Greater Lions Club **[12]**, Albany, IL
Rock River AIFA **[19969]**, Watertown, WI
Rock River Human Rsrcs. Professional Assn. **[1483]**, Dixon, IL
Rock River Speleological Soc. **[17948]**, Evansville, WI
Rock River Valley Pheasants Forever **[18262]**, Janesville, WI
Rock Valley Coll. Students In Free Enterprise **[3302]**, Rockford, IL
Rock Valley Innovators and Entrepreneurs Gp. **[20161]**, Whitewater, WI
Rock Valley Youth for Christ **[17617]**, Beloit, WI
Rocketry Club; Jackson Model **[8381]**, Jackson, MI
Rockford AIFA **[3303]**, Rockford, IL
Rockford Aikikai **[3304]**, Rockford, IL
Rockford Area Assn. of Realtors **[3305]**, Rockford, IL
Rockford Area Chamber of Commerce **[★3309]**
Rockford Area Chamber of Commerce **[9528]**, Rockford, MI
Rockford Area Chamber of Commerce Bus. Women's Coun. **[★3310]**
Rockford Area Chap. of the Amer. Payroll Assn. **[3306]**, Rockford, IL
Rockford Area Coin Club **[587]**, Cherry Valley, IL
Rockford Area Convention and Visitors Bur. **[3307]**, Rockford, IL
Rockford Area Habitat for Humanity **[2353]**, Loves Park, IL
Rockford Area Libertarians **[3308]**, Rockford, IL
Rockford Area Soc. for Human Rsrc. Mgt. **[2354]**, Loves Park, IL
Rockford "Noon" Lions Club **[2355]**, Loves Park, IL
Rockford Regional Chamber of Commerce **[3309]**, Rockford, IL
Rockford Regional Chamber of Commerce Bus. Women's Coun. **[3310]**, Rockford, IL
Rockford Sail and Power Squadron **[3311]**, Rockford, IL
Rockford Skeet Club **[3312]**, Rockford, IL
Rockford Sportsman's Club **[9529]**, Rockford, MI
Rockford Table Tennis Club **[3313]**, Rockford, IL
Rockford - Wyldlife **[3314]**, Rockford, IL
Rockfordland Youth for Christ **[3315]**, Rockford, IL
Rockport Chamber of Commerce **[★6129]**
Rockton Chamber of Commerce **[3336]**, Rockton, IL
Rockville Lions Club **[12202]**, Rockville, MN
Rockwood Lions Club **[7706]**, Flat Rock, MI
Rocky River Chamber of Commerce **[16548]**, Rocky River, OH
Rocky River High School - Young Life **[17236]**, Westlake, OH
Rocky River Power Squadron **[13277]**, Bay Village, OH
Rod and Gun Club; Charlevoix **[7116]**, Charlevoix, MI
Rod Warriors Cruisin' Club **[13524]**, Canal Winchester, OH
Rodeo
  Illinois Gay Rodeo Association **[942]**, Chicago, IL
  Miss Rodeo Wisconsin Pageant Assn. **[19729]**, Shiocton, WI
  North Star Gay Rodeo Assn. **[12555]**, St. Paul, MN
Rodeo Assn; North Star Gay **[12555]**, St. Paul, MN
Rodeo Cowboys Association; Wisconsin **[19907]**, Tomah, WI
Rodeo Wisconsin Pageant Assn; Miss **[19729]**, Shiocton, WI
Rogers Area Chamber of Commerce **[★12203]**
Rogers Area Lions Club - Minnesota **[12204]**, Rogers, MN
Rogers Area Youth Basketball Assn. **[12205]**, Rogers, MN
Rogers City Chamber of Commerce **[9543]**, Rogers City, MI
Rogers-Dayton Chamber of Commerce **[★12203]**
Rogers Park Community Action Network **[1168]**, Chicago, IL
Rogers Park Cricket Club **[164]**, Bartlett, IL
Rogers Park/West Ridge Historical Soc. **[1169]**, Chicago, IL
Rolling Meadows Chamber of Commerce **[3344]**, Rolling Meadows, IL
Rolling Prairie Corvette Club **[1406]**, Decatur, IL
Rolling Readers of Duluth **[10851]**, Duluth, MN
Rolling Readers USA Mid-Michigan Chap. **[8499]**, Laingsburg, MI
Rollingstone Area Jaycees **[12206]**, Rollingstone, MN
Romance Writers of Am., Windy City Chap. **[2303]**, Lisle, IL
Romeo-Washington Chamber of Commerce **[9546]**, Romeo, MI
Romeoville Chamber of Commerce **[3347]**, Romeoville, IL
Roofing Contractors Assn; Michigan **[10071]**, Warren, MI
Roofing Distributors Assn; Chicago **[828]**, Chicago, IL
Roofing Indus. Promotion Fund **[★10071]**
Roosevelt - Wyldlife **[16741]**, Springfield, OH
Rootstown Area Chamber of Commerce **[16551]**, Rootstown, OH
Rootstown Lions Club **[16552]**, Rootstown, OH
Rootstown Soccer Club **[16553]**, Rootstown, OH
Roscoe Village Found. **[14804]**, Coshocton, OH
Roscommon County United Way **[9557]**, Roscommon, MI
Roseau County Historical Soc. **[12209]**, Roseau, MN
Roseau Lions Club **[12210]**, Roseau, MN
Roseland Bus. Development Coun. **[1170]**, Chicago, IL
Roselle Chamber of Commerce and Indus. **[3355]**, Roselle, IL
Roselle Historical Found. **[3356]**, Roselle, IL
Roselle Historical Soc. **[★3356]**
Roselle Lions Club **[3357]**, Roselle, IL
Rosendale Historical Society **[19649]**, Rosendale, WI
Rosenwald Harlanites **[8789]**, Lathrup Village, MI
Roseville Figure Skating Club **[12246]**, Roseville, MN
Roseville - Young Life **[12247]**, Roseville, MN
Ross Co. Radio Pat. Svr REACT **[13672]**, Chillicothe, OH
Ross County Genealogical Society **[13673]**, Chillicothe, OH
Ross Lions Club **[15400]**, Hamilton, OH
Ross - Young Life **[15168]**, Fairfield, OH
Rossford HS - Young Life **[15917]**, Maumee, OH
Rotaract Club of Flint, Michigan **[7755]**, Flint, MI
Rotary Club of Cardington, Ohio **[13597]**, Cardington, OH
Rotary Club of Cincinnati **[13978]**, Cincinnati, OH
Rotary Club of Darien, Illinois **[1365]**, Darien, IL
Rotary Club Found; Toledo **[16976]**, Toledo, OH
Rotary Club of Indianapolis **[5468]**, Indianapolis, IN
Rotary Club of Madison **[18608]**, Madison, WI
Rotary Intl. **[1673]**, Evanston, IL
Rough Rangers Off Road club **[16255]**, Northfield, OH
Round Lake Area Chamber of Commerce and Indus. **[3365]**, Round Lake Beach, IL
Route 66 Assn. of Illinois **[3669]**, Springfield, IL

Rowing
Camp Randall Rowing Club **[18494]**, Madison, WI
Detroit Women's Rowing Assn. **[8080]**, Grosse Pointe, MI
Rowing Assn; Detroit Women's **[8080]**, Grosse Pointe, MI
Rowing Club; Camp Randall **[18494]**, Madison, WI
Rowsburg Lions Club **[13173]**, Ashland, OH
Royal Oak Coin Club **[9591]**, Royal Oak, MI
Royalton Hills Lions Club **[16249]**, North Royalton, OH
RSVP Akron **[13085]**, Akron, OH
RSVP of Ashtabula County **[15547]**, Kent, OH
RSVP-Athens/Hockings County **[13217]**, Athens, OH
RSVP of Bay County **[6894]**, Bay City, MI
RSVP of Belmont County **[16573]**, St. Clairsville, OH
RSVP of Brown County **[18129]**, Green Bay, WI
RSVP Champaign, Douglas, Piatt Counties **[553]**, Champaign, IL
RSVP of Clark County, Ohio **[16742]**, Springfield, OH
RSVP Clay/Effingham/Moultrie/Shelby **[1573]**, Effingham, IL
RSVP Cleveland **[14212]**, Cleveland, OH
RSVP of Columbiana County **[15681]**, Lisbon, OH
RSVP of Crawford and Roscommon Counties **[6650]**, Alpena, MI
RSVP of Dane County **[18609]**, Madison, WI
RSVP of Daviess County Indiana **[6460]**, Washington, IN
RSVP of Dekalb/Noble/Steuben Counties **[4143]**, Auburn, IN
RSVP of Delaware County **[5897]**, Muncie, IN
RSVP Franklin County **[14723]**, Columbus, OH
RSVP of Fulton County **[6126]**, Rochester, IN
RSVP of Genesee and Shiawassee Counties **[7756]**, Flint, MI
RSVP of Hancock, Henry, and Rush **[5940]**, New Castle, IN
RSVP of Hull House Chicago **[1171]**, Chicago, IL
RSVP-Ingham/Eaton/Clinton County **[8756]**, Lansing, MI
RSVP of Iron and Dickinson Counties **[8324]**, Iron Mountain, MI
RSVP of Jackson County **[8396]**, Jackson, MI
RSVP of Jefferson County **[5720]**, Madison, IN
RSVP of Joliet Area **[2119]**, Joliet, IL
RSVP Kalamazoo County **[8464]**, Kalamazoo, MI
RSVP of Laporte/Starke Counties **[5792]**, Michigan City, IN
RSVP of Macomb **[7187]**, Clinton Township, MI
RSVP of Mahoning and Southern Trumbull Counties **[17413]**, Youngstown, OH
RSVP Mecosta/Lake/Osceola **[6951]**, Big Rapids, MI
RSVP Menominee/Delta/Schoolcraft **[7618]**, Escanaba, MI
RSVP Monroe County **[9911]**, Temperance, MI
RSVP of Monroe and Owen Counties **[4254]**, Bloomington, IN
RSVP of Northern Cook and Northern Dupage Counties **[82]**, Arlington Heights, IL
RSVP Northwest Illinois **[1753]**, Freeport, IL
RSVP of Northwest Michigan **[9950]**, Traverse City, MI
RSVP of Northwestern Ohio **[16957]**, Toledo, OH
RSVP of Otsego County **[7823]**, Gaylord, MI
RSVP Outagamie County **[17522]**, Appleton, WI
RSVP of the Pennisula **[2146]**, Karnak, IL
RSVP of Portage County **[15548]**, Kent, OH
RSVP of Red River Valley **[10738]**, Crookston, MN
RSVP Richland County **[15793]**, Mansfield, OH
RSVP of Saint Clair County **[1552]**, East St. Louis, IL
RSVP of Saint Joseph County **[6258]**, South Bend, IN
RSVP of Sangamon, Menard and Logan Counties **[3670]**, Springfield, IL
RSVP of Scioto County **[16474]**, Portsmouth, OH
RSVP of Scott IA and Rock Island IL **[3258]**, Rock Island, IL
RSVP of Southwest Minnesota **[12992]**, Worthington, MN
RSVP of Stark County **[13580]**, Canton, OH
RSVP Todd/Wadena/Otter Tail/Wilkin **[11891]**, New York Mills, MN
RSVP Volunteer Resources of Madison County **[4119]**, Anderson, IN
RSVP Volunteer Sers. **[10519]**, Brainerd, MN
RSVP Volunteers United **[11947]**, Ortonville, MN
RSVP of Washtenaw County **[6761]**, Ann Arbor, MI
RSVP Wayne County **[7426]**, Detroit, MI
RSVP Western Egyptian EOC **[3700]**, Steeleville, IL
RSVP of Winnebago/Boone Counties **[3316]**, Rockford, IL
RSVP of Woodford, Marshall, and Livingston Counties **[1645]**, Eureka, IL
Rudolph Volunteer Fire Dept. **[19653]**, Rudolph, WI
Ruffed Grouse Soc., Agazzi Chap. **[12747]**, Thief River Falls, MN
Ruffed Grouse Soc., Aikit Area Chap. **[10246]**, Aitkin, MN
Ruffed Grouse Soc., Al Litzenburger Chap. **[9370]**, Petoskey, MI
Ruffed Grouse Soc., Andy Ammann Chap. **[8397]**, Jackson, MI
Ruffed Grouse Soc., Ann Arbor Chap. **[7072]**, Canton, MI
Ruffed Grouse Soc., Beaver Creek Chap. **[16588]**, Salem, OH
Ruffed Grouse Soc., Benay of the Lakes Chap. **[10783]**, Detroit Lakes, MN
Ruffed Grouse Soc., Blackduck Chap. **[10447]**, Blackduck, MN
Ruffed Grouse Soc., Blackhawk Area Chap. **[18263]**, Janesville, WI
Ruffed Grouse Soc., Central Upper Peninsula Chap. **[7619]**, Escanaba, MI
Ruffed Grouse Soc., Chequamegon Chap. **[17547]**, Ashland, WI
Ruffed Grouse Soc., Chippewa Valley Chap. **[17893]**, Eau Claire, WI
Ruffed Grouse Soc., Coulee Region Chap. **[18376]**, La Crosse, WI
Ruffed Grouse Soc., Crazy Flight Chap. **[10957]**, Ely, MN
Ruffed Grouse Soc., David Salsman Chap. **[12806]**, Virginia, MN
Ruffed Grouse Soc., David V. Uihlein Chap. **[19111]**, Milwaukee, WI
Ruffed Grouse Soc., Deep Portage Chap. **[10371]**, Backus, MN
Ruffed Grouse Soc., Drumming Log Chap. **[10520]**, Brainerd, MN
Ruffed Grouse Soc., Duluth/Superior Chap. **[19875]**, Superior, WI
Ruffed Grouse Soc., Durand Area Chap. **[17936]**, Elmwood, WI
Ruffed Grouse Soc., Eastern Up Chap. **[9670]**, St. Ignace, MI
Ruffed Grouse Soc., Flambeau River Chap. **[19426]**, Park Falls, WI
Ruffed Grouse Soc., Gilbert R. Symons Chap. **[16322]**, Owensville, OH
Ruffed Grouse Soc., Grand Rapids, Michigan Chap. **[8006]**, Grand Rapids, MI
Ruffed Grouse Soc., Grand Rapids, Minnesota Chap. **[12698]**, Squaw Lake, MN
Ruffed Grouse Soc., Hocking River Valley Chap. **[17160]**, Wellston, OH
Ruffed Grouse Soc., Hoosier Chap. **[5793]**, Michigan City, IN
Ruffed Grouse Soc., Indiana Chap. **[5585]**, Kokomo, IN
Ruffed Grouse Soc., Jim Foote Chap. **[8807]**, Lewiston, MI
Ruffed Grouse Soc., John M. Keener Chap. **[18610]**, Madison, WI
Ruffed Grouse Soc., Keith Davis Chap. **[7194]**, Clio, MI
Ruffed Grouse Soc., Kettle Moraine Chap. **[17825]**, Delafield, WI
Ruffed Grouse Soc., Lake Shore Chap. **[18329]**, Kohler, WI
Ruffed Grouse Soc., Lake of the Woods Chap. **[12844]**, Warroad, MN
Ruffed Grouse Soc., Lakeland Area Chap. **[19658]**, St. Germain, WI
Ruffed Grouse Soc., Langlade Chap. **[17819]**, Deerbrook, WI
Ruffed Grouse Soc., Le Grand Traverse Chap. **[9951]**, Traverse City, MI
Ruffed Grouse Soc., Lincoln County Chap. **[19910]**, Tomahawk, WI
Ruffed Grouse Soc., Marinette County Chap. **[18804]**, Marinette, WI
Ruffed Grouse Soc., Michigan Chap. **[6998]**, Boyne Falls, MI
Ruffed Grouse Soc., Mid Up Chap. **[8958]**, Marquette, MI
Ruffed Grouse Soc., Missa-Croix Chap. **[11129]**, Hastings, MN
Ruffed Grouse Soc., Nicolet Wild River Chap. **[17539]**, Armstrong Creek, WI
Ruffed Grouse Soc., North Shore Chap. **[11078]**, Grand Marais, MN
Ruffed Grouse Soc., Northcentral Minnesota Chap. **[10425]**, Bemidji, MN
Ruffed Grouse Soc., Northeastern Wisconsin Chap. **[18130]**, Green Bay, WI
Ruffed Grouse Soc., Northern Ohio Chap. **[13086]**, Akron, OH
Ruffed Grouse Soc., Northwest Ohio Chap. **[16105]**, Neapolis, OH
Ruffed Grouse Soc., Ohio Chap. **[14724]**, Columbus, OH
Ruffed Grouse Soc., Ohio Hills Chap. **[16040]**, Millersport, OH
Ruffed Grouse Soc., Pine County Chap. **[12734]**, Sturgeon Lake, MN
Ruffed Grouse Soc., Rib Mountain Chap. **[20045]**, Wausau, WI
Ruffed Grouse Soc., Robert J. Lytle Chap. **[9490]**, Richmond, MI
Ruffed Grouse Soc., Roy W. Strickland Chap. **[6999]**, Boyne Falls, MI
Ruffed Grouse Soc., Rum River Chap. **[11230]**, Isanti, MN
Ruffed Grouse Soc., Saginaw Valley Chap. **[7782]**, Frankenmuth, MI
Ruffed Grouse Soc., St. Croix Valley Chap. **[18225]**, Hudson, WI
Ruffed Grouse Soc., Shawano Area Chap. **[19682]**, Shawano, WI
Ruffed Grouse Soc., South Central Michigan Chap. **[7583]**, Eaton Rapids, MI
Ruffed Grouse Soc., Southwest Wisconsin Chap. **[19258]**, Muscoda, WI
Ruffed Grouse Soc., Southwestern Michigan Chap. **[6605]**, Allegan, MI
Ruffed Grouse Soc., Superior Chap. **[8341]**, Ironwood, MI
Ruffed Grouse Soc., T. Stanton Armour Chap. **[1952]**, Harvard, IL
Ruffed Grouse Soc., Three Rivers Chap. **[17443]**, Zanesville, OH
Ruffed Grouse Soc., Twin Cities Chap. **[12662]**, Shoreview, MN
Ruffed Grouse Soc., Voyageur Chap. **[11219]**, International Falls, MN
Ruffed Grouse Soc., West Central Minnesota Chap. **[12297]**, St. Cloud, MN
Ruffed Grouse Soc., West Central Wisconsin Chap. **[19281]**, Neillsville, WI
Ruffed Grouse Soc., Wilderness Wings Chap. **[18199]**, Hayward, WI
Ruffed Grouse Soc., Winnebago Land Chap. **[19404]**, Oshkosh, WI
Ruffed Grouse Soc., Wisconsin Chap. **[19876]**, Superior, WI
Ruffed Grouse Soc., Woods/Meadow Chap. **[19947]**, Warrens, WI
Rugby
Detroit Rugby Football Club of Metropolitan Detroit **[9502]**, Rochester, MI
Rugby Football Club of Metropolitan Detroit; Detroit **[9502]**, Rochester, MI
Rugby Football Club; Oakland Highlanders **[9588]**, Royal Oak, MI
Rum River Cycling Team **[12047]**, Princeton, MN
Runaways
Pathfinders **[19088]**, Milwaukee, WI
Rural Appraisers Indiana Chap; Amer. Soc. of Farm Managers and **[★6424]**
Rural Hea. Clinics Org; Michigan **[7799]**, Fremont, MI
Rural Land Alliance **[16708]**, Springboro, OH
Rural Rental Housing Assn. of Indiana **[5469]**, Indianapolis, IN
Rural Youth
Indiana 4-H Found. **[5158]**, Indianapolis, IN
Rush County Chamber of Commerce **[6145]**, Rushville, IN

Rushford Lions Club **[12257]**, Rushford, MN
Rushville Area Chamber of Commerce and Main St. **[3371]**, Rushville, IL
Rushville Area C.O.C. and Main St. **[3372]**, Rushville, IL
Rushville Chamber of Commerce **[★3371]**
Rustbelt 4x4 Trailriders Assn. **[15465]**, Homerville, OH

S

Sabin Lions Club **[12261]**, Sabin, MN
Sacred Heart Lions Club **[12263]**, Sacred Heart, MN
Sacred Heart-St. Elizabeth Community Development Corp. **[7427]**, Detroit, MI
Safe Community Coalition of Madison and Dane County **[18611]**, Madison, WI
Safe Haven Humane Soc. for Jo Daviess County **[1604]**, Elizabeth, IL
Safety
City of Greensburg Public Safety Facilities Building Corp. **[4840]**, Greensburg, IN
Constr. Safety Coun. **[2005]**, Hillside, IL
Dayton/Miami Valley Safety Coun. **[14878]**, Dayton, OH
Michigan Safety Conf. **[6591]**, Albion, MI
Michigan Women's Bowling Assn. **[8386]**, Jackson, MI
Minnesota Safety Coun. **[12515]**, St. Paul, MN
Mothers Against Drunk Driving, Allen/Putnam Counties **[15663]**, Lima, OH
Mothers Against Drunk Driving, Becker County **[10780]**, Detroit Lakes, MN
Mothers Against Drunk Driving, Blue Earth/Nicollet **[12535]**, St. Paul, MN
Mothers Against Drunk Driving, Brown/Marinette Counties **[18115]**, Green Bay, WI
Mothers Against Drunk Driving, Carver County **[12536]**, St. Paul, MN
Mothers Against Drunk Driving, Chisago/Isanti Counties **[12700]**, Stacy, MN
Mothers Against Drunk Driving, Delaware County **[15009]**, Delaware, OH
Mothers Against Drunk Driving, Dupage County **[2301]**, Lisle, IL
Mothers Against Drunk Driving, East Central Indiana **[4112]**, Anderson, IN
Mothers Against Drunk Driving, Eau Claire County **[17886]**, Eau Claire, WI
Mothers Against Drunk Driving, Fayette County **[3847]**, Vandalia, IL
Mothers Against Drunk Driving, Fayette/Pickaway Counties **[17130]**, Washington Court House, OH
Mothers Against Drunk Driving, Franklin County **[14508]**, Columbus, OH
Mothers Against Drunk Driving, Freeborn County **[11123]**, Hartland, MN
Mothers Against Drunk Driving, Fulton County **[405]**, Canton, IL
Mothers Against Drunk Driving, Greater Toledo Area **[16826]**, Sylvania, OH
Mothers Against Drunk Driving, Greene County **[17374]**, Xenia, OH
Mothers Against Drunk Driving, Heartland Chapter **[1543]**, East Peoria, IL
Mothers Against Drunk Driving, Illinois State **[3651]**, Springfield, IL
Mothers Against Drunk Driving, Indiana State **[4184]**, Beech Grove, IN
Mothers Against Drunk Driving, Kane County **[183]**, Batavia, IL
Mothers Against Drunk Driving, La Crosse County **[18370]**, La Crosse, WI
Mothers Against Drunk Driving, Macomb County **[9091]**, Mount Clemens, MI
Mothers Against Drunk Driving, McHenry County **[1328]**, Crystal Lake, IL
Mothers Against Drunk Driving, McLean County **[298]**, Bloomington, IL
Mothers Against Drunk Driving, Mercer County **[2434]**, Matherville, IL
Mothers Against Drunk Driving, Michigan State **[8733]**, Lansing, MI
Mothers Against Drunk Driving, North Coast Chap. **[14166]**, Cleveland, OH
Mothers Against Drunk Driving, Oakland County **[10088]**, Waterford, MI
Mothers Against Drunk Driving, Ohio **[14509]**, Columbus, OH
Mothers Against Drunk Driving, Ohio Valley Chap. **[16763]**, Steubenville, OH
Mothers Against Drunk Driving, Otter Tail County **[12537]**, St. Paul, MN
Mothers Against Drunk Driving, Portage County **[16499]**, Ravenna, OH
Mothers Against Drunk Driving, Quinsippi Chap. **[3154]**, Quincy, IL
Mothers Against Drunk Driving, Rock/Walworth Counties **[17613]**, Beloit, WI
Mothers Against Drunk Driving, St. Clair/Sanilac Counties **[8975]**, Marysville, MI
Mothers Against Drunk Driving, Sauk County **[19590]**, Reedsburg, WI
Mothers Against Drunk Driving, Shelby County **[3466]**, Shelbyville, IL
Mothers Against Drunk Driving, Southwestern Ohio **[13912]**, Cincinnati, OH
Mothers Against Drunk Driving, Stark County **[13117]**, Alliance, OH
Mothers Against Drunk Driving, State Off. **[12538]**, St. Paul, MN
Mothers Against Drunk Driving, Upper Fox Valley **[17502]**, Appleton, WI
Mothers Against Drunk Driving, Washington County **[20123]**, West Bend, WI
Mothers Against Drunk Driving, Washtenaw County **[6739]**, Ann Arbor, MI
Mothers Against Drunk Driving, Waukesha County **[19991]**, Waukesha, WI
Mothers Against Drunk Driving, Wayne County **[10140]**, Westland, MI
Mothers Against Drunk Driving, Western Reserve **[16336]**, Painesville, OH
Mothers Against Drunk Driving, Winnebago County **[20173]**, Winneconne, WI
Mothers Against Drunk Driving, Winona County **[12956]**, Winona, MN
Mothers Against Drunk Driving, Wisconsin State **[17503]**, Appleton, WI
Natl. Safety Coun., Chicago Chap. **[2068]**, Itasca, IL
Natl. Safety Coun., Northern Ohio Chap. **[17407]**, Youngstown, OH
Oper. Lifesaver, Indiana **[5443]**, Indianapolis, IN
Oper. Lifesaver, Michigan **[8749]**, Lansing, MI
Oper. Lifesaver, Ohio **[14705]**, Columbus, OH
Operation Lifesaver, Wisconsin **[18591]**, Madison, WI
Safe Community Coalition of Madison and Dane County **[18611]**, Madison, WI
Safety Coun. of Northwest Ohio **[16256]**, Northwood, OH
Safety Coun. for Southeast Michigan **[9818]**, Southfield, MI
Toby Tire Safety and Illinois Not-for-Profit Org. **[3688]**, Springfield, IL
Wisconsin Coun. of Safety **[18692]**, Madison, WI
Safety Assn. of Michigan; Traffic **[★8704]**
Safety Coun; Constr. **[2005]**, Hillside, IL
Safety Coun; Dayton/Miami Valley **[14878]**, Dayton, OH
Safety Coun; Minnesota **[12515]**, St. Paul, MN
Safety Coun. of Northwest Ohio **[16256]**, Northwood, OH
Safety Coun. for Southeast Michigan **[9818]**, Southfield, MI
Safety Coun; Toledo Lucas County **[★16256]**
Safety Coun. for West Michigan **[8465]**, Kalamazoo, MI
Safety Facilities Building Corp; City of Greensburg Public **[4840]**, Greensburg, IN
Safety and Illinois Not-for-Profit Org; Toby Tire **[3688]**, Springfield, IL
SAGE/Milwaukee **[19112]**, Milwaukee, WI
Saginaw Alliance for the Mentally Ill **[7149]**, Chesaning, MI
Saginaw Area IDA Collaborative **[9628]**, Saginaw, MI
Saginaw Bay Rsrc. Conservation and Development Coun. **[6895]**, Bay City, MI
Saginaw Bd. of Realtors **[9629]**, Saginaw, MI
Saginaw County Chamber of Commerce **[9630]**, Saginaw, MI
Saginaw County Convention and Visitors Bur. **[9631]**, Saginaw, MI
Saginaw County Medical Soc. **[9632]**, Saginaw, MI
Saginaw Future **[9633]**, Saginaw, MI
Saginaw Gun Club **[9634]**, Saginaw, MI
Saginaw Habitat for Humanity **[9635]**, Saginaw, MI
Saginaw Valley Convention and Visitors Bur. **[★9631]**
Saginaw Valley District Dental Soc. **[9636]**, Saginaw, MI
Saginaw Valley Orchid Soc. **[7203]**, Coleman, MI
Saginaw Valley Railroad Historical Soc. **[9637]**, Saginaw, MI
Saginaw West Lions Club **[9638]**, Saginaw, MI
Sailing Assn; North Coast Women's **[15589]**, Lakewood, OH
Sailing Club; Alpena Youth **[6640]**, Alpena, MI
St. Anthony Wyldlife **[12248]**, Roseville, MN
Saint Bernard Club of Greater Detroit **[10093]**, Waterford, MI
St. Bernard Club; Greater Milwaukee **[19325]**, North Prairie, WI
Saint Bernard Club of Greater St. Louis **[3063]**, Peoria, IL
St. Bonifacius Lions Club **[12265]**, St. Bonifacius, MN
St. Charles Area Chamber of Commerce **[3392]**, St. Charles, IL
St. Charles Chamber of Commerce **[★3392]**
St. Charles Illinois Convention and Visitors Bur. **[3393]**, St. Charles, IL
St. Charles Lions Club **[12267]**, St. Charles, MN
St. Charles Lions Club - Michigan **[9650]**, St. Charles, MI
St. Charles Sportsmen Club **[3394]**, St. Charles, IL
St. Charles - Young Life **[1800]**, Geneva, IL
St. Clair County Convention and Visitors Bureau **[9439]**, Port Huron, MI
St. Clair County Medical Soc. **[210]**, Belleville, IL
St. Clair County Medical Soc. - Michigan **[9440]**, Port Huron, MI
St. Clair County Youth for Christ **[9441]**, Port Huron, MI
St. Clair District Dental Soc. **[2431]**, Mascoutah, IL
St. Clair Numismatic Soc. **[★207]**
St. Clair Shores Figure Skating Club **[9665]**, St. Clair Shores, MI
St. Cloud Area Chamber of Commerce **[12298]**, St. Cloud, MN
St. Cloud Area Planning Org. **[12299]**, St. Cloud, MN
St. Cloud Builders Exchange **[12300]**, St. Cloud, MN
St. Cloud Extraordinary Pseudoscience Teaching Investigations and Community Service **[12301]**, St. Cloud, MN
St. Cloud Figure Skating Club **[12302]**, St. Cloud, MN
Saint Cloud Jaycees **[12303]**, St. Cloud, MN
St. Cloud Lions Club **[12304]**, St. Cloud, MN
St. Cloud State Univ. Natl. Org. for the Reform of Marijuana Laws **[12305]**, St. Cloud, MN
St. Cloud - Young Life **[12306]**, St. Cloud, MN
St. Croix Area United Way **[12724]**, Stillwater, MN
St. Croix County Historical Soc. **[18226]**, Hudson, WI
St. Croix Falls Chamber of Commerce **[19656]**, St. Croix Falls, WI
St. Croix Valley Angus Assn. **[19321]**, New Richmond, WI
St. Croix Valley Brittany Club **[12900]**, White Bear Lake, MN
St. Croix Valley District Nurses Assn. - No. 13 **[17561]**, Baldwin, WI
St. Croix Valley Kennel Club **[10242]**, Afton, MN
St. Croix Valley Kennel Club **[12573]**, St. Paul, MN
St. Croix Valley Lions Club **[12725]**, Stillwater, MN
St. Francis Lions Club **[12320]**, St. Francis, MN
St. Germain Chamber of Commerce **[19659]**, St. Germain, WI
St. Germain PrimeTimers **[19660]**, St. Germain, WI
St. Henry Academic Promoters **[16576]**, St. Henry, OH
St. Hilaire Lions Club **[12748]**, Thief River Falls, MN
St. Ignace Area Convention and Visitors Bur. **[9671]**, St. Ignace, MI
St. Ignace Chamber of Commerce **[9672]**, St. Ignace, MI
Saint Joe Valley Conservation **[6152]**, St. Joe, IN
St. Joe - Young Life **[9689]**, St. Joseph, MI
St. John Chamber of Commerce **[6153]**, St. John, IN

St. Johns Area Chamber of Commerce [9678], St. Johns, MI
St. Johns Lions Club [9679], St. Johns, MI
St. Joseph Chamber of Commerce [12327], St. Joseph, MN
St. Joseph County Assn. of Realtors [7110], Centreville, MI
Saint Joseph County Conservation [9881], Sturgis, MI
St. Joseph County Medical Soc. [6259], South Bend, IN
St. Joseph County United Way, Michigan [7111], Centreville, MI
St. Joseph Lions Club [9690], St. Joseph, MI
Saint Joseph, Michigan Kiwanis Club [9691], St. Joseph, MI
St. Joseph River Basin Commn. [6260], South Bend, IN
St. Joseph River Valley Fly Fishers [6261], South Bend, IN
St. Joseph Valley Beagle Club [5985], North Liberty, IN
St. Joseph Valley REACT [6262], South Bend, IN
St. Joseph's Ridge Lions Club [19369], Onalaska, WI
St. Kloud ESP Teaching Investigation Committee [★12301]
St. Leo Preservation Society [14725], Columbus, OH
St. Louis Chamber [★6632]
St. Louis County Promotional Bureau [11046], Gilbert, MN
St. Louis Lions Club [9697], St. Louis, MI
St. Louis Park Lions Club [10558], Brooklyn Park, MN
St. Louis River Citizens Action Comm. [10852], Duluth, MN
St. Mary's Preparatory Moms and Dads Club [9312], Orchard Lake, MI
St. Paul African Methodist Episcopal Church [7428], Detroit, MI
Saint Paul Area Assn. of Realtors [12574], St. Paul, MN
St. Paul Area Chamber of Commerce [12575], St. Paul, MN
St. Paul Assn. of Responsible Landlords [12576], St. Paul, MN
St. Paul Audubon Soc. [12726], Stillwater, MN
St. Paul; Better Bus. Bur. of [★12392]
Saint Paul Chap. IAAP [12577], St. Paul, MN
St. Paul Chap. Natl. Elecl. Contractors Assn. [12578], St. Paul, MN
St. Paul Community Development Corp. [★7428]
St. Paul Convention and Visitors Bur. [12579], St. Paul, MN
St. Paul District Dental Soc. [12580], St. Paul, MN
St. Paul East Parks Lions Club [11421], Maplewood, MN
St. Paul Figure Skating Club [12581], St. Paul, MN
Saint Paul Jaycees [12582], St. Paul, MN
St. Paul Liberty Coin Club [12583], St. Paul, MN
St. Paul Ostomy Assn. [12584], St. Paul, MN
St. Paul Sail and Power Squadron [11422], Maplewood, MN
St. Paul Urban League [12585], St. Paul, MN
St. Peter Area Chamber of Commerce [12620], St. Peter, MN
St. Stephan's Community Lions Club [8757], Lansing, MI
St. Xavier - Young Life [15169], Fairfield, OH
Saladin Shriners [8007], Grand Rapids, MI
Salamonie AIFA [5742], Marion, IN
Salem Area Chamber of Commerce [16589], Salem, OH
Salem Chamber of Commerce [★3409]
Salem Community Center [16590], Salem, OH
Salem Community Center Assn. [★16590]
Salem Lions Club - Ohio [16591], Salem, OH
Sales
- Elec. Ser. Dealers Assn. of Illinois [883], Chicago, IL
- Illinois Assn. of Tobacco and Candy Distributors [3581], Springfield, IL
- Indiana Assn. of Beverage Retailers [5165], Indianapolis, IN
- Indiana Fireworks Distributors Assn. [5878], Muncie, IN
- Northalsted Area Merchants Association [1105], Chicago, IL
- Sales and Marketing Executives Intl., Greater Milwaukee [19113], Milwaukee, WI
- Sales and Marketing Executives of Madison [19210], Monona, WI
- Sales and Marketing Executives, Minneapolis/St. Paul [10543], Brooklyn Center, MN
- United Sales Associates [14016], Cincinnati, OH

Sales and Marketing Executives [16093], Munroe Falls, OH
Sales and Marketing Executives Intl., Greater Milwaukee [19113], Milwaukee, WI
Sales and Marketing Executives of Madison [19210], Monona, WI
Sales and Marketing Executives, Minneapolis/St. Paul [10543], Brooklyn Center, MN
Saline Area Chamber of Commerce [9703], Saline, MI
Saline Area Lions Club [9704], Saline, MI
Saline County Chamber of Commerce [1940], Harrisburg, IL
Saline High - Young Life [6762], Ann Arbor, MI
Salmon Unlimited [1172], Chicago, IL
Salt Creek Beagle Club [17444], Zanesville, OH
Salt Creek Watershed Network [354], Brookfield, IL
Saluki Club of Am. [19342], Oconomowoc, WI
Samoyed Assn. of Minneapolis-St. Paul [10486], Bloomington, MN
Sand County Found. [18612], Madison, WI
Sand Lake Lions Club [9706], Sand Lake, MI
Sandhill Soaring Club [6763], Ann Arbor, MI
Sandhill Water and Sewer Assn. [15830], Marietta, OH
Sandstone Chamber of Commerce [12626], Sandstone, MN
Sandstone Lions Club [12627], Sandstone, MN
Sandusky County Builders Assn. [15252], Fremont, OH
Sandusky County Convention and Visitors Bureau [15253], Fremont, OH
Sandusky/Erie County Convention and Visitors Bur. [16617], Sandusky, OH
Sandusky Lions Club [16618], Sandusky, OH
Sandusky Main St. Assn. [16619], Sandusky, OH
Sandusky River Basin LUA [15254], Fremont, OH
Sandusky Valley Amateur Astronomy Club [16860], Tiffin, OH
Sandwich Chamber of Commerce [3416], Sandwich, IL
SANE/FREEZE of Greater Cleveland [★14101]
Sanford Lions Club - Michigan [9712], Sanford, MI
Sangamon Astronomical Soc. [3671], Springfield, IL
Sangamon County Medical Soc. [3672], Springfield, IL
Sangamon - Menard County Agricultural Educ. Partnership [3673], Springfield, IL
Sanitarians; Indiana Assn. of [★5231]
Sanitation
- Amer. Soc. of Sanitary Engg., Central Ohio Chap. [14310], Columbus, OH
- Amer. Soc. of Sanitary Engg., Illinois Chap. [2194], Lake Forest, IL
- Amer. Soc. of Sanitary Engg., Michigan Chap. [7322], Detroit, MI
- Amer. Soc. of Sanitary Engg., Minnesota Chap. [11519], Minneapolis, MN
- Amer. Soc. of Sanitary Engg., Northern Ohio Chap. [13649], Chesterland, OH
- Amer. Soc. of Sanitary Engg., Region No. 2 - North Central [10462], Bloomington, MN
- Amer. Soc. of Sanitary Engg., Region No. 6 - East [15494], Independence, OH

Santiago Lions Club [10396], Becker, MN
Sassafras Audubon Soc. [4255], Bloomington, IN
Sassafras Star Sailing Soc. No. 160 [14950], Dayton, OH
Saugatuck-Douglas Art Club [9716], Saugatuck, MI
Saugatuck - Young Life [8219], Holland, MI
Sauk Centre Area Chamber of Commerce [12633], Sauk Centre, MN
Sauk Centre Lions Club [12634], Sauk Centre, MN
Sauk County Fed. of Labor [★18619]
Sauk County Historical Soc. [17577], Baraboo, WI
Sauk County Personnel Assn. [20179], Wisconsin Dells, WI
Sauk Prairie Area Chamber of Commerce [19532], Prairie Du Sac, WI
Sauk Prairie Lions Club [19533], Prairie Du Sac, WI
Sauk Prairie Trap and Skeet [19534], Prairie Du Sac, WI
Sauk-Prairie United Way [19535], Prairie Du Sac, WI
Sauk Rapids Riverside Lions Club [12637], Sauk Rapids, MN
Sauk Trails Rsrc. Conservation and Development Coun. [8466], Kalamazoo, MI
Sauk Valley Area Chamber of Commerce [3703], Sterling, IL
Sauk Valley Assn. of Realtors [3704], Sterling, IL
Saukville Chamber of Commerce [19667], Saukville, WI
Saukville Lions Club [19668], Saukville, WI
Sault Area Arts Coun. [9724], Sault Ste. Marie, MI
Sault Area Chamber of Commerce [9725], Sault Ste. Marie, MI
Sault Convention and Visitors Bur. [★9726]
Sault Ste. Marie Convention and Visitors Bur. [9726], Sault Ste. Marie, MI
Sault Ste. Marie District Dental Soc. [9727], Sault Ste. Marie, MI
Savage Chamber of Commerce [12643], Savage, MN
Savage Wyldlife [10607], Burnsville, MN
Savanna Chamber of Commerce [3421], Savanna, IL
Savannah Lions Club - Ohio [16659], Shiloh, OH
Save the Animals Found. [13979], Cincinnati, OH
Save Cedar Lake Park [★11540]
Save the Dunes Coun. [5794], Michigan City, IN
Save the Valley [5721], Madison, IN
Sayner-Starlake Chamber of Commerce [19669], Sayner, WI
SBC Pioneers Illinois Chap. [1601], Elgin, IL
SBC Pioneers Ohio Chap. [13431], Broadview Heights, OH
SBC Pioneers Wisconsin Chap. [17894], Eau Claire, WI
Scam Victims United [10487], Bloomington, MN
Scarab Club [7429], Detroit, MI
SCDAA - Ohio Sickle Cell and Hea. Assn. [13980], Cincinnati, OH
Scenic Illinois [1468], Des Plaines, IL
Scenic Michigan [9371], Petoskey, MI
Scenic Ohio [13087], Akron, OH
Schaumburg Bus. Assn. [3445], Schaumburg, IL
Schaumburg Table Tennis Club [3446], Schaumburg, IL
Schererville Chamber of Commerce [6168], Schererville, IN
Scholars Foundation; Evans [★1878]
Scholars and Students Association; United Chinese [1215], Chicago, IL
Scholars; Wisconsin [19180], Milwaukee, WI
Scholarship
- Aurora Community Stud. Circles [112], Aurora, IL
- Biltmore Country Club Scholarship Found. [2744], North Barrington, IL

Scholarship Alumni
- Bellevue High School Alumni Assn. [13328], Bellevue, OH

Scholarship Found; Biltmore Country Club [2744], North Barrington, IL
Scholarship and Guidance Assn. [1173], Chicago, IL
School Administrators; Michigan Assn. of [8626], Lansing, MI
School Administrators; Ohio Assn. of Elementary [14552], Columbus, OH
School Administrators; Ohio Assn. of Secondary [14566], Columbus, OH
School Association; Nativity Home and [6059], Portage, IN
School Assn; Ohio Middle [14638], Columbus, OH
School Band and Orchestra Assn; Michigan [9291], Okemos, MI
School Boards
- Illinois Assn. of School Bds. [3580], Springfield, IL
- Indiana School Bds. Assn. [5294], Indianapolis, IN
- Michigan Assn. of School Bds. [8627], Lansing, MI
- Minnesota School Bds. Assn. [12617], St. Peter, MN
- Wisconsin Assn. of School Bds. [18663], Madison, WI

School Bds. Assn; Ohio [14670], Columbus, OH
School Bds; Illinois Assn. of [3580], Springfield, IL

School Bus. Officials; Illinois Assn. of **[1434]**, De-Kalb, IL
School Bus. Officials; Michigan **[8709]**, Lansing, MI
School Bus. Officials; Ohio Assn. of **[14565]**, Columbus, OH
School Bus. Officials; Wisconsin Assn. of **[18664]**, Madison, WI
School Chess Club; North Boone High **[3125]**, Poplar Grove, IL
School Coaches Assn; Michigan High **[8993]**, Mears, MI
School Couns; Wisconsin Assn. of **[18665]**, Madison, WI
School District Communications Governance Comm; West Bloomfield **[★10126]**
School District Parent Communications Network; West Bloomfield **[10126]**, West Bloomfield, MI
School Investment Assn; Michigan **[8710]**, Lansing, MI
School Lib. Media Assn; Illinois **[404]**, Canton, IL
School of Missionary Aviation Tech. **[8866]**, Lowell, MI
School Nurse Org. of Minnesota **[12064]**, Ramsey, MN
School Nutrition Assn. of Michigan **[9040]**, Midland, MI
School Principals; Michigan Assn. of Secondary **[8628]**, Lansing, MI
School Principals; Ohio Assn. of Elementary **[★14552]**
School Psychologists Assn; Ohio **[15270]**, Gahanna, OH
School Public Relations Assn., Michigan; Natl. **[★8711]**
School Public Relations Assn; Minnesota **[12242]**, Roseville, MN
School Public Relations Assn., Wisconsin; Natl. **[★18751]**
School Security
Michigan Assn. of Campus Law Enforcement Administrators **[10027]**, University Center, MI
Minnesota Chap. of Intl. Assn. of Campus Law Enforcement Administrators **[12615]**, St. Peter, MN
School Services
Natl. Assn. of Coll. Auxiliary Services, Central **[2724]**, Normal, IL
Troy Special Services Parent Teacher Org. **[10014]**, Troy, MI
School Trans. Assn; Illinois **[2437]**, Matteson, IL
School Volunteers of District 220 **[★144]**
Schoolcraft County Chamber of Commerce **[8919]**, Manistique, MI
Schools
Amer. Schools Assn. **[720]**, Chicago, IL
Assn. of Illinois Middle-Level Schools **[501]**, Champaign, IL
Home School Children's Club **[3181]**, Rantoul, IL
Schools Assn. of the Central States; Independent **[974]**, Chicago, IL
Schools; Assn. of Lutheran Secondary **[18885]**, Mequon, WI
Schools; Michigan Assn. of Non-Public **[8621]**, Lansing, MI
Schools; North Central Conf. on Summer **[19642]**, River Falls, WI
Schools Organization; Alfordsville-Reeve Township **[5701]**, Loogootee, IN
Schrems West Michigan Trout Unlimited **[8008]**, Grand Rapids, MI
Science
Amer. Assn. of Pharmaceutical Scientists, Univ. of Michigan Student Chap. **[6655]**, Ann Arbor, MI
Assn. for Women in Sci., Bloomington **[4201]**, Bloomington, IN
Assn. for Women in Sci., Central Ohio **[14333]**, Columbus, OH
Assn. for Women in Sci., Detroit **[6683]**, Ann Arbor, MI
Assn. for Women in Sci., Heart of Illinois **[264]**, Bloomington, IL
Association for Women in Science, Indianapolis **[5051]**, Indianapolis, IN
Assn. for Women in Sci., Miami Valley **[14857]**, Dayton, OH
Assn. for Women in Sci., Univ. of Michigan-Ann Arbor **[6684]**, Ann Arbor, MI
Assn. for Women in Sci., Washtenaw Community Coll. **[6685]**, Ann Arbor, MI
Chicago Catalysis Club **[1455]**, Des Plaines, IL
Hoosier Assn. of Sci. Teachers **[5137]**, Indianapolis, IN
Illinois Sci. Teachers Assn. **[121]**, Aurora, IL
Metropolitan Detroit Sci. Teachers Assn. **[7389]**, Detroit, MI
Michigan Catalysis Soc. **[9746]**, Shelby Township, MI
Minnesota Sci. Teachers Assn. **[12518]**, St. Paul, MN
Ohio Acad. of Sci. **[14534]**, Columbus, OH
Ohio Sci. Educ. and Res. Assn. **[15061]**, Dublin, OH
Sci. Educ. Coun. of Ohio **[16646]**, Sharon Center, OH
Tri-State Catalysis Club **[14011]**, Cincinnati, OH
Wisconsin Chap. Triangle Fraternity **[18680]**, Madison, WI
Wisconsin Soc. of Sci. Teachers **[19411]**, Oshkosh, WI
Sci., Arts, and Letters; Michigan Acad. of **[6633]**, Alma, MI
Sci., Detroit; Assn. for Women in **[6683]**, Ann Arbor, MI
Sci. Educ. Coun. of Ohio **[16646]**, Sharon Center, OH
Sci; Ohio Acad. of **[14534]**, Columbus, OH
Scis. Alumni Assn; Mayo School of Hea.-Related **[12154]**, Rochester, MN
Sci. Educ. and Res. Assn; Ohio **[15061]**, Dublin, OH
Sci. Societies; Akron Coun. of Engg. and **[13020]**, Akron, OH
Scioto County Chap. of the Ohio Genealogical Soc. **[16475]**, Portsmouth, OH
Scioto River Hunting Club **[16560]**, Roundhead, OH
Scioto Soc. **[13674]**, Chillicothe, OH
Sclerosis Soc., Indiana State Chap; Natl. Multiple **[5428]**, Indianapolis, IN
SCORE Akron **[13088]**, Akron, OH
SCORE Anderson **[4120]**, Anderson, IN
SCORE Ann Arbor Area **[★6764]**
SCORE Ann Arbor Area Chap. **[6764]**, Ann Arbor, MI
SCORE Bloomington **[4256]**, Bloomington, IN
SCORE Cadillac **[7049]**, Cadillac, MI
SCORE Central Area (St. Cloud) **[12307]**, St. Cloud, MN
SCORE Central Illinois **[311]**, Bloomington, IL
SCORE Central Wisconsin **[18823]**, Marshfield, WI
SCORE Chap. 28, Milwaukee, WI **[19114]**, Milwaukee, WI
SCORE Chap. 50 **[4714]**, Fort Wayne, IN
SCORE Chap. 107 **[14951]**, Dayton, OH
SCORE Chicago **[1174]**, Chicago, IL
SCORE Counselors to Am'.s Small Bus. **[12183]**, Rochester, MN
SCORE Decatur **[1407]**, Decatur, IL
SCORE Detroit **[7430]**, Detroit, MI
SCORE Eau Claire **[17895]**, Eau Claire, WI
SCORE Elkhart **[4506]**, Elkhart, IN
SCORE Evansville **[4571]**, Evansville, IN
SCORE Fox Cities **[17523]**, Appleton, WI
SCORE Fox Valley **[130]**, Aurora, IL
SCORE Grand Rapids **[8009]**, Grand Rapids, MI
SCORE Green Bay **[18131]**, Green Bay, WI
SCORE Kokomo/Howard Counties **[5586]**, Kokomo, IN
SCORE La Crosse **[18377]**, La Crosse, WI
SCORE Logansport **[5698]**, Logansport, IN
SCORE Madison **[18613]**, Madison, WI
SCORE Marion/Grant Co **[5743]**, Marion, IN
SCORE Minneapolis **[11733]**, Minneapolis, MN
SCORE Muskegon **[9160]**, Muskegon, MI
SCORE New Ulm Area **[11887]**, New Ulm, MN
SCORE Northern Illinois **[3317]**, Rockford, IL
SCORE Peoria **[3064]**, Peoria, IL
SCORE Petoskey **[9372]**, Petoskey, MI
SCORE Quad Cities **[2533]**, Moline, IL
SCORE Quincy Tri-State **[3172]**, Quincy, IL
SCORE St. Paul **[12586]**, St. Paul, MN
SCORE South Bend **[6263]**, South Bend, IN
SCORE South Central Indiana **[5923]**, New Albany, IN
SCORE South East Indiana **[4406]**, Columbus, IN
SCORE South Metro **[10608]**, Burnsville, MN
SCORE Southern Illinois **[430]**, Carbondale, IL
SCORE Springfield **[3674]**, Springfield, IL
SCORE Superior **[19877]**, Superior, WI
SCORE SW Illinois **[1876]**, Godfrey, IL
SCORE Traverse City **[9952]**, Traverse City, MI
SCORE Wausau **[20046]**, Wausau, WI
Scott AFB Rod and Gun Club **[3789]**, Troy, IL
Scottish
Scottish Rite Valley of Cleveland **[14213]**, Cleveland, OH
Valley of Cincinnati, Ancient Accepted Scottish Rite **[14021]**, Cincinnati, OH
Wisconsin Scottish **[20111]**, West Allis, WI
Scottish Rite Valley of Cleveland **[14213]**, Cleveland, OH
Scottish Terrier Club of Northern Ohio **[14833]**, Dalton, OH
Scottville Area Chamber of Commerce **[9736]**, Scottville, MI
Scout Coun; Michigan Metro Girl **[9998]**, Troy, MI
Scouting
Boy Scouts of Am., Chippewa Valley Coun. **[17868]**, Eau Claire, WI
Boy Scouts of Am. - Dan Beard Coun. **[13763]**, Cincinnati, OH
Boy Scouts of Am., Gamehaven Coun. **[12130]**, Rochester, MN
Boy Scouts of Am., Glacier's Edge Coun. **[18493]**, Madison, WI
Boy Scouts of Am.-Great Sauk Trail Coun. **[6688]**, Ann Arbor, MI
Covered Bridge Girl Scout Coun. **[6318]**, Terre Haute, IN
Drifting Dunes Girl Scout Coun. **[5769]**, Merrillville, IN
Girl Scout Coun. of Cannon Valley **[11914]**, Northfield, MN
Girl Scout Coun. of Greater Minneapolis **[10536]**, Brooklyn Center, MN
Girl Scout Coun. of Kenosha County **[18298]**, Kenosha, WI
Girl Scout Coun. of River Trails **[12143]**, Rochester, MN
Girl Scout Coun. of St. Croix Valley **[12417]**, St. Paul, MN
Girl Scouts of Appleseed Ridge **[15653]**, Lima, OH
Girl Scouts of Badger Coun. **[17607]**, Beloit, WI
Girl Scouts of Black Hawk Coun. **[18515]**, Madison, WI
Girl Scouts of Buckeye Trails Coun. **[14886]**, Dayton, OH
Girl Scouts of Chicago **[902]**, Chicago, IL
Girl Scouts of Crooked Tree **[9930]**, Traverse City, MI
Girl Scouts of DuPage County Coun. **[2295]**, Lisle, IL
Girl Scouts Fair Winds Coun. **[7739]**, Flint, MI
Girl Scouts of the Fox River Area **[17498]**, Appleton, WI
Girl Scouts - Fox Valley Coun. **[117]**, Aurora, IL
Girl Scouts of Glowing Embers Coun. **[8427]**, Kalamazoo, MI
Girl Scouts - Great Blue Heron Coun. **[19984]**, Waukesha, WI
Girl Scouts-Great Rivers Coun. **[13836]**, Cincinnati, OH
Girl Scouts - Great Trail Coun. **[16216]**, North Canton, OH
Girl Scouts - Green Meadows Coun. **[3817]**, Urbana, IL
Girl Scouts - Heart of Ohio **[17438]**, Zanesville, OH
Girl Scouts of Heritage Trails Coun. **[15767]**, Mansfield, OH
Girl Scouts of Hoosier Capital Coun. **[5121]**, Indianapolis, IN
Girl Scouts - Illinois Crossroads Coun. **[3853]**, Vernon Hills, IL
Girl Scouts - Irish Hills Coun. **[8364]**, Jackson, MI
Girl Scouts-Kickapoo Coun. **[3021]**, Peoria, IL
Girl Scouts of Lake Erie Coun. **[14126]**, Cleveland, OH
Girl Scouts of Lake to River Coun. **[16205]**, Niles, OH
Girl Scouts - Land of Lakes Coun. **[12826]**, Waite Park, MN
Girl Scouts, Land of Lincoln Coun. **[3553]**, Springfield, IL

Girl Scouts of Limberlost Coun. [4666], Fort Wayne, IN
Girl Scouts of Macomb County - Otsikita Coun. [7176], Clinton Township, MI
Girl Scouts of Manitou Coun. [19695], Sheboygan, WI
Girl Scouts of Michigan Trails [7941], Grand Rapids, MI
Girl Scouts of Milwaukee Area [19014], Milwaukee, WI
Girl Scouts Peacepipe Coun. [12094], Redwood Falls, MN
Girl Scouts of Riverland Coun. [18346], La Crosse, WI
Girl Scouts - Rock River Valley [3280], Rockford, IL
Girl Scouts - Seal of Ohio Coun. [14442], Columbus, OH
Girl Scouts of Shagbark Coun. [1973], Herrin, IL
Girl Scouts of Singing Sands Coun. [6228], South Bend, IN
Girl Scouts of South Cook County [2047], Homewood, IL
Girl Scouts - Sybaquay Coun. [1591], Elgin, IL
Girl Scouts of Sycamore Coun. [5611], Lafayette, IN
Girl Scouts of The Calumet Coun. [4911], Highland, IN
Girl Scouts of The Mississippi Valley [3244], Rock Island, IL
Girl Scouts of The Western Reserve [13053], Akron, OH
Girl Scouts of Treaty Line Coun. [6091], Richmond, IN
Girl Scouts of Tulip Trace Coun. [4220], Bloomington, IN
Girl Scouts of Two Rivers Coun. [3150], Quincy, IL
Girl Scouts of Wapehani Coun. [4441], Daleville, IN
Girl Scouts of Whispering Oaks Coun. [352], Brookfield, IL
Girl Scouts of Woodland Council - Central Wisconsin [20184], Wisconsin Rapids, WI
Indiana Lakeland Girl Scout Coun. [4799], Goshen, IN
Michigan Capitol Girl Scout Coun. [8242], Holt, MI
Michigan Metro Girl Scout Coun. [9998], Troy, MI
Scouts of Am., Gamehaven Coun; Boy [12130], Rochester, MN
Scouts; Fayette County Girl [★6091]
Scouts of Treaty Line Coun; Girl [6091], Richmond, IN
Scouts; Wayne County Girl [★6091]
Sculpture
Hamilton, Ohio City of Sculpture [15386], Hamilton, OH
Sculpture; Hamilton, Ohio City of [15386], Hamilton, OH
SE Michigan TSCA [9519], Rochester Hills, MI
Search and Rescue; Eastern Upper Peninsula [9196], Newberry, MI
Seas Educ. Assn; Inland [9886], Suttons Bay, MI
Seaway Gun Club [9161], Muskegon, MI
Sebewaing Chamber of Commerce [9740], Sebewaing, MI
Sebring Lions Club [16625], Sebring, OH
Second Chance Animal Rescue [12901], White Bear Lake, MN
Secondary School Administrators; Ohio Assn. of [14566], Columbus, OH
Secondary School Principals; Michigan Assn. of [8628], Lansing, MI
Secret Victoria's No. 190 [16958], Toledo, OH
Secretaries of Am; Beer Distributors [★11630]
Secretaries; Natl. Assn. of State Beer Assn. [★11630]
Secretaries; State Beer Wholesalers [★11630]
Secrets of Speed Soc. [13271], Batavia, OH
Secular Humanist Soc. of Chicago [1175], Chicago, IL
Securities
Chicago Bd. Options Exchange [794], Chicago, IL
Chicago Stock Exchange [832], Chicago, IL
Midwest Securities Transfer Assn. [1057], Chicago, IL
Security
Minnesota Electronic Security and Tech. Assn. [12480], St. Paul, MN
Ohio Assn. of Security and Investigation Services [14567], Columbus, OH
Ohio Burglar and Fire Alarm Assn. [14574], Columbus, OH
Wisconsin Burglar and Fire Alarm Assn. [20107], West Allis, WI
Security Analysts; Cleveland Soc. of [14104], Cleveland, OH
Seed
Flint - North Central Weed and Seed [7733], Flint, MI
Illinois Seed Trade Assn. [529], Champaign, IL
Michigan Crop Improvement Assn. [8655], Lansing, MI
Minnesota Crop Improvement Assn. [12474], St. Paul, MN
Ohio Seed Improvement Assn. [15062], Dublin, OH
Seguin Retarded Citizens Assn. [239], Berwyn, IL
SEIU Local 73 [1176], Chicago, IL
Self-Help for Hard of Hearing; Central Minnesota [12117], Robbinsdale, MN
Self Insurers Assn; Ohio [14671], Columbus, OH
Self Insurers' Gp. of Ohio [14214], Cleveland, OH
Selfhelp
Northeast Ohio CoDA Community [17015], Twinsburg, OH
Semcac RSVP [12258], Rushford, MN
Seneca County Genealogical Soc. [16861], Tiffin, OH
Seneca County Home Builders Assn. [16862], Tiffin, OH
Seneca Habitat for Humanity [16863], Tiffin, OH
Seneca Lions Club - Wisconsin [19673], Seneca, WI
The Senior Alliance (Area Agency on Aging 1-C in Michigan) [10101], Wayne, MI
Senior Services Assn. of Cook County; Community Nutrition Network and [855], Chicago, IL
Seniors Learning Together [10324], Apple Valley, MN
Sentinel Police Assn. [13981], Cincinnati, OH
Sentry Cares [19805], Stevens Point, WI
SER - Jobs for Progress, Central States [1177], Chicago, IL
SER - Jobs for Progress, Lake County [3931], Waukegan, IL
SER - Jobs for Progress, Metro Detroit [7431], Detroit, MI
SER - Jobs for Progress, Milwaukee [19115], Milwaukee, WI
Sertoma 700 Club Of Rochester [12184], Rochester, MN
Service
Albion Volunteer Ser. Org. [6588], Albion, MI
Intl. Customer Ser. Assn., Chicago [987], Chicago, IL
Intl. Customer Ser. Assn., Cleveland/Northcoast [14146], Cleveland, OH
Intl. Customer Ser. Assn., Greater Cincinnati [15875], Mason, OH
Minnesota Historical Soc. - Field Ser. Dept. [12488], St. Paul, MN
Ohio Car Wash Assn. [13574], Canton, OH
SEIU Local 73 [1176], Chicago, IL
Ser. Employees Intl. Union, AFL-CIO, CLC - Illinois Coun. [1178], Chicago, IL
Ser. Employees Intl. Union, AFL-CIO, CLC - Local Union 4 [1179], Chicago, IL
Ser. Employees Intl. Union, AFL-CIO, CLC - School Ser. Local Union 284 [12683], South St. Paul, MN
Ser. Employees Intl. Union Local 880 [1180], Chicago, IL
Ser. Assn; Indiana Electronic [4818], Greencastle, IN
Ser. Assn., Indianhead Chap; Wisconsin Electronic [17910], Eau Claire, WI
Service Clubs
Ada Lions Club - Minnesota [10235], Ada, MN
Adams Lions Club [10238], Adams, MN
Adena Lions Club [13011], Adena, OH
Adrian Breakfast Lions Club [6560], Adrian, MI
Adrian Evening Lions Club [6561], Adrian, MI
Albertville Lions Club [10269], Albertville, MN
Allen Park Lions Club [7243], Dearborn, MI
Altura Lions Club [10288], Altura, MN
Alvarado Lions Club [10289], Alvarado, MN
AMBUCS - Alive After Five [9731], Schoolcraft, MI
AMBUCS - Greater Twin Cities [12657], Shoreview, MN
AMBUCS, Pekin Club [2982], Pekin, IL
Amherst Lions Club - Ohio [13132], Amherst, OH
Andover Lions Club [10295], Andover, MN
Ann Arbor Evening Lions Club [6672], Ann Arbor, MI
Ann Arbor Host Lions Club [7138], Chelsea, MI
Apple Creek Lions Club [17312], Wooster, OH
Apple Valley Lions Club [10317], Apple Valley, MN
Appleton Lions Club [10330], Appleton, MN
Appleton Noon Lions Club [17487], Appleton, WI
Arcadia Lions Club [6796], Arcadia, MI
Argyle Lions Club [10334], Argyle, MN
Arlington Heights Lions Club [66], Arlington Heights, IL
Arlington Lions Club - Minnesota [10338], Arlington, MN
Ashby Lions Club [10342], Ashby, MN
Ashland Evening Lions Club [13162], Ashland, OH
Ashland Lions Club - Wisconsin [17544], Ashland, WI
Ashland Noon Lions Club [13163], Ashland, OH
Ashley Lions Club [6799], Ashley, MI
Assistance League of Chicagoland West [2014], Hinsdale, IL
Assistance League of Fort Wayne [4641], Fort Wayne, IN
Assistance League of Greater Cincinnati [13748], Cincinnati, OH
Assistance League of Indianapolis [5039], Indianapolis, IN
Assistance League of Metro Columbus [14317], Columbus, OH
Assistance League of Minneapolis/St. Paul [11523], Minneapolis, MN
Assistance League of Southeastern Michigan [9512], Rochester Hills, MI
Astoria Lions Club [96], Astoria, IL
Athens-Union City Lions Club [10020], Union City, MI
Attica Lions Club [13224], Attica, OH
Atwater Lions Club [10345], Atwater, MN
Atwater Lions Club - Ohio [13227], Atwater, OH
Auburn Lions Club - Michigan [6808], Auburn, MI
Aurora Lions Club [10348], Aurora, MN
Austin Lions Club [10354], Austin, MN
Austintown Lions Club [13236], Austintown, OH
Avon Lions Club - Ohio [13241], Avon, OH
Babbit Lions Club [10368], Babbitt, MN
Bagley Lions Club [10373], Bagley, MN
Baldwin Lions Club - Michigan [6823], Baldwin, MI
Baltic Lions Club [13249], Baltic, OH
Bancroft Lions Club [6824], Bancroft, MI
Bangor Lions Club [6827], Bangor, MI
Bangor Lions Club - Wisconsin [17567], Bangor, WI
Baraboo Lions Club [17573], Baraboo, WI
Barnesville Lions Club [10378], Barnesville, MN
Barnesville Lions Club - Ohio [13260], Barnesville, OH
Barnesville Thursday Nite Lions Club [10379], Barnesville, MN
Baroda Lions Club [6832], Baroda, MI
Barre-Coed Lions Club [20136], West Salem, WI
Barryton Lions Club [8500], Lake, MI
Bartlett Lions Club [162], Bartlett, IL
Bartonville Lions Club [168], Bartonville, IL
Bascom Lions Club [15229], Fostoria, OH
Bath Township Lions Club [6835], Bath, MI
Battle Creek Host Lions Club [6853], Battle Creek, MI
Battle Creek Lakeview Lions Club [6854], Battle Creek, MI
Battle Lake Lions Club [10384], Battle Lake, MN
Bay City Lions Club [6884], Bay City, MI
Beach City Lions Club [13280], Beach City, OH
Bear Lake Lions Club [6900], Bear Lake, MI
Bedford Lions Club [7483], Dowling, MI
Bedford Township Lions Club [8523], Lambertville, MI
Beecher Lions Club [9321], Otisville, MI
Bellaire Lions Club [13311], Bellaire, OH
Bellevue Lions Club [13329], Bellevue, OH
Bellevue Lions Club - Michigan [6912], Bellevue, MI
Bellville Lions Club - Ohio [13337], Bellville, OH

Belpre Lions Club **[13342]**, Belpre, OH
Belvidere Lions Club **[221]**, Belvidere, IL
Bemidji First City Lions Club **[10409]**, Bemidji, MN
Bemidji Jaycees **[10410]**, Bemidji, MN
Bemidji Lions Club **[10411]**, Bemidji, MN
Ben Davis High School Key Club **[5056]**, Indianapolis, IN
Benson Lions Club **[10433]**, Benson, MN
Bexley Lions Club **[15261]**, Gahanna, OH
Big Bend-Vernon Lions Club **[17626]**, Big Bend, WI
Big Falls Lions Club **[10438]**, Big Falls, MN
Big Fork Lions Club **[10931]**, Effie, MN
Big Rapids Lions Club **[6941]**, Big Rapids, MI
Big Walnut Breakfast Lions Club **[16811]**, Sunbury, OH
Birch Run Lions Club **[6959]**, Birch Run, MI
Bird Island Lions Club **[10443]**, Bird Island, MN
Blackduck Lions Club **[10446]**, Blackduck, MN
Blaine Jaycees **[10448]**, Blaine, MN
Blissfield Area Lions Club **[6974]**, Blissfield, MI
Bloom Carroll Lions Club **[13602]**, Carroll, OH
Bloomingdale/Gobles (KalHaven Trail) Lions Club **[6994]**, Bloomingdale, MI
Bloomington Lions Club, IL **[265]**, Bloomington, IL
Bloomington Lions Club - Minnesota **[11408]**, Maple Grove, MN
Bloomville Lions Club **[16851]**, Tiffin, OH
Boardman Lions Club **[13372]**, Boardman, OH
Boaz Area Lions Club **[19622]**, Richland Center, WI
Bolivar Lions Club **[13377]**, Bolivar, OH
Borup Lions Club **[10237]**, Ada, MN
Bourbon Lions Club **[4281]**, Bourbon, IN
Brandon Lions Club - Minnesota **[10525]**, Brandon, MN
Bretton Woods Lions Club **[8555]**, Lansing, MI
Brice Prairie Lions Club **[19362]**, Onalaska, WI
Bridgeport Lions Club - Michigan **[9604]**, Saginaw, MI
Bridgeview Lions Club **[341]**, Bridgeview, IL
Bridgman Lions Club **[7003]**, Bridgman, MI
Brighton Lions Club **[7011]**, Brighton, MI
Brilliant Lions Club **[13421]**, Brilliant, OH
Brimfield Lions Club **[16053]**, Mogadore, OH
Broadview Heights Lions Club **[13426]**, Broadview Heights, OH
Brooklyn Center Lions Club **[10546]**, Brooklyn Park, MN
Brooklyn Park Lady Lions Club **[10548]**, Brooklyn Park, MN
Brooklyn Park Lions Club **[10549]**, Brooklyn Park, MN
Brown County Lions Club **[5913]**, Nashville, IN
Brownstown Lions Club **[7032]**, Brownstown, MI
Brownsville Lions Club **[10566]**, Brownsville, MN
Bucyrus Lions Club **[13466]**, Bucyrus, OH
Buena Vista Lions Club - Michigan **[9605]**, Saginaw, MI
Buffalo Lake Lions Club **[10582]**, Buffalo Lake, MN
Burlington Lions Club **[17697]**, Burlington, WI
Butler Lions Club **[13475]**, Butler, OH
Butler Lions Club - Wisconsin **[17699]**, Butler, WI
Byron Area Lions Club **[7038]**, Byron, MI
Byron Lions Club, IL **[384]**, Byron, IL
Cadillac Lions Club **[7046]**, Cadillac, MI
Cadiz Lions Club **[13480]**, Cadiz, OH
Calcutta Lions Club **[13484]**, Calcutta, OH
Caledonia Lions Club **[11361]**, Mabel, MN
Cambridge Lioness Club **[13495]**, Cambridge, OH
Cambridge Lions Club - Ohio **[13496]**, Cambridge, OH
Camden Lions Club **[11537]**, Minneapolis, MN
Camden Lions Club - Ohio **[13505]**, Camden, OH
Camp Douglas Lions Club **[17714]**, Camp Douglas, WI
Canal Fulton Lions Club **[13512]**, Canal Fulton, OH
Canal Winchester Lions Club **[13517]**, Canal Winchester, OH
Canfield Lions Club **[13530]**, Canfield, OH
Canton Lions Club - Michigan **[7062]**, Canton, MI
Canton Lions Club - Ohio **[13556]**, Canton, OH
Canton South Lions Club **[13558]**, Canton, OH
Carlinville Lions Club **[439]**, Carlinville, IL
Carlisle Lions Club - Ohio **[13601]**, Carlisle, OH
Carlos Lions Club **[10274]**, Alexandria, MN
Carlton Lions Club **[10381]**, Barnum, MN
Caro Lions Club **[7083]**, Caro, MI
Carrollton Lions Club **[13605]**, Carrollton, OH
Carrollton Lions Club - Michigan **[9606]**, Saginaw, MI
Carson City Lions Club **[7089]**, Carson City, MI
Cashton Lions Club **[17722]**, Cashton, WI
Cass City Lions Club **[7094]**, Cass City, MI
Cassopolis (Central Cass) Lions Club **[7100]**, Cassopolis, MI
Cassville Lions Club **[17724]**, Cassville, WI
Castalia Lions Club **[13606]**, Castalia, OH
Cedar-Maple City Lions Club **[8921]**, Maple City, MI
Cedar Mills Lions Club **[11205]**, Hutchinson, MN
Cedarburg Lions Club **[17728]**, Cedarburg, WI
Centerville Lions Club, IN **[4340]**, Centerville, IN
Centreville Lions Club - Michigan **[7108]**, Centreville, MI
Centerville Lions Club - Minnesota **[10639]**, Centerville, MN
Cereal City Lions Club **[6857]**, Battle Creek, MI
Champion Lions Club **[17099]**, Warren, OH
Champlin Lions Club **[10642]**, Champlin, MN
Chanhassen Lions Club **[10646]**, Chanhassen, MN
Charlotte Lions Club **[7120]**, Charlotte, MI
Chaseburg Lions Club **[17736]**, Chaseburg, WI
Chaska Area Jaycees **[10651]**, Chaska, MN
Chaska Lions Club **[10652]**, Chaska, MN
Chatfield Lions Club **[10656]**, Chatfield, MN
Chelsea Lions Club **[7141]**, Chelsea, MI
Chesaning Lions Club **[7146]**, Chesaning, MI
Chesterhill Lions Club **[13648]**, Chesterhill, OH
Cheviot Westwood Lions Club **[13768]**, Cincinnati, OH
Chicago Beverly Ridge Lions Club **[1681]**, Evergreen Park, IL
Chippewa Lake Lions Club **[9536]**, Rodney, MI
Cincinnati Host Lions Club **[13789]**, Cincinnati, OH
Cincinnati-Kenwood Lions Club **[13790]**, Cincinnati, OH
Cincinnati-Western Hills Lions Club **[13802]**, Cincinnati, OH
Circle Pines - Lexington Lions Club **[10663]**, Circle Pines, MN
Clara City Lions Club **[10669]**, Clara City, MN
Clarendon Hills Lions Club **[1266]**, Clarendon Hills, IL
Clarklake Lions Club **[7157]**, Clarklake, MI
Clayland Lions Club **[15019]**, Dennison, OH
Cleveland Southeast Lions Club **[16544]**, Rocky River, OH
Clio Lions Club **[7189]**, Clio, MI
Coal Valley Lions Club **[1279]**, Coal Valley, IL
Cokato Lions Club **[10697]**, Cokato, MN
Col. Crawford Lions Club **[16872]**, Tiro, OH
Colchester Lions Club **[1282]**, Colchester, IL
Cold Spring Home Pride Lions Club **[10700]**, Cold Spring, MN
Coleman Lions Club **[7202]**, Coleman, MI
Coloma Lions Club **[7206]**, Coloma, MI
Columbiana Area Lions Club **[14261]**, Columbiana, OH
Columbus Beechcroft Lions Club **[17209]**, Westerville, OH
Columbus Downtown Lions Club **[14384]**, Columbus, OH
Columbus Hilltop Lions Club **[14387]**, Columbus, OH
Columbus Inner City Lions Club **[14389]**, Columbus, OH
Columbus Lions Club, IN **[4397]**, Columbus, IN
Columbus Northeast Lions Club **[14395]**, Columbus, OH
Columbus Northern Lions Club **[14396]**, Columbus, OH
Columbus Northland Lions Club **[14397]**, Columbus, OH
Columbus Southeast Lions Club **[15635]**, Lewis Center, OH
Columbus Southern Pines Lions Club **[14403]**, Columbus, OH
Concord Lions Club - Michigan **[7217]**, Concord, MI
Connersville Lions Club **[4413]**, Connersville, IN
Cook Lions Club **[10706]**, Cook, MN
Coolville Lions Club **[14786]**, Coolville, OH
Coon Rapids Cardinal Lions Club **[10708]**, Coon Rapids, MN
Coon Rapids Lions Club **[10709]**, Coon Rapids, MN
Coon Valley Lions Club **[17785]**, Coon Valley, WI
Corcoran Lions Club **[10720]**, Corcoran, MN
Cortland Lions Club **[14789]**, Cortland, OH
Corydon Noon Lions Club **[4419]**, Corydon, IN
Coshocton Lions Club **[14801]**, Coshocton, OH
Cosmos Lions Club **[11326]**, Litchfield, MN
Countryside Lions Club **[1305]**, Countryside, IL
Covert Township Lions Club **[7227]**, Covert, MI
Crestline Lions Club - Ohio **[14809]**, Crestline, OH
Creston Lions Club **[14813]**, Creston, OH
Crestwood Lions Club **[15799]**, Mantua, OH
Crete Lions Club **[1315]**, Crete, IL
Crookston Dawn To Dusk Lions Club **[10734]**, Crookston, MN
Crookston Lions Club **[10736]**, Crookston, MN
Cross Plains Lions Club **[17793]**, Cross Plains, WI
Crosslake-Ideal Lions Club **[10742]**, Crosslake, MN
Crystal Lake Lions Club **[1322]**, Crystal Lake, IL
Crystal Lions Club **[10573]**, Buffalo, MN
Crystal Lions Club - Michigan **[7230]**, Crystal, MI
Dalton Lions Club - Ohio **[14830]**, Dalton, OH
Danube Lions Club **[10749]**, Danube, MN
Darien Lions Club, IL **[1359]**, Darien, IL
Darwin Lions Club **[10751]**, Darwin, MN
Dawson Lions Club **[10756]**, Dawson, MN
Dayton Downtown Lions Club **[14876]**, Dayton, OH
Dayton Lions Club **[10759]**, Dayton, MN
De Soto Area Lions Club **[17816]**, De Soto, WI
Dearborn Heights Lions Club **[7282]**, Dearborn Heights, MI
Dearborn Lions Club **[7256]**, Dearborn, MI
Decatur AMBUCS **[2605]**, Mount Zion, IL
Deer River Avenue of Pines Lions Club **[10764]**, Deer River, MN
Deer River Lions Club **[10766]**, Deer River, MN
Delaware Community Lions Club **[15003]**, Delaware, OH
Delaware Lions Club **[17211]**, Westerville, OH
Dennison Lions Club **[11859]**, Nerstrand, MN
Detroit Downtown Lions Club **[7344]**, Detroit, MI
Detroit Eastside-Friendship Lions Club **[9865]**, Sterling Heights, MI
Detroit Hispanic Lions Club **[7259]**, Dearborn, MI
Detroit Medical Center Lions Club **[7787]**, Fraser, MI
Detroit Mid-City Lions Club **[8788]**, Lathrup Village, MI
Detroit New Center Lions Club **[7352]**, Detroit, MI
Detroit North Central Lions Club **[9798]**, Southfield, MI
Detroit Northwest Lions Club **[7353]**, Detroit, MI
Detroit Renaissance Lions Club **[7356]**, Detroit, MI
Detroit University/New Gratiot Lions Club **[8295]**, Huntington Woods, MI
DeWitt Breakfast Lions Club **[8564]**, Lansing, MI
DeWitt Host Lions Club **[7461]**, DeWitt, MI
Dexter Lions Club **[10166]**, Whitmore Lake, MI
Dillonvale-Mt. Pleasant Lions Club **[16076]**, Mount Pleasant, OH
Dilworth Lions Club **[10787]**, Dilworth, MN
Dimondale Lions Club **[7472]**, Dimondale, MI
Dodge Center Lions Club **[10790]**, Dodge Center, MN
Dover Lions Club - Ohio **[16149]**, New Philadelphia, OH
Dowagiac Lions Club **[7480]**, Dowagiac, MI
Doylestown Lions Club **[16537]**, Rittman, OH
Dublin Lions Club - Ohio **[16032]**, Milford Center, OH
Duluth Lions Club **[10819]**, Duluth, MN
Duluth Spirit Valley Lions Club **[10821]**, Duluth, MN
Duncan Falls-Philo Lions Club **[17437]**, Zanesville, OH
Durand Lions Club **[7491]**, Durand, MI
East Canton Lions Club **[15071]**, East Canton, OH

East Flint Lions Club **[7723]**, Flint, MI
East Grand Forks Lions Club **[10883]**, East Grand Forks, MN
East Jackson Lions Club **[8363]**, Jackson, MI
East Knox Lions Club **[15467]**, Howard, OH
East Lansing-Meridian Lions Club **[9268]**, Okemos, MI
East Liverpool Lions Club **[15079]**, East Liverpool, OH
Eaton Rapids Lions Club **[7581]**, Eaton Rapids, MI
Eau Claire Lions Club **[7587]**, Eau Claire, MI
Ecorse-River Rouge Lions Club **[9492]**, River Rouge, MI
Eden Prairie Lions Club **[10893]**, Eden Prairie, MN
Eden Valley Lions Club **[10904]**, Eden Valley, MN
Edina Lions Club **[10909]**, Edina, MN
Edinburgh Lions Club **[4480]**, Edinburgh, IN
Edmore Lions Club **[6970]**, Blanchard, MI
Edwardsburg Lions Club **[9205]**, Niles, MI
Eitzen Lions Club **[10933]**, Eitzen, MN
Elbow Lake Lions Club **[10935]**, Elbow Lake, MN
Elburn Lions Club **[1579]**, Elburn, IL
Eldorado Lions Club **[15096]**, Eldorado, OH
Elgin Lions Club **[10941]**, Elgin, MN
Elk River Lions Club **[10946]**, Elk River, MN
Elkhart Lions Club **[4496]**, Elkhart, IN
Elmore Lions Club **[15101]**, Elmore, OH
Elroy Lions Club **[17941]**, Elroy, WI
Elsie Lions Club **[7599]**, Elsie, MI
Ely Lions Club **[10955]**, Ely, MN
Elyria Evening Lions Club **[15110]**, Elyria, OH
Empire Lions Club **[7603]**, Empire, MI
Erskine Lions Club **[10964]**, Erskine, MN
Esko Lions Club **[10823]**, Duluth, MN
Essexville-Hampton Lions Club **[7625]**, Essexville, MI
Evart Lions Club **[7629]**, Evart, MI
Eveleth Lions Club **[10968]**, Eveleth, MN
Evergreen Park Lions Club **[1683]**, Evergreen Park, IL
Exchange Club of Detroit **[9988]**, Troy, MI
Exchange Club of Grayslake **[1892]**, Grayslake, IL
Exchange Club of Speedway **[5111]**, Indianapolis, IN
Exchange Club of Terre Haute **[6319]**, Terre Haute, IN
Fairfax Lions Club **[10974]**, Fairfax, MN
Fairgrove Lions Club **[7633]**, Fairgrove, MI
Falcon Heights-Lauderdale Lions Club **[12226]**, Roseville, MN
Fenton Lions Club **[7684]**, Fenton, MI
Fertile Lions Club **[11008]**, Fertile, MN
Firelands Lions Club **[15111]**, Elyria, OH
Flint Downtown Host Lions Club **[9514]**, Rochester Hills, MI
Flint Inner City Lions Club **[7730]**, Flint, MI
Flint Township Lions Club **[7764]**, Flushing, MI
Flom and Area Lions Club **[12763]**, Twin Valley, MN
Floodwood Area Lions Club **[11011]**, Floodwood, MN
Flushing Lions Club **[7767]**, Flushing, MI
Forada Lions Club **[10276]**, Alexandria, MN
Fosston-Lengby Lions Club **[11023]**, Fosston, MN
Fostoria Lions Club **[15231]**, Fostoria, OH
Fowler Lions Club **[9675]**, St. Johns, MI
Frankenmuth Lions Club **[7780]**, Frankenmuth, MI
Frankfort Lions Club **[7786]**, Frankfort, MI
Franklin Lions Club - Minnesota **[11027]**, Franklin, MN
Franklin Park Manila Lions Club **[1738]**, Franklin Park, IL
Fremont Lions Club - Michigan **[7797]**, Fremont, MI
Fremont Noon Lions Club **[15247]**, Fremont, OH
French Island Lions Club **[18344]**, La Crosse, WI
Fridley Lions Club **[11033]**, Fridley, MN
Gahanna Lions Club **[15264]**, Gahanna, OH
Gaines Area Lions Club **[7804]**, Gaines, MI
Galion Lions Club **[15283]**, Galion, OH
Garden City Lions Club - Michigan **[7812]**, Garden City, MI
Garrettsville Lions Club **[15305]**, Garrettsville, OH
Gary Lions Club **[11040]**, Gary, MN
Gays Mills Lions Club **[18031]**, Gays Mills, WI
Genesee Lions Club **[7826]**, Genesee, MI
Geneva Lions Club **[1794]**, Geneva, IL
Genoa City Lions Club **[18035]**, Genoa City, WI
Genoa Lions Club - Wisconsin **[19825]**, Stoddard, WI
Germantown Lions Club **[15316]**, Germantown, OH
Girard Lions Club **[15322]**, Girard, OH
Glen Ellyn Lions Club **[1830]**, Glen Ellyn, IL
Glen Ellyn Lions Found. **[1831]**, Glen Ellyn, IL
Glendale Heights Barangay Lions Club **[1851]**, Glendale Heights, IL
Glenwood Lions Club - Minnesota **[11053]**, Glenwood, MN
Glyndon Lions Club **[11057]**, Glyndon, MN
Golden Valley Lions Club **[11868]**, New Hope, MN
Goodhue Lions Club **[11068]**, Goodhue, MN
Goodrich Lions Club **[7238]**, Davison, MI
Goodridge Lion Tamers Club **[11070]**, Goodridge, MN
Goodridge Lions Club **[12741]**, Thief River Falls, MN
Goshen Lions Club **[15332]**, Goshen, OH
Grafton Lions Club - Wisconsin **[18064]**, Grafton, WI
Grand Ledge Lions Club **[7872]**, Grand Ledge, MI
Grand Marais Lions Club **[11076]**, Grand Marais, MN
Grand Rapids Cap Baker Lions Club **[11427]**, Marcell, MN
Grand Rapids Lions Club **[20185]**, Wisconsin Rapids, WI
Grand Rapids Star of the North Lions Club **[11086]**, Grand Rapids, MN
Grant Lions Club **[8051]**, Grant, MI
Grass Lake Lions Club **[8055]**, Grass Lake, MI
Greater Greenfield Lions Club **[19017]**, Milwaukee, WI
Green Camp Lions Club **[16486]**, Prospect, OH
Green Springs Lions Club **[15352]**, Green Springs, OH
Greenbush Lions Club **[11099]**, Greenbush, MN
Greendale Lions Club **[18151]**, Greendale, WI
Greenville Lions Club - Michigan **[8068]**, Greenville, MI
Greenville Lions Club - Wisconsin **[18164]**, Greenville, WI
Greenway Lions Club **[10499]**, Bovey, MN
Grosse Ile Lions Club **[8074]**, Grosse Ile, MI
Grosse Pointe Lions Club **[8083]**, Grosse Pointe, MI
Grove City Lions Club **[11101]**, Grove City, MN
Grove City Lions Club - Ohio **[15369]**, Grove City, OH
Grove City Noon Lions Club **[17213]**, Westerville, OH
Groveport Madison Lions Club **[13518]**, Canal Winchester, OH
Grygla Lions Club **[11103]**, Grygla, MN
Hagerstown Lions Club **[4863]**, Hagerstown, IN
Hallock Lions Club **[11108]**, Hallock, MN
Halstad Lions Club **[11110]**, Halstad, MN
Hamel Lions Club **[11114]**, Hamel, MN
Hancock Lions Club **[11115]**, Hancock, MN
Hanover-Horton Lions Club **[8367]**, Jackson, MI
Harmony Lions Club **[11119]**, Harmony, MN
Harper Woods Lions Club **[9658]**, St. Clair Shores, MI
Harrison Lions Club - Michigan **[8127]**, Harrison, MI
Hart Lions Club **[8136]**, Hart, MI
Hartford Lions Club - Michigan **[8139]**, Hartford, MI
Hartland Lions Club **[8143]**, Hartland, MI
Hartville Lions Club **[15410]**, Hartville, OH
Hawley Lions Club **[11135]**, Hawley, MN
Hayesville Lions Club **[16452]**, Polk, OH
Hayfield Lions Club **[11137]**, Hayfield, MN
Heath Lions Club **[15413]**, Heath, OH
Hector Lions Club - Minnesota **[11140]**, Hector, MN
Hemlock Lions Club **[8162]**, Hemlock, MI
Hesperia Lions Club **[8166]**, Hesperia, MI
Hibbing Lions Club **[11160]**, Hibbing, MN
Highland Park Lions Club - Michigan **[8172]**, Highland Park, MI
Hilliard Lions Club **[14457]**, Columbus, OH
Hillsboro Lions Club - Wisconsin **[18207]**, Hillsboro, WI
Hillsdale Lions Club **[8178]**, Hillsdale, MI
Hitterdal Lions Club **[11172]**, Hitterdal, MN
Hoffman Lions Club **[11147]**, Herman, MN
Hokah Lions Club **[11265]**, La Crescent, MN
Holmen Lions Club **[19364]**, Onalaska, WI
Holt Lions Club **[8240]**, Holt, MI
Homer Lions Club - Michigan **[8246]**, Homer, MI
Homeworth Lions Club **[13339]**, Beloit, OH
Hononegah High School Key Club **[3335]**, Rockton, IL
Honor Lions Club **[8247]**, Honor, MI
Hopkins Area Jaycees **[11184]**, Hopkins, MN
Hopkins Evening Lions Club **[11787]**, Minnetonka, MN
Hopkins Noontime Lions Club **[10948]**, Elk River, MN
Houston Lions Club - Minnesota **[11198]**, Houston, MN
Howard City Lions Club **[8266]**, Howard City, MI
Howell Lions Club **[8276]**, Howell, MI
Hoyt Lakes Lions Club **[11201]**, Hoyt Lakes, MN
Hubbard Lions Club **[15471]**, Hubbard, OH
Hudson Lions Club - Wisconsin **[18224]**, Hudson, WI
Huron Lions Club **[15492]**, Huron, OH
Huron Valley Sunrise Lions Club **[10208]**, Ypsilanti, MI
Hutchinson Jaycees **[11209]**, Hutchinson, MN
Illinois Assn. of County Engineers **[3568]**, Springfield, IL
Indianapolis Chapel Hill Lions Club **[5341]**, Indianapolis, IN
Indianapolis Franklin Township Lions Club **[5349]**, Indianapolis, IN
Inter-Lakes Lions Club **[8368]**, Jackson, MI
Intl. Falls Lions Club **[11217]**, International Falls, MN
Ithaca Lions Club - Michigan **[8352]**, Ithaca, MI
Ithaca Lions Club - Wisconsin **[18429]**, Lone Rock, WI
Jackson Cascades Lions Club **[8372]**, Jackson, MI
Jackson Eye Openers Lions Club **[8379]**, Jackson, MI
Jackson Host Lions Club **[8380]**, Jackson, MI
Jackson Township Lions Club **[15885]**, Massillon, OH
Jeromesville Lions Club **[15528]**, Jeromesville, OH
Jonesville Lions Club **[8410]**, Jonesville, MI
Junior League of Cincinnati **[13877]**, Cincinnati, OH
Junior League of Detroit **[8090]**, Grosse Pointe Farms, MI
Junior League of Grand Rapids **[7971]**, Grand Rapids, MI
Junior League of Indianapolis **[5384]**, Indianapolis, IN
Junior League of Milwaukee **[19040]**, Milwaukee, WI
Junior League of St. Paul **[12435]**, St. Paul, MN
Kalamazoo Downtown Lions Club **[8440]**, Kalamazoo, MI
Kalamazoo West Side Lions Club **[9318]**, Oshtemo, MI
Kaleva Lions Club **[8474]**, Kaleva, MI
Karlstad Lions Club **[11241]**, Karlstad, MN
Kasson-Mantorville Lions Club **[11245]**, Kasson, MN
Kellogg Lions Club **[11250]**, Kellogg, MN
Kendall Lions Club **[18291]**, Kendall, WI
Kensington Lions Club **[11252]**, Kensington, MN
Kent Lions Club **[15543]**, Kent, OH
Kenyon Lions Club **[11254]**, Kenyon, MN
Kerkhoven Lions Club **[11258]**, Kerkhoven, MN
Kettering Lions Club **[15560]**, Kettering, OH
Kewaskum Lions Club **[18317]**, Kewaskum, WI
Kingston Lions Club - Michigan **[8495]**, Kingston, MI
Kingston Lions Club - Minnesota **[10754]**, Dassel, MN
Kiwanis Club of Indianapolis **[5387]**, Indianapolis, IN
Kochville Lions Club **[9612]**, Saginaw, MI
La Crosse Lions Club **[18360]**, La Crosse, WI

La Crosse North Lions Club **[18361]**, La Crosse, WI
La Farge Lions Club **[18384]**, La Farge, WI
La Rue Lions Club **[15576]**, La Rue, OH
LaCrescent Lions Club **[11267]**, La Crescent, MN
Lafayette Lions Club, IN **[5620]**, Lafayette, IN
LaGrange Lions Club - Ohio **[15115]**, Elyria, OH
Laingsburg Lions Club **[8497]**, Laingsburg, MI
Lake Ann Lions Club **[8502]**, Lake Ann, MI
Lake Bronson Lions Club **[11272]**, Lake Bronson, MN
Lake City Lions Club **[11276]**, Lake City, MN
Lake Delton Lions Club **[20177]**, Wisconsin Dells, WI
Lake Elmo Jaycees **[11281]**, Lake Elmo, MN
Lake Elmo Minnesota Lions Club **[11282]**, Lake Elmo, MN
Lake Mills Lions Club **[18404]**, Lake Mills, WI
Lakeview Lions Club - Michigan **[8519]**, Lakeview, MI
Lancaster Lions Club - Minnesota **[11300]**, Lancaster, MN
Lanesboro Lions Club **[11302]**, Lanesboro, MN
Lansing Delta Lions Club **[8589]**, Lansing, MI
Lansing Host Lions Club **[8590]**, Lansing, MI
Lawrenceburg Lions Club **[5659]**, Lawrenceburg, IN
Lawton Lions Club **[8793]**, Lawton, MI
Leader Area Lions Club **[12784]**, Verndale, MN
Lebanon Lions Club - Ohio **[15622]**, Lebanon, OH
Lenawee Noon Lions Club **[6578]**, Adrian, MI
Lennon Lions Club **[8798]**, Lennon, MI
Leslie Lions Club **[8802]**, Leslie, MI
Lewisburg Lions Club **[15637]**, Lewisburg, OH
Lexington Lions Club - Ohio **[15770]**, Mansfield, OH
LHS Key Club **[5660]**, Lawrenceburg, IN
Lib. Coun. of Southeastern Wisconsin **[19042]**, Milwaukee, WI
Lima Exchange Club **[15661]**, Lima, OH
Limaville Lions Club **[13115]**, Alliance, OH
Lincoln Park Lions Club - Michigan **[8814]**, Lincoln Park, MI
Linden Lions Club - Michigan **[8820]**, Linden, MI
Lindsey Lions Club **[15675]**, Lindsey, OH
Lions Club of Alliance **[13116]**, Alliance, OH
Lisbon Lions Club - Ohio **[15679]**, Lisbon, OH
Litchfield Lions Club **[11329]**, Litchfield, MN
Little Fork Lions Club **[11342]**, Littlefork, MN
Livonia Hi-Nooners Lions Club **[8843]**, Livonia, MI
Livonia Lamplighter Lions Club **[9477]**, Redford, MI
Livonia Lions Club **[12999]**, Zimmerman, MN
Lockport Area Exchange Club **[2315]**, Lockport, IL
Loda Lions Club **[2321]**, Loda, IL
London Lions Club **[15694]**, London, OH
Lorain Harbor Lions Club **[13136]**, Amherst, OH
Lorain Lions Club **[15707]**, Lorain, OH
Lordstown Lions Club **[17105]**, Warren, OH
Loretto Lions Club **[11349]**, Loretto, MN
Loudonville Lions Club **[15714]**, Loudonville, OH
Louisville Lions Club - Ohio **[15719]**, Louisville, OH
Loves Park Lions Club **[2350]**, Loves Park, IL
Lowry Lions Club **[11351]**, Lowry, MN
Lucas Lions Club **[15734]**, Lucas, OH
Ludington Lions Club **[8874]**, Ludington, MI
Luther Lions Club **[8881]**, Luther, MI
Lyle Lions Club **[11358]**, Lyle, MN
Lyons Lions Club, IL **[2361]**, Lyons, IL
Mabel Lions Club **[10636]**, Canton, MN
Madison Lions Club - Minnesota **[11367]**, Madison, MN
Madison Township Lions Club **[15735]**, Lucas, OH
Magnolia Lions Club - Ohio **[15751]**, Magnolia, OH
Mahnomen Lions Club **[11371]**, Mahnomen, MN
Manistee Lions Club **[8913]**, Manistee, MI
Mansfield Evening Lions Club **[15773]**, Mansfield, OH
Mansfield Noon Lions **[15774]**, Mansfield, OH
Maple Grove Dande Lions Club **[11412]**, Maple Grove, MN
Maple Grove Lions Club **[11413]**, Maple Grove, MN
Maple Plain Lions Club **[11416]**, Maple Plain, MN
Maple Valley Lions Club **[9354]**, Perrinton, MI
Maplewood-Oakdale Lions Club **[11928]**, Oakdale, MN
Marblehead Peninsula Lions Club **[15579]**, Lakeside, OH
Marion Evening Lions Club **[15845]**, Marion, OH
Marion Noon Lions Club **[15846]**, Marion, OH
Marlboro Lions Club - Ohio **[15720]**, Louisville, OH
Marquette County Exchange Club **[8941]**, Marquette, MI
Marshall Lions Club - Wisconsin **[18815]**, Marshall, WI
Marshfield Lions Club - Wisconsin **[18820]**, Marshfield, WI
Mason Lions Club **[15876]**, Mason, OH
Mason Lions Club - Michigan **[8979]**, Mason, MI
Massillon Lions Club **[15888]**, Massillon, OH
Mattawan Lions Club **[8987]**, Mattawan, MI
Mauston Lions Club **[18439]**, Lyndon Station, WI
Maynard Lions Club **[11444]**, Maynard, MN
Mayville Lions Club **[8989]**, Mayville, MI
Mazeppa Lions Club **[11446]**, Mazeppa, MN
McDonald Lions Club **[15935]**, McDonald, OH
Mecosta Lions Club **[8996]**, Mecosta, MI
Merrill Lions Club **[9006]**, Merrill, MI
Mesick Lions Club **[9010]**, Mesick, MI
Metro Airport Lions Club **[7664]**, Farmington Hills, MI
Miamisburg Lion Club **[15988]**, Miamisburg, OH
Michigan Center Lions Club **[9014]**, Michigan Center, MI
Michigan City Exchange Club **[5787]**, Michigan City, IN
Michigan District of Kiwanis Intl. **[8980]**, Mason, MI
Middleton Key Club **[18910]**, Middleton, WI
Midland Lions Club **[9710]**, Sanford, MI
Midview High School Key Club **[15333]**, Grafton, OH
Mifflin Lions Club **[13167]**, Ashland, OH
Milan Edison Lions Club **[16022]**, Milan, OH
Milan Lions Club - Minnesota **[11468]**, Milan, MN
Millington Lions Club - Michigan **[9055]**, Millington, MI
Miltona Lions Club **[10280]**, Alexandria, MN
Mindoro Lions Club **[19193]**, Mindoro, WI
Minneapolis Ambassadores Lions Club **[11609]**, Minneapolis, MN
Minneapolis Central Lions Club **[12978]**, Woodbury, MN
Minneapolis Fort Snelling Lions Club **[12334]**, St. Louis Park, MN
Minneapolis Hiawatha Lions Club **[11614]**, Minneapolis, MN
Minneapolis Lyn Lake Lions Club **[12335]**, St. Louis Park, MN
Minneapolis North Lions Club **[11616]**, Minneapolis, MN
Minneapolis Northeast Lions Club **[11617]**, Minneapolis, MN
Minneapolis Riverview Lions Club **[10551]**, Brooklyn Park, MN
Minneapolis Southwest Lions Club **[10594]**, Burnsville, MN
Minneapolis Twin City Airport Lions Club **[12448]**, St. Paul, MN
Minnesota Jaycees **[10598]**, Burnsville, MN
Minnetonka South Lions Club **[11190]**, Hopkins, MN
Monroe Golden Lions Club **[9071]**, Monroe, MI
Monroe Lions Club - Ohio **[16055]**, Monroe, OH
Montevideo Lions Club **[11803]**, Montevideo, MN
Monticello Lions Club, IL **[2549]**, Monticello, IL
Montrose Lions Club - Michigan **[9079]**, Montrose, MI
Moorhead Midday-Central Lions Club **[11826]**, Moorhead, MN
Mora Lions Club **[11834]**, Mora, MN
Mormon Coulee Lions Club **[18369]**, La Crosse, WI
Morrice Lions Club **[9084]**, Morrice, MI
Morris Lions Club **[11839]**, Morris, MN
Morton Lions Club **[11845]**, Morton, MN
Mount Gilead Lions Club - Ohio **[16071]**, Mount Gilead, OH
Mt. Morris Lions Club **[9094]**, Mount Morris, MI
Mount Pleasant Lions Club - Michigan **[9117]**, Mount Pleasant, MI
Mountain Iron Lions Club **[11228]**, Iron, MN
Mulliken Lions Club **[9127]**, Mulliken, MI
Munith Lions Club **[9133]**, Munith, MI
Naperville Noon Lions Club **[2652]**, Naperville, IL
Napoleon Lions Club **[8388]**, Jackson, MI
Necedah Lions Club **[19264]**, Necedah, WI
Neosho-Rubicon Lions Club **[19284]**, Neosho, WI
Nevada Lions Club - Ohio **[16111]**, Nevada, OH
New Albany Lions Club **[16113]**, New Albany, OH
New Berlin Indus. Lions Club **[19294]**, New Berlin, WI
New Berlin Lions Club **[19295]**, New Berlin, WI
New Buffalo Lions Club **[10022]**, Union Pier, MI
New Goshen-West Vigo Lions Club **[5942]**, New Goshen, IN
New Hope Lions Club **[11870]**, New Hope, MN
New Lebanon Lions Club **[16131]**, New Lebanon, OH
New Lisbon Lions Club **[19312]**, New Lisbon, WI
New London Lions Club **[11873]**, New London, MN
New Lothrop Lions Club **[9190]**, New Lothrop, MI
New Middletown Lions Club **[16142]**, New Middletown, OH
New Paris Lions Club **[5954]**, New Paris, IN
New Waterford Lions Club **[16163]**, New Waterford, OH
Newaygo Lions Club **[9194]**, Newaygo, MI
Newberry High School Key Club **[9200]**, Newberry, MI
Newcomers Club of Saginaw **[9622]**, Saginaw, MI
Newfolden Lions Club **[11893]**, Newfolden, MN
Newton Falls Lions Club **[14791]**, Cortland, OH
Niles Lions Club **[16207]**, Niles, OH
Niles Lions Club - Michigan **[9212]**, Niles, MI
North Adams Lions Club **[9214]**, North Adams, MI
North Aurora Lions Club **[2743]**, North Aurora, IL
North Bend Lions Club **[17944]**, Ettrick, WI
North Br. Lions Club **[11901]**, North Branch, MN
North Canton Lions Club **[16220]**, North Canton, OH
North Coast Lions Club **[17276]**, Willoughby, OH
North Fairfield Lions Club **[16227]**, North Fairfield, OH
North Jackson Lions Club **[8392]**, Jackson, MI
North Lansing Lions Club **[7562]**, East Lansing, MI
North Ridgeville Lions Club **[16243]**, North Ridgeville, OH
North Royalton Lions Club **[16247]**, North Royalton, OH
Northeastern Lions Club **[16321]**, Owensville, OH
Northmont Lions Club **[15132]**, Englewood, OH
Northport Lions Club **[9218]**, Northport, MI
Northville Lions Club **[9228]**, Northville, MI
Northwest Lions Club **[15892]**, Massillon, OH
Northwest Tonka Lions Club **[12666]**, Shorewood, MN
Norwalk Lions Club **[16263]**, Norwalk, OH
Norwalk Lions Club - Wisconsin **[19327]**, Norwalk, WI
Nova Lions Club **[16268]**, Nova, OH
Oak Harbor Lions Club **[16274]**, Oak Harbor, OH
Oakdale Lions Club **[19905]**, Tomah, WI
Oconomowoc Lions Club **[19341]**, Oconomowoc, WI
Oconto Falls Lions Club **[19352]**, Oconto Falls, WI
Ohio State Buckeye Univ. Lions Club **[14681]**, Columbus, OH
Ohio State Univ. Lions Club **[14685]**, Columbus, OH
Old Fort Lions Club **[16294]**, Old Fort, OH
Olivet Lions Club **[9302]**, Olivet, MI
Olivia Lions Club **[11937]**, Olivia, MN
Onalaska Lions Club **[19367]**, Onalaska, WI
Onekama Lions Club **[9305]**, Onekama, MI
Ontario Area Lions Club **[20169]**, Wilton, WI
Ontario Lions Club **[14810]**, Crestline, OH
Oregon Lions Club **[2870]**, Oregon, IL
Orono District Lions Club **[11344]**, Long Lake, MN
Orr Lions Club **[11943]**, Orr, MN
Ortonville Lions Club **[11946]**, Ortonville, MN
Osakis Lions Club **[11949]**, Osakis, MN
Oslo Lions Club **[11951]**, Oslo, MN
Osseo Lions Club **[12032]**, Plymouth, MN
Ostrander Lions Club **[11955]**, Ostrander, MN

Otisville Lions Club [9322], Otisville, MI
Ottawa Lions Club [16319], Ottawa, OH
Ovid Lions Club [9331], Ovid, MI
Owosso/Corunna Lions Club [9334], Owosso, MI
Oxford Lions Club - Ohio [16327], Oxford, OH
Palatine Lions Club [2924], Palatine, IL
Paris Lions Club - Ohio [16350], Paris, OH
Parma-Spring Arbor Lions Club [9344], Parma, MI
Paw Paw Lions Club [9347], Paw Paw, MI
Paxton Lions Club [2976], Paxton, IL
Pekin Lions Club [2990], Pekin, IL
Pennfield Lions Club [6866], Battle Creek, MI
Pennock Lions Club [11989], Pennock, MN
Peoria Lions Club [3054], Peoria, IL
Perry Township Lions Club [13577], Canton, OH
Perrysville Lions Club [16415], Perrysville, OH
Petersburg-Summerfield Lions Club [9358], Petersburg, MI
Pierz Lions Club [11998], Pierz, MN
Pinckney Lions Club [9382], Pinckney, MI
Pinconning Lions Club [9384], Pinconning, MI
Pine Island Lions Club [12005], Pine Island, MN
Pittsfield Lions Club [3096], Pittsfield, IL
Pittsford Area Lions Club [9320], Osseo, MI
Plain City Lions Club [16443], Plain City, OH
Plain Lions Club [19461], Plain, WI
Plainview Lions Club [12014], Plainview, MN
Pleasant Lions Club [15852], Marion, OH
Plummer Lions Club [12018], Plummer, MN
Plummers Lions Too Club [12019], Plummer, MN
Plymouth Lions Club - Michigan [9408], Plymouth, MI
Plymouth Lions Club - Minnesota [12033], Plymouth, MN
Plymouth Lions Club - Ohio [17265], Willard, OH
Poland Lions Club [16450], Poland, OH
Polk Lions Club [16453], Polk, OH
Port Clinton Lions Club [16461], Port Clinton, OH
Portage Exchange Club [6060], Portage, IN
Portage Lions Club [13397], Bowling Green, OH
Portage Lions Club - Michigan [9453], Portage, MI
Potterville Lions Club [9460], Potterville, MI
Prairie du Chien Lions Club [19528], Prairie Du Chien, WI
Prior Lake Lions Club [12056], Prior Lake, MN
Proctor Lions Club [12058], Proctor, MN
Prospect Lions Club - Ohio [16488], Prospect, OH
Quincy Exchange Club [3165], Quincy, IL
Quincy Lions Club - Michigan [9468], Quincy, MI
Racine Lions Club [12061], Racine, MN
Ramsey Lions Club [12063], Ramsey, MN
Randolph Lions Club - Ohio [16054], Mogadore, OH
Rankin Lions Club - Michigan [7850], Grand Blanc, MI
Ravenna Lions Club [15546], Kent, OH
Raymond Lions Club - Minnesota [12069], Raymond, MN
Red Lake Falls Lions Club [12074], Red Lake Falls, MN
Redford Township Lions Club [7268], Dearborn, MI
Reed City Lions Club [9484], Reed City, MI
Reedsburg Lions Club [18387], La Valle, WI
Remus Lions Club [9858], Stanwood, MI
Reno Lions Club [15829], Marietta, OH
Renville Lions Club [12102], Renville, MN
Republic Lions Club [16511], Republic, OH
Reynoldsburg Lions Club [15416], Hebron, OH
Richland Center Lions Club [19626], Richland Center, WI
Ridgedale Lions Club [15854], Marion, OH
Riley Township Lions Club [6117], Riley, IN
River Valley Lions Club [13490], Caledonia, OH
Riverview Lions Club [8815], Lincoln Park, MI
Robbinsdale Lions Club [10745], Crystal, MN
Roberts Lions Club [19648], Roberts, WI
Rochester Host Lions Club [12178], Rochester, MN
Rock Island Greater Lions Club [12], Albany, IL
Rockford "Noon" Lions Club [2355], Loves Park, IL
Rockville Lions Club [12202], Rockville, MN
Rockwood Lions Club [7706], Flat Rock, MI
Rogers Area Lions Club - Minnesota [12204], Rogers, MN
Rollingstone Area Jaycees [12206], Rollingstone, MN
Rootstown Lions Club [16552], Rootstown, OH
Roseau Lions Club [12210], Roseau, MN
Roselle Lions Club [3357], Roselle, IL
Ross Lions Club [15400], Hamilton, OH
Rotary Club of Cardington, Ohio [13597], Cardington, OH
Rotary Club of Cincinnati [13978], Cincinnati, OH
Rotary Club of Indianapolis [5468], Indianapolis, IN
Rotary Club of Madison [18608], Madison, WI
Rotary Intl. [1673], Evanston, IL
Rowsburg Lions Club [13173], Ashland, OH
Royalton Hills Lions Club [16249], North Royalton, OH
Rushford Lions Club [12257], Rushford, MN
Sabin Lions Club [12261], Sabin, MN
Sacred Heart Lions Club [12263], Sacred Heart, MN
Saginaw West Lions Club [9638], Saginaw, MI
St. Bonifacius Lions Club [12265], St. Bonifacius, MN
St. Charles Lions Club [12267], St. Charles, MN
St. Charles Lions Club - Michigan [9650], St. Charles, MI
Saint Cloud Jaycees [12303], St. Cloud, MN
St. Cloud Lions Club [12304], St. Cloud, MN
St. Croix Valley Lions Club [12725], Stillwater, MN
St. Francis Lions Club [12320], St. Francis, MN
St. Hilaire Lions Club [12748], Thief River Falls, MN
St. Johns Lions Club [9679], St. Johns, MI
St. Joseph Lions Club [9690], St. Joseph, MI
St. Joseph's Ridge Lions Club [19369], Onalaska, WI
St. Louis Lions Club [9697], St. Louis, MI
St. Louis Park Lions Club [10558], Brooklyn Park, MN
St. Paul East Parks Lions Club [11421], Maplewood, MN
Saint Paul Jaycees [12582], St. Paul, MN
St. Stephan's Community Lions Club [8757], Lansing, MI
Salem Lions Club - Ohio [16591], Salem, OH
Saline Area Lions Club [9704], Saline, MI
Sand Lake Lions Club [9706], Sand Lake, MI
Sandstone Lions Club [12627], Sandstone, MN
Sandusky Lions Club [16618], Sandusky, OH
Sanford Lions Club - Michigan [9712], Sanford, MI
Santiago Lions Club [10396], Becker, MN
Sauk Centre Lions Club [12634], Sauk Centre, MN
Sauk Prairie Lions Club [19533], Prairie Du Sac, WI
Sauk Rapids Riverside Lions Club [12637], Sauk Rapids, MN
Saukville Lions Club [19668], Saukville, WI
Savannah Lions Club - Ohio [16659], Shiloh, OH
Sebring Lions Club [16625], Sebring, OH
Seneca Lions Club - Wisconsin [19673], Seneca, WI
Shakopee Jaycees [12653], Shakopee, MN
Shakopee Valley Lions Club [12654], Shakopee, MN
Sheboygan Noon Lions Club [19713], Sheboygan, WI
Sheffield Lions Club [15710], Lorain, OH
Shepherd Lions Club [9750], Shepherd, MI
Sheridan Lions Club - Michigan [9752], Sheridan, MI
Shields Lions Club [9639], Saginaw, MI
Shorewood Kiwanis Club [9567], Roseville, MI
Six Lakes Lions Club [8268], Howard City, MI
Soldiers Grove Lions Club [18032], Gays Mills, WI
South Bend Lions Club [6267], South Bend, IN
South Elgin Lions Club [3499], South Elgin, IL
South Haven - Black River Lions Club [9765], South Haven, MI
South St. Paul Lions Club [12684], South St. Paul, MN
South Shore Lions Club [10971], Excelsior, MN
Southgate Lions Club [9843], Southgate, MI
Sparta Lions Club - Wisconsin [19756], Sparta, WI
Speedway Lions Club [6279], Speedway, IN
Spicer Sunrise Lions Club [12687], Spicer, MN
Spring Green Lions Club [19769], Spring Green, WI
Spring Grove Lions Club [12690], Spring Grove, MN
Springboro Lions Club [16710], Springboro, OH
Springdale-Forest Park Lions Club [16711], Springdale, OH
Springfield Exchange Club [16749], Springfield, OH
Springport Lions Club [9851], Springport, MI
Stanton Lions Club - Michigan [9856], Stanton, MI
Stanwood Lions Club [6953], Big Rapids, MI
Star Prairie Lions Club [19775], Star Prairie, WI
Starbuck Lions Club [12707], Starbuck, MN
Stephen Lions Club [12710], Stephen, MN
Stewartville Lions Club [12715], Stewartville, MN
Stockbridge Lions Club [9878], Stockbridge, MI
Stoddard Lions Club [19827], Stoddard, WI
Streator Lions Club [3732], Streator, IL
Struthers Lions Club [17110], Warren, OH
Suffield Lions Club [16843], Tallmadge, OH
Sullivan Lions Club [16807], Sullivan, OH
Sunbury Lions Club [16815], Sunbury, OH
Sunfield Lions Club [9884], Sunfield, MI
Sussex Lions Club [19886], Sussex, WI
Swartz Creek Lions Club [9896], Swartz Creek, MI
Sycamore Lions Club [16822], Sycamore, OH
Taylor Lions Club - Michigan [10142], Westland, MI
Tekonsha Lions Club [9909], Tekonsha, MI
Thief River Falls Lions Club [12752], Thief River Falls, MN
Thiensville Mequon Lions Club [19893], Thiensville, WI
Three Rivers Lions Club [9919], Three Rivers, MI
Tiffin Lions Club [16865], Tiffin, OH
Tomah Lions Club [19906], Tomah, WI
Tower-Soudan Lions Club [10959], Ely, MN
Traverse City Lions Club [9960], Traverse City, MI
Trenton Lions Club - Michigan [9967], Trenton, MI
Trenton Lions Club - Ohio [16991], Trenton, OH
Tri-Village Lions Club [14746], Columbus, OH
Tri-Village Noon Lions Club [14747], Columbus, OH
Troy Lions Club - Ohio [17009], Troy, OH
Tuslaw Lions Club [15895], Massillon, OH
Twin Valley Lions Club [12765], Twin Valley, MN
Two Harbors Lions Club [12776], Two Harbors, MN
Ulen Lions Club [12779], Ulen, MN
Uniontown Lions Club [17022], Uniontown, OH
Univ. of Wisconsin - La Crosse Br. Lions Club [18380], La Crosse, WI
Upper Sandusky Lions Club [17034], Upper Sandusky, OH
Vadnais Heights Lions Club [12782], Vadnais Heights, MN
Valparaiso High School Key Club [6394], Valparaiso, IN
Vandercook Lake Lions Club [8400], Jackson, MI
Vassar Lions Club [10043], Vassar, MI
Vermilion Lions Club [17067], Vermilion, OH
Vermontville Lions Club [10046], Vermontville, MI
Vestaburg Lions Club [10047], Vestaburg, MI
Virginia Lions Club [12809], Virginia, MN
Viroqua Lions Club [19943], Viroqua, WI
Wacousta Lions Club [7469], DeWitt, MI
Wakeman Lions Club [17083], Wakeman, OH
Wannaska Lions Club [12212], Roseau, MN
Warren Lions Club - Minnesota [12842], Warren, MN
Warren Lions Club - Ohio [17118], Warren, OH
Warrens Lions Club [19948], Warrens, WI
Warroad Lions Club [12845], Warroad, MN
Waterford Lions Club - Wisconsin [19957], Waterford, WI
Waterloo Lions Club [3904], Waterloo, IL
Waterman Lions Club [3906], Waterman, IL
Watertown Lions Club - Minnesota [12853], Watertown, MN
Watson Lions Club [12855], Watson, MN
Waukesha Noon Lions Club [20007], Waukesha, WI
Wauwatosa Lions Club [20082], Wauwatosa, WI

Wauzeka Lions Club **[20092]**, Wauzeka, WI
Wayne-Fall Lions Club **[5981]**, Noblesville, IN
Wayne Lions Club **[10104]**, Wayne, MI
Waynesville Lions Club **[17154]**, Waynesville, OH
Wayzata Lions Club **[12863]**, Wayzata, MN
Webberville Lions Club **[10106]**, Webberville, MI
Weidman Lions Club **[10109]**, Weidman, MI
Wellsville Lions Club **[17162]**, Wellsville, OH
Wendell Lions Club **[12871]**, Wendell, MN
West Alexandria Lions Club **[17165]**, West Alexandria, OH
West Point Lions Club - Ohio **[15682]**, Lisbon, OH
West Salem Lions Club **[20139]**, West Salem, WI
Westby Lions Club **[20144]**, Westby, WI
Westerville Lions Club **[17224]**, Westerville, OH
Westland Breakfast Lions Club **[10143]**, Westland, MI
Westland Host Lions Club **[10147]**, Westland, MI
Westwood Heights Lions Club **[9323]**, Otisville, MI
Wharton Lions Club **[17244]**, Wharton, OH
Wheaton Lions Club **[4002]**, Wheaton, IL
Wheaton Lions Club - Minnesota **[12887]**, Wheaton, MN
White Cloud Lions Club **[10154]**, White Cloud, MI
White Pigeon Lions Club **[10160]**, White Pigeon, MI
Whitefish Area Lions Club **[10743]**, Crosslake, MN
Whitehall Area Lions Club **[16520]**, Reynoldsburg, OH
Williams Bay Lions Club **[20166]**, Williams Bay, WI
Williamston Lions Club - Michigan **[10176]**, Williamston, MI
Willmar Evening Lions Club **[12930]**, Willmar, MN
Willmar Jaycees **[12931]**, Willmar, MN
Willmar Noon Lions Club **[12934]**, Willmar, MN
Willowbrook Key Club **[3867]**, Villa Park, IL
Wilton Lions Club - Wisconsin **[20170]**, Wilton, WI
Wind Lake Lions Club **[20171]**, Wind Lake, WI
Windham Lions Club - Ohio **[17299]**, Windham, OH
Winger Lions Club **[12942]**, Winger, MN
Winona Noon Lions Club **[12963]**, Winona, MN
Winona Rivertown Lions Club **[12964]**, Winona, MN
Woodbury Jaycees **[12988]**, Woodbury, MN
Worthington Lions Club **[14768]**, Columbus, OH
Wyandotte Lions Club - Michigan **[9844]**, Southgate, MI
Wykoff Lions Club **[12996]**, Wykoff, MN
Youngstown Lions Club **[17426]**, Youngstown, OH
Youngstown South Side Lions Club **[13238]**, Austintown, OH
Ypsilanti Lions Club **[10222]**, Ypsilanti, MI
Zilwaukee Lions Club **[9648]**, Saginaw, MI
Zionsville Lions Club **[6555]**, Zionsville, IN
Zumbro Falls Lions Club **[13003]**, Zumbro Falls, MN
Zumbrota Lions Club **[13006]**, Zumbrota, MN
Ser. Corps of Retired Executives-Chapter 6 **[5470]**, Indianapolis, IN
Ser. Couns. of Michigan; Automotive **[9395]**, Plymouth, MI
Ser. Employees AFL-CIO, Indiana/Iowa, D 1199 **[★1176]**
Ser. Employees Intl. Union, AFL-CIO, CLC - Illinois Coun. **[1178]**, Chicago, IL
Ser. Employees Intl. Union, AFL-CIO, CLC - Local Union 4 **[1179]**, Chicago, IL
Ser. Employees Intl. Union, AFL-CIO, CLC - School Ser. Local Union 284 **[12683]**, South St. Paul, MN
Ser. Employees Intl. Union Local 880 **[1180]**, Chicago, IL
Service Sororities
Alpha Kappa Alpha, Alpha Mu Omega **[4968]**, Indianapolis, IN
Alpha Kappa Alpha, Theta Lambda Omega **[10110]**, West Bloomfield, MI
Delta Sigma Phi Fraternity, SDSU **[5101]**, Indianapolis, IN
Sigma Alpha Epsilon **[1675]**, Evanston, IL
Ser. Sta. Dealers Assn. of Indiana **[5471]**, Indianapolis, IN
Ser. Sta. Dealers Assn. of Michigan **[8758]**, Lansing, MI
Servicemen's Union; Vending Machine **[4461]**, Dillsboro, IN
Settlers Assn; Early **[★3134]**
Sexual Abuse
Comfort House **[5805]**, Milltown, IN
Seymour Main Street **[6186]**, Seymour, IN
Shakamak Chamber of Commerce **[5522]**, Jasonville, IN
Shaker Figure Skating Club **[16640]**, Shaker Heights, OH
Shaker Historical Soc. **[16641]**, Shaker Heights, OH
Shaker Square Area Development **[14215]**, Cleveland, OH
Shaker Youth Soccer Assn. **[16642]**, Shaker Heights, OH
Shakopee Chamber of Commerce **[12652]**, Shakopee, MN
Shakopee Jaycees **[12653]**, Shakopee, MN
Shakopee Valley Convention and Visitors Bur. **[★12652]**
Shakopee Valley Lions Club **[12654]**, Shakopee, MN
Shakura Ensemble **[★1181]**
Shakura Ensemble Ritual Theatre **[1181]**, Chicago, IL
Shamrock Club of Wisconsin **[19116]**, Milwaukee, WI
Shar-Pei Rescue Gp; Rasp, Chinese **[★4308]**
Share Found. with the Handicapped **[6136]**, Rolling Prairie, IN
Share the Vision **[★14726]**
Share the Vision of Ohio **[14726]**, Columbus, OH
Sharonville Chamber of Commerce **[16648]**, Sharonville, OH
Sharonville Federated Woman's Club **[13982]**, Cincinnati, OH
Shaw Land Conservancy **[16046]**, Minerva, OH
Shawano Area Chamber of Commerce **[19683]**, Shawano, WI
Shawnee Hills Appaloosa Horse Club **[3411]**, Salem, IL
Shawnee Muskie Hunters **[1443]**, DeKalb, IL
Shawnee Rsrc. Conservation and Development Coun. **[2410]**, Marion, IL
Shawnee - Young Life **[16743]**, Springfield, OH
Sheboygan AIFA **[19706]**, Sheboygan, WI
Sheboygan Area Chap. of the Soc. for Human Rsrc. Mgt. **[19707]**, Sheboygan, WI
Sheboygan Area United Way **[19708]**, Sheboygan, WI
Sheboygan Astronomical Soc. **[19378]**, Oostburg, WI
Sheboygan Coin Club **[19709]**, Sheboygan, WI
Sheboygan County Chamber of Commerce and Convention and Visitors Bur. **[19710]**, Sheboygan, WI
Sheboygan County Estate Planning Coun. **[19711]**, Sheboygan, WI
Sheboygan County Historical Soc. **[19712]**, Sheboygan, WI
Sheboygan Falls Chamber Main Street **[19719]**, Sheboygan Falls, WI
Sheboygan Kennel Club **[19720]**, Sheboygan Falls, WI
Sheboygan Noon Lions Club **[19713]**, Sheboygan, WI
Sheboygan Space Soc. **[18323]**, Kiel, WI
Sheep
Illinois Suffolk Sheep Assn. **[2421]**, Marseilles, IL
Indiana Suffolk Sheep Assn. **[6070]**, Princeton, IN
Mid-States Woolgrowers Cooperative Assn. **[13519]**, Canal Winchester, OH
Minnesota Lamb and Wool Producers Assn. **[11877]**, New Prague, MN
Ohio Sheep Improvement Assn. **[14672]**, Columbus, OH
Ohio Suffolk Sheep Assn. **[17091]**, Wapakoneta, OH
Wisconsin Club Lamb Assn. **[19650]**, Rosholt, WI
Wisconsin Suffolk Sheep Assn. **[19337]**, Oakfield, WI
Sheepdog
Old English Sheepdog Club of Am. **[18055]**, Glendale, WI
Sheet Metal and Air Conditioning Contractors Assn. **[19117]**, Milwaukee, WI
Sheet Metal and Air Conditioning Contractors' Natl. Assn. - Cleveland **[16250]**, North Royalton, OH
Sheet Metal and Air Conditioning Contractors Natl. Assn. Metropolitan Detroit Chap. **[10009]**, Troy, MI
Sheet Metal and Air Conditioning Contractors' Natl. Assn. of Michiana **[6264]**, South Bend, IN
Sheet Metal and Air Conditioning Contractors' Natl. Assn. of Minnesota **[11734]**, Minneapolis, MN
Sheet Metal and Air Conditioning Contractors' Natl. Assn. of North Central Ohio **[14216]**, Cleveland, OH
Sheet Metal and Air Conditioning Contractors' Natl. Assn. of Northern Illinois **[3318]**, Rockford, IL
Sheet Metal Contractors Assn. of Central Indiana **[5472]**, Indianapolis, IN
Sheet Metal Contractors Assn. of Evansville **[4572]**, Evansville, IN
Sheet Metal Contractors Assn. of Greater Cincinnati **[13983]**, Cincinnati, OH
Sheet Metal Contractors Assn; Northeastern Illinois **[1598]**, Elgin, IL
Sheet Metal Contractors Assn. of Nortwest Ohio **[16959]**, Toledo, OH
Sheet Metal and Roofing Contractors Assn. of Miami Valley **[14952]**, Dayton, OH
Sheet Metal Workers AFL-CIO, LU 80 **[9819]**, Southfield, MI
Sheet Metal Workers AFL-CIO, LU 183 **[★13984]**
Sheet Metal Workers' Intl. Assn., AFL-CIO, CFL - Local Union 10 **[11423]**, Maplewood, MN
Sheet Metal Workers' Intl. Assn., Local Union 265 **[452]**, Carol Stream, IL
Sheet Metal Workers Intl. Assn. LU 183/AFL-CIO **[13984]**, Cincinnati, OH
Sheet Metal Workers' Local Union 33 Cleveland District **[14217]**, Cleveland, OH
Sheet Metal Workers' Union Local 73, AFL-CIO **[2007]**, Hillside, IL
Sheffield Lions Club **[15710]**, Lorain, OH
Shelby Chamber of Commerce **[16655]**, Shelby, OH
Shelby County Chamber of Commerce **[6195]**, Shelbyville, IN
Shelby County Coin Club **[16667]**, Sidney, OH
Shelby County Historical Soc. **[16668]**, Sidney, OH
Shelby County United Way **[16669]**, Sidney, OH
Shelbyville Area Chamber of Commerce **[3467]**, Shelbyville, IL
Shell Lake Chamber of Commerce **[19725]**, Shell Lake, WI
Shelter
Mattoon Public Action to Deliver Shelter **[2444]**, Mattoon, IL
Shenango Valley Beagle Club **[16451]**, Poland, OH
Shepherd Lions Club **[9750]**, Shepherd, MI
Shepherd Rescue Alliance of Wisconsin; German **[18514]**, Madison, WI
Sherburne County Historical Soc. **[10397]**, Becker, MN
Sheridan Chamber Players **[1674]**, Evanston, IL
Sheridan Lions Club - Michigan **[9752]**, Sheridan, MI
Sheridan Neighborhood Org. **[11735]**, Minneapolis, MN
Sheriff Reserve Deputy Corps; Hancock County **[466]**, Carthage, IL
Sheriffs' Assn; Michigan **[8712]**, Lansing, MI
Sheriffs Dept. Chaplaincy; Hamilton County **[5973]**, Noblesville, IN
Shiawassee Family and Friends Alliance for the Mentally Ill **[9335]**, Owosso, MI
Shiawassee Regional Bd. of Realtors **[9336]**, Owosso, MI
Shiawassee Regional Chamber of Commerce **[9337]**, Owosso, MI
Shiawassee United Way **[9338]**, Owosso, MI
Shields Lions Club **[9639]**, Saginaw, MI
Shooting
3M Trap and Skeet Club **[11925]**, Oakdale, MN
Albany Sportsmen's Club **[10250]**, Albany, MN
Bald Eagle Sportsmen's Assn. **[12892]**, White Bear Lake, MN
Bay County Conservation Club **[8822]**, Linwood, MI
Bemidji Trap and Skeet Club **[10412]**, Bemidji, MN
Bi-State Sportsman's Assn. **[1294]**, Colona, IL
Broken Bird Rod and Gun Club **[13156]**, Arlington, OH
Brown County Sportsmen's Club **[18091]**, Green Bay, WI
Camp Perry Shooting Club **[16458]**, Port Clinton, OH

Cass City Gun Club **[9377]**, Pigeon, MI
Clinton County Farmers and Sportsman's Assn. **[17289]**, Wilmington, OH
Crooked Creek Conservation and Gun Club **[5970]**, Noblesville, IN
Daleville Skeet and Trap Club **[6031]**, Peru, IN
Decatur Gun Club **[1388]**, Decatur, IL
Del-Tone/Luth Gun Club **[12284]**, St. Cloud, MN
Detroit Gun Club **[10055]**, Walled Lake, MI
East View Rod and Gun Club **[16360]**, Parma, OH
Edgar County Sportsman's Club **[2948]**, Paris, IL
Elk Rapids Sportsman's Club **[7596]**, Elk Rapids, MI
Evansville Gun Club **[4906]**, Haubstadt, IN
Fairfield Sportsmen's Assn. **[13824]**, Cincinnati, OH
Fort Thunder PSC **[11992]**, Perham, MN
Frankfort Sportsman Club **[2508]**, Mokena, IL
Gateway Sportsmen's Club **[10025]**, Unionville, MI
Genesee Sportsman's Club **[7768]**, Flushing, MI
Ghetto Grouse Gun Club **[5798]**, Milan, IN
GK Riverbottom Hunt Club **[16060]**, Montpelier, OH
Grand Blanc Huntsman's Club **[7839]**, Goodrich, MI
Grand Rapids Gun Club **[11085]**, Grand Rapids, MN
Grayling Sportsmen's Club **[8062]**, Grayling, MI
Gun River Skeet and Trap **[9386]**, Plainwell, MI
Hawthorne Valley Skeet Club **[13231]**, Aurora, OH
Howell Shooting Club **[4074]**, Yorkville, IL
Hunting Valley Gun Club **[16396]**, Pepper Pike, OH
Illinois Skeet Assn. **[1395]**, Decatur, IL
Illinois Sporting Clay Assn. **[2691]**, New Lenox, IL
Illinois State Rifle Assn. **[582]**, Chatsworth, IL
Indian Hill Shooting Club **[13865]**, Cincinnati, OH
Indiana Skeet Shooting Assn. **[6148]**, Russiaville, IN
Indiana Sporting Clays Assn. **[4554]**, Evansville, IN
Indiana State Rifle and Pistol Assn. **[5323]**, Indianapolis, IN
Kent County Conservation League **[6558]**, Ada, MI
Knollwood Gun Club **[2891]**, Oswego, IL
Kosko Conservation **[6448]**, Warsaw, IN
Loda Sportsmen's Club **[2358]**, Ludlow, IL
Michigan Rifle and Pistol Assn. **[8971]**, Marshall, MI
Michigan Skeet Assn. **[10042]**, Vassar, MI
Mid-up Shooters **[8095]**, Gwinn, MI
Milford Gun Club **[13904]**, Cincinnati, OH
Minneapolis Gun Club **[12052]**, Prior Lake, MN
Minnesota Rifle and Revolver Assn. **[11794]**, Minnetonka, MN
Minnetonka Game and Fish Club **[10308]**, Anoka, MN
Mosinee Sportsmen's Alliance **[19230]**, Mosinee, WI
North Bristol Sportsman's Club **[19862]**, Sun Prairie, WI
North Macomb Sportsman Club **[10078]**, Washington, MI
North Ottawa Rod and Gun Club **[7864]**, Grand Haven, MI
Northbrook Sports Club **[1896]**, Grayslake, IL
Ohio Rifle and Pistol Assn. **[16138]**, New London, OH
Ohio State Skeet Assn. **[16222]**, North Canton, OH
Ohio State Trapshooting Found. **[15371]**, Grove City, OH
Olive Br. Farm Skeet Club **[15065]**, Dublin, OH
Palos Sportsman's Club **[1730]**, Frankfort, IL
Peoria Skeet and Trap **[1546]**, East Peoria, IL
Quincy Gun Club **[3166]**, Quincy, IL
Racine County Line Rifle Club **[19334]**, Oak Creek, WI
Riverside Skeet Club **[20178]**, Wisconsin Dells, WI
Rockford Skeet Club **[3312]**, Rockford, IL
Rockford Sportsman's Club **[9529]**, Rockford, MI
Saginaw Gun Club **[9634]**, Saginaw, MI
St. Charles Sportsmen Club **[3394]**, St. Charles, IL
Saint Joe Valley Conservation **[6152]**, St. Joe, IN
Saint Joseph County Conservation **[9881]**, Sturgis, MI
Sauk Prairie Trap and Skeet **[19534]**, Prairie Du Sac, WI
Scioto River Hunting Club **[16560]**, Roundhead, OH
Scott AFB Rod and Gun Club **[3789]**, Troy, IL
Seaway Gun Club **[9161]**, Muskegon, MI
Southern Michigan Gun Club **[8469]**, Kalamazoo, MI
Tri-County Coonhunters Conservation Club **[4162]**, Batesville, IN
Twin Oak Sporting Clays **[2503]**, Mode, IL
Upland Hunt Club and Sporting Clays **[1367]**, Davis Junction, IL
Van Dyne Sportsmen's Club **[19930]**, Van Dyne, WI
Waukesha Gun Club **[20006]**, Waukesha, WI
Wausau Skeet and Trap Club **[20056]**, Wausau, WI
Wayne County Sportsman's Club **[10103]**, Wayne, MI
Wealthwood Rod and Gun Club **[10247]**, Aitkin, MN
West Walker Sportsman's Club **[8025]**, Grand Rapids, MI
Wisconsin Rifle and Pistol Assn. **[17659]**, Bristol, WI
Wisconsin Skeet Shooting Assn. **[19887]**, Sussex, WI
Wisconsin Sporting Clays Assn. **[17733]**, Cedarburg, WI
Shooting Club; Howell **[4074]**, Yorkville, IL
Shoreline Amateur Astronomy Assn. **[8220]**, Holland, MI
Shorewood Kiwanis Club **[9567]**, Roseville, MI
Shorewood Table Tennis Club **[19733]**, Shorewood, WI
Short North Bus. Assn. **[14727]**, Columbus, OH
Showbiz Players **[13985]**, Cincinnati, OH
Shrine Club; Kokomo **[5577]**, Kokomo, IN
SHRM Ohio State Coun. **[13986]**, Cincinnati, OH
Siberian Husky Club of Greater Cleveland **[13349]**, Berea, OH
Siberian Husky Club of Greater Detroit **[7021]**, Brighton, MI
Siberian Husky Club of the Twin Cities **[10675]**, Clear Lake, MN
Siberian Rescue; Free Spirit **[1949]**, Harvard, IL
Sibley County Pheasants Forever **[10340]**, Arlington, MN
Sickle Cell Anemia
Sickle Cell Disease Assn. of Illinois **[1182]**, Chicago, IL
Sickle Cell Awareness Gp. **[13987]**, Cincinnati, OH
Sickle Cell Awareness Gp. of Greater Cincinnati **[13988]**, Cincinnati, OH
Sickle Cell Disease Assn. of Am. - Michigan **[7432]**, Detroit, MI
Sickle Cell Disease Assn. of Illinois **[1182]**, Chicago, IL
Sidney-Shelby County Young Men's Christian Association **[16670]**, Sidney, OH
Sierra Club - Hoosier Chapter - Dunelands Group **[4930]**, Hobart, IN
Sierra Club - Illinois Chap. - Blackhawk Gp. **[3319]**, Rockford, IL
Sierra Club - Illinois Chap. - Chicago Gp. **[1183]**, Chicago, IL
Sierra Club - Illinois Chap. - Piasa Palisades Gp. **[44]**, Alton, IL
Sierra Club - John Muir Chap. **[18614]**, Madison, WI
Sierra Club - John Muir Chap. - Chippewa Valley Gp. **[17896]**, Eau Claire, WI
Sierra Club - John Muir Chap. - Great Waters Gp. **[19118]**, Milwaukee, WI
Sierra Club - Mackinac Chap. **[8759]**, Lansing, MI
Sierra Club - Mackinac Chap. - Crossroads Gp. **[7022]**, Brighton, MI
Sierra Club - Mackinac Chap. - Huron Valley Gp. **[6765]**, Ann Arbor, MI
Sierra Club - Midwest Off. **[18615]**, Madison, WI
Sierra Club, Ohio Chap. **[14728]**, Columbus, OH
Sigma Alpha Epsilon **[1675]**, Evanston, IL
Sigma Gamma Epsilon, Zeta Sigma Chap., Western Michigan Univ. **[8467]**, Kalamazoo, MI
Sigma Theta Tau Intl. Honor Soc. of Nursing **[5473]**, Indianapolis, IN
Silent Film
Silent Film Soc. of Chicago **[1184]**, Chicago, IL
Silent Film Soc. of Chicago **[1184]**, Chicago, IL
Silver Bay Area Chamber of Commerce **[★12770]**
Silver Creek Beagle Club **[4149]**, Austin, IN
Silver Lake Sand Dunes Area Chamber of Commerce **[8994]**, Mears, MI
Silvercreek Glider Club **[2683]**, New Douglas, IL
Single Volunteers of Lake County **[15978]**, Mentor, OH
Single Volunteers of Twin Cities **[11736]**, Minneapolis, MN
Singles
Single Volunteers of Lake County **[15978]**, Mentor, OH
Single Volunteers of Twin Cities **[11736]**, Minneapolis, MN
Singles Pleasing the Lord **[3447]**, Schaumburg, IL
Singles Pleasing the Lord **[3447]**, Schaumburg, IL
Sinnissippi Audubon Soc. **[3320]**, Rockford, IL
Sister Cities Assn. of Greater Cincinnati **[13989]**, Cincinnati, OH
Sister Cities of Vandalia **[17060]**, Vandalia, OH
Sisters of the Moon **[18616]**, Madison, WI
Sisters of Ozaukee County; Big Bros. and **[18062]**, Grafton, WI
Six Lakes Lions Club **[8268]**, Howard City, MI
Sk8 Bay Figure Skating Club **[6896]**, Bay City, MI
Skate Company Skating Club **[10186]**, Wyandotte, MI
Skaters Edge of West Michigan **[8221]**, Holland, MI
Skating
Albert Lea Figure Skating Club **[10253]**, Albert Lea, MN
Ann Arbor Figure Skating Club **[6674]**, Ann Arbor, MI
Ann Arbor Huron Highschool Skating Club **[6676]**, Ann Arbor, MI
Arctic Figure Skating Club **[7060]**, Canton, MI
Babbitt Figure Skating Club **[10369]**, Babbitt, MN
Bemidji Figure Skating Club **[10408]**, Bemidji, MN
Black River Falls Figure Skating Club **[17632]**, Black River Falls, WI
Bowling Green Skating Club **[13383]**, Bowling Green, OH
Braemar-City of Lakes Figure Skating Club **[10907]**, Edina, MN
Brooklyn Park Figure Skating Club **[10547]**, Brooklyn Park, MN
Burnsville-Minnesota Valley Figure Skating Club **[10589]**, Burnsville, MN
Center Ice Skating Club **[13562]**, Canton, OH
Chicago Figure Skating Club **[1607]**, Elk Grove Village, IL
Chiller Figure Skating Club **[15045]**, Dublin, OH
Coll. of St. Scholastica Figure Skating Club **[10809]**, Duluth, MN
Columbus Figure Skating Club **[14385]**, Columbus, OH
Crookston Figure Skating Club **[10735]**, Crookston, MN
Crystal Ice Figure Skating Club **[19787]**, Stevens Point, WI
Dearborn Figure Skating Club **[7255]**, Dearborn, MI
Duluth Figure Skating Club **[10818]**, Duluth, MN
DuPage Figure Skating Club **[2196]**, Lake Forest, IL
Eagan-Heights Figure Skating Club **[10319]**, Apple Valley, MN
Eagle River Figure Skating Club **[19964]**, Watersmeet, WI
Eau Claire Figure Skating Club **[17877]**, Eau Claire, WI
Eden Prairie Figure Skating Club **[10892]**, Eden Prairie, MN
Escanaba Areas Figure Skating Club **[7613]**, Escanaba, MI
Euclid Blade and Edge Figure Skating Club **[15140]**, Euclid, OH
Farmington Hills Figure Skating Club **[7641]**, Farmington, MI
Figure Skating Club of Bloomington **[10467]**, Bloomington, MN
Figure Skating Club of Cincinnati **[13828]**, Cincinnati, OH

Figure Skating Club of Minneapolis **[11559]**, Minneapolis, MN
Figure Skating Club of Rochester **[12141]**, Rochester, MN
Figure Skating Club of Rockford **[3277]**, Rockford, IL
Flint 4 Seasons Figure Skating Club **[9894]**, Swartz Creek, MI
Fond du Lac Blue Line Figure Skating **[17976]**, Fond du Lac, WI
Forestwood Figure Skating Club of Parma Ohio **[16245]**, North Royalton, OH
Fraser Figure Skating Club **[7790]**, Fraser, MI
Garfield Heights Figure Skating Club **[13472]**, Burton, OH
Gilmour Acad. Figure Skating Club **[16678]**, Solon, OH
Glenwood Figure Skating Club **[1707]**, Flossmoor, IL
Greater Cleveland Coun. Figure Skating Club **[16241]**, North Ridgeville, OH
Greater Evansville Figure Skating Club **[4549]**, Evansville, IN
Greater Grand Rapids Figure Skating Club **[7959]**, Grand Rapids, MI
Greater Green Bay Figure Skating Club **[18101]**, Green Bay, WI
Greater Milwaukee Figure Skating Club **[19251]**, Mukwonago, WI
Hayward Figure Skating Club **[18196]**, Hayward, WI
Hibbing Figure Skating Club **[11158]**, Hibbing, MN
Houghton-Portage Township Highschool Skating Club **[8253]**, Houghton, MI
Ice Skating Club of Indianapolis **[4321]**, Carmel, IN
Ice Zone Figure Skating Club **[13373]**, Boardman, OH
Illinois Valley Figure Skating Club **[3028]**, Peoria, IL
Indiana Univ. Figure Skating Club **[4234]**, Bloomington, IN
Janesville Figure Skating Club **[18251]**, Janesville, WI
Kalamazoo Figure Skating Club **[8441]**, Kalamazoo, MI
Kent Figure Skating Club **[15486]**, Hudson, OH
Kettle Moraine Figure Skating Club **[20120]**, West Bend, WI
Lansing Skating Club **[7526]**, East Lansing, MI
Lincoln Center Figure Skating Club **[4402]**, Columbus, IN
Lincoln High School Figure Skating Club **[12742]**, Thief River Falls, MN
Little Traverse Figure Skating Club **[9364]**, Petoskey, MI
Manitowoc County Figure Skating Club **[18783]**, Manitowoc, WI
Mankato Figure Skating Club **[11385]**, Mankato, MN
Maplewood Figure Skating Club **[11927]**, Oakdale, MN
Marquette Figure Skating Club **[8946]**, Marquette, MI
Melvindale Figure Skating Club **[8998]**, Melvindale, MI
Mentor Figure Skating Club **[15971]**, Mentor, OH
Michiana Figure Skating Club **[9209]**, Niles, MI
Michigan State Univ. Figure Skating Club **[7553]**, East Lansing, MI
Michigan Technological Univ. Synchronized Skating Club **[8257]**, Houghton, MI
Mid-Am. Speed Skating - The Long Track Club of USA **[2756]**, Northbrook, IL
Midland Figure Skating Club **[9037]**, Midland, MI
Monroe Figure Skating Club **[9070]**, Monroe, MI
Mt. Pleasant Figure Skating Club **[9116]**, Mount Pleasant, MI
Muskegon Lakeshore Figure Skating Club **[9155]**, Muskegon, MI
New Prague Figure Skating Club **[11879]**, New Prague, MN
New Ulm Figure Skating Club **[11886]**, New Ulm, MN
North Star Figure Skating Assn. **[7135]**, Cheboygan, MI
Northern Blades Figure Skating Club **[10451]**, Blaine, MN
Northern Ice Skating Club **[2882]**, Orland Park, IL
Northern Michigan Univ. Figure Skating Club **[8955]**, Marquette, MI
Northwoods Figure Skating Club **[19724]**, Shell Lake, WI
Novi High School Skating Club **[9242]**, Novi, MI
Ohio Speedskating Assn. **[17235]**, Westlake, OH
Ontonagon Area High School Skating Club **[9310]**, Ontonagon, MI
Owatonna Figure Skating Club **[11965]**, Owatonna, MN
Port Huron Northern High School Skating Club **[7774]**, Fort Gratiot, MI
Queen City Figure Skating Club **[13970]**, Cincinnati, OH
Rhinelander Figure Skating Club **[19605]**, Rhinelander, WI
Riverbend Skating Club **[1566]**, Edwardsville, IL
Roseville Figure Skating Club **[12246]**, Roseville, MN
St. Clair Shores Figure Skating Club **[9665]**, St. Clair Shores, MI
St. Cloud Figure Skating Club **[12302]**, St. Cloud, MN
St. Paul Figure Skating Club **[12581]**, St. Paul, MN
Shaker Figure Skating Club **[16640]**, Shaker Heights, OH
Sk8 Bay Figure Skating Club **[6896]**, Bay City, MI
Skate Company Skating Club **[10186]**, Wyandotte, MI
Skaters Edge of West Michigan **[8221]**, Holland, MI
Skokie Valley Skating Club **[1423]**, Deerfield, IL
South Dayton Figure Skating Club **[15565]**, Kettering, OH
South Metro Shores Figure Skating Club **[9842]**, Southgate, MI
Southern Wisconsin Figure Skating Club **[18842]**, McFarland, WI
Southport Skating Club **[1925]**, Gurnee, IL
Southwest Michigan Skating Club **[9454]**, Portage, MI
Sparta Area Figure Skating Club **[20138]**, West Salem, WI
Springfield Figure Skating Club **[3677]**, Springfield, IL
Starlight Ice Dance Club **[10902]**, Eden Prairie, MN
Strongsville Skating Club **[16799]**, Strongsville, OH
Summit Skating Club of Michigan **[8244]**, Holt, MI
Superior Figure Skating Club **[19881]**, Superior, WI
Swan City Ice Skaters **[17596]**, Beaver Dam, WI
Sycamore Ice Skating Club **[5486]**, Indianapolis, IN
Timberline Skating Club **[20049]**, Wausau, WI
Tri-County Figure Skating Club **[10991]**, Farmington, MN
Troy Skating Club **[17011]**, Troy, OH
Twin Bays Skating Club **[9962]**, Traverse City, MI
Twin City Figure Skating Assn. **[12599]**, St. Paul, MN
Univ. of Illinois At Urbana-Champaign Figure Skating Club **[555]**, Champaign, IL
Univ. of Michigan Skating Club **[6778]**, Ann Arbor, MI
Univ. of Wisconsin Ice Skating Club - Eau Claire **[17905]**, Eau Claire, WI
Vacationland Figure Skating Club **[10522]**, Brainerd, MN
Wagon Wheel Figure Skating Club **[154]**, Barrington, IL
Waupun Figure Skating Club **[20029]**, Waupun, WI
Western Michigan Univ. Skating Club **[8471]**, Kalamazoo, MI
Westland Figure Skating Club **[10145]**, Westland, MI
Willmar Diamond Edge Figure Skating Club **[10454]**, Blomkest, MN
Winter Club of Indianapolis **[5501]**, Indianapolis, IN
Winterhurst Figure Skating Club **[15592]**, Lakewood, OH
Wisconsin Figure Skating Club **[19169]**, Milwaukee, WI
Wisconsin Rapids Figure Skating Club **[20198]**, Wisconsin Rapids, WI
Woodbury Figure Skating Club **[12987]**, Woodbury, MN
Skating Club of Rochester; Figure **[12141]**, Rochester, MN
Skating Club; South Dayton Figure **[15565]**, Kettering, OH
Skeptics and Agnostics for Christian Culture **[14729]**, Columbus, OH
Skiing
Central Ohio Alpine Ski Troop **[14352]**, Columbus, OH
Chicago Ski Twisters **[830]**, Chicago, IL
Chicago Sno-Gophers Ski Club **[831]**, Chicago, IL
Chicago Trendsetters **[834]**, Chicago, IL
Corbeau Ski Club **[13810]**, Cincinnati, OH
Ebony Ice Ski Club **[19003]**, Milwaukee, WI
Esprit The Ultimate Ski and Sports Club **[14115]**, Cleveland, OH
Flint Snowbirds SkiClub **[7734]**, Flint, MI
Gelende Ski Club **[11568]**, Minneapolis, MN
Gem City Gliders Ski and Bike Club **[14885]**, Dayton, OH
Jim Dandy Ski Club **[7383]**, Detroit, MI
Pathfinders Ski Club **[3040]**, Peoria, IL
Umoja Ski Club **[9643]**, Saginaw, MI
Skills USA, Albert Lea High School **[10261]**, Albert Lea, MN
Skills USA, Anoka-Hennepin Tech. Coll. **[10311]**, Anoka, MN
Skills USA, Anoka High School **[10312]**, Anoka, MN
Skills USA, Austin High School **[10358]**, Austin, MN
Skills USA, Blaine High School **[10452]**, Blaine, MN
Skills USA, Cambridge High School **[10626]**, Cambridge, MN
Skills USA, Carver-Scott Educal. Cooperative **[10654]**, Chaska, MN
Skills USA, Century High School **[12185]**, Rochester, MN
Skills USA, Champlin Park High School **[10644]**, Champlin, MN
Skills USA, Chisago Lakes High School **[11317]**, Lindstrom, MN
Skills USA, Coon Rapids High School **[10717]**, Coon Rapids, MN
Skills USA, Cottonwood River Cooperative Center **[12696]**, Springfield, MN
Skills USA, Dakota County Tech. Center **[12217]**, Rosemount, MN
Skills USA, Duluth Secondary Tech. Center **[10853]**, Duluth, MN
Skills USA, East Grand Forks High School **[10885]**, East Grand Forks, MN
Skills USA, Edison High School **[11737]**, Minneapolis, MN
Skills USA, Fergus Falls High School **[11003]**, Fergus Falls, MN
Skills USA, Hennepin Tech. Coll. **[10559]**, Brooklyn Park, MN
Skills USA, Hopkins High School **[11796]**, Minnetonka, MN
Skills USA, Independent District 287 **[10901]**, Eden Prairie, MN
Skills USA, John F. Kennedy High School **[10488]**, Bloomington, MN
Skills USA, John Marshall High School **[12186]**, Rochester, MN
Skills USA, Lakeville High School **[11296]**, Lakeville, MN
Skills USA, Mankato West High School **[11399]**, Mankato, MN
Skills USA, Mayo High School **[12187]**, Rochester, MN
Skills USA, Minneapolis Public Schools **[11738]**, Minneapolis, MN
Skills USA, North Community High School **[11739]**, Minneapolis, MN
Skills USA, Owatonna High School **[11968]**, Owatonna, MN
Skills USA, Patrick Henry High School **[11740]**, Minneapolis, MN
Skills USA, Proctor High School **[12059]**, Proctor, MN
Skills USA, Red Wing Central High School **[12085]**, Red Wing, MN
Skills USA, Roosevelt High School **[11741]**, Minneapolis, MN

Skills USA, Roseau High School **[12211]**, Roseau, MN
Skills USA, St. Francis High School **[12321]**, St. Francis, MN
Skills USA, South High School **[11742]**, Minneapolis, MN
Skills USA, Southwest High School **[11743]**, Minneapolis, MN
Skills USA, S.T.E.P. - Secondary Tech. Educ. Prog. **[10313]**, Anoka, MN
Skills USA, Tartan High School **[11929]**, Oakdale, MN
Skills USA, Tech. High School **[12308]**, St. Cloud, MN
Skills USA-VICA, Indiana **[★5298]**
Skills USA-VICA, Michigan **[★9530]**
Skills USA, Washburn High School **[11744]**, Minneapolis, MN
Skills USA, Wayzata High School **[12035]**, Plymouth, MN
Skills USA, Work Opportunity Center **[11745]**, Minneapolis, MN
Skills USA, Wright Tech. Center **[10578]**, Buffalo, MN
SkillsUSA Illinois **[2511]**, Mokena, IL
SkillsUSA Michigan **[9530]**, Rockford, MI
SkillsUSA Minnesota **[11746]**, Minneapolis, MN
Skokie Chamber of Commerce **[3490]**, Skokie, IL
Skokie Valley Astronomers **[3879]**, Warrenville, IL
Skokie Valley Kennel Club **[3358]**, Roselle, IL
Skokie Valley Kennel Club **[3773]**, Tinley Park, IL
Skokie Valley Skating Club **[1423]**, Deerfield, IL
Skyscraper Club of Cleveland **[15505]**, Independence, OH
Slayton Area Chamber of Commerce **[12671]**, Slayton, MN
Sleeping Bear Area Chamber of Commerce **[7838]**, Glen Arbor, MI
Sleepy Eye Area Chamber of Commerce **[12673]**, Sleepy Eye, MN
Slovak
First Catholic Slovak Ladies Assn. - Beachwood Junior Br. HO **[13287]**, Beachwood, OH
First Catholic Slovak Ladies Assn. - Beachwood Senior Br. ZJ **[13288]**, Beachwood, OH
First Catholic Slovak Ladies Assn. - Bedford Junior Br. 380 **[13470]**, Burton, OH
First Catholic Slovak Ladies Assn. - Bedford Senior Br. 475 **[13471]**, Burton, OH
First Catholic Slovak Ladies Assn. - Berwyn Junior Br. 426 **[1360]**, Darien, IL
First Catholic Slovak Ladies Assn. - Berwyn Senior Br. 503 **[1361]**, Darien, IL
First Catholic Slovak Ladies Assn. - Campbell Junior Br. 250 **[13508]**, Campbell, OH
First Catholic Slovak Ladies Assn. - Canton Junior Br. 143 **[13564]**, Canton, OH
First Catholic Slovak Ladies Assn. - Canton Senior Br. 301 **[13565]**, Canton, OH
First Catholic Slovak Ladies Assn. - Chicago Junior Br. 174 **[1316]**, Crete, IL
First Catholic Slovak Ladies Assn. - Chicago Junior Br. 308 **[2938]**, Palos Hills, IL
First Catholic Slovak Ladies Assn. - Chicago Junior Br. 370 **[1981]**, Hickory Hills, IL
First Catholic Slovak Ladies Assn. - Chicago Senior Br. 225 **[1982]**, Hickory Hills, IL
First Catholic Slovak Ladies Assn. - Chicago Senior Br. 352 **[2939]**, Palos Hills, IL
First Catholic Slovak Ladies Assn. - Chicago Senior Br. 421 **[4012]**, Willowbrook, IL
First Catholic Slovak Ladies Assn. - Cleveland Junior Br. 014 **[13434]**, Brook Park, OH
First Catholic Slovak Ladies Assn. - Cleveland Junior Br. 057 **[16361]**, Parma, OH
First Catholic Slovak Ladies Assn. - Cleveland Junior Br. 240 **[14121]**, Cleveland, OH
First Catholic Slovak Ladies Assn. - Cleveland Junior Br. 441 **[16362]**, Parma, OH
First Catholic Slovak Ladies Assn. - Cleveland Junior Br. 453 **[17255]**, Wickliffe, OH
First Catholic Slovak Ladies Assn. - Cleveland Junior Br. 461 **[15740]**, Lyndhurst, OH
First Catholic Slovak Ladies Assn. - Cleveland Junior Br. 481 **[16363]**, Parma, OH
First Catholic Slovak Ladies Assn. - Cleveland Junior Br. 483 **[16676]**, Solon, OH
First Catholic Slovak Ladies Assn. - Cleveland Junior Br. 485 **[16364]**, Parma, OH
First Catholic Slovak Ladies Assn. - Cleveland Junior Br. 503 **[15994]**, Middleburg Heights, OH
First Catholic Slovak Ladies Assn. - Cleveland Senior Br. 010 **[14122]**, Cleveland, OH
First Catholic Slovak Ladies Assn. - Cleveland Senior Br. 141 **[16365]**, Parma, OH
First Catholic Slovak Ladies Assn. - Cleveland Senior Br. 176 **[17014]**, Twinsburg, OH
First Catholic Slovak Ladies Assn. - Cleveland Senior Br. 221 **[16366]**, Parma, OH
First Catholic Slovak Ladies Assn. - Cleveland Senior Br. 238 **[16367]**, Parma, OH
First Catholic Slovak Ladies Assn. - Cleveland Senior Br. 360 **[14123]**, Cleveland, OH
First Catholic Slovak Ladies Assn. - Cleveland Senior Br. 378 **[15741]**, Lyndhurst, OH
First Catholic Slovak Ladies Assn. - Cleveland Senior Br. 517 **[16380]**, Parma Heights, OH
First Catholic Slovak Ladies Assn. - Cleveland Senior Br. 522 **[17256]**, Wickliffe, OH
First Catholic Slovak Ladies Assn. - Cleveland Senior Br. 530 **[14124]**, Cleveland, OH
First Catholic Slovak Ladies Assn. - Cleveland Senior Br. 555 **[16677]**, Solon, OH
First Catholic Slovak Ladies Assn. - Cleveland Senior Br. 557 **[16368]**, Parma, OH
First Catholic Slovak Ladies Assn. - Cleveland Senior Br. 578 **[15995]**, Middleburg Heights, OH
First Catholic Slovak Ladies Assn. - Detroit Junior Br. 232 **[6610]**, Allen Park, MI
First Catholic Slovak Ladies Assn. - Detroit Junior Br. 327 **[7788]**, Fraser, MI
First Catholic Slovak Ladies Assn. - Detroit Senior Br. 334 **[6611]**, Allen Park, MI
First Catholic Slovak Ladies Assn. - Detroit Senior Br. 403 **[7789]**, Fraser, MI
First Catholic Slovak Ladies Assn. - Elyria Junior Br. 478 **[16281]**, Oberlin, OH
First Catholic Slovak Ladies Assn. - Elyria Senior Br. 476 **[16282]**, Oberlin, OH
First Catholic Slovak Ladies Assn. - Joliet Senior Br. 053 **[2105]**, Joliet, IL
First Catholic Slovak Ladies Assn. - Lakewood Junior Br. 088 **[16788]**, Strongsville, OH
First Catholic Slovak Ladies Assn. - Lakewood Junior Br. 429 **[15581]**, Lakewood, OH
First Catholic Slovak Ladies Assn. - Lakewood Junior Br. 457 **[16369]**, Parma, OH
First Catholic Slovak Ladies Assn. - Lakewood Senior Br. 432 **[15582]**, Lakewood, OH
First Catholic Slovak Ladies Assn. - Lakewood Senior Br. 524 **[16370]**, Parma, OH
First Catholic Slovak Ladies Assn. - Lorain Senior Br. 114 **[15704]**, Lorain, OH
First Catholic Slovak Ladies Assn. - Milwaukee Junior Br. 130 **[19260]**, Muskego, WI
First Catholic Slovak Ladies Assn. - Milwaukee Senior Br. 023 **[19261]**, Muskego, WI
First Catholic Slovak Ladies Assn. - Milwaukee Senior Br. 376 **[19010]**, Milwaukee, WI
First Catholic Slovak Ladies Assn. - Mount Olive Junior Br. 140 **[2580]**, Mount Olive, IL
First Catholic Slovak Ladies Assn. - Mount Olive Senior Br. 049 **[2581]**, Mount Olive, IL
First Catholic Slovak Ladies Assn. - Muskegon Heights Senior Br. 445 **[9170]**, Muskegon Heights, MI
First Catholic Slovak Ladies Assn. - Muskegon Junior Br. 357 **[9171]**, Muskegon Heights, MI
First Catholic Slovak Ladies Assn. - North Olmsted Junior Br. 499 **[16297]**, Olmsted Falls, OH
First Catholic Slovak Ladies Assn. - North Olmsted Senior Br. 573 **[16298]**, Olmsted Falls, OH
First Catholic Slovak Ladies Assn. - Streator Junior Br. 077 **[3726]**, Streator, IL
First Catholic Slovak Ladies Assn. - Streator Senior Br. 007 **[3727]**, Streator, IL
First Catholic Slovak Ladies Assn. - Streator Senior Br. 066 **[3728]**, Streator, IL
First Catholic Slovak Ladies Assn. - Struthers Junior Br. 066 **[15470]**, Hubbard, OH
First Catholic Slovak Ladies Assn. - Toledo Junior Br. 149 **[16916]**, Toledo, OH
First Catholic Slovak Ladies Assn. - Youngstown Junior Br. 029 **[17398]**, Youngstown, OH
First Catholic Slovak Ladies Assn. - Youngstown Junior Br. 192 **[17399]**, Youngstown, OH
First Catholic Slovak Ladies Assn. - Youngstown Senior Br. 030 **[17400]**, Youngstown, OH
SMA Support **[5587]**, Kokomo, IN
Small Business
Buckeye SCORE **[13551]**, Canton, OH
Citizens Utility Bd. **[18497]**, Madison, WI
Columbus SCORE **[14401]**, Columbus, OH
Coun. of Small Bus. Executives **[18998]**, Milwaukee, WI
Family Firm Inst., Cincinnati Study Group **[13825]**, Cincinnati, OH
Family Firm Inst., Midwest (Chicago) Study Group **[1421]**, Deerfield, IL
Greater Wabash Valley SCORE **[6322]**, Terre Haute, IN
Illinois Small Bus. Development Center **[3634]**, Springfield, IL
Indiana Grocery and Convenience Store Assn. **[5241]**, Indianapolis, IN
Indiana Small Bus. Coun. **[5299]**, Indianapolis, IN
Indiana Small Bus. Development Center **[5300]**, Indianapolis, IN
Minnesota Small Bus. Development Center **[12520]**, St. Paul, MN
Natl. Fed. of Independent Bus. - Illinois **[3654]**, Springfield, IL
Natl. Fed. of Independent Bus. - Indiana **[5426]**, Indianapolis, IN
Natl. Fed. of Independent Bus. - Minnesota **[12550]**, St. Paul, MN
Natl. Fed. of Independent Bus. - Ohio **[14521]**, Columbus, OH
National Federation of Independent Business - Wisconsin **[18578]**, Madison, WI
North Central Ohio SCORE **[15780]**, Mansfield, OH
Owatonna Bus. Incubator **[11964]**, Owatonna, MN
SCORE Akron **[13088]**, Akron, OH
SCORE Anderson **[4120]**, Anderson, IN
SCORE Ann Arbor Area Chap. **[6764]**, Ann Arbor, MI
SCORE Bloomington **[4256]**, Bloomington, IN
SCORE Cadillac **[7049]**, Cadillac, MI
SCORE Central Area (St. Cloud) **[12307]**, St. Cloud, MN
SCORE Central Illinois **[311]**, Bloomington, IL
SCORE Central Wisconsin **[18823]**, Marshfield, WI
SCORE Chap. 28, Milwaukee, WI **[19114]**, Milwaukee, WI
SCORE Chap. 50 **[4714]**, Fort Wayne, IN
SCORE Chap. 107 **[14951]**, Dayton, OH
SCORE Chicago **[1174]**, Chicago, IL
SCORE Counselors to Am'.s Small Bus. **[12183]**, Rochester, MN
SCORE Decatur **[1407]**, Decatur, IL
SCORE Detroit **[7430]**, Detroit, MI
SCORE Eau Claire **[17895]**, Eau Claire, WI
SCORE Elkhart **[4506]**, Elkhart, IN
SCORE Evansville **[4571]**, Evansville, IN
SCORE Fox Cities **[17523]**, Appleton, WI
SCORE Fox Valley **[130]**, Aurora, IL
SCORE Grand Rapids **[8009]**, Grand Rapids, MI
SCORE Green Bay **[18131]**, Green Bay, WI
SCORE Kokomo/Howard Counties **[5586]**, Kokomo, IN
SCORE La Crosse **[18377]**, La Crosse, WI
SCORE Logansport **[5698]**, Logansport, IN
SCORE Madison **[18613]**, Madison, WI
SCORE Marion/Grant Co **[5743]**, Marion, IN
SCORE Minneapolis **[11733]**, Minneapolis, MN
SCORE Muskegon **[9160]**, Muskegon, MI
SCORE New Ulm Area **[11887]**, New Ulm, MN
SCORE Northern Illinois **[3317]**, Rockford, IL
SCORE Peoria **[3064]**, Peoria, IL
SCORE Petoskey **[9372]**, Petoskey, MI
SCORE Quad Cities **[2533]**, Moline, IL
SCORE Quincy Tri-State **[3172]**, Quincy, IL
SCORE St. Paul **[12586]**, St. Paul, MN
SCORE South Bend **[6263]**, South Bend, IN
SCORE South Central Indiana **[5923]**, New Albany, IN
SCORE South East Indiana **[4406]**, Columbus, IN
SCORE South Metro **[10608]**, Burnsville, MN
SCORE Southern Illinois **[430]**, Carbondale, IL

SCORE Springfield **[3674]**, Springfield, IL
SCORE Superior **[19877]**, Superior, WI
SCORE SW Illinois **[1876]**, Godfrey, IL
SCORE Traverse City **[9952]**, Traverse City, MI
SCORE Wausau **[20046]**, Wausau, WI
Ser. Corps of Retired Executives-Chapter 6 **[5470]**, Indianapolis, IN
Small Bus. Assn. of Michigan **[8760]**, Lansing, MI
South Bend SCORE **[6269]**, South Bend, IN
Wisconsin Small Bus. Development Center **[18752]**, Madison, WI
Youngstown SCORE **[17429]**, Youngstown, OH
Small Bus. Assn. of Michigan **[8760]**, Lansing, MI
Small Bus. Development Center **[★13612]**
Small Bus. Development Center Network **[6108]**, Richmond, IN
Small Bus. Development Center; Wisconsin **[18752]**, Madison, WI
SMART Recovery **[★15961]**
Snow Sports
Baxter Snowmobile Club **[12000]**, Pillager, MN
J-Sak Snowboarding **[13133]**, Amherst, OH
Snowboarding; J-Sak **[13133]**, Amherst, OH
Snowmobile Club; Baxter **[12000]**, Pillager, MN
Snowmobile Club; Brule River Riders **[19495]**, Poplar, WI
Snowmobile Club; Driftskippers **[7208]**, Coloma, MI
Snowmobile Club; Longville Lakes Area **[11347]**, Longville, MN
Snowmobile Club; Riverbend Benders **[475]**, Cary, IL
Snowmobile Clubs; Assn. of Wisconsin **[17488]**, Appleton, WI
Snowmobilers Assn; Minnesota United **[10554]**, Brooklyn Park, MN
Snowmobiles
Brule River Riders Snowmobile Club **[19495]**, Poplar, WI
Driftskippers Snowmobile Club **[7208]**, Coloma, MI
Michigan Snowmobile Assn. **[7983]**, Grand Rapids, MI
So. Mn. Albert Lea REACT **[10262]**, Albert Lea, MN
Soccer
Chicago SCORES **[829]**, Chicago, IL
Dearborn Soccer Club **[7257]**, Dearborn, MI
Highland Soccer Club **[4913]**, Highland, IN
Kickers Soccer Club **[122]**, Aurora, IL
Magic Soccer Club **[18558]**, Madison, WI
Rootstown Soccer Club **[16553]**, Rootstown, OH
Shaker Youth Soccer Assn. **[16642]**, Shaker Heights, OH
Tri-Cities Strikers Soccer Club **[9849]**, Spring Lake, MI
Wisconsin Youth Soccer Assn. **[20112]**, West Allis, WI
Soccer Assn; Shaker Youth **[16642]**, Shaker Heights, OH
Soccer Assn; Wisconsin Youth **[20112]**, West Allis, WI
Soccer Club; Dearborn **[7257]**, Dearborn, MI
Soccer Club; Highland **[4913]**, Highland, IN
Soccer Club; Kickers **[122]**, Aurora, IL
Soccer Club; Magic **[18558]**, Madison, WI
Soccer Club; Rootstown **[16553]**, Rootstown, OH
Soccer Club; Tri-Cities Strikers **[9849]**, Spring Lake, MI
Social Action
Gary-East Chicago-Hammond Empowerment Zone **[4779]**, Gary, IN
Social Clubs
Alpine Kiwanis of Rockford, Illinois **[585]**, Cherry Valley, IL
Apple Siders of Cincinnati **[13744]**, Cincinnati, OH
Bay de Noc Kiwanis Golden K of Escanaba **[7608]**, Escanaba, MI
Columbus Evening Kiwanis Club **[4396]**, Columbus, IN
Danville Kiwanis' Clubs, Breakfast Club **[1346]**, Danville, IL
Danville Kiwanis' Clubs, Golden K Club **[1347]**, Danville, IL
Danville Kiwanis' Clubs, Noon Club **[1348]**, Danville, IL
Detroit Kiwanis Club No. 1, Michigan **[7349]**, Detroit, MI
Downtown Kiwanis Club of Bloomington **[4214]**, Bloomington, IN
Downtown Kiwanis Club of Jackson, Michigan **[8362]**, Jackson, MI
Escanaba Kiwanis Club **[7614]**, Escanaba, MI
Flat Rock Kiwanis **[7703]**, Flat Rock, MI
Gathering of Southeast Wisconsin **[19012]**, Milwaukee, WI
Golden K Kiwanis Club of Grand Rapids, Michigan **[7942]**, Grand Rapids, MI
Goshen Noon Kiwanis Club **[4797]**, Goshen, IN
Indy West Daybreakers Kiwanis Club **[5363]**, Indianapolis, IN
Janesville Noon Kiwanis Club **[18253]**, Janesville, WI
Kiwanis Club of Addison **[9]**, Addison, IL
Kiwanis Club of Adrian **[6571]**, Adrian, MI
Kiwanis Club of Ann Arbor **[6713]**, Ann Arbor, MI
Kiwanis Club of Baraboo **[17574]**, Baraboo, WI
Kiwanis Club of Beloit Stateline Golden K **[17612]**, Beloit, WI
Kiwanis Club of Bensenville-Wood Dale **[227]**, Bensenville, IL
Kiwanis Club of Bloomington, Illinois **[294]**, Bloomington, IL
Kiwanis Club of Brookfield, IL **[353]**, Brookfield, IL
Kiwanis Club of Brookfield, Wisconsin **[17671]**, Brookfield, WI
Kiwanis Club of Champaign-Urbana **[534]**, Champaign, IL
Kiwanis Club of Chandler **[4345]**, Chandler, IN
Kiwanis Club of Chatham **[580]**, Chatham, IL
Kiwanis Club of Chesaning, Michigan **[7147]**, Chesaning, MI
Kiwanis Club of Clinton Township, Michigan **[7178]**, Clinton Township, MI
Kiwanis Club of Columbia, Illinois **[1298]**, Columbia, IL
Kiwanis Club of Darien-Westmont **[1362]**, Darien, IL
Kiwanis Club Delphi Chap. **[4455]**, Delphi, IN
Kiwanis Club of Des Plaines, Illinois **[1463]**, Des Plaines, IL
Kiwanis Club of East Lansing **[7525]**, East Lansing, MI
Kiwanis Club of Elkhorn, Wisconsin **[17928]**, Elkhorn, WI
Kiwanis Club of Fishers Sta. **[4609]**, Fishers, IN
Kiwanis Club of Glen Ellyn **[1836]**, Glen Ellyn, IL
Kiwanis Club of Holland **[8884]**, Macatawa, MI
Kiwanis Club of Jacksonville, Illinois **[2082]**, Jacksonville, IL
Kiwanis Club of Kaukauna **[18288]**, Kaukauna, WI
Kiwanis Club of La Grange, Illinois **[2170]**, La Grange, IL
Kiwanis Club of Lombard **[2336]**, Lombard, IL
Kiwanis Club of Menomonee Falls **[18876]**, Menomonee Falls, WI
Kiwanis Club of Milwaukee **[19041]**, Milwaukee, WI
Kiwanis Club of Mt. Vernon **[2600]**, Mount Vernon, IL
Kiwanis Club of Park Ridge - Noon **[2963]**, Park Ridge, IL
Kiwanis Club of Plainfield **[3100]**, Plainfield, IL
Kiwanis Club of Plover **[19484]**, Plover, WI
Kiwanis Club of Potowatomi-South Bend **[6236]**, South Bend, IN
Kiwanis Club of Rockford **[3285]**, Rockford, IL
Kiwanis Club of Shelbyville **[6194]**, Shelbyville, IN
Kiwanis Club of Sparta **[19752]**, Sparta, WI
Kiwanis Club of Streamwood **[3720]**, Streamwood, IL
Kiwanis Club of Tinley Park **[3770]**, Tinley Park, IL
Kiwanis Club of Traverse City **[9934]**, Traverse City, MI
La Crosse Kiwanis Club **[18359]**, La Crosse, WI
Lake County Merry Makers **[8305]**, Idlewild, MI
Lebanon Kiwanis **[5670]**, Lebanon, IN
Madison West Kiwanis Club **[18557]**, Madison, WI
Manistique Area Kiwanis Club **[8918]**, Manistique, MI
Quincy Noon Kiwanis **[3167]**, Quincy, IL
Saint Joseph, Michigan Kiwanis Club **[9691]**, St. Joseph, MI
Skyscraper Club of Cleveland **[15505]**, Independence, OH
Speedway Kiwanis Club **[6278]**, Speedway, IN
West Bend Noon Kiwanis Club (Wisconsin) **[20131]**, West Bend, WI
Zionsville Kiwanis Club **[6554]**, Zionsville, IN
Social Fraternities
Acacia, Indiana Chap. **[4194]**, Bloomington, IN
Acacia, St. Cloud State Chap. **[12269]**, St. Cloud, MN
Acacia, Wisconsin Chap. **[18442]**, Madison, WI
FarmHouse Fraternity - Illinois FarmHouse **[3814]**, Urbana, IL
FarmHouse Fraternity - Michigan State Farm-House **[7519]**, East Lansing, MI
FarmHouse Fraternity - Minnesota FarmHouse **[12412]**, St. Paul, MN
FarmHouse Fraternity - Univ. of Wisconsin Platteville **[19464]**, Platteville, WI
FarmHouse - Purdue Univ. Chap. **[6481]**, West Lafayette, IN
Illinois State Univ. FarmHouse Fraternity **[2721]**, Normal, IL
Theta Xi, Alpha Sigma Chap. — Bradley Univ. **[3066]**, Peoria, IL
Theta Xi Fraternity, Beta Delta Chap. **[435]**, Carbondale, IL
Theta Xi Fraternity, Kappa Sigma Chap. **[7758]**, Flint, MI
Theta Xi Fraternity, Sigma Chap. **[6774]**, Ann Arbor, MI
Theta Xi Fraternity, Theta Chap. **[6501]**, West Lafayette, IN
Theta Xi, Gamma Kappa Chap. — Univ. of Illinois-Chicago **[1207]**, Chicago, IL
Theta Xi, Kappa Chap. — Rose-Hulman Inst. of Tech. **[6346]**, Terre Haute, IN
Theta Xi, Kappa Kappa Chap. — Ball State Univ. **[5898]**, Muncie, IN
Social Issues
Policy Matters Ohio **[14206]**, Cleveland, OH
Social Justice
Wisconsin Citizen Action **[18683]**, Madison, WI
Social Responsibility, Grand Rapids Chap; Educators for **[7927]**, Grand Rapids, MI
Social Security
Chicago Social Security Mgt. Assn. **[3950]**, West Frankfort, IL
Social Security Mgt. Assn; Chicago **[3950]**, West Frankfort, IL
Social Service
Cambodian Assn. of Illinois **[774]**, Chicago, IL
Character Coun. of Indiana **[5083]**, Indianapolis, IN
Chinese Amer. Ser. League **[846]**, Chicago, IL
Coll. Democrats of Minnesota **[12404]**, St. Paul, MN
Ekklesia Development Corp. **[13818]**, Cincinnati, OH
Faith in Action in Dodge County **[11244]**, Kasson, MN
Faith in Action of McHenry County **[1323]**, Crystal Lake, IL
First Call for Help **[4399]**, Columbus, IN
Friendship Circle **[10113]**, West Bloomfield, MI
Hull House Assn. **[920]**, Chicago, IL
Illinois Young Democrats **[2544]**, Montgomery, IL
Indiana Univ. Coll. Democrats **[4232]**, Bloomington, IN
Indiana Young Democrats **[4236]**, Bloomington, IN
Interfaith Volunteer Caregivers of Portage County **[19791]**, Stevens Point, WI
InWord Resources **[16009]**, Middletown, OH
Lake County Democratic Party **[15968]**, Mentor, OH
Levy Cares **[1027]**, Chicago, IL
Lutherans Concerned/Great Lakes **[6714]**, Ann Arbor, MI
Michigan County Social Ser. Assn. **[8654]**, Lansing, MI
Minnesota Social Ser. Assn. **[12521]**, St. Paul, MN
Montgomery County, Ohio - Young Democrats **[14924]**, Dayton, OH
Oak Tree Corner **[14935]**, Dayton, OH
Ohio Young Democrats **[14701]**, Columbus, OH
Phantom Lake Young Men's Christian Association **[19254]**, Mukwonago, WI
Protestants for the Common Good **[1147]**, Chicago, IL
Soc. of St. Vincent de Paul **[13995]**, Cincinnati, OH

Toledo Rotary Club Found. **[16976]**, Toledo, OH
Tuscarawas County Young Democrats **[16156]**, New Philadelphia, OH
Volunteers of Am.-Minnesota **[11066]**, Golden Valley, MN
Wisconsin Intergenerational Network **[18716]**, Madison, WI
Social Ser. Assn; Michigan County **[8654]**, Lansing, MI
Social Services; Friends of Southern Illinois Regional **[418]**, Carbondale, IL

Social Studies
Michigan Coun. for the Social Stud. **[9109]**, Mount Pleasant, MI
Minnesota Coun. for the Social Stud. **[12236]**, Roseville, MN
Ohio Coun. for the Social Stud. **[15439]**, Hilliard, OH
Wisconsin Coun. for the Social Stud. **[19847]**, Sturgeon Bay, WI

Social Welfare
Al-Anon Family Gp. **[1370]**, Decatur, IL
Amer. Friends Ser. Comm., Ann Arbor **[6658]**, Ann Arbor, MI
Amer. Friends Ser. Comm., Chicago **[620]**, Chicago, IL
Amer. Friends Ser. Comm. - Dayton, Ohio **[14841]**, Dayton, OH
Amer. Friends Ser. Comm., Northeast Ohio **[13029]**, Akron, OH
Amer. Red Cross, Hamilton County Ser. Center **[5969]**, Noblesville, IN
Amer. Red Cross of Ottawa County **[8192]**, Holland, MI
Brainerd Area Sertoma Club **[10506]**, Brainerd, MN
Buckeye Sertoma Club **[14344]**, Columbus, OH
Focus: HOPE **[7363]**, Detroit, MI
Franciscan Outreach Assn. **[896]**, Chicago, IL
Hamilton County Sertoma Club **[5972]**, Noblesville, IN
Lancaster Sertoma Club **[15605]**, Lancaster, OH
Org. of the North East **[1117]**, Chicago, IL
Overflowing Cup Total Life Center **[17615]**, Beloit, WI
Powell Sertoma Club **[16481]**, Powell, OH
Sertoma 700 Club Of Rochester **[12184]**, Rochester, MN
Union and League of RSA **[16240]**, North Olmsted, OH
Volunteers of Am. of Central Ohio **[14760]**, Columbus, OH
Volunteers of Am. of Illinois **[1224]**, Chicago, IL
Volunteers of Am. of Indiana **[5496]**, Indianapolis, IN
Volunteers of Am. Michigan **[9830]**, Southfield, MI
Volunteers of Am. of Minnesota **[11774]**, Minneapolis, MN
Volunteers of Am. of Northeast and North Central Ohio **[14235]**, Cleveland, OH
Volunteers of Am. Ohio River Valley **[14023]**, Cincinnati, OH
Young Women's Christian Association of Kalamazoo **[8473]**, Kalamazoo, MI

Social Work
Assn. for Community Org. and Social Admin., Midwest Region **[14321]**, Columbus, OH
Lamplighter's Civic and Social Org. **[17321]**, Wooster, OH
Natl. Assn. of Social Workers, Illinois Chap. **[1077]**, Chicago, IL
Natl. Assn. of Social Workers, Minnesota Chap. **[12545]**, St. Paul, MN
Natl. Assn. of Social Workers - Ohio Chap. **[14518]**, Columbus, OH
Natl. Assn. of Social Workers - Wisconsin Chap. **[18575]**, Madison, WI

Social Workers
Friends of Southern Illinois Regional Social Services **[418]**, Carbondale, IL
Natl. Assn. of Social Workers - Michigan Chap. **[8737]**, Lansing, MI
Social Workers; Chicago Chap. of the Natl. Assn. of Black **[801]**, Chicago, IL
Social Workers, Illinois Chap; Natl. Assn. of **[1077]**, Chicago, IL
Social Workers - Ohio Chap; Natl. Assn. of **[14518]**, Columbus, OH
Social Workers - Wisconsin Chap; Natl. Assn. of **[18575]**, Madison, WI

Socialism
Chicago Democratic Socialists of Am. **[806]**, Chicago, IL
Democratic Socialists of America, Columbus **[14422]**, Columbus, OH
Democratic Socialists of Am., Madison **[18905]**, Middleton, WI
Democratic Socialists of Am., Twin Cities **[12407]**, St. Paul, MN
Society of the 173D Airborne Brigade, Midwest Chapter XVII **[14730]**, Columbus, OH
Soc. for the Advancement of Material and Process Engg., Chicago Chap. **[1676]**, Evanston, IL
Soc. for the Advancement of Material and Process Engg., Michigan Chap. **[7792]**, Fraser, MI
Soc. for the Advancement of Material and Process Engg., Midwest Chap. **[14953]**, Dayton, OH
Soc. for the Advancement of Material and Process Engg., Northern Ohio Chap. **[15549]**, Kent, OH
Soc. of Amer. Foresters, Headwaters Chap. **[11220]**, International Falls, MN
Soc. of Amer. Foresters, Illinois Chap. **[1941]**, Harrisburg, IL
Soc. of Amer. Foresters, Lake Superior Chap. **[12937]**, Willow River, MN
Soc. of Amer. Foresters, Minnesota **[10932]**, Effie, MN
Soc. of Amer. Foresters, Ohio **[14731]**, Columbus, OH
Soc. of Amer. Foresters, Southeast Illinois Student Chap. **[1942]**, Harrisburg, IL
Soc. of Amer. Foresters, Southern Chap. **[12188]**, Rochester, MN
Soc. of Amer. Foresters, Southern Illinois Univ. Student Chap. **[2621]**, Murphysboro, IL
Soc. of Amer. Foresters, Univ. of Illinois Student Chap. **[3833]**, Urbana, IL
Soc. of Amer. Foresters, Univ. of Minnesota Student Chap. **[12587]**, St. Paul, MN
Soc. of Amer. Foresters, Vermilion Community Coll. Student Chap. **[10958]**, Ely, MN
Soc. of Amer. Military Engineers, Chicago Post **[1185]**, Chicago, IL
Soc. of Amer. Military Engineers, Cincinnati Post **[13990]**, Cincinnati, OH
Soc. of Amer. Military Engineers, Detroit Post **[7433]**, Detroit, MI
Soc. of Amer. Military Engineers, Rock Island Post **[3259]**, Rock Island, IL
Soc. of Amer. Registered Architects - Minnesota Coun. **[10854]**, Duluth, MN
Soc. of Amer. Registered Architects - Northern Ohio Chap. **[14218]**, Cleveland, OH
Soc. of Antique Modelers - Flyers 79 **[16574]**, St. Clairsville, OH
Soc. of Antique Modelers - Heart of Ohio Chap. **[17029]**, Upper Arlington, OH
Soc. of Antique Modelers - Illinois 117 **[3107]**, Plainfield, IL
Soc. of Antique Modelers - Indiana 112, Hoosier Bombers **[4175]**, Bedford, IN
Soc. of Antique Modelers - Michigan 4 **[10193]**, Wyoming, MI
Soc. of Antique Modelers - Michigan 40 **[6766]**, Ann Arbor, MI
Soc. of Antique Modelers - Ohio 6 **[14732]**, Columbus, OH
Soc. of Antique Modelers - Ohio 39 **[16620]**, Sandusky, OH
Soc. of Antique Modelers - Old Fort Flyers **[4715]**, Fort Wayne, IN
Soc. of Antique Modelers - Springfield Antique Modelers **[15137]**, Enon, OH
Soc. of Antique Modelers - Variety Gp. **[4176]**, Bedford, IN
Soc. of Antique Modelers - Western Ohio Oldtimers **[14954]**, Dayton, OH
Soc. for Applied Spectroscopy, Chicago **[2268]**, Libertyville, IL
Soc. for Applied Spectroscopy, Cincinnati **[13991]**, Cincinnati, OH
Soc. for Applied Spectroscopy, Detroit **[7434]**, Detroit, MI
Soc. for Applied Spectroscopy, Indiana **[4257]**, Bloomington, IN
Soc. for Applied Spectroscopy, Mid-Michigan **[9041]**, Midland, MI
Soc. for Applied Spectroscopy, Minnesota **[11424]**, Maplewood, MN
Soc. for Applied Spectroscopy, Ohio Valley **[17361]**, Wright-Patterson AFB, OH
Soc. for Applied Spectroscopy, Toledo **[15918]**, Maumee, OH
Soc. of Architectural Historians - Chicago Chap. **[1186]**, Chicago, IL
Soc. of Architectural Historians - Wisconsin Chap. **[19119]**, Milwaukee, WI
Soc. of Automotive Engineers - Indiana State Univ.-Terre Haute **[6343]**, Terre Haute, IN
Soc. of Automotive Engineers - Northern Michigan Univ. **[9511]**, Rochester, MI
Soc. of Automotive Engineers - Univ. of Illinois-Chicago **[1187]**, Chicago, IL
Soc. of Automotive Engineers - Univ. of Michigan-Dearborn **[7269]**, Dearborn, MI
Society of Bioprocessing Professionals **[5474]**, Indianapolis, IN
Soc. of Broadcast Engineers, Chap. 24 Madison Wisconsin **[18617]**, Madison, WI
Soc. of Broadcast Engineers, Chap. 25, Indianapolis **[5475]**, Indianapolis, IN
Soc. of Broadcast Engineers, Chap. 28 Milwaukee **[19120]**, Milwaukee, WI
Soc. of Broadcast Engineers, Chap. 33 - Southwest Ohio **[13992]**, Cincinnati, OH
Soc. of Broadcast Engineers, Chap. 35 - Kentucky **[5924]**, New Albany, IN
Soc. of Broadcast Engineers, Chap. 70 - Northeast Ohio **[13305]**, Bedford, OH
Soc. of Broadcast Engineers, Chap. 112 - Western Wisconsin **[17897]**, Eau Claire, WI
Soc. for Coll. and Univ. Planning, Illinois **[1188]**, Chicago, IL
Soc. of Consumer Affairs Professionals in Bus., Chicago Chap. **[3348]**, Romeoville, IL
Soc. of Consumer Affairs Professionals in Bus., Great Lakes Chap. **[10010]**, Troy, MI
Soc. of Consumer Affairs Professionals in Bus., Indiana Chap. **[5476]**, Indianapolis, IN
Soc. of Consumer Affairs Professionals in Bus., Minnesota Chap. **[11747]**, Minneapolis, MN
Soc. of Consumer Affairs Professionals in Bus., Ohio Chap. **[13089]**, Akron, OH
Soc. of Consumer Affairs Professionals in Bus., Wisconsin Chap. **[17730]**, Cedarburg, WI
Soc. of Consumer Affairs Professionals in Bus., Wisconsin Chap. **[19275]**, Neenah, WI
Soc. of Financial Ser. Professionals - Columbus, Ohio Chap. **[14733]**, Columbus, OH
Soc. of Fire Protection Engineers - Minnesota **[12036]**, Plymouth, MN
Soc. of Fire Protection Engineers - Northeast Ohio Chap. **[16382]**, Parma Heights, OH
Soc. For The Handicapped Of Medina County **[16632]**, Seville, OH
Soc. for Healthcare Consumer Advocacy of the Amer. Hosp. Assn. **[1189]**, Chicago, IL
Society for Healthcare Consumer Advocacy of the American Hospital Association **[4030]**, Winfield, IL
Soc. for Hea.care Consumer Advocacy of the Amer. Hosp. Assn., Wisconsin **[19217]**, Monroe, WI
Soc. for Hea.care Consumer Advocacy, Illinois **[3834]**, Urbana, IL
Soc. for Hea.care Consumer Advocacy, Indiana **[5744]**, Marion, IN
Soc. for Human Rsrc. Mgt. - Chippewa Valley Chap. **[17898]**, Eau Claire, WI
Soc. for Human Rsrc. Mgt. - Dodge County Chap. **[17595]**, Beaver Dam, WI
Soc. for Human Rsrc. Mgt. - Fond du Lac Chap. **[17992]**, Fond du Lac, WI
Soc. for Human Rsrc. Mgt. - Fox Valley Chap. **[17524]**, Appleton, WI
Soc. for Human Rsrc. Mgt. - Green Bay Area **[18132]**, Green Bay, WI
Soc. for Human Rsrc. Mgt. - La Crosse Chap. **[18378]**, La Crosse, WI
Soc. for Human Rsrc. Mgt. - Lake/Geauga Chap. **[15979]**, Mentor, OH
Soc. for Human Rsrc. Mgt. - Northwest Indiana Chap. **[6169]**, Schererville, IN
Soc. for Human Rsrc. Mgt. - Tuscora Chap. **[15032]**, Dover, OH

Soc. of Human Rsrc. Professionals **[1190]**, Chicago, IL
Soc. of Incentive and Travel Executives, Chicago Chap. **[3448]**, Schaumburg, IL
Soc. of Indiana Pioneers **[5477]**, Indianapolis, IN
Soc. for Indus. Archeology **[8261]**, Houghton, MI
Soc. of Indus. Archeology, Northern Ohio Chap. **[17414]**, Youngstown, OH
Soc. for Info. Mgt., Chicago **[1191]**, Chicago, IL
Soc. for Info. Mgt., Evansville Area **[4573]**, Evansville, IN
Soc. of Mfg. Engineers - Baker Coll. U159 **[6816]**, Auburn Hills, MI
Soc. of Mfg. Engineers - Bemidji State Univ. S182 **[10426]**, Bemidji, MN
Soc. of Mfg. Engineers - Bowling Green State Univ. S102 **[13399]**, Bowling Green, OH
Soc. of Mfg. Engineers - Central State Univ. S307 **[17261]**, Wilberforce, OH
Soc. of Mfg. Engineers - Chippewa Valley Technological Coll. S170 **[17899]**, Eau Claire, WI
Soc. of Mfg. Engineers - Columbus State Community Coll. S092 **[14734]**, Columbus, OH
Soc. of Mfg. Engineers - Delta Coll. U185 **[10032]**, University Center, MI
Soc. of Mfg. Engineers - Eastern Illinois Univ. S151 **[572]**, Charleston, IL
Soc. of Mfg. Engineers - Eastern Michigan Univ. S111 **[10215]**, Ypsilanti, MI
Soc. of Mfg. Engineers - Ferris State Univ. S129 **[6952]**, Big Rapids, MI
Soc. of Mfg. Engineers - Focus-Hope Center for Advanced Technologies S279 **[7435]**, Detroit, MI
Soc. of Mfg. Engineers - Grand Valley State Univ. S283 **[8010]**, Grand Rapids, MI
Soc. of Mfg. Engineers, Henry Ford Community Coll. Student Chap. S-331 **[7270]**, Dearborn, MI
Soc. of Mfg. Engineers - Illinois State Univ. S203 **[2732]**, Normal, IL
Soc. of Mfg. Engineers - Indiana Inst. of Tech. S345 **[4716]**, Fort Wayne, IN
Soc. of Mfg. Engineers - Indiana Purdue Univ.-Ft. Wayne S292 **[4717]**, Fort Wayne, IN
Soc. of Mfg. Engineers - ITT - Ft. Wayne S214 **[4718]**, Fort Wayne, IN
Soc. of Mfg. Engineers - ITT - Indianapolis S178 **[5478]**, Indianapolis, IN
Soc. of Mfg. Engineers - ITT Tech. Inst. S347 **[18133]**, Green Bay, WI
Soc. of Mfg. Engineers - Ivy Tech State Coll. S265 **[4719]**, Fort Wayne, IN
Soc. of Mfg. Engineers - James A. Rhodes State Coll. S226 **[15669]**, Lima, OH
Soc. of Mfg. Engineers - Kent State Univ. - Ashtabula U165 **[13186]**, Ashtabula, OH
Soc. of Mfg. Engineers - Kent State Univ. S050 **[15550]**, Kent, OH
Soc. of Mfg. Engineers - Kent State Univ. - Tuscarawas S180 **[16153]**, New Philadelphia, OH
Soc. of Mfg. Engineers - Kettering Univ. S041 **[7757]**, Flint, MI
Soc. of Mfg. Engineers - Lake Superior State Univ. S082 **[9728]**, Sault Ste. Marie, MI
Soc. of Mfg. Engineers - Lawrence Technological Univ. S011 **[9820]**, Southfield, MI
Soc. of Mfg. Engineers - Lorain County Community Coll. S254 **[15125]**, Elyria, OH
Soc. of Mfg. Engineers - Macomb Community Coll. S071 **[10073]**, Warren, MI
Soc. of Mfg. Engineers - Miami Univ. S076 **[16328]**, Oxford, OH
Soc. of Mfg. Engineers - Michigan State Univ. S329 **[7567]**, East Lansing, MI
Soc. of Mfg. Engineers - Michigan Technological Univ. S077 **[8262]**, Houghton, MI
Soc. of Mfg. Engineers - Minnesota State Univ. Moorhead S189 **[11828]**, Moorhead, MN
Soc. of Mfg. Engineers - Moraine Park Tech. Coll. S234 **[17993]**, Fond du Lac, WI
Soc. of Mfg. Engineers - Morrison Inst. of Tech. S321 **[2560]**, Morrison, IL
Soc. of Mfg. Engineers - Northcentral Tech. Coll. S237 **[20047]**, Wausau, WI
Soc. of Mfg. Engineers - Northern Illinois Univ. S210 **[1444]**, DeKalb, IL
Soc. of Mfg. Engineers - Oakland County Community Coll. S144 **[6817]**, Auburn Hills, MI
Soc. of Mfg. Engineers - Ohio State Univ. S205 **[14735]**, Columbus, OH
Soc. of Mfg. Engineers - Ohio Univ. S087 **[13218]**, Athens, OH
Soc. of Mfg. Engineers - Owens Community Coll. S217 **[15214]**, Findlay, OH
Soc. of Mfg. Engineers - Purdue Univ. - Calumet S161 **[4895]**, Hammond, IN
Soc. of Mfg. Engineers - Purdue Univ. - Indianapolis S098 **[5479]**, Indianapolis, IN
Soc. of Mfg. Engineers - Purdue Univ. - Lafayette S006 **[6499]**, West Lafayette, IN
Soc. of Mfg. Engineers - Purdue Univ. - New Albany S351 **[5925]**, New Albany, IN
Soc. of Mfg. Engineers - Riverland Community Coll. U164 **[10359]**, Austin, MN
Soc. of Mfg. Engineers - Rock Valley Coll. S269 **[3321]**, Rockford, IL
Soc. of Mfg. Engineers - St. Cloud State Univ. - S225 **[12309]**, St. Cloud, MN
Soc. of Mfg. Engineers - St. Paul Tech. Coll. S207 **[12588]**, St. Paul, MN
Soc. of Mfg. Engineers - Sinclair Community Coll. U156 **[14955]**, Dayton, OH
Soc. of Mfg. Engineers - Southern Illinois Univ. Edwardsville S349 **[1567]**, Edwardsville, IL
Soc. of Mfg. Engineers - Stark State Coll. U172 **[13581]**, Canton, OH
Soc. of Mfg. Engineers - Tri-State Univ. U173 **[4129]**, Angola, IN
Soc. of Mfg. Engineers - Trumbull Career and Tech. Center S301 **[17109]**, Warren, OH
Soc. of Mfg. Engineers - Univ. of Cincinnati S145 **[13993]**, Cincinnati, OH
Soc. of Mfg. Engineers - Univ. of Dayton S070 **[14956]**, Dayton, OH
Soc. of Mfg. Engineers - Univ. of Detroit - Mercy S081 **[7436]**, Detroit, MI
Soc. of Mfg. Engineers - Univ. of Illinois S219 **[3835]**, Urbana, IL
Soc. of Mfg. Engineers - Univ. of Michigan - Dearborn S326 **[7271]**, Dearborn, MI
Soc. of Mfg. Engineers - Univ. of Michigan S001 **[6767]**, Ann Arbor, MI
Soc. of Mfg. Engineers - Univ. of Toledo S319 **[16960]**, Toledo, OH
Soc. of Mfg. Engineers - Univ. of Wisconsin - Madison S133 **[18618]**, Madison, WI
Soc. of Mfg. Engineers - Univ. of Wisconsin - Milwaukee S152 **[19121]**, Milwaukee, WI
Soc. for Marketing Professional Services, Chicago Chap. **[1614]**, Elk Grove Village, IL
Soc. for Marketing Professional Sers./Columbus Chap. **[14736]**, Columbus, OH
Soc. for Marketing Professional Sers./Michigan **[9821]**, Southfield, MI
Soc. for Marketing Professional Services/Northeast Ohio **[14219]**, Cleveland, OH
Soc. for Marketing Professional Services/Twin Cities Chap. **[11748]**, Minneapolis, MN
Soc. of Minnesota Inventors **[10718]**, Coon Rapids, MN
Soc. for Mitral Valve Prolapse Syndrome **[2069]**, Itasca, IL
Soc. for Neuroscience, Chicago Chap. **[2746]**, North Chicago, IL
Soc. for Neuroscience, Indiana Univ., Bloomington Chap. **[★4222]**
Soc. for Neuroscience, Southern Minnesota Chap. **[12189]**, Rochester, MN
Soc. for Nonprofit Orgs. **[7073]**, Canton, MI
Soc. of Northern Ohio Professional Photographers **[14220]**, Cleveland, OH
Soc. of Nuclear Medicine - Southeastern Chaps. **[13994]**, Cincinnati, OH
Soc. of Otorhinolaryngology and Head/Neck Nurses - Chicago Chap. **[240]**, Berwyn, IL
Soc. of Otorhinolaryngology and Head/Neck Nurses - Grand Rapids Chap. **[8011]**, Grand Rapids, MI
Soc. of Otorhinolaryngology and Head/Neck Nurses - Greater Cleveland Area Chap. **[16398]**, Pepper Pike, OH
Soc. of Otorhinolaryngology and Head/Neck Nurses - Wisconsin Chap. **[19305]**, New Glarus, WI
Soc. of Petrophysicists and Well Log Analysts - Ohio Chap. **[14979]**, Deerfield, OH
Soc. of Physics Students - Carthage Coll. Chap. No. 1015 **[18311]**, Kenosha, WI
Soc. of Physics Students - Cleveland State Univ. Chap. No. 1247 **[14221]**, Cleveland, OH
Soc. of Physics Students - John Carroll Univ. Chap. No. 3329 **[17027]**, University Heights, OH
Soc. of Physics Students - Ohio State Univ. Chap. No. 5175 **[14737]**, Columbus, OH
Soc. of Physics Students - Otterbein Coll. Chap. No. 5413 **[17221]**, Westerville, OH
Soc. of Physics Students - St. Cloud State Univ. Chap. No. 6122 **[12310]**, St. Cloud, MN
Soc. of Physics Students - Sauk Valley Coll. Chap. No. 6390 **[1484]**, Dixon, IL
Soc. of Physics Students - Southwest Minnesota State Univ. Chap. No. 6666 **[11440]**, Marshall, MN
Soc. of Physics Students - Univ. of Wisconsin-Eau Claire Chap. No. 8289 **[17900]**, Eau Claire, WI
Soc. of Physics Students - Univ. of Wisconsin-Platteville Chap. No. 8316 **[19470]**, Platteville, WI
Soc. of Physics Students - Wittenberg Univ. Chap. No. 8379 **[16744]**, Springfield, OH
Soc. for the Preservation of Old Mills, Great Lakes Chap. **[9531]**, Rockford, MI
Soc. of Professional Jour.ists **[5480]**, Indianapolis, IN
Soc. of Professional Jour.ists, Greater Philadelphia Chap. **[★5480]**
Soc. for Protective Coatings, North Central **[11749]**, Minneapolis, MN
Soc. of Reliability Engineer, Southeastern Michigan Chap. **[10124]**, West Bloomfield, MI
Soc. of St. Vincent de Paul **[13995]**, Cincinnati, OH
Soc. of Stud. of Male Psychology **[16063]**, Montpelier, OH
Soc. for Tech. Commun., Central Illinois Chap. **[3836]**, Urbana, IL
Soc. for Tech. Commun., Chicago Chap. **[2928]**, Palatine, IL
Soc. for Tech. Commun., Quad Cities Chap. **[2534]**, Moline, IL
Soc. for Tech. Commun., St. Joseph Valley Chap. **[5955]**, New Paris, IN
Soc. for Tech. Commun., Southeastern Michigan Chap. **[6768]**, Ann Arbor, MI
Soc. for Tech. Commun., Wisconsin Chap. **[19999]**, Waukesha, WI
Soc. of Tribologists and Lubrication Engineers - Canton Sect. **[13582]**, Canton, OH
Soc. of Tribologists and Lubrication Engineers - Central Illinois Sect. **[2364]**, Mackinaw, IL
Soc. of Tribologists and Lubrication Engineers - Chicago Sect. **[1628]**, Elmhurst, IL
Soc. of Tribologists and Lubrication Engineers - Cincinnati Sect. **[13996]**, Cincinnati, OH
Soc. of Tribologists and Lubrication Engineers - Cleveland Sect. **[16628]**, Seven Hills, OH
Soc. of Tribologists and Lubrication Engineers - Dayton Sect. **[17362]**, Wright-Patterson AFB, OH
Soc. of Tribologists and Lubrication Engineers - Detroit Sect. **[9822]**, Southfield, MI
Soc. of Tribologists and Lubrication Engineers - Twin Cities Sect. **[12589]**, St. Paul, MN
Soft Drink Assn; Michigan **[8718]**, Lansing, MI
Softball
Amer. Youth Soccer Org., Region 115 **[586]**, Cherry Valley, IL
Amer. Youth Soccer Org., Region 163 **[2195]**, Lake Forest, IL
Amer. Youth Soccer Org., Region 190 **[9864]**, Sterling Heights, MI
Amer. Youth Soccer Org., Region 300 **[3960]**, Western Springs, IL
Amer. Youth Soccer Org., Region 362 **[1858]**, Glenview, IL
Amer. Youth Soccer Org., Region 372 **[2611]**, Mundelein, IL
Amer. Youth Soccer Org., Region 418 **[730]**, Chicago, IL
Amer. Youth Soccer Org., Region 425 **[4033]**, Winnetka, IL
Amer. Youth Soccer Org., Region 458 **[2238]**, Lemont, IL
Amer. Youth Soccer Org., Region 726 **[4054]**, Woodstock, IL
Amer. Youth Soccer Org., Region 1007 **[1416]**, Deerfield, IL
Amer. Youth Soccer Org., Region 1196 **[8154]**, Hastings, MI
Columbus Softball Assn. **[14402]**, Columbus, OH

Dayton Amateur Softball Assn. **[15315]**, Germantown, OH
Illinois Amateur Softball Assn. **[1393]**, Decatur, IL
Indiana Amateur Softball Assn. **[6324]**, Terre Haute, IN
Indiana Amateur Softball Assn., Region 1 **[4431]**, Crown Point, IN
Indiana Amateur Softball Assn., Region 2 **[4810]**, Granger, IN
Indiana Amateur Softball Assn., Region 3 **[4671]**, Fort Wayne, IN
Indiana Amateur Softball Assn., Region 4 **[4426]**, Crawfordsville, IN
Indiana Amateur Softball Assn., Region 5 **[5691]**, Logansport, IN
Indiana Amateur Softball Assn., Region 6 **[4091]**, Alexandria, IN
Indiana Amateur Softball Assn., Region 7 **[6325]**, Terre Haute, IN
Indiana Amateur Softball Assn., Region 8 **[4153]**, Avon, IN
Indiana Amateur Softball Assn., Region 9 **[6156]**, St. Paul, IN
Indiana Amateur Softball Assn., Region 10 **[5816]**, Mitchell, IN
Indiana Amateur Softball Assn., Region 11 **[6170]**, Scipio, IN
Indiana Amateur Softball Assn., Region 12 **[4552]**, Evansville, IN
Metro Cincinnati Amateur Softball Assn. **[13898]**, Cincinnati, OH
Metro Cleveland Amateur Softball Assn. **[14164]**, Cleveland, OH
Metro Detroit Amateur Softball Assn. **[9270]**, Okemos, MI
Michigan Amateur Softball Assn. **[9029]**, Midland, MI
Minneapolis Amateur Softball Assn. **[11608]**, Minneapolis, MN
Minnesota Sports Fed. Amateur Softball Assn. **[12691]**, Spring Lake Park, MN
Natl. Softball Assn. - Illinois **[539]**, Champaign, IL
Natl. Softball Assn. - Michigan **[7690]**, Fenton, MI
Natl. Softball Assn. - Minnesota **[12553]**, St. Paul, MN
Natl. Softball Assn. - Northern Indiana **[5599]**, La Porte, IN
Natl. Softball Assn. - Ohio **[13438]**, Brooklyn, OH
Natl. Softball Assn. - Southern Indiana **[5432]**, Indianapolis, IN
Ohio Amateur Softball Assn. **[13169]**, Ashland, OH
Softball Assn. of Am., Michigan; Amateur **[★9029]**
Softball Assn; Columbus **[14402]**, Columbus, OH
Softball Assn; Metro Detroit Amateur **[9270]**, Okemos, MI
Softball; Hartford Youth Baseball and **[15408]**, Hartford, OH
Soil Conservation
Izaak Walton League of Am. - Ohio Div. **[15393]**, Hamilton, OH
Minnesota Assn. of Soil and Water Conservation Districts **[12459]**, St. Paul, MN
ParkLands Found. **[303]**, Bloomington, IL
Soil and Water Conservation Soc. of Am. **[19806]**, Stevens Point, WI
Sokaogon-Chippewa Comm. **[17790]**, Crandon, WI
Solar Energy
Illinois Solar Energy Assn. **[3989]**, Wheaton, IL
Minnesota Renewable Energy Soc. **[11672]**, Minneapolis, MN
Solar Energy Assn; Illinois **[3989]**, Wheaton, IL
Soldiers Grove Lions Club **[18032]**, Gays Mills, WI
Solid Waste Assn. of North Am., Illinois Land of Lincoln Chap. **[1841]**, Glen Ellyn, IL
Solid Waste Assn. of North Am., Minnesota Land of Lakes Chap. **[11425]**, Maplewood, MN
Solid Waste Assn. of North Am., Ohio Buckeye Chap. **[13997]**, Cincinnati, OH
Solid Waste Assn. of North Am., Wisconsin Badger Chap. **[18134]**, Green Bay, WI
Solon Chamber of Commerce **[16684]**, Solon, OH
Somerset Area Chamber of Commerce **[19746]**, Somerset, WI
Song of the Lakes Sweet Adelines Chorus **[7239]**, Davison, MI
Songwriters and Poets Critique **[14738]**, Columbus, OH
Sons of the Amer. Legion, Post 44 **[13583]**, Canton, OH
Sons of the Amer. Revolution, Illinois Soc. **[3322]**, Rockford, IL
Sons of the Amer. Revolution - Ohio Soc. **[16345]**, Painesville, OH
Sons of the Desert; Dancing Cuckoos, Metropolitan Detroit Tent of the Intl. **[7063]**, Canton, MI
Sons of the Desert, Tree in a Test Tube Soc. **[165]**, Bartlett, IL
Sons of Italy **[13187]**, Ashtabula, OH
Sons of Norway, Arctic Circle Lodge 5-662 **[13120]**, Alliance, OH
Sons of Norway, Askeladden Lodge 5-610 **[8468]**, Kalamazoo, MI
Sons of Norway, Bemidji Lodge 1-500 **[10427]**, Bemidji, MN
Sons of Norway, Birkebeiner Lodge 5-611 **[17588]**, Bayfield, WI
Sons of Norway, Bjorgvin Lodge 1-10 **[10435]**, Benson, MN
Sons of Norway, Christian Radich Lodge 5-568 **[9219]**, Northport, MI
Sons of Norway, Circle City Lodge 5-614 **[6553]**, Zionsville, IN
Sons of Norway, Cleng Peerson Lodge 5-525 **[2900]**, Ottawa, IL
Sons of Norway, Dovre Lodge 5-353 **[19630]**, Ridgeland, WI
Sons of Norway, Draxten Lodge 1-464 **[12590]**, St. Paul, MN
Sons of Norway, Edvard Grieg Lodge 5-657 **[16446]**, Pleasant Plain, OH
Sons of Norway, Elvedal Lodge 5-556 **[19283]**, Nekoosa, WI
Sons of Norway, Elvesund Lodge 5-593 **[3963]**, Western Springs, IL
Sons of Norway, Elvesvingen Lodge 1-582 **[11400]**, Mankato, MN
Sons of Norway, Elvidal Lodge 1-509 **[10673]**, Clarkfield, MN
Sons of Norway, Fagernes Lodge 5-616 **[17638]**, Blair, WI
Sons of Norway, Fedraheimen Lodge 1-59 **[12927]**, Willmar, MN
Sons of Norway, Fjell Syn Lodge 1-667 **[12591]**, St. Paul, MN
Sons of Norway, Fjordland Lodge 5-606 **[2462]**, McHenry, IL
Sons of Norway, F.M. Christiansen Lodge 5-624 **[19520]**, Porterfield, WI
Sons of Norway, Fosselyngen Lodge 5-82 **[19122]**, Milwaukee, WI
Sons of Norway, Fossen Lodge 5-534 **[17634]**, Black River Falls, WI
Sons of Norway, Gjemtedal Lodge 5-639 **[19627]**, Richland Center, WI
Sons of Norway, Granlund Lodge 1-240 **[11105]**, Gully, MN
Sons of Norway, Gronnvik Lodge 5-632 **[18135]**, Green Bay, WI
Sons of Norway, H R Holand Lodge 5-549 **[19844]**, Sturgeon Bay, WI
Sons of Norway, Haarfager Lodge 1-40 **[12807]**, Virginia, MN
Sons of Norway, Hafrsfjord Lodge 5-206 **[18312]**, Kenosha, WI
Sons of Norway, Heimbygda Lodge 1-376 **[11303]**, Lanesboro, MN
Sons of Norway, Heimskringla Lodge 1-12 **[11004]**, Fergus Falls, MN
Sons of Norway, Heimsyn Lodge 1-15 **[10965]**, Esko, MN
Sons of Norway, Henrik Ibsen Lodge 4-565 **[10792]**, Doran, MN
Sons of Norway, Hjemkomst Lodge 1-599 **[11130]**, Hastings, MN
Sons of Norway, Idun Lodge 5-74 **[19863]**, Sun Prairie, WI
Sons of Norway, Jaabaek Lodge 1-264 **[11805]**, Montevideo, MN
Sons of Norway, Jotunheimen Lodge 5-286 **[19942]**, Viroqua, WI
Sons of Norway, Kenyon Viking Lodge 1-487 **[11255]**, Kenyon, MN
Sons of Norway, Knute Rockne Lodge 5-634 **[6265]**, South Bend, IN
Sons of Norway, Kristiania Lodge 1-47 **[12190]**, Rochester, MN
Sons of Norway, Lauris Norstad Lodge 1-558 **[12086]**, Red Wing, MN
Sons of Norway, Leif Erikson Lodge 1-32 **[12790]**, Vining, MN
Sons of Norway, Leif Erikson Lodge 5-97 **[1512]**, Downers Grove, IL
Sons of Norway, Lin-Hans-Rud Lodge 1-479 **[11401]**, Mankato, MN
Sons of Norway, Lincolnland Lodge 5-598 **[3471]**, Sherman, IL
Sons of Norway, Loven Lodge 5-29 **[17901]**, Eau Claire, WI
Sons of Norway, Midnatsolen Lodge 1-58 **[11988]**, Pengilly, MN
Sons of Norway, Mjosen Lodge 1-175 **[11055]**, Glenwood, MN
Sons of Norway, Morgensol Lodge 1-458 **[10739]**, Crookston, MN
Sons of Norway, Myrmarken Lodge 5-609 **[18824]**, Marshfield, WI
Sons of Norway, Nidaros Lodge 1-1 **[10298]**, Andover, MN
Sons of Norway, Nor-Win Lodge 1-505 **[12958]**, Winona, MN
Sons of Norway, Nordkap Lodge 5-378 **[6769]**, Ann Arbor, MI
Sons of Norway, Nordland Lodge 1-492 **[12764]**, Twin Valley, MN
Sons of Norway, Nordlandet Lodge 5-620 **[18201]**, Hazelhurst, WI
Sons of Norway, Nordlys Lodge 1-498 **[12837]**, Wannaska, MN
Sons of Norway, Nordlyset Lodge 5-183 **[19573]**, Racine, WI
Sons of Norway, Nordmarka Lodge 1-585 **[10987]**, Faribault, MN
Sons of Norway, Nordskogen Lodge 1-626 **[11980]**, Park Rapids, MN
Sons of Norway, Nordstjernen Lodge 1-563 **[11428]**, Marcell, MN
Sons of Norway, Normanna Lodge 1-52 **[10263]**, Albert Lea, MN
Sons of Norway, Nornen Lodge 1-41 **[11368]**, Madison, MN
Sons of Norway, Norrona Lodge 5-27 **[19749]**, South Range, WI
Sons of Norway, Norse Valley Lodge 5-491 **[17525]**, Appleton, WI
Sons of Norway, Norsemen Of Lakes Lodge 5-650 **[19830]**, Stoughton, WI
Sons of Norway, Norskeland Lodge 5-580 **[18236]**, Iola, WI
Sons of Norway, Norskfodt Lodge 1-590 **[11842]**, Morris, MN
Sons of Norway, Norsota Lodge 1-602 **[12592]**, St. Paul, MN
Sons of Norway, Nortun Lodge 1-16 **[10855]**, Duluth, MN
Sons of Norway, Norumbega Lodge 1-217 **[10609]**, Burnsville, MN
Sons of Norway, Oslo Lodge 1-2 **[11750]**, Minneapolis, MN
Sons of Norway, Ostestaden Lodge 5-642 **[19218]**, Monroe, WI
Sons of Norway, Polar Star Lodge 5-472 **[131]**, Aurora, IL
Sons of Norway, Rib Fjell Lodge 5-496 **[20048]**, Wausau, WI
Sons of Norway, Runic Vennskap Lodge 1-530 **[10285]**, Alexandria, MN
Sons of Norway, Sagatun Lodge 1-18 **[10521]**, Brainerd, MN
Sons of Norway, Samhold Lodge 5-473 **[10094]**, Waterford, MI
Sons of Norway, Scandiana Lodge 5-600 **[6390]**, Valparaiso, IN
Sons of Norway, Sjoland Lodge 5-635 **[17764]**, Clear Lake, WI
Sons of Norway, Skjold Lodge 5-100 **[83]**, Arlington Heights, IL
Sons of Norway, Skogvannet Lodge 1-658 **[11021]**, Fort Benedict, MN
Sons of Norway, Snorre Lodge 1-70 **[12749]**, Thief River Falls, MN
Sons of Norway, Sognefjord Lodge 5-523 **[9162]**, Muskegon, MI

Sons of Norway, Solheim Lodge 5-278 **[17653]**, Boyceville, WI
Sons of Norway, Solvang Lodge 5-457 **[20143]**, Westby, WI
Sons of Norway, Sonja Henie Lodge 5-490 **[8761]**, Lansing, MI
Sons of Norway, Sor Vest Viskonsin Lodge 5-629 **[17958]**, Fennimore, WI
Sons of Norway, Stavanger Lodge 1-538 **[11153]**, Heron Lake, MN
Sons of Norway, Stenlandet Lodge 1-640 **[10905]**, Edgerton, MN
Sons of Norway, Storting Lodge 1-519 **[10360]**, Austin, MN
Sons of Norway, Synnove-Nordkap Lodge 1-8 **[12663]**, Shoreview, MN
Sons of Norway, Syttende Mai Lodge 1-517 **[12817]**, Waconia, MN
Sons of Norway, Terje Viken Lodge 1-17 **[12773]**, Two Harbors, MN
Sons of Norway, Tordenskjold Lodge 1-55 **[11111]**, Halstad, MN
Sons of Norway, Tre Elver Lodge 5-628 **[4720]**, Fort Wayne, IN
Sons of Norway, Trollhaugen Lodge 5-417 **[6391]**, Valparaiso, IN
Sons of Norway, Trollheim Lodge 1-511 **[11339]**, Little Falls, MN
Sons of Norway, Trygvason Lodge 5-220 **[19413]**, Osseo, WI
Sons of Norway, Tusenvann Lodge 1-659 **[11231]**, Isle, MN
Sons of Norway, Vakkertland Lodge 5-570 **[19515]**, Portage, WI
Sons of Norway, Valheim Lodge 1-364 **[12689]**, Spring Grove, MN
Sons of Norway, Valkyrien Lodge 5-53 **[20208]**, Woodville, WI
Sons of Norway, Vennekretsen Lodge 1-559 **[10719]**, Coon Rapids, MN
Sons of Norway, Vennelag Lodge 1-546 **[11318]**, Lindstrom, MN
Sons of Norway, Vennelag Lodge 5-513 **[19934]**, Verona, WI
Sons of Norway, Vennligfolk Lodge 5-627 **[19807]**, Stevens Point, WI
Sons of Norway, Vennskap Lodge 1-554 **[10629]**, Canby, MN
Sons of Norway, Vennskap Lodge 5-622 **[19714]**, Sheboygan, WI
Sons of Norway, Vestland Lodge 1-601 **[11193]**, Hopkins, MN
Sons of Norway, Viking Lodge 5-625 **[19205]**, Mondovi, WI
Sons of Norway, Vikingland Lodge 1-495 **[10784]**, Detroit Lakes, MN
Sons of Norway, Vinland Lodge 1-193 **[10439]**, Big Falls, MN
Sons of Norway, Vonheim Lodge 1-108 **[10873]**, Eagan, MN
Sons of Norway, Wergeland Lodge 5-28 **[19370]**, Onalaska, WI
Sophisticated Gents **[15711]**, Lorain, OH
Sotos Syndrome Support Assn. **[3998]**, Wheaton, IL
South Bend-Elkhart Audubon Soc. **[5813]**, Mishawaka, IN
South Bend Fed. of Musicians - Local 278, Amer. Fed. of Musicians **[6266]**, South Bend, IN
South Bend Lions Club **[6267]**, South Bend, IN
South Bend/Mishawaka Convention and Visitors Bur. **[6268]**, South Bend, IN
South Bend SCORE **[6269]**, South Bend, IN
South Bend Table Tennis Club **[6270]**, South Bend, IN
South of the Border Chap. of Muskies **[2463]**, McHenry, IL
South Carolina Component Manufacturers Assn. **[★18767]**
South Central Fed. of Labor, AFL-CIO **[18619]**, Madison, WI
South Central Human Rsrcs. Mgt. Assn. **[8398]**, Jackson, MI
South Central Illinois Regional Planning and Development Commn. **[3412]**, Salem, IL
South Central Indiana AIFA **[5544]**, Jeffersonville, IN
South Central Indiana Corvette Club **[6196]**, Shelbyville, IN
South Central Indiana RSVP **[5926]**, New Albany, IN
South Central Minnesota Youth for Christ **[10264]**, Albert Lea, MN
South Central Ohio AIFA **[13675]**, Chillicothe, OH
South Central Ohio Angus Assn. **[17132]**, Washington Court House, OH
South Central Ohio Minority Bus. Coun. **[13998]**, Cincinnati, OH
South Central Professional Photographers Assn. **[17618]**, Beloit, WI
South Central Sect. of the Amer. Urological Assn. **[3449]**, Schaumburg, IL
South Central Wisconsin AIFA **[17578]**, Baraboo, WI
South Central Wisconsin Builders Assn. **[18264]**, Janesville, WI
South Central Wisconsin Building Authority **[★18264]**
South Central Wisconsin Optometric Soc. **[18831]**, Mauston, WI
South Chicago Parents And Friends Of Retarded Children **[1192]**, Chicago, IL
South Christian - Young Life **[8012]**, Grand Rapids, MI
South Dayton Figure Skating Club **[15565]**, Kettering, OH
South East Wisconsin Optometric Soc. **[19477]**, Pleasant Prairie, WI
South Eastern Chamber United in Bus. **[19335]**, Oak Creek, WI
South Eastern Michigan Bromeliad Soc. **[9229]**, Northville, MI
South Eastern Minnesota Angus Assn. **[12713]**, Stewartville, MN
South Eastern Wisconsin Helicopter Assn. **[19123]**, Milwaukee, WI
South Elgin Lions Club **[3499]**, South Elgin, IL
South Gibson Wrestling Boosters Club **[★6072]**
South Gibson Wrestling Club **[6072]**, Princeton, IN
South Haven - Black River Lions Club **[9765]**, South Haven, MI
South Haven Visitors Bur. **[9766]**, South Haven, MI
South Holland Bus. Assn. **[3507]**, South Holland, IL
South Holland Historical Soc. **[3508]**, South Holland, IL
South Holland Professional Firefighters Assn. **[3509]**, South Holland, IL
South Lyon Area Chamber of Commerce **[9774]**, South Lyon, MI
South Macomb Assn. of Plumbing Contractors **[8522]**, Lakeville, MI
South Metro ALU **[12818]**, Waconia, MN
South Metro Dayton Area Chamber of Commerce **[★14957]**
South Metro Regional Chamber of Commerce **[14957]**, Dayton, OH
South Metro Shores Figure Skating Club **[9842]**, Southgate, MI
South Metropolitan Planning Coun. **[18620]**, Madison, WI
South St. Paul-Inver Grove Heights Chamber of Commerce **[★11227]**
South St. Paul Lions Club **[12684]**, South St. Paul, MN
South Shore Coin Club **[19124]**, Milwaukee, WI
South Shore Lions Club **[10971]**, Excelsior, MN
South Shore Lung Assn. **[★16259]**
South Side Muskie Hawks **[369]**, Burbank, IL
South Suburban Mayors and Managers Assn. **[1535]**, East Hazel Crest, IL
South Town Points **[19125]**, Milwaukee, WI
South West Wisconsin Optometric Soc. **[17807]**, Darlington, WI
South Western Ohio Dairy Goat Assn. **[15861]**, Martinsville, OH
South Wisconsin District, The Lutheran Church-Missouri Synod **[19126]**, Milwaukee, WI
South - Young Life **[4258]**, Bloomington, IN
Southcentral Ohio Acad. of Family Physicians **[13676]**, Chillicothe, OH
Southeast Chicago Commn. **[1193]**, Chicago, IL
Southeast Indiana Healthy Mothers, Healthy Babies Coalition **[5662]**, Lawrenceburg, IN
Southeast Indiana Young Life **[4161]**, Batesville, IN
Southeast Michigan Air Conditioning Contractors of Am. **[8857]**, Livonia, MI
Southeast Michigan Census Coun. **[9823]**, Southfield, MI
Southeast Michigan Coun. of Governments **[7437]**, Detroit, MI
Southeast Michigan Jobs with Justice **[7438]**, Detroit, MI
Southeast Minnesota Agriculture Alliance **[12015]**, Plainview, MN
Southeast Minnesota Assn. of Realtors **[12191]**, Rochester, MN
Southeast MMBA **[9411]**, Plymouth, MI
Southeast Wisconsin FreeThinkers **[18889]**, Mequon, WI
Southeastern Butler County Chamber of Commerce **[17179]**, West Chester, OH
Southeastern District Dental Soc., Minnesota **[10361]**, Austin, MN
Southeastern Franklin County Chamber of Commerce **[15374]**, Groveport, OH
Southeastern Illinois AIFA **[2861]**, Olney, IL
Southeastern Illinois Beagle Club **[2041]**, Homer, IL
Southeastern Illinois Regional Planning and Development Commn. **[1943]**, Harrisburg, IL
Southeastern Indiana Angus Assn. **[4837]**, Greenfield, IN
Southeastern Indiana Bd. of Realtors **[4148]**, Aurora, IN
Southeastern Michigan Angus Assn. **[9705]**, Saline, MI
Southeastern Michigan Chap., MOAA **[8132]**, Harrison Township, MI
Southeastern Michigan Chap., Natl. Elecl. Contractors Assn. **[9824]**, Southfield, MI
Southeastern Michigan Cmpt. Org. **[6991]**, Bloomfield Hills, MI
Southeastern Michigan Mortgage Lenders Assn. **[8084]**, Grosse Pointe, MI
Southeastern Michigan Soc. of Health-System Pharmacists **[9260]**, Oak Park, MI
Southeastern Minnesota Flying Club **[12192]**, Rochester, MN
Southeastern Minnesota Historic Bluff Country **[11120]**, Harmony, MN
Southeastern Ohio Angus Assn. **[13359]**, Bidwell, OH
Southeastern Ohio Dairy Goat Assn. **[16184]**, Newark, OH
Southeastern Ohio Young Life **[13500]**, Cambridge, OH
Southeastern Sect. of the Amer. Urological Assn. **[3450]**, Schaumburg, IL
Southeastern Sheet Metal Contractors Assn. of Wisconsin **[19127]**, Milwaukee, WI
Southeastern Swim Club **[4611]**, Fishers, IN
Southeastern Wisconsin Alpine Team Racing **[19255]**, Mukwonago, WI
Southeastern Wisconsin Assn. of Diabetes Educators **[19128]**, Milwaukee, WI
Southeastern Wisconsin Chap. - MOAA **[19129]**, Milwaukee, WI
Southeastern Wisconsin Professional Photographers Assn. **[20104]**, West Allis, WI
Southeastern Wisconsin Youth for Christ **[19574]**, Racine, WI
Southeastern - Young Life **[16745]**, Springfield, OH
Southern Anoka County Chamber of Commerce **[★11848]**
Southern District Dental Soc., Minnesota **[11307]**, Le Center, MN
Southern Hills Youth for Christ **[4259]**, Bloomington, IN
Southern Illinois Chap. for Healthcare Engg. **[431]**, Carbondale, IL
Southern Illinois Chap. for Hosp. Engg. **[★431]**
Southern Illinois Coll. Conf. **[★2059]**
Southern Illinois Dental Soc. **[3861]**, Vienna, IL
Southern Illinois District, The Lutheran Church-Missouri Synod **[211]**, Belleville, IL
Southern Illinois Fellowship of Christian Athletes **[432]**, Carbondale, IL
Southern Illinois Haflinger Assn. **[3902]**, Waterloo, IL
Southern Illinois Hea. Info. Mgt. Assn. **[3406]**, St. Peter, IL
Southern Illinois Healthcare Materials Mgt. Assn. **[2092]**, Jerseyville, IL
Southern Illinois Libertarians **[433]**, Carbondale, IL
Southern Illinois Sheet Metal Contractors Org. **[1568]**, Edwardsville, IL
Southern Illinois Stamp Club **[434]**, Carbondale, IL

Southern Indiana Angus Assn. **[6374]**, Vallonia, IN
Southern Indiana Beagle Club **[4574]**, Evansville, IN
Southern Indiana Chamber of Commerce **[5927]**, New Albany, IN
Southern Indiana Chap. Natl. Elecl. Contractors Assn. **[4575]**, Evansville, IN
Southern Indiana, Clark-Floyd Counties Convention and Tourism Bur. **[★5541]**
Southern Indiana Daylily, Hosta, Daffodil, and Iris Soc. **[4260]**, Bloomington, IN
Southern Indiana, Natl. Assn. of Women Bus. Owners **[5481]**, Indianapolis, IN
Southern Indiana Realtors Assn. **[4368]**, Clarksville, IN
Southern Indiana Regional Alliance to Prevent Exploitation **[★5805]**
Southern Indiana Table Tennis Assn. **[5928]**, New Albany, IN
Southern Local - Young Life **[16596]**, Salineville, OH
Southern Michigan Beagle Club **[7171]**, Clinton, MI
Southern Michigan Gun Club **[8469]**, Kalamazoo, MI
Southern Michigan Northern Ohio Assn. for Computing Machinery SIGCHI **[6770]**, Ann Arbor, MI
Southern Michigan Obedience Training Club **[9520]**, Rochester Hills, MI
Southern Michigan Orienteering Club **[6771]**, Ann Arbor, MI
Southern Minnesota Area Human Rsrc. Assn. **[11402]**, Mankato, MN
Southern Minnesota Healthcare Engineers Assn. **[12193]**, Rochester, MN
Southern Minnesota Hunting Retriever Assn. **[11969]**, Owatonna, MN
Southern Ohio Assn. of Realtors **[13999]**, Cincinnati, OH
Southern Ohio Beagle Club **[15401]**, Hamilton, OH
Southern Ohio Bd. of Realtors **[14000]**, Cincinnati, OH
Southern Ohio Chap. of the Human Factors and Ergonomics Soc. **[14958]**, Dayton, OH
Southern Ohio Coun. of Teachers of English **[13219]**, Athens, OH
Southern Ohio Draft Horse Assn. **[15451]**, Hillsboro, OH
Southern Ohio Growth Partnership **[16476]**, Portsmouth, OH
Southern Seven Workforce Investment Bd. **[5929]**, New Albany, IN
Southern Thoracic Surgical Assn. **[1194]**, Chicago, IL
Southern Tri-County RSVP **[10265]**, Albert Lea, MN
Southern Twin Cities Assn. of Realtors **[10874]**, Eagan, MN
Southern Wayne County Chamber of Commerce **[★9905]**
Southern Wayne County Regional Chamber **[9905]**, Taylor, MI
Southern Wisconsin AIFA **[17828]**, Delavan, WI
Southern Wisconsin Appaloosa Horse Club **[17930]**, Elkhorn, WI
Southern Wisconsin Chap. - MOAA **[19864]**, Sun Prairie, WI
Southern Wisconsin Figure Skating Club **[18842]**, McFarland, WI
Southern Wisconsin Sporting Spaniel Club **[20162]**, Whitewater, WI
Southernmost Illinois Tourism Bur. **[52]**, Anna, IL
Southfield Area Chamber of Commerce **[9825]**, Southfield, MI
Southfield Chamber of Commerce **[★9825]**
Southgate Lions Club **[9843]**, Southgate, MI
Southlake Young Men's Christian Association **[4437]**, Crown Point, IN
Southport Skating Club **[1925]**, Gurnee, IL
Southview - Young Life **[16832]**, Sylvania, OH
Southwest Badger Rsrc. Conservation and Development Coun. **[19471]**, Platteville, WI
Southwest Chain Gang Bicycle Club **[17839]**, Dodgeville, WI
Southwest Detroit Business Association **[7439]**, Detroit, MI
Southwest Detroit Enval. Vision **[7440]**, Detroit, MI
Southwest Guaranteed Home Equity Program **[1195]**, Chicago, IL
Southwest Indiana Coun. of Teachers of Mathematics **[4576]**, Evansville, IN
Southwest Michigan Associates of Health Underwriters **[9319]**, Oshtemo, MI
Southwest Michigan Skating Club **[9454]**, Portage, MI
Southwest Michigan Youth for Christ **[9882]**, Sturgis, MI
Southwest Minnesota State Univ. Students In Free Enterprise **[11441]**, Marshall, MN
Southwest MMBA **[6818]**, Augusta, MI
Southwest Ohio Enval. Balancing Bur. **[14001]**, Cincinnati, OH
Southwest Ohio Senior Olympics **[14002]**, Cincinnati, OH
Southwest Suburban United Way **[2885]**, Orland Park, IL
Southwest Women Working Together **[1196]**, Chicago, IL
Southwestern Auglaize County Chamber of Commerce **[16119]**, New Bremen, OH
Southwestern District Dental Soc., Michigan **[6869]**, Battle Creek, MI
Southwestern Illinois Angus Breeders Assn. **[3132]**, Prairie du Rocher, IL
Southwestern Illinois Rsrc. Conservation and Development Coun. **[2432]**, Mascoutah, IL
Southwestern Illinois RSVP **[212]**, Belleville, IL
Southwestern Indiana AIFA **[4577]**, Evansville, IN
Southwestern Indiana Angus Assn. **[4338]**, Centerpoint, IN
Southwestern Indiana Daylily Soc. **[4578]**, Evansville, IN
Southwestern Indiana Master Gardener Assn. **[4579]**, Evansville, IN
Southwestern Indiana Regional Coun. on Aging **[4580]**, Evansville, IN
Southwestern Madison County Chamber of Commerce **[1885]**, Granite City, IL
Southwestern Michigan Assn. of Realtors **[9692]**, St. Joseph, MI
Southwestern Michigan Estate Planning Coun. **[9693]**, St. Joseph, MI
Southwestern Michigan Tourist Coun. **[6922]**, Benton Harbor, MI
Southwestern Michigan Urban League **[6870]**, Battle Creek, MI
Southwestern Minnesota AIFA **[11356]**, Luverne, MN
Southwestern Surgical Cong. **[1197]**, Chicago, IL
Southwestern Wisconsin AIFA **[19196]**, Mineral Point, WI
Southwestern Wisconsin Angus Assn. **[17959]**, Fennimore, WI
Southwestern Wisconsin Regional Planning Commn. **[19472]**, Platteville, WI

Space

Ann Arbor Space Soc. **[6678]**, Ann Arbor, MI
Central Indiana Natl. Space Soc. **[5078]**, Indianapolis, IN
Chicago Soc. for Space Stud. **[2748]**, North Riverside, IL
Chicago Space Frontier L5 Soc. **[180]**, Batavia, IL
Cuyahoga Valley Space Soc. **[16359]**, Parma, OH
Illini Space Development Soc. **[3820]**, Urbana, IL
Illinois North Shore North Shore Soc. **[4038]**, Winnetka, IL
Lunar Reclamation Soc. **[19044]**, Milwaukee, WI
Minnesota Space Frontier Soc. **[11673]**, Minneapolis, MN
Natl. Space Soc. Southwest Michigan Chap. **[7806]**, Galesburg, MI
Sheboygan Space Soc. **[18323]**, Kiel, WI

Space Inst; Wisconsin **[18754]**, Madison, WI
Sparta Area Chamber of Commerce **[3514]**, Sparta, IL
Sparta Area Chamber of Commerce **[19755]**, Sparta, WI
Sparta Area Figure Skating Club **[20138]**, West Salem, WI
Sparta Chamber of Commerce **[★3514]**
Sparta Lions Club - Wisconsin **[19756]**, Sparta, WI
Speakers, Midwest; Org. of Islamic **[2660]**, Naperville, IL

Special Education

Coun. for Exceptional Children, Illinois **[862]**, Chicago, IL
Coun. for Exceptional Children, Indiana **[4648]**, Fort Wayne, IN
Coun. for Exceptional Children, Ohio **[14415]**, Columbus, OH
Coun. for Exceptional Children, Wisconsin **[17872]**, Eau Claire, WI
Michigan Found. for Exceptional Children **[6726]**, Ann Arbor, MI
Minnesota Coun. for Exceptional Children **[12160]**, Rochester, MN

Special Forces

Special Forces Assn. Chap. XXXVII **[2886]**, Orland Park, IL

Special Forces Assn. Chap. XXXVII **[2886]**, Orland Park, IL
Special Kids **[19130]**, Milwaukee, WI
Special Libraries Assn., Central Ohio Chap. **[14739]**, Columbus, OH
Special Libraries Assn., Cincinnati Chap. **[14003]**, Cincinnati, OH
Special Libraries Assn., Cleveland Chap. **[13090]**, Akron, OH
Special Libraries Assn., Illinois Chap. **[1198]**, Chicago, IL
Special Libraries Assn., Indiana Chap. **[5482]**, Indianapolis, IN
Special Libraries Assn., Michigan Chap. **[6772]**, Ann Arbor, MI
Special Libraries Assn., Michigan - Western/Upper Peninsula **[476]**, Cary, IL
Special Libraries Assn., Minnesota Chap. **[11751]**, Minneapolis, MN
Special Libraries Assn., Wisconsin Chap. **[18621]**, Madison, WI
Special Needs Network **[3855]**, Vernon Hills, IL
Special Olympics Illinois **[2733]**, Normal, IL
Special Olympics Indiana **[5483]**, Indianapolis, IN
Special Olympics Michigan **[9124]**, Mount Pleasant, MI
Special Olympics Minnesota **[11752]**, Minneapolis, MN
Special Olympics, Ohio **[14740]**, Columbus, OH
Special Olympics Wisconsin **[18622]**, Madison, WI
Special Wish Found., Chicago Chap. **[1199]**, Chicago, IL
Special Wish Found., Dayton **[14959]**, Dayton, OH
Special Wish Found., Newark **[16185]**, Newark, OH

Spectroscopy

Soc. for Applied Spectroscopy, Chicago **[2268]**, Libertyville, IL
Soc. for Applied Spectroscopy, Cincinnati **[13991]**, Cincinnati, OH
Soc. for Applied Spectroscopy, Detroit **[7434]**, Detroit, MI
Soc. for Applied Spectroscopy, Indiana **[4257]**, Bloomington, IN
Soc. for Applied Spectroscopy, Mid-Michigan **[9041]**, Midland, MI
Soc. for Applied Spectroscopy, Minnesota **[11424]**, Maplewood, MN
Soc. for Applied Spectroscopy, Ohio Valley **[17361]**, Wright-Patterson AFB, OH
Soc. for Applied Spectroscopy, Toledo **[15918]**, Maumee, OH

Speech

Michigan Interscholastic Forensic Assn. **[6728]**, Ann Arbor, MI
Natl. Assn. of Urban Debate Leagues **[1078]**, Chicago, IL

Speech Coaches; Michigan **[9999]**, Troy, MI

Speech and Hearing

Columbus Chap. of the Natl. Stuttering Assn. **[14378]**, Columbus, OH
Illinois Speech-Language-Hearing Assn. **[968]**, Chicago, IL
Michigan Speech Coaches **[9999]**, Troy, MI
Minnesota Speech-Language-Hearing Assn. **[12337]**, St. Louis Park, MN

Speech-Language-Hearing Assn; Michigan **[7549]**, East Lansing, MI
Speech-Language-Hearing Assn; Minnesota **[12337]**, St. Louis Park, MN
Speech Sers; Michigan Assn. for Deaf, Hearing and **[8612]**, Lansing, MI
Speed Skating - The Long Track Club of USA; Mid-Am. **[2756]**, Northbrook, IL
Speedskating Assn; Ohio **[17235]**, Westlake, OH
Speedway Kiwanis Club **[6278]**, Speedway, IN
Speedway Lions Club **[6279]**, Speedway, IN

Speleology

Natl. Speleological Soc., Bloomington, Indiana Grotto **[4248]**, Bloomington, IN
Natl. Speleological Soc., Central Indiana Grotto **[5434]**, Indianapolis, IN

Natl. Speleological Soc., Central Ohio Grotto [15275], Galena, OH
Natl. Speleological Soc., Cleveland Grotto [17232], Westlake, OH
Natl. Speleological Soc., Dayton Underground Grotto [14932], Dayton, OH
Natl. Speleological Soc., Detroit Urban Grotto [7143], Chelsea, MI
Natl. Speleological Soc., Eastern Indiana Grotto [4756], Franklin, IN
Natl. Speleological Soc., Evansville Metropolitan Grotto [5532], Jasper, IN
Natl. Speleological Soc., Greater Cincinnati Grotto [13269], Batavia, OH
Natl. Speleological Soc., Harrison-Crawford Grotto [4790], Georgetown, IN
Natl. Speleological Soc., Little Egypt Grotto [425], Carbondale, IL
Natl. Speleological Soc., Miami Valley Grotto [16075], Mount Orab, OH
Natl. Speleological Soc., Michigan Interlakes Grotto [10021], Union Lake, MI
Natl. Speleological Soc., Minnesota Speleological Survey [12682], South St. Paul, MN
Natl. Speleological Soc., Near Normal Grotto [2726], Normal, IL
Natl. Speleological Soc., Northern Indiana Grotto [4357], Churubusco, IN
Natl. Speleological Soc., Ohio Cavers and Climbers [17191], West Salem, OH
Natl. Speleological Soc., Pinckney Area Grotto [7492], Durand, MI
Natl. Speleological Soc., Red-Eye Karst Team [15729], Loveland, OH
Natl. Speleological Soc., St. Joseph Valley Grotto [4812], Granger, IN
Natl. Speleological Soc., Shady Grove Grotto [14528], Columbus, OH
Natl. Speleological Soc., Standing Stone Grotto [16803], Sugar Grove, OH
Natl. Speleological Soc., Sub-Urban Chicago Grotto [3878], Warrenville, IL
Natl. Speleological Soc., West Michigan Grotto [9481], Reed City, MI
Natl. Speleological Soc., Windy City Grotto [2919], Palatine, IL
Rock River Speleological Soc. [17948], Evansville, WI
Wisconsin Speleological Soc. [19717], Sheboygan, WI
Wittenberg Univ. Speleological Soc. [16755], Springfield, OH
Spencer Area Chamber of Commerce [19759], Spencer, WI
Spencer Chamber of Commerce [★6282]
Spencer County ARC [6128], Rockport, IN
Spencer County REACT [4355], Chrisney, IN
Spencer County Regional Chamber of Commerce [6129], Rockport, IN
Spencer County Tourism Commission [6161], Santa Claus, IN
Spencer-Owen Chamber of Commerce [★6282]
Spicer Sunrise Lions Club [12687], Spicer, MN
Spill Planning Prevention and Emergency Response Assn; Ohio [14677], Columbus, OH
Spina Bifida
Illinois Spina Bifida Assn. [2297], Lisle, IL
Spina Bifida Assn. of the Upper Peninsula of Michigan [8350], Ishpeming, MI
Spina Bifida Assn. of Wisconsin, Inc. [20080], Wauwatosa, WI
Spina Bifida Assn. of the Upper Peninsula of Michigan [8350], Ishpeming, MI
Spina Bifida Assn. of Wisconsin, Inc. [20080], Wauwatosa, WI
Spinal Cord Injury Assn. of Illinois [2172], La Grange, IL
Spinal Injury
Natl. Spinal Cord Injury Assn. - Calumet Region Chap. [4784], Gary, IN
Natl. Spinal Cord Injury Assn. - Greater Milwaukee Area Chap. [19082], Milwaukee, WI
Natl. Spinal Cord Injury Assn. - Northwest Ohio Chap. [16409], Perrysburg, OH
Spinal Cord Injury Assn. of Illinois [2172], La Grange, IL
Spiritual Empowerment; Christian Athletes United for [11543], Minneapolis, MN
Spiritual Fellowship [5841], Morgantown, IN
Spiritualist
Michigan State Spiritualists Assn. [9760], South Branch, MI
Spiritual Fellowship [5841], Morgantown, IN
Sponsors; Fox Valley German Amer. Team of Educal. [449], Carol Stream, IL
Spoon River Valley Pheasants Forever [2344], London Mills, IL
Spooner Area Chamber of Commerce [19763], Spooner, WI
Sport Fishing Coun; Great Lakes [1621], Elmhurst, IL
Sports
Akron Turner Club [16838], Tallmadge, OH
Auburn Duesey Walkers [4937], Huntertown, IN
Bedford Hiking Club [4169], Bedford, IN
Birmingham Athletic Club [6978], Bloomfield Hills, MI
Blanchard Valley Volkssporters [15196], Findlay, OH
Bloomington FlyingFish Walking Club [4207], Bloomington, IN
Buckeye Wander Freunde [14346], Columbus, OH
Bulls Run Ramblers [16005], Middletown, OH
Columbus Wellness Walkers [4398], Columbus, IN
Gemutlich Wanderers [16538], Rittman, OH
German Village Wander Volk [15284], Galion, OH
Goodtime Trailblazers [5125], Indianapolis, IN
Heart of Ohio Hikers 522 [14452], Columbus, OH
Illinois High School Assn. [285], Bloomington, IL
Indiana High School Athletic Assn. [5245], Indianapolis, IN
Indiana Volkssport Assn. [4400], Columbus, IN
Indy 'G' Walkers [5360], Indianapolis, IN
Kettering Kilometer Climbers [13623], Centerville, OH
Lebanon Cedar Cruisers [2678], New Baden, IL
Mackinaw Walkers Volkssport Club [205], Belleville, IL
Madison Area Volkssport Assn. [18814], Marshall, WI
Maumee Valley Volkssporters [15913], Maumee, OH
Miami Indian Trekkers [15394], Hamilton, OH
Michigan Disability Sports Alliance [7538], East Lansing, MI
Michigan High School Athletic Assn. [7540], East Lansing, MI
Michigan Sports Unlimited [9617], Saginaw, MI
Minnesota Volkssport Assn. [11682], Minneapolis, MN
NorthStar Trail Travelers [11714], Minneapolis, MN
Ohio Browns Boosters [15936], McDonald, OH
Ohio High School Athletic Assn. [14623], Columbus, OH
Ohio Volkssports Assn. [17377], Xenia, OH
Packer Country Sports and Ports [18126], Green Bay, WI
Peoria Girls Sports League [3052], Peoria, IL
Purple Penquins [13302], Beavercreek, OH
Queen City Skywalkers [13971], Cincinnati, OH
Railsplitter Wanderers [1404], Decatur, IL
Ridgewalkers Walking Club [552], Champaign, IL
River City Ramblers [4569], Evansville, IN
Riverbend Striders Volksmarch Club [11908], North Mankato, MN
Sister Cities of Vandalia [17060], Vandalia, OH
Tecumseh Trailblazers [17043], Urbana, OH
Twin Cities Volkssport [10494], Bloomington, MN
Valley Vagabonds [16800], Strongsville, OH
Vandalia Butler Pee Wee Youth Sports Assn. [17061], Vandalia, OH
Wabash Wanderers [5637], Lafayette, IN
Wabasha-Kellogg Area Chamber/CVB [12813], Wabasha, MN
Wandering Wheels Volkssports Club [6110], Richmond, IN
White River Ramblers [5900], Muncie, IN
Whitewater Valley Wanderers [6113], Richmond, IN
Windy City Walkers [2802], Oak Lawn, IL
Wisconsin Apartment Assn. [18645], Madison, WI
Wisconsin Ice Arena Mgt. Assn. [19278], Neenah, WI
Zinzinnati Wanderers [14029], Cincinnati, OH
Sports Assn; Vandalia Butler Pee Wee Youth [17061], Vandalia, OH
Sports Assn; Wisconsin Intramural Recreational [19819], Stevens Point, WI
Sports Assn; Women's Outdoor [6898], Bay City, MI
Sports Owners Assn; Illinois [1325], Crystal Lake, IL
Sports and Ports; Packer Country [18126], Green Bay, WI
Sports Unlimited; Michigan [9617], Saginaw, MI
Sportsman's Club; Hardwood Country [12256], Rushford, MN
Sportsmen Off-Road Vehicle Association [8325], Iron Mountain, MI
Sportsmen's Club; Commonwealth [17966], Florence, WI
Spring Green Area Chamber of Commerce [19768], Spring Green, WI
Spring Green Lions Club [19769], Spring Green, WI
Spring Grove Lions Club [12690], Spring Grove, MN
Spring Lake Animal Shelter [8326], Iron Mountain, MI
Spring Lake Humane Soc. [★8326]
Spring Lake - Young Life [7866], Grand Haven, MI
Spring Valley Area Chamber of Commerce [16703], Spring Valley, OH
Spring Valley Mine and Historical Society [3518], Spring Valley, IL
Springboard for the Arts [12593], St. Paul, MN
Springboro Chamber of Commerce [16709], Springboro, OH
Springboro Lions Club [16710], Springboro, OH
Springboro - Young Life [16019], Middletown, OH
Springdale-Forest Park Lions Club [16711], Springdale, OH
Springfield Area Chamber of Commerce [12697], Springfield, MN
Springfield Area Chamber of Commerce [★16747]
Springfield Area Mountain Bike Assn. [3675], Springfield, IL
Springfield Assn. for Retarded Citizens [3676], Springfield, IL
Springfield Bd. of Realtors [16746], Springfield, OH
Springfield Chap. of the Natl. Comm. on Planned Giving [★16748]
Springfield-Clark County Chamber of Commerce [16747], Springfield, OH
Springfield Coun. of the Natl. Comm. on Planned Giving [16748], Springfield, OH
Springfield Exchange Club [16749], Springfield, OH
Springfield Figure Skating Club [3677], Springfield, IL
Springfield Home Builders Assn. [3678], Springfield, IL
Springfield Human Resources Mgt. Assn. [16750], Springfield, OH
Springfield Illinois Convention and Visitors Bur. [3679], Springfield, IL
Springfield Jaycees [3680], Springfield, IL
Springfield Jewish Fed. [3681], Springfield, IL
Springfield Milers BMW Motorcycle Club No. 121 [3682], Springfield, IL
Springfield North - Young Life [16751], Springfield, OH
Springfield Parents for Public Schools [3683], Springfield, IL
Springfield and Vicinity Sheet Metal Contractors' Assn. [3684], Springfield, IL
Springfield - Young Life [16833], Sylvania, OH
Springport Lions Club [9851], Springport, MI
Square Dance Assn. of Wisconsin [19865], Sun Prairie, WI
St Cloud REACT [12311], St. Cloud, MN
Staff Coun; IUB Latino Faculty and [4238], Bloomington, IN
Stamp Club; Euclid [15143], Euclid, OH
Standards
Tire and Rim Assn. [13098], Akron, OH
Stanton Lions Club - Michigan [9856], Stanton, MI
Stanwood Lions Club [6953], Big Rapids, MI
Star Prairie Lions Club [19775], Star Prairie, WI
Star Trek
STARFLEET Region 6 [12644], Savage, MN
STARFLEET Region 13 [7775], Fort Gratiot, MI
STARFLEET: Shuttle Armageddon [5633], Lafayette, IN
STARFLEET: USS Arizona [13121], Alliance, OH

STARFLEET: USS Asgard **[15611]**, Lancaster, OH
STARFLEET: USS Black Hawk **[3323]**, Rockford, IL
STARFLEET: USS Bortas **[3837]**, Urbana, IL
STARFLEET: USS Columbus **[14741]**, Columbus, OH
STARFLEET: USS Czar'ak **[12114]**, Richfield, MN
STARFLEET: USS Empress **[9748]**, Shelby Township, MI
STARFLEET: USS Gallifrey **[15126]**, Elyria, OH
STARFLEET: USS Indiana **[4369]**, Clarksville, IN
STARFLEET: USS Intrepid **[15794]**, Mansfield, OH
STARFLEET: USS Lagrange **[14825]**, Cuyahoga Falls, OH
STARFLEET: USS Liberator **[13091]**, Akron, OH
STARFLEET: USS Ohio **[13257]**, Barberton, OH
STARFLEET: USS Parallax **[8858]**, Livonia, MI
STARFLEET: USS Renegade **[17415]**, Youngstown, OH
STARFLEET: USS Sinclair **[10095]**, Waterford, MI
STARFLEET: USS Valkyrie **[7168]**, Clawson, MI
STARFLEET: USS White Star **[7776]**, Fort Gratiot, MI
Starbuck Lions Club **[12707]**, Starbuck, MN
Starfire Coun. of Greater Cincinnati **[14004]**, Cincinnati, OH
STARFLEET Region 6 **[12644]**, Savage, MN
STARFLEET Region 13 **[7775]**, Fort Gratiot, MI
STARFLEET: Shuttle Armageddon **[5633]**, Lafayette, IN
STARFLEET: USS Arizona **[13121]**, Alliance, OH
STARFLEET: USS Asgard **[15611]**, Lancaster, OH
STARFLEET: USS Black Hawk **[3323]**, Rockford, IL
STARFLEET: USS Bortas **[3837]**, Urbana, IL
STARFLEET: USS Columbus **[14741]**, Columbus, OH
STARFLEET: USS Czar'ak **[12114]**, Richfield, MN
STARFLEET: USS Empress **[9748]**, Shelby Township, MI
STARFLEET: USS Gallifrey **[15126]**, Elyria, OH
STARFLEET: USS Indiana **[4369]**, Clarksville, IN
STARFLEET: USS Intrepid **[15794]**, Mansfield, OH
STARFLEET: USS Lagrange **[14825]**, Cuyahoga Falls, OH
STARFLEET: USS Liberator **[13091]**, Akron, OH
STARFLEET: USS Ohio **[13257]**, Barberton, OH
STARFLEET: USS Parallax **[8858]**, Livonia, MI
STARFLEET: USS Renegade **[17415]**, Youngstown, OH
STARFLEET: USS Sinclair **[10095]**, Waterford, MI
STARFLEET: USS Valkyrie **[7168]**, Clawson, MI
STARFLEET: USS White Star **[7776]**, Fort Gratiot, MI
Stark County Assn. of Realtors Charitable Found. **[13584]**, Canton, OH
Stark County Auto. Dealers Assn. **[13585]**, Canton, OH
Stark County Dental Soc. **[13586]**, Canton, OH
Stark County Farm Bur. **[13587]**, Canton, OH
Stark County Human Rsrc. Assn. **[13588]**, Canton, OH
Stark County Medical Soc. **[13589]**, Canton, OH
Stark County Young Life **[13590]**, Canton, OH
Starke County Chamber of Commerce **[5561]**, Knox, IN
Starke/Pulaski Bd. of Realtors **[5562]**, Knox, IN
Starlight Children's Found. Midwest **[1200]**, Chicago, IL
Starlight Ice Dance Club **[10902]**, Eden Prairie, MN
State Bar of Michigan **[8762]**, Lansing, MI
State Bar of Wisconsin **[18623]**, Madison, WI
State Beer Assn. of Executives of Am. **[★11630]**
State Beer Assn. Secretaries; Natl. Assn. of **[★11630]**
State Beer Wholesalers Secretaries **[★11630]**
State Florist Assn. of Indiana **[5820]**, Monrovia, IN
State Government
Coun. of State Governments Midwestern Off. **[2330]**, Lombard, IL
Midwestern Governors Assn. **[2340]**, Lombard, IL
State Guard Assn. of the U.S., Indiana **[5484]**, Indianapolis, IN
State Guard Assn. of the U.S., Michigan **[7023]**, Brighton, MI
State Guard Assn. of the U.S., Ohio **[14960]**, Dayton, OH
Stateline Soc. for Human Rsrc. Mgt. **[1333]**, Crystal Lake, IL
Stateline United Way **[17619]**, Beloit, WI
Statistical Assn., Central Indiana Chap; Amer. **[5026]**, Indianapolis, IN
Statistical Assn., Columbus Chap; Amer. **[14312]**, Columbus, OH
Statistics
Amer. Statistical Assn., Ann Arbor Chap. **[6666]**, Ann Arbor, MI
Amer. Statistical Assn., Central Indiana Chap. **[5026]**, Indianapolis, IN
Amer. Statistical Assn., Chicago Chap. **[2906]**, Palatine, IL
Amer. Statistical Assn., Cincinnati Chap. **[13736]**, Cincinnati, OH
Amer. Statistical Assn., Cleveland Chap. **[14068]**, Cleveland, OH
Amer. Statistical Assn., Columbus Chap. **[14312]**, Columbus, OH
Amer. Statistical Assn., Dayton Chap. **[16719]**, Springfield, OH
Amer. Statistical Assn., Detroit Chap. **[9500]**, Rochester, MI
Amer. Statistical Assn., Milwaukee Chap. **[19267]**, Neenah, WI
Amer. Statistical Assn., Northeastern Illinois Chap. **[2283]**, Lincolnshire, IL
Amer. Statistical Assn., Northwest Ohio Chap. **[13382]**, Bowling Green, OH
Amer. Statistical Assn., Southwest Michigan Chap. **[8419]**, Kalamazoo, MI
Amer. Statistical Assn., Twin Cities Minnesota Chap. **[11015]**, Forest Lake, MN
Staunton Chamber of Commerce **[3697]**, Staunton, IL
Staunton Main St. USA **[3698]**, Staunton, IL
Stearns-Benton County Medical Soc. **[12312]**, St. Cloud, MN
Stearns County Historical Soc. **[★12313]**
Stearns County History Museum **[★12313]**
Stearns History Museum **[12313]**, St. Cloud, MN
Steele County Astronomical Soc. **[11970]**, Owatonna, MN
Steinmetz HS JROTC Pathfinders **[1201]**, Chicago, IL
Step 1 All-Stars **[14742]**, Columbus, OH
Stephen Lions Club **[12710]**, Stephen, MN
Stephenson County Historical Soc. **[1754]**, Freeport, IL
Sterling Area Chamber of Commerce **[★3703]**
Sterling Heights Area Chamber of Commerce **[9870]**, Sterling Heights, MI
Sterling Heights Cmpt. Club **[9871]**, Sterling Heights, MI
Steuben County United Way **[4130]**, Angola, IN
Steubenville AIFA **[17302]**, Wintersville, OH
Steubenville Area Bd. of Realtors **[17303]**, Wintersville, OH
Stevens Point Area Genealogical Soc. **[19808]**, Stevens Point, WI
Stevens Point Area Human Rsrc. Assn. **[19809]**, Stevens Point, WI
Stevens Point PTSA **[19810]**, Stevens Point, WI
Stewartville Chamber of Commerce **[12714]**, Stewartville, MN
Stewartville Lions Club **[12715]**, Stewartville, MN
Stiga Shaker Heights Table Tennis Club **[16643]**, Shaker Heights, OH
Stillwater Leisure Sport Assn. **[17006]**, Troy, OH
Stillwater Stargazers **[17007]**, Troy, OH
Stittsville Beagle Club **[10134]**, West Branch, MI
Stock Exchange; Chicago **[832]**, Chicago, IL
Stock Exchange; Midwest **[★832]**
Stockbridge Lions Club **[9878]**, Stockbridge, MI
Stoddard Lions Club **[19827]**, Stoddard, WI
Stone
Indiana Limestone Inst. of Am. **[4172]**, Bedford, IN
Michigan Indus. Sand Assn. **[8676]**, Lansing, MI
Stone Acad. PTA **[1202]**, Chicago, IL
Stone Belt Arc - Monroe County **[4261]**, Bloomington, IN
Stonebelt Stargazers **[4177]**, Bedford, IN
Stopping Woman Abuse Now **[2862]**, Olney, IL
Stormwater Mgt; Indiana Assn. for Floodplain and **[5172]**, Indianapolis, IN
Stoughton Chamber of Commerce **[19831]**, Stoughton, WI
Stow-Munroe Falls Chamber of Commerce **[16778]**, Stow, OH
Straits Area Home Builders Assn. **[7136]**, Cheboygan, MI
Strait's of Mackinac Beagle Club **[9081]**, Moran, MI
Stratford Area Chamber of Commerce **[19834]**, Stratford, WI
Streamwood Chamber of Commerce **[3721]**, Streamwood, IL
Streamwood Guns 'n Hoses Assn. **[3722]**, Streamwood, IL
Streator Area Chamber of Commerce **[3730]**, Streator, IL
Streator Area Chamber of Commerce and Indus. **[★3730]**
Streator Area United Way **[3731]**, Streator, IL
Streator Lions Club **[3732]**, Streator, IL
Streeterville Org. of Active Residents **[1203]**, Chicago, IL
Sts.boro Chamber of Commerce **[16782]**, Streetsboro, OH
Striders **[★4859]**
String Teachers Assn., Michigan Chap; Amer. **[10111]**, West Bloomfield, MI
Stroke
Ingalls Stroke Club **[1955]**, Harvey, IL
Natl. Stroke Assn., Minnesota Chap. **[11704]**, Minneapolis, MN
Strongsville Area Chamber of Commerce **[★16798]**
Strongsville Chamber of Commerce **[16798]**, Strongsville, OH
Strongsville Skating Club **[16799]**, Strongsville, OH
Structural Engineers Assn; Indiana **[5771]**, Merrillville, IN
Struthers Lions Club **[17110]**, Warren, OH
Studebaker Driver's Club, Black Hawk Chap. **[1204]**, Chicago, IL
Studebakers Driver's Club, Big Six River Bend Chap. **[2535]**, Moline, IL
Studebakers Driver's Club, Crossroads Zone **[9848]**, Spring Lake, MI
Studebakers Driver's Club, Indy Chap. **[5838]**, Mooresville, IN
Studebakers Driver's Club, North Star Chap. **[10332]**, Arden Hills, MN
Student Assn; Indiana Univ. **[4235]**, Bloomington, IN
Student Environment Network; Illinois **[3825]**, Urbana, IL
Student Org; Pennfield Parent Teacher and **[6867]**, Battle Creek, MI
Student Org; Plainfield South High School Parent Teacher **[3106]**, Plainfield, IL
Student Personnel Administrators, NASPA Region IV-East; Natl. Assn. of **[20160]**, Whitewater, WI
Student Services
School Nutrition Assn. of Michigan **[9040]**, Midland, MI
Students
Amer. Acad. of Pediatrics, Ohio Chap. **[17338]**, Worthington, OH
Assoc. Students of Madison **[18480]**, Madison, WI
Detroit Historical Soc. **[7347]**, Detroit, MI
Hawks Inn Historical Soc. **[17823]**, Delafield, WI
Historical Soc. of Michigan **[7522]**, East Lansing, MI
Illinois School Lib. Media Assn. **[404]**, Canton, IL
Indiana Univ. Student Assn. **[4235]**, Bloomington, IN
Intl. Assn. of Elecl. Inspectors, Ohio Chap. **[16661]**, Shreve, OH
Islamic Soc. - Northern Illinois Univ. **[1437]**, DeKalb, IL
Jewish Historical Soc. of Michigan **[10116]**, West Bloomfield, MI
Minnesota State Univ. Student Assn. **[12527]**, St. Paul, MN
Muslim-cultural Students Assn. - Northwestern Univ. **[1670]**, Evanston, IL
Muslim Student Assn. - Purdue Univ. **[6492]**, West Lafayette, IN
Muslim Student Assn. - Southern Illinois Univ. at Carbondale **[422]**, Carbondale, IL
Muslim Student Assn. - Univ. of Illinois - Chicago **[1957]**, Harwood Heights, IL
Muslim Student Assn., Univ. of Minnesota **[11687]**, Minneapolis, MN
Muslim Student Union - Indiana Univ., Bloomington **[4243]**, Bloomington, IN

Muslim Student's Assn. of Cleveland State Univ. [14168], Cleveland, OH
Muslim Students' Assn. - Hiram Coll. [15453], Hiram, OH
Muslim Students' Assn. - Loyola Univ. of Chicago [1061], Chicago, IL
Muslim Students' Assn. of Michigan State Univ. [7555], East Lansing, MI
Muslim Students' Assn. - Northeastern Illinois Univ. [1062], Chicago, IL
Muslim Students' Assn. - Ohio State Univ. [14511], Columbus, OH
Muslim Students Assn. - Ohio Univ. at Athens [13207], Athens, OH
Muslim Students' Assn. - Univ. of Akron [13067], Akron, OH
Muslim Students Assn. - Univ. of Illinois at Urbana-Champaign [3828], Urbana, IL
Muslim Students' Assn. - Univ. of Michigan - Ann Arbor [6740], Ann Arbor, MI
Muslim Students' Assn. - Univ. of Toledo [16932], Toledo, OH
Northville Historical Soc. [9227], Northville, MI
Tauheed (Islamic Soc.) - Ohio Wesleyan Univ. [15011], Delaware, OH
United Council of University of Wisconsin Students [18629], Madison, WI
Wisconsin Assn. of School Couns. [18665], Madison, WI
Wisconsin Scholars [19180], Milwaukee, WI
Youngstown AFL-CIO Coun. [17421], Youngstown, OH
Students Association; United Chinese Scholars and [1215], Chicago, IL
Students for Individual Liberty - Univ. of Illinois, Urbana/Champaign [3838], Urbana, IL
Students Org; Clague Middle School Parent-Teachers- [6691], Ann Arbor, MI
Stud. Circles; Aurora Community [112], Aurora, IL
Sturgeon Creek Beagle Club [9860], Sterling, MI
Sturgeon for Tomorrow; Black Lake Chap. of [7130], Cheboygan, MI
Sturgis Area Chamber of Commerce [9883], Sturgis, MI
Stuttering Assn; Columbus Chap. of the Natl. [14378], Columbus, OH
Subcontractors Assn. of Northeast Ohio [13092], Akron, OH
Substance Abuse
Addiction Rsrc. Coun. [19975], Waukesha, WI
Al-Anon/Alateen of Central Oakland County [10079], Waterford, MI
Al-Anon Family Groups of Metro Detroit [9474], Redford, MI
Alcohol and Addictions Rsrc. Center [6208], South Bend, IN
Alcohol and Drug Abuse Self-Help Network, d.b.a. SMART Recovery [15961], Mentor, OH
Alcohol and Other Drugs Coun. of Kenosha County [18293], Kenosha, WI
Alcoholics Anonymous, Cincinnati Intergroup Off. [13695], Cincinnati, OH
Alcoholics Anonymous, Indianapolis Intergroup [4967], Indianapolis, IN
Alcoholics Anonymous, Intergroup Assn. of Minneapolis and Suburban Area [12329], St. Louis Park, MN
Alcoholics Anonymous, Kent County Central Off. [7880], Grand Rapids, MI
Alcoholics Anonymous, Michiana Central Ser. Off. [6209], South Bend, IN
Alcoholics Anonymous, Southwestern Indiana Central Off. [4516], Evansville, IN
Alcoholics Anonymous, Wabash Valley Intergroup [6304], Terre Haute, IN
Alcoholics Anonymous World Services, Akron Intergroup Coun. [13026], Akron, OH
Alcoholics Anonymous World Sers., Bloomington/Normal Intergroup [252], Bloomington, IL
Alcoholics Anonymous World Services, Canton Area Intergroup Coun. [13539], Canton, OH
Alcoholics Anonymous World Services, Central Ohio Fellowship Intergroup [14272], Columbus, OH
Alcoholics Anonymous World Services, Chicago Area Ser. Off. [602], Chicago, IL
Alcoholics Anonymous World Services, Cleveland District Off. [14042], Cleveland, OH
Alcoholics Anonymous World Sers., Comite De Intergrupos [603], Chicago, IL
Alcoholics Anonymous World Sers., Detroit and Wayne County Off. [7296], Detroit, MI
Alcoholics Anonymous World Sers., District 11 Central Off. [9920], Traverse City, MI
Alcoholics Anonymous World Sers., District 91 Central Off. [1766], Galesburg, IL
Alcoholics Anonymous World Sers., East Central Illinois Intergroup [494], Champaign, IL
Alcoholics Anonymous World Sers., Fort Wayne Area Intergroup [4620], Fort Wayne, IN
Alcoholics Anonymous World Sers., Fox Valley Central Off. [18854], Menasha, WI
Alcoholics Anonymous World Services, Illowa Intergroup [2513], Moline, IL
Alcoholics Anonymous World Sers., Intergroup Off. [16164], Newark, OH
Alcoholics Anonymous World Services, Lansing Central Off. [8527], Lansing, MI
Alcoholics Anonymous World Sers., Lorain County Central Off. [15698], Lorain, OH
Alcoholics Anonymous World Sers., Madison Area Intergroup/Central Off. [18446], Madison, WI
Alcoholics Anonymous World Sers., Madison County Intergroup [4094], Anderson, IN
Alcoholics Anonymous World Services, Midland Area Unity Coun. Intergroup [9018], Midland, MI
Alcoholics Anonymous World Sers., North Central Ohio Area Intergroup [16600], Sandusky, OH
Alcoholics Anonymous World Sers., Northwest Ohio and Southeastern Michigan Central Off. [16873], Toledo, OH
Alcoholics Anonymous World Sers., Original Recipe Intergroup [5953], New Paris, IN
Alcoholics Anonymous World Sers., Peoria Area Intergroup Assn. [2999], Peoria, IL
Alcoholics Anonymous World Sers., Racine Area Central Off. [19548], Racine, WI
Alcoholics Anonymous World Sers., Rockford Area Intergroup [3261], Rockford, IL
Alcoholics Anonymous World Services, Springfield Intergroup [3520], Springfield, IL
Alcoholics Anonymous World Sers., Twin Ports Area Intergroup [10795], Duluth, MN
Alcoholics Anonymous World Sers., Winnebago Land Central Off. [17967], Fond du Lac, WI
Alcoholics Anonymous World Sers., Youngstown Area Intergroup [17384], Youngstown, OH
Alcoholism Coun. of the Cincinnati Area, Natl. Coun. on Alcoholism and Drug Dependence [13696], Cincinnati, OH
Amer. Alcohol and Drug Info. Found. [8528], Lansing, MI
Amer. Soc. of Addiction Medicine, Michigan [7505], East Lansing, MI
Carver County Historical Soc. [12816], Waconia, MN
Central East Alcoholism and Drug Coun. [564], Charleston, IL
Chicagoland Region of Narcotics Anonymous [2808], Oak Park, IL
Coun. on Alcohol and Other Drug Abuse of Washington County [20117], West Bend, WI
Detroit East Area Narcotics Anonymous [7345], Detroit, MI
Drug-Free Marion County [5104], Indianapolis, IN
Flint Area Narcotics Anonymous [7728], Flint, MI
Greater Indianapolis Coun. on Alcoholism and Drug Dependence [5129], Indianapolis, IN
Huron Valley Area Intergroup [10207], Ypsilanti, MI
Illinois Alcoholism and Drug Dependence Assn. [3562], Springfield, IL
Indiana Counselors Assn. on Alcohol and Drug Abuse [5220], Indianapolis, IN
Jackson County Historical Soc. [11290], Lakefield, MN
Michigan Assn. of Alcoholism and Drug Abuse Counselors [7067], Canton, MI
Michigan Assn. of Substance Abuse Coordinating Agencies [7535], East Lansing, MI
Minnesota Region of Narcotics Anonymous [11671], Minneapolis, MN
Mothers Against Drunk Driving, Kent County Chap. [7986], Grand Rapids, MI
Mothers Against Drunk Driving, Marathon/Portage [19794], Stevens Point, WI
Mothers Against Drunk Driving, Wabash Valley Chap. [6335], Terre Haute, IN
Natl. Coun. on Alcoholism and Addictions-Greater Flint Area [7749], Flint, MI
Natl. Coun. on Alcoholism and Drug Dependence, Greater Detroit Area [7411], Detroit, MI
Natl. Coun. on Alcoholism and Drug Dependence of Michigan [8739], Lansing, MI
Natl. Coun. on Alcoholism/Lansing Regional Area [8740], Lansing, MI
Northwoods Area of Narcotics Anonymous [7221], Conway, MI
Ohio Assn. of Alcoholism and Drug Abuse Counselors [14541], Columbus, OH
Ohio Region of Narcotics Anonymous [14666], Columbus, OH
Only One Promise Area of Narcotics Anonymous [1400], Decatur, IL
Primary Purpose Area of Narcotics Anonymous [549], Champaign, IL
Racine Coun. on Alcohol and Other Drug Abuse [19567], Racine, WI
Substance Abuse Prevention Coalition of Southeast Michigan [9826], Southfield, MI
Wisconsin Assn. of Alcohol and Drug Abuse Counselors [19408], Oshkosh, WI
Wisconsin Assn. on Alcohol and Other Drug Abuse [18649], Madison, WI
Substance Abuse Coordinating Agencies; Michigan Assn. of [7535], East Lansing, MI
Substance Abuse Prevention Coalition of Southeast Michigan [9826], Southfield, MI
Suburban Chicago Planned Giving Coun. [2151], Kenilworth, IL
Suburban Corvettes of Minnesota [12594], St. Paul, MN
Suburban Northwest Builders Assn. [10949], Elk River, MN
Sudden Infant Death Syndrome
Tomorrow's Child/Michigan Sudden Infant Death Syndrome [8764], Lansing, MI
Le Sueur Area Chamber of Commerce [11310], Le Sueur, MN
Le Sueur Area United Way [11311], Le Sueur, MN
Suffield Lions Club [16843], Tallmadge, OH
Sugar Creek Protection Society [15102], Elmore, OH
Suicide
Amer. Found. for Suicide Prevention of Northeast Ohio [14049], Cleveland, OH
Community for Hope of Greater Oshkosh [19391], Oshkosh, WI
Suicide Awareness Voices of Educ. [11753], Minneapolis, MN
Suicide Awareness Voices of Educ. [11753], Minneapolis, MN
Suicide Prevention; Marinette and Menominee Counties Youth [18800], Marinette, WI
Sullivan Area Chamber of Commerce [★3741]
Sullivan Chamber and Economic Development [3741], Sullivan, IL
Sullivan County Chamber of Commerce [6287], Sullivan, IN
Sullivan Lions Club [16807], Sullivan, OH
Sullivan Soc; Midwestern Gilbert and [2742], North Aurora, IL
Summer School
North Central Conf. on Summer Schools [19642], River Falls, WI
Summit Beagle Club [17180], West Farmington, OH
Summit County Chap. of Ohio Genealogical Soc. [13093], Akron, OH
Summit County Historical Soc. [13094], Akron, OH
Summit County REACT [13095], Akron, OH
Summit Educ. Initiative [13096], Akron, OH
Summit Skating Club of Michigan [8244], Holt, MI
Sun Prairie Wyldlife [19242], Mount Horeb, WI
Sun Prairie Young Life [19243], Mount Horeb, WI
Sunbeam Registry; Midwest [12051], Prior Lake, MN
Sunburst Corvette Club [1334], Crystal Lake, IL
Sunbury - Big Walnut Area Chamber of Commerce [16814], Sunbury, OH
Sunbury Lions Club [16815], Sunbury, OH
Sundowners African Violet Club [19935], Verona, WI
Sunfield Lions Club [9884], Sunfield, MI
Superior Curling Club [19878], Superior, WI

Superior District Dental Soc. **[8959]**, Marquette, MI
Superior - Douglas County Chamber of Commerce **[19879]**, Superior, WI
Superior/Douglas RSVP **[19880]**, Superior, WI
Superior Figure Skating Club **[19881]**, Superior, WI
Superior Hiking Trail Assn. **[12774]**, Two Harbors, MN
Superiorland Chap. of Human Rsrc. Professionals **[10177]**, Wilson, MI
Supervision and Curriculum Development; Michigan Assn. for **[8629]**, Lansing, MI
Supervision and Curriculum Development; Wisconsin Assn. for **[19895]**, Thiensville, WI
Support Gp; Cincinnati Celiac **[15383]**, Hamilton, OH
Support Gp; Mecosta County **[6949]**, Big Rapids, MI
Support Groups
Amazon Africa Aid Org. **[6654]**, Ann Arbor, MI
Barefoot Connections **[9495]**, Riverview, MI
Cincinnati Celiac Support Gp. **[15383]**, Hamilton, OH
Compassionate Friends - Central Ohio Chap. **[14412]**, Columbus, OH
Compassionate Friends - Cuyahoga/Geauga Counties Chap. **[13643]**, Chardon, OH
Compassionate Friends - East Central Indiana Chap. **[4477]**, Economy, IN
Compassionate Friends - Flint, Michigan Chap. **[7720]**, Flint, MI
Compassionate Friends - Greater Cincinnati-East Chap. **[13808]**, Cincinnati, OH
Compassionate Friends - Lafayette, Indiana Chap. **[5610]**, Lafayette, IN
Compassionate Friends - Lake Porter County Chap. **[6525]**, Whiting, IN
Compassionate Friends - Lakes Area Chap. **[10054]**, Walled Lake, MI
Compassionate Friends - Livonia, Michigan Chap. **[10138]**, Westland, MI
The Compassionate Friends - Miami Valley, Ohio Chap. **[15559]**, Kettering, OH
Compassionate Friends - Miami-WhiteWater Chap. **[4478]**, Economy, IN
Compassionate Friends - Minneapolis Chap. **[11549]**, Minneapolis, MN
Compassionate Friends - Northern Lake County Illinois Chap. **[1901]**, Green Oaks, IL
Compassionate Friends - Pekin Area Chap. **[2386]**, Manito, IL
Compassionate Friends - Southern Indiana Chap. **[4538]**, Evansville, IN
The Compassionate Friends U.S.A. Natl. Org. **[2770]**, Oak Brook, IL
GriefNet **[6703]**, Ann Arbor, MI
Griefshare **[3819]**, Urbana, IL
Mecosta County Support Gp. **[6949]**, Big Rapids, MI
Racing for Recovery **[16831]**, Sylvania, OH
Scam Victims United **[10487]**, Bloomington, MN
Sickle Cell Awareness Gp. **[13987]**, Cincinnati, OH
Surgery
Amer. Coll. of Surgeons - Michigan Chap. **[7502]**, East Lansing, MI
Ohio Chap. of the Amer. Coll. of Surgeons **[14579]**, Columbus, OH
Toledo Surgical Soc. **[16978]**, Toledo, OH
Surgical Soc; Toledo **[16978]**, Toledo, OH
Surveying
Illinois Professional Land Surveyors Assn. **[3230]**, Rochester, IL
Indiana Soc. of Professional Land Surveyors **[5307]**, Indianapolis, IN
Michigan Soc. of Professional Surveyors **[8717]**, Lansing, MI
Minnesota Soc. of Professional Surveyors **[10601]**, Burnsville, MN
Professional Land Surveyors of Ohio **[14713]**, Columbus, OH
Wisconsin Soc. of Land Surveyors **[20013]**, Waukesha, WI
Surveyors Assn; Illinois Professional Land **[3230]**, Rochester, IL
Suspender Wearers Assn. of Am. **[9827]**, Southfield, MI
Sussex Area Chamber of Commerce **[19885]**, Sussex, WI
Sussex Lions Club **[19886]**, Sussex, WI
Sustainable Farming Assn. of Minnesota **[12708]**, Starbuck, MN
Sustainable Farming Assn. of Minnesota - Cannon River **[11256]**, Kenyon, MN
Sustainable Farming Assn. of Minnesota - South Central **[10266]**, Albert Lea, MN
Sustainable Racine **[19575]**, Racine, WI
Suttons Bay Chamber of Commerce **[9889]**, Suttons Bay, MI
SW Suburban RSVP **[13436]**, Brook Park, OH
Swan City Ice Skaters **[17596]**, Beaver Dam, WI
Swansea Chamber of Commerce **[3744]**, Swansea, IL
Swanton Area Chamber of Commerce **[16819]**, Swanton, OH
Swartz Creek Lions Club **[9896]**, Swartz Creek, MI
Swedish
Swedish Amer. Museum Assn. of Chicago **[1205]**, Chicago, IL
Swedish American Chamber of Commerce - Detroit Chapter **[6968]**, Birmingham, MI
Swedish Amer. Museum Assn. of Chicago **[1205]**, Chicago, IL
Swedish Museum and Cultural Center **[★1205]**
Sweet Adelines Intl., Alexienne Chap. **[10286]**, Alexandria, MN
Sweet Adelines Intl., Battle Creek Chap. **[6871]**, Battle Creek, MI
Sweet Adelines Intl., Capital City Chorus **[5485]**, Indianapolis, IN
Sweet Adelines Intl., Capitol Showcase Chap. **[14743]**, Columbus, OH
Sweet Adelines Intl., Center Point Chap. **[19811]**, Stevens Point, WI
Sweet Adelines Intl., Chippewa Valley Chap. **[17902]**, Eau Claire, WI
Sweet Adelines Intl., Choral-Aires Chorus **[2782]**, Oak Brook, IL
Sweet Adelines Intl., City of Flags Chorus **[13591]**, Canton, OH
Sweet Adelines Intl., County Connection Chorus **[10216]**, Ypsilanti, MI
Sweet Adelines Intl., Crosstown Harmony Chorus **[19131]**, Milwaukee, WI
Sweet Adelines Intl., Danville Chap. **[1352]**, Danville, IL
Sweet Adelines Intl., Dogwood Blossoms Chap. **[16089]**, Mount Vernon, OH
Sweet Adelines Intl., Edge O' Town Chap. **[1206]**, Chicago, IL
Sweet Adelines Intl., Fenton Lakes Chorus **[7691]**, Fenton, MI
Sweet Adelines Intl., Fox Valley Chorus **[17526]**, Appleton, WI
Sweet Adelines Intl., French Colony Chap. **[15295]**, Gallipolis, OH
Sweet Adelines Intl., Friendship VII Chap. **[16127]**, New Concord, OH
Sweet Adelines Intl., Gem City Chorus **[13626]**, Centerville, OH
Sweet Adelines Intl., Granite City Sound Chap. **[12314]**, St. Cloud, MN
Sweet Adelines Intl., Great Lakes Chorus **[9872]**, Sterling Heights, MI
Sweet Adelines Intl., Greater Cleveland Chorus **[15506]**, Independence, OH
Sweet Adelines Intl., Harmony of the Hill Chap. **[18221]**, Hubertus, WI
Sweet Adelines Intl., Heart of Illinois Chorus **[3891]**, Washington, IL
Sweet Adelines Intl., Heart of Michigan Chap. **[9751]**, Shepherd, MI
Sweet Adelines Intl., Heart O' Wisconsin Chap. **[18825]**, Marshfield, WI
Sweet Adelines Intl., Heart of Ohio Show Chorus **[16094]**, Munroe Falls, OH
Sweet Adelines Intl., Hocking Valley Chap. **[13220]**, Athens, OH
Sweet Adelines Intl., Irish Hills Chap. **[6584]**, Adrian, MI
Sweet Adelines Intl., Lake Country Chorus **[12902]**, White Bear Lake, MN
Sweet Adelines Intl., Lake Ridge Chorus **[15127]**, Elyria, OH
Sweet Adelines Intl., Lakes Area Chap. **[12997]**, Wyoming, MN
Sweet Adelines Intl., Little River Chap. **[4131]**, Angola, IN
Sweet Adelines Intl., Maple Mountain Chap. **[15980]**, Mentor, OH
Sweet Adelines Intl., Melodeers Chorus **[2762]**, Northbrook, IL
Sweet Adelines Intl., Menominee River Chap. **[9005]**, Menominee, MI
Sweet Adelines Intl., Michigan Northern Lights Chap. **[7824]**, Gaylord, MI
Sweet Adelines Intl., Milwaukee Showcase Chorus **[19132]**, Milwaukee, WI
Sweet Adelines Intl., Minnesota Valley Chap. **[11403]**, Mankato, MN
Sweet Adelines Intl., Newark Chap. **[16186]**, Newark, OH
Sweet Adelines Intl., Northern Buckeye Chap. **[13333]**, Bellevue, OH
Sweet Adelines Intl., Ohio Heartland Chap. **[17222]**, Westerville, OH
Sweet Adelines Intl., Opus 2000 Chap. **[19576]**, Racine, WI
Sweet Adelines Intl., Prairie Echoes Chap. **[1445]**, DeKalb, IL
Sweet Adelines Intl., Queen City Chorus **[17363]**, Wyoming, OH
Sweet Adelines Intl., Red Cedar Sounds Chap. **[17779]**, Colfax, WI
Sweet Adelines Intl., Rhythm of the River Chap. **[17635]**, Black River Falls, WI
Sweet Adelines Intl., River Bend Chorus **[6271]**, South Bend, IN
Sweet Adelines Intl., River City Sound Chap. **[3324]**, Rockford, IL
Sweet Adelines Intl., Sauk Trail Sound Chap. **[7201]**, Coldwater, MI
Sweet Adelines Intl., Scioto Valley Chorus **[15066]**, Dublin, OH
Sweet Adelines Intl., Seven Hills Show Chorus **[14005]**, Cincinnati, OH
Sweet Adelines Intl., Shawano Wolf River Harmony Chap. **[19684]**, Shawano, WI
Sweet Adelines Intl., Shoreline Sound Chap. **[9592]**, Royal Oak, MI
Sweet Adelines Intl., Sisters in Song Chap. **[15670]**, Lima, OH
Sweet Adelines Intl., Sound Celebration Chorus **[3685]**, Springfield, IL
Sweet Adelines Intl., Sound of Madison Chap. **[18624]**, Madison, WI
Sweet Adelines Intl., Spirit of Detroit Chap. **[7674]**, Farmington Hills, MI
Sweet Adelines Intl., Spirit of Evansville Chap. **[4581]**, Evansville, IN
Sweet Adelines Intl., Spirit of the Lakes Chorus **[18399]**, Lake Geneva, WI
Sweet Adelines Intl., Spirit of the Valley Chap. **[17416]**, Youngstown, OH
Sweet Adelines Intl., Spring Valley Chorus **[166]**, Bartlett, IL
Sweet Adelines Intl., Towns of Harmony Chap. **[4721]**, Fort Wayne, IN
Sweet Adelines Intl., Tri-City Chap. **[6810]**, Auburn, MI
Sweet Adelines Intl., Twin Cities Show Chorus **[10610]**, Burnsville, MN
Sweet Adelines Intl., Vallee de Croix Chorus **[12727]**, Stillwater, MN
Sweet Adelines Intl., Vermillion Valley Show Chap. **[3121]**, Pontiac, IL
Sweet Adelines Intl., Westosha Lakes Chorus **[58]**, Antioch, IL
Sweet Adelines Intl., Yahara River Chap. **[18625]**, Madison, WI
Sweet Adelines Intl., Zumbro Valley Chorus **[12194]**, Rochester, MN
Sweetwater Alliance **[10856]**, Duluth, MN
Swim Club; Blue Devil **[1916]**, Gurnee, IL
Swimming
Barrington Swim Club **[145]**, Barrington, IL
Blue Devil Swim Club **[1916]**, Gurnee, IL
Howard/Suamico Storm Breakers **[19850]**, Suamico, WI
Southeastern Swim Club **[4611]**, Fishers, IN
Swine
Illinois Pork Producers Assn. **[3627]**, Springfield, IL
Ohio Pork Producers Coun. **[14654]**, Columbus, OH

Swing Club; Madison West Coast **[18556]**, Madison, WI
Switzerland of Ohio Chamber of Commerce **[★17306]**
SWM - Wyldlife **[9694]**, St. Joseph, MI
Sycamore Audubon Soc. **[5634]**, Lafayette, IN
Sycamore Audubon Soc. **[6500]**, West Lafayette, IN
Sycamore Chamber of Commerce **[3748]**, Sycamore, IL
Sycamore Ice Skating Club **[5486]**, Indianapolis, IN
Sycamore Lions Club **[16822]**, Sycamore, OH
Sycamore Trails Rsrc. Conservation and Development Coun. **[4826]**, Greencastle, IN
Sycamore - Young Life **[14006]**, Cincinnati, OH
Sylvan Lake Bocce Club **[9897]**, Sylvan Lake, MI
Sylvania Area Chamber of Commerce **[16834]**, Sylvania, OH
Synagogue Lib. Assn., Metro Detroit Chap; Church and **[7250]**, Dearborn, MI
Syndrome Camping Org; Tourette **[1208]**, Chicago, IL
Syracuse Municipal Building Corp. **[6292]**, Syracuse, IN
Syracuse-Wawasee Chamber of Commerce **[6293]**, Syracuse, IN
Syrian Shriners **[14007]**, Cincinnati, OH
Syrup Producers Assn; Wisconsin Maple **[18900]**, Merrill, WI
Systems of Help Unlimited **[17417]**, Youngstown, OH

T

T and O Outreach **[★6082]**
Table Tennis
Canton Table Tennis Club **[13560]**, Canton, OH
Chicago Table Tennis Club at Evanston **[1653]**, Evanston, IL
Chicago Table Tennis Club at Franklin **[1736]**, Franklin Park, IL
Chicago Table Tennis Club at Glenview **[1862]**, Glenview, IL
Chicago Table Tennis Club at La Grange **[2169]**, La Grange, IL
Chicago Table Tennis Club at Northern Illinois Univ. **[1429]**, DeKalb, IL
Cincinnati Table Tennis Club **[13800]**, Cincinnati, OH
City Limits Table Tennis Club **[16115]**, New Boston, OH
Cleveland Table Tennis Assn. **[14105]**, Cleveland, OH
Columbus Area Table Tennis Assn. **[4394]**, Columbus, IN
Columbus Table Tennis Club **[14404]**, Columbus, OH
Davison Athletic Club **[7237]**, Davison, MI
Dayton Table Tennis Club **[14881]**, Dayton, OH
Fenton/Flint Table Tennis Club **[8818]**, Linden, MI
Flint Table Tennis Club **[7735]**, Flint, MI
Fort Wayne Table Tennis Club **[4660]**, Fort Wayne, IN
Highland Table Tennis Club **[4914]**, Highland, IN
Hudson Premier Table Tennis Club **[15484]**, Hudson, OH
Killerspin Multiplex Table Tennis Club **[1013]**, Chicago, IL
Kokomo Table Tennis Club **[5578]**, Kokomo, IN
McHenry County Table Tennis Club **[2461]**, McHenry, IL
Minnesota Table Tennis Fed. **[11295]**, Lakeville, MN
Net and Paddle Club **[1098]**, Chicago, IL
New Berlin Table Tennis Club **[19296]**, New Berlin, WI
Newark Table Tennis Club **[16179]**, Newark, OH
Oshkosh Table Tennis Org. **[19402]**, Oshkosh, WI
Park Forest Table Tennis Club **[2955]**, Park Forest, IL
Rochester Table Tennis Club **[12182]**, Rochester, MN
Rockford Table Tennis Club **[3313]**, Rockford, IL
Schaumburg Table Tennis Club **[3446]**, Schaumburg, IL
Shorewood Table Tennis Club **[19733]**, Shorewood, WI
South Bend Table Tennis Club **[6270]**, South Bend, IN
Southern Indiana Table Tennis Assn. **[5928]**, New Albany, IN
Stiga Shaker Heights Table Tennis Club **[16643]**, Shaker Heights, OH
Table Tennis Club of Indianapolis **[5487]**, Indianapolis, IN
Table Tennis Club at UWM **[19133]**, Milwaukee, WI
Table Tennis Minnesota - Bloomington **[10489]**, Bloomington, MN
Table Tennis Minnesota - Fridley **[11036]**, Fridley, MN
Table Tennis Minnesota - Plymouth **[12037]**, Plymouth, MN
Table Tennis/Traverse City **[9953]**, Traverse City, MI
Three Rivers Table Tennis Club **[4726]**, Fort Wayne, IN
Wausau Table Tennis Club **[20057]**, Wausau, WI
Xilin Table Tennis Club **[2667]**, Naperville, IL
Table Tennis Club of Indianapolis **[5487]**, Indianapolis, IN
Table Tennis Club at UWM **[19133]**, Milwaukee, WI
Table Tennis Minnesota - Bloomington **[10489]**, Bloomington, MN
Table Tennis Minnesota - Fridley **[11036]**, Fridley, MN
Table Tennis Minnesota - Plymouth **[12037]**, Plymouth, MN
Table Tennis/Traverse City **[9953]**, Traverse City, MI
Tadmor Shriners **[13097]**, Akron, OH
Tails a' Waggin' Rescue **[6522]**, Whitestown, IN
Talawanda - Young Life **[15170]**, Fairfield, OH
Tall Club of Milwaukee **[19134]**, Milwaukee, WI
Tallmadge Chamber of Commerce **[16844]**, Tallmadge, OH
Tallness
Columbus High Soc. Tall Club **[14386]**, Columbus, OH
Fort Wayne Hi-Lites **[4658]**, Fort Wayne, IN
High Cincinnatians Tall Club **[13862]**, Cincinnati, OH
Mad Town Talls **[18542]**, Madison, WI
Minnesota Heartland Tall Soc. **[11650]**, Minneapolis, MN
Paramount Tall Club of Chicago **[1121]**, Chicago, IL
Rivercity High Soc. **[4570]**, Evansville, IN
Tall Club of Milwaukee **[19134]**, Milwaukee, WI
Tip Toppers Club of Detroit **[9593]**, Royal Oak, MI
Twin Cities Tall Club **[11763]**, Minneapolis, MN
Tammy's Loyal Companions **[8013]**, Grand Rapids, MI
Tango Soc. of Minnesota **[10927]**, Edina, MN
Tapestry Folkdance Center **[11754]**, Minneapolis, MN
Taping Contractors Assn; Northern Ohio Painting and **[15998]**, Middleburg Heights, OH
Tasters Guild Intl. - Akron, Chap. No. 079 **[16257]**, Norton, OH
Tasters Guild Intl. - Ann Arbor, Chap. No. 037 **[6773]**, Ann Arbor, MI
Tasters Guild Intl. - Cleveland, Chap. No. 070 **[14250]**, Cleveland Heights, OH
Tasters Guild Intl. - Grand Rapids, Chap. No. 007 **[8014]**, Grand Rapids, MI
Tasters Guild Intl. - Grand Traverse, Chap. No. 018 **[9954]**, Traverse City, MI
Tasters Guild Intl. - Harbor Springs/Petoskey, Chap. No. 096 **[8119]**, Harbor Springs, MI
Tasters Guild Intl. - Kalamazoo, Chap. No. 038 **[10051]**, Vicksburg, MI
Tasters Guild Intl. - Lansing, Chap. No. 039 **[7467]**, DeWitt, MI
Tasters Guild Intl. - Lapeer, Chap. No. 076 **[8783]**, Lapeer, MI
Tasters Guild Intl. - Michigan Lakeshore, Chap. No. 057 **[9216]**, North Muskegon, MI
Tasters Guild Intl. - Milwaukee, Chap. No. 017 **[17678]**, Brookfield, WI
Tasters Guild Intl. - Oakland County, Chap. No. 040 **[7675]**, Farmington Hills, MI
Tauheed (Islamic Soc.) - Ohio Wesleyan Univ. **[15011]**, Delaware, OH
Tavern League of Wisconsin **[18626]**, Madison, WI
Tawas Area Chamber of Commerce **[9898]**, Tawas City, MI
Tax Club **[19135]**, Milwaukee, WI
Tax Practitioners; Michigan Chap. of Natl. Assn. of **[8237]**, Holly, MI
Tax Practitioners; Minnesota Chap. of Natl. Assn. of **[12158]**, Rochester, MN
Taxation
Illinois Chap. of Natl. Assn. of Tax Professionals **[120]**, Aurora, IL
Illinois Soc. of Enrolled Agents **[2458]**, McHenry, IL
Illinois Soc. of Enrolled Agents - Northwest Chap. **[361]**, Buffalo Grove, IL
Illinois Soc. of Enrolled Agents - Southern Chap. **[488]**, Centralia, IL
Illinois Soc. of Enrolled Agents - Tri-Counties Chap. **[965]**, Chicago, IL
Indiana Chap. of Natl. Assn. of Tax Professionals **[6276]**, South Milford, IN
Indiana Soc. of Enrolled Agents **[4446]**, Danville, IN
Michigan Chap. of Natl. Assn. of Tax Practitioners **[8237]**, Holly, MI
Michigan Soc. of EAs **[9333]**, Owosso, MI
Minnesota Chap. of Natl. Assn. of Tax Practitioners **[12158]**, Rochester, MN
Minnesota Chapter of National Association of Tax Professionals **[12159]**, Rochester, MN
Minnesota Soc. of Enrolled Agents **[10678]**, Clearwater, MN
Minnesota Taxpayers Assn. **[12528]**, St. Paul, MN
Ohio Chap. Natl. Assn. of Tax Professionals **[15030]**, Dover, OH
Ohio State Soc. of Enrolled Agents - Greater Cleveland Chap. **[16795]**, Strongsville, OH
Ohio State Soc. of Enrolled Agents - Greater Columbus Chap. **[15300]**, Galloway, OH
Ohio State Soc. of Enrolled Agents - Greater Dayton Chap. **[14942]**, Dayton, OH
Quality for Indiana Taxpayers **[5465]**, Indianapolis, IN
Tax Club **[19135]**, Milwaukee, WI
Taxpayers' Fed. of Illinois **[3686]**, Springfield, IL
Taxpayers Network **[18136]**, Green Bay, WI
Wisconsin Chap. of Natl. Assn. of Tax Professionals **[19372]**, Onalaska, WI
Taxpayers Alliance; Wisconsin **[18758]**, Madison, WI
Taxpayers' Fed. of Illinois **[3686]**, Springfield, IL
Taxpayers Network **[18136]**, Green Bay, WI
Tayanoka Coun. of Camp Fire **[16592]**, Salem, OH
Taylor Lions Club - Michigan **[10142]**, Westland, MI
Taylor - Young Life **[15171]**, Fairfield, OH
Taylorville Main Street **[3756]**, Taylorville, IL
Tazewell County Genealogical and Historical Soc. **[2993]**, Pekin, IL
Tazewell County S.T.A.R. (Student-Tutor-Adult Reading) **[2994]**, Pekin, IL
Tazewell Numismatic Soc. **[3065]**, Peoria, IL
Teacher Education
Michigan Coun. of Teachers of English **[9505]**, Rochester, MI
Teacher Org; Barnard Elementary School Parent **[9977]**, Troy, MI
Teacher Org; Chagrin Falls Parent **[13631]**, Chagrin Falls, OH
Teacher Org; Columbus Parent **[11016]**, Forest Lake, MN
Teacher Organization; East China Consolidated Parent **[7152]**, China, MI
Teacher Org; Hoover-Wood Elementary School Parent **[181]**, Batavia, IL
Teacher Org; Liberty Benton Parent **[15205]**, Findlay, OH
Teacher Organization; Lily Lake Elementary Parent **[12721]**, Stillwater, MN
Teacher Org; Meadowlawn Parent **[5825]**, Monticello, IN
Teacher Organization; Oconto Elementary School Parent **[19349]**, Oconto, WI
Teacher Org; Owen Marsh Elementary School Parent **[3658]**, Springfield, IL
Teacher Org; Troy Special Services Parent **[10014]**, Troy, MI
Teacher Organization; University Avenue Parent **[10453]**, Blaine, MN
Teacher and Student Org; Pennfield Parent **[6867]**, Battle Creek, MI
Teacher Student Org; Plainfield South High School Parent **[3106]**, Plainfield, IL

Teachers
Gay, Lesbian and Straight Educ. Network, Ann Arbor-Ypsilanti Area **[6696]**, Ann Arbor, MI
Green Bay Educ. Assn. **[18106]**, Green Bay, WI
Illinois Coun. of Teachers of Mathematics **[937]**, Chicago, IL
Illinois Fed. of Teachers **[3970]**, Westmont, IL
Indiana Professional Educators **[5282]**, Indianapolis, IN
Indiana State Teachers Assn. **[5324]**, Indianapolis, IN
Michigan Coun. of Teachers of Mathematics **[6723]**, Ann Arbor, MI
Michigan Sci. Teachers Assn. **[6734]**, Ann Arbor, MI
Minnesota Coun. of Teachers of Mathematics **[11863]**, New Brighton, MN
Newark Teacher's Assn. **[16180]**, Newark, OH
North Eastern Ohio Educ. Assn. **[16381]**, Parma Heights, OH
Ohio Fed. of Teachers **[14609]**, Columbus, OH
We Are Traverse City **[9964]**, Traverse City, MI
Wisconsin Retired Educators' Assn. **[18916]**, Middleton, WI
Teachers Assn., Michigan Chap; Amer. String **[10111]**, West Bloomfield, MI
Teachers of English; Illinois Assn. of **[2716]**, Normal, IL
Teachers of English; Minnesota Coun. of **[10712]**, Coon Rapids, MN
Teachers of English; New Mexico Coun. of **[3832]**, Urbana, IL
Teachers Saving Children **[14834]**, Damascus, OH
Teachers-Students Org; Clague Middle School Parent- **[6691]**, Ann Arbor, MI
Teachers, Wisconsin Sect; Amer. Assn. of Physics **[17861]**, Eau Claire, WI
Teamsters AFL-CIO, LU 916 **[★3687]**
Teamsters for a Democratic Union **[7441]**, Detroit, MI
Teamsters Local 916 **[3687]**, Springfield, IL
Teamsters Local Union 563 **[17527]**, Appleton, WI
Tebala Shriners **[3325]**, Rockford, IL
Tech Corps Wisconsin **[19577]**, Racine, WI
Tech. Assn. of the Pulp and Paper Indus. - Chicago Sect. **[4011]**, Willow Springs, IL
Tech. Assn. of the Pulp and Paper Indus. - Ohio Sect. **[14961]**, Dayton, OH
Technical Consulting
Natl. Results Coun. **[12552]**, St. Paul, MN
Technical Education
Northeast Wisconsin Tech. Coll. **[18123]**, Green Bay, WI
Tech. Educ; Illinois Assn. for Career and **[3565]**, Springfield, IL
Technical Honor Soc., Mahoning County Career and Tech. Center; Natl. Vocational- **[13537]**, Canfield, OH
Technologists; Illinois State Soc. of Radiologic **[291]**, Bloomington, IL
Technology
Global Grid Forum **[2240]**, Lemont, IL
Intl. Fac. Mgt. Assn., Mid-Michigan **[9027]**, Midland, MI
MiCTA **[9112]**, Mount Pleasant, MI
MIT Enterprise Forum of Chicago **[1058]**, Chicago, IL
MIT Enterprise Forum of the Great Lakes **[6738]**, Ann Arbor, MI
Tech Corps Wisconsin **[19577]**, Racine, WI
Tech. Plus of Mankato **[11404]**, Mankato, MN
Tech; Community Economic Development and Info. **[9699]**, Saline, MI
Tech. Plus of Mankato **[11404]**, Mankato, MN
Tech. Student Assn., Illinois **[2609]**, Mulberry Grove, IL
Tecumseh Trailblazers **[17043]**, Urbana, OH
Tecumseh - Young Life **[6585]**, Adrian, MI
Tecumseh - Young Life **[16752]**, Springfield, OH
Teen Straight Talk **[17071]**, Vienna, OH
Teens Aiding the Cancer Community **[9245]**, Novi, MI
Tekonsha Lions Club **[9909]**, Tekonsha, MI
Telecommunications
IEEE Communications Soc., Chicago Chap. **[2638]**, Naperville, IL
IEEE Communs. Soc., Columbus Chap. **[16513]**, Reynoldsburg, OH
IEEE Communs. Soc., Milwaukee Chap. **[18872]**, Menomonee Falls, WI
IEEE Communs. Soc., Southeastern Michigan Chap. **[9401]**, Plymouth, MI
IEEE Communs. Soc., Southern Minnesota Chap. **[12148]**, Rochester, MN
IEEE Communs. Soc., Twin Cities Chap. **[11582]**, Minneapolis, MN
Illinois Chap. of the Natl. Assn. of Telecommunications Officers and Advisors **[1661]**, Evanston, IL
Illinois Telecommunications Assn. **[3643]**, Springfield, IL
Indiana Cable Telecommunications Assn. **[5202]**, Indianapolis, IN
Indiana Telecommunications Assn. **[5328]**, Indianapolis, IN
Minnesota Assn. of Community Telecommunications Administrators **[12234]**, Roseville, MN
Minnesota Telecom Alliance **[12529]**, St. Paul, MN
Natl. Assn. of Telecommunications Off.rs and Advisors, Michigan **[9813]**, Southfield, MI
Natl. Assn. of Telecommunications Off.rs and Advisors, Ohio **[15972]**, Mentor, OH
Ohio Cable Telecommunications Assn. **[14575]**, Columbus, OH
Telecommunications Assn. of Michigan **[8763]**, Lansing, MI
Wisconsin State Telecommunications Assn. **[18756]**, Madison, WI
Telecommunications Assn. of Michigan **[8763]**, Lansing, MI
Telecommunications Assn; Wisconsin State **[18756]**, Madison, WI
Telecommunications Officers and Advisors; Illinois Chap. of the Natl. Assn. of **[1661]**, Evanston, IL
Telephone Assn; Ohio Independent **[★14688]**
Telephone Service
Ohio Telecom Assn. **[14688]**, Columbus, OH
Teleprofessional Managers Assn. - Minnesota **[12595]**, St. Paul, MN
Ten Thousand Villages of Cincinnati **[14008]**, Cincinnati, OH
Ten Thousand Villages-Minnesota **[12596]**, St. Paul, MN
Tennis
Evanston Community Tennis Assn. **[3487]**, Skokie, IL
Terrace Park Historical Soc. **[16848]**, Terrace Park, OH
Terre Haute Area Assn. of Realtors, Indiana **[6344]**, Terre Haute, IN
Terre Haute Convention and Visitors Bur. **[6345]**, Terre Haute, IN
Terre Haute Kennel Club **[4285]**, Brazil, IN
Terrorism
Minnesotans Against Terrorism **[11189]**, Hopkins, MN
Terrorism; Minnesotans Against **[11189]**, Hopkins, MN
Testing
Chicago Chap. of the Intl. Soc. for Performance Improvement **[2294]**, Lisle, IL
ISPI Michigan Chap. **[9583]**, Royal Oak, MI
Minnesota Chap. of the Intl. Soc. for Performance Improvement **[11636]**, Minneapolis, MN
NIRS Forage and Feed Testing Consortium **[18584]**, Madison, WI
Ohio Heartland Chap. of the Intl. Soc. for Performance Improvement **[13523]**, Canal Winchester, OH
Wisconsin Chap. of the Intl. Soc. for Performance Improvement **[19162]**, Milwaukee, WI
Testing Consortium; NIRS Forage and Feed **[18584]**, Madison, WI
Textiles
Illinois State Fabricare Assn. **[971]**, Chicago, IL
Ohio Assn. of Textile Sers. **[14568]**, Columbus, OH
Theater Company; Walkabout **[1226]**, Chicago, IL
Theaters; League of Professionally Managed **[5390]**, Indianapolis, IN
Theatre
Friends of the Broadway **[9104]**, Mount Pleasant, MI
Milford Theatre Guilde **[16028]**, Milford, OH
Palace Cultural Arts Assn. **[15850]**, Marion, OH
Performance Network Theatre **[6752]**, Ann Arbor, MI
Prairie Ensemble **[547]**, Champaign, IL
Project Danztheatre Company **[1146]**, Chicago, IL
Rivendell Theatre Ensemble **[1166]**, Chicago, IL
Shakura Ensemble Ritual Theatre **[1181]**, Chicago, IL
Showbiz Players **[13985]**, Cincinnati, OH
Walkabout Theater Company **[1226]**, Chicago, IL
Theatre Guilde; Milford **[16028]**, Milford, OH
Theosophical
Theosophical Soc. in Am. **[3999]**, Wheaton, IL
Theosophical Soc. in Detroit **[6933]**, Berkley, MI
Theosophical Soc. - Milwaukee Br. **[19136]**, Milwaukee, WI
Theosophical Soc. in Am. **[3999]**, Wheaton, IL
Theosophical Soc. in Detroit **[6933]**, Berkley, MI
Theosophical Soc. - Milwaukee Br. **[19136]**, Milwaukee, WI
Therapy
Amer. Physical Therapy Assn., Minnesota Chap. **[12220]**, Roseville, MN
Illinois Occupational Therapy Assn. **[2814]**, Oak Park, IL
Illinois Physical Therapy Assn. **[2780]**, Oak Brook, IL
Indiana Occupational Therapy Assn. **[6485]**, West Lafayette, IN
Infusion Nurses Soc., Buckeye **[14894]**, Dayton, OH
Infusion Nurses Soc., Capital **[8147]**, Haslett, MI
Infusion Nurses Soc., Great Lakes **[9902]**, Taylor, MI
Infusion Nurses Soc., Illinois **[3990]**, Wheaton, IL
Infusion Nurses Soc., Mid-Michigan **[6901]**, Beaverton, MI
Infusion Nurses Soc., Southern Wisconsin **[17670]**, Brookfield, WI
Infusion Nurses Soc., Upper Midwest **[10592]**, Burnsville, MN
Minnesota Occupational Therapy Assn. **[12504]**, St. Paul, MN
Ohio Occupational Therapy Assn. **[14648]**, Columbus, OH
Ohio Physical Therapy Assn. **[15269]**, Gahanna, OH
Wisconsin Occupational Therapy Assn. **[18738]**, Madison, WI
Therapy Assn., Indiana Chap; Amer. Physical **[5016]**, Indianapolis, IN
Therapy Assn; Michigan Occupational **[8691]**, Lansing, MI
Therapy Assn., Minnesota Chap; Amer. Physical **[12220]**, Roseville, MN
Theta Xi, Alpha Sigma Chap. — Bradley Univ. **[3066]**, Peoria, IL
Theta Xi Fraternity, Beta Delta Chap. **[435]**, Carbondale, IL
Theta Xi Fraternity, Kappa Sigma Chap. **[7758]**, Flint, MI
Theta Xi Fraternity, Sigma Chap. **[6774]**, Ann Arbor, MI
Theta Xi Fraternity, Theta Chap. **[6501]**, West Lafayette, IN
Theta Xi, Gamma Kappa Chap. — Univ. of Illinois-Chicago **[1207]**, Chicago, IL
Theta Xi, Kappa Chap. — Rose-Hulman Inst. of Tech. **[6346]**, Terre Haute, IN
Theta Xi, Kappa Kappa Chap. — Ball State Univ. **[5898]**, Muncie, IN
Thief River Falls Area United Way **[12750]**, Thief River Falls, MN
Thief River Falls Chamber of Commerce **[12751]**, Thief River Falls, MN
Thief River Falls Lions Club **[12752]**, Thief River Falls, MN
Thiensville Mequon Lions Club **[19893]**, Thiensville, WI
Thimble Collectors Intl., Dairyland **[20192]**, Wisconsin Rapids, WI
Thimble Collectors Intl., Great Lakes **[6775]**, Ann Arbor, MI
Thimble Collectors Intl., ILMO Thimblers **[1879]**, Goreville, IL
Thimblefools of Northern Illinois **[2545]**, Montgomery, IL
Thomas - Young Life **[14744]**, Columbus, OH
Thoracic Medicine
Chicago Thoracic Soc. **[833]**, Chicago, IL

Illinois Thoracic Soc. **[3644]**, Springfield, IL
Indiana Thoracic Soc. **[5329]**, Indianapolis, IN
Massachusetts Thoracic Soc. **[8603]**, Lansing, MI
Ohio Thoracic Soc. **[15667]**, Lima, OH
Wisconsin Thoracic Soc. **[17688]**, Brookfield, WI
Thorn Creek Audubon Soc. **[2956]**, Park Forest, IL
Thornwood High School - Young Life **[3510]**, South Holland, IL
Thoroughbred Ex-Racehorses; Communication Alliance to Network **[249]**, Bloomingdale, IL
Three Lakes Info. Bur. **[19899]**, Three Lakes, WI
Three Meadows Home Owners Assn. **[16412]**, Perrysburg, OH
Three Rivers Area Chamber of Commerce **[9918]**, Three Rivers, MI
Three Rivers Assn. of Realtors **[2120]**, Joliet, IL
Three Rivers Fly Fishers **[4722]**, Fort Wayne, IN
Three Rivers Gem and Mineral Soc. **[4723]**, Fort Wayne, IN
Three Rivers Lions Club **[9919]**, Three Rivers, MI
Three Rivers Orchid Society, Fort Wayne **[4724]**, Fort Wayne, IN
Three Rivers Strollers **[4725]**, Fort Wayne, IN
Three Rivers Table Tennis Club **[4726]**, Fort Wayne, IN
Three Rivers Velo Sport **[★4617]**
Three Trackers of Ohio **[14222]**, Cleveland, OH
Thumb Area RSVP **[7086]**, Caro, MI
Thunderbird Midwest **[12038]**, Plymouth, MN
Thurgood Marshall Law Soc. **[14962]**, Dayton, OH
Ties, Needles, and Threads Guild **[1822]**, Glen Carbon, IL
Tiffin Area Chamber of Commerce **[16864]**, Tiffin, OH
Tiffin Lions Club **[16865]**, Tiffin, OH
Tiffin-Seneca United Way **[16866]**, Tiffin, OH
Tiger Cricket Club **[3451]**, Schaumburg, IL
Timber Producers Assn. of Michigan and Wisconsin **[19607]**, Rhinelander, WI
Timber Wolf Preservation Soc. **[18152]**, Greendale, WI
Timberland Rsrc. Conservation and Development Coun. **[7215]**, Comstock Park, MI
Timberline Skating Club **[20049]**, Wausau, WI
Timbermen; Michigan Assn. of **[9197]**, Newberry, MI
Time Out 4 Youth **[6082]**, Richland, IN
Timothy Christian - Young Life **[2024]**, Hinsdale, IL
Tinkers Creek Land Conservancy **[17017]**, Twinsburg, OH
Tinley Park Chamber of Commerce **[3774]**, Tinley Park, IL
Tip of the Mitt Watershed Coun. **[9373]**, Petoskey, MI
Tip Toppers Club of Detroit **[9593]**, Royal Oak, MI
TIPCOA **[★5635]**
Tipp City Area Chamber of Commerce **[16870]**, Tipp City, OH
Tipp City Area United Way **[16871]**, Tipp City, OH
Tippecanoe Audubon Soc. **[5801]**, Milford, IN
Tippecanoe Audubon Soc. **[5991]**, North Manchester, IN
Tippecanoe County Historical Assn. - Alameda McCollough Lib. **[5635]**, Lafayette, IN
Tipton County Chamber of Commerce **[6358]**, Tipton, IN
Tire and Rim Assn. **[13098]**, Akron, OH
Tire Safety and Illinois Not-for-Profit Org; Toby **[3688]**, Springfield, IL
Tire Soc. **[13099]**, Akron, OH
Tires
Ohio Tire Dealers and Retreaders Assn. **[14689]**, Columbus, OH
Tire Soc. **[13099]**, Akron, OH
T.L. Gilmer Dental Soc. **[3373]**, Rushville, IL
Toastmasters Intl.-District 62 **[8015]**, Grand Rapids, MI
Tobacco
Tobacco-Free Dane County Coalition **[18627]**, Madison, WI
Tobacco and Candy Distributors; Ohio Assn. of **[★14698]**
Tobacco-Free Dane County Coalition **[18627]**, Madison, WI
Toby Tire Safety and Illinois Not-for-Profit Org. **[3688]**, Springfield, IL
Toledo AIFA **[16961]**, Toledo, OH
Toledo Area Chamber of Commerce **[16962]**, Toledo, OH
Toledo Area Human Rsrcs. Assn. **[16963]**, Toledo, OH
Toledo Area Military Officers Assn. of Am. **[16964]**, Toledo, OH
Toledo Area Planned Giving Coun. **[16965]**, Toledo, OH
Toledo Area Theatre Organ Soc. **[16966]**, Toledo, OH
Toledo Auto. Dealers Assn. **[16967]**, Toledo, OH
Toledo Bar Assn. **[16968]**, Toledo, OH
Toledo Bd. of Realtors **[16969]**, Toledo, OH
Toledo Chap. Natl. Elecl. Contractors Assn. **[16558]**, Rossford, OH
Toledo Dental Soc. **[16970]**, Toledo, OH
Toledo District Golf Assn. **[16971]**, Toledo, OH
Toledo Estate Planning Coun. **[16972]**, Toledo, OH
Toledo Fed. of Musicians - Local 15-286, Amer. Fed. of Musicians **[★16953]**
Toledo Indus. Recreation and Employee Services Coun. **[16304]**, Oregon, OH
Toledo Jazz Soc. **[16973]**, Toledo, OH
Toledo Kennel Club **[13363]**, Bloomdale, OH
Toledo Lucas County Safety Coun. **[★16256]**
Toledo Police Patrolman's Assn. **[16974]**, Toledo, OH
Toledo Power Squadron **[16975]**, Toledo, OH
Toledo Rotary Club Found. **[16976]**, Toledo, OH
Toledo Senior Olympics **[16977]**, Toledo, OH
Toledo South Side - Young Life **[15919]**, Maumee, OH
Toledo Surgical Soc. **[16978]**, Toledo, OH
Toledo Youth for Christ **[15459]**, Holland, OH
Tomah Lions Club **[19906]**, Tomah, WI
Tomahawk Regional Chamber of Commerce **[19911]**, Tomahawk, WI
Tomorrow's Child/Michigan SIDS Alliance **[★8764]**
Tomorrow's Child/Michigan Sudden Infant Death Syndrome **[8764]**, Lansing, MI
Tomorrow's Hope **[18274]**, Jefferson, WI
Tooling Assn; Michigan **[7671]**, Farmington Hills, MI
Tooling and Mfg. Assn. **[2965]**, Park Ridge, IL
Toronto - Young Life **[16989]**, Toronto, OH
Tourette Syndrome Assn. of Illinois **[1842]**, Glen Ellyn, IL
Tourette Syndrome Assn. of Minnesota Chap. **[11797]**, Minnetonka, MN
Tourette Syndrome Association of Ohio **[14745]**, Columbus, OH
Tourette Syndrome Camping Org. **[1208]**, Chicago, IL
Touring Assn; Gold Wing **[5124]**, Indianapolis, IN
Tourism
Alton Regional Convention and Visitors Bur. **[37]**, Alton, IL
Aurora Area Convention and Tourism Coun. **[111]**, Aurora, IL
Brown County Convention and Visitors Bur. **[5912]**, Nashville, IN
Canton and Stark County Convention and Visitors Bur. **[13559]**, Canton, OH
Chicago Convention and Tourism Bur. **[805]**, Chicago, IL
Chicago Southland Convention and Visitors Bur. **[2216]**, Lansing, IL
Chippewa County Tourism Coun. **[17748]**, Chippewa Falls, WI
Chippewa Valley Convention and Visitors Bur. **[17870]**, Eau Claire, WI
Collinsville Convention and Visitors Bur. **[1288]**, Collinsville, IL
Danville Area Convention and Visitors Bur. **[1344]**, Danville, IL
Dayton and Montgomery County Convention and Visitors Bur. **[14879]**, Dayton, OH
Decatur Area Convention and Visitors Bur. **[1382]**, Decatur, IL
Duluth Convention and Visitors Bur. **[10816]**, Duluth, MN
DuPage Convention and Visitors Bur. **[2771]**, Oak Brook, IL
Experience Columbus **[14431]**, Columbus, OH
Fergus Falls Convention and Visitors Bur. **[10997]**, Fergus Falls, MN
Flint Area Convention and Visitors Bur. **[7727]**, Flint, MI
Fort Wayne/Allen County Convention and Visitors Bur. **[4651]**, Fort Wayne, IN
Fox Cities Convention and Visitors Bur. **[17491]**, Appleton, WI
Galena and Jo Daviess County Convention and Visitors Bur. **[1762]**, Galena, IL
Greater Cincinnati Convention and Visitors Bur. **[13842]**, Cincinnati, OH
Greater Madison Convention and Visitors Bur. **[18518]**, Madison, WI
Greater Woodfield Convention and Visitors Bur. **[3436]**, Schaumburg, IL
Greene County Convention and Visitors Bur. **[13297]**, Beavercreek, OH
Hutchinson Area Convention and Visitors Bur. **[11208]**, Hutchinson, MN
Intl. Visitors Coun. - Columbus **[14476]**, Columbus, OH
Intl. Visitors Coun. of Metropolitan Detroit **[6814]**, Auburn Hills, MI
Knox County Convention and Visitors Bur. **[16083]**, Mount Vernon, OH
Lake County Illinois Convention and Visitors Bur. **[1922]**, Gurnee, IL
Lake of the Woods Tourism **[10387]**, Baudette, MN
Lorain County Visitors Bur. **[13135]**, Amherst, OH
Ludington Area Convention and Visitors Bur. **[8872]**, Ludington, MI
Mansfield and Richland County Convention and Visitors Bur. **[15777]**, Mansfield, OH
Marshall Convention and Visitors Bur. **[11435]**, Marshall, MN
Ohio Division of Travel and Tourism **[14597]**, Columbus, OH
Ohio Travel Assn. **[14691]**, Columbus, OH
Orange County Convention and Visitor's Bur. **[4764]**, French Lick, IN
Pickaway County Visitors Bur. **[14037]**, Circleville, OH
Quad Cities Convention and Visitors Bur., Illinois-Iowa **[2529]**, Moline, IL
Rockford Area Convention and Visitors Bur. **[3307]**, Rockford, IL
St. Louis County Promotional Bureau **[11046]**, Gilbert, MN
Sandusky/Erie County Convention and Visitors Bur. **[16617]**, Sandusky, OH
Sheboygan County Chamber of Commerce and Convention and Visitors Bur. **[19710]**, Sheboygan, WI
Southernmost Illinois Tourism Bur. **[52]**, Anna, IL
Spencer County Tourism Commission **[6161]**, Santa Claus, IN
Springfield Illinois Convention and Visitors Bur. **[3679]**, Springfield, IL
Upper Peninsula Travel and Recreation Assn. **[8328]**, Iron Mountain, MI
Washington County Convention and Visitors Bur. **[20129]**, West Bend, WI
Tourism Assn; Newberry Area **[9199]**, Newberry, MI
Tourism Bur; Br. County **[7199]**, Coldwater, MI
Tourism Bur; Hastings Area Chamber of Commerce and **[11125]**, Hastings, MN
Tourism Bur; Hudson Area Chamber of Commerce and **[18223]**, Hudson, WI
Tourism Bur. of Logan County; Abraham Lincoln **[2270]**, Lincoln, IL
Tourism Bur; River Country **[9880]**, Sturgis, MI
Tourism Bur; Southern Indiana, Clark-Floyd Counties Convention and **[★5541]**
Tourism Bur; Southernmost Illinois **[52]**, Anna, IL
Tourism Bur; Westmont Chamber of Commerce and **[3974]**, Westmont, IL
Tourism Bureau; Williamson County **[2413]**, Marion, IL
Tourism; Center for Commerce **[19377]**, Oostburg, WI
Tourism Commission; Spencer County **[6161]**, Santa Claus, IN
Tourism Coun; Chippewa County **[17748]**, Chippewa Falls, WI
Tourism; East Peoria Chamber of Commerce and **[1542]**, East Peoria, IL
Tourism and Economic Development; Metropolis Area Chamber of Commerce, **[★2484]**
Tourism; Four Flags Area Coun. on **[9207]**, Niles, MI
Tourism; Lake of the Woods **[10387]**, Baudette, MN
Tourism; Owatonna Area Chamber of Commerce and **[11962]**, Owatonna, MN

Tourism; Paris Area Chamber of Commerce and **[2950]**, Paris, IL
Tourism; Redwood Area Chamber and **[12097]**, Redwood Falls, MN
Tourism and Trade District Assn; Milwaukee Intl. **[★19125]**
Tourist Assn; Upper Michigan **[★8328]**
Tourist Assn; West Michigan **[8024]**, Grand Rapids, MI
Tourist Bur; Jackson Convention and **[8373]**, Jackson, MI
Tourist Coun; Southwestern Michigan **[6922]**, Benton Harbor, MI
Tourist and Recreation Assn; Baraga County **[6795]**, L'Anse, MI
Tower-Soudan Lions Club **[10959]**, Ely, MN
Towersoudan Chamber of Commerce **[★12755]**
Towing Assn; Michigan **[9225]**, Northville, MI
Towing and Recovery Operators of Illinois; Professional **[2992]**, Pekin, IL
Town and Country African Violet Club **[6992]**, Bloomfield Hills, MI
Town and Country African Violet Soc. **[16346]**, Painesville, OH
Town and Country Beagle Club **[19343]**, Oconomowoc, WI
Town and Country Rsrc. Conservation and Development Coun. **[20128]**, West Bend, WI
Towns; Indiana Assn. of Cities and **[5167]**, Indianapolis, IN
Township Officials of Illinois **[3689]**, Springfield, IL
Townships Assn; Michigan **[8722]**, Lansing, MI
Townships; Minnesota Assn. of **[12341]**, St. Michael, MN
Track Club; Warren Striders **[17120]**, Warren, OH

Track and Field
- Indiana U.S.A. Track and Field **[4590]**, Fairland, IN
- Lake Erie Assn., USA Track and Field **[16372]**, Parma, OH
- U.S.A. Track and Field, Illinois **[2304]**, Lisle, IL
- USA Track and Field, Indiana **[4591]**, Fairland, IN
- U.S.A. Track and Field Lake Erie **[16378]**, Parma, OH
- U.S.A. Track and Field, Michigan **[7450]**, Detroit, MI
- USA Track and Field Minnesota **[12667]**, Shorewood, MN
- U.S.A. Track and Field, Wisconsin **[18636]**, Madison, WI
- USATF Ohio Assn. **[14966]**, Dayton, OH
- Warren Striders Track Club **[17120]**, Warren, OH

Track and Field, Illinois; U.S.A. **[2304]**, Lisle, IL
Track and Field, Michigan; U.S.A. **[7450]**, Detroit, MI
Track and Field, Wisconsin Top; U.S.A. **[★18636]**
Tracy Area Chamber of Commerce **[12757]**, Tracy, MN

Trade
- Franklinton Bd. of Trade **[14436]**, Columbus, OH
- Indiana Seed Trade Assn. **[5295]**, Indianapolis, IN

Trade Assn. Executives; Ohio **[★17351]**
Trade Association; Indiana Marine **[4126]**, Angola, IN
Trade; Byesville Bd. of **[13478]**, Byesville, OH
Trade Club of Chicago; Intl. **[★993]**
Trade Coun; Michigan Food **[★10070]**
Trade District Assn; Milwaukee Intl. Tourism and **[★19125]**
Trade; Franklinton Bd. of **[14436]**, Columbus, OH

Traffic
- Minnesota State Patrol Troopers Assn. **[12111]**, Richfield, MN

Traffic Safety Assn. of Michigan **[★8704]**
Trail Riders Assn; Michigan **[9877]**, Stockbridge, MI
Trail Riders; Illinois **[1561]**, Edwardsville, IL
Trail of Tears Assn. - Illinois Chap. **[1292]**, Collinsville, IL
Trail Trolls **[15134]**, Englewood, OH
Trail Users Rights Found. **[★3711]**

Trails
- Hiawatha Bicycling Club **[11577]**, Minneapolis, MN
- Hoosier Hikers Coun. **[5754]**, Martinsville, IN
- Ice Age Park and Trail Found. **[19024]**, Milwaukee, WI
- Kekekabic Trail Club **[11593]**, Minneapolis, MN
- North Country Trail Assn. **[8864]**, Lowell, MI
- Trail of Tears Assn. - Illinois Chap. **[1292]**, Collinsville, IL

Trails Association; Turf and Tundra **[20094]**, Webb Lake, WI

Trainers
- Great Lakes Athletic Trainers Assn. **[8935]**, Marquette, MI
- Illinois Athletic Trainers' Assn. **[1660]**, Evanston, IL
- Indiana Athletic Trainers' Assn. **[5190]**, Indianapolis, IN
- Michigan Athletic Trainers' Soc. **[6722]**, Ann Arbor, MI
- Minnesota Athletic Trainers' Assn. **[10475]**, Bloomington, MN
- Ohio Athletic Trainers' Assn. **[15299]**, Galloway, OH
- Wisconsin Athletic Trainers' Assn. **[18669]**, Madison, WI
- Wisconsin Athletic Trainers' Assn., Northeast **[17815]**, De Pere, WI
- Wisconsin Athletic Trainers' Assn., Southeast **[19336]**, Oak Creek, WI
- Wisconsin Athletic Trainers' Assn., Southwest **[18670]**, Madison, WI

Training Assn; MARO Employment and **[8602]**, Lansing, MI
Training and Development Corp; Urban Solutions **[7449]**, Detroit, MI
Training and Development, Rock Valley Chap; Amer. Soc. for **[1476]**, Dixon, IL
Training and Development, Southeast Wisconsin Chap; Amer. Soc. for **[18961]**, Milwaukee, WI
Training Sers; Wisconsin Procurement Inst. Educ. and **[19176]**, Milwaukee, WI
Transformation Cincinnati and Northern Kentucky **[14009]**, Cincinnati, OH
Transit Assn; Michigan Public **[7546]**, East Lansing, MI
Transition of Prisoners **[7442]**, Detroit, MI

Translation
- Chicago Area Translators and Interpreters Assn. **[785]**, Chicago, IL
- Michigan Translators/Interpreters Network **[9240]**, Novi, MI
- Northeast Ohio Translators Assn. **[16681]**, Solon, OH
- Upper Midwest Translators and Interpreters Assn. **[11772]**, Minneapolis, MN

Transport Workers Union of Am., AFL-CIO - Local Union 521 **[9552]**, Romulus, MI
Transport Workers Union of Am., AFL-CIO - Local Union 543 **[10490]**, Bloomington, MN
Transport Workers Union of Am., AFL-CIO - Local Union 572 **[1469]**, Des Plaines, IL

Transportation
- County Road Assn. of Michigan **[8563]**, Lansing, MI
- Downtown Minneapolis Trans. Mgt. Org. **[11555]**, Minneapolis, MN
- East West Corporate Corridor Assn. **[2634]**, Naperville, IL
- I-69 Mid-Continent Highway Coalition **[5153]**, Indianapolis, IN
- Illinois Public Airports Assn. **[3631]**, Springfield, IL
- Illinois Road and Trans. Builders Assn. **[2067]**, Itasca, IL
- Illinois School Trans. Assn. **[2437]**, Matteson, IL
- Indiana Trans. Assn. **[4231]**, Bloomington, IN
- Intl. Brotherhood of Teamsters, Chauffeurs, Warehousemen and Helpers of Am., AFL-CIO - Local Union 24 **[13060]**, Akron, OH
- Intl. Brotherhood of Teamsters, Chauffeurs, Warehousemen and Helpers of Am., AFL-CIO - Local Union 200 **[19034]**, Milwaukee, WI
- Intl. Brotherhood of Teamsters, Chauffeurs, Warehousemen and Helpers of Am., AFL-CIO - Local Union 580 **[8579]**, Lansing, MI
- Intl. Brotherhood of Teamsters, Chauffeurs, Warehousemen and Helpers of Am., AFL-CIO - Local Union 637 **[17439]**, Zanesville, OH
- Intl. Brotherhood of Teamsters, Chauffeurs, Warehousemen and Helpers of Am., AFL-CIO - Local Union 662 **[17881]**, Eau Claire, WI
- Intl. Brotherhood of Teamsters, Chauffeurs, Warehousemen and Helpers of Am., AFL-CIO - Local Union 710 **[986]**, Chicago, IL
- Intl. Brotherhood of Teamsters, Chauffeurs, Warehousemen and Helpers of Am., AFL-CIO - Local Union 714 **[238]**, Berwyn, IL
- Michigan Assn. for Pupil Trans. **[8624]**, Lansing, MI
- Michigan Movers Assn. **[8687]**, Lansing, MI
- Michigan Public Transit Assn. **[7546]**, East Lansing, MI
- Michigan Rsrc. Center for Hea. and Safety **[8704]**, Lansing, MI
- Michigan Road Builders Assn. **[8708]**, Lansing, MI
- Michigan Trucking Assn. **[8725]**, Lansing, MI
- Michigan's Heavy Constr. Assn. **[9294]**, Okemos, MI
- Mid-West Truckers Assn. **[3648]**, Springfield, IL
- Minnesota Transport Services Assn. **[12530]**, St. Paul, MN
- Minnesota Trucking Assn. **[12244]**, Roseville, MN
- Ohio Assn. of Movers **[14559]**, Columbus, OH
- Ohio Contractors Assn. **[14587]**, Columbus, OH
- Ohio Trucking Assn. **[14692]**, Columbus, OH
- Transport Workers Union of Am., AFL-CIO - Local Union 521 **[9552]**, Romulus, MI
- Transport Workers Union of Am., AFL-CIO - Local Union 543 **[10490]**, Bloomington, MN
- Transport Workers Union of Am., AFL-CIO - Local Union 572 **[1469]**, Des Plaines, IL
- Trans. Riders United **[7443]**, Detroit, MI
- Wisconsin Milk Haulers Assn. **[18728]**, Madison, WI
- Wisconsin Motor Carriers Assn. **[18730]**, Madison, WI
- Wisconsin Movers Assn. **[18731]**, Madison, WI
- Wisconsin Trans. Builders Assn. **[18759]**, Madison, WI

Trans. Assn; Illinois School **[2437]**, Matteson, IL
Trans. Riders United **[7443]**, Detroit, MI

Trappers
- Indiana State Trappers Assn. **[5547]**, Kempton, IN
- Minnesota Trappers Assn. **[10569]**, Bruno, MN
- Wisconsin Trappers Assn. **[18069]**, Grand Marsh, WI

Trapping
- Ohio State Trappers Assn. **[14832]**, Dalton, OH

Trapshooting Found; Ohio State **[15371]**, Grove City, OH

Trauma
- Amer. Trauma Soc., Wisconsin **[18474]**, Madison, WI

Travel
- Akron Summit Convention and Visitors Bur. **[13024]**, Akron, OH
- Ann Arbor Area Convention and Visitors Bur. **[6669]**, Ann Arbor, MI
- Blue Water Area Convention and Visitors Bur. **[9430]**, Port Huron, MI
- Br. County Tourism Bur. **[7199]**, Coldwater, MI
- Clare County Visitor and Convention Bur. **[7154]**, Clare, MI
- Convention and Visitors Bur. of Greater Cleveland **[14107]**, Cleveland, OH
- Fond du Lac Area Convention and Visitors Bur. **[17973]**, Fond du Lac, WI
- Greater Toledo Convention and Visitors Bur. **[16919]**, Toledo, OH
- La Crosse Area Convention and Visitors Bur. **[18353]**, La Crosse, WI
- Midwest Bus. Travel Assn. **[1054]**, Chicago, IL
- North Central Bus. Travel Assn. **[11709]**, Minneapolis, MN
- Ohio Valley Bus. Travel Assn. **[13946]**, Cincinnati, OH
- Peoria Area Convention and Visitors Bur. **[3045]**, Peoria, IL
- Porter County Convention Bur. **[4354]**, Chesterton, IN
- Quincy Area Convention and Visitors Bur. **[3162]**, Quincy, IL
- Saginaw County Convention and Visitors Bur. **[9631]**, Saginaw, MI
- St. Charles Illinois Convention and Visitors Bur. **[3393]**, St. Charles, IL
- St. Paul Convention and Visitors Bur. **[12579]**, St. Paul, MN
- Soc. of Incentive and Travel Executives, Chicago Chap. **[3448]**, Schaumburg, IL
- Terre Haute Convention and Visitors Bur. **[6345]**, Terre Haute, IN
- Trumbull County Convention and Visitors Bur. **[16208]**, Niles, OH

VISIT Milwaukee [19148], Milwaukee, WI
Warren County Convention and Visitors Bur. [15624], Lebanon, OH
Willmar Lakes Area Convention and Visitors Bur. [12933], Willmar, MN
Worthington Convention and Visitors Bur. [17353], Worthington, OH
Travel Assn; Ohio [14691], Columbus, OH
Travel and Recreation Assn; Upper Peninsula [8328], Iron Mountain, MI
Travel and Visitors Bur; West Branch-Ogemaw County [10136], West Branch, MI
Traverse Area Assn. of Realtors [9955], Traverse City, MI
Traverse Area Human Rsrcs. Assn. [9956], Traverse City, MI
Traverse Bay Area Central Labor Coun. [9957], Traverse City, MI
Traverse City Area Chamber of Commerce [9958], Traverse City, MI
Traverse City At-Risk Boxing [9959], Traverse City, MI
Traverse City Lions Club [9960], Traverse City, MI
Treasurers Assn. of Ohio; County [14420], Columbus, OH
Trees
Michigan Christmas Tree Assn. [8282], Howell, MI
Wisconsin Arborist Assn. [18890], Mequon, WI
Wisconsin Christmas Tree Producers Assn. [19516], Portage, WI
Trees and Shrubs
Illinois Christmas Tree Assn. [3403], St. Libory, IL
Indiana Christmas Tree Growers Assn. [6284], Springport, IN
Natl. Christmas Tree Assn., Mid Am. [2066], Irving, IL
Ohio Christmas Tree Assn. [14581], Columbus, OH
Trenton Lions Club - Michigan [9967], Trenton, MI
Trenton Lions Club - Ohio [16991], Trenton, OH
Tri-Cities Area Chamber of Commerce [★1885]
Tri-Cities Dog Training Club of Saginaw Michigan [9640], Saginaw, MI
Tri-Cities Strikers Soccer Club [9849], Spring Lake, MI
Tri-City Area United Way [18805], Marinette, WI
Tri-City Curling Club [20193], Wisconsin Rapids, WI
Tri-City REACT [329], Bourbonnais, IL
Tri City REACT [18265], Janesville, WI
Tri-County AIFA [6197], Shelbyville, IN
Tri County AIFA [11971], Owatonna, MN
Tri-County Community Advocates for People with Developmental Disabilities [8765], Lansing, MI
Tri-County Contractors Assn. [19578], Racine, WI
Tri-County Coonhunters Conservation Club [4162], Batesville, IN
Tri-County Coun. on Domestic Violence and Sexual Assault [19608], Rhinelander, WI
Tri-County Estate Planning Coun. [13501], Cambridge, OH
Tri-County Figure Skating Club [10991], Farmington, MN
Tri-County Natl. Assn. of The Remodeling Indus. [13100], Akron, OH
Tri-County REACT [4727], Fort Wayne, IN
Tri-County Regional Planning Commn. [3067], Peoria, IL
Tri-County Youth for Christ [9641], Saginaw, MI
Tri-Lakes Home Builders Assn. [9558], Roscommon, MI
Tri-Moraine Audubon Soc. [15671], Lima, OH
Tri-Rivers Educ. Assn. [15855], Marion, OH
Tri-State Athletics [14010], Cincinnati, OH
Tri State Beagle Club [4582], Evansville, IN
Tri-State Better Bus. Bur. [4583], Evansville, IN
Tri-State Catalysis Club [14011], Cincinnati, OH
Tri-State Corvette Club [5964], Newburgh, IN
Tri-State Manufacturers' Assn. [★10937]
Tri-State Pilots Assn. [16697], South Point, OH
Tri-State Soc. for Healthcare Engineerings [14012], Cincinnati, OH
Tri-State Soc. for Healthcare Engineers [14013], Cincinnati, OH
Tri-Village Lions Club [14746], Columbus, OH
Tri-Village Noon Lions Club [14747], Columbus, OH
Trial Advocacy
Amer. Bd. of Trial Advocates - Cincinnati [13705], Cincinnati, OH
Amer. Bd. of Trial Advocates - Illinois [3377], St. Charles, IL
Amer. Bd. of Trial Advocates - Indiana [4195], Bloomington, IN
Amer. Bd. of Trial Advocates - Michigan [7886], Grand Rapids, MI
Amer. Bd. of Trial Advocates - Minnesota [11484], Minneapolis, MN
Amer. Bd. of Trial Advocates - Ohio [14275], Columbus, OH
Amer. Bd. of Trial Advocates - Wisconsin [18930], Milwaukee, WI
Trial Attorneys; Ohio Assn. of Civil [14547], Columbus, OH
Trial Counsel of Wisconsin; Civil [18993], Milwaukee, WI
Triangle Found. [7444], Detroit, MI
Trillium Land Conservancy [4507], Elkhart, IN
Trimble High School - Young Life [13221], Athens, OH
Triple R Club [17475], Antigo, WI
Tripoli Shriners [19137], Milwaukee, WI
Trips for Kids-Fox Valley [3500], South Elgin, IL
Trips for Kids- Twin Cities [★12600]
TriState Habitat for Humanity [15402], Hamilton, OH
Triumph
South Town Points [19125], Milwaukee, WI
TROA Coun. of MN Chapters [11131], Hastings, MN
TROA Coun. of MN Chapters - Military Officers Assn. of Am. [10611], Burnsville, MN
Troopers Lodge 41 [3690], Springfield, IL
Trotwood Chamber of Commerce [16993], Trotwood, OH
Trotwood-Madison Historical Soc. [16994], Trotwood, OH
Trout Unlimited - Adams Chap. [9961], Traverse City, MI
Trout Unlimited - Aldo Leopold Chap. [17597], Beaver Dam, WI
Trout Unlimited - Ann Arbor Chap. 127 [6776], Ann Arbor, MI
Trout Unlimited - Antigo Chap. [17476], Antigo, WI
Trout Unlimited - Arnold J. Copeland Chap. [7626], Essexville, MI
Trout Unlimited, Blackhawk [17918], Edgerton, WI
Trout Unlimited - Central Wisconsin Chap. [20174], Winneconne, WI
Trout Unlimited, Challenge Chap. [6993], Bloomfield Hills, MI
Trout Unlimited - Challenge Chap. [9342], Oxford, MI
Trout Unlimited, Clear Fork River 667 [17326], Wooster, OH
Trout Unlimited - Copper County Chap. [8111], Hancock, MI
Trout Unlimited, Coulee Region [18379], La Crosse, WI
Trout Unlimited, Elliott Donnelley [1209], Chicago, IL
Trout Unlimited - Emerald Necklace Chapter [17237], Westlake, OH
Trout Unlimited, Fox Valley [17528], Appleton, WI
Trout Unlimited - Fox Valley Chap. [18865], Menasha, WI
Trout Unlimited, Frank Hornberg 624 [19812], Stevens Point, WI
Trout Unlimited - Gitche Gumee Chap. [11151], Hermantown, MN
Trout Unlimited - Green Bay Chap. [18137], Green Bay, WI
Trout Unlimited - Harry and Laura Nohr Chap. [19223], Montfort, WI
Trout Unlimited - Headwaters Chap. [10039], Vanderbilt, MI
Trout Unlimited - Headwaters Chap. [10428], Bemidji, MN
Trout Unlimited - Hiawatha Chapter [12195], Rochester, MN
Trout Unlimited - Illinois Coun. [2783], Oak Brook, IL
Trout Unlimited, Kiap Tu Wish 168 [★12977]
Trout Unlimited - Lakeshore Chap. [18791], Manitowoc, WI
Trout Unlimited, Lansing [★8567]
Trout Unlimited - Lansing Chap. [7468], DeWitt, MI
Trout Unlimited - Lee Wulff Chapter [151], Barrington, IL
Trout Unlimited - Leon P. Martuch Chapter [9042], Midland, MI
Trout Unlimited - Madmen [14963], Dayton, OH
Trout Unlimited - Marinette County Chap. [18806], Marinette, WI
Trout Unlimited - Menominee Range Chap. [8334], Iron River, MI
Trout Unlimited - Mid-Minnesota Chap. [12631], Sartell, MN
Trout Unlimited, Minnesota [10491], Bloomington, MN
Trout Unlimited - Muskegon White River Chap. [9217], North Muskegon, MI
Trout Unlimited, Northwoods 256 [19609], Rhinelander, WI
Trout Unlimited - Oak Brook Chap. [2784], Oak Brook, IL
Trout Unlimited - Oconto River Chap. [★18049]
Trout Unlimited - Oconto River Watershed 385 [18049], Gillett, WI
Trout Unlimited - Ohio Coun. [14964], Dayton, OH
Trout Unlimited - Ojibleau Chap. [17903], Eau Claire, WI
Trout Unlimited - Ottawa Chap. [8342], Ironwood, MI
Trout Unlimited - Paul Bunyan Chap. [10492], Bloomington, MN
Trout Unlimited - Paul H. Young Chap. [10011], Troy, MI
Trout Unlimited - Pine River Chap. [10018], Tustin, MI
Trout Unlimited - Shaw-Paca Chap. [18772], Manawa, WI
Trout Unlimited - Southeastern Wisconsin Chap. [19138], Milwaukee, WI
Trout Unlimited - Southern Wisconsin Chap. [18628], Madison, WI
Trout Unlimited - Two Heart Chap. [9201], Newberry, MI
Trout Unlimited, Vanguard [9547], Romeo, MI
Trout Unlimited - Wa Hue Chap. [12087], Red Wing, MN
Trout Unlimited, Waybinahbe 650 [11093], Grand Rapids, MN
Trout Unlimited - West Michigan Chapter [6915], Belmont, MI
Trout Unlimited - Wild Rivers Chap. [17548], Ashland, WI
Trout Unlimited - William B. Mershon Chapter [9642], Saginaw, MI
Trout Unlimited - Wisconsin River Valley Chap. [20050], Wausau, WI
Trout Unlimited, Wolf River [20154], White Lake, WI
Troy Area Chamber of Commerce [3790], Troy, IL
Troy Area Chamber of Commerce [17008], Troy, OH
Troy Chamber of Commerce [★3790]
Troy Chamber of Commerce [10012], Troy, MI
Troy Community Found. [10013], Troy, MI
Troy Lions Club - Ohio [17009], Troy, OH
Troy Main St. [17010], Troy, OH
Troy Skating Club [17011], Troy, OH
Troy Soldiers Miniatures Club [9594], Royal Oak, MI
Troy Special Services Parent Teacher Org. [10014], Troy, MI
Truck Educ. Assn; Wisconsin Automotive and [20059], Wausau, WI
Truckers Assn; Mid-West [3648], Springfield, IL
Trucking
Continental Trucking Assn. [18276], Johnson Creek, WI
Michigan Truck Stop Operators Assn. [8724], Lansing, MI
Trucks
Amer. Truck Historical Soc., Auburn Heritage Truck Chap. [4137], Auburn, IN
Amer. Truck Historical Soc., Beer City Chap. [19330], Oak Creek, WI
Amer. Truck Historical Soc., Black Swamp Chap. [16510], Republic, OH
Amer. Truck Historical Soc., Buckeye Vintage Haulers [16384], Pataskala, OH
Amer. Truck Historical Soc., Central Illinois Chap. [1817], Glasford, IL
Amer. Truck Historical Soc., Greater Cincinnati Chap. [13739], Cincinnati, OH
Amer. Truck Historical Soc., Hiawathaland Chap. [10256], Albert Lea, MN
Amer. Truck Historical Soc., Lincoln Trail Chap. [1368], Dawson, IL
Amer. Truck Historical Soc., Mark Twain Chap. [156], Barry, IL

Amer. Truck Historical Soc., Minnesota Metro Chap. **[12891]**, White Bear Lake, MN
Amer. Truck Historical Soc., Motor City Chap. **[9261]**, Oakland, MI
Amer. Truck Historical Soc., Northeast Ohio Chap. **[13240]**, Avon, OH
Amer. Truck Historical Soc., Northwest Illinois Chap. **[93]**, Ashton, IL
Amer. Truck Historical Soc., Northwest Indiana Chap. **[6218]**, South Bend, IN
Amer. Truck Historical Soc., Southeast Michigan Chap. **[6667]**, Ann Arbor, MI
Amer. Truck Historical Soc., Wabash Valley Chap. **[5944]**, New Harmony, IN
Amer. Truck Historical Soc., West Michigan Chap. **[7853]**, Grand Haven, MI
Amer. Truck Historical Soc., Windy City Chap. **[3959]**, Western Springs, IL
Trufant Area Chamber of Commerce **[10015]**, Trufant, MI
Trumbull County Bar Assn. **[17111]**, Warren, OH
Trumbull County Convention and Visitors Bur. **[16208]**, Niles, OH
Trumbull County Genealogical Soc. **[17112]**, Warren, OH
Trumbull County Medical Soc. **[17113]**, Warren, OH
The Trumpeter Swan Soc. **[12039]**, Plymouth, MN
Trustees Assn; Illinois Community Coll. **[3595]**, Springfield, IL
TSCA of Wisconsin **[19845]**, Sturgeon Bay, WI
Turf and Tundra Trails Association **[20094]**, Webb Lake, WI
Turfgrass
Ohio Turfgrass Found. **[17441]**, Zanesville, OH
Turkey Growers Assn; Minnesota **[10576]**, Buffalo, MN
Turkey Market Development Council **[6502]**, West Lafayette, IN
Turkish
Turkish Amer. Assn. of Central Ohio **[15067]**, Dublin, OH
Turkish Amer. Assn. of Minnesota **[10325]**, Apple Valley, MN
Turkish Amer. Cultural Alliance of Chicago **[1211]**, Chicago, IL
Turkish Amer. Cultural Assn. of Michigan **[7676]**, Farmington Hills, MI
Turkish Amer. Assn. of Central Ohio **[15067]**, Dublin, OH
Turkish Amer. Assn. of Minnesota **[10325]**, Apple Valley, MN
Turkish Amer. Chamber of Commerce **[1210]**, Chicago, IL
Turkish Amer. Cultural Alliance of Chicago **[1211]**, Chicago, IL
Turkish Amer. Cultural Assn. of Michigan **[7676]**, Farmington Hills, MI
Turn Off the Violence **[11755]**, Minneapolis, MN
Turnaround Mgt. Assn; Chicago - Midwest Chap. of the **[★1722]**
Turnaround Mgt. Assn; Chicago/Midwest Chap. of the **[1722]**, Frankfort, IL
Turner Club; Akron **[16838]**, Tallmadge, OH
Tuscarawas and Carroll REACT **[13592]**, Canton, OH
Tuscarawas County ALU **[15033]**, Dover, OH
Tuscarawas County Chamber of Commerce **[16154]**, New Philadelphia, OH
Tuscarawas County Coin Club **[15034]**, Dover, OH
Tuscarawas County Rabbit Breeders Assn. **[16155]**, New Philadelphia, OH
Tuscarawas County Young Democrats **[16156]**, New Philadelphia, OH
Tuscola Chamber of Commerce **[3796]**, Tuscola, IL
Tuslaw Lions Club **[15895]**, Massillon, OH
TV Broadcast Engineers Intl. Brotherhood of Electrical Workers AFL-CIO, LU 1220; Radio and **[★984]**
Twin Bays Skating Club **[9962]**, Traverse City, MI
Twin Bluff - Wyldlife **[12088]**, Red Wing, MN
Twin Cities Area Yorkshire Terrier Club **[12728]**, Stillwater, MN
Twin Cities Assn. for Computing Machinery SIGAda **[10493]**, Bloomington, MN
Twin Cities Black Journalists **[11756]**, Minneapolis, MN
Twin Cities Chap. of Muskies **[11757]**, Minneapolis, MN
Twin Cities Chap. of the Soc. of Financial Ser. Professionals **[12903]**, White Bear Lake, MN
Twin Cities Compensation Network **[12597]**, St. Paul, MN
Twin Cities Fencing Club **[12598]**, St. Paul, MN
Twin Cities German Wirehair Pointer Club **[10875]**, Eagan, MN
Twin Cities Habitat for Humanity **[11758]**, Minneapolis, MN
Twin Cities Human Rsrc. Assn. **[10326]**, Apple Valley, MN
Twin Cities Irish Water Spaniel Club **[12729]**, Stillwater, MN
Twin Cities Musicians Union, Local 30-73 **[11759]**, Minneapolis, MN
Twin Cities North Chamber of Commerce **[11848]**, Mounds View, MN
Twin Cities Obedience Training Club **[11760]**, Minneapolis, MN
Twin Cities Piping Indus. Assn. **[★12534]**
Twin Cities Poodle Club **[11761]**, Minneapolis, MN
Twin Cities Professional Photographers of Am. **[11194]**, Hopkins, MN
Twin Cities Quorum **[11762]**, Minneapolis, MN
Twin Cities Tall Club **[11763]**, Minneapolis, MN
Twin Cities Vizsla Club **[10327]**, Apple Valley, MN
Twin Cities Volkssport **[10494]**, Bloomington, MN
Twin City Amateur Astronomers **[2734]**, Normal, IL
Twin City Chamber of Commerce **[17020]**, Uhrichsville, OH
Twin City Figure Skating Assn. **[12599]**, St. Paul, MN
Twin City Healthcare Engg. Assn. **[10928]**, Edina, MN
Twin Oak Sporting Clays **[2503]**, Mode, IL
Twin Ports-Arrowhead Chap. Natl. Elecl. Contractors Assn. **[10857]**, Duluth, MN
Twin Valley Lions Club **[12765]**, Twin Valley, MN
Twinsburg Chamber of Commerce **[17018]**, Twinsburg, OH
TwinWest Chamber of Commerce **[11798]**, Minnetonka, MN
Two Harbors Area Chamber of Commerce **[12775]**, Two Harbors, MN
Two Harbors Lions Club **[12776]**, Two Harbors, MN
Two Rivers Historical Soc. **[19920]**, Two Rivers, WI
Two Rivers Jeep Club **[4028]**, Winchester, IL
Two Rivers Main St. **[19921]**, Two Rivers, WI
Two Trackers Four Wheel Drive Club **[8490]**, Kentwood, MI
Two Wheel View/Trips for Kids - Twin Cities **[12600]**, St. Paul, MN

U

U.A. Local 370 **[★7771]**
UAW Local 602 **[8766]**, Lansing, MI
UFO Network, Indiana; Mutual **[6417]**, Vincennes, IN
UFO Network; Michigan Mutual **[8487]**, Kentwood, MI
Ulen Lions Club **[12779]**, Ulen, MN
ULS - Wyldlife **[18186]**, Hartland, WI
Umoja Ski Club **[9643]**, Saginaw, MI
Underground Contractors Assn. **[2070]**, Itasca, IL
Underwater Preserves Coun; Michigan **[9669]**, St. Ignace, MI
Underwriters; Dayton Assn. of Life **[★14870]**
Underwriters; Indiana State Assn. of Life **[★5176]**
UNICEF, Columbus Chap. **[14748]**, Columbus, OH
Union Avenue Wyld Life - Wyldlife **[1212]**, Chicago, IL
Union City Chamber of Commerce **[6364]**, Union City, IN
Union County Chamber of Commerce **[53]**, Anna, IL
Union County Chamber of Commerce **[15867]**, Marysville, OH
Union Grove Chamber of Commerce **[★19926]**
Union and League of RSA **[16240]**, North Olmsted, OH
Unions
AFSME Coun. 31 **[598]**, Chicago, IL
Constr. Labor-Mgt. Assn. **[18502]**, Madison, WI
IAMAW Air Transport District Lodge 141 **[1608]**, Elk Grove Village, IL
Uniontown Lions Club **[17022]**, Uniontown, OH
United Assn. of Journeymen and Apprentices of the Plumbing and Pipe Fitting Indus. of the U.S. and Canada - Local Union 15 **[11764]**, Minneapolis, MN
United Assn. of Journeymen and Apprentices of the Plumbing and Pipe Fitting Indus. of the U.S. and Canada - Local Union 136 **[4584]**, Evansville, IN
United Assn. of Journeymen and Apprentices of the Plumbing and Pipe Fitting Indus. of the U.S. and Canada - Local Union 183 **[18878]**, Menomonee Falls, WI
United Assn. of Journeymen and Apprentices of the Plumbing and Pipe Fitting Indus. of the U.S. and Canada - Local Union 370 **[7772]**, Flushing, MI
United Assn. of Journeymen and Apprentices of the Plumbing and Pipe Fitting Indus. of the U.S. and Canada - Local Union 392 **[14014]**, Cincinnati, OH
United Assn. of Journeymen and Apprentices of the Plumbing and Pipe Fitting Indus. of the U.S. and Canada - Local Union 434 **[19232]**, Mosinee, WI
United Assn. of Journeymen and Apprentices of the Plumbing and Pipe Fitting Indus. of the U.S. and Canada - Local Union 501 **[132]**, Aurora, IL
United Assn. of Journeymen and Apprentices of the Plumbing and Pipe Fitting Indus. of the U.S. and Canada - Local Union 597 **[1213]**, Chicago, IL
United Assn. of Journeymen and Apprentices of the Plumbing and Pipe Fitting Indus. of the U.S. and Canada - Local Union 636 **[7677]**, Farmington Hills, MI
United Assn. of Journeymen and Apprentices of the Plumbing and Pipe Fitting Indus. of the U.S. and Canada - Steamfitters Local Union 601 **[19139]**, Milwaukee, WI
United Auto Workers Local No. 599 Enval. Comm. **[7759]**, Flint, MI
United Brotherhood of Carpenters and Joiners of Am., Chicago Local Union No. 1185 **[2025]**, Hinsdale, IL
United Brotherhood of Carpenters and Joiners of Am., Chicago Local Union No. 9074 **[2026]**, Hinsdale, IL
United Brotherhood of Carpenters and Joiners of Am., Chicago Regional Coun. of Carpenters **[1214]**, Chicago, IL
United Brotherhood of Carpenters and Joiners of Am., Cleveland Local Union No. 21 **[14223]**, Cleveland, OH
United Brotherhood of Carpenters and Joiners of Am., Cleveland Local Union No. 509 **[14224]**, Cleveland, OH
United Brotherhood of Carpenters and Joiners of Am., Heartland Regional Coun. of Carpenters 4274 **[3705]**, Sterling, IL
United Brotherhood of Carpenters and Joiners of Am., Hobart Local Union No. 1005 **[4931]**, Hobart, IN
United Brotherhood of Carpenters and Joiners of Am., Lakes and Plains Regional Coun. 4020 **[12601]**, St. Paul, MN
United Brotherhood of Carpenters and Joiners of Am., Mankato Local Union No. 464 **[11405]**, Mankato, MN
United Brotherhood of Carpenters and Joiners of Am., Marshfield Local Union No. 2958 **[17551]**, Auburndale, WI
United Brotherhood of Carpenters and Joiners of Am., Michigan Regional Coun. 4085 **[★7445]**
United Brotherhood of Carpenters and Joiners of Am., Michigan Regional Coun. of Carpenters and Millwrights **[7445]**, Detroit, MI
United Brotherhood of Carpenters and Joiners of Am., Mid-Central Illinois District Coun. 4281 **[★3691]**
United Brotherhood of Carpenters and Joiners of Am., Mid-Central Illinois Regional Coun. of Carpenters **[3691]**, Springfield, IL
United Brotherhood of Carpenters and Joiners of Am., Midwestern Coun. of Indus. Workers 4021 **[19405]**, Oshkosh, WI
United Brotherhood of Carpenters and Joiners of Am., Milwaukee and Southeast Wisconsin Regional Coun. 4288 **[★1214]**
United Brotherhood of Carpenters and Joiners of Am., Northern Wisconsin Regional Coun. of Carpenters 4183 **[18289]**, Kaukauna, WI
United Brotherhood of Carpenters and Joiners of Am., Ohio and Vicinity Regional Coun. of Carpenters **[14225]**, Cleveland, OH
United Brotherhood of Carpenters and Joiners of Am., Ohio and Vicinity Regional Coun. of Carpenters 4046 **[★14225]**

United Brotherhood of Carpenters and Joiners of Am., Toledo Local Union No. 248 **[16559]**, Rossford, OH
United Brotherhood of Carpenters and Joiners of Am., Youngstown Local Union No. 171 **[17418]**, Youngstown, OH
United Cerebral Palsy Assn. of Central Minnesota **[12315]**, St. Cloud, MN
United Cerebral Palsy Assn. of Greater Cleveland **[14226]**, Cleveland, OH
United Cerebral Palsy Assn. of Greater Indiana **[5488]**, Indianapolis, IN
United Cerebral Palsy Assn. of Metropolitan Detroit **[9828]**, Southfield, MI
United Cerebral Palsy Assn., Michigan **[8767]**, Lansing, MI
United Cerebral Palsy Assn. of Minnesota **[12602]**, St. Paul, MN
United Cerebral Palsy of Illinois **[3692]**, Springfield, IL
United Cerebral Palsy of Southeastern Wisconsin **[19140]**, Milwaukee, WI
United Cerebral Palsy of Southern Illinois **[2603]**, Mount Vernon, IL
United Cerebral Palsy of Will County **[2121]**, Joliet, IL
United Chinese Scholars and Students Association **[1215]**, Chicago, IL
United Coalition for Animals **[14015]**, Cincinnati, OH
United Council of University of Wisconsin Students **[18629]**, Madison, WI
United Counties Coun. of Illinois **[3693]**, Springfield, IL
United Cricket Club **[3345]**, Rolling Meadows, IL
United Elecl., Radio and Machine Workers of Am., Local 1111 **[19141]**, Milwaukee, WI
United Fed. of Doll Clubs - Region 5 **[10429]**, Bemidji, MN
United Fed. of Doll Clubs - Region 10 **[19866]**, Sun Prairie, WI
United Fed. of Doll Clubs - Region 12 **[5489]**, Indianapolis, IN
United Food and Commercial Workers AFL-CIO, Local 951 **[8016]**, Grand Rapids, MI
United Food and Commercial Workers AFL-CIO, LU 665T **[19922]**, Two Rivers, WI
United Food and Commercial Workers Intl. Union, AFL-CIO, CLC - Local Union 6 **[10267]**, Albert Lea, MN
United Food and Commercial Workers Intl. Union, AFL-CIO, CLC -Local Union 9 **[10362]**, Austin, MN
United Food and Commercial Workers Intl. Union, AFL-CIO, CLC - Local Union 789 **[12685]**, South St. Paul, MN
United Food and Commercial Workers Intl. Union, AFL-CIO, CLC - Local Union 880 **[14227]**, Cleveland, OH
United Food and Commercial Workers Intl. Union, AFL-CIO, CLC -Local Union 881, Northcentral Region **[3360]**, Rosemont, IL
United Food and Commercial Workers, Local 12A, Northcentral Region **[10858]**, Duluth, MN
United Food and Commercial Workers, Local 78T, Northcentral Region **[17529]**, Appleton, WI
United Food and Commercial Workers, Local 200T, Northcentral Region **[3723]**, Streamwood, IL
United Food and Commercial Workers, Local 236T, Northcentral Region **[19923]**, Two Rivers, WI
United Food and Commercial Workers, Local 245, Northcentral Region **[19676]**, Seymour, WI
United Food and Commercial Workers, Local 335, Northcentral Region **[12089]**, Red Wing, MN
United Food and Commercial Workers, Local 527, Northcentral Region **[12090]**, Red Wing, MN
United Food and Commercial Workers, Local 536, Northcentral Region **[3068]**, Peoria, IL
United Food and Commercial Workers, Local 580T, Northcentral Region **[1470]**, Des Plaines, IL
United Food and Commercial Workers, Local 653, Northcentral Region **[12040]**, Plymouth, MN
United Food and Commercial Workers, Local 688, Northcentral Region **[18898]**, Merrill, WI
United Food and Commercial Workers, Local 717, Northcentral Region **[17739]**, Chili, WI
United Food and Commercial Workers, Local 876, Central Region **[8901]**, Madison Heights, MI
United Food and Commercial Workers, Local 911 **[15460]**, Holland, OH
United Food and Commercial Workers, Local 1059, Central Region **[14749]**, Columbus, OH
United Food and Commercial Workers, Local 1099, Central Region **[16056]**, Monroe, OH
United Food and Commercial Workers, Local 1116, Northcentral Region **[10859]**, Duluth, MN
United Food and Commercial Workers, Local 1281P, Northcentral Region **[2143]**, Kankakee, IL
United Food and Commercial Workers, Local 1444, Northcentral Region **[19142]**, Milwaukee, WI
United Fund of Switzerland County **[6406]**, Vevay, IN
United Hispanic-Americans **[4728]**, Fort Wayne, IN
United Jewish Fund and Coun. **[12603]**, St. Paul, MN
The United; Madison Gay/Lesbian Rsrc. Center **[★18594]**
United Ostomy Assn; Kokomo Area Chap. of the **[5573]**, Kokomo, IN
United Sales Associates **[14016]**, Cincinnati, OH
United Sales Assn. **[★14016]**
U.S. Army Warrant Off.rs Assn., Fort McCoy Chap. **[19757]**, Sparta, WI
U.S. Army Warrant Officers Assn., St. Louis Gateway Chap. 0312/3312 **[1823]**, Glen Carbon, IL
U.S. Elec. Wheelchair Hockey Assn. **[11765]**, Minneapolis, MN
U.S. Grant Dental Soc. **[1755]**, Freeport, IL
U.S. Harness Writers Assn., Ohio Chap. **[14750]**, Columbus, OH
U.S. Naval Sea Cadet Corps - Aurora Div. **[133]**, Aurora, IL
U.S. Naval Sea Cadet Corps - Badger Div. **[18630]**, Madison, WI
U.S. Naval Sea Cadet Corps - Battleship Wisconsin Div. **[19344]**, Oconomowoc, WI
U.S. Naval Sea Cadet Corps - Carl G. Stockholm Battalion **[1216]**, Chicago, IL
U.S. Naval Sea Cadet Corps - Chosin Div. **[9125]**, Mount Pleasant, MI
U.S. Naval Sea Cadet Corps - Cincinnati Div. **[14017]**, Cincinnati, OH
U.S. Naval Sea Cadet Corps - Cleveland Div. **[14228]**, Cleveland, OH
U.S. Naval Sea Cadet Corps - Cruiser Indianapolis (CA 35) Div. **[5490]**, Indianapolis, IN
U.S. Naval Sea Cadet Corps - Darter-Dace Div. **[8096]**, Gwinn, MI
U.S. Naval Sea Cadet Corps - Dayton Div. **[15478]**, Huber Heights, OH
U.S. Naval Sea Cadet Corps - Gen. Colin L. Powell Div. **[3212]**, Riverdale, IL
U.S. Naval Sea Cadet Corps - HR Doud Div. **[9644]**, Saginaw, MI
U.S. Naval Sea Cadet Corps - James M. Hannan Div. **[7446]**, Detroit, MI
U.S. Naval Sea Cadet Corps - Maj. Gen. John L. Borling Div. **[3326]**, Rockford, IL
U.S. Naval Sea Cadet Corps - Manatra Div. **[152]**, Barrington, IL
U.S. Naval Sea Cadet Corps - Michigan Sea Tigers Div. **[9729]**, Sault Ste. Marie, MI
U.S. Naval Sea Cadet Corps - Tomcat Squadron **[9741]**, Selfridge, MI
U.S. Naval Sea Cadet Corps - U.S. Div. **[8768]**, Lansing, MI
U.S. Naval Sea Cadet Corps - VADM James H. Flatley, Jr. Div. **[18138]**, Green Bay, WI
U.S. Naval Sea Cadet Corps - West Michigan Div. **[9163]**, Muskegon, MI
U.S. Naval Sea Cadet Corps, Windward Div. **[6872]**, Battle Creek, MI
U.S. Power Squadrons - District 10 **[12862]**, Wayzata, MN
U.S. Power Squadrons - District 20 **[2056]**, Huntley, IL
U.S. Power Squadrons - District 29 **[14751]**, Columbus, OH
U.S. Psychiatric Rehabilitation Assn. - Minnesota **[11766]**, Minneapolis, MN
U.S. Psychiatric Rehabilitation Assn. - Ohio Chap. **[15612]**, Lancaster, OH
United Steelworkers of Am., AFL-CIO-CLC - Local Union 77 **[★17123]**
United Steelworkers of Am., Sub District Off. **[17123]**, Warrensville Heights, OH
United Synagogue of Conservative Judaism, Great Lakes and Rivers Region **[16644]**, Shaker Heights, OH
United Synagogue of Conservative Judaism, Mid-Continent Region **[11767]**, Minneapolis, MN
United Synagogue Youth **[★2753]**
United Trans. Union, AFL-CIO - Local Union 322 **[18012]**, Franklin, WI
United Trans. Union, AFL-CIO - Local Union 469 **[1886]**, Granite City, IL
United Trans. Union, AFL-CIO - Local Union 1258 **[3452]**, Schaumburg, IL
United Trans. Union, AFL-CIO - Local Union 1397 **[14752]**, Columbus, OH
United Trans. Union, AFL-CIO - Wisconsin State Legislative Bd. 56 **[18631]**, Madison, WI
United Union Roofers, Waterproofers and Allied Workers, 96 **[11768]**, Minneapolis, MN
United Way of 1000 Lakes **[11094]**, Grand Rapids, MN
United Way of Adams County **[3173]**, Quincy, IL
United Way of Adams County, Indiana **[4452]**, Decatur, IN
United Way of Allen County **[4729]**, Fort Wayne, IN
United Way of Ashland County **[13174]**, Ashland, OH
United Way of Ashtabula County **[13188]**, Ashtabula, OH
United Way of Auglaize County **[16581]**, St. Marys, OH
United Way of Austin **[★10363]**
United Way of Bartholomew County **[4407]**, Columbus, IN
United Way of Bay County **[6897]**, Bay City, MI
United Way of Becker County **[10785]**, Detroit Lakes, MN
United Way of Bemidji Area **[10430]**, Bemidji, MN
United Way of Bluffton, Beaverdam, and Richland Township **[13369]**, Bluffton, OH
United Way of Boone County, Illinois **[223]**, Belvidere, IL
United Way of Brown County, Illinois **[2592]**, Mount Sterling, IL
United Way of Bryan **[★13458]**
United Way; Butler County **[15382]**, Hamilton, OH
United Way of Carlton County **[10693]**, Cloquet, MN
United Way of Cass County **[5699]**, Logansport, IN
United Way of Central Illinois **[3694]**, Springfield, IL
United Way of Central Indiana **[5491]**, Indianapolis, IN
United Way of Central Minnesota **[12316]**, St. Cloud, MN
United Way of Central Ohio **[14753]**, Columbus, OH
United Way of Champaign County **[554]**, Champaign, IL
United Way of the Charlotte-Potterville Area **[★7122]**
United Way of Chippewa County **[9730]**, Sault Ste. Marie, MI
United Way of Christian County **[3757]**, Taylorville, IL
United Way of Clark and Champaign Counties **[16753]**, Springfield, OH
United Way for Clinton County **[4745]**, Frankfort, IN
United Way of Clinton County **[17294]**, Wilmington, OH
United Way of Coles County **[2447]**, Mattoon, IL
United Way Community Ser. of Monroe County **[4262]**, Bloomington, IN
United Way; Copper Country **[8252]**, Houghton, MI
United Way of Coshocton County **[14805]**, Coshocton, OH
United Way of Crookston **[10740]**, Crookston, MN
United Way of Dane County **[18632]**, Madison, WI
United Way of the Danville Area **[1353]**, Danville, IL
United Way of Daviess County **[6461]**, Washington, IN
United Way of Decatur/Macon County **[1408]**, Decatur, IL
United Way of Decatur and Mid Illinois **[1409]**, Decatur, IL
United Way of Defiance County **[14993]**, Defiance, OH
United Way of DeKalb County **[4144]**, Auburn, IN
United Way of Delavan-Darien **[17829]**, Delavan, WI
United Way of Delaware County, Indiana **[5899]**, Muncie, IN
United Way of Delaware County, Ohio **[15012]**, Delaware, OH
United Way of Delta County **[7620]**, Escanaba, MI
United Way of the Detroit Lakes Area **[★10785]**
United Way of Dickinson County **[8327]**, Iron Mountain, MI

United Way of Dodge County, Minnesota [10791], Dodge Center, MN
United Way of Dodge County, Wisconsin [17598], Beaver Dam, WI
United Way of Door County [19846], Sturgeon Bay, WI
United Way of Dunn County [18882], Menomonie, WI
United Way of the DuPage Area [2785], Oak Brook, IL
United Way of Eastern La Salle County [2901], Ottawa, IL
United Way of Edgar County [2951], Paris, IL
United Way of Effingham County [1574], Effingham, IL
United Way of Elgin [1602], Elgin, IL
United Way of Elkhart County [4508], Elkhart, IN
United Way of Erie County, Ohio [16621], Sandusky, OH
United Way of Fairfield County, Ohio [15613], Lancaster, OH
United Way of Fairmont [10981], Fairmont, MN
United Way of Faribault [10988], Faribault, MN
United Way of Fayette County, Indiana [4416], Connersville, IN
United Way of Fayette County, Ohio [17133], Washington Court House, OH
United Way of Fostoria [15232], Fostoria, OH
United Way Fox Cities [18866], Menasha, WI
United Way of Franklin County, Indiana [4300], Brookville, IN
United Way of Freeborn County [10268], Albert Lea, MN
United Way of Fulton County, Ohio [17141], Wauseon, OH
United Way of Gallia County [15296], Gallipolis, OH
United Way of Genesee County [7760], Flint, MI
United Way of Genesee and Lapeer Counties [★7760]
United Way of Gibson County [6073], Princeton, IN
United Way of Gladwin County [7837], Gladwin, MI
United Way of Grant County, Indiana [5745], Marion, IN
United Way of Grant County, Wisconsin [18412], Lancaster, WI
United Way of Gratiot County [6636], Alma, MI
United Way of Greater Battle Creek [6873], Battle Creek, MI
United Way of Greater Beardstown [189], Beardstown, IL
United Way of Greater Cincinnati [14018], Cincinnati, OH
United Way of the Greater Dayton Area [14965], Dayton, OH
United Way of Greater Duluth [10860], Duluth, MN
United Way of Greater Eau Claire [17904], Eau Claire, WI
United Way of Greater La Porte County [5603], La Porte, IN
United Way of Greater Lafayette [5636], Lafayette, IN
United Way of Greater Lima [15672], Lima, OH
United Way of Greater Lorain County [15712], Lorain, OH
United Way of Greater Milwaukee [19143], Milwaukee, WI
United Way of Greater Niles [9213], Niles, MI
United Way of Greater Stark County [13593], Canton, OH
United Way of Greater Toledo [16979], Toledo, OH
United Way of Greater Toledo Ottawa County Off. [16462], Port Clinton, OH
United Way of Greater Toledo Wood County Off. [13400], Bowling Green, OH
United Way of the Greater Union City Area [★6537]
United Way of the Greater Winona Area [12959], Winona, MN
United Way of Green County [19219], Monroe, WI
United Way of Grundy County, Illinois [2555], Morris, IL
United Way of Guernsey and Noble County [13502], Cambridge, OH
United Way of the Hamilton Fairfield, Ohio Area and Vicinity [★15382]
United Way of Hancock County [15215], Findlay, OH
United Way of Hardin County [15554], Kenton, OH
United Way of Hastings, Minnesota [11132], Hastings, MN
United Way of Henry County [16100], Napoleon, OH
United Way of Hibbing [11163], Hibbing, MN
United Way of Hocking County [15691], Logan, OH
United Way of Howard County [5588], Kokomo, IN
United Way of Huntington County [4955], Huntington, IN
United Way of the Hutchinson Area [11213], Hutchinson, MN
United Way of Illinois [2786], Oak Brook, IL
United Way of Illinois Valley [2183], La Salle, IL
United Way of Ionia County [8318], Ionia, MI
United Way of Isabella County [9126], Mount Pleasant, MI
United Way of Jackson County [8399], Jackson, MI
United Way of Jay County [6066], Portland, IN
United Way of Jefferson County, Illinois [2604], Mount Vernon, IL
United Way of Jefferson County, Ohio [16769], Steubenville, OH
United Way of Jefferson and North Walworth Counties [18001], Fort Atkinson, WI
United Way of Johnson County, Indiana [4757], Franklin, IN
United Way of Kandiyohi County [12928], Willmar, MN
United Way of Kankakee County [2144], Kankakee, IL
United Way of Kenosha County [18313], Kenosha, WI
United Way of Knox County, Illinois [1782], Galesburg, IL
United Way of Knox County, Indiana [6422], Vincennes, IN
United Way of Knox County, Ohio [16090], Mount Vernon, OH
United Way of Kosciusko County [6454], Warsaw, IN
United Way of the La Crosse Area [19371], Onalaska, WI
United Way of Lake County, Illinois [1926], Gurnee, IL
United Way of Lake County, Ohio [15981], Mentor, OH
United Way; Land of Blackhawk Chap. of the [★18001]
United Way of Langlade County [17477], Antigo, WI
United Way of Lawrence County, Indiana [4178], Bedford, IN
United Way of Lee County, Illinois [1485], Dixon, IL
United Way of the Lenawee Area [★6579]
United Way of Licking County [16187], Newark, OH
United Way of Livingston County [7024], Brighton, MI
United Way of Logan County [2281], Lincoln, IL
United Way of Logan County, Ohio [13326], Bellefontaine, OH
United Way of Lyon County [★11442]
United Way of Madison County [4121], Anderson, IN
United Way of Manistee County [8916], Manistee, MI
United Way of Manitowoc County [18792], Manitowoc, WI
United Way of Marathon County [20051], Wausau, WI
United Way Marion County [15856], Marion, OH
United Way of Marquette County [8960], Marquette, MI
United Way of Marshall [★11442]
United Way of Marshall County, Indiana [6053], Plymouth, IN
United Way of Mason County [8876], Ludington, MI
United Way of McHenry County [2464], McHenry, IL
United Way of McLean County [312], Bloomington, IL
United Way of Medina County [15957], Medina, OH
United Way of Merrill [18899], Merrill, WI
United Way of Metropolitan Chicago [1217], Chicago, IL
United Way of Miami County [6034], Peru, IN
United Way of Midland County [9043], Midland, MI
United Way of Montcalm County [8071], Greenville, MI
United Way of Morrow County [16074], Mount Gilead, OH
United Way of Mower County [10363], Austin, MN
United Way of Muskegon County [9164], Muskegon, MI
United Way of Muskingum, Perry, and Morgan Counties [17445], Zanesville, OH
United Way of New London [19316], New London, WI
United Way of New Ulm [11888], New Ulm, MN
United Way of Newaygo County [7801], Fremont, MI
United Way of Noble County [4087], Albion, IN
United Way of North East Carlton County [★10693]
United Way of North Rock County [18266], Janesville, WI
United Way of the North Shore [2205], Lake Forest, IL
United Way of Northeast Michigan [6651], Alpena, MI
United Way of Northeastern Minnesota [10661], Chisholm, MN
United Way of Northern Ozaukee County [19503], Port Washington, WI
United Way of Northwest Illinois [1756], Freeport, IL
United Way of Northwest Michigan [9963], Traverse City, MI
United Way of Oak Park, River Forest and Forest Park [2827], Oak Park, IL
United Way of Olmsted County [12196], Rochester, MN
United Way of Otter Tail County [11005], Fergus Falls, MN
United Way of Oxford, Ohio and Vicinity [16329], Oxford, OH
United Way of Pekin [2995], Pekin, IL
United Way of Perry County [6300], Tell City, IN
United Way of Pickaway County [14038], Circleville, OH
United Way of Pike County, Indiana [6039], Petersburg, IN
United Way - Pipestone, Ihlen, Woodstock, Holland, Ruthton [12012], Pipestone, MN
United Way of Platteville [19473], Platteville, WI
United Way of Pontiac [3122], Pontiac, IL
United Way of Portage County [19813], Stevens Point, WI
United Way of Porter County Indiana [6392], Valparaiso, IN
United Way of Posey County [5858], Mount Vernon, IN
United Way of the Prairie Du Chien Area [19531], Prairie Du Chien, WI
United Way of Putnam County, Indiana [4827], Greencastle, IN
United Way of Putnam County, Ohio [16320], Ottawa, OH
United Way of Racine County [19579], Racine, WI
United Way of Randolph County [6537], Winchester, IN
United Way of Rice Lake [19618], Rice Lake, WI
United Way of Richland County [15795], Mansfield, OH
United Way of River Falls [19645], River Falls, WI
United Way of Rock River Valley [3327], Rockford, IL
United Way of Ross County [13677], Chillicothe, OH
United Way of Saginaw County [9645], Saginaw, MI
United Way of St. Charles and Elburn [3395], St. Charles, IL
United Way of St. Clair County [9442], Port Huron, MI
United Way of the St. Cloud Area [★12316]
United Way of St. Croix County [18227], Hudson, WI
United Way of St. Joseph County [6272], South Bend, IN
United Way of St. Peter [12621], St. Peter, MN
United Way of Sandusky County [15255], Fremont, OH
United Way of Sanilac County [8809], Lexington, MI
United Way of Scioto County [16477], Portsmouth, OH
United Way of Scott County [6174], Scottsburg, IN
United Way Services of Geauga County [13645], Chardon, OH
United Way Services of Greater Cleveland [14229], Cleveland, OH
United Way Services of Northern Columbiana County [16593], Salem, OH
United Way of Shawano County [19685], Shawano, WI
United Way of the Sheboygan Area [★19708]
United Way of Sheboygan Falls [19721], Sheboygan Falls, WI
United Way of South Wood County [20194], Wisconsin Rapids, WI

United Way for Southeastern Michigan **[7447]**, Detroit, MI
United Way of Southern Columbiana County **[15082]**, East Liverpool, OH
United Way of Southern Illinois **[2411]**, Marion, IL
United Way of Southwest Michigan **[6923]**, Benton Harbor, MI
United Way of Southwest Minnesota **[11442]**, Marshall, MN
United Way of Southwestern Indiana **[4585]**, Evansville, IN
United Way for Spoon River Country **[407]**, Canton, IL
United Way of Steele County **[11972]**, Owatonna, MN
United Way of Summit County **[13101]**, Akron, OH
United Way of Superior-Douglas County **[19882]**, Superior, WI
United Way of Taylor County **[18849]**, Medford, WI
United Way of Troy, Ohio **[17012]**, Troy, OH
United Way of Trumbull County **[17114]**, Warren, OH
United Way of Tuscarawas County **[16157]**, New Philadelphia, OH
United Way of Tuscola County **[7096]**, Cass City, MI
United Way of Union County, Ohio **[15868]**, Marysville, OH
United Way of Upper Sandusky and Pitt Township **[17032]**, Upper Sandusky, OH
United Way of Van Wert County **[17053]**, Van Wert, OH
United Way and Volunteer Center of Clare County **[7155]**, Clare, MI
United Way of the Wabash Valley **[6347]**, Terre Haute, IN
United Way of Wadena Area **[12824]**, Wadena, MN
United Way of Watertown **[19970]**, Watertown, WI
United Way in Waukesha County **[20000]**, Waukesha, WI
United Way of Wayne and Holmes Counties **[17327]**, Wooster, OH
United Way of Wells County **[4270]**, Bluffton, IN
United Way of Wexford County **[7050]**, Cadillac, MI
United Way of Whiteside County **[3706]**, Sterling, IL
United Way of Whitewater Valley **[6109]**, Richmond, IN
United Way of Whitley County **[4385]**, Columbia City, IN
United Way of Will County **[2122]**, Joliet, IL
United Way of Williams County **[13458]**, Bryan, OH
United Way of Wisconsin **[18633]**, Madison, WI
Unity Christian High - Young Life **[6629]**, Allendale, MI
Universities; Wisconsin Assn. of Independent Colleges and **[18657]**, Madison, WI
University Avenue Parent Teacher Organization **[10453]**, Blaine, MN
Univ. of Detroit-Mercy Assn. for Computing Machinery **[7448]**, Detroit, MI
Univ. of Illinois At Urbana-Champaign Figure Skating Club **[555]**, Champaign, IL
Univ. of Illinois - Comm. on Natural Areas **[556]**, Champaign, IL
Univ. of Illinois Urbana Champaign Natl. Org. for the Reform of Marijuana Laws **[3839]**, Urbana, IL
Univ. of Michigan ACM SIGGRAPH Student Chap. **[6777]**, Ann Arbor, MI
Univ. of Michigan-Dearborn - Student Environmental Assn. **[7272]**, Dearborn, MI
Univ. of Michigan Skating Club **[6778]**, Ann Arbor, MI
Univ. of Minnesota - Civil Engg. Dept. - Enval. Engg. Soc. **[11769]**, Minneapolis, MN
Univ. of Minnesota-Duluth Literary Guild **[10861]**, Duluth, MN
Univ. Musical Soc. **[6779]**, Ann Arbor, MI
Univ. of Oklahoma Assn. - OU Club of Wisconsin **[20105]**, West Allis, WI
Univ. Park Bus. League Chamber of Commerce **[★2438]**
Univ. Professors; Michigan Conf. of the Amer. Assn. of **[8649]**, Lansing, MI
Univ. of Toledo Police Patrolman's Assn. **[16980]**, Toledo, OH
Univ. of Wisconsin Aikido **[18634]**, Madison, WI
Univ. of Wisconsin at Fox Valley Natl. Org. for the Reform of Marijuana Laws **[18867]**, Menasha, WI
Univ. of Wisconsin Ice Skating Club - Eau Claire **[17905]**, Eau Claire, WI
Univ. of Wisconsin - La Crosse Br. Lions Club **[18380]**, La Crosse, WI
Univ. of Wisconsin-Milwaukee; Center for Consumer Affairs, **[18990]**, Milwaukee, WI
Univ. of Wisconsin, Milwaukee - Student Enval. Action Coalition **[19144]**, Milwaukee, WI
Univ. of Wisconsin, Stevens Point - Wildlife Soc. - Student Chap. **[19814]**, Stevens Point, WI
Univ. of Wisconsin, Stevens Point - Wisconsin Parks and Recreation Assn. **[19815]**, Stevens Point, WI
Univ. Women, Grand Rapids Br; Amer. Assn. of **[7885]**, Grand Rapids, MI
Unmanned Vehicle Syss. Intl., Wright Kettering Chap; Assn. for **[17356]**, Wright-Patterson AFB, OH
Upgrade Cycle **[1218]**, Chicago, IL
Upland Chamber of Commerce **[6371]**, Upland, IN
Upland Chap. of Pheasants Forever **[20052]**, Wausau, WI
Upland Hunt Club and Sporting Clays **[1367]**, Davis Junction, IL
Upper Arlington Area Chamber of Commerce **[17030]**, Upper Arlington, OH
Upper Arlington Community Orchestra **[14754]**, Columbus, OH
Upper Arlington - Young Life **[14755]**, Columbus, OH
Upper Michigan Tourist Assn. **[★8328]**
Upper Midwest ACH Assn. **[10560]**, Brooklyn Park, MN
Upper Midwest Automated CH Assn. **[10561]**, Brooklyn Park, MN
Upper Midwest Booksellers Assn. **[11770]**, Minneapolis, MN
Upper Midwest Chap. of the Acoustical Soc. of Am. **[11771]**, Minneapolis, MN
Upper Midwest Dairy Indus. Assn. **[11849]**, Mounds View, MN
Upper Midwest Horseshoer's Assn. No. 21 **[3196]**, Ringwood, IL
Upper Midwest Translators and Interpreters Assn. **[11772]**, Minneapolis, MN
Upper Mississippi River Conservation Comm. **[3260]**, Rock Island, IL
Upper Mississippi River Refuges; Friends of the **[12950]**, Winona, MN
Upper Peninsula Assn. of Realtors **[8961]**, Marquette, MI
Upper Peninsula Development Bur. **[★8328]**
Upper Peninsula Environmental Coalition **[8263]**, Houghton, MI
Upper Peninsula Mountain Bike Club **[8962]**, Marquette, MI
Upper Peninsula Publishers and Authors Assn. **[8513]**, Lake Linden, MI
Upper Peninsula Rsrc. Conservation and Development Coun. **[8963]**, Marquette, MI
Upper Peninsula Travel and Recreation Assn. **[8328]**, Iron Mountain, MI
Upper Peninsula Youth for Christ **[8964]**, Marquette, MI
Upper Sandusky Area Chamber of Commerce **[17033]**, Upper Sandusky, OH
Upper Sandusky Lions Club **[17034]**, Upper Sandusky, OH
Upper Sugar River Watershed Assn. **[19244]**, Mount Horeb, WI
Uptown Chamber of Commerce **[1219]**, Chicago, IL
Urban Affairs
Corp. for Natl. and Community Ser. - Kansas **[858]**, Chicago, IL
Corp. for Natl. and Community Ser. - Missouri **[11550]**, Minneapolis, MN
Corp. for Natl. and Community Ser. - Oklahoma **[14414]**, Columbus, OH
Corp. for Natl. and Community Ser. - Wisconsin **[18997]**, Milwaukee, WI
Heritage Ohio **[14453]**, Columbus, OH
Urban Counties Coun. of Illinois **[★3693]**
Urban Enterprise Zone; City of La Porte **[5595]**, La Porte, IN
Urban League of Champaign County **[557]**, Champaign, IL
Urban League; Detroit **[7357]**, Detroit, MI
Urban League of Flint **[7761]**, Flint, MI
Urban League of Greater Cincinnati **[14019]**, Cincinnati, OH
Urban League of Greater Cleveland **[14230]**, Cleveland, OH
Urban League of Greater Madison **[18635]**, Madison, WI
Urban League of Greater Muskegon **[9165]**, Muskegon, MI
Urban League of Madison County **[4122]**, Anderson, IN
Urban League of NW Indiana **[4787]**, Gary, IN
Urban League; Quad County **[129]**, Aurora, IL
Urban League of Racine and Kenosha **[19580]**, Racine, WI
Urban League of South Bend and St. Joseph County **[6273]**, South Bend, IN
Urban Solutions Training and Development Corp. **[7449]**, Detroit, MI
Urbana - Champaign County Chamber of Commerce **[★17040]**
Urbana Country Dancers **[558]**, Champaign, IL
Urbana Free Lib. Found. **[3840]**, Urbana, IL
Urology
Florida Urological Soc. **[3435]**, Schaumburg, IL
Minnesota Urological Soc. **[11292]**, Lakeland, MN
North Central Sect. of the Amer. Urological Assn. **[3440]**, Schaumburg, IL
Ohio Urological Soc. **[3442]**, Schaumburg, IL
South Central Sect. of the Amer. Urological Assn. **[3449]**, Schaumburg, IL
Southeastern Sect. of the Amer. Urological Assn. **[3450]**, Schaumburg, IL
USA Dance - Central Michigan Chap. No. 2037 **[8769]**, Lansing, MI
USA Dance - Chap. 2015 **[17115]**, Warren, OH
USA Dance - Chicagoland Chap. **[250]**, Bloomingdale, IL
USA Dance - Greater Fox Valley of Illinois Chap. No. 2042 **[4064]**, Woodstock, IL
USA Dance - Heartland Chap. **[4263]**, Bloomington, IN
USA Dance - North Coast Ohio **[15982]**, Mentor, OH
USA Dance - Southern Minnesota Chap. No. 2017 **[12197]**, Rochester, MN
USA Diving - Dive Cincinnati **[16030]**, Milford, OH
USA Diving - Fox Valley Dive Team **[19276]**, Neenah, WI
USA Diving - Indiana Diving **[4264]**, Bloomington, IN
USA Diving - Jeff Arnold Diving Enterprises **[17277]**, Willoughby, OH
USA Diving - No. 19 Wisconsin **[17693]**, Brown Deer, WI
USA Diving - No. 21 Minnesota **[12692]**, Spring Lake Park, MN
USA Diving - Rock Solid Diving **[9532]**, Rockford, MI
U.S.A. Track and Field, Illinois **[2304]**, Lisle, IL
USA Track and Field, Indiana **[4591]**, Fairland, IN
U.S.A. Track and Field Lake Erie **[16378]**, Parma, OH
U.S.A. Track and Field, Michigan **[7450]**, Detroit, MI
U.S.A. Track and Field, Michigan Top **[★7450]**
USA Track and Field Minnesota **[12667]**, Shorewood, MN
U.S.A. Track and Field, Wisconsin **[18636]**, Madison, WI
U.S.A. Track and Field, Wisconsin Top **[★18636]**
U.S.A. Volleyball Badger Region **[19145]**, Milwaukee, WI
U.S.A. Volleyball Great Lakes Region **[1471]**, Des Plaines, IL
U.S.A. Volleyball Hoosier Region **[4509]**, Elkhart, IN
U.S.A. Volleyball Michiana Region **[★4509]**
U.S.A. Volleyball Ohio Valley Region **[15551]**, Kent, OH
USA Weightlifting - Amer. Coll. of Modern Weightlifting **[16845]**, Tallmadge, OH
USA Weightlifting - Armstrong Falcons **[12041]**, Plymouth, MN
USA Weightlifting - Atomic Athletic Club **[8285]**, Howell, MI
USA Weightlifting - Aurora Weightlifting Club **[134]**, Aurora, IL
USA Weightlifting - Charleston **[573]**, Charleston, IL
USA Weightlifting - Cougars **[7568]**, East Lansing, MI
USA Weightlifting - Dearborn **[14020]**, Cincinnati, OH
USA Weightlifting - Dynamic Fitness **[8859]**, Livonia, MI
USA Weightlifting - Farmington **[10992]**, Farmington, MN

USA Weightlifting - Fox Valley [135], Aurora, IL
USA Weightlifting - Glencoe [11049], Glencoe, MN
USA Weightlifting - Husky Power Training [9455], Portage, MI
USA Weightlifting - Lakeville [11297], Lakeville, MN
USA Weightlifting - Lynch's Gym [6274], South Bend, IN
USA Weightlifting - Northfield [11920], Northfield, MN
USA Weightlifting - Olympic Hea. Club [14231], Cleveland, OH
USA Weightlifting - Power Sports Athletic Center [17833], Denmark, WI
USA Weightlifting - Power X-Treme [9343], Oxford, MI
USA Weightlifting - Ramsey Ridge Lifters [1410], Decatur, IL
USA Weightlifting - Red Wing [12091], Red Wing, MN
USA Weightlifting - Rosemount Weightlifting Club [10612], Burnsville, MN
USA Weightlifting - Sayre Park [1220], Chicago, IL
USA Weightlifting - Team Body Club [574], Charleston, IL
USA Weightlifting - Team Cannon Weightlifting [10634], Cannon Falls, MN
USA Weightlifting - Team Janz [17906], Eau Claire, WI
USA Weightlifting - Team Pendragon [14792], Cortland, OH
USA Weightlifting - Team Velocity Willowbrook [4014], Willowbrook, IL
USA Weightlifting - Toledo [16981], Toledo, OH
USA Weightlifting - Town and Country Lifting Club [19345], Oconomowoc, WI
USA Weightlifting - Twin City Barbell [12249], Roseville, MN
USA Weightlifting - West Park YMCA [14232], Cleveland, OH
USA Weightlifting - Windy City [2269], Libertyville, IL
USA Wrestling-Ohio [13102], Akron, OH
USABDA Minnesota Chap. [12339], St. Louis Park, MN
USATF Ohio Assn. [14966], Dayton, OH
USO of Central Ohio [17248], Whitehall, OH
USO of Northern Ohio [13432], Broadview Heights, OH
Utica Police Off.rs Assn. [10038], Utica, MI
Utilities
Elec. League of Indiana [5106], Indianapolis, IN
Illinois Municipal Utilities Assn. [3619], Springfield, IL
Indiana Statewide Assn. of Rural Elec. Cooperatives [5325], Indianapolis, IN
Michigan Elec. and Gas Assn. [8660], Lansing, MI
Michigan Municipal Elec. Assn. [8688], Lansing, MI
Minnesota Municipal Utilities Assn. [12026], Plymouth, MN
Natl. Exchange Carrier Assn., Midwest [1080], Chicago, IL
North Central Elec. League [10484], Bloomington, MN
Ohio Elec. Utility Inst. [14603], Columbus, OH
Utility Workers Union of Am., AFL-CIO - Buildings and Properties Div. Local Union 223 [7273], Dearborn, MI
Utility Workers Union of Am., AFL-CIO - Local Union 116 [15896], Massillon, OH
Utility Workers Union of Am., AFL-CIO - Meter Reading-Detroit Div. Local Union 223 [7274], Dearborn, MI
Utility Workers Union of Am., AFL-CIO - Off., Professional and Tech. Div. Local Union 223 [7275], Dearborn, MI
Utility Workers Union of Am., AFL-CIO - Substation Div. Local Union 223 [7276], Dearborn, MI
Wisconsin Utilities Assn. [18760], Madison, WI
Utilities Assn; Wisconsin [18760], Madison, WI
Utility Contractors Assn; Minnesota [12981], Woodbury, MN
Utility Workers Union of Am., AFL-CIO - Buildings and Properties Div. Local Union 223 [7273], Dearborn, MI
Utility Workers Union of Am., AFL-CIO - Local Union 116 [15896], Massillon, OH
Utility Workers Union of Am., AFL-CIO - Meter Reading-Detroit Div. Local Union 223 [7274], Dearborn, MI
Utility Workers Union of Am., AFL-CIO - Off., Professional and Tech. Div. Local Union 223 [7275], Dearborn, MI
Utility Workers Union of Am., AFL-CIO - Substation Div. Local Union 223 [7276], Dearborn, MI

V

Vacationland Corvairs [16347], Painesville, OH
Vacationland District Dental Soc. [9374], Petoskey, MI
Vacationland Figure Skating Club [10522], Brainerd, MN
Vaccine Awareness Coalition; Illinois [2816], Oak Park, IL
Vacuum Soc., Prairie Chap; Amer. [2237], Lemont, IL
Vacuum Technology
Amer. Vacuum Soc., Prairie Chap. [2237], Lemont, IL
Vadnais Heights Lions Club [12782], Vadnais Heights, MN
Vadnais Lake Area Water Mgt. Org. [12904], White Bear Lake, MN
Valley of Cincinnati, Ancient Accepted Scottish Rite [14021], Cincinnati, OH
Valley of Cincinnati, Scottish Rite [★14021]
Valley City Chamber of Commerce [17046], Valley City, OH
Valley Indus. Development Corp. [★11378]
Valley Soc. for Human Rsrc. Mgt. [9646], Saginaw, MI
Valley Vagabonds [16800], Strongsville, OH
Valparaiso Community Festivals and Events [6393], Valparaiso, IN
Valparaiso High School Key Club [6394], Valparaiso, IN
Valparaiso RSVP [6395], Valparaiso, IN
Van Buren Chamber of Commerce [6397], Van Buren, IN
Van Buren County United Way [9348], Paw Paw, MI
Van Buren Regional Genealogical Soc. [7287], Decatur, MI
Van Dyne Sportsmen's Club [19930], Van Dyne, WI
Van Wert Area County Chamber of Commerce [17054], Van Wert, OH
Van Wert County Historical Soc. [17055], Van Wert, OH
Vandalia Butler Pee Wee Youth Sports Assn. [17061], Vandalia, OH
Vandalia Chamber of Commerce [3849], Vandalia, IL
Vandalia Main St. Prog. [3850], Vandalia, IL
Vanderburgh County 4-H Coun. [4586], Evansville, IN
Vanderburgh County Medical Soc. [4587], Evansville, IN
Vanderburgh County REACT [4588], Evansville, IN
Vanderburgh County RSVP [4589], Evansville, IN
Vandercook Lake Lions Club [8400], Jackson, MI
Vanezetti Hamilton Bar Assn. [6780], Ann Arbor, MI
Variety of Detroit [9829], Southfield, MI
Variety of Illinois [1221], Chicago, IL
Variety of Indiana [5492], Indianapolis, IN
Variety of Western Michigan [8047], Grandville, MI
Variety of Wisconsin [19146], Milwaukee, WI
Vascular System
Chicago Area Vascular Assn. [178], Batavia, IL
Northern Ohio Vascular Assn. [14188], Cleveland, OH
Ohio Northern Kentucky Indiana Vascular Technologists [13941], Cincinnati, OH
Vassar Lions Club [10043], Vassar, MI
Vaulting
Amer. Vaulting Assn. - Agape Vaulters [7586], Eau Claire, MI
Amer. Vaulting Assn. - Blue Moon Vaulters [7160], Clarkston, MI
Amer. Vaulting Assn. - Diamond E Vaulters [9914], Three Rivers, MI
Amer. Vaulting Assn. - MSU Vaulters [7161], Clarkston, MI
Amer. Vaulting Assn. - Sunshine Vaulters [9222], Northville, MI
Amer. Vaulting Assn. - Univ. of Findlay Vaulters [15194], Findlay, OH
Amer. Vaulting Assn. - Victory Vaulters [9776], South Rockwood, MI
Vegans in Motion [★8902]
Vegetable Growers Association; Wisconsin Potato and [17480], Antigo, WI
Vegetables
Canned Vegetable Coun. [18422], Lodi, WI
Chicago Vegetarian Soc. [1995], Highwood, IL
Michigan Bean Commn. [9676], St. Johns, MI
Michigan Potato Indus. Commn. [7464], DeWitt, MI
Michigan Vegetable Coun. [7606], Erie, MI
Minnesota Dry Edible Bean Res. and Promotion Coun. [11993], Perham, MN
Northarvest Bean Growers Assn. [11029], Frazee, MN
Ohio Soybean Coun. [14676], Columbus, OH
Vegetarian Advocates [★16639]
Vegetarian Advocates; Ohio [16639], Shaker Heights, OH
Vegetarian Soc. of the Greater Dayton Area [14967], Dayton, OH
Vegetarianism
Go Veggie! [903], Chicago, IL
Milwaukee Area Rsrcs. For Vegetarians [19732], Shorewood, WI
Ohio Vegetarian Advocates [16639], Shaker Heights, OH
Vegetarian Soc. of the Greater Dayton Area [14967], Dayton, OH
Veggies in Motion [8902], Madison Heights, MI
Veggies in Motion [8902], Madison Heights, MI
Vehicle Assn; Ohio Mobile Home and Recreational [★15058]
Vehicle Association; Sportsmen Off-Road [8325], Iron Mountain, MI
Vehicle Syss. Intl., Wright Kettering Chap; Assn. for Unmanned [17356], Wright-Patterson AFB, OH
Vehicles and Campgrounds; Michigan Assn. of Recreational [9273], Okemos, MI
Vending
Coin Laundry Assn. [1500], Downers Grove, IL
Illinois Coin Machine Operators Assn. [3593], Springfield, IL
Ohio Automatic Merchandising Association [14571], Columbus, OH
Ohio Coin Machine Assn. [14584], Columbus, OH
Vending Machine Servicemen's Union [4461], Dillsboro, IN
Vendors Assn; Michigan Distributors and [8659], Lansing, MI
Venice Cemetery Assn. [15172], Fairfield, OH
Vermilion Advantage-Chamber of Commerce Div. [1354], Danville, IL
Vermilion AIFA [1355], Danville, IL
Vermilion Chamber of Commerce [17066], Vermilion, OH
Vermilion County Museum Soc. [1356], Danville, IL
Vermilion Lions Club [17067], Vermilion, OH
Vermillion County Chamber of Commerce [4372], Clinton, IN
Vermontville Lions Club [10046], Vermontville, MI
Verona Area Chamber of Commerce [19936], Verona, WI
Versailles Area Genealogical and Historical Soc. [3856], Versailles, IL
Vessel Owners Assn; Cleveland [★14153]
Vestaburg Lions Club [10047], Vestaburg, MI
Veteran Motor Car Club of Am. - Battle Creek Chap. [6874], Battle Creek, MI
Veteran Motor Car Club of Am. - Black Swamp Chap. [17252], Whitehouse, OH
Veteran Motor Car Club of Am. - Blue Water Chap. [9443], Port Huron, MI
Veteran Motor Car Club of Am. - Brass and Gas Chap. [6798], Armada, MI
Veteran Motor Car Club of Am. - Brighton Chap. [12828], Waite Park, MN
Veteran Motor Car Club of Am. - Buckeye-Keystone Region [16780], Strasburg, OH
Veteran Motor Car Club of Am. - Coulee Chap. [18028], Galesville, WI
Veteran Motor Car Club of Am. - Defiance Chap. [14994], Defiance, OH
Veteran Motor Car Club of Am. - Detroit Chap. [9873], Sterling Heights, MI
Veteran Motor Car Club of Am. - Great Lakes Region [16413], Perrysburg, OH
Veteran Motor Car Club of Am. - Hall of Fame Chap. [13513], Canal Fulton, OH

Veteran Motor Car Club of Am. - Huron Valley Chap. **[9313]**, Orchard Lake, MI
Veteran Motor Car Club of Am. - Jackson Cascades Chap. **[6593]**, Albion, MI
Veteran Motor Car Club of Am. - Lakeshore Chap. **[9666]**, St. Clair Shores, MI
Veteran Motor Car Club of Am. - Lansing Chap. **[8984]**, Mason, MI
Veteran Motor Car Club of Am. - Nickel Age Touring Chap. **[16594]**, Salem, OH
Veteran Motor Car Club of Am. - Reagan Country Classics Chap. **[1486]**, Dixon, IL
Veteran Motor Car Club of Am. - Steel Valley Chap. **[17304]**, Wintersville, OH
Veteran Motor Car Club of Am. - Toledo Chap. **[16414]**, Perrysburg, OH
Veteran Motor Car Club of Am. - Tri-State Region **[16770]**, Steubenville, OH
Veteran Motor Car Club of Am. - Upper Mississippi Region **[18029]**, Galesville, WI
Veterans
Amer. Legion, Coon Rapids Post No. 334 Social Club **[10707]**, Coon Rapids, MN
Amer. Legion of Indiana **[4997]**, Indianapolis, IN
AMVETS, Big Rapids **[6940]**, Big Rapids, MI
AMVETS, Bloomington Post 2000 **[4199]**, Bloomington, IN
AMVETS, Cadillac Post 110 **[7043]**, Cadillac, MI
AMVETS, Celina Post 91 **[13611]**, Celina, OH
AMVETS, Elyria Post 32 **[15107]**, Elyria, OH
AMVETS, Fisher Post 52 **[1702]**, Fisher, IL
AMVETS, Knoxville Post 8 **[2166]**, Knoxville, IL
AMVETS, Manitowoc Post 99 **[18776]**, Manitowoc, WI
AMVETS, Marion Post 5 **[5727]**, Marion, IN
AMVETS, Mount Vernon Post 4 **[2594]**, Mount Vernon, IL
AMVETS, Muncie Post 12 **[5867]**, Muncie, IN
AMVETS, Oak Creek Post 60 **[19331]**, Oak Creek, WI
AMVETS, Ottawa Post 30 **[2896]**, Ottawa, IL
AMVETS, Richfield Post 176 **[16521]**, Richfield, OH
AMVETS, Rockville Post 61 **[6132]**, Rockville, IN
AMVETS, Toledo Post 222 **[16899]**, Toledo, OH
AMVETS, Waverly Post 58 **[17145]**, Waverly, OH
AMVETS, West Harrison Post 13 **[6466]**, West Harrison, IN
Carmel Clay Veterans Memorial Corp. **[4318]**, Carmel, IN
Central Minnesota Chap. 115, The Retired Enlisted Assn. **[11810]**, Monticello, MN
Memorial Rifle Squad, Minnesota State Veterans Cemetery **[11167]**, Hillman, MN
Red River Valley Fighter Pilot Assn. - Cincinnati, Ohio **[13974]**, Cincinnati, OH
Red River Valley Fighter Pilot Assn. - Michigan **[10123]**, West Bloomfield, MI
Red River Valley Fighter Pilot Assn. - Minnesota **[10606]**, Burnsville, MN
Red River Valley Fighter Pilot Assn. - Wright Patterson AFB/Dayton, Ohio **[15564]**, Kettering, OH
Retired Enlisted Assn., 77 **[17892]**, Eau Claire, WI
Retired Enlisted Assn., 90 **[3930]**, Waukegan, IL
Retired Enlisted Assn., 119 **[19874]**, Superior, WI
The Retired Enlisted Assn. Chap. 66 **[17521]**, Appleton, WI
The Retired Enlisted Assn. Chap. 96 **[11162]**, Hibbing, MN
The Retired Enlisted Assn., Chap., 115 **[12296]**, St. Cloud, MN
Society of the 173D Airborne Brigade, Midwest Chapter XVII **[14730]**, Columbus, OH
Veterans of Foreign Wars **[16463]**, Port Clinton, OH
Veterans Affairs Physician Asst. Assn. **[8329]**, Iron Mountain, MI
Veterans of Am. Chap. No. 10; Vietnam **[14022]**, Cincinnati, OH
Veterans of Am., Michigan Chap; Paralyzed **[9244]**, Novi, MI
Veterans of Am., Vaughan Chap; Paralyzed **[3957]**, Westchester, IL
Veterans of America; Wisconsin Paralyzed **[20110]**, West Allis, WI
Veterans Cemetery; Memorial Rifle Squad, Minnesota State **[11167]**, Hillman, MN
Veterans For Peace - Chap. 93 **[10217]**, Ypsilanti, MI
Veterans of Foreign Wars **[575]**, Charleston, IL
Veterans of Foreign Wars **[16463]**, Port Clinton, OH
Veterans of Foreign Wars **[18850]**, Medford, WI
Veterans of Foreign Wars
Veterans of Foreign Wars 351 **[16067]**, Morrow, OH
Veterans of Foreign Wars 1148 **[13401]**, Bowling Green, OH
Veterans of Foreign Wars 2595 **[16348]**, Painesville, OH
Veterans of Foreign Wars 3288 **[13443]**, Brookville, OH
Veterans of Foreign Wars 3320 **[15869]**, Marysville, OH
Veterans of Foreign Wars 3341 **[15335]**, Grafton, OH
Veterans of Foreign Wars 3424 **[14756]**, Columbus, OH
Veterans of Foreign Wars 3430 **[17266]**, Willard, OH
Veteran's of Foreign Wars 3494 **[15796]**, Mansfield, OH
Veterans of Foreign Wars 4027 **[16091]**, Mount Vernon, OH
Veterans of Foreign Wars 4358 **[17280]**, Willoughby Hills, OH
Veterans of Foreign Wars 5299 **[15926]**, McArthur, OH
Veterans of Foreign Wars 5434 **[15135]**, Englewood, OH
Veterans of Foreign Wars 5645 **[15216]**, Findlay, OH
Veterans of Foreign Wars 7079 **[15566]**, Killbuck, OH
Veterans of Foreign Wars 7174 **[16444]**, The Plains, OH
Veterans of Foreign Wars 8218 **[16101]**, Napoleon, OH
Veterans of Foreign Wars 8402 **[15516]**, Jackson, OH
Veterans of Foreign Wars 8598 **[16820]**, Swanton, OH
Veterans of Foreign Wars 8899 **[13468]**, Bucyrus, OH
Veterans of Foreign Wars 9816 **[16305]**, Oregon, OH
Veterans of Foreign Wars 9893 **[13106]**, Albany, OH
Veterans of Foreign Wars 9942 **[13293]**, Beaver, OH
Veterans of Foreign Wars/Auxiliary Unit 6448 **[4469]**, Dyer, IN
Veterans of Foreign Wars/Griffith Memorial Auxiliary Unit 9982 **[4860]**, Griffith, IN
Veterans of Foreign Wars/Hobart Post 5365 **[4932]**, Hobart, IN
Veterans of Foreign Wars, Indiana Dept. **[5493]**, Indianapolis, IN
Veterans of Foreign Wars/Memorial Post 7881 **[4896]**, Hammond, IN
Veterans of Foreign Wars, Post 5713 **[13616]**, Celina, OH
Veterans of Foreign Wars/Post 6841 **[5706]**, Lowell, IN
Veterans of Foreign Wars/Post 9323 **[5645]**, Lake Station, IN
Veterans of Foreign Wars Post 9622 **[15878]**, Mason, OH
Veterans of Foreign Wars 351 **[16067]**, Morrow, OH
Veterans of Foreign Wars 870 **[16530]**, Richwood, OH
Veterans of Foreign Wars 1148 **[13401]**, Bowling Green, OH
Veterans of Foreign Wars 2595 **[16348]**, Painesville, OH
Veterans of Foreign Wars 3288 **[13443]**, Brookville, OH
Veterans of Foreign Wars 3320 **[15869]**, Marysville, OH
Veterans of Foreign Wars 3341 **[15335]**, Grafton, OH
Veterans of Foreign Wars 3424 **[14756]**, Columbus, OH
Veterans of Foreign Wars 3430 **[17266]**, Willard, OH
Veteran's of Foreign Wars 3494 **[15796]**, Mansfield, OH
Veterans of Foreign Wars 4027 **[16091]**, Mount Vernon, OH
Veterans of Foreign Wars 4358 **[17280]**, Willoughby Hills, OH
Veterans of Foreign Wars 4906 **[16982]**, Toledo, OH
Veterans of Foreign Wars 5299 **[15926]**, McArthur, OH
Veterans of Foreign Wars 5434 **[15135]**, Englewood, OH
Veterans of Foreign Wars 5645 **[15216]**, Findlay, OH
Veterans of Foreign Wars 7079 **[15566]**, Killbuck, OH
Veterans of Foreign Wars 7174 **[16444]**, The Plains, OH
Veterans of Foreign Wars 7424 **[17142]**, Wauseon, OH
Veterans of Foreign Wars 7496 **[15190]**, Felicity, OH
Veterans of Foreign Wars 8218 **[16101]**, Napoleon, OH
Veterans of Foreign Wars 8402 **[15516]**, Jackson, OH
Veterans of Foreign Wars 8598 **[16820]**, Swanton, OH
Veterans of Foreign Wars 8899 **[13468]**, Bucyrus, OH
Veterans of Foreign Wars 9816 **[16305]**, Oregon, OH
Veterans of Foreign Wars 9893 **[13106]**, Albany, OH
Veterans of Foreign Wars 9942 **[13293]**, Beaver, OH
Veterans of Foreign Wars/Auxiliary Unit 6448 **[4469]**, Dyer, IN
Veterans of Foreign Wars/Griffith Memorial Auxiliary Unit 9982 **[4860]**, Griffith, IN
Veterans of Foreign Wars/Hobart Post 5365 **[4932]**, Hobart, IN
Veterans of Foreign Wars, Indiana Dept. **[5493]**, Indianapolis, IN
Veterans of Foreign Wars/Memorial Post 7881 **[4896]**, Hammond, IN
Veterans of Foreign Wars, Post 5713 **[13616]**, Celina, OH
Veterans of Foreign Wars/Post 6841 **[5706]**, Lowell, IN
Veterans of Foreign Wars/Post 9323 **[5645]**, Lake Station, IN
Veterans of Foreign Wars Post 9622 **[15878]**, Mason, OH
Veterans Memorial Committee; Wayne County **[6112]**, Richmond, IN
Veterans Memorial Corp; Carmel Clay **[4318]**, Carmel, IN
Veterinary Medicine
Amer. Assn. of Bovine Practitioners, District 4 **[17308]**, Wooster, OH
Amer. Assn. of Bovine Practitioners, District 5 **[17769]**, Clintonville, WI
Indiana Veterinary Medical Assn. **[5333]**, Indianapolis, IN
Michigan Veterinary Medical Assn. **[9293]**, Okemos, MI
Minnesota Veterinary Medical Assn. **[12681]**, South St. Paul, MN
Ohio Veterinary Medical Assn. **[14697]**, Columbus, OH
Wisconsin Veterinary Medical Assn. **[18761]**, Madison, WI
Vicksburg - Young Life **[8470]**, Kalamazoo, MI
Victims
Hidden Victims Support Gp. **[1392]**, Decatur, IL
Victor C Neumann Assn. **[1222]**, Chicago, IL
Victorian Village Soc. **[14757]**, Columbus, OH
Vietnam Veterans
Vietnam Veterans of Am. Chap. No. 10 **[14022]**, Cincinnati, OH
Vietnam Veterans of Am.-State of Michigan Coun. **[7451]**, Detroit, MI
Vietnam Veterans of Am., Buckeye State Coun. **[14758]**, Columbus, OH
Vietnam Veterans of Am., Central Minnesota - Chap. 290 **[12317]**, St. Cloud, MN
Vietnam Veterans of Am., Chap. 154 **[9568]**, Roseville, MI
Vietnam Veterans of Am., Chap. 237 **[9131]**, Munising, MI
Vietnam Veterans of Am., Chap. 267 **[7277]**, Dearborn, MI
Vietnam Veterans of Am., Chap. 295 **[5494]**, Indianapolis, IN

Vietnam Veterans of Am., Chap. 351 **[17530]**, Appleton, WI
Vietnam Veterans of Am., Chap. 380 **[9179]**, Negaunee, MI
Vietnam Veterans of Am. Chap. No. 10 **[14022]**, Cincinnati, OH
Vietnam Veterans of Am., Chap. No. 34 **[14826]**, Cuyahoga Falls, OH
Vietnam Veterans of Am., Chap. No. 35 **[16983]**, Toledo, OH
Vietnam Veterans of Am., Chap. No. 40 **[17134]**, Washingtonville, OH
Vietnam Veterans of Am., Chap. No. 42 **[17446]**, Zanesville, OH
Vietnam Veterans of Am., Chap. No. 55 **[16188]**, Newark, OH
Vietnam Veterans of Am., Chap. No. 73 **[8222]**, Holland, MI
Vietnam Veterans of Am., Chap. No. 89 LZ-Lima **[15673]**, Lima, OH
Vietnam Veterans of Am., Chap. No. 97 Miami Valley **[14968]**, Dayton, OH
Vietnam Veterans of Am., Chap. No. 135 **[17419]**, Youngstown, OH
Vietnam Veterans of Am., Chap. No. 199 **[13594]**, Canton, OH
Vietnam Veterans of Am., Chap. No. 231 **[13189]**, Ashtabula, OH
Vietnam Veterans of Am., Chap. No. 249 **[13278]**, Bay Village, OH
Vietnam Veterans of Am., Chap. No. 255 **[17328]**, Wooster, OH
Vietnam Veterans of Am., Chap. No. 281 **[13678]**, Chillicothe, OH
Vietnam Veterans of Am., Chap. No. 400 **[15233]**, Fostoria, OH
Vietnam Veterans of Am., Chap. No. 440 **[15234]**, Fostoria, OH
Vietnam Veterans of Am., Chap. No. 532 - Roger D. Lewis Memorial **[16198]**, Newcomerstown, OH
Vietnam Veterans of Am., Chap. No. 559 **[15336]**, Grafton, OH
Vietnam Veterans of Am., Chap. No. 616 **[15797]**, Mansfield, OH
Vietnam Veterans of Am., Chap. No. 634 **[15517]**, Jackson, OH
Vietnam Veterans of Am., Chap. No. 645 **[13679]**, Chillicothe, OH
Vietnam Veterans of Am., Chap. No. 646 - Western Stark County **[15897]**, Massillon, OH
Vietnam Veterans of Am., Chap. No. 649 - Clermont County **[13272]**, Batavia, OH
Vietnam Veterans of Am., Chap. No. 670 **[14759]**, Columbus, OH
Vietnam Veterans of Am., Chap. No. 676 **[16109]**, Nelsonville, OH
Vietnam Veterans of Am., Chap. No. 709 **[15297]**, Gallipolis, OH
Vietnam Veterans of Am., Chap. No. 717 **[14827]**, Cuyahoga Falls, OH
Vietnam Veterans of Am., Chap. No. 746 **[15697]**, London, OH
Vietnam Veterans of Am., Chap. No. 783 **[13617]**, Celina, OH
Vietnam Veterans of Am., Chap. No. 822 - Col. Harold F. Lyon Memorial **[15857]**, Marion, OH
Vietnam Veterans of Am., Chap. No. 857 - New Philadelphia **[16158]**, New Philadelphia, OH
Vietnam Veterans of Am., Chap. No. 882 **[8099]**, Hale, MI
Vietnam Veterans of Am., Greater Cleveland - Chap. No. 15 **[14233]**, Cleveland, OH
Vietnam Veterans of Am., Medina County - Chap. No. 385 **[15958]**, Medina, OH
Vietnam Veterans of Am., Monroe County - Chap. 142 **[9074]**, Monroe, MI
Vietnam Veterans of Am., Region 5 **[16984]**, Toledo, OH
Vietnam Veterans of Am., Region 6 **[20022]**, Waupaca, WI
Vietnam Veterans of Am., Ross County - Chap. No. 810 **[13680]**, Chillicothe, OH
Vietnam Veterans of Am.-State of Michigan Coun. **[7451]**, Detroit, MI
Vietnam Veterans of Am., Washtenaw County - Chap. 310 **[6781]**, Ann Arbor, MI
Vietnam War
  Vietnam Veterans of Am., Buckeye State Coun. **[14758]**, Columbus, OH
  Vietnam Veterans of Am., Central Minnesota - Chap. 290 **[12317]**, St. Cloud, MN
  Vietnam Veterans of Am., Chap. 154 **[9568]**, Roseville, MI
  Vietnam Veterans of Am., Chap. 237 **[9131]**, Munising, MI
  Vietnam Veterans of Am., Chap. 267 **[7277]**, Dearborn, MI
  Vietnam Veterans of Am., Chap. 295 **[5494]**, Indianapolis, IN
  Vietnam Veterans of Am., Chap. 351 **[17530]**, Appleton, WI
  Vietnam Veterans of Am., Chap. 380 **[9179]**, Negaunee, MI
  Vietnam Veterans of Am., Chap. No. 34 **[14826]**, Cuyahoga Falls, OH
  Vietnam Veterans of Am., Chap. No. 35 **[16983]**, Toledo, OH
  Vietnam Veterans of Am., Chap. No. 40 **[17134]**, Washingtonville, OH
  Vietnam Veterans of Am., Chap. No. 42 **[17446]**, Zanesville, OH
  Vietnam Veterans of Am., Chap. No. 55 **[16188]**, Newark, OH
  Vietnam Veterans of Am., Chap. No. 73 **[8222]**, Holland, MI
  Vietnam Veterans of Am., Chap. No. 89 LZ-Lima **[15673]**, Lima, OH
  Vietnam Veterans of Am., Chap. No. 97 Miami Valley **[14968]**, Dayton, OH
  Vietnam Veterans of Am., Chap. No. 135 **[17419]**, Youngstown, OH
  Vietnam Veterans of Am., Chap. No. 199 **[13594]**, Canton, OH
  Vietnam Veterans of Am., Chap. No. 231 **[13189]**, Ashtabula, OH
  Vietnam Veterans of Am., Chap. No. 249 **[13278]**, Bay Village, OH
  Vietnam Veterans of Am., Chap. No. 255 **[17328]**, Wooster, OH
  Vietnam Veterans of Am., Chap. No. 281 **[13678]**, Chillicothe, OH
  Vietnam Veterans of Am., Chap. No. 400 **[15233]**, Fostoria, OH
  Vietnam Veterans of Am., Chap. No. 440 **[15234]**, Fostoria, OH
  Vietnam Veterans of Am., Chap. No. 532 - Roger D. Lewis Memorial **[16198]**, Newcomerstown, OH
  Vietnam Veterans of Am., Chap. No. 559 **[15336]**, Grafton, OH
  Vietnam Veterans of Am., Chap. No. 616 **[15797]**, Mansfield, OH
  Vietnam Veterans of Am., Chap. No. 634 **[15517]**, Jackson, OH
  Vietnam Veterans of Am., Chap. No. 645 **[13679]**, Chillicothe, OH
  Vietnam Veterans of Am., Chap. No. 646 - Western Stark County **[15897]**, Massillon, OH
  Vietnam Veterans of Am., Chap. No. 649 - Clermont County **[13272]**, Batavia, OH
  Vietnam Veterans of Am., Chap. No. 670 **[14759]**, Columbus, OH
  Vietnam Veterans of Am., Chap. No. 676 **[16109]**, Nelsonville, OH
  Vietnam Veterans of Am., Chap. No. 709 **[15297]**, Gallipolis, OH
  Vietnam Veterans of Am., Chap. No. 717 **[14827]**, Cuyahoga Falls, OH
  Vietnam Veterans of Am., Chap. No. 746 **[15697]**, London, OH
  Vietnam Veterans of Am., Chap. No. 783 **[13617]**, Celina, OH
  Vietnam Veterans of Am., Chap. No. 822 - Col. Harold F. Lyon Memorial **[15857]**, Marion, OH
  Vietnam Veterans of Am., Chap. No. 857 - New Philadelphia **[16158]**, New Philadelphia, OH
  Vietnam Veterans of Am., Chap. No. 882 **[8099]**, Hale, MI
  Vietnam Veterans of Am., Greater Cleveland - Chap. No. 15 **[14233]**, Cleveland, OH
  Vietnam Veterans of Am., Medina County - Chap. No. 385 **[15958]**, Medina, OH
  Vietnam Veterans of Am., Monroe County - Chap. 142 **[9074]**, Monroe, MI
  Vietnam Veterans of Am., Region 5 **[16984]**, Toledo, OH
  Vietnam Veterans of Am., Region 6 **[20022]**, Waupaca, WI
  Vietnam Veterans of Am., Ross County - Chap. No. 810 **[13680]**, Chillicothe, OH
  Vietnam Veterans of Am., Washtenaw County - Chap. 310 **[6781]**, Ann Arbor, MI
Views on Learning; Learning Society of Elkhart/ **[★4805]**
Views on Learning/The Learning Society **[4805]**, Goshen, IN
Vigo Parke Vermillion Medical Soc. **[6348]**, Terre Haute, IN
Vilas County Chamber of Commerce **[17850]**, Eagle River, WI
Villa Park Chamber of Commerce **[3866]**, Villa Park, IL
Village Cycle Sport MTB Club **[1615]**, Elk Grove Village, IL
Village of Itasca Chamber of Commerce **[2071]**, Itasca, IL
Village of Mt. Zion Chamber of Commerce **[★2606]**
Village of Turner Trace **[5495]**, Indianapolis, IN
Village of Turner Trace Property Owners Assn. **[★5495]**
Vincennes Area Chamber of Commerce **[★6413]**
Vintage Chevrolet Club of Am., Central Illinois Region No. 7 **[3194]**, Ridge Farm, IL
Vintage Chevrolet Club of Am., Glass Capitol Region No. 7 **[16306]**, Oregon, OH
Vintage Chevrolet Club of Am., Great Lakes Region No. 7 **[2662]**, Naperville, IL
Vintage Chevrolet Club of Am., Indiana Region No. 7 **[5757]**, Martinsville, IN
Vintage Chevrolet Club of Am., Lake Erie (Ohio) Region No. 7 **[15638]**, Lexington, OH
Vintage Chevrolet Club of Am., Lower Michigan Region No. 7 **[8784]**, Lapeer, MI
Vintage Chevrolet Club of Am., Northern Illinois Region No. 7 **[153]**, Barrington, IL
Vintage Chevrolet Club of Am., Packerland Region No. 4 **[18793]**, Manitowoc, WI
Vintage Chevrolet Club of Am., Viking Region No. 4 **[10579]**, Buffalo, MN
Vintage Chevrolet Club of Am., Wisconsin Region No. 4 **[19147]**, Milwaukee, WI
Vintage Thunderbird Club of Indiana **[4304]**, Brownsburg, IN
Vintage Triumphs of Wisconsin **[18187]**, Hartland, WI
Vinton County Chamber of Commerce **[15927]**, McArthur, OH
Vinton County Convention and Visitors Bur. **[15928]**, McArthur, OH
Violence
  Asian Women United of Minnesota **[12385]**, St. Paul, MN
  End Violent Encounters **[8566]**, Lansing, MI
  Help Against Violent Encounters Now **[9418]**, Pontiac, MI
  Turn Off the Violence **[11755]**, Minneapolis, MN
Violence; Citizens Against Domestic **[16007]**, Middletown, OH
Violence; Hoosiers Concerned about Gun **[5148]**, Indianapolis, IN
Violence; Indiana Coalition Against Domestic **[5213]**, Indianapolis, IN
Violence Task Force of Gibson County; Domestic **[6069]**, Princeton, IN
Violence; Turn Off the **[11755]**, Minneapolis, MN
Viper Owners; Motor City **[6988]**, Bloomfield Hills, MI
Virginia Area Historical Soc. **[12808]**, Virginia, MN
Virginia Chamber of Commerce **[★12795]**
Virginia Lake PTA **[2929]**, Palatine, IL
Virginia Lions Club **[12809]**, Virginia, MN
Virginia Mountain Iron Gilbert Area Chamber of Commerce **[★12795]**
Viroqua Lions Club **[19943]**, Viroqua, WI
VISIT Milwaukee **[19148]**, Milwaukee, WI
Visiting Nurse Assn. of Greater Youngstown **[17420]**, Youngstown, OH
Visiting Nurse Assn. Hea.Care and Partners of Ohio **[14234]**, Cleveland, OH
Visiting Nurse Assn. of Ohio **[★14234]**
Visiting Nurse Assn. of West Michigan **[8017]**, Grand Rapids, MI
Visiting Nurses Assn. **[3328]**, Rockford, IL
Visiting Nurses Assn. First **[4015]**, Willowbrook, IL

Visitor Bur., Charlotte Chicago, Illinois; Intl. Assn. of Convention and **[980]**, Chicago, IL
Visitor Burs., Kansas City - Palatine, Illinois; Intl. Assn. of Convention and **[2914]**, Palatine, IL
Visitor and Convention Bur; Clare County **[7154]**, Clare, MI
Visitor and Convention Bur; Wisconsin Dells **[20181]**, Wisconsin Dells, WI
Visitors Bur; Albert Lea Convention and **[10252]**, Albert Lea, MN
Visitors Bur; Alpena Area Convention and **[6639]**, Alpena, MI
Visitors Bur; Ann Arbor Area Convention and **[6669]**, Ann Arbor, MI
Visitors Bur; Bay Area Convention and **[6882]**, Bay City, MI
Visitors Bur; Bloomington Convention and **[4206]**, Bloomington, IN
Visitors Bur; Bloomington Convention and **[10465]**, Bloomington, MN
Visitors Bur; Boyne Country Convention and **[★9367]**
Visitors Bur; Cadillac Area **[7045]**, Cadillac, MI
Visitors Bur; Collinsville Convention and **[1288]**, Collinsville, IL
Visitors Bur; Decatur Area Convention and **[1382]**, Decatur, IL
Visitors Bur; Elgin Area Convention and **[1588]**, Elgin, IL
Visitors Bur; Evansville Convention and **[4546]**, Evansville, IN
Visitors Bur; Fairmont Convention and **[10978]**, Fairmont, MN
Visitors Bur; Fort Wayne/Allen County Convention and **[4651]**, Fort Wayne, IN
Visitors Bur; Galesburg Area Convention and **[1772]**, Galesburg, IL
Visitors Bureau; Grand Haven-Spring Lake Convention and **[7858]**, Grand Haven, MI
Visitors Bur; Grant County Convention and **[★5739]**
Visitors Bur; Greater Hamilton Convention and **[15385]**, Hamilton, OH
Visitors Bur; Greater Lafayette Convention and **[★5623]**
Visitors Bur; Greater Lansing Convention and **[8573]**, Lansing, MI
Visitors Bur; Greater Milwaukee Convention and **[★19148]**
Visitors Bur; Greater Monticello Chamber of Commerce and **[5823]**, Monticello, IN
Visitors Bur; Knox County Convention and **[16083]**, Mount Vernon, OH
Visitors Bur; Kosciusko County Convention and **[6446]**, Warsaw, IN
Visitors Bur; Lake Benton Area Chamber of Commerce and Convention and **[11270]**, Lake Benton, MN
Visitors Bur; Lake County Convention and **[4885]**, Hammond, IN
Visitors Bur; Lakeshore Convention and **[★9766]**
Visitors Bur; LaPorte County Convention and **[5785]**, Michigan City, IN
Visitors Bur; Lenawee County Conf. and **[6577]**, Adrian, MI
Visitors Bur; Livingston County **[★8280]**
Visitors Bur; Ludington Area Convention and **[8872]**, Ludington, MI
Visitors Bur; Marion-Grant County Convention and **[5739]**, Marion, IN
Visitors Bur; Marshall County Convention and **[6048]**, Plymouth, IN
Visitors Bur; Mecosta County Convention and **[6948]**, Big Rapids, MI
Visitors Bur; Medina County Convention and **[15946]**, Medina, OH
Visitors Bur; Middletown Convention and **[16014]**, Middletown, OH
Visitors Bur; Oak Park **[★2821]**
Visitor's Bur; Orange County Convention and **[4764]**, French Lick, IN
Visitor's Bureau; Perry County Convention and **[6298]**, Tell City, IN
Visitors Bur; Petoskey-Harbor Springs-Boyne Country **[9367]**, Petoskey, MI
Visitors Bur; Pickaway County **[14037]**, Circleville, OH
Visitors Bur; Rochester Convention and **[12176]**, Rochester, MN
Visitors Bur; Rockford Area Convention and **[3307]**, Rockford, IL
Visitors Bur; South Bend/Mishawaka Convention and **[6268]**, South Bend, IN
Visitors Bur; Vinton County Convention and **[15928]**, McArthur, OH
Visitors Bur; Washington County Convention and **[20129]**, West Bend, WI
Visitors Bur; West Branch-Ogemaw County Travel and **[10136]**, West Branch, MI
Visitors Bur; Western U.P. Convention and **[8343]**, Ironwood, MI
Visitors Bur; Windom Area Chamber of Commerce and **[12940]**, Windom, MN
Visitors Bureau; Wisconsin Rapids Area Convention and **[20197]**, Wisconsin Rapids, WI
Visitors Commission; Howard County Convention and **[5568]**, Kokomo, IN
Visitors and Convention Bur; Anderson/Madison County **[4100]**, Anderson, IN
Visitors and Convention Bureau; Bemidji **[10413]**, Bemidji, MN
Visitors and Convention Bur; Red Wing **[12084]**, Red Wing, MN
Visitors Council; Grayling Area **[8060]**, Grayling, MI
Visually Impaired
Amer. Coun. of the Blind of Indiana **[4978]**, Indianapolis, IN
Amer. Coun. of the Blind of Minnesota **[11487]**, Minneapolis, MN
Amer. Coun. of the Blind of Ohio **[14279]**, Columbus, OH
Amer. Coun. of the Blind of Ohio **[14280]**, Columbus, OH
Assn. for Educ. and Rehabilitation of the Blind and Visually Impaired, Wisconsin Chap. **[19909]**, Tomahawk, WI
Badger Assn. of the Blind and Visually Impaired **[18976]**, Milwaukee, WI
Cincinnati Assn. for the Blind and Visually Impaired **[13776]**, Cincinnati, OH
Illinois Assn. for Parents of Children with Visual Impairments **[3574]**, Springfield, IL
Illinois Coun. of the Blind **[3599]**, Springfield, IL
Illinois Parents of Blind Children **[954]**, Chicago, IL
Illinois Soc. for the Prevention of Blindness **[967]**, Chicago, IL
Indiana Parents of Blind Children **[5274]**, Indianapolis, IN
Michigan Coun. of the Blind and Visually Impaired **[9435]**, Port Huron, MI
Michigan Parents of Blind Children **[7102]**, Cedar, MI
Minnesota Parents of Blind Children **[11665]**, Minneapolis, MN
Natl. Fed. of the Blind, Greater Summit County **[13071]**, Akron, OH
Natl. Fed. of the Blind of Illinois **[2084]**, Jacksonville, IL
Natl. Fed. of the Blind of Michigan **[8742]**, Lansing, MI
Natl. Fed. of the Blind of Ohio **[16285]**, Oberlin, OH
Natl. Fed. of the Blind, Rock County Chap. **[18257]**, Janesville, WI
Natl. Fed. of the Blind of Wisconsin **[18258]**, Janesville, WI
Ohio Parents of Blind Children **[13324]**, Bellefontaine, OH
Ohio Parents of Children with Visual Impairments **[15954]**, Medina, OH
Prevent Blindness Am., Illinois Div. **[1143]**, Chicago, IL
Prevent Blindness Indiana **[5457]**, Indianapolis, IN
Prevent Blindness Ohio **[14711]**, Columbus, OH
Prevent Blindness Wisconsin **[19098]**, Milwaukee, WI
Share the Vision of Ohio **[14726]**, Columbus, OH
Wisconsin Parents of Blind Children **[17732]**, Cedarburg, WI
Viticulture - Eastern Sect; Amer. Soc. for Enology and **[6474]**, West Lafayette, IN
Vocational Assn; Ohio **[★14545]**
Vocational Education
Bus. Professionals of Am., Michigan Assn. **[10201]**, Ypsilanti, MI
Cincinnati Master Plumbers' Assn. **[13791]**, Cincinnati, OH
Illinois Assn. for Career and Tech. Educ. **[3565]**, Springfield, IL
Indiana Assn. of Private Career Schools **[5180]**, Indianapolis, IN
Michigan Chap. of Assn. for Career and Tech. Educ. **[10086]**, Waterford, MI
Minnesota Assn. for Career and Tech. Educ. **[12233]**, Roseville, MN
Natl. Tech. Honor Soc. - Alma High School - Michigan **[6634]**, Alma, MI
Natl. Tech. Honor Soc. - Calhoun Area Tech. Center Michigan **[6865]**, Battle Creek, MI
Natl. Tech. Honor Soc. - Career Quest Cmpt. Learning Center and Staffing Ser. - Michigan **[7561]**, East Lansing, MI
Natl. Tech. Honor Soc. - Career and Tech. Educ. Centers - Ohio **[16176]**, Newark, OH
Natl. Tech. Honor Soc. - Central Nine Career Center - Indiana **[4851]**, Greenwood, IN
Natl. Tech. Honor Soc. - CTEC Satellite Progs. - Ohio **[16177]**, Newark, OH
Natl. Tech. Honor Soc. - Diamond Oaks - Ohio **[13933]**, Cincinnati, OH
Natl. Tech. Honor Soc. - ITT Tech. Inst. - Canton Michigan **[7071]**, Canton, MI
Natl. Tech. Honor Soc. - ITT Tech. Inst. - Dayton Ohio **[14933]**, Dayton, OH
Natl. Tech. Honor Soc. - ITT Tech. Inst. - Grand Rapids - Michigan **[7993]**, Grand Rapids, MI
Natl. Tech. Honor Soc. - ITT Tech. Inst. - Indiana **[5435]**, Indianapolis, IN
Natl. Tech. Honor Soc. - Jackson Area Career Center - Michigan **[8391]**, Jackson, MI
Natl. Tech. Honor Soc. - John H. Hinds Career Center - Indiana **[4514]**, Elwood, IN
Natl. Tech. Honor Soc. - Mt. Pleasant Area Tech. Center Michigan **[9120]**, Mount Pleasant, MI
Natl. Tech. Honor Soc. - Mt. Vernon High School - Indiana **[4733]**, Fortville, IN
Natl. Tech. Honor Soc. - Northwest Career Center - Ohio **[15051]**, Dublin, OH
Natl. Tech. Honor Soc. - Oakland Schools Tech Campus Northeast - Michigan **[9421]**, Pontiac, MI
Natl. Tech. Honor Soc. - Oakland Schools Tech Campus Northwest - Michigan **[7164]**, Clarkston, MI
Natl. Tech. Honor Soc. - Oakland Schools Tech Campus Soutwest - Michigan **[10180]**, Wixom, MI
Natl. Tech. Honor Soc. - Ohio Valley and Tech. Center Ohio **[17198]**, West Union, OH
Natl. Tech. Honor Soc. - Pankow Vocational Tech. Center Michigan **[7185]**, Clinton Township, MI
Natl. Tech. Honor Soc. - Pickaway-Ross Career and Tech. Center - Ohio **[13669]**, Chillicothe, OH
Natl. Tech. Honor Soc. - The Career Center - Ohio **[15825]**, Marietta, OH
Natl. Tech. Honor Soc. - Tuscola Tech. Center - Michigan **[7085]**, Caro, MI
Natl. Tech. Honor Soc. - Vanguard-Sentinel Career Centers Ohio **[16856]**, Tiffin, OH
Natl. Tech. Honor Soc. - Vantage Career Center - Ohio **[17050]**, Van Wert, OH
Natl. Tech. Honor Soc. - Wisconsin Lutheran High School Wisconsin **[19083]**, Milwaukee, WI
Natl. Tech. Honor Soc. - Wright State Univ. Lake Campus Ohio **[13615]**, Celina, OH
Natl. Technological Honor Soc. - Batavia High School - Illinois **[185]**, Batavia, IL
Natl. Technological Honor Soc. - Bloomington Area Vocational Center - Illinois **[301]**, Bloomington, IL
Natl. Technological Honor Soc. - Capital Area Career Center Illinois **[3656]**, Springfield, IL
Natl. Technological Honor Soc. - East Aurora High School - Illinois **[125]**, Aurora, IL
Natl. Technological Honor Soc. - Elgin High School - Illinois **[1597]**, Elgin, IL
Natl. Technological Honor Soc. - Fox Valley Career Center Illinois **[2393]**, Maple Park, IL
Natl. Technological Honor Soc. - Geneva Community High School Illinois **[1799]**, Geneva, IL
Natl. Technological Honor Soc. - Illinois Central Coll. Illinois **[3039]**, Peoria, IL

Natl. Technological Honor Soc. - Joliet Junior Coll. - Illinois **[2116]**, Joliet, IL
Natl. Technological Honor Soc. - Kaneland High School - Illinois **[2394]**, Maple Park, IL
Natl. Technological Honor Soc. - Oswego High School - Illinois **[2892]**, Oswego, IL
Natl. Technological Honor Soc. - Paw Paw High School - Illinois **[2969]**, Paw Paw, IL
Natl. Technological Honor Soc. - Vatterrott Coll. - Quincy Illinois **[3156]**, Quincy, IL
Natl. Technological Honor Soc. - West Aurora High School - Illinois **[126]**, Aurora, IL
Natl. Technological Honor Soc. - West Leyden High School - Illinois **[2765]**, Northlake, IL
Natl. Vocational-Technical Honor Soc., Mahoning County Career and Tech. Center **[13537]**, Canfield, OH
Ohio Assn. for Career and Tech. Educ. **[14545]**, Columbus, OH
Ohio Valley Constr. Educ. Found. **[16705]**, Springboro, OH
Wisconsin Assn. for Career and Tech. Educ. **[18650]**, Madison, WI
Vocational-Technical Honor Soc., Mahoning County Career and Tech. Center; Natl. **[13537]**, Canfield, OH
Voice of the Retarded, Illinois **[2735]**, Normal, IL
Voice of the Retarded, Michigan **[8770]**, Lansing, MI
Voice of the Retarded, Minnesota **[11773]**, Minneapolis, MN
Voice of the Retarded, Ohio **[17447]**, Zanesville, OH
Voice of the Retarded, Wisconsin **[18178]**, Hartford, WI
Voices for Illinois Children **[1223]**, Chicago, IL
Volcanology
Natl. Tech. Honor Soc. - Auburn Career Center - Ohio **[16337]**, Painesville, OH
Natl. Tech. Honor Soc. - Remington Coll. - Cleveland Campus - Ohio **[14177]**, Cleveland, OH
Natl. Tech. Honor Soc. - Scioto County JVS - Ohio **[15737]**, Lucasville, OH
Volkssport Assn; Minnesota State **[★11682]**
Volleyball
North Country Region USA Volleyball **[10653]**, Chaska, MN
U.S.A. Volleyball Badger Region **[19145]**, Milwaukee, WI
U.S.A. Volleyball Great Lakes Region **[1471]**, Des Plaines, IL
U.S.A. Volleyball Hoosier Region **[4509]**, Elkhart, IN
U.S.A. Volleyball Ohio Valley Region **[15551]**, Kent, OH
Volleyball Badger Region; U.S.A. **[19145]**, Milwaukee, WI
Volleyball Great Lakes Region; U.S.A. **[1471]**, Des Plaines, IL
Volleyball; North Country Region USA **[10653]**, Chaska, MN
Volleyball Ohio Valley Region; U.S.A. **[15551]**, Kent, OH
Voluntarism
Adams County RSVP **[3145]**, Quincy, IL
Aitkin-Carlton County RSVP **[10685]**, Cloquet, MN
Amer. Soc. of Directors of Volunteer Ser. **[723]**, Chicago, IL
Anoka County RSVP **[10305]**, Anoka, MN
Arrowhead RSVP **[12793]**, Virginia, MN
Big Bros. Big Sisters for Milwaukee and Waukesha Counties **[18982]**, Milwaukee, WI
Bloomington Volunteer Network **[4210]**, Bloomington, IN
Bus. Volunteers Unlimited **[14085]**, Cleveland, OH
Champaign/Douglas/Piatt RSVP **[509]**, Champaign, IL
Cincinnati Area RSVP **[13775]**, Cincinnati, OH
Coles County RSVP **[568]**, Charleston, IL
Common Good RSVP **[12949]**, Winona, MN
Community Hea. Charities of Illinois **[854]**, Chicago, IL
Coulee Region RSVP **[18343]**, La Crosse, WI
Crawford/Perry/Spencer RSVP **[6296]**, Tell City, IN
Dearborn County RSVP **[5657]**, Lawrenceburg, IN
Decatur Area RSVP **[1383]**, Decatur, IL
Dubois/Pike and Warrick County RSVP **[5527]**, Jasper, IN
East Central Minnesota RSVP **[11832]**, Mora, MN
Eldercircle RSVP **[11083]**, Grand Rapids, MN
Elkhart County RSVP **[4494]**, Elkhart, IN
Gallia/Jackson/Vinton Counties RSVP **[15512]**, Jackson, OH
Global Citizens Network **[12418]**, St. Paul, MN
Greater Saint Cloud RSVP **[12286]**, St. Cloud, MN
Harcatus RSVP **[16150]**, New Philadelphia, OH
Indianapolis Ambassadors **[5338]**, Indianapolis, IN
Indianapolis RSVP **[5355]**, Indianapolis, IN
Kane/McHenry Counties RSVP **[2459]**, McHenry, IL
Kenosha County RSVP **[18301]**, Kenosha, WI
Kno Ho County RSVP **[16081]**, Mount Vernon, OH
Knox County RSVP **[6414]**, Vincennes, IN
Lake County RSVP **[3928]**, Waukegan, IL
Lorain County RSVP **[15120]**, Elyria, OH
Mahube RSVP **[10778]**, Detroit Lakes, MN
Marion and Crawford Counties RSVP **[15844]**, Marion, OH
Marquette County RSVP **[8945]**, Marquette, MI
McLean County RSVP **[2723]**, Normal, IL
Meigs RSVP **[16456]**, Pomeroy, OH
Miami Valley RSVP **[15363]**, Greenville, OH
Milwaukee RSVP **[19067]**, Milwaukee, WI
Minnesota Assn. for Volunteer Admin. **[11420]**, Maplewood, MN
Montgomery/Greene Counties RSVP **[14925]**, Dayton, OH
Northeastern Wisconsin RSVP **[19600]**, Rhinelander, WI
Northwest RSVP **[17545]**, Ashland, WI
Oakland County RSVP **[9815]**, Southfield, MI
Perry County RSVP **[16135]**, New Lexington, OH
Points of Light Found. - Volunteer Center of Door County **[19843]**, Sturgeon Bay, WI
Points of Light Found. - Volunteer Center of East Central Wisconsin **[17516]**, Appleton, WI
Points of Light Found. - Volunteer Center of Fond du Lac County **[17991]**, Fond du Lac, WI
Points of Light Found. - Volunteer Center Of Greater Kalamazoo **[8461]**, Kalamazoo, MI
Points of Light Found. - Volunteer Center of South Wood County **[20190]**, Wisconsin Rapids, WI
Points of Light Found. - Volunteer Center of Waukesha County **[19442]**, Pewaukee, WI
Points of Light Found. - Volunteer Rsrc. Center **[11725]**, Minneapolis, MN
Portage County RSVP **[19804]**, Stevens Point, WI
Retired and Senior Volunteer Prog. of Peoria and Tazewell Counties **[3062]**, Peoria, IL
Retired and Senior Volunteer Prog. of Racine **[19572]**, Racine, WI
Retired and Senior Volunteer Prog. of Rock County **[17616]**, Beloit, WI
Retired and Senior Volunteer Prog. of South Central Minnesota **[11398]**, Mankato, MN
Retired and Senior Volunteer Prog. of Waukesha County **[19998]**, Waukesha, WI
RSVP Akron **[13085]**, Akron, OH
RSVP of Ashtabula County **[15547]**, Kent, OH
RSVP-Athens/Hockings County **[13217]**, Athens, OH
RSVP of Bay County **[6894]**, Bay City, MI
RSVP of Belmont County **[16573]**, St. Clairsville, OH
RSVP of Brown County **[18129]**, Green Bay, WI
RSVP Champaign, Douglas, Piatt Counties **[553]**, Champaign, IL
RSVP of Clark County, Ohio **[16742]**, Springfield, OH
RSVP Clay/Effingham/Moultrie/Shelby **[1573]**, Effingham, IL
RSVP Cleveland **[14212]**, Cleveland, OH
RSVP of Columbiana County **[15681]**, Lisbon, OH
RSVP of Crawford and Roscommon Counties **[6650]**, Alpena, MI
RSVP of Dane County **[18609]**, Madison, WI
RSVP of Daviess County Indiana **[6460]**, Washington, IN
RSVP of Dekalb/Noble/Steuben Counties **[4143]**, Auburn, IN
RSVP of Delaware County **[5897]**, Muncie, IN
RSVP Franklin County **[14723]**, Columbus, OH
RSVP of Fulton County **[6126]**, Rochester, IN
RSVP of Genesee and Shiawassee Counties **[7756]**, Flint, MI
RSVP of Hancock, Henry, and Rush **[5940]**, New Castle, IN
RSVP of Hull House Chicago **[1171]**, Chicago, IL
RSVP-Ingham/Eaton/Clinton County **[8756]**, Lansing, MI
RSVP of Iron and Dickinson Counties **[8324]**, Iron Mountain, MI
RSVP of Jackson County **[8396]**, Jackson, MI
RSVP of Jefferson County **[5720]**, Madison, IN
RSVP of Joliet Area **[2119]**, Joliet, IL
RSVP Kalamazoo County **[8464]**, Kalamazoo, MI
RSVP of Laporte/Starke Counties **[5792]**, Michigan City, IN
RSVP of Macomb **[7187]**, Clinton Township, MI
RSVP of Mahoning and Southern Trumbull Counties **[17413]**, Youngstown, OH
RSVP Mecosta/Lake/Osceola **[6951]**, Big Rapids, MI
RSVP Menominee/Delta/Schoolcraft **[7618]**, Escanaba, MI
RSVP Monroe County **[9911]**, Temperance, MI
RSVP of Monroe and Owen Counties **[4254]**, Bloomington, IN
RSVP of Northern Cook and Northern Dupage Counties **[82]**, Arlington Heights, IL
RSVP Northwest Illinois **[1753]**, Freeport, IL
RSVP of Northwest Michigan **[9950]**, Traverse City, MI
RSVP of Northwestern Ohio **[16957]**, Toledo, OH
RSVP of Otsego County **[7823]**, Gaylord, MI
RSVP Outagamie County **[17522]**, Appleton, WI
RSVP of the Pennisula **[2146]**, Karnak, IL
RSVP of Portage County **[15548]**, Kent, OH
RSVP of Red River Valley **[10738]**, Crookston, MN
RSVP Richland County **[15793]**, Mansfield, OH
RSVP of Saint Clair County **[1552]**, East St. Louis, IL
RSVP of Saint Joseph County **[6258]**, South Bend, IN
RSVP of Sangamon, Menard and Logan Counties **[3670]**, Springfield, IL
RSVP of Scioto County **[16474]**, Portsmouth, OH
RSVP of Scott IA and Rock Island IL **[3258]**, Rock Island, IL
RSVP of Southwest Minnesota **[12992]**, Worthington, MN
RSVP of Stark County **[13580]**, Canton, OH
RSVP Todd/Wadena/Otter Tail/Wilkin **[11891]**, New York Mills, MN
RSVP Volunteer Resources of Madison County **[4119]**, Anderson, IN
RSVP Volunteer Sers. **[10519]**, Brainerd, MN
RSVP Volunteers United **[11947]**, Ortonville, MN
RSVP of Washtenaw County **[6761]**, Ann Arbor, MI
RSVP Wayne County **[7426]**, Detroit, MI
RSVP Western Egyptian EOC **[3700]**, Steeleville, IL
RSVP of Winnebago/Boone Counties **[3316]**, Rockford, IL
RSVP of Woodford, Marshall, and Livingston Counties **[1645]**, Eureka, IL
Semcac RSVP **[12258]**, Rushford, MN
South Central Indiana RSVP **[5926]**, New Albany, IN
Southern Tri-County RSVP **[10265]**, Albert Lea, MN
Southwestern Illinois RSVP **[212]**, Belleville, IL
Superior/Douglas RSVP **[19880]**, Superior, WI
SW Suburban RSVP **[13436]**, Brook Park, OH
Thumb Area RSVP **[7086]**, Caro, MI
Valparaiso RSVP **[6395]**, Valparaiso, IN
Vanderburgh County RSVP **[4589]**, Evansville, IN
Volunteer Muskegon RSVP **[9166]**, Muskegon, MI
Walworth County RSVP **[20163]**, Whitewater, WI
Warren County Retired and Senior Volunteer Prog. **[15627]**, Lebanon, OH
Washington County RSVP **[15832]**, Marietta, OH
Wayne County RSVP **[6111]**, Richmond, IN
West Central Illinois RSVP **[467]**, Carthage, IL
West Central Minnesota RSVP **[10939]**, Elbow Lake, MN
West Suburban Cook and Southern Du Page County RSVP **[3208]**, River Grove, IL

Western Dairyland RSVP [17907], Eau Claire, WI
Western Upper Peninsula RSVP [8112], Hancock, MI
WICAA RSVP in Clay/Putnam and Vigo Counties [6353], Terre Haute, IN
Voluntary Hea. Agencies in Illinois; Natl. [★854]
Volunteer Bur. of Barrington [★144]
Volunteer Caregivers of Portage County; Interfaith [19791], Stevens Point, WI
Volunteer Fire Department; Benton Township of Monroe County [6367], Unionville, IN
Volunteer Fire Dept; Prairie Township [15463], Holmesville, OH
Volunteer Firefighters Association; Marseilles [2422], Marseilles, IL
Volunteer Guardianship Prog. of Lorain County [15128], Elyria, OH
Volunteer Impact [10125], West Bloomfield, MI
Volunteer Muskegon RSVP [9166], Muskegon, MI
Volunteer Network; Bloomington [4210], Bloomington, IN
Volunteer Resources of Madison County; RSVP [4119], Anderson, IN
Volunteer Sers. of Bartholomew County [★4399]
Volunteer Sers./Info. and Referral [★4399]
Volunteers of Am. of Central Ohio [14760], Columbus, OH
Volunteers of Am. of Illinois [1224], Chicago, IL
Volunteers of Am. of Indiana [5496], Indianapolis, IN
Volunteers of Am. Michigan [9830], Southfield, MI
Volunteers of Am.-Minnesota [11066], Golden Valley, MN
Volunteers of Am. of Minnesota [11774], Minneapolis, MN
Volunteers of Am. of Northeast and North Central Ohio [14235], Cleveland, OH
Volunteers of Am. Ohio River Valley [14023], Cincinnati, OH
Volunteers of Am. of Wisconsin [17679], Brookfield, WI
Voters of the Cleveland Area; League of Women [14155], Cleveland, OH
Voters of the Greater Dayton Area; League of Women [14904], Dayton, OH
Voters of Illinois Education Fund; League of Women [★1026]
Voters of Illinois; League of Women [1026], Chicago, IL
Voters of the Lansing Area; League of Women [8596], Lansing, MI
Voyageurs Natl. Park Assn. [11775], Minneapolis, MN
Voyageurs National Park; Friends of [11215], International Falls, MN
VSA Arts of Michigan [7452], Detroit, MI
VSA Arts of Ohio/Cleveland Area Ser. Div. [14236], Cleveland, OH
VSA arts of Indiana [5497], Indianapolis, IN
VSA arts of Minnesota [11776], Minneapolis, MN
VSA arts of Wisconsin [18637], Madison, WI

W

W. North - Young Life [14761], Columbus, OH
W. South - Young Life [14762], Columbus, OH
Wabash Area Chamber of Commerce [6426], Wabash, IN
Wabash County Bd. of Realtors [6427], Wabash, IN
Wabash County Chamber of Commerce [2575], Mount Carmel, IL
Wabash Marketplace [6428], Wabash, IN
Wabash Regional Planning Commn; Greater [15], Albion, IL
Wabash River Dental Soc. [3413], Salem, IL
Wabash Valley Angus Assn. [3743], Sumner, IL
Wabash Valley Antique Glass and Pottery Club [4593], Farmersburg, IN
Wabash Valley Astronomical Soc. [6503], West Lafayette, IN
Wabash Valley Audubon Soc. [6349], Terre Haute, IN
Wabash Valley Coin Club [6350], Terre Haute, IN
Wabash Valley Gem and Mineral Soc. [4456], Delphi, IN
Wabash Valley REACT [6351], Terre Haute, IN
Wabash Valley Rsrc. Conservation and Development Coun. [2227], Lawrenceville, IL
Wabash Valley Youth for Christ [6352], Terre Haute, IN
Wabash Wanderers [5637], Lafayette, IN
Wabasha-Kellogg Area Chamber of Commerce [12812], Wabasha, MN
Wabasha-Kellogg Area Chamber/CVB [12813], Wabasha, MN
Wabasha River Walkers [★12813]
WACHA - The Premier Payments Rsrc. [18044], Germantown, WI
Waconia Area Chamber of Commerce [12819], Waconia, MN
Wacousta Lions Club [7469], DeWitt, MI
Wadsworth Area Chamber of Commerce [17079], Wadsworth, OH
Wadsworth School PTA [4861], Griffith, IN
Wadsworth - Young Life [17080], Wadsworth, OH
Wagon Wheel Figure Skating Club [154], Barrington, IL
Wakarusa Chamber of Commerce [6431], Wakarusa, IN
Wakeman Lions Club [17083], Wakeman, OH
Walk and Roll Chicago - Amer. Cancer Soc. [1225], Chicago, IL
Walkabout Theater Company [1226], Chicago, IL
Walkacross America for Mother Earth/Ohio Peace March [★14411]
Walkerton Area Chamber of Commerce [6437], Walkerton, IN
Walkerton Chamber of Commerce [★6437]
Walking
Amer. Volkssport Assn., Mid-Am. Region [13740], Cincinnati, OH
Amer. Volkssport Assn., North Central Region [18903], Middleton, WI
Cuyahoga Valley Spaziergangers [14822], Cuyahoga Falls, OH
Germania Volksmarch Gruppe [13834], Cincinnati, OH
Hearty Sole Walkers [17983], Fond du Lac, WI
Illinois Trekkers Volkssport Club [3457], Scott AFB, IL
Illinois Volkssport Assn. [530], Champaign, IL
Manitowoc City Centre Assn. [18782], Manitowoc, WI
Michigan Pathfinders [9868], Sterling Heights, MI
Ohio Volkssport Assn. [15133], Englewood, OH
Pelican Rapids CC Walking Club [11987], Pelican Rapids, MN
Stillwater Leisure Sport Assn. [17006], Troy, OH
Three Rivers Strollers [4725], Fort Wayne, IN
Trail Trolls [15134], Englewood, OH
Zeeland Volk's Corp. [10233], Zeeland, MI
Walled Lake Chamber of Commerce [★10056]
Wally Byam Caravan Club Intl., Region 7 [20180], Wisconsin Dells, WI
Walnut Chamber of Commerce [3875], Walnut, IL
Walnut Coun. [6504], West Lafayette, IN
Walt Durbahn Tool Museum [★1990]
Walworth County Genealogical Soc. [17830], Delavan, WI
Walworth County Land Conservancy [17931], Elkhorn, WI
Walworth County RSVP [20163], Whitewater, WI
Wandering Wheels Volkssports Club [6110], Richmond, IN
Wannaska Lions Club [12212], Roseau, MN
Wapakoneta Area Chamber of Commerce [17094], Wapakoneta, OH
Warder Literacy Center [★16725]
Warehouse District Bus. Assn. [11777], Minneapolis, MN
Warren Area Miniature Club [17116], Warren, OH
Warren Area Stamp Club [17117], Warren, OH
Warren Arts and Educ. Found. [5498], Indianapolis, IN
Warren Astronomical Soc. [10074], Warren, MI
Warren - Center Line - Sterling Heights Chamber of Commerce [★10068]
Warren County Community Found. [6529], Williamsport, IN
Warren County Convention and Visitors Bur. [15624], Lebanon, OH
Warren County Historical Soc. [15625], Lebanon, OH
Warren County Kennel Club of Ohio [15626], Lebanon, OH
Warren County Local Economic Development Org. [6530], Williamsport, IN
Warren County Retired and Senior Volunteer Prog. [15627], Lebanon, OH
Warren County United Way, Illinois [2543], Monmouth, IL
Warren County United Way, Ohio [15628], Lebanon, OH
Warren Jaycees [10075], Warren, MI
Warren Lions Club - Minnesota [12842], Warren, MN
Warren Lions Club - Ohio [17118], Warren, OH
Warren, OH 9to5 [17119], Warren, OH
Warren Striders Track Club [17120], Warren, OH
Warren - Trumbull Urban League [17121], Warren, OH
Warren West Resident Coun. [7453], Detroit, MI
Warrens Lions Club [19948], Warrens, WI
Warrensville Heights Coin Club [16685], Solon, OH
Warrensville Heights Reserve Police Color Guard [13639], Chagrin Falls, OH
Warrenville Firemen [3880], Warrenville, IL
Warrick County Chamber of Commerce [4276], Boonville, IN
Warroad Lions Club [12845], Warroad, MN
Warsaw Astronomical Soc. [6541], Winona Lake, IN
Warsaw - Kosciusko County Chamber of Commerce [6455], Warsaw, IN
Waseca Area Chamber of Commerce [12847], Waseca, MN
Waseca Area United Way [12848], Waseca, MN
Waseca County Chap., Amer. Red Cross [12849], Waseca, MN
Waseca Sleigh and Cutter Festival Assn. [12850], Waseca, MN
Washburn Area Chamber of Commerce [19951], Washburn, WI
Washington - Central Illinois - Young Life [3892], Washington, IL
Washington Chamber of Commerce [3893], Washington, IL
Washington County Convention and Visitors Bur. [20129], West Bend, WI
Washington County Historical Soc. [12730], Stillwater, MN
Washington County (Ohio) Habitat for Humanity [15831], Marietta, OH
Washington County RSVP [15832], Marietta, OH
Washington Island Chamber of Commerce [19953], Washington Island, WI
Washtenaw Bicycling and Walking Coalition [6782], Ann Arbor, MI
Washtenaw Contractors Assn. [6783], Ann Arbor, MI
Washtenaw County Bar Assn. [6784], Ann Arbor, MI
Washtenaw County Coalition on Gender Violence and Safety [6785], Ann Arbor, MI
Washtenaw County Historical Soc. [6786], Ann Arbor, MI
Washtenaw County Medical Soc. [6787], Ann Arbor, MI
Washtenaw County Pheasants Forever [6788], Ann Arbor, MI
Washtenaw District Dental Soc. [6789], Ann Arbor, MI
Washtenaw Historical Soc. [★6786]
Washtenaw Literacy [10218], Ypsilanti, MI
Washtenaw Sierra Club Inner City Outings [6790], Ann Arbor, MI
Washtenaw United Way [6791], Ann Arbor, MI
Waste
Illinois Assn. of Wastewater Agencies [3583], Springfield, IL
Illinois Recycling Assn. [2815], Oak Park, IL
Indiana Recycling Coalition [4229], Bloomington, IN
Metropolitan Sewer District of Greater Cincinnati [13899], Cincinnati, OH
Michigan Recycling Coalition [8703], Lansing, MI
Solid Waste Assn. of North Am., Illinois Land of Lincoln Chap. [1841], Glen Ellyn, IL
Solid Waste Assn. of North Am., Minnesota Land of Lakes Chap. [11425], Maplewood, MN
Solid Waste Assn. of North Am., Ohio Buckeye Chap. [13997], Cincinnati, OH
Solid Waste Assn. of North Am., Wisconsin Badger Chap. [18134], Green Bay, WI
Wisconsin Liquid Waste Carriers Assn. [18722], Madison, WI

Wisconsin Onsite Waste Disposal Assn. **[18179]**, Hartford, WI
Wisconsin Waste Fac. Siting Bd. **[18762]**, Madison, WI
Wastenaws Atari Users Gp. **[★6792]**
Wastewater Assn; Ohio Onsite **[15757]**, Manchester, OH
Water
Clean Water Action of Clinton Township **[7174]**, Clinton Township, MI
Friends of the St. Joe River Assn. **[6800]**, Athens, MI
Illinois Assn. of Groundwater Professionals **[3202]**, River Forest, IL
Illinois Groundwater Assn. **[2369]**, Macomb, IL
Indiana Ground Water Assn. **[5242]**, Indianapolis, IN
Michigan Ground Water Assn. **[8909]**, Manchester, MI
Minnesota Rural Water Assn. **[10938]**, Elbow Lake, MN
Minnesota Water Well Assn. **[12531]**, St. Paul, MN
Ohio Onsite Wastewater Assn. **[15757]**, Manchester, OH
Ohio Water Well Assn. **[15398]**, Hamilton, OH
Sandhill Water and Sewer Assn. **[15830]**, Marietta, OH
Sweetwater Alliance **[10856]**, Duluth, MN
Wisconsin Rural Water Assn. **[19485]**, Plover, WI
Water Conservation
Clean Water Action of Michigan **[7919]**, Grand Rapids, MI
Fox-Wolf Watershed Alliance **[17494]**, Appleton, WI
Friends of the Mississippi River **[12414]**, St. Paul, MN
Friends of the White River **[5120]**, Indianapolis, IN
Huff Run Watershed Restoration Partnership **[16043]**, Mineral City, OH
Michigan Lake and Stream Associations **[9916]**, Three Rivers, MI
Portage River Basin Council **[16951]**, Toledo, OH
St. Louis River Citizens Action Comm. **[10852]**, Duluth, MN
Wawasee Area Conservancy Found. **[6294]**, Syracuse, IN
Water Resources
Amer. Water Resources Assn., Michigan State Sect. **[8547]**, Lansing, MI
Amer. Water Rsrcs. Assn. - UWSP Student Chap. **[19782]**, Stevens Point, WI
Amer. Water Rsrcs. Assn., Wisconsin Sect. **[18904]**, Middleton, WI
Amer. Water Resources Assn. Wisconsin State Sect. **[19783]**, Stevens Point, WI
Chagrin River Watershed Partners **[17272]**, Willoughby, OH
Freshwater Soc. **[10970]**, Excelsior, MN
Friends of the Kettle Ponds **[18906]**, Middleton, WI
Heartland Water Rsrcs. Coun. **[3027]**, Peoria, IL
Huron River Watershed Coun. **[6707]**, Ann Arbor, MI
Indiana Water Resources Assn. **[5334]**, Indianapolis, IN
Inland Sea Soc. **[19950]**, Washburn, WI
Lower Kaskaskia Stakeholders, Inc. **[3185]**, Red Bud, IL
Michigan Rural Water Assn. **[8129]**, Harrison, MI
Mississippi Corridor Neighborhood Coalition **[11685]**, Minneapolis, MN
Ohio and Erie Canalway Coalition **[13076]**, Akron, OH
Ohio River Valley Water Sanitation Commn. **[13943]**, Cincinnati, OH
Trout Unlimited - Challenge Chap. **[9342]**, Oxford, MI
Upper Sugar River Watershed Assn. **[19244]**, Mount Horeb, WI
Vadnais Lake Area Water Mgt. Org. **[12904]**, White Bear Lake, MN
Water Rsrcs. Assn., Wisconsin Sect; Amer. **[18904]**, Middleton, WI
Water Wonderland Bd. of Realtors **[7825]**, Gaylord, MI
Water Wonderland Thunderbirds **[6616]**, Allen Park, MI
Waterford Area Chamber of Commerce **[19956]**, Waterford, WI
Waterford Lions Club - Wisconsin **[19957]**, Waterford, WI
Waterford Township Historical Soc. **[10096]**, Waterford, MI
Waterfowl Assn; Wisconsin **[18189]**, Hartland, WI
Waterfowlers Assn; Wisconsin **[★18189]**
Waterloo Chamber of Commerce **[3903]**, Waterloo, IL
Waterloo Chamber of Commerce **[19961]**, Waterloo, WI
Waterloo Lions Club **[3904]**, Waterloo, IL
Waterman Lions Club **[3906]**, Waterman, IL
Watershed Assn; Upper Sugar River **[19244]**, Mount Horeb, WI
Watershed Coun; Mill Creek **[13907]**, Cincinnati, OH
Watershed Flow; Friends of the Lower Olentangy **[★14439]**
Watershed; Friends of the Lower Olentangy **[14439]**, Columbus, OH
Watershed Network; Salt Creek **[354]**, Brookfield, IL
Watershed Partnership; Central Lake Superior **[8934]**, Marquette, MI
Watershed Restoration Partnership; Huff Run **[16043]**, Mineral City, OH
Watertown Area Chamber of Commerce **[19971]**, Watertown, WI
Watertown Historical Soc. **[19972]**, Watertown, WI
Watertown Lions Club - Minnesota **[12853]**, Watertown, MN
Waterville Area Chamber of Commerce **[17136]**, Waterville, OH
Watonwan County Humane Soc. **[12323]**, St. James, MN
Watrousville-Caro Area Historical Soc. **[7087]**, Caro, MI
Watseka Area Chamber of Commerce **[3911]**, Watseka, IL
Watson Lions Club **[12855]**, Watson, MN
Waubonsie Valley Young Life **[2663]**, Naperville, IL
Wauconda Chamber of Commerce **[3916]**, Wauconda, IL
WAUG **[6792]**, Ann Arbor, MI
Waukegan Chamber of Commerce **[★1921]**
Waukegan/Lake County **[★1921]**
Waukegan Main St. **[3932]**, Waukegan, IL
Waukegan-North Chicago Area Chamber of Commerce **[★1921]**
Waukegan-North Chicago Chamber of Commerce **[★1921]**
Waukesha Area Chamber of Commerce **[★20003]**
Waukesha Area REACT **[20001]**, Waukesha, WI
Waukesha Coin Club **[20002]**, Waukesha, WI
Waukesha County Chamber of Commerce **[20003]**, Waukesha, WI
Waukesha County Fair Assn. **[19445]**, Pewaukee, WI
Waukesha County Historical Soc. **[20004]**, Waukesha, WI
Waukesha County Medical Soc. **[19446]**, Pewaukee, WI
Waukesha County Philatelic Soc. **[20005]**, Waukesha, WI
Waukesha District Nurses Assn. - No. 16 **[19346]**, Oconomowoc, WI
Waukesha Gun Club **[20006]**, Waukesha, WI
Waukesha Kennel Club **[17680]**, Brookfield, WI
Waukesha Noon Lions Club **[20007]**, Waukesha, WI
Waunakee Area Chamber of Commerce **[★20019]**
Waunakee/Westport Chamber of Commerce **[20019]**, Waunakee, WI
Waupaca Area Assn. of Commerce **[★20023]**
Waupaca Area Chamber of Commerce **[20023]**, Waupaca, WI
Waupaca Conservation League **[20024]**, Waupaca, WI
Waupaca Curling Club **[20025]**, Waupaca, WI
Waupaca Historical Society **[20026]**, Waupaca, WI
Waupun Area Chamber of Commerce **[20028]**, Waupun, WI
Waupun Figure Skating Club **[20029]**, Waupun, WI
Wausau Area Apartment Assn. **[20053]**, Wausau, WI
Wausau Curling Club **[20054]**, Wausau, WI
Wausau/Marathon County Chamber of Commerce **[20055]**, Wausau, WI
Wausau Skeet and Trap Club **[20056]**, Wausau, WI
Wausau Table Tennis Club **[20057]**, Wausau, WI
Wausaukee Area Bus. Assn. **[20062]**, Wausaukee, WI
Wauseon Chamber of Commerce **[17143]**, Wauseon, OH
Wauseon Commerce Club **[★17143]**
Waushara Area Chamber of Commerce **[20065]**, Wautoma, WI
Wauwatosa Curling Club **[20081]**, Wauwatosa, WI
Wauwatosa Lions Club **[20082]**, Wauwatosa, WI
Wauwatosa Neighborhood Watch Steering Comm. **[20083]**, Wauwatosa, WI
Wauwatosa West PTA **[20084]**, Wauwatosa, WI
Wauwatosa Woman's Club **[20085]**, Wauwatosa, WI
Wauzeka Lions Club **[20092]**, Wauzeka, WI
Waverly Lawn Bowling Club **[17148]**, Waverly, OH
Wawasee Area Conservancy Found. **[6294]**, Syracuse, IN
Wayne Area Human Rsrcs. Assn. **[17329]**, Wooster, OH
Wayne Chamber of Commerce **[10102]**, Wayne, MI
Wayne County Coun. for Arts, History, and Humanities **[8085]**, Grosse Pointe, MI
Wayne County Genealogical Soc. **[17331]**, Wooster, OH
Wayne County Genealogical Soc. **[17330]**, Wooster, OH
Wayne County Girl Scouts **[★6091]**
Wayne County Historical Soc. **[17332]**, Wooster, OH
Wayne County Medical Soc. of Southeast Michigan **[7454]**, Detroit, MI
Wayne County RSVP **[6111]**, Richmond, IN
Wayne County Sportsman's Club **[10103]**, Wayne, MI
Wayne County Veterans Memorial Committee **[6112]**, Richmond, IN
Wayne-Fall Lions Club **[5981]**, Noblesville, IN
Wayne-Holmes Assn. of Realtors **[17333]**, Wooster, OH
Wayne Lions Club **[10104]**, Wayne, MI
Wayne Oakland Region of Interlibrary Cooperation **[9831]**, Southfield, MI
Wayne-Westland Alliance for the Mentally Ill **[7278]**, Dearborn, MI
Waynesville Area Chamber of Commerce **[17152]**, Waynesville, OH
Waynesville Historical Preservation Bd. **[17153]**, Waynesville, OH
Waynesville Lions Club **[17154]**, Waynesville, OH
Waynesville - Young Life **[14969]**, Dayton, OH
Wayzata Lions Club **[12863]**, Wayzata, MN
We Are Traverse City **[9964]**, Traverse City, MI
We Can Make a Difference **[6924]**, Benton Harbor, MI
Wealthwood Rod and Gun Club **[10247]**, Aitkin, MN
Webberville Lions Club **[10106]**, Webberville, MI
Webster Area Chamber of Commerce **[20096]**, Webster, WI
Webster Musky Club **[6001]**, North Webster, IN
Wedgwood - Other **[8018]**, Grand Rapids, MI
Wee 'c' Mini Club **[3131]**, Prairie Grove, IL
Wehr Astronomical Soc. **[18013]**, Franklin, WI
Weidman Lions Club **[10109]**, Weidman, MI
Weightlifting
Columbus Weightlifting Club **[14406]**, Columbus, OH
Midwest Weightlifting **[4435]**, Crown Point, IN
USA Weightlifting - Amer. Coll. of Modern Weightlifting **[16845]**, Tallmadge, OH
USA Weightlifting - Armstrong Falcons **[12041]**, Plymouth, MN
USA Weightlifting - Atomic Athletic Club **[8285]**, Howell, MI
USA Weightlifting - Aurora Weightlifting Club **[134]**, Aurora, IL
USA Weightlifting - Charleston **[573]**, Charleston, IL
USA Weightlifting - Cougars **[7568]**, East Lansing, MI
USA Weightlifting - Dearborn **[14020]**, Cincinnati, OH
USA Weightlifting - Dynamic Fitness **[8859]**, Livonia, MI
USA Weightlifting - Farmington **[10992]**, Farmington, MN
USA Weightlifting - Fox Valley **[135]**, Aurora, IL
USA Weightlifting - Glencoe **[11049]**, Glencoe, MN

USA Weightlifting - Husky Power Training [9455], Portage, MI
USA Weightlifting - Lakeville [11297], Lakeville, MN
USA Weightlifting - Lynch's Gym [6274], South Bend, IN
USA Weightlifting - Northfield [11920], Northfield, MN
USA Weightlifting - Olympic Hea. Club [14231], Cleveland, OH
USA Weightlifting - Power Sports Athletic Center [17833], Denmark, WI
USA Weightlifting - Power X-Treme [9343], Oxford, MI
USA Weightlifting - Ramsey Ridge Lifters [1410], Decatur, IL
USA Weightlifting - Red Wing [12091], Red Wing, MN
USA Weightlifting - Rosemount Weightlifting Club [10612], Burnsville, MN
USA Weightlifting - Sayre Park [1220], Chicago, IL
USA Weightlifting - Team Body Club [574], Charleston, IL
USA Weightlifting - Team Cannon Weightlifting [10634], Cannon Falls, MN
USA Weightlifting - Team Janz [17906], Eau Claire, WI
USA Weightlifting - Team Pendragon [14792], Cortland, OH
USA Weightlifting - Team Velocity Willowbrook [4014], Willowbrook, IL
USA Weightlifting - Toledo [16981], Toledo, OH
USA Weightlifting - Town and Country Lifting Club [19345], Oconomowoc, WI
USA Weightlifting - Twin City Barbell [12249], Roseville, MN
USA Weightlifting - West Park YMCA [14232], Cleveland, OH
USA Weightlifting - Windy City [2269], Libertyville, IL
Weightlifting Club; Columbus [14406], Columbus, OH
Weightlifting; Midwest [4435], Crown Point, IN
Weimaraner Club of Columbus [15372], Grove City, OH

Weimaraners
Greater Cincinnati Weimaraner Club [13857], Cincinnati, OH
Northstar Weimaraner Club [11224], Inver Grove Heights, MN

Welding
Amer. Welding Soc., Arrowhead [12792], Virginia, MN
Amer. Welding Soc., Blackhawk Sect. 113 [3270], Rockford, IL
Amer. Welding Soc., Central Michigan [7506], East Lansing, MI
Amer. Welding Soc., Chicago Sect. [4188], Beverly Shores, IN
Amer. Welding Soc., Chicago Sect. 002 [2311], Lockport, IL
Amer. Welding Soc., Cleveland Sect. 006 [14069], Cleveland, OH
Amer. Welding Soc., Columbus Sect. 036 [14313], Columbus, OH
Amer. Welding Soc., Dayton [17166], West Carrollton, OH
Amer. Welding Soc., Detroit Sect. 011 [9863], Sterling Heights, MI
Amer. Welding Soc., Fox Valley Sect. [17485], Appleton, WI
Amer. Welding Soc., J.A.K. Sect. [2130], Kankakee, IL
Amer. Welding Soc., Johnny Appleseed Sect. 191 [17048], Van Wert, OH
Amer. Welding Soc., Milwaukee Sect. [18009], Franklin, WI
Amer. Welding Soc., Mississippi Valley Sect. 194 [3148], Quincy, IL
Amer. Welding Soc., Northern Michigan Sect. 158 [7700], Fife Lake, MI
Amer. Welding Soc., Northwest Ohio Sect. 046 [15349], Graytown, OH
Amer. Welding Soc., Racine Kenosha Sect. 132 [18296], Kenosha, WI
Amer. Welding Soc., Sangamon Valley Sect. 070 [2273], Lincoln, IL
Amer. Welding Soc., Stark Central Sect. 085 [15409], Hartville, OH
Amer. Welding Soc., Tri-River Sect. 107 [4528], Evansville, IN
Amer. Welding Soc., Western Michigan [7854], Grand Haven, MI
Amer. Welding Soc., Whitmer Career and Tech. Center [16898], Toledo, OH
Welding Soc., Central Michigan; Amer. [7506], East Lansing, MI
Welding Soc., Chicago Sect; Amer. [4188], Beverly Shores, IN
Welding Soc., Dayton; Amer. [17166], West Carrollton, OH
Welding Soc., J.A.K. Sect; Amer. [2130], Kankakee, IL
Welding Soc., Western Michigan; Amer. [7854], Grand Haven, MI
Wellington Area Chamber of Commerce [17157], Wellington, OH
Wellington Education Association [17158], Wellington, OH
Wellness Coun. of Indiana [5779], Merrillville, IN
Wellness Coun. of Northwest Indiana [★5779]
Wellness Found; Austin-Bailey Hea. and [13548], Canton, OH
Wells Area Chamber of Commerce [12869], Wells, MN
Wells County Chamber of Commerce [4271], Bluffton, IN
Wellsville Lions Club [17162], Wellsville, OH
Wendell Lions Club [12871], Wendell, MN
WesMin Rsrc. Conservation and Development Coun. [10287], Alexandria, MN
West Alexandria Lions Club [17165], West Alexandria, OH
West Allis Chamber of Commerce [★20106]
West Allis/West Milwaukee Chamber of Commerce [20106], West Allis, WI
West Bend Area Chamber of Commerce [20130], West Bend, WI
West Bend Noon Kiwanis Club (Wisconsin) [20131], West Bend, WI
West Bloomfield Chamber of Commerce [★10114]
West Bloomfield School District Communications Governance Comm. [★10126]
West Bloomfield School District Parent Communications Network [10126], West Bloomfield, MI
West Br. Area Chamber of Commerce [10135], West Branch, MI
West Branch-Ogemaw County Travel and Visitors Bur. [10136], West Branch, MI
West Central Antique Power Collectors [11874], New London, MN
West Central Association [1227], Chicago, IL
West Central Assn. of Realtors, Ohio [15674], Lima, OH
West Central Builders Assn. [11875], New London, MN
West Central District Dental Soc., Minnesota [10523], Brainerd, MN
West Central Hea. Info. Mgt. Assn. [14785], Convoy, OH
West Central Illinois AIFA [3174], Quincy, IL
West Central Illinois Assn. of Realtors [1783], Galesburg, IL
West Central Illinois RSVP [467], Carthage, IL
West Central Indiana Angus Assn. [6523], Whitestown, IN
West Central Minnesota RSVP [10939], Elbow Lake, MN
West Central Minnesota Youth for Christ [12929], Willmar, MN
West Central Ohio ALU [16582], St. Marys, OH
West Central Ohio Angus Assn. [15098], Elida, OH
West Central - Young Life [14763], Columbus, OH
West Chatham Improvement Association [1228], Chicago, IL
West Chicago Chamber of Commerce [★3943]
West Chicago Chamber of Commerce and Indus. [3943], West Chicago, IL
West Creek Preservation Comm. [16379], Parma, OH
West Highland White Terrier Club of Northern Illinois [2801], Oak Lawn, IL
West Highland White Terrier Club of Northern Ohio [16224], North Canton, OH
West Highland White Terrier Club of Southeastern Michigan [7471], Dexter, MI

West Indian
Columbus West Indian Assn. [14407], Columbus, OH

West Lafayette High School Alumni Assn. [6505], West Lafayette, IN
West Lafayette High School - Young Life [6506], West Lafayette, IN
West Lawn Chamber of Commerce [1229], Chicago, IL
West Madison/Verona Young Life [19245], Mount Horeb, WI
West Michigan Angus Assn. [8867], Lowell, MI
West Michigan Artificial Reef Soc. [9167], Muskegon, MI
West Michigan Beagle Club [7600], Elwell, MI
West Michigan Bonsai Club [8072], Greenville, MI
West Michigan Chap. of the APA [8223], Holland, MI
West Michigan Cochlear Implant Club [8019], Grand Rapids, MI
West Michigan Corvair Club [9472], Ravenna, MI
West Michigan District Dental Soc. [8020], Grand Rapids, MI
West Michigan District of Precision Metalforming Assn. [8224], Holland, MI
West Michigan Enval. Action Coun. [8021], Grand Rapids, MI
West Michigan Golf Course Superintendents Assn. [9533], Rockford, MI
West Michigan Lakeshore Assn. of Realtors [7867], Grand Haven, MI
West Michigan Mycological Soc. [8877], Ludington, MI
West Michigan Regional Planning Commn. [8022], Grand Rapids, MI
West Michigan Shoreline Regional Development Commn. [9168], Muskegon, MI
West Michigan Soc. for Healthcare Engg. [8023], Grand Rapids, MI
West Michigan Tourist Assn. [8024], Grand Rapids, MI
West Ohio Development Coun. [16671], Sidney, OH
West Ottawa - Wyldlife [8225], Holland, MI
West Ottawa Young Life [8226], Holland, MI
West Point Lions Club - Ohio [15682], Lisbon, OH
West Portage Park Neighborhood Improvement Assn. [1230], Chicago, IL
West Salem Lions Club [20139], West Salem, WI
West Shore Chamber of Commerce [17238], Westlake, OH
West Shore Chorus of Sweet Adelines Intl. [7868], Grand Haven, MI
West Shore Orchid Soc. [15591], Lakewood, OH
West Shore Rock and Mineral Club [8878], Ludington, MI
West Shore Youth for Christ [8879], Ludington, MI
West Suburban Access News Assn. [2828], Oak Park, IL
West Suburban ALANO Club [3973], Westmont, IL
West Suburban Bar Assn. [1715], Forest Park, IL
West Suburban Chamber of Commerce [★2173]
West Suburban Chamber of Commerce [20086], Wauwatosa, WI
West Suburban Chamber of Commerce and Indus. [2173], La Grange, IL
West Suburban Chicago Chap., MOAA [2174], La Grange, IL
West Suburban Cook and Southern Du Page County RSVP [3208], River Grove, IL
West Suburban Stamp Club [9412], Plymouth, MI
West Suburban United Way [2177], La Grange Park, IL
West Suburbs REACT [2829], Oak Park, IL
West Towns Bd. of Realtors [1262], Cicero, IL
West Union Firemens' Building Assn. [17199], West Union, OH
West Unity Area Chamber of Commerce [17201], West Unity, OH
West Unity Chamber of Commerce [★17201]
West Virginia Quarter Horse Assn. [17247], Wheelersburg, OH
West Walker Sportsman's Club [8025], Grand Rapids, MI
West Wisconsin Dressage Assn. [17923], Elk Mound, WI
Westby Lions Club [20144], Westby, WI

Westchester Chamber of Commerce **[3958]**, Westchester, IL
Western Beagle Club **[5589]**, Kokomo, IN
Western Buckeye Rottweiler Club **[16754]**, Springfield, OH
Western Cuyahoga Audubon Soc. **[14237]**, Cleveland, OH
Western Dairyland RSVP **[17907]**, Eau Claire, WI
Western Golf Assn. **[1878]**, Golf, IL
Western Illinois Youth for Christ **[2377]**, Macomb, IL
Western Lake Superior Flying and Hiking Soc. **[10694]**, Cloquet, MN
Western Lights Chorus of Sweet Adelines Intl. **[2027]**, Hinsdale, IL
Western Michigan Appaloosa Horse Club **[7220]**, Constantine, MI
Western Michigan Assn. of Insurance and Financial Advisors **[9169]**, Muskegon, MI
Western Michigan Chap. of Amer. Soc. of Plumbing Engineers **[8026]**, Grand Rapids, MI
Western Michigan Compensation Assn. **[8868]**, Lowell, MI
Western Michigan Estate Planning Coun. **[8027]**, Grand Rapids, MI
Western Michigan Genealogical Soc. **[8028]**, Grand Rapids, MI
Western Michigan Model Yacht Assn No. 103 **[8406]**, Jenison, MI
Western Michigan Mortgage Lenders Assn. **[8029]**, Grand Rapids, MI
Western Michigan Planned Giving Gp. **[8227]**, Holland, MI
Western Michigan Thunderbird Club **[8048]**, Grandville, MI
Western Michigan Univ. Skating Club **[8471]**, Kalamazoo, MI
Western MMBA **[8049]**, Grandville, MI
Western Ohio Chap., Natl. Elecl. Contractors Assn. **[14970]**, Dayton, OH
Western Reserve Amateur Radio Association **[16201]**, Newton Falls, OH
Western Reserve Carriage Assn. **[14828]**, Cuyahoga Falls, OH
Western Reserve Dairy Goat Assn. **[13474]**, Burton, OH
Western Reserve Historical Soc. **[14238]**, Cleveland, OH
Western Reserve Insulator Club **[16251]**, North Royalton, OH
Western Reserve Kennel Club **[16194]**, Newbury, OH
Western Reserve Numismatic Club **[16629]**, Seven Hills, OH
Western Reserve of Ohio Teachers of English **[13510]**, Campbell, OH
Western U.P. Convention and Visitors Bur. **[8343]**, Ironwood, MI
Western Upper Peninsula RSVP **[8112]**, Hancock, MI
Western Waukesha County Dog Training Club **[18240]**, Ixonia, WI
Western Wayne Oakland County Assn. of Realtors **[7649]**, Farmington, MI
Western Wisconsin AFL-CIO **[18381]**, La Crosse, WI
Westerville Area Chamber of Commerce **[17223]**, Westerville, OH
Westerville Lions Club **[17224]**, Westerville, OH
Westfield Chamber of Commerce **[20148]**, Westfield, WI
Westfield Washington Chamber of Commerce **[6513]**, Westfield, IN
Westland Breakfast Lions Club **[10143]**, Westland, MI
Westland Chamber of Commerce **[10144]**, Westland, MI
Westland Figure Skating Club **[10145]**, Westland, MI
Westland Fire Fighters Public Awareness Comm. **[10146]**, Westland, MI
Westland Host Lions Club **[10147]**, Westland, MI
Westland Lawn Bowling Club **[10148]**, Westland, MI
Westland - Young Life **[14764]**, Columbus, OH
Westmont Chamber of Commerce and Tourism Bur. **[3974]**, Westmont, IL
Westridge Chamber of Commerce **[1231]**, Chicago, IL
Westville Area Chamber of Commerce **[6518]**, Westville, IN
Westwood Heights Lions Club **[9323]**, Otisville, MI
Wetlands
Wisconsin Wetlands Assn. **[18763]**, Madison, WI
Wexford County Habitat for Humanity **[7051]**, Cadillac, MI
Wexford County Historical Soc. and Museum **[7052]**, Cadillac, MI
Weyauwega Area Chamber of Commerce **[20151]**, Weyauwega, WI
Wharton Lions Club **[17244]**, Wharton, OH
Wheaton Area Chamber of Commerce **[12886]**, Wheaton, MN
Wheaton Chamber of Commerce **[4000]**, Wheaton, IL
Wheaton Chamber of Commerce **[★12886]**
Wheaton Junior Woman's Club **[4001]**, Wheaton, IL
Wheaton Lions Club **[4002]**, Wheaton, IL
Wheaton Lions Club - Minnesota **[12887]**, Wheaton, MN
Wheel Fast Racing **[2664]**, Naperville, IL
Wheeling - Prospect Heights Area Chamber of Commerce and Indus. **[4006]**, Wheeling, IL
Wheelmen, Illinois **[1232]**, Chicago, IL
Wheelmen, Indiana **[6044]**, Plainfield, IN
Wheelmen, Michigan **[10149]**, Westland, MI
Wheelmen, Minnesota **[11778]**, Minneapolis, MN
Wheelmen, Ohio **[15217]**, Findlay, OH
Wheelmen, Wisconsin **[19149]**, Milwaukee, WI
White Bear Area Chamber of Commerce **[12905]**, White Bear Lake, MN
White Bear Lake Area Chamber of Commerce **[★12905]**
White Bear Lake/Mahtomedi - Wyldlife **[12906]**, White Bear Lake, MN
White Bear Lake - Young Life **[12907]**, White Bear Lake, MN
White Cloud Area Chamber of Commerce **[10153]**, White Cloud, MI
White Cloud Lions Club **[10154]**, White Cloud, MI
White County Assn. of Realtors **[5828]**, Monticello, IN
White County United Way **[5829]**, Monticello, IN
White Lake Area Chamber of Commerce **[10165]**, Whitehall, MI
White Pigeon Lions Club **[10160]**, White Pigeon, MI
White Pine Wildlife Rehabilitation Center **[17953]**, Fall Creek, WI
White River Chap. MOAA **[4333]**, Carmel, IN
White River Humane Soc. **[4179]**, Bedford, IN
White River Ramblers **[5900]**, Muncie, IN
White River Rsrc. Conservation and Development Coun. **[4180]**, Bedford, IN
White River Sound Chorus of Sweet Adelines Intl. **[5499]**, Indianapolis, IN
Whitefish Area Lions Club **[10743]**, Crosslake, MN
Whitefish Bay Young Life **[19150]**, Milwaukee, WI
Whitehall Area Chamber of Commerce **[17249]**, Whitehall, OH
Whitehall Area Chamber of Commerce **[20158]**, Whitehall, WI
Whitehall Area Lions Club **[16520]**, Reynoldsburg, OH
Whiteside Co. Emergency REACT **[3707]**, Sterling, IL
Whiteside-Lee County Dental Soc. **[3708]**, Sterling, IL
Whitewater Area Chamber of Commerce **[20164]**, Whitewater, WI
Whitewater Assn; Chicago **[2327]**, Lombard, IL
Whitewater Valley Wanderers **[6113]**, Richmond, IN
Whiting - Robertsdale Chamber of Commerce **[6526]**, Whiting, IN
Whitley County Literacy Coun. **[4386]**, Columbia City, IN
Wholesale
Indiana Wholesale Distributors **[5335]**, Indianapolis, IN
Ohio Assn. of Wholesale Distributors **[14569]**, Columbus, OH
Ohio Wholesale Marketers Assn. **[14698]**, Columbus, OH
Wholesale Beer Assn. Executives of Am. **[★11630]**
Wholesale Beer and Wine Assn. of Ohio **[14765]**, Columbus, OH
Wholesale Distribution
Middle-Atlantic Wholesalers Assn. **[1050]**, Chicago, IL
Wholesalers Secretaries; State Beer **[★11630]**
WICAA RSVP in Clay/Putnam and Vigo Counties **[6353]**, Terre Haute, IN
Wickliffe Area Chamber of Commerce **[17258]**, Wickliffe, OH
Wild River Audubon Soc. **[10638]**, Center City, MN
Wildcats Cricket Club **[3453]**, Schaumburg, IL
Wildflower Grass Producers Assn; Minnesota Native **[12955]**, Winona, MN
Wildlife
Amer. Bear Assn. - Minnesota **[11941]**, Orr, MN
Fish Point Wildlife Assn. **[10024]**, Unionville, MI
Michigan Natl. Wild Turkey Fed., Alpena Longbeards **[6643]**, Alpena, MI
Michigan Natl. Wild Turkey Fed., Arenac County **[6806]**, Au Gres, MI
Michigan Natl. Wild Turkey Fed., Bay De Noc Gobblers **[7615]**, Escanaba, MI
Michigan Natl. Wild Turkey Fed., Beards and Spurs Chap. **[9867]**, Sterling Heights, MI
Michigan Natl. Wild Turkey Fed., Beaver Creek Chap. **[9554]**, Roscommon, MI
Michigan Natl. Wild Turkey Fed., Berrien County **[9685]**, St. Joseph, MI
Michigan Natl. Wild Turkey Fed., Black Mountain Chap. **[8159]**, Hawks, MI
Michigan Natl. Wild Turkey Fed., Blue Water Chap. **[8307]**, Imlay City, MI
Michigan Natl. Wild Turkey Fed., Br. County Longbeards **[7028]**, Bronson, MI
Michigan Natl. Wild Turkey Fed., Cass River Chap. **[8927]**, Marlette, MI
Michigan Natl. Wild Turkey Fed., Clam River Gobblers **[8992]**, McBain, MI
Michigan Natl. Wild Turkey Fed., Dowagiac River Chap. **[9210]**, Niles, MI
Michigan Natl. Wild Turkey Fed., Dune Drummers Chap. **[10164]**, Whitehall, MI
Michigan Natl. Wild Turkey Fed., Elk Country Gobblers **[6804]**, Atlanta, MI
Michigan Natl. Wild Turkey Fed., Flat Rock Longbeards **[7705]**, Flat Rock, MI
Michigan Natl. Wild Turkey Fed., Flint River Chap. **[7747]**, Flint, MI
Michigan Natl. Wild Turkey Fed., Freemont Area Chap. **[7798]**, Fremont, MI
Michigan Natl. Wild Turkey Fed., Gateway Gobblers **[9709]**, Sanford, MI
Michigan Natl. Wild Turkey Fed., Grand River Longbeards **[10045]**, Vermontville, MI
Michigan Natl. Wild Turkey Fed., Grand Valley Chap. **[8043]**, Grandville, MI
Michigan Natl. Wild Turkey Fed., Grant Gobblers **[8052]**, Grant, MI
Michigan Natl. Wild Turkey Fed., Highbanks Chap. **[9387]**, Plainwell, MI
Michigan Natl. Wild Turkey Fed., Hillsdale Chap. **[9076]**, Montgomery, MI
Michigan Natl. Wild Turkey Fed., Houghton Lake Longbeards **[8265]**, Houghton Lake, MI
Michigan Natl. Wild Turkey Fed., Huron Valley Chap. **[7814]**, Garden City, MI
Michigan Natl. Wild Turkey Fed., Kalamazoo Chap. **[10169]**, Williamsburg, MI
Michigan Natl. Wild Turkey Fed., Kalkaska Gobblers **[8477]**, Kalkaska, MI
Michigan Natl. Wild Turkey Fed., Lapeer Longbeards **[8781]**, Lapeer, MI
Michigan Natl. Wild Turkey Fed., Lenawee Limbhangers **[6975]**, Blissfield, MI
Michigan Natl. Wild Turkey Fed., Little Traverse Bay Gobbler Chap. **[9366]**, Petoskey, MI
Michigan Natl. Wild Turkey Fed., Livingston Longbeards **[8284]**, Howell, MI
Michigan Natl. Wild Turkey Fed., Macomb Lost Gobblers **[8122]**, Harper Woods, MI
Michigan Natl. Wild Turkey Fed., Mecosta County Strutters Chap. **[9110]**, Mount Pleasant, MI
Michigan Natl. Wild Turkey Fed., Menominee Strutting Chap. **[7079]**, Carney, MI
Michigan Natl. Wild Turkey Fed., Mountain Top Gobblers **[9111]**, Mount Pleasant, MI
Michigan Natl. Wild Turkey Fed., Newaygo Valley Gobblers **[9857]**, Stanwood, MI
Michigan Natl. Wild Turkey Fed., North Kent Chap. **[9527]**, Rockford, MI
Michigan Natl. Wild Turkey Fed., North Oakland Gobblers **[8238]**, Holly, MI

Michigan Natl. Wild Turkey Fed., North Ottawa Toms Chap. **[10228]**, Zeeland, MI
Michigan Natl. Wild Turkey Fed., Northern Snow Shoe Toms Chap. **[7802]**, Gaastra, MI
Michigan Natl. Wild Turkey Fed., Ogemaw Hills Chap. **[10130]**, West Branch, MI
Michigan Natl. Wild Turkey Fed., Presque Isle Longbeards **[9542]**, Rogers City, MI
Michigan Natl. Wild Turkey Fed., Rabbit River Chap. **[7476]**, Dorr, MI
Michigan Natl. Wild Turkey Fed., River Raisin Chap. **[9908]**, Tecumseh, MI
Michigan Natl. Wild Turkey Fed., St. Joe Valley Limbhangers **[9917]**, Three Rivers, MI
Michigan Natl. Wild Turkey Fed., Sebawaing Gobblers **[9738]**, Sebewaing, MI
Michigan Natl. Wild Turkey Fed., Shiawasse River Strutters Chap. **[7148]**, Chesaning, MI
Michigan Natl. Wild Turkey Fed., Southwestern Michigan Chap. **[10050]**, Vicksburg, MI
Michigan Natl. Wild Turkey Fed., Superior Turkey Trackers Chap. **[8951]**, Marquette, MI
Michigan Natl. Wild Turkey Fed., Sycamore Creek Chap. **[7124]**, Charlotte, MI
Michigan Natl. Wild Turkey Fed., Tamarock Toms Chap. **[8520]**, Lakeview, MI
Michigan Natl. Wild Turkey Fed., Thornapple Valley Chap. **[9173]**, Nashville, MI
Michigan Natl. Wild Turkey Fed., Three Corners Habitat Chap. **[10017]**, Tustin, MI
Michigan Natl. Wild Turkey Fed., Timber Ghost Gobblers **[9355]**, Perry, MI
Michigan Natl. Wild Turkey Fed., Tri-Valley Gobblers **[9007]**, Merrill, MI
Michigan Natl. Wild Turkey Fed., Tuscola Longbeards **[9739]**, Sebewaing, MI
Michigan Natl. Wild Turkey Fed., U.P. Snow Gobblers **[7232]**, Curtis, MI
Michigan Natl. Wild Turkey Fed., Upper Thumb Gobblers **[7701]**, Filion, MI
Michigan Natl. Wild Turkey Fed., Vanburen Longbeards **[6828]**, Bangor, MI
Michigan Natl. Wild Turkey Fed., Washtenaw County Chap. **[8910]**, Manchester, MI
Michigan Natl. Wild Turkey Fed., Waterloo Longbeards **[8056]**, Grass Lake, MI
Michigan Natl. Wild Turkey Fed., Western U.P. Tommy Knockers Chap. **[6928]**, Bergland, MI
Michigan Natl. Wild Turkey Fed., White River Longbeards **[10152]**, White Cloud, MI
Michigan Natl. Wild Turkey Fed., Whiteford Valley Chap. **[9357]**, Petersburg, MI
Univ. of Wisconsin, Stevens Point - Wildlife Soc. - Student Chap. **[19814]**, Stevens Point, WI
Willowbrook Wildlife Found. **[1843]**, Glen Ellyn, IL
Wildlife Agencies; Assn. of Midwest Fish and **[★19599]**
Wildlife Assn; Fish Point **[10024]**, Unionville, MI
Wildlife Commissioners; Assn. of Midwest Fish and **[★19599]**
Wildlife Conservation
Anoka County Chap. of Pheasants Forever **[11320]**, Lino Lakes, MN
Berrien County Chap. of Pheasants Forever **[7205]**, Coloma, MI
Blue Earth County Chap. of Pheasants Forever **[11376]**, Mankato, MN
Bluebird Restoration Assn. of Wisconsin **[19480]**, Plover, WI
Brown County Bluebird Soc. **[5910]**, Nashville, IN
Calhoun County Michigan Chap. of Pheasants Forever **[8967]**, Marshall, MI
Clinton Valley Trout Unlimited **[9501]**, Rochester, MI
Darke County Pheasants Forever **[16555]**, Rossburg, OH
East Central Illinois Bluebird Soc. **[2946]**, Paris, IL
Frank Bob Perrin - Lansing, Michigan Chap. of Trout Unlimited **[8567]**, Lansing, MI
Great Lakes Indian Fish and Wildlife Commn. **[19353]**, Odanah, WI
Indiana Bluebird Soc. **[6078]**, Rensselaer, IN
Kandiyohi County Pheasants Forever **[12917]**, Willmar, MN
Kiap Tu Wish Chap. of Trout Unlimited **[12977]**, Woodbury, MN
Livingston County Pheasants Forever **[8281]**, Howell, MI
Miami Valley Pheasants Forever **[13506]**, Camden, OH
Michigan Bluebird Soc. **[8384]**, Jackson, MI
Michigan Coun. Trout Unlimited **[7979]**, Grand Rapids, MI
Michigan Loon Preservation Association/Michigan Loonwatch **[9749]**, Shepherd, MI
Michigan Wildlife Conservancy **[6839]**, Bath, MI
Midwest Assn. of Fish and Wildlife Agencies **[19599]**, Rhinelander, WI
Natl. Audubon Soc. - Minnesota River Valley Audubon Chap. **[10483]**, Bloomington, MN
Ohio Bluebird Soc. **[13935]**, Cincinnati, OH
Pheasants Forever of Ashland Ohio **[13171]**, Ashland, OH
Pheasants Forever Bay/Midland Chap. of Michigan **[9039]**, Midland, MI
Pheasants Forever Central Indiana Chap. **[4331]**, Carmel, IN
Pheasants Forever Central Indiana, Clinton County **[4616]**, Forest, IN
Pheasants Forever Central Indiana, Coal Greek **[4427]**, Crawfordsville, IN
Pheasants Forever Central Indiana, Door Prairie **[5601]**, La Porte, IN
Pheasants Forever Central Indiana, Eel River **[4384]**, Columbia City, IN
Pheasants Forever Central Indiana, Elkhart County **[4292]**, Bristol, IN
Pheasants Forever Central Indiana, Fulton County **[6124]**, Rochester, IN
Pheasants Forever Central Indiana, Iroquois River **[4459]**, Demotte, IN
Pheasants Forever Central Indiana, Lagrange County **[5642]**, Lagrange, IN
Pheasants Forever Central Indiana, Marshall County **[4289]**, Bremen, IN
Pheasants Forever Central Indiana, Northeast Indiana **[5649]**, Laotto, IN
Pheasants Forever Central Indiana, Sagamore **[6495]**, West Lafayette, IN
Pheasants Forever Central Indiana, Tippe River Basin **[6452]**, Warsaw, IN
Pheasants Forever Central Indiana, Twin Lakes **[5827]**, Monticello, IN
Pheasants Forever Central Indiana, Wabash Valley **[6338]**, Terre Haute, IN
Pheasants Forever Central Indiana, Wildcat Creek **[5580]**, Kokomo, IN
Pheasants Forever Fox River Valley Chap. **[19403]**, Oshkosh, WI
Pheasants Forever Illinois Pioneer Chap. **[2977]**, Paxton, IL
Pheasants Forever Ionia County Chap. 161 **[8317]**, Ionia, MI
Pheasants Forever Lake Michigan Chap. 75 **[9764]**, South Haven, MI
Pheasants Forever, Macomb County **[9488]**, Richmond, MI
Pheasants Forever - Mchenry County Chap. **[1331]**, Crystal Lake, IL
Pheasants Forever Northeast Indiana Chap. 182 **[4142]**, Auburn, IN
Pheasants Forever Ozaukee County **[18067]**, Grafton, WI
Pheasants Forever Southeastern Wisconsin Chap. **[19297]**, New Berlin, WI
Prairie Rivers Network **[548]**, Champaign, IL
Quail Unlimited, Butler County Chap. **[15989]**, Miamisburg, OH
Quail Unlimited, Northern Indiana Chap. **[4505]**, Elkhart, IN
Quail Unlimited, Ohio Valley Chap. **[15610]**, Lancaster, OH
Quail Unlimited, Patoka Hills **[4942]**, Huntingburg, IN
Quail Unlimited, Quad County Chap. **[3473]**, Shipman, IL
Quail Unlimited, Shawnee Chap. **[2408]**, Marion, IL
Quail Unlimited, Skillet Fork Chap. **[3410]**, Salem, IL
Quail Unlimited, Southeast Wisconsin Chap. **[19914]**, Trevor, WI
Quail Unlimited, Southern Indiana Chap. **[4791]**, Georgetown, IN
Quail Unlimited, Sullivan County Chap. **[5686]**, Linton, IN
Rivers Coun. of Minnesota **[12636]**, Sauk Rapids, MN
Rock Island County Chap. of Pheasants Forever **[3257]**, Rock Island, IL
Rock River Valley Pheasants Forever **[18262]**, Janesville, WI
Ruffed Grouse Soc., Agazzi Chap. **[12747]**, Thief River Falls, MN
Ruffed Grouse Soc., Aikit Area Chap. **[10246]**, Aitkin, MN
Ruffed Grouse Soc., Al Litzenburger Chap. **[9370]**, Petoskey, MI
Ruffed Grouse Soc., Andy Ammann Chap. **[8397]**, Jackson, MI
Ruffed Grouse Soc., Ann Arbor Chap. **[7072]**, Canton, MI
Ruffed Grouse Soc., Beaver Creek Chap. **[16588]**, Salem, OH
Ruffed Grouse Soc., Benay of the Lakes Chap. **[10783]**, Detroit Lakes, MN
Ruffed Grouse Soc., Blackduck Chap. **[10447]**, Blackduck, MN
Ruffed Grouse Soc., Blackhawk Area Chap. **[18263]**, Janesville, WI
Ruffed Grouse Soc., Central Upper Peninsula Chap. **[7619]**, Escanaba, MI
Ruffed Grouse Soc., Chequamegon Chap. **[17547]**, Ashland, WI
Ruffed Grouse Soc., Chippewa Valley Chap. **[17893]**, Eau Claire, WI
Ruffed Grouse Soc., Coulee Region Chap. **[18376]**, La Crosse, WI
Ruffed Grouse Soc., Crazy Flight Chap. **[10957]**, Ely, MN
Ruffed Grouse Soc., David Salsman Chap. **[12806]**, Virginia, MN
Ruffed Grouse Soc., David V. Uihlein Chap. **[19111]**, Milwaukee, WI
Ruffed Grouse Soc., Deep Portage Chap. **[10371]**, Backus, MN
Ruffed Grouse Soc., Drumming Log Chap. **[10520]**, Brainerd, MN
Ruffed Grouse Soc., Duluth/Superior Chap. **[19875]**, Superior, WI
Ruffed Grouse Soc., Durand Area Chap. **[17936]**, Elmwood, WI
Ruffed Grouse Soc., Eastern Up Chap. **[9670]**, St. Ignace, MI
Ruffed Grouse Soc., Flambeau River Chap. **[19426]**, Park Falls, WI
Ruffed Grouse Soc., Gilbert R. Symons Chap. **[16322]**, Owensville, OH
Ruffed Grouse Soc., Grand Rapids, Michigan Chap. **[8006]**, Grand Rapids, MI
Ruffed Grouse Soc., Grand Rapids, Minnesota Chap. **[12698]**, Squaw Lake, MN
Ruffed Grouse Soc., Hocking River Valley Chap. **[17160]**, Wellston, OH
Ruffed Grouse Soc., Hoosier Chap. **[5793]**, Michigan City, IN
Ruffed Grouse Soc., Indiana Chap. **[5585]**, Kokomo, IN
Ruffed Grouse Soc., Jim Foote Chap. **[8807]**, Lewiston, MI
Ruffed Grouse Soc., John M. Keener Chap. **[18610]**, Madison, WI
Ruffed Grouse Soc., Keith Davis Chap. **[7194]**, Clio, MI
Ruffed Grouse Soc., Kettle Moraine Chap. **[17825]**, Delafield, WI
Ruffed Grouse Soc., Lake Shore Chap. **[18329]**, Kohler, WI
Ruffed Grouse Soc., Lake of the Woods Chap. **[12844]**, Warroad, MN
Ruffed Grouse Soc., Lakeland Area Chap. **[19658]**, St. Germain, WI
Ruffed Grouse Soc., Langlade Chap. **[17819]**, Deerbrook, WI
Ruffed Grouse Soc., Le Grand Traverse Chap. **[9951]**, Traverse City, MI
Ruffed Grouse Soc., Lincoln County Chap. **[19910]**, Tomahawk, WI
Ruffed Grouse Soc., Marinette County Chap. **[18804]**, Marinette, WI
Ruffed Grouse Soc., Michigan Chap. **[6998]**, Boyne Falls, MI
Ruffed Grouse Soc., Mid Up Chap. **[8958]**, Marquette, MI

Ruffed Grouse Soc., Missa-Croix Chap. **[11129]**, Hastings, MN
Ruffed Grouse Soc., Nicolet Wild River Chap. **[17539]**, Armstrong Creek, WI
Ruffed Grouse Soc., North Shore Chap. **[11078]**, Grand Marais, MN
Ruffed Grouse Soc., Northcentral Minnesota Chap. **[10425]**, Bemidji, MN
Ruffed Grouse Soc., Northeastern Wisconsin Chap. **[18130]**, Green Bay, WI
Ruffed Grouse Soc., Northern Ohio Chap. **[13086]**, Akron, OH
Ruffed Grouse Soc., Northwest Ohio Chap. **[16105]**, Neapolis, OH
Ruffed Grouse Soc., Ohio Chap. **[14724]**, Columbus, OH
Ruffed Grouse Soc., Ohio Hills Chap. **[16040]**, Millersport, OH
Ruffed Grouse Soc., Pine County Chap. **[12734]**, Sturgeon Lake, MN
Ruffed Grouse Soc., Rib Mountain Chap. **[20045]**, Wausau, WI
Ruffed Grouse Soc., Robert J. Lytle Chap. **[9490]**, Richmond, MI
Ruffed Grouse Soc., Roy W. Strickland Chap. **[6999]**, Boyne Falls, MI
Ruffed Grouse Soc., Rum River Chap. **[11230]**, Isanti, MN
Ruffed Grouse Soc., Saginaw Valley Chap. **[7782]**, Frankenmuth, MI
Ruffed Grouse Soc., St. Croix Valley Chap. **[18225]**, Hudson, WI
Ruffed Grouse Soc., Shawano Area Chap. **[19682]**, Shawano, WI
Ruffed Grouse Soc., South Central Michigan Chap. **[7583]**, Eaton Rapids, MI
Ruffed Grouse Soc., Southwest Wisconsin Chap. **[19258]**, Muscoda, WI
Ruffed Grouse Soc., Southwestern Michigan Chap. **[6605]**, Allegan, MI
Ruffed Grouse Soc., Superior Chap. **[8341]**, Ironwood, MI
Ruffed Grouse Soc., T. Stanton Armour Chap. **[1952]**, Harvard, IL
Ruffed Grouse Soc., Three Rivers Chap. **[17443]**, Zanesville, OH
Ruffed Grouse Soc., Twin Cities Chap. **[12662]**, Shoreview, MN
Ruffed Grouse Soc., Voyageur Chap. **[11219]**, International Falls, MN
Ruffed Grouse Soc., West Central Minnesota Chap. **[12297]**, St. Cloud, MN
Ruffed Grouse Soc., West Central Wisconsin Chap. **[19281]**, Neillsville, WI
Ruffed Grouse Soc., Wilderness Wings Chap. **[18199]**, Hayward, WI
Ruffed Grouse Soc., Winnebago Land Chap. **[19404]**, Oshkosh, WI
Ruffed Grouse Soc., Wisconsin Chap. **[19876]**, Superior, WI
Ruffed Grouse Soc., Woods/Meadow Chap. **[19947]**, Warrens, WI
Schrems West Michigan Trout Unlimited **[8008]**, Grand Rapids, MI
Sibley County Pheasants Forever **[10340]**, Arlington, MN
Spoon River Valley Pheasants Forever **[2344]**, London Mills, IL
Timber Wolf Preservation Soc. **[18152]**, Greendale, WI
Trout Unlimited - Adams Chap. **[9961]**, Traverse City, MI
Trout Unlimited - Aldo Leopold Chap. **[17597]**, Beaver Dam, WI
Trout Unlimited - Antigo Chap. **[17476]**, Antigo, WI
Trout Unlimited - Arnold J. Copeland Chap. **[7626]**, Essexville, MI
Trout Unlimited, Blackhawk **[17918]**, Edgerton, WI
Trout Unlimited - Central Wisconsin Chap. **[20174]**, Winneconne, WI
Trout Unlimited, Challenge Chap. **[6993]**, Bloomfield Hills, MI
Trout Unlimited, Clear Fork River 667 **[17326]**, Wooster, OH
Trout Unlimited - Copper County Chap. **[8111]**, Hancock, MI
Trout Unlimited, Coulee Region **[18379]**, La Crosse, WI
Trout Unlimited, Elliott Donnelley **[1209]**, Chicago, IL
Trout Unlimited, Fox Valley **[17528]**, Appleton, WI
Trout Unlimited - Fox Valley Chap. **[18865]**, Menasha, WI
Trout Unlimited, Frank Hornberg 624 **[19812]**, Stevens Point, WI
Trout Unlimited - Gitche Gumee Chap. **[11151]**, Hermantown, MN
Trout Unlimited - Green Bay Chap. **[18137]**, Green Bay, WI
Trout Unlimited - Harry and Laura Nohr Chap. **[19223]**, Montfort, WI
Trout Unlimited - Headwaters Chap. **[10428]**, Bemidji, MN
Trout Unlimited - Illinois Coun. **[2783]**, Oak Brook, IL
Trout Unlimited - Lakeshore Chap. **[18791]**, Manitowoc, WI
Trout Unlimited - Lansing Chap. **[7468]**, DeWitt, MI
Trout Unlimited - Madmen **[14963]**, Dayton, OH
Trout Unlimited - Marinette County Chap. **[18806]**, Marinette, WI
Trout Unlimited - Mid-Minnesota Chap. **[12631]**, Sartell, MN
Trout Unlimited, Minnesota **[10491]**, Bloomington, MN
Trout Unlimited - Muskegon White River Chap. **[9217]**, North Muskegon, MI
Trout Unlimited, Northwoods 256 **[19609]**, Rhinelander, WI
Trout Unlimited - Oak Brook Chap. **[2784]**, Oak Brook, IL
Trout Unlimited - Oconto River Watershed 385 **[18049]**, Gillett, WI
Trout Unlimited - Ohio Coun. **[14964]**, Dayton, OH
Trout Unlimited - Ojibleau Chap. **[17903]**, Eau Claire, WI
Trout Unlimited - Paul Bunyan Chap. **[10492]**, Bloomington, MN
Trout Unlimited - Paul H. Young Chap. **[10011]**, Troy, MI
Trout Unlimited - Pine River Chap. **[10018]**, Tustin, MI
Trout Unlimited - Shaw-Paca Chap. **[18772]**, Manawa, WI
Trout Unlimited - Southeastern Wisconsin Chap. **[19138]**, Milwaukee, WI
Trout Unlimited - Southern Wisconsin Chap. **[18628]**, Madison, WI
Trout Unlimited - Two Heart Chap. **[9201]**, Newberry, MI
Trout Unlimited, Vanguard **[9547]**, Romeo, MI
Trout Unlimited - Wa Hue Chap. **[12087]**, Red Wing, MN
Trout Unlimited, Waybinahbe 650 **[11093]**, Grand Rapids, MN
Trout Unlimited - Wild Rivers Chap. **[17548]**, Ashland, WI
Trout Unlimited - William B. Mershon Chapter **[9642]**, Saginaw, MI
Trout Unlimited - Wisconsin River Valley Chap. **[20050]**, Wausau, WI
Trout Unlimited, Wolf River **[20154]**, White Lake, WI
The Trumpeter Swan Soc. **[12039]**, Plymouth, MN
Upland Chap. of Pheasants Forever **[20052]**, Wausau, WI
Washtenaw County Pheasants Forever **[6788]**, Ann Arbor, MI
White Pine Wildlife Rehabilitation Center **[17953]**, Fall Creek, WI
Wildlife Soc. - Illinois Chap. **[1961]**, Havana, IL
Wildlife Soc. - Indiana Chap. **[4265]**, Bloomington, IN
Wildlife Soc. - Minnesota Chap. **[12060]**, Proctor, MN
Wildlife Soc. - Southern Illinois Univ. Student Chap. **[436]**, Carbondale, IL
Wildlife Soc. - Wisconsin Chap. **[19427]**, Park Falls, WI
Winnebago County Pheasants Forever **[4032]**, Winnebago, IL
Wisconsin Wildlife Fed. **[19539]**, Prescott, WI
Zoological Soc. of Milwaukee **[19191]**, Milwaukee, WI
Wildlife Fed; Indiana **[4328]**, Carmel, IN
Wildlife Rehabilitation Center; White Pine **[17953]**, Fall Creek, WI
Wildlife Soc. - Illinois Chap. **[1961]**, Havana, IL
Wildlife Soc. - Indiana Chap. **[4265]**, Bloomington, IN
Wildlife Soc. - Minnesota Chap. **[12060]**, Proctor, MN
Wildlife Soc. - Southern Illinois Univ. Student Chap. **[436]**, Carbondale, IL
Wildlife Soc. - Student Chap; Univ. of Wisconsin, Stevens Point - **[19814]**, Stevens Point, WI
Wildlife Soc. - Wisconsin Chap. **[19427]**, Park Falls, WI
Wilkin County Agricultural Soc. **[10527]**, Breckenridge, MN
Wilkin County Historical Soc. **[10528]**, Breckenridge, MN
Will County Center for Economic Development **[2123]**, Joliet, IL
Will County Chamber of Commerce **[★2123]**
Will County Coin Club **[2694]**, New Lenox, IL
Will County Dental Soc. **[2124]**, Joliet, IL
Will-Grundy Home Builders Association **[1311]**, Crest Hill, IL
Willard Area Chamber of Commerce **[17267]**, Willard, OH
Williams Bay Lions Club **[20166]**, Williams Bay, WI
Williams County Area Crime Stoppers **[16064]**, Montpelier, OH
Williamson County Events Commission Corp. **[2412]**, Marion, IL
Williamson County Tourism Bureau **[2413]**, Marion, IL
Williamston Area Chamber of Commerce **[10175]**, Williamston, MI
Williamston Lions Club - Michigan **[10176]**, Williamston, MI
Williamston Middle School - Wyldlife **[7569]**, East Lansing, MI
Williamston - Young Life **[7570]**, East Lansing, MI
Williana Clumber Spaniel Club **[2319]**, Lockport, IL
Willmar Convention and Visitors Bur. **[★12933]**
Willmar Diamond Edge Figure Skating Club **[10454]**, Blomkest, MN
Willmar Evening Lions Club **[12930]**, Willmar, MN
Willmar Jaycees **[12931]**, Willmar, MN
Willmar Lakes Area Chamber of Commerce **[12932]**, Willmar, MN
Willmar Lakes Area Convention and Visitors Bur. **[12933]**, Willmar, MN
Willmar Noon Lions Club **[12934]**, Willmar, MN
Willoughby Area Chamber of Commerce **[17278]**, Willoughby, OH
Willoughby South High Instrumental Music Boosters **[17279]**, Willoughby, OH
Willoughby South Instrumental Music Boosters **[★17279]**
Willow Ridge Elementary PTA **[7876]**, Grand Ledge, MI
Willowbrook - Burr Ridge Chamber of Commerce and Indus. **[378]**, Burr Ridge, IL
Willowbrook Key Club **[3867]**, Villa Park, IL
Willowbrook Wildlife Found. **[1843]**, Glen Ellyn, IL
Willowick Chamber of Commerce **[17284]**, Willowick, OH
Wilmette Chamber of Commerce **[4023]**, Wilmette, IL
Wilmette Golf Club **[4024]**, Wilmette, IL
Wilmington Chamber of Commerce **[4026]**, Wilmington, IL
Wilmington - Clinton County Chamber of Commerce **[17295]**, Wilmington, OH
Wilmington Illinois Beagle Club **[2341]**, Lombard, IL
Wilson's Disease Assn. **[17334]**, Wooster, OH
Wilton Lions Club - Wisconsin **[20170]**, Wilton, WI
Winchester Area Chamber of Commerce **[6538]**, Winchester, IN
Wind - Akron Chap; Women in the **[13103]**, Akron, OH
Wind Lake Lions Club **[20171]**, Wind Lake, WI
Wind; Women in the **[16985]**, Toledo, OH
Windham Lions Club - Ohio **[17299]**, Windham, OH
Windians Cricket Club **[10929]**, Edina, MN
Windjammers Sailing Club **[19852]**, Suamico, WI
Windom Area Chamber of Commerce **[★12940]**
Windom Area Chamber of Commerce and Visitors Bur. **[12940]**, Windom, MN

Windy City Corvettes **[2887]**, Orland Park, IL
Windy City Matchcover Club **[4003]**, Wheaton, IL
Windy City Miniature Club **[1233]**, Chicago, IL
Windy City Soaring Assn. **[2010]**, Hinckley, IL
Windy City Walkers **[2802]**, Oak Lawn, IL
Windy City Women's Charity Club **[1234]**, Chicago, IL
Windy City Z Club **[2665]**, Naperville, IL
Wine
Amer. Wine Soc. - Bloomington-Normal **[262]**, Bloomington, IL
Amer. Wine Soc. - Cincinnati **[13741]**, Cincinnati, OH
Amer. Wine Soc. - Cleveland **[14779]**, Concord Twp, OH
Amer. Wine Soc. - Columbus **[15042]**, Dublin, OH
Amer. Wine Soc. - Cork Club Chicago **[2207]**, Lake in the Hills, IL
Amer. Wine Soc. - Covered Bridge **[15747]**, Madison, OH
Amer. Wine Soc. - Dayton **[13295]**, Beavercreek, OH
Amer. Wine Soc. - Metropolitan Detroit **[9548]**, Romulus, MI
Amer. Wine Soc. - Springfield **[16720]**, Springfield, OH
Amer. Wine Soc. - Suburban Cook County **[2013]**, Hinsdale, IL
Amer. Wine Soc. - Tippie Tasters **[6475]**, West Lafayette, IN
American Wine Society - Wabash Valley Chapter **[6131]**, Rockville, IN
Ohio Wine Producers Assn. **[13234]**, Austinburg, OH
Wine and Spirits Wholesalers of Indiana **[5500]**, Indianapolis, IN
Wisconsin Wine and Spirit Inst. **[18764]**, Madison, WI
Wine Society - Wabash Valley Chapter; American **[6131]**, Rockville, IN
Wine and Spirits Wholesalers of Indiana **[5500]**, Indianapolis, IN
Winfield Chamber of Commerce **[4031]**, Winfield, IL
Winger Lions Club **[12942]**, Winger, MN
Winnebago Audubon Soc. **[19406]**, Oshkosh, WI
Winnebago County Dental Soc. - Illinois **[3329]**, Rockford, IL
Winnebago County Medical Soc. **[3330]**, Rockford, IL
Winnebago County Pheasants Forever **[4032]**, Winnebago, IL
Winnebago Home Builders Assn. **[19407]**, Oshkosh, WI
Winnetka Chamber of Commerce **[4040]**, Winnetka, IL
Winona AIFA **[11071]**, Goodview, MN
Winona Area Chamber of Commerce **[12960]**, Winona, MN
Winona Area Mountain Bikers **[12961]**, Winona, MN
Winona County Historical Soc. **[12962]**, Winona, MN
Winona Noon Lions Club **[12963]**, Winona, MN
Winona Rivertown Lions Club **[12964]**, Winona, MN
Winona Senior High School PTSA **[12965]**, Winona, MN
Winona Soc. for Human Rsrc. Mgt. **[12966]**, Winona, MN
Winona - Young Life **[12967]**, Winona, MN
Winter Club of Indianapolis **[5501]**, Indianapolis, IN
Winterhurst Figure Skating Club **[15592]**, Lakewood, OH
Winthrop Area Chamber of Commerce **[12971]**, Winthrop, MN
Wisconsin 4-H Found. **[18638]**, Madison, WI
Wisconsin 4WD Assn. **[19277]**, Neenah, WI
Wisconsin Acad. of Family Physicians **[19894]**, Thiensville, WI
Wisconsin Acad. of Physician Assistants **[18639]**, Madison, WI
Wisconsin Acad. of Trial Lawyers **[18640]**, Madison, WI
Wisconsin Agri-Service Assn. **[18641]**, Madison, WI
Wisconsin Agribusiness Coun. **[18642]**, Madison, WI
Wisconsin Alliance of Cities **[18643]**, Madison, WI
Wisconsin Alliance of Hearing Professionals **[18644]**, Madison, WI
Wisconsin Amateur Field Trial Club **[19715]**, Sheboygan, WI
Wisconsin Amateur Field Trial Club **[19890]**, Theresa, WI
Wisconsin Amateur Hockey Assn. **[17851]**, Eagle River, WI
Wisconsin Amusement and Music Operators Assn. **[18912]**, Middleton, WI
Wisconsin Angus Assn. **[18424]**, Lodi, WI
Wisconsin Apartment Assn. **[18645]**, Madison, WI
Wisconsin Apple Growers Assn. **[19962]**, Waterloo, WI
Wisconsin Arborist Assn. **[18890]**, Mequon, WI
Wisconsin Art Educ. Assn. **[20058]**, Wausau, WI
Wisconsin Art Therapy Assn. **[19151]**, Milwaukee, WI
Wisconsin Arts Bd. **[18646]**, Madison, WI
Wisconsin Asphalt Pavement Assn. **[18647]**, Madison, WI
Wisconsin Assisted Living Assn. **[18648]**, Madison, WI
Wisconsin Assn. of Academic Librarians **[19152]**, Milwaukee, WI
Wisconsin Assn. of Accountants **[19646]**, River Falls, WI
Wisconsin Assn. African-Amer. Attorneys **[19153]**, Milwaukee, WI
Wisconsin Assn. of Agricultural Educators **[18004]**, Fox Lake, WI
Wisconsin Assn. of Alcohol and Drug Abuse Counselors **[19408]**, Oshkosh, WI
Wisconsin Assn. on Alcohol and Other Drug Abuse **[18649]**, Madison, WI
Wisconsin Assn. for Biomedical Res. and Educ. **[19154]**, Milwaukee, WI
Wisconsin Assn. for Career and Tech. Educ. **[18650]**, Madison, WI
Wisconsin Assn. of Central Ser. Professionals **[18651]**, Madison, WI
Wisconsin Assn. of Coll. Stores **[19409]**, Oshkosh, WI
Wisconsin Assn. of Collegiate Registrars and Admissions Officers **[19816]**, Stevens Point, WI
Wisconsin Assn. of Consulting Engineers **[★18457]**
Wisconsin Assn. of Criminal Defense Lawyers **[19211]**, Monona, WI
Wisconsin Assn. of Educational Opportunity Prog. Personnel **[19155]**, Milwaukee, WI
Wisconsin Assn. for Environmental Educ. **[19817]**, Stevens Point, WI
Wisconsin Assn. of Family and Children's Agencies **[18652]**, Madison, WI
Wisconsin Assn. for Food Protection **[19867]**, Sun Prairie, WI
Wisconsin Assn. of Hea. Plans **[18653]**, Madison, WI
Wisconsin Assn. of Hea. Underwriters **[18654]**, Madison, WI
Wisconsin Assn. for Healthcare Quality **[18655]**, Madison, WI
Wisconsin Assn. of Homes and Services for the Aging **[18656]**, Madison, WI
Wisconsin Assn. for Identification **[19156]**, Milwaukee, WI
Wisconsin Assn. of Independent Colleges and Universities **[18657]**, Madison, WI
Wisconsin Assn. of Insurance and Financial Advisors **[18658]**, Madison, WI
Wisconsin Assn. of Lakes **[18659]**, Madison, WI
Wisconsin Assn. of Legal Administrators **[19298]**, New Berlin, WI
Wisconsin Assn. of Life Underwriters **[★18658]**
Wisconsin Assn. of Local Hea. Dept. and Boards **[18147]**, Green Lake, WI
Wisconsin Assn. of Manufacturers' Agents **[19157]**, Milwaukee, WI
Wisconsin Assn. of Meat Processors **[17643]**, Bloomington, WI
Wisconsin Assn. of Mortgage Brokers **[18660]**, Madison, WI
Wisconsin Assn. of Parliamentarians **[18661]**, Madison, WI
Wisconsin Assn. for Perinatal Care **[18662]**, Madison, WI
Wisconsin Assn. of Scholars **[19158]**, Milwaukee, WI
Wisconsin Assn. of School Bds. **[18663]**, Madison, WI
Wisconsin Assn. of School Bus. Officials **[18664]**, Madison, WI
Wisconsin Assn. of School Couns. **[18665]**, Madison, WI
Wisconsin Assn. of School District Administrators **[18666]**, Madison, WI
Wisconsin Assn. of School Nurses **[18325]**, Kimberly, WI
Wisconsin Assn. of Student Financial Aid Administrators **[18667]**, Madison, WI
Wisconsin Assn. for Supervision and Curriculum Development **[19895]**, Thiensville, WI
Wisconsin Assn. for Talented and Gifted **[17531]**, Appleton, WI
Wisconsin Assn. of Textile Sers. **[18159]**, Greenfield, WI
Wisconsin Assn. of Women Police **[18668]**, Madison, WI
Wisconsin Athletic Trainers' Assn. **[18669]**, Madison, WI
Wisconsin Athletic Trainers' Assn., Northeast **[17815]**, De Pere, WI
Wisconsin Athletic Trainers' Assn., Southeast **[19336]**, Oak Creek, WI
Wisconsin Athletic Trainers' Assn., Southwest **[18670]**, Madison, WI
Wisconsin Auctioneers Assn. **[18913]**, Middleton, WI
Wisconsin Audiovisual Assn. **[★17649]**
Wisconsin Auto Collision Technicians Assn. **[20008]**, Waukesha, WI
Wisconsin Auto. and Truck Dealers Assn. **[18671]**, Madison, WI
Wisconsin Automotive and Truck Educ. Assn. **[20059]**, Wausau, WI
Wisconsin Bakers Assn. **[19159]**, Milwaukee, WI
Wisconsin Bankers Assn. **[18672]**, Madison, WI
Wisconsin Beagle Club **[18837]**, Mazomanie, WI
Wisconsin Beef Coun. **[18673]**, Madison, WI
Wisconsin Beef Improvement **[★19306]**
Wisconsin Beef Improvement Assn. **[19306]**, New Glarus, WI
Wisconsin Berry Growers Assn. **[19963]**, Waterloo, WI
Wisconsin Black Media Assn. **[19160]**, Milwaukee, WI
Wisconsin BMW Motorcycle Club No. 10 **[19419]**, Palmyra, WI
Wisconsin Boer Goat Assn. **[18400]**, Lake Geneva, WI
Wisconsin Broadcasters Assn. **[18674]**, Madison, WI
Wisconsin Burglar and Fire Alarm Assn. **[20107]**, West Allis, WI
Wisconsin Bus. Women's Coalition **[18675]**, Madison, WI
Wisconsin Cable Communs. Assn. **[18676]**, Madison, WI
Wisconsin Capital Model T Ford Club **[19832]**, Stoughton, WI
Wisconsin Center for the Book **[18677]**, Madison, WI
Wisconsin Chap. of the Amer. Coll. of Cardiology **[19161]**, Milwaukee, WI
Wisconsin Chap. of the Amer. Planning Assn. **[18678]**, Madison, WI
Wisconsin Chap. of Amer. Soc. of Plumbing Engineers **[20087]**, Wauwatosa, WI
Wisconsin Chap. of the Intl. Soc. for Performance Improvement **[19162]**, Milwaukee, WI
Wisconsin Chap., Leukemia and Lymphoma Soc. **[17681]**, Brookfield, WI
Wisconsin Chap. of the Myasthenia Gravis Found. **[20108]**, West Allis, WI
Wisconsin Chap. of the Natl. Alliance of Methadone Advocates **[19163]**, Milwaukee, WI
Wisconsin Chap. of Natl. Assn. of Tax Professionals **[19372]**, Onalaska, WI
Wisconsin Chap. Natl. Elecl. Contractors Assn. **[18679]**, Madison, WI
Wisconsin Chap. of the Natl. Emergency Number Assn. **[18382]**, La Crosse, WI
Wisconsin Chap. of RESOLVE **[20088]**, Wauwatosa, WI
Wisconsin Chap. of the Tourette Syndrome Assn. **[17994]**, Fond du Lac, WI
Wisconsin Chap. Triangle Fraternity **[18680]**, Madison, WI
Wisconsin Checkered Giant Rabbit Club **[20195]**, Wisconsin Rapids, WI
Wisconsin Cheese Makers' Assn. **[18681]**, Madison, WI
Wisconsin Chihuahua Rescue **[19226]**, Monticello, WI

Wisconsin Chiropractic Assn. [18682], Madison, WI
Wisconsin Choral Directors Assn. [17451], Abrams, WI
Wisconsin Christmas Tree Producers Assn. [19516], Portage, WI
Wisconsin Citizen Action [18683], Madison, WI
Wisconsin City/County Mgt. Assn. [19164], Milwaukee, WI
Wisconsin Club Lamb Assn. [19650], Rosholt, WI
Wisconsin Coalition Against Domestic Violence [18684], Madison, WI
Wisconsin Collectors Assn. [18267], Janesville, WI
Wisconsin Coll. Personnel Assn. [18685], Madison, WI
Wisconsin Concrete Masonry Assn. [19165], Milwaukee, WI
Wisconsin Concrete Pipe Assn. [19222], Montello, WI
Wisconsin Conservation Cong. [18686], Madison, WI
Wisconsin Coordinating Coun. on Nicaragua [18687], Madison, WI
Wisconsin Corn Growers Assn. [19420], Palmyra, WI
Wisconsin Corn Promotion Bd. [19421], Palmyra, WI
Wisconsin Coun. of African Violet Clubs [19410], Oshkosh, WI
Wisconsin Coun. on Children and Families [18688], Madison, WI
Wisconsin Coun. of County and Municipal Employees AFSCME, Coun. 40 AFL-CIO [18689], Madison, WI
Wisconsin Coun. on Developmental Disabilities [18690], Madison, WI
Wisconsin Coun. of Hostelling Intl. - Amer. Youth Hostels [18691], Madison, WI
Wisconsin Coun. on Problem Gambling [18139], Green Bay, WI
Wisconsin Coun. of Safety [18692], Madison, WI
Wisconsin Coun. for the Social Stud. [19847], Sturgeon Bay, WI
Wisconsin Coun. of Teachers of English Language Arts [17908], Eau Claire, WI
Wisconsin Counties Assn. [18693], Madison, WI
Wisconsin Court Reporters Assn. [18694], Madison, WI
Wisconsin Creameries Assn. [★18914]
Wisconsin Credit Assn. [19299], New Berlin, WI
Wisconsin Credit Union League [19447], Pewaukee, WI
Wisconsin Crop Improvement Assn. [18695], Madison, WI
Wisconsin Curling Assn. [19517], Portage, WI
Wisconsin Curling Assn. - Arlington Curling Club [17538], Arlington, WI
Wisconsin Curling Assn. - Clintonville Curling Club [17772], Clintonville, WI
Wisconsin Curling Assn. - Kettle Moraine Curling Club [18188], Hartland, WI
Wisconsin Curling Assn. - Loch Wissota Curling Club [17909], Eau Claire, WI
Wisconsin Curling Assn. - Lodi Curling Club [18425], Lodi, WI
Wisconsin Curling Assn. - Milwaukee Curling Club [18891], Mequon, WI
Wisconsin Curling Assn. - Portage Curling Club [19518], Portage, WI
Wisconsin Curling Assn. - Rice Lake Curling Club [19619], Rice Lake, WI
Wisconsin Curling Assn. - Waukesha Curling Club [20009], Waukesha, WI
Wisconsin Dairy Foods Assn. [★18914]
Wisconsin Dairy Products Assn. [18914], Middleton, WI
Wisconsin Dells Regional Chamber of Commerce [★20181]
Wisconsin Dells Visitor and Convention Bur. [20181], Wisconsin Dells, WI
Wisconsin Dental Assn. [19166], Milwaukee, WI
Wisconsin Dietary Managers Assn. [18017], Franksville, WI
Wisconsin Dietetic Assn. [19758], Sparta, WI
Wisconsin Direct Marketing Assn. [19167], Milwaukee, WI
Wisconsin District of Precision Metalforming Assn. [18834], Mayville, WI
Wisconsin Division of the Intl. Assn. of Administrative Professionals [20010], Waukesha, WI
Wisconsin Draft Horse Breeders [18205], Hilbert, WI
Wisconsin Dressage and Combined Training Assn. [20132], West Bend, WI
Wisconsin Early Childhood Assn. [18696], Madison, WI
Wisconsin Economic Development Assn. [18697], Madison, WI
Wisconsin Edsel Club [19581], Racine, WI
Wisconsin Educ. Assn. Coun. [18698], Madison, WI
Wisconsin Educational Media Assn. [17649], Boscobel, WI
Wisconsin Educational Media Assn. [17960], Fennimore, WI
Wisconsin Elec. Cooperative Assn. [18699], Madison, WI
Wisconsin Electronic Sales and Ser. Assn., Indianhead Chap. [★17910]
Wisconsin Electronic Ser. Assn., Indianhead Chap. [17910], Eau Claire, WI
Wisconsin Elks Assn. [19672], Schofield, WI
Wisconsin Energy Conservation Corp. [18700], Madison, WI
Wisconsin English Springer Spaniel Assn. [17858], East Troy, WI
Wisconsin Enval. Balancing Bur. [19168], Milwaukee, WI
Wisconsin Environmental Educ. Bd. [19818], Stevens Point, WI
Wisconsin Fabricare Inst. [18160], Greenfield, WI
Wisconsin Family Ties [18701], Madison, WI
Wisconsin Farm Bur. Fed. [18702], Madison, WI
Wisconsin Farmers Union [17758], Chippewa Falls, WI
Wisconsin Fathers for Children and Families [18703], Madison, WI
Wisconsin Fathers for Equal Justice [★18703]
Wisconsin Fed. of Cooperatives [18704], Madison, WI
Wisconsin Fed. of Republican Women [20011], Waukesha, WI
Wisconsin Fed. of Stamp Clubs [18915], Middleton, WI
Wisconsin Fed. of Teachers [★18443]
Wisconsin Fertilizer and Chem. Assn. [18705], Madison, WI
Wisconsin Figure Skating Club [19169], Milwaukee, WI
Wisconsin Financial Sers. Assn. [18706], Madison, WI
Wisconsin Forest Productivity Council [19610], Rhinelander, WI
Wisconsin Forum for Healthcare Strategy [18707], Madison, WI
Wisconsin Fox Valley Sheet Metal Contractors Assn. [17532], Appleton, WI
Wisconsin Funeral Directors Assn. [20089], Wauwatosa, WI
Wisconsin Geological and Natural History Survey [18708], Madison, WI
Wisconsin Golf Course Superintendents Assn. [17682], Brookfield, WI
Wisconsin Grocers Assn. [18709], Madison, WI
Wisconsin Hea. Care Assn. [18710], Madison, WI
Wisconsin Hea. Care Assn., District 1 [18314], Kenosha, WI
Wisconsin Hea. Care Assn., District 2 [19868], Sun Prairie, WI
Wisconsin Hea. Care Assn., District 3 [19665], Sauk City, WI
Wisconsin Hea. Care Assn., District 5 [18172], Hales Corners, WI
Wisconsin Hea. Care Assn., District 6 [17731], Cedarburg, WI
Wisconsin Hea. Care Assn., District 7 [17478], Antigo, WI
Wisconsin Hea. Care Assn., District 8 [18140], Green Bay, WI
Wisconsin Hea. Care Assn., District 9 [17639], Blair, WI
Wisconsin Hea. Care Assn., District 10 [17911], Eau Claire, WI
Wisconsin Hea. Care Assn., District 11 [19451], Phelps, WI
Wisconsin Hea. Care Assn., District 12 [18852], Mellen, WI
Wisconsin Hea. Info. Mgt. Assn. [18383], La Crosse, WI
Wisconsin Healthcare Engg. Assn. [19170], Milwaukee, WI
Wisconsin Hea.care Public Relations and Marketing Soc. [20196], Wisconsin Rapids, WI
Wisconsin Healthcare Purchasing and Materials Mgt. Assn. [19171], Milwaukee, WI
Wisconsin Healthy Mothers, Healthy Babies Coalition [20109], West Allis, WI
Wisconsin Historical Soc. [18711], Madison, WI
Wisconsin Holstein Assn. [17579], Baraboo, WI
Wisconsin Homecare Org. [18712], Madison, WI
Wisconsin Hosp. Assn. [18713], Madison, WI
Wisconsin House Rabbit Soc. [18714], Madison, WI
Wisconsin Housing Alliance [18715], Madison, WI
Wisconsin Humane Soc. [19172], Milwaukee, WI
Wisconsin Ice Arena Mgt. Assn. [19278], Neenah, WI
Wisconsin-Illinois-Indiana-Michigan State Assn. of Emblem Club [190], Beardstown, IL
Wisconsin/Illinois Show Horse Soc. [17859], East Troy, WI
Wisconsin Indianhead Chap. of Assoc. Locksmiths of Am. [17759], Chippewa Falls, WI
Wisconsin Innkeepers Assn. [17683], Brookfield, WI
Wisconsin Inst. of Certified Public Accountants [17684], Brookfield, WI
Wisconsin Intergenerational Network [18716], Madison, WI
Wisconsin Interlibrary Services [18717], Madison, WI
Wisconsin Intramural Recreational Sports Assn. [19819], Stevens Point, WI
Wisconsin Jaguars [20133], West Bend, WI
Wisconsin Jersey Breeders Assn. [18808], Marion, WI
Wisconsin Jewelers Assn. [18718], Madison, WI
Wisconsin Land Title Assn. [20140], West Salem, WI
Wisconsin Land and Water Conservation Assn. [18719], Madison, WI
Wisconsin Landscape Contractors Assn. [20012], Waukesha, WI
Wisconsin Landscape Contractors Assn. of Metro-Milwaukee [★20012]
Wisconsin Landscape Federation [18161], Greenfield, WI
Wisconsin League for Nursing [18430], Long Lake, WI
Wisconsin Lib. Assn. [18720], Madison, WI
Wisconsin Lib. Services [18721], Madison, WI
Wisconsin Liquid Waste Carriers Assn. [18722], Madison, WI
Wisconsin Lung Assn. [★17665]
Wisconsin Manufactured Housing Assn. [★18715]
Wisconsin Manufacturers and Commerce [18723], Madison, WI
Wisconsin Maple Syrup Producers Assn. [18900], Merrill, WI
Wisconsin Marine Historical Soc. [19173], Milwaukee, WI
Wisconsin Mathematical Assn. of Two-Year Colleges [18724], Madison, WI
Wisconsin Mathematics Coun. [18045], Germantown, WI
Wisconsin Medical Gp. Mgt. Assn. [18725], Madison, WI
Wisconsin Medical Soc. [18726], Madison, WI
Wisconsin Merchants Fed. [18727], Madison, WI
Wisconsin Metro Audubon Soc. [18014], Franklin, WI
Wisconsin Milk Haulers Assn. [18728], Madison, WI
Wisconsin-Milwaukee; Center for Consumer Affairs, Univ. of [18990], Milwaukee, WI
Wisconsin Mint Bd. [17479], Antigo, WI
Wisconsin Morgan Horse Club [19227], Monticello, WI
Wisconsin Mortgage Bankers Assn. [18729], Madison, WI
Wisconsin Motor Carriers Assn. [18730], Madison, WI
Wisconsin Movers Assn. [18731], Madison, WI
Wisconsin Music Educators Assn. [20020], Waunakee, WI
Wisconsin Mycological Soc. [19300], New Berlin, WI
Wisconsin Natl. Barrel Horse Assn. [20168], Wilson, WI
Wisconsin Natl. Cong. of Parents and Teachers [18732], Madison, WI
Wisconsin Natl. Guard Assn. [18733], Madison, WI

Wisconsin Natl. Org. for the Reform of Marijuana Laws **[18141]**, Green Bay, WI
Wisconsin Network for Peace and Justice **[18734]**, Madison, WI
Wisconsin Neurosurgical Soc. **[18735]**, Madison, WI
Wisconsin Newspaper Assn. **[18736]**, Madison, WI
Wisconsin NFA Shooters **[19973]**, Watertown, WI
Wisconsin/Nicaragua Partners of the Ams. **[19820]**, Stevens Point, WI
Wisconsin Nursery Assn. **[18162]**, Greenfield, WI
Wisconsin Nurses' Assn. **[18737]**, Madison, WI
Wisconsin Nurses Assn., Northwest District - No. 11 **[19764]**, Spooner, WI
Wisconsin Nurses Assn., Southwest District - No. 2 **[19474]**, Platteville, WI
Wisconsin Occupational Therapy Assn. **[18738]**, Madison, WI
Wisconsin Off-Road Bicycling Assn. **[17934]**, Elm Grove, WI
Wisconsin Onsite Waste Disposal Assn. **[18179]**, Hartford, WI
Wisconsin Optometric Assn. **[18739]**, Madison, WI
Wisconsin Orchid Soc. **[18892]**, Mequon, WI
Wisconsin Org. of Nurse Executives **[18142]**, Green Bay, WI
Wisconsin Outdoor Access **[18275]**, Jefferson, WI
Wisconsin Paralyzed Veterans of America **[20110]**, West Allis, WI
Wisconsin Parents of Blind Children **[17732]**, Cedarburg, WI
Wisconsin Park and Recreation Assn. **[18153]**, Greendale, WI
Wisconsin Parking Assn. **[19174]**, Milwaukee, WI
Wisconsin Parkinson Assn. **[19175]**, Milwaukee, WI
Wisconsin Physical Therapy Assn. **[18740]**, Madison, WI
Wisconsin Planned Giving Coun. **[18741]**, Madison, WI
Wisconsin Polygraph Assn. **[19433]**, Peshtigo, WI
Wisconsin Pony of the Americas Club **[19939]**, Vesper, WI
Wisconsin Pork Assn. **[18413]**, Lancaster, WI
Wisconsin Potato and Vegetable Growers Association **[17480]**, Antigo, WI
Wisconsin Pottery Assn. **[18742]**, Madison, WI
Wisconsin Primary Hea. Care Assn. **[18743]**, Madison, WI
Wisconsin Procurement Inst. Educ. and Training Sers. **[19176]**, Milwaukee, WI
Wisconsin Professional Police Assn. **[18744]**, Madison, WI
Wisconsin Professional Policemen's Assn. **[★18744]**
Wisconsin Psychiatric Assn. **[18745]**, Madison, WI
Wisconsin Psychoanalytic Soc. **[19177]**, Milwaukee, WI
Wisconsin Psychological Assn. **[18746]**, Madison, WI
Wisconsin Public Hea. Assn. **[18747]**, Madison, WI
Wisconsin Public Interest Res. Gp. **[18748]**, Madison, WI
Wisconsin Quarter Horse Assn. **[19309]**, New Holstein, WI
Wisconsin Racquetball Assn. **[19448]**, Pewaukee, WI
Wisconsin Radiological Soc. **[19178]**, Milwaukee, WI
Wisconsin Rapids Area Convention and Visitors Bureau **[20197]**, Wisconsin Rapids, WI
Wisconsin Rapids Figure Skating Club **[20198]**, Wisconsin Rapids, WI
Wisconsin Rapids Independent Development Comm. **[★20186]**
Wisconsin Rapids Kennel Club **[19497]**, Port Edwards, WI
Wisconsin Rapids River Cities Development Corp. **[★20186]**
Wisconsin Ready Mixed Concrete Assn. **[18749]**, Madison, WI
Wisconsin Recreation Assn. **[★18153]**
Wisconsin Regional Lily Soc. **[17760]**, Chippewa Falls, WI
Wisconsin Regional Planning Commn; Southwestern **[19472]**, Platteville, WI
Wisconsin Regional Writers' Assn. **[17533]**, Appleton, WI
Wisconsin Restaurant Assn. **[18750]**, Madison, WI
Wisconsin Retail Lumber Assn. **[18046]**, Germantown, WI
Wisconsin Retired Educators' Assn. **[18916]**, Middleton, WI
Wisconsin Rifle and Pistol Assn. **[17659]**, Bristol, WI
Wisconsin Right to Life **[19179]**, Milwaukee, WI
Wisconsin Rodeo Cowboys Association **[19907]**, Tomah, WI
Wisconsin Rottweiler Performance Club **[19869]**, Sun Prairie, WI
Wisconsin Rural Water Assn. **[19485]**, Plover, WI
Wisconsin Scholars **[19180]**, Milwaukee, WI
Wisconsin School-Age Care Alliance **[18268]**, Janesville, WI
Wisconsin School Bus Assn. **[19716]**, Sheboygan, WI
Wisconsin School Psychologists Assn. **[19686]**, Shawano, WI
Wisconsin School Public Relations Assn. **[18751]**, Madison, WI
Wisconsin Scottish **[20111]**, West Allis, WI
Wisconsin Self-Service Laundry Assn. **[17685]**, Brookfield, WI
Wisconsin Self Storage Assn. **[19181]**, Milwaukee, WI
Wisconsin Senior Olympics **[17686]**, Brookfield, WI
Wisconsin Shoreline Skippers No. 102 **[19279]**, Neenah, WI
Wisconsin Skeet Shooting Assn. **[19887]**, Sussex, WI
Wisconsin Small Bus. Development Center **[18752]**, Madison, WI
Wisconsin Snowmobile Clubs; Assn. of **[17488]**, Appleton, WI
Wisconsin Soaring Soc. **[20090]**, Wauwatosa, WI
Wisconsin Soc. of Assn. Executives **[19182]**, Milwaukee, WI
Wisconsin Soc. of Clinical Hypnosis **[18753]**, Madison, WI
Wisconsin Soc. of Enrolled Agents **[18794]**, Manitowoc, WI
Wisconsin Soc. of Land Surveyors **[20013]**, Waukesha, WI
Wisconsin Soc. of PeriAnesthesia Nurses **[19870]**, Sun Prairie, WI
Wisconsin Soc. of Podiatric Medicine **[19974]**, Watertown, WI
Wisconsin Soc. of Radiologic Technologists **[19582]**, Racine, WI
Wisconsin Soc. for Respiratory Care **[18879]**, Menomonee Falls, WI
Wisconsin Soc. of Sci. Teachers **[19411]**, Oshkosh, WI
Wisconsin Space Inst. **[18754]**, Madison, WI
Wisconsin Speleological Soc. **[19717]**, Sheboygan, WI
Wisconsin Sporting Clays Assn. **[17733]**, Cedarburg, WI
Wisconsin State AFL-CIO **[19183]**, Milwaukee, WI
Wisconsin State B.A.S.S. Fed. **[20149]**, Weston, WI
Wisconsin State Cranberry Growers Association **[20199]**, Wisconsin Rapids, WI
Wisconsin State Genealogical Soc. **[18755]**, Madison, WI
Wisconsin State Golf Assn. **[17687]**, Brookfield, WI
Wisconsin State Grange **[18269]**, Janesville, WI
Wisconsin State Reading Assn. **[19587]**, Randolph, WI
Wisconsin State Telecommunications Assn. **[18756]**, Madison, WI
Wisconsin Stewardship Network **[18757]**, Madison, WI
Wisconsin Suffolk Sheep Assn. **[19337]**, Oakfield, WI
Wisconsin Supreme Court Historical Soc. **[19184]**, Milwaukee, WI
Wisconsin Taxpayers Alliance **[18758]**, Madison, WI
Wisconsin Thoracic Soc. **[17688]**, Brookfield, WI
Wisconsin Timberline Hare Beagle Club **[18392]**, Ladysmith, WI
Wisconsin Towns Assn. **[19687]**, Shawano, WI
Wisconsin Toy Fox Terrier Assn. **[19185]**, Milwaukee, WI
Wisconsin Trans. Builders Assn. **[18759]**, Madison, WI
Wisconsin Trappers Assn. **[18069]**, Grand Marsh, WI
Wisconsin Underground Contractors Assn. **[19186]**, Milwaukee, WI
Wisconsin User Gp. of Applied Systems **[19187]**, Milwaukee, WI
Wisconsin Utilities Assn. **[18760]**, Madison, WI
Wisconsin Valley Optometric Soc. **[20060]**, Wausau, WI
Wisconsin Veterinary Medical Assn. **[18761]**, Madison, WI
Wisconsin Waste Fac. Siting Bd. **[18762]**, Madison, WI
Wisconsin Waterfowl Assn. **[18189]**, Hartland, WI
Wisconsin Waterfowlers Assn. **[★18189]**
Wisconsin Wetlands Assn. **[18763]**, Madison, WI
Wisconsin Wildlife Fed. **[19539]**, Prescott, WI
Wisconsin Wine and Spirit Inst. **[18764]**, Madison, WI
Wisconsin Women in Higher Educ. Leadership **[19188]**, Milwaukee, WI
Wisconsin Women's Network **[18765]**, Madison, WI
Wisconsin Woodland Owners Assn., Bad Axe Chap. **[19628]**, Richland Center, WI
Wisconsin Woodland Owners Assn., Black River Chap. **[18432]**, Loyal, WI
Wisconsin Woodland Owners Assn., Blackhawk Chap. **[17711]**, Cambridge, WI
Wisconsin Woodland Owners Assn., Central Sands Chap. **[17537]**, Arkdale, WI
Wisconsin Woodland Owners Assn., Chippewa Valley Chap. **[19373]**, Onalaska, WI
Wisconsin Woodland Owners Assn., Kettle Moraine Chap. **[19821]**, Stevens Point, WI
Wisconsin Woodland Owners Assn., NEWFO Chap. **[18437]**, Luxemburg, WI
Wisconsin Woodland Owners Assn., North Central Chap. **[20202]**, Wittenberg, WI
Wisconsin Woodland Owners Assn., Northwest Chap. **[18393]**, Ladysmith, WI
Wisconsin Woodland Owners Assn., Penokee Chap. **[19431]**, Pence, WI
Wisconsin Woodland Owners Assn., Phoenix Falls Chap. **[19301]**, New Berlin, WI
Wisconsin Woodland Owners Assn., West Central Chap. **[20205]**, Woodbury, WI
Wisconsin Woodland Owners Assn., Winnebagoland Chap. **[19379]**, Oostburg, WI
Wisconsin Woodland Owners Assn., Wolf River Chap. **[18219]**, Hortonville, WI
Wisconsin Wrestling Fed. **[19647]**, River Falls, WI
Wisconsin Youth Soccer Assn. **[20112]**, West Allis, WI
Wisillin Winds Radio Controlled Yacht Club No. 80 **[19583]**, Racine, WI
Wissota Appaloosa Horse Club **[12874]**, West Concord, MN
Wittenberg Area Chamber of Commerce **[20203]**, Wittenberg, WI
Wittenberg Chamber of Commerce **[★20203]**
Wittenberg Univ. Speleological Soc. **[16755]**, Springfield, OH
Wolverine Bar Assn. **[7455]**, Detroit, MI
Wolverine Beagle Club **[8158]**, Hastings, MI
Wolverine Morgan Horse Assn. **[8479]**, Kalkaska, MI
Woman Abuse Now; Stopping **[2862]**, Olney, IL
Woman's Club of Adena **[13013]**, Adena, OH
Woman's Club; Oconomowoc Junior **[19340]**, Oconomowoc, WI
Woman's Club; Wauwatosa **[20085]**, Wauwatosa, WI
Women
African Amer. Women Evolving **[597]**, Chicago, IL
Amer. Assn. of Univ. Women, Grand Rapids Br. **[7885]**, Grand Rapids, MI
Amer. Assn. of Univ. Women - Illinois **[1414]**, Deerfield, IL
Amer. Assn. of Univ. Women - Minnesota State **[12075]**, Red Wing, MN
Amer. Assn. of Univ. Women - Wisconsin **[19387]**, Oshkosh, WI
Amer. Assn. for Women in Community Colleges, Coll. of DuPage **[1824]**, Glen Ellyn, IL
Amer. Assn. for Women in Community Colleges, Region V **[2095]**, Joliet, IL
Antioch Woman's Club **[57]**, Antioch, IL
Assn. for the Advancement of Hmong Women in Minnesota **[11524]**, Minneapolis, MN
Bowling Green Woman's Club **[13385]**, Bowling Green, OH
Chagrin Valley Women's League **[13634]**, Chagrin Falls, OH
Champaign-Urbana Junior Woman's Club **[513]**, Champaign, IL
Chicago Abused Women Coalition **[779]**, Chicago, IL

Chicago Found. for Women **[811]**, Chicago, IL
Chicago Women in Bus. **[836]**, Chicago, IL
Eastlake Women's Club **[15085]**, Eastlake, OH
Gallipolis Junior Woman's Club **[15292]**, Gallipolis, OH
Germantown Junior Women's Club **[18040]**, Germantown, WI
GFWC Indiana **[4430]**, Crown Point, IN
GFWC of Minnesota **[11890]**, New York Mills, MN
GFWC/Ohio Fed. of Women's Clubs **[13835]**, Cincinnati, OH
GFWC Upper Peninsula District No. 5 **[8323]**, Iron Mountain, MI
Glendale Heights Junior Woman's Club **[1852]**, Glendale Heights, IL
Grand Rapids Opportunities for Women **[7951]**, Grand Rapids, MI
Junior Woman's Club of Des Plaines **[1462]**, Des Plaines, IL
Junior Woman's Club of Waukesha **[19987]**, Waukesha, WI
Lansing Junior Woman's Club **[2221]**, Lansing, IL
Lemont Junior Woman's Club **[2246]**, Lemont, IL
Libertyville Junior Woman's Club **[2262]**, Libertyville, IL
Lincoln Junior Woman's Club **[2275]**, Lincoln, IL
Madeira Woman's Club **[13889]**, Cincinnati, OH
McNabb Magnolia Junior Woman's Club **[2467]**, McNabb, IL
Michigan Women's Commn. **[8727]**, Lansing, MI
Michigan Women's Stud. Assn. **[8728]**, Lansing, MI
Minnesota Women of Today **[10307]**, Anoka, MN
Minnesota Women's Consortium **[12532]**, St. Paul, MN
Montgomery Women's Club **[13910]**, Cincinnati, OH
Naperville Junior Woman's Club **[2651]**, Naperville, IL
Natl. Assn. of Women Bus. Owners, Wisconsin **[17508]**, Appleton, WI
Natl. Org. for Women - Chicago **[1088]**, Chicago, IL
Network of Women Entrepreneurs **[1099]**, Chicago, IL
Newborn Lifeline Network **[6022]**, Pekin, IN
Oconomowoc Junior Woman's Club **[19340]**, Oconomowoc, WI
Ohio Agri-Women **[14936]**, Dayton, OH
Ohio Women's Bus. Rsrc. Network **[14699]**, Columbus, OH
Peotone Woman's Club **[3072]**, Peotone, IL
Plymouth Junior Womans' Club **[19493]**, Plymouth, WI
Rochester Junior Woman's Club **[9510]**, Rochester, MI
Sharonville Federated Woman's Club **[13982]**, Cincinnati, OH
Southwest Women Working Together **[1196]**, Chicago, IL
Wauwatosa Woman's Club **[20085]**, Wauwatosa, WI
Wheaton Junior Woman's Club **[4001]**, Wheaton, IL
Wisconsin Women's Network **[18765]**, Madison, WI
Woman's Club of Adena **[13013]**, Adena, OH
Women for Humanity **[3069]**, Peoria, IL
Women Making a Difference **[2050]**, Hoopeston, IL
Women in the Trades **[12604]**, St. Paul, MN
Women of Westland **[10150]**, Westland, MI
Women's Circuit **[14025]**, Cincinnati, OH
Women's Shelter **[12198]**, Rochester, MN
WomenVenture **[12607]**, St. Paul, MN
Woodridge Junior Woman's Club **[4051]**, Woodridge, IL
YWCA St. Paul **[12610]**, St. Paul, MN
Women Accountants, Anderson/Muncie Chap. No. 077; Amer. Soc. of **[5933]**, New Castle, IN
Women Accountants, Cleveland Chap. No. 013; Amer. Soc. of **[16356]**, Parma, OH
Women Accountants, Indianapolis Chap. No. 001; Amer. Soc. of **[5025]**, Indianapolis, IN
Women Bus. Owners, Wisconsin; Natl. Assn. of **[17508]**, Appleton, WI
Women Clubs; Illinois Fed. of Bus. and Professional **[3604]**, Springfield, IL
Women in Community Ser., Midwest Region **[7456]**, Detroit, MI
Women Contractors; Fed. of **[891]**, Chicago, IL
Women in Direct Marketing Intl., Chicago Chap. **[1634]**, Elmwood Park, IL
Women in the Director's Chair of Chicago **[1235]**, Chicago, IL
Women Employed **[1236]**, Chicago, IL
Women Evolving; African Amer. **[597]**, Chicago, IL
Women in Focus **[18766]**, Madison, WI
Women, Grand Rapids Br; Amer. Assn. of Univ. **[7885]**, Grand Rapids, MI
Women Hea. Executives Network **[2152]**, Kenilworth, IL
Women in Hea.Care; Executive **[5112]**, Indianapolis, IN
Women in Higher Educ. Leadership; Wisconsin **[19188]**, Milwaukee, WI
Women for Humanity **[3069]**, Peoria, IL
Women - Illinois; Amer. Assn. of Univ. **[1414]**, Deerfield, IL
Women In Film Chicago **[1237]**, Chicago, IL
Women in Insurance and Financial Sers., Cincinnati Chap. **[15731]**, Loveland, OH
Women Making a Difference **[2050]**, Hoopeston, IL
Women Police, Region 6; Intl. Assn. of **[4883]**, Hammond, IN
Women of Reform Judaism: Isaac M. Wise Temple Sisterhood **[14024]**, Cincinnati, OH
Women of Reform Judaism: Temple Israel Sisterhood, Columbus **[14766]**, Columbus, OH
Women in Sci., Detroit; Assn. for **[6683]**, Ann Arbor, MI
Women in the Trades **[12604]**, St. Paul, MN
Women Voters of the Cleveland Area; League of **[14155]**, Cleveland, OH
Women Voters of the Greater Dayton Area; League of **[14904]**, Dayton, OH
Women Voters of Illinois Education Fund; League of **[★1026]**
Women Voters of Illinois; League of **[1026]**, Chicago, IL
Women Voters of the Lansing Area; League of **[8596]**, Lansing, MI
Women of Westland **[10150]**, Westland, MI
Women on Wheels **[12605]**, St. Paul, MN
Women in the Wind **[16985]**, Toledo, OH
Women in the Wind - Akron Chap. **[13103]**, Akron, OH
Women in the Wind, Milwaukee Area **[20113]**, West Allis, WI
Women in the Wind, Toledo Chap. **[★16985]**
Women - Wisconsin; Amer. Assn. of Univ. **[19387]**, Oshkosh, WI
Women's Action for New Directions, Michigan **[9832]**, Southfield, MI
Women's Art Alliance **[★3663]**
Women's Art Registry of Minnesota **[12606]**, St. Paul, MN
Women's Bar Assn. of Illinois **[1238]**, Chicago, IL
Women's Bowling Assn; Madison **[19208]**, Monona, WI
Women's Bowling Assn; Michigan **[8386]**, Jackson, MI
Women's Chorus; Grand Rapids **[7953]**, Grand Rapids, MI
Women's Circuit **[14025]**, Cincinnati, OH
Women's Club; Barrington **[146]**, Barrington, IL
Women's Coalition; Wisconsin Bus. **[18675]**, Madison, WI
Women's Commn; Michigan **[8727]**, Lansing, MI
Women's Consortium; Minnesota **[12532]**, St. Paul, MN
Women's Division of the Lancaster Chamber of Commerce **[15614]**, Lancaster, OH
Women's Economic Club **[★7377]**
Women's Entrepreneurial Network **[15920]**, Maumee, OH
Women's Hall of Fame and Women's Historical Center **[★8728]**
Women's Historical Center; Women's Hall of Fame and **[★8728]**
Women's Intl. League for Peace and Freedom - Ann Arbor/Ypsilanti **[6793]**, Ann Arbor, MI
Women's League; Chagrin Valley **[13634]**, Chagrin Falls, OH
Women's Natl. Book Assn., Detroit Chap. **[10151]**, Westland, MI
Women's Network **[13104]**, Akron, OH
Women's Network; Wisconsin **[18765]**, Madison, WI
Women's Outdoor Sports Assn. **[6898]**, Bay City, MI
Women's Peace Presence to Stop Proj. Elf **[★19089]**
Women's Rights
League of Women Voters in the Akron Area **[13063]**, Akron, OH
Natl. Org. for Women-Milwaukee **[19079]**, Milwaukee, WI
Women Employed **[1236]**, Chicago, IL
Women's Action for New Directions, Michigan **[9832]**, Southfield, MI
YWCA of Minneapolis **[11780]**, Minneapolis, MN
Women's Sailing Assn; North Coast **[15589]**, Lakewood, OH
Women's Shelter **[12198]**, Rochester, MN
Women's Studies
Friends of Women's Stud. **[13833]**, Cincinnati, OH
Women's Stud. Assn; Michigan **[8728]**, Lansing, MI
WomenVenture **[12607]**, St. Paul, MN
Woo YL Club - Young Life **[17335]**, Wooster, OH
Wood County Historical Soc. **[13402]**, Bowling Green, OH
Wood Dale Chamber of Commerce **[4044]**, Wood Dale, IL
Wood-Land-Lakes Rsrc. Conservation and Development Coun. **[4132]**, Angola, IN
Wood Trades
Wisconsin Woodland Owners Assn., Bad Axe Chap. **[19628]**, Richland Center, WI
Wisconsin Woodland Owners Assn., Black River Chap. **[18432]**, Loyal, WI
Wisconsin Woodland Owners Assn., Blackhawk Chap. **[17711]**, Cambridge, WI
Wisconsin Woodland Owners Assn., Central Sands Chap. **[17537]**, Arkdale, WI
Wisconsin Woodland Owners Assn., Chippewa Valley Chap. **[19373]**, Onalaska, WI
Wisconsin Woodland Owners Assn., Kettle Moraine Chap. **[19821]**, Stevens Point, WI
Wisconsin Woodland Owners Assn., NEWFO Chap. **[18437]**, Luxemburg, WI
Wisconsin Woodland Owners Assn., North Central Chap. **[20202]**, Wittenberg, WI
Wisconsin Woodland Owners Assn., Northwest Chap. **[18393]**, Ladysmith, WI
Wisconsin Woodland Owners Assn., Penokee Chap. **[19431]**, Pence, WI
Wisconsin Woodland Owners Assn., Phoenix Falls Chap. **[19301]**, New Berlin, WI
Wisconsin Woodland Owners Assn., West Central Chap. **[20205]**, Woodbury, WI
Wisconsin Woodland Owners Assn., Winnebago-land Chap. **[19379]**, Oostburg, WI
Wisconsin Woodland Owners Assn., Wolf River Chap. **[18219]**, Hortonville, WI
Wood Truss Coun. of Am. **[18767]**, Madison, WI
Wood Truss Coun. of Am. - Illinois **[3331]**, Rockford, IL
Wood Truss Coun. of Am. Ohio Chap. Assn. **[13595]**, Canton, OH
Wood Truss Coun. of Michigan **[9647]**, Saginaw, MI
Woodbury Chamber of Commerce **[12986]**, Woodbury, MN
Woodbury Figure Skating Club **[12987]**, Woodbury, MN
Woodbury Jaycees **[12988]**, Woodbury, MN
Woodbury Young Life **[12989]**, Woodbury, MN
Wooden Canoe Heritage Assn., Illinois **[477]**, Cary, IL
Wooden Canoe Heritage Assn., Indiana **[5502]**, Indianapolis, IN
Wooden Canoe Heritage Assn., Michigan **[7584]**, Eaton Rapids, MI
Wooden Canoe Heritage Assn., Minnesota **[11850]**, Mounds View, MN
Wooden Canoe Heritage Assn., Wisconsin **[18283]**, Juneau, WI
Woodland Lakes Assn. of Realtors **[19912]**, Tomahawk, WI
Woodlands Lib. Cooperative **[6594]**, Albion, MI
Woodridge Area Chamber of Commerce **[4050]**, Woodridge, IL
Woodridge Junior Woman's Club **[4051]**, Woodridge, IL
Woodstock Chamber of Commerce and Indus. **[4065]**, Woodstock, IL

Wool
Illinois Lamb and Wool Producers **[380]**, Bushnell, IL
Wooster Area Chamber of Commerce **[17336]**, Wooster, OH
Workers
Southeast Michigan Jobs with Justice **[7438]**, Detroit, MI
UAW Local 602 **[8766]**, Lansing, MI
Workers; Chicago Chap. of the Natl. Assn. of Black Social **[801]**, Chicago, IL
Workforce Development Network; Employers **[18096]**, Green Bay, WI
Workforce Opportunities Rsrc. Consortium **[576]**, Charleston, IL
Works in Progress **[12638]**, Sauk Rapids, MN
World Affairs Coun. of Greater Cincinnati **[14026]**, Cincinnati, OH
World of Children **[14767]**, Columbus, OH
World Future Soc., Akron (Northeastern Ohio) **[13105]**, Akron, OH
World Future Soc., Cincinnati **[16031]**, Milford, OH
World Future Soc., Columbus **[17225]**, Westerville, OH
World Future Soc., Detroit **[8161]**, Hazel Park, MI
World Future Soc., Madison **[19833]**, Stoughton, WI
World Future Soc., Minneapolis-St. Paul **[11779]**, Minneapolis, MN
World Future Soc., Pekin **[2996]**, Pekin, IL
World Notables
Edison Birthplace Assn. **[16021]**, Milan, OH
Worthington Area Chamber of Commerce **[12993]**, Worthington, MN
Worthington Area Chamber of Commerce **[17352]**, Worthington, OH
Worthington Area United Way **[12994]**, Worthington, MN
Worthington Convention and Visitors Bur. **[17353]**, Worthington, OH
Worthington Lions Club **[14768]**, Columbus, OH
Wrestling
Illinois USA Wrestling **[451]**, Carol Stream, IL
Indiana State Wrestling Assn. **[4182]**, Beech Grove, IN
Michigan Wrestling Fed. **[7183]**, Clinton Township, MI
Minnesota USA Wrestling **[11679]**, Minneapolis, MN
Rich Rattlers Wrestling Club **[2439]**, Matteson, IL
South Gibson Wrestling Club **[6072]**, Princeton, IN
USA Wrestling-Ohio **[13102]**, Akron, OH
Wisconsin Wrestling Fed. **[19647]**, River Falls, WI
Wrestling Boosters Club; South Gibson **[★6072]**
Wrestling Club; Rich Rattlers **[2439]**, Matteson, IL
Wrestling Club; South Gibson **[6072]**, Princeton, IN
Wright County Area United Way **[11812]**, Monticello, MN
Wright County Chap., Amer. Red Cross **[10580]**, Buffalo, MN
Wright County Minnesota Kennel Club **[11813]**, Monticello, MN
Wright Dunbar **[14971]**, Dayton, OH
Wright State Univ. Area Coun. of Teachers of Mathematics **[14972]**, Dayton, OH
Wrightwood Community Development Corp. **[1239]**, Chicago, IL
Wrinkled Rescue/Chinese Shar-Pei Rescue **[13123]**, Amanda, OH
Wrinkled Rescue, Chinese Shar-Rescue Gp. **[★13123]**
Writers
Chicago-North Romance Writers of Am. **[67]**, Arlington Heights, IL
Greater Detroit Romance Writers of Am. **[7163]**, Clarkston, MI
Heart and Scroll Romance Writers of Am. **[2713]**, Normal, IL
Indiana Romance Writers of Am. **[5292]**, Indianapolis, IN
Mid-Michigan Chap. of Romance Writers of Am. **[8451]**, Kalamazoo, MI
Midwest Fiction Writers **[11605]**, Minneapolis, MN
Mystery Writers of Am., Midwest Chap. **[4019]**, Wilmette, IL
Natl. Writers Union - Chicago Chap. **[1090]**, Chicago, IL
Natl. Writers Union, Southeast Michigan **[7415]**, Detroit, MI
Natl. Writers Union, Twin Cities Chap. **[11705]**, Minneapolis, MN
Northeast Ohio Romance Writers of Am. **[17233]**, Westlake, OH
Prairie Hearts Romance Writers of Am. Chap. 43 **[3401]**, St. Joseph, IL
Romance Writers of Am., Windy City Chap. **[2303]**, Lisle, IL
Writers of Am., Windy City Chap; Romance **[2303]**, Lisle, IL
Writers Union, Southeast Michigan; Natl. **[7415]**, Detroit, MI
Writers Union, Twin Cities Chap; Natl. **[11705]**, Minneapolis, MN
Writing
Songwriters and Poets Critique **[14738]**, Columbus, OH
Wisconsin Regional Writers' Assn. **[17533]**, Appleton, WI
Wurtland Beagle Club **[15509]**, Ironton, OH
Wyandot County Humane Soc. **[17035]**, Upper Sandusky, OH
Wyandotte Lions Club - Michigan **[9844]**, Southgate, MI
Wyanet Chamber of Commerce **[4071]**, Wyanet, IL
Wycliffe Bible Translators, North Central **[3944]**, West Chicago, IL
Wykoff Lions Club **[12996]**, Wykoff, MN
WyldLife - Morton, Illinois **[3894]**, Washington, IL
WyldLife Naperville and Aurora **[2666]**, Naperville, IL
WyldLife Northville **[9246]**, Novi, MI
WyldLife Novi **[9247]**, Novi, MI
Wyldlife South Lyon **[9248]**, Novi, MI
WyldLife Walled Lake **[9249]**, Novi, MI
WyldLife - Washington, Illinois **[3895]**, Washington, IL
WyldLife - Whitefish Bay **[19189]**, Milwaukee, WI
Wyoming Kentwood Area Chamber of Commerce **[10194]**, Wyoming, MI
Wyoming - Young Life **[15173]**, Fairfield, OH

X

Xenia Area Chamber of Commerce **[17378]**, Xenia, OH
Xenia - Young Life **[17379]**, Xenia, OH
Xi Sigma Pi - Natural Resources Honor Society **[19822]**, Stevens Point, WI
Xilin Table Tennis Club **[2667]**, Naperville, IL

Y

Yellow Bike Coalition **[12608]**, St. Paul, MN
Yellow Springs Chamber of Commerce **[17383]**, Yellow Springs, OH
YL Cleveland Young Lives **[14239]**, Cleveland, OH
YL of Dubois Co - Young Life **[5536]**, Jasper, IN
YMCA - Arthur Jordan **[5503]**, Indianapolis, IN
YMCA - Benjamin Harrison Br. **[5504]**, Indianapolis, IN
YMCA of Cleveland **[★14240]**
YMCA of Greater Cleveland **[14240]**, Cleveland, OH
YMCA Training Alliance **[1240]**, Chicago, IL
Yoga
BKS Iyengar Yoga Assn. of the Midwest Bioregions **[6687]**, Ann Arbor, MI
BKS Iyengar Yoga Assn. Minnesota **[11531]**, Minneapolis, MN
York and Willowbrook - Young Life **[2028]**, Hinsdale, IL
York - Young Life **[2029]**, Hinsdale, IL
Yorkville Area Chamber of Commerce **[4077]**, Yorkville, IL
Young Audiences of Greater Cleveland **[14241]**, Cleveland, OH
Young Audiences of Indiana **[5505]**, Indianapolis, IN
Young Audiences of Michigan **[7457]**, Detroit, MI
Young Audiences of Minnesota **[12609]**, St. Paul, MN
Young Audiences of the Upper Midwest **[★12609]**
Young Entomologists' Soc. **[8771]**, Lansing, MI
Young Life Athens County **[13222]**, Athens, OH
Young Life Boonville **[4277]**, Boonville, IN
Young Life Buckeye Region **[15068]**, Dublin, OH
Young Life Carmel **[5506]**, Indianapolis, IN
Young Life Central Grand Rapids **[8030]**, Grand Rapids, MI
Young Life Central Illinois **[3896]**, Washington, IL
Young Life Chicago Northside **[1241]**, Chicago, IL
Young Life Chicago South **[3511]**, South Holland, IL
Young Life Chicagoland Region **[2668]**, Naperville, IL
Young Life Chippewa Valley **[17912]**, Eau Claire, WI
Young Life Cincinnati Metro **[14027]**, Cincinnati, OH
Young Life Clearwater Cove Development **[8507]**, Lake City, MI
Young Life Cleveland Metro **[14242]**, Cleveland, OH
Young Life Cleveland South **[16252]**, North Royalton, OH
Young Life Cleveland West Shore **[17239]**, Westlake, OH
Young Life Columbiana County **[16597]**, Salineville, OH
Young Life Columbus North **[14769]**, Columbus, OH
Young Life Columbus Northeast **[14770]**, Columbus, OH
Young Life Columbus Northwest **[14771]**, Columbus, OH
Young Life Columbus Southeast **[14772]**, Columbus, OH
Young Life Columbus Southwest **[14773]**, Columbus, OH
Young Life County Line **[17081]**, Wadsworth, OH
Young Life Dayton North **[14973]**, Dayton, OH
Young Life Dayton, OH **[14974]**, Dayton, OH
Young Life Detroit **[7458]**, Detroit, MI
Young Life Eastern Cincinnati **[14028]**, Cincinnati, OH
Young Life Eastern DuPage **[2030]**, Hinsdale, IL
Young Life Eastern Great Lakes Region **[8772]**, Lansing, MI
Young Life Ely **[10960]**, Ely, MN
Young Life Fort Wayne **[4730]**, Fort Wayne, IN
Young Life Geneva Lakes **[18401]**, Lake Geneva, WI
Young Life Glenbard South **[1844]**, Glen Ellyn, IL
Young Life Glenbard West **[1845]**, Glen Ellyn, IL
Young Life Grand Rapids Urban **[8031]**, Grand Rapids, MI
Young Life Grand Rapids West **[8050]**, Grandville, MI
Young Life Greater Cincinnati **[15174]**, Fairfield, OH
Young Life Greater Lansing **[7571]**, East Lansing, MI
Young Life Greater Muncie **[5507]**, Indianapolis, IN
Young Life Greater Richmond **[6114]**, Richmond, IN
Young Life Greencastle **[5508]**, Indianapolis, IN
Young Life Grosse Pointe **[8086]**, Grosse Pointe, MI
Young Life Hamilton-Southeastern **[5509]**, Indianapolis, IN
Young Life Heartland Region **[19246]**, Mount Horeb, WI
Young Life Henry County **[5941]**, New Castle, IN
Young Life Hillsdale **[8185]**, Hillsdale, MI
Young Life Holland **[8228]**, Holland, MI
Young Life Indiana Camp **[5747]**, Marshall, IN
Young Life Indiana-Kentucky Region **[5965]**, Newburgh, IN
Young Life Indiana Region **[5510]**, Indianapolis, IN
Young Life Indianapolis Urban Initiative **[5511]**, Indianapolis, IN
Young Life Jasper **[5537]**, Jasper, IN
Young Life Kalamazoo **[8472]**, Kalamazoo, MI
Young Life Kane County **[1801]**, Geneva, IL
Young Life LaCrosse **[19374]**, Onalaska, WI
Young Life Lake Country **[18190]**, Hartland, WI
Young Life Lake County **[2191]**, Lake Bluff, IL
Young Life Lake Erie West Region **[13403]**, Bowling Green, OH
Young Life Lakeshore - Grand Haven **[7869]**, Grand Haven, MI
Young Life LaSalle St. **[1242]**, Chicago, IL
Young Life Lawrence **[5512]**, Indianapolis, IN
Young Life Lenawee County **[6586]**, Adrian, MI
Young Life Licking County **[15347]**, Granville, OH
Young Life Lincoln-Way **[1731]**, Frankfort, IL
Young Life Lorain County **[13246]**, Avon Lake, OH
Young Life McHenry **[3949]**, West Dundee, IL
Young Life McLean County **[313]**, Bloomington, IL
Young Life Metro SW **[3964]**, Western Springs, IL
Young Life Miami-Shelby County **[16441]**, Piqua, OH
Young Life Michiana **[6275]**, South Bend, IN
Young Life Midland **[9044]**, Midland, MI

Young Life Milwaukee North Shore **[19190]**, Milwaukee, WI
Young Life Mt. Horeb **[19247]**, Mount Horeb, WI
Young Life MW Multicultural/Urban **[1243]**, Chicago, IL
Young Life Naperville and Aurora **[2669]**, Naperville, IL
Young Life Newburgh **[5966]**, Newburgh, IN
Young Life North Central Michigan **[6954]**, Big Rapids, MI
Young Life North Coast Development **[17240]**, Westlake, OH
Young Life North Coast Region **[17241]**, Westlake, OH
Young Life Northern Dakota County **[10876]**, Eagan, MN
Young Life Northern Lakes **[8508]**, Lake City, MI
Young Life Northern States Region **[11195]**, Hopkins, MN
Young Life Northville **[9250]**, Novi, MI
Young Life Northwest Chicago **[1244]**, Chicago, IL
Young Life Northwest DuPage **[1846]**, Glen Ellyn, IL
Young Life Northwest Indianapolis **[5513]**, Indianapolis, IN
Young Life Novi **[9251]**, Novi, MI
Young Life NW Suburban Chicago **[2930]**, Palatine, IL
Young Life NW Suburban Detroit **[9252]**, Novi, MI
Young Life Oak Park and River Forest **[2830]**, Oak Park, IL
Young Life Ohio Valley West **[15522]**, Jacobsburg, OH
Young Life Ottertail County **[11006]**, Fergus Falls, MN
Young Life Owatonna **[11973]**, Owatonna, MN
Young Life Plymouth-Canton and Clarenceville **[9413]**, Plymouth, MI
Young Life Quincy **[3175]**, Quincy, IL
Young Life Red Wing **[12092]**, Red Wing, MN
Young Life Ripon **[18812]**, Markesan, WI
Young Life Rock Island County **[2536]**, Moline, IL
Young Life Rockford **[3332]**, Rockford, IL
Young Life St. Cloud **[12318]**, St. Cloud, MN
Young Life St. Croix Valley **[12731]**, Stillwater, MN
Young Life South Central Indiana **[4408]**, Columbus, IN
Young Life South Grand Rapids **[8032]**, Grand Rapids, MI
Young Life South Lyon **[9253]**, Novi, MI
Young Life Southeast Cincinnati **[13129]**, Amelia, OH
Young Life Southern Hills **[4266]**, Bloomington, IN
Young Life Southwest Michigan **[9695]**, St. Joseph, MI
Young Life Springfield **[16756]**, Springfield, OH
Young Life Stevens Point **[19823]**, Stevens Point, WI
Young Life SW Cleveland **[13350]**, Berea, OH
Young Life Timber Wolf Lake **[8509]**, Lake City, MI
Young Life Tri State **[371]**, Burnside, IL
Young Life Tuscarawas County **[16806]**, Sugarcreek, OH
Young Life Union Ave. **[1245]**, Chicago, IL
Young Life Upper Jefferson Cnty **[16990]**, Toronto, OH
Young Life Urban Growth Proj. **[11196]**, Hopkins, MN
Young Life Walled Lake **[9254]**, Novi, MI
Young Life Washington Township **[5514]**, Indianapolis, IN
Young Life Washtenaw County **[6794]**, Ann Arbor, MI
Young Life Wayne and Ashland Counties **[17337]**, Wooster, OH
Young Life West Ottawa-Zeeland **[8229]**, Holland, MI
Young Life West Toledo **[16835]**, Sylvania, OH
Young Life Western Cincinnati Urban **[15175]**, Fairfield, OH
Young Life Western Great Lakes Region **[8033]**, Grand Rapids, MI
Young Life Western Reserve **[15488]**, Hudson, OH
Young Life Wheaton North **[1847]**, Glen Ellyn, IL
Young Life Wheaton Warrenville South **[1848]**, Glen Ellyn, IL
Young Life White Bear Lake - Mahtomedi Area **[12908]**, White Bear Lake, MN
Young Life Winona **[12968]**, Winona, MN
Young Life Wood County **[13404]**, Bowling Green, OH
Young Life Xenia/Fairborn **[17380]**, Xenia, OH
Young Life Youth Center St. Charles - Department of Corrections **[1802]**, Geneva, IL
Young Life - Youth Farm **[3897]**, Washington, IL
Young Life Ypsilanti **[10219]**, Ypsilanti, MI
Young Life Zionsville **[5515]**, Indianapolis, IN
Young Men's Bus. Assn. **[★3160]**
Young Men's Christian Association; Cleveland **[★14240]**
Young Men's Christian Association; Defiance Area **[14985]**, Defiance, OH
Young Men's Christian Association of Findlay, Ohio **[15218]**, Findlay, OH
Young Men's Christian Association; Phantom Lake **[19254]**, Mukwonago, WI
Young Men's Christian Association; Sidney-Shelby County **[16670]**, Sidney, OH
Young Men's Christian Association; Southlake **[4437]**, Crown Point, IN
Young Women's Christian Association of Indianapolis **[5516]**, Indianapolis, IN
Young Women's Christian Association of Kalamazoo **[8473]**, Kalamazoo, MI
YoungLife Green Bay **[18143]**, Green Bay, WI
YoungLife Northern Twin Cities **[12250]**, Roseville, MN
Youngstown AFL-CIO Coun. **[17421]**, Youngstown, OH
Youngstown Aikikai **[17422]**, Youngstown, OH
Youngstown Air Reserve Base Community Council **[16209]**, Niles, OH
Youngstown All Breed Training Club **[16230]**, North Jackson, OH
Youngstown Area Grocers Assn. **[17423]**, Youngstown, OH
Youngstown BMW No. 120 **[17424]**, Youngstown, OH
Youngstown Columbiana Assn. of Realtors **[17425]**, Youngstown, OH
Youngstown Diocesan Confed. of Teachers **[13375]**, Boardman, OH
Youngstown Lions Club **[17426]**, Youngstown, OH
Youngstown/Mahoning Valley United Way **[17427]**, Youngstown, OH
Youngstown Numismatic Club **[17428]**, Youngstown, OH
Youngstown SCORE **[17429]**, Youngstown, OH
Youngstown South Side Lions Club **[13238]**, Austintown, OH
Youngstown State Univ. Students In Free Enterprise **[17430]**, Youngstown, OH
Youngstown-Warren Inventors Assn. **[17431]**, Youngstown, OH
Youngstown/Warren Regional Chamber of Commerce **[17432]**, Youngstown, OH
Youth
Adams, Jay and Wells County Youth for Christ **[4267]**, Bluffton, IN
Adams - Young Life **[6207]**, South Bend, IN
Adrian - Young Life **[6562]**, Adrian, MI
Alexander High School - Young Life **[13192]**, Athens, OH
Allendale Middle School - Wyldlife **[6618]**, Allendale, MI
Amelia - Young Life **[13124]**, Amelia, OH
Anderson - Young Life **[13126]**, Amelia, OH
Anthony Wayne HS - Young Life **[15901]**, Maumee, OH
Anthony Wayne Wyldlife **[15902]**, Maumee, OH
Apple Valley - Young Life **[10586]**, Burnsville, MN
Appleton Young Life **[19268]**, Neenah, WI
Arrowhead Young Life **[18181]**, Hartland, WI
Ash YL club - Young Life **[17313]**, Wooster, OH
Athens High School - Young Life **[13199]**, Athens, OH
Athens Middle School - YoungLife **[13200]**, Athens, OH
Awana Clubs Intl. **[3718]**, Streamwood, IL
Baldwin St. MS - Wyldlife **[6619]**, Allendale, MI
Batesville - Wyld Life **[4158]**, Batesville, IN
Batesville - Young Life **[4159]**, Batesville, IN
Bay Port High School - Young Life **[18084]**, Green Bay, WI
Beavercreek - Young Life **[14859]**, Dayton, OH
Bedford - Young Life **[8299]**, Ida, MI
Bellbrook - Young Life **[14860]**, Dayton, OH
Belmont County - Young Life **[15520]**, Jacobsburg, OH
Bemidji Area Youth for Christ **[10405]**, Bemidji, MN
Big Bros. and Big Sisters of Metropolitan Detroit **[9792]**, Southfield, MI
Big Rapids - Wyldlife **[6942]**, Big Rapids, MI
Big Rapids - Young Life **[6943]**, Big Rapids, MI
Bloom-Carroll - Young Life **[14337]**, Columbus, OH
Bloomington - Wyldlife **[4211]**, Bloomington, IN
Bloomington Wyldlife **[11180]**, Hopkins, MN
Bloomington Wyldlife - Wyldlife **[2711]**, Normal, IL
Bloomington - Young Life **[2712]**, Normal, IL
Bloomington Young Life **[11181]**, Hopkins, MN
Bluewater Thumb Youth for Christ **[9376]**, Pigeon, MI
Bowling Green - Young Life **[13386]**, Bowling Green, OH
Bowsher HS - Young Life **[15904]**, Maumee, OH
Boys and Girls Club of Cass County **[7099]**, Cassopolis, MI
Boys and Girls Club of Greater Holland **[8194]**, Holland, MI
Boys and Girls Club of Hancock County **[4832]**, Greenfield, IN
Boys and Girls Club of Indianapolis **[5060]**, Indianapolis, IN
Boys and Girls Club of Lansing **[8554]**, Lansing, MI
Boys and Girls Club of Sandusky **[16606]**, Sandusky, OH
Boys and Girls Club of South Oakland County **[9577]**, Royal Oak, MI
Boys and Girls Club of Troy **[9978]**, Troy, MI
Boys and Girls Club of Zionsville **[6549]**, Zionsville, IN
Boys and Girls Clubs **[20032]**, Wausau, WI
Boys and Girls Clubs of Chicago **[769]**, Chicago, IL
Boys and Girls Clubs of Northwest Indiana **[4776]**, Gary, IN
Boys and Girls Clubs of Porter County **[6380]**, Valparaiso, IN
Boys' Village - Young Life **[17316]**, Wooster, OH
Breakfast Discipleship - Young Life **[16431]**, Piqua, OH
Brebeuf - Young Life **[5062]**, Indianapolis, IN
Bridgman - Young Life **[9682]**, St. Joseph, MI
Brown County 4-H and Youth Prog. **[18087]**, Green Bay, WI
Buffet - Wyldlife **[12717]**, Stillwater, MN
Burnsville Young Life **[10590]**, Burnsville, MN
Cadillac - Young Life **[8504]**, Lake City, MI
Caledonia - Young Life **[7915]**, Grand Rapids, MI
Calvin Christian High School - Young Life **[8035]**, Grandville, MI
Calvin Christian Middle School - Wyldlife **[8036]**, Grandville, MI
Cambridge-Isanti - Young Life **[10619]**, Cambridge, MN
Cambridge - Young Life **[13497]**, Cambridge, OH
Camp Fire Boys and Girls Tayanoka Coun. **[16585]**, Salem, OH
Camp Fire USA Greater Dayton Area Coun. **[14865]**, Dayton, OH
Camp Fire USA Illinois Prairie Coun. **[2326]**, Lombard, IL
Camp Fire USA Indiana Heartland Coun. **[5066]**, Indianapolis, IN
Camp Fire USA Metropolitan Chicago Coun. **[775]**, Chicago, IL
Camp Fire USA North Oakland Coun. **[10080]**, Waterford, MI
Camp Fire USA Northeast Ohio Coun. **[13529]**, Canfield, OH
Camp Fire USA Northern Star Coun. **[11821]**, Moorhead, MN
Camp Fire USA Northwest Ohio Coun. **[15197]**, Findlay, OH
Camp Fire USA Oneida Coun. **[19597]**, Rhinelander, WI
Camp Fire USA River Bend Coun. **[6222]**, South Bend, IN
Camp Fire USA Wathana Coun. **[9794]**, Southfield, MI
Camp Fire USA West Michigan Coun. **[7916]**, Grand Rapids, MI
Canal Winchester - Young Life **[14349]**, Columbus, OH

Canterbury - Wyldlife **[4647]**, Fort Wayne, IN
Canton/Plymouth/Salem - Young Life **[9396]**, Plymouth, MI
Carmel High School - Young Life **[5067]**, Indianapolis, IN
Carmel - Wyldlife **[5068]**, Indianapolis, IN
Centerville High School - Young Life **[6089]**, Richmond, IN
Central Indiana Youth for Christ **[5082]**, Indianapolis, IN
Central Michigan Youth for Christ **[6631]**, Alma, MI
Central Minnesota Youth for Christ **[12283]**, St. Cloud, MN
Central Ohio Youth for Christ **[14364]**, Columbus, OH
Champaign Area Young Life **[507]**, Champaign, IL
Champaign WyldLife **[516]**, Champaign, IL
Champaign Young Life **[517]**, Champaign, IL
CHCA Young Life **[13767]**, Cincinnati, OH
Chippewa Valley Young Life Club **[17871]**, Eau Claire, WI
Chippewa Wyldlife **[12224]**, Roseville, MN
City High School - Young Life **[7918]**, Grand Rapids, MI
Clarenceville - Young Life **[9397]**, Plymouth, MI
Clark - YoungLife **[16727]**, Springfield, OH
Clay - Young Life **[6227]**, South Bend, IN
Colerain - Young Life **[15154]**, Fairfield, OH
Copley - Young Life **[17074]**, Wadsworth, OH
County Line - Wyldlife **[17075]**, Wadsworth, OH
Crow River Area Youth for Christ **[11327]**, Litchfield, MN
Darke County Youth for Christ **[15361]**, Greenville, OH
Defiance Area Young Men's Christian Association **[14985]**, Defiance, OH
Defiance Area Youth for Christ **[14986]**, Defiance, OH
Detroit Urban - Young Life **[7358]**, Detroit, MI
Detroit Youth for Christ **[7359]**, Detroit, MI
Dexter HS - Young Life **[6693]**, Ann Arbor, MI
Dexter - Wyldlife **[6694]**, Ann Arbor, MI
Dow/Midland - Young Life **[9024]**, Midland, MI
Dublin Coffman/Jerome - Young Life **[14424]**, Columbus, OH
Dublin Scioto - Young Life **[14425]**, Columbus, OH
Dunlap - Central Illinois - Young Life **[3886]**, Washington, IL
Dunlap Wyldlife - Wyldlife **[3887]**, Washington, IL
East Aurora Young Life **[2633]**, Naperville, IL
East Central Illinois Youth for Christ **[519]**, Champaign, IL
East Central Indiana Youth for Christ **[4105]**, Anderson, IN
East Central Minnesota Young Life **[10621]**, Cambridge, MN
East Central Wyldlife **[10622]**, Cambridge, MN
East Grand Rapids High - Young Life **[7924]**, Grand Rapids, MI
East Grand Rapids Middle School - Wyldlife **[7925]**, Grand Rapids, MI
East Lansing - Young Life **[7517]**, East Lansing, MI
East Peoria - Young Life **[3888]**, Washington, IL
Eastern (Greene) - Young Life **[4216]**, Bloomington, IN
Eastern Ottawa Young Life **[6621]**, Allendale, MI
Eastern - Young Life **[4217]**, Bloomington, IN
Eastwood - Wyldlife **[5105]**, Indianapolis, IN
Eastwood - Young Life **[13388]**, Bowling Green, OH
Eaton Rapids Middle School - Wyldlife **[7926]**, Grand Rapids, MI
Eaton Rapids - Young Life **[7518]**, East Lansing, MI
Eden Prairie - Young Life **[11182]**, Hopkins, MN
Edgewood - Young Life **[4218]**, Bloomington, IN
Edina - Young Life **[11183]**, Hopkins, MN
Elkhart County Youth for Christ **[4495]**, Elkhart, IN
Elmwood - Young Life **[13389]**, Bowling Green, OH
Erie Mason - Young Life **[8300]**, Ida, MI
Fariborn High School - Young Life **[17368]**, Xenia, OH
Farmington Wyldlife **[7642]**, Farmington, MI
Farmington Wyldlife **[10591]**, Burnsville, MN
Farmington Young Life **[7643]**, Farmington, MI
Fed. Hocking High School - Young Life **[13204]**, Athens, OH
Findlay Area Youth for Christ **[15200]**, Findlay, OH
Finneytown - Young Life **[15156]**, Fairfield, OH
Five-Os Young Life - Oconomowoc **[18182]**, Hartland, WI
Fond du Lac Area Youth for Christ **[17975]**, Fond du Lac, WI
Forest Hills Central High School - Young Life **[7932]**, Grand Rapids, MI
Forest Hills Central Middle School - Wyldlife **[7933]**, Grand Rapids, MI
Forest Hills Eastern High School - Young Life **[7934]**, Grand Rapids, MI
Forest Hills Eastern Middle School - Wyldlife **[7935]**, Grand Rapids, MI
Forest Hills Northern High School - Young Life **[7936]**, Grand Rapids, MI
Forest Hills Northern Middle School - Wyldlife **[7937]**, Grand Rapids, MI
Forsythe - Wyldlife **[6695]**, Ann Arbor, MI
Fort Wayne Area Youth for Christ **[4653]**, Fort Wayne, IN
Ft. Wayne Young Life Club **[4662]**, Fort Wayne, IN
Fox Valley WyldLife **[19270]**, Neenah, WI
Fox Valley Young Life **[19271]**, Neenah, WI
Fremd - Young Life **[2909]**, Palatine, IL
Gahanna - Young Life **[14441]**, Columbus, OH
Garaway Young Life **[16805]**, Sugarcreek, OH
Gateway - Wyldlife **[15905]**, Maumee, OH
Geneva - Young Life **[1795]**, Geneva, IL
Girls Incorporated of Monroe County **[4221]**, Bloomington, IN
Girls Incorporated of Shelbyville and Shelby County **[6192]**, Shelbyville, IN
Glen Crest Wyld Life - Wyldlife **[1828]**, Glen Ellyn, IL
Gr. Cleveland YoungLives - YoungLives **[14127]**, Cleveland, OH
Grand Haven - Young Life **[7859]**, Grand Haven, MI
Grand Rapids Area Youth for Christ **[8404]**, Jenison, MI
Grand Rapids Christian High - Young Life **[7947]**, Grand Rapids, MI
Grand Rapids Christian Middle School - Wyldlife **[7948]**, Grand Rapids, MI
Grandview High School - Young Life **[14444]**, Columbus, OH
Grandville High School - Young Life **[8039]**, Grandville, MI
Grandville Middle School - Wyldlife **[8040]**, Grandville, MI
Granville - Young Life **[15342]**, Granville, OH
Great Lakes Region Youth for Christ **[5127]**, Indianapolis, IN
Greater Cleveland Youth for Christ **[14135]**, Cleveland, OH
Greater Lafayette Young Life **[6482]**, West Lafayette, IN
Greater Madison Young Life **[19236]**, Mount Horeb, WI
Greater Wheeling Area Youth Outreach **[2586]**, Mount Prospect, IL
Grove City, OH - Young Life **[14449]**, Columbus, OH
Guernsey - Wyldlife **[13498]**, Cambridge, OH
Hadley Wyld Life **[1833]**, Glen Ellyn, IL
Hamilton - Young Life **[8199]**, Holland, MI
Hamilton - Young Life **[15160]**, Fairfield, OH
Harrison High School - Young Life **[6483]**, West Lafayette, IN
Hayward - YoungLife **[16730]**, Springfield, OH
Head of the Lakes Youth for Christ **[10824]**, Duluth, MN
Hea.y Communities Hea.y Youth **[1919]**, Gurnee, IL
Heath High School - Young Life **[15343]**, Granville, OH
Highview Wyldlife **[12229]**, Roseville, MN
Hilliard Darby - Young Life **[14455]**, Columbus, OH
Hilliard Davidson - Young Life **[14456]**, Columbus, OH
Hillsdale - Wyldlife **[8179]**, Hillsdale, MI
Hillsdale - Young Life **[8180]**, Hillsdale, MI
Hinsdale Central - Young Life **[2016]**, Hinsdale, IL
Hinsdale South - Young Life **[2018]**, Hinsdale, IL
Hinsdale WyldLife **[2019]**, Hinsdale, IL
Holland Christian - Young Life **[8201]**, Holland, MI
Holland High - Young Life **[8203]**, Holland, MI
Holland - Wyldlife **[8204]**, Holland, MI
Homewood-Flossmoor - Young Life **[3504]**, South Holland, IL
Hopkins - Young Life **[8205]**, Holland, MI
Hopkins Young Life **[11185]**, Hopkins, MN
Hudson - Young Life **[15485]**, Hudson, OH
Hudsonville High - Young Life **[6623]**, Allendale, MI
Huron High - Young Life **[6706]**, Ann Arbor, MI
Hyde Park Young Life **[922]**, Chicago, IL
Ida - Young Life **[8301]**, Ida, MI
Indian Hill Young Life **[13866]**, Cincinnati, OH
Indiana Lakes Area Youth for Christ **[6443]**, Warsaw, IN
Indiana School-Age Consortium **[5293]**, Indianapolis, IN
Indiana Youth Inst. **[5337]**, Indianapolis, IN
Interfaith Youth Core **[978]**, Chicago, IL
Irondale Young Life **[12231]**, Roseville, MN
Iroquois Valley Youth for Christ **[3909]**, Watseka, IL
Itasca Youth for Christ **[11090]**, Grand Rapids, MN
Jackson - Young Life **[8382]**, Jackson, MI
Jasper - Wyldlife **[5529]**, Jasper, IN
Jefferson High School - Young Life **[6488]**, West Lafayette, IN
Jenison High - Young Life **[6624]**, Allendale, MI
Jenison Junior High - Wyldlife **[6625]**, Allendale, MI
John Young - Wyldlife **[6235]**, South Bend, IN
Jonathan Alder - Young Life **[14481]**, Columbus, OH
Jonesville Wyld Life - Wyldlife **[8182]**, Hillsdale, MI
Kalamazoo Area Youth for Christ **[8434]**, Kalamazoo, MI
Kalamazoo Christian - Young Life **[8437]**, Kalamazoo, MI
Kaleidoscope Youth Coalition **[14483]**, Columbus, OH
Kankakee Area Youth for Christ **[327]**, Bourbonnais, IL
Karrer MS - Wyldlife **[14484]**, Columbus, OH
Kenowa Hills High School - Young Life **[8041]**, Grandville, MI
Kenton Ridge - Young Life **[16732]**, Springfield, OH
Kentwood - Young Life **[7973]**, Grand Rapids, MI
Kettering - Young Life **[14903]**, Dayton, OH
Kettle Moraine Young Life **[18184]**, Hartland, WI
Kilbourne - Young Life **[14486]**, Columbus, OH
Kings Young Life **[13880]**, Cincinnati, OH
La Porte County 4-H Coun. **[5597]**, La Porte, IN
LaGrange - Wyldlife **[3961]**, Western Springs, IL
Lakes Area Young Life **[10775]**, Detroit Lakes, MN
Lakeshore - Young Life **[9683]**, St. Joseph, MI
Lakeshore Youth for Christ **[9146]**, Muskegon, MI
Lakeville HS - Young Life **[10593]**, Burnsville, MN
Lakewood Wyldlife **[17230]**, Westlake, OH
Lakota East - Young Life **[15162]**, Fairfield, OH
Lakota West - Young Life **[15163]**, Fairfield, OH
Lane Middle School - Wyldlife **[4687]**, Fort Wayne, IN
Lane Tech - Young Life **[1020]**, Chicago, IL
Lansing Youth for Christ **[8594]**, Lansing, MI
LaSalle St. Young Lives - YoungLives **[1021]**, Chicago, IL
Lauj Youth Soc. of Minnesota **[12439]**, St. Paul, MN
Leadership Fort Wayne **[4688]**, Fort Wayne, IN
Lebanon - Young Life **[16010]**, Middletown, OH
Lee High School - Young Life **[8042]**, Grandville, MI
Lesbian/Gay Community Center of Greater Cleveland **[14157]**, Cleveland, OH
Logan High School - Young Life **[13206]**, Athens, OH
LW Central - Young Life **[1727]**, Frankfort, IL
LW East - Young Life **[1728]**, Frankfort, IL
Lyons Township Young Life **[3962]**, Western Springs, IL

Madiera Young Life **[13890]**, Cincinnati, OH
Madison Central City - Young Life **[19237]**, Mount Horeb, WI
Mahtomedi - Young Life **[12897]**, White Bear Lake, MN
Mariemont Young Life **[13893]**, Cincinnati, OH
Marinette and Menominee Counties Youth Suicide Prevention **[18800]**, Marinette, WI
Martin's Ferry/Bridgeport - Young Life **[15521]**, Jacobsburg, OH
Mason Middle School - Wyldlife **[7527]**, East Lansing, MI
Mason - Young Life **[7528]**, East Lansing, MI
Mason Young Life **[13894]**, Cincinnati, OH
Massillon HS - Young Life **[13571]**, Canton, OH
Mattawan - Young Life **[8447]**, Kalamazoo, MI
Maumee HS - Young Life **[15911]**, Maumee, OH
McCutcheon High School - Young Life **[6489]**, West Lafayette, IN
Mchenry Wyldlife **[3946]**, West Dundee, IL
McKinley Jr. High - Wyldlife **[3505]**, South Holland, IL
Medina County Youth for Christ **[13450]**, Brunswick, OH
Mentoring Partnership of Minnesota **[11601]**, Minneapolis, MN
Mesabi Range Youth for Christ **[12796]**, Virginia, MN
Metro Chicago Youth for Christ **[3991]**, Wheaton, IL
Metro Columbus - Young Life **[14500]**, Columbus, OH
Michigan State Univ. Extension 4-H Youth Programs **[7552]**, East Lansing, MI
Michigan Youth in Govt. **[9466]**, Quincy, MI
Middletown - Young Life **[16016]**, Middletown, OH
Milford - Young Life **[13905]**, Cincinnati, OH
Minneapolis South Young Life **[11186]**, Hopkins, MN
Minnehaha Acad. - Wyldlife **[11187]**, Hopkins, MN
Minnesota Valley Young Life **[10603]**, Burnsville, MN
Mishawaka - Young Life **[6245]**, South Bend, IN
Moline - Young Life **[2524]**, Moline, IL
Monroe County Young Life **[8302]**, Ida, MI
Monroe - Young Life **[8303]**, Ida, MI
Morton - Central Illinois - Young Life **[3889]**, Washington, IL
Moundsview - Young Life **[12245]**, Roseville, MN
Mt. Healthy - Young Life **[15164]**, Fairfield, OH
Mt. Horeb Jr. High - Wyldlife **[19239]**, Mount Horeb, WI
Mt. Horeb Sr. High - Young Life **[19240]**, Mount Horeb, WI
Mt. Vernon - Young Life **[5852]**, Mount Vernon, IN
Muncie Area Youth for Christ **[5886]**, Muncie, IN
Muncie - Young Life **[5890]**, Muncie, IN
Naperville Central Young Life **[2650]**, Naperville, IL
Naperville North Young Life **[2653]**, Naperville, IL
Natl. Youth Leadership Coun. **[12554]**, St. Paul, MN
Neenah Young Life **[19274]**, Neenah, WI
Neighborhood Boys and Girls Club **[1097]**, Chicago, IL
Nelsonville York - Young Life **[13211]**, Athens, OH
Neuqua Valley Young Life **[2657]**, Naperville, IL
New Albany - Young Life **[14530]**, Columbus, OH
New Castle Area - Young Life **[5938]**, New Castle, IN
New Knoxville - Young Life **[16434]**, Piqua, OH
New Richmond - Young Life **[13128]**, Amelia, OH
Newburgh - Wyldlife **[5962]**, Newburgh, IN
Normal Wyldlife - Wyldlife **[2727]**, Normal, IL
Normal - Young Life **[302]**, Bloomington, IL
North Central Indiana Youth for Christ **[5740]**, Marion, IN
North Central Ohio Youth for Christ **[15781]**, Mansfield, OH
North Central - Young Life **[5441]**, Indianapolis, IN
North Royalton - Young Life **[16248]**, North Royalton, OH
North - Young Life **[4249]**, Bloomington, IN
Northeast Grand Rapids Young Life **[7995]**, Grand Rapids, MI
Northeast Indiana Youth for Christ **[4141]**, Auburn, IN
Northside Wyldlife - Wyldlife **[1108]**, Chicago, IL
Northview - Wyldlife **[5442]**, Indianapolis, IN
Northview - Young Life **[16827]**, Sylvania, OH
Northwest Indiana Youth for Christ **[6386]**, Valparaiso, IN
Northwestern - Young Life **[16736]**, Springfield, OH
Norwayne - Young Life **[17323]**, Wooster, OH
Oak Hills - Young Life **[15165]**, Fairfield, OH
Oak Park/River Forest - Young Life **[2825]**, Oak Park, IL
Olentangy Liberty - Young Life **[14703]**, Columbus, OH
Olentangy - Young Life **[14704]**, Columbus, OH
Onalaska - Young Life **[19368]**, Onalaska, WI
Ottawa and Allegan Counties Youth for Christ **[8214]**, Holland, MI
Ottertail County - Young Life **[11001]**, Fergus Falls, MN
Our Lady of the Rosary - Young Life **[15166]**, Fairfield, OH
Owatonna Wyldlife **[11966]**, Owatonna, MN
Owatonna Young Life **[11967]**, Owatonna, MN
Palatine/Fremd - Young Life **[2922]**, Palatine, IL
PC - WyldLife **[9403]**, Plymouth, MI
Penn - Young Life **[6251]**, South Bend, IN
Peoria Area Youth for Christ **[3048]**, Peoria, IL
Perrysburg HS - Young Life **[15915]**, Maumee, OH
Perrysburg - Wyldlife **[15916]**, Maumee, OH
Pike - Young Life **[5451]**, Indianapolis, IN
Pinewood Middle - Wyldlife **[7998]**, Grand Rapids, MI
Pioneer High - Young Life **[6755]**, Ann Arbor, MI
Piqua Jr. High - Wyldlife **[16439]**, Piqua, OH
Piqua - Young Life **[16440]**, Piqua, OH
Portage - Young Life **[8462]**, Kalamazoo, MI
Posey County Young Life **[5856]**, Mount Vernon, IN
Princeton - Young Life **[15167]**, Fairfield, OH
Private School B - Young Life **[11191]**, Hopkins, MN
Quad City Area Youth for Christ **[2530]**, Moline, IL
Quincy Wyldlife - Wyldlife **[3169]**, Quincy, IL
Quincy Young Lives - YoungLives **[3170]**, Quincy, IL
Red Wing High School - Young Life **[12083]**, Red Wing, MN
Richfield - Young Life **[11192]**, Hopkins, MN
Richmond - Young Life **[6107]**, Richmond, IN
Richwoods - Central Illinois - Young Life **[3890]**, Washington, IL
Riley St. MS - Wyldlife **[6628]**, Allendale, MI
Riley - Young Life **[6257]**, South Bend, IN
Ripon Jr. High - Wyldlife **[18810]**, Markesan, WI
Ripon Sr. High - Young Life **[18811]**, Markesan, WI
River Valley Youth for Christ **[19767]**, Spring Green, WI
Rock Valley Youth for Christ **[17617]**, Beloit, WI
Rockford - Wyldlife **[3314]**, Rockford, IL
Rockfordland Youth for Christ **[3315]**, Rockford, IL
Rocky River High School - Young Life **[17236]**, Westlake, OH
Roosevelt - Wyldlife **[16741]**, Springfield, OH
Roseville - Young Life **[12247]**, Roseville, MN
Ross - Young Life **[15168]**, Fairfield, OH
Rossford HS - Young Life **[15917]**, Maumee, OH
St. Anthony Wyldlife **[12248]**, Roseville, MN
St. Charles - Young Life **[1800]**, Geneva, IL
St. Clair County Youth for Christ **[9441]**, Port Huron, MI
St. Cloud - Young Life **[12306]**, St. Cloud, MN
St. Joe - Young Life **[9689]**, St. Joseph, MI
St. Xavier - Young Life **[15169]**, Fairfield, OH
Saline High - Young Life **[6762]**, Ann Arbor, MI
Saugatuck - Young Life **[8219]**, Holland, MI
Savage Wyldlife **[10607]**, Burnsville, MN
Scholarship and Guidance Assn. **[1173]**, Chicago, IL
Shawnee - Young Life **[16743]**, Springfield, OH
Sidney-Shelby County Young Men's Christian Association **[16670]**, Sidney, OH
South Central Minnesota Youth for Christ **[10264]**, Albert Lea, MN
South Christian - Young Life **[8012]**, Grand Rapids, MI
South - Young Life **[4258]**, Bloomington, IN
Southeast Indiana Young Life **[4161]**, Batesville, IN
Southeastern Ohio Young Life **[13500]**, Cambridge, OH
Southeastern Wisconsin Youth for Christ **[19574]**, Racine, WI
Southeastern - Young Life **[16745]**, Springfield, OH
Southern Hills Youth for Christ **[4259]**, Bloomington, IN
Southern Local - Young Life **[16596]**, Salineville, OH
Southview - Young Life **[16832]**, Sylvania, OH
Southwest Michigan Youth for Christ **[9882]**, Sturgis, MI
Spring Lake - Young Life **[7866]**, Grand Haven, MI
Springboro - Young Life **[16019]**, Middletown, OH
Springfield North - Young Life **[16751]**, Springfield, OH
Springfield - Young Life **[16833]**, Sylvania, OH
Stark County Young Life **[13590]**, Canton, OH
Sun Prairie Wyldlife **[19242]**, Mount Horeb, WI
Sun Prairie Young Life **[19243]**, Mount Horeb, WI
SWM - Wyldlife **[9694]**, St. Joseph, MI
Sycamore - Young Life **[14006]**, Cincinnati, OH
Talawanda - Young Life **[15170]**, Fairfield, OH
Tayanoka Coun. of Camp Fire **[16592]**, Salem, OH
Taylor - Young Life **[15171]**, Fairfield, OH
Tecumseh - Young Life **[6585]**, Adrian, MI
Tecumseh - Young Life **[16752]**, Springfield, OH
Teen Straight Talk **[17071]**, Vienna, OH
Thomas - Young Life **[14744]**, Columbus, OH
Thornwood High School - Young Life **[3510]**, South Holland, IL
Timothy Christian - Young Life **[2024]**, Hinsdale, IL
Toledo South Side - Young Life **[15919]**, Maumee, OH
Toledo Youth for Christ **[15459]**, Holland, OH
Toronto - Young Life **[16989]**, Toronto, OH
Tri-County Youth for Christ **[9641]**, Saginaw, MI
Trimble High School - Young Life **[13221]**, Athens, OH
Twin Bluff - Wyldlife **[12088]**, Red Wing, MN
ULS - Wyldlife **[18186]**, Hartland, WI
Union Avenue Wyld Life - Wyldlife **[1212]**, Chicago, IL
Unity Christian High - Young Life **[6629]**, Allendale, MI
Upper Arlington - Young Life **[14755]**, Columbus, OH
Upper Peninsula Youth for Christ **[8964]**, Marquette, MI
Vicksburg - Young Life **[8470]**, Kalamazoo, MI
W. North - Young Life **[14761]**, Columbus, OH
W. South - Young Life **[14762]**, Columbus, OH
Wabash Valley Youth for Christ **[6352]**, Terre Haute, IN
Wadsworth - Young Life **[17080]**, Wadsworth, OH
Washington - Central Illinois - Young Life **[3892]**, Washington, IL
Waubonsie Valley Young Life **[2663]**, Naperville, IL
Waynesville - Young Life **[14969]**, Dayton, OH
Wedgwood - Other **[8018]**, Grand Rapids, MI
West Central Minnesota Youth for Christ **[12929]**, Willmar, MN
West Central - Young Life **[14763]**, Columbus, OH
West Lafayette High School - Young Life **[6506]**, West Lafayette, IN
West Madison/Verona Young Life **[19245]**, Mount Horeb, WI
West Ottawa - Wyldlife **[8225]**, Holland, MI
West Ottawa Young Life **[8226]**, Holland, MI
West Shore Youth for Christ **[8879]**, Ludington, MI
Western Illinois Youth for Christ **[2377]**, Macomb, IL
Westland - Young Life **[14764]**, Columbus, OH
White Bear Lake/Mahtomedi - Wyldlife **[12906]**, White Bear Lake, MN
White Bear Lake - Young Life **[12907]**, White Bear Lake, MN
Whitefish Bay Young Life **[19150]**, Milwaukee, WI
Williamston Middle School - Wyldlife **[7569]**, East Lansing, MI

Williamston - Young Life **[7570]**, East Lansing, MI
Winona - Young Life **[12967]**, Winona, MN
Wisconsin 4-H Found. **[18638]**, Madison, WI
Woo YL Club - Young Life **[17335]**, Wooster, OH
Woodbury Young Life **[12989]**, Woodbury, MN
WyldLife - Morton, Illinois **[3894]**, Washington, IL
WyldLife Naperville and Aurora **[2666]**, Naperville, IL
WyldLife Northville **[9246]**, Novi, MI
WyldLife Novi **[9247]**, Novi, MI
Wyldlife South Lyon **[9248]**, Novi, MI
WyldLife Walled Lake **[9249]**, Novi, MI
WyldLife - Washington, Illinois **[3895]**, Washington, IL
WyldLife - Whitefish Bay **[19189]**, Milwaukee, WI
Wyoming - Young Life **[15173]**, Fairfield, OH
Xenia - Young Life **[17379]**, Xenia, OH
YL Cleveland Young Lives **[14239]**, Cleveland, OH
YL of Dubois Co - Young Life **[5536]**, Jasper, IN
YMCA of Greater Cleveland **[14240]**, Cleveland, OH
York and Willowbrook - Young Life **[2028]**, Hinsdale, IL
York - Young Life **[2029]**, Hinsdale, IL
Young Life Athens County **[13222]**, Athens, OH
Young Life Boonville **[4277]**, Boonville, IN
Young Life Buckeye Region **[15068]**, Dublin, OH
Young Life Carmel **[5506]**, Indianapolis, IN
Young Life Central Grand Rapids **[8030]**, Grand Rapids, MI
Young Life Central Illinois **[3896]**, Washington, IL
Young Life Chicago Northside **[1241]**, Chicago, IL
Young Life Chicago South **[3511]**, South Holland, IL
Young Life Chicagoland Region **[2668]**, Naperville, IL
Young Life Chippewa Valley **[17912]**, Eau Claire, WI
Young Life Cincinnati Metro **[14027]**, Cincinnati, OH
Young Life Clearwater Cove Development **[8507]**, Lake City, MI
Young Life Cleveland Metro **[14242]**, Cleveland, OH
Young Life Cleveland South **[16252]**, North Royalton, OH
Young Life Cleveland West Shore **[17239]**, Westlake, OH
Young Life Columbiana County **[16597]**, Salineville, OH
Young Life Columbus North **[14769]**, Columbus, OH
Young Life Columbus Northeast **[14770]**, Columbus, OH
Young Life Columbus Northwest **[14771]**, Columbus, OH
Young Life Columbus Southeast **[14772]**, Columbus, OH
Young Life Columbus Southwest **[14773]**, Columbus, OH
Young Life County Line **[17081]**, Wadsworth, OH
Young Life Dayton North **[14973]**, Dayton, OH
Young Life Dayton, OH **[14974]**, Dayton, OH
Young Life Detroit **[7458]**, Detroit, MI
Young Life Eastern Cincinnati **[14028]**, Cincinnati, OH
Young Life Eastern DuPage **[2030]**, Hinsdale, IL
Young Life Eastern Great Lakes Region **[8772]**, Lansing, MI
Young Life Ely **[10960]**, Ely, MN
Young Life Fort Wayne **[4730]**, Fort Wayne, IN
Young Life Geneva Lakes **[18401]**, Lake Geneva, WI
Young Life Glenbard South **[1844]**, Glen Ellyn, IL
Young Life Glenbard West **[1845]**, Glen Ellyn, IL
Young Life Grand Rapids Urban **[8031]**, Grand Rapids, MI
Young Life Grand Rapids West **[8050]**, Grandville, MI
Young Life Greater Cincinnati **[15174]**, Fairfield, OH
Young Life Greater Lansing **[7571]**, East Lansing, MI
Young Life Greater Muncie **[5507]**, Indianapolis, IN
Young Life Greater Richmond **[6114]**, Richmond, IN
Young Life Greencastle **[5508]**, Indianapolis, IN
Young Life Grosse Pointe **[8086]**, Grosse Pointe, MI
Young Life Hamilton-Southeastern **[5509]**, Indianapolis, IN
Young Life Heartland Region **[19246]**, Mount Horeb, WI
Young Life Henry County **[5941]**, New Castle, IN
Young Life Hillsdale **[8185]**, Hillsdale, MI
Young Life Holland **[8228]**, Holland, MI
Young Life Indiana Camp **[5747]**, Marshall, IN
Young Life Indiana-Kentucky Region **[5965]**, Newburgh, IN
Young Life Indiana Region **[5510]**, Indianapolis, IN
Young Life Indianapolis Urban Initiative **[5511]**, Indianapolis, IN
Young Life Jasper **[5537]**, Jasper, IN
Young Life Kalamazoo **[8472]**, Kalamazoo, MI
Young Life Kane County **[1801]**, Geneva, IL
Young Life LaCrosse **[19374]**, Onalaska, WI
Young Life Lake Country **[18190]**, Hartland, WI
Young Life Lake County **[2191]**, Lake Bluff, IL
Young Life Lake Erie West Region **[13403]**, Bowling Green, OH
Young Life Lakeshore - Grand Haven **[7869]**, Grand Haven, MI
Young Life LaSalle St. **[1242]**, Chicago, IL
Young Life Lawrence **[5512]**, Indianapolis, IN
Young Life Lenawee County **[6586]**, Adrian, MI
Young Life Licking County **[15347]**, Granville, OH
Young Life Lincoln-Way **[1731]**, Frankfort, IL
Young Life Lorain County **[13246]**, Avon Lake, OH
Young Life McHenry **[3949]**, West Dundee, IL
Young Life McLean County **[313]**, Bloomington, IL
Young Life Metro SW **[3964]**, Western Springs, IL
Young Life Miami-Shelby County **[16441]**, Piqua, OH
Young Life Michiana **[6275]**, South Bend, IN
Young Life Midland **[9044]**, Midland, MI
Young Life Milwaukee North Shore **[19190]**, Milwaukee, WI
Young Life Mt. Horeb **[19247]**, Mount Horeb, WI
Young Life MW Multicultural/Urban **[1243]**, Chicago, IL
Young Life Naperville and Aurora **[2669]**, Naperville, IL
Young Life Newburgh **[5966]**, Newburgh, IN
Young Life North Central Michigan **[6954]**, Big Rapids, MI
Young Life North Coast Development **[17240]**, Westlake, OH
Young Life North Coast Region **[17241]**, Westlake, OH
Young Life Northern Dakota County **[10876]**, Eagan, MN
Young Life Northern Lakes **[8508]**, Lake City, MI
Young Life Northern States Region **[11195]**, Hopkins, MN
Young Life Northville **[9250]**, Novi, MI
Young Life Northwest Chicago **[1244]**, Chicago, IL
Young Life Northwest DuPage **[1846]**, Glen Ellyn, IL
Young Life Northwest Indianapolis **[5513]**, Indianapolis, IN
Young Life Novi **[9251]**, Novi, MI
Young Life NW Suburban Chicago **[2930]**, Palatine, IL
Young Life NW Suburban Detroit **[9252]**, Novi, MI
Young Life Oak Park and River Forest **[2830]**, Oak Park, IL
Young Life Ohio Valley West **[15522]**, Jacobsburg, OH
Young Life Ottertail County **[11006]**, Fergus Falls, MN
Young Life Owatonna **[11973]**, Owatonna, MN
Young Life Plymouth-Canton and Clarenceville **[9413]**, Plymouth, MI
Young Life Quincy **[3175]**, Quincy, IL
Young Life Red Wing **[12092]**, Red Wing, MN
Young Life Ripon **[18812]**, Markesan, WI
Young Life Rock Island County **[2536]**, Moline, IL
Young Life Rockford **[3332]**, Rockford, IL
Young Life St. Cloud **[12318]**, St. Cloud, MN
Young Life St. Croix Valley **[12731]**, Stillwater, MN
Young Life South Central Indiana **[4408]**, Columbus, IN
Young Life South Grand Rapids **[8032]**, Grand Rapids, MI
Young Life South Lyon **[9253]**, Novi, MI
Young Life Southeast Cincinnati **[13129]**, Amelia, OH
Young Life Southern Hills **[4266]**, Bloomington, IN
Young Life Southwest Michigan **[9695]**, St. Joseph, MI
Young Life Springfield **[16756]**, Springfield, OH
Young Life Stevens Point **[19823]**, Stevens Point, WI
Young Life SW Cleveland **[13350]**, Berea, OH
Young Life Timber Wolf Lake **[8509]**, Lake City, MI
Young Life Tri State **[371]**, Burnside, IL
Young Life Tuscarawas County **[16806]**, Sugarcreek, OH
Young Life Union Ave. **[1245]**, Chicago, IL
Young Life Upper Jefferson Cnty **[16990]**, Toronto, OH
Young Life Urban Growth Proj. **[11196]**, Hopkins, MN
Young Life Walled Lake **[9254]**, Novi, MI
Young Life Washington Township **[5514]**, Indianapolis, IN
Young Life Washtenaw County **[6794]**, Ann Arbor, MI
Young Life Wayne and Ashland Counties **[17337]**, Wooster, OH
Young Life West Ottawa-Zeeland **[8229]**, Holland, MI
Young Life West Toledo **[16835]**, Sylvania, OH
Young Life Western Cincinnati Urban **[15175]**, Fairfield, OH
Young Life Western Great Lakes Region **[8033]**, Grand Rapids, MI
Young Life Western Reserve **[15488]**, Hudson, OH
Young Life Wheaton North **[1847]**, Glen Ellyn, IL
Young Life Wheaton Warrenville South **[1848]**, Glen Ellyn, IL
Young Life White Bear Lake - Mahtomedi Area **[12908]**, White Bear Lake, MN
Young Life Winona **[12968]**, Winona, MN
Young Life Wood County **[13404]**, Bowling Green, OH
Young Life Xenia/Fairborn **[17380]**, Xenia, OH
Young Life Youth Center St. Charles - Department of Corrections **[1802]**, Geneva, IL
Young Life - Youth Farm **[3897]**, Washington, IL
Young Life Ypsilanti **[10219]**, Ypsilanti, MI
Young Life Zionsville **[5515]**, Indianapolis, IN
Young Men's Christian Association of Findlay, Ohio **[15218]**, Findlay, OH
YoungLife Green Bay **[18143]**, Green Bay, WI
YoungLife Northern Twin Cities **[12250]**, Roseville, MN
Youth for Christ of Southeast Indiana **[4301]**, Brookville, IN
Youth for Christ/West Central Ohio **[17056]**, Van Wert, OH
Youth Development Corp. **[8773]**, Lansing, MI
YWCA of Dayton **[14975]**, Dayton, OH
YWCA of Grand Rapids **[8034]**, Grand Rapids, MI
YWCA of Greater Cleveland **[14243]**, Cleveland, OH
YWCA of Rockford **[3333]**, Rockford, IL
Zeeland - Wyldlife **[8230]**, Holland, MI
Zeeland - Young Life **[8231]**, Holland, MI
Youth Baseball and Softball; Hartford **[15408]**, Hartford, OH
Youth Basketball Assn; Rogers Area **[12205]**, Rogers, MN
Youth Basketball; Lakota Thunderbird **[13882]**, Cincinnati, OH
Youth Cheerleading Assn; Carol Stream **[446]**, Carol Stream, IL
Youth for Christ of Southeast Indiana **[4301]**, Brookville, IN
Youth for Christ; Southwest Michigan **[9882]**, Sturgis, MI
Youth for Christ/West Central Ohio **[17056]**, Van Wert, OH
Youth Development Corp. **[8773]**, Lansing, MI
Youth Football League; Fairfield County **[15599]**, Lancaster, OH
Youth Football League; Midland Area **[9034]**, Midland, MI

Youth Gp; Indiana **[5336]**, Indianapolis, IN
Youth; Hea.y Communities Hea.y **[1919]**, Gurnee, IL
Youth Hockey Assn; Bowling Green **[13387]**, Bowling Green, OH
Youth Hockey Assn; Peoria **[3057]**, Peoria, IL
Youth Hostels-Northeast Ohio Coun; Amer. **[★16394]**
Youth Inst; Indiana **[5337]**, Indianapolis, IN
Youth Mentoring of Princeton; Kinship **[12045]**, Princeton, MN
Youth Outreach; Greater Wheeling Area **[2586]**, Mount Prospect, IL
Youth Sailing Club; Alpena **[6640]**, Alpena, MI
Youth Ser. Bur. of Huntington County **[4956]**, Huntington, IN
Youth Soccer Assn; Shaker **[16642]**, Shaker Heights, OH
Youth Soccer Assn; Wisconsin **[20112]**, West Allis, WI
Youth Sports Assn; Vandalia Butler Pee Wee **[17061]**, Vandalia, OH
Youth Suicide Prevention; Marinette and Menominee Counties **[18800]**, Marinette, WI
Ypsilanti Area Chamber of Commerce **[10220]**, Ypsilanti, MI
Ypsilanti Convention and Visitors Bur. **[10221]**, Ypsilanti, MI
Ypsilanti Lions Club **[10222]**, Ypsilanti, MI
YWCA of Dayton **[14975]**, Dayton, OH
YWCA of Grand Rapids **[8034]**, Grand Rapids, MI
YWCA of Greater Cleveland **[14243]**, Cleveland, OH
YWCA of Metropolitan Chicago **[1246]**, Chicago, IL
YWCA of Minneapolis **[11780]**, Minneapolis, MN
YWCA of Rockford **[3333]**, Rockford, IL
YWCA St. Paul **[12610]**, St. Paul, MN
YWCA Student Tutor Adult Reading **[★2994]**

Z

Z Assn. of Cleveland, Ohio **[16686]**, Solon, OH
Z Car Club of Ohio **[15176]**, Fairfield, OH
Z Car and Roadster Owner Club **[14774]**, Columbus, OH
Z Owners of Minnesota **[12864]**, Wayzata, MN
Zanesville Area AIFA **[17448]**, Zanesville, OH
Zanesville - Muskingum County Chamber of Commerce **[17449]**, Zanesville, OH
Zeeland Chamber of Commerce **[10232]**, Zeeland, MI
Zeeland Volk's Corp. **[10233]**, Zeeland, MI
Zeeland - Wyldlife **[8230]**, Holland, MI
Zeeland - Young Life **[8231]**, Holland, MI
Zeitgeist Detroit **[7459]**, Detroit, MI
Zenobia Shriners **[16986]**, Toledo, OH
Zeta Beta Tau Fraternity **[5517]**, Indianapolis, IN
Zilwaukee Lions Club **[9648]**, Saginaw, MI
Zinzinnati Wanderers **[14029]**, Cincinnati, OH
Zion Chamber of Commerce **[4081]**, Zion, IL
Zionsville Kiwanis Club **[6554]**, Zionsville, IN
Zionsville Lions Club **[6555]**, Zionsville, IN
Zoological Gardens
Lincoln Park Zoo **[1031]**, Chicago, IL
Zoological Soc. of Milwaukee **[19191]**, Milwaukee, WI
Zoological Soc. of Milwaukee County **[★19191]**
Zoology
Brookfield Zoo/Chicago Zoological Soc. **[350]**, Brookfield, IL
Indianapolis Zoo **[5358]**, Indianapolis, IN
Zor Shriners **[18768]**, Madison, WI
Zorah Shriners **[6354]**, Terre Haute, IN
Zuhrah Shriners **[11781]**, Minneapolis, MN
Zumbro Falls Lions Club **[13003]**, Zumbro Falls, MN
Zumbro Valley Audubon Soc. **[12199]**, Rochester, MN
Zumbro Valley Medical Soc. **[12200]**, Rochester, MN
Zumbrota Chamber of Commerce **[13005]**, Zumbrota, MN
Zumbrota Lions Club **[13006]**, Zumbrota, MN